# THE SPORT AMERICANA®

# PRICE GUIDE

By
# DR. JAMES BECKETT

# NUMBER 11

## EDGEWATER BOOK COMPANY · CLEVELAND

*SPORT AMERICANA is a registered trademark*

**EDGEWATER BOOK COMPANY**
**P.O. BOX 40238**
**CLEVELAND, OHIO 44140**

BECKETT is a registered trademark of

BECKETT PUBLICATIONS
DALLAS, TEXAS

Manufactured in the United States of America

First Printing

ISBN 0-937424-75-7

# The Sport Americana Football Card Price Guide

## Table of Contents

About the Author ..................8
How to Use This Book ............8
1993 Football Year In Review ....10
Introduction ...................18
How To Collect ................18
  Obtaining Cards .............20
  Perserving Your Cards .......20
  Collecting vs. Investing .....20
Terminology ...................22
Glossary/Legend ..............22
Understanding Card Value ......29
  Determining Card Value ......29
  Regional Variation ..........29
  Set Prices ..................30
  Scarce Series ...............30
Grading Your Cards ............30
  Centering ..................30
  Corner Wear ...............33
  Creases ...................33
  Alterations ................33
  Categorization of Defects ....33
Condition Guide ..............34
  Grades ...................34
Selling Your Cards ............35
Interesting Notes .............35
Advertising ..................35
Additional Reading ...........36
Prices in this Guide ..........37
History of Football Cards ......37
Acknowledgments ..........1112

## American Football
Action Packed
  1989 Prototypes ...........39
  1989 Test ................39
  1990 ....................39
  1990 Rookie Update ......41
  1990 All-Madden .........42
  1991 NFLPA Awards ......43
  1991 Whizzer White Award ...44
  1991 Prototypes ..........44
  1991 ....................44
  1991 24K Gold ...........47
  1991 Rookie Update ......47
  1991 Rookies 24K Gold ....48
  1991 All-Madden .........49
  1992 24K NFLPA/MDA Awards ...50
  1992 Mackey Award .......50
  1992 Prototypes ..........50
  1992 ....................50
  1992 24K Gold ...........52
  1992 Rookie Update ......53
  1992 Rookies 24K Gold ....54
  1992 All-Madden .........55
  1993 NFLPA Awards ......56
  1993 Troy Aikman Promos ...56
  1993 Emmitt Smith Promos ..56
  1993 Prototypes ..........57
  1993 ....................57
  1993 24K Gold ...........60
  1993 Moving Targets ......60
  1993 QB Club ............61
  1993 Rushers ............61
  1993 Rookies Previews ....62
  1993 All-Madden Prototype ..62
  1993 All-Madden .........62
  1993 All-Madden 24K Gold ..63
  1993 ABC MNF Prototypes ..63
  1993 ABC MNF ..........63
  1994 Prototypes ..........65
  1994 Mammoth Prototype ..65
All World
  1991 Troy Aikman Promos ..65
  1992 NFL Promo ..........66
  1992 ....................66
  1992 Greats/Rookies ......69
  1992 Legends/Rookies .....70
American Oil
  1966 All-Pro .............70
  1968 Mr. and Mrs. .......71
Arena Cleveland Thunderbolts ..71
Athletes in Action * ..........72
A1 Masters of the Grill ......72
Bazooka
  1959 ....................72
  1971 ....................73
  1972 Official Signals ......73
Bears Coke Discs ............74
Bills

1960 Team Issue ............74
1963 Jones Dairy ...........75
1965 Super Duper Markets ...75
1967 Jones-Rich Milk .......75
1974 Team Issue ...........75
1976 McDonald's ..........76
1979 Bell's Market .........76
1980 Bell's Market .........76
1986 Sealtest .............76
Bleachers
  1993-94 Troy Aikman Promos ...77
  1994 23K Troy Aikman .....77
Blitz Chicago ...............77
Bowman
  1948 ....................77
  1950 ....................79
  1951 ....................80
  1952 Large ..............82
  1952 Small ..............84
  1953 ....................86
  1954 ....................87
  1955 ....................88
  1991 ....................90
  1992 ....................94
  1993 ...................100
Bread for Health ...........105
Breyers Bookmarks .........106
British Petroleum ..........106
Broncos
  1984 KOA ..............107
  1987 Orange Crush ......107
Brownell Heisman .........108
Browns
  1950 Team Issue ........108
  1951 White Border ......109
  1954-55 White Border ...109
  1955 Carling Beer .......109
  1955 Color Postcards ....109
  1959 Carling Beer .......109
  1961 Carling Beer .......110
  1961 National City Bank ..110
  1961 White Border ......110
  1963 White Border ......111
  1985 Coke/Mr. Hero ....111
  1987 Louis Rich ........111
  1992 Sunoco ..........112
Buccaneers Shell ..........112
Buckmans Discs ..........112
Cardinals
  1960 Mayrose Franks ...113
  1961 Jay Publishing ....113
  1965 Big Red Biographies ..113
Cardz Flintstones
  1993 Promos ..........114
  1993 NFL .............114
CBS Television Announcers ..115
Chargers
  1961 Golden Tulip ......115
  1962 Union Oil ........116
  1966 White Border ......116
  1985 Kodak ...........117
  1986 Kodak ...........117
  1987 Junior Coke Tickets ..117
  1989 Junior Ralph's Tickets ..117
  1991 Vons ............118
  1992 Louis Rich ........118
Chiefs
  1964-69 Fairmont Dairy ..118
  1969 Kroger ...........119
  1971 Team Issue .......119
  1984 QuikTrip .........119
Chiquita NFL Slides ........119
Clark Volpe ..............120
Classic
  1991 Draft Promos .....120
  1991 Draft ............121
  1992 Draft Promos .....121
  1992 Draft Foil ........121
  1992 Draft Blister ......123
  1992 Draft LPs ........124
  1992 NFL Game .......124
  1993 Draft Preview .....125
  1993 C3 Presidential Promo ..125
  1993 Draft Gold Promos ..125
  1993 Draft ............127
  1993 Draft Gold ......127
  1993 Draft Stars ......127
  1993 Draft LPs ......127
  1993 ProLine Previews ..128

1993 Superhero Comic .....128
1993 TONX ..............128
1994 Draft Promos .......130
1994 Draft Football Previews ..130
1994 Draft ..............130
1994 Draft Gold .........131
1994 Draft LPs ..........132
1994 Draft Stars .........132
1994 NFL Experience Promos ..132
1994 NFL Experience .....133
1994 NFL Experience LPs ..133
1994 ProLine Previews ....134
1994 ROY Sweepstakes ...134
Coke
  1964 Caps All-Stars AFL ..135
  1964 Caps All-Stars NFL ..135
  1964 Caps Browns ......136
  1964 Caps Chargers .....136
  1964 Caps Lions ........136
  1964 Caps Patriots ......137
  1964 Caps Team Emblems NFL ..137
  1965 Caps All-Stars NFL ..137
  1965 Caps Bills .........138
  1965 Caps Giants .......138
  1965 Caps Jets .........138
  1965 Caps Lions ........139
  1965 Caps Redskins .....139
  1966 Caps All-Stars AFL ..139
  1966 Caps All-Stars NFL ..140
  1966 Caps Bills .........140
  1966 Caps Browns ......141
  1966 Caps Cardinals .....141
  1966 Caps Chiefs .......141
  1966 Caps Colts ........142
  1966 Caps Cowboys .....142
  1966 Caps Falcons ......142
  1966 Caps 49ers ........143
  1966 Caps Giants .......143
  1966 Caps Jets .........143
  1966 Caps National NFL ..144
  1966 Caps Oilers .......144
  1966 Caps Patriots ......145
  1966 Caps Rams ........145
  1966 Caps Steelers .....145
  1971 Caps Packers .....146
  1981 ...................146
  1994 Monsters of the Gridiron ..147
Collector's Edge
  1992 Prototypes ........147
  1992 ...................148
  1992 RU Prototypes ....150
  1992 Special ...........150
  1993 Prototypes ........150
  1993 RU Prototypes ....151
  1993 ...................151
  1993 Checklists ........153
  1993 Varsity Prisms ....154
  1993 Rookies FX Prototypes ..154
  1993 Rookies FX .......154
  1994 Boss Squad Promos ..155
  1994 Excalibur Elway Promos ..155
  1994 Excalibur ........155
  1994 Excalibur EdgeQuest ..156
  1994 Excalibur FX ......156
  1994 Excalibur 22K Gold ..156
Colts
  1961 Jay Publishing ....157
  1967 Johnny Pro .......157
  1978 Team Issue .......157
  1985 Kroger ..........158
Courtside
  1992 Draft Pix Promos ..158
  1992 ..................158
  1992 Foilgrams ........160
  1992 Inserts ..........160
  1993 Sean Dawkins .....161
  1993 Russell White .....161
Cowboys
  1969 Team Issue .......161
  1971 Team Issue .......161
  1982 Carrollton Park ....162
  1985 Frito Lay .........162
Crane Discs ...............162
DairyPak Cartons ..........163
Dell ......................164
Diamond Stickers .........164
Dog Tags
  1992 ..................165
  1993 ..................166

Dolphins
  1967 Royal Castle ......167
  1974 All-Pro Graphics ...168
Domino's Quarterbacks ....168
Eagles
  1959 Jay Publishing ....169
  1960 White Border ......169
  1961 Jay Publishing ....169
  1971 Team Issue .......169
  1983 Frito Lay .........170
  1985 Team Issue .......170
  1989 Daily News .......171
  1990 Sealtest ..........171
English
  1987 Bears ............171
  1987 Broncos .........171
  1987 Cowboys .........172
  1987 Dolphins .........172
  1987 49ers ............173
  1987 Giants ...........173
  1987 Jets .............173
  1987 Lions ............174
  1987 Packers .........174
  1987 Rams ...........174
  1987 Redskins ........175
  1987 Seahawks .......175
ENOR Pro Football HOF
  1991 Promos ..........175
  1991 .................176
Eskimo Pie ..............177
Exhibit W468 Football .....177
FACT
  1990 Pro Set Cincinnati ..178
  1991 Pro Set Mobil .....181
  1992 NFL Properties ....182
  1993 Fleer Shell .......182
Falcons Kinnett Dairies .....184
FCA Super Bowl ..........184
Fleer
  1960 .................184
  1960 AFL Team Decals ..186
  1960 College Pennant Decals ..186
  1961 .................186
  1961 Blue Inserts .....188
  1962 .................188
  1963 .................189
  1968 Big Signs .......190
  1972 Quiz ...........190
  1973 Pro Bowl Scouting Report ..191
  1974 Big Signs .......191
  1974 Hall of Fame .....191
  1975 Hall of Fame .....192
  1976 Team Action .....192
  1977 Team Action .....193
  1978 Team Action .....195
  1979 Team Action .....196
  1980 Team Action .....197
  1981 Team Action .....198
  1982 Team Action .....199
  1983 Team Action .....201
  1984 Team Action .....202
  1985 Team Action .....204
  1986 Team Action .....205
  1987 Team Action .....207
  1988 Team Action .....209
  1990 .................210
  1990 All-Pros .........213
  1990 Stars'n'Stripes ...213
  1990 Update ..........215
  1991 .................216
  1991 All-Pros .........218
  1991 Pro-Visions ......219
  1991 Stars'n'Stripes ...219
  1992 Prototypes .......220
  1992 .................220
  1992 All-Pros .........223
  1992 Rookie Sensations ..224
  1992 Mark Rypien .....224
  1992 Team Leaders ....225
  1993 Promo Panel .....225
  1993 .................225
  1993 All-Pros .........231
  1993 Prospects .......232
  1993 Rookie Sensations ..232
  1993 Team Leaders ....232
  1993 Steve Young .....233
  1993 Fruit of the Loom ..233
  1994 .................234
  1994 All-Pros .........237

1994 Award Winners 237
1994 Jerome Bettis 237
1994 League Leaders 238
1994 Living Legends 238
1994 Prospects 238
1994 Pro-Visions 239
1994 Rookie Sensations 239
1994 Scoring Machines 239
**Football Heroes Sticker Book** 240
**Football Immortals** 240
**49ers**
1955 White Border 241
1956 White Border 242
1957 White Border 242
1958 White Border 243
1959 White Border 244
1960 White Border 244
1968 White Border 245
1972 Redwood City Tribune 245
1975 246
1990-91 SF Examiner 246
1992 FBI 246
**GameDay**
1992 Draft Day Promos 247
1992 National 247
1992 248
1992 Box Tops 253
1992-93 SB Program 254
1992-93 Gamebreakers 254
1993 254
1993 Gamebreakers 260
1993 Rookie Standouts 260
1993 Second-Year Stars 260
**GTE Super Bowl Theme Art** 261
**Giants**
1956 Team Issue 261
1957 Team Issue 262
1959 Shell/Riger Posters 262
1960 Jay Publishing 262
1961 Jay Publishing 262
1973 Color Litho 262
**Glendale Stamps** 262
**Goal Line HOF** 264
**Gridiron Greats Blotters** 266
**Gridiron**
1992 Promos 266
1992 266
**Hall of Fame Stickers** 267
**Heads and Tails SB XXVII** 268
**Heisman Collection**
1991 I 269
1992 II 269
**Hi-C Mini-Posters** 269
**Highland Mint** 270
**Hoby SEC Stars**
1991 270
1991 Signature 272
**Holsum**
1987 Dolphins 273
1988 Cardinals 273
1988 Dolphins 273
1988 Patriots 274
1989 Cardinals 274
**Homers** 274
**Intimidator Bio Sheets** 274
**Jeno's Pizza** 275
**Kahn's**
1959 276
1960 276
1961 277
1962 277
1963 278
1964 279
**Kellogg's**
1970 280
1971 281
1982 Panels 282
1982 Teams 282
**King B Disc**
1989 283
1990 283
1991 283
1992 284
1993 284
**Knudsen**
1989 Raiders 285
1990 Chargers 285
1990 49ers 285
1990 Sealtest Patriots 286
1990 Rams 286
1991 286
**Laughlin Flaky Football** 287
**Leaf**
1948 287
1949 288
**Lions**
1961 Jay Publishing 289
1964 White Border 289
1966 Marathon Oil 289
1993 60th Season Comm. 290
**Little Big Leaguers** 290
**Marketcom**
1978-79 Test 290
1980 291
1981 292
1982 292
**Mattel Mini-Records** 293
**Mayo N302** 294
**McDonald's**
1975 Quarterbacks 294
1985 Bears 294
1986 All-Stars 295
1986 Bears 295
1986 Bengals 296
1986 Bills 296
1986 Broncos 296
1986 Browns 297
1986 Buccaneers 297
1986 Cardinals 297
1986 Chargers 298
1986 Chiefs 298
1986 Colts 299
1986 Cowboys 299
1986 Dolphins 299
1986 Eagles 300
1986 Falcons 300
1986 49ers 300
1986 Giants 301
1986 Jets 301
1986 Lions 302
1986 Oilers 302
1986 Packers 302
1986 Patriots 303
1986 Raiders 303
1986 Rams 303
1986 Redskins 304
1986 Saints 304
1986 Seahawks 304
1986 Steelers 305
1986 Vikings 305
1993 GameDay 306
**Metallic Images**
1992 Tins 309
1993 QB Legends 309
**Miller Lite Beer** 310
**Monte Gum** 310
**MSA**
1981 Holsum Discs 311
1990 Superstars 312
**National Chicle** 312
**NewSport** 313
**NFL Experience** 313
**NFLPA**
1972 Vinyl Stickers 314
1972 Fabric Cards 314
1971-72 Won. World Stamps 315
1979 Pennant Stickers 317
**NFL Properties**
1993 Santa Claus 318
1993 Show Redemption Cards 319
**Nu-Card**
1961 319
1961 Pennant Inserts 320
**Oilers**
1961 Jay Publishing 322
1964-65 Color Team Issue 322
1969 323
1971 323
1973 McDonald's 323
**Pacific**
1984 Legends 324
1989 Steve Largent 324
1991 Prototypes 325
1991 325
1991 Checklists 330
1991 Picks The Pros 331
1991 Flash Cards 331
1992 Prototypes 333
1992 333
1992 Checklists 337
1992 Bob Griese 337
1992 Steve Largent 337
1992 Picks The Pros 337
1992 Prism Inserts 338
1992 Statistical Leaders 338
1992 Triple Folders 339
1993 Prototypes 339
1993 340
1993 Checklists 342
1993 Picks the Pros Gold 343
1993 Silver Prism Inserts 343
1993 Prism Promos 344
1993 Prisms 344
1993 Triple Folders 345
1993 Triple Folder Rookies/Superstars 345
1994 Prisms 346
1994 Prisms Team Helmets 347
**Packers**
1961 Lake to Lake 347
1969 Drenks Potato Chip Pins 348
1972 Team Issue 348
1990 25th Anniversary 349
1991 Super Bowl II 349
1992 Hall of Fame 350
1993 Archives Postcards 350
**Panini Stickers**
1988 351
1989 354
1990 356
**Parker Brothers**
1974 Pro Draft 358
1989 Talking Football 359
**Payton Commemorative** 360
**Pepsi Discs** 361
**Philadelphia**
1964 362
1965 364
1966 365
1967 367
**Pinnacle**
1991 Promo Emmitt Smith 368
1991 Promo Panels 368
1991 369
1992 Samples 374
1992 SB XXVII Promo Panel 374
1992 374
1992 Team Pinnacle 378
1992 Team 2000 379
1993 Samples 379
1993 379
1993 Men of Autumn 383
1993 Rookies 384
1993 Super Bowl XXVII 385
1993 Team Pinnacle 385
1993 Team 2001 385
1994 Sportflics Super Bowl 386
1994 Canton Bound Promo 386
1994 Canton Bound 386
**Playoff**
1992 Promos 387
1992 387
1993 Promos 389
1993 389
1993 Checklists 393
1993 Club 393
1993 Brett Favre 393
1993 Ricky Watters 394
1993 Headliners Redemption 394
1993 Promo Inserts 394
1993 Rookie Roundup Redem. 395
1993 Contenders Promos 395
1993 Contenders 395
1993 Contenders Rick Mirer 397
1993 Contenders Rookie Cont. 397
1994 Super Bowl Promos 398
1994 Prototypes 398
1994 398
1994 Jerome Bettis 402
1994 Checklists 402
1994 Club 402
**Police**
1979 Chiefs 403
1979 Cowboys 403
1979 Seahawks 403
1980 Broncos Stamps 403
1980 Buccaneers 404
1980 Cardinals 404
1980 Chiefs 405
1980 Cowboys 405
1980 Dolphins 405
1980 Falcons 405
1980 Oilers 406
1980 Rams 406
1980 Seahawks 406
1981 Bears 407
1981 Chargers 407
1981 Chiefs 407
1981 Cowboys 408
1981 Cowboys Thousand Oaks 408
1981 Dolphins 408
1981 Falcons 409
1981 Jets 409
1981 Steelers 409
1982 Broncos 410
1982 Chargers 410
1982 Chiefs 410
1982 Dolphins 410
1982 Redskins 411
1982 Seahawks 411
1982 Steelers 411
1983 Chiefs 412
1983 Cowboys 412
1983 Dolphins 412
1983 Latrobe 413
1983 Packers 413
1983 Redskins 413
1983 Steelers 414
1983 Vikings 414
1984 Buccaneers 414
1984 Chiefs 415
1984 Dolphins 415
1984 Eagles 415
1984 49ers 416
1984 Packers 416
1984 Redskins 416
1984 Steelers 416
1984 Vikings 417
1985 Chiefs 417
1985 Dolphins 417
1985 Eagles 418
1985 49ers 418
1985 Packers 418
1985 Raiders/Rams 418
1985 Redskins 419
1985 Seahawks 419
1985 Steelers 419
1985 Vikings 420
1986 Bears/Patriots 420
1986 Chiefs 420
1986 Dolphins 421
1986 Eagles 421
1986 Lions 421
1986 Packers 421
1986 Redskins 422
1986 Seahawks 422
1986 Steelers 422
1986 Vikings 423
1987 Bills 423
1987 Chargers 423
1987 Chiefs 424
1987 Dolphins 424
1987 Eagles 424
1987 Giants 424
1987 Lions 425
1987 Packers 425
1987 Redskins 425
1987 Seahawks 426
1987 Steelers 426
1987 Vikings 426
1988 Bills 427
1988 Chargers 427
1988 Chiefs 427
1988 Colts 427
1988 Eagles 428
1988 49ers 428
1988 Giants 428
1988 Lions 428
1988 Packers 429
1988 Raiders 429
1988 Redskins 429
1988 Seahawks 429
1988 Steelers 430
1988 Vikings 430
1989 Bills 430
1989 Buccaneers 431
1989 Cardinals 431
1989 Chargers 431
1989 Chiefs 431
1989 Colts 432
1989 Eagles 432
1989 Lions 432
1989 Packers 432
1989 Rams 433
1989 Redskins 433
1989 Seahawks 433
1989 Steelers 434
1989 Vikings 434
1990 Bills 434
1990 Cardinals 434
1990 Chargers 435
1990 Colts 435
1990 Eagles 435
1990 Giants 435
1990 Lions 436
1990 Packers 436

1990 Redskins ....436
1990 Seahawks ....437
1990 Steelers ....437
1990 Vikings ....437
1991 Bills ....437
1991 Lions ....438
1991 Packers ....438
1991 Raiders ....438
1991 Redskins ....439
1991 Steelers ....439
1991 Surge WLAF ....439
1991 Vikings ....440
1992 Bills ....440
1992 Cardinals ....440
1992 Giants ....440
1992 Redskins ....441
1992 Steelers ....441
1992 Vikings ....441
1993 Packers ....442
1993 Redskins ....442
1993 Steelers ....442
1993 Vikings ....442
**Popsicle Teams** ....443
**Post**
1962 Cereal ....443
1962 Booklets ....444
**Pottsville Maroons** ....445
**Power**
1992 ....445
1992 Combos ....449
1992-93 Emmitt Smith ....449
1993 Prototypes ....449
1993 ....450
1993 All-Power Defense ....452
1993 Combos ....453
1993 Draft Picks ....453
1993 Moves ....454
1993 Update Combos ....454
1993 Update Impact Rookies ....455
1993 Update Moves ....455
1993 Update Prospects ....456
**Press Pass SB Photo Board** ....457
**Pro Athletes Outreach** ....457
**ProLine**
1990-91 Samples ....457
1991 Portraits ....458
1991 Portraits Autographs ....461
1991 Portraits Collectibles ....463
1991 Portraits Collectible Auto. ....463
1991 Portraits Wives ....463
1991 Portraits Wives Autograph ....464
1991 Punt& Pass& and Kick ....464
1991-92 Profiles Anthony Munoz ....464
1992 Draft Day ....464
1992 Prototypes ....465
1992 Portraits ....465
1992 Portraits Autographs ....467
1992 Portraits Checklists ....468
1992 Portraits Collectibles ....468
1992 Portraits Collectibles Auto. ....469
1992 Portraits QB Gold ....469
1992 Portraits Rookie Gold ....469
1992 Portraits Team NFL ....470
1992 Portraits Team NFL Auto. ....470
1992 Portraits Wives ....470
1992 Portraits Wives Auto. ....471
1992 Profiles ....471
1992 Profile Autographs ....478
1992 Mobil ....478
1992-93 SB Program ....479
1993 Live Draft Day NYC ....479
1993 Live Draft Day QVC ....480
1993 Live Promo ....480
1993 Live ....480
1993 Live Autographs ....482
1993 Live Future Stars ....483
1993 Live Illustrated ....483
1993 Live LPs ....484
1993 Live Tonx ....484
1993 Portraits ....484
1993 Portraits Wives ....485
1993 Profiles ....485
1994 Live Draft Day Prototypes ....487
1994 Live ....487
1994 Live Basketball Previews ....491
**Pro Set**
1988 Test Designs ....492
1988 Test ....492
1989 ....492
1989 Super Bowl Logos ....497
1989 Announcers ....497
1989 Promos ....498
1989-90 GTE SB Album ....498
1990 Draft Day ....498
1990 ....499
1990 Theme Art ....507
1990 Inserts ....508
1990 Super Bowl MVP's ....508
1990 Collect-A-Books ....508
1990-91 Super Bowl 160 ....509
1990-91 Super Bowl Binder ....510
1990-91 Pro Bowl 106 ....511
1991 Draft Day ....513
1991 National Banquet ....513
1991 Promos ....513
1991 ....513
1991 Inserts ....521
1991 UK Sheets ....521
1991 WLAF Helmets ....522
1991 WLAF Inserts ....522
1991 WLAF Combo 43 ....523
1991 WLAF 150 ....523
1991 Cinderella Story ....524
1991 Platinum ....525
1991 Platinum PC ....527
1991 Spanish ....528
1991-92 Super Bowl Binder ....530
1992 Pro Set ....530
1992 HOF Inductees ....536
1992 Gold MVPs ....536
1992 Ground Force ....537
1992 HOF 2000 ....537
1992 Emmitt Smith Holograms ....538
1992 Club ....538
1992-93 Super Bowl XXVII ....538
1993 Promos ....539
1993 ....539
1993 All-Rookies ....542
1993 College Connections ....542
1993 Rookie Quarterbacks ....543
1993 Rookie Running Backs ....543
1994 National Promos * ....543
**Quarterback Legends 1991** ....544
**Quarterback Greats GE** ....544
**Quarterback Legends 1993** ....545
**R311-2 Premium Photos** ....545
**Raiders**
1985 Shell Oil Posters ....546
1989 Swanson ....546
1990-91 Main Street Dairy ....546
1991-92 Adohr Farms Dairy ....547
1993-94 Adohr Farms Dairy ....547
**Rams**
1950 Admiral ....547
1953 Black Border ....548
1954 Black Border ....548
1955 Black Border ....549
1956 White Border ....549
1957 Black Border ....550
1959 Bell Brand ....550
1960 Bell Brand ....551
1987 Jello/General Foods ....551
1987 Oscar Mayer ....551
1992 Carl's Jr. ....552
**Redskins**
1969 High's Dairy ....552
1991 Mobil Schedules ....552
1992 Mobil Schedules ....552
1993 Mobil Schedules ....553
**Rice Council *** ....553
**Saints**
1974 Circle Inset ....553
1979 Coke ....554
1992 McDag ....554
**Salada Coins** ....554
**San Giorgio Flipbooks** ....556
**Score**
1989 Promos ....556
1989 ....556
1989 Supplemental ....560
1989-90 Franco Harris ....562
1990 Promos ....562
1990 ....562
1990 Hot Card ....570
1990 Supplemental ....570
1990 Young Superstars ....571
1990 100 Hottest ....572
1990-91 Franco Harris ....573
1991 Prototypes ....573
1991 ....574
1991 Hot Rookie ....581
1991 Young Superstars ....582
1991 National 10 ....582
1991 Supplemental ....583
1992 ....584
1992 Dream Team ....590
1992 Gridiron Stars ....590
1992 Young Superstars ....591
1993 Samples ....592
1993 ....592
1993 Dream Team ....597
1993 Franchise ....597
1993 Ore-Ida QB Club ....598
1994 Samples ....598
1994 ....598
1994 Gold ....602
**Seahawks**
1977 Fred Meyer ....602
1977 Team Issue ....603
1978-80 Nalley's ....603
1980 7-Up ....603
1981 7-Up ....603
1982 7-Up ....604
1984 GTE ....604
1984 Nalley's ....604
1987 Snyder's/Franz ....604
1988 Domino's ....605
1988 GTE ....605
1988 Snyder's/Franz ....605
1989 Oroweat ....606
1990 Oroweat ....606
1991 Oroweat ....606
1992 Oroweat ....607
1993 Oroweat ....607
**Sears-Roebuck** ....608
**Select**
1993 ....608
1993 Gridiron Skills ....610
1993 Young Stars ....610
**7-Eleven**
1960 Dallas Texans ....610
1983 Coins ....612
1984 Coins ....612
**Shell Posters** ....613
**Signature Rookies**
1994 ....613
1994 Signatures ....614
**SkyBox**
1992 Impel Promos ....614
1992 Impact Promos ....615
1992 Impact ....615
1992 Impact Holograms ....619
1992 Impact Major Impact ....619
1992 Primetime Previews ....620
1992 Primetime ....620
1992 Primetime Poster Cards ....624
1993 Impact Promos ....625
1993 Promo Sheet ....625
1993 Celebrity Cycle Proto.* ....625
1993 ....626
1993 Poster Cards ....629
1993 Rookies ....629
1993 Thunder and Lightning ....629
1993 Impact ....630
1993 Impact Kelly/Magic ....633
1993 Impact Colors ....633
1993 Impact Rookie Redemption ....633
1993 Impact Update ....634
1994 Impact Super Bowl Promo ....634
1994 Impact Promos ....635
1994 Impact ....635
1994 Impact Instant Impact ....638
1994 Impact Ultimate Impact ....638
**Slam**
1992 Thurman Thomas ....639
1993 Jerome Bettis ....639
**Slim Jim** ....639
**Smokey**
1984 Invaders ....640
1985 49ers ....640
1985 Raiders ....641
1985 Rams ....641
1987 Chargers ....641
1987 Raiders Color-Grams ....642
1988 Chargers ....642
1988 49ers ....643
1988 Raiders ....643
1989 Chargers ....643
1989 Eagles ....644
1990 Chargers ....644
1990 Raiders ....645
**Sport Decks**
1992 Promo Aces ....645
1992 ....645
**Stadium Club**
1991 ....646
1992 Promo Sheet ....652
1992 ....652
1992 No.1 Draft Picks ....659
1992 QB Legends ....659
1993 Promo Sheet ....660
1993 ....660
1993 First Day Production ....666
1993 Master Photos I ....667
1993 Master Photos II ....667
1993 Super Team ....667
1993 Super Bowl Redemption ....668
1993 Master Photos Bills ....668
1993 AFC Winner Bills ....668
1993 Master Photos Cowboys ....669
1993 NFC Winner Cowboys ....669
1993 Division Winner Chiefs ....669
1993 Division Winner 49ers ....670
1993 Division Winner Lions ....670
1993 Division Winner Oilers ....670
**Stancraft Playing Cards** ....671
**Star-Cal Decals**
1989 ....671
1990 ....672
**Star Pics**
1991 Promos ....673
1991 ....673
1992 ....675
1992 StarStat Bonus ....676
**Steelers**
1961 Jay Publishing ....676
1963 IDL ....677
1968 KDKA ....677
1972 Photo Sheets ....678
**Stop'N'Go**
1979 ....678
1980 ....678
**Sunbeam NFL Helmet Die-Cuts** ....679
**Sunkist Fun Fruits** ....680
**Sunoco Stamps**
1972 ....680
1972 Update ....683
**Swell Greats**
1988 ....684
1989 ....685
1990 ....686
**TCMA**
1981 Greats ....688
1987 Update CMC ....688
**Titans Jay Publishing** ....688
**Topps**
1950 Felt Backs ....689
1951 Magic ....690
1955 All-American ....691
1956 ....692
1957 ....694
1958 ....696
1959 ....698
1960 ....700
1960 Metallic Inserts ....701
1961 ....702
1961 Flocked Stickers ....703
1962 ....704
1962 Bucks ....705
1963 ....706
1964 ....707
1964 Pennant Stickers ....708
1965 ....708
1965 Magic Rub-Off Inserts ....710
1966 ....710
1967 ....711
1967 Comic Pennants ....712
1968 ....712
1968 Posters ....715
1968 Stand-Ups ....715
1968 Test Teams ....716
1968 Team Patch/Stickers ....716
1969 ....716
1969 Four-in-One ....719
1969 Mini-Albums ....721
1970 ....721
1970 Super ....724
1970 Glossy ....725
1970 Poster Inserts ....725
1971 ....726
1971 Game ....729
1971 Posters ....730
1972 ....730
1973 ....734
1973 Team Checklists ....740
1974 ....740
1974 Team Checklists ....746
1975 ....747
1975 Team Checklists ....753
1976 ....753
1976 Team Checklists ....759
1977 ....759
1977 Team Checklists ....765
1977 Holsum Packers/Vikings ....765
1978 ....766
1978 Holsum ....772

1979 ... 772
1980 ... 778
1980 Super ... 785
1981 ... 785
1982 ... 791
1983 ... 795
1983 Sticker Inserts ... 798
1984 ... 799
1984 Glossy Send-In ... 801
1984 Glossy Inserts ... 802
1984 USFL ... 802
1985 ... 803
1985 Box Bottoms ... 806
1985 Glossy Inserts ... 806
1985 USFL ... 807
1985 USFL Generals ... 808
1986 ... 808
1986 Box Bottoms ... 811
1986 1000 Yard Club ... 811
1987 ... 812
1987 Box Bottoms ... 815
1987 1000 Yard Club ... 815
1987 American/UK ... 816
1988 ... 816
1988 Box Bottoms ... 819
1988 1000 Yard Club ... 820
1989 ... 820
1989 Box Bottoms ... 823
1989 1000 Yard Club ... 823
1989 Traded ... 824
1989 American/UK ... 825
1990 ... 826
1990 Box Bottoms ... 829
1990 1000 Yard Club ... 830
1990 Traded ... 830
1991 ... 832
1991 1000 Yard Club ... 836
1992 ... 836
1992 Gold ... 845
1992 No.1 Draft Picks ... 845
1992 Finest ... 845
1992 1000 Yard Club ... 846
1993 ... 846
1993 Black Gold ... 854
1993 FantaSports ... 854
1993 Gold ... 857
1994 ... 857
1994 Special Effects ... 861
1994 Finest Inserts ... 862
1994 Finest ... 862
1994 Finest Refractors ... 865
1994 Finest Rookie Jumbos ... 865
1994 Archives 1956 ... 866
1994 Archives 1957 ... 866
**Topps Album Stickers**
1981 ... 867
1981 Red Border ... 869
1982 "Coming Soon" ... 870
1982 ... 870
1983 Boxes ... 872
1983 ... 873
1984 ... 875
1985 "Coming Soon" ... 877
1985 ... 878
1986 ... 880
1987 ... 882
1988 ... 884
1988 Backs ... 886
**Touchdown Club** ... 886
**Tresler Comet Bengals** ... 887
**TV-4 NFL Quarterbacks** ... 887
**Ultimate**
1992 WLAF ... 888
1992 WLAF Logo Holograms ... 889
**Ultra**
1991 ... 890
1991 All-Stars ... 892
1991 Performances ... 892
1991 Update ... 892
1992 ... 893
1992 Award Winners ... 896
1992 Chris Miller ... 896
1992 Reggie White ... 897
1993 ... 897
1993 All-Rookies ... 900
1993 Award Winners ... 900
1993 Michael Irvin ... 900
1993 League Leaders ... 901
1993 Stars ... 901
1993 Touchdown Kings ... 901
**Upper Deck**
1991 Promos ... 902
1991 ... 902
1991 Heroes Joe Montana ... 910
1991 Heroes Montana Box ... 910
1991 Game Breaker Holograms ... 910
1991 Heroes Joe Namath ... 911
1991 Heroes Namath Box ... 911
1991 Sheets ... 911
1992 SCD Sheets ... 911
1992 NFL Sheets ... 912
1992 ... 913
1992 Coach's Report ... 919
1992 Fanimation ... 920
1992 Game Breaker Holograms ... 920
1992 Gold ... 921
1992 Heroes Dan Marino ... 921
1992 Heroes Marino Box ... 922
1992 Heroes Walter Payton ... 922
1992 Heroes Payton Box ... 922
1992 Pro Bowl ... 922
1992-93 NFL Experience ... 923
1993 ... 924
1993 America's Team ... 929
1993 Future Heroes ... 930
1993 Montana Box Bottom ... 930
1993 Pro Bowl ... 930
1993 Rookie Exchange ... 931
1993 Team MVPs ... 931
1993 SP Promo ... 931
1993 SP ... 932
1993 SP All-Pros ... 933
1993 Team Chiefs ... 934
1993 Team Cowboys ... 934
1993 Team 49ers ... 934
1993-94 Miller Lite SB ... 935
1994 Collector's Choice Proto ... 935
1994 National Samples ... 935
1994 Collector's Choice ... 936
1994 Collector's Choice Silver ... 940
**U.S. Playing Cards**
**Ditka's Picks** ... 940
**Vikings**
1967-68 ... 941
1971 Photos ... 941
1971 Postcards ... 941
1978 Country Kitchen ... 942
1989 Taystee Discs ... 942
**Wagon Wheel** ... 942
**Wheaties**
1964 Stamps ... 943
1987 ... 944
**Wild Card**
1991 National Promos ... 944
1991 Draft ... 944
1991 NFL Prototypes ... 946
1991 ... 947
1991 NFL Redemption Cards ... 949
1991 NFL Super Bowl Promos ... 949
1991-92 Redemption Proto ... 949
1992 NFL Prototypes ... 949
1992 ... 950
1992 Field Force ... 954
1992 Pro Picks ... 954
1992 Red Hot Rookies ... 955
1992 Running Wild Silver ... 955
1992 Stat Smashers ... 956
1992 WLAF ... 957
1992 Class Back Attack ... 958
1992 NASDAM ... 958
1992 NASDAM/SCAI Miami ... 958
1992 Sacramento CardFest ... 959
1992-93 San Francisco ... 959
1993 NFL Prototypes ... 959
1993 ... 959
1993 Bomb Squad ... 961
1993 Bomb Squad B/B ... 962
1993 Field Force ... 962
1993 Field Force Superchrome ... 964
1993 Red Hot Rookies ... 964
1993 Red Hot Rookies Superchrome ... 965
1993 Superchrome FF/RHR B/B ... 965
1993 Stat Smashers ... 965
1993 Stat Smashers Rookies ... 966
1993 Superchrome Promos ... 967
1993 Superchrome Rookies Promos ... 967
1993 Superchrome Rookies ... 967
1993 Superchrome Rookies B/B ... 968
**Ted Williams**
1994 Promos ... 969
1994 ... 969
1994 Auckland Collection ... 970
1994 Etched In Stone Unitas ... 970
1994 Instant Replays ... 970
1994 Path to Greatness ... 971
1994 Walter Payton ... 971
1994 POG Cards ... 971
**Wonder Bread**
1974 ... 972
1975 ... 972
1976 ... 973
**Wranglers Carl's Jr.** ... 973


## College Football


**Air Force Smokey** ... 974
**Alabama**
1972 ... 974
1973 ... 974
1988 Winners ... 975
1989 Coke 20 ... 975
1989 Coke 580 ... 976
1992 Greats Hoby ... 979
**Arizona**
1980 Police ... 979
1981 Police ... 980
1982 Police ... 980
1983 Police ... 980
1984 Police ... 981
1985 Police ... 981
1986 Police ... 981
1987 Police ... 982
1988 Police ... 982
1989 Police ... 982
1992 Police ... 983
**Army Smokey** ... 983
**Auburn**
1972 Tigers ... 983
1973 Tigers ... 984
1989 Coke 20 ... 984
1989 Coke 580 ... 985
1991 Hoby ... 988
**Baylor** ... 988
**BYU**
1984 All-Time Greats ... 989
1990 Safety ... 989
1991 Safety ... 989
1992 Safety ... 990
1993 ... 990
**California**
1988 Smokey ... 990
1989 Smokey ... 991
1990 Smokey ... 991
1991 Smokey ... 991
1992 Smokey ... 991
1993 Smokey ... 992
**Clemson** ... 992
**C.O.P. Betsy Ross** ... 992
**Colorado**
1990 Smokey ... 993
1993 Pepsi ... 993
1993 Smokey ... 993
1973 State ... 994
**Duke Police** ... 994
**Florida**
1988 Burger King ... 994
1989 ... 994
1989 Smokey ... 995
1990 Smokey ... 995
1991 Smokey ... 995
1993 State ... 996
**Fresno State**
1987 Burger King ... 996
1990 Smokey ... 996
**Georgia**
1988 McDag ... 996
1989 200 ... 997
1989 Police ... 998
1990 Police ... 998
1991 Police ... 998
1992 Police ... 999
1993 Police ... 999
1991 Southern ... 999
**Hawaii**
1989 ... 1000
1990 7-Eleven ... 1000
**Houston Motion Sports** ... 1001
**Humboldt State Smokey** ... 1001
**Idaho** ... 1001
**Illinois**
1990 Centennial ... 1002
1992 ... 1002
**Indiana State Police** ... 1003
**Iowa**
1984 ... 1003
1987 ... 1004
1988 ... 1004
1989 ... 1005
1993 ... 1005
**Kansas**
1989 ... 1006
1992 ... 1006
**Louisville**
1981 Police ... 1007
1990 Smokey ... 1008
1992 Kraft ... 1008
1993 Kraft ... 1008
**LSU**
1983 Sunbeam ... 1009
1985 Police ... 1009
1986 Police ... 1010
1987 Police ... 1010
1988 Police ... 1010
1989 Police ... 1010
1992 McDag ... 1011
**Maryland HS Big 33** ... 1011
**McNeese State McDag/Police**
1988 ... 1012
1989 ... 1012
1990 ... 1012
1991 ... 1012
1992 ... 1013
**Miami**
1990 Smokey ... 1013
1991 Police ... 1013
1992 Safety ... 1014
1993 Bumble Bee ... 1014
**Michigan**
1977 ... 1014
1989 ... 1015
**Mississippi Hoby** ... 1015
**Mississippi State** ... 1015
**Nebraska** ... 1016
**North Carolina Schedules** ... 1016
**North Carolina State** ... 1017
**North Texas McDag**
1989 ... 1017
1990 ... 1018
**Northwestern Louisiana State** ... 1018
**Notre Dame**
1988 ... 1018
1988 Smokey* ... 1019
1989 1903-32* ... 1019
1989 1935-59 ... 1019
1989 1964-87 ... 1020
1990 Promos ... 1020
1990 200 ... 1020
1990 60 ... 1022
1990 Greats ... 1022
1992 ... 1022
1993 ... 1023
**Oberlin College Heisman Club** ... 1023
**Ohio State**
1979 Greats ... 1024
1988 ... 1024
1989 ... 1024
1990 ... 1025
**Oklahoma**
1982 ... 1025
1986 ... 1025
1986 McDag ... 1026
1987 Police ... 1026
1988 Greats ... 1026
1988 Police ... 1027
1989 Police ... 1027
1991 Police ... 1027
**Oregon**
1953 ... 1027
1956 ... 1028
1958 ... 1028
1991 Smokey ... 1028
**Oregon State**
1988 Smokey ... 1028
1990 Smokey ... 1028
1991 Smokey ... 1029
1992 Smokey ... 1029
**Penn State**
1988 Police ... 1029
1989 Police ... 1030
1990 Police ... 1030
1991-92 Legends ... 1030
1992 Police ... 1031
1993 ... 1031
**Pennsylvania HS Big 33** ... 1031
**Pittsburgh**
1989 ... 1032
1990 Foodland ... 1032
1991 Foodland ... 1032
**Pitt State**
1991 ... 1033
1992 ... 1033
**Purdue Legends Smokey** ... 1033
**Rice**
1990 Aetna ... 1034
1991 Aetna ... 1034

1992 Taco Cabana.................1034
1993 Taco Cabana.................1034
**San Jose State Smokey**.............1035
**Southern Cal**
1974 Discs........................1035
1988 Smokey......................1035
1988 Winners.....................1036
1989 Smokey......................1036
1991 College Classics*...........1037
1991 Smokey......................1038
1992 Smokey......................1038
**Southwestern Louisiana 1988**.1038
**Stanford**
1991 All-Century.................1039
1992............................1039
1993............................1040
**Syracuse**
1989 Burger King.................1040
1991 Program Cards...............1040
**Tennessee**
1980 Police......................1041
1990 Centennial..................1041
1991 Hoby........................1043
**Texas HS Legends**.................1043
**Texas Taco Bell**..................1044
**Texas A and M**....................1044
**UNLV**.............................1045
**Versailles HS**....................1045
**Virginia**
1990............................1046
1992 Coca-Cola...................1046
1993 Coca-Cola...................1046
**Washington**
1973 KFC.........................1047
1988 Smokey......................1047
1990 Smokey *....................1047
1991 Smokey *....................1048
1992 Pay Less....................1048
1992 Greats/Pacific..............1048
1993 Safeway.....................1049
**Washington State Smokey**
1988............................1049
1990 *..........................1050
1991 *..........................1050
1992 *..........................1050
**West Virginia**
1974............................1051
1988............................1051
1990 Program Cards...............1051
1991 ATG........................1052
1991 Program Cards...............1052
1992 Program Cards...............1053
1993............................1053

**Wisconsin Program Cards**.........1054
**Wyoming Smokey**
1990............................1054
1993............................1054
**Youngstown State**.................1055

## Canadian Football
**All World**
1991 Promo.......................1055
1991............................1055
1992 Promos......................1057
1992............................1057
**Bantam/FBI CFL Discs**.............1058
**Blue Ribbon Tea CFL**..............1058
**Bootlegger B.C. Lions**............1059
**Chiquita CFL All-Stars**...........1059
**CKNW B.C. Lions**
1961............................1060
1962............................1060
**Coke Caps CFL**....................1060
**Crown Brand**......................1062
**Dairy Lids Saskatchewan Roughriders**......................1062
**Dream Cards Winnipeg Bombers**............................1062
**Edmonton Journal Eskimos**
1981............................1063
1984............................1063
**JOGO**
1981 B/W.........................1063
1982 Ottawa......................1064
1982-84 Ottawa Past..............1064
1983 Quarterbacks................1064
1983 Hall of Fame A..............1065
1983 Hall of Fame B..............1065
1983 Limited.....................1066
1984............................1067
1985............................1068
1985 Ottawa Program Inserts......1068
1986............................1068
1987............................1070
1988............................1070
1988 League......................1071
1989............................1072
1990............................1073
1991 Ismail Promo................1075
1991............................1075
1991 Stamp Card Inserts..........1077
1992 Promos......................1077
1992 Charlton Inserts............1077
1992............................1077
1992 Missing Years...............1079
1992 Stamp Cards.................1079

1993............................1079
1993 Missing Years...............1081
1994 Caravan.....................1081
**KFC Calgary**
1989............................1082
1990............................1082
**McDonald's Ottawa**................1082
**Mohawk B.C. Lions**
1983............................1082
1984............................1083
1985............................1083
**Nalley's**
1963 Coins.......................1083
1964 Coins.......................1084
1976 Chips.......................1085
**O-Pee-Chee**
1968............................1086
1968 Poster Inserts..............1086
1970............................1087
1970 Push-Out Inserts............1088
1971............................1088
1971 Poster Inserts..............1089
1972............................1089
1972 Trio Sticker Inserts........1090
**Parkhurst**
1952............................1091
1956............................1092
**Police**
1982 Hamilton....................1092
1982 Saskatchewan................1092
1982 Winnipeg....................1093
1983 Hamilton....................1093
1983 Saskatchewan................1093
1984 Ottawa......................1094
1985 Ottawa......................1094
**Post Cereal**
1962............................1094
1963............................1095
**Queen's University**...............1096
**Red Lobster**
1981 Calgary Stampeders..........1097
1981 Edmonton Eskimos............1097
**Royal Bank B.C. Lions**
1971............................1098
1972............................1098
1973............................1098
1974............................1099
1975............................1099
1976............................1099
1977............................1099
1978............................1099
**Sargent Promotions Stamps**.......1100
**Shredded Wheat**...................1101

**Topps**
1958............................1102
1959............................1102
1960............................1103
1961............................1104
1962............................1105
1963............................1106
1964............................1107
1965............................1107
**Vachon**
1988............................1108
1989............................1109
**Wheaties**.........................1110

## Index to Advertisers
Athleticards........................23
AU Sports Memorabilia...............23
Beverly Hills Baseball............1118
Mike Blaisdell....................1113
Blandford Cards & Stuff...........1118
Brewart Coins & Stamps............1118
Don Chubey.........................21
Joe Colabella......................11
Collector's World.................1118
Columbia City Collectibles..........9
Cornell & Finkelmeier.............1116
Dave & Alex's.....................1118
Bill Dodge.........................19
Rick Donohoo......................1117
First Base.........................25
Foot's Hobbies & Collectibles......27
Four C's..........................1118
Larry Fritsch......................13
JEM Associates.....................17
JOGO, Inc.........................1119
Oldies and Goodies................1115
Bob Pauly.........................1118
Portland Sports Card Co...........1115
Ragtime...........................1118
Randy's Sportscards...............1118
Reno Sports Cards..................25
Slam Trading Cards.................21
Smokey's...........................15
Sports Fever......................1118
Bob Swick.........................1118
Touchdown Cards...................1117
Two Capitals Card Co..............1118
University Trading Cards..........1118
Whiz Kid Promotions...............1113
Zindler's Baseball Card Co.........27

# About the Author

Jim Beckett, the leading authority on sport card values in the United States, maintains a wide range of activities in the world of sports. He possesses one of the finest collections of sports cards and autographs in the world, has made numerous appearances on radio and television, and has been frequently cited in many national publications. He was awarded the first "Special Achievement Award" for Contributions to the Hobby by the National Sports Collectors Convention in 1980, the "Jock-Jaspersen Award" for Hobby Dedication in 1983, and the "Buck Barker, Spirit of the Hobby" Award in 1991.

Dr. Beckett is the author of *The Sport Americana Baseball Card Price Guide, The Official Price Guide to Baseball Cards, The Sport Americana Price Guide to Baseball Collectibles, The Sport Americana Baseball Memorabilia and Autograph Price Guide, The Sport Americana Football Card Price Guide, The Official Price Guide to Football Cards, The Sport Americana Hockey Card Price Guide, The Official Price Guide to Hockey Cards, The Sport Americana Basketball Card Price Guide and Alphabetical Checklist, The Official Price Guide to Basketball Cards, and The Sport Americana Baseball Card Alphabetical Checklist.* In addition, he is the founder, publisher, and editor of *Beckett Baseball Card Monthly, Beckett Basketball Monthly, Beckett Football Card Monthly, Beckett Hockey Monthly, Beckett Focus on Future Stars, Beckett Tribute:,* and *Beckett Racing Monthly* magazines.

Jim Beckett received his Ph.D. in Statistics from Southern Methodist University in 1975. Prior to starting Beckett Publications in 1984, Dr. Beckett served as an Associate Professor of Statistics at Bowling Green State University and as a Vice President of a consulting firm in Dallas, Texas. He currently resides in Dallas with his wife, Patti, and their daughters, Christina, Rebecca, and Melissa.

## How To Use This Book

Isn't it great? Every year this book gets bigger and bigger with all the new sets coming out. But even more exciting is that every year there are more attractive choices and, subsequently, more interest in the cards we love so much. This edition

has been enhanced and expanded from the previous edition. The cards you collect — who appears on them, what they look like, where they are from, and (most important to most of you) what their current values are — enumerated within. Many of the features contained in the other *Beckett Price Guides* have been incorporated into this volume since condition grading, terminology, and many other aspects of collecting are common to the card hobby in general. We hope you find the book both interesting and useful in your collecting pursuits.

The *Beckett Guide* has been successful where other attempts have failed because it is complete, current, and valid. This Price Guide contains not just one, but three prices by condition for all the football cards listed. These account for most of the football cards in existence. The prices were added to the card lists just prior to printing and reflect not the author's opinions or desires but the going retail prices for each card, based on the marketplace (sports memorabilia conventions and shows, sports card shops, hobby papers, current mail-order catalogs, local club meetings, auction results, and other firsthand reportings of actually realized prices).

What is the best price guide available on the market today? Of course card sellers will prefer the price guide with the highest prices, while card buyers will naturally prefer the one with the lowest prices. Accuracy, however, is the true test. Use the price guide used by more collectors and dealers than all the others combined. Look for the Beckett name. I won't put my name on anything I won't stake my reputation on. Not the lowest and not the highest — but the most accurate, with integrity.

To facilitate your use of this book, read the complete introductory section on the following pages before going to the pricing pages. Every collectible field has its own terminology; we've tried to capture most of these terms and definitions in our glossary. Please read carefully the section on grading and the condition of your cards, as you will not be able to determine which price column is appropriate for a given card without first knowing its condition.

*Jim Beckett*

# 1993 Football Cards Year in Review

## by James E. Smith

Another year passed during which hobbyists found themselves torn between two extremes. They divided their time protesting the overabundance of football trading card sets while, at the same time, chasing the most beautiful cards our hobby has ever seen.

The crowded market spurred predictions that cardmakers finally would begin to fall by the wayside. The concern seemed warranted: A daunting array of 1993-94 listings in *Beckett Football Card Monthly* included 24 sets with more than 8,500 regular cards and 3,000 inserts. The choices became more than tough for some collectors; they became impossible. It was the collector, and not the cardmaker, who seemed prepared to take a powder.

Given the crowded playing field, all 12 licensed cardmakers faced the challenge of grabbing some attention and securing a solid foothold. By season's end, one manufacturer was fighting for its NFL life. Wild Card, which joined football's expansion fleet in 1991, was embroiled in a licensing dispute with NFL Properties and the NFL Players Association.

## Technical Knockouts

What kept collectors buying products and opening packs was an impressive lineup of tempting issues that stretched the limits of technology and imagination. Manufacturers followed a new strategy of lowering production and adding bells and whistles. It was hard to find a set that didn't incorporate at least one new technological touch.

Techniques such as gold-embossing, UV-coating and full-bleed photography, now the rule rather than the exception, were joined by chromium accents, Tekchrome processes and ghosting effects. Indeed, it became questionable as to how much board was actually used

**Upper Deck SP and its insert set stretched the playing field in '93.**

in the cardboard images of 1993.

Content matched form, as NFL Properties and the Players Association resolved an ongoing disagreement that had limited the availability of players in most sets. For the first time since 1990, manufacturers by and large enjoyed equal access to the full complement of players.

Some of the established cardmakers brought popular issues from other sports into the field of play. Upper Deck's top line, SP, played to rave reviews and enticed collectors with a 15-card All-Pros insert set. Topps brought back Bowman for a second run after watching the late-breaking 1992 debut series fly off the shelves in early '93.

## Chasing a Dream

Insert cards again caught the eyes of collectors. Among the most imaginative were the Super Team cards from Stadium Club, a gimmick which saw the values of the cards fluctuate on a weekly basis based on the performances of the teams. Stadium Club scored another victory with its hard-to-pull First Day Production cards.

Playoff, a second-year player with its thicker stock and Tekchrome processing, produced one of the widest assortments of sets, including Playoff Club, Contenders, Rookie Contenders and a pair of redemption card offers. Action Packed once again claimed the richest set in the hobby with its 24K gold cards.

ProLine, taken over by Classic Games in 1993, had 35 players autograph varying numbers of cards that were randomly inserted in packs of its regular product. Fleer gave collectors a bigger choice by taking over the oversized GameDay line. Wild Card caused a controversy by releasing its much-publicized Superchrome cards in the early days of its licensing dispute with the NFL.

There was no shortage of special issue sets. Action Packed produced Monday Night Football and the 10th Anniversary All-Madden Team; Classic Games had the NFL Experience Super Bowl set; Coca-Cola produced Monsters of the Gridiron; Pacific Trading Cards repeated production of Triple Folders; Pinnacle Brands

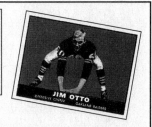

# JOE COLABELLA

*Specializing In Mail Order*

P. O. Box 4186-Z
Clearlake, CA 95422
Phone / Fax (707) 995-1157

*Want Lists Solicited*

## SPECIALIZING IN FOOTBALL CARDS

1935-1967 National Chicle, Leaf, Bowman, Topps, Fleer, Philadelphia

## SELLING

Fill in the missing numbers in your collections from my extensive — always changing inventory — most conditions are available from very good for the average collector to EX-MT for the quality buyer.

**SEND YOUR WANT LISTS!**

## BUYING

I am always interested in buying sets and accumulations of early football cards-ship via registered mail for my offer — all lots are kept intact pending your approval!

# 1 9 9 3

## HOT

1. Emmitt Smith
2. Troy Aikman
3. Barry Sanders
4. Brett Favre
5. Ricky Watters
6. Michael Irvin
7. Barry Foster
8. Dan Marino
9. Joe Montana
10. Sterling Sharpe
11. Steve Young
12. Jerry Rice
13. Thurman Thomas
14. Deion Sanders
15. Reggie White
16. Art Monk
17. Junior Seau
18. Randall Cunningham
19. Dallas Cowboys
20. Drew Bledsoe

## COLD

1. Mark Rypien
2. Bo Jackson
3. John Elway
4. Jim Kelly
5. Joe Montana
6. Boomer Esiason
7. Barry Sanders
8. Dan McGwire
9. Thurman Thomas
   Jeff George
10. Todd Marinovich

Above are the cumulative "Weather Report" rankings from the 1993 issues of *Beckett Football Card Monthly*. Readers' votes determine rankings, which are good indicators of players' popularity and, to a lesser extent, card values. The Hottest and Coldest players are ranked No. 1.

After a successful 1992, Bowman made another run at collectors.

trotted out a Young Stars Collection; and GameDay hooked up with McDonald's Restaurants for a special promotional set.

NFL Properties even got into the act. With the cooperation of its major licensees, the NFL released a 13-card Santa Claus mail-in set that many collectors may have missed. The Ted Williams Card Company expanded into football using Roger Staubach as its signal caller. Country crooner Hank Williams Jr., who sang the popular lyric "Are You Ready For Some Football," was added to Action Packed's Monday Night Football set as a special mail-in offer.

### The Old Guard

To label the vintage card market (pre-1981) soft would be misleading. Prices always have been reasonable for early football issues and that trend continued through 1993.

While older cards in Good to Fair condition could be purchased for bargain-basement prices, the same could not be said of the higher grades, which held their values in most cases. Collectors looking for cards of popular Hall of Famers like Jim Brown, Johnny Unitas and Joe Namath had to search hard for good deals. There was renewed interest in the cards of footballer-turned-politician Jack Kemp.

Several older sets improved their places in the hobby, among them 1963 Fleer featuring Len Dawson's Rookie Card and oversized 1965 Topps sporting Namath's debut card.

Unlike baseball, which exploded in the 1980s and saw its popularity begin to wane in the '90s, football has never occupied the dizzying heights and therefore has not had to cope with radi-

cal change. Vintage football sets remain steady performers, and their defensive stars still are considered underrated by some collectors.

The first year of free agency (1993) dramatically altered the individual makeup of NFL teams, and trading cards provided a fitting platform from which to view the changing landscape. With big-name players changing teams and colors like never before, cards kept collectors in touch with the transactions. It's not always easy to accept the reality that a superstar like Joe Montana will not be forever cast in a 49ers uniform, or that a dominating defenseman like Reggie White will not always be the featured attraction in Philly.

**Action Packed and Bettis turned in 24-karat performances.**

The truth is professional sports is big business, and NFL fans in 1993 got a first-hand view of the once unthinkable: Joe as a Chief and Reggie as a Packer. Trading cards helped us assimilate the changes and eased the transition to this season, which will show such unfamiliar sights as Warren Moon in a Minnesota uniform.

## The Drawing Cards

Some exciting new players provided hobbyists with a nice blend of rookie and veteran stars to follow and collect. Here's a look at some of the dynamos who drove the hobby:

**Emmitt Smith** held out the first two games, then picked up where he left off in 1992 by leading the league in rushing for the third straight season and helping the Cowboys repeat as Super Bowl champs. Smith's cards, particularly his two best 1990 update issues (Fleer Update #U40 and Score Supplemental #101T), have been wildfire.

**Troy Aikman** enjoyed another year of productivity and popularity, and while quarterbacking the Cowboys clean

**Playoff's glitz captured flashy rookies like the Pats' Bledsoe.**

through the NFL once again, was awarded the richest quarterback contract in NFL history.

**Jerome Bettis**, who nearly ended Smith's rushing title reign, carried the Rams with seven 100-yard games and 1,429 yards overall, numbers that earned him Rookie of the Year honors and sent collectors scurrying for his cards.

**Drew Bledsoe** and **Rick Mirer**, the first two selections of the 1993 draft, have been hard to separate. Both performed admirably for rookie quarterbacks thrown into the fire, Bledsoe with the rebuilding New England Patriots and Mirer in Seattle. Instantly popular with collectors, these stars could rise with the improvement of their respective teams.

**Barry Sanders**, sidelined by injury the final five games of the regular season, still became the third back in NFL history to gain 1,000 yards in his first five seasons (he finished with 1,115 in '93). The 1989 Score Rookie Cards of Sanders (#257) and Aikman (#270) remain the benchmarks of an extremely popular release.

The play that knocked Sanders and the Lions out of the playoffs gave a boost to a pair of popular Packers. **Brett Favre**, who suffered through a hot-cold second year in Green Bay, reminded hobbyists of his Starr-like potential with a lightning strike to **Sterling Sharpe**, the NFL's most productive receiver. While Favre's early cards from 1991 remain available at lower-level prices, Sharpe's 1989 Score Supplemental Rookie (#333S) — like Sterling himself — continues its strong performance.

**Barry Foster** of Pittsburgh let his actions do most of the talking. Despite missing seven games due to injury, Foster garnered Pro Bowl honors while sparking interest in his Rookie issues, particularly his 1990 Score Supplemental (#110T).

**Michael Irvin**, yet another of the exciting rookies featured in 1989 Score (#18), remained in the spotlight as Aikman's primary target on the Super Bowl champions. Only Sharpe and Jerry Rice caught more passes than Irvin among NFL receivers.

On a somber note, **O.J. Simpson** made hobby news for all the wrong reasons. All of the Hall of Famer's issues, including his Rookie Card (1970 Topps #90), fluctuated wildly, mostly upward, during the media blitz covering the stabbing deaths of Nicole Simpson and Ronald Goldman.

The beat went on for a handful of veteran quarterbacks who spent the season padding their impressive credentials. **Joe Montana** not only looked good in his new Arrowhead helmet; he played well enough to earn Pro Bowl honors. His 1981 Topps Rookie (#216) is one of the most coveted cards in the hobby, and his new cards in K.C. colors were hotly pursued in Kansas and Missouri.

**Steve Young** made the most of Montana's old target, **Jerry Rice**, who finished the season just two touchdowns short of Jim Brown's NFL record of 126. Both Pro Bowlers continued their productive ways while driving their cards to new levels of popularity. The 1986 Topps set contains the first NFL issues of both players, although Young's debut is in the popular and pricey 1984 Topps USFL (#52) set.

**Jim Kelly** and **Dan Marino** maintained their lofty positions in the hobby despite unrelated misfortunes. Kelly and the Bills lost another Super Bowl, while Marino went down with a season-ending injury in the fifth game. Marino, in fact, cut across hobby currents by gaining in popularity during his absence.

**John Elway** had a spectacular season, passing for more than 4,000 yards to earn AFC Player of the Year honors.

**Chief Joe and his Rookie Card continued their classic ways.**

As Elway moved into third place in career passing yardage among active quarterbacks, his 1984 Topps Rookie Card (#63) nudged upward in value.

## A Look Ahead

The hobby may have lost some football collectors in the 1990s, but those who have hung on have been rewarded with the best quality and assortment of cards ever put on shelves. Any predictions of further slippage are counteracted by two positive factors: The popularity of the sport and the continuing efforts of cardmakers to invent appealing products.

That quest for market share continues in 1994 with the debut of three major sets: the superpremium Topps Finest and Collector's Edge Excalibur and Upper Deck's base brand, Collector's Choice.

Football has the biggest audience among the professional team sports. It continues to provide great theatre as it showcases some of the world's most exciting athletes. While that doesn't automatically translate into more collectors, it's a solid foundation from which to grow and unquestionably the reason why manufacturers continue to invest heavily in the sport.

Because of that, guarded optimism reigned in 1993 and seems sure to color our hobby in the near future. The NFL's liberal licensing policy may have fostered a competitive environment that now listens intently to collectors, but it also created a crowded playing field.

No one knows how long it will take before a balance is struck and hobbyists can focus again solely on the joys of collecting. Fortunately, more and more segments of our hobby are becoming willing partners in that challenge.

**A third rushing crown stoked Emmitt's 1990 update issues.**

*James E. Smith is a freelance writer based in the Twin Cities.*

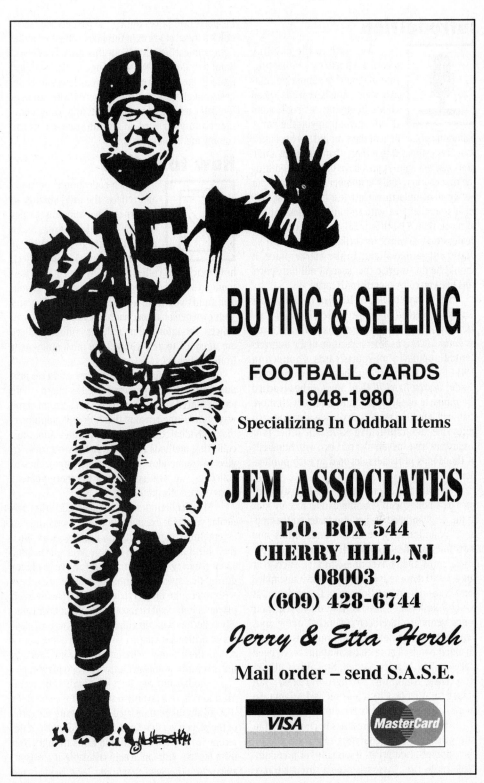

# Introduction

Welcome to the exciting world of sports card collecting, one of America's most popular avocations. You have made a good choice in buying this book, since it will open up to you the entire panorama of this field in the simplest, most concise way. It is estimated that more than a third of a million different sports cards have been issued during the past century. And the number of total cards put out by all manufacturers last year has been estimated at several billion, with an initial wholesale price of more than $1 billion. Sales of older cards by dealers may account for a like amount. With all that cardboard available in the marketplace, it should be no surprise that several million sports fans like you collect sports cards today.

The growth of *Beckett Baseball Card Monthly*, *Beckett Basketball Monthly*, *Beckett Football Card Monthly*, *Beckett Hockey Monthly*, and *Beckett Focus on Future Stars* is another indication of the unprecedented popularity of sports cards. Founded in 1984 by Dr. James Beckett, the author of this Price Guide, *Beckett Baseball Card Monthly* has reached the pinnacle of the sports card hobby, with more than half a million readers anxiously awaiting each enjoyable and informative issue. The other four magazines have met similar success, with hundreds of thousands of readers devoted to each publication.

So collecting sports cards — while still pursued as a hobby with youthful exuberance by kids in the neighborhood — has also taken on the trappings of an industry, with thousands of full- and part-time card dealers, as well as vendors of supplies, clubs and conventions. In fact, each year since 1980 thousands of hobbyists have assembled for a National Sports Collectors Convention, at which hundreds of dealers have displayed their wares, seminars have been conducted, autographs penned by sports notables, and millions of cards changed hands. These colossal affairs have been staged in Los Angeles, Detroit, St. Louis, Chicago, New York, Anaheim, Arlington (Texas), San Francisco, Atlantic City, Houston and Atlanta. So sports card collecting really is national in scope!

This increasing interest has been reflected in card values. As more collectors compete for available supplies, card prices (especially for premium-grade cards) rise. There has been a strong advance in sports card prices during the past decade, and a quick perusal of prices in this book compared to the figures in earlier editions of this Price Guide will demonstrate this. Which brings us back around again to the book you have in your hands. It is the best annual guide available to this exciting world of football cards. Read it and use it. May your enjoyment and your card collection increase in the coming months and years.

# How to Collect

Each collection is personal and reflects the individuality of its owner. There are no set rules on how to collect cards. Since card collecting is a hobby or leisure pastime, what you collect, how much you collect, and how much time and money you spend collecting are entirely up to you. The funds you have available for collecting and your own personal taste should determine how you collect. The information and ideas presented here are intended to help you get the most enjoyment from this hobby.

It is impossible to collect every card ever produced. Therefore, beginners as well as intermediate and advanced collectors usually specialize in some way. One of the reasons this hobby is popular is that individual collectors can define and tailor their collecting methods to match their own tastes. To give you some ideas of the various approaches to collecting, we will list some of the more popular areas of specialization.

Many collectors select complete sets from particular years. For example, they may concentrate on assembling complete sets from all the years since their birth or since they became avid sports fans. They may try to collect a card for every player during that specified period of time. Many others wish to acquire only certain players. Usually such players are the superstars of the sport, but occasionally collectors will specialize in all the cards of players who attended a particular college or came from a certain town. Some collectors are only interested in the first cards or Rookie Cards of certain players.

Another fun way to collect cards is by team. Most fans have a favorite team, and it is natural for that loyalty to be translated into a desire for cards of the players on that favorite team. For most of the recent years, team sets (all the cards from a given team for that year) are readily available at a reasonable price. *The Sport Americana Team Football and*

# Football Sets & Wax Boxes

## Football Sets

| | |
|---|---|
| 1993 Topps (660) | $35.00 |
| 1991 Topps (660) | 20.00 |
| 1990 Topps (528) | 16.00 |
| 1992 Collectors Edge (175) | 85.00 |
| 1992 Fleer (480) | 12.00 |
| 1991 Fleer (432) | 10.00 |
| 1991 Fleer Ultra (400) | 15.00 |
| 1991 Pacific Series 1 (550) | 10.00 |
| 1994 Pro Line (405) | 25.00 |
| 1993 Pro Line (450) | 30.00 |
| 1992 Pro Line (687) | 18.00 |
| 1990 Pro Set Series 1 (377) | 10.00 |
| 1990 Pro Set Series 2 (392) | 10.00 |
| 1991 Score (690) | 10.00 |
| 1990 Score (665) | 10.00 |
| 1992 Upper Deck Lo No. (400) | 20.00 |
| 1991 Upper Deck (700) | 30.00 |

## Football Traded Sets

| | |
|---|---|
| 1993 Stadium Club High Series (51) | 18.00 |
| 1992 Topps Series 3 (113) | 20.00 |
| 1990 Topps (132) | 20.00 |
| 1989 Topps (132) | 12.00 |
| 1991 Upper Deck Hi No. (200) | 8.00 |
| 1991 Score (110) | 10.00 |
| 1990 Score (110) | 100.00 |
| 1989 Score (110) | 30.00 |
| 1990 Fleer Update (120) | 55.00 |
| 1991 Fleer Ultra Update (110) | 30.00 |
| 1991 Action Packed Rookies (84) | 27.00 |

## Football Specialty Sets

| | |
|---|---|
| Barry Sanders Arena Hologram (1) | 5.00 |
| Joe Montana Arena Hologram (1) | 5.00 |
| 1991 Pro Set World League (32) | 15.00 |
| Collect-A-Books (36) | 7.00 |
| Pro Set Super Bowl XXV Commemorative (160) | 5.00 |
| 1990 Score Young Superstars (40) | 6.00 |
| 1991 Star Pics (113) | 8.00 |
| 1991 Upper Deck/Domino's QB (50) | 10.00 |
| 1992 Upper Deck NFL Experience (50) | 17.00 |
| 1980 Topps Supers (30) | 15.00 |
| 1991 Wild Card Collegiate (160) | 12.00 |

## Football Wax Boxes

| | |
|---|---|
| 1994 Topps Series 1 (432) | 31.00 |
| 1993 Topps Series 1 (576) | 25.00 |
| 1993 Topps Series 2 (576) | 25.00 |

| | |
|---|---|
| 1992 Topps Series 2 (540) | 25.00 |
| 1992 Topps Series 3 (540) | 35.00 |
| 1992 Stadium Club Series 2 (540) | 35.00 |
| 1991 Stadium Club (432) | 160.00 |
| 1991 Action Packed Rookies (144) | 45.00 |
| 1991 Action Packed All Madden (144) | 30.00 |
| 1993 Bowman (336) | 50.00 |
| 1994 Classic Draft Pick (360) | 40.00 |
| 1992 Classic Draft Pick (360) | 25.00 |
| 1993 Collectors Edge (144) | 50.00 |
| 1992 Collectors Edge (144) | 50.00 |
| 1992 Fleer (612) | 15.00 |
| 1990 Fleer (540) | 12.00 |
| 1991 Fleer Ultra (504) | 13.00 |
| 1993 Roger Staubach (360) | 49.00 |
| 1994 Pro Line (360) | 45.00 |
| 1993 Pro Line (432) | 30.00 |
| 1992 Pro Line (432) | 15.00 |
| 1991 Score Pinnacle (432) | 45.00 |
| 1993 Score Select (432) | 145.00 |
| 1993 Skybox Premium (360) | 40.00 |
| 1994 Upper Deck Collectors Choice (432) | 35.00 |
| 1991 Upper Deck Lo (432) | 18.00 |
| 1991 Upper Deck Hi (432) | 18.00 |

## Pro Line Autographs

**Each autographed card is certified authentic by the NFL.**

Over 1,000 different cards in stock.
Call or write for prices.
INCLUDES 1991 THRU 1994

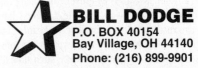

*Basketball Card Checklist* will open up this field to the collector.

## Obtaining Cards

Several avenues are open to card collectors. Cards still can be purchased in the traditional way: by the pack at the local discount, grocery or convenience stores. But there are also thousands of card shops across the country that specialize in selling cards individually or by the pack, box, or set. Another alternative is the thousands of card shows held each month around the country, which feature anywhere from five to 800 tables of sports cards and memorabilia for sale.

For many years, it has been possible to purchase complete sets of cards through mail-order advertisers found in traditional sports media publications, such as *The Sporting News, Football Digest, Street & Smith* yearbooks, and others. These sets also are advertised in the card collecting periodicals. Many collectors will begin by subscribing to at least one of the hobby periodicals, all with good up-to-date information. In fact, subscription offers can be found in the advertising section of this book.

Most serious card collectors obtain old (and new) cards from one or more of several main sources: (1) trading or buying from other collectors or dealers; (2) responding to sale or auction ads in the hobby publications; (3) buying at a local hobby store; and/or (4) attending sports collectibles shows or conventions.

We advise that you try all four methods since each has its own distinct advantages: (1) trading is a great way to make new friends; (2) hobby periodicals help you keep up with what's going on in the hobby (including when and where the conventions are happening); (3) stores provide the opportunity to enjoy personalized service and consider a great diversity of material in a relaxed sports-oriented atmosphere; and (4) shows allow you to choose from multiple dealers and thousands of cards under one roof in a competitive situation.

## Preserving Your Cards

Cards are fragile. They must be handled properly in order to retain their value. Careless handling can easily result in creased or bent cards. It is, however, not recommended that tweezers or tongs be used to pick up your cards since such utensils might mar or indent card surfaces and thus reduce those cards' conditions and values. In general, your cards should be handled directly as little as possible. This is sometimes easier to say than to do.

Although there are still many who use custom boxes, storage trays, or even shoe boxes, plastic sheets are the preferred method of many collectors for storing cards. A collection stored in plastic pages in a three-ring album allows you to view your collection at any time without the need to touch the card itself. Cards can also be kept in single holders (of various types and thickness) designed for the enjoyment of each card individually. For a large collection, some collectors may use a combination of the above methods. When purchasing plastic sheets for your cards, be sure that you find the pocket size that fits the cards snugly. Don't put your 1951 Bowmans in a sheet designed to fit 1981 Topps.

Most hobby and collectibles shops and virtually all collectors' conventions will have these plastic pages available in quantity for the various sizes offered, or you can purchase them directly from the advertisers in this book. Also, remember that pocket size isn't the only factor to consider when looking for plastic sheets. Other factors such as safety, economy, appearance, availability, or personal preference also may indicate which types of sheets a collector may want to buy.

Damp, sunny and/or hot conditions — no, this is not a weather forecast — are three elements to avoid in extremes if you are interested in preserving your collection. Too much (or too little) humidity can cause gradual deterioration of a card. Direct, bright sun (or fluorescent light) over time will bleach out the color of a card. Extreme heat accelerates the decomposition of the card. On the other hand, many cards have lasted more than 50 years without much scientific intervention. So be cautious, even if the above factors typically present a problem only when present in the extreme. It never hurts to be prudent.

## Collecting vs. Investing

Collecting individual players and collecting complete sets are both popular vehicles for investment and speculation. Most investors and speculators stock up on complete sets or on quantities of players they think have good investment potential.

There is obviously no guarantee in this book, or anywhere else for that matter, that cards will outperform the stock market or other investment alternatives in the future. After all, football cards do not pay quarterly dividends and cards cannot be

sold at their "current values" as easily as stocks or bonds.

Nevertheless, investors have noticed a favorable long-term trend in the past performance of sports collectibles, and certain cards and sets have outperformed just about any other investment in some years. Many hobbyists maintain that the best investment is and always will be the building of a collection, which traditionally has held up better than outright speculation.

Some of the obvious questions are: Which cards? When to buy? When to sell? The best investment you can make is in your own education. The more you know about your collection and the hobby, the more informed the decisions you will be able to make. We're not selling investment tips. We're selling information about the current value of football cards. It's up to you to use that information to your best advantage.

# Terminology

Each hobby has its own language to describe its area of interest. The terminology traditionally used for trading cards is derived from the *American Card Catalog*, published in 1960 by Nostalgia Press. That catalog, written by Jefferson Burdick (who is called the "Father of Card Collecting" for his pioneering work), uses letter and number designations for each separate set of cards. The letter used in the ACC designation refers to the generic type of card. While both sport and non-sport issues are classified in the ACC, we shall confine ourselves to the sport issues. The following list defines the letters and their meanings as used by the *American Card Catalog*, as applied to football cards:

> **(none) or N** - 19th Century U.S. Tobacco
> **F** - Food Inserts
> **H** - Advertising
> **M** - Periodicals
> **N** - 19th Century U.S. Tobacco
> **PC** - Postcards
> **R** - Recent Candy and Gum Cards, 1930 to Present
> **UO** - Gas and Oil Inserts
> **V** - Canadian Candy
> **W** - Exhibits, Strip Cards, Team Cards

Following the letter prefix and an optional hyphen are one-, two-, or three-digit numbers, R(-)999. These typically represent the company or

entity issuing the cards. In several cases, the ACC number is extended by an additional hyphen and another one- or two-digit numerical suffix. For example, the 1957 Topps regular-series football card issue carries an ACC designation of R415-5. The "R" indicates a Candy or Gum card produced since 1930. The "415" is the ACC designation for the 1957 regular issue (Topps fifth football set).

Like other traditional methods of identification, this system provides order to the process of cataloging cards; however, most serious collectors learn the ACC designation of the popular sets by repetition and familiarity, rather than by attempting to "figure out" what they might or should be. From 1948 forward, collectors and dealers commonly refer to all sets by their year, maker, type of issue, and any other distinguishing characteristic. For example, such a characteristic could be an unusual issue or one of several regular issues put out by a specific maker in a single year. Regional issues are usually referred to by year, maker, and sometimes by title or theme of the set.

## Glossary/Legend

Our glossary defines terms frequently used in the card collecting hobby. Many of these terms are also common to other types of sports memorabilia collecting. Some terms may have several meanings depending on use and context.

**ACC** - Acronym for American Card Catalog.

**AFC** - American Football Conference.

**AFL** - American Football League.

**AP** - All-Pro card. A card that portrays an All-Pro player of the previous year, that says "All Pro" on its face.

**AR** - Archrivals.

**AS** - All-Star.

**AT** - Aerial Threats.

**ATG** - All Time Great card.

**INSERT** - A special card or other collectible (often a poster or sticker) contained in the same package along with cards of a major set. Sometimes called a CHASE CARD.

**BOX** - Card issued on a box.

**BRICK** - A group or "lot" or cards, usually 50 or more having common characteristics, that is intended to be bought, sold, or traded as a unit.

**C** - Center.

**C90** - Class of 1990.

**CB** - Cornerback.

**CC** - Crunch Crew.

**CFL** - Canadian Football League.

**CL** - Checklist card. A card that lists in order the cards and players in the set or series. Older checklist cards in Mint condition that have not been checked off are very desirable and command large premiums.

**CO** - Coach card.

**COIN** - A small disc of metal or plastic portraying a player in its center.

**COLLECTOR** - A person who engages in the hobby of collecting cards primarily for his own enjoyment, with any profit motive being secondary.

**COLLECTOR ISSUE** - A set produced for the sake of the card itself, with no product or service sponsor. It derives its name from the fact that most of these sets are produced for sale directly to the hobby market.

**COMBINATION CARD** - A single card depicting two or more players (not including team cards).

**COMMON CARD** - The typical card of any set; it has no premium value accruing from subject matter, numerical scarcity, popular demand, or anomaly.

**CONVENTION** - A large gathering of dealers and collectors at a single location for the purpose of buying, selling, and sometimes trading sports memorabilia items. Conventions are open to the public and sometimes also feature autograph guests, door prizes, films, contests, etc. More commonly called "shows."

**COR** - Corrected card. A version of an error card that was fixed by the manufacturer.

**COUPON** - See Tab.

**DB** - Defensive back.

**DD** - Draft Day.

**DEALER** - A person who engages in buying, selling, and trading sports collectibles or supplies. A dealer may also be a collector, but as a dealer, he anticipates a profit.

**DIE-CUT** - A card with part of its stock partially cut, allowing one or more parts to be folded or removed. After removal or appropriate folding, the remaining part of the card can frequently be made to stand up.

**DISC** - A circular-shaped card.

**DISPLAY SHEET** - A clear, plastic page that is punched for insertion into a binder (with standard three-ring spacing) containing pockets for displaying cards. Many different styles of sheets exist with pockets of varying sizes to

hold the many differing card formats. The vast majority of current cards measure 2 1/2 by 3 1/2 inches and fit in nine-pocket sheets.

**DP** - Double Print. A card that was printed in approximately double the quantity compared to other cards in the same series, or draft pick card.

**D-ROY** - Defensive Rookie of the Year.

**DT** - Defensive tackle or Dream Team.

**ERR** - Error card. A card with erroneous information, spelling, or depiction on either side of the card. Most errors are never corrected by the producing card company.

**EXHIBIT** - The generic name given to thick stock, postcard-size cards with single-color, obverse pictures. The name is derived from the Exhibit Supply Co. of Chicago, the principal manufacturer of this type of card. These are also known as Arcade cards since they were found in many arcades.

**FB** - Fullback.

**FDP** - First (round) draft pick.

**FG** - Field goal.

**FOIL** - A special type of sticker with a metallic-looking surface.

**FULL SHEET** - A complete sheet of cards that has not been cut into individual cards by the manufacturer. Also called an uncut sheet.

**G** - Guard.

**GF** - Ground Force.

**GG** - Greats of the Game.

**GW** - Game Winners.

**HG** - Hot Gun.

**HH** - Head to Head.

**HIGH NUMBER** - The cards in the last series of number, in a year in which such higher-numbered cards were printed or distributed in significantly lesser amount than the lower-numbered cards. The high-number designation refers to a scarcity of the high-numbered cards. Many (pre-1973) older football card sets have high numbers in terms of this definition.

**HIT** - Hot Hitters.

**HL** - Highlight card, for example from the 1978 Topps subset.

**HOF** - Hall of Fame, or Hall of Famer (also abbreviated HOFer).

**HOR** - Horizontal pose on a card as opposed to the standard vertical orientation found on most cards.

**IA** - In Action card. A special type of card depicting

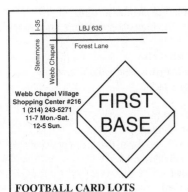

## ORDERING INSTRUCTIONS

Offers expire Sept. 1995, while supply lasts. Please include $3.00 per order for postage and handling.

Send orders to:

### FIRST BASE
216 Webb Chapel Village
Dallas, Texas 75229
(214) 243-5271

Our current price lists sent free with orders. To receive price lists without ordering send $1.00 or a **large** self addressed stamped (75¢ in stamps) envelope to the above address.

## FOOTBALL CARD LOTS
*Our Choice - No Superstars*

1969 Topps 25 diff (f-vg) ............$7.95
1970 Topps 25 diff (f-vg) ...............6.95
1971 Topps 25 diff (f-vg) ...............4.95
1972 Topps 25 diff (f-vg) ...............4.95
1973 Topps 25 diff (f-vg) ...............4.95
1974 Topps 25 diff (f-vg) ...............3.50
1975 Topps 25 diff (f-vg) ...............3.50
1976 Topps 25 diff (f-vg) ...............3.50
1977 Topps 25 diff (f-vg) ...............2.50
1978 Topps 50 diff (f-vg) ...............3.00
1979 Topps 50 diff (f-vg) ...............3.00
1980 Topps 50 diff (f-vg) ...............2.50

## SPECIAL OFFERS

**#1:** Type Set: One card from each year of Topps football 1956 through 1990, our choice of cards, Good to EX, 35 cards for $20.00.
**#2:** Super Bowl XX game program — $10.00.
**#3:** 1986 McDonald's NFL All-Stars Football Card Set of 24 — $3.95
**#4:** 1991 ProSet 10-card "Think About It" set — $5.00
**#5:** 1990 Topps Football complete set — $12.00
**#6:** 1991 Upper Deck Football - 100 different (our choice) cards — $2.50
**#7:** 1990 Score Football – 12 unopened packs — $6.00 or 100 different cards (our choice) — $2.00

# RENO SPORTS CARDS
## Your #1 Dealer for Police, Smokey Bear/Safety Sets

1979 Dallas Cowboys (14) .....................9.95
1979 Kansas City Chiefs (10) .............10.95
1980 Tampa Bay Bucs (56).................99.95
1980 Los Angeles Rams (14) .............14.95
1980 Atlanta Falcons (30) ..................49.95
1980 Dallas Cowboys (14) ...................9.95
1981 Pittsburgh Steelers (16) .............19.95

1981 Miami Dolphins (16) .................19.95
1983 Minnesota Vikings (17) ...............9.95
1984 San Francisco 49ers (12) ..........14.95
1984 Green Bay Packers (25) ..............9.95
1986 Bears/Patriots Super Bowl (17) 17.95
1987 San Diego Chargers (21) ...........24.95
1988 L.A. Raiders (14) (Smokey) ......14.95

We have hundreds of other sets in stock from different years and sports, professional or college. Specializing only in complete and NrMT–MT Police/Smokey Bear Safety sets.

Please include $2.00 postage with order.
Texas residents please add 7.75% sales tax to all orders.

Buying Police/Smokey Bear Safety Sets

# RENO SPORTS CARDS
### 6315 Lamar Road, Paris, TX 75462
### (903) 784-7710 (10am-6pm CST) • (903) 785-4926 (after 6pm)

a player in an action photo, such as the 1982 Topps cards.

**ID** - Idols.

**IL** - Inside linebacker.

**INSERT** - A card of a different type, e.g., a poster, or any other sports collectible contained and sold in the same package along with a card or cards of a major set.

**IR** - Instant Replay card. Similar to In Action and Super Action cards.

**ISSUE** - Synonymous with set, but usually used in conjunction with a manufacturer, e.g., a Topps issue.

**K** - Kicker.

**KP** - Kid Picture card.

**LAYERING** - The separation or peeling of one or more layers of the card stock, usually at the corner of the card. Also see the Condition Guide.

**LB** - Linebacker.

**LEGITIMATE ISSUE** - A set produced to promote or boost sales of a product or service, e.g., bubble gum, cereal, cigarettes, etc. Most collector issues are not legitimate issues in this sense.

**LID** - A circular-shaped card (possibly with tab) that forms the top of the container for the product being promoted.

**LL** - League leader card. A card depicting the leader or leaders in a specific statistical category form the previous season. Not to be confused with team leader (TL).

**LOGO** - NFLPA logo on card.

**LP** - Longest plays.

**MAJOR SET** - A set produced by a national manufacturer of cards, containing a large number of cards. Usually 100 or more different cards comprise a major set.

**MEM** - Memorial.

**MINI** - A small card or stamp (specifically the 1969 Topps Four-in-One football inserts or the 1987 Topps mini football set issued for the United Kingdom).

**ML** - Milestone.

**MN** - Magic Numbers.

**MVP** - Most Valuable Player.

**NEW** - Newsreel cards.

**NFLPA** - National Football League Players Association.

**NO LOGO** - No NFLPA logo on card.

**NO TR** - No trade reference on card.

**NPO** - No position.

**NT** - Nose tackle.

**NUM** - Numerical checklist on card.

**OBVERSE** - The front, face, or pictured side of the card.

**OFF** - Officials cards.

**O-ROY** - Offensive Rookie of the Year.

**OT** - Offensive tackle.

**P** - Punter.

**P1** - First Printing.

**P2** - Second Printing.

**PANEL** - An extended card that is composed of multiple individual cards.

**PB** - Pro Bowl.

**PC** - Poster Card.

**PERIPHERAL SET** - A loosely defined term that applies to any non-regular issue set. This term most often is used to describe food issue, giveaway, regional or sendaway sets that contain a fairly small number of cards and are not accepted by the hobby as major sets.

**PL** - Playoff Team Leaders.

**POY** - Player of the Year.

**PP** - Platinum Performer.

**PRED** - Predator.

**PREMIUM CARDS** - A class of products introduced recently, intended to have higher quality card stock and photography than regular cards, but more limited production and higher cost. Defining what is and isn't a premium card is somewhat subjective.

**PREMIUM** - A card, sometimes on photographic stock, that is purchased or obtained in conjunction with (or redeemed for) another card or product. This term applies mainly to older products, as newer cards distributed in this manner are generally lumped together as peripheral sets.

**PROMOTIONAL SET** - A set, usually containing a small number of cards, issued by a national card producer and distributed in limited quantities or to a select group of people, such as major show attendees or dealers with wholesale accounts. Presumably, the purpose of a promo set is to stir up demand for an upcoming set. Also called a preview, prototype or test set.

**QB** - Quarterback.

**RARE** - A card or series of cards of very limited availability. Unfortunately, "rare" is a subjective term sometimes used indiscriminately. Using the strict definitions, rare cards are harder to obtain than scarce cards.

**RB** - Record Breaker card or running back.

**RC** - Rookie Card. A player's first appearance on a regular issue card from one of the major card companies. Each company has only one regular issue set per season, and that is the widely available traditional set. With a few exceptions, each player has only one RC in any given set. A Rookie Card cannot be an All-Star, Highlight, In Action, league leader, Super Action or team leader card. It can, however, be a coach card or draft pick card.

**REGIONAL** - A card issued and distributed only in a limited geographical area of the country. The producer may or may not be a major, national producer of trading cards. The key is whether the set was distributed nationally in any form or not.

**REP** - Replay cards.

**RET** - Retired.

**REVERSE** - The back or narrative side of the card.

**REV NEG** - Reversed or flopped photo side of the card. This is a major type of error card, but only some are corrected.

**RM** - Rocket Man.

**ROY** - Rookie of the Year.

**RS** - Rookie Superstar.

**S** - Safety.

**SA** - Super Action card. Similar to an In Action card.

**SACK** - Sack Attack.

**SB** - Super Bowl.

**SBK** - Scrapbook.

**SCARCE** - A card or series of cards of limited availability. This subjective term is sometimes used indiscriminately to promote or hype value. Using strict definitions, scarce cards are easier to obtain than rare cards.

**SEMI-HIGH** - A card from the next-to-last series of a sequentially issued set. It has more value than an average card and generally less value than a high number. A card is not called a semi-high unless its next-to-last series has an additional premium attached to it.

**SERIES** - The entire set of cards issued by a particular producer in a particular year, e.g., the 1978 Topps series. Also, within a particular set, series can refer to a group of (consecutively numbered) cards printed at the same time, e.g., the first series of the 1948 Leaf set (#1 through #49).

**SET** - One each of an entire run of cards of the same type, produced by a particular manufacturer during a single season. In other words, if you have a complete set of 1975 Topps football cards, then you have every card from #1 up to and including #528; i.e., all the different cards that were produced.

**SHOW** - A large gathering of dealers and collectors at a single location for the purpose of buying, selling, and trading sorts cards and memorabilia. Conventions are open to the public and sometimes also feature autograph guests, door prizes, films, contests, etc.

**SIDE** - Sidelines.

**SKIP-NUMBERED** - A set that has many unissued card numbers between the lowest number in the set and the highest number in the set, e.g., the 1949 Leaf football set contains 49 cards skip-numbered from number 1-144. A major set in which a few numbers were not printed is not considered to be skip-numbered.

**SL** - Season Leaders.

**SP** - Single or Short Print. A card which was printed in lesser quantity compared to the other cards in the same series (also see DP). This term only can be used in a relative sense and in reference to one particular set. For instance, the 1989 Pro Set Pete Rozelle SP is less common than the other cards in that set, but it isn't necessarily scarcer than regular cards of any other set.

**SPD** - Speedburner.

**SPECIAL CARD** - A card that portrays something other than a single player or team; for example, the 1990 Fleer Joe Montana/Jerry Rice Super Bowl MVPs card #397.

**SR** - Super Rookie.

**STAMP** - Adhesive-backed papers depicting a player. The stamp may be individual or in a sheet of many stamps. Moisture must be applied to the adhesive in order for the stamp to be attached to another surface.

**STAR CARD** - A card that portrays a player of some repute, usually determined by his ability, but sometimes referring to sheer popularity.

**STICKER** - A card-like item with a removable layer that can be affixed to another surface. Example: 1983 Topps inserts.

**STOCK** - The cardboard or paper on which the card is printed.

**SUPER ACTION** - A card type similar to In Action. Abbreviated in the Price Guide as SA.

**SUPERSTAR CARD** - A card that portrays a superstar, e.g., a Hall of Fame member or a player whose current performance may eventually warrant serious Hall of Fame consideration.

**TAB** - A card portion set off from the rest of the card, usually with perforations, that may be removed without damaging the central character or event depicted by the card.

**TC** - Team card or team checklist card.

**TEAM CARD** - A card that depicts an entire team.

**TECH** - Technicians.

**TL** - Team leader card or Top Leader.

**TM** - Team MVPs.

**TR** - Trade reference on card.

**TRIMMED** - A card cut down from its original size. Trimmed cards are undesirable to most collectors, and are therefore less valuable than otherwise identical, untrimmed cards. Also see the Condition Guide.

**UER** - Uncorrected error card.

**USFL** - United States Football League.

**VAR** - Variation card. One of two or more cards from the same series, with the same card number (or player with identical pose, if the series is unnumbered) differing from one another in some aspect, from the printing, stock or other feature of the card. This is often caused when the manufacturer of the cards notices an error in a particular card, corrects the error and then resumes the print run. In this case there will be two versions or variations of the same card. Sometimes one of the variations is relatively scarce. Variations also can result from accidental or deliberate design changes, information updates, photo substitutions, etc.

**VERT** - Vertical pose on a card.

**WFL** - World Football League.

**WLAF** - World League of American Football.

**WR** - Wide receiver.

**XRC** - Extended Rookie Card. A player's first appearance on a card, but issued in a set that was not distributed nationally nor in packs. In football sets, this term generally refers to the 1984 and 1985 Topps USFL sets.

**90** - Ninety-plus.

# Understanding Card Values

### Determining Value

Why are some cards more valuable than others? Obviously, the economic laws of supply and demand are applicable to card collecting just as they are to any other field where a commodity is bought, sold or traded in a free, unregulated market.

Supply (the number of cards available on the market) is less than the total number of cards originally produced since attrition diminishes that original quantity. Each year a percentage of cards is typically thrown away, destroyed or otherwise lost to collectors. This percentage is much, much smaller today than it was in the past because more and more people have become increasingly aware of the value of their cards.

For those who collect only Mint condition cards, the supply of older cards can be quite small indeed. Until recently, collectors were not so conscious of the need to preserve the condition of their cards. For this reason, it is difficult to know exactly how many 1962 Topps are currently available, Mint or otherwise. It is generally accepted that there are fewer 1962 Topps available than 1972, 1982 or 1992 Topps cards. If demand were equal for each of these sets, the law of supply and demand would increase the price for the least available sets.

Demand, however, is never equal for all sets, so price correlations can be complicated. The demand for a card is influenced by many factors. These include: (1) the age of the card; (2) the number of cards printed; (3) the player(s) portrayed on the card; (4) the attractiveness and popularity of the set; and (5) the physical condition of the card.

In general, (1) the older the card, (2) the fewer the number of the cards printed, (3) the more famous, popular and talented the player, (4) the more attractive and popular the set, and (5) the better the condition of the card, the higher the value of the card will be. There are exceptions to all but one of these factors: the condition of the card. Given two cards similar in all respects except condition, the one in the best condition will always be valued higher.

While those guidelines help to establish the value of a card, the countless exceptions and peculiarities make any simple, direct mathematical formula to determine card values impossible.

### Regional Variation

Since the market varies from region to region, card prices of local players may be higher. This is known as a regional premium. How significant the premium is — and if there is any premium at all — depends on the local popularity of the team and the player.

The largest regional premiums usually do not apply to superstars, who often are so well known nationwide that the prices of their key cards are too high for local dealers to realize a premium.

Lesser stars often command the strongest premiums. Their popularity is concentrated in their home region, creating local demand that greatly exceeds overall demand.

Regional premiums can apply to popular retired players and sometimes can be found in the areas where the players grew up or starred in college.

A regional discount is the converse of a regional premium. Regional discounts occur when a player has been so popular in his region for so long that local collectors and dealers have accumulated quantities of his cards. The abundant supply may make the cards available in that area at the lowest prices anywhere.

## Set Prices

A somewhat paradoxical situation exists in the price of a complete set vs. the combined cost of the individual cards in the set. In nearly every case, the sum of the prices for the individual cards is higher than the cost for the complete set. This is prevalent especially in the cards of the past few years. The reasons for this apparent anomaly stem from the habits of collectors and from the carrying costs to dealers. Today, each card in a set normally is produced in the same quantity as all others in its set.

Many collectors pick up only stars, superstars and particular teams. As a result, the dealer is left with a shortage of certain player cards and an abundance of others. He therefore incurs an expense in simply "carrying" these less desirable cards in stock. On the other hand, if he sells a complete set, he gets rid of large numbers of cards at one time. For this reason, he generally is willing to receive less money for a complete set. By doing this, he recovers all of his costs and also makes a profit.

Set prices do not include rare card varieties, unless specifically stated. Of course, the prices for sets do include one example of each type for the given set, but this is the least expensive variety.

## Scarce Series

Scarce series occur because cards issued before 1973 were made available to the public each year in several series of finite numbers of cards, rather than all cards of the set being available for purchase at one time. At some point during the season, interest in current year cards waned. Consequently, the manufacturers produced smaller numbers of these later-series cards. Nearly all nationwide issues from post-World War II manufacturers (1948 to 1972) exhibit these series variations.

In the past, Topps, for example, may have issued series consisting of many different numbers of cards, including 55, 66, 80, 88, 110 and others. However, after 1968, the sheet size generally has been 132. Despite Topps' standardization of the sheet size, the company double-printed one sheet in 1983 and possibly in 1984 and 1985, too. This was apparently an effort to induce collectors to buy more packs.

We are always looking for information or photographs of printing sheets of cards for research. Each year, we try to update the hobby's knowledge of distribution anomalies. Please let us know at the address in this book if you have first-hand knowledge that would be helpful in this pursuit.

# Grading Your Cards

Each hobby has its own grading terminology — stamps, coins, comic books, record collecting, etc. Collectors of sports cards are no exception. The one invariable criterion for determining the value of a card is its condition: the better the condition of the card, the more valuable it is. Condition grading, however, is subjective. Individual card dealers and collectors differ in the strictness of their grading, but the stated condition of a card should be determined without regard to whether it is being bought or sold.

No allowance is made for age. A 1952 card is judged by the same standards as a 1992 card. But there are specific sets and cards that are condition sensitive (marked with "!" in the Price Guide) because of their border color, consistently poor centering, etc. Such cards and sets sometimes command premiums above the listed percentages in Mint condition.

## Centering

Current centering terminology uses numbers representing the percentage of border on either side of the main design. Obviously, centering is diminished in importance for borderless cards such as

# Centering

**Well-centered**

**Slightly Off-centered**

**Off-centered**

**Badly Off-centered**

**Miscut**

# Corner Wear

The partial cards shown at right have been photographed at 300%. This was done in order to magnify each card's corner wear to such a degree that differences could be shown on a printed page.

*This 1985 Topps Fred Quillan card has a fuzzy corner. Notice the extremely slight fraying on the corner.*

*This 1985 Topps Fred Smerlas card has a slightly rounded corner. Notice that there is no longer a sharp corner but heavy wear.*

*This 1985 Topps Daryl Turner card has a rounded corner evident by the lack of a sharp point and heavy wear on both edges.*

*This 1985 Topps Kim Bokamper card displays a badly rounded corner. Notice a large portion of missing cardboard accompanied by heavy wear and excessive fraying.*

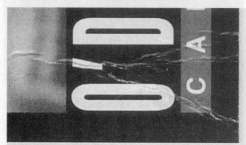

*This 1985 Topps Neil O'Donaghue card displays creases of varying degrees. Light creases (left side of the card) may not break the card's surface, while heavy creases (right side) will.*

Stadium Club.

**Slightly Off-Center** (60/40): A slightly off-center card is one that upon close inspection is found to have one border bigger than the opposite border. This degree once was offensive to only purists, but now some hobbyists try to avoid cards that are anything other than perfectly centered.

**Off-Center** (70/30): An off-center card has one border that is noticeably more than twice as wide as the opposite border.

**Badly Off-Center** (80/20 or worse): A badly off-center card has virtually no border on one side of the card.

**Miscut**: A miscut card actually shows part of the adjacent card in its larger border and consequently a corresponding amount of its card is cut off.

## Corner Wear

Corner wear is the most scrutinized grading criteria in the hobby. These are the major categories of corner wear:

**Corner with a slight touch of wear**: The corner still is sharp, but there is a slight touch of wear showing. On a dark-bordered card, this shows as a dot of white.

**Fuzzy corner**: The corner still comes to a point, but the point has just begun to fray. A slightly "dinged" corner is considered the same as a fuzzy corner.

**Slightly rounded corner**: The fraying of the corner has increased to where there is only a hint of a point. Mild layering may be evident. A "dinged" corner is considered the same as a slightly rounded corner.

**Rounded corner**: The point is completely gone. Some layering is noticeable.

**Badly rounded corner**: The corner is completely round and rough. Severe layering is evident.

## Creases

A third common defect is the crease. The degree of creasing in a card is difficult to show in a drawing or picture. On giving the specific condition of an expensive card for sale, the seller should note any creases additionally. Creases can be categorized as to severity according to the following scale.

**Light Crease**: A light crease is a crease that is barely noticeable upon close inspection. In fact, when cards are in plastic sheets or holders, a light crease may not be seen (until the card is taken out

of the holder). A light crease on the front is much more serious than a light crease on the card back only.

**Medium Crease**: A medium crease is noticeable when held and studied at arm's length by the naked eye, but does not overly detract from the appearance of the card. It is an obvious crease, but not one that breaks the picture surface of the card.

**Heavy Crease**: A heavy crease is one that has torn or broken through the card's picture surface, e.g., puts a tear in the photo surface.

## Alterations

**Deceptive Trimming**: This occurs when someone alters the card in order (1) to shave off edge wear, (2) to improve the sharpness of the corners, or (3) to improve centering — obviously their objective is to falsely increase the perceived value of the card to an unsuspecting buyer. The shrinkage usually is evident only if the trimmed card is compared to an adjacent full-sized card or if the trimmed card is itself measured.

**Obvious Trimming**: Obvious trimming is noticeable and unfortunate. It is usually performed by non-collectors who give no thought to the present or future value of their cards.

**Deceptively Retouched Borders**: This occurs when the borders (especially on those cards with dark borders) are touched up on the edges and corners with magic marker or crayons of appropriate color in order to make the card appear to be Mint.

## Categorization of Defects
### Miscellaneous Flaws

The following are common minor flaws that, depending on severity, lower a card's condition by one to four grades and often render it no better than Excellent-Mint: bubbles (lumps in surface), gum and wax stains, diamond cutting (slanted borders), notching, off-centered backs, paper wrinkles, scratched-off cartoons or puzzles on back, rubber band marks, scratches, surface impressions and warping.

The following are common serious flaws that, depending on severity, lower a card's condition at least four grades and often render it no better than Good: chemical or sun fading, erasure marks, mildew, miscutting (severe off-centering), holes, bleached or retouched borders, tape marks, tears, trimming, water or coffee stains and writing.

# Condition Guide

## Grades

**Mint** (Mt) - A card with no flaws or wear. The card has four perfect corners, 60/40 or better centering from top to bottom and from left to right, original gloss, smooth edges and original color borders. A Mint card does not have print spots, color or focus imperfections.

**Near Mint-Mint** (NrMt-Mt) - A card with one minor flaw. Any one of the following would lower a Mint card to Near Mint-Mint: one corner with a slight touch of wear, barely noticeable print spots, color or focus imperfections. The card must have 60/40 or better centering in both directions, original gloss, smooth edges and original color borders.

**Near Mint** (NrMt) - A card with one minor flaw. Any one of the following would lower a Mint card to Near Mint: one fuzzy corner or two to four corners with slight touches of wear, 70/30 to 60/40 centering, slightly rough edges, minor print spots, color or focus imperfections. The card must have original gloss and original color borders.

**Excellent-Mint** (ExMt) - A card with two or three fuzzy, but not rounded, corners and centering no worse than 80/20. The card may have no more than two of the following: slightly rough edges, very slightly discolored borders, minor print spots, color or focus imperfections. The card must have original gloss.

**Excellent** (Ex) - A card with four fuzzy but definitely not rounded corners and centering no worse than 80/20. The card may have a small amount of original gloss lost, rough edges, slightly discolored borders and minor print spots, color or focus imperfections.

**Very Good** (Vg) - A card that has been handled but not abused: slightly rounded corners with slight layering, slight notching on edges, a significant amount of gloss lost from the surface but no scuffing and moderate discoloration of borders. The card may have a few light creases.

**Good** (G), **Fair** (F), **Poor** (P) - A well-worn, mishandled or abused card: badly rounded and layered corners, scuffing, most or all original gloss missing, seriously discolored borders, moderate or heavy creases, and one or more serious flaws. The grade of Good, Fair or Poor depends on the severity of wear and flaws. Good, Fair and Poor cards gener-

ally are used only as fillers.

The most widely used grades are defined above. Obviously, many cards will not perfectly fit one of the definitions.

Therefore, categories between the major grades known as in-between grades are used, such as Good to Very Good (G-Vg), Very Good to Excellent (VgEx), and Excellent-Mint to Near Mint (ExMt-NrMt). Such grades indicate a card with all qualities of the lower category but with at least a few qualities of the higher category.

The *Sport Americana Football Card Price Guide* lists each card and set in three grades, with the middle grade valued at about 40-45% of the top grade, and the bottom grade valued at about 10-15% of the top grade.

The value of cards that fall between the listed columns can also be calculated using a percentage of the top grade. For example, a card that falls between the top and middle grades (Ex, ExMt or NrMt in most cases) will generally be valued at anywhere from 50% to 90% of the top grade.

Similarly, a card that falls between the middle and bottom grades (G-Vg, Vg or VgEx in most cases) will generally be valued at anywhere from 20% to 40% of the top grade.

There are also cases where cards are in better condition than the top grade or worse than the bottom grade. Cards that grade worse than the lowest grade are generally valued at 5-10% of the top grade.

When a card exceeds the top grade by one — such as NrMt-Mt when the top grade is NrMt, or Mint when the top grade is NrMt-Mt — a premium of up to 50% is possible, with 10-20% the usual norm.

When a card exceeds the top grade by two — such as Mint when the top grade is NrMt, or NrMt-Mt when the top grade is ExMt — a premium of 25-50% is the usual norm. But certain condition sensitive cards or sets, particularly those from the pre-war era, can bring premiums of up to 100% or even more.

Unopened packs, boxes and factory-collated sets are considered Mint in their unknown (and presumed perfect) state. Once opened, however, each card can be graded (and valued) in its own right by taking into account any defects that may be present in spite of the fact that the card has never been handled.

# Selling Your Cards

Just about every collector sells cards or will sell cards eventually. Someday you may be interested in selling your duplicates or maybe even your whole collection. You may sell to other collectors, friends or dealers. You may even sell cards you purchased from a certain dealer back to that same dealer. In any event, it helps to know some of the mechanics of the typical transaction between buyer and seller.

Dealers will buy cards in order to resell them to other collectors who are interested in the cards. Dealers will always pay a higher percentage for items that (in their opinion) can be resold quickly, and a much lower percentage for those items that are perceived as having low demand and hence are slow moving. In either case, dealers must buy at a price that allows for the expense of doing business and a margin for profit.

If you have cards for sale, the best advice we can give is that you get several offers for your cards — either from card shops or at a card show — and take the best offer, all things considered. Note, the "best" offer may not be the one for the highest amount. And remember, if a dealer really wants your cards, he won't let you get away without making his best competitive offer. Another alternative is to place your cards in an auction as one or several lots.

Many people think nothing of going into a department store and paying $15 for an item of clothing for which the store paid $5. But if you were selling your $15 card to a dealer and he offered you $5 for it, you might think his mark-up unreasonable. To complete the analogy: most department stores (and card dealers) that consistently pay $10 for $15 items eventually go out of business. An exception is when the dealer has lined up a willing buyer for the item(s) you are attempting to sell, or if the cards are so Hot that it's likely he'll have to hold the cards for only a short period of time.

In those cases, an offer of up to 75 percent of book value still will allow the dealer to make a reasonable profit considering the short time he will need to hold the merchandise. In general, however, most cards and collections will bring offers in the range of 25 to 50 percent of retail price. Also consider that most material from the past five to 10 years is plentiful. If that's what you're selling, don't be surprised if your best offer is well below that range.

# Interesting Notes

The first card numerically of an issue is the single card most likely to obtain excessive wear. Consequently, you typically will find the price on the #1 card (in NrMt or Mint condition) somewhat higher than might otherwise be the case. Similarly, but to a lesser extent (because normally the less important, reverse side of the card is the one exposed), the last card numerically in an issue also is prone to abnormal wear. This extra wear and tear occurs because the first and last cards are exposed to the elements (human element included) more than any other cards. They are generally end cards in any brick formations, rubber bandings, stackings on wet surfaces, and like activities.

Sports cards have no intrinsic value. The value of a card, like the value of other collectibles, can be determined only by you and your enjoyment in viewing and possessing these cardboard treasures.

Remember, the buyer ultimately determines the price of each card. You are the determining price factor because you have the ability to say "No" to the price of any card by not exchanging your hard-earned money for a given card. When the cost of a trading card exceeds the enjoyment you will receive from it, your answer should be "No." We assess and report the prices. You set them!

We are always interested in receiving the price input of collectors and dealers from around the country. We happily credit major contributors. We welcome your opinions, since your contributions assist us in ensuring a better guide each year. If you would like to join our survey list for the next editions of this book and others authored by Dr. Beckett, please send your name and address to Dr. James Beckett, 15850 Dallas Parkway, Dallas, Texas 75248.

# Advertising

Within this Price Guide you will find advertisements for sports memorabilia material, mail order, and retail sports collectibles establishments. All advertisements were accepted in good faith based on the reputation of the advertiser; however, neither the author, the publisher, the distributors, nor the other advertisers in this Price Guide accept any responsibility for any particular advertiser not complying with the terms of his or her ad.

Readers also should be aware that prices in advertisements are subject to change over the annual period before a new edition of this volume is issued each spring. When replying to an advertisement late in the football year, the reader should take this into account, and contact the dealer by phone or in writing for up-to-date price information. Should you come into contact with any of the advertisers in this guide as a result of their advertisement herein, please mention this source as your contact.

# Additional Reading

 With the increase in popularity of the hobby in recent years, there has been a corresponding increase in available literature. Below is a list of the books and periodicals that receive our highest recommendation and that we hope will further advance your knowledge and enjoyment of our great hobby.

*The Sport Americana Baseball Card Price Guide* by Dr. James Beckett (Sixteenth Edition, $16.95, released 1994, published by Edgewater Book Company) — the most comprehensive Price Guide and checklist ever issued on baseball cards.

*The Official Price Guide to Baseball Cards* by Dr. James Beckett (Fourteenth Edition, $6.99, released 1994, published by The House of Collectibles) — an abridgment of *The Sport Americana Price Guide* in a convenient and economical pocket-size format providing Dr. Beckett's pricing of the major baseball sets since 1948.

*The Official Price Guide to Football Cards* by Dr. James Beckett (Fourteenth Edition, $6.99, released 1994, published by The House of Collectibles) — an abridgment of *The Sport Americana Price Guide No.11* in a convenient and economical pocket-size format providing Dr. Beckett's pricing of the major football sets since 1948.

*The Sport Americana Hockey Card Price Guide* by Dr. James Beckett (Third Edition, $14.95, released 1994, published by Edgewater Book Company) — the most comprehensive Price Guide

and checklist ever issued on hockey cards.

*The Official Price Guide to Hockey Cards* by Dr. James Beckett (Third Edition, $6.99, released 1993, published by The House of Collectibles) — an abridgment of *The Sport Americana Price Guide* listed above in a convenient and economical pocket-size format providing Dr. Beckett's pricing of the major hockey sets since 1951.

*The Sport Americana Basketball Card Price Guide and Alphabetical Checklist* by Dr. James Beckett (Third Edition, $14.95, released 1993, published by Edgewater Book Company) — the most comprehensive combination Price Guide and alphabetical checklist ever issued on basketball cards.

*The Official Price Guide to Basketball Cards* by Dr. James Beckett (Third Edition, $6.99, released 1993, published by The House of Collectibles) — an abridgment of *The Sport Americana Price Guide* listed above in a convenient and economical pocket-size format providing Dr. Beckett's pricing of the major basketball sets since 1948.

*The Sport Americana Baseball Card Alphabetical Checklist* by Dr. James Beckett (Sixth Edition, $15.95, released 1994, published by Edgewater Book Company) — an alphabetical listing, by the last name of the player portrayed on the card, of virtually all baseball cards (major league and minor league) produced up through the 1994 major sets.

*The Sport Americana Price Guide to the Non-Sports Cards 1930-1960* by Christopher Benjamin (Second Edition, $14.95, released 1993, published by Edgewater Book Company) — the definitive guide to virtually all popular non-sports American tobacco and bubblegum cards issued between 1930 and 1960. In addition to cards, illustrations and prices for wrappers also are included.

*The Sport Americana Price Guide to the Non-Sports Cards* by Christopher Benjamin (Fourth Edition, $14.95, released 1992, published by Edgewater Book Company) — the definitive guide to all popular non-sports American cards. In addition to cards, illustrations and prices for wrappers also are included. This volume covers non-sports cards from 1961 to 1992.

*The Sport Americana Baseball Address List* by Jack Smalling (Seventh Edition, $12.95, released 1992, published by Edgewater Book Company) — the definitive guide for autograph hunters, giving addresses and deceased information for virtually all Major League Baseball players past and present.

*The Sport Americana Team Baseball Card Checklist* by Jeff Fritsch (Sixth Edition, $12.95, released 1992, published by Edgewater Book Company) — includes all Topps, Bowman, Donruss, Fleer, Score, Play Ball, Goudey, and Upper Deck cards, with the players portrayed on the cards listed with the teams for whom they played. The book is invaluable to the collector who specializes in an individual team because it is the most complete baseball card team checklist available.

*The Sport Americana Team Football and Basketball Card Checklist* by Jeff Fritsch and Jane Fritsch-Gavin (Second Edition, $12.95, released 1993, published by Edgewater Book Company) — the book is invaluable to the collector who specializes in an individual team because it is the most complete football and basketball card team checklist available.

*The Encyclopedia of Baseball Cards, Volume I: 19th Century Cards* by Lew Lipset ($11.95, released 1983, published by the author) — everything you ever wanted to know about 19th century cards.

*The Encyclopedia of Baseball Cards, Volume II: Early Gum and Candy Cards* by Lew Lipset ($10.95, released 1984, published by the author) — everything you ever wanted to know about early candy and gum cards.

*The Encyclopedia of Baseball Cards, Volume III: 20th Century Tobacco Cards, 1909-1932* by Lew Lipset ($12.95, released 1986, published by the author) — everything you ever wanted to know about old tobacco cards.

## Prices in this Guide

Prices found in this guide reflect current retail rates just prior to the printing of this book. They do not reflect the FOR SALE prices of the author, the publisher, the distributors, the advertisers, or any card dealers associated with this guide. No one is obligated in any way to buy, sell or trade his or her cards based on these prices. The price listings were compiled by the author from actual buy/sell transactions at sports conventions, sports card shops, buy/sell advertisements in the hobby papers, for sale prices from dealer catalogs and price lists, and discussions with leading hobbyists in the U.S. and Canada. All prices are in U.S. dollars.

# History of Football Cards

Until the 1930s, the first and only set which featured football players was the Mayo N302 set. The first bubblegum issue dedicated entirely to football players did not appear until the National Chicle issue of 1935. Before this, athletes from several sports were pictured in the multi-sport Goudey Sport Kings issue of 1933. In that set, football was represented by three legends whose fame has not diminished through the years: Red Grange, Knute Rockne and Jim Thorpe.

But it was not until 1948, and the post-war bubblegum boom, that the next football issues appeared. Bowman and Leaf Gum companies both issued football card sets in that year. From this point on, football cards have been issued annually by one company or another up to the present time, with Topps being the only major card producer until 1989, when Pro Set and Score debuted and sparked a football card boom.

Football cards depicting players from the Canadian Football League (CFL) did not appear until Parkhurst issued a 100-card set in 1952. Four years later, Parkhurst issued another CFL set with 50 small cards this time. Topps began issuing CFL sets in 1958 and continued annually until 1965, although from 1961 to 1965 these cards were printed in Canada by O-Pee-Chee. Post Cereal issued two CFL sets in 1962 and 1963; these cards formed the backs of boxes of Post Cereals distributed in Canada. The O-Pee-Chee company, which has maintained a working relationship with the Topps Gum Company, issued four CFL sets in the years 1968, 1970, 1971, and 1972. Since 1981, the JOGO Novelties Company has been producing a number of CFL sets depicting past and present players.

Returning to American football issues, Bowman resumed its football cards (by then with full-color fronts) from 1950 to 1955. The company twice increased the size of its card during that period. Bowman was unopposed during most of the early 1950s as the sole producer of cards featuring pro football players.

Topps issued its first football card set in 1950 with a group of very small, felt-back cards. In 1951 Topps issued what is referred to as the "Magic Football Card" set. This set of 75 has a scratch-off section on the back which answers a football quiz. Topps did not issue another football set until 1955 when its All-American Football set paid tribute to past college football greats. In January of 1956, Topps Gum Company (of Brooklyn) purchased the Bowman Company (of Philadelphia).

After the purchase, Topps issued sets of National Football League (NFL) players up until 1963. The 1961 Topps football set also included American Football League (AFL) players in the high number series (133-198). Topps sets from 1964 to 1967 contained AFL players only. From 1968 to the present, Topps has issued a major set of football cards each year.

When the AFL was founded in 1960, Fleer produced a 132-card set of AFL players and coaches. In 1961, Fleer issued a 220-card set (even larger than the Topps issue of that year) featuring players from both the NFL and AFL. Apparently, for that one year, Topps and Fleer tested a reciprocal arrangement, trading the card printing rights to each other's contracted players. The 1962 and 1963 Fleer sets feature only AFL players. Both sets are relatively small at 88 cards each.

Post Cereal issued a 200-card set of National League football players in 1962 which contains numerous scarcities, namely those players appearing on unpopular varieties of Post Cereal. From 1964 to 1967, the Philadelphia Gum company issued four 198-card NFL player sets.

In 1984 and 1985, Topps produced a set for the now defunct United States Football League, in addition to its annual NFL set. The 1984 set in particular is quite scarce, due to both low distribution and the high demand for the extended Rookie Cards of current NFL superstars Jim Kelly and Reggie White, among others.

In 1986, the McDonald's Restaurants generated the most excitement in football cards in many years. McDonald's created a nationwide football card promotion in which customers could receive a card or two per food purchase, upon request. However, the cards distributed were only of the local team, or of the "McDonald's All-Stars" for areas not near NFL cities. Also, each set was produced with four possible color tabs: blue, black, gold, and green. The tab color distributed depended on the week of the promotion. In general, cards with blue tabs are the scarcest, although for some teams the cards with black tabs are the hardest to find. The tabs were intended to be scratched off and removed by customers to be redeemed for food and other prizes, but among collectors, cards with scratched or removed tabs are categorized as having a major defect, and therefore are valued considerably less.

The entire set, including four color tabs for all 29 subsets, totals over 2800 different cards. The hoopla over the McDonald's cards fell off precipitously after 1988, as collector interest shifted to the new 1989 Score and Pro Set issues.

The popularity of football cards has continued to grow since 1986. Topps introduced "Super Rookie" cards in 1987. Card companies other than Topps noticed the burgeoning interest in football cards, resulting in the two landmark 1989 football sets: a 330-card Score issue, and a 440-card Pro Set release. Score later produced a self-contained 110-card supplemental set, while Pro Set printed 100 Series II cards and a 21-card "Final Update" set. Topps, Pro Set and Score all improved card quality and increased the size of their sets for 1990. That season also marked Fleer's return to football cards and Action Packed's first major set.

In 1991, Pacific, Pro Line, Upper Deck and Wild Card joined a market that is now at least as competitive as the baseball card market. And the premium card trend that began in baseball cards spilled over to the gridiron in the form of Fleer Ultra, Pro Set Platinum, Score Pinnacle, and Topps Stadium Club sets.

The year 1992 brought even more growth with the debuts of All World, Collectors Edge, GameDay, Playoff, Pro Set Power, SkyBox Impact and SkyBox Primetime. Collectors now have more choices than ever.

The football card market stabilized somewhat in 1993 thanks to an agreement between the long-fueding NFL licensing bodies, NFL Properties and the NFL Players Association. Also helping the stabilization was the emergence of several promising rookies, including Drew Bledsoe, Jerome Bettis and Rick Mirer. Limited production became the industry buzzword in sports cards, and football was no exception. The result was the success of three new product lines: 1993 Select, 1993 Upper Deck SP and 1994 Topps Finest.

# 1989 Action Packed Prototypes

These two prototype cards were issued before the 1989 Test issue was released to show the style of Action Packed cards. The cards were folded by hand when they were made, which is why there is no seam on the back of the card as is typical of other Action Packed cards. The standard-size (2 1/2" by 3 1/2") cards feature on the fronts embossed color photos bordered in gold. The horizontally oriented backs have a mugshot, biography, statistics, and an "Action Note" in the form of a caption to the action shot on the front. The cards are numbered on the back. The primary stylistic difference between these prototype cards and the test set issued later that year is the location of the card number.

|  | MINT | EXC | G-VG |
|---|---|---|---|
| COMPLETE SET (2) | 60.00 | 24.00 | 6.00 |
| COMMON PLAYER | 35.00 | 14.00 | 3.50 |
| ☐ 72 Freeman McNeil<br>New York Jets | 35.00 | 14.00 | 3.50 |
| ☐ 101 Phil Simms<br>New York Giants | 40.00 | 16.00 | 4.00 |

# 1989 Action Packed Test

The 1989 Action Packed Football Test set contains 30 standard-size (2 1/2" by 3 1/2") cards. The cards have rounded corners and gold borders. The fronts have "raised" color action shots, and the horizontally-oriented backs feature mug shots and complete stats. The set, which includes ten players each from the Chicago Bears, New York Giants, and Washington Redskins, was packaged in six-card poly packs. These cards were not packaged very well; many cards come creased or bent out of packs, and a typical box will yield quite a few duplicates. Although this was supposed to be a limited test issue, the test apparently was successful as there were reports that more than 4300 cases were produced of these cards. Factory sets packaged in small dull-gold colored boxes were also available on a limited basis. The cards are copyrighted by Hi-Pro Marketing of Northbrook, Illinois and the packs are labeled "Action Packed." On the card back of number 6 Dan Hampton it lists his uniform number as 95 which is actually Richard Dent's number; Hampton wears 99 for the Bears. The cards are numbered in alphabetical order within teams, Chicago Bears (1-10), New York Giants (11-20), and Washington Redskins (21-30). Since this set was a test issue, the cards of Dave Meggett and Mark Rypien are not considered true Rookie Cards.

|  | MINT | EXC | G-VG |
|---|---|---|---|
| COMPLETE SET (30) | 20.00 | 8.00 | 2.00 |
| COMMON PLAYER (1-30) | .50 | .20 | .05 |

| ☐ 1 Neal Anderson | 1.50 | .60 | .15 |
|---|---|---|---|
| ☐ 2 Trace Armstrong | .50 | .20 | .05 |
| ☐ 3 Kevin Butler | .50 | .20 | .05 |
| ☐ 4 Richard Dent | .75 | .30 | .07 |
| ☐ 5 Dennis Gentry | .50 | .20 | .05 |
| ☐ 6 Dan Hampton UER<br>(Wrong uniform<br>number on back) | .75 | .30 | .07 |
| ☐ 7 Jay Hilgenberg | .50 | .20 | .05 |
| ☐ 8 Thomas Sanders | .50 | .20 | .05 |
| ☐ 9 Mike Singletary | .75 | .30 | .07 |
| ☐ 10 Mike Tomczak | .75 | .30 | .07 |
| ☐ 11 Raul Allegre | .50 | .20 | .05 |
| ☐ 12 Ottis Anderson | .75 | .30 | .07 |
| ☐ 13 Mark Bavaro | .60 | .24 | .06 |
| ☐ 14 Terry Kinard | .50 | .20 | .05 |
| ☐ 15 Lionel Manuel | .60 | .24 | .06 |
| ☐ 16 Leonard Marshall | .60 | .24 | .06 |
| ☐ 17 Dave Meggett | 1.50 | .60 | .15 |
| ☐ 18 Joe Morris | .75 | .30 | .07 |
| ☐ 19 Phil Simms | 1.00 | .40 | .10 |
| ☐ 20 Lawrence Taylor<br>(Mark Rypien<br>in background) | 1.50 | .60 | .15 |
| ☐ 21 Kelvin Bryant | .75 | .30 | .07 |
| ☐ 22 Darrell Green | .75 | .30 | .07 |
| ☐ 23 Dexter Manley | .60 | .24 | .06 |
| ☐ 24 Charles Mann | .60 | .24 | .06 |
| ☐ 25 Wilber Marshall | .75 | .30 | .07 |
| ☐ 26 Art Monk | 1.25 | .50 | .12 |
| ☐ 27 Jamie Morris | .50 | .20 | .05 |
| ☐ 28 Tracy Rocker | .50 | .20 | .05 |
| ☐ 29 Mark Rypien UER<br>(Born 10/2/52,<br>should be 10/2/62) | 2.50 | 1.00 | .25 |
| ☐ 30 Ricky Sanders | 1.00 | .40 | .10 |

# 1990 Action Packed

This 280-card set was issued in two skip-numbered series. The cards are the same style as previous year's "test" issue and are standard size, 2 1/2" by 3 1/2". The set is organized numerically in alphabetical order within team and teams themselves are in alphabetical order by city name, Atlanta Falcons (1-10), Buffalo Bills (11-20), Chicago Bears (21-30), Cincinnati Bengals (31-40), Cleveland Browns (41-50), Dallas Cowboys (51-60), Denver Broncos (61-70), Detroit Lions (71-80), Green Bay Packers (81-90), Houston Oilers (91-100), Indianapolis Colts (101-110), Kansas City Chiefs (111-120), Los Angeles Raiders (121-130), Los Angeles Rams (131-140), Miami Dolphins (141-150), Minnesota Vikings (151-160), New England Patriots (161-170), New Orleans Saints (171-180), New York Giants (181-190), New York Jets (191-200), Philadelphia Eagles (201-210), Phoenix Cardinals (211-220), Pittsburgh Steelers (221-230), San Diego Chargers (231-240), San Francisco 49ers (241-250), Seattle Seahawks (251-260), Tampa Bay Buccaneers (261-270), and Washington Redskins (271-280). For cards numbered 3, 26, 193, and 222, the action note on the card back does not correspond with the picture on the card front. Later in the year Action Packed released these cards in the form of pre-packed ten-card complete team sets. A special Braille-backed card of Jim Plunkett was also released as an insert with complete 281-card factory sets.

|  | MINT | EXC | G-VG |
|---|---|---|---|
| COMPLETE SET (280) | 50.00 | 23.00 | 6.25 |
| COMPLETE FACT.SET (281) | 55.00 | 25.00 | 7.00 |
| COMMON PLAYER (1-280) | .15 | .07 | .02 |
| ☐ 1 Aundray Bruce UER<br>(Andre on back) | .15 | .07 | .02 |
| ☐ 2 Scott Case | .15 | .07 | .02 |
| ☐ 3 Tony Casillas | .15 | .07 | .02 |
| ☐ 4 Shawn Collins | .15 | .07 | .02 |
| ☐ 5 Marcus Cotton | .15 | .07 | .02 |

| | | | |
|---|---|---|---|
| ☐ 6 Bill Fralic | .20 | .09 | .03 |
| ☐ 7 Tim Green | .15 | .07 | .02 |
| ☐ 8 Chris Miller | .40 | .18 | .05 |
| ☐ 9 Deion Sanders | 1.00 | .45 | .13 |
| ☐ 10 John Settle | .15 | .07 | .02 |
| ☐ 11 Cornelius Bennett | .25 | .11 | .03 |
| ☐ 12 Shane Conlan | .20 | .09 | .03 |
| ☐ 13 Kent Hill | .15 | .07 | .02 |
| ☐ 14 Jim Kelly | 1.00 | .45 | .13 |
| ☐ 15 Mark Kelso | .15 | .07 | .02 |
| ☐ 16 Scott Norwood | .15 | .07 | .02 |
| ☐ 17 Andre Reed | .40 | .18 | .05 |
| ☐ 18 Fred Smerlas | .15 | .07 | .02 |
| ☐ 19 Bruce Smith | .25 | .11 | .03 |
| ☐ 20 Thurman Thomas | 2.00 | .90 | .25 |
| ☐ 21 Neal Anderson UER | .20 | .09 | .03 |
| (Action note begins, "Neil ...") | | | |
| ☐ 22 Kevin Butler | .15 | .07 | .02 |
| ☐ 23 Richard Dent | .20 | .09 | .03 |
| ☐ 24 Dennis Gentry | .15 | .07 | .02 |
| ☐ 25 Dan Hampton | .20 | .09 | .03 |
| ☐ 26 Jay Hilgenberg | .20 | .09 | .03 |
| ☐ 27 Steve McMichael | .20 | .09 | .03 |
| ☐ 28 Brad Muster | .20 | .09 | .03 |
| ☐ 29 Mike Singletary | .25 | .11 | .03 |
| ☐ 30 Mike Tomczak | .20 | .09 | .03 |
| ☐ 31 James Brooks | .20 | .09 | .03 |
| ☐ 32 Rickey Dixon | .15 | .07 | .02 |
| ☐ 33 Boomer Esiason | .40 | .18 | .05 |
| ☐ 34 David Fulcher | .20 | .09 | .03 |
| ☐ 35 Rodney Holman | .15 | .07 | .02 |
| ☐ 36 Tim Krumrie | .15 | .07 | .02 |
| ☐ 37 Tim McGee | .20 | .09 | .03 |
| ☐ 38 Anthony Munoz UER | .20 | .09 | .03 |
| (Action note says he's blocking Howie Long, but jersey begins with a nine) | | | |
| ☐ 39 Reggie Williams | .15 | .07 | .02 |
| ☐ 40 Ickey Woods | .15 | .07 | .02 |
| ☐ 41 Thane Gash | .20 | .09 | .03 |
| ☐ 42 Mike Johnson | .15 | .07 | .02 |
| ☐ 43 Bernie Kosar | .25 | .11 | .03 |
| ☐ 44 Reggie Langhorne | .20 | .09 | .03 |
| ☐ 45 Clay Matthews | .20 | .09 | .03 |
| ☐ 46 Eric Metcalf | .40 | .18 | .05 |
| ☐ 47 Frank Minnifield | .15 | .07 | .02 |
| ☐ 48 Ozzie Newsome | .25 | .11 | .03 |
| ☐ 49 Webster Slaughter | .20 | .09 | .03 |
| ☐ 50 Felix Wright | .15 | .07 | .02 |
| ☐ 51 Troy Aikman | 5.00 | 2.30 | .60 |
| ☐ 52 James Dixon | .15 | .07 | .02 |
| ☐ 53 Michael Irvin | 2.25 | 1.00 | .30 |
| ☐ 54 Jim Jeffcoat | .15 | .07 | .02 |
| ☐ 55 Ed Too Tall Jones | .25 | .11 | .03 |
| ☐ 56 Eugene Lockhart | .15 | .07 | .02 |
| ☐ 57 Danny Noonan | .15 | .07 | .02 |
| ☐ 58 Paul Palmer | .15 | .07 | .02 |
| ☐ 59 Everson Walls | .20 | .09 | .03 |
| ☐ 60 Steve Walsh | .15 | .07 | .02 |
| ☐ 61 Steve Atwater | .25 | .11 | .03 |
| ☐ 62 Tyrone Braxton | .15 | .07 | .02 |
| ☐ 63 John Elway | 1.25 | .55 | .16 |
| ☐ 64 Bobby Humphrey | .20 | .09 | .03 |
| ☐ 65 Mark Jackson | .20 | .09 | .03 |
| ☐ 66 Vance Johnson | .20 | .09 | .03 |
| ☐ 67 Greg Kragen | .15 | .07 | .02 |
| ☐ 68 Karl Mecklenburg | .20 | .09 | .03 |
| ☐ 69 Dennis Smith | .20 | .09 | .03 |
| ☐ 70 David Treadwell | .15 | .07 | .02 |
| ☐ 71 Jim Arnold | .15 | .07 | .02 |
| ☐ 72 Jerry Ball | .20 | .09 | .03 |
| ☐ 73 Bennie Blades | .15 | .07 | .02 |
| ☐ 74 Mel Gray | .20 | .09 | .03 |
| ☐ 75 Richard Johnson | .15 | .07 | .02 |
| ☐ 76 Eddie Murray | .20 | .09 | .03 |
| ☐ 77 Rodney Peete UER | .25 | .11 | .03 |
| (On back, squeaker misspelled as squeeker) | | | |
| ☐ 78 Barry Sanders | 4.00 | 1.80 | .50 |
| ☐ 79 Chris Spielman | .20 | .09 | .03 |
| ☐ 80 Walter Stanley | .15 | .07 | .02 |
| ☐ 81 Dave Brown | .15 | .07 | .02 |
| ☐ 82 Brent Fullwood | .15 | .07 | .02 |
| ☐ 83 Tim Harris | .20 | .09 | .03 |
| ☐ 84 Johnny Holland | .15 | .07 | .02 |
| ☐ 85 Don Majkowski | .20 | .09 | .03 |
| ☐ 86 Tony Mandarich | .15 | .07 | .02 |
| ☐ 87 Mark Murphy | .15 | .07 | .02 |
| ☐ 88 Brian Noble UER | .15 | .07 | .02 |
| (Fumble recovery stats show 9 instead of 7) | | | |
| ☐ 89 Ken Ruettgers | .15 | .07 | .02 |
| ☐ 90 Sterling Sharpe UER | 2.25 | 1.00 | .30 |
| (Born Glenville, Ga., should be Chicago) | | | |
| ☐ 91 Ray Childress | .20 | .09 | .03 |
| ☐ 92 Ernest Givins | .20 | .09 | .03 |
| ☐ 93 Alonzo Highsmith | .15 | .07 | .02 |
| ☐ 94 Drew Hill | .25 | .11 | .03 |
| ☐ 95 Bruce Matthews | .20 | .09 | .03 |
| ☐ 96 Bubba McDowell | .15 | .07 | .02 |
| ☐ 97 Warren Moon | .75 | .35 | .09 |
| ☐ 98 Mike Munchak | .20 | .09 | .03 |
| ☐ 99 Allen Pinkett | .15 | .07 | .02 |
| ☐ 100 Mike Rozier | .20 | .09 | .03 |
| ☐ 101 Albert Bentley | .15 | .07 | .02 |
| ☐ 102 Duane Bickett | .15 | .07 | .02 |
| ☐ 103 Bill Brooks | .20 | .09 | .03 |
| ☐ 104 Chris Chandler | .20 | .09 | .03 |
| ☐ 105 Ray Donaldson | .15 | .07 | .02 |
| ☐ 106 Chris Hinton | .20 | .09 | .03 |
| ☐ 107 Andre Rison | 1.00 | .45 | .13 |
| ☐ 108 Keith Taylor | .15 | .07 | .02 |
| ☐ 109 Clarence Verdin | .15 | .07 | .02 |
| ☐ 110 Fredd Young | .15 | .07 | .02 |
| ☐ 111 Deron Cherry | .20 | .09 | .03 |
| ☐ 112 Steve DeBerg | .20 | .09 | .03 |
| ☐ 113 Dino Hackett | .15 | .07 | .02 |
| ☐ 114 Albert Lewis | .20 | .09 | .03 |
| ☐ 115 Nick Lowery | .20 | .09 | .03 |
| ☐ 116 Christian Okoye | .20 | .09 | .03 |
| ☐ 117 Stephone Paige | .20 | .09 | .03 |
| ☐ 118 Kevin Ross | .20 | .09 | .03 |
| ☐ 119 Derrick Thomas | 1.00 | .45 | .13 |
| ☐ 120 Mike Webster | .20 | .09 | .03 |
| ☐ 121 Marcus Allen | .35 | .16 | .04 |
| ☐ 122 Eddie Anderson | .25 | .11 | .03 |
| ☐ 123 Steve Beuerlein | .60 | .25 | .08 |
| ☐ 124 Tim Brown | 1.00 | .45 | .13 |
| ☐ 125 Mervyn Fernandez | .15 | .07 | .02 |
| ☐ 126 Willie Gault | .20 | .09 | .03 |
| ☐ 127 Bob Golic | .15 | .07 | .02 |
| ☐ 128 Bo Jackson UER | 1.25 | .55 | .16 |
| (Final column in stats has LG, should be TD) | | | |
| ☐ 129 Howie Long | .20 | .09 | .03 |
| ☐ 130 Greg Townsend | .20 | .09 | .03 |
| ☐ 131 Flipper Anderson | .20 | .09 | .03 |
| ☐ 132 Greg Bell | .20 | .09 | .03 |
| ☐ 133 Robert Delpino | .20 | .09 | .03 |
| ☐ 134 Henry Ellard | .20 | .09 | .03 |
| ☐ 135 Jim Everett | .20 | .09 | .03 |
| ☐ 136 Jerry Gray | .15 | .07 | .02 |
| ☐ 137 Kevin Greene | .20 | .09 | .03 |
| ☐ 138 Tom Newberry | .15 | .07 | .02 |
| ☐ 139 Jackie Slater | .20 | .09 | .03 |
| ☐ 140 Doug Smith | .20 | .09 | .03 |
| ☐ 141 Mark Clayton | .20 | .09 | .03 |
| ☐ 142 Jeff Cross | .15 | .07 | .02 |
| ☐ 143 Mark Duper | .20 | .09 | .03 |
| ☐ 144 Ferrell Edmunds | .15 | .07 | .02 |
| ☐ 145 Jim C.Jensen | .15 | .07 | .02 |
| ☐ 146 Dan Marino | 2.25 | 1.00 | .30 |
| ☐ 147 John Offerdahl | .20 | .09 | .03 |
| ☐ 148 Louis Oliver | .20 | .09 | .03 |
| ☐ 149 Reggie Roby | .20 | .09 | .03 |
| ☐ 150 Sammie Smith | .15 | .07 | .02 |
| ☐ 151 Joey Browner | .20 | .09 | .03 |
| ☐ 152 Anthony Carter | .25 | .11 | .03 |
| ☐ 153 Chris Doleman | .20 | .09 | .03 |
| ☐ 154 Steve Jordan | .20 | .09 | .03 |
| ☐ 155 Carl Lee | .15 | .07 | .02 |
| ☐ 156 Randall McDaniel | .15 | .07 | .02 |
| ☐ 157 Keith Millard | .20 | .09 | .03 |
| ☐ 158 Herschel Walker | .25 | .11 | .03 |
| ☐ 159 Wade Wilson | .20 | .09 | .03 |
| ☐ 160 Gary Zimmerman | .20 | .09 | .03 |
| ☐ 161 Hart Lee Dykes | .15 | .07 | .02 |
| ☐ 162 Irving Fryar | .20 | .09 | .03 |
| ☐ 163 Steve Grogan | .20 | .09 | .03 |
| ☐ 164 Maurice Hurst | .15 | .07 | .02 |
| ☐ 165 Fred Marion | .15 | .07 | .02 |
| ☐ 166 Stanley Morgan | .20 | .09 | .03 |
| ☐ 167 Robert Perryman | .15 | .07 | .02 |
| ☐ 168 John Stephens UER | .20 | .09 | .03 |
| (Taking handoff from Eason, not Grogan) | | | |
| ☐ 169 Andre Tippett | .20 | .09 | .03 |
| ☐ 170 Brent Williams | .15 | .07 | .02 |
| ☐ 171 John Fourcade | .15 | .07 | .02 |
| ☐ 172 Bobby Hebert | .40 | .18 | .05 |
| ☐ 173 Dalton Hilliard | .20 | .09 | .03 |
| ☐ 174 Rickey Jackson | .20 | .09 | .03 |
| ☐ 175 Vaughan Johnson | .20 | .09 | .03 |
| ☐ 176 Eric Martin | .20 | .09 | .03 |
| ☐ 177 Robert Massey | .15 | .07 | .02 |
| ☐ 178 Rueben Mayes UER | .20 | .09 | .03 |
| (Final column in stats has LG, should be TD) | | | |
| ☐ 179 Sam Mills | .20 | .09 | .03 |
| ☐ 180 Pat Swilling | .25 | .11 | .03 |
| ☐ 181 Ottis Anderson | .20 | .09 | .03 |

| | | | |
|---|---|---|---|
| ☐ 182 Carl Banks | .20 | .09 | .03 |
| ☐ 183 Mark Bavaro | .20 | .09 | .03 |
| ☐ 184 Mark Collins | .15 | .07 | .02 |
| ☐ 185 Leonard Marshall | .20 | .09 | .03 |
| ☐ 186 Dave Meggett | .25 | .11 | .03 |
| ☐ 187 Gary Reasons | .15 | .07 | .02 |
| ☐ 188 Phil Simms | .25 | .11 | .03 |
| ☐ 189 Lawrence Taylor | .35 | .16 | .04 |
| ☐ 190 Odessa Turner | .30 | .14 | .04 |
| ☐ 191 Kyle Clifton | .15 | .07 | .02 |
| ☐ 192 James Hasty | .15 | .07 | .02 |
| ☐ 193 Johnny Hector | .15 | .07 | .02 |
| ☐ 194 Jeff Lageman | .15 | .07 | .02 |
| ☐ 195 Pat Leahy | .20 | .09 | .03 |
| ☐ 196 Erik McMillan | .15 | .07 | .02 |
| ☐ 197 Ken O'Brien | .20 | .09 | .03 |
| ☐ 198 Mickey Shuler | .15 | .07 | .02 |
| ☐ 199 Al Toon | .20 | .09 | .03 |
| ☐ 200 Jo Jo Townsell | .15 | .07 | .02 |
| ☐ 201 Eric Allen UER | .20 | .09 | .03 |
| (Card has 24 passes de- | | | |
| fended, Eagles say 25) | | | |
| ☐ 202 Jerome Brown | .20 | .09 | .03 |
| ☐ 203 Keith Byars UER | .20 | .09 | .03 |
| (LG column shows TD's, | | | |
| not longest run) | | | |
| ☐ 204 Cris Carter | .60 | .25 | .08 |
| ☐ 205 Wes Hopkins | .15 | .07 | .02 |
| (Photo from 1985 season) | | | |
| ☐ 206 Keith Jackson UER | .75 | .35 | .09 |
| (Born AK, should be AR) | | | |
| ☐ 207 Seth Joyner | .20 | .09 | .03 |
| (Photo not from an | | | |
| Eagle home game) | | | |
| ☐ 208 Mike Quick | .15 | .07 | .02 |
| (Photo is from a | | | |
| pre-1985 game) | | | |
| ☐ 209 Andre Waters | .20 | .09 | .03 |
| ☐ 210 Reggie White | .50 | .23 | .06 |
| ☐ 211 Rich Camarillo | .15 | .07 | .02 |
| ☐ 212 Roy Green | .20 | .09 | .03 |
| ☐ 213 Ken Harvey | .40 | .18 | .05 |
| ☐ 214 Gary Hogeboom | .20 | .09 | .03 |
| ☐ 215 Tim McDonald | .20 | .09 | .03 |
| ☐ 216 Stump Mitchell | .20 | .09 | .03 |
| ☐ 217 Luis Sharpe | .15 | .07 | .02 |
| ☐ 218 Vai Sikahema | .20 | .09 | .03 |
| ☐ 219 J.T. Smith | .15 | .07 | .02 |
| ☐ 220 Ron Wolfley | .15 | .07 | .02 |
| ☐ 221 Gary Anderson | .15 | .07 | .02 |
| ☐ 222 Bubby Brister UER | .25 | .11 | .03 |
| (Stats say 0 TD passes | | | |
| in 1989, should be 9) | | | |
| ☐ 223 Merril Hoge | .20 | .09 | .03 |
| ☐ 224 Tunch Ilkin | .15 | .07 | .02 |
| ☐ 225 Louis Lipps | .20 | .09 | .03 |
| ☐ 226 David Little | .15 | .07 | .02 |
| ☐ 227 Greg Lloyd | .15 | .07 | .02 |
| ☐ 228 Dwayne Woodruff | .15 | .07 | .02 |
| ☐ 229 Rod Woodson | .60 | .25 | .08 |
| (AJR patch is from | | | |
| 1988 season, not 1989) | | | |
| ☐ 230 Tim Worley | .20 | .09 | .03 |
| ☐ 231 Marion Butts | .25 | .11 | .03 |
| ☐ 232 Gill Byrd | .20 | .09 | .03 |
| ☐ 233 Burt Grossman | .15 | .07 | .02 |
| ☐ 234 Jim McMahon | .25 | .11 | .03 |
| ☐ 235 Anthony Miller UER | 1.00 | .45 | .13 |
| (Text says 76 catches, | | | |
| stats say 75) | | | |
| ☐ 236 Leslie O'Neal UER | .25 | .11 | .03 |
| (Born AK, should be AR) | | | |
| ☐ 237 Gary Plummer | .15 | .07 | .02 |
| ☐ 238 Billy Ray Smith | .15 | .07 | .02 |
| (Action note begins, | | | |
| "Bily Ray ...") | | | |
| ☐ 239 Tim Spencer | .15 | .07 | .02 |
| ☐ 240 Lee Williams | .20 | .09 | .03 |
| ☐ 241 Mike Cofer | .15 | .07 | .02 |
| ☐ 242 Roger Craig | .25 | .11 | .03 |
| ☐ 243 Charles Haley | .20 | .09 | .03 |
| ☐ 244 Ronnie Lott | .15 | .07 | .02 |
| ☐ 245 Guy McIntyre | .20 | .09 | .03 |
| ☐ 246 Joe Montana | 2.50 | 1.15 | .30 |
| ☐ 247 Tom Rathman | .20 | .09 | .03 |
| ☐ 248 Jerry Rice | 2.00 | .90 | .25 |
| ☐ 249 John Taylor | .40 | .18 | .05 |
| ☐ 250 Michael Walter | .15 | .07 | .02 |
| ☐ 251 Brian Blades | .35 | .16 | .04 |
| ☐ 252 Jacob Green | .15 | .07 | .02 |
| ☐ 253 Dave Krieg | .20 | .09 | .03 |
| ☐ 254 Steve Largent | .75 | .35 | .09 |
| ☐ 255 Joe Nash | .15 | .07 | .02 |
| ☐ 256 Rufus Porter | .15 | .07 | .02 |
| ☐ 257 Eugene Robinson | .15 | .07 | .02 |
| ☐ 258 Paul Skansi | .25 | .11 | .03 |
| ☐ 259 Curt Warner UER | .20 | .09 | .03 |

| | | | |
|---|---|---|---|
| (Yards and attempts | | | |
| are reversed in text) | | | |
| ☐ 260 John L. Williams | .20 | .09 | .03 |
| ☐ 261 Mark Carrier | .15 | .07 | .02 |
| ☐ 262 Reuben Davis | .15 | .07 | .02 |
| ☐ 263 Harry Hamilton | .15 | .07 | .02 |
| ☐ 264 Bruce Hill | .15 | .07 | .02 |
| ☐ 265 Donald Igwebuike | .15 | .07 | .02 |
| ☐ 266 Eugene Marve | .15 | .07 | .02 |
| ☐ 267 Kevin Murphy | .15 | .07 | .02 |
| ☐ 268 Mark Robinson | .15 | .07 | .02 |
| ☐ 269 Lars Tate | .15 | .07 | .02 |
| ☐ 270 Vinny Testaverde | .25 | .11 | .03 |
| ☐ 271 Gary Clark | .25 | .11 | .03 |
| ☐ 272 Monte Coleman | .15 | .07 | .02 |
| ☐ 273 Darrell Green | .20 | .09 | .03 |
| ☐ 274 Charles Mann UER | .20 | .09 | .03 |
| (CA is not alpha- | | | |
| betized on back) | | | |
| ☐ 275 Wilber Marshall | .20 | .09 | .03 |
| ☐ 276 Art Monk | .25 | .11 | .03 |
| ☐ 277 Gerald Riggs | .20 | .09 | .03 |
| ☐ 278 Mark Rypien | .35 | .16 | .04 |
| ☐ 279 Ricky Sanders | .20 | .09 | .03 |
| ☐ 280 Alvin Walton | .15 | .07 | .02 |
| ☐ NNO Jim Plunkett BR | 5.00 | 2.30 | .60 |
| (Braille on card back) | | | |

## 1990 Action Packed Rookie Update

This 84-card standard size set (2 1/2" by 3 1/2") was issued to feature most of the rookies who made an impact in the 1990 season that Action Packed did not issue in their regular set. The first 64 cards in the set are 1990 rookies while the last 20 cards are either players who were traded during the off-season or players such as Randall Cunningham who were not included in the regular set. The key Rookie Cards in the set are Fred Barnett, Reggie Cobb, Barry Foster, Jeff George, Harold Green, Rodney Hampton, Johnny Johnson, Cortez Kennedy, Scott Mitchell, Rob Moore, Junior Seau, Emmitt Smith, and Blair Thomas. The set was released through both the Action Packed dealer network and via traditional retail outlets and was available both in wax packs and as collated factory sets.

| | MINT | EXC | G-VG |
|---|---|---|---|
| COMPLETE SET (84) | 35.00 | 16.00 | 4.40 |
| COMPLETE FACT.SET (84) | 38.00 | 17.00 | 4.70 |
| COMMON PLAYER (1-64) | .15 | .07 | .02 |
| COMMON PLAYER (65-84) | .15 | .07 | .02 |
| | | | |
| ☐ 1 Jeff George | 2.25 | 1.00 | .30 |
| Indianapolis Colts | | | |
| ☐ 2 Richmond Webb | .50 | .23 | .06 |
| Miami Dolphins | | | |
| ☐ 3 James Williams | .30 | .14 | .04 |
| Buffalo Bills | | | |
| ☐ 4 Tony Bennett | 1.00 | .45 | .13 |
| Green Bay Packers | | | |
| ☐ 5 Darrell Thompson | .50 | .23 | .06 |
| Green Bay Packers | | | |
| ☐ 6 Steve Broussard | .25 | .11 | .03 |
| Atlanta Falcons | | | |
| ☐ 7 Rodney Hampton | 5.00 | 2.30 | .60 |
| New York Giants | | | |
| ☐ 8 Rob Moore | 1.00 | .45 | .13 |
| New York Jets | | | |
| ☐ 9 Alton Montgomery | .20 | .09 | .03 |
| Denver Broncos | | | |
| ☐ 10 LeRoy Butler | .40 | .18 | .05 |
| Green Bay Packers | | | |
| ☐ 11 Anthony Johnson | .35 | .16 | .04 |
| Indianapolis Colts | | | |
| ☐ 12 Scott Mitchell | 5.00 | 2.30 | .60 |
| Miami Dolphins | | | |
| ☐ 13 Mike Fox | .15 | .07 | .02 |

New York Giants
| ☐ 14 Robert Blackmon | .20 | .09 | .03 |
|---|---|---|---|

Seattle Seahawks
| ☐ 15 Blair Thomas | .30 | .14 | .04 |
|---|---|---|---|

New York Jets
| ☐ 16 Tony Stargell | .25 | .11 | .03 |
|---|---|---|---|

New York Jets
| ☐ 17 Peter Tom Willis | .35 | .16 | .04 |
|---|---|---|---|

Chicago Bears
| ☐ 18 Harold Green | 1.00 | .45 | .13 |
|---|---|---|---|

Cincinnati Bengals
| ☐ 19 Bernard Clark | .15 | .07 | .02 |
|---|---|---|---|

Cincinnati Bengals
| ☐ 20 Aaron Wallace | .30 | .14 | .04 |
|---|---|---|---|

Los Angeles Raiders
| ☐ 21 Dennis Brown | .25 | .11 | .03 |
|---|---|---|---|

San Francisco 49ers
| ☐ 22 Johnny Johnson | 2.50 | 1.15 | .30 |
|---|---|---|---|

Phoenix Cardinals
| ☐ 23 Chris Calloway | .25 | .11 | .03 |
|---|---|---|---|

Pittsburgh Steelers
| ☐ 24 Walter Wilson | .15 | .07 | .02 |
|---|---|---|---|

San Diego Chargers
| ☐ 25 Dexter Carter | .40 | .18 | .05 |
|---|---|---|---|

San Francisco 49ers
| ☐ 26 Percy Snow | .15 | .07 | .02 |
|---|---|---|---|

Kansas City Chiefs
| ☐ 27 Johnny Bailey | .50 | .23 | .06 |
|---|---|---|---|

Chicago Bears
| ☐ 28 Mike Bellamy | .15 | .07 | .02 |
|---|---|---|---|

Philadelphia Eagles
| ☐ 29 Ben Smith | .20 | .09 | .03 |
|---|---|---|---|

Philadelphia Eagles
| ☐ 30 Mark Carrier UER | .50 | .23 | .06 |
|---|---|---|---|

Chicago Bears
(stats say 54 yards
in '89, text has 58)
| ☐ 31 James Francis | .40 | .18 | .05 |
|---|---|---|---|

Cincinnati Bengals
| ☐ 32 Lamar Lathon | .40 | .18 | .05 |
|---|---|---|---|

Houston Oilers
| ☐ 33 Bern Brostek | .15 | .07 | .02 |
|---|---|---|---|

Los Angeles Rams
| ☐ 34 Emmitt Smith UER | 20.00 | 9.00 | 2.50 |
|---|---|---|---|

Dallas Cowboys
(Career yardage on
back is 4232,
should be 3928)
| ☐ 35 Andre Collins UER | .35 | .16 | .04 |
|---|---|---|---|

Washington Redskins
(born '86, should
be '66)
| ☐ 36 Alexander Wright | .30 | .14 | .04 |
|---|---|---|---|

Dallas Cowboys
| ☐ 37 Fred Barnett | 1.25 | .55 | .16 |
|---|---|---|---|

Philadelphia Eagles
| ☐ 38 Junior Seau | 3.00 | 1.35 | .40 |
|---|---|---|---|

San Diego Chargers
| ☐ 39 Cortez Kennedy | 2.00 | .90 | .25 |
|---|---|---|---|

Seattle Seahawks
| ☐ 40 Terry Wooden | .20 | .09 | .03 |
|---|---|---|---|

Seattle Seahawks
| ☐ 41 Eric Davis | .30 | .14 | .04 |
|---|---|---|---|

San Francisco 49ers
| ☐ 42 Fred Washington | .15 | .07 | .02 |
|---|---|---|---|

Chicago Bears
| ☐ 43 Reggie Cobb | 2.25 | 1.00 | .30 |
|---|---|---|---|

Tampa Bay Buccaneers
| ☐ 44 Andre Ware | .60 | .25 | .08 |
|---|---|---|---|

Detroit Lions
| ☐ 45 Anthony Smith | .75 | .35 | .09 |
|---|---|---|---|

Los Angeles Raiders
| ☐ 46 Shannon Sharpe | 5.00 | 2.30 | .60 |
|---|---|---|---|

Denver Broncos
| ☐ 47 Harlon Barnett | .25 | .11 | .03 |
|---|---|---|---|

Cleveland Browns
| ☐ 48 Greg McMurtry | .35 | .16 | .04 |
|---|---|---|---|

New England Patriots
| ☐ 49 Stacey Simmons | .15 | .07 | .02 |
|---|---|---|---|

Indianapolis Colts
| ☐ 50 Calvin Williams | 1.75 | .80 | .22 |
|---|---|---|---|

Philadelphia Eagles
| ☐ 51 Anthony Thompson | .25 | .11 | .03 |
|---|---|---|---|

Phoenix Cardinals
| ☐ 52 Ricky Proehl | 1.00 | .45 | .13 |
|---|---|---|---|

Phoenix Cardinals
| ☐ 53 Tony Jones | .35 | .16 | .04 |
|---|---|---|---|

Houston Oilers
| ☐ 54 Ray Agnew | .15 | .07 | .02 |
|---|---|---|---|

New England Patriots
| ☐ 55 Tommy Hodson | .25 | .11 | .03 |
|---|---|---|---|

New England Patriots
| ☐ 56 Ron Cox | .15 | .07 | .02 |
|---|---|---|---|

Chicago Bears
| ☐ 57 Leroy Hoard | .40 | .18 | .05 |
|---|---|---|---|

Cleveland Browns
| ☐ 58 Eric Green UER | 1.50 | .65 | .19 |
|---|---|---|---|

Pittsburgh Steelers

(Back photo reversed)
| ☐ 59 Barry Foster | 5.00 | 2.30 | .60 |
|---|---|---|---|

Pittsburgh Steelers
| ☐ 60 Keith McCants | .30 | .14 | .04 |
|---|---|---|---|

Tampa Bay Buccaneers
| ☐ 61 Oliver Barnett | .30 | .14 | .04 |
|---|---|---|---|

Atlanta Falcons
| ☐ 62 Chris Warren | 2.50 | 1.15 | .30 |
|---|---|---|---|

Seattle Seahawks
| ☐ 63 Pat Terrell | .25 | .11 | .03 |
|---|---|---|---|

Los Angeles Rams
| ☐ 64 Renaldo Turnbull | 1.00 | .45 | .13 |
|---|---|---|---|

New Orleans Saints
| ☐ 65 Chris Chandler | .15 | .07 | .02 |
|---|---|---|---|

Tampa Bay Buccaneers
| ☐ 66 Everson Walls | .20 | .09 | .03 |
|---|---|---|---|

New York Giants
| ☐ 67 Alonzo Highsmith | .15 | .07 | .02 |
|---|---|---|---|

Dallas Cowboys
| ☐ 68 Gary Anderson | .20 | .09 | .03 |
|---|---|---|---|

Tampa Bay Buccaneers
| ☐ 69 Fred Smerlas | .15 | .07 | .02 |
|---|---|---|---|

San Francisco 49ers
| ☐ 70 Jim McMahon | .25 | .11 | .03 |
|---|---|---|---|

Philadelphia Eagles
| ☐ 71 Curt Warner | .20 | .09 | .03 |
|---|---|---|---|

Los Angeles Rams
| ☐ 72 Stan Humphries | .20 | .09 | .03 |
|---|---|---|---|

Indianapolis Colts
| ☐ 73 Dave Waymer | .15 | .07 | .02 |
|---|---|---|---|

San Francisco 49ers
| ☐ 74 Billy Joe Tolliver | .15 | .07 | .02 |
|---|---|---|---|

San Diego Chargers
| ☐ 75 Tony Eason | .15 | .07 | .02 |
|---|---|---|---|

New York Jets
| ☐ 76 Max Montoya | .15 | .07 | .02 |
|---|---|---|---|

Los Angeles Raiders
| ☐ 77 Greg Bell | .20 | .09 | .03 |
|---|---|---|---|

Los Angeles Raiders
| ☐ 78 Dennis McKinnon | .15 | .07 | .02 |
|---|---|---|---|

Dallas Cowboys
| ☐ 79 Raymond Clayborn | .20 | .09 | .03 |
|---|---|---|---|

Cleveland Browns
| ☐ 80 Broderick Thomas | .15 | .07 | .02 |
|---|---|---|---|

Tampa Bay Buccaneers
| ☐ 81 Timm Rosenbach | .15 | .07 | .02 |
|---|---|---|---|

Phoenix Cardinals
| ☐ 82 Tim McKyer | .20 | .09 | .03 |
|---|---|---|---|

Miami Dolphins
| ☐ 83 Andre Rison | 1.00 | .45 | .13 |
|---|---|---|---|

Atlanta Falcons
| ☐ 84 Randall Cunningham | .50 | .23 | .06 |
|---|---|---|---|

Philadelphia Eagles

# 1990 Action Packed All-Madden

This 58-card (2 1/2" by 3 1/2") set honors the members of the annual team selected by CBS analyst John Madden. This set features a borderless design on the front and an action shot of the player and a brief description on the back about what qualifies the player to be on the All-Madden Team. The back also features a portrait shot of the player and a portrait shot of John Madden as well. The set also has some of the features standard in Action Packed sets, rounded corners, and the All-Madden Team logo in embossed, raised letters as well as the players' photos being raised. The set was issued in both six-card foil packs and in factory set form. The Neal Anderson prototype (12A) is not included in the complete set as it was passed out to dealers prior to the mass distribution of the set. The Anderson prototype was also available as a special magazine insert in SCD.

| | MINT | EXC | G-VG |
|---|---|---|---|
| COMPLETE SET (58) | 20.00 | 8.00 | 2.00 |
| COMMON CARD (1-58) | .25 | .10 | .02 |

| | | | |
|---|---|---|---|
| ☐ 1 Joe Montana | 4.00 | 1.60 | .40 |
| San Francisco 49ers | | | |
| ☐ 2 Jerry Rice | 2.00 | .80 | .20 |
| San Francisco 49ers | | | |
| ☐ 3 Charles Haley | .35 | .14 | .03 |
| San Francisco 49ers | | | |
| ☐ 4 Steve Wisniewski | .25 | .10 | .02 |
| Los Angeles Raiders | | | |
| ☐ 5 Dave Meggett | .35 | .14 | .03 |
| New York Giants | | | |
| ☐ 6 Ottis Anderson | .35 | .14 | .03 |
| New York Giants | | | |
| ☐ 7 Nate Newton | .35 | .14 | .03 |
| Dallas Cowboys | | | |
| ☐ 8 Warren Moon | 1.00 | .40 | .10 |
| Houston Oilers | | | |
| ☐ 9 Emmitt Smith | 5.00 | 2.00 | .50 |
| Dallas Cowboys | | | |
| ☐ 10 Jackie Slater | .25 | .10 | .02 |
| Los Angeles Rams | | | |
| ☐ 11 Pepper Johnson | .25 | .10 | .02 |
| New York Giants | | | |
| ☐ 12A Neal Anderson | 5.00 | 2.00 | .50 |
| Chicago Bears | | | |
| (Prototype) | | | |
| ☐ 12B Lawrence Taylor | .75 | .30 | .07 |
| New York Giants | | | |
| ☐ 13 Sterling Sharpe | 1.50 | .60 | .15 |
| Green Bay Packers | | | |
| ☐ 14 Sean Landeta | .25 | .10 | .02 |
| New York Giants | | | |
| ☐ 15 Richard Dent | .50 | .20 | .05 |
| Chicago Bears | | | |
| (tackling Jim Kelly) | | | |
| ☐ 16 Neal Anderson | .50 | .20 | .05 |
| Chicago Bears | | | |
| ☐ 17 Bruce Matthews | .25 | .10 | .02 |
| Houston Oilers | | | |
| ☐ 18 Matt Millen | .25 | .10 | .02 |
| San Francisco 49ers | | | |
| ☐ 19 Reggie White | .75 | .30 | .07 |
| Philadelphia Eagles | | | |
| ☐ 20 Greg Townsend | .25 | .10 | .02 |
| Los Angeles Raiders | | | |
| ☐ 21 Troy Aikman | 4.00 | 1.60 | .40 |
| Dallas Cowboys | | | |
| ☐ 22 Don Mosebar | .25 | .10 | .02 |
| Los Angeles Raiders | | | |
| ☐ 23 Jeff Zimmerman | .25 | .10 | .02 |
| Dallas Cowboys | | | |
| ☐ 24 Rod Woodson | .50 | .20 | .05 |
| Pittsburgh Steelers | | | |
| ☐ 25 Keith Byars | .35 | .14 | .03 |
| Philadelphia Eagles | | | |
| ☐ 26 Randall Cunningham | 1.00 | .40 | .10 |
| Philadelphia Eagles | | | |
| ☐ 27 Reyna Thompson | .25 | .10 | .02 |
| New York Giants | | | |
| ☐ 28 Marcus Allen | .75 | .30 | .07 |
| Los Angeles Raiders | | | |
| ☐ 29 Gary Clark | .50 | .20 | .05 |
| Washington Redskins | | | |
| ☐ 30 Anthony Carter | .35 | .14 | .03 |
| Minnesota Vikings | | | |
| ☐ 31 Bubba Paris | .25 | .10 | .02 |
| San Francisco 49ers | | | |
| ☐ 32 Ronnie Lott | .50 | .20 | .05 |
| San Francisco 49ers | | | |
| ☐ 33 Erik Howard | .25 | .10 | .02 |
| New York Giants | | | |
| ☐ 34 Ernest Givins | .50 | .20 | .05 |
| Houston Oilers | | | |
| ☐ 35 Mike Munchak | .35 | .14 | .03 |
| Houston Oilers | | | |
| ☐ 36 Jim Lachey | .35 | .14 | .03 |
| Washington Redskins | | | |
| ☐ 37 Merril Hoge UER | .35 | .14 | .03 |
| Pittsburgh Steelers | | | |
| (Back photo reversed) | | | |
| ☐ 38 Darrell Green | .50 | .20 | .05 |
| Washington Redskins | | | |
| ☐ 39 Pierce Holt | .50 | .20 | .05 |
| San Francisco 49ers | | | |
| ☐ 40 Jerome Brown | .35 | .14 | .03 |
| Philadelphia Eagles | | | |
| ☐ 41 William Perry UER | .50 | .20 | .05 |
| Chicago Bears | | | |
| (Back photo reversed) | | | |
| ☐ 42 Michael Carter | .35 | .14 | .03 |
| San Francisco 49ers | | | |
| ☐ 43 Keith Jackson | .75 | .30 | .07 |
| Philadelphia Eagles | | | |
| ☐ 44 Kevin Fagan | .25 | .10 | .02 |
| San Francisco 49ers | | | |
| ☐ 45 Mark Carrier | .35 | .14 | .03 |
| Chicago Bears | | | |
| ☐ 46 Fred Barnett | .75 | .30 | .07 |

| | | | |
|---|---|---|---|
| Philadelphia Eagles | | | |
| ☐ 47 Barry Sanders | 2.50 | 1.00 | .25 |
| Detroit Lions | | | |
| ☐ 48 Pat Swilling and | .50 | .20 | .05 |
| Rickey Jackson | | | |
| New Orleans Saints | | | |
| ☐ 49 Sam Mills and | .35 | .14 | .03 |
| and Vaughan Johnson | | | |
| New Orleans Saints | | | |
| ☐ 50 Jacob Green | .25 | .10 | .02 |
| Seattle Seahawks | | | |
| ☐ 51 Stan Brock | .25 | .10 | .02 |
| New Orleans Saints | | | |
| ☐ 52 Dan Hampton | .50 | .20 | .05 |
| Chicago Bears | | | |
| ☐ 53 Brian Noble | .25 | .10 | .02 |
| Green Bay Packers | | | |
| ☐ 54 John Elliott | .25 | .10 | .02 |
| New York Giants | | | |
| ☐ 55 Matt Bahr | .25 | .10 | .02 |
| New York Giants | | | |
| ☐ 56 Bill Parcells CO | .35 | .14 | .03 |
| New York Giants | | | |
| ☐ 57 Art Shell CO | .35 | .14 | .03 |
| Los Angeles Raiders | | | |
| ☐ 58 All-Madden Team Trophy | .25 | .10 | .02 |

# 1991 Action Packed NFLPA Awards

This 16-card standard size (2 1/2" by 3 1/2") set was produced by Action Packed to honor the athletes who earned various awards in the 1990 NFL season. There were 5,000 sets issued each in their own attractive solid black box; these boxes were individually numbered on the back. The box has the inscription NFLPA/MDA Awards Dinner March 12, 1991 on it. The cards are in the 1991 Action Packed design with a raised, 3-D like photo on the front and a hockey-stick like frame going down the left side of the card and on the bottom identifying the player. The card backs feature a portrait of the player along with biographical information and statistical information where applicable. The cards feature the now-traditional Action Packed rounded corners.

| | MINT | EXC | G-VG |
|---|---|---|---|
| COMPLETE SET (16) | 75.00 | 30.00 | 7.50 |
| COMMON PLAYER (1-16) | 4.00 | 1.60 | .40 |
| | | | |
| ☐ 1 Jim Lachey | 4.00 | 1.60 | .40 |
| Washington Redskins | | | |
| NFC Offensive Lineman | | | |
| ☐ 2 Anthony Munoz | 6.00 | 2.40 | .60 |
| Cincinnati Bengals | | | |
| AFC Offensive Lineman | | | |
| ☐ 3 Bruce Smith | 6.00 | 2.40 | .60 |
| Buffalo Bills | | | |
| AFC Defensive Lineman | | | |
| ☐ 4 Reggie White | 7.50 | 3.00 | .75 |
| Philadelphia Eagles | | | |
| NFC Defensive Lineman | | | |
| ☐ 5 Charles Haley | 5.00 | 2.00 | .50 |
| San Francisco 49ers | | | |
| NFC Linebacker | | | |
| ☐ 6 Derrick Thomas | 7.50 | 3.00 | .75 |
| Kansas City Chiefs | | | |
| AFC Linebacker | | | |
| ☐ 7 Albert Lewis | 4.00 | 1.60 | .40 |
| Kansas City Chiefs | | | |
| AFC Defensive Back | | | |
| ☐ 8 Mark Carrier | 5.00 | 2.00 | .50 |
| Chicago Bears | | | |
| NFC Defensive Back | | | |
| ☐ 9 Reyna Thompson | 4.00 | 1.60 | .40 |
| New York Giants | | | |
| NFC Special Teams | | | |
| ☐ 10 Steve Tasker | 4.00 | 1.60 | .40 |
| Buffalo Bills | | | |

| | | MINT | EXC | G-VG |
|---|---|---|---|---|
| | AFC Special Teams | | | |
| ☐ 11 | James Francis | 5.00 | 2.00 | .50 |
| | Cincinnati Bengals | | | |
| | AFC Defensive Rookie | | | |
| ☐ 12 | Mark Carrier | 5.00 | 2.00 | .50 |
| | Chicago Bears | | | |
| | NFC Defensive Rookie | | | |
| ☐ 13 | Johnny Johnson | 9.00 | 3.75 | .90 |
| | Phoenix Cardinals | | | |
| | NFC Offensive Rookie | | | |
| ☐ 14 | Eric Green | 6.00 | 2.40 | .60 |
| | Pittsburgh Steelers | | | |
| | AFC Offensive Rookie | | | |
| ☐ 15 | Warren Moon | 10.00 | 4.00 | 1.00 |
| | Houston Oilers | | | |
| | AFC MVP | | | |
| ☐ 16 | Randall Cunningham | 10.00 | 4.00 | 1.00 |
| | Philadelphia Eagles | | | |
| | NFC MVP | | | |

| | | MINT | EXC | G-VG |
|---|---|---|---|---|
| | Pittsburgh Steelers | | | |
| ☐ 17 | Doug Dieken | 2.00 | .80 | .20 |
| | Cleveland Browns | | | |
| ☐ 18 | Rolf Benirschke | 2.00 | .80 | .20 |
| | San Diego Chargers | | | |
| ☐ 19 | Reggie Williams | 3.00 | 1.20 | .30 |
| | Cincinnati Bengals | | | |
| ☐ 20 | Nat Moore | 2.00 | .80 | .20 |
| | Miami Dolphins | | | |
| ☐ 21 | George Martin | 2.00 | .80 | .20 |
| | New York Giants | | | |
| ☐ 22 | Deron Cherry | 2.00 | .80 | .20 |
| | Kansas City Chiefs | | | |
| ☐ 23 | Mike Singletary | 5.00 | 2.00 | .50 |
| | Chicago Bears | | | |
| ☐ 24 | Ozzie Newsome | 4.00 | 1.60 | .40 |
| | Cleveland Browns | | | |
| ☐ 25 | Mike Kenn | 2.00 | .80 | .20 |
| | Atlanta Falcons | | | |

## 1991 Action Packed Whizzer White Award

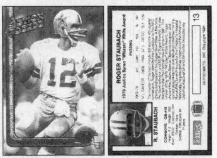

At the silver anniversary NFLPA/Mackey Awards banquet in Chicago (June 23, 1991), Action Packed presented this 25-card commemorative set in honor of the 25 winners of the Justice Byron "Whizzer" White Humanitarian Award from 1967-91. Reportedly 3,500 sets were distributed at the dinner and another 5,000 numbered boxed sets were produced for sale into the hobby. The front design features a color embossed action photo, with indicia in silver and the award year inscribed on a silver helmet. The backs have a color head shot, biographical information, career statistics, and a tribute to the player's professional career and community contributions. The cards are numbered on the back and are standard size, 2 1/2" by 3 1/2". The card numbering follows chronologically the order in which the award was won, 1967 through 1991, inclusive.

| | | MINT | EXC | G-VG |
|---|---|---|---|---|
| | COMPLETE SET (25) | 75.00 | 30.00 | 7.50 |
| | COMMON PLAYER (1-25) | 2.00 | .80 | .20 |
| ☐ 1 | Bart Starr | 12.50 | 5.00 | 1.25 |
| | Green Bay Packers | | | |
| ☐ 2 | Willie Davis | 4.00 | 1.60 | .40 |
| | Green Bay Packers | | | |
| ☐ 3 | Ed Meador | 2.00 | .80 | .20 |
| | Los Angeles Rams | | | |
| ☐ 4 | Gale Sayers | 12.50 | 5.00 | 1.25 |
| | Chicago Bears | | | |
| ☐ 5 | Kermit Alexander | 2.00 | .80 | .20 |
| | Los Angeles Rams | | | |
| ☐ 6 | Ray May | 2.00 | .80 | .20 |
| | Baltimore Colts | | | |
| ☐ 7 | Andy Russell | 3.00 | 1.20 | .30 |
| | Pittsburgh Steelers | | | |
| ☐ 8 | Floyd Little | 4.00 | 1.60 | .40 |
| | Denver Broncos | | | |
| ☐ 9 | Rocky Bleier | 4.00 | 1.60 | .40 |
| | Pittsburgh Steelers | | | |
| ☐ 10 | Jim Hart | 3.00 | 1.20 | .30 |
| | St. Louis Cardinals | | | |
| ☐ 11 | Lyle Alzado | 4.00 | 1.60 | .40 |
| | Denver Broncos | | | |
| ☐ 12 | Archie Manning | 4.00 | 1.60 | .40 |
| | New Orleans Saints | | | |
| ☐ 13 | Roger Staubach | 25.00 | 10.00 | 2.50 |
| | Dallas Cowboys | | | |
| ☐ 14 | Gene Upshaw | 4.00 | 1.60 | .40 |
| | Oakland Raiders | | | |
| ☐ 15 | Ken Houston | 4.00 | 1.60 | .40 |
| | Washington Redskins | | | |
| ☐ 16 | Franco Harris | 10.00 | 4.00 | 1.00 |

## 1991 Action Packed Prototypes

These standard size (2 1/2" by 3 1/2") cards were issued during the year to show the various styles of Action Packed's football sets. The differences between the Randall Cunningham regular issue (204) and the unnumbered Randall Cunningham prototype are the presence of a black border around the gold strip and the presence of a football player above the Action Packed logo. The back of the Cunningham prototype card has a gold border with black highlighting the gold around the photo.

| | MINT | EXC | G-VG |
|---|---|---|---|
| COMPLETE SET (2) | 20.00 | 8.00 | 2.00 |
| COMMON PLAYER | 7.50 | 3.00 | .75 |
| ☐ NNO Randall Cunningham | 7.50 | 3.00 | .75 |
| (Prototype) | | | |
| Philadelphia Eagles | | | |
| ☐ NNO Emmitt Smith | 15.00 | 6.00 | 1.50 |
| (Rookie prototype) | | | |
| Dallas Cowboys | | | |

## 1991 Action Packed

This 280-card standard size set (2 1/2" by 3 1/2") marked the third year Action Packed issued football cards. This set is basically arranged by alphabetical order within alphabetical team order. The set looks as if there is less relief on the card as in previous years and the action photos on the front of the cards are framed in gold along the left side and on the bottom of the card. The cards feature sharp photography on the front while the backs feature complete biographical information, a portrait shot of the player as well as the last five seasons stats and some career highlights. There is also a small space on the bottom for the players signature. The differences between the Randall Cunningham regular issue (204) and the unnumbered Randall Cunningham prototype are the presence of a black border around the gold strip and the absence of the football player above the Action Packed logo. The back of the Cunningham prototype card has a gold border with black highlighting the gold around the photo. The Cunningham prototype is not included as part of the complete set. The cards are arranged by team: Atlanta Falcons (1-10), Buffalo Bills (11-20), Chicago Bears (21-30), Cincinnati Bengals (31-40), Cleveland Browns (41-50), Dallas Cowboys (51-60), Denver Broncos (61-70), Detroit Lions (71-80), Green Bay Packers (81-90), Houston Oilers (91-100), Indianapolis Colts (101-110), Kansas City Chiefs (111-120), Los Angeles Raiders (121-130), Los Angeles Rams (131-140), Miami Dolphins (141-150), Minnesota Vikings (151-160), New England Patriots (161-170), New Orleans Saints (171-180), New York Giants (181-190), New York Jets (191-200), Philadelphia Eagles (201-210), Phoenix Cardinals (211-220), Pittsburgh Steelers (221-230), San Diego Chargers (231-240), San Francisco 49ers (241-250), Seattle Seahawks (251-260), Tampa Bay Buccaneers (261-270), Washington Redskins (271-280). The 1991 Action Packed factory sets also included an exclusive subset of 8 Braille cards. Card numbers 281-288 feature the category leaders of the AFC and NFC. They have the same front design as the regular issue, but different borderless embossed color player photos. The player cards have horizontally oriented backs written in Braille. Two logo cards and an unnumbered checklist card complete the set. The cards are numbered on the back.

|  | MINT | EXC | G-VG |
|---|---|---|---|
| COMPLETE SET (280) | 45.00 | 20.00 | 5.75 |
| COMPLETE FACT.SET (291) | 50.00 | 23.00 | 6.25 |
| COMMON PLAYER (1-280) | .15 | .07 | .02 |
| COMMON BRAILLE (281-288) | .60 | .25 | .08 |
| COMMON LOGOS (289-290) | .25 | .11 | .03 |

| | | | |
|---|---|---|---|
| ☐ 1 Steve Broussard | .20 | .09 | .03 |
| ☐ 2 Scott Case | .15 | .07 | .02 |
| ☐ 3 Brian Jordan | .30 | .14 | .04 |
| ☐ 4 Darion Conner | .15 | .07 | .02 |
| ☐ 5 Tim Green | .15 | .07 | .02 |
| ☐ 6 Chris Miller | .25 | .11 | .03 |
| ☐ 7 Andre Rison | .50 | .23 | .06 |
| ☐ 8 Mike Rozier | .20 | .09 | .03 |
| ☐ 9 Deion Sanders | .50 | .23 | .06 |
| ☐ 10 Jessie Tuggle | .15 | .07 | .02 |
| ☐ 11 Leonard Smith | .15 | .07 | .02 |
| ☐ 12 Shane Conlan | .20 | .09 | .03 |
| ☐ 13 Kent Hull | .15 | .07 | .02 |
| ☐ 14 Keith McKeller | .15 | .07 | .02 |
| ☐ 15 James Lofton | .25 | .11 | .03 |
| ☐ 16 Andre Reed | .35 | .16 | .04 |
| ☐ 17 Bruce Smith | .25 | .11 | .03 |
| ☐ 18 Darryl Talley | .20 | .09 | .03 |
| ☐ 19 Steve Tasker | .20 | .09 | .03 |
| ☐ 20 Thurman Thomas | 1.25 | .55 | .16 |
| ☐ 21 Neal Anderson | .20 | .09 | .03 |
| ☐ 22 Trace Armstrong | .15 | .07 | .02 |
| ☐ 23 Mark Bortz | .15 | .07 | .02 |
| ☐ 24 Mark Carrier | .20 | .09 | .03 |
| ☐ 25 Wendell Davis | .15 | .07 | .02 |
| ☐ 26 Richard Dent | .20 | .09 | .03 |
| ☐ 27 Jim Harbaugh | .20 | .09 | .03 |
| ☐ 28 Jay Hilgenberg | .20 | .09 | .03 |
| ☐ 29 Brad Muster | .20 | .09 | .03 |
| ☐ 30 Mike Singletary | .25 | .11 | .03 |
| ☐ 31 Harold Green | .30 | .14 | .04 |
| ☐ 32 James Brooks | .20 | .09 | .03 |
| ☐ 33 Eddie Brown | .15 | .07 | .02 |
| ☐ 34 Boomer Esiason | .40 | .18 | .05 |
| ☐ 35 James Francis | .20 | .09 | .03 |
| ☐ 36 David Fulcher | .15 | .07 | .02 |
| ☐ 37 Rodney Holman | .15 | .07 | .02 |
| ☐ 38 Tim McGee | .20 | .09 | .03 |
| ☐ 39 Anthony Munoz | .20 | .09 | .03 |
| ☐ 40 Ickey Woods | .15 | .07 | .02 |
| ☐ 41 Rob Burnett | .50 | .23 | .06 |
| ☐ 42 Thane Gash | .15 | .07 | .02 |
| ☐ 43 Mike Johnson | .15 | .07 | .02 |
| ☐ 44 Brian Brennan | .15 | .07 | .02 |
| ☐ 45 Reggie Langhorne | .20 | .09 | .03 |
| ☐ 46 Kevin Mack | .20 | .09 | .03 |
| ☐ 47 Clay Matthews | .20 | .09 | .03 |
| ☐ 48 Eric Metcalf | .25 | .11 | .03 |
| ☐ 49 Anthony Pleasant | .15 | .07 | .02 |
| ☐ 50 Ozzie Newsome | .25 | .11 | .03 |
| ☐ 51 Troy Aikman | 4.00 | 1.80 | .50 |
| ☐ 52 Issiac Holt | .15 | .07 | .02 |
| ☐ 53 Michael Irvin | 1.50 | .65 | .19 |
| ☐ 54 Jimmie Jones | .15 | .07 | .02 |
| ☐ 55 Eugene Lockhart | .15 | .07 | .02 |
| ☐ 56 Kelvin Martin | .20 | .09 | .03 |
| ☐ 57 Ken Norton Jr. | .25 | .11 | .03 |

| | | | |
|---|---|---|---|
| ☐ 58 Jay Novacek | .50 | .23 | .06 |
| ☐ 59 Emmitt Smith | 6.00 | 2.70 | .75 |
| ☐ 60 Daniel Stubbs | .15 | .07 | .02 |
| ☐ 61 Steve Atwater | .25 | .11 | .03 |
| ☐ 62 Michael Brooks | .15 | .07 | .02 |
| ☐ 63 John Elway | 1.00 | .45 | .13 |
| ☐ 64 Simon Fletcher | .20 | .09 | .03 |
| ☐ 65 Bobby Humphrey | .20 | .09 | .03 |
| ☐ 66 Mark Jackson | .20 | .09 | .03 |
| ☐ 67 Vance Johnson | .20 | .09 | .03 |
| ☐ 68 Karl Mecklenburg | .20 | .09 | .03 |
| ☐ 69 Dennis Smith | .20 | .09 | .03 |
| ☐ 70 Greg Kragen UER | .15 | .07 | .02 |
| (NT, not DT) | | | |
| ☐ 71 Jerry Ball | .20 | .09 | .03 |
| ☐ 72 Lomas Brown | .15 | .07 | .02 |
| ☐ 73 Robert Clark | .15 | .07 | .02 |
| ☐ 74 Michael Cofer | .15 | .07 | .02 |
| ☐ 75 Mel Gray | .20 | .09 | .03 |
| ☐ 76 Richard Johnson | .15 | .07 | .02 |
| ☐ 77 Rodney Peete | .20 | .09 | .03 |
| ☐ 78 Barry Sanders | 2.50 | 1.15 | .30 |
| ☐ 79 Chris Spielman | .20 | .09 | .03 |
| ☐ 80 Andre Ware | .25 | .11 | .03 |
| ☐ 81 Matt Brock | .15 | .07 | .02 |
| ☐ 82 LeRoy Butler | .15 | .07 | .02 |
| ☐ 83 Tim Harris | .20 | .09 | .03 |
| ☐ 84 Perry Kemp | .15 | .07 | .02 |
| ☐ 85 Don Majkowski | .20 | .09 | .03 |
| ☐ 86 Mark Murphy | .15 | .07 | .02 |
| ☐ 87 Brian Noble | .15 | .07 | .02 |
| ☐ 88 Sterling Sharpe | 1.50 | .65 | .19 |
| ☐ 89 Darrell Thompson | .20 | .09 | .03 |
| ☐ 90 Ed West | .15 | .07 | .02 |
| ☐ 91 Ray Childress | .20 | .09 | .03 |
| ☐ 92 Ernest Givins | .20 | .09 | .03 |
| ☐ 93 Drew Hill | .20 | .09 | .03 |
| ☐ 94 Haywood Jeffires | .75 | .35 | .09 |
| ☐ 95 Richard Johnson | .15 | .07 | .02 |
| ☐ 96 Sean Jones | .20 | .09 | .03 |
| ☐ 97 Bruce Matthews | .20 | .09 | .03 |
| ☐ 98 Warren Moon | .75 | .35 | .09 |
| ☐ 99 Mike Munchak | .20 | .09 | .03 |
| ☐ 100 Lorenzo White | .25 | .11 | .03 |
| ☐ 101 Albert Bentley | .15 | .07 | .02 |
| ☐ 102 Duane Bickett | .15 | .07 | .02 |
| ☐ 103 Bill Brooks | .20 | .09 | .03 |
| ☐ 104 Jeff George | .50 | .23 | .06 |
| ☐ 105 Jon Hand | .15 | .07 | .02 |
| ☐ 106 Jeff Herrod | .15 | .07 | .02 |
| ☐ 107 Jessie Hester | .20 | .09 | .03 |
| ☐ 108 Mike Prior UER | .15 | .07 | .02 |
| (Did not play in '86) | | | |
| ☐ 109 Rohn Stark | .15 | .07 | .02 |
| ☐ 110 Clarence Verdin | .15 | .07 | .02 |
| ☐ 111 Steve DeBerg | .20 | .09 | .03 |
| ☐ 112 Dan Saleaumua UER | .15 | .07 | .02 |
| (NT, not DT) | | | |
| ☐ 113 Albert Lewis | .20 | .09 | .03 |
| ☐ 114 Nick Lowery | .20 | .09 | .03 |
| ☐ 115 Christian Okoye | .20 | .09 | .03 |
| ☐ 116 Stephone Paige | .20 | .09 | .03 |
| ☐ 117 Kevin Ross | .20 | .09 | .03 |
| ☐ 118 Dino Hackett | .15 | .07 | .02 |
| ☐ 119 Derrick Thomas UER | .50 | .23 | .06 |
| (Drafted in '89, not '90) | | | |
| ☐ 120 Barry Word UER | .25 | .11 | .03 |
| (Bio says 1105 yards, stats say 1015) | | | |
| ☐ 121 Marcus Allen | .30 | .14 | .04 |
| ☐ 122 Mervyn Fernandez UER | .15 | .07 | .02 |
| (Drafted by Raiders) | | | |
| ☐ 123 Willie Gault | .20 | .09 | .03 |
| ☐ 124 Bo Jackson | 1.00 | .45 | .13 |
| ☐ 125 Terry McDaniel | .15 | .07 | .02 |
| ☐ 126 Don Mosebar | .15 | .07 | .02 |
| ☐ 127 Jay Schroeder | .20 | .09 | .03 |
| ☐ 128 Greg Townsend UER | .15 | .07 | .02 |
| (B in DeBerg not in caps) | | | |
| ☐ 129 Aaron Wallace | .15 | .07 | .02 |
| ☐ 130 Steve Wisniewski | .15 | .07 | .02 |
| ☐ 131 Flipper Anderson | .20 | .09 | .03 |
| ☐ 132 Henry Ellard | .20 | .09 | .03 |
| ☐ 133 Jim Everett | .20 | .09 | .03 |
| ☐ 134 Cleveland Gary | .20 | .09 | .03 |
| ☐ 135 Jerry Gray | .15 | .07 | .02 |
| ☐ 136 Kevin Greene | .20 | .09 | .03 |
| ☐ 137 Buford McGee | .15 | .07 | .02 |
| ☐ 138 Vince Newsome | .15 | .07 | .02 |
| ☐ 139 Jackie Slater | .20 | .09 | .03 |
| ☐ 140 Frank Stams | .15 | .07 | .02 |
| ☐ 141 Jeff Cross | .15 | .07 | .02 |
| ☐ 142 Mark Duper | .20 | .09 | .03 |
| ☐ 143 Ferrell Edmunds | .15 | .07 | .02 |
| ☐ 144 Dan Marino | 2.00 | .90 | .25 |
| ☐ 145 Louis Oliver | .20 | .09 | .03 |

|  |  | | | |
|---|---|---|---|---|
| ☐ 146 | John Offerdahl | .20 | .09 | .03 |
| ☐ 147 | Tony Paige | .15 | .07 | .02 |
| ☐ 148 | Sammie Smith | .15 | .07 | .02 |
| ☐ 149 | Richmond Webb | .20 | .09 | .03 |
| ☐ 150 | Jarvis Williams | .15 | .07 | .02 |
| ☐ 151 | Joey Browner | .15 | .07 | .02 |
| ☐ 152 | Anthony Carter | .20 | .09 | .03 |
| ☐ 153 | Chris Doleman | .20 | .09 | .03 |
| ☐ 154 | Hassan Jones | .15 | .07 | .02 |
| ☐ 155 | Steve Jordan | .20 | .09 | .03 |
| ☐ 156 | Carl Lee | .15 | .07 | .02 |
| ☐ 157 | Randall McDaniel | .15 | .07 | .02 |
| ☐ 158 | Mike Merriweather | .15 | .07 | .02 |
| ☐ 159 | Herschel Walker | .25 | .11 | .03 |
| ☐ 160 | Wade Wilson | .20 | .09 | .03 |
| ☐ 161 | Ray Agnew | .15 | .07 | .02 |
| ☐ 162 | Bruce Armstrong | .15 | .07 | .02 |
| ☐ 163 | Marv Cook | .15 | .07 | .02 |
| ☐ 164 | Hart Lee Dykes | .15 | .07 | .02 |
| ☐ 165 | Irving Fryar | .20 | .09 | .03 |
| ☐ 166 | Tommy Hodson | .15 | .07 | .02 |
| ☐ 167 | Ronnie Lippett | .15 | .07 | .02 |
| ☐ 168 | Fred Marion | .15 | .07 | .02 |
| ☐ 169 | John Stephens | .20 | .09 | .03 |
| ☐ 170 | Brent Williams | .15 | .07 | .02 |
| ☐ 171A | Morten Andersen ERR (Back photo has white emblem, should be black) | .20 | .09 | .03 |
| ☐ 171B | Morten Andersen COR | .20 | .09 | .03 |
| ☐ 172A | Gene Atkins ERR (Back photo has white emblem, should be black) | .15 | .07 | .02 |
| ☐ 172B | Gene Atkins COR | .15 | .07 | .02 |
| ☐ 173A | Craig Heyward ERR (Back photo has white emblem, should be black) | .15 | .07 | .02 |
| ☐ 173B | Craig Heyward COR | .15 | .07 | .02 |
| ☐ 174A | Rickey Jackson ERR (Back photo has white emblem, should be black) | .20 | .09 | .03 |
| ☐ 174B | Rickey Jackson COR | .20 | .09 | .03 |
| ☐ 175A | Vaughan Johnson ERR (Back photo has white emblem, should be black) | .20 | .09 | .03 |
| ☐ 175B | Vaughan Johnson COR | .20 | .09 | .03 |
| ☐ 176A | Eric Martin ERR (Back photo has white emblem, should be black) | .20 | .09 | .03 |
| ☐ 176B | Eric Martin COR | .20 | .09 | .03 |
| ☐ 177A | Rueben Mayes ERR (Back photo has white emblem, should be black; would have been fifth season, not sixth) | .15 | .07 | .02 |
| ☐ 177B | Rueben Mayes COR | .15 | .07 | .02 |
| ☐ 178A | Pat Swilling ERR (Back photo has white emblem, should be black) | .30 | .14 | .04 |
| ☐ 178B | Pat Swilling COR | .30 | .14 | .04 |
| ☐ 179A | Renaldo Turnbull ERR (Back photo has white emblem, should be black) | .15 | .07 | .02 |
| ☐ 179B | Renaldo Turnbull COR | .15 | .07 | .02 |
| ☐ 180A | Steve Walsh ERR (Back photo has white emblem, should be black) | .15 | .07 | .02 |
| ☐ 180B | Steve Walsh COR | .15 | .07 | .02 |
| ☐ 181 | Ottis Anderson | .20 | .09 | .03 |
| ☐ 182 | Rodney Hampton | 1.50 | .65 | .19 |
| ☐ 183 | Jeff Hostetler | .50 | .23 | .06 |
| ☐ 184 | Pepper Johnson | .20 | .09 | .03 |
| ☐ 185 | Sean Landeta | .15 | .07 | .02 |
| ☐ 186 | Dave Meggett | .25 | .11 | .03 |
| ☐ 187 | Bart Oates | .15 | .07 | .02 |
| ☐ 188 | Phil Simms | .25 | .11 | .03 |
| ☐ 189 | Lawrence Taylor | .35 | .16 | .04 |
| ☐ 190 | Reyna Thompson | .15 | .07 | .02 |
| ☐ 191 | Brad Baxter | .20 | .09 | .03 |
| ☐ 192 | Dennis Byrd | .20 | .09 | .03 |
| ☐ 193 | Kyle Clifton | .15 | .07 | .02 |
| ☐ 194 | James Hasty | .15 | .07 | .02 |
| ☐ 195 | Pat Leahy | .20 | .09 | .03 |
| ☐ 196 | Erik McMillan | .15 | .07 | .02 |
| ☐ 197 | Rob Moore | .25 | .11 | .03 |
| ☐ 198 | Ken O'Brien | .20 | .09 | .03 |
| ☐ 199 | Mark Boyer | .15 | .07 | .02 |
| ☐ 200 | Al Toon | .20 | .09 | .03 |
| ☐ 201 | Fred Barnett | .35 | .16 | .04 |
| ☐ 202 | Jerome Brown | .20 | .09 | .03 |
| ☐ 203 | Keith Byars | .20 | .09 | .03 |
| ☐ 204 | Randall Cunningham | .50 | .23 | .06 |
| ☐ 205 | Wes Hopkins | .15 | .07 | .02 |
| ☐ 206 | Keith Jackson | .50 | .23 | .06 |
| ☐ 207 | Seth Joyner | .20 | .09 | .03 |
| ☐ 208 | Heath Sherman | .20 | .09 | .03 |
| ☐ 209 | Reggie White | .40 | .18 | .05 |
| ☐ 210 | Calvin Williams | .50 | .23 | .06 |

|  |  | | | |
|---|---|---|---|---|
| ☐ 211 | Roy Green | .20 | .09 | .03 |
| ☐ 212 | Ken Harvey UER (Tackling Rodney Hampton, not Howard Cross) | .15 | .07 | .02 |
| ☐ 213 | Luis Sharpe | .15 | .07 | .02 |
| ☐ 214 | Ernie Jones | .15 | .07 | .02 |
| ☐ 215 | Tim McDonald | .20 | .09 | .03 |
| ☐ 216 | Freddie Joe Nunn | .15 | .07 | .02 |
| ☐ 217 | Ricky Proehl | .25 | .11 | .03 |
| ☐ 218 | Timm Rosenbach | .20 | .09 | .03 |
| ☐ 219 | Anthony Thompson | .15 | .07 | .02 |
| ☐ 220 | Lonnie Young | .15 | .07 | .02 |
| ☐ 221 | Gary Anderson | .15 | .07 | .02 |
| ☐ 222 | Bubby Brister | .25 | .11 | .03 |
| ☐ 223 | Eric Green | .30 | .14 | .04 |
| ☐ 224 | Merril Hoge | .20 | .09 | .03 |
| ☐ 225 | Carnell Lake | .15 | .07 | .02 |
| ☐ 226 | Louis Lipps | .20 | .09 | .03 |
| ☐ 227 | David Little | .15 | .07 | .02 |
| ☐ 228 | Greg Lloyd | .15 | .07 | .02 |
| ☐ 229 | Gerald Williams | .15 | .07 | .02 |
| ☐ 230 | Rod Woodson | .25 | .11 | .03 |
| ☐ 231 | Marion Butts | .25 | .11 | .03 |
| ☐ 232 | Gill Byrd | .20 | .09 | .03 |
| ☐ 233 | Burt Grossman | .15 | .07 | .02 |
| ☐ 234 | Courtney Hall | .15 | .07 | .02 |
| ☐ 235 | Ronnie Harmon | .15 | .07 | .02 |
| ☐ 236 | Anthony Miller | .40 | .18 | .05 |
| ☐ 237 | Leslie O'Neal | .20 | .09 | .03 |
| ☐ 238 | Junior Seau | 1.00 | .45 | .13 |
| ☐ 239 | Billy Joe Tolliver | .20 | .09 | .03 |
| ☐ 240 | Lee Williams | .20 | .09 | .03 |
| ☐ 241 | Dexter Carter | .20 | .09 | .03 |
| ☐ 242 | Kevin Fagan | .15 | .07 | .02 |
| ☐ 243 | Charles Haley | .20 | .09 | .03 |
| ☐ 244 | Brent Jones | .25 | .11 | .03 |
| ☐ 245 | Ronnie Lott | .25 | .11 | .03 |
| ☐ 246 | Guy McIntyre | .20 | .09 | .03 |
| ☐ 247 | Joe Montana | 2.00 | .90 | .25 |
| ☐ 248 | Jerry Rice | 1.75 | .80 | .22 |
| ☐ 249 | John Taylor | .25 | .11 | .03 |
| ☐ 250 | Roger Craig | .25 | .11 | .03 |
| ☐ 251 | Brian Blades | .25 | .11 | .03 |
| ☐ 252 | Derrick Fenner | .20 | .09 | .03 |
| ☐ 253 | Nesby Glasgow UER ('91 was his 13th season, not 12th) | .15 | .07 | .02 |
| ☐ 254 | Jacob Green | .15 | .07 | .02 |
| ☐ 255 | Tommy Kane | .15 | .07 | .02 |
| ☐ 256 | Dave Krieg | .20 | .09 | .03 |
| ☐ 257 | Rufus Porter | .15 | .07 | .02 |
| ☐ 258 | Eugene Robinson | .15 | .07 | .02 |
| ☐ 259 | Cortez Kennedy | .75 | .35 | .09 |
| ☐ 260 | John L. Williams | .20 | .09 | .03 |
| ☐ 261 | Gary Anderson | .15 | .07 | .02 |
| ☐ 262 | Mark Carrier | .20 | .09 | .03 |
| ☐ 263 | Steve Christie | .15 | .07 | .02 |
| ☐ 264 | Reggie Cobb | .60 | .25 | .08 |
| ☐ 265 | Paul Gruber | .20 | .09 | .03 |
| ☐ 266 | Wayne Haddix | .15 | .07 | .02 |
| ☐ 267 | Bruce Hill | .15 | .07 | .02 |
| ☐ 268 | Keith McCants | .15 | .07 | .02 |
| ☐ 269 | Vinny Testaverde | .25 | .11 | .03 |
| ☐ 270 | Broderick Thomas | .20 | .09 | .03 |
| ☐ 271 | Earnest Byner | .25 | .11 | .03 |
| ☐ 272 | Gary Clark | .25 | .11 | .03 |
| ☐ 273 | Darrell Green | .20 | .09 | .03 |
| ☐ 274 | Jim Lachey | .15 | .07 | .02 |
| ☐ 275 | Chip Lohmiller | .20 | .09 | .03 |
| ☐ 276 | Charles Mann | .20 | .09 | .03 |
| ☐ 277 | Wilber Marshall | .20 | .09 | .03 |
| ☐ 278 | Art Monk | .25 | .11 | .03 |
| ☐ 279 | Mark Rypien | .25 | .11 | .03 |
| ☐ 280 | Alvin Walton | .15 | .07 | .02 |
| ☐ 281 | Randall Cunningham BR NFC Passing Leader Philadelphia Eagles | 1.00 | .45 | .13 |
| ☐ 282 | Warren Moon BR AFC Passing Leader Houston Oilers | 1.25 | .55 | .16 |
| ☐ 283 | Barry Sanders BR NFC Rushing Leader Detroit Lions | 4.00 | 1.80 | .50 |
| ☐ 284 | Thurman Thomas BR AFC Rushing Leader Buffalo Bills | 2.25 | 1.00 | .30 |
| ☐ 285 | Jerry Rice BR NFC Receiving Leader San Francisco 49ers | 2.50 | 1.15 | .30 |
| ☐ 286 | Haywood Jeffires BR AFC Receiving Leader Houston Oilers | 1.00 | .45 | .13 |
| ☐ 287 | Charles Haley BR NFC Sack Leader San Francisco 49ers | .60 | .25 | .08 |
| ☐ 288 | Derrick Thomas BR AFC Sack Leader | 1.00 | .45 | .13 |

Kansas City Chiefs

| | | MINT | EXC | G-VG |
|---|---|---|---|---|
| ☐ 289 | NFC Logo Card | .25 | .11 | .03 |
| ☐ 290 | AFC Logo Card | .25 | .11 | .03 |
| ☐ NNO | Checklist Card | .50 | .07 | .02 |
| | (Double fold) | | | |

## 1991 Action Packed 24K Gold

This 42-card set consists of 24K gold-stamped superstar cards that were randomly inserted in foil packs. The fronts of these standard-size (2 1/2" by 3 1/2") cards feature borderless embossed color player photos, with gold indicia bordered in black. The team logo appears in the lower right corner. In a horizontal format, the gold-bordered backs have color head shots, biographical information, statistics, and an "Action Note" in the form of a caption to the action shot on the card front. The cards are numbered on the back. The set numbering follows an alphabetical team order. Also distributed was an 18K version of Randall Cunningham; only 23 were produced.

| | | MINT | EXC | G-VG |
|---|---|---|---|---|
| COMPLETE SET (42) | | 1500.00 | 700.00 | 190.00 |
| COMMON PLAYER (1G-42G) | | 20.00 | 9.00 | 2.50 |
| ☐ 1G | Andre Rison | 40.00 | 18.00 | 5.00 |
| | Atlanta Falcons | | | |
| ☐ 2G | Deion Sanders | 40.00 | 18.00 | 5.00 |
| | Atlanta Falcons | | | |
| ☐ 3G | Andre Reed | 30.00 | 13.50 | 3.80 |
| | Buffalo Bills | | | |
| ☐ 4G | Bruce Smith | 25.00 | 11.50 | 3.10 |
| | Buffalo Bills | | | |
| ☐ 5G | Thurman Thomas | 60.00 | 27.00 | 7.50 |
| | Buffalo Bills | | | |
| ☐ 6G | Neal Anderson | 22.00 | 10.00 | 2.80 |
| | Chicago Bears | | | |
| ☐ 7G | Mark Carrier | 20.00 | 9.00 | 2.50 |
| | Chicago Bears | | | |
| ☐ 8G | Mike Singletary | 22.00 | 10.00 | 2.80 |
| | Chicago Bears | | | |
| ☐ 9G | Boomer Esiason | 30.00 | 13.50 | 3.80 |
| | Cincinnati Bengals | | | |
| ☐ 10G | James Francis | 20.00 | 9.00 | 2.50 |
| | Cincinnati Bengals | | | |
| ☐ 11G | Anthony Munoz | 22.00 | 10.00 | 2.80 |
| | Cincinnati Bengals | | | |
| ☐ 12G | Troy Aikman | 160.00 | 70.00 | 20.00 |
| | Dallas Cowboys | | | |
| ☐ 13G | Emmitt Smith | 200.00 | 90.00 | 25.00 |
| | Dallas Cowboys | | | |
| ☐ 14G | John Elway | 75.00 | 34.00 | 9.50 |
| | Denver Broncos | | | |
| ☐ 15G | Bobby Humphrey | 20.00 | 9.00 | 2.50 |
| | Denver Broncos | | | |
| ☐ 16G | Barry Sanders | 100.00 | 45.00 | 12.50 |
| | Detroit Lions | | | |
| ☐ 17G | Don Majkowski | 20.00 | 9.00 | 2.50 |
| | Green Bay Packers | | | |
| ☐ 18G | Sterling Sharpe | 80.00 | 36.00 | 10.00 |
| | Green Bay Packers | | | |
| ☐ 19G | Warren Moon | 40.00 | 18.00 | 5.00 |
| | Houston Oilers | | | |
| ☐ 20G | Jeff George | 40.00 | 18.00 | 5.00 |
| | Indianapolis Colts | | | |
| ☐ 21G | Christian Okoye | 20.00 | 9.00 | 2.50 |
| | Kansas City Chiefs | | | |
| ☐ 22G | Derrick Thomas | 40.00 | 18.00 | 5.00 |
| | Kansas City Chiefs | | | |
| ☐ 23G | Barry Word | 20.00 | 9.00 | 2.50 |
| | Kansas City Chiefs | | | |
| ☐ 24G | Marcus Allen | 20.00 | 9.00 | 2.50 |
| | Los Angeles Raiders | | | |
| ☐ 25G | Bo Jackson | 60.00 | 27.00 | 7.50 |
| | Los Angeles Raiders | | | |
| ☐ 26G | Jim Everett | 22.00 | 10.00 | 2.80 |
| | Los Angeles Rams | | | |
| ☐ 27G | Cleveland Gary | 20.00 | 9.00 | 2.50 |
| | Los Angeles Rams | | | |
| ☐ 28G | Dan Marino | 100.00 | 45.00 | 12.50 |
| | Miami Dolphins | | | |
| ☐ 29G | Herschel Walker | 20.00 | 9.00 | 2.50 |
| | Minnesota Vikings | | | |
| ☐ 30G | Ottis Anderson | 22.00 | 10.00 | 2.80 |
| | New York Giants | | | |
| ☐ 31G | Rodney Hampton | 70.00 | 32.00 | 8.75 |
| | New York Giants | | | |
| ☐ 32G | Dave Meggett | 22.00 | 10.00 | 2.80 |
| | New York Giants | | | |
| ☐ 33G | Marion Butts | 22.00 | 10.00 | 2.80 |
| | San Diego Chargers | | | |
| ☐ 34G | Randall Cunningham | 25.00 | 11.50 | 3.10 |
| | Philadelphia Eagles | | | |
| ☐ 35G | Reggie White | 30.00 | 13.50 | 3.80 |
| | Philadelphia Eagles | | | |
| ☐ 36G | Jerry Rice | 100.00 | 45.00 | 12.50 |
| | San Francisco 49ers | | | |
| ☐ 37G | Eric Green | 22.00 | 10.00 | 2.80 |
| | Pittsburgh Steelers | | | |
| ☐ 38G | Charles Haley | 20.00 | 9.00 | 2.50 |
| | San Francisco 49ers | | | |
| ☐ 39G | Ronnie Lott | 25.00 | 11.50 | 3.10 |
| | San Francisco 49ers | | | |
| ☐ 40G | Joe Montana | 160.00 | 70.00 | 20.00 |
| | San Francisco 49ers | | | |
| ☐ 41G | Vinny Testaverde | 25.00 | 11.50 | 3.10 |
| | Tampa Bay Buccaneers | | | |
| ☐ 42G | Gary Clark | 25.00 | 11.50 | 3.10 |
| | Washington Redskins | | | |

## 1991 Action Packed Rookie Update

This 84-card standard size (2 1/2" by 3 1/2") set marks the second year that Action Packed has issued a Rookie Update set. Cards were issued in foil packs as well as in collated factory sets. The set contains 74 Rookie Cards (including the 26 1st round draft picks) plus ten traded and update cards. The front design consists of embossed color player photos, with an embossed red helmet with a white "R". The gold indicia and logo are bordered in red instead of black as on the regular set. In red print, the horizontally oriented backs have the player's college regular season and career statistics. The Emmitt Smith rookie prototype card was included as a bonus with each case of 1991 Action Packed Rookie Update foil or sets ordered. The Emmitt Smith prototype is not included in the complete set price below. The cards are numbered on the back. The key Rookie Cards in this set are Nick Bell, Bryan Cox, Ricky Ervins, Brett Favre, Alvin Harper, Mark Higgs, Randal Hill, Todd Marinovich, Herman Moore, Russell Maryland, Dan McGwire, Browning Nagle, Mike Pritchard, Leonard Russell, Ricky Watters, and Harvey Williams.

| | | MINT | EXC | G-VG |
|---|---|---|---|---|
| COMPLETE SET (84) | | 20.00 | 9.00 | 2.50 |
| COMPLETE FACT.SET (84) | | 22.00 | 10.00 | 2.80 |
| COMMON ROOKIE (1-74) | | .15 | .07 | .02 |
| COMMON PLAYER (75-84) | | .15 | .07 | .02 |
| ☐ 1 | Herman Moore | 2.00 | .90 | .25 |
| | Detroit Lions | | | |
| ☐ 2 | Eric Turner | .40 | .18 | .05 |
| | Cleveland Browns | | | |
| ☐ 3 | Mike Croel | .40 | .18 | .05 |
| | Denver Broncos | | | |
| ☐ 4 | Alfred Williams | .35 | .16 | .04 |
| | Cincinnati Bengals | | | |
| ☐ 5 | Stanley Richard | .25 | .11 | .03 |
| | San Diego Chargers | | | |
| ☐ 6 | Russell Maryland | .75 | .35 | .09 |
| | Dallas Cowboys | | | |
| ☐ 7 | Pat Harlow | .25 | .11 | .03 |

| | | | |
|---|---|---|---|
| New England Patriots | | | |
| ☐ 8 Alvin Harper | 2.00 | .90 | .25 |
| Dallas Cowboys | | | |
| ☐ 9 Mike Pritchard | 1.50 | .65 | .19 |
| Atlanta Falcons | | | |
| ☐ 10 Leonard Russell | 2.00 | .90 | .25 |
| New England Patriots | | | |
| ☐ 11 Jarrod Bunch | .35 | .16 | .04 |
| New York Giants | | | |
| ☐ 12 Dan McGwire | .30 | .14 | .04 |
| Seattle Seahawks | | | |
| ☐ 13 Bobby Wilson | .20 | .09 | .03 |
| Washington Redskins | | | |
| ☐ 14 Vinnie Clark | .15 | .07 | .02 |
| Green Bay Packers | | | |
| ☐ 15 Kelvin Pritchett | .15 | .07 | .02 |
| Detroit Lions | | | |
| ☐ 16 Harvey Williams | .40 | .18 | .05 |
| Kansas City Chiefs | | | |
| ☐ 17 Stan Thomas | .15 | .07 | .02 |
| Chicago Bears | | | |
| ☐ 18 Todd Marinovich | .25 | .11 | .03 |
| Los Angeles Raiders | | | |
| ☐ 19 Antone Davis | .15 | .07 | .02 |
| Philadelphia Eagles | | | |
| ☐ 20 Greg Lewis | .15 | .07 | .02 |
| Denver Broncos | | | |
| ☐ 21 Brett Favre | 5.00 | 2.30 | .60 |
| Atlanta Falcons | | | |
| ☐ 22 Wesley Carroll | .35 | .16 | .04 |
| New Orleans Saints | | | |
| ☐ 23 Ed McCaffrey | .30 | .14 | .04 |
| New York Giants | | | |
| ☐ 24 Reggie Barrett | .15 | .07 | .02 |
| Detroit Lions | | | |
| ☐ 25 Chris Zorich | .40 | .18 | .05 |
| Chicago Bears | | | |
| ☐ 26 Kenny Walker | .15 | .07 | .02 |
| Denver Broncos | | | |
| ☐ 27 Aaron Craver | .15 | .07 | .02 |
| Miami Dolphins | | | |
| ☐ 28 Browning Nagle | .40 | .18 | .05 |
| New York Jets | | | |
| ☐ 29 Nick Bell | .40 | .18 | .05 |
| Los Angeles Raiders | | | |
| ☐ 30 Anthony Morgan | .30 | .14 | .04 |
| Chicago Bears | | | |
| ☐ 31 Jesse Campbell | .25 | .11 | .03 |
| Philadelphia Eagles | | | |
| ☐ 32 Eric Bieniemy | .30 | .14 | .04 |
| San Diego Chargers | | | |
| ☐ 33 Ricky Ervins UER | .40 | .18 | .05 |
| Washington Redskins | | | |
| (Totals don't add up) | | | |
| ☐ 34 Kanavis McGhee | .25 | .11 | .03 |
| New York Giants | | | |
| ☐ 35 Shawn Moore | .50 | .23 | .06 |
| Denver Broncos | | | |
| ☐ 36 Todd Lyght | .25 | .11 | .03 |
| Los Angeles Rams | | | |
| ☐ 37 Eric Swann | .50 | .23 | .06 |
| Phoenix Cardinals | | | |
| ☐ 38 Henry Jones | .50 | .23 | .06 |
| Buffalo Bills | | | |
| ☐ 39 Ted Washington | .15 | .07 | .02 |
| San Francisco 49ers | | | |
| ☐ 40 Charles McRae | .15 | .07 | .02 |
| Tampa Bay Buccaneers | | | |
| ☐ 41 Randal Hill | .75 | .35 | .09 |
| Phoenix Cardinals | | | |
| ☐ 42 Huey Richardson | .15 | .07 | .02 |
| Pittsburgh Steelers | | | |
| ☐ 43 Roman Phifer | .20 | .09 | .03 |
| Los Angeles Rams | | | |
| ☐ 44 Ricky Watters | 4.00 | 1.80 | .50 |
| San Francisco 49ers | | | |
| ☐ 45 Esera Tuaolo | .15 | .07 | .02 |
| Green Bay Packers | | | |
| ☐ 46 Michael Jackson | 1.25 | .55 | .16 |
| Cleveland Browns | | | |
| ☐ 47 Shawn Jefferson | .25 | .11 | .03 |
| San Diego Chargers | | | |
| ☐ 48 Tim Barnett | .40 | .18 | .05 |
| Kansas City Chiefs | | | |
| ☐ 49 Chuck Webb | .15 | .07 | .02 |
| Green Bay Packers | | | |
| ☐ 50 Moe Gardner | .20 | .09 | .03 |
| Atlanta Falcons | | | |
| ☐ 51 Mo Lewis | .20 | .09 | .03 |
| New York Jets | | | |
| ☐ 52 Mike Dumas | .15 | .07 | .02 |
| Houston Oilers | | | |
| ☐ 53 Jon Vaughn | .50 | .23 | .06 |
| New England Patriots | | | |
| ☐ 54 Jerome Henderson | .15 | .07 | .02 |
| New England Patriots | | | |
| ☐ 55 Harry Colon | .15 | .07 | .02 |
| New England Patriots | | | |
| ☐ 56 David Daniels | .15 | .07 | .02 |
| Seattle Seahawks | | | |
| ☐ 57 Phil Hansen | .30 | .14 | .04 |
| Buffalo Bills | | | |
| ☐ 58 Ernie Mills | .30 | .14 | .04 |
| Pittsburgh Steelers | | | |
| ☐ 59 John Kasay | .30 | .14 | .04 |
| Seattle Seahawks | | | |
| ☐ 60 Darren Lewis | .35 | .16 | .04 |
| Chicago Bears | | | |
| ☐ 61 James Joseph | .40 | .18 | .05 |
| Philadelphia Eagles | | | |
| ☐ 62 Robert Wilson | .15 | .07 | .02 |
| Tampa Bay Buccaneers | | | |
| ☐ 63 Lawrence Dawsey | .40 | .18 | .05 |
| Tampa Bay Buccaneers | | | |
| ☐ 64 Mike Jones | .15 | .07 | .02 |
| Phoenix Cardinals | | | |
| ☐ 65 Dave McCloughan | .15 | .07 | .02 |
| Indianapolis Colts | | | |
| ☐ 66 Erric Pegram | 2.50 | 1.15 | .30 |
| Atlanta Falcons | | | |
| ☐ 67 Aeneas Williams | .30 | .14 | .04 |
| Phoenix Cardinals | | | |
| ☐ 68 Reggie Johnson | .50 | .23 | .06 |
| Denver Broncos | | | |
| ☐ 69 Todd Scott | .40 | .18 | .05 |
| Minnesota Vikings | | | |
| ☐ 70 James Jones | .30 | .14 | .04 |
| Cleveland Browns | | | |
| ☐ 71 Lamar Rogers | .15 | .07 | .02 |
| Cincinnati Bengals | | | |
| ☐ 72 Darryll Lewis | .25 | .11 | .03 |
| Houston Oilers | | | |
| ☐ 73 Bryan Cox | .75 | .35 | .09 |
| Miami Dolphins | | | |
| ☐ 74 Leroy Thompson | .50 | .23 | .06 |
| Pittsburgh Steelers | | | |
| ☐ 75 Mark Higgs | 1.25 | .55 | .16 |
| Miami Dolphins | | | |
| ☐ 76 John Friesz | .35 | .16 | .04 |
| San Diego Chargers | | | |
| ☐ 77 Tim McKyer | .15 | .07 | .02 |
| Atlanta Falcons | | | |
| ☐ 78 Roger Craig | .25 | .11 | .03 |
| Los Angeles Raiders | | | |
| ☐ 79 Ronnie Lott | .15 | .07 | .02 |
| Los Angeles Raiders | | | |
| ☐ 80 Steve Young | 1.00 | .45 | .13 |
| San Francisco 49ers | | | |
| ☐ 81 Percy Snow | .15 | .07 | .02 |
| Kansas City Chiefs | | | |
| ☐ 82 Cornelius Bennett | .15 | .07 | .02 |
| Buffalo Bills | | | |
| ☐ 83 Johnny Johnson | .60 | .25 | .08 |
| Phoenix Cardinals | | | |
| ☐ 84 Blair Thomas | .25 | .11 | .03 |
| New York Jets | | | |

## 1991 Action Packed Rookies 24K Gold

This 26-card set measures the standard size (2 1/2" by 3 1/2") and was issued in honor of the first round draft picks. These special cards are identified by "24K" stamped on the card front, and they were randomly inserted in 1991 Rookie Update foil packs. Like the other Rookie Update cards, the fronts have borderless embossed color player photos, with gold indicia and logo bordered in red. In a horizontal format, the backs have the player's collegiate regular season and career statistics in red print. The cards are numbered on the back. The set numbering order is according to NFL draft order.

|  | MINT | EXC | G-VG |
|---|---|---|---|
| COMPLETE SET (26).................... | 1000.00 | 450.00 | 125.00 |
| COMMON PLAYER (1G-26G)............ | 20.00 | 9.00 | 2.50 |
| ☐ 1G Russell Maryland.................... Dallas Cowboys | 30.00 | 13.50 | 3.80 |
| ☐ 2G Eric Turner.......................... Cleveland Browns | 30.00 | 13.50 | 3.80 |
| ☐ 3G Mike Croel .......................... Denver Broncos | 20.00 | 9.00 | 2.50 |
| ☐ 4G Todd Lyght .......................... Los Angeles Rams | 20.00 | 9.00 | 2.50 |
| ☐ 5G Eric Swann .......................... Phoenix Cardinals | 30.00 | 13.50 | 3.80 |
| ☐ 6G Charles McRae ...................... Tampa Bay Buccaneers | 20.00 | 9.00 | 2.50 |
| ☐ 7G Antone Davis ....................... Philadelphia Eagles | 20.00 | 9.00 | 2.50 |
| ☐ 8G Stanley Richard ..................... San Diego Chargers | 20.00 | 9.00 | 2.50 |
| ☐ 9G Herman Moore ...................... Detroit Lions | 90.00 | 40.00 | 11.50 |
| ☐ 10G Pat Harlow.......................... New England Patriots | 20.00 | 9.00 | 2.50 |
| ☐ 11G Alvin Harper ....................... Dallas Cowboys | 90.00 | 40.00 | 11.50 |
| ☐ 12G Mike Pritchard ..................... Atlanta Falcons | 60.00 | 27.00 | 7.50 |
| ☐ 13G Leonard Russell.................... New England Patriots | 60.00 | 27.00 | 7.50 |
| ☐ 14G Huey Richardson ................... Pittsburgh Steelers | 20.00 | 9.00 | 2.50 |
| ☐ 15G Dan McGwire ...................... Seattle Seahawks | 20.00 | 9.00 | 2.50 |
| ☐ 16G Bobby Wilson ...................... Washington Redskins | 20.00 | 9.00 | 2.50 |
| ☐ 17G Alfred Williams .................... Cincinnati Bengals | 30.00 | 13.50 | 3.80 |
| ☐ 18G Vinnie Clark ....................... Green Bay Packers | 20.00 | 9.00 | 2.50 |
| ☐ 19G Kelvin Pritchett .................... Detroit Lions | 20.00 | 9.00 | 2.50 |
| ☐ 20G Harvey Williams.................... Kansas City Chiefs | 30.00 | 13.50 | 3.80 |
| ☐ 21G Stan Thomas ....................... Chicago Bears | 20.00 | 9.00 | 2.50 |
| ☐ 22G Randal Hill ......................... Phoenix Cardinals | 40.00 | 18.00 | 5.00 |
| ☐ 23G Todd Marinovich.................... Los Angeles Raiders | 20.00 | 9.00 | 2.50 |
| ☐ 24G Ted Washington .................... San Francisco 49ers | 20.00 | 9.00 | 2.50 |
| ☐ 25G Henry Jones ........................ Buffalo Bills | 30.00 | 13.50 | 3.80 |
| ☐ 26G Jarrod Bunch ....................... New York Giants | 20.00 | 9.00 | 2.50 |

## 1991 Action Packed All-Madden

In its second year, this 52-card standard-size (2 1/2" by 3 1/2") set honors the selections to the All-Madden Team. The fronts feature borderless embossed color player photos, accented by gold and aqua border stripes running down either the left or right side of the card face. The All-Madden Team logo appears in the upper left corner, with the team helmet, player's name, and position printed at the card bottom. Between aqua border stripes, the horizontally oriented backs carry player profile, a color head shot, and a diagram of a football play. The cards are numbered on the back. The cards were issued in foil packs as well as in factory sets. Each of the cards in the set was also available on a very limited basis in Action Packed's increasingly popular 24K version. These 24K All-Madden cards are valued at approximately 50 to 100 times the corresponding values below.

|  | MINT | EXC | G-VG |
|---|---|---|---|
| COMPLETE SET (52)...................... | 18.00 | 7.25 | 1.80 |
| COMMON CARD (1-52) .................. | .25 | .10 | .02 |
| ☐ 1 Mark Rypien .......................... Washington Redskins | .35 | .14 | .03 |
| ☐ 2 Erik Kramer .......................... Detroit Lions | .50 | .20 | .05 |
| ☐ 3 Jim McMahon ........................ Philadelphia Eagles | .50 | .20 | .05 |
| ☐ 4 Jesse Sapolu.......................... San Francisco 49ers | .25 | .10 | .02 |
| ☐ 5 Jay Hilgenberg ....................... Chicago Bears | .25 | .10 | .02 |
| ☐ 6 Howard Ballard ...................... Buffalo Bills | .25 | .10 | .02 |
| ☐ 7 Lomas Brown.......................... Detroit Lions | .25 | .10 | .02 |
| ☐ 8 John Elliott............................ New York Giants | .25 | .10 | .02 |
| ☐ 9 Joe Jacoby ........................... Washington Redskins | .25 | .10 | .02 |
| ☐ 10 Jim Lachey........................... Washington Redskins | .35 | .14 | .03 |
| ☐ 11 Anthony Munoz....................... Cincinnati Bengals | .50 | .20 | .05 |
| ☐ 12 Nate Newton ........................ Dallas Cowboys | .35 | .14 | .03 |
| ☐ 13 Will Wolford ......................... Buffalo Bills | .25 | .10 | .02 |
| ☐ 14 Jerry Ball ............................ Detroit Lions | .25 | .10 | .02 |
| ☐ 15 Jerome Brown........................ Philadelphia Eagles | .35 | .14 | .03 |
| ☐ 16 William Perry ........................ Chicago Bears | .50 | .20 | .05 |
| ☐ 17 Charles Mann........................ Washington Redskins | .25 | .10 | .02 |
| ☐ 18 Clyde Simmons...................... Philadelphia Eagles | .25 | .10 | .02 |
| ☐ 19 Reggie White........................ Philadelphia Eagles | .75 | .30 | .07 |
| ☐ 20 Eric Allen............................ Philadelphia Eagles | .25 | .10 | .02 |
| ☐ 21 Darrell Green ........................ Washington Redskins | .50 | .20 | .05 |
| ☐ 22 Bennie Blades ....................... Detroit Lions | .35 | .14 | .03 |
| ☐ 23 Chuck Cecil .......................... Green Bay Packers | .25 | .10 | .02 |
| ☐ 24 Rickey Dixon ........................ Cincinnati Bengals | .35 | .14 | .03 |
| ☐ 25 David Fulcher ........................ Cincinnati Bengals | .35 | .14 | .03 |
| ☐ 26 Ronnie Lott .......................... Los Angeles Raiders | .50 | .20 | .05 |
| ☐ 27 Emmitt Smith........................ Dallas Cowboys | 5.00 | 2.00 | .50 |
| ☐ 28 Neal Anderson........................ Chicago Bears | .50 | .20 | .05 |
| ☐ 29 Robert Delpino ....................... Los Angeles Rams | .35 | .14 | .03 |
| ☐ 30 Barry Sanders ........................ Detroit Lions | 2.00 | .80 | .20 |
| ☐ 31 Thurman Thomas...................... Buffalo Bills | 1.25 | .50 | .12 |
| ☐ 32 Cornelius Bennett..................... Buffalo Bills | .50 | .20 | .05 |
| ☐ 33 Rickey Jackson ....................... New Orleans Saints | .35 | .14 | .03 |
| ☐ 34 Seth Joyner .......................... Philadelphia Eagles | .35 | .14 | .03 |
| ☐ 35 Wilber Marshall....................... Washington Redskins | .35 | .14 | .03 |
| ☐ 36 Clay Matthews........................ Cleveland Browns | .35 | .14 | .03 |
| ☐ 37 Chris Spielman........................ Detroit Lions | .35 | .14 | .03 |
| ☐ 38 Pat Swilling .......................... New Orleans Saints | .35 | .14 | .03 |
| ☐ 39 Fred Barnett ......................... Philadelphia Eagles | .75 | .30 | .07 |
| ☐ 40 Gary Clark ........................... Washington Redskins | .50 | .20 | .05 |
| ☐ 41 Michael Irvin......................... Dallas Cowboys | 1.50 | .60 | .15 |
| ☐ 42 Art Monk.............................. Washington Redskins | .75 | .30 | .07 |
| ☐ 43 Jerry Rice............................. San Francisco 49ers | 2.00 | .80 | .20 |
| ☐ 44 John Taylor........................... San Francisco 49ers | .50 | .20 | .05 |
| ☐ 45 Tom Waddle........................... Chicago Bears | .50 | .20 | .05 |
| ☐ 46 Kevin Butler.......................... Chicago Bears | .25 | .10 | .02 |
| ☐ 47 Bill Bates ............................ Dallas Cowboys | .35 | .14 | .03 |

| | | | |
|---|---|---|---|
| ☐ 48 Greg Manusky | .25 | .10 | .02 |
| Minnesota Vikings | | | |
| ☐ 49 Elvis Patterson | .25 | .10 | .02 |
| Los Angeles Raiders | | | |
| ☐ 50 Steve Tasker | .25 | .10 | .02 |
| Buffalo Bills | | | |
| ☐ 51 John Daly | 1.00 | .40 | .10 |
| (Golfer) | | | |
| ☐ 52 All-Madden Team Trophy | .35 | .14 | .03 |

# 1992 Action Packed 24K NFLPA/MDA Awards

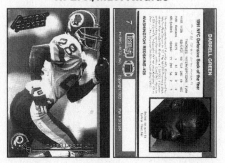

This 16-card, 24K gold standard-size (2 1/2" by 3 1/2") set was produced by Action Packed to honor NFL Players of the Year for the 1991 season. Cards come packed in an attractive black box imprinted on front with NFLPA/MDA Awards Dinner, March 5, 1992. Only 1,000 sets were produced, and banquet attendees each received a set stamped "Banquet Edition." Card fronts feature a raised-print player photo and team helmet. The Action Packed logo appears in the upper left corner of red cards (AFC) and in the upper right on blue cards (NFC). Players' names appear at the lower right or left of each card offsetting the logo. Handsomely designed with 24K gold borders and lettering, horizontally designed backs feature biographical and statistical information and a head shot of each player within a 24K gold box. Featuring the traditional rounded corners, cards are numbered in the lower left corner.

| | MINT | EXC | G-VG |
|---|---|---|---|
| COMPLETE SET (16) | 300.00 | 120.00 | 30.00 |
| COMMON PLAYER (1-16) | 12.00 | 5.00 | 1.20 |
| ☐ 1 Steve Wisniewski | 12.00 | 5.00 | 1.20 |
| Los Angeles Raiders | | | |
| ☐ 2 Jim Lachey | 15.00 | 6.00 | 1.50 |
| Washington Redskins | | | |
| ☐ 3 Reggie White | 30.00 | 12.00 | 3.00 |
| Philadelphia Eagles | | | |
| ☐ 4 William Fuller | 15.00 | 6.00 | 1.50 |
| Houston Oilers | | | |
| ☐ 5 Derrick Thomas | 30.00 | 12.00 | 3.00 |
| Kansas City Chiefs | | | |
| ☐ 6 Pat Swilling | 15.00 | 6.00 | 1.50 |
| New Orleans Saints | | | |
| ☐ 7 Darrell Green | 15.00 | 6.00 | 1.50 |
| Washington Redskins | | | |
| ☐ 8 Ronnie Lott | 20.00 | 8.00 | 2.00 |
| Los Angeles Raiders | | | |
| ☐ 9 Steve Tasker | 15.00 | 6.00 | 1.50 |
| Buffalo Bills | | | |
| ☐ 10 Mel Gray | 12.00 | 5.00 | 1.20 |
| Detroit Lions | | | |
| ☐ 11 Aeneas Williams | 12.00 | 5.00 | 1.20 |
| Phoenix Cardinals | | | |
| ☐ 12 Mike Croel | 18.00 | 7.25 | 1.80 |
| Denver Broncos | | | |
| ☐ 13 Leonard Russell | 30.00 | 12.00 | 3.00 |
| New England Patriots | | | |
| ☐ 14 Lawrence Dawsey | 20.00 | 8.00 | 2.00 |
| Tampa Bay Buccaneers | | | |
| ☐ 15 Barry Sanders | 75.00 | 30.00 | 7.50 |
| Detroit Lions | | | |
| ☐ 16 Thurman Thomas | 50.00 | 20.00 | 5.00 |
| Buffalo Bills | | | |

# 1992 Action Packed Mackey Award

Only 2,000 numbered sets of these three 24K gold cards were produced for the attendees at the 1992 NFLPA Mackey Awards Banquet. The cards measure the standard size, 2 1/2" by 3 1/2".

| | MINT | EXC | G-VG |
|---|---|---|---|
| COMPLETE SET (3) | 90.00 | 36.00 | 9.00 |
| COMMON PLAYER | 20.00 | 8.00 | 2.00 |
| ☐ 92W Reggie White | 30.00 | 12.00 | 3.00 |
| ☐ HOF John Mackey | 20.00 | 8.00 | 2.00 |
| ☐ HUD Jack Kemp | 60.00 | 24.00 | 6.00 |

# 1992 Action Packed Prototypes

The 1992 Action Packed Prototype set contains three cards measuring the standard size (2 1/2" by 3 1/2"). The card design is very similar to the 1992 Action Packed regular issue cards. The cards were first distributed at the Super Bowl Show in Minneapolis in January, 1992. The cards are overstamped "Prototype" on the back. The Barry Sanders card seems to be a little more difficult to find than the other two cards.

| | MINT | EXC | G-VG |
|---|---|---|---|
| COMPLETE SET (3) | 25.00 | 10.00 | 2.50 |
| COMMON PLAYER | 5.00 | 2.00 | .50 |
| ☐ 92A Thurman Thomas | 5.00 | 2.00 | .50 |
| Buffalo Bills | | | |
| ☐ 92N Emmitt Smith | 15.00 | 6.00 | 1.50 |
| Dallas Cowboys | | | |
| ☐ 92P Barry Sanders | 12.00 | 5.00 | 1.20 |
| Detroit Lions | | | |

# 1992 Action Packed

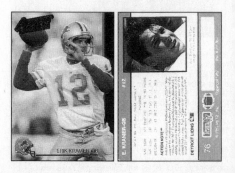

The 1992 Action Packed football set contains 280 cards measuring the standard size (2 1/2" by 3 1/2"). The fronts feature borderless embossed color player photos, accented by either gold and aqua (NFC) or gold and red (AFC) border stripes running down either the left or right side of the card face. The team helmet appears in the lower left or right corner, with the player's name and position printed at the card bottom. The horizontally oriented backs carry biography, player profile, a color head shot, and an "Action Note" in the form of an extended caption to the photo on the front. The cards are numbered on the back and checklisted below alphabetically according to teams as follows: Atlanta Falcons (1-10), Buffalo Bills (11-20), Chicago Bears (21-30), Cincinnati Bengals (31-40), Cleveland Browns (41-50), Dallas Cowboys (51-60), Denver Broncos (61-70), Detroit Lions (71-80), Green Bay Packers (81-90), Houston Oilers (91-100), Indianapolis Colts (101-110), Kansas City Chiefs (111-120), Los Angeles Raiders (121-130), Los Angeles Rams (131-140), Miami Dolphins (141-150), Minnesota Vikings (151-160), New England Patriots (161-170), New Orleans Saints (171-180), New York Giants (181-190), New York Jets (191-200), Philadelphia Eagles (201-210), Phoenix Cardinals (211-220), Pittsburgh Steelers (221-230), San Diego Chargers (231-240), San Francisco 49ers (241-250), Seattle Seahawks (251-260), Tampa Bay Buccaneers (261-270), and Washington Redskins (271-280). To show support for their injured teammate, a special "thumbs up" logo with Mike Utley's number 60 was placed on the back of all Detroit Lions' cards. The factory set closes with a Braille subset (281-288) and Logo cards (289-290). The inside lid of the factory set box has the set printed on it. The eight Braille cards, available this year in foil packs as well as factory sets, feature category leaders in their division. Action Packed also made 26 18K solid gold Tiffany-designed cards of Barry Sanders, the Action Packed Player of the Year, and certificates for a chance to win these cards were randomly inserted in the regular series foil packs. Action Packed also produced a 288-card "Mint" version of the regular set. Action Packed produced only 500 "Mint" versions of each player card, and each "Mint" card was individually numbered (1/500, 2/500, etc.). Twenty-four six-card packs were packaged in a gold, velour-lined box, and purchase of an even-numbered box and an odd-numbered box guaranteed receipt of the complete 288-card set. Sets were offered for sale beginning on July 7, 1992 at a special reception during the 13th Annual National Sports Card Convention in Atlanta, Georgia, and collectors who placed an order on that day received a free Barry Sanders prototype card. The player's image on the front is embossed and accented by 24K gold leaf, and the card edges are black. The "Mint" version cards are currently valued at 100 to 200 times the regular issue value of the respective card.

| | MINT | EXC | G-VG |
|---|---|---|---|
| COMPLETE SET (280) | 50.00 | 23.00 | 6.25 |
| COMPLETE FACT.SET (292) | 90.00 | 40.00 | 11.50 |
| COMMON PLAYER (1-280) | .15 | .07 | .02 |
| COMMON BRAILLE (281-288) | .75 | .35 | .09 |
| COMMON LOGO (289-290) | .35 | .16 | .04 |
| B. SANDERS GOLD (43G/44G) | 25.00 | 11.50 | 3.10 |

| | | | |
|---|---|---|---|
| ☐ 1 Steve Broussard | .20 | .09 | .03 |
| ☐ 2 Michael Haynes | .75 | .35 | .09 |
| ☐ 3 Tim McKyer | .20 | .09 | .03 |
| ☐ 4 Chris Miller | .25 | .11 | .03 |
| ☐ 5 Andre Rison | .50 | .23 | .06 |
| ☐ 6 Jessie Tuggle | .15 | .07 | .02 |
| ☐ 7 Mike Pritchard | .60 | .25 | .08 |
| ☐ 8 Moe Gardner | .15 | .07 | .02 |
| ☐ 9 Brian Jordan | .20 | .09 | .03 |
| ☐ 10 Mike Kenn and | .20 | .09 | .03 |
| Chris Hinton | | | |
| ☐ 11 Steve Tasker | .20 | .09 | .03 |
| ☐ 12 Cornelius Bennett | .25 | .11 | .03 |
| ☐ 13 Shane Conlan | .20 | .09 | .03 |
| ☐ 14 Darryl Talley | .20 | .09 | .03 |
| ☐ 15 Thurman Thomas | 1.00 | .45 | .13 |
| ☐ 16 James Lofton | .25 | .11 | .03 |
| ☐ 17 Don Beebe | .25 | .11 | .03 |
| ☐ 18 Jim Ritcher | .15 | .07 | .02 |
| ☐ 19 Keith McKeller | .15 | .07 | .02 |
| ☐ 20 Nate Odomes | .25 | .11 | .03 |
| ☐ 21 Mark Carrier USC | .20 | .09 | .03 |
| ☐ 22 Wendell Davis | .15 | .07 | .02 |
| ☐ 23 Richard Dent | .20 | .09 | .03 |
| ☐ 24 Jim Harbaugh | .20 | .09 | .03 |
| ☐ 25 Jay Hilgenberg | .20 | .09 | .03 |
| ☐ 26 Steve McMichael | .20 | .09 | .03 |
| ☐ 27 Tom Waddle | .25 | .11 | .03 |
| ☐ 28 Neal Anderson | .20 | .09 | .03 |
| ☐ 29 Brad Muster | .20 | .09 | .03 |
| ☐ 30 Shaun Gayle | .15 | .07 | .02 |
| ☐ 31 Jim Breech | .15 | .07 | .02 |
| ☐ 32 James Brooks | .20 | .09 | .03 |
| ☐ 33 James Francis | .20 | .09 | .03 |
| ☐ 34 David Fulcher | .15 | .07 | .02 |
| ☐ 35 Harold Green | .15 | .07 | .02 |
| ☐ 36 Rodney Holman | .15 | .07 | .02 |
| ☐ 37 Anthony Munoz | .20 | .09 | .03 |
| ☐ 38 Tim Krumrie | .15 | .07 | .02 |
| ☐ 39 Tim McGee | .15 | .07 | .02 |
| ☐ 40 Eddie Brown | .15 | .07 | .02 |
| ☐ 41 Kevin Mack | .20 | .09 | .03 |
| ☐ 42 James Jones | .15 | .07 | .02 |
| ☐ 43 Vince Newsome | .15 | .07 | .02 |
| ☐ 44 Ed King | .15 | .07 | .02 |
| ☐ 45 Eric Metcalf | .25 | .11 | .03 |
| ☐ 46 Leroy Hoard | .20 | .09 | .03 |
| ☐ 47 Stephen Braggs | .15 | .07 | .02 |
| ☐ 48 Clay Matthews | .20 | .09 | .03 |
| ☐ 49 David Brandon | .15 | .07 | .02 |
| ☐ 50 Rob Burnett | .15 | .07 | .02 |
| ☐ 51 Larry Brown | .15 | .07 | .02 |
| ☐ 52 Alvin Harper | .75 | .35 | .09 |
| ☐ 53 Michael Irvin | 1.25 | .55 | .16 |
| ☐ 54 Ken Norton Jr. | .25 | .11 | .03 |
| ☐ 55 Jay Novacek | .50 | .23 | .06 |
| ☐ 56 Emmitt Smith | 6.00 | 2.70 | .75 |
| ☐ 57 Tony Tolbert | .15 | .07 | .02 |
| ☐ 58 Nate Newton | .15 | .07 | .02 |
| ☐ 59 Steve Beuerlein | .35 | .16 | .04 |
| ☐ 60 Tony Casillas | .15 | .07 | .02 |
| ☐ 61 Steve Atwater | .20 | .09 | .03 |
| ☐ 62 Mike Croel | .20 | .09 | .03 |
| ☐ 63 Gaston Green | .20 | .09 | .03 |
| ☐ 64 Mark Jackson | .20 | .09 | .03 |
| ☐ 65 Greg Kragen | .15 | .07 | .02 |
| ☐ 66 Karl Mecklenburg | .20 | .09 | .03 |
| ☐ 67 Dennis Smith | .20 | .09 | .03 |
| ☐ 68 Steve Sewell | .15 | .07 | .02 |
| ☐ 69 John Elway | 1.00 | .45 | .13 |
| ☐ 70 Simon Fletcher | .20 | .09 | .03 |
| ☐ 71 Mel Gray | .20 | .09 | .03 |
| ☐ 72 Barry Sanders | 2.50 | 1.15 | .30 |
| ☐ 73 Jerry Ball | .20 | .09 | .03 |
| ☐ 74 Bennie Blades | .15 | .07 | .02 |
| ☐ 75 Lomas Brown | .15 | .07 | .02 |
| ☐ 76 Erik Kramer | .35 | .16 | .04 |
| ☐ 77 Chris Spielman | .20 | .09 | .03 |
| ☐ 78 Ray Crockett | .15 | .07 | .02 |
| ☐ 79 Willie Green | .15 | .07 | .02 |
| ☐ 80 Rodney Peete | .20 | .09 | .03 |
| ☐ 81 Sterling Sharpe | 1.25 | .55 | .16 |
| ☐ 82 Tony Bennett | .20 | .09 | .03 |
| ☐ 83 Chuck Cecil | .15 | .07 | .02 |
| ☐ 84 Perry Kemp | .15 | .07 | .02 |
| ☐ 85 Brian Noble | .15 | .07 | .02 |
| ☐ 86 Darrell Thompson | .20 | .09 | .03 |
| ☐ 87 Mike Tomczak | .15 | .07 | .02 |
| ☐ 88 Vince Workman | .20 | .09 | .03 |
| ☐ 89 Esera Tuaolo | .15 | .07 | .02 |
| ☐ 90 Mark Murphy | .15 | .07 | .02 |
| ☐ 91 William Fuller | .15 | .07 | .02 |
| ☐ 92 Ernest Givins | .20 | .09 | .03 |
| ☐ 93 Drew Hill | .20 | .09 | .03 |
| ☐ 94 Al Smith | .15 | .07 | .02 |
| ☐ 95 Ray Childress | .20 | .09 | .03 |
| ☐ 96 Haywood Jeffires | .25 | .11 | .03 |
| ☐ 97 Cris Dishman | .20 | .09 | .03 |
| ☐ 98 Warren Moon | .50 | .23 | .06 |
| ☐ 99 Lamar Lathon | .15 | .07 | .02 |
| ☐ 100 Mike Munchak and | .20 | .09 | .03 |
| Bruce Matthews | | | |
| ☐ 101 Bill Brooks | .20 | .09 | .03 |
| ☐ 102 Duane Bickett | .15 | .07 | .02 |
| ☐ 103 Eugene Daniel | .15 | .07 | .02 |
| ☐ 104 Jeff Herrod | .15 | .07 | .02 |
| ☐ 105 Jessie Hester | .15 | .07 | .02 |
| ☐ 106 Donnell Thompson | .15 | .07 | .02 |
| ☐ 107 Anthony Johnson | .15 | .07 | .02 |
| ☐ 108 Jon Hand | .15 | .07 | .02 |
| ☐ 109 Rohn Stark | .15 | .07 | .02 |
| ☐ 110 Clarence Verdin | .15 | .07 | .02 |
| ☐ 111 Derrick Thomas | .60 | .25 | .08 |
| ☐ 112 Steve DeBerg | .20 | .09 | .03 |
| ☐ 113 Deron Cherry | .15 | .07 | .02 |
| ☐ 114 Chris Martin | .15 | .07 | .02 |
| ☐ 115 Christian Okoye | .20 | .09 | .03 |
| ☐ 116 Dan Saleaumua | .15 | .07 | .02 |
| ☐ 117 Neil Smith | .25 | .11 | .03 |
| ☐ 118 Barry Word | .25 | .11 | .03 |
| ☐ 119 Tim Barnett | .20 | .09 | .03 |
| ☐ 120 Albert Lewis | .20 | .09 | .03 |
| ☐ 121 Ronnie Lott | .25 | .11 | .03 |
| ☐ 122 Marcus Allen | .20 | .09 | .03 |
| ☐ 123 Todd Marinovich | .15 | .07 | .02 |
| ☐ 124 Nick Bell | .15 | .07 | .02 |
| ☐ 125 Tim Brown | .60 | .25 | .08 |
| ☐ 126 Ethan Horton | .15 | .07 | .02 |
| ☐ 127 Greg Townsend | .15 | .07 | .02 |
| ☐ 128 Jeff Gossett and | .15 | .07 | .02 |
| Jeff Jaeger | | | |
| ☐ 129 Scott Davis | .15 | .07 | .02 |
| ☐ 130 Steve Wisniewski and | .15 | .07 | .02 |

Don Mosebar

| | | | |
|---|---|---|---|
| ☐ 131 Kevin Greene | .20 | .09 | .03 |
| ☐ 132 Roman Phifer | .15 | .07 | .02 |
| ☐ 133 Tony Zendejas | .15 | .07 | .02 |
| ☐ 134 Pat Terrell | .15 | .07 | .02 |
| ☐ 135 Flipper Anderson | .20 | .09 | .03 |
| ☐ 136 Robert Delpino | .20 | .09 | .03 |
| ☐ 137 Jim Everett | .20 | .09 | .03 |
| ☐ 138 Larry Kelm | .15 | .07 | .02 |
| ☐ 139 Todd Lyght | .15 | .07 | .02 |
| ☐ 140 Henry Ellard | .20 | .09 | .03 |
| ☐ 141 Mark Clayton | .20 | .09 | .03 |
| ☐ 142 Jeff Cross | .15 | .07 | .02 |
| ☐ 143 Mark Duper | .20 | .09 | .03 |
| ☐ 144 John Offerdahl | .20 | .09 | .03 |
| ☐ 145 Louis Oliver | .20 | .09 | .03 |
| ☐ 146 Pete Stoyanovich | .20 | .09 | .03 |
| ☐ 147 Richmond Webb | .20 | .09 | .03 |
| ☐ 148 Mark Higgs | .30 | .14 | .04 |
| ☐ 149 Tony Paige | .15 | .07 | .02 |
| ☐ 150 Bryan Cox | .15 | .07 | .02 |
| ☐ 151 Anthony Carter | .20 | .09 | .03 |
| ☐ 152 Cris Carter | .25 | .11 | .03 |
| ☐ 153 Rich Gannon | .20 | .09 | .03 |
| ☐ 154 Steve Jordan | .20 | .09 | .03 |
| ☐ 155 Mike Merriweather | .15 | .07 | .02 |
| ☐ 156 Henry Thomas | .15 | .07 | .02 |
| ☐ 157 Herschel Walker | .15 | .07 | .02 |
| ☐ 158 Randall McDaniel | .15 | .07 | .02 |
| ☐ 159 Terry Allen | .50 | .23 | .06 |
| ☐ 160 Joey Browner | .15 | .07 | .02 |
| ☐ 161 Leonard Russell | .75 | .35 | .09 |
| ☐ 162 Bruce Armstrong | .15 | .07 | .02 |
| ☐ 163 Vincent Brown | .15 | .07 | .02 |
| ☐ 164 Hugh Millen | .15 | .07 | .02 |
| ☐ 165 Andre Tippett | .20 | .09 | .03 |
| ☐ 166 Jon Vaughn | .15 | .07 | .02 |
| ☐ 167 Pat Harlow | .15 | .07 | .02 |
| ☐ 168 Marv Cook | .20 | .09 | .03 |
| ☐ 169 Irving Fryar | .20 | .09 | .03 |
| ☐ 170 Maurice Hurst | .15 | .07 | .02 |
| ☐ 171 Pat Swilling | .20 | .09 | .03 |
| ☐ 172 Vince Buck | .15 | .07 | .02 |
| ☐ 173 Rickey Jackson | .20 | .09 | .03 |
| ☐ 174 Sam Mills | .20 | .09 | .03 |
| ☐ 175 Bobby Hebert | .25 | .11 | .03 |
| ☐ 176 Vaughan Johnson | .20 | .09 | .03 |
| ☐ 177 Floyd Turner | .15 | .07 | .02 |
| ☐ 178 Fred McAfee | .35 | .16 | .04 |
| ☐ 179 Morten Andersen | .20 | .09 | .03 |
| ☐ 180 Eric Martin | .20 | .09 | .03 |
| ☐ 181 Rodney Hampton | 1.25 | .55 | .16 |
| ☐ 182 Pepper Johnson | .20 | .09 | .03 |
| ☐ 183 Leonard Marshall | .20 | .09 | .03 |
| ☐ 184 Stephen Baker | .15 | .07 | .02 |
| ☐ 185 Mark Ingram | .20 | .09 | .03 |
| ☐ 186 Dave Meggett | .20 | .09 | .03 |
| ☐ 187 Bart Oates | .15 | .07 | .02 |
| ☐ 188 Mark Collins | .15 | .07 | .02 |
| ☐ 189 Myron Guyton | .15 | .07 | .02 |
| ☐ 190 Jeff Hostetler | .40 | .18 | .05 |
| ☐ 191 Jeff Lageman | .15 | .07 | .02 |
| ☐ 192 Brad Baxter | .20 | .09 | .03 |
| ☐ 193 Mo Lewis | .15 | .07 | .02 |
| ☐ 194 Chris Burkett | .15 | .07 | .02 |
| ☐ 195 James Hasty | .15 | .07 | .02 |
| ☐ 196 Rob Moore | .25 | .11 | .03 |
| ☐ 197 Kyle Clifton | .15 | .07 | .02 |
| ☐ 198 Terance Mathis | .15 | .07 | .02 |
| ☐ 199 Marvin Washington | .15 | .07 | .02 |
| ☐ 200 Lonnie Young | .15 | .07 | .02 |
| ☐ 201 Reggie White | .30 | .14 | .04 |
| ☐ 202 Eric Allen | .20 | .09 | .03 |
| ☐ 203 Fred Barnett | .25 | .11 | .03 |
| ☐ 204 Keith Byars | .20 | .09 | .03 |
| ☐ 205 Seth Joyner | .20 | .09 | .03 |
| ☐ 206 Clyde Simmons | .20 | .09 | .03 |
| ☐ 207 Jerome Brown | .20 | .09 | .03 |
| ☐ 208 Wes Hopkins | .15 | .07 | .02 |
| ☐ 209 Keith Jackson | .25 | .11 | .03 |
| ☐ 210 Calvin Williams | .25 | .11 | .03 |
| ☐ 211 Aeneas Williams | .15 | .07 | .02 |
| ☐ 212 Ken Harvey | .15 | .07 | .02 |
| ☐ 213 Ernie Jones | .15 | .07 | .02 |
| ☐ 214 Freddie Joe Nunn | .15 | .07 | .02 |
| ☐ 215 Rich Camarillo | .15 | .07 | .02 |
| ☐ 216 Johnny Johnson | .35 | .16 | .04 |
| ☐ 217 Tim McDonald | .20 | .09 | .03 |
| ☐ 218 Eric Swann | .20 | .09 | .03 |
| ☐ 219 Eric Hill | .15 | .07 | .02 |
| ☐ 220 Anthony Thompson | .15 | .07 | .02 |
| ☐ 221 Hardy Nickerson | .15 | .07 | .02 |
| ☐ 222 Barry Foster | 1.00 | .45 | .13 |
| ☐ 223 Louis Lipps | .20 | .09 | .03 |
| ☐ 224 Greg Lloyd | .15 | .07 | .02 |
| ☐ 225 Neil O'Donnell | 1.00 | .45 | .13 |
| ☐ 226 Jerrol Williams | .15 | .07 | .02 |
| ☐ 227 Eric Green | .25 | .11 | .03 |

| | | | |
|---|---|---|---|
| ☐ 228 Rod Woodson | .25 | .11 | .03 |
| ☐ 229 Carnell Lake | .15 | .07 | .02 |
| ☐ 230 Dwight Stone | .15 | .07 | .02 |
| ☐ 231 Marion Butts | .25 | .11 | .03 |
| ☐ 232 John Friesz | .20 | .09 | .03 |
| ☐ 233 Burt Grossman | .15 | .07 | .02 |
| ☐ 234 Ronnie Harmon | .15 | .07 | .02 |
| ☐ 235 Gill Byrd | .20 | .09 | .03 |
| ☐ 236 Rod Bernstine | .20 | .09 | .03 |
| ☐ 237 Courtney Hall | .15 | .07 | .02 |
| ☐ 238 Nate Lewis | .20 | .09 | .03 |
| ☐ 239 Joe Phillips | .15 | .07 | .02 |
| ☐ 240 Henry Rolling | .15 | .07 | .02 |
| ☐ 241 Keith Henderson | .15 | .07 | .02 |
| ☐ 242 Guy McIntyre | .20 | .09 | .03 |
| ☐ 243 Bill Romanowski | .15 | .07 | .02 |
| ☐ 244 Don Griffin | .15 | .07 | .02 |
| ☐ 245 Dexter Carter | .20 | .09 | .03 |
| ☐ 246 Charles Haley | .20 | .09 | .03 |
| ☐ 247 Brent Jones | .25 | .11 | .03 |
| ☐ 248 John Taylor | .25 | .11 | .03 |
| ☐ 249 Steve Young | 1.00 | .45 | .13 |
| ☐ 250 Larry Roberts | .15 | .07 | .02 |
| ☐ 251 Brian Blades | .20 | .09 | .03 |
| ☐ 252 Jacob Green | .15 | .07 | .02 |
| ☐ 253 John Kasay | .15 | .07 | .02 |
| ☐ 254 Cortez Kennedy | .35 | .16 | .04 |
| ☐ 255 Rufus Porter | .15 | .07 | .02 |
| ☐ 256 John L. Williams | .20 | .09 | .03 |
| ☐ 257 Tommy Kane | .15 | .07 | .02 |
| ☐ 258 Eugene Robinson | .15 | .07 | .02 |
| ☐ 259 Terry Wooden | .15 | .07 | .02 |
| ☐ 260 Chris Warren | .75 | .35 | .09 |
| ☐ 261 Lawrence Dawsey | .25 | .11 | .03 |
| ☐ 262 Mark Carrier | .20 | .09 | .03 |
| ☐ 263 Keith McCants | .15 | .07 | .02 |
| ☐ 264 Jesse Solomon | .15 | .07 | .02 |
| ☐ 265 Vinny Testaverde | .25 | .11 | .03 |
| ☐ 266 Ricky Reynolds | .15 | .07 | .02 |
| ☐ 267 Broderick Thomas | .15 | .07 | .02 |
| ☐ 268 Gary Anderson | .15 | .07 | .02 |
| ☐ 269 Reggie Cobb | .15 | .07 | .02 |
| ☐ 270 Tony Covington | .15 | .07 | .02 |
| ☐ 271 Darrell Green | .20 | .09 | .03 |
| ☐ 272 Charles Mann | .20 | .09 | .03 |
| ☐ 273 Wilber Marshall | .20 | .09 | .03 |
| ☐ 274 Gary Clark | .20 | .09 | .03 |
| ☐ 275 Chip Lohmiller | .20 | .09 | .03 |
| ☐ 276 Earnest Byner | .20 | .09 | .03 |
| ☐ 277 Jim Lachey | .15 | .07 | .02 |
| ☐ 278 Art Monk | .25 | .11 | .03 |
| ☐ 279 Mark Rypien | .25 | .11 | .03 |
| ☐ 280 Mark Schlereth | .25 | .11 | .03 |
| ☐ 281 Mark Rypien BR<br>Washington Redskins<br>NFC Passing Yardage<br>Leader | .75 | .35 | .09 |
| ☐ 282 Warren Moon BR<br>Houston Oilers<br>AFC Passing Yardage<br>Leader | 1.25 | .55 | .16 |
| ☐ 283 Emmitt Smith BR<br>Dallas Cowboys<br>NFC Rushing Leader | 8.00 | 3.60 | 1.00 |
| ☐ 284 Thurman Thomas BR<br>Buffalo Bills<br>AFC Rushing Leader | 2.50 | 1.15 | .30 |
| ☐ 285 Michael Irvin BR<br>Dallas Cowboys<br>NFC Receiving Leader | 3.00 | 1.35 | .40 |
| ☐ 286 Haywood Jeffires BR<br>Houston Oilers<br>AFC Receiving Leader | .75 | .35 | .09 |
| ☐ 287 Pat Swilling BR<br>New Orleans Saints<br>NFC Sack Leader | .75 | .35 | .09 |
| ☐ 288 Ronnie Lott BR<br>Los Angeles Raiders<br>AFC Interception<br>Leader | .75 | .35 | .09 |
| ☐ 289 NFC Logo<br>(Only available in<br>factory sets) | .35 | .16 | .04 |
| ☐ 290 AFC Logo<br>(Only available in<br>factory sets) | .35 | .16 | .04 |
| ☐ NNO Barry Sanders<br>(18K version)<br>Detroit Lions | 500.00 | 230.00 | 65.00 |

# 1992 Action Packed 24K Gold

This 42-card set consists of 24K gold-stamped cards that were randomly inserted in foil packs. Barry Sanders (card number 13G) autographed 1,000 of his cards. The cards measure the standard size

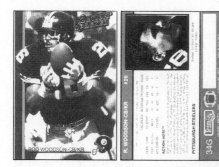

| | 33G Eric Green | 22.00 | 10.00 | 2.80 |
|---|---|---|---|---|
| | Pittsburgh Steelers | | | |
| | 34G Rod Woodson | 25.00 | 11.50 | 3.10 |
| | Pittsburgh Steelers | | | |
| | 35G Marion Butts | 20.00 | 9.00 | 2.50 |
| | San Diego Chargers | | | |
| | 36G Charles Haley | 20.00 | 9.00 | 2.50 |
| | San Francisco 49ers | | | |
| | 37G John Taylor | 20.00 | 9.00 | 2.50 |
| | San Francisco 49ers | | | |
| | 38G Steve Young | 70.00 | 32.00 | 8.75 |
| | San Francisco 49ers | | | |
| | 39G Earnest Byner | 22.00 | 10.00 | 2.80 |
| | Washington Redskins | | | |
| | 40G Gary Clark | 20.00 | 9.00 | 2.50 |
| | Washington Redskins | | | |
| | 41G Art Monk | 20.00 | 9.00 | 2.50 |
| | Washington Redskins | | | |
| | 42G Mark Rypien | 20.00 | 9.00 | 2.50 |
| | Washington Redskins | | | |

(2 1/2" by 3 1/2"). The cards are numbered on the back. The set numbering follows alphabetical order of team names. The fronts feature borderless embossed color player photos with gold indicia. The horizontally oriented backs have a mugshot, biography, statistics, and an "Action Note" in the form of a caption to the action shot on the front. The style of the cards is very similar to that of the 1992 Action Packed regular issue cards.

| | MINT | EXC | G-VG |
|---|---|---|---|
| COMPLETE SET (42) | 1600.00 | 700.00 | 200.00 |
| COMMON PLAYER (1G-42G) | 20.00 | 9.00 | 2.50 |

| | 1G Michael Haynes | 50.00 | 23.00 | 6.25 |
|---|---|---|---|---|
| | Atlanta Falcons | | | |
| | 2G Chris Miller | 20.00 | 9.00 | 2.50 |
| | Atlanta Falcons | | | |
| | 3G Andre Rison | 40.00 | 18.00 | 5.00 |
| | Atlanta Falcons | | | |
| | 4G Cornelius Bennett | 22.00 | 10.00 | 2.80 |
| | Buffalo Bills | | | |
| | 5G James Lofton | 20.00 | 9.00 | 2.50 |
| | Buffalo Bills | | | |
| | 6G Thurman Thomas | 70.00 | 32.00 | 8.75 |
| | Buffalo Bills | | | |
| | 7G Neal Anderson | 20.00 | 9.00 | 2.50 |
| | Chicago Bears | | | |
| | 8G Michael Irvin | 75.00 | 34.00 | 9.50 |
| | Dallas Cowboys | | | |
| | 9G Emmitt Smith | 225.00 | 100.00 | 28.00 |
| | Dallas Cowboys | | | |
| | 10G Mike Croel | 20.00 | 9.00 | 2.50 |
| | Denver Broncos | | | |
| | 11G John Elway | 75.00 | 34.00 | 9.50 |
| | Denver Broncos | | | |
| | 12G Gaston Green | 20.00 | 9.00 | 2.50 |
| | Denver Broncos | | | |
| | 13G Barry Sanders | 125.00 | 57.50 | 15.50 |
| | Detroit Lions | | | |
| | 14G Sterling Sharpe | 75.00 | 34.00 | 9.50 |
| | Green Bay Packers | | | |
| | 15G Ernest Givins | 20.00 | 9.00 | 2.50 |
| | Houston Oilers | | | |
| | 16G Drew Hill | 20.00 | 9.00 | 2.50 |
| | Houston Oilers | | | |
| | 17G Haywood Jeffires | 40.00 | 18.00 | 5.00 |
| | Houston Oilers | | | |
| | 18G Warren Moon | 40.00 | 18.00 | 5.00 |
| | Houston Oilers | | | |
| | 19G Christian Okoye | 20.00 | 9.00 | 2.50 |
| | Kansas City Chiefs | | | |
| | 20G Derrick Thomas | 40.00 | 18.00 | 5.00 |
| | Kansas City Chiefs | | | |
| | 21G Ronnie Lott | 25.00 | 11.50 | 3.10 |
| | Los Angeles Raiders | | | |
| | 22G Todd Marinovich | 20.00 | 9.00 | 2.50 |
| | Los Angeles Raiders | | | |
| | 23G Henry Ellard | 20.00 | 9.00 | 2.50 |
| | Los Angeles Rams | | | |
| | 24G Mark Clayton | 22.00 | 10.00 | 2.80 |
| | Miami Dolphins | | | |
| | 25G Herschel Walker | 20.00 | 9.00 | 2.50 |
| | Minnesota Vikings | | | |
| | 26G Irving Fryar | 20.00 | 9.00 | 2.50 |
| | New England Patriots | | | |
| | 27G Leonard Russell | 40.00 | 18.00 | 5.00 |
| | New England Patriots | | | |
| | 28G Pat Swilling | 20.00 | 9.00 | 2.50 |
| | New Orleans Saints | | | |
| | 29G Rodney Hampton | 70.00 | 32.00 | 8.75 |
| | New York Giants | | | |
| | 30G Rob Moore | 20.00 | 9.00 | 2.50 |
| | New York Jets | | | |
| | 31G Seth Joyner | 22.00 | 10.00 | 2.80 |
| | Philadelphia Eagles | | | |
| | 32G Reggie White | 40.00 | 18.00 | 5.00 |
| | Philadelphia Eagles | | | |

# 1992 Action Packed Rookie Update

This 84-card standard-size (2 1/2" by 3 1/2") set features 25 first round draft choices pictured in their NFL uniforms and some of the league's outstanding veteran players. Action Packed guaranteed one 1st round draft pick in each seven-card foil pack. The foil packs also included randomly inserted 24K gold cards of the quarterbacks and 1st round draft choices as well as a special "Neon Deion Sanders" card featuring neon fluorescent orange and numbered "84N". No factory sets were made. The fronts feature full-bleed embossed color player photos that are edged on one side by black and gold foil stripes. The player's name and position are gold-foil stamped at the bottom alongside a representation of the team helmet. The horizontal backs display a color head shot, biography, statistics, and career summary. A black stripe at the bottom carries the card number and an autograph slot. Action Packed also produced a 24K gold "Mint" rookie/update set. The 24K gold "Mint" cards were sold in six-card packs, with some packs to a box. Each box was numbered 1 through 500, and the purchase of an even-numbered and an odd-numbered box produced a complete set of cards. Moreover, each of the 250 "Mint" cards of each player were individually numbered (1/250, 2/250, etc.). The "Mint" version cards are currently valued at 100 to 200 times the regular issue value of the respective card. Rookie Cards in this set include Edgar Bennett, Terrell Buckley, Marco Coleman, Quentin Coryatt, Steve Emtman, David Klingler, Tommy Maddox, Johnny Mitchell and Tony Smith.

| | MINT | EXC | G-VG |
|---|---|---|---|
| COMPLETE SET (84) | 25.00 | 11.50 | 3.10 |
| COMMON ROOKIES (1-52) | .15 | .07 | .02 |
| COMMON PLAYER (53-84) | .15 | .07 | .02 |

| | 1 Steve Emtman | .40 | .18 | .05 |
|---|---|---|---|---|
| | Indianapolis Colts | | | |
| | 2 Quentin Coryatt | .75 | .35 | .09 |
| | Indianapolis Colts | | | |
| | 3 Sean Gilbert | 1.00 | .45 | .13 |
| | Los Angeles Rams | | | |
| | 4 John Fina | .15 | .07 | .02 |
| | Buffalo Bills | | | |
| | 5 Alonzo Spellman | .50 | .23 | .06 |
| | Chicago Bears | | | |
| | 6 Amp Lee | .50 | .23 | .06 |
| | San Francisco 49ers | | | |
| | 7 Robert Porcher | .60 | .25 | .08 |
| | Detroit Lions | | | |
| | 8 Jason Hanson | .35 | .16 | .04 |
| | Detroit Lions | | | |
| | 9 Ty Detmer | .20 | .09 | .03 |
| | Green Bay Packers | | | |

| | | | |
|---|---|---|---|
| ☐ 10 Ray Roberts | .15 | .07 | .02 |
| Seattle Seahawks | | | |
| ☐ 11 Bob Whitfield | .25 | .11 | .03 |
| Atlanta Falcons | | | |
| ☐ 12 Greg Skrepenak | .25 | .11 | .03 |
| Los Angeles Raiders | | | |
| ☐ 13 Vaughn Dunbar | .50 | .23 | .06 |
| New Orleans Saints | | | |
| ☐ 14 Siran Stacy | .30 | .14 | .04 |
| Philadelphia Eagles | | | |
| ☐ 15 Mark D'Onofrio | .15 | .07 | .02 |
| Green Bay Packers | | | |
| ☐ 16 Tony Sacca | .40 | .18 | .05 |
| Phoenix Cardinals | | | |
| ☐ 17 Dana Hall | .35 | .16 | .04 |
| San Francisco 49ers | | | |
| ☐ 18 Courtney Hawkins | .60 | .25 | .08 |
| Tampa Bay Buccaneers | | | |
| ☐ 19 Shane Collins | .40 | .18 | .05 |
| Washington Redskins | | | |
| ☐ 20 Tony Smith | .50 | .23 | .06 |
| Atlanta Falcons | | | |
| ☐ 21 Rod Smith | .25 | .11 | .03 |
| New England Patriots | | | |
| ☐ 22 Troy Auzenne | .15 | .07 | .02 |
| Chicago Bears | | | |
| ☐ 23 David Klingler | 1.75 | .80 | .22 |
| Cincinnati Bengals | | | |
| ☐ 24 Darryl Williams | .40 | .18 | .05 |
| Cincinnati Bengals | | | |
| ☐ 25 Carl Pickens | .75 | .35 | .09 |
| Cincinnati Bengals | | | |
| ☐ 26 Ricardo McDonald | .30 | .14 | .04 |
| Cincinnati Bengals | | | |
| ☐ 27 Tommy Vardell | .60 | .25 | .08 |
| Cleveland Browns | | | |
| ☐ 28 Kevin Smith | .75 | .35 | .09 |
| Dallas Cowboys | | | |
| ☐ 29 Rodney Culver | .30 | .14 | .04 |
| Indianapolis Colts | | | |
| ☐ 30 Jimmy Smith | .30 | .14 | .04 |
| Dallas Cowboys | | | |
| ☐ 31 Robert Jones | .35 | .16 | .04 |
| Dallas Cowboys | | | |
| ☐ 32 Tommy Maddox | 1.25 | .55 | .16 |
| Denver Broncos | | | |
| ☐ 33 Shane Dronett | .50 | .23 | .06 |
| Denver Broncos | | | |
| ☐ 34 Terrell Buckley | .60 | .25 | .08 |
| Green Bay Packers | | | |
| ☐ 35 Santana Dotson | .60 | .25 | .08 |
| Tampa Bay Buccaneers | | | |
| ☐ 36 Edgar Bennett | 1.00 | .45 | .13 |
| Green Bay Packers | | | |
| ☐ 37 Ashley Ambrose | .25 | .11 | .03 |
| Indianapolis Colts | | | |
| ☐ 38 Dale Carter | .50 | .23 | .06 |
| Kansas City Chiefs | | | |
| ☐ 39 Chester McGlockton | .35 | .16 | .04 |
| Los Angeles Raiders | | | |
| ☐ 40 Steve Israel | .15 | .07 | .02 |
| Los Angeles Rams | | | |
| ☐ 41 Marc Boutte | .15 | .07 | .02 |
| Los Angeles Rams | | | |
| ☐ 42 Marco Coleman | 1.00 | .45 | .13 |
| Miami Dolphins | | | |
| ☐ 43 Troy Vincent | .35 | .16 | .04 |
| Miami Dolphins | | | |
| ☐ 44 Mark Wheeler | .30 | .14 | .04 |
| Tampa Bay Buccaneers | | | |
| ☐ 45 Darren Perry | .35 | .16 | .04 |
| Pittsburgh Steelers | | | |
| ☐ 46 Eugene Chung | .15 | .07 | .02 |
| New England Patriots | | | |
| ☐ 47 Derek Brown | .30 | .14 | .04 |
| New York Giants | | | |
| ☐ 48 Phillippi Sparks | .15 | .07 | .02 |
| New York Giants | | | |
| ☐ 49 Johnny Mitchell | 1.50 | .65 | .19 |
| New York Jets | | | |
| ☐ 50 Kurt Barber | .25 | .11 | .03 |
| New York Jets | | | |
| ☐ 51 Leon Searcy | .15 | .07 | .02 |
| Pittsburgh Steelers | | | |
| ☐ 52 Chris Mims | .50 | .23 | .06 |
| San Diego Chargers | | | |
| ☐ 53 Keith Jackson | .25 | .11 | .03 |
| Miami Dolphins | | | |
| ☐ 54 Charles Haley | .20 | .09 | .03 |
| Dallas Cowboys | | | |
| ☐ 55 Dave Krieg | .20 | .09 | .03 |
| Kansas City Chiefs | | | |
| ☐ 56 Dan McGwire | .20 | .09 | .03 |
| Seattle Seahawks | | | |
| ☐ 57 Phil Simms | .25 | .11 | .03 |
| New York Giants | | | |
| ☐ 58 Bobby Humphrey | .20 | .09 | .03 |

| | | | |
|---|---|---|---|
| Miami Dolphins | | | |
| ☐ 59 Jerry Rice | 1.75 | .80 | .22 |
| San Francisco 49ers | | | |
| ☐ 60 Joe Montana | 2.50 | 1.15 | .30 |
| San Francisco 49ers | | | |
| ☐ 61 Junior Seau | .35 | .16 | .04 |
| San Diego Chargers | | | |
| ☐ 62 Leslie O'Neal | .20 | .09 | .03 |
| San Diego Chargers | | | |
| ☐ 63 Anthony Miller | .40 | .18 | .05 |
| San Diego Chargers | | | |
| ☐ 64 Timm Rosenbach | .15 | .07 | .02 |
| Phoenix Cardinals | | | |
| ☐ 65 Herschel Walker | .20 | .09 | .03 |
| Philadelphia Eagles | | | |
| ☐ 66 Randal Hill | .25 | .11 | .03 |
| Phoenix Cardinals | | | |
| ☐ 67 Randall Cunningham | .35 | .16 | .04 |
| Philadelphia Eagles | | | |
| ☐ 68 Al Toon | .20 | .09 | .03 |
| New York Jets | | | |
| ☐ 69 Browning Nagle | .20 | .09 | .03 |
| New York Jets | | | |
| ☐ 70 Lawrence Taylor | .30 | .14 | .04 |
| New York Giants | | | |
| ☐ 71 Dan Marino | 2.00 | .90 | .25 |
| Miami Dolphins | | | |
| ☐ 72 Eric Dickerson | .30 | .14 | .04 |
| Los Angeles Raiders | | | |
| ☐ 73 Harvey Williams | .25 | .11 | .03 |
| Kansas City Chiefs | | | |
| ☐ 74 Jeff George | .50 | .23 | .06 |
| Indianapolis Colts | | | |
| ☐ 75 Russell Maryland | .30 | .14 | .04 |
| Dallas Cowboys | | | |
| ☐ 76 Troy Aikman | 4.00 | 1.80 | .50 |
| Dallas Cowboys | | | |
| ☐ 77 Michael Dean Perry | .25 | .11 | .03 |
| Cleveland Browns | | | |
| ☐ 78 Bernie Kosar | .25 | .11 | .03 |
| Cleveland Browns | | | |
| ☐ 79 Boomer Esiason | .25 | .11 | .03 |
| Cincinnati Bengals | | | |
| ☐ 80 Mike Singletary | .25 | .11 | .03 |
| Chicago Bears | | | |
| ☐ 81 Bruce Smith | .25 | .11 | .03 |
| Buffalo Bills | | | |
| ☐ 82 Andre Reed | .20 | .09 | .03 |
| Buffalo Bills | | | |
| ☐ 83 Jim Kelly | .75 | .35 | .09 |
| Buffalo Bills | | | |
| ☐ 84 Deion Sanders | .50 | .23 | .06 |
| Atlanta Falcons | | | |
| ☐ 84N Neon Deion Sanders | 20.00 | 9.00 | 2.50 |
| Atlanta Falcons | | | |

## 1992 Action Packed Rookies 24K Gold

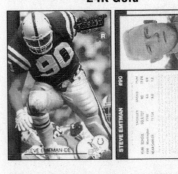

The players selected by Action Packed for this 24K set include eight NFL quarterbacks (26-33) and first round draft picks in the regular Rookie/Update set. These rounded-corner cards are standard size, 2 1/2" by 3 1/2".

| | MINT | EXC | G-VG |
|---|---|---|---|
| COMPLETE SET (35) | 1400.00 | 650.00 | 180.00 |
| COMMON PLAYER (1G-35G) | 20.00 | 9.00 | 2.50 |
| ☐ 1G Steve Emtman | 30.00 | 13.50 | 3.80 |
| Indianapolis Colts | | | |
| ☐ 2G Quentin Coryatt | 40.00 | 18.00 | 5.00 |
| Indianapolis Colts | | | |
| ☐ 3G Sean Gilbert | 40.00 | 18.00 | 5.00 |
| Los Angeles Rams | | | |

| | | | |
|---|---|---|---|
| ☐ 4G Terrell Buckley | 30.00 | 13.50 | 3.80 |
| Green Bay Packers | | | |
| ☐ 5G David Klingler | 70.00 | 32.00 | 8.75 |
| Cincinnati Bengals | | | |
| ☐ 6G Troy Vincent | 30.00 | 13.50 | 3.80 |
| Miami Dolphins | | | |
| ☐ 7G Tommy Vardell | 40.00 | 18.00 | 5.00 |
| Cleveland Browns | | | |
| ☐ 8G Leon Searcy | 20.00 | 9.00 | 2.50 |
| Pittsburgh Steelers | | | |
| ☐ 9G Marco Coleman | 40.00 | 18.00 | 5.00 |
| Miami Dolphins | | | |
| ☐ 10G Eugene Chung | 20.00 | 9.00 | 2.50 |
| New England Patriots | | | |
| ☐ 11G Derek Brown | 30.00 | 13.50 | 3.80 |
| New York Giants | | | |
| ☐ 12G Johnny Mitchell | 40.00 | 18.00 | 5.00 |
| New York Jets | | | |
| ☐ 13G Chester McGlockton | 20.00 | 9.00 | 2.50 |
| Los Angeles Raiders | | | |
| ☐ 14G Kevin Smith | 30.00 | 13.50 | 3.80 |
| Dallas Cowboys | | | |
| ☐ 15G Dana Hall | 20.00 | 9.00 | 2.50 |
| San Francisco 49ers | | | |
| ☐ 16G Tony Smith | 30.00 | 13.50 | 3.80 |
| Atlanta Falcons | | | |
| ☐ 17G Dale Carter | 30.00 | 13.50 | 3.80 |
| Kansas City Chiefs | | | |
| ☐ 18G Vaughn Dunbar | 30.00 | 13.50 | 3.80 |
| New Orleans Saints | | | |
| ☐ 19G Alonzo Spellman | 30.00 | 13.50 | 3.80 |
| Chicago Bears | | | |
| ☐ 20G Chris Mims | 30.00 | 13.50 | 3.80 |
| San Diego Chargers | | | |
| ☐ 21G Robert Jones | 20.00 | 9.00 | 2.50 |
| Dallas Cowboys | | | |
| ☐ 22G Tommy Maddox | 40.00 | 18.00 | 5.00 |
| Denver Broncos | | | |
| ☐ 23G Robert Porcher | 30.00 | 13.50 | 3.80 |
| Detroit Lions | | | |
| ☐ 24G John Fina | 20.00 | 9.00 | 2.50 |
| Buffalo Bills | | | |
| ☐ 25G Darryl Williams | 20.00 | 9.00 | 2.50 |
| Cincinnati Bengals | | | |
| ☐ 26G Jim Kelly | 70.00 | 32.00 | 8.75 |
| Buffalo Bills | | | |
| ☐ 27G Randall Cunningham | 40.00 | 18.00 | 5.00 |
| Philadelphia Eagles | | | |
| ☐ 28G Dan Marino | 100.00 | 45.00 | 12.50 |
| Miami Dolphins | | | |
| ☐ 29G Troy Aikman | 185.00 | 85.00 | 23.00 |
| Dallas Cowboys | | | |
| ☐ 30G Boomer Esiason | 30.00 | 13.50 | 3.80 |
| Cincinnati Bengals | | | |
| ☐ 31G Bernie Kosar | 22.00 | 10.00 | 2.80 |
| Cleveland Browns | | | |
| ☐ 32G Jeff George | 40.00 | 18.00 | 5.00 |
| Indianapolis Colts | | | |
| ☐ 33G Phil Simms | 22.00 | 10.00 | 2.80 |
| New York Giants | | | |
| ☐ 34G Ray Roberts | 20.00 | 9.00 | 2.50 |
| Seattle Seahawks | | | |
| ☐ 35G Bob Whitfield | 20.00 | 9.00 | 2.50 |
| Atlanta Falcons | | | |

# 1992 Action Packed All-Madden

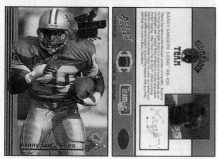

For the third consecutive year, Action Packed has issued a 55-card set to honor the toughest players in the game as picked by sportscaster John Madden. For hobby dealers only, Action Packed inserted two prototype cards of upcoming products in each display box of All-Madden Team foil packs. Moreover, 24K gold leaf versions of each card were randomly inserted in the foil packs. These 24K All-Madden cards are valued at approximately 50 to 100 times the corresponding

values below. The cards measure the standard size (2 1/2" by 3 1/2"). The fronts display full-bleed embossed color player photos that are edged on one side by turquoise and variegated gold foil stripes. The player's name and position are gold-foil stamped at the bottom alongside a representation of the team helmet. The horizontal backs display a color head shot, player profile in the form of a quote by Madden, and a play diagram. The card number appears in a turquoise stripe at the bottom.

| | MINT | EXC | G-VG |
|---|---|---|---|
| COMPLETE SET (55) | 18.00 | 7.25 | 1.80 |
| COMMON PLAYER (1-55) | .25 | .10 | .02 |
| | | | |
| ☐ 1 Emmitt Smith | 4.00 | 1.60 | .40 |
| Dallas Cowboys | | | |
| ☐ 2 Reggie White | .75 | .30 | .07 |
| Philadelphia Eagles | | | |
| ☐ 3 Deion Sanders | .75 | .30 | .07 |
| Atlanta Falcons | | | |
| ☐ 4 Wilber Marshall | .35 | .14 | .03 |
| Washington Redskins | | | |
| ☐ 5 Barry Sanders | 2.00 | .80 | .20 |
| Detroit Lions | | | |
| ☐ 6 Derrick Thomas | .75 | .30 | .07 |
| Kansas City Chiefs | | | |
| ☐ 7 Troy Aikman | 3.00 | 1.20 | .30 |
| Dallas Cowboys | | | |
| ☐ 8 Eric Allen | .25 | .10 | .02 |
| Philadelphia Eagles | | | |
| ☐ 9 Cris Carter | .35 | .14 | .03 |
| Minnesota Vikings | | | |
| ☐ 10 Jerry Rice | 2.00 | .80 | .20 |
| San Francisco 49ers | | | |
| ☐ 11 Rickey Jackson | .35 | .14 | .03 |
| New Orleans Saints | | | |
| ☐ 12 Bubba McDowell | .25 | .10 | .02 |
| Houston Oilers | | | |
| ☐ 13 Jack Del Rio | .25 | .10 | .02 |
| Minnesota Vikings | | | |
| ☐ 14 Nate Newton | .35 | .14 | .03 |
| Dallas Cowboys | | | |
| ☐ 15 John Elliott | .25 | .10 | .02 |
| New York Giants | | | |
| ☐ 16 Fred Barnett | .50 | .20 | .05 |
| Philadelphia Eagles | | | |
| ☐ 17 Mike Singletary | .50 | .20 | .05 |
| Chicago Bears | | | |
| ☐ 18 Lawrence Taylor | .75 | .30 | .07 |
| New York Giants | | | |
| ☐ 19 Bruce Matthews | .25 | .10 | .02 |
| Houston Oilers | | | |
| ☐ 20 Pat Swilling | .35 | .14 | .03 |
| New Orleans Saints | | | |
| ☐ 21 Charles Haley | .35 | .14 | .03 |
| Dallas Cowboys | | | |
| ☐ 22 Andre Rison | .75 | .30 | .07 |
| Atlanta Falcons | | | |
| ☐ 23 Seth Joyner | .35 | .14 | .03 |
| Philadelphia Eagles | | | |
| ☐ 24 Steve Young | 1.25 | .50 | .12 |
| San Francisco 49ers | | | |
| ☐ 25 Gary Clark | .50 | .20 | .05 |
| Washington Redskins | | | |
| ☐ 26 Jerry Ball | .25 | .10 | .02 |
| Detroit Lions | | | |
| ☐ 27 Michael Irvin | 1.00 | .40 | .10 |
| Dallas Cowboys | | | |
| ☐ 28 Haywood Jeffires | .75 | .30 | .07 |
| Houston Oilers | | | |
| ☐ 29 Kevin Ross | .25 | .10 | .02 |
| Kansas City Chiefs | | | |
| ☐ 30 Chris Doleman | .35 | .14 | .03 |
| Minnesota Vikings | | | |
| ☐ 31 Vai Sikahema | .25 | .10 | .02 |
| Philadelphia Eagles | | | |
| ☐ 32 Ricky Watters | 1.25 | .50 | .12 |
| San Francisco 49ers | | | |
| ☐ 33 Henry Thomas | .25 | .10 | .02 |
| Minnesota Vikings | | | |
| ☐ 34 Mike Kenn | .25 | .10 | .02 |
| Atlanta Falcons | | | |
| ☐ 35 Erik Williams | .25 | .10 | .02 |
| Dallas Cowboys | | | |
| ☐ 36 Neil Smith | .35 | .14 | .03 |
| Kansas City Chiefs | | | |
| ☐ 37 Mark Schlereth | .25 | .10 | .02 |
| Washington Redskins | | | |
| ☐ 38 Steve Wallace | .25 | .10 | .02 |
| San Francisco 49ers | | | |
| ☐ 39 Randall McDaniel | .25 | .10 | .02 |
| Minnesota Vikings | | | |
| ☐ 40 Kurt Gouveia | .25 | .10 | .02 |
| Washington Redskins | | | |
| ☐ 41 Al Noga | .35 | .14 | .03 |
| Minnesota Vikings | | | |
| ☐ 42 Tom Rathman | .35 | .14 | .03 |

| | | MINT | EXC | G-VG |
|---|---|---|---|---|
| San Francisco 49ers | | | | |
| ☐ 43 Harris Barton | .25 | .10 | .02 |
| San Francisco 49ers | | | | |
| ☐ 44 Mel Gray | .25 | .10 | .02 |
| Detroit Lions | | | | |
| ☐ 45 Keith Byars | .35 | .14 | .03 |
| Philadelphia Eagles | | | | |
| ☐ 46 Todd Scott | .25 | .10 | .02 |
| Minnesota Vikings | | | | |
| ☐ 47 Brent Jones | .35 | .14 | .03 |
| San Francisco 49ers | | | | |
| ☐ 48 Audray McMillian | .25 | .10 | .02 |
| Minnesota Vikings | | | | |
| ☐ 49 Ray Childress | .35 | .14 | .03 |
| Houston Oilers | | | | |
| ☐ 50 Dennis Smith | .25 | .10 | .02 |
| Denver Broncos | | | | |
| ☐ 51 Mark McMillian | .25 | .10 | .02 |
| Philadelphia Eagles | | | | |
| ☐ 52 Sean Gilbert | .50 | .20 | .05 |
| Los Angeles Rams | | | | |
| ☐ 53 Pierce Holt | .35 | .14 | .03 |
| San Francisco 49ers | | | | |
| ☐ 54 Daryl Johnston | .75 | .30 | .07 |
| Dallas Cowboys | | | | |
| ☐ 55 Madden Cruiser (Bus) | .35 | .14 | .03 |

## 1993 Action Packed NFLPA Awards

Held on March 4, 1993 in Washington, D.C., and sponsored by Action Packed, the 20th annual NFLPA banquet honored outstanding professional football players from the 1992 season. The set was produced to benefit the District of Columbia's Special Olympics. Reportedly less than 2,000 sets were produced. This 17-card set features the players selected as the best at their position by their peers. The standard size (2 1/2" by 3 1/2") cards were issued in a special black box. The fronts feature an embossed action player photo overlapping a black-bordered gold stripe. The backs have a player photo and the award recipient's statistics. The cards are numbered on the back.

| | MINT | EXC | G-VG |
|---|---|---|---|
| COMPLETE SET (17) | 75.00 | 30.00 | 7.50 |
| COMMON PLAYER (1-17) | 4.00 | 1.60 | .40 |
| | | | |
| ☐ 1 Randall McDaniel | 4.00 | 1.60 | .40 |
| Minnesota Vikings | | | |
| ☐ 2 Bruce Matthews | 4.00 | 1.60 | .40 |
| Houston Oilers | | | |
| ☐ 3 Richmond Webb | 4.00 | 1.60 | .40 |
| Miami Dolphins | | | |
| ☐ 4 Cortez Kennedy | 8.00 | 3.25 | .80 |
| Seattle Seahawks | | | |
| ☐ 5 Clyde Simmons | 4.00 | 1.60 | .40 |
| Philadelphia Eagles | | | |
| ☐ 6 Wilber Marshall | 5.00 | 2.00 | .50 |
| Washington Redskins | | | |
| ☐ 7 Junior Seau | 8.00 | 3.25 | .80 |
| San Diego Chargers | | | |
| ☐ 8 Henry Jones | 5.00 | 2.00 | .50 |
| Buffalo Bills | | | |
| ☐ 9 Audray McMillian | 4.00 | 1.60 | .40 |
| Minnesota Vikings | | | |
| ☐ 10 Mel Gray | 4.00 | 1.60 | .40 |
| Detroit Lions | | | |
| ☐ 11 Steve Tasker | 4.00 | 1.60 | .40 |
| Buffalo Bills | | | |
| ☐ 12 Marco Coleman | 8.00 | 3.25 | .80 |
| Miami Dolphins | | | |
| ☐ 13 Santana Dotson | 6.00 | 2.40 | .60 |
| Tampa Bay Buccaneers | | | |
| ☐ 14 Vaughn Dunbar | 8.00 | 3.25 | .80 |
| New Orleans Saints | | | |
| ☐ 15 Carl Pickens | 8.00 | 3.25 | .80 |

| | | MINT | EXC | G-VG |
|---|---|---|---|---|
| Cincinnati Bengals | | | | |
| ☐ 16 Barry Foster | 12.00 | 5.00 | 1.20 |
| Pittsburgh Steelers | | | | |
| ☐ 17 Steve Young | 10.00 | 4.00 | 1.00 |
| San Francisco 49ers | | | | |

## 1993 Action Packed Troy Aikman Promos

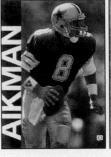

This two-card set measures the standard size (2 1/2" by 3 1/2") and honors Cowboys' quarterback, Troy Aikman. The fronts feature borderless embossed color player photos, accented by a gold border stripe running down either the right or left side of the card face. The stripe is printed with the player's name in large white block letters. The horizontal backs display a color cut-out image from the waist up of Aikman against a green football field background. The player's name and team name are printed in red above biographical information, statistics, and career highlights. Sponsor logos appear in the green margin at the bottom. The phrase "1993 Prototype" are printed in gray across the text. The cards are numbered on the back. The cards were produced on a prototype sheet which included eleven different Aikmans, TA1 through TA11; however only TA2 and TA3 were formally released.

| | MINT | EXC | G-VG |
|---|---|---|---|
| COMPLETE SET (2) | 60.00 | 24.00 | 6.00 |
| COMMON PLAYER (TA2-TA3) | 30.00 | 12.00 | 3.00 |
| | | | |
| ☐ TA2 Troy Aikman | 30.00 | 12.00 | 3.00 |
| (Running with ball) | | | |
| ☐ TA3 Troy Aikman | 30.00 | 12.00 | 3.00 |
| (Pitching the ball) | | | |

## 1993 Action Packed Emmitt Smith Promos

This five-card set measures the standard size (2 1/2" by 3 1/2") and was issued to promote the 1993 Action Packed All-Madden Team set. The fronts feature borderless embossed color player photos, accented by gold and aqua border stripes running down the right side of the card face. The All-Madden Team logo appears in the upper left corner, with the team helmet, player's name, and position printed at the card bottom. Between aqua border stripes, the horizontal backs carry player profile, a color headshot, and a diagram of a football play. The word "Prototype" is printed across the text. Two of these cards (ES1 and ES4) were given out at the 1993 Super Bowl Card Show. The ES5 card was a give-away to members of the Tuff Stuff Buyers Club. All the cards are numbered on the back.

| | MINT | EXC | G-VG |
|---|---|---|---|
| COMPLETE SET (5)............................ | 50.00 | 20.00 | 5.00 |
| COMMON PLAYER (ES1-ES5) .......... | 7.50 | 3.00 | .75 |
| ☐ ES1 Emmitt Smith........................ | 7.50 | 3.00 | .75 |
| (Receiving handoff from quarterback; side view) | | | |
| ☐ ES2 Emmitt Smith........................ | 15.00 | 6.00 | 1.50 |
| ☐ ES3 Emmitt Smith........................ | 15.00 | 6.00 | 1.50 |
| ☐ ES4 Emmitt Smith........................ | 7.50 | 3.00 | .75 |
| (Cutting to right to elude tackler; ball cradled in left arm) | | | |
| ☐ ES5 Emmitt Smith........................ | 10.00 | 4.00 | 1.00 |
| (Running to right; ball in left arm) | | | |

## 1993 Action Packed Prototypes

These six standard-size (2 1/2" by 3 1/2") cards were issued to show the design of the 1993 Action Packed regular series. The fronts feature the traditional full-bleed embossed color player photos. The player's last name is printed vertically in gold-foil block lettering running down one of the sides. On a green football field design, the horizontal backs carry biography, 1992 season and career statistics, and an "Action Note". The disclaimer "1993 Prototype" is printed diagonally across the back. A black stripe edged by gold foil has an autograph slot and the card number.

| | MINT | EXC | G-VG |
|---|---|---|---|
| COMPLETE SET (6)............................ | 40.00 | 16.00 | 4.00 |
| COMMON PLAYER (FB1-FB6)........... | 6.00 | 2.40 | .60 |
| ☐ FB1 Emmitt Smith........................ | 15.00 | 6.00 | 1.50 |
| Dallas Cowboys | | | |
| ☐ FB2 Thurman Thomas.................. | 6.00 | 2.40 | .60 |
| Buffalo Bills | | | |
| ☐ FB3 Steve Young........................ | 7.50 | 3.00 | .75 |
| San Francisco 49ers | | | |
| ☐ FB4 Barry Sanders ...................... | 9.00 | 3.75 | .90 |
| Detroit Lions | | | |
| ☐ FB5 Barry Foster........................ | 6.00 | 2.40 | .60 |
| Pittsburgh Steelers | | | |
| ☐ FB6 Warren Moon........................ | 7.50 | 3.00 | .75 |
| Houston Oilers | | | |

## 1993 Action Packed

The 1993 Action Packed football set consists of 222 cards. In addition, three individually numbered topical subsets totalling 42 cards were also randomly inserted in packs. Randomly inserted certificates entitled the collector to a trip to the Super Bowl. Moreover, 24K equivalents of the topical subset cards were seeded throughout the packs. Certificates for one of the individually numbered gold mint Quarterback Club cards were also randomly inserted, but only in hobby foil packs. Five hundred of each gold mint QB cards were produced. Finally, Braille versions of the Quarterback Club cards were also randomly packed, and two Chiptopper preview cards were packed only in hobby boxes. The cards measure the standard size (2 1/2" by 3 1/2"). The full-bleed color action photos on the fronts have the player's name etched in a two-tone gold foil running down the side. The backs have a playing field with the team helmet in the center and player information, statistics, an Action Note, and a head shot. The foil packs feature six different collectible player photos, Barry Foster, Rodney Hampton, Michael Irvin, Andre Rison, Sterling Sharpe, and Ricky Watters. The individually numbered topical subsets are Quarterback Club (QB1-QB18), Moving Targets (MT1-MT12), and 1,000 Yard Rushers (RB1-RB12). The cards are numbered on the back. A 60-card Rookie Update series begins at card number 163, where the first series leaves off. It features players selected in the early rounds of the NFL draft wearing their NFL uniforms. The fronts feature an embossed color player cut-out against a full-bleed background that consists of a tilted colored panel bordered on two sides by foil. Depending on the round the player was drafted, the foil varies from gold (first round, 163-192); to silver (second round, 193-210); to bronze (third round, 211-216). Players drafted after the third round have their panels bordered in a non-foil sky blue color (cards 217-222). The horizontal backs carry a color close-up photo, '92 college season and NCAA career statistics, biography, and college career highlights. The cards are numbered on the back. Rookie Cards include Drew Bledsoe, Garrison Hearst, Terry Kirby, O.J. McDuffie, Natrone Means, Rick Mirer, Glyn Milburn, Jerome Bettis and Reggie Brooks.

| | MINT | EXC | G-VG |
|---|---|---|---|
| COMPLETE SET (222)...................... | 70.00 | 32.00 | 8.75 |
| COMPLETE SERIES 1 (162)............. | 45.00 | 20.00 | 5.75 |
| COMPLETE SERIES 2 (60).............. | 25.00 | 11.50 | 3.10 |
| COMMON PLAYER (1-162)............. | .15 | .07 | .02 |
| COMMON PLAYER (163-222)........... | .15 | .07 | .02 |
| ☐ 1 Michael Haynes......................... | .50 | .23 | ·.06 |
| Atlanta Falcons | | | |
| ☐ 2 Chris Miller ............................ | .25 | .11 | .03 |
| Atlanta Falcons | | | |
| ☐ 3 Andre Rison ............................ | .50 | .23 | .06 |
| Atlanta Falcons | | | |
| ☐ 4 Jim Kelly .............................. | 1.00 | .45 | .13 |
| Buffalo Bills | | | |
| ☐ 5 Andre Reed ............................ | .25 | .11 | .03 |
| Buffalo Bills | | | |
| ☐ 6 Thurman Thomas....................... | 1.00 | .45 | .13 |
| Buffalo Bills | | | |
| ☐ 7 Jim Harbaugh .......................... | .20 | .09 | .03 |
| Chicago Bears | | | |
| ☐ 8 Harold Green ........................... | .20 | .09 | .03 |
| Cincinnati Bengals | | | |
| ☐ 9 David Klingler.......................... | .60 | .25 | .08 |
| Cincinnati Bengals | | | |
| ☐ 10 Bernie Kosar........................... | .25 | .11 | .03 |
| Cleveland Browns | | | |
| ☐ 11 Troy Aikman........................... | 4.00 | 1.80 | .50 |
| Dallas Cowboys | | | |
| ☐ 12 Michael Irvin ......................... | 1.50 | .65 | .19 |
| Dallas Cowboys | | | |
| ☐ 13 Emmitt Smith......................... | 6.00 | 2.70 | .75 |
| Dallas Cowboys | | | |
| ☐ 14 John Elway............................ | 1.00 | .45 | .13 |
| Denver Broncos | | | |
| ☐ 15 Barry Sanders ........................ | 2.25 | 1.00 | .30 |
| Detroit Lions | | | |
| ☐ 16 Brett Favre............................ | 2.00 | .90 | .25 |
| Green Bay Packers | | | |
| ☐ 17 Sterling Sharpe ...................... | 1.50 | .65 | .19 |
| Green Bay Packers | | | |
| ☐ 18 Ernest Givins......................... | .20 | .09 | .03 |
| Houston Oilers | | | |
| ☐ 19 Haywood Jeffires ................... | .25 | .11 | .03 |
| Houston Oilers | | | |
| ☐ 20 Warren Moon.......................... | .50 | .23 | .06 |
| Houston Oilers | | | |
| ☐ 21 Lorenzo White......................... | .20 | .09 | .03 |
| Houston Oilers | | | |
| ☐ 22 Jeff George ............................ | .50 | .23 | .06 |
| Indianapolis Colts | | | |
| ☐ 23 Joe Montana .......................... | 3.00 | 1.35 | .40 |
| Kansas City Chiefs | | | |
| ☐ 24 Jim Everett ............................ | .15 | .07 | .02 |
| Los Angeles Rams | | | |
| ☐ 25 Cleveland Gary ....................... | .20 | .09 | .03 |
| Los Angeles Rams | | | |
| ☐ 26 Dan Marino ........................... | 2.50 | 1.15 | .30 |
| Miami Dolphins | | | |

| | | | |
|---|---|---|---|
| ☐ 27 Terry Allen | .25 | .11 | .03 |
| Minnesota Vikings | | | |
| ☐ 28 Rodney Hampton | 1.00 | .45 | .13 |
| New York Giants | | | |
| ☐ 29 Phil Simms | .25 | .11 | .03 |
| New York Giants | | | |
| ☐ 30 Fred Barnett | .25 | .11 | .03 |
| Philadelphia Eagles | | | |
| ☐ 31 Randall Cunningham | .30 | .14 | .04 |
| Philadelphia Eagles | | | |
| ☐ 32 Gary Clark | .20 | .09 | .03 |
| Phoenix Cardinals | | | |
| ☐ 33 Barry Foster | 1.00 | .45 | .13 |
| Pittsburgh Steelers | | | |
| ☐ 34 Neil O'Donnell | 1.00 | .45 | .13 |
| Pittsburgh Steelers | | | |
| ☐ 35 Stan Humphries | .25 | .11 | .03 |
| San Diego Chargers | | | |
| ☐ 36 Anthony Miller | .40 | .18 | .05 |
| San Diego Chargers | | | |
| ☐ 37 Jerry Rice | 1.75 | .80 | .22 |
| San Francisco 49ers | | | |
| ☐ 38 Ricky Watters | .75 | .35 | .09 |
| San Francisco 49ers | | | |
| ☐ 39 Steve Young | 1.00 | .45 | .13 |
| San Francisco 49ers | | | |
| ☐ 40 Chris Warren | .40 | .18 | .05 |
| Seattle Seahawks | | | |
| ☐ 41 Reggie Cobb | .25 | .11 | .03 |
| Tampa Bay Buccaneers | | | |
| ☐ 42 Mark Rypien | .20 | .09 | .03 |
| Washington Redskins | | | |
| ☐ 43 Deion Sanders | .50 | .23 | .06 |
| Atlanta Falcons | | | |
| ☐ 44 Henry Jones | .15 | .07 | .02 |
| Buffalo Bills | | | |
| ☐ 45 Bruce Smith | .25 | .11 | .03 |
| Buffalo Bills | | | |
| ☐ 46 Richard Dent | .20 | .09 | .03 |
| Chicago Bears | | | |
| ☐ 47 Tommy Vardell | .20 | .09 | .03 |
| Cleveland Browns | | | |
| ☐ 48 Charles Haley | .20 | .09 | .03 |
| Dallas Cowboys | | | |
| ☐ 49 Ken Norton Jr. | .20 | .09 | .03 |
| Dallas Cowboys | | | |
| ☐ 50 Jay Novacek | .15 | .07 | .02 |
| Dallas Cowboys | | | |
| ☐ 51 Simon Fletcher | .20 | .09 | .03 |
| Denver Broncos | | | |
| ☐ 52 Pat Swilling | .20 | .09 | .03 |
| Detroit Lions | | | |
| ☐ 53 Tony Bennett | .15 | .07 | .02 |
| Green Bay Packers | | | |
| ☐ 54 Reggie White | .40 | .18 | .05 |
| Green Bay Packers | | | |
| ☐ 55 Ray Childress | .15 | .07 | .02 |
| Houston Oilers | | | |
| ☐ 56 Quentin Coryatt | .15 | .07 | .02 |
| Indianapolis Colts | | | |
| ☐ 57 Steve Emtman | .20 | .09 | .03 |
| Indianapolis Colts | | | |
| ☐ 58 Derrick Thomas | .40 | .18 | .05 |
| Kansas City Chiefs | | | |
| ☐ 59 James Lofton | .25 | .11 | .03 |
| Los Angeles Raiders | | | |
| ☐ 60 Marco Coleman | .20 | .09 | .03 |
| Miami Dolphins | | | |
| ☐ 61 Bryan Cox | .20 | .09 | .03 |
| Miami Dolphins | | | |
| ☐ 62 Troy Vincent | .15 | .07 | .02 |
| Miami Dolphins | | | |
| ☐ 63 Chris Doleman | .20 | .09 | .03 |
| Minnesota Vikings | | | |
| ☐ 64 Audray McMillian | .15 | .07 | .02 |
| Minnesota Vikings | | | |
| ☐ 65 Vaughn Dunbar | .20 | .09 | .03 |
| New Orleans Saints | | | |
| ☐ 66 Rickey Jackson | .20 | .09 | .03 |
| New Orleans Saints | | | |
| ☐ 67 Lawrence Taylor | .30 | .14 | .04 |
| New York Giants | | | |
| ☐ 68 Ronnie Lott | .25 | .11 | .03 |
| New York Jets | | | |
| ☐ 69 Rob Moore | .25 | .11 | .03 |
| New York Jets | | | |
| ☐ 70 Browning Nagle | .20 | .09 | .03 |
| New York Jets | | | |
| ☐ 71 Eric Allen | .20 | .09 | .03 |
| Philadelphia Eagles | | | |
| ☐ 72 Tim Harris | .15 | .07 | .02 |
| Philadelphia Eagles | | | |
| ☐ 73 Clyde Simmons | .20 | .09 | .03 |
| Philadelphia Eagles | | | |
| ☐ 74 Steve Beuerlein | .30 | .14 | .04 |
| Phoenix Cardinals | | | |
| ☐ 75 Randal Hill | .25 | .11 | .03 |
| Phoenix Cardinals | | | |
| ☐ 76 Darren Perry | .15 | .07 | .02 |
| Pittsburgh Steelers | | | |
| ☐ 77 Rod Woodson | .25 | .11 | .03 |
| Pittsburgh Steelers | | | |
| ☐ 78 Marion Butts | .25 | .11 | .03 |
| San Diego Chargers | | | |
| ☐ 79 Chris Mims | .15 | .07 | .02 |
| San Diego Chargers | | | |
| ☐ 80 Junior Seau | .25 | .11 | .03 |
| San Diego Chargers | | | |
| ☐ 81 Cortez Kennedy | .25 | .11 | .03 |
| Seattle Seahawks | | | |
| ☐ 82 Santana Dotson | .15 | .07 | .02 |
| Tampa Bay Buccaneers | | | |
| ☐ 83 Earnest Byner | .20 | .09 | .03 |
| Washington Redskins | | | |
| ☐ 84 Charles Mann | .20 | .09 | .03 |
| Washington Redskins | | | |
| ☐ 85 Pierce Holt | .15 | .07 | .02 |
| Atlanta Falcons | | | |
| ☐ 86 Mike Pritchard | .25 | .11 | .03 |
| Atlanta Falcons | | | |
| ☐ 87 Cornelius Bennett | .25 | .11 | .03 |
| Buffalo Bills | | | |
| ☐ 88 Neal Anderson | .20 | .09 | .03 |
| Chicago Bears | | | |
| ☐ 89 Carl Pickens | .30 | .14 | .04 |
| Cincinnati Bengals | | | |
| ☐ 90 Eric Metcalf | .25 | .11 | .03 |
| Cleveland Browns | | | |
| ☐ 91 Michael Dean Perry | .25 | .11 | .03 |
| Cleveland Browns | | | |
| ☐ 92 Alvin Harper | .75 | .35 | .09 |
| Dallas Cowboys | | | |
| ☐ 93 Robert Jones | .15 | .07 | .02 |
| Dallas Cowboys | | | |
| ☐ 94 Steve Atwater | .20 | .09 | .03 |
| Denver Broncos | | | |
| ☐ 95 Rod Bernstine | .20 | .09 | .03 |
| Denver Broncos | | | |
| ☐ 96 Herman Moore | .75 | .35 | .09 |
| Detroit Lions | | | |
| ☐ 97 Chris Spielman | .15 | .07 | .02 |
| Detroit Lions | | | |
| ☐ 98 Terrell Buckley | .15 | .07 | .02 |
| Green Bay Packers | | | |
| ☐ 99 Dale Carter | .15 | .07 | .02 |
| Kansas City Chiefs | | | |
| ☐ 100 Terry McDaniel | .15 | .07 | .02 |
| Los Angeles Raiders | | | |
| ☐ 101 Tim Brown | .50 | .23 | .06 |
| Los Angeles Raiders | | | |
| ☐ 102 Gaston Green | .20 | .09 | .03 |
| Los Angeles Raiders | | | |
| ☐ 103 Howie Long | .20 | .09 | .03 |
| Los Angeles Raiders | | | |
| ☐ 104 Todd Marinovich | .15 | .07 | .02 |
| Los Angeles Raiders | | | |
| ☐ 105 Anthony Smith | .15 | .07 | .02 |
| Los Angeles Raiders | | | |
| ☐ 106 Flipper Anderson | .20 | .09 | .03 |
| Los Angeles Rams | | | |
| ☐ 107 Henry Ellard | .20 | .09 | .03 |
| Los Angeles Rams | | | |
| ☐ 108 Mark Higgs | .15 | .07 | .02 |
| Miami Dolphins | | | |
| ☐ 109 Keith Jackson | .25 | .11 | .03 |
| Miami Dolphins | | | |
| ☐ 110 Irving Fryar | .20 | .09 | .03 |
| Miami Dolphins | | | |
| ☐ 111 Cris Carter | .25 | .11 | .03 |
| Minnesota Vikings | | | |
| ☐ 112 Leonard Russell | .15 | .07 | .02 |
| New England Patriots | | | |
| ☐ 113 Wayne Martin | .15 | .07 | .02 |
| New Orleans Saints | | | |
| ☐ 114 Mark Jackson | .20 | .09 | .03 |
| New York Giants | | | |
| ☐ 115 David Meggett | .20 | .09 | .03 |
| New York Giants | | | |
| ☐ 116 Brad Baxter | .20 | .09 | .03 |
| New York Jets | | | |
| ☐ 117 Boomer Esiason | .35 | .16 | .04 |
| New York Jets | | | |
| ☐ 118 Johnny Johnson | .25 | .11 | .03 |
| New York Jets | | | |
| ☐ 119 Seth Joyner | .20 | .09 | .03 |
| Philadelphia Eagles | | | |
| ☐ 120 Kevin Greene | .15 | .07 | .02 |
| Pittsburgh Steelers | | | |
| ☐ 121 Greg Lloyd | .15 | .07 | .02 |
| Pittsburgh Steelers | | | |
| ☐ 122 Brent Jones | .25 | .11 | .03 |
| San Francisco 49ers | | | |
| ☐ 123 Amp Lee | .20 | .09 | .03 |
| San Francisco 49ers | | | |
| ☐ 124 Tim McDonald | .15 | .07 | .02 |

| | | | | |
|---|---|---|---|---|
| | San Francisco 49ers | | | |
| ☐ 125 | Darrell Green | .20 | .09 | .03 |
| | Washington Redskins | | | |
| ☐ 126 | Art Monk | .25 | .11 | .03 |
| | Washington Redskins | | | |
| ☐ 127 | Tony Smith | .15 | .07 | .02 |
| | Atlanta Falcons | | | |
| ☐ 128 | Bill Brooks | .20 | .09 | .03 |
| | Buffalo Bills | | | |
| ☐ 129 | Kenneth Davis | .20 | .09 | .03 |
| | Buffalo Bills | | | |
| ☐ 130 | Donnell Woolford | .15 | .07 | .02 |
| | Chicago Bears | | | |
| ☐ 131 | Derrick Fenner | .15 | .07 | .02 |
| | Cincinnati Bengals | | | |
| ☐ 132 | Michael Jackson | .25 | .11 | .03 |
| | Cleveland Browns | | | |
| ☐ 133 | Mark Clayton | .20 | .09 | .03 |
| | Green Bay Packers | | | |
| ☐ 134 | Al Smith | .15 | .07 | .02 |
| | Houston Oilers | | | |
| ☐ 135 | Curtis Duncan | .20 | .09 | .03 |
| | Houston Oilers | | | |
| ☐ 136 | Rodney Culver | .20 | .09 | .03 |
| | Indianapolis Colts | | | |
| ☐ 137 | Harvey Williams | .25 | .11 | .03 |
| | Kansas City Chiefs | | | |
| ☐ 138 | Neil Smith | .25 | .11 | .03 |
| | Kansas City Chiefs | | | |
| ☐ 139 | Marcus Allen | .20 | .09 | .03 |
| | Kansas City Chiefs | | | |
| ☐ 140 | Eric Dickerson | .25 | .11 | .03 |
| | Los Angeles Raiders | | | |
| ☐ 141 | Sean Gilbert | .20 | .09 | .03 |
| | Los Angeles Rams | | | |
| ☐ 142 | Shane Conlan | .15 | .07 | .02 |
| | Los Angeles Rams | | | |
| ☐ 143 | Todd Scott | .15 | .07 | .02 |
| | Minnesota Vikings | | | |
| ☐ 144 | Vincent Brown | .15 | .07 | .02 |
| | New England Patriots | | | |
| ☐ 145 | Andre Tippett | .15 | .07 | .02 |
| | New England Patriots | | | |
| ☐ 146 | Jon Vaughn | .15 | .07 | .02 |
| | New England Patriots | | | |
| ☐ 147 | Marv Cook | .15 | .07 | .02 |
| | New England Patriots | | | |
| ☐ 148 | Morten Andersen | .20 | .09 | .03 |
| | New Orleans Saints | | | |
| ☐ 149 | Sam Mills | .20 | .09 | .03 |
| | New Orleans Saints | | | |
| ☐ 150 | Mark Collins | .15 | .07 | .02 |
| | New York Giants | | | |
| ☐ 151 | Heath Sherman | .15 | .07 | .02 |
| | Philadelphia Eagles | | | |
| ☐ 152 | Johnny Bailey | .15 | .07 | .02 |
| | Phoenix Cardinals | | | |
| ☐ 153 | Eric Green | .25 | .11 | .03 |
| | Pittsburgh Steelers | | | |
| ☐ 154 | Ronnie Harmon | .20 | .09 | .03 |
| | San Diego Chargers | | | |
| ☐ 155 | Gill Byrd | .20 | .09 | .03 |
| | San Diego Chargers | | | |
| ☐ 156 | Leslie O'Neal | .20 | .09 | .03 |
| | San Diego Chargers | | | |
| ☐ 157 | Rufus Porter | .15 | .07 | .02 |
| | Seattle Seahawks | | | |
| ☐ 158 | Eugene Robinson | .15 | .07 | .02 |
| | Seattle Seahawks | | | |
| ☐ 159 | Broderick Thomas | .15 | .07 | .02 |
| | Tampa Bay Buccaneers | | | |
| ☐ 160 | Lawrence Dawsey | .25 | .11 | .03 |
| | Tampa Bay Buccaneers | | | |
| ☐ 161 | Anthony Munoz | .20 | .09 | .03 |
| | Tampa Bay Buccaneers | | | |
| ☐ 162 | Wilber Marshall | .20 | .09 | .03 |
| | Washington Redskins | | | |
| ☐ 163 | Drew Bledsoe | 8.00 | 3.60 | 1.00 |
| | New England Patriots | | | |
| ☐ 164 | Rick Mirer | 8.00 | 3.60 | 1.00 |
| | Seattle Seahawks | | | |
| ☐ 165 | Garrison Hearst | 2.25 | 1.00 | .30 |
| | Phoenix Cardinals | | | |
| ☐ 166 | Marvin Jones | .50 | .23 | .06 |
| | New York Jets | | | |
| ☐ 167 | John Copeland | .75 | .35 | .09 |
| | Cincinnati Bengals | | | |
| ☐ 168 | Eric Curry | .75 | .35 | .09 |
| | Tampa Bay Buccaneers | | | |
| ☐ 169 | Curtis Conway | 1.50 | .65 | .19 |
| | Chicago Bears | | | |
| ☐ 170 | William Roaf | .35 | .16 | .04 |
| | New Orleans Saints | | | |
| ☐ 171 | Lincoln Kennedy | .40 | .18 | .05 |
| | Atlanta Falcons | | | |
| ☐ 172 | Jerome Bettis | 8.00 | 3.60 | 1.00 |
| | Los Angeles Rams | | | |
| ☐ 173 | Dan Williams | .40 | .18 | .05 |
| | Denver Broncos | | | |
| ☐ 174 | Patrick Bates | .40 | .18 | .05 |
| | Los Angeles Raiders | | | |
| ☐ 175 | Brad Hopkins | .30 | .14 | .04 |
| | Houston Oilers | | | |
| ☐ 176 | Steve Everitt | .30 | .14 | .04 |
| | Cleveland Browns | | | |
| ☐ 177 | Wayne Simmons UER | .30 | .14 | .04 |
| | Green Bay Packers | | | |
| | (College touchdowns and yards are in wrong columns) | | | |
| ☐ 178 | Tom Carter | .50 | .23 | .06 |
| | Washington Redskins | | | |
| ☐ 179 | Ernest Dye | .25 | .11 | .03 |
| | Phoenix Cardinals | | | |
| ☐ 180 | Lester Holmes | .15 | .07 | .02 |
| | Philadelphia Eagles | | | |
| ☐ 181 | Irv Smith | .50 | .23 | .06 |
| | New Orleans Saints | | | |
| ☐ 182 | Robert Smith | 1.00 | .45 | .13 |
| | Minnesota Vikings | | | |
| ☐ 183 | Darrien Gordon | .60 | .25 | .08 |
| | San Diego Chargers | | | |
| ☐ 184 | Deon Figures | .35 | .16 | .04 |
| | Pittsburgh Steelers | | | |
| ☐ 185 | Leonard Renfro | .25 | .11 | .03 |
| | Philadelphia Eagles | | | |
| ☐ 186 | O.J. McDuffie | 3.00 | 1.35 | .40 |
| | Miami Dolphins | | | |
| ☐ 187 | Dana Stubblefield | 1.25 | .55 | .16 |
| | San Francisco 49ers | | | |
| ☐ 188 | Todd Kelly | .25 | .11 | .03 |
| | San Francisco 49ers | | | |
| ☐ 189 | Thomas Smith | .35 | .16 | .04 |
| | Buffalo Bills | | | |
| ☐ 190 | George Teague | .40 | .18 | .05 |
| | Green Bay Packers | | | |
| ☐ 191 | Wilber Marshall | .20 | .09 | .03 |
| | Houston Oilers | | | |
| ☐ 192 | Reggie White | .40 | .18 | .05 |
| | Green Bay Packers | | | |
| ☐ 193 | Carlton Gray | .40 | .18 | .05 |
| | Seattle Seahawks | | | |
| ☐ 194 | Chris Slade | .75 | .35 | .09 |
| | New England Patriots | | | |
| ☐ 195 | Ben Coleman | .20 | .09 | .03 |
| | Phoenix Cardinals | | | |
| ☐ 196 | Ryan McNeil | .40 | .18 | .05 |
| | Detroit Lions | | | |
| ☐ 197 | Demetrius DuBose | .40 | .18 | .05 |
| | Tampa Bay Buccaneers | | | |
| ☐ 198 | Coleman Rudolph | .25 | .11 | .03 |
| | New York Jets | | | |
| ☐ 199 | Tony McGee | .40 | .18 | .05 |
| | Cincinnati Bengals | | | |
| ☐ 200 | Troy Drayton | .50 | .23 | .06 |
| | Los Angeles Rams | | | |
| ☐ 201 | Natrone Means | 3.00 | 1.35 | .40 |
| | San Diego Chargers | | | |
| ☐ 202 | Glyn Milburn | 2.50 | 1.15 | .30 |
| | Denver Broncos | | | |
| ☐ 203 | Chad Brown | .30 | .14 | .04 |
| | Pittsburgh Steelers | | | |
| ☐ 204 | Reggie Brooks | 4.00 | 1.80 | .50 |
| | Washington Redskins | | | |
| ☐ 205 | Kevin Williams | 1.75 | .80 | .22 |
| | Dallas Cowboys | | | |
| ☐ 206 | Micheal Barrow | .15 | .07 | .02 |
| | Houston Oilers | | | |
| ☐ 207 | Roosevelt Potts | .75 | .35 | .09 |
| | Indianapolis Colts | | | |
| ☐ 208 | Victor Bailey | .75 | .35 | .09 |
| | Philadelphia Eagles | | | |
| ☐ 209 | Qadry Ismail | 1.25 | .55 | .16 |
| | Minnesota Vikings | | | |
| ☐ 210 | Vincent Brisby | 1.25 | .55 | .16 |
| | New England Patriots | | | |
| ☐ 211 | Billy Joe Hobert | .75 | .35 | .09 |
| | Los Angeles Raiders | | | |
| ☐ 212 | Lamar Thomas | .75 | .35 | .09 |
| | Tampa Bay Buccaneers | | | |
| ☐ 213 | Jason Elam | .25 | .11 | .03 |
| | Denver Broncos | | | |
| ☐ 214 | Andre Hastings | .50 | .23 | .06 |
| | Pittsburgh Steelers | | | |
| ☐ 215 | Terry Kirby | 3.00 | 1.35 | .40 |
| | Miami Dolphins | | | |
| ☐ 216 | Joe Montana | 4.00 | 1.80 | .50 |
| | Kansas City | | | |
| ☐ 217 | Derrick Lassic | .50 | .23 | .06 |
| | Dallas Cowboys | | | |
| ☐ 218 | Mark Brunell | .75 | .35 | .09 |
| | Green Bay Packers | | | |
| ☐ 219 | Vaughn Hebron | .75 | .35 | .09 |
| | Philadelphia Eagles | | | |
| ☐ 220 | Troy Brown | .30 | .14 | .04 |
| | New England Patriots | | | |
| ☐ 221 | Derek Brown | 2.25 | 1.00 | .30 |

New Orleans Saints
☐ 222 Raghib Ismail ........................ 1.00 .45 .13
Los Angeles Raiders

## 1993 Action Packed 24K Gold

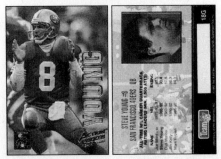

Randomly inserted throughout the foil packs, this 72-card standard-size (2 1/2" by 3 1/2") set features 24K versions of the Quarterback Club (1-18), Moving Targets (19-30), and 1000 YD Rushers (31-42). In design, the backs and fronts of these cards are identical to the regular series; their fronts are easily distinguished by the 24K notation beneath the Action Packed logo. The cards are numbered on the back with a "G" suffix.

| | MINT | EXC | G-VG |
|---|---|---|---|
| COMPLETE SET (72)........................ | 2500.00 | 1150.00 | 325.00 |
| COMPLETE SERIES 1 (42)................ | 1600.00 | 700.00 | 200.00 |
| COMPLETE SERIES 2 (30)................ | 900.00 | 400.00 | 115.00 |
| COMMON PLAYER (1G-42G).......... | 25.00 | 11.50 | 3.10 |
| COMMON PLAYER (43G-72G).......... | 25.00 | 11.50 | 3.10 |

| | | | |
|---|---|---|---|
| ☐ 1G Troy Aikman ........................ | 150.00 | 70.00 | 19.00 |
| Dallas Cowboys | | | |
| ☐ 2G Randall Cunningham .............. | 30.00 | 13.50 | 3.80 |
| Philadelphia Eagles | | | |
| ☐ 3G John Elway ........................ | 75.00 | 34.00 | 9.50 |
| Denver Broncos | | | |
| ☐ 4G Jim Everett ........................ | 30.00 | 13.50 | 3.80 |
| Los Angeles Rams | | | |
| ☐ 5G Brett Favre ........................ | 120.00 | 55.00 | 15.00 |
| Green Bay Packers | | | |
| ☐ 6G Jim Harbaugh ........................ | 25.00 | 11.50 | 3.10 |
| Chicago Bears | | | |
| ☐ 7G Jeff Hostetler ........................ | 30.00 | 13.50 | 3.80 |
| Los Angeles Raiders | | | |
| ☐ 8G Jim Kelly ........................ | 60.00 | 27.00 | 7.50 |
| Buffalo Bills | | | |
| ☐ 9G David Klingler ........................ | 35.00 | 16.00 | 4.40 |
| Cincinnati Bengals | | | |
| ☐ 10G Bernie Kosar ........................ | 25.00 | 11.50 | 3.10 |
| Cleveland Browns | | | |
| ☐ 11G Dan Marino ........................ | 120.00 | 55.00 | 15.00 |
| Miami Dolphins | | | |
| ☐ 12G Chris Miller ........................ | 30.00 | 13.50 | 3.80 |
| Atlanta Falcons | | | |
| ☐ 13G Boomer Esiason ................ | 30.00 | 13.50 | 3.80 |
| New York Jets | | | |
| ☐ 14G Warren Moon ........................ | 40.00 | 18.00 | 5.00 |
| Houston Oilers | | | |
| ☐ 15G Neil O'Donnell ................ | 35.00 | 16.00 | 4.40 |
| Pittsburgh Steelers | | | |
| ☐ 16G Mark Rypien ........................ | 30.00 | 13.50 | 3.80 |
| Washington Redskins | | | |
| ☐ 17G Phil Simms ........................ | 30.00 | 13.50 | 3.80 |
| New York Giants | | | |
| ☐ 18G Steve Young ........................ | 60.00 | 27.00 | 7.50 |
| San Francisco 49ers | | | |
| ☐ 19G Fred Barnett........................ | 25.00 | 11.50 | 3.10 |
| Philadelphia Eagles | | | |
| ☐ 20G Gary Clark ........................ | 30.00 | 13.50 | 3.80 |
| Washington Redskins | | | |
| ☐ 21G Mark Clayton ........................ | 25.00 | 11.50 | 3.10 |
| Miami Dolphins | | | |
| ☐ 22G Ernest Givins ........................ | 25.00 | 11.50 | 3.10 |
| Houston Oilers | | | |
| ☐ 23G Michael Haynes ................ | 35.00 | 16.00 | 4.40 |
| Atlanta Falcons | | | |
| ☐ 24G Michael Irvin ........................ | 75.00 | 34.00 | 9.50 |
| Dallas Cowboys | | | |
| ☐ 25G Haywood Jeffires................ | 25.00 | 11.50 | 3.10 |
| Houston Oilers | | | |
| ☐ 26G Anthony Miller ................ | 35.00 | 16.00 | 4.40 |
| San Diego Chargers | | | |
| ☐ 27G Andre Reed........................ | 30.00 | 13.50 | 3.80 |
| Atlanta Falcons | | | |

| | | | |
|---|---|---|---|
| ☐ 28G Jerry Rice ........................ | 100.00 | 45.00 | 12.50 |
| San Francisco 49ers | | | |
| ☐ 29G Andre Rison........................ | 50.00 | 23.00 | 6.25 |
| Atlanta Falcons | | | |
| ☐ 30G Sterling Sharpe................ | 75.00 | 34.00 | 9.50 |
| Green Bay Packers | | | |
| ☐ 31G Terry Allen ........................ | 30.00 | 13.50 | 3.80 |
| Minnesota Vikings | | | |
| ☐ 32G Reggie Cobb........................ | 30.00 | 13.50 | 3.80 |
| Tampa Bay Buccaneers | | | |
| ☐ 33G Barry Foster ........................ | 60.00 | 27.00 | 7.50 |
| Pittsburgh Steelers | | | |
| ☐ 34G Cleveland Gary................ | 25.00 | 11.50 | 3.10 |
| Los Angeles Rams | | | |
| ☐ 35G Harold Green ................ | 25.00 | 11.50 | 3.10 |
| Cincinnati Bengals | | | |
| ☐ 36G Rodney Hampton ................ | 60.00 | 27.00 | 7.50 |
| New York Giants | | | |
| ☐ 37G Barry Sanders................ | 100.00 | 45.00 | 12.50 |
| Detroit Lions | | | |
| ☐ 38G Emmitt Smith ................ | 185.00 | 85.00 | 23.00 |
| Dallas Cowboys | | | |
| ☐ 39G Thurman Thomas ................ | 70.00 | 32.00 | 8.75 |
| Buffalo Bills | | | |
| ☐ 40G Chris Warren ................ | 30.00 | 13.50 | 3.80 |
| Seattle Seahawks | | | |
| ☐ 41G Rickey Watters ................ | 60.00 | 27.00 | 7.50 |
| San Francisco 49ers | | | |
| ☐ 42G Lorenzo White ................ | 25.00 | 11.50 | 3.10 |
| Houston Oilers | | | |
| ☐ 43G Drew Bledsoe ................ | 120.00 | 55.00 | 15.00 |
| New England Patriots | | | |
| ☐ 44G Rick Mirer........................ | 120.00 | 55.00 | 15.00 |
| Seattle Seahawks | | | |
| ☐ 45G Garrison Hearst ................ | 50.00 | 23.00 | 6.25 |
| Phoenix Cardinals | | | |
| ☐ 46G Marvin Jones........................ | 30.00 | 13.50 | 3.80 |
| New York Jets | | | |
| ☐ 47G John Copeland................ | 35.00 | 16.00 | 4.40 |
| Cincinnati Bengals | | | |
| ☐ 48G Eric Curry ........................ | 35.00 | 16.00 | 4.40 |
| Tampa Bay Buccaneers | | | |
| ☐ 49G Curtis Conway ................ | 60.00 | 27.00 | 7.50 |
| Chicago Bears | | | |
| ☐ 50G William Roaf ................ | 25.00 | 11.50 | 3.10 |
| New Orleans Saints | | | |
| ☐ 51G Lincoln Kennedy ................ | 25.00 | 11.50 | 3.10 |
| Atlanta Falcons | | | |
| ☐ 52G Jerome Bettis ................ | 120.00 | 55.00 | 15.00 |
| Los Angeles Rams | | | |
| ☐ 53G Dan Williams ................ | 25.00 | 11.50 | 3.10 |
| Denver Broncos | | | |
| ☐ 54G Patrick Bates................ | 30.00 | 13.50 | 3.80 |
| Los Angeles Raiders | | | |
| ☐ 55G Brad Hopkins ................ | 25.00 | 11.50 | 3.10 |
| Houston Oilers | | | |
| ☐ 56G Steve Everitt ................ | 25.00 | 11.50 | 3.10 |
| Cleveland Browns | | | |
| ☐ 57G Wayne Simmons ................ | 25.00 | 11.50 | 3.10 |
| Green Bay Packers | | | |
| ☐ 58G Tom Carter ................ | 30.00 | 13.50 | 3.80 |
| Washington Redskins | | | |
| ☐ 59G Ernest Dye ................ | 25.00 | 11.50 | 3.10 |
| Phoenix Cardinals | | | |
| ☐ 60G Lester Holmes ................ | 25.00 | 11.50 | 3.10 |
| Philadelphia Eagles | | | |
| ☐ 61G Irv Smith ........................ | 30.00 | 13.50 | 3.80 |
| New Orleans Saints | | | |
| ☐ 62G Robert Smith ................ | 40.00 | 18.00 | 5.00 |
| Minnesota Vikings | | | |
| ☐ 63G Darrien Gordon................ | 30.00 | 13.50 | 3.80 |
| San Diego Chargers | | | |
| ☐ 64G Deon Figures ................ | 30.00 | 13.50 | 3.80 |
| Pittsburgh Steelers | | | |
| ☐ 65G Leonard Renfro................ | 25.00 | 11.50 | 3.10 |
| Philadelphia Eagles | | | |
| ☐ 66G O.J. McDuffie................ | 60.00 | 27.00 | 7.50 |
| Miami Dolphins | | | |
| ☐ 67G Dana Stubblefield ................ | 35.00 | 16.00 | 4.40 |
| San Francisco 49ers | | | |
| ☐ 68G Todd Kelly ................ | 25.00 | 11.50 | 3.10 |
| San Francisco 49ers | | | |
| ☐ 69G Thomas Smith ................ | 30.00 | 13.50 | 3.80 |
| Buffalo Bills | | | |
| ☐ 70G George Teague ................ | 30.00 | 13.50 | 3.80 |
| Green Bay Packers | | | |
| ☐ 71G Wilber Marshall ................ | 25.00 | 11.50 | 3.10 |
| Houston Oilers | | | |
| ☐ 72G Reggie White ................ | 30.00 | 13.50 | 3.80 |
| Green Bay Packers | | | |

## 1993 Action Packed Moving Targets

This 12-card subset was collated in the boxes the same as the regular cards. Moreover, 24K equivalents were randomly inserted throughout

the packs in limited quantities. These gold cards carry a "G" suffix after the number. The full-bleed embossed player photos on the fronts have the player's name printed in gold foil running down the left edge. The "Moving Targets" logo appears in the lower right corner. On a background consisting of an oil painting of a football scene depicting the position featured, the backs show a color head shot and charts highlighting the player's accomplishment. A black stripe carrying an autograph slot and the card number (with a "MT" prefix) round out the back.

|  | MINT | EXC | G-VG |
|---|---|---|---|
| COMPLETE SET (12) | 15.00 | 6.75 | 1.90 |
| COMMON PLAYER (MT1-MT12) | .50 | .23 | .06 |
| ☐ MT1 Fred Barnett | .50 | .23 | .06 |
| Philadelphia Eagles |  |  |  |
| ☐ MT2 Gary Clark | .75 | .35 | .09 |
| Washington Redskins |  |  |  |
| ☐ MT3 Mark Clayton | .50 | .23 | .06 |
| Miami Dolphins |  |  |  |
| ☐ MT4 Ernest Givins | .75 | .35 | .09 |
| Houston Oilers |  |  |  |
| ☐ MT5 Michael Haynes | 1.00 | .45 | .13 |
| Atlanta Falcons |  |  |  |
| ☐ MT6 Michael Irvin | 4.00 | 1.80 | .50 |
| Dallas Cowboys |  |  |  |
| ☐ MT7 Haywood Jeffires | .75 | .35 | .09 |
| Houston Oilers |  |  |  |
| ☐ MT8 Anthony Miller | .75 | .35 | .09 |
| San Diego Chargers |  |  |  |
| ☐ MT9 Andre Reed | .75 | .35 | .09 |
| Atlanta Falcons |  |  |  |
| ☐ MT10 Jerry Rice | 4.00 | 1.80 | .50 |
| San Francisco 49ers |  |  |  |
| ☐ MT11 Andre Rison | 1.25 | .55 | .16 |
| Atlanta Falcons |  |  |  |
| ☐ MT12 Sterling Sharpe | 4.00 | 1.80 | .50 |
| Green Bay Packers |  |  |  |

## 1993 Action Packed QB Club

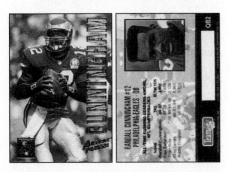

This 18-card subset was collated in the boxes the same as the regular cards. Moreover, 24K equivalents were randomly inserted throughout the packs in limited quantities. These gold cards carry a "G" suffix after the number. The Quarterback Club cards were also done in braille; these cards have a "B" prefix after the number, and some were donated to over 400 schools for the blind. Finally, certificates for mint versions (which are totally 24K gold leaf) of these cards were randomly packed in hobby boxes. Five hundred of each card were produced and individually numbered. The regular cards are numbered on the back with a "QB" prefix.

|  | MINT | EXC | G-VG |
|---|---|---|---|
| COMPLETE SET (18) | 20.00 | 9.00 | 2.50 |
| COMMON PLAYER (QB1-QB18) | .50 | .23 | .06 |
| *BRAILLE VERSIONS: 2X to 3X VALUE |  |  |  |
| ☐ QB1 Troy Aikman | 7.00 | 3.10 | .85 |
| Dallas Cowboys |  |  |  |
| ☐ QB2 Randall Cunningham | .75 | .35 | .09 |
| Philadelphia Eagles |  |  |  |
| ☐ QB3 John Elway | 4.00 | 1.80 | .50 |
| Denver Broncos |  |  |  |
| ☐ QB4 Jim Everett | .50 | .23 | .06 |
| Los Angeles Rams |  |  |  |
| ☐ QB5 Brett Favre | 4.00 | 1.80 | .50 |
| Green Bay Packers |  |  |  |
| ☐ QB6 Jim Harbaugh | .50 | .23 | .06 |
| Chicago Bears |  |  |  |
| ☐ QB7 Jeff Hostetler | .50 | .23 | .06 |
| Los Angeles Raiders |  |  |  |
| ☐ QB8 Jim Kelly | 2.25 | 1.00 | .30 |
| Buffalo Bills |  |  |  |
| ☐ QB9 David Klingler | 1.50 | .65 | .19 |
| Cincinnati Bengals |  |  |  |
| ☐ QB10 Bernie Kosar | .50 | .23 | .06 |
| Cleveland Browns |  |  |  |
| ☐ QB11 Dan Marino | 5.00 | 2.30 | .60 |
| Miami Dolphins |  |  |  |
| ☐ QB12 Chris Miller | .50 | .23 | .06 |
| Atlanta Falcons |  |  |  |
| ☐ QB13 Boomer Esiason | .75 | .35 | .09 |
| New York Jets |  |  |  |
| ☐ QB14 Warren Moon | 1.25 | .55 | .16 |
| Houston Oilers |  |  |  |
| ☐ QB15 Neil O'Donnell | 1.00 | .45 | .13 |
| Pittsburgh Steelers |  |  |  |
| ☐ QB16 Mark Rypien | .50 | .23 | .06 |
| Washington Redskins |  |  |  |
| ☐ QB17 Phil Simms | .75 | .35 | .09 |
| New York Giants |  |  |  |
| ☐ QB18 Steve Young | 2.25 | 1.00 | .30 |
| San Francisco 49ers |  |  |  |

## 1993 Action Packed Rushers

Featuring outstanding running backs, this 12-card subset was collated in the boxes the same as the regular cards. Moreover, 24K equivalents were randomly inserted throughout the packs in limited quantities. These gold cards carry a "G" suffix after the number. The fronts display full-bleed, embossed color action player photos, with a special "1000 Yard Rushers" logo in one of the lower corners. The player's last name is gold-foil stamped in block lettering and runs parallel to the side of the card. On a background consisting of an oil painting of a runner breaking through the line, the horizontal backs carry a color head shot and statistics on all-time single-season rushing leaders for the player's team. A black stripe at the bottom with a white slot for autograph rounds out the back. The cards are numbered on the back with an "RB" prefix.

|  | MINT | EXC | G-VG |
|---|---|---|---|
| COMPLETE SET (12) | 16.00 | 7.25 | 2.00 |
| COMMON PLAYER (RB1-RB12) | .50 | .23 | .06 |
| ☐ RB1 Terry Allen | .50 | .23 | .06 |
| Minnesota Vikings |  |  |  |
| ☐ RB2 Reggie Cobb | .50 | .23 | .06 |
| Tampa Bay Buccaneers |  |  |  |
| ☐ RB3 Barry Foster | 1.50 | .65 | .19 |
| Pittsburgh Steelers |  |  |  |
| ☐ RB4 Cleveland Gary | .50 | .23 | .06 |
| Los Angeles Rams |  |  |  |
| ☐ RB5 Harold Green | .50 | .23 | .06 |
| Cincinnati Bengals |  |  |  |
| ☐ RB6 Rodney Hampton | 2.00 | .90 | .25 |
| New York Giants |  |  |  |

| | | | |
|---|---|---|---|
| ☐ RB7 Barry Sanders | 4.00 | 1.80 | .50 |
| Detroit Lions | | | |
| ☐ RB8 Emmitt Smith | 8.00 | 3.60 | 1.00 |
| Dallas Cowboys | | | |
| ☐ RB9 Thurman Thomas | 1.50 | .65 | .19 |
| Buffalo Bills | | | |
| ☐ RB10 Chris Warren | .75 | .35 | .09 |
| Seattle Seahawks | | | |
| ☐ RB11 Ricky Watters | 1.50 | .65 | .19 |
| San Francisco 49ers | | | |
| ☐ RB12 Lorenzo White | .50 | .23 | .06 |
| Houston Oilers | | | |

## 1993 Action Packed Rookies Previews

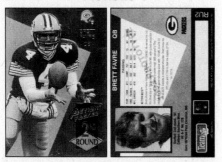

These three standard-size (2 1/2" by 3 1/2") cards preview the design of the 1993 Action Packed set. Card numbers 1-3 represent quarterbacks taken in the first three rounds of various NFL drafts. The fronts feature a color player cut-out against a full-bleed background that consists of a tilted colored panel bordered on two sides by foil. Depending on the round the player was drafted, the foil varies from gold (first round) to silver (second round) and then to bronze (third round). The horizontal backs carry a color close-up photo, '92 and career passing statistics, biography, and an "Action Note" that describes the game situation portrayed by the front picture before summarizing the player's performance. The cards are numbered on the back with an "RU" prefix.

| | MINT | EXC | G-VG |
|---|---|---|---|
| COMPLETE SET (3) | 10.00 | 4.50 | 1.25 |
| COMMON PLAYER (RU1-RU3) | 2.00 | .90 | .25 |
| ☐ RU1 Troy Aikman | 5.00 | 2.30 | .60 |
| Dallas Cowboys | | | |
| ☐ RU2 Brett Favre | 4.00 | 1.80 | .50 |
| Green Bay Packers | | | |
| ☐ RU3 Neil O'Donnell | 2.00 | .90 | .25 |
| Pittsburgh Steelers | | | |

## 1993 Action Packed All-Madden Prototype

This standard-size prototype card was issued to promote the December release of the 1993 Action Packed 10th Anniversary All-Madden Team set. The front features an embossed color action shot of Aikman that is borderless, except at the top, where an irregular gray lithic margin set off by a wavy black line carries his name in embossed

gold foil. The 10th Anniversary logo rests at the lower left. On a background of a mountainous rocky slope, the horizontal back carries a color head shot toward the upper right. Aikman's career highlights appear in a white rectangle to the left of the photo, with the word "prototype" printed diagonally across it in gray lettering. His name and position appear in gold foil across the top. The card is numbered on the back.

| | MINT | EXC | G-VG |
|---|---|---|---|
| COMPLETE SET (1) | 8.00 | 3.25 | .80 |
| COMMON PLAYER | 8.00 | 3.25 | .80 |
| ☐ 1 Troy Aikman | 8.00 | 3.25 | .80 |
| Dallas Cowboys | | | |

## 1993 Action Packed All-Madden

This 42-card standard-size set marks the fourth consecutive year Action Packed has honored the toughest players in the game as picked by sportscaster John Madden, and commemorates the 10th anniversary of his All-Madden Team by featuring his all-time favorites from the last 10 years. Action Packed produced 1,000 numbered cases and distributed them only through hobby distributors and dealers. Every case contained a certificate for an uncut sheet of the set autographed by John Madden. Also, 24K gold versions of 12 of these cards were randomly inserted in packs. The fronts feature embossed color player action shots that are borderless, except at the top, where an irregular gray lithic margin set off by a wavy black line carries the player's name in embossed gold foil. The 10th Anniversary logo rests at the lower left. On a background of a mountainous rocky slope, the horizontal back carries a color player head shot toward the upper right. The player's career highlights appear in a white rectangle to the left of the photo. His name and position appear in gold foil across the top. The cards are numbered on the back.

| | MINT | EXC | G-VG |
|---|---|---|---|
| COMPLETE SET (42) | 12.00 | 5.00 | 1.20 |
| COMMON PLAYER (1-42) | .15 | .06 | .01 |
| ☐ 1 Troy Aikman | 2.50 | 1.00 | .25 |
| Dallas Cowboys | | | |
| ☐ 2 Bill Bates | .15 | .06 | .01 |
| Dallas Cowboys | | | |
| ☐ 3 Mark Bavaro | .15 | .06 | .01 |
| New York Giants | | | |
| ☐ 4 Jim Burt | .15 | .06 | .01 |
| San Francisco 49ers | | | |
| ☐ 5 Gary Clark | .25 | .10 | .02 |
| Washington Redskins | | | |
| ☐ 6 Richard Dent | .25 | .10 | .02 |
| Chicago Bears | | | |
| ☐ 7 Gary Fencik | .15 | .06 | .01 |
| Chicago Bears | | | |
| ☐ 8 Darrell Green | .25 | .10 | .02 |
| Washington Redskins | | | |
| ☐ 9 Roy Green | .25 | .10 | .02 |
| St. Louis Cardinals | | | |
| ☐ 10 Russ Grimm | .15 | .06 | .01 |
| Washington Redskins | | | |
| ☐ 11 Charles Haley | .15 | .06 | .01 |
| Dallas Cowboys | | | |
| ☐ 12 Dan Hampton | .25 | .10 | .02 |
| Chicago Bears | | | |
| ☐ 13 Lester Hayes | .25 | .10 | .02 |
| Los Angeles Raiders | | | |
| ☐ 14 Mike Haynes | .25 | .10 | .02 |
| Los Angeles Raiders | | | |
| ☐ 15 Jay Hilgenberg | .15 | .06 | .01 |
| Chicago Bears | | | |
| ☐ 16 Michael Irvin | .75 | .30 | .07 |
| Dallas Cowboys | | | |
| ☐ 17 Joe Jacoby | .15 | .06 | .01 |

| | | | |
|---|---|---|---|
| Washington Redskins | | | |
| ☐ 18 Steve Largent | .50 | .20 | .05 |
| Seattle Seahawks | | | |
| ☐ 19 Howie Long | .25 | .10 | .02 |
| Los Angeles Raiders | | | |
| ☐ 20 Ronnie Lott | .35 | .14 | .03 |
| New York Jets | | | |
| ☐ 21 Dan Marino | 1.50 | .60 | .15 |
| Miami Dolphins | | | |
| ☐ 22 Jim McMahon | .35 | .14 | .03 |
| Chicago Bears | | | |
| ☐ 23 Matt Millen | .15 | .06 | .01 |
| Los Angeles Raiders | | | |
| ☐ 24 Art Monk | .35 | .14 | .03 |
| Washington Redskins | | | |
| ☐ 25 Joe Montana | 2.50 | 1.00 | .25 |
| Kansas City Chiefs | | | |
| ☐ 26 Anthony Munoz | .25 | .10 | .02 |
| Cincinnati Bengals | | | |
| ☐ 27 Nate Newton | .25 | .10 | .02 |
| Dallas Cowboys | | | |
| ☐ 28 Walter Payton | 1.50 | .60 | .15 |
| Chicago Bears | | | |
| ☐ 29 William Perry | .25 | .10 | .02 |
| Chicago Bears | | | |
| ☐ 30 Jack Reynolds | .15 | .06 | .01 |
| San Francisco 49ers | | | |
| ☐ 31 Jerry Rice | 1.00 | .40 | .10 |
| San Francisco 49ers | | | |
| ☐ 32 Barry Sanders | 1.00 | .40 | .10 |
| Detroit Lions | | | |
| ☐ 33 Sterling Sharpe | .75 | .30 | .07 |
| Green Bay Packers | | | |
| ☐ 34 Mike Singletary | .25 | .10 | .02 |
| Chicago Bears | | | |
| ☐ 35 Jackie Slater | .15 | .06 | .01 |
| Los Angeles Rams | | | |
| ☐ 36 Emmitt Smith | 3.00 | 1.20 | .30 |
| Dallas Cowboys | | | |
| ☐ 37 Pat Summerall | .25 | .10 | .02 |
| New York Giants | | | |
| ☐ 38 Lawrence Taylor | .50 | .20 | .05 |
| New York Giants | | | |
| ☐ 39 Jeff Van Note | .15 | .06 | .01 |
| Atlanta Falcons | | | |
| ☐ 40 Reggie White | .35 | .14 | .03 |
| Philadelphia Eagles | | | |
| ☐ 41 Otis Wilson | .15 | .06 | .01 |
| Chicago Bears | | | |
| ☐ 42 Jack Youngblood | .25 | .10 | .02 |
| Los Angeles Rams | | | |

## 1993 Action Packed All-Madden 24K Gold

These twelve 24K gold cards were randomly inserted in packs of 1993 Action Packed 10th Anniversary All-Madden Team. The cards measure the standard size (2 1/2" by 3 1/2"). Except for the richer tone of the 24K gold foil and the words "24 Kt. Gold" stamped on the front in gold foil, the design is identical to the regular 10th Anniversary All-Madden cards. The cards are numbered on the back with a "G" suffix.

| | MINT | EXC | G-VG |
|---|---|---|---|
| COMPLETE SET (12) | 400.00 | 180.00 | 45.00 |
| COMMON PLAYER (1-12) | 25.00 | 10.00 | 2.50 |
| ☐ 1G Troy Aikman | 100.00 | 40.00 | 10.00 |
| Dallas Cowboys | | | |
| ☐ 2G Michael Irvin | 50.00 | 20.00 | 5.00 |
| Dallas Cowboys | | | |
| ☐ 3G Ronnie Lott | 25.00 | 10.00 | 2.50 |
| New York Jets | | | |
| ☐ 4G Dan Marino | 75.00 | 30.00 | 7.50 |

| | | | |
|---|---|---|---|
| Miami Dolphins | | | |
| ☐ 5G Joe Montana | 100.00 | 40.00 | 10.00 |
| Kansas City Chiefs | | | |
| ☐ 6G Walter Payton | 50.00 | 20.00 | 5.00 |
| Chicago Bears | | | |
| ☐ 7G Jerry Rice | 60.00 | 24.00 | 6.00 |
| San Francisco 49ers | | | |
| ☐ 8G Barry Sanders | 60.00 | 24.00 | 6.00 |
| Detroit Lions | | | |
| ☐ 9G Sterling Sharpe | 50.00 | 20.00 | 5.00 |
| Green Bay Packers | | | |
| ☐ 10G Emmitt Smith | 125.00 | 50.00 | 12.50 |
| Dallas Cowboys | | | |
| ☐ 11G Lawrence Taylor | 25.00 | 10.00 | 2.50 |
| New York Giants | | | |
| ☐ 12G Reggie White | 25.00 | 10.00 | 2.50 |
| Philadelphia Eagles | | | |

## 1993 Action Packed ABC MNF Prototypes

These six standard-size (2 1/2" by 3 1/2") cards were issued to show the design of the 1993 Action Packed ABC Monday Night Football series. On a gold-foil background with black borders, the horizontal fronts feature cut-out embossed color player photos. The set title "ABC's Monday Night Football" is printed across the top between two helmets representing the teams that played. The cards highlight two of the 1992 season's best games. The date of the game is given in each side border, while the player's name is printed in the bottom black border. On the back, a gold foil border stripe carrying the words "ABC's Monday Night Football" edges the left side of the card. The rest of the back consists of a rose-colored panel that displays a color head shot, the scoring broken down by quarter, a summary of the player's performance, and various logos. The disclaimer "1993 Prototype" is printed diagonally across the back. The cards are numbered on the back.

| | MINT | EXC | G-VG |
|---|---|---|---|
| COMPLETE SET (6) | 40.00 | 16.00 | 4.00 |
| COMMON PLAYER (MN1-MN6) | 7.50 | 3.00 | .75 |
| ☐ MN1 Barry Sanders | 10.00 | 4.00 | 1.00 |
| Detroit Lions | | | |
| ☐ MN2 Steve Young | 10.00 | 4.00 | 1.00 |
| San Francisco 49ers | | | |
| ☐ MN3 Emmitt Smith | 15.00 | 6.00 | 1.50 |
| Dallas Cowboys | | | |
| ☐ MN4 Thurman Thomas | 7.50 | 3.00 | .75 |
| Buffalo Bills | | | |
| ☐ MN5 Barry Foster | 7.50 | 3.00 | .75 |
| Pittsburgh Steelers | | | |
| ☐ MN6 Warren Moon | 10.00 | 4.00 | 1.00 |
| Houston Oilers | | | |

## 1993 Action Packed ABC MNF

Previewing the top players and match-ups for the 1993 games, this 81-card set consists of cards for each game of the 1993 Monday Night Football schedule. In addition to featuring the top players in the games, the set also includes a card for each of the three ABC Monday Night Football announcers and a card with all three announcers together. Moreover, 250 individually numbered gold mint cards of each card were produced. and winning certificates for these were randomly inserted in the foil packs. Certificates entitling the collector to an all-expense paid trip to the Pro Bowl were also randomly inserted in the packs. A limited number of 24K gold leaf equivalents of all the cards was randomly inserted throughout the foil packs. These 24K Monday Night Football cards are valued at approximately 50 to

100 times the corresponding values below. Finally, Chiptopper preview cards were packed two per hobby box. The cards measure the standard-size (2 1/2" by 3 1/2"). On a gold-foil background with black borders, the horizontal fronts feature cut-out embossed color player photos. The set title "ABC's Monday Night Football" is printed across the top between two helmets representing the teams that played. The date of the game is given in each side border, while the player's name is printed in the bottom black border. On the back, a gold foil border stripe carrying the words "ABC's Monday Night Football" edges the left side of the card. The rest of the back consists of a rose-colored panel that displays a color head shot, the date of the upcoming game, and a game preview focusing on that player's performances versus the future opponent. Also a special "Monday Night Fact" highlights a record set during a Monday Night Football matchup by a player who shares the position of the player on the card. The cards are numbered on the back. The set numbering is chronological Dallas at Washington, September 6, 1993 (1-4), San Francisco at Cleveland, September 13, 1993 (5-8), Denver at Kansas City, September 20, 1993 (9-12), Pittsburgh at Atlanta, September 27, 1993, (13-16), Washington at Miami, October 4, 1993 (17-20), Houston at Buffalo, October 11, 1993 (21-25), L.A. Raiders at Denver, October 18, 1993 (26-29), Minnesota at Chicago, October 25, 1993 (30-33), Washington at Buffalo, November 1, 1993 (34-37), Green Bay at Kansas City, November 8, 1993 (38-42), Buffalo at Pittsburgh, November 15, 1993 (43-46), New Orleans at San Francisco, November 22, 1993 (47-50), San Diego at Indianapolis, November 29, 1993 (51-55), Philadelphia at Dallas, December 6, 1993 (56-61), Pittsburgh at Miami, December 13, 1993 (62-65), N.Y. Giants at New Orleans, December 20, 1993 (66-70), Miami at San Diego, December 27, 1993 (71-74), Philadelphia at San Francisco, January 3, 1993 (75-78), and Announcers (79-81).

|  | MINT | EXC | G-VG |
|---|---|---|---|
| COMPLETE SET (81) | 20.00 | 8.00 | 2.00 |
| COMMON PLAYER (1-81) | .15 | .06 | .01 |
| ☐ 1 Michael Irvin | .75 | .30 | .07 |
| Dallas Cowboys |  |  |  |
| ☐ 2 Charles Haley | .15 | .06 | .01 |
| San Francisco 49ers |  |  |  |
| ☐ 3 Art Monk | .35 | .14 | .03 |
| Washington Redskins |  |  |  |
| ☐ 4 Earnest Byner | .15 | .06 | .01 |
| Washington Redskins |  |  |  |
| ☐ 5 Tom Rathman | .25 | .10 | .02 |
| San Francisco 49ers |  |  |  |
| ☐ 6 John Taylor | .25 | .10 | .02 |
| San Francisco 49ers |  |  |  |
| ☐ 7 Bernie Kosar | .35 | .14 | .03 |
| Cleveland Browns |  |  |  |
| ☐ 8 Clay Matthews | .25 | .10 | .02 |
| Cleveland Browns |  |  |  |
| ☐ 9 Simon Fletcher | .15 | .06 | .01 |
| Denver Broncos |  |  |  |
| ☐ 10 John Elway | 1.00 | .40 | .10 |
| Denver Broncos |  |  |  |
| ☐ 11 Joe Montana | 2.50 | 1.00 | .25 |
| Kansas City Chiefs |  |  |  |
| ☐ 12 Derrick Thomas | .50 | .20 | .05 |
| Kansas City Chiefs |  |  |  |
| ☐ 13 Rod Woodson | .35 | .14 | .03 |
| Pittsburgh Steelers |  |  |  |
| ☐ 14 Gary Anderson | .15 | .06 | .01 |
| Pittsburgh Steelers |  |  |  |
| ☐ 15 Chris Miller | .25 | .10 | .02 |
| Atlanta Falcons |  |  |  |
| ☐ 16 Andre Rison | .50 | .20 | .05 |
| Atlanta Falcons |  |  |  |
| ☐ 17 Mark Rypien | .25 | .10 | .02 |
| Washington Redskins |  |  |  |
| ☐ 18 Charles Mann | .15 | .06 | .01 |
| Washington Redskins |  |  |  |
| ☐ 19 John Offerdahl | .15 | .06 | .01 |
| Miami Dolphins |  |  |  |
| ☐ 20 Pete Stoyanovich | .15 | .06 | .01 |
| Miami Dolphins |  |  |  |
| ☐ 21 Warren Moon | .75 | .30 | .07 |
| Houston Oilers |  |  |  |
| ☐ 22 Lorenzo White | .25 | .10 | .02 |
| Houston Oilers |  |  |  |
| ☐ 23 Haywood Jeffires | .35 | .14 | .03 |
| Houston Oilers |  |  |  |
| ☐ 24 Andre Reed | .35 | .14 | .03 |
| Buffalo Bills |  |  |  |
| ☐ 25 Darryl Talley | .25 | .10 | .02 |
| Buffalo Bills |  |  |  |
| ☐ 26 Tim Brown | .50 | .20 | .05 |
| Los Angeles Raiders |  |  |  |
| ☐ 27 Howie Long | .25 | .10 | .02 |
| Los Angeles Raiders |  |  |  |
| ☐ 28 Steve Atwater | .15 | .06 | .01 |
| Denver Broncos |  |  |  |
| ☐ 29 Karl Mecklenburg | .25 | .10 | .02 |
| Denver Broncos |  |  |  |
| ☐ 30 Chris Doleman | .25 | .10 | .02 |
| Minnesota Vikings |  |  |  |
| ☐ 31 Terry Allen | .50 | .20 | .05 |
| Minnesota Vikings |  |  |  |
| ☐ 32 Richard Dent | .25 | .10 | .02 |
| Chicago Bears |  |  |  |
| ☐ 33 Neal Anderson | .25 | .10 | .02 |
| Chicago Bears |  |  |  |
| ☐ 34 Darrell Green | .25 | .10 | .02 |
| Washington Redskins |  |  |  |
| ☐ 35 Chip Lohmiller | .15 | .06 | .01 |
| Washington Redskins |  |  |  |
| ☐ 36 Jim Kelly | .75 | .30 | .07 |
| Buffalo Bills |  |  |  |
| ☐ 37 Cornelius Bennett | .35 | .14 | .03 |
| Buffalo Bills |  |  |  |
| ☐ 38 Brett Favre | 1.25 | .50 | .12 |
| Green Bay Packers |  |  |  |
| ☐ 39 Sterling Sharpe | .75 | .30 | .07 |
| Green Bay Packers |  |  |  |
| ☐ 40 Reggie White | .50 | .20 | .05 |
| Green Bay Packers |  |  |  |
| ☐ 41 Neil Smith | .25 | .10 | .02 |
| Kansas City Chiefs |  |  |  |
| ☐ 42 Nick Lowery | .15 | .06 | .01 |
| Kansas City Chiefs |  |  |  |
| ☐ 43 Thurman Thomas | .75 | .30 | .07 |
| Buffalo Bills |  |  |  |
| ☐ 44 Bruce Smith | .35 | .14 | .03 |
| Buffalo Bills |  |  |  |
| ☐ 45 Barry Foster | .50 | .20 | .05 |
| Pittsburgh Steelers |  |  |  |
| ☐ 46 Neil O'Donnell | .50 | .20 | .05 |
| Pittsburgh Steelers |  |  |  |
| ☐ 47 Rickey Jackson | .25 | .10 | .02 |
| New Orleans Saints |  |  |  |
| ☐ 48 Morten Andersen | .15 | .06 | .01 |
| New Orleans Saints |  |  |  |
| ☐ 49 Brent Jones | .25 | .10 | .02 |
| San Francisco 49ers |  |  |  |
| ☐ 50 Ricky Watters | .75 | .30 | .07 |
| San Francisco 49ers |  |  |  |
| ☐ 51 Leslie O'Neal | .25 | .10 | .02 |
| San Diego Chargers |  |  |  |
| ☐ 52 Marion Butts | .35 | .14 | .03 |
| San Diego Chargers |  |  |  |
| ☐ 53 Anthony Miller | .50 | .20 | .05 |
| San Diego Chargers |  |  |  |
| ☐ 54 Jeff George | .50 | .20 | .05 |
| Indianapolis Colts |  |  |  |
| ☐ 55 Steve Emtman | .35 | .14 | .03 |
| Indianapolis Colts |  |  |  |
| ☐ 56 Herschel Walker | .35 | .14 | .03 |
| Philadelphia Eagles |  |  |  |
| ☐ 57 Randall Cunningham | .75 | .30 | .07 |
| Philadelphia Eagles |  |  |  |
| ☐ 58 Clyde Simmons | .15 | .06 | .01 |
| Philadelphia Eagles |  |  |  |
| ☐ 59 Emmitt Smith | 4.00 | 1.60 | .40 |
| Dallas Cowboys |  |  |  |
| ☐ 60 Ken Norton Jr. | .25 | .10 | .02 |
| Dallas Cowboys |  |  |  |
| ☐ 61 Troy Aikman | 3.00 | 1.20 | .30 |
| Dallas Cowboys |  |  |  |
| ☐ 62 Eric Green | .25 | .10 | .02 |
| Pittsburgh Steelers |  |  |  |
| ☐ 63 Greg Lloyd | .15 | .06 | .01 |
| Pittsburgh Steelers |  |  |  |
| ☐ 64 Bryan Cox | .25 | .10 | .02 |
| Miami Dolphins |  |  |  |
| ☐ 65 Mark Higgs | .35 | .14 | .03 |
| Miami Dolphins |  |  |  |
| ☐ 66 Phil Simms | .35 | .14 | .03 |
| New York Giants |  |  |  |
| ☐ 67 Lawrence Taylor | .35 | .14 | .03 |
| New York Giants |  |  |  |
| ☐ 68 Rodney Hampton | .50 | .20 | .05 |

| | | | |
|---|---|---|---|
| New York Giants | | | |
| ☐ 69 Wayne Martin | .15 | .06 | .01 |
| New Orleans Saints | | | |
| ☐ 70 Vaughn Dunbar | .25 | .10 | .02 |
| New Orleans Saints | | | |
| ☐ 71 Keith Jackson | .35 | .14 | .03 |
| Miami Dolphins | | | |
| ☐ 72 Dan Marino | 2.00 | .80 | .20 |
| Miami Dolphins | | | |
| ☐ 73 Junior Seau | .35 | .14 | .03 |
| San Diego Chargers | | | |
| ☐ 74 Stan Humphries | .35 | .14 | .03 |
| San Diego Chargers | | | |
| ☐ 75 Fred Barnett | .35 | .14 | .03 |
| Philadelphia Eagles | | | |
| ☐ 76 Seth Joyner | .25 | .10 | .02 |
| Philadelphia Eagles | | | |
| ☐ 77 Steve Young | .75 | .30 | .07 |
| San Francisco 49ers | | | |
| ☐ 78 Jerry Rice | 1.00 | .40 | .10 |
| San Francisco 49ers | | | |
| ☐ 79 Dan Dierdorf ANN | .25 | .10 | .02 |
| ☐ 80 Frank Gifford ANN | .50 | .20 | .05 |
| ☐ 81 Al Michaels ANN | .15 | .06 | .01 |
| ☐ HW1 Hank Williams Jr. | .25 | .10 | .02 |

## 1994 Action Packed Prototypes

The 1994 Action Packed Prototype set consists of 12 standard-size (2 1/2" by 3 1/2") cards with rounded corners. An 11-card set (without Barry Foster) was distributed in a black cardboard display frame which held three cards horizontally down the middle and four cards vertically on either side. The display frame is packaged with a black cardboard sleeve with the gold-stamped Action Packed logo and lettering. The prototypes were made available to dealers. The cards were also given out at the Super Bowl XXVIII card show. The set includes: one regular issue 1994 Action Packed card; one "Quarterback Challenge" subset card; one "Catching the Fire" subset card that honors NFL's best receivers; and one "Warp Speed" subset card featuring the fastest running backs. Also included in the set are one "Rookie Update" card, two "The Golden Domers Class of '93" subset cards featuring Notre Dame players who made it to the 1993 NFL rookie class, one Monday Night Football card, and two "Monday Night Moment" subset cards. Each card carries its number and the word "Prototype" on the back.

| | MINT | EXC | G-VG |
|---|---|---|---|
| COMPLETE SET (12) | 60.00 | 24.00 | 6.00 |
| COMMON PLAYER | 2.50 | 1.00 | .25 |
| | | | |
| ☐ FB941 Troy Aikman | 12.00 | 5.00 | 1.20 |
| Dallas Cowboys | | | |
| 1994 Action Packed | | | |
| ☐ FB942 Jeff Hostetler | 2.50 | 1.00 | .25 |
| Oakland Raiders | | | |
| Quarterback Challenge | | | |
| ☐ FB943 Emmitt Smith | 12.00 | 5.00 | 1.20 |
| Dallas Cowboys | | | |
| Warp Speed | | | |
| ☐ FB944 Jerry Rice | 5.00 | 2.00 | .50 |
| San Francisco 49ers | | | |
| Catching Fire | | | |
| ☐ FB945 Barry Foster | 3.50 | 1.40 | .35 |
| Pittsburgh Steelers | | | |
| Fantasy Forecast Subset | | | |
| ☐ MNF941 Steve Young | 3.50 | 1.40 | .35 |
| San Francisco 49ers | | | |
| Sept. 12, 1994 | | | |
| S.F. at Cleveland | | | |
| Monday Night Football | | | |
| ☐ MNF942 Steve Young | 3.50 | 1.40 | .35 |
| San Francisco 49ers | | | |
| Monday Night Moment | | | |
| ☐ MNF943 Barry Foster | 3.50 | 1.40 | .35 |

| | | | |
|---|---|---|---|
| Pittsburgh Steelers | | | |
| Monday Night Moment | | | |
| ☐ RU941 Drew Bledsoe | 9.00 | 3.75 | .90 |
| New England Patriots | | | |
| Rookie Update | | | |
| ☐ RU942 Derrick Lassic | 2.50 | 1.00 | .25 |
| Dallas Cowboys | | | |
| Rookie Update | | | |
| ☐ RU943 Rick Mirer | 9.00 | 3.75 | .90 |
| Seattle Seahawks | | | |
| (Golden Domers) | | | |
| ☐ RU944 Jerome Bettis | 9.00 | 3.75 | .90 |
| Los Angeles Rams | | | |
| (Golden Domers) | | | |

## 1994 Action Packed Mammoth Prototype

To herald the introduction of Action Packed's newest product (the Mammoth card), this 7 1/2" by 10 1/2" prototype card was issued with the press release. The front displays a full-bleed embossed color action player photo, with the player's name printed on a gold foil curve in an upper corner. On a pastel purple background, the horizontal backs carry biography, the 1993 season and career statistics, an Action Note, and a color cutout. Separated by thin gold foil stripe, the bottom dark purple stripe has logos and the card letter.

| | MINT | EXC | G-VG |
|---|---|---|---|
| COMPLETE SET (1) | 15.00 | 6.00 | 1.50 |
| COMMON PLAYER | 15.00 | 6.00 | 1.50 |
| | | | |
| ☐ MMP Troy Aikman | 15.00 | 6.00 | 1.50 |
| Dallas Cowboys | | | |

## 1991 All World Troy Aikman Promos

 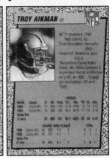

This set consists of six standard-size (2 1/2" by 3 1/2") cards. The cards feature the same color action photo of Aikman, with ball cocked behind head ready to pass. On the first three cards, the top of the photo is oval-shaped and framed by yellow stripes. The space above the oval as well as the stripe at the bottom carrying player information are purple. The outer border is green. Inside green borders, the horizontal back has a color close-up photo, biography (there were French, Spanish, and English versions), and statistics. On the second three cards listed below, the player photo is tilted slightly to the right and framed by a thin green border. Yellow stripes above and below the picture carry information, and the outer border is black-and-white speckled. The backs have a similar design and display a close-up color head shot and biographical and statistical information on a pastel green panel. All versions use the same color action photo, picturing Aikman with the ball behind his head ready to pass. They differ in that the photo is cropped differently on the green-border cards compared to the speckled-border cards. All cards are numbered on the back as number 1.

|  | MINT | EXC | G-VG |
|---|---|---|---|
| COMPLETE SET (6) | 18.00 | 7.25 | 1.80 |
| COMMON PLAYER (1A-1F) | 4.00 | 1.60 | .40 |
| ☐ 1A Troy Aikman | 4.00 | 1.60 | .40 |
| Dallas Cowboys (Green border; English bio) | | | |
| ☐ 1B Troy Aikman | 4.00 | 1.60 | .40 |
| Dallas Cowboys (Green border; French bio) | | | |
| ☐ 1C Troy Aikman | 4.00 | 1.60 | .40 |
| Dallas Cowboys (Green border; Spanish bio) | | | |
| ☐ 1D Troy Aikman | 4.00 | 1.60 | .40 |
| Dallas Cowboys (Speckled border; English bio) | | | |
| ☐ 1E Troy Aikman | 4.00 | 1.60 | .40 |
| Dallas Cowboys (Speckled border; French bio) | | | |
| ☐ 1F Troy Aikman | 4.00 | 1.60 | .40 |
| Dallas Cowboys (Speckled border; Spanish bio) | | | |

## 1992 All World NFL Promo

This standard-size (2 1/2" by 3 1/2") promo card was issued to show the design of the 1992 All World NFL card series. The front design features a glossy color player photo of Howard, bordered on top by a full-bleed American flag and by white on the remaining three sides. The backs have a second color player photo, with player information (biography and player profile) in a horizontally oriented box alongside the picture. The card is lettered "P" on the back.

|  | MINT | EXC | G-VG |
|---|---|---|---|
| COMPLETE SET (1) | 3.00 | 1.20 | .30 |
| COMMON PLAYER | 3.00 | 1.20 | .30 |
| ☐ P Desmond Howard | 3.00 | 1.20 | .30 |
| Washington Redskins | | | |

## 1992 All World

The 1992 All World NFL football set contains 300 standard-size (2 1/2 by 3 1/2") cards. The production run was reported to be 8,000 foil cases. However, there is strong speculation that fewer cases than the announced figure were produced. The front design features glossy color player photos, bordered on top by a full-bleed American flag and by white on the remaining three sides. Ten Rookie Cards and ten "Legends in the Making" cards, embossed with gold-foil stars, were randomly inserted in the foil packs. Likewise, autographed cards by Joe Namath (1,000), Jim Brown (1,000), and Desmond Howard (2,500) were inserted in both foil and rack packs. Although the player's name is not printed on the front, his autograph and number do appear. A special double-fold card (TR1) of the three autographed cards was inserted only in the rack packs. It is distinguished from the regular issue triple cards by foil-stamping. The regular card backs have a second color player photo, with player information (biography and player profile) in a horizontally oriented box alongside the picture. Topical subsets featured include Legends in the Making (1-10) and Greats of the Game (266-300). The cards are numbered on the back and checklisted below accordingly. The key Rookie Cards in this set are Edgar Bennett, Steve Bono, Terrell Buckley, Dale Carter, Marco Coleman, Quentin Coryatt, Vaughn Dunbar, Steve Emtman, Desmond Howard, David Klingler, Tommy Maddox, Carl Pickens, and Tommy Vardell.

|  | MINT | EXC | G-VG |
|---|---|---|---|
| COMPLETE SET (300) | 18.00 | 8.00 | 2.30 |
| COMMON PLAYER (1-300) | .05 | .02 | .01 |
| ☐ 1 Emmitt Smith LM | 1.25 | .55 | .16 |
| Dallas Cowboys | | | |
| ☐ 2 Thurman Thomas LM | .25 | .11 | .03 |
| Buffalo Bills | | | |
| ☐ 3 Deion Sanders LM | .10 | .05 | .01 |
| Atlanta Falcons | | | |
| ☐ 4 Randall Cunningham LM | .10 | .05 | .01 |
| Philadelphia Eagles | | | |
| ☐ 5 Michael Irvin LM | .25 | .11 | .03 |
| Dallas Cowboys | | | |
| ☐ 6 Bruce Smith LM | .10 | .05 | .01 |
| Buffalo Bills | | | |
| ☐ 7 Jeff George LM | .10 | .05 | .01 |
| Indianapolis Colts | | | |
| ☐ 8 Derrick Thomas LM | .10 | .05 | .01 |
| Kansas City Chiefs | | | |
| ☐ 9 Andre Rison LM | .10 | .05 | .01 |
| Atlanta Falcons | | | |
| ☐ 10 Troy Aikman LM | .75 | .35 | .09 |
| Dallas Cowboys | | | |
| ☐ 11 Quentin Coryatt | .30 | .14 | .04 |
| Indianapolis Colts | | | |
| ☐ 12 Carl Pickens | .40 | .18 | .05 |
| Cincinnati Bengals | | | |
| ☐ 13 Steve Emtman | .15 | .07 | .02 |
| Indianapolis Colts | | | |
| ☐ 14 Derek Brown | .10 | .05 | .01 |
| New York Giants | | | |
| ☐ 15 Desmond Howard | 3.00 | 1.35 | .40 |
| Washington Redskins | | | |
| ☐ 16 Troy Vincent | .10 | .05 | .01 |
| Miami Dolphins | | | |
| ☐ 17 David Klingler | .50 | .23 | .06 |
| Cincinnati Bengals | | | |
| ☐ 18 Vaughn Dunbar | .25 | .11 | .03 |
| New Orleans Saints | | | |
| ☐ 19 Terrell Buckley | .25 | .11 | .03 |
| Green Bay Packers | | | |
| ☐ 20 Jimmy Smith | .10 | .05 | .01 |
| Dallas Cowboys | | | |
| ☐ 21 Marquez Pope | .10 | .05 | .01 |
| San Diego Chargers | | | |
| ☐ 22 Kurt Barber | .10 | .05 | .01 |
| New York Jets | | | |
| ☐ 23 Robert Harris | .05 | .02 | .01 |
| Minnesota Vikings | | | |
| ☐ 24 Tony Sacca | .15 | .07 | .02 |
| Phoenix Cardinals | | | |
| ☐ 25 Alonzo Spellman | .20 | .09 | .03 |
| Chicago Bears | | | |
| ☐ 26 Shane Collins | .15 | .07 | .02 |
| Washington Redskins | | | |
| ☐ 27 Chris Mims | .25 | .11 | .03 |
| San Diego Chargers | | | |
| ☐ 28 Siran Stacy | .10 | .05 | .01 |
| Philadelphia Eagles | | | |
| ☐ 29 Edgar Bennett | .30 | .14 | .04 |
| Green Bay Packers | | | |
| ☐ 30 Sean Gilbert | .30 | .14 | .04 |
| Los Angeles Rams | | | |
| ☐ 31 Eugene Chung | .05 | .02 | .01 |
| New England Patriots | | | |
| ☐ 32 Lorenzo Kirkland | .15 | .07 | .02 |
| Pittsburgh Steelers | | | |
| ☐ 33 Chuck Smith | .10 | .05 | .01 |
| Atlanta Falcons | | | |

|  |  |  | | | |
|---|--------|------|----|----|----|
| ☐ 34 | Chester McGlockton | Los Angeles Raiders | .20 | .09 | .03 |
| ☐ 35 | Ashley Ambrose | Indianapolis Colts | .10 | .05 | .01 |
| ☐ 36 | Phillippi Sparks | New York Giants | .05 | .02 | .01 |
| ☐ 37 | Darryl Williams | Cincinnati Bengals | .20 | .09 | .03 |
| ☐ 38 | Tracy Scroggins | Detroit Lions | .20 | .09 | .03 |
| ☐ 39 | Mike Gaddis | Minnesota Vikings | .05 | .02 | .01 |
| ☐ 40 | Tony Brooks | Philadelphia Eagles | .05 | .02 | .01 |
| ☐ 41 | Steve Israel | Los Angeles Rams | .05 | .02 | .01 |
| ☐ 42 | Patrick Rowe | Cleveland Browns | .10 | .05 | .01 |
| ☐ 43 | Shane Dronett | Denver Broncos | .20 | .09 | .03 |
| ☐ 44 | Mike Pawlawski | Tampa Bay Buccaneers | .10 | .05 | .01 |
| ☐ 45 | Dale Carter | Kansas City Chiefs | .25 | .11 | .03 |
| ☐ 46 | Tyji Armstrong | Tampa Bay Buccaneers | .15 | .07 | .02 |
| ☐ 47 | Kevin Smith | Dallas Cowboys | .25 | .11 | .03 |
| ☐ 48 | Courtney Hawkins | Tampa Bay Buccaneers | .25 | .11 | .03 |
| ☐ 49 | Marco Coleman | Miami Dolphins | .30 | .14 | .04 |
| ☐ 50 | Tommy Vardell | Cleveland Browns | .30 | .14 | .04 |
| ☐ 51 | Ray Ethridge | San Diego Chargers | .05 | .02 | .01 |
| ☐ 52 | Robert Porcher | Detroit Lions | .20 | .09 | .03 |
| ☐ 53 | Todd Collins | New England Patriots | .12 | .05 | .02 |
| ☐ 54 | Robert Jones | Dallas Cowboys | .12 | .05 | .02 |
| ☐ 55 | Tommy Maddox | Denver Broncos | .50 | .23 | .06 |
| ☐ 56 | Dana Hall | San Francisco 49ers | .15 | .07 | .02 |
| ☐ 57 | Leon Searcy | Pittsburgh Steelers | .05 | .02 | .01 |
| ☐ 58 | Robert Brooks | Green Bay Packers | .20 | .09 | .03 |
| ☐ 59 | Darren Woodson | Dallas Cowboys | .20 | .09 | .03 |
| ☐ 60 | Jeremy Lincoln | Chicago Bears | .15 | .07 | .02 |
| ☐ 61 | Sean Jones | Houston Oilers | .05 | .02 | .01 |
| ☐ 62 | Howie Long | Los Angeles Raiders | .08 | .04 | .01 |
| ☐ 63 | Rich Gannon | Minnesota Vikings | .08 | .04 | .01 |
| ☐ 64 | Keith Byars | Philadelphia Eagles | .08 | .04 | .01 |
| ☐ 65 | John Taylor | San Francisco 49ers | .10 | .05 | .01 |
| ☐ 66 | Burt Grossman | San Diego Chargers | .05 | .02 | .01 |
| ☐ 67 | Chris Hinton | Atlanta Falcons | .05 | .02 | .01 |
| ☐ 68 | Brad Muster | Chicago Bears | .08 | .04 | .01 |
| ☐ 69 | Cris Dishman | Houston Oilers | .08 | .04 | .01 |
| ☐ 70 | Russell Maryland | Dallas Cowboys | .15 | .07 | .02 |
| ☐ 71 | Harvey Williams | Kansas City Chiefs | .10 | .05 | .01 |
| ☐ 72 | Broderick Thomas | Tampa Bay Buccaneers | .05 | .02 | .01 |
| ☐ 73 | Louis Lipps | Pittsburgh Steelers | .08 | .04 | .01 |
| ☐ 74 | Erik Kramer | Detroit Lions | .15 | .07 | .02 |
| ☐ 75 | David Fulcher | Cincinnati Bengals | .05 | .02 | .01 |
| ☐ 76 | Andre Tippett | New England Patriots | .08 | .04 | .01 |
| ☐ 77 | Timm Rosenbach | Phoenix Cardinals | .05 | .02 | .01 |
| ☐ 78 | Mark Rypien | Washington Redskins | .10 | .05 | .01 |
| ☐ 79 | James Lofton | Buffalo Bills | .10 | .05 | .01 |
| ☐ 80 | Dan Saleaumua | Kansas City Chiefs | .05 | .02 | .01 |
| ☐ 81 | John L. Williams | Seattle Seahawks | .08 | .04 | .01 |
| ☐ 82 | Kevin Fagan | San Francisco 49ers | .05 | .02 | .01 |
| ☐ 83 | Flipper Anderson | Los Angeles Rams | .08 | .04 | .01 |
| ☐ 84 | Michael Dean Perry | Cleveland Browns | .10 | .05 | .01 |
| ☐ 85 | Mark Higgs | Miami Dolphins | .10 | .05 | .01 |
| ☐ 86 | Pat Swilling | New Orleans Saints | .08 | .04 | .01 |
| ☐ 87 | Pierce Holt | San Francisco 49ers | .05 | .02 | .01 |
| ☐ 88 | John Elway | Denver Broncos | .40 | .18 | .05 |
| ☐ 89 | Bill Brooks | Indianapolis Colts | .08 | .04 | .01 |
| ☐ 90 | Rob Moore | New York Jets | .10 | .05 | .01 |
| ☐ 91 | Junior Seau | San Diego Chargers | .15 | .07 | .02 |
| ☐ 92 | Wendell Davis | Chicago Bears | .05 | .02 | .01 |
| ☐ 93 | Brian Noble | Green Bay Packers | .05 | .02 | .01 |
| ☐ 94 | Ernest Givins | Houston Oilers | .08 | .04 | .01 |
| ☐ 95 | Phil Simms | New York Giants | .10 | .05 | .01 |
| ☐ 96 | Eric Dickerson | Los Angeles Raiders | .10 | .05 | .01 |
| ☐ 97 | Bennie Blades | Detroit Lions | .05 | .02 | .01 |
| ☐ 98 | Gary Anderson | Tampa Bay Buccaneers | .08 | .04 | .01 |
| ☐ 99 | Erric Pegram | Atlanta Falcons | .40 | .18 | .05 |
| ☐ 100 | Hart Lee Dykes | New England Patriots | .05 | .02 | .01 |
| ☐ 101 | Charles Haley | San Francisco 49ers | .08 | .04 | .01 |
| ☐ 102 | Bruce Smith | Buffalo Bills | .10 | .05 | .01 |
| ☐ 103 | Nick Lowery | Kansas City Chiefs | .08 | .04 | .01 |
| ☐ 104 | Webster Slaughter | Cleveland Browns | .08 | .04 | .01 |
| ☐ 105 | Ray Childress | Houston Oilers | .08 | .04 | .01 |
| ☐ 106 | Gene Atkins | New Orleans Saints | .05 | .02 | .01 |
| ☐ 107 | Bruce Armstrong | New England Patriots | .05 | .02 | .01 |
| ☐ 108 | Anthony Miller | San Diego Chargers | .15 | .07 | .02 |
| ☐ 109 | Eric Thomas | Cincinnati Bengals | .05 | .02 | .01 |
| ☐ 110 | Greg Townsend | Los Angeles Raiders | .05 | .02 | .01 |
| ☐ 111 | Anthony Carter | Minnesota Vikings | .08 | .04 | .01 |
| ☐ 112 | James Hasty | New York Jets | .05 | .02 | .01 |
| ☐ 113 | Chris Miller | Atlanta Falcons | .10 | .05 | .01 |
| ☐ 114 | Sammie Smith | Denver Broncos | .05 | .02 | .01 |
| ☐ 115 | Bubby Brister | Pittsburgh Steelers | .08 | .04 | .01 |
| ☐ 116 | Mark Clayton | Miami Dolphins | .08 | .04 | .01 |
| ☐ 117 | Richard Johnson | Houston Oilers | .05 | .02 | .01 |
| ☐ 118 | Bernie Kosar | Cleveland Browns | .10 | .05 | .01 |
| ☐ 119 | Lionel Washington | Los Angeles Raiders | .05 | .02 | .01 |
| ☐ 120 | Gary Clark | Washington Redskins | .08 | .04 | .01 |
| ☐ 121 | Anthony Munoz | Cincinnati Bengals | .08 | .04 | .01 |
| ☐ 122 | Brent Jones | San Francisco 49ers | .10 | .05 | .01 |
| ☐ 123 | Thurman Thomas | Buffalo Bills | .40 | .18 | .05 |
| ☐ 124 | Lee Williams | Houston Oilers | .08 | .04 | .01 |
| ☐ 125 | Jessie Hester | Indianapolis Colts | .05 | .02 | .01 |
| ☐ 126 | Andre Ware | Detroit Lions | .08 | .04 | .01 |
| ☐ 127 | Patrick Hunter | Seattle Seahawks | .05 | .02 | .01 |
| ☐ 128 | Erik Howard | New York Giants | .05 | .02 | .01 |
| ☐ 129 | Keith Jackson | Philadelphia Eagles | .10 | .05 | .01 |
| ☐ 130 | Troy Aikman | Dallas Cowboys | 1.25 | .55 | .16 |
| ☐ 131 | Mike Singletary | | .10 | .05 | .01 |

| | | | |
|---|---|---|---|
| Chicago Bears | | | |
| ☐ 132 Carnell Lake | .05 | .02 | .01 |
| Pittsburgh Steelers | | | |
| ☐ 133 Jeff Hostetler | .20 | .09 | .03 |
| New York Giants | | | |
| ☐ 134 Alonzo Highsmith | .05 | .02 | .01 |
| Tampa Bay Buccaneers | | | |
| ☐ 135 Vaughan Johnson | .08 | .04 | .01 |
| New Orleans Saints | | | |
| ☐ 136 Louis Oliver | .08 | .04 | .01 |
| Miami Dolphins | | | |
| ☐ 137 Mel Gray | .08 | .04 | .01 |
| Detroit Lions | | | |
| ☐ 138 Al Toon | .08 | .04 | .01 |
| New York Jets | | | |
| ☐ 139 Bubba McDowell | .05 | .02 | .01 |
| Houston Oilers | | | |
| ☐ 140 Ronnie Lott | .10 | .05 | .01 |
| Los Angeles Raiders | | | |
| ☐ 141 Deion Sanders | .20 | .09 | .03 |
| Atlanta Falcons | | | |
| ☐ 142 Jim Harbaugh | .08 | .04 | .01 |
| Chicago Bears | | | |
| ☐ 143 Gary Zimmerman | .05 | .02 | .01 |
| Minnesota Vikings | | | |
| ☐ 144 Ernie Jones | .05 | .02 | .01 |
| Phoenix Cardinals | | | |
| ☐ 145 Cortez Kennedy | .10 | .05 | .01 |
| Seattle Seahawks | | | |
| ☐ 146 Jeff Cross | .05 | .02 | .01 |
| Miami Dolphins | | | |
| ☐ 147 Floyd Turner UER | .05 | .02 | .01 |
| (Bio says he was | | | |
| drafted in 4th round) | | | |
| New Orleans Saints | | | |
| ☐ 148 Mike Tomczak | .05 | .02 | .01 |
| Green Bay Packers | | | |
| ☐ 149 Lorenzo White | .08 | .04 | .01 |
| Houston Oilers | | | |
| ☐ 150 Mark Carrier | .08 | .04 | .01 |
| Chicago Bears | | | |
| ☐ 151 John Stephens | .08 | .04 | .01 |
| New England Patriots | | | |
| ☐ 152 Jerry Rice | .50 | .23 | .06 |
| San Francisco 49ers | | | |
| ☐ 153 Jim Kelly | .25 | .11 | .03 |
| Buffalo Bills | | | |
| ☐ 154 Al Smith | .05 | .02 | .01 |
| Houston Oilers | | | |
| ☐ 155 Duane Bickett | .05 | .02 | .01 |
| Indianapolis Colts | | | |
| ☐ 156 Brett Perriman | .08 | .04 | .01 |
| Detroit Lions | | | |
| ☐ 157 Boomer Esiason | .15 | .07 | .02 |
| Cincinnati Bengals | | | |
| ☐ 158 Neil Smith | .10 | .05 | .01 |
| Kansas City Chiefs | | | |
| ☐ 159 Eddie Anderson | .05 | .02 | .01 |
| Los Angeles Raiders | | | |
| ☐ 160 Browning Nagle | .08 | .04 | .01 |
| New York Jets | | | |
| ☐ 161 John Friesz | .08 | .04 | .01 |
| San Diego Chargers | | | |
| ☐ 162 Robert Delpino | .08 | .04 | .01 |
| Los Angeles Rams | | | |
| ☐ 163 Darren Lewis | .05 | .02 | .01 |
| Chicago Bears | | | |
| ☐ 164 Roger Craig | .08 | .04 | .01 |
| Minnesota Vikings | | | |
| ☐ 165 Keith McCants | .05 | .02 | .01 |
| Tampa Bay Buccaneers | | | |
| ☐ 166 Stephone Paige | .08 | .04 | .01 |
| Kansas City Chiefs | | | |
| ☐ 167 Steve Broussard | .08 | .04 | .01 |
| Atlanta Falcons | | | |
| ☐ 168 Gaston Green | .08 | .04 | .01 |
| Denver Broncos | | | |
| ☐ 169 Ethan Horton | .05 | .02 | .01 |
| Los Angeles Raiders | | | |
| ☐ 170 Lewis Billups | .05 | .02 | .01 |
| Green Bay Packers | | | |
| ☐ 171 Mike Merriweather | .05 | .02 | .01 |
| Minnesota Vikings | | | |
| ☐ 172 Randall Cunningham | .05 | .02 | .01 |
| Philadelphia Eagles | | | |
| ☐ 173 Leonard Marshall | .08 | .04 | .01 |
| New York Giants | | | |
| ☐ 174 Jay Novacek | .15 | .07 | .02 |
| Dallas Cowboys | | | |
| ☐ 175 Irving Fryar | .08 | .04 | .01 |
| New England Patriots | | | |
| ☐ 176 Randal Hill | .10 | .05 | .01 |
| Phoenix Cardinals | | | |
| ☐ 177 Keith Henderson | .05 | .02 | .01 |
| San Francisco 49ers | | | |
| ☐ 178 Brad Baxter | .08 | .04 | .01 |
| New York Jets | | | |
| ☐ 179 William Fuller | .05 | .02 | .01 |

| | | | |
|---|---|---|---|
| Houston Oilers | | | |
| ☐ 180 Leslie O'Neal | .08 | .04 | .01 |
| San Diego Chargers | | | |
| ☐ 181 Steve Smith | .08 | .04 | .01 |
| Los Angeles Raiders | | | |
| ☐ 182 Joe Montana UER | 1.00 | .45 | .13 |
| (Born 1956, not 1965) | | | |
| San Francisco 49ers | | | |
| ☐ 183 Eric Green | .10 | .05 | .01 |
| Pittsburgh Steelers | | | |
| ☐ 184 Rodney Peete | .08 | .04 | .01 |
| Detroit Lions | | | |
| ☐ 185 Lawrence Dawsey | .10 | .05 | .01 |
| Tampa Bay Buccaneers | | | |
| ☐ 186 Brian Mitchell | .08 | .04 | .01 |
| Washington Redskins | | | |
| ☐ 187 Rickey Jackson | .08 | .04 | .01 |
| New Orleans Saints | | | |
| ☐ 188 Christian Okoye | .08 | .04 | .01 |
| Kansas City Chiefs | | | |
| ☐ 189 David Wyman | .05 | .02 | .01 |
| Seattle Seahawks | | | |
| ☐ 190 Jessie Tuggle | .05 | .02 | .01 |
| Atlanta Falcons | | | |
| ☐ 191 Ronnie Harmon | .05 | .02 | .01 |
| San Diego Chargers | | | |
| ☐ 192 Andre Reed | .10 | .05 | .01 |
| Buffalo Bills | | | |
| ☐ 193 Chris Doleman | .08 | .04 | .01 |
| Minnesota Vikings | | | |
| ☐ 194 Leroy Hoard | .08 | .04 | .01 |
| Cleveland Browns | | | |
| ☐ 195 Mark Ingram | .08 | .04 | .01 |
| New York Giants | | | |
| ☐ 196 Willie Gault | .08 | .04 | .01 |
| Los Angeles Raiders | | | |
| ☐ 197 Eugene Lockhart | .05 | .02 | .01 |
| New England Patriots | | | |
| ☐ 198 Jim Everett | .08 | .04 | .01 |
| Los Angeles Rams | | | |
| ☐ 199 Doug Smith | .05 | .02 | .01 |
| Houston Oilers | | | |
| ☐ 200 Clarence Verdin | .05 | .02 | .01 |
| Indianapolis Colts | | | |
| ☐ 201 Steve Bono | .50 | .23 | .06 |
| San Francisco 49ers | | | |
| ☐ 202 Mark Vlasic | .08 | .04 | .01 |
| Kansas City Chiefs | | | |
| ☐ 203 Fred Barnett | .10 | .05 | .01 |
| Philadelphia Eagles | | | |
| ☐ 204 Henry Thomas | .05 | .02 | .01 |
| Minnesota Vikings | | | |
| ☐ 205 Shaun Gayle | .05 | .02 | .01 |
| Chicago Bears | | | |
| ☐ 206 Rod Bernstine | .08 | .04 | .01 |
| San Diego Chargers | | | |
| ☐ 207 Harold Green | .05 | .02 | .01 |
| Cincinnati Bengals | | | |
| ☐ 208 Dan McGwire | .08 | .04 | .01 |
| Seattle Seahawks | | | |
| ☐ 209 Marv Cook | .08 | .04 | .01 |
| New England Patriots | | | |
| ☐ 210 Emmitt Smith | 2.00 | .90 | .25 |
| Dallas Cowboys | | | |
| ☐ 211 Merril Hoge | .08 | .04 | .01 |
| Pittsburgh Steelers | | | |
| ☐ 212 Darion Conner | .05 | .02 | .01 |
| Atlanta Falcons | | | |
| ☐ 213 Mike Sherrard | .08 | .04 | .01 |
| San Francisco 49ers | | | |
| ☐ 214 Jeff George | .20 | .09 | .03 |
| Indianapolis Colts | | | |
| ☐ 215 Craig Heyward | .05 | .02 | .01 |
| New Orleans Saints | | | |
| ☐ 216 Henry Ellard | .08 | .04 | .01 |
| Los Angeles Rams | | | |
| ☐ 217 Lawrence Taylor | .10 | .05 | .01 |
| New York Giants | | | |
| ☐ 218 Jerry Ball | .08 | .04 | .01 |
| Detroit Lions | | | |
| ☐ 219 Tom Rathman | .08 | .04 | .01 |
| San Francisco 49ers | | | |
| ☐ 220 Warren Moon | .20 | .09 | .03 |
| Houston Oilers | | | |
| ☐ 221 Ricky Proehl | .10 | .05 | .01 |
| Phoenix Cardinals | | | |
| ☐ 222 Sterling Sharpe | .50 | .23 | .06 |
| Green Bay Packers | | | |
| ☐ 223 Earnest Byner | .08 | .04 | .01 |
| Washington Redskins | | | |
| ☐ 224 Jay Schroeder | .08 | .04 | .01 |
| Los Angeles Raiders | | | |
| ☐ 225 Vance Johnson | .08 | .04 | .01 |
| Denver Broncos | | | |
| ☐ 226 Cornelius Bennett | .10 | .05 | .01 |
| Buffalo Bills | | | |
| ☐ 227 Ken O'Brien | .08 | .04 | .01 |
| New York Jets | | | |

| | | | | |
|---|---|---|---|---|
| ☐ 228 Ferrell Edmunds | | .05 | .02 | .01 |
| Miami Dolphins | | | | |
| ☐ 229 Eric Allen | | .08 | .04 | .01 |
| Philadelphia Eagles | | | | |
| ☐ 230 Derrick Thomas | | .15 | .07 | .02 |
| Kansas City Chiefs | | | | |
| ☐ 231 Cris Carter | | .10 | .05 | .01 |
| Minnesota Vikings | | | | |
| ☐ 232 Jon Vaughn | | .05 | .02 | .01 |
| New England Patriots | | | | |
| ☐ 233 Eric Metcalf | | .10 | .05 | .01 |
| Cleveland Browns | | | | |
| ☐ 234 William Perry | | .08 | .04 | .01 |
| Chicago Bears | | | | |
| ☐ 235 Vinny Testaverde | | .10 | .05 | .01 |
| Tampa Bay Buccaneers | | | | |
| ☐ 236 Chip Banks | | .05 | .02 | .01 |
| Indianapolis Colts | | | | |
| ☐ 237 Brian Blades | | .08 | .04 | .01 |
| Seattle Seahawks | | | | |
| ☐ 238 Calvin Williams | | .10 | .05 | .01 |
| Philadelphia Eagles | | | | |
| ☐ 239 Andre Rison | | .25 | .11 | .03 |
| Atlanta Falcons | | | | |
| ☐ 240 Neil O'Donnell | | .50 | .23 | .06 |
| Pittsburgh Steelers | | | | |
| ☐ 241 Michael Irvin | | .50 | .23 | .06 |
| Dallas Cowboys | | | | |
| ☐ 242 Gary Plummer | | .05 | .02 | .01 |
| San Diego Chargers | | | | |
| ☐ 243 Nick Bell | | .05 | .02 | .01 |
| Los Angeles Raiders | | | | |
| ☐ 244 Ray Crockett | | .05 | .02 | .01 |
| Detroit Lions | | | | |
| ☐ 245 Sam Mills | | .08 | .04 | .01 |
| New Orleans Saints | | | | |
| ☐ 246 Haywood Jeffires | | .10 | .05 | .01 |
| Houston Oilers | | | | |
| ☐ 247 Steve Young | | .35 | .16 | .04 |
| San Francisco 49ers | | | | |
| ☐ 248 Martin Bayless | | .05 | .02 | .01 |
| Kansas City Chiefs | | | | |
| ☐ 249 Dan Marino | | .75 | .35 | .09 |
| Miami Dolphins | | | | |
| ☐ 250 Carl Banks | | .08 | .04 | .01 |
| New York Giants | | | | |
| ☐ 251 Keith McKeller | | .05 | .02 | .01 |
| Buffalo Bills | | | | |
| ☐ 252 Aaron Wallace | | .05 | .02 | .01 |
| Los Angeles Raiders | | | | |
| ☐ 253 Lamar Lathon | | .05 | .02 | .01 |
| Houston Oilers | | | | |
| ☐ 254 Derrick Fenner | | .08 | .04 | .01 |
| Cincinnati Bengals | | | | |
| ☐ 255 Vai Sikahema | | .08 | .04 | .01 |
| Philadelphia Eagles | | | | |
| ☐ 256 Keith Sims | | .05 | .02 | .01 |
| Miami Dolphins | | | | |
| ☐ 257 Rohn Stark | | .05 | .02 | .01 |
| Indianapolis Colts | | | | |
| ☐ 258 Reggie Roby | | .05 | .02 | .01 |
| Miami Dolphins | | | | |
| ☐ 259 Tony Zendejas | | .05 | .02 | .01 |
| Los Angeles Rams | | | | |
| ☐ 260 Harris Barton | | .05 | .02 | .01 |
| San Francisco 49ers | | | | |
| ☐ 261 Checklist 1-100 | | .05 | .02 | .01 |
| ☐ 262 Checklist 101-200 | | .05 | .02 | .01 |
| ☐ 263 Checklist 201-300 | | .05 | .02 | .01 |
| ☐ 264 Rookies Checklist | | .05 | .02 | .01 |
| ☐ 265 Greats Checklist | | .05 | .02 | .01 |
| ☐ 266 Joe Namath GG | | .15 | .07 | .02 |
| ☐ 267 Joe Namath GG | | .15 | .07 | .02 |
| ☐ 268 Joe Namath GG | | .15 | .07 | .02 |
| ☐ 269 Joe Namath GG | | .15 | .07 | .02 |
| ☐ 270 Joe Namath GG | | .15 | .07 | .02 |
| ☐ 271 Jim Brown GG | | .15 | .07 | .02 |
| ☐ 272 Jim Brown GG | | .15 | .07 | .02 |
| ☐ 273 Jim Brown GG | | .15 | .07 | .02 |
| ☐ 274 Jim Brown GG | | .15 | .07 | .02 |
| ☐ 275 Jim Brown GG | | .15 | .07 | .02 |
| ☐ 276 Vince Lombardi GG | | .10 | .05 | .01 |
| ☐ 277 Jim Thorpe GG | | .10 | .05 | .01 |
| ☐ 278 Tom Fears GG | | .05 | .02 | .01 |
| ☐ 279 John Henry Johnson GG | | .05 | .02 | .01 |
| ☐ 280 Gale Sayers GG | | .10 | .05 | .01 |
| ☐ 281 Willie Brown GG | | .05 | .02 | .01 |
| ☐ 282 Doak Walker GG | | .05 | .02 | .01 |
| ☐ 283 Dick Lane GG | | .05 | .02 | .01 |
| ☐ 284 Otto Graham GG | | .10 | .05 | .01 |
| ☐ 285 Hugh McElhenny GG | | .05 | .02 | .01 |
| ☐ 286 Roger Staubach GG | | .15 | .07 | .02 |
| ☐ 287 Steve Largent GG | | .10 | .05 | .01 |
| ☐ 288 Otis Taylor GG | | .05 | .02 | .01 |
| ☐ 289 Sam Huff GG | | .05 | .02 | .01 |
| ☐ 290 Harold Carmichael GG | | .05 | .02 | .01 |
| ☐ 291 Steve Van Buren GG | | .05 | .02 | .01 |
| ☐ 292 Gino Marchetti GG | | .05 | .02 | .01 |
| ☐ 293 Tony Dorsett GG | | .05 | .02 | .01 |
| ☐ 294 Leo Nomellini GG | | .05 | .02 | .01 |
| ☐ 295 Jack Lambert GG | | .05 | .02 | .01 |
| ☐ 296 Joe Theismann GG | | .05 | .02 | .01 |
| ☐ 297 Bobby Layne GG | | .10 | .05 | .01 |
| ☐ 298 John Stallworth GG | | .05 | .02 | .01 |
| ☐ 299 Paul Hornung GG | | .10 | .05 | .01 |
| ☐ 300 Don Maynard GG | | .05 | .02 | .01 |
| ☐ A1 Desmond Howard AU | | 80.00 | 36.00 | 10.00 |
| (Certified autograph) | | | | |
| Washington Redskins | | | | |
| ☐ A2 Jim Brown AU | | 100.00 | 45.00 | 12.50 |
| (Certified autograph) | | | | |
| Cleveland Browns | | | | |
| ☐ A3 Joe Namath AU | | 175.00 | 80.00 | 22.00 |
| (Certified autograph) | | | | |
| New York Jets | | | | |
| ☐ TRI Howard/Brown/Namath | | 15.00 | 6.75 | 1.90 |
| (Triplefolder) | | | | |

# 1992 All World Greats/Rookies

One of these 20 standard size (2 1/2" by 3 1/2") cards was inserted into every 1992 All World rack pack. The fronts display borderless color or black-and-white player photos, with the U.S. flag blazing across the top. Those cards of current players are color. Those of older players are black-and-white. The first ten have gold foil-embossed stars on the flag and the player's name is gold foil-embossed in script across the bottom of the card. The second ten have the same design but have silver embossing instead. The backs carry a full-bleed ghosted photo of the player with biography printed over the picture. The player's name appears at the bottom in black script that is similar to that on the front. The cards are numbered on the back. Reportedly, only 60,000 of each card were produced. The cards are numbered with an "SG" prefix.

| | MINT | EXC | G-VG |
|---|---|---|---|
| COMPLETE SET (20) | 14.00 | 6.25 | 1.75 |
| COMMON GREATS (SG1-SG10) | .30 | .14 | .04 |
| COMMON ROOKIES (SG11-SG20) | .30 | .14 | .04 |
| ☐ SG1 Troy Aikman | 3.50 | 1.55 | .45 |
| Dallas Cowboys | | | |
| ☐ SG2 Thurman Thomas | 1.50 | .65 | .19 |
| Buffalo Bills | | | |
| ☐ SG3 Andre Rison | .50 | .23 | .06 |
| Atlanta Falcons | | | |
| ☐ SG4 Emmitt Smith | 5.00 | 2.30 | .60 |
| Dallas Cowboys | | | |
| ☐ SG5 Derrick Thomas | .50 | .23 | .06 |
| Kansas City Chiefs | | | |
| ☐ SG6 Joe Namath | .50 | .23 | .06 |
| New York Jets | | | |
| ☐ SG7 Jim Brown | .50 | .23 | .06 |
| Cleveland Browns | | | |
| ☐ SG8 Roger Staubach | .60 | .25 | .08 |
| Dallas Cowboys | | | |
| ☐ SG9 Gale Sayers | .30 | .14 | .04 |
| Chicago Bears | | | |
| ☐ SG10 Jim Thorpe | .30 | .14 | .04 |
| ☐ SG11 Quentin Coryatt | .75 | .35 | .09 |
| Indianapolis Colts | | | |
| ☐ SG12 Carl Pickens | .60 | .25 | .08 |
| Cincinnati Bengals | | | |
| ☐ SG13 Steve Emtman | .30 | .14 | .04 |
| Indianapolis Colts | | | |
| ☐ SG14 Derek Brown | .50 | .23 | .06 |
| New York Giants | | | |
| ☐ SG15 Desmond Howard | 1.50 | .65 | .19 |
| Washington Redskins | | | |
| ☐ SG16 Troy Vincent | .30 | .14 | .04 |
| Miami Dolphins | | | |

| | MINT | EXC | G-VG |
|---|---|---|---|
| ☐ SG17 David Klinger | 1.00 | .45 | .13 |
| Cincinnati Bengals | | | |
| ☐ SG18 Vaughn Dunbar | .50 | .23 | .06 |
| New Orleans Saints | | | |
| ☐ SG19 Terrell Buckley | .50 | .23 | .06 |
| Green Bay Packers | | | |
| ☐ SG20 Jimmy Smith | .30 | .14 | .04 |
| Dallas Cowboys | | | |

## 1992 All World Legends/Rookies

Randomly inserted in the foil packs, this subset consists of ten Legends in the Making cards (1-10) and ten Rookie (11-20) cards. The cards measure the standard size (2 1/2" by 3 1/2"). All the fronts display borderless color player photos, with gold foil stars on the U.S. flag draped across the top of the card. Also a row of gold foil stars appears in the shape of a crescent at the lower right corner of the picture. The top of the backs of the Legends cards feature a gold plaque with the words "Legends in the Making" superimposed on navy blue with white stars of the American flag. On the other hand, the Rookie cards have a red circular "92 Rookie" logo superimposed on red and white stripes of the American flag. Beneath these decorative elements, both backs present biographical information and, in a two-column format, career summary. The cards are numbered on the back. Reportedly, only 5000 of each card were produced. The cards were numbered with an "I" prefix.

| | MINT | EXC | G-VG |
|---|---|---|---|
| COMPLETE SET (20) | 40.00 | 18.00 | 5.00 |
| COMMON LEGENDS (L1-L10) | 1.00 | .45 | .13 |
| COMMON ROOKIES (L11-L20) | 1.00 | .45 | .13 |
| ☐ L1 Emmitt Smith | 10.00 | 4.50 | 1.25 |
| Dallas Cowboys | | | |
| ☐ L2 Thurman Thomas | 3.00 | 1.35 | .40 |
| Buffalo Bills | | | |
| ☐ L3 Deion Sanders | 1.50 | .65 | .19 |
| Atlanta Falcons | | | |
| ☐ L4 Randall Cunningham | 1.25 | .55 | .16 |
| Philadelphia Eagles | | | |
| ☐ L5 Michael Irvin | 4.00 | 1.80 | .50 |
| Dallas Cowboys | | | |
| ☐ L6 Bruce Smith | 1.00 | .45 | .13 |
| Buffalo Bills | | | |
| ☐ L7 Jeff George | 1.50 | .65 | .19 |
| Indianapolis Colts | | | |
| ☐ L8 Derrick Thomas | 1.25 | .55 | .16 |
| Kansas City Chiefs | | | |
| ☐ L9 Andre Rison | 1.50 | .65 | .19 |
| Atlanta Falcons | | | |
| ☐ L10 Troy Aikman | 7.00 | 3.10 | .85 |
| Dallas Cowboys | | | |
| ☐ L11 Quentin Coryatt | 1.50 | .65 | .19 |
| Indianapolis Colts | | | |
| ☐ L12 Carl Pickens | 1.50 | .65 | .19 |
| Cincinnati Bengals | | | |
| ☐ L13 Steve Emtman | 1.00 | .45 | .13 |
| Indianapolis Colts | | | |
| ☐ L14 Derek Brown | 1.25 | .55 | .16 |
| New York Giants | | | |
| ☐ L15 Desmond Howard | 3.00 | 1.35 | .40 |
| Washington Redskins | | | |
| ☐ L16 Troy Vincent | 1.00 | .45 | .13 |
| Miami Dolphins | | | |
| ☐ L17 David Klinger | 2.25 | 1.00 | .30 |
| Cincinnati Bengals | | | |
| ☐ L18 Vaughn Dunbar | 1.00 | .45 | .13 |
| New Orleans Saints | | | |
| ☐ L19 Terrell Buckley | 1.00 | .45 | .13 |
| Green Bay Packers | | | |
| ☐ L20 Jimmy Smith | 1.00 | .45 | .13 |
| Dallas Cowboys | | | |

## 1966 American Oil All-Pro

The 1966 American Oil All-Pro set featured 20 stamps, each measuring approximately 15/16" by 1 1/8". To participate in the contest, the consumer needed to acquire an 8 1/2" by 11" collection sheet from a participating American Oil dealer. This sheet is horizontally oriented and presents rules governing the contest as well as 20 slots in which to paste the stamps. The 20 slots are arranged in five rows in the shape of an inverted triangle (6, 5, 4, 3, and 2 stamps per row as one moves from top to bottom) with the prizes listed to the left of each row. The consumer also received envelopes from participating dealers that contained small sheets of three perforated player stamps each. These stamps feature crude color head shots with the players' wearing their helmets. After separating the stamps, the consumer was instructed to paste them on the matching squares of the collection sheet. If all the stamps in a particular prize group row were collected, the consumer won that particular prize. Top prize for all six stamps in the top group was a 1967 Ford Mustang. The other prizes were 250.00, 25.00, 5.00, and 1.00 for five-, four-, three-, and two-stamp prize groups respectively. Prizes were to be redeemed within 15 days after the closing of the promotion, but no later than March 1, 1967 in any event. The stamps are blank backed and unnumbered, and they have been checklisted below alphabetically. Wayne Walker and Tommy Nobis were required to win 1.00; Herb Adderley and Dave Parks and Lenny Moore were required to win 5.00; John Unitas and Dave Jones, Mick Tingelhoff, and Alex Karras were required to win 25.00; Dick Butkus and Charley Johnson, Gary Ballman, Frank Ryan, and Willie Davis were required to win 250.00; and Gary Collins and Tucker Frederickson, Pete Retzlaff, Sam Huff, Gale Sayers, and Bob Lilly were required to win the 1967 Mustang. The winner cards indicated below are not priced (and not considered necessary for a complete set) since each was the particular scarce card that made that specific prize a serious challenge.

| | NRMT | VG-E | GOOD |
|---|---|---|---|
| COMPLETE SET (15) | 150.00 | 60.00 | 15.00 |
| COMMON PLAYER (1-20) | 6.00 | 2.40 | .60 |
| ☐ 1 Herb Adderley | .00 | .00 | .00 |
| Green Bay Packers | | | |
| (Winner 5.00) | | | |
| ☐ 2 Gary Ballman | 6.00 | 2.40 | .60 |
| Pittsburgh Steelers | | | |
| ☐ 3 Dick Butkus | .00 | .00 | .00 |
| Chicago Bears | | | |
| (Winner 250.00) | | | |
| ☐ 4 Gary Collins | .00 | .00 | .00 |
| Cleveland Browns | | | |
| (Winner Car) | | | |
| ☐ 5 Willie Davis | 12.00 | 5.00 | 1.20 |
| Green Bay Packers | | | |
| ☐ 6 Tucker Frederickson | 7.50 | 3.00 | .75 |
| New York Giants | | | |
| ☐ 7 Sam Huff | 15.00 | 6.00 | 1.50 |
| Washington Redskins | | | |
| ☐ 8 Charley Johnson | 9.00 | 3.75 | .90 |
| St. Louis Cardinals | | | |
| ☐ 9 Deacon Jones | 12.00 | 5.00 | 1.20 |
| Los Angeles Rams | | | |
| ☐ 10 Alex Karras | 15.00 | 6.00 | 1.50 |
| Detroit Lions | | | |
| ☐ 11 Bob Lilly | 15.00 | 6.00 | 1.50 |
| Dallas Cowboys | | | |
| ☐ 12 Lenny Moore | 15.00 | 6.00 | 1.50 |
| Baltimore Colts | | | |
| ☐ 13 Tommy Nobis | 12.00 | 5.00 | 1.20 |
| Atlanta Falcons | | | |
| ☐ 14 Dave Parks | 7.50 | 3.00 | .75 |
| San Francisco 49ers | | | |
| ☐ 15 Pete Retzlaff | 7.50 | 3.00 | .75 |
| Philadelphia Eagles | | | |
| ☐ 16 Frank Ryan | 9.00 | 3.75 | .90 |

| | | | |
|---|---|---|---|
| ☐ 17 Gale Sayers ............................ | 40.00 | 16.00 | 4.00 |
| Chicago Bears | | | |
| ☐ 18 Mick Tingelhoff ...................... | 7.50 | 3.00 | .75 |
| Minnesota Vikings | | | |
| ☐ 19 John Unitas ............................ | .00 | .00 | .00 |
| Baltimore Colts | | | |
| (Winner 25.00) | | | |
| ☐ 20 Wayne Walker ........................ | .00 | .00 | .00 |
| Detroit Lions | | | |
| (Winner 1.00) | | | |

## 1968 American Oil Mr. and Mrs.

This 32-card set was produced by Glendinning Companies and distributed by the American Oil Company. The cards measure approximately 2 1/8" by 3 7/16". The set is made up of 16 player cards and 16 wife/family cards that were originally connected by perforation in pairs. The cards were distributed as pieces of the "Mr. and Mrs. NFL" game. If a matched pair (i.e. a player card and his wife/family card) were obtained, the holder was an instant winner of either a 1969 Ford (choice of Mustang Mach I or Country Squire), 500.00, 100.00, 10.00, 5.00, 1.00, or 50 cents. The cards are most frequently found as detached halves. The horizontally oriented fronts feature action color player photos or color family photos featuring the wife. On the player card, the player's name is printed above the picture. On the wife card, the woman's married name (i.e. Mrs. Bobby Mitchell) and a caption defining the activity shown are above the picture. Each card is bordered in a different color and the prize corresponding to that card is printed in the border. The backs of the cards vary. In each pair that were originally connected, the wife card back features contest rules in a blue box on a red background with darker red car silhouettes. The player card back carries the game title (Mr. and Mrs. NFL), the American Oil Company logo, and the words "Win 1969 Fords and Cash" on the same background. In addition, attached to each pair at either end and forming a 12" strip, two more cardlike pieces contained further information and a game piece for predicting the 1969 Super Bowl scores. The smaller of the two (approximately 1 7/8" by 2 1/8") is printed with the NFL players and the corresponding prizes. The larger of the two (2 1/8" by 3 1/4") is the game piece for the second part of the contest with blanks for recording a score prediction for one NFL and one AFL team. This piece was mailed in to Super Bowl Scoreboard in New York. Each correct entry would share equally in the 100,000.00 Super Bowl Scoreboard cash prize. The cards are checklisted below alphabetically. The prize corresponding to each married couple is listed under the tougher of the pair. Prices listed are for single cards. Complete two-card panels are valued at approximately double the value of the individual cards. Card numbers 1, 4, 5, 7, 10, 11, 14, 16, 17, 19, 21, 23, 26, 28, 29, and 32 are the 16 tougher pieces and are not considered necessary for a complete set.

| | NRMT | VG-E | GOOD |
|---|---|---|---|
| COMPLETE SET (16) ........................ | 60.00 | 24.00 | 6.00 |
| COMMON PLAYER (1-32) ................. | 4.00 | 1.60 | .40 |
| COMMON WIFE (2/6/8/12/18) .......... | 2.00 | .80 | .20 |
| COMMON WIFE (22/24/30) ............... | 2.00 | .80 | .20 |

| | | | |
|---|---|---|---|
| ☐ 1 Kermit Alexander ...................... | .00 | .00 | .00 |
| San Francisco 49ers | | | |
| (Winner 100.00) | | | |
| ☐ 2 Mrs. Kermit Alexander .............. | 2.00 | .80 | .20 |
| Jogging with Family | | | |
| ☐ 3 Jim Bakken ............................. | 4.00 | 1.60 | .40 |
| St. Louis Cardinals | | | |
| ☐ 4 Mrs. Jim Bakken ...................... | .00 | .00 | .00 |
| (Winner 1.00) | | | |
| ☐ 5 Gary Collins ............................ | .00 | .00 | .00 |
| Cleveland Browns | | | |
| (Winner 500.00) | | | |
| ☐ 6 Mrs. Gary Collins ..................... | 2.00 | .80 | .20 |

| | | | |
|---|---|---|---|
| Enjoying the Outdoors | | | |
| ☐ 7 Earl Gros ................................ | .00 | .00 | .00 |
| Pittsburgh Steelers | | | |
| (Winner 1.00) | | | |
| ☐ 8 Mrs. Earl Gros ......................... | 2.00 | .80 | .20 |
| At the Park | | | |
| ☐ 9 Deacon Jones .......................... | 9.00 | 3.75 | .90 |
| Los Angeles Rams | | | |
| ☐ 10 Mrs. Deacon Jones ................. | .00 | .00 | .00 |
| (Winner 500.00) | | | |
| ☐ 11 Billy Lothridge ...................... | .00 | .00 | .00 |
| Atlanta Falcons | | | |
| (Winner 10.00) | | | |
| ☐ 12 Mrs. Billy Lothridge ............... | 2.00 | .80 | .20 |
| And Baby Daughter | | | |
| ☐ 13 Tom Matte ............................ | 6.00 | 2.40 | .60 |
| Baltimore Colts | | | |
| ☐ 14 Mrs. Tom Matte ..................... | .00 | .00 | .00 |
| (Winner 50 cents) | | | |
| ☐ 15 Joe Morrison .......................... | 5.00 | 2.00 | .50 |
| New York Giants | | | |
| ☐ 16 Mrs. Joe Morrison .................. | .00 | .00 | .00 |
| (Winner 1969 Ford) | | | |
| ☐ 17 Dan Reeves ........................... | .00 | .00 | .00 |
| Dallas Cowboys | | | |
| (Winner 50 cents) | | | |
| ☐ 18 Mrs. Dan Reeves .................... | 2.00 | .80 | .20 |
| Enjoying the Children | | | |
| ☐ 19 Norm Snead .......................... | .00 | .00 | .00 |
| Philadelphia Eagles | | | |
| (Winner 1.00) | | | |
| ☐ 20 Mrs. Norm Snead ................... | 2.00 | .80 | .20 |
| On the Family Boat | | | |
| ☐ 21 Wayne Walker ....................... | .00 | .00 | .00 |
| Detroit Lions | | | |
| (Winner 50 cents) | | | |
| ☐ 22 Mrs. Wayne Walker ................ | 2.00 | .80 | .20 |
| At a Family Picnic | | | |
| ☐ 23 Bobby Mitchell ...................... | .00 | .00 | .00 |
| Cleveland Browns | | | |
| (Winner 5.00) | | | |
| ☐ 24 Mrs. Bobby Mitchell ............... | 2.00 | .80 | .20 |
| At a Backyard Barbecue | | | |
| ☐ 25 Steve Stonebreaker ................ | 4.00 | 1.60 | .40 |
| New Orleans Saints | | | |
| ☐ 26 Mrs. Steve ............................ | .00 | .00 | .00 |
| Stonebreaker | | | |
| (Winner 10.00) | | | |
| ☐ 27 Dave Osborn .......................... | 5.00 | 2.00 | .50 |
| Minnesota Vikings | | | |
| ☐ 28 Mrs. Dave Osborn .................. | .00 | .00 | .00 |
| (Winner 5.00) | | | |
| ☐ 29 Jim Grabowski ....................... | .00 | .00 | .00 |
| Green Bay Packers | | | |
| (Winner 1969 Ford) | | | |
| ☐ 30 Mrs. Jim Grabowski ............... | 2.00 | .80 | .20 |
| At the Fireside | | | |
| ☐ 31 Gale Sayers .......................... | 15.00 | 6.00 | 1.50 |
| Chicago Bears | | | |
| ☐ 32 Mrs. Gale Sayers ................... | .00 | .00 | .00 |
| (Winner 100.00) | | | |

## 1992 Arena Cleveland Thunderbolts

Printed on plain white card stock, these 24 cards are irregularly cut and so vary in size, but are close to standard size (2 1/2" by 3 1/2"). Framed by a purple line, the fronts feature coarsely screened posed black-and-white player photos of the Arena Football League's (AFL) Cleveland Thunderbolts. The player's name and position, along with the logo of the sponsor, Area Temps, appear below the photo. The backs carry the player's name at the top, followed by the team logo, position, jersey number, biography, and career highlights. The cards are unnumbered and checklisted below in alphabetical order.

|  | MINT | EXC | G-VG |
|---|---|---|---|
| COMPLETE SET (24)......................... | 15.00 | 6.00 | 1.50 |
| COMMON PLAYER (1-24)................... | .50 | .20 | .05 |

| | | | |
|---|---|---|---|
| ☐ 1 Eric Anderson ........................... | .75 | .30 | .07 |
| ☐ 2 Robert Banks ............................ | .75 | .30 | .07 |
| ☐ 3 Bobby Bounds.......................... | .50 | .20 | .05 |
| ☐ 4 Marvin Bowman ........................ | .50 | .20 | .05 |
| ☐ 5 George Cooper .......................... | .50 | .20 | .05 |
| ☐ 6 Michael Denbrock ACO ............ | .50 | .20 | .05 |
| ☐ 7 Chris Drennan .......................... | .50 | .20 | .05 |
| ☐ 8 Dennis Fitzgerald ACO............. | .50 | .20 | .05 |
| ☐ 9 John Fletcher ........................... | .50 | .20 | .05 |
| ☐ 10 Andre Giles ............................ | .50 | .20 | .05 |
| ☐ 11 Chris Harkness....................... | .50 | .20 | .05 |
| ☐ 12 Major Harris........................... | 7.50 | 3.00 | .75 |
| ☐ 13 Luther Johnson ...................... | .50 | .20 | .05 |
| ☐ 14 Marvin Mattox........................ | .75 | .30 | .07 |
| ☐ 15 Cedric McKinnon..................... | .50 | .20 | .05 |
| ☐ 16 Cleo Miller ACO...................... | .75 | .30 | .07 |
| ☐ 17 Tony Missick........................... | .50 | .20 | .05 |
| ☐ 18 Anthony Newsom..................... | .50 | .20 | .05 |
| ☐ 19 Phil Poirier............................. | .75 | .30 | .07 |
| ☐ 20 Alvin Powell ........................... | .50 | .20 | .05 |
| ☐ 21 Ray Puryear ........................... | .50 | .20 | .05 |
| ☐ 22 Dave Whinham CO .................. | .50 | .20 | .05 |
| ☐ 23 Brian Williams........................ | .50 | .20 | .05 |
| ☐ 24 Kennedy Wilson....................... | .50 | .20 | .05 |

## 1988 Athletes in Action *

Doug Cosbie - Dallas Cowboys -- #11 of 12

The set features six Texas Rangers (1-6) and six Dallas Cowboys (7-12). The cards are standard size, 2 1/2" by 3 1/2". The fronts display color action player photos bordered in white. The words "Athletes in Action" are printed in black across the lower edge of the picture. The backs carry a player quote, a salvation message, and the player's favorite Scripture. The cards are numbered on the back.

|  | MINT | EXC | G-VG |
|---|---|---|---|
| COMPLETE SET (12)......................... | 6.00 | 2.40 | .60 |
| COMMON PLAYER (1-6).................... | .50 | .20 | .05 |
| COMMON PLAYER (7-12).................. | .50 | .20 | .05 |

| | | | |
|---|---|---|---|
| ☐ 1 Pete O'Brien ............................ | .50 | .20 | .05 |
| ☐ 2 Scott Fletcher .......................... | .60 | .24 | .06 |
| ☐ 3 Oddibe McDowell ..................... | .60 | .24 | .06 |
| ☐ 4 Steve Buechele......................... | .60 | .24 | .06 |
| ☐ 5 Jerry Browne ........................... | .50 | .20 | .05 |
| ☐ 6 Larry Parrish ........................... | .50 | .20 | .05 |
| ☐ 7 Tom Landry CO......................... | 2.00 | .80 | .20 |
| ☐ 8 Steve Pelluer ........................... | .60 | .24 | .06 |
| ☐ 9 Gordon Banks .......................... | .50 | .20 | .05 |
| ☐ 10 Bill Bates .............................. | .75 | .30 | .07 |
| ☐ 11 Doug Cosbie .......................... | .50 | .20 | .05 |
| ☐ 12 Herschel Walker...................... | 1.00 | .40 | .10 |

## 1994 A1 Masters of the Grill

Sponsored by A.1. Steak Sauce, this 28-card standard-size (2 1/2" by 3 1/2") set is actually a recipe card set. Inside gold and black borders, the fronts display a football player wearing his team's jersey, an apron, a hat with A.1. on it, and holding either A.1. steak sauce or barbeque utensils. The player's facsimile autograph appears in one of the upper corners, with player's name and team name immediately below. The backs present a picture of a prepared dish as well as recipe instructions for its preparing the food. The cards are unnumbered and checklisted below in alphabetical order.

|  | MINT | EXC | G-VG |
|---|---|---|---|
| COMPLETE SET (28)........................ | 20.00 | 8.00 | 2.00 |
| COMMON PLAYER (1-28)................. | .60 | .24 | .06 |

| | | | |
|---|---|---|---|
| ☐ 1 Harris Barton.......................... | .60 | .24 | .06 |
|     San Francisco 49ers | | | |
| ☐ 2 Jerome Bettis .......................... | 4.00 | 1.60 | .40 |
|     Los Angeles Rams | | | |
| ☐ 3 Ray Childress .......................... | .75 | .30 | .07 |
|     Houston Oilers | | | |
| ☐ 4 Eugene Chung .......................... | .60 | .24 | .06 |
|     New England Patriots | | | |
| ☐ 5 Jamie Dukes ........................... | .60 | .24 | .06 |
|     Atlanta Falcons | | | |
| ☐ 6 Steve Emtman.......................... | .75 | .30 | .07 |
|     Indianapolis Colts | | | |
| ☐ 7 Burt Grossman......................... | .60 | .24 | .06 |
|     Philadelphia Eagles | | | |
| ☐ 8 Ken Harvey ............................. | .60 | .24 | .06 |
|     Washington Redskins | | | |
| ☐ 9 Courtney Hall .......................... | .60 | .24 | .06 |
|     San Diego Chargers | | | |
| ☐ 10 Chris Hinton .......................... | .75 | .30 | .07 |
|     Minnesota Vikings | | | |
| ☐ 11 Kent Hull .............................. | .60 | .24 | .06 |
|     Buffalo Bills | | | |
| ☐ 12 Keith Jackson ........................ | 1.00 | .40 | .10 |
|     Miami Dolphins | | | |
| ☐ 13 Rickey Jackson ...................... | .75 | .30 | .07 |
|     New Orleans Saints | | | |
| ☐ 14 Cortez Kennedy ...................... | 1.25 | .50 | .12 |
|     Seattle Seahawks | | | |
| ☐ 15 Tim Krumrie ......................... | .60 | .24 | .06 |
|     Cincinnati Bengals | | | |
| ☐ 16 Jeff Lageman ......................... | .60 | .24 | .06 |
|     New York Jets | | | |
| ☐ 17 Greg Lloyd ............................ | .75 | .30 | .07 |
|     Pittsburgh Steelers | | | |
| ☐ 18 Howie Long............................ | 1.00 | .40 | .10 |
|     Los Angeles Raiders | | | |
| ☐ 19 Hardy Nickerson ..................... | .75 | .30 | .07 |
|     Tampa Bay Buccaneers | | | |
| ☐ 20 Bart Oates ............................ | .75 | .30 | .07 |
|     New York Giants | | | |
| ☐ 21 Ken Ruettgers........................ | .60 | .24 | .06 |
|     Green Bay Packers | | | |
| ☐ 22 Dan Saleaumua....................... | .60 | .24 | .06 |
|     Kansas City Chiefs | | | |
| ☐ 23 Alonzo Spellman ..................... | .75 | .30 | .07 |
|     Chicago Bears | | | |
| ☐ 24 Eric Swann............................ | .75 | .30 | .07 |
|     Phoenix Cardinals | | | |
| ☐ 25 Pat Swilling ........................... | 1.00 | .40 | .10 |
|     Detroit Lions | | | |
| ☐ 26 Tommy Vardell........................ | 1.00 | .40 | .10 |
|     Cleveland Browns | | | |
| ☐ 27 Erik Williams ......................... | .60 | .24 | .06 |
|     Dallas Cowboys | | | |
| ☐ 28 Gary Zimmerman..................... | .60 | .24 | .06 |
|     Denver Broncos | | | |

## 1959 Bazooka

The 1959 Bazooka football cards made up the back of the Bazooka Bubble Gum boxes of that year. The cards are blank backed and measure approximately 2 13/16" by 4 15/16". Comparable to the Bazooka baseball cards of that year, they are relatively difficult to obtain and fairly attractive considering they form part of the box. The cards are unnumbered but have been numbered alphabetically in the checklist below for your convenience. The cards marked with SP in the checklist below were apparently printed in shorter supply and are more difficult to find. The catalog number for this set is R414-15A. The value of complete intact boxes would be 50 percent greater than the prices listed below.

|  | NRMT | VG-E | GOOD |
|---|---|---|---|
| COMPLETE SET (18)........................ | 5000.00 | 2250.00 | 600.00 |
| COMMON PLAYER (1-18)................. | 150.00 | 60.00 | 15.00 |

JIMMY BROWN
FULLBACK · CLEVELAND BROWNS

| | | | | |
|---|---|---|---|---|
| ☐ 1 Alan Ameche | 175.00 | 70.00 | 18.00 |
| Baltimore Colts | | | |
| ☐ 2 Jon Arnett | 150.00 | 60.00 | 15.00 |
| Los Angeles Rams | | | |
| ☐ 3 Jim Brown | 600.00 | 240.00 | 60.00 |
| Cleveland Browns | | | |
| ☐ 4 Rick Casares | 150.00 | 60.00 | 15.00 |
| Chicago Bears | | | |
| ☐ 5A Charley Conerly SP | 450.00 | 180.00 | 45.00 |
| ERR (Baltimore Colts) | | | |
| ☐ 5B Charley Conerly SP | 300.00 | 120.00 | 30.00 |
| COR (New York Giants) | | | |
| ☐ 6 Howard Ferguson | 150.00 | 60.00 | 15.00 |
| Pittsburgh Steelers | | | |
| ☐ 7 Frank Gifford | 450.00 | 180.00 | 45.00 |
| New York Giants | | | |
| ☐ 8 Lou Groza SP | 450.00 | 180.00 | 45.00 |
| Cleveland Browns | | | |
| ☐ 9 Bobby Layne | 300.00 | 120.00 | 30.00 |
| Pittsburgh Steelers | | | |
| ☐ 10 Eddie LeBaron | 175.00 | 70.00 | 18.00 |
| Washington Redskins | | | |
| ☐ 11 Woodley Lewis | 150.00 | 60.00 | 15.00 |
| Chicago Cardinals | | | |
| ☐ 12 Ollie Matson | 250.00 | 100.00 | 25.00 |
| Chicago Cardinals | | | |
| ☐ 13 Joe Perry | 250.00 | 100.00 | 25.00 |
| San Francisco 49ers | | | |
| ☐ 14 Pete Retzlaff | 150.00 | 60.00 | 15.00 |
| Philadelphia Eagles | | | |
| ☐ 15 Tobin Rote | 150.00 | 60.00 | 15.00 |
| Green Bay Packers | | | |
| ☐ 16 Y.A. Tittle | 300.00 | 120.00 | 30.00 |
| San Francisco 49ers | | | |
| ☐ 17 Tom Tracy SP | 300.00 | 120.00 | 30.00 |
| Pittsburgh Steelers | | | |
| ☐ 18 Johnny Unitas | 500.00 | 200.00 | 50.00 |
| Baltimore Colts | | | |

## 1971 Bazooka

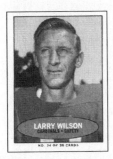

LARRY WILSON
CARDINALS · SAFETY

NO. 34 OF 36 CARDS

The 1971 Bazooka football cards were issued as twelve panels of three on the backs of Bazooka Bubble Gum boxes. Consequently, cards are seen in panels of three or as individual cards which have been cut from panels of three. The individual cards measure approximtely 1 15/16" by 2 5/8" and the panels of three measure 2 5/8" by 5 7/8". The 36 individual blank-backed cards are numbered on the card front. The checklist below presents prices for the individual cards. Complete panels are worth 25 percent more than the sum of the individual players making up the panel; complete boxes are worth approximately

50 percent more (i.e., an additional 25 percent premium) than the sum of the three players on the box. With regard to cut single cards, the mid-panel cards (2, 5, 8, ...) seem to be somewhat easier to find in nice shape.

| | NRMT | VG-E | GOOD |
|---|---|---|---|
| COMPLETE SET (36) | 200.00 | 80.00 | 20.00 |
| COMMON PLAYER (1-36) | 3.00 | 1.20 | .30 |
| ☐ 1 Joe Namath | 35.00 | 14.00 | 3.50 |
| New York Jets | | | |
| ☐ 2 Larry Brown | 4.00 | 1.60 | .40 |
| Washington Redskins | | | |
| ☐ 3 Bobby Bell | 5.00 | 2.00 | .50 |
| Kansas City Chiefs | | | |
| ☐ 4 Dick Butkus | 12.00 | 5.00 | 1.20 |
| Chicago Bears | | | |
| ☐ 5 Charlie Sanders | 3.00 | 1.20 | .30 |
| Detroit Lions | | | |
| ☐ 6 Chuck Howley | 4.00 | 1.60 | .40 |
| Dallas Cowboys | | | |
| ☐ 7 Gale Gillingham | 3.00 | 1.20 | .30 |
| Green Bay Packers | | | |
| ☐ 8 Leroy Kelly | 6.00 | 2.40 | .60 |
| Cleveland Browns | | | |
| ☐ 9 Floyd Little | 5.00 | 2.00 | .50 |
| Denver Broncos | | | |
| ☐ 10 Dan Abramowicz | 3.00 | 1.20 | .30 |
| New Orleans Saints | | | |
| ☐ 11 Sonny Jurgensen | 12.00 | 5.00 | 1.20 |
| Washington Redskins | | | |
| ☐ 12 Andy Russell | 3.00 | 1.20 | .30 |
| Pittsburgh Steelers | | | |
| ☐ 13 Tommy Nobis | 4.00 | 1.60 | .40 |
| Atlanta Falcons | | | |
| ☐ 14 O.J. Simpson | 35.00 | 14.00 | 3.50 |
| Buffalo Bills | | | |
| ☐ 15 Tom Woodeshick | 3.00 | 1.20 | .30 |
| Philadelphia Eagles | | | |
| ☐ 16 Roman Gabriel | 4.00 | 1.60 | .40 |
| Los Angeles Rams | | | |
| ☐ 17 Claude Humphrey | 3.00 | 1.20 | .30 |
| Atlanta Falcons | | | |
| ☐ 18 Merlin Olsen | 9.00 | 3.75 | .90 |
| Los Angeles Rams | | | |
| ☐ 19 Daryle Lamonica | 5.00 | 2.00 | .50 |
| Oakland Raiders | | | |
| ☐ 20 Fred Cox | 3.00 | 1.20 | .30 |
| Minnesota Vikings | | | |
| ☐ 21 Bart Starr | 15.00 | 6.00 | 1.50 |
| Green Bay Packers | | | |
| ☐ 22 John Brodie | 9.00 | 3.75 | .90 |
| San Francisco 49ers | | | |
| ☐ 23 Jim Nance | 3.00 | 1.20 | .30 |
| New England Patriots | | | |
| ☐ 24 Gary Garrison | 3.00 | 1.20 | .30 |
| San Diego Chargers | | | |
| ☐ 25 Fran Tarkenton | 20.00 | 8.00 | 2.00 |
| New York Giants | | | |
| ☐ 26 Johnny Robinson | 3.00 | 1.20 | .30 |
| Kansas City Chiefs | | | |
| ☐ 27 Gale Sayers | 20.00 | 8.00 | 2.00 |
| Chicago Bears | | | |
| ☐ 28 John Unitas | 25.00 | 10.00 | 2.50 |
| Baltimore Colts | | | |
| ☐ 29 Jerry LeVias | 3.00 | 1.20 | .30 |
| Houston Oilers | | | |
| ☐ 30 Virgil Carter | 3.00 | 1.20 | .30 |
| Cincinnati Bengals | | | |
| ☐ 31 Bill Nelsen | 3.00 | 1.20 | .30 |
| Cleveland Browns | | | |
| ☐ 32 Dave Osborn | 3.00 | 1.20 | .30 |
| Minnesota Vikings | | | |
| ☐ 33 Matt Snell | 3.00 | 1.20 | .30 |
| New York Jets | | | |
| ☐ 34 Larry Wilson | 6.00 | 2.40 | .60 |
| St. Louis Cardinals | | | |
| ☐ 35 Bob Griese | 15.00 | 6.00 | 1.50 |
| Miami Dolphins | | | |
| ☐ 36 Lance Alworth | 9.00 | 3.75 | .90 |
| San Diego Chargers | | | |

## 1972 Bazooka Official Signals

This 12-card set was issued on the bottom of Bazooka Bubble Gum boxes. The box bottom measures approximately 6 1/4" by 2 7/8". The bottoms are numbered in the upper left corner and the text appears between cartoon characters on the sides of the bottom. The material is entitled "A children's guide to TV football," having been extracted from the book Football Lingo. Cards 1-8 provide definitions of numerous terms associated with football. Card number 9 lists the six different officials and describes their responsibilities. Cards 10-12 picture the officials' signals and explain their meanings. The value of complete intact boxes would be 50 percent greater than the prices listed below.

|  | NRMT | VG-E | GOOD |
|---|---|---|---|
| COMPLETE SET (12) | 75.00 | 30.00 | 7.50 |
| COMMON PANEL (1-12) | 7.50 | 3.00 | .75 |
| ☐ 1 Football Lingo<br>Automatic through<br>Bread and Butter Play | 7.50 | 3.00 | .75 |
| ☐ 2 Football Lingo<br>Broken-Field Runner<br>through Dive | 7.50 | 3.00 | .75 |
| ☐ 3 Football Lingo<br>Double-Coverage<br>through Interference | 7.50 | 3.00 | .75 |
| ☐ 4 Football Lingo<br>Game Plan through<br>Lateral Pass | 7.50 | 3.00 | .75 |
| ☐ 5 Football Lingo<br>Interception through<br>Man-to-Man Coverage | 7.50 | 3.00 | .75 |
| ☐ 6 Football Lingo<br>Killing the Clock<br>through Punt | 7.50 | 3.00 | .75 |
| ☐ 7 Football Lingo<br>Belly Series through<br>Quick Whistle | 7.50 | 3.00 | .75 |
| ☐ 8 Football Lingo<br>Prevent Defense through<br>Primary Receiver | 7.50 | 3.00 | .75 |
| ☐ 9 Officials' Duties<br>Referee through<br>Line Judge | 7.50 | 3.00 | .75 |
| ☐ 10 Officials' Duties | 7.50 | 3.00 | .75 |
| ☐ 11 Officials' Signals | 7.50 | 3.00 | .75 |
| ☐ 12 Officials' Signals | 7.50 | 3.00 | .75 |

# 1976 Bears Coke Discs

The cards in this 22-player disc set are unnumbered so they are listed below alphabetically. All players in the set are members of the Chicago Bears suggesting that these cards were issued as part of a local Chicago Coca-Cola promotion. The discs measure approximately 3 3/8" in diameter but with the hang tab intact the whole card is 5 1/4" long. There are two versions of the Doug Plank disc (green and yellow) and two versions of Clemons (yellow and orange); both of these variations were printed in the same quantities as all the other cards in the set and hence are not that difficult to find. The discs were

produced by Mike Schechter Associates (MSA). These cards are frequently found with their hang tabs intact and hence they are priced that way in the list below. The back of each disc contains the phrase, "Coke adds life to ... halftime fun." The set price below includes all the variation cards. The set is also noteworthy in that it contains another card (albeit round) of Walter Payton in 1976, the same year as his Topps Rookie Card.

|  | NRMT | VG-E | GOOD |
|---|---|---|---|
| COMPLETE SET (24) | 50.00 | 20.00 | 5.00 |
| COMMON PLAYER (1-22) | 1.25 | .50 | .12 |
| ☐ 1 Lionel Antoine | 1.25 | .50 | .12 |
| ☐ 2 Bob Avellini | 2.00 | .80 | .20 |
| ☐ 3 Waymond Bryant | 1.50 | .60 | .15 |
| ☐ 4 Doug Buffone | 2.00 | .80 | .20 |
| ☐ 5 Wally Chambers | 2.00 | .80 | .20 |
| ☐ 6A Craig Clemons<br>(Yellow border) | 1.25 | .50 | .12 |
| ☐ 6B Craig Clemons<br>(Orange border) | 1.25 | .50 | .12 |
| ☐ 7 Allan Ellis | 1.25 | .50 | .12 |
| ☐ 8 Roland Harper | 2.00 | .80 | .20 |
| ☐ 9 Mike Hartenstine | 1.25 | .50 | .12 |
| ☐ 10 Noah Jackson | 1.50 | .60 | .15 |
| ☐ 11 Virgil Livers | 1.25 | .50 | .12 |
| ☐ 12 Jim Osborne | 1.25 | .50 | .12 |
| ☐ 13 Bob Parsons | 1.25 | .50 | .12 |
| ☐ 14 Walter Payton | 30.00 | 12.00 | 3.00 |
| ☐ 15 Dan Peiffer | 1.25 | .50 | .12 |
| ☐ 16A Doug Plank<br>(Yellow border) | 1.50 | .60 | .15 |
| ☐ 16B Doug Plank<br>(Green border) | 1.50 | .60 | .15 |
| ☐ 17 Bo Rather | 1.50 | .60 | .15 |
| ☐ 18 Don Rives | 1.25 | .50 | .12 |
| ☐ 19 Jeff Sevy | 1.25 | .50 | .12 |
| ☐ 20 Ron Shanklin | 1.50 | .60 | .15 |
| ☐ 21 Revie Sorey | 1.50 | .60 | .15 |
| ☐ 22 Roger Stillwell | 1.25 | .50 | .12 |

# 1960 Bills Team Issue

Issued by the team, this set of 40 black-and-white (approximately) 5" by 7" pictures was given to each 1960 Bills season ticketholder. The photos are unnumbered and checklisted below in alphabetical order. The photos are frequently found personally autographed.

|  | NRMT | VG-E | GOOD |
|---|---|---|---|
| COMPLETE SET (40) | 150.00 | 60.00 | 15.00 |
| COMMON PLAYER (1-40) | 4.00 | 1.60 | .40 |
| ☐ 1 Bill Atkins | 5.00 | 2.00 | .50 |
| ☐ 2 Bob Barrett | 4.00 | 1.60 | .40 |
| ☐ 3 Phil Blazer | 4.00 | 1.60 | .40 |
| ☐ 4 Bob Brodhead | 4.00 | 1.60 | .40 |
| ☐ 5 Dick Brubacher | 4.00 | 1.60 | .40 |
| ☐ 6 Bernie Burzinski | 4.00 | 1.60 | .40 |
| ☐ 7 Wray Carlton | 6.00 | 2.40 | .60 |
| ☐ 8 Don Chelf | 4.00 | 1.60 | .40 |
| ☐ 9 Monte Crockett | 5.00 | 2.00 | .50 |
| ☐ 10 Bob Dove | 4.00 | 1.60 | .40 |
| ☐ 11 Elbert Dubenion | 7.50 | 3.00 | .75 |
| ☐ 12 Fred Ford | 4.00 | 1.60 | .40 |
| ☐ 13 Dick Gallagher | 4.00 | 1.60 | .40 |
| ☐ 14 Darrell Harper | 4.00 | 1.60 | .40 |
| ☐ 15 Harvey Johnson | 5.00 | 2.00 | .50 |
| ☐ 16 John Johnson | 4.00 | 1.60 | .40 |
| ☐ 17 Billy Kinard | 5.00 | 2.00 | .50 |
| ☐ 18 Joe Kulbacki | 4.00 | 1.60 | .40 |
| ☐ 19 John Laraway | 4.00 | 1.60 | .40 |
| ☐ 20 Richie Lucas | 7.50 | 3.00 | .75 |
| ☐ 21 Archie Matsos | 6.00 | 2.40 | .60 |
| ☐ 22 Richie McCabe | 6.00 | 2.40 | .60 |
| ☐ 23 Dan McGrew | 5.00 | 2.00 | .50 |
| ☐ 24 Chuck McMurtry | 4.00 | 1.60 | .40 |
| ☐ 25 Ed Meyer | 4.00 | 1.60 | .40 |
| ☐ 26 Ed Muelhaupt | 4.00 | 1.60 | .40 |
| ☐ 27 Tommy O'Connell | 5.00 | 2.00 | .50 |
| ☐ 28 Harold Olson | 4.00 | 1.60 | .40 |
| ☐ 29 Buster Ramsey CO | 5.00 | 2.00 | .50 |
| ☐ 30 Breezy Reid | 4.00 | 1.60 | .40 |
| ☐ 31 Tom Rychlec | 5.00 | 2.00 | .50 |
| ☐ 32 Joe Schaeffer | 4.00 | 1.60 | .40 |
| ☐ 33 John Scott | 4.00 | 1.60 | .40 |
| ☐ 34 Bob Sedlock | 4.00 | 1.60 | .40 |
| ☐ 35 Carl Smith | 4.00 | 1.60 | .40 |
| ☐ 36 Jim Sorey | 4.00 | 1.60 | .40 |
| ☐ 37 Laverne Torczon | 5.00 | 2.00 | .50 |
| ☐ 38 Jim Wagstaff | 4.00 | 1.60 | .40 |
| ☐ 39 Ralph Wilson OWN | 6.00 | 2.40 | .60 |
| ☐ 40 Mack Yoho | 5.00 | 2.00 | .50 |

## 1963 Bills Jones Dairy

This set of 40 crude drawings features members of the Buffalo Bills. These "cards" are actually cardboard cut from the side of the milk cartons. These circular cards measure approximately 1" in diameter and are frequently found miscut, i.e., off-centered. The catalog designation for this set is F118-1. This unnumbered set is listed alphabetically below for convenience.

|  | NRMT | VG-E | GOOD |
|---|---|---|---|
| COMPLETE SET (40) | 750.00 | 300.00 | 75.00 |
| COMMON PLAYER (1-40) | 15.00 | 6.00 | 1.50 |
|  |  |  |  |
| ☐ 1 Ray Abruzzese | 15.00 | 6.00 | 1.50 |
| ☐ 2 Art Baker | 15.00 | 6.00 | 1.50 |
| ☐ 3 Stew Barber | 18.00 | 7.25 | 1.80 |
| ☐ 4 Glenn Bass | 18.00 | 7.25 | 1.80 |
| ☐ 5 Dave Behrman | 18.00 | 7.25 | 1.80 |
| ☐ 6 Al Bemiller | 15.00 | 6.00 | 1.50 |
| ☐ 7 Wray Carlton | 20.00 | 8.00 | 2.00 |
| ☐ 8 Carl Charon | 15.00 | 6.00 | 1.50 |
| ☐ 9 Monte Crockett | 18.00 | 7.25 | 1.80 |
| ☐ 10 Wayne Crow | 15.00 | 6.00 | 1.50 |
| ☐ 11 Tom Day | 15.00 | 6.00 | 1.50 |
| ☐ 12 Elbert Dubenion | 20.00 | 8.00 | 2.00 |
| ☐ 13 Jim Dunaway | 18.00 | 7.25 | 1.80 |
| ☐ 14 Booker Edgerson | 15.00 | 6.00 | 1.50 |
| ☐ 15 Cookie Gilchrist | 30.00 | 12.00 | 3.00 |
| ☐ 16 Dick Hudson | 18.00 | 7.25 | 1.80 |
| ☐ 17 Frank Jackunas | 15.00 | 6.00 | 1.50 |
| ☐ 18 Harry Jacobs | 18.00 | 7.25 | 1.80 |
| ☐ 19 Jack Kemp | 300.00 | 120.00 | 30.00 |
| ☐ 20 Roger Kochman | 15.00 | 6.00 | 1.50 |
| ☐ 21 Daryle Lamonica | 50.00 | 20.00 | 5.00 |
| ☐ 22 Charley Leo | 15.00 | 6.00 | 1.50 |
| ☐ 23 Marv Matuszak | 18.00 | 7.25 | 1.80 |
| ☐ 24 Bill Miller | 15.00 | 6.00 | 1.50 |
| ☐ 25 Leroy Moore | 15.00 | 6.00 | 1.50 |
| ☐ 26 Harold Olson | 15.00 | 6.00 | 1.50 |
| ☐ 27 Herb Paterra | 15.00 | 6.00 | 1.50 |
| ☐ 28 Ken Rice | 15.00 | 6.00 | 1.50 |
| ☐ 29 Henry Rivera | 15.00 | 6.00 | 1.50 |
| ☐ 30 Ed Rutkowski | 18.00 | 7.25 | 1.80 |
| ☐ 31 George Saimes | 20.00 | 8.00 | 2.00 |
| ☐ 32 Tom Sestak | 20.00 | 8.00 | 2.00 |
| ☐ 33 Billy Shaw | 20.00 | 8.00 | 2.00 |
| ☐ 34 Mike Stratton | 20.00 | 8.00 | 2.00 |
| ☐ 35 Gene Sykes | 15.00 | 6.00 | 1.50 |
| ☐ 36 John Tracey | 18.00 | 7.25 | 1.80 |
| ☐ 37 Ernie Warlick | 18.00 | 7.25 | 1.80 |
| ☐ 38 Willie West | 20.00 | 8.00 | 2.00 |
| ☐ 39 Mack Yoho | 18.00 | 7.25 | 1.80 |
| ☐ 40 Sid Youngelman | 18.00 | 7.25 | 1.80 |

## 1965 Bills Super Duper Markets

Super Duper Food Markets offered these black-and-white approximately 8 1/2" by 11" Buffalo Bills player photos to shoppers during the fall of 1965. The photos were a weekly giveaway during the football season by Super Duper markets in western New York. The photos are unnumbered and checklisted below in alphabetical order.

|  | NRMT | VG-E | GOOD |
|---|---|---|---|
| COMPLETE SET (10) | 150.00 | 60.00 | 15.00 |
| COMMON PLAYER (1-10) | 6.00 | 2.40 | .60 |
|  |  |  |  |
| ☐ 1 Glenn Bass | 6.00 | 2.40 | .60 |
| ☐ 2 Elbert Dubenion | 9.00 | 3.75 | .90 |
| ☐ 3 Billy Joe | 9.00 | 3.75 | .90 |
| ☐ 4 Jack Kemp | 75.00 | 30.00 | 7.50 |
| ☐ 5 Daryle Lamonica | 15.00 | 6.00 | 1.50 |
| ☐ 6 Tom Sestak | 6.00 | 2.40 | .60 |
| ☐ 7 Billy Shaw | 7.50 | 3.00 | .75 |
| ☐ 8 Mike Stratton | 6.00 | 2.40 | .60 |
| ☐ 9 Ernie Warlick | 6.00 | 2.40 | .60 |
| ☐ 10 Team Photo | 25.00 | 10.00 | 2.50 |

## 1967 Bills Jones-Rich Milk

Through a special mail-in offer, Jones-Rich Milk Co. offered this set of six Buffalo Bills' highlight action photos from the 1965 and 1966 seasons. These black-and-white photos measure approximately 8 1/2" by 11".

|  | NRMT | VG-E | GOOD |
|---|---|---|---|
| COMPLETE SET (6) | 75.00 | 30.00 | 7.50 |
| COMMON PLAYER (1-6) | 12.00 | 5.00 | 1.20 |
|  |  |  |  |
| ☐ 1 Butch Byrd | 15.00 | 6.00 | 1.50 |
| ☐ 2 Wray Carlton | 15.00 | 6.00 | 1.50 |
| ☐ 3 Hagood Clarke | 12.00 | 5.00 | 1.20 |
| ☐ 4 Paul Costa | 15.00 | 6.00 | 1.50 |
| ☐ 5 Jim Dunaway | 15.00 | 6.00 | 1.50 |
| ☐ 6 Jack Spikes | 15.00 | 6.00 | 1.50 |

## 1974 Bills Team Issue

Measuring approximately 8 1/2" by 11", this set of 12 team-issued Buffalo Bills color player photos was sold at the concession stands in Rich Stadium in Buffalo during the 1974 season.

|  | NRMT | VG-E | GOOD |
|---|---|---|---|
| COMPLETE SET (12) | 60.00 | 24.00 | 6.00 |
| COMMON PLAYER (1-12) | 3.00 | 1.20 | .30 |
|  |  |  |  |
| ☐ 1 Jim Braxton | 4.00 | 1.60 | .40 |
| ☐ 2 Bob Chandler | 6.00 | 2.40 | .60 |
| ☐ 3 Jim Cheyunski | 4.00 | 1.60 | .40 |
| ☐ 4 Earl Edwards | 3.00 | 1.20 | .30 |
| ☐ 5 Joe Ferguson | 7.50 | 3.00 | .75 |
| ☐ 6 Dave Foley | 3.00 | 1.20 | .30 |

| | | | |
|---|---|---|---|
| ☐ 7 Robert James | 3.00 | 1.20 | .30 |
| ☐ 8 Reggie McKenzie | 5.00 | 2.00 | .50 |
| ☐ 9 Jerry Patton | 3.00 | 1.20 | .30 |
| ☐ 10 Walt Patulski | 4.00 | 1.60 | .40 |
| ☐ 11 John Skorupan | 4.00 | 1.60 | .40 |
| ☐ 12 O.J. Simpson | 35.00 | 14.00 | 3.50 |

## 1976 Bills McDonald's

This set of three photos was sponsored by McDonald's in conjunction with WBEN-TV. These "Player of the Week" photos were given away free with the purchase of a Quarter Pounder at participating McDonald's restaurants of Western New York. The offer was valid while supplies lasted but ended Nov. 28, 1976. Each photo measures approximately 8" by 10" and features a posed color close-up photo bordered in white. The player's name and team name are printed in black in the bottom white border, and his facsimile autograph is inscribed across the photo toward the lower right corner. The top portion of the back has biographical information, career summary, and career statistics (except the McKenzie back omits statistics). Inside a rectangle, the bottom portion describes the promotion and presents the 1976-77 football schedule on WBEN-TV. The photos are unnumbered and are checklisted below alphabetically.

| | NRMT | VG-E | GOOD |
|---|---|---|---|
| COMPLETE SET (3) | 20.00 | 8.00 | 2.00 |
| COMMON PLAYER (1-3) | 7.50 | 3.00 | .75 |
| ☐ 1 Bob Chandler | 7.50 | 3.00 | .75 |
| ☐ 2 Joe Ferguson | 10.00 | 4.00 | 1.00 |
| ☐ 3 Reggie McKenzie | 7.50 | 3.00 | .75 |

## 1979 Bills Bell's Market

The 1979 Bell's Market Buffalo Bills set contains 11 photos which were issued one per week, with purchase, at Bell's Markets during the football season. The cards measure approximately 7 5/8" by 10" and were printed on thin stock. The Bills' logo as well as the Bell's Markets logo appears on the back along with information and statistics about the players. The cards show the player portrayed in action in full color. The photos are unnumbered and are listed below in alphabetical order by name.

| | NRMT | VG-E | GOOD |
|---|---|---|---|
| COMPLETE SET (11) | 30.00 | 12.00 | 3.00 |
| COMMON PLAYER (1-11) | 3.00 | 1.20 | .30 |
| ☐ 1 Curtis Brown | 3.00 | 1.20 | .30 |
| ☐ 2 Bob Chandler | 5.00 | 2.00 | .50 |
| ☐ 3 Joe DeLamielleure | 4.00 | 1.60 | .40 |
| ☐ 4 Joe Ferguson | 6.00 | 2.40 | .60 |
| ☐ 5 Reuben Gant | 4.00 | 1.60 | .40 |
| ☐ 6 Dee Hardison | 3.00 | 1.20 | .30 |
| ☐ 7 Frank Lewis | 4.00 | 1.60 | .40 |
| ☐ 8 Reggie McKenzie | 4.00 | 1.60 | .40 |
| ☐ 9 Terry Miller | 4.00 | 1.60 | .40 |
| ☐ 10 Shane Nelson | 3.00 | 1.20 | .30 |
| ☐ 11 Lucius Sanford | 3.00 | 1.20 | .30 |

## 1980 Bills Bell's Market

The 1980 Bell's Market Buffalo Bills cards were available in ten strips of two (connected together by a perforation) or singly as 20 individual cards. The individual cards measure approximately 2 1/2" by 3 1/2". The cards are in full color and contain a red frame line on the front. The back features blue printing listing player biographies, statistics

and the Bell's Markets logo. The prices below are for the individual cards. The value of a connected pair is approximately 20 percent more than the sum of the two individual cards listed below. The pairings were as follows: 1-2, 3-4, 5-6, 7-8, 9-10, 11-12, 13-14, 15-16, 17-18, and 19-20.

| | MINT | EXC | G-VG |
|---|---|---|---|
| COMPLETE SET (20) | 10.00 | 4.00 | 1.00 |
| COMMON PLAYER (1-20) | .50 | .20 | .05 |
| ☐ 1 Curtis Brown | .50 | .20 | .05 |
| ☐ 2 Shane Nelson | .50 | .20 | .05 |
| ☐ 3 Jerry Butler | .75 | .30 | .07 |
| ☐ 4 Joe Ferguson | 1.25 | .50 | .12 |
| ☐ 5 Joe Cribbs | 1.00 | .40 | .10 |
| ☐ 6 Reggie McKenzie | .75 | .30 | .07 |
| ☐ 7 Joe Devlin | .60 | .24 | .06 |
| ☐ 8 Ken Jones | .50 | .20 | .05 |
| ☐ 9 Steve Freeman | .50 | .20 | .05 |
| ☐ 10 Mike Kadish | .50 | .20 | .05 |
| ☐ 11 Jim Haslett | .50 | .20 | .05 |
| ☐ 12 Isiah Robertson | .75 | .30 | .07 |
| ☐ 13 Frank Lewis | .75 | .30 | .07 |
| ☐ 14 Jeff Nixon | .50 | .20 | .05 |
| ☐ 15 Nick Mike-Mayer | .50 | .20 | .05 |
| ☐ 16 Jim Ritcher | .75 | .30 | .07 |
| ☐ 17 Charles Romes | .50 | .20 | .05 |
| ☐ 18 Fred Smerlas | 1.00 | .40 | .10 |
| ☐ 19 Ben Williams | .50 | .20 | .05 |
| ☐ 20 Roland Hooks | .50 | .20 | .05 |

## 1986 Bills Sealtest

These panels were issued on the sides of half-gallon Sealtest milk cartons. The Freeman and Marve panels were issued on the sides of vitamin D cartons, and the Kelly and Romes panels appeared on two percent lowfat cartons. The panels measure approximately 3 5/8" by 7 5/8" and feature a black and white head shot of the player, biographical information, statistics, and career highlights, all in black lettering. The panels are unnumbered and listed below in alphabetical order.

| | MINT | EXC | G-VG |
|---|---|---|---|
| COMPLETE SET (6) | 20.00 | 8.00 | 2.00 |
| COMMON PLAYER (1-6) | 1.25 | .50 | .12 |
| ☐ 1 Greg Bell SP | 5.00 | 2.00 | .50 |
| ☐ 2 Jerry Butler SP | 4.00 | 1.60 | .40 |
| ☐ 3 Steve Freeman | 1.25 | .50 | .12 |
| ☐ 4 Jim Kelly | 12.00 | 5.00 | 1.20 |
| ☐ 5 Eugene Marve | 1.25 | .50 | .12 |
| ☐ 6 Charles Romes | 1.25 | .50 | .12 |

## 1993-94 Bleachers Troy Aikman Promos

Issued to herald the release of the three-card 23K Gold Border Troy Aikman set, these standard-size (2 1/2" by 3 1/2") promo cards feature a borderless color photo of Aikman in his UCLA uniform. The Bleachers logo at the upper right is highlighted by gold-foil bars above and below. The words "1 of 10,000 Promos" appears vertically in gold foil near the right edge. The back carries Aikman's career highlights over a ghosted black-and-white version of the front photo. The cards are unnumbered. A special version of this promo was produced by Bleachers for Tri-Star's Houston show with the words "Houston 1994" printed in 23K gold lettering on the left edge.

|  | MINT | EXC | G-VG |
|---|---|---|---|
| COMPLETE SET (4) | 15.00 | 6.00 | 1.50 |
| COMMON PLAYER (1-4) | 5.00 | 2.00 | .50 |
| ☐ 1 Troy Aikman | 5.00 | 2.00 | .50 |
| Dallas Cowboys | | | |
| (Exclusive promo) | | | |
| ☐ 2 Troy Aikman | 5.00 | 2.00 | .50 |
| UCLA | | | |
| ☐ 3 Troy Aikman | 5.00 | 2.00 | .50 |
| UCLA | | | |
| (Comicfest '93) | | | |
| ☐ 4 Troy Aikman | 5.00 | 2.00 | .50 |
| UCLA | | | |
| (Houston '94) | | | |

## 1994 Bleachers 23K Troy Aikman

These three standard-size (2 1/2" by 3 1/2") cards feature on their fronts color photos of Aikman with wide gold outer borders, and colored and gold-foil inner borders. Aikman's name, team, and position are stamped in gold foil near the bottom. The back carries at the top the set's production number out of a total of 10,000 produced. Below are Aikman's name, biography, and stats and highlights the team Aikman is pictured playing for on the front. A facsimile Aikman autograph appears in gold foil at the bottom. The cards are numbered on the back as "X of 3."

|  | MINT | EXC | G-VG |
|---|---|---|---|
| COMPLETE SET (3) | 24.00 | 10.00 | 2.40 |
| COMMON PLAYER (1-3) | 10.00 | 4.00 | 1.00 |
| ☐ 1 Troy Aikman | 10.00 | 4.00 | 1.00 |
| Oklahoma | | | |
| ☐ 2 Troy Aikman | 10.00 | 4.00 | 1.00 |
| UCLA | | | |
| ☐ 3 Troy Aikman | 10.00 | 4.00 | 1.00 |
| Dallas Cowboys | | | |

## 1983 Blitz Chicago

Each of these sheets measures approximately 10" by 8" and features two rows with four players per row. The first sheet presents the coaching staff, while the other seven sheets feature players. The individual photos measure 2 1/4" by 2 1/2" and have white borders. The photos are head-and-shoulders shots, with player information immediately below. A title between two team logos running across the bottom of the sheets completes them. The sheets are unnumbered and checklisted below in alphabetical order.

|  | MINT | EXC | G-VG |
|---|---|---|---|
| COMPLETE SET (8) | 40.00 | 16.00 | 4.00 |
| COMMON PLAYER (1-8) | 5.00 | 2.00 | .50 |
| ☐ 1 Coaching Staff | 7.50 | 3.00 | .75 |
| George Allen | | | |
| Joe Haering | | | |
| Paul Lanham | | | |
| John Payne | | | |
| John Teerlink | | | |
| Dick Walker | | | |
| Charlie Waller | | | |
| Ray Wietecha | | | |
| ☐ 2 Luther Bradley | 6.00 | 2.40 | .60 |
| Eddie Brown | | | |
| Virgil Livers | | | |
| Frank Minnifield | | | |
| Lance Sheilds | | | |
| Don Schwartz | | | |
| Maurice Tyler | | | |
| Ted Walton | | | |
| ☐ 3 Mack Boatner | 6.00 | 2.40 | .60 |
| Frank Collins | | | |
| Frank Corral | | | |
| Doug Cozen | | | |
| Doug Dennison | | | |
| John Roveto | | | |
| Jim Stone | | | |
| Tim Wrightman | | | |
| ☐ 4 Robert Barnes | 5.00 | 2.00 | .50 |
| Bruce Branch | | | |
| Nick Eyre | | | |
| Tim Norman | | | |
| Wally Pesuit | | | |
| Mark Stevenson | | | |
| Rob Taylor | | | |
| Steve Tobin | | | |
| ☐ 5 Junior Ah You | 5.00 | 2.00 | .50 |
| Mark Buben | | | |
| Bob Cobb | | | |
| Joe Ehrmann | | | |
| Kit Lathrop | | | |
| Karl Lorch | | | |
| Troy Thomas | | | |
| ☐ 6 Jim Fahnhorst | 6.00 | 2.40 | .60 |
| Joe Federspiel | | | |
| Doak Field | | | |
| Bruce Gheesling | | | |
| Andy Melontree | | | |
| Ed Smith | | | |
| Stan White | | | |
| Kari Yli-Renko | | | |
| ☐ 7 Marcus Anderson | 5.00 | 2.00 | .50 |
| Larry Douglas | | | |
| Marc May | | | |
| Pat Schmidt | | | |
| Lenny Willis | | | |
| Warren Anderson | | | |
| Chris Pagnucco | | | |
| Bruce Allen GM | | | |
| ☐ 8 Wamon Buggs | 7.50 | 3.00 | .75 |
| Trumaine Johnson | | | |
| Tim Koegel | | | |
| Greg Landry | | | |
| Kevin Long | | | |
| Paul Ricker | | | |
| Tom Rozantz | | | |
| Tim Spencer | | | |

## 1948 Bowman

The 1948 Bowman set is considered the first football set of the modern era. The set is complete at 108 cards; each measures 2 1/16" by 2 1/2". The cards were printed in three sheets; the third sheet (containing all the card numbers divisible by three, i.e., 3, 6, 9, 12, 15, etc.) being printed in much lesser quantities. Hence, cards with numbers divisible by three are substantially more valuable than the

other cards in the set. The second sheet (numbers 2, 5, 8, 11, 14, etc.) is also regarded as slightly tougher to obtain than the first sheet (numbers 1, 4, 7, 10, 13, etc.) which contains the most plentiful cards. The key Rookie Cards in this set are Sammy Baugh, Charley Conerly, Sid Luckman, Johnny Lujack, Steve Van Buren, and Bob Waterfield.

| | NRMT | VG-E | GOOD |
|---|---|---|---|
| COMPLETE SET (108) | 6300.00 | 2800.00 | 800.00 |
| COMMON PLAYER (1-108) | 18.00 | 8.00 | 2.30 |
| ☐ 1 Joe Tereshinski | 140.00 | 35.00 | 11.00 |
| Washington Redskins | | | |
| ☐ 2 Larry Olsonoski | 18.00 | 8.00 | 2.30 |
| Green Bay Packers | | | |
| ☐ 3 John Lujack SP | 260.00 | 115.00 | 33.00 |
| Chicago Bears | | | |
| ☐ 4 Ray Poole | 18.00 | 8.00 | 2.30 |
| New York Giants | | | |
| ☐ 5 Bill DeCorrevont | 18.00 | 8.00 | 2.30 |
| Chicago Cardinals | | | |
| ☐ 6 Paul Briggs SP | 100.00 | 45.00 | 12.50 |
| Detroit Lions | | | |
| ☐ 7 Steve Van Buren | 160.00 | 70.00 | 20.00 |
| Philadelphia Eagles | | | |
| ☐ 8 Kenny Washington | 48.00 | 22.00 | 6.00 |
| Los Angeles Rams | | | |
| ☐ 9 Nolan Luhn SP | 100.00 | 45.00 | 12.50 |
| Green Bay Packers | | | |
| ☐ 10 Chris Iversen | 18.00 | 8.00 | 2.30 |
| New York Giants | | | |
| ☐ 11 Jack Wiley | 18.00 | 8.00 | 2.30 |
| Pittsburgh Steelers | | | |
| ☐ 12 Charley Conerly SP | 250.00 | 115.00 | 31.00 |
| New York Giants | | | |
| ☐ 13 Hugh Taylor | 27.00 | 12.00 | 3.40 |
| Washington Redskins | | | |
| ☐ 14 Frank Seno | 18.00 | 8.00 | 2.30 |
| Boston Yanks | | | |
| ☐ 15 Gil Bouley SP | 100.00 | 45.00 | 12.50 |
| Los Angeles Rams | | | |
| ☐ 16 Tommy Thompson | 35.00 | 16.00 | 4.40 |
| Philadelphia Eagles | | | |
| ☐ 17 Charley Trippi | 110.00 | 50.00 | 14.00 |
| Chicago Cardinals | | | |
| ☐ 18 Vince Banonis SP | 110.00 | 50.00 | 14.00 |
| Chicago Cardinals | | | |
| ☐ 19 Art Faircloth | 18.00 | 8.00 | 2.30 |
| New York Giants | | | |
| ☐ 20 Clyde Goodnight | 18.00 | 8.00 | 2.30 |
| Green Bay Packers | | | |
| ☐ 21 Bill Chipley SP | 100.00 | 45.00 | 12.50 |
| Boston Yanks | | | |
| ☐ 22 Sammy Baugh | 300.00 | 135.00 | 38.00 |
| Washington Redskins | | | |
| ☐ 23 Don Kindt | 18.00 | 8.00 | 2.30 |
| Chicago Bears | | | |
| ☐ 24 John Koniszewski SP | 100.00 | 45.00 | 12.50 |
| Washington Redskins | | | |
| ☐ 25 Pat McHugh | 18.00 | 8.00 | 2.30 |
| Philadelphia Eagles | | | |
| ☐ 26 Bob Waterfield | 200.00 | 90.00 | 25.00 |
| Los Angeles Rams | | | |
| ☐ 27 Tony Compagno SP | 100.00 | 45.00 | 12.50 |
| Pittsburgh Steelers | | | |
| ☐ 28 Paul Governali | 18.00 | 8.00 | 2.30 |
| New York Giants | | | |
| ☐ 29 Pat Harder | 45.00 | 20.00 | 5.75 |
| Chicago Cardinals | | | |
| ☐ 30 Vic Lindskog SP | 100.00 | 45.00 | 12.50 |
| Philadelphia Eagles | | | |
| ☐ 31 Salvatore Rosato | 18.00 | 8.00 | 2.30 |
| Washington Redskins | | | |
| ☐ 32 John Mastrangelo | 18.00 | 8.00 | 2.30 |
| Pittsburgh Steelers | | | |
| ☐ 33 Fred Gehrke SP | 100.00 | 45.00 | 12.50 |
| Los Angeles Rams | | | |
| ☐ 34 Bosh Pritchard | 18.00 | 8.00 | 2.30 |
| Philadelphia Eagles | | | |
| ☐ 35 Mike Micka | 18.00 | 8.00 | 2.30 |
| Boston Yanks | | | |
| ☐ 36 Bulldog Turner SP | 200.00 | 90.00 | 25.00 |
| Chicago Bears | | | |
| ☐ 37 Len Younce | 18.00 | 8.00 | 2.30 |
| New York Giants | | | |
| ☐ 38 Pat West | 18.00 | 8.00 | 2.30 |
| Los Angeles Rams | | | |
| ☐ 39 Russ Thomas SP | 100.00 | 45.00 | 12.50 |
| Detroit Lions | | | |
| ☐ 40 James Peebles | 18.00 | 8.00 | 2.30 |
| Washington Redskins | | | |
| ☐ 41 Bob Skoglund | 18.00 | 8.00 | 2.30 |
| Green Bay Packers | | | |
| ☐ 42 Walt Stickle SP | 100.00 | 45.00 | 12.50 |
| Chicago Bears | | | |
| ☐ 43 Whitey Wistert | 25.00 | 11.50 | 3.10 |
| Philadelphia Eeagles | | | |
| ☐ 44 Paul Christman | 40.00 | 18.00 | 5.00 |
| Chicago Cardinals | | | |
| ☐ 45 Jay Rhodemyre SP | 100.00 | 45.00 | 12.50 |
| Green Bay Packers | | | |
| ☐ 46 Skip Minisi | 18.00 | 8.00 | 2.30 |
| New York Giants | | | |
| ☐ 47 Bob Mann | 18.00 | 8.00 | 2.30 |
| Detroit Lions | | | |
| ☐ 48 Mal Kutner SP | 100.00 | 45.00 | 12.50 |
| Chicago Cardinals | | | |
| ☐ 49 Dick Poillon | 18.00 | 8.00 | 2.30 |
| Washington Redskins | | | |
| ☐ 50 Charles Cherundolo | 18.00 | 8.00 | 2.30 |
| Pittsburgh Steelers | | | |
| ☐ 51 Gerald Cowhig SP | 100.00 | 45.00 | 12.50 |
| Los Angeles Rams | | | |
| ☐ 52 Neil Armstrong | 27.00 | 12.00 | 3.40 |
| Philadelphia Eagles | | | |
| ☐ 53 Frank Maznicki | 18.00 | 8.00 | 2.30 |
| Boston Yanks | | | |
| ☐ 54 John Sanchez SP | 100.00 | 45.00 | 12.50 |
| Washington Redskins | | | |
| ☐ 55 Frank Reagan | 18.00 | 8.00 | 2.30 |
| New York Giants | | | |
| ☐ 56 Jim Hardy | 18.00 | 8.00 | 2.30 |
| Los Angeles Rams | | | |
| ☐ 57 John Badaczewski SP | 100.00 | 45.00 | 12.50 |
| Boston Yanks | | | |
| ☐ 58 Robert Nussbaumer | 18.00 | 8.00 | 2.30 |
| Washington Redskins | | | |
| ☐ 59 Marvin Pregulman | 18.00 | 8.00 | 2.30 |
| Detroit Lions | | | |
| ☐ 60 Elbert Nickel SP | 125.00 | 57.50 | 15.50 |
| Pittsburgh Steelers | | | |
| ☐ 61 Alex Wojciechowicz | 100.00 | 45.00 | 12.50 |
| Philadelphia Eagles | | | |
| ☐ 62 Walt Schlinkman | 18.00 | 8.00 | 2.30 |
| Green Bay Packers | | | |
| ☐ 63 Pete Pihos SP | 200.00 | 90.00 | 25.00 |
| Philadelphia Eagles | | | |
| ☐ 64 Joseph Sulaitis | 18.00 | 8.00 | 2.30 |
| New York Giants | | | |
| ☐ 65 Mike Holovak | 45.00 | 20.00 | 5.75 |
| Chicago Bears | | | |
| ☐ 66 Cecil Souders SP | 100.00 | 45.00 | 12.50 |
| Detroit Lions | | | |
| ☐ 67 Paul McKee | 18.00 | 8.00 | 2.30 |
| Washington Redskins | | | |
| ☐ 68 Bill Moore | 18.00 | 8.00 | 2.30 |
| Pittsburgh Steelers | | | |
| ☐ 69 Frank Minini SP | 100.00 | 45.00 | 12.50 |
| Chicago Bears | | | |
| ☐ 70 Jack Ferrante | 18.00 | 8.00 | 2.30 |
| Philadelphia Eagles | | | |
| ☐ 71 Leslie Horvath | 45.00 | 20.00 | 5.75 |
| Los Angeles Rams | | | |
| ☐ 72 Ted Fritsch Sr. SP | 110.00 | 50.00 | 14.00 |
| Green Bay Packers | | | |
| ☐ 73 Tex Coulter | 20.00 | 9.00 | 2.50 |
| New York Giants | | | |
| ☐ 74 Boley Dancewicz | 18.00 | 8.00 | 2.30 |
| Boston Yanks | | | |
| ☐ 75 Dante Mangani SP | 100.00 | 45.00 | 12.50 |
| Los Angeles Rams | | | |
| ☐ 76 James Hefti | 18.00 | 8.00 | 2.30 |
| Washington Redskins | | | |
| ☐ 77 Paul Sarringhaus | 18.00 | 8.00 | 2.30 |
| Detroit Lions | | | |
| ☐ 78 Joe Scott SP | 100.00 | 45.00 | 12.50 |
| New York Giants | | | |
| ☐ 79 Bucko Kilroy | 30.00 | 13.50 | 3.80 |
| Philadelphia Eagles | | | |
| ☐ 80 Bill Dudley | 100.00 | 45.00 | 12.50 |
| Detroit Lions | | | |
| ☐ 81 Marshall Goldberg SP | 100.00 | 45.00 | 12.50 |
| Chicago Cardinals | | | |
| ☐ 82 John Cannady | 18.00 | 8.00 | 2.30 |
| New York Giants | | | |
| ☐ 83 Perry Moss | 18.00 | 8.00 | 2.30 |
| Green Bay Packers | | | |
| ☐ 84 Harold Crisler SP | 100.00 | 45.00 | 12.50 |

Boston Yanks
| | | | |
|---|---|---|---|
| ☐ 85 Bill Gray | 18.00 | 8.00 | 2.30 |

Washington Redskins
| | | | |
|---|---|---|---|
| ☐ 86 John Clement | 18.00 | 8.00 | 2.30 |

Pittsburgh Steelers
| | | | |
|---|---|---|---|
| ☐ 87 Dan Sandifer SP | 100.00 | 45.00 | 12.50 |

Washington Redskins
| | | | |
|---|---|---|---|
| ☐ 88 Ben Kish | 18.00 | 8.00 | 2.30 |

Philadelphia Eagles
| | | | |
|---|---|---|---|
| ☐ 89 Herbert Banta | 18.00 | 8.00 | 2.30 |

Los Angeles Rams
| | | | |
|---|---|---|---|
| ☐ 90 Bill Garnaas SP | 100.00 | 45.00 | 12.50 |

Pittsburgh Steelers
| | | | |
|---|---|---|---|
| ☐ 91 Jim White | 18.00 | 8.00 | 2.30 |

New York Giants
| | | | |
|---|---|---|---|
| ☐ 92 Frank Barzilauskas | 18.00 | 8.00 | 2.30 |

Boston Yanks
| | | | |
|---|---|---|---|
| ☐ 93 Vic Sears SP | 100.00 | 45.00 | 12.50 |

Philadelphia Eagles
| | | | |
|---|---|---|---|
| ☐ 94 John Adams | 18.00 | 8.00 | 2.30 |

Washington Redskins
| | | | |
|---|---|---|---|
| ☐ 95 George McAfee | 100.00 | 45.00 | 12.50 |

Chicago Bears
| | | | |
|---|---|---|---|
| ☐ 96 Ralph Heywood SP | 100.00 | 45.00 | 12.50 |

Detroit Lions
| | | | |
|---|---|---|---|
| ☐ 97 Joe Muha | 18.00 | 8.00 | 2.30 |

Philadelphia Eagles
| | | | |
|---|---|---|---|
| ☐ 98 Fred Enke | 18.00 | 8.00 | 2.30 |

Detroit Lions
| | | | |
|---|---|---|---|
| ☐ 99 Harry Gilmer SP | 150.00 | 70.00 | 19.00 |

Washington Redskins
| | | | |
|---|---|---|---|
| ☐ 100 Bill Miklich | 18.00 | 8.00 | 2.30 |

New York Giants
| | | | |
|---|---|---|---|
| ☐ 101 Joe Gottlieb | 18.00 | 8.00 | 2.30 |

Pittsburgh Steelers
| | | | |
|---|---|---|---|
| ☐ 102 Bud Angsman SP | 100.00 | 45.00 | 12.50 |

Chicago Cardinals
| | | | |
|---|---|---|---|
| ☐ 103 Tom Farmer | 18.00 | 8.00 | 2.30 |

Washington Redskins
| | | | |
|---|---|---|---|
| ☐ 104 Bruce Smith | 35.00 | 16.00 | 4.40 |

Green Bay Packers
| | | | |
|---|---|---|---|
| ☐ 105 Bob Cifers SP | 100.00 | 45.00 | 12.50 |

Pittsburgh Steelers
| | | | |
|---|---|---|---|
| ☐ 106 Ernie Steele | 18.00 | 8.00 | 2.30 |

Philadelphia Eagles
| | | | |
|---|---|---|---|
| ☐ 107 Sid Luckman | 210.00 | 95.00 | 26.00 |

Chicago Bears
| | | | |
|---|---|---|---|
| ☐ 108 Buford Ray SP | 350.00 | 90.00 | 28.00 |

Green Bay Packers

## 1950 Bowman

The 1950 Bowman set is Bowman's first color football set. The color quality on the cards is superior to previous Bowman sports' issues. The set is complete at 144 cards; the cards measure approximately 2 1/16" by 2 1/2". The card backs feature black printing except for the player's name and the logo for the "5-Star Bowman Picture Card Collectors Club" which are in red. The set features the "Rookie cards" of Tony Canadeo, Glenn Davis, Tom Fears, Otto Graham, Lou Groza, Elroy Hirsch, Dante Lavelli, Marion Motley, Joe Perry, and Y.A. Tittle. With a few exceptions the set numbering is arranged so that trios of players from the same team are numbered in sequence.

| | NRMT | VG-E | GOOD |
|---|---|---|---|
| COMPLETE SET (144) | 3800.00 | 1700.00 | 475.00 |
| COMMON PLAYER (1-36) | 18.00 | 8.00 | 2.30 |
| COMMON PLAYER (37-72) | 18.00 | 8.00 | 2.30 |
| COMMON PLAYER (73-108) | 18.00 | 8.00 | 2.30 |
| COMMON PLAYER (109-144) | 18.00 | 8.00 | 2.30 |
| | | | |
| ☐ 1 Doak Walker | 150.00 | 38.00 | 12.00 |

Detroit Lions
| | | | |
|---|---|---|---|
| ☐ 2 John Greene | 18.00 | 8.00 | 2.30 |

Detroit Lions
| | | | |
|---|---|---|---|
| ☐ 3 Bob Nowasky | 18.00 | 8.00 | 2.30 |

Baltimore Colts
| | | | |
|---|---|---|---|
| ☐ 4 Jonathan Jenkins | 18.00 | 8.00 | 2.30 |

Baltimore Colts
| | | | |
|---|---|---|---|
| ☐ 5 Y.A. Tittle | 260.00 | 115.00 | 33.00 |

Baltimore Colts
| | | | |
|---|---|---|---|
| ☐ 6 Lou Groza | 175.00 | 80.00 | 22.00 |

Cleveland Browns
| | | | |
|---|---|---|---|
| ☐ 7 Alex Agase | 28.00 | 12.50 | 3.50 |

Cleveland Browns
| | | | |
|---|---|---|---|
| ☐ 8 Mac Speedie | 35.00 | 16.00 | 4.40 |

Cleveland Browns
| | | | |
|---|---|---|---|
| ☐ 9 Tony Canadeo | 50.00 | 23.00 | 6.25 |

Green Bay Packers
| | | | |
|---|---|---|---|
| ☐ 10 Larry Craig | 18.00 | 8.00 | 2.30 |

Green Bay Packers
| | | | |
|---|---|---|---|
| ☐ 11 Ted Fritsch Sr. | 20.00 | 9.00 | 2.50 |

Green Bay Packers
| | | | |
|---|---|---|---|
| ☐ 12 Joe Goldring | 18.00 | 8.00 | 2.30 |

New York Yanks
| | | | |
|---|---|---|---|
| ☐ 13 Martin Ruby | 18.00 | 8.00 | 2.30 |

New York Yanks
| | | | |
|---|---|---|---|
| ☐ 14 George Taliaferro | 20.00 | 9.00 | 2.50 |

New York Yanks
| | | | |
|---|---|---|---|
| ☐ 15 Tank Younger | 40.00 | 18.00 | 5.00 |

Los Angeles Rams
| | | | |
|---|---|---|---|
| ☐ 16 Glenn Army Davis | 125.00 | 57.50 | 15.50 |

Los Angeles Rams
| | | | |
|---|---|---|---|
| ☐ 17 Bob Waterfield | 70.00 | 32.00 | 8.75 |

Los Angeles Rams
| | | | |
|---|---|---|---|
| ☐ 18 Val Jansante | 18.00 | 8.00 | 2.30 |

Pittsburgh Steelers
| | | | |
|---|---|---|---|
| ☐ 19 Joe Geri | 18.00 | 8.00 | 2.30 |

Pittsburgh Steelers
| | | | |
|---|---|---|---|
| ☐ 20 Jerry Nuzum | 18.00 | 8.00 | 2.30 |

Pittsburgh Steelers
| | | | |
|---|---|---|---|
| ☐ 21 Elmer Angsman | 18.00 | 8.00 | 2.30 |

Chicago Cardinals
| | | | |
|---|---|---|---|
| ☐ 22 Billy Dewell | 18.00 | 8.00 | 2.30 |

Chicago Cardinals
| | | | |
|---|---|---|---|
| ☐ 23 Steve Van Buren | 60.00 | 27.00 | 7.50 |

Philadelphia Eagles
| | | | |
|---|---|---|---|
| ☐ 24 Cliff Patton | 18.00 | 8.00 | 2.30 |

Philadelphia Eagles
| | | | |
|---|---|---|---|
| ☐ 25 Bosh Pritchard | 18.00 | 8.00 | 2.30 |

Philadelphia Eagles
| | | | |
|---|---|---|---|
| ☐ 26 John Lujack | 60.00 | 27.00 | 7.50 |

Chicago Bears
| | | | |
|---|---|---|---|
| ☐ 27 Sid Luckman | 75.00 | 34.00 | 9.50 |

Chicago Bears
| | | | |
|---|---|---|---|
| ☐ 28 Bulldog Turner | 40.00 | 18.00 | 5.00 |

Chicago Bears
| | | | |
|---|---|---|---|
| ☐ 29 Bill Dudley | 35.00 | 16.00 | 4.40 |

Washington Redskins
| | | | |
|---|---|---|---|
| ☐ 30 Hugh Taylor | 20.00 | 9.00 | 2.50 |

Washington Redskins
| | | | |
|---|---|---|---|
| ☐ 31 George Thomas | 18.00 | 8.00 | 2.30 |

Washington Redskins
| | | | |
|---|---|---|---|
| ☐ 32 Ray Poole | 18.00 | 8.00 | 2.30 |

New York Giants
| | | | |
|---|---|---|---|
| ☐ 33 Travis Tidwell | 18.00 | 8.00 | 2.30 |

New York Giants
| | | | |
|---|---|---|---|
| ☐ 34 Gail Bruce | 18.00 | 8.00 | 2.30 |

San Francisco 49ers
| | | | |
|---|---|---|---|
| ☐ 35 Joe Perry | 150.00 | 70.00 | 19.00 |

San Francisco 49ers
| | | | |
|---|---|---|---|
| ☐ 36 Frankie Albert | 40.00 | 18.00 | 5.00 |

San Francisco 49ers
| | | | |
|---|---|---|---|
| ☐ 37 Bobby Layne | 140.00 | 65.00 | 17.50 |

Detroit Lions
| | | | |
|---|---|---|---|
| ☐ 38 Leon Hart | 28.00 | 12.50 | 3.50 |

Detroit Lions
| | | | |
|---|---|---|---|
| ☐ 39 Bob Hoernschemeyer | 20.00 | 9.00 | 2.50 |

Detroit Lions
| | | | |
|---|---|---|---|
| ☐ 40 Dick Barwegan | 20.00 | 9.00 | 2.50 |

Baltimore Colts
| | | | |
|---|---|---|---|
| ☐ 41 Adrian Burk | 20.00 | 9.00 | 2.50 |

Baltimore Colts
| | | | |
|---|---|---|---|
| ☐ 42 Barry French | 18.00 | 8.00 | 2.30 |

Baltimore Colts
| | | | |
|---|---|---|---|
| ☐ 43 Marion Motley | 95.00 | 42.50 | 12.00 |

Cleveland Browns
| | | | |
|---|---|---|---|
| ☐ 44 Jim Martin | 20.00 | 9.00 | 2.50 |

Cleveland Browns
| | | | |
|---|---|---|---|
| ☐ 45 Otto Graham | 425.00 | 190.00 | 52.50 |

Cleveland Browns
| | | | |
|---|---|---|---|
| ☐ 46 Al Baldwin | 18.00 | 8.00 | 2.30 |

Green Bay Packers
| | | | |
|---|---|---|---|
| ☐ 47 Larry Coutre | 18.00 | 8.00 | 2.30 |

Green Bay Packers
| | | | |
|---|---|---|---|
| ☐ 48 John Rauch | 18.00 | 8.00 | 2.30 |

New York Yanks
| | | | |
|---|---|---|---|
| ☐ 49 Sam Tamburo | 18.00 | 8.00 | 2.30 |

New York Yanks
| | | | |
|---|---|---|---|
| ☐ 50 Mike Swistowicz | 18.00 | 8.00 | 2.30 |

New York Yanks
| | | | |
|---|---|---|---|
| ☐ 51 Tom Fears | 80.00 | 36.00 | 10.00 |

Los Angeles Rams
| | | | |
|---|---|---|---|
| ☐ 52 Elroy Hirsch | 150.00 | 70.00 | 19.00 |

Los Angeles Rams
| | | | |
|---|---|---|---|
| ☐ 53 Dick Huffman | 18.00 | 8.00 | 2.30 |

| | | | |
|---|---|---|---|
| Los Angeles Rams | | | |
| ☐ 54 Bob Gage | 18.00 | 8.00 | 2.30 |
| Pittsburgh Steelers | | | |
| ☐ 55 Bob Tinsley | 18.00 | 8.00 | 2.30 |
| Los Angeles Rams | | | |
| ☐ 56 Bill Blackburn | 18.00 | 8.00 | 2.30 |
| Chicago Cardinals | | | |
| ☐ 57 John Cochran | 18.00 | 8.00 | 2.30 |
| Chicago Cardinals | | | |
| ☐ 58 Bill Fischer | 18.00 | 8.00 | 2.30 |
| Chicago Cardinals | | | |
| ☐ 59 Whitey Wistert | 20.00 | 9.00 | 2.50 |
| Philadelphia Eagles | | | |
| ☐ 60 Clyde Scott | 18.00 | 8.00 | 2.30 |
| Philadelphia Eagles | | | |
| ☐ 61 Walter Barnes | 18.00 | 8.00 | 2.30 |
| Philadelphia Eagles | | | |
| ☐ 62 Bob Perina | 18.00 | 8.00 | 2.30 |
| Baltimore Colts | | | |
| ☐ 63 Bill Wightkin | 18.00 | 8.00 | 2.30 |
| Chicago Bears | | | |
| ☐ 64 Bob Goode | 18.00 | 8.00 | 2.30 |
| Washington Redskins | | | |
| ☐ 65 Al Demao | 18.00 | 8.00 | 2.30 |
| Washington Redskins | | | |
| ☐ 66 Harry Gilmer | 20.00 | 9.00 | 2.50 |
| Washington Redskins | | | |
| ☐ 67 Bill Austin | 18.00 | 8.00 | 2.30 |
| New York Giants | | | |
| ☐ 68 Joe Scott | 18.00 | 8.00 | 2.30 |
| New York Giants | | | |
| ☐ 69 Tex Coulter | 18.00 | 8.00 | 2.30 |
| New York Giants | | | |
| ☐ 70 Paul Salata | 18.00 | 8.00 | 2.30 |
| San Francisco 49ers | | | |
| ☐ 71 Emil Sitko | 20.00 | 9.00 | 2.50 |
| San Francisco 49ers | | | |
| ☐ 72 Bill Johnson | 18.00 | 8.00 | 2.30 |
| San Francisco 49ers | | | |
| ☐ 73 Don Doll | 20.00 | 9.00 | 2.50 |
| Detroit Lions | | | |
| ☐ 74 Dan Sandifer | 18.00 | 8.00 | 2.30 |
| Detroit Lions | | | |
| ☐ 75 John Panelli | 18.00 | 8.00 | 2.30 |
| Detroit Lions | | | |
| ☐ 76 Bill Leonard | 18.00 | 8.00 | 2.30 |
| Baltimore Colts | | | |
| ☐ 77 Bob Kelly | 18.00 | 8.00 | 2.30 |
| Baltimore Colts | | | |
| ☐ 78 Dante Lavelli | 75.00 | 34.00 | 9.50 |
| Cleveland Browns | | | |
| ☐ 79 Tony Adamle | 20.00 | 9.00 | 2.50 |
| Cleveland Browns | | | |
| ☐ 80 Dick Wildung | 18.00 | 8.00 | 2.30 |
| Green Bay Packers | | | |
| ☐ 81 Tobin Rote | 40.00 | 18.00 | 5.00 |
| Green Bay Packers | | | |
| ☐ 82 Paul Burris | 18.00 | 8.00 | 2.30 |
| Green Bay Packers | | | |
| ☐ 83 Lowell Tew | 18.00 | 8.00 | 2.30 |
| New York Yanks | | | |
| ☐ 84 Barney Poole | 18.00 | 8.00 | 2.30 |
| New York Yanks | | | |
| ☐ 85 Fred Naumetz | 18.00 | 8.00 | 2.30 |
| Los Angeles Rams | | | |
| ☐ 86 Dick Hoerner | 18.00 | 8.00 | 2.30 |
| Los Angeles Rams | | | |
| ☐ 87 Bob Reinhard | 18.00 | 8.00 | 2.30 |
| Los Angeles Rams | | | |
| ☐ 88 Howard Hartley | 18.00 | 8.00 | 2.30 |
| Pittsburgh Steelers | | | |
| ☐ 89 Darrell Hogan | 18.00 | 8.00 | 2.30 |
| Pittsburgh Steelers | | | |
| ☐ 90 Jerry Shipkey | 18.00 | 8.00 | 2.30 |
| Pittsburgh Steelers | | | |
| ☐ 91 Frank Tripucka | 25.00 | 11.50 | 3.10 |
| Chicago Cardinals | | | |
| ☐ 92 Garrard Ramsey | 20.00 | 9.00 | 2.50 |
| Chicago Cardinals | | | |
| ☐ 93 Pat Harder | 20.00 | 9.00 | 2.50 |
| Chicago Cardinals | | | |
| ☐ 94 Vic Sears | 18.00 | 8.00 | 2.30 |
| Philadelphia Eagles | | | |
| ☐ 95 Tommy Thompson | 20.00 | 9.00 | 2.50 |
| Philadelphia Eagles | | | |
| ☐ 96 Bucko Kilroy | 20.00 | 9.00 | 2.50 |
| Philadelphia Eagles | | | |
| ☐ 97 George Connor | 30.00 | 13.50 | 3.80 |
| Chicago Bears | | | |
| ☐ 98 Fred Morrison | 18.00 | 8.00 | 2.30 |
| Chicago Bears | | | |
| ☐ 99 Jim Keane | 18.00 | 8.00 | 2.30 |
| Chicago Bears | | | |
| ☐ 100 Sammy Baugh | 150.00 | 70.00 | 19.00 |
| Washington Redskins | | | |
| ☐ 101 Harry Ulinski | 18.00 | 8.00 | 2.30 |
| Washington Redskins | | | |
| ☐ 102 Frank Spaniel | 18.00 | 8.00 | 2.30 |

| | | | |
|---|---|---|---|
| Washington Redskins | | | |
| ☐ 103 Charley Conerly | 60.00 | 27.00 | 7.50 |
| New York Giants | | | |
| ☐ 104 Dick Hensley | 18.00 | 8.00 | 2.30 |
| New York Giants | | | |
| ☐ 105 Eddie Price | 20.00 | 9.00 | 2.50 |
| New York Giants | | | |
| ☐ 106 Ed Carr | 18.00 | 8.00 | 2.30 |
| San Francisco 49ers | | | |
| ☐ 107 Leo Nomellini | 45.00 | 20.00 | 5.75 |
| San Francisco 49ers | | | |
| ☐ 108 Verl Lillywhite | 18.00 | 8.00 | 2.30 |
| San Francisco 49ers | | | |
| ☐ 109 Wallace Triplett | 18.00 | 8.00 | 2.30 |
| Detroit Lions | | | |
| ☐ 110 Joe Watson | 18.00 | 8.00 | 2.30 |
| Detroit Lions | | | |
| ☐ 111 Cloyce Box | 22.00 | 10.00 | 2.80 |
| Detroit Lions | | | |
| ☐ 112 Billy Stone | 18.00 | 8.00 | 2.30 |
| Baltimore Colts | | | |
| ☐ 113 Earl Murray | 18.00 | 8.00 | 2.30 |
| Baltimore Colts | | | |
| ☐ 114 Chet Mutryn | 20.00 | 9.00 | 2.50 |
| Baltimore Colts | | | |
| ☐ 115 Ken Carpenter | 18.00 | 8.00 | 2.30 |
| Cleveland Browns | | | |
| ☐ 116 Lou Rymkus | 22.00 | 10.00 | 2.80 |
| Cleveland Browns | | | |
| ☐ 117 Dub Jones | 30.00 | 13.50 | 3.80 |
| Cleveland Browns | | | |
| ☐ 118 Clayton Tonnemaker | 18.00 | 8.00 | 2.30 |
| Green Bay Packers | | | |
| ☐ 119 Walt Schlinkman | 18.00 | 8.00 | 2.30 |
| Green Bay Packers | | | |
| ☐ 120 Billy Grimes | 18.00 | 8.00 | 2.30 |
| Green Bay Packers | | | |
| ☐ 121 George Ratterman | 27.00 | 12.00 | 3.40 |
| New York Yanks | | | |
| ☐ 122 Bob Mann | 18.00 | 8.00 | 2.30 |
| New York Yanks | | | |
| ☐ 123 Buddy Young | 40.00 | 18.00 | 5.00 |
| New York Yanks | | | |
| ☐ 124 Jack Zilly | 18.00 | 8.00 | 2.30 |
| Los Angeles Rams | | | |
| ☐ 125 Tom Kalmanir | 18.00 | 8.00 | 2.30 |
| Los Angeles Rams | | | |
| ☐ 126 Frank Sinkovitz | 18.00 | 8.00 | 2.30 |
| Pittsburgh Steelers | | | |
| ☐ 127 Elbert Nickel | 18.00 | 8.00 | 2.30 |
| Pittsburgh Steelers | | | |
| ☐ 128 Jim Finks | 35.00 | 16.00 | 4.40 |
| Pittsburgh Steelers | | | |
| ☐ 129 Charley Trippi | 38.00 | 17.00 | 4.70 |
| Chicago Cardinals | | | |
| ☐ 130 Tom Wham | 18.00 | 8.00 | 2.30 |
| Chicago Cardinals | | | |
| ☐ 131 Ventan Yablonski | 18.00 | 8.00 | 2.30 |
| Chicago Cardinals | | | |
| ☐ 132 Chuck Bednarik | 60.00 | 27.00 | 7.50 |
| Philadelphia Eagles | | | |
| ☐ 133 Joe Muha | 18.00 | 8.00 | 2.30 |
| Philadelphia Eagles | | | |
| ☐ 134 Pete Pihos | 35.00 | 16.00 | 4.40 |
| Philadelphia Eagles | | | |
| ☐ 135 Washington Serini | 18.00 | 8.00 | 2.30 |
| Chicago Bears | | | |
| ☐ 136 George Gulyanics | 18.00 | 8.00 | 2.30 |
| Chicago Bears | | | |
| ☐ 137 Ken Kavanaugh | 22.00 | 10.00 | 2.80 |
| Chicago Bears | | | |
| ☐ 138 Howie Livingston | 18.00 | 8.00 | 2.30 |
| Washington Redskins | | | |
| ☐ 139 Joe Tereshinski | 18.00 | 8.00 | 2.30 |
| Washington Redskins | | | |
| ☐ 140 Jim White | 18.00 | 8.00 | 2.30 |
| New York Giants | | | |
| ☐ 141 Gene Roberts | 18.00 | 8.00 | 2.30 |
| New York Giants | | | |
| ☐ 142 William Swiacki | 20.00 | 9.00 | 2.50 |
| New York Giants | | | |
| ☐ 143 Norm Standlee | 20.00 | 9.00 | 2.50 |
| San Francisco 49ers | | | |
| ☐ 144 Knox Ramsey | 45.00 | 9.00 | 2.70 |
| Chicago Cardinals | | | |

# 1951 Bowman

The 1951 Bowman set of 144 numbered cards witnessed an increase in card size from previous Bowman football sets. The cards were enlarged from the previous year to 2 1/16" by 3 1/8". The 144-card set is very similar in format to the baseball card set of that year. The card backs are printed in maroon and blue on gray card stock. The set features the "Rookie cards" of Tom Landry, Emlen Tunnell, and Norm Van Brocklin. The Bill Walsh in this set went to Notre Dame and is not

the Bill Walsh who coached the San Francisco 49ers in the 1980s. The set numbering is arranged so that two, three, or four players from the same team are numbered together in sequence.

|  | NRMT | VG-E | GOOD |
|---|---|---|---|
| COMPLETE SET (144) | 3300.00 | 1500.00 | 425.00 |
| COMMON PLAYER (1-144) | 16.00 | 7.25 | 2.00 |

| | NRMT | VG-E | GOOD |
|---|---|---|---|
| ☐ 1 Weldon Humble | 50.00 | 10.00 | 3.00 |
| Cleveland Browns | | | |
| ☐ 2 Otto Graham | 125.00 | 57.50 | 15.50 |
| Cleveland Browns | | | |
| ☐ 3 Mac Speedie | 20.00 | 9.00 | 2.50 |
| Cleveland Browns | | | |
| ☐ 4 Norm Van Brocklin | 210.00 | 95.00 | 26.00 |
| Los Angeles Rams | | | |
| ☐ 5 Woodley Lewis | 20.00 | 9.00 | 2.50 |
| Los Angeles Rams | | | |
| ☐ 6 Tom Fears | 35.00 | 16.00 | 4.40 |
| Los Angeles Rams | | | |
| ☐ 7 George Musacco | 16.00 | 7.25 | 2.00 |
| New York Yanks | | | |
| ☐ 8 George Taliaferro | 18.00 | 8.00 | 2.30 |
| New York Yanks | | | |
| ☐ 9 Barney Poole | 16.00 | 7.25 | 2.00 |
| New York Yanks | | | |
| ☐ 10 Steve Van Buren | 45.00 | 20.00 | 5.75 |
| Philadelphia Eagles | | | |
| ☐ 11 Whitey Wistert | 18.00 | 8.00 | 2.30 |
| Philadelphia Eagles | | | |
| ☐ 12 Chuck Bednarik | 45.00 | 20.00 | 5.75 |
| Philadelphia Eagles | | | |
| ☐ 13 Bulldog Turner | 32.00 | 14.50 | 4.00 |
| Chicago Bears | | | |
| ☐ 14 Bob Williams | 16.00 | 7.25 | 2.00 |
| Chicago Bears | | | |
| ☐ 15 John Lujack | 45.00 | 20.00 | 5.75 |
| Chicago Bears | | | |
| ☐ 16 Roy Rebel Steiner | 16.00 | 7.25 | 2.00 |
| Green Bay Packers | | | |
| ☐ 17 Earl Jug Girard | 16.00 | 7.25 | 2.00 |
| Green Bay Packers | | | |
| ☐ 18 Bill Neal | 16.00 | 7.25 | 2.00 |
| Green Bay Packers | | | |
| ☐ 19 Travis Tidwell | 16.00 | 7.25 | 2.00 |
| New York Giants | | | |
| ☐ 20 Tom Landry | 500.00 | 230.00 | 65.00 |
| New York Giants | | | |
| ☐ 21 Arnie Weinmeister | 45.00 | 20.00 | 5.75 |
| New York Giants | | | |
| ☐ 22 Joe Geri | 16.00 | 7.25 | 2.00 |
| Pittsburgh Steelers | | | |
| ☐ 23 Bill Walsh | 25.00 | 11.50 | 3.10 |
| Pittsburgh Steelers | | | |
| ☐ 24 Fran Rogel | 16.00 | 7.25 | 2.00 |
| Pittsburgh Steelers | | | |
| ☐ 25 Doak Walker | 45.00 | 20.00 | 5.75 |
| Detroit Lions | | | |
| ☐ 26 Leon Hart | 22.00 | 10.00 | 2.80 |
| Detroit Lions | | | |
| ☐ 27 Thurman McGraw | 16.00 | 7.25 | 2.00 |
| Detroit Lions | | | |
| ☐ 28 Buster Ramsey | 18.00 | 8.00 | 2.30 |
| Chicago Cardinals | | | |
| ☐ 29 Frank Tripucka | 20.00 | 9.00 | 2.50 |
| Chicago Cardinals | | | |
| ☐ 30 Don Paul | 16.00 | 7.25 | 2.00 |
| Chicago Cardinals | | | |
| ☐ 31 Alex Loyd | 16.00 | 7.25 | 2.00 |
| San Francisco 49ers | | | |
| ☐ 32 Y.A. Tittle | 100.00 | 45.00 | 12.50 |
| San Francisco 49ers | | | |
| ☐ 33 Verl Lillywhite | 16.00 | 7.25 | 2.00 |
| San Francisco 49ers | | | |
| ☐ 34 Sammy Baugh | 125.00 | 57.50 | 15.50 |
| Washington Redskins | | | |
| ☐ 35 Chuck Drazenovich | 16.00 | 7.25 | 2.00 |

| | | | |
|---|---|---|---|
| Washington Redskins | | | |
| ☐ 36 Bob Goode | 16.00 | 7.25 | 2.00 |
| Washington Redskins | | | |
| ☐ 37 Horace Gillom | 16.00 | 7.25 | 2.00 |
| Cleveland Browns | | | |
| ☐ 38 Lou Rymkus | 18.00 | 8.00 | 2.30 |
| Cleveland Browns | | | |
| ☐ 39 Ken Carpenter | 16.00 | 7.25 | 2.00 |
| Cleveland Browns | | | |
| ☐ 40 Bob Waterfield | 55.00 | 25.00 | 7.00 |
| Los Angeles Rams | | | |
| ☐ 41 Vitamin Smith | 16.00 | 7.25 | 2.00 |
| Los Angeles Rams | | | |
| ☐ 42 Glenn Army Davis | 45.00 | 20.00 | 5.75 |
| Los Angeles Rams | | | |
| ☐ 43 Dan Edwards | 16.00 | 7.25 | 2.00 |
| New York Yanks | | | |
| ☐ 44 John Rauch | 16.00 | 7.25 | 2.00 |
| New York Yanks | | | |
| ☐ 45 Zollie Toth | 16.00 | 7.25 | 2.00 |
| New York Yanks | | | |
| ☐ 46 Pete Pihos | 30.00 | 13.50 | 3.80 |
| Philadelphia Eagles | | | |
| ☐ 47 Russ Craft | 16.00 | 7.25 | 2.00 |
| Philadelphia Eagles | | | |
| ☐ 48 Walter Barnes | 16.00 | 7.25 | 2.00 |
| Philadelphia Eagles | | | |
| ☐ 49 Fred Morrison | 16.00 | 7.25 | 2.00 |
| Chicago Bears | | | |
| ☐ 50 Ray Bray | 16.00 | 7.25 | 2.00 |
| Chicago Bears | | | |
| ☐ 51 Ed Sprinkle | 22.00 | 10.00 | 2.80 |
| Chicago Bears | | | |
| ☐ 52 Floyd Reid | 16.00 | 7.25 | 2.00 |
| Green Bay Packers | | | |
| ☐ 53 Billy Grimes | 16.00 | 7.25 | 2.00 |
| Green Bay Packers | | | |
| ☐ 54 Ted Fritsch Sr. | 18.00 | 8.00 | 2.30 |
| Green Bay Packers | | | |
| ☐ 55 Al DeRogatis | 18.00 | 8.00 | 2.30 |
| New York Giants | | | |
| ☐ 56 Charley Conerly | 45.00 | 20.00 | 5.75 |
| New York Giants | | | |
| ☐ 57 Jon Baker | 16.00 | 7.25 | 2.00 |
| New York Giants | | | |
| ☐ 58 Tom McWilliams | 16.00 | 7.25 | 2.00 |
| Pittsburgh Steelers | | | |
| ☐ 59 Jerry Shipkey | 16.00 | 7.25 | 2.00 |
| Pittsburgh Steelers | | | |
| ☐ 60 Lynn Chandnois | 16.00 | 7.25 | 2.00 |
| Pittsburgh Steelers | | | |
| ☐ 61 Don Doll | 18.00 | 8.00 | 2.30 |
| Detroit Lions | | | |
| ☐ 62 Lou Creekmur | 22.00 | 10.00 | 2.80 |
| Detroit Lions | | | |
| ☐ 63 Bob Hoernschemeyer | 18.00 | 8.00 | 2.30 |
| Detroit Lions | | | |
| ☐ 64 Tom Wham | 16.00 | 7.25 | 2.00 |
| Chicago Cardinals | | | |
| ☐ 65 Bill Fischer | 16.00 | 7.25 | 2.00 |
| Chicago Cardinals | | | |
| ☐ 66 Robert Nussbaumer | 16.00 | 7.25 | 2.00 |
| Green Bay Packers | | | |
| ☐ 67 Gordon Soltau | 16.00 | 7.25 | 2.00 |
| San Francisco 49ers | | | |
| ☐ 68 Visco Grgich | 16.00 | 7.25 | 2.00 |
| San Francisco 49ers | | | |
| ☐ 69 John Strzykalski | 16.00 | 7.25 | 2.00 |
| San Francisco 49ers | | | |
| ☐ 70 Pete Stout | 16.00 | 7.25 | 2.00 |
| Washington Redskins | | | |
| ☐ 71 Paul Lipscomb | 16.00 | 7.25 | 2.00 |
| Washington Redskins | | | |
| ☐ 72 Harry Gilmer | 18.00 | 8.00 | 2.30 |
| Washington Redskins | | | |
| ☐ 73 Dante Lavelli | 35.00 | 16.00 | 4.40 |
| Cleveland Browns | | | |
| ☐ 74 Dub Jones | 18.00 | 8.00 | 2.30 |
| Cleveland Browns | | | |
| ☐ 75 Lou Groza | 75.00 | 34.00 | 9.50 |
| Cleveland Browns | | | |
| ☐ 76 Elroy Hirsch | 60.00 | 27.00 | 7.50 |
| Los Angeles Rams | | | |
| ☐ 77 Tom Kalmanir | 16.00 | 7.25 | 2.00 |
| Los Angeles Rams | | | |
| ☐ 78 Jack Zilly | 16.00 | 7.25 | 2.00 |
| Los Angeles Rams | | | |
| ☐ 79 Bruce Alford | 16.00 | 7.25 | 2.00 |
| New York Yanks | | | |
| ☐ 80 Art Weiner | 16.00 | 7.25 | 2.00 |
| New York Yanks | | | |
| ☐ 81 Brad Ecklund | 16.00 | 7.25 | 2.00 |
| New York Yanks | | | |
| ☐ 82 Bosh Pritchard | 16.00 | 7.25 | 2.00 |
| Philadelphia Eagles | | | |
| ☐ 83 John Green | 16.00 | 7.25 | 2.00 |
| Philadelphia Eagles | | | |
| ☐ 84 H. Ebert Van Buren | 16.00 | 7.25 | 2.00 |

| | | | |
|---|---|---|---|
| Philadelphia Eagles | | | |
| ☐ 85 Julie Rykovich | 16.00 | 7.25 | 2.00 |
| Chicago Bears | | | |
| ☐ 86 Fred Davis | 16.00 | 7.25 | 2.00 |
| Chicago Bears | | | |
| ☐ 87 John Hoffman | 16.00 | 7.25 | 2.00 |
| Chicago Bears | | | |
| ☐ 88 Tobin Rote | 22.00 | 10.00 | 2.80 |
| Green Bay Packers | | | |
| ☐ 89 Paul Burris | 16.00 | 7.25 | 2.00 |
| Green Bay Packers | | | |
| ☐ 90 Tony Canadeo | 27.00 | 12.00 | 3.40 |
| Green Bay Packers | | | |
| ☐ 91 Emlen Tunnell | 80.00 | 36.00 | 10.00 |
| New York Giants | | | |
| ☐ 92 Otto Schnellbacher | 20.00 | 9.00 | 2.50 |
| New York Giants | | | |
| ☐ 93 Ray Poole | 16.00 | 7.25 | 2.00 |
| New York Giants | | | |
| ☐ 94 Darrell Hogan | 16.00 | 7.25 | 2.00 |
| Pittsburgh Steelers | | | |
| ☐ 95 Frank Sinkovitz | 16.00 | 7.25 | 2.00 |
| Pittsburgh Steelers | | | |
| ☐ 96 Ernie Stautner | 70.00 | 32.00 | 8.75 |
| Pittsburgh Steelers | | | |
| ☐ 97 Elmer Angsman | 16.00 | 7.25 | 2.00 |
| Chicago Cardinals | | | |
| ☐ 98 Jack Jennings | 16.00 | 7.25 | 2.00 |
| Chicago Cardinals | | | |
| ☐ 99 Jerry Groom | 16.00 | 7.25 | 2.00 |
| Chicago Cardinals | | | |
| ☐ 100 John Prchlik | 16.00 | 7.25 | 2.00 |
| Detroit Lions | | | |
| ☐ 101 J. Robert Smith | 18.00 | 8.00 | 2.30 |
| Detroit Lions | | | |
| ☐ 102 Bobby Layne | 90.00 | 40.00 | 11.50 |
| Detroit Lions | | | |
| ☐ 103 Frankie Albert | 22.00 | 10.00 | 2.80 |
| San Francisco 49ers | | | |
| ☐ 104 Gail Bruce | 16.00 | 7.25 | 2.00 |
| San Francisco 49ers | | | |
| ☐ 105 Joe Perry | 60.00 | 27.00 | 7.50 |
| San Francisco 49ers | | | |
| ☐ 106 Leon Heath | 16.00 | 7.25 | 2.00 |
| Washington Redskins | | | |
| ☐ 107 Ed Quirk | 16.00 | 7.25 | 2.00 |
| Washington Redskins | | | |
| ☐ 108 Hugh Taylor | 18.00 | 8.00 | 2.30 |
| Washington Redskins | | | |
| ☐ 109 Marion Motley | 45.00 | 20.00 | 5.75 |
| Cleveland Browns | | | |
| ☐ 110 Tony Adamle | 16.00 | 7.25 | 2.00 |
| Cleveland Browns | | | |
| ☐ 111 Alex Agase | 18.00 | 8.00 | 2.30 |
| Cleveland Browns | | | |
| ☐ 112 Tank Younger | 22.00 | 10.00 | 2.80 |
| Los Angeles Rams | | | |
| ☐ 113 Bob Boyd | 16.00 | 7.25 | 2.00 |
| Los Angeles Rams | | | |
| ☐ 114 Jerry Williams | 16.00 | 7.25 | 2.00 |
| Los Angeles Rams | | | |
| ☐ 115 Joe Golding | 16.00 | 7.25 | 2.00 |
| New York Yanks | | | |
| ☐ 116 Sherman Howard | 16.00 | 7.25 | 2.00 |
| New York Yanks | | | |
| ☐ 117 John Wozniak | 16.00 | 7.25 | 2.00 |
| New York Yanks | | | |
| ☐ 118 Frank Reagan | 16.00 | 7.25 | 2.00 |
| Philadelphia Eagles | | | |
| ☐ 119 Vic Sears | 16.00 | 7.25 | 2.00 |
| Philadelphia Eagles | | | |
| ☐ 120 Clyde Scott | 16.00 | 7.25 | 2.00 |
| Philadelphia Eagles | | | |
| ☐ 121 George Gulyanics | 16.00 | 7.25 | 2.00 |
| Chicago Bears | | | |
| ☐ 122 Bill Wightkin | 16.00 | 7.25 | 2.00 |
| Chicago Bears | | | |
| ☐ 123 Chuck Hunsinger | 16.00 | 7.25 | 2.00 |
| Chicago Bears | | | |
| ☐ 124 Jack Cloud | 16.00 | 7.25 | 2.00 |
| Green Bay Packers | | | |
| ☐ 125 Abner Wimberly | 16.00 | 7.25 | 2.00 |
| Green Bay Packers | | | |
| ☐ 126 Dick Wildung | 16.00 | 7.25 | 2.00 |
| Green Bay Packers | | | |
| ☐ 127 Eddie Price | 16.00 | 7.25 | 2.00 |
| New York Giants | | | |
| ☐ 128 Joe Scott | 16.00 | 7.25 | 2.00 |
| New York Giants | | | |
| ☐ 129 Jerry Nuzum | 16.00 | 7.25 | 2.00 |
| Pittsburgh Steelers | | | |
| ☐ 130 Jim Finks | 20.00 | 9.00 | 2.50 |
| Pittsburgh Steelers | | | |
| ☐ 131 Bob Gage | 16.00 | 7.25 | 2.00 |
| Pittsburgh Steelers | | | |
| ☐ 132 William Swiacki | 18.00 | 8.00 | 2.30 |
| Detroit Lions | | | |
| ☐ 133 Joe Watson | 16.00 | 7.25 | 2.00 |

| | | | |
|---|---|---|---|
| Detroit Lions | | | |
| ☐ 134 Ollie Cline | 16.00 | 7.25 | 2.00 |
| Detroit Lions | | | |
| ☐ 135 Jack Lininger | 16.00 | 7.25 | 2.00 |
| Detroit Lions | | | |
| ☐ 136 Fran Polsfoot | 16.00 | 7.25 | 2.00 |
| Chicago Cardinals | | | |
| ☐ 137 Charley Trippi | 35.00 | 16.00 | 4.40 |
| Chicago Cardinals | | | |
| ☐ 138 Ventan Yablonski | 16.00 | 7.25 | 2.00 |
| Chicago Cardinals | | | |
| ☐ 139 Emil Sitko | 18.00 | 8.00 | 2.30 |
| Chicago Cardinals | | | |
| ☐ 140 Leo Nomellini | 38.00 | 17.00 | 4.70 |
| San Francisco 49ers | | | |
| ☐ 141 Norm Standlee | 16.00 | 7.25 | 2.00 |
| San Francisco 49ers | | | |
| ☐ 142 Eddie Saenz | 16.00 | 7.25 | 2.00 |
| Washington Redskins | | | |
| ☐ 143 Al Demao | 16.00 | 7.25 | 2.00 |
| Washington Redskins | | | |
| ☐ 144 Bill Dudley | 60.00 | 15.00 | 4.80 |
| Washington Redskins | | | |

## 1952 Bowman Large

The 1952 Bowman set contains 144 numbered cards, each of both a small and large size. The small cards measure 2 1/16" by 3 1/8" whereas the large cards measure 2 1/2" by 3 3/4". The fronts and backs of both sets are identical except for size. The checklist below lists prices for the "large" set. Certain numbers were systematically printed in lesser quantities due to the fact that Bowman apparently could not fit all the cards in the series (of 72) on one sheet; the affected numbers are those which are divisible by nine and those which are "one more" than those divisible by nine. These shorter-printed (lesser quantity produced) cards are marked in the checklist below by SP. The set features the "Rookie Cards" of Paul Brown, Jack Christiansen, Art Donovan, Frank Gifford, George Halas, Yale Lary, Gino Marchetti, Ollie Matson, Hugh McElhenny, and Andy Robustelli. The last card in the set, No. 144 Jim Lansford, is among the toughest football cards to acquire. It is generally accepted among hobbyists that the card was located at the bottom right corner of the production sheet and was subject to much abuse including numerous poor cuts. The problem was such that many cards never made it out of the factory as they were discarded.

| | NRMT | VG-E | GOOD |
|---|---|---|---|
| COMPLETE SET (144) | 12000. | 5400. | 1500. |
| COMMON PLAYER (1-72) | 25.00 | 11.50 | 3.10 |
| COMMON PLAYER (73-144) | 40.00 | 18.00 | 5.00 |
| | | | |
| ☐ 1 Norm Van Brocklin | 350.00 | 105.00 | 35.00 |
| Los Angeles Rams | | | |
| ☐ 2 Otto Graham | 200.00 | 90.00 | 25.00 |
| Cleveland Browns | | | |
| ☐ 3 Doak Walker | 60.00 | 27.00 | 7.50 |
| Detroit Lions | | | |
| ☐ 4 Steve Owen CO | 50.00 | 23.00 | 6.25 |
| New York Giants | | | |
| ☐ 5 Frankie Albert | 32.00 | 14.50 | 4.00 |
| San Francisco 49ers | | | |
| ☐ 6 Laurie Niemi | 25.00 | 11.50 | 3.10 |
| Washington Redskins | | | |
| ☐ 7 Chuck Hunsinger | 25.00 | 11.50 | 3.10 |
| Chicago Bears | | | |
| ☐ 8 Ed Modzelewski | 27.50 | 12.50 | 3.40 |
| Pittsburgh Steelers | | | |
| ☐ 9 Joe Spencer SP | 60.00 | 27.00 | 7.50 |
| Green Bay Packers | | | |
| ☐ 10 Chuck Bednarik SP | 125.00 | 57.50 | 15.50 |
| Philadelphia Eagles | | | |
| ☐ 11 Barney Poole | 25.00 | 11.50 | 3.10 |

| No. / Player | | | |
|---|---|---|---|
| Dallas Texans | | | |
| ☐ 12 Charley Trippi | 50.00 | 23.00 | 6.25 |
| Chicago Cardinals | | | |
| ☐ 13 Tom Fears | 50.00 | 23.00 | 6.25 |
| Los Angeles Rams | | | |
| ☐ 14 Paul Brown CO | 135.00 | 60.00 | 17.00 |
| Cleveland Browns | | | |
| ☐ 15 Leon Hart | 32.00 | 14.50 | 4.00 |
| Detroit Lions | | | |
| ☐ 16 Frank Gifford | 500.00 | 230.00 | 65.00 |
| New York Giants | | | |
| ☐ 17 Y.A. Tittle | 125.00 | 57.50 | 15.50 |
| San Francisco 49ers | | | |
| ☐ 18 Charlie Justice SP | 150.00 | 70.00 | 19.00 |
| Washington Redskins | | | |
| ☐ 19 George Connor SP | 85.00 | 38.00 | 10.50 |
| Chicago Bears | | | |
| ☐ 20 Lynn Chandnois | 25.00 | 11.50 | 3.10 |
| Pittsburgh Steelers | | | |
| ☐ 21 Bill Howton | 40.00 | 18.00 | 5.00 |
| Green Bay Packers | | | |
| ☐ 22 Kenneth Snyder | 25.00 | 11.50 | 3.10 |
| Philadelphia Eagles | | | |
| ☐ 23 Gino Marchetti | 135.00 | 60.00 | 17.00 |
| Dallas Texans | | | |
| ☐ 24 John Karras | 25.00 | 11.50 | 3.10 |
| Chicago Cardinals | | | |
| ☐ 25 Tank Younger | 30.00 | 13.50 | 3.80 |
| Los Angeles Rams | | | |
| ☐ 26 Tommy Thompson | 30.00 | 13.50 | 3.80 |
| Cleveland Browns | | | |
| ☐ 27 Bob Miller SP | 250.00 | 115.00 | 31.00 |
| Detroit Lions | | | |
| ☐ 28 Kyle Rote SP | 150.00 | 70.00 | 19.00 |
| New York Giants | | | |
| ☐ 29 Hugh McElhenny | 175.00 | 80.00 | 22.00 |
| San Francisco 49ers | | | |
| ☐ 30 Sammy Baugh | 300.00 | 135.00 | 38.00 |
| Washington Redskins | | | |
| ☐ 31 Jim Dooley | 35.00 | 16.00 | 4.40 |
| Chicago Bears | | | |
| ☐ 32 Ray Mathews | 25.00 | 11.50 | 3.10 |
| Pittsburgh Steelers | | | |
| ☐ 33 Fred Cone | 27.50 | 12.50 | 3.40 |
| Green Bay Packers | | | |
| ☐ 34 Al Pollard | 25.00 | 11.50 | 3.10 |
| Philadelphia Eagles | | | |
| ☐ 35 Brad Ecklund | 25.00 | 11.50 | 3.10 |
| Dallas Texans | | | |
| ☐ 36 John Lee Hancock SP | 250.00 | 115.00 | 31.00 |
| Chicago Cardinals | | | |
| ☐ 37 Elroy Hirsch SP | 125.00 | 57.50 | 15.50 |
| Los Angeles Rams | | | |
| ☐ 38 Keever Jankovich | 25.00 | 11.50 | 3.10 |
| Cleveland Browns | | | |
| ☐ 39 Emlen Tunnell | 60.00 | 27.00 | 7.50 |
| New York Giants | | | |
| ☐ 40 Steve Dowden | 25.00 | 11.50 | 3.10 |
| Green Bay Packers | | | |
| ☐ 41 Claude Hipps | 25.00 | 11.50 | 3.10 |
| Pittsburgh Steelers | | | |
| ☐ 42 Norm Standlee | 25.00 | 11.50 | 3.10 |
| San Francisco 49ers | | | |
| ☐ 43 Dick Todd CO | 25.00 | 11.50 | 3.10 |
| Washington Redskins | | | |
| ☐ 44 Babe Parilli | 35.00 | 16.00 | 4.40 |
| Green Bay Packers | | | |
| ☐ 45 Steve Van Buren SP | 185.00 | 85.00 | 23.00 |
| Philadelphia Eagles | | | |
| ☐ 46 Art Donovan SP | 225.00 | 100.00 | 28.00 |
| Dallas Texans | | | |
| ☐ 47 Bill Fischer | 25.00 | 11.50 | 3.10 |
| Chicago Cardinals | | | |
| ☐ 48 George Halas CO | 175.00 | 80.00 | 22.00 |
| Chicago Bears | | | |
| ☐ 49 Jerrell Price | 25.00 | 11.50 | 3.10 |
| Chicago Cardinals | | | |
| ☐ 50 John Sandusky | 30.00 | 13.50 | 3.80 |
| Cleveland Browns | | | |
| ☐ 51 Ray Beck | 25.00 | 11.50 | 3.10 |
| New York Giants | | | |
| ☐ 52 Jim Martin | 27.50 | 12.50 | 3.40 |
| Detroit Lions | | | |
| ☐ 53 Joe Bach CO UER | 25.00 | 11.50 | 3.10 |
| (Misspelled Back) | | | |
| Pittsburgh Steelers | | | |
| ☐ 54 Glen Christian SP | 60.00 | 27.00 | 7.50 |
| San Francisco 49ers | | | |
| ☐ 55 Andy Davis SP | 60.00 | 27.00 | 7.50 |
| Washington Redskins | | | |
| ☐ 56 Tobin Rote | 30.00 | 13.50 | 3.80 |
| Green Bay Packers | | | |
| ☐ 57 Wayne Millner CO | 70.00 | 32.00 | 8.75 |
| Philadelphia Eagles | | | |
| ☐ 58 Zollie Toth | 25.00 | 11.50 | 3.10 |
| Dallas Texans | | | |
| ☐ 59 Jack Jennings | 25.00 | 11.50 | 3.10 |
| Chicago Cardinals | | | |
| ☐ 60 Bill McColl | 25.00 | 11.50 | 3.10 |
| Chicago Bears | | | |
| ☐ 61 Les Richter | 30.00 | 13.50 | 3.80 |
| Los Angeles Rams | | | |
| ☐ 62 Walt Michaels | 35.00 | 16.00 | 4.40 |
| Cleveland Browns | | | |
| ☐ 63 Charley Conerly SP | 425.00 | 190.00 | 52.50 |
| New York Giants | | | |
| ☐ 64 Howard Hartley SP | 60.00 | 27.00 | 7.50 |
| Pittsburgh Steelers | | | |
| ☐ 65 Jerome Smith | 25.00 | 11.50 | 3.10 |
| San Francisco 49ers | | | |
| ☐ 66 James Clark | 25.00 | 11.50 | 3.10 |
| Washington Redskins | | | |
| ☐ 67 Dick Logan | 25.00 | 11.50 | 3.10 |
| Cleveland Browns | | | |
| ☐ 68 Wayne Robinson | 25.00 | 11.50 | 3.10 |
| Philadelphia Eagles | | | |
| ☐ 69 James Hammond | 25.00 | 11.50 | 3.10 |
| Dallas Texans | | | |
| ☐ 70 Gene Schroeder | 25.00 | 11.50 | 3.10 |
| Chicago Bears | | | |
| ☐ 71 Tex Coulter | 25.00 | 11.50 | 3.10 |
| New York Giants | | | |
| ☐ 72 John Schweder SP | 350.00 | 160.00 | 45.00 |
| Pittsburgh Steelers | | | |
| ☐ 73 Vitamin Smith SP | 100.00 | 45.00 | 12.50 |
| Los Angeles Rams | | | |
| ☐ 74 Joe Campanella | 40.00 | 18.00 | 5.00 |
| Cleveland Browns | | | |
| ☐ 75 Joe Kuharich CO | 45.00 | 20.00 | 5.75 |
| Chicago Cardinals | | | |
| ☐ 76 Herman Clark | 40.00 | 18.00 | 5.00 |
| Chicago Bears | | | |
| ☐ 77 Dan Edwards | 40.00 | 18.00 | 5.00 |
| Dallas Texans | | | |
| ☐ 78 Bobby Layne | 150.00 | 70.00 | 19.00 |
| Detroit Lions | | | |
| ☐ 79 Bob Hoernschemeyer | 42.50 | 19.00 | 5.25 |
| Detroit Lions | | | |
| ☐ 80 John Carr Blount | 40.00 | 18.00 | 5.00 |
| Philadelphia Eagles | | | |
| ☐ 81 John Kastan SP | 100.00 | 45.00 | 12.50 |
| New York Giants | | | |
| ☐ 82 Harry Minarik SP | 125.00 | 57.50 | 15.50 |
| Pittsburgh Steelers | | | |
| ☐ 83 Joe Perry | 80.00 | 36.00 | 10.00 |
| San Francisco 49ers | | | |
| ☐ 84 Ray(Buddy) Parker CO | 45.00 | 20.00 | 5.75 |
| Detroit Lions | | | |
| ☐ 85 Andy Robustelli | 160.00 | 70.00 | 20.00 |
| Los Angeles Rams | | | |
| ☐ 86 Dub Jones | 40.00 | 18.00 | 5.00 |
| Cleveland Browns | | | |
| ☐ 87 Mal Cook | 40.00 | 18.00 | 5.00 |
| Chicago Cardinals | | | |
| ☐ 88 Billy Stone | 40.00 | 18.00 | 5.00 |
| Chicago Bears | | | |
| ☐ 89 George Taliaferro | 42.50 | 19.00 | 5.25 |
| Dallas Texans | | | |
| ☐ 90 Thomas Johnson SP | 100.00 | 45.00 | 12.50 |
| Green Bay Packers | | | |
| ☐ 91 Leon Heath SP | 80.00 | 36.00 | 10.00 |
| Washington Redskins | | | |
| ☐ 92 Pete Pihos | 55.00 | 25.00 | 7.00 |
| Philadelphia Eagles | | | |
| ☐ 93 Fred Benners | 40.00 | 18.00 | 5.00 |
| New York Giants | | | |
| ☐ 94 George Tarasovic | 40.00 | 18.00 | 5.00 |
| Pittsburgh Steelers | | | |
| ☐ 95 Lawr. (Buck) Shaw CO | 40.00 | 18.00 | 5.00 |
| San Francisco 49ers | | | |
| ☐ 96 Bill Wightkin | 40.00 | 18.00 | 5.00 |
| Chicago Bears | | | |
| ☐ 97 John Wozniak | 40.00 | 18.00 | 5.00 |
| Dallas Texans | | | |
| ☐ 98 Bobby Dillon | 45.00 | 20.00 | 5.75 |
| Green Bay Packers | | | |
| ☐ 99 Joe Stydahar CO SP | 450.00 | 200.00 | 57.50 |
| Los Angeles Rams | | | |
| ☐ 100 Dick Alban SP | 100.00 | 45.00 | 12.50 |
| Washington Redskins | | | |
| ☐ 101 Arnie Weinmeister | 55.00 | 25.00 | 7.00 |
| New York Giants | | | |
| ☐ 102 Robert Joe Cross | 40.00 | 18.00 | 5.00 |
| Chicago Bears | | | |
| ☐ 103 Don Paul | 40.00 | 18.00 | 5.00 |
| Chicago Cardinals | | | |
| ☐ 104 Buddy Young | 45.00 | 20.00 | 5.75 |
| Dallas Texans | | | |
| ☐ 105 Lou Groza | 100.00 | 45.00 | 12.50 |
| Cleveland Browns | | | |
| ☐ 106 Ray Pelfrey | 40.00 | 18.00 | 5.00 |
| Green Bay Packers | | | |
| ☐ 107 Maurice Nipp | 40.00 | 18.00 | 5.00 |
| Philadelphia Eagles | | | |
| ☐ 108 Hubert Johnston SP | 375.00 | 170.00 | 47.50 |

| | | NRMT | VG-E | GOOD |
|---|---|---|---|---|
| ☐ 109 | Volney Quinlan SP | 80.00 | 36.00 | 10.00 |
| | Washington Redskins | | | |
| ☐ 110 | Jack Simmons | 40.00 | 18.00 | 5.00 |
| | Los Angeles Rams | | | |
| ☐ 111 | George Ratterman | 42.50 | 19.00 | 5.25 |
| | Chicago Cardinals | | | |
| ☐ 112 | John Badaczewski | 40.00 | 18.00 | 5.00 |
| | Cleveland Browns | | | |
| ☐ 113 | Bill Reichardt | 40.00 | 18.00 | 5.00 |
| | Washington Redskins | | | |
| ☐ 114 | Art Weiner | 40.00 | 18.00 | 5.00 |
| | Green Bay Packers | | | |
| ☐ 115 | Keith Flowers | 40.00 | 18.00 | 5.00 |
| | Dallas Texans | | | |
| ☐ 116 | Russ Craft | 40.00 | 18.00 | 5.00 |
| | Detroit Lions | | | |
| ☐ 117 | Jim O'Donahue SP | 100.00 | 45.00 | 12.50 |
| | Philadelphia Eagles | | | |
| ☐ 118 | Darrell Hogan SP | 80.00 | 36.00 | 10.00 |
| | San Francisco 49ers | | | |
| ☐ 119 | Frank Ziegler | 40.00 | 18.00 | 5.00 |
| | Pittsburgh Steelers | | | |
| ☐ 120 | Deacon Dan Towler | 45.00 | 20.00 | 5.75 |
| | Philadelphia Eagles | | | |
| ☐ 121 | Fred Williams | 40.00 | 18.00 | 5.00 |
| | Los Angeles Rams | | | |
| ☐ 122 | Jimmy Phelan CO | 40.00 | 18.00 | 5.00 |
| | Chicago Bears | | | |
| ☐ 123 | Eddie Price | 40.00 | 18.00 | 5.00 |
| | Dallas Texans | | | |
| ☐ 124 | Chet Ostrowski | 40.00 | 18.00 | 5.00 |
| | New York Giants | | | |
| ☐ 125 | Leo Nomellini | 60.00 | 27.00 | 7.50 |
| | Washington Redskins | | | |
| ☐ 126 | Steve Romanik SP | 300.00 | 135.00 | 38.00 |
| | San Francisco 49ers | | | |
| ☐ 127 | Ollie Matson SP | 250.00 | 115.00 | 31.00 |
| | Chicago Bears | | | |
| ☐ 128 | Dante Lavelli | 60.00 | 27.00 | 7.50 |
| | Chicago Cardinals | | | |
| ☐ 129 | Jack Christiansen | 135.00 | 60.00 | 17.00 |
| | Cleveland Browns | | | |
| ☐ 130 | Dom Moselle | 40.00 | 18.00 | 5.00 |
| | Detroit Lions | | | |
| ☐ 131 | John Rapacz | 40.00 | 18.00 | 5.00 |
| | Green Bay Packers | | | |
| ☐ 132 | Chuck Ortman UER | 40.00 | 18.00 | 5.00 |
| | (Avg. gain 9.4, should be 4.8) New York Giants | | | |
| ☐ 133 | Bob Williams | 40.00 | 18.00 | 5.00 |
| | Pittsburgh Steelers | | | |
| ☐ 134 | Chuck Ulrich | 40.00 | 18.00 | 5.00 |
| | Chicago Bears | | | |
| ☐ 135 | Gene Ronzani CO SP | 400.00 | 180.00 | 50.00 |
| | Chicago Cardinals | | | |
| ☐ 136 | Bert Rechichar SP | 80.00 | 36.00 | 10.00 |
| | Green Bay Packers | | | |
| ☐ 137 | Bob Waterfield | 100.00 | 45.00 | 12.50 |
| | Cleveland Browns | | | |
| ☐ 138 | Bobby Walston | 45.00 | 20.00 | 5.75 |
| | Los Angeles Rams | | | |
| ☐ 139 | Jerry Shipkey | 40.00 | 18.00 | 5.00 |
| | Philadelphia Eagles | | | |
| ☐ 140 | Yale Lary | 135.00 | 60.00 | 17.00 |
| | Pittsburgh Steelers | | | |
| ☐ 141 | Gordon Soltau | 40.00 | 18.00 | 5.00 |
| | Detroit Lions | | | |
| ☐ 142 | Tom Landry | 525.00 | 240.00 | 65.00 |
| | San Francisco 49ers | | | |
| ☐ 143 | John Papit | 40.00 | 18.00 | 5.00 |
| | New York Giants | | | |
| ☐ 144 | Jim Lansford SP | 2000.00 | 600.00 | 200.00 |
| | Washington Redskins | | | |
| | Dallas Texans | | | |

## 1952 Bowman Small

The 1952 Bowman set contains 144 numbered cards, each of both a small and large size. The small cards measure approximately 2 1/16" by 3 1/8" whereas the large cards measure 2 1/2" by 3 3/4". The fronts and backs of both sets are identical except for size. The checklist below lists prices for the "small" set. The set features the "Rookie cards" of Paul Brown, Jack Christiansen, Art Donovan, Frank Gifford, George Halas, Yale Lary, Gino Marchetti, Ollie Matson, Hugh McElhenny, and Andy Robustelli.

| | NRMT | VG-E | GOOD |
|---|---|---|---|
| COMPLETE SET (144) | 4500.00 | 2000.00 | 575.00 |
| COMMON PLAYER (1-72) | 20.00 | 9.00 | 2.50 |
| COMMON PLAYER (73-144) | 25.00 | 11.50 | 3.10 |

| | | NRMT | VG-E | GOOD |
|---|---|---|---|---|
| ☐ 1 | Norm Van Brocklin | 175.00 | 45.00 | 14.00 |
| | Los Angeles Rams | | | |
| ☐ 2 | Otto Graham | 135.00 | 60.00 | 17.00 |
| | Cleveland Browns | | | |
| ☐ 3 | Doak Walker | 35.00 | 16.00 | 4.40 |
| | Detroit Lions | | | |
| ☐ 4 | Steve Owen CO | 30.00 | 13.50 | 3.80 |
| | New York Giants | | | |
| ☐ 5 | Frankie Albert | 22.00 | 10.00 | 2.80 |
| | San Francisco 49ers | | | |
| ☐ 6 | Laurie Niemi | 20.00 | 9.00 | 2.50 |
| | Washington Redskins | | | |
| ☐ 7 | Chuck Hunsinger | 20.00 | 9.00 | 2.50 |
| | Chicago Bears | | | |
| ☐ 8 | Ed Modzelewski | 22.00 | 10.00 | 2.80 |
| | Pittsburgh Steelers | | | |
| ☐ 9 | Joe Spencer | 20.00 | 9.00 | 2.50 |
| | Green Bay Packers | | | |
| ☐ 10 | Chuck Bednarik | 45.00 | 20.00 | 5.75 |
| | Philadelphia Eagles | | | |
| ☐ 11 | Barney Poole | 20.00 | 9.00 | 2.50 |
| | Dallas Texans | | | |
| ☐ 12 | Charley Trippi | 32.00 | 14.50 | 4.00 |
| | Chicago Cardinals | | | |
| ☐ 13 | Tom Fears | 32.00 | 14.50 | 4.00 |
| | Los Angeles Rams | | | |
| ☐ 14 | Paul Brown CO | 80.00 | 36.00 | 10.00 |
| | Cleveland Browns | | | |
| ☐ 15 | Leon Hart | 22.00 | 10.00 | 2.80 |
| | Detroit Lions | | | |
| ☐ 16 | Frank Gifford | 425.00 | 190.00 | 52.50 |
| | New York Giants | | | |
| ☐ 17 | Y.A. Tittle | 100.00 | 45.00 | 12.50 |
| | San Francisco 49ers | | | |
| ☐ 18 | Charlie Justice | 30.00 | 13.50 | 3.80 |
| | Washington Redskins | | | |
| ☐ 19 | George Connor | 30.00 | 13.50 | 3.80 |
| | Chicago Bears | | | |
| ☐ 20 | Lynn Chandnois | 20.00 | 9.00 | 2.50 |
| | Pittsburgh Steelers | | | |
| ☐ 21 | Bill Howton | 28.00 | 12.50 | 3.50 |
| | Green Bay Packers | | | |
| ☐ 22 | Kenneth Snyder | 20.00 | 9.00 | 2.50 |
| | Philadelphia Eagles | | | |
| ☐ 23 | Gino Marchetti | 100.00 | 45.00 | 12.50 |
| | Dallas Texans | | | |
| ☐ 24 | John Karras | 20.00 | 9.00 | 2.50 |
| | Chicago Cardinals | | | |
| ☐ 25 | Tank Younger | 25.00 | 11.50 | 3.10 |
| | Los Angeles Rams | | | |
| ☐ 26 | Tommy Thompson | 22.00 | 10.00 | 2.80 |
| | Cleveland Browns | | | |
| ☐ 27 | Bob Miller | 20.00 | 9.00 | 2.50 |
| | Detroit Lions | | | |
| ☐ 28 | Kyle Rote | 50.00 | 23.00 | 6.25 |
| | New York Giants | | | |
| ☐ 29 | Hugh McElhenny | 125.00 | 57.50 | 15.50 |
| | San Francisco 49ers | | | |
| ☐ 30 | Sammy Baugh | 160.00 | 70.00 | 20.00 |
| | Washington Redskins | | | |
| ☐ 31 | Jim Dooley | 24.00 | 11.00 | 3.00 |
| | Chicago Bears | | | |
| ☐ 32 | Ray Mathews | 20.00 | 9.00 | 2.50 |
| | Pittsburgh Steelers | | | |
| ☐ 33 | Fred Cone | 22.00 | 10.00 | 2.80 |
| | Green Bay Packers | | | |
| ☐ 34 | Al Pollard | 20.00 | 9.00 | 2.50 |
| | Philadelphia Eagles | | | |
| ☐ 35 | Brad Ecklund | 20.00 | 9.00 | 2.50 |
| | Dallas Texans | | | |
| ☐ 36 | John Lee Hancock | 20.00 | 9.00 | 2.50 |
| | Chicago Cardinals | | | |
| ☐ 37 | Elroy Hirsch | 45.00 | 20.00 | 5.75 |
| | Los Angeles Rams | | | |
| ☐ 38 | Keever Jankovich | 20.00 | 9.00 | 2.50 |
| | Cleveland Browns | | | |
| ☐ 39 | Emlen Tunnell | 35.00 | 16.00 | 4.40 |
| | New York Giants | | | |
| ☐ 40 | Steve Dowden | 20.00 | 9.00 | 2.50 |
| | Green Bay Packers | | | |

| | | | |
|---|---|---|---|
| ☐ 41 Claude Hipps | 20.00 | 9.00 | 2.50 |
| Pittsburgh Steelers | | | |
| ☐ 42 Norm Standlee | 20.00 | 9.00 | 2.50 |
| San Francisco 49ers | | | |
| ☐ 43 Dick Todd CO | 20.00 | 9.00 | 2.50 |
| Washington Redskins | | | |
| ☐ 44 Babe Parilli | 27.00 | 12.00 | 3.40 |
| Green Bay Packers | | | |
| ☐ 45 Steve Van Buren | 45.00 | 20.00 | 5.75 |
| Philadelphia Eagles | | | |
| ☐ 46 Art Donovan | 100.00 | 45.00 | 12.50 |
| Dallas Texans | | | |
| ☐ 47 Bill Fischer | 20.00 | 9.00 | 2.50 |
| Chicago Cardinals | | | |
| ☐ 48 George Halas CO | 80.00 | 36.00 | 10.00 |
| Chicago Bears | | | |
| ☐ 49 Jerrell Price | 20.00 | 9.00 | 2.50 |
| Chicago Cardinals | | | |
| ☐ 50 John Sandusky | 22.00 | 10.00 | 2.80 |
| Cleveland Browns | | | |
| ☐ 51 Ray Beck | 20.00 | 9.00 | 2.50 |
| New York Giants | | | |
| ☐ 52 Jim Martin | 22.00 | 10.00 | 2.80 |
| Detroit Lions | | | |
| ☐ 53 Joe Bach CO UER | 20.00 | 9.00 | 2.50 |
| (Misspelled Back) | | | |
| Pittsburgh Steelers | | | |
| ☐ 54 Glen Christian | 20.00 | 9.00 | 2.50 |
| San Francisco 49ers | | | |
| ☐ 55 Andy Davis | 20.00 | 9.00 | 2.50 |
| Washington Redskins | | | |
| ☐ 56 Tobin Rote | 24.00 | 11.00 | 3.00 |
| Green Bay Packers | | | |
| ☐ 57 Wayne Millner CO | 35.00 | 16.00 | 4.40 |
| Philadelphia Eagles | | | |
| ☐ 58 Zollie Toth | 20.00 | 9.00 | 2.50 |
| Dallas Texans | | | |
| ☐ 59 Jack Jennings | 20.00 | 9.00 | 2.50 |
| Chicago Cardinals | | | |
| ☐ 60 Bill McColl | 20.00 | 9.00 | 2.50 |
| Chicago Bears | | | |
| ☐ 61 Les Richter | 24.00 | 11.00 | 3.00 |
| Los Angeles Rams | | | |
| ☐ 62 Walt Michaels | 25.00 | 11.50 | 3.10 |
| Cleveland Browns | | | |
| ☐ 63 Charley Conerly | 45.00 | 20.00 | 5.75 |
| New York Giants | | | |
| ☐ 64 Howard Hartley | 20.00 | 9.00 | 2.50 |
| Pittsburgh Steelers | | | |
| ☐ 65 Jerome Smith | 20.00 | 9.00 | 2.50 |
| San Francisco 49ers | | | |
| ☐ 66 James Clark | 20.00 | 9.00 | 2.50 |
| Washington Redskins | | | |
| ☐ 67 Dick Logan | 20.00 | 9.00 | 2.50 |
| Cleveland Browns | | | |
| ☐ 68 Wayne Robinson | 20.00 | 9.00 | 2.50 |
| Philadelphia Eagles | | | |
| ☐ 69 James Hammond | 20.00 | 9.00 | 2.50 |
| Dallas Texans | | | |
| ☐ 70 Gene Schroeder | 20.00 | 9.00 | 2.50 |
| Chicago Bears | | | |
| ☐ 71 Tex Coulter | 20.00 | 9.00 | 2.50 |
| New York Giants | | | |
| ☐ 72 John Schweder | 20.00 | 9.00 | 2.50 |
| Pittsburgh Steelers | | | |
| ☐ 73 Vitamin Smith | 25.00 | 11.50 | 3.10 |
| Los Angeles Rams | | | |
| ☐ 74 Joe Campanella | 25.00 | 11.50 | 3.10 |
| Cleveland Browns | | | |
| ☐ 75 Joe Kuharich CO | 27.00 | 12.00 | 3.40 |
| Chicago Cardinals | | | |
| ☐ 76 Herman Clark | 25.00 | 11.50 | 3.10 |
| Chicago Bears | | | |
| ☐ 77 Dan Edwards | 25.00 | 11.50 | 3.10 |
| Dallas Texans | | | |
| ☐ 78 Bobby Layne | 90.00 | 40.00 | 11.50 |
| Detroit Lions | | | |
| ☐ 79 Bob Hoernschemeyer | 27.50 | 12.50 | 3.40 |
| Detroit Lions | | | |
| ☐ 80 John Carr Blount | 25.00 | 11.50 | 3.10 |
| Philadelphia Eagles | | | |
| ☐ 81 John Kastan | 25.00 | 11.50 | 3.10 |
| New York Giants | | | |
| ☐ 82 Harry Minarik | 25.00 | 11.50 | 3.10 |
| Pittsburgh Steelers | | | |
| ☐ 83 Joe Perry | 50.00 | 23.00 | 6.25 |
| San Francisco 49ers | | | |
| ☐ 84 Ray(Buddy) Parker CO | 28.00 | 12.50 | 3.50 |
| Detroit Lions | | | |
| ☐ 85 Andy Robustelli | 100.00 | 45.00 | 12.50 |
| Los Angeles Rams | | | |
| ☐ 86 Dub Jones | 25.00 | 11.50 | 3.10 |
| Cleveland Browns | | | |
| ☐ 87 Mal Cook | 25.00 | 11.50 | 3.10 |
| Chicago Cardinals | | | |
| ☐ 88 Billy Stone | 25.00 | 11.50 | 3.10 |
| Chicago Bears | | | |
| ☐ 89 George Taliaferro | 27.50 | 12.50 | 3.40 |
| Dallas Texans | | | |
| ☐ 90 Thomas Johnson | 25.00 | 11.50 | 3.10 |
| Green Bay Packers | | | |
| ☐ 91 Leon Heath | 25.00 | 11.50 | 3.10 |
| Washington Redskins | | | |
| ☐ 92 Pete Pihos | 40.00 | 18.00 | 5.00 |
| Philadelphia Eagles | | | |
| ☐ 93 Fred Benners | 25.00 | 11.50 | 3.10 |
| New York Giants | | | |
| ☐ 94 George Tarasovic | 25.00 | 11.50 | 3.10 |
| Pittsburgh Steelers | | | |
| ☐ 95 Lawr. (Buck) Shaw CO | 25.00 | 11.50 | 3.10 |
| San Francisco 49ers | | | |
| ☐ 96 Bill Wightkin | 25.00 | 11.50 | 3.10 |
| Chicago Bears | | | |
| ☐ 97 John Wozniak | 25.00 | 11.50 | 3.10 |
| Dallas Texans | | | |
| ☐ 98 Bobby Dillon | 27.00 | 12.00 | 3.40 |
| Green Bay Packers | | | |
| ☐ 99 Joe Stydahar CO | 40.00 | 18.00 | 5.00 |
| Los Angeles Rams | | | |
| ☐ 100 Dick Alban | 25.00 | 11.50 | 3.10 |
| Washington Redskins | | | |
| ☐ 101 Arnie Weinmeister | 35.00 | 16.00 | 4.40 |
| New York Giants | | | |
| ☐ 102 Robert Joe Cross | 25.00 | 11.50 | 3.10 |
| Chicago Bears | | | |
| ☐ 103 Don Paul | 25.00 | 11.50 | 3.10 |
| Chicago Cardinals | | | |
| ☐ 104 Buddy Young | 27.00 | 12.00 | 3.40 |
| Dallas Texans | | | |
| ☐ 105 Lou Groza | 45.00 | 20.00 | 5.75 |
| Cleveland Browns | | | |
| ☐ 106 Ray Pelfrey | 25.00 | 11.50 | 3.10 |
| Green Bay Packers | | | |
| ☐ 107 Maurice Nipp | 25.00 | 11.50 | 3.10 |
| Philadelphia Eagles | | | |
| ☐ 108 Hubert Johnston | 25.00 | 11.50 | 3.10 |
| Washington Redskins | | | |
| ☐ 109 Volney Quinlan | 25.00 | 11.50 | 3.10 |
| Los Angeles Rams | | | |
| ☐ 110 Jack Simmons | 25.00 | 11.50 | 3.10 |
| Chicago Cardinals | | | |
| ☐ 111 George Ratterman | 27.50 | 12.50 | 3.40 |
| Cleveland Browns | | | |
| ☐ 112 John Badaczewski | 25.00 | 11.50 | 3.10 |
| Washington Redskins | | | |
| ☐ 113 Bill Reichardt | 25.00 | 11.50 | 3.10 |
| Green Bay Packers | | | |
| ☐ 114 Art Weiner | 25.00 | 11.50 | 3.10 |
| Dallas Texans | | | |
| ☐ 115 Keith Flowers | 25.00 | 11.50 | 3.10 |
| Detroit Lions | | | |
| ☐ 116 Russ Craft | 25.00 | 11.50 | 3.10 |
| Philadelphia Eagles | | | |
| ☐ 117 Jim O'Donahue | 25.00 | 11.50 | 3.10 |
| San Francisco 49ers | | | |
| ☐ 118 Darrell Hogan | 25.00 | 11.50 | 3.10 |
| Pittsburgh Steelers | | | |
| ☐ 119 Frank Ziegler | 25.00 | 11.50 | 3.10 |
| Philadelphia Eagles | | | |
| ☐ 120 Deacon Dan Towler | 27.00 | 12.00 | 3.40 |
| Los Angeles Rams | | | |
| ☐ 121 Fred Williams | 25.00 | 11.50 | 3.10 |
| Chicago Bears | | | |
| ☐ 122 Jimmy Phelan CO | 25.00 | 11.50 | 3.10 |
| Dallas Texans | | | |
| ☐ 123 Eddie Price | 25.00 | 11.50 | 3.10 |
| New York Giants | | | |
| ☐ 124 Chet Ostrowski | 25.00 | 11.50 | 3.10 |
| Washington Redskins | | | |
| ☐ 125 Leo Nomellini | 40.00 | 18.00 | 5.00 |
| San Francisco 49ers | | | |
| ☐ 126 Steve Romanik | 25.00 | 11.50 | 3.10 |
| Chicago Bears | | | |
| ☐ 127 Ollie Matson | 115.00 | 52.50 | 14.50 |
| Chicago Cardinals | | | |
| ☐ 128 Dante Lavelli | 40.00 | 18.00 | 5.00 |
| Cleveland Browns | | | |
| ☐ 129 Jack Christiansen | 75.00 | 34.00 | 9.50 |
| Detroit Lions | | | |
| ☐ 130 Dom Moselle | 25.00 | 11.50 | 3.10 |
| Green Bay Packers | | | |
| ☐ 131 John Rapacz | 25.00 | 11.50 | 3.10 |
| New York Giants | | | |
| ☐ 132 Chuck Ortman UER | 25.00 | 11.50 | 3.10 |
| (Avg. gain 9.4, | | | |
| should be 4.8) | | | |
| Pittsburgh Steelers | | | |
| ☐ 133 Bob Williams | 25.00 | 11.50 | 3.10 |
| Chicago Bears | | | |
| ☐ 134 Chuck Ulrich | 25.00 | 11.50 | 3.10 |
| Chicago Cardinals | | | |
| ☐ 135 Gene Ronzani CO | 27.00 | 12.00 | 3.40 |
| Green Bay Packers | | | |
| ☐ 136 Bert Rechichar | 27.50 | 12.50 | 3.40 |

|  | NRMT | VG-E | GOOD |
|---|---|---|---|
| Cleveland Browns | | | |
| ☐ 137 Bob Waterfield | 55.00 | 25.00 | 7.00 |
| Los Angeles Rams | | | |
| ☐ 138 Bobby Walston | 27.00 | 12.00 | 3.40 |
| Philadelphia Eagles | | | |
| ☐ 139 Jerry Shipkey | 25.00 | 11.50 | 3.10 |
| Pittsburgh Steelers | | | |
| ☐ 140 Yale Lary | 75.00 | 34.00 | 9.50 |
| Detroit Lions | | | |
| ☐ 141 Gordon Soltau | 25.00 | 11.50 | 3.10 |
| San Francisco 49ers | | | |
| ☐ 142 Tom Landry | 300.00 | 135.00 | 38.00 |
| New York Giants | | | |
| ☐ 143 John Papit | 25.00 | 11.50 | 3.10 |
| Washington Redskins | | | |
| ☐ 144 Jim Lansford | 90.00 | 23.00 | 7.25 |
| Dallas Texans | | | |

# 1953 Bowman

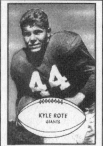 

The 1953 Bowman set of 96 cards continued the new, larger card size. The cards measure approximately 2 1/2" by 3 3/4". The set is somewhat smaller in number than would be thought since Bowman was the only major producer of football cards during this year. There are 24 cards marked SP in the checklist below which are considered in shorter supply than the other cards in the set. The Bill Walsh in this set went to Notre Dame and is not the Bill Walsh who coached the San Francisco 49ers in the 1980s. The most notable Rookie Card in this set is Eddie LeBaron.

|  | NRMT | VG-E | GOOD |
|---|---|---|---|
| COMPLETE SET (96) | 2500.00 | 1150.00 | 325.00 |
| COMMON PLAYER (1-96) | 20.00 | 9.00 | 2.50 |
| ☐ 1 Eddie LeBaron | 100.00 | 25.00 | 8.00 |
| Washington Redskins | | | |
| ☐ 2 John Dottley | 20.00 | 9.00 | 2.50 |
| Chicago Bears | | | |
| ☐ 3 Babe Parilli | 24.00 | 11.00 | 3.00 |
| Green Bay Packers | | | |
| ☐ 4 Bucko Kilroy | 22.00 | 10.00 | 2.80 |
| Philadelphia Eagles | | | |
| ☐ 5 Joe Tereshinski | 20.00 | 9.00 | 2.50 |
| Washington Redskins | | | |
| ☐ 6 Doak Walker | 40.00 | 18.00 | 5.00 |
| Detroit Lions | | | |
| ☐ 7 Fran Polsfoot | 20.00 | 9.00 | 2.50 |
| Chicago Cardinals | | | |
| ☐ 8 Sisto Averno | 20.00 | 9.00 | 2.50 |
| Baltimore Colts | | | |
| ☐ 9 Marion Motley | 40.00 | 18.00 | 5.00 |
| Cleveland Browns | | | |
| ☐ 10 Pat Brady | 20.00 | 9.00 | 2.50 |
| Pittsburgh Steelers | | | |
| ☐ 11 Norm Van Brocklin | 75.00 | 34.00 | 9.50 |
| Los Angeles Rams | | | |
| ☐ 12 Bill McColl | 20.00 | 9.00 | 2.50 |
| Chicago Bears | | | |
| ☐ 13 Jerry Groom | 20.00 | 9.00 | 2.50 |
| Chicago Cardinals | | | |
| ☐ 14 Al Pollard | 20.00 | 9.00 | 2.50 |
| Philadelphia Eagles | | | |
| ☐ 15 Dante Lavelli | 35.00 | 16.00 | 4.40 |
| Cleveland Browns | | | |
| ☐ 16 Eddie Price | 20.00 | 9.00 | 2.50 |
| New York Giants | | | |
| ☐ 17 Charley Trippi | 35.00 | 16.00 | 4.40 |
| Chicago Cardinals | | | |
| ☐ 18 Elbert Nickel | 20.00 | 9.00 | 2.50 |
| Pittsburgh Steelers | | | |
| ☐ 19 George Taliaferro | 22.00 | 10.00 | 2.80 |
| Baltimore Colts | | | |
| ☐ 20 Charley Conerly | 45.00 | 20.00 | 5.75 |
| New York Giants | | | |

|  | NRMT | VG-E | GOOD |
|---|---|---|---|
| ☐ 21 Bobby Layne | 80.00 | 36.00 | 10.00 |
| Detroit Lions | | | |
| ☐ 22 Elroy Hirsch | 50.00 | 23.00 | 6.25 |
| Los Angeles Rams | | | |
| ☐ 23 Jim Finks | 20.00 | 9.00 | 2.50 |
| Pittsburgh Steelers | | | |
| ☐ 24 Chuck Bednarik | 45.00 | 20.00 | 5.75 |
| Philadelphia Eagles | | | |
| ☐ 25 Kyle Rote | 30.00 | 13.50 | 3.80 |
| New York Giants | | | |
| ☐ 26 Otto Graham | 125.00 | 57.50 | 15.50 |
| Cleveland Browns | | | |
| ☐ 27 Harry Gilmer | 22.00 | 10.00 | 2.80 |
| Washington Redskins | | | |
| ☐ 28 Tobin Rote | 22.00 | 10.00 | 2.80 |
| Green Bay Packers | | | |
| ☐ 29 Billy Stone | 20.00 | 9.00 | 2.50 |
| Chicago Bears | | | |
| ☐ 30 Buddy Young | 30.00 | 13.50 | 3.80 |
| Baltimore Colts | | | |
| ☐ 31 Leon Hart | 22.00 | 10.00 | 2.80 |
| Detroit Lions | | | |
| ☐ 32 Hugh McElhenny | 60.00 | 27.00 | 7.50 |
| San Francisco 49ers | | | |
| ☐ 33 Dale Samuels | 20.00 | 9.00 | 2.50 |
| Chicago Cardinals | | | |
| ☐ 34 Lou Creekmur | 22.00 | 10.00 | 2.80 |
| Detroit Lions | | | |
| ☐ 35 Tom Catlin | 20.00 | 9.00 | 2.50 |
| Cleveland Browns | | | |
| ☐ 36 Tom Fears | 35.00 | 16.00 | 4.40 |
| Los Angeles Rams | | | |
| ☐ 37 George Connor | 30.00 | 13.50 | 3.80 |
| Chicago Bears | | | |
| ☐ 38 Bill Walsh | 20.00 | 9.00 | 2.50 |
| Pittsburgh Steelers | | | |
| ☐ 39 Leo Sanford SP | 32.00 | 14.50 | 4.00 |
| Chicago Cardinals | | | |
| ☐ 40 Horace Gillom | 20.00 | 9.00 | 2.50 |
| Cleveland Browns | | | |
| ☐ 41 John Schweder SP | 32.00 | 14.50 | 4.00 |
| Pittsburgh Steelers | | | |
| ☐ 42 Tom O'Connell | 20.00 | 9.00 | 2.50 |
| Chicago Bears | | | |
| ☐ 43 Frank Gifford SP | 350.00 | 160.00 | 45.00 |
| New York Giants | | | |
| ☐ 44 Frank Continetti SP | 32.00 | 14.50 | 4.00 |
| Baltimore Colts | | | |
| ☐ 45 John Olszewski SP | 32.00 | 14.50 | 4.00 |
| Chicago Cardinals | | | |
| ☐ 46 Dub Jones | 20.00 | 9.00 | 2.50 |
| Cleveland Browns | | | |
| ☐ 47 Don Paul SP | 32.00 | 14.50 | 4.00 |
| Los Angeles Rams | | | |
| ☐ 48 Gerald Weatherly | 20.00 | 9.00 | 2.50 |
| Chicago Bears | | | |
| ☐ 49 Fred Bruney SP | 32.00 | 14.50 | 4.00 |
| San Francisco 49ers | | | |
| ☐ 50 Jack Scarbath | 20.00 | 9.00 | 2.50 |
| Washington Redskins | | | |
| ☐ 51 John Karras | 20.00 | 9.00 | 2.50 |
| Chicago Cardinals | | | |
| ☐ 52 Al Conway | 20.00 | 9.00 | 2.50 |
| Philadelphia Eagles | | | |
| ☐ 53 Emlen Tunnell SP | 60.00 | 27.00 | 7.50 |
| New York Giants | | | |
| ☐ 54 Gern Nagler SP | 32.00 | 14.50 | 4.00 |
| Baltimore Colts | | | |
| ☐ 55 Kenneth Snyder SP | 32.00 | 14.50 | 4.00 |
| Philadelphia Eagles | | | |
| ☐ 56 Y.A. Tittle | 90.00 | 40.00 | 11.50 |
| San Francisco 49ers | | | |
| ☐ 57 John Rapacz SP | 32.00 | 14.50 | 4.00 |
| New York Giants | | | |
| ☐ 58 Harley Sewell SP | 35.00 | 16.00 | 4.40 |
| Detroit Lions | | | |
| ☐ 59 Don Bingham | 20.00 | 9.00 | 2.50 |
| Chicago Bears | | | |
| ☐ 60 Darrell Hogan | 20.00 | 9.00 | 2.50 |
| Pittsburgh Steelers | | | |
| ☐ 61 Tony Curcillo | 20.00 | 9.00 | 2.50 |
| Chicago Cardinals | | | |
| ☐ 62 Ray Renfro SP | 40.00 | 18.00 | 5.00 |
| Cleveland Browns | | | |
| ☐ 63 Leon Heath | 20.00 | 9.00 | 2.50 |
| Washington Redskins | | | |
| ☐ 64 Tex Coulter SP | 32.00 | 14.50 | 4.00 |
| New York Giants | | | |
| ☐ 65 Dewayne Douglas | 20.00 | 9.00 | 2.50 |
| New York Giants | | | |
| ☐ 66 J. Robert Smith SP | 32.00 | 14.50 | 4.00 |
| Detroit Lions | | | |
| ☐ 67 Bob McChesney SP | 32.00 | 14.50 | 4.00 |
| New York Giants | | | |
| ☐ 68 Dick Alban SP | 32.00 | 14.50 | 4.00 |
| Washington Redskins | | | |
| ☐ 69 Andy Kozar | 20.00 | 9.00 | 2.50 |

| | Chicago Bears | NRMT | VG-E | GOOD |
|---|---|---|---|---|
| ☐ 70 | Merwin Hodel SP | 32.00 | 14.50 | 4.00 |
| | New York Giants | | | |
| ☐ 71 | Thurman McGraw | 20.00 | 9.00 | 2.50 |
| | Detroit Lions | | | |
| ☐ 72 | Cliff Anderson | 20.00 | 9.00 | 2.50 |
| | Chicago Cardinals | | | |
| ☐ 73 | Pete Pihos | 35.00 | 16.00 | 4.40 |
| | Philadelphia Eagles | | | |
| ☐ 74 | Julie Rykovich | 20.00 | 9.00 | 2.50 |
| | Washington Redskins | | | |
| ☐ 75 | John Kreamcheck SP | 32.00 | 14.50 | 4.00 |
| | Chicago Bears | | | |
| ☐ 76 | Lynn Chandnois | 20.00 | 9.00 | 2.50 |
| | Pittsburgh Steelers | | | |
| ☐ 77 | Cloyce Box SP | 32.00 | 14.50 | 4.00 |
| | Detroit Lions | | | |
| ☐ 78 | Ray Mathews | 20.00 | 9.00 | 2.50 |
| | Pittsburgh Steelers | | | |
| ☐ 79 | Bobby Walston | 22.00 | 10.00 | 2.80 |
| | Philadelphia Eagles | | | |
| ☐ 80 | Jim Dooley | 22.00 | 10.00 | 2.80 |
| | Chicago Bears | | | |
| ☐ 81 | Pat Harder SP | 35.00 | 16.00 | 4.40 |
| | Detroit Lions | | | |
| ☐ 82 | Jerry Shipkey | 20.00 | 9.00 | 2.50 |
| | Pittsburgh Steelers | | | |
| ☐ 83 | Bobby Thomason | 22.00 | 10.00 | 2.80 |
| | Philadelphia Eagles | | | |
| ☐ 84 | Hugh Taylor | 22.00 | 10.00 | 2.80 |
| | Washington Redskins | | | |
| ☐ 85 | George Ratterman | 22.00 | 10.00 | 2.80 |
| | Cleveland Browns | | | |
| ☐ 86 | Don Stonesifer | 20.00 | 9.00 | 2.50 |
| | Chicago Cardinals | | | |
| ☐ 87 | John Williams SP | 32.00 | 14.50 | 4.00 |
| | Washington Redskins | | | |
| ☐ 88 | Leo Nomellini | 35.00 | 16.00 | 4.40 |
| | San Francisco 49ers | | | |
| ☐ 89 | Frank Ziegler | 20.00 | 9.00 | 2.50 |
| | Philadelphia Eagles | | | |
| ☐ 90 | Don Paul UER | 20.00 | 9.00 | 2.50 |
| | (19th in punt returns, should be 9th) | | | |
| | Chicago Cardinals | | | |
| ☐ 91 | Tom Dublinski | 20.00 | 9.00 | 2.50 |
| | Baltimore Colts | | | |
| ☐ 92 | Ken Carpenter | 20.00 | 9.00 | 2.50 |
| | Cleveland Browns | | | |
| ☐ 93 | Ted Marchibroda | 35.00 | 16.00 | 4.40 |
| | Pittsburgh Steelers | | | |
| ☐ 94 | Chuck Drazenovich | 20.00 | 9.00 | 2.50 |
| | Washington Redskins | | | |
| ☐ 95 | Lou Groza SP | 75.00 | 34.00 | 9.50 |
| | Cleveland Browns | | | |
| ☐ 96 | William Cross SP | 65.00 | 16.50 | 5.25 |
| | Chicago Cardinals | | | |

## 1954 Bowman

GEORGE BLANDA
CHICAGO BEARS

The 1954 Bowman set of 128 cards was produced in four series of 32; the third series (65-96) being somewhat more difficult to obtain. The cards measure 2 1/2" by 3 3/4". The card backs feature the player's name in black print inside a red outline of a football. A "football quiz" question with upside-down answer is also given on the back. The player's statistical information from the previous season is summarized on the right-hand side of the back of the card. The "Whizzer" White in the set (125) is not Byron White, the Supreme Court Justice, but Wilford White, the father of former Dallas Cowboys' quarterback, Danny White. The Bill Walsh in this set went to Notre Dame and is not the Bill Walsh who coached the San Francisco 49ers in the 1980s. Prominent "Rookie Cards" included in this set are Doug Atkins and George Blanda.

| | | NRMT | VG-E | GOOD |
|---|---|---|---|---|
| | COMPLETE SET (128) | 1600.00 | 700.00 | 200.00 |
| | COMMON PLAYER (1-64) | 6.00 | 2.70 | .75 |
| | COMMON PLAYER (65-96) | 16.00 | 7.25 | 2.00 |
| | COMMON PLAYER (97-128) | 6.00 | 2.70 | .75 |
| ☐ 1 | Ray Mathews | 25.00 | 5.00 | 1.50 |
| | Pittsburgh Steelers | | | |
| ☐ 2 | John Huzvar | 6.00 | 2.70 | .75 |
| | Baltimore Colts | | | |
| ☐ 3 | Jack Scarbath | 6.00 | 2.70 | .75 |
| | Washington Redskins | | | |
| ☐ 4 | Doug Atkins | 45.00 | 20.00 | 5.75 |
| | Cleveland Browns | | | |
| ☐ 5 | Bill Stits | 6.00 | 2.70 | .75 |
| | Detroit Lions | | | |
| ☐ 6 | Joe Perry | 30.00 | 13.50 | 3.80 |
| | San Francisco 49ers | | | |
| ☐ 7 | Kyle Rote | 15.00 | 6.75 | 1.90 |
| | New York Giants | | | |
| ☐ 8 | Norm Van Brocklin | 42.00 | 19.00 | 5.25 |
| | Los Angeles Rams | | | |
| ☐ 9 | Pete Pihos | 22.00 | 10.00 | 2.80 |
| | Philadelphia Eagles | | | |
| ☐ 10 | Babe Parilli | 10.00 | 4.50 | 1.25 |
| | Green Bay Packers | | | |
| ☐ 11 | Zeke Bratkowski | 25.00 | 11.50 | 3.10 |
| | Chicago Bears | | | |
| ☐ 12 | Ollie Matson | 25.00 | 11.50 | 3.10 |
| | Chicago Cardinals | | | |
| ☐ 13 | Pat Brady | 6.00 | 2.70 | .75 |
| | Pittsburgh Steelers | | | |
| ☐ 14 | Fred Enke | 6.00 | 2.70 | .75 |
| | Baltimore Colts | | | |
| ☐ 15 | Harry Ulinski | 6.00 | 2.70 | .75 |
| | Washington Redskins | | | |
| ☐ 16 | Bobby Garrett | 6.00 | 2.70 | .75 |
| | Cleveland Browns | | | |
| ☐ 17 | Bill Bowman | 6.00 | 2.70 | .75 |
| | Detroit Lions | | | |
| ☐ 18 | Leo Rucka | 6.00 | 2.70 | .75 |
| | San Francisco 49ers | | | |
| ☐ 19 | John Cannady | 6.00 | 2.70 | .75 |
| | New York Giants | | | |
| ☐ 20 | Tom Fears | 20.00 | 9.00 | 2.50 |
| | Los Angeles Rams | | | |
| ☐ 21 | Norm Willey | 6.00 | 2.70 | .75 |
| | Philadelphia Eagles | | | |
| ☐ 22 | Floyd Reid | 6.00 | 2.70 | .75 |
| | Green Bay Packers | | | |
| ☐ 23 | George Blanda | 200.00 | 90.00 | 25.00 |
| | Chicago Bears | | | |
| ☐ 24 | Don Doheney | 6.00 | 2.70 | .75 |
| | Chicago Cardinals | | | |
| ☐ 25 | John Schweder | 6.00 | 2.70 | .75 |
| | Pittsburgh Steelers | | | |
| ☐ 26 | Bert Rechichar | 6.00 | 2.70 | .75 |
| | Baltimore Colts | | | |
| ☐ 27 | Harry Dowda | 6.00 | 2.70 | .75 |
| | Philadelphia Eagles | | | |
| ☐ 28 | John Sandusky | 7.00 | 3.10 | .85 |
| | Cleveland Browns | | | |
| ☐ 29 | Les Bingaman | 10.00 | 4.50 | 1.25 |
| | Detroit Lions | | | |
| ☐ 30 | Joe Arenas | 6.00 | 2.70 | .75 |
| | San Francisco 49ers | | | |
| ☐ 31 | Ray Wietecha | 8.00 | 3.60 | 1.00 |
| | New York Giants | | | |
| ☐ 32 | Elroy Hirsch | 30.00 | 13.50 | 3.80 |
| | Los Angeles Rams | | | |
| ☐ 33 | Harold Giancanelli | 6.00 | 2.70 | .75 |
| | Philadelphia Eagles | | | |
| ☐ 34 | Bill Howton | 10.00 | 4.50 | 1.25 |
| | Green Bay Packers | | | |
| ☐ 35 | Fred Morrison | 6.00 | 2.70 | .75 |
| | Chicago Bears | | | |
| ☐ 36 | Bobby Cavazos | 6.00 | 2.70 | .75 |
| | Chicago Cardinals | | | |
| ☐ 37 | Darrell Hogan | 6.00 | 2.70 | .75 |
| | Pittsburgh Steelers | | | |
| ☐ 38 | Buddy Young | 7.00 | 3.10 | .85 |
| | Baltimore Colts | | | |
| ☐ 39 | Charlie Justice | 12.00 | 5.50 | 1.50 |
| | Washington Redskins | | | |
| ☐ 40 | Otto Graham | 75.00 | 34.00 | 9.50 |
| | Cleveland Browns | | | |
| ☐ 41 | Doak Walker | 25.00 | 11.50 | 3.10 |
| | Detroit Lions | | | |
| ☐ 42 | Y.A. Tittle | 55.00 | 25.00 | 7.00 |
| | San Francisco 49ers | | | |
| ☐ 43 | Buford Long | 6.00 | 2.70 | .75 |
| | New York Giants | | | |
| ☐ 44 | Volney Quinlan | 6.00 | 2.70 | .75 |
| | Los Angeles Rams | | | |
| ☐ 45 | Bobby Thomason | 7.00 | 3.10 | .85 |
| | Philadelphia Eagles | | | |
| ☐ 46 | Fred Cone | 7.00 | 3.10 | .85 |
| | Green Bay Packers | | | |

| | | | |
|---|---|---|---|
| ☐ 47 Gerald Weatherly | 6.00 | 2.70 | .75 |
| Chicago Bears | | | |
| ☐ 48 Don Stonesifer | 6.00 | 2.70 | .75 |
| Chicago Cardinals | | | |
| ☐ 49 Lynn Chandnois | 6.00 | 2.70 | .75 |
| Pittsburgh Steelers | | | |
| ☐ 50 George Taliaferro | 7.00 | 3.10 | .85 |
| Baltimore Colts | | | |
| ☐ 51 Dick Alban | 6.00 | 2.70 | .75 |
| Washington Redskins | | | |
| ☐ 52 Lou Groza | 30.00 | 13.50 | 3.80 |
| Cleveland Browns | | | |
| ☐ 53 Bobby Layne | 50.00 | 23.00 | 6.25 |
| Detroit Lions | | | |
| ☐ 54 Hugh McElhenny | 30.00 | 13.50 | 3.80 |
| San Francisco 49ers | | | |
| ☐ 55 Frank Gifford UER | 125.00 | 57.50 | 15.50 |
| (Avg. gain 7.83, should be 3.1) | | | |
| New York Giants | | | |
| ☐ 56 Leon McLaughlin | 6.00 | 2.70 | .75 |
| Los Angeles Rams | | | |
| ☐ 57 Chuck Bednarik | 28.00 | 12.50 | 3.50 |
| Philadelphia Eagles | | | |
| ☐ 58 Art Hunter | 6.00 | 2.70 | .75 |
| Green Bay Packers | | | |
| ☐ 59 Bill McColl | 6.00 | 2.70 | .75 |
| Chicago Bears | | | |
| ☐ 60 Charley Trippi | 22.00 | 10.00 | 2.80 |
| Chicago Cardinals | | | |
| ☐ 61 Jim Finks | 6.00 | 2.70 | .75 |
| Pittsburgh Steelers | | | |
| ☐ 62 Bill Lange | 6.00 | 2.70 | .75 |
| Baltimore Colts | | | |
| ☐ 63 Laurie Niemi | 6.00 | 2.70 | .75 |
| Washington Redskins | | | |
| ☐ 64 Ray Renfro | 7.00 | 3.10 | .85 |
| Cleveland Browns | | | |
| ☐ 65 Dick Chapman | 16.00 | 7.25 | 2.00 |
| Detroit Lions | | | |
| ☐ 66 Bob Hantla | 16.00 | 7.25 | 2.00 |
| San Francisco 49ers | | | |
| ☐ 67 Ralph Starkey | 16.00 | 7.25 | 2.00 |
| New York Giants | | | |
| ☐ 68 Don Paul | 16.00 | 7.25 | 2.00 |
| Los Angeles Rams | | | |
| ☐ 69 Kenneth Snyder | 16.00 | 7.25 | 2.00 |
| Philadelphia Eagles | | | |
| ☐ 70 Tobin Rote | 18.00 | 8.00 | 2.30 |
| Green Bay Packers | | | |
| ☐ 71 Arthur DeCarlo | 16.00 | 7.25 | 2.00 |
| Pittsburgh Steelers | | | |
| ☐ 72 Tom Keane | 16.00 | 7.25 | 2.00 |
| Baltimore Colts | | | |
| ☐ 73 Hugh Taylor | 17.00 | 7.75 | 2.10 |
| Washington Redskins | | | |
| ☐ 74 Warren Lahr | 20.00 | 9.00 | 2.50 |
| Cleveland Browns | | | |
| ☐ 75 Jim Neal | 16.00 | 7.25 | 2.00 |
| Detroit Lions | | | |
| ☐ 76 Leo Nomellini | 45.00 | 20.00 | 5.75 |
| San Francisco 49ers | | | |
| ☐ 77 Dick Yelvington | 16.00 | 7.25 | 2.00 |
| New York Giants | | | |
| ☐ 78 Les Richter | 17.00 | 7.75 | 2.10 |
| Los Angeles Rams | | | |
| ☐ 79 Bucko Kilroy | 17.00 | 7.75 | 2.10 |
| Philadelphia Eagles | | | |
| ☐ 80 John Martinkovic | 16.00 | 7.25 | 2.00 |
| Green Bay Packers | | | |
| ☐ 81 Dale Dodrill | 20.00 | 9.00 | 2.50 |
| Pittsburgh Steelers | | | |
| ☐ 82 Ken Jackson | 16.00 | 7.25 | 2.00 |
| Baltimore Colts | | | |
| ☐ 83 Paul Lipscomb | 16.00 | 7.25 | 2.00 |
| Washington Redskins | | | |
| ☐ 84 John Bauer | 16.00 | 7.25 | 2.00 |
| Cleveland Browns | | | |
| ☐ 85 Lou Creekmur | 17.00 | 7.75 | 2.10 |
| Detroit Lions | | | |
| ☐ 86 Eddie Price | 16.00 | 7.25 | 2.00 |
| New York Giants | | | |
| ☐ 87 Kenneth Farragut | 16.00 | 7.25 | 2.00 |
| Philadelphia Eagles | | | |
| ☐ 88 Dave Hanner | 20.00 | 9.00 | 2.50 |
| Green Bay Packers | | | |
| ☐ 89 Don Boll | 16.00 | 7.25 | 2.00 |
| Washington Redskins | | | |
| ☐ 90 Chet Hanulak | 16.00 | 7.25 | 2.00 |
| Cleveland Browns | | | |
| ☐ 91 Thurman McGraw | 16.00 | 7.25 | 2.00 |
| Detroit Lions | | | |
| ☐ 92 Don Heinrich | 20.00 | 9.00 | 2.50 |
| New York Giants | | | |
| ☐ 93 Dan McKown | 16.00 | 7.25 | 2.00 |
| Philadelphia Eagles | | | |
| ☐ 94 Bob Fleck | 16.00 | 7.25 | 2.00 |

| | | | |
|---|---|---|---|
| Green Bay Packers | | | |
| ☐ 95 Jerry Hilgenberg | 16.00 | 7.25 | 2.00 |
| Cleveland Browns | | | |
| ☐ 96 Bill Walsh | 16.00 | 7.25 | 2.00 |
| Pittsburgh Steelers | | | |
| ☐ 97A Tom Finnin ERR | 30.00 | 13.50 | 3.80 |
| Baltimore Colts | | | |
| ☐ 97B Tom Finnan COR | 6.00 | 2.70 | .75 |
| Baltimore Colts | | | |
| ☐ 98 Paul Barry | 6.00 | 2.70 | .75 |
| Washington Redskins | | | |
| ☐ 99 Harry Jagade | 6.00 | 2.70 | .75 |
| Cleveland Browns | | | |
| ☐ 100 Jack Christiansen | 20.00 | 9.00 | 2.50 |
| Detroit Lions | | | |
| ☐ 101 Gordon Soltau | 6.00 | 2.70 | .75 |
| San Francisco 49ers | | | |
| ☐ 102 Emlen Tunnell | 20.00 | 9.00 | 2.50 |
| New York Giants | | | |
| ☐ 103 Stan West | 6.00 | 2.70 | .75 |
| Los Angeles Rams | | | |
| ☐ 104 Jerry Williams | 6.00 | 2.70 | .75 |
| Philadelphia Eagles | | | |
| ☐ 105 Veryl Switzer | 6.00 | 2.70 | .75 |
| Green Bay Packers | | | |
| ☐ 106 Billy Stone | 6.00 | 2.70 | .75 |
| Chicago Bears | | | |
| ☐ 107 Jerry Watford | 6.00 | 2.70 | .75 |
| Chicago Cardinals | | | |
| ☐ 108 Elbert Nickel | 6.00 | 2.70 | .75 |
| Pittsburgh Steelers | | | |
| ☐ 109 Ed Sharkey | 6.00 | 2.70 | .75 |
| Baltimore Colts | | | |
| ☐ 110 Steve Meilinger | 6.00 | 2.70 | .75 |
| Washington Redskins | | | |
| ☐ 111 Dante Lavelli | 20.00 | 9.00 | 2.50 |
| Cleveland Browns | | | |
| ☐ 112 Leon Hart | 10.00 | 4.50 | 1.25 |
| Detroit Lions | | | |
| ☐ 113 Charley Conerly | 30.00 | 13.50 | 3.80 |
| New York Giants | | | |
| ☐ 114 Richard Lemmon | 6.00 | 2.70 | .75 |
| Philadelphia Eagles | | | |
| ☐ 115 Al Carmichael | 6.00 | 2.70 | .75 |
| Green Bay Packers | | | |
| ☐ 116 George Connor | 18.00 | 8.00 | 2.30 |
| Chicago Bears | | | |
| ☐ 117 John Olszewski | 6.00 | 2.70 | .75 |
| Chicago Cardinals | | | |
| ☐ 118 Ernie Stautner | 22.00 | 10.00 | 2.80 |
| Pittsburgh Steelers | | | |
| ☐ 119 Ray Smith | 6.00 | 2.70 | .75 |
| Chicago Bears | | | |
| ☐ 120 Neil Worden | 6.00 | 2.70 | .75 |
| Philadelphia Eagles | | | |
| ☐ 121 Jim Dooley | 7.00 | 3.10 | .85 |
| Chicago Bears | | | |
| ☐ 122 Arnold Galiffa | 10.00 | 4.50 | 1.25 |
| New York Giants | | | |
| ☐ 123 Kline Gilbert | 6.00 | 2.70 | .75 |
| Chicago Bears | | | |
| ☐ 124 Bob Hoernschemeyer | 7.00 | 3.10 | .85 |
| Detroit Lions | | | |
| ☐ 125 Whizzer White | 15.00 | 6.75 | 1.90 |
| Chicago Bears | | | |
| ☐ 126 Art Spinney | 6.00 | 2.70 | .75 |
| Baltimore Colts | | | |
| ☐ 127 Joe Koch | 6.00 | 2.70 | .75 |
| Chicago Bears | | | |
| ☐ 128 John Lattner | 60.00 | 12.00 | 3.60 |
| Pittsburgh Steelers | | | |

# 1955 Bowman

The 1955 Bowman set of 160 cards was Bowman's last sports issue before the company was purchased by Topps in January of 1956. Numbers above 64 are somewhat more difficult to obtain. The cards measure approximately 2 1/2" by 3 3/4". On the bottom of most of the card backs is found a play diagram. Card backs are printed in red and blue on gray card stock. The notable Rookie Cards in this set are Alan Ameche, Len Ford, Frank Gatski, John Henry Johnson, Mike McCormack, Jim Ringo, Bob St. Clair, and Pat Summerall.

| | NRMT | VG-E | GOOD |
|---|---|---|---|
| COMPLETE SET (160) | 1500.00 | 700.00 | 190.00 |
| COMMON PLAYER (1-64) | 4.50 | 2.00 | .55 |
| COMMON PLAYER (65-160) | 6.00 | 2.70 | .75 |
| ☐ 1 Doak Walker | 50.00 | 10.00 | 3.00 |
| Detroit Lions | | | |
| ☐ 2 Mike McCormack | 30.00 | 13.50 | 3.80 |
| Cleveland Browns | | | |
| ☐ 3 John Olszewski | 4.50 | 2.00 | .55 |
| Chicago Cardinals | | | |
| ☐ 4 Dorne Dibble | 5.00 | 2.30 | .60 |
| Detroit Lions | | | |
| ☐ 5 Lindon Crow | 4.50 | 2.00 | .55 |
| Chicago Cardinals | | | |
| ☐ 6 Hugh Taylor UER | 5.00 | 2.30 | .60 |
| (First word in bio should be Bones) Washington Redskins | | | |
| ☐ 7 Frank Gifford | 90.00 | 40.00 | 11.50 |
| New York Giants | | | |
| ☐ 8 Alan Ameche | 30.00 | 13.50 | 3.80 |
| Baltimore Colts | | | |
| ☐ 9 Don Stonesifer | 4.50 | 2.00 | .55 |
| Chicago Cardinals | | | |
| ☐ 10 Pete Pihos | 12.00 | 5.50 | 1.50 |
| Philadelphia Eagles | | | |
| ☐ 11 Bill Austin | 4.50 | 2.00 | .55 |
| New York Giants | | | |
| ☐ 12 Dick Alban | 4.50 | 2.00 | .55 |
| Washington Redskins | | | |
| ☐ 13 Bobby Walston | 5.00 | 2.30 | .60 |
| Philadelphia Eagles | | | |
| ☐ 14 Len Ford | 30.00 | 13.50 | 3.80 |
| Cleveland Browns | | | |
| ☐ 15 Jug Girard | 5.00 | 2.30 | .60 |
| Detroit Lions | | | |
| ☐ 16 Charley Conerly | 24.00 | 11.00 | 3.00 |
| New York Giants | | | |
| ☐ 17 Volney Peters | 4.50 | 2.00 | .55 |
| Washington Redskins | | | |
| ☐ 18 Max Boydston | 4.50 | 2.00 | .55 |
| Chicago Cardinals | | | |
| ☐ 19 Leon Hart | 7.00 | 3.10 | .85 |
| Detroit Lions | | | |
| ☐ 20 Bert Rechichar | 4.50 | 2.00 | .55 |
| Baltimore Colts | | | |
| ☐ 21 Lee Riley | 4.50 | 2.00 | .55 |
| Detroit Lions | | | |
| ☐ 22 Johnny Carson | 4.50 | 2.00 | .55 |
| Washington Redskins | | | |
| ☐ 23 Harry Thompson | 4.50 | 2.00 | .55 |
| Los Angeles Rams | | | |
| ☐ 24 Ray Wietecha | 4.50 | 2.00 | .55 |
| New York Giants | | | |
| ☐ 25 Ollie Matson | 24.00 | 11.00 | 3.00 |
| Chicago Cardinals | | | |
| ☐ 26 Eddie LeBaron | 10.00 | 4.50 | 1.25 |
| Washington Redskins | | | |
| ☐ 27 Jack Simmons | 4.50 | 2.00 | .55 |
| Chicago Cardinals | | | |
| ☐ 28 Jack Christiansen | 14.00 | 6.25 | 1.75 |
| Detroit Lions | | | |
| ☐ 29 Bucko Kilroy | 5.00 | 2.30 | .60 |
| Philadelphia Eagles | | | |
| ☐ 30 Tom Keane | 4.50 | 2.00 | .55 |
| Chicago Cardinals | | | |
| ☐ 31 Dave Leggett | 4.50 | 2.00 | .55 |
| Chicago Cardinals | | | |
| ☐ 32 Norm Van Brocklin | 35.00 | 16.00 | 4.40 |
| Los Angeles Rams | | | |
| ☐ 33 Harlon Hill | 10.00 | 4.50 | 1.25 |
| Chicago Bears | | | |
| ☐ 34 Robert Haner | 4.50 | 2.00 | .55 |
| Washington Redskins | | | |
| ☐ 35 Veryl Switzer | 4.50 | 2.00 | .55 |
| Green Bay Packers | | | |
| ☐ 36 Dick Stanfel | 8.00 | 3.60 | 1.00 |
| Detroit Lions | | | |
| ☐ 37 Lou Groza | 25.00 | 11.50 | 3.10 |
| Cleveland Browns | | | |
| ☐ 38 Tank Younger | 5.00 | 2.30 | .60 |
| Los Angeles Rams | | | |
| ☐ 39 Dick Flanagan | 4.50 | 2.00 | .55 |
| Pittsburgh Steelers | | | |
| ☐ 40 Jim Dooley | 5.00 | 2.30 | .60 |
| Chicago Bears | | | |
| ☐ 41 Ray Collins | 4.50 | 2.00 | .55 |
| New York Giants | | | |
| ☐ 42 John Henry Johnson | 40.00 | 18.00 | 5.00 |
| San Francisco 49ers | | | |
| ☐ 43 Tom Fears | 15.00 | 6.75 | 1.90 |
| Los Angeles Rams | | | |
| ☐ 44 Joe Perry | 24.00 | 11.00 | 3.00 |
| San Francisco 49ers | | | |
| ☐ 45 Gene Brito | 6.00 | 2.70 | .75 |
| Washington Redskins | | | |
| ☐ 46 Bill Johnson | 4.50 | 2.00 | .55 |
| San Francisco 49ers | | | |
| ☐ 47 Deacon Dan Towler | 8.00 | 3.60 | 1.00 |
| Los Angeles Rams | | | |
| ☐ 48 Dick Moegle | 5.00 | 2.30 | .60 |
| San Francisco 49ers | | | |
| ☐ 49 Kline Gilbert | 4.50 | 2.00 | .55 |
| Chicago Bears | | | |
| ☐ 50 Les Gobel | 4.50 | 2.00 | .55 |
| Chicago Cardinals | | | |
| ☐ 51 Ray Krouse | 5.00 | 2.30 | .60 |
| New York Giants | | | |
| ☐ 52 Pat Summerall | 50.00 | 23.00 | 6.25 |
| Chicago Cardinals | | | |
| ☐ 53 Ed Brown | 10.00 | 4.50 | 1.25 |
| Chicago Bears | | | |
| ☐ 54 Lynn Chandnois | 4.50 | 2.00 | .55 |
| Pittsburgh Steelers | | | |
| ☐ 55 Joe Heap | 4.50 | 2.00 | .55 |
| New York Giants | | | |
| ☐ 56 John Hoffman | 4.50 | 2.00 | .55 |
| Chicago Bears | | | |
| ☐ 57 Howard Ferguson | 4.50 | 2.00 | .55 |
| Green Bay Packers | | | |
| ☐ 58 Bobby Watkins | 4.50 | 2.00 | .55 |
| Chicago Bears | | | |
| ☐ 59 Charlie Ane | 5.00 | 2.30 | .60 |
| Detroit Lions | | | |
| ☐ 60 Ken MacAfee | 7.00 | 3.10 | .85 |
| New York Giants | | | |
| ☐ 61 Ralph Guglielmi | 7.00 | 3.10 | .85 |
| Washington Redskins | | | |
| ☐ 62 George Blanda | 80.00 | 36.00 | 10.00 |
| Chicago Bears | | | |
| ☐ 63 Kenneth Snyder | 4.50 | 2.00 | .55 |
| Philadelphia Eagles | | | |
| ☐ 64 Chet Ostrowski | 4.50 | 2.00 | .55 |
| Washington Redskins | | | |
| ☐ 65 Buddy Young | 7.00 | 3.10 | .85 |
| Baltimore Colts | | | |
| ☐ 66 Gordon Soltau | 6.00 | 2.70 | .75 |
| San Francisco 49ers | | | |
| ☐ 67 Eddie Bell | 6.00 | 2.70 | .75 |
| Philadelphia Eagles | | | |
| ☐ 68 Ben Agajanian | 8.00 | 3.60 | 1.00 |
| New York Giants | | | |
| ☐ 69 Tom Dahms | 6.00 | 2.70 | .75 |
| Los Angeles Rams | | | |
| ☐ 70 Jim Ringo | 35.00 | 16.00 | 4.40 |
| Green Bay Packers | | | |
| ☐ 71 Bobby Layne | 45.00 | 20.00 | 5.75 |
| Detroit Lions | | | |
| ☐ 72 Y.A. Tittle | 50.00 | 23.00 | 6.25 |
| San Francisco 49ers | | | |
| ☐ 73 Bob Gaona | 6.00 | 2.70 | .75 |
| Pittsburgh Steelers | | | |
| ☐ 74 Tobin Rote | 8.00 | 3.60 | 1.00 |
| Green Bay Packers | | | |
| ☐ 75 Hugh McElhenny | 25.00 | 11.50 | 3.10 |
| San Francisco 49ers | | | |
| ☐ 76 John Kreamcheck | 6.00 | 2.70 | .75 |
| Chicago Bears | | | |
| ☐ 77 Al Dorow | 6.00 | 2.70 | .75 |
| Washington Redskins | | | |
| ☐ 78 Bill Wade | 10.00 | 4.50 | 1.25 |
| Los Angeles Rams | | | |
| ☐ 79 Dale Dodrill | 6.00 | 2.70 | .75 |
| Pittsburgh Steelers | | | |
| ☐ 80 Chuck Drazenovich | 6.00 | 2.70 | .75 |
| Washington Redskins | | | |
| ☐ 81 Billy Wilson | 10.00 | 4.50 | 1.25 |
| San Francisco 49ers | | | |
| ☐ 82 Les Richter | 7.00 | 3.10 | .85 |
| Los Angeles Rams | | | |
| ☐ 83 Pat Brady | 6.00 | 2.70 | .75 |
| Pittsburgh Steelers | | | |
| ☐ 84 Bob Hoernschemeyer | 7.00 | 3.10 | .85 |
| Detroit Lions | | | |
| ☐ 85 Joe Arenas | 6.00 | 2.70 | .75 |
| San Francisco 49ers | | | |
| ☐ 86 Len Szafaryn UER | 6.00 | 2.70 | .75 |
| Green Bay Packers (Listed as Ben on front) | | | |
| ☐ 87 Rick Casares | 16.00 | 7.25 | 2.00 |
| Chicago Bears | | | |
| ☐ 88 Leon McLaughlin | 6.00 | 2.70 | .75 |
| Los Angeles Rams | | | |

| | | | |
|---|---|---|---|
| ☐ 89 Charley Toogood | 6.00 | 2.70 | .75 |
| Los Angeles Rams | | | |
| ☐ 90 Tom Bettis | 6.00 | 2.70 | .75 |
| Green Bay Packers | | | |
| ☐ 91 John Sandusky | 7.00 | 3.10 | .85 |
| Cleveland Browns | | | |
| ☐ 92 Bill Wightkin | 6.00 | 2.70 | .75 |
| Chicago Bears | | | |
| ☐ 93 Darrell Brewster | 6.00 | 2.70 | .75 |
| Cleveland Browns | | | |
| ☐ 94 Marion Campbell | 10.00 | 4.50 | 1.25 |
| San Francisco 49ers | | | |
| ☐ 95 Floyd Reid | 6.00 | 2.70 | .75 |
| Green Bay Packers | | | |
| ☐ 96 Harry Jagade | 6.00 | 2.70 | .75 |
| Chicago Bears | | | |
| ☐ 97 George Taliaferro | 7.00 | 3.10 | .85 |
| Philadelphia Eagles | | | |
| ☐ 98 Carleton Massey | 6.00 | 2.70 | .75 |
| Cleveland Browns | | | |
| ☐ 99 Fran Rogel | 6.00 | 2.70 | .75 |
| Pittsburgh Steelers | | | |
| ☐ 100 Alex Sandusky | 6.00 | 2.70 | .75 |
| Baltimore Colts | | | |
| ☐ 101 Bob St. Clair | 35.00 | 16.00 | 4.40 |
| San Francisco 49ers | | | |
| ☐ 102 Al Carmichael | 6.00 | 2.70 | .75 |
| Green Bay Packers | | | |
| ☐ 103 Carl Taseff | 8.00 | 3.60 | 1.00 |
| Baltimore Colts | | | |
| ☐ 104 Leo Nomellini | 18.00 | 8.00 | 2.30 |
| San Francisco 49ers | | | |
| ☐ 105 Tom Scott | 6.00 | 2.70 | .75 |
| Philadelphia Eagles | | | |
| ☐ 106 Ted Marchibroda | 10.00 | 4.50 | 1.25 |
| Pittsburgh Steelers | | | |
| ☐ 107 Art Spinney | 6.00 | 2.70 | .75 |
| Baltimore Colts | | | |
| ☐ 108 Wayne Robinson | 6.00 | 2.70 | .75 |
| Philadelphia Eagles | | | |
| ☐ 109 Jim Ricca | 6.00 | 2.70 | .75 |
| Detroit Lions | | | |
| ☐ 110 Lou Ferry | 6.00 | 2.70 | .75 |
| Pittsburgh Steelers | | | |
| ☐ 111 Roger Zatkoff | 6.00 | 2.70 | .75 |
| Green Bay Packers | | | |
| ☐ 112 Lou Creekmur | 7.00 | 3.10 | .85 |
| Detroit Lions | | | |
| ☐ 113 Kenny Konz | 7.00 | 3.10 | .85 |
| Cleveland Browns | | | |
| ☐ 114 Doug Eggers | 6.00 | 2.70 | .75 |
| Baltimore Colts | | | |
| ☐ 115 Bobby Thomason | 7.00 | 3.10 | .85 |
| Philadelphia Eagles | | | |
| ☐ 116 Bill McPeak | 6.00 | 2.70 | .75 |
| Pittsburgh Steelers | | | |
| ☐ 117 William Brown | 6.00 | 2.70 | .75 |
| Green Bay Packers | | | |
| ☐ 118 Royce Womble | 6.00 | 2.70 | .75 |
| Baltimore Colts | | | |
| ☐ 119 Frank Gatski | 30.00 | 13.50 | 3.80 |
| Cleveland Browns | | | |
| ☐ 120 Jim Finks | 6.00 | 2.70 | .75 |
| Pittsburgh Steelers | | | |
| ☐ 121 Andy Robustelli | 20.00 | 9.00 | 2.50 |
| Los Angeles Rams | | | |
| ☐ 122 Bobby Dillon | 6.00 | 2.70 | .75 |
| Green Bay Packers | | | |
| ☐ 123 Leo Sanford | 6.00 | 2.70 | .75 |
| Chicago Cardinals | | | |
| ☐ 124 Elbert Nickel | 6.00 | 2.70 | .75 |
| Pittsburgh Steelers | | | |
| ☐ 125 Wayne Hansen | 6.00 | 2.70 | .75 |
| Chicago Bears | | | |
| ☐ 126 Buck Lansford | 6.00 | 2.70 | .75 |
| Philadelphia Eagles | | | |
| ☐ 127 Gern Nagler | 6.00 | 2.70 | .75 |
| Chicago Cardinals | | | |
| ☐ 128 Jim Salsbury | 6.00 | 2.70 | .75 |
| Detroit Lions | | | |
| ☐ 129 Dale Atkeson | 6.00 | 2.70 | .75 |
| Washington Redskins | | | |
| ☐ 130 John Schweder | 6.00 | 2.70 | .75 |
| Pittsburgh Steelers | | | |
| ☐ 131 Dave Hanner | 7.00 | 3.10 | .85 |
| Green Bay Packers | | | |
| ☐ 132 Eddie Price | 6.00 | 2.70 | .75 |
| New York Giants | | | |
| ☐ 133 Vic Janowicz | 18.00 | 8.00 | 2.30 |
| Washington Redskins | | | |
| ☐ 134 Ernie Stautner | 20.00 | 9.00 | 2.50 |
| Pittsburgh Steelers | | | |
| ☐ 135 James Parmer | 6.00 | 2.70 | .75 |
| Philadelphia Eagles | | | |
| ☐ 136 Emlen Tunnell UER | 20.00 | 9.00 | 2.50* |
| New York Giants | | | |
| (Misspelled Tunnel | | | |

| | | | |
|---|---|---|---|
| on card front) | | | |
| ☐ 137 Kyle Rote UER | 15.00 | 6.75 | 1.90 |
| (Longest gain 1.8 yards, | | | |
| should be 18 yards) | | | |
| New York Giants | | | |
| ☐ 138 Norm Willey | 6.00 | 2.70 | .75 |
| Philadelphia Eagles | | | |
| ☐ 139 Charley Trippi | 18.00 | 8.00 | 2.30 |
| Chicago Cardinals | | | |
| ☐ 140 Bill Howton | 8.00 | 3.60 | 1.00 |
| Green Bay Packers | | | |
| ☐ 141 Bobby Clatterbuck | 6.00 | 2.70 | .75 |
| New York Giants | | | |
| ☐ 142 Bob Boyd | 6.00 | 2.70 | .75 |
| Los Angeles Rams | | | |
| ☐ 143 Bob Toneff | 8.00 | 3.60 | 1.00 |
| San Francisco 49ers | | | |
| ☐ 144 Jerry Helluin | 6.00 | 2.70 | .75 |
| Green Bay Packers | | | |
| ☐ 145 Adrian Burk | 6.00 | 2.70 | .75 |
| Philadelphia Eagles | | | |
| ☐ 146 Walt Michaels | 8.00 | 3.60 | 1.00 |
| Cleveland Browns | | | |
| ☐ 147 Zollie Toth | 6.00 | 2.70 | .75 |
| Baltimore Colts | | | |
| ☐ 148 Frank Varrichione | 8.00 | 3.60 | 1.00 |
| Pittsburgh Steelers | | | |
| ☐ 149 Dick Bielski | 7.00 | 3.10 | .85 |
| Philadelphia Eagles | | | |
| ☐ 150 George Ratterman | 7.00 | 3.10 | .85 |
| Cleveland Browns | | | |
| ☐ 151 Mike Jarmoluk | 6.00 | 2.70 | .75 |
| Philadelphia Eagles | | | |
| ☐ 152 Tom Landry | 175.00 | 80.00 | 22.00 |
| New York Giants | | | |
| ☐ 153 Ray Renfro | 7.00 | 3.10 | .85 |
| Cleveland Browns | | | |
| ☐ 154 Zeke Bratkowski | 8.00 | 3.60 | 1.00 |
| Chicago Bears | | | |
| ☐ 155 Jerry Norton | 6.00 | 2.70 | .75 |
| Philadelphia Eagles | | | |
| ☐ 156 Maurice Bassett | 6.00 | 2.70 | .75 |
| Cleveland Browns | | | |
| ☐ 157 Volney Quinlan | 6.00 | 2.70 | .75 |
| Los Angeles Rams | | | |
| ☐ 158 Chuck Bednarik | 25.00 | 11.50 | 3.10 |
| Philadelphia Eagles | | | |
| ☐ 159 Don Colo | 7.00 | 3.10 | .85 |
| Cleveland Browns | | | |
| ☐ 160 L.G. Dupre | 30.00 | 6.00 | 1.80 |
| Baltimore Colts | | | |

# 1991 Bowman

The premier edition of the 1991 Bowman Football set was produced by Topps and contains 561 cards. The cards measure the standard size (2 1/2" by 3 1/2"). The cards were available in wax packs, jumbo packs, and factory set form. The fronts feature color player photos, with blue and orange borders on a white card face. The player's name appears in white lettering in a purple stripe below the picture. The backs are printed in black and green on gray and present biography, player profile, and last season's statistics. The cards are numbered on the back and checklisted below alphabetically according to teams as follows: Atlanta Falcons (12-29), Buffalo Bills (30-50), Chicago Bears (51-71), Cincinnati Bengals (72-88), Cleveland Browns (89-103), Dallas Cowboys (104-122), Denver Broncos (123-142), Detroit Lions (143-158), Green Bay Packers (159-178), Houston Oilers (179-197), Indianapolis Colts (198-214), Kansas City Chiefs (215-234), Los Angeles Raiders (235-253), Los Angeles Rams (254-283), Miami Dolphins (284-302), Minnesota Vikings (303-320), New England Patriots (321-336), New Orleans Saints (337-355), New York Giants (356-375), New York Jets (376-394), Philadelphia Eagles (395-413), Phoenix Cardinals (414-431), Pittsburgh Steelers (432-449), San

Diego Chargers (450-468), San Francisco 49ers (469-490), Seattle Seahawks (491-509), Tampa Bay Buccaneers (510-527), and Washington Redskins (528-546). Subsets within this set include Rookie Superstars (1-11), League Leaders (273-283), and Road to Super Bowl XXV (547-557). These 33 cards are gold foil embossed, and each pack contains one of these foil cards. The cards are numbered on the back. The key Rookie Cards in this set are Nick Bell, Mike Croel, Ricky Ervins, Alvin Harper, Randal Hill, Todd Marinovich, Dan McGwire, Herman Moore, Browning Nagle, Mike Pritchard, Ricky Watters, and Harvey Williams.

| | MINT | EXC | G-VG |
|---|---|---|---|
| COMPLETE SET (561) | 10.00 | 4.50 | 1.25 |
| COMPLETE FACT.SET (561) | 10.00 | 4.50 | 1.25 |
| COMMON PLAYER (1-561) | .04 | .02 | .01 |
| | | | |
| ☐ 1 Jeff George RS | .15 | .07 | .02 |
| ☐ 2 Richmond Webb RS | .04 | .02 | .01 |
| ☐ 3 Emmitt Smith RS | 1.00 | .45 | .13 |
| ☐ 4 Mark Carrier RS UER | .80 | .40 | .01 |
| (Chambers was rookie in '73, not '74) | | | |
| ☐ 5 Steve Christie RS | .04 | .02 | .01 |
| ☐ 6 Keith Sims RS | .04 | .02 | .01 |
| ☐ 7 Rob Moore RS UER | .08 | .04 | .01 |
| (Yards misspelled as yarders on back) | | | |
| ☐ 8 Johnny Johnson RS | .12 | .05 | .02 |
| ☐ 9 Eric Green RS | .08 | .04 | .01 |
| ☐ 10 Ben Smith RS | .04 | .02 | .01 |
| ☐ 11 Tory Epps RS | .04 | .02 | .01 |
| ☐ 12 Andre Rison | .25 | .11 | .03 |
| ☐ 13 Shawn Collins | .04 | .02 | .01 |
| ☐ 14 Chris Hinton | .04 | .02 | .01 |
| ☐ 15 Deion Sanders UER | .25 | .11 | .03 |
| (Bio says he played for Georgia, College listed should be Florida State) | | | |
| ☐ 16 Darion Conner | .04 | .02 | .01 |
| ☐ 17 Michael Haynes | .30 | .14 | .04 |
| ☐ 18 Chris Miller | .10 | .05 | .01 |
| ☐ 19 Jessie Tuggle | .04 | .02 | .01 |
| ☐ 20 Scott Fulhage | .04 | .02 | .01 |
| ☐ 21 Bill Fralic | .04 | .02 | .01 |
| ☐ 22 Floyd Dixon | .04 | .02 | .01 |
| ☐ 23 Oliver Barnett | .04 | .02 | .01 |
| ☐ 24 Mike Rozier | .08 | .04 | .01 |
| ☐ 25 Tory Epps | .04 | .02 | .01 |
| ☐ 26 Tim Green | .04 | .02 | .01 |
| ☐ 27 Steve Broussard | .08 | .04 | .01 |
| ☐ 28 Bruce Pickens | .10 | .05 | .01 |
| ☐ 29 Mike Pritchard | .75 | .35 | .09 |
| ☐ 30 Andre Reed | .10 | .05 | .01 |
| ☐ 31 Darryl Talley | .08 | .04 | .01 |
| ☐ 32 Nate Odomes | .10 | .05 | .01 |
| ☐ 33 Jamie Mueller | .04 | .02 | .01 |
| ☐ 34 Leon Seals | .04 | .02 | .01 |
| ☐ 35 Keith McKeller | .04 | .02 | .01 |
| ☐ 36 Al Edwards | .04 | .02 | .01 |
| ☐ 37 Butch Rolle | .04 | .02 | .01 |
| ☐ 38 Jeff Wright | .10 | .05 | .01 |
| ☐ 39 Will Wolford | .04 | .02 | .01 |
| ☐ 40 James Williams | .04 | .02 | .01 |
| ☐ 41 Kent Hull | .04 | .02 | .01 |
| ☐ 42 James Lofton | .10 | .05 | .01 |
| ☐ 43 Frank Reich | .10 | .05 | .01 |
| ☐ 44 Bruce Smith | .10 | .05 | .01 |
| ☐ 45 Thurman Thomas | .40 | .18 | .05 |
| ☐ 46 Leonard Smith | .04 | .02 | .01 |
| ☐ 47 Shane Conlan | .08 | .04 | .01 |
| ☐ 48 Steve Tasker | .08 | .04 | .01 |
| ☐ 49 Ray Bentley | .04 | .02 | .01 |
| ☐ 50 Cornelius Bennett | .10 | .05 | .01 |
| ☐ 51 Stan Thomas | .04 | .02 | .01 |
| ☐ 52 Shaun Gayle | .04 | .02 | .01 |
| ☐ 53 Wendell Davis | .04 | .02 | .01 |
| ☐ 54 James Thornton | .04 | .02 | .01 |
| ☐ 55 Mark Carrier | .08 | .04 | .01 |
| ☐ 56 Richard Dent | .08 | .04 | .01 |
| ☐ 57 Ron Morris | .04 | .02 | .01 |
| ☐ 58 Mike Singletary | .10 | .05 | .01 |
| ☐ 59 Jay Hilgenberg | .08 | .04 | .01 |
| ☐ 60 Donnell Woolford | .04 | .02 | .01 |
| ☐ 61 Jim Covert | .04 | .02 | .01 |
| ☐ 62 Jim Harbaugh | .08 | .04 | .01 |
| ☐ 63 Neal Anderson | .08 | .04 | .01 |
| ☐ 64 Brad Muster | .08 | .04 | .01 |
| ☐ 65 Kevin Butler | .04 | .02 | .01 |
| ☐ 66 Trace Armstrong UER | .04 | .02 | .01 |
| (Bio says 80 tackles in '90, stats say 82) | | | |
| ☐ 67 Ron Cox | .04 | .02 | .01 |
| ☐ 68 Peter Tom Willis | .04 | .02 | .01 |
| ☐ 69 Johnny Bailey | .08 | .04 | .01 |
| ☐ 70 Mark Bortz UER | .04 | .02 | .01 |
| (Bio has 6th round, but was 8th round) | | | |
| ☐ 71 Chris Zorich | .25 | .11 | .03 |
| ☐ 72 Lamar Rogers | .04 | .02 | .01 |
| ☐ 73 David Grant UER | .04 | .02 | .01 |
| (Listed as DE, but should be NT) | | | |
| ☐ 74 Lewis Billups | .04 | .02 | .01 |
| ☐ 75 Harold Green | .10 | .05 | .01 |
| ☐ 76 Ickey Woods | .04 | .02 | .01 |
| ☐ 77 Eddie Brown | .04 | .02 | .01 |
| ☐ 78 David Fulcher | .04 | .02 | .01 |
| ☐ 79 Anthony Munoz | .08 | .04 | .01 |
| ☐ 80 Carl Zander | .04 | .02 | .01 |
| ☐ 81 Rodney Holman | .04 | .02 | .01 |
| ☐ 82 James Brooks | .08 | .04 | .01 |
| ☐ 83 Tim McGee | .04 | .02 | .01 |
| ☐ 84 Boomer Esiason | .15 | .07 | .02 |
| ☐ 85 Leon White | .04 | .02 | .01 |
| ☐ 86 James Francis UER | .08 | .04 | .01 |
| (Ron is CB, card says he's LB) | | | |
| ☐ 87 Mitchell Price | .04 | .02 | .01 |
| ☐ 88 Ed King | .04 | .02 | .01 |
| ☐ 89 Eric Turner | .20 | .09 | .03 |
| ☐ 90 Rob Burnett | .15 | .07 | .02 |
| ☐ 91 Leroy Hoard | .08 | .04 | .01 |
| ☐ 92 Kevin Mack UER | .08 | .04 | .01 |
| (Height 6-2, should be 6-0) | | | |
| ☐ 93 Thane Gash UER | .04 | .02 | .01 |
| (Comma omitted after name in bio) | | | |
| ☐ 94 Gregg Rakoczy | .04 | .02 | .01 |
| ☐ 95 Clay Matthews | .08 | .04 | .01 |
| ☐ 96 Eric Metcalf | .10 | .05 | .01 |
| ☐ 97 Stephen Braggs | .04 | .02 | .01 |
| ☐ 98 Frank Minnifield | .04 | .02 | .01 |
| ☐ 99 Reggie Langhorne | .08 | .04 | .01 |
| ☐ 100 Mike Johnson | .04 | .02 | .01 |
| ☐ 101 Brian Brennan | .04 | .02 | .01 |
| ☐ 102 Anthony Pleasant | .04 | .02 | .01 |
| ☐ 103 Godfrey Myles UER | .10 | .05 | .01 |
| (Vertical misspelled as verticle) | | | |
| ☐ 104 Russell Maryland | .40 | .18 | .05 |
| ☐ 105 James Washington | .20 | .09 | .03 |
| ☐ 106 Nate Newton | .04 | .02 | .01 |
| ☐ 107 Jimmie Jones | .04 | .02 | .01 |
| ☐ 108 Jay Novacek | .15 | .07 | .02 |
| ☐ 109 Alexander Wright | .08 | .04 | .01 |
| ☐ 110 Jack Del Rio | .04 | .02 | .01 |
| ☐ 111 Jim Jeffcoat | .04 | .02 | .01 |
| ☐ 112 Mike Saxon | .04 | .02 | .01 |
| ☐ 113 Troy Aikman | 1.25 | .55 | .16 |
| ☐ 114 Issiac Holt | .04 | .02 | .01 |
| ☐ 115 Ken Norton | .10 | .05 | .01 |
| ☐ 116 Kelvin Martin | .08 | .04 | .01 |
| ☐ 117 Emmitt Smith | 2.00 | .90 | .25 |
| ☐ 118 Ken Willis | .04 | .02 | .01 |
| ☐ 119 Daniel Stubbs | .04 | .02 | .01 |
| ☐ 120 Michael Irvin | .50 | .23 | .06 |
| ☐ 121 Danny Noonan | .04 | .02 | .01 |
| ☐ 122 Alvin Harper UER | 1.00 | .45 | .13 |
| (Drafted in first round, not second) | | | |
| ☐ 123 Reggie Johnson | .15 | .07 | .02 |
| ☐ 124 Vance Johnson | .08 | .04 | .01 |
| ☐ 125 Steve Atwater | .10 | .05 | .01 |
| ☐ 126 Greg Kragen | .04 | .02 | .01 |
| ☐ 127 John Elway | .35 | .16 | .04 |
| ☐ 128 Simon Fletcher | .08 | .04 | .01 |
| ☐ 129 Wymon Henderson | .04 | .02 | .01 |
| ☐ 130 Ricky Nattiel | .04 | .02 | .01 |
| ☐ 131 Shannon Sharpe | .60 | .25 | .08 |
| ☐ 132 Ron Holmes | .04 | .02 | .01 |
| ☐ 133 Karl Mecklenburg | .08 | .04 | .01 |
| ☐ 134 Bobby Humphrey | .08 | .04 | .01 |
| ☐ 135 Clarence Kay | .04 | .02 | .01 |
| ☐ 136 Dennis Smith | .08 | .04 | .01 |
| ☐ 137 Jim Juriga | .04 | .02 | .01 |
| ☐ 138 Melvin Bratton | .04 | .02 | .01 |
| ☐ 139 Mark Jackson UER | .08 | .04 | .01 |
| (Apostrophe placed in front of longest) | | | |
| ☐ 140 Michael Brooks | .04 | .02 | .01 |
| ☐ 141 Alton Montgomery | .04 | .02 | .01 |
| ☐ 142 Mike Croel | .20 | .09 | .03 |
| ☐ 143 Mel Gray | .08 | .04 | .01 |
| ☐ 144 Michael Cofer | .04 | .02 | .01 |
| ☐ 145 Jeff Campbell | .04 | .02 | .01 |
| ☐ 146 Dan Owens | .04 | .02 | .01 |
| ☐ 147 Robert Clark UER | .04 | .02 | .01 |
| (Drafted in '87, not '89) | | | |
| ☐ 148 Jim Arnold | .04 | .02 | .01 |
| ☐ 149 William White | .04 | .02 | .01 |
| ☐ 150 Rodney Peete | .08 | .04 | .01 |
| ☐ 151 Jerry Ball | .08 | .04 | .01 |

| | | | |
|---|---|---|---|
| ☐ 152 Bennie Blades | .04 | .02 | .01 |
| ☐ 153 Barry Sanders UER | .75 | .35 | .09 |
| (Drafted in '89, not '88) | | | |
| ☐ 154 Andre Ware | .10 | .05 | .01 |
| ☐ 155 Lomas Brown | .04 | .02 | .01 |
| ☐ 156 Chris Spielman | .08 | .04 | .01 |
| ☐ 157 Kelvin Pritchett | .04 | .02 | .01 |
| ☐ 158 Herman Moore | 1.00 | .45 | .13 |
| ☐ 159 Chris Jacke | .04 | .02 | .01 |
| ☐ 160 Tony Mandarich | .04 | .02 | .01 |
| ☐ 161 Perry Kemp | .04 | .02 | .01 |
| ☐ 162 Johnny Holland | .04 | .02 | .01 |
| ☐ 163 Mark Lee | .04 | .02 | .01 |
| ☐ 164 Anthony Dilweg | .08 | .04 | .01 |
| ☐ 165 Scott Stephen | .04 | .02 | .01 |
| ☐ 166 Ed West | .04 | .02 | .01 |
| ☐ 167 Mark Murphy | .04 | .02 | .01 |
| ☐ 168 Darrell Thompson | .08 | .04 | .01 |
| ☐ 169 James Campen | .04 | .02 | .01 |
| ☐ 170 Jeff Query | .04 | .02 | .01 |
| ☐ 171 Brian Noble | .04 | .02 | .01 |
| ☐ 172 Sterling Sharpe UER | .50 | .23 | .06 |
| (Card says he gained 3314 yards in 1990) | | | |
| ☐ 173 Robert Brown | .04 | .02 | .01 |
| ☐ 174 Tim Harris | .08 | .04 | .01 |
| ☐ 175 LeRoy Butler | .04 | .02 | .01 |
| ☐ 176 Don Majkowski | .08 | .04 | .01 |
| ☐ 177 Vinnie Clark | .04 | .02 | .01 |
| ☐ 178 Esera Tuaolo | .04 | .02 | .01 |
| ☐ 179 Lorenzo White UER | .08 | .04 | .01 |
| (Bio says 3rd year, actually 4th year) | | | |
| ☐ 180 Warren Moon | .20 | .09 | .03 |
| ☐ 181 Sean Jones | .08 | .04 | .01 |
| ☐ 182 Curtis Duncan | .08 | .04 | .01 |
| ☐ 183 Al Smith | .04 | .02 | .01 |
| ☐ 184 Richard Johnson | .04 | .02 | .01 |
| ☐ 185 Tony Jones | .04 | .02 | .01 |
| ☐ 186 Bubba McDowell | .04 | .02 | .01 |
| ☐ 187 Bruce Matthews | .08 | .04 | .01 |
| ☐ 188 Ray Childress | .08 | .04 | .01 |
| ☐ 189 Haywood Jeffires | .15 | .07 | .02 |
| ☐ 190 Ernest Givins | .08 | .04 | .01 |
| ☐ 191 Mike Munchak | .08 | .04 | .01 |
| ☐ 192 Greg Montgomery | .04 | .02 | .01 |
| ☐ 193 Cody Carlson | .75 | .35 | .09 |
| ☐ 194 Johnny Meads | .04 | .02 | .01 |
| ☐ 195 Drew Hill UER | .08 | .04 | .01 |
| (Age listed as 24, should be 34) | | | |
| ☐ 196 Mike Dumas | .04 | .02 | .01 |
| ☐ 197 Darryll Lewis | .10 | .05 | .01 |
| ☐ 198 Rohn Stark | .04 | .02 | .01 |
| ☐ 199 Clarence Verdin UER | .04 | .02 | .01 |
| (Played 2 seasons in USFL, not one) | | | |
| ☐ 200 Mike Prior | .04 | .02 | .01 |
| ☐ 201 Eugene Daniel | .04 | .02 | .01 |
| ☐ 202 Dean Biasucci | .04 | .02 | .01 |
| ☐ 203 Jeff Herrod | .04 | .02 | .01 |
| ☐ 204 Keith Taylor | .04 | .02 | .01 |
| ☐ 205 Jon Hand | .04 | .02 | .01 |
| ☐ 206 Pat Beach | .04 | .02 | .01 |
| ☐ 207 Duane Bickett | .04 | .02 | .01 |
| ☐ 208 Jessie Hester UER | .08 | .04 | .01 |
| (Bio confuses Hester's NFL history) | | | |
| ☐ 209 Chip Banks | .04 | .02 | .01 |
| ☐ 210 Ray Donaldson | .04 | .02 | .01 |
| ☐ 211 Bill Brooks | .08 | .04 | .01 |
| ☐ 212 Jeff George | .25 | .11 | .03 |
| ☐ 213 Tony Siragusa | .04 | .02 | .01 |
| ☐ 214 Albert Bentley | .04 | .02 | .01 |
| ☐ 215 Joe Valerio | .04 | .02 | .01 |
| ☐ 216 Chris Martin | .04 | .02 | .01 |
| ☐ 217 Christian Okoye | .08 | .04 | .01 |
| ☐ 218 Stephone Paige | .08 | .04 | .01 |
| ☐ 219 Percy Snow | .04 | .02 | .01 |
| ☐ 220 David Szott | .04 | .02 | .01 |
| ☐ 221 Derrick Thomas | .25 | .11 | .03 |
| ☐ 222 Todd McNair | .04 | .02 | .01 |
| ☐ 223 Albert Lewis | .08 | .04 | .01 |
| ☐ 224 Neil Smith | .10 | .05 | .01 |
| ☐ 225 Barry Word | .10 | .05 | .01 |
| ☐ 226 Robb Thomas | .04 | .02 | .01 |
| ☐ 227 John Alt | .04 | .02 | .01 |
| ☐ 228 Jonathan Hayes | .04 | .02 | .01 |
| ☐ 229 Kevin Ross | .08 | .04 | .01 |
| ☐ 230 Nick Lowery | .08 | .04 | .01 |
| ☐ 231 Tim Grunhard | .04 | .02 | .01 |
| ☐ 232 Dan Saleaumua | .04 | .02 | .01 |
| ☐ 233 Steve DeBerg | .08 | .04 | .01 |
| ☐ 234 Harvey Williams | .25 | .11 | .03 |
| ☐ 235 Nick Bell UER | .20 | .09 | .03 |
| (Lives in Nevada, not California) | | | |
| ☐ 236 Mervyn Fernandez UER | .04 | .02 | .01 |
| (Drafted in '83, not FA '87 as on card) | | | |
| ☐ 237 Howie Long | .08 | .04 | .01 |
| ☐ 238 Marcus Allen | .15 | .07 | .02 |
| ☐ 239 Eddie Anderson | .04 | .02 | .01 |
| ☐ 240 Ethan Horton | .04 | .02 | .01 |
| ☐ 241 Lionel Washington | .04 | .02 | .01 |
| ☐ 242 Steve Wisniewski UER | .04 | .02 | .01 |
| (Drafted, should be traded to) | | | |
| ☐ 243 Bo Jackson UER | .35 | .16 | .04 |
| (Drafted by Raiders, should say drafted by Tampa Bay in '86) | | | |
| ☐ 244 Greg Townsend | .04 | .02 | .01 |
| ☐ 245 Jeff Jaeger | .04 | .02 | .01 |
| ☐ 246 Aaron Wallace | .04 | .02 | .01 |
| ☐ 247 Garry Lewis | .04 | .02 | .01 |
| ☐ 248 Steve Smith | .08 | .04 | .01 |
| ☐ 249 Willie Gault UER | .08 | .04 | .01 |
| ('90 stats 839 yards, should be 985) | | | |
| ☐ 250 Scott Davis | .04 | .02 | .01 |
| ☐ 251 Jay Schroeder | .08 | .04 | .01 |
| ☐ 252 Don Mosebar | .04 | .02 | .01 |
| ☐ 253 Todd Marinovich | .08 | .04 | .01 |
| ☐ 254 Irv Pankey | .04 | .02 | .01 |
| ☐ 255 Flipper Anderson | .08 | .04 | .01 |
| ☐ 256 Tom Newberry | .04 | .02 | .01 |
| ☐ 257 Kevin Greene | .08 | .04 | .01 |
| ☐ 258 Mike Wilcher | .04 | .02 | .01 |
| ☐ 259 Bern Brostek | .04 | .02 | .01 |
| ☐ 260 Buford McGee | .04 | .02 | .01 |
| ☐ 261 Cleveland Gary | .08 | .04 | .01 |
| ☐ 262 Jackie Slater | .08 | .04 | .01 |
| ☐ 263 Henry Ellard | .08 | .04 | .01 |
| ☐ 264 Alvin Wright | .04 | .02 | .01 |
| ☐ 265 Darryl Henley | .04 | .02 | .01 |
| ☐ 266 Damone Johnson | .04 | .02 | .01 |
| ☐ 267 Frank Stams | .04 | .02 | .01 |
| ☐ 268 Jerry Gray | .04 | .02 | .01 |
| ☐ 269 Jim Everett | .08 | .04 | .01 |
| ☐ 270 Pat Terrell | .04 | .02 | .01 |
| ☐ 271 Todd Lyght | .10 | .05 | .01 |
| ☐ 272 Aaron Cox | .04 | .02 | .01 |
| ☐ 273 Barry Sanders LL Rushing Leader | .35 | .16 | .04 |
| ☐ 274 Jerry Rice LL Receiving Leader | .35 | .16 | .04 |
| ☐ 275 Derrick Thomas LL Sack Leader | .12 | .05 | .02 |
| ☐ 276 Mark Carrier LL Interception Leader | .04 | .02 | .01 |
| ☐ 277 Warren Moon LL Passing Yardage Leader | .10 | .05 | .01 |
| ☐ 278 Randall Cunningham LL Rushing Average Leader | .08 | .04 | .01 |
| ☐ 279 Nick Lowery LL Scoring Leader | .04 | .02 | .01 |
| ☐ 280 Clarence Verdin LL Punt Return Leader | .04 | .02 | .01 |
| ☐ 281 Thurman Thomas LL Yards From Scrimmage Leader | .20 | .09 | .03 |
| ☐ 282 Mike Horan LL Punting Average Leader | .04 | .02 | .01 |
| ☐ 283 Flipper Anderson LL Receiving Average Leader | .04 | .02 | .01 |
| ☐ 284 John Offerdahl | .08 | .04 | .01 |
| ☐ 285 Dan Marino UER | .75 | .35 | .09 |
| (2637 yards gained, should be 3563) | | | |
| ☐ 286 Mark Clayton | .08 | .04 | .01 |
| ☐ 287 Tony Paige | .04 | .02 | .01 |
| ☐ 288 Keith Sims | .04 | .02 | .01 |
| ☐ 289 Jeff Cross | .04 | .02 | .01 |
| ☐ 290 Pete Stoyanovich | .08 | .04 | .01 |
| ☐ 291 Ferrell Edmunds | .04 | .02 | .01 |
| ☐ 292 Reggie Roby | .04 | .02 | .01 |
| ☐ 293 Louis Oliver | .08 | .04 | .01 |
| ☐ 294 Jarvis Williams | .04 | .02 | .01 |
| ☐ 295 Sammie Smith | .04 | .02 | .01 |
| ☐ 296 Richmond Webb | .08 | .04 | .01 |
| ☐ 297 J.B. Brown | .04 | .02 | .01 |
| ☐ 298 Jim Jensen | .04 | .02 | .01 |
| ☐ 299 Mark Duper | .08 | .04 | .01 |
| ☐ 300 David Griggs | .04 | .02 | .01 |
| ☐ 301 Randal Hill | .30 | .14 | .04 |
| ☐ 302 Aaron Craver | .04 | .02 | .01 |
| (See also 320) | | | |
| ☐ 303 Keith Millard | .08 | .04 | .01 |
| ☐ 304 Steve Jordan | .08 | .04 | .01 |
| ☐ 305 Anthony Carter | .08 | .04 | .01 |
| ☐ 306 Mike Merriweather | .04 | .02 | .01 |
| ☐ 307 Audray McMillian UER | .30 | .14 | .04 |
| (Front Audray, | | | |

|  |  | | | |
|---|--------|---|---|---|
| | (back Audrey) | | | |
| ☐ 308 | Randall McDaniel | .04 | .02 | .01 |
| ☐ 309 | Gary Zimmerman | .04 | .02 | .01 |
| ☐ 310 | Carl Lee | .04 | .02 | .01 |
| ☐ 311 | Reggie Rutland | .04 | .02 | .01 |
| ☐ 312 | Hassan Jones | .04 | .02 | .01 |
| ☐ 313 | Kirk Lowdermilk UER | .04 | .02 | .01 |
| | (Reversed negative) | | | |
| ☐ 314 | Herschel Walker | .10 | .05 | .01 |
| ☐ 315 | Chris Doleman | .08 | .04 | .01 |
| ☐ 316 | Joey Browner | .04 | .02 | .01 |
| ☐ 317 | Wade Wilson | .08 | .04 | .01 |
| ☐ 318 | Henry Thomas | .04 | .02 | .01 |
| ☐ 319 | Rich Gannon | .08 | .04 | .01 |
| ☐ 320 | Al Noga UER | .04 | .02 | .01 |
| | (Numbered incorrectly as 302 on card) | | | |
| ☐ 321 | Pat Harlow | .10 | .05 | .01 |
| ☐ 322 | Bruce Armstrong | .04 | .02 | .01 |
| ☐ 323 | Maurice Hurst | .04 | .02 | .01 |
| ☐ 324 | Brent Williams | .04 | .02 | .01 |
| ☐ 325 | Chris Singleton | .04 | .02 | .01 |
| ☐ 326 | Jason Staurovsky | .04 | .02 | .01 |
| ☐ 327 | Marvin Allen | .04 | .02 | .01 |
| ☐ 328 | Hart Lee Dykes | .04 | .02 | .01 |
| ☐ 329 | Johnny Rembert | .04 | .02 | .01 |
| ☐ 330 | Andre Tippett | .08 | .04 | .01 |
| ☐ 331 | Greg McMurtry | .04 | .02 | .01 |
| ☐ 332 | John Stephens | .08 | .04 | .01 |
| ☐ 333 | Ray Agnew | .04 | .02 | .01 |
| ☐ 334 | Tommy Hodson | .04 | .02 | .01 |
| ☐ 335 | Ronnie Lippett | .04 | .02 | .01 |
| ☐ 336 | Marv Cook | .04 | .02 | .01 |
| ☐ 337 | Tommy Barnhardt | .04 | .02 | .01 |
| ☐ 338 | Dalton Hilliard | .04 | .02 | .01 |
| ☐ 339 | Sam Mills | .08 | .04 | .01 |
| ☐ 340 | Morten Andersen | .08 | .04 | .01 |
| ☐ 341 | Stan Brock | .04 | .02 | .01 |
| ☐ 342 | Brett Maxie | .04 | .02 | .01 |
| ☐ 343 | Steve Walsh | .04 | .02 | .01 |
| ☐ 344 | Vaughan Johnson | .08 | .04 | .01 |
| ☐ 345 | Rickey Jackson | .08 | .04 | .01 |
| ☐ 346 | Renaldo Turnbull | .08 | .04 | .01 |
| ☐ 347 | Joel Hilgenberg | .04 | .02 | .01 |
| ☐ 348 | Toi Cook | .04 | .02 | .01 |
| ☐ 349 | Robert Massey | .04 | .02 | .01 |
| ☐ 350 | Pat Swilling | .08 | .04 | .01 |
| ☐ 351 | Eric Martin | .08 | .04 | .01 |
| ☐ 352 | Rueben Mayes UER | .04 | .02 | .01 |
| | (Bio says 2nd round, should be 3rd) | | | |
| ☐ 353 | Vince Buck | .04 | .02 | .01 |
| ☐ 354 | Brett Perriman | .10 | .05 | .01 |
| ☐ 355 | Wesley Carroll | .10 | .05 | .01 |
| ☐ 356 | Jarrod Bunch | .15 | .07 | .02 |
| ☐ 357 | Pepper Johnson | .08 | .04 | .01 |
| ☐ 358 | Dave Meggett | .10 | .05 | .01 |
| ☐ 359 | Mark Collins | .04 | .02 | .01 |
| ☐ 360 | Sean Landeta | .04 | .02 | .01 |
| ☐ 361 | Maurice Carthon | .04 | .02 | .01 |
| ☐ 362 | Mike Fox UER | .04 | .02 | .01 |
| | (Listed as DE, should say DT) | | | |
| ☐ 363 | Jeff Hostetler | .25 | .11 | .03 |
| ☐ 364 | Phil Simms | .10 | .05 | .01 |
| ☐ 365 | Leonard Marshall | .08 | .04 | .01 |
| ☐ 366 | Gary Reasons | .04 | .02 | .01 |
| ☐ 367 | Rodney Hampton | .75 | .35 | .09 |
| ☐ 368 | Greg Jackson | .10 | .05 | .01 |
| ☐ 369 | Jumbo Elliott | .04 | .02 | .01 |
| ☐ 370 | Bob Kratch | .10 | .05 | .01 |
| ☐ 371 | Lawrence Taylor | .10 | .05 | .01 |
| ☐ 372 | Erik Howard | .04 | .02 | .01 |
| ☐ 373 | Carl Banks | .08 | .04 | .01 |
| ☐ 374 | Stephen Baker | .04 | .02 | .01 |
| ☐ 375 | Mark Ingram | .08 | .04 | .01 |
| ☐ 376 | Browning Nagle | .20 | .09 | .03 |
| ☐ 377 | Jeff Lageman | .04 | .02 | .01 |
| ☐ 378 | Ken O'Brien | .08 | .04 | .01 |
| ☐ 379 | Al Toon | .08 | .04 | .01 |
| ☐ 380 | Joe Prokop | .04 | .02 | .01 |
| ☐ 381 | Tony Stargell | .04 | .02 | .01 |
| ☐ 382 | Blair Thomas | .08 | .04 | .01 |
| ☐ 383 | Erik McMillan | .04 | .02 | .01 |
| ☐ 384 | Dennis Byrd | .08 | .04 | .01 |
| ☐ 385 | Freeman McNeil | .04 | .02 | .01 |
| ☐ 386 | Brad Baxter | .08 | .04 | .01 |
| ☐ 387 | Mark Boyer | .04 | .02 | .01 |
| ☐ 388 | Terance Mathis | .04 | .02 | .01 |
| ☐ 389 | Jim Sweeney | .04 | .02 | .01 |
| ☐ 390 | Kyle Clifton | .04 | .02 | .01 |
| ☐ 391 | Pat Leahy | .08 | .04 | .01 |
| ☐ 392 | Rob Moore | .10 | .05 | .01 |
| ☐ 393 | James Hasty | .04 | .02 | .01 |
| ☐ 394 | Blaise Bryant | .04 | .02 | .01 |
| ☐ 395A | Jesse Campbell ERR | 1.50 | .65 | .19 |
| | (Photo actually Dan McGwire; see 509) | | | |
| ☐ 395B | Jesse Campbell COR | .10 | .05 | .01 |
| ☐ 396 | Keith Jackson | .15 | .07 | .02 |
| ☐ 397 | Jerome Brown | .08 | .04 | .01 |
| ☐ 398 | Keith Byars | .08 | .04 | .01 |
| ☐ 399 | Seth Joyner | .08 | .04 | .01 |
| ☐ 400 | Mike Bellamy | .04 | .02 | .01 |
| ☐ 401 | Fred Barnett | .15 | .07 | .02 |
| ☐ 402 | Reggie Singletary | .04 | .02 | .01 |
| ☐ 403 | Reggie White | .15 | .07 | .02 |
| ☐ 404 | Randall Cunningham | .10 | .05 | .01 |
| ☐ 405 | Byron Evans | .08 | .04 | .01 |
| ☐ 406 | Wes Hopkins | .04 | .02 | .01 |
| ☐ 407 | Ben Smith | .04 | .02 | .01 |
| ☐ 408 | Roger Ruzek | .04 | .02 | .01 |
| ☐ 409 | Eric Allen UER | .08 | .04 | .01 |
| | (Comparative misspelled as comparate) | | | |
| ☐ 410 | Anthony Toney UER | .04 | .02 | .01 |
| | (Heath Sherman was rookie in '89, not '90) | | | |
| ☐ 411 | Clyde Simmons | .08 | .04 | .01 |
| ☐ 412 | Andre Waters | .04 | .02 | .01 |
| ☐ 413 | Calvin Williams | .20 | .09 | .03 |
| ☐ 414 | Eric Swann | .20 | .09 | .03 |
| ☐ 415 | Eric Hill | .04 | .02 | .01 |
| ☐ 416 | Tim McDonald | .08 | .04 | .01 |
| ☐ 417 | Luis Sharpe | .04 | .02 | .01 |
| ☐ 418 | Ernie Jones UER | .04 | .02 | .01 |
| | (Photo actually Steve Jordan) | | | |
| ☐ 419 | Ken Harvey | .04 | .02 | .01 |
| ☐ 420 | Ricky Proehl | .10 | .05 | .01 |
| ☐ 421 | Johnny Johnson | .25 | .11 | .03 |
| ☐ 422 | Anthony Bell | .04 | .02 | .01 |
| ☐ 423 | Timm Rosenbach | .08 | .04 | .01 |
| ☐ 424 | Rich Camarillo | .04 | .02 | .01 |
| ☐ 425 | Walter Reeves | .04 | .02 | .01 |
| ☐ 426 | Freddie Joe Nunn | .04 | .02 | .01 |
| ☐ 427 | Anthony Thompson UER | .04 | .02 | .01 |
| | (40 touchdowns, sic) | | | |
| ☐ 428 | Bill Lewis | .04 | .02 | .01 |
| ☐ 429 | Jim Wahler | .10 | .05 | .01 |
| ☐ 430 | Cedric Mack | .04 | .02 | .01 |
| ☐ 431 | Michael Jones | .10 | .05 | .01 |
| ☐ 432 | Ernie Mills | .10 | .05 | .01 |
| ☐ 433 | Tim Worley | .08 | .04 | .01 |
| ☐ 434 | Greg Lloyd | .04 | .02 | .01 |
| ☐ 435 | Dermontti Dawson | .04 | .02 | .01 |
| ☐ 436 | Louis Lipps | .08 | .04 | .01 |
| ☐ 437 | Eric Green | .15 | .07 | .02 |
| ☐ 438 | Donald Evans | .04 | .02 | .01 |
| ☐ 439 | David Johnson | .04 | .02 | .01 |
| ☐ 440 | Tunch Ilkin | .04 | .02 | .01 |
| ☐ 441 | Bubby Brister | .08 | .04 | .01 |
| ☐ 442 | Chris Calloway | .04 | .02 | .01 |
| ☐ 443 | David Little | .04 | .02 | .01 |
| ☐ 444 | Thomas Everett | .04 | .02 | .01 |
| ☐ 445 | Carnell Lake | .04 | .02 | .01 |
| ☐ 446 | Rod Woodson | .10 | .05 | .01 |
| ☐ 447 | Gary Anderson | .08 | .04 | .01 |
| ☐ 448 | Merril Hoge | .08 | .04 | .01 |
| ☐ 449 | Gerald Williams | .04 | .02 | .01 |
| ☐ 450 | Eric Moten | .04 | .02 | .01 |
| ☐ 451 | Marion Butts | .10 | .05 | .01 |
| ☐ 452 | Leslie O'Neal | .08 | .04 | .01 |
| ☐ 453 | Ronnie Harmon | .04 | .02 | .01 |
| ☐ 454 | Gill Byrd | .08 | .04 | .01 |
| ☐ 455 | Junior Seau | .25 | .11 | .03 |
| ☐ 456 | Nate Lewis | .25 | .11 | .03 |
| ☐ 457 | Leo Goeas | .04 | .02 | .01 |
| ☐ 458 | Burt Grossman | .04 | .02 | .01 |
| ☐ 459 | Courtney Hall | .04 | .02 | .01 |
| ☐ 460 | Anthony Miller | .20 | .09 | .03 |
| ☐ 461 | Gary Plummer | .04 | .02 | .01 |
| ☐ 462 | Billy Joe Tolliver | .08 | .04 | .01 |
| ☐ 463 | Lee Williams | .08 | .04 | .01 |
| ☐ 464 | Arthur Cox | .04 | .02 | .01 |
| ☐ 465 | John Kidd UER | .04 | .02 | .01 |
| | (Stron gleg, sic) | | | |
| ☐ 466 | Frank Cornish | .04 | .02 | .01 |
| ☐ 467 | John Carney | .04 | .02 | .01 |
| ☐ 468 | Eric Bieniemy | .15 | .07 | .02 |
| ☐ 469 | Don Griffin | .04 | .02 | .01 |
| ☐ 470 | Jerry Rice | .75 | .35 | .09 |
| ☐ 471 | Keith DeLong | .04 | .02 | .01 |
| ☐ 472 | John Taylor | .10 | .05 | .01 |
| ☐ 473 | Brent Jones | .10 | .05 | .01 |
| ☐ 474 | Pierce Holt | .04 | .02 | .01 |
| ☐ 475 | Kevin Fagan | .04 | .02 | .01 |
| ☐ 476 | Bill Romanowski | .04 | .02 | .01 |
| ☐ 477 | Dexter Carter | .08 | .04 | .01 |
| ☐ 478 | Guy McIntyre | .08 | .04 | .01 |
| ☐ 479 | Joe Montana | 1.00 | .45 | .13 |
| ☐ 480 | Charles Haley | .08 | .04 | .01 |
| ☐ 481 | Mike Cofer | .04 | .02 | .01 |
| ☐ 482 | Jesse Sapolu | .04 | .02 | .01 |
| ☐ 483 | Eric Davis | .04 | .02 | .01 |

| | | | |
|---|---|---|---|
| ☐ 484 Mike Sherrard | .08 | .04 | .01 |
| ☐ 485 Steve Young | .50 | .23 | .06 |
| ☐ 486 Darryl Pollard | .04 | .02 | .01 |
| ☐ 487 Tom Rathman | .08 | .04 | .01 |
| ☐ 488 Michael Carter | .04 | .02 | .01 |
| ☐ 489 Ricky Watters | 1.25 | .55 | .16 |
| ☐ 490 John Johnson | .04 | .02 | .01 |
| ☐ 491 Eugene Robinson | .04 | .02 | .01 |
| ☐ 492 Andy Heck | .04 | .02 | .01 |
| ☐ 493 John L. Williams | .08 | .04 | .01 |
| ☐ 494 Norm Johnson | .04 | .02 | .01 |
| ☐ 495 David Wyman | .04 | .02 | .01 |
| ☐ 496 Derrick Fenner UER | .08 | .04 | .01 |
| (Drafted in '88, should be '89) | | | |
| ☐ 497 Rick Donnelly | .04 | .02 | .01 |
| ☐ 498 Tony Woods | .04 | .02 | .01 |
| ☐ 499 Derek Loville UER | .04 | .02 | .01 |
| (Ahmad Rashad is misspelled Ahmed) | | | |
| ☐ 500 Dave Krieg | .08 | .04 | .01 |
| ☐ 501 Joe Nash | .04 | .02 | .01 |
| ☐ 502 Brian Blades | .10 | .05 | .01 |
| ☐ 503 Cortez Kennedy | .25 | .11 | .03 |
| ☐ 504 Jeff Bryant | .04 | .02 | .01 |
| ☐ 505 Tommy Kane | .04 | .02 | .01 |
| ☐ 506 Travis McNeal | .04 | .02 | .01 |
| ☐ 507 Terry Wooden | .04 | .02 | .01 |
| ☐ 508 Chris Warren | .30 | .14 | .04 |
| ☐ 509A Dan McGwire ERR | .75 | .35 | .09 |
| (Photo actually Jesse Campbell; see 395) | | | |
| ☐ 509B Dan McGwire COR | .15 | .07 | .02 |
| ☐ 510 Mark Robinson | .04 | .02 | .01 |
| ☐ 511 Ron Hall | .04 | .02 | .01 |
| ☐ 512 Paul Gruber | .08 | .04 | .01 |
| ☐ 513 Harry Hamilton | .04 | .02 | .01 |
| ☐ 514 Keith McCants | .04 | .02 | .01 |
| ☐ 515 Reggie Cobb | .25 | .11 | .03 |
| ☐ 516 Steve Christie UER | .04 | .02 | .01 |
| (Listed as Californian, should be Canadian) | | | |
| ☐ 517 Broderick Thomas | .08 | .04 | .01 |
| ☐ 518 Mark Carrier | .08 | .04 | .01 |
| ☐ 519 Vinny Testaverde | .10 | .05 | .01 |
| ☐ 520 Ricky Reynolds | .04 | .02 | .01 |
| ☐ 521 Jesse Anderson | .04 | .02 | .01 |
| ☐ 522 Reuben Davis | .04 | .02 | .01 |
| ☐ 523 Wayne Haddix | .04 | .02 | .01 |
| ☐ 524 Gary Anderson UER | .08 | .04 | .01 |
| (Photo actually Don Mosebar) | | | |
| ☐ 525 Bruce Hill | .04 | .02 | .01 |
| ☐ 526 Kevin Murphy | .04 | .02 | .01 |
| ☐ 527 Lawrence Dawsey | .20 | .09 | .03 |
| ☐ 528 Ricky Ervins | .20 | .09 | .03 |
| ☐ 529 Charles Mann | .08 | .04 | .01 |
| ☐ 530 Jim Lachey | .04 | .02 | .01 |
| ☐ 531 Mark Rypien UER | .10 | .05 | .01 |
| (No stat for percentage; 2,0703 yards, sic) | | | |
| ☐ 532 Darrell Green | .08 | .04 | .01 |
| ☐ 533 Stan Humphries | .20 | .09 | .03 |
| ☐ 534 Jeff Bostic UER | .04 | .02 | .01 |
| (Age listed as 32 in stats and 33 in bio) | | | |
| ☐ 535 Earnest Byner | .08 | .04 | .01 |
| ☐ 536 Art Monk UER | .10 | .05 | .01 |
| (Bio says 718 receptions, should be 730) | | | |
| ☐ 537 Don Warren | .04 | .02 | .01 |
| ☐ 538 Darryl Grant | .04 | .02 | .01 |
| ☐ 539 Wilber Marshall | .08 | .04 | .01 |
| ☐ 540 Kurt Gouveia | .20 | .09 | .03 |
| ☐ 541 Markus Koch | .04 | .02 | .01 |
| ☐ 542 Andre Collins | .04 | .02 | .01 |
| ☐ 543 Chip Lohmiller | .08 | .04 | .01 |
| ☐ 544 Alvin Walton | .04 | .02 | .01 |
| ☐ 545 Gary Clark | .08 | .04 | .01 |
| ☐ 546 Ricky Sanders | .08 | .04 | .01 |
| ☐ 547 Redskins vs. Eagles | .08 | .04 | .01 |
| (Gary Clark) | | | |
| ☐ 548 Bengals vs. Oilers | .04 | .02 | .01 |
| (Cody Carlson) | | | |
| ☐ 549 Dolphins vs. Chiefs | .04 | .02 | .01 |
| (Mark Clayton) | | | |
| ☐ 550 Bears vs. Saints UER | .04 | .02 | .01 |
| (Neal Anderson; Name misspelled Andersen on back) | | | |
| ☐ 551 Bills vs. Dolphins | .15 | .07 | .02 |
| (Thurman Thomas) | | | |
| ☐ 552 49ers vs. Redskins | .04 | .02 | .01 |
| (Line play) | | | |
| ☐ 553 Giants vs. Bears | .04 | .02 | .01 |
| (Ottis Anderson) | | | |
| ☐ 554 Raiders vs. Bengals | .15 | .07 | .02 |

| | | | |
|---|---|---|---|
| (Bo Jackson) | | | |
| ☐ 555 AFC Championship | .08 | .04 | .01 |
| (Andre Reed) | | | |
| ☐ 556 NFC Championship | .08 | .04 | .01 |
| (Jeff Hostetler) | | | |
| ☐ 557 Super Bowl XXV | .08 | .04 | .01 |
| (Ottis Anderson) | | | |
| ☐ 558 Checklist 1-140 | .04 | .02 | .01 |
| ☐ 559 Checklist 141-280 | .04 | .02 | .01 |
| ☐ 560 Checklist 281-420 UER | .04 | .02 | .01 |
| (301 Randall Hill) | | | |
| ☐ 561 Checklist 421-561 UER | .04 | .02 | .01 |

# 1992 Bowman

 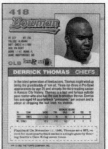

The 1992 Bowman football set consists of 573 standard-size (2 1/2" by 3 1/2") cards. The set includes a 45-card subset that consists of 28 Team Leader cards, 12 Playoff Star cards, and five special player cards commemorating the longest plays of the 1991 season (field goal, run, reception, kick return, and punt). Each of these cards has a gold-foil engraved border, and one is found in every 15-card pack. The cards measure the standard size (2 1/2" by 3 1/2"). The fronts feature color action player photos with white borders. A red "B" for Bowman overlays a short green stripe at the upper left corner, while the player's name appears in a orange-yellow stripe superimposed on the bottom edge of the picture. The only notable Rookie Card in the set is Steve Bono.

| | MINT | EXC | G-VG |
|---|---|---|---|
| COMPLETE SET (573) | 250.00 | 115.00 | 31.00 |
| COMMON PLAYER (1-573) | .20 | .09 | .03 |
| ☐ 1 Reggie White | 1.00 | .45 | .13 |
| Philadelphia Eagles | | | |
| ☐ 2 Johnny Meads | .20 | .09 | .03 |
| Houston Oilers | | | |
| ☐ 3 Chip Lohmiller | .25 | .11 | .03 |
| Washington Redskins | | | |
| ☐ 4 James Lofton | .30 | .14 | .04 |
| Buffalo Bills | | | |
| ☐ 5 Ray Horton | .20 | .09 | .03 |
| Dallas Cowboys | | | |
| ☐ 6 Rich Moran | .20 | .09 | .03 |
| Green Bay Packers | | | |
| ☐ 7 Howard Cross | .20 | .09 | .03 |
| New York Giants | | | |
| ☐ 8 Mike Horan | .20 | .09 | .03 |
| Denver Broncos | | | |
| ☐ 9 Erik Kramer | 1.75 | .80 | .22 |
| Detroit Lions | | | |
| ☐ 10 Steve Wisniewski | .20 | .09 | .03 |
| Los Angeles Raiders | | | |
| ☐ 11 Michael Haynes | 1.50 | .65 | .19 |
| Atlanta Falcons | | | |
| ☐ 12 Donald Evans | .20 | .09 | .03 |
| Pittsburgh Steelers | | | |
| ☐ 13 Michael Irvin | 8.00 | 3.60 | 1.00 |
| PL FOIL | | | |
| Dallas Cowboys | | | |
| ☐ 14 Gary Zimmerman | .20 | .09 | .03 |
| Minnesota Vikings | | | |
| ☐ 15 John Friesz | .25 | .11 | .03 |
| San Diego Chargers | | | |
| ☐ 16 Mark Carrier | .25 | .11 | .03 |
| Tampa Bay Buccaneers | | | |
| ☐ 17 Mark Duper | .25 | .11 | .03 |
| Miami Dolphins | | | |
| ☐ 18 James Thornton | .20 | .09 | .03 |
| Chicago Bears | | | |
| ☐ 19 Jon Hand | .20 | .09 | .03 |
| Indianapolis Colts | | | |
| ☐ 20 Sterling Sharpe | 6.00 | 2.70 | .75 |
| Green Bay Packers | | | |

| | | | |
|---|---|---|---|
| ☐ 21 Jacob Green | .20 | .09 | .03 |
| Seattle Seahawks | | | |
| ☐ 22 Wesley Carroll | .25 | .11 | .03 |
| New Orleans Saints | | | |
| ☐ 23 Clay Matthews | .25 | .11 | .03 |
| Cleveland Browns | | | |
| ☐ 24 Kevin Greene | .25 | .11 | .03 |
| Los Angeles Rams | | | |
| ☐ 25 Brad Baxter | .25 | .11 | .03 |
| New York Jets | | | |
| ☐ 26 Don Griffin | .20 | .09 | .03 |
| San Francisco 49ers | | | |
| ☐ 27 Robert Delpino | 4.00 | 1.80 | .50 |
| TL FOIL SP | | | |
| Los Angeles Rams | | | |
| ☐ 28 Lee Johnson | .20 | .09 | .03 |
| Cincinnati Bengals | | | |
| ☐ 29 Jim Wahler | .20 | .09 | .03 |
| Phoenix Cardinals | | | |
| ☐ 30 Leonard Russell | 3.00 | 1.35 | .40 |
| New England Patriots | | | |
| ☐ 31 Eric Moore | .20 | .09 | .03 |
| New York Giants | | | |
| ☐ 32 Dino Hackett | .20 | .09 | .03 |
| Kansas City Chiefs | | | |
| ☐ 33 Simon Fletcher | .25 | .11 | .03 |
| Denver Broncos | | | |
| ☐ 34 Al Edwards | .20 | .09 | .03 |
| Buffalo Bills | | | |
| ☐ 35 Brad Edwards | .20 | .09 | .03 |
| Washington Redskins | | | |
| ☐ 36 James Joseph | .20 | .09 | .03 |
| Philadelphia Eagles | | | |
| ☐ 37 Rodney Peete | .25 | .11 | .03 |
| Detroit Lions | | | |
| ☐ 38 Ricky Reynolds | .20 | .09 | .03 |
| Tampa Bay Buccaneers | | | |
| ☐ 39 Eddie Anderson | .20 | .09 | .03 |
| Los Angeles Raiders | | | |
| ☐ 40 Ken Clarke | .20 | .09 | .03 |
| Minnesota Vikings | | | |
| ☐ 41 Tony Bennett | 1.00 | .45 | .13 |
| TL FOIL | | | |
| Green Bay Packers | | | |
| ☐ 42 Larry Brown | .20 | .09 | .03 |
| Dallas Cowboys | | | |
| ☐ 43 Ray Childress | .25 | .11 | .03 |
| Houston Oilers | | | |
| ☐ 44 Mike Kenn | .25 | .11 | .03 |
| Atlanta Falcons | | | |
| ☐ 45 Vestee Jackson | .20 | .09 | .03 |
| Miami Dolphins | | | |
| ☐ 46 Neil O'Donnell | 2.50 | 1.15 | .30 |
| Pittsburgh Steelers | | | |
| ☐ 47 Bill Brooks | .25 | .11 | .03 |
| Indianapolis Colts | | | |
| ☐ 48 Kevin Butler | .20 | .09 | .03 |
| Chicago Bears | | | |
| ☐ 49 Joe Phillips | .20 | .09 | .03 |
| San Diego Chargers | | | |
| ☐ 50 Cortez Kennedy | .75 | .35 | .09 |
| Seattle Seahawks | | | |
| ☐ 51 Rickey Jackson | .25 | .11 | .03 |
| New Orleans Saints | | | |
| ☐ 52 Vinnie Clark | .20 | .09 | .03 |
| Green Bay Packers | | | |
| ☐ 53 Michael Jackson | .75 | .35 | .09 |
| Cleveland Browns | | | |
| ☐ 54 Ernie Jones | .20 | .09 | .03 |
| Phoenix Cardinals | | | |
| ☐ 55 Tom Newberry | .20 | .09 | .03 |
| Los Angeles Rams | | | |
| ☐ 56 Pat Harlow | .20 | .09 | .03 |
| New England Patriots | | | |
| ☐ 57 Craig Taylor | .20 | .09 | .03 |
| Cincinnati Bengals | | | |
| ☐ 58 Joe Prokop | .20 | .09 | .03 |
| San Francisco 49ers | | | |
| ☐ 59 Warren Moon | 6.00 | 2.70 | .75 |
| PL FOIL SP | | | |
| Houston Oilers | | | |
| ☐ 60 Jeff Lageman | .20 | .09 | .03 |
| New York Jets | | | |
| ☐ 61 Neil Smith | .30 | .14 | .04 |
| Kansas City Chiefs | | | |
| ☐ 62 Jim Jeffcoat | .20 | .09 | .03 |
| Dallas Cowboys | | | |
| ☐ 63 Bill Fralic | .20 | .09 | .03 |
| Atlanta Falcons | | | |
| ☐ 64 Mark Schlereth | .30 | .14 | .04 |
| Washington Redskins | | | |
| ☐ 65 Keith Byars | .25 | .11 | .03 |
| Philadelphia Eagles | | | |
| ☐ 66 Jeff Hostetler | .75 | .35 | .09 |
| New York Giants | | | |
| ☐ 67 Joey Browner | .20 | .09 | .03 |
| Minnesota Vikings | | | |

| | | | |
|---|---|---|---|
| ☐ 68 Bobby Hebert | 4.00 | 1.80 | .50 |
| PL FOIL SP | | | |
| New Orleans Saints | | | |
| ☐ 69 Keith Sims | .20 | .09 | .03 |
| Miami Dolphins | | | |
| ☐ 70 Warren Moon | 1.50 | .65 | .19 |
| Houston Oilers | | | |
| ☐ 71 Pio Sagapolutele | .35 | .16 | .04 |
| Cleveland Browns | | | |
| ☐ 72 Cornelius Bennett | .30 | .14 | .04 |
| Buffalo Bills | | | |
| ☐ 73 Greg Davis | .20 | .09 | .03 |
| Phoenix Cardinals | | | |
| ☐ 74 Ronnie Harmon | .20 | .09 | .03 |
| San Diego Chargers | | | |
| ☐ 75 Ron Hall | .20 | .09 | .03 |
| Tampa Bay Buccaneers | | | |
| ☐ 76 Howie Long | .25 | .11 | .03 |
| Los Angeles Raiders | | | |
| ☐ 77 Greg Lewis | .20 | .09 | .03 |
| Denver Broncos | | | |
| ☐ 78 Carnell Lake | .20 | .09 | .03 |
| Pittsburgh Steelers | | | |
| ☐ 79 Ray Crockett | .20 | .09 | .03 |
| Detroit Lions | | | |
| ☐ 80 Tom Waddle | .30 | .14 | .04 |
| Chicago Bears | | | |
| ☐ 81 Vincent Brown | .20 | .09 | .03 |
| New England Patriots | | | |
| ☐ 82 Bill Brooks | 1.00 | .45 | .13 |
| TL FOIL | | | |
| Indianapolis Colts | | | |
| ☐ 83 John L. Williams | .25 | .11 | .03 |
| Seattle Seahawks | | | |
| ☐ 84 Floyd Turner | .20 | .09 | .03 |
| New Orleans Saints | | | |
| ☐ 85 Scott Radecic | .20 | .09 | .03 |
| Indianapolis Colts | | | |
| ☐ 86 Anthony Munoz | .25 | .11 | .03 |
| Cincinnati Bengals | | | |
| ☐ 87 Lonnie Young | .20 | .09 | .03 |
| New York Jets | | | |
| ☐ 88 Dexter Carter | .25 | .11 | .03 |
| San Francisco 49ers | | | |
| ☐ 89 Tony Zendejas | .20 | .09 | .03 |
| Los Angeles Rams | | | |
| ☐ 90 Tim Jorden | .20 | .09 | .03 |
| Phoenix Cardinals | | | |
| ☐ 91 LeRoy Butler | .20 | .09 | .03 |
| Green Bay Packers | | | |
| ☐ 92 Richard Brown | .20 | .09 | .03 |
| Cleveland Browns | | | |
| ☐ 93 Erric Pegram | 2.50 | 1.15 | .30 |
| Atlanta Falcons | | | |
| ☐ 94 Sean Landeta | .20 | .09 | .03 |
| New York Giants | | | |
| ☐ 95 Clyde Simmons | .25 | .11 | .03 |
| Philadelphia Eagles | | | |
| ☐ 96 Martin Mayhew | .20 | .09 | .03 |
| Washington Redskins | | | |
| ☐ 97 Jarvis Williams | .20 | .09 | .03 |
| Miami Dolphins | | | |
| ☐ 98 Barry Word | .30 | .14 | .04 |
| LP FOIL | | | |
| Kansas City Chiefs | | | |
| ☐ 99 John Taylor | 1.50 | .65 | .19 |
| San Francisco 49ers | | | |
| ☐ 100 Emmitt Smith | 30.00 | 13.50 | 3.80 |
| Dallas Cowboys | | | |
| ☐ 101 Leon Seals | .20 | .09 | .03 |
| Buffalo Bills | | | |
| ☐ 102 Marion Butts | .30 | .14 | .04 |
| San Diego Chargers | | | |
| ☐ 103 Mike Merriweather | .20 | .09 | .03 |
| Minnesota Vikings | | | |
| ☐ 104 Ernest Givins | .25 | .11 | .03 |
| Houston Oilers | | | |
| ☐ 105 Wymon Henderson | .20 | .09 | .03 |
| Denver Broncos | | | |
| ☐ 106 Robert Wilson | .20 | .09 | .03 |
| Tampa Bay Buccaneers | | | |
| ☐ 107 Bobby Hebert | .30 | .14 | .04 |
| New Orleans Saints | | | |
| ☐ 108 Terry McDaniel | .20 | .09 | .03 |
| Los Angeles Raiders | | | |
| ☐ 109 Jerry Ball | .25 | .11 | .03 |
| Detroit Lions | | | |
| ☐ 110 John Taylor | .30 | .14 | .04 |
| San Francisco 49ers | | | |
| ☐ 111 Rob Moore | .30 | .14 | .04 |
| New York Jets | | | |
| ☐ 112 Thurman Thomas | 6.00 | 2.70 | .75 |
| TL FOIL | | | |
| Buffalo Bills | | | |
| ☐ 113 Checklist 1-115 | .20 | .09 | .03 |
| ☐ 114 Brian Blades | .25 | .11 | .03 |
| Seattle Seahawks | | | |

| | | | |
|---|---|---|---|
| ☐ 115 Larry Kelm | .20 | .09 | .03 |
| Los Angeles Rams | | | |
| ☐ 116 James Francis | .25 | .11 | .03 |
| Cincinnati Bengals | | | |
| ☐ 117 Rod Woodson | .60 | .25 | .08 |
| Pittsburgh Steelers | | | |
| ☐ 118 Trace Armstrong | .20 | .09 | .03 |
| Chicago Bears | | | |
| ☐ 119 Eugene Daniel | .20 | .09 | .03 |
| Indianapolis Colts | | | |
| ☐ 120 Andre Tippett | .25 | .11 | .03 |
| New England Patriots | | | |
| ☐ 121 Chris Jacke | .20 | .09 | .03 |
| Green Bay Packers | | | |
| ☐ 122 Jessie Tuggle | .20 | .09 | .03 |
| Atlanta Falcons | | | |
| ☐ 123 Chris Chandler | .25 | .11 | .03 |
| Phoenix Cardinals | | | |
| ☐ 124 Tim Johnson | .20 | .09 | .03 |
| Washington Redskins | | | |
| ☐ 125 Mark Collins | .20 | .09 | .03 |
| New York Giants | | | |
| ☐ 126 Aeneas Williams | 4.00 | 1.80 | .50 |
| TL FOIL SP | | | |
| Phoenix Cardinals | | | |
| ☐ 127 James Jones | .20 | .09 | .03 |
| Cleveland Browns | | | |
| ☐ 128 George Jamison | .20 | .09 | .03 |
| Detroit Lions | | | |
| ☐ 129 Deron Cherry | .20 | .09 | .03 |
| Kansas City Chiefs | | | |
| ☐ 130 Mark Clayton | .20 | .09 | .03 |
| Miami Dolphins | | | |
| ☐ 131 Keith DeLong | .20 | .09 | .03 |
| San Francisco 49ers | | | |
| ☐ 132 Marcus Allen | .75 | .35 | .09 |
| Los Angeles Raiders | | | |
| ☐ 133 Joe Walter | .30 | .14 | .04 |
| Cincinnati Bengals | | | |
| ☐ 134 Reggie Rutland | .20 | .09 | .03 |
| Minnesota Vikings | | | |
| ☐ 135 Kent Hull | .20 | .09 | .03 |
| Buffalo Bills | | | |
| ☐ 136 Jeff Feagles | .20 | .09 | .03 |
| Philadelphia Eagles | | | |
| ☐ 137 Ronnie Lott | 4.50 | 2.00 | .55 |
| TL FOIL SP | | | |
| Los Angeles Raiders | | | |
| ☐ 138 Henry Rolling | .20 | .09 | .03 |
| San Diego Chargers | | | |
| ☐ 139 Gary Anderson | .20 | .09 | .03 |
| Tampa Bay Buccaneers | | | |
| ☐ 140 Morten Andersen | .25 | .11 | .03 |
| New Orleans Saints | | | |
| ☐ 141 Cris Dishman | .25 | .11 | .03 |
| Houston Oilers | | | |
| ☐ 142 David Treadwell | .20 | .09 | .03 |
| Denver Broncos | | | |
| ☐ 143 Kevin Gogan | .20 | .09 | .03 |
| Dallas Cowboys | | | |
| ☐ 144 James Hasty | .20 | .09 | .03 |
| New York Jets | | | |
| ☐ 145 Robert Delpino | .25 | .11 | .03 |
| Los Angeles Rams | | | |
| ☐ 146 Patrick Hunter | .20 | .09 | .03 |
| Seattle Seahawks | | | |
| ☐ 147 Gary Anderson | .25 | .11 | .03 |
| Pittsburgh Steelers | | | |
| ☐ 148 Chip Banks | .20 | .09 | .03 |
| Indianapolis Colts | | | |
| ☐ 149 Dan Fike | .20 | .09 | .03 |
| Cleveland Browns | | | |
| ☐ 150 Chris Miller | .30 | .14 | .04 |
| Atlanta Falcons | | | |
| ☐ 151 Hugh Millen | .25 | .11 | .03 |
| New England Patriots | | | |
| ☐ 152 Courtney Hall | .20 | .09 | .03 |
| San Diego Chargers | | | |
| ☐ 153 Gary Clark | .30 | .14 | .04 |
| Washington Redskins | | | |
| ☐ 154 Michael Brooks | .20 | .09 | .03 |
| Denver Broncos | | | |
| ☐ 155 Jay Hilgenberg | .25 | .11 | .03 |
| Chicago Bears | | | |
| ☐ 156 Tim McDonald | .25 | .11 | .03 |
| Phoenix Cardinals | | | |
| ☐ 157 Andre Tippett | 1.00 | .45 | .13 |
| TL FOIL | | | |
| New England Patriots | | | |
| ☐ 158 Doug Riesenberg | .20 | .09 | .03 |
| New York Giants | | | |
| ☐ 159 Bill Maas | .20 | .09 | .03 |
| Kansas City Chiefs | | | |
| ☐ 160 Fred Barnett | .50 | .23 | .06 |
| Philadelphia Eagles | | | |
| ☐ 161 Pierce Holt | .20 | .09 | .03 |
| San Francisco 49ers | | | |

| | | | |
|---|---|---|---|
| ☐ 162 Brian Noble | .20 | .09 | .03 |
| Green Bay Packers | | | |
| ☐ 163 Harold Green | .30 | .14 | .04 |
| Cincinnati Bengals | | | |
| ☐ 164 Joel Hilgenberg | .20 | .09 | .03 |
| New Orleans Saints | | | |
| ☐ 165 Mervyn Fernandez | .20 | .09 | .03 |
| Los Angeles Raiders | | | |
| ☐ 166 John Offerdahl | .25 | .11 | .03 |
| Miami Dolphins | | | |
| ☐ 167 Shane Conlan | .25 | .11 | .03 |
| Buffalo Bills | | | |
| ☐ 168 Mark Higgs | 5.00 | 2.30 | .60 |
| TL FOIL SP | | | |
| Miami Dolphins | | | |
| ☐ 169 Bubba McDowell | .20 | .09 | .03 |
| Houston Oilers | | | |
| ☐ 170 Barry Sanders | 8.00 | 3.60 | 1.00 |
| Detroit Lions | | | |
| ☐ 171 Larry Roberts | .20 | .09 | .03 |
| San Francisco 49ers | | | |
| ☐ 172 Herschel Walker | .30 | .14 | .04 |
| Philadelphia Eagles | | | |
| ☐ 173 Steve McMichael | .25 | .11 | .03 |
| Chicago Bears | | | |
| ☐ 174 Kelly Stouffer | .20 | .09 | .03 |
| Seattle Seahawks | | | |
| ☐ 175 Louis Lipps | .25 | .11 | .03 |
| Pittsburgh Steelers | | | |
| ☐ 176 Jim Everett | .25 | .11 | .03 |
| Los Angeles Rams | | | |
| ☐ 177 Tony Tolbert | .20 | .09 | .03 |
| Dallas Cowboys | | | |
| ☐ 178 Mike Baab | .20 | .09 | .03 |
| Cleveland Browns | | | |
| ☐ 179 Eric Swann | .25 | .11 | .03 |
| Phoenix Cardinals | | | |
| ☐ 180 Emmitt Smith | 110.00 | 50.00 | 14.00 |
| TL FOIL SP | | | |
| Dallas Cowboys | | | |
| ☐ 181 Tim Brown | 1.25 | .55 | .16 |
| Los Angeles Raiders | | | |
| ☐ 182 Dennis Smith | .25 | .11 | .03 |
| Denver Broncos | | | |
| ☐ 183 Moe Gardner | .20 | .09 | .03 |
| Atlanta Falcons | | | |
| ☐ 184 Derrick Walker | .20 | .09 | .03 |
| San Diego Chargers | | | |
| ☐ 185 Reyna Thompson | .20 | .09 | .03 |
| New York Giants | | | |
| ☐ 186 Esera Tuaolo | .20 | .09 | .03 |
| Green Bay Packers | | | |
| ☐ 187 Jeff Wright | .20 | .09 | .03 |
| Buffalo Bills | | | |
| ☐ 188 Mark Rypien | .30 | .14 | .04 |
| Washington Redskins | | | |
| ☐ 189 Quinn Early | .25 | .11 | .03 |
| New Orleans Saints | | | |
| ☐ 190 Christian Okoye | .25 | .11 | .03 |
| Kansas City Chiefs | | | |
| ☐ 191 Keith Jackson | .75 | .35 | .09 |
| Philadelphia Eagles | | | |
| ☐ 192 Doug Smith | .20 | .09 | .03 |
| Houston Oilers | | | |
| ☐ 193 John Elway | 5.00 | 2.30 | .60 |
| PL FOIL | | | |
| Denver Broncos | | | |
| ☐ 194 Reggie Cobb | .50 | .23 | .06 |
| Tampa Bay Buccaneers | | | |
| ☐ 195 Reggie Roby | .20 | .09 | .03 |
| Miami Dolphins | | | |
| ☐ 196 Clarence Verdin | .20 | .09 | .03 |
| Indianapolis Colts | | | |
| ☐ 197 Jim Breech | .20 | .09 | .03 |
| Cincinnati Bengals | | | |
| ☐ 198 Jim Sweeney | .20 | .09 | .03 |
| New York Jets | | | |
| ☐ 199 Marv Cook | .25 | .11 | .03 |
| New England Patriots | | | |
| ☐ 200 Ronnie Lott | .30 | .14 | .04 |
| Los Angeles Raiders | | | |
| ☐ 201 Mel Gray | .25 | .11 | .03 |
| Detroit Lions | | | |
| ☐ 202 Maury Buford | .20 | .09 | .03 |
| Chicago Bears | | | |
| ☐ 203 Lorenzo Lynch | .20 | .09 | .03 |
| Phoenix Cardinals | | | |
| ☐ 204 Jesse Sapolu | .20 | .09 | .03 |
| San Francisco 49ers | | | |
| ☐ 205 Steve Jordan | .25 | .11 | .03 |
| Minnesota Vikings | | | |
| ☐ 206 Don Majkowski | .25 | .11 | .03 |
| Green Bay Packers | | | |
| ☐ 207 Flipper Anderson | .25 | .11 | .03 |
| Los Angeles Rams | | | |
| ☐ 208 Ed King | .20 | .09 | .03 |
| Cleveland Browns | | | |

| | | | | |
|---|---|---|---|---|
| ☐ 209 Tony Woods........................ | .20 | .09 | .03 | |
| Seattle Seahawks | | | | |
| ☐ 210 Ron Heller........................... | .20 | .09 | .03 | |
| Philadelphia Eagles | | | | |
| ☐ 211 Greg Kragen........................ | .20 | .09 | .03 | |
| Denver Broncos | | | | |
| ☐ 212 Scott Case.......................... | .20 | .09 | .03 | |
| Atlanta Falcons | | | | |
| ☐ 213 Tommy Barnhardt................. | .20 | .09 | .03 | |
| New Orleans Saints | | | | |
| ☐ 214 Charles Mann...................... | .25 | .11 | .03 | |
| Washington Redskins | | | | |
| ☐ 215 David Griggs....................... | .20 | .09 | .03 | |
| Miami Dolphins | | | | |
| ☐ 216 Kenneth Davis..................... | 4.00 | 1.80 | .50 | |
| LP FOIL SP | | | | |
| Buffalo Bills | | | | |
| ☐ 217 Lamar Lathon...................... | .20 | .09 | .03 | |
| Houston Oilers | | | | |
| ☐ 218 Nate Odomes...................... | .30 | .14 | .04 | |
| Buffalo Bills | | | | |
| ☐ 219 Vinny Testaverde................. | .30 | .14 | .04 | |
| Tampa Bay Buccaneers | | | | |
| ☐ 220 Rod Bernstine..................... | .25 | .11 | .03 | |
| San Diego Chargers | | | | |
| ☐ 221 Barry Sanders..................... | 16.00 | 7.25 | 2.00 | |
| TL FOIL | | | | |
| Detroit Lions | | | | |
| ☐ 222 Carlton Haselrig.................. | .35 | .16 | .04 | |
| Pittsburgh Steelers | | | | |
| ☐ 223 Steve Beuerlein................... | .75 | .35 | .09 | |
| Dallas Cowboys | | | | |
| ☐ 224 John Alt............................. | .20 | .09 | .03 | |
| Kansas City Chiefs | | | | |
| ☐ 225 Pepper Johnson................... | .25 | .11 | .03 | |
| New York Giants | | | | |
| ☐ 226 Checklist 116-230................ | .20 | .09 | .03 | |
| ☐ 227 Irv Eatman.......................... | .20 | .09 | .03 | |
| New York Jets | | | | |
| ☐ 228 Greg Townsend.................... | .20 | .09 | .03 | |
| Los Angeles Raiders | | | | |
| ☐ 229 Mark Jackson...................... | .25 | .11 | .03 | |
| Denver Broncos | | | | |
| ☐ 230 Robert Blackmon................. | .20 | .09 | .03 | |
| Seattle Seahawks | | | | |
| ☐ 231 Terry Allen......................... | 1.25 | .55 | .16 | |
| Minnesota Vikings | | | | |
| ☐ 232 Bennie Blades..................... | .20 | .09 | .03 | |
| Detroit Lions | | | | |
| ☐ 233 Sam Mills.......................... | 1.00 | .45 | .13 | |
| TL FOIL | | | | |
| New Orleans Saints | | | | |
| ☐ 234 Richmond Webb................... | .25 | .11 | .03 | |
| Miami Dolphins | | | | |
| ☐ 235 Richard Dent...................... | .25 | .11 | .03 | |
| Chicago Bears | | | | |
| ☐ 236 Alonzo Mitz........................ | .20 | .09 | .03 | |
| Cincinnati Bengals | | | | |
| ☐ 237 Steve Young........................ | 3.00 | 1.35 | .40 | |
| San Francisco 49ers | | | | |
| ☐ 238 Pat Swilling........................ | .25 | .11 | .03 | |
| New Orleans Saints | | | | |
| ☐ 239 James Campen..................... | .20 | .09 | .03 | |
| Green Bay Packers | | | | |
| ☐ 240 Earnest Byner..................... | .30 | .14 | .04 | |
| Washington Redskins | | | | |
| ☐ 241 Pat Terrell......................... | .20 | .09 | .03 | |
| Los Angeles Rams | | | | |
| ☐ 242 Carwell Gardner.................. | .20 | .09 | .03 | |
| Buffalo Bills | | | | |
| ☐ 243 Charles McRae.................... | .20 | .09 | .03 | |
| Tampa Bay Buccaneers | | | | |
| ☐ 244 Vince Newsome................... | .20 | .09 | .03 | |
| Cleveland Browns | | | | |
| ☐ 245 Eric Hill............................ | .20 | .09 | .03 | |
| Phoenix Cardinals | | | | |
| ☐ 246 Steve Young........................ | 5.00 | 2.30 | .60 | |
| TL FOIL | | | | |
| San Francisco 49ers | | | | |
| ☐ 247 Nate Lewis......................... | .25 | .11 | .03 | |
| San Diego Chargers | | | | |
| ☐ 248 William Fuller..................... | .25 | .11 | .03 | |
| Houston Oilers | | | | |
| ☐ 249 Andre Waters...................... | .20 | .09 | .03 | |
| Philadelphia Eagles | | | | |
| ☐ 250 Dean Biasucci..................... | .20 | .09 | .03 | |
| Indianapolis Colts | | | | |
| ☐ 251 Andre Rison........................ | 1.25 | .55 | .16 | |
| Atlanta Falcons | | | | |
| ☐ 252 Brent Williams.................... | .20 | .09 | .03 | |
| New England Patriots | | | | |
| ☐ 253 Todd McNair....................... | .20 | .09 | .03 | |
| Kansas City Chiefs | | | | |
| ☐ 254 Jeff Davidson...................... | .20 | .09 | .03 | |
| Denver Broncos | | | | |
| ☐ 255 Art Monk............................ | .30 | .14 | .04 | |
| Washington Redskins | | | | |

| | | | |
|---|---|---|---|
| ☐ 256 Kirk Lowdermilk.................. | .20 | .09 | .03 |
| Minnesota Vikings | | | |
| ☐ 257 Bob Golic........................... | .20 | .09 | .03 |
| Los Angeles Raiders | | | |
| ☐ 258 Michael Irvin...................... | 6.00 | 2.70 | .75 |
| Dallas Cowboys | | | |
| ☐ 259 Eric Green.......................... | .30 | .14 | .04 |
| Pittsburgh Steelers | | | |
| ☐ 260 David Fulcher...................... | 1.00 | .45 | .13 |
| TL FOIL | | | |
| Cincinnati Bengals | | | |
| ☐ 261 Damone Johnson.................. | .20 | .09 | .03 |
| Los Angeles Rams | | | |
| ☐ 262 Marc Spindler..................... | .20 | .09 | .03 |
| Detroit Lions | | | |
| ☐ 263 Alfred Williams................... | .20 | .09 | .03 |
| Cincinnati Bengals | | | |
| ☐ 264 Donnie Elder....................... | .20 | .09 | .03 |
| San Diego Chargers | | | |
| ☐ 265 Keith McKeller.................... | .20 | .09 | .03 |
| Buffalo Bills | | | |
| ☐ 266 Steve Bono......................... | 3.00 | 1.35 | .40 |
| San Francisco 49ers | | | |
| ☐ 267 Jumbo Elliott...................... | .20 | .09 | .03 |
| New York Giants | | | |
| ☐ 268 Randy Hilliard..................... | .20 | .09 | .03 |
| Cleveland Browns | | | |
| ☐ 269 Rufus Porter....................... | .20 | .09 | .03 |
| Seattle Seahawks | | | |
| ☐ 270 Neal Anderson..................... | .25 | .11 | .03 |
| Chicago Bears | | | |
| ☐ 271 Dalton Hilliard.................... | .20 | .09 | .03 |
| New Orleans Saints | | | |
| ☐ 272 Michael Zordich................... | .20 | .09 | .03 |
| Phoenix Cardinals | | | |
| ☐ 273 Cornelius Bennett................ | 1.50 | .65 | .19 |
| PL FOIL | | | |
| Buffalo Bills | | | |
| ☐ 274 Louie Aguiar....................... | .20 | .09 | .03 |
| New York Jets | | | |
| ☐ 275 Aaron Craver...................... | .20 | .09 | .03 |
| Miami Dolphins | | | |
| ☐ 276 Tony Bennett...................... | .25 | .11 | .03 |
| Green Bay Packers | | | |
| ☐ 277 Terry Wooden...................... | .20 | .09 | .03 |
| Seattle Seahawks | | | |
| ☐ 278 Mike Munchak..................... | .25 | .11 | .03 |
| Houston Oilers | | | |
| ☐ 279 Chris Hinton....................... | .20 | .09 | .03 |
| Atlanta Falcons | | | |
| ☐ 280 John Elway......................... | 3.00 | 1.35 | .40 |
| Denver Broncos | | | |
| ☐ 281 Randall McDaniel................ | .20 | .09 | .03 |
| Minnesota Vikings | | | |
| ☐ 282 Brad Baxter........................ | 1.00 | .45 | .13 |
| TL FOIL | | | |
| New York Jets | | | |
| ☐ 283 Wes Hopkins....................... | .20 | .09 | .03 |
| Philadelphia Eagles | | | |
| ☐ 284 Scott Davis......................... | .20 | .09 | .03 |
| Los Angeles Raiders | | | |
| ☐ 285 Mark Tuinei........................ | .20 | .09 | .03 |
| Dallas Cowboys | | | |
| ☐ 286 Broderick Thompson............. | .20 | .09 | .03 |
| San Diego Chargers | | | |
| ☐ 287 Henry Ellard....................... | .25 | .11 | .03 |
| Los Angeles Rams | | | |
| ☐ 288 Adrian Cooper..................... | .20 | .09 | .03 |
| Pittsburgh Steelers | | | |
| ☐ 289 Don Warren........................ | .20 | .09 | .03 |
| Washington Redskins | | | |
| ☐ 290 Rodney Hampton.................. | 2.50 | 1.15 | .30 |
| New York Giants | | | |
| ☐ 291 Kevin Ross......................... | .25 | .11 | .03 |
| Kansas City Chiefs | | | |
| ☐ 292 Mark Carrier....................... | .25 | .11 | .03 |
| Chicago Bears | | | |
| ☐ 293 Ian Beckles........................ | .20 | .09 | .03 |
| Tampa Bay Buccaneers | | | |
| ☐ 294 Gene Atkins........................ | .20 | .09 | .03 |
| New Orleans Saints | | | |
| ☐ 295 Mark Rypien....................... | 1.50 | .65 | .19 |
| PL FOIL | | | |
| Washington Redskins | | | |
| ☐ 296 Eric Metcalf........................ | .30 | .14 | .04 |
| Cleveland Browns | | | |
| ☐ 297 Howard Ballard.................... | .20 | .09 | .03 |
| Buffalo Bills | | | |
| ☐ 298 Nate Newton....................... | .20 | .09 | .03 |
| Dallas Cowboys | | | |
| ☐ 299 Dan Owens......................... | .20 | .09 | .03 |
| Detroit Lions | | | |
| ☐ 300 Tim McGee......................... | .20 | .09 | .03 |
| Cincinnati Bengals | | | |
| ☐ 301 Greg McMurtry................... | .20 | .09 | .03 |
| New England Patriots | | | |
| ☐ 302 Walter Reeves..................... | .20 | .09 | .03 |

| | | | |
|---|---|---|---|
| Phoenix Cardinals | | | |
| ☐ 303 Jeff Herrod | .20 | .09 | .03 |
| Indianapolis Colts | | | |
| ☐ 304 Darren Comeaux | .20 | .09 | .03 |
| Seattle Seahawks | | | |
| ☐ 305 Pete Stoyanovich | .25 | .11 | .03 |
| Miami Dolphins | | | |
| ☐ 306 Johnny Holland | .20 | .09 | .03 |
| Green Bay Packers | | | |
| ☐ 307 Jay Novacek | .75 | .35 | .09 |
| Dallas Cowboys | | | |
| ☐ 308 Steve Broussard | .25 | .11 | .03 |
| Atlanta Falcons | | | |
| ☐ 309 Darrell Green | .20 | .09 | .03 |
| Washington Redskins | | | |
| ☐ 310 Sam Mills | .25 | .11 | .03 |
| New Orleans Saints | | | |
| ☐ 311 Tim Barnett | .25 | .11 | .03 |
| Kansas City Chiefs | | | |
| ☐ 312 Steve Atwater | .25 | .11 | .03 |
| Denver Broncos | | | |
| ☐ 313 Tom Waddle | 1.00 | .45 | .13 |
| PL FOIL | | | |
| Chicago Bears | | | |
| ☐ 314 Felix Wright | .20 | .09 | .03 |
| Minnesota Vikings | | | |
| ☐ 315 Sean Jones | .25 | .11 | .03 |
| Houston Oilers | | | |
| ☐ 316 Jim Harbaugh | .25 | .11 | .03 |
| Chicago Bears | | | |
| ☐ 317 Eric Allen | .25 | .11 | .03 |
| Philadelphia Eagles | | | |
| ☐ 318 Don Mosebar | .20 | .09 | .03 |
| Los Angeles Raiders | | | |
| ☐ 319 Rob Taylor | .20 | .09 | .03 |
| Tampa Bay Buccaneers | | | |
| ☐ 320 Terance Mathis | .20 | .09 | .03 |
| New York Jets | | | |
| ☐ 321 Leroy Hoard | .25 | .11 | .03 |
| Cleveland Browns | | | |
| ☐ 322 Kenneth Davis | .20 | .09 | .03 |
| Buffalo Bills | | | |
| ☐ 323 Guy McIntyre | .25 | .11 | .03 |
| San Francisco 49ers | | | |
| ☐ 324 Deron Cherry | 1.00 | .45 | .13 |
| PL FOIL | | | |
| Kansas City Chiefs | | | |
| ☐ 325 Tunch Ilkin | .20 | .09 | .03 |
| Pittsburgh Steelers | | | |
| ☐ 326 Willie Green | .20 | .09 | .03 |
| Detroit Lions | | | |
| ☐ 327 Darryl Henley | .20 | .09 | .03 |
| Los Angeles Rams | | | |
| ☐ 328 Shawn Jefferson | .20 | .09 | .03 |
| San Diego Chargers | | | |
| ☐ 329 Greg Jackson | .20 | .09 | .03 |
| New York Giants | | | |
| ☐ 330 John Roper | .20 | .09 | .03 |
| Chicago Bears | | | |
| ☐ 331 Bill Lewis | .20 | .09 | .03 |
| Phoenix Cardinals | | | |
| ☐ 332 Rodney Holman | .20 | .09 | .03 |
| Cincinnati Bengals | | | |
| ☐ 333 Bruce Armstrong | .20 | .09 | .03 |
| New England Patriots | | | |
| ☐ 334 Robb Thomas | .20 | .09 | .03 |
| Kansas City Chiefs | | | |
| ☐ 335 Alvin Harper | 3.00 | 1.35 | .40 |
| Dallas Cowboys | | | |
| ☐ 336 Brian Jordan | .30 | .14 | .04 |
| Atlanta Falcons | | | |
| ☐ 337 Morten Andersen | 1.00 | .45 | .13 |
| LP FOIL | | | |
| New Orleans Saints | | | |
| ☐ 338 Dermontti Dawson | .20 | .09 | .03 |
| Pittsburgh Steelers | | | |
| ☐ 339 Checklist 231-345 | .20 | .09 | .03 |
| ☐ 340 Louis Oliver | .25 | .11 | .03 |
| Miami Dolphins | | | |
| ☐ 341 Paul McJulien | .20 | .09 | .03 |
| Green Bay Packers | | | |
| ☐ 342 Karl Mecklenburg | .25 | .11 | .03 |
| Denver Broncos | | | |
| ☐ 343 Lawrence Dawsey | .30 | .14 | .04 |
| Tampa Bay Buccaneers | | | |
| ☐ 344 Kyle Clifton | .20 | .09 | .03 |
| New York Jets | | | |
| ☐ 345 Jeff Bostic | .20 | .09 | .03 |
| Washington Redskins | | | |
| ☐ 346 Cris Carter | .30 | .14 | .04 |
| Minnesota Vikings | | | |
| ☐ 347 Al Smith | .20 | .09 | .03 |
| Houston Oilers | | | |
| ☐ 348 Mark Kelso | .20 | .09 | .03 |
| Buffalo Bills | | | |
| ☐ 349 Art Monk | 1.50 | .65 | .19 |
| TL FOIL | | | |
| Washington Redskins | | | |

| | | | |
|---|---|---|---|
| ☐ 350 Michael Carter | .20 | .09 | .03 |
| San Francisco 49ers | | | |
| ☐ 351 Ethan Horton | .20 | .09 | .03 |
| Los Angeles Raiders | | | |
| ☐ 352 Andy Heck | .20 | .09 | .03 |
| Seattle Seahawks | | | |
| ☐ 353 Gill Fenerty | .20 | .09 | .03 |
| New Orleans Saints | | | |
| ☐ 354 David Brandon | .20 | .09 | .03 |
| Cleveland Browns | | | |
| ☐ 355 Anthony Johnson | .20 | .09 | .03 |
| Indianapolis Colts | | | |
| ☐ 356 Mike Golic | .20 | .09 | .03 |
| Philadelphia Eagles | | | |
| ☐ 357 Ferrell Edmunds | .20 | .09 | .03 |
| Miami Dolphins | | | |
| ☐ 358 Dennis Gibson | .20 | .09 | .03 |
| Detroit Lions | | | |
| ☐ 359 Gill Byrd | .25 | .11 | .03 |
| San Diego Chargers | | | |
| ☐ 360 Todd Lyght | .20 | .09 | .03 |
| Los Angeles Rams | | | |
| ☐ 361 Jayice Pearson | .20 | .09 | .03 |
| Kansas City Chiefs | | | |
| ☐ 362 John Rade | .20 | .09 | .03 |
| Atlanta Falcons | | | |
| ☐ 363 Keith Van Horne | .20 | .09 | .03 |
| Chicago Bears | | | |
| ☐ 364 John Kasay | .20 | .09 | .03 |
| Seattle Seahawks | | | |
| ☐ 365 Broderick Thomas | 4.00 | 1.80 | .50 |
| TL FOIL SP | | | |
| Tampa Bay Buccaneers | | | |
| ☐ 366 Ken Harvey | .20 | .09 | .03 |
| Phoenix Cardinals | | | |
| ☐ 367 Rich Gannon | .25 | .11 | .03 |
| Minnesota Vikings | | | |
| ☐ 368 Darrell Thompson | .25 | .11 | .03 |
| Green Bay Packers | | | |
| ☐ 369 Jon Vaughn | .20 | .09 | .03 |
| New England Patriots | | | |
| ☐ 370 Jesse Solomon | .20 | .09 | .03 |
| Tampa Bay Buccaneers | | | |
| ☐ 371 Erik McMillan | .20 | .09 | .03 |
| New York Jets | | | |
| ☐ 372 Bruce Matthews | .25 | .11 | .03 |
| Houston Oilers | | | |
| ☐ 373 Wilber Marshall | .25 | .11 | .03 |
| Washington Redskins | | | |
| ☐ 374 Brian Blades | 4.00 | 1.80 | .50 |
| TL FOIL SP | | | |
| Seattle Seahawks | | | |
| ☐ 375 Vance Johnson | .25 | .11 | .03 |
| Denver Broncos | | | |
| ☐ 376 Eddie Brown | .20 | .09 | .03 |
| Cincinnati Bengals | | | |
| ☐ 377 Don Beebe | .30 | .14 | .04 |
| Buffalo Bills | | | |
| ☐ 378 Brent Jones | .30 | .14 | .04 |
| San Francisco 49ers | | | |
| ☐ 379 Matt Bahr | .20 | .09 | .03 |
| New York Giants | | | |
| ☐ 380 Dwight Stone | .20 | .09 | .03 |
| Pittsburgh Steelers | | | |
| ☐ 381 Tony Casillas | .20 | .09 | .03 |
| Dallas Cowboys | | | |
| ☐ 382 Jay Schroeder | .25 | .11 | .03 |
| Los Angeles Raiders | | | |
| ☐ 383 Byron Evans | .25 | .11 | .03 |
| Philadelphia Eagles | | | |
| ☐ 384 Dan Saleaumua | .20 | .09 | .03 |
| Kansas City Chiefs | | | |
| ☐ 385 Wendell Davis | .20 | .09 | .03 |
| Chicago Bears | | | |
| ☐ 386 Ron Holmes | .20 | .09 | .03 |
| Denver Broncos | | | |
| ☐ 387 George Thomas | .30 | .14 | .04 |
| Atlanta Falcons | | | |
| ☐ 388 Ray Berry | .20 | .09 | .03 |
| Minnesota Vikings | | | |
| ☐ 389 Eric Martin | .25 | .11 | .03 |
| New Orleans Saints | | | |
| ☐ 390 Kevin Mack | .25 | .11 | .03 |
| Cleveland Browns | | | |
| ☐ 391 Natu Tuatagaloa | .40 | .18 | .05 |
| Cincinnati Bengals | | | |
| ☐ 392 Bill Romanowski | .20 | .09 | .03 |
| San Francisco 49ers | | | |
| ☐ 393 Nick Bell | 5.00 | 2.30 | .60 |
| PL FOIL SP | | | |
| Los Angeles Raiders | | | |
| ☐ 394 Grant Feasel | .20 | .09 | .03 |
| Seattle Seahawks | | | |
| ☐ 395 Eugene Lockhart | .20 | .09 | .03 |
| New England Patriots | | | |
| ☐ 396 Lorenzo White | .25 | .11 | .03 |
| Houston Oilers | | | |

|  |  | | | |
|---|---|---|---|---|
| ☐ 397 | Mike Farr / Detroit Lions | .20 | .09 | .03 |
| ☐ 398 | Eric Bieniemy / San Diego Chargers | .25 | .11 | .03 |
| ☐ 399 | Kevin Murphy / Tampa Bay Buccaneers | .20 | .09 | .03 |
| ☐ 400 | Luis Sharpe / Phoenix Cardinals | .20 | .09 | .03 |
| ☐ 401 | Jessie Tuggle / PL FOIL SP / Atlanta Falcons | 4.00 | 1.80 | .50 |
| ☐ 402 | Cleveland Gary / Los Angeles Rams | .25 | .11 | .03 |
| ☐ 403 | Tony Mandarich / Green Bay Packers | .20 | .09 | .03 |
| ☐ 404 | Bryan Cox / Miami Dolphins | .25 | .11 | .03 |
| ☐ 405 | Marvin Washington / New York Jets | .20 | .09 | .03 |
| ☐ 406 | Fred Stokes / Washington Redskins | .20 | .09 | .03 |
| ☐ 407 | Duane Bickett / Indianapolis Colts | .20 | .09 | .03 |
| ☐ 408 | Leonard Marshall / New York Giants | .25 | .11 | .03 |
| ☐ 409 | Barry Foster / Pittsburgh Steelers | 4.00 | 1.80 | .50 |
| ☐ 410 | Thurman Thomas / Buffalo Bills | 4.50 | 2.00 | .55 |
| ☐ 411 | Willie Gault / Los Angeles Raiders | .25 | .11 | .03 |
| ☐ 412 | Vinson Smith / Dallas Cowboys | .40 | .18 | .05 |
| ☐ 413 | Mark Bortz / Chicago Bears | .20 | .09 | .03 |
| ☐ 414 | Johnny Johnson / Phoenix Cardinals | .40 | .18 | .05 |
| ☐ 415 | Rodney Hampton / TL FOIL / New York Giants | 6.00 | 2.70 | .75 |
| ☐ 416 | Steve Wallace / San Francisco 49ers | .20 | .09 | .03 |
| ☐ 417 | Fuad Reveiz / Minnesota Vikings | .20 | .09 | .03 |
| ☐ 418 | Derrick Thomas / Kansas City Chiefs | 1.00 | .45 | .13 |
| ☐ 419 | Jackie Harris / Green Bay Packers | 4.00 | 1.80 | .50 |
| ☐ 420 | Derek Russell / Denver Broncos | .25 | .11 | .03 |
| ☐ 421 | David Grant / Cincinnati Bengals | .20 | .09 | .03 |
| ☐ 422 | Tommy Kane / Seattle Seahawks | .20 | .09 | .03 |
| ☐ 423 | Stan Brock / New Orleans Saints | .20 | .09 | .03 |
| ☐ 424 | Haywood Jeffires / Houston Oilers | .50 | .23 | .06 |
| ☐ 425 | Broderick Thomas / Tampa Bay Buccaneers | .20 | .09 | .03 |
| ☐ 426 | John Kidd / San Diego Chargers | .20 | .09 | .03 |
| ☐ 427 | Shawn McCarthy / LP FOIL / New England Patriots | 1.00 | .45 | .13 |
| ☐ 428 | Jim Arnold / Detroit Lions | .20 | .09 | .03 |
| ☐ 429 | Scott Fulhage / Atlanta Falcons | .20 | .09 | .03 |
| ☐ 430 | Jackie Slater / Los Angeles Rams | .25 | .11 | .03 |
| ☐ 431 | Scott Galbraith / Cleveland Browns | .20 | .09 | .03 |
| ☐ 432 | Roger Ruzek / Philadelphia Eagles | .20 | .09 | .03 |
| ☐ 433 | Irving Fryar / New England Patriots | .25 | .11 | .03 |
| ☐ 434A | Derrick Thomas ERR / TL FOIL (Misnumbered 494) / Kansas City Chiefs | 3.00 | 1.35 | .40 |
| ☐ 434B | Derrick Thomas COR / TL FOIL (Numbered 434) | 3.00 | 1.35 | .40 |
| ☐ 435 | David Johnson / Pittsburgh Steelers | .20 | .09 | .03 |
| ☐ 436 | Jim Jensen / Miami Dolphins | .20 | .09 | .03 |
| ☐ 437 | James Washington / Dallas Cowboys | .20 | .09 | .03 |
| ☐ 438 | Phil Hansen / Buffalo Bills | .20 | .09 | .03 |
| ☐ 439 | Rohn Stark / Indianapolis Colts | .20 | .09 | .03 |
| ☐ 440 | Jarrod Bunch / New York Giants | .20 | .09 | .03 |
| ☐ 441 | Todd Marinovich / Los Angeles Raiders | .20 | .09 | .03 |
| ☐ 442 | Brett Perriman / Detroit Lions | .40 | .18 | .05 |
| ☐ 443 | Eugene Robinson / Seattle Seahawks | .20 | .09 | .03 |
| ☐ 444 | Robert Massey / Phoenix Cardinals | .20 | .09 | .03 |
| ☐ 445 | Nick Lowery / Kansas City Chiefs | .25 | .11 | .03 |
| ☐ 446 | Rickey Dixon / Cincinnati Bengals | .20 | .09 | .03 |
| ☐ 447 | Jim Lachey / Washington Redskins | .20 | .09 | .03 |
| ☐ 448 | Johnny Hector / PL FOIL / New York Jets | 1.00 | .45 | .13 |
| ☐ 449 | Gary Plummer / San Diego Chargers | .20 | .09 | .03 |
| ☐ 450 | Robert Brown / Green Bay Packers | .20 | .09 | .03 |
| ☐ 451 | Gaston Green / Denver Broncos | .25 | .11 | .03 |
| ☐ 452 | Checklist 346-459 | .20 | .09 | .03 |
| ☐ 453 | Darion Conner / Atlanta Falcons | .20 | .09 | .03 |
| ☐ 454 | Mike Cofer / San Francisco 49ers | .20 | .09 | .03 |
| ☐ 455 | Craig Heyward / New Orleans Saints | .20 | .09 | .03 |
| ☐ 456 | Anthony Carter / Minnesota Vikings | .25 | .11 | .03 |
| ☐ 457 | Pat Coleman / Houston Oilers | .30 | .14 | .04 |
| ☐ 458 | Jeff Bryant / Seattle Seahawks | .20 | .09 | .03 |
| ☐ 459 | Mark Gunn / New York Jets | .30 | .14 | .04 |
| ☐ 460 | Stan Thomas / Chicago Bears | .20 | .09 | .03 |
| ☐ 461 | Simon Fletcher / TL FOIL SP / Denver Broncos | 4.00 | 1.80 | .50 |
| ☐ 462 | Ray Agnew / New England Patriots | .20 | .09 | .03 |
| ☐ 463 | Jessie Hester / Indianapolis Colts | .20 | .09 | .03 |
| ☐ 464 | Rob Burnett / Cleveland Browns | .20 | .09 | .03 |
| ☐ 465 | Mike Croel / Denver Broncos | .25 | .11 | .03 |
| ☐ 466 | Mike Pitts / Philadelphia Eagles | .20 | .09 | .03 |
| ☐ 467 | Darryl Talley / Buffalo Bills | .25 | .11 | .03 |
| ☐ 468 | Rich Camarillo / Phoenix Cardinals | .20 | .09 | .03 |
| ☐ 469 | Reggie White / TL FOIL / Philadelphia Eagles | 2.50 | 1.15 | .30 |
| ☐ 470 | Nick Bell / Los Angeles Raiders | .40 | .18 | .05 |
| ☐ 471 | Tracy Hayworth / Detroit Lions | .20 | .09 | .03 |
| ☐ 472 | Eric Thomas / Cincinnati Bengals | .20 | .09 | .03 |
| ☐ 473 | Paul Gruber / Tampa Bay Buccaneers | .25 | .11 | .03 |
| ☐ 474 | David Richards / San Diego Chargers | .20 | .09 | .03 |
| ☐ 475 | T.J. Turner / Miami Dolphins | .20 | .09 | .03 |
| ☐ 476 | Mark Ingram / New York Giants | .25 | .11 | .03 |
| ☐ 477 | Tim Grunhard / Kansas City Chiefs | .20 | .09 | .03 |
| ☐ 478 | Marion Butts / TL FOIL / San Diego Chargers | 1.50 | .65 | .19 |
| ☐ 479 | Tom Rathman / San Francisco 49ers | .25 | .11 | .03 |
| ☐ 480 | Brian Mitchell / Washington Redskins | .30 | .14 | .04 |
| ☐ 481 | Bryce Paup / Green Bay Packers | .20 | .09 | .03 |
| ☐ 482 | Mike Pritchard / Atlanta Falcons | .75 | .35 | .09 |
| ☐ 483 | Ken Norton Jr. / Dallas Cowboys | .30 | .14 | .04 |
| ☐ 484 | Roman Phifer / Los Angeles Rams | .20 | .09 | .03 |
| ☐ 485 | Greg Lloyd / Pittsburgh Steelers | .20 | .09 | .03 |
| ☐ 486 | Brett Maxie / New Orleans Saints | .20 | .09 | .03 |
| ☐ 487 | Richard Dent / TL FOIL SP / Chicago Bears | 4.50 | 2.00 | .55 |
| ☐ 488 | Curtis Duncan / Houston Oilers | .25 | .11 | .03 |
| ☐ 489 | Chris Burkett | .20 | .09 | .03 |

New York Jets
| ☐ 490 | Travis McNeal | .20 | .09 | .03 |
|---|---|---|---|---|

Seattle Seahawks
| ☐ 491 | Carl Lee | .20 | .09 | .03 |
|---|---|---|---|---|

Minnesota Vikings
| ☐ 492 | Clarence Kay | .20 | .09 | .03 |
|---|---|---|---|---|

Denver Broncos
| ☐ 493 | Tom Thayer | .20 | .09 | .03 |
|---|---|---|---|---|

Chicago Bears
| ☐ 494 | Erik Kramer | 7.00 | 3.10 | .85 |
|---|---|---|---|---|

PL FOIL SP (See also 434A)
Detroit Lions
| ☐ 495 | Perry Kemp | .20 | .09 | .03 |
|---|---|---|---|---|

Green Bay Packers
| ☐ 496 | Jeff Jaeger | .20 | .09 | .03 |
|---|---|---|---|---|

Los Angeles Raiders
| ☐ 497 | Eric Sanders | .20 | .09 | .03 |
|---|---|---|---|---|

Detroit Lions
| ☐ 498 | Burt Grossman | .20 | .09 | .03 |
|---|---|---|---|---|

San Diego Chargers
| ☐ 499 | Ben Smith | .20 | .09 | .03 |
|---|---|---|---|---|

Philadelphia Eagles
| ☐ 500 | Keith McCants | .20 | .09 | .03 |
|---|---|---|---|---|

Tampa Bay Buccaneers
| ☐ 501 | John Stephens | .25 | .11 | .03 |
|---|---|---|---|---|

New England Patriots
| ☐ 502 | John Rienstra | .20 | .09 | .03 |
|---|---|---|---|---|

Cleveland Browns
| ☐ 503 | Jim Ritcher | .20 | .09 | .03 |
|---|---|---|---|---|

Buffalo Bills
| ☐ 504 | Harris Barton | .20 | .09 | .03 |
|---|---|---|---|---|

San Francisco 49ers
| ☐ 505 | Andre Rison | 7.00 | 3.10 | .85 |
|---|---|---|---|---|

TL FOIL SP
Atlanta Falcons
| ☐ 506 | Chris Martin | .20 | .09 | .03 |
|---|---|---|---|---|

Kansas City Chiefs
| ☐ 507 | Freddie Joe Nunn | .20 | .09 | .03 |
|---|---|---|---|---|

Phoenix Cardinals
| ☐ 508 | Mark Higgs | .75 | .35 | .09 |
|---|---|---|---|---|

Miami Dolphins
| ☐ 509 | Norm Johnson | .20 | .09 | .03 |
|---|---|---|---|---|

Atlanta Falcons
| ☐ 510 | Stephen Baker | .20 | .09 | .03 |
|---|---|---|---|---|

New York Giants
| ☐ 511 | Ricky Sanders | .20 | .09 | .03 |
|---|---|---|---|---|

Washington Redskins
| ☐ 512 | Ray Donaldson | .20 | .09 | .03 |
|---|---|---|---|---|

Indianapolis Colts
| ☐ 513 | David Fulcher | .20 | .09 | .03 |
|---|---|---|---|---|

Cincinnati Bengals
| ☐ 514 | Gerald Williams | .20 | .09 | .03 |
|---|---|---|---|---|

Pittsburgh Steelers
| ☐ 515 | Toi Cook | .20 | .09 | .03 |
|---|---|---|---|---|

New Orleans Saints
| ☐ 516 | Chris Warren | 1.25 | .55 | .16 |
|---|---|---|---|---|

Seattle Seahawks
| ☐ 517 | Jeff Gossett | .20 | .09 | .03 |
|---|---|---|---|---|

Los Angeles Raiders
| ☐ 518 | Ken Lanier | .20 | .09 | .03 |
|---|---|---|---|---|

Denver Broncos
| ☐ 519 | Haywood Jeffires | 5.00 | 2.30 | .60 |
|---|---|---|---|---|

TL FOIL SP
Houston Oilers
| ☐ 520 | Kevin Glover | .20 | .09 | .03 |
|---|---|---|---|---|

Detroit Lions
| ☐ 521 | Mo Lewis | .20 | .09 | .03 |
|---|---|---|---|---|

New York Jets
| ☐ 522 | Bern Brostek | .20 | .09 | .03 |
|---|---|---|---|---|

Los Angeles Rams
| ☐ 523 | Bo Orlando | .40 | .18 | .05 |
|---|---|---|---|---|

Houston Oilers
| ☐ 524 | Mike Saxon | .20 | .09 | .03 |
|---|---|---|---|---|

Dallas Cowboys
| ☐ 525 | Seth Joyner | .25 | .11 | .03 |
|---|---|---|---|---|

Philadelphia Eagles
| ☐ 526 | John Carney | .20 | .09 | .03 |
|---|---|---|---|---|

San Diego Chargers
| ☐ 527 | Jeff Cross | .20 | .09 | .03 |
|---|---|---|---|---|

Miami Dolphins
| ☐ 528 | Gary Anderson | 4.00 | 1.80 | .50 |
|---|---|---|---|---|

TL FOIL SP
Pittsburgh Steelers
| ☐ 529 | Chuck Cecil | .20 | .09 | .03 |
|---|---|---|---|---|

Green Bay Packers
| ☐ 530 | Tim Green | .20 | .09 | .03 |
|---|---|---|---|---|

Atlanta Falcons
| ☐ 531 | Kevin Porter | .20 | .09 | .03 |
|---|---|---|---|---|

Kansas City Chiefs
| ☐ 532 | Chris Spielman | .25 | .11 | .03 |
|---|---|---|---|---|

Detroit Lions
| ☐ 533 | Willie Drewrey | .20 | .09 | .03 |
|---|---|---|---|---|

Tampa Bay Buccaneers
| ☐ 534 | Chris Singleton UER | .20 | .09 | .03 |
|---|---|---|---|---|

(Card has wrong score
for Super Bowl XX)
New England Patriots
| ☐ 535 | Matt Stover | .20 | .09 | .03 |
|---|---|---|---|---|

Cleveland Browns
| ☐ 536 | Andre Collins | .20 | .09 | .03 |
|---|---|---|---|---|

Washington Redskins
| ☐ 537 | Erik Howard | .20 | .09 | .03 |
|---|---|---|---|---|

New York Giants
| ☐ 538 | Steve Tasker | .25 | .11 | .03 |
|---|---|---|---|---|

Buffalo Bills
| ☐ 539 | Anthony Thompson | .20 | .09 | .03 |
|---|---|---|---|---|

Phoenix Cardinals
| ☐ 540 | Charles Haley | .25 | .11 | .03 |
|---|---|---|---|---|

San Francisco 49ers
| ☐ 541 | Mike Merriweather | 1.00 | .45 | .13 |
|---|---|---|---|---|

TL FOIL
Minnesota Vikings
| ☐ 542 | Henry Thomas | .20 | .09 | .03 |
|---|---|---|---|---|

Minnesota Vikings
| ☐ 543 | Scott Stephen | .20 | .09 | .03 |
|---|---|---|---|---|

Green Bay Packers
| ☐ 544 | Bruce Kozerski | .20 | .09 | .03 |
|---|---|---|---|---|

Cincinnati Bengals
| ☐ 545 | Tim McKyer | .25 | .11 | .03 |
|---|---|---|---|---|

Atlanta Falcons
| ☐ 546 | Chris Doleman | .25 | .11 | .03 |
|---|---|---|---|---|

Minnesota Vikings
| ☐ 547 | Riki Ellison | .20 | .09 | .03 |
|---|---|---|---|---|

Los Angeles Raiders
| ☐ 548 | Mike Prior | .20 | .09 | .03 |
|---|---|---|---|---|

Indianapolis Colts
| ☐ 549 | Dwayne Harper | .20 | .09 | .03 |
|---|---|---|---|---|

Seattle Seahawks
| ☐ 550 | Bubby Brister | .25 | .11 | .03 |
|---|---|---|---|---|

Pittsburgh Steelers
| ☐ 551 | Dave Meggett | .25 | .11 | .03 |
|---|---|---|---|---|

New York Giants
| ☐ 552 | Greg Montgomery | .20 | .09 | .03 |
|---|---|---|---|---|

Houston Oilers
| ☐ 553 | Kevin Mack | 1.00 | .45 | .13 |
|---|---|---|---|---|

TL FOIL
Cleveland Browns
| ☐ 554 | Mark Stepnoski | .20 | .09 | .03 |
|---|---|---|---|---|

Dallas Cowboys
| ☐ 555 | Kenny Walker | .20 | .09 | .03 |
|---|---|---|---|---|

Denver Broncos
| ☐ 556 | Eric Moten | .20 | .09 | .03 |
|---|---|---|---|---|

San Diego Chargers
| ☐ 557 | Michael Stewart | .20 | .09 | .03 |
|---|---|---|---|---|

Los Angeles Rams
| ☐ 558 | Calvin Williams | .50 | .23 | .06 |
|---|---|---|---|---|

Philadelphia Eagles
| ☐ 559 | Johnny Hector | .20 | .09 | .03 |
|---|---|---|---|---|

New York Jets
| ☐ 560 | Tony Paige | .20 | .09 | .03 |
|---|---|---|---|---|

Miami Dolphins
| ☐ 561 | Tim Newton | .20 | .09 | .03 |
|---|---|---|---|---|

Tampa Bay Buccaneers
| ☐ 562 | Brad Muster | .25 | .11 | .03 |
|---|---|---|---|---|

Chicago Bears
| ☐ 563 | Aeneas Williams | .20 | .09 | .03 |
|---|---|---|---|---|

Phoenix Cardinals
| ☐ 564 | Herman Moore | 3.00 | 1.35 | .40 |
|---|---|---|---|---|

Detroit Lions
| ☐ 565 | Checklist 460-573 | .20 | .09 | .03 |
|---|---|---|---|---|
| ☐ 566 | Jerome Henderson | .20 | .09 | .03 |

New England Patriots
| ☐ 567 | Danny Copeland | .20 | .09 | .03 |
|---|---|---|---|---|

Washington Redskins
| ☐ 568 | Alexander Wright | 1.00 | .45 | .13 |
|---|---|---|---|---|

LP FOIL
Dallas Cowboys
| ☐ 569 | Tim Harris | .25 | .11 | .03 |
|---|---|---|---|---|

San Francisco 49ers
| ☐ 570 | Jonathan Hayes | .20 | .09 | .03 |
|---|---|---|---|---|

Kansas City Chiefs
| ☐ 571 | Tony Jones | .20 | .09 | .03 |
|---|---|---|---|---|

Cleveland Browns
| ☐ 572 | Carlton Bailey | .75 | .35 | .09 |
|---|---|---|---|---|

Buffalo Bills
| ☐ 573 | Vaughan Johnson | .25 | .11 | .03 |
|---|---|---|---|---|

New Orleans Saints

# 1993 Bowman

The 423 standard-size (2 1/2" by 3 1/2") cards comprising the 1993 Bowman set feature on their fronts white-bordered color player action shots. The player's name appears at the lower right. Several cards are bordered in prismatic foil. The multicolored horizontal back is borderless at the top and bottom, and has white borders on the left and right sides. A small player photo that carries his position in its lower right corner appears below the player's name on the left side. His biography, career highlights, and other comments appear on the right. The cards are numbered on the back. Rookie Cards include Jerome Bettis, Drew Bledsoe, Reggie Brooks, Garrison Hearst, O.J. McDuffie, Natrone Means and Rick Mirer.

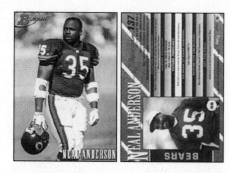

| | MINT | EXC | G-VG |
|---|---|---|---|
| COMPLETE SET (423) | 70.00 | 32.00 | 8.75 |
| COMMON PLAYER (1-423) | .15 | .07 | .02 |
| ☐ 1 Troy Aikman FOIL | 8.00 | 3.60 | 1.00 |
| Dallas Cowboys | | | |
| ☐ 2 John Parella | .25 | .11 | .03 |
| Buffalo Bills | | | |
| ☐ 3 Dana Stubblefield | 1.25 | .55 | .16 |
| San Francisco 49ers | | | |
| ☐ 4 Mark Higgs | .25 | .11 | .03 |
| Miami Dolphins | | | |
| ☐ 5 Tom Carter | .60 | .25 | .08 |
| Washington Redskins | | | |
| ☐ 6 Nate Lewis | .20 | .09 | .03 |
| San Diego Chargers | | | |
| ☐ 7 Vaughn Hebron | 1.00 | .45 | .13 |
| Philadelphia Eagles | | | |
| ☐ 8 Ernest Givins | .20 | .09 | .03 |
| Houston Oilers | | | |
| ☐ 9 Vince Buck | .25 | .11 | .03 |
| New Orleans Saints | | | |
| ☐ 10 Levon Kirkland | .15 | .07 | .02 |
| Pittsburgh Steelers | | | |
| ☐ 11 J.J. Birden | .20 | .09 | .03 |
| Kansas City Chiefs | | | |
| ☐ 12 Steve Jordan | .20 | .09 | .03 |
| Minnesota Vikings | | | |
| ☐ 13 Simon Fletcher | .20 | .09 | .03 |
| Denver Broncos | | | |
| ☐ 14 Willie Green | .20 | .09 | .03 |
| Detroit Lions | | | |
| ☐ 15 Pepper Johnson | .15 | .07 | .02 |
| Cleveland Browns | | | |
| ☐ 16 Roger Harper | .35 | .16 | .04 |
| Atlanta Falcons | | | |
| ☐ 17 Rob Moore | .25 | .11 | .03 |
| New York Jets | | | |
| ☐ 18 David Lang | .15 | .07 | .02 |
| Los Angeles Rams | | | |
| ☐ 19 David Klingler | .50 | .23 | .06 |
| Cincinnati Bengals | | | |
| ☐ 20 Garrison Hearst FOIL | 2.25 | 1.00 | .30 |
| Phoenix Cardinals | | | |
| ☐ 21 Anthony Johnson | .15 | .07 | .02 |
| Indianapolis Colts | | | |
| ☐ 22 Eric Curry FOIL | .75 | .35 | .09 |
| Tampa Bay Buccaneers | | | |
| ☐ 23 Nolan Harrison | .15 | .07 | .02 |
| Los Angeles Raiders | | | |
| ☐ 24 Earl Dotson | .20 | .09 | .03 |
| Green Bay Packers | | | |
| ☐ 25 Leonard Russell | .20 | .09 | .03 |
| New England Patriots | | | |
| ☐ 26 Doug Riesenberg | .15 | .07 | .02 |
| New York Giants | | | |
| ☐ 27 Dwayne Harper | .15 | .07 | .02 |
| Seattle Seahawks | | | |
| ☐ 28 Richard Dent | .20 | .09 | .03 |
| Chicago Bears | | | |
| ☐ 29 Victor Bailey | 1.00 | .45 | .13 |
| Philadelphia Eagles | | | |
| ☐ 30 Junior Seau | .25 | .11 | .03 |
| San Diego Chargers | | | |
| ☐ 31 Steve Tasker | .15 | .07 | .02 |
| Buffalo Bills | | | |
| ☐ 32 Kurt Gouveia | .15 | .07 | .02 |
| Washington Redskins | | | |
| ☐ 33 Renaldo Turnbull UER | .20 | .09 | .03 |
| New Orleans Saints | | | |
| (Listed as wide receiver) | | | |
| ☐ 34 Dale Carter | .25 | .11 | .03 |
| Kansas City Chiefs | | | |
| ☐ 35 Russell Maryland | .25 | .11 | .03 |
| Dallas Cowboys | | | |
| ☐ 36 Dana Hall | .15 | .07 | .02 |
| San Francisco 49ers | | | |
| ☐ 37 Marco Coleman | .20 | .09 | .03 |
| Miami Dolphins | | | |
| ☐ 38 Greg Montgomery | .15 | .07 | .02 |
| Houston Oilers | | | |
| ☐ 39 Deon Figures | .50 | .23 | .06 |
| Pittsburgh Steelers | | | |
| ☐ 40 Troy Drayton | .75 | .35 | .09 |
| Los Angeles Rams | | | |
| ☐ 41 Eric Metcalf | .25 | .11 | .03 |
| Cleveland Browns | | | |
| ☐ 42 Michael Husted | .25 | .11 | .03 |
| Tampa Bay Buccaneers | | | |
| ☐ 43 Harry Newsome | .15 | .07 | .02 |
| Minnesota Vikings | | | |
| ☐ 44 Kelvin Pritchett | .15 | .07 | .02 |
| Detroit Lions | | | |
| ☐ 45 Andre Rison FOIL | .50 | .23 | .06 |
| Atlanta Falcons | | | |
| ☐ 46 John Copeland | .75 | .35 | .09 |
| Cincinnati Bengals | | | |
| ☐ 47 Greg Biekert | .30 | .14 | .04 |
| Los Angeles Raiders | | | |
| ☐ 48 Johnny Johnson | .25 | .11 | .03 |
| New York Jets | | | |
| ☐ 49 Chuck Cecil | .15 | .07 | .02 |
| Phoenix Cardinals | | | |
| ☐ 50 Rick Mirer FOIL | 10.00 | 4.50 | 1.25 |
| Seattle Seahawks | | | |
| ☐ 51 Rod Bernstine | .20 | .09 | .03 |
| Denver Broncos | | | |
| ☐ 52 Steve McMichael | .15 | .07 | .02 |
| Chicago Bears | | | |
| ☐ 53 Roosevelt Potts | .75 | .35 | .09 |
| Indianapolis Colts | | | |
| ☐ 54 Mike Sherrard | .15 | .07 | .02 |
| New York Giants | | | |
| ☐ 55 Terrell Buckley | .25 | .11 | .03 |
| Green Bay Packers | | | |
| ☐ 56 Eugene Chung | .15 | .07 | .02 |
| New England Patriots | | | |
| ☐ 57 Kimble Anders | .75 | .35 | .09 |
| Kansas City Chiefs | | | |
| ☐ 58 Daryl Johnston | .25 | .11 | .03 |
| Dallas Cowboys | | | |
| ☐ 59 Harris Barton | .15 | .07 | .02 |
| San Francisco 49ers | | | |
| ☐ 60 Thurman Thomas FOIL | 1.75 | .80 | .22 |
| Buffalo Bills | | | |
| ☐ 61 Eric Martin | .20 | .09 | .03 |
| New Orleans Saints | | | |
| ☐ 62 Reggie Brooks FOIL | 7.00 | 3.10 | .85 |
| Washington Redskins | | | |
| ☐ 63 Eric Bieniemy | .20 | .09 | .03 |
| San Diego Chargers | | | |
| ☐ 64 John Offerdahl | .15 | .07 | .02 |
| Miami Dolphins | | | |
| ☐ 65 Wilber Marshall | .20 | .09 | .03 |
| Houston Oilers | | | |
| ☐ 66 Mark Carrier WR | .20 | .09 | .03 |
| Cleveland Browns | | | |
| ☐ 67 Merril Hoge | .15 | .07 | .02 |
| Pittsburgh Steelers | | | |
| ☐ 68 Cris Carter | .25 | .11 | .03 |
| Minnesota Vikings | | | |
| ☐ 69 Marty Thompson | .30 | .14 | .04 |
| Detroit Lions | | | |
| ☐ 70 Randall Cunningham FOIL | .40 | .18 | .05 |
| Philadelphia Eagles | | | |
| ☐ 71 Winston Moss | .15 | .07 | .02 |
| Los Angeles Raiders | | | |
| ☐ 72 Doug Pelfrey | .20 | .09 | .03 |
| Cincinnati Bengals | | | |
| ☐ 73 Jackie Slater | .15 | .07 | .02 |
| Los Angeles Raiders | | | |
| ☐ 74 Pierce Holt | .15 | .07 | .02 |
| Atlanta Falcons | | | |
| ☐ 75 Hardy Nickerson | .15 | .07 | .02 |
| Tampa Bay Buccaneers | | | |
| ☐ 76 Chris Burkett | .15 | .07 | .02 |
| New York Jets | | | |
| ☐ 77 Michael Brandon | .15 | .07 | .02 |
| New York Giants | | | |
| ☐ 78 Tom Waddle | .25 | .11 | .03 |
| Chicago Bears | | | |
| ☐ 79 Walter Reeves | .15 | .07 | .02 |
| Phoenix Cardinals | | | |
| ☐ 80 Lawrence Taylor FOIL | .40 | .18 | .05 |
| New York Giants | | | |
| ☐ 81 Wayne Simmons | .30 | .14 | .04 |
| Philadelphia Eagles | | | |
| ☐ 82 Brent Williams | .15 | .07 | .02 |
| New England Patriots | | | |
| ☐ 83 Shannon Sharpe | .75 | .35 | .09 |
| Denver Broncos | | | |
| ☐ 84 Robert Blackmon | .15 | .07 | .02 |
| Seattle Seahawks | | | |
| ☐ 85 Keith Jackson | .25 | .11 | .03 |

Miami Dolphins
| | | | |
|---|---|---|---|
| ☐ 86 A.J. Johnson | .15 | .07 | .02 |

Pittsburgh Steelers
| | | | |
|---|---|---|---|
| ☐ 87 Ryan McNeil | .40 | .18 | .05 |

Detroit Lions
| | | | |
|---|---|---|---|
| ☐ 88 Michael Dean Perry | .25 | .11 | .03 |

Cleveland Browns
| | | | |
|---|---|---|---|
| ☐ 89 Russell Copeland | .35 | .16 | .04 |

Buffalo Bills
| | | | |
|---|---|---|---|
| ☐ 90 Sam Mills | .20 | .09 | .03 |

New Orleans Saints
| | | | |
|---|---|---|---|
| ☐ 91 Courtney Hall | .15 | .07 | .02 |

San Diego Chargers
| | | | |
|---|---|---|---|
| ☐ 92 Gino Torretta | .75 | .35 | .09 |

Minnesota Vikings
| | | | |
|---|---|---|---|
| ☐ 93 Artie Smith | .35 | .16 | .04 |

San Francisco 49ers
| | | | |
|---|---|---|---|
| ☐ 94 David Whitmore | .15 | .07 | .02 |

Kansas City Chiefs
| | | | |
|---|---|---|---|
| ☐ 95 Charles Haley | .20 | .09 | .03 |

Dallas Cowboys
| | | | |
|---|---|---|---|
| ☐ 96 Rod Woodson | .25 | .11 | .03 |

Pittsburgh Steelers
| | | | |
|---|---|---|---|
| ☐ 97 Lorenzo White | .20 | .09 | .03 |

Houston Oilers
| | | | |
|---|---|---|---|
| ☐ 98 Tom Scott | .20 | .09 | .03 |

Cincinnati Bengals
| | | | |
|---|---|---|---|
| ☐ 99 Tyji Armstrong | .15 | .07 | .02 |

Tampa Bay Buccaneers
| | | | |
|---|---|---|---|
| ☐ 100 Boomer Esiason | .35 | .16 | .04 |

New York Jets
| | | | |
|---|---|---|---|
| ☐ 101 Raghib Ismail FOIL | 1.00 | .45 | .13 |

Los Angeles Raiders
| | | | |
|---|---|---|---|
| ☐ 102 Mark Carrier USC | .20 | .09 | .03 |

Chicago Bears
| | | | |
|---|---|---|---|
| ☐ 103 Broderick Thompson | .15 | .07 | .02 |

Tampa Bay Buccaneers
| | | | |
|---|---|---|---|
| ☐ 104 Bob Whitfield | .15 | .07 | .02 |

Atlanta Falcons
| | | | |
|---|---|---|---|
| ☐ 105 Ben Coleman | .20 | .09 | .03 |

Phoenix Cardinals
| | | | |
|---|---|---|---|
| ☐ 106 Jon Vaughn | .15 | .07 | .02 |

New England Patriots
| | | | |
|---|---|---|---|
| ☐ 107 Marcus Buckley | .25 | .11 | .03 |

New York Giants
| | | | |
|---|---|---|---|
| ☐ 108 Cleveland Gary | .20 | .09 | .03 |

Los Angeles Rams
| | | | |
|---|---|---|---|
| ☐ 109 Ashley Ambrose | .15 | .07 | .02 |

Indianapolis Colts
| | | | |
|---|---|---|---|
| ☐ 110 Reggie White FOIL | .50 | .23 | .06 |

Green Bay Packers
| | | | |
|---|---|---|---|
| ☐ 111 Arthur Marshall | .50 | .23 | .06 |

Denver Broncos
| | | | |
|---|---|---|---|
| ☐ 112 Greg McMurtry | .15 | .07 | .02 |

New England Patriots
| | | | |
|---|---|---|---|
| ☐ 113 Mike Johnson | .15 | .07 | .02 |

Cleveland Browns
| | | | |
|---|---|---|---|
| ☐ 114 Tim McGee | .15 | .07 | .02 |

Washington Redskins
| | | | |
|---|---|---|---|
| ☐ 115 John Carney | .15 | .07 | .02 |

San Diego Chargers
| | | | |
|---|---|---|---|
| ☐ 116 Neil Smith | .25 | .11 | .03 |

Kansas City Chiefs
| | | | |
|---|---|---|---|
| ☐ 117 Mark Stepnoski | .15 | .07 | .02 |

Dallas Cowboys
| | | | |
|---|---|---|---|
| ☐ 118 Don Beebe | .25 | .11 | .03 |

Buffalo Bills
| | | | |
|---|---|---|---|
| ☐ 119 Scott Mitchell | 2.00 | .90 | .25 |

Miami Dolphins
| | | | |
|---|---|---|---|
| ☐ 120 Randall McDaniel | .15 | .07 | .02 |

Minnesota Vikings
| | | | |
|---|---|---|---|
| ☐ 121 Chidi Ahanotu | .20 | .09 | .03 |

Tampa Bay Buccaneers
| | | | |
|---|---|---|---|
| ☐ 122 Ray Childress | .15 | .07 | .02 |

Houston Oilers
| | | | |
|---|---|---|---|
| ☐ 123 Tony McGee | .50 | .23 | .06 |

Cincinnati Bengals
| | | | |
|---|---|---|---|
| ☐ 124 Marc Boutte | .15 | .07 | .02 |

Los Angeles Raiders
| | | | |
|---|---|---|---|
| ☐ 125 Ronnie Lott | .25 | .11 | .03 |

New York Jets
| | | | |
|---|---|---|---|
| ☐ 126 Jason Elam | .30 | .14 | .04 |

Denver Broncos
| | | | |
|---|---|---|---|
| ☐ 127 Martin Harrison | .40 | .18 | .05 |

San Francisco 49ers
| | | | |
|---|---|---|---|
| ☐ 128 Leonard Renfro | .25 | .11 | .03 |

Philadelphia Eagles
| | | | |
|---|---|---|---|
| ☐ 129 Jesse Armstead | .30 | .14 | .04 |

New York Giants
| | | | |
|---|---|---|---|
| ☐ 130 Quentin Coryatt | .25 | .11 | .03 |

Indianapolis Colts
| | | | |
|---|---|---|---|
| ☐ 131 Luis Sharpe | .15 | .07 | .02 |

Phoenix Cardinals
| | | | |
|---|---|---|---|
| ☐ 132 Bill Maas | .15 | .07 | .02 |

Green Bay Packers
| | | | |
|---|---|---|---|
| ☐ 133 Jesse Solomon | .15 | .07 | .02 |

Atlanta Falcons
| | | | |
|---|---|---|---|
| ☐ 134 Kevin Greene | .15 | .07 | .02 |

Pittsburgh Steelers
| | | | |
|---|---|---|---|
| ☐ 135 Derek Brown RB | 2.25 | 1.00 | .30 |

New Orleans Saints
| | | | |
|---|---|---|---|
| ☐ 136 Greg Townsend | .15 | .07 | .02 |

Los Angeles Raiders
| | | | |
|---|---|---|---|
| ☐ 137 Neal Anderson | .20 | .09 | .03 |

Chicago Bears
| | | | |
|---|---|---|---|
| ☐ 138 John L. Williams | .20 | .09 | .03 |

Seattle Seahawks
| | | | |
|---|---|---|---|
| ☐ 139 Vincent Brisby | 2.00 | .90 | .25 |

New England Patriots
| | | | |
|---|---|---|---|
| ☐ 140 Barry Sanders FOIL | 2.50 | 1.15 | .30 |

Detroit Lions
| | | | |
|---|---|---|---|
| ☐ 141 Charles Mann | .15 | .07 | .02 |

Washington Redskins
| | | | |
|---|---|---|---|
| ☐ 142 Ken Norton | .20 | .09 | .03 |

Dallas Cowboys
| | | | |
|---|---|---|---|
| ☐ 143 Eric Moten | .15 | .07 | .02 |

San Diego Chargers
| | | | |
|---|---|---|---|
| ☐ 144 John Alt | .15 | .07 | .02 |

Kansas City Chiefs
| | | | |
|---|---|---|---|
| ☐ 145 Dan Footman | .40 | .18 | .05 |

Cleveland Browns
| | | | |
|---|---|---|---|
| ☐ 146 Bill Brooks | .15 | .07 | .02 |

Buffalo Bills
| | | | |
|---|---|---|---|
| ☐ 147 James Thornton | .15 | .07 | .02 |

New York Jets
| | | | |
|---|---|---|---|
| ☐ 148 Martin Mayhew | .15 | .07 | .02 |

Tampa Bay Buccaneers
| | | | |
|---|---|---|---|
| ☐ 149 Andy Harmon | .15 | .07 | .02 |

Philadelphia Eagles
| | | | |
|---|---|---|---|
| ☐ 150 Dan Marino FOIL | 5.00 | 2.30 | .60 |

Miami Dolphins
| | | | |
|---|---|---|---|
| ☐ 151 Micheal Barrow | .15 | .07 | .02 |

Houston Oilers
| | | | |
|---|---|---|---|
| ☐ 152 Flipper Anderson | .20 | .09 | .03 |

Los Angeles Rams
| | | | |
|---|---|---|---|
| ☐ 153 Jackie Harris | 1.00 | .45 | .13 |

Green Bay Packers
| | | | |
|---|---|---|---|
| ☐ 154 Todd Kelly | .30 | .14 | .04 |

San Francisco 49ers
| | | | |
|---|---|---|---|
| ☐ 155 Dan Williams | .40 | .18 | .05 |

Denver Broncos
| | | | |
|---|---|---|---|
| ☐ 156 Harold Green | .20 | .09 | .03 |

Cincinnati Bengals
| | | | |
|---|---|---|---|
| ☐ 157 David Treadwell | .15 | .07 | .02 |

New York Giants
| | | | |
|---|---|---|---|
| ☐ 158 Chris Doleman | .20 | .09 | .03 |

Minnesota Vikings
| | | | |
|---|---|---|---|
| ☐ 159 Eric Hill | .15 | .07 | .02 |

Phoenix Cardinals
| | | | |
|---|---|---|---|
| ☐ 160 Lincoln Kennedy | .50 | .23 | .06 |

Atlanta Falcons
| | | | |
|---|---|---|---|
| ☐ 161 Devon McDonald | .20 | .09 | .03 |

Indianapolis Colts
| | | | |
|---|---|---|---|
| ☐ 162 Natrone Means | 3.50 | 1.55 | .45 |

San Diego Chargers
| | | | |
|---|---|---|---|
| ☐ 163 Rick Hamilton | .20 | .09 | .03 |

Washington Redskins
| | | | |
|---|---|---|---|
| ☐ 164 Kelvin Martin | .15 | .07 | .02 |

Seattle Seahawks
| | | | |
|---|---|---|---|
| ☐ 165 Jeff Hostetler | .25 | .11 | .03 |

Los Angeles Raiders
| | | | |
|---|---|---|---|
| ☐ 166 Mark Brunell | .75 | .35 | .09 |

New York Giants
| | | | |
|---|---|---|---|
| ☐ 167 Tim Barnett | .20 | .09 | .03 |

Kansas City Chiefs
| | | | |
|---|---|---|---|
| ☐ 168 Ray Crockett | .15 | .07 | .02 |

Detroit Lions
| | | | |
|---|---|---|---|
| ☐ 169 William Perry | .15 | .07 | .02 |

Chicago Bears
| | | | |
|---|---|---|---|
| ☐ 170 Michael Irvin | 2.25 | 1.00 | .30 |

Dallas Cowboys
| | | | |
|---|---|---|---|
| ☐ 171 Marvin Washington | .15 | .07 | .02 |

New York Jets
| | | | |
|---|---|---|---|
| ☐ 172 Irving Fryar | .15 | .07 | .02 |

Miami Dolphins
| | | | |
|---|---|---|---|
| ☐ 173 Scott Sisson | .25 | .11 | .03 |

New England Patriots
| | | | |
|---|---|---|---|
| ☐ 174 Gary Anderson | .15 | .07 | .02 |

Pittsburgh Steelers
| | | | |
|---|---|---|---|
| ☐ 175 Bruce Smith | .25 | .11 | .03 |

Buffalo Bills
| | | | |
|---|---|---|---|
| ☐ 176 Clyde Simmons | .20 | .09 | .03 |

Philadelphia Eagles
| | | | |
|---|---|---|---|
| ☐ 177 Russell White | .40 | .18 | .05 |

Los Angeles Rams
| | | | |
|---|---|---|---|
| ☐ 178 Irv Smith | .60 | .25 | .08 |

New Orleans Saints
| | | | |
|---|---|---|---|
| ☐ 179 Mark Wheeler | .15 | .07 | .02 |

Tampa Bay Buccaneers
| | | | |
|---|---|---|---|
| ☐ 180 Warren Moon | .60 | .25 | .08 |

Houston Oilers
| | | | |
|---|---|---|---|
| ☐ 181 Del Speer | .25 | .11 | .03 |

Cleveland Browns
| | | | |
|---|---|---|---|
| ☐ 182 Henry Thomas | .15 | .07 | .02 |

Minnesota Vikings
| | | | |
|---|---|---|---|
| ☐ 183 Keith Kartz | .15 | .07 | .02 |

| | | | | |
|---|---|---|---|---|
| Denver Broncos | | | | |
| ☐ 184 Ricky Ervins | .20 | .09 | .03 | |
| Washington Redskins | | | | |
| ☐ 185 Phil Simms | .25 | .11 | .03 | |
| New York Giants | | | | |
| ☐ 186 Tim Brown | .60 | .25 | .08 | |
| Los Angeles Raiders | | | | |
| ☐ 187 Willis Peguese | .15 | .07 | .02 | |
| Indianapolis Colts | | | | |
| ☐ 188 Rich Moran | .15 | .07 | .02 | |
| Green Bay Packers | | | | |
| ☐ 189 Robert Jones | .15 | .07 | .02 | |
| Dallas Cowboys | | | | |
| ☐ 190 Craig Heyward | .15 | .07 | .02 | |
| Chicago Bears | | | | |
| ☐ 191 Ricky Watters | 1.00 | .45 | .13 | |
| San Francisco 49ers | | | | |
| ☐ 192 Stan Humphries | .25 | .11 | .03 | |
| San Diego Chargers | | | | |
| ☐ 193 Larry Webster | .15 | .07 | .02 | |
| Miami Dolphins | | | | |
| ☐ 194 Brad Baxter | .20 | .09 | .03 | |
| New York Jets | | | | |
| ☐ 195 Randal Hill | .25 | .11 | .03 | |
| Phoenix Cardinals | | | | |
| ☐ 196 Robert Porcher | .20 | .09 | .03 | |
| Detroit Lions | | | | |
| ☐ 197 Patrick Robinson | .30 | .14 | .04 | |
| Cincinnati Bengals | | | | |
| ☐ 198 Ferrell Edmunds | .15 | .07 | .02 | |
| Seattle Seahawks | | | | |
| ☐ 199 Melvin Jenkins | .15 | .07 | .02 | |
| Atlanta Falcons | | | | |
| ☐ 200 Joe Montana FOIL | 7.00 | 3.10 | .85 | |
| Kansas City Chiefs | | | | |
| ☐ 201 Marv Cook | .15 | .07 | .02 | |
| New England Patriots | | | | |
| ☐ 202 Henry Ellard | .20 | .09 | .03 | |
| Los Angeles Rams | | | | |
| ☐ 203 Calvin Williams | .25 | .11 | .03 | |
| Philadelphia Eagles | | | | |
| ☐ 204 Craig Erickson | .25 | .11 | .03 | |
| Tampa Bay Buccaneers | | | | |
| ☐ 205 Steve Atwater | .20 | .09 | .03 | |
| Denver Broncos | | | | |
| ☐ 206 Najee Mustafaa | .15 | .07 | .02 | |
| Cleveland Browns | | | | |
| ☐ 207 Darryl Talley | .15 | .07 | .02 | |
| Buffalo Bills | | | | |
| ☐ 208 Jarrod Bunch | .15 | .07 | .02 | |
| New York Giants | | | | |
| ☐ 209 Tim McDonald | .15 | .07 | .02 | |
| San Francisco 49ers | | | | |
| ☐ 210 Patrick Bates | .40 | .18 | .05 | |
| Los Angeles Raiders | | | | |
| ☐ 211 Sean Jones | .15 | .07 | .02 | |
| Houston Oilers | | | | |
| ☐ 212 Leslie O'Neal | .20 | .09 | .03 | |
| San Diego Chargers | | | | |
| ☐ 213 Mike Golic | .15 | .07 | .02 | |
| Miami Dolphins | | | | |
| ☐ 214 Mark Clayton | .15 | .07 | .02 | |
| Green Bay Packers | | | | |
| ☐ 215 Leonard Marshall | .15 | .07 | .02 | |
| Washington Redskins | | | | |
| ☐ 216 Curtis Conway | 1.50 | .65 | .19 | |
| Chicago Bears | | | | |
| ☐ 217 Andre Hastings | .60 | .25 | .08 | |
| Pittsburgh Steelers | | | | |
| ☐ 218 Barry Word | .25 | .11 | .03 | |
| Minnesota Vikings | | | | |
| ☐ 219 Will Wolford | .15 | .07 | .02 | |
| Indianapolis Colts | | | | |
| ☐ 220 Desmond Howard | .75 | .35 | .09 | |
| Washington Redskins | | | | |
| ☐ 221 Rickey Jackson | .20 | .09 | .03 | |
| New Orleans Saints | | | | |
| ☐ 222 Alvin Harper | 1.00 | .45 | .13 | |
| Dallas Cowboys | | | | |
| ☐ 223 William White | .15 | .07 | .02 | |
| Detroit Lions | | | | |
| ☐ 224 Steve Broussard | .15 | .07 | .02 | |
| Atlanta Falcons | | | | |
| ☐ 225 Aeneas Williams | .15 | .07 | .02 | |
| Phoenix Cardinals | | | | |
| ☐ 226 Michael Brooks | .15 | .07 | .02 | |
| New York Giants | | | | |
| ☐ 227 Reggie Cobb | .25 | .11 | .03 | |
| Tampa Bay Buccaneers | | | | |
| ☐ 228 Derrick Walker | .15 | .07 | .02 | |
| San Diego Chargers | | | | |
| ☐ 229 Marcus Allen | .40 | .18 | .05 | |
| Kansas City Chiefs | | | | |
| ☐ 230 Jerry Ball | .15 | .07 | .02 | |
| Cleveland Browns | | | | |
| ☐ 231 J.B. Brown | .15 | .07 | .02 | |
| Miami Dolphins | | | | |
| ☐ 232 Terry McDaniel | .15 | .07 | .02 | |

| | | | | |
|---|---|---|---|---|
| Los Angeles Raiders | | | | |
| ☐ 233 LeRoy Butler | .15 | .07 | .02 | |
| Green Bay Packers | | | | |
| ☐ 234 Kyle Clifton | .15 | .07 | .02 | |
| New York Jets | | | | |
| ☐ 235 Henry Jones | .15 | .07 | .02 | |
| Buffalo Bills | | | | |
| ☐ 236 Shane Conlan | .15 | .07 | .02 | |
| Los Angeles Rams | | | | |
| ☐ 237 Michael Bates | .60 | .25 | .08 | |
| Seattle Seahawks | | | | |
| ☐ 238 Vincent Brown | .15 | .07 | .02 | |
| New England Patriots | | | | |
| ☐ 239 William Fuller | .15 | .07 | .02 | |
| Houston Oilers | | | | |
| ☐ 240 Ricardo McDonald | .15 | .07 | .02 | |
| Cincinnati Bengals | | | | |
| ☐ 241 Gary Zimmerman | .15 | .07 | .02 | |
| Denver Broncos | | | | |
| ☐ 242 Fred Barnett | .25 | .11 | .03 | |
| Philadelphia Eagles | | | | |
| ☐ 243 Elvis Grbac | 1.25 | .55 | .16 | |
| San Francisco 49ers | | | | |
| ☐ 244 Myron Baker | .40 | .18 | .05 | |
| Chicago Bears | | | | |
| ☐ 245 Steve Emtman | .20 | .09 | .03 | |
| Indianapolis Colts | | | | |
| ☐ 246 Mike Compton | .30 | .14 | .04 | |
| Detroit Lions | | | | |
| ☐ 247 Mark Jackson | .20 | .09 | .03 | |
| New York Giants | | | | |
| ☐ 248 Santo Stephens | .20 | .09 | .03 | |
| Kansas City Chiefs | | | | |
| ☐ 249 Tommie Agee | .15 | .07 | .02 | |
| Dallas Cowboys | | | | |
| ☐ 250 Broderick Thomas | .15 | .07 | .02 | |
| Tampa Bay Buccaneers | | | | |
| ☐ 251 Fred Baxter | .20 | .09 | .03 | |
| New York Jets | | | | |
| ☐ 252 Andre Collins | .15 | .07 | .02 | |
| Washington Redskins | | | | |
| ☐ 253 Ernest Dye | .25 | .11 | .03 | |
| Phoenix Cardinals | | | | |
| ☐ 254 Raylee Johnson | .30 | .14 | .04 | |
| San Diego Chargers | | | | |
| ☐ 255 Rickey Dixon | .15 | .07 | .02 | |
| Los Angeles Raiders | | | | |
| ☐ 256 Ron Heller | .15 | .07 | .02 | |
| Miami Dolphins | | | | |
| ☐ 257 Joel Steed | .15 | .07 | .02 | |
| Pittsburgh Steelers | | | | |
| ☐ 258 Everett Lindsay | .20 | .09 | .03 | |
| Minnesota Vikings | | | | |
| ☐ 259 Tony Smith | .15 | .07 | .02 | |
| Atlanta Falcons | | | | |
| ☐ 260 Sterling Sharpe UER | 2.50 | 1.15 | .30 | |
| Green Bay Packers | | | | |
| (Edgar Bennett is pictured on front) | | | | |
| ☐ 261 Tommy Vardell | .20 | .09 | .03 | |
| Cleveland Browns | | | | |
| ☐ 262 Morten Andersen | .20 | .09 | .03 | |
| New Orleans Saints | | | | |
| ☐ 263 Eddie Robinson | .15 | .07 | .02 | |
| Houston Oilers | | | | |
| ☐ 264 Jerome Bettis | 10.00 | 4.50 | 1.25 | |
| Los Angeles Rams | | | | |
| ☐ 265 Alonzo Spellman | .20 | .09 | .03 | |
| Detroit Lions | | | | |
| ☐ 266 Harvey Williams | .25 | .11 | .03 | |
| Kansas City Chiefs | | | | |
| ☐ 267 Jason Belser | .20 | .09 | .03 | |
| Indianapolis Colts | | | | |
| ☐ 268 Derek Russell | .20 | .09 | .03 | |
| Denver Broncos | | | | |
| ☐ 269 Derrick Lassic | .50 | .23 | .06 | |
| Dallas Cowboys | | | | |
| ☐ 270 Steve Young FOIL | 1.50 | .65 | .19 | |
| San Francisco 49ers | | | | |
| ☐ 271 Adrian Murrell | .30 | .14 | .04 | |
| New York Jets | | | | |
| ☐ 272 Lewis Tillman | .20 | .09 | .03 | |
| New York Giants | | | | |
| ☐ 273 O.J. McDuffie | 4.00 | 1.80 | .50 | |
| Miami Dolphins | | | | |
| ☐ 274 Marty Carter | .15 | .07 | .02 | |
| Tampa Bay Buccaneers | | | | |
| ☐ 275 Ray Seals | .15 | .07 | .02 | |
| Tampa Bay Buccaneers | | | | |
| ☐ 276 Earnest Byner | .20 | .09 | .03 | |
| Washington Redskins | | | | |
| ☐ 277 Marion Butts | .25 | .11 | .03 | |
| San Diego Chargers | | | | |
| ☐ 278 Chris Spielman | .15 | .07 | .02 | |
| Detroit Lions | | | | |
| ☐ 279 Carl Pickens | .30 | .14 | .04 | |
| Cincinnati Bengals | | | | |
| ☐ 280 Drew Bledsoe FOIL | 10.00 | 4.50 | 1.25 | |
| New England Patriots | | | | |

| | | | | |
|---|---|---|---|---|
| ☐ 281 Mark Kelso | .15 | .07 | .02 |
| Buffalo Bills | | | |
| ☐ 282 Eugene Robinson | .15 | .07 | .02 |
| Seattle Seahawks | | | |
| ☐ 283 Eric Allen | .20 | .09 | .03 |
| Philadelphia Eagles | | | |
| ☐ 284 Ethan Horton | .15 | .07 | .02 |
| Los Angeles Raiders | | | |
| ☐ 285 Greg Lloyd | .15 | .07 | .02 |
| Pittsburgh Steelers | | | |
| ☐ 286 Anthony Carter | .20 | .09 | .03 |
| Minnesota Vikings | | | |
| ☐ 287 Edgar Bennett | .25 | .11 | .03 |
| Green Bay Packers | | | |
| ☐ 288 Bobby Hebert | .25 | .11 | .03 |
| Atlanta Falcons | | | |
| ☐ 289 Haywood Jeffires | .25 | .11 | .03 |
| Houston Oilers | | | |
| ☐ 290 Glyn Milburn | 2.50 | 1.15 | .30 |
| Denver Broncos | | | |
| ☐ 291 Bernie Kosar | .25 | .11 | .03 |
| Cleveland Browns | | | |
| ☐ 292 Jumbo Elliott | .15 | .07 | .02 |
| New York Giants | | | |
| ☐ 293 Jessie Hester | .15 | .07 | .02 |
| Indianapolis Colts | | | |
| ☐ 294 Brent Jones | .25 | .11 | .03 |
| San Francisco 49ers | | | |
| ☐ 295 Carl Banks | .15 | .07 | .02 |
| Washington Redskins | | | |
| ☐ 296 Brian Washington | .15 | .07 | .02 |
| New York Jets | | | |
| ☐ 297 Steve Beuerlein | .40 | .18 | .05 |
| Phoenix Cardinals | | | |
| ☐ 298 John Lynch | .25 | .11 | .03 |
| Tampa Bay Buccaneers | | | |
| ☐ 299 Troy Vincent | .20 | .09 | .03 |
| Miami Dolphins | | | |
| ☐ 300 Emmitt Smith FOIL | 10.00 | 4.50 | 1.25 |
| Dallas Cowboys | | | |
| ☐ 301 Chris Zorich | .20 | .09 | .03 |
| Chicago Bears | | | |
| ☐ 302 Wade Wilson | .20 | .09 | .03 |
| New Orleans Saints | | | |
| ☐ 303 Darrien Gordon | .60 | .25 | .08 |
| San Diego Chargers | | | |
| ☐ 304 Fred Stokes | .15 | .07 | .02 |
| Los Angeles Rams | | | |
| ☐ 305 Nick Lowery | .15 | .07 | .02 |
| Kansas City Chiefs | | | |
| ☐ 306 Rodney Peete | .20 | .09 | .03 |
| Detroit Lions | | | |
| ☐ 307 Chris Warren | .50 | .23 | .06 |
| Seattle Seahawks | | | |
| ☐ 308 Herschel Walker | .25 | .11 | .03 |
| Philadelphia Eagles | | | |
| ☐ 309 Aundray Bruce | .15 | .07 | .02 |
| Los Angeles Raiders | | | |
| ☐ 310 Barry Foster FOIL | 1.00 | .45 | .13 |
| Pittsburgh Steelers | | | |
| ☐ 311 George Teague | .50 | .23 | .06 |
| Green Bay Packers | | | |
| ☐ 312 Darryl Williams | .20 | .09 | .03 |
| Cincinnati Bengals | | | |
| ☐ 313 Thomas Smith | .40 | .18 | .05 |
| Buffalo Bills | | | |
| ☐ 314 Dennis Brown | .15 | .07 | .02 |
| San Francisco 49ers | | | |
| ☐ 315 Marvin Jones FOIL | .50 | .23 | .06 |
| New York Jets | | | |
| ☐ 316 Andre Tippett | .15 | .07 | .02 |
| New England Patriots | | | |
| ☐ 317 Demetrius DuBose | .50 | .23 | .06 |
| Tampa Bay Buccaneers | | | |
| ☐ 318 Kirk Lowdermilk | .15 | .07 | .02 |
| Minnesota Vikings | | | |
| ☐ 319 Shane Dronett | .15 | .07 | .02 |
| Denver Broncos | | | |
| ☐ 320 Terry Kirby | 4.00 | 1.80 | .50 |
| Miami Dolphins | | | |
| ☐ 321 Qadry Ismail | 1.50 | .65 | .19 |
| Minnesota Vikings | | | |
| ☐ 322 Lorenzo Lynch | .15 | .07 | .02 |
| Phoenix Cardinals | | | |
| ☐ 323 Willie Drewrey | .15 | .07 | .02 |
| Houston Oilers | | | |
| ☐ 324 Jessie Tuggle | .15 | .07 | .02 |
| Atlanta Falcons | | | |
| ☐ 325 Leroy Hoard | .20 | .09 | .03 |
| Cleveland Browns | | | |
| ☐ 326 Mark Collins | .15 | .07 | .02 |
| New York Giants | | | |
| ☐ 327 Darrell Green | .20 | .09 | .03 |
| Washington Redskins | | | |
| ☐ 328 Anthony Miller | .50 | .23 | .06 |
| San Diego Chargers | | | |
| ☐ 329 Brad Muster | .20 | .09 | .03 |
| New Orleans Saints | | | |
| ☐ 330 Jim Kelly FOIL | 1.00 | .45 | .13 |
| Buffalo Bills | | | |
| ☐ 331 Sean Gilbert | .20 | .09 | .03 |
| Los Angeles Rams | | | |
| ☐ 332 Tim McKyer | .20 | .09 | .03 |
| Detroit Lions | | | |
| ☐ 333 Scott Mersereau | .15 | .07 | .02 |
| New York Jets | | | |
| ☐ 334 Willie Davis | .40 | .18 | .05 |
| Kansas City Chiefs | | | |
| ☐ 335 Brett Favre FOIL | 4.00 | 1.80 | .50 |
| Green Bay Packers | | | |
| ☐ 336 Kevin Gogan | .15 | .07 | .02 |
| Dallas Cowboys | | | |
| ☐ 337 Jim Harbaugh | .20 | .09 | .03 |
| Chicago Bears | | | |
| ☐ 338 James Trapp | .30 | .14 | .04 |
| Los Angeles Raiders | | | |
| ☐ 339 Pete Stoyanovich | .15 | .07 | .02 |
| Miami Dolphins | | | |
| ☐ 340 Jerry Rice FOIL | 3.00 | 1.35 | .40 |
| San Francisco 49ers | | | |
| ☐ 341 Gary Anderson | .20 | .09 | .03 |
| Tampa Bay Buccaneers | | | |
| ☐ 342 Carlton Gray | .50 | .23 | .06 |
| Seattle Seahawks | | | |
| ☐ 343 Dermontti Dawson | .15 | .07 | .02 |
| Pittsburgh Steelers | | | |
| ☐ 344 Ray Buchanan | .25 | .11 | .03 |
| Indianapolis Colts | | | |
| ☐ 345 Derrick Fenner | .15 | .07 | .02 |
| Cincinnati Bengals | | | |
| ☐ 346 Dennis Smith | .15 | .07 | .02 |
| Denver Broncos | | | |
| ☐ 347 Todd Rucci | .25 | .11 | .03 |
| New England Patriots | | | |
| ☐ 348 Seth Joyner | .20 | .09 | .03 |
| Philadelphia Eagles | | | |
| ☐ 349 Jim McMahon | .25 | .11 | .03 |
| Minnesota Vikings | | | |
| ☐ 350 Rodney Hampton | 1.00 | .45 | .13 |
| New York Giants | | | |
| ☐ 351 Al Smith | .15 | .07 | .02 |
| Houston Oilers | | | |
| ☐ 352 Steve Everitt | .30 | .14 | .04 |
| Cleveland Browns | | | |
| ☐ 353 Vinnie Clark | .15 | .07 | .02 |
| Atlanta Falcons | | | |
| ☐ 354 Eric Swann | .20 | .09 | .03 |
| Phoenix Cardinals | | | |
| ☐ 355 Brian Mitchell | .20 | .09 | .03 |
| Washington Redskins | | | |
| ☐ 356 Will Shields | .25 | .11 | .03 |
| Kansas City Chiefs | | | |
| ☐ 357 Cornelius Bennett | .25 | .11 | .03 |
| Buffalo Bills | | | |
| ☐ 358 Darrin Smith | 1.00 | .45 | .13 |
| Dallas Cowboys | | | |
| ☐ 359 Chris Mims | .20 | .09 | .03 |
| San Diego Chargers | | | |
| ☐ 360 Blair Thomas | .20 | .09 | .03 |
| New York Jets | | | |
| ☐ 361 Dennis Gibson | .15 | .07 | .02 |
| Detroit Lions | | | |
| ☐ 362 Santana Dotson | .25 | .11 | .03 |
| Tampa Bay Buccaneers | | | |
| ☐ 363 Mark Ingram | .20 | .09 | .03 |
| Miami Dolphins | | | |
| ☐ 364 Don Mosebar | .15 | .07 | .02 |
| Los Angeles Raiders | | | |
| ☐ 365 Ty Detmer | .20 | .09 | .03 |
| Green Bay Packers | | | |
| ☐ 366 Bob Christian | .35 | .16 | .04 |
| Chicago Bears | | | |
| ☐ 367 Adrian Hardy | .15 | .07 | .02 |
| San Francisco 49ers | | | |
| ☐ 368 Vaughan Johnson | .15 | .07 | .02 |
| New Orleans Saints | | | |
| ☐ 369 Jim Everett | .15 | .07 | .02 |
| Los Angeles Rams | | | |
| ☐ 370 Ricky Sanders | .20 | .09 | .03 |
| Washington Redskins | | | |
| ☐ 371 Jonathan Hayes | .15 | .07 | .02 |
| Kansas City Chiefs | | | |
| ☐ 372 Bruce Matthews | .20 | .09 | .03 |
| Houston Oilers | | | |
| ☐ 373 Darren Drozdov | .30 | .14 | .04 |
| Denver Broncos | | | |
| ☐ 374 Scott Brumfield | .20 | .09 | .03 |
| Cincinnati Bengals | | | |
| ☐ 375 Cortez Kennedy | .25 | .11 | .03 |
| Seattle Seahawks | | | |
| ☐ 376 Tim Harris | .15 | .07 | .02 |
| Philadelphia Eagles | | | |
| ☐ 377 Neil O'Donnell | 1.00 | .45 | .13 |
| Pittsburgh Steelers | | | |
| ☐ 378 Robert Smith | 1.25 | .55 | .16 |

Minnesota Vikings
| | | | |
|---|---|---|---|
| ☐ 379 Mike Caldwell | .30 | .14 | .04 |

Cleveland Browns
| | | | |
|---|---|---|---|
| ☐ 380 Burt Grossman | .15 | .07 | .02 |

San Diego Chargers
| | | | |
|---|---|---|---|
| ☐ 381 Corey Miller | .15 | .07 | .02 |

New York Giants
| | | | |
|---|---|---|---|
| ☐ 382 Kevin Williams FOIL | 1.75 | .80 | .22 |

Dallas Cowboys
| | | | |
|---|---|---|---|
| ☐ 383 Ken Harvey | .15 | .07 | .02 |

Phoenix Cardinals
| | | | |
|---|---|---|---|
| ☐ 384 Greg Robinson | 2.25 | 1.00 | .30 |

Los Angeles Raiders
| | | | |
|---|---|---|---|
| ☐ 385 Harold Alexander | .20 | .09 | .03 |

Atlanta Falcons
| | | | |
|---|---|---|---|
| ☐ 386 Andre Reed | .25 | .11 | .03 |

Buffalo Bills
| | | | |
|---|---|---|---|
| ☐ 387 Reggie Langhorne | .20 | .09 | .03 |

Indianapolis Colts
| | | | |
|---|---|---|---|
| ☐ 388 Courtney Hawkins | .20 | .09 | .03 |

Tampa Bay Buccaneers
| | | | |
|---|---|---|---|
| ☐ 389 James Hasty | .15 | .07 | .02 |

New York Jets
| | | | |
|---|---|---|---|
| ☐ 390 Pat Swilling | .20 | .09 | .03 |

Detroit Lions
| | | | |
|---|---|---|---|
| ☐ 391 Chris Slade | .75 | .35 | .09 |

New England Patriots
| | | | |
|---|---|---|---|
| ☐ 392 Keith Byars | .20 | .09 | .03 |

Miami Dolphins
| | | | |
|---|---|---|---|
| ☐ 393 Dalton Hilliard | .15 | .07 | .02 |

New Orleans Saints
| | | | |
|---|---|---|---|
| ☐ 394 David Williams | .15 | .07 | .02 |

Houston Oilers
| | | | |
|---|---|---|---|
| ☐ 395 Terry Obee | .50 | .23 | .06 |

Chicago Bears
| | | | |
|---|---|---|---|
| ☐ 396 Heath Sherman | .15 | .07 | .02 |

Philadelphia Eagles
| | | | |
|---|---|---|---|
| ☐ 397 John Taylor | .25 | .11 | .03 |

San Francisco 49ers
| | | | |
|---|---|---|---|
| ☐ 398 Irv Eatman | .15 | .07 | .02 |

Los Angeles Raiders
| | | | |
|---|---|---|---|
| ☐ 399 Johnny Holland | .15 | .07 | .02 |

Green Bay Packers
| | | | |
|---|---|---|---|
| ☐ 400 John Elway FOIL | 1.50 | .65 | .19 |

Denver Broncos
| | | | |
|---|---|---|---|
| ☐ 401 Clay Matthews | .20 | .09 | .03 |

Cleveland Browns
| | | | |
|---|---|---|---|
| ☐ 402 Dave Meggett | .20 | .09 | .03 |

New York Giants
| | | | |
|---|---|---|---|
| ☐ 403 Eric Green | .15 | .07 | .02 |

Pittsburgh Steelers
| | | | |
|---|---|---|---|
| ☐ 404 Bryan Cox | .20 | .09 | .03 |

Miami Dolphins
| | | | |
|---|---|---|---|
| ☐ 405 Jay Novacek | .25 | .11 | .03 |

Dallas Cowboys
| | | | |
|---|---|---|---|
| ☐ 406 Kenneth Davis | .15 | .07 | .02 |

Buffalo Bills
| | | | |
|---|---|---|---|
| ☐ 407 Lamar Thomas | .75 | .35 | .09 |

Tampa Bay Buccaneers
| | | | |
|---|---|---|---|
| ☐ 408 Lance Gunn | .30 | .14 | .04 |

Cincinnati Bengals
| | | | |
|---|---|---|---|
| ☐ 409 Audray McMillian | .15 | .07 | .02 |

Minnesota Vikings
| | | | |
|---|---|---|---|
| ☐ 410 Derrick Thomas FOIL | .40 | .18 | .05 |

Kansas City Chiefs
| | | | |
|---|---|---|---|
| ☐ 411 Rufus Porter | .15 | .07 | .02 |

Seattle Seahawks
| | | | |
|---|---|---|---|
| ☐ 412 Coleman Rudolph | .25 | .11 | .03 |

New York Jets
| | | | |
|---|---|---|---|
| ☐ 413 Mark Rypien | .20 | .09 | .03 |

Washington Redskins
| | | | |
|---|---|---|---|
| ☐ 414 Duane Bickett | .15 | .07 | .02 |

Indianapolis Colts
| | | | |
|---|---|---|---|
| ☐ 415 Chris Singleton | .15 | .07 | .02 |

New England Patriots
| | | | |
|---|---|---|---|
| ☐ 416 Mitch Lyons | .30 | .14 | .04 |

Atlanta Falcons
| | | | |
|---|---|---|---|
| ☐ 417 Bill Fralic | .15 | .07 | .02 |

Detroit Lions
| | | | |
|---|---|---|---|
| ☐ 418 Gary Plummer | .15 | .07 | .02 |

San Diego Chargers
| | | | |
|---|---|---|---|
| ☐ 419 Ricky Proehl | .20 | .09 | .03 |

Phoenix Cardinals
| | | | |
|---|---|---|---|
| ☐ 420 Howie Long | .20 | .09 | .03 |

Los Angeles Raiders
| | | | |
|---|---|---|---|
| ☐ 421 Willie Roaf FOIL | .35 | .16 | .04 |

New Orleans Saints
| | | | |
|---|---|---|---|
| ☐ 422 Checklist 1-212 | .15 | .07 | .02 |
| ☐ 423 Checklist 213-423 | .15 | .07 | .02 |

# 1950 Bread for Health

The 1950 Bread for Health football card (actually bread end labels) set contains 32 bread-end labels of players in the National Football League. The cards (actually paper thin labels) measure approximately

2 3/4" by 2 3/4". These labels are not usually found in top condition due to the difficulty in removing them from the bread package. While all the bakeries who issued this set are not presently known, Fisher's Bread in the New Jersey, New York and Pennsylvania area and NBC Bread in the Michigan area are two of the bakeries that have been confirmed to date. As with many of the bread label sets of the early 1950's, an album to house the set was probably issued. Each label contains the B.E.B. copyright found on so many of the labels of this period. Labels which contain "Bread for Energy" at the bottom are not a part of the set but part of a series of movie, western and sport stars issued during the same approximate time period. The catalog designation for this set is D290-15. The cards are unnumbered but are arranged alphabetically below for convenience.

| | NRMT | VG-E | GOOD |
|---|---|---|---|
| COMPLETE SET (32) | 7000.00 | 3000.00 | 800.00 |
| COMMON PLAYER (1-32) | 125.00 | 50.00 | 12.50 |
| ☐ 1 Frankie Albert | 150.00 | 60.00 | 15.00 |
| San Francisco 49ers | | | |
| ☐ 2 Elmer Angsman | 125.00 | 50.00 | 12.50 |
| Chicago Cardinals | | | |
| ☐ 3 Dick Barwegen | 125.00 | 50.00 | 12.50 |
| Baltimore Colts | | | |
| ☐ 4 Sammy Baugh | 600.00 | 240.00 | 60.00 |
| Washington Redskins | | | |
| ☐ 5 Charley Conerly | 300.00 | 120.00 | 30.00 |
| New York Giants | | | |
| ☐ 6 Glenn Davis | 250.00 | 100.00 | 25.00 |
| Los Angeles Rams | | | |
| ☐ 7 Don Doll | 125.00 | 50.00 | 12.50 |
| Detroit Lions | | | |
| ☐ 8 Tom Fears | 250.00 | 100.00 | 25.00 |
| Los Angeles Rams | | | |
| ☐ 9 Harry Gilmer | 150.00 | 60.00 | 15.00 |
| Washington Redskins | | | |
| ☐ 10 Otto Graham | 750.00 | 300.00 | 75.00 |
| Cleveland Browns | | | |
| ☐ 11 Pat Harder | 175.00 | 70.00 | 18.00 |
| Chicago Cardinals | | | |
| ☐ 12 Bobby Layne | 500.00 | 200.00 | 50.00 |
| Detroit Lions | | | |
| ☐ 13 Sid Luckman | 400.00 | 160.00 | 40.00 |
| Chicago Bears | | | |
| ☐ 14 Johnny Lujack | 350.00 | 140.00 | 35.00 |
| Chicago Bears | | | |
| ☐ 15 John Panelli | 125.00 | 50.00 | 12.50 |
| Detroit Lions | | | |
| ☐ 16 Barney Poole | 125.00 | 50.00 | 12.50 |
| New York Yankees | | | |
| ☐ 17 George Ratterman | 150.00 | 60.00 | 15.00 |
| New York Yankees | | | |
| ☐ 18 Tobin Rote | 175.00 | 70.00 | 18.00 |
| Green Bay Packers | | | |
| ☐ 19 Jack Russell | 125.00 | 50.00 | 12.50 |
| New York Yankees | | | |
| ☐ 20 Lou Rymkus | 150.00 | 60.00 | 15.00 |
| Cleveland Browns | | | |
| ☐ 21 Joe Signiago | 125.00 | 50.00 | 12.50 |
| New York Yankees | | | |
| ☐ 22 Mac Speedie | 175.00 | 70.00 | 18.00 |
| Cleveland Browns | | | |
| ☐ 23 Bill Swiacki | 150.00 | 60.00 | 15.00 |
| New York Giants | | | |
| ☐ 24 Tommy Thompson | 175.00 | 70.00 | 18.00 |
| Philadelphia Eagles | | | |
| ☐ 25 Y.A. Tittle | 750.00 | 300.00 | 75.00 |
| Baltimore Colts | | | |
| ☐ 26 Clayton Tonnemaker | 125.00 | 50.00 | 12.50 |
| Green Bay Packers | | | |
| ☐ 27 Charley Trippi | 250.00 | 100.00 | 25.00 |
| Chicago Cardinals | | | |
| ☐ 28 Clyde Turner | 300.00 | 120.00 | 30.00 |
| Chicago Bears | | | |
| ☐ 29 Steve Van Buren | 350.00 | 140.00 | 35.00 |
| Philadelphia Eagles | | | |

| | MINT | EXC | G-VG |
|---|---|---|---|
| ☐ 30 Bill Walsh | 150.00 | 60.00 | 15.00 |
| Pittsburgh Steelers | | | |
| ☐ 31 Bob Waterfield | 400.00 | 160.00 | 40.00 |
| Los Angeles Rams | | | |
| ☐ 32 Jim White | 125.00 | 50.00 | 12.50 |
| New York Giants | | | |

## 1992 Breyers Bookmarks

This 66-card set (of bookmarks) was produced by Breyers to promote reading in the home cities of eleven NFL teams. The bookmarks measure approximately 2" by 8". The fronts feature a cut-out player photo superimposed on a yellow background decorated with open books. A lighter yellow panel above the player contains a player profile and a biography. The player's name appears in a black stripe that borders the panel. The Breyers logo and the words "Reading Team" appear on an electronic billboard design. The backs list book selections found at the library, the American Library Association logo, and the sponsor logo. The cards are numbered on the front and are arranged in team order as follows: Los Angeles Raiders (1-6), San Francisco 49ers (7-12), San Diego Chargers (13-18), Seattle Seahawks (19-24), New Orleans Saints (25-30), Kansas City Chiefs (31-36), Minnesota Vikings (37-42), Pittsburgh Steelers (43-48), Indianapolis Colts (49-54), Dallas Cowboys (55-60), and Cleveland Browns (61-66).

| | MINT | EXC | G-VG |
|---|---|---|---|
| COMPLETE SET (66) | 100.00 | 40.00 | 10.00 |
| COMMON PLAYER (1-66) | 1.25 | .50 | .12 |
| | | | |
| ☐ 1 Greg Townsend | 1.25 | .50 | .12 |
| ☐ 2 Steve Wisniewski | 1.25 | .50 | .12 |
| ☐ 3 Art Shell CO | 2.50 | 1.00 | .25 |
| ☐ 4 Jeff Jaeger | 1.25 | .50 | .12 |
| ☐ 5 Lisa O'Day | 2.00 | .80 | .20 |
| (Cheerleader) | | | |
| ☐ 6 Los Angeles Raiders | 1.25 | .50 | .12 |
| Helmet and SB trophies | | | |
| ☐ 7 Jerry Rice | 9.00 | 3.75 | .90 |
| ☐ 8 Don Griffin | 1.25 | .50 | .12 |
| ☐ 9 John Taylor | 2.00 | .80 | .20 |
| ☐ 10 Joe Montana | 15.00 | 6.00 | 1.50 |
| ☐ 11 Mike Walter | 1.25 | .50 | .12 |
| ☐ 12 San Francisco 49ers | 1.25 | .50 | .12 |
| ☐ 13 Junior Seau | 2.50 | 1.00 | .25 |
| ☐ 14 John Friesz | 2.00 | .80 | .20 |
| ☐ 15 Ronnie Harmon | 2.00 | .80 | .20 |
| ☐ 16 Marion Butts | 2.00 | .80 | .20 |
| ☐ 17 Gill Byrd | 1.25 | .50 | .12 |
| ☐ 18 San Diego Chargers | 1.25 | .50 | .12 |
| Helmet | | | |
| ☐ 19 Kelly Stouffer | 1.25 | .50 | .12 |
| ☐ 20 John Kasay | 1.25 | .50 | .12 |
| ☐ 21 Andy Heck | 1.25 | .50 | .12 |
| ☐ 22 Jacob Green | 1.50 | .60 | .15 |
| ☐ 23 Eugene Robinson | 1.25 | .50 | .12 |
| ☐ 24 Seattle Seahawks | 1.25 | .50 | .12 |
| Helmet | | | |
| ☐ 25 Pat Swilling | 1.50 | .60 | .15 |
| ☐ 26 Vaughan Johnson | 1.25 | .50 | .12 |
| ☐ 27 Bobby Hebert | 1.50 | .60 | .15 |
| ☐ 28 Floyd Turner | 1.25 | .50 | .12 |
| ☐ 29 Rickey Jackson | 1.50 | .60 | .15 |
| ☐ 30 New Orleans Saints | 1.25 | .50 | .12 |
| Helmet | | | |
| ☐ 31 Harvey Williams | 2.00 | .80 | .20 |
| ☐ 32 Derrick Thomas | 3.00 | 1.20 | .30 |
| ☐ 33 Bill Maas | 1.25 | .50 | .12 |
| ☐ 34 Tim Grunhard | 1.25 | .50 | .12 |
| ☐ 35 Jonathan Hayes | 1.25 | .50 | .12 |
| ☐ 36 Kansas City Chiefs | 1.25 | .50 | .12 |
| Mascot | | | |
| ☐ 37 Rich Gannon | 1.50 | .60 | .15 |
| ☐ 38 Tim Irwin | 1.25 | .50 | .12 |
| ☐ 39 Audray McMillian | 1.25 | .50 | .12 |
| ☐ 40 Gary Zimmerman | 1.25 | .50 | .12 |
| ☐ 41 Hassan Jones | 1.25 | .50 | .12 |
| ☐ 42 Minnesota Vikings | 1.25 | .50 | .12 |
| Helmet | | | |
| ☐ 43 Eric Green | 1.50 | .60 | .15 |
| ☐ 44 Louis Lipps | 1.50 | .60 | .15 |
| ☐ 45 Rod Woodson | 2.00 | .80 | .20 |
| ☐ 46 Merril Hoge | 1.50 | .60 | .15 |
| ☐ 47 Gary Anderson | 1.25 | .50 | .12 |
| ☐ 48 Pittsburgh Steelers | 1.25 | .50 | .12 |
| 60-Season Emblem | | | |
| ☐ 49 Anthony Johnson | 1.50 | .60 | .15 |
| ☐ 50 Bill Brooks | 2.00 | .80 | .20 |
| ☐ 51 Jeff Herrod | 1.25 | .50 | .12 |
| ☐ 52 Mike Prior | 1.25 | .50 | .12 |
| ☐ 53 Jeff George | 3.00 | 1.20 | .30 |
| ☐ 54 Indianapolis Colts | 1.25 | .50 | .12 |
| Ted Marchibroda CO | | | |
| ☐ 55 Troy Aikman | 15.00 | 6.00 | 1.50 |
| ☐ 56 Jay Novacek | 2.50 | 1.00 | .25 |
| ☐ 57 Emmitt Smith | 15.00 | 6.00 | 1.50 |
| ☐ 58 Michael Irvin | 6.00 | 2.40 | .60 |
| ☐ 59 Dorie Braddy | 2.00 | .80 | .20 |
| (Cheerleader) | | | |
| ☐ 60 Dallas Cowboys | 1.25 | .50 | .12 |
| Super Bowl trophy | | | |
| ☐ 61 Clay Matthews | 1.50 | .60 | .15 |
| ☐ 62 Tommy Vardell | 2.00 | .80 | .20 |
| ☐ 63 Eric Turner | 1.50 | .60 | .15 |
| ☐ 64 Mike Johnson | 1.25 | .50 | .12 |
| ☐ 65 James Jones | 1.25 | .50 | .12 |
| ☐ 66 Cleveland Browns | 1.25 | .50 | .12 |
| Helmet | | | |

## 1990 British Petroleum

This 36-card standard size (2 1/2" by 3 1/2") set was issued two cards at a time by British Petroleum gas stations throughout California in association with Talent Network Inc. of Skokie, Illinois. There were five winning player cards issued in the following quantities. Andre Tippett: 5.00 - 990 cards, Freeman McNeil: 10.00 - 325 cards, Clay Matthews: 100.00 - 18 cards, Tim Harris: 1,000.00 - three cards, and Deion Sanders 10,000.00 - one card. These winning cards are not valued as collectibles in the checklist below as they were more valuable as prize winners. The set has multiple players numbered 1, 3, 6, 8, and 10, and we have arranged each group of same-numbered cards into alphabetical order. Each game piece was two NFL football cards inside a cardboard frame, with full-color head shots in uniform of the player. Cards are frequently found in less than Mint condition due to the fact that glue was applied to the obverses of the cards in the manufacturing process. There were 36 cards in the set, and the object of the game was to collect two adjacent numbers, 1-2, 3-4, 5-6, 7-8, or 9-10. One number was easy to get, but the other was difficult. The game redemptions expired in October of 1991.

| | MINT | EXC | G-VG |
|---|---|---|---|
| COMPLETE SET (36) | 30.00 | 12.00 | 3.00 |
| COMMON PLAYER (1-10) | .50 | .20 | .05 |
| | | | |
| ☐ 1A John Elway | 2.50 | 1.00 | .25 |
| Denver Broncos | | | |
| ☐ 1B Boomer Esiason | 1.00 | .40 | .10 |
| Cincinnati Bengals | | | |
| ☐ 1C Jim Everett | .75 | .30 | .07 |
| Los Angeles Rams | | | |
| ☐ 1D Bernie Kosar | 1.00 | .40 | .10 |
| Cleveland Browns | | | |

| | | | |
|---|---|---|---|
| ☐ 1E Karl Mecklenburg ..................<br>Denver Broncos | .50 | .20 | .05 |
| ☐ 1F Bruce Smith ..........................<br>Buffalo Bills | .75 | .30 | .07 |
| ☐ 2 Deion Sanders........................<br>Atlanta Falcons<br>(Winning card) | .00 | .00 | .00 |
| ☐ 3A Roger Craig..........................<br>San Francisco 49ers | .75 | .30 | .07 |
| ☐ 3B Randall Cunningham..............<br>Philadelphia Eagles | 1.25 | .50 | .12 |
| ☐ 3C Keith Jackson .......................<br>Philadelphia Eagles | .75 | .30 | .07 |
| ☐ 3D Dan Marino ..........................<br>Miami Dolphins | 4.00 | 1.60 | .40 |
| ☐ 3E Freddie Joe Nunn ..................<br>Phoenix Cardinals | .50 | .20 | .05 |
| ☐ 3F Jerry Rice ............................<br>San Francisco 49ers | 2.50 | 1.00 | .25 |
| ☐ 3G Vinny Testaverde ..................<br>Tampa Bay Buccaneers | .75 | .30 | .07 |
| ☐ 3H John L. Williams ...................<br>Seattle Seahawks | .75 | .30 | .07 |
| ☐ 4 Tim Harris ............................<br>Green Bay Packers<br>(Winning card) | .00 | .00 | .00 |
| ☐ 5 Clay Matthews .......................<br>Cleveland Browns<br>(Winning card) | .00 | .00 | .00 |
| ☐ 6A Neal Anderson ......................<br>Chicago Bears | .75 | .30 | .07 |
| ☐ 6B Duane Bickett.......................<br>Indianapolis Colts | .50 | .20 | .05 |
| ☐ 6C Ronnie Lott ..........................<br>San Francisco 49ers | .75 | .30 | .07 |
| ☐ 6D Anthony Munoz .....................<br>Cincinnati Bengals | .75 | .30 | .07 |
| ☐ 6E Christian Okoye.....................<br>Kansas City Chiefs | .75 | .30 | .07 |
| ☐ 6F Barry Sanders .......................<br>Detroit Lions | 3.00 | 1.20 | .30 |
| ☐ 7 Freeman McNeil .....................<br>New York Jets<br>(Winning card) | .00 | .00 | .00 |
| ☐ 8A Cornelius Bennett ..................<br>Buffalo Bills | .75 | .30 | .07 |
| ☐ 8B Anthony Carter......................<br>Minnesota Vikings | .50 | .20 | .05 |
| ☐ 8C Jim Kelly ............................<br>Buffalo Bills | 1.50 | .60 | .15 |
| ☐ 8D Louis Lipps ..........................<br>Pittsburgh Steelers | .50 | .20 | .05 |
| ☐ 8E Phil Simms ..........................<br>New York Giants | 1.00 | .40 | .10 |
| ☐ 8F Billy Ray Smith......................<br>San Diego Chargers | .50 | .20 | .05 |
| ☐ 8G Lawrence Taylor ...................<br>New York Giants | 1.00 | .40 | .10 |
| ☐ 9 Andre Tippett .........................<br>New England Patriots<br>(Winning card) | .00 | .00 | .00 |
| ☐ 10A Bo Jackson .........................<br>Los Angeles Raiders | 1.50 | .60 | .15 |
| ☐ 10B Howie Long .........................<br>Los Angeles Raiders | .50 | .20 | .05 |
| ☐ 10C Don Majkowski ....................<br>Green Bay Packers | .50 | .20 | .05 |
| ☐ 10D Art Monk ...........................<br>Washington Redskins | .75 | .30 | .07 |
| ☐ 10E Warren Moon .......................<br>Houston Oilers | 1.25 | .50 | .12 |
| ☐ 10F Mike Singletary ...................<br>Chicago Bears | .75 | .30 | .07 |
| ☐ 10G Al Toon .............................<br>New York Jets | .50 | .20 | .05 |
| ☐ 10H Herschel Walker ..................<br>Minnesota Vikings | .75 | .30 | .07 |
| ☐ 10I Reggie White .......................<br>Philadelphia Eagles | 1.00 | .40 | .10 |

## 1984 Broncos KOA

These cards were issued as part of a KOA "Match 'N Win" and KOA/Denver Broncos Silver Anniversary Sweepstakes. They were distributed at any participating Dairy Queen or Safeway in the Metro Denver area between September 17 and November 11, 1984. The cards measure approximately 2" by 4", with a tab at the bottom (measuring 1 1/8" in length). The front has a black and white photo of the player from the waist up. Above the card reads "KOA Official Denver Broncos Memory Series" in blue print with white outlining. The lower portion of the photo is covered over by three items: 1) player number, name, and position; 2) a logo of the original American Football League and the sponsor's name or logo (Rocky

Mountain News, Kodak, Dairy Queen, Wood Bros. Homes, KMGH-TV-7 Denver, Safeway, and Armour). The picture and these items are enframed by a color border on a color background. There were three each of eight different color schemes used. The tab portion of the card has three silver footballs that were to be scratched off with a coin. The back lists the rules governing the sweepstakes. There are four players marked as SP in the checklist below who are supposedly tougher to find than the others; they are Bobby Anderson, Randy Gradishar, Floyd Little, and Claudie Minor. The cards are unnumbered but are listed below in uniform number order. The prices listed refer to unscratch cards.

| | MINT | EXC | G-VG |
|---|---|---|---|
| COMPLETE SET (24)......................... | 50.00 | 20.00 | 5.00 |
| COMMON PLAYER (1-24)................ | 1.25 | .50 | .12 |

| | | | |
|---|---|---|---|
| ☐ 7 Craig Morton........................... | 3.50 | 1.40 | .35 |
| ☐ 11 Bobby Anderson SP............... | 7.50 | 3.00 | .75 |
| ☐ 12 Charlie Johnson..................... | 3.00 | 1.20 | .30 |
| ☐ 15 Jim Turner ........................... | 2.50 | 1.00 | .25 |
| ☐ 21 Gene Mingo .......................... | 1.25 | .50 | .12 |
| ☐ 22 Fran Lynch ........................... | 1.25 | .50 | .12 |
| ☐ 23 Goose Gonsoulin.................... | 1.50 | .60 | .15 |
| ☐ 24 Otis Armstrong ...................... | 4.00 | 1.60 | .40 |
| ☐ 24 Willie Brown.......................... | 4.00 | 1.60 | .40 |
| ☐ 25 Haven Moses ........................ | 2.50 | 1.00 | .25 |
| ☐ 36 Billy Thompson ...................... | 2.50 | 1.00 | .25 |
| ☐ 42 Bill Van Heusen ..................... | 1.25 | .50 | .12 |
| ☐ 44 Floyd Little SP....................... | 10.00 | 4.00 | 1.00 |
| ☐ 53 Randy Gradishar SP............... | 10.00 | 4.00 | 1.00 |
| ☐ 71 Claudie Minor SP.................... | 6.00 | 2.40 | .60 |
| ☐ 72 Sam Brunelli ......................... | 1.25 | .50 | .12 |
| ☐ 74 Mike Current ........................ | 1.25 | .50 | .12 |
| ☐ 75 Eldon Danenhauer .................. | 1.25 | .50 | .12 |
| ☐ 78 Marv Montgomery ................. | 1.25 | .50 | .12 |
| ☐ 81 Billy Masters ........................ | 1.25 | .50 | .12 |
| ☐ 82 Bob Scarpitto ....................... | 1.25 | .50 | .12 |
| ☐ 87 Lionel Taylor ........................ | 2.50 | 1.00 | .25 |
| ☐ 87 Rich Jackson......................... | 1.25 | .50 | .12 |
| ☐ 88 Riley Odoms ........................ | 2.50 | 1.00 | .25 |

## 1987 Broncos Orange Crush

This nine-card set of Denver Broncos' ex-players was sponsored by Orange Crush and KOA Radio. The cards are standard size, 2 1/2" by 3 1/2", and feature black and white photos inside a blue and orange frame. The set is a salute to the "Ring of Famers," Denver's best players in its history as a franchise. Card backs (written in black, orange, and blue on white card stock) feature a capsule biography and indicate the year of induction into the Ring of Fame. Reportedly 1.35 million cards were distributed over a three-week period at participating 7-Eleven and Albertsons stores in Denver and surrounding areas.

|  | MINT | EXC | G-VG |
|---|---|---|---|
| COMPLETE SET (9) | 4.00 | 1.60 | .40 |
| COMMON PLAYER (1-9) | .50 | .20 | .05 |
| ☐ 1 Billy Thompson | .60 | .24 | .06 |
| ☐ 2 Lionel Taylor | .60 | .24 | .06 |
| ☐ 3 Goose Gonsoulin | .50 | .20 | .05 |
| ☐ 4 Paul Smith | .50 | .20 | .05 |
| ☐ 5 Rich Jackson | .50 | .20 | .05 |
| ☐ 6 Charlie Johnson | .75 | .30 | .07 |
| ☐ 7 Floyd Little | 1.25 | .50 | .12 |
| ☐ 8 Frank Tripucka | .60 | .24 | .06 |
| ☐ 9 Gerald Phipps | .50 | .20 | .05 |
| (Owner 1960-1981) | | | |

## 1986 Brownell Heisman

This large-sized black and white set features drawings of past Heisman Trophy winners by Art Brownell. The set was originally available as part of a promotion. They are unnumbered and blank backed so they are numbered below in chronological order according to when each player won the Heisman Trophy starting with Jay Berwanger of Chicago in 1935. Since Archie Griffin of Ohio State won the Heisman in both 1974 and 1975 there is only one card for him. The cards measure approximately 7 15/16" by 10".

|  | MINT | EXC | G-VG |
|---|---|---|---|
| COMPLETE SET (50) | 200.00 | 80.00 | 20.00 |
| COMMON PLAYER (1-50) | 4.00 | 1.60 | .40 |
| ☐ 1 Jay Berwanger | 5.00 | 2.00 | .50 |
| Chicago | | | |
| ☐ 2 Larry Kelley | 4.00 | 1.60 | .40 |
| Yale | | | |
| ☐ 3 Clint Frank | 4.00 | 1.60 | .40 |
| Yale | | | |
| ☐ 4 Davey O'Brien | 5.00 | 2.00 | .50 |
| TCU | | | |
| ☐ 5 Nile Kinnick | 6.00 | 2.40 | .60 |
| Iowa | | | |
| ☐ 6 Tom Harmon | 5.00 | 2.00 | .50 |
| Michigan | | | |
| ☐ 7 Bruce Smith | 4.00 | 1.60 | .40 |
| Minnesota | | | |
| ☐ 8 Frank Sinkwich | 4.00 | 1.60 | .40 |
| Georgia | | | |
| ☐ 9 Angelo Bertelli | 5.00 | 2.00 | .50 |
| Notre Dame | | | |
| ☐ 10 Les Horvath | 5.00 | 2.00 | .50 |
| Ohio State | | | |
| ☐ 11 Doc Blanchard | 5.00 | 2.00 | .50 |
| Army | | | |
| ☐ 12 Glenn Davis | 5.00 | 2.00 | .50 |
| Army | | | |
| ☐ 13 Johnny Lujack | 7.50 | 3.00 | .75 |
| Notre Dame | | | |
| ☐ 14 Doak Walker | 7.50 | 3.00 | .75 |
| SMU | | | |
| ☐ 15 Leon Hart | 5.00 | 2.00 | .50 |
| Notre Dame | | | |
| ☐ 16 Vic Janowicz | 5.00 | 2.00 | .50 |
| Ohio State | | | |
| ☐ 17 Dick Kazmaier | 5.00 | 2.00 | .50 |
| Princeton | | | |
| ☐ 18 Bill Vessels | 5.00 | 2.00 | .50 |
| Oklahoma | | | |
| ☐ 19 John Lattner | 5.00 | 2.00 | .50 |
| Notre Dame | | | |
| ☐ 20 Alan Ameche | 4.00 | 1.60 | .40 |
| Wisconsin | | | |
| ☐ 21 Howard Cassady | 4.00 | 1.60 | .40 |
| Ohio State | | | |
| ☐ 22 Paul Hornung | 7.50 | 3.00 | .75 |

| | | | |
|---|---|---|---|
| Notre Dame | | | |
| ☐ 23 John David Crow | 4.00 | 1.60 | .40 |
| Texas A and M | | | |
| ☐ 24 Pete Dawkins | 5.00 | 2.00 | .50 |
| Army | | | |
| ☐ 25 Billy Cannon | 4.00 | 1.60 | .40 |
| LSU | | | |
| ☐ 26 Joe Bellino | 4.00 | 1.60 | .40 |
| Navy | | | |
| ☐ 27 Ernie Davis | 20.00 | 8.00 | 2.00 |
| Syracuse | | | |
| ☐ 28 Terry Baker | 4.00 | 1.60 | .40 |
| Oregon State | | | |
| ☐ 29 Roger Staubach | 20.00 | 8.00 | 2.00 |
| Navy | | | |
| ☐ 30 John Huarte | 4.00 | 1.60 | .40 |
| Notre Dame | | | |
| ☐ 31 Mike Garrett | 4.00 | 1.60 | .40 |
| USC | | | |
| ☐ 32 Steve Spurrier | 6.00 | 2.40 | .60 |
| Florida | | | |
| ☐ 33 Gary Beban | 4.00 | 1.60 | .40 |
| UCLA | | | |
| ☐ 34 O.J. Simpson | 20.00 | 8.00 | 2.00 |
| USC | | | |
| ☐ 35 Steve Owens | 4.00 | 1.60 | .40 |
| Oklahoma | | | |
| ☐ 36 Jim Plunkett | 5.00 | 2.00 | .50 |
| Stanford | | | |
| ☐ 37 Pat Sullivan | 4.00 | 1.60 | .40 |
| Auburn | | | |
| ☐ 38 Johnny Rodgers | 4.00 | 1.60 | .40 |
| Nebraska | | | |
| ☐ 39 John Cappelletti | 4.00 | 1.60 | .40 |
| Penn State | | | |
| ☐ 40 Archie Griffin | 5.00 | 2.00 | .50 |
| Ohio State | | | |
| ☐ 41 Tony Dorsett | 7.50 | 3.00 | .75 |
| Pittsburgh | | | |
| ☐ 42 Earl Campbell | 7.50 | 3.00 | .75 |
| Texas | | | |
| ☐ 43 Billy Sims | 4.00 | 1.60 | .40 |
| Oklahoma | | | |
| ☐ 44 Charles White | 4.00 | 1.60 | .40 |
| USC | | | |
| ☐ 45 George Rogers | 4.00 | 1.60 | .40 |
| South Carolina | | | |
| ☐ 46 Marcus Allen | 6.00 | 2.40 | .60 |
| USC | | | |
| ☐ 47 Herschel Walker | 6.00 | 2.40 | .60 |
| Georgia | | | |
| ☐ 48 Mike Rozier | 4.00 | 1.60 | .40 |
| Nebraska | | | |
| ☐ 49 Doug Flutie | 5.00 | 2.00 | .50 |
| Boston College | | | |
| ☐ 50 Bo Jackson | 7.50 | 3.00 | .75 |
| Auburn | | | |

## 1950 Browns Team Issue

This set of team-issued photos measures approximately 6 1/2" by 9" and is printed on thin paper stock. The fronts feature black-and-white posed action shots framed by white borders. The player's name appears in script across the photo. The backs are blank. The photos are unnumbered and checklisted below in alphabetical order.

|  | NRMT | VG-E | GOOD |
|---|---|---|---|
| COMPLETE SET (5) | 50.00 | 20.00 | 5.00 |
| COMMON PLAYER (1-5) | 7.50 | 3.00 | .75 |
| ☐ 1 Frank Gatski | 15.00 | 6.00 | 1.50 |
| ☐ 2 Tommy James | 7.50 | 3.00 | .75 |
| ☐ 3 Don Moselle | 7.50 | 3.00 | .75 |
| ☐ 4 Marion Motley | 20.00 | 8.00 | 2.00 |
| ☐ 5 Derrell F. Palmer | 7.50 | 3.00 | .75 |

# 1951 Browns White Border

This set of team-issued photos measures approximately 6 1/2" by 9" and features black and white posed action shots framed by white borders. The set was distributed in an attractive off-white envelope with orange and brown trim titled "Cleveland Browns Photographs". The year of issue is postulated based on the presence of Ken Gorgal and Weldon Humble whose last year with the Browns was 1950 and from the fact that several of the photos were also used in the 1951 Bowman set. The player's name appears in script across the top of the photo. The backs are blank. The cards are unnumbered and checklisted below in alphabetical order.

|  | NRMT | VG-E | GOOD |
|---|---|---|---|
| COMPLETE SET (25) | 150.00 | 60.00 | 15.00 |
| COMMON PLAYER (1-25) | 5.00 | 2.00 | .50 |
| ☐ 1 Tony Adamle | 6.00 | 2.40 | .60 |
| ☐ 2 Alex Agase | 6.00 | 2.40 | .60 |
| ☐ 3 Rex Bumgardner | 5.00 | 2.00 | .50 |
| ☐ 4 Emerson Cole | 5.00 | 2.00 | .50 |
| ☐ 5 Len Ford | 10.00 | 4.00 | 1.00 |
| ☐ 6 Frank Gatski | 10.00 | 4.00 | 1.00 |
| ☐ 7 Horace Gillom | 5.00 | 2.00 | .50 |
| ☐ 8 Ken Gorgal | 5.00 | 2.00 | .50 |
| ☐ 9 Otto Graham | 30.00 | 12.00 | 3.00 |
| ☐ 10 Forrest Grigg | 5.00 | 2.00 | .50 |
| ☐ 11 Lou Groza | 20.00 | 8.00 | 2.00 |
| ☐ 12 Hal Herring | 5.00 | 2.00 | .50 |
| ☐ 13 Lin Houston | 5.00 | 2.00 | .50 |
| ☐ 14 Weldon Humble | 5.00 | 2.00 | .50 |
| ☐ 15 Tommy James | 5.00 | 2.00 | .50 |
| ☐ 16 Dub Jones | 7.50 | 3.00 | .75 |
| ☐ 17 Warren Lahr | 5.00 | 2.00 | .50 |
| ☐ 18 Dante Lavelli | 10.00 | 4.00 | 1.00 |
| ☐ 19 Cliff Lewis | 5.00 | 2.00 | .50 |
| ☐ 20 Marion Motley | 12.50 | 5.00 | 1.25 |
| ☐ 21 Lou Rymkus | 6.00 | 2.40 | .60 |
| ☐ 22 Mac Speedie | 7.50 | 3.00 | .75 |
| ☐ 23 Tommy Thompson | 6.00 | 2.40 | .60 |
| ☐ 24 Bill Willis | 7.50 | 3.00 | .75 |
| ☐ 25 George Young | 7.50 | 3.00 | .75 |

# 1954-55 Browns White Border

This set consists of twenty 8 1/2" by 10" posed player photos, with white borders and blank backs. Most of the photos are poses shot from the waist up; a few (Colo, Ford, and Lahr) picture the player in an action pose. The player's name and position are printed in the bottom white border. The photos are unnumbered and checklisted below in alphabetical order.

|  | NRMT | VG-E | GOOD |
|---|---|---|---|
| COMPLETE SET (20) | 100.00 | 40.00 | 10.00 |
| COMMON PLAYER (1-20) | 4.00 | 1.60 | .40 |
| ☐ 1 Maurice Bassett | 4.00 | 1.60 | .40 |
| ☐ 2 Harold Bradley | 4.00 | 1.60 | .40 |
| ☐ 3 Darrell(Pete) Brewster | 4.00 | 1.60 | .40 |
| ☐ 4 Don Colo | 4.00 | 1.60 | .40 |
| ☐ 5 Len Ford | 8.00 | 3.25 | .80 |
| ☐ 6 Bob Gain | 5.00 | 2.00 | .50 |
| ☐ 7 Frank Gatski | 8.00 | 3.25 | .80 |
| ☐ 8 Abe Gibron | 6.00 | 2.40 | .60 |
| ☐ 9 Tom James | 4.00 | 1.60 | .40 |
| ☐ 10 Dub Jones | 6.00 | 2.40 | .60 |
| ☐ 11 Ken Konz | 5.00 | 2.00 | .50 |
| ☐ 12 Warren Lahr | 5.00 | 2.00 | .50 |
| ☐ 13 Dante Lavelli | 8.00 | 3.25 | .80 |
| ☐ 14 Carlton Massey | 4.00 | 1.60 | .40 |

| ☐ 15 Mike McCormack | 8.00 | 3.25 | .80 |
|---|---|---|---|
| ☐ 16 Walt Michaels | 5.00 | 2.00 | .50 |
| ☐ 17 Chuck Noll | 12.00 | 5.00 | 1.20 |
| ☐ 18 Don Paul | 4.00 | 1.60 | .40 |
| ☐ 19 Ray Renfro | 5.00 | 2.00 | .50 |
| ☐ 20 George Ratterman | 5.00 | 2.00 | .50 |

# 1955 Browns Carling Beer

This set of ten black and white posed action shots was sponsored by Carling Black Label Beer and features members of the Cleveland Browns. The pictures measure approximately 8 1/2" by 11 1/2" and have white borders. The sponsor's name and the team name appear below the picture in black lettering. The cards are unnumbered and the backs are blank. The serial number in the lower right corner on the fronts lists "DBL 54". The photos were shot against a background of an open field with trees.

|  | NRMT | VG-E | GOOD |
|---|---|---|---|
| COMPLETE SET (10) | 250.00 | 100.00 | 25.00 |
| COMMON PLAYER (1-10) | 15.00 | 6.00 | 1.50 |
| ☐ 1 Darrell(Pete) Brewster | 15.00 | 6.00 | 1.50 |
| ☐ 2 Tom Catlin | 15.00 | 6.00 | 1.50 |
| ☐ 3 Len Ford | 30.00 | 12.00 | 3.00 |
| ☐ 4 Otto Graham | 60.00 | 24.00 | 6.00 |
| ☐ 5 Lou Groza | 45.00 | 18.00 | 4.50 |
| ☐ 6 Kenny Konz | 15.00 | 6.00 | 1.50 |
| ☐ 7 Dante Lavelli | 35.00 | 14.00 | 3.50 |
| ☐ 8 Mike McCormack | 30.00 | 12.00 | 3.00 |
| ☐ 9 Fred Morrison | 15.00 | 6.00 | 1.50 |
| ☐ 10 Chuck Noll | 75.00 | 30.00 | 7.50 |

# 1955 Browns Color Postcards

Measuring approximately 6" by 9", these color postcards feature Cleveland Browns players. The cards have rounded corners.

|  | NRMT | VG-E | GOOD |
|---|---|---|---|
| COMPLETE SET (6) | 100.00 | 40.00 | 10.00 |
| COMMON PLAYER (1-6) | 10.00 | 4.00 | 1.00 |
| ☐ 1 Mo Bassett | 10.00 | 4.00 | 1.00 |
| ☐ 2 Don Colo | 10.00 | 4.00 | 1.00 |
| ☐ 3 Frank Gatski | 20.00 | 8.00 | 2.00 |
| ☐ 4 Lou Groza | 50.00 | 20.00 | 5.00 |
| ☐ 5 Dante Lavelli | 25.00 | 10.00 | 2.50 |
| ☐ 6 George Ratterman | 12.50 | 5.00 | 1.25 |

# 1959 Browns Carling Beer

This set of nine black and white posed action shots was sponsored by Carling Black Label Beer and features members of the Cleveland Browns. The pictures measure approximately 8 1/2" by 11 1/2" and have white borders. The sponsor's name and the team name appear below the picture in black lettering. The backs are typically blank, but are sometimes found with a rubber-stamped identification that reads "Henry M. Barr Studios, Berea, Ohio BE4-1330." The pictures are numbered in the lower right corner on the fronts, with the exception of Jim Brown's picture. The photos were shot against a background of an open field with trees. The set is dated by the fact that Billy Howton's last year with Cleveland was 1959. This set was illegally reprinted in the late 1980's; the reprints are on thinner paper and typically show the Henry M. Barr stamp on the back. In fact the Jimmy Brown photo is apparently only available in the reprint set.

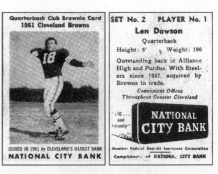

| | NRMT | VG-E | GOOD |
|---|---|---|---|
| COMPLETE SET (9) | 150.00 | 60.00 | 15.00 |
| COMMON PLAYER (302A-302K) | 15.00 | 6.00 | 1.50 |
| ☐ 302A Leroy Bolden | 15.00 | 6.00 | 1.50 |
| ☐ 302B Vince Costello | 15.00 | 6.00 | 1.50 |
| ☐ 302C Galen Fiss | 15.00 | 6.00 | 1.50 |
| ☐ 302E Lou Groza | 45.00 | 18.00 | 4.50 |
| ☐ 302F Walt Michaels | 20.00 | 8.00 | 2.00 |
| ☐ 302G Bobby Mitchell | 35.00 | 14.00 | 3.50 |
| ☐ 302J Bob Gain | 15.00 | 6.00 | 1.50 |
| ☐ 302K Billy Howton | 20.00 | 8.00 | 2.00 |
| ☐ NNO Jim Brown DP | 5.00 | 2.00 | .50 |

# 1961 Browns Carling Beer

This set of ten black and white posed action shots was sponsored by Carling Black Label Beer and features members of the Cleveland Browns. The pictures measure approximately 8 1/2" by 11 1/2" and have white borders. The sponsor's name and the team name appear below the picture in black lettering. The banks are blank. The pictures are numbered in the lower right corner on the fronts. The set is dated by the fact that Jim Houston's first year was 1960 and Bobby Mitchell and Milt Plum's last year with the Browns was 1961.

| | NRMT | VG-E | GOOD |
|---|---|---|---|
| COMPLETE SET (10) | 200.00 | 80.00 | 20.00 |
| COMMON PLAYER (439A-439L) | 15.00 | 6.00 | 1.50 |
| ☐ 439A Milt Plum | 20.00 | 8.00 | 2.00 |
| ☐ 439B Mike McCormack | 25.00 | 10.00 | 2.50 |
| ☐ 439C Bob Gain | 15.00 | 6.00 | 1.50 |
| ☐ 439D John Morrow | 15.00 | 6.00 | 1.50 |
| ☐ 439E Jim Brown | 75.00 | 30.00 | 7.50 |
| ☐ 439F Bobby Mitchell | 30.00 | 12.00 | 3.00 |
| ☐ 439G Bobby Franklin | 15.00 | 6.00 | 1.50 |
| ☐ 439H Jim Ray Smith | 15.00 | 6.00 | 1.50 |
| ☐ 439K Jim Houston | 20.00 | 8.00 | 2.00 |
| ☐ 439L Ray Renfro | 20.00 | 8.00 | 2.00 |

# 1961 Browns National City Bank

The 1961 National City Bank Cleveland Browns football card set contains 36 brown and white cards each measuring approximately 2 1/2" by 3 9/16". The cards were issued in sheets of six cards, with each sheet of six given a set number and each individual card within the sheet given a player number. In the checklist below the cards have been numbered consecutively from one to 36. On the actual card, set number one will appear on cards 1 through 6, set number two on cards 7 through 12, etc. The front of the card states that the card is a "Quarterback Club Brownie Card". The backs of the cards contain the card number, a short biography and an ad for the National City Bank. Cards still in their uncut (sheet of six) state are valued at 50 percent higher than the prices listed below. Len Dawson's card predates his 1963 Fleer Rookie Card by two years.

| | NRMT | VG-E | GOOD |
|---|---|---|---|
| COMPLETE SET (36) | 2000.00 | 900.00 | 250.00 |
| COMMON PLAYER (1-36) | 35.00 | 14.00 | 3.50 |
| ☐ 1 Mike McCormack | 65.00 | 26.00 | 6.50 |
| ☐ 2 Jim Brown | 500.00 | 200.00 | 50.00 |
| ☐ 3 Leon Clarke | 40.00 | 16.00 | 4.00 |
| ☐ 4 Walt Michaels | 40.00 | 16.00 | 4.00 |
| ☐ 5 Jim Ray Smith | 35.00 | 14.00 | 3.50 |
| ☐ 6 Quarterback Club Membership Card | 200.00 | 80.00 | 20.00 |
| ☐ 7 Len Dawson | 250.00 | 100.00 | 25.00 |
| ☐ 8 John Morrow | 35.00 | 14.00 | 3.50 |
| ☐ 9 Bernie Parrish | 35.00 | 14.00 | 3.50 |
| ☐ 10 Floyd Peters | 40.00 | 16.00 | 4.00 |
| ☐ 11 Paul Wiggin | 40.00 | 16.00 | 4.00 |
| ☐ 12 John Wooten | 40.00 | 16.00 | 4.00 |
| ☐ 13 Ray Renfro | 40.00 | 16.00 | 4.00 |
| ☐ 14 Galen Fiss | 35.00 | 14.00 | 3.50 |
| ☐ 15 Dave Lloyd | 35.00 | 14.00 | 3.50 |
| ☐ 16 Dick Schafrath | 40.00 | 16.00 | 4.00 |
| ☐ 17 Ross Fichtner | 35.00 | 14.00 | 3.50 |
| ☐ 18 Gern Nagler | 35.00 | 14.00 | 3.50 |
| ☐ 19 Rich Kreitling | 35.00 | 14.00 | 3.50 |
| ☐ 20 Duane Putnam | 35.00 | 14.00 | 3.50 |
| ☐ 21 Vince Costello | 35.00 | 14.00 | 3.50 |
| ☐ 22 Jim Shofner | 40.00 | 16.00 | 4.00 |
| ☐ 23 Sam Baker | 40.00 | 16.00 | 4.00 |
| ☐ 24 Bob Gain | 35.00 | 14.00 | 3.50 |
| ☐ 25 Lou Groza | 100.00 | 40.00 | 10.00 |
| ☐ 26 Don Fleming | 50.00 | 20.00 | 5.00 |
| ☐ 27 Tom Watkins | 35.00 | 14.00 | 3.50 |
| ☐ 28 Jim Houston | 40.00 | 16.00 | 4.00 |
| ☐ 29 Larry Stephens | 35.00 | 14.00 | 3.50 |
| ☐ 30 Bobby Mitchell | 90.00 | 36.00 | 9.00 |
| ☐ 31 Bobby Franklin | 35.00 | 14.00 | 3.50 |
| ☐ 32 Charley Ferguson | 35.00 | 14.00 | 3.50 |
| ☐ 33 Johnny Brewer | 35.00 | 14.00 | 3.50 |
| ☐ 34 Bob Crespino | 35.00 | 14.00 | 3.50 |
| ☐ 35 Milt Plum | 45.00 | 18.00 | 4.50 |
| ☐ 36 Preston Powell | 35.00 | 14.00 | 3.50 |

# 1961 Browns White Border

These 20 large photo cards are an unnumbered, blank-backed, team issue set of black and white photographs of the Cleveland Browns measuring approximately 8 1/2" by 10 1/2". The set features posed action shots of players whose name and position appear in a white reverse-out block burned into the bottom of each picture. Team players are listed alphabetically for convenience.

| | NRMT | VG-E | GOOD |
|---|---|---|---|
| COMPLETE SET (20) | 125.00 | 50.00 | 12.50 |
| COMMON PLAYER (1-20) | 3.50 | 1.40 | .35 |
| | | | |
| ☐ 1 Jim Brown | 60.00 | 24.00 | 6.00 |
| ☐ 2 Galen Fiss | 3.50 | 1.40 | .35 |
| ☐ 3 Don Fleming | 6.00 | 2.40 | .60 |
| ☐ 4 Bobby Franklin | 3.50 | 1.40 | .35 |
| ☐ 5 Bob Gain | 3.50 | 1.40 | .35 |
| ☐ 6 Jim Houston | 5.00 | 2.00 | .50 |
| ☐ 7 Rich Kreitling | 3.50 | 1.40 | .35 |
| ☐ 8 Dave Lloyd | 3.50 | 1.40 | .35 |
| ☐ 9 Mike McCormack | 7.50 | 3.00 | .75 |
| ☐ 10 Bobby Mitchell | 12.00 | 5.00 | 1.20 |
| ☐ 11 John Morrow | 3.50 | 1.40 | .35 |
| ☐ 12 Bernie Parrish | 5.00 | 2.00 | .50 |
| ☐ 13 Milt Plum | 6.00 | 2.40 | .60 |
| ☐ 14 Ray Renfro | 5.00 | 2.00 | .50 |
| ☐ 15 Dick Schafrath | 5.00 | 2.00 | .50 |
| ☐ 16 Jim Shofner | 5.00 | 2.00 | .50 |
| ☐ 17 Jim Ray Smith | 3.50 | 1.40 | .35 |
| ☐ 18 Tom Watkins | 3.50 | 1.40 | .35 |
| ☐ 19 Paul Wiggin | 5.00 | 2.00 | .50 |
| ☐ 20 John Wooten | 5.00 | 2.00 | .50 |

## 1963 Browns White Border

The large photo cards are approximately 7 1/2" by 9 1/2", black-and-white, blank backed, printed on glossy heavy paper or thin cardboard. The cards are unnumbered and checklisted below in alphabetical order. The year of issue of this set is dated by the presence of Ken Webb in the set, who was only active with the Cleveland Browns during the 1963 season.

| | MINT | EXC | G-VG |
|---|---|---|---|
| COMPLETE SET (26) | 100.00 | 40.00 | 10.00 |
| COMMON PLAYER (1-26) | 3.00 | 1.20 | .30 |
| | | | |
| ☐ 1 Johnny Brewer | 3.00 | 1.20 | .30 |
| ☐ 2 Monte Clark | 5.00 | 2.00 | .50 |
| ☐ 3 Gary Collins | 5.00 | 2.00 | .50 |
| ☐ 4 Vince Costello | 4.00 | 1.60 | .40 |
| ☐ 5 Bob Crespino | 3.00 | 1.20 | .30 |
| ☐ 6 Ross Fichtner | 3.00 | 1.20 | .30 |
| ☐ 7 Galen Fiss | 3.00 | 1.20 | .30 |
| ☐ 8 Bob Gain | 3.00 | 1.20 | .30 |
| ☐ 9 Bill Glass | 6.00 | 2.40 | .60 |
| ☐ 10 Ernie Green | 5.00 | 2.00 | .50 |
| ☐ 11 Lou Groza | 12.00 | 5.00 | 1.20 |
| ☐ 12 Gene Hickerson | 4.00 | 1.60 | .40 |
| ☐ 13 Jim Houston | 4.00 | 1.60 | .40 |
| ☐ 14 Tom Hutchinson | 3.00 | 1.20 | .30 |
| ☐ 15 Rich Kreitling | 3.00 | 1.20 | .30 |
| ☐ 16 Mike Lucci | 5.00 | 2.00 | .50 |
| ☐ 17 John Morrow | 3.00 | 1.20 | .30 |
| ☐ 18 Jim Ninowski | 4.00 | 1.60 | .40 |
| ☐ 19 Frank Parker | 3.00 | 1.20 | .30 |
| ☐ 20 Bernie Parrish | 4.00 | 1.60 | .40 |
| ☐ 21 Ray Renfro | 4.00 | 1.60 | .40 |
| ☐ 22 Dick Schafrath | 4.00 | 1.60 | .40 |
| ☐ 23 Jim Shofner | 4.00 | 1.60 | .40 |
| ☐ 24 Ken Webb | 3.00 | 1.20 | .30 |
| ☐ 25 Paul Wiggin | 4.00 | 1.60 | .40 |
| ☐ 26 John Wooten | 4.00 | 1.60 | .40 |

## 1985 Browns Coke/Mr. Hero

This 48-card set was issued as six sheets of eight cards each featuring players on the Cleveland Browns. Each card measures approximately 2 3/4" by 3 1/4". Each sheet was numbered; the sheet number is given after each player in the checklist below. The cards are otherwise unnumbered except for uniform number as they are listed below. The bottom of each sheet had coupons for discounts on food and drink from the sponsors.

| | MINT | EXC | G-VG |
|---|---|---|---|
| COMPLETE SET (48) | 25.00 | 10.00 | 2.50 |
| COMMON PLAYER | .60 | .24 | .06 |
| | | | |
| ☐ 7 Jeff Gossett 4 | .75 | .30 | .07 |
| ☐ 9 Matt Bahr 1 | .75 | .30 | .07 |
| ☐ 16 Paul McDonald 4 | .75 | .30 | .07 |
| ☐ 18 Gary Danielson 5 | .75 | .30 | .07 |
| ☐ 19 Bernie Kosar 6 | 7.50 | 3.00 | .75 |
| ☐ 20 Don Rogers 4 | .75 | .30 | .07 |
| ☐ 22 Felix Wright 2 | .75 | .30 | .07 |
| ☐ 26 Greg Allen 3 | .60 | .24 | .06 |
| ☐ 27 Al Gross 2 | .60 | .24 | .06 |
| ☐ 29 Hanford Dixon 5 | .75 | .30 | .07 |
| ☐ 30 Boyce Green 1 | .60 | .24 | .06 |
| ☐ 31 Frank Minnifield 1 | .75 | .30 | .07 |
| ☐ 34 Kevin Mack 3 | 1.00 | .40 | .10 |
| ☐ 37 Chris Rockins 1 | .60 | .24 | .06 |
| ☐ 38 Johnny Davis 5 | .75 | .30 | .07 |
| ☐ 44 Earnest Byner 2 | 1.50 | .60 | .15 |
| ☐ 47 Larry Braziel 4 | .60 | .24 | .06 |
| ☐ 50 Tom Cousineau 6 | 1.00 | .40 | .10 |
| ☐ 51 Eddie Johnson 2 | .60 | .24 | .06 |
| ☐ 55 Curtis Weathers 1 | .60 | .24 | .06 |
| ☐ 56 Chip Banks 6 | .75 | .30 | .07 |
| ☐ 57 Clay Matthews 5 | 1.25 | .50 | .12 |
| ☐ 58 Scott Nicolas 1 | .60 | .24 | .06 |
| ☐ 61 Mike Baab 4 | .75 | .30 | .07 |
| ☐ 62 George Lilja 5 | .60 | .24 | .06 |
| ☐ 63 Cody Risien 6 | .75 | .30 | .07 |
| ☐ 65 Mark Krerowicz 3 | .60 | .24 | .06 |
| ☐ 68 Robert Jackson 4 | .75 | .30 | .07 |
| ☐ 69 Dan Fike 2 | .60 | .24 | .06 |
| ☐ 72 Dave Puzzuoli 1 | .60 | .24 | .06 |
| ☐ 74 Paul Farren 2 | .60 | .24 | .06 |
| ☐ 77 Rickey Bolden 3 | .60 | .24 | .06 |
| ☐ 78 Carl Hairston 2 | .75 | .30 | .07 |
| ☐ 79 Bob Golic 6 | .90 | .36 | .09 |
| ☐ 80 Willis Adams 1 | .60 | .24 | .06 |
| ☐ 81 Harry Holt 3 | .60 | .24 | .06 |
| ☐ 82 Ozzie Newsome 3 | 2.00 | .80 | .20 |
| ☐ 83 Fred Banks 3 | .75 | .30 | .07 |
| ☐ 84 Glen Young 1 | .60 | .24 | .06 |
| ☐ 85 Clarence Weathers 6 | .60 | .24 | .06 |
| ☐ 86 Brian Brennan 5 | .75 | .30 | .07 |
| ☐ 87 Travis Tucker 6 | .60 | .24 | .06 |
| ☐ 88 Reggie Langhorne 5 | .75 | .30 | .07 |
| ☐ 89 John Jefferson 4 | 1.00 | .40 | .10 |
| ☐ 91 Sam Clancy 4 | .75 | .30 | .07 |
| ☐ 96 Reggie Camp 5 | .60 | .24 | .06 |
| ☐ 99 Keith Baldwin 6 | .60 | .24 | .06 |
| ☐ xx Action Photo 3 | 1.25 | .50 | .12 |
| (Clay Matthews tackling Eric Dickerson) | | | |

## 1987 Browns Louis Rich

This five-card set was originally produced as a food product insert for Louis Rich products. Apparently, the promotion was canceled, and collectors were known to have acquired these cards directly from the Cleveland office of Oscar Meyer, which produces the Louis Rich brand. On card number 4 below, the player was unidentified as a question mark, and it is rumored that this was intended to be part of a contest in the promotion. Both Dante Lavelli and Dub Jones wore number 86. Jones wore uniform number 86 in his earlier years with the Browns, in 1952 he began to wear number 40. Also that same year Lavelli changed from wearing number 56 to number 86, Jones' former uniform number. The plastic helmet dates the photo as after 1952 since the Browns changed to this type of helmet in 1952. Therefore, Dante Lavelli appears to be the correct identification. The oversized cards measure approximately 5" by 7 1/8" and are printed on heavy white card stock. The fronts feature full-bleed sepia-toned player photos. An orange diagonal cuts across the lower left corner and carries the set title ("Memorable Moments by Louis Rich"), uniform number, and player's name. The backs are blank. The cards are unnumbered and checklisted below in alphabetical order.

| | MINT | EXC | G-VG |
|---|---|---|---|
| COMPLETE SET (5) | 35.00 | 14.00 | 3.50 |
| COMMON PLAYER (1-5) | 4.00 | 1.60 | .40 |
| ☐ 1 Jim Brown and Bobby Mitchell | 12.00 | 5.00 | 1.20 |
| ☐ 2 Otto Graham | 10.00 | 4.00 | 1.00 |
| ☐ 3 Lou Groza | 8.00 | 3.25 | .80 |
| ☐ 4 Dante Lavelli (Question Mark) | 4.00 | 1.60 | .40 |
| ☐ 5 Marion Motley | 6.00 | 2.40 | .60 |

## 1992 Browns Sunoco

Featuring Cleveland Browns' Hall of Famers, this 24-card set was produced by NFL Properties for an Ohio-area promotion sponsored by Sunoco. Two AM radio stations, WMMS 100.7 and WHK 14.20, cosponsored the set. The cards were available in cello packs that contained a cover card, a player card, and an official sweepstakes entry blank. Some packs contained autograph cards of featured players who were still living. The grand prize offered to the winner was a trip for two to the Super Bowl in Pasadena, California. One player card shown at the Pro Football Hall of Fame would entitle the holder to receive up to three complimentary admissions when up to three admissions were purchased. The offer expired August 31, 1993. The fronts of the cover cards have the words "The Cleveland Browns' Collection" printed in black near the top. A Browns helmet is near the center with the player's name printed below it. The words "Hall of Famer Limited Edition" are printed at the bottom with the Sunoco logo. The backs are simple showing only the Pro Football Hall of Fame logo and sponsors' logos. The player cards exhibit a mix of color and black-and-white full-bleed photos with the player's last name printed in oversized orange letters at the bottom. The Sunoco logo is superimposed on the player's name. The backs are sandstone-textured in varying pastel shades and display a ghosted picture of the player. A career summary and the year the player was inducted into the Hall of Fame are overprinted in black. The player cards are numbered on the back. The cover cards are unnumbered but are checklisted below as they appear in the set and assigned corresponding card numbers with a "C" suffix. There was also an album produced for this set.

| | MINT | EXC | G-VG |
|---|---|---|---|
| COMPLETE SET (24) | 15.00 | 6.00 | 1.50 |
| COMMON PLAYER (1-12) | .60 | .24 | .06 |
| ☐ 1 Otto Graham (Player card) | 2.00 | .80 | .20 |
| ☐ 1C Otto Graham (Cover card) | .75 | .30 | .07 |
| ☐ 2 Paul Brown CO (Player card) | 1.50 | .60 | .15 |
| ☐ 2C Paul Brown CO (Cover card) | .75 | .30 | .07 |
| ☐ 3 Marion Motley (Player card) | 1.25 | .50 | .12 |
| ☐ 3C Marion Motley (Cover card) | .75 | .30 | .07 |
| ☐ 4 Jim Brown (Player card) | 5.00 | 2.00 | .50 |
| ☐ 4C Jim Brown (Cover card) | 2.00 | .80 | .20 |
| ☐ 5 Lou Groza (Player card) | 1.50 | .60 | .15 |
| ☐ 5C Lou Groza (Cover card) | .75 | .30 | .07 |
| ☐ 6 Dante Lavelli | 1.25 | .50 | .12 |
| (Player card) | | | |
| ☐ 6C Dante Lavelli (Cover card) | .75 | .30 | .07 |
| ☐ 7 Len Ford (Player card) | 1.00 | .40 | .10 |
| ☐ 7C Len Ford (Cover card) | .60 | .24 | .06 |
| ☐ 8 Bill Willis (Player card) | .75 | .30 | .07 |
| ☐ 8C Bill Willis (Cover card) | .60 | .24 | .06 |
| ☐ 9 Bobby Mitchell (Player card) | 1.25 | .50 | .12 |
| ☐ 9C Bobby Mitchell (Cover card) | .75 | .30 | .07 |
| ☐ 10 Paul Warfield (Player card) | 1.50 | .60 | .15 |
| ☐ 10C Paul Warfield (Cover card) | .75 | .30 | .07 |
| ☐ 11 Mike McCormack (Player card) | 1.00 | .40 | .10 |
| ☐ 11C Mike McCormack (Cover card) | .60 | .24 | .06 |
| ☐ 12 Frank Gatski (Player card) | 1.00 | .40 | .10 |
| ☐ 12C Frank Gatski (Cover card) | .60 | .24 | .06 |

## 1982 Buccaneers Shell

Sponsored by Shell Oil Co., these 32 paper-thin blank-backed cards measure approximately 1 1/2" by 2 1/2" and feature color action player photos. The photos are borderless, except at the bottom, where the player's name, his team's helmet, and the Shell logo appear in a white margin. The cards are unnumbered and checklisted below in alphabetical order.

| | MINT | EXC | G-VG |
|---|---|---|---|
| COMPLETE SET (32) | 20.00 | 8.00 | 2.00 |
| COMMON PLAYER (1-32) | .60 | .24 | .06 |
| ☐ 1 Theo Bell | 1.00 | .40 | .10 |
| ☐ 2 Scott Brantley | .75 | .30 | .07 |
| ☐ 3 Cedric Brown | .60 | .24 | .06 |
| ☐ 4 Bill Capece | .60 | .24 | .06 |
| ☐ 5 Neal Colzie | 1.00 | .40 | .10 |
| ☐ 6 Mark Cotney | .60 | .24 | .06 |
| ☐ 7 Hugh Culverhouse OWN | 1.00 | .40 | .10 |
| ☐ 8 Jeff Davis | .75 | .30 | .07 |
| ☐ 9 Jerry Eckwood | 1.25 | .50 | .12 |
| ☐ 10 Sean Farrell | .75 | .30 | .07 |
| ☐ 11 Jimmie Giles | 1.00 | .40 | .10 |
| ☐ 12 Hugh Green | 1.25 | .50 | .12 |
| ☐ 13 Charley Hannah | .75 | .30 | .07 |
| ☐ 14 Andy Hawkins | .60 | .24 | .06 |
| ☐ 15 John Holt | .60 | .24 | .06 |
| ☐ 16 Kevin House | 1.00 | .40 | .10 |
| ☐ 17 Gordon Jones | .75 | .30 | .07 |
| ☐ 18 Cecil Johnson | .60 | .24 | .06 |
| ☐ 19 David Logan | .75 | .30 | .07 |
| ☐ 20 John McKay CO | 1.00 | .40 | .10 |
| ☐ 21 James Owens | 1.00 | .40 | .10 |
| ☐ 22 Greg Roberts | .60 | .24 | .06 |
| ☐ 23 Gene Sanders | .60 | .24 | .06 |
| ☐ 24 Lee Roy Selmon | 2.00 | .80 | .20 |
| ☐ 25 Ray Snell | .60 | .24 | .06 |
| ☐ 26 Larry Swider | .60 | .24 | .06 |
| ☐ 27 Norris Thomas | .60 | .24 | .06 |
| ☐ 28 Mike Washington | .60 | .24 | .06 |
| ☐ 29 James Wilder | 1.25 | .50 | .12 |
| ☐ 30 Doug Williams | 1.50 | .60 | .15 |
| ☐ 31 Steve Wilson | .60 | .24 | .06 |
| ☐ 32 Richard Wood | 1.00 | .40 | .10 |

## 1976 Buckmans Discs

The 1976 Buckmans football disc set of 20 is unnumbered and features star players from the National Football League. The circular cards measure approximately 3 3/8" in diameter. The players' pictures are in black and white with a colored arc serving as the disc border. Four stars complete the border. The backs contain the address of the Buckmans ice cream outlet in Rochester, New York. The MSA marking, signifying Michael Schechter Associates, is also contained on the reverse. Since the set is unnumbered, the cards are ordered below alphabetically by player's name.

| | NRMT | VG-E | GOOD |
|---|---|---|---|
| COMPLETE SET (20) | 30.00 | 12.00 | 3.00 |
| COMMON PLAYER (1-20) | .75 | .30 | .07 |
| ☐ 1 Otis Armstrong<br>Denver Broncos | 1.00 | .40 | .10 |
| ☐ 2 Steve Bartkowski<br>Atlanta Falcons | 1.50 | .60 | .15 |
| ☐ 3 Terry Bradshaw<br>Pittsburgh Steelers | 7.50 | 3.00 | .75 |
| ☐ 4 Doug Buffone<br>Chicago Bears | .75 | .30 | .07 |
| ☐ 5 Wally Chambers<br>Chicago Bears | .75 | .30 | .07 |
| ☐ 6 Chuck Foreman<br>Minnesota Vikings | 1.00 | .40 | .10 |
| ☐ 7 Roman Gabriel<br>Philadelphia Eagles | 1.25 | .50 | .12 |
| ☐ 8 Mel Gray<br>St. Louis Cardinals | 1.00 | .40 | .10 |
| ☐ 9 Franco Harris<br>Pittsburgh Steelers | 7.50 | 3.00 | .75 |
| ☐ 10 James Harris<br>Los Angeles Rams | 1.00 | .40 | .10 |
| ☐ 11 Jim Hart<br>St. Louis Cardinals | 1.00 | .40 | .10 |
| ☐ 12 Gary Huff<br>Chicago Bears | .75 | .30 | .07 |
| ☐ 13 Billy Kilmer<br>Washington Redskins | 1.25 | .50 | .12 |
| ☐ 14 Terry Metcalf<br>St. Louis Cardinals | 1.00 | .40 | .10 |
| ☐ 15 Jim Otis<br>St. Louis Cardinals | .75 | .30 | .07 |
| ☐ 16 Jim Plunkett<br>New England Patriots | 1.25 | .50 | .12 |
| ☐ 17 Greg Pruitt<br>Cleveland Browns | 1.00 | .40 | .10 |
| ☐ 18 Roger Staubach<br>Dallas Cowboys | 10.00 | 4.00 | 1.00 |
| ☐ 19 Jan Stenerud<br>Kansas City Chiefs | 2.00 | .80 | .20 |
| ☐ 20 Roger Wehrli<br>St. Louis Cardinals | .75 | .30 | .07 |

## 1960 Cardinals Mayrose Franks

The Mayrose Franks set of 11 cards features players on the St. Louis (Football) Cardinals. The cards are plastic coated (they were intended as inserts in hot dog and bacon packages) with slightly rounded corners and are numbered. The cards measure approximately 2 1/2" by 3 1/2". The fronts, with a black and white photograph of the player and a red background, contain the card number, player statistics and the Cardinal's logo. The backs contain a description of the Big Mayrose Football Contest.

| | NRMT | VG-E | GOOD |
|---|---|---|---|
| COMPLETE SET (11) | 85.00 | 34.00 | 8.50 |
| COMMON PLAYER (1-11) | 8.00 | 3.25 | .80 |
| ☐ 1 Don Gillis | 8.00 | 3.25 | .80 |
| ☐ 2 Frank Fuller | 8.00 | 3.25 | .80 |

| | | | |
|---|---|---|---|
| ☐ 3 George Izo | 10.00 | 4.00 | 1.00 |
| ☐ 4 Woodley Lewis | 8.00 | 3.25 | .80 |
| ☐ 5 King Hill | 10.00 | 4.00 | 1.00 |
| ☐ 6 John David Crow | 15.00 | 6.00 | 1.50 |
| ☐ 7 Bill Stacy | 8.00 | 3.25 | .80 |
| ☐ 8 Ted Bates | 8.00 | 3.25 | .80 |
| ☐ 9 Mike McGee | 8.00 | 3.25 | .80 |
| ☐ 10 Bobby Joe Conrad | 10.00 | 4.00 | 1.00 |
| ☐ 11 Ken Panfil | 8.00 | 3.25 | .80 |

## 1961 Cardinals Jay Publishing

This 12-card set features (approximately) 5" by 7" black-and-white player photos. The pictures show players in traditional poses with the quarterback preparing to throw, the runner heading downfield, and the defensive player ready for the tackle. These cards were packaged 12 to a packet and originally sold for 25 cents. The backs are blank. The cards are unnumbered and checklisted below in alphabetical order.

| | NRMT | VG-E | GOOD |
|---|---|---|---|
| COMPLETE SET (12) | 60.00 | 24.00 | 6.00 |
| COMMON PLAYER (1-12) | 5.00 | 2.00 | .50 |
| ☐ 1 Joe Childress | 5.00 | 2.00 | .50 |
| ☐ 2 Sam Etcheverry | 7.50 | 3.00 | .75 |
| ☐ 3 Ed Henke | 5.00 | 2.00 | .50 |
| ☐ 4 Jimmy Hill | 5.00 | 2.00 | .50 |
| ☐ 5 Bill Koman | 5.00 | 2.00 | .50 |
| ☐ 6 Roland McDole | 6.00 | 2.40 | .60 |
| ☐ 7 Mike McGee | 5.00 | 2.00 | .50 |
| ☐ 8 Dale Meinert | 5.00 | 2.00 | .50 |
| ☐ 9 Jerry Norton | 5.00 | 2.00 | .50 |
| ☐ 10 Sonny Randle | 6.00 | 2.40 | .60 |
| ☐ 11 Joe Robb | 5.00 | 2.00 | .50 |
| ☐ 12 Billy Stacy | 5.00 | 2.00 | .50 |

## 1965 Cardinals Big Red Biographies

This set was featured during the 1965 football season as the side panels of half-gallon milk cartons from Adams Dairy in St. Louis. When cut, the cards measure approximately 3 1/16" by 5 9/16". The printing on the cards is in purple and orange. All cards feature members of the St. Louis Cardinals. The catalog designation for this set is F112. The list below contains those cards known at this time; any additions to the list would be most welcome. The cards have blank backs as is the case with most milk carton issues. Complete milk cartons would be valued at double the prices listed below.

| | NRMT | VG-E | GOOD |
|---|---|---|---|
| COMPLETE SET (17) | 1000.00 | 450.00 | 125.00 |
| COMMON PLAYER (1-17) | 60.00 | 24.00 | 6.00 |
| ☐ 1 Monk Bailey | 60.00 | 24.00 | 6.00 |
| ☐ 2 Jim Bakken | 90.00 | 36.00 | 9.00 |
| ☐ 3 Jim Burson | 60.00 | 24.00 | 6.00 |
| ☐ 4 Willis Crenshaw | 75.00 | 30.00 | 7.50 |
| ☐ 5 Bob DeMarco | 75.00 | 30.00 | 7.50 |
| ☐ 6 Pat Fischer | 90.00 | 36.00 | 9.00 |
| ☐ 7 Billy Gambrell | 60.00 | 24.00 | 6.00 |
| ☐ 8 Ken Gray | 75.00 | 30.00 | 7.50 |
| ☐ 9 Irv Goode | 60.00 | 24.00 | 6.00 |
| ☐ 10 Mike Melinkovich | 60.00 | 24.00 | 6.00 |
| ☐ 11 Bob Reynolds | 60.00 | 24.00 | 6.00 |
| ☐ 12 Marion Rushing | 60.00 | 24.00 | 6.00 |
| ☐ 13 Carl Silvestri | 60.00 | 24.00 | 6.00 |
| ☐ 14 Dave Simmons | 75.00 | 30.00 | 7.50 |
| ☐ 15 Jackie Smith | 125.00 | 50.00 | 12.50 |
| ☐ 16 Bill(Thunder) Thornton | 60.00 | 24.00 | 6.00 |
| ☐ 17 Herschel Turner | 60.00 | 24.00 | 6.00 |

# 1993 Cardz Flintstones Promos

This six-card promo set measures the standard size (2 1/2" by 3 1/2") and features color cartoons of Flintstones characters in NFL uniforms. The characters are set against a sky blue background with white borders. The team name appears in large print in team colors. The backs display statistics and team records for 1992 against team-colored backgrounds with white borders. The cards are numbered on the back, and the word prototype appears next to the card number.

|  | MINT | EXC | G-VG |
|---|---|---|---|
| COMPLETE SET (6) | 7.50 | 3.00 | .75 |
| COMMON PLAYER (1-6) | 1.50 | .60 | .15 |
| ☐ 1 Fred Flintstone<br>Miami Dolphins | 1.50 | .60 | .15 |
| ☐ 2 Fred Flintstone<br>San Francisco 49ers | 1.50 | .60 | .15 |
| ☐ 3 Fred and Barney<br>Buffalo Bills | 1.50 | .60 | .15 |
| ☐ 4 Fred and Barney<br>Dallas Cowboys | 1.50 | .60 | .15 |
| ☐ 5 Fred Flintstone<br>Philadelphia Eagles | 1.50 | .60 | .15 |
| ☐ 6 Fred, Barney and Dino<br>San Diego Chargers | 1.50 | .60 | .15 |

## 1993 Cardz Flintstones NFL

This 110-card set measures the standard size (2 1/2" by 3 1/2") and was produced by CARDZ under license granted by Turner Home Entertainment and the NFL. Randomly packed in eight-card foil packs were three holograms and one Tekchrome card. The fronts feature color action shots of Fred Flintstone, Barney, and other Flintstones characters in NFL colors and uniforms against a light blue background with white borders. The team name and logo also appear on the front. The backs carry either statistics, trivia questions, team records, or team schedules on team-colored backgrounds. Four bonus cards are randomly inserted in the eight-card foil packs: three holograms and one Tekchrome card. The cards are numbered on the back and are divided into the categories of Team Draft Picks (1-28), Team Schedules (29-56), Team Stats (57-84), Stone Age Signals (85-100), Activity Cards (101-110), and Bonus Cards (H1-H3, T1). The cards are checklisted below accordingly.

|  | MINT | EXC | G-VG |
|---|---|---|---|
| COMPLETE SET (114) | 12.00 | 5.00 | 1.20 |
| COMMON CARD (1-110) | .10 | .04 | .01 |
| ☐ 1 Atlanta Falcons<br>1993 Draft Picks | .10 | .04 | .01 |
| ☐ 2 Buffalo Bills<br>1993 Draft Picks | .10 | .04 | .01 |
| ☐ 3 Chicago Bears<br>1993 Draft Picks | .10 | .04 | .01 |
| ☐ 4 Cincinnati Bengals<br>1993 Draft Picks | .10 | .04 | .01 |
| ☐ 5 Cleveland Browns<br>1993 Draft Picks | .10 | .04 | .01 |
| ☐ 6 Dallas Cowboys<br>1993 Draft Picks | .10 | .04 | .01 |
| ☐ 7 Denver Broncos<br>1993 Draft Picks | .10 | .04 | .01 |
| ☐ 8 Detroit Lions<br>1993 Draft Picks | .10 | .04 | .01 |
| ☐ 9 Green Bay Packers<br>1993 Draft Picks | .10 | .04 | .01 |
| ☐ 10 Houston Oilers<br>1993 Draft Picks | .10 | .04 | .01 |
| ☐ 11 Indianapolis Colts<br>1993 Draft Picks | .10 | .04 | .01 |
| ☐ 12 Kansas City Chiefs<br>1993 Draft Picks | .10 | .04 | .01 |
| ☐ 13 Los Angeles Raiders<br>1993 Draft Picks | .10 | .04 | .01 |
| ☐ 14 Los Angeles Rams<br>1993 Draft Picks | .10 | .04 | .01 |
| ☐ 15 Miami Dolphins<br>1993 Draft Picks | .10 | .04 | .01 |
| ☐ 16 Minnesota Vikings<br>1993 Draft Picks | .10 | .04 | .01 |
| ☐ 17 New England Patriots<br>1993 Draft Picks | .10 | .04 | .01 |
| ☐ 18 New Orleans Saints<br>1993 Draft Picks | .10 | .04 | .01 |
| ☐ 19 New York Giants<br>1993 Draft Picks | .10 | .04 | .01 |
| ☐ 20 New York Jets<br>1993 Draft Picks | .10 | .04 | .01 |
| ☐ 21 Philadelphia Eagles<br>1993 Draft Picks | .10 | .04 | .01 |
| ☐ 22 Phoenix Cardinals<br>1993 Draft Picks | .10 | .04 | .01 |
| ☐ 23 Pittsburgh Steelers<br>1993 Draft Picks | .10 | .04 | .01 |
| ☐ 24 San Diego Chargers<br>1993 Draft Picks | .10 | .04 | .01 |
| ☐ 25 San Francisco 49ers<br>1993 Draft Picks | .10 | .04 | .01 |
| ☐ 26 Seattle Seahawks<br>1993 Draft Picks | .10 | .04 | .01 |
| ☐ 27 Tampa Bay Buccaneers<br>1993 Draft Picks | .10 | .04 | .01 |
| ☐ 28 Washington Redskins<br>1993 Draft Picks | .10 | .04 | .01 |
| ☐ 29 Atlanta Falcons<br>1993 Schedule | .10 | .04 | .01 |
| ☐ 30 Buffalo Bills<br>1993 Schedule | .10 | .04 | .01 |
| ☐ 31 Chicago Bears<br>1993 Schedule | .10 | .04 | .01 |
| ☐ 32 Cincinnati Bengals<br>1993 Schedule | .10 | .04 | .01 |
| ☐ 33 Cleveland Browns<br>1993 Schedule | .10 | .04 | .01 |
| ☐ 34 Dallas Cowboys<br>1993 Schedule | .10 | .04 | .01 |
| ☐ 35 Denver Broncos<br>1993 Schedule | .10 | .04 | .01 |
| ☐ 36 Detroit Lions<br>1993 Schedule | .10 | .04 | .01 |
| ☐ 37 Green Bay Packers<br>1993 Schedule | .10 | .04 | .01 |
| ☐ 38 Houston Oilers<br>1993 Schedule | .10 | .04 | .01 |
| ☐ 39 Indianapolis Colts<br>1993 Schedule | .10 | .04 | .01 |
| ☐ 40 Kansas City Chiefs<br>1993 Schedule | .10 | .04 | .01 |
| ☐ 41 Los Angeles Raiders<br>1993 Schedule | .10 | .04 | .01 |
| ☐ 42 Los Angeles Rams<br>1993 Schedule | .10 | .04 | .01 |
| ☐ 43 Miami Dolphins<br>1993 Schedule | .10 | .04 | .01 |
| ☐ 44 Minnesota Vikings<br>1993 Schedule | .10 | .04 | .01 |
| ☐ 45 New England Patriots<br>1993 Schedule | .10 | .04 | .01 |
| ☐ 46 New Orleans Saints<br>1993 Schedule | .10 | .04 | .01 |
| ☐ 47 New York Giants<br>1993 Schedule | .10 | .04 | .01 |
| ☐ 48 New York Jets<br>1993 Schedule | .10 | .04 | .01 |
| ☐ 49 Philadelphia Eagles<br>1993 Schedule | .10 | .04 | .01 |
| ☐ 50 Phoenix Cardinals | .10 | .04 | .01 |

|  |  |  |  |
|---|---|---|---|
| 1993 Schedule |  |  |  |
| ☐ 51 Pittsburgh Steelers | .10 | .04 | .01 |
| 1993 Schedule |  |  |  |
| ☐ 52 San Diego Chargers | .10 | .04 | .01 |
| 1993 Schedule |  |  |  |
| ☐ 53 San Francisco 49ers | .10 | .04 | .01 |
| 1993 Schedule |  |  |  |
| ☐ 54 Seattle Seahawks | .10 | .04 | .01 |
| 1993 Schedule |  |  |  |
| ☐ 55 Tampa Bay Buccaneers | .10 | .04 | .01 |
| 1993 Schedule |  |  |  |
| ☐ 56 Washington Redskins | .10 | .04 | .01 |
| 1993 Schedule |  |  |  |
| ☐ 57 Atlanta Falcons | .10 | .04 | .01 |
| 1992 Team Stats |  |  |  |
| ☐ 58 Buffalo Bills | .10 | .04 | .01 |
| 1992 Team Stats |  |  |  |
| ☐ 59 Chicago Bears | .10 | .04 | .01 |
| 1992 Team Stats |  |  |  |
| ☐ 60 Cincinnati Bengals | .10 | .04 | .01 |
| 1992 Team Stats |  |  |  |
| ☐ 61 Cleveland Browns | .10 | .04 | .01 |
| 1992 Team Stats |  |  |  |
| ☐ 62 Dallas Cowboys | .10 | .04 | .01 |
| 1992 Team Stats |  |  |  |
| ☐ 63 Denver Broncos | .10 | .04 | .01 |
| 1992 Team Stats |  |  |  |
| ☐ 64 Detroit Lions | .10 | .04 | .01 |
| 1992 Team Stats |  |  |  |
| ☐ 65 Green Bay Packers | .10 | .04 | .01 |
| 1992 Team Stats |  |  |  |
| ☐ 66 Houston Oilers | .10 | .04 | .01 |
| 1992 Team Stats |  |  |  |
| ☐ 67 Indianapolis Colts | .10 | .04 | .01 |
| 1992 Team Stats |  |  |  |
| ☐ 68 Kansas City Chiefs | .10 | .04 | .01 |
| 1992 Team Stats |  |  |  |
| ☐ 69 Los Angeles Raiders | .10 | .04 | .01 |
| 1992 Team Stats |  |  |  |
| ☐ 70 Los Angeles Rams | .10 | .04 | .01 |
| 1992 Team Stats |  |  |  |
| ☐ 71 Miami Dolphins | .10 | .04 | .01 |
| 1992 Team Stats |  |  |  |
| ☐ 72 Minnesota Vikings | .10 | .04 | .01 |
| 1992 Team Stats |  |  |  |
| ☐ 73 New England Patriots | .10 | .04 | .01 |
| 1992 Team Stats |  |  |  |
| ☐ 74 New Orleans Saints | .10 | .04 | .01 |
| 1992 Team Stats |  |  |  |
| ☐ 75 New York Giants | .10 | .04 | .01 |
| 1992 Team Stats |  |  |  |
| ☐ 76 New York Jets | .10 | .04 | .01 |
| 1992 Team Stats |  |  |  |
| ☐ 77 Philadelphia Eagles | .10 | .04 | .01 |
| 1992 Team Stats |  |  |  |
| ☐ 78 Phoenix Cardinals | .10 | .04 | .01 |
| 1992 Team Stats |  |  |  |
| ☐ 79 Pittsburgh Steelers | .10 | .04 | .01 |
| 1992 Team Stats |  |  |  |
| ☐ 80 San Diego Chargers | .10 | .04 | .01 |
| 1992 Team Stats |  |  |  |
| ☐ 81 San Francisco 49ers | .10 | .04 | .01 |
| 1992 Team Stats |  |  |  |
| ☐ 82 Seattle Seahawks | .10 | .04 | .01 |
| 1992 Team Stats |  |  |  |
| ☐ 83 Tampa Bay Buccaneers | .10 | .04 | .01 |
| 1992 Team Stats |  |  |  |
| ☐ 84 Washington Redskins | .10 | .04 | .01 |
| 1992 Team Stats |  |  |  |
| ☐ 85 Stone Age Signals | .10 | .04 | .01 |
| Touchdown |  |  |  |
| ☐ 86 Stone Age Signals | .10 | .04 | .01 |
| Time Out |  |  |  |
| ☐ 87 Stone Age Signals | .10 | .04 | .01 |
| First Down |  |  |  |
| ☐ 88 Stone Age Signals | .10 | .04 | .01 |
| Personal Foul |  |  |  |
| ☐ 89 Stone Age Signals | .10 | .04 | .01 |
| Delay of Game |  |  |  |
| ☐ 90 Stone Age Signals | .10 | .04 | .01 |
| Offside or Encroachment |  |  |  |
| ☐ 91 Stone Age Signals | .10 | .04 | .01 |
| Holding |  |  |  |
| ☐ 92 Stone Age Signals | .10 | .04 | .01 |
| Illegal Motion at Snap |  |  |  |
| ☐ 93 Stone Age Signals | .10 | .04 | .01 |
| Unsportsmanlike Conduct |  |  |  |
| ☐ 94 Stone Age Signals | .10 | .04 | .01 |
| Blocking Below the Waist |  |  |  |
| ☐ 95 Stone Age Signals | .10 | .04 | .01 |
| Intentional Grounding of Pass |  |  |  |
| ☐ 96 Stone Age Signals | .10 | .04 | .01 |
| Illegal Contact |  |  |  |
| ☐ 97 Stone Age Signals | .10 | .04 | .01 |
| False Start |  |  |  |
| ☐ 98 Stone Age Signals | .10 | .04 | .01 |

|  |  |  |  |
|---|---|---|---|
| Illegal Use of Hands, Arms, or Body |  |  |  |
| ☐ 99 Stone Age Signals | .10 | .04 | .01 |
| Interference with Forward Pass |  |  |  |
| ☐ 100 Stone Age Signals | .10 | .04 | .01 |
| Incomplete Pass or Refused Penalty |  |  |  |
| ☐ 101 NFL Football Facts I | .10 | .04 | .01 |
| ☐ 102 NFL Football Facts II | .10 | .04 | .01 |
| ☐ 103 NFL Football Facts III | .10 | .04 | .01 |
| ☐ 104 A Team Scramble | .10 | .04 | .01 |
| ☐ 105 Lost in the Pocket | .10 | .04 | .01 |
| ☐ 106 The NFL Position | .10 | .04 | .01 |
| Condition |  |  |  |
| ☐ 107 AFC Match Game | .10 | .04 | .01 |
| ☐ 108 NFC Match Game | .10 | .04 | .01 |
| ☐ 109 A-Mazing | .10 | .04 | .01 |
| ☐ 110 It's a Mad Scramble | .10 | .04 | .01 |
| ☐ H1 A Decade of Super | 1.50 | .60 | .15 |
| Bowl Champions |  |  |  |
| ☐ H2 The 1993 NFC Pro Bowl | 1.50 | .60 | .15 |
| Lineup |  |  |  |
| ☐ H3 The 1993 AFC Pro Bowl | 1.50 | .60 | .15 |
| Lineups |  |  |  |
| ☐ T1 Super Bowl XXVII | 3.00 | 1.20 | .30 |
| Champions |  |  |  |

## 1989 CBS Television Announcers

This ten-card set (with cards measuring approximately 2 3/4" by 3 7/8") features those members of the 1989 CBS Football Announcing team who had been involved in professional football. The front of the card features a color action shot from the person's professional career bordered in orange and superimposed over a green football field with a white yard stripe. The words "Going the extra yard" appear in red block lettering at the card top, while the words "NFL on CBS" appear in the lower right corner. The backs are horizontally oriented and have a black and white studio portrait head shot of the announcer. Biography and career highlights are bordered in red. It has been reported that 500 sets were distributed to various CBS outlets and publication sources. The set was split into two series of five announcers each and are unnumbered.

|  | MINT | EXC | G-VG |
|---|---|---|---|
| COMPLETE SET (10) | 150.00 | 60.00 | 15.00 |
| COMMON CARD (1-5) | 7.50 | 3.00 | .75 |
| COMMON CARD (6-10) | 7.50 | 3.00 | .75 |
| ☐ 1 Terry Bradshaw | 50.00 | 20.00 | 5.00 |
| ☐ 2 Dick Butkus | 30.00 | 12.00 | 3.00 |
| ☐ 3 Irv Cross | 7.50 | 3.00 | .75 |
| ☐ 4 Dan Fouts | 25.00 | 10.00 | 2.50 |
| ☐ 5 Pat Summerall | 15.00 | 6.00 | 1.50 |
| ☐ 6 Gary Fencik | 7.50 | 3.00 | .75 |
| ☐ 7 Dan Jiggetts | 7.50 | 3.00 | .75 |
| ☐ 8 John Madden | 30.00 | 12.00 | 3.00 |
| ☐ 9 Ken Stabler | 30.00 | 12.00 | 3.00 |
| ☐ 10 Hank Stram | 12.00 | 5.00 | 1.20 |

## 1961 Chargers Golden Tulip

The 1961 Golden Tulip Chips football card set contains 22 black and white cards featuring San Diego (Los Angeles in 1960) Chargers AFL players. The cards measure approximately 2" by 3". The fronts contain the player's name, a short biography, and vital statistics. The backs, which are the same for all cards, contain an ad for XETV television, a premium offer for (approximately) 8" by 10" photos and an ad for a free ticket contest. The cards are unnumbered but have been numbered in alphabetical order in the checklist below for your convenience. The catalog designation for this set is F395.

SAM DeLUCA, Charger offensive
tackle from South Carolina. Very
strong 6' 2", 245 lbs., 25 years old.

|  | NRMT | VG-E | GOOD |
|---|---|---|---|
| COMPLETE SET (22) | 1000.00 | 450.00 | 125.00 |
| COMMON PLAYER (1-22) | 30.00 | 12.00 | 3.00 |
| ☐ 1 Ron Botchan | 30.00 | 12.00 | 3.00 |
| ☐ 2 Howard Clark | 30.00 | 12.00 | 3.00 |
| ☐ 3 Fred Cole | 30.00 | 12.00 | 3.00 |
| ☐ 4 Sam DeLuca | 35.00 | 14.00 | 3.50 |
| ☐ 5 Orlando Ferrante | 30.00 | 12.00 | 3.00 |
| ☐ 6 Charlie Flowers | 35.00 | 14.00 | 3.50 |
| ☐ 7 Dick Harris | 30.00 | 12.00 | 3.00 |
| ☐ 8 Emil Karas | 30.00 | 12.00 | 3.00 |
| ☐ 9 Jack Kemp | 400.00 | 160.00 | 40.00 |
| ☐ 10 Dave Kocourek | 35.00 | 14.00 | 3.50 |
| ☐ 11 Bob Laraba | 30.00 | 12.00 | 3.00 |
| ☐ 12 Paul Lowe | 50.00 | 20.00 | 5.00 |
| ☐ 13 Paul Maguire | 50.00 | 20.00 | 5.00 |
| ☐ 14 Charlie McNeil | 35.00 | 14.00 | 3.50 |
| ☐ 15 Ron Mix | 60.00 | 24.00 | 6.00 |
| ☐ 16 Ron Nery | 30.00 | 12.00 | 3.00 |
| ☐ 17 Don Norton | 30.00 | 12.00 | 3.00 |
| ☐ 18 Volney Peters | 30.00 | 12.00 | 3.00 |
| ☐ 19 Don Rogers | 30.00 | 12.00 | 3.00 |
| ☐ 20 Maury Schleicher | 30.00 | 12.00 | 3.00 |
| ☐ 21 Ernie Wright | 30.00 | 12.00 | 3.00 |
| ☐ 22 Bob Zeman | 30.00 | 12.00 | 3.00 |

## 1962 Chargers Union Oil

The set was sponsored by Union 76. All players featured in the set are members of the San Diego Chargers. They are derived from sketches by the artist, Patrick. The cards are black and white, approximately 6" by 8" with player biography and Union Oil logo on backs. The catalog designation for the set is UO35-2. The cards were reportedly issued with an album with 24 spaces for the photos. The key cards in this set are quarterback Jack Kemp, who would later gain fame as the Secretary of House, Education and Welfare as well as cards issued during the rookie season of future Hall of Famer Lance Alworth and star quarterback John Hadl.

|  | NRMT | VG-E | GOOD |
|---|---|---|---|
| COMPLETE SET (14) | 300.00 | 120.00 | 30.00 |
| COMMON PLAYER (1-14) | 9.00 | 3.75 | .90 |
| ☐ 1 Chuck Allen | 9.00 | 3.75 | .90 |
| ☐ 2 Lance Alworth | 50.00 | 20.00 | 5.00 |
| ☐ 3 John Hadl | 25.00 | 10.00 | 2.50 |
| ☐ 4 Dick Harris | 12.00 | 5.00 | 1.20 |
| ☐ 5 Bill Hudson | 9.00 | 3.75 | .90 |
| ☐ 6 Jack Kemp | 150.00 | 60.00 | 15.00 |
| ☐ 7 Dave Kocourek | 12.00 | 5.00 | 1.20 |

| ☐ 8 Ernie Ladd | 25.00 | 10.00 | 2.50 |
|---|---|---|---|
| ☐ 9 Keith Lincoln | 20.00 | 8.00 | 2.00 |
| ☐ 10 Paul Lowe | 20.00 | 8.00 | 2.00 |
| ☐ 11 Charlie McNeil | 12.00 | 5.00 | 1.20 |
| ☐ 12 Ron Mix | 25.00 | 10.00 | 2.50 |
| ☐ 13 Ron Nery | 9.00 | 3.75 | .90 |
| ☐ 14 Team Photo | 20.00 | 8.00 | 2.00 |

## 1966 Chargers White Border

This team issue set, with cards measuring approximately 5 1/2" by 8 1/2", features black and white close-up player photos on off-white linen weave paper. Player's facsimile autograph is centered beneath each picture above team name. The photo of George Gross has biographical information on the back. The other pictures have blank backs. Because the set is unnumbered, players and coaches are listed alphabetically for convenience.

|  | NRMT | VG-E | GOOD |
|---|---|---|---|
| COMPLETE SET (50) | 175.00 | 70.00 | 18.00 |
| COMMON CARD (1-50) | 3.00 | 1.20 | .30 |
| ☐ 1 Chuck Allen | 3.00 | 1.20 | .30 |
| ☐ 2 James Allison | 3.00 | 1.20 | .30 |
| ☐ 3 Lance Alworth | 25.00 | 10.00 | 2.50 |
| ☐ 4 Tom Bass | 3.00 | 1.20 | .30 |
| ☐ 5 Joe Beauchamp | 3.00 | 1.20 | .30 |
| ☐ 6 Frank Buncom | 4.00 | 1.60 | .40 |
| ☐ 7 Richard Degen | 3.00 | 1.20 | .30 |
| ☐ 8 Steve DeLong | 4.00 | 1.60 | .40 |
| ☐ 9 Les(Speedy) Duncan | 4.00 | 1.60 | .40 |
| ☐ 10 John Farris | 3.00 | 1.20 | .30 |
| ☐ 11 Gene Foster | 3.00 | 1.20 | .30 |
| ☐ 12 Willie Frazier | 4.00 | 1.60 | .40 |
| ☐ 13 Gary Garrison | 5.00 | 2.00 | .50 |
| ☐ 14 Sid Gillman CO | 10.00 | 4.00 | 1.00 |
| ☐ 15 Kenny Graham | 3.00 | 1.20 | .30 |
| ☐ 16 George Gross | 4.00 | 1.60 | .40 |
| ☐ 17 Sam Gruineisen | 3.00 | 1.20 | .30 |
| ☐ 18 Walt Hackett CO | 3.00 | 1.20 | .30 |
| ☐ 19 John Hadl | 12.00 | 5.00 | 1.20 |
| ☐ 20 Dick Harris | 4.00 | 1.60 | .40 |
| ☐ 21 Dan Henning | 12.00 | 5.00 | 1.20 |
| ☐ 22 Bob Horton | 3.00 | 1.20 | .30 |
| ☐ 23 Harry Johnston CO | 3.00 | 1.20 | .30 |
| ☐ 24 Howard Kindig | 3.00 | 1.20 | .30 |
| ☐ 25 Keith Lincoln | 6.00 | 2.40 | .60 |
| ☐ 26 Paul Lowe | 6.00 | 2.40 | .60 |
| ☐ 27 Jacque MacKinnon | 4.00 | 1.60 | .40 |
| ☐ 28 Joseph Madro CO | 3.00 | 1.20 | .30 |
| ☐ 29 Ed Mitchell | 3.00 | 1.20 | .30 |
| ☐ 30 Bob Mitinger | 3.00 | 1.20 | .30 |
| ☐ 31 Ron Mix | 10.00 | 4.00 | 1.00 |
| ☐ 32 Fred Moore | 3.00 | 1.20 | .30 |
| ☐ 33 Don Norton | 3.00 | 1.20 | .30 |
| ☐ 34 Terry Owen | 3.00 | 1.20 | .30 |
| ☐ 35 Bob Petrich | 3.00 | 1.20 | .30 |
| ☐ 36 Dave Plump | 3.00 | 1.20 | .30 |
| ☐ 37 Rick Redman | 4.00 | 1.60 | .40 |
| ☐ 38 Houston Ridge | 3.00 | 1.20 | .30 |
| ☐ 39 Pat Shea | 3.00 | 1.20 | .30 |
| ☐ 40 Walt Sweeney | 4.00 | 1.60 | .40 |
| ☐ 41 Sammy Taylor | 3.00 | 1.20 | .30 |
| ☐ 42 Steve Tensi | 6.00 | 2.40 | .60 |
| ☐ 43 Herb Travenio | 3.00 | 1.20 | .30 |
| ☐ 44 John Travis | 3.00 | 1.20 | .30 |
| ☐ 45 Dick Van Raaphorst | 3.00 | 1.20 | .30 |
| ☐ 46 Charlie Waller CO | 3.00 | 1.20 | .30 |
| ☐ 47 Bud Whitehead | 3.00 | 1.20 | .30 |
| ☐ 48 Nat Whitmyer | 3.00 | 1.20 | .30 |
| ☐ 49 Ernie Wright | 4.00 | 1.60 | .40 |
| ☐ 50 Bob Zeman | 3.00 | 1.20 | .30 |

## 1985 Chargers Kodak

This 15-card set was sponsored by Kodak and measures approximately 5 1/2" by 8 1/2". The fronts have white borders and action color photos. The player's name, position, and a Chargers helmet icon appear below the picture. The backs have biographical information. The set is listed below in alphabetical order by player's name.

|  | MINT | EXC | G-VG |
|---|---|---|---|
| COMPLETE SET (15) | 30.00 | 12.00 | 3.00 |
| COMMON PLAYER (1-15) | 2.00 | .80 | .20 |
| ☐ 1 Carlos Bradley | 2.00 | .80 | .20 |
| ☐ 2 Wes Chandler | 4.00 | 1.60 | .40 |
| ☐ 3 Chuck Ehin | 2.00 | .80 | .20 |
| ☐ 4 Mike Green | 2.00 | .80 | .20 |
| ☐ 5 Pete Holohan | 2.50 | 1.00 | .25 |
| ☐ 6 Lionel James | 2.50 | 1.00 | .25 |
| ☐ 7 Charlie Joiner | 10.00 | 4.00 | 1.00 |
| ☐ 8 Woodrow Lowe | 2.50 | 1.00 | .25 |
| ☐ 9 Dennis McKnight | 2.00 | .80 | .20 |
| ☐ 10 Miles McPherson | 2.00 | .80 | .20 |
| ☐ 11 Derrie Nelson | 2.00 | .80 | .20 |
| ☐ 12 Vince Osby | 2.00 | .80 | .20 |
| ☐ 13 Billy Ray Smith | 2.50 | 1.00 | .25 |
| ☐ 14 Danny Walters | 2.00 | .80 | .20 |
| ☐ 15 Ed White | 2.50 | 1.00 | .25 |

## 1986 Chargers Kodak

This set of 36 photos featuring the San Diego Chargers was sponsored by Kodak and measures approximately 5 1/2" by 8 1/2". The fronts feature color action photos with white borders. Biographical information is given below the photo between the Chargers' helmet on the left and the Kodak logo on the right. The backs are blank. The photos are unnumbered and checklisted below in alphabetical order.

|  | MINT | EXC | G-VG |
|---|---|---|---|
| COMPLETE SET (36) | 60.00 | 24.00 | 6.00 |
| COMMON PLAYER (1-36) | 2.00 | .80 | .20 |
| ☐ 1 Curtis Adams | 2.00 | .80 | .20 |
| ☐ 2 Gary Anderson | 5.00 | 2.00 | .50 |
| ☐ 3 Jesse Bendross | 2.50 | 1.00 | .25 |
| ☐ 4 Gill Byrd | 3.00 | 1.20 | .30 |
| ☐ 5 Sam Claphan | 2.00 | .80 | .20 |
| ☐ 6 Don Coryell CO | 3.00 | 1.20 | .30 |
| ☐ 7 Jeff Dale | 2.00 | .80 | .20 |
| ☐ 8 Wayne Davis | 2.00 | .80 | .20 |
| ☐ 9 Jerry Doerger | 2.00 | .80 | .20 |
| ☐ 10 Chris Faulkner | 2.00 | .80 | .20 |
| ☐ 11 Mark Fellows | 2.00 | .80 | .20 |
| ☐ 12 Dan Fouts | 10.00 | 4.00 | 1.00 |
| ☐ 13 Mike Guendling | 2.00 | .80 | .20 |
| ☐ 14 John Hendy | 2.00 | .80 | .20 |
| ☐ 15 Mark Herrmann | 2.50 | 1.00 | .25 |
| ☐ 16 Lionel James | 2.50 | 1.00 | .25 |
| ☐ 17 Trumaine Johnson | 2.50 | 1.00 | .25 |
| ☐ 18 David King | 2.00 | .80 | .20 |
| ☐ 19 Linden King | 2.00 | .80 | .20 |
| ☐ 20 Jim Lachey | 4.00 | 1.60 | .40 |
| ☐ 21 Don Macek | 2.00 | .80 | .20 |
| ☐ 22 Buford McGee | 2.00 | .80 | .20 |
| ☐ 23 Dennis McKnight | 2.00 | .80 | .20 |
| ☐ 24 Ralf Mojsiejenko | 2.00 | .80 | .20 |
| ☐ 25 Ron O'Bard | 2.00 | .80 | .20 |
| ☐ 26 Fred Robinson | 2.00 | .80 | .20 |
| ☐ 27 Eric Sievers | 2.50 | 1.00 | .25 |
| ☐ 28 Tony Simmons | 2.00 | .80 | .20 |
| ☐ 29 Billy Ray Smith | 2.50 | 1.00 | .25 |
| ☐ 30 Lucious Smith | 2.00 | .80 | .20 |
| ☐ 31 Alex G. Spanos PRES | 2.50 | 1.00 | .25 |
| ☐ 32 Tim Spencer | 2.50 | 1.00 | .25 |
| ☐ 33 Rich Umphrey | 2.00 | .80 | .20 |
| ☐ 34 Ed White | 2.50 | 1.00 | .25 |
| ☐ 35 Lee Williams | 4.00 | 1.60 | .40 |
| ☐ 36 Earl Wilson | 2.00 | .80 | .20 |

## 1987 Chargers Junior Coke Tickets

This 11" by 8 1/2" perforated sheet features two rows of six coupons each. The coupons resemble tickets, with each coupon measuring approximately 1 7/8" by 4 1/4". They were given to members of the Coca-Cola Junior Chargers club. Edged below by a mustard stripe, a powder blue strip at the top carries the coupon's subtitle. The large middle panel of the ticket carries a color action player photo with white borders and the player's name immediately below. Another powder blue stripe at the bottom of the coupon reads "Sec. Row Seat" in imitation of an actual ticket. The horizontal backs vary in their content, consisting of either a membership card, season schedule, Coca-Cola Junior Chargers club, preseason pass, or various coupons to attractions in the San Diego area. The coupons are unnumbered and are listed below in alphabetical order by subject.

|  | MINT | EXC | G-VG |
|---|---|---|---|
| COMPLETE SET (12) | 15.00 | 6.00 | 1.50 |
| COMMON PLAYER (1-12) | 1.00 | .40 | .10 |
| ☐ 1 Gary Anderson | 2.00 | .80 | .20 |
| ☐ 2 Rolf Benirschke | 1.50 | .60 | .15 |
| ☐ 3 Wes Chandler | 3.00 | 1.20 | .30 |
| ☐ 4 Jeffery Dale | 1.00 | .40 | .10 |
| ☐ 5 Dan Fouts | 5.00 | 2.00 | .50 |
| ☐ 6 Pete Holohan | 1.00 | .40 | .10 |
| ☐ 7 Lionel James | 1.50 | .60 | .15 |
| ☐ 8 Don Macek | 1.00 | .40 | .10 |
| ☐ 9 Dennis McKnight | 1.00 | .40 | .10 |
| ☐ 10 Al Saunders CO | 1.00 | .40 | .10 |
| ☐ 11 Billy Ray Smith | 2.00 | .80 | .20 |
| ☐ 12 Kellen Winslow | 3.00 | 1.20 | .30 |

## 1989 Chargers Junior Ralph's Tickets

This perforated sheet features two rows of six cards each. If the cards were separated, they would measure 1 7/8" by 3 5/8". The color action player photos are bordered in white. A bonus gift is listed at the top of each card and the player's name printed below the photo. The set was sponsored by Ralph's and XTRA. The backs contain information about the bonus gift or discount available to the ticket holder. The coupons are unnumbered and are listed below in alphabetical order by subject.

|  | MINT | EXC | G-VG |
|---|---|---|---|
| COMPLETE SET (12) | 12.00 | 5.00 | 1.20 |
| COMMON PLAYER (1-12) | 1.00 | .40 | .10 |
| ☐ 1 Gary Anderson | 2.00 | .80 | .20 |
| ☐ 2 Gill Byrd | 1.50 | .60 | .15 |
| ☐ 3 Quinn Early | 2.00 | .80 | .20 |
| ☐ 4 Vencie Glenn | 1.00 | .40 | .10 |
| ☐ 5 Jamie Holland | 1.00 | .40 | .10 |
| ☐ 6 Don Macek | 1.00 | .40 | .10 |
| ☐ 7 Dennis McKnight | 1.00 | .40 | .10 |
| ☐ 8 Anthony Miller | 5.00 | 2.00 | .50 |
| ☐ 9 Ralf Mojsiejenko | 1.00 | .40 | .10 |
| ☐ 10 Leslie O'Neal | 3.00 | 1.20 | .30 |
| ☐ 11 Billy Ray Smith | 1.50 | .60 | .15 |
| ☐ 12 Lee Williams | 1.50 | .60 | .15 |

# 1991 Chargers Vons

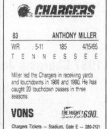

The 12-card Vons Chargers set was issued on panels measuring approximately 6 5/8" by 3 1/2". Two perforated lines divide the panels into three sections: a standard size (2 1/2" by 3 1/2") player card, a 1991 Junior Charger Official Membership Card, and a Sea World of California discount coupon. The player cards have color action player photos on the fronts, with yellow borders on a white card face. A Charger helmet and the words "Junior Chargers" appear at the top of the card. In a horizontal format with dark blue print, the back has biography, career highlights, and sponsors' logos. The cards are unnumbered and checklisted below in alphabetical order.

|  | MINT | EXC | G-VG |
|---|---|---|---|
| COMPLETE SET (12) | 7.50 | 3.00 | .75 |
| COMMON PLAYER (1-12) | .60 | .24 | .06 |
| | | | |
| ☐ 1 Rod Bernstine | 1.00 | .40 | .10 |
| ☐ 2 Gill Byrd | .75 | .30 | .07 |
| ☐ 3 Burt Grossman | .75 | .30 | .07 |
| ☐ 4 Ronnie Harmon | .75 | .30 | .07 |
| ☐ 5 Anthony Miller | 1.25 | .50 | .12 |
| ☐ 6 Leslie O'Neal | 1.00 | .40 | .10 |
| ☐ 7 Gary Plummer | .60 | .24 | .06 |
| ☐ 8 Junior Seau | 1.25 | .50 | .12 |
| ☐ 9 Billy Ray Smith | .75 | .30 | .07 |
| ☐ 10 Broderick Thompson | .60 | .24 | .06 |
| ☐ 11 Billy Joe Tolliver | .75 | .30 | .07 |
| ☐ 12 Lee Williams | .75 | .30 | .07 |

# 1992 Chargers Louis Rich

Sponsored by Louis Rich, this 52-card oversized set measures approximately 5" by 8". The fronts feature full-bleed glossy color action photos that are framed by a thin white line. The player's jersey number, name, and position appear at the lower left corner, while the sponsor logo and a replica of the team helmet are printed in the lower right corner. In addition to biographical information, the backs are dominated by a large advertisement for Louis Rich products. The cards are unnumbered and checklisted below in alphabetical order.

|  | MINT | EXC | G-VG |
|---|---|---|---|
| COMPLETE SET (52) | 30.00 | 12.00 | 3.00 |
| COMMON PLAYER (1-52) | .60 | .24 | .06 |
| | | | |
| ☐ 1 Sam Anno | .60 | .24 | .06 |
| ☐ 2 Johnnie Barnes | .60 | .24 | .06 |
| ☐ 3 Rod Bernstine | 1.00 | .40 | .10 |
| ☐ 4 Eric Bieniemy | 1.00 | .40 | .10 |

| ☐ 5 Anthony Blaylock | .60 | .24 | .06 |
|---|---|---|---|
| ☐ 6 Brian Brennan | .60 | .24 | .06 |
| ☐ 7 Marion Butts | 1.25 | .50 | .12 |
| ☐ 8 Gill Byrd | .75 | .30 | .07 |
| ☐ 9 John Carney | .75 | .30 | .07 |
| ☐ 10 Darren Carrington | .60 | .24 | .06 |
| ☐ 11 Robert Claborne | 2.00 | .80 | .20 |
| ☐ 12 Floyd Fields | .60 | .24 | .06 |
| ☐ 13 Donald Frank | .60 | .24 | .06 |
| ☐ 14 Bob Gagliano | .75 | .30 | .07 |
| ☐ 15 Leo Goeas | .60 | .24 | .06 |
| ☐ 16 Burt Grossman | .75 | .30 | .07 |
| ☐ 17 Courtney Hall | .75 | .30 | .07 |
| ☐ 18 Delton Hall | .60 | .24 | .06 |
| ☐ 19 Ronnie Harmon | 1.00 | .40 | .10 |
| ☐ 20 Steve Hendrickson | .75 | .30 | .07 |
| ☐ 21 Stan Humphries | 2.00 | .80 | .20 |
| ☐ 22 Shawn Jefferson | .75 | .30 | .07 |
| ☐ 23 John Kidd | .60 | .24 | .06 |
| ☐ 24 Shawn Lee | .60 | .24 | .06 |
| ☐ 25 Nate Lewis | .75 | .30 | .07 |
| ☐ 26 Eugene Marve | .60 | .24 | .06 |
| ☐ 27 Deems May | .60 | .24 | .06 |
| ☐ 28 Anthony Miller | 1.50 | .60 | .15 |
| ☐ 29 Chris Mims | 1.25 | .50 | .12 |
| ☐ 30 Eric Moten | .60 | .24 | .06 |
| ☐ 31 Kevin Murphy | .60 | .24 | .06 |
| ☐ 32 Pat O'Hara | .60 | .24 | .06 |
| ☐ 33 Leslie O'Neal | 1.00 | .40 | .10 |
| ☐ 34 Gary Plummer | .60 | .24 | .06 |
| ☐ 35 Marquez Pope | .60 | .24 | .06 |
| ☐ 36 Alfred Pupunu | .60 | .24 | .06 |
| ☐ 37 Stanley Richard | .75 | .30 | .07 |
| ☐ 38 David Richards | .60 | .24 | .06 |
| ☐ 39 Henry Rolling | .60 | .24 | .06 |
| ☐ 40 Bobby Ross CO | 1.25 | .50 | .12 |
| ☐ 41 Junior Seau | 1.50 | .60 | .15 |
| ☐ 42 Harry Swayne | .75 | .30 | .07 |
| ☐ 43 Broderick Thompson | .60 | .24 | .06 |
| ☐ 44 George Thornton | .60 | .24 | .06 |
| ☐ 45 Peter Tuipulotu | .60 | .24 | .06 |
| ☐ 46 Sean Vanhorse | .60 | .24 | .06 |
| ☐ 47 Derrick Walker | .60 | .24 | .06 |
| ☐ 48 Reggie E. White | .60 | .24 | .06 |
| ☐ 49 Curtis Whitley | .60 | .24 | .06 |
| ☐ 50 Blaise Winter | .75 | .30 | .07 |
| ☐ 51 Duane Young | .60 | .24 | .06 |
| ☐ 52 Mike Zandofsky | .60 | .24 | .06 |

# 1964-69 Chiefs Fairmont Dairy

These cards were featured as the side panels of half-gallon milk cartons in the Kansas City area by Fairmont Dairy. The cards were apparently issued during more than one season as there are several styles with different sizes and colors. The cards may have been issued as early as 1964 and as late as 1969. When cut, the cards measure approximately 3 3/8" by 2 3/8" (red) or 3 7/16" by 1 9/16" (black). The printing on the cards is either in black or red depending apparently on the year of issue. The fronts feature close-up player photos with the player's team, name, position, jersey number, and biographical information appearing to the right. All cards feature members of the Kansas City Chiefs. The catalog designation for this set is F120. This list below are those known at this time. We expect that there are others in the set. Additions would be welcomed, please contact the author at the address given in the introduction of this book. The cards have blank backs as is the case with most milk carton issues. Complete milk cartons would be valued at double the prices listed below.

|  | NRMT | VG-E | GOOD |
|---|---|---|---|
| COMPLETE SET (18) | 1400.00 | 650.00 | 150.00 |
| COMMON PLAYER (1-18) | 65.00 | 26.00 | 6.50 |

| | | | |
|---|---|---|---|
| ☐ 1 Fred Arbanas | 75.00 | 30.00 | 7.50 |
| (Red printing) | | | |
| ☐ 2 Bobby Bell | 125.00 | 50.00 | 12.50 |
| (Red printing) | | | |
| ☐ 3 Buck Buchanan | 125.00 | 50.00 | 12.50 |
| (Black print) | | | |
| ☐ 4 Chris Burford | 75.00 | 30.00 | 7.50 |
| (Red printing) | | | |
| ☐ 5 Len Dawson | 200.00 | 80.00 | 20.00 |
| (Red printing) | | | |
| ☐ 6 Dave Grayson | 65.00 | 26.00 | 6.50 |
| (Red printing) | | | |
| ☐ 7 Abner Haynes | 100.00 | 40.00 | 10.00 |
| (Red printing) | | | |
| ☐ 8 Sherrill Headrick | 75.00 | 30.00 | 7.50 |
| (Red printing) | | | |
| ☐ 9 Bobby Hunt | 65.00 | 26.00 | 6.50 |
| (Red printing) | | | |
| ☐ 10 Frank Jackson | 65.00 | 26.00 | 6.50 |
| (Red printing) | | | |
| ☐ 11 Curtis McClinton | 75.00 | 30.00 | 7.50 |
| (Red printing) | | | |
| ☐ 12 Bobby Ply | 65.00 | 26.00 | 6.50 |
| (Red printing) | | | |
| ☐ 13 Al Reynolds | 65.00 | 26.00 | 6.50 |
| (Red printing) | | | |
| ☐ 14 Johnny Robinson | 100.00 | 40.00 | 10.00 |
| (Red printing) | | | |
| ☐ 15 Noland Smith | 65.00 | 26.00 | 6.50 |
| ☐ 16 Smokey Stover | 65.00 | 26.00 | 6.50 |
| (Red printing) | | | |
| ☐ 17 Otis Taylor | 100.00 | 40.00 | 10.00 |
| ☐ 18 Jim Tyrer | 75.00 | 30.00 | 7.50 |
| (Red printing) | | | |

## 1969 Chiefs Kroger

This eight-card, unnumbered set was sponsored by Kroger and measures approximately 8" by 9 3/4". The front features a color painting of the player by artist John Wheeldon, with the player's name inscribed across the bottom of the picture. The back has biographical and statistical information about the player and a brief note about the artist.

| | NRMT | VG-E | GOOD |
|---|---|---|---|
| COMPLETE SET (8) | 45.00 | 18.00 | 4.50 |
| COMMON PLAYER (1-8) | 4.00 | 1.60 | .40 |
| | | | |
| ☐ 1 Buck Buchanan | 8.00 | 3.25 | .80 |
| ☐ 2 Len Dawson | 15.00 | 6.00 | 1.50 |
| ☐ 3 Mike Garrett | 6.00 | 2.40 | .60 |
| ☐ 4 Willie Lanier | 12.00 | 5.00 | 1.20 |
| ☐ 5 Jerry Mays | 4.00 | 1.60 | .40 |
| ☐ 6 Johnny Robinson | 6.00 | 2.40 | .60 |
| ☐ 7 Jan Stenerud | 8.00 | 3.25 | .80 |
| ☐ 8 Jim Tyrer | 4.00 | 1.60 | .40 |

## 1971 Chiefs Team Issue

This set of ten photos is a team-issued set. Each photo measures approximately 7" by 10" and features a black-and-white head shot bordered in white. The player's name and team name are printed in the lower white border, while the player's facsimile autograph is inscribed across the picture. The backs carry biography and career summary; some of the backs also have statistics. The photos are unnumbered and checklisted below in alphabetical order.

| | MINT | EXC | G-VG |
|---|---|---|---|
| COMPLETE SET (10) | 40.00 | 16.00 | 4.00 |
| COMMON PLAYER (1-10) | 3.50 | 1.40 | .35 |
| | | | |
| ☐ 1 Bobby Bell | 7.50 | 3.00 | .75 |
| ☐ 2 Wendell Hayes | 5.00 | 2.00 | .50 |

| | | | |
|---|---|---|---|
| ☐ 3 Ed Lothamer | 3.50 | 1.40 | .35 |
| ☐ 4 Jim Lynch | 5.00 | 2.00 | .50 |
| ☐ 5 Jack Rudnay | 5.00 | 2.00 | .50 |
| ☐ 6 Sid Smith | 3.50 | 1.40 | .35 |
| ☐ 7 Bob Stein | 3.50 | 1.40 | .35 |
| ☐ 8 Jan Stenerud | 7.50 | 3.00 | .75 |
| ☐ 9 Otis Taylor | 6.00 | 2.40 | .60 |
| ☐ 10 Jim Tyrer | 5.00 | 2.00 | .50 |

## 1984 Chiefs QuikTrip

This 16-card set was sponsored by QuikTrip and measures approximately 5" by 7". The front features a black and white posed photo of the player and the back is blank.

| | MINT | EXC | G-VG |
|---|---|---|---|
| COMPLETE SET (16) | 30.00 | 12.00 | 3.00 |
| COMMON PLAYER (1-16) | 1.50 | .60 | .15 |
| | | | |
| ☐ 1 Mike Bell | 2.00 | .80 | .20 |
| ☐ 2 Todd Blackledge | 2.50 | 1.00 | .25 |
| ☐ 3 Brad Budde | 2.00 | .80 | .20 |
| ☐ 4 Lloyd Burruss | 1.50 | .60 | .15 |
| ☐ 5 Carlos Carson | 2.00 | .80 | .20 |
| ☐ 6 Gary Green | 1.50 | .60 | .15 |
| ☐ 7 Anthony Hancock | 2.00 | .80 | .20 |
| ☐ 8 Eric Harris | 1.50 | .60 | .15 |
| ☐ 9 Lamar Hunt OWN | 5.00 | 2.00 | .50 |
| ☐ 10 Bill Kenney | 2.00 | .80 | .20 |
| ☐ 11 Ken Kremer | 1.50 | .60 | .15 |
| ☐ 12 Nick Lowery | 3.00 | 1.20 | .30 |
| ☐ 13 John Mackovic CO | 2.50 | 1.00 | .25 |
| ☐ 14 J.T. Smith | 2.50 | 1.00 | .25 |
| ☐ 15 Gary Spani | 1.50 | .60 | .15 |
| ☐ 16 Art Still | 2.00 | .80 | .20 |

## 1972 Chiquita NFL Slides

This set consists of 13 slides and a yellow plastic viewer for viewing the slides. Each slide measures approximately 3 9/16" by 1 3/4" and features two players (one on each side); each of the 26 NFL teams is represented by one player. Each side has a player summary on its middle portion, with two small color action slides at each end stacked one above the other. When the slide is placed in the viewer, the two bottom slides, which are identical, reveal the first player. Flipping the slide over reveals the other player biography and enables one to view the other two slides, which show the second player. Each side of the slides is numbered as listed below. The set is considered complete without the yellow viewer.

| | NRMT | VG-E | GOOD |
|---|---|---|---|
| COMPLETE SET (13) | 200.00 | 80.00 | 20.00 |
| COMMON PAIR | 15.00 | 6.00 | 1.50 |
| | | | |
| ☐ 1 Joe Greene | 50.00 | 20.00 | 5.00 |
| Pittsburgh Steelers | | | |
| 2 Bob Lilly | | | |
| Dallas Cowboys | | | |
| ☐ 3 Bill Bergey | 15.00 | 6.00 | 1.50 |
| Cincinnati Bengals | | | |
| 4 Gary Collins | | | |
| Cleveland Browns | | | |
| ☐ 5 Walt Sweeney | 20.00 | 8.00 | 2.00 |
| San Diego Chargers | | | |
| 6 Bubba Smith | | | |
| Baltimore Colts | | | |
| ☐ 7 Larry Wilson | 20.00 | 8.00 | 2.00 |
| St. Louis Cardinals | | | |
| 8 Fred Carr | | | |
| Green Bay Packers | | | |
| ☐ 9 Mac Percival | 20.00 | 8.00 | 2.00 |

|  | NRMT | VG-E | GOOD |
|---|---|---|---|
| Chicago Bears | | | |
| 10 John Brodie | | | |
| San Francisco 49ers | | | |
| ☐ 11 Lem Barney | 20.00 | 8.00 | 2.00 |
| Detroit Lions | | | |
| 12 Ron Yary | | | |
| Minnesota Vikings | | | |
| ☐ 13 Curt Knight | 15.00 | 6.00 | 1.50 |
| Washington Redskins | | | |
| 14 Alvin Haymond | | | |
| Los Angeles Rams | | | |
| ☐ 15 Floyd Little | 15.00 | 6.00 | 1.50 |
| Denver Broncos | | | |
| 16 Gerry Philbin | | | |
| New York Jets | | | |
| ☐ 17 Jim Mitchell | 15.00 | 6.00 | 1.50 |
| Atlanta Falcons | | | |
| 18 Paul Costa | | | |
| Buffalo Bills | | | |
| ☐ 19 Jake Kupp | 15.00 | 6.00 | 1.50 |
| New Orleans Saints | | | |
| 20 Ben Hawkins | | | |
| Philadelphia Eagles | | | |
| ☐ 21 Johnny Robinson | 15.00 | 6.00 | 1.50 |
| Kansas City Chiefs | | | |
| 22 George Webster | | | |
| Houston Oilers | | | |
| ☐ 23 Mercury Morris | 25.00 | 10.00 | 2.50 |
| Miami Dolphins | | | |
| 24 Willie Brown | | | |
| Oakland Raiders | | | |
| ☐ 25 Ron Johnson | 15.00 | 6.00 | 1.50 |
| New York Giants | | | |
| 26 Jon Morris | | | |
| New England Patriots | | | |
| ☐ xx Yellow Viewer | 40.00 | 16.00 | 4.00 |

## 1970 Clark Volpe

This 66-card set is actually a collection of team sets. Each team subset contains between six and nine cards. These unnumbered cards are listed below alphabetically by player within team as follows: Chicago Bears (1-8), Cincinnati Bengals (9-14), Cleveland Browns (15-21), Detroit Lions (22-30), Green Bay Packers (31-39), Kansas City Chiefs (40-48), Minnesota Vikings (49-57), St. Louis Cardinals (58-66). The cards measure approximately 7 1/2" by 9 15/16" (or 7 1/2" by 14" with mail-in tab intact). The back of the (top) drawing portion describes the mail-in offers for tumblers, posters, etc. The bottom tab is a business-reply mail-in card addressed to Clark Oil and Refining Corporation to the attention of Alex Karras. The artist for these drawings was Nicholas Volpe. The cards are typically found with tabs intact and hence they are priced that way below.

|  | NRMT | VG-E | GOOD |
|---|---|---|---|
| COMPLETE SET (66) | 350.00 | 140.00 | 35.00 |
| COMMON PLAYER (1-66) | 4.00 | 1.60 | .40 |
| | | | |
| ☐ 1 Ron Bull | 4.00 | 1.60 | .40 |
| ☐ 2 Dick Butkus | 20.00 | 8.00 | 2.00 |
| ☐ 3 Lee Roy Caffey | 4.00 | 1.60 | .40 |
| ☐ 4 Bobby Douglass | 5.00 | 2.00 | .50 |
| ☐ 5 Dick Gordon | 4.00 | 1.60 | .40 |
| ☐ 6 Bennie McRae | 4.00 | 1.60 | .40 |
| ☐ 7 Ed O'Bradovich | 4.00 | 1.60 | .40 |
| ☐ 8 George Seals | 4.00 | 1.60 | .40 |
| ☐ 9 Bill Bergey | 7.50 | 3.00 | .75 |
| ☐ 10 Jess Phillips | 4.00 | 1.60 | .40 |
| ☐ 11 Mike Reid | 9.00 | 3.75 | .90 |
| ☐ 12 Paul Robinson | 5.00 | 2.00 | .50 |
| ☐ 13 Bob Trumpy | 9.00 | 3.75 | .90 |
| ☐ 14 Sam Wyche | 12.00 | 5.00 | 1.20 |
| ☐ 15 Erich Barnes | 4.00 | 1.60 | .40 |
| ☐ 16 Gary Collins | 5.00 | 2.00 | .50 |
| ☐ 17 Gene Hickerson | 4.00 | 1.60 | .40 |
| ☐ 18 Jim Houston | 4.00 | 1.60 | .40 |
| ☐ 19 Leroy Kelly | 9.00 | 3.75 | .90 |
| ☐ 20 Ernie Kellerman | 4.00 | 1.60 | .40 |
| ☐ 21 Bill Nelsen | 5.00 | 2.00 | .50 |
| ☐ 22 Lem Barney | 10.00 | 4.00 | 1.00 |
| ☐ 23 Mel Farr | 5.00 | 2.00 | .50 |
| ☐ 24 Larry Hand | 4.00 | 1.60 | .40 |
| ☐ 25 Alex Karras | 9.00 | 3.75 | .90 |
| ☐ 26 Mike Lucci | 5.00 | 2.00 | .50 |
| ☐ 27 Bill Munson | 5.00 | 2.00 | .50 |
| ☐ 28 Charlie Sanders | 5.00 | 2.00 | .50 |
| ☐ 29 Tommy Vaughn | 4.00 | 1.60 | .40 |
| ☐ 30 Wayne Walker | 5.00 | 2.00 | .50 |
| ☐ 31 Lionel Aldridge | 4.00 | 1.60 | .40 |
| ☐ 32 Donny Anderson | 5.00 | 2.00 | .50 |
| ☐ 33 Ken Bowman | 4.00 | 1.60 | .40 |
| ☐ 34 Carroll Dale | 5.00 | 2.00 | .50 |
| ☐ 35 Jim Grabowski | 5.00 | 2.00 | .50 |
| ☐ 36 Ray Nitschke | 10.00 | 4.00 | 1.00 |
| ☐ 37 Dave Robinson | 5.00 | 2.00 | .50 |
| ☐ 38 Travis Williams | 4.00 | 1.60 | .40 |
| ☐ 39 Willie Wood | 9.00 | 3.75 | .90 |
| ☐ 40 Fred Arbanas | 5.00 | 2.00 | .50 |
| ☐ 41 Bobby Bell | 9.00 | 3.75 | .90 |
| ☐ 42 Aaron Brown | 4.00 | 1.60 | .40 |
| ☐ 43 Buck Buchanan | 9.00 | 3.75 | .90 |
| ☐ 44 Len Dawson | 12.00 | 5.00 | 1.20 |
| ☐ 45 Jim Marsalis | 4.00 | 1.60 | .40 |
| ☐ 46 Jerry Mays | 4.00 | 1.60 | .40 |
| ☐ 47 Johnny Robinson | 5.00 | 2.00 | .50 |
| ☐ 48 Jim Tyrer | 5.00 | 2.00 | .50 |
| ☐ 49 Bill Brown | 5.00 | 2.00 | .50 |
| ☐ 50 Fred Cox | 4.00 | 1.60 | .40 |
| ☐ 51 Gary Cuozzo | 5.00 | 2.00 | .50 |
| ☐ 52 Carl Eller | 9.00 | 3.75 | .90 |
| ☐ 53 Jim Marshall | 9.00 | 3.75 | .90 |
| ☐ 54 Dave Osborn | 5.00 | 2.00 | .50 |
| ☐ 55 Alan Page | 9.00 | 3.75 | .90 |
| ☐ 56 Mick Tingelhoff | 6.00 | 2.40 | .60 |
| ☐ 57 Gene Washington | 5.00 | 2.00 | .50 |
| ☐ 58 Pete Beathard | 5.00 | 2.00 | .50 |
| ☐ 59 John Gilliam | 5.00 | 2.00 | .50 |
| ☐ 60 Jim Hart | 7.50 | 3.00 | .75 |
| ☐ 61 Johnny Roland | 5.00 | 2.00 | .50 |
| ☐ 62 Jackie Smith | 9.00 | 3.75 | .90 |
| ☐ 63 Larry Stallings | 5.00 | 2.00 | .50 |
| ☐ 64 Roger Wehrli | 5.00 | 2.00 | .50 |
| ☐ 65 Dave Williams | 4.00 | 1.60 | .40 |
| ☐ 66 Larry Wilson | 9.00 | 3.75 | .90 |

## 1991 Classic Draft Promos

These 1991 Classic Football Draft Pick promos measure the standard 2 1/2" by 3 1/2". The front features an action color photo on a two-toned spotted gray background of the player with his name below in aqua or black print. The borders are a white and gray spotty pattern, with "Premiere Classic Edition" in the upper left hand corner and "'91" in the upper right hand corner. The back states that these cards are for promotional purposes only. These five player cards (minus the "B" variations) were also issued as an unperforated promo sheet that measures approximately 7 1/2" by 7 1/8". The sheets were given away during the 1991 12th National Sports Collectors Convention in Anaheim (July 2nd-7th). The promo sheets bear a unique serial number("X of 10,000"). The backs have the warning "For Promotional Use Only" plastered over the Premier Classic Edition logo.

|  | MINT | EXC | G-VG |
|---|---|---|---|
| COMPLETE SET (7) | 15.00 | 6.00 | 1.50 |
| COMMON PLAYER (1-5) | 1.50 | .60 | .15 |
| | | | |
| ☐ 1 Antone Davis | 1.50 | .60 | .15 |
| Tennessee | | | |

| | MINT | EXC | G-VG |
|---|---|---|---|
| ☐ 2A Raghib Rocket Ismail.............. (Black print on front) Notre Dame | 5.00 | 2.00 | .50 |
| ☐ 2B Raghib Rocket Ismail.............. (Black print on front) Notre Dame | 5.00 | 2.00 | .50 |
| ☐ 3A Todd Lyght ......................... (Blue print on front) Notre Dame | 2.00 | .80 | .20 |
| ☐ 3B Todd Lyght ......................... (Black print on front) Notre Dame | 2.00 | .80 | .20 |
| ☐ 4 Russell Maryland ................... (Blue print on front) Miami | 2.00 | .80 | .20 |
| ☐ 5 Eric Turner .............................. (Black print on front) UCLA | 2.00 | .80 | .20 |
| (Black print on front) | | | |

## 1991 Classic Draft

Russell Maryland    DT

This 50-card standard size, 2 1/2" by 3 1/2", set was issued by Classic Cards and featured most of the early picks of the 1991 National Football League draft. No team names or colleges are mentioned on the cards. Among the players in the set are number one pick Russell Maryland, Brett Favre, Alvin Harper, Raghib Ismail, Browning Nagle, and Ricky Watters. The set has a gray wallpaper type border which surrounds a small photo of the player.

| | MINT | EXC | G-VG |
|---|---|---|---|
| COMPLETE SET (50)...................... | 5.00 | 2.00 | .50 |
| COMMON PLAYER (1-50)................. | .04 | .02 | .00 |
| ☐ 1 Raghib(Rocket) Ismail .............. | 1.75 | .70 | .17 |
| ☐ 2 Russell Maryland ..................... | .40 | .16 | .04 |
| ☐ 3 Eric Turner ............................. | .20 | .08 | .02 |
| ☐ 4 Bruce Pickens ........................ | .10 | .04 | .01 |
| ☐ 5 Mike Croel ............................. | .25 | .10 | .02 |
| ☐ 6 Todd Lyght............................. | .25 | .10 | .02 |
| ☐ 7 Eric Swann ............................ | .30 | .12 | .03 |
| ☐ 8 Antone Davis ......................... | .10 | .04 | .01 |
| ☐ 9 Stanley Richard....................... | .25 | .10 | .02 |
| ☐ 10 Pat Harlow ........................... | .10 | .04 | .01 |
| ☐ 11 Alvin Harper ......................... | .90 | .36 | .09 |
| ☐ 12 Mike Pritchard....................... | .75 | .30 | .07 |
| ☐ 13 Leonard Russell ..................... | .75 | .30 | .07 |
| ☐ 14 Dan McGwire ........................ | .15 | .06 | .01 |
| ☐ 15 Bobby Wilson ........................ | .10 | .04 | .01 |
| ☐ 16 Alfred Williams....................... | .15 | .06 | .01 |
| ☐ 17 Vinnie Clark.......................... | .12 | .05 | .01 |
| ☐ 18 Kelvin Pritchett...................... | .15 | .06 | .01 |
| ☐ 19 Harvey Williams ..................... | .25 | .10 | .02 |
| ☐ 20 Stan Thomas ......................... | .10 | .04 | .01 |
| ☐ 21 Randal Hill............................ | .50 | .20 | .05 |
| ☐ 22 Todd Marinovich ..................... | .10 | .04 | .01 |
| ☐ 23 Henry Jones .......................... | .30 | .12 | .03 |
| ☐ 24 Jarrod Bunch ......................... | .25 | .10 | .02 |
| ☐ 25 Mike Dumas .......................... | .10 | .04 | .01 |
| ☐ 26 Ed King ............................... | .10 | .04 | .01 |
| ☐ 27 Reggie Johnson ...................... | .12 | .05 | .01 |
| ☐ 28 Roman Phifer ........................ | .15 | .06 | .01 |
| ☐ 29 Mike Jones ........................... | .12 | .05 | .01 |
| ☐ 30 Brett Favre............................ | 1.75 | .70 | .17 |
| ☐ 31 Browning Nagle....................... | .12 | .05 | .01 |
| ☐ 32 Esera Tuaolo ......................... | .10 | .04 | .01 |
| ☐ 33 George Thornton..................... | .04 | .02 | .00 |
| ☐ 34 Dixon Edwards....................... | .15 | .06 | .01 |
| ☐ 35 Darryll Lewis UER .................. (Misspelled Darryl) | .10 | .04 | .01 |
| ☐ 36 Eric Bieniemy ........................ | .20 | .08 | .02 |
| ☐ 37 Shane Curry .......................... | .04 | .02 | .00 |
| ☐ 38 Jerome Henderson.................. | .10 | .04 | .01 |
| ☐ 39 Wesley Carroll ....................... | .10 | .04 | .01 |
| ☐ 40 Nick Bell .............................. | .25 | .10 | .02 |
| ☐ 41 John Flannery ........................ | .04 | .02 | .00 |
| ☐ 42 Ricky Watters ........................ | 1.25 | .50 | .12 |
| ☐ 43 Jeff Graham .......................... | .30 | .12 | .03 |
| ☐ 44 Eric Moten............................ | .10 | .04 | .01 |
| ☐ 45 Jesse Campbell ...................... | .10 | .04 | .01 |
| ☐ 46 Chris Zorich.......................... | .35 | .14 | .03 |
| ☐ 47 Doug Thomas ........................ | .15 | .06 | .01 |
| ☐ 48 Phil Hansen........................... | .20 | .08 | .02 |
| ☐ 49 Kanavis McGhee ..................... | .10 | .04 | .01 |
| ☐ 50 Reggie Barrett........................ | .10 | .04 | .01 |

## 1992 Classic Draft Promos

This six-card standard-size (2 1/2" by 3 1/2") set was issued by Classic to preview the forthcoming draft pick issue. As with the regular issue foil and blister pack cards, the fronts have glossy color player photos enclosed by thin black borders. However, the color player photos on these promo cards differ from those used in the regular issue set. The Classic logo in the lower left corner is superimposed over a blue bottom stripe that includes player information. For background, the backs display the same unfocused image of a ball carrier breaking through the line in the deep, rich purple and maroon of the blister-pack cards. The backs present biography, but only the headings of the college stat categories appear. Further, the color close-up photos are also different, and the career summary has been replaced by a "News Flash" in the form of an advertisement for the draft pick set. Finally, the disclaimer "For Promotional Purposes Only" is stamped where the statistics would have been listed. The cards are numbered on the back.

| | MINT | EXC | G-VG |
|---|---|---|---|
| COMPLETE SET (6)........................... | 12.00 | 5.00 | 1.20 |
| COMMON PLAYER (1-6)................... | 1.00 | .40 | .10 |
| ☐ 1 Desmond Howard ..................... Michigan | 5.00 | 2.00 | .50 |
| ☐ 2 David Klingler.......................... Houston | 5.00 | 2.00 | .50 |
| ☐ 3 Quentin Coryatt ....................... Texas A and M | 2.00 | .80 | .20 |
| ☐ 4 Carl Pickens ........................... Tennessee | 2.00 | .80 | .20 |
| ☐ 5 Derek Brown ........................... Notre Dame | 1.50 | .60 | .15 |
| ☐ 6 Casey Weldon .......................... Florida State | 1.00 | .40 | .10 |

## 1992 Classic Draft Foil

Terrell Buckley    CB

The 1992 Classic Draft Picks Foil set contains 100 cards featuring the highest rated football players eligible for the 1992 NFL draft. The production run of the foil was limited to 14,000, ten-box cases, and to 40,000 of each bonus card. The cards measure the standard size (2 1/2" by 3 1/2"). The fronts have glossy color player photos enclosed by thin black borders. A Classic logo in the lower left corner is superimposed over a blue bottom stripe that includes player information. Against the background of an unfocused image of a ball carrier breaking through the line, the backs have biography, college statistics, and career summary, with a color head shot in the lower left corner. This 100-card set can be distinguished from the 60-card set sold in blister packs only. Although both sets are identical in design, the photos displayed on the fronts are different, as are the head shots on the backs. On some of the cards, the career summary also differs. However, the most distinctive feature is that the backgrounds on the backs of the foil-pack cards are ghosted, whereas the same backgrounds on the blister-pack cards exhibit a deep, rich purple and maroon. The cards are numbered on the back. The key cards in the set are Edgar Bennett, Marco Coleman, Quinton Coryatt, Sean Gilbert, Desmond Howard, David Klingler, Johnny Mitchell, and Carl Pickens.

|  | MINT | EXC | G-VG |
|---|---|---|---|
| COMPLETE SET (100) | 10.00 | 4.00 | 1.00 |
| COMMON PLAYER (1-100) | .05 | .02 | .00 |
| ☐ 1 Desmond Howard<br>Michigan | .90 | .36 | .09 |
| ☐ 2 David Klingler<br>Houston | .90 | .36 | .09 |
| ☐ 3 Quentin Coryatt<br>Texas A and M | .90 | .36 | .09 |
| ☐ 4 Bill Johnson<br>Michigan State | .10 | .04 | .01 |
| ☐ 5 Eugene Chung<br>Virginia Tech | .12 | .05 | .01 |
| ☐ 6 Derek Brown<br>Notre Dame | .50 | .20 | .05 |
| ☐ 7 Carl Pickens<br>Tennessee | 1.00 | .40 | .10 |
| ☐ 8 Chris Mims<br>Tennessee | .30 | .12 | .03 |
| ☐ 9 Charles Davenport<br>NC State | .15 | .06 | .01 |
| ☐ 10 Ray Roberts<br>Virginia | .12 | .05 | .01 |
| ☐ 11 Chuck Smith<br>Tennessee | .12 | .05 | .01 |
| ☐ 12 Joe Bowden<br>Oklahoma | .10 | .04 | .01 |
| ☐ 13 Mirko Jurkovic<br>Notre Dame | .05 | .02 | .00 |
| ☐ 14 Tony Smith RB<br>Southern Mississippi | .25 | .10 | .02 |
| ☐ 15 Ken Swilling<br>Georgia Tech | .05 | .02 | .00 |
| ☐ 16 Greg Skrepenak<br>Michigan | .12 | .05 | .01 |
| ☐ 17 Phillippi Sparks<br>Arizona State | .10 | .04 | .01 |
| ☐ 18 Alonzo Spellman<br>Ohio State | .20 | .08 | .02 |
| ☐ 19 Bernard Dafney<br>Tennessee | .10 | .04 | .01 |
| ☐ 20 Edgar Bennett<br>Florida State | 1.25 | .50 | .12 |
| ☐ 21 Shane Dronett<br>Texas | .20 | .08 | .02 |
| ☐ 22 Jeremy Lincoln<br>Tennessee | .15 | .06 | .01 |
| ☐ 23 Dion Lambert<br>UCLA | .10 | .04 | .01 |
| ☐ 24 Siran Stacy<br>Alabama | .10 | .04 | .01 |
| ☐ 25 Tony Sacca<br>Penn State | .15 | .06 | .01 |
| ☐ 26 Sean Lumpkin<br>Minnesota | .10 | .04 | .01 |
| ☐ 27 Tommy Vardell<br>Stanford | .60 | .24 | .06 |
| ☐ 28 Keith Hamilton<br>Pittsburgh | .30 | .12 | .03 |
| ☐ 29 Ashley Ambrose<br>Mississippi Valley | .15 | .06 | .01 |
| ☐ 30 Sean Gilbert<br>Pittsburgh | .90 | .36 | .09 |
| ☐ 31 Casey Weldon<br>Florida State | .30 | .12 | .03 |
| ☐ 32 Marc Boutte<br>LSU | .15 | .06 | .01 |
| ☐ 33 Santana Dotson<br>Baylor | .30 | .12 | .03 |
| ☐ 34 Ronnie West<br>Pittsburg State | .05 | .02 | .00 |
| ☐ 35 Michael Bankston<br>Sam Houston | .12 | .05 | .01 |
| ☐ 36 Mike Pawlawski<br>California | .05 | .02 | .00 |
| ☐ 37 Dale Carter<br>Tennessee | .25 | .10 | .02 |
| ☐ 38 Carlos Snow<br>Ohio State | .05 | .02 | .00 |
| ☐ 39 Corey Barlow<br>Auburn | .10 | .04 | .01 |
| ☐ 40 Mark D'Onofrio<br>Penn State | .10 | .04 | .01 |
| ☐ 41 Matt Blundin<br>Virginia | .30 | .12 | .03 |
| ☐ 42 George Rooks<br>Syracuse | .05 | .02 | .00 |
| ☐ 43 Patrick Rowe<br>San Diego State | .10 | .04 | .01 |
| ☐ 44 Dwight Hollier<br>North Carolina | .15 | .06 | .01 |
| ☐ 45 Joel Steed<br>Colorado | .10 | .04 | .01 |
| ☐ 46 Erick Anderson<br>Michigan | .12 | .05 | .01 |
| ☐ 47 Rodney Culver<br>Notre Dame | .25 | .10 | .02 |
| ☐ 48 Chris Hakel<br>William and Mary | .10 | .04 | .01 |
| ☐ 49 Luke Fisher<br>East Carolina | .05 | .02 | .00 |
| ☐ 50 Kevin Smith<br>Texas A and M | .30 | .12 | .03 |
| ☐ 51 Robert Brooks<br>South Carolina | .15 | .06 | .01 |
| ☐ 52 Bucky Richardson<br>Texas A and M | .25 | .10 | .02 |
| ☐ 53 Steve Israel<br>Pittsburgh | .10 | .04 | .01 |
| ☐ 54 Marco Coleman<br>Georgia Tech | .90 | .36 | .09 |
| ☐ 55 Johnny Mitchell<br>Nebraska | 1.00 | .40 | .10 |
| ☐ 56 Scottie Graham<br>Ohio State | .60 | .24 | .06 |
| ☐ 57 Keith Goganious<br>Penn State | .10 | .04 | .01 |
| ☐ 58 Tommy Maddox<br>UCLA | .60 | .24 | .06 |
| ☐ 59 Terrell Buckley<br>Florida State | .60 | .24 | .06 |
| ☐ 60 Dana Hall<br>Washington | .15 | .06 | .01 |
| ☐ 61 Ty Detmer<br>BYU | .50 | .20 | .05 |
| ☐ 62 Darryl Williams<br>Miami | .20 | .08 | .02 |
| ☐ 63 Jason Hanson<br>Washington State | .35 | .14 | .03 |
| ☐ 64 Leon Searcy<br>Miami | .12 | .05 | .01 |
| ☐ 65 Gene McGuire<br>Notre Dame | .10 | .04 | .01 |
| ☐ 66 Will Furrer<br>Virginia Tech | .30 | .12 | .03 |
| ☐ 67 Darren Woodson<br>Arizona State | .25 | .10 | .02 |
| ☐ 68 Tracy Scroggins<br>Tulsa | .15 | .06 | .01 |
| ☐ 69 Corey Widmer<br>Montana State | .10 | .04 | .01 |
| ☐ 70 Robert Harris<br>Southern | .10 | .04 | .01 |
| ☐ 71 Larry Tharpe<br>Tennessee State | .10 | .04 | .01 |
| ☐ 72 Lance Olberding<br>Randolph Oilers<br>(Eastern Football<br>League) | .05 | .02 | .00 |
| ☐ 73 Stacey Dillard<br>Oklahoma | .10 | .04 | .01 |
| ☐ 74 Troy Auzenne<br>California | .05 | .02 | .00 |
| ☐ 75 Tommy Jeter<br>Texas | .10 | .04 | .01 |
| ☐ 76 Mike Evans<br>Michigan | .05 | .02 | .00 |
| ☐ 77 Shane Collins<br>Arizona State | .10 | .04 | .01 |
| ☐ 78 Mark Thomas<br>North Carolina State | .10 | .04 | .01 |
| ☐ 79 Chester McGlockton<br>Clemson | .15 | .06 | .01 |
| ☐ 80 Robert Porcher<br>South Carolina State | .15 | .06 | .01 |
| ☐ 81 Marquez Pope<br>Fresno State | .15 | .06 | .01 |
| ☐ 82 Rico Smith<br>Colorado | .10 | .04 | .01 |
| ☐ 83 Tyrone Williams<br>Western Ontario | .10 | .04 | .01 |
| ☐ 84 Rod Smith | .10 | .04 | .01 |

Notre Dame
☐ 85 Tyrone Legette ........................ .10 .04 .01
Nebraska
☐ 86 Wayne Hawkins ....................... .05 .02 .00
Southwest Minnesota
☐ 87 Derrick Moore .......................... .25 .10 .02
Northeastern State
☐ 88 Tim Lester ............................... .12 .05 .01
Eastern Kentucky
☐ 89 Calvin Holmes ......................... .05 .02 .00
USC
☐ 90 Reggie Dwight .......................... .05 .02 .00
Troy State
☐ 91 Eddie Robinson ....................... .20 .08 .02
Alabama State
☐ 92 Robert Jones ........................... .20 .08 .02
East Carolina
☐ 93 Ricardo McDonald .................. .10 .04 .01
Pittsburgh
☐ 94 Howard Dinkins ....................... .10 .04 .01
Florida State
☐ 95 Todd Collins ............................ .15 .06 .01
Carson-Newman
☐ 96 Eddie Blake ............................. .10 .04 .01
Auburn
☐ 97 Classic Quarterbacks .............. .30 .12 .03
Matt Blundin
David Klingler
Tommy Maddox
Mike Pawlawski
Tony Sacca
Casey Weldon
☐ 98 Back to Back ........................... .30 .12 .03
Ty Detmer
Desmond Howard
☐ NNO Checklist 1 ........................... .05 .02 .00
☐ NNO Checklist 2 ........................... .05 .02 .00

## 1992 Classic Draft Blister

The 1992 Classic Draft Picks Blister set contains 60 cards featuring the highest rated football players eligible for the 1992 NFL draft. These cards were sold only in blister packs bearing unique set numbers, with a production run reportedly of 300,000 sets. The cards measure the standard size (2 1/2" by 3 1/2"). The fronts have glossy color player photos enclosed by thin black borders. A Classic logo in the lower left corner is superimposed over a blue bottom stripe that includes player information. Against the background of an unfocused image of a ball carrier breaking through the line, the backs have biography, college statistics, and career summary, with a color head shot in the lower left corner. This 60-card set can be distinguished from the 100-card set sold in foil packs only. Though the first 60 cards of both sets are identical in player selection and design, the photos displayed on the fronts are different, as are the head shots on the backs. On some of the cards, the career summary also differs. However, the most distinctive feature is that the backgrounds on the backs of the blister-pack cards exhibit a deep, rich purple and maroon, whereas the same backgrounds on the foil-pack cards are ghosted. The cards are numbered on the back.

|  | MINT | EXC | G-VG |
| --- | --- | --- | --- |
| COMPLETE SET (60) ........................ | 8.00 | 3.25 | .80 |
| COMMON PLAYER (1-60) ................ | .05 | .02 | .00 |
| ☐ 1 Desmond Howard .................... | .90 | .36 | .09 |
| Michigan |  |  |  |
| ☐ 2 David Klingler .......................... | .90 | .36 | .09 |
| Houston |  |  |  |
| ☐ 3 Quentin Coryatt ....................... | .90 | .36 | .09 |
| Texas A and M |  |  |  |
| ☐ 4 Bill Johnson ........................... | .10 | .04 | .01 |
| Michigan State |  |  |  |

☐ 5 Eugene Chung .......................... .12 .05 .01
Virginia Tech
☐ 6 Derek Brown ............................ .50 .20 .05
Notre Dame
☐ 7 Carl Pickens ........................... 1.00 .40 .10
Tennessee
☐ 8 Chris Mims .............................. .30 .12 .03
Tennessee
☐ 9 Charles Davenport .................... .15 .06 .01
NC State
☐ 10 Ray Roberts ........................... .12 .05 .01
Virginia
☐ 11 Chuck Smith .......................... .12 .05 .01
Tennessee
☐ 12 Joe Bowden ........................... .10 .04 .01
Oklahoma
☐ 13 Mirko Jurkovic ...................... .05 .02 .00
Notre Dame
☐ 14 Tony Smith (RB) .................... .25 .10 .02
Southern Mississippi
☐ 15 Ken Swilling ........................... .05 .02 .00
Georgia Tech
☐ 16 Greg Skrepenak ..................... .12 .05 .01
Michigan
☐ 17 Phillippi Sparks ..................... .10 .04 .01
Arizona State
☐ 18 Alonzo Spellman .................... .20 .08 .02
Ohio State
☐ 19 Bernard Dafney ...................... .10 .04 .01
Tennessee
☐ 20 Edgar Bennett ........................ 1.25 .50 .12
Florida State
☐ 21 Shane Dronett ........................ .20 .08 .02
Texas
☐ 22 Jeremy Lincoln ...................... .15 .06 .01
Tennessee
☐ 23 Dion Lambert ......................... .10 .04 .01
UCLA
☐ 24 Siran Stacy ............................ .10 .04 .01
Alabama
☐ 25 Tony Sacca ............................ .15 .06 .01
Penn State
☐ 26 Sean Lumpkin ........................ .10 .04 .01
Minnesota
☐ 27 Tommy Vardell ....................... .60 .24 .06
Stanford
☐ 28 Keith Hamilton ....................... .30 .12 .03
Pittsburgh
☐ 29 Ashley Ambrose ..................... .15 .06 .01
Mississippi Valley
☐ 30 John Rays .............................. .10 .04 .01
West Virginia
☐ 31 Casey Weldon ........................ .50 .20 .05
Florida State
☐ 32 Marc Boutte ........................... .15 .06 .01
LSU
☐ 33 Santana Dotson ...................... .30 .12 .03
Baylor
☐ 34 Ronnie West ........................... .05 .02 .00
Pittsburgh State
☐ 35 Michael Bankston .................... .12 .05 .01
Sam Houston
☐ 36 Mike Pawlawski ...................... .05 .02 .00
California
☐ 37 Dale Carter ............................ .25 .10 .02
Tennessee
☐ 38 Carlos Snow ........................... .05 .02 .00
Ohio State
☐ 39 Corey Barlow .......................... .10 .04 .01
Auburn
☐ 40 Mark D'Onofrio ...................... .10 .04 .01
Penn State
☐ 41 Matt Blundin ........................... .30 .12 .03
Virginia
☐ 42 George Rooks ......................... .05 .02 .00
Syracuse
☐ 43 Patrick Rowe .......................... .10 .04 .01
San Diego State
☐ 44 Dwight Hollier ........................ .15 .06 .01
North Carolina
☐ 45 Joel Steed .............................. .10 .04 .01
Colorado
☐ 46 Erick Anderson ....................... .12 .05 .01
Michigan
☐ 47 Rodney Culver ........................ .25 .10 .02
Notre Dame
☐ 48 Chris Hakel ............................ .10 .04 .01
William and Mary
☐ 49 Luke Fisher ............................ .05 .02 .00
East Carolina
☐ 50 Kevin Smith ............................ .30 .12 .03
Texas A and M
☐ 51 Robert Brooks ........................ .15 .06 .01
South Carolina
☐ 52 Bucky Richardson ................... .25 .10 .02
Texas A and M
☐ 53 Steve Israel ............................ .10 .04 .01

Pittsburgh
| | | | |
|---|---|---|---|
| ☐ 54 Tyrone Ashley | .05 | .02 | .00 |
| Mississippi | | | |
| ☐ 55 Johnny Mitchell | 1.00 | .40 | .10 |
| Nebraska | | | |
| ☐ 56 Scottie Graham | .60 | .24 | .06 |
| Ohio State | | | |
| ☐ 57 Keith Goganious | .10 | .04 | .01 |
| Penn State | | | |
| ☐ 58 Tommy Maddox | .60 | .24 | .06 |
| UCLA | | | |
| ☐ 59 Terrell Buckley | .60 | .24 | .06 |
| Florida State | | | |
| ☐ 60 Dana Hall | .15 | .06 | .01 |
| Washington | | | |

## 1992 Classic Draft LPs

The 1992 Classic Draft Picks Gold LPs Insert set contains ten cards featuring the highest rated football players eligible for the 1992 NFL draft. These ten gold foil stamped bonus cards were randomly inserted in foil packs. The production run of the foil was limited to 14,000, ten-box cases, and to 40,000 of each bonus card. The cards measure the standard size (2 1/2" by 3 1/2"). The cards are numbered on the back.

| | MINT | EXC | G-VG |
|---|---|---|---|
| COMPLETE SET (10) | 12.00 | 5.00 | 1.20 |
| COMMON PLAYER (LP1-LP10) | 1.00 | .40 | .10 |
| ☐ LP1 Desmond Howard | 4.00 | 1.60 | .40 |
| Michigan | | | |
| ☐ LP2 David Klingler | 4.00 | 1.60 | .40 |
| Houston | | | |
| ☐ LP3 Siran Stacy | 1.00 | .40 | .10 |
| Alabama | | | |
| ☐ LP4 Casey Weldon | 1.50 | .60 | .15 |
| Florida State | | | |
| ☐ LP5 Sean Gilbert | 4.00 | 1.60 | .40 |
| Pittsburgh | | | |
| ☐ LP6 Matt Blundin | 1.75 | .70 | .17 |
| Virginia | | | |
| ☐ LP7 Tommy Maddox | 3.50 | 1.40 | .35 |
| UCLA | | | |
| ☐ LP8 Derek Brown | 3.00 | 1.20 | .30 |
| Notre Dame | | | |
| ☐ LP9 Tony Smith RB | 1.50 | .60 | .15 |
| Southern Mississippi | | | |
| ☐ LP10 Tony Sacca | 1.00 | .40 | .10 |
| Penn State | | | |

## 1992 Classic NFL Game

The 1992 Classic NFL Game football set consists of 60 cards, a travel game board, player piece and die, rules, and scoreboard. The game board included with each 60-card blister pack featured a football field and a list of plays at each end with the outcome of each play determining by a roll of the die. The board is folded in half and measures approximately 15 1/2" by 6" after unfolding. The rules for the game are printed on the backs of the Andre Ware and Cris Dishman cards. The cards measure the standard size (2 1/2" by 3 1/2"). The fronts feature color player photos with a dusty rose inner border and a dark blue outer border. The player's name and position appear in a black bar at the lower right corner. The horizontal backs are white and carry a second color player photo, a "personal bio" feature, and five trivia questions with answers. The cards are numbered on the back.

| | MINT | EXC | G-VG |
|---|---|---|---|
| COMPLETE SET (62) | 10.00 | 4.00 | 1.00 |
| COMMON PLAYER (1-60) | .15 | .06 | .01 |
| ☐ 1 Steve Atwater | .15 | .06 | .01 |
| Denver Broncos | | | |
| ☐ 2 Louis Oliver | .15 | .06 | .01 |
| Miami Dolphins | | | |
| ☐ 3 Ronnie Lott | .25 | .10 | .02 |
| Los Angeles Raiders | | | |
| ☐ 4 Reggie White | .50 | .20 | .05 |
| Philadelphia Eagles | | | |
| ☐ 5 Cortez Kennedy | .35 | .14 | .03 |
| Seattle Seahawks | | | |
| ☐ 6 Derrick Thomas | .50 | .20 | .05 |
| Kansas City Chiefs | | | |
| ☐ 7 Pat Swilling | .15 | .06 | .01 |
| New Orleans Saints | | | |
| ☐ 8 Cornelius Bennett | .25 | .10 | .02 |
| Buffalo Bills | | | |
| ☐ 9 Mark Rypien | .25 | .10 | .02 |
| Washington Redskins | | | |
| ☐ 10 Todd Marinovich | .15 | .06 | .01 |
| Los Angeles Raiders | | | |
| ☐ 11 Steve Young | .75 | .30 | .07 |
| San Francisco 49ers | | | |
| ☐ 12 Warren Moon | .35 | .14 | .03 |
| Houston Oilers | | | |
| ☐ 13 Mirko Jurkovic | .15 | .06 | .01 |
| Chicago Bears | | | |
| ☐ 14 Hugh Millen | .15 | .06 | .01 |
| New England Patriots | | | |
| ☐ 15 John Friesz | .25 | .10 | .02 |
| San Diego Chargers | | | |
| ☐ 16 John Elway | .75 | .30 | .07 |
| Denver Broncos | | | |
| ☐ 17 Chris Miller | .25 | .10 | .02 |
| Atlanta Falcons | | | |
| ☐ 18 Jim Everett | .25 | .10 | .02 |
| Los Angeles Rams | | | |
| ☐ 19 Emmitt Smith | 2.00 | .80 | .20 |
| Dallas Cowboys | | | |
| ☐ 20 Johnny Johnson | .35 | .14 | .03 |
| Phoenix Cardinals | | | |
| ☐ 21 Thurman Thomas | .75 | .30 | .07 |
| Buffalo Bills | | | |
| ☐ 22 Leonard Russell | .50 | .20 | .05 |
| New England Patriots | | | |
| ☐ 23 Rodney Hampton | .50 | .20 | .05 |
| New York Giants | | | |
| ☐ 24 Marion Butts | .25 | .10 | .02 |
| San Diego Chargers | | | |
| ☐ 25 Neal Anderson | .25 | .10 | .02 |
| Chicago Bears | | | |
| ☐ 26 Barry Sanders | 1.00 | .40 | .10 |
| Detroit Lions | | | |
| ☐ 27 Dexter Carter | .15 | .06 | .01 |
| San Francisco 49ers | | | |
| ☐ 28 Gaston Green | .15 | .06 | .01 |
| Denver Broncos | | | |
| ☐ 29 Barry Word | .25 | .10 | .02 |
| Kansas City Chiefs | | | |
| ☐ 30 Eric Bieniemy | .15 | .06 | .01 |
| San Diego Chargers | | | |
| ☐ 31 Nick Bell | .35 | .14 | .03 |
| Los Angeles Raiders | | | |
| ☐ 32 Reggie Cobb | .50 | .20 | .05 |
| Tampa Bay Buccaneers | | | |
| ☐ 33 Jay Novacek | .35 | .14 | .03 |
| Dallas Cowboys | | | |
| ☐ 34 Keith Jackson | .35 | .14 | .03 |
| Philadelphia Eagles | | | |
| ☐ 35 Eric Green | .25 | .10 | .02 |
| Pittsburgh Steelers | | | |
| ☐ 36 Lawrence Dawsey | .25 | .10 | .02 |
| Tampa Bay Buccaneers | | | |
| ☐ 37 Mike Pritchard | .35 | .14 | .03 |
| Atlanta Falcons | | | |
| ☐ 38 Michael Haynes | .35 | .14 | .03 |
| Atlanta Falcons | | | |
| ☐ 39 James Lofton | .25 | .10 | .02 |
| Buffalo Bills | | | |

| | MINT | EXC | G-VG |
|---|---|---|---|
| ☐ 40 Art Monk | .25 | .10 | .02 |
| Washington Redskins | | | |
| ☐ 41 Herman Moore | .50 | .20 | .05 |
| Detroit Lions | | | |
| ☐ 42 Andre Rison | .35 | .14 | .03 |
| Atlanta Falcons | | | |
| ☐ 43 Wendell Davis | .25 | .10 | .02 |
| Chicago Bears | | | |
| ☐ 44 Sterling Sharpe | .75 | .30 | .07 |
| Green Bay Packers | | | |
| ☐ 45 Fred Barnett | .35 | .14 | .03 |
| Philadelphia Eagles | | | |
| ☐ 46 Rob Moore | .35 | .14 | .03 |
| New York Jets | | | |
| ☐ 47 Gary Clark | .25 | .10 | .02 |
| Washington Redskins | | | |
| ☐ 48 Wesley Carroll | .15 | .06 | .01 |
| New Orleans Saints | | | |
| ☐ 49 Michael Irvin | .75 | .30 | .07 |
| Dallas Cowboys | | | |
| ☐ 50 John Taylor | .25 | .10 | .02 |
| San Francisco 49ers | | | |
| ☐ 51 Robert Brooks | .15 | .06 | .01 |
| Green Bay Packers | | | |
| ☐ 52 Ray Bentley | .15 | .06 | .01 |
| Cincinnati Bengals | | | |
| ☐ 53 Eric Swann | .25 | .10 | .02 |
| Phoenix Cardinals | | | |
| ☐ 54 Amp Lee | .35 | .14 | .03 |
| San Francisco 49ers | | | |
| ☐ 55 Darryl Williams | .25 | .10 | .02 |
| Cincinnati Bengals | | | |
| ☐ 56 Wilber Marshall | .25 | .10 | .02 |
| Washington Redskins | | | |
| ☐ 57 Siran Stacy | .15 | .06 | .01 |
| Philadelphia Eagles | | | |
| ☐ 58 Chip Lohmiller | .15 | .06 | .01 |
| Washington Redskins | | | |
| ☐ 59 Rodney Culver | .25 | .10 | .02 |
| Indianapolis Colts | | | |
| ☐ 60 Tommy Vardell | .50 | .20 | .05 |
| Cleveland Browns | | | |
| ☐ NNO Cris Dishman | .15 | .06 | .01 |
| Houston Oilers | | | |
| (Rules on back) | | | |
| ☐ NNO Andre Ware | .25 | .10 | .02 |
| Detroit Lions | | | |
| (Rules on back) | | | |

## 1993 Classic Draft Preview

This standard-size (2 1/2" by 3 1/2") card was issued to preview the design of the 1993 Classic Football Draft Picks series. The front features a color action player photo with bluish-gray variegated borders. The player's name, position, and the Classic 1993 Draft emblem appear in the mustard stripe that edges the bottom of the picture. The horizontal back carries a second color action photo, biography, player profile, and complete collegiate statistics. The card is numbered on the back.

| | MINT | EXC | G-VG |
|---|---|---|---|
| COMPLETE SET (1) | 5.00 | 2.00 | .50 |
| COMMON PLAYER | 5.00 | 2.00 | .50 |
| | | | |
| ☐ PR1 Drew Bledsoe | 5.00 | 2.00 | .50 |
| Washington State | | | |

## 1993 Classic C3 Presidential Promo

Reportedly 5,000 of this standard-size (2 1/2" by 3 1/2") card were produced for charter members of the Classic Presidential Club. The horizontal fronts feature a color action photo of each player bordered

in white. The players' names are printed below the pictures, and C3 Presidential is gold foil stamped at the upper left. The back design is similar, with two more color player photos and biography displayed in a ghosted stripe running across the pictures. The importance of these two players for their respective teams is highlighted beneath the pictures. The card is unnumbered.

| | MINT | EXC | G-VG |
|---|---|---|---|
| COMPLETE SET (1) | 5.00 | 2.00 | .50 |
| COMMON PLAYER | 5.00 | 2.00 | .50 |
| | | | |
| ☐ NNO Drew Bledsoe | 5.00 | 2.00 | .50 |
| Rick Mirer | | | |

## 1993 Classic Draft Gold Promos

These standard-size (2 1/2" by 3 1/2") promo cards were sent to Classic Collectors Club members. The fronts feature color action player photos. The player's name, the word "Gold," and his position are gold foil stamped in a black stripe at the bottom. The production run "1 of 5,000" is gold foil stamped above this black stripe. The gold foil Classic logo at the upper left rounds out the front. On a blue-gray variegated background, the horizontal back has a narrowly cropped action photo, biography, and player profile. A tan pebble-grain panel designed for college statistics carries the disclaimer "For Promotional Purposes Only." The card is numbered on the back with a "PR" prefix.

| | MINT | EXC | G-VG |
|---|---|---|---|
| COMPLETE SET (2) | 7.50 | 3.00 | .75 |
| COMMON PLAYER (1-2) | 2.50 | 1.00 | .25 |
| | | | |
| ☐ PR1 Terry Kirby | 2.50 | 1.00 | .25 |
| Virginia | | | |
| ☐ PR2 Jerome Bettis | 5.00 | 2.00 | .50 |
| Notre Dame | | | |

## 1993 Classic Draft

The 1993 Classic Football Draft Picks set consists of 100 standard-size (2 1/2" by 3 1/2") cards. Randomly inserted throughout the foil packs were ten limited-print foil stamped cards, 1993 Classic Basketball Draft Pick Preview cards, 1993 Classic NFL Pro Line Preview cards, and 1,000 autographed cards by Super Bowl MVP Troy Aikman. Cards of number one pick Drew Bledsoe and number two pick Rick Mirer were exclusive to Classic until these players signed their NFL contracts. Other noteworthy cards in the set are Jerome Bettis and Terry Kirby. The production figures were 15,000 ten-box sequentially numbered cases, with 36 ten-card packs per box. The fronts feature color action player photos with blue stone-textured borders. The player's name and position is printed in a mustard bar at

the bottom of the picture. The Classic Draft Picks logo overlaps the bar and the photo slightly to the right of center. The horizontal backs carry a small action photo, biographical information, statistics, and a player profile. The cards are numbered on the back.

| | MINT | EXC | G-VG |
|---|---|---|---|
| COMPLETE SET (100) | 8.00 | 3.25 | .80 |
| COMMON PLAYER (1-100) | .05 | .02 | .00 |
| ☐ 1 Drew Bledsoe | 1.50 | .60 | .15 |
| Washington State | | | |
| ☐ 2 Rick Mirer | 1.50 | .60 | .15 |
| Notre Dame | | | |
| ☐ 3 Garrison Hearst | .40 | .16 | .04 |
| Georgia | | | |
| ☐ 4 Marvin Jones | .25 | .10 | .02 |
| Florida State | | | |
| ☐ 5 John Copeland | .25 | .10 | .02 |
| Alabama | | | |
| ☐ 6 Eric Curry | .25 | .10 | .02 |
| Alabama | | | |
| ☐ 7 Curtis Conway | .40 | .16 | .04 |
| USC | | | |
| ☐ 8 Willie Roaf | .35 | .14 | .03 |
| Louisiana Tech | | | |
| ☐ 9 Lincoln Kennedy | .15 | .06 | .01 |
| Washington | | | |
| ☐ 10 Jerome Bettis | 1.75 | .70 | .17 |
| Notre Dame | | | |
| ☐ 11 Mike Compton | .10 | .04 | .01 |
| West Virginia | | | |
| ☐ 12 John Gerak | .10 | .04 | .01 |
| Penn State | | | |
| ☐ 13 Will Shields | .12 | .05 | .01 |
| Nebraska | | | |
| ☐ 14 Ben Coleman | .10 | .04 | .01 |
| Wake Forest | | | |
| ☐ 15 Ernest Dye | .12 | .05 | .01 |
| South Carolina | | | |
| ☐ 16 Lester Holmes | .12 | .05 | .01 |
| Jackson State | | | |
| ☐ 17 Brad Hopkins | .12 | .05 | .01 |
| Illinois | | | |
| ☐ 18 Everett Lindsay | .10 | .04 | .01 |
| Mississippi | | | |
| ☐ 19 Todd Rucci | .10 | .04 | .01 |
| Penn State | | | |
| ☐ 20 Lance Gunn | .10 | .04 | .01 |
| Texas | | | |
| ☐ 21 Elvis Grbac | .25 | .10 | .02 |
| Michigan | | | |
| ☐ 22 Shane Matthews | .20 | .08 | .02 |
| Florida | | | |
| ☐ 23 Rudy Harris | .12 | .05 | .01 |
| Clemson | | | |
| ☐ 24 Richie Anderson | .15 | .06 | .01 |
| Penn State | | | |
| ☐ 25 Derek Brown RB | .50 | .20 | .05 |
| Nebraska | | | |
| ☐ 26 Roger Harper | .15 | .06 | .01 |
| Ohio State | | | |
| ☐ 27 Terry Kirby | 1.00 | .40 | .10 |
| Virginia | | | |
| ☐ 28 Natrone Means | .90 | .36 | .09 |
| North Carolina | | | |
| ☐ 29 Glyn Milburn | .60 | .24 | .06 |
| Stanford | | | |
| ☐ 30 Adrian Murrell | .12 | .05 | .01 |
| West Virginia | | | |
| ☐ 31 Lorenzo Neal | .25 | .10 | .02 |
| Fresno State | | | |
| ☐ 32 Roosevelt Potts | .60 | .24 | .06 |
| NE Louisiana | | | |
| ☐ 33 Kevin Williams RB | .15 | .06 | .01 |
| UCLA | | | |
| ☐ 34 Russell Copeland | .25 | .10 | .02 |
| Memphis State | | | |
| ☐ 35 Fred Baxter | .12 | .05 | .01 |
| Auburn | | | |
| ☐ 36 Troy Drayton | .20 | .08 | .02 |
| Penn State | | | |
| ☐ 37 Chris Gedney | .12 | .05 | .01 |
| Syracuse | | | |
| ☐ 38 Irv Smith | .15 | .06 | .01 |
| Notre Dame | | | |
| ☐ 39 Olanda Truitt | .15 | .06 | .01 |
| Mississippi State | | | |
| ☐ 40 Victor Bailey | .40 | .16 | .04 |
| Missouri | | | |
| ☐ 41 Horace Copeland | .40 | .16 | .04 |
| Miami | | | |
| ☐ 42 Ron Dickerson Jr. | .10 | .04 | .01 |
| Arkansas | | | |
| ☐ 43 Willie Harris | .05 | .02 | .00 |
| Mississippi State | | | |
| ☐ 44 Tyrone Hughes | .35 | .14 | .03 |
| Nebraska | | | |
| ☐ 45 Qadry Ismail | .60 | .24 | .06 |
| Syracuse | | | |
| ☐ 46 Reggie Brooks | 1.00 | .40 | .10 |
| Notre Dame | | | |
| ☐ 47 Sean LaChapelle | .15 | .06 | .01 |
| UCLA | | | |
| ☐ 48 O.J. McDuffie UER | .75 | .30 | .07 |
| Penn State | | | |
| ☐ 49 Larry Ryans | .05 | .02 | .00 |
| Clemson | | | |
| ☐ 50 Kenny Shedd | .05 | .02 | .00 |
| Northern Iowa | | | |
| ☐ 51 Brian Stablein | .05 | .02 | .00 |
| Ohio State | | | |
| ☐ 52 Lamar Thomas | .30 | .12 | .03 |
| Miami | | | |
| ☐ 53 Kevin Williams WR | .60 | .24 | .06 |
| Miami | | | |
| ☐ 54 Othello Henderson | .10 | .04 | .01 |
| UCLA | | | |
| ☐ 55 Kevin Henry | .10 | .04 | .01 |
| Mississippi State | | | |
| ☐ 56 Todd Kelly | .12 | .05 | .01 |
| Tennessee | | | |
| ☐ 57 Devon McDonald | .10 | .04 | .01 |
| Notre Dame | | | |
| ☐ 58 Michael Strahan | .10 | .04 | .01 |
| Texas Southern | | | |
| ☐ 59 Dan Williams | .10 | .04 | .01 |
| Toledo | | | |
| ☐ 60 Gilbert Brown | .10 | .04 | .01 |
| Kansas | | | |
| ☐ 61 Mark Caesar | .05 | .02 | .00 |
| Miami | | | |
| ☐ 62 Ronnie Dixon | .10 | .04 | .01 |
| Cincinnati | | | |
| ☐ 63 John Parrella | .10 | .04 | .01 |
| Nebraska | | | |
| ☐ 64 Leonard Renfro | .12 | .05 | .01 |
| Colorado | | | |
| ☐ 65 Coleman Rudolph | .12 | .05 | .01 |
| Georgia Tech | | | |
| ☐ 66 Ronnie Bradford | .12 | .05 | .01 |
| Colorado | | | |
| ☐ 67 Tom Carter | .25 | .10 | .02 |
| Notre Dame | | | |
| ☐ 68 Deon Figures | .25 | .10 | .02 |
| Colorado | | | |
| ☐ 69 Derrick Frazier | .10 | .04 | .01 |
| Texas A and M | | | |
| ☐ 70 Darrien Gordon | .25 | .10 | .02 |
| Stanford | | | |
| ☐ 71 Carlton Gray | .12 | .05 | .01 |
| UCLA | | | |
| ☐ 72 Adrian Hardy | .10 | .04 | .01 |
| North West State | | | |
| ☐ 73 Mike Reid | .10 | .04 | .01 |
| North Carolina St. | | | |
| ☐ 74 Thomas Smith | .10 | .04 | .01 |
| North Carolina | | | |
| ☐ 75 Robert O'Neal | .10 | .04 | .01 |
| Clemson | | | |
| ☐ 76 Chad Brown | .10 | .04 | .01 |
| Colorado | | | |
| ☐ 77 Demetrius DuBose | .15 | .06 | .01 |
| Notre Dame | | | |
| ☐ 78 Reggie Givens | .05 | .02 | .00 |
| Penn State | | | |
| ☐ 79 Travis Hill | .05 | .02 | .00 |
| Nebraska | | | |
| ☐ 80 Rich McKenzie | .10 | .04 | .01 |
| Penn State | | | |
| ☐ 81 Barry Minter | .05 | .02 | .00 |
| Tulsa | | | |
| ☐ 82 Darrin Smith | .25 | .10 | .02 |
| Miami | | | |
| ☐ 83 Steve Tovar | .15 | .06 | .01 |

Ohio State
☐ 84 Patrick Bates .......................... .15 .06 .01
Texas A and M
☐ 85 Dan Footman .......................... .12 .05 .01
Florida State
☐ 86 Ryan McNeil .......................... .15 .06 .01
Miami
☐ 87 Danan Hughes .......................... .15 .06 .01
Iowa
☐ 88 Mark Brunell .......................... .25 .10 .02
Washington
☐ 89 Ron Moore .......................... .75 .30 .07
Pittsburgh State
☐ 90 Antonio London .......................... .12 .05 .01
Alabama
☐ 91 Steve Everitt .......................... .15 .06 .01
Michigan
☐ 92 Wayne Simmons .......................... .12 .05 .01
Clemson
☐ 93 Robert Smith .......................... .40 .16 .04
Ohio State
☐ 94 Dana Stubblefield .......................... .30 .12 .03
Kansas
☐ 95 George Teague .......................... .25 .10 .02
Alabama
☐ 96 Carl Simpson .......................... .10 .04 .01
Florida State
☐ 97 Billy Joe Hobert .......................... .30 .12 .03
Washington
☐ 98 Gino Torretta .......................... .30 .12 .03
Miami
☐ 99 Checklist 1 .......................... .05 .02 .00
☐ 100 Checklist 2 .......................... .05 .02 .00
☐ AU Troy Aikman AU/1000 .......... 200.00 80.00 20.00
(Certified autograph)

## 1993 Classic Draft Gold

This set was essentially a factory set of gold versions of the regular 100-card Classic Football Draft. Moreover, individual, sequentially numbered autographed cards of Drew Bledsoe and Rick Mirer were also included in the set. The set is accompanied by a Certificate of Authenticity and a sequentially numbered, brass labeled display box; 5,000 sets were produced. Star cards are valued at three to six times the values of the regular cards. Members of the Classic Collectors Club who purchased the 100-card 1993 Classic Draft Pick Gold set also received one of only 2,000 100-card uncut sheet of the set.

|  | MINT | EXC | G-VG |
| --- | --- | --- | --- |
| COMPLETE SET (102) | 175.00 | 70.00 | 18.00 |
| COMMON PLAYER (1-100) | .30 | .12 | .03 |
| ☐ AU Drew Bledsoe AU/5000 | 60.00 | 24.00 | 6.00 |
| (Certified autograph) |  |  |  |
| ☐ AU Rick Mirer AU/5000 | 60.00 | 24.00 | 6.00 |
| (Certified autograph) |  |  |  |

## 1993 Classic Draft Stars

These standard-size (2 1/2" by 3 1/2") cards were issued one per jumbo pack. This 20-card set features "Draft Stars". The cards have a "DS" prefix on the card numbers. There was reportedly approximately one Bledsoe/Mirer "Jumbo card" in every other box.

|  | MINT | EXC | G-VG |
| --- | --- | --- | --- |
| COMPLETE SET (20) | 25.00 | 10.00 | 2.50 |
| COMMON PLAYER (DS1-DS20) | .50 | .20 | .05 |
| ☐ DS1 Drew Bledsoe | 5.00 | 2.00 | .50 |
| Washington State |  |  |  |
| ☐ DS2 Rick Mirer | 5.00 | 2.00 | .50 |
| Notre Dame |  |  |  |
| ☐ DS3 Garrison Hearst | 1.25 | .50 | .12 |
| Georgia |  |  |  |
| ☐ DS4 Marvin Jones | .75 | .30 | .07 |
| Florida State |  |  |  |
| ☐ DS5 John Copeland | .75 | .30 | .07 |
| Alabama |  |  |  |
| ☐ DS6 Eric Curry | .75 | .30 | .07 |
| Alabama |  |  |  |
| ☐ DS7 Curtis Conway | 1.25 | .50 | .12 |
| Southern Cal |  |  |  |
| ☐ DS8 Jerome Bettis | 6.00 | 2.40 | .60 |
| Notre Dame |  |  |  |
| ☐ DS9 Patrick Bates | .50 | .20 | .05 |
| Texas A and M |  |  |  |
| ☐ DS10 Tom Carter | .75 | .30 | .07 |
| Notre Dame |  |  |  |
| ☐ DS11 Irv Smith | .50 | .20 | .05 |
| Notre Dame |  |  |  |
| ☐ DS12 Robert Smith | 1.25 | .50 | .12 |
| Ohio State |  |  |  |
| ☐ DS13 O.J. McDuffie | 2.00 | .80 | .20 |
| Penn State |  |  |  |
| ☐ DS14 Roosevelt Potts | 1.75 | .70 | .17 |
| NE Louisiana |  |  |  |
| ☐ DS15 Natrone Means | 2.50 | 1.00 | .25 |
| North Carolina |  |  |  |
| ☐ DS16 Glyn Milburn | 1.75 | .70 | .17 |
| Stanford |  |  |  |
| ☐ DS17 Reggie Brooks | 3.00 | 1.20 | .30 |
| Notre Dame |  |  |  |
| ☐ DS18 Kevin Williams WR | 1.75 | .70 | .17 |
| Miami |  |  |  |
| ☐ DS19 Qadry Ismail | 1.75 | .70 | .17 |
| Syracuse |  |  |  |
| ☐ DS20 Billy Joe Hobert | .90 | .36 | .09 |
| Washington |  |  |  |
| ☐ NNO Bledsoe/Mirer | 10.00 | 4.00 | 1.00 |
| Jumbo Card |  |  |  |

## 1993 Classic Draft LPs

These limited print, foil-stamped cards were randomly inserted in 1993 Classic Football Draft Pick foil packs. The cards measure the standard size (2 1/2" by 3 1/2"), and just 45,000 of each card were produced. The fronts feature color action player photos with bluish-gray variegated borders. The player's name, position, and the Classic 1993 Draft emblem appear in the golden foil stripe that edges the bottom of the picture. In addition, "1 of 45,000" and "LP" are gold foil stamped just above the stripe. On a bluish-gray background, the horizontal back carries a second color action photo and player profile. The cards are numbered on the back.

|  | MINT | EXC | G-VG |
| --- | --- | --- | --- |
| COMPLETE SET (10) | 40.00 | 16.00 | 4.00 |
| COMMON PLAYER (LP1-LP10) | 2.00 | .80 | .20 |
| ☐ LP1 Drew Bledsoe | 9.00 | 3.75 | .90 |
| Washington State |  |  |  |
| ☐ LP2 Rick Mirer | 9.00 | 3.75 | .90 |
| Notre Dame |  |  |  |
| ☐ LP3 Garrison Hearst | 3.00 | 1.20 | .30 |
| Georgia |  |  |  |
| ☐ LP4 Marvin Jones | 2.00 | .80 | .20 |
| Florida State |  |  |  |
| ☐ LP5 John Copeland | 2.00 | .80 | .20 |
| Alabama |  |  |  |
| ☐ LP6 Eric Curry | 2.00 | .80 | .20 |
| Alabama |  |  |  |
| ☐ LP7 Curtis Conway | 3.00 | 1.20 | .30 |
| Southern Cal |  |  |  |
| ☐ LP8 Jerome Bettis | 10.00 | 4.00 | 1.00 |
| Notre Dame |  |  |  |
| ☐ LP9 Reggie Brooks | 6.00 | 2.40 | .60 |
| Notre Dame |  |  |  |
| ☐ LP10 Qadry Ismail | 4.00 | 1.60 | .40 |
| Syracuse |  |  |  |

## 1993 Classic ProLine Previews

Featuring the last five number one NFL Draft Picks, these five cards were randomly inserted in 1993 Classic Football Draft Pick foil packs. The cards measure the standard size (2 1/2" by 3 1/2"), and just 12,000 of each card were produced. The fronts from the Classic ProLine Live, Profiles and Portraits sets appear in this preview of ProLine's main sets. The backs, however, are more or less the same, featuring the set logo, year and player who was selected the number one draft pick, all printed on a gray background of diagonal Team NFL logos. The NFL and Classic logos appear in the bottom corners. The production number is shown at the bottom. The cards are numbered on the back.

|  | MINT | EXC | G-VG |
|---|---|---|---|
| COMPLETE SET (5) | 55.00 | 22.00 | 5.50 |
| COMMON PLAYER (PL1-PL5) | 3.00 | 1.20 | .30 |
| ☐ PL1 Troy Aikman<br>Dallas Cowboys | 30.00 | 12.00 | 3.00 |
| ☐ PL2 Jeff George<br>Indianapolis Colts | 6.00 | 2.40 | .60 |
| ☐ PL3 Russell Maryland<br>Dallas Cowboys | 10.00 | 4.00 | 1.00 |
| ☐ PL4 Steve Emtman<br>Indianapolis Colts | 3.00 | 1.20 | .30 |
| ☐ PL5 Drew Bledsoe<br>Portrait | 18.00 | 7.25 | 1.80 |

## 1993 Classic Superhero Comic

Illustrated by Neal Adams of Deathwatch 2,000 fame, these four comic cards were randomly inserted in 1993 Classic Football Draft Pick foil packs. The cards measure the standard size (2 1/2" by 3 1/2"), and just 15,000 of each card were produced. The fronts feature full-bleed color comic-style action poses of the player. The player's name and position appear in a mustard stripe toward the bottom of the picture. Over a ghosted version of the front photo, the horizontal backs carry a small color action photo and a summary of the player's performance. The cards are numbered on the back with an "SH" prefix.

|  | MINT | EXC | G-VG |
|---|---|---|---|
| COMPLETE SET (4) | 60.00 | 24.00 | 6.00 |
| COMMON PLAYER (SS1-SS4) | 8.00 | 3.25 | .80 |
| ☐ SS1 Troy Aikman | 30.00 | 12.00 | 3.00 |
| ☐ SS2 Drew Bledsoe | 18.00 | 7.25 | 1.80 |
| ☐ SS3 Rick Mirer | 18.00 | 7.25 | 1.80 |
| ☐ SS4 Garrison Hearst | 8.00 | 3.25 | .80 |

## 1993 Classic TONX

These 150 tonx (or player caps) were sold in a clear plastic bag; the attached paper display tag advertises that 123 players and 27 quarterbacks from all NFL teams are featured in the set. Each tonx measures approximately 1 5/8" in diameter and features a full-bleed color action player photo. The Classic logo at the bottom rounds out the front. The backs have a black background bisected by a purple stripe carrying the player's name. The tonx number, the team helmet, and logos fill out the back.

|  | MINT | EXC | G-VG |
|---|---|---|---|
| COMPLETE SET (150) | 10.00 | 4.00 | 1.00 |
| COMMON PLAYER (1-150) | .05 | .02 | .00 |
| ☐ 1 Troy Aikman<br>Dallas Cowboys | 1.00 | .40 | .10 |
| ☐ 2 Eric Allen<br>Philadelphia Eagles | .05 | .02 | .00 |
| ☐ 3 Terry Allen<br>Minnesota Vikings | .10 | .04 | .01 |
| ☐ 4 Morten Andersen<br>New Orleans Saints | .05 | .02 | .00 |
| ☐ 5 Neal Anderson<br>Chicago Bears | .10 | .04 | .01 |
| ☐ 6 Flipper Anderson<br>Los Angeles Rams | .05 | .02 | .00 |
| ☐ 7 Steve Atwater<br>Denver Broncos | .05 | .02 | .00 |
| ☐ 8 Carl Banks<br>Washington Redskins | .05 | .02 | .00 |
| ☐ 9 Patrick Bates<br>Los Angeles Raiders | .05 | .02 | .00 |
| ☐ 10 Cornelius Bennett<br>Buffalo Bills | .10 | .04 | .01 |
| ☐ 11 Rod Bernstine<br>Denver Broncos | .05 | .02 | .00 |
| ☐ 12 Jerome Bettis<br>Los Angeles Rams | 1.00 | .40 | .10 |
| ☐ 13 Steve Beuerlein<br>Phoenix Cardinals | .10 | .04 | .01 |
| ☐ 14 Bennie Blades<br>Detroit Lions | .05 | .02 | .00 |
| ☐ 15 Brian Blades<br>Seattle Seahawks | .10 | .04 | .01 |
| ☐ 16 Drew Bledsoe<br>New England Patriots | 1.00 | .40 | .10 |
| ☐ 17 Tim Brown<br>Los Angeles Raiders | .15 | .06 | .01 |
| ☐ 18 Terrell Buckley<br>Green Bay Packers | .10 | .04 | .01 |
| ☐ 19 Marion Butts<br>San Diego Chargers | .10 | .04 | .01 |
| ☐ 20 Mark Carrier<br>Chicago Bears | .05 | .02 | .00 |
| ☐ 21 Anthony Carter<br>Minnesota Vikings | .10 | .04 | .01 |
| ☐ 22 Cris Carter<br>Minnesota Vikings | .10 | .04 | .01 |
| ☐ 23 Dale Carter<br>Kansas City Chiefs | .10 | .04 | .01 |
| ☐ 24 Ray Childress<br>Houston Oilers | .10 | .04 | .01 |
| ☐ 25 Gary Clark<br>Phoenix Cardinals | .10 | .04 | .01 |
| ☐ 26 Reggie Cobb<br>Tampa Bay Buccaneers | .10 | .04 | .01 |
| ☐ 27 Marco Coleman<br>Miami Dolphins | .10 | .04 | .01 |
| ☐ 28 Curtis Conway<br>Chicago Bears | .15 | .06 | .01 |
| ☐ 29 John Copeland<br>Cincinnati Bengals | .10 | .04 | .01 |
| ☐ 30 Quentin Coryatt<br>Indianapolis Colts | .10 | .04 | .01 |
| ☐ 31 Randall Cunningham<br>Philadelphia Eagles | .15 | .06 | .01 |
| ☐ 32 Eric Curry<br>Tampa Bay Buccaneers | .10 | .04 | .01 |
| ☐ 33 Lawrence Dawsey<br>Tampa Bay Buccaneers | .10 | .04 | .01 |
| ☐ 34 Chris Doleman<br>Minnesota Vikings | .05 | .02 | .00 |
| ☐ 35 Vaughn Dunbar<br>New Orleans Saints | .10 | .04 | .01 |
| ☐ 36 Henry Ellard<br>Los Angeles Rams | .05 | .02 | .00 |
| ☐ 37 John Elway<br>Denver Broncos | .35 | .14 | .03 |
| ☐ 38 Steve Emtman<br>Indianapolis Colts | .10 | .04 | .01 |
| ☐ 39 Ricky Ervins<br>Washington Redskins | .10 | .04 | .01 |
| ☐ 40 Jim Everett<br>Los Angeles Rams | .10 | .04 | .01 |
| ☐ 41 Brett Favre<br>Green Bay Packers | .35 | .14 | .03 |
| ☐ 42 Barry Foster | .15 | .06 | .01 |

| | | | |
|---|---|---|---|
| Pittsburgh Steelers | | | |
| ☐ 43 Cleveland Gary | .05 | .02 | .00 |
| Los Angeles Rams | | | |
| ☐ 44 Jeff George | .15 | .06 | .01 |
| Indianapolis Colts | | | |
| ☐ 45 Sean Gilbert | .10 | .04 | .01 |
| Los Angeles Rams | | | |
| ☐ 46 Ernest Givins | .10 | .04 | .01 |
| Houston Oilers | | | |
| ☐ 47 Harold Green | .10 | .04 | .01 |
| Cincinnati Bengals | | | |
| ☐ 48 Kevin Greene | .05 | .02 | .00 |
| Pittsburgh Steelers | | | |
| ☐ 49 Paul Gruber | .05 | .02 | .00 |
| Tampa Bay Buccaneers | | | |
| ☐ 50 Charles Haley | .05 | .02 | .00 |
| Dallas Cowboys | | | |
| ☐ 51 Rodney Hampton | .20 | .08 | .02 |
| New York Giants | | | |
| ☐ 52 Jim Harbaugh | .10 | .04 | .01 |
| Chicago Bears | | | |
| ☐ 53 Ronnie Harmon | .05 | .02 | .00 |
| San Diego Chargers | | | |
| ☐ 54 Michael Haynes | .10 | .04 | .01 |
| Atlanta Falcons | | | |
| ☐ 55 Garrison Hearst | .25 | .10 | .02 |
| Phoenix Cardinals | | | |
| ☐ 56 Randal Hill | .10 | .04 | .01 |
| Phoenix Cardinals | | | |
| ☐ 57 Merril Hoge | .05 | .02 | .00 |
| Pittsburgh Steelers | | | |
| ☐ 58 Pierce Holt | .05 | .02 | .00 |
| Atlanta Falcons | | | |
| ☐ 59 Jeff Hostetler | .15 | .06 | .01 |
| Los Angeles Raiders | | | |
| ☐ 60 Stan Humphries | .10 | .04 | .01 |
| San Diego Chargers | | | |
| ☐ 61 Michael Irvin | .35 | .14 | .03 |
| Dallas Cowboys | | | |
| ☐ 62 Keith Jackson | .15 | .06 | .01 |
| Miami Dolphins | | | |
| ☐ 63 Rickey Jackson | .05 | .02 | .00 |
| New Orleans Saints | | | |
| ☐ 64 Haywood Jeffires | .10 | .04 | .01 |
| Miami Dolphins | | | |
| ☐ 65 Pepper Johnson | .05 | .02 | .00 |
| New York Giants | | | |
| ☐ 66 Brent Jones | .10 | .04 | .01 |
| San Francisco 49ers | | | |
| ☐ 67 Marvin Jones | .10 | .04 | .01 |
| New York Jets | | | |
| ☐ 68 Seth Joyner | .10 | .04 | .01 |
| Philadelphia Eagles | | | |
| ☐ 69 Jim Kelly | .30 | .12 | .03 |
| Buffalo Bills | | | |
| ☐ 70 Cortez Kennedy | .15 | .06 | .01 |
| Seattle Seahawks | | | |
| ☐ 71 David Klingler | .20 | .08 | .02 |
| Cincinnati Bengals | | | |
| ☐ 72 Bernie Kosar | .15 | .06 | .01 |
| Cleveland Browns | | | |
| ☐ 73 Reggie Langhorne | .05 | .02 | .00 |
| Indianapolis Colts | | | |
| ☐ 74 Mo Lewis | .10 | .04 | .01 |
| New York Jets | | | |
| ☐ 75 Howie Long | .10 | .04 | .01 |
| Los Angeles Raiders | | | |
| ☐ 76 Ronnie Lott | .15 | .06 | .01 |
| New York Jets | | | |
| ☐ 77 Charles Mann | .10 | .04 | .01 |
| Washington Redskins | | | |
| ☐ 78 Dan Marino | .75 | .30 | .07 |
| Miami Dolphins | | | |
| ☐ 79 Todd Marinovich | .10 | .04 | .01 |
| Los Angeles Raiders | | | |
| ☐ 80 Eric Martin | .10 | .04 | .01 |
| New Orleans Saints | | | |
| ☐ 81 Clay Matthews | .10 | .04 | .01 |
| Cleveland Browns | | | |
| ☐ 82 Ed McCaffrey | .10 | .04 | .01 |
| New York Giants | | | |
| ☐ 83 O.J. McDuffie | .25 | .10 | .02 |
| Miami Dolphins | | | |
| ☐ 84 Steve McMichael | .10 | .04 | .01 |
| Chicago Bears | | | |
| ☐ 85 Audray McMillian | .05 | .02 | .00 |
| Minnesota Vikings | | | |
| ☐ 86 Greg McMurtry | .10 | .04 | .01 |
| New England Patriots | | | |
| ☐ 87 Karl Mecklenburg | .10 | .04 | .01 |
| Denver Broncos | | | |
| ☐ 88 Dave Meggett | .10 | .04 | .01 |
| New York Giants | | | |
| ☐ 89 Eric Metcalf | .10 | .04 | .01 |
| Cleveland Browns | | | |
| ☐ 90 Anthony Miller | .10 | .04 | .01 |
| San Diego Chargers | | | |
| ☐ 91 Chris Miller | .15 | .06 | .01 |

| | | | |
|---|---|---|---|
| Atlanta Falcons | | | |
| ☐ 92 Sam Mills | .05 | .02 | .00 |
| New Orleans Saints | | | |
| ☐ 93 Rick Mirer | 1.00 | .40 | .10 |
| Seattle Seahawks | | | |
| ☐ 94 Johnny Mitchell | .15 | .06 | .01 |
| New York Jets | | | |
| ☐ 95 Art Monk | .15 | .06 | .01 |
| Washington Redskins | | | |
| ☐ 96 Joe Montana | 1.00 | .40 | .10 |
| Kansas City Chiefs | | | |
| ☐ 97 Warren Moon | .25 | .10 | .02 |
| Houston Oilers | | | |
| ☐ 98 Rob Moore | .15 | .06 | .01 |
| New York Jets | | | |
| ☐ 99 Brad Muster | .10 | .04 | .01 |
| New Orleans Saints | | | |
| ☐ 100 Browning Nagle | .10 | .04 | .01 |
| New York Jets | | | |
| ☐ 101 Ken Norton Jr. | .10 | .04 | .01 |
| Dallas Cowboys | | | |
| ☐ 102 Jay Novacek | .10 | .04 | .01 |
| Dallas Cowboys | | | |
| ☐ 103 Neil O'Donnell | .20 | .08 | .02 |
| Pittsburgh Steelers | | | |
| ☐ 104 Leslie O'Neal | .10 | .04 | .01 |
| San Diego Chargers | | | |
| ☐ 105 Louis Oliver | .05 | .02 | .00 |
| Miami Dolphins | | | |
| ☐ 106 Rodney Peete | .10 | .04 | .01 |
| Detroit Lions | | | |
| ☐ 107 Michael Dean Perry | .10 | .04 | .01 |
| Cleveland Browns | | | |
| ☐ 108 Carl Pickens | .15 | .06 | .01 |
| Cincinnati Bengals | | | |
| ☐ 109 Ricky Proehl | .10 | .04 | .01 |
| Phoenix Cardinals | | | |
| ☐ 110 Andre Reed | .15 | .06 | .01 |
| Buffalo Bills | | | |
| ☐ 111 Jerry Rice | .50 | .20 | .05 |
| San Francisco 49ers | | | |
| ☐ 112 Andre Rison | .25 | .10 | .02 |
| Atlanta Falcons | | | |
| ☐ 113 Leonard Russell | .15 | .06 | .01 |
| New England Patriots | | | |
| ☐ 114 Mark Rypien | .10 | .04 | .01 |
| Washington Redskins | | | |
| ☐ 115 Barry Sanders | .50 | .20 | .05 |
| Detroit Lions | | | |
| ☐ 116 Deion Sanders | .25 | .10 | .02 |
| Atlanta Falcons | | | |
| ☐ 117 Junior Seau | .15 | .06 | .01 |
| San Diego Chargers | | | |
| ☐ 118 Shannon Sharpe | .25 | .10 | .02 |
| Denver Broncos | | | |
| ☐ 119 Sterling Sharpe | .35 | .14 | .03 |
| Green Bay Packers | | | |
| ☐ 120 Clyde Simmons | .10 | .04 | .01 |
| Philadelphia Eagles | | | |
| ☐ 121 Wayne Simmons | .10 | .04 | .01 |
| Green Bay Packers | | | |
| ☐ 122 Phil Simms | .20 | .08 | .02 |
| New York Giants | | | |
| ☐ 123 Bruce Smith | .15 | .06 | .01 |
| Buffalo Bills | | | |
| ☐ 124 Emmitt Smith | 1.00 | .40 | .10 |
| Dallas Cowboys | | | |
| ☐ 126 Alonzo Spellman | .10 | .04 | .01 |
| Chicago Bears | | | |
| ☐ 127 Pat Swilling | .10 | .04 | .01 |
| Detroit Lions | | | |
| ☐ 128 John Taylor | .10 | .04 | .01 |
| San Francisco 49ers | | | |
| ☐ 129 Lawrence Taylor | .25 | .10 | .02 |
| New York Giants | | | |
| ☐ 130 Broderick Thomas | .10 | .04 | .01 |
| Tampa Bay Buccaneers | | | |
| ☐ 131 Derrick Thomas | .25 | .10 | .02 |
| Kansas City Chiefs | | | |
| ☐ 132 Thurman Thomas | .35 | .14 | .03 |
| Buffalo Bills | | | |
| ☐ 133 Andre Tippett | .10 | .04 | .01 |
| New England Patriots | | | |
| ☐ 134 Jessie Tuggle | .05 | .02 | .00 |
| Atlanta Falcons | | | |
| ☐ 135 Tommy Vardell | .15 | .06 | .01 |
| Cleveland Browns | | | |
| ☐ 136 Jon Vaughn | .10 | .04 | .01 |
| New England Patriots | | | |
| ☐ 137 Clarence Verdin | .05 | .02 | .00 |
| Indianapolis Colts | | | |
| ☐ 138 Herschel Walker | .15 | .06 | .01 |
| Philadelphia Eagles | | | |
| ☐ 139 Andre Ware | .15 | .06 | .01 |
| Detroit Lions | | | |
| ☐ 140 Chris Warren | .10 | .04 | .01 |
| Seattle Seahawks | | | |
| ☐ 141 Ricky Watters | .20 | .08 | .02 |

| | MINT | EXC | G-VG |
|---|---|---|---|
| San Francisco 49ers | | | |
| ☐ 142 Lorenzo White | .10 | .04 | .01 |
| Houston Oilers | | | |
| ☐ 143 Reggie White | .20 | .08 | .02 |
| Green Bay Packers | | | |
| ☐ 144 Alfred Williams | .10 | .04 | .01 |
| Cincinnati Bengals | | | |
| ☐ 145 Calvin Williams | .10 | .04 | .01 |
| Philadelphia Eagles | | | |
| ☐ 146 Harvey Williams | .20 | .08 | .02 |
| Kansas City Chiefs | | | |
| ☐ 147 John L. Williams | .10 | .04 | .01 |
| Seattle Seahawks | | | |
| ☐ 148 Rod Woodson | .15 | .06 | .01 |
| Pittsburgh Steelers | | | |
| ☐ 149 Barry Word | .15 | .06 | .01 |
| Kansas City Chiefs | | | |
| ☐ 150 Steve Young | .35 | .14 | .03 |
| San Francisco 49ers | | | |

## 1994 Classic Draft Promos

These standard-size (2 1/2" by 3 1/2") cards were issued to preview the design of the 1994 Classic Football Draft Picks series. The fronts feature color action shots of the players in their college uniforms. The photos are borderless, except for a royal blue lower corner that carries the player's position. The player's name is printed in the other lower corner. The borderless back carries a player action shot that is ghosted, with the exception of the area around the player's head. Player biography, statistics, and career highlights round out the back. Along the bottom are the words, "For promotional purposes only." The cards are numbered on the back with a "PR" prefix.

| | MINT | EXC | G-VG |
|---|---|---|---|
| COMPLETE SET (3) | 15.00 | 6.00 | 1.50 |
| COMMON PLAYER (PR1-PR3) | 5.00 | 2.00 | .50 |
| ☐ PR1 Marshall Faulk | 5.00 | 2.00 | .50 |
| San Diego State | | | |
| ☐ PR2 Heath Shuler | 7.50 | 3.00 | .75 |
| Tennessee | | | |
| ☐ PR3 Heath Shuler | 7.50 | 3.00 | .75 |
| Tennessee | | | |

## 1994 Classic Draft Football Previews

Randomly inserted in Images packs, this five-card standard-size (2 1/2" by 3 1/2") set features color player action shots on the fronts. These photos are borderless, except for the blue triangle in a lower

corner that carries the player's position in white lettering. The player's name appears in the other corner. The back carries a borderless color player action shot, which is ghosted, except for the area around the player's head. A congratulatory message at the bottom gives the number of sets produced: 1,950. The cards are numbered on the back with a "PR" prefix.

| | MINT | EXC | G-VG |
|---|---|---|---|
| COMPLETE SET (5) | 90.00 | 36.00 | 9.00 |
| COMMON PLAYER (PR1-PR5) | 8.00 | 3.25 | .80 |
| ☐ PR1 Heath Shuler | 50.00 | 20.00 | 5.00 |
| Tennessee | | | |
| ☐ PR2 Trent Dilfer | 25.00 | 10.00 | 2.50 |
| Fresno State | | | |
| ☐ PR3 Dan Wilkinson | 12.00 | 5.00 | 1.20 |
| Ohio State | | | |
| ☐ PR4 David Palmer | 12.00 | 5.00 | 1.20 |
| Alabama | | | |
| ☐ PR5 Johnnie Morton | 8.00 | 3.25 | .80 |
| USC | | | |

## 1994 Classic Draft

This 105-card standard-size (2 1/2" by 3 1/2") set features color player action shots on the fronts. These photos are borderless, except for the blue triangle in a lower corner that carries the player's position in white lettering. The draftee's name and his new NFL team helmet logo appear in the other corner. The back carries a borderless color player action shot, which is ghosted, except for the area around the player's head. The player's statistics, brief biography, and career highlights round out the back. The cards are numbered on the back.

| | MINT | EXC | G-VG |
|---|---|---|---|
| COMPLETE SET (105) | 10.00 | 4.00 | 1.00 |
| COMMON PLAYER (1-105) | .05 | .02 | .00 |
| ☐ 1 Heath Shuler | 2.00 | .80 | .20 |
| Tennessee | | | |
| ☐ 2 Trent Dilfer | 2.00 | .80 | .20 |
| Fresno State | | | |
| ☐ 3 Marshall Faulk | 1.50 | .60 | .15 |
| San Diego State | | | |
| ☐ 4 Errict Rhett | .50 | .20 | .05 |
| Florida | | | |
| ☐ 5 Charlie Garner | .25 | .10 | .02 |
| Tennessee | | | |
| ☐ 6 Sam Adams | .15 | .06 | .01 |
| Texas A and M | | | |
| ☐ 7 Shante Carver | .15 | .06 | .01 |
| Arizona State | | | |
| ☐ 8 Dwayne Chandler | .05 | .02 | .00 |
| Kansas | | | |
| ☐ 9 Andre Coleman | .15 | .06 | .01 |
| Kansas State | | | |
| ☐ 10 Carlester Crumpler | .10 | .04 | .01 |
| East Carolina | | | |
| ☐ 11 Charles Johnson | .50 | .20 | .05 |
| Colorado | | | |
| ☐ 12 David Palmer | .50 | .20 | .05 |
| Alabama | | | |
| ☐ 13 Dan Wilkinson | .50 | .20 | .05 |
| Ohio State | | | |
| ☐ 14 LeShon Johnson | .20 | .08 | .02 |
| Northern Illinois | | | |
| ☐ 15 Mario Bates | .25 | .10 | .02 |
| Arizona State | | | |
| ☐ 16 Glenn Foley | .20 | .08 | .02 |
| Boston College | | | |
| ☐ 17 William Gaines | .10 | .04 | .01 |
| Florida | | | |

| | | | |
|---|---|---|---|
| ☐ 18 Wayne Gandy | .12 | .05 | .01 |
| Auburn | | | |
| ☐ 19 Jason Gildon | .10 | .04 | .01 |
| Oklahoma State | | | |
| ☐ 20 Eric Gant | .10 | .04 | .01 |
| Grambling | | | |
| ☐ 21 Tre Johnson | .10 | .04 | .01 |
| Temple | | | |
| ☐ 22 Calvin Jones | .25 | .10 | .02 |
| Nebraska | | | |
| ☐ 23 Jake Kelchner | .12 | .05 | .01 |
| West Virginia | | | |
| ☐ 24 Perry Klein | .20 | .08 | .02 |
| C.W. Post | | | |
| ☐ 25 Chuck Levy | .30 | .12 | .03 |
| Arizona | | | |
| ☐ 26 Corey Louchiey | .10 | .04 | .01 |
| South Carolina | | | |
| ☐ 27 Chris Maumalanga | .10 | .04 | .01 |
| Kansas | | | |
| ☐ 28 Jamir Miller | .20 | .08 | .02 |
| UCLA | | | |
| ☐ 29 Jim Miller | .15 | .06 | .01 |
| Michigan State | | | |
| ☐ 30 Johnnie Morton | .30 | .12 | .03 |
| USC | | | |
| ☐ 31 Doug Nussmeier | .20 | .08 | .02 |
| Idaho | | | |
| ☐ 32 Vaughn Parker | .10 | .04 | .01 |
| UCLA | | | |
| ☐ 33 Darnay Scott | .25 | .10 | .02 |
| San Diego State | | | |
| ☐ 34 Fernando Smith | .10 | .04 | .01 |
| Jackson State | | | |
| ☐ 35 Lamar Smith | .15 | .06 | .01 |
| Houston | | | |
| ☐ 36 Marcus Spears | .10 | .04 | .01 |
| Northwestern State | | | |
| ☐ 37 Irving Spikes | .10 | .04 | .01 |
| N.E. Louisiana | | | |
| ☐ 38 Todd Steussie | .12 | .05 | .01 |
| California | | | |
| ☐ 39 Aaron Taylor | .12 | .05 | .01 |
| Notre Dame | | | |
| ☐ 40 John Thierry | .15 | .06 | .01 |
| Alcorn State | | | |
| ☐ 41 DeWayne Washington | .12 | .05 | .01 |
| North Carolina State | | | |
| ☐ 42 Jason Winrow | .05 | .02 | .00 |
| Ohio State | | | |
| ☐ 43 Ronnie Woolfork | .10 | .04 | .01 |
| Colorado | | | |
| ☐ 44 Bryant Young | .20 | .08 | .02 |
| Notre Dame | | | |
| ☐ 45 Arthur Bussie | .05 | .02 | .00 |
| N.E. Louisiana | | | |
| ☐ 46 Derrick Alexander | .25 | .10 | .02 |
| Michigan | | | |
| ☐ 47 Larry Allen | .10 | .04 | .01 |
| Sonoma State | | | |
| ☐ 48 Aubrey Beavers | .12 | .05 | .01 |
| Oklahoma | | | |
| ☐ 49 James Bostic | .15 | .06 | .01 |
| Auburn | | | |
| ☐ 50 Jeff Burris | .25 | .10 | .02 |
| Notre Dame | | | |
| ☐ 51 Lindsey Chapman | .10 | .04 | .01 |
| California | | | |
| ☐ 52 Isaac Davis | .15 | .06 | .01 |
| Arkansas | | | |
| ☐ 53 Lake Dawson | .25 | .10 | .02 |
| Notre Dame | | | |
| ☐ 54 Tyronne Drakeford | .10 | .04 | .01 |
| Virginia Tech | | | |
| ☐ 55 William Floyd | .35 | .14 | .03 |
| Florida State | | | |
| ☐ 56 Henry Ford | .10 | .04 | .01 |
| Arkansas | | | |
| ☐ 57 Rob Fredrickson | .12 | .05 | .01 |
| Michigan State | | | |
| ☐ 58 Aaron Glenn | .15 | .06 | .01 |
| Texas A and M | | | |
| ☐ 59 Shelby Hill | .10 | .04 | .01 |
| Syracuse | | | |
| ☐ 60 Willie Jackson | .20 | .08 | .02 |
| Florida | | | |
| ☐ 61 Joe Johnson | .15 | .06 | .01 |
| Louisville | | | |
| ☐ 62 Aaron Laing | .10 | .04 | .01 |
| New Mexico State | | | |
| ☐ 63 Kevin Lee | .20 | .08 | .02 |
| Alabama | | | |
| ☐ 64 Eric Mahlum | .10 | .04 | .01 |
| California | | | |
| ☐ 65 Steve Matthews | .15 | .06 | .01 |
| Memphis State | | | |
| ☐ 66 Willie McGinest | .20 | .08 | .02 |
| USC | | | |
| ☐ 67 Kevin Mitchell | .10 | .04 | .01 |
| Syracuse | | | |
| ☐ 68 Byron Morris | .20 | .08 | .02 |
| Texas Tech | | | |
| ☐ 69 Thomas Randolph | .10 | .04 | .01 |
| Kansas State | | | |
| ☐ 70 Tony Richardson | .10 | .04 | .01 |
| Auburn | | | |
| ☐ 71 Corey Sawyer | .12 | .05 | .01 |
| Florida State | | | |
| ☐ 72 Jason Sehorn | .10 | .04 | .01 |
| USC | | | |
| ☐ 73 Rob Waldrop | .10 | .04 | .01 |
| Arizona | | | |
| ☐ 74 Jay Walker | .15 | .06 | .01 |
| Howard | | | |
| ☐ 75 Bernard Williams | .12 | .05 | .01 |
| Georgia | | | |
| ☐ 76 Marvin Goodwin | .10 | .04 | .01 |
| UCLA | | | |
| ☐ 77 Romeo Bandison | .10 | .04 | .01 |
| Oregon | | | |
| ☐ 78 Bucky Brooks | .15 | .06 | .01 |
| North Carolina | | | |
| ☐ 79 James Folston | .10 | .04 | .01 |
| N.E. Louisiana | | | |
| ☐ 80 Donnell Bennett | .15 | .06 | .01 |
| Miami | | | |
| ☐ 81 Charlie Ward | .75 | .30 | .07 |
| Florida State | | | |
| ☐ 82 Antonio Langham | .20 | .08 | .02 |
| Alabama | | | |
| ☐ 83 Greg Hill | .35 | .14 | .03 |
| Texas A and M | | | |
| ☐ 84 Anthony Phillips | .10 | .04 | .01 |
| Texas A and M | | | |
| ☐ 85 Winfred Tubbs | .10 | .04 | .01 |
| Texas | | | |
| ☐ 86 Trev Alberts | .25 | .10 | .02 |
| Nebraska | | | |
| ☐ 87 Tim Bowens | .12 | .05 | .01 |
| Mississippi | | | |
| ☐ 88 Thomas Lewis | .20 | .08 | .02 |
| Indiana | | | |
| ☐ 89 Allen Aldridge | .10 | .04 | .01 |
| Houston | | | |
| ☐ 90 Bert Emanuel | .15 | .06 | .01 |
| Rice | | | |
| ☐ 91 Ryan Yarborough | .15 | .06 | .01 |
| Wyoming | | | |
| ☐ 92 Lonnie Johnson | .10 | .04 | .01 |
| Florida State | | | |
| ☐ 93 Isaac Bruce | .15 | .06 | .01 |
| Memphis State | | | |
| ☐ 94 Checklist 1 | .05 | .02 | .00 |
| ☐ 95 Checklist 2 | .05 | .02 | .00 |
| ☐ 96 Troy Aikman FLB | .60 | .24 | .06 |
| Dallas Cowboys | | | |
| ☐ 97 Steve Young FLB | .15 | .06 | .01 |
| Tampa Bay Buccaneers | | | |
| ☐ 98 Rick Mirer FLB | .30 | .12 | .03 |
| Seattle Seahawks | | | |
| ☐ 99 Drew Bledsoe FLB | .30 | .12 | .03 |
| New England Patriots | | | |
| ☐ 100 Jerry Rice FLB | .25 | .10 | .02 |
| San Francisco 49ers | | | |
| ☐ 101 Heath Shuler COMIC | 1.25 | .50 | .12 |
| Tennessee | | | |
| ☐ 102 Marshall Faulk COMIC | .90 | .36 | .09 |
| San Diego State | | | |
| ☐ 103 Trent Dilfer COMIC | .60 | .24 | .06 |
| Fresno State | | | |
| ☐ 104 Dan Wilkinson COMIC | .30 | .12 | .03 |
| Ohio State | | | |
| ☐ 105 David Palmer COMIC | .25 | .10 | .02 |
| Alabama | | | |
| ☐ NNO Jerry Rice Special | 15.00 | 6.00 | 1.50 |
| San Francisco 49ers | | | |
| ☐ NNO Jerry Rice AU/1994 | 100.00 | 40.00 | 10.00 |
| San Francisco 49ers | | | |

## 1994 Classic Draft Gold

Inserted one per '94 Classic Draft pack, this 105-card standard-size (2 1/2" by 3 1/2") parallel set features color player action shots on the card fronts. These photos are borderless, except for the gold-foil triangle in a lower corner that carries the player's position in white lettering. The draftee's name and his new NFL team helmet logo appear in the other corner. The set logo appears in gold foil in an upper corner. The back carries a borderless color player action shot, which is ghosted, except for the area around the player's head. The player's statistics, brief biography, and career highlights round out the

back. The cards are numbered on the back. The individual gold card values are valued at two to four times the values of the regular issue counterparts.

|  | MINT | EXC | G-VG |
|---|---|---|---|
| COMPLETE SET (105) | 40.00 | 16.00 | 4.00 |
| COMMON GOLD (1-105) | .15 | .06 | .01 |

## 1994 Classic Draft LPs

Randomly inserted in packs, these five standard-size (2 1/2" by 3 1/2") cards have borderless fronts featuring color action player cutouts set on textured metallic backgrounds. The player's name appears in an upper corner in colored metallic lettering. The back carries a borderless ghosted color player action shot. A color headshot appears in a lower corner. Career highlights appear near the top and a brief player biography appears near the bottom. A message in blue lettering states that production was limited to 20,000 of each card. The cards are numbered on the back with an "LP" prefix.

|  | MINT | EXC | G-VG |
|---|---|---|---|
| COMPLETE SET (5) | 45.00 | 18.00 | 4.50 |
| COMMON PLAYER (LP1-LP5) | 4.00 | 1.60 | .40 |
| ☐ LP1 Heath Shuler<br>Tennessee | 18.00 | 7.25 | 1.80 |
| ☐ LP2 Trent Dilfer<br>Fresno State | 9.00 | 3.75 | .90 |
| ☐ LP3 Johnnie Morton<br>USC | 4.00 | 1.60 | .40 |
| ☐ LP4 David Palmer<br>Alabama | 6.00 | 2.40 | .60 |
| ☐ LP5 Marshall Faulk<br>San Diego State | 14.00 | 5.75 | 1.40 |

## 1994 Classic Draft Stars

Inserted one per jumbo pack, this 20-card standard-size (2 1/2" by 3 1/2") set features some of the NFL's top draft picks. The full-bleed color action photos on the fronts have a metallic sheen to them. The player's name, position, and the helmet of the team which drafted him are printed toward the bottom. A second color photo appears on the back. A diagonal line divides the photo into two, and on the lower ghosted portion appears biographical information. The cards are numbered on the back "X of 20."

|  | MINT | EXC | G-VG |
|---|---|---|---|
| COMPLETE SET (20) | 15.00 | 6.00 | 1.50 |
| COMMON PLAYER (1-20) | .30 | .12 | .03 |
| ☐ 1 Trev Alberts<br>Nebraska | .50 | .20 | .05 |
| ☐ 2 Jeff Burris<br>Notre Dame | .50 | .20 | .05 |
| ☐ 3 Shante Carver<br>Arizona State | .30 | .12 | .03 |
| ☐ 4 Trent Dilfer<br>Fresno State | 2.00 | .80 | .20 |
| ☐ 5 Marshall Faulk<br>San Diego State | 3.00 | 1.20 | .30 |
| ☐ 6 William Floyd<br>Florida State | .75 | .30 | .07 |
| ☐ 7 Aaron Glenn<br>Texas A and M | .30 | .12 | .03 |
| ☐ 8 Greg Hill<br>Texas A and M | .75 | .30 | .07 |
| ☐ 9 Charles Johnson<br>Colorado | 1.00 | .40 | .10 |
| ☐ 10 Calvin Jones<br>Nebraska | .50 | .20 | .05 |
| ☐ 11 Antonio Langham<br>Alabama | .40 | .16 | .04 |
| ☐ 12 Thomas Lewis<br>Indiana | .40 | .16 | .04 |
| ☐ 13 Willie McGinest<br>USC | .40 | .16 | .04 |
| ☐ 14 Jamir Miller<br>UCLA | .40 | .16 | .04 |
| ☐ 15 Johnnie Morton<br>USC | .60 | .24 | .06 |
| ☐ 16 David Palmer<br>Alabama | 1.00 | .40 | .10 |
| ☐ 17 Darnay Scott<br>San Diego State | .50 | .20 | .05 |
| ☐ 18 Heath Shuler<br>Tennessee | 4.00 | 1.60 | .40 |
| ☐ 19 Dan Wilkinson<br>Ohio State | 1.00 | .40 | .10 |
| ☐ 20 Bryant Young<br>Notre Dame | .40 | .16 | .04 |

## 1994 Classic NFL Experience Promos

Issued to herald the release of the 100-card 1994 Classic NFL Experience set, these six standard-size (2 1/2" by 3 1/2") cards were given away at the NFL Experience Card show during Super Bowl weekend. The fronts feature borderless color player action shots. The player's name appears within a ghosted bar near the bottom. The backs also feature borderless color player action photos. The player's name, team, and position, along with highlights from the first half of the 1993 season, appear within a ghosted panel toward the bottom. The promotional disclaimer appears in white lettering across the top. The back of the Smith card differs; instead of a player photo, it has an advertisement for the Super Bowl Card Show V on a gray screened background of Super Bowl XXVIII logos. The cards are numbered on the back as "X of 6."

| | MINT | EXC | G-VG |
|---|---|---|---|
| COMPLETE SET (6)................... | 20.00 | 8.00 | 2.00 |
| COMMON PLAYER (1-6)............. | 2.00 | .80 | .20 |
| | | | |
| ☐ 1 Troy Aikman..................... | 8.00 | 3.25 | .80 |
| Dallas Cowboys | | | |
| ☐ 2 Jerry Rice........................ | 5.00 | 2.00 | .50 |
| San Francisco 49ers | | | |
| ☐ 3 Emmitt Smith................... | 8.00 | 3.25 | .80 |
| Dallas Cowboys | | | |
| ☐ 4 Derrick Thomas................ | 2.00 | .80 | .20 |
| Kansas City Chiefs | | | |
| ☐ 5 Thurman Thomas.............. | 3.00 | 1.20 | .30 |
| Buffalo Bills | | | |
| ☐ 6 Rod Woodson................... | 2.00 | .80 | .20 |
| Pittsburgh Steelers | | | |

# 1994 Classic NFL Experience

These 100 standard-size (2 1/2" by 3 1/2") cards were released by Classic Games in celebration of Super Bowl XXVIII. Classic produced 1,500 sequentially numbered cases that were offered to hobby dealers only. Cards from the 10-card 1993 Classic Rookies set and 1,994 Troy Aikman Super Bowl XXVII MVP cards were randomly inserted in the eight-card foil packs. The fronts feature full-bleed color action player photos, with the player's name displayed on a ghosted dark stripe near the bottom. The NFL Experience logo overlays the picture at one of the upper corners. The backs carries a second full-bleed action photo, with game highlights summarized on a ghosted panel toward the bottom. The cards are numbered on the back, checklisted alphabetically according to teams, and arranged alphabetically within teams as follows: Atlanta Falcons (3-6), Buffalo Bills (7-11), Chicago Bears (12-13), Cincinnati Bengals (14-16), Cleveland Browns (17-20), Dallas Cowboys (21-24), Denver Broncos (25-27), Detroit Lions (28-31), Green Bay Packers (32-34), Houston Oilers (35-38), Indianapolis Colts (39-41), Kansas City Chiefs (42-45), Los Angeles Raiders (46-49), Los Angeles Rams (50-52), Miami Dolphins (53-57), Minnesota Vikings (58-60), New England Patriots (61-62), New Orleans Saints (63-66), New York Giants (67-69), New York Jets (70-74), Philadelphia Eagles (75-77), Phoenix Cardinals (78-81), Pittsburgh Steelers (82-85), San Diego Chargers (86-88), San Francisco 49ers (89-91), Seattle Seahawks (92-94), Tampa Bay Buccaneers (95-97), and Washington Redskins (98-100).

| | MINT | EXC | G-VG |
|---|---|---|---|
| COMPLETE SET (100)................. | 20.00 | 9.00 | 2.50 |
| COMMON PLAYER (1-100)............. | .08 | .04 | .01 |
| | | | |
| ☐ 1 Checklist 1 ..................... | .08 | .04 | .01 |
| ☐ 2 Checklist 2 ..................... | .08 | .04 | .01 |
| ☐ 3 Bobby Hebert .................. | .08 | .04 | .01 |
| ☐ 4 Erric Pegram ................... | .25 | .11 | .03 |
| ☐ 5 Andre Rison .................... | .20 | .09 | .03 |
| ☐ 6 Deion Sanders ................. | .15 | .07 | .02 |
| ☐ 7 Cornelius Bennett ............ | .10 | .05 | .01 |
| ☐ 8 Jim Kelly ....................... | .25 | .11 | .03 |
| ☐ 9 Andre Reed ..................... | .12 | .05 | .02 |
| ☐ 10 Bruce Smith .................. | .12 | .05 | .02 |
| ☐ 11 Thurman Thomas.............. | .35 | .16 | .04 |
| ☐ 12 Curtis Conway ................ | .20 | .09 | .03 |
| ☐ 13 Jim Harbaugh ................ | .10 | .05 | .01 |

| | | | |
|---|---|---|---|
| ☐ 14 John Copeland ................ | .08 | .04 | .01 |
| ☐ 15 David Klingler ................ | .15 | .07 | .02 |
| ☐ 16 Carl Pickens .................. | .10 | .05 | .01 |
| ☐ 17 Eric Metcalf .................. | .10 | .05 | .01 |
| ☐ 18 Vinny Testaverde ............ | .12 | .05 | .02 |
| ☐ 19 Eric Turner ................... | .08 | .04 | .01 |
| ☐ 20 Tommy Vardell ............... | .10 | .05 | .01 |
| ☐ 21 Troy Aikman ................... | 1.25 | .55 | .16 |
| ☐ 22 Michael Irvin ................. | .30 | .14 | .04 |
| ☐ 23 Emmitt Smith ................. | 1.75 | .80 | .22 |
| ☐ 24 Kevin Williams ............... | .10 | .05 | .01 |
| ☐ 25 John Elway .................... | .35 | .16 | .04 |
| ☐ 26 Glyn Milburn .................. | .20 | .09 | .03 |
| ☐ 27 Shannon Sharpe .............. | .10 | .05 | .01 |
| ☐ 28 Herman Moore ................ | .25 | .11 | .03 |
| ☐ 29 Rodney Peete ................. | .08 | .04 | .01 |
| ☐ 30 Barry Sanders ................ | .60 | .25 | .08 |
| ☐ 31 Pat Swilling ................... | .10 | .05 | .01 |
| ☐ 32 Brett Favre .................... | .50 | .23 | .06 |
| ☐ 33 Sterling Sharpe ............... | .30 | .14 | .04 |
| ☐ 34 Reggie White .................. | .15 | .07 | .02 |
| ☐ 35 Haywood Jeffires ............. | .12 | .05 | .02 |
| ☐ 36 Warren Moon .................. | .15 | .07 | .02 |
| ☐ 37 Webster Slaughter ............ | .10 | .05 | .01 |
| ☐ 38 Lorenzo White ................. | .10 | .05 | .01 |
| ☐ 39 Quentin Coryatt .............. | .10 | .05 | .01 |
| ☐ 40 Jeff George ................... | .10 | .05 | .01 |
| ☐ 41 Roosevelt Potts .............. | .10 | .05 | .01 |
| ☐ 42 Marcus Allen .................. | .12 | .05 | .02 |
| ☐ 43 Joe Montana .................. | 1.25 | .55 | .16 |
| ☐ 44 Neil Smith .................... | .08 | .04 | .01 |
| ☐ 45 Derrick Thomas............... | .15 | .07 | .02 |
| ☐ 46 Tim Brown ..................... | .20 | .09 | .03 |
| ☐ 47 Jeff Hostetler ................ | .10 | .05 | .01 |
| ☐ 48 Raghib Ismail ................ | .15 | .07 | .02 |
| ☐ 49 Anthony Smith ............... | .08 | .04 | .01 |
| ☐ 50 Jerome Bettis ................. | 2.25 | 1.00 | .30 |
| ☐ 51 Jim Everett ................... | .12 | .05 | .02 |
| ☐ 52 T.J. Rubley .................... | .75 | .35 | .09 |
| ☐ 53 Keith Jackson ................ | .12 | .05 | .02 |
| ☐ 54 Terry Kirby .................... | .50 | .23 | .06 |
| ☐ 55 Dan Marino .................... | .75 | .35 | .09 |
| ☐ 56 O.J. McDuffie ................. | .25 | .11 | .03 |
| ☐ 57 Scott Mitchell ................ | .40 | .18 | .05 |
| ☐ 58 Cris Carter ................... | .10 | .05 | .01 |
| ☐ 59 Chris Doleman ................ | .08 | .04 | .01 |
| ☐ 60 Robert Smith .................. | .10 | .05 | .01 |
| ☐ 61 Drew Bledsoe................... | 2.25 | 1.00 | .30 |
| ☐ 62 Vincent Brisby ................ | .30 | .14 | .04 |
| ☐ 63 Derek Brown ................... | .20 | .09 | .03 |
| ☐ 64 Willie Roaf ................... | .08 | .04 | .01 |
| ☐ 65 Irv Smith ..................... | .10 | .05 | .01 |
| ☐ 66 Renaldo Turnbull............. | .08 | .04 | .01 |
| ☐ 67 Rodney Hampton ............. | .25 | .11 | .03 |
| ☐ 68 Phil Simms .................... | .10 | .05 | .01 |
| ☐ 69 Lawrence Taylor .............. | .12 | .05 | .02 |
| ☐ 70 Boomer Esiason ............... | .12 | .05 | .02 |
| ☐ 71 Marvin Jones .................. | .08 | .04 | .01 |
| ☐ 72 Ronnie Lott ................... | .12 | .05 | .02 |
| ☐ 73 Johnny Mitchell .............. | .10 | .05 | .01 |
| ☐ 74 Rob Moore ..................... | .10 | .05 | .01 |
| ☐ 75 Victor Bailey .................. | .08 | .04 | .01 |
| ☐ 76 Randall Cunningham.......... | .12 | .05 | .02 |
| ☐ 77 Ken O'Brien .................. | .08 | .04 | .01 |
| ☐ 78 Steve Beuerlein .............. | .12 | .05 | .02 |
| ☐ 79 Garrison Hearst .............. | .20 | .09 | .03 |
| ☐ 80 Ron Moore ..................... | .50 | .23 | .06 |
| ☐ 81 Ricky Proehl .................. | .10 | .05 | .01 |
| ☐ 82 Deon Figures ................. | .08 | .04 | .01 |
| ☐ 83 Barry Foster .................. | .20 | .09 | .03 |
| ☐ 84 Neil O'Donnell ............... | .15 | .07 | .02 |
| ☐ 85 Rod Woodson.................. | .12 | .05 | .02 |
| ☐ 86 Natrone Means................ | .25 | .11 | .03 |
| ☐ 87 Anthony Miller ............... | .20 | .09 | .03 |
| ☐ 88 Junior Seau ................... | .10 | .05 | .01 |
| ☐ 89 Jerry Rice .................... | .60 | .25 | .08 |
| ☐ 90 Ricky Watters ................ | .20 | .09 | .03 |
| ☐ 91 Steve Young ................... | .20 | .09 | .03 |
| ☐ 92 Brian Blades .................. | .10 | .05 | .01 |
| ☐ 93 Cortez Kennedy ............... | .12 | .05 | .02 |
| ☐ 94 Rick Mirer ..................... | 2.25 | 1.00 | .30 |
| ☐ 95 Reggie Cobb .................. | .10 | .05 | .01 |
| ☐ 96 Eric Curry .................... | .08 | .04 | .01 |
| ☐ 97 Craig Erickson ............... | .10 | .05 | .01 |
| ☐ 98 Reggie Brooks ................ | .75 | .35 | .09 |
| ☐ 99 Desmond Howard ............. | .10 | .05 | .01 |
| ☐ 100 Mark Rypien ................. | .10 | .05 | .01 |
| ☐ SP1 Troy Aikman ................ | 100.00 | 45.00 | 12.50 |
| Dallas Cowboys | | | |

# 1994 Classic NFL Experience LPs

Randomly inserted in 1994 Classic NFL Experience packs, these ten standard-size (2 1/2" by 3 1/2") cards feature 1993 first-year players.

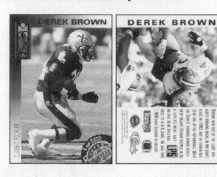

Card fronts feature color action player photos with fading blue borders on the left and above the photo. Reportedly only 2,400 of each card were produced. Each card includes embossed gold-foil Super Bowl XXVIII logo. The cards are numbered on the back with an "LP" prefix.

| | MINT | EXC | G-VG |
|---|---|---|---|
| COMPLETE SET (10) | 175.00 | 80.00 | 22.00 |
| COMMON PLAYER (LP1-LP10) | 10.00 | 4.50 | 1.25 |
| ☐ LP1 Jerome Bettis | 40.00 | 18.00 | 5.00 |
| Los Angeles Rams | | | |
| ☐ LP2 Drew Bledsoe | 40.00 | 18.00 | 5.00 |
| New England Patriots | | | |
| ☐ LP3 Reggie Brooks | 20.00 | 9.00 | 2.50 |
| Washington Redskins | | | |
| ☐ LP4 Garrison Hearst | 10.00 | 4.50 | 1.25 |
| Phoenix Cardinals | | | |
| ☐ LP5 Derek Brown | 10.00 | 4.50 | 1.25 |
| New Orleans Saints | | | |
| ☐ LP6 Terry Kirby | 15.00 | 6.75 | 1.90 |
| Miami Dolphins | | | |
| ☐ LP7 Natrone Means | 12.50 | 5.75 | 1.55 |
| San Diego Chargers | | | |
| ☐ LP8 Glyn Milburn | 12.50 | 5.75 | 1.55 |
| Denver Broncos | | | |
| ☐ LP9 Rick Mirer | 40.00 | 18.00 | 5.00 |
| Seattle Seahawks | | | |
| ☐ LP10 Robert Smith | 10.00 | 4.50 | 1.25 |
| Minnesota Vikings | | | |

# 1994 Classic ProLine Previews

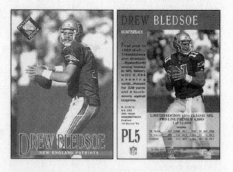

Randomly inserted in packs, the five standard-size (2 1/2" by 3 1/2") cards comprising this set feature borderless color player action shots on their fronts. The player's name in upper case lettering, along with his team's name in a colored stripe, appears at the bottom. The back carries a color player action shot with colored borders above and on one side. The player's name and position appear in the margin above the photo; career highlights and a brief biography appear in the margin alongside. Player statistics appear within a ghosted band near the bottom of the photo. A message in black lettering states that production was limited to 12,000 of each card. The cards are numbered on the back with a "PL" prefix.

| | MINT | EXC | G-VG |
|---|---|---|---|
| COMPLETE SET (5) | 50.00 | 20.00 | 5.00 |
| COMMON PLAYER (PL1-PL5) | 5.00 | 2.00 | .50 |

| | | MINT | EXC | G-VG |
|---|---|---|---|---|
| ☐ PL1 Troy Aikman | | 18.00 | 7.25 | 1.80 |
| | Dallas Cowboys | | | |
| ☐ PL2 Jerry Rice | | 10.00 | 4.00 | 1.00 |
| | San Francisco 49ers | | | |
| ☐ PL3 Steve Young | | 5.00 | 2.00 | .50 |
| | San Francisco 49ers | | | |
| ☐ PL4 Rick Mirer | | 12.00 | 5.00 | 1.20 |
| | Seattle Seahawks | | | |
| ☐ PL5 Drew Bledsoe | | 12.00 | 5.00 | 1.20 |
| | New England Patriots | | | |

# 1994 Classic ROY Sweepstakes

Randomly inserted in packs, these 20 cards feature candidates for the '94 NFL offensive Rookie of the Year. The card of the player who won the award was redeemable for a football signed by the player. The white-bordered fronts feature color action player cutouts set on an image of a football. The player's name appears in red lettering within the margin above the photo. The question, "Rookie of the Year" appears in the margin below the picture. The production run of 2,500 appears in gold foil within an upper corner of the photo. The white horizontal back carries sweepstake rules and set checklist. The player's ghosted NFL team helmet also appears. The cards are numbered on the back with a "ROY" prefix.

| | MINT | EXC | G-VG |
|---|---|---|---|
| COMPLETE SET (20) | 150.00 | 60.00 | 15.00 |
| COMMON PLAYER (1-20) | 5.00 | 2.00 | .50 |
| ☐ 1 Trent Dilfer | 25.00 | 10.00 | 2.50 |
| Fresno State | | | |
| ☐ 2 Mario Bates | 6.00 | 2.40 | .60 |
| Arizona State | | | |
| ☐ 3 Darnay Scott | 6.00 | 2.40 | .60 |
| San Diego State | | | |
| ☐ 4 Johnnie Morton | 8.00 | 3.25 | .80 |
| USC | | | |
| ☐ 5 William Floyd | 9.00 | 3.75 | .90 |
| Florida State | | | |
| ☐ 6 Errict Rhett | 12.00 | 5.00 | 1.20 |
| Florida | | | |
| ☐ 7 Greg Hill | 9.00 | 3.75 | .90 |
| Texas A and M | | | |
| ☐ 8 Lake Dawson | 6.00 | 2.40 | .60 |
| Notre Dame | | | |
| ☐ 9 Charlie Garner | 6.00 | 2.40 | .60 |
| Tennessee | | | |
| ☐ 10 Heath Shuler | 50.00 | 20.00 | 5.00 |
| Tennessee | | | |
| ☐ 11 Derrick Alexander | 6.00 | 2.40 | .60 |
| Michigan | | | |
| ☐ 12 LeShon Johnson | 5.00 | 2.00 | .50 |
| Northern Illinois | | | |
| ☐ 13 Kevin Lee | 5.00 | 2.00 | .50 |
| Alabama | | | |
| ☐ 14 David Palmer | 12.00 | 5.00 | 1.20 |
| Alabama | | | |
| ☐ 15 Charles Johnson | 12.00 | 5.00 | 1.20 |
| Colorado | | | |
| ☐ 16 Chuck Levy | 8.00 | 3.25 | .80 |
| Arizona | | | |
| ☐ 17 Calvin Jones | 6.00 | 2.40 | .60 |
| Nebraska | | | |
| ☐ 18 Thomas Lewis | 5.00 | 2.00 | .50 |
| Indiana | | | |
| ☐ 19 Marshall Faulk | 35.00 | 14.00 | 3.50 |
| San Diego State | | | |
| ☐ 20 Field Card | 5.00 | 2.00 | .50 |

# 1964 Coke Caps All-Stars AFL

These caps were issued in AFL cities (and some other cities as well) along with the local team caps. The AFL city Cap Saver sheets had separate sections in which to affix both the local team's caps and the All-Stars' caps. The caps measure approximately 1 1/8" in diameter and have the Coke logo and a football on the outside, while the inside has the player's face printed in black, with text surrounding the face. A Cap Saver sheet was issued to aid in collecting the bottle caps. The consumer could turn in his completed sheet to receive various prizes. The caps are unnumbered and checklisted below in alphabetical order. These "Coke" caps were typically also available with other Coca-Cola products such as Fresca and Tab.

| | NRMT | VG-E | GOOD |
|---|---|---|---|
| COMPLETE SET (44) | 150.00 | 60.00 | 15.00 |
| COMMON PLAYER (1-44) | 3.00 | 1.20 | .30 |
| ☐ 1 Tom Addison<br>Boston Patriots | 3.00 | 1.20 | .30 |
| ☐ 2 Dalva Allen<br>Oakland Raiders | 3.00 | 1.20 | .30 |
| ☐ 3 Lance Alworth<br>San Diego Chargers | 15.00 | 6.00 | 1.50 |
| ☐ 4 Houston Antwine<br>Boston Patriots | 3.00 | 1.20 | .30 |
| ☐ 5 Fred Arbanas<br>Kansas City Chiefs | 4.00 | 1.60 | .40 |
| ☐ 6 Tony Banfield<br>Houston Oilers | 3.00 | 1.20 | .30 |
| ☐ 7 Stew Barber<br>Buffalo Bills | 3.00 | 1.20 | .30 |
| ☐ 8 George Blair<br>San Diego Chargers | 3.00 | 1.20 | .30 |
| ☐ 9 Mel Branch<br>Kansas City Chiefs | 3.00 | 1.20 | .30 |
| ☐ 10 Nick Buoniconti<br>Boston Patriots | 10.00 | 4.00 | 1.00 |
| ☐ 11 Doug Cline<br>Houston Oilers | 3.00 | 1.20 | .30 |
| ☐ 12 Eldon Danenhauer<br>Denver Broncos | 3.00 | 1.20 | .30 |
| ☐ 13 Clem Daniels<br>Oakland Raiders | 4.00 | 1.60 | .40 |
| ☐ 14 Larry Eisenhauer<br>Boston Patriots | 3.00 | 1.20 | .30 |
| ☐ 15 Earl Faison<br>San Diego Chargers | 3.00 | 1.20 | .30 |
| ☐ 16 Cookie Gilchrist<br>Buffalo Bills | 6.00 | 2.40 | .60 |
| ☐ 17 Fred Glick<br>Houston Oilers | 3.00 | 1.20 | .30 |
| ☐ 18 Larry Grantham<br>New York Jets | 4.00 | 1.60 | .40 |
| ☐ 19 Ron Hall<br>Boston Patriots | 3.00 | 1.20 | .30 |
| ☐ 20 Charlie Hennigan<br>Houston Oilers | 5.00 | 2.00 | .50 |
| ☐ 21 E.J. Holub<br>Kansas City Chiefs | 4.00 | 1.60 | .40 |
| ☐ 22 Ed Husmann<br>Houston Oilers | 3.00 | 1.20 | .30 |
| ☐ 23 Jack Kemp<br>Buffalo Bills | 30.00 | 12.00 | 3.00 |
| ☐ 24 Dave Kocourek<br>San Diego Chargers | 3.00 | 1.20 | .30 |
| ☐ 25 Keith Lincoln<br>San Diego Chargers | 5.00 | 2.00 | .50 |
| ☐ 26 Charley Long<br>Boston Patriots | 3.00 | 1.20 | .30 |
| ☐ 27 Paul Lowe<br>San Diego Chargers | 5.00 | 2.00 | .50 |
| ☐ 28 Archie Matsos<br>Oakland Raiders | 3.00 | 1.20 | .30 |
| ☐ 29 Jerry Mays<br>Kansas City Chiefs | 4.00 | 1.60 | .40 |
| ☐ 30 Ron Mix<br>San Diego Chargers | 7.50 | 3.00 | .75 |
| ☐ 31 Tom Morrow<br>Oakland Raiders | 3.00 | 1.20 | .30 |
| ☐ 32 Billy Neighbors<br>Boston Patriots | 4.00 | 1.60 | .40 |
| ☐ 33 Jim Otto<br>Oakland Raiders | 7.50 | 3.00 | .75 |
| ☐ 34 Art Powell<br>Oakland Raiders | 4.00 | 1.60 | .40 |
| ☐ 35 Johnny Robinson<br>Kansas City Chiefs | 5.00 | 2.00 | .50 |
| ☐ 36 Tobin Rote<br>San Diego Chargers | 5.00 | 2.00 | .50 |
| ☐ 37 Bob Schmidt<br>Houston Oilers | 3.00 | 1.20 | .30 |
| ☐ 38 Tom Sestak<br>Buffalo Bills | 3.00 | 1.20 | .30 |
| ☐ 39 Billy Shaw | 3.00 | 1.20 | .30 |

| | | | |
|---|---|---|---|
| Buffalo Bills | | | |
| ☐ 40 Bob Talamini<br>Houston Oilers | 3.00 | 1.20 | .30 |
| ☐ 41 Lionel Taylor<br>Denver Broncos | 5.00 | 2.00 | .50 |
| ☐ 42 Jim Tyrer<br>Kansas City Chiefs | 4.00 | 1.60 | .40 |
| ☐ 43 Dick Westmoreland<br>San Diego Chargers | 3.00 | 1.20 | .30 |
| ☐ 44 Fred Williamson<br>Oakland Raiders | 6.00 | 2.40 | .60 |

# 1964 Coke Caps All-Stars NFL

These caps were issued in NFL cities (and some other cities as well) along with the local team caps. The NFL city Cap Saver sheets had separate sections in which to affix both the local team's caps and the All-Stars' caps. The caps measure approximately 1 1/8" in diameter and have the Coke logo and a football on the outside, while the inside has the player's face printed in black, with text surrounding the face. A Cap Saver sheet was issued to aid in collecting the bottle caps. The consumer could turn in his completed sheet to receive various prizes. The caps are unnumbered and checklisted below in alphabetical order. These "Coke" caps were typically also available with other Coca-Cola products such as Fresca and Tab.

| | NRMT | VG-E | GOOD |
|---|---|---|---|
| COMPLETE SET (44) | 200.00 | 80.00 | 20.00 |
| COMMON PLAYER (1-44) | 3.00 | 1.20 | .30 |
| ☐ 1 Doug Atkins<br>Chicago Bears | 7.50 | 3.00 | .75 |
| ☐ 2 Terry Barr<br>Detroit Lions | 3.00 | 1.20 | .30 |
| ☐ 3 Jim Brown<br>Cleveland Browns | 25.00 | 10.00 | 2.50 |
| ☐ 4 Roger Brown<br>Detroit Lions | 4.00 | 1.60 | .40 |
| ☐ 5 Roosevelt Brown<br>New York Giants | 7.50 | 3.00 | .75 |
| ☐ 6 Timmy Brown<br>Philadelphia Eagles | 5.00 | 2.00 | .50 |
| ☐ 7 Bobby Joe Conrad<br>St. Louis Cardinals | 4.00 | 1.60 | .40 |
| ☐ 8 Willie Davis<br>Green Bay Packers | 7.50 | 3.00 | .75 |
| ☐ 9 Bob DeMarco<br>St. Louis Cardinals | 3.00 | 1.20 | .30 |
| ☐ 10 Darrell Dess<br>New York Giants | 3.00 | 1.20 | .30 |
| ☐ 11 Mike Ditka<br>Chicago Bears | 15.00 | 6.00 | 1.50 |
| ☐ 12 Bill Forester<br>Green Bay Packers | 4.00 | 1.60 | .40 |
| ☐ 13 Joe Fortunato<br>Chicago Bears | 3.00 | 1.20 | .30 |
| ☐ 14 Bill George<br>Chicago Bears | 7.50 | 3.00 | .75 |
| ☐ 15 Ken Gray<br>St. Louis Cardinals | 4.00 | 1.60 | .40 |
| ☐ 16 Forrest Gregg<br>Green Bay Packers | 7.50 | 3.00 | .75 |
| ☐ 17 Roosevelt Grier<br>Los Angeles Rams | 6.00 | 2.40 | .60 |
| ☐ 18 Henry Jordan<br>Green Bay Packers | 5.00 | 2.00 | .50 |
| ☐ 19 Jim Katcavage<br>New York Giants | 3.00 | 1.20 | .30 |
| ☐ 20 Jerry Kramer<br>Green Bay Packers | 6.00 | 2.40 | .60 |
| ☐ 21 Ron Kramer<br>Green Bay Packers | 4.00 | 1.60 | .40 |
| ☐ 22 Dick Lane<br>Detroit Lions | 7.50 | 3.00 | .75 |
| ☐ 23 Dick Lynch<br>New York Giants | 4.00 | 1.60 | .40 |
| ☐ 24 Gino Marchetti<br>Baltimore Colts | 7.50 | 3.00 | .75 |
| ☐ 25 Tommy Mason | 4.00 | 1.60 | .40 |

Minnesota Vikings
| | | | |
|---|---|---|---|
| ☐ 26 Ed Meador | 4.00 | 1.60 | .40 |

Los Angeles Rams
| | | | |
|---|---|---|---|
| ☐ 27 Bobby Mitchell | 7.50 | 3.00 | .75 |

Washington Redskins
| | | | |
|---|---|---|---|
| ☐ 28 Larry Morris | 3.00 | 1.20 | .30 |

Chicago Bears
| | | | |
|---|---|---|---|
| ☐ 29 Merlin Olsen | 7.50 | 3.00 | .75 |

Los Angeles Rams
| | | | |
|---|---|---|---|
| ☐ 30 Jim Parker | 7.50 | 3.00 | .75 |

Baltimore Colts
| | | | |
|---|---|---|---|
| ☐ 31 Jim Patton | 4.00 | 1.60 | .40 |

New York Giants
| | | | |
|---|---|---|---|
| ☐ 32 Myron Pottios | 4.00 | 1.60 | .40 |

Pittsburgh Steelers
| | | | |
|---|---|---|---|
| ☐ 33 Jim Ringo | 7.50 | 3.00 | .75 |

Green Bay Packers
| | | | |
|---|---|---|---|
| ☐ 34 Dick Schafrath | 4.00 | 1.60 | .40 |

Cleveland Browns
| | | | |
|---|---|---|---|
| ☐ 35 Joe Schmidt | 7.50 | 3.00 | .75 |

Detroit Lions
| | | | |
|---|---|---|---|
| ☐ 36 Del Shofner | 5.00 | 2.00 | .50 |

New York Giants
| | | | |
|---|---|---|---|
| ☐ 37 Bob St. Clair | 7.50 | 3.00 | .75 |

San Francisco 49ers
| | | | |
|---|---|---|---|
| ☐ 38 Jim Taylor | 10.00 | 4.00 | 1.00 |

Green Bay Packers
| | | | |
|---|---|---|---|
| ☐ 39 Roosevelt Taylor | 3.00 | 1.20 | .30 |

Chicago Bears
| | | | |
|---|---|---|---|
| ☐ 40 Y.A. Tittle | 12.00 | 5.00 | 1.20 |

New York Giants
| | | | |
|---|---|---|---|
| ☐ 41 John Unitas | 20.00 | 8.00 | 2.00 |

Baltimore Colts
| | | | |
|---|---|---|---|
| ☐ 42 Larry Wilson | 7.50 | 3.00 | .75 |

St. Louis Cardinals
| | | | |
|---|---|---|---|
| ☐ 43 Willie Wood | 7.50 | 3.00 | .75 |

Green Bay Packers
| | | | |
|---|---|---|---|
| ☐ 44 Abe Woodson | 4.00 | 1.60 | .40 |

San Francisco 49ers

## 1964 Coke Caps Browns

This set of 35 Coke caps was issued on bottled soft drinks in Ohio and featured Cleveland Browns players. Collectors who assembled the entire set could redeem it (before the expiration date) at one of several redemption centers listed on the Cap-Saver sheet and receive a prize. The caps measure approximately 1 1/8" in diameter. The cap top is stamped with a picture of a football, and inside the cap under the cork is a likeness of a Browns player. The caps are unnumbered and checklisted below in alphabetical order. There is a cap issued of Paul Warfield during his rookie season. These "Coke" caps were typically also available with other Coca-Cola products such as Fresca and Tab.

| | NRMT | VG-E | GOOD |
|---|---|---|---|
| COMPLETE SET (35) | 125.00 | 50.00 | 12.50 |
| COMMON PLAYER (1-35) | 3.00 | 1.20 | .30 |
| | | | |
| ☐ 1 Walter Beach | 3.00 | 1.20 | .30 |
| ☐ 2 Larry Benz | 3.00 | 1.20 | .30 |
| ☐ 3 Johnny Brewer | 3.00 | 1.20 | .30 |
| ☐ 4 Jim Brown | 25.00 | 10.00 | 2.50 |
| ☐ 5 John Brown | 3.00 | 1.20 | .30 |
| ☐ 6 Monte Clark | 5.00 | 2.00 | .50 |
| ☐ 7 Gary Collins | 5.00 | 2.00 | .50 |
| ☐ 8 Vince Costello | 4.00 | 1.60 | .40 |
| ☐ 9 Ross Fichtner | 3.00 | 1.20 | .30 |
| ☐ 10 Galen Fiss | 3.00 | 1.20 | .30 |
| ☐ 11 Bob Franklin | 3.00 | 1.20 | .30 |
| ☐ 12 Bob Gain | 3.00 | 1.20 | .30 |
| ☐ 13 Bill Glass | 5.00 | 2.00 | .50 |
| ☐ 14 Ernie Green | 4.00 | 1.60 | .40 |
| ☐ 15 Lou Groza | 10.00 | 4.00 | 1.00 |
| ☐ 16 Gene Hickerson | 4.00 | 1.60 | .40 |
| ☐ 17 Jim Houston | 4.00 | 1.60 | .40 |
| ☐ 18 Tom Hutchinson | 3.00 | 1.20 | .30 |
| ☐ 19 Jim Kanicki | 3.00 | 1.20 | .30 |
| ☐ 20 Mike Lucci | 4.00 | 1.60 | .40 |
| ☐ 21 Dick Modzelewski | 4.00 | 1.60 | .40 |
| ☐ 22 John Morrow | 3.00 | 1.20 | .30 |
| ☐ 23 Jim Ninowski | 4.00 | 1.60 | .40 |
| ☐ 24 Frank Parker | 3.00 | 1.20 | .30 |
| ☐ 25 Bernie Parrish | 4.00 | 1.60 | .40 |
| ☐ 26 Frank Ryan | 6.00 | 2.40 | .60 |
| ☐ 27 Charley Scales | 3.00 | 1.20 | .30 |
| ☐ 28 Dick Schafrath | 4.00 | 1.60 | .40 |
| ☐ 29 Roger Shoals | 3.00 | 1.20 | .30 |
| ☐ 30 Jim Shorter | 3.00 | 1.20 | .30 |
| ☐ 31 Billy Truax | 4.00 | 1.60 | .40 |
| ☐ 32 Paul Warfield | 15.00 | 6.00 | 1.50 |
| ☐ 33 Ken Webb | 3.00 | 1.20 | .30 |
| ☐ 34 Paul Wiggin | 4.00 | 1.60 | .40 |
| ☐ 35 John Wooten | 4.00 | 1.60 | .40 |

## 1964 Coke Caps Chargers

This set of 35 Coke caps was issued on bottled soft drinks in the San Diego area and featured San Diego Chargers players. Collectors who assembled the entire set could redeem it (before the expiration date) at a redemption center shown on the Cap-Saver sheet and receive a prize. The caps measure approximately 1 1/8" in diameter. The cap top is stamped with a picture of a football, and inside the cap under the cork is a likeness of a Chargers player. The caps are unnumbered and checklisted below in alphabetical order. These "Coke" caps were typically also available with other Coca-Cola products such as Fresca and Tab.

| | NRMT | VG-E | GOOD |
|---|---|---|---|
| COMPLETE SET (35) | 100.00 | 40.00 | 10.00 |
| COMMON PLAYER (1-35) | 3.00 | 1.20 | .30 |
| | | | |
| ☐ 1 Chuck Allen | 3.00 | 1.20 | .30 |
| ☐ 2 Lance Alworth | 15.00 | 6.00 | 1.50 |
| ☐ 3 George Blair | 3.00 | 1.20 | .30 |
| ☐ 4 Frank Buncom | 4.00 | 1.60 | .40 |
| ☐ 5 Earl Faison | 4.00 | 1.60 | .40 |
| ☐ 6 Ken Graham | 3.00 | 1.20 | .30 |
| ☐ 7 George Gross | 3.00 | 1.20 | .30 |
| ☐ 8 Sam Gruneisen | 3.00 | 1.20 | .30 |
| ☐ 9 John Hadl | 10.00 | 4.00 | 1.00 |
| ☐ 10 Dick Harris | 4.00 | 1.60 | .40 |
| ☐ 11 Bob Jackson | 3.00 | 1.20 | .30 |
| ☐ 12 Emil Karas | 3.00 | 1.20 | .30 |
| ☐ 13 Dave Kocourek | 4.00 | 1.60 | .40 |
| ☐ 14 Ernie Ladd | 7.50 | 3.00 | .75 |
| ☐ 15 Bobby Lane | 3.00 | 1.20 | .30 |
| ☐ 16 Keith Lincoln | 6.00 | 2.40 | .60 |
| ☐ 17 Paul Lowe | 6.00 | 2.40 | .60 |
| ☐ 18 Jacque MacKinnon | 4.00 | 1.60 | .40 |
| ☐ 19 Gerry McDougall | 3.00 | 1.20 | .30 |
| ☐ 20 Charley McNeil | 5.00 | 2.00 | .50 |
| ☐ 21 Bob Mitinger | 3.00 | 1.20 | .30 |
| ☐ 22 Ron Mix | 7.50 | 3.00 | .75 |
| ☐ 23 Don Norton | 4.00 | 1.60 | .40 |
| ☐ 24 Ernie Park | 3.00 | 1.20 | .30 |
| ☐ 25 Bob Petrich | 3.00 | 1.20 | .30 |
| ☐ 26 Jerry Robinson | 3.00 | 1.20 | .30 |
| ☐ 27 Don Rogers | 4.00 | 1.60 | .40 |
| ☐ 28 Tobin Rote | 5.00 | 2.00 | .50 |
| ☐ 29 Henry Schmidt | 3.00 | 1.20 | .30 |
| ☐ 30 Pat Shea | 3.00 | 1.20 | .30 |
| ☐ 31 Walt Sweeney | 4.00 | 1.60 | .40 |
| ☐ 32 Jimmy Warren | 3.00 | 1.20 | .30 |
| ☐ 33 Dick Westmoreland | 3.00 | 1.20 | .30 |
| ☐ 34 Bud Whitehead | 3.00 | 1.20 | .30 |
| ☐ 35 Ernie Wright | 3.00 | 1.20 | .30 |

## 1964 Coke Caps Lions

This set of 35 Coke caps was issued on bottled soft drinks in Michigan and featured Detroit Lions players. Collectors who assembled the entire set could redeem it (before the expiration date) at a redemption center shown on the Cap-Saver sheet and receive a prize. The caps measure approximately 1 1/8" in diameter. The cap top is stamped with a picture of a football, and inside the cap under the cork is a likeness of a Lions player. The caps are unnumbered and checklisted below in alphabetical order. These "Coke" caps were typically also available with other Coca-Cola products such as Fresca and Tab.

| | NRMT | VG-E | GOOD |
|---|---|---|---|
| COMPLETE SET (35) | 100.00 | 40.00 | 10.00 |
| COMMON PLAYER (1-35) | 3.00 | 1.20 | .30 |
| | | | |
| ☐ 1 Terry Barr | 4.00 | 1.60 | .40 |
| ☐ 2 Carl Brettschneider | 3.00 | 1.20 | .30 |
| ☐ 3 Roger Brown | 4.00 | 1.60 | .40 |
| ☐ 4 Mike Bundra | 3.00 | 1.20 | .30 |
| ☐ 5 Ernie Clark | 3.00 | 1.20 | .30 |
| ☐ 6 Gail Cogdill | 4.00 | 1.60 | .40 |
| ☐ 7 Larry Ferguson | 3.00 | 1.20 | .30 |
| ☐ 8 Dennis Gaubatz | 3.00 | 1.20 | .30 |
| ☐ 9 Jim Gibbons | 4.00 | 1.60 | .40 |
| ☐ 10 John Gonzaga | 3.00 | 1.20 | .30 |
| ☐ 11 John Gordy | 4.00 | 1.60 | .40 |
| ☐ 12 Tom Hall | 3.00 | 1.20 | .30 |
| ☐ 13 Alex Karras | 9.00 | 3.75 | .90 |
| ☐ 14 Dick Lane | 7.50 | 3.00 | .75 |
| ☐ 15 Dan LaRose | 3.00 | 1.20 | .30 |
| ☐ 16 Yale Lary | 7.50 | 3.00 | .75 |
| ☐ 17 Dick LeBeau | 5.00 | 2.00 | .50 |
| ☐ 18 Dan Lewis | 3.00 | 1.20 | .30 |
| ☐ 19 Garry Lowe | 3.00 | 1.20 | .30 |
| ☐ 20 Bruce Maher | 3.00 | 1.20 | .30 |
| ☐ 21 Darris McCord | 3.00 | 1.20 | .30 |
| ☐ 22 Max Messner | 3.00 | 1.20 | .30 |
| ☐ 23 Earl Morrall | 6.00 | 2.40 | .60 |

| | | | |
|---|---|---|---|
| ☐ 24 Nick Pietrosante | 5.00 | 2.00 | .50 |
| ☐ 25 Milt Plum | 5.00 | 2.00 | .50 |
| ☐ 26 Daryl Sanders | 3.00 | 1.20 | .30 |
| ☐ 27 Joe Schmidt | 7.50 | 3.00 | .75 |
| ☐ 28 Bob Scholtz | 3.00 | 1.20 | .30 |
| ☐ 29 J.D. Smith | 3.00 | 1.20 | .30 |
| ☐ 30 Pat Studstill | 5.00 | 2.00 | .50 |
| ☐ 31 Larry Vargo | 3.00 | 1.20 | .30 |
| ☐ 32 Wayne Walker | 4.00 | 1.60 | .40 |
| ☐ 33 Tom Watkins | 4.00 | 1.60 | .40 |
| ☐ 34 Bob Whitlow | 3.00 | 1.20 | .30 |
| ☐ 35 Sam Williams | 3.00 | 1.20 | .30 |

## 1964 Coke Caps Patriots

This set of 36 Coke caps was issued on bottled soft drinks in New England and featured Patriots players. Collectors who assembled the entire set could redeem it (before the expiration date) at a redemption center shown on the Cap-Saver sheet and receive a prize. The caps measure approximately 1 1/8" in diameter. The cap top is stamped with a picture of a football, and inside the cap under the cork is a likeness of a Patriots player. The caps are unnumbered and checklisted below in alphabetical order. These "Coke" caps were typically also available with other Coca-Cola products such as Fresca and Tab. At this time the identification of players for 9, 13, 14, 23, 30, and 34 is unknown; any help from readers would be appreciated.

| | NRMT | VG-E | GOOD |
|---|---|---|---|
| COMPLETE SET (36) | 100.00 | 40.00 | 10.00 |
| COMMON PLAYER (1-36) | 3.00 | 1.20 | .30 |
| | | | |
| ☐ 1 Jon Morris | 4.00 | 1.60 | .40 |
| ☐ 2 Don Webb | 3.00 | 1.20 | .30 |
| ☐ 3 Charles Long | 4.00 | 1.60 | .40 |
| ☐ 4 Tony Romeo | 3.00 | 1.20 | .30 |
| ☐ 5 Bob Dee | 3.00 | 1.20 | .30 |
| ☐ 6 Tom Addison | 4.00 | 1.60 | .40 |
| ☐ 7 Bob Yates | 3.00 | 1.20 | .30 |
| ☐ 8 Ron Hall | 3.00 | 1.20 | .30 |
| ☐ 10 Jack Rudolph | 3.00 | 1.20 | .30 |
| ☐ 11 Don Oakes | 3.00 | 1.20 | .30 |
| ☐ 12 Tom Yewcic | 3.00 | 1.20 | .30 |
| ☐ 15 Larry Garron | 4.00 | 1.60 | .40 |
| ☐ 16 Dave Watson | 3.00 | 1.20 | .30 |
| ☐ 17 Art Graham | 3.00 | 1.20 | .30 |
| ☐ 18 Babe Parilli | 5.00 | 2.00 | .50 |
| ☐ 19 Jim Hunt | 3.00 | 1.20 | .30 |
| ☐ 20 Don McKinnon | 3.00 | 1.20 | .30 |
| ☐ 21 Houston Antwine | 4.00 | 1.60 | .40 |
| ☐ 22 Nick Buoniconti | 7.50 | 3.00 | .75 |
| ☐ 24 Gino Cappelletti | 5.00 | 2.00 | .50 |
| ☐ 25 Chuck Shonta | 3.00 | 1.20 | .30 |
| ☐ 26 Dick Felt | 3.00 | 1.20 | .30 |
| ☐ 27 Mike Dukes | 3.00 | 1.20 | .30 |
| ☐ 28 Larry Eisenhauer | 4.00 | 1.60 | .40 |
| ☐ 29 Bob Schmidt | 3.00 | 1.20 | .30 |
| ☐ 31 J.D. Garrett | 3.00 | 1.20 | .30 |
| ☐ 32 Jim Whalen | 3.00 | 1.20 | .30 |
| ☐ 33 Jim Nance | 5.00 | 2.00 | .50 |
| ☐ 35 Lonnie Farmer | 3.00 | 1.20 | .30 |
| ☐ 36 Boston Patriots Logo | 3.00 | 1.20 | .30 |

## 1964 Coke Caps Team Emblems NFL

Each 1964 Coke Caps saver sheet had a section for collecting caps featuring the team emblem for all fourteen NFL teams. The caps are unnumbered and checklisted below in alphabetical order. These "Coke" caps were typically also available with other Coca-Cola products such as Fresca and Tab.

| | NRMT | VG-E | GOOD |
|---|---|---|---|
| COMPLETE SET (14) | 60.00 | 24.00 | 6.00 |
| COMMON TEAM (1-14) | 5.00 | 2.00 | .50 |
| | | | |
| ☐ 1 Baltimore Colts | 5.00 | 2.00 | .50 |
| ☐ 2 Chicago Bears | 5.00 | 2.00 | .50 |
| ☐ 3 Cleveland Browns | 5.00 | 2.00 | .50 |
| ☐ 4 Dallas Cowboys | 6.00 | 2.40 | .60 |
| ☐ 5 Detroit Lions | 5.00 | 2.00 | .50 |
| ☐ 6 Green Bay Packers | 6.00 | 2.40 | .60 |
| ☐ 7 Los Angeles Rams | 5.00 | 2.00 | .50 |
| ☐ 8 Minnesota Vikings | 5.00 | 2.00 | .50 |
| ☐ 9 New York Giants | 6.00 | 2.40 | .60 |
| ☐ 10 Philadelphia Eagles | 5.00 | 2.00 | .50 |
| ☐ 11 Pittsburgh Steelers | 5.00 | 2.00 | .50 |
| ☐ 12 San Francisco 49ers | 5.00 | 2.00 | .50 |
| ☐ 13 St. Louis Cardinals | 5.00 | 2.00 | .50 |
| ☐ 14 Washington Redskins | 5.00 | 2.00 | .50 |

## 1965 Coke Caps All-Stars NFL

This is a 34-player set of Coca-Cola bottle caps featuring NFL All-Stars. These caps were issued in NFL cities (and some other cities as well) along with the local team caps. The NFL city Cap Saver sheets had separate sections in which to affix both the local team's caps and the All-Stars' caps. The caps measure approximately 1 1/8" in diameter and have the Coke logo and a football on the outside, while the inside has the player's face printed in black, with text surrounding the face. A Cap Saver sheet was issued to aid in collecting the bottle caps. The consumer could turn in his completed sheet to receive various prizes. The caps are numbered with a "C" prefix. These "Coke" caps were typically also available with other Coca-Cola products such as Fresca and Tab.

| | MINT | EXC | G-VG |
|---|---|---|---|
| COMPLETE SET (34) | 125.00 | 50.00 | 12.50 |
| COMMON PLAYER (C37-C70) | 3.00 | 1.20 | .30 |
| | | | |
| ☐ C37 Sonny Jurgensen<br>Washington Redskins | 7.50 | 3.00 | .75 |
| ☐ C38 Fran Tarkenton<br>Minnesota Vikings | 12.00 | 5.00 | 1.20 |
| ☐ C39 Frank Ryan<br>Cleveland Browns | 4.00 | 1.60 | .40 |
| ☐ C40 John Unitas<br>Baltimore Colts | 12.00 | 5.00 | 1.20 |
| ☐ C41 Tommy Mason<br>Minnesota Vikings | 4.00 | 1.60 | .40 |
| ☐ C42 Mel Renfro<br>Dallas Cowboys | 5.00 | 2.00 | .50 |
| ☐ C43 Ed Meador<br>Los Angeles Rams | 3.00 | 1.20 | .30 |
| ☐ C44 Paul Krause<br>Washington Redskins | 5.00 | 2.00 | .50 |
| ☐ C45 Irv Cross<br>Philadelphia Eagles | 4.00 | 1.60 | .40 |
| ☐ C46 Bill Brown<br>Minnesota Vikings | 4.00 | 1.60 | .40 |
| ☐ C47 Joe Fortunato<br>Chicago Bears | 3.00 | 1.20 | .30 |
| ☐ C48 Jim Taylor<br>Green Bay Packers | 7.50 | 3.00 | .75 |
| ☐ C49 John Henry Johnson<br>Pittsburgh Steelers | 7.50 | 3.00 | .75 |
| ☐ C50 Pat Fischer<br>St. Louis Cardinals | 3.00 | 1.20 | .30 |
| ☐ C51 Bobby Boyd<br>Baltimore Colts | 3.00 | 1.20 | .30 |
| ☐ C52 Terry Barr<br>Detroit Lions | 3.00 | 1.20 | .30 |
| ☐ C53 Charley Taylor<br>Washington Redskins | 9.00 | 3.75 | .90 |
| ☐ C54 Paul Warfield<br>Cleveland Browns | 9.00 | 3.75 | .90 |
| ☐ C55 Pete Retzlaff<br>Philadelphia Eagles | 4.00 | 1.60 | .40 |
| ☐ C56 Maxie Baughan<br>Philadelphia Eagles | 4.00 | 1.60 | .40 |
| ☐ C57 Matt Hazeltine<br>San Francisco 49ers | 3.00 | 1.20 | .30 |
| ☐ C58 Ken Gray<br>St. Louis Cardinals | 3.00 | 1.20 | .30 |
| ☐ C59 Ray Nitschke<br>Green Bay Packers | 7.50 | 3.00 | .75 |
| ☐ C60 Myron Pottios<br>Pittsburgh Steelers | 3.00 | 1.20 | .30 |
| ☐ C61 Charlie Krueger<br>San Francisco 49ers | 3.00 | 1.20 | .30 |
| ☐ C62 Deacon Jones<br>Los Angeles Rams | 7.50 | 3.00 | .75 |
| ☐ C63 Bob Lilly<br>Dallas Cowboys | 9.00 | 3.75 | .90 |
| ☐ C64 Merlin Olsen<br>Los Angeles Rams | 7.50 | 3.00 | .75 |
| ☐ C65 Jim Parker<br>Baltimore Colts | 7.50 | 3.00 | .75 |
| ☐ C66 Roosevelt Brown<br>New York Giants | 7.50 | 3.00 | .75 |

| | NRMT | VG-E | GOOD |
|---|---|---|---|
| ☐ C67 Jim Gibbons | 3.00 | 1.20 | .30 |
| Detroit Lions | | | |
| ☐ C68 Mike Ditka | 12.00 | 5.00 | 1.20 |
| Chicago Bears | | | |
| ☐ C69 Willie Davis | 7.50 | 3.00 | .75 |
| Green Bay Packers | | | |
| ☐ C70 Aaron Thomas | 3.00 | 1.20 | .30 |
| New York Giants | | | |

## 1965 Coke Caps Bills

This set of 35 Coke caps was issued on bottled soft drinks in Western New York and featured Buffalo Bills players. Collectors who assembled the entire set could redeem it at a Coca-Cola bottling company and receive a prize of either a Bills' miniature megaphone, miniature plastic helmets of all the AFL teams, or an AFL leather-grain football. The caps measure approximately 1 1/8" in diameter. The cap top is stamped with a picture of a football and inside the cap under the cork is a likeness of a Bills player. The Coca-Cola Company issued a Cap Saver sheet for mounting the caps. These "Coke" caps were typically also available with other Coca-Cola products such as Fresca and Tab.

| | NRMT | VG-E | GOOD |
|---|---|---|---|
| COMPLETE SET (35) | 100.00 | 40.00 | 10.00 |
| COMMON PLAYER (B1-B35) | 3.00 | 1.20 | .30 |
| ☐ B1 Ray Abbruzzese | 3.00 | 1.20 | .30 |
| ☐ B2 Joe Auer | 3.00 | 1.20 | .30 |
| ☐ B3 Stew Barber | 4.00 | 1.60 | .40 |
| ☐ B4 Glenn Bass | 3.00 | 1.20 | .30 |
| ☐ B5 Dave Behrman | 3.00 | 1.20 | .30 |
| ☐ B6 Al Bemiller | 3.00 | 1.20 | .30 |
| ☐ B7 Butch Byrd | 4.00 | 1.60 | .40 |
| ☐ B8 Wray Carlton | 4.00 | 1.60 | .40 |
| ☐ B9 Hagood Clarke | 3.00 | 1.20 | .30 |
| ☐ B10 Jack Kemp | 35.00 | 14.00 | 3.50 |
| ☐ B11 Oliver Dobbins | 3.00 | 1.20 | .30 |
| ☐ B12 Elbert Dubenion | 6.00 | 2.40 | .60 |
| ☐ B13 Jim Dunaway | 4.00 | 1.60 | .40 |
| ☐ B14 Booker Edgerson | 3.00 | 1.20 | .30 |
| ☐ B15 George Flint | 3.00 | 1.20 | .30 |
| ☐ B16 Pete Gogolak | 5.00 | 2.00 | .50 |
| ☐ B17 Dick Hudson | 4.00 | 1.60 | .40 |
| ☐ B18 Harry Jacobs | 4.00 | 1.60 | .40 |
| ☐ B19 Tom Keating | 4.00 | 1.60 | .40 |
| ☐ B20 Tom Day | 4.00 | 1.60 | .40 |
| ☐ B21 Daryle Lamonica | 8.00 | 3.25 | .80 |
| ☐ B22 Paul Maguire | 6.00 | 2.40 | .60 |
| ☐ B23 Roland McDole | 4.00 | 1.60 | .40 |
| ☐ B24 Dudley Meredith | 3.00 | 1.20 | .30 |
| ☐ B25 Joe O'Donnell | 3.00 | 1.20 | .30 |
| ☐ B26 Willie Ross | 3.00 | 1.20 | .30 |
| ☐ B27 Ed Rutkowski | 3.00 | 1.20 | .30 |
| ☐ B28 George Saimes | 4.00 | 1.60 | .40 |
| ☐ B29 Tom Sestak | 4.00 | 1.60 | .40 |
| ☐ B30 Billy Shaw | 5.00 | 2.00 | .50 |
| ☐ B31 Bob Smith | 3.00 | 1.20 | .30 |
| ☐ B32 Mike Stratton | 4.00 | 1.60 | .40 |
| ☐ B33 Gene Sykes | 3.00 | 1.20 | .30 |
| ☐ B34 John Tracey | 4.00 | 1.60 | .40 |
| ☐ B35 Ernie Warlick | 4.00 | 1.60 | .40 |

## 1965 Coke Caps Giants

This set of 35 Coke caps was issued on bottled soft drinks in the New York metropolitan area and featured New York Giants players. Collectors who assembled the entire set could redeem it at a Coca-Cola bottling company and receive a prize of either a Giants' miniature megaphone, miniature plastic helmets of all the NFL teams, or an NFL leather-grain football. The caps measure approximately 1 1/8" in diameter. The cap top is stamped with a picture of a football and inside the cap under the cork is a likeness of a Giants player. The Coca-Cola Company issued a Cap Saver sheet for mounting the caps. These "Coke" caps were typically also available with other Coca-Cola products such as Fresca and Tab.

| | NRMT | VG-E | GOOD |
|---|---|---|---|
| COMPLETE SET (35) | 100.00 | 40.00 | 10.00 |
| COMMON PLAYER (G1-G35) | 3.00 | 1.20 | .30 |
| ☐ G1 Joe Morrison | 4.00 | 1.60 | .40 |
| ☐ G2 Dick Lynch | 4.00 | 1.60 | .40 |
| ☐ G3 Andy Stynchula | 3.00 | 1.20 | .30 |
| ☐ G4 Clarence Childs | 3.00 | 1.20 | .30 |
| ☐ G5 Aaron Thomas | 3.00 | 1.20 | .30 |
| ☐ G6 Mickey Walker | 3.00 | 1.20 | .30 |
| ☐ G7 Bill Winter | 3.00 | 1.20 | .30 |
| ☐ G8 Bookie Bolin | 3.00 | 1.20 | .30 |
| ☐ G9 Tom Scott | 3.00 | 1.20 | .30 |
| ☐ G10 John Lovetere | 3.00 | 1.20 | .30 |
| ☐ G11 Jim Patton | 4.00 | 1.60 | .40 |
| ☐ G12 Darrell Dess | 3.00 | 1.20 | .30 |
| ☐ G13 Dick James | 3.00 | 1.20 | .30 |
| ☐ G14 Jerry Hillebrand | 3.00 | 1.20 | .30 |
| ☐ G15 Dick Pesonen | 3.00 | 1.20 | .30 |
| ☐ G16 Del Shofner | 5.00 | 2.00 | .50 |
| ☐ G17 Erich Barnes | 4.00 | 1.60 | .40 |
| ☐ G18 Roosevelt Brown | 7.50 | 3.00 | .75 |
| ☐ G19 Greg Larson | 3.00 | 1.20 | .30 |
| ☐ G20 Jim Katcavage | 4.00 | 1.60 | .40 |
| ☐ G21 Frank Lasky | 3.00 | 1.20 | .30 |
| ☐ G22 Lou Slaby | 3.00 | 1.20 | .30 |
| ☐ G23 Jim Moran | 3.00 | 1.20 | .30 |
| ☐ G24 Roger Anderson | 3.00 | 1.20 | .30 |
| ☐ G25 Steve Thurlow | 3.00 | 1.20 | .30 |
| ☐ G26 Ernie Wheelwright | 4.00 | 1.60 | .40 |
| ☐ G27 Gary Wood | 4.00 | 1.60 | .40 |
| ☐ G28 Tony Dimidio | 3.00 | 1.20 | .30 |
| ☐ G29 John Contoulis | 3.00 | 1.20 | .30 |
| ☐ G30 Tucker Frederickson | 5.00 | 2.00 | .50 |
| ☐ G31 Bob Timberlake | 4.00 | 1.60 | .40 |
| ☐ G32 Chuck Mercein | 4.00 | 1.60 | .40 |
| ☐ G33 Ernie Koy | 5.00 | 2.00 | .50 |
| ☐ G34 Tom Costello | 3.00 | 1.20 | .30 |
| ☐ G35 Homer Jones | 5.00 | 2.00 | .50 |

## 1965 Coke Caps Jets

This set of 35 Coke caps was issued on bottled soft drinks in the New York metropolitan area and featured New York Jets players. Collectors who assembled the entire set could redeem it at a Coca-Cola bottling company and receive a prize of either a Jets' miniature megaphone, miniature plastic helmets of all the AFL teams, or an AFL leather-grain football. The caps measure approximately 1 1/8" in diameter. The cap top is stamped with a picture of a football and inside the cap under the cork is a likeness of a Jets player. The Coca-Cola Company issued a Cap Saver sheet for mounting the caps. These "Coke" caps were typically also available with other Coca-Cola products such as Fresca and Tab.

| | NRMT | VG-E | GOOD |
|---|---|---|---|
| COMPLETE SET (35) | 125.00 | 50.00 | 12.50 |
| COMMON PLAYER (J1-J35) | 3.00 | 1.20 | .30 |
| ☐ J1 Don Maynard | 7.50 | 3.00 | .75 |
| ☐ J2 George Sauer | 5.00 | 2.00 | .50 |
| ☐ J3 Cosmo Iacavazzi | 4.00 | 1.60 | .40 |
| ☐ J4 Jim O'Mahoney | 3.00 | 1.20 | .30 |
| ☐ J5 Matt Snell | 5.00 | 2.00 | .50 |
| ☐ J6 Clyde Washington | 3.00 | 1.20 | .30 |
| ☐ J7 Jim Turner | 4.00 | 1.60 | .40 |
| ☐ J8 Mike Taliaferro | 4.00 | 1.60 | .40 |
| ☐ J9 Marshall Starks | 3.00 | 1.20 | .30 |
| ☐ J10 Mark Smolinski | 3.00 | 1.20 | .30 |
| ☐ J11 Bob Schweickert | 3.00 | 1.20 | .30 |
| ☐ J12 Paul Rochester | 3.00 | 1.20 | .30 |
| ☐ J13 Sherman Plunkett | 4.00 | 1.60 | .40 |
| ☐ J14 Gerry Philbin | 4.00 | 1.60 | .40 |
| ☐ J15 Pete Perreault | 3.00 | 1.20 | .30 |
| ☐ J16 Dainard Paulson | 3.00 | 1.20 | .30 |
| ☐ J17 Joe Namath | 50.00 | 20.00 | 5.00 |
| ☐ J18 Winston Hill | 4.00 | 1.60 | .40 |
| ☐ J19 Dee Mackey | 3.00 | 1.20 | .30 |
| ☐ J20 Curley Johnson | 4.00 | 1.60 | .40 |

| | | | |
|---|---|---|---|
| ☐ J21 Mike Hudock | 3.00 | 1.20 | .30 |
| ☐ J22 John Huarte | 5.00 | 2.00 | .50 |
| ☐ J23 Gordy Holz | 3.00 | 1.20 | .30 |
| ☐ J24 Gene Heeter | 5.00 | 2.00 | .50 |
| ☐ J25 Larry Grantham | 4.00 | 1.60 | .40 |
| ☐ J26 Dan Ficca | 3.00 | 1.20 | .30 |
| ☐ J27 Sam DeLuca | 3.00 | 1.20 | .30 |
| ☐ J28 Bill Baird | 3.00 | 1.20 | .30 |
| ☐ J29 Ralph Baker | 3.00 | 1.20 | .30 |
| ☐ J30 Wahoo McDaniel | 7.50 | 3.00 | .75 |
| ☐ J31 Jim Evans | 3.00 | 1.20 | .30 |
| ☐ J32 Dave Herman | 3.00 | 1.20 | .30 |
| ☐ J33 John Schmitt | 3.00 | 1.20 | .30 |
| ☐ J34 Jim Harris | 3.00 | 1.20 | .30 |
| ☐ J35 Bake Turner | 4.00 | 1.60 | .40 |

## 1965 Coke Caps Lions

This is a 36-player set of Coca-Cola bottle caps featuring members of the Detroit Lions. The Coke logo and a football are on the outside, while the player's face printed in black and his name below the picture appear on the inside. The caps measure approximately 1 1/8" in diameter. A Cap-Saver sheet was also issued to aid in collecting the bottle caps, and the collector could turn in his completed sheet to receive various prizes. The 1965 Coke Caps All-Stars NFL set was also to be mounted on this same Cap-Saver sheet. The caps are numbered with a "C" prefix. These "Coke" caps were typically also available with other Coca-Cola products such as Fresca and Tab.

| | MINT | EXC | G-VG |
|---|---|---|---|
| COMPLETE SET (36) | 100.00 | 40.00 | 10.00 |
| COMMON PLAYER (C1-C36) | 3.00 | 1.20 | .30 |
| | | | |
| ☐ C1 Pat Studstill | 5.00 | 2.00 | .50 |
| ☐ C2 Bob Whitlow | 3.00 | 1.20 | .30 |
| ☐ C3 Wayne Walker | 4.00 | 1.60 | .40 |
| ☐ C4 Tom Watkins | 4.00 | 1.60 | .40 |
| ☐ C5 Jim Simon | 3.00 | 1.20 | .30 |
| ☐ C6 Sam Williams | 3.00 | 1.20 | .30 |
| ☐ C7 Terry Barr | 4.00 | 1.60 | .40 |
| ☐ C8 Jerry Rush | 3.00 | 1.20 | .30 |
| ☐ C9 Roger Brown | 4.00 | 1.60 | .40 |
| ☐ C10 Tom Nowatzke | 4.00 | 1.60 | .40 |
| ☐ C11 Dick Lane | 7.50 | 3.00 | .75 |
| ☐ C12 Dick Compton | 3.00 | 1.20 | .30 |
| ☐ C13 Yale Lary | 7.50 | 3.00 | .75 |
| ☐ C14 Dick Lebeau | 5.00 | 2.00 | .50 |
| ☐ C15 Dan Lewis | 4.00 | 1.60 | .40 |
| ☐ C16 Wally Hilgenburg | 4.00 | 1.60 | .40 |
| ☐ C17 Bruce Maher | 3.00 | 1.20 | .30 |
| ☐ C18 Darris McCord | 4.00 | 1.60 | .40 |
| ☐ C19 Hugh McInnis | 3.00 | 1.20 | .30 |
| ☐ C20 Ernie Clark | 3.00 | 1.20 | .30 |
| ☐ C21 Gail Cogdill | 4.00 | 1.60 | .40 |
| ☐ C22 Wayne Rasmussen | 3.00 | 1.20 | .30 |
| ☐ C23 Joe Don Looney | 15.00 | 6.00 | 1.50 |
| ☐ C24 Jim Gibbons | 4.00 | 1.60 | .40 |
| ☐ C25 John Gonzaga | 3.00 | 1.20 | .30 |
| ☐ C26 John Gordy | 4.00 | 1.60 | .40 |
| ☐ C27 Bobby Thompson | 4.00 | 1.60 | .40 |
| ☐ C28 J.D. Smith | 4.00 | 1.60 | .40 |
| ☐ C29 Earl Morrall | 6.00 | 2.40 | .60 |
| ☐ C30 Alex Karras | 7.50 | 3.00 | .75 |
| ☐ C31 Nick Pietrosante | 5.00 | 2.00 | .50 |
| ☐ C32 Milt Plum | 5.00 | 2.00 | .50 |
| ☐ C33 Daryl Sanders | 3.00 | 1.20 | .30 |
| ☐ C34 Joe Schmidt | 7.50 | 3.00 | .75 |
| ☐ C35 Bob Scholtz | 3.00 | 1.20 | .30 |
| ☐ C36 Team Logo | 3.00 | 1.20 | .30 |

## 1965 Coke Caps Redskins

This set of 36 Coke caps was issued on bottled soft drinks in the Washington, D.C. area and featured Washington Redskins players. Collectors who assembled the entire set could redeem it at a Coca-Cola bottling company and receive a prize. The caps measure approximately 1 1/8" in diameter. The cap top is stamped with a picture of a football and inside the cap under the cork is a likeness of a Redskins player. The Coca-Cola Company issued a Cap Saver sheet for mounting the caps. These "Coke" caps were typically also available with other Coca-Cola products such as Fresca and Tab. At this time the identification of players for C1, C14, C16, C18, C19, C20, C25, C27, and C33 is unknown; any help from readers would be appreciated.

| | NRMT | VG-E | GOOD |
|---|---|---|---|
| COMPLETE SET (27) | 75.00 | 30.00 | 7.50 |
| COMMON PLAYER (C1-C36) | 3.00 | 1.20 | .30 |
| | | | |
| ☐ C2 Fred Mazurek | 3.00 | 1.20 | .30 |
| ☐ C3 Lonnie Sanders | 3.00 | 1.20 | .30 |
| ☐ C4 Jim Steffen | 3.00 | 1.20 | .30 |
| ☐ C5 John Nisby | 3.00 | 1.20 | .30 |
| ☐ C6 George Izo | 5.00 | 2.00 | .50 |
| ☐ C7 Vince Promuto | 3.00 | 1.20 | .30 |
| ☐ C8 John Sample | 4.00 | 1.60 | .40 |
| ☐ C9 Pat Richter | 4.00 | 1.60 | .40 |
| ☐ C10 Preston Carpenter | 3.00 | 1.20 | .30 |
| ☐ C11 Sam Huff | 7.50 | 3.00 | .75 |
| ☐ C12 Pervis Atkins | 4.00 | 1.60 | .40 |
| ☐ C13 Fred Barnett | 3.00 | 1.20 | .30 |
| ☐ C15 Bill Anderson | 3.00 | 1.20 | .30 |
| ☐ C17 George Seals | 3.00 | 1.20 | .30 |
| ☐ C21 John Paluck | 3.00 | 1.20 | .30 |
| ☐ C22 Fran O'Brien | 3.00 | 1.20 | .30 |
| ☐ C23 Joe Rutgens | 3.00 | 1.20 | .30 |
| ☐ C24 Rod Breedlove | 3.00 | 1.20 | .30 |
| ☐ C26 Bob Jencks | 4.00 | 1.60 | .40 |
| ☐ C28 Sonny Jurgensen | 10.00 | 4.00 | 1.00 |
| ☐ C29 Bob Toneff | 3.00 | 1.20 | .30 |
| ☐ C30 Charley Taylor | 7.50 | 3.00 | .75 |
| ☐ C31 Bob Shiner | 3.00 | 1.20 | .30 |
| ☐ C32 Bob Williams | 3.00 | 1.20 | .30 |
| ☐ C34 Ron Snidow | 3.00 | 1.20 | .30 |
| ☐ C35 Paul Krause | 5.00 | 2.00 | .50 |
| ☐ C36 Team Logo | 3.00 | 1.20 | .30 |

## 1966 Coke Caps All-Stars AFL

These caps were issued in NFL cities (and some other cities as well) along with the local team caps. Some NFL city Cap Saver sheets had separate sections in which to affix both the local team's caps and the All-Stars' (or National NFL) caps. The caps measure approximately 1 1/8" in diameter and have the Coke logo and a football on the outside, while the inside has the player's face printed in black, with text surrounding the face. A Cap-Saver sheet was issued to aid in collecting the bottle caps. The consumer could turn in his completed sheet to receive various prizes. The numbering of the caps below reflects that of the Cap-Saver sheet. These "Coke" caps were typically also available with other Coca-Cola products such as Fresca and Tab.

| | NRMT | VG-E | GOOD |
|---|---|---|---|
| COMPLETE SET (34) | 125.00 | 50.00 | 12.50 |
| COMMON PLAYER (C37-C70) | 3.00 | 1.20 | .30 |
| | | | |
| ☐ C37 Babe Parilli | 4.00 | 1.60 | .40 |
| Boston Patriots | | | |
| ☐ C38 Mike Stratton | 3.00 | 1.20 | .30 |
| Buffalo Bills | | | |
| ☐ C39 Jack Kemp | 20.00 | 8.00 | 2.00 |
| Buffalo Bills | | | |
| ☐ C40 Len Dawson | 9.00 | 3.75 | .90 |
| Kansas City Chiefs | | | |
| ☐ C41 Fred Arbanas | 3.00 | 1.20 | .30 |
| Kansas City Chiefs | | | |
| ☐ C42 Bobby Bell | 6.00 | 2.40 | .60 |
| Kansas City Chiefs | | | |
| ☐ C43 Willie Brown | 6.00 | 2.40 | .60 |
| Oakland Raiders | | | |
| ☐ C44 Buck Buchanan | 6.00 | 2.40 | .60 |
| Kansas City Chiefs | | | |
| ☐ C45 Frank Buncom | 3.00 | 1.20 | .30 |
| San Diego Chargers | | | |

| | NRMT | VG-E | GOOD |
|---|---|---|---|
| ☐ C46 Nick Buoniconti | 5.00 | 2.00 | .50 |
| Boston Patriots | | | |
| ☐ C47 Gino Cappelletti | 4.00 | 1.60 | .40 |
| Boston Patriots | | | |
| ☐ C48 Eldon Danenhauer | 3.00 | 1.20 | .30 |
| Denver Broncos | | | |
| ☐ C49 Clem Daniels | 4.00 | 1.60 | .40 |
| Oakland Raiders | | | |
| ☐ C50 Leslie Duncan | 4.00 | 1.60 | .40 |
| San Diego Chargers | | | |
| ☐ C51 Willie Frazier | 4.00 | 1.60 | .40 |
| Kansas City Chiefs | | | |
| ☐ C52 Cookie Gilchrist | 5.00 | 2.00 | .50 |
| Miami Dolphins | | | |
| ☐ C53 Dave Grayson | 3.00 | 1.20 | .30 |
| Oakland Raiders | | | |
| ☐ C54 John Hadl | 5.00 | 2.00 | .50 |
| San Diego Chargers | | | |
| ☐ C55 Wayne Hawkins | 3.00 | 1.20 | .30 |
| Oakland Raiders | | | |
| ☐ C56 Sherrill Headrick | 3.00 | 1.20 | .30 |
| Kansas City Chiefs | | | |
| ☐ C57 Charlie Hennigan | 4.00 | 1.60 | .40 |
| Houston Oilers | | | |
| ☐ C58 E.J. Holub | 4.00 | 1.60 | .40 |
| Kansas City Chiefs | | | |
| ☐ C59 Curley Johnson | 3.00 | 1.20 | .30 |
| New York Jets | | | |
| ☐ C60 Keith Lincoln | 4.00 | 1.60 | .40 |
| San Diego Chargers | | | |
| ☐ C61 Paul Lowe | 4.00 | 1.60 | .40 |
| San Diego Chargers | | | |
| ☐ C62 Don Maynard | 6.00 | 2.40 | .60 |
| New York Jets | | | |
| ☐ C63 Jon Morris | 3.00 | 1.20 | .30 |
| Boston Patriots | | | |
| ☐ C64 Joe Namath | 25.00 | 10.00 | 2.50 |
| New York Jets | | | |
| ☐ C65 Jim Otto | 6.00 | 2.40 | .60 |
| Oakland Raiders | | | |
| ☐ C66 Dainard Paulson | 3.00 | 1.20 | .30 |
| New York Jets | | | |
| ☐ C67 Art Powell | 4.00 | 1.60 | .40 |
| Oakland Raiders | | | |
| ☐ C68 Walt Sweeney | 3.00 | 1.20 | .30 |
| San Diego Chargers | | | |
| ☐ C69 Bob Talamini | 3.00 | 1.20 | .30 |
| Houston Oilers | | | |
| ☐ C70 Lance Alworth UER | 9.00 | 3.75 | .90 |
| San Diego Chargers | | | |
| (Name misspelled | | | |
| Alsworth) | | | |

# 1966 Coke Caps All-Stars NFL

These caps were issued in NFL cities (and some other cities as well) along with the local team caps. Some NFL city Cap Saver sheets had separate sections in which to affix both the local team's caps and the All-Stars' (or National NFL) caps. The caps measure approximately 1 1/8" in diameter and have the Coke logo and a football on the outside, while the inside has the player's face printed in black, with text surrounding the face. A Cap-Saver sheet was issued to aid in collecting the bottle caps. The consumer could turn in his completed sheet to receive various prizes. The numbering of the caps below reflects that of the Cap-Saver sheet. These "Coke" caps were typically also available with other Coca-Cola products such as Fresca and Tab.

| | NRMT | VG-E | GOOD |
|---|---|---|---|
| COMPLETE SET (34) | 125.00 | 50.00 | 12.50 |
| COMMON PLAYER (C37-C70) | 3.00 | 1.20 | .30 |
| ☐ C37 Frank Ryan | 4.00 | 1.60 | .40 |
| Cleveland Browns | | | |
| ☐ C38 Timmy Brown | 4.00 | 1.60 | .40 |
| Philadelphia Eagles | | | |
| ☐ C39 Tucker Frederickson | 4.00 | 1.60 | .40 |
| New York Giants | | | |
| ☐ C40 Cornell Green | 4.00 | 1.60 | .40 |
| Dallas Cowboys | | | |

| | NRMT | VG-E | GOOD |
|---|---|---|---|
| ☐ C41 Bob Hayes | 5.00 | 2.00 | .50 |
| Dallas Cowboys | | | |
| ☐ C42 Charley Taylor | 6.00 | 2.40 | .60 |
| Washington Redskins | | | |
| ☐ C43 Pete Retzlaff | 4.00 | 1.60 | .40 |
| Philadelphia Eagles | | | |
| ☐ C44 Jim Ringo | 6.00 | 2.40 | .60 |
| Philadelphia Eagles | | | |
| ☐ C45 John Wooten | 3.00 | 1.20 | .30 |
| Cleveland Browns | | | |
| ☐ C46 Dale Meinert | 3.00 | 1.20 | .30 |
| St. Louis Cardinals | | | |
| ☐ C47 Bob Lilly | 9.00 | 3.75 | .90 |
| Dallas Cowboys | | | |
| ☐ C48 Sam Silas | 3.00 | 1.20 | .30 |
| St. Louis Cardinals | | | |
| ☐ C49 Roosevelt Brown | 6.00 | 2.40 | .60 |
| New York Giants | | | |
| ☐ C50 Gary Ballman | 4.00 | 1.60 | .40 |
| Pittsburgh Steelers | | | |
| ☐ C51 Gary Collins | 4.00 | 1.60 | .40 |
| Cleveland Browns | | | |
| ☐ C52 Sonny Randle | 4.00 | 1.60 | .40 |
| St. Louis Cardinals | | | |
| ☐ C53 Charlie Johnson | 4.00 | 1.60 | .40 |
| St. Louis Cardinals | | | |
| ☐ C54 Herb Adderley | 6.00 | 2.40 | .60 |
| Green Bay Packers | | | |
| ☐ C55 Doug Atkins | 6.00 | 2.40 | .60 |
| Chicago Bears | | | |
| ☐ C56 Roger Brown | 4.00 | 1.60 | .40 |
| Detroit Lions | | | |
| ☐ C57 Dick Butkus | 12.00 | 5.00 | 1.20 |
| Chicago Bears | | | |
| ☐ C58 Willie Davis | 6.00 | 2.40 | .60 |
| Green Bay Packers | | | |
| ☐ C59 Tommy McDonald | 4.00 | 1.60 | .40 |
| Los Angeles Rams | | | |
| ☐ C60 Alex Karras | 7.50 | 3.00 | .75 |
| Detroit Lions | | | |
| ☐ C61 John Mackey | 6.00 | 2.40 | .60 |
| Baltimore Colts | | | |
| ☐ C62 Ed Meador | 4.00 | 1.60 | .40 |
| Los Angeles Rams | | | |
| ☐ C63 Merlin Olsen | 7.50 | 3.00 | .75 |
| Los Angeles Rams | | | |
| ☐ C64 Dave Parks | 4.00 | 1.60 | .40 |
| San Francisco 49ers | | | |
| ☐ C65 Gale Sayers | 20.00 | 8.00 | 2.00 |
| Chicago Bears | | | |
| ☐ C66 Fran Tarkenton | 10.00 | 4.00 | 1.00 |
| Minnesota Vikings | | | |
| ☐ C67 Mick Tingelhoff | 4.00 | 1.60 | .40 |
| Minnesota Vikings | | | |
| ☐ C68 Ken Willard | 4.00 | 1.60 | .40 |
| San Francisco 49ers | | | |
| ☐ C69 Willie Wood | 6.00 | 2.40 | .60 |
| Green Bay Packers | | | |
| ☐ C70 Bill Brown | 4.00 | 1.60 | .40 |
| Minnesota Vikings | | | |

# 1966 Coke Caps Bills

This set of 36 Coke caps was issued on bottled soft drinks in Western New York and featured Buffalo Bills players. The caps measure approximately 1 1/8" in diameter. The cap top is stamped with a picture of a football and inside the cap under the clear plastic cover is an image of a Bills player. This plastic cover distinguishes the 1966 issue from the 1965 issue. Otherwise, the Cap Saver checklist (which provides the numbering) is the only way to distinguish the two issues. These "Coke" caps were typically also available with other Coca-Cola products such as Fresca and Tab.

| | NRMT | VG-E | GOOD |
|---|---|---|---|
| COMPLETE SET (36) | 100.00 | 40.00 | 10.00 |
| COMMON PLAYER (B1-B36) | 3.00 | 1.20 | .30 |
| ☐ B1 Bill Laskey | 3.00 | 1.20 | .30 |
| ☐ B2 Marty Schottenheimer | 7.50 | 3.00 | .75 |
| ☐ B3 Stew Barber | 4.00 | 1.60 | .40 |
| ☐ B4 Glenn Bass | 3.00 | 1.20 | .30 |
| ☐ B5 Remi Prudhomme | 3.00 | 1.20 | .30 |
| ☐ B6 Al Bemiller | 3.00 | 1.20 | .30 |
| ☐ B7 Butch Byrd | 4.00 | 1.60 | .40 |
| ☐ B8 Wray Carlton | 4.00 | 1.60 | .40 |
| ☐ B9 Hagood Clarke | 3.00 | 1.20 | .30 |
| ☐ B10 Jack Kemp | 30.00 | 12.00 | 3.00 |
| ☐ B11 Charley Warner | 3.00 | 1.20 | .30 |
| ☐ B12 Elbert Dubenion | 6.00 | 2.40 | .60 |
| ☐ B13 Jim Dunaway | 4.00 | 1.60 | .40 |
| ☐ B14 Booker Edgerson | 3.00 | 1.20 | .30 |

| | | | |
|---|---|---|---|
| ☐ B15 Paul Costa | 4.00 | 1.60 | .40 |
| ☐ B16 Henry Schmidt | 3.00 | 1.20 | .30 |
| ☐ B17 Dick Hudson | 4.00 | 1.60 | .40 |
| ☐ B18 Harry Jacobs | 4.00 | 1.60 | .40 |
| ☐ B19 Tom Janik | 3.00 | 1.20 | .30 |
| ☐ B20 Tom Day | 4.00 | 1.60 | .40 |
| ☐ B21 Daryle Lamonica | 7.50 | 3.00 | .75 |
| ☐ B22 Paul Maguire | 6.00 | 2.40 | .60 |
| ☐ B23 Roland McDole | 4.00 | 1.60 | .40 |
| ☐ B24 Dudley Meredith | 3.00 | 1.20 | .30 |
| ☐ B25 Joe O'Donnell | 3.00 | 1.20 | .30 |
| ☐ B26 Charley Ferguson | 3.00 | 1.20 | .30 |
| ☐ B27 Ed Rutkowski | 4.00 | 1.60 | .40 |
| ☐ B28 George Saimes | 4.00 | 1.60 | .40 |
| ☐ B29 Tom Sestak | 4.00 | 1.60 | .40 |
| ☐ B30 Billy Shaw | 4.00 | 1.60 | .40 |
| ☐ B31 Bob Smith | 3.00 | 1.20 | .30 |
| ☐ B32 Mike Stratton | 4.00 | 1.60 | .40 |
| ☐ B33 Gene Sykes | 3.00 | 1.20 | .30 |
| ☐ B34 John Tracey | 4.00 | 1.60 | .40 |
| ☐ B35 Ernie Warlick | 4.00 | 1.60 | .40 |
| ☐ B36 Bills Logo | 3.00 | 1.20 | .30 |

# 1966 Coke Caps Browns

As part of an advertising promotion, Coca-Cola issued 21 sets of bottle caps, covering the 14 NFL cities, the six (separate) AFL cities, and a separate All-Star promotion for cities not reached by the leagues. The caps measure approximately 1 1/8" in diameter. They have the Coke logo and a football on the outside, while the inside has the player's face printed in black, with text surrounding the face. A Cap-Saver sheet was also issued to aid in collecting the bottle caps, and the consumer could turn in his completed sheet to receive various prizes. The numbering of the caps below reflects that of the Cap-Saver sheet. Each team had 36 caps issued plus the same 34 all-stars. These "Coke" caps were typically also available with other Coca-Cola products such as Fresca and Tab.

| | NRMT | VG-E | GOOD |
|---|---|---|---|
| COMPLETE SET (36) | 100.00 | 40.00 | 10.00 |
| COMMON PLAYER (C1-C36) | 3.00 | 1.20 | .30 |
| | | | |
| ☐ C1 Jim Ninowski | 4.00 | 1.60 | .40 |
| ☐ C2 Leroy Kelly | 7.50 | 3.00 | .75 |
| ☐ C3 Lou Groza | 7.50 | 3.00 | .75 |
| ☐ C4 Gary Collins | 4.00 | 1.60 | .40 |
| ☐ C5 Bill Glass | 4.00 | 1.60 | .40 |
| ☐ C6 Dale Lindsey | 3.00 | 1.20 | .30 |
| ☐ C7 Galen Fiss | 3.00 | 1.20 | .30 |
| ☐ C8 Ross Fichtner | 3.00 | 1.20 | .30 |
| ☐ C9 John Wooten | 3.00 | 1.20 | .30 |
| ☐ C10 Clifton McNeil | 4.00 | 1.60 | .40 |
| ☐ C11 Paul Wiggin | 4.00 | 1.60 | .40 |
| ☐ C12 Gene Hickerson | 4.00 | 1.60 | .40 |
| ☐ C13 Ernie Green | 4.00 | 1.60 | .40 |
| ☐ C14 Mike Howell | 3.00 | 1.20 | .30 |
| ☐ C15 Dick Schafrath | 4.00 | 1.60 | .40 |
| ☐ C16 Sidney Williams | 3.00 | 1.20 | .30 |
| ☐ C17 Frank Ryan | 5.00 | 2.00 | .50 |
| ☐ C18 Bernie Parrish | 4.00 | 1.60 | .40 |
| ☐ C19 Vince Costello | 3.00 | 1.20 | .30 |
| ☐ C20 John Brown OT | 3.00 | 1.20 | .30 |
| ☐ C21 Monte Clark | 4.00 | 1.60 | .40 |
| ☐ C22 Walt Roberts | 3.00 | 1.20 | .30 |
| ☐ C23 Johnny Brewer | 3.00 | 1.20 | .30 |
| ☐ C24 Walter Beach | 3.00 | 1.20 | .30 |
| ☐ C25 Dick Modzelewski | 4.00 | 1.60 | .40 |
| ☐ C26 Gary Lane | 3.00 | 1.20 | .30 |
| ☐ C27 Jim Houston | 4.00 | 1.60 | .40 |
| ☐ C28 Milt Morin | 4.00 | 1.60 | .40 |
| ☐ C29 Erich Barnes | 4.00 | 1.60 | .40 |
| ☐ C30 Tom Hutchinson | 3.00 | 1.20 | .30 |
| ☐ C31 John Morrow | 3.00 | 1.20 | .30 |
| ☐ C32 Jim Kanicki | 3.00 | 1.20 | .30 |
| ☐ C33 Paul Warfield | 7.50 | 3.00 | .75 |
| ☐ C34 Jim Garcia | 3.00 | 1.20 | .30 |

| | | | |
|---|---|---|---|
| ☐ C35 Walter Johnson | 4.00 | 1.60 | .40 |
| ☐ C36 Browns Logo | 3.00 | 1.20 | .30 |

# 1966 Coke Caps Cardinals

As part of an advertising promotion, Coca-Cola issued 21 sets of bottle caps, covering the 14 NFL cities, the six (separate) AFL cities, and a separate All-Star promotion for cities not reached by the leagues. The caps measure approximately 1 1/8" in diameter. They have the Coke logo and a football on the outside, while the inside has the player's face printed in black, with text surrounding the face. A Cap-Saver sheet was also issued to aid in collecting the bottle caps, and the consumer could turn in his completed sheet to receive various prizes. The numbering of the caps below reflects that of the Cap-Saver sheet. Each team had 36 caps issued plus the same 34 all-stars. These "Coke" caps were typically also available with other Coca-Cola products such as Fresca and Tab.

| | NRMT | VG-E | GOOD |
|---|---|---|---|
| COMPLETE SET (36) | 100.00 | 40.00 | 10.00 |
| COMMON PLAYER (C1-C36) | 3.00 | 1.20 | .30 |
| | | | |
| ☐ C1 Pat Fischer | 4.00 | 1.60 | .40 |
| ☐ C2 Sonny Randle | 4.00 | 1.60 | .40 |
| ☐ C3 Joe Childress | 3.00 | 1.20 | .30 |
| ☐ C4 Dave Meggysey UER | 5.00 | 2.00 | .50 |
| (Name misspelled Meggyesy) | | | |
| ☐ C5 Joe Robb | 3.00 | 1.20 | .30 |
| ☐ C6 Jerry Stovall | 4.00 | 1.60 | .40 |
| ☐ C7 Ernie McMillan | 4.00 | 1.60 | .40 |
| ☐ C8 Dale Meinert | 3.00 | 1.20 | .30 |
| ☐ C9 Irv Goode | 3.00 | 1.20 | .30 |
| ☐ C10 Bob DeMarco | 4.00 | 1.60 | .40 |
| ☐ C11 Mal Hammack | 3.00 | 1.20 | .30 |
| ☐ C12 Jim Bakken | 5.00 | 2.00 | .50 |
| ☐ C13 Bill Thornton | 3.00 | 1.20 | .30 |
| ☐ C14 Buddy Humphrey | 3.00 | 1.20 | .30 |
| ☐ C15 Bill Koman | 3.00 | 1.20 | .30 |
| ☐ C16 Larry Wilson | 7.50 | 3.00 | .75 |
| ☐ C17 Charles Walker | 3.00 | 1.20 | .30 |
| ☐ C18 Prentice Gautt | 5.00 | 2.00 | .50 |
| ☐ C19 Charlie Johnson UER | 5.00 | 2.00 | .50 |
| (Name misspelled Charley) | | | |
| ☐ C20 Ken Gray | 4.00 | 1.60 | .40 |
| ☐ C21 Dave Simmons | 4.00 | 1.60 | .40 |
| ☐ C22 Sam Silas | 3.00 | 1.20 | .30 |
| ☐ C23 Larry Stallings | 4.00 | 1.60 | .40 |
| ☐ C24 Don Brumm | 3.00 | 1.20 | .30 |
| ☐ C25 Bobby Joe Conrad | 4.00 | 1.60 | .40 |
| ☐ C26 Bill Triplett | 3.00 | 1.20 | .30 |
| ☐ C27 Luke Owens | 3.00 | 1.20 | .30 |
| ☐ C28 Jackie Smith | 6.00 | 2.40 | .60 |
| ☐ C29 Bob Reynolds | 3.00 | 1.20 | .30 |
| ☐ C30 Abe Woodson | 4.00 | 1.60 | .40 |
| ☐ C31 Jimmy Burson | 3.00 | 1.20 | .30 |
| ☐ C32 Willis Crenshaw | 3.00 | 1.20 | .30 |
| ☐ C33 Billy Gambrell | 3.00 | 1.20 | .30 |
| ☐ C34 Ray Ogden | 3.00 | 1.20 | .30 |
| ☐ C35 Herschel Turner | 3.00 | 1.20 | .30 |
| ☐ C36 Cardinals Logo | 3.00 | 1.20 | .30 |

# 1966 Coke Caps Chiefs

As part of an advertising promotion, Coca-Cola issued 21 sets of bottle caps, covering the 14 NFL cities, the six (separate) AFL cities, and a separate All-Star promotion for cities not reached by the leagues. The caps measure approximately 1 1/8" in diameter. They have the Coke logo and a football on the outside, while the inside has the player's face printed in black, with text surrounding the face. A Cap-Saver sheet was also issued to aid in collecting the bottle caps, and the consumer could turn in his completed sheet to receive various prizes. The numbering of the caps below reflects that of the Cap-Saver sheet. Each team had 36 caps issued plus the same 34 all-stars. These "Coke" caps were typically also available with other Coca-Cola products such as Fresca and Tab.

| | NRMT | VG-E | GOOD |
|---|---|---|---|
| COMPLETE SET (36) | 100.00 | 40.00 | 10.00 |
| COMMON PLAYER (1-36) | 3.00 | 1.20 | .30 |
| ☐ C1 E.J. Holub | 4.00 | 1.60 | .40 |
| ☐ C2 Al Reynolds | 3.00 | 1.20 | .30 |
| ☐ C3 Buck Buchanan | 7.50 | 3.00 | .75 |
| ☐ C4 Curt Merz SP | 10.00 | 4.00 | 1.00 |
| ☐ C5 David Hill | 3.00 | 1.20 | .30 |
| ☐ C6 Bobby Hunt | 3.00 | 1.20 | .30 |
| ☐ C7 Jerry Mays | 4.00 | 1.60 | .40 |
| ☐ C8 Jon Gilliam | 4.00 | 1.60 | .40 |
| ☐ C9 Walt Corey | 3.00 | 1.20 | .30 |
| ☐ C10 Solomon Brannan | 3.00 | 1.20 | .30 |
| ☐ C11 Aaron Brown | 4.00 | 1.60 | .40 |
| ☐ C12 Bert Coan | 4.00 | 1.60 | .40 |
| ☐ C13 Ed Budde | 4.00 | 1.60 | .40 |
| ☐ C14 Tommy Brooker | 4.00 | 1.60 | .40 |
| ☐ C15 Bobby Bell | 7.50 | 3.00 | .75 |
| ☐ C16 Smokey Stover | 3.00 | 1.20 | .30 |
| ☐ C17 Curtis McClinton | 4.00 | 1.60 | .40 |
| ☐ C18 Jerrel Wilson | 5.00 | 2.00 | .50 |
| ☐ C19 Ron Burton | 4.00 | 1.60 | .40 |
| ☐ C20 Mike Garrett | 7.50 | 3.00 | .75 |
| ☐ C21 Jim Tyrer | 4.00 | 1.60 | .40 |
| ☐ C22 Johnny Robinson | 5.00 | 2.00 | .50 |
| ☐ C23 Bobby Ply | 3.00 | 1.20 | .30 |
| ☐ C24 Frank Pitts | 3.00 | 1.20 | .30 |
| ☐ C25 Ed Lothamer | 3.00 | 1.20 | .30 |
| ☐ C26 Sherrill Headrick | 4.00 | 1.60 | .40 |
| ☐ C27 Fred Williamson | 6.00 | 2.40 | .60 |
| ☐ C28 Chris Burford | 4.00 | 1.60 | .40 |
| ☐ C29 Willie Mitchell | 3.00 | 1.20 | .30 |
| ☐ C30 Otis Taylor | 7.50 | 3.00 | .75 |
| ☐ C31 Fred Arbanas | 4.00 | 1.60 | .40 |
| ☐ C32 Hatch Rosdahl | 3.00 | 1.20 | .30 |
| ☐ C33 Reg Carolan | 3.00 | 1.20 | .30 |
| ☐ C34 Len Dawson | 10.00 | 4.00 | 1.00 |
| ☐ C35 Pete Beathard | 5.00 | 2.00 | .50 |
| ☐ C36 Chiefs Logo | 3.00 | 1.20 | .30 |

## 1966 Coke Caps Colts

As part of an advertising promotion, Coca-Cola issued 21 sets of bottle caps, covering the 14 NFL cities, the six (separate) AFL cities, and a separate All-Star promotion for cities not reached by the leagues. The caps measure approximately 1 1/8" in diameter. They have the Coke logo and a football on the outside, while the inside has the player's face printed in black, with text surrounding the face. A Cap-Saver sheet was also issued to aid in collecting the bottle caps, and the consumer could turn in his completed sheet to receive various prizes. The numbering of the caps below reflects that of the Cap-Saver sheet. Each team had 36 caps issued plus the same 34 all-stars. These "Coke" caps were typically also available with other Coca-Cola products such as Fresca and Tab.

| | NRMT | VG-E | GOOD |
|---|---|---|---|
| COMPLETE SET (36) | 100.00 | 40.00 | 10.00 |
| COMMON PLAYER (1-36) | 3.00 | 1.20 | .30 |
| ☐ C1 Ted Davis | 3.00 | 1.20 | .30 |
| ☐ C2 Bobby Boyd | 3.00 | 1.20 | .30 |
| ☐ C3 Lenny Moore | 7.50 | 3.00 | .75 |
| ☐ C4 Jackie Burkett | 4.00 | 1.60 | .40 |
| ☐ C5 Jimmy Orr | 5.00 | 2.00 | .50 |
| ☐ C6 Andy Stynchula | 3.00 | 1.20 | .30 |
| ☐ C7 Mike Curtis | 5.00 | 2.00 | .50 |
| ☐ C8 Jerry Logan | 3.00 | 1.20 | .30 |
| ☐ C9 Steve Stonebreaker | 4.00 | 1.60 | .40 |
| ☐ C10 John Mackey | 6.00 | 2.40 | .60 |
| ☐ C11 Dennis Gaubatz | 3.00 | 1.20 | .30 |
| ☐ C12 Don Shinnick | 4.00 | 1.60 | .40 |
| ☐ C13 Dick Szymanski | 3.00 | 1.20 | .30 |
| ☐ C14 Ordell Braase | 3.00 | 1.20 | .30 |
| ☐ C15 Len Lyles | 3.00 | 1.20 | .30 |
| ☐ C16 Rick Kestner | 3.00 | 1.20 | .30 |
| ☐ C17 Dan Sullivan | 3.00 | 1.20 | .30 |
| ☐ C18 Lou Michaels | 4.00 | 1.60 | .40 |
| ☐ C19 Gary Cuozzo | 4.00 | 1.60 | .40 |
| ☐ C20 Butch Wilson | 3.00 | 1.20 | .30 |
| ☐ C21 Willie Richardson | 4.00 | 1.60 | .40 |
| ☐ C22 Jim Welch | 3.00 | 1.20 | .30 |
| ☐ C23 Tony Lorick | 4.00 | 1.60 | .40 |
| ☐ C24 Billy Ray Smith | 4.00 | 1.60 | .40 |
| ☐ C25 Fred Miller | 3.00 | 1.20 | .30 |

| | NRMT | VG-E | GOOD |
|---|---|---|---|
| ☐ C26 Tom Matte | 5.00 | 2.00 | .50 |
| ☐ C27 John Unitas | 15.00 | 6.00 | 1.50 |
| ☐ C28 Glenn Ressler | 3.00 | 1.20 | .30 |
| ☐ C29 Alvin Haymond | 3.00 | 1.20 | .30 |
| ☐ C30 Jim Parker | 6.00 | 2.40 | .60 |
| ☐ C31 Butch Allison | 3.00 | 1.20 | .30 |
| ☐ C32 Bob Vogel | 3.00 | 1.20 | .30 |
| ☐ C33 Jerry Hill | 3.00 | 1.20 | .30 |
| ☐ C34 Raymond Berry | 7.50 | 3.00 | .75 |
| ☐ C35 Sam Ball | 3.00 | 1.20 | .30 |
| ☐ C36 Colts Team Logo | 3.00 | 1.20 | .30 |

## 1966 Coke Caps Cowboys

As part of an advertising promotion, Coca-Cola issued 21 sets of bottle caps, covering the 14 NFL cities, the six (separate) AFL cities, and a separate All-Star promotion for cities not reached by the leagues. The caps measure approximately 1 1/8" in diameter. They have the Coke logo and a football on the outside, while the inside has the player's face printed in black, with text surrounding the face. A Cap-Saver sheet was also issued to aid in collecting the bottle caps, and the consumer could turn in his completed sheet to receive various prizes. The numbering of the caps below reflects that of the Cap-Saver sheet. Each team had 36 caps issued plus the same 34 all-stars. These "Coke" caps were typically also available with other Coca-Cola products such as Fresca and Tab.

| | NRMT | VG-E | GOOD |
|---|---|---|---|
| COMPLETE SET (36) | 100.00 | 40.00 | 10.00 |
| COMMON PLAYER (C1-C36) | 3.00 | 1.20 | .30 |
| ☐ C1 Mike Connelly | 3.00 | 1.20 | .30 |
| ☐ C2 Tony Liscio | 3.00 | 1.20 | .30 |
| ☐ C3 Jethro Pugh | 5.00 | 2.00 | .50 |
| ☐ C4 Larry Stephens | 3.00 | 1.20 | .30 |
| ☐ C5 Jim Colvin | 3.00 | 1.20 | .30 |
| ☐ C6 Malcolm Walker | 3.00 | 1.20 | .30 |
| ☐ C7 Danny Villanueva | 4.00 | 1.60 | .40 |
| ☐ C8 Frank Clarke | 4.00 | 1.60 | .40 |
| ☐ C9 Don Meredith | 12.00 | 5.00 | 1.20 |
| ☐ C10 George Andrie | 4.00 | 1.60 | .40 |
| ☐ C11 Mel Renfro | 6.00 | 2.40 | .60 |
| ☐ C12 Pettis Norman | 4.00 | 1.60 | .40 |
| ☐ C13 Buddy Dial | 4.00 | 1.60 | .40 |
| ☐ C14 Pete Gent | 4.00 | 1.60 | .40 |
| ☐ C15 Jerry Rhome | 4.00 | 1.60 | .40 |
| ☐ C16 Bob Hayes | 6.00 | 2.40 | .60 |
| ☐ C17 Mike Gaechter | 3.00 | 1.20 | .30 |
| ☐ C18 Joe Bob Isbell | 3.00 | 1.20 | .30 |
| ☐ C19 Harold Hays | 3.00 | 1.20 | .30 |
| ☐ C20 Craig Morton | 5.00 | 2.00 | .50 |
| ☐ C21 Jake Kupp | 3.00 | 1.20 | .30 |
| ☐ C22 Cornell Green | 4.00 | 1.60 | .40 |
| ☐ C23 Dan Reeves | 10.00 | 4.00 | 1.00 |
| ☐ C24 Leon Donohue | 3.00 | 1.20 | .30 |
| ☐ C25 Dave Manders | 4.00 | 1.60 | .40 |
| ☐ C26 Warren Livingston | 3.00 | 1.20 | .30 |
| ☐ C27 Bob Lilly | 7.50 | 3.00 | .75 |
| ☐ C28 Chuck Howley | 5.00 | 2.00 | .50 |
| ☐ C29 Don Bishop | 3.00 | 1.20 | .30 |
| ☐ C30 Don Perkins | 4.00 | 1.60 | .40 |
| ☐ C31 Jim Boeke | 3.00 | 1.20 | .30 |
| ☐ C32 Dave Edwards | 3.00 | 1.20 | .30 |
| ☐ C33 Lee Roy Jordan | 6.00 | 2.40 | .60 |
| ☐ C34 Obert Logan | 3.00 | 1.20 | .30 |
| ☐ C35 Ralph Neely | 4.00 | 1.60 | .40 |
| ☐ C36 Cowboys Logo | 3.00 | 1.20 | .30 |

## 1966 Coke Caps Falcons

As part of an advertising promotion, Coca-Cola issued 21 sets of bottle caps, covering the 14 NFL cities, the six (separate) AFL cities, and a separate All-Star promotion for cities not reached by the leagues. The caps measure approximately 1 1/8" in diameter. They have the Coke logo and a football on the outside, while the inside has the player's face printed in black, with text surrounding the face. A Cap-Saver sheet was also issued to aid in collecting the bottle caps, and the consumer could turn in his completed sheet to receive various prizes. The numbering of the caps below reflects that of the Cap-Saver sheet. Each team had 36 caps issued plus the same 34 all-stars. These "Coke" caps were typically also available with other Coca-Cola products such as Fresca and Tab.

| | NRMT | VG-E | GOOD |
|---|---|---|---|
| COMPLETE SET (36) | 100.00 | 40.00 | 10.00 |
| COMMON PLAYER (C1-C36) | 3.00 | 1.20 | .30 |

| | NRMT | VG-E | GOOD |
|---|---|---|---|
| ☐ C1 Tommy Nobis | 7.50 | 3.00 | .75 |
| ☐ C2 Ernie Wheelwright | 4.00 | 1.60 | .40 |
| ☐ C3 Lee Calland | 3.00 | 1.20 | .30 |
| ☐ C4 Chuck Sieminski | 3.00 | 1.20 | .30 |
| ☐ C5 Dennis Claridge | 3.00 | 1.20 | .30 |
| ☐ C6 Ralph Heck | 3.00 | 1.20 | .30 |
| ☐ C7 Alex Hawkins | 4.00 | 1.60 | .40 |
| ☐ C8 Dan Grimm | 3.00 | 1.20 | .30 |
| ☐ C9 Marion Rushing | 3.00 | 1.20 | .30 |
| ☐ C10 Bobbie Johnson | 3.00 | 1.20 | .30 |
| ☐ C11 Bobby Franklin | 3.00 | 1.20 | .30 |
| ☐ C12 Bill McWatters | 3.00 | 1.20 | .30 |
| ☐ C13 Billy Lothridge | 4.00 | 1.60 | .40 |
| ☐ C14 Billy Martin | 3.00 | 1.20 | .30 |
| ☐ C15 Tom Wilson | 3.00 | 1.20 | .30 |
| ☐ C16 Dennis Murphy | 3.00 | 1.20 | .30 |
| ☐ C17 Randy Johnson | 4.00 | 1.60 | .40 |
| ☐ C18 Guy Reese | 3.00 | 1.20 | .30 |
| ☐ C19 Frank Marchlewski | 3.00 | 1.20 | .30 |
| ☐ C20 Don Talbert | 4.00 | 1.60 | .40 |
| ☐ C21 Errol Linden | 3.00 | 1.20 | .30 |
| ☐ C22 Dan Lewis | 3.00 | 1.20 | .30 |
| ☐ C23 Ed Cook | 3.00 | 1.20 | .30 |
| ☐ C24 Hugh McInnis | 3.00 | 1.20 | .30 |
| ☐ C25 Frank Lasky | 3.00 | 1.20 | .30 |
| ☐ C26 Bob Jencks | 3.00 | 1.20 | .30 |
| ☐ C27 Bill Jobko | 3.00 | 1.20 | .30 |
| ☐ C28 Nick Rassas | 3.00 | 1.20 | .30 |
| ☐ C29 Bob Riggle | 3.00 | 1.20 | .30 |
| ☐ C30 Ken Reaves | 3.00 | 1.20 | .30 |
| ☐ C31 Bob Sanders | 3.00 | 1.20 | .30 |
| ☐ C32 Steve Sloan | 7.50 | 3.00 | .75 |
| ☐ C33 Ron Smith | 4.00 | 1.60 | .40 |
| ☐ C34 Bob Whitlow | 3.00 | 1.20 | .30 |
| ☐ C35 Roger Anderson | 3.00 | 1.20 | .30 |
| ☐ C36 Falcons Logo | 3.00 | 1.20 | .30 |

## 1966 Coke Caps 49ers

As part of an advertising promotion, Coca-Cola issued 21 sets of bottle caps, covering the 14 NFL cities, the six (separate) AFL cities, and a separate All-Star promotion for cities not reached by the leagues. The caps measure approximately 1 1/8" in diameter. They have the Coke logo and a football on the outside, while the inside has the player's face printed in black, with text surrounding the face. A Cap-Saver sheet was also issued to aid in collecting the bottle caps, and the consumer could turn in his completed sheet to receive various prizes. The numbering of the caps below reflects that of the Cap-Saver sheet. Each team had 36 caps issued plus the same 34 all-stars. These "Coke" caps were typically also available with other Coca-Cola products such as Fresca and Tab.

| | NRMT | VG-E | GOOD |
|---|---|---|---|
| COMPLETE SET (36) | 100.00 | 40.00 | 10.00 |
| COMMON PLAYER (C1-C36) | 3.00 | 1.20 | .30 |
| ☐ C1 Bernie Casey | 5.00 | 2.00 | .50 |
| ☐ C2 Bruce Bosley | 4.00 | 1.60 | .40 |
| ☐ C3 Kermit Alexander | 4.00 | 1.60 | .40 |
| ☐ C4 John Brodie | 9.00 | 3.75 | .90 |
| ☐ C5 Dave Parks | 4.00 | 1.60 | .40 |
| ☐ C6 Len Rohde | 3.00 | 1.20 | .30 |
| ☐ C7 Walter Rock | 3.00 | 1.20 | .30 |
| ☐ C8 George Mira | 5.00 | 2.00 | .50 |
| ☐ C9 Karl Rubke | 3.00 | 1.20 | .30 |
| ☐ C10 Ken Willard | 4.00 | 1.60 | .40 |
| ☐ C11 John David Crow UER | 5.00 | 2.00 | .50 |
| (Name misspelled Crowe) | | | |
| ☐ C12 George Donnelly | 3.00 | 1.20 | .30 |
| ☐ C13 Dave Wilcox | 5.00 | 2.00 | .50 |
| ☐ C14 Vern Burke | 3.00 | 1.20 | .30 |
| ☐ C15 Wayne Swinford | 3.00 | 1.20 | .30 |
| ☐ C16 Elbert Kimbrough | 3.00 | 1.20 | .30 |
| ☐ C17 Clark Miller | 3.00 | 1.20 | .30 |
| ☐ C18 Dave Kopay | 4.00 | 1.60 | .40 |
| ☐ C19 Joe Cerne | 3.00 | 1.20 | .30 |
| ☐ C20 Roland Lakes | 3.00 | 1.20 | .30 |
| ☐ C21 Charlie Krueger | 4.00 | 1.60 | .40 |
| ☐ C22 Billy Kilmer | 6.00 | 2.40 | .60 |
| ☐ C23 Jim Johnson | 6.00 | 2.40 | .60 |
| ☐ C24 Matt Hazeltine | 3.00 | 1.20 | .30 |
| ☐ C25 Mike Dowdle | 3.00 | 1.20 | .30 |
| ☐ C26 Jim Wilson | 3.00 | 1.20 | .30 |
| ☐ C27 Tommy Davis | 4.00 | 1.60 | .40 |
| ☐ C28 Jim Norton | 3.00 | 1.20 | .30 |
| ☐ C29 Jack Chapple | 3.00 | 1.20 | .30 |
| ☐ C30 Ed Beard | 3.00 | 1.20 | .30 |
| ☐ C31 John Thomas | 3.00 | 1.20 | .30 |
| ☐ C32 Monty Stickles | 4.00 | 1.60 | .40 |
| ☐ C33 Kay McFarland | 4.00 | 1.60 | .40 |
| ☐ C34 Gary Lewis | 3.00 | 1.20 | .30 |
| ☐ C35 Howard Mudd | 3.00 | 1.20 | .30 |
| ☐ C36 49ers Logo | 3.00 | 1.20 | .30 |

## 1966 Coke Caps Giants

As part of an advertising promotion, Coca-Cola issued 21 sets of bottle caps, covering the 14 NFL cities, the six (separate) AFL cities, and a separate All-Star promotion for cities not reached by the leagues. The caps measure approximately 1 1/8" in diameter. They have the Coke logo and a football on the outside, while the inside has the player's face printed in black, with text surrounding the face. A cap-saver sheet was also issued to aid in collecting the bottle caps, and the consumer could turn in his completed sheet to receive various prizes. The numbering of the caps below reflects that of the cap-saver sheet. Each team had 35 player caps issued plus the same 34 all-stars. These "Coke" caps were typically also available with other Coca-Cola products such as Fresca and Tab. Much of the set corresponds closely with the set from the previous year; the following cap numbers are different from the 1965 Giants set: G3, G6, G7, G9, G12, G13, G15, G17, G21, G24, G26, G28, and G29.

| | NRMT | VG-E | GOOD |
|---|---|---|---|
| COMPLETE SET (35) | 100.00 | 40.00 | 10.00 |
| COMMON PLAYER (G1-G35) | 3.00 | 1.20 | .30 |
| ☐ G1 Joe Morrison | 4.00 | 1.60 | .40 |
| ☐ G2 Dick Lynch | 4.00 | 1.60 | .40 |
| ☐ G3 Pete Case | 3.00 | 1.20 | .30 |
| ☐ G4 Clarence Childs | 3.00 | 1.20 | .30 |
| ☐ G5 Aaron Thomas | 3.00 | 1.20 | .30 |
| ☐ G6 Jim Carroll | 3.00 | 1.20 | .30 |
| ☐ G7 Henry Carr | 4.00 | 1.60 | .40 |
| ☐ G8 Bookie Bolin | 3.00 | 1.20 | .30 |
| ☐ G9 Roosevelt Davis | 3.00 | 1.20 | .30 |
| ☐ G10 John Lovetere | 3.00 | 1.20 | .30 |
| ☐ G11 Jim Patton | 4.00 | 1.60 | .40 |
| ☐ G12 Wendell Harris | 3.00 | 1.20 | .30 |
| ☐ G13 Roger LaLonde | 3.00 | 1.20 | .30 |
| ☐ G14 Jerry Hillebrand | 3.00 | 1.20 | .30 |
| ☐ G15 Carl Lockhart | 4.00 | 1.60 | .40 |
| ☐ G16 Del Shofner | 5.00 | 2.00 | .50 |
| ☐ G17 Earl Morrall | 6.00 | 2.40 | .60 |
| ☐ G18 Roosevelt Brown | 6.00 | 2.40 | .60 |
| ☐ G19 Greg Larson | 3.00 | 1.20 | .30 |
| ☐ G20 Jim Katcavage | 4.00 | 1.60 | .40 |
| ☐ G21 Smith Reed | 3.00 | 1.20 | .30 |
| ☐ G22 Lou Slaby | 3.00 | 1.20 | .30 |
| ☐ G23 Jim Moran | 3.00 | 1.20 | .30 |
| ☐ G24 Bill Swain | 3.00 | 1.20 | .30 |
| ☐ G25 Steve Thurlow | 3.00 | 1.20 | .30 |
| ☐ G26 Olen Underwood | 3.00 | 1.20 | .30 |
| ☐ G27 Gary Wood | 4.00 | 1.60 | .40 |
| ☐ G28 Larry Vargo | 3.00 | 1.20 | .30 |
| ☐ G29 Jim Prestel | 3.00 | 1.20 | .30 |
| (Cap saver sheet reads Ed Prestel) | | | |
| ☐ G30 Tucker Frederickson | 4.00 | 1.60 | .40 |
| ☐ G31 Bob Timberlake | 4.00 | 1.60 | .40 |
| ☐ G32 Chuck Mercein | 4.00 | 1.60 | .40 |
| ☐ G33 Ernie Koy | 4.00 | 1.60 | .40 |
| ☐ G34 Tom Costello | 3.00 | 1.20 | .30 |
| ☐ G35 Homer Jones | 4.00 | 1.60 | .40 |

## 1966 Coke Caps Jets

As part of an advertising promotion, Coca-Cola issued 21 sets of bottle caps, covering the 14 NFL cities, the six (separate) AFL cities, and a separate All-Star promotion for cities not reached by the leagues. The caps measure approximately 1 1/8" in diameter. They have the Coke logo and a football on the outside, while the inside has the player's face printed in black, with text surrounding the face. A cap-saver sheet was also issued to aid in collecting the bottle caps, and the consumer could turn in his completed sheet to receive various prizes. The numbering of the caps below reflects that of the cap-saver sheet. Each team had 35 player caps issued plus the same 34 all-stars. These "Coke" caps were typically also available with other Coca-Cola products such as Fresca and Tab.

|  | NRMT | VG-E | GOOD |
|---|---|---|---|
| COMPLETE SET (35) | 100.00 | 40.00 | 10.00 |
| COMMON PLAYER (J1-J35) | 3.00 | 1.20 | .30 |
| ☐ J1 Don Maynard | 6.00 | 2.40 | .60 |
| ☐ J2 George Sauer | 4.00 | 1.60 | .40 |
| ☐ J3 Paul Crane | 3.00 | 1.20 | .30 |
| ☐ J4 Jim Colclough | 3.00 | 1.20 | .30 |
| ☐ J5 Matt Snell | 5.00 | 2.00 | .50 |
| ☐ J6 Sherman Lewis | 4.00 | 1.60 | .40 |
| ☐ J7 Jim Turner | 4.00 | 1.60 | .40 |
| ☐ J8 Mike Taliaferro | 4.00 | 1.60 | .40 |
| ☐ J9 Cornell Gordon | 3.00 | 1.20 | .30 |
| ☐ J10 Mark Smolinski | 3.00 | 1.20 | .30 |
| ☐ J11 Al Atkinson | 4.00 | 1.60 | .40 |
| ☐ J12 Paul Rochester | 3.00 | 1.20 | .30 |
| ☐ J13 Sherman Plunkett | 3.00 | 1.20 | .30 |
| ☐ J14 Gerry Philbin | 4.00 | 1.60 | .40 |
| ☐ J15 Pete Lammons | 4.00 | 1.60 | .40 |
| ☐ J16 Dainard Paulson | 3.00 | 1.20 | .30 |
| ☐ J17 Joe Namath | 30.00 | 12.00 | 3.00 |
| ☐ J18 Winston Hill | 3.00 | 1.20 | .30 |
| ☐ J19 Dee Mackey | 3.00 | 1.20 | .30 |
| ☐ J20 Curley Johnson | 3.00 | 1.20 | .30 |
| ☐ J21 Verlon Biggs | 4.00 | 1.60 | .40 |
| ☐ J22 Bill Mathis | 4.00 | 1.60 | .40 |
| ☐ J23 Carl McAdams | 3.00 | 1.20 | .30 |
| ☐ J24 Bert Wilder | 3.00 | 1.20 | .30 |
| ☐ J25 Larry Grantham | 4.00 | 1.60 | .40 |
| ☐ J26 Bill Yearby | 3.00 | 1.20 | .30 |
| ☐ J27 Sam DeLuca | 3.00 | 1.20 | .30 |
| ☐ J28 Bill Baird | 3.00 | 1.20 | .30 |
| ☐ J29 Ralph Baker | 3.00 | 1.20 | .30 |
| ☐ J30 Ray Abruzzese | 3.00 | 1.20 | .30 |
| ☐ J31 Jim Hudson | 3.00 | 1.20 | .30 |
| ☐ J32 Dave Herman | 3.00 | 1.20 | .30 |
| ☐ J33 John Schmitt | 3.00 | 1.20 | .30 |
| ☐ J34 Jim Harris | 3.00 | 1.20 | .30 |
| ☐ J35 Bake Turner | 4.00 | 1.60 | .40 |

## 1966 Coke Caps National NFL

These caps were issued in NFL cities (and some other cities as well) along with the local team caps. Some NFL city Cap Saver sheets had separate sections in which to affix both the local team's caps and the All-Stars' (or National NFL) caps. The caps measure approximately 1 1/8" in diameter. They have the Coke logo and a football on the outside, while the inside has the player's face printed in black, with text surrounding the face. A Cap-Saver sheet was also issued to aid in collecting the bottle caps, and the consumer could turn in his completed sheet to receive various prizes. The numbering of the caps below reflects that of the Cap-Saver sheet. These "Coke" caps were typically also available with other Coca-Cola products such as Fresca and Tab.

|  | MINT | EXC | G-VG |
|---|---|---|---|
| COMPLETE SET (70) | 200.00 | 80.00 | 20.00 |
| COMMON PLAYER (1-70) | 3.00 | 1.20 | .30 |
| ☐ 1 Larry Wilson | 6.00 | 2.40 | .60 |
| ☐ 2 Frank Ryan | 4.00 | 1.60 | .40 |
| ☐ 3 Norm Snead | 4.00 | 1.60 | .40 |
| ☐ 4 Mel Renfro | 5.00 | 2.00 | .50 |
| ☐ 5 Timmy Brown | 4.00 | 1.60 | .40 |
| ☐ 6 Tucker Frederickson | 3.00 | 1.20 | .30 |
| ☐ 7 Jim Bakken | 3.00 | 1.20 | .30 |
| ☐ 8 Paul Krause | 5.00 | 2.00 | .50 |
| ☐ 9 Irv Cross | 4.00 | 1.60 | .40 |
| ☐ 10 Cornell Green | 3.00 | 1.20 | .30 |
| ☐ 11 Pat Fischer | 3.00 | 1.20 | .30 |
| ☐ 12 Bob Hayes | 5.00 | 2.00 | .50 |
| ☐ 13 Charley Taylor | 6.00 | 2.40 | .60 |
| ☐ 14 Pete Retzlaff | 3.00 | 1.20 | .30 |
| ☐ 15 Jim Ringo | 6.00 | 2.40 | .60 |
| ☐ 16 Maxie Baughan | 4.00 | 1.60 | .40 |
| ☐ 17 Chuck Howley | 4.00 | 1.60 | .40 |
| ☐ 18 John Wooten | 3.00 | 1.20 | .30 |
| ☐ 19 Bob DeMarco | 3.00 | 1.20 | .30 |
| ☐ 20 Dale Meinert | 3.00 | 1.20 | .30 |
| ☐ 21 Gene Hickerson | 3.00 | 1.20 | .30 |
| ☐ 22 George Andrie | 3.00 | 1.20 | .30 |
| ☐ 23 Joe Rutgens | 3.00 | 1.20 | .30 |
| ☐ 24 Bob Lilly | 7.50 | 3.00 | .75 |
| ☐ 25 Sam Silas | 3.00 | 1.20 | .30 |
| ☐ 26 Bob Brown | 4.00 | 1.60 | .40 |
| ☐ 27 Dick Schafrath | 3.00 | 1.20 | .30 |
| ☐ 28 Roosevelt Brown | 6.00 | 2.40 | .60 |
| ☐ 29 Jim Houston | 3.00 | 1.20 | .30 |
| ☐ 30 Paul Wiggin | 3.00 | 1.20 | .30 |
| ☐ 31 Gary Ballman | 3.00 | 1.20 | .30 |
| ☐ 32 Gary Collins | 4.00 | 1.60 | .40 |
| ☐ 33 Sonny Randle | 4.00 | 1.60 | .40 |
| ☐ 34 Charlie Johnson | 4.00 | 1.60 | .40 |
| ☐ 35 Cleveland Browns Logo | 3.00 | 1.20 | .30 |
| ☐ 36 Green Bay Packers Logo | 3.00 | 1.20 | .30 |
| ☐ 37 Herb Adderley | 6.00 | 2.40 | .60 |
| ☐ 38 Grady Alderman | 3.00 | 1.20 | .30 |
| ☐ 39 Doug Atkins | 6.00 | 2.40 | .60 |
| ☐ 40 Bruce Bosley | 3.00 | 1.20 | .30 |
| ☐ 41 John Brodie | 7.50 | 3.00 | .75 |
| ☐ 42 Roger Brown | 3.00 | 1.20 | .30 |
| ☐ 43 Bill Brown | 4.00 | 1.60 | .40 |
| ☐ 44 Dick Butkus | 10.00 | 4.00 | 1.00 |
| ☐ 45 Lee Roy Caffey | 3.00 | 1.20 | .30 |
| ☐ 46 John David Crow | 4.00 | 1.60 | .40 |
| ☐ 47 Willie Davis | 6.00 | 2.40 | .60 |
| ☐ 48 Mike Ditka | 10.00 | 4.00 | 1.00 |
| ☐ 49 Joe Fortunato | 3.00 | 1.20 | .30 |
| ☐ 50 John Gordy | 3.00 | 1.20 | .30 |
| ☐ 51 Deacon Jones | 6.00 | 2.40 | .60 |
| ☐ 52 Alex Karras | 6.00 | 2.40 | .60 |
| ☐ 53 Dick LeBeau | 3.00 | 1.20 | .30 |
| ☐ 54 Jerry Logan | 3.00 | 1.20 | .30 |
| ☐ 55 John Mackey | 6.00 | 2.40 | .60 |
| ☐ 56 Ed Meador | 3.00 | 1.20 | .30 |
| ☐ 57 Tommy McDonald | 4.00 | 1.60 | .40 |
| ☐ 58 Merlin Olsen | 6.00 | 2.40 | .60 |
| ☐ 59 Jimmy Orr | 4.00 | 1.60 | .40 |
| ☐ 60 Jim Parker | 6.00 | 2.40 | .60 |
| ☐ 61 Dave Parks | 4.00 | 1.60 | .40 |
| ☐ 62 Walter Rock | 3.00 | 1.20 | .30 |
| ☐ 63 Gale Sayers | 12.00 | 5.00 | 1.20 |
| ☐ 64 Pat Studstill | 3.00 | 1.20 | .30 |
| ☐ 65 Fran Tarkenton | 10.00 | 4.00 | 1.00 |
| ☐ 66 Mick Tingelhoff | 4.00 | 1.60 | .40 |
| ☐ 67 Bob Vogel | 3.00 | 1.20 | .30 |
| ☐ 68 Wayne Walker | 4.00 | 1.60 | .40 |
| ☐ 69 Ken Willard | 4.00 | 1.60 | .40 |
| ☐ 70 Willie Wood | 6.00 | 2.40 | .60 |

## 1966 Coke Caps Oilers

As part of an advertising promotion, Coca-Cola issued 21 sets of bottle caps, covering the 14 NFL cities, the six (separate) AFL cities, and a separate All-Star promotion for cities not reached by the leagues. The caps measure approximately 1 1/8" in diameter. They have the Coke logo and a football on the outside, while the inside has the player's face printed in black, with text surrounding the face. A Cap-Saver sheet was also issued to aid in collecting the bottle caps, and the consumer could turn in his completed sheet to receive various prizes. The numbering of the caps below reflects that of the Cap-Saver sheet. Each team had 36 caps issued plus the same 34 all-stars. These "Coke" caps were typically also available with other Coca-Cola products such as Fresca and Tab.

|  | NRMT | VG-E | GOOD |
|---|---|---|---|
| COMPLETE SET (36) | 100.00 | 40.00 | 10.00 |
| COMMON PLAYER (C1-C36) | 3.00 | 1.20 | .30 |
| ☐ C1 Scott Appleton | 4.00 | 1.60 | .40 |
| ☐ C2 George Allen | 4.00 | 1.60 | .40 |
| ☐ C3 Don Floyd | 4.00 | 1.60 | .40 |
| ☐ C4 Ronnie Caveness | 3.00 | 1.20 | .30 |
| ☐ C5 Jim Norton | 3.00 | 1.20 | .30 |
| ☐ C6 Jackie Lee | 4.00 | 1.60 | .40 |
| ☐ C7 George Blanda | 12.00 | 5.00 | 1.20 |
| ☐ C8 Tony Banfield | 4.00 | 1.60 | .40 |
| ☐ C9 George Rice | 3.00 | 1.20 | .30 |
| ☐ C10 Charley Tolar | 4.00 | 1.60 | .40 |

| | NRMT | VG-E | GOOD |
|---|---|---|---|
| ☐ C11 Bobby Jancik | 4.00 | 1.60 | .40 |
| ☐ C12 Fred Glick | 3.00 | 1.20 | .30 |
| ☐ C13 Ode Burrell | 3.00 | 1.20 | .30 |
| ☐ C14 Walt Suggs | 3.00 | 1.20 | .30 |
| ☐ C15 Bob McLeod | 3.00 | 1.20 | .30 |
| ☐ C16 Johnny Baker | 3.00 | 1.20 | .30 |
| ☐ C17 Danny Bradshaw | 3.00 | 1.20 | .30 |
| ☐ C18 Gary Cutsinger | 3.00 | 1.20 | .30 |
| ☐ C19 Doug Cline | 3.00 | 1.20 | .30 |
| ☐ C20 Hoyle Granger | 4.00 | 1.60 | .40 |
| ☐ C21 Bob Talamini | 3.00 | 1.20 | .30 |
| ☐ C22 Don Trull | 4.00 | 1.60 | .40 |
| ☐ C23 Charlie Hennigan | 4.00 | 1.60 | .40 |
| ☐ C24 Sid Blanks | 4.00 | 1.60 | .40 |
| ☐ C25 Pat Holmes | 3.00 | 1.20 | .30 |
| ☐ C26 John Frongillo | 3.00 | 1.20 | .30 |
| ☐ C27 John Whitehorn | 3.00 | 1.20 | .30 |
| ☐ C28 George Kinney | 3.00 | 1.20 | .30 |
| ☐ C29 Charles Frazier | 4.00 | 1.60 | .40 |
| ☐ C30 Ernie Ladd | 6.00 | 2.40 | .60 |
| ☐ C31 W.K. Hicks | 3.00 | 1.20 | .30 |
| ☐ C32 Sonny Bishop | 3.00 | 1.20 | .30 |
| ☐ C33 Larry Elkins | 4.00 | 1.60 | .40 |
| ☐ C34 Glen Ray Hines | 4.00 | 1.60 | .40 |
| ☐ C35 Bobby Maples | 4.00 | 1.60 | .40 |
| ☐ C36 Oilers Logo | 3.00 | 1.20 | .30 |

# 1966 Coke Caps Patriots

As part of an advertising promotion, Coca-Cola issued 21 sets of bottle caps, covering the 14 NFL cities, the six (separate) AFL cities, and a separate All-Star promotion for cities not reached by the leagues. The caps measure approximately 1 1/8" in diameter. They have the Coke logo and a football on the outside, while the inside has the player's face printed in black, with text surrounding the face. A Cap-Saver sheet was also issued to aid in collecting the bottle caps, and the consumer could turn in his completed sheet to receive various prizes. The numbering of the caps below reflects that of the Cap-Saver sheet. Each team had 36 caps issued plus the same 34 all-stars. These "Coke" caps were typically also available with other Coca-Cola products such as Fresca and Tab.

| | NRMT | VG-E | GOOD |
|---|---|---|---|
| COMPLETE SET (36) | 100.00 | 40.00 | 10.00 |
| COMMON PLAYER (C1-C36) | 3.00 | 1.20 | .30 |
| | | | |
| ☐ C1 Jon Morris | 3.00 | 1.20 | .30 |
| ☐ C2 Don Webb | 3.00 | 1.20 | .30 |
| ☐ C3 Charles Long | 3.00 | 1.20 | .30 |
| ☐ C4 Tony Romeo | 3.00 | 1.20 | .30 |
| ☐ C5 Bob Dee | 3.00 | 1.20 | .30 |
| ☐ C6 Tom Addison | 3.00 | 1.20 | .30 |
| ☐ C7 Tom Neville | 3.00 | 1.20 | .30 |
| ☐ C8 Ron Hall | 3.00 | 1.20 | .30 |
| ☐ C9 White Graves | 3.00 | 1.20 | .30 |
| ☐ C10 Ellis Johnson | 3.00 | 1.20 | .30 |
| ☐ C11 Don Oakes | 3.00 | 1.20 | .30 |
| ☐ C12 Tom Yewcic | 3.00 | 1.20 | .30 |
| ☐ C13 Tom Hennessey | 3.00 | 1.20 | .30 |
| ☐ C14 Jay Cunningham | 3.00 | 1.20 | .30 |
| ☐ C15 Larry Garron | 3.00 | 1.20 | .30 |
| ☐ C16 Justin Canale | 3.00 | 1.20 | .30 |
| ☐ C17 Art Graham | 3.00 | 1.20 | .30 |
| ☐ C18 Babe Parilli | 4.00 | 1.60 | .40 |
| ☐ C19 Jim Hunt | 3.00 | 1.20 | .30 |
| ☐ C20 Karl Singer | 3.00 | 1.20 | .30 |
| ☐ C21 Houston Antwine | 4.00 | 1.60 | .40 |
| ☐ C22 Nick Buoniconti | 6.00 | 2.40 | .60 |
| ☐ C23 John Huarte | 5.00 | 2.00 | .50 |
| ☐ C24 Gino Cappelletti | 4.00 | 1.60 | .40 |
| ☐ C25 Chuck Shonta | 3.00 | 1.20 | .30 |
| ☐ C26 Dick Felt | 3.00 | 1.20 | .30 |
| ☐ C27 Mike Dukes | 3.00 | 1.20 | .30 |
| ☐ C28 Larry Eisenhauer | 4.00 | 1.60 | .40 |
| ☐ C29 Jim Fraser | 3.00 | 1.20 | .30 |
| ☐ C30 Len St. Jean | 3.00 | 1.20 | .30 |
| ☐ C31 J.D. Garrett | 3.00 | 1.20 | .30 |
| ☐ C32 Jim Whalen | 4.00 | 1.60 | .40 |
| ☐ C33 Jim Nance | 5.00 | 2.00 | .50 |

| | NRMT | VG-E | GOOD |
|---|---|---|---|
| ☐ C34 Dick Arrington | 3.00 | 1.20 | .30 |
| ☐ C35 Lonnie Farmer | 3.00 | 1.20 | .30 |
| ☐ C36 Patriots Logo | 3.00 | 1.20 | .30 |

# 1966 Coke Caps Rams

As part of an advertising promotion, Coca-Cola issued 21 sets of bottle caps, covering the 14 NFL cities, the six (separate) AFL cities, and a separate All-Star promotion for cities not reached by the leagues. The caps measure approximately 1 1/8" in diameter. They have the Coke logo and a football on the outside, while the inside has the player's face printed in black, with text surrounding the face. A Cap-Saver sheet was also issued to aid in collecting the bottle caps, and the consumer could turn in his completed sheet to receive various prizes. The numbering of the caps below reflects that of the Cap-Saver sheet. Each team had 36 caps issued plus the same 34 all-stars. These "Coke" caps were typically also available with other Coca-Cola products such as Fresca and Tab.

| | NRMT | VG-E | GOOD |
|---|---|---|---|
| COMPLETE SET (36) | 100.00 | 40.00 | 10.00 |
| COMMON PLAYER (C1-C36) | 3.00 | 1.20 | .30 |
| | | | |
| ☐ C1 Tom Mack | 4.00 | 1.60 | .40 |
| ☐ C2 Tom Moore | 4.00 | 1.60 | .40 |
| ☐ C3 Bill Munson | 4.00 | 1.60 | .40 |
| ☐ C4 Bill George | 6.00 | 2.40 | .60 |
| ☐ C5 Joe Carollo | 3.00 | 1.20 | .30 |
| ☐ C6 Dick Bass | 4.00 | 1.60 | .40 |
| ☐ C7 Ken Iman | 3.00 | 1.20 | .30 |
| ☐ C8 Charlie Cowan | 4.00 | 1.60 | .40 |
| ☐ C9 Terry Baker | 5.00 | 2.00 | .50 |
| ☐ C10 Don Chuy | 3.00 | 1.20 | .30 |
| ☐ C11 Jack Pardee | 5.00 | 2.00 | .50 |
| ☐ C12 Lamar Lundy | 4.00 | 1.60 | .40 |
| ☐ C13 Bill Anderson | 3.00 | 1.20 | .30 |
| ☐ C14 Roman Gabriel | 6.00 | 2.40 | .60 |
| ☐ C15 Roosevelt Grier | 5.00 | 2.00 | .50 |
| ☐ C16 Billy Truax | 4.00 | 1.60 | .40 |
| ☐ C17 Merlin Olsen | 6.00 | 2.40 | .60 |
| ☐ C18 Deacon Jones | 6.00 | 2.40 | .60 |
| ☐ C19 Joe Scibelli | 3.00 | 1.20 | .30 |
| ☐ C20 Marlin McKeever | 4.00 | 1.60 | .40 |
| ☐ C21 Doug Woodlief | 3.00 | 1.20 | .30 |
| ☐ C22 Chuck Lamson | 3.00 | 1.20 | .30 |
| ☐ C23 Dan Currie | 3.00 | 1.20 | .30 |
| ☐ C24 Maxie Baughan | 4.00 | 1.60 | .40 |
| ☐ C25 Bruce Gossett | 4.00 | 1.60 | .40 |
| ☐ C26 Les Josephson | 4.00 | 1.60 | .40 |
| ☐ C27 Ed Meador | 4.00 | 1.60 | .40 |
| ☐ C28 Anthony Guillory | 3.00 | 1.20 | .30 |
| ☐ C29 Irv Cross | 4.00 | 1.60 | .40 |
| ☐ C30 Tommy McDonald | 4.00 | 1.60 | .40 |
| ☐ C31 Bucky Pope | 4.00 | 1.60 | .40 |
| ☐ C32 Jack Snow | 5.00 | 2.00 | .50 |
| ☐ C33 Joe Wendryhoski | 3.00 | 1.20 | .30 |
| ☐ C34 Clancy Williams | 4.00 | 1.60 | .40 |
| ☐ C35 Ben Wilson | 3.00 | 1.20 | .30 |
| ☐ C36 Rams Logo | 3.00 | 1.20 | .30 |

# 1966 Coke Caps Steelers

As part of an advertising promotion, Coca-Cola issued 21 sets of bottle caps, covering the 14 NFL cities, the six (separate) AFL cities, and a separate All-Star promotion for cities not reached by the leagues. The caps measure approximately 1 1/8" in diameter. They have the Coke logo and a football on the outside, while the inside has the player's face printed in black, with text surrounding the face. A Cap-Saver sheet was also issued to aid in collecting the bottle caps, and the consumer could turn in his completed sheet to receive various prizes. The numbering of the caps below reflects that of the Cap-Saver sheet. Each team had 36 caps issued plus the same 34 all-stars. These "Coke" caps were typically also available with other Coca-Cola products such as Fresca and Tab.

| | NRMT | VG-E | GOOD |
|---|---|---|---|
| COMPLETE SET (36)................. | 100.00 | 40.00 | 10.00 |
| COMMON PLAYER (C1-C36)........... | 3.00 | 1.20 | .30 |

| | | | |
|---|---|---|---|
| ☐ C1 John Baker........................ | 3.00 | 1.20 | .30 |
| ☐ C2 Mike Lind.......................... | 4.00 | 1.60 | .40 |
| ☐ C3 Ken Kortas........................ | 3.00 | 1.20 | .30 |
| ☐ C4 Willie Daniel...................... | 3.00 | 1.20 | .30 |
| ☐ C5 Roy Jefferson.................... | 5.00 | 2.00 | .50 |
| ☐ C6 Bob Hohn.......................... | 3.00 | 1.20 | .30 |
| ☐ C7 Dan James........................ | 3.00 | 1.20 | .30 |
| ☐ C8 Gary Ballman..................... | 4.00 | 1.60 | .40 |
| ☐ C9 Brady Keys........................ | 3.00 | 1.20 | .30 |
| ☐ C10 Charley Bradshaw............ | 4.00 | 1.60 | .40 |
| ☐ C11 Jim Bradshaw.................. | 3.00 | 1.20 | .30 |
| ☐ C12 Jim Butler........................ | 3.00 | 1.20 | .30 |
| ☐ C13 Paul Martha.................... | 5.00 | 2.00 | .50 |
| ☐ C14 Mike Clark....................... | 3.00 | 1.20 | .30 |
| ☐ C15 Ray Lemek...................... | 3.00 | 1.20 | .30 |
| ☐ C16 Clarence Peaks................ | 4.00 | 1.60 | .40 |
| ☐ C17 Theron Sapp.................... | 4.00 | 1.60 | .40 |
| ☐ C18 Ray Mansfield.................. | 3.00 | 1.20 | .30 |
| ☐ C19 Chuck Hinton.................... | 3.00 | 1.20 | .30 |
| ☐ C20 Bill Nelsen....................... | 5.00 | 2.00 | .50 |
| ☐ C21 Rod Breedlove.................. | 3.00 | 1.20 | .30 |
| ☐ C22 Frank Lambert.................. | 3.00 | 1.20 | .30 |
| ☐ C23 Ben McGee...................... | 3.00 | 1.20 | .30 |
| ☐ C24 Myron Pottios................... | 4.00 | 1.60 | .40 |
| ☐ C25 John Campbell.................. | 3.00 | 1.20 | .30 |
| ☐ C26 Andy Russell.................... | 5.00 | 2.00 | .50 |
| ☐ C27 Mike Sandusky................. | 3.00 | 1.20 | .30 |
| ☐ C28 Bob Schmitz..................... | 3.00 | 1.20 | .30 |
| ☐ C29 Riley Gunnels................... | 3.00 | 1.20 | .30 |
| ☐ C30 Clendon Thomas............... | 4.00 | 1.60 | .40 |
| ☐ C31 Tommy Wade.................... | 3.00 | 1.20 | .30 |
| ☐ C32 Dick Hoak........................ | 4.00 | 1.60 | .40 |
| ☐ C33 Marv Woodson.................. | 3.00 | 1.20 | .30 |
| ☐ C34 Bob Nichols...................... | 3.00 | 1.20 | .30 |
| ☐ C35 John Henry Johnson........... | 7.50 | 3.00 | .75 |
| ☐ C36 Steelers Logo................... | 3.00 | 1.20 | .30 |

## 1971 Coke Caps Packers

This is a 22-player set of Coca-Cola bottle caps featuring members of the Green Bay Packers. They have the Coke logo and a football on the outside, while the inside has the player's face printed in black, with the player's name below the picture. The caps measure approximately 1 1/8" in diameter. A cap-saver sheet was also issued to aid in collecting the bottle caps, and the consumer could turn in his completed sheet to receive various prizes. The caps are unnumbered and therefore listed below alphabetically. The caps were also produced in a twist-off version which is valued at double the listings below.

| | NRMT | VG-E | GOOD |
|---|---|---|---|
| COMPLETE SET (22)..................... | 30.00 | 12.00 | 3.00 |
| COMMON PLAYER (1-22)............... | 1.50 | .60 | .15 |

| | | | |
|---|---|---|---|
| ☐ 1 Ken Bowman....................... | 1.50 | .60 | .15 |
| ☐ 2 John Brockington................. | 3.00 | 1.20 | .30 |
| ☐ 3 Bob Brown.......................... | 2.00 | .80 | .20 |
| ☐ 4 Fred Carr............................ | 2.00 | .80 | .20 |
| ☐ 5 Jim Carter........................... | 1.50 | .60 | .15 |
| ☐ 6 Carroll Dale........................ | 2.00 | .80 | .20 |
| ☐ 7 Ken Ellis............................ | 1.50 | .60 | .15 |
| ☐ 8 Gale Gillingham................... | 2.00 | .80 | .20 |
| ☐ 9 Dave Hampton..................... | 2.00 | .80 | .20 |
| ☐ 10 Doug Hart......................... | 1.50 | .60 | .15 |
| ☐ 11 Jim Hill............................. | 1.50 | .60 | .15 |
| ☐ 12 Dick Himes........................ | 1.50 | .60 | .15 |
| ☐ 13 Scott Hunter...................... | 2.00 | .80 | .20 |
| ☐ 14 MacArthur Lane.................. | 3.00 | 1.20 | .30 |
| ☐ 15 Bill Lueck.......................... | 1.50 | .60 | .15 |
| ☐ 16 Al Matthews...................... | 1.50 | .60 | .15 |
| ☐ 17 Rich McGeorge................... | 1.50 | .60 | .15 |
| ☐ 18 Ray Nitschke..................... | 5.00 | 2.00 | .50 |
| ☐ 19 Francis Peay...................... | 1.50 | .60 | .15 |
| ☐ 20 Dave Robinson................... | 2.00 | .80 | .20 |

| | | | |
|---|---|---|---|
| ☐ 21 Alden Roche...................... | 1.50 | .60 | .15 |
| ☐ 22 Bart Starr......................... | 9.00 | 3.75 | .90 |

## 1981 Coke

The 1981 Coca-Cola/Topps football set of 84 cards contains 11 player cards and one header card each from seven National Football League teams. The cards are actually numbered on the back in alphabetical order within team from 1-11; however in the checklist below the cards are numbered 1-77 alphabetically by team, i.e., Baltimore Colts (1-11), Dallas Cowboys (12-22), Houston Oilers (23-33), New York Giants (34-44), St. Louis Cardinals (45-55), San Diego Chargers (56-66), and Washington Redskins (67-77). The backs of the header cards carried an offer to receive one (of four) uncut sheet(s) of the 1981 Topps regular series. Similar in design to the Topps cards of that year, these cards contain the Coke logo on both the front and the back. The cards measure standard size, 2 1/2" by 3 1/2". Key cards in the set are Art Monk and Kellen Winslow, both appearing in their "Rookie" year for cards.

| | MINT | EXC | G-VG |
|---|---|---|---|
| COMPLETE SET (84)...................... | 45.00 | 18.00 | 4.50 |
| COMMON PLAYER (1-77)................. | .25 | .10 | .02 |

| | | | |
|---|---|---|---|
| ☐ 1 Raymond Butler.................... | .50 | .20 | .05 |
| ☐ 2 Roger Carr.......................... | .35 | .14 | .03 |
| ☐ 3 Curtis Dickey....................... | .50 | .20 | .05 |
| ☐ 4 Nesby Glasgow.................... | .25 | .10 | .02 |
| ☐ 5 Bert Jones.......................... | 1.25 | .50 | .12 |
| ☐ 6 Bruce Laird........................ | .25 | .10 | .02 |
| ☐ 7 Greg Landry........................ | .50 | .20 | .05 |
| ☐ 8 Reese McCall...................... | .25 | .10 | .02 |
| ☐ 9 Don McCauley...................... | .25 | .10 | .02 |
| ☐ 10 Herb Orvis......................... | .25 | .10 | .02 |
| ☐ 11 Ed Simonini....................... | .25 | .10 | .02 |
| ☐ 12 Pat Donovan...................... | .25 | .10 | .02 |
| ☐ 13 Tony Dorsett...................... | 3.50 | 1.40 | .35 |
| ☐ 14 Billy Joe DuPree................. | .50 | .20 | .05 |
| ☐ 15 Tony Hill........................... | .50 | .20 | .05 |
| ☐ 16 Ed "Too Tall" Jones............. | 1.25 | .50 | .12 |
| ☐ 17 Harvey Martin.................... | .50 | .20 | .05 |
| ☐ 18 Robert Newhouse................ | .50 | .20 | .05 |
| ☐ 19 Drew Pearson.................... | .50 | .20 | .05 |
| ☐ 20 Charlie Waters................... | .50 | .20 | .05 |
| ☐ 21 Danny White...................... | .75 | .30 | .07 |
| ☐ 22 Randy White...................... | 1.25 | .50 | .12 |
| ☐ 23 Mike Barber....................... | .35 | .14 | .03 |
| ☐ 24 Elvin Bethea...................... | .50 | .20 | .05 |
| ☐ 25 Gregg Bingham................... | .25 | .10 | .02 |
| ☐ 26 Robert Brazile.................... | .50 | .20 | .05 |
| ☐ 27 Ken Burrough..................... | .50 | .20 | .05 |
| ☐ 28 Rob Carpenter.................... | .35 | .14 | .03 |
| ☐ 29 Leon Gray......................... | .35 | .14 | .03 |
| ☐ 30 Vernon Perry...................... | .25 | .10 | .02 |
| ☐ 31 Mike Renfro....................... | .35 | .14 | .03 |
| ☐ 32 Carl Roaches..................... | .35 | .14 | .03 |
| ☐ 33 Morris Towns...................... | .25 | .10 | .02 |
| ☐ 34 Harry Carson...................... | .75 | .30 | .07 |
| ☐ 35 Mike Dennis....................... | .25 | .10 | .02 |
| ☐ 36 Mike Friede....................... | .25 | .10 | .02 |
| ☐ 37 Earnest Gray...................... | .25 | .10 | .02 |
| ☐ 38 Dave Jennings.................... | .25 | .10 | .02 |
| ☐ 39 Gary Jeter......................... | .35 | .14 | .03 |
| ☐ 40 George Martin.................... | .35 | .14 | .03 |
| ☐ 41 Roy Simmons..................... | .25 | .10 | .02 |
| ☐ 42 Phil Simms........................ | 4.00 | 1.60 | .40 |
| ☐ 43 Billy Taylor........................ | .25 | .10 | .02 |
| ☐ 44 Brad Van Pelt.................... | .35 | .14 | .03 |
| ☐ 45 Ottis Anderson................... | 1.50 | .60 | .15 |
| ☐ 46 Rush Brown....................... | .25 | .10 | .02 |
| ☐ 47 Theotis Brown.................... | .35 | .14 | .03 |
| ☐ 48 Dan Dierdorf..................... | .50 | .20 | .05 |
| ☐ 49 Mel Gray.......................... | .50 | .20 | .05 |

| | | | | |
|---|---|---|---|---|
| ☐ 50 Ken Greene | | .25 | .10 | .02 |
| ☐ 51 Jim Hart | | .50 | .20 | .05 |
| ☐ 52 Doug Marsh | | .25 | .10 | .02 |
| ☐ 53 Wayne Morris | | .25 | .10 | .02 |
| ☐ 54 Pat Tilley | | .25 | .10 | .02 |
| ☐ 55 Roger Wehrli | | .35 | .14 | .03 |
| ☐ 56 Rolf Benirschke | | .35 | .14 | .03 |
| ☐ 57 Fred Dean | | .35 | .14 | .03 |
| ☐ 58 Dan Fouts | | 2.00 | .80 | .20 |
| ☐ 59 John Jefferson | | .50 | .20 | .05 |
| ☐ 60 Gary Johnson | | .35 | .14 | .03 |
| ☐ 61 Charlie Joiner | | 1.00 | .40 | .10 |
| ☐ 62 Louie Kelcher | | .35 | .14 | .03 |
| ☐ 63 Chuck Muncie | | .50 | .20 | .05 |
| ☐ 64 Doug Wilkerson | | .25 | .10 | .02 |
| ☐ 65 Clarence Williams | | .25 | .10 | .02 |
| ☐ 66 Kellen Winslow | | 2.00 | .80 | .20 |
| ☐ 67 Coy Bacon | | .25 | .10 | .02 |
| ☐ 68 Wilbur Jackson | | .35 | .14 | .03 |
| ☐ 69 Karl Lorch | | .25 | .10 | .02 |
| ☐ 70 Rich Milot | | .25 | .10 | .02 |
| ☐ 71 Art Monk | | 15.00 | 6.00 | 1.50 |
| ☐ 72 Mark Moseley | | .35 | .14 | .03 |
| ☐ 73 Mike Nelms | | .35 | .14 | .03 |
| ☐ 74 Lemar Parrish | | .35 | .14 | .03 |
| ☐ 75 Joe Theismann | | 2.00 | .80 | .20 |
| ☐ 76 Ricky Thompson | | .25 | .10 | .02 |
| ☐ 77 Joe Washington | | .35 | .14 | .03 |
| ☐ NNO Header Card | | .25 | .10 | .02 |
| Baltimore Colts | | | | |
| ☐ NNO Header Card | | .25 | .10 | .02 |
| Dallas Cowboys | | | | |
| ☐ NNO Header Card | | .25 | .10 | .02 |
| Houston Oilers | | | | |
| ☐ NNO Header Card | | .25 | .10 | .02 |
| New York Giants | | | | |
| ☐ NNO Header Card | | .25 | .10 | .02 |
| St. Louis Cardinals | | | | |
| ☐ NNO Header Card | | .25 | .10 | .02 |
| San Diego Chargers | | | | |
| ☐ NNO Header Card | | .25 | .10 | .02 |
| Washington Redskins | | | | |

## 1994 Coke Monsters of the Gridiron

Sponsored by Coca-Cola, this 30-card standard-size (2 1/2" by 3 1/2") set was released at the Super Bowl Card Show V, January 27-30, 1994 in Atlanta. The set was available to the first 10,000 fans at the redemption booth in exchange for ten wrappers from any 1993 NFL-licensed trading card packs. The fronts feature on their fronts borderless color studio shots of NFL players posed in their uniforms. The players are also dressed in horror costumes and made up to look like "monsters." Three of the cards (10, 19, and 20) feature fanciful color paintings of the players instead of photos. The white back carries the player's name and "monstrous" nickname at the top, followed below by career highlights. The cards are numbered on the back. Television ads featuring Randall Cunningham helped promote this set.

| | MINT | EXC | G-VG |
|---|---|---|---|
| COMPLETE SET (30) | 12.50 | 5.00 | 1.25 |
| COMMON PLAYER (1-30) | .25 | .10 | .02 |

| | | | |
|---|---|---|---|
| ☐ 1 Title Card | .35 | .14 | .03 |
| Checklist | | | |
| ☐ 2 Cornelius Bennett | .35 | .14 | .03 |
| Big Bear | | | |
| Buffalo Bills | | | |
| ☐ 3 Terrell Buckley | .35 | .14 | .03 |
| Tiger | | | |
| Green Bay Packers | | | |
| ☐ 4 Tony Casillas | .25 | .10 | .02 |
| Conde (Count) | | | |

| | | | |
|---|---|---|---|
| Dallas Cowboys | | | |
| ☐ 5 Reggie Cobb | .75 | .30 | .07 |
| Crossbones | | | |
| Tampa Bay Buccaneers | | | |
| ☐ 6 Marco Coleman | .35 | .14 | .03 |
| Cobra | | | |
| Miami Dolphins | | | |
| ☐ 7 Shane Conlan | .25 | .10 | .02 |
| Conlan The Barbarian | | | |
| Los Angeles Rams | | | |
| ☐ 8 Randall Cunningham | 1.00 | .40 | .10 |
| Rocket Man | | | |
| Philadelphia Eagles | | | |
| ☐ 9 Chris Doleman | .25 | .10 | .02 |
| Dr. Doomsday | | | |
| Minnesota Vikings | | | |
| ☐ 10 Steve Emtman | .35 | .14 | .03 |
| Beast-Man | | | |
| Indianapolis Colts | | | |
| ☐ 11 Harold Green | .50 | .20 | .05 |
| Slime | | | |
| Cincinnati Bengals | | | |
| ☐ 12 Michael Haynes | .50 | .20 | .05 |
| Moonlight Flyer | | | |
| Atlanta Falcons | | | |
| ☐ 13 Garrison Hearst | 1.00 | .40 | .10 |
| Hearse | | | |
| Phoenix Cardinals | | | |
| ☐ 14 Craig Heyward | .25 | .10 | .02 |
| Iron Head | | | |
| Chicago Bears | | | |
| ☐ 15 Rickey Jackson | .35 | .14 | .03 |
| The Jackal | | | |
| New Orleans Saints | | | |
| ☐ 16 Joe Jacoby | .25 | .10 | .02 |
| Frankenstein | | | |
| Washington Redskins | | | |
| ☐ 17 Sean Jones | .25 | .10 | .02 |
| Ghost | | | |
| Houston Oilers | | | |
| ☐ 18 Cortez Kennedy | .50 | .20 | .05 |
| Tez Rex | | | |
| Seattle Seahawks | | | |
| ☐ 19 Howie Long | .35 | .14 | .03 |
| Howlin' | | | |
| Los Angeles Raiders | | | |
| ☐ 20 Ronnie Lott | .50 | .20 | .05 |
| The Rattler | | | |
| New York Jets | | | |
| ☐ 21 Karl Mecklenburg | .25 | .10 | .02 |
| Midnight Marauder | | | |
| Denver Broncos | | | |
| ☐ 22 Neil O'Donnell | .75 | .30 | .07 |
| Knight Raider | | | |
| Pittsburgh Steelers | | | |
| ☐ 23 Tom Rathman | .35 | .14 | .03 |
| Psycho | | | |
| San Francisco 49ers | | | |
| ☐ 24 Junior Seau | .50 | .20 | .05 |
| Stealth | | | |
| San Diego Chargers | | | |
| ☐ 25 Emmitt Smith | 3.50 | 1.40 | .35 |
| Lone Star Sheriff | | | |
| Dallas Cowboys | | | |
| ☐ 26 Pat Swilling | .35 | .14 | .03 |
| Chillin' | | | |
| Detroit Lions | | | |
| ☐ 27 Lawrence Taylor | .75 | .30 | .07 |
| Six Gun | | | |
| New York Giants | | | |
| ☐ 28 Derrick Thomas | .75 | .30 | .07 |
| Attack Cat | | | |
| Kansas City Chiefs | | | |
| ☐ 29 Andre Tippett | .25 | .10 | .02 |
| Andre The Terrible | | | |
| New England Patriots | | | |
| ☐ 30 Eric Turner | .25 | .10 | .02 |
| Bad Bone | | | |
| Cleveland Browns | | | |

## 1992 Collector's Edge Prototypes

These six prototype cards were issued before the 1992 regular issue was released to show the design of Collector's Edge cards. The standard-size (2 1/2" by 3 1/2") cards feature on the fronts color action photos bordered in black. The team helmet appears in the lower right corner. Inside a dark green border, the backs have a head shot, biography, and statistics against a ghosted reproduction of the front photo. The cards were issued in two different styles, with slightly sticky backs with a removable paper protective cover backing or with a non-sticky back. The paper-covered back versions are somewhat more difficult to find. The production figures were reportedly 8,000 for each card. The cards are numbered on the back.

|  | MINT | EXC | G-VG |
|---|---|---|---|
| COMPLETE SET (6) | 25.00 | 10.00 | 2.50 |
| COMMON PLAYER (1-6) | 2.50 | 1.00 | .25 |
| ☐ 1 Jim Kelly | 5.00 | 2.00 | .50 |
| Buffalo Bills |  |  |  |
| ☐ 2 Randall Cunningham | 3.50 | 1.40 | .35 |
| Philadelphia Eagles |  |  |  |
| ☐ 3 Warren Moon | 3.50 | 1.40 | .35 |
| Houston Oilers |  |  |  |
| ☐ 4 John Elway | 6.00 | 2.40 | .60 |
| Denver Broncos |  |  |  |
| ☐ 5 Dan Marino | 9.00 | 3.75 | .90 |
| Miami Dolphins |  |  |  |
| ☐ 6 Bernie Kosar | 2.50 | 1.00 | .25 |
| Cleveland Browns |  |  |  |

## 1992 Collector's Edge

 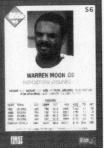

This 250-card football set was produced by Collector's Edge. The set was issued in two series of 175 and 75 cards, respectively. The cards are printed on plastic stock and production quantities were limited to 100,000 of each card, with every card individually numbered. Two thousand five hundred cards autographed by John Elway and Ken O'Brien were randomly inserted in foil packs and factory sets. The standard-size (2 1/2" by 3 1/2") cards feature on the fronts color action photos bordered in black. The team helmet appears in the lower right corner. Inside a dark green border, the backs have a head shot, biography, and statistics against a ghosted reproduction of the front photo. The cards are numbered on the back and checklisted below alphabetically according to teams as follows: Atlanta Falcons (1-6), Buffalo Bills (7-12), Chicago Bears (13-18), Cincinnati Bengals (19-24), Cleveland Browns (25-30), Dallas Cowboys (31-36), Denver Broncos (37-43), Detroit Lions (44-49), Green Bay Packers (50-55), Houston Oilers (56-62), Indianapolis Colts (63-69), Kansas City Chiefs (70-76), Los Angeles Raiders (77-83), Los Angeles Rams (84-89), Miami Dolphins (90-96), Minnesota Vikings (97-102), New England Patriots (103-109), New Orleans Saints (110-115), New York Giants (116-121), New York Jets (122-127), Philadelphia Eagles (128-133), Phoenix Cardinals (134-139), Pittsburgh Steelers (140-145), San Diego Chargers (146-151), San Francisco 49ers (152-157), Seattle Seahawks (158-163), Tampa Bay Buccaneers (164-169), and Washington Redskins (170-175). The second series (Rookies) also included 2,500 signed Ronnie Lott cards. There are a few cards in the set which were apparently late additions; 242 Neal Anderson apparently replaced Mark Bavaro and Bavaro cards have been found with a big "X" on the back and actual serial numbers just like regular cards. Similarly 182 Tony Casillas replaced Ray Roberts, 188 Brad Muster replaced Casey Weldon, 241 Russell Maryland replaced Bobby Humphrey, and 247 Ricky Ervins replaced Marion Butts, as they have

also been found with a big red "X" on the back. Card number 179 was also changed. The key Rookie Cards in this second series are Steve Bono, Terrell Buckley, Dale Carter, Marco Coleman, Quentin Coryatt, Vaughn Dunbar, Steve Emtman, Sean Gilbert, Courtney Hawkins, David Klingler, Chris Mims, Johnny Mitchell, Tommy Maddox, Carl Pickens, Robert Procher, Kevin Smith, Alonzo Spellman and Tommy Vardell.

|  | MINT | EXC | G-VG |
|---|---|---|---|
| COMPLETE SET (250) | 70.00 | 32.00 | 8.75 |
| COMPLETE SERIES 1 (175) | 40.00 | 18.00 | 5.00 |
| COMPLETE FACT.SER.1 (175) | 60.00 | 27.00 | 7.50 |
| COMPLETE SERIES 2 (75) | 30.00 | 13.50 | 3.80 |
| COMPLETE FACT.SER.2 (75) | 30.00 | 13.50 | 3.80 |
| COMMON PLAYER (1-175) | .20 | .09 | .03 |
| COMMON PLAYER (176-250) | .20 | .09 | .03 |
| ☐ 1 Chris Miller | .30 | .14 | .04 |
| ☐ 2 Steve Broussard | .25 | .11 | .03 |
| ☐ 3 Mike Pritchard | 1.00 | .45 | .13 |
| ☐ 4 Tim Green | .20 | .09 | .03 |
| ☐ 5 Andre Rison | .60 | .25 | .08 |
| ☐ 6 Deion Sanders | .75 | .35 | .09 |
| ☐ 7 Jim Kelly | 1.00 | .45 | .13 |
| ☐ 8 James Lofton | .30 | .14 | .04 |
| ☐ 9 Andre Reed | .30 | .14 | .04 |
| ☐ 10 Bruce Smith | .30 | .14 | .04 |
| ☐ 11 Thurman Thomas | 1.25 | .55 | .16 |
| ☐ 12 Cornelius Bennett | .30 | .14 | .04 |
| ☐ 13 Jim Harbaugh | .25 | .11 | .03 |
| ☐ 14 William Perry | .25 | .11 | .03 |
| ☐ 15 Mike Singletary | .30 | .14 | .04 |
| ☐ 16 Mark Carrier | .25 | .11 | .03 |
| ☐ 17 Kevin Butler | .20 | .09 | .03 |
| ☐ 18 Tom Waddle | .30 | .14 | .04 |
| ☐ 19 Boomer Esiason | .40 | .18 | .05 |
| ☐ 20 David Fulcher | .20 | .09 | .03 |
| ☐ 21 Anthony Munoz | .25 | .11 | .03 |
| ☐ 22 Tim McGee | .20 | .09 | .03 |
| ☐ 23 Harold Green | .25 | .11 | .03 |
| ☐ 24 Rickey Dixon | .20 | .09 | .03 |
| ☐ 25 Bernie Kosar | .30 | .14 | .04 |
| ☐ 26 Michael Dean Perry | .30 | .14 | .04 |
| ☐ 27 Mike Baab | .20 | .09 | .03 |
| ☐ 28 Brian Brennan | .20 | .09 | .03 |
| ☐ 29 Michael Jackson | .50 | .23 | .06 |
| ☐ 30 Eric Metcalf | .30 | .14 | .04 |
| ☐ 31 Troy Aikman | 7.00 | 3.10 | .85 |
| ☐ 32 Emmitt Smith | 10.00 | 4.50 | 1.25 |
| ☐ 33 Michael Irvin | 3.00 | 1.35 | .40 |
| ☐ 34 Jay Novacek | .50 | .23 | .06 |
| ☐ 35 Issiac Holt | .20 | .09 | .03 |
| ☐ 36 Ken Norton | .25 | .11 | .03 |
| ☐ 37 John Elway | 1.75 | .80 | .22 |
| ☐ 38 Gaston Green | .25 | .11 | .03 |
| ☐ 39 Charles Dimry | .20 | .09 | .03 |
| ☐ 40 Vance Johnson | .25 | .11 | .03 |
| ☐ 41 Dennis Smith | .25 | .11 | .03 |
| ☐ 42 David Treadwell | .20 | .09 | .03 |
| ☐ 43 Michael Young | .20 | .09 | .03 |
| ☐ 44 Bennie Blades | .20 | .09 | .03 |
| ☐ 45 Mel Gray | .25 | .11 | .03 |
| ☐ 46 Andre Ware | .25 | .11 | .03 |
| ☐ 47 Rodney Peete | .25 | .11 | .03 |
| ☐ 48 Toby Caston | .20 | .09 | .03 |
| ☐ 49 Herman Moore | 2.00 | .90 | .25 |
| ☐ 50 Brian Noble | .20 | .09 | .03 |
| ☐ 51 Sterling Sharpe | 3.00 | 1.35 | .40 |
| ☐ 52 Mike Tomczak | .20 | .09 | .03 |
| ☐ 53 Vinnie Clark | .20 | .09 | .03 |
| ☐ 54 Tony Mandarich | .20 | .09 | .03 |
| ☐ 55 Ed West | .20 | .09 | .03 |
| ☐ 56 Warren Moon | 1.00 | .45 | .13 |
| ☐ 57 Ray Childress | .25 | .11 | .03 |
| ☐ 58 Haywood Jeffires | .30 | .14 | .04 |
| ☐ 59 Al Smith | .20 | .09 | .03 |
| ☐ 60 Cris Dishman | .25 | .11 | .03 |
| ☐ 61 Ernest Givins | .25 | .11 | .03 |
| ☐ 62 Richard Johnson | .20 | .09 | .03 |
| ☐ 63 Eric Dickerson | .30 | .14 | .04 |
| ☐ 64 Jessie Hester | .20 | .09 | .03 |
| ☐ 65 Rohn Stark | .20 | .09 | .03 |
| ☐ 66 Clarence Verdin | .20 | .09 | .03 |
| ☐ 67 Dean Biasucci | .20 | .09 | .03 |
| ☐ 68 Duane Bickett | .20 | .09 | .03 |
| ☐ 69 Jeff George | .75 | .35 | .09 |
| ☐ 70 Christian Okoye | .25 | .11 | .03 |
| ☐ 71 Derrick Thomas | .60 | .25 | .08 |
| ☐ 72 Stephone Paige | .25 | .11 | .03 |
| ☐ 73 Dan Saleaumua | .20 | .09 | .03 |
| ☐ 74 Deron Cherry | .20 | .09 | .03 |
| ☐ 75 Kevin Ross | .25 | .11 | .03 |
| ☐ 76 Barry Word | .30 | .14 | .04 |
| ☐ 77 Ronnie Lott | .30 | .14 | .04 |
| ☐ 78 Greg Townsend | .20 | .09 | .03 |
| ☐ 79 Willie Gault | .25 | .11 | .03 |
| ☐ 80 Howie Long | .25 | .11 | .03 |

| | | | |
|---|---|---|---|
| ☐ 81 Winston Moss | .20 | .09 | .03 |
| ☐ 82 Steve Smith | .25 | .11 | .03 |
| ☐ 83 Jay Schroeder | .25 | .11 | .03 |
| ☐ 84 Jim Everett | .25 | .11 | .03 |
| ☐ 85 Flipper Anderson | .25 | .11 | .03 |
| ☐ 86 Henry Ellard | .25 | .11 | .03 |
| ☐ 87 Tony Zendejas | .20 | .09 | .03 |
| ☐ 88 Robert Delpino | .25 | .11 | .03 |
| ☐ 89 Pat Terrell | .20 | .09 | .03 |
| ☐ 90 Dan Marino | 3.50 | 1.55 | .45 |
| ☐ 91 Mark Clayton | .25 | .11 | .03 |
| ☐ 92 Jim Jensen | .20 | .09 | .03 |
| ☐ 93 Reggie Roby | .20 | .09 | .03 |
| ☐ 94 Sammie Smith | .20 | .09 | .03 |
| ☐ 95 Tony Martin | .20 | .09 | .03 |
| ☐ 96 Jeff Cross | .20 | .09 | .03 |
| ☐ 97 Anthony Carter | .25 | .11 | .03 |
| ☐ 98 Chris Doleman | .25 | .11 | .03 |
| ☐ 99 Wade Wilson | .25 | .11 | .03 |
| ☐ 100 Cris Carter | .30 | .14 | .04 |
| ☐ 101 Mike Merriweather | .20 | .09 | .03 |
| ☐ 102 Gary Zimmerman | .20 | .09 | .03 |
| ☐ 103 Chris Singleton | .20 | .09 | .03 |
| ☐ 104 Bruce Armstrong | .20 | .09 | .03 |
| ☐ 105 Marv Cook | .25 | .11 | .03 |
| ☐ 106 Andre Tippett | .25 | .11 | .03 |
| ☐ 107 Tommy Hodson | .20 | .09 | .03 |
| ☐ 108 Greg McMurtry | .20 | .09 | .03 |
| ☐ 109 Jon Vaughn | .20 | .09 | .03 |
| ☐ 110 Vaughan Johnson | .25 | .11 | .03 |
| ☐ 111 Craig Heyward | .20 | .09 | .03 |
| ☐ 112 Floyd Turner | .20 | .09 | .03 |
| ☐ 113 Pat Swilling | .25 | .11 | .03 |
| ☐ 114 Rickey Jackson | .25 | .11 | .03 |
| ☐ 115 Steve Walsh | .20 | .09 | .03 |
| ☐ 116 Phil Simms | .30 | .14 | .04 |
| ☐ 117 Carl Banks | .25 | .11 | .03 |
| ☐ 118 Mark Ingram | .25 | .11 | .03 |
| ☐ 119 Bart Oates | .20 | .09 | .03 |
| ☐ 120 Lawrence Taylor | .40 | .18 | .05 |
| ☐ 121 Jeff Hostetler | .50 | .23 | .06 |
| ☐ 122 Rob Moore | .30 | .14 | .04 |
| ☐ 123 Ken O'Brien | .25 | .11 | .03 |
| ☐ 124 Bill Pickel | .20 | .09 | .03 |
| ☐ 125 Irv Eatman | .20 | .09 | .03 |
| ☐ 126 Browning Nagle | .25 | .11 | .03 |
| ☐ 127 Al Toon | .25 | .11 | .03 |
| ☐ 128 Randall Cunningham | .50 | .23 | .06 |
| ☐ 129 Eric Allen | .25 | .11 | .03 |
| ☐ 130 Mike Golic | .20 | .09 | .03 |
| ☐ 131 Fred Barnett | .30 | .14 | .04 |
| ☐ 132 Keith Byars | .25 | .11 | .03 |
| ☐ 133 Calvin Williams | .30 | .14 | .04 |
| ☐ 134 Randal Hill | .30 | .14 | .04 |
| ☐ 135 Ricky Proehl | .30 | .14 | .04 |
| ☐ 136 Lance Smith | .20 | .09 | .03 |
| ☐ 137 Ernie Jones | .20 | .09 | .03 |
| ☐ 138 Timm Rosenbach | .20 | .09 | .03 |
| ☐ 139 Anthony Thompson | .20 | .09 | .03 |
| ☐ 140 Bubby Brister | .25 | .11 | .03 |
| ☐ 141 Merril Hoge | .25 | .11 | .03 |
| ☐ 142 Louis Lipps | .25 | .11 | .03 |
| ☐ 143 Eric Green | .30 | .14 | .04 |
| ☐ 144 Gary Anderson | .20 | .09 | .03 |
| ☐ 145 Neil O'Donnell | 1.50 | .65 | .19 |
| ☐ 146 Rod Bernstine | .25 | .11 | .03 |
| ☐ 147 John Friesz | .25 | .11 | .03 |
| ☐ 148 Anthony Miller | .60 | .25 | .08 |
| ☐ 149 Junior Seau | .50 | .23 | .06 |
| ☐ 150 Leslie O'Neal | .25 | .11 | .03 |
| ☐ 151 Nate Lewis | .25 | .11 | .03 |
| ☐ 152 Steve Young | 1.25 | .55 | .16 |
| ☐ 153 Kevin Fagan | .20 | .09 | .03 |
| ☐ 154 Charles Haley | .25 | .11 | .03 |
| ☐ 155 Tom Rathman | .25 | .11 | .03 |
| ☐ 156 Jerry Rice | 2.50 | 1.15 | .30 |
| ☐ 157 John Taylor | .30 | .14 | .04 |
| ☐ 158 Brian Blades | .25 | .11 | .03 |
| ☐ 159 Patrick Hunter | .20 | .09 | .03 |
| ☐ 160 Cortez Kennedy | .50 | .23 | .06 |
| ☐ 161 Vann McElroy | .20 | .09 | .03 |
| ☐ 162 Dan McGwire | .25 | .11 | .03 |
| ☐ 163 John L. Williams | .25 | .11 | .03 |
| ☐ 164 Gary Anderson | .25 | .11 | .03 |
| ☐ 165 Broderick Thomas | .20 | .09 | .03 |
| ☐ 166 Vinny Testaverde | .30 | .14 | .04 |
| ☐ 167 Lawrence Dawsey | .30 | .14 | .04 |
| ☐ 168 Paul Gruber | .20 | .09 | .03 |
| ☐ 169 Keith McCants | .20 | .09 | .03 |
| ☐ 170 Mark Rypien | .20 | .09 | .03 |
| ☐ 171 Gary Clark | .25 | .11 | .03 |
| ☐ 172 Earnest Byner | .25 | .11 | .03 |
| ☐ 173 Brian Mitchell | .25 | .11 | .03 |
| ☐ 174 Monte Coleman | .20 | .09 | .03 |
| ☐ 175 Joe Jacoby | .20 | .09 | .03 |
| ☐ 176 Tommy Vardell | 1.00 | .45 | .13 |
|    Cleveland Browns | | | |
| ☐ 177 Troy Vincent | .40 | .18 | .05 |
|    Miami Dolphins | | | |
| ☐ 178 Robert Jones | .50 | .23 | .06 |
|    Dallas Cowboys | | | |
| ☐ 179 Marc Boutte | .20 | .09 | .03 |
|    Los Angeles Rams | | | |
| ☐ 180 Marco Coleman | 1.25 | .55 | .16 |
|    Miami Dolphins | | | |
| ☐ 181 Chris Mims | .50 | .23 | .06 |
|    San Diego Chargers | | | |
| ☐ 182 Tony Casillas | .20 | .09 | .03 |
|    Dallas Cowboys | | | |
| ☐ 183 Shane Dronett | .50 | .23 | .06 |
|    Denver Broncos | | | |
| ☐ 184 Sean Gilbert | 1.25 | .55 | .16 |
|    Los Angeles Rams | | | |
| ☐ 185 Siran Stacy | .40 | .18 | .05 |
|    Philadelphia Eagles | | | |
| ☐ 186 Tommy Maddox | 1.50 | .65 | .19 |
|    Denver Broncos | | | |
| ☐ 187 Steve Israel | .20 | .09 | .03 |
|    Los Angeles Rams | | | |
| ☐ 188 Brad Muster | .25 | .11 | .03 |
|    Chicago Bears | | | |
| ☐ 189 Shane Collins | .40 | .18 | .05 |
|    Washington Redskins | | | |
| ☐ 190 Terrell Buckley | .75 | .35 | .09 |
|    Green Bay Packers | | | |
| ☐ 191 Eugene Chung | .20 | .09 | .03 |
|    New England Patriots | | | |
| ☐ 192 Leon Searcy | .20 | .09 | .03 |
|    Pittsburgh Steelers | | | |
| ☐ 193 Chuck Smith | .30 | .14 | .04 |
|    Atlanta Falcons | | | |
| ☐ 194 Patrick Rowe | .30 | .14 | .04 |
|    Cleveland Browns | | | |
| ☐ 195 Bill Johnson | .35 | .16 | .04 |
|    Cleveland Browns | | | |
| ☐ 196 Gerald Dixon | .30 | .14 | .04 |
|    Cleveland Browns | | | |
| ☐ 197 Robert Porcher | .75 | .35 | .09 |
|    Detroit Lions | | | |
| ☐ 198 Tracy Scroggins | .75 | .35 | .09 |
|    Detroit Lions | | | |
| ☐ 199 Jason Hanson | .35 | .16 | .04 |
|    Detroit Lions | | | |
| ☐ 200 Corey Harris | .30 | .14 | .04 |
|    Houston Oilers | | | |
| ☐ 201 Eddie Robinson | .30 | .14 | .04 |
|    Houston Oilers | | | |
| ☐ 202 Steve Emtman | .40 | .18 | .05 |
|    Indianapolis Colts | | | |
| ☐ 203 Ashley Ambrose | .30 | .14 | .04 |
|    Indianapolis Colts | | | |
| ☐ 204 Greg Skrepenak | .30 | .14 | .04 |
|    Los Angeles Raiders | | | |
| ☐ 205 Todd Collins | .60 | .25 | .08 |
|    New England Patriots | | | |
| ☐ 206 Derek Brown | .30 | .14 | .04 |
|    New York Giants | | | |
| ☐ 207 Kurt Barber | .30 | .14 | .04 |
|    New York Jets | | | |
| ☐ 208 Tony Sacca | .50 | .23 | .06 |
|    Phoenix Cardinals | | | |
| ☐ 209 Mark Wheeler | .30 | .14 | .04 |
|    Tampa Bay Buccaneers | | | |
| ☐ 210 Kevin Smith | 1.00 | .45 | .13 |
|    Dallas Cowboys | | | |
| ☐ 211 John Fina | .20 | .09 | .03 |
|    Buffalo Bills | | | |
| ☐ 212 Johnny Mitchell | 2.00 | .90 | .25 |
|    New York Jets | | | |
| ☐ 213 Dale Carter | 1.00 | .45 | .13 |
|    Kansas City Chiefs | | | |
| ☐ 214 Bobby Spitulski | .30 | .14 | .04 |
|    Seattle Seahawks | | | |
| ☐ 215 Phillippi Sparks | .20 | .09 | .03 |
|    New York Giants | | | |
| ☐ 216 Levon Kirkland | .30 | .14 | .04 |
|    Pittsburgh Steelers | | | |
| ☐ 217 Mike Sherrard | .25 | .11 | .03 |
|    San Francisco 49ers | | | |
| ☐ 218 Marquez Pope | .30 | .14 | .04 |
|    San Diego Chargers | | | |
| ☐ 219 Courtney Hawkins | 1.00 | .45 | .13 |
|    Tampa Bay Buccaneers | | | |
| ☐ 220 Tyji Armstrong | .30 | .14 | .04 |
|    Tampa Bay Buccaneers | | | |
| ☐ 221 Keith Jackson | .30 | .14 | .04 |
|    Miami Dolphins | | | |
| ☐ 222 Clayton Holmes | .20 | .09 | .03 |
|    Dallas Cowboys | | | |
| ☐ 223 Quentin Coryatt | 1.25 | .55 | .16 |
|    Indianapolis Colts | | | |
| ☐ 224 Troy Auzenne | .20 | .09 | .03 |
|    Chicago Bears | | | |
| ☐ 225 David Klingler | 2.25 | 1.00 | .30 |

| | | MINT | EXC | G-VG |
|---|---|---|---|---|
| | Cincinnati Bengals | | | |
| ☐ 226 | Darryl Williams | .75 | .35 | .09 |
| | Cincinnati Bengals | | | |
| ☐ 227 | Carl Pickens | 1.25 | .55 | .16 |
| | Cincinnati Bengals | | | |
| ☐ 228 | Jimmy Smith | .25 | .11 | .03 |
| | Dallas Cowboys | | | |
| ☐ 229 | Chester McGlockton | .40 | .18 | .05 |
| | Los Angeles Raiders | | | |
| ☐ 230 | Robert Brooks | .40 | .18 | .05 |
| | Green Bay Packers | | | |
| ☐ 231 | Alonzo Spellman | .60 | .25 | .08 |
| | Chicago Bears | | | |
| ☐ 232 | Darren Woodson | .50 | .23 | .06 |
| | Dallas Cowboys | | | |
| ☐ 233 | Lewis Billups | .20 | .09 | .03 |
| | Green Bay Packers | | | |
| ☐ 234 | Edgar Bennett | 1.00 | .45 | .13 |
| | Green Bay Packers | | | |
| ☐ 235 | Vaughn Dunbar | .75 | .35 | .09 |
| | New Orleans Saints | | | |
| ☐ 236 | Steve Bono | 1.50 | .65 | .19 |
| | San Francisco 49ers | | | |
| ☐ 237 | Clarence Kay | .20 | .09 | .03 |
| | Denver Broncos | | | |
| ☐ 238 | Chris Hinton | .20 | .09 | .03 |
| | Atlanta Falcons | | | |
| ☐ 239 | Jimmie Jones | .20 | .09 | .03 |
| | Dallas Cowboys | | | |
| ☐ 240 | Vai Sikahema | .25 | .11 | .03 |
| | Philadelphia Eagles | | | |
| ☐ 241 | Russell Maryland | .40 | .18 | .05 |
| | Dallas Cowboys | | | |
| ☐ 242 | Neal Anderson | .25 | .11 | .03 |
| | Chicago Bears | | | |
| ☐ 243 | Charles Mann | .25 | .11 | .03 |
| | Washington Redskins | | | |
| ☐ 244 | Hugh Millen | .25 | .11 | .03 |
| | New England Patriots | | | |
| ☐ 245 | Roger Craig | .25 | .11 | .03 |
| | Minnesota Vikings | | | |
| ☐ 246 | Rich Gannon | .25 | .11 | .03 |
| | Minnesota Vikings | | | |
| ☐ 247 | Ricky Ervins | .25 | .11 | .03 |
| | Washington Redskins | | | |
| ☐ 248 | Leonard Marshall | .25 | .11 | .03 |
| | New York Giants | | | |
| ☐ 249 | Eric Dickerson | .30 | .14 | .04 |
| | Los Angeles Raiders | | | |
| ☐ 250 | Joe Montana | 5.00 | 2.30 | .60 |
| | San Francisco 49ers | | | |
| ☐ AU37 | John Elway | 125.00 | 57.50 | 15.50 |
| | (2,500 signed) | | | |
| ☐ AU77 | Ronnie Lott Bonus | 60.00 | 27.00 | 7.50 |
| | (2,500 signed) | | | |
| ☐ AU123 | Ken O'Brien | 25.00 | 11.50 | 3.10 |
| | (2,500 signed) | | | |

## 1992 Collector's Edge RU Prototypes

These two Collector's Edge Rookie/Update prototypes cards measure the standard size (2 1/2" by 3 1/2"). The fronts have color action player photos inside a gold frame and black borders. The upper left corner of the picture is cut off. The player's name and position appear in the bottom border, and the team helmet is superimposed at the lower right corner of the picture. Within green borders, the backs carry a color head shot, draft information, biography, and collegiate statistics on a ghosted version of the front photo. The cards are numbered on the back and have a serial number in the bottom border. The production figures were 20,000 for each card.

| | MINT | EXC | G-VG |
|---|---|---|---|
| COMPLETE SET (2) | 6.00 | 2.40 | .60 |
| COMMON PLAYER (RU1-RU2) | 3.00 | 1.20 | .30 |

| | | MINT | EXC | G-VG |
|---|---|---|---|---|
| ☐ RU1 | Terrell Buckley | 3.00 | 1.20 | .30 |
| | Green Bay Packers | | | |
| ☐ RU2 | Tommy Maddox | 4.00 | 1.60 | .40 |
| | Denver Broncos | | | |

## 1992 Collector's Edge Special

This four-card set was issued to promote the Tuff Stuff Buyer's Club. The Elway card was distributed in all copies of the November issue of Tuff Stuff. More than 250,000 cards were printed; only about 40,000 each of the remaining three cards were printed. One of these was given away with each paid membership in the Buyers Club. The Elway card was printed also with the designations "Proto 1," "Elway Foundation," and "John Elway Dealerships"; the number of these additional cards is less than 50,000. The fronts of these standard-size (2 1/2" by 3 1/2") promo cards have a color action player photo inside a gold frame and dark blue borders. The upper left corner of the picture is cut off. The player's name and position appear in the bottom border, and the team helmet is superimposed at the lower right corner of the picture. Within bright blue borders, the backs carry a color head shot, biography, and statistics on a ghosted version of the front photo. The cards are numbered on the back, and each has a serial number in the bottom border.

| | MINT | EXC | G-VG |
|---|---|---|---|
| COMPLETE SET (4) | 10.00 | 4.00 | 1.00 |
| COMMON PLAYER (TS1-TS4) | 3.00 | 1.20 | .30 |

| | | MINT | EXC | G-VG |
|---|---|---|---|---|
| ☐ NNO | Elway Foundation, Elway Dealerships | 25.00 | 10.00 | 2.50 |
| ☐ PROT1 | John Elway | 10.00 | 4.00 | 1.00 |
| | Denver Broncos | | | |
| ☐ TS1 | John Elway | 3.00 | 1.20 | .30 |
| | Denver Broncos | | | |
| ☐ TS2 | Ronnie Lott | 4.00 | 1.60 | .40 |
| | Los Angeles Raiders | | | |
| ☐ TS3 | Jim Everett | 4.00 | 1.60 | .40 |
| | Los Angeles Rams | | | |
| ☐ TS4 | Bernie Kosar | 3.00 | 1.20 | .30 |
| | Cleveland Browns | | | |

## 1993 Collector's Edge Prototypes

These six prototype cards were issued before the 1993 regular issue set was released to show the design of the 1993 Collector's Edge regular series. Forty thousand six-card sets were produced, with each card serial-numbered from 00001 to 40,000 on the backs. The standard-size (2 1/2" by 3 1/2") cards feature color action photos with blue marbleized borders on their fronts. The team helmet appears in the lower right corner. Inside a green marbleized border, the backs have a head shot, biography, and statistics placed on a three-dimensional style gray granite panel. The cards are numbered on the back "Proto X." Also, 8 1/2" by 11" versions of these prototypes were packed in dealer cases. The oversized cards are unnumbered, and the production number is handwritten on the back in a gold-colored permanent marker. Otherwise, the cards are identical to their standard-size counterparts but are valued at two to four times the corresponding values listed below.

|  | MINT | EXC | G-VG |
|---|---|---|---|
| COMPLETE SET (6) | 20.00 | 8.00 | 2.00 |
| COMMON PLAYER (1-6) | 3.00 | 1.20 | .30 |
| ☐ 1 John Elway<br>Denver Broncos | 6.00 | 2.40 | .60 |
| ☐ 2 Derrick Thomas<br>Kansas City Chiefs | 3.00 | 1.20 | .30 |
| ☐ 3 Randall Cunningham<br>Philadelphia Eagles | 4.00 | 1.60 | .40 |
| ☐ 4 Thurman Thomas<br>Buffalo Bills | 5.00 | 2.00 | .50 |
| ☐ 5 Warren Moon<br>Houston Oilers | 4.00 | 1.60 | .40 |
| ☐ 6 Barry Sanders<br>Detroit Lions | 7.50 | 3.00 | .75 |

## 1993 Collector's Edge RU Prototypes

These five prototypes were issued to herald the design of the regular 1993 Collector's Edge Rookie/Update set. Each card carries a production number on its back. The standard-size (2 1/2" by 3 1/2") cards feature on their fronts color player action shots framed by a thin red line and having blue marbleized borders. The backgrounds of the photos are slightly ghosted, making the image of the featured player stand out. The player's name and position, as well as the team helmet, rest at the bottom. The back has a gray lithic design with green marbleized borders. A color player head shot appears at the upper left. His name, team name and logo, position, and uniform number are shown alongside to the right. Biography and statistics appear below. The cards are numbered on the back with an "RU" prefix.

|  | MINT | EXC | G-VG |
|---|---|---|---|
| COMPLETE SET (5) | 5.00 | 2.00 | .50 |
| COMMON PLAYER (RU1-RU5) | 1.00 | .40 | .10 |
| ☐ RU1 Garrison Hearst<br>Phoenix Cardinals | 1.50 | .60 | .15 |
| ☐ RU2 Reggie White<br>Green Bay Packers | 1.50 | .60 | .15 |
| ☐ RU3 Boomer Esiason<br>New York Jets | 1.50 | .60 | .15 |
| ☐ RU4 Rod Bernstine<br>Denver Broncos | 1.00 | .40 | .10 |
| ☐ RU5 Dana Stubblefield<br>San Francisco 49ers | 1.00 | .40 | .10 |

## 1993 Collector's Edge

The 1993 Collector's Edge football set consists of 325 cards. The standard-size (2 1/2" by 3 1/2") cards feature on their fronts color action shots with blue marbleized borders. The player's name and position appear at the lower left; the team helmet appears at the lower right. Inside a green marbleized border, the backs have a head shot, biography, and statistics placed on a gray, simulated three-dimensional granite panel. The production run was limited to 100,000 of each type, with each card serially numbered from 000001 to 100,000. In this year's issue, the cards were printed on heavier, 20-mil, thick plastic stock. Also this year's set added new Team Cards that depict whole-team portraits of the 28 NFL teams. The cards are

numbered on the back and checklisted below according to teams as follows: Atlanta Falcons (1-9), Buffalo Bills (10-18), Chicago Bears (19-27), Cincinnati Bengals (28-34), Cleveland Browns (35-42), Dallas Cowboys (43-52), Denver Broncos (53-62), Detroit Lions (63-72), Green Bay Packers (73-81), Houston Oilers (82-90), Indianapolis Colts (91-98), Kansas City Chiefs (99-109), Miami Dolphins (110-120), Minnesota Vikings (121-129), New England Patriots (130-136), New Orleans Saints (137-144), New York Giants (145-152), New York Jets (153-161), Philadelphia Eagles (162-170), Phoenix Cardinals (171-179), Pittsburgh Steelers (180-186), Los Angeles Raiders (187-195), Los Angeles Rams (196-203), San Diego Chargers (204-214), San Francisco 49ers (215-221), Seattle Seahawks (222-231), Tampa Bay Buccaneers (232-242), and Washington Redskins (243-250). Cards 251-325 comprise the Rookie Update series. Randomly inserted in the foil packs was a factory redemption card that entitled the holder to redeem the card for a factory set, in which every card had the same serial number. The offer expired at noon on February 28, 1994. Two cards commemorating the newest expansion teams in the NFL, the Jacksonville Jaguars and the Carolina Panthers, were produced. The cards were originally numbered 326 and 327, but since only 4,000 were produced, which is fewer than the regular issue, the company produced a second version and adjusted the numbering by adding a prefix "M". The cards were available by mail and cost 3.95, with only 25,000 produced. The purple marbleized fronts have a grey granite panel with a welcome to the new expansion team. The team logo appears in the lower right corner. Rookie Cards include Drew Bledsoe, Vincent Brisby, Reggie Brooks, Curtis Conway, Garrison Hearst, Billy Jo Hobert, Qadry Ismail, Glyn Milburn, Rick Mirer, Roosevelt Potts, Robert Smith and Dana Stubblefield.

|  | MINT | EXC | G-VG |
|---|---|---|---|
| COMPLETE SET (325) | 40.00 | 18.00 | 5.00 |
| COMPLETE SERIES 1 (250) | 20.00 | 9.00 | 2.50 |
| COMPLETE SERIES 2 (75) | 20.00 | 9.00 | 2.50 |
| COMMON PLAYER (1-250) | .10 | .05 | .01 |
| COMMON PLAYER (251-325) | .15 | .07 | .02 |
| ☐ 1 Falcons Team Photo | .10 | .05 | .01 |
| ☐ 2 Michael Haynes | .50 | .23 | .06 |
| ☐ 3 Chris Miller | .20 | .09 | .03 |
| ☐ 4 Mike Pritchard | .20 | .09 | .03 |
| ☐ 5 Andre Rison | .50 | .23 | .06 |
| ☐ 6 Deion Sanders | .50 | .23 | .06 |
| ☐ 7 Chuck Smith | .10 | .05 | .01 |
| ☐ 8 Drew Hill | .15 | .07 | .02 |
| ☐ 9 Bobby Hebert | .20 | .09 | .03 |
| ☐ 10 Bills Team Photo | .10 | .05 | .01 |
| ☐ 11 Matt Darby | .10 | .05 | .01 |
| ☐ 12 John Fina | .10 | .05 | .01 |
| ☐ 13 Jim Kelly | .75 | .35 | .09 |
| ☐ 14 Marvcus Patton | .25 | .11 | .03 |
| ☐ 15 Andre Reed | .20 | .09 | .03 |
| ☐ 16 Thurman Thomas | .75 | .35 | .09 |
| ☐ 17 James Lofton | .20 | .09 | .03 |
| ☐ 18 Bruce Smith | .20 | .09 | .03 |
| ☐ 19 Bears Team Photo | .10 | .05 | .01 |
| ☐ 20 Neal Anderson | .15 | .07 | .02 |
| ☐ 21 Troy Auzenne | .10 | .05 | .01 |
| ☐ 22 Jim Harbaugh | .15 | .07 | .02 |
| ☐ 23 Alonzo Spellman | .15 | .07 | .02 |
| ☐ 24 Tom Waddle | .20 | .09 | .03 |
| ☐ 25 Darren Lewis | .10 | .05 | .01 |
| ☐ 26 Wendell Davis | .10 | .05 | .01 |
| ☐ 27 Will Furrer | .10 | .05 | .01 |
| ☐ 28 Bengals Team Photo | .10 | .05 | .01 |
| ☐ 29 David Klingler | .50 | .23 | .06 |
| ☐ 30 Ricardo McDonald | .10 | .05 | .01 |
| ☐ 31 Carl Pickens | .25 | .11 | .03 |
| ☐ 32 Harold Green | .15 | .07 | .02 |
| ☐ 33 Anthony Munoz | .10 | .05 | .01 |
| ☐ 34 Darryl Williams | .15 | .07 | .02 |
| ☐ 35 Browns Team Photo | .10 | .05 | .01 |
| ☐ 36 Michael Jackson | .20 | .09 | .03 |

| | | | | | | | |
|---|---|---|---|---|---|---|---|
| ☐ 37 Pio Sagapolutele | .10 | .05 | .01 | ☐ 134 Leonard Russell | .15 | .07 | .02 |
| ☐ 38 Tommy Vardell | .15 | .07 | .02 | ☐ 135 Jon Vaughn | .10 | .05 | .01 |
| ☐ 39 Bernie Kosar | .20 | .09 | .03 | ☐ 136 Andre Tippett | .10 | .05 | .01 |
| ☐ 40 Michael Dean Perry | .20 | .09 | .03 | ☐ 137 Saints Team Photo | .10 | .05 | .01 |
| ☐ 41 Bill Johnson | .10 | .05 | .01 | ☐ 138 Wesley Carroll | .10 | .05 | .01 |
| ☐ 42 Vinny Testaverde | .10 | .05 | .01 | ☐ 139 Richard Cooper | .10 | .05 | .01 |
| ☐ 43 Cowboys Team Photo | .10 | .05 | .01 | ☐ 140 Vaughn Dunbar | .15 | .07 | .02 |
| ☐ 44 Troy Aikman | 3.50 | 1.55 | .45 | ☐ 141 Fred McAfee | .10 | .05 | .01 |
| ☐ 45 Alvin Harper | .75 | .35 | .09 | ☐ 142 Torrance Small | .10 | .05 | .01 |
| ☐ 46 Michael Irvin | 1.25 | .55 | .16 | ☐ 143 Steve Walsh | .10 | .05 | .01 |
| ☐ 47 Russell Maryland | .20 | .09 | .03 | ☐ 144 Vaughan Johnson | .10 | .05 | .01 |
| ☐ 48 Emmitt Smith | 4.00 | 1.80 | .50 | ☐ 145 Giants Team Photo | .10 | .05 | .01 |
| ☐ 49 Kenneth Gant | .10 | .05 | .01 | ☐ 146 Jarrod Bunch | .10 | .05 | .01 |
| ☐ 50 Jay Novacek | .20 | .09 | .03 | ☐ 147 Phil Simms | .20 | .09 | .03 |
| ☐ 51 Robert Jones | .10 | .05 | .01 | ☐ 148 Carl Banks | .10 | .05 | .01 |
| ☐ 52 Clayton Holmes | .10 | .05 | .01 | ☐ 149 Lawrence Taylor | .30 | .14 | .04 |
| ☐ 53 Broncos Team Photo | .10 | .05 | .01 | ☐ 150 Rodney Hampton | .75 | .35 | .09 |
| ☐ 54 Mike Croel | .15 | .07 | .02 | ☐ 151 Phillippi Sparks | .10 | .05 | .01 |
| ☐ 55 Shane Dronett | .10 | .05 | .01 | ☐ 152 Derek Brown | .15 | .07 | .02 |
| ☐ 56 Kenny Walker | .10 | .05 | .01 | ☐ 153 Jets Team Photo | .10 | .05 | .01 |
| ☐ 57 Tommy Maddox | .50 | .23 | .06 | ☐ 154 Boomer Esiason | .35 | .16 | .04 |
| ☐ 58 Dennis Smith | .10 | .05 | .01 | ☐ 155 Johnny Mitchell | .50 | .23 | .06 |
| ☐ 59 John Elway | 1.00 | .45 | .13 | ☐ 156 Rob Moore | .20 | .09 | .03 |
| ☐ 60 Karl Mecklenburg | .10 | .05 | .01 | ☐ 157 Ronnie Lott | .20 | .09 | .03 |
| ☐ 61 Steve Atwater | .15 | .07 | .02 | ☐ 158 Browning Nagle | .15 | .07 | .02 |
| ☐ 62 Vance Johnson | .15 | .07 | .02 | ☐ 159 Johnny Johnson | .20 | .09 | .03 |
| ☐ 63 Lions Team Photo | .10 | .05 | .01 | ☐ 160 Dwayne White | .10 | .05 | .01 |
| ☐ 64 Barry Sanders | 2.00 | .90 | .25 | ☐ 161 Blair Thomas | .15 | .07 | .02 |
| ☐ 65 Andre Ware | .15 | .07 | .02 | ☐ 162 Eagles Team Photo | .10 | .05 | .01 |
| ☐ 66 Pat Swilling | .15 | .07 | .02 | ☐ 163 Randall Cunningham | .30 | .14 | .04 |
| ☐ 67 Jason Hanson | .10 | .05 | .01 | ☐ 164 Fred Barnett | .20 | .09 | .03 |
| ☐ 68 Willie Green | .15 | .07 | .02 | ☐ 165 Siran Stacy | .10 | .05 | .01 |
| ☐ 69 Herman Moore | .75 | .35 | .09 | ☐ 166 Keith Byars | .15 | .07 | .02 |
| ☐ 70 Rodney Peete | .15 | .07 | .02 | ☐ 167 Calvin Williams | .20 | .09 | .03 |
| ☐ 71 Erik Kramer | .25 | .11 | .03 | ☐ 168 Jeff Sydner | .10 | .05 | .01 |
| ☐ 72 Robert Porcher | .15 | .07 | .02 | ☐ 169 Tommy Jeter | .10 | .05 | .01 |
| ☐ 73 Packers Team Photo | .10 | .05 | .01 | ☐ 170 Andre Waters | .10 | .05 | .01 |
| ☐ 74 Terrell Buckley | .20 | .09 | .03 | ☐ 171 Phoenix Team Photo | .10 | .05 | .01 |
| ☐ 75 Reggie White | .40 | .18 | .05 | ☐ 172 Steve Beuerlein | .30 | .14 | .04 |
| ☐ 76 Brett Favre | 2.00 | .90 | .25 | ☐ 173 Randal Hill | .20 | .09 | .03 |
| ☐ 77 Don Majkowski | .15 | .07 | .02 | ☐ 174 Timm Rosenbach | .10 | .05 | .01 |
| ☐ 78 Edgar Bennett | .25 | .11 | .03 | ☐ 175 Ed Cunningham | .10 | .05 | .01 |
| ☐ 79 Ty Detmer | .15 | .07 | .02 | ☐ 176 Walter Reeves | .10 | .05 | .01 |
| ☐ 80 Sanjay Beach | .10 | .05 | .01 | ☐ 177 Michael Zordich | .10 | .05 | .01 |
| ☐ 81 Sterling Sharpe | 1.25 | .55 | .16 | ☐ 178 Gary Clark | .15 | .07 | .02 |
| ☐ 82 Oilers Team Photo | .10 | .05 | .01 | ☐ 179 Ken Harvey | .10 | .05 | .01 |
| ☐ 83 Gary Brown | 1.75 | .80 | .22 | ☐ 180 Steelers Team Photo | .10 | .05 | .01 |
| ☐ 84 Ernest Givins | .15 | .07 | .02 | ☐ 181 Barry Foster | .75 | .35 | .09 |
| ☐ 85 Haywood Jeffires | .20 | .09 | .03 | ☐ 182 Neil O'Donnell | .60 | .25 | .08 |
| ☐ 86 Corey Harris | .10 | .05 | .01 | ☐ 183 Leon Searcy | .10 | .05 | .01 |
| ☐ 87 Warren Moon | .50 | .23 | .06 | ☐ 184 Bubby Brister | .10 | .05 | .01 |
| ☐ 88 Eddie Robinson | .10 | .05 | .01 | ☐ 185 Merril Hoge | .10 | .05 | .01 |
| ☐ 89 Lorenzo White | .15 | .07 | .02 | ☐ 186 Joel Steed | .10 | .05 | .01 |
| ☐ 90 Bo Orlando | .10 | .05 | .01 | ☐ 187 Raiders Team Photo | .10 | .05 | .01 |
| ☐ 91 Colts Team Photo | .10 | .05 | .01 | ☐ 188 Nick Bell | .15 | .07 | .02 |
| ☐ 92 Quentin Coryatt | .20 | .09 | .03 | ☐ 189 Eric Dickerson | .20 | .09 | .03 |
| ☐ 93 Steve Emtman | .15 | .07 | .02 | ☐ 190 Nolan Harrison | .10 | .05 | .01 |
| ☐ 94 Jeff George | .40 | .18 | .05 | ☐ 191 Todd Marinovich | .10 | .05 | .01 |
| ☐ 95 Jessie Hester | .10 | .05 | .01 | ☐ 192 Greg Skrepenak | .10 | .05 | .01 |
| ☐ 96 Rohn Stark | .10 | .05 | .01 | ☐ 193 Howie Long | .15 | .07 | .02 |
| ☐ 97 Ashley Ambrose | .10 | .05 | .01 | ☐ 194 Jay Schroeder | .10 | .05 | .01 |
| ☐ 98 John Baylor | .10 | .05 | .01 | ☐ 195 Chester McGlockton | .10 | .05 | .01 |
| ☐ 99 Chiefs Team Photo | .10 | .05 | .01 | ☐ 196 Rams Team Photo | .10 | .05 | .01 |
| ☐ 100 Tim Barnett | .15 | .07 | .02 | ☐ 197 Jim Everett | .10 | .05 | .01 |
| ☐ 101 Derrick Thomas | .40 | .18 | .05 | ☐ 198 Sean Gilbert | .15 | .07 | .02 |
| ☐ 102 Barry Word | .20 | .09 | .03 | ☐ 199 Steve Isreal | .10 | .05 | .01 |
| ☐ 103 Dale Carter | .20 | .09 | .03 | ☐ 200 Marc Boutte | .10 | .05 | .01 |
| ☐ 104 Jayice Pearson | .10 | .05 | .01 | ☐ 201 Joe Milinichick | .10 | .05 | .01 |
| ☐ 105 Tracy Simien | .10 | .05 | .01 | ☐ 202 Henry Ellard | .15 | .07 | .02 |
| ☐ 106 Harvey Williams | .20 | .09 | .03 | ☐ 203 Jackie Slater | .10 | .05 | .01 |
| ☐ 107 Dave Krieg | .15 | .07 | .02 | ☐ 204 Chargers Team Photo | .10 | .05 | .01 |
| ☐ 108 Christian Okoye | .15 | .07 | .02 | ☐ 205 Eric Bieniemy | .15 | .07 | .02 |
| ☐ 109 Joe Montana | 3.00 | 1.35 | .40 | ☐ 206 Marion Butts | .20 | .09 | .03 |
| ☐ 110 Dolphins Team Photo | .10 | .05 | .01 | ☐ 207 Nate Lewis | .15 | .07 | .02 |
| ☐ 111 J.B. Brown | .10 | .05 | .01 | ☐ 208 Junior Seau | .20 | .09 | .03 |
| ☐ 112 Marco Coleman | .15 | .07 | .02 | ☐ 209 Steve Hendrickson | .10 | .05 | .01 |
| ☐ 113 Dan Marino | 2.00 | .90 | .25 | ☐ 210 Chris Mims | .15 | .07 | .02 |
| ☐ 114 Mark Clayton | .10 | .05 | .01 | ☐ 211 Harry Swayne | .10 | .05 | .01 |
| ☐ 115 Mark Higgs | .20 | .09 | .03 | ☐ 212 Marquez Pope | .10 | .05 | .01 |
| ☐ 116 Bryan Cox | .15 | .07 | .02 | ☐ 213 Donald Frank | .10 | .05 | .01 |
| ☐ 117 Chuck Klingbeil | .10 | .05 | .01 | ☐ 214 Anthony Miller | .40 | .18 | .05 |
| ☐ 118 Troy Vincent | .15 | .07 | .02 | ☐ 215 Seahawks Team Photo | .10 | .05 | .01 |
| ☐ 119 Keith Jackson | .20 | .09 | .03 | ☐ 216 Cortez Kennedy | .20 | .09 | .03 |
| ☐ 120 Bruce Alexander | .10 | .05 | .01 | ☐ 217 Dan McGwire | .15 | .07 | .02 |
| ☐ 121 Vikings Team Photo | .10 | .05 | .01 | ☐ 218 Kelly Stouffer | .10 | .05 | .01 |
| ☐ 122 Terry Allen | .20 | .09 | .03 | ☐ 219 Chris Warren | .40 | .18 | .05 |
| ☐ 123 Rich Gannon | .15 | .07 | .02 | ☐ 220 Brian Blades | .15 | .07 | .02 |
| ☐ 124 Todd Scott | .10 | .05 | .01 | ☐ 221 Rod Stephens | .30 | .14 | .04 |
| ☐ 125 Cris Carter | .20 | .09 | .03 | ☐ 222 49ers Team Photo | .10 | .05 | .01 |
| ☐ 126 Sean Salisbury | .15 | .07 | .02 | ☐ 223 Jerry Rice | 1.50 | .65 | .19 |
| ☐ 127 Jack Del Rio | .10 | .05 | .01 | ☐ 224 Ricky Watters | .75 | .35 | .09 |
| ☐ 128 Chris Doleman | .15 | .07 | .02 | ☐ 225 Steve Young | .60 | .25 | .08 |
| ☐ 129 Anthony Carter | .15 | .07 | .02 | ☐ 226 Tom Rathman | .15 | .07 | .02 |
| ☐ 130 Patriots Team Photo | .10 | .05 | .01 | ☐ 227 Dana Hall | .10 | .05 | .01 |
| ☐ 131 Eugene Chung | .10 | .05 | .01 | ☐ 228 Amp Lee | .15 | .07 | .02 |
| ☐ 132 Todd Collins | .10 | .05 | .01 | ☐ 229 Brian Bollinger | .10 | .05 | .01 |
| ☐ 133 Tommy Hodson | .10 | .05 | .01 | ☐ 230 Keith DeLong | .10 | .05 | .01 |

| | | | |
|---|---|---|---|
| ☐ 231 John Taylor | .20 | .09 | .03 |
| ☐ 232 Buccaneers Team Photo | .10 | .05 | .01 |
| ☐ 233 Tyji Armstrong | .10 | .05 | .01 |
| ☐ 234 Lawrence Dawsey | .20 | .09 | .03 |
| ☐ 235 Mark Wheeler | .10 | .05 | .01 |
| ☐ 236 Vince Workman | .10 | .05 | .01 |
| ☐ 237 Reggie Cobb | .20 | .09 | .03 |
| ☐ 238 Tony Mayberry | .10 | .05 | .01 |
| ☐ 239 Marty Carter | .10 | .05 | .01 |
| ☐ 240 Courtney Hawkins | .15 | .07 | .02 |
| ☐ 241 Ray Seals | .10 | .05 | .01 |
| ☐ 242 Mark Carrier | .15 | .07 | .02 |
| ☐ 243 Redskins Team Photo | .10 | .05 | .01 |
| ☐ 244 Mark Rypien | .15 | .07 | .02 |
| ☐ 245 Ricky Ervins | .15 | .07 | .02 |
| ☐ 246 Gerald Riggs | .10 | .05 | .01 |
| ☐ 247 Art Monk | .20 | .09 | .03 |
| ☐ 248 Mark Schlereth | .10 | .05 | .01 |
| ☐ 249 Monte Coleman | .10 | .05 | .01 |
| ☐ 250 Wilber Marshall | .15 | .07 | .02 |
| ☐ 251 Ben Coleman | .20 | .09 | .03 |
| Phoenix Cardinals | | | |
| ☐ 252 Curtis Conway | 1.00 | .45 | .13 |
| Chicago Bears | | | |
| ☐ 253 Ernest Dye | .20 | .09 | .03 |
| Phoenix Cardinals | | | |
| ☐ 254 Todd Kelly | .30 | .14 | .04 |
| San Francisco 49ers | | | |
| ☐ 255 Patrick Bates | .30 | .14 | .04 |
| Los Angeles Raiders | | | |
| ☐ 256 George Teague | .40 | .18 | .05 |
| Green Bay Packers | | | |
| ☐ 257 Mark Brunell | .50 | .23 | .06 |
| Green Bay Packers | | | |
| ☐ 258 Adrian Hardy | .15 | .07 | .02 |
| San Francisco 49ers | | | |
| ☐ 259 Dana Stubblefield | 1.00 | .45 | .13 |
| San Francisco 49ers | | | |
| ☐ 260 William Roaf | .35 | .16 | .04 |
| New Orleans Saints | | | |
| ☐ 261 Irv Smith | .50 | .23 | .06 |
| New Orleans Saints | | | |
| ☐ 262 Drew Bledsoe | 6.00 | 2.70 | .75 |
| New England Patriots | | | |
| ☐ 263 Dan Williams | .40 | .18 | .05 |
| Denver Broncos | | | |
| ☐ 264 Jerry Ball | .15 | .07 | .02 |
| Cleveland Browns | | | |
| ☐ 265 Mark Clayton | .15 | .07 | .02 |
| Green Bay Packers | | | |
| ☐ 266 John Stephens | .15 | .07 | .02 |
| Green Bay Packers | | | |
| ☐ 267 Reggie White | .30 | .14 | .04 |
| Green Bay Packers | | | |
| ☐ 268 Jeff Hostetler | .25 | .11 | .03 |
| Los Angeles Raiders | | | |
| ☐ 269 Boomer Esiason | .35 | .16 | .04 |
| New York Jets | | | |
| ☐ 270 Wade Wilson | .20 | .09 | .03 |
| New Orleans Saints | | | |
| ☐ 271 Steve Beuerlein | .30 | .14 | .04 |
| Phoenix Cardinals | | | |
| ☐ 272 Tim McDonald | .15 | .07 | .02 |
| San Francisco 49ers | | | |
| ☐ 273 Craig Heyward | .15 | .07 | .02 |
| Chicago Bears | | | |
| ☐ 274 Everson Walls | .15 | .07 | .02 |
| Cleveland Browns | | | |
| ☐ 275 Stan Humphries | .25 | .11 | .03 |
| San Diego Chargers | | | |
| ☐ 276 Carl Banks | .15 | .07 | .02 |
| Washington Redskins | | | |
| ☐ 277 Brad Muster | .20 | .09 | .03 |
| New Orleans Saints | | | |
| ☐ 278 Tim Harris | .15 | .07 | .02 |
| Philadelphia Eagles | | | |
| ☐ 279 Gary Clark | .20 | .09 | .03 |
| Phoenix Cardinals | | | |
| ☐ 280 Joe Milinichik | .15 | .07 | .02 |
| San Diego Chargers | | | |
| ☐ 281 Leonard Marshall | .15 | .07 | .02 |
| New York Jets | | | |
| ☐ 282 Joe Montana | 3.50 | 1.55 | .45 |
| Kansas City Chiefs | | | |
| ☐ 283 Rod Bernstine | .20 | .09 | .03 |
| Denver Broncos | | | |
| ☐ 284 Mark Carrier | .20 | .09 | .03 |
| Cleveland Browns | | | |
| ☐ 285 Michael Brooks | .15 | .07 | .02 |
| New York Giants | | | |
| ☐ 286 Marvin Jones | .40 | .18 | .05 |
| New York Jets | | | |
| ☐ 287 John Copeland | .75 | .35 | .09 |
| Cincinnati Bengals | | | |
| ☐ 288 Eric Curry | .50 | .23 | .06 |
| Tampa Bay Buccaneers | | | |
| ☐ 289 Steve Everitt | .30 | .14 | .04 |

| | | | |
|---|---|---|---|
| Cleveland Browns | | | |
| ☐ 290 Tom Carter | .50 | .23 | .06 |
| Washington Redskins | | | |
| ☐ 291 Deon Figures | .40 | .18 | .05 |
| Pittsburgh Steelers | | | |
| ☐ 292 Leonard Renfro | .20 | .09 | .03 |
| Philadelphia Eagles | | | |
| ☐ 293 Thomas Smith | .35 | .16 | .04 |
| Buffalo Bills | | | |
| ☐ 294 Carlton Gray | .40 | .18 | .05 |
| Seattle Seahawks | | | |
| ☐ 295 Demetrius DuBose | .35 | .16 | .04 |
| Tampa Bay Buccaneers | | | |
| ☐ 296 Coleman Rudolph | .20 | .09 | .03 |
| New York Jets | | | |
| ☐ 297 John Parella | .20 | .09 | .03 |
| Buffalo Bills | | | |
| ☐ 298 Glyn Milburn | 1.75 | .80 | .22 |
| Denver Broncos | | | |
| ☐ 299 Reggie Brooks | 4.00 | 1.80 | .50 |
| Washington Redskins | | | |
| ☐ 300 Garrison Hearst | 1.25 | .55 | .16 |
| Phoenix Cardinals | | | |
| ☐ 301 John Elway | .75 | .35 | .09 |
| Denver Broncos | | | |
| ☐ 302 Brad Hopkins | .25 | .11 | .03 |
| Houston Oilers | | | |
| ☐ 303 Darrien Gordon UER | .50 | .23 | .06 |
| San Diego Chargers | | | |
| Card states he was drafted 12th | | | |
| instead of 22nd | | | |
| ☐ 304 Robert Smith | .75 | .35 | .09 |
| Minnesota Vikings | | | |
| ☐ 305 Chris Slade | .60 | .25 | .08 |
| New England Patriots | | | |
| ☐ 306 Ryan McNeil | .35 | .16 | .04 |
| Detroit Lions | | | |
| ☐ 307 Micheal Barrow | .15 | .07 | .02 |
| Houston Oilers | | | |
| ☐ 308 Roosevelt Potts | .75 | .35 | .09 |
| Indianapolis Colts | | | |
| ☐ 309 Qadry Ismail | 1.00 | .45 | .13 |
| Minnesota Vikings | | | |
| ☐ 310 Reggie Freeman | .20 | .09 | .03 |
| New Orleans Saints | | | |
| ☐ 311 Vincent Brisby | 1.25 | .55 | .16 |
| New England Patriots | | | |
| ☐ 312 Rick Mirer | 6.00 | 2.70 | .75 |
| Seattle Seahawks | | | |
| ☐ 313 Billy Joe Hobert | .60 | .25 | .08 |
| Los Angeles Raiders | | | |
| ☐ 314 Natrone Means | 2.00 | .90 | .25 |
| San Diego Chargers | | | |
| ☐ 315 Gary Zimmerman | .15 | .07 | .02 |
| Denver Broncos | | | |
| ☐ 316 Bobby Hebert | .25 | .11 | .03 |
| Atlanta Falcons | | | |
| ☐ 317 Don Beebe | .25 | .11 | .03 |
| Buffalo Bills | | | |
| ☐ 318 Wilber Marshall | .20 | .09 | .03 |
| Houston Oilers | | | |
| ☐ 319 Marcus Allen | .20 | .09 | .03 |
| Kansas City Chiefs | | | |
| ☐ 320 Ronnie Lott | .25 | .11 | .03 |
| New York Jets | | | |
| ☐ 321 Ricky Sanders | .20 | .09 | .03 |
| Washington Redskins | | | |
| ☐ 322 Charles Mann | .15 | .07 | .02 |
| Washington Redskins | | | |
| ☐ 323 Simon Fletcher | .20 | .09 | .03 |
| Denver Broncos | | | |
| ☐ 324 Johnny Johnson | .25 | .11 | .03 |
| New York Jets | | | |
| ☐ 325 Gary Plummer | .15 | .07 | .02 |
| San Diego Chargers | | | |
| ☐ 326 Carolina Panthers | 40.00 | 18.00 | 5.00 |
| Insert | | | |
| ☐ M326 Carolina Panthers | 3.50 | 1.55 | .45 |
| Send Away | | | |
| ☐ M327 Jacksonville Jaguars | 3.50 | 1.55 | .45 |
| Send Away | | | |
| ☐ NNO Factory Set Redemption | 5.00 | 2.30 | .60 |
| Card (Expired) | | | |
| ☐ NNO John Elway Auto | 100.00 | 45.00 | 12.50 |
| (Certified autograph) | | | |

# 1993 Collector's Edge Checklists

Randomly inserted in Collector's Edge packs, the 1993 Collector's Edge Checklist set consists of five standard-size (2 1/2" by 3 1/2") cards. The fronts have a light purple marbleized border around a light gray simulated stone panel edged in red. The similarly designed backs have a green marbleized border. The cards are numbered on the back "Checklist X".

|  | MINT | EXC | G-VG |
|---|---|---|---|
| COMPLETE SET (5) | 3.00 | 1.35 | .40 |
| COMMON CARD (1-5) | .75 | .35 | .09 |
| ☐ 1 Checklist 1 | .75 | .35 | .09 |
| ☐ 2 Checklist 2 | .75 | .35 | .09 |
| ☐ 3 Checklist 3 | .75 | .35 | .09 |
| ☐ 4 Checklist 4 | .75 | .35 | .09 |
| ☐ 5 Checklist 5 | .75 | .35 | .09 |

## 1993 Collector's Edge Elway Prisms

Randomly inserted in 1993 Collector's Edge packs, these five standard-size (2 1/2" by 3 1/2") cards feature blue-bordered prismatic foil fronts that carry color cut-outs of John Elway in action against a silver prismatic background. The Collector's Edge logo appears at the upper left, and a Bronco helmet rests at the lower right. The gray lithic back, which has a blue marbleized border, carries the same Elway photo at the top, but this time with its original on-field background. The production number appears below and, further below, career highlights. The cards are numbered on the back with an "E" prefix. There are two versions of each card. Tougher to find early packs contained cards with the serial number starting with "S" and cards found in packs released later had the serieal number start with "E". A noted difference between the two versions are the prismatic backgrounds. Every collector who purchased All Star Collection Manager software direct from Taurus Technologies received a free Collector's Edge five-card John Elway (E-prefix) prism set. Just 500 sets were available through this offer. Titled the "Two Minute Warning" set, these standard-size (2 1/2" by 3 1/2") cards highlight some of Elway's greatest two-minute marches.

|  | MINT | EXC | G-VG |
|---|---|---|---|
| COMPLETE E SET (5) | 10.00 | 4.50 | 1.25 |
| COMPLETE S SET (5) | 75.00 | 34.00 | 9.50 |
| COMMON ELWAY (E1-E5) | 2.50 | 1.15 | .30 |
| COMMON ELWAY (S1-S5) | 15.00 | 6.75 | 1.90 |
| ☐ E1 John Elway (Both arms outstretched) | 2.50 | 1.15 | .30 |
| ☐ E2 John Elway (Passing, orange jersey) | 2.50 | 1.15 | .30 |
| ☐ E3 John Elway (Running, orange jersey) | 2.50 | 1.15 | .30 |
| ☐ E4 John Elway (Passing, white jersey) | 2.50 | 1.15 | .30 |
| ☐ E5 John Elway (Running, white jersey) | 2.50 | 1.15 | .30 |
| ☐ PRO1 John Elway AU/3000 | 100.00 | 45.00 | 12.50 |
| ☐ S1 John Elway (Both arms outstretched) | 15.00 | 6.75 | 1.90 |
| ☐ S2 John Elway | 15.00 | 6.75 | 1.90 |
| (Passing, orange jersey) | | | |
| ☐ S3 John Elway | 15.00 | 6.75 | 1.90 |
| (Running, orange jersey) | | | |
| ☐ S4 John Elway | 15.00 | 6.75 | 1.90 |
| (Passing, white jersey) | | | |
| ☐ S5 John Elway | 15.00 | 6.75 | 1.90 |
| (Running, white jersey) | | | |

## 1993 Collector's Edge Rookies FX Prototypes

These two standard-size (2 1/2" by 3 1/2") cards were issued by Collector's Edge to preview the design of the 1993 Rookies FX series. Both clear plastic cards feature the same color action shot of Bledsoe. Other than their numbers, the only distinction between the two cards is the color of their inner borders; the outer borders are clear. The fronts are textured with a diffraction grating. The player's name and position appear at the upper right in white lettering. The team helmet is printed in the lower right corner. The backs are blank, or rather, clear, allowing the reverse image of the front to show through. The cards are numbered on the front with a "P" prefix.

|  | MINT | EXC | G-VG |
|---|---|---|---|
| COMPLETE SET (2) | 8.00 | 3.25 | .80 |
| COMMON PLAYER (P1-P2) | 5.00 | 2.00 | .50 |
| ☐ P2 Drew Bledsoe New England Patriots (Gray checkered border) | 5.00 | 2.00 | .50 |
| ☐ P2 Drew Bledsoe New England Patriots (Red border) | 5.00 | 2.00 | .50 |

## 1993 Collector's Edge Rookies FX

One of these 25 standard-size (2 1/2" by 3 1/2") cards was inserted in each Rookie/Update foil pack. Each clear plastic card has its front textured with a diffraction grating and features a color action player shot within a wide maroon inner border. The player's name and position appear at the upper right in white lettering. The team helmet is printed at the lower right. The backs are blank, or rather, clear, allowing the reverse image of the front to show through. The cards are numbered on the front with an "F/X" prefix. Gold-colored background versions of these cards are valued at 10 to 20 times the regular cards.

|  | MINT | EXC | G-VG |
|---|---|---|---|
| COMPLETE SET (25) | 25.00 | 11.50 | 3.10 |
| COMMON PLAYER (1-25) | .30 | .14 | .04 |
| *GOLD CARDS: 10X to 20X VALUE . | | | |

| | | | |
|---|---|---|---|
| ☐ 1 Garrison Hearst | 1.25 | .55 | .16 |
| Arizona Cardinals | | | |
| ☐ 2 Glyn Milburn | 1.50 | .65 | .19 |
| Denver Broncos | | | |
| ☐ 3 Demetrius DuBose | .40 | .18 | .05 |
| Tampa Bay Buccaneers | | | |
| ☐ 4 Joe Montana | 4.00 | 1.80 | .50 |
| Kansas City Chiefs | | | |
| ☐ 5 Thomas Smith | .40 | .18 | .05 |
| Buffalo Bills | | | |
| ☐ 6 Mark Clayton | .30 | .14 | .04 |
| Green Bay Packers | | | |
| ☐ 7 Curtis Conway | 1.00 | .45 | .13 |
| Chicago Bears | | | |
| ☐ 8 Drew Bledsoe | 5.00 | 2.30 | .60 |
| New England Patriots | | | |
| ☐ 9 Todd Kelly | .30 | .14 | .04 |
| San Francisco 49ers | | | |
| ☐ 10 Stan Humphries | .30 | .14 | .04 |
| San Diego Chargers | | | |
| ☐ 11 John Elway | 1.50 | .65 | .19 |
| Denver Broncos | | | |
| ☐ 12 Troy Aikman | 5.00 | 2.30 | .60 |
| Dallas Cowboys | | | |
| ☐ 13 Marion Butts | .35 | .16 | .04 |
| San Diego Chargers | | | |
| ☐ 14 Alvin Harper | 1.00 | .45 | .13 |
| Dallas Cowboys | | | |
| ☐ 15 Drew Hill | .30 | .14 | .04 |
| Atlanta Falcons | | | |
| ☐ 16 Michael Irvin | 1.75 | .80 | .22 |
| Dallas Cowboys | | | |
| ☐ 17 Warren Moon | .60 | .25 | .08 |
| Houston Oilers | | | |
| ☐ 18 Andre Reed | .35 | .16 | .04 |
| Buffalo Bills | | | |
| ☐ 19 Andre Rison | .75 | .35 | .09 |
| Atlanta Falcons | | | |
| ☐ 20 Emmitt Smith | 8.00 | 3.60 | 1.00 |
| Dallas Cowboys | | | |
| ☐ 21 Thurman Thomas | 1.50 | .65 | .19 |
| Buffalo Bills | | | |
| ☐ 22 Ricky Watters | 1.50 | .65 | .19 |
| San Francisco 49ers | | | |
| ☐ 23 Calvin Williams | .35 | .16 | .04 |
| Philadelphia Eagles | | | |
| ☐ 24 Steve Young | 1.25 | .55 | .16 |
| San Francisco 49ers | | | |
| ☐ 25 Howie Long | .30 | .14 | .04 |
| Los Angeles Raiders | | | |

# 1994 Collector's Edge Boss Squad Promos

These six standard-size (2 1/2" by 3 1/2") clear plastic cards feature on their fronts color action player cutouts set on backgrounds of parallel and converging lines. The player's name appears in orange-yellow lettering within a blue bar near the bottom. The back allows the reverse image of the front photo to show through. The cards are numbered on the front with a "Boss" prefix.

| | MINT | EXC | G-VG |
|---|---|---|---|
| COMPLETE SET (6) | 12.00 | 5.00 | 1.20 |
| COMMON PLAYER (1-6) | 2.00 | .80 | .20 |
| ☐ 1 Marshall Faulk | 5.00 | 2.00 | .50 |
| Indianapolis Colts | | | |
| ☐ 2 Jerome Bettis | 4.00 | 1.60 | .40 |
| Los Angeles Rams | | | |
| ☐ 3 Erric Pegram | 2.00 | .80 | .20 |
| Atlanta Falcons | | | |
| ☐ 4 Sterling Sharpe | 3.00 | 1.20 | .30 |
| Green Bay Packers | | | |

| | | | |
|---|---|---|---|
| ☐ 5 Shannon Sharpe | 2.50 | 1.00 | .25 |
| Denver Broncos | | | |
| ☐ 6 Leonard Russell | 2.00 | .80 | .20 |
| New England Patriots | | | |

# 1994 Collector's Edge Excalibur Elway Promos

These three standard-size (2 1/2" by 3 1/2") cards were issued to promote the 1994 Excalibur design and feature borderless color action shots of John Elway. The Excalibur logo appears in silver foil at the top; the player's name and position, also in silver foil, appear at the bottom. The back carries a color head shot of Elway in an heraldic shield at the upper left, and his name (preceded by a "Sir") and team logo in another shield at the upper right. A photo of an armored knight holding sword and football forms the background. Elway's career and 1993 stats appear in a ghosted strip below the shields. The "X of 3" numbering on the back is preceded by an "SL" prefix.

| | MINT | EXC | G-VG |
|---|---|---|---|
| COMPLETE SET (3) | 15.00 | 6.00 | 1.50 |
| COMMON PLAYER (SL1-SL3) | 5.00 | 2.00 | .50 |
| ☐ SL1 John Elway | 7.50 | 3.00 | .75 |
| Denver Broncos | | | |
| ☐ SL2 John Elway | 5.00 | 2.00 | .50 |
| Denver Broncos (Looking to pass) | | | |
| ☐ SL3 John Elway | 5.00 | 2.00 | .50 |
| Denver Broncos (Running with football) | | | |

# 1994 Collector's Edge Excalibur

The 1994 Collector's Edge Excalibur set consists of 75 standard-size (2 1/2" by 3 1/2") cards based on the medieval theme of "Excalibur", the silver sword pulled from the stone in the legend of King Arthur. The fronts feature full-bleed color action player photos. The Excalibur logo, player name and position are stamped in bright silver foil. The backs carry player information and a head shot framed in medieval shields at the top with a knight ghosted in the background. Stats for 1993 and NFL career totals appear just below the player commentary by Dick Butkus. Just 1,500 cases were produced, and every NFL team is represented with the exception of the Minnesota Vikings. The cards are numbered on the back and checklisted below alphabetically according to teams as follows: Atlanta Falcons (1-3), Buffalo Bills (4-8), Chicago Bears (9-11), Dallas Cowboys (12-15), Denver Broncos (16-20), Detroit Lions (21), Green Bay Packers (22-25), Houston

Oilers (26-29), Indianapolis Colts (30-32), Kansas City Chiefs (33-36), Los Angeles Raiders (37-40), Los Angeles Rams (41), Miami Dolphins (42-44), New England Patriots (45-46), New Orleans Saints (47-48), New York Giants (49-51), New York Jets (52-54), Philadelphia Eagles (55), Pittsburgh Steelers (56-58), San Diego Chargers (59-62), San Francisco 49ers (63-68), Seattle Seahawks (69-71), and Washington Redskins (72-75).

|  | MINT | EXC | G-VG |
|---|---|---|---|
| COMPLETE SET (75) | 35.00 | 16.00 | 4.40 |
| COMMON PLAYER (1-75) | .20 | .09 | .03 |
| ☐ 1 Bobby Hebert | .20 | .09 | .03 |
| ☐ 2 Deion Sanders | .60 | .25 | .08 |
| ☐ 3 Andre Rison | .60 | .25 | .08 |
| ☐ 4 Cornelius Bennett | .25 | .11 | .03 |
| ☐ 5 Jim Kelly | .75 | .35 | .09 |
| ☐ 6 Andre Reed | .30 | .14 | .04 |
| ☐ 7 Bruce Smith | .30 | .14 | .04 |
| ☐ 8 Thurman Thomas | 1.00 | .45 | .13 |
| ☐ 9 Curtis Conway | .50 | .23 | .06 |
| ☐ 10 Richard Dent | .25 | .11 | .03 |
| ☐ 11 Jim Harbaugh | .25 | .11 | .03 |
| ☐ 12 Troy Aikman | 4.00 | 1.80 | .50 |
| ☐ 13 Michael Irvin | 1.50 | .65 | .19 |
| ☐ 14 Russell Maryland | .20 | .09 | .03 |
| ☐ 15 Emmitt Smith | 6.00 | 2.70 | .75 |
| ☐ 16 Steve Atwater | .20 | .09 | .03 |
| ☐ 17 Rod Bernstine | .25 | .11 | .03 |
| ☐ 18 John Elway | 1.25 | .55 | .16 |
| ☐ 19 Glyn Milburn | .75 | .35 | .09 |
| ☐ 20 Shannon Sharpe | .60 | .25 | .08 |
| ☐ 21 Barry Sanders | 2.00 | .90 | .25 |
| ☐ 22 Edgar Bennett | .20 | .09 | .03 |
| ☐ 23 Brett Favre | 2.00 | .90 | .25 |
| ☐ 24 Sterling Sharpe | 1.50 | .65 | .19 |
| ☐ 25 Reggie White | .60 | .25 | .08 |
| ☐ 26 Warren Moon | .40 | .18 | .05 |
| ☐ 27 Wilber Marshall | .20 | .09 | .03 |
| ☐ 28 Haywood Jeffires | .30 | .14 | .04 |
| ☐ 29 Lorenzo White | .25 | .11 | .03 |
| ☐ 30 Quentin Coryatt | .25 | .11 | .03 |
| ☐ 31 Roosevelt Potts | .25 | .11 | .03 |
| ☐ 32 Jeff George | .25 | .11 | .03 |
| ☐ 33 Joe Montana | 4.00 | 1.80 | .50 |
| ☐ 34 Neil Smith | .20 | .09 | .03 |
| ☐ 35 Marcus Allen | .30 | .14 | .04 |
| ☐ 36 Derrick Thomas | .50 | .23 | .06 |
| ☐ 37 Jeff Hostetler | .25 | .11 | .03 |
| ☐ 38 Tim Brown | .60 | .25 | .08 |
| ☐ 39 Raghib Ismail | .60 | .25 | .08 |
| ☐ 40 Howie Long | .25 | .11 | .03 |
| ☐ 41 Jerome Bettis | 4.00 | 1.80 | .50 |
| ☐ 42 Dan Marino | 2.50 | 1.15 | .30 |
| ☐ 43 Keith Jackson | .30 | .14 | .04 |
| ☐ 44 O.J. McDuffie | .75 | .35 | .09 |
| ☐ 45 Drew Bledsoe | 4.00 | 1.80 | .50 |
| ☐ 46 Leonard Russell | .25 | .11 | .03 |
| ☐ 47 Wade Wilson | .20 | .09 | .03 |
| ☐ 48 Eric Martin | .20 | .09 | .03 |
| ☐ 49 Phil Simms | .25 | .11 | .03 |
| ☐ 50 Lawrence Taylor | .30 | .14 | .04 |
| ☐ 51 Rodney Hampton | .75 | .35 | .09 |
| ☐ 52 Boomer Esiason | .30 | .14 | .04 |
| ☐ 53 Johnny Johnson | .25 | .11 | .03 |
| ☐ 54 Ronnie Lott | .30 | .14 | .04 |
| ☐ 55 Fred Barnett | .25 | .11 | .03 |
| ☐ 56 Leroy Thompson | .25 | .11 | .03 |
| ☐ 57 Barry Foster | .60 | .25 | .08 |
| ☐ 58 Neil O'Donnell | .50 | .23 | .06 |
| ☐ 59 Stan Humphries | .25 | .11 | .03 |
| ☐ 60 Marion Butts | .25 | .11 | .03 |
| ☐ 61 Anthony Miller | .50 | .23 | .06 |
| ☐ 62 Natrone Means | 1.00 | .45 | .13 |
| ☐ 63 Dana Stubblefield | .35 | .16 | .04 |
| ☐ 64 John Taylor | .25 | .11 | .03 |
| ☐ 65 Ricky Watters | .60 | .25 | .08 |
| ☐ 66 Steve Young | .75 | .35 | .09 |
| ☐ 67 Jerry Rice | 2.00 | .90 | .25 |
| ☐ 68 Tom Rathman | .20 | .09 | .03 |
| ☐ 69 Rick Mirer | 4.00 | 1.80 | .50 |
| ☐ 70 Chris Warren | .25 | .11 | .03 |
| ☐ 71 Cortez Kennedy | .30 | .14 | .04 |
| ☐ 72 Mark Rypien | .25 | .11 | .03 |
| ☐ 73 Desmond Howard | .50 | .23 | .06 |
| ☐ 74 Art Monk | .30 | .14 | .04 |
| ☐ 75 Reggie Brooks | 2.50 | 1.15 | .30 |

## 1994 Collector's Edge Excalibur EdgeQuest

This nine-card standard-size (2 1/2" by 3 1/2") set constitutes a new redemption card game titled EdgeQuest. Each card bears one of nine

letters rather than a card number, and the object of the game is to spell out E-X-C-A-L-I-B-U-R with the cards. Five of the nine game pieces (X, A, I, B, and R) are randomly inserted into foil packs; the odds of finding these are one per nine packs. The other four game pieces (E, C, L, and U) are provided free to hobby dealers who purchased a case of Edge Excalibur. For collectors who failed to complete the whole set, any single EdgeQuest card could be redeemed before December 31, 1994 for an Edge prototype card from upcoming issues. A collector who completed the set of all nine cards could win either an F/X subset or an uncut press sheet.

|  | MINT | EXC | G-VG |
|---|---|---|---|
| COMPLETE SET (9) | 40.00 | 18.00 | 5.00 |
| COMMON INSERT (A/B/I/R) | 4.00 | 1.80 | .50 |
| COMMON DEALER (C/E/L/U) | 4.00 | 1.80 | .50 |
| *GOLD CARDS: 2.5X TO 5X VALUE.. | | | |
| ☐ A A | 4.00 | 1.80 | .50 |
| (Foil pack insert) | | | |
| ☐ B B | 4.00 | 1.80 | .50 |
| (Foil pack insert) | | | |
| ☐ C C | 4.00 | 1.80 | .50 |
| (Dealer promo) | | | |
| ☐ E E | 4.00 | 1.80 | .50 |
| (Dealer promo) | | | |
| ☐ I I | 4.00 | 1.80 | .50 |
| (Foil pack insert) | | | |
| ☐ L L | 4.00 | 1.80 | .50 |
| (Dealer promo) | | | |
| ☐ R R | 4.00 | 1.80 | .50 |
| (Foil pack insert) | | | |
| ☐ U U | 4.00 | 1.80 | .50 |
| (Dealer promo) | | | |
| ☐ X X | 25.00 | 11.50 | 3.10 |
| (Foil pack insert) | | | |

## 1994 Collector's Edge Excalibur FX

This 7-card standard-size (2 1/2" by 3 1/2") set was randomly inserted in foil packs. An acetate design, the player emerges from a cutout of a shield. The player's name, position and card number appear in a team colored label at the bottom right of the shield. A team helmet appears at the bottom of the card.

|  | MINT | EXC | G-VG |
|---|---|---|---|
| COMPLETE SET (7) | 80.00 | 36.00 | 10.00 |
| COMMON PLAYER (1-7) | 6.00 | 2.70 | .75 |
| *GOLD CARDS: 5X TO 10X VALUE... | | | |
| ☐ 1 Emmitt Smith | 20.00 | 9.00 | 2.50 |
| Dallas Cowboys | | | |
| ☐ 2 Rodney Hampton | 6.00 | 2.70 | .75 |
| New York Giants | | | |
| ☐ 3 Jerome Bettis | 16.00 | 7.25 | 2.00 |
| Los Angeles Rams | | | |
| ☐ 4 Steve Young | 6.00 | 2.70 | .75 |
| San Francisco 49ers | | | |
| ☐ 5 Rick Mirer | 16.00 | 7.25 | 2.00 |
| Seattle Seahawks | | | |
| ☐ 6 John Elway | 9.00 | 4.00 | 1.15 |
| Denver Broncos | | | |
| ☐ 7 Troy Aikman | 16.00 | 7.25 | 2.00 |
| Dallas Cowboys | | | |

## 1994 Collector's Edge Excalibur 22K Gold

Randomly inserted in packs, this 25-card standard-size (2 1/2" by 3 1/2") set is randomly inserted in foil packs. The card fronts feature a color photo of the player with part of a knight in shining armour as a

background. The top of the card features a gold sword and the player's name and position are at the bottom. The card back depicts a knight with a sword and shield with the player's name and team logo superimposed over the knight.

|  | MINT | EXC | G-VG |
|---|---|---|---|
| COMPLETE SET (25) | 100.00 | 45.00 | 12.50 |
| COMMON PLAYER (1-25) | 1.00 | .45 | .13 |
| ☐ 1 Troy Aikman | 16.00 | 7.25 | 2.00 |
| Dallas Cowboys |  |  |  |
| ☐ 2 Michael Irvin | 5.00 | 2.30 | .60 |
| Dallas Cowboys |  |  |  |
| ☐ 3 Emmitt Smith | 20.00 | 9.00 | 2.50 |
| Dallas Cowboys |  |  |  |
| ☐ 4 Edgar Bennett | 1.00 | .45 | .13 |
| Green Bay Packers |  |  |  |
| ☐ 5 Brett Favre | 6.00 | 2.70 | .75 |
| Green Bay Packers |  |  |  |
| ☐ 6 Sterling Sharpe | 5.00 | 2.30 | .60 |
| Green Bay Packers |  |  |  |
| ☐ 7 Rodney Hampton | 3.00 | 1.35 | .40 |
| New York Giants |  |  |  |
| ☐ 8 Jerome Bettis | 16.00 | 7.25 | 2.00 |
| Los Angeles Rams |  |  |  |
| ☐ 9 Jerry Rice | 8.00 | 3.60 | 1.00 |
| San Francisco 49ers |  |  |  |
| ☐ 10 Steve Young | 2.50 | 1.15 | .30 |
| San Francisco 49ers |  |  |  |
| ☐ 11 Ricky Watters | 2.25 | 1.00 | .30 |
| San Francisco 49ers |  |  |  |
| ☐ 12 Thurman Thomas | 3.00 | 1.35 | .40 |
| Buffalo Bills |  |  |  |
| ☐ 13 John Elway | 6.00 | 2.70 | .75 |
| Denver Broncos |  |  |  |
| ☐ 14 Shannon Sharpe | 2.25 | 1.00 | .30 |
| Denver Broncos |  |  |  |
| ☐ 15 Joe Montana | 16.00 | 7.25 | 2.00 |
| Kansas City Chiefs |  |  |  |
| ☐ 16 Marcus Allen | 1.25 | .55 | .16 |
| Kansas City Chiefs |  |  |  |
| ☐ 17 Tim Brown | 1.25 | .55 | .16 |
| Los Angeles Raiders |  |  |  |
| ☐ 18 Raghib Ismael | 2.25 | 1.00 | .30 |
| Los Angeles Raiders |  |  |  |
| ☐ 19 Barry Foster | 2.25 | 1.00 | .30 |
| Pittsburgh Steelers |  |  |  |
| ☐ 20 Natrone Means | 3.00 | 1.35 | .40 |
| San Diego Chargers |  |  |  |
| ☐ 21 Rick Mirer | 16.00 | 7.25 | 2.00 |
| Seattle Seahawks |  |  |  |
| ☐ 22 Dan Marino | 10.00 | 4.50 | 1.25 |
| Miami Dolphins |  |  |  |
| ☐ 23 AFC Card | 1.00 | .45 | .13 |
| ☐ 24 NFC Card | 1.00 | .45 | .13 |
| ☐ 25 Excalibur Card | 1.00 | .45 | .13 |

## 1961 Colts Jay Publishing

This 12-card set features (approximately) 5" by 7" black-and-white player photos. The photos show players in traditional poses with the quarterback preparing to throw, the runner heading downfield, and the defenseman ready for the tackle. These cards were packaged 12 to a packet and originally sold for 25 cents. The backs are blank. The cards are unnumbered and checklisted below in alphabetical order.

|  | NRMT | VG-E | GOOD |
|---|---|---|---|
| COMPLETE SET (12) | 75.00 | 30.00 | 7.50 |
| COMMON PLAYER (1-12) | 5.00 | 2.00 | .50 |
| ☐ 1 Ray Berry | 12.00 | 5.00 | 1.20 |
| ☐ 2 Art Donovan | 12.00 | 5.00 | 1.20 |
| ☐ 3 Weeb Ewbank CO | 6.00 | 2.40 | .60 |
| ☐ 4 Alex Hawkins | 6.00 | 2.40 | .60 |

| ☐ 5 Gino Marchetti | 10.00 | 4.00 | 1.00 |
|---|---|---|---|
| ☐ 6 Lenny Moore | 12.00 | 5.00 | 1.20 |
| ☐ 7 Jim Mutscheller | 5.00 | 2.00 | .50 |
| ☐ 8 Steve Myhra | 5.00 | 2.00 | .50 |
| ☐ 9 Jimmy Orr | 6.00 | 2.40 | .60 |
| ☐ 10 Jim Parker | 10.00 | 4.00 | 1.00 |
| ☐ 11 Joe Perry | 12.00 | 5.00 | 1.20 |
| ☐ 12 Johnny Unitas | 25.00 | 10.00 | 2.50 |

## 1967 Colts Johnny Pro

These 41 die-cut punchouts were issued (six or seven per page) in an album which itself measured approximately 11" by 14". Each punchout is approximately 4 1/8" tall and 2 7/8" wide at its base. A stand came with each punchout, and by inserting the punchout in it, the player stood upright. Each punchout consisted of a color player photo against a green grass background. The player's jersey number, name, and position are printed in a white box toward the bottom. The punchouts are unnumbered and checklisted below in alphabetical order.

|  | NRMT | VG-E | GOOD |
|---|---|---|---|
| COMPLETE SET (41) | 700.00 | 280.00 | 70.00 |
| COMMON PLAYER (1-41) | 12.50 | 5.00 | 1.25 |
| ☐ 1 Sam Ball | 12.50 | 5.00 | 1.25 |
| ☐ 2 Raymond Berry | 35.00 | 14.00 | 3.50 |
| ☐ 3 Bob Boyd | 15.00 | 6.00 | 1.50 |
| ☐ 4 Ordell Braase | 12.50 | 5.00 | 1.25 |
| ☐ 5 Barry Brown | 12.50 | 5.00 | 1.25 |
| ☐ 6 Bill Curry | 25.00 | 10.00 | 2.50 |
| ☐ 7 Mike Curtis | 20.00 | 8.00 | 2.00 |
| ☐ 8 Norman Davis | 12.50 | 5.00 | 1.25 |
| ☐ 9 Jim Detwiler | 12.50 | 5.00 | 1.25 |
| ☐ 10 Dennis Gaubatz | 12.50 | 5.00 | 1.25 |
| ☐ 11 Alvin Haymond | 15.00 | 6.00 | 1.50 |
| ☐ 12 Jerry Hill | 12.50 | 5.00 | 1.25 |
| ☐ 13 Roy Hilton | 12.50 | 5.00 | 1.25 |
| ☐ 14 David Lee | 12.50 | 5.00 | 1.25 |
| ☐ 15 Jerry Logan | 12.50 | 5.00 | 1.25 |
| ☐ 16 Tony Lorick | 15.00 | 6.00 | 1.50 |
| ☐ 17 Lenny Lyles | 12.50 | 5.00 | 1.25 |
| ☐ 18 John Mackey | 30.00 | 12.00 | 3.00 |
| ☐ 19 Tom Matte | 20.00 | 8.00 | 2.00 |
| ☐ 20 Lou Michaels | 15.00 | 6.00 | 1.50 |
| ☐ 21 Fred Miller | 12.50 | 5.00 | 1.25 |
| ☐ 22 Lenny Moore | 35.00 | 14.00 | 3.50 |
| ☐ 23 Jimmy Orr | 18.00 | 7.25 | 1.80 |
| ☐ 24 Jim Parker | 25.00 | 10.00 | 2.50 |
| ☐ 25 Ray Perkins | 30.00 | 12.00 | 3.00 |
| ☐ 26 Glenn Ressler | 12.50 | 5.00 | 1.25 |
| ☐ 27 Willie Richardson | 15.00 | 6.00 | 1.50 |
| ☐ 28 Don Shinnick | 12.50 | 5.00 | 1.25 |
| ☐ 29 Billy Ray Smith | 15.00 | 6.00 | 1.50 |
| ☐ 30 Bubba Smith | 30.00 | 12.00 | 3.00 |
| ☐ 31 Charles Stukes | 12.50 | 5.00 | 1.25 |
| ☐ 32 Andy Stynchula | 12.50 | 5.00 | 1.25 |
| ☐ 33 Dan Sullivan | 12.50 | 5.00 | 1.25 |
| ☐ 34 Dick Szymanski | 12.50 | 5.00 | 1.25 |
| ☐ 35 Johnny Unitas | 75.00 | 30.00 | 7.50 |
| ☐ 36 Bob Vogel | 15.00 | 6.00 | 1.50 |
| ☐ 37 Rick Volk | 15.00 | 6.00 | 1.50 |
| ☐ 38 Bob Wade | 12.50 | 5.00 | 1.25 |
| ☐ 39 Jim Ward | 12.50 | 5.00 | 1.25 |
| ☐ 40 Jim Welch | 12.50 | 5.00 | 1.25 |
| ☐ 41 Butch Wilson | 12.50 | 5.00 | 1.25 |

## 1978 Colts Team Issue

This set of 28 photos was issued by the Baltimore Colts. Each photo measures approximately 5" by 7". The fronts display player portrait photos with player name, postion, and team below the photo. The photos are blank backed. The photos are unnumbered and checklisted below in alphabetical order. The set is dated by the fact that Don Morrison and Calvin O'Neal were only with the Baltimore Colts in 1978.

|  | MINT | EXC | G-VG |
|---|---|---|---|
| COMPLETE SET (28).................. | 45.00 | 18.00 | 4.50 |
| COMMON PLAYER (1-28)............ | 1.50 | .60 | .15 |
| ☐ 1 Mack Alston ..................... | 2.00 | .80 | .20 |
| ☐ 2 Ron Baker......................... | 1.50 | .60 | .15 |
| ☐ 3 Mike Barnes .................... | 1.50 | .60 | .15 |
| ☐ 4 Tim Baylor........................ | 1.50 | .60 | .15 |
| ☐ 5 Randy Burke ................... | 1.50 | .60 | .15 |
| ☐ 6 Glenn Doughty ................ | 2.00 | .80 | .20 |
| ☐ 7 Joe Ehrmann................... | 2.00 | .80 | .20 |
| ☐ 8 Wade Griffin ................... | 1.50 | .60 | .15 |
| ☐ 9 Don Hardeman ................ | 1.50 | .60 | .15 |
| ☐ 10 Dwight Harrison ............ | 1.50 | .60 | .15 |
| ☐ 11 Ken Huff....................... | 1.50 | .60 | .15 |
| ☐ 12 Marshall Johnson .......... | 1.50 | .60 | .15 |
| ☐ 13 Bert Jones .................... | 4.00 | 1.60 | .40 |
| ☐ 14 Bruce Laird ................... | 1.50 | .60 | .15 |
| ☐ 15 Roosevelt Leaks ........... | 2.50 | 1.00 | .25 |
| ☐ 16 David Lee ..................... | 1.50 | .60 | .15 |
| ☐ 17 Ron Lee ........................ | 1.50 | .60 | .15 |
| ☐ 18 Toni Linhart................... | 1.50 | .60 | .15 |
| ☐ 19 Derrel Luce ................... | 1.50 | .60 | .15 |
| ☐ 20 Reese McCall ................ | 1.50 | .60 | .15 |
| ☐ 21 Ken Mendenhall ............ | 1.50 | .60 | .15 |
| ☐ 22 Don Morrison................. | 1.50 | .60 | .15 |
| ☐ 23 Lloyd Mumphord ........... | 1.50 | .60 | .15 |
| ☐ 24 Calvin O'Neal ................ | 1.50 | .60 | .15 |
| ☐ 25 Robert Pratt .................. | 1.50 | .60 | .15 |
| ☐ 26 Mike Siani .................... | 2.00 | .80 | .20 |
| ☐ 27 Bill Troup ..................... | 1.50 | .60 | .15 |
| ☐ 28 Stan White .................... | 2.00 | .80 | .20 |

## 1985 Colts Kroger

This set of 17 photos was sponsored by Kroger. Each photo measures approximately 5 1/2" by 8 1/2". The fronts display color action player photos with white borders. Player identification is given below the photo between the Colts' helmet on the left and the Kroger logo on the right. In navy blue print on a white background, the backs carry biographical information, the NFL logo, and the Kroger emblem. The photos are unnumbered and checklisted below in alphabetical order.

|  | MINT | EXC | G-VG |
|---|---|---|---|
| COMPLETE SET (17)................. | 20.00 | 8.00 | 2.00 |
| COMMON PLAYER (1-17)............ | 1.00 | .40 | .10 |
| ☐ 1 Karl Baldischwiler ............ | 1.00 | .40 | .10 |
| ☐ 2 Pat Beach...................... | 1.50 | .60 | .15 |
| ☐ 3 Albert Bentley................. | 2.50 | 1.00 | .25 |
| ☐ 4 Duane Bickett ................ | 2.00 | .80 | .20 |
| ☐ 5 Matt Bouza .................... | 1.00 | .40 | .10 |
| ☐ 6 Nesby Glasgow .............. | 1.50 | .60 | .15 |
| ☐ 7 Chris Hinton ................... | 2.00 | .80 | .20 |
| ☐ 8 Lamonte Hunley .............. | 1.00 | .40 | .10 |
| ☐ 9 Barry Krauss .................. | 1.50 | .60 | .15 |
| ☐ 10 Orlando Lowry ............... | 1.00 | .40 | .10 |
| ☐ 11 Tate Randle .................. | 1.00 | .40 | .10 |
| ☐ 12 Tim Sherwin.................. | 1.00 | .40 | .10 |
| ☐ 13 Ron Solt....................... | 1.50 | .60 | .15 |
| ☐ 14 Rohn Stark ................... | 1.50 | .60 | .15 |
| ☐ 15 Ben Utt ........................ | 1.00 | .40 | .10 |
| ☐ 16 Brad White.................... | 1.00 | .40 | .10 |
| ☐ 17 Anthony Young .............. | 1.50 | .60 | .15 |

## 1992 Courtside Draft Pix Promos

The 1992 Courtside Draft Pix Promo set contains eight player cards. These promos are sometimes found with red overprint stamps on the back commemorating the show where they were available as give-aways. The style of these promo cards is very similar to that of the 1992 Courtside regular issue cards. All these promo cards are marked

on the back clearly with "Promotion Not For Sale". Two number 20's were issued. The cards are standard-size (2 1/2" by 3 1/2") and feature glossy color action photos bordered in white. The cards are numbered on the back.

|  | MINT | EXC | G-VG |
|---|---|---|---|
| COMPLETE SET (8)................... | 12.00 | 5.00 | 1.20 |
| COMMON PLAYER..................... | 1.50 | .60 | .15 |
| ☐ 20A Tony Brooks ................ | 1.50 | .60 | .15 |
| Notre Dame |  |  |  |
| ☐ 20B Amp Lee .................... | 2.50 | 1.00 | .25 |
| Florida State |  |  |  |
| ☐ 22 Terrell Buckley .............. | 2.00 | .80 | .20 |
| Florida State |  |  |  |
| ☐ 30 Tommy Vardell............... | 2.00 | .80 | .20 |
| Stanford |  |  |  |
| ☐ 40 Carl Pickens ................. | 2.00 | .80 | .20 |
| Tennessee |  |  |  |
| ☐ 44 Quentin Coryatt ............. | 2.00 | .80 | .20 |
| Texas A and M |  |  |  |
| ☐ 50 Mike Gaddis .................. | 1.50 | .60 | .15 |
| Oklahoma |  |  |  |
| ☐ 60 Steve Emtman................ | 2.00 | .80 | .20 |
| Washington |  |  |  |
| (No statistics or |  |  |  |
| bio on card back) |  |  |  |

## 1992 Courtside

The 1992 Courtside Draft Pix football set contains 140 player cards. Ten short printed insert cards (five Award Winner and five All-America) were randomly inserted in the foil packs. This set also includes a foilgram card featuring Steve Emtman. Fifty thousand foilgram cards were printed, and collectors could receive one by sending in ten foil pack wrappers. Moreover, one set of foilgram cards and 20 free promo cards were offered to dealers for each case order. It has been reported that the production run was limited to 7,500 numbered cases, and that no factory sets were issued. Gold, silver, and bronze foil versions of the regular cards were randomly inserted within the foil cases in quantities of 1,000, 2,000, and 3,000 respectively. Reportedly more than 70,000 autographed cards were also inserted. Bronze versions are valued three to five times the values below; silver versions are valued six to ten times the values below; gold versions are valued ten to 20 times the values below. Autographed cards are valued approximately 25 to 50 times the corresponding player's card value. The standard-size (2 1/2" by 3 1/2") card feature on the fronts glossy color action photos bordered in white (some of the cards are oriented horizontally). The player's name and position appear in a gold stripe cutting across the bottom. On the backs, the upper half has a color close-up photo, with biography and collegiate statistics below. The cards are numbered on the back. The key players in this set are Quentin Coryatt, Amp Lee, Johnny Mitchell, Carl Pickens, and Tommy Vardell.

| | MINT | EXC | G-VG |
|---|---|---|---|
| COMPLETE SET (140) | 7.00 | 2.80 | .70 |
| COMMON PLAYER (1-140) | .05 | .02 | .00 |
| ☐ 1 Steve Emtman<br>Washington | .10 | .04 | .01 |
| ☐ 2 Quentin Coryatt<br>Texas A and M | .90 | .36 | .09 |
| ☐ 3 Ken Swilling<br>Georgia Tech | .05 | .02 | .00 |
| ☐ 4 Jay Leeuwenburg<br>Colorado | .10 | .04 | .01 |
| ☐ 5 Mazio Royster<br>USC | .15 | .06 | .01 |
| ☐ 6 Matt Veatch<br>San Diego State | .05 | .02 | .00 |
| ☐ 7A Scott Lockwood ERR<br>(No career totals)<br>USC | .10 | .04 | .01 |
| ☐ 7B Scott Lockwood COR<br>USC | .50 | .20 | .05 |
| ☐ 8 Todd Collins<br>Carson-Newman | .15 | .06 | .01 |
| ☐ 9 Gene McGuire<br>Notre Dame | .10 | .04 | .01 |
| ☐ 10 Dale Carter<br>Tennessee | .25 | .10 | .02 |
| ☐ 11 Michael Bankston<br>Sam Houston | .12 | .05 | .01 |
| ☐ 12 Jeremy Lincoln<br>Tennessee | .15 | .06 | .01 |
| ☐ 13A Troy Auzenne ERR<br>(Misspelled Auzene)<br>California | .10 | .04 | .01 |
| ☐ 13B Troy Auzenne COR<br>California | 3.00 | 1.20 | .30 |
| ☐ 14 Rod Smith<br>Notre Dame | .10 | .04 | .01 |
| ☐ 15 Andy Kelly<br>Tennessee | .05 | .02 | .00 |
| ☐ 16 Chris Holder<br>Tuskegee | .05 | .02 | .00 |
| ☐ 17 Rico Smith<br>Colorado | .10 | .04 | .01 |
| ☐ 18 Chris Pedersen<br>Iowa State | .05 | .02 | .00 |
| ☐ 19 Brian Treggs<br>California | .05 | .02 | .00 |
| ☐ 20 Eugene Chung<br>Virginia Tech | .12 | .05 | .01 |
| ☐ 21 Joel Steed<br>Colorado | .10 | .04 | .01 |
| ☐ 22 Ricardo McDonald<br>Pittsburgh | .10 | .04 | .01 |
| ☐ 23 Nate Turner<br>Nebraska | .10 | .04 | .01 |
| ☐ 24 Sean Lumpkin<br>Minnesota | .10 | .04 | .01 |
| ☐ 25 Ty Detmer<br>BYU | .50 | .20 | .05 |
| ☐ 26 Matt Darby<br>UCLA | .15 | .06 | .01 |
| ☐ 27 Michael Warfield<br>Catawba | .05 | .02 | .00 |
| ☐ 28 Tracy Scroggins<br>Tulsa | .15 | .06 | .01 |
| ☐ 29 Carl Pickens<br>Tennessee | 1.00 | .40 | .10 |
| ☐ 30 Chris Mims<br>Tennessee | .30 | .12 | .03 |
| ☐ 31 Mark D'Onofrio<br>Penn State | .10 | .04 | .01 |
| ☐ 32 Dwight Hollier<br>North Carolina | .15 | .06 | .01 |
| ☐ 33 Siupeli Malamala<br>Washington | .10 | .04 | .01 |
| ☐ 34A Mark Barsotti ERR<br>(Back stats jumbled<br>with no career totals)<br>Fresno State | .10 | .04 | .01 |
| ☐ 34B Mark Barsotti COR<br>Fresno State | .50 | .20 | .05 |
| ☐ 35 Charles Davenport<br>NC State | .15 | .06 | .01 |
| ☐ 36 Brian Bollinger<br>North Carolina | .10 | .04 | .01 |
| ☐ 37 Willie McClendon<br>Florida | .05 | .02 | .00 |
| ☐ 38 Calvin Holmes<br>USC | .05 | .02 | .00 |
| ☐ 39 Phillippi Sparks<br>Arizona State | .10 | .04 | .01 |
| ☐ 40 Darryl Williams | .20 | .08 | .02 |

| | | | |
|---|---|---|---|
| Miami | | | |
| ☐ 41 Greg Skrepenak<br>Michigan | .12 | .05 | .01 |
| ☐ 42 Larry Webster<br>Maryland | .12 | .05 | .01 |
| ☐ 43 Dion Lambert<br>UCLA | .10 | .04 | .01 |
| ☐ 44 Sam Gash<br>Penn State | .15 | .06 | .01 |
| ☐ 45 Patrick Rowe<br>San Diego State | .10 | .04 | .01 |
| ☐ 46 Scottie Graham<br>Ohio State | .60 | .24 | .06 |
| ☐ 47 Darian Hagan<br>Colorado | .05 | .02 | .00 |
| ☐ 48 Arthur Marshall<br>Georgia | .25 | .10 | .02 |
| ☐ 49 Amp Lee<br>Florida State | .50 | .20 | .05 |
| ☐ 50 Tommy Vardell<br>Stanford | .60 | .24 | .06 |
| ☐ 51 Robert Porcher<br>South Carolina State | .15 | .06 | .01 |
| ☐ 52 Reggie Dwight<br>Troy State | .05 | .02 | .00 |
| ☐ 53 Torrance Small<br>Alcorn State | .15 | .06 | .01 |
| ☐ 54 Ronnie West<br>Pittsburgh State | .05 | .02 | .00 |
| ☐ 55 Tony Brooks<br>Notre Dame | .05 | .02 | .00 |
| ☐ 56 Anthony McDowell<br>Texas Tech | .10 | .04 | .01 |
| ☐ 57 Chris Hakel<br>William and Mary | .10 | .04 | .01 |
| ☐ 58 Ed Cunningham<br>Washington | .10 | .04 | .01 |
| ☐ 59 Ashley Ambrose<br>Mississippi Valley St. | .15 | .06 | .01 |
| ☐ 60 Alonzo Spellman<br>Ohio State | .20 | .08 | .02 |
| ☐ 61 Harold Heath<br>Jackson State | .05 | .02 | .00 |
| ☐ 62 Ron Lopez<br>Utah State | .05 | .02 | .00 |
| ☐ 63 Bill Johnson<br>Michigan State | .10 | .04 | .01 |
| ☐ 64 Kent Graham<br>Ohio State | .40 | .16 | .04 |
| ☐ 65 Aaron Pierce<br>Washington | .15 | .06 | .01 |
| ☐ 66 Bucky Richardson<br>Texas A and M | .25 | .10 | .02 |
| ☐ 67A Todd Kinchen ERR<br>(Long reception for '91<br>is on a different line)<br>LSU | .10 | .04 | .01 |
| ☐ 67B Todd Kinchen COR<br>(Stats are properly<br>arranged)<br>LSU | .50 | .20 | .05 |
| ☐ 68 Ken Ealy<br>Central Michigan | .05 | .02 | .00 |
| ☐ 69 Carlos Snow<br>Ohio State | .05 | .02 | .00 |
| ☐ 70 Dana Hall<br>Washington | .15 | .06 | .01 |
| ☐ 71 Matt Rodgers<br>Iowa | .05 | .02 | .00 |
| ☐ 72 Howard Dinkins<br>Florida State | .10 | .04 | .01 |
| ☐ 73 Tim Lester<br>Eastern Kentucky | .12 | .05 | .01 |
| ☐ 74 Mark Chmura<br>Boston College | .10 | .04 | .01 |
| ☐ 75 Johnny Mitchell<br>Nebraska | 1.00 | .40 | .10 |
| ☐ 76 Mirko Jurkovic<br>Notre Dame | .05 | .02 | .00 |
| ☐ 77 Anthony Lynn<br>Texas Tech | .10 | .04 | .01 |
| ☐ 78 Roosevelt Collins<br>TCU | .05 | .02 | .00 |
| ☐ 79 Tony Sands<br>Kansas | .05 | .02 | .00 |
| ☐ 80 Kevin Smith<br>Texas A and M | .30 | .12 | .03 |
| ☐ 81 Tony Brown<br>Fresno State | .10 | .04 | .01 |
| ☐ 82 Bobby Fuller<br>South Carolina | .05 | .02 | .00 |
| ☐ 83 Darryl Ashmore<br>Northwestern | .10 | .04 | .01 |
| ☐ 84 Tyrone Legette<br>Nebraska | .10 | .04 | .01 |
| ☐ 85 Mike Gaddis<br>Oklahoma | .05 | .02 | .00 |
| ☐ 86A Cal Dixon ERR | .15 | .06 | .01 |

(Should be number 101)

| | | | | |
|---|---|---|---|---|
| South Carolina | | | | |
| ☐ 86B Gerald Dixon COR | 1.00 | .40 | .10 | |
| South Carolina | | | | |
| ☐ 87 T.J. Rubley | .50 | .20 | .05 | |
| Tulsa | | | | |
| ☐ 88 Mark Thomas | .10 | .04 | .01 | |
| NC State | | | | |
| ☐ 89 Corey Widmer | .10 | .04 | .01 | |
| Montana State | | | | |
| ☐ 90 Robert Jones | .20 | .08 | .02 | |
| East Carolina | | | | |
| ☐ 91 Eddie Robinson | .20 | .08 | .02 | |
| Alabama State | | | | |
| ☐ 92 Rob Tomlinson | .05 | .02 | .00 | |
| Cal State-Chico | | | | |
| ☐ 93 Russ Campbell | .05 | .02 | .00 | |
| Kansas State | | | | |
| ☐ 94 Keith Goganious | .10 | .04 | .01 | |
| Penn State | | | | |
| ☐ 95 Rod Moore | .05 | .02 | .00 | |
| Utah State | | | | |
| ☐ 96 Jerry Ostroski | .05 | .02 | .00 | |
| Tulsa | | | | |
| ☐ 97 Tyji Armstrong | .15 | .06 | .01 | |
| Mississippi | | | | |
| ☐ 98 Ronald Humphrey | .05 | .02 | .00 | |
| Mississippi Valley St. | | | | |
| ☐ 99 Corey Harris | .10 | .04 | .01 | |
| Vanderbilt | | | | |
| ☐ 100 Terrell Buckley | .60 | .24 | .06 | |
| Florida State | | | | |
| ☐ 101 Cal Dixon | .10 | .04 | .01 | |
| (See card number 86A) | | | | |
| Florida | | | | |
| ☐ 102 Tyrone Williams | .10 | .04 | .01 | |
| Western Ontario | | | | |
| ☐ 103 Joe Bowden | .10 | .04 | .01 | |
| Oklahoma | | | | |
| ☐ 104 Santana Dotson | .30 | .12 | .03 | |
| Baylor | | | | |
| ☐ 105 Jeff Blake | .20 | .08 | .02 | |
| East Carolina | | | | |
| ☐ 106 Erick Anderson | .12 | .05 | .01 | |
| Michigan | | | | |
| ☐ 107 Steve Israel | .10 | .04 | .01 | |
| Pittsburgh | | | | |
| ☐ 108 Chad Roghair | .05 | .02 | .00 | |
| Princeton | | | | |
| ☐ 109 Todd Harrison | .05 | .02 | .00 | |
| NC State | | | | |
| ☐ 110 Chester McGlockton | .15 | .06 | .01 | |
| Clemson | | | | |
| ☐ 111 Marquez Pope | .15 | .06 | .01 | |
| Fresno State | | | | |
| ☐ 112 George Rooks | .05 | .02 | .00 | |
| Syracuse | | | | |
| ☐ 113 Dion Johnson | .05 | .02 | .00 | |
| East Carolina | | | | |
| ☐ 114 Tim Simpson | .05 | .02 | .00 | |
| Illinois | | | | |
| ☐ 115 Chris Walsh | .10 | .04 | .01 | |
| Stanford | | | | |
| ☐ 116 Marc Boutte | .15 | .06 | .01 | |
| LSU | | | | |
| ☐ 117 Jamie Gill | .05 | .02 | .00 | |
| Texas Tech | | | | |
| ☐ 118 Willie Clay | .12 | .05 | .01 | |
| Georgia Tech | | | | |
| ☐ 119 Tim Paulk | .05 | .02 | .00 | |
| Florida | | | | |
| ☐ 120 Ray Roberts | .12 | .05 | .01 | |
| Virginia | | | | |
| ☐ 121 Jeff Thomason | .05 | .02 | .00 | |
| Oregon | | | | |
| ☐ 122 Leodis Flowers | .05 | .02 | .00 | |
| Nebraska | | | | |
| ☐ 123 Robert Brooks | .15 | .06 | .01 | |
| South Carolina | | | | |
| ☐ 124 Jeff Ellis | .05 | .02 | .00 | |
| Ohio State | | | | |
| ☐ 125 John Fina | .10 | .04 | .01 | |
| Arizona | | | | |
| ☐ 126A Michael Smith ERR | .10 | .04 | .01 | |
| (Back stats jumbled | | | | |
| with no career totals) | | | | |
| Kansas State | | | | |
| ☐ 126B Michael Smith COR | .50 | .20 | .05 | |
| Kansas State | | | | |
| ☐ 127 Mike Saunders | .05 | .02 | .00 | |
| Iowa | | | | |
| ☐ 128 John Brown III | .05 | .02 | .00 | |
| Houston | | | | |
| ☐ 129 Reggie Yarbrough | .05 | .02 | .00 | |
| Cal State-Fullerton | | | | |
| ☐ 130 Leon Searcy | .12 | .05 | .01 | |
| Miami | | | | |
| ☐ 131 Marcus Woods | .05 | .02 | .00 | |

| | | | |
|---|---|---|---|
| Oregon | | | |
| ☐ 132 Shane Collins | .10 | .04 | .01 |
| Arizona State | | | |
| ☐ 133 Chuck Smith | .12 | .05 | .01 |
| Tennessee | | | |
| ☐ 134 Keith Hamilton | .30 | .12 | .03 |
| Pittsburgh | | | |
| ☐ 135 Rodney Blackshear | .05 | .02 | .00 |
| Texas Tech | | | |
| ☐ 136 Corey Barlow | .10 | .04 | .01 |
| Auburn | | | |
| ☐ 137 Robert Harris | .10 | .04 | .01 |
| Southern-Baton Rouge | | | |
| ☐ 138 Tony Smith WR | .05 | .02 | .00 |
| Southern Mississippi | | | |
| ☐ 139 Checklist 1 | .05 | .02 | .00 |
| ☐ 140 Checklist 2 | .05 | .02 | .00 |

## 1992 Courtside Foilgrams

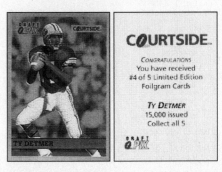

These five special foilgram cards were redeemable by mail via a wrapper offer. The cards are standard-size, 2 1/2" by 3 1/2". The cards are numbered on the back.

| | MINT | EXC | G-VG |
|---|---|---|---|
| COMPLETE SET (5) | 4.00 | 1.60 | .40 |
| COMMON PLAYER (1-5) | .25 | .10 | .02 |
| ☐ 1 Steve Emtman | .25 | .10 | .02 |
| Washington | | | |
| ☐ 2 Tommy Vardell | 1.25 | .50 | .12 |
| Stanford | | | |
| ☐ 3 Terrell Buckley | 1.25 | .50 | .12 |
| Florida State | | | |
| ☐ 4 Ty Detmer | 1.00 | .40 | .10 |
| Brigham Young | | | |
| ☐ 5 Amp Lee | 1.00 | .40 | .10 |
| Florida State | | | |

## 1992 Courtside Inserts

These ten special insert cards were included as random inserts within foil cases of 1992 Courtside Draft Pix football. They consist of five Award Winners and five All-America cards. The fronts of these standard-size (2 1/2" by 3 1/2") cards have glossy color action photos enclosed by white borders. The player's name and position appear in a stripe that cuts across the top of the picture; a football icon with the words "All-America" or the award won appears in the lower left corner. The backs have a close-up player photo, with player profile printed on a color box alongside the picture. The cards are numbered on the back.

|  | MINT | EXC | G-VG |
|---|---|---|---|
| COMPLETE SET (10) ........................ | 18.00 | 7.25 | 1.80 |
| COMMON PLAYER (AA1-AA5) ......... | 1.00 | .40 | .10 |
| COMMON PLAYER (AW1-AW5) ........ | .60 | .24 | .06 |
| ☐ AA1 Carl Pickens ........................... | 5.00 | 2.00 | .50 |
| Tennessee |  |  |  |
| ☐ AA2 Dale Carter ............................ | 1.75 | .70 | .17 |
| Tennessee |  |  |  |
| ☐ AA3 Tommy Vardell .................... | 3.50 | 1.40 | .35 |
| Stanford |  |  |  |
| ☐ AA4 Amp Lee ............................... | 2.50 | 1.00 | .25 |
| Florida State |  |  |  |
| ☐ AA5 Leon Searcy .......................... | 1.00 | .40 | .10 |
| Miami |  |  |  |
| ☐ AW1 Steve Emtman ...................... | .60 | .24 | .06 |
| Washington |  |  |  |
| Outland Trophy |  |  |  |
| ☐ AW2 Ty Detmer ............................ | 3.00 | 1.20 | .30 |
| Brigham Young |  |  |  |
| '90 Heisman Trophy |  |  |  |
| ☐ AW3 Steve Emtman ...................... | .60 | .24 | .06 |
| Washington |  |  |  |
| Lombardi Award |  |  |  |
| ☐ AW4 Terrell Buckley ..................... | 3.00 | 1.20 | .30 |
| Florida State |  |  |  |
| Jim Thorpe Award |  |  |  |
| ☐ AW5 Erick Anderson ................... | 1.00 | .40 | .10 |
| Michigan |  |  |  |
| Dick Butkus Award |  |  |  |

# 1993 Courtside Sean Dawkins

Sean Dawkins, who was drafted in the first round by the Indianapolis Colts, is showcased in this five-card, standard-size (2 1/2" by 3 1/2") set. Only 20,000 sets of each player were produced, and Dawkins personally autographed 5,000 cards for random insertion within the sets. The fronts display full-bleed glossy action photos, with the backgrounds blurred to highlight the player. Each card has a color bar carrying a gold foil football icon, the words "Draft Pix," and the player's name in gold foil lettering. On a background reflecting the same color as the front bar, the backs have a second color action photo and either biography, statistics, player profile, or highlights. The cards are numbered on the back. The complete set price below is a sealed price since it is not known if there is an autograph sealed inside. Card number 3 was also issued as a promo which was identical to the regular issue, except that the disclaimer "Promotional Not for Sale" is stamped on the front in a circular format, and the words "Authentic Signature" are printed in silver lettering toward the bottom of the front.

|  | MINT | EXC | G-VG |
|---|---|---|---|
| COMPLETE SET (5) .......................... | 10.00 | 4.00 | 1.00 |
| COMMON PLAYER (1-5) .................. | 1.75 | .70 | .17 |
| ☐ 1 Sean Dawkins ............................ | 1.75 | .70 | .17 |
| (Ball cradled in right |  |  |  |
| arm; running up field) |  |  |  |
| ☐ 2 Sean Dawkins ............................ | 1.75 | .70 | .17 |
| (Hands outstretched |  |  |  |
| to catch ball) |  |  |  |
| ☐ 3 Sean Dawkins ............................ | 1.75 | .70 | .17 |
| (Being handchecked |  |  |  |
| by cornerback) |  |  |  |
| ☐ 4 Sean Dawkins ............................ | 1.75 | .70 | .17 |
| (Kneeling pose) |  |  |  |
| ☐ 5 Sean Dawkins ............................ | 1.75 | .70 | .17 |
| (Dressed in tuxedo) |  |  |  |
| ☐ AU Sean Dawkins AU/5000 .......... | 15.00 | 6.00 | 1.50 |
| (Certified autograph) |  |  |  |

# 1993 Courtside Russell White

Russell White, who was drafted in the third round by the Los Angeles Rams, is showcased in this five-card, standard-size (2 1/2" by 3 1/2") set. Just 20,000 sets of each player were produced, and White personally autographed 5,000 cards for random insertion within the sets. The fronts display full-bleed glossy action photos, with the backgrounds blurred to highlight the player. Each card has a color bar carrying a gold foil football icon, the words "Draft Pix," and the player's name in gold foil lettering. On a background reflecting the same color as the front bar, the backs have a second color action photo and either biography, statistics, player profile, or highlights. The cards are numbered on the back. The complete set price below is a sealed price since it is not known if there is an autograph sealed inside. Card numbers 3-5 were also issued as promos. They are identical to their regular issues, except that the disclaimer "Promotional Not for Sale" is stamped on their fronts in a circular format, and the words "Authentic Signature" are printed in silver lettering toward the bottom of the front.

|  | MINT | EXC | G-VG |
|---|---|---|---|
| COMPLETE SET (5) .......................... | 7.00 | 2.80 | .70 |
| COMMON PLAYER (1-5) .................. | 1.75 | .70 | .17 |
| ☐ 1 Russell White ............................. | 1.75 | .70 | .17 |
| (Running almost |  |  |  |
| straight head) |  |  |  |
| ☐ 2 Russell White ............................. | 1.75 | .70 | .17 |
| (Running toward |  |  |  |
| the right) |  |  |  |
| ☐ 3 Russell White ............................. | 1.75 | .70 | .17 |
| (Running toward |  |  |  |
| defensive player |  |  |  |
| number 78) |  |  |  |
| ☐ 4 Russell White ............................. | 1.75 | .70 | .17 |
| (Running upfield; |  |  |  |
| side view) |  |  |  |
| ☐ 5 Russell White ............................. | 1.75 | .70 | .17 |
| (Dressed in tuxedo) |  |  |  |
| ☐ AU Russell White AU/5000 .......... | 10.00 | 4.00 | 1.00 |
| (Certified autograph) |  |  |  |

# 1969 Cowboys Team Issue

Measuring approximately 7" by 10", these five color action photos of Dallas Cowboys have rounded-corner black borders on thin white paper. The player's name and team are printed below the picture in the white margin. The backs are blank. The photos are unnumbered and checklisted below in alphabetical order.

|  | NRMT | VG-E | GOOD |
|---|---|---|---|
| COMPLETE SET (5) .......................... | 25.00 | 10.00 | 2.50 |
| COMMON PLAYER (1-5) .................. | 4.00 | 1.60 | .40 |
| ☐ 1 Walt Garrison ............................ | 6.00 | 2.40 | .60 |
| ☐ 2 Lee Roy Jordan ......................... | 6.00 | 2.40 | .60 |
| ☐ 3 Bob Lilly .................................... | 8.00 | 3.25 | .80 |
| ☐ 4 Dave Manders ........................... | 4.00 | 1.60 | .40 |
| ☐ 5 Mel Renfro ................................ | 6.00 | 2.40 | .60 |

# 1971 Cowboys Team Issue

This team-issued 40-card set features black-and-white posed action player photos with white borders. Each photo measures approximately 5" by 6 1/2". A wider white border at the bottom contains the player's name and team. These cards are printed on thin card stock and have blank backs. The cards are unnumbered and checklisted below in alphabetical order.

CHARLIE WATERS • DALLAS COWBOYS

|  | NRMT | VG-E | GOOD |
|---|---|---|---|
| COMPLETE SET (40) | 100.00 | 40.00 | 10.00 |
| COMMON PLAYER (1-40) | 2.00 | .80 | .20 |
| ☐ 1 Herb Adderley | 6.00 | 2.40 | .60 |
| ☐ 2 Lance Alworth | 10.00 | 4.00 | 1.00 |
| ☐ 3 George Andrie | 3.00 | 1.20 | .30 |
| ☐ 4 Mike Clark | 2.00 | .80 | .20 |
| ☐ 5 Larry Cole | 3.00 | 1.20 | .30 |
| ☐ 6 Mike Ditka | 15.00 | 6.00 | 1.50 |
| ☐ 7 Dave Edwards | 3.00 | 1.20 | .30 |
| ☐ 8 John Fitzgerald | 2.00 | .80 | .20 |
| ☐ 9 Toni Frisch | 2.00 | .80 | .20 |
| ☐ 10 Walt Garrison | 4.00 | 1.60 | .40 |
| ☐ 11 Cornell Green | 3.00 | 1.20 | .30 |
| ☐ 12 Bill Gregory | 2.00 | .80 | .20 |
| ☐ 13 Cliff Harris | 4.00 | 1.60 | .40 |
| ☐ 14 Bob Hayes | 5.00 | 2.00 | .50 |
| ☐ 15 Calvin Hill | 5.00 | 2.00 | .50 |
| ☐ 16 Chuck Howley | 4.00 | 1.60 | .40 |
| ☐ 17 Lee Roy Jordan | 5.00 | 2.00 | .50 |
| ☐ 18 D.D. Lewis | 3.00 | 1.20 | .30 |
| ☐ 19 Bob Lilly | 10.00 | 4.00 | 1.00 |
| ☐ 20 Tony Liscio | 2.00 | .80 | .20 |
| ☐ 21 Dave Manders | 2.00 | .80 | .20 |
| ☐ 22 Craig Morton | 6.00 | 2.40 | .60 |
| ☐ 23 Ralph Neely | 3.00 | 1.20 | .30 |
| ☐ 24 John Niland | 2.00 | .80 | .20 |
| ☐ 25 Jethro Pugh | 3.00 | 1.20 | .30 |
| ☐ 26 Dan Reeves | 10.00 | 4.00 | 1.00 |
| ☐ 27 Mel Renfro | 6.00 | 2.40 | .60 |
| ☐ 28 Gloster Richardson | 2.00 | .80 | .20 |
| ☐ 29 Tody Smith | 2.00 | .80 | .20 |
| ☐ 30 Roger Staubach | 30.00 | 12.00 | 3.00 |
| ☐ 31 Don Talbert | 2.00 | .80 | .20 |
| ☐ 32 Duane Thomas | 5.00 | 2.00 | .50 |
| ☐ 33 Isaac Thomas | 2.00 | .80 | .20 |
| ☐ 34 Pat Toomay | 2.00 | .80 | .20 |
| ☐ 35 Billy Truax | 3.00 | 1.20 | .30 |
| ☐ 36 Rodney Wallace | 2.00 | .80 | .20 |
| ☐ 37 Mark Washington | 2.00 | .80 | .20 |
| ☐ 38 Charlie Waters | 4.00 | 1.60 | .40 |
| ☐ 39 Claxton Welch | 2.00 | .80 | .20 |
| ☐ 40 Ron Widby | 2.00 | .80 | .20 |

## 1982 Cowboys Carrollton Park

CARROLLTON PARK MALL

The 1982 Carrollton Park Mall Cowboys set contains six photo cards in black and white with the words "Carrollton Park Mall" in blue at the bottom of the card front. The cards measure approximately 3" by 4". The backs contain the 1982 Cowboys schedule and brief career statistics of the player portrayed. The cards are numbered on the back and the set is available as an uncut sheet with no difference in value.

|  | MINT | EXC | G-VG |
|---|---|---|---|
| COMPLETE SET (6) | 5.00 | 2.00 | .50 |
| COMMON PLAYER (1-6) | .50 | .20 | .05 |
| ☐ 1 Roger Staubach | 2.50 | 1.00 | .25 |
| ☐ 2 Danny White | .75 | .30 | .07 |
| ☐ 3 Tony Dorsett | 1.25 | .50 | .12 |
| ☐ 4 Randy White | 1.00 | .40 | .10 |
| ☐ 5 Charlie Waters | .60 | .24 | .06 |
| ☐ 6 Billy Joe DuPree | .50 | .20 | .05 |

## 1985 Cowboys Frito Lay

77 ★ Jim Jeffcoat
DEFENSIVE END • 6-5 • 263 • ARIZONA ST.

The 1985 Cowboys Frito Lay set contains 41 photo cards. The cards measure approximately 4" by 5 1/2" and are printed on photographic quality paper stock. The white-bordered fronts display black-and-white player photos. The player's name, position, a brief biography, and team number appear on a wider lower border. The Frito Lay logo in the lower right corner rounds out the front. The backs are blank. The cards are unnumbered and checklisted below alphabetically. Roger Staubach is included in the set even though he retired in 1979.

|  | MINT | EXC | G-VG |
|---|---|---|---|
| COMPLETE SET (41) | 30.00 | 12.00 | 3.00 |
| COMMON PLAYER (1-41) | .60 | .24 | .06 |
| ☐ 1 Vince Albritton | .60 | .24 | .06 |
| ☐ 2 Brian Baldinger | .60 | .24 | .06 |
| ☐ 3 Dexter Clinkscale | .60 | .24 | .06 |
| ☐ 4 Jim Cooper | .60 | .24 | .06 |
| ☐ 5 Fred Cornwell | .60 | .24 | .06 |
| ☐ 6 Doug Cosbie | .75 | .30 | .07 |
| ☐ 7 Steve DeOssie | .75 | .30 | .07 |
| ☐ 8 John Dutton | .75 | .30 | .07 |
| ☐ 9 Ricky Easmon | .60 | .24 | .06 |
| ☐ 10 Ron Fellows | .60 | .24 | .06 |
| ☐ 11 Leon Gonzalez | .60 | .24 | .06 |
| ☐ 12 Gary Hogeboom | 1.00 | .40 | .10 |
| ☐ 13 Jim Jeffcoat | 1.50 | .60 | .15 |
| ☐ 14 Ed Too Tall Jones | 2.50 | 1.00 | .25 |
| ☐ 15 James Jones | .75 | .30 | .07 |
| ☐ 16 Crawford Ker | .60 | .24 | .06 |
| ☐ 17 Robert Lavette | .60 | .24 | .06 |
| ☐ 18 Eugene Lockhart | 1.00 | .40 | .10 |
| ☐ 19 Timmy Newsome | .75 | .30 | .07 |
| ☐ 20 Drew Pearson ACO | 1.50 | .60 | .15 |
| ☐ 21 Steve Pelluer | 1.00 | .40 | .10 |
| ☐ 22 Jesse Penn | .60 | .24 | .06 |
| ☐ 23 Kurt Petersen | .60 | .24 | .06 |
| ☐ 24 Karl Powe | .60 | .24 | .06 |
| ☐ 25 Phil Pozderac | .60 | .24 | .06 |
| ☐ 26 Tom Rafferty | .75 | .30 | .07 |
| ☐ 27 Mike Renfro | 1.00 | .40 | .10 |
| ☐ 28 Howard Richards | .60 | .24 | .06 |
| ☐ 29 Jeff Rohrer | .60 | .24 | .06 |
| ☐ 30 Mike Saxon | 1.00 | .40 | .10 |
| ☐ 31 Victor Scott | .60 | .24 | .06 |
| ☐ 32 Rafael Septien | .75 | .30 | .07 |
| ☐ 33 Don Smerek | .60 | .24 | .06 |
| ☐ 34 Roger Staubach | 7.50 | 3.00 | .75 |
| ☐ 35 Broderick Thompson | .60 | .24 | .06 |
| ☐ 36 Dennis Thurman | .75 | .30 | .07 |
| ☐ 37 Glen Titensor | .60 | .24 | .06 |
| ☐ 38 Mark Tuinei | 1.00 | .40 | .10 |
| ☐ 39 Everson Walls | 1.00 | .40 | .10 |
| ☐ 40 John Williams | .60 | .24 | .06 |
| ☐ 41 Team Photo | 1.50 | .60 | .15 |

## 1976 Crane Discs

The 1976 Crane football disc set of 30 cards contains a black and white photo of the player surrounded by a colored border. These circular cards measure 3 3/8" in diameter. The word Crane completes the circle of the border. The backs contain a Crane advertisement and

# 1986 DairyPak Cartons

the letters MSA, signifying Michael Schechter Associates. The set has benefited in recent years from the presence of Walter Payton in the set; Payton's 1976 Topps card is his Rookie Card and this Crane disc is one of the few other football cards or items of Payton from 1976. These discs were available as a mail-in offer but were not inserted in the Crane Potato Chip bags; consequently they are normally found in nice condition. There are 12 discs that were produced in shorter supply than the other 18; these are noted by SP in the checklist below. These extras found their way into the hobby when Crane sold their leftovers to major midwestern dealer Paul Marchant. Since the cards are unnumbered, they are ordered below alphabetically. The discs are also sometimes found with other back sponsors, e.g., Saga Philadelphia School District; there should be a slight premium attached to these non-Crane disc sets.

|  | NRMT | VG-E | GOOD |
|---|---|---|---|
| COMPLETE SET (30) | 16.00 | 6.50 | 1.60 |
| COMMON PLAYER (1-30) | .15 | .06 | .01 |
| COMMON SP (5/16/26) | .35 | .14 | .03 |
| ☐ 1 Ken Anderson<br>Cincinnati Bengals | .50 | .20 | .05 |
| ☐ 2 Otis Armstrong<br>Denver Broncos | .25 | .10 | .02 |
| ☐ 3 Steve Bartkowski<br>Atlanta Falcons | .35 | .14 | .03 |
| ☐ 4 Terry Bradshaw<br>Pittsburgh Steelers | 2.00 | .80 | .20 |
| ☐ 5 John Brockington SP<br>Green Bay Packers | .35 | .14 | .03 |
| ☐ 6 Doug Buffone<br>Chicago Bears | .15 | .06 | .01 |
| ☐ 7 Wally Chambers<br>Chicago Bears | .15 | .06 | .01 |
| ☐ 8 Isaac Curtis SP<br>Cincinnati Bengals | .50 | .20 | .05 |
| ☐ 9 Chuck Foreman<br>Minnesota Vikings | .25 | .10 | .02 |
| ☐ 10 Roman Gabriel SP<br>Philadelphia Eagles | .75 | .30 | .07 |
| ☐ 11 Mel Gray<br>St. Louis Cardinals | .15 | .06 | .01 |
| ☐ 12 Joe Greene<br>Pittsburgh Steelers | 1.00 | .40 | .10 |
| ☐ 13 James Harris SP<br>Los Angeles Rams | .50 | .20 | .05 |
| ☐ 14 Jim Hart<br>St. Louis Cardinals | .25 | .10 | .02 |
| ☐ 15 Billy Kilmer<br>Washington Redskins | .25 | .10 | .02 |
| ☐ 16 Greg Landry SP<br>Detroit Lions | .35 | .14 | .03 |
| ☐ 17 Ed Marinaro SP<br>Minnesota Vikings | .75 | .30 | .07 |
| ☐ 18 Lawrence McCutcheon SP<br>Los Angeles Rams | .50 | .20 | .05 |
| ☐ 19 Terry Metcalf<br>St. Louis Cardinals | .15 | .06 | .01 |
| ☐ 20 Lydell Mitchell SP<br>Baltimore Colts | .50 | .20 | .05 |
| ☐ 21 Jim Otis<br>St. Louis Cardinals | .15 | .06 | .01 |
| ☐ 22 Alan Page<br>Minnesota Vikings | .50 | .20 | .05 |
| ☐ 23 Walter Payton SP<br>Chicago Bears | 12.50 | 5.00 | 1.25 |
| ☐ 24 Greg Pruitt SP<br>Cleveland Browns | .50 | .20 | .05 |
| ☐ 25 Charlie Sanders SP<br>Detroit Lions | .50 | .20 | .05 |
| ☐ 26 Ron Shanklin SP<br>Chicago Bears | .35 | .14 | .03 |
| ☐ 27 Roger Staubach<br>Dallas Cowboys | 3.00 | 1.20 | .30 |
| ☐ 28 Jan Stenerud<br>Kansas City Chiefs | .50 | .20 | .05 |
| ☐ 29 Charley Taylor<br>Washington Redskins | .50 | .20 | .05 |
| ☐ 30 Roger Wehrli<br>St. Louis Cardinals | .15 | .06 | .01 |

This set of 24 numbered cards was issued as the side panel on half-gallon cartons of various brands of milk all over the country. Depending on the sponsoring milk company, the cards can be found in black, brown, red, green, dark blue, light blue, aqua, orange, or lavender. The actual pictures of the players on the cards are in black and white. Each player's card also contains a facsimile autograph above or to the side of his head. The prices listed below are for cards cut from the carton. Complete carton prices are 50 percent greater than the prices listed below. The cards, when cut on the dotted line, measure approximately 3 1/4" by 4 7/16". The set was only licensed by the NFL Players Association and hence team logos are not shown, i.e., the players are pictured without helmets. The bottom of the panel details an offer to receive a 24" by 32" poster (featuring the card fronts of the 24 NFL Superstars featured in this set) for 1.95 and two proofs-of-purchase. The Lofton card was supposedly withdrawn at some time during the promotion; however there does not appear to be any drastic shortage of Lofton cards needed for complete sets.

|  | MINT | EXC | G-VG |
|---|---|---|---|
| COMPLETE SET (24) | 60.00 | 24.00 | 6.00 |
| COMMON PLAYER (1-24) | 1.00 | .40 | .10 |
| ☐ 1 Joe Montana<br>San Francisco 49ers | 15.00 | 6.00 | 1.50 |
| ☐ 2 Marcus Allen<br>Los Angeles Raiders | 2.50 | 1.00 | .25 |
| ☐ 3 Art Monk<br>Washington Redskins | 2.50 | 1.00 | .25 |
| ☐ 4 Mike Quick<br>Philadelphia Eagles | 1.00 | .40 | .10 |
| ☐ 5 John Elway<br>Denver Broncos | 6.00 | 2.40 | .60 |
| ☐ 6 Eric Hipple<br>Detroit Lions | 1.00 | .40 | .10 |
| ☐ 7 Louis Lipps<br>Pittsburgh Steelers | 1.50 | .60 | .15 |
| ☐ 8 Dan Fouts<br>San Diego Chargers | 2.00 | .80 | .20 |
| ☐ 9 Phil Simms<br>New York Giants | 2.00 | .80 | .20 |
| ☐ 10 Mike Rozier<br>Houston Oilers | 1.00 | .40 | .10 |
| ☐ 11 Greg Bell<br>Buffalo Bills | 1.00 | .40 | .10 |
| ☐ 12 Ottis Anderson<br>St. Louis Cardinals | 1.50 | .60 | .15 |
| ☐ 13 Dave Krieg<br>Seattle Seahawks | 1.50 | .60 | .15 |
| ☐ 14 Anthony Carter<br>Minnesota Vikings | 1.50 | .60 | .15 |
| ☐ 15 Freeman McNeil<br>New York Jets | 1.50 | .60 | .15 |
| ☐ 16 Doug Cosbie<br>Dallas Cowboys | 1.00 | .40 | .10 |
| ☐ 17 James Lofton SP<br>Green Bay Packers | 6.00 | 2.40 | .60 |
| ☐ 18 Dan Marino<br>Miami Dolphins | 10.00 | 4.00 | 1.00 |
| ☐ 19 James Wilder<br>Tampa Bay Buccaneers | 1.00 | .40 | .10 |
| ☐ 20 Cris Collinsworth UER<br>(Name misspelled Chris)<br>Cincinnati Bengals | 1.00 | .40 | .10 |
| ☐ 21 Eric Dickerson<br>Los Angeles Rams | 3.00 | 1.20 | .30 |
| ☐ 22 Walter Payton<br>Chicago Bears | 6.00 | 2.40 | .60 |
| ☐ 23 Ozzie Newsome<br>Cleveland Browns | 2.00 | .80 | .20 |
| ☐ 24 Chris Hinton<br>Indianapolis Colts | 1.00 | .40 | .10 |

## 1971-72 Dell

MERLIN OLSEN
Los Angeles

JAMES LOFTON

Measuring approximately 8 1/4" by 10 3/4", the 1971-72 Dell Pro Football Guide features a center insert that unfolds to display 48 color player photos that are framed by black and yellow border stripes. Each picture measures approximately 1 3/4" by 3" and is not perforated. The player's name and team name are printed beneath the picture. The backs have various color action shots that are framed by a black-and-white film type pattern. Biographies on the NFL stars featured on the insert are found throughout the guide. The pictures are unnumbered and checklisted below in alphabetical order.

|  | NRMT | VG-E | GOOD |
|---|---|---|---|
| COMPLETE SET (48) | 75.00 | 30.00 | 7.50 |
| COMMON PLAYER (1-48) | 1.00 | .40 | .10 |
| ☐ 1 Dan Abramowicz | 1.00 | .40 | .10 |
| ☐ 2 Herb Adderley | 2.00 | .80 | .20 |
| ☐ 3 Lem Barney | 2.00 | .80 | .20 |
| ☐ 4 Bobby Bell | 2.00 | .80 | .20 |
| ☐ 5 George Blanda | 3.00 | 1.20 | .30 |
| ☐ 6 Terry Bradshaw | 7.50 | 3.00 | .75 |
| ☐ 7 John Brodie | 3.00 | 1.20 | .30 |
| ☐ 8 Larry Brown | 1.50 | .60 | .15 |
| ☐ 9 Dick Butkus | 5.00 | 2.00 | .50 |
| ☐ 10 Fred Carr | 1.00 | .40 | .10 |
| ☐ 11 Virgil Carter | 1.00 | .40 | .10 |
| ☐ 12 Mike Curtis | 1.00 | .40 | .10 |
| ☐ 13 Len Dawson | 3.00 | 1.20 | .30 |
| ☐ 14 Carl Eller | 2.00 | .80 | .20 |
| ☐ 15 Mel Farr | 1.00 | .40 | .10 |
| ☐ 16 Roman Gabriel | 2.00 | .80 | .20 |
| ☐ 17 Gary Garrison | 1.00 | .40 | .10 |
| ☐ 18 Dick Gordon | 1.00 | .40 | .10 |
| ☐ 19 Bob Griese | 5.00 | 2.00 | .50 |
| ☐ 20 Bob Hayes | 1.50 | .60 | .15 |
| ☐ 21 Rich Jackson | 1.00 | .40 | .10 |
| ☐ 22 Charley Johnson | 1.50 | .60 | .15 |
| ☐ 23 Ron Johnson | 1.00 | .40 | .10 |
| ☐ 24 Deacon Jones | 2.00 | .80 | .20 |
| ☐ 25 Sonny Jurgensen | 3.00 | 1.20 | .30 |
| ☐ 26 Leroy Kelly | 2.00 | .80 | .20 |
| ☐ 27 Daryle Lamonica | 1.50 | .60 | .15 |
| ☐ 28 MacArthur Lane | 1.00 | .40 | .10 |
| ☐ 29 Willie Lanier | 2.00 | .80 | .20 |
| ☐ 30 Bob Lilly | 3.00 | 1.20 | .30 |
| ☐ 31 Floyd Little | 2.00 | .80 | .20 |
| ☐ 32 Mike Lucci | 1.00 | .40 | .10 |
| ☐ 33 Don Maynard | 3.00 | 1.20 | .30 |
| ☐ 34 Joe Namath | 15.00 | 6.00 | 1.50 |
| ☐ 35 Tommy Nobis | 2.00 | .80 | .20 |
| ☐ 36 Merlin Olsen | 3.00 | 1.20 | .30 |
| ☐ 37 Alan Page | 2.00 | .80 | .20 |
| ☐ 38 Gerry Philbin | 1.00 | .40 | .10 |
| ☐ 39 Jim Plunkett | 2.00 | .80 | .20 |
| ☐ 40 Tim Rossovich | 1.00 | .40 | .10 |
| ☐ 41 Gayle Sayers | 5.00 | 2.00 | .50 |
| ☐ 42 Dennis Shaw | 1.00 | .40 | .10 |
| ☐ 43 O.J. Simpson | 15.00 | 6.00 | 1.50 |
| ☐ 44 Fran Tarkenton | 6.00 | 2.40 | .60 |
| ☐ 45 John Unitas | 7.50 | 3.00 | .75 |
| ☐ 46 Paul Warfield | 3.00 | 1.20 | .30 |
| ☐ 47 Gene Washington | 1.00 | .40 | .10 |
| ☐ 48 Larry Wilson | 2.00 | .80 | .20 |

## 1992 Diamond Stickers

Produced by Diamond Publishing Inc., the first series of NFL Superstar stickers consists of 160 stickers, each measuring approximately 1 15/16" by 2 15/16". The stickers were sold in six-sticker packets and could be pasted in a 36-page sticker album. Eight hundred autographed stickers were randomly inserted throughout the packs; apparently, each of the featured stars (Mark Carrier, Cornelius

Bennett, Chris Miller, and Rob Moore) signed 200 each. The fronts feature action color player photos framed by a team-color coded inner border and a white outer border. The team name appears in the team's accent color within the top border. The horizontally oriented backs are white with purple print and carry biographical and statistical information. The stickers are numbered on the back and checklisted below alphabetically according to teams in the AFC and NFC as follows: Buffalo Bills (3-7), Cincinnati Bengals (8-12), Cleveland Browns (13-17), Denver Broncos (18-22), Houston Oilers (23-27), Indianapolis Colts (28-32), Kansas City Chiefs (33-37), Los Angeles Raiders (38-42), Miami Dolphins (43-47), New England Patriots (48-52), New York Jets (53-57), Pittsburgh Steelers (58-62), San Diego Chargers (63-67), Seattle Seahawks (68-72), Atlanta Falcons (87-91), Chicago Bears (92-96), Dallas Cowboys (97-101), Detroit Lions (102-106), Green Bay Packers (107-111), Los Angeles Rams (112-116), Minnesota Vikings (117-121), New Orleans Saints (122-126), New York Giants (127-131), Philadelphia Eagles (132-136), Phoenix Cardinals (137-141), San Francisco 49ers (142-146), Tampa Bay Buccaneers (147-151), and Washington Redskins (152-156). The set includes an All Pro (75-84) subset and closes with a Super Bowl XXVI (157-160) subset.

|  | MINT | EXC | G-VG |
|---|---|---|---|
| COMPLETE SET (160) | 15.00 | 6.00 | 1.50 |
| COMMON PLAYER (1-160) | .10 | .04 | .01 |
| ☐ 1 Super Bowl XXVI logo | .10 | .04 | .01 |
| (Top portion) | | | |
| ☐ 2 Super Bowl XXVI logo | .10 | .04 | .01 |
| (Bottom portion) | | | |
| ☐ 3 Jim Kelly | .25 | .10 | .02 |
| ☐ 4 Thurman Thomas | .30 | .12 | .03 |
| ☐ 5 Andre Reed | .20 | .08 | .02 |
| ☐ 6 James Lofton | .15 | .06 | .01 |
| ☐ 7 Cornelius Bennett | .15 | .06 | .01 |
| ☐ 8 Boomer Esiason | .15 | .06 | .01 |
| ☐ 9 Harold Green | .20 | .08 | .02 |
| ☐ 10 Anthony Munoz | .15 | .06 | .01 |
| ☐ 11 Mitchell Price | .10 | .04 | .01 |
| ☐ 12 Louis Billups | .10 | .04 | .01 |
| ☐ 13 Bernie Kosar | .20 | .08 | .02 |
| ☐ 14 Eric Metcalf | .15 | .06 | .01 |
| ☐ 15 Michael Dean Perry | .15 | .06 | .01 |
| ☐ 16 Van Waiters | .10 | .04 | .01 |
| ☐ 17 Brian Brennan | .10 | .04 | .01 |
| ☐ 18 John Elway | .50 | .20 | .05 |
| ☐ 19 Gaston Green | .10 | .04 | .01 |
| ☐ 20 Vance Johnson | .10 | .04 | .01 |
| ☐ 21 Dennis Smith | .10 | .04 | .01 |
| ☐ 22 Clarence Kay | .10 | .04 | .01 |
| ☐ 23 Warren Moon | .25 | .10 | .02 |
| ☐ 24 Haywood Jeffires | .20 | .08 | .02 |
| ☐ 25 Cris Dishman | .10 | .04 | .01 |
| ☐ 26 Bubba McDowell | .10 | .04 | .01 |
| ☐ 27 Ray Childress | .10 | .04 | .01 |
| ☐ 28 Eric Dickerson | .20 | .08 | .02 |
| ☐ 29 Jesse Hester | .10 | .04 | .01 |
| ☐ 30 Clarence Verdin | .10 | .04 | .01 |
| ☐ 31 Bill Brooks | .10 | .04 | .01 |
| ☐ 32 Albert Bentley | .10 | .04 | .01 |
| ☐ 33 Christian Okoye | .10 | .04 | .01 |
| ☐ 34 Derrick Thomas | .25 | .10 | .02 |
| ☐ 35 Dino Hackett | .10 | .04 | .01 |
| ☐ 36 Deron Cherry | .10 | .04 | .01 |
| ☐ 37 Bill Maas | .10 | .04 | .01 |
| ☐ 38 Todd Marinovich | .10 | .04 | .01 |
| ☐ 39 Roger Craig | .15 | .06 | .01 |
| ☐ 40 Greg Townsend | .10 | .04 | .01 |
| ☐ 41 Ronnie Lott | .15 | .06 | .01 |
| ☐ 42 Howie Long | .15 | .06 | .01 |
| ☐ 43 Dan Marino | 1.00 | .40 | .10 |
| ☐ 44 Mark Clayton | .15 | .06 | .01 |
| ☐ 45 Sammie Smith | .10 | .04 | .01 |
| ☐ 46 Jim Jensen | .10 | .04 | .01 |

| | | | | |
|---|---|---|---|---|
| ☐ 47 Reggie Roby | .10 | .04 | .01 |
| ☐ 48 Brent Williams | .10 | .04 | .01 |
| ☐ 49 Andre Tippett | .10 | .04 | .01 |
| ☐ 50 John Stephens | .15 | .06 | .01 |
| ☐ 51 Johnny Rembert | .10 | .04 | .01 |
| ☐ 52 Irving Fryar | .15 | .06 | .01 |
| ☐ 53 Ken O'Brien | .10 | .04 | .01 |
| ☐ 54 Al Toon | .15 | .06 | .01 |
| ☐ 55 Brad Baxter | .20 | .08 | .02 |
| ☐ 56 James Hasty | .10 | .04 | .01 |
| ☐ 57 Rob Moore | .25 | .10 | .02 |
| ☐ 58 Neil O'Donnell | .35 | .14 | .03 |
| ☐ 59 Bubby Brister | .10 | .04 | .01 |
| ☐ 60 Louis Lipps | .10 | .04 | .01 |
| ☐ 61 Merril Hoge | .10 | .04 | .01 |
| ☐ 62 Gary Anderson | .10 | .04 | .01 |
| ☐ 63 John Friesz | .20 | .08 | .02 |
| ☐ 64 Junior Seau | .25 | .10 | .02 |
| ☐ 65 Leslie O'Neal | .15 | .06 | .01 |
| ☐ 66 Rod Bernstine | .15 | .06 | .01 |
| ☐ 67 Burt Grossman | .10 | .04 | .01 |
| ☐ 68 Brian Blades | .15 | .06 | .01 |
| ☐ 69 Cortez Kennedy | .25 | .10 | .02 |
| ☐ 70 Dave Wyman | .10 | .04 | .01 |
| ☐ 71 John L. Williams | .15 | .06 | .01 |
| ☐ 72 Robert Blackmon | .10 | .04 | .01 |
| ☐ 73 Checklist 33-48 | .15 | .06 | .01 |
|    Jim Kelly | | | |
|    Buffalo Bills | | | |
| ☐ 74 Checklist 49-64 | .15 | .06 | .01 |
|    Ronnie Lott | | | |
|    Los Angeles Raiders | | | |
| ☐ 75 Jerry Rice | .25 | .10 | .02 |
|    San Francisco 49ers | | | |
|    Andre Reed | | | |
|    Buffalo Bills | | | |
| ☐ 76 Jay Novacek | .15 | .06 | .01 |
|    Dallas Cowboys | | | |
|    Dennis Smith | | | |
|    Denver Broncos | | | |
| ☐ 77 Mark Rypien | .20 | .08 | .02 |
|    Washington Redskins | | | |
|    Jim Kelly | | | |
|    Buffalo Bills | | | |
| ☐ 78 Pat Swilling | .15 | .06 | .01 |
|    New Orleans Saints | | | |
|    Derrick Thomas | | | |
|    Kansas City Chiefs | | | |
| ☐ 79 Deion Sanders | .15 | .06 | .01 |
|    Atlanta Falcons | | | |
|    Cris Dishman | | | |
|    Houston Oilers | | | |
| ☐ 80 Mel Gray | .10 | .04 | .01 |
|    Detroit Lions | | | |
|    Gaston Green | | | |
|    Denver Broncos | | | |
| ☐ 81 Earnest Byner | .10 | .04 | .01 |
|    Washington Redskins | | | |
|    Christian Okoye | | | |
|    Kansas City Chiefs | | | |
| ☐ 82 Eric Allen | .15 | .06 | .01 |
|    Philadelphia Eagles | | | |
|    Ronnie Lott | | | |
|    Los Angeles Raiders | | | |
| ☐ 83 Mike Singletary | .15 | .06 | .01 |
|    Chicago Bears | | | |
|    Junior Seau | | | |
|    San Diego Chargers | | | |
| ☐ 84 Andre Rison | .20 | .08 | .02 |
|    Atlanta Falcons | | | |
|    Haywood Jeffires | | | |
|    Houston Oilers | | | |
| ☐ 85 Checklist 65-80 | .20 | .08 | .02 |
|    Steve Young | | | |
|    San Francisco 49ers | | | |
| ☐ 86 Checklist 81-96 | .10 | .04 | .01 |
|    Pat Swilling | | | |
|    New Orleans Saints | | | |
| ☐ 87 Chris Miller | .15 | .06 | .01 |
| ☐ 88 Andre Rison | .25 | .10 | .02 |
| ☐ 89 Deion Sanders | .25 | .10 | .02 |
| ☐ 90 Michael Haynes | .20 | .08 | .02 |
| ☐ 91 Tim Green | .10 | .04 | .01 |
| ☐ 92 Jim Harbaugh | .15 | .06 | .01 |
| ☐ 93 Mark Carrier USC | .15 | .06 | .01 |
| ☐ 94 Mike Singletary | .15 | .06 | .01 |
| ☐ 95 William Perry | .15 | .06 | .01 |
| ☐ 96 Donnell Woolford | .10 | .04 | .01 |
| ☐ 97 Troy Aikman | 1.00 | .40 | .10 |
| ☐ 98 Michael Irvin | .35 | .14 | .03 |
| ☐ 99 Russell Maryland | .25 | .10 | .02 |
| ☐ 100 Jay Novacek | .20 | .08 | .02 |
| ☐ 101 Ken Norton Jr | .15 | .06 | .01 |
| ☐ 102 Mel Gray | .10 | .04 | .01 |
| ☐ 103 Bennie Blades | .10 | .04 | .01 |
| ☐ 104 Rodney Peete | .15 | .06 | .01 |
| ☐ 105 Brett Perriman | .10 | .04 | .01 |
| ☐ 106 William White | .10 | .04 | .01 |
| ☐ 107 Vai Sikahema | .10 | .04 | .01 |
| ☐ 108 Vince Workman | .15 | .06 | .01 |
| ☐ 109 Jeff Query | .15 | .06 | .01 |
| ☐ 110 Sterling Sharpe | .35 | .14 | .03 |
| ☐ 111 Tony Mandarich | .10 | .04 | .01 |
| ☐ 112 Jim Everett | .15 | .06 | .01 |
| ☐ 113 Flipper Anderson | .15 | .06 | .01 |
| ☐ 114 Robert Delpino | .15 | .06 | .01 |
| ☐ 115 Darryl Henley | .10 | .04 | .01 |
| ☐ 116 Henry Ellard | .15 | .06 | .01 |
| ☐ 117 Wade Wilson | .15 | .06 | .01 |
| ☐ 118 Anthony Carter | .15 | .06 | .01 |
| ☐ 119 Chris Doleman | .15 | .06 | .01 |
| ☐ 120 Cris Carter | .15 | .06 | .01 |
| ☐ 121 Henry Thomas | .10 | .04 | .01 |
| ☐ 122 Steve Walsh | .15 | .06 | .01 |
| ☐ 123 Pat Swilling | .15 | .06 | .01 |
| ☐ 124 Dalton Hilliard | .15 | .06 | .01 |
| ☐ 125 Floyd Turner | .10 | .04 | .01 |
| ☐ 126 Craig Heyward | .15 | .06 | .01 |
| ☐ 127 Jeff Hostetler | .20 | .08 | .02 |
| ☐ 128 Phil Simms | .20 | .08 | .02 |
| ☐ 129 Lawrence Taylor | .25 | .10 | .02 |
| ☐ 130 Mark Ingram | .15 | .06 | .01 |
| ☐ 131 Leonard Marshall | .10 | .04 | .01 |
| ☐ 132 Randall Cunningham | .25 | .10 | .02 |
| ☐ 133 Eric Allen | .10 | .04 | .01 |
| ☐ 134 Keith Byars | .15 | .06 | .01 |
| ☐ 135 Fred Barnett | .20 | .08 | .02 |
| ☐ 136 Wes Hopkins | .10 | .04 | .01 |
| ☐ 137 Ernie Jones | .15 | .06 | .01 |
| ☐ 138 Johnny Johnson | .30 | .12 | .03 |
| ☐ 139 Anthony Thompson | .15 | .06 | .01 |
| ☐ 140 Timm Rosenbach | .15 | .06 | .01 |
| ☐ 141 Randal Hill | .25 | .10 | .02 |
| ☐ 142 Steve Young | .35 | .14 | .03 |
| ☐ 143 Jerry Rice | .50 | .20 | .05 |
| ☐ 144 Tom Rathman | .15 | .06 | .01 |
| ☐ 145 Charles Haley | .10 | .04 | .01 |
| ☐ 146 John Taylor | .15 | .06 | .01 |
| ☐ 147 Vinny Testaverde | .20 | .08 | .02 |
| ☐ 148 Gary Anderson | .15 | .06 | .01 |
| ☐ 149 Broderick Thomas | .10 | .04 | .01 |
| ☐ 150 Mark Carrier | .15 | .06 | .01 |
| ☐ 151 Ian Beckles | .10 | .04 | .01 |
| ☐ 152 Mark Rypien | .15 | .06 | .01 |
| ☐ 153 Earnest Byner | .10 | .04 | .01 |
| ☐ 154 Gary Clark | .15 | .06 | .01 |
| ☐ 155 Monte Coleman | .10 | .04 | .01 |
| ☐ 156 Ricky Ervins | .15 | .06 | .01 |
| ☐ 157 Earnest Byner | .10 | .04 | .01 |
| ☐ 158 Jim Kelly | .15 | .06 | .01 |
|    Fred Stokes | | | |
|    James Geathers | | | |
| ☐ 159 Checklist 129-144 | .10 | .04 | .01 |
|    Mark Rypien | | | |
|    Washington Redskins | | | |
| ☐ 160 Mark Rypien | .15 | .06 | .01 |
|    Washington Redskins | | | |

## 1992 Dog Tags

Produced by Chris Martin Enterprises, Inc., this boxed set consists of 81 dog tags. Made of durable plastic, each tag measures approximately 2 1/8" by 3 3/8" and, with its rounded corners, resembles a credit card. All the tags are bordered on each end by white stripes, and in the top stripe, a hole was bore through so that it could be worn on a chain. The team tags are horizontally oriented and display a picture of the team's stadium on their fronts. The backs present a variety of information, including individual career record holders and pictures of the team's uniform, logo, and helmet. The regular player tags have a color action player photo on their fronts. The backs have biography, 1991 season summary, 1991 statistics, color head shot, and autograph slot. The rookie tags are identical to the regular player tags, except that their top border stripe is gold foil; they are distinguished in the checklist below by an R prefix which is not present on the cards themselves. The set subdivides into three groups: team tags (1-28), regular player tags (29-76), and rookie tags (R1-R5). The cards are numbered on both sides.

|  | MINT | EXC | G-VG |
|---|---|---|---|
| COMPLETE SET (81) | 75.00 | 30.00 | 7.50 |
| COMMON TEAM (1-28) | .50 | .20 | .05 |
| COMMON PLAYER (29-76) | .75 | .30 | .07 |
| COMMON ROOKIE (R1-R5) | 1.50 | .60 | .15 |
| ☐ 1 Atlanta Falcons | .50 | .20 | .05 |
| ☐ 2 Buffalo Bills | .50 | .20 | .05 |
| ☐ 3 Chicago Bears | .50 | .20 | .05 |
| ☐ 4 Cincinnati Bengals | .50 | .20 | .05 |
| ☐ 5 Cleveland Browns | .50 | .20 | .05 |
| ☐ 6 Dallas Cowboys | .75 | .30 | .07 |
| ☐ 7 Denver Broncos | .50 | .20 | .05 |
| ☐ 8 Detroit Lions | .50 | .20 | .05 |
| ☐ 9 Green Bay Packers | .50 | .20 | .05 |
| ☐ 10 Houston Oilers | .50 | .20 | .05 |
| ☐ 11 Indianapolis Colts | .50 | .20 | .05 |
| ☐ 12 Kansas City Chiefs | .50 | .20 | .05 |
| ☐ 13 Los Angeles Raiders | .75 | .30 | .07 |
| ☐ 14 Los Angeles Rams | .50 | .20 | .05 |
| ☐ 15 Miami Dolphins | .75 | .30 | .07 |
| ☐ 16 Minnesota Vikings | .50 | .20 | .05 |
| ☐ 17 New England Patriots | .50 | .20 | .05 |
| ☐ 18 New Orleans Saints | .50 | .20 | .05 |
| ☐ 19 New York Giants | .50 | .20 | .05 |
| ☐ 20 New York Jets | .50 | .20 | .05 |
| ☐ 21 Philadelphia Eagles | .50 | .20 | .05 |
| ☐ 22 Phoenix Cardinals | .50 | .20 | .05 |
| ☐ 23 Pittsburgh Steelers | .50 | .20 | .05 |
| ☐ 24 San Diego Chargers | .50 | .20 | .05 |
| ☐ 25 San Francisco 49ers | .50 | .20 | .05 |
| ☐ 26 Seattle Seahawks | .50 | .20 | .05 |
| ☐ 27 Tampa Bay Buccaneers | .50 | .20 | .05 |
| ☐ 28 Washington Redskins | .50 | .20 | .05 |
| ☐ 29 Chris Martin | 1.00 | .40 | .10 |
| Kansas City Chiefs |  |  |  |
| ☐ 30 Dan Marino | 5.00 | 2.00 | .50 |
| Miami Dolphins |  |  |  |
| ☐ 31 Chris Miller | 1.25 | .50 | .12 |
| Atlanta Falcons |  |  |  |
| ☐ 32 Deion Sanders | 2.50 | 1.00 | .25 |
| Atlanta Falcons |  |  |  |
| ☐ 33 Jim Kelly | 2.50 | 1.00 | .25 |
| Buffalo Bills |  |  |  |
| ☐ 34 Thurman Thomas | 3.00 | 1.20 | .30 |
| Buffalo Bills |  |  |  |
| ☐ 35 Jim Harbaugh | 1.00 | .40 | .10 |
| Chicago Bears |  |  |  |
| ☐ 36 Mike Singletary | 1.00 | .40 | .10 |
| Chicago Bears |  |  |  |
| ☐ 37 Boomer Esiason | 1.00 | .40 | .10 |
| Cincinnati Bengals |  |  |  |
| ☐ 38 Anthony Munoz | 1.00 | .40 | .10 |
| Cincinnati Bengals |  |  |  |
| ☐ 39 Bernie Kosar | 1.00 | .40 | .10 |
| Cleveland Browns |  |  |  |
| ☐ 40 Troy Aikman | 6.00 | 2.40 | .60 |
| Dallas Cowboys |  |  |  |
| ☐ 41 Michael Irvin | 3.00 | 1.20 | .30 |
| Dallas Cowboys |  |  |  |
| ☐ 42 Emmitt Smith | 7.50 | 3.00 | .75 |
| Dallas Cowboys |  |  |  |
| ☐ 43 John Elway | 3.00 | 1.20 | .30 |
| Denver Broncos |  |  |  |
| ☐ 44 Rodney Peete | 1.00 | .40 | .10 |
| Detroit Lions |  |  |  |
| ☐ 45 Sterling Sharpe | 3.00 | 1.20 | .30 |
| Green Bay Packers |  |  |  |
| ☐ 46 Haywood Jeffires | 2.00 | .80 | .20 |
| Houston Oilers |  |  |  |
| ☐ 47 Warren Moon | 2.00 | .80 | .20 |
| Houston Oilers |  |  |  |
| ☐ 48 Jeff George | 1.50 | .60 | .15 |
| Indianapolis Colts |  |  |  |
| ☐ 49 Christian Okoye | 1.00 | .40 | .10 |
| Kansas City Chiefs |  |  |  |
| ☐ 50 Derrick Thomas | 2.00 | .80 | .20 |
| Kansas City Chiefs |  |  |  |
| ☐ 51 Howie Long | 1.00 | .40 | .10 |
| Los Angeles Raiders |  |  |  |
| ☐ 52 Ronnie Lott | 1.25 | .50 | .12 |
| Los Angeles Raiders |  |  |  |
| ☐ 53 Jim Everett | 1.00 | .40 | .10 |
| Los Angeles Rams |  |  |  |
| ☐ 54 Mark Clayton | 1.00 | .40 | .10 |
| Miami Dolphins |  |  |  |
| ☐ 55 Anthony Carter | 1.00 | .40 | .10 |
| Minnesota Vikings |  |  |  |
| ☐ 56 Chris Doleman | .75 | .30 | .07 |
| Minnesota Vikings |  |  |  |

| ☐ 57 Andre Tippett | .75 | .30 | .07 |
|---|---|---|---|
| New England Patriots |  |  |  |
| ☐ 58 Pat Swilling | 1.00 | .40 | .10 |
| New Orleans Saints |  |  |  |
| ☐ 59 Jeff Hostetler | 1.50 | .60 | .15 |
| New York Giants |  |  |  |
| ☐ 60 Lawrence Taylor | 1.50 | .60 | .15 |
| New York Giants |  |  |  |
| ☐ 61 Rob Moore | 1.50 | .60 | .15 |
| New York Jets |  |  |  |
| ☐ 62 Ken O'Brien | .75 | .30 | .07 |
| New York Jets |  |  |  |
| ☐ 63 Keith Byars | 1.00 | .40 | .10 |
| Philadelphia Eagles |  |  |  |
| ☐ 64 Randall Cunningham | 2.00 | .80 | .20 |
| Philadelphia Eagles |  |  |  |
| ☐ 65 Johnny Johnson | 2.00 | .80 | .20 |
| Phoenix Cardinals |  |  |  |
| ☐ 66 Timm Rosenbach | .75 | .30 | .07 |
| Phoenix Cardinals |  |  |  |
| ☐ 67 Bubby Brister | .75 | .30 | .07 |
| Pittsburgh Steelers |  |  |  |
| ☐ 68 John Friesz | 1.25 | .50 | .12 |
| San Diego Chargers |  |  |  |
| ☐ 69 Jerry Rice | 3.00 | 1.20 | .30 |
| San Francisco 49ers |  |  |  |
| ☐ 70 Steve Young | 2.50 | 1.00 | .25 |
| San Francisco 49ers |  |  |  |
| ☐ 71 Dan McGwire | .75 | .30 | .07 |
| Seattle Seahawks |  |  |  |
| ☐ 72 Broderick Thomas | .75 | .30 | .07 |
| Tampa Bay Buccaneers |  |  |  |
| ☐ 73 Vinny Testaverde | 1.00 | .40 | .10 |
| Tampa Bay Buccaneers |  |  |  |
| ☐ 74 Gary Clark | 1.00 | .40 | .10 |
| Washington Redskins |  |  |  |
| ☐ 75 Mark Rypien | 1.25 | .50 | .12 |
| Washington Redskins |  |  |  |
| ☐ 76 Neil Smith | 1.00 | .40 | .10 |
| Kansas City Chiefs |  |  |  |
| ☐ R1 Dale Carter | 1.50 | .60 | .15 |
| Kansas City Chiefs |  |  |  |
| ☐ R2 Steve Emtman | 1.50 | .60 | .15 |
| Indianapolis Colts |  |  |  |
| ☐ R3 David Klingler | 3.00 | 1.20 | .30 |
| Cincinnati Bengals |  |  |  |
| ☐ R4 Tommy Maddox | 2.50 | 1.00 | .25 |
| Denver Broncos |  |  |  |
| ☐ R5 Vaughn Dunbar | 2.00 | .80 | .20 |
| New Orleans Saints |  |  |  |

# 1993 Dog Tags

Produced by Chris Martin Enterprises, Inc., this set of "Dog Tags Plus" consists of 110 individual player tags and 28 team tags. Two tags, numbers 48 and 138, were not produced. The dog tags were originally distributed in random assortments but later as comllkete steam sets. The only two teams not included in the team set packaging were the Atlanta Falcons and the Los Angeles Raiders. There were also 25,000 sequentially numbered Joe Montana limited edition bonus tags. The collector could obtain one of these Montana tags through a mail-in offer for 5.00 and three proofs of purchase. Reportedly 50,000 of each tag were produced, with each one sequentially numbered. Autographed tags were randomly inserted throughout the cases. Also collectors could enter a contest to win a seven-point diamond tag and a 14K gold bead chain. Made of durable plastic, each tag measures approximately 2 1/8" by 3 3/8" and, with its rounded corners, resembles a credit card. The player tags show a full-bleed action photo on their fronts. The year "1993" and the word "Plus" are gold foil stamped at the top, while the player's name appears on a short bar toward the bottom. On a team color-coded background, the backs have a color close-up photo, biography, player profile, 1992 stats, and an autograph slot. The tags are numbered on the back. After team logo tags (1-28), the set is arranged alphabetically within teams and checklisted below alphabetically according to teams as follows: Atlanta Falcons (29-32), Buffalo Bills (33-36), Chicago Bears (37-40), Cincinnati Bengals (41-44), Cleveland Browns (45-47), Dallas Cowboys (49-52), Denver Broncos (53-56), Detroit Lions (57-60), Green Bay Packers (61-64), Houston Oilers (65-68), Indianapolis Colts (69-72), Kansas City Chiefs (73-76), Los Angeles Raiders (77-80), Los Angeles Rams (81-84), Miami Dolphins (85-88), Minnesota Vikings (89-92), New England Patriots (93-96), New Orleans Saints (97-100), New York Giants (101-104), New York Jets (105-108), Philadelphia Eagles (109-112), Phoenix Cardinals (113-116), Pittsburgh Steelers (117-120), San Diego Chargers (121-124), San Francisco 49ers (125-128), Seattle Seahawks (129-132), Tampa Bay Buccaneers (133-136), and Washington Redskins (137, 139-140).

| | MINT | EXC | G-VG |
|---|---|---|---|
| COMPLETE SET (138) | 125.00 | 50.00 | 12.50 |
| COMMON TEAM (1-28) | .50 | .20 | .05 |
| COMMON PLAYER (29-140) | .75 | .30 | .07 |
| ☐ 1 Atlanta Falcons | .50 | .20 | .05 |
| ☐ 2 Buffalo Bills | .50 | .20 | .05 |
| ☐ 3 Chicago Bears | .50 | .20 | .05 |
| ☐ 4 Cincinnati Bengals | .50 | .20 | .05 |
| ☐ 5 Cleveland Browns | .50 | .20 | .05 |
| ☐ 6 Dallas Cowboys | .75 | .30 | .07 |
| ☐ 7 Denver Broncos | .50 | .20 | .05 |
| ☐ 8 Detroit Lions | .50 | .20 | .05 |
| ☐ 9 Green Bay Packers | .50 | .20 | .05 |
| ☐ 10 Houston Oilers | .50 | .20 | .05 |
| ☐ 11 Indianapolis Colts | .50 | .20 | .05 |
| ☐ 12 Kansas City Chiefs | .50 | .20 | .05 |
| ☐ 13 Los Angeles Raiders | .75 | .30 | .07 |
| ☐ 14 Los Angeles Rams | .50 | .20 | .05 |
| ☐ 15 Miami Dolphins | .75 | .30 | .07 |
| ☐ 16 Minnesota Vikings | .50 | .20 | .05 |
| ☐ 17 New England Patriots | .50 | .20 | .05 |
| ☐ 18 New Orleans Saints | .50 | .20 | .05 |
| ☐ 19 New York Giants | .50 | .20 | .05 |
| ☐ 20 New York Jets | .50 | .20 | .05 |
| ☐ 21 Philadelphia Eagles | .50 | .20 | .05 |
| ☐ 22 Phoenix Cardinals | .50 | .20 | .05 |
| ☐ 23 Pittsburgh Steelers | .50 | .20 | .05 |
| ☐ 24 San Diego Chargers | .50 | .20 | .05 |
| ☐ 25 San Fransico 49ers | .50 | .20 | .05 |
| ☐ 26 Seattle Seahawks | .50 | .20 | .05 |
| ☐ 27 Tampa Bay Buccaneers | .50 | .20 | .05 |
| ☐ 28 Washington Redskins | .50 | .20 | .05 |
| ☐ 29 Steve Broussard | .50 | .20 | .05 |
| ☐ 30 Chris Miller | 1.00 | .40 | .10 |
| ☐ 31 Andre Rison | 1.50 | .60 | .15 |
| ☐ 32 Deion Sanders | 2.00 | .80 | .20 |
| ☐ 33 Cornelius Bennett | 1.00 | .40 | .10 |
| ☐ 34 Jim Kelly | 2.50 | 1.00 | .25 |
| ☐ 35 Bruce Smith | 1.25 | .50 | .12 |
| ☐ 36 Thurman Thomas | 2.50 | 1.00 | .25 |
| ☐ 37 Neal Anderson | .75 | .30 | .07 |
| ☐ 38 Mark Carrier | .50 | .20 | .05 |
| ☐ 39 Jim Harbaugh | .75 | .30 | .07 |
| ☐ 40 Alonzo Spellman | .75 | .30 | .07 |
| ☐ 41 David Fulcher | .50 | .20 | .05 |
| ☐ 42 Harold Green | .75 | .30 | .07 |
| ☐ 43 David Klingler | 1.50 | .60 | .15 |
| ☐ 44 Carl Pickens | 1.25 | .50 | .12 |
| ☐ 45 Bernie Kosar | 1.00 | .40 | .10 |
| ☐ 46 Clay Matthews | 1.00 | .40 | .10 |
| ☐ 47 Eric Metcalf | 1.00 | .40 | .10 |
| ☐ 49 Troy Aikman | 5.00 | 2.00 | .50 |
| ☐ 50 Michael Irvin | 2.50 | 1.00 | .25 |
| ☐ 51 Russell Maryland | 1.00 | .40 | .10 |
| ☐ 52 Emmitt Smith | 6.00 | 2.40 | .60 |
| ☐ 53 Steve Atwater | .50 | .20 | .05 |
| ☐ 54 John Elway | 4.00 | 1.60 | .40 |
| ☐ 55 Tommy Maddox | 1.25 | .50 | .12 |
| ☐ 56 Shannon Sharpe | 1.25 | .50 | .12 |
| ☐ 57 Herman Moore | 1.25 | .50 | .12 |
| ☐ 58 Rodney Peete | .75 | .30 | .07 |
| ☐ 59 Barry Sanders | 4.00 | 1.60 | .40 |
| ☐ 60 Andre Ware | .75 | .30 | .07 |
| ☐ 61 Terrell Buckley | .75 | .30 | .07 |
| ☐ 62 Brett Favre | 2.50 | 1.00 | .25 |
| ☐ 63 Sterling Sharpe | 3.00 | 1.20 | .30 |
| ☐ 64 Reggie White | 1.50 | .60 | .15 |
| ☐ 65 Ray Childress | .75 | .30 | .07 |
| ☐ 66 Haywood Jeffires | 1.25 | .50 | .12 |
| ☐ 67 Warren Moon | 2.50 | 1.00 | .25 |
| ☐ 68 Lorenzo White | .75 | .30 | .07 |
| ☐ 69 Duane Bickett | .75 | .30 | .07 |
| ☐ 70 Quentin Coryatt | 1.00 | .40 | .10 |
| ☐ 71 Steve Emtman | .75 | .30 | .07 |
| ☐ 72 Jeff George | 1.50 | .60 | .15 |
| ☐ 73 Dale Carter | .75 | .30 | .07 |
| ☐ 74 Neil Smith | .75 | .30 | .07 |
| ☐ 75 Derrick Thomas | 2.00 | .80 | .20 |
| ☐ 76 Harvey Williams | 1.25 | .50 | .12 |
| ☐ 77 Eric Dickerson | 1.25 | .50 | .12 |
| ☐ 78 Howie Long | .75 | .30 | .07 |
| ☐ 79 Todd Marinovich | .75 | .30 | .07 |
| ☐ 80 Alexander Wright | .75 | .30 | .07 |
| ☐ 81 Flipper Anderson | .50 | .20 | .05 |
| ☐ 82 Jim Everett | .75 | .30 | .07 |
| ☐ 83 Cleveland Gary | .50 | .20 | .05 |
| ☐ 84 Chris Martin | .75 | .30 | .07 |
| ☐ 85 Irving Fryar | .75 | .30 | .07 |
| ☐ 86 Keith Jackson | 1.25 | .50 | .12 |
| ☐ 87 Dan Marino | 5.00 | 2.00 | .50 |
| ☐ 88 Louis Oliver | .50 | .20 | .05 |
| ☐ 89 Terry Allen | 1.00 | .40 | .10 |
| ☐ 90 Anthony Carter | .75 | .30 | .07 |
| ☐ 91 Chris Doleman | .75 | .30 | .07 |
| ☐ 92 Rich Gannon | .75 | .30 | .07 |
| ☐ 93 Eugene Chung | .50 | .20 | .05 |
| ☐ 94 Marv Cook | .50 | .20 | .05 |
| ☐ 95 Leonard Russell | 1.00 | .40 | .10 |
| ☐ 96 Andre Tippett | .75 | .30 | .07 |
| ☐ 97 Morten Anderson | .50 | .20 | .05 |
| ☐ 98 Vaughn Dunbar | .75 | .30 | .07 |
| ☐ 99 Rickey Jackson | .75 | .30 | .07 |
| ☐ 100 Sam Mills | .50 | .20 | .05 |
| ☐ 101 Derek Brown | .75 | .30 | .07 |
| ☐ 102 Lawrence Taylor | 1.50 | .60 | .15 |
| ☐ 103 Rodney Hampton | 2.00 | .80 | .20 |
| ☐ 104 Phil Simms | 1.25 | .50 | .12 |
| ☐ 105 Johnny Mitchell | 1.25 | .50 | .12 |
| ☐ 106 Rob Moore | 1.00 | .40 | .10 |
| ☐ 107 Blair Thomas | .75 | .30 | .07 |
| ☐ 108 Browning Nagle | 1.00 | .40 | .10 |
| ☐ 109 Eric Allen | .50 | .20 | .05 |
| ☐ 110 Fred Barnett | 1.25 | .50 | .12 |
| ☐ 111 Randall Cunningham | 2.00 | .80 | .20 |
| ☐ 112 Herschel Walker | 1.00 | .40 | .10 |
| ☐ 113 Chris Chandler | .75 | .30 | .07 |
| ☐ 114 Randal Hill | 1.00 | .40 | .10 |
| ☐ 115 Ricky Proehl | .75 | .30 | .07 |
| ☐ 116 Eric Swann | .75 | .30 | .07 |
| ☐ 117 Barry Foster | 1.50 | .60 | .15 |
| ☐ 118 Eric Green | 1.00 | .40 | .10 |
| ☐ 119 Neil O'Donnell | 1.50 | .60 | .15 |
| ☐ 120 Rod Woodson | 1.00 | .40 | .10 |
| ☐ 121 Marion Butts | 1.00 | .40 | .10 |
| ☐ 122 Stan Humphries | 1.25 | .50 | .12 |
| ☐ 123 Anthony Miller | 1.00 | .40 | .10 |
| ☐ 124 Junior Seau | 1.50 | .60 | .15 |
| ☐ 125 Amp Lee | 1.00 | .40 | .10 |
| ☐ 126 Jerry Rice | 4.00 | 1.60 | .40 |
| ☐ 127 Ricky Watters | 2.00 | .80 | .20 |
| ☐ 128 Steve Young | 2.50 | 1.00 | .25 |
| ☐ 129 Brian Blades | .75 | .30 | .07 |
| ☐ 130 Cortez Kennedy | 1.00 | .40 | .10 |
| ☐ 131 Dan McGwire | 1.00 | .40 | .10 |
| ☐ 132 John L. Williams | .75 | .30 | .07 |
| ☐ 133 Reggie Cobb | 1.00 | .40 | .10 |
| ☐ 134 Steve DeBerg | .75 | .30 | .07 |
| ☐ 135 Keith McCants | .75 | .30 | .07 |
| ☐ 136 Broderick Thomas | .75 | .30 | .07 |
| ☐ 137 Earnest Byner | .75 | .30 | .07 |
| ☐ 139 Mark Rypien | .75 | .30 | .07 |
| ☐ 140 Ricky Sanders | .75 | .30 | .07 |

## 1967 Dolphins Royal Castle

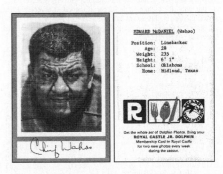

This 27-card set was issued by Royal Castle, a south Florida hamburger stand, at a rate of two new cards every week during the season. These unnumbered cards measure approximately 3" by 4 3/8". The front features a black and white (almost sepia-toned) posed photo of the player enframed by an orange border, with the player's signature below the photo. Biographical information is given on the back (including player's nickname where appropriate), along with the logos for the Miami Dolphins and Royal Castle. This set features a card of Bob Griese during his rookie season. There may be a 28th card: George Wilson Jr. There are 16 cards that are easier than the others; rather than calling these double prints, the other eleven cards are marked as SP's in the checklist below.

|  | NRMT | VG-E | GOOD |
|---|---|---|---|
| COMPLETE SET (27) | 2000.00 | 900.00 | 250.00 |
| COMMON PLAYER (1-27) | 15.00 | 6.00 | 1.50 |
| COMMON PLAYER SP | 90.00 | 36.00 | 9.00 |
| ☐ 1 Joseph Auer SP | 90.00 | 36.00 | 9.00 |
| ☐ 2 Tom Beier | 15.00 | 6.00 | 1.50 |
| ☐ 3 Mel Branch | 20.00 | 8.00 | 2.00 |
| ☐ 4 Jon Brittenum | 25.00 | 10.00 | 2.50 |
| ☐ 5 George Chesser | 15.00 | 6.00 | 1.50 |
| ☐ 6 Edward Cooke | 15.00 | 6.00 | 1.50 |
| ☐ 7 Frank Emanuel SP | 90.00 | 36.00 | 9.00 |
| ☐ 8 Norm Erlandson SP | 90.00 | 36.00 | 9.00 |
| ☐ 9 Norm Evans SP | 125.00 | 50.00 | 12.50 |
| ☐ 10 Bob Griese SP | 600.00 | 240.00 | 60.00 |
| ☐ 11 Abner Haynes SP | 125.00 | 50.00 | 12.50 |
| ☐ 12 Jerry Hopkins SP | 90.00 | 36.00 | 9.00 |
| ☐ 13 Frank Jackson | 15.00 | 6.00 | 1.50 |
| ☐ 14 Billy Joe | 20.00 | 8.00 | 2.00 |
| ☐ 15 Wahoo McDaniel | 75.00 | 30.00 | 7.50 |
| ☐ 16 Robert Neff | 15.00 | 6.00 | 1.50 |
| ☐ 17 Billy Neighbors | 20.00 | 8.00 | 2.00 |
| ☐ 18 Rick Norton | 15.00 | 6.00 | 1.50 |
| ☐ 19 Robert Petrich | 15.00 | 6.00 | 1.50 |
| ☐ 20 Jim Riley | 15.00 | 6.00 | 1.50 |
| ☐ 21 John Stofa SP | 125.00 | 50.00 | 12.50 |
| ☐ 22 Laverne Torczon | 15.00 | 6.00 | 1.50 |
| ☐ 23 Howard Twilley | 60.00 | 24.00 | 6.00 |
| ☐ 24 Jimmy Warren SP | 90.00 | 36.00 | 9.00 |
| ☐ 25 Richard Westmoreland | 15.00 | 6.00 | 1.50 |
| ☐ 26 Maxie Williams SP | 200.00 | 80.00 | 20.00 |
| ☐ 27 George Wilson Sr. SP | 125.00 | 50.00 | 12.50 |
| (Head Coach) | | | |

# 1974 Dolphins All-Pro Graphics

Each of these ten photos measures approximately 8 1/4" by 10 3/4". The fronts feature color action photos bordered in white. The player's name, position, and team name appear in the top border, while the copyright year (1974) and the manufacturer "All Pro Graphics, Inc." are printed in the bottom white border at the left. It is reported that several of these photos do not have the tagline in the lower left corner. The backs are blank. The photos are unnumbered and checklisted below in alphabetical order.

|  | NRMT | VG-E | GOOD |
|---|---|---|---|
| COMPLETE SET (10) | 75.00 | 30.00 | 7.50 |
| COMMON PLAYER (1-10) | 5.00 | 2.00 | .50 |
| ☐ 1 Dick Anderson | 7.50 | 3.00 | .75 |
| ☐ 2 Nick Buoniconti | 10.00 | 4.00 | 1.00 |
| (1974 All-Pro Graphics) | | | |
| ☐ 3 Larry Csonka | 15.00 | 6.00 | 1.50 |
| ☐ 4 Manny Fernandez | 6.00 | 2.40 | .60 |
| ☐ 5 Bob Griese | 20.00 | 8.00 | 2.00 |
| ☐ 6 Jim Kiick | 7.50 | 3.00 | .75 |
| ☐ 7 Earl Morrall | 10.00 | 4.00 | 1.00 |
| ☐ 8 Mercury Morris | 7.50 | 3.00 | .75 |
| ☐ 9 Jake Scott | 6.00 | 2.40 | .60 |
| ☐ 10 Garo Yepremian | 5.00 | 2.00 | .50 |
| (1974 All-Pro Graphics) | | | |

# 1991 Domino's Quarterbacks

This 50-card NFL quarterback set was produced by Upper Deck and sponsored by Domino's Pizza in conjunction with Coca-Cola and NFL Properties. These standard-size (2 1/2" by 3 1/2") cards were part of a national promotion that was kicked off during the August 3, 1991, "NBC Sportsworld" telecast of "NFL Quarterback Challenge". The cards were distributed through the 5,000 Domino's restaurants across the country. During August, or while supplies lasted, customers who ordered the Domino's Pizza NFL Kick-off Deal received two medium cheese pizzas, four cans of Coke, Diet Coke, or Coke Classic, and one free foil pack with four NFL Quarterback cards, all for 9.99. The front design has color action player photos bordered in white, with the words "Quarterback Challenge" inscribed across the top of the card in a black stripe. The Domino's logo, the player's name, and the team logo appear across the bottom of the card face. The backs picture smaller color action shots, statistics, and career highlights. The cards are numbered on the back. The first 32 cards in the set are active quarterbacks arranged in alphabetical order by teams. Cards 33-46 feature retired quarterbacks in alphabetical order by player name and cards 47-49 depict quarterback duos from the same team but different eras.

|  | MINT | EXC | G-VG |
|---|---|---|---|
| COMPLETE SET (50) | 6.00 | 2.40 | .60 |
| COMMON PLAYER (1-50) | .10 | .04 | .01 |
| ☐ 1 Chris Miller | .15 | .06 | .01 |
| Atlanta Falcons | | | |
| ☐ 2 Jim Kelly | .35 | .14 | .03 |
| Buffalo Bills | | | |
| ☐ 3 Jim Harbaugh | .15 | .06 | .01 |
| Chicago Bears | | | |
| ☐ 4 Boomer Esiason | .20 | .08 | .02 |
| Cincinnati Bengals | | | |
| ☐ 5 Bernie Kosar | .25 | .10 | .02 |
| Cleveland Browns | | | |
| ☐ 6 Troy Aikman | 1.00 | .40 | .10 |
| Dallas Cowboys | | | |
| ☐ 7 John Elway | .50 | .20 | .05 |
| Denver Broncos | | | |
| ☐ 8 Rodney Peete | .10 | .04 | .01 |
| Detroit Lions | | | |
| ☐ 9 Andre Ware | .15 | .06 | .01 |
| Detroit Lions | | | |
| ☐ 10 Anthony Dilweg | .10 | .04 | .01 |
| Green Bay Packers | | | |
| ☐ 11 Warren Moon | .30 | .12 | .03 |
| Houston Oilers | | | |
| ☐ 12 Jeff George | .30 | .12 | .03 |
| Indianapolis Colts | | | |
| ☐ 13 Jim Everett | .15 | .06 | .01 |
| Los Angeles Rams | | | |
| ☐ 14 Jay Schroeder | .10 | .04 | .01 |
| Los Angeles Raiders | | | |
| ☐ 15 Wade Wilson | .15 | .06 | .01 |
| Minnesota Vikings | | | |
| ☐ 16 Dan Marino | .75 | .30 | .07 |
| Miami Dolphins | | | |
| ☐ 17 Phil Simms | .15 | .06 | .01 |
| New York Giants | | | |
| ☐ 18 Jeff Hostetler | .15 | .06 | .01 |
| New York Giants | | | |
| ☐ 19 Ken O'Brien | .10 | .04 | .01 |
| New York Jets | | | |
| ☐ 20 Timm Rosenbach | .10 | .04 | .01 |
| Phoenix Cardinals | | | |
| ☐ 21 Bubby Brister | .10 | .04 | .01 |
| Pittsburgh Steelers | | | |
| ☐ 22 Steve DeBerg | .15 | .06 | .01 |
| Kansas City Chiefs | | | |
| ☐ 23 Randall Cunningham | .30 | .12 | .03 |
| Philadelphia Eagles | | | |

| | | | |
|---|---|---|---|
| ☐ 24 Steve Walsh | .15 | .06 | .01 |
| New Orleans Saints | | | |
| ☐ 25 Billy Joe Tolliver | .10 | .04 | .01 |
| San Diego Chargers | | | |
| ☐ 26 Steve Young | .35 | .14 | .03 |
| San Francisco 49ers | | | |
| ☐ 27 Dave Krieg | .15 | .06 | .01 |
| Seattle Seahawks | | | |
| ☐ 28 Dan McGwire | .15 | .06 | .01 |
| Seattle Seahawks | | | |
| ☐ 29 Vinny Testaverde | .15 | .06 | .01 |
| Tampa Bay Buccaneers | | | |
| ☐ 30 Stan Humphries | .20 | .08 | .02 |
| Washington Redskins | | | |
| ☐ 31 Mark Rypien | .15 | .06 | .01 |
| Washington Redskins | | | |
| ☐ 32 Terry Bradshaw | .50 | .20 | .05 |
| Pittsburgh Steelers | | | |
| ☐ 33 John Brodie | .15 | .06 | .01 |
| San Francisco 49ers | | | |
| ☐ 34 Len Dawson | .20 | .08 | .02 |
| Kansas City Chiefs | | | |
| ☐ 35 Dan Fouts | .25 | .10 | .02 |
| San Diego Chargers | | | |
| ☐ 36 Otto Graham | .40 | .16 | .04 |
| Cleveland Browns | | | |
| ☐ 37 Bob Griese | .25 | .10 | .02 |
| Miami Dolphins | | | |
| ☐ 38 Sonny Jurgensen | .25 | .10 | .02 |
| Washington Redskins | | | |
| ☐ 39 Daryle Lamonica | .15 | .06 | .01 |
| Oakland Raiders | | | |
| ☐ 40 Archie Manning | .20 | .08 | .02 |
| New Orleans Saints | | | |
| ☐ 41 Jim Plunkett | .15 | .06 | .01 |
| Oakland Raiders | | | |
| ☐ 42 Bart Starr | .35 | .14 | .03 |
| Green Bay Packers | | | |
| ☐ 43 Roger Staubach | .75 | .30 | .07 |
| Dallas Cowboys | | | |
| ☐ 44 Joe Theismann | .25 | .10 | .02 |
| Washington Redskins | | | |
| ☐ 45 Y.A. Tittle | .25 | .10 | .02 |
| New York Giants | | | |
| ☐ 46 Johnny Unitas | .50 | .20 | .05 |
| Baltimore Colts | | | |
| ☐ 47 Cowboy Gunslingers | .60 | .24 | .06 |
| Troy Aikman | | | |
| Roger Staubach | | | |
| Dallas Cowboys | | | |
| ☐ 48 Cajun Connection | .30 | .12 | .03 |
| Bubby Brister | | | |
| Terry Bradshaw | | | |
| Pittsburgh Steelers | | | |
| ☐ 49 Dolphin Duo | .40 | .16 | .04 |
| Dan Marino | | | |
| Bob Griese | | | |
| Miami Dolphins | | | |
| ☐ 50 Checklist Card | .10 | .04 | .01 |

## 1959 Eagles Jay Publishing

This 12-card set features (approximately) 5" by 7" black-and-white player photos. The photos show players in traditional poses with the quarterback preparing to throw, the runner heading downfield, and the defenseman ready for the tackle. These cards were packaged 12 to a packet and originally sold for 25 cents. The backs are blank. The cards are unnumbered and checklisted below in alphabetical order.

| | NRMT | VG-E | GOOD |
|---|---|---|---|
| COMPLETE SET (12) | 60.00 | 24.00 | 6.00 |
| COMMON PLAYER (1-12) | 5.00 | 2.00 | .50 |
| | | | |
| ☐ 1 Billy Barnes | 5.00 | 2.00 | .50 |
| ☐ 2 Chuck Bednarik | 10.00 | 4.00 | 1.00 |
| ☐ 3 Tom Brookshier | 6.00 | 2.40 | .60 |
| ☐ 4 Marion Campbell | 6.00 | 2.40 | .60 |
| ☐ 5 Ted Dean | 5.00 | 2.00 | .50 |
| ☐ 6 Tommy McDonald | 7.50 | 3.00 | .75 |
| ☐ 7 Clarence Peaks | 5.00 | 2.00 | .50 |
| ☐ 8 Pete Retzlaff | 7.50 | 3.00 | .75 |
| ☐ 9 Jess Richardson | 5.00 | 2.00 | .50 |
| ☐ 10 Norm Van Brocklin | 10.00 | 4.00 | 1.00 |
| ☐ 11 Bobby Walston | 6.00 | 2.40 | .60 |
| ☐ 12 Chuck Weber | 5.00 | 2.00 | .50 |

## 1960 Eagles White Border

This 11-card team-issued set measures approximately 5" by 7" and is printed on thin, slick card stock. The fronts feature black-and-white posed action player photos with white borders. The player's name is printed in black below the picture. The backs are blank. The cards are unnumbered and checklisted below in alphabetical order.

MAXIE BAUGHAN, Eagles

| | NRMT | VG-E | GOOD |
|---|---|---|---|
| COMPLETE SET (11) | 45.00 | 18.00 | 4.50 |
| COMMON PLAYER (1-11) | 5.00 | 2.00 | .50 |
| | | | |
| ☐ 1 Maxie Baughan | 7.50 | 3.00 | .75 |
| ☐ 2 Chuck Bednarik | 10.00 | 4.00 | 1.00 |
| ☐ 3 Don Burroughs | 5.00 | 2.00 | .50 |
| ☐ 4 Jimmy Carr | 6.00 | 2.40 | .60 |
| ☐ 5 Howard Keys | 5.00 | 2.00 | .50 |
| ☐ 6 Ed Khayat | 5.00 | 2.00 | .50 |
| ☐ 7 Jim McCusker | 5.00 | 2.00 | .50 |
| ☐ 8 John Nocera | 5.00 | 2.00 | .50 |
| ☐ 9 Nick Skorich | 6.00 | 2.40 | .60 |
| ☐ 10 J.D. Smith | 6.00 | 2.40 | .60 |
| ☐ 11 John Wittenborn | 5.00 | 2.00 | .50 |

## 1961 Eagles Jay Publishing

This 12-card set features (approximately) 5" by 7" black-and-white player photos. The photos show players in traditional poses with the quarterback preparing to throw, the runner heading downfield, and the defenseman ready for the tackle. These cards were packaged 12 to a packet and originally sold for 25 cents. The backs are blank. The cards are unnumbered and checklisted below in alphabetical order.

| | NRMT | VG-E | GOOD |
|---|---|---|---|
| COMPLETE SET (12) | 50.00 | 20.00 | 5.00 |
| COMMON PLAYER (1-12) | 5.00 | 2.00 | .50 |
| | | | |
| ☐ 1 Maxie Baughan | 7.50 | 3.00 | .75 |
| ☐ 2 Jim McCusker | 5.00 | 2.00 | .50 |
| ☐ 3 Tommy McDonald | 7.50 | 3.00 | .75 |
| ☐ 4 Bob Pellegrini | 5.00 | 2.00 | .50 |
| ☐ 5 Pete Retzlaff | 7.50 | 3.00 | .75 |
| ☐ 6 Jess Richardson | 5.00 | 2.00 | .50 |
| ☐ 7 Joe Robb | 5.00 | 2.00 | .50 |
| ☐ 8 Theron Sapp | 5.00 | 2.00 | .50 |
| ☐ 9 J.D. Smith | 6.00 | 2.40 | .60 |
| ☐ 10 Bobby Walston | 6.00 | 2.40 | .60 |
| ☐ 11 Jerry Williams ACO | 5.00 | 2.00 | .50 |
| ☐ 12 John Wittenborn | 5.00 | 2.00 | .50 |

## 1971 Eagles Team Issue

GARY BALLMAN          PHILADELPHIA EAGLES

This 16-card set measures approximately 4 1/4" by 5 1/2" and features posed action, black-and-white player photos with white borders. The player's name and team are printed in black in the bottom white margin. The backs are blank. The cards are unnumbered and checklisted below in alphabetical order. The set's date is defined by the fact that Jim Ward's only year with the Eagles was 1971, Lee Bougess' last year with the Eagles was 1971, and Kent Kramer and

Tom McNeill's first year with the Eagles was 1971. Norm Snead's last year with the Eagles was 1970, but he was traded to the Minnesota Vikings during the off-season.

|  | MINT | EXC | G-VG |
|---|---|---|---|
| COMPLETE SET (16) | 30.00 | 12.00 | 3.00 |
| COMMON PLAYER (1-16) | 2.00 | .80 | .20 |
| ☐ 1 Gary Ballman | 2.50 | 1.00 | .25 |
| ☐ 2 Lee Bouggess | 2.00 | .80 | .20 |
| ☐ 3 Kent Kramer | 2.50 | 1.00 | .25 |
| ☐ 4 Tom McNeill | 2.00 | .80 | .20 |
| ☐ 5 Mark Nordquist | 2.00 | .80 | .20 |
| ☐ 6 Ron Porter | 2.00 | .80 | .20 |
| ☐ 7 Steve Preece | 2.00 | .80 | .20 |
| ☐ 8 Tim Rossovich | 3.00 | 1.20 | .30 |
| (Facing right edge of card) | | | |
| ☐ 9 Tim Rossovich | 3.00 | 1.20 | .30 |
| (Facing left edge of card) | | | |
| ☐ 10 Jim Skaggs | 2.00 | .80 | .20 |
| ☐ 11 Norm Snead | 3.00 | 1.20 | .30 |
| ☐ 12 Jim Thrower | 2.00 | .80 | .20 |
| ☐ 13 Mel Tom | 2.50 | 1.00 | .25 |
| ☐ 14 Jim Ward | 2.00 | .80 | .20 |
| ☐ 15 Adrian Young | 2.00 | .80 | .20 |
| ☐ 16 Don Zimmerman | 2.00 | .80 | .20 |

## 1983 Eagles Frito Lay

This 37-card set measures approximately 4 1/4" by 5 1/2" and features an action player shot and facsimile autograph enclosed in a white border. The team name and mascot appear in the top border while the player's name, position, and Frito Lay logo appear in the bottom border. The backs of card numbers 5, 27, and 31 are in the postcard format, while the rest of the backs are blank. Because this set is unnumbered, the cards are listed alphabetically.

|  | MINT | EXC | G-VG |
|---|---|---|---|
| COMPLETE SET (37) | 40.00 | 16.00 | 4.00 |
| COMMON PLAYER (1-37) | 1.00 | .40 | .10 |
| ☐ 1 Harvey Armstrong | 1.00 | .40 | .10 |
| ☐ 2 Ron Baker | 1.00 | .40 | .10 |
| ☐ 3 Greg Brown | 1.00 | .40 | .10 |
| ☐ 4 Marion Campbell CO | 1.50 | .60 | .15 |
| ☐ 5 Harold Carmichael | 2.50 | 1.00 | .25 |
| ☐ 6 Ken Clarke | 1.00 | .40 | .10 |
| ☐ 7 Dennis DeVaughn | 1.00 | .40 | .10 |
| ☐ 8 Herman Edwards | 1.25 | .50 | .12 |
| ☐ 9 Ray Ellis | 1.00 | .40 | .10 |
| ☐ 10 Major Everett | 1.50 | .60 | .15 |
| ☐ 11 Anthony Griggs | 1.00 | .40 | .10 |
| ☐ 12 Michael Haddix | 1.25 | .50 | .12 |
| ☐ 13 Perry Harrington | 1.00 | .40 | .10 |
| ☐ 14 Dennis Harrison | 1.00 | .40 | .10 |
| ☐ 15 Wes Hopkins | 1.50 | .60 | .15 |
| ☐ 16 Ron Jaworski | 3.00 | 1.20 | .30 |
| ☐ 17 Ron Johnson | 1.00 | .40 | .10 |
| ☐ 18 Vyto Kab | 1.25 | .50 | .12 |
| ☐ 19 Steve Kenney | 1.00 | .40 | .10 |
| ☐ 20 Dean Miraldi | 1.00 | .40 | .10 |
| ☐ 21 Leonard Mitchell | 1.00 | .40 | .10 |
| ☐ 22 Wilbert Montgomery | 3.00 | 1.20 | .30 |
| ☐ 23 Hubie Oliver | 1.00 | .40 | .10 |
| ☐ 24 Joe Pisarcik | 1.50 | .60 | .15 |
| ☐ 25 Mike Quick | 2.50 | 1.00 | .25 |
| ☐ 26 Jerry Robinson | 2.00 | .80 | .20 |
| ☐ 27 Max Runager | 1.00 | .40 | .10 |
| ☐ 28 Buddy Ryan CO | 4.00 | 1.60 | .40 |
| ☐ 29 Lawrence Sampleton | 1.25 | .50 | .12 |
| ☐ 30 Jody Schulz | 1.00 | .40 | .10 |
| ☐ 31 Jerry Sisemore | 1.25 | .50 | .12 |

|  | MINT | EXC | G-VG |
|---|---|---|---|
| ☐ 32 John Spagnola | 1.50 | .60 | .15 |
| ☐ 33 Reggie Wilkes | 1.00 | .40 | .10 |
| ☐ 34 Mike Williams | 1.00 | .40 | .10 |
| ☐ 35 Tony Woodruff | 1.00 | .40 | .10 |
| ☐ 36 Glen Young | 1.00 | .40 | .10 |
| ☐ 37 Roynell Young | 1.50 | .60 | .15 |

## 1985 Eagles Team Issue

RON JAWORSKI    QB    7

RON JAWORSKI    QB    7

This 53-card team-issued set measures approximately 2 15/16" by 3 7/8". The fronts feature glossy color player photos bordered in white. The wider bottom border contains the player's name, position, and jersey number. Player information again appears on the top of the backs in green print; the career summary is printed in a black box that fills the rest of the backs. The cards are unnumbered and checklisted below alphabetically, with the miscellaneous cards listed at the end.

|  | MINT | EXC | G-VG |
|---|---|---|---|
| COMPLETE SET (53) | 50.00 | 20.00 | 5.00 |
| COMMON PLAYER (1-53) | 1.00 | .40 | .10 |
| ☐ 1 Harvey Armstrong | 1.00 | .40 | .10 |
| ☐ 2 Ron Baker | 1.00 | .40 | .10 |
| ☐ 3 Norman Braman PRES | 1.50 | .60 | .15 |
| ☐ 4 Greg Brown | 1.00 | .40 | .10 |
| ☐ 5 Marion Campbell CO | 1.50 | .60 | .15 |
| ☐ 6 Jeff Christensen | 1.00 | .40 | .10 |
| ☐ 7 Ken Clarke | 1.00 | .40 | .10 |
| ☐ 8 Evan Cooper | 1.00 | .40 | .10 |
| ☐ 9 Byron Darby | 1.00 | .40 | .10 |
| ☐ 10 Mark Dennard | 1.00 | .40 | .10 |
| ☐ 11 Herman Edwards | 1.25 | .50 | .12 |
| ☐ 12 Ray Ellis | 1.00 | .40 | .10 |
| ☐ 13 Major Everett | 1.25 | .50 | .12 |
| ☐ 14 Gerry Feehery | 1.00 | .40 | .10 |
| ☐ 15 Elbert Foules | 1.00 | .40 | .10 |
| ☐ 16 Gregg Garrity | 1.25 | .50 | .12 |
| ☐ 17 Anthony Griggs | 1.00 | .40 | .10 |
| ☐ 18 Michael Haddix | 1.25 | .50 | .12 |
| ☐ 19 Andre Hardy | 1.00 | .40 | .10 |
| ☐ 20 Dennis Harrison | 1.00 | .40 | .10 |
| ☐ 21 Joe Hayes | 1.00 | .40 | .10 |
| ☐ 22 Melvin Hoover | 1.00 | .40 | .10 |
| ☐ 23 Wes Hopkins | 1.50 | .60 | .15 |
| ☐ 24 Mike Horan | 1.00 | .40 | .10 |
| ☐ 25 Kenny Jackson | 1.25 | .50 | .12 |
| ☐ 26 Ron Jaworski | 3.00 | 1.20 | .30 |
| ☐ 27 Vyto Kab | 1.25 | .50 | .12 |
| ☐ 28 Steve Kenney | 1.00 | .40 | .10 |
| ☐ 29 Rich Kraynak | 1.00 | .40 | .10 |
| ☐ 30 Dean May | 1.00 | .40 | .10 |
| ☐ 31 Paul McFadden | 1.00 | .40 | .10 |
| ☐ 32 Dean Miraldi | 1.00 | .40 | .10 |
| ☐ 33 Leonard Mitchell | 1.00 | .40 | .10 |
| ☐ 34 Wilbert Montgomery | 3.00 | 1.20 | .30 |
| ☐ 35 Hubie Oliver | 1.00 | .40 | .10 |
| ☐ 36 Mike Quick | 2.00 | .80 | .20 |
| ☐ 37 Mike Reichenbach | 1.25 | .50 | .12 |
| ☐ 38 Jerry Robinson | 1.50 | .60 | .15 |
| ☐ 39 Rusty Russell | 1.00 | .40 | .10 |
| ☐ 40 Lawrence Sampleton | 1.25 | .50 | .12 |
| ☐ 41 Jody Schulz | 1.00 | .40 | .10 |
| ☐ 42 John Spagnola | 1.50 | .60 | .15 |
| ☐ 43 Tom Strauthers | 1.00 | .40 | .10 |
| ☐ 44 Andre Waters | 2.00 | .80 | .20 |
| ☐ 45 Reggie Wilkes | 1.25 | .50 | .12 |
| ☐ 46 Joel Williams | 1.00 | .40 | .10 |
| ☐ 47 Michael Williams | 1.00 | .40 | .10 |
| ☐ 48 Brenard Wilson | 1.00 | .40 | .10 |
| ☐ 49 Tony Woodruff | 1.00 | .40 | .10 |
| ☐ 50 Roynell Young | 1.50 | .60 | .15 |
| ☐ 51 Logo Card | 1.50 | .60 | .15 |
| (Eagle holding football on both sides) | | | |

| | MINT | EXC | G-VG |
|---|---|---|---|
| ☐ 52 1985 Schedule Card................ | 1.50 | .60 | .15 |
| (Both sides) | | | |
| ☐ 53 Title Card 1985-86 ................. | 1.50 | .60 | .15 |
| (Eagles' helmet) | | | |

## 1989 Eagles Daily News

This 24-card set which measures approximately 5 9/16" by 4 1/4" features black and white portrait photos of the players. Above the player's photo is the Eagle logo and the Philadelphia Eagles team name while underneath are advertisements for McDonald's, radio station KYW, and the Philadelphia Daily News. The backs are blank. This was the third season that the Eagles had participated in this project. We have checklisted this set in alphabetical order.

| | MINT | EXC | G-VG |
|---|---|---|---|
| COMPLETE SET (24)........................ | 25.00 | 10.00 | 2.50 |
| COMMON PLAYER (1-23)................. | 1.00 | .40 | .10 |
| ☐ 1 Eric Allen................................. | 1.00 | .40 | .10 |
| ☐ 2 Jerome Brown.......................... | 2.00 | .80 | .20 |
| ☐ 3 Keith Byars............................. | 2.00 | .80 | .20 |
| ☐ 4 Cris Carter UER....................... | 2.50 | 1.00 | .25 |
| (Name misspelled | | | |
| Chris on front) | | | |
| ☐ 5 Randall Cunningham................. | 5.00 | 2.00 | .50 |
| ☐ 6 Matt Darwin............................ | 1.00 | .40 | .10 |
| ☐ 7 Gerry Feehery.......................... | 1.00 | .40 | .10 |
| ☐ 8 Ron Heller.............................. | 1.00 | .40 | .10 |
| ☐ 9A Terry Hoage........................... | 1.50 | .60 | .15 |
| (Solid color jersey) | | | |
| ☐ 9B Terry Hoage........................... | 1.50 | .60 | .15 |
| (With white collar | | | |
| or undershirt) | | | |
| ☐ 10 Wes Hopkins.......................... | 1.50 | .60 | .15 |
| ☐ 11 Keith Jackson......................... | 3.00 | 1.20 | .30 |
| ☐ 12 Seth Joyner........................... | 2.50 | 1.00 | .25 |
| ☐ 13 Mike Pitts............................. | 1.00 | .40 | .10 |
| ☐ 14 Mike Quick............................ | 1.50 | .60 | .15 |
| ☐ 15 Mike Reichenbach................... | 1.00 | .40 | .10 |
| ☐ 16 Clyde Simmons....................... | 2.00 | .80 | .20 |
| ☐ 17 John Spagnola........................ | 1.25 | .50 | .12 |
| ☐ 18 Junior Tautalatasi................... | 1.00 | .40 | .10 |
| ☐ 19 John Teltschik........................ | 1.00 | .40 | .10 |
| ☐ 20 Anthony Toney........................ | 1.00 | .40 | .10 |
| ☐ 21 Andre Waters......................... | 1.50 | .60 | .15 |
| ☐ 22 Reggie White.......................... | 4.00 | 1.60 | .40 |
| ☐ 23 Luis Zendejas......................... | 1.00 | .40 | .10 |

## 1990 Eagles Sealtest

This six-card set (of bookmarks) which measures approximately 2" by 8" was produced by Sealtest to promote reading among children in Philadelphia. Apparently they were given out at The Free Library of Philadelphia on a weekly basis. The basic design of these bookmarks is identical to the 1990 Knudsen Chargers and 49ers bookmark sets. The color action player cut-out overlays a football stadium design. A box at the bottom whose color varies per bookmark gives biographical information and player profile. The backs have sponsor logos and describe two books that are available at the public library. The bookmarks are unnumbered and checklisted below in alphabetical order.

| | MINT | EXC | G-VG |
|---|---|---|---|
| COMPLETE SET (6)........................ | 15.00 | 6.00 | 1.50 |
| COMMON PLAYER (1-6)................... | 2.50 | 1.00 | .25 |
| ☐ 1 David Alexander ...................... | 2.50 | 1.00 | .25 |
| ☐ 2 Eric Allen............................... | 3.00 | 1.20 | .30 |
| ☐ 3 Keith Byars............................ | 3.50 | 1.40 | .35 |
| ☐ 4 Randall Cunningham................ | 6.00 | 2.40 | .60 |
| ☐ 5 Mike Pitts.............................. | 2.50 | 1.00 | .25 |
| ☐ 6 Mike Quick............................. | 3.00 | 1.20 | .30 |

## 1987 English Bears

This 33-card set was made in West Germany (by Ace Fact Pack) for distribution in England. The cards measure the standard size (2 1/2" by 3 1/2") and feature rounded corners and a playing card type design on the back. The 22 player cards in the set have been checklisted below in alphabetical order.

| | MINT | EXC | G-VG |
|---|---|---|---|
| COMPLETE SET (33)........................ | 150.00 | 60.00 | 15.00 |
| COMMON PLAYER (1-33)................. | 3.50 | 1.40 | .35 |
| ☐ 1 Todd Bell............................... | 5.00 | 2.00 | .50 |
| ☐ 2 Mark Bortz............................. | 3.50 | 1.40 | .35 |
| ☐ 3 Kevin Butler........................... | 5.00 | 2.00 | .50 |
| ☐ 4 Jim Covert............................. | 5.00 | 2.00 | .50 |
| ☐ 5 Richard Dent........................... | 9.00 | 3.75 | .90 |
| ☐ 6 Dave Duerson ......................... | 3.50 | 1.40 | .35 |
| ☐ 7 Gary Fencik............................ | 5.00 | 2.00 | .50 |
| ☐ 8 Willie Gault............................ | 7.50 | 3.00 | .75 |
| ☐ 9 Dan Hampton.......................... | 9.00 | 3.75 | .90 |
| ☐ 10 Jay Hilgenberg....................... | 3.50 | 1.40 | .35 |
| ☐ 11 Wilber Marshall...................... | 6.00 | 2.40 | .60 |
| ☐ 12 Jim McMahon........................ | 10.00 | 4.00 | 1.00 |
| ☐ 13 Steve McMichael..................... | 5.00 | 2.00 | .50 |
| ☐ 14 Emery Moorehead................... | 3.50 | 1.40 | .35 |
| ☐ 15 Keith Ortega.......................... | 3.50 | 1.40 | .35 |
| ☐ 16 Walter Payton........................ | 50.00 | 20.00 | 5.00 |
| ☐ 17 William Perry......................... | 7.50 | 3.00 | .75 |
| ☐ 18 Mike Richardson..................... | 3.50 | 1.40 | .35 |
| ☐ 19 Mike Singletary....................... | 10.00 | 4.00 | 1.00 |
| ☐ 20 Matt Suhey............................ | 5.00 | 2.00 | .50 |
| ☐ 21 Keith Van Horne...................... | 3.50 | 1.40 | .35 |
| ☐ 22 Otis Wilson............................ | 5.00 | 2.00 | .50 |
| ☐ 23 Bears Helmet......................... | 3.50 | 1.40 | .35 |
| ☐ 24 Bears Information.................... | 3.50 | 1.40 | .35 |
| ☐ 25 Bears Uniform........................ | 3.50 | 1.40 | .35 |
| ☐ 26 Game Record Holders............. | 3.50 | 1.40 | .35 |
| ☐ 27 Season Record Holders........... | 3.50 | 1.40 | .35 |
| ☐ 28 Career Record Holders............ | 3.50 | 1.40 | .35 |
| ☐ 29 Record 1967-86...................... | 3.50 | 1.40 | .35 |
| ☐ 30 1986 Team Statistics .............. | 3.50 | 1.40 | .35 |
| ☐ 31 All-Time Greats ...................... | 3.50 | 1.40 | .35 |
| ☐ 32 Roll of Honour ....................... | 3.50 | 1.40 | .35 |
| ☐ 33 Soldier Field.......................... | 3.50 | 1.40 | .35 |

## 1987 English Broncos

This 33-card set measures approximately 2 1/4" by 3 5/8". This set consists of 22 player cards and 11 organizational cards. These cards, which were issued in Great Britain and made in West Germany (by Ace

Fact Pack), have a playing card design on the back. The cards are checklisted below in alphabetical order.

|  | MINT | EXC | G-VG |
|---|---|---|---|
| COMPLETE SET (33) | 150.00 | 60.00 | 15.00 |
| COMMON PLAYER (1-33) | 3.50 | 1.40 | .35 |

| | | MINT | EXC | G-VG |
|---|---|---|---|---|
| ☐ 1 | Keith Bishop | 3.50 | 1.40 | .35 |
| ☐ 2 | Bill Bryan | 3.50 | 1.40 | .35 |
| ☐ 3 | Mark Cooper | 3.50 | 1.40 | .35 |
| ☐ 4 | John Elway | 50.00 | 20.00 | 5.00 |
| ☐ 5 | Steve Foley | 5.00 | 2.00 | .50 |
| ☐ 6 | Mike Harden | 3.50 | 1.40 | .35 |
| ☐ 7 | Rick Hunley | 3.50 | 1.40 | .35 |
| ☐ 8 | Vance Johnson | 5.00 | 2.00 | .50 |
| ☐ 9 | Rulon Jones | 5.00 | 2.00 | .50 |
| ☐ 10 | Rich Karlis | 3.50 | 1.40 | .35 |
| ☐ 11 | Clarence Kay | 5.00 | 2.00 | .50 |
| ☐ 12 | Ken Lanier | 5.00 | 2.00 | .50 |
| ☐ 13 | Karl Mecklenburg | 7.50 | 3.00 | .75 |
| ☐ 14 | Chris Norman | 3.50 | 1.40 | .35 |
| ☐ 15 | Jim Ryan | 3.50 | 1.40 | .35 |
| ☐ 16 | Dennis Smith | 5.00 | 2.00 | .50 |
| ☐ 17 | Dave Studdard | 3.50 | 1.40 | .35 |
| ☐ 18 | Andre Townsend | 3.50 | 1.40 | .35 |
| ☐ 19 | Steve Watson | 5.00 | 2.00 | .50 |
| ☐ 20 | Gerald Wilhite | 3.50 | 1.40 | .35 |
| ☐ 21 | Sammy Winder | 5.00 | 2.00 | .50 |
| ☐ 22 | Louis Wright | 5.00 | 2.00 | .50 |
| ☐ 23 | Broncos Helmet | 3.50 | 1.40 | .35 |
| ☐ 24 | Broncos Information | 3.50 | 1.40 | .35 |
| ☐ 25 | Broncos Uniform | 3.50 | 1.40 | .35 |
| ☐ 26 | Game Record Holders | 3.50 | 1.40 | .35 |
| ☐ 27 | Season Record Holders | 3.50 | 1.40 | .35 |
| ☐ 28 | Career Record Holders | 3.50 | 1.40 | .35 |
| ☐ 29 | Record 1967-86 | 3.50 | 1.40 | .35 |
| ☐ 30 | 1986 Team Statistics | 3.50 | 1.40 | .35 |
| ☐ 31 | All-Time Greats | 3.50 | 1.40 | .35 |
| ☐ 32 | Roll of Honour | 3.50 | 1.40 | .35 |
| ☐ 33 | Denver Mile High Stadium | 3.50 | 1.40 | .35 |

## 1987 English Cowboys

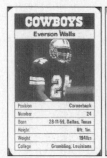

This 33-card set measures approximately 2 1/4" by 3 5/8". This set, which was printed in West Germany (by Ace Fact Pack) for release in Great Britain, has rounded corners and a playing type card back. There were 22 players in this set which we have checklisted alphabetically.

|  | MINT | EXC | G-VG |
|---|---|---|---|
| COMPLETE SET (33) | 150.00 | 60.00 | 15.00 |
| COMMON PLAYER (1-33) | 3.50 | 1.40 | .35 |

| | | MINT | EXC | G-VG |
|---|---|---|---|---|
| ☐ 1 | Bill Bates | 5.00 | 2.00 | .50 |
| ☐ 2 | Doug Cosbie | 5.00 | 2.00 | .50 |
| ☐ 3 | Tony Dorsett | 20.00 | 8.00 | 2.00 |
| ☐ 4 | Michael Downs | 3.50 | 1.40 | .35 |
| ☐ 5 | John Dutton | 5.00 | 2.00 | .50 |
| ☐ 6 | Ron Fellows | 3.50 | 1.40 | .35 |
| ☐ 7 | Mike Hegman | 3.50 | 1.40 | .35 |
| ☐ 8 | Tony Hill | 6.00 | 2.40 | .60 |
| ☐ 9 | Jim Jeffcoat | 5.00 | 2.00 | .50 |
| ☐ 10 | Ed Too Tall Jones | 10.00 | 4.00 | 1.00 |
| ☐ 11 | Crawford Ker | 3.50 | 1.40 | .35 |
| ☐ 12 | Eugene Lockhart | 5.00 | 2.00 | .50 |
| ☐ 13 | Phil Pozderac | 3.50 | 1.40 | .35 |
| ☐ 14 | Tom Rafferty | 5.00 | 2.00 | .50 |
| ☐ 15 | Jeff Rohrer | 3.50 | 1.40 | .35 |
| ☐ 16 | Mike Sherrard | 6.00 | 2.40 | .60 |
| ☐ 17 | Glen Titensor | 3.50 | 1.40 | .35 |
| ☐ 18 | Mark Tuinei | 5.00 | 2.00 | .50 |
| ☐ 19 | Herschel Walker | 12.00 | 5.00 | 1.20 |
| ☐ 20 | Everson Walls | 5.00 | 2.00 | .50 |
| ☐ 21 | Danny White | 7.50 | 3.00 | .75 |
| ☐ 22 | Randy White | 10.00 | 4.00 | 1.00 |
| ☐ 23 | Cowboys Helmet | 3.50 | 1.40 | .35 |
| ☐ 24 | Cowboys Information | 3.50 | 1.40 | .35 |
| ☐ 25 | Cowboys Uniform | 3.50 | 1.40 | .35 |
| ☐ 26 | Game Record Holders | 3.50 | 1.40 | .35 |
| ☐ 27 | Season Record Holders | 3.50 | 1.40 | .35 |
| ☐ 28 | Career Record Holders | 3.50 | 1.40 | .35 |
| ☐ 29 | Record 1967-86 | 3.50 | 1.40 | .35 |
| ☐ 30 | 1986 Team Statistics | 3.50 | 1.40 | .35 |
| ☐ 31 | All-Time Greats | 3.50 | 1.40 | .35 |
| ☐ 32 | Roll of Honour | 3.50 | 1.40 | .35 |
| ☐ 33 | Texas Stadium | 3.50 | 1.40 | .35 |

## 1987 English Dolphins

This 33-card set measures approximately 2 1/4" by 3 5/8". The set was printed in West Germany (by Ace Fact Pack) for release in Great Britain. This set features members of the Miami Dolphins and the set has rounded corners on the front and a design for Ace (looks like a playing card) on the back. We have checklisted the set in alphabetical order.

|  | MINT | EXC | G-VG |
|---|---|---|---|
| COMPLETE SET (33) | 150.00 | 60.00 | 15.00 |
| COMMON PLAYER (1-33) | 3.50 | 1.40 | .35 |

| | | MINT | EXC | G-VG |
|---|---|---|---|---|
| ☐ 1 | Bob Baumhower | 5.00 | 2.00 | .50 |
| ☐ 2 | Woody Bennett | 3.50 | 1.40 | .35 |
| ☐ 3 | Doug Betters | 5.00 | 2.00 | .50 |
| ☐ 4 | Glenn Blackwood | 5.00 | 2.00 | .50 |
| ☐ 5 | Bud Brown | 3.50 | 1.40 | .35 |
| ☐ 6 | Bob Brudzinksi | 3.50 | 1.40 | .35 |
| ☐ 7 | Mark Clayton | 7.50 | 3.00 | .75 |
| ☐ 8 | Mark Duper | 6.00 | 2.40 | .60 |
| ☐ 9 | Roy Foster | 3.50 | 1.40 | .35 |
| ☐ 10 | Jon Giesler | 3.50 | 1.40 | .35 |
| ☐ 11 | Hugh Green | 6.00 | 2.40 | .60 |
| ☐ 12 | Lorenzo Hampton | 5.00 | 2.00 | .50 |
| ☐ 13 | Bruce Hardy | 3.50 | 1.40 | .35 |
| ☐ 14 | William Judson | 3.50 | 1.40 | .35 |
| ☐ 15 | Greg Koch | 3.50 | 1.40 | .35 |
| ☐ 16 | Paul Lankford | 3.50 | 1.40 | .35 |
| ☐ 17 | George Little | 3.50 | 1.40 | .35 |
| ☐ 18 | Dan Marino | 75.00 | 30.00 | 7.50 |
| ☐ 19 | John Offerdahl | 5.00 | 2.00 | .50 |
| ☐ 20 | Dwight Stephenson | 5.00 | 2.00 | .50 |
| ☐ 21 | Don Strock | 5.00 | 2.00 | .50 |
| ☐ 22 | T.J. Turner | 3.50 | 1.40 | .35 |
| ☐ 23 | Dolphins Helmet | 3.50 | 1.40 | .35 |
| ☐ 24 | Dolphins Information | 3.50 | 1.40 | .35 |
| ☐ 25 | Dolphins Uniform | 3.50 | 1.40 | .35 |
| ☐ 26 | Game Record Holders | 3.50 | 1.40 | .35 |
| ☐ 27 | Season Record Holders | 3.50 | 1.40 | .35 |

| | MINT | EXC | G-VG |
|---|---|---|---|
| ☐ 28 Career Record Holders............ | 3.50 | 1.40 | .35 |
| ☐ 29 Record 1967-86...................... | 3.50 | 1.40 | .35 |
| ☐ 30 1986 Team Statistics .............. | 3.50 | 1.40 | .35 |
| ☐ 31 All-Time Greats ...................... | 3.50 | 1.40 | .35 |
| ☐ 32 Roll of Honour ....................... | 3.50 | 1.40 | .35 |
| ☐ 33 Joe Robbie Stadium................ | 3.50 | 1.40 | .35 |

## 1987 English 49ers

 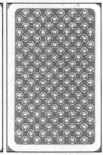

This 33-card set measures approximately 2 1/4" by 3 5/8". This set was manufactured in West Germany (by Ace Fact Pack) for release in Great Britain and features rounded corners and a playing card type of design on the back. There are 22 player cards in this set and we have checklisted those cards in alphabetical order.

| | MINT | EXC | G-VG |
|---|---|---|---|
| COMPLETE SET (33)...................... | 225.00 | 90.00 | 22.00 |
| COMMON PLAYER (1-33)................ | 3.50 | 1.40 | .35 |
| | | | |
| ☐ 1 John Ayers............................. | 3.50 | 1.40 | .35 |
| ☐ 2 Dwaine Board......................... | 3.50 | 1.40 | .35 |
| ☐ 3 Michael Carter........................ | 6.00 | 2.40 | .60 |
| ☐ 4 Dwight Clark .......................... | 10.00 | 4.00 | 1.00 |
| ☐ 5 Roger Craig ........................... | 10.00 | 4.00 | 1.00 |
| ☐ 6 Joe Cribbs............................. | 5.00 | 2.00 | .50 |
| ☐ 7 Randy Cross .......................... | 5.00 | 2.00 | .50 |
| ☐ 8 Riki Ellison ............................ | 3.50 | 1.40 | .35 |
| ☐ 9 Jim Fahnhorst ........................ | 3.50 | 1.40 | .35 |
| ☐ 10 Keith Fahnhorst.................... | 3.50 | 1.40 | .35 |
| ☐ 11 Russ Francis ........................ | 5.00 | 2.00 | .50 |
| ☐ 12 Don Griffin .......................... | 5.00 | 2.00 | .50 |
| ☐ 13 Ronnie Lott .......................... | 12.00 | 5.00 | 1.20 |
| ☐ 14 Milt McColl .......................... | 3.50 | 1.40 | .35 |
| ☐ 15 Tim McKyer ......................... | 5.00 | 2.00 | .50 |
| ☐ 16 Joe Montana ........................ | 90.00 | 36.00 | 9.00 |
| ☐ 17 Bubba Paris.......................... | 3.50 | 1.40 | .35 |
| ☐ 18 Fred Quillan ......................... | 3.50 | 1.40 | .35 |
| ☐ 19 Jerry Rice ............................ | 45.00 | 18.00 | 4.50 |
| ☐ 20 Manu Tuiasosopo ................. | 3.50 | 1.40 | .35 |
| ☐ 21 Keena Turner ....................... | 5.00 | 2.00 | .50 |
| ☐ 22 Carlton Williamson................. | 3.50 | 1.40 | .35 |
| ☐ 23 49ers Helmet........................ | 3.50 | 1.40 | .35 |
| ☐ 24 49ers Information .................. | 3.50 | 1.40 | .35 |
| ☐ 25 49ers Uniform ...................... | 3.50 | 1.40 | .35 |
| ☐ 26 Game Record Holders............ | 3.50 | 1.40 | .35 |
| ☐ 27 Season Record Holders .......... | 3.50 | 1.40 | .35 |
| ☐ 28 Career Record Holders............ | 3.50 | 1.40 | .35 |
| ☐ 29 Record 1967-86...................... | 3.50 | 1.40 | .35 |
| ☐ 30 1986 Team Statistics .............. | 3.50 | 1.40 | .35 |
| ☐ 31 All-Time Greats ...................... | 3.50 | 1.40 | .35 |
| ☐ 32 Roll of Honour ....................... | 3.50 | 1.40 | .35 |
| ☐ 33 Candlestick Park .................... | 3.50 | 1.40 | .35 |

## 1987 English Giants

This 33-card set, which measures approximately 2 1/4" by 3 5/8", was made in West Germany (by Ace Fact Pack) for distribution in England. This set features rounded corners and the back says "Ace" as if they were playing cards. We have checklisted the players in the set in alphabetical order.

| | MINT | EXC | G-VG |
|---|---|---|---|
| COMPLETE SET (33)...................... | 125.00 | 50.00 | 12.50 |
| COMMON PLAYER (1-33)................ | 3.50 | 1.40 | .35 |
| | | | |
| ☐ 1 Billy Ard............................... | 3.50 | 1.40 | .35 |
| ☐ 2 Carl Banks............................ | 6.00 | 2.40 | .60 |
| ☐ 3 Mark Bavaro.......................... | 5.00 | 2.00 | .50 |
| ☐ 4 Brad Benson .......................... | 3.50 | 1.40 | .35 |
| ☐ 5 Harry Carson.......................... | 6.00 | 2.40 | .60 |
| ☐ 6 Maurice Carthon UER............... | 5.00 | 2.00 | .50 |
| (Misspelled Morris) | | | |
| ☐ 7 Mark Collins .......................... | 5.00 | 2.00 | .50 |
| ☐ 8 Chris Godfrey......................... | 3.50 | 1.40 | .35 |
| ☐ 9 Kenny Hill.............................. | 3.50 | 1.40 | .35 |
| ☐ 10 Erik Howard ......................... | 5.00 | 2.00 | .50 |
| ☐ 11 Bobby Johnson ..................... | 3.50 | 1.40 | .35 |
| ☐ 12 Leonard Marshall ................... | 6.00 | 2.40 | .60 |
| ☐ 13 George Martin ....................... | 5.00 | 2.00 | .50 |
| ☐ 14 Joe Morris............................ | 5.00 | 2.00 | .50 |
| ☐ 15 Karl Nelson .......................... | 3.50 | 1.40 | .35 |
| ☐ 16 Bart Oates UER ..................... | 5.00 | 2.00 | .50 |
| (Misspelled Oakes) | | | |
| ☐ 17 Gary Reasons........................ | 5.00 | 2.00 | .50 |
| ☐ 18 Stacy Robinson...................... | 3.50 | 1.40 | .35 |
| ☐ 19 Phil Simms........................... | 15.00 | 6.00 | 1.50 |
| ☐ 20 Lawrence Taylor..................... | 25.00 | 10.00 | 2.50 |
| ☐ 21 Herb Welch .......................... | 3.50 | 1.40 | .35 |
| ☐ 22 Perry Williams....................... | 3.50 | 1.40 | .35 |
| ☐ 23 Giants Helmet ....................... | 3.50 | 1.40 | .35 |
| ☐ 24 Giants Information .................. | 3.50 | 1.40 | .35 |
| ☐ 25 Giants Uniforms .................... | 3.50 | 1.40 | .35 |
| ☐ 26 Game Record Holders............. | 3.50 | 1.40 | .35 |
| ☐ 27 Season Record Holders .......... | 3.50 | 1.40 | .35 |
| ☐ 28 Career Record Holders........... | 3.50 | 1.40 | .35 |
| ☐ 29 Record 1967-86..................... | 3.50 | 1.40 | .35 |
| ☐ 30 1986 Team Statistics .............. | 3.50 | 1.40 | .35 |
| ☐ 31 All-Time Greats ..................... | 3.50 | 1.40 | .35 |
| ☐ 32 Roll of Honour ...................... | 3.50 | 1.40 | .35 |
| ☐ 33 Giants Stadium ..................... | 3.50 | 1.40 | .35 |

## 1987 English Jets

 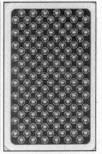

This 33-card set was made in West Germany (by Ace Fact Pack) for sale in England. This set measures approximately 2 1/4" by 3 5/8" and features members of the New York Jets. This set features cards with rounded corners; the card backs have a design for "Ace" like a playing card. We have checklisted the 22 players in the set in alphabetical order.

| | MINT | EXC | G-VG |
|---|---|---|---|
| COMPLETE SET (33)...................... | 100.00 | 40.00 | 10.00 |
| COMMON PLAYER (1-33)................ | 3.50 | 1.40 | .35 |
| | | | |
| ☐ 1 Dan Alexander ....................... | 3.50 | 1.40 | .35 |
| ☐ 2 Tom Baldwin .......................... | 3.50 | 1.40 | .35 |
| ☐ 3 Barry Bennett ......................... | 3.50 | 1.40 | .35 |
| ☐ 4 Russell Carter ........................ | 5.00 | 2.00 | .50 |
| ☐ 5 Kyle Clifton........................... | 5.00 | 2.00 | .50 |
| ☐ 6 Bob Crable ............................ | 3.50 | 1.40 | .35 |
| ☐ 7 Joe Fields ............................. | 5.00 | 2.00 | .50 |
| ☐ 8 Rusty Guilbeau ...................... | 3.50 | 1.40 | .35 |
| ☐ 9 Harry Hamilton........................ | 5.00 | 2.00 | .50 |
| ☐ 10 Johnny Hector....................... | 6.00 | 2.40 | .60 |
| ☐ 11 Jerry Holmes ........................ | 3.50 | 1.40 | .35 |
| ☐ 12 Gordon King ......................... | 3.50 | 1.40 | .35 |
| ☐ 13 Lester Lyles .......................... | 3.50 | 1.40 | .35 |
| ☐ 14 Marty Lyons.......................... | 5.00 | 2.00 | .50 |
| ☐ 15 Kevin McArthur ..................... | 3.50 | 1.40 | .35 |

| | | | |
|---|---|---|---|
| ☐ 16 Freeman McNeil | 7.50 | 3.00 | .75 |
| ☐ 17 Ken O'Brien | 7.50 | 3.00 | .75 |
| ☐ 18 Tony Paige | 6.00 | 2.40 | .60 |
| ☐ 19 Mickey Shuler | 5.00 | 2.00 | .50 |
| ☐ 20 Jim Sweeney | 3.50 | 1.40 | .35 |
| ☐ 21 Al Toon | 7.50 | 3.00 | .75 |
| ☐ 22 Wesley Walker | 7.50 | 3.00 | .75 |
| ☐ 23 Jets Helmet | 3.50 | 1.40 | .35 |
| ☐ 24 Jets Information | 3.50 | 1.40 | .35 |
| ☐ 25 Jets Uniform | 3.50 | 1.40 | .35 |
| ☐ 26 Game Record Holders | 3.50 | 1.40 | .35 |
| ☐ 27 Season Record Holders | 3.50 | 1.40 | .35 |
| ☐ 28 Career Record Holders | 3.50 | 1.40 | .35 |
| ☐ 29 Record 1967-86 | 3.50 | 1.40 | .35 |
| ☐ 30 1986 Team Statistics | 3.50 | 1.40 | .35 |
| ☐ 31 All-Time Greats | 3.50 | 1.40 | .35 |
| ☐ 32 Roll of Honour | 3.50 | 1.40 | .35 |
| ☐ 33 Giants Stadium | 3.50 | 1.40 | .35 |

## 1987 English Lions

This 33 card set measures approximately 2 1/4" by 3 5/8". This set features members of the Detroit Lions and has rounded corners. The back of the cards features a design for "Ace" like a playing card. These cards were manufactured in West Germany (by Ace Fact Pack) and we have checklisted this set alphabetically.

| | MINT | EXC | G-VG |
|---|---|---|---|
| COMPLETE SET (33) | 100.00 | 40.00 | 10.00 |
| COMMON PLAYER (1-33) | 3.50 | 1.40 | .35 |

| | | | |
|---|---|---|---|
| ☐ 1 Carl Bland | 3.50 | 1.40 | .35 |
| ☐ 2 Lomas Brown | 5.00 | 2.00 | .50 |
| ☐ 3 Jeff Chadwick | 5.00 | 2.00 | .50 |
| ☐ 4 Mike Cofer | 5.00 | 2.00 | .50 |
| ☐ 5 Keith Dorney | 3.50 | 1.40 | .35 |
| ☐ 6 Keith Ferguson | 3.50 | 1.40 | .35 |
| ☐ 7 William Gay | 5.00 | 2.00 | .50 |
| ☐ 8 James Harrell | 3.50 | 1.40 | .35 |
| ☐ 9 Eric Hipple | 5.00 | 2.00 | .50 |
| ☐ 10 Garry James | 5.00 | 2.00 | .50 |
| ☐ 11 Demetrious Johnson | 3.50 | 1.40 | .35 |
| ☐ 12 James Jones | 5.00 | 2.00 | .50 |
| ☐ 13 Chuck Long | 5.00 | 2.00 | .50 |
| ☐ 14 Vernon Maxwell | 5.00 | 2.00 | .50 |
| ☐ 15 Bruce McNorton | 3.50 | 1.40 | .35 |
| ☐ 16 Devon Mitchell | 3.50 | 1.40 | .35 |
| ☐ 17 Steve Lott | 3.50 | 1.40 | .35 |
| ☐ 18 Eddie Murray | 5.00 | 2.00 | .50 |
| ☐ 19 Harvey Salem | 3.50 | 1.40 | .35 |
| ☐ 20 Rich Stenger | 3.50 | 1.40 | .35 |
| ☐ 21 Eric Williams | 3.50 | 1.40 | .35 |
| ☐ 22 Jimmy Williams | 3.50 | 1.40 | .35 |
| ☐ 23 Lions Helmet | 3.50 | 1.40 | .35 |
| ☐ 24 Lions Information | 3.50 | 1.40 | .35 |
| ☐ 25 Lions Uniform | 3.50 | 1.40 | .35 |
| ☐ 26 Game Record Holders | 3.50 | 1.40 | .35 |
| ☐ 27 Season Record Holders | 3.50 | 1.40 | .35 |
| ☐ 28 Career Record Holders | 3.50 | 1.40 | .35 |
| ☐ 29 Record 1967-86 | 3.50 | 1.40 | .35 |
| ☐ 30 1986 Team Statistics | 3.50 | 1.40 | .35 |
| ☐ 31 All-Time Greats | 3.50 | 1.40 | .35 |
| ☐ 32 Championship Seasons | 3.50 | 1.40 | .35 |
| ☐ 33 Pontiac Silverdome | 3.50 | 1.40 | .35 |

## 1987 English Packers

This 33-card set measures approximately 2 1/4" by 3 5/8". These cards feature rounded corners and a playing card type design on the back. There were 22 player cards issued which we have checklisted alphabetically. These cards were made in West Germany (by Ace Fact Pack) for release in Great Britain to capitalize on the popularity of

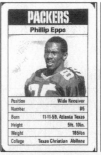 

American Football overseas. The set contains members of the Green Bay Packers.

| | MINT | EXC | G-VG |
|---|---|---|---|
| COMPLETE SET (33) | 100.00 | 40.00 | 10.00 |
| COMMON PLAYER (1-33) | 3.50 | 1.40 | .35 |

| | | | |
|---|---|---|---|
| ☐ 1 John Anderson | 5.00 | 2.00 | .50 |
| ☐ 2 Robbie Bosco | 5.00 | 2.00 | .50 |
| ☐ 3 Don Bracken | 3.50 | 1.40 | .35 |
| ☐ 4 John Cannon | 5.00 | 2.00 | .50 |
| ☐ 5 Alphonso Carreker | 3.50 | 1.40 | .35 |
| ☐ 6 Kenneth Davis | 7.50 | 3.00 | .75 |
| ☐ 7 Al Del Greco | 3.50 | 1.40 | .35 |
| ☐ 8 Gary Ellerson | 3.50 | 1.40 | .35 |
| ☐ 9 Gerry Ellis | 3.50 | 1.40 | .35 |
| ☐ 10 Phillip Epps | 5.00 | 2.00 | .50 |
| ☐ 11 Ron Hallstrom | 3.50 | 1.40 | .35 |
| ☐ 12 Mark Lee | 5.00 | 2.00 | .50 |
| ☐ 13 Bobby Leopold | 3.50 | 1.40 | .35 |
| ☐ 14 Charles Martin | 3.50 | 1.40 | .35 |
| ☐ 15 Brian Noble | 5.00 | 2.00 | .50 |
| ☐ 16 Ken Ruettgers | 5.00 | 2.00 | .50 |
| ☐ 17 Randy Scott | 3.50 | 1.40 | .35 |
| ☐ 18 Walter Stanley | 5.00 | 2.00 | .50 |
| ☐ 19 Ken Stills | 3.50 | 1.40 | .35 |
| ☐ 20 Keith Uecker | 3.50 | 1.40 | .35 |
| ☐ 21 Ed West | 5.00 | 2.00 | .50 |
| ☐ 22 Randy Wright | 5.00 | 2.00 | .50 |
| ☐ 23 Packers Helmet | 3.50 | 1.40 | .35 |
| ☐ 24 Packers Information | 3.50 | 1.40 | .35 |
| ☐ 25 Packers Uniform | 3.50 | 1.40 | .35 |
| ☐ 26 Game Record Holders | 3.50 | 1.40 | .35 |
| ☐ 27 Season Record Holders | 3.50 | 1.40 | .35 |
| ☐ 28 Career Record Holders | 3.50 | 1.40 | .35 |
| ☐ 29 Record 1967-86 | 3.50 | 1.40 | .35 |
| ☐ 30 1986 Team Statistics | 3.50 | 1.40 | .35 |
| ☐ 31 All-Time Greats | 3.50 | 1.40 | .35 |
| ☐ 32 Roll of Honour | 3.50 | 1.40 | .35 |
| ☐ 33 Lambeau Field/<br>Milwaukee County<br>Stadium | 3.50 | 1.40 | .35 |

## 1987 English Rams

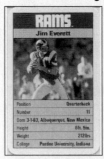 

This 33-card set measures approximately 2 1/4" by 3 5/8" and has rounded corners. This set was manufactured in West Germany (by Ace Fact Pack) for release in Great Britain. There are 22 player cards in the set, checklisted below in alphabetical order. The backs of the cards feature a playing card design. The set contains members of the Los Angeles Rams.

| | MINT | EXC | G-VG |
|---|---|---|---|
| COMPLETE SET (33) | 100.00 | 40.00 | 10.00 |
| COMMON PLAYER (1-33) | 3.50 | 1.40 | .35 |

| | MINT | EXC | G-VG |
|---|---|---|---|
| ☐ 1 Nolan Cromwell | 6.00 | 2.40 | .60 |
| ☐ 2 Eric Dickerson | 15.00 | 6.00 | 1.50 |
| ☐ 3 Reggie Doss | 3.50 | 1.40 | .35 |
| ☐ 4 Carl Ekern | 3.50 | 1.40 | .35 |
| ☐ 5 Henry Ellard | 7.50 | 3.00 | .75 |
| ☐ 6 Jim Everett | 10.00 | 4.00 | 1.00 |
| ☐ 7 Jerry Gray | 5.00 | 2.00 | .50 |
| ☐ 8 Dennis Harrah | 5.00 | 2.00 | .50 |
| ☐ 9 David Hill | 3.50 | 1.40 | .35 |
| ☐ 10 Kevin House | 5.00 | 2.00 | .50 |
| ☐ 11 LeRoy Irvin | 5.00 | 2.00 | .50 |
| ☐ 12 Mark Jerue | 3.50 | 1.40 | .35 |
| ☐ 13 Shawn Miller | 3.50 | 1.40 | .35 |
| ☐ 14 Tom Newberry | 5.00 | 2.00 | .50 |
| ☐ 15 Vince Newsome | 3.50 | 1.40 | .35 |
| ☐ 16 Mel Owens | 5.00 | 2.00 | .50 |
| ☐ 17 Irv Pankey | 3.50 | 1.40 | .35 |
| ☐ 18 Doug Reed | 3.50 | 1.40 | .35 |
| ☐ 19 Doug Smith | 5.00 | 2.00 | .50 |
| ☐ 20 Jackie Slater | 6.00 | 2.40 | .60 |
| ☐ 21 Charles White | 6.00 | 2.40 | .60 |
| ☐ 22 Mike Wilcher | 3.50 | 1.40 | .35 |
| ☐ 23 Rams Helmet | 3.50 | 1.40 | .35 |
| ☐ 24 Rams Information | 3.50 | 1.40 | .35 |
| ☐ 25 Rams Uniform | 3.50 | 1.40 | .35 |
| ☐ 26 Game Record Holders | 3.50 | 1.40 | .35 |
| ☐ 27 Season Record Holders | 3.50 | 1.40 | .35 |
| ☐ 28 Career Record Holders | 3.50 | 1.40 | .35 |
| ☐ 29 Record 1967-86 | 3.50 | 1.40 | .35 |
| ☐ 30 1986 Team Statistics | 3.50 | 1.40 | .35 |
| ☐ 31 All-Time Greats | 3.50 | 1.40 | .35 |
| ☐ 32 Roll of Honour | 3.50 | 1.40 | .35 |
| ☐ 33 Anaheim Stadium | 3.50 | 1.40 | .35 |

## 1987 English Redskins

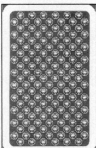

This 33-card set measures approximately 2 1/4" by 3 5/8" and features members of the Washington Redskins. This set was made in West Germany (by Ace Fact Pack) and the card design features rounded corners. We have checklisted the players portrayed in the set in alphabetical order. There are also many informative cards which are part of the set.

| | MINT | EXC | G-VG |
|---|---|---|---|
| COMPLETE SET (33) | 100.00 | 40.00 | 10.00 |
| COMMON PLAYER (1-33) | 3.50 | 1.40 | .35 |
| ☐ 1 Jeff Bostic | 5.00 | 2.00 | .50 |
| ☐ 2 Dave Butz | 6.00 | 2.40 | .60 |
| ☐ 3 Gary Clark | 9.00 | 3.75 | .90 |
| ☐ 4 Monte Coleman | 5.00 | 2.00 | .50 |
| ☐ 5 Vernon Dean | 3.50 | 1.40 | .35 |
| ☐ 6 Clint Didier | 5.00 | 2.00 | .50 |
| ☐ 7 Darryl Grant | 3.50 | 1.40 | .35 |
| ☐ 8 Darrell Green | 7.50 | 3.00 | .75 |
| ☐ 9 Russ Grimm | 6.00 | 2.40 | .60 |
| ☐ 10 Joe Jacoby | 6.00 | 2.40 | .60 |
| ☐ 11 Curtis Jordan | 3.50 | 1.40 | .35 |
| ☐ 12 Dexter Manley | 5.00 | 2.00 | .50 |
| ☐ 13 Charles Mann | 6.00 | 2.40 | .60 |
| ☐ 14 Mark May | 5.00 | 2.00 | .50 |
| ☐ 15 Rich Milot | 3.50 | 1.40 | .35 |
| ☐ 16 Art Monk | 15.00 | 6.00 | 1.50 |
| ☐ 17 Neal Olkewicz | 3.50 | 1.40 | .35 |
| ☐ 18 George Rogers | 7.50 | 3.00 | .75 |
| ☐ 19 Jay Schroeder | 7.50 | 3.00 | .75 |
| ☐ 20 R.C. Thielemann | 3.50 | 1.40 | .35 |
| ☐ 21 Alvin Walton | 3.50 | 1.40 | .35 |
| ☐ 22 Don Warren | 5.00 | 2.00 | .50 |
| ☐ 23 Redskins Helmet | 3.50 | 1.40 | .35 |
| ☐ 24 Redskins Information | 3.50 | 1.40 | .35 |
| ☐ 25 Redskins Uniform | 3.50 | 1.40 | .35 |
| ☐ 26 Game Record Holders | 3.50 | 1.40 | .35 |
| ☐ 27 Season Record Holders | 3.50 | 1.40 | .35 |

| | MINT | EXC | G-VG |
|---|---|---|---|
| ☐ 28 Career Record Holders | 3.50 | 1.40 | .35 |
| ☐ 29 Record 1967-86 | 3.50 | 1.40 | .35 |
| ☐ 30 1986 Team Statistics | 3.50 | 1.40 | .35 |
| ☐ 31 All-Time Greats | 3.50 | 1.40 | .35 |
| ☐ 32 Roll of Honour | 3.50 | 1.40 | .35 |
| ☐ 33 Robert F. Kennedy Stadium | 3.50 | 1.40 | .35 |

## 1987 English Seahawks

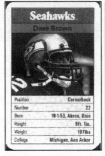
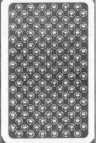

This 33-card set measures approximately 2 1/4" by 3 5/8". This set consists of 33 cards of which 22 are player cards and we have checklisted those cards alphabetically. The cards have rounded corners and a playing card type of design on the back. These cards were manufactured in West Germany (by Ace Fact Pack) and released in Great Britain. The set contains members of the Seattle Seahawks.

| | MINT | EXC | G-VG |
|---|---|---|---|
| COMPLETE SET (33) | 125.00 | 50.00 | 12.50 |
| COMMON PLAYER (1-33) | 3.50 | 1.40 | .35 |
| ☐ 1 Edwin Bailey | 3.50 | 1.40 | .35 |
| ☐ 2 Dave Brown | 5.00 | 2.00 | .50 |
| ☐ 3 Jeff Bryant | 3.50 | 1.40 | .35 |
| ☐ 4 Blair Bush | 5.00 | 2.00 | .50 |
| ☐ 5 Keith Butler | 3.50 | 1.40 | .35 |
| ☐ 6 Kenny Easley | 5.00 | 2.00 | .50 |
| ☐ 7 Greg Gaines | 3.50 | 1.40 | .35 |
| ☐ 8 Jacob Green | 6.00 | 2.40 | .60 |
| ☐ 9 Norm Johnson | 5.00 | 2.00 | .50 |
| ☐ 10 Dave Krieg | 7.50 | 3.00 | .75 |
| ☐ 11 Steve Largent | 25.00 | 10.00 | 2.50 |
| ☐ 12 Reggie Kinlaw | 3.50 | 1.40 | .35 |
| ☐ 13 Ron Mattes | 3.50 | 1.40 | .35 |
| ☐ 14 Bryan Millard | 3.50 | 1.40 | .35 |
| ☐ 15 Eugene Robinson | 5.00 | 2.00 | .50 |
| ☐ 16 Bruce Scholtz | 3.50 | 1.40 | .35 |
| ☐ 17 Terry Taylor | 3.50 | 1.40 | .35 |
| ☐ 18 Mike Tice | 5.00 | 2.00 | .50 |
| ☐ 19 Daryl Turner | 5.00 | 2.00 | .50 |
| ☐ 20 Curt Warner | 6.00 | 2.40 | .60 |
| ☐ 21 John L. Williams | 10.00 | 4.00 | 1.00 |
| ☐ 22 Fredd Young | 5.00 | 2.00 | .50 |
| ☐ 23 Seahawks Helmet | 3.50 | 1.40 | .35 |
| ☐ 24 Seahawks Information | 3.50 | 1.40 | .35 |
| ☐ 25 Seahawks Uniform | 3.50 | 1.40 | .35 |
| ☐ 26 Game Record Holders | 3.50 | 1.40 | .35 |
| ☐ 27 Season Record Holders | 3.50 | 1.40 | .35 |
| ☐ 28 Career Record Holders | 3.50 | 1.40 | .35 |
| ☐ 29 Record 1977-86 | 3.50 | 1.40 | .35 |
| ☐ 30 1986 Team Statistics | 3.50 | 1.40 | .35 |
| ☐ 31 All-Time Greats | 3.50 | 1.40 | .35 |
| ☐ 32 Roll of Honour | 3.50 | 1.40 | .35 |
| ☐ 33 Kingdome | 3.50 | 1.40 | .35 |

## 1991 ENOR Pro Football HOF Promos

This six-card standard-size (2 1/2" by 3 1/2") promo set was issued to preview the 160-card 1991 ENOR Pro Football Hall of Fame set. Apart from a slightly different shade of colors and card numbering differences, these promo cards differ from their counterparts in that the Team NFL logo on their card backs is black and white, while on the regular series cards, it is red, white, and blue. The cards are numbered on the back.

| | MINT | EXC | G-VG |
|---|---|---|---|
| COMPLETE SET (6) | 5.00 | 2.00 | .50 |
| COMMON PLAYER (1-6) | 1.00 | .40 | .10 |

| | MINT | EXC | G-VG |
|---|---|---|---|
| ☐ 1 Pro Football Hall....................... of Fame (Building) (Regular issue card number is also 1) | 1.00 | .40 | .10 |
| ☐ 2 Earl Campbell............................ (Regular issue card number is 23) | 3.00 | 1.20 | .30 |
| ☐ 3 John Hannah............................. (Regular issue card number is 57) | 1.00 | .40 | .10 |
| ☐ 4 Stan Jones ............................... (Regular issue card number is 74) | 1.00 | .40 | .10 |
| ☐ 5 Jan Stenerud............................ (Regular issue card number is 131) | 1.00 | .40 | .10 |
| ☐ 6 Tex Schramm ADM................. (Regular issue card number is 127) | 1.00 | .40 | .10 |

## 1991 ENOR Pro Football HOF

The 1991 Pro Football Hall of Fame set contains 160 cards measuring the standard size (2 1/2" by 3 1/2"). The set, which includes this year's inductees, was issued in factory sets and wax packs. The fronts feature a mix of color or black and white player photos, with black and gold borders (the photos were obtained from the NFL's extensive archives). The player's position and name are given in a black stripe below the picture. A purple box with the words "Pro Football Hall of Fame" in white appears at the lower right corner of the card face. The backs have biography, career summary, and the year the individual was inducted. The backs are predominantly orange in color and have a picture of the Hall of Fame building at the bottom. The cards are numbered on the back. The numbering is essentially in alphabetical order by subject. Randomly inserted throughout the packs were coupon cards that entitled the collector to receive a free Hall of Fame Album and free admission to the Pro Football Hall of Fame (offer expired December 31, 1993). The front design of the Free Admission card shows four different scenes of the Hall of Fame.

| | MINT | EXC | G-VG |
|---|---|---|---|
| COMPLETE SET (160)...................... | 8.00 | 3.25 | .80 |
| COMMON CARD (1-160) ................. | .10 | .04 | .01 |
| ☐ 1 Pro Football Hall of ................... Fame (Canton, OH) | .10 | .04 | .01 |
| ☐ 1A Free Admission........................ Pro Football Hall of Fame (Canton, OH) | 1.00 | .40 | .10 |

| | | | |
|---|---|---|---|
| ☐ 2 Herb Adderley ........................... | .15 | .06 | .01 |
| ☐ 3 Lance Alworth ........................... | .20 | .08 | .02 |
| ☐ 4 Doug Atkins .............................. | .10 | .04 | .01 |
| ☐ 5 Morris(Red) Badgro .................. | .10 | .04 | .01 |
| ☐ 6 Cliff Battles.............................. | .10 | .04 | .01 |
| ☐ 7 Sammy Baugh........................... | .40 | .16 | .04 |
| ☐ 8 Chuck Bednarik ........................ | .20 | .08 | .02 |
| ☐ 9A Bert Bell FOUND/OWN ........... (Factory set version in coat and tie) | .25 | .10 | .02 |
| ☐ 9B Bert Bell FOUND/OWN ........... (Wax pack version in Steelers tee shirt) | .25 | .10 | .02 |
| ☐ 10 Bobby Bell.............................. | .15 | .06 | .01 |
| ☐ 11 Raymond Berry ....................... | .20 | .08 | .02 |
| ☐ 12 Charles W. Bidwill OWN ......... | .10 | .04 | .01 |
| ☐ 13 Fred Biletnikoff ....................... | .20 | .08 | .02 |
| ☐ 14 George Blanda ........................ | .25 | .10 | .02 |
| ☐ 15 Mel Blount .............................. | .15 | .06 | .01 |
| ☐ 16 Terry Bradshaw ....................... | .50 | .20 | .05 |
| ☐ 17 Jim Brown ............................... | .50 | .20 | .05 |
| ☐ 18 Paul Brown CO/OWN/ ............ FOUND | .10 | .04 | .01 |
| ☐ 19 Roosevelt Brown ..................... | .15 | .06 | .01 |
| ☐ 20 Willie Brown ............................ | .15 | .06 | .01 |
| ☐ 21 Buck Buchanan ....................... | .15 | .06 | .01 |
| ☐ 22 Dick Butkus ............................ | .30 | .12 | .03 |
| ☐ 23 Earl Campbell .......................... | .50 | .20 | .05 |
| ☐ 24 Tony Canadeo ......................... | .10 | .04 | .01 |
| ☐ 25 Joe Carr PRES ........................ | .10 | .04 | .01 |
| ☐ 26 Guy Chamberlin ...................... | .10 | .04 | .01 |
| ☐ 27 Jack Christiansen .................... | .10 | .04 | .01 |
| ☐ 28 Earl(Dutch) Clark .................... | .10 | .04 | .01 |
| ☐ 29 George Connor ........................ | .10 | .04 | .01 |
| ☐ 30 Jimmy Conzelman .................... | .10 | .04 | .01 |
| ☐ 31 Larry Csonka ........................... | .30 | .12 | .03 |
| ☐ 32 Willie Davis ............................. | .15 | .06 | .01 |
| ☐ 33 Len Dawson ............................ | .25 | .10 | .02 |
| ☐ 34 Mike Ditka .............................. | .50 | .20 | .05 |
| ☐ 35 Art Donovan ........................... | .20 | .08 | .02 |
| ☐ 36 John(Paddy) Driscoll ............... | .10 | .04 | .01 |
| ☐ 37 Bill Dudley .............................. | .10 | .04 | .01 |
| ☐ 38 Turk Edwards .......................... | .10 | .04 | .01 |
| ☐ 39 Weeb Ewbank CO .................... | .10 | .04 | .01 |
| ☐ 40 Tom Fears .............................. | .15 | .06 | .01 |
| ☐ 41 Ray Flaherty CO ...................... | .10 | .04 | .01 |
| ☐ 42 Len Ford ................................. | .10 | .04 | .01 |
| ☐ 43 Dan Fortmann .......................... | .10 | .04 | .01 |
| ☐ 44 Frank Gatski ........................... | .10 | .04 | .01 |
| ☐ 45 Bill George .............................. | .10 | .04 | .01 |
| ☐ 46 Frank Gifford ........................... | .40 | .16 | .04 |
| ☐ 47 Sid Gillman CO ........................ | .10 | .04 | .01 |
| ☐ 48 Otto Graham ........................... | .30 | .12 | .03 |
| ☐ 49 Harold(Red) Grange ................. | .35 | .14 | .03 |
| ☐ 50 Joe Greene ............................. | .25 | .10 | .02 |
| ☐ 51 Forrest Gregg .......................... | .15 | .06 | .01 |
| ☐ 52 Bob Griese .............................. | .30 | .12 | .03 |
| ☐ 53 Lou Groza .............................. | .25 | .10 | .02 |
| ☐ 54 Joe Guyon .............................. | .10 | .04 | .01 |
| ☐ 55 George Halas CO/OWN............ FOUND | .20 | .08 | .02 |
| ☐ 56 Jack Ham ............................... | .20 | .08 | .02 |
| ☐ 57 John Hannah ........................... | .15 | .06 | .01 |
| ☐ 58 Franco Harris .......................... | .30 | .12 | .03 |
| ☐ 59 Ed Healey .............................. | .10 | .04 | .01 |
| ☐ 60 Mel Hein ................................ | .10 | .04 | .01 |
| ☐ 61 Ted Hendricks ......................... | .15 | .06 | .01 |
| ☐ 62 Pete(Fats) Henry ..................... | .10 | .04 | .01 |
| ☐ 63 Arnie Herber ........................... | .10 | .04 | .01 |
| ☐ 64 Bill Hewitt............................... | .10 | .04 | .01 |
| ☐ 65 Clarke Hinkle .......................... | .10 | .04 | .01 |
| ☐ 66 Elroy Hirsch ............................ | .20 | .08 | .02 |
| ☐ 67 Ken Houston ........................... | .15 | .06 | .01 |
| ☐ 68 Cal Hubbard ........................... | .10 | .04 | .01 |
| ☐ 69 Sam Huff ............................... | .20 | .08 | .02 |
| ☐ 70 Lamar Hunt OWN/FOUND ........ | .15 | .06 | .01 |
| ☐ 71 Don Hutson ............................ | .20 | .08 | .02 |
| ☐ 72 John Henry Johnson ............... | .20 | .08 | .02 |
| ☐ 73 Deacon Jones .......................... | .20 | .08 | .02 |
| ☐ 74 Stan Jones ............................. | .10 | .04 | .01 |
| ☐ 75 Sonny Jurgensen ..................... | .25 | .10 | .02 |
| ☐ 76 Walt Kiesling ........................... | .10 | .04 | .01 |
| ☐ 77 Frank(Bruiser) Kinard .............. | .10 | .04 | .01 |
| ☐ 78 Earl(Curly) Lambeau ............... CO/OWN/FOUND | .10 | .04 | .01 |
| ☐ 79 Jack Lambert .......................... | .30 | .12 | .03 |
| ☐ 80 Tom Landry CO ....................... | .35 | .14 | .03 |
| ☐ 81 Dick Lane .............................. | .15 | .06 | .01 |
| ☐ 82 Jim Langer .............................. | .15 | .06 | .01 |
| ☐ 83 Willie Lanier ............................ | .15 | .06 | .01 |
| ☐ 84 Yale Lary ............................... | .15 | .06 | .01 |
| ☐ 85 Dante Lavelli ........................... | .10 | .04 | .01 |
| ☐ 86 Bobby Layne ........................... | .30 | .12 | .03 |
| ☐ 87 Tuffy Leemans ........................ | .10 | .04 | .01 |
| ☐ 88 Bob Lilly ................................ | .25 | .10 | .02 |
| ☐ 89 Sid Luckman ........................... | .20 | .08 | .02 |
| ☐ 90 William Roy Lyman.................. | .10 | .04 | .01 |

| | | | |
|---|---|---|---|
| ☐ 91 Tim Mara FOUND/OWN | .10 | .04 | .01 |
| ☐ 92 Gino Marchetti | .20 | .08 | .02 |
| ☐ 93 Geo.Preston Marshall FOUND/OWN | .10 | .04 | .01 |
| ☐ 94 Don Maynard | .25 | .10 | .02 |
| ☐ 95 George McAfee | .10 | .04 | .01 |
| ☐ 96 Mike McCormack | .15 | .06 | .01 |
| ☐ 97 Johnny(Blood) McNally | .10 | .04 | .01 |
| ☐ 98 Mike Michalske | .10 | .04 | .01 |
| ☐ 99 Wayne Millner | .10 | .04 | .01 |
| ☐ 100 Bobby Mitchell | .20 | .08 | .02 |
| ☐ 101 Ron Mix | .15 | .06 | .01 |
| ☐ 102 Lenny Moore | .20 | .08 | .02 |
| ☐ 103 Marion Motley (See also 130) | .20 | .08 | .02 |
| ☐ 104 George Musso | .10 | .04 | .01 |
| ☐ 105 Bronko Nagurski | .30 | .12 | .03 |
| ☐ 106 Earle(Greasy) Neale CO | .10 | .04 | .01 |
| ☐ 107 Ernie Nevers | .20 | .08 | .02 |
| ☐ 108 Ray Nitschke | .20 | .08 | .02 |
| ☐ 109 Leo Nomellini | .20 | .08 | .02 |
| ☐ 110 Merlin Olsen | .25 | .10 | .02 |
| ☐ 111 Jim Otto | .20 | .08 | .02 |
| ☐ 112 Steve Owen CO | .10 | .04 | .01 |
| ☐ 113 Alan Page | .15 | .06 | .01 |
| ☐ 114 Clarence(Ace) Parker | .10 | .04 | .01 |
| ☐ 115 Jim Parker | .15 | .06 | .01 |
| ☐ 116 1958 NFL Championship | .10 | .04 | .01 |
| ☐ 117 Pete Pihos | .10 | .04 | .01 |
| ☐ 118 Hugh(Shorty) Ray OFF | .10 | .04 | .01 |
| ☐ 119 Dan Reeves OWN | .10 | .04 | .01 |
| ☐ 120 Jim Ringo | .15 | .06 | .01 |
| ☐ 121 Andy Robustelli | .15 | .06 | .01 |
| ☐ 122 Art Rooney FOUND/ADMIN | .10 | .04 | .01 |
| ☐ 123 Pete Rozelle COMM | .25 | .10 | .02 |
| ☐ 124 Bob St.Clair | .15 | .06 | .01 |
| ☐ 125 Gale Sayers | .30 | .12 | .03 |
| ☐ 126 Joe Schmidt | .20 | .08 | .02 |
| ☐ 127 Tex Schramm ADM | .10 | .04 | .01 |
| ☐ 128 Art Shell | .25 | .10 | .02 |
| ☐ 129 Roger Staubach | .60 | .24 | .06 |
| ☐ 130 Ernie Stautner UER (Numbered as 103) | .20 | .08 | .02 |
| ☐ 131 Jan Stenerud | .15 | .06 | .01 |
| ☐ 132 Ken Strong | .10 | .04 | .01 |
| ☐ 133 Joe Stydahar | .10 | .04 | .01 |
| ☐ 134 Fran Tarkenton | .35 | .14 | .03 |
| ☐ 135 Charley Taylor | .20 | .08 | .02 |
| ☐ 136 Jim Taylor | .20 | .08 | .02 |
| ☐ 137 Jim Thorpe | .50 | .20 | .05 |
| ☐ 138 Y.A. Tittle | .30 | .12 | .03 |
| ☐ 139 George Trafton | .10 | .04 | .01 |
| ☐ 140 Charley Trippi | .20 | .08 | .02 |
| ☐ 141 Emlen Tunnell | .20 | .08 | .02 |
| ☐ 142 Clyde(Bulldog) Turner | .20 | .08 | .02 |
| ☐ 143 Johnny Unitas | .50 | .20 | .05 |
| ☐ 144 Gene Upshaw | .20 | .08 | .02 |
| ☐ 145 Norm Van Brocklin | .30 | .12 | .03 |
| ☐ 146 Steve Van Buren | .25 | .10 | .02 |
| ☐ 147 Doak Walker | .20 | .08 | .02 |
| ☐ 148 Paul Warfield | .25 | .10 | .02 |
| ☐ 149 Bob Waterfield | .25 | .10 | .02 |
| ☐ 150 Arnie Weinmeister | .10 | .04 | .01 |
| ☐ 151 Bill Willis | .10 | .04 | .01 |
| ☐ 152 Larry Wilson | .20 | .08 | .02 |
| ☐ 153 Alex Wojciechowicz | .10 | .04 | .01 |
| ☐ 154 Willie Wood | .15 | .06 | .01 |
| ☐ 155 Enshrinement Day Hall of Fame Induction Ceremony | .10 | .04 | .01 |
| ☐ 156 Mementoes Exhibit Enshrinee Mementoes Room | .10 | .04 | .01 |
| ☐ 157 Checklist 1 The Beginning | .10 | .04 | .01 |
| ☐ 158 Checklist 2 The Early Years | .10 | .04 | .01 |
| ☐ 159 Checklist 3 The Modern Era | .10 | .04 | .01 |
| ☐ 160 Checklist 4 Evolution of Uniform | .10 | .04 | .01 |

## 1969 Eskimo Pie

The 1969 Eskimo Pie football card set contains 15 panel pairs of American Football League players. The panels measure approximately 2 1/2" by 3". The cards are actually stickers which could be removed from the cardboard to which they are attached. There are two players per panel. The panels and the players pictured are unnumbered and in color. Numbers have been provided in the checklist below, alphabetically according to the last name of the player on the left since the cards are most commonly found in panels. The names are reversed on the card containing Jim Otto and Len Dawson (card number 14). The catalog designation for this set is F73.

| | NRMT | VG-E | GOOD |
|---|---|---|---|
| COMPLETE SET (15) | 1100.00 | 500.00 | 125.00 |
| COMMON CARD (1-15) | 60.00 | 24.00 | 6.00 |
| ☐ 1 Lance Alworth and John Charles | 125.00 | 50.00 | 12.50 |
| ☐ 2 Al Atkinson and George Goeddeke | 60.00 | 24.00 | 6.00 |
| ☐ 3 Marlin Briscoe and Billy Shaw | 75.00 | 30.00 | 7.50 |
| ☐ 4 Gino Cappelletti and Dale Livingston | 60.00 | 24.00 | 6.00 |
| ☐ 5 Eric Crabtree and Jim Dunaway | 60.00 | 24.00 | 6.00 |
| ☐ 6 Ben Davidson and Bob Griese | 150.00 | 60.00 | 15.00 |
| ☐ 7 Hewritt Dixon and Pete Beathard | 75.00 | 30.00 | 7.50 |
| ☐ 8 Mike Garrett and Bob Hunt | 60.00 | 24.00 | 6.00 |
| ☐ 9 Daryle Lamonica and Willie Frazier | 75.00 | 30.00 | 7.50 |
| ☐ 10 Jim Lynch and John Hadl | 75.00 | 30.00 | 7.50 |
| ☐ 11 Kent McCloughan and Tom Regner | 60.00 | 24.00 | 6.00 |
| ☐ 12 Jim Nance and Billy Neighbors | 60.00 | 24.00 | 6.00 |
| ☐ 13 Rick Norton and Paul Costa | 60.00 | 24.00 | 6.00 |
| ☐ 14 Jim Otto and Len Dawson UER (Names reversed) | 150.00 | 60.00 | 15.00 |
| ☐ 15 Matt Snell and Dick Post | 60.00 | 24.00 | 6.00 |

## 1948-52 Exhibit W468 Football

Produced by the Exhibit Supply Company of Chicago, the 1948-52 Football Exhibit cards are unnumbered, blank-backed, thick-stocked cards issued in various colors in vending machines. Advertising panels on the front of these machines displayed from one to three cards and the price for one card, originally one cent, but later raised to two cents. The cards were originally issued in black and white; in subsequent years, the cards were issued in green, red, blue, yellow, and sepia. The cards measure approximately 3 1/4" by 5 3/8" and feature pro and college players. Cards marked with an * in the checklist below have the same photo as in the Exhibit Sports Champions set of 1948; however, cards in this series do not have the single agate line of type describing the player at the bottom of the card. The cards were issued in three groups of 32 at a time during 1948, 1950, and 1951. The 1951 group is the most plentiful as they were reissued intact in a sepia tone in 1952 (and perhaps 1953 as well). Some veteran collectors believe the second group may have been issued in 1949 rather than 1950. Cards issued during and after 1951 are marked as DP's as they are quite common compared to the other cards in the set. Those remaining unmarked (16) cards are those that were dropped before the 1951 mass production (but after 1948). Several players, such as Creekmur, Houck, and Martin, are rumored to exist, but they have not been verified and are assumed not to exist in the checklist below. The American Card Catalog designation is W468. A football exhibit checklist card has also been found but was apparently produced in very limited quantity in 1950 only. This checklist card is known to exist in green and black-and-white and is identical to the Bednarik card but has the 32 players from the 1950 set listed on its front. In the first 32-card printing (1948), the words "Made In USA" measure 5/8". Eleven of these original cards were single prints (Cifers, Comp, Coulter, Horvath, Jacobs, Johnson, LeForce, Mastrangelo, Pritko, Schlinkman, and Wedemeyer) and marked as SP48 below since they were only issued in 1948. These single print cards are much rarer than the six single print cards issued in 1950 (Bednarik, Davis, Hoerner, Justice, Perry, and Ruby) and marked as SP50 below. In the second printing (1950), 11 new cards were produced to replace the original 11 single prints; on these new cards, the words "Made In USA" measure 7/16". The third printing (1951) consisted of only 16 cards; the six single print cards from 1950 and ten cards from 1948 were dropped. In this third printing, the words "Made In USA" measure 1/2".

| | NRMT | VG-E | GOOD |
|---|---|---|---|
| COMPLETE SET (59) | 3300.00 | 1400.00 | 375.00 |
| COMMON PLAYER DP | 7.50 | 3.00 | .75 |
| COMMON PLAYER | 30.00 | 12.00 | 3.00 |
| COMMON PLAYER SP48 | 175.00 | 70.00 | 18.00 |
| COMMON PLAYER SP50 | 60.00 | 24.00 | 6.00 |
| ☐ 1 Frankie Albert DP | 9.00 | 3.75 | .90 |
| ☐ 2 Dick Barwegan DP | 7.50 | 3.00 | .75 |
| ☐ 3 Sammy Baugh * DP | 40.00 | 16.00 | 4.00 |
| ☐ 4 Chuck Bednarik SP50 | 100.00 | 40.00 | 10.00 |
| ☐ 5 Tony Canadeo DP | 12.00 | 5.00 | 1.20 |
| ☐ 6 Paul Christman | 35.00 | 14.00 | 3.50 |
| ☐ 7 Bob Cifers SP48 | 175.00 | 70.00 | 18.00 |
| ☐ 8 Irv Comp SP48 | 175.00 | 70.00 | 18.00 |
| ☐ 9 Charley Conerly DP | 15.00 | 6.00 | 1.50 |
| ☐ 10 George Connor DP | 12.00 | 5.00 | 1.20 |
| ☐ 11 Dewitt Coulter SP48 | 175.00 | 70.00 | 18.00 |
| ☐ 12 Glenn Davis SP50 | 90.00 | 36.00 | 9.00 |
| ☐ 13 Glen Dobbs * | 50.00 | 20.00 | 5.00 |
| ☐ 14 John Dottley DP | 7.50 | 3.00 | .75 |
| ☐ 15 Bill Dudley | 50.00 | 20.00 | 5.00 |
| ☐ 16 Tom Fears DP | 12.00 | 5.00 | 1.20 |
| ☐ 17 Joe Geri DP | 7.50 | 3.00 | .75 |
| ☐ 18 Otto Graham * DP | 40.00 | 16.00 | 4.00 |
| ☐ 19 Pat Harder * | 40.00 | 16.00 | 4.00 |
| ☐ 20 Elroy Hirsch DP | 15.00 | 6.00 | 1.50 |
| ☐ 21 Dick Hoerner SP50 | 60.00 | 24.00 | 6.00 |
| ☐ 22 Bob Hoernschemeyer DP | 7.50 | 3.00 | .75 |
| ☐ 23 Les Horvath SP48 | 200.00 | 80.00 | 20.00 |
| ☐ 24 Jack Jacobs * SP48 | 175.00 | 70.00 | 18.00 |
| ☐ 25 Nate Johnson SP48 | 175.00 | 70.00 | 18.00 |
| ☐ 26 Charlie Justice SP50 | 75.00 | 30.00 | 7.50 |
| ☐ 27 Bobby Layne DP | 25.00 | 10.00 | 2.50 |
| ☐ 28 Clyde LeForce SP48 | 175.00 | 70.00 | 18.00 |
| ☐ 29 Sid Luckman * | 75.00 | 30.00 | 7.50 |
| ☐ 30 John Lujack * | 60.00 | 24.00 | 6.00 |
| ☐ 31 John Mastrangelo SP48 | 175.00 | 70.00 | 18.00 |
| ☐ 32 Ollie Matson DP | 15.00 | 6.00 | 1.50 |
| ☐ 33 Bill McColl DP | 7.50 | 3.00 | .75 |
| ☐ 34 Fred Morrison DP | 7.50 | 3.00 | .75 |
| ☐ 35 Marion Motley * DP | 20.00 | 8.00 | 2.00 |
| ☐ 36 Chuck Ortmann DP | 7.50 | 3.00 | .75 |
| ☐ 37 Joe Perry SP50 | 75.00 | 30.00 | 7.50 |
| ☐ 38 Pete Pihos | 50.00 | 20.00 | 5.00 |
| ☐ 39 Steve Pritko SP48 | 175.00 | 70.00 | 18.00 |
| ☐ 40 George Ratterman DP | 9.00 | 3.75 | .90 |
| ☐ 41 Jay Rhodemyre DP | 7.50 | 3.00 | .75 |
| ☐ 42 Martin Ruby SP50 | 60.00 | 24.00 | 6.00 |
| ☐ 43 Julie Rykovich DP | 7.50 | 3.00 | .75 |
| ☐ 44 Walt Schlinkman SP48 | 200.00 | 80.00 | 20.00 |
| ☐ 45 Emil(Red) Sitko * DP | 7.50 | 3.00 | .75 |
| ☐ 46 Vitamin Smith DP | 7.50 | 3.00 | .75 |
| ☐ 47 Norm Standlee | 35.00 | 14.00 | 3.50 |
| ☐ 48 George Taliaferro DP | 7.50 | 3.00 | .75 |
| ☐ 49 Y.A. Tittle HOR | 75.00 | 30.00 | 7.50 |
| ☐ 50 Charley Trippi DP | 15.00 | 6.00 | 1.50 |
| ☐ 51 Frank Tripucka DP | 9.00 | 3.75 | .90 |
| ☐ 52 Emlen Tunnell DP | 12.00 | 5.00 | 1.20 |
| ☐ 53 Bulldog Turner DP | 12.00 | 5.00 | 1.20 |
| ☐ 54 Steve Van Buren * | 60.00 | 24.00 | 6.00 |
| ☐ 55 Bob Waterfield * DP | 20.00 | 8.00 | 2.00 |
| ☐ 56 Herm Wedemeyer SP48 | 500.00 | 200.00 | 50.00 |
| ☐ 57 Bob Williams DP | 7.50 | 3.00 | .75 |
| ☐ 58 Claude Buddy Young DP | 9.00 | 3.75 | .90 |
| (passing) | | | |
| ☐ 59 Tank Younger * DP | 9.00 | 3.75 | .90 |
| ☐ xx Checklist Card SP50 | 500.00 | 200.00 | 50.00 |

# 1990 FACT Pro Set Cincinnati

The 1990 Pro Set FACT (Football and Academics: A Cincinnati Team) set was aimed at fourth graders in 29 schools in the Cincinnati school system. The special cards were used as motivational learning tools to promote public health and education. Twenty-five cards per week were issued in 25-card cello packs for fifteen consecutive weeks beginning October 1990. Moreover, a Teacher Instructional Game Plan, measuring approximately 8 1/2" by 11" and containing answers to all of the questions, was also issued. The standard-size (2 1/2" by 3 1/2") cards are identical to first series cards, with the exception that the backs have interactive educational (Math, grammar, and science) questions instead of player information. Each 1990 Pro Set first series card was reprinted. The cards are numbered on the back. Each cello-wrapped pack led off with a header card which indicated the "week" number at the bottom. The missing numbers from the first series are 338, 376, and 377.

| | MINT | EXC | G-VG |
|---|---|---|---|
| COMPLETE SET (375) | 500.00 | 200.00 | 50.00 |
| COMMON PLAYER (1-375) | .75 | .30 | .07 |
| ☐ 1 Barry Sanders W1 | 10.00 | 4.00 | 1.00 |
| ☐ 2 Joe Montana W1 | 25.00 | 10.00 | 2.50 |
| ☐ 3 Lindy Infante W1 UER | .75 | .30 | .07 |
| Coach of the Year | | | |
| (missing Coach next | | | |
| to Packers) | | | |
| ☐ 4 Warren Moon W1 UER | 2.50 | 1.00 | .25 |
| Man of the Year | | | |
| (missing R symbol) | | | |
| ☐ 5 Keith Millard W1 | .75 | .30 | .07 |
| Defensive Player | | | |
| of the Year | | | |
| ☐ 6 Derrick Thomas W1 UER | 2.50 | 1.00 | .25 |
| Defensive Rookie | | | |
| of the Year | | | |
| (no 1989 on front | | | |
| banner of card) | | | |
| ☐ 7 Ottis Anderson W1 | 1.25 | .50 | .12 |
| Comeback Player | | | |
| of the Year | | | |
| ☐ 8 Joe Montana W2 | 20.00 | 8.00 | 2.00 |
| Passing Leader | | | |
| ☐ 9 Christian Okoye W2 | 1.00 | .40 | .10 |
| Rushing Leader | | | |
| ☐ 10 Thurman Thomas W2 | 5.00 | 2.00 | .50 |
| Total Yardage Leader | | | |
| ☐ 11 Mike Cofer W2 | .75 | .30 | .07 |
| Kick Scoring Leader | | | |
| ☐ 12 Dalton Hilliard W2 UER | .75 | .30 | .07 |
| TD Scoring Leader | | | |
| (O.J. Simpson not | | | |
| listed in stats, but | | | |
| is mentioned in text) | | | |
| ☐ 13 Sterling Sharpe W2 | 5.00 | 2.00 | .50 |
| Receiving Leader | | | |
| ☐ 14 Rich Camarillo W3 | .75 | .30 | .07 |
| Punting Leader | | | |
| ☐ 15 Walter Stanley W3 | 1.00 | .40 | .10 |
| Punt Return Leader | | | |
| ☐ 16 Rod Woodson W3 | 1.50 | .60 | .15 |
| Kickoff Return Leader | | | |
| ☐ 17 Felix Wright W3 | .75 | .30 | .07 |
| Interception Leader | | | |
| ☐ 18 Chris Doleman W3 | 1.00 | .40 | .10 |
| Sack Leader | | | |
| ☐ 19 Andre Ware W3 | 1.00 | .40 | .10 |
| Heisman Trophy | | | |
| ☐ 20 Mohammed Elewonibi W4 | .75 | .30 | .07 |
| Outland Trophy | | | |
| ☐ 21 Percy Snow W4 | .75 | .30 | .07 |
| Lombardi Award | | | |
| ☐ 22 Anthony Thompson W4 | .75 | .30 | .07 |
| Maxwell Award | | | |

| |  | | |
|---|---|---|---|
| ☐ 23 Buck Buchanan W4 | 1.00 | .40 | .10 |
| (Sacking Bart Starr) 1990 HOF Selection | | | |
| ☐ 24 Bob Griese W4 | 1.50 | .60 | .15 |
| 1990 HOF Selection | | | |
| ☐ 25 Franco Harris W5 | 1.50 | .60 | .15 |
| 1990 HOF Selection | | | |
| ☐ 26 Ted Hendricks W4 | 1.00 | .40 | .10 |
| 1990 HOF Selection | | | |
| ☐ 27 Jack Lambert W5 | 1.00 | .40 | .10 |
| 1990 HOF Selection | | | |
| ☐ 28 Tom Landry W5 | 2.00 | .80 | .20 |
| 1990 HOF Selection | | | |
| ☐ 29 Bob St.Clair W5 | 1.00 | .40 | .10 |
| 1990 HOF Selection | | | |
| ☐ 30 Aundray Bruce W5 UER | .75 | .30 | .07 |
| (Stats say Falcons) | | | |
| ☐ 31 Tony Casillas W5 UER | .75 | .30 | .07 |
| (Stats say Falcons) | | | |
| ☐ 32 Shawn Collins W5 | .75 | .30 | .07 |
| ☐ 33 Marcus Cotton W6 | .75 | .30 | .07 |
| ☐ 34 Bill Fralic W6 | .75 | .30 | .07 |
| ☐ 35 Chris Miller W6 | 2.50 | 1.00 | .25 |
| ☐ 36 Deion Sanders W6 UER | 3.00 | 1.20 | .30 |
| (Stats say Falcons) | | | |
| ☐ 37 John Settle W6 | .75 | .30 | .07 |
| ☐ 38 Jerry Glanville CO W6 | 1.00 | .40 | .10 |
| ☐ 39 Cornelius Bennett W7 | 1.00 | .40 | .10 |
| ☐ 40 Jim Kelly W7 | 3.00 | 1.20 | .30 |
| ☐ 41 Mark Kelso W7 UER | .75 | .30 | .07 |
| (No fumble rec. in '88; mentioned in '89) | | | |
| ☐ 42 Scott Norwood W7 | .75 | .30 | .07 |
| ☐ 43 Nate Odomes W7 | .75 | .30 | .07 |
| ☐ 44 Scott Radecic W7 | .75 | .30 | .07 |
| ☐ 45 Jim Ritcher W8 | .75 | .30 | .07 |
| ☐ 46 Leonard Smith W8 | .75 | .30 | .07 |
| ☐ 47 Darryl Talley W8 | 1.00 | .40 | .10 |
| ☐ 48 Marv Levy CO W8 | .75 | .30 | .07 |
| ☐ 49 Neal Anderson W8 | 1.00 | .40 | .10 |
| ☐ 50 Kevin Butler W8 | .75 | .30 | .07 |
| ☐ 51 Jim Covert W8 | .75 | .30 | .07 |
| ☐ 52 Richard Dent W9 | 1.00 | .40 | .10 |
| ☐ 53 Jay Hilgenberg W9 | .75 | .30 | .07 |
| ☐ 54 Steve McMichael W9 | .75 | .30 | .07 |
| ☐ 55 Ron Morris W9 | .75 | .30 | .07 |
| ☐ 56 John Roper W9 | .75 | .30 | .07 |
| ☐ 57 Mike Singletary W9 | 1.00 | .40 | .10 |
| ☐ 58 Keith Van Horne W10 | .75 | .30 | .07 |
| ☐ 59 Mike Ditka CO W10 | 1.50 | .60 | .15 |
| ☐ 60 Lewis Billups W10 | .75 | .30 | .07 |
| ☐ 61 Eddie Brown W10 | 1.00 | .40 | .10 |
| ☐ 62 Jason Buck W10 | .75 | .30 | .07 |
| ☐ 63 Rickey Dixon W10 | 1.00 | .40 | .10 |
| ☐ 64 Tim McGee W11 | 1.00 | .40 | .10 |
| ☐ 65 Eric Thomas W11 | .75 | .30 | .07 |
| ☐ 66 Ickey Woods W11 | 1.00 | .40 | .10 |
| ☐ 67 Carl Zander W11 | .75 | .30 | .07 |
| ☐ 68 Sam Wyche CO W11 | 1.00 | .40 | .10 |
| ☐ 69 Paul Farren W11 | .75 | .30 | .07 |
| ☐ 70 Thane Gash W12 | .75 | .30 | .07 |
| ☐ 71 David Grayson W12 | .75 | .30 | .07 |
| ☐ 72 Bernie Kosar W12 | 2.00 | .80 | .20 |
| ☐ 73 Reggie Langhorne W12 | .75 | .30 | .07 |
| ☐ 74 Eric Metcalf W12 | 1.50 | .60 | .15 |
| ☐ 75 Ozzie Newsome W12 | 1.50 | .60 | .15 |
| ☐ 76 Felix Wright W13 | .75 | .30 | .07 |
| ☐ 77 Bud Carson CO W13 | .75 | .30 | .07 |
| ☐ 78 Troy Aikman W13 | 20.00 | 8.00 | 2.00 |
| ☐ 79 Michael Irvin W13 | 5.00 | 2.00 | .50 |
| ☐ 80 Jim Jeffcoat W13 | .75 | .30 | .07 |
| ☐ 81 Crawford Ker W13 | .75 | .30 | .07 |
| ☐ 82 Eugene Lockhart W13 | .75 | .30 | .07 |
| ☐ 83 Kelvin Martin W14 | 1.00 | .40 | .10 |
| ☐ 84 Ken Norton Jr. W14 | 1.50 | .60 | .15 |
| ☐ 85 Jimmy Johnson CO W14 | 1.00 | .40 | .10 |
| ☐ 86 Steve Atwater W14 | 1.00 | .40 | .10 |
| ☐ 87 Tyrone Braxton W14 | .75 | .30 | .07 |
| ☐ 88 John Elway W14 | 7.50 | 3.00 | .75 |
| ☐ 89 Simon Fletcher W15 | 1.00 | .40 | .10 |
| ☐ 90 Ron Holmes W15 | .75 | .30 | .07 |
| ☐ 91 Bobby Humphrey W15 | 1.00 | .40 | .10 |
| ☐ 92 Vance Johnson W15 | 1.00 | .40 | .10 |
| ☐ 93 Ricky Nattiel W15 | 1.00 | .40 | .10 |
| ☐ 94 Dan Reeves CO W15 | 1.00 | .40 | .10 |
| ☐ 95 Jim Arnold W1 | .75 | .30 | .07 |
| ☐ 96 Jerry Ball W1 | .75 | .30 | .07 |
| ☐ 97 Bennie Blades W1 | 1.00 | .40 | .10 |
| ☐ 98 Lomas Brown W1 | .75 | .30 | .07 |
| ☐ 99 Michael Cofer W1 | .75 | .30 | .07 |
| ☐ 100 Richard Johnson W4 | .75 | .30 | .07 |
| ☐ 101 Eddie Murray W4 | .75 | .30 | .07 |
| ☐ 102 Barry Sanders W2 | 10.00 | 4.00 | 1.00 |
| ☐ 103 Chris Spielman W2 | 1.00 | .40 | .10 |
| ☐ 104 William White W2 | .75 | .30 | .07 |
| ☐ 105 Eric Williams W2 | .75 | .30 | .07 |
| ☐ 106 Wayne Fontes CO W3 UER | .75 | .30 | .07 |
| (Says born in MO, actually born in MA) | | | |
| ☐ 107 Brent Fullwood W3 | .75 | .30 | .07 |
| ☐ 108 Ron Hallstrom W3 | .75 | .30 | .07 |
| ☐ 109 Tim Harris W8 | 1.00 | .40 | .10 |
| ☐ 110 Johnny Holland W8 | 1.00 | .40 | .10 |
| ☐ 111 Perry Kemp W8 | 1.00 | .40 | .10 |
| ☐ 112 Don Majkowski W9 | 1.00 | .40 | .10 |
| ☐ 113 Mark Murphy W9 | .75 | .30 | .07 |
| ☐ 114 Sterling Sharpe W9 | 5.00 | 2.00 | .50 |
| ☐ 115 Ed West W9 | 1.00 | .40 | .10 |
| ☐ 116 Lindy Infante CO W9 | .75 | .30 | .07 |
| ☐ 117 Steve Brown W9 | .75 | .30 | .07 |
| ☐ 118 Ray Childress W10 | 1.00 | .40 | .10 |
| ☐ 119 Ernest Givins W10 | 1.50 | .60 | .15 |
| ☐ 120 John Grimsley W10 | .75 | .30 | .07 |
| ☐ 121 Alonzo Highsmith W10 | 1.00 | .40 | .10 |
| ☐ 122 Drew Hill W10 | 1.00 | .40 | .10 |
| ☐ 123 Bubba McDowell W10 | .75 | .30 | .07 |
| ☐ 124 Dean Steinkuhler W10 | .75 | .30 | .07 |
| ☐ 125 Lorenzo White W11 | 1.00 | .40 | .10 |
| ☐ 126 Tony Zendejas W11 | .75 | .30 | .07 |
| ☐ 127 Jack Pardee CO W11 | .75 | .30 | .07 |
| ☐ 128 Albert Bentley W11 | 1.00 | .40 | .10 |
| ☐ 129 Dean Biasucci W11 | .75 | .30 | .07 |
| ☐ 130 Duane Bickett W11 | 1.00 | .40 | .10 |
| ☐ 131 Bill Brooks W12 | 1.00 | .40 | .10 |
| ☐ 132 Jon Hand W12 | 1.00 | .40 | .10 |
| ☐ 133 Mike Prior W12 | .75 | .30 | .07 |
| ☐ 134 Andre Rison W12 | 3.00 | 1.20 | .30 |
| ☐ 135 Rohn Stark W12 | .75 | .30 | .07 |
| ☐ 136 Donnell Thompson W12 | .75 | .30 | .07 |
| ☐ 137 Clarence Verdin W13 | 1.00 | .40 | .10 |
| ☐ 138 Fredd Young W13 | .75 | .30 | .07 |
| ☐ 139 Ron Meyer CO W14 | .75 | .30 | .07 |
| ☐ 140 John Alt W14 | .75 | .30 | .07 |
| ☐ 141 Steve DeBerg W14 | 1.00 | .40 | .10 |
| ☐ 142 Irv Eatman W1 | .75 | .30 | .07 |
| ☐ 143 Dino Hackett W2 | .75 | .30 | .07 |
| ☐ 144 Nick Lowery W2 | 1.00 | .40 | .10 |
| ☐ 145 Bill Maas W2 | .75 | .30 | .07 |
| ☐ 146 Stephone Paige W5 | 1.00 | .40 | .10 |
| ☐ 147 Neil Smith W3 | 1.00 | .40 | .10 |
| ☐ 148 Marty Schottenheimer CO W3 | .75 | .30 | .07 |
| ☐ 149 Steve Beuerlein W3 | 2.00 | .80 | .20 |
| ☐ 150 Tim Brown W4 | 4.00 | 1.60 | .40 |
| ☐ 151 Mike Dyal W4 | .75 | .30 | .07 |
| ☐ 152 Mervyn Fernandez W4 | 1.00 | .40 | .10 |
| ☐ 153 Willie Gault W4 | 1.00 | .40 | .10 |
| ☐ 154 Bob Golic W5 | .75 | .30 | .07 |
| ☐ 155 Bo Jackson W5 | 4.00 | 1.60 | .40 |
| ☐ 156 Don Mosebar W5 | .75 | .30 | .07 |
| ☐ 157 Steve Smith W5 | .75 | .30 | .07 |
| ☐ 158 Greg Townsend W5 | 1.00 | .40 | .10 |
| ☐ 159 Bruce Wilkerson W6 | .75 | .30 | .07 |
| ☐ 160 Steve Wisniewski W6 | .75 | .30 | .07 |
| (Blocking for Bo Jackson) | | | |
| ☐ 161 Art Shell CO W6 | 1.25 | .50 | .12 |
| ☐ 162 Flipper Anderson W6 | 1.00 | .40 | .10 |
| ☐ 163 Greg Bell W6 UER | 1.00 | .40 | .10 |
| (Stats have 5 catches, should be 9) | | | |
| ☐ 164 Henry Ellard W6 | 1.00 | .40 | .10 |
| ☐ 165 Jim Everett W6 | 1.00 | .40 | .10 |
| ☐ 166 Jerry Gray W7 | .75 | .30 | .07 |
| ☐ 167 Kevin Greene W7 | 1.00 | .40 | .10 |
| ☐ 168 Pete Holohan W13 | .75 | .30 | .07 |
| ☐ 169 Larry Kelm W13 | .75 | .30 | .07 |
| ☐ 170 Tom Newberry W13 | .75 | .30 | .07 |
| ☐ 171 Vince Newsome W13 | .75 | .30 | .07 |
| ☐ 172 Irv Pankey W14 | .75 | .30 | .07 |
| ☐ 173 Jackie Slater W14 | 1.00 | .40 | .10 |
| ☐ 174 Fred Strickland W14 | .75 | .30 | .07 |
| ☐ 175 Mike Wilcher W14 UER | .75 | .30 | .07 |
| (Fumble rec. number different from 1989 Pro Set card) | | | |
| ☐ 176 John Robinson CO W7 UER (Stats say Rams, should say L.A. Rams) | .75 | .30 | .07 |
| ☐ 177 Mark Clayton W7 | 1.00 | .40 | .10 |
| ☐ 178 Roy Foster W7 | .75 | .30 | .07 |
| ☐ 179 Harry Galbreath W7 | .75 | .30 | .07 |
| ☐ 180 Jim C. Jensen W8 | .75 | .30 | .07 |
| ☐ 181 Dan Marino W15 | 15.00 | 6.00 | 1.50 |
| ☐ 182 Louis Oliver W15 | 1.00 | .40 | .10 |
| ☐ 183 Sammie Smith W15 | 1.00 | .40 | .10 |
| ☐ 184 Brian Sochia W15 | .75 | .30 | .07 |
| ☐ 185 Don Shula CO W15 | 1.25 | .50 | .12 |
| ☐ 186 Joey Browner W8 | 1.00 | .40 | .10 |
| ☐ 187 Anthony Carter W15 | 1.00 | .40 | .10 |
| ☐ 188 Chris Doleman W15 | 1.00 | .40 | .10 |
| ☐ 189 Steve Jordan W4 | 1.00 | .40 | .10 |
| ☐ 190 Carl Lee W4 | 1.00 | .40 | .10 |
| ☐ 191 Randall McDaniel W5 | .75 | .30 | .07 |
| ☐ 192 Mike Merriweather W5 | .75 | .30 | .07 |
| ☐ 193 Keith Millard W14 | 1.00 | .40 | .10 |

|  | | | |
|---|---|---|---|
| ☐ 194 Al Noga W12 | .75 | .30 | .07 |
| ☐ 195 Scott Studwell W5 | .75 | .30 | .07 |
| ☐ 196 Henry Thomas W12 | .75 | .30 | .07 |
| ☐ 197 Herschel Walker W5 | 1.00 | .40 | .10 |
| ☐ 198 Wade Wilson W5 | 1.00 | .40 | .10 |
| ☐ 199 Gary Zimmerman W5 | .75 | .30 | .07 |
| ☐ 200 Jerry Burns CO W6 | .75 | .30 | .07 |
| ☐ 201 Vincent Brown W6 | 1.00 | .40 | .10 |
| ☐ 202 Hart Lee Dykes W14 | 1.00 | .40 | .10 |
| ☐ 203 Sean Farrell W6 | .75 | .30 | .07 |
| ☐ 204 Fred Marion W6 | .75 | .30 | .07 |
| ☐ 205 Stanley Morgan W15 UER | 1.00 | .40 | .10 |
| (Text says he reached 10,000 yards fastest; 3 players did it in 10 seasons) | | | |
| ☐ 206 Eric Sievers W6 | 1.00 | .40 | .10 |
| ☐ 207 John Stephens W15 | 1.25 | .50 | .12 |
| ☐ 208 Andre Tippett W15 | 1.00 | .40 | .10 |
| ☐ 209 Rod Rust CO W15 | .75 | .30 | .07 |
| ☐ 210 Morten Andersen W6 | 1.00 | .40 | .10 |
| ☐ 211 Brad Edelman W12 | .75 | .30 | .07 |
| ☐ 212 John Fourcade W12 | 1.00 | .40 | .10 |
| ☐ 213 Dalton Hilliard W13 | 1.00 | .40 | .10 |
| ☐ 214 Rickey Jackson W13 | 1.00 | .40 | .10 |
| (Forcing Jim Kelly fumble) | | | |
| ☐ 215 Vaughan Johnson W13 | 1.00 | .40 | .10 |
| ☐ 216 Eric Martin W13 | 1.00 | .40 | .10 |
| ☐ 217 Sam Mills W7 | 1.00 | .40 | .10 |
| ☐ 218 Pat Swilling W7 UER | 1.00 | .40 | .10 |
| (Total fumble recoveries listed as 4, should be 5) | | | |
| ☐ 219 Frank Warren W7 | 1.00 | .40 | .10 |
| ☐ 220 Jim Wilks W7 | .75 | .30 | .07 |
| ☐ 221 Jim Mora CO W7 | 1.00 | .40 | .10 |
| ☐ 222 Raul Allegre W2 | .75 | .30 | .07 |
| ☐ 223 Carl Banks W1 | 1.00 | .40 | .10 |
| ☐ 224 John Elliott W1 | .75 | .30 | .07 |
| ☐ 225 Erik Howard W7 | .75 | .30 | .07 |
| ☐ 226 Pepper Johnson W2 | 1.00 | .40 | .10 |
| ☐ 227 Leonard Marshall W7 | 1.00 | .40 | .10 |
| UER (In Super Bowl XXI, George Martin had the safety) | | | |
| ☐ 228 Dave Meggett W2 | 1.00 | .40 | .10 |
| ☐ 229 Bart Oates W3 | 1.00 | .40 | .10 |
| ☐ 230 Phil Simms W8 | 1.50 | .60 | .15 |
| ☐ 231 Lawrence Taylor W8 | 2.50 | 1.00 | .25 |
| ☐ 232 Bill Parcells CO W8 | 1.00 | .40 | .10 |
| ☐ 233 Troy Benson W8 | .75 | .30 | .07 |
| ☐ 234 Kyle Clifton W8 UER | .75 | .30 | .07 |
| (Born: Onley, should be Olney) | | | |
| ☐ 235 Johnny Hector W8 | 1.00 | .40 | .10 |
| ☐ 236 Jeff Lageman W9 | 1.00 | .40 | .10 |
| ☐ 237 Pat Leahy W9 | .75 | .30 | .07 |
| ☐ 238 Freeman McNeil W9 | 1.00 | .40 | .10 |
| ☐ 239 Ken O'Brien W9 | 1.00 | .40 | .10 |
| ☐ 240 Al Toon W9 | 1.00 | .40 | .10 |
| ☐ 241 Jo Jo Townsell W9 | .75 | .30 | .07 |
| ☐ 242 Bruce Coslet CO W10 | .75 | .30 | .07 |
| ☐ 243 Eric Allen W10 | 1.00 | .40 | .10 |
| ☐ 244 Jerome Brown W10 | 1.00 | .40 | .10 |
| ☐ 245 Keith Byars W10 | 1.00 | .40 | .10 |
| ☐ 246 Cris Carter W10 | 1.50 | .60 | .15 |
| ☐ 247 Randall Cunningham W13 | 3.00 | 1.20 | .30 |
| ☐ 248 Keith Jackson W14 | 1.50 | .60 | .15 |
| ☐ 249 Mike Quick W14 | 1.00 | .40 | .10 |
| ☐ 250 Clyde Simmons W14 | 1.00 | .40 | .10 |
| ☐ 251 Andre Waters W14 | 1.00 | .40 | .10 |
| ☐ 252 Reggie White W15 | 2.00 | .80 | .20 |
| ☐ 253 Buddy Ryan CO W15 | 1.00 | .40 | .10 |
| ☐ 254 Rich Camarillo W15 | .75 | .30 | .07 |
| ☐ 255 Earl Ferrell W10 | .75 | .30 | .07 |
| (No mention of retirement on card front) | | | |
| ☐ 256 Roy Green W10 | 1.00 | .40 | .10 |
| ☐ 257 Ken Harvey W3 | 1.00 | .40 | .10 |
| ☐ 258 Ernie Jones W1 | 1.00 | .40 | .10 |
| ☐ 259 Tim McDonald W11 | 1.00 | .40 | .10 |
| ☐ 260 Timm Rosenbach W11 UER | 1.00 | .40 | .10 |
| (Born '67, should be '66) | | | |
| ☐ 261 Luis Sharpe W3 | 1.00 | .40 | .10 |
| ☐ 262 Vai Sikahema W3 | 1.00 | .40 | .10 |
| ☐ 263 J.T. Smith W1 | 1.00 | .40 | .10 |
| ☐ 264 Ron Wolfley W1 UER | .75 | .30 | .07 |
| (Born Blaisdel, should be Blasdel) | | | |
| ☐ 265 Joe Bugel CO W11 | .75 | .30 | .07 |
| ☐ 266 Gary Anderson W11 | .75 | .30 | .07 |
| ☐ 267 Bubby Brister W1 | 1.00 | .40 | .10 |
| ☐ 268 Merril Hoge W11 | 1.00 | .40 | .10 |
| ☐ 269 Carnell Lake W2 | .75 | .30 | .07 |
| ☐ 270 Louis Lipps W11 | 1.00 | .40 | .10 |
| ☐ 271 David Little W3 | 1.00 | .40 | .10 |
| ☐ 272 Greg Lloyd W3 | 1.00 | .40 | .10 |
| ☐ 273 Keith Willis W11 | .75 | .30 | .07 |
| ☐ 274 Tim Worley W3 | 1.00 | .40 | .10 |
| ☐ 275 Chuck Noll CO W4 | 1.00 | .40 | .10 |
| ☐ 276 Marion Butts W4 | 1.25 | .50 | .12 |
| ☐ 277 Gill Byrd W2 | 1.00 | .40 | .10 |
| ☐ 278 Vencie Glenn W2 UER | .75 | .30 | .07 |
| (Sack total should be 2, not 2.5) | | | |
| ☐ 279 Burt Grossman W4 | 1.00 | .40 | .10 |
| ☐ 280 Gary Plummer W4 | .75 | .30 | .07 |
| ☐ 281 Billy Ray Smith W12 | 1.00 | .40 | .10 |
| ☐ 282 Billy Joe Tolliver W12 | 1.00 | .40 | .10 |
| ☐ 283 Dan Henning CO W1 | .75 | .30 | .07 |
| ☐ 284 Harris Barton W1 | .75 | .30 | .07 |
| ☐ 285 Michael Carter W1 | 1.00 | .40 | .10 |
| ☐ 286 Mike Cofer W1 | .75 | .30 | .07 |
| ☐ 287 Roger Craig W1 | 1.50 | .60 | .15 |
| ☐ 288 Don Griffin W1 | .75 | .30 | .07 |
| ☐ 289 Charles Haley W2 | 1.00 | .40 | .10 |
| ☐ 290 Pierce Holt W2 | 1.00 | .40 | .10 |
| ☐ 291 Ronnie Lott W2 | 1.50 | .60 | .15 |
| ☐ 292 Guy McIntyre W2 | 1.00 | .40 | .10 |
| ☐ 293 Joe Montana W2 | 25.00 | 10.00 | 2.50 |
| ☐ 294 Tom Rathman W2 | 1.00 | .40 | .10 |
| ☐ 295 Jerry Rice W3 | 15.00 | 6.00 | 1.50 |
| ☐ 296 Jesse Sapolu W3 | .75 | .30 | .07 |
| ☐ 297 John Taylor W3 | 1.50 | .60 | .15 |
| ☐ 298 Michael Walter W3 | .75 | .30 | .07 |
| ☐ 299 George Seifert CO W3 | .75 | .30 | .07 |
| ☐ 300 Jeff Bryant W3 | .75 | .30 | .07 |
| ☐ 301 Jacob Green W4 | 1.00 | .40 | .10 |
| ☐ 302 Norm Johnson W4 UER | 1.00 | .40 | .10 |
| (Card shop not in Garden Grove, should say Fullerton) | | | |
| ☐ 303 Bryan Millard W4 | .75 | .30 | .07 |
| ☐ 304 Joe Nash W4 | .75 | .30 | .07 |
| ☐ 305 Eugene Robinson W4 | 1.00 | .40 | .10 |
| ☐ 306 John L. Williams W14 | 1.00 | .40 | .10 |
| ☐ 307 Dave Wyman W14 | .75 | .30 | .07 |
| (NFL EXP is in caps, inconsistent with rest of the set) | | | |
| ☐ 308 Chuck Knox CO W14 | .75 | .30 | .07 |
| ☐ 309 Mark Carrier W14 | 1.00 | .40 | .10 |
| ☐ 310 Paul Gruber W14 | 1.00 | .40 | .10 |
| ☐ 311 Harry Hamilton W15 | 1.00 | .40 | .10 |
| ☐ 312 Bruce Hill W15 | .75 | .30 | .07 |
| ☐ 313 Donald Igwebuike W15 | .75 | .30 | .07 |
| ☐ 314 Kevin Murphy W15 | .75 | .30 | .07 |
| ☐ 315 Ervin Randle W12 | .75 | .30 | .07 |
| ☐ 316 Mark Robinson W12 | .75 | .30 | .07 |
| ☐ 317 Lars Tate W12 | .75 | .30 | .07 |
| ☐ 318 Vinny Testaverde W12 | 1.25 | .50 | .12 |
| ☐ 319 Ray Perkins CO W12 | 1.50 | .60 | .15 |
| ☐ 320 Earnest Byner W12 | 1.00 | .40 | .10 |
| ☐ 321 Gary Clark W12 | 1.25 | .50 | .12 |
| (Randall Cunningham looking on from sidelines) | | | |
| ☐ 322 Darryl Grant W13 | .75 | .30 | .07 |
| ☐ 323 Darrell Green W13 | 1.00 | .40 | .10 |
| ☐ 324 Jim Lachey W13 | 1.00 | .40 | .10 |
| ☐ 325 Charles Mann W13 | 1.00 | .40 | .10 |
| ☐ 326 Wilber Marshall W13 | 1.00 | .40 | .10 |
| ☐ 327 Ralf Mojsiejenko W13 | .75 | .30 | .07 |
| ☐ 328 Art Monk W15 | 1.25 | .50 | .12 |
| ☐ 329 Gerald Riggs W15 | 1.00 | .40 | .10 |
| ☐ 330 Mark Rypien W14 | 1.00 | .40 | .10 |
| ☐ 331 Ricky Sanders W4 | 1.00 | .40 | .10 |
| ☐ 332 Alvin Walton W4 | .75 | .30 | .07 |
| ☐ 333 Joe Gibbs CO W5 | 1.00 | .40 | .10 |
| ☐ 334 Aloha Stadium W5 | .75 | .30 | .07 |
| Site of Pro Bowl | | | |
| ☐ 335 Brian Blades PB W5 | .75 | .30 | .07 |
| ☐ 336 James Brooks PB W5 | .75 | .30 | .07 |
| ☐ 337 Shane Conlan PB W5 | .75 | .30 | .07 |
| ☐ 339 Ray Donaldson PB W5 | .75 | .30 | .07 |
| ☐ 340 Ferrell Edmunds PB W6 | .75 | .30 | .07 |
| ☐ 341 Boomer Esiason PB W6 | 1.00 | .40 | .10 |
| ☐ 342 David Fulcher PB W6 | .75 | .30 | .07 |
| ☐ 343 Chris Hinton PB W6 | 1.00 | .40 | .10 |
| ☐ 344 Rodney Holman PB W6 | .75 | .30 | .07 |
| ☐ 345 Kent Hull PB W6 | .75 | .30 | .07 |
| ☐ 346 Tunch Ilkin PB W7 | .75 | .30 | .07 |
| ☐ 347 Mike Johnson PB W7 | .75 | .30 | .07 |
| ☐ 348 Greg Kragen PB W7 | .75 | .30 | .07 |
| ☐ 349 Dave Krieg PB W7 | 1.00 | .40 | .10 |
| ☐ 350 Albert Lewis PB W7 | .75 | .30 | .07 |
| ☐ 351 Howie Long PB W7 | 1.00 | .40 | .10 |
| ☐ 352 Bruce Matthews PB W8 | .75 | .30 | .07 |
| ☐ 353 Clay Matthews PB W8 | 1.00 | .40 | .10 |
| ☐ 354 Erik McMillan PB W8 | .75 | .30 | .07 |
| ☐ 355 Karl Mecklenburg PB W8 | .75 | .30 | .07 |
| ☐ 356 Anthony Miller PB W8 | 1.00 | .40 | .10 |
| ☐ 357 Frank Minnifield PB W8 | .75 | .30 | .07 |
| ☐ 358 Max Montoya PB W8 | .75 | .30 | .07 |
| ☐ 359 Warren Moon PB W10 | 2.00 | .80 | .20 |

| | | | |
|---|---|---|---|
| ☐ 360 Mike Munchak PB W9 | 1.00 | .40 | .10 |
| ☐ 361 Anthony Munoz PB W9 | 1.00 | .40 | .10 |
| ☐ 362 John Offerdahl PB W9 | .75 | .30 | .07 |
| ☐ 363 Christian Okoye PB W9 | 1.00 | .40 | .10 |
| ☐ 364 Leslie O'Neal PB W9 | 1.00 | .40 | .10 |
| ☐ 365 Rufus Porter PB W9 UER | .75 | .30 | .07 |
| (TM logo missing) | | | |
| ☐ 366 Andre Reed PB W10 | 1.00 | .40 | .10 |
| ☐ 367 Johnny Rembert PB W10 | .75 | .30 | .07 |
| ☐ 368 Reggie Roby PB W10 | .75 | .30 | .07 |
| ☐ 369 Kevin Ross PB W10 | .75 | .30 | .07 |
| ☐ 370 Webster Slaughter PB W10 | 1.00 | .40 | .10 |
| ☐ 371 Bruce Smith PB W11 | 1.00 | .40 | .10 |
| ☐ 372 Dennis Smith PB W11 | .75 | .30 | .07 |
| ☐ 373 Derrick Thomas PB W11 | 2.00 | .80 | .20 |
| ☐ 374 Thurman Thomas PB W11 | 2.50 | 1.00 | .25 |
| ☐ 375 David Treadwell PB W11 | .75 | .30 | .07 |
| ☐ 376 Lee Williams PB W11 | .75 | .30 | .07 |

# 1991 FACT Pro Set Mobil

Sponsored by Pro Set and Mobil Oil, the 1991 Pro Set FACT (Football and Academics: A Championship Team) set marks the second year that Pro Set produced cards to serve as motivational learning tools to promote public health and education. This year's program was expanded to include all 26 NFL cities and to target 200,000 fourth grade students in low socio-economic areas. Six monthly lessons were featured in the set, and each lesson had an educational theme. Teachers utilized in-classroom educational materials and distributed a set of 17 Pro Set cards (along with one title/header card) each month, with the reverse sides carrying specific educational lessons corresponding to the educational theme. The standard-size (2 1/2" by 3 1/2") cards are identical to first series cards, with the exception that the backs have interactive educational questions instead of player information. The cards are numbered on the back. The particular set in which the card was issued is indicated below by S for set number.

| | MINT | EXC | G-VG |
|---|---|---|---|
| COMPLETE SET (108) | 100.00 | 40.00 | 10.00 |
| COMMON PLAYER | .75 | .30 | .07 |
| ☐ 3 Joe Montana S1 | 15.00 | 6.00 | 1.50 |
| San Francisco 49ers | | | |
| ☐ 5 Mike Singletary S2 | 1.00 | .40 | .10 |
| Chicago Bears | | | |
| ☐ 12 Jay Novacek S3 | 1.50 | .60 | .15 |
| Dallas Cowboys | | | |
| ☐ 20 Ottis Anderson S2 | 1.00 | .40 | .10 |
| New York Giants | | | |
| ☐ 40 Tim Brown S1 | 1.50 | .60 | .15 |
| Los Angeles Raiders | | | |
| ☐ 44 Herschel Walker S1 | 1.25 | .50 | .12 |
| Minnesota Vikings | | | |
| ☐ 59 Eric Dorsey S3 | .75 | .30 | .07 |
| New York Giants | | | |
| ☐ 60 John Elliott S1 | .75 | .30 | .07 |
| New York Giants | | | |
| ☐ 63 Jeff Hostetler S2 | 1.25 | .50 | .12 |
| New York Giants | | | |
| ☐ 69 Eric Moore S4 | .75 | .30 | .07 |
| New York Giants | | | |
| ☐ 70 Bart Oates S3 | .75 | .30 | .07 |
| New York Giants | | | |
| ☐ 71 Gary Reasons S4 | .75 | .30 | .07 |
| New York Giants | | | |
| ☐ 75 Shane Conlan S3 | 1.00 | .40 | .10 |
| Buffalo Bills | | | |
| ☐ 78 Jim Kelly S4 | 4.00 | 1.60 | .40 |
| Buffalo Bills | | | |
| ☐ 84 Darryl Talley S6 | 1.00 | .40 | .10 |
| Buffalo Bills | | | |
| ☐ 90 Marv Levy CO S1 | .75 | .30 | .07 |
| Buffalo Bills | | | |

| | | | |
|---|---|---|---|
| ☐ 94 Tim Green S2 | .75 | .30 | .07 |
| Atlanta Falcons | | | |
| ☐ 99 Jerry Glanville CO S3 | .75 | .30 | .07 |
| Atlanta Falcons | | | |
| ☐ 101 Mark Carrier S3 | 1.00 | .40 | .10 |
| Chicago Bears | | | |
| ☐ 104 Jim Harbaugh S6 | 1.25 | .50 | .12 |
| Chicago Bears | | | |
| ☐ 105 Brad Muster S4 | 1.00 | .40 | .10 |
| Chicago Bears | | | |
| ☐ 107 Keith Van Horne S6 | .75 | .30 | .07 |
| Chicago Bears | | | |
| ☐ 111 Boomer Esiason S1 | 1.25 | .50 | .12 |
| Cincinnati Bengals | | | |
| ☐ 116 Anthony Munoz S2 | 1.25 | .50 | .12 |
| Cincinnati Bengals | | | |
| ☐ 117 Sam Wyche CO S4 | 1.00 | .40 | .10 |
| Cincinnati Bengals | | | |
| ☐ 118 Paul Farren S6 | .75 | .30 | .07 |
| Cleveland Browns | | | |
| ☐ 119 Thane Gash S3 | .75 | .30 | .07 |
| Cleveland Browns | | | |
| ☐ 122 Clay Matthews S2 | 1.25 | .50 | .12 |
| Cleveland Browns | | | |
| ☐ 123 Eric Metcalf S6 | 1.50 | .60 | .15 |
| Cleveland Browns | | | |
| ☐ 127 Tommie Agee S4 | .75 | .30 | .07 |
| Dallas Cowboys | | | |
| ☐ 128 Troy Aikman S6 | 12.00 | 5.00 | 1.20 |
| Dallas Cowboys | | | |
| ☐ 132 Michael Irvin S6 | 5.00 | 2.00 | .50 |
| Dallas Cowboys | | | |
| ☐ 134 Daniel Stubbs S6 | .75 | .30 | .07 |
| Dallas Cowboys | | | |
| ☐ 136 Steve Atwater S1 | 1.00 | .40 | .10 |
| Denver Broncos | | | |
| ☐ 138 John Elway S2 | 6.00 | 2.40 | .60 |
| Denver Broncos | | | |
| ☐ 141 Mark Jackson S6 | 1.00 | .40 | .10 |
| Denver Broncos | | | |
| ☐ 142 Karl Mecklenburg S3 | 1.00 | .40 | .10 |
| Denver Broncos | | | |
| ☐ 143 Doug Widell S2 | .75 | .30 | .07 |
| Denver Broncos | | | |
| ☐ 153 Wayne Fontes CO S2 | .75 | .30 | .07 |
| Detroit Lions | | | |
| ☐ 156 Don Majkowski S1 | 1.00 | .40 | .10 |
| Green Bay Packers | | | |
| ☐ 157 Tony Mandarich S6 | .75 | .30 | .07 |
| Green Bay Packers | | | |
| ☐ 158 Mark Murphy S6 | .75 | .30 | .07 |
| Green Bay Packers | | | |
| ☐ 161 Sterling Sharpe S4 | 5.00 | 2.00 | .50 |
| Green Bay Packers | | | |
| ☐ 162 Lindy Infante CO S3 | .75 | .30 | .07 |
| Green Bay Packers | | | |
| ☐ 163 Ray Childress S6 | 1.00 | .40 | .10 |
| Houston Oilers | | | |
| ☐ 166 Bruce Matthews S3 | 1.00 | .40 | .10 |
| Houston Oilers | | | |
| ☐ 167 Warren Moon S6 | 3.00 | 1.20 | .30 |
| Houston Oilers | | | |
| ☐ 168 Mike Munchak S4 | 1.00 | .40 | .10 |
| Houston Oilers | | | |
| ☐ 169 Al Smith S6 | .75 | .30 | .07 |
| Houston Oilers | | | |
| ☐ 174 Bill Brooks S1 | 1.00 | .40 | .10 |
| Indianapolis Colts | | | |
| ☐ 179 Clarence Verdin S3 | .75 | .30 | .07 |
| Indianapolis Colts | | | |
| ☐ 182 Steve DeBerg S1 | 1.00 | .40 | .10 |
| Kansas City Chiefs | | | |
| ☐ 185 Christian Okoye S3 | 1.00 | .40 | .10 |
| Kansas City Chiefs | | | |
| ☐ 189 M.Schottenheimer CO S1 | .75 | .30 | .07 |
| Kansas City Chiefs | | | |
| ☐ 191 Howie Long S2 | 1.00 | .40 | .10 |
| Los Angeles Raiders | | | |
| ☐ 194 Steve Smith S4 | 1.00 | .40 | .10 |
| Los Angeles Raiders | | | |
| ☐ 196 Lionel Washington S6 | .75 | .30 | .07 |
| Los Angeles Raiders | | | |
| ☐ 198 Art Shell CO S3 | 1.25 | .50 | .12 |
| Los Angeles Raiders | | | |
| ☐ 203 Buford McGee S2 | .75 | .30 | .07 |
| Los Angeles Rams | | | |
| ☐ 204 Tom Newberry S6 | .75 | .30 | .07 |
| Los Angeles Rams | | | |
| ☐ 205 Frank Stams S1 | .75 | .30 | .07 |
| Los Angeles Rams | | | |
| ☐ 210 Dan Marino S4 | 7.50 | 3.00 | .75 |
| Miami Dolphins | | | |
| ☐ 212 John Offerdahl S1 | 1.00 | .40 | .10 |
| Miami Dolphins | | | |
| ☐ 216 Don Shula CO S4 | 1.25 | .50 | .12 |
| Miami Dolphins | | | |
| ☐ 217 Darrell Fullington S6 | .75 | .30 | .07 |

| | | MINT | EXC | G-VG |
|---|---|---|---|---|
| | Minnesota Vikings | | | |
| ☐ 218 | Tim Irwin S2 | .75 | .30 | .07 |
| | Minnesota Vikings | | | |
| ☐ 219 | Mike Merriweather S3 | .75 | .30 | .07 |
| | Minnesota Vikings | | | |
| ☐ 231 | Ed Reynolds S3 | .75 | .30 | .07 |
| | New England Patriots | | | |
| ☐ 238 | Robert Massey S4 | .75 | .30 | .07 |
| | New Orleans Saints | | | |
| ☐ 246 | James Hasty S1 | .75 | .30 | .07 |
| | New York Jets | | | |
| ☐ 247 | Erik McMillan S2 | .75 | .30 | .07 |
| | New York Jets | | | |
| ☐ 249 | Ken O'Brien S4 | 1.00 | .40 | .10 |
| | New York Jets | | | |
| ☐ 260 | Andre Waters S2 | 1.00 | .40 | .10 |
| | Philadelphia Eagles | | | |
| ☐ 270 | Joe Bugel CO S2 | .75 | .30 | .07 |
| | Phoenix Cardinals | | | |
| ☐ 271 | Gary Anderson S1 | .75 | .30 | .07 |
| | Pittsburgh Steelers | | | |
| ☐ 272 | Dermontti Dawson S4 | .75 | .30 | .07 |
| | Pittsburgh Steelers | | | |
| ☐ 275 | Tunch Ilkin S2 | .75 | .30 | .07 |
| | Pittsburgh Steelers | | | |
| ☐ 282 | Gill Byrd S4 | .75 | .30 | .07 |
| | San Diego Chargers | | | |
| ☐ 290 | Michael Carter S2 | 1.00 | .40 | .10 |
| | San Francisco 49ers | | | |
| ☐ 292 | Pierce Holt S3 | 1.00 | .40 | .10 |
| | San Francisco 49ers | | | |
| ☐ 297 | George Seifert CO S1 | 1.00 | .40 | .10 |
| | San Francisco 49ers | | | |
| ☐ 306 | Chuck Knox CO S3 | .75 | .30 | .07 |
| | Seattle Seahawks | | | |
| ☐ 310 | Harry Hamilton S4 | 1.00 | .40 | .10 |
| | Tampa Bay Buccaneers | | | |
| ☐ 321 | Martin Mayhew S4 | .75 | .30 | .07 |
| | Washington Redskins | | | |
| ☐ 322 | Mark Rypien S1 | 1.25 | .50 | .12 |
| | Washington Redskins | | | |
| ☐ xx | S1 Title Card | .75 | .30 | .07 |
| | Stay Fit | | | |
| ☐ xx | S2 Title Card | .75 | .30 | .07 |
| | Eat Smart | | | |
| ☐ xx | S3 Title Card | .75 | .30 | .07 |
| | Stay Off Drugs | | | |
| ☐ xx | S4 Title Card | .75 | .30 | .07 |
| | Stay In Tune | | | |
| ☐ xx | S5 Title Card | .75 | .30 | .07 |
| | Stay True to Yourself | | | |
| ☐ xx | S6 Title Card | .75 | .30 | .07 |
| | Stay In School | | | |

## 1992 FACT NFL Properties

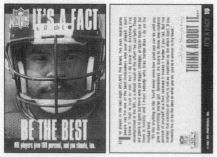

Sponsored by NFL Properties, Inc., this 18-card FACT (Football and Academics: A Championship Team) set measures the standard-size (2 1/2" by 3 1/2") and features NFL star players. The color photos on the fronts are full-bleed on the sides but bordered by black above and below. In white block lettering, the top of each card reads "It's A Fact," while the bottom slogan varies from card to card. On a white background with "It's A Fact" printed in pale blue, the horizontal backs have an extended player quote on the theme of the card. The cards are numbered on the back.

| | | MINT | EXC | G-VG |
|---|---|---|---|---|
| | COMPLETE SET (18) | 25.00 | 10.00 | 2.50 |
| | COMMON PLAYER (1-18) | 1.00 | .40 | .10 |
| ☐ 1 | Warren Moon | 2.50 | 1.00 | .25 |
| | Crack Kills | | | |
| ☐ 2 | Boomer Esiason | 2.00 | .80 | .20 |
| | Think Before You Drink | | | |
| ☐ 3 | Troy Aikman | 7.50 | 3.00 | .75 |

| | | MINT | EXC | G-VG |
|---|---|---|---|---|
| | Play It Straight | | | |
| ☐ 4 | Anthony Munoz | 1.25 | .50 | .12 |
| | Quedate en la Escuela | | | |
| ☐ 5 | Charles Mann | 1.00 | .40 | .10 |
| | Steroids Destroy | | | |
| ☐ 6 | Earnest Byner | 1.25 | .50 | .12 |
| | Never Give Up | | | |
| ☐ 7 | Joe Jacoby | 1.00 | .40 | .10 |
| | Don't Pollute | | | |
| ☐ 8 | Howie Long | 1.50 | .60 | .15 |
| | Aids Kills | | | |
| ☐ 9 | Dan Marino | 6.00 | 2.40 | .60 |
| | School's The Ticket | | | |
| ☐ 10 | Mike Singletary | 1.50 | .60 | .15 |
| | Be The Best | | | |
| ☐ 11 | Cornelius Bennett | 1.50 | .60 | .15 |
| | Chill | | | |
| ☐ 12 | Chris Doleman | 1.00 | .40 | .10 |
| | Turn It Off | | | |
| ☐ 13 | Jim Harbaugh | 1.50 | .60 | .15 |
| | Eat To Win | | | |
| ☐ 14 | Chris Hinton | 1.00 | .40 | .10 |
| | Say It Don't Spray It | | | |
| ☐ 15 | Nick Lowery | 1.00 | .40 | .10 |
| | Heal The Planet | | | |
| ☐ 16 | Rodney Peete | 1.50 | .60 | .15 |
| | Respect The Law | | | |
| ☐ 17 | Pat Swilling | 1.25 | .50 | .12 |
| | Vote | | | |
| ☐ 18 | Jim Everett | 1.50 | .60 | .15 |
| | Study | | | |

## 1993 FACT Fleer Shell

This 108-card set was issued by Fleer and co-sponsored by Shell and Russell Athletic. The FACT (Football and Academics: A Championship Team) sets were originally produced by Pro Set to serve as motivational learning tool to promote public health and education. Teachers utilized in-classroom educational materials and distributed a set of 18 Fleer cards each month, with the reverse sides carrying specific educational lessons corresponding to the educational theme. The standard-size (2 1/2" by 3 1/2") cards are identical to the regular 1993 Fleer set, with the exception that the backs include interactive educational questions along with player information. The cards are numbered on the back with 1-18 being in set 1, 19-36 in set 2, 37-54 in set 3, etc.

| | | MINT | EXC | G-VG |
|---|---|---|---|---|
| | COMPLETE SET (108) | 60.00 | 24.00 | 6.00 |
| | COMMON PLAYER (1-108) | .50 | .20 | .05 |
| ☐ 1 | Stay in School | .50 | .20 | .05 |
| | Scorecard | | | |
| ☐ 2 | Andre Rison | 1.00 | .40 | .10 |
| | Atlanta Falcons | | | |
| ☐ 3 | Jim Kelly | 2.00 | .80 | .20 |
| | Buffalo Bills | | | |
| ☐ 4 | Mark Carrier | .75 | .30 | .07 |
| | Chicago Bears | | | |
| ☐ 5 | David Fulcher | .50 | .20 | .05 |
| | Cincinnati Bengals | | | |
| ☐ 6 | Eric Metcalf | .75 | .30 | .07 |
| | Cleveland Browns | | | |
| ☐ 7 | Emmitt Smith | 7.50 | 3.00 | .75 |
| | Dallas Cowboys | | | |
| ☐ 8 | John Elway | 4.00 | 1.60 | .40 |
| | Denver Broncos | | | |
| ☐ 9 | Rodney Peete | .75 | .30 | .07 |
| | Detroit Lions | | | |
| ☐ 10 | Brett Favre | 3.00 | 1.20 | .30 |
| | Green Bay Packers | | | |
| ☐ 11 | Warren Moon | 1.50 | .60 | .15 |
| | Houson Oilers | | | |

| | | | |
|---|---|---|---|
| ☐ 12 Reggie Langhorne | .75 | .30 | .07 |
| Indianapolis Colts | | | |
| ☐ 13 Christian Okoye | .75 | .30 | .07 |
| Kansas City Chiefs | | | |
| ☐ 14 Nick Bell | .75 | .30 | .07 |
| Los Angeles Raiders | | | |
| ☐ 15 Jim Everett | 1.00 | .40 | .10 |
| Los Angeles Rams | | | |
| ☐ 16 Dan Marino | 6.00 | 2.40 | .60 |
| Miami Dolphins | | | |
| ☐ 17 Chris Doleman | .75 | .30 | .07 |
| Minnesota Vikings | | | |
| ☐ 18 Leonard Russell | 1.00 | .40 | .10 |
| New England Patriots | | | |
| ☐ 19 Stay Fit | .50 | .20 | .05 |
| Scorecard | | | |
| ☐ 20 Sam Mills | .50 | .20 | .05 |
| New Orleans Saints | | | |
| ☐ 21 Rodney Hampton | 1.25 | .50 | .12 |
| New York Giants | | | |
| ☐ 22 Rob Moore | 1.00 | .40 | .10 |
| New York Jets | | | |
| ☐ 23 Seth Joyner | .75 | .30 | .07 |
| Philadelphia Eagles | | | |
| ☐ 24 Chris Chandler | .75 | .30 | .07 |
| Phoenix Cardinals | | | |
| ☐ 25 Barry Foster | 1.25 | .50 | .12 |
| Pittsburgh Steelers | | | |
| ☐ 26 Stan Humphries | .75 | .30 | .07 |
| San Diego Chargers | | | |
| ☐ 27 Steve Young | 2.00 | .80 | .20 |
| San Francisco 49ers | | | |
| ☐ 28 Cortez Kennedy | 1.00 | .40 | .10 |
| Seattle Seahawks | | | |
| ☐ 29 Reggie Cobb | 1.00 | .40 | .10 |
| Tampa Bay Buccaneers | | | |
| ☐ 30 Mark Rypien | .75 | .30 | .07 |
| Washington Redskins | | | |
| ☐ 31 Michael Haynes | 1.00 | .40 | .10 |
| Atlanta Falcons | | | |
| ☐ 32 Thurman Thomas | 1.50 | .60 | .15 |
| Buffalo Bills | | | |
| ☐ 33 Tom Waddle | .75 | .30 | .07 |
| Chicago Bears | | | |
| ☐ 34 Harold Green | .75 | .30 | .07 |
| Cincinnati Bengals | | | |
| ☐ 35 Tommy Vardell | .75 | .30 | .07 |
| Cleveland Browns | | | |
| ☐ 36 Michael Irwin | 2.00 | .80 | .20 |
| Dallas Cowboys | | | |
| ☐ 37 Eat Smart | .50 | .20 | .05 |
| Scorecard | | | |
| ☐ 38 Mike Croel | .75 | .30 | .07 |
| Denver Broncos | | | |
| ☐ 39 Barry Sanders | 3.00 | 1.20 | .30 |
| Detroit Lions | | | |
| ☐ 40 Sterling Sharpe | 2.00 | .80 | .20 |
| Green Bay Packers | | | |
| ☐ 41 Haywood Jeffires | 1.00 | .40 | .10 |
| Houston Oilers | | | |
| ☐ 42 Duane Bickett | .75 | .30 | .07 |
| Indianapolis Colts | | | |
| ☐ 43 Nick Lowery | .50 | .20 | .05 |
| Kansas City Chiefs | | | |
| ☐ 44 Greg Townsend | .75 | .30 | .07 |
| Los Angeles Raiders | | | |
| ☐ 45 Todd Lyght | .75 | .30 | .07 |
| Los Angeles Rams | | | |
| ☐ 46 Richmond Webb | .75 | .30 | .07 |
| Miami Dolphins | | | |
| ☐ 47 Cris Carter | 1.00 | .40 | .10 |
| Minnesota Vikings | | | |
| ☐ 48 Marv Cook | .50 | .20 | .05 |
| New England Patriots | | | |
| ☐ 49 Vaughan Johnson | .50 | .20 | .05 |
| New Orleans Saints | | | |
| ☐ 50 Pepper Johnson | .50 | .20 | .05 |
| New York Giants | | | |
| ☐ 51 Kyle Clifton | .50 | .20 | .05 |
| New York Jets | | | |
| ☐ 52 Fred Barnett | 1.25 | .50 | .12 |
| Philadelphia Eagles | | | |
| ☐ 53 Ken Harvey | .75 | .30 | .07 |
| Phoenix Cardinals | | | |
| ☐ 54 Rod Woodson | 1.00 | .40 | .10 |
| Pittsburgh Steelers | | | |
| ☐ 55 Stay in Tune | .50 | .20 | .05 |
| Scorecard | | | |
| ☐ 56 Marion Butts | .75 | .30 | .07 |
| San Diego Chargers | | | |
| ☐ 57 Ricky Watters | 1.50 | .60 | .15 |
| San Francisco 49ers | | | |
| ☐ 58 Brian Blades | .75 | .30 | .07 |
| Seattle Seahawks | | | |
| ☐ 59 Broderick Thomas | .75 | .30 | .07 |
| Tampa Bay Buccaneers | | | |
| ☐ 60 Charles Mann | .50 | .20 | .05 |
| Washington Redskins | | | |
| ☐ 61 Chris Hinton | .50 | .20 | .05 |
| Atlanta Falcons | | | |
| ☐ 62 Cornelius Bennett | .75 | .30 | .07 |
| Buffalo Bills | | | |
| ☐ 63 Jim Harbaugh | 1.00 | .40 | .10 |
| Chicago Bears | | | |
| ☐ 64 Tim Krumrie | .50 | .20 | .05 |
| Cincinnati Bengals | | | |
| ☐ 65 Bernie Kosar | 1.25 | .50 | .12 |
| Cleveland Browns | | | |
| ☐ 66 Troy Aikman | 7.50 | 3.00 | .75 |
| Dallas Cowboys | | | |
| ☐ 67 Shannon Sharpe | 1.25 | .50 | .12 |
| Denver Broncos | | | |
| ☐ 68 Chris Spielman | .50 | .20 | .05 |
| Detroit Lions | | | |
| ☐ 69 Brian Noble | .50 | .20 | .05 |
| Green Bay Packers | | | |
| ☐ 70 Curtis Duncan | .50 | .20 | .05 |
| Houston Oilers | | | |
| ☐ 71 Quentin Coryatt | .75 | .30 | .07 |
| Indianapolis Colts | | | |
| ☐ 72 Derrick Thomas | 1.50 | .60 | .15 |
| Kansas City Chiefs | | | |
| ☐ 73 Stay off Drugs | .50 | .20 | .05 |
| Scorecard | | | |
| ☐ 74 Tim Brown | 1.50 | .60 | .15 |
| Los Angeles Raiders | | | |
| ☐ 75 Jackie Slater | .50 | .20 | .05 |
| Los Angeles Rams | | | |
| ☐ 76 Keith Jackson | 1.25 | .50 | .12 |
| Miami Dolphins | | | |
| ☐ 77 Terry Allen | 1.50 | .60 | .15 |
| Minnesota Vikings | | | |
| ☐ 78 Andre Tippett | .75 | .30 | .07 |
| New England Patriots | | | |
| ☐ 79 Morten Andersen | .60 | .24 | .06 |
| New Orleans Saints | | | |
| ☐ 80 Phil Simms | 1.25 | .50 | .12 |
| New York Giants | | | |
| ☐ 81 Jeff Lageman | .50 | .20 | .05 |
| New York Jets | | | |
| ☐ 82 Randall Cunningham | 1.50 | .60 | .15 |
| Philadelphia Eagles | | | |
| ☐ 83 Randal Hill | 1.00 | .40 | .10 |
| Phoenix Cardinals | | | |
| ☐ 84 Neil O'Donnell | 1.50 | .60 | .15 |
| Pittsburgh Steelers | | | |
| ☐ 85 Gill Byrd | .50 | .20 | .05 |
| San Diego Chargers | | | |
| ☐ 86 John Taylor | .75 | .30 | .07 |
| San Francisco 49ers | | | |
| ☐ 87 Eugene Robinson | .50 | .20 | .05 |
| Seattle Seahawks | | | |
| ☐ 88 Paul Gruber | .50 | .20 | .05 |
| Tampa Bay Buccaneers | | | |
| ☐ 89 Andre Collins | .50 | .20 | .05 |
| Washington Redskins | | | |
| ☐ 90 Chris Miller | 1.00 | .40 | .10 |
| Atlanta Falcons | | | |
| ☐ 91 Stay True to Yourself | .50 | .20 | .05 |
| Scorecard | | | |
| ☐ 92 Andre Reed | .75 | .30 | .07 |
| Buffalo Bills | | | |
| ☐ 93 Richard Dent | .75 | .30 | .07 |
| Chicago Bears | | | |
| ☐ 94 David Klingler | 1.00 | .40 | .10 |
| Cincinnati Bengals | | | |
| ☐ 95 Jay Novacek | .75 | .30 | .07 |
| Dallas Cowboys | | | |
| ☐ 96 Steve Atwater | .50 | .20 | .05 |
| Denver Broncos | | | |
| ☐ 97 Bennie Blades | .50 | .20 | .05 |
| Detroit Lions | | | |
| ☐ 98 Terrell Buckley | .75 | .30 | .07 |
| Green Bay Packers | | | |
| ☐ 99 Ray Childress | .50 | .20 | .05 |
| Houston Oilers | | | |
| ☐ 100 Harvey Williams | 1.00 | .40 | .10 |
| Kansas City Chiefs | | | |
| ☐ 101 Howie Long | .75 | .30 | .07 |
| Los Angeles Raiders | | | |
| ☐ 102 Lawrence Taylor | 1.50 | .60 | .15 |
| New York Giants | | | |
| ☐ 103 Johnny Mitchell | 1.00 | .40 | .10 |
| New York Jets | | | |
| ☐ 104 Carnell Lake | .50 | .20 | .05 |
| Pittsburgh Steelers | | | |
| ☐ 105 Junior Seau | 1.25 | .50 | .12 |
| San Diego Chargers | | | |
| ☐ 106 Kevin Fagan | .50 | .20 | .05 |
| San Francisco 49ers | | | |
| ☐ 107 Lawrence Dawsey | .75 | .30 | .07 |
| Tampa Bay Buccaneers | | | |
| ☐ 108 Art Monk | 1.25 | .50 | .12 |
| Washington Redskins | | | |

## 1978 Falcons Kinnett Dairies

These six blank-backed white panels measure approximately 4 1/4" by 6" and feature four black-and-white player headshots per panel, all framed by a thin red line. A narrow strip running across the center of the panel contains the sponsor name, the words "Atlanta Player Cards," and the NFLPA logo. The cards are unnumbered and checklisted below in the alphabetical order of the players shown in the upper left corners.

|  | NRMT | VG-E | GOOD |
|---|---|---|---|
| COMPLETE SET (6) | 25.00 | 10.00 | 2.50 |
| COMMON PANEL (1-6) | 3.50 | 1.40 | .35 |
| ☐ 1 William Andrews | 5.00 | 2.00 | .50 |
| Jeff Yeates | | | |
| Wilson Faumuina | | | |
| Phil McKinnely | | | |
| ☐ 2 Warren Bryant | 7.50 | 3.00 | .75 |
| R.C. Thieleman | | | |
| Steve Bartkowski | | | |
| Frank Reed | | | |
| ☐ 3 Wallace Francis | 5.00 | 2.00 | .50 |
| Jim Mitchell | | | |
| Jeff Van Note | | | |
| Ray Easterling | | | |
| ☐ 4 Dewey McClain | 3.50 | 1.40 | .35 |
| Billy Ryckman | | | |
| Paul Ryczek | | | |
| Bubba Bean | | | |
| ☐ 5 Robert Pennywell | 3.50 | 1.40 | .35 |
| Dave Scott | | | |
| Jim Bailey | | | |
| John James | | | |
| ☐ 6 Haskel Stanback | 3.50 | 1.40 | .35 |
| Rick Byas | | | |
| Mike Esposito | | | |
| Tom Moriarty | | | |

## 1993 FCA Super Bowl

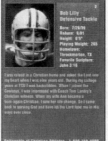

This six-card set measures the standard size (2 1/2" by 3 1/2") and features color player photos on a gradated blue background. The pictures are bordered on three sides by a thin hot pink line. The left side is bordered by a gradated blue border that also runs across the the bottom creating a double hot pink and blue bottom border. At the upper left of the picture is the FCA (Fellowship of Christian Athletes) emblem. The player's name appears in the bottom border, while his position is printed in the bottom margin. A hot pink stripe on the left edge contains the words "Professional Football." The backs are blue and display a color close-up photo, biographical information (including favorite scripture), and the player's testimony in yellow print. The cards are numbered on the back.

|  | MINT | EXC | G-VG |
|---|---|---|---|
| COMPLETE SET (6) | 5.00 | 2.00 | .50 |
| COMMON PLAYER (1-5) | 1.00 | .40 | .10 |
| ☐ 1 Alfred Anderson | 1.00 | .40 | .10 |
| Minnesota Vikings | | | |
| ☐ 2 Bob Lilly | 2.50 | 1.00 | .25 |
| Dallas Cowboys | | | |
| ☐ 3 Tom Landry CO | 2.00 | .80 | .20 |
| Dallas Cowboys | | | |
| ☐ 4 Brent Jones | 1.50 | .60 | .15 |
| San Francisco 49ers | | | |
| ☐ 5 Bruce Matthews | 1.00 | .40 | .10 |
| Houston Oilers | | | |
| ☐ 6 Title Card | 1.00 | .40 | .10 |

## 1960 Fleer

The 1960 Fleer set of 132 cards was Fleer's first venture into football card production. The cards measure the standard 2 1/2" by 3 1/2". This set features players of the American Football League's debut season. Several well-known coaches are featured in the set; the set is the last regular issue set to feature coaches (on their own speciufic card) until the 1989 Pro Set release. The card backs are printed in red and black. The key card in the set is Jack Kemp's Rookie Card. Other Rookie Cards include Sid Gillman and Ron Mix. The cards are frequently found off-centered as Fleer's first effort into the football card market left much to be desired in the area of quality control.

|  | NRMT | VG-E | GOOD |
|---|---|---|---|
| COMPLETE SET (132) | 750.00 | 350.00 | 95.00 |
| COMMON PLAYER (1-132) | 3.00 | 1.35 | .40 |
| ☐ 1 Harvey White | 20.00 | 4.00 | 1.20 |
| Boston Patriots | | | |
| ☐ 2 Tom"Corky" Tharp | 3.00 | 1.35 | .40 |
| New York Titans | | | |
| ☐ 3 Dan McGrew | 3.00 | 1.35 | .40 |
| Buffalo Bills | | | |
| ☐ 4 Bob White | 3.50 | 1.55 | .45 |
| Houston Oilers | | | |
| ☐ 5 Dick Jamieson | 3.00 | 1.35 | .40 |
| Dallas Texans | | | |
| ☐ 6 Sam Salerno | 3.00 | 1.35 | .40 |
| Denver Broncos | | | |
| ☐ 7 Sid Gillman CO | 15.00 | 6.75 | 1.90 |
| Los Angeles Chargers | | | |
| ☐ 8 Ben Preston | 3.00 | 1.35 | .40 |
| Los Angeles Chargers | | | |
| ☐ 9 George Blanch | 3.00 | 1.35 | .40 |
| Oakland Raiders | | | |
| ☐ 10 Bob Stransky | 3.00 | 1.35 | .40 |
| Denver Broncos | | | |
| ☐ 11 Fran Curci | 3.50 | 1.55 | .45 |
| Dallas Texans | | | |
| ☐ 12 George Shirkey | 3.00 | 1.35 | .40 |
| Houston Oilers | | | |
| ☐ 13 Paul Larson | 3.00 | 1.35 | .40 |
| Oakland Raiders | | | |
| ☐ 14 John Stolte | 3.00 | 1.35 | .40 |
| Los Angeles Chargers | | | |
| ☐ 15 Serafino(Foge) Fazio | 3.50 | 1.55 | .45 |
| Boston Patriots | | | |
| ☐ 16 Tom Dimitroff | 3.00 | 1.35 | .40 |
| Boston Patriots | | | |
| ☐ 17 Elbert Dubenion | 7.00 | 3.10 | .85 |
| Buffalo Bills | | | |
| ☐ 18 Hogan Wharton | 3.00 | 1.35 | .40 |
| Houston Oilers | | | |
| ☐ 19 Tom O'Connell | 3.00 | 1.35 | .40 |
| Buffalo Bills | | | |
| ☐ 20 Sammy Baugh CO | 32.00 | 14.50 | 4.00 |
| New York Titans | | | |
| ☐ 21 Tony Sardisco | 3.00 | 1.35 | .40 |
| Boston Patriots | | | |
| ☐ 22 Alan Cann | 3.00 | 1.35 | .40 |

| | | | | | | | |
|---|---|---|---|---|---|---|---|
| Boston Patriots | | | | Houston Oilers | | | |
| ☐ 23 Mike Hudock | 3.00 | 1.35 | .40 | ☐ 71 Gerhard Schwedes | 3.00 | 1.35 | .40 |
| New York Titans | | | | Boston Patriots | | | |
| ☐ 24 Bill Atkins | 3.00 | 1.35 | .40 | ☐ 72 Thurlow Cooper | 3.00 | 1.35 | .40 |
| Buffalo Bills | | | | New York Titans | | | |
| ☐ 25 Charlie Jackson | 3.00 | 1.35 | .40 | ☐ 73 Abner Haynes | 15.00 | 6.75 | 1.90 |
| Dallas Texans | | | | Dallas Texans | | | |
| ☐ 26 Frank Tripucka | 4.00 | 1.80 | .50 | ☐ 74 Billy Shoemake | 3.00 | 1.35 | .40 |
| Denver Broncos | | | | Denver Broncos | | | |
| ☐ 27 Tony Teresa | 3.00 | 1.35 | .40 | ☐ 75 Marv Lasater | 3.00 | 1.35 | .40 |
| Oakland Raiders | | | | Oakland Raiders | | | |
| ☐ 28 Joe Amstutz | 3.00 | 1.35 | .40 | ☐ 76 Paul Lowe | 15.00 | 6.75 | 1.90 |
| Oakland Raiders | | | | Los Angeles Chargers | | | |
| ☐ 29 Bob Fee | 3.00 | 1.35 | .40 | ☐ 77 Bruce Hartman | 3.00 | 1.35 | .40 |
| Boston Patriots | | | | Boston Patriots | | | |
| ☐ 30 Jim Baldwin | 3.00 | 1.35 | .40 | ☐ 78 Blanche Martin | 3.00 | 1.35 | .40 |
| New York Titans | | | | New York Titans | | | |
| ☐ 31 Jim Yates | 3.00 | 1.35 | .40 | ☐ 79 Gene Grabosky | 3.00 | 1.35 | .40 |
| Houston Oilers | | | | Buffalo Bills | | | |
| ☐ 32 Don Flynn | 3.00 | 1.35 | .40 | ☐ 80 Lou Rymkus CO | 3.00 | 1.35 | .40 |
| Dallas Texans | | | | Houston Oilers | | | |
| ☐ 33 Ken Adamson | 3.00 | 1.35 | .40 | ☐ 81 Chris Burford | 5.00 | 2.30 | .60 |
| Denver Broncos | | | | Dallas Texans | | | |
| ☐ 34 Ron Drzewiecki | 3.00 | 1.35 | .40 | ☐ 82 Don Allen | 3.00 | 1.35 | .40 |
| Oakland Raiders | | | | Denver Broncos | | | |
| ☐ 35 J.W. Slack | 3.00 | 1.35 | .40 | ☐ 83 Bob Nelson | 3.00 | 1.35 | .40 |
| Los Angeles Chargers | | | | Oakland Raiders | | | |
| ☐ 36 Bob Yates | 3.00 | 1.35 | .40 | ☐ 84 Jim Woodard | 3.00 | 1.35 | .40 |
| Boston Patriots | | | | Oakland Raiders | | | |
| ☐ 37 Gary Cobb | 3.00 | 1.35 | .40 | ☐ 85 Tom Rychlec | 3.00 | 1.35 | .40 |
| Buffalo Bills | | | | Buffalo Bills | | | |
| ☐ 38 Jacky Lee | 4.00 | 1.80 | .50 | ☐ 86 Bob Cox | 3.00 | 1.35 | .40 |
| Houston Oilers | | | | Boston Patriots | | | |
| ☐ 39 Jack Spikes | 3.50 | 1.55 | .45 | ☐ 87 Jerry Cornelison | 3.00 | 1.35 | .40 |
| Dallas Texans | | | | Dallas Texans | | | |
| ☐ 40 Jim Padgett | 3.00 | 1.35 | .40 | ☐ 88 Jack Work | 3.00 | 1.35 | .40 |
| Denver Broncos | | | | Denver Broncos | | | |
| ☐ 41 Jack Larsheid | 3.00 | 1.35 | .40 | ☐ 89 Sam DeLuca | 3.00 | 1.35 | .40 |
| Oakland Raiders | | | | Los Angeles Chargers | | | |
| ☐ 42 Bob Reifsnyder | 3.00 | 1.35 | .40 | ☐ 90 Rommie Loudd | 3.00 | 1.35 | .40 |
| Los Angeles Chargers | | | | Los Angeles Chargers | | | |
| ☐ 43 Fran Rogel | 3.00 | 1.35 | .40 | ☐ 91 Teddy Edmondson | 3.00 | 1.35 | .40 |
| New York Titans | | | | New York Titans | | | |
| ☐ 44 Ray Moss | 3.00 | 1.35 | .40 | ☐ 92 Buster Ramsey CO | 3.50 | 1.55 | .45 |
| Buffalo Bills | | | | Buffalo Bills | | | |
| ☐ 45 Tony Banfield | 3.00 | 1.35 | .40 | ☐ 93 Doug Asad | 3.00 | 1.35 | .40 |
| Houston Oilers | | | | Houston Oilers | | | |
| ☐ 46 George Herring | 3.00 | 1.35 | .40 | ☐ 94 Jimmy Harris | 3.00 | 1.35 | .40 |
| Denver Broncos | | | | Dallas Texans | | | |
| ☐ 47 Willie Smith | 3.00 | 1.35 | .40 | ☐ 95 Larry Cundiff | 3.00 | 1.35 | .40 |
| Denver Broncos | | | | Denver Broncos | | | |
| ☐ 48 Buddy Allen | 3.00 | 1.35 | .40 | ☐ 96 Richie Lucas | 3.50 | 1.55 | .45 |
| Oakland Raiders | | | | Buffalo Bills | | | |
| ☐ 49 Bill Brown | 3.00 | 1.35 | .40 | ☐ 97 Don Norwood | 3.00 | 1.35 | .40 |
| Boston Patriots | | | | Boston Patriots | | | |
| ☐ 50 Ken Ford | 3.00 | 1.35 | .40 | ☐ 98 Larry Grantham | 4.00 | 1.80 | .50 |
| New York Titans | | | | New York Titans | | | |
| ☐ 51 Billy Kinard | 3.00 | 1.35 | .40 | ☐ 99 Bill Mathis | 4.00 | 1.80 | .50 |
| Buffalo Bills | | | | Houston Oilers | | | |
| ☐ 52 Buddy Mayfield | 3.00 | 1.35 | .40 | ☐ 100 Mel Branch | 4.00 | 1.80 | .50 |
| Houston Oilers | | | | Dallas Texans | | | |
| ☐ 53 Bill Krisher | 3.50 | 1.55 | .45 | ☐ 101 Marvin Terrell | 3.00 | 1.35 | .40 |
| Dallas Texans | | | | Dallas Texans | | | |
| ☐ 54 Frank Bernardi | 3.00 | 1.35 | .40 | ☐ 102 Charlie Flowers | 3.50 | 1.55 | .45 |
| Denver Broncos | | | | Los Angeles Chargers | | | |
| ☐ 55 Lou Saban CO | 3.50 | 1.55 | .45 | ☐ 103 John McMullan | 3.00 | 1.35 | .40 |
| Boston Patriots | | | | New York Titans | | | |
| ☐ 56 Gene Cockrell | 3.00 | 1.35 | .40 | ☐ 104 Charlie Kaaihue | 3.00 | 1.35 | .40 |
| New York Titans | | | | Oakland Raiders | | | |
| ☐ 57 Sam Sanders | 3.00 | 1.35 | .40 | ☐ 105 Joe Schaffer | 3.00 | 1.35 | .40 |
| Buffalo Bills | | | | Buffalo Bills | | | |
| ☐ 58 George Blanda | 40.00 | 18.00 | 5.00 | ☐ 106 Al Day | 3.00 | 1.35 | .40 |
| Houston Oilers | | | | Denver Broncos | | | |
| ☐ 59 Sherrill Headrick | 5.00 | 2.30 | .60 | ☐ 107 Johnny Carson | 3.00 | 1.35 | .40 |
| Dallas Texans | | | | Houston Oilers | | | |
| ☐ 60 Carl Larpenter | 3.00 | 1.35 | .40 | ☐ 108 Alan Goldstein | 3.00 | 1.35 | .40 |
| Denver Broncos | | | | Oakland Raiders | | | |
| ☐ 61 Gene Prebola | 3.00 | 1.35 | .40 | ☐ 109 Doug Cline | 3.00 | 1.35 | .40 |
| Oakland Raiders | | | | Houston Oilers | | | |
| ☐ 62 Dick Chorovich | 3.00 | 1.35 | .40 | ☐ 110 Al Carmichael | 3.00 | 1.35 | .40 |
| Los Angeles Chargers | | | | Denver Broncos | | | |
| ☐ 63 Bob McNamara | 3.00 | 1.35 | .40 | ☐ 111 Bob Dee | 3.00 | 1.35 | .40 |
| Boston Patriots | | | | Boston Patriots | | | |
| ☐ 64 Tom Saidock | 3.00 | 1.35 | .40 | ☐ 112 John Bredice | 3.00 | 1.35 | .40 |
| New York Titans | | | | New York Titans | | | |
| ☐ 65 Willie Evans | 3.00 | 1.35 | .40 | ☐ 113 Don Floyd | 3.50 | 1.55 | .45 |
| Buffalo Bills | | | | Houston Oilers | | | |
| ☐ 66 Billy Cannon UER | 15.00 | 6.75 | 1.90 | ☐ 114 Ronnie Cain | 3.00 | 1.35 | .40 |
| Houston Oilers | | | | Denver Broncos | | | |
| (Hometown: Istruma, | | | | ☐ 115 Stan Flowers | 3.00 | 1.35 | .40 |
| should be Istrouma) | | | | Boston Patriots | | | |
| ☐ 67 Sam McCord | 3.00 | 1.35 | .40 | ☐ 116 Hank Stram CO | 20.00 | 9.00 | 2.50 |
| Oakland Raiders | | | | Dallas Texans | | | |
| ☐ 68 Mike Simmons | 3.00 | 1.35 | .40 | ☐ 117 Bob Dougherty | 3.00 | 1.35 | .40 |
| New York Titans | | | | Oakland Raiders | | | |
| ☐ 69 Jim Swink | 3.50 | 1.55 | .45 | ☐ 118 Ron Mix | 35.00 | 16.00 | 4.40 |
| Dallas Texans | | | | Los Angeles Chargers | | | |
| ☐ 70 Don Hitt | 3.00 | 1.35 | .40 | ☐ 119 Roger Ellis | 3.00 | 1.35 | .40 |

| | NRMT | VG-E | GOOD |
|---|---|---|---|
| New York Titans | | | |
| ☐ 120 Elvin Caldwell | 3.00 | 1.35 | .40 |
| Boston Patriots | | | |
| ☐ 121 Bill Kimber | 3.00 | 1.35 | .40 |
| Los Angeles Chargers | | | |
| ☐ 122 Jim Matheny | 3.00 | 1.35 | .40 |
| Houston Oilers | | | |
| ☐ 123 Curley Johnson | 3.50 | 1.55 | .45 |
| Dallas Texans | | | |
| ☐ 124 Jack Kemp | 450.00 | 200.00 | 57.50 |
| Los Angeles Chargers | | | |
| ☐ 125 Ed Denk | 3.00 | 1.35 | .40 |
| Boston Patriots | | | |
| ☐ 126 Jerry McFarland | 3.00 | 1.35 | .40 |
| New York Titans | | | |
| ☐ 127 Dan Lanphear | 3.00 | 1.35 | .40 |
| Houston Oilers | | | |
| ☐ 128 Paul Maguire | 15.00 | 6.75 | 1.90 |
| Los Angeles Chargers | | | |
| ☐ 129 Ray Collins | 3.00 | 1.35 | .40 |
| Dallas Texans | | | |
| ☐ 130 Ron Burton | 5.00 | 2.30 | .60 |
| Boston Patriots | | | |
| ☐ 131 Eddie Erdelatz CO | 3.50 | 1.55 | .45 |
| Oakland Raiders | | | |
| ☐ 132 Ron Beagle | 15.00 | 3.00 | .90 |
| Oakland Raiders | | | |

## 1960 Fleer AFL Team Decals

This set of nine logo decals was inserted with the 1960 Fleer regular issue inaugural AFL football set. These inserts measure approximately 2 1/4" by 3" and one decal was to be inserted in each wax pack. The decals are unnumbered and are ordered below alphabetically by team name for convenience. There is one decal for each of the eight AFL teams as well as a decal with the league logo. The backs of the decal backing contained instructions on the proper application of the decal.

| | NRMT | VG-E | GOOD |
|---|---|---|---|
| COMPLETE SET (9) | 125.00 | 50.00 | 12.50 |
| COMMON PLAYER (1-9) | 12.00 | 5.00 | 1.20 |
| | | | |
| ☐ 1 AFL Logo | 20.00 | 8.00 | 2.00 |
| ☐ 2 Boston Patriots | 12.00 | 5.00 | 1.20 |
| ☐ 3 Buffalo Bills | 15.00 | 6.00 | 1.50 |
| ☐ 4 Dallas Texans | 20.00 | 8.00 | 2.00 |
| ☐ 5 Denver Broncos | 15.00 | 6.00 | 1.50 |
| ☐ 6 Houston Oilers | 12.00 | 5.00 | 1.20 |
| ☐ 7 Los Angeles Chargers | 15.00 | 6.00 | 1.50 |
| ☐ 8 New York Titans | 15.00 | 6.00 | 1.50 |
| ☐ 9 Oakland Raiders | 25.00 | 10.00 | 2.50 |

## 1960 Fleer College Pennant Decals

This set of 19 pennant decal pairs was distributed as an insert with the 1960 Fleer regular issue inaugural AFL football set along with and at the same time as the AFL Team Decals described immediately above. Some dealers feel that these college decals are tougher to find than the AFL team decals. These inserts were approximately 2 1/4" by 3" and one decal was to be inserted in each wax pack. The decals are unnumbered and are ordered below alphabetically according to the lower alphabetically of each college pair. The backs of the decal backing contained instructions on the proper application of the decal printed in very light blue.

| | NRMT | VG-E | GOOD |
|---|---|---|---|
| COMPLETE SET (19) | 125.00 | 50.00 | 12.50 |
| COMMON PLAYER (1-19) | 7.00 | 2.80 | .70 |
| | | | |
| ☐ 1 Alabama/Yale | 10.00 | 4.00 | 1.00 |
| ☐ 2 Army/Mississippi | 8.00 | 3.25 | .80 |
| ☐ 3 California/Indiana | 8.00 | 3.25 | .80 |
| ☐ 4 Duke/Notre Dame | 15.00 | 6.00 | 1.50 |
| ☐ 5 Florida St./Kentucky | 8.00 | 3.25 | .80 |
| ☐ 6 Georgia/Oklahoma | 12.00 | 5.00 | 1.20 |
| ☐ 7 Houston/Iowa | 8.00 | 3.25 | .80 |
| ☐ 8 Idaho St./Penn | 7.00 | 2.80 | .70 |
| ☐ 9 Iowa St./Penn State | 7.00 | 2.80 | .70 |
| ☐ 10 Kansas/UCLA | 8.00 | 3.25 | .80 |
| ☐ 11 Marquette/New Mexico | 7.00 | 2.80 | .70 |
| ☐ 12 Maryland/Missouri | 8.00 | 3.25 | .80 |
| ☐ 13 Miss.South./N.Carolina | 7.00 | 2.80 | .70 |
| ☐ 14 Navy/Stanford | 9.00 | 3.75 | .90 |
| ☐ 15 Nebraska/Purdue | 9.00 | 3.75 | .90 |
| ☐ 16 Pittsburgh/Utah | 7.00 | 2.80 | .70 |
| ☐ 17 SMU/West Virginia | 7.00 | 2.80 | .70 |
| ☐ 18 So.Carolina/USC | 7.00 | 2.80 | .70 |
| ☐ 19 Wake Forest/Wisconsin | 7.00 | 2.80 | .70 |

## 1961 Fleer

The 1961 Fleer football set contains 220 cards. The cards measure 2 1/2" by 3 1/2". Most of the players are pictured in action with a background. The set contains NFL (1-132) and AFL (133-220) players. The cards are grouped alphabetically by team nicknames within league, e.g., Chicago Bears (1-9), Cleveland Browns (10-19), St. Louis Cardinals (20-29), Baltimore Colts (30-39), Dallas Cowboys (40-48), Philadelphia Eagles (49-58), San Francisco 49ers (59-67), New York Giants (68-77), Detroit Lions (78-87), Green Bay Packers (88-97), Los Angeles Rams (98-107), Washington Redskins (108-116), Pittsburgh Steelers (117-125), Minnesota Vikings (126-132), Buffalo Bills (133-143), Denver Broncos (144-154), Los Angeles Chargers (155-165), Houston Oilers (166-176), Boston Patriots (177-187), Oakland Raiders (188-198), Dallas Texans (199-209), and New York Titans (210-220). The backs are printed in black and lime green on a white card stock. The key Rookie Cards in this set are John Brodie, Don Maynard, Don Meredith, and Jim Otto.

| | NRMT | VG-E | GOOD |
|---|---|---|---|
| COMPLETE SET (220) | 1550.00 | 700.00 | 190.00 |
| COMMON PLAYER (1-132) | 3.50 | 1.55 | .45 |
| COMMON PLAYER (133-220) | 5.50 | 2.50 | .70 |
| | | | |
| ☐ 1 Ed Brown | 10.00 | 2.00 | .60 |
| ☐ 2 Rick Casares | 3.75 | 1.70 | .45 |
| ☐ 3 Willie Galimore | 3.75 | 1.70 | .45 |
| ☐ 4 Jim Dooley | 3.75 | 1.70 | .45 |
| ☐ 5 Harlon Hill | 3.75 | 1.70 | .45 |
| ☐ 6 Stan Jones | 5.00 | 2.30 | .60 |
| ☐ 7 J.C. Caroline | 3.50 | 1.55 | .45 |
| ☐ 8 Joe Fortunato | 3.75 | 1.70 | .45 |
| ☐ 9 Doug Atkins | 6.00 | 2.70 | .75 |
| ☐ 10 Milt Plum | 3.75 | 1.70 | .45 |
| ☐ 11 Jim Brown | 125.00 | 57.50 | 15.50 |
| ☐ 12 Bobby Mitchell | 8.00 | 3.60 | 1.00 |

|  |  | | | |
|---|--------|------|------|------|
| ☐ 13 | Ray Renfro | 3.75 | 1.70 | .45 |
| ☐ 14 | Gern Nagler | 3.50 | 1.55 | .45 |
| ☐ 15 | Jim Shofner | 3.75 | 1.70 | .45 |
| ☐ 16 | Vince Costello | 3.50 | 1.55 | .45 |
| ☐ 17 | Galen Fiss | 3.50 | 1.55 | .45 |
| ☐ 18 | Walt Michaels | 3.75 | 1.70 | .45 |
| ☐ 19 | Bob Gain | 3.50 | 1.55 | .45 |
| ☐ 20 | Mal Hammack | 3.50 | 1.55 | .45 |
| ☐ 21 | Frank Mestnick | 3.50 | 1.55 | .45 |
| ☐ 22 | Bobby Joe Conrad | 3.75 | 1.70 | .45 |
| ☐ 23 | John David Crow | 4.00 | 1.80 | .50 |
| ☐ 24 | Sonny Randle | 4.00 | 1.80 | .50 |
| ☐ 25 | Don Gillis | 3.50 | 1.55 | .45 |
| ☐ 26 | Jerry Norton | 3.50 | 1.55 | .45 |
| ☐ 27 | Bill Stacy | 3.50 | 1.55 | .45 |
| ☐ 28 | Leo Sugar | 3.50 | 1.55 | .45 |
| ☐ 29 | Frank Fuller | 3.50 | 1.55 | .45 |
| ☐ 30 | John Unitas | 75.00 | 34.00 | 9.50 |
| ☐ 31 | Alan Ameche | 4.50 | 2.00 | .55 |
| ☐ 32 | Lenny Moore | 9.00 | 4.00 | 1.15 |
| ☐ 33 | Raymond Berry | 10.00 | 4.50 | 1.25 |
| ☐ 34 | Jim Mutscheller | 3.50 | 1.55 | .45 |
| ☐ 35 | Jim Parker | 6.00 | 2.70 | .75 |
| ☐ 36 | Bill Pellington | 3.50 | 1.55 | .45 |
| ☐ 37 | Gino Marchetti | 6.00 | 2.70 | .75 |
| ☐ 38 | Gene Lipscomb | 4.00 | 1.80 | .50 |
| ☐ 39 | Art Donovan | 6.00 | 2.70 | .75 |
| ☐ 40 | Eddie LeBaron | 4.00 | 1.80 | .50 |
| ☐ 41 | Don Meredith | 160.00 | 70.00 | 20.00 |
| ☐ 42 | Don McIlhenny | 3.75 | 1.70 | .45 |
| ☐ 43 | L.G. Dupre | 3.75 | 1.70 | .45 |
| ☐ 44 | Fred Dugan | 3.50 | 1.55 | .45 |
| ☐ 45 | Bill Howton | 3.75 | 1.70 | .45 |
| ☐ 46 | Duane Putnam | 3.50 | 1.55 | .45 |
| ☐ 47 | Gene Cronin | 3.50 | 1.55 | .45 |
| ☐ 48 | Jerry Tubbs | 3.75 | 1.70 | .45 |
| ☐ 49 | Clarence Peaks | 3.50 | 1.55 | .45 |
| ☐ 50 | Ted Dean | 4.00 | 1.80 | .50 |
| ☐ 51 | Tommy McDonald | 3.75 | 1.70 | .45 |
| ☐ 52 | Bill Barnes | 3.50 | 1.55 | .45 |
| ☐ 53 | Pete Retzlaff | 3.75 | 1.70 | .45 |
| ☐ 54 | Bobby Walston | 3.75 | 1.70 | .45 |
| ☐ 55 | Chuck Bednarik | 10.00 | 4.50 | 1.25 |
| ☐ 56 | Maxie Baughan | 5.00 | 2.30 | .60 |
| ☐ 57 | Bob Pellegrini | 3.50 | 1.55 | .45 |
| ☐ 58 | Jesse Richardson | 3.50 | 1.55 | .45 |
| ☐ 59 | John Brodie | 75.00 | 34.00 | 9.50 |
| ☐ 60 | J.D. Smith | 3.75 | 1.70 | .45 |
| ☐ 61 | Ray Norton | 4.00 | 1.80 | .50 |
| ☐ 62 | Monty Stickles | 3.50 | 1.55 | .45 |
| ☐ 63 | Bob St. Clair | 5.00 | 2.30 | .60 |
| ☐ 64 | Dave Baker | 3.50 | 1.55 | .45 |
| ☐ 65 | Abe Woodson | 3.75 | 1.70 | .45 |
| ☐ 66 | Matt Hazeltine | 3.50 | 1.55 | .45 |
| ☐ 67 | Leo Nomellini | 6.00 | 2.70 | .75 |
| ☐ 68 | Charley Conerly | 12.00 | 5.50 | 1.50 |
| ☐ 69 | Kyle Rote | 4.50 | 2.00 | .55 |
| ☐ 70 | Jack Stroud | 3.50 | 1.55 | .45 |
| ☐ 71 | Roosevelt Brown | 5.00 | 2.30 | .60 |
| ☐ 72 | Jim Patton | 3.75 | 1.70 | .45 |
| ☐ 73 | Erich Barnes | 3.75 | 1.70 | .45 |
| ☐ 74 | Sam Huff | 10.00 | 4.50 | 1.25 |
| ☐ 75 | Andy Robustelli | 6.00 | 2.70 | .75 |
| ☐ 76 | Dick Modzelewski | 3.75 | 1.70 | .45 |
| ☐ 77 | Roosevelt Grier | 5.00 | 2.30 | .60 |
| ☐ 78 | Earl Morrall | 5.00 | 2.30 | .60 |
| ☐ 79 | Jim Ninowski | 3.75 | 1.70 | .45 |
| ☐ 80 | Nick Pietrosante | 4.00 | 1.80 | .50 |
| ☐ 81 | Howard Cassady | 3.75 | 1.70 | .45 |
| ☐ 82 | Jim Gibbons | 3.50 | 1.55 | .45 |
| ☐ 83 | Gail Cogdill | 4.00 | 1.80 | .50 |
| ☐ 84 | Dick Lane | 6.00 | 2.70 | .75 |
| ☐ 85 | Yale Lary | 6.00 | 2.70 | .75 |
| ☐ 86 | Joe Schmidt | 6.00 | 2.70 | .75 |
| ☐ 87 | Darris McCord | 3.50 | 1.55 | .45 |
| ☐ 88 | Bart Starr | 50.00 | 23.00 | 6.25 |
| ☐ 89 | Jim Taylor | 32.00 | 14.50 | 4.00 |
| ☐ 90 | Paul Hornung | 40.00 | 18.00 | 5.00 |
| ☐ 91 | Tom Moore | 5.00 | 2.30 | .60 |
| ☐ 92 | Boyd Dowler | 7.50 | 3.40 | .95 |
| ☐ 93 | Max McGee | 4.00 | 1.80 | .50 |
| ☐ 94 | Forrest Gregg | 8.50 | 3.80 | 1.05 |
| ☐ 95 | Jerry Kramer | 7.00 | 3.10 | .85 |
| ☐ 96 | Jim Ringo | 6.00 | 2.70 | .75 |
| ☐ 97 | Bill Forester | 3.75 | 1.70 | .45 |
| ☐ 98 | Frank Ryan | 4.00 | 1.80 | .50 |
| ☐ 99 | Ollie Matson | 9.00 | 4.00 | 1.15 |
| ☐ 100 | Jon Arnett | 3.75 | 1.70 | .45 |
| ☐ 101 | Dick Bass | 4.00 | 1.80 | .50 |
| ☐ 102 | Jim Phillips | 3.75 | 1.70 | .45 |
| ☐ 103 | Del Shofner | 3.75 | 1.70 | .45 |
| ☐ 104 | Art Hunter | 3.50 | 1.55 | .45 |
| ☐ 105 | Lindon Crow | 3.50 | 1.55 | .45 |
| ☐ 106 | Les Richter | 3.75 | 1.70 | .45 |
| ☐ 107 | Lou Michaels | 3.50 | 1.55 | .45 |
| ☐ 108 | Ralph Guglielmi | 3.75 | 1.70 | .45 |
| ☐ 109 | Don Bosseler | 3.50 | 1.55 | .45 |
| ☐ 110 | John Olszewski | 3.50 | 1.55 | .45 |
| ☐ 111 | Bill Anderson | 3.50 | 1.55 | .45 |
| ☐ 112 | Joe Walton | 3.50 | 1.55 | .45 |
| ☐ 113 | Jim Schrader | 3.50 | 1.55 | .45 |
| ☐ 114 | Gary Glick | 3.50 | 1.55 | .45 |
| ☐ 115 | Ralph Felton | 3.50 | 1.55 | .45 |
| ☐ 116 | Bob Toneff | 3.50 | 1.55 | .45 |
| ☐ 117 | Bobby Layne | 24.00 | 11.00 | 3.00 |
| ☐ 118 | John Henry Johnson | 7.00 | 3.10 | .85 |
| ☐ 119 | Tom Tracy | 3.75 | 1.70 | .45 |
| ☐ 120 | Jimmy Orr | 6.00 | 2.70 | .75 |
| ☐ 121 | John Nisby | 3.50 | 1.55 | .45 |
| ☐ 122 | Dean Derby | 3.50 | 1.55 | .45 |
| ☐ 123 | John Reger | 3.50 | 1.55 | .45 |
| ☐ 124 | George Tarasovic | 3.50 | 1.55 | .45 |
| ☐ 125 | Ernie Stautner | 6.00 | 2.70 | .75 |
| ☐ 126 | George Shaw | 3.75 | 1.70 | .45 |
| ☐ 127 | Hugh McElhenny | 9.00 | 4.00 | 1.15 |
| ☐ 128 | Dick Haley | 3.50 | 1.55 | .45 |
| ☐ 129 | Dave Middleton | 3.50 | 1.55 | .45 |
| ☐ 130 | Perry Richards | 3.50 | 1.55 | .45 |
| ☐ 131 | Gene Johnson | 3.50 | 1.55 | .45 |
| ☐ 132 | Don Joyce | 4.00 | 1.80 | .50 |
| ☐ 133 | John(Chuck) Green | 6.00 | 2.70 | .75 |
| ☐ 134 | Wray Carlton | 6.00 | 2.70 | .75 |
| ☐ 135 | Richie Lucas | 6.00 | 2.70 | .75 |
| ☐ 136 | Elbert Dubenion | 6.00 | 2.70 | .75 |
| ☐ 137 | Tom Rychlec | 5.50 | 2.50 | .70 |
| ☐ 138 | Mack Yoho | 5.50 | 2.50 | .70 |
| ☐ 139 | Phil Blazer | 5.50 | 2.50 | .70 |
| ☐ 140 | Dan McGrew | 5.50 | 2.50 | .70 |
| ☐ 141 | Bill Atkins | 5.50 | 2.50 | .70 |
| ☐ 142 | Archie Matsos | 6.00 | 2.70 | .75 |
| ☐ 143 | Gene Grabosky | 5.50 | 2.50 | .70 |
| ☐ 144 | Frank Tripucka | 6.00 | 2.70 | .75 |
| ☐ 145 | Al Carmichael | 5.50 | 2.50 | .70 |
| ☐ 146 | Bob McNamara | 5.50 | 2.50 | .70 |
| ☐ 147 | Lionel Taylor | 12.00 | 5.50 | 1.50 |
| ☐ 148 | Eldon Danenhauer | 6.00 | 2.70 | .75 |
| ☐ 149 | Willie Smith | 5.50 | 2.50 | .70 |
| ☐ 150 | Carl Larpenter | 5.50 | 2.50 | .70 |
| ☐ 151 | Ken Adamson | 5.50 | 2.50 | .70 |
| ☐ 152 | Goose Gonsoulin | 6.00 | 2.70 | .75 |
| ☐ 153 | Joe Young | 5.50 | 2.50 | .70 |
| ☐ 154 | Gordy Holz | 5.50 | 2.50 | .70 |
| ☐ 155 | Jack Kemp | 275.00 | 125.00 | 34.00 |
| ☐ 156 | Charlie Flowers | 5.50 | 2.50 | .70 |
| ☐ 157 | Paul Lowe | 7.00 | 3.10 | .85 |
| ☐ 158 | Don Norton | 5.50 | 2.50 | .70 |
| ☐ 159 | Howard Clark | 5.50 | 2.50 | .70 |
| ☐ 160 | Paul Maguire | 7.00 | 3.10 | .85 |
| ☐ 161 | Ernie Wright | 6.00 | 2.70 | .75 |
| ☐ 162 | Ron Mix | 15.00 | 6.75 | 1.90 |
| ☐ 163 | Fred Cole | 5.50 | 2.50 | .70 |
| ☐ 164 | Jim Sears | 5.50 | 2.50 | .70 |
| ☐ 165 | Volney Peters | 5.50 | 2.50 | .70 |
| ☐ 166 | George Blanda | 40.00 | 18.00 | 5.00 |
| ☐ 167 | Jacky Lee | 6.00 | 2.70 | .75 |
| ☐ 168 | Bob White | 5.50 | 2.50 | .70 |
| ☐ 169 | Doug Cline | 5.50 | 2.50 | .70 |
| ☐ 170 | Dave Smith | 5.50 | 2.50 | .70 |
| ☐ 171 | Billy Cannon | 8.00 | 3.60 | 1.00 |
| ☐ 172 | Bill Groman | 6.00 | 2.70 | .75 |
| ☐ 173 | Al Jamison | 5.50 | 2.50 | .70 |
| ☐ 174 | Jim Norton | 5.50 | 2.50 | .70 |
| ☐ 175 | Dennit Morris | 5.50 | 2.50 | .70 |
| ☐ 176 | Don Floyd | 6.00 | 2.70 | .75 |
| ☐ 177 | Butch Songin | 6.00 | 2.70 | .75 |
| ☐ 178 | Billy Lott | 6.00 | 2.70 | .75 |
| ☐ 179 | Ron Burton | 6.00 | 2.70 | .75 |
| ☐ 180 | Jim Colclough | 5.50 | 2.50 | .70 |
| ☐ 181 | Charley Leo | 5.50 | 2.50 | .70 |
| ☐ 182 | Walt Cudzik | 5.50 | 2.50 | .70 |
| ☐ 183 | Fred Bruney | 5.50 | 2.50 | .70 |
| ☐ 184 | Ross O'Hanley | 5.50 | 2.50 | .70 |
| ☐ 185 | Tony Sardisco | 5.50 | 2.50 | .70 |
| ☐ 186 | Harry Jacobs | 5.50 | 2.50 | .70 |
| ☐ 187 | Bob Dee | 5.50 | 2.50 | .70 |
| ☐ 188 | Tom Flores | 35.00 | 16.00 | 4.40 |
| ☐ 189 | Jack Larsheid | 5.50 | 2.50 | .70 |
| ☐ 190 | Dick Christy | 5.50 | 2.50 | .70 |
| ☐ 191 | Alan Miller | 5.50 | 2.50 | .70 |
| ☐ 192 | Jim Smith | 5.50 | 2.50 | .70 |
| ☐ 193 | Gerald Burch | 5.50 | 2.50 | .70 |
| ☐ 194 | Gene Prebola | 5.50 | 2.50 | .70 |
| ☐ 195 | Alan Goldstein | 5.50 | 2.50 | .70 |
| ☐ 196 | Don Manoukian | 5.50 | 2.50 | .70 |
| ☐ 197 | Jim Otto | 60.00 | 27.00 | 7.50 |
| ☐ 198 | Wayne Crow | 5.50 | 2.50 | .70 |
| ☐ 199 | Cotton Davidson | 6.00 | 2.70 | .75 |
| ☐ 200 | Randy Duncan | 6.00 | 2.70 | .75 |
| ☐ 201 | Jack Spikes | 6.00 | 2.70 | .75 |
| ☐ 202 | Johnny Robinson | 10.00 | 4.50 | 1.25 |
| ☐ 203 | Abner Haynes | 8.00 | 3.60 | 1.00 |
| ☐ 204 | Chris Burford | 6.00 | 2.70 | .75 |
| ☐ 205 | Bill Krisher | 5.50 | 2.50 | .70 |
| ☐ 206 | Marvin Terrell | 5.50 | 2.50 | .70 |

| | NRMT | VG-E | GOOD |
|---|---|---|---|
| ☐ 207 Jimmy Harris | 5.50 | 2.50 | .70 |
| ☐ 208 Mel Branch | 6.00 | 2.70 | .75 |
| ☐ 209 Paul Miller | 5.50 | 2.50 | .70 |
| ☐ 210 Al Dorow | 5.50 | 2.50 | .70 |
| ☐ 211 Dick Jamieson | 5.50 | 2.50 | .70 |
| ☐ 212 Pete Hart | 5.50 | 2.50 | .70 |
| ☐ 213 Bill Shockley | 5.50 | 2.50 | .70 |
| ☐ 214 Dewey Bohling | 5.50 | 2.50 | .70 |
| ☐ 215 Don Maynard | 90.00 | 40.00 | 11.50 |
| ☐ 216 Bob Mischak | 5.50 | 2.50 | .70 |
| ☐ 217 Mike Hudock | 5.50 | 2.50 | .70 |
| ☐ 218 Bob Reifsnyder | 6.00 | 2.70 | .75 |
| ☐ 219 Tom Saidock | 5.50 | 2.50 | .70 |
| ☐ 220 Sid Youngelman | 20.00 | 4.00 | 1.20 |

## 1961 Fleer Magic Message Blue Inserts

This unattractive set contains 40 cards that were inserted in 1961 Fleer football wax packs. The cards are light blue in color and measure approximately 3" by 2 1/8". The fronts feature a question and a crude line drawing. For the answer, the collector is instructed to "Turn card and wet; when dry, wet again." A tag line at the bottom of the front indicates that the cards were printed by Business Service of Long Island, New York. The backs are blank, and the cards are numbered on the front in the lower right corner.

| | NRMT | VG-E | GOOD |
|---|---|---|---|
| COMPLETE SET (40) | 100.00 | 40.00 | 10.00 |
| COMMON PLAYER (1-40) | 3.00 | 1.20 | .30 |
| ☐ 1 When was the first Sugar Bowl game played | 3.00 | 1.20 | .30 |
| ☐ 2 Which school was famous for its Point-A-Minute team | 3.00 | 1.20 | .30 |
| ☐ 3 What famous coach was known as Gloomy Gil | 3.00 | 1.20 | .30 |
| ☐ 4 Which college coach holds the longest record for years coached | 3.00 | 1.20 | .30 |
| ☐ 5 What is meant by two Platoon System | 3.00 | 1.20 | .30 |
| ☐ 6 When was the only Sudden Death playoff in NFL history | 3.00 | 1.20 | .30 |
| ☐ 7 What is a Sudden Death playoff in professional football | 3.00 | 1.20 | .30 |
| ☐ 8 What is the longest field goal kicked in pro football (place kick) | 3.00 | 1.20 | .30 |
| ☐ 9 What famous Colorado All-American now holds a key position in President Kennedy's administration (Whizzer White) | 4.00 | 1.60 | .40 |
| ☐ 10 What Michigan All-American has gained added fame as a radio and television sportscaster (Tom Harmon) | 4.00 | 1.60 | .40 |
| ☐ 11 The North-South game has become an annual classic. Do you know where it was first played | 3.00 | 1.20 | .30 |
| ☐ 12 The Army-Navy game has become an annual classic. Do you know when it was first played | 3.00 | 1.20 | .30 |
| ☐ 13 What slugging major league outfielder was | 4.00 | 1.60 | .40 |
| an All-American back during his college days | | | |
| ☐ 14 What All-Americans were known as Mr. Inside and Mr. Outside (Glenn Davis and Doc Blanchard) | 4.00 | 1.60 | .40 |
| ☐ 15 Which team was called the Thundering Herd | 3.00 | 1.20 | .30 |
| ☐ 16 When was the first championship playoff in the National Football League | 3.00 | 1.20 | .30 |
| ☐ 17 What is the record for field goals dropkicked in a single game | 3.00 | 1.20 | .30 |
| ☐ 18 What is the longest winning streak in college football | 3.00 | 1.20 | .30 |
| ☐ 19 Who was the first collegian gained by draft in the National Football League | 3.00 | 1.20 | .30 |
| ☐ 20 Which team was the first to use the huddle | 3.00 | 1.20 | .30 |
| ☐ 21 Who was the first Intercollegiate Champion | 3.00 | 1.20 | .30 |
| ☐ 22 When was the first broadcast of a football game | 3.00 | 1.20 | .30 |
| ☐ 23 What is the longest field goal (placement kick) on record | 3.00 | 1.20 | .30 |
| ☐ 24 What is the origin of the tackling dummy | 3.00 | 1.20 | .30 |
| ☐ 25 What player was selected in 1950 as Greatest Player in the half-century (Jim Thorpe) | 4.00 | 1.60 | .40 |
| ☐ 26 What is the record for the most touchdowns in a game | 3.00 | 1.20 | .30 |
| ☐ 27 What player ran the wrong way in a bowl game | 3.00 | 1.20 | .30 |
| ☐ 28 When was the first field goal attempted in college football | 3.00 | 1.20 | .30 |
| ☐ 29 When and by whom was the first All-American team selected | 3.00 | 1.20 | .30 |
| ☐ 30 When was the forward pass first used | 3.00 | 1.20 | .30 |
| ☐ 31 What was the first college to put numbers on player's jerseys | 3.00 | 1.20 | .30 |
| ☐ 32 When was the first professional football game played | 3.00 | 1.20 | .30 |
| ☐ 33 Where is the Football Hall of Fame to be erected (Canton, Ohio) | 3.00 | 1.20 | .30 |
| ☐ 34 Who were the Four Horsemen | 4.00 | 1.60 | .40 |
| ☐ 35 When was the first Rose Bowl game played | 3.00 | 1.20 | .30 |
| ☐ 36 Who holds the record for the most forward passes attempted in a professional game | 3.00 | 1.20 | .30 |
| ☐ 37 Who was known as the Galloping Ghost (Red Grange) | 4.00 | 1.60 | .40 |
| ☐ 38 Has the Rose Bowl always been played in California | 3.00 | 1.20 | .30 |
| ☐ 39 Which team featured the Seven Blocks of Granite (Fordham) | 3.00 | 1.20 | .30 |
| ☐ 40 Where and when was the first football game played in the United States | 3.00 | 1.20 | .30 |

## 1962 Fleer

The 1962 Fleer football set contains 88 cards featuring AFL players only. Card numbering is by team city name order, e.g., Boston Patriots (1-11), Buffalo Bills (12-22), Dallas Texans (23-33), Denver Broncos (34-44), Houston Oilers (45-55), New York Titans (56-66), Oakland

Raiders (67-77), and San Diego Chargers (78-88). The cards measure 2 1/2" by 3 1/2". The card backs are printed in black and blue on a white card stock. Key Rookie Cards in this set are Gino Cappelletti, Ernie Ladd and Fred Williamson.

| | NRMT | VG-E | GOOD |
|---|---|---|---|
| COMPLETE SET (88) | 750.00 | 350.00 | 95.00 |
| COMMON PLAYER (1-88) | 6.00 | 2.70 | .75 |

| | | NRMT | VG-E | GOOD |
|---|---|---|---|---|
| ☐ 1 | Billy Lott | 15.00 | 3.00 | .90 |
| ☐ 2 | Ron Burton | 6.50 | 2.90 | .80 |
| ☐ 3 | Gino Cappelletti | 16.00 | 7.25 | 2.00 |
| ☐ 4 | Babe Parilli | 6.50 | 2.90 | .80 |
| ☐ 5 | Jim Colclough | 6.00 | 2.70 | .75 |
| ☐ 6 | Tony Sardisco | 6.00 | 2.70 | .75 |
| ☐ 7 | Walt Cudzik | 6.00 | 2.70 | .75 |
| ☐ 8 | Bob Dee | 6.00 | 2.70 | .75 |
| ☐ 9 | Tommy Addison | 6.00 | 2.70 | .75 |
| ☐ 10 | Harry Jacobs | 6.00 | 2.70 | .75 |
| ☐ 11 | Ross O'Hanley | 6.00 | 2.70 | .75 |
| ☐ 12 | Art Baker | 6.00 | 2.70 | .75 |
| ☐ 13 | John"Chuck" Green | 6.00 | 2.70 | .75 |
| ☐ 14 | Elbert Dubenion | 6.50 | 2.90 | .80 |
| ☐ 15 | Tom Rychlec | 6.00 | 2.70 | .75 |
| ☐ 16 | Billy Shaw | 8.00 | 3.60 | 1.00 |
| ☐ 17 | Ken Rice | 6.00 | 2.70 | .75 |
| ☐ 18 | Bill Atkins | 6.00 | 2.70 | .75 |
| ☐ 19 | Richie Lucas | 6.50 | 2.90 | .80 |
| ☐ 20 | Archie Matsos | 6.50 | 2.90 | .80 |
| ☐ 21 | Laverne Torczon | 6.00 | 2.70 | .75 |
| ☐ 22 | Warren Rabb | 6.00 | 2.70 | .75 |
| ☐ 23 | Jack Spikes | 6.50 | 2.90 | .80 |
| ☐ 24 | Cotton Davidson | 6.50 | 2.90 | .80 |
| ☐ 25 | Abner Haynes | 9.00 | 4.00 | 1.15 |
| ☐ 26 | Jimmy Saxton | 6.50 | 2.90 | .80 |
| ☐ 27 | Chris Burford | 6.50 | 2.90 | .80 |
| ☐ 28 | Bill Miller | 6.00 | 2.70 | .75 |
| ☐ 29 | Sherrill Headrick | 6.50 | 2.90 | .80 |
| ☐ 30 | E.J. Holub | 9.00 | 4.00 | 1.15 |
| ☐ 31 | Jerry Mays | 9.00 | 4.00 | 1.15 |
| ☐ 32 | Mel Branch | 6.50 | 2.90 | .80 |
| ☐ 33 | Paul Rochester | 6.00 | 2.70 | .75 |
| ☐ 34 | Frank Tripucka | 7.00 | 3.10 | .85 |
| ☐ 35 | Gene Mingo | 6.00 | 2.70 | .75 |
| ☐ 36 | Lionel Taylor | 9.00 | 4.00 | 1.15 |
| ☐ 37 | Ken Adamson | 6.00 | 2.70 | .75 |
| ☐ 38 | Eldon Danenhauer | 6.50 | 2.90 | .80 |
| ☐ 39 | Goose Gonsoulin | 6.50 | 2.90 | .80 |
| ☐ 40 | Gordy Holz | 6.00 | 2.70 | .75 |
| ☐ 41 | Bud McFadin | 6.00 | 2.70 | .75 |
| ☐ 42 | Jim Stinnette | 6.00 | 2.70 | .75 |
| ☐ 43 | Bob Hudson | 6.00 | 2.70 | .75 |
| ☐ 44 | George Herring | 6.00 | 2.70 | .75 |
| ☐ 45 | Charley Tolar | 7.00 | 3.10 | .85 |
| ☐ 46 | George Blanda | 50.00 | 23.00 | 6.25 |
| ☐ 47 | Billy Cannon | 9.00 | 4.00 | 1.15 |
| ☐ 48 | Charlie Hennigan | 15.00 | 6.75 | 1.90 |
| ☐ 49 | Bill Groman | 6.50 | 2.90 | .80 |
| ☐ 50 | Al Jamison | 6.00 | 2.70 | .75 |
| ☐ 51 | Tony Banfield | 6.00 | 2.70 | .75 |
| ☐ 52 | Jim Norton | 6.00 | 2.70 | .75 |
| ☐ 53 | Dennit Morris | 6.00 | 2.70 | .75 |
| ☐ 54 | Don Floyd | 6.00 | 2.70 | .75 |
| ☐ 55 | Ed Husmann UER | 6.00 | 2.70 | .75 |
| | (Misspelled Hussman on both sides) | | | |
| ☐ 56 | Robert Brooks | 6.00 | 2.70 | .75 |
| ☐ 57 | Al Dorow | 6.00 | 2.70 | .75 |
| ☐ 58 | Dick Christy | 6.00 | 2.70 | .75 |
| ☐ 59 | Don Maynard | 35.00 | 16.00 | 4.40 |
| ☐ 60 | Art Powell | 9.00 | 4.00 | 1.15 |
| ☐ 61 | Mike Hudock | 6.00 | 2.70 | .75 |
| ☐ 62 | Bill Mathis | 6.00 | 2.70 | .75 |
| ☐ 63 | Butch Songin | 6.50 | 2.90 | .80 |
| ☐ 64 | Larry Grantham | 6.50 | 2.90 | .80 |
| ☐ 65 | Nick Mumley | 6.00 | 2.70 | .75 |
| ☐ 66 | Tom Saidock | 6.00 | 2.70 | .75 |
| ☐ 67 | Alan Miller | 6.00 | 2.70 | .75 |
| ☐ 68 | Tom Flores | 18.00 | 8.00 | 2.30 |
| ☐ 69 | Bob Coolbaugh | 6.00 | 2.70 | .75 |
| ☐ 70 | George Fleming | 6.00 | 2.70 | .75 |
| ☐ 71 | Wayne Hawkins | 7.00 | 3.10 | .85 |
| ☐ 72 | Jim Otto | 24.00 | 11.00 | 3.00 |
| ☐ 73 | Wayne Crow | 6.00 | 2.70 | .75 |
| ☐ 74 | Fred Williamson | 20.00 | 9.00 | 2.50 |
| ☐ 75 | Tom Louderback | 6.00 | 2.70 | .75 |
| ☐ 76 | Volney Peters | 6.00 | 2.70 | .75 |
| ☐ 77 | Charley Powell | 6.00 | 2.70 | .75 |
| ☐ 78 | Don Norton | 6.00 | 2.70 | .75 |
| ☐ 79 | Jack Kemp | 225.00 | 100.00 | 28.00 |
| ☐ 80 | Paul Lowe | 9.00 | 4.00 | 1.15 |
| ☐ 81 | Dave Kocourek | 6.50 | 2.90 | .80 |
| ☐ 82 | Ron Mix | 12.00 | 5.50 | 1.50 |
| ☐ 83 | Ernie Wright | 6.00 | 2.70 | .75 |
| ☐ 84 | Dick Harris | 6.00 | 2.70 | .75 |
| ☐ 85 | Bill Hudson | 6.00 | 2.70 | .75 |
| ☐ 86 | Ernie Ladd | 28.00 | 12.50 | 3.50 |
| ☐ 87 | Earl Faison | 7.00 | 3.10 | .85 |
| ☐ 88 | Ron Nery | 12.00 | 2.40 | .70 |

# 1963 Fleer

The 1963 Fleer football set of 88 cards features AFL players only. Card numbers follow team order, Boston Patriots (1-11), New York Titans (12-22), Buffalo Bills (23-33), Houston Oilers (34-44), Kansas City Chiefs (45-55), Oakland Raiders (56-66), San Diego Chargers (67-77), and Denver Broncos (78-88). Card numbers 6 and 64 are more difficult to obtain than the other cards in the set; their shortage is believed to be attributable to their possible replacement on the printing sheet by the unnumbered checklist. The cards measure 2 1/2" by 3 1/2". The card backs are printed in red and black on a white card stock. The set price below does include the checklist card. Cards with numbers divisible by four can be found with or without a red stripe on the bottom of the card back; it is thought that those without the red stripe are in lesser supply. The key Rookie Cards in this set are Lance Alworth, Nick Buoniconti, and Len Dawson.

| | NRMT | VG-E | GOOD |
|---|---|---|---|
| COMPLETE SET (89) | 2000.00 | 900.00 | 250.00 |
| COMMON PLAYER (1-88) | 8.50 | 3.80 | 1.05 |

| | | NRMT | VG-E | GOOD |
|---|---|---|---|---|
| ☐ 1 | Larry Garron | 18.00 | 3.60 | 1.10 |
| ☐ 2 | Babe Parilli | 9.00 | 4.00 | 1.15 |
| ☐ 3 | Ron Burton | 9.00 | 4.00 | 1.15 |
| ☐ 4 | Jim Colclough | 8.50 | 3.80 | 1.05 |
| ☐ 5 | Gino Cappelletti | 10.00 | 4.50 | 1.25 |
| ☐ 6 | Charles Long SP | 225.00 | 100.00 | 28.00 |
| ☐ 7 | Bill Neighbors | 10.00 | 4.50 | 1.25 |
| ☐ 8 | Dick Felt | 8.50 | 3.80 | 1.05 |
| ☐ 9 | Tommy Addison | 8.50 | 3.80 | 1.05 |
| ☐ 10 | Nick Buoniconti | 75.00 | 34.00 | 9.50 |
| ☐ 11 | Larry Eisenhauer | 10.00 | 4.50 | 1.25 |
| ☐ 12 | Bill Mathis | 9.00 | 4.00 | 1.15 |
| ☐ 13 | Lee Grosscup | 10.00 | 4.50 | 1.25 |
| ☐ 14 | Dick Christy | 8.50 | 3.80 | 1.05 |
| ☐ 15 | Don Maynard | 45.00 | 20.00 | 5.75 |
| ☐ 16 | Alex Kroll | 10.00 | 4.50 | 1.25 |
| ☐ 17 | Bob Mischak | 8.50 | 3.80 | 1.05 |
| ☐ 18 | Dainard Paulson | 8.50 | 3.80 | 1.05 |
| ☐ 19 | Lee Riley | 8.50 | 3.80 | 1.05 |
| ☐ 20 | Larry Grantham | 9.00 | 4.00 | 1.15 |
| ☐ 21 | Hubert Bobo | 8.50 | 3.80 | 1.05 |
| ☐ 22 | Nick Mumley | 8.50 | 3.80 | 1.05 |
| ☐ 23 | Cookie Gilchrist | 35.00 | 16.00 | 4.40 |
| ☐ 24 | Jack Kemp | 250.00 | 115.00 | 31.00 |
| ☐ 25 | Wray Carlton | 9.00 | 4.00 | 1.15 |
| ☐ 26 | Elbert Dubenion | 9.00 | 4.00 | 1.15 |
| ☐ 27 | Ernie Warlick | 9.00 | 4.00 | 1.15 |
| ☐ 28 | Billy Shaw | 8.50 | 3.80 | 1.05 |
| ☐ 29 | Ken Rice | 8.50 | 3.80 | 1.05 |
| ☐ 30 | Booker Edgerson | 8.50 | 3.80 | 1.05 |

| | | | |
|---|---|---|---|
| ☐ 31 Ray Abruzzese | 8.50 | 3.80 | 1.05 |
| ☐ 32 Mike Stratton | 10.00 | 4.50 | 1.25 |
| ☐ 33 Tom Sestak | 10.00 | 4.50 | 1.25 |
| ☐ 34 Charley Tolar | 8.50 | 3.80 | 1.05 |
| ☐ 35 Dave Smith | 8.50 | 3.80 | 1.05 |
| ☐ 36 George Blanda | 55.00 | 25.00 | 7.00 |
| ☐ 37 Billy Cannon | 10.00 | 4.50 | 1.25 |
| ☐ 38 Charlie Hennigan | 12.00 | 5.50 | 1.50 |
| ☐ 39 Bob Talamini | 10.00 | 4.50 | 1.25 |
| ☐ 40 Jim Norton | 8.50 | 3.80 | 1.05 |
| ☐ 41 Tony Banfield | 8.50 | 3.80 | 1.05 |
| ☐ 42 Doug Cline | 8.50 | 3.80 | 1.05 |
| ☐ 43 Don Floyd | 8.50 | 3.80 | 1.05 |
| ☐ 44 Ed Husmann | 8.50 | 3.80 | 1.05 |
| ☐ 45 Curtis McClinton | 12.00 | 5.50 | 1.50 |
| ☐ 46 Jack Spikes | 9.00 | 4.00 | 1.15 |
| ☐ 47 Len Dawson | 250.00 | 115.00 | 31.00 |
| ☐ 48 Abner Haynes | 10.00 | 4.50 | 1.25 |
| ☐ 49 Chris Burford | 9.00 | 4.00 | 1.15 |
| ☐ 50 Fred Arbanas | 12.00 | 5.50 | 1.50 |
| ☐ 51 Johnny Robinson | 9.00 | 4.00 | 1.15 |
| ☐ 52 E.J. Holub | 9.00 | 4.00 | 1.15 |
| ☐ 53 Sherrill Headrick | 9.00 | 4.00 | 1.15 |
| ☐ 54 Mel Branch | 9.00 | 4.00 | 1.15 |
| ☐ 55 Jerry Mays | 9.00 | 4.00 | 1.15 |
| ☐ 56 Cotton Davidson | 9.00 | 4.00 | 1.15 |
| ☐ 57 Clem Daniels | 16.00 | 7.25 | 2.00 |
| ☐ 58 Bo Roberson | 8.50 | 3.80 | 1.05 |
| ☐ 59 Art Powell | 10.00 | 4.50 | 1.25 |
| ☐ 60 Bob Coolbaugh | 8.50 | 3.80 | 1.05 |
| ☐ 61 Wayne Hawkins | 8.50 | 3.80 | 1.05 |
| ☐ 62 Jim Otto | 30.00 | 13.50 | 3.80 |
| ☐ 63 Fred Williamson | 10.00 | 4.50 | 1.25 |
| ☐ 64 Bob Dougherty SP | 225.00 | 100.00 | 28.00 |
| ☐ 65 Dalva Allen | 8.50 | 3.80 | 1.05 |
| ☐ 66 Chuck McMurtry | 8.50 | 3.80 | 1.05 |
| ☐ 67 Gerry McDougall | 8.50 | 3.80 | 1.05 |
| ☐ 68 Tobin Rote | 9.00 | 4.00 | 1.15 |
| ☐ 69 Paul Lowe | 10.00 | 4.50 | 1.25 |
| ☐ 70 Keith Lincoln | 24.00 | 11.00 | 3.00 |
| ☐ 71 Dave Kocourek | 9.00 | 4.00 | 1.15 |
| ☐ 72 Lance Alworth | 250.00 | 115.00 | 31.00 |
| ☐ 73 Ron Mix | 20.00 | 9.00 | 2.50 |
| ☐ 74 Charles McNeil | 10.00 | 4.50 | 1.25 |
| ☐ 75 Emil Karas | 8.50 | 3.80 | 1.05 |
| ☐ 76 Ernie Ladd | 18.00 | 8.00 | 2.30 |
| ☐ 77 Earl Faison | 9.00 | 4.00 | 1.15 |
| ☐ 78 Jim Stinnette | 8.50 | 3.80 | 1.05 |
| ☐ 79 Frank Tripucka | 10.00 | 4.50 | 1.25 |
| ☐ 80 Don Stone | 8.50 | 3.80 | 1.05 |
| ☐ 81 Bob Scarpitto | 8.50 | 3.80 | 1.05 |
| ☐ 82 Lionel Taylor | 10.00 | 4.50 | 1.25 |
| ☐ 83 Jerry Tarr | 8.50 | 3.80 | 1.05 |
| ☐ 84 Eldon Danenhauer | 9.00 | 4.00 | 1.15 |
| ☐ 85 Goose Gonsoulin | 9.00 | 4.00 | 1.15 |
| ☐ 86 Jim Fraser | 8.50 | 3.80 | 1.05 |
| ☐ 87 Chuck Gavin | 8.50 | 3.80 | 1.05 |
| ☐ 88 Bud McFadin | 16.00 | 3.20 | .95 |
| ☐ NNO Checklist Card SP | 360.00 | 90.00 | 36.00 |

## 1968 Fleer Big Signs

This set of 26 "Big Signs" was produced by Fleer in 1968. They are blank backed and measure approximately 7 3/4" by 11 1/2" with rounded corners. They are unnumbered so they are listed below alphabetically by team city name. They are credited at the bottom as 1968 in roman numerals. As another point of reference in dating the set, the New England Patriots changed their name from Boston in 1970. There were two distinct versions of this set, with each version including all 26 teams. The 1968 version was issued in a green box, while the 1974 version was issued in a brown box. Both boxes carry a 1968 copyright date; however, 1974 is generally considered to be the issue date of the second series. Though they are considerably different

in design, the size of the collectibles is similar. The generic drawings (of a faceless player from each team) are in color with a white border. The set was licensed by NFL Properties so there are no players identifiably shown.

| | NRMT | VG-E | GOOD |
|---|---|---|---|
| COMPLETE SET (26) | 100.00 | 40.00 | 10.00 |
| COMMON TEAM (1-26) | 6.00 | 2.40 | .60 |
| | | | |
| ☐ 1 Atlanta Falcons | 6.00 | 2.40 | .60 |
| ☐ 2 Baltimore Colts | 6.00 | 2.40 | .60 |
| ☐ 3 Buffalo Bills | 6.00 | 2.40 | .60 |
| ☐ 4 Chicago Bears | 7.50 | 3.00 | .75 |
| ☐ 5 Cincinnati Bengals | 6.00 | 2.40 | .60 |
| ☐ 6 Cleveland Browns | 6.00 | 2.40 | .60 |
| ☐ 7 Dallas Cowboys | 7.50 | 3.00 | .75 |
| ☐ 8 Denver Broncos | 6.00 | 2.40 | .60 |
| ☐ 9 Detroit Lions | 6.00 | 2.40 | .60 |
| ☐ 10 Green Bay Packers | 6.00 | 2.40 | .60 |
| ☐ 11 Houston Oilers | 6.00 | 2.40 | .60 |
| ☐ 12 Kansas City Chiefs | 6.00 | 2.40 | .60 |
| ☐ 13 Los Angeles Rams | 6.00 | 2.40 | .60 |
| ☐ 14 Miami Dolphins | 6.00 | 2.40 | .60 |
| ☐ 15 Minnesota Vikings | 6.00 | 2.40 | .60 |
| ☐ 16 New England Patriots | 6.00 | 2.40 | .60 |
| ☐ 17 New Orleans Saints | 6.00 | 2.40 | .60 |
| ☐ 18 New York Giants | 6.00 | 2.40 | .60 |
| ☐ 19 New York Jets | 6.00 | 2.40 | .60 |
| ☐ 20 Oakland Raiders | 7.50 | 3.00 | .75 |
| ☐ 21 Philadelphia Eagles | 6.00 | 2.40 | .60 |
| ☐ 22 Pittsburgh Steelers | 7.50 | 3.00 | .75 |
| ☐ 23 St. Louis Cardinals | 6.00 | 2.40 | .60 |
| ☐ 24 San Diego Chargers | 6.00 | 2.40 | .60 |
| ☐ 25 San Francisco 49ers | 6.00 | 2.40 | .60 |
| ☐ 26 Washington Redskins | 7.50 | 3.00 | .75 |

## 1972 Fleer Quiz

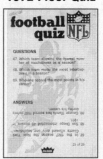

The 28 cards in this set measure approximately 2 1/2" by 4" and feature three questions and (upside down) answers about football players and events. The words "Official Football Quiz" are printed at the top and are accented by the NFL logo. The backs are blank. The cards are numbered in the lower right hand corner.

| | NRMT | VG-E | GOOD |
|---|---|---|---|
| COMPLETE SET (28) | 50.00 | 20.00 | 5.00 |
| COMMON PLAYER (1-28) | 2.00 | .80 | .20 |
| ☐ 1 Questions 1-3 | 2.50 | 1.00 | .25 |
| ☐ 2 Questions 4-6 | 2.00 | .80 | .20 |
| ☐ 3 Questions 7-9 | 2.00 | .80 | .20 |
| ☐ 4 Questions 10-12 | 2.00 | .80 | .20 |
| ☐ 5 Questions 13-15 | 2.00 | .80 | .20 |
| ☐ 6 Questions 16-18 | 2.00 | .80 | .20 |
| ☐ 7 Questions 19-21 | 2.00 | .80 | .20 |
| ☐ 8 Questions 22-24 | 2.00 | .80 | .20 |
| ☐ 9 Questions 25-27 | 2.00 | .80 | .20 |
| ☐ 10 Questions 28-30 | 2.00 | .80 | .20 |
| ☐ 11 Questions 31-33 | 2.00 | .80 | .20 |
| ☐ 12 Questions 34-36 | 2.00 | .80 | .20 |
| ☐ 13 Questions 37-39 | 2.00 | .80 | .20 |
| ☐ 14 Questions 40-42 | 2.00 | .80 | .20 |
| ☐ 15 Questions 43-45 | 2.00 | .80 | .20 |
| ☐ 16 Questions 46-48 | 2.00 | .80 | .20 |
| ☐ 17 Questions 49-51 | 2.00 | .80 | .20 |
| ☐ 18 Questions 52-54 | 2.00 | .80 | .20 |
| ☐ 19 Questions 55-57 | 2.00 | .80 | .20 |
| ☐ 20 Questions 58-60 | 2.00 | .80 | .20 |
| ☐ 21 Questions 61-63 | 2.00 | .80 | .20 |
| ☐ 22 Questions 64-66 | 2.00 | .80 | .20 |
| ☐ 23 Questions 67-69 | 2.00 | .80 | .20 |
| ☐ 24 Questions 70-72 | 2.00 | .80 | .20 |
| ☐ 25 Questions 73-75 | 2.00 | .80 | .20 |
| ☐ 26 Questions 76-78 | 2.00 | .80 | .20 |
| ☐ 27 Questions 79-81 | 2.00 | .80 | .20 |
| ☐ 28 Questions 82-84 | 2.50 | 1.00 | .25 |

# 1973 Fleer Pro Bowl Scouting Report

The 14 cards in this set measure approximately 2 1/2" by 4" and feature an explanation of the ideal size, responsibilities, and assignments of each player on the team. Each card shows a different position. Color artwork illustrates examples of how a player might appear. A diagram shows the position on the field. The words "AFC-NFC Pro Bowl Scouting Cards" are printed at the top and are accented by the NFL logo and underscored by a blue stripe. The backs are blank. The cards are unnumbered and checklisted below in alphabetical order. The cards came one per pack with two cloth football logo patches that are dated 1972. It appears that the same cloth patches were sold each year from 1972 to 1975. In the first year, they were sold alone in packs, while in the following years, they were sold again through packs with the Scouting Report and Hall of Fame issues, respectively.

|  | NRMT | VG-E | GOOD |
|---|---|---|---|
| COMPLETE SET (14)........................ | 40.00 | 16.00 | 4.00 |
| COMMON PLAYER (1-14)................. | 3.50 | 1.40 | .35 |
| ☐ 1 Center ................................... | 4.00 | 1.60 | .40 |
| ☐ 2 Cornerback............................... | 3.50 | 1.40 | .35 |
| ☐ 3 Defensive End .......................... | 3.50 | 1.40 | .35 |
| ☐ 4 Defensive Tackle ..................... | 3.50 | 1.40 | .35 |
| ☐ 5 Guard..................................... | 3.50 | 1.40 | .35 |
| ☐ 6 Kicker..................................... | 3.50 | 1.40 | .35 |
| ☐ 7 Linebacker ............................. | 3.50 | 1.40 | .35 |
| ☐ 8 Offensive Tackle ..................... | 3.50 | 1.40 | .35 |
| ☐ 9 Punter..................................... | 3.50 | 1.40 | .35 |
| ☐ 10 Quarterback........................... | 4.00 | 1.60 | .40 |
| ☐ 11 Running Back......................... | 4.00 | 1.60 | .40 |
| ☐ 12 Safety.................................... | 3.50 | 1.40 | .35 |
| ☐ 13 Tight End............................... | 3.50 | 1.40 | .35 |
| ☐ 14 Wide Receiver ....................... | 4.00 | 1.60 | .40 |

# 1974 Fleer Big Signs

This set of 26 "Big Signs" was produced by Fleer in 1974. They are blank backed and measure approximately 7 3/4" by 11 1/2" with rounded corners. They are unnumbered so they are listed below alphabetically by team city name. They are credited at the bottom as 1968 in roman numerals, but in fact were probably issued several years later, perhaps as late as 1974. As another point of reference in dating the set, the New England Patriots changed their name from Boston in 1970. There were two distinct versions of this set, with each version including all 26 teams. The 1968 version was issued in a green box, while the 1974 version was issued in a brown box. Both boxes carry a 1968 copyright date; however, 1974 is generally considered to be the issue date of this second series. Though they are

considerably different in design, the size of the collectibles is similar. The generic drawings (of a faceless player from each team) are in color with a white border. The set was licensed by NFL Properties so there are no players identifiably shown.

|  | NRMT | VG-E | GOOD |
|---|---|---|---|
| COMPLETE SET (26)........................ | 60.00 | 24.00 | 6.00 |
| COMMON TEAM (1-26) ................. | 4.00 | 1.60 | .40 |
| ☐ 1 Atlanta Falcons........................ | 4.00 | 1.60 | .40 |
| ☐ 2 Baltimore Colts ........................ | 4.00 | 1.60 | .40 |
| ☐ 3 Buffalo Bills ............................ | 4.00 | 1.60 | .40 |
| ☐ 4 Chicago Bears ......................... | 5.00 | 2.00 | .50 |
| ☐ 5 Cincinnati Bengals.................... | 4.00 | 1.60 | .40 |
| ☐ 6 Cleveland Browns ..................... | 4.00 | 1.60 | .40 |
| ☐ 7 Dallas Cowboys........................ | 5.00 | 2.00 | .50 |
| ☐ 8 Denver Broncos ....................... | 4.00 | 1.60 | .40 |
| ☐ 9 Detroit Lions ........................... | 4.00 | 1.60 | .40 |
| ☐ 10 Green Bay Packers.................. | 4.00 | 1.60 | .40 |
| ☐ 11 Houston Oilers ....................... | 4.00 | 1.60 | .40 |
| ☐ 12 Kansas City Chiefs ................. | 4.00 | 1.60 | .40 |
| ☐ 13 Los Angeles Rams .................. | 4.00 | 1.60 | .40 |
| ☐ 14 Miami Dolphins....................... | 4.00 | 1.60 | .40 |
| ☐ 15 Minnesota Vikings................... | 4.00 | 1.60 | .40 |
| ☐ 16 New England Patriots............... | 4.00 | 1.60 | .40 |
| ☐ 17 New Orleans Saints ................. | 4.00 | 1.60 | .40 |
| ☐ 18 New York Giants ..................... | 4.00 | 1.60 | .40 |
| ☐ 19 New York Jets ........................ | 4.00 | 1.60 | .40 |
| ☐ 20 Oakland Raiders...................... | 5.00 | 2.00 | .50 |
| ☐ 21 Philadelphia Eagles ................ | 4.00 | 1.60 | .40 |
| ☐ 22 Pittsburgh Steelers ................. | 5.00 | 2.00 | .50 |
| ☐ 23 St. Louis Cardinals.................. | 4.00 | 1.60 | .40 |
| ☐ 24 San Diego Chargers ................ | 4.00 | 1.60 | .40 |
| ☐ 25 San Francisco 49ers................ | 4.00 | 1.60 | .40 |
| ☐ 26 Washington Redskins ............. | 5.00 | 2.00 | .50 |

# 1974 Fleer Hall of Fame

The 1974 Fleer Hall of Fame football card set contains 50 players inducted into the Pro Football Hall of Fame in Canton, Ohio. The cards measure approximately 2 1/2" by 4". The fronts feature black and white photos, white borders, and a cartoon head of a football player flanked by the words "The Immortal Role." The backs contain biographical data and a stylized Pro Football Hall of Fame logo. The cards are unnumbered and can be distinguished from cards of the 1975 Fleer Hall of Fame set by this lack of numbering. The cards are arranged and numbered below alphabetically by player's name for convenience. The cards were originally issued in wax packs with one Hall of Fame card and two cloth team logo stickers.

|  | NRMT | VG-E | GOOD |
|---|---|---|---|
| COMPLETE SET (50)........................ | 40.00 | 16.00 | 4.00 |
| COMMON PLAYER (1-50)................. | .75 | .30 | .07 |
| ☐ 1 Cliff Battles............................. | .75 | .30 | .07 |
| ☐ 2 Sammy Baugh .......................... | 1.50 | .60 | .15 |
| ☐ 3 Chuck Bednarik ....................... | 1.00 | .40 | .10 |
| ☐ 4 Bert Bell COMM/OWN .... | .75 | .30 | .07 |
| ☐ 5 Paul Brown CO/OWN/FOUND.... | 1.00 | .40 | .10 |
| ☐ 6 Joe Carr PRES ........................ | .75 | .30 | .07 |
| ☐ 7 Guy Chamberlin ....................... | .75 | .30 | .07 |
| ☐ 8 Earl(Dutch) Clark...................... | .75 | .30 | .07 |
| ☐ 9 Jimmy Conzelman...................... | .75 | .30 | .07 |
| ☐ 10 Art Donovan ........................... | 1.00 | .40 | .10 |
| ☐ 11 John(Paddy) Driscoll ............. | .75 | .30 | .07 |
| ☐ 12 Bill Dudley............................. | .75 | .30 | .07 |
| ☐ 13 Dan Fortmann ........................ | .75 | .30 | .07 |
| ☐ 14 Otto Graham .......................... | 1.50 | .60 | .15 |
| ☐ 15 Red Grange ........................... | 2.00 | .80 | .20 |
| ☐ 16 George Halas CO/OWN/ .......... | 1.00 | .40 | .10 |

FOUND

| | NRMT | VG-E | GOOD |
|---|---|---|---|
| ☐ 17 Mel Hein | .75 | .30 | .07 |
| ☐ 18 Fats Henry | .75 | .30 | .07 |
| ☐ 19 Bill Hewitt | .75 | .30 | .07 |
| ☐ 20 Clarke Hinkle | .75 | .30 | .07 |
| ☐ 21 Elroy(Crazylegs) Hirsch | 1.00 | .40 | .10 |
| ☐ 22 Robert(Cal) Hubbard | .75 | .30 | .07 |
| ☐ 23 Lamar Hunt OWN/FOUND | 1.00 | .40 | .10 |
| ☐ 24 Don Hutson | 1.00 | .40 | .10 |
| ☐ 25 Earl(Curly) Lambeau CO/ OWN/FOUND | .75 | .30 | .07 |
| ☐ 26 Bobby Layne | 1.00 | .40 | .10 |
| ☐ 27 Vince Lombardi CO | 1.50 | .60 | .15 |
| ☐ 28 Sid Luckman | 1.00 | .40 | .10 |
| ☐ 29 Gino Marchetti | 1.00 | .40 | .10 |
| ☐ 30 Ollie Matson | 1.00 | .40 | .10 |
| ☐ 31 George McAfee | .75 | .30 | .07 |
| ☐ 32 Hugh McElhenny | 1.00 | .40 | .10 |
| ☐ 33 Johnny(Blood) McNally | .75 | .30 | .07 |
| ☐ 34 Marion Motley | 1.00 | .40 | .10 |
| ☐ 35 Bronko Nagurski | 1.50 | .60 | .15 |
| ☐ 36 Ernie Nevers | 1.00 | .40 | .10 |
| ☐ 37 Leo Nomellini | .75 | .30 | .07 |
| ☐ 38 Steve Owen CO | .75 | .30 | .07 |
| ☐ 39 Joe Perry | 1.00 | .40 | .10 |
| ☐ 40 Pete Pihos | .75 | .30 | .07 |
| ☐ 41 Andy Robustelli | .75 | .30 | .07 |
| ☐ 42 Ken Strong | .75 | .30 | .07 |
| ☐ 43 Jim Thorpe | 2.00 | .80 | .20 |
| ☐ 44 Y.A. Tittle | 1.00 | .40 | .10 |
| ☐ 45 Charley Trippi | .75 | .30 | .07 |
| ☐ 46 Emlen Tunnell | .75 | .30 | .07 |
| ☐ 47 Clyde(Bulldog) Turner | 1.00 | .40 | .10 |
| ☐ 48 Norm Van Brocklin | 1.00 | .40 | .10 |
| ☐ 49 Steve Van Buren | 1.00 | .40 | .10 |
| ☐ 50 Bob Waterfield | 1.00 | .40 | .10 |

| | | | |
|---|---|---|---|
| ☐ 21 Ken Strong | .50 | .20 | .05 |
| ☐ 22 Chuck Bednarik | .75 | .30 | .07 |
| ☐ 23 Bert Bell COMM/OWN | .50 | .20 | .05 |
| ☐ 24 Paul Brown CO/OWN/FOUND | .75 | .30 | .07 |
| ☐ 25 Art Donovan | .75 | .30 | .07 |
| ☐ 26 Bill Dudley | .50 | .20 | .05 |
| ☐ 27 Otto Graham | 1.25 | .50 | .12 |
| ☐ 28 Fats Henry | .50 | .20 | .05 |
| ☐ 29 Elroy Hirsch | .75 | .30 | .07 |
| ☐ 30 Lamar Hunt OWN/FOUND | .75 | .30 | .07 |
| ☐ 31 Earl(Curly) Lambeau CO/ OWN/FOUND | .50 | .20 | .05 |
| ☐ 32 Vince Lombardi CO | 1.00 | .40 | .10 |
| ☐ 33 Sid Luckman | 1.00 | .40 | .10 |
| ☐ 34 Gino Marchetti | .75 | .30 | .07 |
| ☐ 35 Ollie Matson | .75 | .30 | .07 |
| ☐ 36 Hugh McElhenny | .75 | .30 | .07 |
| ☐ 37 Marion Motley | .75 | .30 | .07 |
| ☐ 38 Leo Nomellini | .50 | .20 | .05 |
| ☐ 39 Joe Perry | .75 | .30 | .07 |
| ☐ 40 Andy Robustelli | .50 | .20 | .05 |
| ☐ 41 Pete Pihos | .50 | .20 | .05 |
| ☐ 42 Y.A. Tittle | .75 | .30 | .07 |
| ☐ 43 Charley Trippi | .50 | .20 | .05 |
| ☐ 44 Emlen Tunnell | .50 | .20 | .05 |
| ☐ 45 Clyde(Bulldog) Turner | .50 | .20 | .05 |
| ☐ 46 Norm Van Brocklin | .75 | .30 | .07 |
| ☐ 47 Steve Van Buren | .75 | .30 | .07 |
| ☐ 48 Bob Waterfield | 1.00 | .40 | .10 |
| ☐ 49 Bobby Layne | .75 | .30 | .07 |
| ☐ 50 Sammy Baugh | 1.25 | .50 | .12 |
| ☐ 51 Joe Guyon | .50 | .20 | .05 |
| ☐ 52 Roy(Link) Lyman | .50 | .20 | .05 |
| ☐ 53 George Trafton | .50 | .20 | .05 |
| ☐ 54 Glen(Turk) Edwards | .50 | .20 | .05 |
| ☐ 55 Ed Healey | .50 | .20 | .05 |
| ☐ 56 Mike Michalske | .50 | .20 | .05 |
| ☐ 57 Alex Wojciechowicz | .50 | .20 | .05 |
| ☐ 58 Dante Lavelli | .50 | .20 | .05 |
| ☐ 59 George Connor | .50 | .20 | .05 |
| ☐ 60 Wayne Millner | .50 | .20 | .05 |
| ☐ 61 Jack Christiansen | .50 | .20 | .05 |
| ☐ 62 Roosevelt Brown | .50 | .20 | .05 |
| ☐ 63 Joe Stydahar | .50 | .20 | .05 |
| ☐ 64 Ernie Stautner | .75 | .30 | .07 |
| ☐ 65 Jim Parker | .75 | .30 | .07 |
| ☐ 66 Raymond Berry | .75 | .30 | .07 |
| ☐ 67 Geo.Preston Marshall | .50 | .20 | .05 |

OWN/FOUND

| | | | |
|---|---|---|---|
| ☐ 68 Clarence(Ace) Parker | .75 | .30 | .07 |
| ☐ 69 Earle(Greasy) Neale CO | .50 | .20 | .05 |
| ☐ 70 Tim Mara OWN/FOUND | .50 | .20 | .05 |
| ☐ 71 Hugh(Shorty) Ray OFF | .50 | .20 | .05 |
| ☐ 72 Tom Fears | .75 | .30 | .07 |
| ☐ 73 Arnie Herber | .50 | .20 | .05 |
| ☐ 74 Walt Kiesling | .50 | .20 | .05 |
| ☐ 75 Frank(Bruiser) Kinard | .50 | .20 | .05 |
| ☐ 76 Tony Canadeo | .50 | .20 | .05 |
| ☐ 77 Bill George | .50 | .20 | .05 |
| ☐ 78 Art Rooney FOUND/OWN | .75 | .30 | .07 |

ADMIN

| | | | |
|---|---|---|---|
| ☐ 79 Joe Schmidt | .75 | .30 | .07 |
| ☐ 80 Dan Reeves OWN | .50 | .20 | .05 |
| ☐ 81 Lou Groza | .75 | .30 | .07 |
| ☐ 82 Charles W. Bidwill OWN | .50 | .20 | .05 |
| ☐ 83 Lenny Moore | .75 | .30 | .07 |
| ☐ 84 Dick(Night Train) Lane | .75 | .30 | .07 |

## 1975 Fleer Hall of Fame

The 1975 Fleer Hall of Fame football card set contains 84 cards. The cards measure 2 1/2" by 4". Except for the change in border color from white to brown and the different set numbering contained on the backs of the cards, fifty of the cards in this set are similar to the cards in the 1974 Fleer set. Thirty-four additional cards have been added to this set in comparison to the 1974 Fleer set. These cards are numbered and were issued in wax packs with cloth team logo stickers.

| | NRMT | VG-E | GOOD |
|---|---|---|---|
| COMPLETE SET (84) | 40.00 | 16.00 | 4.00 |
| COMMON PLAYER (1-84) | .50 | .20 | .05 |
| ☐ 1 Jim Thorpe | 1.50 | .60 | .15 |
| ☐ 2 Cliff Battles | .50 | .20 | .05 |
| ☐ 3 Bronko Nagurski | 1.00 | .40 | .10 |
| ☐ 4 Harold Grange | 1.50 | .60 | .15 |
| ☐ 5 Guy Chamberlin | .50 | .20 | .05 |
| ☐ 6 Joe Carr PRES | .50 | .20 | .05 |
| ☐ 7 George Halas CO/OWN/ FOUND | .75 | .30 | .07 |
| ☐ 8 Jimmy Conzelman | .50 | .20 | .05 |
| ☐ 9 George McAfee | .50 | .20 | .05 |
| ☐ 10 Clarke Hinkle | .50 | .20 | .05 |
| ☐ 11 John(Paddy) Driscoll | .50 | .20 | .05 |
| ☐ 12 Mel Hein | .50 | .20 | .05 |
| ☐ 13 Johnny(Blood) McNally | .50 | .20 | .05 |
| ☐ 14 Earl(Dutch) Clark | .50 | .20 | .05 |
| ☐ 15 Steve Owen CO | .50 | .20 | .05 |
| ☐ 16 Bill Hewitt | .50 | .20 | .05 |
| ☐ 17 Robert(Cal) Hubbard | .50 | .20 | .05 |
| ☐ 18 Don Hutson | .75 | .30 | .07 |
| ☐ 19 Ernie Nevers | .75 | .30 | .07 |
| ☐ 20 Dan Fortmann | .50 | .20 | .05 |

## 1976 Fleer Team Action

This 66-card set contains cards picturing action scenes with two cards for every NFL team and then a card for each previous Super Bowl. The first card in each team pair, i.e., the odd-numbered card, is an offensive card; the even-numbered cards are defensive scenes. The cards measure 2 1/2" by 3 1/2". The cards are numbered on the back.

Cards have a white border with a red outline on the front; the backs are printed with black ink on white cardboard stock with a light blue NFL emblem superimposed in the middle of the write-up on the back of the card. These cards are actually stickers as they may be peeled and stuck. The instructions on the back of the sticker say, "For use as sticker, bend corner and peel." The cards were issued in four-card packs with no inserts, unlike earlier Fleer football issues.

|  | NRMT | VG-E | GOOD |
|---|---|---|---|
| COMPLETE SET (66) | 400.00 | 160.00 | 40.00 |
| COMMON CARD (1-56) | 6.00 | 2.40 | .60 |
| COMMON SB CARD (57-66) | 10.00 | 4.00 | 1.00 |

| | NRMT | VG-E | GOOD |
|---|---|---|---|
| ☐ 1 Baltimore Colts<br>High Scorers | 7.50 | 3.00 | .75 |
| ☐ 2 Baltimore Colts<br>Effective Tackle | 6.00 | 2.40 | .60 |
| ☐ 3 Buffalo Bills<br>Perfect Blocking | 6.00 | 2.40 | .60 |
| ☐ 4 Buffalo Bills<br>The Sack | 6.00 | 2.40 | .60 |
| ☐ 5 Cincinnati Bengals<br>Being Hit Behind<br>The Runner | 6.00 | 2.40 | .60 |
| ☐ 6 Cincinnati Bengals<br>A Little Help<br>(Tackling Franco Harris) | 10.00 | 4.00 | 1.00 |
| ☐ 7 Cleveland Browns<br>Blocking Tight End | 6.00 | 2.40 | .60 |
| ☐ 8 Cleveland Browns<br>Stopping the<br>Double Threat | 6.00 | 2.40 | .60 |
| ☐ 9 Denver Broncos<br>The Swing Pass | 6.00 | 2.40 | .60 |
| ☐ 10 Denver Broncos<br>The Gang Tackle | 6.00 | 2.40 | .60 |
| ☐ 11 Houston Oilers<br>Short Zone Flood<br>(Dan Pastorini passing) | 7.50 | 3.00 | .75 |
| ☐ 12 Houston Oilers<br>Run Stoppers<br>(Franco Harris running) | 10.00 | 4.00 | 1.00 |
| ☐ 13 Kansas City Chiefs<br>Off On the Ball | 6.00 | 2.40 | .60 |
| ☐ 14 Kansas City Chiefs<br>Forcing the Scramble | 6.00 | 2.40 | .60 |
| ☐ 15 Miami Dolphins<br>Pass Protection<br>(Bob Griese) | 12.00 | 5.00 | 1.20 |
| ☐ 16 Miami Dolphins<br>Natural Turf | 7.50 | 3.00 | .75 |
| ☐ 17 New England Patriots<br>Quicker Than the Eye | 6.00 | 2.40 | .60 |
| ☐ 18 New England Patriots<br>The Rugby Touch | 6.00 | 2.40 | .60 |
| ☐ 19 New York Jets<br>They Run, Too<br>(John Riggins and<br>Joe Namath) | 15.00 | 6.00 | 1.50 |
| ☐ 20 New York Jets<br>The Buck Stops Here<br>(O.J.Simpson tackled) | 15.00 | 6.00 | 1.50 |
| ☐ 21 Oakland Raiders<br>A Strong Offense | 7.50 | 3.00 | .75 |
| ☐ 22 Oakland Raiders<br>High and Low | 7.50 | 3.00 | .75 |
| ☐ 23 Pittsburgh Steelers<br>The Pitch-Out<br>(Terry Bradshaw,<br>Franco Harris, and<br>Rocky Bleier) | 15.00 | 6.00 | 1.50 |
| ☐ 24 Pittsburgh Steelers<br>The Takeaway<br>(Jack Lambert) | 15.00 | 6.00 | 1.50 |
| ☐ 25 San Diego Chargers<br>Run to Daylight | 6.00 | 2.40 | .60 |
| ☐ 26 San Diego Chargers<br>The Swarm | 6.00 | 2.40 | .60 |
| ☐ 27 Tampa Bay Buccaneers<br>Stadium | 6.00 | 2.40 | .60 |
| ☐ 28 Tampa Bay Buccaneers<br>Buccaneers Uniform | 6.00 | 2.40 | .60 |
| ☐ 29 Atlanta Falcons<br>A Key Block | 6.00 | 2.40 | .60 |
| ☐ 30 Atlanta Falcons<br>Breakthrough<br>(Robert Newhouse) | 6.00 | 2.40 | .60 |
| ☐ 31 Chicago Bears<br>An Inside Look | 6.00 | 2.40 | .60 |
| ☐ 32 Chicago Bears<br>Defensive Emphasis | 6.00 | 2.40 | .60 |
| ☐ 33 Dallas Cowboys<br>Eight-Yard Burst<br>(Robert Newhouse) | 7.50 | 3.00 | .75 |
| ☐ 34 Dallas Cowboys<br>The Big Return<br>(Cliff Harris) | 7.50 | 3.00 | .75 |

| | NRMT | VG-E | GOOD |
|---|---|---|---|
| ☐ 35 Detroit Lions<br>Power Sweep | 6.00 | 2.40 | .60 |
| ☐ 36 Detroit Lions<br>A Tough Defense | 6.00 | 2.40 | .60 |
| ☐ 37 Green Bay Packers<br>Tearaway Gain | 6.00 | 2.40 | .60 |
| ☐ 38 Green Bay Packers<br>Good Support | 6.00 | 2.40 | .60 |
| ☐ 39 Los Angeles Rams<br>(Cullen Bryant) | 6.00 | 2.40 | .60 |
| ☐ 40 Los Angeles Rams<br>Low-Point Defense | 6.00 | 2.40 | .60 |
| ☐ 41 Minnesota Vikings<br>The Running Guards<br>(Fran Tarkenton and<br>Chuck Foreman) | 10.00 | 4.00 | 1.00 |
| ☐ 42 Minnesota Vikings<br>A Stingy Defense | 6.00 | 2.40 | .60 |
| ☐ 43 New York Giants<br>The Quick Opener | 6.00 | 2.40 | .60 |
| ☐ 44 New York Giants<br>Defending a Tradition | 6.00 | 2.40 | .60 |
| ☐ 45 New Orleans Saints<br>Head for the Hole<br>(Archie Manning) | 7.50 | 3.00 | .75 |
| ☐ 46 New Orleans Saints<br>The Contain Man | 6.00 | 2.40 | .60 |
| ☐ 47 Philadelphia Eagles<br>Line Signals | 6.00 | 2.40 | .60 |
| ☐ 48 Philadelphia Eagles<br>Don't Take Sides | 6.00 | 2.40 | .60 |
| ☐ 49 San Francisco 49ers<br>The Clues | 6.00 | 2.40 | .60 |
| ☐ 50 San Francisco 49ers<br>Goal-Line Stand | 6.00 | 2.40 | .60 |
| ☐ 51 St. Louis Cardinals<br>Nonskid Handoff<br>(Jim Hart) | 7.50 | 3.00 | .75 |
| ☐ 52 St. Louis Cardinals<br>Strong Pursuit | 6.00 | 2.40 | .60 |
| ☐ 53 Seattle Seahawks<br>Stadium | 7.50 | 3.00 | .75 |
| ☐ 54 Seattle Seahawks<br>Uniform | 7.50 | 3.00 | .75 |
| ☐ 55 Washington Redskins<br>A Fancy Passing<br>(Billy Kilmer) | 7.50 | 3.00 | .75 |
| ☐ 56 Washington Redskins<br>Let's Go Defense<br>(Chris Hanburger) | 6.00 | 2.40 | .60 |
| ☐ 57 Super Bowl I<br>Green Bay NFL 35<br>Kansas City AFL 10<br>(Jim Taylor) | 10.00 | 4.00 | 1.00 |
| ☐ 58 Super Bowl II<br>Green Bay NFL 33<br>Oakland AFL 14<br>(Ben Davidson) | 10.00 | 4.00 | 1.00 |
| ☐ 59 Super Bowl III<br>New York AFL 16<br>Baltimore NFL 7 | 10.00 | 4.00 | 1.00 |
| ☐ 60 Super Bowl IV<br>Kansas City AFL 23<br>Minnesota NFL 7 | 10.00 | 4.00 | 1.00 |
| ☐ 61 Super Bowl V<br>Baltimore AFC 16<br>Dallas NFC 13 | 10.00 | 4.00 | 1.00 |
| ☐ 62 Super Bowl VI<br>Dallas NFC 24<br>Miami AFC 3<br>(Walt Garrison and<br>Roger Staubach) | 15.00 | 6.00 | 1.50 |
| ☐ 63 Super Bowl VII<br>Miami AFC 14<br>Washington NFC 7<br>(Larry Csonka) | 12.00 | 5.00 | 1.20 |
| ☐ 64 Super Bowl VIII<br>Miami AFC 24<br>Minnesota NFC 7<br>(Larry Csonka diving) | 12.00 | 5.00 | 1.20 |
| ☐ 65 Super Bowl IX<br>Pittsburgh AFC 16<br>Minnesota NFC 6 | 10.00 | 4.00 | 1.00 |
| ☐ 66 Super Bowl X<br>Pittsburgh AFC 21<br>Dallas NFC 17<br>(Terry Bradshaw and<br>Franco Harris) | 20.00 | 8.00 | 2.00 |

# 1977 Fleer Team Action

The 1977 Fleer Teams in Action football set contains 67 cards depicting action scenes. The cards measure 2 1/2" by 3 1/2". There are two cards for each NFL team and one card for each Super Bowl. The first card in each team pair, i.e., the odd-numbered card, is an

offensive card; the even-numbered cards are defensive scenes. The cards have white borders and the backs are printed in dark blue ink on gray stock. The cards are numbered and contain a 1977 copyright date. The cards were issued in four-card wax packs along with four team logo stickers.

|  | NRMT | VG-E | GOOD |
|---|---|---|---|
| COMPLETE SET (67) | 70.00 | 28.00 | 7.00 |
| COMMON CARD (1-56) | 1.00 | .40 | .10 |
| COMMON SB CARD (57-67) | 1.50 | .60 | .15 |

| | NRMT | VG-E | GOOD |
|---|---|---|---|
| ☐ 1 Baltimore Colts<br>The Easy Chair<br>(Bert Jones) | 2.50 | 1.00 | .25 |
| ☐ 2 Baltimore Colts<br>A Handy Solution | 1.00 | .40 | .10 |
| ☐ 3 Buffalo Bills<br>Blocking Tight End | 1.00 | .40 | .10 |
| ☐ 4 Buffalo Bills<br>Search And Destroy | 1.00 | .40 | .10 |
| ☐ 5 Cincinnati Bengals<br>Cutting on a Rug<br>(Ken Anderson hand off) | 2.00 | .80 | .20 |
| ☐ 6 Cincinnati Bengals<br>Strength in<br>the Middle | 1.00 | .40 | .10 |
| ☐ 7 Cleveland Browns<br>Snap, Drop, Set<br>(Brian Sipe) | 1.50 | .60 | .15 |
| ☐ 8 Cleveland Browns<br>High and Low | 1.00 | .40 | .10 |
| ☐ 9 Denver Broncos<br>Green Light | 1.50 | .60 | .15 |
| ☐ 10 Denver Broncos<br>Help From Behind | 1.50 | .60 | .15 |
| ☐ 11 Houston Oilers<br>Room to Move | 1.00 | .40 | .10 |
| ☐ 12 Houston Oilers<br>For The Defense | 1.00 | .40 | .10 |
| ☐ 13 Kansas City Chiefs<br>Chance to Motor | 1.00 | .40 | .10 |
| ☐ 14 Kansas City Chiefs<br>From the Ground Up | 1.00 | .40 | .10 |
| ☐ 15 Miami Dolphins<br>Eye of the Storm | 1.50 | .60 | .15 |
| ☐ 16 Miami Dolphins<br>When Man Takes<br>Flight | 1.50 | .60 | .15 |
| ☐ 17 New England Patriots<br>Turning the Corner | 1.00 | .40 | .10 |
| ☐ 18 New England Patriots<br>A Matter of Inches | 1.00 | .40 | .10 |
| ☐ 19 New York Jets<br>Keeping Him Clean<br>(Joe Namath) | 7.50 | 3.00 | .75 |
| ☐ 20 New York Jets<br>Plugging the Leaks | 1.00 | .40 | .10 |
| ☐ 21 Oakland Raiders<br>On Solid Ground | 1.50 | .60 | .15 |
| ☐ 22 Oakland Raiders<br>3-4, Shut The Door | 1.50 | .60 | .15 |
| ☐ 23 Pittsburgh Steelers<br>Daylight Saving<br>Time (Rocky Bleier) | 1.50 | .60 | .15 |
| ☐ 24 Pittsburgh Steelers<br>A Controlled Swarm | 1.50 | .60 | .15 |
| ☐ 25 San Diego Chargers<br>Youth on the Move<br>(Dan Fouts) | 3.00 | 1.20 | .30 |
| ☐ 26 San Diego Chargers<br>A Rude Housewarming | 1.00 | .40 | .10 |
| ☐ 27 Seattle Seahawks<br>Play Action Pass<br>(Jim Zorn faking) | 2.50 | 1.00 | .25 |
| ☐ 28 Seattle Seahawks<br>Birds of Prey | 1.50 | .60 | .15 |
| ☐ 29 Atlanta Falcons | 1.00 | .40 | .10 |

| | | | |
|---|---|---|---|
| Ad-Libbing<br>on Offense | | | |
| ☐ 30 Atlanta Falcons<br>A Futile Chase | 1.00 | .40 | .10 |
| ☐ 31 Chicago Bears<br>Follow Me<br>(Walter Payton blocking) | 4.00 | 1.60 | .40 |
| ☐ 32 Chicago Bears<br>A Nose for<br>the Ball | 1.00 | .40 | .10 |
| ☐ 33 Dallas Cowboys<br>The Plunge | 1.50 | .60 | .15 |
| ☐ 34 Dallas Cowboys<br>Unassisted Sack<br>(Ed Too Tall Jones) | 2.50 | 1.00 | .25 |
| ☐ 35 Detroit Lions<br>Motor City Might | 1.00 | .40 | .10 |
| ☐ 36 Detroit Lions<br>Block Party | 1.00 | .40 | .10 |
| ☐ 37 Green Bay Packers<br>Another Era | 1.00 | .40 | .10 |
| ☐ 38 Green Bay Packers<br>Face-to-Face<br>(Walter Payton tackled) | 4.00 | 1.60 | .40 |
| ☐ 39 Los Angeles Rams<br>Personal Escort | 1.00 | .40 | .10 |
| ☐ 40 Los Angeles Rams<br>A Closed Case | 1.00 | .40 | .10 |
| ☐ 41 Minnesota Vikings<br>Nothing Fancy | 1.00 | .40 | .10 |
| ☐ 42 Minnesota Vikings<br>Lending A Hand | 1.00 | .40 | .10 |
| ☐ 43 New Orleans Saints<br>Ample Protection | 1.00 | .40 | .10 |
| ☐ 44 New Orleans Saints<br>Well-Timed Contact | 1.00 | .40 | .10 |
| ☐ 45 New York Giants<br>Quick Pitch | 1.00 | .40 | .10 |
| ☐ 46 New York Giants<br>In A Pinch | 1.00 | .40 | .10 |
| ☐ 47 Philadelphia Eagles<br>When to Fly | 1.00 | .40 | .10 |
| ☐ 48 Philadelphia Eagles<br>Swooping Defense | 1.00 | .40 | .10 |
| ☐ 49 St. Louis Cardinals<br>Speed Outside<br>(Jim Hart) | 1.50 | .60 | .15 |
| ☐ 50 St. Louis Cardinals<br>The Circle Tightens | 1.00 | .40 | .10 |
| ☐ 51 San Francisco 49ers<br>Sideline Route<br>(Gene Washington) | 1.50 | .60 | .15 |
| ☐ 52 San Francisco 49ers<br>The Gold Rush | 1.00 | .40 | .10 |
| ☐ 53 Tampa Bay Buccaneers<br>A Rare Occasion | 1.00 | .40 | .10 |
| ☐ 54 Tampa Bay Buccaneers<br>Expansion Blues | 1.00 | .40 | .10 |
| ☐ 55 Washington Redskins<br>Splitting the Seam<br>(Joe Theismann passing) | 2.50 | 1.00 | .25 |
| ☐ 56 Washington Redskins<br>The Hands of Time | 1.00 | .40 | .10 |
| ☐ 57 Super Bowl I<br>Green Bay NFL 35<br>Kansas City AFL 10 | 1.50 | .60 | .15 |
| ☐ 58 Super Bowl II<br>Green Bay NFL 33<br>Oakland AFL 14 | 1.50 | .60 | .15 |
| ☐ 59 Super Bowl III<br>New York AFL 16<br>Baltimore NFL 7<br>(Tom Matte running) | 1.50 | .60 | .15 |
| ☐ 60 Super Bowl IV<br>Kansas City AFL 23<br>Minnesota NFL 7 | 1.50 | .60 | .15 |
| ☐ 61 Super Bowl V<br>Baltimore AFC 16<br>Dallas NFC 13 | 1.50 | .60 | .15 |
| ☐ 62 Super Bowl VI<br>Dallas NFC 24<br>Miami AFC 3<br>(Walt Garrison<br>running; Roger Staubach<br>also shown) | 3.00 | 1.20 | .30 |
| ☐ 63 Super Bowl VII<br>Miami AFC 14<br>Washington NFC 7<br>(Larry Csonka<br>running) | 2.50 | 1.00 | .25 |
| ☐ 64 Super Bowl VIII<br>Miami AFC 24<br>Minnesota NFC 7<br>(Larry Csonka<br>running) | 2.50 | 1.00 | .25 |
| ☐ 65 Super Bowl IX<br>Pittsburgh AFC 16<br>Minnesota NFC 6 | 1.50 | .60 | .15 |

| | NRMT | VG-E | GOOD |
|---|---|---|---|
| ☐ 66 Super Bowl X | 3.00 | 1.20 | .30 |
| Pittsburgh AFC 21 | | | |
| Dallas NFC 17 | | | |
| (Terry Bradshaw | | | |
| and Franco Harris) | | | |
| ☐ 67 Super Bowl XI | 3.00 | 1.20 | .30 |
| Oakland AFC 32 | | | |
| Minnesota NFC 14 | | | |
| (Ken Stabler) | | | |

# 1978 Fleer Team Action

The 1978 Fleer Teams in Action football set contains 68 action scenes. The cards measure 2 1/2" by 3 1/2". As in the previous year, each team is depicted on two cards and each Super Bowl is depicted on one card. The additional card in comparison to last year's set comes from the additional Super Bowl which was played during the year. The fronts have yellow borders. The card backs are printed with black ink on gray stock. The cards are numbered and feature a 1978 copyright date. Cards were issued in wax packs of seven team cards plus four team logo stickers.

| | NRMT | VG-E | GOOD |
|---|---|---|---|
| COMPLETE SET (68) | 40.00 | 16.00 | 4.00 |
| COMMON CARD (1-56) | .60 | .24 | .06 |
| COMMON SB CARD (57-68) | .75 | .30 | .07 |
| | | | |
| ☐ 1 Atlanta Falcons | 1.25 | .50 | .12 |
| Sticking to Basics | | | |
| ☐ 2 Atlanta Falcons | .60 | .24 | .06 |
| In Pursuit | | | |
| ☐ 3 Baltimore Colts | .60 | .24 | .06 |
| Forward Plunge | | | |
| ☐ 4 Baltimore Colts | .60 | .24 | .06 |
| Stacking It Up | | | |
| ☐ 5 Buffalo Bills | .60 | .24 | .06 |
| Daylight Breakers | | | |
| ☐ 6 Buffalo Bills | .60 | .24 | .06 |
| Swarming Defense | | | |
| ☐ 7 Chicago Bears | 5.00 | 2.00 | .50 |
| Up The Middle | | | |
| (Walter Payton | | | |
| running) | | | |
| ☐ 8 Chicago Bears | .60 | .24 | .06 |
| Rejuvenated Defense | | | |
| ☐ 9 Cincinnati Bengals | 1.50 | .60 | .15 |
| Poise and Execution | | | |
| (Ken Anderson) | | | |
| ☐ 10 Cincinnati Bengals | .60 | .24 | .06 |
| Down-to-Earth | | | |
| ☐ 11 Cleveland Browns | 1.00 | .40 | .10 |
| Breakaway | | | |
| (Greg Pruitt) | | | |
| ☐ 12 Cleveland Browns | 1.00 | .40 | .10 |
| Red Dogs | | | |
| (Ken Anderson tackled) | | | |
| ☐ 13 Dallas Cowboys | 6.00 | 2.40 | .60 |
| Up and Over | | | |
| (Tony Dorsett) | | | |
| ☐ 14 Dallas Cowboys | 1.00 | .40 | .10 |
| Doomsday II | | | |
| ☐ 15 Denver Broncos | .75 | .30 | .07 |
| Mile-High Offense | | | |
| ☐ 16 Denver Broncos | 2.50 | 1.00 | .25 |
| Orange Crush | | | |
| (Walter Payton tackled) | | | |
| ☐ 17 Detroit Lions | .60 | .24 | .06 |
| End-Around | | | |
| ☐ 18 Detroit Lions | .60 | .24 | .06 |
| Special Teams | | | |
| ☐ 19 Green Bay Packers | .60 | .24 | .06 |
| Running Strong | | | |
| ☐ 20 Green Bay Packers | .60 | .24 | .06 |
| Tearin' em Down | | | |

| | NRMT | VG-E | GOOD |
|---|---|---|---|
| ☐ 21 Houston Oilers | .60 | .24 | .06 |
| Goal-Line Drive | | | |
| ☐ 22 Houston Oilers | .60 | .24 | .06 |
| Interception | | | |
| ☐ 23 Kansas City Chiefs | .75 | .30 | .07 |
| Running Wide | | | |
| (Ed Podolak) | | | |
| ☐ 24 Kansas City Chiefs | .60 | .24 | .06 |
| Armed Defense | | | |
| ☐ 25 Los Angeles Rams | .60 | .24 | .06 |
| Rushing Power | | | |
| ☐ 26 Los Angeles Rams | .60 | .24 | .06 |
| Backing the Line | | | |
| ☐ 27 Miami Dolphins | 2.50 | 1.00 | .25 |
| Protective Pocket | | | |
| (Bob Griese passing) | | | |
| ☐ 28 Miami Dolphins | .75 | .30 | .07 |
| Life in the Pit | | | |
| ☐ 29 Minnesota Vikings | 1.00 | .40 | .10 |
| Storm Breakers | | | |
| (Foreman in snow) | | | |
| ☐ 30 Minnesota Vikings | .60 | .24 | .06 |
| Blocking the Kick | | | |
| ☐ 31 New England Patriots | .60 | .24 | .06 |
| Clearing The Way | | | |
| ☐ 32 New England Patriots | .60 | .24 | .06 |
| One-on-One | | | |
| ☐ 33 New Orleans Saints | .60 | .24 | .06 |
| Extra Yardage | | | |
| ☐ 34 New Orleans Saints | .60 | .24 | .06 |
| Drag-Down Defense | | | |
| ☐ 35 New York Giants | .60 | .24 | .06 |
| Ready, Aim, Fire | | | |
| ☐ 36 New York Giants | .60 | .24 | .06 |
| Meeting of Minds | | | |
| ☐ 37 New York Jets | .60 | .24 | .06 |
| Take-Off | | | |
| ☐ 38 New York Jets | .60 | .24 | .06 |
| Ambush | | | |
| ☐ 39 Oakland Raiders | 1.00 | .40 | .10 |
| Power 31 Left | | | |
| ☐ 40 Oakland Raiders | 1.00 | .40 | .10 |
| Welcoming Committee | | | |
| ☐ 41 Philadelphia Eagles | .60 | .24 | .06 |
| Taking Flight | | | |
| ☐ 42 Philadelphia Eagles | .60 | .24 | .06 |
| Soaring High | | | |
| ☐ 43 Pittsburgh Steelers | .75 | .30 | .07 |
| Ironclad Offense | | | |
| ☐ 44 Pittsburgh Steelers | 1.50 | .60 | .15 |
| Curtain Closes | | | |
| (Jack Lambert) | | | |
| ☐ 45 St. Louis Cardinals | .60 | .24 | .06 |
| A Good Bet | | | |
| ☐ 46 St. Louis Cardinals | .60 | .24 | .06 |
| Gang Tackle | | | |
| ☐ 47 San Diego Chargers | .60 | .24 | .06 |
| Circus Catch | | | |
| ☐ 48 San Diego Chargers | .60 | .24 | .06 |
| Charge | | | |
| ☐ 49 San Francisco 49ers | .60 | .24 | .06 |
| Follow the Block | | | |
| ☐ 50 San Francisco 49ers | .60 | .24 | .06 |
| Goal-Line Stand | | | |
| ☐ 51 Seattle Seahawks | .75 | .30 | .07 |
| Finding Daylight | | | |
| ☐ 52 Seattle Seahawks | .75 | .30 | .07 |
| Rushing The Pass | | | |
| ☐ 53 Tampa Bay Buccaneers | .60 | .24 | .06 |
| Play Action | | | |
| ☐ 54 Tampa Bay Buccaneers | .60 | .24 | .06 |
| Youth on the Move | | | |
| ☐ 55 Washington Redskins | .60 | .24 | .06 |
| Renegade Runners | | | |
| ☐ 56 Washington Redskins | .60 | .24 | .06 |
| Dual Action | | | |
| ☐ 57 Super Bowl I | 2.00 | .80 | .20 |
| Green Bay NFL 35 | | | |
| Kansas City AFL 10 | | | |
| (Bart Starr) | | | |
| ☐ 58 Super Bowl II | .75 | .30 | .07 |
| Green Bay NFL 33 | | | |
| Oakland AFL 14 | | | |
| ☐ 59 Super Bowl III | .75 | .30 | .07 |
| New York AFL 16 | | | |
| Baltimore NFL 7 | | | |
| ☐ 60 Super Bowl IV | .75 | .30 | .07 |
| Kansas City AFL 23 | | | |
| Minnesota NFL 7 | | | |
| ☐ 61 Super Bowl V | .75 | .30 | .07 |
| Baltimore AFC 16 | | | |
| Dallas NFC 13 | | | |
| ☐ 62 Super Bowl VI | .75 | .30 | .07 |
| Dallas NFC 24 | | | |
| Miami AFC 3 | | | |
| ☐ 63 Super Bowl VII | .75 | .30 | .07 |
| Miami AFC 14 | | | |

Washington NFC 7

| | NRMT | VG-E | GOOD |
|---|---|---|---|
| ☐ 64 Super Bowl VIII | 2.00 | .80 | .20 |
| Miami AFC 24 | | | |
| Minnesota NFC 7 | | | |
| (Larry Csonka | | | |
| running) | | | |
| ☐ 65 Super Bowl IX | 2.50 | 1.00 | .25 |
| Pittsburgh AFC 16 | | | |
| Minnesota NFC 6 | | | |
| (Terry Bradshaw | | | |
| and Franco Harris) | | | |
| ☐ 66 Super Bowl X | .75 | .30 | .07 |
| Pittsburgh AFC 21 | | | |
| Dallas NFC 17 | | | |
| ☐ 67 Super Bowl XI | 1.50 | .60 | .15 |
| Oakland AFC 32 | | | |
| Minnesota NFC 14 | | | |
| (Ken Stabler hand off) | | | |
| ☐ 68 Super Bowl XII | 3.00 | 1.20 | .30 |
| Dallas NFC 27 | | | |
| Denver AFC 10 | | | |
| (Roger Staubach and | | | |
| Tony Dorsett) | | | |

# 1979 Fleer Team Action

The 1979 Fleer Teams in Action football set mirrors the previous two sets in design (colorful action scenes with specific players not identified) and contains an additional card for the most recent Super Bowl making a total of 69 cards in the set. The cards measure 2 1/2" by 3 1/2". The fronts have white borders, and the backs are printed in black ink on gray stock. Cards are numbered on the back and feature a 1979 copyright date. The card numbering follows team name alphabetical order followed by Super Bowl cards in chronological order. Cards were issued in wax packs of seven team cards plus three team logo stickers.

| | NRMT | VG-E | GOOD |
|---|---|---|---|
| COMPLETE SET (69) | 35.00 | 14.00 | 3.50 |
| COMMON CARD (1-56) | .50 | .20 | .05 |
| COMMON SB CARD (57-69) | .60 | .24 | .06 |
| | | | |
| ☐ 1 Atlanta Falcons | 1.00 | .40 | .10 |
| What's Up | | | |
| Front Counts | | | |
| ☐ 2 Atlanta Falcons | .50 | .20 | .05 |
| Following The | | | |
| Bouncing Ball | | | |
| ☐ 3 Baltimore Colts | .50 | .20 | .05 |
| Big Enough To Drive | | | |
| A Truck Through | | | |
| ☐ 4 Baltimore Colts | .50 | .20 | .05 |
| When The Defense | | | |
| Becomes The Offense | | | |
| ☐ 5 Buffalo Bills | .50 | .20 | .05 |
| Full Steam Ahead | | | |
| ☐ 6 Buffalo Bills | .50 | .20 | .05 |
| Three's A Crowd | | | |
| ☐ 7 Chicago Bears | .50 | .20 | .05 |
| Moving Out As One | | | |
| ☐ 8 Chicago Bears | .50 | .20 | .05 |
| Stack 'Em Up | | | |
| ☐ 9 Cincinnati Bengals | .50 | .20 | .05 |
| Out In The | | | |
| Open Field | | | |
| ☐ 10 Cincinnati Bengals | .50 | .20 | .05 |
| Sandwiched | | | |
| ☐ 11 Cleveland Browns | .50 | .20 | .05 |
| Protective Pocket | | | |
| ☐ 12 Cleveland Browns | .50 | .20 | .05 |
| Shake Rattle | | | |
| And Roll | | | |
| ☐ 13 Dallas Cowboys | 3.00 | 1.20 | .30 |
| Paving The Way | | | |

| | NRMT | VG-E | GOOD |
|---|---|---|---|
| (Tony Dorsett running) | | | |
| ☐ 14 Dallas Cowboys | .60 | .24 | .06 |
| The Right Place | | | |
| At The Right Time | | | |
| ☐ 15 Denver Broncos | .60 | .24 | .06 |
| A Stable Of Runners | | | |
| ☐ 16 Denver Broncos | .60 | .24 | .06 |
| Orange Crush | | | |
| ☐ 17 Detroit Lions | .50 | .20 | .05 |
| Through The Line | | | |
| ☐ 18 Detroit Lions | .50 | .20 | .05 |
| Tracked Down | | | |
| ☐ 19 Green Bay Packers | .50 | .20 | .05 |
| Power Play | | | |
| ☐ 20 Green Bay Packers | .50 | .20 | .05 |
| Four-To-One Odds | | | |
| ☐ 21 Houston Oilers | 8.00 | 3.25 | .80 |
| Offensive Gusher | | | |
| (Earl Campbell running) | | | |
| ☐ 22 Houston Oilers | .50 | .20 | .05 |
| Gotcha | | | |
| ☐ 23 Kansas City Chiefs | .50 | .20 | .05 |
| Get Wings | | | |
| ☐ 24 Kansas City Chiefs | .50 | .20 | .05 |
| Ambushed | | | |
| ☐ 25 Los Angeles Rams | .50 | .20 | .05 |
| Men In The Middle | | | |
| ☐ 26 Los Angeles Rams | .50 | .20 | .05 |
| Nowhere To Go | | | |
| But Down | | | |
| ☐ 27 Miami Dolphins | .60 | .24 | .06 |
| Escort Service | | | |
| ☐ 28 Miami Dolphins | .60 | .24 | .06 |
| All For One | | | |
| ☐ 29 Minnesota Vikings | .50 | .20 | .05 |
| Up And Over | | | |
| ☐ 30 Minnesota Vikings | .50 | .20 | .05 |
| The Purple Gang | | | |
| ☐ 31 New England Patriots | .50 | .20 | .05 |
| Prepare For Takeoff | | | |
| ☐ 32 New England Patriots | .50 | .20 | .05 |
| Dept. Of Defense | | | |
| ☐ 33 New Orleans Saints | 1.00 | .40 | .10 |
| Bombs Away | | | |
| (Archie Manning) | | | |
| ☐ 34 New Orleans Saints | .50 | .20 | .05 |
| Duel In The Dome | | | |
| ☐ 35 New York Giants | .50 | .20 | .05 |
| Battle Of The Line | | | |
| Of Scrimmage | | | |
| ☐ 36 New York Giants | .50 | .20 | .05 |
| Piled Up | | | |
| ☐ 37 New York Jets | .50 | .20 | .05 |
| Hitting The Hole | | | |
| ☐ 38 New York Jets | .50 | .20 | .05 |
| Making Sure | | | |
| ☐ 39 Oakland Raiders | 1.50 | .60 | .15 |
| Left-Handed | | | |
| Strength | | | |
| (Kenny Stabler) | | | |
| ☐ 40 Oakland Raiders | .75 | .30 | .07 |
| Black Sunday | | | |
| ☐ 41 Philadelphia Eagles | .50 | .20 | .05 |
| Ready Aim Fire | | | |
| ☐ 42 Philadelphia Eagles | .50 | .20 | .05 |
| Closing In | | | |
| ☐ 43 Pittsburgh Steelers | .60 | .24 | .06 |
| Anchor Man | | | |
| ☐ 44 Pittsburgh Steelers | .75 | .30 | .07 |
| The Steel Curtain | | | |
| ☐ 45 St. Louis Cardinals | .75 | .30 | .07 |
| High Altitude Bomber | | | |
| (Jim Hart) | | | |
| ☐ 46 St. Louis Cardinals | .50 | .20 | .05 |
| Three On One | | | |
| ☐ 47 San Diego Chargers | .50 | .20 | .05 |
| Charge | | | |
| ☐ 48 San Diego Chargers | .50 | .20 | .05 |
| Special Teams Shot | | | |
| ☐ 49 San Francisco 49ers | .50 | .20 | .05 |
| In For The Score | | | |
| ☐ 50 San Francisco 49ers | .50 | .20 | .05 |
| Nothing But | | | |
| Red Shirts | | | |
| ☐ 51 Seattle Seahawks | .60 | .24 | .06 |
| North-South Runner | | | |
| ☐ 52 Seattle Seahawks | .60 | .24 | .06 |
| The Sting | | | |
| ☐ 53 Tampa Bay Buccaneers | .50 | .20 | .05 |
| Hitting Paydirt | | | |
| ☐ 54 Tampa Bay Buccaneers | .50 | .20 | .05 |
| Making 'Em Pay | | | |
| The Price | | | |
| ☐ 55 Washington Redskins | .50 | .20 | .05 |
| On The Warpath | | | |
| ☐ 56 Washington Redskins | .50 | .20 | .05 |
| Drawing A Crowd | | | |
| ☐ 57 Super Bowl I | 1.00 | .40 | .10 |

Green Bay NFL 35
Kansas City AFL 10
(Jim Taylor running)
☐ 58 Super Bowl II ......................... 1.25 .50 .12
Green Bay NFL 33
Oakland AFL 14
(Bart Starr passing)
☐ 59 Super Bowl III ........................ .60 .24 .06
New York AFL 16
Baltimore NFL 7
☐ 60 Super Bowl IV ........................ .60 .24 .06
Kansas City AFL 23
Minnesota NFL 7
☐ 61 Super Bowl V ......................... .60 .24 .06
Baltimore AFC 16
Dallas NFC 13
☐ 62 Super Bowl VI ........................ 2.00 .80 .20
Dallas NFC 24
Miami AFC 3
(Bob Griese
and Bob Lilly)
☐ 63 Super Bowl VII ....................... .60 .24 .06
Miami AFC 14
Washington NFC 7
☐ 64 Super Bowl VIII ..................... 2.00 .80 .20
Miami AFC 24
Minnesota NFC 7
(Bob Griese and
Larry Csonka)
☐ 65 Super Bowl IX ........................ 2.50 1.00 .25
Pittsburgh AFC 16
Minnesota NFC 6
(Terry Bradshaw and
Franco Harris)
☐ 66 Super Bowl X ......................... .60 .24 .06
Pittsburgh AFC 21
Dallas NFC 17
☐ 67 Super Bowl XI ........................ .60 .24 .06
Oakland AFC 32
Minnesota NFC 14
☐ 68 Super Bowl XII ....................... .60 .24 .06
Dallas NFC 27
Denver AFC 10
☐ 69 Super Bowl XIII ...................... 1.25 .50 .12
Pittsburgh AFC 35
Dallas NFC 31

## 1980 Fleer Team Action

The 1980 Fleer Teams in Action football set continues the tradition of earlier sets but has one additional card for the most recent Super Bowl, i.e., now 70 cards in the set. The cards are in full color and measure 2 1/2" by 3 1/2". The fronts have white borders and the backs are printed in black on gray stock. The cards are numbered on back and feature a 1980 copyright date. The card numbering follows team name alphabetical order followed by Super Bowl cards in chronological order. Cards were issued in seven-card wax packs along with three team logo stickers.

|  | MINT | EXC | G-VG |
|---|---|---|---|
| COMPLETE SET (70) ...................... | 30.00 | 12.00 | 3.00 |
| COMMON CARD (1-56) ...................... | .40 | .16 | .04 |
| COMMON SB CARD (57-70) ............ | .50 | .20 | .05 |

☐ 1 Atlanta Falcons .......................... 1.00 .40 .10
Getting The
Extra Yards
☐ 2 Atlanta Falcons ......................... .40 .16 .04
Falcons Get
Their Prey
☐ 3 Baltimore Colts .......................... .60 .24 .06
Looking For Daylight
(Joe Washington)
☐ 4 Baltimore Colts .......................... .40 .16 .04

Ready If Needed
☐ 5 Buffalo Bills ................................ .40 .16 .04
You Block For Me and
I'll Block For You
☐ 6 Buffalo Bills ................................ .40 .16 .04
Stand Em Up And
Push 'Em Back
☐ 7 Chicago Bears ........................... 4.00 1.60 .40
Coming Through
(Walter Payton)
☐ 8 Chicago Bears ........................... .40 .16 .04
Four On One
☐ 9 Cincinnati Bengals ..................... .40 .16 .04
Power Running
☐ 10 Cincinnati Bengals ................... .40 .16 .04
Out Of Running Room
☐ 11 Cleveland Browns ..................... 2.00 .80 .20
End Around
(Ozzie Newsome)
☐ 12 Cleveland Browns .................... .40 .16 .04
Rubber Band Defense
☐ 13 Dallas Cowboys ........................ 2.00 .80 .20
Point Of Attack
(Tony Dorsett)
☐ 14 Dallas Cowboys ........................ .60 .24 .06
Man In The Middle
(Bob Breunig)
☐ 15 Denver Broncos ........................ .50 .20 .05
Strong And Steady
☐ 16 Denver Broncos ........................ .50 .20 .05
Orange Power
☐ 17 Detroit Lions ............................. .40 .16 .04
On The March
☐ 18 Detroit Lions ............................. .40 .16 .04
The Silver Rush
☐ 19 Green Bay Packers ................... .40 .16 .04
Getting Underway
☐ 20 Green Bay Packers ................... .40 .16 .04
The Best Offense
Is A Good Defense
☐ 21 Houston Oilers .......................... .40 .16 .04
Airborne
☐ 22 Houston Oilers .......................... .40 .16 .04
Search And Destroy
☐ 23 Kansas City Chiefs ................... .40 .16 .04
Blazing The Trail
☐ 24 Kansas City Chiefs ................... .40 .16 .04
Making Sure
☐ 25 Los Angeles Rams .................... .40 .16 .04
One Good Turn
Deserves Another
☐ 26 Los Angeles Rams .................... .40 .16 .04
Shedding The Block
☐ 27 Miami Dolphins ......................... .50 .20 .05
Sweeping The Flanks
☐ 28 Miami Dolphins ......................... .50 .20 .05
Keep 'Em Busy
☐ 29 Minnesota Vikings ..................... .40 .16 .04
One Man To Beat
☐ 30 Minnesota Vikings ..................... .40 .16 .04
Purple People
Eaters II
☐ 31 New England Patriots ............. .40 .16 .04
Hitting The Hole
☐ 32 New England Patriots ............. .40 .16 .04
Getting To The Ball
☐ 33 New Orleans Saints ................. .40 .16 .04
Splitting The
Defenders
☐ 34 New Orleans Saints ................. 1.50 .60 .15
Don't Let Him
Get Outside
(Joe Theismann)
☐ 35 New York Giants ..................... 4.00 1.60 .40
Audible
(Phil Simms)
☐ 36 New York Giants ..................... .40 .16 .04
Wrong Side Up
☐ 37 New York Jets ......................... .40 .16 .04
Make Him Miss
☐ 38 New York Jets ......................... .50 .20 .05
The Only Way To
Play (Mark Gastineau)
☐ 39 Oakland Raiders ...................... .75 .30 .07
Pulling Out All
The Stops
☐ 40 Oakland Raiders ...................... .75 .30 .07
Right On
☐ 41 Philadelphia Eagles ................ .40 .16 .04
Not Pretty, But
Still Points
☐ 42 Philadelphia Eagles ................ .40 .16 .04
Applying The Clamps
☐ 43 Pittsburgh Steelers ................. 2.00 .80 .20
All Systems Go
(Franco Harris sweep)
☐ 44 Pittsburgh Steelers ................. .75 .30 .07
Still The Steel

Curtain
| | | | |
|---|---|---|---|
| ☐ 45 St. Louis Cardinals | 2.00 | .80 | .20 |
| On The Move | | | |
| (Ottis Anderson) | | | |
| ☐ 46 St. Louis Cardinals | .40 | .16 | .04 |
| Long Gone | | | |
| ☐ 47 San Diego Chargers | .40 | .16 | .04 |
| Short-Range Success | | | |
| ☐ 48 San Diego Chargers | .40 | .16 | .04 |
| Pursuit | | | |
| ☐ 49 San Francisco 49ers | .40 | .16 | .04 |
| Getting Field Position | | | |
| ☐ 50 San Francisco 49ers | .40 | .16 | .04 |
| Finding A Nugget | | | |
| ☐ 51 Seattle Seahawks | .50 | .20 | .05 |
| They'll Try | | | |
| Anything Once | | | |
| ☐ 52 Seattle Seahawks | .50 | .20 | .05 |
| Paying The Price | | | |
| ☐ 53 Tampa Bay Buccaneers | .40 | .16 | .04 |
| Coming Of Age | | | |
| ☐ 54 Tampa Bay Buccaneers | 3.00 | 1.20 | .30 |
| 3-4 Shut The Door | | | |
| (Walter Payton | | | |
| tackled) | | | |
| ☐ 55 Washington Redskins | .40 | .16 | .04 |
| Wide Open | | | |
| ☐ 56 Washington Redskins | .40 | .16 | .04 |
| Rude Reception | | | |
| ☐ 57 Super Bowl I | .50 | .20 | .05 |
| Green Bay NFL 35 | | | |
| Kansas City AFL 10 | | | |
| ☐ 58 Super Bowl II | 1.00 | .40 | .10 |
| Green Bay NFL 33 | | | |
| Oakland AFL 14 | | | |
| (Bart Starr) | | | |
| ☐ 59 Super Bowl III | 3.00 | 1.20 | .30 |
| New York AFL 16 | | | |
| Baltimore NFL 7 | | | |
| (Joe Namath) | | | |
| ☐ 60 Super Bowl IV | .50 | .20 | .05 |
| Kansas City AFL 23 | | | |
| Minnesota NFL 7 | | | |
| ☐ 61 Super Bowl V | .50 | .20 | .05 |
| Baltimore AFC 16 | | | |
| Dallas NFC 13 | | | |
| ☐ 62 Super Bowl VI | 2.50 | 1.00 | .25 |
| Dallas NFC 24 | | | |
| Miami AFC 3 | | | |
| (Roger Staubach) | | | |
| ☐ 63 Super Bowl VII | .50 | .20 | .05 |
| Miami AFC 14 | | | |
| Washington NFC 7 | | | |
| ☐ 64 Super Bowl VIII | .50 | .20 | .05 |
| Miami AFC 24 | | | |
| Minnesota NFC 7 | | | |
| ☐ 65 Super Bowl IX | 1.50 | .60 | .15 |
| Pittsburgh AFC 16 | | | |
| Minnesota NFC 6 | | | |
| (Bradshaw/Bleier) | | | |
| ☐ 66 Super Bowl X | 1.00 | .40 | .10 |
| Pittsburgh AFC 21 | | | |
| Dallas NFC 17 | | | |
| (Jack Lambert) | | | |
| ☐ 67 Super Bowl XI | .60 | .24 | .06 |
| Oakland AFC 44 | | | |
| Minnesota NFC 14 | | | |
| (Chuck Foreman) | | | |
| ☐ 68 Super Bowl XII | .50 | .20 | .05 |
| Dallas NFC 27 | | | |
| Denver AFC 10 | | | |
| ☐ 69 Super Bowl XIII | 2.00 | .80 | .20 |
| Pittsburgh AFC 35 | | | |
| Dallas NFC 31 | | | |
| (Terry Bradshaw) | | | |
| ☐ 70 Super Bowl XIV | 1.50 | .60 | .15 |
| Pittsburgh AFC 31 | | | |
| Los Angeles NFC 19 | | | |
| (Franco Harris) | | | |

# 1981 Fleer Team Action

The 1981 Fleer Teams in Action football set deviates from previous years in that, while each team is depicted on two cards and each Super Bowl is depicted on one card, an additional group of cards (72-88) have been added to make the set number 88 cards, no doubt to accomodate the press sheet size. The card numbering follows team name alphabetical order followed by Super Bowl cards in chronological order and the last group of miscellaneous cards. The cards measure 2 1/2" by 3 1/2". The card fronts are in full color with white borders, and the card backs are printed in blue and red on white stock. The cards are numbered on the backs and contain a 1981 copyright. Cards were issued in eight-card wax packs along with three team logo stickers.

| | MINT | EXC | G-VG |
|---|---|---|---|
| COMPLETE SET (88) | 25.00 | 10.00 | 2.50 |
| COMMON CARD (1-88) | .30 | .12 | .03 |
| ☐ 1 Atlanta Falcons | .75 | .30 | .07 |
| Out In The Open | | | |
| (William Andrews) | | | |
| ☐ 2 Atlanta Falcons | .30 | .12 | .03 |
| Grits Blitz | | | |
| ☐ 3 Baltimore Colts | .30 | .12 | .03 |
| Sprung Through | | | |
| The Line | | | |
| ☐ 4 Baltimore Colts | .30 | .12 | .03 |
| Human Pyramid | | | |
| ☐ 5 Buffalo Bills | .30 | .12 | .03 |
| Buffalo Bills' | | | |
| Wild West Show | | | |
| ☐ 6 Buffalo Bills | .30 | .12 | .03 |
| Buffaloed | | | |
| ☐ 7 Chicago Bears | 3.00 | 1.20 | .30 |
| About To Hit Paydirt | | | |
| (Walter Payton) | | | |
| ☐ 8 Chicago Bears | .30 | .12 | .03 |
| Bear Trap | | | |
| ☐ 9 Cincinnati Bengals | .40 | .16 | .04 |
| Behind The Wall | | | |
| (Pete Johnson) | | | |
| ☐ 10 Cincinnati Bengals | .30 | .12 | .03 |
| Black Cloud | | | |
| ☐ 11 Cleveland Browns | .50 | .20 | .05 |
| Point Of Attack | | | |
| (Mike Pruitt) | | | |
| ☐ 12 Cleveland Browns | .60 | .24 | .06 |
| The Only Way To | | | |
| Go Is Down | | | |
| (Rocky Bleier tackled) | | | |
| ☐ 13 Dallas Cowboys | .50 | .20 | .05 |
| Big O In Big D | | | |
| (Ron Springs fumble) | | | |
| ☐ 14 Dallas Cowboys | .50 | .20 | .05 |
| Headed Off At The Pass | | | |
| ☐ 15 Denver Broncos | .40 | .16 | .04 |
| Man Versus Elements | | | |
| (Craig Morton in snow) | | | |
| ☐ 16 Denver Broncos | .40 | .16 | .04 |
| The Old High-Low | | | |
| Treatment | | | |
| ☐ 17 Detroit Lions | .75 | .30 | .07 |
| Play Action | | | |
| (Billy Sims) | | | |
| ☐ 18 Detroit Lions | .30 | .12 | .03 |
| Into The Lions' Den | | | |
| ☐ 19 Green Bay Packers | .30 | .12 | .03 |
| A Packer Packs | | | |
| The Pigskin | | | |
| ☐ 20 Green Bay Packers | .30 | .12 | .03 |
| Sandwiched | | | |
| ☐ 21 Houston Oilers | .30 | .12 | .03 |
| Wait A Minute | | | |
| ☐ 22 Houston Oilers | .30 | .12 | .03 |
| 3-4 Shut The Door | | | |
| ☐ 23 Kansas City Chiefs | .30 | .12 | .03 |
| On The Ball | | | |
| ☐ 24 Kansas City Chiefs | .30 | .12 | .03 |
| Seeing Red | | | |
| ☐ 25 Los Angeles Rams | .30 | .12 | .03 |
| The Point Of Attack | | | |
| ☐ 26 Los Angeles Rams | .30 | .12 | .03 |
| Get Your Hands Up | | | |
| ☐ 27 Miami Dolphins | .50 | .20 | .05 |
| Plenty Of Time | | | |
| (David Woodley) | | | |
| ☐ 28 Miami Dolphins | .40 | .16 | .04 |
| Pursuit | | | |
| ☐ 29 Minnesota Vikings | .30 | .12 | .03 |
| Tough Yardage | | | |
| ☐ 30 Minnesota Vikings | .40 | .16 | .04 |

| | | | |
|---|---|---|---|
| Purple Avalanche | | | |
| (Pete Johnson) | | | |
| ☐ 31 New England Patriots | .30 | .12 | .03 |
| In High Gear | | | |
| ☐ 32 New England Patriots | 1.00 | .40 | .10 |
| Keep 'Em Covered | | | |
| (Ken Stabler) | | | |
| ☐ 33 New Orleans Saints | .60 | .24 | .06 |
| Setting Up | | | |
| (Archie Manning) | | | |
| ☐ 34 New Orleans Saints | .30 | .12 | .03 |
| Air Ball | | | |
| ☐ 35 New York Giants | .30 | .12 | .03 |
| Off Tackle | | | |
| ☐ 36 New York Giants | .30 | .12 | .03 |
| In The Land Of | | | |
| The Giants | | | |
| ☐ 37 New York Jets | .40 | .16 | .04 |
| Cleared For Lauching | | | |
| (Richard Todd) | | | |
| ☐ 38 New York Jets | .30 | .12 | .03 |
| Airborne | | | |
| ☐ 39 Oakland Raiders | .50 | .20 | .05 |
| Off And Running | | | |
| ☐ 40 Oakland Raiders | .50 | .20 | .05 |
| Block That Kick | | | |
| ☐ 41 Philadelphia Eagles | .30 | .12 | .03 |
| About To Take Flight | | | |
| ☐ 42 Philadelphia Eagles | .50 | .20 | .05 |
| Birds Of Prey | | | |
| (Robert Newhouse) | | | |
| ☐ 43 Pittsburgh Steelers | 1.25 | .50 | .12 |
| Here Come The | | | |
| Infantry | | | |
| (Franco Harris) | | | |
| ☐ 44 Pittsburgh Steelers | .40 | .16 | .04 |
| Like A Steel Trap | | | |
| ☐ 45 St. Louis Cardinals | .30 | .12 | .03 |
| Run To Daylight | | | |
| ☐ 46 St. Louis Cardinals | .30 | .12 | .03 |
| Stacked Up And Up | | | |
| ☐ 47 San Diego Chargers | .30 | .12 | .03 |
| Straight-Ahead Power | | | |
| ☐ 48 San Diego Chargers | .30 | .12 | .03 |
| Stonewalled | | | |
| ☐ 49 San Francisco 49ers | .30 | .12 | .03 |
| Follow The Leader | | | |
| ☐ 50 San Francisco 49ers | .30 | .12 | .03 |
| Search And Destroy | | | |
| ☐ 51 Seattle Seahawks | .30 | .12 | .03 |
| Short-Range Success | | | |
| ☐ 52 Seattle Seahawks | .30 | .12 | .03 |
| Take Down | | | |
| ☐ 53 Tampa Bay Buccaneers | .40 | .16 | .04 |
| Orange Blossom Special | | | |
| (Jerry Eckwood) | | | |
| ☐ 54 Tampa Bay Buccaneers | .30 | .12 | .03 |
| Tropical Storm Buc | | | |
| ☐ 55 Washington Redskins | .30 | .12 | .03 |
| Alone For A Moment | | | |
| ☐ 56 Washington Redskins | .30 | .12 | .03 |
| Ambushed | | | |
| ☐ 57 Super Bowl I | .60 | .24 | .06 |
| Green Bay NFL 35 | | | |
| Kansas City AFL 10 | | | |
| (Jim Taylor) | | | |
| ☐ 58 Super Bowl II | .30 | .12 | .03 |
| Green Bay NFL 35 | | | |
| Oakland AFL 14 | | | |
| ☐ 59 Super Bowl III | .30 | .12 | .03 |
| New York AFL 16 | | | |
| Baltimore NFL 7 | | | |
| ☐ 60 Super Bowl IV | .30 | .12 | .03 |
| Kansas City AFL 23 | | | |
| Minnesota NFL 7 | | | |
| ☐ 61 Super Bowl V | .30 | .12 | .03 |
| Baltimore AFC 16 | | | |
| Dallas NFC 13 | | | |
| ☐ 62 Super Bowl VI | .30 | .12 | .03 |
| Dallas NFC 24 | | | |
| Miami AFC 3 | | | |
| ☐ 63 Super Bowl VII | .30 | .12 | .03 |
| Miami AFC 14 | | | |
| Washington NFC 7 | | | |
| ☐ 64 Super Bowl VIII | 1.00 | .40 | .10 |
| Miami AFC 24 | | | |
| Minnesota NFC 7 | | | |
| (Larry Csonka | | | |
| running) | | | |
| ☐ 65 Super Bowl IX | 1.25 | .50 | .12 |
| Pittsburgh AFC 16 | | | |
| Minnesota NFC 6 | | | |
| (Franco Harris) | | | |
| ☐ 66 Super Bowl X | .40 | .16 | .04 |
| Pittsburgh AFC 21 | | | |
| Dallas NFC 17 | | | |
| ☐ 67 Super Bowl XI | .75 | .30 | .07 |
| Oakland AFC 32 | | | |

| | | | |
|---|---|---|---|
| Minnesota NFC 14 | | | |
| (Kenny Stabler) | | | |
| ☐ 68 Super Bowl XII | 2.00 | .80 | .20 |
| Dallas NFC 27 | | | |
| Denver AFC 10 | | | |
| (Roger Staubach | | | |
| and Tony Dorsett) | | | |
| ☐ 69 Super Bowl XIII | 2.00 | .80 | .20 |
| Pittsburgh AFC 35 | | | |
| Dallas NFC 31 | | | |
| (Roger Staubach | | | |
| and Tony Dorsett) | | | |
| ☐ 70 Super Bowl XIV | 1.25 | .50 | .12 |
| Pittsburgh AFC 31 | | | |
| Los Angeles NFC 19 | | | |
| (Franco Harris) | | | |
| ☐ 71 Super Bowl XV | .60 | .24 | .06 |
| Oakland AFC 27 | | | |
| Philadelphia NFC 10 | | | |
| (Jim Plunkett) | | | |
| ☐ 72 Training Camp | .60 | .24 | .06 |
| (Steelers) | | | |
| (Chuck Noll) | | | |
| ☐ 73 Practice Makes | .30 | .12 | .03 |
| Perfect | | | |
| ☐ 74 Airborn Carrier | .30 | .12 | .03 |
| ☐ 75 The National Anthem | .30 | .12 | .03 |
| Chargers | | | |
| ☐ 76 Filling Up | .30 | .12 | .03 |
| (Stadium) | | | |
| ☐ 77 Away In Time | 1.50 | .60 | .15 |
| (Terry Bradshaw) | | | |
| ☐ 78 Flat Out | .30 | .12 | .03 |
| ☐ 79 Halftime | .30 | .12 | .03 |
| (Band playing) | | | |
| ☐ 80 Warm Ups Patriots | .30 | .12 | .03 |
| ☐ 81 Getting To The | .30 | .12 | .03 |
| Bottom Of It | | | |
| ☐ 82 Souvenir (Crowd) | .30 | .12 | .03 |
| ☐ 83 A Game Of Inches | .30 | .12 | .03 |
| (Officials measuring) | | | |
| ☐ 84 The Overview | .30 | .12 | .03 |
| ☐ 85 The Dropback | .30 | .12 | .03 |
| ☐ 86 Pregame Huddle | .30 | .12 | .03 |
| (Redskins) | | | |
| ☐ 87 Every Way But Loose UER | .30 | .12 | .03 |
| (Giants helmet on back, | | | |
| should be Rams) | | | |
| ☐ 88 Mudders UER | .75 | .30 | .07 |
| (Redskins helmet on | | | |
| back, should be 49ers) | | | |

# 1982 Fleer Team Action

The 1982 Fleer Teams in Action football set is very similar to the 1981 set (with again 88 cards) and other Fleer Teams in Action sets of previous years. The cards measure 2 1/2" by 3 1/2". The backs are printed in yellow and gray on a white stock. Cards are numbered on back and feature a 1982 copyright date. The card numbering follows team name alphabetical order followed by Super Bowl cards in chronological order and NFL Team Highlights cards. Cards were issued in wax packs of seven team cards along with three team logo stickers.

| | MINT | EXC | G-VG |
|---|---|---|---|
| COMPLETE SET (88) | 50.00 | 20.00 | 5.00 |
| COMMON CARD (1-88) | .30 | .12 | .03 |
| | | | |
| ☐ 1 Atlanta Falcons | .60 | .24 | .06 |
| Running to Daylight | | | |
| (William Andrews) | | | |
| ☐ 2 Atlanta Falcons | .30 | .12 | .03 |
| Airborne Falcons | | | |
| ☐ 3 Baltimore Colts | .50 | .20 | .05 |

Plenty of Time To Throw (Bert Jones and Mark Gastineau)
☐ 4 Baltimore Colts ... .30 .12 .03

Lassoing the Opponent
☐ 5 Buffalo Bills ... .50 .20 .05

Point of Attack (Joe Ferguson)
☐ 6 Buffalo Bills ... .30 .12 .03

Capturing the Enemy
☐ 7 Chicago Bears ... 2.50 1.00 .25

Three on One (Walter Payton)
☐ 8 Chicago Bears ... .30 .12 .03

Stretched Out
☐ 9 Cincinnati Bengals ... .40 .16 .04

About to Hit Paydirt (Pete Johnson)
☐ 10 Cincinnati Bengals ... .30 .12 .03

Tiger-Striped Attack
☐ 11 Cleveland Browns ... .50 .20 .05

Reading the Field (Brian Sipe)
☐ 12 Cleveland Browns ... .30 .12 .03

Covered From All Angles
☐ 13 Dallas Cowboys ... 1.25 .50 .12

Blocking Convoy (Tony Dorsett)
☐ 14 Dallas Cowboys ... .50 .20 .05

Encircled
☐ 15 Denver Broncos ... .50 .20 .05

Springing Into Action (Craig Morton)
☐ 16 Denver Broncos ... .40 .16 .04

High and Low
☐ 17 Detroit Lions ... .30 .12 .03

Setting Up The Screen Pass
☐ 18 Detroit Lions ... .40 .16 .04

Poised and Ready To Attack (Doug Williams)
☐ 19 Green Bay Packers ... .30 .12 .03

Flying Through The Air
☐ 20 Green Bay Packers ... .30 .12 .03

Hitting The Pack
☐ 21 Houston Oilers ... 4.00 1.60 .40

Waiting For The Hole To Open (Gifford Nielsen and Earl Campbell)
☐ 22 Houston Oilers ... .30 .12 .03

Biting The Dust
☐ 23 Kansas City Chiefs ... .30 .12 .03

Going In Untouched
☐ 24 Kansas City Chiefs ... .30 .12 .03

No Place To Go
☐ 25 Los Angeles Rams ... .40 .16 .04

Getting To The Outside (Wendell Tyler)
☐ 26 Los Angeles Rams ... .75 .30 .07

Double Team, Double Trouble (Riggins tackled)
☐ 27 Miami Dolphins ... .50 .20 .05

Cutting Back Against The Grain (Tony Nathan)
☐ 28 Miami Dolphins ... .40 .16 .04

Taking Two Down
☐ 29 Minnesota Vikings ... .30 .12 .03

Running Inside For Tough Yardage
☐ 30 Minnesota Vikings ... .30 .12 .03

Bowling Over The Opponent
☐ 31 New England Patriots ... .30 .12 .03

Leaping For The First Down
☐ 32 New England Patriots ... .30 .12 .03

Gang Tackling
☐ 33 New Orleans Saints ... .50 .20 .05

Breaking Into The Clear (George Rogers)
☐ 34 New Orleans Saints ... .30 .12 .03

Double Jeopardy
☐ 35 New York Giants ... .30 .12 .03

Getting Ready To Hit The Opening
☐ 36 New York Giants ... 1.25 .50 .12

Negative Yardage (Tony Dorsett)
☐ 37 New York Jets ... 1.00 .40 .10

Off To The Races (Freeman McNeil)
☐ 38 New York Jets ... .30 .12 .03

Sandwiched
☐ 39 Oakland Raiders ... .50 .20 .05

Throwing The Down and Out (Marc Wilson)
☐ 40 Oakland Raiders ... .50 .20 .05

The Second Wave Is On The Way
☐ 41 Philadelphia Eagles ... .50 .20 .05

Blasting Up The Middle (Ron Jaworski)
☐ 42 Philadelphia Eagles ... .75 .30 .07

Triple-Teaming (Carl Hairston and John Riggins)
☐ 43 Pittsburgh Steelers ... .40 .16 .04

Stretching For A Score
☐ 44 Pittsburgh Steelers ... .40 .16 .04

Rising Above The Crowd
☐ 45 St. Louis Cardinals ... .50 .20 .05

Sweeping To The Right (Jim Hart)
☐ 46 St. Louis Cardinals ... .30 .12 .03

No Place To Go But Down
☐ 47 San Diego Chargers ... .30 .12 .03

Looking For Someone To Block
☐ 48 San Diego Chargers ... .30 .12 .03

Being In The Right Place
☐ 49 San Francisco 49ers ... 20.00 8.00 2.00

Giving Second Effort (Joe Montana)
☐ 50 San Francisco 49ers ... .60 .24 .06

In Your Face (Steve Bartkowski)
☐ 51 Seattle Seahawks ... .75 .30 .07

Nothing But Open Space (Jack Lambert)
☐ 52 Seattle Seahawks ... .50 .20 .05

Attacking From The Blind Side (Brian Sipe)
☐ 53 Tampa Bay Buccaneers ... .40 .16 .04

Everyone In Motion (Doug Williams)
☐ 54 Tampa Bay Buccaneers ... .30 .12 .03

Ring Around The Running Back
☐ 55 Washington Redskins ... .75 .30 .07

Knocking Them Down One-By-One (Joe Theismann)
☐ 56 Washington Redskins ... .30 .12 .03

Coming From All Directions
☐ 57 Super Bowl I ... .60 .24 .06
Green Bay NFL 35
Kansas City AFL 10
(Jim Taylor)
☐ 58 Super Bowl II ... .30 .12 .03
Green Bay NFL 33
Oakland AFL 14
☐ 59 Super Bowl III ... .30 .12 .03
New York AFL 16
Baltimore NFL 7
☐ 60 Super Bowl IV ... .30 .12 .03
Kansas City AFL 23
Minnesota NFL 7
☐ 61 Super Bowl V ... .30 .12 .03
Baltimore AFC 16
Dallas NFC 13
☐ 62 Super Bowl VI ... 1.00 .40 .10
Dallas NFC 24
Miami AFC 3
(Bob Griese and Bob Lilly)
☐ 63 Super Bowl VII ... .75 .30 .07
Miami AFC 14
Washington NFC 7
(Larry Csonka running)
☐ 64 Super Bowl VIII ... 1.00 .40 .10
Miami AFC 24
Minnesota NFC 7
(Larry Csonka and Paul Warfield)
☐ 65 Super Bowl IX ... .30 .12 .03
Pittsburgh AFC 16
Minnesota NFC 6

| | | | |
|---|---|---|---|
| ☐ 66 Super Bowl X | 2.00 | .80 | .20 |
| Pittsburgh AFC 21 | | | |
| Dallas NFC 17 | | | |
| (Roger Staubach) | | | |
| ☐ 67 Super Bowl XI | .40 | .16 | .04 |
| Oakland AFC 32 | | | |
| Minnesota NFC 14 | | | |
| (Mark Van Eeghen) | | | |
| ☐ 68 Super Bowl XII | 2.00 | .80 | .20 |
| Dallas NFC 27 | | | |
| Denver AFC 10 | | | |
| (Roger Staubach) | | | |
| ☐ 69 Super Bowl XIII | 1.25 | .50 | .12 |
| Pittsburgh AFC 35 | | | |
| Dallas NFC 31 | | | |
| (Lynn Swann) | | | |
| ☐ 70 Super Bowl XIV | .30 | .12 | .03 |
| Pittsburgh AFC 31 | | | |
| Los Angeles NFC 19 | | | |
| ☐ 71 Super Bowl XV | .50 | .20 | .05 |
| Oakland AFC 27 | | | |
| Philadelphia NFC 10 | | | |
| (Jim Plunkett) | | | |
| ☐ 72 Super Bowl XVI | 1.00 | .40 | .10 |
| San Francisco NFC 26 | | | |
| Cincinnati AFC 21 | | | |
| (Dwight Clark) | | | |
| ☐ 73 NFL Team Highlights | 10.00 | 4.00 | 1.00 |
| 1982 AFC-NFC | | | |
| Pro Bowl Action | | | |
| (Montana rolling) | | | |
| ☐ 74 NFL Team Highlights | 1.00 | .40 | .10 |
| 1982 AFC-NFC | | | |
| Pro Bowl Action | | | |
| (Ken Anderson and | | | |
| Anthony Munoz) | | | |
| ☐ 75 NFL Team Highlights | .30 | .12 | .03 |
| Aloha Stadium | | | |
| ☐ 76 NFL Team Highlights | .30 | .12 | .03 |
| On The Field Meeting | | | |
| ☐ 77 NFL Team Highlights | .75 | .30 | .07 |
| First Down | | | |
| (Joe Theismann) | | | |
| ☐ 78 NFL Team Highlights | .30 | .12 | .03 |
| The Man In Charge | | | |
| (Jerry Markbright) | | | |
| ☐ 79 NFL Team Highlights | .30 | .12 | .03 |
| Coming Onto | | | |
| The Field | | | |
| ☐ 80 NFL Team Highlights | .40 | .16 | .04 |
| In The Huddle | | | |
| (Bill Kenney and | | | |
| Carlos Carson) | | | |
| ☐ 81 NFL Team Highlights | .30 | .12 | .03 |
| Lying In Wait | | | |
| (Atlanta defense) | | | |
| ☐ 82 NFL Team Highlights | .30 | .12 | .03 |
| Celebration | | | |
| ☐ 83 NFL Team Highlights | .30 | .12 | .03 |
| Men In Motion | | | |
| ☐ 84 NFL Team Highlights | .30 | .12 | .03 |
| Shotgun Formation | | | |
| ☐ 85 NFL Team Highlights | .30 | .12 | .03 |
| Training Camp | | | |
| ☐ 86 NFL Team Highlights | 1.00 | .40 | .10 |
| Halftime Instructions | | | |
| (Bill Walsh in | | | |
| locker room) | | | |
| ☐ 87 NFL Team Highlights | .40 | .16 | .04 |
| Field Goal Attempt | | | |
| (Rolf Benirschke) | | | |
| ☐ 88 NFL Team Highlights | .60 | .24 | .06 |
| Free Kick | | | |

# 1983 Fleer Team Action

The 1983 Fleer Teams in Action football set contains 88 cards. There are two cards numbered 67, one of which was obviously intended to be card number 66. The cards measure 2 1/2" by 3 1/2". The backs are printed in blue on white card stock. Cards are numbered on the back and feature a 1983 copyright date. The card numbering follows team name alphabetical order followed by Super Bowl cards in chronological order and NFL Team Highlights cards. Cards were issued in seven-card packs along with three team logo stickers.

| | MINT | EXC | G-VG |
|---|---|---|---|
| COMPLETE SET (88) | 22.00 | 9.00 | 2.20 |
| COMMON CARD (1-88) | .25 | .10 | .02 |
| | | | |
| ☐ 1 Atlanta Falcons | 1.25 | .50 | .12 |
| Breaking Away | | | |
| to Daylight | | | |
| (Ronnie Lott) | | | |
| ☐ 2 Atlanta Falcons | .25 | .10 | .02 |
| Piled Up | | | |
| ☐ 3 Baltimore Colts | .25 | .10 | .02 |
| Cutting Back | | | |
| to Daylight | | | |
| ☐ 4 Baltimore Colts | .35 | .14 | .03 |
| Pressuring the QB | | | |
| (Joe Ferguson) | | | |
| ☐ 5 Buffalo Bills | .35 | .14 | .03 |
| Moving to the Outside | | | |
| (Roosevelt Leaks running) | | | |
| ☐ 6 Buffalo Bills | .25 | .10 | .02 |
| Buffalo Stampede | | | |
| ☐ 7 Chicago Bears | 2.50 | 1.00 | .25 |
| Ready to Let It Fly | | | |
| (Jim McMahon and | | | |
| Walter Payton) | | | |
| ☐ 8 Chicago Bears | .25 | .10 | .02 |
| Jump Ball | | | |
| ☐ 9 Cincinnati Bengals | .25 | .10 | .02 |
| Hurdling Into Open | | | |
| ☐ 10 Cincinnati Bengals | .25 | .10 | .02 |
| Hands Up | | | |
| ☐ 11 Cleveland Browns | .35 | .14 | .03 |
| An Open Field Ahead | | | |
| (Mike Pruitt) | | | |
| ☐ 12 Cleveland Browns | .25 | .10 | .02 |
| Reacting to the | | | |
| Ball Carrier | | | |
| ☐ 13 Dallas Cowboys | 1.25 | .50 | .12 |
| Mid-Air Ballet | | | |
| (Tony Dorsett) | | | |
| ☐ 14 Dallas Cowboys | .35 | .14 | .03 |
| 3, 2, 1 Takeoff | | | |
| ☐ 15 Denver Broncos | .35 | .14 | .03 |
| Clear Sailing | | | |
| ☐ 16 Denver Broncos | .35 | .14 | .03 |
| Stacking Up Offense | | | |
| ☐ 17 Detroit Lions | .25 | .10 | .02 |
| Hitting the Wall | | | |
| ☐ 18 Detroit Lions | .25 | .10 | .02 |
| Snapping into Action | | | |
| ☐ 19 Green Bay Packers | .75 | .30 | .07 |
| Fingertip Control | | | |
| (Ed Too Tall Jones) | | | |
| ☐ 20 Green Bay Packers | .25 | .10 | .02 |
| QB Sack | | | |
| ☐ 21 Houston Oilers | .25 | .10 | .02 |
| Sweeping to Outside | | | |
| ☐ 22 Houston Oilers | .50 | .20 | .05 |
| Halting Forward | | | |
| Progress | | | |
| (Freeman McNeil) | | | |
| ☐ 23 Kansas City Chiefs | .25 | .10 | .02 |
| Waiting for | | | |
| the Key Block | | | |
| ☐ 24 Kansas City Chiefs | .60 | .24 | .06 |
| Going Head to Head | | | |
| (John Hannah) | | | |
| ☐ 25 Los Angeles Raiders | .50 | .20 | .05 |
| Bombs Away | | | |
| (Plunkett passing) | | | |
| ☐ 26 Los Angeles Raiders | .50 | .20 | .05 |
| Caged Bengal | | | |
| ☐ 27 Los Angeles Rams | .25 | .10 | .02 |
| Clearing Out Middle | | | |
| ☐ 28 Los Angeles Rams | .25 | .10 | .02 |
| One on One Tackle | | | |
| ☐ 29 Miami Dolphins | .35 | .14 | .03 |
| Skating through Hole | | | |
| ☐ 30 Miami Dolphins | .35 | .14 | .03 |
| Follow the Bounc- | | | |
| ing Ball | | | |
| ☐ 31 Minnesota Vikings | .35 | .14 | .03 |
| Dropping into Pocket | | | |
| (Tommy Kramer) | | | |
| ☐ 32 Minnesota Vikings | .25 | .10 | .02 |
| Attacking from | | | |
| All Angles | | | |

☐ 33 New England Patriots.............. .25 .10 .02
Touchdown
☐ 34 New England Patriots.............. 2.00 .80 .20
Pouncing Patriots
(W.Payton tackled)
☐ 35 New Orleans Saints................ .25 .10 .02
Only One Man to Beat
☐ 36 New Orleans Saints................ 1.25 .50 .12
Closing In
(Tony Dorsett)
☐ 37 New York Giants.................... .25 .10 .02
Setting Up to Pass
☐ 38 New York Giants.................... .25 .10 .02
In Pursuit
☐ 39 New York Jets...................... .25 .10 .02
Just Enough Room
☐ 40 New York Jets...................... .25 .10 .02
Wrapping Up Runner
☐ 41 Philadelphia Eagles............... .35 .14 .03
Play Action Fakers
(Ron Jaworski and
Harry Carson)
☐ 42 Philadelphia Eagles............... .50 .20 .05
Step Away from Sack
(Archie Manning)
☐ 43 Pittsburgh Steelers............... 1.25 .50 .12
Exploding Through a
Hole (Franco Harris
and Terry Bradshaw)
☐ 44 Pittsburgh Steelers............... .75 .30 .07
Outnumbered
(Jack Lambert)
☐ 45 St. Louis Cardinals................ .25 .10 .02
Keeping His Balance
☐ 46 St. Louis Cardinals................ .25 .10 .02
Waiting for the
Reinforcements
☐ 47 San Diego Chargers.............. .25 .10 .02
Supercharged Charger
☐ 48 San Diego Chargers.............. .25 .10 .02
Triple Team Tackle
☐ 49 San Francisco 49ers............. .25 .10 .02
There's No Stopping
Him Now
☐ 50 San Francisco 49ers............. .35 .14 .03
Heading 'Em Off
at the Pass
☐ 51 Seattle Seahawks.................. .50 .20 .05
Calling the Signals
(Jim Zorn)
☐ 52 Seattle Seahawks.................. .35 .14 .03
The Hands Have It
☐ 53 Tampa Bay Buccaneers.......... .25 .10 .02
Off to the Races
☐ 54 Tampa Bay Buccaneers.......... .25 .10 .02
Buccaneer Sandwich
☐ 55 Washington Redskins............. .25 .10 .02
Looking for Daylight
☐ 56 Washington Redskins............. .25 .10 .02
Smothering the
Ball Carrier
☐ 57 Super Bowl I........................ .75 .30 .07
Green Bay NFL 35
Kansas City AFL 10
(Jim Taylor)
☐ 58 Super Bowl II....................... .25 .10 .02
Green Bay NFL 33
Oakland AFL 14
☐ 59 Super Bowl III...................... .25 .10 .02
New York AFL 16
Baltimore NFL 7
☐ 60 Super Bowl IV...................... .25 .10 .02
Kansas City AFL 23
Minnesota NFL 7
☐ 61 Super Bowl V....................... 1.50 .60 .15
Baltimore AFC 16
Dallas NFC 13
(Johnny Unitas)
☐ 62 Super Bowl VI...................... 1.00 .40 .10
Dallas NFC 24
Miami AFC 3
(Bob Griese and
Bob Lilly)
☐ 63 Super Bowl VII..................... .35 .14 .03
Miami AFC 14
Washington NFC 7
(Manny Fernandez)
☐ 64 Super Bowl VIII.................... .75 .30 .07
Miami AFC 24
Minnesota NFC 7
(Larry Csonka diving)
☐ 65 Super Bowl IX...................... 1.00 .40 .10
Pittsburgh AFC 16
Minnesota NFC 6
(Franco Harris)
☐ 66 Super Bowl X UER ................ 1.50 .60 .15
Pittsburgh AFC 21

Dallas NFC 17
(Terry Bradshaw;
number on back 67)
☐ 67 Super Bowl XI...................... .50 .20 .05
Oakland AFC 32
Minnesota NFC 14
(see also card 66)
☐ 68 Super Bowl XII..................... .25 .10 .02
Dallas NFC 27
Denver AFC 10
☐ 69 Super Bowl XIII.................... 1.25 .50 .12
Pittsburgh AFC 35
Dallas NFC 31
(Terry Bradshaw
passing)
☐ 70 Super Bowl XIV.................... .35 .14 .03
Pittsburgh AFC 31
Los Angeles NFC 19
(Vince Ferragamo
passing)
☐ 71 Super Bowl XV..................... .25 .10 .02
Oakland AFC 27
Philadelphia NFC 10
☐ 72 Super Bowl XVI.................... .25 .10 .02
San Francisco NFC 26
Cincinnati AFC 21
☐ 73 Super Bowl XVII................... .75 .30 .07
Washington NFC 27
Miami AFC 17
(John Riggins running)
☐ 74 NFL Team Highlights............. 1.00 .40 .10
1983 AFC-NFC
Pro Bowl (Dan Fouts)
☐ 75 NFL Team Highlights............. .25 .10 .02
Super Bowl XVII
Spectacular
☐ 76 NFL Team Highlights............. .25 .10 .02
Tampa Stadium: Super
Bowl XVIII
☐ 77 NFL Team Highlights............. .25 .10 .02
Up, Up, and Away
☐ 78 NFL Team Highlights............. .35 .14 .03
Sideline Conference
(Steve Bartkowski)
☐ 79 NFL Team Highlights............. .25 .10 .02
Barefoot Follow-
Through
(Mike Lansford)
☐ 80 NFL Team Highlights............. .25 .10 .02
Fourth and Long
(Max Runager punting)
☐ 81 NFL Team Highlights............. .25 .10 .02
Blocked Punt
☐ 82 NFL Team Highlights............. .25 .10 .02
Fumble
☐ 83 NFL Team Highlights............. .35 .14 .03
National Anthem
☐ 84 NFL Team Highlights............. .25 .10 .02
Concentrating on the
Ball (Tony Franklin)
☐ 85 NFL Team Highlights............. .35 .14 .03
Splashing Around
☐ 86 NFL Team Highlights............. .25 .10 .02
Loading in Shotgun
☐ 87 NFL Team Highlights............. .25 .10 .02
Taking the Snap
☐ 88 NFL Team Highlights............. .50 .20 .05
Line of Scrimmage

# 1984 Fleer Team Action

The 1984 Fleer Teams in Action football card set contains 88 cards. The cards measure 2 1/2" by 3 1/2". The cards are numbered on the back and feature a 1984 copyright date. The cards show action scenes with specific players not identified. There is a green border on the fronts of the cards with the title of the card inside a yellow strip; the backs are red and white. The card fronts are in full color. The card numbering follows team name alphabetical order (with the exception of the Indianapolis Colts whose last-minute move from Baltimore aparently put them out of order) followed by Super Bowl cards in chronological order and NFL Team Highlights cards. Cards were issued in seven-card wax packs along with three team logo stickers.

| | MINT | EXC | G-VG |
|---|---|---|---|
| COMPLETE SET (88) | 18.00 | 7.25 | 1.80 |
| COMMON CARD (1-88) | .25 | .10 | .02 |
| ☐ 1 Atlanta Falcons | .50 | .20 | .05 |
| ☐ 2 Atlanta Falcons | .25 | .10 | .02 |
| Gang Tackle | | | |
| ☐ 3 Indianapolis Colts | .25 | .10 | .02 |
| About to Break Free | | | |
| ☐ 4 Indianapolis Colts | .25 | .10 | .02 |
| Cutting Off All | | | |
| the Angles | | | |
| ☐ 5 Buffalo Bills | .25 | .10 | .02 |
| Cracking the First | | | |
| Line of Defense | | | |
| ☐ 6 Buffalo Bills | .25 | .10 | .02 |
| Getting Help From | | | |
| A Friend | | | |
| ☐ 7 Chicago Bears | 1.50 | .60 | .15 |
| Over the Top | | | |
| (Jim McMahon | | | |
| and Walter Payton) | | | |
| ☐ 8 Chicago Bears | .25 | .10 | .02 |
| You Grab Him High | | | |
| I'll Grab Him Low | | | |
| ☐ 9 Cincinnati Bengals | .25 | .10 | .02 |
| Skipping Through | | | |
| an Opening | | | |
| ☐ 10 Cincinnati Bengals | .35 | .14 | .03 |
| Saying Hello to a QB | | | |
| (Joe Ferguson) | | | |
| ☐ 11 Cleveland Browns | .35 | .14 | .03 |
| Free Sailing into | | | |
| the End Zone | | | |
| (Greg Pruitt) | | | |
| ☐ 12 Cleveland Browns | .25 | .10 | .02 |
| Making Sure of | | | |
| the Tackle | | | |
| ☐ 13 Dallas Cowboys | .50 | .20 | .05 |
| (Danny White) | | | |
| ☐ 14 Dallas Cowboys | .60 | .24 | .06 |
| Cowboy's Corral | | | |
| (Ed Too Tall Jones) | | | |
| ☐ 15 Denver Broncos | .35 | .14 | .03 |
| Sprinting into the Open | | | |
| ☐ 16 Denver Broncos | .50 | .20 | .05 |
| Ready to Pounce | | | |
| (Curt Warner) | | | |
| ☐ 17 Detroit Lions | .50 | .20 | .05 |
| Lion on the Prowl | | | |
| (Billy Sims) | | | |
| ☐ 18 Detroit Lions | .60 | .24 | .06 |
| Stacking Up | | | |
| the Ball Carrier | | | |
| (John Riggins) | | | |
| ☐ 19 Green Bay Packers | .25 | .10 | .02 |
| Waiting For the | | | |
| Hole to Open | | | |
| ☐ 20 Green Bay Packers | .25 | .10 | .02 |
| Packing Up | | | |
| Your Opponent | | | |
| ☐ 21 Houston Oilers | 4.00 | 1.60 | .40 |
| Nothing But Open | | | |
| Spaces Ahead | | | |
| (Earl Campbell) | | | |
| ☐ 22 Houston Oilers | .25 | .10 | .02 |
| Meeting Him Head On | | | |
| ☐ 23 Kansas City Chiefs | .25 | .10 | .02 |
| Going Outside for | | | |
| Extra Yardage | | | |
| ☐ 24 Kansas City Chiefs | .25 | .10 | .02 |
| A Running Back | | | |
| in Trouble | | | |
| ☐ 25 Los Angeles Raiders | 1.50 | .60 | .15 |
| No Defenders in Sight | | | |
| (Marcus Allen) | | | |
| ☐ 26 Los Angeles Raiders | 1.25 | .50 | .12 |
| Rampaging Raiders | | | |
| (Howie Long and | | | |
| John Riggins) | | | |
| ☐ 27 Los Angeles Rams | .25 | .10 | .02 |
| Making the Cut | | | |
| ☐ 28 Los Angeles Rams | .25 | .10 | .02 |
| Caught From Behind | | | |
| ☐ 29 Miami Dolphins | .35 | .14 | .03 |
| Sliding Down the Line | | | |
| ☐ 30 Miami Dolphins | .35 | .14 | .03 |
| Making Sure | | | |
| ☐ 31 Minnesota Vikings | .25 | .10 | .02 |
| Stretching For | | | |

| | MINT | EXC | G-VG |
|---|---|---|---|
| Touchdown | | | |
| ☐ 32 Minnesota Vikings | .25 | .10 | .02 |
| Hitting the Wall | | | |
| ☐ 33 New England Patriots | .50 | .20 | .05 |
| Straight Up the Middle | | | |
| (Steve Grogan) | | | |
| ☐ 34 New England Patriots | 2.50 | 1.00 | .25 |
| Come here and | | | |
| Give Me a Hug | | | |
| (Earl Campbell tackled) | | | |
| ☐ 35 New Orleans Saints | .25 | .10 | .02 |
| One Defender to Beat | | | |
| ☐ 36 New Orleans Saints | .25 | .10 | .02 |
| Saints Sandwich | | | |
| ☐ 37 New York Giants | .25 | .10 | .02 |
| A Six Point Landing | | | |
| ☐ 38 New York Giants | .25 | .10 | .02 |
| Leaping to the Aid | | | |
| of a Teammate | | | |
| ☐ 39 New York Jets | .25 | .10 | .02 |
| Galloping through | | | |
| Untouched | | | |
| ☐ 40 New York Jets | .25 | .10 | .02 |
| Capturing the Enemy | | | |
| ☐ 41 Philadelphia Eagles | .25 | .10 | .02 |
| One More Block and | | | |
| He's Gone | | | |
| ☐ 42 Philadelphia Eagles | .25 | .10 | .02 |
| Meeting an Opponent | | | |
| With Open Arms | | | |
| ☐ 43 Pittsburgh Steelers | .35 | .14 | .03 |
| The Play Begins | | | |
| to Develop | | | |
| ☐ 44 Pittsburgh Steelers | .35 | .14 | .03 |
| Rally Around the | | | |
| Ball Carrier | | | |
| ☐ 45 St. Louis Cardinals | .25 | .10 | .02 |
| Sprinting Around | | | |
| the Corner | | | |
| ☐ 46 St. Louis Cardinals | .25 | .10 | .02 |
| Overmatched | | | |
| ☐ 47 San Diego Chargers | .25 | .10 | .02 |
| Up, Up, and Away | | | |
| ☐ 48 San Diego Chargers | .25 | .10 | .02 |
| Engulfing the Opponent | | | |
| ☐ 49 San Francisco 49ers | .35 | .14 | .03 |
| Tunneling Up | | | |
| the Middle | | | |
| (Wendell Tyler) | | | |
| ☐ 50 San Francisco 49ers | .60 | .24 | .06 |
| Nowhere to Go but | | | |
| Down (John Riggins) | | | |
| ☐ 51 Seattle Seahawks | .50 | .20 | .05 |
| Letting the Ball Fly | | | |
| (Jim Zorn) | | | |
| ☐ 52 Seattle Seahawks | .35 | .14 | .03 |
| Handing Out | | | |
| Some Punishment | | | |
| ☐ 53 Tampa Bay Buccaneers | .25 | .10 | .02 |
| When he Hits the | | | |
| Ground He's Gone | | | |
| ☐ 54 Tampa Bay Buccaneers | .25 | .10 | .02 |
| One Leg Takedown | | | |
| ☐ 55 Washington Redskins | .60 | .24 | .06 |
| Plenty of Room to Run | | | |
| (John Riggins) | | | |
| ☐ 56 Washington Redskins | .25 | .10 | .02 |
| Squashing the Opponent | | | |
| ☐ 57 Super Bowl I | .60 | .24 | .06 |
| Green Bay NFL 35 | | | |
| Kansas City AFL 10 | | | |
| (Jim Taylor) | | | |
| ☐ 58 Super Bowl II | .75 | .30 | .07 |
| Green Bay NFL 33 | | | |
| Oakland AFL 14 | | | |
| (Bart Starr) | | | |
| ☐ 59 Super Bowl III | .25 | .10 | .02 |
| New York AFL 16 | | | |
| Baltimore NFL 7 | | | |
| ☐ 60 Super Bowl IV | .25 | .10 | .02 |
| Kansas City AFL 23 | | | |
| Minnesota NFL 7 | | | |
| ☐ 61 Super Bowl V | .75 | .30 | .07 |
| Baltimore AFC 16 | | | |
| Dallas NFC 13 | | | |
| (Earl Morrall) | | | |
| ☐ 62 Super Bowl VI | 1.25 | .50 | .12 |
| Dallas NFC 24 | | | |
| Miami AFC 3 | | | |
| (Roger Staubach) | | | |
| ☐ 63 Super Bowl VII | .50 | .20 | .05 |
| Miami AFC 14 | | | |
| Washington NFC 7 | | | |
| (Jim Kiick and | | | |
| Bob Griese) | | | |
| ☐ 64 Super Bowl VIII | .75 | .30 | .07 |
| Miami AFC 24 | | | |
| Minnesota NFC 7 | | | |

(Larry Csonka diving)
| | | | | |
|---|---|---|---|---|
| ☐ 65 Super Bowl IX | 1.25 | .50 | .12 |
| Pittsburgh AFC 16 | | | |
| Minnesota NFC 6 | | | |
| (Terry Bradshaw) | | | |
| ☐ 66 Super Bowl X | .75 | .30 | .07 |
| Pittsburgh AFC 21 | | | |
| Dallas NFC 17 | | | |
| (Franco Harris) | | | |
| ☐ 67 Super Bowl XI | .25 | .10 | .02 |
| Oakland AFC 32 | | | |
| Minnesota NFC 14 | | | |
| ☐ 68 Super Bowl XII | 1.00 | .40 | .10 |
| Dallas NFC 27 | | | |
| Denver AFC 10 | | | |
| (Tony Dorsett) | | | |
| ☐ 69 Super Bowl XIII | .75 | .30 | .07 |
| Pittsburgh AFC 35 | | | |
| Dallas NFC 31 | | | |
| (Franco Harris) | | | |
| ☐ 70 Super Bowl XIV | .75 | .30 | .07 |
| Pittsburgh AFC 31 | | | |
| Los Angeles NFC 19 | | | |
| (Franco Harris) | | | |
| ☐ 71 Super Bowl XV | .35 | .14 | .03 |
| Oakland AFC 27 | | | |
| Philadelphia NFC 10 | | | |
| (Jim Plunkett) | | | |
| ☐ 72 Super Bowl XVI | .25 | .10 | .02 |
| San Francisco NFC 26 | | | |
| Cincinnati AFC 21 | | | |
| ☐ 73 Super Bowl XVII | .25 | .10 | .02 |
| Washington NFC 27 | | | |
| Miami AFC 17 | | | |
| ☐ 74 Super Bowl XVIII | .60 | .24 | .06 |
| Los Angeles AFC 38 | | | |
| Washington NFC 9 | | | |
| (Howie Long) | | | |
| ☐ 75 NFL Team Highlights | .25 | .10 | .02 |
| Official's Conference | | | |
| ☐ 76 NFL Team Highlights | .25 | .10 | .02 |
| Leaping for the | | | |
| Ball Carrier | | | |
| ☐ 77 NFL Team Highlights | .35 | .14 | .03 |
| Setting Up in the | | | |
| Passing Pocket | | | |
| (Jim Plunkett) | | | |
| ☐ 78 NFL Team Highlights | .25 | .10 | .02 |
| Field Goal Block | | | |
| ☐ 79 NFL Team Highlights | .35 | .14 | .03 |
| Stopped For No Gain | | | |
| (Steve Grogan) | | | |
| ☐ 80 NFL Team Highlights | .25 | .10 | .02 |
| Double Team Block | | | |
| ☐ 81 NFL Team Highlights | .25 | .10 | .02 |
| Kickoff | | | |
| ☐ 82 NFL Team Highlights | .25 | .10 | .02 |
| Punt Block | | | |
| ☐ 83 NFL Team Highlights | .25 | .10 | .02 |
| Coaches Signals | | | |
| ☐ 84 NFL Team Highlights | .25 | .10 | .02 |
| Training Camp | | | |
| ☐ 85 NFL Team Highlights | .50 | .20 | .05 |
| Fumble | | | |
| (Dwight Stephenson) | | | |
| ☐ 86 NFL Team Highlights | .25 | .10 | .02 |
| 1984 AFC-NFC Pro Bowl | | | |
| ☐ 87 NFL Team Highlights | .50 | .20 | .05 |
| Cheerleaders | | | |
| ☐ 88 NFL Team Highlights | .75 | .30 | .07 |
| In the Huddle | | | |
| (Joe Theismann) | | | |

## 1985 Fleer Team Action

This 88-card set, entitled Fleer Teams in Action, is essentially organized alphabetically by the name of the team. There are three

cards for each team, the first subtitled "On Offense" with offensive team statistics on the back, the second "On Defense" with defensive team statistics on the back, and the third "In Action" with a team schedule for the upcoming 1985 season. The last four cards feature highlights of the previous three Super Bowls and Pro Bowl. The cards are standard size 2 1/2" by 3 1/2" and are typically oriented horizontally. The cards are numbered on the back and feature a 1985 copyright date. The cards show full-color action scenes with specific players not identified. The card backs are printed in orange and black on white card stock. Cards were issued in wax packs of 15 cards and one sticker.

| | MINT | EXC | G-VG |
|---|---|---|---|
| COMPLETE SET (88) | 18.00 | 7.25 | 1.80 |
| COMMON PLAYER (1-88) | .25 | .10 | .02 |
| | | | |
| ☐ 1 Atlanta Falcons | .50 | .20 | .05 |
| Nothing But Open | | | |
| Spaces Ahead | | | |
| ☐ 2 Atlanta Falcons | .25 | .10 | .02 |
| Leveling Ball Carrier | | | |
| ☐ 3 Atlanta Falcons | .60 | .24 | .06 |
| Flying Falcon | | | |
| (John Riggins) | | | |
| ☐ 4 Buffalo Bills | .25 | .10 | .02 |
| Ducking Under | | | |
| the Pressure | | | |
| ☐ 5 Buffalo Bills | .25 | .10 | .02 |
| Swallowing Up | | | |
| the Opponent | | | |
| ☐ 6 Buffalo Bills | .25 | .10 | .02 |
| Avoiding Late Hit | | | |
| ☐ 7 Chicago Bears | 2.00 | .80 | .20 |
| Picking His Spot | | | |
| (Walter Payton) | | | |
| ☐ 8 Chicago Bears | .25 | .10 | .02 |
| C'Mon Guys, Give Me | | | |
| Some Room to Breathe | | | |
| ☐ 9 Chicago Bears | 1.25 | .50 | .12 |
| Just Hanging Around | | | |
| in Case They're Needed | | | |
| (Richard Dent) | | | |
| ☐ 10 Cincinnati Bengals | .25 | .10 | .02 |
| Struggling for | | | |
| Every Extra Yard | | | |
| ☐ 11 Cincinnati Bengals | .25 | .10 | .02 |
| Making Opponent Pay | | | |
| ☐ 12 Cincinnati Bengals | .25 | .10 | .02 |
| Just Out of the | | | |
| Reach of the Defender | | | |
| ☐ 13 Cleveland Browns | .25 | .10 | .02 |
| Plenty of Time to | | | |
| Fire the Ball | | | |
| ☐ 14 Cleveland Browns | .25 | .10 | .02 |
| Hitting the Wall | | | |
| ☐ 15 Cleveland Browns | .25 | .10 | .02 |
| Look What We Found | | | |
| ☐ 16 Dallas Cowboys | 1.00 | .40 | .10 |
| Waiting for the Right | | | |
| Moment to Burst Upfield | | | |
| (Tony Dorsett and | | | |
| Wilber Marshall) | | | |
| ☐ 17 Dallas Cowboys | 1.50 | .60 | .15 |
| Sorry Buddy, This is | | | |
| the End of the Line | | | |
| (Ed Too Tall Jones | | | |
| tackling Walter Payton) | | | |
| ☐ 18 Dallas Cowboys | .60 | .24 | .06 |
| Following Through | | | |
| for Three Points | | | |
| (Ed Too Tall Jones) | | | |
| ☐ 19 Denver Broncos | .35 | .14 | .03 |
| Blasting Up the Middle | | | |
| ☐ 20 Denver Broncos | .35 | .14 | .03 |
| Finishing Off | | | |
| the Tackle | | | |
| ☐ 21 Denver Broncos | .35 | .14 | .03 |
| About to Hit Paydirt | | | |
| ☐ 22 Detroit Lions | .35 | .14 | .03 |
| Waiting to Throw | | | |
| Until the Last Second | | | |
| (Dexter Manley) | | | |
| ☐ 23 Detroit Lions | .25 | .10 | .02 |
| Double Trouble on | | | |
| the Tackle | | | |
| ☐ 24 Detroit Lions | .25 | .10 | .02 |
| Quick Pitch | | | |
| ☐ 25 Green Bay Packers | .50 | .20 | .05 |
| Unleashing the | | | |
| Long Bomb | | | |
| (Steve McMichael) | | | |
| ☐ 26 Green Bay Packers | .75 | .30 | .07 |
| Encircling the | | | |
| Ball Carrier | | | |
| (Marcus Allen) | | | |
| ☐ 27 Green Bay Packers | .25 | .10 | .02 |

| | | | |
|---|---|---|---|
| Piggy-Back Ride | | | |
| ☐ 28 Houston Oilers ........................ | 5.00 | 2.00 | .50 |
| Retreating into the Pocket (Warren Moon and Earl Campbell) | | | |
| ☐ 29 Houston Oilers ........................ | .25 | .10 | .02 |
| Punishing the Enemy | | | |
| ☐ 30 Houston Oilers ........................ | .25 | .10 | .02 |
| No Chance to Block This One | | | |
| ☐ 31 Indianapolis Colts ................... | .25 | .10 | .02 |
| Getting Ready to Let It Fly | | | |
| ☐ 32 Indianapolis Colts ................... | .25 | .10 | .02 |
| Pushing the Ball Carrier Backward | | | |
| ☐ 33 Indianapolis Colts ................... | .25 | .10 | .02 |
| Nowhere to Go | | | |
| ☐ 34 Kansas City Chiefs .................. | .25 | .10 | .02 |
| Cutting Back for Extra Yardage | | | |
| ☐ 35 Kansas City Chiefs .................. | .25 | .10 | .02 |
| Reaching for the Deflection | | | |
| ☐ 36 Kansas City Chiefs .................. | .25 | .10 | .02 |
| Rising to the Occasion | | | |
| ☐ 37 Los Angeles Raiders .............. | .35 | .14 | .03 |
| Hurdling Into the Open Field | | | |
| ☐ 38 Los Angeles Raiders .............. | .25 | .10 | .02 |
| No Place To Go | | | |
| ☐ 39 Los Angeles Raiders .............. | .25 | .10 | .02 |
| Standing Tall In the Pocket | | | |
| ☐ 40 Los Angeles Rams ................. | 2.00 | .80 | .20 |
| One More Barrier and He's Off to the Races (Eric Dickerson) | | | |
| ☐ 41 Los Angeles Rams ................. | .25 | .10 | .02 |
| Driving A Shoulder Into the Opponent | | | |
| ☐ 42 Los Angeles Rams ................. | .25 | .10 | .02 |
| The Kickoff | | | |
| ☐ 43 Miami Dolphins ...................... | .50 | .20 | .05 |
| Sidestepping Trouble (Tony Nathan) | | | |
| ☐ 44 Miami Dolphins ...................... | .35 | .14 | .03 |
| Hold On, We're Coming | | | |
| ☐ 45 Miami Dolphins ...................... | 6.00 | 2.40 | .60 |
| The Release Point (Dan Marino) | | | |
| ☐ 46 Minnesota Vikings .................. | .35 | .14 | .03 |
| Putting As Much As He Has Into the Pass (Tommy Kramer) | | | |
| ☐ 47 Minnesota Vikings .................. | .25 | .10 | .02 |
| Gang Tackling | | | |
| ☐ 48 Minnesota Vikings .................. | .25 | .10 | .02 |
| You're Not Getting Away From Me This Time | | | |
| ☐ 49 New England Patriots ............. | .35 | .14 | .03 |
| Throwing On the Run (Tony Eason) | | | |
| ☐ 50 New England Patriots ............. | .25 | .10 | .02 |
| The Only Place to Go Is Down | | | |
| ☐ 51 New England Patriots ............. | .25 | .10 | .02 |
| Standing the Ball Carrier Up | | | |
| ☐ 52 New Orleans Saints ................ | .25 | .10 | .02 |
| Going Up the Middle Under A Full Head of Steam | | | |
| ☐ 53 New Orleans Saints ................ | .25 | .10 | .02 |
| Putting Everything They've Got Into the Tackle | | | |
| ☐ 54 New Orleans Saints ................ | .25 | .10 | .02 |
| Getting Off the Ground to Block the Kick | | | |
| ☐ 55 New York Giants .................... | .25 | .10 | .02 |
| Over the Top | | | |
| ☐ 56 New York Giants .................... | .25 | .10 | .02 |
| Rallying Around the Opposition | | | |
| ☐ 57 New York Giants .................... | .60 | .24 | .06 |
| The Huddle (Phil Simms) | | | |
| ☐ 58 New York Jets ........................ | .25 | .10 | .02 |
| Following His Blockers | | | |
| ☐ 59 New York Jets ........................ | .25 | .10 | .02 |
| This Is As Far As You Go | | | |
| ☐ 60 New York Jets ........................ | .25 | .10 | .02 |
| Looking Over the Defense | | | |
| ☐ 61 Philadelphia Eagles ................ | .25 | .10 | .02 |

| | | | |
|---|---|---|---|
| Going Through the Opening Untouched | | | |
| ☐ 62 Philadelphia Eagles ................ | .25 | .10 | .02 |
| Squashing the Enemy | | | |
| ☐ 63 Philadelphia Eagles ................ | .25 | .10 | .02 |
| There's No Room Here, So Let's Go Outside | | | |
| ☐ 64 Pittsburgh Steelers ................ | .35 | .14 | .03 |
| Sprinting Around the End | | | |
| ☐ 65 Pittsburgh Steelers ................ | .35 | .14 | .03 |
| Mismatch | | | |
| ☐ 66 Pittsburgh Steelers ................ | .35 | .14 | .03 |
| About to Be Thrown Back | | | |
| ☐ 67 St.Louis Cardinals .................. | .25 | .10 | .02 |
| In for Six | | | |
| ☐ 68 St.Louis Cardinals .................. | .25 | .10 | .02 |
| Piling Up the Ball Carrier | | | |
| ☐ 69 St.Louis Cardinals .................. | .75 | .30 | .07 |
| Causing the Fumble (Joe Theismann tackled) | | | |
| ☐ 70 San Diego Chargers ............... | .25 | .10 | .02 |
| Plenty of Open Space Ahead | | | |
| ☐ 71 San Diego Chargers ............... | .25 | .10 | .02 |
| Ready to Be Swallowed Up | | | |
| ☐ 72 San Diego Chargers ............... | .25 | .10 | .02 |
| A Quarterback in Serious Trouble | | | |
| ☐ 73 San Francisco 49ers................ | .25 | .10 | .02 |
| Reading the Hole and Exploding Through It | | | |
| ☐ 74 San Francisco 49ers................ | .25 | .10 | .02 |
| Burying the Opponent | | | |
| ☐ 75 San Francisco 49ers................ | 5.00 | 2.00 | .50 |
| Waiting to Throw Until His Receiver Breaks Free (Joe Montana and Russ Francis) | | | |
| ☐ 76 Seattle Seahawks ................... | .50 | .20 | .05 |
| Getting Just Enough Time to Pass (Dave Krieg) | | | |
| ☐ 77 Seattle Seahawks ................... | .50 | .20 | .05 |
| Capturing the Enemy (Craig James tackled) | | | |
| ☐ 78 Seattle Seahawks ................... | .35 | .14 | .03 |
| It's Going to Be A Footrace Now | | | |
| ☐ 79 Tampa Bay Buccaneers........... | .25 | .10 | .02 |
| Heading Outside Away From Trouble | | | |
| ☐ 80 Tampa Bay Buccaneers........... | .25 | .10 | .02 |
| One-On-One Tackle | | | |
| ☐ 81 Tampa Bay Buccaneers........... | 1.00 | .40 | .10 |
| A Buccaneers Sandwich (Dickerson tackled) | | | |
| ☐ 82 Washington Redskins ............. | .60 | .24 | .06 |
| Just Enough Room To Get Through (John Riggins) | | | |
| ☐ 83 Washington Redskins ............. | .25 | .10 | .02 |
| Wrapping Up the Opponent | | | |
| ☐ 84 Washington Redskins ............. | .35 | .14 | .03 |
| Field-Goal Attempt (Mark Moseley) | | | |
| ☐ 85 Super Bowl XIX ...................... | .75 | .30 | .07 |
| San Francisco NFC 38 Miami AFC 16 (Roger Craig running) | | | |
| ☐ 86 Super Bowl XIX ...................... | 3.50 | 1.40 | .35 |
| San Francisco NFC 38 Miami AFC 16 (Joe Montana passing) | | | |
| ☐ 87 Super Bowl XIX ...................... | .35 | .14 | .03 |
| San Francisco NFC 38 Miami AFC 16 (Tony Nathan tackled) | | | |
| ☐ 88 1985 Pro Bowl ...................... | .50 | .20 | .05 |
| AFC 22, NFC 14 (Runner stopped) | | | |

# 1986 Fleer Team Action

This 88-card set, entitled "Live Action Football," is essentially organized alphabetically by the name of the team. There are three cards for each team; the first subtitled "On Offense" with offensive team statistics on the back, the second "On Defense" with defensive team statistics on the back, and the third "In Action" with a team

schedule for the upcoming 1986 season. The last four cards feature highlights of the previous three Super Bowls and Pro Bowl. The cards are standard size 2 1/2" by 3 1/2" and are typically oriented horizontally. The cards are numbered on the back and feature a 1986 copyright date. The cards show full-color action scenes (with a light blue border around the photo) with specific players not identified. The card backs are printed in blue and black on white card stock. Cards were issued in wax packs of seven team action cards and three team logo stickers.

|  | MINT | EXC | G-VG |
|---|---|---|---|
| COMPLETE SET (88) | 20.00 | 8.00 | 2.00 |
| COMMON CARD (1-88) | .25 | .10 | .02 |
| ☐ 1 Atlanta Falcons<br>Preparing to Make Cut | .50 | .20 | .05 |
| ☐ 2 Atlanta Falcons<br>Everybody Gets<br>Into the Act | .25 | .10 | .02 |
| ☐ 3 Atlanta Falcons<br>Where Do You Think<br>You're Going | .25 | .10 | .02 |
| ☐ 4 Buffalo Bills<br>Turning On the<br>After-Burners | .25 | .10 | .02 |
| ☐ 5 Buffalo Bills<br>Running Into a<br>Wall of Blue | .25 | .10 | .02 |
| ☐ 6 Buffalo Bills<br>Up and Over | .25 | .10 | .02 |
| ☐ 7 Chicago Bears<br>Pocket Forms Around<br>Passer (Jim McMahon<br>and Walter Payton) | 1.50 | .60 | .15 |
| ☐ 8 Chicago Bears<br>Monsters of the<br>Midway II (Richard<br>Dent and Dan Hampton) | 1.00 | .40 | .10 |
| ☐ 9 Chicago Bears<br>Blitz in a Blizzard<br>(Mike Singletary) | 1.00 | .40 | .10 |
| ☐ 10 Cincinnati Bengals<br>Plowing through<br>Defense<br>(Dave Rimington<br>and Anthony Munoz) | .60 | .24 | .06 |
| ☐ 11 Cincinnati Bengals<br>Zeroing In for the Hit | .25 | .10 | .02 |
| ☐ 12 Cincinnati Bengals<br>Oh, No You Don't<br>(Marcus Allen) | 1.00 | .40 | .10 |
| ☐ 13 Cleveland Browns<br>Looking for a Hole<br>to Develop<br>(Bernie Kosar<br>and Kevin Mack) | 2.00 | .80 | .20 |
| ☐ 14 Cleveland Browns<br>Buried by the Browns | .25 | .10 | .02 |
| ☐ 15 Cleveland Browns<br>Another Runner<br>Pounded Into the Turf | .25 | .10 | .02 |
| ☐ 16 Dallas Cowboys<br>Hole You Could Drive<br>Truck Through<br>(Tony Dorsett) | 1.00 | .40 | .10 |
| ☐ 17 Dallas Cowboys<br>We've Got You<br>Surrounded<br>(Jim Jeffcoat) | .50 | .20 | .05 |
| ☐ 18 Dallas Cowboys<br>Giving the Referee<br>Some Help<br>(Randy White) | .75 | .30 | .07 |
| ☐ 19 Denver Broncos<br>The Blockers Spring<br>Into Action (John Elway) | 3.00 | 1.20 | .30 |
| ☐ 20 Denver Broncos<br>The Orange Crush<br>Shows Its Stuff | .50 | .20 | .05 |
| ☐ 21 Denver Broncos<br>A Stampede to Block<br>the Kick | .35 | .14 | .03 |
| ☐ 22 Detroit Lions<br>A Runner's Eye View<br>of the Situation | .25 | .10 | .02 |
| ☐ 23 Detroit Lions<br>Levelling the<br>Ball Carrier | .25 | .10 | .02 |
| ☐ 24 Detroit Lions<br>Going All Out to Get<br>the Quarterback | .25 | .10 | .02 |
| ☐ 25 Green Bay Packers<br>Sweeping Around<br>the Corner | .25 | .10 | .02 |
| ☐ 26 Green Bay Packers<br>Not Afraid to Go<br>Head to Head | .25 | .10 | .02 |
| ☐ 27 Green Bay Packers<br>Taking the Snap | .25 | .10 | .02 |
| ☐ 28 Houston Oilers<br>Plunging for that<br>Extra Yard | .25 | .10 | .02 |
| ☐ 29 Houston Oilers<br>Tightening the Vise | .25 | .10 | .02 |
| ☐ 30 Houston Oilers<br>Launching a Field Goal | .25 | .10 | .02 |
| ☐ 31 Indianapolis Colts<br>Galloping Out of<br>an Arm-Tackle | .25 | .10 | .02 |
| ☐ 32 Indianapolis Colts<br>Ball Is Knocked Loose | .25 | .10 | .02 |
| ☐ 33 Indianapolis Colts<br>Busting Out of the<br>Backfield | .25 | .10 | .02 |
| ☐ 34 Kansas City Chiefs<br>About to Head Upfield | .25 | .10 | .02 |
| ☐ 35 Kansas City Chiefs<br>On the Warpath | .25 | .10 | .02 |
| ☐ 36 Kansas City Chiefs<br>Getting the Point<br>Across | .25 | .10 | .02 |
| ☐ 37 Los Angeles Raiders<br>Looks Like Clear<br>Sailing Ahead | .35 | .14 | .03 |
| ☐ 38 Los Angeles Raiders<br>Surrounded by<br>Unfriendly Faces | .35 | .14 | .03 |
| ☐ 39 Los Angeles Raiders<br>Vaulting for Six Points | .35 | .14 | .03 |
| ☐ 40 Los Angeles Rams<br>Breaking into an Open<br>Field (Eric Dickerson) | 1.25 | .50 | .12 |
| ☐ 41 Los Angeles Rams<br>Swept Away By a<br>Wave of Rams | .25 | .10 | .02 |
| ☐ 42 Los Angeles Rams<br>Alertly Scooping<br>Up a Fumble | .25 | .10 | .02 |
| ☐ 43 Miami Dolphins<br>Clearing a Path for<br>the Running Back | .35 | .14 | .03 |
| ☐ 44 Miami Dolphins<br>Teaching a Painful<br>Lesson | .35 | .14 | .03 |
| ☐ 45 Miami Dolphins<br>Trying for a Piece<br>of the Ball | .35 | .14 | .03 |
| ☐ 46 Minnesota Vikings<br>All Day to Throw<br>(Tommy Kramer) | .50 | .20 | .05 |
| ☐ 47 Minnesota Vikings<br>The Moment before<br>Impact (Walter Payton<br>tackled) | 1.50 | .60 | .15 |
| ☐ 48 Minnesota Vikings<br>Leaving the<br>Competition Behind | .25 | .10 | .02 |
| ☐ 49 New England Patriots<br>Solid Line of Blockers | .25 | .10 | .02 |
| ☐ 50 New England Patriots<br>Surprise Attack from<br>the Rear | .25 | .10 | .02 |
| ☐ 51 New England Patriots<br>Getting a Grip on<br>the Opponent | .25 | .10 | .02 |
| ☐ 52 New Orleans Saints<br>Look Out, I'm Coming<br>Through | .25 | .10 | .02 |
| ☐ 53 New Orleans Saints<br>A Furious Assault | .25 | .10 | .02 |
| ☐ 54 New Orleans Saints<br>Line of Scrimmage | .25 | .10 | .02 |
| ☐ 55 New York Giants | .75 | .30 | .07 |

Pass Play Develops
(Phil Simms
and Joe Morris)

| | | | | |
|---|---|---|---|---|
| ☐ 56 New York Giants | | .25 | .10 | .02 |

Putting Squeeze on
Offense

| | | | | |
|---|---|---|---|---|
| ☐ 57 New York Giants | | .25 | .10 | .02 |

Using a Great Block
to Turn Corner

| | | | | |
|---|---|---|---|---|
| ☐ 58 New York Jets | | .25 | .10 | .02 |

The Runner Spots Lane

| | | | | |
|---|---|---|---|---|
| ☐ 59 New York Jets | | .25 | .10 | .02 |

About to Deliver
a Headache

| | | | | |
|---|---|---|---|---|
| ☐ 60 New York Jets | | .25 | .10 | .02 |

Flying Formation

| | | | | |
|---|---|---|---|---|
| ☐ 61 Philadelphia Eagles | | 1.00 | .40 | .10 |

Slipping a Tackle
(Keith Byars)

| | | | | |
|---|---|---|---|---|
| ☐ 62 Philadelphia Eagles | | .25 | .10 | .02 |

Airborne Eagles
Break Up Pass

| | | | | |
|---|---|---|---|---|
| ☐ 63 Philadelphia Eagles | | .50 | .20 | .05 |

Connecting on Toss
Over Middle
(Ron Jaworski passing)

| | | | | |
|---|---|---|---|---|
| ☐ 64 Pittsburgh Steelers | | .25 | .10 | .02 |

Letting Big Guy
Lead The Way

| | | | | |
|---|---|---|---|---|
| ☐ 65 Pittsburgh Steelers | | .25 | .10 | .02 |

Converging From
Every Direction

| | | | | |
|---|---|---|---|---|
| ☐ 66 Pittsburgh Steelers | | .35 | .14 | .03 |

All Eyes Are on
the Football
(Gary Anderson)

| | | | | |
|---|---|---|---|---|
| ☐ 67 St.Louis Cardinals | | .35 | .14 | .03 |

Calmly Dropping Back
to Pass (Neil Lomax
and Jim Burt)

| | | | | |
|---|---|---|---|---|
| ☐ 68 St.Louis Cardinals | | .25 | .10 | .02 |

Applying Some Bruises

| | | | | |
|---|---|---|---|---|
| ☐ 69 St.Louis Cardinals | | .25 | .10 | .02 |

Looking for Yardage
on Interception Return

| | | | | |
|---|---|---|---|---|
| ☐ 70 San Diego Chargers UER | | .50 | .20 | .05 |

Human Cannonball
(reverse negative)

| | | | | |
|---|---|---|---|---|
| ☐ 71 San Diego Chargers | | .50 | .20 | .05 |

Another One Bites
the Dust
(Dave Krieg)

| | | | | |
|---|---|---|---|---|
| ☐ 72 San Diego Chargers | | .25 | .10 | .02 |

A Clean Steal by
the Defense

| | | | | |
|---|---|---|---|---|
| ☐ 73 San Francisco 49ers | | 4.00 | 1.60 | .40 |

Looking for Safe
Passage
(Joe Montana
handing off)

| | | | | |
|---|---|---|---|---|
| ☐ 74 San Francisco 49ers | | .25 | .10 | .02 |

An Uplifting Experience

| | | | | |
|---|---|---|---|---|
| ☐ 75 San Francisco 49ers | | .50 | .20 | .05 |

In Hot Pursuit
(Danny White)

| | | | | |
|---|---|---|---|---|
| ☐ 76 Seattle Seahawks | | .35 | .14 | .03 |

Preparing for Collision

| | | | | |
|---|---|---|---|---|
| ☐ 77 Seattle Seahawks | | .35 | .14 | .03 |

A Group Effort

| | | | | |
|---|---|---|---|---|
| ☐ 78 Seattle Seahawks | | .75 | .30 | .07 |

Forcing a Hurried Throw
(Dan Fouts)

| | | | | |
|---|---|---|---|---|
| ☐ 79 Tampa Bay Buccaneers | | .25 | .10 | .02 |

Protecting Quarterback
at All Costs

| | | | | |
|---|---|---|---|---|
| ☐ 80 Tampa Bay Buccaneers | | .25 | .10 | .02 |

Dishing Out Some
Punishment

| | | | | |
|---|---|---|---|---|
| ☐ 81 Tampa Bay Buccaneers | | .25 | .10 | .02 |

No Trespassing

| | | | | |
|---|---|---|---|---|
| ☐ 82 Washington Redskins | | .25 | .10 | .02 |

Squaring Off in the
Trenches

| | | | | |
|---|---|---|---|---|
| ☐ 83 Washington Redskins | | .50 | .20 | .05 |

Pouncing on the
Passer (Danny White)

| | | | | |
|---|---|---|---|---|
| ☐ 84 Washington Redskins | | .25 | .10 | .02 |

Two Hits Are Better
Than One

| | | | | |
|---|---|---|---|---|
| ☐ 85 Super Bowl XX | | 1.50 | .60 | .15 |

Chicago NFC 46
New England AFC 10
(Walter Payton running)

| | | | | |
|---|---|---|---|---|
| ☐ 86 Super Bowl XX | | .75 | .30 | .07 |

Chicago NFC 46
New England AFC 10
(Jim McMahon passing)

| | | | | |
|---|---|---|---|---|
| ☐ 87 Super Bowl XX | | .35 | .14 | .03 |

Chicago NFC 46
New England AFC 10
(Bears defense)

| | | | | |
|---|---|---|---|---|
| ☐ 88 Pro Bowl 1986 | | 1.00 | .40 | .10 |

NFC 28, AFC 24
(Marcus Allen running)

# 1987 Fleer Team Action

This 88-card set, entitled "Live Action Football," is essentially organized alphabetically by the name of the team. There are two cards for each team; basically odd-numbered cards feature the team's offense and even-numbered cards feature the team's defense. The cards are standard size 2 1/2" by 3 1/2" and are typically oriented horizontally. The cards are numbered on the back and feature a 1987 copyright date. The cards show full-color action scenes (with a yellow and black border around the photo) with specific players not identified. The card backs are printed in gold and black on white card stock. Cards were issued in wax packs of seven team action cards and three team logo stickers.

| | MINT | EXC | G-VG |
|---|---|---|---|
| COMPLETE SET (88) | 15.00 | 6.00 | 1.50 |
| COMMON CARD (1-88) | .20 | .08 | .02 |

| | | | | |
|---|---|---|---|---|
| ☐ 1 Atlanta Falcons | | .40 | .16 | .04 |

A Clear View Downfield

| | | | | |
|---|---|---|---|---|
| ☐ 2 Atlanta Falcons | | .40 | .16 | .04 |

Pouncing on a Runner
(Roger Craig tackled)

| | | | | |
|---|---|---|---|---|
| ☐ 3 Buffalo Bills | | .20 | .08 | .02 |

Buffalo Stampede

| | | | | |
|---|---|---|---|---|
| ☐ 4 Buffalo Bills UER | | .20 | .08 | .02 |

Double Bill
(Bengals and Oilers
pictured)

| | | | | |
|---|---|---|---|---|
| ☐ 5 Chicago Bears | | 1.00 | .40 | .10 |

Stay Out of Our Way
(Walter Payton)

| | | | | |
|---|---|---|---|---|
| ☐ 6 Chicago Bears | | .40 | .16 | .04 |

Quarterback's Night-
mare (Dan Hampton)

| | | | | |
|---|---|---|---|---|
| ☐ 7 Cincinnati Bengals | | .40 | .16 | .04 |

Irresistible Force
(Eddie Brown)

| | | | | |
|---|---|---|---|---|
| ☐ 8 Cincinnati Bengals UER | | .20 | .08 | .02 |

Bengals on the Prowl
(Bills defense
tackling Bengal)

| | | | | |
|---|---|---|---|---|
| ☐ 9 Cleveland Browns | | .20 | .08 | .02 |

Following the
Lead Blocker

| | | | | |
|---|---|---|---|---|
| ☐ 10 Cleveland Browns | | .20 | .08 | .02 |

Block That Kick

| | | | | |
|---|---|---|---|---|
| ☐ 11 Dallas Cowboys | | .30 | .12 | .03 |

Next Stop...End Zone

| | | | | |
|---|---|---|---|---|
| ☐ 12 Dallas Cowboys | | .30 | .12 | .03 |

Ride 'em Cowboys

| | | | | |
|---|---|---|---|---|
| ☐ 13 Denver Broncos | | 1.50 | .60 | .15 |

Pitchout in Progress
(John Elway)

| | | | | |
|---|---|---|---|---|
| ☐ 14 Denver Broncos | | .30 | .12 | .03 |

Broncos' Busters

| | | | | |
|---|---|---|---|---|
| ☐ 15 Detroit Lions | | .20 | .08 | .02 |

Off to the Races

| | | | | |
|---|---|---|---|---|
| ☐ 16 Detroit Lions | | .20 | .08 | .02 |

Entering the Lions' Den

| | | | | |
|---|---|---|---|---|
| ☐ 17 Green Bay Packers | | .20 | .08 | .02 |

Setting the Wheels
in Motion

| | | | | |
|---|---|---|---|---|
| ☐ 18 Green Bay Packers | | .20 | .08 | .02 |

Stack of Packers

| | | | | |
|---|---|---|---|---|
| ☐ 19 Houston Oilers | | .20 | .08 | .02 |

Making a Cut at the
Line of Scrimmage

| | | | |
|---|---|---|---|
| ☐ 20 Houston Oilers ....................... | .20 | .08 | .02 |
| Hit Parade | | | |
| ☐ 21 Indianapolis Colts ................... | .20 | .08 | .02 |
| The Horses Up Front | | | |
| ☐ 22 Indianapolis Colts ................... | .20 | .08 | .02 |
| Stopping the Runner in His Tracks | | | |
| ☐ 23 Kansas City Chiefs ................. | .20 | .08 | .02 |
| It's a Snap | | | |
| ☐ 24 Kansas City Chiefs ................. | 1.50 | .60 | .15 |
| Nowhere to Hide (Bo Jackson getting tackled) | | | |
| ☐ 25 Los Angeles Raiders ............... | 2.50 | 1.00 | .25 |
| Looking for Daylight (Bo Jackson running) | | | |
| ☐ 26 Los Angeles Raiders ............... | .30 | .12 | .03 |
| Wrapped Up by Raiders | | | |
| ☐ 27 Los Angeles Rams ................. | 1.00 | .40 | .10 |
| Movers and Shakers (Jim Everett) | | | |
| ☐ 28 Los Angeles Rams ................. | .20 | .08 | .02 |
| In the Quarter- back's Face | | | |
| ☐ 29 Miami Dolphins ...................... | .30 | .12 | .03 |
| Full Speed Ahead | | | |
| ☐ 30 Miami Dolphins ...................... | .30 | .12 | .03 |
| Acrobatic Interception | | | |
| ☐ 31 Minnesota Vikings.................. | .30 | .12 | .03 |
| Solid Line of Protection (Tommy Kramer) | | | |
| ☐ 32 Minnesota Vikings.................. | .20 | .08 | .02 |
| Bearing a Heavy Load | | | |
| ☐ 33 New England Patriots............. | .40 | .16 | .04 |
| The Blockers Fan Out (Craig James) | | | |
| ☐ 34 New England Patriots............. | .20 | .08 | .02 |
| Converging Linebackers | | | |
| ☐ 35 New Orleans Saints................ | .40 | .16 | .04 |
| Saints Go Diving In (Dalton Hilliard and Jim Burt) | | | |
| ☐ 36 New Orleans Saints................ | .20 | .08 | .02 |
| Crash Course | | | |
| ☐ 37 New York Giants .................... | .40 | .16 | .04 |
| Armed and Dangerous (Phil Simms) | | | |
| ☐ 38 New York Giants .................... | .75 | .30 | .07 |
| A Giant-sized Hit (Lawrence Taylor) | | | |
| ☐ 39 New York Jets........................ | .30 | .12 | .03 |
| Jets Prepare for Takeoff (Ken O'Brien) | | | |
| ☐ 40 New York Jets........................ | .20 | .08 | .02 |
| Showing No Mercy | | | |
| ☐ 41 Philadelphia Eagles ............... | .20 | .08 | .02 |
| Taking It Straight Up the Middle | | | |
| ☐ 42 Philadelphia Eagles ............... | 1.00 | .40 | .10 |
| The Strong Arm of the Defense (Reggie White) | | | |
| ☐ 43 Pittsburgh Steelers ................ | .20 | .08 | .02 |
| Double-team Trouble | | | |
| ☐ 44 Pittsburgh Steelers ................ | .20 | .08 | .02 |
| Caught in a Steel Trap | | | |
| ☐ 45 St. Louis Cardinals................. | .20 | .08 | .02 |
| The kick is up and...it's good | | | |
| ☐ 46 St. Louis Cardinals................. | .20 | .08 | .02 |
| Seeing Red | | | |
| ☐ 47 San Diego Chargers .............. | .20 | .08 | .02 |
| Blast Off | | | |
| ☐ 48 San Diego Chargers .............. | .40 | .16 | .04 |
| Lightning Strikes (Todd Christensen tackled) | | | |
| ☐ 49 San Francisco 49ers UER........ | .75 | .30 | .07 |
| The Rush Is On (reverse negative photo on front) | | | |
| ☐ 50 San Francisco 49ers............... | .20 | .08 | .02 |
| Shoulder to Shoulder | | | |
| ☐ 51 Seattle Seahawks .................. | .30 | .12 | .03 |
| Not a Defender in Sight (Curt Warner) | | | |
| ☐ 52 Seattle Seahawks .................. | .20 | .08 | .02 |
| Hard Knocks | | | |
| ☐ 53 Tampa Bay Buccaneers........... | 1.50 | .60 | .15 |
| Rolling Out Against the Grain (Steve Young) | | | |
| ☐ 54 Tampa Bay Buccaneers........... | .20 | .08 | .02 |
| Crunch Time | | | |
| ☐ 55 Washington Redskins ............. | .40 | .16 | .04 |

| | | | |
|---|---|---|---|
| Getting the Drop on the Defense (Jay Schroeder) | | | |
| ☐ 56 Washington Redskins ............. | .20 | .08 | .02 |
| The Blitz Claims Another Victim | | | |
| ☐ 57 AFC Championship Game........ | .20 | .08 | .02 |
| Denver 23, Cleveland 20 (OT) | | | |
| ☐ 58 AFC Divisional Playoff ............ | .20 | .08 | .02 |
| Cleveland 23, New York Jets 20 (OT) | | | |
| ☐ 59 AFC Divisional Playoff ............ | .30 | .12 | .03 |
| Denver 22, New England 17 (Andre Tippett) | | | |
| ☐ 60 AFC Wild Card Game.............. | .20 | .08 | .02 |
| New York Jets 35, Kansas City 15 | | | |
| ☐ 61 NFC Championship ................ | .60 | .24 | .06 |
| New York Giants 17, Washington 0 (Lawrence Taylor) | | | |
| ☐ 62 NFC Divisional Playoff ............ | .30 | .12 | .03 |
| Washington 27, Chicago 13 (William Perry) | | | |
| ☐ 63 NFC Divisional Playoff ............ | .30 | .12 | .03 |
| New York Giants 49, San Francisco 3 (Joe Morris) | | | |
| ☐ 64 NFC Wild Card Game.............. | .75 | .30 | .07 |
| Washington 19, Los Angeles Rams 7 (Eric Dickerson) | | | |
| ☐ 65 Super Bowl I .......................... | .30 | .12 | .03 |
| Green Bay NFL 35 Kansas City AFL 10 | | | |
| ☐ 66 Super Bowl II ......................... | .50 | .20 | .05 |
| Green Bay NFL 33 Oakland AFL 14 (Bart Starr) | | | |
| ☐ 67 Super Bowl III ........................ | .30 | .12 | .03 |
| New York AFL 16 Baltimore NFL 7 (Matt Snell running) | | | |
| ☐ 68 Super Bowl IV ........................ | .20 | .08 | .02 |
| Kansas City AFL 23 Minnesota NFL 7 | | | |
| ☐ 69 Super Bowl V ......................... | .40 | .16 | .04 |
| Baltimore AFC 16 Dallas NFC 13 (Duane Thomas tackled) | | | |
| ☐ 70 Super Bowl VI ........................ | 1.00 | .40 | .10 |
| Dallas NFC 24 Miami AFC 3 (Roger Staubach) | | | |
| ☐ 71 Super Bowl VII ....................... | .60 | .24 | .06 |
| Miami AFC 14 Washington NFC 7 (Bob Griese and Jim Kiick) | | | |
| ☐ 72 Super Bowl VIII...................... | .60 | .24 | .06 |
| Miami AFC 24 Minnesota NFC 7 (Larry Csonka running) | | | |
| ☐ 73 Super Bowl IX ........................ | .75 | .30 | .07 |
| Pittsburgh AFC 16 Minnesota NFC 6 (Fran Tarkenton loose ball) | | | |
| ☐ 74 Super Bowl X ......................... | .75 | .30 | .07 |
| Pittsburgh AFC 21 Dallas NFC 17 (Franco Harris) | | | |
| ☐ 75 Super Bowl XI ........................ | .30 | .12 | .03 |
| Oakland AFC 32 Minnesota NFC 14 (Chuck Foreman tackled) | | | |
| ☐ 76 Super Bowl XII........................ | .60 | .24 | .06 |
| Dallas NFC 27 Denver AFC 10 (Tony Dorsett running) | | | |
| ☐ 77 Super Bowl XIII ...................... | 1.00 | .40 | .10 |
| Pittsburgh AFC 35 Dallas NFC 31 (Terry Bradshaw passing) | | | |
| ☐ 78 Super Bowl XIV...................... | .30 | .12 | .03 |
| Pittsburgh AFC 31 Los Angeles NFC 19 (Cullen Bryant tackled) | | | |
| ☐ 79 Super Bowl XV ....................... | .30 | .12 | .03 |
| Oakland AFC 27, Philadelphia NFC 10 (Jim Plunkett passing) | | | |
| ☐ 80 Super Bowl XVI....................... | .20 | .08 | .02 |

San Francisco NFC 26,
Cincinnati AFC 21
☐ 81 Super Bowl XVII ..................... .20 .08 .02
Washington NFC 27,
Miami AFC 17
☐ 82 Super Bowl XVIII .................... .20 .08 .02
Los Angeles AFC 38,
Washington NFC 9
(Punt blocked)
☐ 83 Super Bowl XIX ..................... 2.00 .80 .20
San Francisco NFC 38,
Miami AFC 16
(Roger Craig and
Joe Montana)
☐ 84 Super Bowl XX ...................... .40 .16 .04
Chicago NFC 46,
New England AFC 10
(Wilber Marshall
and Richard Dent)
☐ 85 Super Bowl XXI ..................... .60 .24 .06
New York NFC 39,
Denver AFC 20
(Lawrence Taylor)
☐ 86 Super Bowl XXI ..................... .40 .16 .04
New York NFC 39,
Denver AFC 20
(Phil Simms)
☐ 87 Super Bowl XXI ..................... .50 .20 .05
Giants erupt in 3rd,
Score 17 points
(Lawrence Taylor
and Carl Banks)
(Checklist 1-44 on back)
☐ 88 Super Bowl XXI ..................... .50 .20 .05
Giants Outrun Broncos
by only 27 yards
(Checklist 45-88
on card back)

# 1988 Fleer Team Action

This 88-card set, entitled "Live Action Football," is essentially organized alphabetically by the nickname of the team within each conference. There are two cards for each team. Basically odd-numbered cards feature the team's offense and even-numbered cards feature the team's defense. The Super Bowl cards included in this set are subtitled "Super Bowls of the Decade." The cards are standard size 2 1/2" by 3 1/2" and are typically oriented horizontally. The cards are numbered on the back and feature a 1988 copyright date. The cards show full-color action scenes with specific players not identified. The card backs are printed in blue and green on white card stock. Cards were issued in wax packs of seven team action cards and three team logo stickers.

| | MINT | EXC | G-VG |
|---|---|---|---|
| COMPLETE SET (88) ...................... | 15.00 | 6.00 | 1.50 |
| COMMON PLAYER (1-88) ............... | .15 | .06 | .01 |

☐ 1 Bengals Offense ...................... .75 .30 .07
A Great Wall
(Boomer Esiason)
☐ 2 Bengals Defense ..................... .15 .06 .01
Stacking the Odds
☐ 3 Bills Offense ........................... 1.25 .50 .12
Play-Action
(Jim Kelly)
☐ 4 Bills Defense ........................... .15 .06 .01
Buffalo Soldiers
☐ 5 Broncos Offense ..................... 1.25 .50 .12
Sneak Attack
(John Elway)
☐ 6 Broncos Defense .................... .15 .06 .01
Crushing the Opposition
☐ 7 Browns Offense ...................... .50 .20 .05

On the Run
(Bernie Kosar
and Kevin Mack)
☐ 8 Browns Defense ..................... .75 .30 .07
Dogs' Day
(Eric Dickerson)
☐ 9 Chargers Offense .................... .25 .10 .02
A Bolt of Blue
(Gary Anderson)
☐ 10 Chargers Defense .................. .15 .06 .01
That's a Wrap
☐ 11 Chiefs Offense ...................... .15 .06 .01
Last Line of Offense
☐ 12 Chiefs Defense ...................... .15 .06 .01
Hard-Hitting in the
Heartland
☐ 13 Colts Offense ........................ .15 .06 .01
An Eye To the End Zone
☐ 14 Colts Defense ....................... .15 .06 .01
Free Ball
☐ 15 Dolphins Offense ................... 2.00 .80 .20
Miami Scoring Machine
(Dan Marino takes snap)
☐ 16 Dolphins Defense .................. .25 .10 .02
No Mercy
☐ 17 Jets Offense ......................... .25 .10 .02
On a Roll
(Ken O'Brien)
☐ 18 Jets Defense ......................... .15 .06 .01
Jets Win a Dogfight
☐ 19 Oilers Offense ...................... 1.00 .40 .10
Well-Oiled Machine
(Warren Moon
hands off)
☐ 20 Oilers Defense ...................... .15 .06 .01
Hard Shoulder
☐ 21 Patriots Offense .................... .25 .10 .02
A Clean Sweep
(Craig James)
☐ 22 Patriots Defense ................... 1.00 .40 .10
A Fall in New England
(Bo Jackson tackled)
☐ 23 Raiders Offense .................... 1.50 .60 .15
Rush Hour in Los
Angeles (Bo Jackson)
☐ 24 Raiders Defense .................... .25 .10 .02
Cut Me Some Slack
(Howie Long)
☐ 25 Seahawks Offense ................. .25 .10 .02
Follow the Leader
(Curt Warner)
☐ 26 Seahawks Defense ................ .35 .14 .03
Pain, But No Gain
(Brian Bosworth)
☐ 27 Steelers Offense .................... .15 .06 .01
Life in the Fast Lane
☐ 28 Steelers Defense ................... .15 .06 .01
No Exit
☐ 29 Bears Offense ....................... .15 .06 .01
Bearly Audible
☐ 30 Bears Defense ....................... .15 .06 .01
Here, Kitty, Kitty
☐ 31 Buccaneers Offense .............. .75 .30 .07
Letting Loose
(Vinny Testaverde)
☐ 32 Buccaneers Defense .............. .15 .06 .01
In The Grasp
☐ 33 Cardinals Offense .................. .25 .10 .02
You've Gotta Hand It
to Him (Neil Lomax)
☐ 34 Cardinals Defense ................. .35 .14 .03
Stack of Cards
(Roger Craig)
☐ 35 Cowboys Offense .................. .60 .24 .06
Take It Away
(Herschel Walker)
☐ 36 Cowboys Defense .................. .35 .14 .03
Howdy, Pardner
(Randy White)
☐ 37 Eagles Offense ...................... .75 .30 .07
Eagle in Flight
(Randall Cunningham)
☐ 38 Eagles Defense ...................... .60 .24 .06
Buffalo Sandwich
(Reggie White)
☐ 39 Falcons Offense .................... .15 .06 .01
Rumbling Runner
☐ 40 Falcons Defense .................... .15 .06 .01
The Brink of Disaster
☐ 41 49ers Offense ....................... .35 .14 .03
Move aside
(Roger Craig)
☐ 42 49ers Defense ....................... .50 .20 .05
Bullies by the Bay
(Ronnie Lott)
☐ 43 Giants Offense ...................... .35 .14 .03
Firing a Fastball
(Phil Simms passing)

☐ 44 Giants Defense .......................... .15 .06 .01
    A Giant Headache
☐ 45 Lions Offense .......................... .15 .06 .01
    Charge Up the Middle
☐ 46 Lions Defense .......................... .15 .06 .01
    Rocking and Rolling
    in Motown
☐ 47 Packers Offense .......................... .25 .10 .02
    Gaining Altitude
    (Carl Lee)
☐ 48 Packers Defense .......................... .15 .06 .01
    This Play is a Hit
☐ 49 Rams Offense .......................... .35 .14 .03
    Rams Lock Horns
    (Jim Everett)
☐ 50 Rams Defense .......................... .15 .06 .01
    Greetings from L.A.
☐ 51 Redskins Offense .......................... .15 .06 .01
    Capital Gains
☐ 52 Redskins Defense .......................... .15 .06 .01
    No More Mr. Nice Guy
☐ 53 Saints Offense .......................... .15 .06 .01
    Roamin' in the Dome
☐ 54 Saints Defense .......................... .15 .06 .01
    He'll Feel This One
    Tomorrow
☐ 55 Vikings Offense .......................... .50 .20 .05
    Passing Fancy
    (Wade Wilson)
☐ 56 Vikings Defense .......................... .15 .06 .01
    A Vikings' Siege
☐ 57 Super Bowl XXII .......................... .25 .10 .02
    Washington 42
    Denver 10
    (Timmy Smith)
☐ 58 Super Bowl Checklist .......................... .25 .10 .02
    (Timmy Smith running;
    Checklist 1-50
    on back)
☐ 59 Super Bowl Checklist .......................... 1.00 .40 .10
    (John Elway sacked;
    Checklist 51-88
    on back)
☐ 60 Super Bowl XXI .......................... .50 .20 .05
    New York Giants 39
    Denver 20
    (Lawrence Taylor
    and Carl Banks)
☐ 61 Super Bowl XX .......................... .75 .30 .07
    Chicago 46
    New England 10
    (Walter Payton)
☐ 62 Super Bowl XIX .......................... .25 .10 .02
    San Francisco 38
    Miami 16
    (Roger Craig running)
☐ 63 Super Bowl XVIII .......................... .50 .20 .05
    L.A. Raiders 38
    Washington 9
    (Marcus Allen running)
☐ 64 Super Bowl XVII .......................... .15 .06 .01
    Washington 27
    Miami 17
☐ 65 Super Bowl XVI .......................... 2.00 .80 .20
    San Francisco 26
    Cincinnati 21
    (Joe Montana pitching)
☐ 66 Super Bowl XV .......................... .25 .10 .02
    Oakland 27
    Philadelphia 10
    (Jim Plunkett)
☐ 67 Super Bowl XIV .......................... .15 .06 .01
    Pittsburgh 31
    Los Angeles Rams 19
☐ 68 NFC Championship .......................... .15 .06 .01
    Washington 17
    Minnesota 10
☐ 69 AFC Championship .......................... 1.00 .40 .10
    Denver 38
    Cleveland 33
    (John Elway)
☐ 70 NFC Playoff Game .......................... 2.00 .80 .20
    Minnesota 36
    San Francisco 24
    (Joe Montana chased)
☐ 71 NFC Playoff Game .......................... .15 .06 .01
    Washington 21
    Chicago 17
☐ 72 AFC Playoff Game .......................... .25 .10 .02
    Cleveland 38
    Indianapolis 21
    (Ozzie Newsome
    and Kevin Mack)
☐ 73 AFC Playoff Game .......................... .15 .06 .01
    Denver 34
    Houston 10
☐ 74 NFC Wild Card Game .......................... .15 .06 .01

    Minnesota 44
    New Orleans 10
☐ 75 AFC Wild Card Game .......................... .15 .06 .01
    Houston 23
    Seattle 20 (OT)
☐ 76 League Leading Team .......................... .25 .10 .02
    Rushing: 49ers
    (Roger Craig running)
☐ 77 League Leading Team .......................... 1.50 .60 .15
    Passing: Dolphins
    (Dan Marino drops back)
☐ 78 League Leading Team .......................... .15 .06 .01
    Interceptions: Saints
☐ 79 League Leading Team .......................... .15 .06 .01
    Fumble Recovery:
    Eagles
☐ 80 League Leading Team .......................... .35 .14 .03
    Sacks: Bears
    (Richard Dent)
☐ 81 League Leading Team .......................... .15 .06 .01
    Defense Against
    Kickoff Returns: Bills
☐ 82 League Leading Team .......................... .15 .06 .01
    Defense Against
    Punt Returns: Jets
☐ 83 League Leading Team .......................... .15 .06 .01
    Punt Returns:
    Cardinals
☐ 84 League Leading Team .......................... .15 .06 .01
    Kickoff Returns:
    Falcons
☐ 85 League Leading Team .......................... .15 .06 .01
    Fewest Fumbles:
    Steelers
☐ 86 League Leading Team .......................... .50 .20 .05
    Fewest Interceptions:
    Browns (Bernie Kosar)
☐ 87 League Leading Team .......................... .15 .06 .01
    Fewest Points Allowed:
    Colts
☐ 88 League Leading Team .......................... .35 .14 .03
    TD's on Returns: Rams
    (Henry Ellard)

## 1990 Fleer

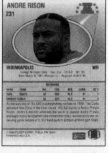

The 1990 Fleer set contains 400 standard-size (2 1/2" by 3 1/2") cards. The fronts have color action photos and team colored inner borders with white outer borders. The vertically oriented backs are multicolored and have stats and color mug shots. The set numbering is according to teams and alphabetical within teams as is the Fleer custom, San Francisco 49ers (1-17), Denver Broncos (18-32), Los Angeles Rams (33-46), Cleveland Browns (47-60), New York Giants (61-77), Philadelphia Eagles (78-93), Minnesota Vikings (94-109), Buffalo Bills (110-124), Houston Oilers (125-138), Pittsburgh Steelers (139-153), Washington Redskins (154-168), Green Bay Packers (169-182), New Orleans Saints (183-196), Kansas City Chiefs (197-209), Cincinnati Bengals (210-223), Indianapolis Colts (224-235), Miami Dolphins (236-248), Los Angeles Raiders (249-262), Seattle Seahawks (263-274), Detroit Lions (275-287), Chicago Bears (288-302), San Diego Chargers (303-316), New England Patriots (317-329), Phoenix Cardinals (330-342), Tampa Bay Buccaneers (343-357), New York Jets (358-370), Atlanta Falcons (371-383), and Dallas Cowboys (384-396). The teams are essentially ordered by their respective order of finish during the 1989 season. The following cards have AFC logo location variations: 18, 20-22, 24, 27-30, 32, 49-56, 58, 60, 110-111, 113-117, 119, 122, 124, 198, 200-211, 213-217, and 221-223. Jim Covert (290) and Mark May (162) can be found with or without a thin line just above the text on the back. The key rookies in this set are Jeff George, Jeff Hostetler, and Blair Thomas.

| | MINT | EXC | G-VG |
|---|---|---|---|
| COMPLETE SET (400)...................... | 8.00 | 3.60 | 1.00 |
| COMMON PLAYER (1-400)............... | .04 | .02 | .01 |
| ☐ 1 Harris Barton............................. | .04 | .02 | .01 |
| ☐ 2 Chet Brooks ............................. | .04 | .02 | .01 |
| ☐ 3 Michael Carter .......................... | .04 | .02 | .01 |
| ☐ 4 Mike Cofer UER........................ | .04 | .02 | .01 |
| (FGA and FGM columns switched) | | | |
| ☐ 5 Roger Craig.............................. | .08 | .04 | .01 |
| ☐ 6 Kevin Fagan ............................ | .04 | .02 | .01 |
| ☐ 7 Charles Haley UER .................. | .08 | .04 | .01 |
| (Fumble recoveries should be 2 in '86 and 5 career, card says 1 and 4) | | | |
| ☐ 8 Pierce Holt .............................. | .15 | .07 | .02 |
| ☐ 9 Ronnie Lott ............................. | .10 | .05 | .01 |
| ☐ 10A Joe Montana ERR ................ | 1.00 | .45 | .13 |
| (31,054 TD's) | | | |
| ☐ 10B Joe Montana COR ................ | 1.00 | .45 | .13 |
| (216 TD's) | | | |
| ☐ 11 Bubba Paris ........................... | .08 | .04 | .01 |
| ☐ 12 Tom Rathman ......................... | .08 | .04 | .01 |
| ☐ 13 Jerry Rice .............................. | .75 | .35 | .09 |
| ☐ 14 John Taylor............................ | .15 | .07 | .02 |
| ☐ 15 Keena Turner .......................... | .08 | .04 | .01 |
| ☐ 16 Mike Walter ........................... | .04 | .02 | .01 |
| ☐ 17 Steve Young ........................... | .40 | .18 | .05 |
| ☐ 18 Steve Atwater ......................... | .10 | .05 | .01 |
| ☐ 19 Tyrone Braxton ....................... | .04 | .02 | .01 |
| ☐ 20 Michael Brooks ....................... | .20 | .09 | .03 |
| ☐ 21 John Elway............................. | .40 | .18 | .05 |
| ☐ 22 Simon Fletcher ........................ | .08 | .04 | .01 |
| ☐ 23 Bobby Humphrey ..................... | .08 | .04 | .01 |
| ☐ 24 Mark Jackson ......................... | .08 | .04 | .01 |
| ☐ 25 Vance Johnson ........................ | .08 | .04 | .01 |
| ☐ 26 Greg Kragen ........................... | .04 | .02 | .01 |
| ☐ 27 Ken Lanier ............................. | .04 | .02 | .01 |
| ☐ 28 Karl Mecklenburg ..................... | .08 | .04 | .01 |
| ☐ 29 Orson Mobley .......................... | .04 | .02 | .01 |
| ☐ 30 Steve Sewell ........................... | .04 | .02 | .01 |
| ☐ 31 Dennis Smith .......................... | .08 | .04 | .01 |
| ☐ 32 David Treadwell........................ | .04 | .02 | .01 |
| ☐ 33 Flipper Anderson...................... | .08 | .04 | .01 |
| ☐ 34 Greg Bell ............................... | .08 | .04 | .01 |
| ☐ 35 Henry Ellard ........................... | .08 | .04 | .01 |
| ☐ 36 Jim Everett ............................. | .08 | .04 | .01 |
| ☐ 37 Jerry Gray ............................. | .04 | .02 | .01 |
| ☐ 38 Kevin Greene .......................... | .08 | .04 | .01 |
| ☐ 39 Pete Holohan .......................... | .04 | .02 | .01 |
| ☐ 40 LeRoy Irvin ............................ | .04 | .02 | .01 |
| ☐ 41 Mike Lansford ......................... | .04 | .02 | .01 |
| ☐ 42 Buford McGee ......................... | .04 | .02 | .01 |
| ☐ 43 Tom Newberry ......................... | .04 | .02 | .01 |
| ☐ 44 Vince Newsome ....................... | .04 | .02 | .01 |
| ☐ 45 Jackie Slater ........................... | .08 | .04 | .01 |
| ☐ 46 Mike Wilcher .......................... | .04 | .02 | .01 |
| ☐ 47 Matt Bahr .............................. | .04 | .02 | .01 |
| ☐ 48 Brian Brennan ......................... | .04 | .02 | .01 |
| ☐ 49 Thane Gash ........................... | .04 | .02 | .01 |
| ☐ 50 Mike Johnson .......................... | .04 | .02 | .01 |
| ☐ 51 Bernie Kosar ........................... | .10 | .05 | .01 |
| ☐ 52 Reggie Langhorne ..................... | .08 | .04 | .01 |
| ☐ 53 Tim Manoa ............................ | .04 | .02 | .01 |
| ☐ 54 Clay Matthews......................... | .08 | .04 | .01 |
| ☐ 55 Eric Metcalf ........................... | .15 | .07 | .02 |
| ☐ 56 Frank Minnifield ....................... | .04 | .02 | .01 |
| ☐ 57 Gregg Rakoczy UER .................. | .04 | .02 | .01 |
| (First line of text calls him Greg) | | | |
| ☐ 58 Webster Slaughter ................... | .08 | .04 | .01 |
| ☐ 59 Bryan Wagner ......................... | .04 | .02 | .01 |
| ☐ 60 Felix Wright ........................... | .04 | .02 | .01 |
| ☐ 61 Raul Allegre ........................... | .04 | .02 | .01 |
| ☐ 62 Ottis Anderson UER .................. | .08 | .04 | .01 |
| (Stats say 9.317 yards, should be 9,317) | | | |
| ☐ 63 Carl Banks ............................. | .08 | .04 | .01 |
| ☐ 64 Mark Bavaro ........................... | .08 | .04 | .01 |
| ☐ 65 Maurice Carthon ...................... | .04 | .02 | .01 |
| ☐ 66 Mark Collins UER ...................... | .04 | .02 | .01 |
| (Total fumble recoveries should be 5, not 3) | | | |
| ☐ 67 Jeff Hostetler.......................... | .50 | .23 | .06 |
| ☐ 68 Erik Howard ........................... | .04 | .02 | .01 |
| ☐ 69 Pepper Johnson ....................... | .08 | .04 | .01 |
| ☐ 70 Sean Landeta ......................... | .08 | .04 | .01 |
| ☐ 71 Lionel Manuel ......................... | .04 | .02 | .01 |
| ☐ 72 Leonard Marshall ..................... | .08 | .04 | .01 |
| ☐ 73 Dave Meggett .......................... | .10 | .05 | .01 |
| ☐ 74 Bart Oates ............................. | .04 | .02 | .01 |
| ☐ 75 Doug Riesenberg ...................... | .04 | .02 | .01 |
| ☐ 76 Phil Simms ............................. | .10 | .05 | .01 |
| ☐ 77 Lawrence Taylor ...................... | .10 | .05 | .01 |
| ☐ 78 Eric Allen ............................. | .08 | .04 | .01 |
| ☐ 79 Jerome Brown.......................... | .08 | .04 | .01 |
| ☐ 80 Keith Byars............................. | .08 | .04 | .01 |
| ☐ 81 Cris Carter ............................. | .20 | .09 | .03 |
| ☐ 82A Byron Evans ERR .................. | .20 | .09 | .03 |
| (should be 83 according to checklist) | | | |
| ☐ 82B Randall Cunningham............... | .15 | .07 | .02 |
| ☐ 83A Ron Heller ERR ...................... | .10 | .05 | .01 |
| (should be 84 according to checklist) | | | |
| ☐ 83B Byron Evans COR.................. | .15 | .07 | .02 |
| ☐ 84 Ron Heller ............................. | .10 | .05 | .01 |
| ☐ 85 Terry Hoage ........................... | .10 | .05 | .01 |
| ☐ 86 Keith Jackson ......................... | .25 | .11 | .03 |
| ☐ 87 Seth Joyner ............................ | .08 | .04 | .01 |
| ☐ 88 Mike Quick ............................ | .08 | .04 | .01 |
| ☐ 89 Mike Schad ............................ | .04 | .02 | .01 |
| ☐ 90 Clyde Simmons ....................... | .08 | .04 | .01 |
| ☐ 91 John Teltschik......................... | .04 | .02 | .01 |
| ☐ 92 Anthony Toney ........................ | .04 | .02 | .01 |
| ☐ 93 Reggie White........................... | .15 | .07 | .02 |
| ☐ 94 Ray Berry .............................. | .04 | .02 | .01 |
| ☐ 95 Joey Browner .......................... | .08 | .04 | .01 |
| ☐ 96 Anthony Carter ........................ | .08 | .04 | .01 |
| ☐ 97 Chris Doleman ........................ | .08 | .04 | .01 |
| ☐ 98 Rick Fenney ........................... | .04 | .02 | .01 |
| ☐ 99 Rich Gannon ........................... | .25 | .11 | .03 |
| ☐ 100 Hassan Jones ........................ | .04 | .02 | .01 |
| ☐ 101 Steve Jordan ........................ | .08 | .04 | .01 |
| ☐ 102 Rich Karlis ........................... | .04 | .02 | .01 |
| ☐ 103 Andre Ware ........................... | .15 | .07 | .02 |
| ☐ 104 Kirk Lowdermilk ...................... | .04 | .02 | .01 |
| ☐ 105 Keith Millard .......................... | .08 | .04 | .01 |
| ☐ 106 Scott Studwell ....................... | .04 | .02 | .01 |
| ☐ 107 Herschel Walker ..................... | .10 | .05 | .01 |
| ☐ 108 Wade Wilson .......................... | .08 | .04 | .01 |
| ☐ 109 Gary Zimmerman .................... | .08 | .04 | .01 |
| ☐ 110 Don Beebe............................ | .15 | .07 | .02 |
| ☐ 111 Cornelius Bennett.................... | .10 | .05 | .01 |
| ☐ 112 Shane Conlan ........................ | .08 | .04 | .01 |
| ☐ 113 Jim Kelly .............................. | .30 | .14 | .04 |
| ☐ 114 Scott Norwood UER .............. | .04 | .02 | .01 |
| (FGA and FGM columns switched) | | | |
| ☐ 115 Mark Kelso UER .................. | .04 | .02 | .01 |
| (Some stats added wrong on back) | | | |
| ☐ 116 Larry Kinnebrew...................... | .04 | .02 | .01 |
| ☐ 117 Pete Metzelaars...................... | .04 | .02 | .01 |
| ☐ 118 Scott Radecic ........................ | .04 | .02 | .01 |
| ☐ 119 Andre Reed ........................... | .15 | .07 | .02 |
| ☐ 120 Jim Ritcher ........................... | .10 | .05 | .01 |
| ☐ 121 Bruce Smith .......................... | .10 | .05 | .01 |
| ☐ 122 Leonard Smith ....................... | .04 | .02 | .01 |
| ☐ 123 Art Still ............................... | .08 | .04 | .01 |
| ☐ 124 Thurman Thomas ..................... | .40 | .18 | .05 |
| ☐ 125 Steve Brown .......................... | .04 | .02 | .01 |
| ☐ 126 Ray Childress......................... | .08 | .04 | .01 |
| ☐ 127 Ernest Givens ........................ | .08 | .04 | .01 |
| ☐ 128 John Grimsley......................... | .04 | .02 | .01 |
| ☐ 129 Alonzo Highsmith..................... | .04 | .02 | .01 |
| ☐ 130 Drew Hill ............................. | .08 | .04 | .01 |
| ☐ 131 Bruce Matthews ...................... | .08 | .04 | .01 |
| ☐ 132 Johnny Meads........................ | .04 | .02 | .01 |
| ☐ 133 Warren Moon UER ................ | .20 | .09 | .03 |
| (186 completions in '87 and 1341 career, should be 184 and 1339) | | | |
| ☐ 134 Mike Munchak......................... | .08 | .04 | .01 |
| ☐ 135 Mike Rozier .......................... | .08 | .04 | .01 |
| ☐ 136 Dean Steinkuhler..................... | .04 | .02 | .01 |
| ☐ 137 Lorenzo White ........................ | .15 | .07 | .02 |
| ☐ 138 Tony Zendejas........................ | .04 | .02 | .01 |
| ☐ 139 Gary Anderson ....................... | .04 | .02 | .01 |
| ☐ 140 Bubby Brister ........................ | .10 | .05 | .01 |
| ☐ 141 Thomas Everett....................... | .04 | .02 | .01 |
| ☐ 142 Derek Hill ............................ | .04 | .02 | .01 |
| ☐ 143 Merril Hoge ........................... | .08 | .04 | .01 |
| ☐ 144 Tim Johnson .......................... | .04 | .02 | .01 |
| ☐ 145 Louis Lipps ........................... | .08 | .04 | .01 |
| ☐ 146 David Little ........................... | .04 | .02 | .01 |
| ☐ 147 Greg Lloyd ........................... | .04 | .02 | .01 |
| ☐ 148 Mike Mularkey........................ | .04 | .02 | .01 |
| ☐ 149 John Rienstra......................... | .04 | .02 | .01 |
| ☐ 150 Gerald Williams UER ............. | .04 | .02 | .01 |
| (Tackles and fumble recovery headers are switched) | | | |
| ☐ 151 Keith Willis UER .................. | .04 | .02 | .01 |
| (Tackles and fumble recovery headers are switched) | | | |
| ☐ 152 Rod Woodson ........................ | .20 | .09 | .03 |
| ☐ 153 Tim Worley ........................... | .08 | .04 | .01 |
| ☐ 154 Gary Clark ........................... | .10 | .05 | .01 |
| ☐ 155 Darryl Grant .......................... | .04 | .02 | .01 |
| ☐ 156 Darrell Green ........................ | .08 | .04 | .01 |
| ☐ 157 Joe Jacoby ........................... | .08 | .04 | .01 |

| | | | | | | | |
|---|---|---|---|---|---|---|---|
| ☐ 158 Jim Lachey | .08 | .04 | .01 | ☐ 251 Steve Beuerlein | .25 | .11 | .03 |
| ☐ 159 Chip Lohmiller | .08 | .04 | .01 | ☐ 252 Mike Dyal | .04 | .02 | .01 |
| ☐ 160 Charles Mann | .08 | .04 | .01 | ☐ 253 Mervyn Fernandez | .04 | .02 | .01 |
| ☐ 161 Wilber Marshall | .08 | .04 | .01 | ☐ 254 Bob Golic | .04 | .02 | .01 |
| ☐ 162 Mark May | .04 | .02 | .01 | ☐ 255 Mike Harden | .04 | .02 | .01 |
| ☐ 163 Ralf Mojsiejenko | .04 | .02 | .01 | ☐ 256 Bo Jackson | .40 | .18 | .05 |
| ☐ 164 Art Monk UER | .10 | .05 | .01 | ☐ 257 Howie Long UER | .08 | .04 | .01 |
| (No explanation of How Acquired) | | | | (Born Sommerville, should be Somerville) | | | |
| ☐ 165 Gerald Riggs | .08 | .04 | .01 | ☐ 258 Don Mosebar | .04 | .02 | .01 |
| ☐ 166 Mark Rypien | .10 | .05 | .01 | ☐ 259 Jay Schroeder | .04 | .02 | .01 |
| ☐ 167 Ricky Sanders | .08 | .04 | .01 | ☐ 260 Steve Smith | .08 | .04 | .01 |
| ☐ 168 Don Warren | .04 | .02 | .01 | ☐ 261 Greg Townsend | .08 | .04 | .01 |
| ☐ 169 Robert Brown | .04 | .02 | .01 | ☐ 262 Lionel Washington | .04 | .02 | .01 |
| ☐ 170 Blair Bush | .04 | .02 | .01 | ☐ 263 Brian Blades | .15 | .07 | .02 |
| ☐ 171 Brent Fullwood | .04 | .02 | .01 | ☐ 264 Jeff Bryant | .04 | .02 | .01 |
| ☐ 172 Tim Harris | .08 | .04 | .01 | ☐ 265 Grant Feasel | .04 | .02 | .01 |
| ☐ 173 Chris Jacke | .04 | .02 | .01 | ☐ 266 Jacob Green | .04 | .02 | .01 |
| ☐ 174 Perry Kemp | .04 | .02 | .01 | ☐ 267 James Jefferson | .04 | .02 | .01 |
| ☐ 175 Don Majkowski | .08 | .04 | .01 | ☐ 268 Norm Johnson | .04 | .02 | .01 |
| ☐ 176 Tony Mandarich | .04 | .02 | .01 | ☐ 269 Dave Krieg UER | .08 | .04 | .01 |
| ☐ 177 Mark Murphy | .04 | .02 | .01 | (Misspelled Kreig on card front) | | | |
| ☐ 178 Brian Noble | .04 | .02 | .01 | | | | |
| ☐ 179 Ken Ruettgers | .04 | .02 | .01 | ☐ 270 Travis McNeal | .04 | .02 | .01 |
| ☐ 180 Sterling Sharpe | .75 | .35 | .09 | ☐ 271 Joe Nash | .04 | .02 | .01 |
| ☐ 181 Ed West | .10 | .05 | .01 | ☐ 272 Rufus Porter | .04 | .02 | .01 |
| ☐ 182 Keith Woodside | .04 | .02 | .01 | ☐ 273 Kelly Stouffer | .04 | .02 | .01 |
| ☐ 183 Morten Andersen | .08 | .04 | .01 | ☐ 274 John L. Williams | .08 | .04 | .01 |
| ☐ 184 Stan Brock | .04 | .02 | .01 | ☐ 275 Jim Arnold | .04 | .02 | .01 |
| ☐ 185 Jim Dombrowski | .10 | .05 | .01 | ☐ 276 Jerry Ball | .08 | .04 | .01 |
| ☐ 186 John Fourcade | .04 | .02 | .01 | ☐ 277 Bennie Blades | .04 | .02 | .01 |
| ☐ 187 Bobby Hebert | .15 | .07 | .02 | ☐ 278 Lomas Brown | .04 | .02 | .01 |
| ☐ 188 Craig Heyward | .08 | .04 | .01 | ☐ 279 Michael Cofer | .04 | .02 | .01 |
| ☐ 189 Dalton Hilliard | .08 | .04 | .01 | ☐ 280 Bob Gagliano | .04 | .02 | .01 |
| ☐ 190 Rickey Jackson | .08 | .04 | .01 | ☐ 281 Richard Johnson | .04 | .02 | .01 |
| ☐ 191 Buford Jordan | .04 | .02 | .01 | ☐ 282 Eddie Murray | .08 | .04 | .01 |
| ☐ 192 Eric Martin | .08 | .04 | .01 | ☐ 283 Rodney Peete | .08 | .04 | .01 |
| ☐ 193 Robert Massey | .04 | .02 | .01 | ☐ 284 Barry Sanders | 1.00 | .45 | .13 |
| ☐ 194 Sam Mills | .08 | .04 | .01 | ☐ 285 Eric Sanders | .04 | .02 | .01 |
| ☐ 195 Pat Swilling | .10 | .05 | .01 | ☐ 286 Chris Spielman | .08 | .04 | .01 |
| ☐ 196 Jim Wilks | .04 | .02 | .01 | ☐ 287 Eric Williams | .10 | .05 | .01 |
| ☐ 197 John Alt | .10 | .05 | .01 | ☐ 288 Neal Anderson | .08 | .04 | .01 |
| ☐ 198 Walker Lee Ashley | .04 | .02 | .01 | ☐ 289A Kevin Butler ERR/ERR | .25 | .11 | .03 |
| ☐ 199 Steve DeBerg | .08 | .04 | .01 | (Listed as Punter on front and back) | | | |
| ☐ 200 Leonard Griffin | .04 | .02 | .01 | | | | |
| ☐ 201 Albert Lewis | .08 | .04 | .01 | ☐ 289B Kevin Butler COR/ERR | .25 | .11 | .03 |
| ☐ 202 Nick Lowery | .08 | .04 | .01 | (Listed as Placekicker on front and Punter on back) | | | |
| ☐ 203 Bill Maas | .08 | .04 | .01 | | | | |
| ☐ 204 Pete Mandley | .04 | .02 | .01 | | | | |
| ☐ 205 Chris Martin | .10 | .05 | .01 | ☐ 289C Kevin Butler ERR/COR | .25 | .11 | .03 |
| ☐ 206 Christian Okoye | .08 | .04 | .01 | (Listed as Punter on front and Placekicker on back) | | | |
| ☐ 207 Stephone Paige | .08 | .04 | .01 | | | | |
| ☐ 208 Kevin Porter | .04 | .02 | .01 | | | | |
| ☐ 209 Derrick Thomas | .25 | .11 | .03 | ☐ 289D Kevin Butler COR/COR | .04 | .02 | .01 |
| ☐ 210 Lewis Billups | .04 | .02 | .01 | (Listed as Placekicker on front and back) | | | |
| ☐ 211 James Brooks | .08 | .04 | .01 | | | | |
| ☐ 212 Jason Buck | .04 | .02 | .01 | ☐ 290 Jim Covert | .04 | .02 | .01 |
| ☐ 213 Rickey Dixon | .04 | .02 | .01 | ☐ 291 Richard Dent | .08 | .04 | .01 |
| ☐ 214 Boomer Esiason | .20 | .09 | .03 | ☐ 292 Dennis Gentry | .04 | .02 | .01 |
| ☐ 215 David Fulcher | .08 | .04 | .01 | ☐ 293 Jim Harbaugh | .10 | .05 | .01 |
| ☐ 216 Rodney Holman | .04 | .02 | .01 | ☐ 294 Jay Hilgenberg | .08 | .04 | .01 |
| ☐ 217 Lee Johnson | .04 | .02 | .01 | ☐ 295 Vestee Jackson | .04 | .02 | .01 |
| ☐ 218 Tim Krumrie | .04 | .02 | .01 | ☐ 296 Steve McMichael | .08 | .04 | .01 |
| ☐ 219 Tim McGee | .08 | .04 | .01 | ☐ 297 Ron Morris | .04 | .02 | .01 |
| ☐ 220 Anthony Munoz | .08 | .04 | .01 | ☐ 298 Brad Muster | .08 | .04 | .01 |
| ☐ 221 Bruce Reimers | .04 | .02 | .01 | ☐ 299 Mike Singletary | .10 | .05 | .01 |
| ☐ 222 Leon White | .04 | .02 | .01 | ☐ 300 James Thornton UER | .04 | .02 | .01 |
| ☐ 223 Ickey Woods | .04 | .02 | .01 | (Missing birthdate) | | | |
| ☐ 224 Harvey Armstrong | .04 | .02 | .01 | ☐ 301 Mike Tomczak | .08 | .04 | .01 |
| ☐ 225 Michael Ball | .04 | .02 | .01 | ☐ 302 Keith Van Horne | .04 | .02 | .01 |
| ☐ 226 Chip Banks | .08 | .04 | .01 | ☐ 303 Chris Bahr UER | .04 | .02 | .01 |
| ☐ 227 Pat Beach | .04 | .02 | .01 | ('86 FGA and FGM stats are reversed) | | | |
| ☐ 228 Duane Bickett | .04 | .02 | .01 | | | | |
| ☐ 229 Bill Brooks | .08 | .04 | .01 | ☐ 304 Martin Bayless | .10 | .05 | .01 |
| ☐ 230 Jon Hand | .04 | .02 | .01 | ☐ 305 Marion Butts | .10 | .05 | .01 |
| ☐ 231 Andre Rison | .25 | .11 | .03 | ☐ 306 Gill Byrd | .08 | .04 | .01 |
| ☐ 232 Rohn Stark | .08 | .04 | .01 | ☐ 307 Arthur Cox | .04 | .02 | .01 |
| ☐ 233 Donnell Thompson | .04 | .02 | .01 | ☐ 308 Burt Grossman | .04 | .02 | .01 |
| ☐ 234 Jack Trudeau | .08 | .04 | .01 | ☐ 309 Jamie Holland | .04 | .02 | .01 |
| ☐ 235 Clarence Verdin | .04 | .02 | .01 | ☐ 310 Jim McMahon | .10 | .05 | .01 |
| ☐ 236 Mark Clayton | .08 | .04 | .01 | ☐ 311 Anthony Miller | .30 | .14 | .04 |
| ☐ 237 Jeff Cross | .04 | .02 | .01 | ☐ 312 Leslie O'Neal | .08 | .04 | .01 |
| ☐ 238 Jeff Dellenbach | .04 | .02 | .01 | ☐ 313 Billy Ray Smith | .08 | .04 | .01 |
| ☐ 239 Mark Duper | .08 | .04 | .01 | ☐ 314 Tim Spencer | .04 | .02 | .01 |
| ☐ 240 Ferrell Edmunds | .04 | .02 | .01 | ☐ 315 Broderick Thompson | .04 | .02 | .01 |
| ☐ 241 Hugh Green UER | .08 | .04 | .01 | ☐ 316 Lee Williams | .08 | .04 | .01 |
| (Back says Traded '86, should be '85) | | | | ☐ 317 Bruce Armstrong | .04 | .02 | .01 |
| | | | | ☐ 318 Tim Goad | .04 | .02 | .01 |
| ☐ 242 E.J. Junior | .04 | .02 | .01 | ☐ 319 Steve Grogan | .08 | .04 | .01 |
| ☐ 243 Marc Logan | .04 | .02 | .01 | ☐ 320 Roland James | .04 | .02 | .01 |
| ☐ 244 Dan Marino | .75 | .35 | .09 | ☐ 321 Cedric Jones | .04 | .02 | .01 |
| ☐ 245 John Offerdahl | .08 | .04 | .01 | ☐ 322 Fred Marion | .04 | .02 | .01 |
| ☐ 246 Reggie Roby | .08 | .04 | .01 | ☐ 323 Stanley Morgan | .08 | .04 | .01 |
| ☐ 247 Sammie Smith | .04 | .02 | .01 | ☐ 324 Robert Perryman | .04 | .02 | .01 |
| ☐ 248 Pete Stoyanovich | .08 | .04 | .01 | (Back says Robert, front says Bob) | | | |
| ☐ 249 Marcus Allen | .15 | .07 | .02 | | | | |
| ☐ 250 Eddie Anderson | .10 | .05 | .01 | ☐ 325 Johnny Rembert | .04 | .02 | .01 |

| | | | | |
|---|---|---|---|---|
| ☐ 326 Ed Reynolds | .04 | .02 | .01 |
| ☐ 327 Kenneth Sims | .04 | .02 | .01 |
| ☐ 328 John Stephens | .08 | .04 | .01 |
| ☐ 329 Danny Villa | .04 | .02 | .01 |
| ☐ 330 Robert Awalt | .04 | .02 | .01 |
| ☐ 331 Anthony Bell | .04 | .02 | .01 |
| ☐ 332 Rich Camarillo | .04 | .02 | .01 |
| ☐ 333 Earl Ferrell | .04 | .02 | .01 |
| ☐ 334 Roy Green | .08 | .04 | .01 |
| ☐ 335 Gary Hogeboom | .08 | .04 | .01 |
| ☐ 336 Cedric Mack | .04 | .02 | .01 |
| ☐ 337 Freddie Joe Nunn | .08 | .04 | .01 |
| ☐ 338 Luis Sharpe | .04 | .02 | .01 |
| ☐ 339 Vai Sikahema | .08 | .04 | .01 |
| ☐ 340 J.T. Smith | .04 | .02 | .01 |
| ☐ 341 Tom Tupa | .10 | .05 | .01 |
| ☐ 342 Percy Snow | .04 | .02 | .01 |
| ☐ 343 Mark Carrier | .04 | .02 | .01 |
| ☐ 344 Randy Grimes | .04 | .02 | .01 |
| ☐ 345 Paul Gruber | .08 | .04 | .01 |
| ☐ 346 Ron Hall | .04 | .02 | .01 |
| ☐ 347 Jeff George | .75 | .35 | .09 |
| ☐ 348 Bruce Hill UER | .04 | .02 | .01 |
| (Photo on back is actually Jerry Bell) | | | |
| ☐ 349 William Howard UER | .04 | .02 | .01 |
| (Yards rec. says 284, should be 285) | | | |
| ☐ 350 Donald Igwebuike | .04 | .02 | .01 |
| ☐ 351 Chris Mohr | .10 | .05 | .01 |
| ☐ 352 Winston Moss | .04 | .02 | .01 |
| ☐ 353 Ricky Reynolds | .04 | .02 | .01 |
| ☐ 354 Mark Robinson | .04 | .02 | .01 |
| ☐ 355 Lars Tate | .04 | .02 | .01 |
| ☐ 356 Vinny Testaverde | .15 | .07 | .02 |
| ☐ 357 Broderick Thomas | .04 | .02 | .01 |
| ☐ 358 Troy Benson | .04 | .02 | .01 |
| ☐ 359 Jeff Criswell | .04 | .02 | .01 |
| ☐ 360 Tony Eason | .04 | .02 | .01 |
| ☐ 361 James Hasty | .04 | .02 | .01 |
| ☐ 362 Johnny Hector | .04 | .02 | .01 |
| ☐ 363 Bobby Humphery UER | .04 | .02 | .01 |
| (Photo on back is actually Bobby Humphrey) | | | |
| ☐ 364 Pat Leahy | .08 | .04 | .01 |
| ☐ 365 Erik McMillan | .04 | .02 | .01 |
| ☐ 366 Freeman McNeil | .08 | .04 | .01 |
| ☐ 367 Ken O'Brien | .08 | .04 | .01 |
| ☐ 368 Ron Stallworth | .04 | .02 | .01 |
| ☐ 369 Al Toon | .08 | .04 | .01 |
| ☐ 370 Blair Thomas | .10 | .05 | .01 |
| ☐ 371 Aundray Bruce | .04 | .02 | .01 |
| ☐ 372 Tony Casillas | .04 | .02 | .01 |
| ☐ 373 Shawn Collins | .04 | .02 | .01 |
| ☐ 374 Evan Cooper | .04 | .02 | .01 |
| ☐ 375 Bill Fralic | .08 | .04 | .01 |
| ☐ 376 Scott Funhage | .04 | .02 | .01 |
| ☐ 377 Mike Gann | .04 | .02 | .01 |
| ☐ 378 Ron Heller | .04 | .02 | .01 |
| ☐ 379 Keith Jones | .04 | .02 | .01 |
| ☐ 380 Mike Kenn | .08 | .04 | .01 |
| ☐ 381 Chris Miller | .15 | .07 | .02 |
| ☐ 382 Deion Sanders UER | .25 | .11 | .03 |
| (Stats say no '89 fumble recoveries, should be 1) | | | |
| ☐ 383 John Settle | .04 | .02 | .01 |
| ☐ 384 Troy Aikman | 1.25 | .55 | .16 |
| ☐ 385 Bill Bates | .04 | .02 | .01 |
| ☐ 386 Willie Broughton | .04 | .02 | .01 |
| ☐ 387 Steve Folsom | .04 | .02 | .01 |
| ☐ 388 Ray Horton UER | .04 | .02 | .01 |
| (Extra line after career totals) | | | |
| ☐ 389 Michael Irvin | .75 | .35 | .09 |
| ☐ 390 Jim Jeffcoat | .04 | .02 | .01 |
| ☐ 391 Eugene Lockhart | .04 | .02 | .01 |
| ☐ 392 Kelvin Martin | .25 | .11 | .03 |
| ☐ 393 Nate Newton | .04 | .02 | .01 |
| ☐ 394 Mike Saxon UER | .04 | .02 | .01 |
| (6 career blocked kicks, stats add up to 4) | | | |
| ☐ 395 Derrick Shepard | .04 | .02 | .01 |
| ☐ 396 Steve Walsh UER | .04 | .02 | .01 |
| (Yards Passing 50.2; Percentage and yards data are switched) | | | |
| ☐ 397 Super Bowl MVP's | .40 | .18 | .05 |
| (Jerry Rice and Joe Montana) HOR | | | |
| ☐ 398 Checklist Card UER | .04 | .02 | .01 |
| (Card 103 not listed) | | | |
| ☐ 399 Checklist Card UER | .04 | .02 | .01 |
| (Bengals misspelled) | | | |
| ☐ 400 Checklist Card | .04 | .02 | .01 |

## 1990 Fleer All-Pros

The 1990 Fleer All-Pro set contains 25 standard-size (2 1/2" by 3 1/2") cards. The fronts are silver with a portrait and an action photo. The vertically oriented backs have detailed career information. These cards were randomly distributed in Fleer poly packs, approximately five per box.

| | MINT | EXC | G-VG |
|---|---|---|---|
| COMPLETE SET (25) | 12.00 | 5.00 | 1.20 |
| COMMON PLAYER (1-25) | .25 | .10 | .02 |
| ☐ 1 Joe Montana | 4.00 | 1.60 | .40 |
| San Francisco 49ers | | | |
| ☐ 2 Jerry Rice UER | 2.50 | 1.00 | .25 |
| San Francisco 49ers (photo on front is actually John Taylor) | | | |
| ☐ 3 Keith Jackson | .50 | .20 | .05 |
| Philadelphia Eagles | | | |
| ☐ 4 Barry Sanders | 2.50 | 1.00 | .25 |
| Detroit Lions | | | |
| ☐ 5 Christian Okoye | .35 | .14 | .03 |
| Kansas City Chiefs | | | |
| ☐ 6 Tom Newberry | .25 | .10 | .02 |
| Los Angeles Rams | | | |
| ☐ 7 Jim Covert | .25 | .10 | .02 |
| Chicago Bears | | | |
| ☐ 8 Anthony Munoz | .35 | .14 | .03 |
| Cincinnati Bengals | | | |
| ☐ 9 Mike Munchak | .25 | .10 | .02 |
| Houston Oilers | | | |
| ☐ 10 Jay Hilgenberg | .25 | .10 | .02 |
| Chicago Bears | | | |
| ☐ 11 Chris Doleman | .25 | .10 | .02 |
| Minnesota Vikings | | | |
| ☐ 12 Keith Millard | .25 | .10 | .02 |
| Minnesota Vikings | | | |
| ☐ 13 Derrick Thomas | .75 | .30 | .07 |
| Kansas City Chiefs | | | |
| ☐ 14 Lawrence Taylor | .75 | .30 | .07 |
| New York Giants | | | |
| ☐ 15 Karl Mecklenburg | .25 | .10 | .02 |
| Denver Broncos | | | |
| ☐ 16 Reggie White | .75 | .30 | .07 |
| Philadelphia Eagles | | | |
| ☐ 17 Tim Harris | .35 | .14 | .03 |
| Green Bay Packers | | | |
| ☐ 18 David Fulcher | .25 | .10 | .02 |
| Cincinnati Bengals | | | |
| ☐ 19 Ronnie Lott | .50 | .20 | .05 |
| San Francisco 49ers | | | |
| ☐ 20 Eric Allen | .25 | .10 | .02 |
| Philadelphia Eagles | | | |
| ☐ 21 Steve Atwater | .35 | .14 | .03 |
| Denver Broncos | | | |
| ☐ 22 Rich Camarillo | .25 | .10 | .02 |
| Phoenix Cardinals | | | |
| ☐ 23 Morten Andersen | .35 | .14 | .03 |
| New Orleans Saints | | | |
| ☐ 24 Andre Reed | .75 | .30 | .07 |
| Buffalo Bills | | | |
| ☐ 25 Rod Woodson | .75 | .30 | .07 |
| Pittsburgh Steelers | | | |

## 1990 Fleer Stars'n'Stripes

This 90-card standard size (2 1/2" by 3 1/2") set was issued by Fleer in conjunction with their subsidiary, the Asher Candy Company, in a packaging which included two red, white, and blue striped candy sticks as well as eight cards. This set features members of the 1990 Pro Bowl teams as well as ten of the leading rookies in the 1990 season. Cards were arranged as follows, AFC Pro Bowlers (1-39), NFC

Pro Bowlers (40-80), and leading draftees (81-90). The fronts of the cards feature an attractive action photo of the player with candy stripes running vertically down each side of the card and the words Stars'n'Stripes on top with the player's name and position underneath the photo and their team identification on the lower right hand corner. While the back of the card is reminiscent of the regular Fleer 1990 issue, the players photo is encased in a star and the identification that this is a Stars'n'Stripes card is also made on the back. Some of the same mistakes made in the regular Fleer set were carried over into the Stars'n'Stripes set including the misspelling of Dave Krieg's name as Kreig. Since this set did not sell that well at the retail level, much of the production was remaindered. However some of these leftover sealed cases are susceptible to damaged cards from the candy "leaking" into or onto the cards.

|  | MINT | EXC | G-VG |
|---|---|---|---|
| COMPLETE SET (90) | 8.00 | 3.25 | .80 |
| COMMON PLAYER (1-90) | .10 | .04 | .01 |
| ☐ 1 Warren Moon | .40 | .16 | .04 |
| Houston Oilers |  |  |  |
| ☐ 2 Reggie Roby | .10 | .04 | .01 |
| Miami Dolphins |  |  |  |
| ☐ 3 David Treadwell | .10 | .04 | .01 |
| Denver Broncos |  |  |  |
| ☐ 4 Dave Krieg UER | .15 | .06 | .01 |
| Seattle Seahawks |  |  |  |
| (Misspelled Kreig) |  |  |  |
| ☐ 5 James Brooks | .15 | .06 | .01 |
| Cincinnati Bengals |  |  |  |
| ☐ 6 Erik McMillan | .10 | .04 | .01 |
| New York Jets |  |  |  |
| ☐ 7 Rod Woodson | .20 | .08 | .02 |
| Pittsburgh Steelers |  |  |  |
| ☐ 8 Albert Lewis | .10 | .04 | .01 |
| Kansas City Chiefs |  |  |  |
| ☐ 9 Kevin Ross | .10 | .04 | .01 |
| Kansas City Chiefs |  |  |  |
| ☐ 10 Frank Minnifield | .10 | .04 | .01 |
| Cleveland Browns |  |  |  |
| ☐ 11 David Fulcher | .10 | .04 | .01 |
| Cincinnati Bengals |  |  |  |
| ☐ 12 Thurman Thomas | .60 | .24 | .06 |
| Buffalo Bills |  |  |  |
| ☐ 13 Christian Okoye | .15 | .06 | .01 |
| Kansas City Chiefs |  |  |  |
| ☐ 14 Dennis Smith | .10 | .04 | .01 |
| Denver Broncos |  |  |  |
| ☐ 15 Johnny Rembert | .10 | .04 | .01 |
| New England Patriots |  |  |  |
| ☐ 16 Ray Donaldson | .10 | .04 | .01 |
| Indianapolis Colts |  |  |  |
| ☐ 17 John Offerdahl | .10 | .04 | .01 |
| Miami Dolphins |  |  |  |
| ☐ 18 Clay Matthews | .15 | .06 | .01 |
| Cleveland Browns |  |  |  |
| ☐ 19 Shane Conlan | .15 | .06 | .01 |
| Buffalo Bills |  |  |  |
| ☐ 20 Derrick Thomas | .35 | .14 | .03 |
| Kansas City Chiefs |  |  |  |
| ☐ 21 Tunch Ilkin | .10 | .04 | .01 |
| Pittsburgh Steelers |  |  |  |
| ☐ 22 Mike Munchak | .10 | .04 | .01 |
| Houston Oilers |  |  |  |
| ☐ 23 Max Montoya | .10 | .04 | .01 |
| Los Angeles Raiders |  |  |  |
| ☐ 24 Kent Hull | .10 | .04 | .01 |
| Buffalo Bills |  |  |  |
| ☐ 25 Greg Kragen | .10 | .04 | .01 |
| Denver Broncos |  |  |  |
| ☐ 26 Bruce Matthews | .10 | .04 | .01 |
| Houston Oilers |  |  |  |
| ☐ 27 Howie Long | .15 | .06 | .01 |
| Los Angeles Raiders |  |  |  |
| ☐ 28 Chris Hinton | .15 | .06 | .01 |
| Atlanta Falcons |  |  |  |

| ☐ 29 Anthony Munoz | .20 | .08 | .02 |
|---|---|---|---|
| Cincinnati Bengals |  |  |  |
| ☐ 30 Bruce Smith | .20 | .08 | .02 |
| Buffalo Bills |  |  |  |
| ☐ 31 Ferrell Edmunds | .10 | .04 | .01 |
| Miami Dolphins |  |  |  |
| ☐ 32 Rodney Holman | .10 | .04 | .01 |
| Cincinnati Bengals |  |  |  |
| ☐ 33 Andre Reed | .20 | .08 | .02 |
| Buffalo Bills |  |  |  |
| ☐ 34 Webster Slaughter | .15 | .06 | .01 |
| Cleveland Browns |  |  |  |
| ☐ 35 Anthony Miller | .30 | .12 | .03 |
| San Diego Chargers |  |  |  |
| ☐ 36 Brian Blades | .15 | .06 | .01 |
| Seattle Seahawks |  |  |  |
| ☐ 37 Leslie O'Neal | .15 | .06 | .01 |
| San Diego Chargers |  |  |  |
| ☐ 38 Rufus Porter | .10 | .04 | .01 |
| Seattle Seahawks |  |  |  |
| ☐ 39 Lee Williams | .15 | .06 | .01 |
| San Diego Chargers |  |  |  |
| ☐ 40 Eddie Murray | .10 | .04 | .01 |
| Detroit Lions |  |  |  |
| ☐ 41 Mark Rypien | .20 | .08 | .02 |
| Washington Redskins |  |  |  |
| ☐ 42 Randall Cunningham | .40 | .16 | .04 |
| Philadelphia Eagles |  |  |  |
| ☐ 43 Rich Camarillo | .10 | .04 | .01 |
| Phoenix Cardinals |  |  |  |
| ☐ 44 Barry Sanders | 1.00 | .40 | .10 |
| Detroit Lions |  |  |  |
| ☐ 45 Dalton Hilliard | .15 | .06 | .01 |
| New Orleans Saints |  |  |  |
| ☐ 46 Eric Allen | .10 | .04 | .01 |
| Philadelphia Eagles |  |  |  |
| ☐ 47 Brent Fullwood | .10 | .04 | .01 |
| Green Bay Packers |  |  |  |
| ☐ 48 Ron Wolfley | .10 | .04 | .01 |
| Phoenix Cardinals |  |  |  |
| ☐ 49 Jerry Gray | .10 | .04 | .01 |
| Los Angeles Rams |  |  |  |
| ☐ 50 Dave Meggett | .15 | .06 | .01 |
| New York Giants |  |  |  |
| ☐ 51 Roger Craig | .25 | .10 | .02 |
| San Francisco 49ers |  |  |  |
| ☐ 52 Carl Lee | .10 | .04 | .01 |
| Minnesota Vikings |  |  |  |
| ☐ 53 Ronnie Lott | .20 | .08 | .02 |
| San Francisco 49ers |  |  |  |
| ☐ 54 Tim McDonald | .15 | .06 | .01 |
| Phoenix Cardinals |  |  |  |
| ☐ 55 Joey Browner | .10 | .04 | .01 |
| Minnesota Vikings |  |  |  |
| ☐ 56 Mike Singletary | .20 | .08 | .02 |
| Chicago Bears |  |  |  |
| ☐ 57 Vaughan Johnson | .10 | .04 | .01 |
| New Orleans Saints |  |  |  |
| ☐ 58 Chris Spielman | .15 | .06 | .01 |
| Detroit Lions |  |  |  |
| ☐ 59 Doug Smith | .10 | .04 | .01 |
| Houston Oilers |  |  |  |
| ☐ 60 Lawrence Taylor | .35 | .14 | .03 |
| New York Giants |  |  |  |
| ☐ 61 Chris Doleman | .15 | .06 | .01 |
| Minnesota Vikings |  |  |  |
| ☐ 62 Guy McIntyre | .10 | .04 | .01 |
| San Francisco 49ers |  |  |  |
| ☐ 63 Jay Hilgenberg | .10 | .04 | .01 |
| Chicago Bears |  |  |  |
| ☐ 64 Randall McDaniel | .10 | .04 | .01 |
| Minnesota Vikings |  |  |  |
| ☐ 65 Gary Zimmerman | .10 | .04 | .01 |
| Minnesota Vikings |  |  |  |
| ☐ 66 Luis Sharpe | .10 | .04 | .01 |
| Phoenix Cardinals |  |  |  |
| ☐ 67 Charles Mann | .15 | .06 | .01 |
| Washington Redskins |  |  |  |
| ☐ 68 Keith Millard | .10 | .04 | .01 |
| Minnesota Vikings |  |  |  |
| ☐ 69 Jackie Slater | .15 | .06 | .01 |
| Los Angeles Rams |  |  |  |
| ☐ 70 Bill Fralic | .15 | .06 | .01 |
| Atlanta Falcons |  |  |  |
| ☐ 71 Henry Ellard | .15 | .06 | .01 |
| Los Angeles Rams |  |  |  |
| ☐ 72 Jerry Rice | .75 | .30 | .07 |
| San Francisco 49ers |  |  |  |
| ☐ 73 Steve Jordan | .15 | .06 | .01 |
| Minnesota Vikings |  |  |  |
| ☐ 74 Sterling Sharpe | .50 | .20 | .05 |
| Green Bay Packers |  |  |  |
| ☐ 75 Keith Jackson | .25 | .10 | .02 |
| Philadelphia Eagles |  |  |  |
| ☐ 76 Mark Carrier | .15 | .06 | .01 |
| Tampa Bay Buccaneers |  |  |  |
| ☐ 77 Kevin Greene | .15 | .06 | .01 |
| Los Angeles Rams |  |  |  |

| | MINT | EXC | G-VG |
|---|---|---|---|
| ☐ 78 Reggie White | .35 | .14 | .03 |
|     Philadelphia Eagles | | | |
| ☐ 79 Jerry Ball | .10 | .04 | .01 |
|     Detroit Lions | | | |
| ☐ 80 Tim Harris | .15 | .06 | .01 |
|     Green Bay Packers | | | |
| ☐ 81 Jeff George | .35 | .14 | .03 |
|     Indianapolis Colts | | | |
| ☐ 82 Blair Thomas | .20 | .08 | .02 |
|     New York Jets | | | |
| ☐ 83 Cortez Kennedy | .35 | .14 | .03 |
|     Seattle Seahawks | | | |
| ☐ 84 Junior Seau | .35 | .14 | .03 |
|     San Diego Chargers | | | |
| ☐ 85 Mark Carrier | .15 | .06 | .01 |
|     Chicago Bears | | | |
| ☐ 86 Andre Ware | .20 | .08 | .02 |
|     Detroit Lions | | | |
| ☐ 87 Chris Singleton | .10 | .04 | .01 |
|     New England Patriots | | | |
| ☐ 88 Percy Snow | .10 | .04 | .01 |
|     Kansas City Chiefs | | | |
| ☐ 89 Steve Broussard | .10 | .04 | .01 |
|     Atlanta Falcons | | | |
| ☐ 90 Rodney Hampton | .60 | .24 | .06 |
|     New York Giants | | | |

## 1990 Fleer Update

This 120-card standard size set (2 1/2" by 3 1/2") was produced and released by Fleer and featured some of the leading rookies and players who switched franchises for the 1990 season. The set was issued in its own box and was distributed through the Fleer dealers. The set is in the same design as the regular issue. Rookie cards include Mark Carrier, Reggie Cobb, Derrick Fenner, Barry Foster, Eric Green, Harold Green, Rodney Hampton, Stan Humphries, Haywood Jeffires, Johnny Johnson, Brent Jones, Cortez Kennedy, Rob Moore, Ken Norton Jr., Junior Seau, Emmitt Smith and Calvin Williams. The set is arranged in team order: Indianapolis Colts (1-4), New England Patriots (5-7), Cincinnati Bengals (8-9), New York Giants (10-14), Philadelphia Eagles (15-19), Washington Redskins (20-24), Pittsburgh Steelers (25-29), Cleveland Browns (30-32), Houston Oilers (33-36), Dallas Cowboys (37-41), Phoenix Cardinals (42-45), San Francisco 49ers (46-51), Los Angeles Rams (52-56), Atlanta Falcons (57-60), New Orleans Saints (61-63), Los Angeles Raiders (64-69), Buffalo Bills (70-73), New York Jets (74-78), Miami Dolphins (79-81), Seattle Seahawks (82-86), Kansas City Chiefs (87-91), Detroit Lions (92), Minnesota Vikings (93-95), Green Bay Packers (96-100), San Diego Chargers (101-104), Tampa Bay Buccaneers (105-108), Chicago Bears (109-115), and Denver Broncos (116-119). The cards are numbered on the back with a "U" prefix.

| | MINT | EXC | G-VG |
|---|---|---|---|
| COMPLETE FACT.SET (120) | 50.00 | 23.00 | 6.25 |
| COMMON PLAYER (U1-U120) | .08 | .04 | .01 |
| | | | |
| ☐ U1 Albert Bentley | .08 | .04 | .01 |
| ☐ U2 Dean Biasucci | .08 | .04 | .01 |
| ☐ U3 Ray Donaldson | .08 | .04 | .01 |
| ☐ U4 Jeff George | 2.50 | 1.15 | .30 |
| ☐ U5 Ray Agnew | .08 | .04 | .01 |
| ☐ U6 Greg McMurtry | .35 | .16 | .04 |
| ☐ U7 Chris Singleton | .20 | .09 | .03 |
| ☐ U8 James Francis | .40 | .18 | .05 |
| ☐ U9 Harold Green | 1.25 | .55 | .16 |
| ☐ U10 John Elliott | .08 | .04 | .01 |
| ☐ U11 Rodney Hampton | 5.00 | 2.30 | .60 |
| ☐ U12 Gary Reasons | .08 | .04 | .01 |
| ☐ U13 Lewis Tillman | .30 | .14 | .04 |
| ☐ U14 Everson Walls | .08 | .04 | .01 |
| ☐ U15 David Alexander | .08 | .04 | .01 |
| ☐ U16 Jim McMahon | .12 | .05 | .02 |
| ☐ U17 Ben Smith | .15 | .07 | .02 |

| | MINT | EXC | G-VG |
|---|---|---|---|
| ☐ U18 Andre Waters | .10 | .05 | .01 |
| ☐ U19 Calvin Williams | 1.75 | .80 | .22 |
| ☐ U20 Earnest Byner | .10 | .05 | .01 |
| ☐ U21 Andre Collins | .35 | .16 | .04 |
| ☐ U22 Russ Grimm | .08 | .04 | .01 |
| ☐ U23 Stan Humphries | 2.00 | .90 | .25 |
| ☐ U24 Martin Mayhew | .20 | .09 | .03 |
| ☐ U25 Barry Foster | 5.00 | 2.30 | .60 |
| ☐ U26 Eric Green | 1.75 | .80 | .22 |
| ☐ U27 Tunch Ilkin | .08 | .04 | .01 |
| ☐ U28 Hardy Nickerson | .10 | .05 | .01 |
| ☐ U29 Jerrol Williams | .08 | .04 | .01 |
| ☐ U30 Mike Baab | .08 | .04 | .01 |
| ☐ U31 Leroy Hoard | .35 | .16 | .04 |
| ☐ U32 Eddie Johnson | .08 | .04 | .01 |
| ☐ U33 William Fuller | .10 | .05 | .01 |
| ☐ U34 Haywood Jeffires | 3.00 | 1.35 | .40 |
| ☐ U35 Don Maggs | .15 | .07 | .02 |
| ☐ U36 Allen Pinkett | .08 | .04 | .01 |
| ☐ U37 Robert Awalt | .08 | .04 | .01 |
| ☐ U38 Dennis McKinnon | .08 | .04 | .01 |
| ☐ U39 Ken Norton | 2.00 | .90 | .25 |
| ☐ U40 Emmitt Smith | 40.00 | 18.00 | 5.00 |
| ☐ U41 Alexander Wright | .30 | .14 | .04 |
| ☐ U42 Eric Hill | .08 | .04 | .01 |
| ☐ U43 Johnny Johnson | 2.50 | 1.15 | .30 |
| ☐ U44 Timm Rosenbach | .08 | .04 | .01 |
| ☐ U45 Anthony Thompson | .25 | .11 | .03 |
| ☐ U46 Dexter Carter | .50 | .23 | .06 |
| ☐ U47 Eric Davis UER | .25 | .11 | .03 |
|     (Listed as WR on | | | |
|     front, DB on back) | | | |
| ☐ U48 Keith DeLong | .08 | .04 | .01 |
| ☐ U49 Brent Jones | 1.00 | .45 | .13 |
| ☐ U50 Darryl Pollard | .08 | .04 | .01 |
| ☐ U51 Steve Wallace | .15 | .07 | .02 |
| ☐ U52 Bern Brostek | .08 | .04 | .01 |
| ☐ U53 Aaron Cox | .08 | .04 | .01 |
| ☐ U54 Cleveland Gary | .15 | .07 | .02 |
| ☐ U55 Fred Strickland | .08 | .04 | .01 |
| ☐ U56 Pat Terrell | .20 | .09 | .03 |
| ☐ U57 Steve Broussard | .25 | .11 | .03 |
| ☐ U58 Scott Case | .08 | .04 | .01 |
| ☐ U59 Brian Jordan | .50 | .23 | .06 |
| ☐ U60 Andre Rison | 1.00 | .45 | .13 |
| ☐ U61 Kevin Haverdink | .08 | .04 | .01 |
| ☐ U62 Rueben Mayes | .10 | .05 | .01 |
| ☐ U63 Steve Walsh | .08 | .04 | .01 |
| ☐ U64 Greg Bell | .08 | .04 | .01 |
| ☐ U65 Tim Brown | 1.00 | .45 | .13 |
| ☐ U66 Willie Gault | .10 | .05 | .01 |
| ☐ U67 Vance Mueller | .08 | .04 | .01 |
| ☐ U68 Bill Pickel | .08 | .04 | .01 |
| ☐ U69 Aaron Wallace | .30 | .14 | .04 |
| ☐ U70 Glenn Parker | .12 | .05 | .02 |
| ☐ U71 Frank Reich | .40 | .18 | .05 |
| ☐ U72 Leon Seals | .20 | .09 | .03 |
| ☐ U73 Darryl Talley | .10 | .05 | .01 |
| ☐ U74 Brad Baxter | .60 | .25 | .08 |
| ☐ U75 Jeff Criswell | .08 | .04 | .01 |
| ☐ U76 Jeff Lageman | .08 | .04 | .01 |
| ☐ U77 Rob Moore | 1.00 | .45 | .13 |
| ☐ U78 Blair Thomas | .30 | .14 | .04 |
| ☐ U79 Louis Oliver | .10 | .05 | .01 |
| ☐ U80 Tony Paige | .08 | .04 | .01 |
| ☐ U81 Richmond Webb | .40 | .18 | .05 |
| ☐ U82 Robert Blackmon | .15 | .07 | .02 |
| ☐ U83 Derrick Fenner | .30 | .14 | .04 |
| ☐ U84 Andy Heck | .08 | .04 | .01 |
| ☐ U85 Cortez Kennedy | 2.50 | 1.15 | .30 |
| ☐ U86 Terry Wooden | .15 | .07 | .02 |
| ☐ U87 Jeff Donaldson | .08 | .04 | .01 |
| ☐ U88 Tim Grunhard | .08 | .04 | .01 |
| ☐ U89 Emile Harry | .08 | .04 | .01 |
| ☐ U90 Dan Saleaumua | .08 | .04 | .01 |
| ☐ U91 Percy Snow | .08 | .04 | .01 |
| ☐ U92 Andre Ware | .40 | .18 | .05 |
| ☐ U93 Darrell Fullington | .08 | .04 | .01 |
| ☐ U94 Mike Merriweather | .10 | .05 | .01 |
| ☐ U95 Henry Thomas | .08 | .04 | .01 |
| ☐ U96 Robert Brown | .08 | .04 | .01 |
| ☐ U97 LeRoy Butler | .40 | .18 | .05 |
| ☐ U98 Anthony Dilweg | .08 | .04 | .01 |
| ☐ U99 Darrell Thompson | .40 | .18 | .05 |
| ☐ U100 Keith Woodside | .08 | .04 | .01 |
| ☐ U101 Gary Plummer | .08 | .04 | .01 |
| ☐ U102 Junior Seau | 3.00 | 1.35 | .40 |
| ☐ U103 Billy Joe Tolliver | .08 | .04 | .01 |
| ☐ U104 Mark Vlasic | .12 | .05 | .02 |
| ☐ U105 Gary Anderson | .10 | .05 | .01 |
| ☐ U106 Ian Beckles | .08 | .04 | .01 |
| ☐ U107 Reggie Cobb | 2.25 | 1.00 | .30 |
| ☐ U108 Keith McCants | .30 | .14 | .04 |
| ☐ U109 Mark Bortz | .10 | .05 | .01 |
| ☐ U110 Maury Buford | .08 | .04 | .01 |
| ☐ U111 Mark Carrier | .50 | .23 | .06 |
| ☐ U112 Dan Hampton | .10 | .05 | .01 |
| ☐ U113 William Perry | .10 | .05 | .01 |

| | MINT | EXC | G-VG |
|---|---|---|---|
| ☐ U114 Ron Rivera | .08 | .04 | .01 |
| ☐ U115 Lemuel Stinson | .08 | .04 | .01 |
| ☐ U116 Melvin Bratton | .08 | .04 | .01 |
| ☐ U117 Gary Kubiak | .25 | .11 | .03 |
| ☐ U118 Alton Montgomery | .20 | .09 | .03 |
| ☐ U119 Ricky Nattiel | .08 | .04 | .01 |
| ☐ U120 Checklist 1-132 | .08 | .04 | .01 |

## 1991 Fleer

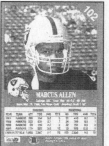

This 432-card standard size (2 1/2" by 3 1/2") set marked Fleer's second year of football sets featuring named players (not including the older AFL/NFL sets they produced between 1960 and 1963). The player cards feature a full-color action shot on the front and the back has a full-color shot along with complete statistics about the player involved. The cards have green borders on both the front and the back. Among the special subsets in the set are NFL Hitters, NFL League Leaders, and a Rookie Subset. The card numbering is alphabetical by player within teams, which are themselves in alphabetical order by conference as follows, Buffalo Bills (1-14), Cincinnati Bengals (15-29), Cleveland Browns (30-42), Denver Broncos (43-57), Houston Oilers (58-73), Indianapolis Colts (74-87), Kansas City Chiefs (88-101), Los Angeles Raiders (102-117), Miami Dolphins (118-133), New England Patriots (134-146), New York Jets (147-154), Pittsburgh Steelers (155-169), San Diego Chargers (170-182), Seattle Seahawks (183-195), Atlanta Falcons (196-211), Chicago Bears (212-226), Dallas Cowboys (227-238), Detroit Lions (239-248), Green Bay Packers (249-263), Los Angeles Rams (264-276), Minnesota Vikings (277-290), New Orleans Saints (291-304), New York Giants (305-321), Philadelphia Eagles (322-337), Phoenix Cardinals (338-351), San Francisco 49ers (352-367), Tampa Bay Buccaneers (368-381), Washington Redskins (382-395), Hot Hitters (396-407), League Leaders (408-419), Rookie Prospects (420-428), and Checklists (429-432). Rookie Cards in this set include Nick Bell, Russell Maryland, Derek Russell and Kenny Walker.

| | MINT | EXC | G-VG |
|---|---|---|---|
| COMPLETE SET (432) | 8.00 | 3.60 | 1.00 |
| COMMON PLAYER (1-432) | .04 | .02 | .01 |
| ☐ 1 Shane Conlan | .08 | .04 | .01 |
| ☐ 2 John Davis | .04 | .02 | .01 |
| ☐ 3 Kent Hull | .04 | .02 | .01 |
| ☐ 4 James Lofton | .10 | .05 | .01 |
| ☐ 5 Keith McKeller | .04 | .02 | .01 |
| ☐ 6 Scott Norwood | .04 | .02 | .01 |
| ☐ 7 Nate Odomes | .10 | .05 | .01 |
| ☐ 8 Andre Reed | .10 | .05 | .01 |
| ☐ 9 Jim Ritcher | .04 | .02 | .01 |
| ☐ 10 Leon Seals | .04 | .02 | .01 |
| ☐ 11 Bruce Smith | .10 | .05 | .01 |
| ☐ 12 Leonard Smith | .04 | .02 | .01 |
| ☐ 13 Steve Tasker | .08 | .04 | .01 |
| ☐ 14 Thurman Thomas | .40 | .18 | .05 |
| ☐ 15 Lewis Billups | .04 | .02 | .01 |
| ☐ 16 James Brooks | .08 | .04 | .01 |
| ☐ 17 Eddie Brown | .04 | .02 | .01 |
| ☐ 18 Carl Carter | .04 | .02 | .01 |
| ☐ 19 Boomer Esiason | .15 | .07 | .02 |
| ☐ 20 James Francis | .08 | .04 | .01 |
| ☐ 21 David Fulcher | .04 | .02 | .01 |
| ☐ 22 Harold Green | .10 | .05 | .01 |
| ☐ 23 Rodney Holman | .04 | .02 | .01 |
| ☐ 24 Bruce Kozerski | .04 | .02 | .01 |
| ☐ 25 Tim McGee | .04 | .02 | .01 |
| ☐ 26 Anthony Munoz | .08 | .04 | .01 |
| ☐ 27 Bruce Reimers | .04 | .02 | .01 |
| ☐ 28 Ickey Woods | .04 | .02 | .01 |
| ☐ 29 Carl Zander | .04 | .02 | .01 |
| ☐ 30 Mike Baab | .04 | .02 | .01 |
| ☐ 31 Brian Brennan | .04 | .02 | .01 |
| ☐ 32 Rob Burnett | .15 | .07 | .02 |

| | MINT | EXC | G-VG |
|---|---|---|---|
| ☐ 33 Paul Farren | .04 | .02 | .01 |
| ☐ 34 Thane Gash | .04 | .02 | .01 |
| ☐ 35 David Grayson | .04 | .02 | .01 |
| ☐ 36 Mike Johnson | .04 | .02 | .01 |
| ☐ 37 Reggie Langhorne | .08 | .04 | .01 |
| ☐ 38 Kevin Mack | .08 | .04 | .01 |
| ☐ 39 Eric Metcalf | .10 | .05 | .01 |
| ☐ 40 Frank Minnifield | .04 | .02 | .01 |
| ☐ 41 Gregg Rakoczy | .04 | .02 | .01 |
| ☐ 42 Felix Wright | .04 | .02 | .01 |
| ☐ 43 Steve Atwater | .10 | .05 | .01 |
| ☐ 44 Michael Brooks | .04 | .02 | .01 |
| ☐ 45 John Elway | .35 | .16 | .04 |
| ☐ 46 Simon Fletcher | .08 | .04 | .01 |
| ☐ 47 Bobby Humphrey | .08 | .04 | .01 |
| ☐ 48 Mark Jackson | .08 | .04 | .01 |
| ☐ 49 Keith Kartz | .04 | .02 | .01 |
| ☐ 50 Clarence Kay | .04 | .02 | .01 |
| ☐ 51 Greg Kragen | .04 | .02 | .01 |
| ☐ 52 Karl Mecklenburg | .08 | .04 | .01 |
| ☐ 53 Warren Powers | .04 | .02 | .01 |
| ☐ 54 Dennis Smith | .08 | .04 | .01 |
| ☐ 55 Jim Szymanski | .04 | .02 | .01 |
| ☐ 56 David Treadwell | .04 | .02 | .01 |
| ☐ 57 Michael Young | .04 | .02 | .01 |
| ☐ 58 Ray Childress | .08 | .04 | .01 |
| ☐ 59 Curtis Duncan | .08 | .04 | .01 |
| ☐ 60 William Fuller | .08 | .04 | .01 |
| ☐ 61 Ernest Givins | .08 | .04 | .01 |
| ☐ 62 Drew Hill | .08 | .04 | .01 |
| ☐ 63 Haywood Jeffires | .15 | .07 | .02 |
| ☐ 64 Richard Johnson | .04 | .02 | .01 |
| ☐ 65 Sean Jones | .08 | .04 | .01 |
| ☐ 66 Don Maggs | .04 | .02 | .01 |
| ☐ 67 Bruce Matthews | .08 | .04 | .01 |
| ☐ 68 Johnny Meads | .04 | .02 | .01 |
| ☐ 69 Greg Montgomery | .04 | .02 | .01 |
| ☐ 70 Warren Moon | .20 | .09 | .03 |
| ☐ 71 Mike Munchak | .08 | .04 | .01 |
| ☐ 72 Allen Pinkett | .04 | .02 | .01 |
| ☐ 73 Lorenzo White | .08 | .04 | .01 |
| ☐ 74 Pat Beach | .04 | .02 | .01 |
| ☐ 75 Albert Bentley | .04 | .02 | .01 |
| ☐ 76 Dean Biasucci | .04 | .02 | .01 |
| ☐ 77 Duane Bickett | .04 | .02 | .01 |
| ☐ 78 Bill Brooks | .08 | .04 | .01 |
| ☐ 79 Sam Clancy | .04 | .02 | .01 |
| ☐ 80 Ray Donaldson | .04 | .02 | .01 |
| ☐ 81 Jeff George | .25 | .11 | .03 |
| ☐ 82 Alan Grant | .04 | .02 | .01 |
| ☐ 83 Jessie Hester | .08 | .04 | .01 |
| ☐ 84 Jeff Herrod | .04 | .02 | .01 |
| ☐ 85 Rohn Stark | .04 | .02 | .01 |
| ☐ 86 Jack Trudeau | .04 | .02 | .01 |
| ☐ 87 Clarence Verdin | .04 | .02 | .01 |
| ☐ 88 John Alt | .04 | .02 | .01 |
| ☐ 89 Steve DeBerg | .08 | .04 | .01 |
| ☐ 90 Tim Grunhard | .04 | .02 | .01 |
| ☐ 91 Dino Hackett | .04 | .02 | .01 |
| ☐ 92 Jonathan Hayes | .04 | .02 | .01 |
| ☐ 93 Albert Lewis | .08 | .04 | .01 |
| ☐ 94 Nick Lowery | .08 | .04 | .01 |
| ☐ 95 Bill Maas UER | .04 | .02 | .01 |
| (Back photo actually David Szott) | | | |
| ☐ 96 Christian Okoye | .08 | .04 | .01 |
| ☐ 97 Stephone Paige | .08 | .04 | .01 |
| ☐ 98 Kevin Porter | .04 | .02 | .01 |
| ☐ 99 David Szott | .04 | .02 | .01 |
| ☐ 100 Derrick Thomas | .25 | .11 | .03 |
| ☐ 101 Barry Word | .10 | .05 | .01 |
| ☐ 102 Marcus Allen | .15 | .07 | .02 |
| ☐ 103 Tom Benson | .04 | .02 | .01 |
| ☐ 104 Tim Brown | .20 | .09 | .03 |
| ☐ 105 Riki Ellison | .04 | .02 | .01 |
| ☐ 106 Mervyn Fernandez | .04 | .02 | .01 |
| ☐ 107 Willie Gault | .08 | .04 | .01 |
| ☐ 108 Bob Golic | .04 | .02 | .01 |
| ☐ 109 Ethan Horton | .04 | .02 | .01 |
| ☐ 110 Bo Jackson | .35 | .16 | .04 |
| ☐ 111 Howie Long | .08 | .04 | .01 |
| ☐ 112 Don Mosebar | .04 | .02 | .01 |
| ☐ 113 Jerry Robinson | .04 | .02 | .01 |
| ☐ 114 Jay Schroeder | .08 | .04 | .01 |
| ☐ 115 Steve Smith | .08 | .04 | .01 |
| ☐ 116 Greg Townsend | .04 | .02 | .01 |
| ☐ 117 Steve Wisniewski | .04 | .02 | .01 |
| ☐ 118 Mark Clayton | .08 | .04 | .01 |
| ☐ 119 Mark Duper | .08 | .04 | .01 |
| ☐ 120 Ferrell Edmunds | .04 | .02 | .01 |
| ☐ 121 Hugh Green | .04 | .02 | .01 |
| ☐ 122 David Griggs | .04 | .02 | .01 |
| ☐ 123 Jim C. Jensen | .04 | .02 | .01 |
| ☐ 124 Dan Marino | .75 | .35 | .09 |
| ☐ 125 Tim McKyer | .08 | .04 | .01 |
| ☐ 126 John Offerdahl | .08 | .04 | .01 |
| ☐ 127 Louis Oliver | .08 | .04 | .01 |
| ☐ 128 Tony Paige | .04 | .02 | .01 |

| | | | |
|---|---|---|---|
| ☐ 129 Reggie Roby | .04 | .02 | .01 |
| ☐ 130 Keith Sims | .04 | .02 | .01 |
| ☐ 131 Sammie Smith | .04 | .02 | .01 |
| ☐ 132 Pete Stoyanovich | .08 | .04 | .01 |
| ☐ 133 Richmond Webb | .08 | .04 | .01 |
| ☐ 134 Bruce Armstrong | .04 | .02 | .01 |
| ☐ 135 Vincent Brown | .04 | .02 | .01 |
| ☐ 136 Hart Lee Dykes | .04 | .02 | .01 |
| ☐ 137 Irving Fryar | .08 | .04 | .01 |
| ☐ 138 Tim Goad | .04 | .02 | .01 |
| ☐ 139 Tommy Hodson | .04 | .02 | .01 |
| ☐ 140 Maurice Hurst | .04 | .02 | .01 |
| ☐ 141 Ronnie Lippett | .04 | .02 | .01 |
| ☐ 142 Greg McMurtry | .04 | .02 | .01 |
| ☐ 143 Ed Reynolds | .04 | .02 | .01 |
| ☐ 144 John Stephens | .08 | .04 | .01 |
| ☐ 145 Andre Tippett | .08 | .04 | .01 |
| ☐ 146 Danny Villa | .04 | .02 | .01 |
| (Old photo wearing | | | |
| retired number) | | | |
| ☐ 147 Brad Baxter | .08 | .04 | .01 |
| ☐ 148 Kyle Clifton | .04 | .02 | .01 |
| ☐ 149 Jeff Criswell | .04 | .02 | .01 |
| ☐ 150 James Hasty | .04 | .02 | .01 |
| ☐ 151 Jeff Lageman | .04 | .02 | .01 |
| ☐ 152 Pat Leahy | .08 | .04 | .01 |
| ☐ 153 Rob Moore | .10 | .05 | .01 |
| ☐ 154 Al Toon | .08 | .04 | .01 |
| ☐ 155 Gary Anderson | .04 | .02 | .01 |
| ☐ 156 Bubby Brister | .08 | .04 | .01 |
| ☐ 157 Chris Calloway | .04 | .02 | .01 |
| ☐ 158 Donald Evans | .04 | .02 | .01 |
| ☐ 159 Eric Green | .15 | .07 | .02 |
| ☐ 160 Bryan Hinkle | .04 | .02 | .01 |
| ☐ 161 Merril Hoge | .08 | .04 | .01 |
| ☐ 162 Tunch Ilkin | .04 | .02 | .01 |
| ☐ 163 Louis Lipps | .08 | .04 | .01 |
| ☐ 164 David Little | .04 | .02 | .01 |
| ☐ 165 Mike Mularkey | .04 | .02 | .01 |
| ☐ 166 Gerald Williams | .04 | .02 | .01 |
| ☐ 167 Warren Williams | .04 | .02 | .01 |
| ☐ 168 Rod Woodson | .10 | .05 | .01 |
| ☐ 169 Tim Worley | .08 | .04 | .01 |
| ☐ 170 Martin Bayless | .04 | .02 | .01 |
| ☐ 171 Marion Butts | .10 | .05 | .01 |
| ☐ 172 Gill Byrd | .08 | .04 | .01 |
| ☐ 173 Frank Cornish | .04 | .02 | .01 |
| ☐ 174 Arthur Cox | .04 | .02 | .01 |
| ☐ 175 Burt Grossman | .04 | .02 | .01 |
| ☐ 176 Anthony Miller | .20 | .09 | .03 |
| ☐ 177 Leslie O'Neal | .08 | .04 | .01 |
| ☐ 178 Gary Plummer | .04 | .02 | .01 |
| ☐ 179 Junior Seau | .25 | .11 | .03 |
| ☐ 180 Billy Joe Tolliver | .08 | .04 | .01 |
| ☐ 181 Derrick Walker | .04 | .02 | .01 |
| ☐ 182 Lee Williams | .08 | .04 | .01 |
| ☐ 183 Robert Blackmon | .04 | .02 | .01 |
| ☐ 184 Brian Blades | .10 | .05 | .01 |
| ☐ 185 Grant Feasel | .04 | .02 | .01 |
| ☐ 186 Derrick Fenner | .08 | .04 | .01 |
| ☐ 187 Andy Heck | .04 | .02 | .01 |
| ☐ 188 Norm Johnson | .04 | .02 | .01 |
| ☐ 189 Tommy Kane | .04 | .02 | .01 |
| ☐ 190 Cortez Kennedy | .25 | .11 | .03 |
| ☐ 191 Dave Krieg | .08 | .04 | .01 |
| ☐ 192 Travis McNeal | .04 | .02 | .01 |
| ☐ 193 Eugene Robinson | .04 | .02 | .01 |
| ☐ 194 Chris Warren | .30 | .14 | .04 |
| ☐ 195 John L. Williams | .08 | .04 | .01 |
| ☐ 196 Steve Broussard | .08 | .04 | .01 |
| ☐ 197 Scott Case | .04 | .02 | .01 |
| ☐ 198 Shawn Collins | .04 | .02 | .01 |
| ☐ 199 Darion Conner UER | .04 | .02 | .01 |
| (Player on back 8 | | | |
| is not Conner 56) | | | |
| ☐ 200 Tory Epps | .04 | .02 | .01 |
| ☐ 201 Bill Fralic | .04 | .02 | .01 |
| ☐ 202 Michael Haynes | .35 | .16 | .04 |
| ☐ 203 Chris Hinton | .04 | .02 | .01 |
| ☐ 204 Keith Jones | .04 | .02 | .01 |
| ☐ 205 Brian Jordan | .10 | .05 | .01 |
| ☐ 206 Mike Kenn | .08 | .04 | .01 |
| ☐ 207 Chris Miller | .10 | .05 | .01 |
| ☐ 208 Andre Rison | .25 | .11 | .03 |
| ☐ 209 Mike Rozier | .08 | .04 | .01 |
| ☐ 210 Deion Sanders | .25 | .11 | .03 |
| ☐ 211 Gary Wilkins | .04 | .02 | .01 |
| ☐ 212 Neal Anderson | .08 | .04 | .01 |
| ☐ 213 Trace Armstrong | .04 | .02 | .01 |
| ☐ 214 Mark Bortz | .04 | .02 | .01 |
| ☐ 215 Kevin Butler | .04 | .02 | .01 |
| ☐ 216 Mark Carrier | .08 | .04 | .01 |
| ☐ 217 Wendell Davis | .04 | .02 | .01 |
| ☐ 218 Richard Dent | .08 | .04 | .01 |
| ☐ 219 Dennis Gentry | .04 | .02 | .01 |
| ☐ 220 Jim Harbaugh | .08 | .04 | .01 |
| ☐ 221 Jay Hilgenberg | .08 | .04 | .01 |
| ☐ 222 Steve McMichael | .08 | .04 | .01 |
| ☐ 223 Ron Morris | .04 | .02 | .01 |
| ☐ 224 Brad Muster | .08 | .04 | .01 |
| ☐ 225 Mike Singletary | .10 | .05 | .01 |
| ☐ 226 James Thornton | .04 | .02 | .01 |
| ☐ 227 Tommie Agee | .04 | .02 | .01 |
| ☐ 228 Troy Aikman | 1.25 | .55 | .16 |
| ☐ 229 Jack Del Rio | .04 | .02 | .01 |
| ☐ 230 Issiac Holt | .04 | .02 | .01 |
| ☐ 231 Ray Horton | .04 | .02 | .01 |
| ☐ 232 Jim Jeffcoat | .04 | .02 | .01 |
| ☐ 233 Eugene Lockhart | .04 | .02 | .01 |
| ☐ 234 Kelvin Martin | .08 | .04 | .01 |
| ☐ 235 Nate Newton | .04 | .02 | .01 |
| ☐ 236 Mike Saxon | .04 | .02 | .01 |
| ☐ 237 Emmitt Smith | 2.00 | .90 | .25 |
| ☐ 238A Danny Stubbs | .10 | .05 | .01 |
| (Danny on back) | | | |
| ☐ 238B Danny Stubbs | .10 | .05 | .01 |
| (Daniel on back) | | | |
| ☐ 239 Jim Arnold | .04 | .02 | .01 |
| ☐ 240 Jerry Ball | .08 | .04 | .01 |
| ☐ 241 Bennie Blades | .04 | .02 | .01 |
| ☐ 242 Lomas Brown | .04 | .02 | .01 |
| ☐ 243 Robert Clark | .04 | .02 | .01 |
| ☐ 244 Mike Cofer | .04 | .02 | .01 |
| ☐ 245 Mel Gray | .08 | .04 | .01 |
| ☐ 246 Rodney Peete | .08 | .04 | .01 |
| ☐ 247 Barry Sanders | .75 | .35 | .09 |
| ☐ 248 Andre Ware | .10 | .05 | .01 |
| ☐ 249 Matt Brock | .04 | .02 | .01 |
| ☐ 250 Robert Brown | .04 | .02 | .01 |
| ☐ 251 Anthony Dilweg | .08 | .04 | .01 |
| ☐ 252 Johnny Holland | .04 | .02 | .01 |
| ☐ 253 Tim Harris | .08 | .04 | .01 |
| ☐ 254 Chris Jacke | .04 | .02 | .01 |
| ☐ 255 Perry Kemp | .04 | .02 | .01 |
| ☐ 256 Don Majkowski UER | .08 | .04 | .01 |
| (1990 attempts should | | | |
| be 264, not 265) | | | |
| ☐ 257 Tony Mandarich | .04 | .02 | .01 |
| ☐ 258 Mark Murphy | .04 | .02 | .01 |
| ☐ 259 Brian Noble | .04 | .02 | .01 |
| ☐ 260 Jeff Query | .04 | .02 | .01 |
| ☐ 261 Sterling Sharpe | .50 | .23 | .06 |
| ☐ 262 Ed West | .04 | .02 | .01 |
| ☐ 263 Keith Woodside | .04 | .02 | .01 |
| ☐ 264 Flipper Anderson | .08 | .04 | .01 |
| ☐ 265 Aaron Cox | .04 | .02 | .01 |
| ☐ 266 Henry Ellard | .08 | .04 | .01 |
| ☐ 267 Jim Everett | .08 | .04 | .01 |
| ☐ 268 Cleveland Gary | .08 | .04 | .01 |
| ☐ 269 Kevin Greene | .08 | .04 | .01 |
| ☐ 270 Pete Holohan | .04 | .02 | .01 |
| ☐ 271 Mike Lansford | .04 | .02 | .01 |
| ☐ 272 Duval Love | .04 | .02 | .01 |
| ☐ 273 Buford McGee | .04 | .02 | .01 |
| ☐ 274 Tom Newberry | .04 | .02 | .01 |
| ☐ 275 Jackie Slater | .08 | .04 | .01 |
| ☐ 276 Frank Stams | .04 | .02 | .01 |
| ☐ 277 Alfred Anderson | .04 | .02 | .01 |
| ☐ 278 Joey Browner | .04 | .02 | .01 |
| ☐ 279 Anthony Carter | .08 | .04 | .01 |
| ☐ 280 Chris Doleman | .08 | .04 | .01 |
| ☐ 281 Rick Fenney | .04 | .02 | .01 |
| ☐ 282 Rich Gannon | .08 | .04 | .01 |
| ☐ 283 Hassan Jones | .04 | .02 | .01 |
| ☐ 284 Steve Jordan | .08 | .04 | .01 |
| ☐ 285 Carl Lee | .04 | .02 | .01 |
| ☐ 286 Randall McDaniel | .04 | .02 | .01 |
| ☐ 287 Keith Millard | .08 | .04 | .01 |
| ☐ 288 Herschel Walker | .10 | .05 | .01 |
| ☐ 289 Wade Wilson | .08 | .04 | .01 |
| ☐ 290 Gary Zimmerman | .04 | .02 | .01 |
| ☐ 291 Morten Andersen | .08 | .04 | .01 |
| ☐ 292 Jim Dombrowski | .04 | .02 | .01 |
| ☐ 293 Gill Fenerty | .08 | .04 | .01 |
| ☐ 294 Craig Heyward | .04 | .02 | .01 |
| ☐ 295 Dalton Hilliard | .04 | .02 | .01 |
| ☐ 296 Rickey Jackson | .08 | .04 | .01 |
| ☐ 297 Vaughan Johnson | .08 | .04 | .01 |
| ☐ 298 Eric Martin | .08 | .04 | .01 |
| ☐ 299 Robert Massey | .04 | .02 | .01 |
| ☐ 300 Rueben Mayes | .04 | .02 | .01 |
| ☐ 301 Sam Mills | .08 | .04 | .01 |
| ☐ 302 Brett Perriman | .10 | .05 | .01 |
| ☐ 303 Pat Swilling | .08 | .04 | .01 |
| ☐ 304 Steve Walsh | .04 | .02 | .01 |
| ☐ 305 Ottis Anderson | .08 | .04 | .01 |
| ☐ 306 Matt Bahr | .04 | .02 | .01 |
| ☐ 307 Mark Bavaro | .08 | .04 | .01 |
| ☐ 308 Maurice Carthon | .04 | .02 | .01 |
| ☐ 309 Mark Collins | .04 | .02 | .01 |
| ☐ 310 John Elliott | .04 | .02 | .01 |
| ☐ 311 Rodney Hampton | .75 | .35 | .09 |
| ☐ 312 Jeff Hostetler | .25 | .11 | .03 |
| ☐ 313 Erik Howard | .04 | .02 | .01 |
| ☐ 314 Pepper Johnson | .08 | .04 | .01 |
| ☐ 315 Sean Landeta | .04 | .02 | .01 |

| | | | |
|---|---|---|---|
| ☐ 316 Dave Meggett | .10 | .05 | .01 |
| ☐ 317 Bart Oates | .04 | .02 | .01 |
| ☐ 318 Phil Simms | .10 | .05 | .01 |
| ☐ 319 Lawrence Taylor | .10 | .05 | .01 |
| ☐ 320 Reyna Thompson | .04 | .02 | .01 |
| ☐ 321 Everson Walls | .04 | .02 | .01 |
| ☐ 322 Eric Allen | .08 | .04 | .01 |
| ☐ 323 Fred Barnett | .15 | .07 | .02 |
| ☐ 324 Jerome Brown | .08 | .04 | .01 |
| ☐ 325 Keith Byars | .08 | .04 | .01 |
| ☐ 326 Randall Cunningham | .10 | .05 | .01 |
| ☐ 327 Byron Evans | .08 | .04 | .01 |
| ☐ 328 Ron Heller | .04 | .02 | .01 |
| ☐ 329 Keith Jackson | .15 | .07 | .02 |
| ☐ 330 Seth Joyner | .08 | .04 | .01 |
| ☐ 331 Heath Sherman | .08 | .04 | .01 |
| ☐ 332 Clyde Simmons | .08 | .04 | .01 |
| ☐ 333 Ben Smith | .04 | .02 | .01 |
| ☐ 334 Anthony Toney | .04 | .02 | .01 |
| ☐ 335 Andre Waters | .04 | .02 | .01 |
| ☐ 336 Reggie White | .15 | .07 | .02 |
| ☐ 337 Calvin Williams | .20 | .09 | .03 |
| ☐ 338 Anthony Bell | .04 | .02 | .01 |
| ☐ 339 Rich Camarillo | .04 | .02 | .01 |
| ☐ 340 Roy Green | .08 | .04 | .01 |
| ☐ 341 Tim Jorden | .04 | .02 | .01 |
| ☐ 342 Cedric Mack | .04 | .02 | .01 |
| ☐ 343 Dexter Manley | .04 | .02 | .01 |
| ☐ 344 Freddie Joe Nunn | .04 | .02 | .01 |
| ☐ 345 Ricky Proehl | .10 | .05 | .01 |
| ☐ 346 Tootie Robbins | .04 | .02 | .01 |
| ☐ 347 Timm Rosenbach | .08 | .04 | .01 |
| ☐ 348 Luis Sharpe | .04 | .02 | .01 |
| ☐ 349 Vai Sikahema | .08 | .04 | .01 |
| ☐ 350 Anthony Thompson | .04 | .02 | .01 |
| ☐ 351 Lonnie Young | .04 | .02 | .01 |
| ☐ 352 Dexter Carter | .08 | .04 | .01 |
| ☐ 353 Mike Cofer | .04 | .02 | .01 |
| ☐ 354 Kevin Fagan | .04 | .02 | .01 |
| ☐ 355 Don Griffin | .04 | .02 | .01 |
| ☐ 356 Charles Haley UER | .08 | .04 | .01 |
| (Total fumbles should be 6, not 5) | | | |
| ☐ 357 Pierce Holt | .04 | .02 | .01 |
| ☐ 358 Brent Jones | .10 | .05 | .01 |
| ☐ 359 Guy McIntyre | .08 | .04 | .01 |
| ☐ 360 Joe Montana | 1.00 | .45 | .13 |
| ☐ 361 Darryl Pollard | .04 | .02 | .01 |
| ☐ 362 Tom Rathman | .08 | .04 | .01 |
| ☐ 363 Jerry Rice | .75 | .35 | .09 |
| ☐ 364 Bill Romanowski | .04 | .02 | .01 |
| ☐ 365 John Taylor | .10 | .05 | .01 |
| ☐ 366 Steve Wallace | .04 | .02 | .01 |
| ☐ 367 Steve Young | .50 | .23 | .06 |
| ☐ 368 Gary Anderson | .08 | .04 | .01 |
| ☐ 369 Ian Beckles | .04 | .02 | .01 |
| ☐ 370 Mark Carrier | .08 | .04 | .01 |
| ☐ 371 Reggie Cobb | .25 | .11 | .03 |
| ☐ 372 Reuben Davis | .04 | .02 | .01 |
| ☐ 373 Randy Grimes | .04 | .02 | .01 |
| ☐ 374 Wayne Haddix | .04 | .02 | .01 |
| ☐ 375 Ron Hall | .04 | .02 | .01 |
| ☐ 376 Harry Hamilton | .04 | .02 | .01 |
| ☐ 377 Bruce Hill | .04 | .02 | .01 |
| ☐ 378 Keith McCants | .04 | .02 | .01 |
| ☐ 379 Bruce Perkins | .04 | .02 | .01 |
| ☐ 380 Vinny Testaverde UER | .10 | .05 | .01 |
| (Misspelled Vinnie on card front) | | | |
| ☐ 381 Broderick Thomas | .08 | .04 | .01 |
| ☐ 382 Jeff Bostic | .04 | .02 | .01 |
| ☐ 383 Earnest Byner | .08 | .04 | .01 |
| ☐ 384 Gary Clark | .08 | .04 | .01 |
| ☐ 385 Darryl Grant | .04 | .02 | .01 |
| ☐ 386 Darrell Green | .08 | .04 | .01 |
| ☐ 387 Stan Humphries | .20 | .09 | .03 |
| ☐ 388 Jim Lachey | .04 | .02 | .01 |
| ☐ 389 Charles Mann | .08 | .04 | .01 |
| ☐ 390 Wilber Marshall | .08 | .04 | .01 |
| ☐ 391 Art Monk | .10 | .05 | .01 |
| ☐ 392 Gerald Riggs | .08 | .04 | .01 |
| ☐ 393 Mark Rypien | .10 | .05 | .01 |
| ☐ 394 Ricky Sanders | .08 | .04 | .01 |
| ☐ 395 Don Warren | .04 | .02 | .01 |
| ☐ 396 Bruce Smith HIT | .08 | .04 | .01 |
| ☐ 397 Reggie White HIT | .08 | .04 | .01 |
| ☐ 398 Lawrence Taylor HIT | .08 | .04 | .01 |
| ☐ 399 David Fulcher HIT | .04 | .02 | .01 |
| ☐ 400 Derrick Thomas HIT | .12 | .05 | .02 |
| ☐ 401 Mark Carrier HIT | .04 | .02 | .01 |
| ☐ 402 Mike Singletary HIT | .08 | .04 | .01 |
| ☐ 403 Charles Haley HIT | .04 | .02 | .01 |
| ☐ 404 Jeff Cross HIT | .04 | .02 | .01 |
| ☐ 405 Leslie O'Neal HIT | .04 | .02 | .01 |
| ☐ 406 Tim Harris HIT | .04 | .02 | .01 |
| ☐ 407 Steve Atwater HIT | .08 | .04 | .01 |
| ☐ 408 Joe Montana LL UER | .50 | .23 | .06 |
| (4th on yardage | | | |

| | | | |
|---|---|---|---|
| list, not 3rd) | | | |
| ☐ 409 Randall Cunningham LL | .08 | .04 | .01 |
| ☐ 410 Warren Moon LL | .10 | .05 | .01 |
| ☐ 411 Andre Rison LL UER | .12 | .05 | .02 |
| (Card incorrectly numbered as 412 and Michigan State misspelled as Stage) | | | |
| ☐ 412 Haywood Jeffires LL | .08 | .04 | .01 |
| (See number 411) | | | |
| ☐ 413 Stephone Paige LL | .04 | .02 | .01 |
| ☐ 414 Phil Simms LL | .08 | .04 | .01 |
| ☐ 415 Barry Sanders LL | .35 | .16 | .04 |
| ☐ 416 Bo Jackson LL | .15 | .07 | .02 |
| ☐ 417 Thurman Thomas LL | .20 | .09 | .03 |
| ☐ 418 Emmitt Smith LL | 1.00 | .45 | .13 |
| ☐ 419 John L. Williams LL | .04 | .02 | .01 |
| ☐ 420 Nick Bell RP | .20 | .09 | .03 |
| ☐ 421 Eric Bieniemy RP | .15 | .07 | .02 |
| ☐ 422 Mike Dumas RP UER | .04 | .02 | .01 |
| (Returned interception vs. Purdue, not Michigan State) | | | |
| ☐ 423 Russell Maryland RP | .40 | .18 | .05 |
| ☐ 424 Derek Russell RP | .25 | .11 | .03 |
| ☐ 425 Chris Smith RP UER | .04 | .02 | .01 |
| (Bengals misspelled as Bengels) | | | |
| ☐ 426 Mike Stonebreaker RP | .04 | .02 | .01 |
| ☐ 427 Patrick Tyrance RP | .04 | .02 | .01 |
| ☐ 428 Kenny Walker RP | .04 | .02 | .01 |
| (How Acquired has a different style) | | | |
| ☐ 429 Checklist 1-108 UER | .04 | .02 | .01 |
| (David Grayson misspelled as Graysor) | | | |
| ☐ 430 Checklist 109-216 | .04 | .02 | .01 |
| ☐ 431 Checklist 217-324 | .04 | .02 | .01 |
| ☐ 432 Checklist 325-432 | .04 | .02 | .01 |

# 1991 Fleer All-Pros

This 26-card standard size (2 1/2" by 3 1/2") set was issued by Fleer as an insert in their 1991 Football packs. The set features attractive full-color photography. The card backs contain the card number but are devoid of statistics.

| | MINT | EXC | G-VG |
|---|---|---|---|
| COMPLETE SET (26) | 6.00 | 2.70 | .75 |
| COMMON PLAYER (1-26) | .10 | .05 | .01 |
| | | | |
| ☐ 1 Andre Reed UER | .25 | .11 | .03 |
| Buffalo Bills | | | |
| (Caught 81 passes in '89, should say 88 passes) | | | |
| ☐ 2 Bobby Humphrey | .10 | .05 | .01 |
| Denver Broncos | | | |
| ☐ 3 Kent Hull | .10 | .05 | .01 |
| Buffalo Bills | | | |
| ☐ 4 Mark Bortz | .10 | .05 | .01 |
| Chicago Bears | | | |
| ☐ 5 Bruce Smith | .10 | .05 | .01 |
| Buffalo Bills | | | |
| ☐ 6 Greg Townsend | .10 | .05 | .01 |
| Los Angeles Raiders | | | |
| ☐ 7 Ray Childress | .10 | .05 | .01 |
| Houston Oilers | | | |
| ☐ 8 Andre Rison | .50 | .23 | .06 |
| Atlanta Falcons | | | |
| ☐ 9 Barry Sanders | 2.00 | .90 | .25 |
| Detroit Lions | | | |
| ☐ 10 Bo Jackson | .75 | .35 | .09 |
| Los Angeles Raiders | | | |

| | | | |
|---|---|---|---|
| ☐ 11 Neal Anderson | .10 | .05 | .01 |
| Chicago Bears | | | |
| ☐ 12 Keith Jackson | .25 | .11 | .03 |
| Philadelphia Eagles | | | |
| ☐ 13 Derrick Thomas | .50 | .23 | .06 |
| Kansas City Chiefs | | | |
| ☐ 14 John Offerdahl | .10 | .05 | .01 |
| Miami Dolphins | | | |
| ☐ 15 Lawrence Taylor | .25 | .11 | .03 |
| New York Giants | | | |
| ☐ 16 Darrell Green | .10 | .05 | .01 |
| Washington Redskins | | | |
| ☐ 17 Mark Carrier UER | .10 | .05 | .01 |
| Chicago Bears | | | |
| (No period in last | | | |
| sentence of bio) | | | |
| ☐ 18 David Fulcher UER | .10 | .05 | .01 |
| Cincinnati Bengals | | | |
| (Bill Wyche, should | | | |
| be Sam) | | | |
| ☐ 19 Joe Montana | 2.00 | .90 | .25 |
| San Francisco 49ers | | | |
| ☐ 20 Jerry Rice | 1.25 | .55 | .16 |
| San Francisco 49ers | | | |
| ☐ 21 Charles Haley | .10 | .05 | .01 |
| San Francisco 49ers | | | |
| ☐ 22 Mike Singletary | .15 | .07 | .02 |
| Chicago Bears | | | |
| ☐ 23 Nick Lowery | .10 | .05 | .01 |
| Kansas City Chiefs | | | |
| ☐ 24 Jim Lachey UER | .10 | .05 | .01 |
| Washington Redskins | | | |
| (Acquired by trade | | | |
| in '87, not '88) | | | |
| ☐ 25 Anthony Munoz | .15 | .07 | .02 |
| Cincinnati Bengals | | | |
| ☐ 26 Thurman Thomas | .75 | .35 | .09 |
| Buffalo Bills | | | |

## 1991 Fleer Pro-Visions

This ten-card standard size (2 1/2" by 3 1/2") set was issued by Fleer as an insert to their 1991 Football packs. The set is in the same basic, attractive design as the Pro-Vision baseball subset. The artworks from which the cards were derived were performed by artist Terry Smith. The card numbering is described on the card backs as 1 of 10, 2 of 10, etc.

| | MINT | EXC | G-VG |
|---|---|---|---|
| COMPLETE SET (10) | 5.00 | 2.30 | .60 |
| COMMON PLAYER (1-10) | .25 | .11 | .03 |
| | | | |
| ☐ 1 Joe Montana | 2.00 | .90 | .25 |
| San Francisco 49ers | | | |
| ☐ 2 Barry Sanders | 1.75 | .80 | .22 |
| Detroit Lions | | | |
| ☐ 3 Lawrence Taylor | .40 | .18 | .05 |
| New York Giants | | | |
| ☐ 4 Mike Singletary | .25 | .11 | .03 |
| Chicago Bears | | | |
| ☐ 5 Dan Marino | 1.75 | .80 | .22 |
| Miami Dolphins | | | |
| ☐ 6 Bo Jackson | .75 | .35 | .09 |
| Los Angeles Raiders | | | |
| ☐ 7 Randall Cunningham | .50 | .23 | .06 |
| Philadelphia Eagles | | | |
| ☐ 8 Bruce Smith | .25 | .11 | .03 |
| Buffalo Bills | | | |
| ☐ 9 Derrick Thomas | .50 | .23 | .06 |
| Kansas City Chiefs | | | |
| ☐ 10 Howie Long | .25 | .11 | .03 |
| Los Angeles Raiders | | | |

## 1991 Fleer Stars'n'Stripes

This 140-card standard size set (2 1/2" by 3 1/2") marked the second year that Fleer, in conjunction with Asher Candy, marketed a set sold with cherry candy sticks. The set features full-color game action shots on the front and a large color portrait (similar to the design used in Fleer Ultra baseball on the back), as well as complete statistical information, on the back. The cards are arranged by alphabetical team order within each conference. Buffalo Bills (1-5), Cincinnati Bengals (6-10), Cleveland Browns (11-14), Denver Broncos (15-19), Houston Oilers (20-24), Indianapolis Colts (25-28), Kansas City Chiefs (29-34), Los Angeles Raiders (35-38), Miami Dolphins (39-42), New England Patriots (43-45), New York Jets (46-48), Pittsburgh Steelers (49-53), San Diego Chargers (54-57), Seattle Seahawks (58-60), Atlanta Falcons (61-63), Chicago Bears (64-68), Dallas Cowboys (69-70), Detroit Lions (71-73), Green Bay Packers (74-76), Los Angeles Rams (77-80), Minnesota Vikings (81-85), New Orleans Saints (86-89), New York Giants (90-96), Philadelphia Eagles (97-100), Phoenix Cardinals (101-104), San Francisco 49ers (105-111), Tampa Bay Buccaneers (112-113), Washington Redskins (114-119), and High Picks (120-140).

| | MINT | EXC | G-VG |
|---|---|---|---|
| COMPLETE SET (140) | 14.00 | 5.75 | 1.40 |
| COMMON PLAYER (1-140) | .10 | .04 | .01 |
| | | | |
| ☐ 1 Shane Conlan | .15 | .06 | .01 |
| ☐ 2 Kent Hull | .10 | .04 | .01 |
| ☐ 3 Andre Reed | .20 | .08 | .02 |
| ☐ 4 Bruce Smith | .20 | .08 | .02 |
| ☐ 5 Thurman Thomas | .50 | .20 | .05 |
| ☐ 6 James Brooks | .15 | .06 | .01 |
| ☐ 7 Boomer Esiason | .25 | .10 | .02 |
| ☐ 8 David Fulcher | .10 | .04 | .01 |
| ☐ 9 Rodney Holman | .10 | .04 | .01 |
| ☐ 10 Anthony Munoz | .20 | .08 | .02 |
| ☐ 11 Reggie Langhorne | .10 | .04 | .01 |
| ☐ 12 Clay Matthews | .15 | .06 | .01 |
| ☐ 13 Eric Metcalf | .20 | .08 | .02 |
| ☐ 14 Gregg Rakoczy | .10 | .04 | .01 |
| ☐ 15 Steve Atwater | .15 | .06 | .01 |
| ☐ 16 John Elway | .60 | .24 | .06 |
| ☐ 17 Bobby Humphrey | .15 | .06 | .01 |
| ☐ 18 Karl Mecklenburg | .15 | .06 | .01 |
| ☐ 19 Dennis Smith | .10 | .04 | .01 |
| ☐ 20 Ray Childress | .15 | .06 | .01 |
| ☐ 21 Ernest Givins | .20 | .08 | .02 |
| ☐ 22 Haywood Jeffires | .25 | .10 | .02 |
| ☐ 23 Warren Moon | .40 | .16 | .04 |
| ☐ 24 Mike Munchak | .15 | .06 | .01 |
| ☐ 25 Albert Bentley | .15 | .06 | .01 |
| ☐ 26 Jeff George | .30 | .12 | .03 |
| ☐ 27 Rohn Stark | .10 | .04 | .01 |
| ☐ 28 Clarence Verdin | .10 | .04 | .01 |
| ☐ 29 Albert Lewis | .10 | .04 | .01 |
| ☐ 30 Nick Lowery | .10 | .04 | .01 |
| ☐ 31 Christian Okoye | .15 | .06 | .01 |
| ☐ 32 Stephone Paige | .10 | .04 | .01 |
| ☐ 33 Derrick Thomas | .30 | .12 | .03 |
| ☐ 34 Barry Word | .20 | .08 | .02 |
| ☐ 35 Bo Jackson | .75 | .30 | .07 |
| ☐ 36 Howie Long | .15 | .06 | .01 |
| ☐ 37 Greg Townsend | .10 | .04 | .01 |
| ☐ 38 Steve Wisniewski UER | .10 | .04 | .01 |
| (Acquired by trade in | | | |
| '89, not draft) | | | |
| ☐ 39 Mark Clayton | .15 | .06 | .01 |
| ☐ 40 Dan Marino | 1.50 | .60 | .15 |
| ☐ 41 John Offerdahl | .10 | .04 | .01 |
| ☐ 42 Richmond Webb | .15 | .06 | .01 |
| ☐ 43 Irving Fryar | .15 | .06 | .01 |
| ☐ 44 Ed Reynolds | .10 | .04 | .01 |
| ☐ 45 John Stephens | .20 | .08 | .02 |

| | | | |
|---|---|---|---|
| ☐ 46 Rob Moore | .35 | .14 | .03 |
| ☐ 47 Ken O'Brien | .15 | .06 | .01 |
| ☐ 48 Al Toon | .15 | .06 | .01 |
| ☐ 49 Bubby Brister | .10 | .04 | .01 |
| ☐ 50 Eric Green | .15 | .06 | .01 |
| ☐ 51 Merril Hoge | .10 | .04 | .01 |
| ☐ 52 David Little | .10 | .04 | .01 |
| ☐ 53 Rod Woodson | .20 | .08 | .02 |
| ☐ 54 Marion Butts | .20 | .08 | .02 |
| ☐ 55 Leslie O'Neal | .15 | .06 | .01 |
| ☐ 56 Junior Seau | .25 | .10 | .02 |
| ☐ 57 Billy Joe Tolliver | .15 | .06 | .01 |
| ☐ 58 Cortez Kennedy | .25 | .10 | .02 |
| ☐ 59 Dave Krieg | .15 | .06 | .01 |
| ☐ 60 John L. Williams | .15 | .06 | .01 |
| ☐ 61 Steve Broussard | .10 | .04 | .01 |
| ☐ 62 Bill Fralic | .15 | .06 | .01 |
| ☐ 63 Andre Rison | .30 | .12 | .03 |
| ☐ 64 Neal Anderson | .15 | .06 | .01 |
| ☐ 65 Mark Carrier | .15 | .06 | .01 |
| ☐ 66 Richard Dent | .15 | .06 | .01 |
| ☐ 67 Jim Harbaugh | .15 | .06 | .01 |
| ☐ 68 Mike Singletary | .20 | .08 | .02 |
| ☐ 69 Troy Aikman | 2.00 | .80 | .20 |
| ☐ 70 Emmitt Smith | 3.00 | 1.20 | .30 |
| ☐ 71 Mel Gray | .10 | .04 | .01 |
| ☐ 72 Rodney Peete | .20 | .08 | .02 |
| ☐ 73 Barry Sanders | 1.50 | .60 | .15 |
| ☐ 74 Tim Harris | .15 | .06 | .01 |
| ☐ 75 Perry Kemp | .10 | .04 | .01 |
| ☐ 76 Sterling Sharpe | .40 | .16 | .04 |
| ☐ 77 Henry Ellard | .15 | .06 | .01 |
| ☐ 78 Jim Everett | .20 | .08 | .02 |
| ☐ 79 Kevin Greene | .15 | .06 | .01 |
| ☐ 80 Jackie Slater | .15 | .06 | .01 |
| ☐ 81 Joey Browner | .10 | .04 | .01 |
| ☐ 82 Chris Doleman | .15 | .06 | .01 |
| ☐ 83 Steve Jordan | .15 | .06 | .01 |
| ☐ 84 Carl Lee | .10 | .04 | .01 |
| ☐ 85 Herschel Walker | .25 | .10 | .02 |
| ☐ 86 Morten Andersen | .15 | .06 | .01 |
| ☐ 87 Dalton Hilliard | .15 | .06 | .01 |
| ☐ 88 Vaughan Johnson | .10 | .04 | .01 |
| ☐ 89 Steve Walsh | .15 | .06 | .01 |
| ☐ 90 Ottis Anderson | .15 | .06 | .01 |
| ☐ 91 John Elliott | .10 | .04 | .01 |
| ☐ 92 Rodney Hampton | .50 | .20 | .05 |
| ☐ 93 Sean Landeta | .10 | .04 | .01 |
| ☐ 94 Dave Meggett | .15 | .06 | .01 |
| ☐ 95 Phil Simms | .25 | .10 | .02 |
| ☐ 96 Lawrence Taylor | .35 | .14 | .03 |
| ☐ 97 Randall Cunningham | .40 | .16 | .04 |
| ☐ 98 Keith Jackson | .25 | .10 | .02 |
| ☐ 99 Seth Joyner | .15 | .06 | .01 |
| ☐ 100 Reggie White | .30 | .12 | .03 |
| ☐ 101 Roy Green | .15 | .06 | .01 |
| ☐ 102 Johnny Johnson | .40 | .16 | .04 |
| ☐ 103 Ricky Proehl | .15 | .06 | .01 |
| ☐ 104 Tootie Robbins | .10 | .04 | .01 |
| ☐ 105 Kevin Fagan UER | .10 | .04 | .01 |
| (4th round pick in | | | |
| '87, not '86) | | | |
| ☐ 106 Charles Haley | .15 | .06 | .01 |
| ☐ 107 Guy McIntyre | .10 | .04 | .01 |
| ☐ 108 Joe Montana | 2.50 | 1.00 | .25 |
| ☐ 109 Tom Rathman | .15 | .06 | .01 |
| ☐ 110 Jerry Rice | 1.25 | .50 | .12 |
| ☐ 111 John Taylor | .20 | .08 | .02 |
| ☐ 112 Wayne Haddix | .10 | .04 | .01 |
| ☐ 113 Vinny Testaverde | .15 | .06 | .01 |
| ☐ 114 Earnest Byner | .15 | .06 | .01 |
| ☐ 115 Gary Clark | .20 | .08 | .02 |
| ☐ 116 Darrell Green | .15 | .06 | .01 |
| ☐ 117 Jim Lachey | .15 | .06 | .01 |
| ☐ 118 Art Monk | .25 | .10 | .02 |
| ☐ 119 Mark Rypien | .20 | .08 | .02 |
| ☐ 120 Nick Bell | .25 | .10 | .02 |
| Los Angeles Raiders | | | |
| ☐ 121 Eric Bieniemy | .20 | .08 | .02 |
| San Diego Chargers | | | |
| ☐ 122 Jarrod Bunch | .20 | .08 | .02 |
| New York Giants | | | |
| ☐ 123 Aaron Craver | .15 | .06 | .01 |
| Miami Dolphins | | | |
| ☐ 124 Lawrence Dawsey | .25 | .10 | .02 |
| Tampa Bay Buccaneers | | | |
| ☐ 125 Mike Dumas | .10 | .04 | .01 |
| Houston Oilers | | | |
| ☐ 126 Jeff Graham | .25 | .10 | .02 |
| Pittsburgh Steelers | | | |
| ☐ 127 Paul Justin | .10 | .04 | .01 |
| Chicago Bears | | | |
| ☐ 128 Darryll Lewis UER | .15 | .06 | .01 |
| Houston Oilers | | | |
| (Darryll misspelled | | | |
| as Darryl) | | | |
| ☐ 129 Todd Marinovich | .15 | .06 | .01 |
| Los Angeles Raiders | | | |

| | | | |
|---|---|---|---|
| ☐ 130 Russell Maryland | .35 | .14 | .03 |
| Dallas Cowboys | | | |
| ☐ 131 Kanavis McGhee | .15 | .06 | .01 |
| New York Giants | | | |
| ☐ 132 Ernie Mills | .15 | .06 | .01 |
| Pittsburgh Steelers | | | |
| ☐ 133 Herman Moore | .50 | .20 | .05 |
| Detroit Lions | | | |
| ☐ 134 Godfrey Myles | .10 | .04 | .01 |
| Dallas Cowboys | | | |
| ☐ 135 Browning Nagle | .20 | .08 | .02 |
| New York Jets | | | |
| ☐ 136 Esera Tuaolo | .10 | .04 | .01 |
| Green Bay Packers | | | |
| ☐ 137 Mark Vander Poel | .10 | .04 | .01 |
| Indianapolis Colts | | | |
| ☐ 138 Harvey Williams | .30 | .12 | .03 |
| Kansas City Chiefs | | | |
| ☐ 139 Chris Zorich | .25 | .10 | .02 |
| Chicago Bears | | | |
| ☐ 140 Checklist Card UER | .10 | .04 | .01 |
| (Darryll Lewis mis- | | | |
| spelled as Darryl) | | | |

## 1992 Fleer Prototypes

The 1992 Fleer Prototype football set contains six cards measuring the standard size (2 1/2" by 3 1/2"). The cards were distributed as two-card and three-card panels or strips in an attempt to show off the new design features of the 1992 Fleer football cards. The cards prominently pronounce "1992 Pre-Production Sample" in the middle of the reverse.

| | MINT | EXC | G-VG |
|---|---|---|---|
| COMPLETE SET (6) | 6.00 | 2.40 | .60 |
| COMMON PLAYER | 1.00 | .40 | .10 |
| ☐ 93 Mike Croel | 1.00 | .40 | .10 |
| Denver Broncos | | | |
| ☐ 191 Tim Brown | 1.25 | .50 | .12 |
| Los Angeles Raiders | | | |
| ☐ 428 Mark Rypien | 1.25 | .50 | .12 |
| Washington Redskins | | | |
| ☐ 435 Terrell Buckley | 1.50 | .60 | .15 |
| Green Bay Packers | | | |
| ☐ 457 Barry Sanders LL | 2.00 | .80 | .20 |
| Detroit Lions | | | |
| ☐ 475 Emmitt Smith PV | 3.00 | 1.20 | .30 |
| Dallas Cowboys | | | |

## 1992 Fleer

The 1992 Fleer football set contains 480 cards measuring the standard size (2 1/2" by 3 1/2"). The cards were available in 17-card wax packs,

42-card rack packs, and 32-card cello packs. The fronts display glossy color action photos bordered in white. The player's name appears in a color stripe at the bottom of the picture, with the team logo in a shield icon at the lower right corner. The backs carry a close-up color photo, with biography and career statistics in a box on the lower portion of the card. The cards are numbered on the back and checklisted below alphabetically according to teams as follows: Atlanta Falcons (1-16), Buffalo Bills (17-34), Chicago Bears (35-52), Cincinnati Bengals (53-62), Cleveland Browns (63-76), Dallas Cowboys (77-91), Denver Broncos (92-108), Detroit Lions (109-125), Green Bay Packers (126-140), Houston Oilers (141-157), Indianapolis Colts (158-168), Kansas City Chiefs (169-187), Los Angeles Raiders (188-206), Los Angeles Rams (207-221), Miami Dolphins (222-237), Minnesota Vikings (238-253), New England Patriots (254-268), New Orleans Saints (269-286), New York Giants (287-302), New York Jets (303-314), Philadelphia Eagles (315-328), Phoenix Cardinals (329-339), Pittsburgh Steelers (340-353), San Diego Chargers (354-369), San Francisco 49ers (370-386), Seattle Seahawks (387-399), Tampa Bay Buccaneers (400-412), and Washington Redskins (413-431). Other subsets included are Prospects (432-451), League Leaders (452-470), Pro-Visions (471-476), and Checklists (477-480). Key Rookie Cards include Edgar Bennett, Steve Bono, Amp Lee and Tomy Vardell.

| | MINT | EXC | G-VG |
|---|---|---|---|
| COMPLETE SET (480) | 10.00 | 4.50 | 1.25 |
| COMMON PLAYER (1-480) | .04 | .02 | .01 |

| | | | |
|---|---|---|---|
| ☐ 1 Steve Broussard | .08 | .04 | .01 |
| ☐ 2 Rick Bryan | .04 | .02 | .01 |
| ☐ 3 Scott Case | .04 | .02 | .01 |
| ☐ 4 Tory Epps | .04 | .02 | .01 |
| ☐ 5 Bill Fralic | .04 | .02 | .01 |
| ☐ 6 Moe Gardner | .04 | .02 | .01 |
| ☐ 7 Michael Haynes | .30 | .14 | .04 |
| ☐ 8 Chris Hinton | .04 | .02 | .01 |
| ☐ 9 Brian Jordan | .08 | .04 | .01 |
| ☐ 10 Mike Kenn | .08 | .04 | .01 |
| ☐ 11 Tim McKyer | .08 | .04 | .01 |
| ☐ 12 Chris Miller | .10 | .05 | .01 |
| ☐ 13 Erric Pegram | .40 | .18 | .05 |
| ☐ 14 Mike Pritchard | .25 | .11 | .03 |
| ☐ 15 Andre Rison | .25 | .11 | .03 |
| ☐ 16 Jessie Tuggle | .04 | .02 | .01 |
| ☐ 17 Carlton Bailey | .20 | .09 | .03 |
| ☐ 18 Howard Ballard | .04 | .02 | .01 |
| ☐ 19 Don Beebe | .10 | .05 | .01 |
| ☐ 20 Cornelius Bennett | .10 | .05 | .01 |
| ☐ 21 Shane Conlan | .08 | .04 | .01 |
| ☐ 22 Kent Hull | .04 | .02 | .01 |
| ☐ 23 Mark Kelso | .04 | .02 | .01 |
| ☐ 24 James Lofton | .10 | .05 | .01 |
| ☐ 25 Keith McKeller | .04 | .02 | .01 |
| ☐ 26 Scott Norwood | .04 | .02 | .01 |
| ☐ 27 Nate Odomes | .08 | .04 | .01 |
| ☐ 28 Frank Reich | .08 | .04 | .01 |
| ☐ 29 Jim Ritcher | .04 | .02 | .01 |
| ☐ 30 Leon Seals | .04 | .02 | .01 |
| ☐ 31 Darryl Talley | .08 | .04 | .01 |
| ☐ 32 Steve Tasker | .08 | .04 | .01 |
| ☐ 33 Thurman Thomas | .40 | .18 | .05 |
| ☐ 34 Will Wolford | .04 | .02 | .01 |
| ☐ 35 Neal Anderson | .08 | .04 | .01 |
| ☐ 36 Trace Armstrong | .04 | .02 | .01 |
| ☐ 37 Mark Carrier | .08 | .04 | .01 |
| ☐ 38 Richard Dent | .08 | .04 | .01 |
| ☐ 39 Shaun Gayle | .04 | .02 | .01 |
| ☐ 40 Jim Harbaugh | .08 | .04 | .01 |
| ☐ 41 Jay Hilgenberg | .08 | .04 | .01 |
| ☐ 42 Darren Lewis | .04 | .02 | .01 |
| ☐ 43 Steve McMichael | .08 | .04 | .01 |
| ☐ 44 Brad Muster | .08 | .04 | .01 |
| ☐ 45 William Perry | .08 | .04 | .01 |
| ☐ 46 John Roper | .04 | .02 | .01 |
| ☐ 47 Lemuel Stinson | .04 | .02 | .01 |
| ☐ 48 Stan Thomas | .04 | .02 | .01 |
| ☐ 49 Keith Van Horne | .04 | .02 | .01 |
| ☐ 50 Tom Waddle | .10 | .05 | .01 |
| ☐ 51 Donnell Woolford | .04 | .02 | .01 |
| ☐ 52 Chris Zorich | .08 | .04 | .01 |
| ☐ 53 Eddie Brown | .04 | .02 | .01 |
| ☐ 54 James Francis | .08 | .04 | .01 |
| ☐ 55 David Fulcher | .04 | .02 | .01 |
| ☐ 56 David Grant | .04 | .02 | .01 |
| ☐ 57 Harold Green | .08 | .04 | .01 |
| ☐ 58 Rodney Holman | .04 | .02 | .01 |
| ☐ 59 Lee Johnson | .04 | .02 | .01 |
| ☐ 60 Tim Krumrie | .04 | .02 | .01 |
| ☐ 61 Anthony Munoz | .08 | .04 | .01 |
| ☐ 62 Joe Walter | .04 | .02 | .01 |
| ☐ 63 Mike Baab | .04 | .02 | .01 |
| ☐ 64 Stephen Braggs | .04 | .02 | .01 |
| ☐ 65 Richard Brown | .04 | .02 | .01 |
| ☐ 66 Dan Fike | .04 | .02 | .01 |
| ☐ 67 Scott Galbraith | .04 | .02 | .01 |
| ☐ 68 Randy Hilliard | .04 | .02 | .01 |
| ☐ 69 Michael Jackson | .10 | .05 | .01 |
| ☐ 70 Tony Jones | .04 | .02 | .01 |
| ☐ 71 Ed King | .04 | .02 | .01 |
| ☐ 72 Kevin Mack | .08 | .04 | .01 |
| ☐ 73 Clay Matthews | .08 | .04 | .01 |
| ☐ 74 Eric Metcalf | .10 | .05 | .01 |
| ☐ 75 Vince Newsome | .04 | .02 | .01 |
| ☐ 76 John Rienstra | .04 | .02 | .01 |
| ☐ 77 Steve Beuerlein | .20 | .09 | .03 |
| ☐ 78 Larry Brown | .04 | .02 | .01 |
| ☐ 79 Tony Casillas | .04 | .02 | .01 |
| ☐ 80 Alvin Harper | .40 | .18 | .05 |
| ☐ 81 Issiac Holt | .04 | .02 | .01 |
| ☐ 82 Ray Horton | .04 | .02 | .01 |
| ☐ 83 Michael Irvin | .50 | .23 | .06 |
| ☐ 84 Daryl Johnston | .10 | .05 | .01 |
| ☐ 85 Kelvin Martin | .08 | .04 | .01 |
| ☐ 86 Nate Newton | .04 | .02 | .01 |
| ☐ 87 Ken Norton | .08 | .04 | .01 |
| ☐ 88 Jay Novacek | .15 | .07 | .02 |
| ☐ 89 Emmitt Smith | 2.00 | .90 | .25 |
| ☐ 90 Vinson Smith | .10 | .05 | .01 |
| ☐ 91 Mark Stepnoski | .04 | .02 | .01 |
| ☐ 92 Steve Atwater | .08 | .04 | .01 |
| ☐ 93 Mike Croel | .08 | .04 | .01 |
| ☐ 94 John Elway | .40 | .18 | .05 |
| ☐ 95 Simon Fletcher | .08 | .04 | .01 |
| ☐ 96 Gaston Green | .08 | .04 | .01 |
| ☐ 97 Mark Jackson | .08 | .04 | .01 |
| ☐ 98 Keith Kartz | .04 | .02 | .01 |
| ☐ 99 Greg Kragen | .04 | .02 | .01 |
| ☐ 100 Greg Lewis | .04 | .02 | .01 |
| ☐ 101 Karl Mecklenburg | .08 | .04 | .01 |
| ☐ 102 Derek Russell | .08 | .04 | .01 |
| ☐ 103 Steve Sewell | .04 | .02 | .01 |
| ☐ 104 Dennis Smith | .08 | .04 | .01 |
| ☐ 105 David Treadwell | .04 | .02 | .01 |
| ☐ 106 Kenny Walker | .04 | .02 | .01 |
| ☐ 107 Doug Widell | .04 | .02 | .01 |
| ☐ 108 Michael Young | .04 | .02 | .01 |
| ☐ 109 Jerry Ball | .08 | .04 | .01 |
| ☐ 110 Bennie Blades | .04 | .02 | .01 |
| ☐ 111 Lomas Brown | .04 | .02 | .01 |
| ☐ 112 Scott Conover | .10 | .05 | .01 |
| ☐ 113 Ray Crockett | .04 | .02 | .01 |
| ☐ 114 Mike Farr | .04 | .02 | .01 |
| ☐ 115 Mel Gray | .08 | .04 | .01 |
| ☐ 116 Willie Green | .04 | .02 | .01 |
| ☐ 117 Tracy Hayworth | .04 | .02 | .01 |
| ☐ 118 Erik Kramer | .15 | .07 | .02 |
| ☐ 119 Herman Moore | .30 | .14 | .04 |
| ☐ 120 Dan Owens | .04 | .02 | .01 |
| ☐ 121 Rodney Peete | .08 | .04 | .01 |
| ☐ 122 Brett Perriman | .08 | .04 | .01 |
| ☐ 123 Barry Sanders | .75 | .35 | .09 |
| ☐ 124 Chris Spielman | .08 | .04 | .01 |
| ☐ 125 Marc Spindler | .04 | .02 | .01 |
| ☐ 126 Tony Bennett | .08 | .04 | .01 |
| ☐ 127 Matt Brock | .04 | .02 | .01 |
| ☐ 128 LeRoy Butler | .04 | .02 | .01 |
| ☐ 129 Johnny Holland | .04 | .02 | .01 |
| ☐ 130 Perry Kemp | .04 | .02 | .01 |
| ☐ 131 Don Majkowski | .08 | .04 | .01 |
| ☐ 132 Mark Murphy | .04 | .02 | .01 |
| ☐ 133 Brian Noble | .04 | .02 | .01 |
| ☐ 134 Bryce Paup | .04 | .02 | .01 |
| ☐ 135 Sterling Sharpe | .50 | .23 | .06 |
| ☐ 136 Scott Stephen | .04 | .02 | .01 |
| ☐ 137 Darrell Thompson | .08 | .04 | .01 |
| ☐ 138 Mike Tomczak | .04 | .02 | .01 |
| ☐ 139 Esera Tuaolo | .04 | .02 | .01 |
| ☐ 140 Keith Woodside | .04 | .02 | .01 |
| ☐ 141 Ray Childress | .08 | .04 | .01 |
| ☐ 142 Cris Dishman | .08 | .04 | .01 |
| ☐ 143 Curtis Duncan | .08 | .04 | .01 |
| ☐ 144 John Flannery | .04 | .02 | .01 |
| ☐ 145 William Fuller | .04 | .02 | .01 |
| ☐ 146 Ernest Givins | .08 | .04 | .01 |
| ☐ 147 Haywood Jeffires | .10 | .05 | .01 |
| ☐ 148 Sean Jones | .04 | .02 | .01 |
| ☐ 149 Lamar Lathon | .04 | .02 | .01 |
| ☐ 150 Bruce Matthews | .08 | .04 | .01 |
| ☐ 151 Bubba McDowell | .04 | .02 | .01 |
| ☐ 152 Johnny Meads | .04 | .02 | .01 |
| ☐ 153 Warren Moon | .20 | .09 | .03 |
| ☐ 154 Mike Munchak | .08 | .04 | .01 |
| ☐ 155 Al Smith | .04 | .02 | .01 |
| ☐ 156 Doug Smith | .04 | .02 | .01 |
| ☐ 157 Lorenzo White | .08 | .04 | .01 |
| ☐ 158 Michael Ball | .04 | .02 | .01 |
| ☐ 159 Chip Banks | .04 | .02 | .01 |
| ☐ 160 Duane Bickett | .04 | .02 | .01 |
| ☐ 161 Bill Brooks | .08 | .04 | .01 |
| ☐ 162 Ken Clark | .04 | .02 | .01 |
| ☐ 163 Jon Hand | .04 | .02 | .01 |
| ☐ 164 Jeff Herrod | .04 | .02 | .01 |
| ☐ 165 Jessie Hester | .04 | .02 | .01 |
| ☐ 166 Scott Radecic | .04 | .02 | .01 |

|  |  | | | |
|---|--------|-----|-----|-----|
| ☐ 167 | Rohn Stark | .04 | .02 | .01 |
| ☐ 168 | Clarence Verdin | .04 | .02 | .01 |
| ☐ 169 | John Alt | .04 | .02 | .01 |
| ☐ 170 | Tim Barnett | .08 | .04 | .01 |
| ☐ 171 | Tim Grunhard | .04 | .02 | .01 |
| ☐ 172 | Dino Hackett | .04 | .02 | .01 |
| ☐ 173 | Jonathan Hayes | .04 | .02 | .01 |
| ☐ 174 | Bill Maas | .04 | .02 | .01 |
| ☐ 175 | Chris Martin | .04 | .02 | .01 |
| ☐ 176 | Christian Okoye | .08 | .04 | .01 |
| ☐ 177 | Stephone Paige | .08 | .04 | .01 |
| ☐ 178 | Jayice Pearson | .04 | .02 | .01 |
| ☐ 179 | Kevin Porter | .04 | .02 | .01 |
| ☐ 180 | Kevin Ross | .08 | .04 | .01 |
| ☐ 181 | Dan Saleaumua | .04 | .02 | .01 |
| ☐ 182 | Tracy Simien | .15 | .07 | .02 |
| ☐ 183 | Neil Smith | .10 | .05 | .01 |
| ☐ 184 | Derrick Thomas | .15 | .07 | .02 |
| ☐ 185 | Robb Thomas | .04 | .02 | .01 |
| ☐ 186 | Mark Vlasic | .08 | .04 | .01 |
| ☐ 187 | Barry Word | .10 | .05 | .01 |
| ☐ 188 | Marcus Allen | .08 | .04 | .01 |
| ☐ 189 | Eddie Anderson | .04 | .02 | .01 |
| ☐ 190 | Nick Bell | .08 | .04 | .01 |
| ☐ 191 | Tim Brown | .25 | .11 | .03 |
| ☐ 192 | Scott Davis | .04 | .02 | .01 |
| ☐ 193 | Riki Ellison | .04 | .02 | .01 |
| ☐ 194 | Mervyn Fernandez | .04 | .02 | .01 |
| ☐ 195 | Willie Gault | .08 | .04 | .01 |
| ☐ 196 | Jeff Gossett | .04 | .02 | .01 |
| ☐ 197 | Ethan Horton | .04 | .02 | .01 |
| ☐ 198 | Jeff Jaeger | .04 | .02 | .01 |
| ☐ 199 | Howie Long | .08 | .04 | .01 |
| ☐ 200 | Ronnie Lott | .10 | .05 | .01 |
| ☐ 201 | Todd Marinovich | .04 | .02 | .01 |
| ☐ 202 | Don Mosebar | .04 | .02 | .01 |
| ☐ 203 | Jay Schroeder | .08 | .04 | .01 |
| ☐ 204 | Greg Townsend | .04 | .02 | .01 |
| ☐ 205 | Lionel Washington | .04 | .02 | .01 |
| ☐ 206 | Steve Wisniewski | .04 | .02 | .01 |
| ☐ 207 | Flipper Anderson | .08 | .04 | .01 |
| ☐ 208 | Bern Brostek | .04 | .02 | .01 |
| ☐ 209 | Robert Delpino | .08 | .04 | .01 |
| ☐ 210 | Henry Ellard | .08 | .04 | .01 |
| ☐ 211 | Jim Everett | .08 | .04 | .01 |
| ☐ 212 | Cleveland Gary | .08 | .04 | .01 |
| ☐ 213 | Kevin Greene | .08 | .04 | .01 |
| ☐ 214 | Darryl Henley | .04 | .02 | .01 |
| ☐ 215 | Damone Johnson | .04 | .02 | .01 |
| ☐ 216 | Larry Kelm | .04 | .02 | .01 |
| ☐ 217 | Todd Lyght | .04 | .02 | .01 |
| ☐ 218 | Jackie Slater | .08 | .04 | .01 |
| ☐ 219 | Michael Stewart | .04 | .02 | .01 |
| ☐ 220 | Pat Terrell UER | .04 | .02 | .01 |
| | (1991 stats have 74 tackles, text has 64) | | | |
| ☐ 221 | Robert Young | .08 | .04 | .01 |
| ☐ 222 | Mark Clayton | .08 | .04 | .01 |
| ☐ 223 | Bryan Cox | .08 | .04 | .01 |
| ☐ 224 | Aaron Craver | .04 | .02 | .01 |
| ☐ 225 | Jeff Cross | .04 | .02 | .01 |
| ☐ 226 | Mark Duper | .08 | .04 | .01 |
| ☐ 227 | Harry Galbreath | .04 | .02 | .01 |
| ☐ 228 | David Griggs | .04 | .02 | .01 |
| ☐ 229 | Mark Higgs | .10 | .05 | .01 |
| ☐ 230 | Vestee Jackson | .04 | .02 | .01 |
| ☐ 231 | John Offerdahl | .08 | .04 | .01 |
| ☐ 232 | Louis Oliver | .08 | .04 | .01 |
| ☐ 233 | Tony Paige | .04 | .02 | .01 |
| ☐ 234 | Reggie Roby | .04 | .02 | .01 |
| ☐ 235 | Sammie Smith | .04 | .02 | .01 |
| ☐ 236 | Pete Stoyanovich | .08 | .04 | .01 |
| ☐ 237 | Richmond Webb | .08 | .04 | .01 |
| ☐ 238 | Terry Allen | .20 | .09 | .03 |
| ☐ 239 | Ray Berry | .04 | .02 | .01 |
| ☐ 240 | Joey Browner | .04 | .02 | .01 |
| ☐ 241 | Anthony Carter | .08 | .04 | .01 |
| ☐ 242 | Cris Carter | .10 | .05 | .01 |
| ☐ 243 | Chris Doleman | .08 | .04 | .01 |
| ☐ 244 | Rich Gannon | .08 | .04 | .01 |
| ☐ 245 | Tim Irwin | .04 | .02 | .01 |
| ☐ 246 | Steve Jordan | .08 | .04 | .01 |
| ☐ 247 | Carl Lee | .04 | .02 | .01 |
| ☐ 248 | Randall McDaniel | .04 | .02 | .01 |
| ☐ 249 | Mike Merriweather | .04 | .02 | .01 |
| ☐ 250 | Harry Newsome | .04 | .02 | .01 |
| ☐ 251 | John Randle | .04 | .02 | .01 |
| ☐ 252 | Henry Thomas | .04 | .02 | .01 |
| ☐ 253 | Herschel Walker | .10 | .05 | .01 |
| ☐ 254 | Ray Agnew | .04 | .02 | .01 |
| ☐ 255 | Bruce Armstrong | .04 | .02 | .01 |
| ☐ 256 | Vincent Brown | .04 | .02 | .01 |
| ☐ 257 | Marv Cook | .08 | .04 | .01 |
| ☐ 258 | Irving Fryar | .08 | .04 | .01 |
| ☐ 259 | Pat Harlow | .04 | .02 | .01 |
| ☐ 260 | Tommy Hodson | .04 | .02 | .01 |
| ☐ 261 | Maurice Hurst | .04 | .02 | .01 |
| ☐ 262 | Ronnie Lippett | .04 | .02 | .01 |
| ☐ 263 | Eugene Lockhart | .04 | .02 | .01 |
| ☐ 264 | Greg McMurtry | .04 | .02 | .01 |
| ☐ 265 | Hugh Millen | .08 | .04 | .01 |
| ☐ 266 | Leonard Russell | .30 | .14 | .04 |
| ☐ 267 | Andre Tippett | .08 | .04 | .01 |
| ☐ 268 | Brent Williams | .04 | .02 | .01 |
| ☐ 269 | Morten Andersen | .08 | .04 | .01 |
| ☐ 270 | Gene Atkins | .04 | .02 | .01 |
| ☐ 271 | Wesley Carroll | .08 | .04 | .01 |
| ☐ 272 | Jim Dombrowski | .04 | .02 | .01 |
| ☐ 273 | Quinn Early | .08 | .04 | .01 |
| ☐ 274 | Gill Fenerty | .04 | .02 | .01 |
| ☐ 275 | Bobby Hebert | .10 | .05 | .01 |
| ☐ 276 | Joel Hilgenberg | .04 | .02 | .01 |
| ☐ 277 | Rickey Jackson | .08 | .04 | .01 |
| ☐ 278 | Vaughan Johnson | .08 | .04 | .01 |
| ☐ 279 | Eric Martin | .08 | .04 | .01 |
| ☐ 280 | Brett Maxie | .04 | .02 | .01 |
| ☐ 281 | Fred McAfee | .15 | .07 | .02 |
| ☐ 282 | Sam Mills | .08 | .04 | .01 |
| ☐ 283 | Pat Swilling | .08 | .04 | .01 |
| ☐ 284 | Floyd Turner | .04 | .02 | .01 |
| ☐ 285 | Steve Walsh | .04 | .02 | .01 |
| ☐ 286 | Frank Warren | .04 | .02 | .01 |
| ☐ 287 | Stephen Baker | .04 | .02 | .01 |
| ☐ 288 | Maurice Carthon | .04 | .02 | .01 |
| ☐ 289 | Mark Collins | .04 | .02 | .01 |
| ☐ 290 | John Elliott | .04 | .02 | .01 |
| ☐ 291 | Myron Guyton | .04 | .02 | .01 |
| ☐ 292 | Rodney Hampton | .40 | .18 | .05 |
| ☐ 293 | Jeff Hostetler | .20 | .09 | .03 |
| ☐ 294 | Mark Ingram | .08 | .04 | .01 |
| ☐ 295 | Pepper Johnson | .08 | .04 | .01 |
| ☐ 296 | Sean Landeta | .04 | .02 | .01 |
| ☐ 297 | Leonard Marshall | .08 | .04 | .01 |
| ☐ 298 | Dave Meggett | .08 | .04 | .01 |
| ☐ 299 | Bart Oates | .04 | .02 | .01 |
| ☐ 300 | Phil Simms | .10 | .05 | .01 |
| ☐ 301 | Reyna Thompson | .04 | .02 | .01 |
| ☐ 302 | Lewis Tillman | .08 | .04 | .01 |
| ☐ 303 | Brad Baxter | .08 | .04 | .01 |
| ☐ 304 | Kyle Clifton | .04 | .02 | .01 |
| ☐ 305 | James Hasty | .04 | .02 | .01 |
| ☐ 306 | Joe Kelly | .04 | .02 | .01 |
| ☐ 307 | Jeff Lageman | .04 | .02 | .01 |
| ☐ 308 | Mo Lewis | .04 | .02 | .01 |
| ☐ 309 | Erik McMillan | .04 | .02 | .01 |
| ☐ 310 | Rob Moore | .10 | .05 | .01 |
| ☐ 311 | Tony Stargell | .04 | .02 | .01 |
| ☐ 312 | Jim Sweeney | .04 | .02 | .01 |
| ☐ 313 | Marvin Washington | .04 | .02 | .01 |
| ☐ 314 | Lonnie Young | .04 | .02 | .01 |
| ☐ 315 | Eric Allen | .08 | .04 | .01 |
| ☐ 316 | Fred Barnett | .10 | .05 | .01 |
| ☐ 317 | Jerome Brown | .08 | .04 | .01 |
| ☐ 318 | Keith Byars | .08 | .04 | .01 |
| ☐ 319 | Wes Hopkins | .04 | .02 | .01 |
| ☐ 320 | Keith Jackson | .10 | .05 | .01 |
| ☐ 321 | James Joseph | .04 | .02 | .01 |
| ☐ 322 | Seth Joyner | .08 | .04 | .01 |
| ☐ 323 | Jeff Kemp | .04 | .02 | .01 |
| ☐ 324 | Roger Ruzek | .04 | .02 | .01 |
| ☐ 325 | Clyde Simmons | .08 | .04 | .01 |
| ☐ 326 | William Thomas | .04 | .02 | .01 |
| ☐ 327 | Reggie White | .15 | .07 | .02 |
| ☐ 328 | Calvin Williams | .10 | .05 | .01 |
| ☐ 329 | Rich Camarillo | .04 | .02 | .01 |
| ☐ 330 | Ken Harvey | .04 | .02 | .01 |
| ☐ 331 | Eric Hill | .04 | .02 | .01 |
| ☐ 332 | Johnny Johnson | .10 | .05 | .01 |
| ☐ 333 | Ernie Jones | .04 | .02 | .01 |
| ☐ 334 | Tim Jorden | .04 | .02 | .01 |
| ☐ 335 | Tim McDonald | .08 | .04 | .01 |
| ☐ 336 | Freddie Joe Nunn | .04 | .02 | .01 |
| ☐ 337 | Luis Sharpe | .04 | .02 | .01 |
| ☐ 338 | Eric Swann | .08 | .04 | .01 |
| ☐ 339 | Aeneas Williams | .04 | .02 | .01 |
| ☐ 340 | Gary Anderson | .04 | .02 | .01 |
| ☐ 341 | Bubby Brister | .08 | .04 | .01 |
| ☐ 342 | Adrian Cooper | .04 | .02 | .01 |
| ☐ 343 | Barry Foster | .35 | .16 | .04 |
| ☐ 344 | Eric Green | .10 | .05 | .01 |
| ☐ 345 | Bryan Hinkle | .04 | .02 | .01 |
| ☐ 346 | Tunch Ilkin | .04 | .02 | .01 |
| ☐ 347 | Carnell Lake | .04 | .02 | .01 |
| ☐ 348 | Louis Lipps | .08 | .04 | .01 |
| ☐ 349 | David Little | .04 | .02 | .01 |
| ☐ 350 | Greg Lloyd | .04 | .02 | .01 |
| ☐ 351 | Neil O'Donnell | .50 | .23 | .06 |
| ☐ 352 | Dwight Stone | .04 | .02 | .01 |
| ☐ 353 | Rod Woodson | .10 | .05 | .01 |
| ☐ 354 | Rod Bernstine | .08 | .04 | .01 |
| ☐ 355 | Eric Bieniemy | .08 | .04 | .01 |
| ☐ 356 | Marion Butts | .10 | .05 | .01 |
| ☐ 357 | Gill Byrd | .08 | .04 | .01 |
| ☐ 358 | John Friesz | .08 | .04 | .01 |
| ☐ 359 | Burt Grossman | .04 | .02 | .01 |
| ☐ 360 | Courtney Hall | .04 | .02 | .01 |

| | | | |
|---|---|---|---|
| ☐ 361 Ronnie Harmon | .04 | .02 | .01 |
| ☐ 362 Shawn Jefferson | .04 | .02 | .01 |
| ☐ 363 Nate Lewis | .08 | .04 | .01 |
| ☐ 364 Craig McEwen | .04 | .02 | .01 |
| ☐ 365 Eric Moten | .04 | .02 | .01 |
| ☐ 366 Joe Phillips | .04 | .02 | .01 |
| ☐ 367 Gary Plummer | .04 | .02 | .01 |
| ☐ 368 Henry Rolling | .04 | .02 | .01 |
| ☐ 369 Broderick Thompson | .04 | .02 | .01 |
| ☐ 370 Harris Barton | .04 | .02 | .01 |
| ☐ 371 Steve Bono | .50 | .23 | .06 |
| ☐ 372 Todd Bowles | .04 | .02 | .01 |
| ☐ 373 Dexter Carter | .08 | .04 | .01 |
| ☐ 374 Michael Carter | .04 | .02 | .01 |
| ☐ 375 Mike Cofer | .04 | .02 | .01 |
| ☐ 376 Keith DeLong | .04 | .02 | .01 |
| ☐ 377 Charles Haley | .08 | .04 | .01 |
| ☐ 378 Merton Hanks | .04 | .02 | .01 |
| ☐ 379 Tim Harris | .08 | .04 | .01 |
| ☐ 380 Brent Jones | .10 | .05 | .01 |
| ☐ 381 Guy McIntyre | .08 | .04 | .01 |
| ☐ 382 Tom Rathman | .08 | .04 | .01 |
| ☐ 383 Bill Romanowski | .04 | .02 | .01 |
| ☐ 384 Jesse Sapolu | .04 | .02 | .01 |
| ☐ 385 John Taylor | .10 | .05 | .01 |
| ☐ 386 Steve Young | .35 | .16 | .04 |
| ☐ 387 Robert Blackmon | .04 | .02 | .01 |
| ☐ 388 Brian Blades | .08 | .04 | .01 |
| ☐ 389 Jacob Green | .04 | .02 | .01 |
| ☐ 390 Dwayne Harper | .04 | .02 | .01 |
| ☐ 391 Andy Heck | .04 | .02 | .01 |
| ☐ 392 Tommy Kane | .04 | .02 | .01 |
| ☐ 393 John Kasay | .04 | .02 | .01 |
| ☐ 394 Cortez Kennedy | .10 | .05 | .01 |
| ☐ 395 Bryan Millard | .04 | .02 | .01 |
| ☐ 396 Rufus Porter | .04 | .02 | .01 |
| ☐ 397 Eugene Robinson | .04 | .02 | .01 |
| ☐ 398 John L. Williams | .08 | .04 | .01 |
| ☐ 399 Terry Wooden | .04 | .02 | .01 |
| ☐ 400 Gary Anderson | .08 | .04 | .01 |
| ☐ 401 Ian Beckles | .04 | .02 | .01 |
| ☐ 402 Mark Carrier | .08 | .04 | .01 |
| ☐ 403 Reggie Cobb | .10 | .05 | .01 |
| ☐ 404 Lawrence Dawsey | .10 | .05 | .01 |
| ☐ 405 Ron Hall | .04 | .02 | .01 |
| ☐ 406 Keith McCants | .04 | .02 | .01 |
| ☐ 407 Charles McRae | .04 | .02 | .01 |
| ☐ 408 Tim Newton | .04 | .02 | .01 |
| ☐ 409 Jesse Solomon | .04 | .02 | .01 |
| ☐ 410 Vinny Testaverde | .10 | .05 | .01 |
| ☐ 411 Broderick Thomas | .04 | .02 | .01 |
| ☐ 412 Robert Wilson | .04 | .02 | .01 |
| ☐ 413 Jeff Bostic | .04 | .02 | .01 |
| ☐ 414 Earnest Byner | .08 | .04 | .01 |
| ☐ 415 Gary Clark | .08 | .04 | .01 |
| ☐ 416 Andre Collins | .04 | .02 | .01 |
| ☐ 417 Brad Edwards | .04 | .02 | .01 |
| ☐ 418 Kurt Gouveia | .04 | .02 | .01 |
| ☐ 419 Darrell Green | .08 | .04 | .01 |
| ☐ 420 Joe Jacoby | .04 | .02 | .01 |
| ☐ 421 Jim Lachey | .04 | .02 | .01 |
| ☐ 422 Chip Lohmiller | .08 | .04 | .01 |
| ☐ 423 Charles Mann | .08 | .04 | .01 |
| ☐ 424 Wilber Marshall | .08 | .04 | .01 |
| ☐ 425 Ron Middleton | .04 | .02 | .01 |
| ☐ 426 Brian Mitchell | .08 | .04 | .01 |
| ☐ 427 Art Monk UER | .10 | .05 | .01 |
| (Born in 1967, should say 1957) | | | |
| ☐ 428 Mark Rypien | .10 | .05 | .01 |
| ☐ 429 Ricky Sanders | .08 | .04 | .01 |
| ☐ 430 Mark Schlereth | .10 | .05 | .01 |
| ☐ 431 Fred Stokes | .04 | .02 | .01 |
| ☐ 432 Edgar Bennett | .30 | .14 | .04 |
| Green Bay Packers | | | |
| ☐ 433 Brian Bollinger | .05 | .02 | .01 |
| San Francisco 49ers | | | |
| ☐ 434 Joe Bowden | .05 | .02 | .01 |
| Houston Oilers | | | |
| ☐ 435 Terrell Buckley | .25 | .11 | .03 |
| Green Bay Packers | | | |
| ☐ 436 Willie Clay | .05 | .02 | .01 |
| Detroit Lions | | | |
| ☐ 437 Steve Gordon | .05 | .02 | .01 |
| New England Patriots | | | |
| ☐ 438 Keith Hamilton | .15 | .07 | .02 |
| New York Giants | | | |
| ☐ 439 Carlos Huerta | .05 | .02 | .01 |
| San Diego Chargers | | | |
| ☐ 440 Matt LaBounty | .05 | .02 | .01 |
| San Francisco 49ers | | | |
| ☐ 441 Amp Lee | .25 | .11 | .03 |
| San Francisco 49ers | | | |
| ☐ 442 Ricardo McDonald | .10 | .05 | .01 |
| Cincinnati Bengals | | | |
| ☐ 443 Chris Mims | .25 | .11 | .03 |
| San Diego Chargers | | | |
| ☐ 444 Michael Mooney | .05 | .02 | .01 |

| | | | |
|---|---|---|---|
| Houston Oilers | | | |
| ☐ 445 Patrick Rowe | .10 | .05 | .01 |
| Cleveland Browns | | | |
| ☐ 446 Leon Searcy | .05 | .02 | .01 |
| Pittsburgh Steelers | | | |
| ☐ 447 Siran Stacy | .10 | .05 | .01 |
| Philadelphia Eagles | | | |
| ☐ 448 Kevin Turner | .20 | .09 | .03 |
| New England Patriots | | | |
| ☐ 449 Tommy Vardell | .30 | .14 | .04 |
| Cleveland Browns | | | |
| ☐ 450 Bob Whitfield | .12 | .05 | .02 |
| Atlanta Falcons | | | |
| ☐ 451 Darryl Williams | .20 | .09 | .03 |
| Cincinnati Bengals | | | |
| ☐ 452 Thurman Thomas LL | .20 | .09 | .03 |
| Buffalo Bills | | | |
| ☐ 453 Emmitt Smith LL UER | .75 | .35 | .09 |
| Dallas Cowboys | | | |
| (Thr at start of second paragraph should be the) | | | |
| ☐ 454 Haywood Jeffires LL | .08 | .04 | .01 |
| Houston Oilers | | | |
| ☐ 455 Michael Irvin LL | .20 | .09 | .03 |
| Dallas Cowboys | | | |
| ☐ 456 Mark Clayton LL | .04 | .02 | .01 |
| Miami Dolphins | | | |
| ☐ 457 Barry Sanders LL | .30 | .14 | .04 |
| Detroit Lions | | | |
| ☐ 458 Pete Stoyanovich LL | .04 | .02 | .01 |
| Miami Dolphins | | | |
| ☐ 459 Chip Lohmiller LL | .04 | .02 | .01 |
| Washington Redskins | | | |
| ☐ 460 William Fuller LL | .04 | .02 | .01 |
| Houston Oilers | | | |
| ☐ 461 Pat Swilling LL | .08 | .04 | .01 |
| New Orleans Saints | | | |
| ☐ 462 Ronnie Lott LL | .08 | .04 | .01 |
| Los Angeles Raiders | | | |
| ☐ 463 Ray Crockett LL | .04 | .02 | .01 |
| Detroit Lions | | | |
| ☐ 464 Tim McKyer LL | .04 | .02 | .01 |
| Atlanta Falcons | | | |
| ☐ 465 Aeneas Williams LL | .04 | .02 | .01 |
| Phoenix Cardinals | | | |
| ☐ 466 Rod Woodson LL | .08 | .04 | .01 |
| Pittsburgh Steelers | | | |
| ☐ 467 Mel Gray LL | .04 | .02 | .01 |
| Detroit Lions | | | |
| ☐ 468 Nate Lewis LL | .04 | .02 | .01 |
| San Diego Chargers | | | |
| ☐ 469 Steve Young LL | .08 | .04 | .01 |
| San Francisco 49ers | | | |
| ☐ 470 Reggie Roby LL | .04 | .02 | .01 |
| Miami Dolphins | | | |
| ☐ 471 John Elway PV | .15 | .07 | .02 |
| Denver Broncos | | | |
| ☐ 472 Ronnie Lott PV | .08 | .04 | .01 |
| Los Angeles Raiders | | | |
| ☐ 473 Art Monk PV UER | .08 | .04 | .01 |
| Washington Redskins | | | |
| (Born in 1967, should say 1957) | | | |
| ☐ 474 Warren Moon PV | .10 | .05 | .01 |
| Houston Oilers | | | |
| ☐ 475 Emmitt Smith PV | .75 | .35 | .09 |
| Dallas Cowboys | | | |
| ☐ 476 Thurman Thomas PV | .20 | .09 | .03 |
| Buffalo Bills | | | |
| ☐ 477 Checklist 1-120 | .04 | .02 | .01 |
| ☐ 478 Checklist 121-240 | .04 | .02 | .01 |
| ☐ 479 Checklist 241-360 | .04 | .02 | .01 |
| ☐ 480 Checklist 361-480 | .04 | .02 | .01 |

# 1992 Fleer All-Pros

This 24-card subset was available in Fleer's wax packs. The cards measure the standard size (2 1/2" by 3 1/2"). On a dark blue card face, the fronts feature color player cut outs superimposed on a red, white, and blue NFL logo emblem. The player's name and position appear in gold foil lettering at the lower left corner. The backs carry a color head shot and player profile on a pink background. The cards are numbered on the back.

| | MINT | EXC | G-VG |
|---|---|---|---|
| COMPLETE SET (24) | 6.00 | 2.70 | .75 |
| COMMON PLAYER (1-24) | .25 | .11 | .03 |
| | | | |
| ☐ 1 Marv Cook | .25 | .11 | .03 |
| New England Patriots | | | |
| ☐ 2 Mike Kenn | .25 | .11 | .03 |
| Atlanta Falcons | | | |
| ☐ 3 Steve Wisniewski | .25 | .11 | .03 |
| Los Angeles Raiders | | | |
| ☐ 4 Jim Ritcher | .25 | .11 | .03 |

| | MINT | EXC | G-VG |
|---|---|---|---|
| COMPLETE SET (20) | 35.00 | 16.00 | 4.40 |
| COMMON PLAYER (1-20) | 2.00 | .90 | .25 |
| ☐ 1 Moe Gardner | 2.00 | .90 | .25 |
| Atlanta Falcons | | | |
| ☐ 2 Mike Pritchard | 7.00 | 3.10 | .85 |
| Atlanta Falcons | | | |
| ☐ 3 Stan Thomas | 2.00 | .90 | .25 |
| Chicago Bears | | | |
| ☐ 4 Larry Brown | 2.50 | 1.15 | .30 |
| Dallas Cowboys | | | |
| ☐ 5 Todd Lyght | 2.50 | 1.15 | .30 |
| Los Angeles Rams | | | |
| ☐ 6 James Joseph | 2.50 | 1.15 | .30 |
| Philadelphia Eagles | | | |
| ☐ 7 Aeneas Williams | 2.00 | .90 | .25 |
| Phoenix Cardinals | | | |
| ☐ 8 Michael Jackson | 3.00 | 1.35 | .40 |
| Cleveland Browns | | | |
| ☐ 9 Ed King | 2.00 | .90 | .25 |
| Cleveland Browns | | | |
| ☐ 10 Mike Croel | 2.50 | 1.15 | .30 |
| Denver Broncos | | | |
| ☐ 11 Kenny Walker | 2.00 | .90 | .25 |
| Denver Broncos | | | |
| ☐ 12 Tim Barnett | 2.50 | 1.15 | .30 |
| Kansas City Chiefs | | | |
| ☐ 13 Nick Bell | 2.50 | 1.15 | .30 |
| Los Angeles Raiders | | | |
| ☐ 14 Todd Marinovich | 2.00 | .90 | .25 |
| Los Angeles Raiders | | | |
| ☐ 15 Leonard Russell | 8.00 | 3.60 | 1.00 |
| New England Patriots | | | |
| ☐ 16 Pat Harlow | 2.00 | .90 | .25 |
| New England Patriots | | | |
| ☐ 17 Mo Lewis | 2.00 | .90 | .25 |
| New York Jets | | | |
| ☐ 18 John Kasay | 2.00 | .90 | .25 |
| Seattle Seahawks | | | |
| ☐ 19 Lawrence Dawsey | 2.50 | 1.15 | .30 |
| Tampa Bay Buccaneers | | | |
| ☐ 20 Charles McRae | 2.00 | .90 | .25 |
| Tampa Bay Buccaneers | | | |

| | | | |
|---|---|---|---|
| Buffalo Bills | | | |
| ☐ 5 Jim Lachey | .25 | .11 | .03 |
| Washington Redskins | | | |
| ☐ 6 Michael Irvin | 1.50 | .65 | .19 |
| Dallas Cowboys | | | |
| ☐ 7 Andre Rison | .60 | .25 | .08 |
| Dallas Cowboys | | | |
| ☐ 8 Thurman Thomas | 1.25 | .55 | .16 |
| Buffalo Bills | | | |
| ☐ 9 Barry Sanders | 2.50 | 1.15 | .30 |
| Detroit Lions | | | |
| ☐ 10 Bruce Matthews | .25 | .11 | .03 |
| Houston Oilers | | | |
| ☐ 11 Mark Rypien | .30 | .14 | .04 |
| Washington Redskins | | | |
| ☐ 12 Jeff Jaeger | .25 | .11 | .03 |
| Los Angeles Raiders | | | |
| ☐ 13 Reggie White | .60 | .25 | .08 |
| Philadelphia Eagles | | | |
| ☐ 14 Clyde Simmons | .30 | .14 | .04 |
| Philadelphia Eagles | | | |
| ☐ 15 Pat Swilling | .25 | .11 | .03 |
| New Orleans Saints | | | |
| ☐ 16 Sam Mills | .25 | .11 | .03 |
| New Orleans Saints | | | |
| ☐ 17 Ray Childress | .25 | .11 | .03 |
| Houston Oilers | | | |
| ☐ 18 Jerry Ball | .25 | .11 | .03 |
| Detroit Lions | | | |
| ☐ 19 Derrick Thomas | .60 | .25 | .08 |
| Kansas City Chiefs | | | |
| ☐ 20 Darrell Green | .25 | .11 | .03 |
| Washington Redskins | | | |
| ☐ 21 Ronnie Lott | .30 | .14 | .04 |
| Los Angeles Raiders | | | |
| ☐ 22 Steve Atwater | .25 | .11 | .03 |
| Denver Broncos | | | |
| ☐ 23 Mark Carrier | .25 | .11 | .03 |
| Chicago Bears | | | |
| ☐ 24 Jeff Gossett | .25 | .11 | .03 |
| Los Angeles Raiders | | | |

## 1992 Fleer Mark Rypien

This 15-card "Performance Highlights" subset chronicles the career of Mark Rypien, Super Bowl XXVI's Most Valuable Player. Rypien autographed over 2,000 of his cards, which were randomly inserted in wax, rack, and cello packs. Moreover, collectors could obtain three additional cards of him by mailing in ten Fleer pack proofs of purchase. The cards measure the standard size (2 1/2" by 3 1/2"). On a dark blue card face, the fronts feature color action photos outlined in the team's colors. The words "Mark Rypien Performance Highlights" appear in gold-foil lettering above the picture. The backs carry capsule summaries of different phases of Rypien's career. The cards are numbered on the back.

| | MINT | EXC | G-VG |
|---|---|---|---|
| COMPLETE SET (15) | 4.00 | 1.80 | .50 |
| COMMON RYPIEN (1-12) | .40 | .18 | .05 |
| COMMON SEND-OFF (13-15) | .60 | .25 | .08 |
| ☐ 1 A Matter of Faith | .40 | .18 | .05 |
| ☐ 2 Mr. Everything | .40 | .18 | .05 |
| ☐ 3 Great Expectations | .40 | .18 | .05 |
| ☐ 4 Hills and Valleys | .40 | .18 | .05 |
| ☐ 5 Breakout Season | .40 | .18 | .05 |
| ☐ 6 The End of the | .40 | .18 | .05 |
| Beginning | | | |
| ☐ 7 Bowled Over | .40 | .18 | .05 |
| ☐ 8 Watching and Waiting | .40 | .18 | .05 |
| ☐ 9 QB Controversy | .40 | .18 | .05 |

## 1992 Fleer Rookie Sensations

This 20-card subset was inserted in 1992 Fleer cello packs. The cards measure the standard size (2 1/2" by 3 1/2"). The color action player photos on the fronts are slightly tilted to the left and have shadow borders on the left and bottom. The card face is designed like a football field, with a green background sectioned off by white yard line markers. At the card top, the words "Rookie Sensations" are accented by gold foil stripes representing the flight of a football, while the player's name appears in gold foil lettering below the picture. The backs have a similar design to the fronts and present a career summary. The cards are numbered on the back.

| | | | |
|---|---|---|---|
| ☐ 10 Redemption | .40 | .18 | .05 |
| ☐ 11 Pain and Pressure | .40 | .18 | .05 |
| ☐ 12 Jubilation | .40 | .18 | .05 |
| ☐ 13 A Year For The Books | .60 | .25 | .08 |
| ☐ 14 No Big Surprise | .60 | .25 | .08 |
| ☐ 15 Father Figure | .60 | .25 | .08 |
| ☐ AU Mark Rypien AU | 35.00 | 16.00 | 4.40 |
| (Certified Autograph) | | | |

## 1992 Fleer Team Leaders

This 24-card subset was inserted in 1992 Fleer rack packs. The cards measure the standard size (2 1/2" by 3 1/2"). The color action player photos on the fronts are bordered in black. The player's name, team, position, and a "Team Leader" logo appear in gold foil lettering toward the bottom of the card face. On a light grayish-blue background, the backs feature a color head shot in an oval frame and present career summary. The cards are numbered on the back.

| | MINT | EXC | G-VG |
|---|---|---|---|
| COMPLETE SET (24) | 175.00 | 80.00 | 22.00 |
| COMMON PLAYER (1-24) | 6.00 | 2.70 | .75 |
| | | | |
| ☐ 1 Chris Miller | 6.50 | 2.90 | .80 |
| Atlanta Falcons | | | |
| ☐ 2 Neal Anderson | 6.50 | 2.90 | .80 |
| Chicago Bears | | | |
| ☐ 3 Emmitt Smith | 100.00 | 45.00 | 12.50 |
| Dallas Cowboys | | | |
| ☐ 4 Chris Spielman | 6.00 | 2.70 | .75 |
| Detroit Lions | | | |
| ☐ 5 Brian Noble | 6.00 | 2.70 | .75 |
| Green Bay Packers | | | |
| ☐ 6 Jim Everett | 6.50 | 2.90 | .80 |
| Los Angeles Rams | | | |
| ☐ 7 Joey Browner | 6.00 | 2.70 | .75 |
| Minnesota Vikings | | | |
| ☐ 8 Sam Mills | 6.00 | 2.70 | .75 |
| New Orleans Saints | | | |
| ☐ 9 Rodney Hampton | 15.00 | 6.75 | 1.90 |
| New York Giants | | | |
| ☐ 10 Reggie White | 10.00 | 4.50 | 1.25 |
| Philadelphia Eagles | | | |
| ☐ 11 Tim McDonald | 6.00 | 2.70 | .75 |
| Phoenix Cardinals | | | |
| ☐ 12 Charles Haley | 6.00 | 2.70 | .75 |
| San Francisco 49ers | | | |
| ☐ 13 Mark Rypien | 6.50 | 2.90 | .80 |
| Washington Redskins | | | |
| ☐ 14 Cornelius Bennett | 6.50 | 2.90 | .80 |
| Buffalo Bills | | | |
| ☐ 15 Clay Matthews | 6.00 | 2.70 | .75 |
| Cleveland Browns | | | |
| ☐ 16 John Elway | 25.00 | 11.50 | 3.10 |
| Denver Broncos | | | |
| ☐ 17 Warren Moon | 10.00 | 4.50 | 1.25 |
| Houston Oilers | | | |
| ☐ 18 Derrick Thomas | 10.00 | 4.50 | 1.25 |
| Kansas City Chiefs | | | |
| ☐ 19 Greg Townsend | 6.00 | 2.70 | .75 |
| Los Angeles Raiders | | | |
| ☐ 20 Bruce Armstrong | 6.00 | 2.70 | .75 |
| New England Patriots | | | |
| ☐ 21 Brad Baxter | 6.00 | 2.70 | .75 |
| New York Jets | | | |
| ☐ 22 Rod Woodson | 6.50 | 2.90 | .80 |
| Pittsburgh Steelers | | | |
| ☐ 23 Marion Butts | 6.50 | 2.90 | .80 |
| San Diego Chargers | | | |
| ☐ 24 Rufus Porter | 6.00 | 2.70 | .75 |
| Seattle Seahawks | | | |

## 1993 Fleer Promo Panel

Measuring approximately 7 1/2" by 10 1/2", this nine-card promo panel was issued to preview the design of the 1993 Fleer football set. The sheet is not perforated, but if the cards were cut, they would measure the standard-size (2 1/2" by 3 1/2"). The fronts feature color action player photos inside silver borders. In transparent block lettering, the player's last name appears at the bottom, with his team name and position below in much smaller print. On a team color-coded background, the horizontal backs have a player cutout, biography, career summary and, on a white panel, statistics. All the cards are numbered "000" and they are listed below beginning in the upper left and proceeding across and down toward the lower right.

| | MINT | EXC | G-VG |
|---|---|---|---|
| COMPLETE SET (1) | 5.00 | 2.00 | .50 |
| COMMON PANEL | 5.00 | 2.00 | .50 |
| | | | |
| ☐ 1 Steve Young | 5.00 | 2.00 | .50 |
| San Francisco 49ers | | | |
| Kenny Walker | | | |
| Denver Broncos | | | |
| Chip Lohmiller | | | |
| Washington Redskins | | | |
| Kevin Greene | | | |
| Los Angeles Rams | | | |
| Fleer Ad Card | | | |
| Craig Heyward | | | |
| New Orleans Saints | | | |
| Ernie Jones | | | |
| Phoenix Cardinals | | | |
| Emmitt Smith | | | |
| Dallas Cowboys | | | |
| Keith Byars | | | |
| Philadelphia Eagles | | | |

## 1993 Fleer

The 1993 Fleer football set consists of 500 cards, each measuring the standard size (2 1/2" by 3 1/2"). The color action player photos on the fronts are UV coated and framed by silver metallic borders. At the bottom of the picture, the player's last name is printed in transparent lettering that has an embossed look. The team affiliation and position appear at the lower right corner. On team color-coded panels, the horizontal backs carry a color close-up photo, biography, player profile, team logo, and statistics. Topical subsets featured are Award Winners (236-240, 253-257), League Leaders (241-243, 258-262), and Pro Visions (246-248, 263-264). The cards are numbered on the back.

| | MINT | EXC | G-VG |
|---|---|---|---|
| COMPLETE SET (500) | 20.00 | 9.00 | 2.50 |
| COMMON PLAYER (1-500) | .05 | .02 | .01 |

| | | | |
|---|---|---|---|
| ☐ 1 Dan Saleaumua | .05 | .02 | .01 |
| Kansas City Chiefs | | | |
| ☐ 2 Bryan Cox | .08 | .04 | .01 |
| Miami Dolphins | | | |
| ☐ 3 Dermontti Dawson | .05 | .02 | .01 |
| Pittsburgh Steelers | | | |
| ☐ 4 Michael Jackson | .10 | .05 | .01 |
| Cleveland Browns | | | |
| ☐ 5 Calvin Williams | .10 | .05 | .01 |
| Philadelphia Eagles | | | |
| ☐ 6 Terry McDaniel | .05 | .02 | .01 |
| Los Angeles Raiders | | | |
| ☐ 7 Jack Del Rio | .05 | .02 | .01 |
| Minnesota Vikings | | | |
| ☐ 8 Steve Atwater | .08 | .04 | .01 |
| Denver Broncos | | | |
| ☐ 9 Ernie Jones | .05 | .02 | .01 |
| Phoenix Cardinals | | | |
| ☐ 10 Brad Muster | .08 | .04 | .01 |
| Chicago Bears | | | |
| (Signed with | | | |
| New Orleans Saints) | | | |
| ☐ 11 Harold Green | .08 | .04 | .01 |
| Cincinnati Bengals | | | |
| ☐ 12 Eric Bieniemy | .08 | .04 | .01 |
| San Diego Chargers | | | |
| ☐ 13 Eric Dorsey | .05 | .02 | .01 |
| New York Giants | | | |
| ☐ 14 Fred Barnett | .10 | .05 | .01 |
| Philadelphia Eagles | | | |
| ☐ 15 Cleveland Gary | .08 | .04 | .01 |
| Los Angeles Rams | | | |
| ☐ 16 Darion Conner | .05 | .02 | .01 |
| Atlanta Falcons | | | |
| ☐ 17 Jerry Ball | .05 | .02 | .01 |
| Detroit Lions | | | |
| (Traded to | | | |
| Cleveland Browns) | | | |
| ☐ 18 Tony Casillas | .05 | .02 | .01 |
| Dallas Cowboys | | | |
| ☐ 19 Brian Blades | .08 | .04 | .01 |
| Seattle Seahawks | | | |
| ☐ 20 Tony Bennett | .05 | .02 | .01 |
| Green Bay Packers | | | |
| ☐ 21 Reggie Cobb | .10 | .05 | .01 |
| Tampa Bay Buccaneers | | | |
| ☐ 22 Kurt Gouveia | .05 | .02 | .01 |
| Washington Redskins | | | |
| ☐ 23 Greg McMurtry | .05 | .02 | .01 |
| New England Patriots | | | |
| ☐ 24 Kyle Clifton | .05 | .02 | .01 |
| New York Jets | | | |
| ☐ 25 Trace Armstrong | .05 | .02 | .01 |
| Chicago Bears | | | |
| ☐ 26 Terry Allen | .10 | .05 | .01 |
| Minnesota Vikings | | | |
| ☐ 27 Steve Bono | .15 | .07 | .02 |
| San Francisco 49ers | | | |
| ☐ 28 Barry Word | .10 | .05 | .01 |
| Kansas City Chiefs | | | |
| ☐ 29 Mark Duper | .08 | .04 | .01 |
| Miami Dolphins | | | |
| ☐ 30 Nate Newton | .05 | .02 | .01 |
| Dallas Cowboys | | | |
| ☐ 31 Will Wolford | .05 | .02 | .01 |
| Buffalo Bills | | | |
| (Signed with | | | |
| Indianapolis Colts) | | | |
| ☐ 32 Curtis Duncan | .08 | .04 | .01 |
| Houston Oilers | | | |
| ☐ 33 Nick Bell | .08 | .04 | .01 |
| Los Angeles Raiders | | | |
| ☐ 34 Don Beebe | .10 | .05 | .01 |
| Buffalo Bills | | | |
| ☐ 35 Mike Croel | .08 | .04 | .01 |
| Denver Broncos | | | |
| ☐ 36 Rich Camarillo | .05 | .02 | .01 |
| Phoenix Cardinals | | | |
| ☐ 37 Wade Wilson | .08 | .04 | .01 |
| Atlanta Falcons | | | |
| (Signed with | | | |
| New Orleans Saints) | | | |
| ☐ 38 John Taylor | .10 | .05 | .01 |
| San Francisco 49ers | | | |
| ☐ 39 Marion Butts | .10 | .05 | .01 |
| San Diego Chargers | | | |
| ☐ 40 Rodney Hampton | .30 | .14 | .04 |
| New York Giants | | | |
| ☐ 41 Seth Joyner | .08 | .04 | .01 |
| Philadelphia Eagles | | | |
| ☐ 42 Wilber Marshall | .08 | .04 | .01 |
| Washington Redskins | | | |
| ☐ 43 Bobby Hebert | .10 | .05 | .01 |
| New Orleans Saints | | | |
| (Signed with | | | |
| Atlanta Falcons) | | | |
| ☐ 44 Bennie Blades | .05 | .02 | .01 |
| Detroit Lions | | | |

| | | | |
|---|---|---|---|
| ☐ 45 Thomas Everett | .05 | .02 | .01 |
| Dallas Cowboys | | | |
| ☐ 46 Ricky Sanders | .08 | .04 | .01 |
| Washington Redskins | | | |
| ☐ 47 Matt Brock | .05 | .02 | .01 |
| Green Bay Packers | | | |
| ☐ 48 Lawrence Dawsey | .10 | .05 | .01 |
| Tampa Bay Buccaneers | | | |
| ☐ 49 Brad Edwards | .05 | .02 | .01 |
| Washington Redskins | | | |
| ☐ 50 Vincent Brown | .05 | .02 | .01 |
| New England Patriots | | | |
| ☐ 51 Jeff Lageman | .05 | .02 | .01 |
| New York Jets | | | |
| ☐ 52 Mark Carrier | .08 | .04 | .01 |
| Chicago Bears | | | |
| ☐ 53 Cris Carter | .10 | .05 | .01 |
| Minnesota Vikings | | | |
| ☐ 54 Brent Jones | .10 | .05 | .01 |
| San Francisco 49ers | | | |
| ☐ 55 Barry Foster | .25 | .11 | .03 |
| Pittsburgh Steelers | | | |
| ☐ 56 Derrick Thomas | .15 | .07 | .02 |
| Kansas City Chiefs | | | |
| ☐ 57 Scott Zolak | .05 | .02 | .01 |
| New England Patriots | | | |
| ☐ 58 Mark Stepnoski | .05 | .02 | .01 |
| Dallas Cowboys | | | |
| ☐ 59 Eric Metcalf | .10 | .05 | .01 |
| Cleveland Browns | | | |
| ☐ 60 Al Smith | .05 | .02 | .01 |
| Houston Oilers | | | |
| ☐ 61 Ronnie Harmon | .08 | .04 | .01 |
| San Diego Chargers | | | |
| ☐ 62 Cornelius Bennett | .10 | .05 | .01 |
| Buffalo Bills | | | |
| ☐ 63 Karl Mecklenburg | .08 | .04 | .01 |
| Denver Broncos | | | |
| ☐ 64 Chris Chandler | .08 | .04 | .01 |
| Phoenix Cardinals | | | |
| ☐ 65 Toi Cook | .05 | .02 | .01 |
| New Orleans Saints | | | |
| ☐ 66 Tim Krumrie | .05 | .02 | .01 |
| Cincinnati Bengals | | | |
| ☐ 67 Gill Byrd | .08 | .04 | .01 |
| San Diego Chargers | | | |
| ☐ 68 Mark Jackson | .08 | .04 | .01 |
| Denver Broncos | | | |
| (Signed with | | | |
| New York Giants) | | | |
| ☐ 69 Tim Harris | .05 | .02 | .01 |
| San Francisco 49ers | | | |
| (Signed with | | | |
| Philadelphia Eagles) | | | |
| ☐ 70 Shane Conlan | .05 | .02 | .01 |
| Buffalo Bills | | | |
| (Signed with | | | |
| Los Angeles Rams) | | | |
| ☐ 71 Moe Gardner | .05 | .02 | .01 |
| Atlanta Falcons | | | |
| ☐ 72 Lomas Brown | .05 | .02 | .01 |
| Detroit Lions | | | |
| ☐ 73 Charles Haley | .08 | .04 | .01 |
| Dallas Cowboys | | | |
| ☐ 74 Mark Rypien | .08 | .04 | .01 |
| Washington Redskins | | | |
| ☐ 75 LeRoy Butler | .05 | .02 | .01 |
| Green Bay Packers | | | |
| ☐ 76 Steve DeBerg | .08 | .04 | .01 |
| Tampa Bay Buccaneers | | | |
| ☐ 77 Darrell Green | .08 | .04 | .01 |
| Washington Redskins | | | |
| ☐ 78 Marv Cook | .05 | .02 | .01 |
| New England Patriots | | | |
| ☐ 79 Chris Burkett | .05 | .02 | .01 |
| New York Jets | | | |
| ☐ 80 Richard Dent | .08 | .04 | .01 |
| Chicago Bears | | | |
| ☐ 81 Roger Craig | .08 | .04 | .01 |
| Minnesota Vikings | | | |
| ☐ 82 Amp Lee | .08 | .04 | .01 |
| San Francisco 49ers | | | |
| ☐ 83 Eric Green | .10 | .05 | .01 |
| Pittsburgh Steelers | | | |
| ☐ 84 Willie Davis | .10 | .05 | .01 |
| Kansas City Chiefs | | | |
| ☐ 85 Mark Higgs | .10 | .05 | .01 |
| Miami Dolphins | | | |
| ☐ 86 Carlton Haselrig | .05 | .02 | .01 |
| Pittsburgh Steelers | | | |
| ☐ 87 Tommy Vardell | .08 | .04 | .01 |
| Cleveland Browns | | | |
| ☐ 88 Haywood Jeffires | .10 | .05 | .01 |
| Houston Oilers | | | |
| ☐ 89 Tim Brown | .25 | .11 | .03 |
| Los Angeles Raiders | | | |
| ☐ 90 Randall McDaniel | .05 | .02 | .01 |
| Minnesota Vikings | | | |

| | | | |
|---|---|---|---|
| ☐ 91 John Elway | .35 | .16 | .04 |
| Denver Broncos | | | |
| ☐ 92 Ken Harvey | .05 | .02 | .01 |
| Phoenix Cardinals | | | |
| ☐ 93 Joel Hilgenberg | .05 | .02 | .01 |
| New Orleans Saints | | | |
| ☐ 94 Steve Wallace | .05 | .02 | .01 |
| San Francisco 49ers | | | |
| ☐ 95 Stan Humphries | .10 | .05 | .01 |
| San Diego Chargers | | | |
| ☐ 96 Greg Jackson | .05 | .02 | .01 |
| New York Giants | | | |
| ☐ 97 Clyde Simmons | .08 | .04 | .01 |
| Philadelphia Eagles | | | |
| ☐ 98 Jim Everett | .05 | .02 | .01 |
| Los Angeles Rams | | | |
| ☐ 99 Michael Haynes | .20 | .09 | .03 |
| Atlanta Falcons | | | |
| ☐ 100 Mel Gray | .08 | .04 | .01 |
| Detroit Lions | | | |
| ☐ 101 Alvin Harper | .25 | .11 | .03 |
| Dallas Cowboys | | | |
| ☐ 102 Art Monk | .10 | .05 | .01 |
| Washington Redskins | | | |
| ☐ 103 Brett Favre | .75 | .35 | .09 |
| Green Bay Packers | | | |
| ☐ 104 Keith McCants | .05 | .02 | .01 |
| Tampa Bay Buccaneers | | | |
| ☐ 105 Charles Mann | .08 | .04 | .01 |
| Washington Redskins | | | |
| ☐ 106 Leonard Russell | .08 | .04 | .01 |
| New England Patriots | | | |
| ☐ 107 Mo Lewis | .05 | .02 | .01 |
| New York Jets | | | |
| ☐ 108 Shaun Gayle | .05 | .02 | .01 |
| Chicago Bears | | | |
| ☐ 109 Chris Doleman | .08 | .04 | .01 |
| Minnesota Vikings | | | |
| ☐ 110 Tim McDonald | .05 | .02 | .01 |
| Phoenix Cardinals | | | |
| (Signed with | | | |
| San Francisco 49ers) | | | |
| ☐ 111 Louis Oliver | .05 | .02 | .01 |
| Miami Dolphins | | | |
| ☐ 112 Greg Lloyd | .05 | .02 | .01 |
| Pittsburgh Steelers | | | |
| ☐ 113 Chip Banks | .05 | .02 | .01 |
| Indianapolis Colts | | | |
| ☐ 114 Sean Jones | .05 | .02 | .01 |
| Houston Oilers | | | |
| ☐ 115 Ethan Horton | .05 | .02 | .01 |
| Los Angeles Raiders | | | |
| ☐ 116 Kenneth Davis | .08 | .04 | .01 |
| Buffalo Bills | | | |
| ☐ 117 Simon Fletcher | .08 | .04 | .01 |
| Denver Broncos | | | |
| ☐ 118 Johnny Johnson | .10 | .05 | .01 |
| Phoenix Cardinals | | | |
| (Traded to | | | |
| New York Jets) | | | |
| ☐ 119 Vaughan Johnson | .05 | .02 | .01 |
| New Orleans Saints | | | |
| ☐ 120 Derrick Fenner | .05 | .02 | .01 |
| Cincinnati Bengals | | | |
| ☐ 121 Nate Lewis | .08 | .04 | .01 |
| San Diego Chargers | | | |
| ☐ 122 Pepper Johnson | .05 | .02 | .01 |
| New York Giants | | | |
| ☐ 123 Heath Sherman | .05 | .02 | .01 |
| Philadelphia Eagles | | | |
| ☐ 124 Darryl Henley | .05 | .02 | .01 |
| Los Angeles Rams | | | |
| ☐ 125 Pierce Holt | .05 | .02 | .01 |
| San Francisco 49ers | | | |
| (Signed with | | | |
| Atlanta Falcons) | | | |
| ☐ 126 Herman Moore | .35 | .16 | .04 |
| Detroit Lions | | | |
| ☐ 127 Michael Irvin | .40 | .18 | .05 |
| Dallas Cowboys | | | |
| ☐ 128 Tommy Kane | .05 | .02 | .01 |
| Seattle Seahawks | | | |
| ☐ 129 Jackie Harris | .30 | .14 | .04 |
| Green Bay Packers | | | |
| ☐ 130 Hardy Nickerson | .05 | .02 | .01 |
| Pittsburgh Steelers | | | |
| (Signed with | | | |
| Tampa Bay Buccaneers) | | | |
| ☐ 131 Chip Lohmiller | .05 | .02 | .01 |
| Washington Redskins | | | |
| ☐ 132 Andre Tippett | .05 | .02 | .01 |
| New England Patriots | | | |
| ☐ 133 Leonard Marshall | .08 | .04 | .01 |
| New York Giants | | | |
| (Signed with | | | |
| New York Jets) | | | |
| ☐ 134 Craig Heyward | .05 | .02 | .01 |
| New Orleans Saints | | | |
| (Signed with | | | |
| Chicago Bears) | | | |
| ☐ 135 Anthony Carter | .08 | .04 | .01 |
| Minnesota Vikings | | | |
| ☐ 136 Tom Rathman | .08 | .04 | .01 |
| San Francisco 49ers | | | |
| ☐ 137 Lorenzo White | .08 | .04 | .01 |
| Houston Oilers | | | |
| ☐ 138 Nick Lowery | .05 | .02 | .01 |
| Kansas City Chiefs | | | |
| ☐ 139 John Offerdahl | .05 | .02 | .01 |
| Miami Dolphins | | | |
| ☐ 140 Neil O'Donnell | .25 | .11 | .03 |
| Pittsburgh Steelers | | | |
| ☐ 141 Clarence Verdin | .05 | .02 | .01 |
| Indianapolis Colts | | | |
| ☐ 142 Ernest Givins | .08 | .04 | .01 |
| Houston Oilers | | | |
| ☐ 143 Todd Marinovich | .05 | .02 | .01 |
| Los Angeles Raiders | | | |
| ☐ 144 Jeff Wright | .05 | .02 | .01 |
| Buffalo Bills | | | |
| ☐ 145 Michael Brooks | .05 | .02 | .01 |
| Denver Broncos | | | |
| ☐ 146 Freddie Joe Nunn | .05 | .02 | .01 |
| Phoenix Cardinals | | | |
| ☐ 147 William Perry | .08 | .04 | .01 |
| Chicago Bears | | | |
| ☐ 148 Daniel Stubbs | .05 | .02 | .01 |
| Cincinnati Bengals | | | |
| ☐ 149 Morten Andersen | .08 | .04 | .01 |
| New Orleans Saints | | | |
| ☐ 150 David Meggett | .08 | .04 | .01 |
| New York Giants | | | |
| ☐ 151 Andre Waters | .05 | .02 | .01 |
| Philadelphia Eagles | | | |
| ☐ 152 Todd Lyght | .05 | .02 | .01 |
| Los Angeles Rams | | | |
| ☐ 153 Chris Miller | .10 | .05 | .01 |
| Atlanta Falcons | | | |
| ☐ 154 Rodney Peete | .08 | .04 | .01 |
| Detroit Lions | | | |
| ☐ 155 Jim Jeffcoat | .05 | .02 | .01 |
| Dallas Cowboys | | | |
| ☐ 156 Cortez Kennedy | .10 | .05 | .01 |
| Seattle Seahawks | | | |
| ☐ 157 Johnny Holland | .05 | .02 | .01 |
| Green Bay Packers | | | |
| ☐ 158 Ricky Reynolds | .05 | .02 | .01 |
| Tampa Bay Buccaneers | | | |
| ☐ 159 Kevin Greene | .05 | .02 | .01 |
| Los Angeles Rams | | | |
| (Signed with | | | |
| Pittsburgh Steelers) | | | |
| ☐ 160 Jeff Herrod | .05 | .02 | .01 |
| Indianapolis Colts | | | |
| ☐ 161 Bruce Matthews | .08 | .04 | .01 |
| Houston Oilers | | | |
| ☐ 162 Anthony Smith | .05 | .02 | .01 |
| Los Angeles Raiders | | | |
| ☐ 163 Henry Jones | .05 | .02 | .01 |
| Buffalo Bills | | | |
| ☐ 164 Rob Burnett | .05 | .02 | .01 |
| Cleveland Browns | | | |
| ☐ 165 Eric Swann | .08 | .04 | .01 |
| Phoenix Cardinals | | | |
| ☐ 166 Tom Waddle | .10 | .05 | .01 |
| Chicago Bears | | | |
| ☐ 167 Alfred Williams | .05 | .02 | .01 |
| Cincinnati Bengals | | | |
| ☐ 168 Darren Carrington | .10 | .05 | .01 |
| San Diego Chargers | | | |
| ☐ 169 Mike Sherrard | .05 | .02 | .01 |
| San Francisco 49ers | | | |
| (Signed with | | | |
| New York Giants) | | | |
| ☐ 170 Frank Reich | .08 | .04 | .01 |
| Buffalo Bills | | | |
| ☐ 171 Anthony Newman | .05 | .02 | .01 |
| Los Angeles Rams | | | |
| ☐ 172 Mike Pritchard | .10 | .05 | .01 |
| Atlanta Falcons | | | |
| ☐ 173 Andre Ware | .08 | .04 | .01 |
| Detroit Lions | | | |
| ☐ 174 Daryl Johnston | .10 | .05 | .01 |
| Dallas Cowboys | | | |
| ☐ 175 Rufus Porter | .05 | .02 | .01 |
| Seattle Seahawks | | | |
| ☐ 176 Reggie White | .15 | .07 | .02 |
| Philadelphia Eagles | | | |
| (Signed with | | | |
| Green Bay Packers) | | | |
| ☐ 177 Charles Mincy | .20 | .09 | .03 |
| Kansas City Chiefs | | | |
| ☐ 178 Pete Stoyanovich | .05 | .02 | .01 |
| Miami Dolphins | | | |
| ☐ 179 Rod Woodson | .10 | .05 | .01 |
| Pittsburgh Steelers | | | |

| | | | | |
|---|---|---|---|---|
| ☐ 180 Anthony Johnson<br>Indianapolis Colts | .05 | .02 | .01 |
| ☐ 181 Cody Carlson<br>Houston Oilers | .20 | .09 | .03 |
| ☐ 182 Gaston Green<br>Denver Broncos<br>(Traded to<br>Los Angeles Raiders) | .08 | .04 | .01 |
| ☐ 183 Audray McMillian<br>Minnesota Vikings | .05 | .02 | .01 |
| ☐ 184 Mike Johnson<br>Cleveland Browns | .05 | .02 | .01 |
| ☐ 185 Aeneas Williams<br>Phoenix Cardinals | .05 | .02 | .01 |
| ☐ 186 Jarrod Bunch<br>New York Giants | .08 | .04 | .01 |
| ☐ 187 Dennis Smith<br>Denver Broncos | .05 | .02 | .01 |
| ☐ 188 Quinn Early<br>New Orleans Saints | .08 | .04 | .01 |
| ☐ 189 James Hasty<br>New York Jets | .05 | .02 | .01 |
| ☐ 190 Darryl Talley<br>Buffalo Bills | .05 | .02 | .01 |
| ☐ 191 Jon Vaughn<br>New England Patriots | .05 | .02 | .01 |
| ☐ 192 Andre Rison<br>Atlanta Falcons | .25 | .11 | .03 |
| ☐ 193 Kelvin Pritchett<br>Detroit Lions | .05 | .02 | .01 |
| ☐ 194 Ken Norton Jr.<br>Dallas Cowboys | .08 | .04 | .01 |
| ☐ 195 Chris Warren<br>Seattle Seahawks | .15 | .07 | .02 |
| ☐ 196 Sterling Sharpe<br>Green Bay Packers | .40 | .18 | .05 |
| ☐ 197 Christian Okoye<br>Kansas City Chiefs | .08 | .04 | .01 |
| ☐ 198 Richmond Webb<br>Miami Dolphins | .05 | .02 | .01 |
| ☐ 199 James Francis<br>Cincinnati Bengals | .05 | .02 | .01 |
| ☐ 200 Reggie Langhorne<br>Indianapolis Colts | .08 | .04 | .01 |
| ☐ 201 J.J. Birden<br>Kansas City Chiefs | .08 | .04 | .01 |
| ☐ 202 Aaron Wallace<br>Los Angeles Raiders | .05 | .02 | .01 |
| ☐ 203 Henry Thomas<br>Minnesota Vikings | .05 | .02 | .01 |
| ☐ 204 Clay Matthews<br>Cleveland Browns | .08 | .04 | .01 |
| ☐ 205 Robert Massey<br>Phoenix Cardinals | .05 | .02 | .01 |
| ☐ 206 Donnell Woolford<br>Chicago Bears | .05 | .02 | .01 |
| ☐ 207 Ricky Watters<br>San Francisco 49ers | .30 | .14 | .04 |
| ☐ 208 Wayne Martin<br>New Orleans Saints | .05 | .02 | .01 |
| ☐ 209 Rob Moore<br>New York Jets | .10 | .05 | .01 |
| ☐ 210 Steve Tasker<br>Buffalo Bills | .05 | .02 | .01 |
| ☐ 211 Jackie Slater<br>Los Angeles Rams | .05 | .02 | .01 |
| ☐ 212 Steve Young<br>San Francisco 49ers | .25 | .11 | .03 |
| ☐ 213 Barry Sanders<br>Detroit Lions | .75 | .35 | .09 |
| ☐ 214 Jay Novacek<br>Dallas Cowboys | .10 | .05 | .01 |
| ☐ 215 Eugene Robinson<br>Seattle Seahawks | .05 | .02 | .01 |
| ☐ 216 Duane Bickett<br>Indianapolis Colts | .05 | .02 | .01 |
| ☐ 217 Broderick Thomas<br>Tampa Bay Buccaneers | .05 | .02 | .01 |
| ☐ 218 David Fulcher<br>Cincinnati Bengals | .05 | .02 | .01 |
| ☐ 219 Rohn Stark<br>Indianapolis Colts | .05 | .02 | .01 |
| ☐ 220 Warren Moon<br>Houston Oilers | .15 | .07 | .02 |
| ☐ 221 Steve Wisniewski<br>Los Angeles Raiders | .05 | .02 | .01 |
| ☐ 222 Nate Odomes<br>Buffalo Bills | .08 | .04 | .01 |
| ☐ 223 Shannon Sharpe<br>Denver Broncos | .20 | .09 | .03 |
| ☐ 224 Byron Evans<br>Philadelphia Eagles | .05 | .02 | .01 |
| ☐ 225 Mark Collins<br>New York Giants | .05 | .02 | .01 |
| ☐ 226 Rod Bernstine<br>San Diego Chargers<br>(Signed with<br>Denver Broncos) | .08 | .04 | .01 |
| ☐ 227 Sam Mills<br>New Orleans Saints | .08 | .04 | .01 |
| ☐ 228 Marvin Washington<br>New York Jets | .05 | .02 | .01 |
| ☐ 229 Thurman Thomas<br>Buffalo Bills | .35 | .16 | .04 |
| ☐ 230 Brent Williams<br>New England Patriots | .05 | .02 | .01 |
| ☐ 231 Jessie Tuggle<br>Atlanta Falcons | .05 | .02 | .01 |
| ☐ 232 Chris Spielman<br>Detroit Lions | .05 | .02 | .01 |
| ☐ 233 Emmitt Smith<br>Dallas Cowboys | 2.00 | .90 | .25 |
| ☐ 234 John L. Williams<br>Seattle Seahawks | .08 | .04 | .01 |
| ☐ 235 Jeff Cross<br>Miami Dolphins | .05 | .02 | .01 |
| ☐ 236 Chris Doleman AW<br>Minnesota Vikings | .05 | .02 | .01 |
| ☐ 237 John Elway AW<br>Denver Broncos | .15 | .07 | .02 |
| ☐ 238 Barry Foster AW<br>Pittsburgh Steelers | .12 | .05 | .02 |
| ☐ 239 Cortez Kennedy AW<br>Seattle Seahawks | .08 | .04 | .01 |
| ☐ 240 Steve Young AW<br>San Francisco 49ers | .12 | .05 | .02 |
| ☐ 241 Barry Foster LL<br>Pittsburgh Steelers | .12 | .05 | .02 |
| ☐ 242 Warren Moon LL<br>Houston Oilers | .10 | .05 | .01 |
| ☐ 243 Sterling Sharpe LL<br>Green Bay Packers | .20 | .09 | .03 |
| ☐ 244 Emmitt Smith LL<br>Dallas Cowboys | .75 | .35 | .09 |
| ☐ 245 Thurman Thomas LL<br>Buffalo Bills | .15 | .07 | .02 |
| ☐ 246 Michael Irvin PV<br>Dallas Cowboys | .20 | .09 | .03 |
| ☐ 247 Steve Young PV<br>San Francisco 49ers | .12 | .05 | .02 |
| ☐ 248 Barry Foster PV<br>Pittsburgh Steelers | .12 | .05 | .02 |
| ☐ 249 Checklist<br>Teams Atlanta<br>through Detroit | .05 | .02 | .01 |
| ☐ 250 Checklist<br>Teams Detroit<br>through Miami | .05 | .02 | .01 |
| ☐ 251 Checklist<br>Teams Minnesota<br>through Pittsburgh | .05 | .02 | .01 |
| ☐ 252 Checklist<br>Teams Pittsburgh<br>through Washington<br>and Specials | .05 | .02 | .01 |
| ☐ 253 Troy Aikman AW<br>Dallas Cowboys | .40 | .18 | .05 |
| ☐ 254 Jason Hanson AW<br>Detroit Lions | .05 | .02 | .01 |
| ☐ 255 Carl Pickens AW<br>Cincinnati Bengals | .08 | .04 | .01 |
| ☐ 256 Santana Dotson AW<br>Tampa Bay Buccaneers | .08 | .04 | .01 |
| ☐ 257 Dale Carter AW<br>Kansas City Chiefs | .08 | .04 | .01 |
| ☐ 258 Clyde Simmons LL<br>Philadelphia Eagles | .05 | .02 | .01 |
| ☐ 259 Audray McMillian LL<br>Minnesota Vikings | .05 | .02 | .01 |
| ☐ 260 Henry Jones LL<br>Buffalo Bills | .05 | .02 | .01 |
| ☐ 261 Deion Sanders LL<br>Atlanta Falcons | .08 | .04 | .01 |
| ☐ 262 Haywood Jeffires LL<br>Houston Oilers | .08 | .04 | .01 |
| ☐ 263 Deion Sanders PV<br>Atlanta Falcons | .08 | .04 | .01 |
| ☐ 264 Andre Reed PV<br>Buffalo Bills | .08 | .04 | .01 |
| ☐ 265 Vince Workman<br>Green Bay Packers<br>(Signed with<br>Tampa Bay Buccaneers) | .05 | .02 | .01 |
| ☐ 266 Robert Brown<br>Green Bay Packers | .05 | .02 | .01 |
| ☐ 267 Ray Agnew<br>New England Patriots | .05 | .02 | .01 |
| ☐ 268 Ronnie Lott<br>Los Angeles Raiders<br>(Signed with<br>New York Jets) | .10 | .05 | .01 |
| ☐ 269 Wesley Carroll<br>New Orleans Saints | .05 | .02 | .01 |
| ☐ 270 John Randle<br>Minnesota Vikings | .05 | .02 | .01 |

| | | | |
|---|---|---|---|
| ☐ 271 Rodney Culver........................ | .08 | .04 | .01 |
| Indianapolis Colts | | | |
| ☐ 272 David Alexander................... | .05 | .02 | .01 |
| Philadelphia Eagles | | | |
| ☐ 273 Troy Aikman........................ | 1.25 | .55 | .16 |
| Dallas Cowboys | | | |
| ☐ 274 Bernie Kosar ....................... | .10 | .05 | .01 |
| Cleveland Browns | | | |
| ☐ 275 Scott Case ........................... | .05 | .02 | .01 |
| Atlanta Falcons | | | |
| ☐ 276 Dan McGwire ...................... | .08 | .04 | .01 |
| Seattle Seahawks | | | |
| ☐ 277 John Alt ............................... | .05 | .02 | .01 |
| Kansas City Chiefs | | | |
| ☐ 278 Dan Marino .......................... | .75 | .35 | .09 |
| Miami Dolphins | | | |
| ☐ 279 Santana Dotson..................... | .10 | .05 | .01 |
| Tampa Bay Buccaneers | | | |
| ☐ 280 Johnny Mitchell.................... | .25 | .11 | .03 |
| New York Jets | | | |
| ☐ 281 Alonzo Spellman ................... | .08 | .04 | .01 |
| Chicago Bears | | | |
| ☐ 282 Adrian Cooper ...................... | .05 | .02 | .01 |
| Pittsburgh Steelers | | | |
| ☐ 283 Gary Clark ........................... | .08 | .04 | .01 |
| Washington Redskins | | | |
| (Signed with | | | |
| Phoenix Cardinals) | | | |
| ☐ 284 Vance Johnson ..................... | .08 | .04 | .01 |
| Denver Broncos | | | |
| ☐ 285 Eric Martin ........................... | .08 | .04 | .01 |
| New Orleans Saints | | | |
| ☐ 286 Jesse Solomon ..................... | .05 | .02 | .01 |
| Atlanta Falcons | | | |
| ☐ 287 Carl Banks........................... | .05 | .02 | .01 |
| New York Giants | | | |
| ☐ 288 Harris Barton ....................... | .05 | .02 | .01 |
| San Francisco 49ers | | | |
| ☐ 289 Jim Harbaugh ....................... | .08 | .04 | .01 |
| Chicago Bears | | | |
| ☐ 290 Bubba McDowell ................... | .05 | .02 | .01 |
| Houston Oilers | | | |
| ☐ 291 Anthony McDowell.............. | .10 | .05 | .01 |
| Tampa Bay Buccaneers | | | |
| ☐ 292 Terrell Buckley .................... | .10 | .05 | .01 |
| Green Bay Packers | | | |
| ☐ 293 Bruce Armstrong.................. | .05 | .02 | .01 |
| New England Patriots | | | |
| ☐ 294 Kurt Barber ......................... | .05 | .02 | .01 |
| New York Jets | | | |
| ☐ 295 Reginald Jones .................... | .05 | .02 | .01 |
| New Orleans Saints | | | |
| ☐ 296 Steve Jordan ....................... | .08 | .04 | .01 |
| Minnesota Vikings | | | |
| ☐ 297 Kerry Cash .......................... | .05 | .02 | .01 |
| Indianapolis Colts | | | |
| ☐ 298 Ray Crockett ....................... | .05 | .02 | .01 |
| Detroit Lions | | | |
| ☐ 299 Keith Byars.......................... | .08 | .04 | .01 |
| Philadelphia Eagles | | | |
| ☐ 300 Russell Maryland .................. | .10 | .05 | .01 |
| Dallas Cowboys | | | |
| ☐ 301 Johnny Bailey....................... | .05 | .02 | .01 |
| Phoenix Cardinals | | | |
| ☐ 302 Vinnie Clark......................... | .05 | .02 | .01 |
| Green Bay Packers | | | |
| (Traded to | | | |
| Atlanta Falcons) | | | |
| ☐ 303 Terry Wooden ...................... | .05 | .02 | .01 |
| Seattle Seahawks | | | |
| ☐ 304 Harvey Williams ................... | .10 | .05 | .01 |
| Kansas City Chiefs | | | |
| ☐ 305 Marco Coleman..................... | .08 | .04 | .01 |
| Miami Dolphins | | | |
| ☐ 306 Mark Wheeler ...................... | .05 | .02 | .01 |
| Tampa Bay Buccaneers | | | |
| ☐ 307 Greg Townsend..................... | .05 | .02 | .01 |
| Los Angeles Raiders | | | |
| ☐ 308 Tim McGee........................... | .05 | .02 | .01 |
| Cincinnati Bengals | | | |
| (Signed with | | | |
| Washington Redskins) | | | |
| ☐ 309 Donald Evans ...................... | .05 | .02 | .01 |
| Pittsburgh Steelers | | | |
| ☐ 310 Randal Hill.......................... | .10 | .05 | .01 |
| Phoenix Cardinals | | | |
| ☐ 311 Kenny Walker ...................... | .05 | .02 | .01 |
| Denver Broncos | | | |
| ☐ 312 Dalton Hilliard...................... | .05 | .02 | .01 |
| New Orleans Saints | | | |
| ☐ 313 Howard Ballard .................... | .05 | .02 | .01 |
| Buffalo Bills | | | |
| ☐ 314 Phil Simms .......................... | .10 | .05 | .01 |
| New York Giants | | | |
| ☐ 315 Jerry Rice............................ | .50 | .23 | .06 |
| San Francisco 49ers | | | |
| ☐ 316 Courtney Hall ...................... | .05 | .02 | .01 |
| San Diego Chargers | | | |
| ☐ 317 Darren Lewis........................ | .08 | .04 | .01 |
| Chicago Bears | | | |
| ☐ 318 Greg Montgomery................. | .05 | .02 | .01 |
| Houston Oilers | | | |
| ☐ 319 Paul Gruber.......................... | .05 | .02 | .01 |
| Tampa Bay Buccaneers | | | |
| ☐ 320 George Koonce ..................... | .15 | .07 | .02 |
| Green Bay Packers | | | |
| ☐ 321 Eugene Chung ...................... | .05 | .02 | .01 |
| New England Patriots | | | |
| ☐ 322 Mike Brim ........................... | .05 | .02 | .01 |
| New York Jets | | | |
| ☐ 323 Patrick Hunter ..................... | .05 | .02 | .01 |
| Seattle Seahawks | | | |
| ☐ 324 Todd Scott .......................... | .05 | .02 | .01 |
| Minnesota Vikings | | | |
| ☐ 325 Steve Emtman....................... | .08 | .04 | .01 |
| Indianapolis Colts | | | |
| ☐ 326 Andy Harmon........................ | .05 | .02 | .01 |
| Philadelphia Eagles | | | |
| ☐ 327 Larry Brown ........................ | .05 | .02 | .01 |
| Dallas Cowboys | | | |
| ☐ 328 Chuck Cecil ......................... | .05 | .02 | .01 |
| Green Bay Packers | | | |
| (Signed with | | | |
| Phoenix Cardinals) | | | |
| ☐ 329 Tim McKyer......................... | .08 | .04 | .01 |
| Atlanta Falcons | | | |
| ☐ 330 Jeff Bryant........................... | .05 | .02 | .01 |
| Seattle Seahawks | | | |
| ☐ 331 Tim Barnett ......................... | .08 | .04 | .01 |
| Kansas City Chiefs | | | |
| ☐ 332 Irving Fryar ......................... | .08 | .04 | .01 |
| New England Patriots | | | |
| (Traded to | | | |
| Miami Dolphins) | | | |
| ☐ 333 Tyji Armstrong .................... | .05 | .02 | .01 |
| Tampa Bay Buccaneers | | | |
| ☐ 334 Brad Baxter ......................... | .08 | .04 | .01 |
| New York Jets | | | |
| ☐ 335 Shane Collins ....................... | .05 | .02 | .01 |
| Washington Redskins | | | |
| ☐ 336 Jeff Graham ......................... | .08 | .04 | .01 |
| Pittsburgh Steelers | | | |
| ☐ 337 Ricky Proehl......................... | .08 | .04 | .01 |
| Phoenix Cardinals | | | |
| ☐ 338 Tommy Maddox.................... | .10 | .05 | .01 |
| Denver Broncos | | | |
| ☐ 339 Jim Dombrowski.................... | .05 | .02 | .01 |
| New Orleans Saints | | | |
| ☐ 340 Bill Brooks........................... | .08 | .04 | .01 |
| Indianapolis Colts | | | |
| (Signed with | | | |
| Buffalo Bills) | | | |
| ☐ 341 Dave Brown......................... | .75 | .35 | .09 |
| New York Giants | | | |
| ☐ 342 Eric Davis............................ | .05 | .02 | .01 |
| San Francisco 49ers | | | |
| ☐ 343 Leslie O'Neal ....................... | .08 | .04 | .01 |
| San Diego Chargers | | | |
| ☐ 344 Jim Morrissey....................... | .05 | .02 | .01 |
| Chicago Bears | | | |
| ☐ 345 Mike Munchak....................... | .08 | .04 | .01 |
| Houston Oilers | | | |
| ☐ 346 Ron Hall ............................. | .05 | .02 | .01 |
| Tampa Bay Buccaneers | | | |
| ☐ 347 Brian Noble .......................... | .05 | .02 | .01 |
| Green Bay Packers | | | |
| ☐ 348 Chris Singleton ................... | .05 | .02 | .01 |
| New England Patriots | | | |
| ☐ 349 Boomer Esiason UER ........... | .15 | .07 | .02 |
| Cincinnati Bengals | | | |
| (Signed with | | | |
| New York Jets) | | | |
| (Card front notes he was | | | |
| signed instead of traded) | | | |
| ☐ 350 Ray Roberts ........................ | .05 | .02 | .01 |
| Seattle Seahawks | | | |
| ☐ 351 Gary Zimmerman ................. | .05 | .02 | .01 |
| Minnesota Vikings | | | |
| ☐ 352 Quentin Coryatt ................... | .10 | .05 | .01 |
| Indianapolis Colts | | | |
| ☐ 353 Willie Green.......................... | .08 | .04 | .01 |
| Detroit Lions | | | |
| ☐ 354 Randall Cunningham.............. | .10 | .05 | .01 |
| Philadelphia Eagles | | | |
| ☐ 355 Kevin Smith ......................... | .08 | .04 | .01 |
| Dallas Cowboys | | | |
| ☐ 356 Michael Dean Perry.............. | .10 | .05 | .01 |
| Cleveland Browns | | | |
| ☐ 357 Tim Green ............................ | .05 | .02 | .01 |
| Atlanta Falcons | | | |
| ☐ 358 Dwayne Harper .................... | .05 | .02 | .01 |
| Seattle Seahawks | | | |
| ☐ 359 Dale Carter .......................... | .10 | .05 | .01 |
| Kansas City Chiefs | | | |
| ☐ 360 Keith Jackson........................ | .10 | .05 | .01 |

| | | | |
|---|---|---|---|
| Miami Dolphins | | | |
| ☐ 361 Martin Mayhew | .05 | .02 | .01 |
| Washington Redskins | | | |
| (Signed with | | | |
| Tampa Bay Buccaneers) | | | |
| ☐ 362 Brian Washington | .05 | .02 | .01 |
| New York Jets | | | |
| ☐ 363 Earnest Byner | .08 | .04 | .01 |
| Washington Redskins | | | |
| ☐ 364 David Johnson | .05 | .02 | .01 |
| Pittsburgh Steelers | | | |
| ☐ 365 Timm Rosenbach | .05 | .02 | .01 |
| Phoenix Cardinals | | | |
| ☐ 366 Doug Widell | .05 | .02 | .01 |
| Denver Broncos | | | |
| ☐ 367 Vaughn Dunbar | .08 | .04 | .01 |
| New Orleans Saints | | | |
| ☐ 368 Phil Hansen | .05 | .02 | .01 |
| Buffalo Bills | | | |
| ☐ 369 Mike Fox | .05 | .02 | .01 |
| New York Giants | | | |
| ☐ 370 Dana Hall | .08 | .04 | .01 |
| San Francisco 49ers | | | |
| ☐ 371 Junior Seau | .10 | .05 | .01 |
| San Diego Chargers | | | |
| ☐ 372 Steve McMichael | .05 | .02 | .01 |
| Chicago Bears | | | |
| ☐ 373 Eddie Robinson | .05 | .02 | .01 |
| Houston Oilers | | | |
| ☐ 374 Milton Mack | .10 | .05 | .01 |
| Tampa Bay Buccaneers | | | |
| ☐ 375 Mike Prior | .05 | .02 | .01 |
| Indianapolis Colts | | | |
| (Signed with | | | |
| Green Bay Packers) | | | |
| ☐ 376 Jerome Henderson | .05 | .02 | .01 |
| New England Patriots | | | |
| ☐ 377 Scott Mersereau | .05 | .02 | .01 |
| New York Jets | | | |
| ☐ 378 Neal Anderson | .08 | .04 | .01 |
| Chicago Bears | | | |
| ☐ 379 Harry Newsome | .05 | .02 | .01 |
| Minnesota Vikings | | | |
| ☐ 380 John Baylor | .05 | .02 | .01 |
| Indianapolis Colts | | | |
| ☐ 381 Bill Fralic | .05 | .02 | .01 |
| Atlanta Falcons | | | |
| (Signed with | | | |
| Detroit Lions) | | | |
| ☐ 382 Mark Bavaro | .08 | .04 | .01 |
| Cleveland Browns | | | |
| (Signed with | | | |
| Philadelphia Eagles) | | | |
| ☐ 383 Robert Jones | .05 | .02 | .01 |
| Dallas Cowboys | | | |
| ☐ 384 Tyronne Stowe | .05 | .02 | .01 |
| Phoenix Cardinals | | | |
| ☐ 385 Deion Sanders | .15 | .07 | .02 |
| Atlanta Falcons | | | |
| ☐ 386 Robert Blackmon | .05 | .02 | .01 |
| Seattle Seahawks | | | |
| ☐ 387 Neil Smith | .10 | .05 | .01 |
| Kansas City Chiefs | | | |
| ☐ 388 Mark Ingram | .08 | .04 | .01 |
| New York Giants | | | |
| (Signed with | | | |
| Miami Dolphins) | | | |
| ☐ 389 Mark Carrier | .08 | .04 | .01 |
| Tampa Bay Buccaneers | | | |
| (Signed with | | | |
| Cleveland Browns) | | | |
| ☐ 390 Browning Nagle | .08 | .04 | .01 |
| New York Jets | | | |
| ☐ 391 Ricky Ervins | .08 | .04 | .01 |
| Washington Redskins | | | |
| ☐ 392 Carnell Lake | .05 | .02 | .01 |
| Pittsburgh Steelers | | | |
| ☐ 393 Luis Sharpe | .05 | .02 | .01 |
| Phoenix Cardinals | | | |
| ☐ 394 Greg Kragen | .05 | .02 | .01 |
| Denver Broncos | | | |
| ☐ 395 Tommy Barnhardt | .05 | .02 | .01 |
| New Orleans Saints | | | |
| ☐ 396 Mark Kelso | .05 | .02 | .01 |
| Buffalo Bills | | | |
| ☐ 397 Kent Graham | .50 | .23 | .06 |
| New York Giants | | | |
| ☐ 398 Bill Romanowski | .05 | .02 | .01 |
| San Francisco 49ers | | | |
| ☐ 399 Anthony Miller | .15 | .07 | .02 |
| San Diego Chargers | | | |
| ☐ 400 John Roper | .05 | .02 | .01 |
| Chicago Bears | | | |
| ☐ 401 Lamar Rogers | .05 | .02 | .01 |
| Cincinnati Bengals | | | |
| ☐ 402 Troy Auzenne | .05 | .02 | .01 |
| Chicago Bears | | | |
| ☐ 403 Webster Slaughter | .08 | .04 | .01 |
| Houston Oilers | | | |
| ☐ 404 David Brandon | .05 | .02 | .01 |
| Cleveland Browns | | | |
| ☐ 405 Chris Hinton | .05 | .02 | .01 |
| Atlanta Falcons | | | |
| ☐ 406 Andy Heck | .05 | .02 | .01 |
| Seattle Seahawks | | | |
| ☐ 407 Tracy Simien | .05 | .02 | .01 |
| Kansas City Chiefs | | | |
| ☐ 408 Troy Vincent | .08 | .04 | .01 |
| Miami Dolphins | | | |
| ☐ 409 Jason Hanson | .05 | .02 | .01 |
| Detroit Lions | | | |
| ☐ 410 Rod Jones | .10 | .05 | .01 |
| Cincinnati Bengals | | | |
| ☐ 411 Al Noga | .05 | .02 | .01 |
| Minnesota Vikings | | | |
| (Signed with | | | |
| Washington Redskins) | | | |
| ☐ 412 Ernie Mills | .05 | .02 | .01 |
| Pittsburgh Steelers | | | |
| ☐ 413 Willie Gault | .08 | .04 | .01 |
| Los Angeles Raiders | | | |
| ☐ 414 Henry Ellard | .08 | .04 | .01 |
| Los Angeles Rams | | | |
| ☐ 415 Rickey Jackson | .08 | .04 | .01 |
| New Orleans Saints | | | |
| ☐ 416 Bruce Smith | .10 | .05 | .01 |
| Buffalo Bills | | | |
| ☐ 417 Derek Brown | .08 | .04 | .01 |
| New York Giants | | | |
| ☐ 418 Kevin Fagan | .05 | .02 | .01 |
| San Francisco 49ers | | | |
| ☐ 419 Gary Plummer | .05 | .02 | .01 |
| San Diego Chargers | | | |
| ☐ 420 Wendell Davis | .08 | .04 | .01 |
| Chicago Bears | | | |
| ☐ 421 Craig Thompson | .05 | .02 | .01 |
| Cincinnati Bengals | | | |
| ☐ 422 Wes Hopkins | .05 | .02 | .01 |
| Philadelphia Eagles | | | |
| ☐ 423 Ray Childress | .05 | .02 | .01 |
| Houston Oilers | | | |
| ☐ 424 Pat Harlow | .05 | .02 | .01 |
| New England Patriots | | | |
| ☐ 425 Howie Long | .08 | .04 | .01 |
| Los Angeles Raiders | | | |
| ☐ 426 Shane Dronett | .05 | .02 | .01 |
| Denver Broncos | | | |
| ☐ 427 Sean Salisbury | .08 | .04 | .01 |
| Minnesota Vikings | | | |
| ☐ 428 Dwight Hollier | .10 | .05 | .01 |
| Miami Dolphins | | | |
| ☐ 429 Brett Perriman | .08 | .04 | .01 |
| Detroit Lions | | | |
| ☐ 430 Donald Hollas | .05 | .02 | .01 |
| Cincinnati Bengals | | | |
| ☐ 431 Jim Lachey | .05 | .02 | .01 |
| Washington Redskins | | | |
| ☐ 432 Darren Perry | .05 | .02 | .01 |
| Pittsburgh Steelers | | | |
| ☐ 433 Lionel Washington | .05 | .02 | .01 |
| Los Angeles Raiders | | | |
| ☐ 434 Sean Gilbert | .08 | .04 | .01 |
| Los Angeles Rams | | | |
| ☐ 435 Gene Atkins | .05 | .02 | .01 |
| New Orleans Saints | | | |
| ☐ 436 Jim Kelly | .25 | .11 | .03 |
| Buffalo Bills | | | |
| ☐ 437 Ed McCaffrey | .05 | .02 | .01 |
| New York Giants | | | |
| ☐ 438 Don Griffin | .05 | .02 | .01 |
| San Francisco 49ers | | | |
| ☐ 439 Jerrol Williams | .05 | .02 | .01 |
| Pittsburgh Steelers | | | |
| (Signed with | | | |
| San Diego Chargers) | | | |
| ☐ 440 Bryce Paup | .05 | .02 | .01 |
| Green Bay Packers | | | |
| ☐ 441 Darryl Williams | .08 | .04 | .01 |
| Cincinnati Bengals | | | |
| ☐ 442 Vai Sikahema | .05 | .02 | .01 |
| Philadelphia Eagles | | | |
| ☐ 443 Cris Dishman | .05 | .02 | .01 |
| Houston Oilers | | | |
| ☐ 444 Kevin Mack | .08 | .04 | .01 |
| Cleveland Browns | | | |
| ☐ 445 Winston Moss | .05 | .02 | .01 |
| Los Angeles Raiders | | | |
| ☐ 446 Tyrone Braxton | .05 | .02 | .01 |
| Denver Broncos | | | |
| ☐ 447 Mike Merriweather | .05 | .02 | .01 |
| Minnesota Vikings | | | |
| ☐ 448 Tony Paige | .05 | .02 | .01 |
| Miami Dolphins | | | |
| ☐ 449 Robert Porcher | .08 | .04 | .01 |
| Detroit Lions | | | |
| ☐ 450 Ricardo McDonald | .05 | .02 | .01 |

Cincinnati Bengals
- [ ] 451 Danny Copeland ........................ .05 .02 .01
  Washington Redskins
- [ ] 452 Tony Tolbert ............................. .05 .02 .01
  Dallas Cowboys
- [ ] 453 Eric Dickerson ......................... .10 .05 .01
  Los Angeles Raiders
- [ ] 454 Flipper Anderson ..................... .08 .04 .01
  Los Angeles Rams
- [ ] 455 Dave Krieg ............................... .08 .04 .01
  Kansas City Chiefs
- [ ] 456 Brad Lamb ............................... .12 .05 .02
  Buffalo Bills
- [ ] 457 Bart Oates ............................... .05 .02 .01
  New York Giants
- [ ] 458 Guy McIntyre ........................... .05 .02 .01
  San Francisco 49ers
- [ ] 459 Stanley Richard ....................... .05 .02 .01
  San Diego Chargers
- [ ] 460 Edgar Bennett .......................... .10 .05 .01
  Green Bay Packers
- [ ] 461 Pat Carter ............................... .05 .02 .01
  Los Angeles Rams
- [ ] 462 Eric Allen ................................. .08 .04 .01
  Philadelphia Eagles
- [ ] 463 William Fuller .......................... .05 .02 .01
  Houston Oilers
- [ ] 464 James Jones ............................ .05 .02 .01
  Cleveland Browns
- [ ] 465 Chester McGlockton ............... .05 .02 .01
  Los Angeles Raiders
- [ ] 466 Charles Dimry ......................... .05 .02 .01
  Denver Broncos
- [ ] 467 Tim Grunhard .......................... .05 .02 .01
  Kansas City Chiefs
- [ ] 468 Jarvis Williams ....................... .05 .02 .01
  Miami Dolphins
- [ ] 469 Tracy Scroggins ...................... .08 .04 .01
  Detroit Lions
- [ ] 470 David Klingler .......................... .15 .07 .02
  Cincinnati Bengals
- [ ] 471 Andre Collins ........................... .05 .02 .01
  Washington Redskins
- [ ] 472 Erik Williams ........................... .05 .02 .01
  Dallas Cowboys
- [ ] 473 Eddie Anderson ....................... .05 .02 .01
  Los Angeles Raiders
- [ ] 474 Marc Boutte ............................. .05 .02 .01
  Los Angeles Rams
- [ ] 475 Joe Montana ............................ 1.00 .45 .13
  Kansas City Chiefs
- [ ] 476 Andre Reed .............................. .10 .05 .01
  Buffalo Bills
- [ ] 477 Lawrence Taylor ...................... .10 .05 .01
  New York Giants
- [ ] 478 Jeff George ............................. .15 .07 .02
  Indianapolis Colts
- [ ] 479 Chris Mims .............................. .08 .04 .01
  San Diego Chargers
- [ ] 480 Ken Ruettgers ......................... .05 .02 .01
  Green Bay Packers
- [ ] 481 Roman Phifer ........................... .05 .02 .01
  Los Angeles Rams
- [ ] 482 William Thomas ....................... .05 .02 .01
  Philadelphia Eagles
- [ ] 483 Lamar Lathon .......................... .05 .02 .01
  Houston Oilers
- [ ] 484 Vinny Testaverde ..................... .10 .05 .01
  Tampa Bay Buccaneers
  (Signed with
  Cleveland Browns)
- [ ] 485 Mike Kenn ............................... .05 .02 .01
  Atlanta Falcons
- [ ] 486 Greg Lewis .............................. .05 .02 .01
  Denver Broncos
- [ ] 487 Chris Martin ............................. .05 .02 .01
  Kansas City Chiefs
  (Traded to
  Los Angeles Rams)
- [ ] 488 Maurice Hurst ......................... .05 .02 .01
  New England Patriots
- [ ] 489 Pat Swilling ............................. .08 .04 .01
  New Orleans Saints
  (Traded to
  Detroit Lions)
- [ ] 490 Carl Pickens ........................... .10 .05 .01
  Cincinnati Bengals
- [ ] 491 Tony Smith .............................. .05 .02 .01
  Atlanta Falcons
- [ ] 492 James Washington ................... .05 .02 .01
  Dallas Cowboys
- [ ] 493 Jeff Hostetler.......................... .10 .05 .01
  New York Giants
  (Signed with
  Los Angeles Raiders)
- [ ] 494 Jeff Chadwic ........................... .05 .02 .01
  Los Angeles Rams
- [ ] 495 Kevin Ross .............................. .05 .02 .01

Kansas City Chiefs
- [ ] 496 Jim Ritcher ............................. .05 .02 .01
  Buffalo Bills
- [ ] 497 Jessie Hester .......................... .05 .02 .01
  Indianapolis Colts
- [ ] 498 Burt Grossman ........................ .05 .02 .01
  San Diego Chargers
- [ ] 499 Keith Van Horne ...................... .05 .02 .01
  Chicago Bears
- [ ] 500 Gerald Robinson ...................... .05 .02 .01
  Los Angeles Rams

# 1993 Fleer All-Pros

Randomly inserted into foil packs, this 25-card standard-size (2 1/2" by 3 1/2") set features the best of the NFL. Inside white borders, the horizontal fronts feature a color player cut out superimposed on a black-and-white action shot of the player. The "Fleer All-Pro" logo and the player's name are gold foil stamped on the picture. On team color-coded panels, the horizontal backs present career summary. The cards are numbered on the back.

|  | MINT | EXC | G-VG |
|---|---|---|---|
| COMPLETE SET (25) ................... | 40.00 | 18.00 | 5.00 |
| COMMON PLAYER (1-25) ................ | 1.00 | .45 | .13 |

- [ ] 1 Steve Atwater ........................... 1.00 .45 .13
  Denver Broncos
- [ ] 2 Rich Camarillo .......................... 1.00 .45 .13
  Phoenix Cardinals
- [ ] 3 Ray Childress .......................... 1.00 .45 .13
  Houston Oilers
- [ ] 4 Chris Doleman ......................... 1.00 .45 .13
  Minnesota Vikings
- [ ] 5 Barry Foster ........................... 3.00 1.35 .40
  Pittsburgh Steelers
- [ ] 6 Henry Jones ............................ 1.00 .45 .13
  Buffalo Bills
- [ ] 7 Cortez Kennedy ....................... 1.25 .55 .16
  Seattle Seahawks
- [ ] 8 Nick Lowery ............................ 1.00 .45 .13
  Kansas City Chiefs
- [ ] 9 Wilber Marshall ....................... 1.00 .45 .13
  Washington Redskins
- [ ] 10 Bruce Matthews ...................... 1.00 .45 .13
  Houston Oilers
- [ ] 11 Randall McDaniel .................... 1.00 .45 .13
  Minnesota Vikings
- [ ] 12 Audray McMillian ................... 1.00 .45 .13
  Minnesota Vikings
- [ ] 13 Sam Mills .............................. 1.00 .45 .13
  New Orleans Saints
- [ ] 14 Jay Novacek ........................... 1.25 .55 .16
  Dallas Cowboys
- [ ] 15 Jerry Rice .............................. 6.00 2.70 .75
  San Francisco 49ers
- [ ] 16 Junior Seau ............................ 1.25 .55 .16
  San Diego Chargers
- [ ] 17 Sterling Sharpe ...................... 5.00 2.30 .60
  Green Bay Packers
- [ ] 18 Clyde Simmons........................ 1.25 .55 .16
  Philadelphia Eagles
- [ ] 19 Emmitt Smith.......................... 25.00 11.50 3.10
  Dallas Cowboys
- [ ] 20 Derrick Thomas........................ 1.25 .55 .16
  Kansas City Chiefs
- [ ] 21 Steve Wallace ......................... 1.00 .45 .13
  San Francisco 49ers
- [ ] 22 Richmond Webb ....................... 1.00 .45 .13
  Miami Dolphins
- [ ] 23 Steve Wisniewski ................... 1.00 .45 .13
  Los Angeles Raiders

| | MINT | EXC | G-VG |
|---|---|---|---|
| ☐ 24 Rod Woodson | 1.25 | .55 | .16 |
| Pittsburgh Steelers | | | |
| ☐ 25 Steve Young | 3.00 | 1.35 | .40 |
| San Francisco 49ers | | | |

## 1993 Fleer Prospects

Drew Bledsoe
1ST ROUND · PATR...

Randomly inserted into foil packs, this 30-card standard-size (2 1/2" by 3 1/2") set features the top 1993 NFL draft picks. The fronts feature color player cut outs on a gold panel with sky blue borders. Gold foil stamped on the picture is Fleer's "1993 NFL Prospect" emblem, the player's name, the round he was drafted, and the team name. The backs reverse the colors on the front and carry player profile and a color close-up shot. The cards are numbered on the back.

| | MINT | EXC | G-VG |
|---|---|---|---|
| COMPLETE SET (30) | 50.00 | 23.00 | 6.25 |
| COMMON PLAYER (1-30) | 1.00 | .45 | .13 |
| ☐ 1 Drew Bledsoe | 12.00 | 5.50 | 1.50 |
| New England Patriots | | | |
| ☐ 2 Garrison Hearst | 3.50 | 1.55 | .45 |
| Phoenix Cardinals | | | |
| ☐ 3 John Copeland | 1.25 | .55 | .16 |
| Cincinnati Bengals | | | |
| ☐ 4 Eric Curry | 1.25 | .55 | .16 |
| Tampa Bay Buccaneers | | | |
| ☐ 5 Curtis Conway | 2.50 | 1.15 | .30 |
| Chicago Bears | | | |
| ☐ 6 Lincoln Kennedy | 1.25 | .55 | .16 |
| Atlanta Falcons | | | |
| ☐ 7 Jerome Bettis | 12.00 | 5.50 | 1.50 |
| Los Angeles Rams | | | |
| ☐ 8 Patrick Bates | 1.25 | .55 | .16 |
| Los Angeles Raiders | | | |
| ☐ 9 Brad Hopkins | 1.00 | .45 | .13 |
| Houston Oilers | | | |
| ☐ 10 Tom Carter | 1.25 | .55 | .16 |
| Washington Redskins | | | |
| ☐ 11 Irv Smith | 1.25 | .55 | .16 |
| New Orleans Saints | | | |
| ☐ 12 Robert Smith | 1.75 | .80 | .22 |
| Minnesota Vikings | | | |
| ☐ 13 Deon Figures | 1.25 | .55 | .16 |
| Pittsburgh Steelers | | | |
| ☐ 14 Leonard Renfro | 1.00 | .45 | .13 |
| Philadelphia Eagles | | | |
| ☐ 15 O.J. McDuffie | 5.00 | 2.30 | .60 |
| Miami Dolphins | | | |
| ☐ 16 Dana Stubblefield | 2.25 | 1.00 | .30 |
| San Francisco 49ers | | | |
| ☐ 17 Todd Kelly | 1.25 | .55 | .16 |
| San Francisco 49ers | | | |
| ☐ 18 George Teague | 1.25 | .55 | .16 |
| Green Bay Packers | | | |
| ☐ 19 Demetrius DuBose | 1.25 | .55 | .16 |
| Tampa Bay Buccaneers | | | |
| ☐ 20 Coleman Rudolph | 1.00 | .45 | .13 |
| New York Jets | | | |
| ☐ 21 Carlton Gray | 1.25 | .55 | .16 |
| Seattle Seahawks | | | |
| ☐ 22 Troy Drayton | 1.25 | .55 | .16 |
| Los Angeles Rams | | | |
| ☐ 23 Natrone Means UER | 6.00 | 2.70 | .75 |
| (San Diego Chargers | | | |
| Receiver spelled Reveiever) | | | |
| ☐ 24 Qadry Ismail | 2.50 | 1.15 | .30 |
| Minnesota Vikings | | | |
| ☐ 25 Gino Torretta | 2.00 | .90 | .25 |
| Minnesota Vikings | | | |
| ☐ 26 Carl Simpson | 1.00 | .45 | .13 |
| Chicago Bears | | | |
| ☐ 27 Glyn Milburn | 5.00 | 2.30 | .60 |
| Denver Broncos | | | |

| | MINT | EXC | G-VG |
|---|---|---|---|
| ☐ 28 Chad Brown | 1.00 | .45 | .13 |
| Pittsburgh Steelers | | | |
| ☐ 29 Reggie Brooks | 8.00 | 3.60 | 1.00 |
| Washington Redskins | | | |
| ☐ 30 Billy Joe Hobert | 2.00 | .90 | .25 |
| Los Angeles Raiders | | | |

## 1993 Fleer Rookie Sensations

EUGENE CHUNG

2 of 20

This 20-card set was distributed as random inserts in 1993 Fleer football jumbo packs only. The cards are standard size, 2 1/2" by 3 1/2". The cards are numbered on the back.

| | MINT | EXC | G-VG |
|---|---|---|---|
| COMPLETE SET (20) | 75.00 | 34.00 | 9.50 |
| COMMON PLAYER (1-20) | 4.00 | 1.80 | .50 |
| ☐ 1 Dale Carter | 4.50 | 2.00 | .55 |
| Kansas City Chiefs | | | |
| ☐ 2 Eugene Chung | 4.00 | 1.80 | .50 |
| New England Patriots | | | |
| ☐ 3 Marco Coleman | 4.50 | 2.00 | .55 |
| Miami Dolphins | | | |
| ☐ 4 Quentin Coryatt | 4.50 | 2.00 | .55 |
| Indianapolis Colts | | | |
| ☐ 5 Santana Dotson | 4.50 | 2.00 | .55 |
| Tampa Bay Buccaneers | | | |
| ☐ 6 Vaughn Dunbar | 4.50 | 2.00 | .55 |
| New Orleans Saints | | | |
| ☐ 7 Steve Emtman | 4.50 | 2.00 | .55 |
| Indianapolis Colts | | | |
| ☐ 8 Sean Gilbert | 4.50 | 2.00 | .55 |
| Los Angeles Rams | | | |
| ☐ 9 Dana Hall | 4.50 | 2.00 | .55 |
| San Francisco 49ers | | | |
| ☐ 10 Jason Hanson | 4.00 | 1.80 | .50 |
| Detroit Lions | | | |
| ☐ 11 Robert Jones | 4.00 | 1.80 | .50 |
| Dallas Cowboys | | | |
| ☐ 12 David Klingler | 6.00 | 2.70 | .75 |
| Cincinnati Bengals | | | |
| ☐ 13 Amp Lee | 4.50 | 2.00 | .55 |
| San Francisco 49ers | | | |
| ☐ 14 Arthur Marshall | 4.50 | 2.00 | .55 |
| Denver Broncos | | | |
| ☐ 15 Ricardo McDonald | 4.00 | 1.80 | .50 |
| Cincinnati Bengals | | | |
| ☐ 16 Chris Mims | 4.50 | 2.00 | .55 |
| San Diego Chargers | | | |
| ☐ 17 Johnny Mitchell | 6.00 | 2.70 | .75 |
| New York Jets | | | |
| ☐ 18 Carl Pickens | 5.00 | 2.30 | .60 |
| Cincinnati Bengals | | | |
| ☐ 19 Darren Perry | 4.00 | 1.80 | .50 |
| Pittsburgh Steelers | | | |
| ☐ 20 Troy Vincent | 4.50 | 2.00 | .55 |
| Miami Dolphins | | | |

## 1993 Fleer Team Leaders

Randomly inserted into foil packs, this five-card standard-size (2 1/2" by 3 1/2") set showcases 1992's brightest stars. On a sky blue background laced with lightning streaks, the fronts feature full-bleed color action player cut outs. The words "Team Leader" and the player's name are gold foil stamped at the bottom. Inside a gold border on a sky blue panel, the backs present a player profile and a second color player cut out. The cards are numbered on the back.

| | MINT | EXC | G-VG |
|---|---|---|---|
| COMPLETE SET (5) | 22.00 | 10.00 | 2.80 |
| COMMON PLAYER (1-5) | 3.00 | 1.35 | .40 |

| | MINT | EXC | G-VG |
|---|---|---|---|
| ☐ 1 Brett Favre....................... | 10.00 | 4.50 | 1.25 |
| Green Bay Packers | | | |
| ☐ 2 Derrick Thomas...................... | 3.00 | 1.35 | .40 |
| Kansas City Chiefs | | | |
| ☐ 3 Steve Young........................ | 6.00 | 2.70 | .75 |
| San Francisco 49ers | | | |
| ☐ 4 John Elway........................ | 8.00 | 3.60 | 1.00 |
| Denver Broncos | | | |
| ☐ 5 Cortez Kennedy...................... | 3.00 | 1.35 | .40 |
| Seattle Seahawks | | | |

## 1993 Fleer Steve Young

Randomly inserted into foil packs, this ten-card standard-size (2 1/2" by 3 1/2") set spotlights Steve Young, the NFL's MVP for the 1992 season. Young autographed more than 2,000 of his cards and, through a mail-in offer for ten 1993 Fleer Football wrappers plus 1.00, the collector could receive three additional Steve Young "Performance Highlights" cards. The fronts feature color action player photos bordered in white. The player's name and "Performance Highlights" are gold-foil stamped at the upper left corner. Inside white borders, a red panel carries a color close-up shot and player profile. The cards are numbered on the back.

| | MINT | EXC | G-VG |
|---|---|---|---|
| COMPLETE SET (13)........................ | 8.00 | 3.60 | 1.00 |
| COMMON INSERT (1-10)................. | .75 | .35 | .09 |
| COMMON SEND-OFF (11-13) ........... | 1.50 | .65 | .19 |
| ☐ 1 Steve Young........................ | .75 | .35 | .09 |
| The Next Natural | | | |
| ☐ 2 Steve Young........................ | .75 | .35 | .09 |
| Judging the Book | | | |
| ☐ 3 Steve Young........................ | .75 | .35 | .09 |
| Understudy to Stardom | | | |
| ☐ 4 Steve Young........................ | .75 | .35 | .09 |
| Express to Success | | | |
| ☐ 5 Steve Young........................ | .75 | .35 | .09 |
| NFL | | | |
| ☐ 6 Steve Young........................ | .75 | .35 | .09 |
| Full-Time Football | | | |
| ☐ 7 Steve Young........................ | .75 | .35 | .09 |
| Learning To Fly | | | |
| ☐ 8 Steve Young........................ | .75 | .35 | .09 |
| Ringbearer | | | |
| ☐ 9 Steve Young........................ | .75 | .35 | .09 |
| Showtime | | | |
| ☐ 10 Steve Young........................ | .75 | .35 | .09 |
| Top Gun | | | |
| ☐ 11 Steve Young........................ | 1.50 | .65 | .19 |
| Man for All Seasons | | | |
| ☐ 12 Steve Young........................ | 1.50 | .65 | .19 |
| Quips and Quotes | | | |
| ☐ 13 Steve Young........................ | 1.50 | .65 | .19 |

| 1992AAMVP | | | |
|---|---|---|---|
| ☐ AU Steve Young AU ................... | 125.00 | 57.50 | 15.50 |
| (Certified autograph) | | | |

## 1993 Fleer Fruit of the Loom

This 50-card set issued by Fleer was sponsored by Fruit of the Loom. Each specially marked underwear package contained six cards. The cards measure standard size (2 1/2" by 3 1/2"). The color action player photos on the fronts are framed with silver metallic borders. At the bottom of the photo, the player's last name is printed in transparent lettering that has an embossed look. The team affiliation and position appear at the lower right corner. Fruit of the Loom's logo is in the upper left corner. On a team color-coded panel, the horizontal backs carry a close-up color shot, biography, player profile, team logo, and statistics. The cards are numbered on the back.

| | MINT | EXC | G-VG |
|---|---|---|---|
| COMPLETE SET (50)........................ | 100.00 | 40.00 | 10.00 |
| COMMON PLAYER (1-50)................. | 1.50 | .60 | .15 |
| ☐ 1 Andre Rison........................ | 4.00 | 1.60 | .40 |
| Atlanta Falcons | | | |
| ☐ 2 Deion Sanders...................... | 5.00 | 2.00 | .50 |
| Atlanta Falcons | | | |
| ☐ 3 Neal Anderson...................... | 2.00 | .80 | .20 |
| Chicago Bears | | | |
| ☐ 4 Jim Harbaugh ..................... | 2.00 | .80 | .20 |
| Chicago Bears | | | |
| ☐ 5 Bernie Kosar ..................... | 2.50 | 1.00 | .25 |
| Cleveland Browns | | | |
| ☐ 6 Eric Metcalf ...................... | 2.00 | .80 | .20 |
| Cleveland Browns | | | |
| ☐ 7 John Elway........................ | 7.50 | 3.00 | .75 |
| Denver Broncos | | | |
| ☐ 8 Karl Mecklenburg.................... | 1.50 | .60 | .15 |
| Denver Broncos | | | |
| ☐ 9 Sterling Sharpe .................... | 6.00 | 2.40 | .60 |
| Green Bay Packers | | | |
| ☐ 10 Reggie White........................ | 3.00 | 1.20 | .30 |
| Philadelphia Eagles | | | |
| (Traded to Green Bay | | | |
| Packers) | | | |
| ☐ 11 Steve Emtman........................ | 2.00 | .80 | .20 |
| Indianapolis Colts | | | |
| ☐ 12 Jeff George ........................ | 3.00 | 1.20 | .30 |
| Indianapolis Colts | | | |
| ☐ 13 Willie Gault........................ | 2.00 | .80 | .20 |
| Los Angeles Raiders | | | |
| ☐ 14 Jim Kelly ........................ | 5.00 | 2.00 | .50 |
| Buffalo Bills | | | |
| ☐ 15 Thurman Thomas.................... | 5.00 | 2.00 | .50 |
| Buffalo Bills | | | |
| ☐ 16 Harold Green........................ | 2.00 | .80 | .20 |
| Cincinnati Bengals | | | |
| ☐ 17 Carl Pickens........................ | 2.50 | 1.00 | .25 |
| Cincinnati Bengals | | | |
| ☐ 18 Troy Aikman........................ | 15.00 | 6.00 | 1.50 |
| Dallas Cowboys | | | |
| ☐ 19 Emmitt Smith........................ | 18.00 | 7.25 | 1.80 |
| Dallas Cowboys | | | |
| ☐ 20 Barry Sanders ........................ | 9.00 | 3.75 | .90 |
| Detroit Lions | | | |
| ☐ 21 Pat Swilling........................ | 2.00 | .80 | .20 |
| New Orleans Saints | | | |
| (Traded to Detroit Lions) | | | |
| ☐ 22 Haywood Jeffires.................... | 2.50 | 1.00 | .25 |
| Houston Oilers | | | |
| ☐ 23 Warren Moon ........................ | 4.00 | 1.60 | .40 |
| Houston Oilers | | | |
| ☐ 24 Derrick Thomas...................... | 4.00 | 1.60 | .40 |
| Kansas City Chiefs | | | |
| ☐ 25 Christian Okoye.................... | 2.00 | .80 | .20 |
| Kansas City Chiefs | | | |
| ☐ 26 Flipper Anderson.................... | 1.50 | .60 | .15 |
| Los Angeles Rams | | | |

| | | | |
|---|---|---|---|
| ☐ 27 Jim Everett | 2.00 | .80 | .20 |
| Los Angeles Rams | | | |
| ☐ 28 Keith Jackson | 2.50 | 1.00 | .25 |
| Miami Dolphins | | | |
| ☐ 29 Dan Marino | 12.50 | 5.00 | 1.25 |
| Miami Dolphins | | | |
| ☐ 30 Andre Tippett | 1.50 | .60 | .15 |
| New England Patriots | | | |
| ☐ 31 Lawrence Taylor | 2.50 | 1.00 | .25 |
| New York Giants | | | |
| ☐ 32 Randall Cunningham | 3.00 | 1.20 | .30 |
| Philadelphia Eagles | | | |
| ☐ 33 Barry Foster | 3.00 | 1.20 | .30 |
| Pittsburgh Steelers | | | |
| ☐ 34 Rod Woodson | 2.50 | 1.00 | .25 |
| Pittsburgh Steelers | | | |
| ☐ 35 Jerry Rice | 7.50 | 3.00 | .75 |
| San Francisco 49ers | | | |
| ☐ 36 Steve Young | 5.00 | 2.00 | .50 |
| San Francisco 49ers | | | |
| ☐ 37 Reggie Cobb | 2.50 | 1.00 | .25 |
| Tampa Bay Buccaneers | | | |
| ☐ 38 Roger Craig | 2.00 | .80 | .20 |
| Minnesota Vikings | | | |
| ☐ 39 Chris Doleman | 1.50 | .60 | .15 |
| Minnesota Vikings | | | |
| ☐ 40 Morten Andersen | 1.50 | .60 | .15 |
| New Orleans Saints | | | |
| ☐ 41 Dalton Hilliard | 1.50 | .60 | .15 |
| New Orleans Saints | | | |
| ☐ 42 Ronnie Lott | 2.50 | 1.00 | .25 |
| Los Angeles Raiders | | | |
| (Traded to New York Jets) | | | |
| ☐ 43 Chris Chandler | 1.50 | .60 | .15 |
| Phoenix Cardinals | | | |
| ☐ 44 Stan Humphries | 2.00 | .80 | .20 |
| San Diego Chargers | | | |
| ☐ 45 Junior Seau | 2.50 | 1.00 | .25 |
| San Diego Chargers | | | |
| ☐ 46 Brian Blades | 2.00 | .80 | .20 |
| Seattle Seahawks | | | |
| ☐ 47 Cortez Kennedy | 2.50 | 1.00 | .25 |
| Seattle Seahawks | | | |
| ☐ 48 Wilber Marshall | 1.50 | .60 | .15 |
| Washington Redskins | | | |
| ☐ 49 Art Monk | 2.50 | 1.00 | .25 |
| Washington Redskins | | | |
| ☐ 50 Checklist Card | 1.50 | .60 | .15 |

# 1994 Fleer

The 1994 Fleer football set consists of 480 standard-size (2 1/2" by 3 1/2") cards. The fronts feature white-bordered color action player photos with a gold-foil stamped player signature, name and position, and team logo. The horizontal backs carry a ghosted action shot, and a close-up color player portrait. Complete stats are printed over the ghosted action photo. The cards are numbered on the back, grouped alphabetically within teams, and checklisted below alphabetically according to teams as follows: Arizona Cardinals (1-17), Atlanta Falcons (18-34), Buffalo Bills (35-53), Chicago Bears (54-72), Cincinnati Bengals (73-91), Cleveland Browns (92-106), Dallas Cowboys (107-127), Denver Broncos (128-145), Detroit Lions (146-163), Green Bay Packers (164-180), Houston Oilers (181-198), Indianapolis Colts (199-214), Kansas City Chiefs (215-230), Los Angeles Raiders (231-250), Los Angeles Rams (251-267), Miami Dolphins (268-286), Minnesota Vikings (287-304), New England Patriots (305-317), New Orleans Saints (318-334), New York Giants (335-350), New York Jets (351-365), Philadelphia Eagles (366-380), Pittsburgh Steelers (381-396), San Diego Chargers (397-409), San Francisco 49ers (410-429), Seattle Seahawks (430-446), Tampa Bay Buccaneers (447-458), and Washington Redskins (459-474). A "Fleer

Hot Pack" has been inserted in about every other box. It looks like a regular pack but it is filled with 15 insert cards. Otherwise, one insert card was included per pack.

| | MINT | EXC | G-VG |
|---|---|---|---|
| COMPLETE SET (480) | 22.00 | 10.00 | 2.80 |
| COMMON PLAYER (1-480) | .05 | .02 | .01 |
| | | | |
| ☐ 1 Michael Bankston | .05 | .02 | .01 |
| ☐ 2 Steve Beuerlein | .10 | .05 | .01 |
| ☐ 3 John Booty | .05 | .02 | .01 |
| ☐ 4 Rich Camarillo | .05 | .02 | .01 |
| ☐ 5 Chuck Cecil | .05 | .02 | .01 |
| ☐ 6 Larry Centers | .05 | .02 | .01 |
| ☐ 7 Gary Clark | .08 | .04 | .01 |
| ☐ 8 Garrison Hearst | .15 | .07 | .02 |
| ☐ 9 Eric Hill | .05 | .02 | .01 |
| ☐ 10 Randal Hill | .10 | .05 | .01 |
| ☐ 11 Ron Moore | .50 | .23 | .06 |
| ☐ 12 Ricky Proehl | .08 | .04 | .01 |
| ☐ 13 Luis Sharpe | .05 | .02 | .01 |
| ☐ 14 Clyde Simmons | .08 | .04 | .01 |
| ☐ 15 Tyronne Stowe | .05 | .02 | .01 |
| ☐ 16 Eric Swann | .08 | .04 | .01 |
| ☐ 17 Aeneas Williams | .05 | .02 | .01 |
| ☐ 18 Darion Conner | .05 | .02 | .01 |
| ☐ 19 Moe Gardner | .05 | .02 | .01 |
| ☐ 20 James Geathers | .05 | .02 | .01 |
| ☐ 21 Jeff George | .10 | .05 | .01 |
| ☐ 22 Roger Harper | .05 | .02 | .01 |
| ☐ 23 Bobby Hebert | .10 | .05 | .01 |
| ☐ 24 Pierce Holt | .05 | .02 | .01 |
| ☐ 25 David Johnson | .05 | .02 | .01 |
| ☐ 26 Mike Kenn | .05 | .02 | .01 |
| ☐ 27 Lincoln Kennedy | .05 | .02 | .01 |
| ☐ 28 Erric Pegram | .25 | .11 | .03 |
| ☐ 29 Mike Pritchard | .10 | .05 | .01 |
| ☐ 30 Andre Rison | .15 | .07 | .02 |
| ☐ 31 Deion Sanders | .15 | .07 | .02 |
| ☐ 32 Tony Smith | .05 | .02 | .01 |
| ☐ 33 Jesse Solomon | .05 | .02 | .01 |
| ☐ 34 Jessie Tuggle | .05 | .02 | .01 |
| ☐ 35 Don Beebe | .10 | .05 | .01 |
| ☐ 36 Cornelius Bennett | .10 | .05 | .01 |
| ☐ 37 Bill Brooks | .05 | .02 | .01 |
| ☐ 38 Kenneth Davis | .05 | .02 | .01 |
| ☐ 39 John Fina | .05 | .02 | .01 |
| ☐ 40 Phil Hansen | .05 | .02 | .01 |
| ☐ 41 Kent Hull | .05 | .02 | .01 |
| ☐ 42 Henry Jones | .05 | .02 | .01 |
| ☐ 43 Jim Kelly | .20 | .09 | .03 |
| ☐ 44 Pete Metzelaars | .05 | .02 | .01 |
| ☐ 45 Marvcus Patton | .05 | .02 | .01 |
| ☐ 46 Andre Reed | .10 | .05 | .01 |
| ☐ 47 Frank Reich | .08 | .04 | .01 |
| ☐ 48 Bruce Smith | .10 | .05 | .01 |
| ☐ 49 Thomas Smith | .05 | .02 | .01 |
| ☐ 50 Darryl Talley | .05 | .02 | .01 |
| ☐ 51 Steve Tasker | .05 | .02 | .01 |
| ☐ 52 Thurman Thomas | .25 | .11 | .03 |
| ☐ 53 Jeff Wright | .05 | .02 | .01 |
| ☐ 54 Neal Anderson | .08 | .04 | .01 |
| ☐ 55 Trace Armstrong | .05 | .02 | .01 |
| ☐ 56 Troy Auzenne | .05 | .02 | .01 |
| ☐ 57 Joe Cain | .05 | .02 | .01 |
| ☐ 58 Mark Carrier | .08 | .04 | .01 |
| ☐ 59 Curtis Conway | .15 | .07 | .02 |
| ☐ 60 Richard Dent | .08 | .04 | .01 |
| ☐ 61 Shaun Gayle | .05 | .02 | .01 |
| ☐ 62 Andy Heck | .05 | .02 | .01 |
| ☐ 63 Dante Jones | .05 | .02 | .01 |
| ☐ 64 Erik Kramer | .15 | .07 | .02 |
| ☐ 65 Steve McMichael | .05 | .02 | .01 |
| ☐ 66 Terry Obee | .15 | .07 | .02 |
| ☐ 67 Vinson Smith | .05 | .02 | .01 |
| ☐ 68 Alonzo Spellman | .08 | .04 | .01 |
| ☐ 69 Tom Waddle | .10 | .05 | .01 |
| ☐ 70 Donnell Woolford | .05 | .02 | .01 |
| ☐ 71 Tim Worley | .05 | .02 | .01 |
| ☐ 72 Chris Zorich | .08 | .04 | .01 |
| ☐ 73 Mike Brim | .05 | .02 | .01 |
| ☐ 74 John Copeland | .05 | .02 | .01 |
| ☐ 75 Derrick Fenner | .05 | .02 | .01 |
| ☐ 76 James Francis | .05 | .02 | .01 |
| ☐ 77 Harold Green | .08 | .04 | .01 |
| ☐ 78 Rod Jones | .05 | .02 | .01 |
| ☐ 79 David Klingler | .15 | .07 | .02 |
| ☐ 80 Bruce Kozerski | .05 | .02 | .01 |
| ☐ 81 Tim Krumrie | .05 | .02 | .01 |
| ☐ 82 Ricardo McDonald | .05 | .02 | .01 |
| ☐ 83 Tim McGee | .05 | .02 | .01 |
| ☐ 84 Tony McGee | .05 | .02 | .01 |
| ☐ 85 Louis Oliver | .05 | .02 | .01 |
| ☐ 86 Carl Pickens | .10 | .05 | .01 |
| ☐ 87 Jeff Query | .05 | .02 | .01 |
| ☐ 88 Daniel Stubbs | .05 | .02 | .01 |
| ☐ 89 Steve Tovar | .05 | .02 | .01 |

|  |  | | | |
|---|--------|---|---|---|
| ☐ 90 | Alfred Williams | .05 | .02 | .01 |
| ☐ 91 | Darryl Williams | .08 | .04 | .01 |
| ☐ 92 | Rob Burnett | .05 | .02 | .01 |
| ☐ 93 | Mark Carrier | .08 | .04 | .01 |
| ☐ 94 | Leroy Hoard | .08 | .04 | .01 |
| ☐ 95 | Michael Jackson | .10 | .05 | .01 |
| ☐ 96 | Mike Johnson | .05 | .02 | .01 |
| ☐ 97 | Pepper Johnson | .05 | .02 | .01 |
| ☐ 98 | Tony Jones | .05 | .02 | .01 |
| ☐ 99 | Clay Matthews | .08 | .04 | .01 |
| ☐ 100 | Eric Metcalf | .10 | .05 | .01 |
| ☐ 101 | Stevon Moore | .05 | .02 | .01 |
| ☐ 102 | Michael Dean Perry | .10 | .05 | .01 |
| ☐ 103 | Anthony Pleasant | .05 | .02 | .01 |
| ☐ 104 | Vinny Testaverde | .10 | .05 | .01 |
| ☐ 105 | Eric Turner | .08 | .04 | .01 |
| ☐ 106 | Tommy Vardell | .08 | .04 | .01 |
| ☐ 107 | Troy Aikman | 1.25 | .55 | .16 |
| ☐ 108 | Larry Brown | .05 | .02 | .01 |
| ☐ 109 | Dixon Edwards | .05 | .02 | .01 |
| ☐ 110 | Charles Haley | .08 | .04 | .01 |
| ☐ 111 | Alvin Harper | .08 | .04 | .01 |
| ☐ 112 | Michael Irvin | .30 | .14 | .04 |
| ☐ 113 | Jim Jeffcoat | .05 | .02 | .01 |
| ☐ 114 | Daryl Johnston | .10 | .05 | .01 |
| ☐ 115 | Leon Lett | .05 | .02 | .01 |
| ☐ 116 | Russell Maryland | .10 | .05 | .01 |
| ☐ 117 | Nate Newton | .05 | .02 | .01 |
| ☐ 118 | Ken Norton Jr. | .08 | .04 | .01 |
| ☐ 119 | Jay Novacek | .10 | .05 | .01 |
| ☐ 120 | Darrin Smith | .05 | .02 | .01 |
| ☐ 121 | Emmitt Smith | 1.75 | .80 | .22 |
| ☐ 122 | Kevin Smith | .08 | .04 | .01 |
| ☐ 123 | Mark Stepnoski | .05 | .02 | .01 |
| ☐ 124 | Tony Tolbert | .05 | .02 | .01 |
| ☐ 125 | Erik Williams | .05 | .02 | .01 |
| ☐ 126 | Kevin Williams | .15 | .07 | .02 |
| ☐ 127 | Darren Woodson | .05 | .02 | .01 |
| ☐ 128 | Steve Atwater | .08 | .04 | .01 |
| ☐ 129 | Rod Bernstine | .08 | .04 | .01 |
| ☐ 130 | Ray Crockett | .05 | .02 | .01 |
| ☐ 131 | Mike Croel | .08 | .04 | .01 |
| ☐ 132 | Robert Delpino | .08 | .04 | .01 |
| ☐ 133 | Shane Dronett | .05 | .02 | .01 |
| ☐ 134 | Jason Elam | .05 | .02 | .01 |
| ☐ 135 | John Elway | .40 | .18 | .05 |
| ☐ 136 | Simon Fletcher | .08 | .04 | .01 |
| ☐ 137 | Greg Kragen | .05 | .02 | .01 |
| ☐ 138 | Karl Mecklenburg | .05 | .02 | .01 |
| ☐ 139 | Glyn Milburn | .20 | .09 | .03 |
| ☐ 140 | Anthony Miller | .15 | .07 | .02 |
| ☐ 141 | Derek Russell | .08 | .04 | .01 |
| ☐ 142 | Shannon Sharpe | .15 | .07 | .02 |
| ☐ 143 | Dennis Smith | .05 | .02 | .01 |
| ☐ 144 | Dan Williams | .05 | .02 | .01 |
| ☐ 145 | Gary Zimmerman | .05 | .02 | .01 |
| ☐ 146 | Bennie Blades | .05 | .02 | .01 |
| ☐ 147 | Lomas Brown | .05 | .02 | .01 |
| ☐ 148 | Bill Fralic | .05 | .02 | .01 |
| ☐ 149 | Mel Gray | .05 | .02 | .01 |
| ☐ 150 | Willie Green | .08 | .04 | .01 |
| ☐ 151 | Jason Hanson | .05 | .02 | .01 |
| ☐ 152 | Robert Massey | .05 | .02 | .01 |
| ☐ 153 | Ryan McNeil | .05 | .02 | .01 |
| ☐ 154 | Scott Mitchell | .30 | .14 | .04 |
| ☐ 155 | Derrick Moore | .08 | .04 | .01 |
| ☐ 156 | Herman Moore | .15 | .07 | .02 |
| ☐ 157 | Brett Perriman | .08 | .04 | .01 |
| ☐ 158 | Robert Porcher | .08 | .04 | .01 |
| ☐ 159 | Kelvin Pritchett | .05 | .02 | .01 |
| ☐ 160 | Barry Sanders | .60 | .25 | .08 |
| ☐ 161 | Tracy Scroggins | .08 | .04 | .01 |
| ☐ 162 | Chris Spielman | .05 | .02 | .01 |
| ☐ 163 | Pat Swilling | .08 | .04 | .01 |
| ☐ 164 | Edgar Bennett | .05 | .02 | .01 |
| ☐ 165 | Robert Brooks | .08 | .04 | .01 |
| ☐ 166 | Terrell Buckley | .10 | .05 | .01 |
| ☐ 167 | LeRoy Butler | .05 | .02 | .01 |
| ☐ 168 | Brett Favre | .50 | .23 | .06 |
| ☐ 169 | Harry Galbreath | .05 | .02 | .01 |
| ☐ 170 | Jackie Harris | .15 | .07 | .02 |
| ☐ 171 | Johnny Holland | .05 | .02 | .01 |
| ☐ 172 | Chris Jacke | .05 | .02 | .01 |
| ☐ 173 | George Koonce | .05 | .02 | .01 |
| ☐ 174 | Bryce Paup | .05 | .02 | .01 |
| ☐ 175 | Ken Ruettgers | .05 | .02 | .01 |
| ☐ 176 | Sterling Sharpe | .30 | .14 | .04 |
| ☐ 177 | Wayne Simmons | .05 | .02 | .01 |
| ☐ 178 | George Teague | .05 | .02 | .01 |
| ☐ 179 | Darrell Thompson | .08 | .04 | .01 |
| ☐ 180 | Reggie White | .15 | .07 | .02 |
| ☐ 181 | Gary Brown | .30 | .14 | .04 |
| ☐ 182 | Cody Carlson | .10 | .05 | .01 |
| ☐ 183 | Ray Childress | .05 | .02 | .01 |
| ☐ 184 | Cris Dishman | .05 | .02 | .01 |
| ☐ 185 | Ernest Givins | .08 | .04 | .01 |
| ☐ 186 | Haywood Jeffires | .10 | .05 | .01 |
| ☐ 187 | Sean Jones | .05 | .02 | .01 |
| ☐ 188 | Lamar Lathon | .05 | .02 | .01 |
| ☐ 189 | Bruce Matthews | .08 | .04 | .01 |
| ☐ 190 | Bubba McDowell | .05 | .02 | .01 |
| ☐ 191 | Glenn Montgomery | .05 | .02 | .01 |
| ☐ 192 | Greg Montgomery | .05 | .02 | .01 |
| ☐ 193 | Warren Moon | .10 | .05 | .01 |
| ☐ 194 | Bo Orlando | .05 | .02 | .01 |
| ☐ 195 | Marcus Robertson | .05 | .02 | .01 |
| ☐ 196 | Eddie Robinson | .05 | .02 | .01 |
| ☐ 197 | Webster Slaughter | .08 | .04 | .01 |
| ☐ 198 | Lorenzo White | .08 | .04 | .01 |
| ☐ 199 | John Baylor | .05 | .02 | .01 |
| ☐ 200 | Jason Belser | .05 | .02 | .01 |
| ☐ 201 | Tony Bennett | .05 | .02 | .01 |
| ☐ 202 | Dean Biasucci | .05 | .02 | .01 |
| ☐ 203 | Ray Buchanan | .05 | .02 | .01 |
| ☐ 204 | Kerry Cash | .05 | .02 | .01 |
| ☐ 205 | Quentin Coryatt | .10 | .05 | .01 |
| ☐ 206 | Eugene Daniel | .05 | .02 | .01 |
| ☐ 207 | Steve Emtman | .08 | .04 | .01 |
| ☐ 208 | Jon Hand | .05 | .02 | .01 |
| ☐ 209 | Jim Harbaugh | .08 | .04 | .01 |
| ☐ 210 | Jeff Herrod | .05 | .02 | .01 |
| ☐ 211 | Anthony Johnson | .05 | .02 | .01 |
| ☐ 212 | Roosevelt Potts | .05 | .02 | .01 |
| ☐ 213 | Rohn Stark | .05 | .02 | .01 |
| ☐ 214 | Will Wolford | .05 | .02 | .01 |
| ☐ 215 | Marcus Allen | .08 | .04 | .01 |
| ☐ 216 | John Alt | .05 | .02 | .01 |
| ☐ 217 | Kimble Anders | .15 | .07 | .02 |
| ☐ 218 | J.J. Birden | .08 | .04 | .01 |
| ☐ 219 | Dale Carter | .10 | .05 | .01 |
| ☐ 220 | Keith Cash | .05 | .02 | .01 |
| ☐ 221 | Tony Casillas | .05 | .02 | .01 |
| ☐ 222 | Willie Davis | .05 | .02 | .01 |
| ☐ 223 | Tim Grunhard | .05 | .02 | .01 |
| ☐ 224 | Nick Lowery | .05 | .02 | .01 |
| ☐ 225 | Charles Mincy | .05 | .02 | .01 |
| ☐ 226 | Joe Montana | 1.25 | .55 | .16 |
| ☐ 227 | Dan Saleaumua | .05 | .02 | .01 |
| ☐ 228 | Tracy Simien | .05 | .02 | .01 |
| ☐ 229 | Neil Smith | .10 | .05 | .01 |
| ☐ 230 | Derrick Thomas | .15 | .07 | .02 |
| ☐ 231 | Eddie Anderson | .05 | .02 | .01 |
| ☐ 232 | Tim Brown | .15 | .07 | .02 |
| ☐ 233 | Nolan Harrison | .05 | .02 | .01 |
| ☐ 234 | Jeff Hostetler | .10 | .05 | .01 |
| ☐ 235 | Raghib Ismail | .15 | .07 | .02 |
| ☐ 236 | Jeff Jaeger | .05 | .02 | .01 |
| ☐ 237 | James Jett | .30 | .14 | .04 |
| ☐ 238 | Joe Kelly | .05 | .02 | .01 |
| ☐ 239 | Albert Lewis | .05 | .02 | .01 |
| ☐ 240 | Terry McDaniel | .05 | .02 | .01 |
| ☐ 241 | Chester McGlockton | .05 | .02 | .01 |
| ☐ 242 | Winston Moss | .05 | .02 | .01 |
| ☐ 243 | Gerald Perry | .05 | .02 | .01 |
| ☐ 244 | Greg Robinson | .10 | .05 | .01 |
| ☐ 245 | Anthony Smith | .05 | .02 | .01 |
| ☐ 246 | Steve Smith | .08 | .04 | .01 |
| ☐ 247 | Greg Townsend | .05 | .02 | .01 |
| ☐ 248 | Lionel Washington | .05 | .02 | .01 |
| ☐ 249 | Steve Wisniewski | .05 | .02 | .01 |
| ☐ 250 | Alexander Wright | .08 | .04 | .01 |
| ☐ 251 | Flipper Anderson | .08 | .04 | .01 |
| ☐ 252 | Jerome Bettis | 2.00 | .90 | .25 |
| ☐ 253 | Marc Boutte | .05 | .02 | .01 |
| ☐ 254 | Shane Conlan | .05 | .02 | .01 |
| ☐ 255 | Troy Drayton | .08 | .04 | .01 |
| ☐ 256 | Henry Ellard | .08 | .04 | .01 |
| ☐ 257 | Sean Gilbert | .08 | .04 | .01 |
| ☐ 258 | Nate Lewis | .08 | .04 | .01 |
| ☐ 259 | Todd Lyght | .05 | .02 | .01 |
| ☐ 260 | Chris Miller | .10 | .05 | .01 |
| ☐ 261 | Anthony Newman | .05 | .02 | .01 |
| ☐ 262 | Roman Phifer | .05 | .02 | .01 |
| ☐ 263 | Henry Rolling | .05 | .02 | .01 |
| ☐ 264 | T.J. Rubley | .75 | .35 | .09 |
| ☐ 265 | Jackie Slater | .08 | .04 | .01 |
| ☐ 266 | Fred Stokes | .05 | .02 | .01 |
| ☐ 267 | Robert Young | .08 | .04 | .01 |
| ☐ 268 | Gene Atkins | .05 | .02 | .01 |
| ☐ 269 | J.B. Brown | .05 | .02 | .01 |
| ☐ 270 | Keith Byars | .08 | .04 | .01 |
| ☐ 271 | Marco Coleman | .08 | .04 | .01 |
| ☐ 272 | Bryan Cox | .08 | .04 | .01 |
| ☐ 273 | Jeff Cross | .05 | .02 | .01 |
| ☐ 274 | Irving Fryar | .05 | .02 | .01 |
| ☐ 275 | Mark Higgs | .10 | .05 | .01 |
| ☐ 276 | Dwight Hollier | .05 | .02 | .01 |
| ☐ 277 | Mark Ingram | .08 | .04 | .01 |
| ☐ 278 | Keith Jackson | .10 | .05 | .01 |
| ☐ 279 | Terry Kirby | .50 | .23 | .06 |
| ☐ 280 | Bernie Kosar | .10 | .05 | .01 |
| ☐ 281 | Dan Marino | .75 | .35 | .09 |
| ☐ 282 | O.J. McDuffie | .25 | .11 | .03 |
| ☐ 283 | Keith Sims | .05 | .02 | .01 |

|  |  | | | |
|---|---|---|---|---|
| 284 | Pete Stoyanovich | .05 | .02 | .01 |
| 285 | Troy Vincent | .08 | .04 | .01 |
| 286 | Richmond Webb | .05 | .02 | .01 |
| 287 | Terry Allen | .10 | .05 | .01 |
| 288 | Anthony Carter | .08 | .04 | .01 |
| 289 | Cris Carter | .10 | .05 | .01 |
| 290 | Jack Del Rio | .05 | .02 | .01 |
| 291 | Chris Doleman | .08 | .04 | .01 |
| 292 | Vencie Glenn | .05 | .02 | .01 |
| 293 | Scottie Graham | .40 | .18 | .05 |
| 294 | Chris Hinton | .05 | .02 | .01 |
| 295 | Qadry Ismail | .15 | .07 | .02 |
| 296 | Carlos Jenkins | .05 | .02 | .01 |
| 297 | Steve Jordan | .08 | .04 | .01 |
| 298 | Carl Lee | .05 | .02 | .01 |
| 299 | Randall McDaniel | .05 | .02 | .01 |
| 300 | John Randle | .05 | .02 | .01 |
| 301 | Todd Scott | .05 | .02 | .01 |
| 302 | Robert Smith | .10 | .05 | .01 |
| 303 | Fred Strickland | .05 | .02 | .01 |
| 304 | Henry Thomas | .05 | .02 | .01 |
| 305 | Bruce Armstrong | .05 | .02 | .01 |
| 306 | Harlon Barnett | .05 | .02 | .01 |
| 307 | Drew Bledsoe | 2.00 | .90 | .25 |
| 308 | Vincent Brown | .05 | .02 | .01 |
| 309 | Ben Coates | .05 | .02 | .01 |
| 310 | Todd Collins | .05 | .02 | .01 |
| 311 | Myron Guyton | .05 | .02 | .01 |
| 312 | Pat Harlow | .05 | .02 | .01 |
| 313 | Maurice Hurst | .05 | .02 | .01 |
| 314 | Leonard Russell | .08 | .04 | .01 |
| 315 | Chris Slade | .05 | .02 | .01 |
| 316 | Michael Timpson | .05 | .02 | .01 |
| 317 | Andre Tippett | .05 | .02 | .01 |
| 318 | Morten Andersen | .08 | .04 | .01 |
| 319 | Derek Brown | .20 | .09 | .03 |
| 320 | Vince Buck | .05 | .02 | .01 |
| 321 | Toi Cook | .05 | .02 | .01 |
| 322 | Quinn Early | .08 | .04 | .01 |
| 323 | Jim Everett | .05 | .02 | .01 |
| 324 | Michael Haynes | .15 | .07 | .02 |
| 325 | Tyrone Hughes | .05 | .02 | .01 |
| 326 | Rickey Jackson | .08 | .04 | .01 |
| 327 | Vaughan Johnson | .05 | .02 | .01 |
| 328 | Eric Martin | .08 | .04 | .01 |
| 329 | Wayne Martin | .05 | .02 | .01 |
| 330 | Sam Mills | .08 | .04 | .01 |
| 331 | Willie Roaf | .05 | .02 | .01 |
| 332 | Irv Smith | .05 | .02 | .01 |
| 333 | Keith Taylor | .05 | .02 | .01 |
| 334 | Renaldo Turnbull | .08 | .04 | .01 |
| 335 | Carlton Bailey | .05 | .02 | .01 |
| 336 | Michael Brooks | .05 | .02 | .01 |
| 337 | Jarrod Bunch | .05 | .02 | .01 |
| 338 | Chris Calloway | .05 | .02 | .01 |
| 339 | Mark Collins | .05 | .02 | .01 |
| 340 | Howard Cross | .05 | .02 | .01 |
| 341 | Stacey Dillard | .15 | .07 | .02 |
| 342 | John Elliott | .05 | .02 | .01 |
| 343 | Rodney Hampton | .25 | .11 | .03 |
| 344 | Greg Jackson | .05 | .02 | .01 |
| 345 | Mark Jackson | .08 | .04 | .01 |
| 346 | Dave Meggett | .08 | .04 | .01 |
| 347 | Corey Miller | .05 | .02 | .01 |
| 348 | Mike Sherrard | .05 | .02 | .01 |
| 349 | Phil Simms | .10 | .05 | .01 |
| 350 | Lewis Tillman | .08 | .04 | .01 |
| 351 | Brad Baxter | .08 | .04 | .01 |
| 352 | Kyle Clifton | .05 | .02 | .01 |
| 353 | Boomer Esiason | .10 | .05 | .01 |
| 354 | James Hasty | .05 | .02 | .01 |
| 355 | Bobby Houston | .05 | .02 | .01 |
| 356 | Johnny Johnson | .10 | .05 | .01 |
| 357 | Jeff Lageman | .05 | .02 | .01 |
| 358 | Mo Lewis | .05 | .02 | .01 |
| 359 | Ronnie Lott | .10 | .05 | .01 |
| 360 | Leonard Marshall | .05 | .02 | .01 |
| 361 | Johnny Mitchell | .10 | .05 | .01 |
| 362 | Rob Moore | .10 | .05 | .01 |
| 363 | Eric Thomas | .05 | .02 | .01 |
| 364 | Brian Washington | .05 | .02 | .01 |
| 365 | Marvin Washington | .05 | .02 | .01 |
| 366 | Eric Allen | .08 | .04 | .01 |
| 367 | Fred Barnett | .10 | .05 | .01 |
| 368 | Bubby Brister | .05 | .02 | .01 |
| 369 | Randall Cunningham | .10 | .05 | .01 |
| 370 | Byron Evans | .05 | .02 | .01 |
| 371 | William Fuller | .05 | .02 | .01 |
| 372 | Andy Harmon | .05 | .02 | .01 |
| 373 | Seth Joyner | .08 | .04 | .01 |
| 374 | William Perry | .08 | .04 | .01 |
| 375 | Leonard Renfro | .05 | .02 | .01 |
| 376 | Heath Sherman | .05 | .02 | .01 |
| 377 | Ben Smith | .05 | .02 | .01 |
| 378 | William Thomas | .05 | .02 | .01 |
| 379 | Herschel Walker | .10 | .05 | .01 |
| 380 | Calvin Williams | .10 | .05 | .01 |
| 381 | Chad Brown | .05 | .02 | .01 |
| 382 | Dermontti Dawson | .05 | .02 | .01 |
| 383 | Deon Figures | .05 | .02 | .01 |
| 384 | Barry Foster | .15 | .07 | .02 |
| 385 | Jeff Graham | .08 | .04 | .01 |
| 386 | Eric Green | .10 | .05 | .01 |
| 387 | Kevin Greene | .05 | .02 | .01 |
| 388 | Carlton Haselrig | .05 | .02 | .01 |
| 389 | Levon Kirkland | .05 | .02 | .01 |
| 390 | Carnell Lake | .05 | .02 | .01 |
| 391 | Greg Lloyd | .05 | .02 | .01 |
| 392 | Neil O'Donnell | .12 | .05 | .02 |
| 393 | Darren Perry | .05 | .02 | .01 |
| 394 | Dwight Stone | .05 | .02 | .01 |
| 395 | Leroy Thompson | .08 | .04 | .01 |
| 396 | Rod Woodson | .10 | .05 | .01 |
| 397 | Marion Butts | .10 | .05 | .01 |
| 398 | John Carney | .05 | .02 | .01 |
| 399 | Darren Carrington | .05 | .02 | .01 |
| 400 | Burt Grossman | .05 | .02 | .01 |
| 401 | Courtney Hall | .05 | .02 | .01 |
| 402 | Ronnie Harmon | .05 | .02 | .01 |
| 403 | Stan Humphries | .10 | .05 | .01 |
| 404 | Shawn Jefferson | .05 | .02 | .01 |
| 405 | Vance Johnson | .08 | .04 | .01 |
| 406 | Chris Mims | .08 | .04 | .01 |
| 407 | Leslie O'Neal | .08 | .04 | .01 |
| 408 | Stanley Richard | .05 | .02 | .01 |
| 409 | Junior Seau | .10 | .05 | .01 |
| 410 | Harris Barton | .05 | .02 | .01 |
| 411 | Dennis Brown | .05 | .02 | .01 |
| 412 | Eric Davis | .05 | .02 | .01 |
| 413 | Merton Hanks | .05 | .02 | .01 |
| 414 | John Johnson | .05 | .02 | .01 |
| 415 | Brent Jones | .10 | .05 | .01 |
| 416 | Marc Logan | .05 | .02 | .01 |
| 417 | Tim McDonald | .05 | .02 | .01 |
| 418 | Gary Plummer | .05 | .02 | .01 |
| 419 | Tom Rathman | .08 | .04 | .01 |
| 420 | Jerry Rice | .50 | .23 | .06 |
| 421 | Bill Romanowski | .05 | .02 | .01 |
| 422 | Jesse Sapolu | .05 | .02 | .01 |
| 423 | Dana Stubblefield | .15 | .07 | .02 |
| 424 | John Taylor | .10 | .05 | .01 |
| 425 | Steve Wallace | .05 | .02 | .01 |
| 426 | Ted Washington | .05 | .02 | .01 |
| 427 | Ricky Watters | .20 | .09 | .03 |
| 428 | Troy Wilson | .15 | .07 | .02 |
| 429 | Steve Young | .15 | .07 | .02 |
| 430 | Howard Ballard | .05 | .02 | .01 |
| 431 | Michael Bates | .05 | .02 | .01 |
| 432 | Robert Blackmon | .05 | .02 | .01 |
| 433 | Brian Blades | .08 | .04 | .01 |
| 434 | Ferrell Edmunds | .05 | .02 | .01 |
| 435 | Carlton Gray | .05 | .02 | .01 |
| 436 | Patrick Hunter | .05 | .02 | .01 |
| 437 | Cortez Kennedy | .10 | .05 | .01 |
| 438 | Kelvin Martin | .05 | .02 | .01 |
| 439 | Rick Mirer | 2.00 | .90 | .25 |
| 440 | Nate Odomes | .08 | .04 | .01 |
| 441 | Ray Roberts | .05 | .02 | .01 |
| 442 | Eugene Robinson | .05 | .02 | .01 |
| 443 | Rod Stephens | .05 | .02 | .01 |
| 444 | Chris Warren | .10 | .05 | .01 |
| 445 | John L. Williams | .08 | .04 | .01 |
| 446 | Terry Wooden | .05 | .02 | .01 |
| 447 | Marty Carter | .05 | .02 | .01 |
| 448 | Reggie Cobb | .10 | .05 | .01 |
| 449 | Lawrence Dawsey | .10 | .05 | .01 |
| 450 | Santana Dotson | .10 | .05 | .01 |
| 451 | Craig Erickson | .10 | .05 | .01 |
| 452 | Thomas Everett | .05 | .02 | .01 |
| 453 | Paul Gruber | .05 | .02 | .01 |
| 454 | Courtney Hawkins | .08 | .04 | .01 |
| 455 | Martin Mayhew | .05 | .02 | .01 |
| 456 | Hardy Nickerson | .05 | .02 | .01 |
| 457 | Ricky Reynolds | .05 | .02 | .01 |
| 458 | Vince Workman | .05 | .02 | .01 |
| 459 | Reggie Brooks | .75 | .35 | .09 |
| 460 | Earnest Byner | .08 | .04 | .01 |
| 461 | Andre Collins | .05 | .02 | .01 |
| 462 | Brad Edwards | .05 | .02 | .01 |
| 463 | Kurt Gouveia | .05 | .02 | .01 |
| 464 | Darrell Green | .08 | .04 | .01 |
| 465 | Ken Harvey | .05 | .02 | .01 |
| 466 | Ethan Horton | .05 | .02 | .01 |
| 467 | A.J. Johnson | .05 | .02 | .01 |
| 468 | Tim Johnson | .05 | .02 | .01 |
| 469 | Jim Lachey | .05 | .02 | .01 |
| 470 | Chip Lohmiller | .05 | .02 | .01 |
| 471 | Art Monk | .10 | .05 | .01 |
| 472 | Sterling Palmer | .15 | .07 | .02 |
| 473 | Mark Rypien | .08 | .04 | .01 |
| 474 | Ricky Sanders | .08 | .04 | .01 |
| 475 | Checklist | .05 | .02 | .01 |
| 476 | Checklist | .05 | .02 | .01 |
| 477 | Checklist | .05 | .02 | .01 |

| | | | |
|---|---|---|---|
| ☐ 478 Checklist | .05 | .02 | .01 |
| ☐ 479 Checklist | .05 | .02 | .01 |
| ☐ 480 Checklist | .05 | .02 | .01 |
| ☐ NNO Rookie Exchange | 25.00 | 11.50 | 3.10 |

## 1994 Fleer All-Pros

Randomly inserted in packs, these 24 standard-size (2 1/2" by 3 1/2") cards present Fleer's choices for leading offensive and defensive players from both conferences. The borderless fronts feature color action player cutouts with multiple ghosted "echoes" of the player's image. The player's name appears vertically in gold foil near the left edge. The borderless back carries a color player closeup surrounded by a colorful "aura." Career highlights appear near the bottom. The cards are numbered on the back as "X of 24."

| | MINT | EXC | G-VG |
|---|---|---|---|
| COMPLETE SET (24) | 30.00 | 13.50 | 3.80 |
| COMMON PLAYER (1-24) | .30 | .14 | .04 |
| ☐ 1 Troy Aikman | 4.00 | 1.80 | .50 |
| Dallas Cowboys | | | |
| ☐ 2 Eric Allen | .30 | .14 | .04 |
| Philadelphia Eagles | | | |
| ☐ 3 Jerome Bettis | 4.00 | 1.80 | .50 |
| Los Angeles Rams | | | |
| ☐ 4 Barry Foster | .75 | .35 | .09 |
| Pittsburgh Steelers | | | |
| ☐ 5 Michael Irvin | 1.25 | .55 | .16 |
| Dallas Cowboys | | | |
| ☐ 6 Cortez Kennedy | .40 | .18 | .05 |
| Seattle Seahawks | | | |
| ☐ 7 Joe Montana | 4.00 | 1.80 | .50 |
| Kansas City Chiefs | | | |
| ☐ 8 Hardy Nickerson | .30 | .14 | .04 |
| Tampa Bay Buccaneers | | | |
| ☐ 9 Jerry Rice | 2.00 | .90 | .25 |
| San Francisco 49ers | | | |
| ☐ 10 Andre Rison | .50 | .23 | .06 |
| Atlanta Falcons | | | |
| ☐ 11 Barry Sanders | 2.00 | .90 | .25 |
| Detroit Lions | | | |
| ☐ 12 Deion Sanders | .50 | .23 | .06 |
| Atlanta Falcons | | | |
| ☐ 13 Junior Seau | .40 | .18 | .05 |
| San Diego Chargers | | | |
| ☐ 14 Shannon Sharpe | .50 | .23 | .06 |
| Denver Broncos | | | |
| ☐ 15 Sterling Sharpe | 1.50 | .65 | .19 |
| Green Bay Packers | | | |
| ☐ 16 Bruce Smith | .40 | .18 | .05 |
| Buffalo Bills | | | |
| ☐ 17 Emmitt Smith | 5.00 | 2.30 | .60 |
| Dallas Cowboys | | | |
| ☐ 18 Neil Smith | .30 | .14 | .04 |
| Kansas City Chiefs | | | |
| ☐ 19 Derrick Thomas | .50 | .23 | .06 |
| Kansas City Chiefs | | | |
| ☐ 20 Thurman Thomas | 1.00 | .45 | .13 |
| Buffalo Bills | | | |
| ☐ 21 Renaldo Turnbull | .30 | .14 | .04 |
| New Orleans Saints | | | |
| ☐ 22 Reggie White | .50 | .23 | .06 |
| Green Bay Packers | | | |
| ☐ 23 Rod Woodson | .40 | .18 | .05 |
| Pittsburgh Steelers | | | |
| ☐ 24 Steve Young | .75 | .35 | .09 |
| San Francisco 49ers | | | |

## 1994 Fleer Award Winners

Randomly inserted in packs, this five-card standard-size (2 1/2" by 3 1/2") set focuses on the Super Bowl MVP, the AFC and NFC Offensive

Rookies of the Year, the NFL Defensive Player of the Year and the NFL Rookie of the Year. Each borderless front features a color action player cutout. This is set on a background of a black-and-white player close-up, which is color-screened near the bottom. The player's name appears in gold foil at the lower left. The borderless back carries a color player action shot, the background of which is faded to black-and-white. Career highlights appear within a color-screened rectangle set off to one side. The cards are numbered on the back as "X of 5."

| | MINT | EXC | G-VG |
|---|---|---|---|
| COMPLETE SET (5) | 6.00 | 2.70 | .75 |
| COMMON PLAYER (1-5) | .30 | .14 | .04 |
| ☐ 1 Jerome Bettis | 2.00 | .90 | .25 |
| Los Angeles Rams | | | |
| ☐ 2 Rick Mirer | 2.00 | .90 | .25 |
| Seattle Seahawks | | | |
| ☐ 3 Deion Sanders | .50 | .23 | .06 |
| Atlanta Falcons | | | |
| ☐ 4 Emmitt Smith | 2.50 | 1.15 | .30 |
| Dallas Cowboys | | | |
| ☐ 5 Dana Stubblefield | .30 | .14 | .04 |
| San Francisco 49ers | | | |

## 1994 Fleer Jerome Bettis

Randomly inserted in packs, this 12-card set details Jerome Bettis' achievements at Notre Dame and as a 1993 rookie star with the Los Angeles Rams. Each standard-size (2 1/2" by 3 1/2") card features a color action player cutout set on a colorized abstract design. The player's name and likeness appear in gold foil at the bottom. A horizontal back features a color action shot of Bettis as well as career highlights. The three mail-in cards could be obtained for 10 1994 Fleer Football wrappers plus 1.50. The cards are numbered on the back.

| | MINT | EXC | G-VG |
|---|---|---|---|
| COMPLETE SET (12) | 10.00 | 4.50 | 1.25 |
| COMMON PLAYER (1-12) | 1.00 | .45 | .13 |
| ☐ 1 Jerome Bettis | 1.00 | .45 | .13 |
| Notre Dame action photo | | | |
| ☐ 2 Jerome Bettis | 1.00 | .45 | .13 |
| Draft day photo | | | |
| ☐ 3 Jerome Bettis | 1.00 | .45 | .13 |
| Rams action photo | | | |
| ☐ 4 Jerome Bettis | 1.00 | .45 | .13 |
| Rams action photo | | | |
| ☐ 5 Jerome Bettis | 1.00 | .45 | .13 |
| Rams action photo | | | |
| ☐ 6 Jerome Bettis | 1.00 | .45 | .13 |
| Rams action photo | | | |
| ☐ 7 Jerome Bettis | 1.00 | .45 | .13 |
| Rams action photo | | | |
| ☐ 8 Jerome Bettis | 1.00 | .45 | .13 |

| | MINT | EXC | G-VG |
|---|---|---|---|
| Rams action photo | | | |
| ☐ 9 Jerome Bettis........................ | 1.00 | .45 | .13 |
| Rams action photo | | | |
| ☐ 10 Jerome Bettis...................... | 1.00 | .45 | .13 |
| Rams action photo | | | |
| ☐ 11 Jerome Bettis...................... | 1.00 | .45 | .13 |
| Rams action photo | | | |
| ☐ 12 Jerome Bettis...................... | 1.00 | .45 | .13 |
| Pro Bowl photo | | | |

## 1994 Fleer League Leaders

The 1994 Fleer League Leaders set highlights top-ranked players in passing, rushing and receiving from the 1993 campaign. The card fronts feature color photos of players that emerge from a blurred background. Player name and the League Leader logo adorn the front. Card backs contain a small color photo and 1993 achievements. The cards were randomly inserted in wax packs.

| | MINT | EXC | G-VG |
|---|---|---|---|
| COMPLETE SET (10)........................ | 12.00 | 5.50 | 1.50 |
| COMMON PLAYER (1-10)................ | .50 | .23 | .06 |
| ☐ 1 Marcus Allen............................. | .75 | .35 | .09 |
| Kansas City Chiefs | | | |
| ☐ 2 Tim Brown................................. | .75 | .35 | .09 |
| Los Angeles Raiders | | | |
| ☐ 3 John Elway................................ | 2.00 | .90 | .25 |
| Denver Broncos | | | |
| ☐ 4 Tyrone Hughes......................... | .50 | .23 | .06 |
| New Orleans Saints | | | |
| ☐ 5 Jerry Rice................................. | 2.50 | 1.15 | .30 |
| San Francisco 49ers | | | |
| ☐ 6 Sterling Sharpe......................... | 2.00 | .90 | .25 |
| Green Bay Packers | | | |
| ☐ 7 Emmitt Smith............................. | 5.00 | 2.30 | .60 |
| Dallas Cowboys | | | |
| ☐ 8 Neil Smith................................. | .50 | .23 | .06 |
| Kansas City Chiefs | | | |
| ☐ 9 Thurman Thomas...................... | 1.50 | .65 | .19 |
| Buffalo Bills | | | |
| ☐ 10 Steve Young............................ | 1.00 | .45 | .13 |
| San Francisco 49ers | | | |

## 1994 Fleer Living Legends

These metallized cards feature NFL stars with long records of achievement in the league. A six-card set, they are randomly inserted

in wax packs. Horizontally designed fronts and backs have color photos with career highlights on the back.

| | MINT | EXC | G-VG |
|---|---|---|---|
| COMPLETE SET (6).......................... | 125.00 | 57.50 | 15.50 |
| COMMON PLAYER (1-6)................... | 10.00 | 4.50 | 1.25 |
| ☐ 1 Marcus Allen............................. | 10.00 | 4.50 | 1.25 |
| Kansas City Chiefs | | | |
| ☐ 2 John Elway................................ | 18.00 | 8.00 | 2.30 |
| Denver Broncos | | | |
| ☐ 3 Joe Montana............................. | 40.00 | 18.00 | 5.00 |
| Kansas City Chiefs | | | |
| ☐ 4 Jerry Rice................................. | 20.00 | 9.00 | 2.50 |
| San Francisco 49ers | | | |
| ☐ 5 Emmitt Smith............................. | 50.00 | 23.00 | 6.25 |
| Dallas Cowboys | | | |
| ☐ 6 Reggie White............................. | 10.00 | 4.50 | 1.25 |
| Green Bay Packers | | | |

## 1994 Fleer Prospects

This 25-card set features college players with a great chance of making it big in the NFL. Pictured in his collegiate uniform, the player is superimposed over a the fiery background of a steel mill. The backs have a smaller player photo with a like background. Collegiate highlights are provided in the text on back.

| | MINT | EXC | G-VG |
|---|---|---|---|
| COMPLETE SET (25)........................ | 35.00 | 16.00 | 4.40 |
| COMMON PLAYER (1-25)................ | .75 | .35 | .09 |
| ☐ 1 Sam Adams.............................. | 1.50 | .65 | .19 |
| Seattle Seahawks | | | |
| ☐ 2 Trev Alberts.............................. | 2.50 | 1.15 | .30 |
| Indianapolis Colts | | | |
| ☐ 3 Derrick Alexander...................... | 2.50 | 1.15 | .30 |
| Cleveland Browns | | | |
| ☐ 4 Mario Bates.............................. | 2.50 | 1.15 | .30 |
| New Orleans Saints | | | |
| ☐ 5 Jeff Burris................................. | 1.50 | .65 | .19 |
| Buffalo Bills | | | |
| ☐ 6 Shante Carver........................... | 1.00 | .45 | .13 |
| Dallas Cowboys | | | |
| ☐ 7 Marshall Faulk........................... | 7.00 | 3.10 | .85 |
| Indianapolis Colts | | | |
| ☐ 8 William Floyd ............................ | 2.50 | 1.15 | .30 |
| San Francisco 49ers | | | |
| ☐ 9 Rob Fredrickson........................ | .75 | .35 | .09 |
| Los Angeles Raiders | | | |
| ☐ 10 Wayne Gandy.......................... | .75 | .35 | .09 |
| Los Angeles Rams | | | |
| ☐ 11 Charlie Garner......................... | 2.50 | 1.15 | .30 |
| Philadelphia Eagles | | | |
| ☐ 12 Aaron Glenn............................ | 1.00 | .45 | .13 |
| New York Jets | | | |
| ☐ 13 Charles Johnson ..................... | 3.00 | 1.35 | .40 |
| Pittsburgh Steelers | | | |
| ☐ 14 Joe Johnson ........................... | .75 | .35 | .09 |
| New Orleans Saints | | | |
| ☐ 15 Tre Johnson ........................... | .75 | .35 | .09 |
| Washington Redskins | | | |
| ☐ 16 Antonio Langham...................... | 1.50 | .65 | .19 |
| Cleveland Browns | | | |
| ☐ 17 Chuck Levy.............................. | 2.50 | 1.15 | .30 |
| Arizona Cardinals | | | |
| ☐ 18 Willie McGinest........................ | 2.25 | 1.00 | .30 |
| New England Patriots | | | |
| ☐ 19 David Palmer........................... | 4.00 | 1.80 | .50 |
| Minnesota Vikings | | | |
| ☐ 20 Errict Rhett.............................. | 4.00 | 1.80 | .50 |
| Tampa Bay Buccaneers | | | |
| ☐ 21 Jason Sehorn........................... | .75 | .35 | .09 |
| New York Giants | | | |

| | | MINT | EXC | G-VG |
|---|---|---|---|---|
| ☐ 22 | Heath Shuler | 10.00 | 4.50 | 1.25 |
| | Washington Redskins | | | |
| ☐ 23 | Charlie Ward | 3.00 | 1.35 | .40 |
| | Not Drafted | | | |
| ☐ 24 | DeWayne Washington | .75 | .35 | .09 |
| | Minnesota Vikings | | | |
| ☐ 25 | Bryant Young | 2.00 | .90 | .25 |
| | San Francisco 49ers | | | |

## 1994 Fleer Pro-Visions

In keeping with the Pro-Visions theme established in prior years, selected stars of the NFL are presented artistically. The back contains career highlights. The nine-card jumbo set was distributed one set per hobby case.

| | MINT | EXC | G-VG |
|---|---|---|---|
| COMPLETE SET (9) | 10.00 | 4.50 | 1.25 |
| COMMON PLAYER (1-9) | .30 | .14 | .04 |
| *JUMBO CARDS: 2X TO 4X VALUE .. | | | |

| | | MINT | EXC | G-VG |
|---|---|---|---|---|
| ☐ 1 | Rodney Hampton | .50 | .23 | .06 |
| | New York Giants | | | |
| ☐ 2 | Ricky Watters | .50 | .23 | .06 |
| | San Francisco 49ers | | | |
| ☐ 3 | Rick Mirer | 2.00 | .90 | .25 |
| | Seattle Seahawks | | | |
| ☐ 4 | Brett Favre | .75 | .35 | .09 |
| | Green Bay Packers | | | |
| ☐ 5 | Troy Aikman | 2.25 | 1.00 | .30 |
| | Dallas Cowboys | | | |
| ☐ 6 | Jerome Bettis | 2.00 | .90 | .25 |
| | Los Angeles Rams | | | |
| ☐ 7 | Joe Montana | 2.25 | 1.00 | .30 |
| | Kansas City Chiefs | | | |
| ☐ 8 | Cornelius Bennett | .30 | .14 | .04 |
| | Buffalo Bills | | | |
| ☐ 9 | Rod Woodson | .30 | .14 | .04 |
| | Pittsburgh Steelers | | | |

## 1994 Fleer Rookie Sensations

Randomly inserted in jumbo packs, the Rookie Sensations set contains 20 cards of players that performed as a rookie in 1993. A color player photo on the front has a wavy background in the dominant color of his team. The backs also have a team colored background with a small player photo and bio.

| | MINT | EXC | G-VG |
|---|---|---|---|
| COMPLETE SET (20) | 200.00 | 90.00 | 25.00 |
| COMMON PLAYER (1-20) | 4.00 | 1.80 | .50 |

| | | MINT | EXC | G-VG |
|---|---|---|---|---|
| ☐ 1 | Jerome Bettis | 40.00 | 18.00 | 5.00 |
| | Los Angeles Rams | | | |
| ☐ 2 | Drew Bledsoe | 40.00 | 18.00 | 5.00 |
| | New England Patriots | | | |
| ☐ 3 | Reggie Brooks | 20.00 | 9.00 | 2.50 |
| | Washington Redskins | | | |
| ☐ 4 | Tom Carter | 4.00 | 1.80 | .50 |
| | Washington Redskins | | | |
| ☐ 5 | John Copeland | 4.00 | 1.80 | .50 |
| | Cincinnati Bengals | | | |
| ☐ 6 | Jason Elam | 4.00 | 1.80 | .50 |
| | Denver Broncos | | | |
| ☐ 7 | Garrison Hearst | 8.00 | 3.60 | 1.00 |
| | Phoenix Cardinals | | | |
| ☐ 8 | Tyrone Hughes | 4.00 | 1.80 | .50 |
| | New Orleans Saints | | | |
| ☐ 9 | James Jett | 8.00 | 3.60 | 1.00 |
| | Los Angeles Raiders | | | |
| ☐ 10 | Lincoln Kennedy | 4.00 | 1.80 | .50 |
| | Atlanta Falcons | | | |
| ☐ 11 | Terry Kirby | 12.00 | 5.50 | 1.50 |
| | Miami Dolphins | | | |
| ☐ 12 | Glyn Milburn | 8.00 | 3.60 | 1.00 |
| | Denver Broncos | | | |
| ☐ 13 | Rick Mirer | 40.00 | 18.00 | 5.00 |
| | Seattle Seahawks | | | |
| ☐ 14 | Ron Moore | 10.00 | 4.50 | 1.25 |
| | Arizona Cardinals | | | |
| ☐ 15 | William Roaf | 4.00 | 1.80 | .50 |
| | New Orleans Saints | | | |
| ☐ 16 | Wayne Simmons | 4.00 | 1.80 | .50 |
| | Green Bay Packers | | | |
| ☐ 17 | Chris Slade | 5.00 | 2.30 | .60 |
| | New England Patriots | | | |
| ☐ 18 | Darrin Smith | 5.00 | 2.30 | .60 |
| | Dallas Cowboys | | | |
| ☐ 19 | Dana Stubblefield | 5.00 | 2.30 | .60 |
| | San Francisco 49ers | | | |
| ☐ 20 | George Teague | 4.00 | 1.80 | .50 |
| | Green Bay Packers | | | |

## 1994 Fleer Scoring Machines

Inserted only in 15-card foil packs, this set highlights top running backs, quarterbacks and receivers. Horizontally designed fronts feature three player photos. The back has a player photo and 1993 highlights.

| | MINT | EXC | G-VG |
|---|---|---|---|
| COMPLETE SET (20) | 200.00 | 90.00 | 25.00 |
| COMMON PLAYER (1-20) | 3.00 | 1.35 | .40 |

| | | MINT | EXC | G-VG |
|---|---|---|---|---|
| ☐ 1 | Marcus Allen | 4.00 | 1.80 | .50 |
| | Kansas City Chiefs | | | |
| ☐ 2 | Natrone Means | 6.00 | 2.70 | .75 |
| | San Diego Chargers | | | |
| ☐ 3 | Jerome Bettis | 25.00 | 11.50 | 3.10 |
| | Los Angeles Rams | | | |
| ☐ 4 | Tim Brown | 5.00 | 2.30 | .60 |
| | Los Angeles Raiders | | | |
| ☐ 5 | Barry Foster | 6.00 | 2.70 | .75 |
| | Pittsburgh Steelers | | | |
| ☐ 6 | Rodney Hampton | 7.00 | 3.10 | .85 |
| | New York Giants | | | |
| ☐ 7 | Michael Irvin | 8.00 | 3.60 | 1.00 |
| | Dallas Cowboys | | | |
| ☐ 8 | Nick Lowery | 3.00 | 1.35 | .40 |
| | Kansas City Chiefs | | | |
| ☐ 9 | Dan Marino | 20.00 | 9.00 | 2.50 |
| | Miami Dolphins | | | |
| ☐ 10 | Joe Montana | 30.00 | 13.50 | 3.80 |
| | Kansas City Chiefs | | | |
| ☐ 11 | Warren Moon | 5.00 | 2.30 | .60 |
| | Houston Oilers | | | |
| ☐ 12 | Andre Reed | 4.00 | 1.80 | .50 |
| | Buffalo Bills | | | |

| | MINT | EXC | G-VG |
|---|---|---|---|
| ☐ 13 Jerry Rice.................... San Francisco 49ers | 16.00 | 7.25 | 2.00 |
| ☐ 14 Andre Rison........................ Atlanta Falcons | 5.00 | 2.30 | .60 |
| ☐ 15 Barry Sanders...................... Detroit Lions | 14.00 | 6.25 | 1.75 |
| ☐ 16 Shannon Sharpe.................. Denver Broncos | 5.00 | 2.30 | .60 |
| ☐ 17 Sterling Sharpe.................... Green Bay Packers | 8.00 | 3.60 | 1.00 |
| ☐ 18 Emmitt Smith........................ Dallas Cowboys | 40.00 | 18.00 | 5.00 |
| ☐ 19 Thurman Thomas.................. Buffalo Bills | 6.00 | 2.70 | .75 |
| ☐ 20 Ricky Watters........................ San Francisco 49ers | 6.00 | 2.70 | .75 |

# 1988 Football Heroes Sticker Book

This sticker book contains 20 pages and measures approximately 9 1/4" by 12 1/2". It serves as an introduction to American football, with a discussion of how the game is played and a glossary of terms. The bulk of the book discusses various positions (e.g., quarterbacks, running backs, tight ends, wide receivers, kickers, offensive linemen, and defensive linemen) and outstanding NFL players who fill these positions. The stickers are approximately 3" in height and issued on two sheets, with 15 stickers per sheet. They are to be pasted on a glossy "Football Heroes" poster, which has an imitation-wood picture frame and slots for only 15 player stickers. The cards are unnumbered and checklisted below in alphabetical order.

| | MINT | EXC | G-VG |
|---|---|---|---|
| COMPLETE SET (30)...................... | 8.00 | 3.25 | .80 |
| COMMON PLAYER (1-30).............. | .25 | .10 | .02 |
| ☐ 1 Marcus Allen........................ Los Angeles Raiders | .50 | .20 | .05 |
| ☐ 2 Gary Anderson...................... Pittsburgh Steelers | .25 | .10 | .02 |
| ☐ 3 Brian Bosworth...................... Seattle Seahawks | .25 | .10 | .02 |
| ☐ 4 Anthony Carter....................... Minnesota Vikings | .35 | .14 | .03 |
| ☐ 5 Deron Cherry......................... Kansas City Chiefs | .25 | .10 | .02 |
| ☐ 6 Eric Dickerson...................... Los Angeles Rams | .50 | .20 | .05 |
| ☐ 7 John Elway.......................... Denver Broncos | 1.00 | .40 | .10 |
| ☐ 8 Bo Jackson.......................... Los Angeles Raiders | .75 | .30 | .07 |
| ☐ 9 Rich Karlis............................ Denver Broncos | .25 | .10 | .02 |
| ☐ 10 Bernie Kosar......................... Cleveland Browns | .50 | .20 | .05 |
| ☐ 11 Steve Largent....................... Seattle Seahawks | .75 | .30 | .07 |
| ☐ 12 Mick Luckhurst.................... Atlanta Falcons | .25 | .10 | .02 |
| ☐ 13 Dexter Manley...................... Washington Redskins | .25 | .10 | .02 |
| ☐ 14 Dan Marino......................... Miami Dolphins | 2.00 | .80 | .20 |
| ☐ 15 Jim McMahon...................... Chicago Bears | .50 | .20 | .05 |
| ☐ 16 Joe Montana........................ San Francisco 49ers | 3.00 | 1.20 | .30 |
| ☐ 17 Joe Morris........................... New York Giants | .25 | .10 | .02 |
| ☐ 18 Anthony Munoz.................... Cincinnati Bengals | .35 | .14 | .03 |
| ☐ 19 Ozzie Newsome.................... Cleveland Browns | .35 | .14 | .03 |
| ☐ 20 Walter Payton....................... Chicago Bears | 2.00 | .80 | .20 |

| | MINT | EXC | G-VG |
|---|---|---|---|
| ☐ 21 William Perry........................ Chicago Bears | .35 | .14 | .03 |
| ☐ 22 Jerry Rice............................ San Francisco 49ers | 2.00 | .80 | .20 |
| ☐ 23 Ricky Sanders..................... Washington Redskins | .35 | .14 | .03 |
| ☐ 24 Phil Simms.......................... New York Giants | .50 | .20 | .05 |
| ☐ 25 Mike Singletary..................... Chicago Bears | .35 | .14 | .03 |
| ☐ 26 Dwight Stephenson................ Miami Dolphins | .25 | .10 | .02 |
| ☐ 27 Lawrence Taylor.................... New York Giants | .50 | .20 | .05 |
| ☐ 28 Herschel Walker................... Dallas Cowboys | .50 | .20 | .05 |
| ☐ 29 Doug Williams...................... Washington Redskins | .35 | .14 | .03 |
| ☐ 30 Kellen Winslow...................... San Diego Chargers | .35 | .14 | .03 |

# 1985-87 Football Immortals

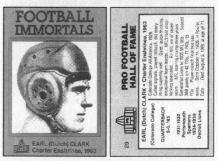

This set was produced in 1985 and 1987; since the majority of the cards in the sets are exactly the same both years, the sets are lumped together below. The 1985 set had 135 cards and the 1987 had 142 cards. In the checklist below the variation cards are listed using the following convention, that the A (or first) variety is from 1985 and the B variety is the version that was released with the 1987 set. Cards 6-128 are essentially in alphabetical order by subject's name. The cards are standard size, 2 1/2" by 3 1/2". The horizontal card backs are light green and black on white card stock. The card photos are in black and white inside two color borders. The outer, thicker border is gold metallic. The inner border is color coded according to the number of the card, red border (1-45), blue border (46-90), green border (91-135), and yellow border (136-142). The set is titled "Football Immortals" at the top of every obverse. Since all members of the set are Football Hall of Famers, their year of induction is given on the front and back of each card. The complete set price below includes all listed variations.

| | MINT | EXC | G-VG |
|---|---|---|---|
| COMPLETE SET (147)...................... | 60.00 | 24.00 | 6.00 |
| COMMON CARD (1-135).............. | .25 | .10 | .02 |
| COMMON CARD (136-142)............ | 1.50 | .60 | .15 |
| ☐ 1 Pete Rozelle........................ | .75 | .30 | .07 |
| ☐ 2 Joe Namath......................... | 1.50 | .60 | .15 |
| ☐ 3 Frank Gatski........................ | .25 | .10 | .02 |
| ☐ 4 O.J. Simpson....................... | 1.50 | .60 | .15 |
| ☐ 5 Roger Staubach.................... | 1.00 | .40 | .10 |
| ☐ 6 Herb Adderley...................... | .25 | .10 | .02 |
| ☐ 7 Lance Alworth...................... | .35 | .14 | .03 |
| ☐ 8 Doug Atkins......................... | .25 | .10 | .02 |
| ☐ 9 Morris(Red) Badgro............... | .25 | .10 | .02 |
| ☐ 10 Cliff Battles.......................... | .25 | .10 | .02 |
| ☐ 11 Sammy Baugh...................... | .50 | .20 | .05 |
| ☐ 12 Raymond Berry.................... | .35 | .14 | .03 |
| ☐ 13 Charles W. Bidwill................ | .25 | .10 | .02 |
| ☐ 14 Chuck Bednarik.................... | .35 | .14 | .03 |
| ☐ 15 Bert Bell............................. | .25 | .10 | .02 |
| ☐ 16 Bobby Bell.......................... | .25 | .10 | .02 |
| ☐ 17 George Blanda..................... | .35 | .14 | .03 |
| ☐ 18 Jim Brown........................... | 1.00 | .40 | .10 |
| ☐ 19 Paul Brown.......................... | .35 | .14 | .03 |
| ☐ 20 Roosevelt Brown.................. | .25 | .10 | .02 |
| ☐ 21 Ray Flaherty........................ | .25 | .10 | .02 |
| ☐ 22 Len Ford............................. | .25 | .10 | .02 |
| ☐ 23 Dan Fortmann...................... | .25 | .10 | .02 |
| ☐ 24 Bill George.......................... | .25 | .10 | .02 |
| ☐ 25 Art Donovan......................... | .25 | .10 | .02 |
| ☐ 26 John(Paddy) Driscoll............. | .25 | .10 | .02 |
| ☐ 27 Jimmy Conzelman................. | .25 | .10 | .02 |

| | | | |
|---|---|---|---|
| ☐ 42 Harold(Red) Grange | .75 | .30 | .07 |
| ☐ 43 Frank Gifford | .75 | .30 | .07 |
| ☐ 44 Sid Gillman | .25 | .10 | .02 |
| ☐ 45 Forrest Gregg | .25 | .10 | .02 |
| ☐ 46 Lou Groza | .35 | .14 | .03 |
| ☐ 47 Joe Guyon | .25 | .10 | .02 |
| ☐ 48 George Halas | .35 | .14 | .03 |
| ☐ 49 Ed Healey | .25 | .10 | .02 |
| ☐ 50 Mel Hein | .25 | .10 | .02 |
| ☐ 51 Fats Henry | .25 | .10 | .02 |
| ☐ 52 Arnie Herber | .25 | .10 | .02 |
| ☐ 53 Bill Hewitt | .25 | .10 | .02 |
| ☐ 54 Clarke Hinkle | .25 | .10 | .02 |
| ☐ 55 Elroy Hirsch | .35 | .14 | .03 |
| (Crazylegs) | | | |
| ☐ 56 Robert(Cal) Hubbard | .25 | .10 | .02 |
| ☐ 57 Sam Huff | .25 | .10 | .02 |
| ☐ 58 Lamar Hunt | .35 | .14 | .03 |
| ☐ 59 Don Hutson | .35 | .14 | .03 |
| ☐ 60 Dave(Deacon) Jones | .25 | .10 | .02 |
| ☐ 61 Sonny Jurgensen | .35 | .14 | .03 |
| ☐ 62 Walt Kiesling | .25 | .10 | .02 |
| ☐ 63 Frank(Bruiser) Kinard | .25 | .10 | .02 |
| ☐ 64 Earl(Curly) Lambeau | .25 | .10 | .02 |
| ☐ 65 Dick(Night Train)Lane | .25 | .10 | .02 |
| ☐ 66 Yale Lary | .25 | .10 | .02 |
| ☐ 67 Dante Lavelli | .25 | .10 | .02 |
| ☐ 68 Bobby Layne | .35 | .14 | .03 |
| ☐ 69 Tuffy Leemans | .25 | .10 | .02 |
| ☐ 70 Bob Lilly | .35 | .14 | .03 |
| ☐ 71 Vince Lombardi | .50 | .20 | .05 |
| ☐ 72 Sid Luckman | .35 | .14 | .03 |
| ☐ 73 Link Lyman | .25 | .10 | .02 |
| ☐ 74 Tim Mara | .25 | .10 | .02 |
| ☐ 75 Gino Marchetti | .25 | .10 | .02 |
| ☐ 76 Geo.Preston Marshall | .25 | .10 | .02 |
| ☐ 77 Ollie Matson | .35 | .14 | .03 |
| ☐ 78 George McAfee | .25 | .10 | .02 |
| ☐ 79 Mike McCormack | .25 | .10 | .02 |
| ☐ 80 Hugh McElhenny | .35 | .14 | .03 |
| ☐ 81 Johnny(Blood) McNally | .25 | .10 | .02 |
| ☐ 82 Mike Michalske | .25 | .10 | .02 |
| ☐ 83 Wayne Millner | .25 | .10 | .02 |
| ☐ 84 Bobby Mitchell | .25 | .10 | .02 |
| ☐ 85 Ron Mix | .25 | .10 | .02 |
| ☐ 86 Lenny Moore | .35 | .14 | .03 |
| ☐ 87 Marion Motley | .35 | .14 | .03 |
| ☐ 88 George Musso | .25 | .10 | .02 |
| ☐ 89 Bronko Nagurski | .50 | .20 | .05 |
| ☐ 90 Earle(Greasy) Neale | .25 | .10 | .02 |
| ☐ 91 Ernie Nevers | .35 | .14 | .03 |
| ☐ 92 Ray Nitschke | .25 | .10 | .02 |
| ☐ 93 Leo Nomellini | .25 | .10 | .02 |
| ☐ 94 Merlin Olsen | .35 | .14 | .03 |
| ☐ 95 Jim Otto | .25 | .10 | .02 |
| ☐ 96 Steve Owen | .25 | .10 | .02 |
| ☐ 97 Clarence(Ace) Parker | .25 | .10 | .02 |
| ☐ 98 Jim Parker | .25 | .10 | .02 |
| ☐ 99 Joe Perry | .35 | .14 | .03 |
| ☐ 100 Pete Pihos | .25 | .10 | .02 |
| ☐ 101 Hugh(Shorty) Ray | .25 | .10 | .02 |
| ☐ 102 Dan Reeves | .25 | .10 | .02 |
| ☐ 103 Jim Ringo | .25 | .10 | .02 |
| ☐ 104 Andy Robustelli | .25 | .10 | .02 |
| ☐ 105 Art Rooney | .25 | .10 | .02 |
| ☐ 106 Gale Sayers | .50 | .20 | .05 |
| ☐ 107 Joe Schmidt | .25 | .10 | .02 |
| ☐ 108 Bart Starr | .50 | .20 | .05 |
| ☐ 109 Ernie Stautner | .25 | .10 | .02 |
| ☐ 110 Ken Strong | .25 | .10 | .02 |
| ☐ 111 Joe Stydahar | .25 | .10 | .02 |
| ☐ 112 Charley Taylor | .25 | .10 | .02 |
| ☐ 113 Jim Taylor | .35 | .14 | .03 |
| ☐ 114 Jim Thorpe | 1.00 | .40 | .10 |
| ☐ 115 Y.A. Tittle | .35 | .14 | .03 |
| ☐ 116 George Trafton | .25 | .10 | .02 |
| ☐ 117 Charley Trippi | .25 | .10 | .02 |
| ☐ 118 Emlen Tunnell | .25 | .10 | .02 |
| ☐ 119 Clyde(Bulldog) Turner | .25 | .10 | .02 |
| ☐ 120 Johnny Unitas | 1.00 | .40 | .10 |
| ☐ 121 Norm Van Brocklin | .50 | .20 | .05 |
| ☐ 122 Steve Van Buren | .35 | .14 | .03 |
| ☐ 123 Paul Warfield | .35 | .14 | .03 |
| ☐ 124 Bob Waterfield | .35 | .14 | .03 |
| ☐ 125 Arnie Weinmeister | .25 | .10 | .02 |
| ☐ 126 Bill Willis | .25 | .10 | .02 |
| ☐ 127 Larry Wilson | .25 | .10 | .02 |
| ☐ 128 Alex Wojciechowicz | .25 | .10 | .02 |
| ☐ 129 Pro Football | .25 | .10 | .02 |
| Hall of Fame | | | |
| (Entrance pictured) | | | |
| ☐ 130A Jim Thorpe Statue | 1.00 | .40 | .10 |
| ☐ 130B Doak Walker | 3.00 | 1.20 | .30 |
| ☐ 131A Enshrinement | .75 | .30 | .07 |
| Galleries | | | |
| ☐ 131B Willie Lanier | 2.50 | 1.00 | .25 |
| ☐ 132 Pro Football | .25 | .10 | .02 |

| | | | |
|---|---|---|---|
| Hall of Fame on | | | |
| Enshrinement Day | | | |
| (Aerial shot of crowd) | | | |
| ☐ 133A Eric Dickerson | 1.00 | .40 | .10 |
| Display | | | |
| ☐ 133B Paul Hornung | 3.50 | 1.40 | .35 |
| ☐ 134A Walter Payton | 1.00 | .40 | .10 |
| Display | | | |
| ☐ 134B Ken Houston | 2.00 | .80 | .20 |
| ☐ 135A Super Bowl Display | .75 | .30 | .07 |
| ☐ 135B Fran Tarkenton | 6.00 | 2.40 | .60 |
| ☐ 136 Don Maynard | 2.50 | 1.00 | .25 |
| ☐ 137 Larry Csonka | 4.00 | 1.60 | .40 |
| ☐ 138 Joe Greene | 4.00 | 1.60 | .40 |
| ☐ 139 Len Dawson | 3.50 | 1.40 | .35 |
| ☐ 140 Gene Upshaw | 2.50 | 1.00 | .25 |
| ☐ 141 Jim Langer | 1.50 | .60 | .15 |
| ☐ 142 John Henry Johnson | 2.50 | 1.00 | .25 |

# 1955 49ers White Border

This 38-card set measures approximately 4 1/4" by 6 1/4". The front features a black and white posed action photo enclosed by a white border, with the player's signature across the bottom portion of the picture. The back of the card lists the player's name, position, height, weight, and college, along with basic biographical information. Many of the cards in this and the other similar team issue sets are only distinguishable as to year by comparing text on the card back; the first few words of text are provided for many of the cards parenthetically below. The set was available direct from the team as part of a package for their fans. The cards are unnumbered and hence are listed alphabetically for convenience.

| | NRMT | VG-E | GOOD |
|---|---|---|---|
| COMPLETE SET (38) | 150.00 | 60.00 | 15.00 |
| COMMON CARD (1-38) | 3.00 | 1.20 | .30 |
| ☐ 1 Frankie Albert CO | 4.00 | 1.60 | .40 |
| (One of Red ...) | | | |
| ☐ 2 Joe Arenas | 3.00 | 1.20 | .30 |
| (The All-Time ...) | | | |
| ☐ 3 Harry Babcock | 3.00 | 1.20 | .30 |
| ☐ 4 Ed Beatty | 3.00 | 1.20 | .30 |
| (After searching ...) | | | |
| ☐ 5 Phil Bengtson CO | 4.00 | 1.60 | .40 |
| (An All-America ...) | | | |
| ☐ 6 Rex Berry | 3.00 | 1.20 | .30 |
| (One of the ...) | | | |
| ☐ 7 Hardy Brown | 6.00 | 2.40 | .60 |
| ☐ 8 Marion Campbell | 5.00 | 2.00 | .50 |
| ☐ 9 Al Carapella | 3.00 | 1.20 | .30 |
| ☐ 10 Paul Carr | 3.00 | 1.20 | .30 |
| (Drafted by ...) | | | |
| ☐ 11 Maury Duncan | 3.00 | 1.20 | .30 |
| ☐ 12 Bob Hantla | 3.00 | 1.20 | .30 |
| ☐ 13 Carroll Hardy | 4.00 | 1.60 | .40 |
| ☐ 14 Matt Hazeltine | 4.00 | 1.60 | .40 |
| (Won All-America ...) | | | |
| ☐ 15 Howard(Red) Hickey CO | 4.00 | 1.60 | .40 |
| (After 14 years ...) | | | |
| ☐ 16 Doug Hogland | 3.00 | 1.20 | .30 |
| ☐ 17 Bill Johnson | 3.00 | 1.20 | .30 |
| (Here's one ... with | | | |
| ten lines of text) | | | |
| ☐ 18 John Henry Johnson | 18.00 | 7.25 | 1.80 |
| ☐ 19 Eldred Kraemer | 3.00 | 1.20 | .30 |
| ☐ 20 Bud Laughlin | 3.00 | 1.20 | .30 |
| ☐ 21 Bobby Luna | 3.00 | 1.20 | .30 |
| ☐ 22 George Maderos | 3.00 | 1.20 | .30 |
| (The greatest ...) | | | |
| ☐ 23 Clay Matthews Sr. | 5.00 | 2.00 | .50 |
| ☐ 24 Hugh McElhenny | 15.00 | 6.00 | 1.50 |

|  | NRMT | VG-E | GOOD |
|---|---|---|---|
| (NFL Commissioner ...) | | | |
| ☐ 25 Dicky Moegle | 4.00 | 1.60 | .40 |
| (25 text lines) | | | |
| ☐ 26 Leo Nomellini | 12.00 | 5.00 | 1.20 |
| (Leo was ...) | | | |
| ☐ 27 Lou Palatella | 3.00 | 1.20 | .30 |
| (Like Eldred ...) | | | |
| ☐ 28 Joe Perry | 15.00 | 6.00 | 1.50 |
| (First man ...) | | | |
| ☐ 29 Charley Powell | 4.00 | 1.60 | .40 |
| (Charley, ...) | | | |
| ☐ 30 Gordy Soltau | 3.00 | 1.20 | .30 |
| (One of the ...) | | | |
| ☐ 31 Bob St. Clair | 15.00 | 6.00 | 1.50 |
| (In two years ...) | | | |
| ☐ 32 Tom Stolhandske | 3.00 | 1.20 | .30 |
| ☐ 33 Roy Storey ANN, | 3.00 | 1.20 | .30 |
| Bob Fouts ANN, | | | |
| and Red Strader CO | | | |
| ☐ 34 Red Strader CO | 3.00 | 1.20 | .30 |
| ☐ 35 Y.A. Tittle | 25.00 | 10.00 | 2.50 |
| (Jinxed by ...) | | | |
| ☐ 36 Bob Toneff | 3.00 | 1.20 | .30 |
| (Rated the ...) | | | |
| ☐ 37 Billy Wilson | 5.00 | 2.00 | .50 |
| (Named the ...) | | | |
| ☐ 38 Sid Youngelman | 3.00 | 1.20 | .30 |

|  | NRMT | VG-E | GOOD |
|---|---|---|---|
| (Bill is one ...) | | | |
| ☐ 15 Bill Johnson | 3.00 | 1.20 | .30 |
| (Here's one ... with | | | |
| nine lines of text) | | | |
| ☐ 16 George Maderos | 3.00 | 1.20 | .30 |
| (A 21st ...) | | | |
| ☐ 17 Dicky Moegle | 4.00 | 1.60 | .40 |
| (San ... with | | | |
| 11 lines of text) | | | |
| ☐ 18 George Morris | 3.00 | 1.20 | .30 |
| ☐ 19 Leo Nomellini | 12.00 | 5.00 | 1.20 |
| (A 49er standby ...) | | | |
| ☐ 20 Lou Palatella | 3.00 | 1.20 | .30 |
| (Most ... | | | |
| same as 1957) | | | |
| ☐ 21 Joe Perry | 15.00 | 6.00 | 1.50 |
| (Joe is ...) | | | |
| ☐ 22 Charley Powell | 4.00 | 1.60 | .40 |
| (Equipped ...) | | | |
| ☐ 23 Leo Rucka | 3.00 | 1.20 | .30 |
| ☐ 24 Ed Sharkey | 3.00 | 1.20 | .30 |
| ☐ 25 Charles Smith | 3.00 | 1.20 | .30 |
| ☐ 26 Gordy Soltau | 3.00 | 1.20 | .30 |
| (No all-time ...) | | | |
| ☐ 27 Bob St. Clair | 12.00 | 5.00 | 1.20 |
| (Tallest man ...) | | | |
| ☐ 28 Bob Toneff | 3.00 | 1.20 | .30 |
| (Another ...) | | | |
| ☐ 29 Billy Wilson | 4.00 | 1.60 | .40 |
| (Billy is ...) | | | |

# 1956 49ers White Border

This 29-card set measures approximately 4 1/8" by 6 1/4". The front features a black and white posed action photo enclosed by a white border, with the player's signature across the bottom portion of the picture. The back of the card lists the player's name, position, height, weight, and college, along with basic biographical information. Many of the cards in this and the other similar team issue sets are only distinguishable as to year by comparing text on the card back; the first few words of text are provided for many of the cards parenthetically below. The set was available direct from the team as part of a package for their fans. The cards are unnumbered and hence are listed alphabetically for convenience.

|  | NRMT | VG-E | GOOD |
|---|---|---|---|
| COMPLETE SET (29) | 100.00 | 40.00 | 10.00 |
| COMMON CARD (1-29) | 3.00 | 1.20 | .30 |
| ☐ 1 Frankie Albert CO | 4.00 | 1.60 | .40 |
| (Frank Culling Albert, | | | |
| who ...) | | | |
| ☐ 2 Ed Beatty | 3.00 | 1.20 | .30 |
| (Traded by ...) | | | |
| ☐ 3 Phil Bengtson CO | 4.00 | 1.60 | .40 |
| (Phil is known ...) | | | |
| ☐ 4 Rex Berry | 3.00 | 1.20 | .30 |
| (Unanimously ...) | | | |
| ☐ 5 Bruce Bosley | 4.00 | 1.60 | .40 |
| (Bosley was ...) | | | |
| ☐ 6 Fred Bruney | 3.00 | 1.20 | .30 |
| ☐ 7 Paul Carr | 3.00 | 1.20 | .30 |
| (A "redshirt" ...) | | | |
| ☐ 8 Clyde Conner | 3.00 | 1.20 | .30 |
| (One of the ...) | | | |
| ☐ 9 Paul Goad | 3.00 | 1.20 | .30 |
| ☐ 10 Matt Hazeltine | 4.00 | 1.60 | .40 |
| (Matt reported ...) | | | |
| ☐ 11 Ed Henke | 3.00 | 1.20 | .30 |
| (After attending ...) | | | |
| ☐ 12 Bill Herchman | 3.00 | 1.20 | .30 |
| (Bill was ...) | | | |
| ☐ 13 Howard(Red) Hickey CO | 4.00 | 1.60 | .40 |
| (Red Hickey ...) | | | |
| ☐ 14 Bill Jessup | 3.00 | 1.20 | .30 |

# 1957 49ers White Border

This 43-card set measures approximatey 4 1/8" by 6 1/4". The front features a black and white posed action photo enclosed by a white border, with the player's signature across the bottom portion of the picture. For those players who were included in the 1956 set, the same photos were used in the 1957 set, with the exception of Bill Johnson, who appears as a coach in the 1957 set. The back lists the player's name, position, height, weight, and college, along with basic biographical information. Many of the cards in this and the other similar team issue sets are only distinguishable as to year by comparing text on the card back; the first few words of text are provided for many of the cards parenthetically below. The set was available direct from the team as part of a package for their fans. The John Brodie card in this set predates his Topps and Fleer Rookie Cards by four years. The cards are unnumbered and hence are listed alphabetically for convenience.

|  | NRMT | VG-E | GOOD |
|---|---|---|---|
| COMPLETE SET (43) | 150.00 | 60.00 | 15.00 |
| COMMON CARD (1-43) | 3.00 | 1.20 | .30 |
| ☐ 1 Frankie Albert CO | 4.00 | 1.60 | .40 |
| (Frank Culling Albert | | | |
| played ... same as 1958) | | | |
| ☐ 2 Joe Arenas | 3.00 | 1.20 | .30 |
| (Again in 1956 ...) | | | |
| ☐ 3 Gene Babb | 3.00 | 1.20 | .30 |
| (Drafted 19th ...) | | | |
| ☐ 4 Larry Barnes | 3.00 | 1.20 | .30 |
| ☐ 5 Phil Bengtson CO | 4.00 | 1.60 | .40 |
| (Beginning his | | | |
| eighth ...) | | | |
| ☐ 6 Bruce Bosley | 4.00 | 1.60 | .40 |
| (After a ... | | | |
| same as 1958) | | | |
| ☐ 7 John Brodie | 30.00 | 12.00 | 3.00 |
| (According to ...) | | | |
| ☐ 8 Paul Carr | 3.00 | 1.20 | .30 |
| (Versatile on ...) | | | |
| ☐ 9 Clyde Conner | 3.00 | 1.20 | .30 |

| | NRMT | VG-E | GOOD |
|---|---|---|---|
| (Football ...) | | | |
| ☐ 10 Ted Connolly .......................... | 3.00 | 1.20 | .30 |
| (The 49er ...) | | | |
| ☐ 11 Bobby Cross .......................... | 3.00 | 1.20 | .30 |
| ☐ 12 Mark Duncan CO .................... | 3.00 | 1.20 | .30 |
| (Mark ... same as 1958) | | | |
| ☐ 13 Bob Fouts ANN, ...................... | 3.00 | 1.20 | .30 |
| Lon Simmons ANN, and Frankie Albert CO (Same as 1958) | | | |
| ☐ 14 John Gonzaga ........................ | 3.00 | 1.20 | .30 |
| (One of the ...) | | | |
| ☐ 15 Tom Harmon ANN.................... | 5.00 | 2.00 | .50 |
| (Kids' ages are 11, 8, and 5) | | | |
| ☐ 16 Matt Hazeltine ........................ | 4.00 | 1.60 | .40 |
| (An All-American ...) | | | |
| ☐ 17 Ed Henke .............................. | 3.00 | 1.20 | .30 |
| (Studious-looking ...) | | | |
| ☐ 18 Bill Herchman ........................ | 3.00 | 1.20 | .30 |
| (The 49ers' ...) | | | |
| ☐ 19 Howard(Red) Hickey CO ........ | 4.00 | 1.60 | .40 |
| (After 14 campaigns ... same as 1958) | | | |
| ☐ 20 Bobby Holladay ...................... | 3.00 | 1.20 | .30 |
| ☐ 21 Bill Jessup ............................ | 3.00 | 1.20 | .30 |
| (One of the ...) | | | |
| ☐ 22 Bill Johnson CO ...................... | 3.00 | 1.20 | .30 |
| (No all-time ... same as 1958) | | | |
| ☐ 23 Marv Matuszak........................ | 4.00 | 1.60 | .40 |
| (Traded to ...) | | | |
| ☐ 24 Hugh McElhenny.................... | 15.00 | 6.00 | 1.50 |
| (Sidelined ...) | | | |
| ☐ 25 Dicky Moegle .......................... | 4.00 | 1.60 | .40 |
| (An ... with 11 lines of text) | | | |
| ☐ 26 Frank Morze .......................... | 3.00 | 1.20 | .30 |
| (The 49ers, used ...) | | | |
| ☐ 27 Leo Nomellini .......................... | 12.00 | 5.00 | 1.20 |
| (He was ...) | | | |
| ☐ 28 R.C. Owens .......................... | 6.00 | 2.40 | .60 |
| (If the ...) | | | |
| ☐ 29 Lou Palatella .......................... | 3.00 | 1.20 | .30 |
| (Most ... same as 1956) | | | |
| ☐ 30 Joe Perry................................ | 15.00 | 6.00 | 1.50 |
| (The greatest ...) | | | |
| ☐ 31 Charley Powell ...................... | 4.00 | 1.60 | .40 |
| (Name almost ...) | | | |
| ☐ 32 Jim Ridlon.............................. | 3.00 | 1.20 | .30 |
| (Teaming with ...) | | | |
| ☐ 33 Karl Rubke ............................ | 3.00 | 1.20 | .30 |
| (The 16th ...) | | | |
| ☐ 34 J.D. Smith .............................. | 4.00 | 1.60 | .40 |
| (J.D.'s football ...) | | | |
| ☐ 35 Gordy Soltau .......................... | 3.00 | 1.20 | .30 |
| (Already listed ...) | | | |
| ☐ 36 Bob St. Clair .......................... | 12.00 | 5.00 | 1.20 |
| (A born leader ...) | | | |
| ☐ 37 Bill Stits................................ | 3.00 | 1.20 | .30 |
| (An All-American ...) | | | |
| ☐ 38 Y.A. Tittle .............................. | 20.00 | 8.00 | 2.00 |
| (For sheer ...) | | | |
| ☐ 39 Bob Toneff ............................ | 3.00 | 1.20 | .30 |
| (After a ...) | | | |
| ☐ 40 Lynn Waldorf .......................... | 3.00 | 1.20 | .30 |
| Director of Personnel (Vertical text, same as 1958) | | | |
| ☐ 41 Val Joe Walker ...................... | 3.00 | 1.20 | .30 |
| ☐ 42 Billy Wilson............................ | 4.00 | 1.60 | .40 |
| (Born on ...) | | | |
| ☐ 43 49ers Coaches ...................... | 4.00 | 1.60 | .40 |
| Bill Johnson Phil Bengtson Frankie Albert Mark Duncan Howard(Red) Hickey (Blank back, same as 1958) | | | |

## 1958 49ers White Border

This 44-card set measures approximately 4 1/8" by 6 1/4". The front features a black and white posed action photo enclosed by a white border, with the player's signature across the bottom portion of the picture. The back lists the player's name, position, height, weight, and college, along with basic biographical information. Many of the cards in this and the other similar team issue sets are only distinguishable as to year by comparing text on the card back; the first few words of text are provided for many of the cards parenthetically below. The set

was available direct from the team as part of a package for their fans. The John Brodie card in this set holds particular interest to some collectors in that it precedes Brodie's Topps and Fleer Rookie Cards by three years. The cards are unnumbered and hence are listed alphabetically for convenience.

| | NRMT | VG-E | GOOD |
|---|---|---|---|
| COMPLETE SET (44)........................ | 150.00 | 60.00 | 15.00 |
| COMMON CARD (1-44) .................. | 3.00 | 1.20 | .30 |
| ☐ 1 Frankie Albert CO ...................... | 4.00 | 1.60 | .40 |
| (Frank Culling Albert played ... same as 1957) | | | |
| ☐ 2 Bill Atkins................................ | 3.00 | 1.20 | .30 |
| (Alabama ...) | | | |
| ☐ 3 Gene Babb.............................. | 3.00 | 1.20 | .30 |
| (A great ...) | | | |
| ☐ 4 Phil Bengtson CO ...................... | 4.00 | 1.60 | .40 |
| (Beginning his 9th ...) | | | |
| ☐ 5 Bruce Bosley .......................... | 4.00 | 1.60 | .40 |
| (After a ... same as 1957) | | | |
| ☐ 6 John Brodie.............................. | 20.00 | 8.00 | 2.00 |
| (With John ...) | | | |
| ☐ 7 Clyde Conner............................ | 3.00 | 1.20 | .30 |
| (In signing ... running pose) | | | |
| ☐ 8 Ted Connolly ............................ | 3.00 | 1.20 | .30 |
| (When Santa Clara ...) | | | |
| ☐ 9 Fred Dugan .............................. | 3.00 | 1.20 | .30 |
| ("Butch" Dugan ...) | | | |
| ☐ 10 Mark Duncan CO .................... | 3.00 | 1.20 | .30 |
| (Mark ... same as 1957) | | | |
| ☐ 11 Bob Fouts ANN........................ | 3.00 | 1.20 | .30 |
| Lon Simmons ANN, and Frankie Albert CO (Same as 1957) | | | |
| ☐ 12 John Gonzaga ........................ | 3.00 | 1.20 | .30 |
| (Recommended ...) | | | |
| ☐ 13 Tom Harmon ANN.................... | 5.00 | 2.00 | .50 |
| (Kids' ages are 12, 9, and 6) | | | |
| ☐ 14 Matt Hazeltine ........................ | 4.00 | 1.60 | .40 |
| (Improved ...) | | | |
| ☐ 15 Ed Henke .............................. | 3.00 | 1.20 | .30 |
| (The "Frank Buck" ...) | | | |
| ☐ 16 Bill Herchman ........................ | 3.00 | 1.20 | .30 |
| (A lineman's ...) | | | |
| ☐ 17 Howard(Red) Hickey CO ........ | 4.00 | 1.60 | .40 |
| (After 14 campaigns ... same as 1957) | | | |
| ☐ 18 Bill Jessup.............................. | 3.00 | 1.20 | .30 |
| (Hard luck ...) | | | |
| ☐ 19 Bill Johnson CO ...................... | 3.00 | 1.20 | .30 |
| (No all-time ... same as 1957) | | | |
| ☐ 20 Marv Matuszak........................ | 4.00 | 1.60 | .40 |
| (The best ...) | | | |
| ☐ 21 Hugh McElhenny .................... | 15.00 | 6.00 | 1.50 |
| (More people ...) | | | |
| ☐ 22 Jerry Mertens........................ | 3.00 | 1.20 | .30 |
| (A 20th draft selection, Jerry ...) | | | |
| ☐ 23 Dicky Moegle .......................... | 4.00 | 1.60 | .40 |
| (13 text lines) | | | |
| ☐ 24 Dennit Morris.......................... | 3.00 | 1.20 | .30 |
| ☐ 25 Frank Morze .......................... | 3.00 | 1.20 | .30 |
| (The 49ers drafted ...) | | | |
| ☐ 26 Leo Nomellini .......................... | 12.00 | 5.00 | 1.20 |
| (Defensive ...) | | | |
| ☐ 27 R.C. Owens .......................... | 5.00 | 2.00 | .50 |
| (There's always ...) | | | |
| ☐ 28 Jim Pace .............................. | 3.00 | 1.20 | .30 |
| ☐ 29 Lou Palatella .......................... | 3.00 | 1.20 | .30 |
| (When ...) | | | |
| ☐ 30 Joe Perry................................ | 15.00 | 6.00 | 1.50 |

| | | NRMT | VG-E | GOOD |
|---|---|---|---|---|
| ☐ 27 R.C. Owens | | 5.00 | 2.00 | .50 |
| (Defensive ...) | | | | |
| (There's always ...) | | | | |
| ☐ 28 Jim Pace | | 3.00 | 1.20 | .30 |
| ☐ 29 Lou Palatella | | 3.00 | 1.20 | .30 |
| (When ...) | | | | |
| ☐ 30 Joe Perry | | 15.00 | 6.00 | 1.50 |
| (The all-time ...) | | | | |
| ☐ 31 Jim Ridlon | | 3.00 | 1.20 | .30 |
| (After a ...) | | | | |
| ☐ 32 Karl Rubke | | 3.00 | 1.20 | .30 |
| (Desperately ...) | | | | |
| ☐ 33 J.D. Smith | | 4.00 | 1.60 | .40 |
| (Used mainly ...) | | | | |
| ☐ 34 Gordy Soltau | | 3.00 | 1.20 | .30 |
| (In his eight ...) | | | | |
| ☐ 35 Bob St. Clair | | 12.00 | 5.00 | 1.20 |
| (The only ...) | | | | |
| ☐ 36 Bill Stits | | 3.00 | 1.20 | .30 |
| (When the ...) | | | | |
| ☐ 37 John Thomas | | 3.00 | 1.20 | .30 |
| (This is ...) | | | | |
| ☐ 38 Y.A. Tittle | | 20.00 | 8.00 | 2.00 |
| (His real ...) | | | | |
| ☐ 39 Bob Toneff | | 3.00 | 1.20 | .30 |
| (A chronic ...) | | | | |
| ☐ 40 Lynn Waldorf | | 3.00 | 1.20 | .30 |
| Director of Personnel | | | | |
| (Vertical text, | | | | |
| same as 1957) | | | | |
| ☐ 41 Billy Wilson | | 4.00 | 1.60 | .40 |
| (Em Tunnell, great ...) | | | | |
| ☐ 42 John Wittenborn | | 3.00 | 1.20 | .30 |
| (John ...) | | | | |
| ☐ 43 Abe Woodson | | 5.00 | 2.00 | .50 |
| (The 49ers ...) | | | | |
| ☐ 44 49ers Coaches | | 4.00 | 1.60 | .40 |
| Bill Johnson | | | | |
| Phil Bengtson | | | | |
| Frankie Albert | | | | |
| Mark Duncan | | | | |
| Howard(Red) Hickey | | | | |
| (Blank back, | | | | |
| same as 1957) | | | | |

| | | NRMT | VG-E | GOOD |
|---|---|---|---|---|
| uniform number 88) | | | | |
| ☐ 8 Ted Connolly | | 3.00 | 1.20 | .30 |
| (Realized his ...) | | | | |
| ☐ 9 Tommy Davis | | 4.00 | 1.60 | .40 |
| ☐ 10 Eddie Dove | | 3.00 | 1.20 | .30 |
| ☐ 11 Fred Dugan | | 3.00 | 1.20 | .30 |
| (Made ...) | | | | |
| ☐ 12 Mark Duncan CO | | 3.00 | 1.20 | .30 |
| (A versatile ...) | | | | |
| ☐ 13 Bob Fouts ANN | | 3.00 | 1.20 | .30 |
| ☐ 14 John Gonzaga | | 3.00 | 1.20 | .30 |
| (One of few ...) | | | | |
| ☐ 15 Bob Harrison | | 3.00 | 1.20 | .30 |
| ☐ 16 Matt Hazeltine | | 4.00 | 1.60 | .40 |
| (One of the ...) | | | | |
| ☐ 17 Ed Henke | | 3.00 | 1.20 | .30 |
| (Suffered a ...) | | | | |
| ☐ 18 Bill Herchman | | 3.00 | 1.20 | .30 |
| (Starting ...) | | | | |
| ☐ 19 Howard(Red) Hickey CO | | 4.00 | 1.60 | .40 |
| (Baseball ...) | | | | |
| ☐ 20 Russ Hodges ANN | | 4.00 | 1.60 | .40 |
| ☐ 21 Bill Johnson CO | | 3.00 | 1.20 | .30 |
| (Bill Johnson ...) | | | | |
| ☐ 22 Charlie Krueger | | 4.00 | 1.60 | .40 |
| ☐ 23 Lenny Lyles | | 3.00 | 1.20 | .30 |
| ☐ 24 Hugh McElhenny | | 15.00 | 6.00 | 1.50 |
| (One of the ...) | | | | |
| ☐ 25 Jerry Mertens | | 3.00 | 1.20 | .30 |
| (A 20th draft | | | | |
| selection last ...) | | | | |
| ☐ 26 Dick Moegle | | 4.00 | 1.60 | .40 |
| (7 text lines) | | | | |
| ☐ 27 Frank Morze | | 3.00 | 1.20 | .30 |
| (Transferred ...) | | | | |
| ☐ 28 Leo Nomellini | | 12.00 | 5.00 | 1.20 |
| (Has never ...) | | | | |
| ☐ 29 Clancy Osborne | | 4.00 | 1.60 | .40 |
| (Have football ...) | | | | |
| ☐ 30 R.C. Owens | | 5.00 | 2.00 | .50 |
| (Football's ...) | | | | |
| ☐ 31 Joe Perry | | 15.00 | 6.00 | 1.50 |
| (Showed ...) | | | | |
| ☐ 32 Jim Ridlon | | 3.00 | 1.20 | .30 |
| (Started his ...) | | | | |
| ☐ 33 Karl Rubke | | 3.00 | 1.20 | .30 |
| (Tallest player ...) | | | | |
| ☐ 34 Bob St.Clair | | 12.00 | 5.00 | 1.20 |
| ☐ 35 Henry Schmidt | | 3.00 | 1.20 | .30 |
| ☐ 36 Bob Shaw CO | | 3.00 | 1.20 | .30 |
| ☐ 37 Lon Simmons ANN | | 3.00 | 1.20 | .30 |
| ☐ 38 J.D. Smith | | 4.00 | 1.60 | .40 |
| (One of the ...) | | | | |
| ☐ 39 John Thomas | | 3.00 | 1.20 | .30 |
| (Didn't make ...) | | | | |
| ☐ 40 Y.A. Tittle | | 20.00 | 8.00 | 2.00 |
| (In 11 years ...) | | | | |
| ☐ 41 Jerry Tubbs | | 5.00 | 2.00 | .50 |
| ☐ 42 Lynn Waldorf | | 3.00 | 1.20 | .30 |
| Director of Personnel | | | | |
| (Horizontal text) | | | | |
| ☐ 43 Billy Wilson | | 4.00 | 1.60 | .40 |
| (Emlen Tunnell, | | | | |
| 12-year ...) | | | | |
| ☐ 44 John Wittenborn | | 3.00 | 1.20 | .30 |
| (Handy ...) | | | | |
| ☐ 45 Abe Woodson | | 4.00 | 1.60 | .40 |
| (Received ...) | | | | |

## 1959 49ers White Border

This 45-card set measures approximately 4 1/8" by 6 1/4". The front features a black and white posed action photo enclosed by a white border, with the player's signature across the bottom portion of the picture. The back lists the player's name, position, height, weight, and college, along with basic biographical information. Many of the cards in this and the other similar team issue sets are only distinguishable as to year by comparing text on the card back; the first few words of text are provided for many of the cards parenthetically below. The set was available direct from the team as part of a package for their fans. The cards are unnumbered and hence are listed alphabetically for convenience.

| | NRMT | VG-E | GOOD |
|---|---|---|---|
| COMPLETE SET (45) | 150.00 | 60.00 | 15.00 |
| COMMON CARD (1-45) | 3.00 | 1.20 | .30 |
| ☐ 1 Bill Atkins | 3.00 | 1.20 | .30 |
| (Played defensive ...) | | | |
| ☐ 2 Dave Baker | 4.00 | 1.60 | .40 |
| ☐ 3 Bruce Bosley | 4.00 | 1.60 | .40 |
| (Starred as ...) | | | |
| ☐ 4 John Brodie | 15.00 | 6.00 | 1.50 |
| (Led NFL ...) | | | |
| ☐ 5 Jack Christiansen CO | 10.00 | 4.00 | 1.00 |
| ☐ 6 Monte Clark | 5.00 | 2.00 | .50 |
| ☐ 7 Clyde Conner | 3.00 | 1.20 | .30 |
| (Standing pose, | | | |

## 1960 49ers White Border

This 44-card set measures approximately 4 1/8" by 6 1/4". The front features a black-and-white posed action photo with white borders. The player's facsimile autograph is inscribed across the picture. The back lists the player's name, position, height, weight, age, college, along with career summary and biographical notes. The set was available direct from the team as part of a package for their fans. The photos are unnumbered and checklisted below in alphabetical order.

|  | NRMT | VG-E | GOOD |
|---|---|---|---|
| COMPLETE SET (44) | 150.00 | 60.00 | 15.00 |
| COMMON PLAYER (1-44) | 3.00 | 1.20 | .30 |
| ☐ 1 Dave Baker | 4.00 | 1.60 | .40 |
| (David Lee Baker ...) | | | |
| ☐ 2 Bruce Bosley | 4.00 | 1.60 | .40 |
| (Born in Fresno ...) | | | |
| ☐ 3 John Brodie | 15.00 | 6.00 | 1.50 |
| (This could be ...) | | | |
| ☐ 4 Jack Christiansen ACO | 10.00 | 4.00 | 1.00 |
| ☐ 5 Monte Clark | 5.00 | 2.00 | .50 |
| (A special chapter ...) | | | |
| ☐ 6 Dan Colchico | 3.00 | 1.20 | .30 |
| (Big Dan ...) | | | |
| ☐ 7 Clyde Conner | 3.00 | 1.20 | .30 |
| (Clyde Raymond ...) | | | |
| ☐ 8 Ted Connolly | 3.00 | 1.20 | .30 |
| (When Theodore ...) | | | |
| ☐ 9 Tommy Davis | 4.00 | 1.60 | .40 |
| (San Francisco ...) | | | |
| ☐ 10 Eddie Dove | 3.00 | 1.20 | .30 |
| (Edward Everett ...) | | | |
| ☐ 11 Mark Duncan ACO | 3.00 | 1.20 | .30 |
| (A versatile ...) | | | |
| ☐ 12 Bob Fouts ANN | 3.00 | 1.20 | .30 |
| ☐ 13 Bob Harrison | 3.00 | 1.20 | .30 |
| (There is no more ...) | | | |
| ☐ 14 Matt Hazeltine | 4.00 | 1.60 | .40 |
| (Matthew Hazeltine ...) | | | |
| ☐ 15 Ed Henke | 3.00 | 1.20 | .30 |
| (Desire and ...) | | | |
| ☐ 16 Howard(Red) Hickey CO | 4.00 | 1.60 | .40 |
| (Baseball ...) | | | |
| ☐ 17 Russ Hodges ANN | 4.00 | 1.60 | .40 |
| ☐ 18 Bill Johnson ACO | 3.00 | 1.20 | .30 |
| (Bill Johnson ...) | | | |
| ☐ 19 Gordon Kelley | 3.00 | 1.20 | .30 |
| (This Southern ...) | | | |
| ☐ 20 Charlie Krueger | 4.00 | 1.60 | .40 |
| (The 49ers' ...) | | | |
| ☐ 21 Lenny Lyles | 3.00 | 1.20 | .30 |
| (Leonard Lyles ...) | | | |
| ☐ 22 Hugh McElhenny | 15.00 | 6.00 | 1.50 |
| (San Francisco's ...) | | | |
| ☐ 23 Mike Magac | 4.00 | 1.60 | .40 |
| (Mike was ...) | | | |
| ☐ 24 Jerry Mertens | 3.00 | 1.20 | .30 |
| (Jerome William ...) | | | |
| ☐ 25 Frank Morze | 3.00 | 1.20 | .30 |
| (Anyone with ...) | | | |
| ☐ 26 Leo Nomellini | 12.00 | 5.00 | 1.20 |
| (Leo Joseph ...) | | | |
| ☐ 27 Clancy Osborne | 4.00 | 1.60 | .40 |
| "Desire" ...) | | | |
| ☐ 28 R.C. Owens | 5.00 | 2.00 | .50 |
| (Few players ...) | | | |
| ☐ 29 Jim Ridlon | 3.00 | 1.20 | .30 |
| (James Ridlon ...) | | | |
| ☐ 30 C.R. Roberts | 3.00 | 1.20 | .30 |
| (After trials ...) | | | |
| ☐ 31 Len Rohde | 3.00 | 1.20 | .30 |
| (Len, a three- ...) | | | |
| ☐ 32 Karl Rubke | 3.00 | 1.20 | .30 |
| (Only 20 years ...) | | | |
| ☐ 33 Bob St.Clair | 12.00 | 5.00 | 1.20 |
| (Robert Bruce ...) | | | |
| ☐ 34 Henry Schmidt | 3.00 | 1.20 | .30 |
| (After two years ...) | | | |
| ☐ 35 Lon Simmons ANN | 3.00 | 1.20 | .30 |
| ☐ 36 J.D. Smith | 4.00 | 1.60 | .40 |
| (In J.D. Smith ...) | | | |
| ☐ 37 Gordy Soltau ANN | 3.00 | 1.20 | .30 |
| ☐ 38 Monty Stickles | 4.00 | 1.60 | .40 |
| (The football ...) | | | |
| ☐ 39 John Thomas | 3.00 | 1.20 | .30 |
| (Noted more ...) | | | |
| ☐ 40 Y.A. Tittle | 20.00 | 8.00 | 2.00 |
| (When Yelberton ...) | | | |
| ☐ 41 Lynn(Pappy) Waldorf | 3.00 | 1.20 | .30 |
| (Director of Personnel) | | | |
| ☐ 42 Bobby Waters | 4.00 | 1.60 | .40 |
| (A smart, ..) | | | |
| ☐ 43 Billy Wilson | 4.00 | 1.60 | .40 |
| (Only Don Hutson ...) | | | |
| ☐ 44 Abe Woodson | 4.00 | 1.60 | .40 |
| (A Big 10 ...) | | | |

## 1968 49ers White Border

This 35-card team issue set measures approximately 8 1/2" by 11" and features black and white posed action photos of the San Francisco

49ers on thin card stock. The backs are blank. The player's name, position, height, and weight are printed in the white lower border in all caps. The team logo/patch also appears in the white border at the bottom. Because this set is unnumbered, the players and coaches are listed alphabetically. Steve Spurrier's card predates his Rookie Card by four years.

|  | NRMT | VG-E | GOOD |
|---|---|---|---|
| COMPLETE SET (35) | 100.00 | 40.00 | 10.00 |
| COMMON CARD (1-35) | 2.50 | 1.00 | .25 |
| ☐ 1 Kermit Alexander | 3.50 | 1.40 | .35 |
| ☐ 2 Cas Banaszek | 2.50 | 1.00 | .25 |
| ☐ 3 Ed Beard | 2.50 | 1.00 | .25 |
| ☐ 4 Forrest Blue | 3.50 | 1.40 | .35 |
| ☐ 5 Bruce Bosley | 2.50 | 1.00 | .25 |
| ☐ 6 John Brodie | 12.00 | 5.00 | 1.20 |
| ☐ 7 Elmer Collett | 2.50 | 1.00 | .25 |
| ☐ 8 Doug Cunningham | 3.50 | 1.40 | .35 |
| ☐ 9 Tommy Davis | 3.50 | 1.40 | .35 |
| ☐ 10 Kevin Hardy | 2.50 | 1.00 | .25 |
| ☐ 11 Matt Hazeltine | 3.50 | 1.40 | .35 |
| ☐ 12 Stan Hindman | 2.50 | 1.00 | .25 |
| ☐ 13 Tom Holzer | 2.50 | 1.00 | .25 |
| ☐ 14 Jim Johnson | 7.50 | 3.00 | .75 |
| ☐ 15 Charlie Krueger | 3.50 | 1.40 | .35 |
| ☐ 16 Roland Lakes | 2.50 | 1.00 | .25 |
| ☐ 17 Gary Lewis | 2.50 | 1.00 | .25 |
| ☐ 18 Kay McFarland | 2.50 | 1.00 | .25 |
| ☐ 19 Clifton McNeil | 3.50 | 1.40 | .35 |
| ☐ 20 George Mira | 5.00 | 2.00 | .50 |
| ☐ 21 Howard Mudd | 2.50 | 1.00 | .25 |
| ☐ 22 Dick Nolan CO | 3.50 | 1.40 | .35 |
| ☐ 23 Frank Nunley | 2.50 | 1.00 | .25 |
| ☐ 24 Don Parker | 2.50 | 1.00 | .25 |
| ☐ 25 Mel Phillips | 3.50 | 1.40 | .35 |
| ☐ 26 Al Randolph | 2.50 | 1.00 | .25 |
| ☐ 27 Len Rohde | 2.50 | 1.00 | .25 |
| ☐ 28 Steve Spurrier | 15.00 | 6.00 | 1.50 |
| ☐ 29 John Thomas | 2.50 | 1.00 | .25 |
| ☐ 30 Bill Tucker | 2.50 | 1.00 | .25 |
| ☐ 31 Dave Wilcox | 5.00 | 2.00 | .50 |
| ☐ 32 Ken Willard | 5.00 | 2.00 | .50 |
| ☐ 33 Bob Windsor | 3.50 | 1.40 | .35 |
| ☐ 34 Dick Witcher | 3.50 | 1.40 | .35 |
| ☐ 35 Team Photo | 10.00 | 4.00 | 1.00 |

## 1972 49ers Redwood City Tribune

This set of six 3" by 5 1/2" autograph cards features black-and-white head shots with white borders. The player's name is printed beneath the picture and in a large space immediately beneath, the card carries the player's signature. The bottom of the front reads "49er autograph card courtesy of Redwood City Tribune." The cards are unnumbered and checklisted below in alphabetical order. The set's date is bracketed by the fact that Frank Edwards last year with the San Francisco 49ers was 1972 and Larry Schreiber's first year with the 49ers was 1971.

|  | MINT | EXC | G-VG |
|---|---|---|---|
| COMPLETE SET (6) | 50.00 | 20.00 | 5.00 |
| COMMON PLAYER (1-6) | 6.00 | 2.40 | .60 |
| ☐ 1 Frank Edwards | 6.00 | 2.40 | .60 |
| ☐ 2 Frank Nunley | 6.00 | 2.40 | .60 |
| ☐ 3 Len Rohde | 6.00 | 2.40 | .60 |
| ☐ 4 Larry Schreiber | 6.00 | 2.40 | .60 |
| ☐ 5 Steve Spurrier | 25.00 | 10.00 | 2.50 |
| ☐ 6 Gene Washington | 9.00 | 3.75 | .90 |

# 1975 49ers

This six-card set measures approximately 7" by 11" and is printed on very thin stock. The fronts feature black-and-white action player photos on a white background. The pictures measure 6 1/4" by 7 1/2." The player's name, biographical information, career highlights, and a personal profile are printed in the white margin at the bottom. The backs are blank. The cards are unnumbered and checklisted below in alphabetical order. The set's date is bracketed by the fact that Windlan Hall, Manfred Moore, and Steve Spurrier's last year with the San Francisco 49ers was 1975, and the first year with the 49ers for Wilbur Jackson and Manfred Moore was 1974.

|  | NRMT | VG-E | GOOD |
|---|---|---|---|
| COMPLETE SET (6) | 30.00 | 12.00 | 3.00 |
| COMMON PLAYER (1-6) | 4.00 | 1.60 | .40 |
|  |  |  |  |
| ☐ 1 Windlan Hall | 4.00 | 1.60 | .40 |
| ☐ 2 Wilbur Jackson | 6.00 | 2.40 | .60 |
| ☐ 3 Manfred Moore | 4.00 | 1.60 | .40 |
| ☐ 4 Mel Phillips | 4.00 | 1.60 | .40 |
| ☐ 5 Steve Spurrier | 15.00 | 6.00 | 1.50 |
| ☐ 6 Gene Washington | 6.00 | 2.40 | .60 |

# 1990-91 49ers SF Examiner

This 16-card San Francisco Examiner 49ers set was issued on two unperforated sheets measuring approximately 14" by 11". Each sheet featured eight cards, with a newspaper headline at the top of the sheet reading "San Francisco Examiner Salutes the 49ers' Finest." If the cards were cut, they would measure approximately 3 1/4" by 4 1/8". The front design has color game shots, with a thin orange border on a red card face. A gold plaque at the card top reads "SF Examiner's Finest," while the gold plaque at the bottom has the player's position and name. The horizontally oriented backs have a black and white head shot, biographical information, statistics, and player profile. The cards are unnumbered and checklisted below in alphabetical order.

|  | MINT | EXC | G-VG |
|---|---|---|---|
| COMPLETE SET (16) | 15.00 | 6.00 | 1.50 |
| COMMON PLAYER (1-16) | .50 | .20 | .05 |
|  |  |  |  |
| ☐ 1 Harris Barton | .50 | .20 | .05 |
| ☐ 2 Michael Carter | .75 | .30 | .07 |
| ☐ 3 Mike Cofer | .50 | .20 | .05 |
| ☐ 4 Roger Craig | 1.00 | .40 | .10 |

| ☐ 5 Kevin Fagan | .50 | .20 | .05 |
|---|---|---|---|
| ☐ 6 Don Griffin | .50 | .20 | .05 |
| ☐ 7 Charles Haley | .75 | .30 | .07 |
| ☐ 8 Pierce Holt | .75 | .30 | .07 |
| ☐ 9 Brent Jones | 1.00 | .40 | .10 |
| ☐ 10 Ronnie Lott | 1.00 | .40 | .10 |
| ☐ 11 Guy McIntyre | .50 | .20 | .05 |
| ☐ 12 Matt Millen | .60 | .24 | .06 |
| ☐ 13 Joe Montana | 6.00 | 2.40 | .60 |
| ☐ 14 Tom Rathman | 1.00 | .40 | .10 |
| ☐ 15 Jerry Rice | 4.00 | 1.60 | .40 |
| ☐ 16 John Taylor | 1.00 | .40 | .10 |

# 1992 49ers FBI

This 40-card set was sponsored by the San Francisco 49ers and the FBI (Federal Bureau of Investigation). According to the title card, a different pack of cards was available free with the 49ers' edition of GameDay Magazine at regular season home games each week at Candlestick Park. The fronts display color action player photos with white borders. In red and white lettering, the player's first and last names are overprinted on the photo at the upper left and lower right corners respectively. The team helmet at the lower left corner rounds out the front. Inside white borders on brick-red background, the backs feature a color close-up photo (inside a football helmet design), biographical information, and a public service message in the form of a player quote. The cards are numbered on the back. The cards measure the standard size (2 1/2" by 3 1/2").

|  | MINT | EXC | G-VG |
|---|---|---|---|
| COMPLETE SET (40) | 35.00 | 14.00 | 3.50 |
| COMMON PLAYER (1-39) | .50 | .20 | .05 |
|  |  |  |  |
| ☐ 1 Michael Carter | .75 | .30 | .07 |
| ☐ 2 Kevin Fagan | .50 | .20 | .05 |
| ☐ 3 Charles Haley | .75 | .30 | .07 |
| ☐ 4 Guy McIntyre | .50 | .20 | .05 |
| ☐ 5 George Seifert CO | .75 | .30 | .07 |
| ☐ 6 Harry Sydney | .50 | .20 | .05 |
| ☐ 7 John Taylor | 1.25 | .50 | .12 |
| ☐ 8 Mike Walter | .50 | .20 | .05 |
| ☐ 9 Steve Young | 4.00 | 1.60 | .40 |
| ☐ 10 Mike Cofer | .50 | .20 | .05 |
| ☐ 11 Keith DeLong | .50 | .20 | .05 |
| ☐ 12 Don Griffin | .50 | .20 | .05 |
| ☐ 13 Pierce Holt | .75 | .30 | .07 |
| ☐ 14 Mike Sherrard | 1.00 | .40 | .10 |
| ☐ 15 Larry Roberts | .50 | .20 | .05 |
| ☐ 16 Bill Romanowski | .50 | .20 | .05 |
| ☐ 17 Tom Rathman | 1.00 | .40 | .10 |
| ☐ 18 Jesse Sapolu | .50 | .20 | .05 |
| ☐ 19 Brent Jones | 1.00 | .40 | .10 |
| ☐ 20 Brian Bollinger | .50 | .20 | .05 |
| ☐ 21 Eric Davis | .50 | .20 | .05 |
| ☐ 22 Antonio Goss | .50 | .20 | .05 |
| ☐ 23 Alan Grant | .50 | .20 | .05 |
| ☐ 24 Harris Barton | .50 | .20 | .05 |
| ☐ 25 Ricky Watters | 3.00 | 1.20 | .30 |
| ☐ 26 Darin Jordan | .50 | .20 | .05 |
| ☐ 27 Odessa Turner | .50 | .20 | .05 |
| ☐ 28 David Wilkins | .50 | .20 | .05 |
| ☐ 29 Merton Hanks | .50 | .20 | .05 |
| ☐ 30 David Whitmore | .50 | .20 | .05 |
| ☐ 31 Joe Montana | 10.00 | 4.00 | 1.00 |
| ☐ 32 Klaus Wilmsmeyer | .50 | .20 | .05 |
| ☐ 33 Tim Harris | .75 | .30 | .07 |
| ☐ 34 Roy Foster | .50 | .20 | .05 |
| ☐ 35 Bill Musgrave | 1.25 | .50 | .12 |
| ☐ 36 Dana Hall | 1.00 | .40 | .10 |
| ☐ 37 Steve Wallace | .75 | .30 | .07 |
| ☐ 38 Steve Bono | 2.00 | .80 | .20 |
| ☐ 39 Jerry Rice | 6.00 | 2.40 | .60 |
| ☐ NNO Title Card | .75 | .30 | .07 |

## 1992 GameDay Draft Day Promos

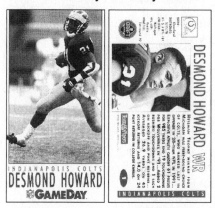

This 13-card promo set was produced by NFL Properties. In the May 1, 1992 edition of USA Today, an ad ran offering to the public 2,500 sets for 50.00 each with the proceeds going to NFL Charities. Other unnumbered sets (originally reported as 10,000 sets but later discovered to be only a small percentage of the original reported amount with many of these other sets missing one player) were also available through various media and dealer channels. The cards were patterned after 1965 Topps football and thus measure approximately 2 1/2" by 4 11/16". Several cards of the same player were issued to reflect different draft day scenarios; 13 different combos existed. Card fronts feature a full-color action picture in a small colored border enclosed by a white border. The team name beneath the photo is in gray lettering, while the player's name appears in block lettering. The title "NFL GameDay" is below the name. Horizontal backs feature the player's team helmet in a box, biography, and the NFL Draft logo in the white border on the far left. A full-color photo is also on the back along with a summary of the player's collegiate career. Although all the cards are numbered "1" on the back, they are checklisted below in alphabetical order according to the player's last name.

|  | MINT | EXC | G-VG |
|---|---|---|---|
| COMPLETE SET (13) | 30.00 | 12.00 | 3.00 |
| COMMON PLAYER (1A-1M) | 2.50 | 1.00 | .25 |
| ☐ 1A Quentin Coryatt<br>Los Angeles Rams | 4.50 | 1.80 | .45 |
| ☐ 1B Vaughn Dunbar<br>Atlanta Falcons | 2.50 | 1.00 | .25 |
| ☐ 1C Vaughn Dunbar<br>San Francisco 49ers | 2.50 | 1.00 | .25 |
| ☐ 1D Vaughn Dunbar<br>Seattle Seahawks | 2.50 | 1.00 | .25 |
| ☐ 1E Steve Emtman<br>Indianapolis Colts | 2.50 | 1.00 | .25 |
| ☐ 1F Steve Emtman<br>Los Angeles Rams | 2.50 | 1.00 | .25 |
| ☐ 1G Desmond Howard<br>Indianapolis Colts | 4.50 | 1.80 | .45 |
| ☐ 1H Desmond Howard<br>Washington Redskins | 4.50 | 1.80 | .45 |
| ☐ 1I David Klingler<br>Kansas City Chiefs | 4.50 | 1.80 | .45 |
| ☐ 1J David Klingler<br>New York Giants | 4.50 | 1.80 | .45 |
| ☐ 1K Troy Vincent<br>Cincinnati Bengals | 3.50 | 1.40 | .35 |
| ☐ 1L Troy Vincent<br>Indianapolis Colts | 3.50 | 1.40 | .35 |
| ☐ 1M Troy Vincent<br>Green Bay Packers | 3.50 | 1.40 | .35 |

## 1992 GameDay National

The cards in this 46-card preview set were given away during the 13th National Sports Card Convention in Atlanta, Georgia. An attractive black vinyl notebook with a cardboard slip cover was available to hold the cards. Like the 1965 Topps football set, these cards measure approximately 2 1/2" by 4 11/16". The players featured on each card front are in color against a black and white background. The horizontally oriented backs have career statistics, biography, and a color head shot. The cards are numbered on the back. Reportedly the cards of Deron Cherry, Mark Rypien, and Deion Sanders were individually distributed in limited quantities at the National in Atlanta.

|  | MINT | EXC | G-VG |
|---|---|---|---|
| COMPLETE SET (46) | 50.00 | 20.00 | 5.00 |
| COMMON PLAYER (1-46) | 1.00 | .40 | .10 |
| ☐ 1 Deion Sanders<br>Atlanta Falcons | 2.00 | .80 | .20 |
| ☐ 2 Jim Kelly<br>Buffalo Bills | 2.50 | 1.00 | .25 |
| ☐ 3 Jim Harbaugh<br>Chicago Bears | 1.25 | .50 | .12 |
| ☐ 4 Boomer Esiason<br>Cincinnati Bengals | 1.50 | .60 | .15 |
| ☐ 5 Bernie Kosar<br>Cleveland Browns | 1.50 | .60 | .15 |
| ☐ 6 Troy Aikman<br>Dallas Cowboys | 9.00 | 3.75 | .90 |
| ☐ 7 John Elway<br>Denver Broncos | 3.50 | 1.40 | .35 |
| ☐ 8 Rodney Peete<br>Detroit Lions | 1.00 | .40 | .10 |
| ☐ 9 Sterling Sharpe<br>Green Bay Packers | 3.00 | 1.20 | .30 |
| ☐ 10 Warren Moon<br>Houston Oilers | 2.00 | .80 | .20 |
| ☐ 11 Jeff George<br>Indianapolis Colts | 2.00 | .80 | .20 |
| ☐ 12 Derrick Thomas<br>Kansas City Chiefs | 2.00 | .80 | .20 |
| ☐ 13 Howie Long<br>Los Angeles Raiders | 1.00 | .40 | .10 |
| ☐ 14 Jim Everett<br>Los Angeles Rams | 1.25 | .50 | .12 |
| ☐ 15 Dan Marino<br>Miami Dolphins | 6.00 | 2.40 | .60 |
| ☐ 16 Chris Doleman<br>Minnesota Vikings | 1.00 | .40 | .10 |
| ☐ 17 Irving Fryar<br>New England Patriots | 1.25 | .50 | .12 |
| ☐ 18 Pat Swilling<br>New Orleans Saints | 1.25 | .50 | .12 |
| ☐ 19 Lawrence Taylor<br>New York Giants | 2.00 | .80 | .20 |
| ☐ 20 Ken O'Brien<br>New York Jets | 1.00 | .40 | .10 |
| ☐ 21 Randall Cunningham<br>Philadelphia Eagles | 2.50 | 1.00 | .25 |
| ☐ 22 Timm Rosenbach<br>Phoenix Cardinals | 1.00 | .40 | .10 |
| ☐ 23 Bubby Brister<br>Pittsburgh Steelers | 1.00 | .40 | .10 |
| ☐ 24 John Friesz<br>San Diego Chargers | 1.50 | .60 | .15 |
| ☐ 25 Joe Montana<br>San Francisco 49ers | 9.00 | 3.75 | .90 |
| ☐ 26 Dan McGwire<br>Seattle Seahawks | 1.00 | .40 | .10 |
| ☐ 27 Vinny Testaverde<br>Tampa Bay Buccaneers | 1.25 | .50 | .12 |
| ☐ 28 Mark Rypien<br>Washington Redskins | 1.25 | .50 | .12 |
| ☐ 29 Ronnie Lott<br>Los Angeles Raiders | 1.50 | .60 | .15 |
| ☐ 30 Marco Coleman<br>Miami Dolphins | 2.00 | .80 | .20 |
| ☐ 31 Rob Moore<br>New York Jets | 2.00 | .80 | .20 |
| ☐ 32 Bill Pickel<br>New York Jets | 1.00 | .40 | .10 |
| ☐ 33 Brad Baxter<br>New York Jets | 1.50 | .60 | .15 |
| ☐ 34 Steve Broussard<br>Atlanta Falcons | 1.25 | .50 | .12 |

| ☐ 35 Darion Conner | 1.25 | .50 | .12 |
|---|---|---|---|
| Atlanta Falcons | | | |
| ☐ 36 Chris Hinton | 1.00 | .40 | .10 |
| Atlanta Falcons | | | |
| ☐ 37 Erric Pegram | 2.00 | .80 | .20 |
| Atlanta Falcons | | | |
| ☐ 38 Jessie Tuggle | 1.00 | .40 | .10 |
| Atlanta Falcons | | | |
| ☐ 39 Billy Joe Tolliver | 1.25 | .50 | .12 |
| Atlanta Falcons | | | |
| ☐ 40 David Klingler | 3.00 | 1.20 | .30 |
| Cincinnati Bengals | | | |
| ☐ 41 Michael Irvin | 3.00 | 1.20 | .30 |
| Dallas Cowboys | | | |
| ☐ 42 Emmitt Smith | 10.00 | 4.00 | 1.00 |
| Dallas Cowboys | | | |
| ☐ 43 Quentin Coryatt | 2.00 | .80 | .20 |
| Indianapolis Colts | | | |
| ☐ 44 Steve Emtman | 1.50 | .60 | .15 |
| Indianapolis Colts | | | |
| ☐ 45 Deron Cherry | 1.00 | .40 | .10 |
| Kansas City Chiefs | | | |
| ☐ 46 Ricky Ervins | 1.25 | .50 | .12 |
| Washington Redskins | | | |

# 1992 GameDay

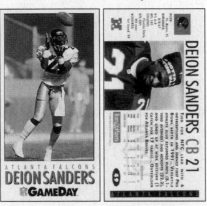

Measuring the same size as the 1965 Topps football issue (2 1/2" by 4 11/16"), this 500-card set has action player photos with the featured player in color against a black-and-white background. According to NFL Properties, only 17,500 16-box cases were produced. The set also includes 14 special "quad" cards, which feature 56 rookies chosen after the third round of the 1992 draft. The card face is white and the photo is bordered in a color coordinating with the team colors. The player's name and "GameDay" are printed at the bottom in team colors. The horizontally oriented backs carry close-up color player photos surrounded by biography, statistics, and career highlights. The player's name, position, uniform number, team name, and helmet icon complete the back and are also team-color coded. The cards are numbered on the back. The key Rookie Cards in this set are Steve Bono, Terrell Buckley, Marco Coleman, Quentin Coryatt, Vaughn Dunbar, Steve Emtman, David Klingler, Tommy Maddox, Johnny Mitchell, Carl Pickens, Tony Smith, and Tommy Vardell.

| | MINT | EXC | G-VG |
|---|---|---|---|
| COMPLETE SET (500) | 45.00 | 20.00 | 5.75 |
| COMMON PLAYER (1-500) | .10 | .05 | .01 |
| | | | |
| ☐ 1 Jim Kelly | .75 | .35 | .09 |
| Buffalo Bills | | | |
| ☐ 2 Mark Ingram | .12 | .05 | .02 |
| New York Giants | | | |
| ☐ 3 Travis McNeal | .10 | .05 | .01 |
| Seattle Seahawks | | | |
| ☐ 4 Ricky Ervins | .12 | .05 | .02 |
| Washington Redskins | | | |
| ☐ 5 Joe Montana | 3.00 | 1.35 | .40 |
| San Francisco 49ers | | | |
| ☐ 6 Broderick Thompson | .10 | .05 | .01 |
| San Diego Chargers | | | |
| ☐ 7 Darion Conner | .10 | .05 | .01 |
| Atlanta Falcons | | | |
| ☐ 8 Jim Harbaugh | .12 | .05 | .02 |
| Chicago Bears | | | |
| ☐ 9 Harvey Williams | .15 | .07 | .02 |
| Kansas City Chiefs | | | |
| ☐ 10 Chip Banks | .10 | .05 | .01 |
| Indianapolis Colts | | | |

| ☐ 11 Henry Thomas | .10 | .05 | .01 |
|---|---|---|---|
| Minnesota Vikings | | | |
| ☐ 12 Derek Brown | .20 | .09 | .03 |
| New York Giants | | | |
| ☐ 13 James Joseph | .10 | .05 | .01 |
| Philadelphia Eagles | | | |
| ☐ 14 Kevin Fagan | .10 | .05 | .01 |
| San Francisco 49ers | | | |
| ☐ 15 Chuck Klingbeil | .25 | .11 | .03 |
| Miami Dolphins | | | |
| ☐ 16 Harlon Barnett | .10 | .05 | .01 |
| Cleveland Browns | | | |
| ☐ 17 Jim Price | .10 | .05 | .01 |
| Los Angeles Rams | | | |
| ☐ 18 Terrell Buckley | .50 | .23 | .06 |
| Green Bay Packers | | | |
| ☐ 19 Paul McJulien | .10 | .05 | .01 |
| Green Bay Packers | | | |
| ☐ 20 James Hasty | .10 | .05 | .01 |
| New York Jets | | | |
| ☐ 21 James Francis | .12 | .05 | .02 |
| Cincinnati Bengals | | | |
| ☐ 22 Andre Tippett | .12 | .05 | .02 |
| New England Patriots | | | |
| ☐ 23 John Elway | 1.00 | .45 | .13 |
| Denver Broncos | | | |
| ☐ 24 Eric Dickerson | .15 | .07 | .02 |
| Los Angeles Raiders | | | |
| ☐ 25 James Jefferson | .10 | .05 | .01 |
| Seattle Seahawks | | | |
| ☐ 26 Danny Noonan | .10 | .05 | .01 |
| Dallas Cowboys | | | |
| ☐ 27 Warren Moon | .35 | .16 | .04 |
| Houston Oilers | | | |
| ☐ 28 Gene Atkins | .10 | .05 | .01 |
| New Orleans Saints | | | |
| ☐ 29 Jessie Hester | .10 | .05 | .01 |
| Indianapolis Colts | | | |
| ☐ 30 Mike Mooney | .25 | .11 | .03 |
| Houston Oilers | | | |
| Kevin Smith RB | | | |
| Los Angeles Raiders | | | |
| Ron Humphrey | | | |
| Indianapolis Colts | | | |
| Tracy Boyd | | | |
| New England Patriots | | | |
| ☐ 31 Toby Caston | .10 | .05 | .01 |
| Detroit Lions | | | |
| ☐ 32 Howard Dinkins | .10 | .05 | .01 |
| Atlanta Falcons | | | |
| ☐ 33 James Patton | .15 | .07 | .02 |
| Buffalo Bills | | | |
| ☐ 34 Walter Reeves | .10 | .05 | .01 |
| Phoenix Cardinals | | | |
| ☐ 35 Johnny Mitchell | 1.25 | .55 | .16 |
| New York Jets | | | |
| ☐ 36 Michael Brim | .10 | .05 | .01 |
| New York Jets | | | |
| ☐ 37 Irving Fryar | .12 | .05 | .02 |
| New England Patriots | | | |
| ☐ 38 Lewis Billups | .10 | .05 | .01 |
| Green Bay Packers | | | |
| ☐ 39 Alonzo Spellman | .40 | .18 | .05 |
| Chicago Bears | | | |
| ☐ 40 John Friesz | .12 | .05 | .02 |
| San Diego Chargers | | | |
| ☐ 41 Patrick Hunter | .10 | .05 | .01 |
| Seattle Seahawks | | | |
| ☐ 42 Reuben Davis | .10 | .05 | .01 |
| Tampa Bay Buccaneers | | | |
| ☐ 43 Tom Myslinski | .15 | .07 | .02 |
| Dallas Cowboys | | | |
| Shawn Harper | | | |
| Los Angeles Rams | | | |
| Mark Thomas | | | |
| San Francisco 49ers | | | |
| Mike Frier | | | |
| Seattle Seahawks | | | |
| ☐ 44 Siran Stacy | .20 | .09 | .03 |
| Philadelphia Eagles | | | |
| ☐ 45 Stephone Paige | .12 | .05 | .02 |
| Kansas City Chiefs | | | |
| ☐ 46 Eddie Robinson | .20 | .09 | .03 |
| Houston Oilers | | | |
| ☐ 47 Tracy Scroggins | .40 | .18 | .05 |
| Detroit Lions | | | |
| ☐ 48 David Klingler | 1.25 | .55 | .16 |
| Cincinnati Bengals | | | |
| ☐ 49A Deion Sanders ERR | .40 | .18 | .05 |
| (Last line of card | | | |
| says outfielder) | | | |
| Atlanta Falcons | | | |
| ☐ 49B Deion Sanders COR | .40 | .18 | .05 |
| (Last line of card | | | |
| says plays outfield) | | | |
| Atlanta Falcons | | | |
| ☐ 50 Tom Waddle | .15 | .07 | .02 |
| Chicago Bears | | | |

| | | | |
|---|---|---|---|
| ☐ 51 Gary Anderson | .12 | .05 | .02 |
| Tampa Bay Buccaneers | | | |
| ☐ 52 Kevin Butler | .10 | .05 | .01 |
| Chicago Bears | | | |
| ☐ 53 Bruce Smith | .15 | .07 | .02 |
| Buffalo Bills | | | |
| ☐ 54 Steve Sewell | .10 | .05 | .01 |
| Denver Broncos | | | |
| ☐ 55 Wesley Walls | .10 | .05 | .01 |
| San Francisco 49ers | | | |
| ☐ 56 Lawrence Taylor | .20 | .09 | .03 |
| New York Giants | | | |
| ☐ 57 Mike Merriweather | .10 | .05 | .01 |
| Minnesota Vikings | | | |
| ☐ 58 Roman Phifer | .10 | .05 | .01 |
| Los Angeles Rams | | | |
| ☐ 59 Shaun Gayle | .10 | .05 | .01 |
| Chicago Bears | | | |
| ☐ 60 Marc Boutte | .10 | .05 | .01 |
| Los Angeles Rams | | | |
| ☐ 61 Tony Mayberry | .10 | .05 | .01 |
| Tampa Bay Buccaneers | | | |
| ☐ 62 Antone Davis UER | .10 | .05 | .01 |
| (Card has 9th pick in | | | |
| '91 draft, was 8th) | | | |
| Philadelphia Eagles | | | |
| ☐ 63 Rod Bernstine | .12 | .05 | .02 |
| San Diego Chargers | | | |
| ☐ 64 Shane Collins | .25 | .11 | .03 |
| Washington Redskins | | | |
| ☐ 65 Martin Bayless | .10 | .05 | .01 |
| Kansas City Chiefs | | | |
| ☐ 66 Corey Harris | .15 | .07 | .02 |
| Houston Oilers | | | |
| ☐ 67 Jason Hanson | .25 | .11 | .03 |
| Detroit Lions | | | |
| ☐ 68 John Fina | .10 | .05 | .01 |
| Buffalo Bills | | | |
| ☐ 69 Cornelius Bennett | .15 | .07 | .02 |
| Buffalo Bills | | | |
| ☐ 70 Mark Bortz | .10 | .05 | .01 |
| Chicago Bears | | | |
| ☐ 71 Gary Anderson | .10 | .05 | .01 |
| Pittsburgh Steelers | | | |
| ☐ 72 Paul Siever | .15 | .07 | .02 |
| Washington Redskins | | | |
| ☐ 73 Flipper Anderson | .12 | .05 | .02 |
| Los Angeles Rams | | | |
| ☐ 74 Shane Dronett | .30 | .14 | .04 |
| Denver Broncos | | | |
| ☐ 75 Brian Noble | .10 | .05 | .01 |
| Green Bay Packers | | | |
| ☐ 76 Tim Green | .10 | .05 | .01 |
| Atlanta Falcons | | | |
| ☐ 77 Percy Snow | .10 | .05 | .01 |
| Kansas City Chiefs | | | |
| ☐ 78 Greg McMurty | .10 | .05 | .01 |
| New England Patriots | | | |
| ☐ 79 Dana Hall | .25 | .11 | .03 |
| San Francisco 49ers | | | |
| ☐ 80 Tyji Armstrong | .20 | .09 | .03 |
| Tampa Bay Buccaneers | | | |
| ☐ 81 Gary Clark | .12 | .05 | .02 |
| Washington Redskins | | | |
| ☐ 82 Steve Emtman | .20 | .09 | .03 |
| Indianapolis Colts | | | |
| ☐ 83 Eric Moore | .10 | .05 | .01 |
| New York Giants | | | |
| ☐ 84 Brent Jones | .15 | .07 | .02 |
| San Francisco 49ers | | | |
| ☐ 85 Ray Seals | .20 | .09 | .03 |
| Tampa Bay Buccaneers | | | |
| ☐ 86 James Jones | .10 | .05 | .01 |
| Cleveland Browns | | | |
| ☐ 87 Jeff Hostetler | .30 | .14 | .04 |
| New York Giants | | | |
| ☐ 88 Keith Jackson | .15 | .07 | .02 |
| Philadelphia Eagles | | | |
| ☐ 89 Gary Plummer | .10 | .05 | .01 |
| San Diego Chargers | | | |
| ☐ 90 Robert Blackmon | .10 | .05 | .01 |
| Seattle Seahawks | | | |
| ☐ 91 Larry Tharpe | .15 | .07 | .02 |
| Detroit Lions | | | |
| Mike Brandon | | | |
| Indianapolis Colts | | | |
| Anthony Hamlet | | | |
| Seattle Seahawks | | | |
| Mike Pawlawski | | | |
| Tampa Bay Buccaneers | | | |
| ☐ 92 Greg Skrepenak | .15 | .07 | .02 |
| Los Angeles Raiders | | | |
| ☐ 93 Kevin Call | .10 | .05 | .01 |
| Indianapolis Colts | | | |
| ☐ 94 Clarence Kay | .10 | .05 | .01 |
| Denver Broncos | | | |
| ☐ 95 William Fuller | .10 | .05 | .01 |
| Houston Oilers | | | |
| ☐ 96 Troy Auzenne | .10 | .05 | .01 |
| Chicago Bears | | | |
| ☐ 97 Carl Pickens | .75 | .35 | .09 |
| Cincinnati Bengals | | | |
| ☐ 98 Lorenzo White | .12 | .05 | .02 |
| Houston Oilers | | | |
| ☐ 99 Doug Smith | .10 | .05 | .01 |
| Houston Oilers | | | |
| ☐ 100 Dale Carter | .50 | .23 | .06 |
| Kansas City Chiefs | | | |
| ☐ 101 Fred McAfee | .25 | .11 | .03 |
| New Orleans Saints | | | |
| ☐ 102 Jack Del Rio | .10 | .05 | .01 |
| Minnesota Vikings | | | |
| ☐ 103 Vaughn Dunbar | .40 | .18 | .05 |
| New Orleans Saints | | | |
| ☐ 104 J.J. Birden | .12 | .05 | .02 |
| Kansas City Chiefs | | | |
| ☐ 105 Harris Barton | .10 | .05 | .01 |
| San Francisco 49ers | | | |
| ☐ 106 Ray Ethridge | .10 | .05 | .01 |
| San Diego Chargers | | | |
| ☐ 107 John Gesek | .10 | .05 | .01 |
| Dallas Cowboys | | | |
| ☐ 108 Mike Singletary | .15 | .07 | .02 |
| Chicago Bears | | | |
| ☐ 109 Mark Rypien | .15 | .07 | .02 |
| Washington Redskins | | | |
| ☐ 110 Robb Thomas | .10 | .05 | .01 |
| Kansas City Chiefs | | | |
| ☐ 111 Joe Kelly | .10 | .05 | .01 |
| New York Jets | | | |
| ☐ 112 Ben Smith | .10 | .05 | .01 |
| Philadelphia Eagles | | | |
| ☐ 113 Neil O'Donnell | 1.00 | .45 | .13 |
| Pittsburgh Steelers | | | |
| ☐ 114 John L. Williams | .12 | .05 | .02 |
| Seattle Seahawks | | | |
| ☐ 115 Mike Sherrard | .12 | .05 | .02 |
| San Francisco 49ers | | | |
| ☐ 116 Chad Hennings | .25 | .11 | .03 |
| Dallas Cowboys | | | |
| ☐ 117 Henry Ellard | .12 | .05 | .02 |
| Los Angeles Rams | | | |
| ☐ 118 Jay Hilgenberg | .12 | .05 | .02 |
| Chicago Bears | | | |
| ☐ 119 Charles Dimry | .10 | .05 | .01 |
| Denver Broncos | | | |
| ☐ 120 Chuck Smith | .20 | .09 | .03 |
| Atlanta Falcons | | | |
| ☐ 121 Brian Mitchell | .12 | .05 | .02 |
| Washington Redskins | | | |
| ☐ 122 Eric Allen | .12 | .05 | .02 |
| Philadelphia Eagles | | | |
| ☐ 123 Nate Lewis | .12 | .05 | .02 |
| San Diego Chargers | | | |
| ☐ 124 Kevin Ross | .12 | .05 | .02 |
| Kansas City Chiefs | | | |
| ☐ 125 Jimmy Smith | .15 | .07 | .02 |
| Dallas Cowboys | | | |
| ☐ 126 Kevin Smith | .50 | .23 | .06 |
| Dallas Cowboys | | | |
| ☐ 127 Larry Webster | .10 | .05 | .01 |
| Miami Dolphins | | | |
| ☐ 128 Marv Cook | .12 | .05 | .02 |
| New England Patriots | | | |
| ☐ 129 Calvin Williams | .15 | .07 | .02 |
| Philadelphia Eagles | | | |
| ☐ 130 Harry Swayne | .15 | .07 | .02 |
| San Diego Chargers | | | |
| ☐ 131 Jimmie Jones | .10 | .05 | .01 |
| Dallas Cowboys | | | |
| ☐ 132 Ethan Horton | .10 | .05 | .01 |
| Los Angeles Raiders | | | |
| ☐ 133 Chris Mims | .40 | .18 | .05 |
| San Diego Chargers | | | |
| ☐ 134 Derrick Thomas | .30 | .14 | .04 |
| Kansas City Chiefs | | | |
| ☐ 135 Gerald Dixon | .25 | .11 | .03 |
| Cleveland Browns | | | |
| ☐ 136 Gary Zimmerman | .10 | .05 | .01 |
| Minnesota Vikings | | | |
| ☐ 137 Robert Jones | .25 | .11 | .03 |
| Dallas Cowboys | | | |
| ☐ 138 Steve Broussard | .12 | .05 | .02 |
| Atlanta Falcons | | | |
| ☐ 139 David Wyman | .10 | .05 | .01 |
| Seattle Seahawks | | | |
| ☐ 140 Ian Beckles | .10 | .05 | .01 |
| Tampa Bay Buccaneers | | | |
| ☐ 141 Steve Bono | 1.00 | .45 | .13 |
| San Francisco 49ers | | | |
| ☐ 142 Cris Carter | .15 | .07 | .02 |
| Minnesota Vikings | | | |
| ☐ 143 Anthony Carter | .12 | .05 | .02 |
| Minnesota Vikings | | | |
| ☐ 144 Greg Townsend | .10 | .05 | .01 |
| Los Angeles Raiders | | | |

|  |  | | | |
|---|---|---|---|---|
| ☐ 145 | Al Smith — Houston Oilers | .10 | .05 | .01 |
| ☐ 146 | Troy Vincent — Miami Dolphins | .15 | .07 | .02 |
| ☐ 147 | Jessie Tuggle — Atlanta Falcons | .10 | .05 | .01 |
| ☐ 148 | David Fulcher — Cincinnati Bengals | .10 | .05 | .01 |
| ☐ 149 | Johnny Rembert — New England Patriots | .10 | .05 | .01 |
| ☐ 150 | Ernie Jones — Phoenix Cardinals | .10 | .05 | .01 |
| ☐ 151 | Mark Royals — Pittsburgh Steelers | .10 | .05 | .01 |
| ☐ 152 | Jeff Bryant — Seattle Seahawks | .10 | .05 | .01 |
| ☐ 153 | Vai Sikahema — Philadelphia Eagles | .12 | .05 | .02 |
| ☐ 154 | Tony Woods — Seattle Seahawks | .10 | .05 | .01 |
| ☐ 155 | Joe Bowden — Houston Oilers; Doug Rigby — Kansas City Chiefs; Marcus Dowdell — New Orleans Saints; Ostell Miles — Cincinnati Bengals | .15 | .07 | .02 |
| ☐ 156 | Mark Carrier — Tampa Bay Buccaneers | .12 | .05 | .02 |
| ☐ 157 | Joe Nash — Seattle Seahawks | .10 | .05 | .01 |
| ☐ 158 | Keith Van Horne — Chicago Bears | .10 | .05 | .01 |
| ☐ 159 | Kelvin Martin — Dallas Cowboys | .12 | .05 | .02 |
| ☐ 160 | Peter Tom Willis — Chicago Bears | .12 | .05 | .02 |
| ☐ 161 | Richard Johnson — Houston Oilers | .10 | .05 | .01 |
| ☐ 162 | Louis Oliver — Miami Dolphins | .12 | .05 | .02 |
| ☐ 163 | Nick Lowery — Kansas City Chiefs | .12 | .05 | .02 |
| ☐ 164 | Ricky Proehl — Phoenix Cardinals | .15 | .07 | .02 |
| ☐ 165 | Terance Mathis — New York Jets | .10 | .05 | .01 |
| ☐ 166 | Keith Sims — Miami Dolphins | .10 | .05 | .01 |
| ☐ 167 | E.J. Junior — Miami Dolphins | .10 | .05 | .01 |
| ☐ 168 | Scott Mersereau — New York Jets | .10 | .05 | .01 |
| ☐ 169 | Tom Rathman — San Francisco 49ers | .12 | .05 | .02 |
| ☐ 170 | Robert Harris — Minnesota Vikings | .10 | .05 | .01 |
| ☐ 171 | Ashley Ambrose — Indianapolis Colts | .15 | .07 | .02 |
| ☐ 172 | David Treadwell — Denver Broncos | .10 | .05 | .01 |
| ☐ 173 | Mark Green — Chicago Bears | .10 | .05 | .01 |
| ☐ 174 | Clayton Holmes — Dallas Cowboys | .10 | .05 | .01 |
| ☐ 175 | Tony Sacca — Phoenix Cardinals | .20 | .09 | .03 |
| ☐ 176 | Wes Hopkins — Philadelphia Eagles | .10 | .05 | .01 |
| ☐ 177 | Mark Wheeler — Tampa Bay Buccaneers | .15 | .07 | .02 |
| ☐ 178 | Robert Clark — Miami Dolphins | .10 | .05 | .01 |
| ☐ 179 | Eugene Daniel — Indianapolis Colts | .10 | .05 | .01 |
| ☐ 180 | Rob Burnett — Cleveland Browns | .10 | .05 | .01 |
| ☐ 181 | Al Edwards — Buffalo Bills | .10 | .05 | .01 |
| ☐ 182 | Clarence Verdin — Indianapolis Colts | .10 | .05 | .01 |
| ☐ 183 | Tom Newberry — Los Angeles Rams | .10 | .05 | .01 |
| ☐ 184 | Mike Jones — Phoenix Cardinals | .10 | .05 | .01 |
| ☐ 185 | Roy Foster — San Francisco 49ers | .10 | .05 | .01 |
| ☐ 186 | Leslie O'Neal — San Diego Chargers | .12 | .05 | .02 |
| ☐ 187 | Izel Jenkins — Philadelphia Eagles | .10 | .05 | .01 |
| ☐ 188 | Willie Clay — Detroit Lions; Ty Detmer — Green Bay Packers; Mike Evans — Kansas City Chiefs | .40 | .18 | .05 |
| | Ed McDaniel — Minnesota Vikings | | | |
| ☐ 189 | Mike Tomczak — Green Bay Packers | .10 | .05 | .01 |
| ☐ 190 | Leonard Wheeler — Cincinnati Bengals | .15 | .07 | .02 |
| ☐ 191 | Gaston Green — Denver Broncos | .12 | .05 | .02 |
| ☐ 192 | Maury Buford — Chicago Bears | .10 | .05 | .01 |
| ☐ 193 | Jeremy Lincoln — Chicago Bears | .20 | .09 | .03 |
| ☐ 194 | Todd Collins — New England Patriots | .25 | .11 | .03 |
| ☐ 195 | Billy Ray Smith — San Diego Chargers | .10 | .05 | .01 |
| ☐ 196 | Renaldo Turnbull — New Orleans Saints | .12 | .05 | .02 |
| ☐ 197 | Michael Carter — San Francisco 49ers | .10 | .05 | .01 |
| ☐ 198 | Rod Milstead — Dallas Cowboys; Dion Lambert — New England Patriots; Hesham Ismail — Pittsburgh Steelers; Reggie E. White — San Diego Chargers | .15 | .07 | .02 |
| ☐ 199 | Shawn Collins — Atlanta Falcons | .10 | .05 | .01 |
| ☐ 200 | Issiac Holt — Dallas Cowboys | .10 | .05 | .01 |
| ☐ 201 | Irv Eatman — New York Jets | .10 | .05 | .01 |
| ☐ 202 | Anthony Thompson — Phoenix Cardinals | .10 | .05 | .01 |
| ☐ 203 | Chester McGlockton — Los Angeles Raiders | .25 | .11 | .03 |
| ☐ 204 | Greg Biggs — Dallas Cowboys; Chris Crooms — Los Angeles Rams; Ephesians Bartley — Philadelphia Eagles; Curtis Whitley — San Diego Chargers | .15 | .07 | .02 |
| ☐ 205 | James Brown — Dallas Cowboys | .15 | .07 | .02 |
| ☐ 206 | Marvin Washington — New York Jets | .10 | .05 | .01 |
| ☐ 207 | Richard Cooper — New Orleans Saints | .15 | .07 | .02 |
| ☐ 208 | Jim C. Jensen — Miami Dolphins | .10 | .05 | .01 |
| ☐ 209 | Sam Seale — Los Angeles Raiders | .10 | .05 | .01 |
| ☐ 210 | Andre Reed — Buffalo Bills | .15 | .07 | .02 |
| ☐ 211 | Thane Gash — San Francisco 49ers | .10 | .05 | .01 |
| ☐ 212 | Randal Hill — Phoenix Cardinals | .15 | .07 | .02 |
| ☐ 213 | Brad Baxter — New York Jets | .12 | .05 | .02 |
| ☐ 214 | Michael Cofer — Detroit Lions | .10 | .05 | .01 |
| ☐ 215 | Ray Crockett — Detroit Lions | .10 | .05 | .01 |
| ☐ 216 | Tony Mandarich — Green Bay Packers | .10 | .05 | .01 |
| ☐ 217 | Warren Williams — Pittsburgh Steelers | .10 | .05 | .01 |
| ☐ 218 | Erik Kramer — Detroit Lions | .20 | .09 | .03 |
| ☐ 219 | Bubby Brister — Pittsburgh Steelers | .12 | .05 | .02 |
| ☐ 220 | Steve Young — San Francisco 49ers | .75 | .35 | .09 |
| ☐ 221 | Jeff George — Indianapolis Colts | .40 | .18 | .05 |
| ☐ 222 | James Washington — Dallas Cowboys | .10 | .05 | .01 |
| ☐ 223 | Bruce Alexander — Miami Dolphins | .10 | .05 | .01 |
| ☐ 224 | Broderick Thomas — Tampa Bay Buccaneers | .10 | .05 | .01 |
| ☐ 225 | Bern Brostek — Los Angeles Rams | .10 | .05 | .01 |
| ☐ 226 | Brian Blades — Seattle Seahawks | .12 | .05 | .02 |
| ☐ 227 | Troy Aikman — Dallas Cowboys | 4.00 | 1.80 | .50 |
| ☐ 228 | Aaron Wallace — Los Angeles Raiders | .10 | .05 | .01 |
| ☐ 229 | Tommy Jeter — Philadelphia Eagles | .15 | .07 | .02 |
| ☐ 230 | Russell Maryland — Dallas Cowboys | .25 | .11 | .03 |

| | | | |
|---|---|---|---|
| ☐ 231 Charles Haley | .12 | .05 | .02 |
| Dallas Cowboys | | | |
| ☐ 232 James Lofton | .15 | .07 | .02 |
| Buffalo Bills | | | |
| ☐ 233 William White | .10 | .05 | .01 |
| Detroit Lions | | | |
| ☐ 234 Tim McGee | .10 | .05 | .01 |
| Cincinnati Bengals | | | |
| ☐ 235 Haywood Jeffires | .15 | .07 | .02 |
| Houston Oilers | | | |
| ☐ 236 Charles Mann | .12 | .05 | .02 |
| Washington Redskins | | | |
| ☐ 237 Robert Lyles | .10 | .05 | .01 |
| Atlanta Falcons | | | |
| ☐ 238 Rohn Stark | .10 | .05 | .01 |
| Indianapolis Colts | | | |
| ☐ 239 Jim Morrissey | .10 | .05 | .01 |
| Chicago Bears | | | |
| ☐ 240 Mel Gray | .12 | .05 | .02 |
| Detroit Lions | | | |
| ☐ 241 Barry Word | .15 | .07 | .02 |
| Kansas City Chiefs | | | |
| ☐ 242 Dave Widell | .15 | .07 | .02 |
| Denver Broncos | | | |
| ☐ 243 Sean Gilbert | .75 | .35 | .09 |
| Los Angeles Rams | | | |
| ☐ 244 Tommy Maddox | 1.00 | .45 | .13 |
| Denver Broncos | | | |
| ☐ 245 Bernie Kosar | .15 | .07 | .02 |
| Cleveland Browns | | | |
| ☐ 246 John Roper | .10 | .05 | .01 |
| Chicago Bears | | | |
| ☐ 247 Mark Higgs | .20 | .09 | .03 |
| Miami Dolphins | | | |
| ☐ 248 Rob Moore | .15 | .07 | .02 |
| New York Jets | | | |
| ☐ 249 Dan Fike | .10 | .05 | .01 |
| Cleveland Browns | | | |
| ☐ 250 Dan Saleaumua | .10 | .05 | .01 |
| Kansas City Chiefs | | | |
| ☐ 251 Tim Krumrie | .10 | .05 | .01 |
| Cincinnati Bengals | | | |
| ☐ 252 Tony Casillas | .10 | .05 | .01 |
| Dallas Cowboys | | | |
| ☐ 253 Jayice Pearson | .10 | .05 | .01 |
| Kansas City Chiefs | | | |
| ☐ 254 Dan Marino | 2.25 | 1.00 | .30 |
| Miami Dolphins | | | |
| ☐ 255 Tony Martin | .10 | .05 | .01 |
| Miami Dolphins | | | |
| ☐ 256 Mike Fox | .10 | .05 | .01 |
| New York Giants | | | |
| ☐ 257 Courtney Hawkins | .60 | .25 | .08 |
| Tampa Bay Buccaneers | | | |
| ☐ 258 Leonard Marshall | .12 | .05 | .02 |
| New York Giants | | | |
| ☐ 259 Willie Gault | .12 | .05 | .02 |
| Los Angeles Raiders | | | |
| ☐ 260 Al Toon | .12 | .05 | .02 |
| New York Jets | | | |
| ☐ 261 Browning Nagle | .12 | .05 | .02 |
| New York Jets | | | |
| ☐ 262 Ronnie Lott | .15 | .07 | .02 |
| Los Angeles Raiders | | | |
| ☐ 263 Sean Jones | .10 | .05 | .01 |
| Houston Oilers | | | |
| ☐ 264 Ernest Givins | .12 | .05 | .02 |
| Houston Oilers | | | |
| ☐ 265 Ray Donaldson | .10 | .05 | .01 |
| Indianapolis Colts | | | |
| ☐ 266 Vaughan Johnson | .12 | .05 | .02 |
| New Orleans Saints | | | |
| ☐ 267 Tom Hodson | .10 | .05 | .01 |
| New England Patriots | | | |
| ☐ 268 Chris Doleman | .12 | .05 | .02 |
| Minnesota Vikings | | | |
| ☐ 269 Pat Swilling | .12 | .05 | .02 |
| New Orleans Saints | | | |
| ☐ 270 Merril Hoge | .12 | .05 | .02 |
| Pittsburgh Steelers | | | |
| ☐ 271 Bill Maas | .10 | .05 | .01 |
| Kansas City Chiefs | | | |
| ☐ 272 Sterling Sharpe | 1.50 | .65 | .19 |
| Green Bay Packers | | | |
| ☐ 273 Mitchell Price | .10 | .05 | .01 |
| Cincinnati Bengals | | | |
| ☐ 274 Richard Brown | .10 | .05 | .01 |
| Cleveland Browns | | | |
| ☐ 275 Randall Cunningham | .20 | .09 | .03 |
| Philadelphia Eagles | | | |
| ☐ 276 Chris Martin | .10 | .05 | .01 |
| Kansas City Chiefs | | | |
| ☐ 277 Courtney Hall | .10 | .05 | .01 |
| San Diego Chargers | | | |
| ☐ 278 Michael Walter | .10 | .05 | .01 |
| San Francisco 49ers | | | |
| ☐ 279 Ricardo McDonald | .25 | .11 | .03 |
| Cincinnati Bengals | | | |

| | | | |
|---|---|---|---|
| David Wilson | | | |
| Minnesota Vikings | | | |
| Sean Lumpkin | | | |
| New Orleans Saints | | | |
| Tony Brooks | | | |
| Philadelphia Eagles | | | |
| ☐ 280 Bill Brooks | .12 | .05 | .02 |
| Indianapolis Colts | | | |
| ☐ 281 Jay Schroeder | .12 | .05 | .02 |
| Los Angeles Raiders | | | |
| ☐ 282 John Stephens | .12 | .05 | .02 |
| New England Patriots | | | |
| ☐ 283 William Perry | .12 | .05 | .02 |
| Chicago Bears | | | |
| ☐ 284 Floyd Turner | .10 | .05 | .01 |
| New Orleans Saints | | | |
| ☐ 285 Carnell Lake | .10 | .05 | .01 |
| Pittsburgh Steelers | | | |
| ☐ 286 Joel Steed | .15 | .07 | .02 |
| Pittsburgh Steelers | | | |
| ☐ 287 Vinnie Clark | .10 | .05 | .01 |
| Green Bay Packers | | | |
| ☐ 288 Ken Norton | .12 | .05 | .02 |
| Dallas Cowboys | | | |
| ☐ 289 Eric Thomas | .10 | .05 | .01 |
| Cincinnati Bengals | | | |
| ☐ 290 Derrick Fenner | .12 | .05 | .02 |
| Cincinnati Bengals | | | |
| ☐ 291 Tony Smith | .40 | .18 | .05 |
| Atlanta Falcons | | | |
| ☐ 292 Eric Metcalf | .15 | .07 | .02 |
| Cleveland Browns | | | |
| ☐ 293 Roger Craig | .12 | .05 | .02 |
| Minnesota Vikings | | | |
| ☐ 294 Leon Searcy | .10 | .05 | .01 |
| Pittsburgh Steelers | | | |
| ☐ 295 Tyrone Legette | .15 | .07 | .02 |
| New Orleans Saints | | | |
| ☐ 296 Rob Taylor | .10 | .05 | .01 |
| Tampa Bay Buccaneers | | | |
| ☐ 297 Eric Williams | .10 | .05 | .01 |
| Washington Redskins | | | |
| ☐ 298 David Little | .10 | .05 | .01 |
| Pittsburgh Steelers | | | |
| ☐ 299 Wayne Martin | .10 | .05 | .01 |
| New Orleans Saints | | | |
| ☐ 300 Eric Martin | .12 | .05 | .02 |
| New Orleans Saints | | | |
| ☐ 301 Jim Everett | .12 | .05 | .02 |
| Los Angeles Rams | | | |
| ☐ 302 Michael Dean Perry | .15 | .07 | .02 |
| Cleveland Browns | | | |
| ☐ 303 Dwayne White | .10 | .05 | .01 |
| New York Jets | | | |
| ☐ 304 Greg Lloyd | .10 | .05 | .01 |
| Pittsburgh Steelers | | | |
| ☐ 305 Ricky Reynolds | .10 | .05 | .01 |
| Tampa Bay Buccaneers | | | |
| ☐ 306 Anthony Smith | .12 | .05 | .02 |
| Los Angeles Raiders | | | |
| ☐ 307 Robert Delpino | .12 | .05 | .02 |
| Los Angeles Rams | | | |
| ☐ 308 Ken Clark | .10 | .05 | .01 |
| Indianapolis Colts | | | |
| ☐ 309 Chris Jacke | .10 | .05 | .01 |
| Green Bay Packers | | | |
| ☐ 310 Reggie Dwight | .15 | .07 | .02 |
| Atlanta Falcons | | | |
| Anthony McCoy | | | |
| Indianapolis Colts | | | |
| Craig Thompson | | | |
| Cincinnati Bengals | | | |
| Klaus Wilmsmeyer | | | |
| Tampa Bay Buccaneers | | | |
| ☐ 311 Doug Widell | .10 | .05 | .01 |
| Denver Broncos | | | |
| ☐ 312 Sammie Smith | .10 | .05 | .01 |
| Denver Broncos | | | |
| ☐ 313 Ken O'Brien | .12 | .05 | .02 |
| New York Jets | | | |
| ☐ 314 Timm Rosenbach | .10 | .05 | .01 |
| Phoenix Cardinals | | | |
| ☐ 315 Jesse Sapolu | .10 | .05 | .01 |
| San Francisco 49ers | | | |
| ☐ 316 Ronnie Harmon | .10 | .05 | .01 |
| San Diego Chargers | | | |
| ☐ 317 Bill Pickel | .10 | .05 | .01 |
| New York Jets | | | |
| ☐ 318 Lonnie Young | .10 | .05 | .01 |
| Philadelphia Eagles | | | |
| ☐ 319 Chris Burkett | .10 | .05 | .01 |
| New York Jets | | | |
| ☐ 320 Ervin Randle | .10 | .05 | .01 |
| Kansas City Chiefs | | | |
| ☐ 321 Ed West | .10 | .05 | .01 |
| Green Bay Packers | | | |
| ☐ 322 Tom Thayer | .10 | .05 | .01 |
| Chicago Bears | | | |

| | | | | | | | | |
|---|---|---|---|---|---|---|---|---|
| ☐ 323 Keith McKeller | .10 | .05 | .01 | ☐ 372 Aundray Bruce | .10 | .05 | .01 |
| Buffalo Bills | | | | Los Angeles Raiders | | | |
| ☐ 324 Webster Slaughter | .12 | .05 | .02 | ☐ 373 Michael Irvin | 1.50 | .65 | .19 |
| Cleveland Browns | | | | Dallas Cowboys | | | |
| ☐ 325 Duane Bickett | .10 | .05 | .01 | ☐ 374 Lemuel Stinson | .10 | .05 | .01 |
| Indianapolis Colts | | | | Chicago Bears | | | |
| ☐ 326 Howie Long | .12 | .05 | .02 | ☐ 375 Billy Joe Tolliver | .12 | .05 | .02 |
| Los Angeles Raiders | | | | Atlanta Falcons | | | |
| ☐ 327 Sam Mills | .12 | .05 | .02 | ☐ 376 Anthony Munoz | .12 | .05 | .02 |
| New Orleans Saints | | | | Cincinnati Bengals | | | |
| ☐ 328 Mike Golic | .10 | .05 | .01 | ☐ 377 Nate Newton | .10 | .05 | .01 |
| Philadelphia Eagles | | | | Dallas Cowboys | | | |
| ☐ 329 Bruce Armstrong | .10 | .05 | .01 | ☐ 378 Steve Smith | .12 | .05 | .02 |
| New England Patriots | | | | Los Angeles Raiders | | | |
| ☐ 330 Pat Terrell | .10 | .05 | .01 | ☐ 379 Eugene Chung | .10 | .05 | .01 |
| Los Angeles Rams | | | | New England Patriots | | | |
| ☐ 331 Mike Pritchard | .50 | .23 | .06 | ☐ 380 Bryan Hinkle | .10 | .05 | .01 |
| Atlanta Falcons | | | | Pittsburgh Steelers | | | |
| ☐ 332 Audray McMillian | .10 | .05 | .01 | ☐ 381 Dan McGwire | .12 | .05 | .02 |
| Minnesota Vikings | | | | Seattle Seahawks | | | |
| ☐ 333 Marquez Pope | .15 | .07 | .02 | ☐ 382 Jeff Cross | .10 | .05 | .01 |
| San Diego Chargers | | | | Miami Dolphins | | | |
| ☐ 334 Pierce Holt | .10 | .05 | .01 | ☐ 383 Ferrell Edmunds | .10 | .05 | .01 |
| San Francisco 49ers | | | | Miami Dolphins | | | |
| ☐ 335 Erik Howard | .10 | .05 | .01 | ☐ 384 Craig Heyward | .10 | .05 | .01 |
| New York Giants | | | | New Orleans Saints | | | |
| ☐ 336 Jerry Rice | 1.50 | .65 | .19 | ☐ 385 Shannon Sharpe | .50 | .23 | .06 |
| San Francisco 49ers | | | | Denver Broncos | | | |
| ☐ 337 Vinny Testaverde | .15 | .07 | .02 | ☐ 386 Anthony Miller | .30 | .14 | .04 |
| Tampa Bay Buccaneers | | | | San Diego Chargers | | | |
| ☐ 338 Bart Oates | .10 | .05 | .01 | ☐ 387 Eugene Lockhart | .10 | .05 | .01 |
| New York Giants | | | | New England Patriots | | | |
| ☐ 339 Nolan Harrison | .15 | .07 | .02 | ☐ 388 Darryl Henley | .10 | .05 | .01 |
| Los Angeles Raiders | | | | Los Angeles Rams | | | |
| ☐ 340 Chris Goode | .10 | .05 | .01 | ☐ 389 LeRoy Butler | .10 | .05 | .01 |
| Indianapolis Colts | | | | Green Bay Packers | | | |
| ☐ 341 Ken Ruettgers | .10 | .05 | .01 | ☐ 390 Scott Fulhage | .10 | .05 | .01 |
| Green Bay Packers | | | | Atlanta Falcons | | | |
| ☐ 342 Brad Muster | .12 | .05 | .02 | ☐ 391 Andre Ware | .12 | .05 | .02 |
| Chicago Bears | | | | Detroit Lions | | | |
| ☐ 343 Paul Farren | .10 | .05 | .01 | ☐ 392 Lionel Washington | .10 | .05 | .01 |
| Cleveland Browns | | | | Los Angeles Raiders | | | |
| ☐ 344 Corey Miller | .25 | .11 | .03 | ☐ 393 Rick Fenney | .10 | .05 | .01 |
| New York Giants | | | | Minnesota Vikings | | | |
| ☐ 345 Brian Washington | .10 | .05 | .01 | ☐ 394 John Taylor | .15 | .07 | .02 |
| New York Jets | | | | San Francisco 49ers | | | |
| ☐ 346 Jim Sweeney | .10 | .05 | .01 | ☐ 395 Chris Singleton | .10 | .05 | .01 |
| New York Jets | | | | New England Patriots | | | |
| ☐ 347 Keith McCants | .10 | .05 | .01 | ☐ 396 Monte Coleman | .10 | .05 | .01 |
| Tampa Bay Buccaneers | | | | Washington Redskins | | | |
| ☐ 348 Louis Lipps | .12 | .05 | .02 | ☐ 397 Brett Perriman | .12 | .05 | .02 |
| Pittsburgh Steelers | | | | Detroit Lions | | | |
| ☐ 349 Keith Byars | .12 | .05 | .02 | ☐ 398 Hugh Millen | .12 | .05 | .02 |
| Philadelphia Eagles | | | | New England Patriots | | | |
| ☐ 350 Steve Walsh | .10 | .05 | .01 | ☐ 399 Dennis Gentry | .10 | .05 | .01 |
| New Orleans Saints | | | | Chicago Bears | | | |
| ☐ 351 Jeff Jaeger | .10 | .05 | .01 | ☐ 400 Eddie Anderson | .10 | .05 | .01 |
| Los Angeles Raiders | | | | Los Angeles Raiders | | | |
| ☐ 352 Christian Okoye | .12 | .05 | .01 | ☐ 401 Lance Olberding | .15 | .07 | .02 |
| Kansas City Chiefs | | | | Cincinnati Bengals | | | |
| ☐ 353 Cris Dishman | .12 | .05 | .02 | Eddie Miller | | | |
| Houston Oilers | | | | Indianapolis Colts | | | |
| ☐ 354 Keith Kartz | .10 | .05 | .01 | Dwayne Sabb | | | |
| Denver Broncos | | | | New England Patriots | | | |
| ☐ 355 Harold Green | .12 | .05 | .02 | Corey Widmer | | | |
| Cincinnati Bengals | | | | New York Giants | | | |
| ☐ 356 Richard Shelton | .15 | .07 | .02 | ☐ 402 Brent Williams | .10 | .05 | .01 |
| Pittsburgh Steelers | | | | New England Patriots | | | |
| ☐ 357 Jacob Green | .10 | .05 | .01 | ☐ 403 Tony Zendejas | .10 | .05 | .01 |
| Seattle Seahawks | | | | Los Angeles Rams | | | |
| ☐ 358 Al Noga | .10 | .05 | .01 | ☐ 404 Donnell Woolford | .10 | .05 | .01 |
| Minnesota Vikings | | | | Chicago Bears | | | |
| ☐ 359 Dean Biasucci | .10 | .05 | .01 | ☐ 405 Boomer Esiason | .20 | .09 | .03 |
| Indianapolis Colts | | | | Cincinnati Bengals | | | |
| ☐ 360 Jeff Herrod | .10 | .05 | .01 | ☐ 406 Gill Fenerty | .10 | .05 | .01 |
| Indianapolis Colts | | | | New Orleans Saints | | | |
| ☐ 361 Bennie Blades | .10 | .05 | .01 | ☐ 407 Kurt Barber | .15 | .07 | .02 |
| Detroit Lions | | | | New York Jets | | | |
| ☐ 362 Mark Vlasic | .12 | .05 | .02 | ☐ 408 William Thomas | .10 | .05 | .01 |
| Kansas City Chiefs | | | | Philadelphia Eagles | | | |
| ☐ 363 Chris Miller | .15 | .07 | .02 | ☐ 409 Keith Henderson | .10 | .05 | .01 |
| Atlanta Falcons | | | | San Francisco 49ers | | | |
| ☐ 364 Bubba McDowell | .10 | .05 | .01 | ☐ 410 Paul Gruber | .10 | .05 | .01 |
| Houston Oilers | | | | Tampa Bay Buccaneers | | | |
| ☐ 365 Tyrone Stowe | .15 | .07 | .02 | ☐ 411 Alfred Oglesby | .10 | .05 | .01 |
| Phoenix Cardinals | | | | Miami Dolphins | | | |
| ☐ 366 Jon Vaughn | .10 | .05 | .01 | ☐ 412 Wendell Davis | .10 | .05 | .01 |
| New England Patriots | | | | Chicago Bears | | | |
| ☐ 367 Winston Moss | .10 | .05 | .01 | ☐ 413 Robert Brooks | .35 | .16 | .04 |
| Los Angeles Raiders | | | | Green Bay Packers | | | |
| ☐ 368 Levon Kirkland | .30 | .14 | .04 | ☐ 414 Ken Willis | .10 | .05 | .01 |
| Pittsburgh Steelers | | | | Tampa Bay Buccaneers | | | |
| ☐ 369 Ted Washington | .10 | .05 | .01 | ☐ 415 Aaron Cox | .10 | .05 | .01 |
| San Francisco 49ers | | | | Los Angeles Rams | | | |
| ☐ 370 Cortez Kennedy | .20 | .09 | .03 | ☐ 416 Thurman Thomas | 1.00 | .45 | .13 |
| Seattle Seahawks | | | | Buffalo Bills | | | |
| ☐ 371 Jeff Feagles | .10 | .05 | .01 | ☐ 417 Alton Montgomery | .10 | .05 | .01 |
| Philadelphia Eagles | | | | Denver Broncos | | | |

| | | | | | | | | |
|---|---|---|---|---|---|---|---|---|
| ☐ 418 Mike Prior<br>Indianapolis Colts | .10 | .05 | .01 | ☐ 467 Alvin Harper<br>Dallas Cowboys | .60 | .25 | .08 |
| ☐ 419 Albert Bentley<br>Indianapolis Colts | .10 | .05 | .01 | ☐ 468 Andre Rison<br>Atlanta Falcons | .40 | .18 | .05 |
| ☐ 420 John Randle<br>Minnesota Vikings | .10 | .05 | .01 | ☐ 469 Rufus Porter<br>Seattle Seahawks | .10 | .05 | .01 |
| ☐ 421 Dermontti Dawson<br>Pittsburgh Steelers | .10 | .05 | .01 | ☐ 470 Robert Wilson<br>Tampa Bay Buccaneers | .10 | .05 | .01 |
| ☐ 422 Phillippi Sparks<br>New York Giants | .10 | .05 | .01 | ☐ 471 Phil Simms<br>New York Giants | .15 | .07 | .02 |
| ☐ 423 Michael Jackson<br>Cleveland Browns | .25 | .11 | .03 | ☐ 472 Art Monk<br>Washington Redskins | .15 | .07 | .02 |
| ☐ 424 Carl Banks<br>New York Giants | .12 | .05 | .02 | ☐ 473 Mike Tice<br>Minnesota Vikings | .10 | .05 | .01 |
| ☐ 425 Chris Zorich<br>Chicago Bears | .12 | .05 | .02 | ☐ 474 Quentin Coryatt<br>Indianapolis Colts | .60 | .25 | .08 |
| ☐ 426 Dwight Stone<br>Pittsburgh Steelers | .10 | .05 | .01 | ☐ 475 Chris Hinton<br>Atlanta Falcons | .10 | .05 | .01 |
| ☐ 427 Bryan Millard<br>Seattle Seahawks | .10 | .05 | .01 | ☐ 476 Vance Johnson<br>Denver Broncos | .12 | .05 | .02 |
| ☐ 428 Neal Anderson<br>Chicago Bears | .12 | .05 | .02 | ☐ 477 Kyle Clifton<br>New York Jets | .10 | .05 | .01 |
| ☐ 429 Michael Haynes<br>Atlanta Falcons | .60 | .25 | .08 | ☐ 478 Garth Jax<br>Phoenix Cardinals | .10 | .05 | .01 |
| ☐ 430 Michael Young<br>Denver Broncos | .10 | .05 | .01 | ☐ 479 Ray Agnew<br>New England Patriots | .10 | .05 | .01 |
| ☐ 431 Dennis Byrd<br>New York Jets | .12 | .05 | .02 | ☐ 480 Patrick Rowe<br>Cleveland Browns | .20 | .09 | .03 |
| ☐ 432 Fred Barnett<br>Philadelphia Eagles | .15 | .07 | .02 | ☐ 481 Joe Jacoby<br>Washington Redskins | .10 | .05 | .01 |
| ☐ 433 Junior Seau<br>San Diego Chargers | .30 | .14 | .04 | ☐ 482 Bruce Pickens<br>Atlanta Falcons | .10 | .05 | .01 |
| ☐ 434 Mark Clayton<br>Miami Dolphins | .12 | .05 | .02 | ☐ 483 Keith DeLong<br>San Francisco 49ers | .10 | .05 | .01 |
| ☐ 435 Marco Coleman<br>Miami Dolphins | .60 | .25 | .08 | ☐ 484 Eric Swann<br>Phoenix Cardinals | .12 | .05 | .02 |
| ☐ 436 Lee Williams<br>Houston Oilers | .12 | .05 | .02 | ☐ 485 Steve McMichael<br>Chicago Bears | .12 | .05 | .02 |
| ☐ 437 Stan Thomas<br>Chicago Bears | .10 | .05 | .01 | ☐ 486 Leroy Hoard<br>Cleveland Browns | .12 | .05 | .02 |
| ☐ 438 Lawrence Dawsey<br>Tampa Bay Buccaneers | .15 | .07 | .02 | ☐ 487 Rickey Dixon<br>Cincinnati Bengals | .10 | .05 | .01 |
| ☐ 439 Tommy Vardell<br>Cleveland Browns | .50 | .23 | .06 | ☐ 488 Robert Perryman<br>Denver Broncos | .10 | .05 | .01 |
| ☐ 440 Steve Israel<br>Los Angeles Rams | .10 | .05 | .01 | ☐ 489 Darryl Williams<br>Cincinnati Bengals | .35 | .16 | .04 |
| ☐ 441 Ray Childress<br>Houston Oilers | .12 | .05 | .02 | ☐ 490 Emmitt Smith<br>Dallas Cowboys | 6.00 | 2.70 | .75 |
| ☐ 442 Darren Woodson<br>Dallas Cowboys | .30 | .14 | .04 | ☐ 491 Dino Hackett<br>Kansas City Chiefs | .10 | .05 | .01 |
| ☐ 443 Lamar Lathon<br>Houston Oilers | .10 | .05 | .01 | ☐ 492 Earnest Byner<br>Washington Redskins | .12 | .05 | .02 |
| ☐ 444 Reggie Roby<br>Miami Dolphins | .10 | .05 | .01 | ☐ 493 Bucky Richardson<br>Houston Oilers<br>Bernard Dafney<br>Houston Oilers<br>Anthony Davis<br>Houston Oilers<br>Tony Brown<br>Houston Oilers | .40 | .18 | .05 |
| ☐ 445 Eric Green<br>Pittsburgh Steelers | .15 | .07 | .02 | | | | |
| ☐ 446 Mark Carrier<br>Chicago Bears | .12 | .05 | .02 | | | | |
| ☐ 447 Kevin Walker<br>Cincinnati Bengals | .10 | .05 | .01 | ☐ 494 Bill Johnson<br>Cleveland Browns | .20 | .09 | .03 |
| ☐ 448 Vince Workman<br>Green Bay Packers | .12 | .05 | .02 | ☐ 495 Darryl Ashmore<br>Los Angeles Rams<br>Joe Campbell<br>Los Angeles Rams<br>Kelvin Harris<br>Los Angeles Rams<br>Tim Lester<br>Los Angeles Rams | .10 | .05 | .01 |
| ☐ 449 Leonard Griffin<br>Kansas City Chiefs | .10 | .05 | .01 | | | | |
| ☐ 450 Robert Porcher<br>Detroit Lions | .40 | .18 | .05 | | | | |
| ☐ 451 Hart Lee Dykes<br>New England Patriots | .10 | .05 | .01 | | | | |
| ☐ 452 Thomas McLemore<br>Detroit Lions | .10 | .05 | .01 | ☐ 496 Nick Bell<br>Los Angeles Raiders | .12 | .05 | .02 |
| ☐ 453 Jamie Dukes<br>Atlanta Falcons | .10 | .05 | .01 | ☐ 497 Jerry Ball<br>Detroit Lions | .12 | .05 | .02 |
| ☐ 454 Bill Romanowski<br>San Francisco 49ers | .10 | .05 | .01 | ☐ 498 Edgar Bennett<br>Green Bay Packers<br>Mark Chmura<br>Green Bay Packers<br>Chris Holder<br>Green Bay Packers<br>Mazio Royster<br>Tampa Bay Buccaneers | .75 | .35 | .09 |
| ☐ 455 Deron Cherry<br>Kansas City Chiefs | .10 | .05 | .01 | | | | |
| ☐ 456 Burt Grossman<br>San Diego Chargers | .10 | .05 | .01 | | | | |
| ☐ 457 Lance Smith<br>Phoenix Cardinals | .10 | .05 | .01 | | | | |
| ☐ 458 Jay Novacek<br>Dallas Cowboys | .25 | .11 | .03 | | | | |
| ☐ 459 Erric Pegram<br>Atlanta Falcons | .75 | .35 | .09 | ☐ 499 Steve Christie<br>Buffalo Bills | .10 | .05 | .01 |
| ☐ 460 Reggie Rutland<br>Minnesota Vikings | .10 | .05 | .01 | ☐ 500 Kenneth Davis<br>Buffalo Bills | .12 | .05 | .02 |
| ☐ 461 Rickey Jackson<br>New Orleans Saints | .12 | .05 | .02 | | | | |
| ☐ 462 Dennis Brown<br>San Francisco 49ers | .10 | .05 | .01 | | | | |
| ☐ 463 Neil Smith<br>Kansas City Chiefs | .15 | .07 | .02 | | | | |
| ☐ 464 Rich Gannon<br>Minnesota Vikings | .12 | .05 | .02 | | | | |
| ☐ 465 Herman Moore<br>Detroit Lions | .60 | .25 | .08 | | | | |
| ☐ 466 Rodney Peete<br>Detroit Lions | .12 | .05 | .02 | | | | |

## 1992 GameDay Box Tops

The GameDay foil pack display boxes featured four different box tops. Each box lid measures approximately 5 1/2" by 11 5/8" and displays four GameDay player cards. While most of the cards featured differ from one box top to another, the Randall Cunningham card is found on all four box tops. The backs of the box tops are blank. The box tops are unnumbered and the individual cards are checklisted below beginning in the upper left corner and ending in the lower right corner.

| | MINT | EXC | G-VG |
|---|---|---|---|
| COMPLETE SET (4)........................ | 2.50 | 1.00 | .25 |
| COMMON PANEL (1-4)................. | .75 | .30 | .07 |

| | MINT | EXC | G-VG |
|---|---|---|---|
| ☐ 1 Randall Cunningham................. | .75 | .30 | .07 |
| Philadelphia Eagles | | | |
| Anthony Munoz | | | |
| Cincinnati Bengals | | | |
| Earnest Byner | | | |
| Washington Redskins | | | |
| Jim Everett | | | |
| Los Angeles Rams | | | |
| ☐ 2 Haywood Jeffires ..................... | .75 | .30 | .07 |
| Houston Oilers | | | |
| Randall Cunningham | | | |
| Philadelphia Eagles | | | |
| Mark Carrier | | | |
| Chicago Bears | | | |
| Vinny Testaverde | | | |
| Tampa Bay Buccaneers | | | |
| ☐ 3 Howie Long.......................... | 1.00 | .40 | .10 |
| Los Angeles Raiders | | | |
| Thurman Thomas | | | |
| Buffalo Bills | | | |
| Randall Cunningham | | | |
| Philadelphia Eagles | | | |
| Jerry Rice | | | |
| San Francisco 49ers | | | |
| ☐ 4 Christian Okoye...................... | .75 | .30 | .07 |
| Kansas City Chiefs | | | |
| Pat Swilling | | | |
| New Orleans Saints | | | |
| Steve Emtman | | | |
| Indianapolis Colts | | | |
| Randall Cunningham | | | |
| Philadelphia Eagles | | | |

## 1992-93 GameDay SB Program

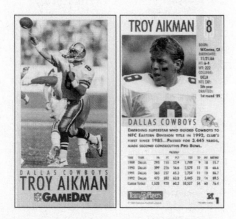

This six-card promo set was inserted one card per 1993 Super Bowl program. Each card measures approximately 2 1/2" by 4 11/16". The fronts feature action player photos with the featured player in color against a black-and-white background. The borders shade from white to the team's dominant color, and the team, name, player's name, and producer's name are printed in the team's second color in the bottom border. The backs carry a color close-up photo, biography, career summary, and season-by-season statistics. The cards are numbered on the back, arranged, in alphabetical order, and identified as promo cards.

| | MINT | EXC | G-VG |
|---|---|---|---|
| COMPLETE SET (6)........................ | 20.00 | 8.00 | 2.00 |
| COMMON PLAYER (1-6)................. | 1.50 | .60 | .15 |

| | MINT | EXC | G-VG |
|---|---|---|---|
| ☐ 1 Troy Aikman............................ | 10.00 | 4.00 | 1.00 |
| Dallas Cowboys | | | |
| ☐ 2 Terry Allen............................. | 2.50 | 1.00 | .25 |
| Minnesota Vikings | | | |
| ☐ 3 Ray Childress.......................... | 1.50 | .60 | .15 |
| Houston Oilers | | | |
| ☐ 4 Marco Coleman........................ | 2.00 | .80 | .20 |
| Miami Dolphins | | | |
| ☐ 5 Barry Foster .......................... | 3.00 | 1.20 | .30 |
| Pittsburgh Steelers | | | |
| ☐ 6 Sterling Sharpe ....................... | 4.00 | 1.60 | .40 |
| Green Bay Packers | | | |

## 1992-93 GameDay Gamebreakers

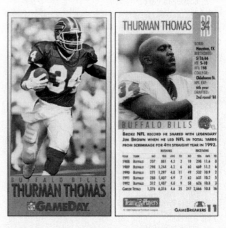

This 14-card set was first made available at the Super Bowl card show to preview the 1993 design. The cards, patterned after 1965 Topps football, measure approximately 2 1/2" by 4 11/16". The checklist card is printed with the individual number of the set and the total number produced (5,000). The fronts feature action player photos with the featured player in color against a black-and-white background. The pictures are bordered by a thin team color-coded line, and they rest on backgrounds that are pale versions of the team color at the bottom and fade to white toward the top. The team name and player's name are printed below the picture in the other team color. The backs carry a close-up player picture bordered on the right and bottom by a pale, team color-coded border that fades to white where they intersect at the team helmet icon. The borders contain the team name and biographical information. Below the picture, on a white background, are career highlights and statistics. The player's name, position, and jersey number appear at the top. The cards are numbered on the back.

| | MINT | EXC | G-VG |
|---|---|---|---|
| COMPLETE SET (14)........................ | 20.00 | 8.00 | 2.00 |
| COMMON PLAYER (1-13)................. | 1.00 | .40 | .10 |

| | MINT | EXC | G-VG |
|---|---|---|---|
| ☐ 1 Marco Coleman......................... | 2.00 | .80 | .20 |
| Miami Dolphins | | | |
| ☐ 2 Bill Cowher CO......................... | 1.00 | .40 | .10 |
| Pittsburgh Steelers | | | |
| ☐ 3 John Elway............................. | 4.00 | 1.60 | .40 |
| Denver Broncos | | | |
| ☐ 4 Barry Foster ........................... | 3.00 | 1.20 | .30 |
| Pittsburgh Steelers | | | |
| ☐ 5 Cortez Kennedy........................ | 2.00 | .80 | .20 |
| Seattle Seahawks | | | |
| ☐ 6 James Lofton .......................... | 1.25 | .50 | .12 |
| Buffalo Bills | | | |
| ☐ 7 Art Monk................................ | 1.50 | .60 | .15 |
| Washington Redskins | | | |
| ☐ 8 Jerry Rice.............................. | 4.00 | 1.60 | .40 |
| San Francisco 49ers | | | |
| ☐ 9 Sterling Sharpe ....................... | 3.00 | 1.20 | .30 |
| Green Bay Packers | | | |
| ☐ 10 Emmitt Smith......................... | 7.50 | 3.00 | .75 |
| Dallas Cowboys | | | |
| ☐ 11 Thurman Thomas.................... | 3.00 | 1.20 | .30 |
| Buffalo Bills | | | |
| ☐ 12 Gino Torretta......................... | 2.00 | .80 | .20 |
| University of Miami | | | |
| ☐ 13 Steve Young.......................... | 2.50 | 1.00 | .25 |
| San Francisco 49ers | | | |
| ☐ 14 Checklist Card ....................... | 1.00 | .40 | .10 |

## 1993 GameDay

The 1993 edition of Fleer's GameDay consists of 480 cards measuring approximately 2 1/2" by 4 3/4". Three subsets were randomly inserted in the 12-card foil packs, including a 20-card "Gamebreakers" set, a 16-card "Second-Year Stars" set, and a 16-card "Rookie Standouts" set. Faded team-colored borders surround the fronts' color action player photos, which are set against black-and-white game-action backgrounds. The team name appears at the bottom of the picture, and the player's name appears in team colors within the lower border. The backs carry close-up color player shots, biography, statistics and career highlights. The cards are numbered on the back. Rookie Cards

include Jerome Bettis, Drew Bledsoe, Reggie Brooks, Curtis Conway, Garrison Hearst, Qadry Ismail, Terry Kirby, O.J. McDuffie, Natrone Means, Glyn Milburn, Rick Mirer, Roosevelt Potts, Dana Stubblefield and Kevin Williams.

|  | MINT | EXC | G-VG |
|---|---|---|---|
| COMPLETE SET (480) | 50.00 | 23.00 | 6.25 |
| COMMON PLAYER (1-480) | .10 | .05 | .01 |
| ☐ 1 Troy Aikman | 3.00 | 1.35 | .40 |
| Dallas Cowboys |  |  |  |
| ☐ 2 Terry Allen | .15 | .07 | .02 |
| Minnesota Vikings |  |  |  |
| ☐ 3 Ray Childress | .10 | .05 | .01 |
| Houston Oilers |  |  |  |
| ☐ 4 Marco Coleman | .12 | .05 | .02 |
| Miami Dolphins |  |  |  |
| ☐ 5 Barry Foster | .50 | .23 | .06 |
| Pittsburgh Steelers |  |  |  |
| ☐ 6 Sterling Sharpe | 1.00 | .45 | .13 |
| Green Bay Packers |  |  |  |
| ☐ 7 Steve McMichael | .10 | .05 | .01 |
| Chicago Bears |  |  |  |
| ☐ 8 Steve Young | .50 | .23 | .06 |
| San Francisco 49ers |  |  |  |
| ☐ 9 Derrick Thomas | .30 | .14 | .04 |
| Kansas City Chiefs |  |  |  |
| ☐ 10 John Elway | .90 | .40 | .11 |
| Denver Broncos |  |  |  |
| ☐ 11 Drew Bledsoe | 9.00 | 4.00 | 1.15 |
| New England Patriots |  |  |  |
| ☐ 12 Jim Kelly | .40 | .18 | .05 |
| Buffalo Bills |  |  |  |
| ☐ 13 Dan Marino | 1.50 | .65 | .19 |
| Miami Dolphins |  |  |  |
| ☐ 14 Mo Lewis | .10 | .05 | .01 |
| New York Jets |  |  |  |
| ☐ 15 David Klingler | .50 | .23 | .06 |
| Cincinnati Bengals |  |  |  |
| ☐ 16 Darrell Green | .12 | .05 | .02 |
| Washington Redskins |  |  |  |
| ☐ 17 James Francis | .10 | .05 | .01 |
| Cincinnati Bengals |  |  |  |
| ☐ 18 John Copeland | .50 | .23 | .06 |
| Cincinnati Bengals |  |  |  |
| ☐ 19 Terry McDaniel | .10 | .05 | .01 |
| Los Angeles Raiders |  |  |  |
| ☐ 20 Barry Sanders | 1.50 | .65 | .19 |
| Detroit Lions |  |  |  |
| ☐ 21 Deion Sanders | .30 | .14 | .04 |
| Atlanta Falcons |  |  |  |
| ☐ 22 Emmitt Smith | 5.00 | 2.30 | .60 |
| Dallas Cowboys |  |  |  |
| ☐ 23 Marion Butts | .15 | .07 | .02 |
| San Diego Chargers |  |  |  |
| ☐ 24 Darryl Talley | .10 | .05 | .01 |
| Buffalo Bills |  |  |  |
| ☐ 25 Randall Cunningham | .20 | .09 | .03 |
| Philadelphia Eagles |  |  |  |
| ☐ 26 Rod Woodson | .15 | .07 | .02 |
| Pittsburgh Steelers |  |  |  |
| ☐ 27 Terrell Buckley | .15 | .07 | .02 |
| Green Bay Packers |  |  |  |
| ☐ 28 Michael Haynes | .40 | .18 | .05 |
| Atlanta Falcons |  |  |  |
| ☐ 29 Tony Jones | .10 | .05 | .01 |
| Atlanta Falcons |  |  |  |
| ☐ 30 Santana Dotson | .15 | .07 | .02 |
| Tampa Bay Buccaneers |  |  |  |
| ☐ 31 Lomas Brown | .10 | .05 | .01 |
| Detroit Lions |  |  |  |
| ☐ 32 Eric Metcalf | .15 | .07 | .02 |
| Cleveland Browns |  |  |  |
| ☐ 33 Morten Andersen | .12 | .05 | .02 |
| New Orleans Saints |  |  |  |
| ☐ 34 Reggie Cobb | .15 | .07 | .02 |
| Tampa Bay Buccaneers |  |  |  |
| ☐ 35 Ferrell Edmunds | .10 | .05 | .01 |
| Seattle Seahawks |  |  |  |
| ☐ 36 Joe Montana | 3.00 | 1.35 | .40 |
| Kansas City Chiefs |  |  |  |
| ☐ 37 Ken Harvey | .10 | .05 | .01 |
| Phoenix Cardinals |  |  |  |
| ☐ 38 Rodney Hampton | .75 | .35 | .09 |
| New York Giants |  |  |  |
| ☐ 39 Kurt Gouveia | .10 | .05 | .01 |
| Washington Redskins |  |  |  |
| ☐ 40 Ken Norton Jr. | .12 | .05 | .02 |
| Dallas Cowboys |  |  |  |
| ☐ 41 Frank Reich | .12 | .05 | .02 |
| Buffalo Bills |  |  |  |
| ☐ 42 Kevin Greene | .10 | .05 | .01 |
| Pittsburgh Steelers |  |  |  |
| ☐ 43 Cleveland Gary | .12 | .05 | .02 |
| Los Angeles Rams |  |  |  |
| ☐ 44 Maurice Hurst | .10 | .05 | .01 |
| New England Patriots |  |  |  |
| ☐ 45 Troy Vincent | .12 | .05 | .02 |
| Miami Dolphins |  |  |  |
| ☐ 46 Eric Curry | .50 | .23 | .06 |
| Tampa Bay Buccaneers |  |  |  |
| ☐ 47 Curtis Conway | 1.00 | .45 | .13 |
| Chicago Bears |  |  |  |
| ☐ 48 Christian Okoye | .12 | .05 | .02 |
| Kansas City Chiefs |  |  |  |
| ☐ 49 Tunch Ilkin | .10 | .05 | .01 |
| Pittsburgh Steelers |  |  |  |
| ☐ 50 Michael Irvin | 1.00 | .45 | .13 |
| Dallas Cowboys |  |  |  |
| ☐ 51 Bart Oates | .10 | .05 | .01 |
| New York Giants |  |  |  |
| ☐ 52 Pepper Johnson | .10 | .05 | .01 |
| New York Giants |  |  |  |
| ☐ 53 Vaughan Johnson | .10 | .05 | .01 |
| New Orleans Saints |  |  |  |
| ☐ 54 Lawrence Taylor | .15 | .07 | .02 |
| New York Giants |  |  |  |
| ☐ 55 Junior Seau | .15 | .07 | .02 |
| San Diego Chargers |  |  |  |
| ☐ 56 Michael Brooks | .10 | .05 | .01 |
| New York Giants |  |  |  |
| ☐ 57 Neal Anderson | .12 | .05 | .02 |
| Chicago Bears |  |  |  |
| ☐ 58 D.J. Johnson | .10 | .05 | .01 |
| Pittsburgh Steelers |  |  |  |
| ☐ 59 Seth Joyner | .12 | .05 | .02 |
| Philadelphia Eagles |  |  |  |
| ☐ 60 Marvin Washington | .10 | .05 | .01 |
| New York Jets |  |  |  |
| ☐ 61 Ernest Givins | .12 | .05 | .02 |
| Houston Oilers |  |  |  |
| ☐ 62 Jaime Fields | .15 | .07 | .02 |
| Kansas City Chiefs |  |  |  |
| ☐ 63 Vincent Brown | .10 | .05 | .01 |
| New England Patriots |  |  |  |
| ☐ 64 Randall McDaniel | .10 | .05 | .01 |
| Minnesota Vikings |  |  |  |
| ☐ 65 Tommy Maddox | .25 | .11 | .03 |
| Denver Broncos |  |  |  |
| ☐ 66 Steve Everitt | .20 | .09 | .03 |
| Cleveland Browns |  |  |  |
| ☐ 67 Brian Noble | .10 | .05 | .01 |
| Green Bay Packers |  |  |  |
| ☐ 68 Bryce Paup | .10 | .05 | .01 |
| Green Bay Packers |  |  |  |
| ☐ 69 Brad Baxter | .12 | .05 | .02 |
| New York Jets |  |  |  |
| ☐ 70 Demetrius DuBose | .35 | .16 | .04 |
| Tampa Bay Buccaneers |  |  |  |
| ☐ 71 Duane Bickett | .10 | .05 | .01 |
| Indianapolis Colts |  |  |  |
| ☐ 72 Mark Rypien | .12 | .05 | .02 |
| Washington Redskins |  |  |  |
| ☐ 73 Harris Barton | .10 | .05 | .01 |
| San Francisco 49ers |  |  |  |
| ☐ 74 Bruce Matthews | .12 | .05 | .02 |
| Houston Oilers |  |  |  |
| ☐ 75 Irving Fryar | .10 | .05 | .01 |
| Miami Dolphins |  |  |  |
| ☐ 76 Steve Wisniewski | .10 | .05 | .01 |
| Los Angeles Raiders |  |  |  |
| ☐ 77 Will Shields | .15 | .07 | .02 |
| Kansas City Chiefs |  |  |  |
| ☐ 78 Tom Carter | .40 | .18 | .05 |
| Washington Redskins |  |  |  |
| ☐ 79 Steve Emtman | .12 | .05 | .02 |
| Indianapolis Colts |  |  |  |
| ☐ 80 Jerry Rice | 1.50 | .65 | .19 |
| San Francisco 49ers |  |  |  |

| | | | | | | | | |
|---|---|---|---|---|---|---|---|---|
| ☐ 81 Art Monk | .15 | .07 | .02 | ☐ 129 Todd Lyght | .10 | .05 | .01 |
| Washington Redskins | | | | Los Angeles Rams | | | |
| ☐ 82 Tony Tolbert | .10 | .05 | .01 | ☐ 130 Rodney Culver | .10 | .05 | .01 |
| Dallas Cowboys | | | | Indianapolis Colts | | | |
| ☐ 83 Johnny Mitchell | .50 | .23 | .06 | ☐ 131 Richmond Webb | .10 | .05 | .01 |
| New York Jets | | | | Miami Dolphins | | | |
| ☐ 84 Deon Figures | .35 | .16 | .04 | ☐ 132 John Parrella | .15 | .07 | .02 |
| Pittsburgh Steelers | | | | Buffalo Bills | | | |
| ☐ 85 Marv Cook | .10 | .05 | .01 | ☐ 133 Reggie Brooks | 4.00 | 1.80 | .50 |
| New England Patriots | | | | Washington Redskins | | | |
| ☐ 86 Darion Conner | .10 | .05 | .01 | ☐ 134 Lincoln Kennedy | .30 | .14 | .04 |
| Atlanta Falcons | | | | Atlanta Falcons | | | |
| ☐ 87 Ricky Proehl | .12 | .05 | .02 | ☐ 135 Tim Johnson | .10 | .05 | .01 |
| Phoenix Cardinals | | | | Washington Redskins | | | |
| ☐ 88 Tony Bennett | .10 | .05 | .01 | ☐ 136 Robert Massey | .10 | .05 | .01 |
| Green Bay Packers | | | | Phoenix Cardinals | | | |
| ☐ 89 Jay Schroeder | .10 | .05 | .01 | ☐ 137 Keith Jackson | .15 | .07 | .02 |
| Washington Redskins | | | | Miami Dolphins | | | |
| ☐ 90 Neil Smith | .15 | .07 | .02 | ☐ 138 Alfred Williams | .10 | .05 | .01 |
| Kansas City Chiefs | | | | Cincinnati Bengals | | | |
| ☐ 91 Jarvis Williams | .10 | .05 | .01 | ☐ 139 Leroy Hoard | .12 | .05 | .02 |
| Miami Dolphins | | | | Cleveland Browns | | | |
| ☐ 92 James Hasty | .10 | .05 | .01 | ☐ 140 Jessie Tuggle | .10 | .05 | .01 |
| New York Jets | | | | Atlanta Falcons | | | |
| ☐ 93 Anthony Miller | .30 | .14 | .04 | ☐ 141 Chris Mims | .12 | .05 | .02 |
| San Diego Chargers | | | | San Diego Chargers | | | |
| ☐ 94 Thomas Smith | .25 | .11 | .03 | ☐ 142 Herschel Walker | .15 | .07 | .02 |
| Buffalo Bills | | | | Philadelphia Eagles | | | |
| ☐ 95 Richard Dent | .12 | .05 | .02 | ☐ 143 Clyde Simmons | .12 | .05 | .02 |
| Chicago Bears | | | | Philadelphia Eagles | | | |
| ☐ 96 Henry Jones | .10 | .05 | .01 | ☐ 144 Dana Hall | .10 | .05 | .01 |
| Buffalo Bills | | | | San Francisco 49ers | | | |
| ☐ 97 Renaldo Turnbull | .12 | .05 | .02 | ☐ 145 Nate Newton | .10 | .05 | .01 |
| New Orleans Saints | | | | Dallas Cowboys | | | |
| ☐ 98 Jason Hanson | .10 | .05 | .01 | ☐ 146 Dennis Smith | .10 | .05 | .01 |
| Detroit Lions | | | | Denver Broncos | | | |
| ☐ 99 Cortez Kennedy | .15 | .07 | .02 | ☐ 147 Rich Camarillo | .10 | .05 | .01 |
| Seattle Seahawks | | | | Phoenix Cardinals | | | |
| ☐ 100 Brett Favre | 1.50 | .65 | .19 | ☐ 148 Chris Spielman | .10 | .05 | .01 |
| Green Bay Packers | | | | Detroit Lions | | | |
| ☐ 101 Anthony Carter | .12 | .05 | .02 | ☐ 149 Jim Dombrowski | .10 | .05 | .01 |
| Minnesota Vikings | | | | New York Giants | | | |
| ☐ 102 Cris Carter | .15 | .07 | .02 | ☐ 150 Steve Beuerlein | .25 | .11 | .03 |
| Minnesota Vikings | | | | Phoenix Cardinals | | | |
| ☐ 103 Dana Stubblefield | 1.00 | .45 | .13 | ☐ 151 Mark Clayton | .10 | .05 | .01 |
| San Francisco 49ers | | | | Green Bay Packers | | | |
| ☐ 104 Nick Bell | .12 | .05 | .02 | ☐ 152 Lee Williams | .10 | .05 | .01 |
| Los Angeles Raiders | | | | Houston Oilers | | | |
| ☐ 105 Marcus Allen | .30 | .14 | .04 | ☐ 153 Robert Smith | .75 | .35 | .09 |
| Kansas City Chiefs | | | | Minnesota Vikings | | | |
| ☐ 106 Neil O'Donnell | .50 | .23 | .06 | ☐ 154 Greg Jackson | .10 | .05 | .01 |
| Pittsburgh Steelers | | | | New York Giants | | | |
| ☐ 107 Steve DeBerg | .12 | .05 | .02 | ☐ 155 Jay Hilgenberg | .10 | .05 | .01 |
| Tampa Bay Buccaneers | | | | Mew York Giants | | | |
| ☐ 108 Leonard Russell | .12 | .05 | .02 | ☐ 156 Howard Ballard | .10 | .05 | .01 |
| New England Patriots | | | | Buffalo Bills | | | |
| ☐ 109 Ethan Horton | .10 | .05 | .01 | ☐ 157 Mike Compton | .20 | .09 | .03 |
| Los Angeles Raiders | | | | Detroit Lions | | | |
| ☐ 110 William Perry | .10 | .05 | .01 | ☐ 158 Brent Williams | .10 | .05 | .01 |
| Chicago Bears | | | | New England Patriots | | | |
| ☐ 111 Don Griffin UER | .10 | .05 | .01 | ☐ 159 Tommy Kane | .10 | .05 | .01 |
| San Francisco 49ers | | | | Seattle Seahawks | | | |
| (104 on back, | | | | ☐ 160 Barry Word | .15 | .07 | .02 |
| 111 does not exist) | | | | Kansas City Chiefs | | | |
| ☐ 112 Clarence Verdin | .10 | .05 | .01 | ☐ 161 Darren Lewis | .10 | .05 | .01 |
| Indianapolis Colts | | | | Chicago Bears | | | |
| ☐ 113 Amp Lee | .12 | .05 | .02 | ☐ 162 Steve Atwater | .12 | .05 | .02 |
| San Francisco 49ers | | | | Denver Broncos | | | |
| ☐ 114 Earnest Byner | .12 | .05 | .02 | ☐ 163 Gary Clark | .12 | .05 | .02 |
| Washington Redskins | | | | Phoenix Cardinals | | | |
| ☐ 115 Ricky Reynolds | .10 | .05 | .01 | ☐ 164 Donnell Woolford | .10 | .05 | .01 |
| Tampa Bay Buccaneers | | | | Pittsburgh Steelers | | | |
| ☐ 116 Tom Waddle | .15 | .07 | .02 | ☐ 165 Henry Thomas | .10 | .05 | .01 |
| Chicago Bears | | | | Minnesota Vikings | | | |
| ☐ 117 Robert Jones | .10 | .05 | .01 | ☐ 166 Tim Brown | .40 | .18 | .05 |
| Dallas Cowboys | | | | Los Angeles Raiders | | | |
| ☐ 118 Willie Davis | .20 | .09 | .03 | ☐ 167 Andre Ware | .12 | .05 | .02 |
| Kansas City Chiefs | | | | Detroit Lions | | | |
| ☐ 119 Chris Miller | .15 | .07 | .02 | ☐ 168 Jackie Harris | .50 | .23 | .06 |
| Atlanta Falcons | | | | Green Bay Packers | | | |
| ☐ 120 Drew Hill | .12 | .05 | .02 | ☐ 169 Browning Nagle | .12 | .05 | .02 |
| Atlanta Falcons | | | | New York Jets | | | |
| ☐ 121 Warren Moon | .30 | .14 | .04 | ☐ 170 Chris Singleton | .10 | .05 | .01 |
| Houston Oilers | | | | New England Patriots | | | |
| ☐ 122 Flipper Anderson | .12 | .05 | .02 | ☐ 171 Ronnie Lott | .15 | .07 | .02 |
| Los Angeles Rams | | | | New York Jets | | | |
| ☐ 123 George Teague | .35 | .16 | .04 | ☐ 172 Leonard Marshall | .10 | .05 | .01 |
| Green Bay Packers | | | | New York Jets | | | |
| ☐ 124 John L. Williams | .12 | .05 | .02 | ☐ 173 Dale Carter | .15 | .07 | .02 |
| Seattle Seahawks | | | | Kansas City Chiefs | | | |
| ☐ 125 Ed McCaffrey | .10 | .05 | .01 | ☐ 174 Bruce Armstrong | .10 | .05 | .01 |
| New York Giants | | | | New England Patriots | | | |
| ☐ 126 Eric Green | .15 | .07 | .02 | ☐ 175 Tommy Vardell | .12 | .05 | .02 |
| Pittsburgh Steelers | | | | Denver Broncos | | | |
| ☐ 127 Scott Mersereau | .10 | .05 | .01 | ☐ 176 Bubba McDowell | .10 | .05 | .01 |
| New York Jets | | | | Houston Oilers | | | |
| ☐ 128 Charles Mann | .10 | .05 | .01 | ☐ 177 Patrick Bates | .25 | .11 | .03 |
| Washington Redskins | | | | New York Jets | | | |

| | | | |
|---|---|---|---|
| ☐ 178 Tyji Armstrong | .10 | .05 | .01 |
| Tampa Bay Buccaneers | | | |
| ☐ 179 Keith Byars | .12 | .05 | .02 |
| Miami Dolphins | | | |
| ☐ 180 Boomer Esiason | .25 | .11 | .03 |
| New York Jets | | | |
| ☐ 181 Ricky Watters | .75 | .35 | .09 |
| San Francisco 49ers | | | |
| ☐ 182 Keith Sims | .10 | .05 | .01 |
| Miami Dolphins | | | |
| ☐ 183 Burt Grossman | .10 | .05 | .01 |
| San Diego Chargers | | | |
| ☐ 184 Richard Cooper | .10 | .05 | .01 |
| New York Giants | | | |
| ☐ 185 Marc Boutte | .10 | .05 | .01 |
| Los Angeles Rams | | | |
| ☐ 186 Shane Conlan | .10 | .05 | .01 |
| Los Angeles Rams | | | |
| ☐ 187 Luis Sharpe | .10 | .05 | .01 |
| Phoenix Cardinals | | | |
| ☐ 188 O.J. McDuffie | 2.50 | 1.15 | .30 |
| Miami Dolphins | | | |
| ☐ 189 Harvey Williams | .15 | .07 | .02 |
| Kansas City Chiefs | | | |
| ☐ 190 Blair Thomas | .12 | .05 | .02 |
| New York Jets | | | |
| ☐ 191 Charles Haley | .12 | .05 | .02 |
| Dallas Cowboys | | | |
| ☐ 192 Chip Lohmiller | .10 | .05 | .01 |
| Washington Redskins | | | |
| ☐ 193 Vinny Testaverde | .10 | .05 | .01 |
| Cleveland Browns | | | |
| ☐ 194 Desmond Howard | .50 | .23 | .06 |
| Washington Redskins | | | |
| ☐ 195 Johnny Johnson | .15 | .07 | .02 |
| New York Jets | | | |
| ☐ 196 Bennie Blades | .10 | .05 | .01 |
| Detroit Lions | | | |
| ☐ 197 Jeff Wright | .10 | .05 | .01 |
| Buffalo Bills | | | |
| ☐ 198 Cody Carlson | .30 | .14 | .04 |
| Houston Oilers | | | |
| ☐ 199 Micheal Barrow | .10 | .05 | .01 |
| Houston Oilers | | | |
| ☐ 200 Pat Swilling | .12 | .05 | .02 |
| Detroit Lions | | | |
| ☐ 201 Willie Roaf | .30 | .14 | .04 |
| New Orleans Saints | | | |
| ☐ 202 Mike Walter | .10 | .05 | .01 |
| San Francisco 49ers | | | |
| ☐ 203 Kevin Fagan | .10 | .05 | .01 |
| San Francisco 49ers | | | |
| ☐ 204 Nate Odomes | .12 | .05 | .02 |
| Buffalo Bills | | | |
| ☐ 205 Michael Dean Perry | .15 | .07 | .02 |
| Cleveland Browns | | | |
| ☐ 206 Bruce Pickens | .10 | .05 | .01 |
| Atlanta Falcons | | | |
| ☐ 207 Mel Gray | .10 | .05 | .01 |
| Detroit Lions | | | |
| ☐ 208 Jack Trudeau | .10 | .05 | .01 |
| Indianapolis Colts | | | |
| ☐ 209 Ricky Sanders | .12 | .05 | .02 |
| Washington Redskins | | | |
| ☐ 210 Bobby Hebert | .15 | .07 | .02 |
| Atlanta Falcons | | | |
| ☐ 211 Craig Heyward | .10 | .05 | .01 |
| Chicago Bears | | | |
| ☐ 212 Eric Bieniemy | .12 | .05 | .02 |
| San Diego Chargers | | | |
| ☐ 213 Andre Rison | .40 | .18 | .05 |
| Atlanta Falcons | | | |
| ☐ 214 Bernie Kosar | .15 | .07 | .02 |
| Cleveland Browns | | | |
| ☐ 215 Lester Holmes | .10 | .05 | .01 |
| Philadelphia Eagles | | | |
| ☐ 216 Marcus Buckley | .15 | .07 | .02 |
| New York Giants | | | |
| ☐ 217 Tony Casillas | .10 | .05 | .01 |
| Dallas Cowboys | | | |
| ☐ 218 Cornelius Bennett | .15 | .07 | .02 |
| Buffalo Bills | | | |
| ☐ 219 Kyle Clifton | .10 | .05 | .01 |
| New York Jets | | | |
| ☐ 220 Kirk Lowdermilk | .10 | .05 | .01 |
| Indianapolis Colts | | | |
| ☐ 221 Leon Searcy | .10 | .05 | .01 |
| Pittsburgh Steelers | | | |
| ☐ 222 Gary Anderson | .10 | .05 | .01 |
| Pittsburgh Steelers | | | |
| ☐ 223 Tim Barnett | .12 | .05 | .02 |
| Kansas City Chiefs | | | |
| ☐ 224 Gene Atkins | .10 | .05 | .01 |
| New York Giants | | | |
| ☐ 225 Jeff Cross | .10 | .05 | .01 |
| Miami Dolphins | | | |
| ☐ 226 Darrin Smith | .60 | .25 | .08 |
| Dallas Cowboys | | | |
| ☐ 227 Rohn Stark | .10 | .05 | .01 |
| Indianapolis Colts | | | |
| ☐ 228 Chris Warren | .30 | .14 | .04 |
| Seattle Seahawks | | | |
| ☐ 229 Eric Allen | .12 | .05 | .02 |
| Philadelphia Eagles | | | |
| ☐ 230 Wayne Simmons | .25 | .11 | .03 |
| Green Bay Packers | | | |
| ☐ 231 Al Smith | .10 | .05 | .01 |
| Houston Oilers | | | |
| ☐ 232 Reggie Rivers | .35 | .16 | .04 |
| Denver Broncos | | | |
| ☐ 233 Kevin Smith | .12 | .05 | .02 |
| Dallas Cowboys | | | |
| ☐ 234 Vince Workman | .10 | .05 | .01 |
| Tampa Bay Buccaneers | | | |
| ☐ 235 Thurman Thomas | .75 | .35 | .09 |
| Buffalo Bills | | | |
| ☐ 236 Kevin Williams | 1.00 | .45 | .13 |
| Dallas Cowboys | | | |
| ☐ 237 Dan McGwire | .12 | .05 | .02 |
| Seattle Seahawks | | | |
| ☐ 238 Greg Lloyd | .10 | .05 | .01 |
| Pittsburgh Steelers | | | |
| ☐ 239 Ray Buchanan | .15 | .07 | .02 |
| Indianapolis Colts | | | |
| ☐ 240 Shannon Sharpe | .35 | .16 | .04 |
| Denver Broncos | | | |
| ☐ 241 Ricardo McDonald | .10 | .05 | .01 |
| Cincinnati Bengals | | | |
| ☐ 242 Aaron Wallace | .10 | .05 | .01 |
| Los Angeles Raiders | | | |
| ☐ 243 Chris Hinton | .10 | .05 | .01 |
| Indianapolis Colts | | | |
| ☐ 244 Bill Romanowski | .10 | .05 | .01 |
| San Francisco 49ers | | | |
| ☐ 245 Randal Hill | .15 | .07 | .02 |
| Phoenix Cardinals | | | |
| ☐ 246 Ray Agnew | .10 | .05 | .01 |
| New England Patriots | | | |
| ☐ 247 Todd Kelly | .20 | .09 | .03 |
| San Francisco 49ers | | | |
| ☐ 248 John Stephens | .10 | .05 | .01 |
| Green Bay Packers | | | |
| ☐ 249 Sean Salisbury | .12 | .05 | .02 |
| Minnesota Vikings | | | |
| ☐ 250 Roger Craig | .12 | .05 | .02 |
| Minnesota Vikings | | | |
| ☐ 251 Dave Krieg | .12 | .05 | .02 |
| Kansas City Chiefs | | | |
| ☐ 252 Brian Blades | .12 | .05 | .02 |
| Seattle Seahawks | | | |
| ☐ 253 Jarrod Bunch | .10 | .05 | .01 |
| New York Giants | | | |
| ☐ 254 Phil Simms | .15 | .07 | .02 |
| New York Giants | | | |
| ☐ 255 Keith Van Horne | .10 | .05 | .01 |
| Chicago Bears | | | |
| ☐ 256 Jim Price | .10 | .05 | .01 |
| Los Angeles Rams | | | |
| ☐ 257 Garrison Hearst | 1.00 | .45 | .13 |
| Phoenix Cardinals | | | |
| ☐ 258 Derrick Walker | .10 | .05 | .01 |
| San Diego Chargers | | | |
| ☐ 259 Mike Pritchard | .15 | .07 | .02 |
| Atlanta Falcons | | | |
| ☐ 260 Leonard Renfro | .15 | .07 | .02 |
| Philadelphia Eagles | | | |
| ☐ 261 Rodney Peete | .12 | .05 | .02 |
| Detroit Lions | | | |
| ☐ 262 Jeff Bryant | .10 | .05 | .01 |
| Seattle Seahawks | | | |
| ☐ 263 Dermontti Dawson | .10 | .05 | .01 |
| Pittsburgh Steelers | | | |
| ☐ 264 Greg McMurtry | .10 | .05 | .01 |
| New England Patriots | | | |
| ☐ 265 Wendell Davis | .10 | .05 | .01 |
| Cleveland Browns | | | |
| ☐ 266 Kerry Cash | .10 | .05 | .01 |
| Indianapolis Colts | | | |
| ☐ 267 Jackie Slater | .10 | .05 | .01 |
| Los Angeles Rams | | | |
| ☐ 268 Sam Mills | .12 | .05 | .02 |
| New Orleans Saints | | | |
| ☐ 269 Carlton Bailey | .10 | .05 | .01 |
| Buffalo Bills | | | |
| ☐ 270 Mark Wheeler | .10 | .05 | .01 |
| Tampa Bay Buccaneers | | | |
| ☐ 271 Darren Perry | .10 | .05 | .01 |
| Pittsburgh Steelers | | | |
| ☐ 272 Todd Scott | .10 | .05 | .01 |
| Minnesota Vikings | | | |
| ☐ 273 Johnny Holland | .10 | .05 | .01 |
| Green Bay Packers | | | |
| ☐ 274 Mike Croel | .12 | .05 | .02 |
| Denver Broncos | | | |
| ☐ 275 Shane Dronett | .10 | .05 | .01 |

| | | | |
|---|---|---|---|
| Denver Broncos | | | |
| ☐ 276 Andre Collins | .10 | .05 | .01 |
| Washington Redskins | | | |
| ☐ 277 Eric Swann | .12 | .05 | .02 |
| Phoenix Cardinals | | | |
| ☐ 278 Jessie Hester | .10 | .05 | .01 |
| Indianapolis Colts | | | |
| ☐ 279 Bryan Cox | .12 | .05 | .02 |
| Miami Dolphins | | | |
| ☐ 280 Mark Jackson | .12 | .05 | .02 |
| New York Giants | | | |
| ☐ 281 Thomas Everett | .10 | .05 | .01 |
| Dallas Cowboys | | | |
| ☐ 282 James Lofton | .15 | .07 | .02 |
| Los Angeles Raiders | | | |
| ☐ 283 Carl Pickens | .15 | .07 | .02 |
| Cincinnati Bengals | | | |
| ☐ 284 Mark Carrier | .12 | .05 | .02 |
| Tampa Bay Buccaneers | | | |
| ☐ 285 Heath Sherman | .10 | .05 | .01 |
| Philadelphia Eagles | | | |
| ☐ 286 Chris Burkett | .10 | .05 | .01 |
| New York Jets | | | |
| ☐ 287 Coleman Rudolph | .25 | .11 | .03 |
| New York Jets | | | |
| ☐ 288 Todd Marinovich | .10 | .05 | .01 |
| Los Angeles Raiders | | | |
| ☐ 289 Nate Lewis | .12 | .05 | .02 |
| San Diego Chargers | | | |
| ☐ 290 Fred Barnett | .15 | .07 | .02 |
| Philadelphia Eagles | | | |
| ☐ 291 Jim Lachey | .10 | .05 | .01 |
| Washington Redskins | | | |
| ☐ 292 Jerry Ball | .10 | .05 | .01 |
| Detroit Lions | | | |
| ☐ 293 Jeff George | .25 | .11 | .03 |
| Indianapolis Colts | | | |
| ☐ 294 William Fuller | .10 | .05 | .01 |
| Houston Oilers | | | |
| ☐ 295 Courtney Hawkins | .12 | .05 | .02 |
| Tampa Bay Buccaneers | | | |
| ☐ 296 Kelvin Martin | .10 | .05 | .01 |
| Seattle Seahawks | | | |
| ☐ 297 Trace Armstrong | .10 | .05 | .01 |
| Chicago Bears | | | |
| ☐ 298 Carl Banks | .10 | .05 | .01 |
| Washington Redskins | | | |
| ☐ 299 Terry Kirby | 2.50 | 1.15 | .30 |
| Miami Dolphins | | | |
| ☐ 300 John Offerdahl | .10 | .05 | .01 |
| Miami Dolphins | | | |
| ☐ 301 Harry Swayne | .10 | .05 | .01 |
| San Diego Chargers | | | |
| ☐ 302 Wilber Marshall | .12 | .05 | .02 |
| Houston Oilers | | | |
| ☐ 303 Guy McIntyre | .10 | .05 | .01 |
| San Francisco 49ers | | | |
| ☐ 304 Steve Wallace | .10 | .05 | .01 |
| San Francisco 49ers | | | |
| ☐ 305 Chris Slade | .50 | .23 | .06 |
| New England Patriots | | | |
| ☐ 306 Anthony Newman | .10 | .05 | .01 |
| Los Angeles Rams | | | |
| ☐ 307 Chip Banks | .10 | .05 | .01 |
| Indianapolis Colts | | | |
| ☐ 308 Carlton Gray | .35 | .16 | .04 |
| Seattle Seahawks | | | |
| ☐ 309 Wayne Martin | .10 | .05 | .01 |
| New York Giants | | | |
| ☐ 310 Tom Rathman | .12 | .05 | .02 |
| San Francisco 49ers | | | |
| ☐ 311 Shaun Gayle | .10 | .05 | .01 |
| Chicago Bears | | | |
| ☐ 312 Billy Joe Hobert | .75 | .35 | .09 |
| Los Angeles Raiders | | | |
| ☐ 313 Matt Brock | .10 | .05 | .01 |
| Green Bay Packers | | | |
| ☐ 314 Arthur Marshall | .40 | .18 | .05 |
| Denver Broncos | | | |
| ☐ 315 Wade Wilson | .12 | .05 | .02 |
| New Orleans Saints | | | |
| ☐ 316 Michael Jackson | .15 | .07 | .02 |
| Cleveland Browns | | | |
| ☐ 317 Bruce Kozerski | .10 | .05 | .01 |
| Cincinnati Bengals | | | |
| ☐ 318 Reggie Langhorne | .12 | .05 | .02 |
| Indianapolis Colts | | | |
| ☐ 319 Jerrol Williams | .10 | .05 | .01 |
| San Diego Chargers | | | |
| ☐ 320 Aeneas Williams | .10 | .05 | .01 |
| Phoenix Cardinals | | | |
| ☐ 321 Tony McGee | .40 | .18 | .05 |
| Cincinnati Bengals | | | |
| ☐ 322 Carl Simpson | .20 | .09 | .03 |
| Chicago Bears | | | |
| ☐ 323 Russell Maryland | .15 | .07 | .02 |
| Dallas Cowboys | | | |
| ☐ 324 Nick Lowery | .10 | .05 | .01 |

| | | | |
|---|---|---|---|
| Kansas City Chiefs | | | |
| ☐ 325 Steve Tasker | .10 | .05 | .01 |
| Buffalo Bills | | | |
| ☐ 326 Alvin Harper | .50 | .23 | .06 |
| Dallas Cowboys | | | |
| ☐ 327 Haywood Jeffires | .15 | .07 | .02 |
| Houston Oilers | | | |
| ☐ 328 Hardy Nickerson | .10 | .05 | .01 |
| Pittsburgh Steelers | | | |
| ☐ 329 Alonzo Spellman | .12 | .05 | .02 |
| Chicago Bears | | | |
| ☐ 330 Eric Dickerson | .15 | .07 | .02 |
| Atlanta Falcons | | | |
| ☐ 331 Scott Zolak | .10 | .05 | .01 |
| New England Patriots | | | |
| ☐ 332 Darryl Henley | .10 | .05 | .01 |
| Los Angeles Rams | | | |
| ☐ 333 Daniel Stubbs | .10 | .05 | .01 |
| Cincinnati Bengals | | | |
| ☐ 334 Andy Heck | .10 | .05 | .01 |
| Atlanta Falcons | | | |
| ☐ 335 Mark May | .10 | .05 | .01 |
| Washington Redskins | | | |
| ☐ 336 Roosevelt Potts | .50 | .23 | .06 |
| Indianapolis Colts | | | |
| ☐ 337 Erik Howard | .10 | .05 | .01 |
| New York Giants | | | |
| ☐ 338 Sean Gilbert | .12 | .05 | .02 |
| Los Angeles Rams | | | |
| ☐ 339 Jerome Bettis | 9.00 | 4.00 | 1.15 |
| Los Angeles Rams | | | |
| ☐ 340 Darren Carrington | .20 | .09 | .03 |
| San Diego Chargers | | | |
| ☐ 341 Gill Byrd | .10 | .05 | .01 |
| San Diego Chargers | | | |
| ☐ 342 John Friesz | .12 | .05 | .02 |
| San Diego Chargers | | | |
| ☐ 343 Roger Harper | .25 | .11 | .03 |
| Atlanta Falcons | | | |
| ☐ 344 Fred Stokes | .10 | .05 | .01 |
| Phoenix Cardinals | | | |
| ☐ 345 Stanley Richard | .10 | .05 | .01 |
| San Diego Chargers | | | |
| ☐ 346 Johnny Bailey | .10 | .05 | .01 |
| Phoenix Cardinals | | | |
| ☐ 347 David Wyman | .10 | .05 | .01 |
| Denver Broncos | | | |
| ☐ 348 Merril Hoge | .10 | .05 | .01 |
| Pittsburgh Steelers | | | |
| ☐ 349 Brett Perriman | .12 | .05 | .02 |
| Detroit Lions | | | |
| ☐ 350 Kelvin Pritchett | .10 | .05 | .01 |
| Detroit Lions | | | |
| ☐ 351 Rod Bernstine | .12 | .05 | .02 |
| Denver Broncos | | | |
| ☐ 352 Jim Ritcher | .10 | .05 | .01 |
| Buffalo Bills | | | |
| ☐ 353 Mark Stepnoski | .10 | .05 | .01 |
| Dallas Cowboys | | | |
| ☐ 354 Jeff Lageman | .10 | .05 | .01 |
| New York Jets | | | |
| ☐ 355 Darrien Gordon | .35 | .16 | .04 |
| San Diego Chargers | | | |
| ☐ 356 Don Mosebar | .10 | .05 | .01 |
| Los Angeles Raiders | | | |
| ☐ 357 Simon Fletcher | .12 | .05 | .02 |
| Denver Broncos | | | |
| ☐ 358 Charles Mincy | .35 | .16 | .04 |
| Kansas City Chiefs | | | |
| ☐ 359 Ron Hall | .10 | .05 | .01 |
| Tampa Bay Buccaneers | | | |
| ☐ 360 Brent Jones | .15 | .07 | .02 |
| San Francisco 49ers | | | |
| ☐ 361 Byron Evans | .10 | .05 | .01 |
| Philadelphia Eagles | | | |
| ☐ 362 Dan Footman | .25 | .11 | .03 |
| Cleveland Browns | | | |
| ☐ 363 Mark Higgs | .15 | .07 | .02 |
| Miami Dolphins | | | |
| ☐ 364 Brian Washington | .10 | .05 | .01 |
| New York Jets | | | |
| ☐ 365 Brad Hopkins | .20 | .09 | .03 |
| Houston Oilers | | | |
| ☐ 366 Tracy Simien | .10 | .05 | .01 |
| Kansas City Chiefs | | | |
| ☐ 367 Derrick Fenner | .10 | .05 | .01 |
| Cincinnati Bengals | | | |
| ☐ 368 Lorenzo White | .12 | .05 | .02 |
| Houston Oilers | | | |
| ☐ 369 Marvin Jones | .40 | .18 | .05 |
| New York Jets | | | |
| ☐ 370 Chris Doleman | .12 | .05 | .02 |
| Minnesota Vikings | | | |
| ☐ 371 Jeff Herrod | .10 | .05 | .01 |
| Indianapolis Colts | | | |
| ☐ 372 Jim Harbaugh | .12 | .05 | .02 |
| Chicago Bears | | | |
| ☐ 373 Jim Jeffcoat | .10 | .05 | .01 |

| | | | | | | | | |
|---|---|---|---|---|---|---|---|---|
| | Dallas Cowboys | | | | | Pittsburgh Steelers | | |
| ☐ 374 | Michael Strahan | .20 | .09 | .03 | ☐ 423 | Clay Matthews | .12 | .05 | .02 |
| | New York Giants | | | | | Cleveland Browns | | |
| ☐ 375 | Ricky Ervins | .12 | .05 | .02 | ☐ 424 | Jay Novacek | .15 | .07 | .02 |
| | Washington Redskins | | | | | Dallas Cowboys | | |
| ☐ 376 | Joel Hilgenberg | .10 | .05 | .01 | ☐ 425 | Phil Hansen | .10 | .05 | .01 |
| | New York Giants | | | | | Buffalo Bills | | |
| ☐ 377 | Curtis Duncan | .10 | .05 | .01 | ☐ 426 | Andre Hastings | .40 | .18 | .05 |
| | Houston Oilers | | | | | Pittsburgh Steelers | | |
| ☐ 378 | Glyn Milburn | 1.75 | .80 | .22 | ☐ 427 | Toi Cook | .10 | .05 | .01 |
| | Denver Broncos | | | | | New York Giants | | |
| ☐ 379 | Jack Del Rio | .10 | .05 | .01 | ☐ 428 | Rufus Porter | .10 | .05 | .01 |
| | Minnesota Vikings | | | | | Seattle Seahawks | | |
| ☐ 380 | Eric Martin | .12 | .05 | .02 | ☐ 429 | Mike Pitts | .10 | .05 | .01 |
| | New York Giants | | | | | New England Patriots | | |
| ☐ 381 | Dave Meggett | .12 | .05 | .02 | ☐ 430 | Eddie Robinson | .10 | .05 | .01 |
| | New York Giants | | | | | Houston Oilers | | |
| ☐ 382 | Jeff Hostetler | .15 | .07 | .02 | ☐ 431 | Herman Moore | .50 | .23 | .06 |
| | Los Angeles Raiders | | | | | Detroit Lions | | |
| ☐ 383 | Greg Townsend | .10 | .05 | .01 | ☐ 432 | Erik Kramer | .25 | .11 | .03 |
| | Los Angeles Raiders | | | | | Detroit Lions | | |
| ☐ 384 | Brad Muster | .12 | .05 | .02 | ☐ 433 | Mark Carrier | .12 | .05 | .02 |
| | New York Giants | | | | | Chicago Bears | | |
| ☐ 385 | Irv Smith | .40 | .18 | .05 | ☐ 434 | Natrone Means | 2.00 | .90 | .25 |
| | New York Giants | | | | | San Diego Chargers | | |
| ☐ 386 | Chris Jacke | .10 | .05 | .01 | ☐ 435 | Carnell Lake | .10 | .05 | .01 |
| | Green Bay Packers | | | | | Pittsburgh Steelers | | |
| ☐ 387 | Ernest Dye | .20 | .09 | .03 | ☐ 436 | Carlton Haselrig | .10 | .05 | .01 |
| | New York Giants | | | | | Pittsburgh Steelers | | |
| ☐ 388 | Henry Ellard | .12 | .05 | .02 | ☐ 437 | John Randle | .10 | .05 | .01 |
| | Los Angeles Rams | | | | | Minnesota Vikings | | |
| ☐ 389 | John Taylor | .15 | .07 | .02 | ☐ 438 | Louis Oliver | .10 | .05 | .01 |
| | San Francisco 49ers | | | | | Miami Dolphins | | |
| ☐ 390 | Chris Chandler | .12 | .05 | .02 | ☐ 439 | Ray Roberts | .10 | .05 | .01 |
| | Phoenix Cardinals | | | | | Seattle Seahawks | | |
| ☐ 391 | Larry Centers | .40 | .18 | .05 | ☐ 440 | Leslie O'Neal | .12 | .05 | .02 |
| | Phoenix Cardinals | | | | | San Diego Chargers | | |
| ☐ 392 | Henry Rolling | .10 | .05 | .01 | ☐ 441 | Reggie White | .25 | .11 | .03 |
| | Buffalo Bills | | | | | Green Bay Packers | | |
| ☐ 393 | Dan Saleaumua | .10 | .05 | .01 | ☐ 442 | Dalton Hilliard | .10 | .05 | .01 |
| | Kansas City Chiefs | | | | | New Orleans Saints | | |
| ☐ 394 | Moe Gardner | .10 | .05 | .01 | ☐ 443 | Tim Krumrie | .10 | .05 | .01 |
| | Atlanta Falcons | | | | | Cincinnati Bengals | | |
| ☐ 395 | Darryl Williams | .12 | .05 | .02 | ☐ 444 | LeRoy Butler | .10 | .05 | .01 |
| | Cincinnati Bengals | | | | | Green Bay Packers | | |
| ☐ 396 | Paul Gruber | .10 | .05 | .01 | ☐ 445 | Greg Kragen | .10 | .05 | .01 |
| | Tampa Bay Buccaneers | | | | | Denver Broncos | | |
| ☐ 397 | Dwayne Harper | .10 | .05 | .01 | ☐ 446 | Anthony Johnson | .10 | .05 | .01 |
| | Seattle Seahawks | | | | | Indianapolis Colts | | |
| ☐ 398 | Pat Harlow | .10 | .05 | .01 | ☐ 447 | Audray McMillian | .10 | .05 | .01 |
| | New England Patriots | | | | | Minnesota Vikings | | |
| ☐ 399 | Rickey Jackson | .12 | .05 | .02 | ☐ 448 | Lawrence Dawsey | .15 | .07 | .02 |
| | New York Giants | | | | | Tampa Bay Buccaneers | | |
| ☐ 400 | Quentin Coryatt | .15 | .07 | .02 | ☐ 449 | Pierce Holt | .10 | .05 | .01 |
| | Indianapolis Colts | | | | | Atlanta Falcons | | |
| ☐ 401 | Steve Jordan | .12 | .05 | .02 | ☐ 450 | Brad Edwards | .10 | .05 | .01 |
| | Minnesota Vikings | | | | | Washington Redskins | | |
| ☐ 402 | Rick Mirer | 9.00 | 4.00 | 1.15 | ☐ 451 | J.J. Birden | .12 | .05 | .02 |
| | Seattle Seahawks | | | | | Kansas City Chiefs | | |
| ☐ 403 | Howard Cross | .10 | .05 | .01 | ☐ 452 | Mike Munchak | .12 | .05 | .02 |
| | New York Giants | | | | | Houston Oilers | | |
| ☐ 404 | Mike Johnson | .10 | .05 | .01 | ☐ 453 | Tracy Scroggins | .12 | .05 | .02 |
| | Cleveland Browns | | | | | Detroit Lions | | |
| ☐ 405 | Broderick Thomas | .10 | .05 | .01 | ☐ 454 | Mike Tomczak | .10 | .05 | .01 |
| | Tampa Bay Buccaneers | | | | | Pittsburgh Steelers | | |
| ☐ 406 | Stan Humphries | .15 | .07 | .02 | ☐ 455 | Harold Green | .12 | .05 | .02 |
| | San Diego Chargers | | | | | Cincinnati Bengals | | |
| ☐ 407 | Ronnie Harmon | .10 | .05 | .01 | ☐ 456 | Vaughn Dunbar | .12 | .05 | .02 |
| | San Diego Chargers | | | | | New Orleans Saints | | |
| ☐ 408 | Andy Harmon | .10 | .05 | .01 | ☐ 457 | Calvin Williams | .15 | .07 | .02 |
| | Philadelphia Eagles | | | | | Philadelphia Eagles | | |
| ☐ 409 | Troy Drayton | .50 | .23 | .06 | ☐ 458 | Pete Stoyanovich | .10 | .05 | .01 |
| | Los Angeles Rams | | | | | Miami Dolphins | | |
| ☐ 410 | Dan Williams | .25 | .11 | .03 | ☐ 459 | Willie Gault | .12 | .05 | .02 |
| | Denver Broncos | | | | | Los Angeles Raiders | | |
| ☐ 411 | Mark Bavaro | .10 | .05 | .01 | ☐ 460 | Ken Ruettgers | .10 | .05 | .01 |
| | Philadelphia Eagles | | | | | Green Bay Packers | | |
| ☐ 412 | Bruce Smith | .15 | .07 | .02 | ☐ 461 | Eugene Robinson | .10 | .05 | .01 |
| | Buffalo Bills | | | | | Seattle Seahawks | | |
| ☐ 413 | Elbert Shelley | .20 | .09 | .03 | ☐ 462 | Larry Brown | .10 | .05 | .01 |
| | Atlanta Falcons | | | | | Dallas Cowboys | | |
| ☐ 414 | Tim McGee | .10 | .05 | .01 | ☐ 463 | Antonio London | .20 | .09 | .03 |
| | Washington Redskins | | | | | Detroit Lions | | |
| ☐ 415 | Tim Harris | .10 | .05 | .01 | ☐ 464 | Andre Reed | .15 | .07 | .02 |
| | Philadelphia Eagles | | | | | Buffalo Bills | | |
| ☐ 416 | Rob Moore | .15 | .07 | .02 | ☐ 465 | Daryl Johnston | .15 | .07 | .02 |
| | New York Jets | | | | | Dallas Cowboys | | |
| ☐ 417 | Rob Burnett | .10 | .05 | .01 | ☐ 466 | Karl Mecklenburg | .10 | .05 | .01 |
| | New York Jets | | | | | Denver Broncos | | |
| ☐ 418 | Howie Long | .12 | .05 | .02 | ☐ 467 | David Lang | .10 | .05 | .01 |
| | Los Angeles Raiders | | | | | Los Angeles Rams | | |
| ☐ 419 | Chuck Cecil | .10 | .05 | .01 | ☐ 468 | Bill Brooks | .10 | .05 | .01 |
| | Phoenix Cardinals | | | | | Buffalo Bills | | |
| ☐ 420 | Carl Lee | .10 | .05 | .01 | ☐ 469 | Jim Everett | .10 | .05 | .01 |
| | Minnesota Vikings | | | | | Los Angeles Rams | | |
| ☐ 421 | Anthony Smith | .10 | .05 | .01 | ☐ 470 | Qadry Ismail | 1.00 | .45 | .13 |
| | Los Angeles Raiders | | | | | Minnesota Vikings | | |
| ☐ 422 | Jeff Graham | .12 | .05 | .02 | ☐ 471 | Vai Sikahema | .10 | .05 | .01 |

Philadelphia Eagles

| | MINT | EXC | G-VG |
|---|---|---|---|
| ☐ 472 Andre Tippett | .10 | .05 | .01 |
| New England Patriots | | | |
| ☐ 473 Eugene Chung | .10 | .05 | .01 |
| New England Patriots | | | |
| ☐ 474 Cris Dishman | .10 | .05 | .01 |
| Houston Oilers | | | |
| ☐ 475 Tim McDonald | .10 | .05 | .01 |
| San Francisco 49ers | | | |
| ☐ 476 Freddie Joe Nunn | .10 | .05 | .01 |
| Phoenix Cardinals | | | |
| ☐ 477 Checklist 1 | .10 | .05 | .01 |
| ☐ 478 Checklist 2 | .10 | .05 | .01 |
| ☐ 479 Checklist 3 | .10 | .05 | .01 |
| ☐ 480 Checklist 4 | .10 | .05 | .01 |

## 1993 GameDay Gamebreakers

Fleer's 1993 GameDay Gamebreakers set consists of 20 cards measuring approximately 2 1/2" by 4 3/4". They were randomly inserted in packs of 1993 GameDay and spotlight 20 top offensive stars like Joe Montana and Troy Aikman. The black-bordered fronts feature color action player photos against black-and-white game-action backgrounds. Stamped in gold foil at the bottom of the picture are the set name and the player's name. The white borderless backs carry a close-up color player picture, the player's name, jersey number, and highlights of the 1992 season. The cards are numbered on the back "X of 20."

| | MINT | EXC | G-VG |
|---|---|---|---|
| COMPLETE SET (20) | 28.00 | 12.50 | 3.50 |
| COMMON PLAYER (1-20) | .40 | .18 | .05 |
| ☐ 1 Troy Aikman | 6.00 | 2.70 | .75 |
| Dallas Cowboys | | | |
| ☐ 2 Brett Favre | 3.50 | 1.55 | .45 |
| Green Bay Packers | | | |
| ☐ 3 Steve Young | 1.00 | .45 | .13 |
| San Francisco 49ers | | | |
| ☐ 4 Dan Marino | 3.00 | 1.35 | .40 |
| Miami Dolphins | | | |
| ☐ 5 Joe Montana | 5.00 | 2.30 | .60 |
| Kansas City Chiefs | | | |
| ☐ 6 Jim Kelly | 1.00 | .45 | .13 |
| Buffalo Bills | | | |
| ☐ 7 Emmitt Smith | 9.00 | 4.00 | 1.15 |
| Dallas Cowboys | | | |
| ☐ 8 Ricky Watters | 1.50 | .65 | .19 |
| San Francisco 49ers | | | |
| ☐ 9 Barry Foster | 1.25 | .55 | .16 |
| Pittsburgh Steelers | | | |
| ☐ 10 Barry Sanders | 2.25 | 1.00 | .30 |
| Detroit Lions | | | |
| ☐ 11 Michael Irvin | 1.50 | .65 | .19 |
| Dallas Cowboys | | | |
| ☐ 12 Thurman Thomas | 1.25 | .55 | .16 |
| Buffalo Bills | | | |
| ☐ 13 Sterling Sharpe | 1.50 | .65 | .19 |
| Green Bay Packers | | | |
| ☐ 14 Jerry Rice | 2.25 | 1.00 | .30 |
| San Francisco 49ers | | | |
| ☐ 15 Andre Rison | .75 | .35 | .09 |
| Atlanta Falcons | | | |
| ☐ 16 Deion Sanders | .75 | .35 | .09 |
| Atlanta Falcons | | | |
| ☐ 17 Harold Green | .40 | .18 | .05 |
| Cincinnati Bengals | | | |

| | MINT | EXC | G-VG |
|---|---|---|---|
| ☐ 18 Lorenzo White | .40 | .18 | .05 |
| Houston Oilers | | | |
| ☐ 19 Terry Allen | .50 | .23 | .06 |
| Minnesota Vikings | | | |
| ☐ 20 Haywood Jeffires | .40 | .18 | .05 |
| Houston Oilers | | | |

## 1993 GameDay Rookie Standouts

Fleer's 1993 GameDay Rookie Standouts set consists of 16 cards measuring approximately 2 1/2" by 4 3/4". They were randomly inserted in packs of 1993 GameDay and spotlight 16 top picks of the 1993 NFL Draft. The dark blue-bordered fronts feature color action player photos against black-and-white game-action backgrounds. Stamped in gold foil at the bottom of the picture are the set name and the player's name. The white borderless backs carry a close-up color player picture, the player's name, jersey number, and highlights of the 1992 season. The cards are numbered on the back "X of 16."

| | MINT | EXC | G-VG |
|---|---|---|---|
| COMPLETE SET (16) | 30.00 | 13.50 | 3.80 |
| COMMON PLAYER (1-16) | .50 | .23 | .06 |
| ☐ 1 Drew Bledsoe | 8.00 | 3.60 | 1.00 |
| New England Patriots | | | |
| ☐ 2 Rick Mirer | 8.00 | 3.60 | 1.00 |
| Seattle Seahawks | | | |
| ☐ 3 Garrison Hearst | 2.50 | 1.15 | .30 |
| Phoenix Cardinals | | | |
| ☐ 4 Jerome Bettis | 8.00 | 3.60 | 1.00 |
| Los Angeles Rams | | | |
| ☐ 5 Marvin Jones | .75 | .35 | .09 |
| New York Jets | | | |
| ☐ 6 Reggie Brooks | 5.00 | 2.30 | .60 |
| Washington Redskins | | | |
| ☐ 7 O.J. McDuffie | 3.00 | 1.35 | .40 |
| Miami Dolphins | | | |
| ☐ 8 Qadry Ismail | 1.25 | .55 | .16 |
| Minnesota Vikings | | | |
| ☐ 9 Glyn Milburn | 3.00 | 1.35 | .40 |
| Denver Broncos | | | |
| ☐ 10 Andre Hastings | .75 | .35 | .09 |
| Pittsburgh Steelers | | | |
| ☐ 11 Curtis Conway | 1.00 | .45 | .13 |
| Chicago Bears | | | |
| ☐ 12 Eric Curry | .75 | .35 | .09 |
| Tampa Bay Buccaneers | | | |
| ☐ 13 John Copeland | .75 | .35 | .09 |
| Cincinnati Bengals | | | |
| ☐ 14 Kevin Williams | 1.50 | .65 | .19 |
| Dallas Cowboys | | | |
| ☐ 15 Patrick Bates | .50 | .23 | .06 |
| Los Angeles Raiders | | | |
| ☐ 16 Lincoln Kennedy | .50 | .23 | .06 |
| Atlanta Falcons | | | |

## 1993 GameDay Second-Year Stars

Fleer's 1993 GameDay Second-Year Stars set consists of 16 cards measuring approximately 2 1/2" by 4 3/4". They were randomly inserted in packs of 1993 GameDay and spotlights 16 hot 1992 rookies including Vaughn Dunbar and Steve Emtman. The green-bordered fronts feature color action player photos against black-and-white game-action backgrounds. Stamped in gold foil at the bottom of the picture are the set name and the player's name. The white

borderless backs carry a close-up color player picture, the player's name, jersey number, and highlights of the 1992 season. The cards are numbered on the back "X of 16."

| | MINT | EXC | G-VG |
|---|---|---|---|
| COMPLETE SET (16) | 8.00 | 3.60 | 1.00 |
| COMMON PLAYER (1-16) | .40 | .18 | .05 |
| ☐ 1 Carl Pickens | .60 | .25 | .08 |
| Cincinnati Bengals | | | |
| ☐ 2 David Klingler | 1.50 | .65 | .19 |
| Cincinnati Bengals | | | |
| ☐ 3 Santana Dotson | .50 | .23 | .06 |
| Tampa Bay Buccaneers | | | |
| ☐ 4 Chris Mims | .50 | .23 | .06 |
| San Diego Chargers | | | |
| ☐ 5 Steve Emtman | .50 | .23 | .06 |
| Indianapolis Colts | | | |
| ☐ 6 Marco Coleman | .40 | .18 | .05 |
| Miami Dolphins | | | |
| ☐ 7 Robert Jones | .40 | .18 | .05 |
| Dallas Cowboys | | | |
| ☐ 8 Dale Carter | .50 | .23 | .06 |
| Kansas City Chiefs | | | |
| ☐ 9 Troy Vincent | .40 | .18 | .05 |
| Miami Dolphins | | | |
| ☐ 10 Tracy Scroggins | .40 | .18 | .05 |
| Detroit Lions | | | |
| ☐ 11 Vaughn Dunbar | .50 | .23 | .06 |
| New Orleans Saints | | | |
| ☐ 12 Quentin Coryatt | .50 | .23 | .06 |
| Indianapolis Colts | | | |
| ☐ 13 Dana Hall | .40 | .18 | .05 |
| San Francisco 49ers | | | |
| ☐ 14 Terrell Buckley | .50 | .23 | .06 |
| Green Bay Packers | | | |
| ☐ 15 Tommy Vardell | .50 | .23 | .06 |
| Cleveland Browns | | | |
| ☐ 16 Johnny Mitchell | 1.00 | .45 | .13 |
| New York Jets | | | |

## 1991 GTE Super Bowl Theme Art

This limited edition set of approximately 4 5/8 by 6" cards was issued on the occasion of Super Bowl XXV and sponsored by GTE, whose company logo appears at the bottom on the front of each card above a full color reproduction of the Super Bowl program cover enframed by black borders. The back includes information on the Super Bowl for that particular year, including location, teams, score, winning coach, MVP, and a GTE Super Bowl Telefact.

| | MINT | EXC | G-VG |
|---|---|---|---|
| COMPLETE SET (25) | 10.00 | 4.00 | 1.00 |
| COMMON PLAYER (1-25) | .75 | .30 | .07 |
| ☐ 1 Super Bowl I | 1.00 | .40 | .10 |
| ☐ 2 Super Bowl II | .75 | .30 | .07 |
| ☐ 3 Super Bowl III | .75 | .30 | .07 |
| ☐ 4 Super Bowl IV | .75 | .30 | .07 |
| ☐ 5 Super Bowl V | .75 | .30 | .07 |
| ☐ 6 Super Bowl VI | .75 | .30 | .07 |
| ☐ 7 Super Bowl VII | .75 | .30 | .07 |
| ☐ 8 Super Bowl VIII | .75 | .30 | .07 |
| ☐ 9 Super Bowl IX | .75 | .30 | .07 |
| ☐ 10 Super Bowl X | .75 | .30 | .07 |
| ☐ 11 Super Bowl XI | .75 | .30 | .07 |
| ☐ 12 Super Bowl XII | .75 | .30 | .07 |
| ☐ 13 Super Bowl XIII | .75 | .30 | .07 |
| ☐ 14 Super Bowl XIV | .75 | .30 | .07 |
| ☐ 15 Super Bowl XV | .75 | .30 | .07 |
| ☐ 16 Super Bowl XVI | .75 | .30 | .07 |
| ☐ 17 Super Bowl XVII | .75 | .30 | .07 |
| ☐ 18 Super Bowl XVIII | .75 | .30 | .07 |
| ☐ 19 Super Bowl XIX | .75 | .30 | .07 |
| ☐ 20 Super Bowl XX | .75 | .30 | .07 |
| ☐ 21 Super Bowl XXI | .75 | .30 | .07 |
| ☐ 22 Super Bowl XXII | .75 | .30 | .07 |
| ☐ 23 Super Bowl XXIII | .75 | .30 | .07 |
| ☐ 24 Super Bowl XXIV | .75 | .30 | .07 |
| ☐ 25 Super Bowl XXV | 1.00 | .40 | .10 |

## 1956 Giants Team Issue

The 1956 Giants Team Issue set contains 36 cards measuring approximately 4 7/8 by 6 7/8". The fronts have black and white posed player photos with white borders. A facsimile autograph appears below the picture. The backs have brief biographical information and career highlights. The cards are unnumbered and checklisted below in alphabetical order.

| | NRMT | VG-E | GOOD |
|---|---|---|---|
| COMPLETE SET (36) | 175.00 | 70.00 | 18.00 |
| COMMON PLAYER (1-36) | 4.00 | 1.60 | .40 |
| ☐ 1 Bill Austin | 5.00 | 2.00 | .50 |
| ☐ 2 Ray Beck | 4.00 | 1.60 | .40 |
| ☐ 3 Roosevelt Brown | 12.00 | 5.00 | 1.20 |
| ☐ 4 Hank Burnine | 4.00 | 1.60 | .40 |
| ☐ 5 Don Chandler | 6.00 | 2.40 | .60 |
| ☐ 6 Bob Clatterbuck | 4.00 | 1.60 | .40 |
| ☐ 7 Charley Conerly | 18.00 | 7.25 | 1.80 |
| ☐ 8 Frank Gifford | 30.00 | 12.00 | 3.00 |
| ☐ 9 Rosey Grier | 12.00 | 5.00 | 1.20 |
| ☐ 10 Don Heinrich | 6.00 | 2.40 | .60 |
| ☐ 11 John Hermann | 4.00 | 1.60 | .40 |
| ☐ 12 Jim Lee Howell CO | 5.00 | 2.00 | .50 |
| ☐ 13 Sam Huff | 15.00 | 6.00 | 1.50 |
| ☐ 14 Ed Hughes | 4.00 | 1.60 | .40 |
| ☐ 15 Gerald Huth | 4.00 | 1.60 | .40 |
| ☐ 16 Jim Katcavage | 6.00 | 2.40 | .60 |
| ☐ 17 Gene Kirby ANN | 4.00 | 1.60 | .40 |
| ☐ 18 Ken MacAfee | 5.00 | 2.00 | .50 |
| ☐ 19 Dick Modzelewski | 5.00 | 2.00 | .50 |
| (Misspelled Modelewski | | | |
| on the reverse) | | | |
| ☐ 20 Henry Moore | 4.00 | 1.60 | .40 |
| ☐ 21 Dick Nolan | 6.00 | 2.40 | .60 |
| ☐ 22 Jimmy Patton | 5.00 | 2.00 | .50 |
| ☐ 23 Andy Robustelli | 12.00 | 5.00 | 1.20 |
| ☐ 24 Kyle Rote | 12.00 | 5.00 | 1.20 |
| ☐ 25 Chris Schenkel ANN | 5.00 | 2.00 | .50 |
| ☐ 26 Bob Schnelker | 5.00 | 2.00 | .50 |
| ☐ 27 Jack Stroud | 4.00 | 1.60 | .40 |
| ☐ 28 Harland Svare | 5.00 | 2.00 | .50 |
| ☐ 29 Bill Svoboda | 4.00 | 1.60 | .40 |
| ☐ 30 Bob Topp | 4.00 | 1.60 | .40 |

| | | NRMT | VG-E | GOOD |
|---|---|---|---|---|
| ☐ 31 | Mel Triplett | 5.00 | 2.00 | .50 |
| ☐ 32 | Emlen Tunnell | 12.00 | 5.00 | 1.20 |
| ☐ 33 | Alex Webster | 6.00 | 2.40 | .60 |
| ☐ 34 | Ray Wietecha | 4.00 | 1.60 | .40 |
| ☐ 35 | Dick Yelvington | 4.00 | 1.60 | .40 |
| ☐ 36 | Walt Yowarsky | 4.00 | 1.60 | .40 |

# 1957 Giants Team Issue

This 40-card set measures approximately 4 7/8" by 6 7/8". The front has a black and white photo on glossy stock with a white border. The back gives biographical and statistical information. This set features one of the earliest Vince Lombardi cards. The cards are unnumbered and checklisted below in alphabetical order.

| | | NRMT | VG-E | GOOD |
|---|---|---|---|---|
| | COMPLETE SET (40) | 250.00 | 100.00 | 25.00 |
| | COMMON PLAYER (1-40) | 4.00 | 1.60 | .40 |
| ☐ 1 | Ben Agajanian | 5.00 | 2.00 | .50 |
| ☐ 2 | Bill Austin | 4.00 | 1.60 | .40 |
| ☐ 3 | Ray Beck | 4.00 | 1.60 | .40 |
| ☐ 4 | John Bookman | 4.00 | 1.60 | .40 |
| ☐ 5 | Roosevelt Brown | 12.00 | 5.00 | 1.20 |
| ☐ 6 | Don Chandler | 6.00 | 2.40 | .60 |
| ☐ 7 | Bob Clatterbuck | 4.00 | 1.60 | .40 |
| ☐ 8 | Charley Conerly | 18.00 | 7.25 | 1.80 |
| ☐ 9 | John Dell Isola CO | 4.00 | 1.60 | .40 |
| ☐ 10 | Gene Filipski | 5.00 | 2.00 | .50 |
| ☐ 11 | Frank Gifford | 30.00 | 12.00 | 3.00 |
| ☐ 12 | Don Heinrich | 6.00 | 2.40 | .60 |
| ☐ 13 | Jim Lee Howell CO | 5.00 | 2.00 | .50 |
| ☐ 14 | Sam Huff | 12.00 | 5.00 | 1.20 |
| ☐ 15 | Ed Hughes | 4.00 | 1.60 | .40 |
| ☐ 16 | Gerald Huth | 4.00 | 1.60 | .40 |
| ☐ 17 | Jim Katcavage | 6.00 | 2.40 | .60 |
| ☐ 18 | Ken Kavanaugh CO | 6.00 | 2.40 | .60 |
| ☐ 19 | Les Keiter ANN | 4.00 | 1.60 | .40 |
| ☐ 20 | Tom Landry CO | 35.00 | 14.00 | 3.50 |
| ☐ 21 | Cliff Livingston | 4.00 | 1.60 | .40 |
| ☐ 22 | Vince Lombardi CO | 35.00 | 14.00 | 3.50 |
| ☐ 23 | Ken MacAfee | 5.00 | 2.00 | .50 |
| ☐ 24 | Dennis Mendyk | 4.00 | 1.60 | .40 |
| ☐ 25 | Dick Modzelewski | 5.00 | 2.00 | .50 |
| ☐ 26 | Dick Nolan | 6.00 | 2.40 | .60 |
| ☐ 27 | Jim Patton | 5.00 | 2.00 | .50 |
| ☐ 28 | Andy Robustelli | 12.00 | 5.00 | 1.20 |
| ☐ 29 | Kyle Rote | 12.00 | 5.00 | 1.20 |
| ☐ 30 | Chris Schenkel ANN | 5.00 | 2.00 | .50 |
| ☐ 31 | Jack Spinks | 4.00 | 1.60 | .40 |
| ☐ 32 | Jack Stroud | 5.00 | 2.00 | .50 |
| ☐ 33 | Harland Svare | 5.00 | 2.00 | .50 |
| ☐ 34 | Bill Svoboda | 4.00 | 1.60 | .40 |
| ☐ 35 | Mel Triplett | 5.00 | 2.00 | .50 |
| ☐ 36 | Emlen Tunnell | 12.00 | 5.00 | 1.20 |
| ☐ 37 | Alex Webster | 6.00 | 2.40 | .60 |
| ☐ 38 | Ray Wietecha | 5.00 | 2.00 | .50 |
| ☐ 39 | Dick Yelvington | 4.00 | 1.60 | .40 |
| ☐ 40 | Walt Yowarsky | 4.00 | 1.60 | .40 |

# 1959 Giants Shell/Riger Posters

This set of nine posters was distributed by Shell Oil in 1959. The pictures are black and white drawings by Robert Riger, and they measure approximately 11 3/4" by 13 3/4". The posters are arranged alphabetically by the player's last name and feature members of the 1959 New York Giants.

| | | NRMT | VG-E | GOOD |
|---|---|---|---|---|
| | COMPLETE SET (9) | 150.00 | 60.00 | 15.00 |
| | COMMON PLAYER (1-9) | 10.00 | 4.00 | 1.00 |
| ☐ 1 | Charley Conerly | 30.00 | 12.00 | 3.00 |
| ☐ 2 | Frank Gifford | 50.00 | 20.00 | 5.00 |
| ☐ 3 | Sam Huff | 20.00 | 8.00 | 2.00 |
| ☐ 4 | Dick Modzelewski | 10.00 | 4.00 | 1.00 |
| ☐ 5 | Jim Patton | 10.00 | 4.00 | 1.00 |
| ☐ 6 | Kyle Rote | 20.00 | 8.00 | 2.00 |
| ☐ 7 | Bob Schnelker | 10.00 | 4.00 | 1.00 |
| ☐ 8 | Pat Summerall | 20.00 | 8.00 | 2.00 |
| ☐ 9 | Alex Webster and | 15.00 | 6.00 | 1.50 |
| | Roosevelt Brown | | | |

# 1960 Giants Jay Publishing

This 12-card set features (approximately) 5" by 7" black-and-white player photos. The photos show players in traditional poses with the

quarterback preparing to throw, the runner heading downfield, and the defenseman ready for the tackle. These cards were packaged 12 to a packet and originally sold for 25 cents. The backs are blank. The cards are unnumbered and checklisted below in alphabetical order. Bob Schnelker's last active year with the New York Giants was 1960.

| | | NRMT | VG-E | GOOD |
|---|---|---|---|---|
| | COMPLETE SET (12) | 60.00 | 24.00 | 6.00 |
| | COMMON PLAYER (1-12) | 5.00 | 2.00 | .50 |
| ☐ 1 | Rosey Brown | 9.00 | 3.75 | .90 |
| ☐ 2 | Don Chandler | 6.00 | 2.40 | .60 |
| ☐ 3 | Charlie Conerly | 10.00 | 4.00 | 1.00 |
| ☐ 4 | Frank Gifford | 20.00 | 8.00 | 2.00 |
| ☐ 5 | Roosevelt Grier | 8.00 | 3.25 | .80 |
| ☐ 6 | Sam Huff | 10.00 | 4.00 | 1.00 |
| ☐ 7 | Phil King | 5.00 | 2.00 | .50 |
| ☐ 8 | Andy Robustelli | 9.00 | 3.75 | .90 |
| ☐ 9 | Kyle Rote | 7.50 | 3.00 | .75 |
| ☐ 10 | Bob Schnelker | 6.00 | 2.40 | .60 |
| ☐ 11 | Pat Summerall | 7.50 | 3.00 | .75 |
| ☐ 12 | Alex Webster | 6.00 | 2.40 | .60 |

# 1961 Giants Jay Publishing

This 12-card set features (approximately) 5" by 7" black-and-white player photos. The photos show players in traditional poses with the quarterback preparing to throw, the runner heading downfield, and the defenseman ready for the tackle. These cards were packaged 12 to a packet and originally sold for 25 cents. The backs are blank. The cards are unnumbered and checklisted below in alphabetical order.

| | | NRMT | VG-E | GOOD |
|---|---|---|---|---|
| | COMPLETE SET (12) | 60.00 | 24.00 | 6.00 |
| | COMMON PLAYER (1-12) | 4.00 | 1.60 | .40 |
| ☐ 1 | Roosevelt Brown | 9.00 | 3.75 | .90 |
| ☐ 2 | Don Chandler | 6.00 | 2.40 | .60 |
| ☐ 3 | Charley Conerly | 10.00 | 4.00 | 1.00 |
| ☐ 4 | Roosevelt Grier | 8.00 | 3.25 | .80 |
| ☐ 5 | Sam Huff | 10.00 | 4.00 | 1.00 |
| ☐ 6 | Dick Modzelewski | 5.00 | 2.00 | .50 |
| ☐ 7 | Jimmy Patton | 5.00 | 2.00 | .50 |
| ☐ 8 | Jim Podoley | 4.00 | 1.60 | .40 |
| ☐ 9 | Andy Robustelli | 9.00 | 3.75 | .90 |
| ☐ 10 | Allie Sherman CO | 5.00 | 2.00 | .50 |
| ☐ 11 | Del Shofner | 6.00 | 2.40 | .60 |
| ☐ 12 | Y.A. Tittle | 15.00 | 6.00 | 1.50 |

# 1973 Giants Color Litho

This set of eight color lithos measures approximately 8 1/2" by 11" and is blank backed with no border and a facsimile autograph in a white triangle in the lower right corner. The set is dated by the fact that Jim Files' last year with the New York Giants was 1973 and Brad Van Pelt's first year was 1973.

| | | NRMT | VG-E | GOOD |
|---|---|---|---|---|
| | COMPLETE SET (8) | 50.00 | 20.00 | 5.00 |
| | COMMON PLAYER (1-8) | 6.00 | 2.40 | .60 |
| ☐ 1 | James Files | 6.00 | 2.40 | .60 |
| ☐ 2 | Jack Gregory | 7.50 | 3.00 | .75 |
| ☐ 3 | Ron Johnson | 9.00 | 3.75 | .90 |
| ☐ 4 | Greg Larson | 7.50 | 3.00 | .75 |
| ☐ 5 | Spider Lockhart | 7.50 | 3.00 | .75 |
| ☐ 6 | Norm Snead | 7.50 | 3.00 | .75 |
| ☐ 7 | Bob Tucker | 7.50 | 3.00 | .75 |
| ☐ 8 | Brad Van Pelt | 7.50 | 3.00 | .75 |

# 1969 Glendale Stamps

This set contains 312 stamps featuring NFL players each measuring approximately 1 13/16" by 2 15/16". The stamps were meant to be pasted in an accompanying album, which itself measures approximately 9" by 12". The stamps and the album positions are unnumbered so the stamps are ordered and numbered below according to the team order that they appear in the book. The team order is alphabetical as well, according to the city name, i.e., Atlanta Falcons (1-12), Baltimore Colts (13-24), Boston Patriots (25-36), Buffalo Bills (37-48), Chicago Bears (49-60), Cincinnati Bengals (61-72), Cleveland Browns (73-84), Dallas Cowboys (85-96), Denver Broncos (97-108), Detroit Lions (109-120), Green Bay Packers (121-132), Houston Oilers (133-144), Kansas City Chiefs (145-156), Los Angeles Rams (157-168), Miami Dolphins (169-180), Minnesota

Dampen strip and affix in album ↑

DETROIT
LIONS

MEL FARR

Vikings (181-192), New Orleans Saints (193-204), New York Giants (205-216), New York Jets (217-228), Oakland Raiders (229-240), Philadelphia Eagles (241-252), Pittsburgh Steelers (253-264), St. Louis Cardinals (265-276), San Diego Chargers (277-288), San Francisco 49ers (289-300), and Washington Redskins (301-312). The stamp of O.J. Simpson predates his 1970 Topps Rookie Card by one year and the stamp of Gene Upshaw predates his Rookie Card by three years.

|  | NRMT | VG-E | GOOD |
|---|---|---|---|
| COMPLETE SET (312) | 175.00 | 70.00 | 18.00 |
| COMMON PLAYER (1-312) | .25 | .10 | .02 |

| | | | |
|---|---|---|---|
| ☐ 1 Bob Berry | .35 | .14 | .03 |
| ☐ 2 Clark Miller | .25 | .10 | .02 |
| ☐ 3 Jim Butler | .25 | .10 | .02 |
| ☐ 4 Junior Coffey | .25 | .10 | .02 |
| ☐ 5 Paul Flatley | .35 | .14 | .03 |
| ☐ 6 Randy Johnson | .35 | .14 | .03 |
| ☐ 7 Charlie Bryant | .25 | .10 | .02 |
| ☐ 8 Billy Lothridge | .25 | .10 | .02 |
| ☐ 9 Tommy Nobis | 1.50 | .60 | .15 |
| ☐ 10 Claude Humphrey | .35 | .14 | .03 |
| ☐ 11 Ken Reaves | .25 | .10 | .02 |
| ☐ 12 Jerry Simmons | .35 | .14 | .03 |
| ☐ 13 Mike Curtis | .50 | .20 | .05 |
| ☐ 14 Dennis Gaubatz | .25 | .10 | .02 |
| ☐ 15 Jerry Logan | .25 | .10 | .02 |
| ☐ 16 Lenny Lyles | .25 | .10 | .02 |
| ☐ 17 John Mackey | 2.00 | .80 | .20 |
| ☐ 18 Tom Matte | .50 | .20 | .05 |
| ☐ 19 Lou Michaels | .35 | .14 | .03 |
| ☐ 20 Jimmy Orr | .50 | .20 | .05 |
| ☐ 21 Willie Richardson | .35 | .14 | .03 |
| ☐ 22 Don Shinnick | .25 | .10 | .02 |
| ☐ 23 Dan Sullivan | .25 | .10 | .02 |
| ☐ 24 Johnny Unitas | 10.00 | 4.00 | 1.00 |
| ☐ 25 Houston Antwine | .25 | .10 | .02 |
| ☐ 26 John Bramlett | .25 | .10 | .02 |
| ☐ 27 Aaron Marsh | .25 | .10 | .02 |
| ☐ 28 R.C. Gamble | .25 | .10 | .02 |
| ☐ 29 Gino Cappelletti | .50 | .20 | .05 |
| ☐ 30 John Charles | .25 | .10 | .02 |
| ☐ 31 Larry Eisenhauer | .35 | .14 | .03 |
| ☐ 32 Jon Morris | .25 | .10 | .02 |
| ☐ 33 Jim Nance | .50 | .20 | .05 |
| ☐ 34 Len St. Jean | .25 | .10 | .02 |
| ☐ 35 Mike Taliaferro | .25 | .10 | .02 |
| ☐ 36 Jim Whalen | .25 | .10 | .02 |
| ☐ 37 Stew Barber | .35 | .14 | .03 |
| ☐ 38 Al Bemiller | .25 | .10 | .02 |
| ☐ 39 George(Butch) Byrd | .35 | .14 | .03 |
| ☐ 40 Booker Edgerson | .25 | .10 | .02 |
| ☐ 41 Harry Jacobs | .35 | .14 | .03 |
| ☐ 42 Jack Kemp | 15.00 | 6.00 | 1.50 |
| ☐ 43 Ron McDole | .35 | .14 | .03 |
| ☐ 44 Joe O'Donnell | .25 | .10 | .02 |
| ☐ 45 John Pitts | .25 | .10 | .02 |
| ☐ 46 George Saimes | .35 | .14 | .03 |
| ☐ 47 Mike Stratton | .35 | .14 | .03 |
| ☐ 48 O.J. Simpson | 30.00 | 12.00 | 3.00 |
| ☐ 49 Ronnie Bull | .35 | .14 | .03 |
| ☐ 50 Dick Butkus | 6.00 | 2.40 | .60 |
| ☐ 51 Jim Cadile | .25 | .10 | .02 |
| ☐ 52 Jack Concannon | .35 | .14 | .03 |
| ☐ 53 Dick Evey | .25 | .10 | .02 |
| ☐ 54 Bennie McRae | .25 | .10 | .02 |
| ☐ 55 Ed O'Bradovich | .25 | .10 | .02 |
| ☐ 56 Brian Piccolo | 10.00 | 4.00 | 1.00 |
| ☐ 57 Mike Pyle | .25 | .10 | .02 |
| ☐ 58 Gale Sayers | 7.50 | 3.00 | .75 |
| ☐ 59 Dick Gordon | .35 | .14 | .03 |
| ☐ 60 Roosevelt Taylor | .35 | .14 | .03 |
| ☐ 61 Al Beauchamp | .25 | .10 | .02 |
| ☐ 62 Dave Middendorf | .25 | .10 | .02 |
| ☐ 63 Harry Gunner | .25 | .10 | .02 |
| ☐ 64 Bobby Hunt | .25 | .10 | .02 |

| | | | |
|---|---|---|---|
| ☐ 65 Bob Johnson | .35 | .14 | .03 |
| ☐ 66 Charley King | .25 | .10 | .02 |
| ☐ 67 Andy Rice | .25 | .10 | .02 |
| ☐ 68 Paul Robinson | .35 | .14 | .03 |
| ☐ 69 Bill Staley | .25 | .10 | .02 |
| ☐ 70 Pat Matson | .25 | .10 | .02 |
| ☐ 71 Bob Trumpy | 1.00 | .40 | .10 |
| ☐ 72 Sam Wyche | 4.00 | 1.60 | .40 |
| ☐ 73 Erich Barnes | .35 | .14 | .03 |
| ☐ 74 Gary Collins | .35 | .14 | .03 |
| ☐ 75 Ben Davis | .25 | .10 | .02 |
| ☐ 76 John Demarie | .25 | .10 | .02 |
| ☐ 77 Gene Hickerson | .35 | .14 | .03 |
| ☐ 78 Jim Houston | .35 | .14 | .03 |
| ☐ 79 Ernie Kellerman | .25 | .10 | .02 |
| ☐ 80 Leroy Kelly | 2.00 | .80 | .20 |
| ☐ 81 Dale Lindsey | .25 | .10 | .02 |
| ☐ 82 Bill Nelsen | .50 | .20 | .05 |
| ☐ 83 Jim Kanicki | .25 | .10 | .02 |
| ☐ 84 Dick Schafrath | .35 | .14 | .03 |
| ☐ 85 George Andrie | .50 | .20 | .05 |
| ☐ 86 Mike Clark | .25 | .10 | .02 |
| ☐ 87 Cornell Green | .50 | .20 | .05 |
| ☐ 88 Bob Hayes | 1.25 | .50 | .12 |
| ☐ 89 Chuck Howley | .75 | .30 | .07 |
| ☐ 90 Lee Roy Jordan | 1.25 | .50 | .12 |
| ☐ 91 Bob Lilly | 2.50 | 1.00 | .25 |
| ☐ 92 Craig Morton | .75 | .30 | .07 |
| ☐ 93 John Niland | .25 | .10 | .02 |
| ☐ 94 Dan Reeves | 5.00 | 2.00 | .50 |
| ☐ 95 Mel Renfro | 1.00 | .40 | .10 |
| ☐ 96 Lance Rentzel | .50 | .20 | .05 |
| ☐ 97 Tom Beer | .25 | .10 | .02 |
| ☐ 98 Billy Van Heusen | .25 | .10 | .02 |
| ☐ 99 Mike Current | .25 | .10 | .02 |
| ☐ 100 Al Denson | .25 | .10 | .02 |
| ☐ 101 Pete Duranko | .25 | .10 | .02 |
| ☐ 102 George Goeddeke | .25 | .10 | .02 |
| ☐ 103 John Huard | .25 | .10 | .02 |
| ☐ 104 Richard Jackson | .25 | .10 | .02 |
| ☐ 105 Pete Jacques | .35 | .14 | .03 |
| ☐ 106 Fran Lynch | .25 | .10 | .02 |
| ☐ 107 Floyd Little | 1.50 | .60 | .15 |
| ☐ 108 Steve Tensi | .50 | .20 | .05 |
| ☐ 109 Lem Barney | 3.00 | 1.20 | .30 |
| ☐ 110 Nick Eddy | .50 | .20 | .05 |
| ☐ 111 Mel Farr | .50 | .20 | .05 |
| ☐ 112 Ed Flanagan | .25 | .10 | .02 |
| ☐ 113 Larry Hand | .25 | .10 | .02 |
| ☐ 114 Alex Karras | 2.00 | .80 | .20 |
| ☐ 115 Dick LeBeau | .35 | .14 | .03 |
| ☐ 116 Mike Lucci | .35 | .14 | .03 |
| ☐ 117 Earl McCullouch | .35 | .14 | .03 |
| ☐ 118 Bill Munson | .35 | .14 | .03 |
| ☐ 119 Jerry Rush | .25 | .10 | .02 |
| ☐ 120 Wayne Walker | .35 | .14 | .03 |
| ☐ 121 Herb Adderley | 1.50 | .60 | .15 |
| ☐ 122 Donny Anderson | .50 | .20 | .05 |
| ☐ 123 Lee Roy Caffey | .25 | .10 | .02 |
| ☐ 124 Carroll Dale | .35 | .14 | .03 |
| ☐ 125 Willie Davis | 1.50 | .60 | .15 |
| ☐ 126 Boyd Dowler | .35 | .14 | .03 |
| ☐ 127 Marv Fleming | .35 | .14 | .03 |
| ☐ 128 Bob Jeter | .35 | .14 | .03 |
| ☐ 129 Henry Jordan | .35 | .14 | .03 |
| ☐ 130 Dave Robinson | .35 | .14 | .03 |
| ☐ 131 Bart Starr | 7.50 | 3.00 | .75 |
| ☐ 132 Willie Wood | 1.50 | .60 | .15 |
| ☐ 133 Pete Beathard | .75 | .30 | .07 |
| ☐ 134 Jim Beirne | .25 | .10 | .02 |
| ☐ 135 Garland Boyette | .25 | .10 | .02 |
| ☐ 136 Woody Campbell | .25 | .10 | .02 |
| ☐ 137 Miller Farr | .25 | .10 | .02 |
| ☐ 138 Hoyle Granger | .25 | .10 | .02 |
| ☐ 139 Mac Haik | .25 | .10 | .02 |
| ☐ 140 Ken Houston | 2.50 | 1.00 | .25 |
| ☐ 141 Bobby Maples | .35 | .14 | .03 |
| ☐ 142 Alvin Reed | .25 | .10 | .02 |
| ☐ 143 Don Trull | .35 | .14 | .03 |
| ☐ 144 George Webster | .50 | .20 | .05 |
| ☐ 145 Bobby Bell | 1.50 | .60 | .15 |
| ☐ 146 Aaron Brown | .25 | .10 | .02 |
| ☐ 147 Buck Buchanan | 1.50 | .60 | .15 |
| ☐ 148 Len Dawson | 4.00 | 1.60 | .40 |
| ☐ 149 Mike Garrett | .50 | .20 | .05 |
| ☐ 150 Robert Holmes | .35 | .14 | .03 |
| ☐ 151 Willie Lanier | 3.00 | 1.20 | .30 |
| ☐ 152 Frank Pitts | .25 | .10 | .02 |
| ☐ 153 Johnny Robinson | .75 | .30 | .07 |
| ☐ 154 Jan Stenerud | 2.50 | 1.00 | .25 |
| ☐ 155 Otis Taylor | .75 | .30 | .07 |
| ☐ 156 Jim Tyrer | .50 | .20 | .05 |
| ☐ 157 Dick Bass | .35 | .14 | .03 |
| ☐ 158 Maxie Baughan | .50 | .20 | .05 |
| ☐ 159 Rich Petitbon | .50 | .20 | .05 |
| ☐ 160 Roger Brown | .35 | .14 | .03 |
| ☐ 161 Roman Gabriel | 1.00 | .40 | .10 |
| ☐ 162 Bruce Gossett | .25 | .10 | .02 |

| | | | |
|---|---|---|---|
| ☐ 163 Deacon Jones | 1.50 | .60 | .15 |
| ☐ 164 Tom Mack | 1.25 | .50 | .12 |
| ☐ 165 Tommy Mason | .50 | .20 | .05 |
| ☐ 166 Ed Meador | .35 | .14 | .03 |
| ☐ 167 Merlin Olsen | 2.50 | 1.00 | .25 |
| ☐ 168 Pat Studstill | .35 | .14 | .03 |
| ☐ 169 Jack Clancy | .25 | .10 | .02 |
| ☐ 170 Maxie Williams | .25 | .10 | .02 |
| ☐ 171 Larry Csonka | 9.00 | 3.75 | .90 |
| ☐ 172 Jimmy Warren | .25 | .10 | .02 |
| ☐ 173 Norm Evans | .35 | .14 | .03 |
| ☐ 174 Rick Norton | .25 | .10 | .02 |
| ☐ 175 Bob Griese | 7.50 | 3.00 | .75 |
| ☐ 176 Howard Twilley | .50 | .20 | .05 |
| ☐ 177 Billy Neighbors | .35 | .14 | .03 |
| ☐ 178 Nick Buoniconti | 1.25 | .50 | .12 |
| ☐ 179 Tom Goode | .25 | .10 | .02 |
| ☐ 180 Dick Westmoreland | .25 | .10 | .02 |
| ☐ 181 Grady Alderman | .25 | .10 | .02 |
| ☐ 182 Bill Brown | .50 | .20 | .05 |
| ☐ 183 Fred Cox | .35 | .14 | .03 |
| ☐ 184 Clint Jones | .35 | .14 | .03 |
| ☐ 185 Joe Kapp | 1.00 | .40 | .10 |
| ☐ 186 Paul Krause | 1.00 | .40 | .10 |
| ☐ 187 Gary Larsen | .25 | .10 | .02 |
| ☐ 188 Jim Marshall | 1.50 | .60 | .15 |
| ☐ 189 Dave Osborn | .25 | .10 | .02 |
| ☐ 190 Alan Page | 3.50 | 1.40 | .35 |
| ☐ 191 Mick Tingelhoff | .75 | .30 | .07 |
| ☐ 192 Roy Winston | .35 | .14 | .03 |
| ☐ 193 Dan Abramowicz | .50 | .20 | .05 |
| ☐ 194 Doug Atkins | 1.50 | .60 | .15 |
| ☐ 195 Bo Burris | .25 | .10 | .02 |
| ☐ 196 John Douglas | .25 | .10 | .02 |
| ☐ 197 Don Shy | .25 | .10 | .02 |
| ☐ 198 Bill Kilmer | .75 | .30 | .07 |
| ☐ 199 Tony Lorick | .25 | .10 | .02 |
| ☐ 200 Dave Parks | .50 | .20 | .05 |
| ☐ 201 Dave Rowe | .25 | .10 | .02 |
| ☐ 202 Monty Stickles | .25 | .10 | .02 |
| ☐ 203 Steve Stonebreaker | .35 | .14 | .03 |
| ☐ 204 Del Williams | .25 | .10 | .02 |
| ☐ 205 Pete Case | .25 | .10 | .02 |
| ☐ 206 Tommy Crutcher | .35 | .14 | .03 |
| ☐ 207 Scott Eaton | .25 | .10 | .02 |
| ☐ 208 Tucker Frederickson | .50 | .20 | .05 |
| ☐ 209 Pete Gogolak | .35 | .14 | .03 |
| ☐ 210 Homer Jones | .35 | .14 | .03 |
| ☐ 211 Ernie Koy | .35 | .14 | .03 |
| ☐ 212 Spider Lockhart | .35 | .14 | .03 |
| ☐ 213 Bruce Maher | .25 | .10 | .02 |
| ☐ 214 Aaron Thomas | .35 | .14 | .03 |
| ☐ 215 Fran Tarkenton | 10.00 | 4.00 | 1.00 |
| ☐ 216 Jim Katcavage | .35 | .14 | .03 |
| ☐ 217 Al Atkinson | .25 | .10 | .02 |
| ☐ 218 Emerson Boozer | .35 | .14 | .03 |
| ☐ 219 John Elliott | .25 | .10 | .02 |
| ☐ 220 Dave Herman | .25 | .10 | .02 |
| ☐ 221 Winston Hill | .35 | .14 | .03 |
| ☐ 222 Jim Hudson | .25 | .10 | .02 |
| ☐ 223 Pete Lammons | .35 | .14 | .03 |
| ☐ 224 Gerry Philbin | .35 | .14 | .03 |
| ☐ 225 George Sauer | .50 | .20 | .05 |
| ☐ 226 Joe Namath | 15.00 | 6.00 | 1.50 |
| ☐ 227 Matt Snell | .50 | .20 | .05 |
| ☐ 228 Jim Turner | .35 | .14 | .03 |
| ☐ 229 Fred Biletnikoff | 2.50 | 1.00 | .25 |
| ☐ 230 Willie Brown | 1.50 | .60 | .15 |
| ☐ 231 Billy Cannon | .50 | .20 | .05 |
| ☐ 232 Dan Conners | .25 | .10 | .02 |
| ☐ 233 Ben Davidson | .75 | .30 | .07 |
| ☐ 234 Hewritt Dixon | .35 | .14 | .03 |
| ☐ 235 Daryle Lamonica | 1.00 | .40 | .10 |
| ☐ 236 Ike Lassiter | .25 | .10 | .02 |
| ☐ 237 Kent McCloughan | .25 | .10 | .02 |
| ☐ 238 Jim Otto | 1.50 | .60 | .15 |
| ☐ 239 Harry Schuh | .25 | .10 | .02 |
| ☐ 240 Gene Upshaw | 2.50 | 1.00 | .25 |
| ☐ 241 Gary Ballman | .35 | .14 | .03 |
| ☐ 242 Joe Carollo | .25 | .10 | .02 |
| ☐ 243 Dave Lloyd | .25 | .10 | .02 |
| ☐ 244 Fred Hill | .25 | .10 | .02 |
| ☐ 245 Al Nelson | .25 | .10 | .02 |
| ☐ 246 Joe Scarpati | .25 | .10 | .02 |
| ☐ 247 Sam Baker | .35 | .14 | .03 |
| ☐ 248 Fred Brown | .25 | .10 | .02 |
| ☐ 249 Floyd Peters | .50 | .20 | .05 |
| ☐ 250 Nate Ramsey | .25 | .10 | .02 |
| ☐ 251 Norm Snead | .50 | .20 | .05 |
| ☐ 252 Tom Woodeshick | .25 | .10 | .02 |
| ☐ 253 John Hilton | .25 | .10 | .02 |
| ☐ 254 Kent Nix | .25 | .10 | .02 |
| ☐ 255 Paul Martha | .50 | .20 | .05 |
| ☐ 256 Ben McGee | .25 | .10 | .02 |
| ☐ 257 Andy Russell | .50 | .20 | .05 |
| ☐ 258 Dick Shiner | .25 | .10 | .02 |
| ☐ 259 J.R. Wilburn | .25 | .10 | .02 |
| ☐ 260 Marv Woodson | .25 | .10 | .02 |
| ☐ 261 Earl Gros | .25 | .10 | .02 |
| ☐ 262 Dick Hoak | .50 | .20 | .05 |
| ☐ 263 Roy Jefferson | .50 | .20 | .05 |
| ☐ 264 Larry Gagner | .25 | .10 | .02 |
| ☐ 265 Johnny Roland | .75 | .30 | .07 |
| ☐ 266 Jackie Smith | 2.00 | .80 | .20 |
| ☐ 267 Jim Bakken | .50 | .20 | .05 |
| ☐ 268 Don Brumm | .25 | .10 | .02 |
| ☐ 269 Bob DeMarco | .35 | .14 | .03 |
| ☐ 270 Irv Goode | .25 | .10 | .02 |
| ☐ 271 Ken Gray | .35 | .14 | .03 |
| ☐ 272 Charlie Johnson | .75 | .30 | .07 |
| ☐ 273 Ernie McMillan | .35 | .14 | .03 |
| ☐ 274 Larry Stallings | .35 | .14 | .03 |
| ☐ 275 Jerry Stovall | .50 | .20 | .05 |
| ☐ 276 Larry Wilson | 1.50 | .60 | .15 |
| ☐ 277 Chuck Allen | .25 | .10 | .02 |
| ☐ 278 Lance Alworth | 2.50 | 1.00 | .25 |
| ☐ 279 Kenny Graham | .25 | .10 | .02 |
| ☐ 280 Steve DeLong | .35 | .14 | .03 |
| ☐ 281 Willie Frazier | .35 | .14 | .03 |
| ☐ 282 Gary Garrison | .35 | .14 | .03 |
| ☐ 283 Sam Gruniesen | .25 | .10 | .02 |
| ☐ 284 John Hadl | .75 | .30 | .07 |
| ☐ 285 Brad Hubbert | .25 | .10 | .02 |
| ☐ 286 Ron Mix | 1.50 | .60 | .15 |
| ☐ 287 Dick Post | .35 | .14 | .03 |
| ☐ 288 Walt Sweeney | .35 | .14 | .03 |
| ☐ 289 Kermit Alexander | .50 | .20 | .05 |
| ☐ 290 Ed Beard | .25 | .10 | .02 |
| ☐ 291 Bruce Bosley | .35 | .14 | .03 |
| ☐ 292 John Brodie | 2.50 | 1.00 | .25 |
| ☐ 293 Stan Hindman | .25 | .10 | .02 |
| ☐ 294 Jim Johnson | 1.50 | .60 | .15 |
| ☐ 295 Charlie Krueger | .35 | .14 | .03 |
| ☐ 296 Clifton McNeil | .35 | .14 | .03 |
| ☐ 297 Gary Lewis | .25 | .10 | .02 |
| ☐ 298 Howard Mudd | .25 | .10 | .02 |
| ☐ 299 Dave Wilcox | .50 | .20 | .05 |
| ☐ 300 Ken Willard | .50 | .20 | .05 |
| ☐ 301 Charlie Gogolak | .35 | .14 | .03 |
| ☐ 302 Len Hauss | .50 | .20 | .05 |
| ☐ 303 Sonny Jurgensen | 2.50 | 1.00 | .25 |
| ☐ 304 Carl Kammerer | .25 | .10 | .02 |
| ☐ 305 Walt Rock | .25 | .10 | .02 |
| ☐ 306 Ray Schoenke | .25 | .10 | .02 |
| ☐ 307 Chris Hanburger | .75 | .30 | .07 |
| ☐ 308 Tom Brown | .50 | .20 | .05 |
| ☐ 309 Sam Huff | 1.50 | .60 | .15 |
| ☐ 310 Bob Long | .25 | .10 | .02 |
| ☐ 311 Vince Promuto | .25 | .10 | .02 |
| ☐ 312 Pat Richter | .35 | .14 | .03 |
| ☐ xx Stamp Album | 20.00 | 8.00 | 2.00 |

## 1989-94 Goal Line HOF

These attractive cards were issued by subscription per series. They were sent out one series at a time in a custom box. The cards are postcard-size drawings (a beautiful full-color action painting) measuring approximately 4" by 6". The card backs contain brief biographical information and are printed in black on white card stock. Each card contains the specific set number out of 5,000 at the bottom of the reverse of every card in the set as well as the player's name, college, position, years, pro team, and the date he was enshrined in the Hall of Fame. The players featured are all members of the Pro Football Hall of Fame in Canton, Ohio. It was reported that 5,000 of the each series were produced and distributed. The second series was produced in 1990, the third series was produced in 1991, the fourth series in 1992, the fifth series in 1993, and the sixth series of 25 cards in 1994. Direct cost to subscribers per series 6 was 54.00 postpaid. Collectors who ordered series five before August 31, 1993, received a free commemorative ticket signed by Pete Elliott (Commissioner of the Pro Football Hall of Fame) and were entered into a drawing for one of three uncut sheets of series five. In total, 50 fifth series uncut sheets were produced, and they were signed and numbered by the artist. Within each series the cards have been numbered alphabetically by the producer. The cards are considered ideal for autographing. Also available directly for sale from the Pro Football Hall of Fame were unnumbered, but autographed, proof cards of many of the subjects. The artist for the set was Gary Thomas. Johnny Unitas (174) apparently did not give his permission for inclusion in the sixth series, thus his card was not issued.

|  | MINT | EXC | G-VG |
|---|---|---|---|
| COMPLETE SET (174) | 375.00 | 150.00 | 45.00 |
| COMMON CARD (1-30) | 2.50 | 1.00 | .25 |
| COMMON CARD (31-60) | 2.00 | .80 | .20 |
| COMMON CARD (61-90) | 2.00 | .80 | .20 |
| COMMON CARD (91-120) | 2.00 | .80 | .20 |
| COMMON CARD (121-150) | 2.00 | .80 | .20 |
| COMMON CARD (151-175) | 2.00 | .80 | .20 |

| | MINT | EXC | G-VG |
|---|---|---|---|
| ☐ 1 Lance Alworth | 5.00 | 2.00 | .50 |
| ☐ 2 Morris(Red) Badgro | 2.50 | 1.00 | .25 |
| ☐ 3 Cliff Battles | 2.50 | 1.00 | .25 |
| ☐ 4 Mel Blount | 2.50 | 1.00 | .25 |
| ☐ 5 Terry Bradshaw | 9.00 | 3.75 | .90 |
| ☐ 6 Jim Brown | 10.00 | 4.00 | 1.00 |
| ☐ 7 George Connor | 2.50 | 1.00 | .25 |
| ☐ 8 Glen(Turk) Edwards | 2.50 | 1.00 | .25 |
| ☐ 9 Tom Fears | 2.50 | 1.00 | .25 |
| ☐ 10 Frank Gifford | 9.00 | 3.75 | .90 |
| ☐ 11 Otto Graham | 6.00 | 2.40 | .60 |
| ☐ 12 Harold(Red) Grange | 5.00 | 2.00 | .50 |
| ☐ 13 George Halas | 3.00 | 1.20 | .30 |
| ☐ 14 Clarke Hinkle | 2.50 | 1.00 | .25 |
| ☐ 15 Robert(Cal) Hubbard | 2.50 | 1.00 | .25 |
| ☐ 16 Sam Huff | 2.50 | 1.00 | .25 |
| ☐ 17 Frank(Bruiser) Kinard | 2.50 | 1.00 | .25 |
| ☐ 18 Dick(Night Train) Lane | 2.50 | 1.00 | .25 |
| ☐ 19 Sid Luckman | 5.00 | 2.00 | .50 |
| ☐ 20 Bobby Mitchell | 2.50 | 1.00 | .25 |
| ☐ 21 Merlin Olsen | 4.00 | 1.60 | .40 |
| ☐ 22 Jim Parker | 2.50 | 1.00 | .25 |
| ☐ 23 Joe Perry | 3.00 | 1.20 | .30 |
| ☐ 24 Pete Rozelle | 3.00 | 1.20 | .30 |
| ☐ 25 Art Shell | 3.00 | 1.20 | .30 |
| ☐ 26 Fran Tarkenton | 8.00 | 3.25 | .80 |
| ☐ 27 Jim Thorpe | 6.00 | 2.40 | .60 |
| ☐ 28 Paul Warfield | 3.00 | 1.20 | .30 |
| ☐ 29 Larry Wilson | 2.50 | 1.00 | .25 |
| ☐ 30 Willie Wood | 2.50 | 1.00 | .25 |
| ☐ 31 Doug Atkins | 2.00 | .80 | .20 |
| ☐ 32 Bobby Bell | 2.00 | .80 | .20 |
| ☐ 33 Raymond Berry | 3.00 | 1.20 | .30 |
| ☐ 34 Paul Brown | 2.00 | .80 | .20 |
| ☐ 35 Guy Chamberlin | 2.00 | .80 | .20 |
| ☐ 36 Earl(Dutch) Clark | 2.00 | .80 | .20 |
| ☐ 37 Jimmy Conzelman | 2.00 | .80 | .20 |
| ☐ 38 Len Dawson | 3.00 | 1.20 | .30 |
| ☐ 39 Mike Ditka | 6.00 | 2.40 | .60 |
| ☐ 40 Dan Fortmann | 2.00 | .80 | .20 |
| ☐ 41 Frank Gatski | 2.00 | .80 | .20 |
| ☐ 42 Bill George | 2.00 | .80 | .20 |
| ☐ 43 Elroy Hirsch | 3.00 | 1.20 | .30 |
| ☐ 44 Paul Hornung | 4.00 | 1.60 | .40 |
| ☐ 45 John Henry Johnson | 2.00 | .80 | .20 |
| ☐ 46 Walt Kiesling | 2.00 | .80 | .20 |
| ☐ 47 Yale Lary | 2.00 | .80 | .20 |
| ☐ 48 Bobby Layne | 3.00 | 1.20 | .30 |
| ☐ 49 Tuffy Leemans | 2.00 | .80 | .20 |
| ☐ 50 Geo. Preston Marshall | 2.00 | .80 | .20 |
| ☐ 51 George McAfee | 2.00 | .80 | .20 |
| ☐ 52 Wayne Millner | 2.00 | .80 | .20 |
| ☐ 53 Bronko Nagurski | 4.00 | 1.60 | .40 |
| ☐ 54 Joe Namath | 10.00 | 4.00 | 1.00 |
| ☐ 55 Ray Nitschke | 3.00 | 1.20 | .30 |
| ☐ 56 Jim Ringo | 2.00 | .80 | .20 |
| ☐ 57 Art Rooney | 2.00 | .80 | .20 |
| ☐ 58 Joe Stydahar | 2.00 | .80 | .20 |
| ☐ 59 Charley Taylor | 2.00 | .80 | .20 |
| ☐ 60 Charley Trippi | 2.00 | .80 | .20 |
| ☐ 61 Fred Biletnikoff | 3.00 | 1.20 | .30 |
| ☐ 62 Buck Buchanan | 2.00 | .80 | .20 |
| ☐ 63 Dick Butkus | 5.00 | 2.00 | .50 |
| ☐ 64 Earl Campbell | 7.50 | 3.00 | .75 |
| ☐ 65 Tony Canadeo | 2.00 | .80 | .20 |
| ☐ 66 Art Donovan | 3.00 | 1.20 | .30 |
| ☐ 67 Ray Flaherty | 2.00 | .80 | .20 |
| ☐ 68 Forrest Gregg | 2.50 | 1.00 | .25 |
| ☐ 69 Lou Groza | 3.00 | 1.20 | .30 |
| ☐ 70 John Hannah | 2.00 | .80 | .20 |
| ☐ 71 Don Hutson | 2.50 | 1.00 | .25 |
| ☐ 72 Deacon Jones | 2.00 | .80 | .20 |
| ☐ 73 Stan Jones | 2.00 | .80 | .20 |
| ☐ 74 Sonny Jurgensen | 3.00 | 1.20 | .30 |
| ☐ 75 Vince Lombardi | 3.00 | 1.20 | .30 |
| ☐ 76 Tim Mara | 2.00 | .80 | .20 |
| ☐ 77 Ollie Matson | 2.00 | .80 | .20 |
| ☐ 78 Mike McCormack | 2.00 | .80 | .20 |
| ☐ 79 Johnny(Blood) McNally | 2.00 | .80 | .20 |
| ☐ 80 Marion Motley | 2.00 | .80 | .20 |
| ☐ 81 George Musso | 2.00 | .80 | .20 |
| ☐ 82 Earle(Greasy) Neale | 2.00 | .80 | .20 |
| ☐ 83 Clarence(Ace) Parker | 2.00 | .80 | .20 |
| ☐ 84 Pete Pihos | 2.00 | .80 | .20 |
| ☐ 85 Tex Schramm | 2.00 | .80 | .20 |
| ☐ 86 Roger Staubach | 10.00 | 4.00 | 1.00 |
| ☐ 87 Jan Stenerud | 2.00 | .80 | .20 |
| ☐ 88 Y.A. Tittle | 3.00 | 1.20 | .30 |
| ☐ 89 Clyde(Bulldog) Turner | 2.00 | .80 | .20 |
| ☐ 90 Steve Van Buren | 2.00 | .80 | .20 |
| ☐ 91 Herb Adderley | 2.00 | .80 | .20 |
| ☐ 92 Lem Barney | 2.00 | .80 | .20 |
| ☐ 93 Sammy Baugh | 4.00 | 1.60 | .40 |
| ☐ 94 Chuck Bednarik | 3.00 | 1.20 | .30 |
| ☐ 95 Charles W. Bidwill | 2.00 | .80 | .20 |
| ☐ 96 Willie Brown | 2.00 | .80 | .20 |
| ☐ 97 Al Davis | 4.00 | 1.60 | .40 |
| ☐ 98 Bill Dudley | 2.00 | .80 | .20 |
| ☐ 99 Weeb Ewbank | 2.00 | .80 | .20 |
| ☐ 100 Len Ford | 2.00 | .80 | .20 |
| ☐ 101 Sid Gillman | 2.00 | .80 | .20 |
| ☐ 102 Jack Ham | 2.00 | .80 | .20 |
| ☐ 103 Mel Hein | 2.00 | .80 | .20 |
| ☐ 104 Bill Hewitt | 2.00 | .80 | .20 |
| ☐ 105 Dante Lavelli | 2.00 | .80 | .20 |
| ☐ 106 Bob Lilly | 3.00 | 1.20 | .30 |
| ☐ 107 John Mackey | 2.00 | .80 | .20 |
| ☐ 108 Hugh McElhenny | 3.00 | 1.20 | .30 |
| ☐ 109 Mike Michalske | 2.00 | .80 | .20 |
| ☐ 110 Ron Mix | 2.00 | .80 | .20 |
| ☐ 111 Leo Nomellini | 2.00 | .80 | .20 |
| ☐ 112 Steve Owen | 2.00 | .80 | .20 |
| ☐ 113 Alan Page | 2.50 | 1.00 | .25 |
| ☐ 114 Dan Reeves | 2.00 | .80 | .20 |
| ☐ 115 John Riggins | 3.00 | 1.20 | .30 |
| ☐ 116 Gale Sayers | 4.00 | 1.60 | .40 |
| ☐ 117 Ken Strong | 2.00 | .80 | .20 |
| ☐ 118 Gene Upshaw | 3.00 | 1.20 | .30 |
| ☐ 119 Norm Van Brocklin | 4.00 | 1.60 | .40 |
| ☐ 120 Alex Wojciechowicz | 2.00 | .80 | .20 |
| ☐ 121 Bert Bell COMM | 2.00 | .80 | .20 |
| ☐ 122 George Blanda | 4.00 | 1.60 | .40 |
| ☐ 123 Joe Carr | 2.00 | .80 | .20 |
| ☐ 124 Larry Csonka | 4.00 | 1.60 | .40 |
| ☐ 125 John(Paddy) Driscoll | 2.00 | .80 | .20 |
| ☐ 126 Dan Fouts | 3.00 | 1.20 | .30 |
| ☐ 127 Bob Griese | 4.00 | 1.60 | .40 |
| ☐ 128 Ed Healey | 2.00 | .80 | .20 |
| ☐ 129 Wilbur(Fats) Henry | 2.00 | .80 | .20 |
| ☐ 130 Ken Houston | 2.00 | .80 | .20 |
| ☐ 131 Lamar Hunt OWN | 2.00 | .80 | .20 |
| ☐ 132 Jack Lambert | 2.50 | 1.00 | .25 |
| ☐ 133 Tom Landry | 4.00 | 1.60 | .40 |
| ☐ 134 Willie Lanier | 2.00 | .80 | .20 |
| ☐ 135 Larry Little | 2.00 | .80 | .20 |
| ☐ 136 Don Maynard | 3.00 | 1.20 | .30 |
| ☐ 137 Lenny Moore | 3.00 | 1.20 | .30 |
| ☐ 138 Chuck Noll CO | 3.00 | 1.20 | .30 |
| ☐ 139 Jim Otto | 2.00 | .80 | .20 |
| ☐ 140 Walter Payton | 8.00 | 3.25 | .80 |
| ☐ 141 Hugh(Shorty) Ray OFF | 2.00 | .80 | .20 |
| ☐ 142 Andy Robustelli | 2.00 | .80 | .20 |
| ☐ 143 Bob St. Clair | 2.00 | .80 | .20 |
| ☐ 144 Joe Schmidt | 3.00 | 1.20 | .30 |
| ☐ 145 Jim Taylor | 3.00 | 1.20 | .30 |
| ☐ 146 Doak Walker | 3.00 | 1.20 | .30 |
| ☐ 147 Bill Walsh CO | 3.00 | 1.20 | .30 |
| ☐ 148 Bob Waterfield | 3.00 | 1.20 | .30 |
| ☐ 149 Arnie Weinmeister | 2.00 | .80 | .20 |
| ☐ 150 Bill Willis | 2.00 | .80 | .20 |
| ☐ 151 Roosevelt Brown | 2.00 | .80 | .20 |
| ☐ 152 Jack Christiansen | 2.00 | .80 | .20 |
| ☐ 153 Willie Davis | 3.00 | 1.20 | .30 |
| ☐ 154 Tony Dorsett | 5.00 | 2.00 | .50 |
| ☐ 155 Bud Grant | 2.00 | .80 | .20 |
| ☐ 156 Joe Greene | 4.00 | 1.60 | .40 |
| ☐ 157 Joe Guyon | 2.00 | .80 | .20 |
| ☐ 158 Franco Harris | 4.00 | 1.60 | .40 |
| ☐ 159 Ted Hendricks | 2.00 | .80 | .20 |
| ☐ 160 Arnie Herber | 2.00 | .80 | .20 |
| ☐ 161 Jimmy Johnson | 2.00 | .80 | .20 |
| ☐ 162 Leroy Kelly | 2.00 | .80 | .20 |
| ☐ 163 Curly Lambeau | 2.00 | .80 | .20 |
| ☐ 164 Jim Langer | 2.00 | .80 | .20 |
| ☐ 165 Link Lyman | 2.00 | .80 | .20 |
| ☐ 166 Gino Marchetti | 3.00 | 1.20 | .30 |
| ☐ 167 Ernie Nevers | 3.00 | 1.20 | .30 |
| ☐ 168 O.J. Simpson | 10.00 | 4.00 | 1.00 |
| ☐ 169 Jackie Smith | 2.00 | .80 | .20 |
| ☐ 170 Bart Starr | 5.00 | 2.00 | .50 |
| ☐ 171 Ernie Stautner | 2.50 | 1.00 | .25 |
| ☐ 172 George Trafton | 2.00 | .80 | .20 |
| ☐ 173 Emlen Tunnell | 2.00 | .80 | .20 |
| ☐ 174 Johnny Unitas (Not issued) | .00 | .00 | .00 |
| ☐ 175 Randy White | 3.00 | 1.20 | .30 |

# 1939 Gridiron Greats Blotters

This set of 12 ink blotters was sponsored by Louis F. Dow Company in honor of great college football players. The legal size blotters measure approximately 9" by 3 7/8" and were issued in a brown paper sleeve. The left portion of the blotter front has a head and shoulders sepia-toned drawing, with the player wearing either a red or a blue jersey. This drawing is superimposed on a football, and the player's college letter appears in a banner below the picture. The right portion of the blotter has a brief player profile, a brand advertisement, and a monthly calendar (a different month on each of the 12 blotters). The backs are blank and done in medium blue. The blotters are numbered on the front.

| | EX-MT | VG-E | GOOD |
|---|---|---|---|
| COMPLETE SET (12) | 1250.00 | 500.00 | 135.00 |
| COMMON PLAYER | 75.00 | 30.00 | 7.50 |
| ☐ B3941 Jim Thorpe | 275.00 | 110.00 | 27.00 |
| ☐ B3942 Walter Eckersall | 100.00 | 40.00 | 10.00 |
| ☐ B3943 Edward Mahan | 75.00 | 30.00 | 7.50 |
| ☐ B3944 Sammy Baugh | 250.00 | 100.00 | 25.00 |
| ☐ B3945 Thomas Shevlin | 75.00 | 30.00 | 7.50 |
| ☐ B3946 Harold(Red) Grange | 275.00 | 110.00 | 27.00 |
| ☐ B3947 Ernie Nevers | 200.00 | 80.00 | 20.00 |
| ☐ B3948 George Gipp | 275.00 | 110.00 | 27.00 |
| ☐ B3949 Pudge Heffelfinger | 150.00 | 60.00 | 15.00 |
| ☐ B3950 Bronko Nagurski | 275.00 | 110.00 | 27.00 |
| ☐ B3951 Willie Heston | 75.00 | 30.00 | 7.50 |
| ☐ B3952 Jay Berwanger | 125.00 | 50.00 | 12.50 |

# 1992 Gridiron Promos

Produced by Lafayette Sportscard Corporation, this four-card promo set was issued to show the design of the 1992 Gridiron set. The cards measure the standard size (2 1/2" by 3 1/2") and feature full-bleed action color player photos. The picture on card number 1P is horizontal. The player's name appears at the lower left in team color-coded lettering; his school and position are at the lower right. On a background of team color-coded panels, the backs display a vertical close-up photo, biography, player profile information, and college statistics. The cards are numbered on the back.

| | MINT | EXC | G-VG |
|---|---|---|---|
| COMPLETE SET (4) | 3.00 | 1.20 | .30 |
| COMMON PLAYER (1P-4P) | 1.00 | .40 | .10 |
| ☐ 1P Siran Stacy | 1.00 | .40 | .10 |
| Alabama | | | |
| ☐ 2P Casey Weldon | 1.25 | .50 | .12 |
| Florida State | | | |
| ☐ 3P Mike Saunders | 1.00 | .40 | .10 |
| Iowa | | | |
| ☐ 4P Jeff Blake | 1.00 | .40 | .10 |
| East Carolina | | | |

# 1992 Gridiron

The 1992 Gridiron football set was produced by Lafayette Sportscard Corporation. The 110 standard-size (2 1/2" by 3 1/2") cards pay tribute to graduating seniors and coaches from the top 25 college teams of 1991. Three players and one coach represent each team. Reportedly the production run was limited to 50,000 sets or 2,500 numbered cases. The full-bleed glossy color photos dominate the card fronts; the producer's logo, player's name, team name, and position are placed in the corners. In addition to a second color player photo, the back carries biography, career highlights, and statistics (1991 and career), on panels reflecting the team colors. The cards are numbered on the back in a helmet icon in the upper left corner. Only the four Desmond Howard cards (13B, 33B, 105B, and 107B) have a letter suffix after the card number.

| | MINT | EXC | G-VG |
|---|---|---|---|
| COMPLETE SET (110) | 25.00 | 10.00 | 2.50 |
| COMMON PLAYER (1-107) | .15 | .06 | .01 |
| ☐ 1 Rob Perez | .15 | .06 | .01 |
| Air Force | | | |
| ☐ 2 Jason Jones | .15 | .06 | .01 |
| Air Force | | | |
| ☐ 3 Jason Christ | .25 | .10 | .02 |
| Air Force | | | |
| ☐ 4 Fisher DeBerry CO | .25 | .10 | .02 |
| Air Force | | | |
| ☐ 5 Danny Woodson | .15 | .06 | .01 |
| Alabama | | | |
| ☐ 6 Siran Stacy | .25 | .10 | .02 |
| Alabama | | | |
| ☐ 7 Robert Stewart | .15 | .06 | .01 |
| Alabama | | | |
| ☐ 8 Gene Stallings CO | .75 | .30 | .07 |
| Alabama | | | |
| ☐ 9 Santana Dotson | .50 | .20 | .05 |
| Baylor | | | |
| ☐ 10 Curtis Hafford | .15 | .06 | .01 |
| Baylor | | | |
| ☐ 11 John Turnpaugh | .15 | .06 | .01 |
| Baylor | | | |
| ☐ 12 Grant Teaff CO | .50 | .20 | .05 |
| Baylor | | | |
| ☐ 13B Desmond Howard | 1.25 | .50 | .12 |
| Michigan | | | |
| ☐ 14 Brian Treggs | .15 | .06 | .01 |
| California | | | |
| ☐ 15 Troy Auzenne | .15 | .06 | .01 |
| California | | | |
| ☐ 16 Bruce Snyder CO | .35 | .14 | .03 |
| California | | | |
| ☐ 17 DeChane Cameron | .15 | .06 | .01 |
| Clemson | | | |
| ☐ 18 Levon Kirkland | .25 | .10 | .02 |
| Clemson | | | |
| ☐ 19 Ed McDaniel | .15 | .06 | .01 |
| Clemson | | | |

| | | | |
|---|---|---|---|
| ☐ 20 Ken Hatfield CO | .35 | .14 | .03 |
| Clemson | | | |
| ☐ 21 Darian Hagan | .25 | .10 | .02 |
| Colorado | | | |
| ☐ 22 Rico Smith | .15 | .06 | .01 |
| Colorado | | | |
| ☐ 23 Joel Steed | .15 | .06 | .01 |
| Colorado | | | |
| ☐ 24 Bill McCartney CO | 1.00 | .40 | .10 |
| Colorado | | | |
| ☐ 25 Jeff Blake | .25 | .10 | .02 |
| East Carolina | | | |
| ☐ 26 David Daniels | .15 | .06 | .01 |
| East Carolina | | | |
| ☐ 27 Robert Jones | .25 | .10 | .02 |
| East Carolina | | | |
| ☐ 28 Bill Lewis CO | .25 | .10 | .02 |
| East Carolina | | | |
| ☐ 29 Tim Paulk | .15 | .06 | .01 |
| Florida | | | |
| ☐ 30 Arden Czyzewski | .15 | .06 | .01 |
| Florida | | | |
| ☐ 31 Cal Dixon | .15 | .06 | .01 |
| Florida | | | |
| ☐ 32 Steve Spurrier CO | 1.00 | .40 | .10 |
| Florida | | | |
| ☐ 33B Desmond Howard | 1.25 | .50 | .12 |
| Michigan | | | |
| ☐ 34 Casey Weldon | .25 | .10 | .02 |
| Florida State | | | |
| ☐ 35 Kirk Carruthers | .15 | .06 | .01 |
| Florida State | | | |
| ☐ 36 Bobby Bowden CO | 1.00 | .40 | .10 |
| Florida State | | | |
| ☐ 37 Mark Barsotti | .25 | .10 | .02 |
| Fresno State | | | |
| ☐ 38 Kelvin Means | .15 | .06 | .01 |
| Fresno State | | | |
| ☐ 39 Marquez Pope | .25 | .10 | .02 |
| Fresno State | | | |
| ☐ 40 Jim Sweeney CO | .35 | .14 | .03 |
| Fresno State | | | |
| ☐ 41 Kameno Bell | .15 | .06 | .01 |
| Illinois | | | |
| ☐ 42 Elbert Turner | .15 | .06 | .01 |
| Illinois | | | |
| ☐ 43 Marlin Primous | .15 | .06 | .01 |
| Illinois | | | |
| ☐ 44 John Mackovic CO | .35 | .14 | .03 |
| Illinois | | | |
| ☐ 45 Matt Rodgers | .25 | .10 | .02 |
| Iowa | | | |
| ☐ 46 Mike Saunders | .15 | .06 | .01 |
| Iowa | | | |
| ☐ 47 John Derby | .15 | .06 | .01 |
| Iowa | | | |
| ☐ 48 Hayden Fry CO | .50 | .20 | .05 |
| Iowa | | | |
| ☐ 49 Carlos Huerta | .25 | .10 | .02 |
| Miami | | | |
| ☐ 50 Leon Searcy | .25 | .10 | .02 |
| Miami | | | |
| ☐ 51 Claude Jones | .15 | .06 | .01 |
| Miami | | | |
| ☐ 52 Dennis Erickson CO | .75 | .30 | .07 |
| Miami | | | |
| ☐ 53 Erick Anderson | .25 | .10 | .02 |
| Michigan | | | |
| ☐ 54 J.D. Carlson | .15 | .06 | .01 |
| Michigan | | | |
| ☐ 55 Greg Skrepenak | .25 | .10 | .02 |
| Michigan | | | |
| ☐ 56 Gary Moeller CO | .50 | .20 | .05 |
| Michigan | | | |
| ☐ 57 Keithen McCant | .35 | .14 | .03 |
| Nebraska | | | |
| ☐ 58 Nate Turner | .15 | .06 | .01 |
| Nebraska | | | |
| ☐ 59 Pat Englebert | .15 | .06 | .01 |
| Nebraska | | | |
| ☐ 60 Tom Osborne CO | 1.00 | .40 | .10 |
| Nebraska | | | |
| ☐ 61 Charles Davenport | .25 | .10 | .02 |
| N. Carolina State | | | |
| ☐ 62 Mark Thomas | .15 | .06 | .01 |
| N. Carolina State | | | |
| ☐ 63 Clyde Hawley | .15 | .06 | .01 |
| N. Carolina State | | | |
| ☐ 64 Dick Sheridan CO | .25 | .10 | .02 |
| N. Carolina State | | | |
| ☐ 65 Derek Brown | .75 | .30 | .07 |
| Notre Dame | | | |
| ☐ 66 Rodney Culver | .50 | .20 | .05 |
| Notre Dame | | | |
| ☐ 67 Tony Smith | .25 | .10 | .02 |
| Notre Dame | | | |
| ☐ 68 Lou Holtz CO | 1.00 | .40 | .10 |
| Notre Dame | | | |

| | | | |
|---|---|---|---|
| ☐ 69 Kent Graham | .75 | .30 | .07 |
| Ohio State | | | |
| ☐ 70 Scottie Graham | .75 | .30 | .07 |
| Ohio State | | | |
| ☐ 71 John Kacherski | .15 | .06 | .01 |
| Ohio State | | | |
| ☐ 72 John Cooper CO | .35 | .14 | .03 |
| Ohio State | | | |
| ☐ 73 Mike Gaddis | .15 | .06 | .01 |
| Oklahoma | | | |
| ☐ 74 Joe Bowden | .25 | .10 | .02 |
| Oklahoma | | | |
| ☐ 75 Mike McKinley | .15 | .06 | .01 |
| Oklahoma | | | |
| ☐ 76 Gary Gibbs CO | .50 | .20 | .05 |
| Oklahoma | | | |
| ☐ 77 Sam Gash | .25 | .10 | .02 |
| Penn State | | | |
| ☐ 78 Keith Goganious | .25 | .10 | .02 |
| Penn State | | | |
| ☐ 79 Darren Perry | .15 | .06 | .01 |
| Penn State | | | |
| ☐ 80 Joe Paterno CO | 1.00 | .40 | .10 |
| Penn State | | | |
| ☐ 81 Steven Israel | .25 | .10 | .02 |
| Pittsburgh | | | |
| ☐ 82 Eric Seaman | .15 | .06 | .01 |
| Pittsburgh | | | |
| ☐ 83 Glen Deveaux | .15 | .06 | .01 |
| Pittsburgh | | | |
| ☐ 84 Paul Hackett CO | .35 | .14 | .03 |
| Pittsburgh | | | |
| ☐ 85 Tommy Vardell | .75 | .30 | .07 |
| Stanford | | | |
| ☐ 86 Chris Walsh | .15 | .06 | .01 |
| Stanford | | | |
| ☐ 87 Jason Palumbis | .15 | .06 | .01 |
| Stanford | | | |
| ☐ 88 Dennis Green CO | .75 | .30 | .07 |
| Stanford | | | |
| ☐ 89 Andy Kelly | .25 | .10 | .02 |
| Tennessee | | | |
| ☐ 90 Dale Carter | .35 | .14 | .03 |
| Tennessee | | | |
| ☐ 91 Shon Walker | .15 | .06 | .01 |
| Tennessee | | | |
| ☐ 92 Johnny Majors CO | .50 | .20 | .05 |
| Tennessee | | | |
| ☐ 93 Bucky Richardson | .25 | .10 | .02 |
| Texas A and M | | | |
| ☐ 94 Quentin Coryatt | .75 | .30 | .07 |
| Texas A and M | | | |
| ☐ 95 Kevin Smith | .35 | .14 | .03 |
| Texas A and M | | | |
| ☐ 96 R.C. Slocum CO | .50 | .20 | .05 |
| Texas A and M | | | |
| ☐ 97 Ed Cunningham | .25 | .10 | .02 |
| Washington | | | |
| ☐ 98 Mario Bailey | .25 | .10 | .02 |
| Washington | | | |
| ☐ 99 Donald Jones | .15 | .06 | .01 |
| Washington | | | |
| ☐ 100 Don James CO | .75 | .30 | .07 |
| Washington | | | |
| ☐ 101 Vaughn Dunbar | .50 | .20 | .05 |
| Indiana | | | |
| ☐ 102 Reggie Yarbrough | .15 | .06 | .01 |
| Cal Fullerton | | | |
| ☐ 103 Matt Blundin | .50 | .20 | .05 |
| Virginia | | | |
| ☐ 104 Tony Sands | .15 | .06 | .01 |
| Kansas | | | |
| ☐ 105B Desmond Howard | 1.25 | .50 | .12 |
| Michigan | | | |
| ☐ 106 Ty Detmer | .50 | .20 | .05 |
| Brigham Young | | | |
| ☐ 107B Desmond Howard | 1.25 | .50 | .12 |
| Michigan | | | |
| ☐ xx Checklist 1 | .25 | .10 | .02 |
| Mario Bailey | | | |
| Washington | | | |
| Jeff Blake | | | |
| East Carolina | | | |
| ☐ xx Checklist 2 | .35 | .14 | .03 |
| Mike Gaddis | | | |
| Oklahoma | | | |
| Tommy Vardell | | | |
| Stanford | | | |
| ☐ xx Title Card | .15 | .06 | .01 |

# 1990 Hall of Fame Stickers

This 80-sticker set is actually part of a book; the individual stickers in the book measure approximately 1 7/8" by 2 1/8". The book was entitled "The Official Pro Football Hall of Fame Fun and Fact Sticker

Jim Thorpe, HB

Book. The original artwork from which the stickers were derived was performed by noted hobbyist Mark Rucker and featured 80 members of the Pro Football Hall of Fame.

| | MINT | EXC | G-VG |
|---|---|---|---|
| COMPLETE SET (80) | 9.00 | 3.75 | .90 |
| COMMON CARD (1-80) | .15 | .06 | .01 |

| | | | |
|---|---|---|---|
| ☐ 1 Wilbur(Fats) Henry | .15 | .06 | .01 |
| ☐ 2 George Trafton | .15 | .06 | .01 |
| ☐ 3 Mike Michalske | .15 | .06 | .01 |
| ☐ 4 Glen(Turk) Edwards | .15 | .06 | .01 |
| ☐ 5 Bill Hewitt | .15 | .06 | .01 |
| ☐ 6 Mel Hein | .15 | .06 | .01 |
| ☐ 7 Joe Stydahar | .15 | .06 | .01 |
| ☐ 8 Dan Fortmann | .15 | .06 | .01 |
| ☐ 9 Alex Wojciechowicz | .15 | .06 | .01 |
| ☐ 10 George Connor | .15 | .06 | .01 |
| ☐ 11 Jim Thorpe | .75 | .30 | .07 |
| ☐ 12 Ernie Nevers | .35 | .14 | .03 |
| ☐ 13 Johnny(Blood) McNally | .15 | .06 | .01 |
| ☐ 14 Ken Strong | .15 | .06 | .01 |
| ☐ 15 Bronko Nagurski | .50 | .20 | .05 |
| ☐ 16 Clarke Hinkle | .15 | .06 | .01 |
| ☐ 17 Clarence(Ace) Parker | .15 | .06 | .01 |
| ☐ 18 Bill Dudley | .15 | .06 | .01 |
| ☐ 19 Don Hutson | .25 | .10 | .02 |
| ☐ 20 Dante Lavelli | .15 | .06 | .01 |
| ☐ 21 Elroy Hirsch | .25 | .10 | .02 |
| ☐ 22 Raymond Berry | .25 | .10 | .02 |
| ☐ 23 Bobby Mitchell | .15 | .06 | .01 |
| ☐ 24 Don Maynard | .25 | .10 | .02 |
| ☐ 25 Mike Ditka | .50 | .20 | .05 |
| ☐ 26 Lance Alworth | .25 | .10 | .02 |
| ☐ 27 Charley Taylor | .15 | .06 | .01 |
| ☐ 28 Paul Warfield | .25 | .10 | .02 |
| ☐ 29 Lou Groza | .35 | .14 | .03 |
| ☐ 30 Art Donovan | .25 | .10 | .02 |
| ☐ 31 Leo Nomellini | .15 | .06 | .01 |
| ☐ 32 Andy Robustelli | .15 | .06 | .01 |
| ☐ 33 Gino Marchetti | .15 | .06 | .01 |
| ☐ 34 Forrest Gregg | .15 | .06 | .01 |
| ☐ 35 Jim Otto | .15 | .06 | .01 |
| ☐ 36 Ron Mix | .15 | .06 | .01 |
| ☐ 37 Deacon Jones | .15 | .06 | .01 |
| ☐ 38 Bob Lilly | .25 | .10 | .02 |
| ☐ 39 Merlin Olsen | .25 | .10 | .02 |
| ☐ 40 Alan Page | .15 | .06 | .01 |
| ☐ 41 Joe Greene | .25 | .10 | .02 |
| ☐ 42 Art Shell | .25 | .10 | .02 |
| ☐ 43 Sammy Baugh | .35 | .14 | .03 |
| ☐ 44 Sid Luckman | .35 | .14 | .03 |
| ☐ 45 Bob Waterfield | .35 | .14 | .03 |
| ☐ 46 Bobby Layne | .25 | .10 | .02 |
| ☐ 47 Norm Van Brocklin | .25 | .10 | .02 |
| ☐ 48 Y.A. Tittle | .25 | .10 | .02 |
| ☐ 49 Johnny Unitas | .50 | .20 | .05 |
| ☐ 50 Bart Starr | .35 | .14 | .03 |
| ☐ 51 Sonny Jurgensen | .25 | .10 | .02 |
| ☐ 52 Joe Namath | .75 | .30 | .07 |
| ☐ 53 Roger Staubach | .75 | .30 | .07 |
| ☐ 54 Terry Bradshaw | .50 | .20 | .05 |
| ☐ 55 Steve Van Buren | .25 | .10 | .02 |
| ☐ 56 Marion Motley | .25 | .10 | .02 |
| ☐ 57 Joe Perry | .25 | .10 | .02 |
| ☐ 58 Hugh McElhenny | .25 | .10 | .02 |
| ☐ 59 Frank Gifford | .50 | .20 | .05 |
| ☐ 60 Jim Brown | .75 | .30 | .07 |
| ☐ 61 Jim Taylor | .25 | .10 | .02 |
| ☐ 62 Gale Sayers | .35 | .14 | .03 |
| ☐ 63 Larry Csonka | .25 | .10 | .02 |
| ☐ 64 Emlen Tunnell | .15 | .06 | .01 |
| ☐ 65 Jack Christiansen | .15 | .06 | .01 |
| ☐ 66 Dick(Night Train) Lane | .15 | .06 | .01 |
| ☐ 67 Sam Huff | .25 | .10 | .02 |
| ☐ 68 Ray Nitschke | .15 | .06 | .01 |
| ☐ 69 Larry Wilson | .15 | .06 | .01 |
| ☐ 70 Willie Wood | .15 | .06 | .01 |
| ☐ 71 Bobby Bell | .15 | .06 | .01 |
| ☐ 72 Willie Brown | .15 | .06 | .01 |
| ☐ 73 Dick Butkus | .35 | .14 | .03 |
| ☐ 74 Jack Ham | .15 | .06 | .01 |
| ☐ 75 George Halas | .15 | .06 | .01 |
| ☐ 76 Steve Owen | .15 | .06 | .01 |
| ☐ 77 Art Rooney | .15 | .06 | .01 |
| ☐ 78 Bert Bell | .15 | .06 | .01 |
| ☐ 79 Paul Brown | .15 | .06 | .01 |
| ☐ 80 Pete Rozelle | .15 | .06 | .01 |

## 1993 Heads and Tails SB XXVII

Designed and produced by Heads and Tails Inc., this 25-card set features the best past and current players that the Super Bowl has to offer as well as some 1993 NFL Pro Bowl picks. The production run was reportedly 200,000 sets, and these sets were sold through Wal-Mart and other retailers. Randomly inserted throughout the product were 10,000 sets featuring gold foil stamping on the words "Rose Bowl" and on the stem of the Rose Bowl insignia. The remaining 190,000 sets have silver foil stamping instead of gold. Gold sets are valued at two to three times the values listed below. Each set was packed in a special box that contained foil packs with over 200 cards from other NFL licensed trading card producers (Topps, Fleer Ultra, GameDay, Proline, and Wild Card). The cards measure the standard size (2 1/2" by 3 1/2") and feature full-bleed color action player photos. The Pro Bowl picks have the player's name embossed in foil at the bottom. The Super Bowl player cards display the player's name in white printed vertically down one edge, a Rose Bowl foil embossed emblem, and an icon showing the Super Bowl they played in. On a background consisting of a ghosted picture of the Rose Bowl, the backs summarize the player's performance. After a checklist/header card, the set is arranged as follows: NFL Salutes (2-3), '93 Pro Bowl Picks (4-7), Super Bowl MVP's of the Past (8-11), AFC Champions Buffalo Bills (12-18), and NFC Champions Dallas Cowboys (19-25). The cards are numbered with an "SB" prefix.

| | MINT | EXC | G-VG |
|---|---|---|---|
| COMPLETE SET (25) | 10.00 | 4.00 | 1.00 |
| COMMON PLAYER (1-25) | .25 | .10 | .02 |

| | | | |
|---|---|---|---|
| ☐ 1 Title Card CL | .35 | .14 | .03 |
| ☐ 2 Lawrence Taylor | .35 | .14 | .03 |
|    New York Giants | | | |
|    Mike Singletary | | | |
|    Chicago Bears | | | |
| ☐ 3 Dennis Byrd | .50 | .20 | .05 |
|    New York Jets | | | |
| ☐ 4 Junior Seau | .35 | .14 | .03 |
|    San Diego Chargers | | | |
| ☐ 5 Steve Young | .75 | .30 | .07 |
|    San Francisco 49ers | | | |
| ☐ 6 Sterling Sharpe | .75 | .30 | .07 |
|    Green Bay Packers | | | |
| ☐ 7 Cortez Kennedy | .35 | .14 | .03 |
|    Seattle Seahawks | | | |
| ☐ 8 Terry Bradshaw | .75 | .30 | .07 |
|    Pittsburgh Steelers | | | |
| ☐ 9 Fred Biletnikoff | .35 | .14 | .03 |
|    Oakland Raiders | | | |
| ☐ 10 John Riggins | .35 | .14 | .03 |
|    Washington Redskins | | | |
| ☐ 11 Phil Simms | .35 | .14 | .03 |
|    New York Giants | | | |
| ☐ 12 Cornelius Bennett | .35 | .14 | .03 |
| ☐ 13 Jim Kelly | .75 | .30 | .07 |
| ☐ 14 Bruce Smith | .35 | .14 | .03 |
| ☐ 15 Andre Reed | .35 | .14 | .03 |
| ☐ 16 Keith McKeller | .25 | .10 | .02 |
| ☐ 17 James Lofton | .35 | .14 | .03 |
| ☐ 18 Thurman Thomas | .75 | .30 | .07 |
| ☐ 19 Emmitt Smith | 2.50 | 1.00 | .25 |
| ☐ 20 Kelvin Martin | .25 | .10 | .02 |
| ☐ 21 Troy Aikman | 2.00 | .80 | .20 |
| ☐ 22 Charles Haley | .35 | .14 | .03 |

| | | | |
|---|---|---|---|
| ☐ 23 Alvin Harper | .75 | .30 | .07 |
| ☐ 24 Michael Irvin | 1.00 | .40 | .10 |
| ☐ 25 Jay Novacek | .50 | .20 | .05 |

## 1991 Heisman Collection I

The first series of the Heisman Collection contains 20 cards honoring former Heisman Trophy winners. The cards are standard size, 2 1/2 by 3 1/2. Only 100,000 sets were produced, and each set contains a title card with a unique serial number. Each of the 1,000 cases (100 sets per case) contained two personally autographed cards from a former Heisman Trophy winner. The front design features a color posed shot of the player, bordered in gold and black. The player's name appears in a black stripe at the bottom of the picture, with a picture of the Heisman Trophy in the lower right corner of the card face. The horizontally oriented back has a larger picture of the Heisman Trophy and a summary of the player's career. The year the player won the trophy is indicated in a gold stripe on the right side of the card back. The cards are skip-numbered and arranged chronologically from older to more recent Heisman trophy winners. There also exists a promo card of Bo Jackson marked "Sample" on the back; it was issued as part of a 10" by 3 1/2" strip with set and ordering information on it.

| | MINT | EXC | G-VG |
|---|---|---|---|
| COMPLETE SET (21) | 8.00 | 3.25 | .80 |
| COMMON PLAYER | .50 | .20 | .05 |
| | | | |
| ☐ 1 Jay Berwanger | .50 | .20 | .05 |
| ☐ 6 Tom Harmon | .75 | .30 | .07 |
| ☐ 9 Angelo Bertelli | .50 | .20 | .05 |
| ☐ 11 Doc Blanchard | .75 | .30 | .07 |
| ☐ 13 John Lujack | .75 | .30 | .07 |
| ☐ 15 Leon Hart | .50 | .20 | .05 |
| ☐ 16 Vic Janowicz | .50 | .20 | .05 |
| ☐ 19 John Lattner | .50 | .20 | .05 |
| ☐ 23 John David Crow | .50 | .20 | .05 |
| ☐ 26 Joe Bellino | .50 | .20 | .05 |
| ☐ 30 John Huarte | .50 | .20 | .05 |
| ☐ 32 Steve Spurrier | 1.00 | .40 | .10 |
| ☐ 36 Jim Plunkett | .75 | .30 | .07 |
| ☐ 40 Archie Griffin | .75 | .30 | .07 |
| ☐ 42 Tony Dorsett | 1.00 | .40 | .10 |
| ☐ 43 Earl Campbell | 2.00 | .80 | .20 |
| ☐ 45 Charles White | .50 | .20 | .05 |
| ☐ 48 Herschel Walker | 1.00 | .40 | .10 |
| ☐ 51 Bo Jackson | 1.50 | .60 | .15 |
| ☐ 53 Tim Brown | 1.00 | .40 | .10 |
| ☐ SAM Bo Jackson | 5.00 | 2.00 | .50 |
| (Sample/Promo) | | | |
| ☐ xx Title card | .50 | .20 | .05 |

## 1992 Heisman Collection II

For the second year, College Classics in association with The Downtown Athletic Club of New York issued a series consisting of 20 cards honoring Heisman Trophy winners. One hundred thousand sets were produced, and each one included a consecutively numbered card from 1-100,000. The set was issued in a sturdy cardboard box with an unnumbered checklist on its back. Two-card strips measuring approximately 3 1/2 by 7 1/2 and featuring either Barry Sanders or Roger Staubach were issued to promote the set. The Sanders and Staubach promos are different in that the card number on the back of the regular issue has been replaced by the word "Sample." The front design features a color player portrait bordered in black and gold. The player's name appears in a black stripe that cuts across the bottom of the picture, intersecting a picture of the Heisman Trophy at the lower right corner. The horizontal back has a larger picture of the Heisman Trophy and a summary of the player's career. The year the player won

the trophy is printed vertically in a gold stripe running down the right side. The cards are skip-numbered and arranged chronologically from older to more recent Heisman trophy winners.

| | MINT | EXC | G-VG |
|---|---|---|---|
| COMPLETE SET (21) | 10.00 | 4.00 | 1.00 |
| COMMON PLAYER | .50 | .20 | .05 |
| | | | |
| ☐ 2 Larry Kelley | .50 | .20 | .05 |
| ☐ 3 Clint Frank | .50 | .20 | .05 |
| ☐ 5 Nile Kinnick | .75 | .30 | .07 |
| ☐ 7 Bruce Smith | .50 | .20 | .05 |
| ☐ 10 Les Horvath | .50 | .20 | .05 |
| ☐ 14 Doak Walker | .75 | .30 | .07 |
| ☐ 17 Dick Kazmaier | .50 | .20 | .05 |
| ☐ 20 Alan Ameche | .50 | .20 | .05 |
| ☐ 21 Howard Cassady | .50 | .20 | .05 |
| ☐ 25 Billy Cannon | .50 | .20 | .05 |
| ☐ 27 Ernie Davis | 1.50 | .60 | .15 |
| ☐ 29 Roger Staubach | 2.50 | 1.00 | .25 |
| ☐ 31 Mike Garrett | .50 | .20 | .05 |
| ☐ 35 Steve Owens | .50 | .20 | .05 |
| ☐ 38 Johnny Rodgers | .50 | .20 | .05 |
| ☐ 39 John Cappelletti | .50 | .20 | .05 |
| ☐ 44 Billy Sims | .75 | .30 | .07 |
| ☐ 50 Doug Flutie | 1.00 | .40 | .10 |
| ☐ 52 Vinny Testaverde | .50 | .20 | .05 |
| ☐ 54 Barry Sanders | 1.50 | .60 | .15 |
| ☐ NNO Title Card | .50 | .20 | .05 |
| ☐ SAM Barry Sanders | 7.50 | 3.00 | .75 |
| ☐ SAM Roger Staubach | 10.00 | 4.00 | 1.00 |

## 1970 Hi-C Mini-Posters

This set of ten posters were the insides of the Hi-C drink can labels. They are numbered very subtly below the player's picture but they are listed here in alphabetical order. The players selected for the set were leaders at their positions during the 1969 season. The mini-posters measure approximately 6 5/8" by 13 3/4".

| | NRMT | VG-E | GOOD |
|---|---|---|---|
| COMPLETE SET (10) | 600.00 | 240.00 | 60.00 |
| COMMON PLAYER (1-10) | 60.00 | 24.00 | 6.00 |
| | | | |
| ☐ 1 Greg Cook | 70.00 | 28.00 | 7.00 |
| ☐ 2 Fred Cox | 60.00 | 24.00 | 6.00 |
| ☐ 3 Sonny Jurgensen | 100.00 | 40.00 | 10.00 |
| ☐ 4 David Lee | 60.00 | 24.00 | 6.00 |
| ☐ 5 Dennis Partee | 60.00 | 24.00 | 6.00 |

| | MINT | EXC | G-VG |
|---|---|---|---|
| ☐ 6 Dick Post | 60.00 | 24.00 | 6.00 |
| ☐ 7 Mel Renfro | 80.00 | 32.00 | 8.00 |
| ☐ 8 Gale Sayers | 150.00 | 60.00 | 15.00 |
| ☐ 9 Emmitt Thomas | 60.00 | 24.00 | 6.00 |
| ☐ 10 Jim Turner | 60.00 | 24.00 | 6.00 |

## 1993-94 Highland Mint

Produced by Highland Mint, these cards measure the standard size (2 1/2" by 3 1/2") and are exact reproductions of Topps football cards. Produced in limited quantities, only 1,000 silver (500 silver for Emmitt Smith) and 2,500 bronze were issued. Highland Mint also issued 40 bronze promos of the Smith card. Each card bears a serial number on its bottom edge. These cards were available only at hobby stores, and were packaged in a lucite display case within an album. Each card came with a sequentially numbered Certificate of Authenticity. The numbering of the cards reflects the actual card numbers from the original Topps issues; however the listing below is ordered alphabetically for convenience. The prices below refer to bronze versions; the silver versions are generally valued at approximately five times the values listed below.

| | MINT | EXC | G-VG |
|---|---|---|---|
| COMPLETE SET (11) | 600.00 | 240.00 | 60.00 |
| COMMON PLAYER (1-11) | 50.00 | 20.00 | 5.00 |
| ☐ 1 Troy Aikman | 75.00 | 30.00 | 7.50 |
| (1989 Topps Traded) | | | |
| ☐ 2 Jerome Bettis | 50.00 | 20.00 | 5.00 |
| (1993 Rookie) | | | |
| ☐ 3 John Elway | 50.00 | 20.00 | 5.00 |
| (1984 Rookie) | | | |
| ☐ 4 Michael Irvin | 50.00 | 20.00 | 5.00 |
| (1989 Rookie) | | | |
| ☐ 5 Jim Kelly | 50.00 | 20.00 | 5.00 |
| (1987 Rookie) | | | |
| ☐ 6 Dan Marino | 75.00 | 30.00 | 7.50 |
| (1984 Rookie) | | | |
| ☐ 7 Jerry Rice | 50.00 | 20.00 | 5.00 |
| (1986 Rookie) | | | |
| ☐ 8 Barry Sanders | 50.00 | 20.00 | 5.00 |
| (1989 Rookie) | | | |
| ☐ 9 Deion Sanders | 50.00 | 20.00 | 5.00 |
| (1989 Rookie) | | | |
| ☐ 10 Emmitt Smith | 100.00 | 40.00 | 10.00 |
| Dallas Cowboys | | | |
| (1990 Topps Traded) | | | |
| ☐ 11 Steve Young | 50.00 | 20.00 | 5.00 |
| (1986 Rookie) | | | |

## 1991 Hoby SEC Stars

The premier edition of Hoby's Stars of the Southeastern Conference football card set contains 396 cards measuring the standard size (2 1/2" by 3 1/2"). Each institution is represented by 36 prominent past players. The front design features a mix of color or black and white, posed or action player photos, with thin white borders on a gold card face. The school logo appears in the lower left corner of the picture, with the player's name in a blue stripe extending to the right. The color of the backs reflects the team's primary color; the backs present biography, statistics, or career highlights. The cards are numbered on the back in the upper right corner. The cards are checklisted below alphabetically according to teams as follows, with athletic director, coach, and checklist cards listed at the end: Alabama (1-36, 361-363), Auburn (37-72, 364-365), Florida (73-108, 381-383), Georgia (109-144, 366-368), Kentucky (145-180, 369-371), Louisiana State (181-216, 372-374), Mississippi State (217-252, 378-380), Mississippi (253-288, 375-377), Tennessee (299-334, 384-386), and Vanderbilt

(325-360, 387-389). The set closes with an SEC Rivalries subset (390-395) and a Commissioner card (396). The numbering below reflects the actual numbering on the cards and checklists. A mistake occurred when Tennessee's players began with 299 rather than 289; thus no cards are numbered 289-298, and both Tennessee and Vanderbilt cards share the numbers 325-334.

| | MINT | EXC | G-VG |
|---|---|---|---|
| COMPLETE SET (396) | 40.00 | 16.00 | 4.00 |
| COMMON CARD (1-396) | .10 | .04 | .01 |
| ☐ 1 Paul(Bear) Bryant CO | 1.00 | .40 | .10 |
| ☐ 2 Johnny Musso | .50 | .20 | .05 |
| ☐ 3 Keith McCants | .20 | .08 | .02 |
| ☐ 4 Cecil Dowdy | .10 | .04 | .01 |
| ☐ 5 Thomas Rayam | .10 | .04 | .01 |
| ☐ 6 Van Tiffin | .10 | .04 | .01 |
| ☐ 7 Efrum Thomas | .10 | .04 | .01 |
| ☐ 8 Jon Hand | .20 | .08 | .02 |
| ☐ 9 David Smith | .10 | .04 | .01 |
| ☐ 10 Larry Rose | .10 | .04 | .01 |
| ☐ 11 Lamonde Russell | .10 | .04 | .01 |
| ☐ 12 Mike Washington | .10 | .04 | .01 |
| ☐ 13 Tommy Cole | .10 | .04 | .01 |
| ☐ 14 Roger Shultz | .10 | .04 | .01 |
| ☐ 15 Spencer Hammond | .10 | .04 | .01 |
| ☐ 16 John Fruhmorgen | .10 | .04 | .01 |
| ☐ 17 Gene Jelks | .20 | .08 | .02 |
| ☐ 18 John Mangum | .10 | .04 | .01 |
| ☐ 19 George Thornton | .10 | .04 | .01 |
| ☐ 20 Billy Neighbors | .20 | .08 | .02 |
| ☐ 21 Howard Cross | .30 | .12 | .03 |
| ☐ 22 Jeremiah Castille | .20 | .08 | .02 |
| ☐ 23 Derrick Thomas | 1.00 | .40 | .10 |
| ☐ 24 Terrill Chatman | .10 | .04 | .01 |
| ☐ 25 Ken Stabler | 1.00 | .40 | .10 |
| ☐ 26 Lee Ozmint | .10 | .04 | .01 |
| ☐ 27 Philip Doyle | .10 | .04 | .01 |
| ☐ 28 Kermit Kendrick | .10 | .04 | .01 |
| ☐ 29 Chris Mohr | .10 | .04 | .01 |
| ☐ 30 Tommy Wilcox | .10 | .04 | .01 |
| ☐ 31 Gary Hollingsworth | .10 | .04 | .01 |
| ☐ 32 Sylvester Croom | .20 | .08 | .02 |
| ☐ 33 Willie Wyatt | .10 | .04 | .01 |
| ☐ 34 Pooley Hubert | .10 | .04 | .01 |
| ☐ 35 Bobby Humphrey | .20 | .08 | .02 |
| ☐ 36 Vaughn Mancha | .10 | .04 | .01 |
| ☐ 37 Reggie Slack | .30 | .12 | .03 |
| ☐ 38 Vince Dooley CO | .30 | .12 | .03 |
| ☐ 39 Ed King | .20 | .08 | .02 |
| ☐ 40 Connie Frederick | .10 | .04 | .01 |
| ☐ 41 Jeff Burger | .20 | .08 | .02 |
| ☐ 42 Monk Gafford | .10 | .04 | .01 |
| ☐ 43 David Rocker | .20 | .08 | .02 |
| ☐ 44 Jim Pyburn | .10 | .04 | .01 |
| ☐ 45 Bob Harris | .10 | .04 | .01 |
| ☐ 46 Travis Tidwell | .10 | .04 | .01 |
| ☐ 47 Shug Jordan CO | .30 | .12 | .03 |
| ☐ 48 Zeke Smith | .10 | .04 | .01 |
| ☐ 49 Terry Beasley | .20 | .08 | .02 |
| ☐ 50 Pat Sullivan | .30 | .12 | .03 |
| ☐ 51 Stacy Danley | .20 | .08 | .02 |
| ☐ 52 Jimmy Hitchcock | .10 | .04 | .01 |
| ☐ 53 John Wiley | .10 | .04 | .01 |
| ☐ 54 Greg Taylor | .10 | .04 | .01 |
| ☐ 55 Lamar Rogers | .10 | .04 | .01 |
| ☐ 56 Rob Selby | .10 | .04 | .01 |
| ☐ 57 James Joseph | .30 | .12 | .03 |
| ☐ 58 Mike Kolen | .10 | .04 | .01 |
| ☐ 59 Kevin Greene | .20 | .08 | .02 |
| ☐ 60 Ben Thomas | .10 | .04 | .01 |
| ☐ 61 Shayne Wasden | .10 | .04 | .01 |
| ☐ 62 Tex Warrington | .10 | .04 | .01 |
| ☐ 63 Tommie Agee | .20 | .08 | .02 |
| ☐ 64 Jimmy Phillips | .20 | .08 | .02 |
| ☐ 65 Lawyer Tillman | .30 | .12 | .03 |
| ☐ 66 Mark Dorminey | .10 | .04 | .01 |

|  |  | | | |
|---|--------|----|----|----|
| ☐ 67 | Steve Wallace | .20 | .08 | .02 |
| ☐ 68 | Ed Dyas | .10 | .04 | .01 |
| ☐ 69 | Alexander Wright | .30 | .12 | .03 |
| ☐ 70 | Lionel James | .20 | .08 | .02 |
| ☐ 71 | Aundray Bruce | .20 | .08 | .02 |
| ☐ 72 | Edmund Nelson | .10 | .04 | .01 |
| ☐ 73 | Jack Youngblood | .50 | .20 | .05 |
| ☐ 74 | Carlos Alvarez | .20 | .08 | .02 |
| ☐ 75 | Ricky Nattiel | .20 | .08 | .02 |
| ☐ 76 | Bill Carr | .10 | .04 | .01 |
| ☐ 77 | Guy Dennis | .10 | .04 | .01 |
| ☐ 78 | Charles Casey | .10 | .04 | .01 |
| ☐ 79 | Louis Oliver | .30 | .12 | .03 |
| ☐ 80 | John Reaves | .20 | .08 | .02 |
| ☐ 81 | Wayne Peace | .20 | .08 | .02 |
| ☐ 82 | Charlie LaPradd | .10 | .04 | .01 |
| ☐ 83 | Wes Chandler | .30 | .12 | .03 |
| ☐ 84 | Richard Trapp | .10 | .04 | .01 |
| ☐ 85 | Ralph Ortega | .10 | .04 | .01 |
| ☐ 86 | Tommy Durrance | .10 | .04 | .01 |
| ☐ 87 | Burton Lawless | .20 | .08 | .02 |
| ☐ 88 | Bruce Bennett | .10 | .04 | .01 |
| ☐ 89 | Huey Richardson | .20 | .08 | .02 |
| ☐ 90 | Larry Smith | .10 | .04 | .01 |
| ☐ 91 | Trace Armstrong | .20 | .08 | .02 |
| ☐ 92 | Nat Moore | .30 | .12 | .03 |
| ☐ 93 | James Jones | .30 | .12 | .03 |
| ☐ 94 | Kay Stephenson | .20 | .08 | .02 |
| ☐ 95 | Scot Brantley | .20 | .08 | .02 |
| ☐ 96 | Ray Criswell | .10 | .04 | .01 |
| ☐ 97 | Steve Tannen | .20 | .08 | .02 |
| ☐ 98 | Ernie Mills | .30 | .12 | .03 |
| ☐ 99 | Bruce Vaughn | .10 | .04 | .01 |
| ☐ 100 | Steve Spurrier | 1.00 | .40 | .10 |
| ☐ 101 | Crawford Ker | .20 | .08 | .02 |
| ☐ 102 | David Galloway | .20 | .08 | .02 |
| ☐ 103 | David Williams | .20 | .08 | .02 |
| ☐ 104 | Lomas Brown | .30 | .12 | .03 |
| ☐ 105 | Fernando Jackson | .10 | .04 | .01 |
| ☐ 106 | Jeff Roth | .10 | .04 | .01 |
| ☐ 107 | Mark Murray | .10 | .04 | .01 |
| ☐ 108 | Kirk Kirkpatrick | .10 | .04 | .01 |
| ☐ 109 | Ray Goff CO | .20 | .08 | .02 |
| ☐ 110 | Quinton Lumpkin | .10 | .04 | .01 |
| ☐ 111 | Royce Smith | .10 | .04 | .01 |
| ☐ 112 | Larry Rakestraw | .20 | .08 | .02 |
| ☐ 113 | Kevin Butler | .20 | .08 | .02 |
| ☐ 114 | Aschel M. Day | .10 | .04 | .01 |
| ☐ 115 | Scott Woerner | .20 | .08 | .02 |
| ☐ 116 | Herb St. John | .10 | .04 | .01 |
| ☐ 117 | Ray Rissmiller | .10 | .04 | .01 |
| ☐ 118 | Buck Belue | .20 | .08 | .02 |
| ☐ 119 | George Collins | .10 | .04 | .01 |
| ☐ 120 | Joel Parrish | .10 | .04 | .01 |
| ☐ 121 | Terry Hoage | .20 | .08 | .02 |
| ☐ 122 | Frank Sinkwich | .30 | .12 | .03 |
| ☐ 123 | Billy Payne | .30 | .12 | .03 |
| ☐ 124 | Zeke Bratkowski | .20 | .08 | .02 |
| ☐ 125 | Herschel Walker | .50 | .20 | .05 |
| ☐ 126 | Pat Dye CO | .30 | .12 | .03 |
| ☐ 127 | Vernon Smith | .10 | .04 | .01 |
| ☐ 128 | Rex Robinson | .10 | .04 | .01 |
| ☐ 129 | Mike Castronis | .10 | .04 | .01 |
| ☐ 130 | Pop Warner CO | .30 | .12 | .03 |
| ☐ 131 | George Patton | .20 | .08 | .02 |
| ☐ 132 | Harry Babcock | .10 | .04 | .01 |
| ☐ 133 | Lindsay Scott | .20 | .08 | .02 |
| ☐ 134 | Bill Stanfill | .20 | .08 | .02 |
| ☐ 135 | Bill Hartman Jr. | .10 | .04 | .01 |
| ☐ 136 | Eddie Weaver | .10 | .04 | .01 |
| ☐ 137 | Tim Worley | .30 | .12 | .03 |
| ☐ 138 | Ben Zambiasi | .30 | .12 | .03 |
| ☐ 139 | Bob McWhorter | .10 | .04 | .01 |
| ☐ 140 | Rodney Hampton | .75 | .30 | .07 |
| ☐ 141 | Len Hauss | .20 | .08 | .02 |
| ☐ 142 | Wallace Butts CO | .20 | .08 | .02 |
| ☐ 143 | Andy Johnson | .20 | .08 | .02 |
| ☐ 144 | I.M. Shiver Jr. | .10 | .04 | .01 |
| ☐ 145 | Clyde Johnson | .10 | .04 | .01 |
| ☐ 146 | Steve Meilenger | .20 | .08 | .02 |
| ☐ 147 | Howard Schnellenberger CO | .30 | .12 | .03 |
| ☐ 148 | Irv Goode | .20 | .08 | .02 |
| ☐ 149 | Sam Ball | .10 | .04 | .01 |
| ☐ 150 | Babe Parilli | .30 | .12 | .03 |
| ☐ 151 | Rick Norton | .20 | .08 | .02 |
| ☐ 152 | Warren Bryant | .20 | .08 | .02 |
| ☐ 153 | Mike Pfeifer | .10 | .04 | .01 |
| ☐ 154 | Sonny Collins | .20 | .08 | .02 |
| ☐ 155 | Mark Higgs | .50 | .20 | .05 |
| ☐ 156 | Randy Holleran | .10 | .04 | .01 |
| ☐ 157 | Bill Ransdell | .10 | .04 | .01 |
| ☐ 158 | Joey Worley | .10 | .04 | .01 |
| ☐ 159 | Jim Kovach | .20 | .08 | .02 |
| ☐ 160 | Joe Federspiel | .20 | .08 | .02 |
| ☐ 161 | Larry Seiple | .20 | .08 | .02 |
| ☐ 162 | Darryl Bishop | .10 | .04 | .01 |
| ☐ 163 | George Blanda | .75 | .30 | .07 |
| ☐ 164 | Oliver Barnett | .10 | .04 | .01 |
| ☐ 165 | Paul Calhoun | .10 | .04 | .01 |
| ☐ 166 | Dicky Lyons | .20 | .08 | .02 |
| ☐ 167 | Tom Hutchinson | .10 | .04 | .01 |
| ☐ 168 | George Adams | .20 | .08 | .02 |
| ☐ 169 | Derrick Ramsey | .20 | .08 | .02 |
| ☐ 170 | Rick Kestner | .10 | .04 | .01 |
| ☐ 171 | Art Still | .30 | .12 | .03 |
| ☐ 172 | Rick Nuzum | .10 | .04 | .01 |
| ☐ 173 | Richard Jaffe | .10 | .04 | .01 |
| ☐ 174 | Rodger Bird | .20 | .08 | .02 |
| ☐ 175 | Jeff Van Note | .30 | .12 | .03 |
| ☐ 176 | Herschel Turner | .10 | .04 | .01 |
| ☐ 177 | Lou Michaels | .20 | .08 | .02 |
| ☐ 178 | Ray Correll | .10 | .04 | .01 |
| ☐ 179 | Doug Moseley | .10 | .04 | .01 |
| ☐ 180 | Bob Gain | .20 | .08 | .02 |
| ☐ 181 | Tommy Casanova | .30 | .12 | .03 |
| ☐ 182 | Mike Anderson | .10 | .04 | .01 |
| ☐ 183 | Craig Burns | .10 | .04 | .01 |
| ☐ 184 | A.J. Duhe | .20 | .08 | .02 |
| ☐ 185 | Lyman White | .10 | .04 | .01 |
| ☐ 186 | Paul Dietzel CO | .30 | .12 | .03 |
| ☐ 187 | Paul Lyons | .10 | .04 | .01 |
| ☐ 188 | Eddie Ray | .10 | .04 | .01 |
| ☐ 189 | Roy Winston | .20 | .08 | .02 |
| ☐ 190 | Brad Davis | .10 | .04 | .01 |
| ☐ 191 | Mike Williams | .10 | .04 | .01 |
| ☐ 192 | Karl Wilson | .10 | .04 | .01 |
| ☐ 193 | Ronnie Estay | .10 | .04 | .01 |
| ☐ 194 | Malcolm Scott | .10 | .04 | .01 |
| ☐ 195 | Greg Jackson | .10 | .04 | .01 |
| ☐ 196 | Willie Teal | .20 | .08 | .02 |
| ☐ 197 | Eddie Fuller | .10 | .04 | .01 |
| ☐ 198 | Ralph Norwood | .10 | .04 | .01 |
| ☐ 199 | Bert Jones | .30 | .12 | .03 |
| ☐ 200 | Y.A. Tittle | .50 | .20 | .05 |
| ☐ 201 | Jerry Stovall | .30 | .12 | .03 |
| ☐ 202 | Henry Thomas | .20 | .08 | .02 |
| ☐ 203 | Lance Smith | .10 | .04 | .01 |
| ☐ 204 | Doug Moreau | .20 | .08 | .02 |
| ☐ 205 | Tyler LaFauci | .10 | .04 | .01 |
| ☐ 206 | George Bevan | .10 | .04 | .01 |
| ☐ 207 | Robert Dugas | .10 | .04 | .01 |
| ☐ 208 | Carlos Carson | .20 | .08 | .02 |
| ☐ 209 | Andy Hamilton | .20 | .08 | .02 |
| ☐ 210 | James Britt | .10 | .04 | .01 |
| ☐ 211 | Wendell Davis | .30 | .12 | .03 |
| ☐ 212 | Ron Sancho | .10 | .04 | .01 |
| ☐ 213 | Johnny Robinson | .30 | .12 | .03 |
| ☐ 214 | Eric Martin | .30 | .12 | .03 |
| ☐ 215 | Michael Brooks | .20 | .08 | .02 |
| ☐ 216 | Toby Caston | .20 | .08 | .02 |
| ☐ 217 | Jesse Anderson | .10 | .04 | .01 |
| ☐ 218 | Jimmy Webb | .10 | .04 | .01 |
| ☐ 219 | Mardye McDole | .20 | .08 | .02 |
| ☐ 220 | David Smith | .10 | .04 | .01 |
| ☐ 221 | Dana Moore | .10 | .04 | .01 |
| ☐ 222 | Cedric Corse | .10 | .04 | .01 |
| ☐ 223 | Louis Clark | .10 | .04 | .01 |
| ☐ 224 | Walter Packer | .20 | .08 | .02 |
| ☐ 225 | George Wonsley | .20 | .08 | .02 |
| ☐ 226 | Billy Jackson | .20 | .08 | .02 |
| ☐ 227 | Bruce Plummer | .10 | .04 | .01 |
| ☐ 228 | Aaron Pearson | .10 | .04 | .01 |
| ☐ 229 | Glen Collins | .10 | .04 | .01 |
| ☐ 230 | Paul Davis CO | .10 | .04 | .01 |
| ☐ 231 | Wayne Jones | .10 | .04 | .01 |
| ☐ 232 | John Bond | .10 | .04 | .01 |
| ☐ 233 | Johnie Cooks | .20 | .08 | .02 |
| ☐ 234 | Robert Young | .10 | .04 | .01 |
| ☐ 235 | Don Smith | .10 | .04 | .01 |
| ☐ 236 | Kent Hull | .30 | .12 | .03 |
| ☐ 237 | Tony Shell | .10 | .04 | .01 |
| ☐ 238 | Steve Freeman | .20 | .08 | .02 |
| ☐ 239 | James Williams | .10 | .04 | .01 |
| ☐ 240 | Tom Goode | .20 | .08 | .02 |
| ☐ 241 | Stan Black | .10 | .04 | .01 |
| ☐ 242 | Bo Russell | .10 | .04 | .01 |
| ☐ 243 | Ricky Byrd | .10 | .04 | .01 |
| ☐ 244 | Frank Dowsing | .10 | .04 | .01 |
| ☐ 245 | Wayne Harris | .30 | .12 | .03 |
| ☐ 246 | Richard Keys | .10 | .04 | .01 |
| ☐ 247 | Artie Cosby | .10 | .04 | .01 |
| ☐ 248 | Dave Marler | .10 | .04 | .01 |
| ☐ 249 | Michael Haddix | .20 | .08 | .02 |
| ☐ 250 | Jerry Clower | .10 | .04 | .01 |
| ☐ 251 | Bill Bell | .10 | .04 | .01 |
| ☐ 252 | Jerry Bouldin | .10 | .04 | .01 |
| ☐ 253 | Parker Hall | .10 | .04 | .01 |
| ☐ 254 | Allen Brown | .10 | .04 | .01 |
| ☐ 255 | Bill Smith | .10 | .04 | .01 |
| ☐ 256 | Freddie Joe Nunn | .20 | .08 | .02 |
| ☐ 257 | John Vaught CO | .20 | .08 | .02 |
| ☐ 258 | Buford McGee | .20 | .08 | .02 |
| ☐ 259 | Kenny Dill | .10 | .04 | .01 |
| ☐ 260 | Jim Miller | .10 | .04 | .01 |
| ☐ 261 | Doug Jacobs | .10 | .04 | .01 |

| | | | |
|---|---|---|---|
| ☐ 262 John Dottley | .20 | .08 | .02 |
| ☐ 263 Willie Green | .30 | .12 | .03 |
| ☐ 264 Tony Bennett | .30 | .12 | .03 |
| ☐ 265 Stan Hindman | .20 | .08 | .02 |
| ☐ 266 Charles Childers | .10 | .04 | .01 |
| ☐ 267 Harry Harrison | .10 | .04 | .01 |
| ☐ 268 Todd Sandroni | .10 | .04 | .01 |
| ☐ 269 Glynn Griffing | .20 | .08 | .02 |
| ☐ 270 Chris Mitchell | .10 | .04 | .01 |
| ☐ 271 Shawn Cobb | .10 | .04 | .01 |
| ☐ 272 Doug Elmore | .10 | .04 | .01 |
| ☐ 273 Dawson Pruett | .10 | .04 | .01 |
| ☐ 274 Warner Alford | .10 | .04 | .01 |
| ☐ 275 Archie Manning | .75 | .30 | .07 |
| ☐ 276 Kelvin Pritchett | .20 | .08 | .02 |
| ☐ 277 Pat Coleman | .10 | .04 | .01 |
| ☐ 278 Stevon Moore | .20 | .08 | .02 |
| ☐ 279 John Darnell | .10 | .04 | .01 |
| ☐ 280 Wesley Walls | .20 | .08 | .02 |
| ☐ 281 Billy Brewer | .20 | .08 | .02 |
| ☐ 282 Mark Young | .10 | .04 | .01 |
| ☐ 283 Andre Townsend | .20 | .08 | .02 |
| ☐ 284 Billy Ray Adams | .10 | .04 | .01 |
| ☐ 285 Jim Dunaway | .20 | .08 | .02 |
| ☐ 286 Paige Cothren | .20 | .08 | .02 |
| ☐ 287 Jake Gibbs | .30 | .12 | .03 |
| ☐ 288 Jim Urbanek | .10 | .04 | .01 |
| ☐ 299 Tony Thompson | .10 | .04 | .01 |
| ☐ 300 Johnny Majors CO | .30 | .12 | .03 |
| ☐ 301 Roland Poles | .10 | .04 | .01 |
| ☐ 302 Alvin Harper | .75 | .30 | .07 |
| ☐ 303 Doug Baird | .10 | .04 | .01 |
| ☐ 304 Greg Burke | .10 | .04 | .01 |
| ☐ 305 Sterling Henton | .10 | .04 | .01 |
| ☐ 306 Preston Warren | .10 | .04 | .01 |
| ☐ 307 Stanley Morgan | .50 | .20 | .05 |
| ☐ 308 Bobby Scott | .20 | .08 | .02 |
| ☐ 309 Doug Atkins | .40 | .16 | .04 |
| ☐ 310 Bill Young | .10 | .04 | .01 |
| ☐ 311 Bob Garmon | .10 | .04 | .01 |
| ☐ 312 Herman Weaver | .20 | .08 | .02 |
| ☐ 313 Dewey Warren | .10 | .04 | .01 |
| ☐ 314 John Boynton | .20 | .08 | .02 |
| ☐ 315 Bob Davis | .10 | .04 | .01 |
| ☐ 316 Pat Ryan | .10 | .04 | .01 |
| ☐ 317 Keith DeLong | .20 | .08 | .02 |
| ☐ 318 Bobby Dodd CO | .20 | .08 | .02 |
| ☐ 319 Ricky Townsend | .10 | .04 | .01 |
| ☐ 320 Eddie Brown | .20 | .08 | .02 |
| ☐ 321 Herman Hickman CO | .20 | .08 | .02 |
| ☐ 322 Nathan Dougherty | .10 | .04 | .01 |
| ☐ 323 Mickey Marvin | .20 | .08 | .02 |
| ☐ 324 Reggie Cobb | .50 | .20 | .05 |
| ☐ 325A Condredge Holloway | .30 | .12 | .03 |
| Tennessee | | | |
| ☐ 325B Josh Cody | .10 | .04 | .01 |
| Vanderbilt | | | |
| ☐ 326A Anthony Hancock | .30 | .12 | .03 |
| Tennessee | | | |
| ☐ 326B Jack Jenkins | .10 | .04 | .01 |
| Vanderbilt | | | |
| ☐ 327A Steve Kiner | .20 | .08 | .02 |
| Tennessee | | | |
| ☐ 327B Bob Goodridge | .20 | .08 | .02 |
| Vanderbilt | | | |
| ☐ 328A Mike Mauck | .10 | .04 | .01 |
| Tennessee | | | |
| ☐ 328B Chris Gaines | .10 | .04 | .01 |
| Vanderbilt | | | |
| ☐ 329A Bill Bates | .40 | .16 | .04 |
| Tennessee | | | |
| ☐ 329B Willie Geny | .10 | .04 | .01 |
| Tennessee | | | |
| ☐ 330A Austin Denney | .20 | .08 | .02 |
| Tennessee | | | |
| ☐ 330B Bob Laws | .10 | .04 | .01 |
| Vanderbilt | | | |
| ☐ 331A Robert Neyland CO | .30 | .12 | .03 |
| Tennessee | | | |
| ☐ 331B Rob Monaco | .10 | .04 | .01 |
| Vanderbilt | | | |
| ☐ 332A Bob Suffridge | .10 | .04 | .01 |
| Tennessee | | | |
| ☐ 332B Chuck Scott | .10 | .04 | .01 |
| Vanderbilt | | | |
| ☐ 333A Abe Shires | .10 | .04 | .01 |
| Tennessee | | | |
| ☐ 333B Hek Wakefield | .10 | .04 | .01 |
| Vanderbilt | | | |
| ☐ 334A Robert Shaw | .20 | .08 | .02 |
| Tennessee | | | |
| ☐ 334B Ken Stone | .10 | .04 | .01 |
| Vanderbilt | | | |
| ☐ 335 Mark Adams | .10 | .04 | .01 |
| ☐ 336 Ed Smith | .10 | .04 | .01 |
| ☐ 337 Dan McGugin CO | .10 | .04 | .01 |
| ☐ 338 Doug Mathews | .10 | .04 | .01 |
| ☐ 339 Whit Taylor | .20 | .08 | .02 |

| | | | |
|---|---|---|---|
| ☐ 340 Gene Moshier | .10 | .04 | .01 |
| ☐ 341 Christie Hauck | .10 | .04 | .01 |
| ☐ 342 Lee Nalley | .10 | .04 | .01 |
| ☐ 343 Wamon Buggs | .10 | .04 | .01 |
| ☐ 344 Jim Arnold | .10 | .04 | .01 |
| ☐ 345 Buford Ray | .20 | .08 | .02 |
| ☐ 346 Will Wolford | .20 | .08 | .02 |
| ☐ 347 Steve Bearden | .10 | .04 | .01 |
| ☐ 348 Frank Mordica | .10 | .04 | .01 |
| ☐ 349 Barry Burton | .10 | .04 | .01 |
| ☐ 350 Bill Wade | .30 | .12 | .03 |
| ☐ 351 Tommy Woodroof | .10 | .04 | .01 |
| ☐ 352 Steve Wade | .10 | .04 | .01 |
| ☐ 353 Preston Brown | .10 | .04 | .01 |
| ☐ 354 Ben Roderick | .10 | .04 | .01 |
| ☐ 355 Charles Horton | .10 | .04 | .01 |
| ☐ 356 DeMond Winston | .20 | .08 | .02 |
| ☐ 357 John North | .10 | .04 | .01 |
| ☐ 358 Don Orr | .10 | .04 | .01 |
| ☐ 359 Art Demmas | .10 | .04 | .01 |
| ☐ 360 Mark Johnson | .10 | .04 | .01 |
| ☐ 361 Hootie Ingram AD | .20 | .08 | .02 |
| Alabama | | | |
| ☐ 362 Gene Stallings CO | .20 | .08 | .02 |
| Alabama | | | |
| ☐ 363 Alabama Checklist | .10 | .04 | .01 |
| ☐ 364 Pat Dye CO | .20 | .08 | .02 |
| Auburn | | | |
| ☐ 365 Auburn Checklist | .10 | .04 | .01 |
| ☐ 366 Vince Dooley AD | .20 | .08 | .02 |
| Georgia | | | |
| ☐ 367 Ray Goff CO | .20 | .08 | .02 |
| Georgia | | | |
| ☐ 368 Georgia Checklist | .10 | .04 | .01 |
| ☐ 369 C.M. Newton AD | .20 | .08 | .02 |
| Kentucky | | | |
| ☐ 370 Bill Curry CO | .20 | .08 | .02 |
| Kentucky | | | |
| ☐ 371 Kentucky Checklist | .10 | .04 | .01 |
| ☐ 372 Joe Dean AD | .10 | .04 | .01 |
| LSU | | | |
| ☐ 373 Curley Hallman CO | .10 | .04 | .01 |
| LSU | | | |
| ☐ 374 LSU Checklist | .10 | .04 | .01 |
| ☐ 375 Warner Alford AD | .10 | .04 | .01 |
| Ole Miss | | | |
| ☐ 376 Billy Brewer CO | .20 | .08 | .02 |
| Ole Miss | | | |
| ☐ 377 Ole Miss Checklist | .10 | .04 | .01 |
| ☐ 378 Larry Templeton AD | .10 | .04 | .01 |
| Mississippi State | | | |
| ☐ 379 Jackie Sherrill CO | .30 | .12 | .03 |
| Mississippi State | | | |
| ☐ 380 Miss. State Checklist | .10 | .04 | .01 |
| ☐ 381 Bill Arnsbarger AD | .20 | .08 | .02 |
| Florida | | | |
| ☐ 382 Steve Spurrier CO | .40 | .16 | .04 |
| Florida | | | |
| ☐ 383 Florida Checklist | .10 | .04 | .01 |
| ☐ 384 Doug Dickey AD | .20 | .08 | .02 |
| Tennessee | | | |
| ☐ 385 Johnny Majors CO | .20 | .08 | .02 |
| Tennessee | | | |
| ☐ 386 Tennessee Checklist | .10 | .04 | .01 |
| ☐ 387 Paul Hoolahan AD | .10 | .04 | .01 |
| Vanderbilt | | | |
| ☐ 388 Gerry DiNardo CO | .20 | .08 | .02 |
| Vanderbilt | | | |
| ☐ 389 Vanderbilt Checklist | .10 | .04 | .01 |
| ☐ 390 The Iron Bowl | .20 | .08 | .02 |
| Alabama vs. Auburn | | | |
| ☐ 391 Largest Outdoor | .20 | .08 | .02 |
| Cocktail Party | | | |
| Florida vs. Georgia | | | |
| ☐ 392 The Egg Bowl | .20 | .08 | .02 |
| Mississippi State | | | |
| vs. Ole Miss | | | |
| ☐ 393 The Beer Barrel | .20 | .08 | .02 |
| Kentucky vs. Tennessee | | | |
| ☐ 394 Drama on Halloween | .20 | .08 | .02 |
| LSU vs. Ole Miss | | | |
| ☐ 395 Tennessee Hoedown | .20 | .08 | .02 |
| Tennessee vs. Vanderbilt | | | |
| ☐ 396 Roy Kramer COMM | .20 | .08 | .02 |

# 1991 Hoby SEC Stars Signature

These ten specially designed signature series cards feature a prominent player from each SEC institution. They were randomly inserted in the 1991 SEC Stars Hoby gold-foil packs. Each player selected autographed 1,000 cards, and each card bears a unique serial number. The cards are identical in size (2 1/2" by 3 1/2") and design with the corresponding player cards in the regular series, with four exceptions: 1) the stripe at the bottom of the card face is left blank for the player's autograph; 2) the numbering of the complete set has been

removed; 3) the pattern of gold and blue borders on the front differs slightly from the regular issue; and 4) the Manning card displays a different photo on the front than its counterpart in the regular set. Since the cards are unnumbered, they are checklisted below in alphabetical order.

|  | MINT | EXC | G-VG |
|---|---|---|---|
| COMPLETE SET (10) | 225.00 | 90.00 | 22.00 |
| COMMON PLAYER (1-10) | 10.00 | 4.00 | 1.00 |
| ☐ 1 Carlos Alvarez | 10.00 | 4.00 | 1.00 |
| Florida |  |  |  |
| ☐ 2 Zeke Bratkowski | 20.00 | 8.00 | 2.00 |
| Georgia |  |  |  |
| ☐ 3 Jerry Clower | 10.00 | 4.00 | 1.00 |
| Mississippi State |  |  |  |
| ☐ 4 Condredge Holloway | 15.00 | 6.00 | 1.50 |
| Tennessee |  |  |  |
| ☐ 5 Bert Jones | 40.00 | 16.00 | 4.00 |
| LSU |  |  |  |
| ☐ 6 Archie Manning | 50.00 | 20.00 | 5.00 |
| Ole Miss |  |  |  |
| ☐ 7 Ken Stabler | 60.00 | 24.00 | 6.00 |
| Alabama |  |  |  |
| ☐ 8 Pat Sullivan | 40.00 | 16.00 | 4.00 |
| Auburn |  |  |  |
| ☐ 9 Jeff Van Note | 15.00 | 6.00 | 1.50 |
| Kentucky |  |  |  |
| ☐ 10 Bill Wade | 20.00 | 8.00 | 2.00 |
| Vanderbilt |  |  |  |

## 1987 Holsum Dolphins

This 22-card set features players of the Miami Dolphins; cards were available only in Holsum Bread packages. The set was co-produced by Mike Schechter Associates on behalf of the NFL Players Association. The cards are standard size, 2 1/2" by 3 1/2", and are done in full color. Card fronts have a color photo within a green border and the backs are printed in black ink on white card stock. Cards are numbered on the back.

|  | MINT | EXC | G-VG |
|---|---|---|---|
| COMPLETE SET (22) | 40.00 | 16.00 | 4.00 |
| COMMON PLAYER (1-22) | 1.25 | .50 | .12 |
| ☐ 1 Bob Baumhower | 1.50 | .60 | .15 |
| ☐ 2 Mark Brown | 1.25 | .50 | .12 |
| ☐ 3 Mark Clayton | 4.00 | 1.60 | .40 |
| ☐ 4 Mark Duper | 2.50 | 1.00 | .25 |
| ☐ 5 Roy Foster | 1.25 | .50 | .12 |
| ☐ 6 Hugh Green | 1.50 | .60 | .15 |
| ☐ 7 Lorenzo Hampton | 1.50 | .60 | .15 |
| ☐ 8 William Judson | 1.25 | .50 | .12 |
| ☐ 9 George Little | 1.25 | .50 | .12 |
| ☐ 10 Dan Marino | 20.00 | 8.00 | 2.00 |

| ☐ 11 Nat Moore | 2.50 | 1.00 | .25 |
|---|---|---|---|
| ☐ 12 Tony Nathan | 2.00 | .80 | .20 |
| ☐ 13 John Offerdahl | 2.00 | .80 | .20 |
| ☐ 14 James Pruitt | 1.25 | .50 | .12 |
| ☐ 15 Fuad Reveiz | 1.25 | .50 | .12 |
| ☐ 16 Dwight Stephenson | 2.00 | .80 | .20 |
| ☐ 17 Glenn Blackwood | 1.50 | .60 | .15 |
| ☐ 18 Bruce Hardy | 1.25 | .50 | .12 |
| ☐ 19 Reggie Roby | 1.50 | .60 | .15 |
| ☐ 20 Bob Brudzinski | 1.50 | .60 | .15 |
| ☐ 21 Ron Jaworski | 2.00 | .80 | .20 |
| ☐ 22 T.J. Turner | 1.50 | .60 | .15 |

## 1988 Holsum Cardinals

This 12-card set features players of the St. Louis Cardinals; cards were available only in Holsum Bread packages. The set was co-produced by Mike Schechter Associates on behalf of the NFL Players Association. Cards are standard size, 2 1/2" by 3 1/2", and are done in full color. Card fronts have a color photo within a green border and the backs are printed in black ink on white card stock. The cards are numbered on the back.

|  | MINT | EXC | G-VG |
|---|---|---|---|
| COMPLETE SET (12) | 45.00 | 18.00 | 4.50 |
| COMMON PLAYER (1-12) | 4.00 | 1.60 | .40 |
| ☐ 1 Roy Green | 6.00 | 2.40 | .60 |
| ☐ 2 Stump Mitchell | 5.00 | 2.00 | .50 |
| ☐ 3 J.T. Smith | 5.00 | 2.00 | .50 |
| ☐ 4 E.J. Junior | 5.00 | 2.00 | .50 |
| ☐ 5 Cedric Mack | 4.00 | 1.60 | .40 |
| ☐ 6 Curtis Greer | 4.00 | 1.60 | .40 |
| ☐ 7 Lonnie Young | 4.00 | 1.60 | .40 |
| ☐ 8 David Galloway | 4.00 | 1.60 | .40 |
| ☐ 9 Luis Sharpe | 5.00 | 2.00 | .50 |
| ☐ 10 Leonard Smith | 4.00 | 1.60 | .40 |
| ☐ 11 Ron Wolfley | 4.00 | 1.60 | .40 |
| ☐ 12 Earl Ferrell | 4.00 | 1.60 | .40 |

## 1988 Holsum Dolphins

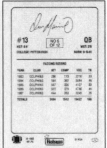

This 12-card set features players of the Miami Dolphins; cards were available only in Holsum Bread packages. The set was co-produced by Mike Schechter Associates on behalf of the NFL Players Association. The cards are standard size, 2 1/2" by 3 1/2", and are done in full color. Card fronts have a color photo within a green border and the backs are printed in black ink on white card stock. The cards are numbered on the back.

|  | MINT | EXC | G-VG |
|---|---|---|---|
| COMPLETE SET (12) | 30.00 | 12.00 | 3.00 |
| COMMON PLAYER (1-12) | 1.50 | .60 | .15 |

| | | | |
|---|---|---|---|
| ☐ 1 Mark Clayton | 3.00 | 1.20 | .30 |
| ☐ 2 Dwight Stephenson | 2.00 | .80 | .20 |
| ☐ 3 Mark Duper | 2.00 | .80 | .20 |
| ☐ 4 John Offerdahl | 2.00 | .80 | .20 |
| ☐ 5 Dan Marino | 15.00 | 6.00 | 1.50 |
| ☐ 6 T.J. Turner | 1.50 | .60 | .15 |
| ☐ 7 Lorenzo Hampton | 1.50 | .60 | .15 |
| ☐ 8 Bruce Hardy | 1.50 | .60 | .15 |
| ☐ 9 Fuad Reveiz | 1.50 | .60 | .15 |
| ☐ 10 Reggie Roby | 2.00 | .80 | .20 |
| ☐ 11 William Judson | 1.50 | .60 | .15 |
| ☐ 12 Bob Brudzinski | 2.00 | .80 | .20 |

## 1988 Holsum Patriots

This 12-card set features players of the New England Patriots; cards were available only in Holsum Bread packages. The set was co-produced by Mike Schechter Associates on behalf of the NFL Players Association. Cards are standard size, 2 1/2" by 3 1/2", and are done in full color. Card fronts have a color photo within a green border and the backs are printed in black ink on white card stock. The cards are numbered on the back.

| | MINT | EXC | G-VG |
|---|---|---|---|
| COMPLETE SET (12) | 40.00 | 16.00 | 4.00 |
| COMMON PLAYER (1-12) | 3.50 | 1.40 | .35 |
| | | | |
| ☐ 1 Andre Tippett | 5.00 | 2.00 | .50 |
| ☐ 2 Stanley Morgan | 6.00 | 2.40 | .60 |
| ☐ 3 Steve Grogan | 6.00 | 2.40 | .60 |
| ☐ 4 Ronnie Lippett | 5.00 | 2.00 | .50 |
| ☐ 5 Kenneth Sims | 3.50 | 1.40 | .35 |
| ☐ 6 Pete Brock | 3.50 | 1.40 | .35 |
| ☐ 7 Sean Farrell | 3.50 | 1.40 | .35 |
| ☐ 8 Garin Veris | 3.50 | 1.40 | .35 |
| ☐ 9 Mosi Tatupu | 5.00 | 2.00 | .50 |
| ☐ 10 Ray Clayborn | 5.00 | 2.00 | .50 |
| ☐ 11 Tony Franklin | 3.50 | 1.40 | .35 |
| ☐ 12 Reggie Dupard | 5.00 | 2.00 | .50 |

## 1989 Holsum Cardinals

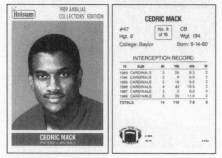

The 1989 Holsum Phoenix Cardinals set features 16 standard-size (2 1/2" by 3 1/2") cards. The set was co-produced by Mike Schechter Associates on behalf of the NFL Players Association. The fronts have helmetless color mug shots; the vertically oriented backs have bios, stats, and card numbers.

| | MINT | EXC | G-VG |
|---|---|---|---|
| COMPLETE SET (16) | 8.00 | 3.25 | .80 |
| COMMON PLAYER (1-16) | .50 | .20 | .05 |

| | | | |
|---|---|---|---|
| ☐ 1 Roy Green | 1.25 | .50 | .12 |
| ☐ 2 J.T. Smith | 1.00 | .40 | .10 |
| ☐ 3 Neil Lomax | 1.25 | .50 | .12 |
| ☐ 4 Stump Mitchell | 1.00 | .40 | .10 |
| ☐ 5 Vai Sikehema | 1.00 | .40 | .10 |
| ☐ 6 Lonnie Young | .60 | .24 | .06 |
| ☐ 7 Robert Awalt | .60 | .24 | .06 |
| ☐ 8 Cedric Mack | .60 | .24 | .06 |
| ☐ 9 Earl Ferrell | .60 | .24 | .06 |
| ☐ 10 Ron Wolfley | .60 | .24 | .06 |
| ☐ 11 Bob Clasby | .50 | .20 | .05 |
| ☐ 12 Luis Sharpe | .60 | .24 | .06 |
| ☐ 13 Steve Alvord | .50 | .20 | .05 |
| ☐ 14 David Galloway | .50 | .20 | .05 |
| ☐ 15 Freddie Joe Nunn | .75 | .30 | .07 |
| ☐ 16 Niko Noga | .60 | .24 | .06 |

## 1991 Homers

This six-card standard-size (2 1/2" by 3 1/2") set was sponsored by Legend Food Products in honor of the listed Hall of Famers. One free card was randomly inserted in either 3 1/2 or 10 oz. boxes of QB's Cookies. The vanilla-flavored cookies came in six player shapes (wide receiver, kicker, linebacker, tackle, running back, and quarterback), with a trivia quiz and secret message featured on each box. The card fronts display sepia-toned photos enclosed by bronze borders on a white card face. The player's name appears in a bronze bar at the lower left corner. The backs present year of induction into the Pro Football Hall of Fame, biography, career highlights, and a checklist for the set. The cards are numbered on the back.

| | MINT | EXC | G-VG |
|---|---|---|---|
| COMPLETE SET (6) | 15.00 | 6.00 | 1.50 |
| COMMON CARD (1-6) | 2.00 | .80 | .20 |
| | | | |
| ☐ 1 Vince Lombardi CO | 3.00 | 1.20 | .30 |
| ☐ 2 Hugh McElhenny | 3.00 | 1.20 | .30 |
| "The King" | | | |
| ☐ 3 Elroy Hirsch | 3.00 | 1.20 | .30 |
| "Crazy Legs" | | | |
| ☐ 4 Jim Thorpe | 5.00 | 2.00 | .50 |
| ☐ 5 Dick Lane | 2.00 | .80 | .20 |
| "Night Train" | | | |
| ☐ 6 Bart Starr | 4.00 | 1.60 | .40 |

## 1992-93 Intimidator Bio Sheets

Produced by Intimidator, each of these 36 bio sheets measures approximately 8 1/2" x 11" and is printed on card stock. The fronts display a large glossy color player photo framed by black and white inner borders. The right side of the photo is edged by a gold foil stripe that presents the player's name, team name, Intimidator logo, and uniform number. The surrounding card face, which constitutes the outer border, is team color-coded. The backs carry two black-and-white player photos, pro career summary, college career summary, and personal as well as biographical information. An autograph slot at the lower right corner rounds out the back. The bio sheets are unnumbered and checklisted below in alphabetical order.

|  | MINT | EXC | G-VG |
|---|---|---|---|
| COMPLETE SET (36) | 60.00 | 24.00 | 6.00 |
| COMMON PLAYER (1-36) | 1.00 | .40 | .10 |
| ☐ 1 Troy Aikman | 12.00 | 5.00 | 1.20 |
| Dallas Cowboys |  |  |  |
| ☐ 2 Jerry Ball | 1.00 | .40 | .10 |
| Detroit Lions |  |  |  |
| ☐ 3 Cornelius Bennett | 1.25 | .50 | .12 |
| Buffalo Bills |  |  |  |
| ☐ 4 Earnest Byner | 1.00 | .40 | .10 |
| Washington Redskins |  |  |  |
| ☐ 5 Randall Cunningham | 2.50 | 1.00 | .25 |
| Philadelphia Eagles |  |  |  |
| ☐ 6 Chris Doleman | 1.00 | .40 | .10 |
| Minnesota Vikings |  |  |  |
| ☐ 7 John Elway | 5.00 | 2.00 | .50 |
| Denver Broncos |  |  |  |
| ☐ 8 Jim Everett | 1.25 | .50 | .12 |
| Los Angeles Rams |  |  |  |
| ☐ 9 Michael Irvin | 4.00 | 1.60 | .40 |
| Dallas Cowboys |  |  |  |
| ☐ 10 Jim Kelly | 3.00 | 1.20 | .30 |
| Buffalo Bills |  |  |  |
| ☐ 11 James Lofton | 1.25 | .50 | .12 |
| Buffalo Bills |  |  |  |
| ☐ 12 Howie Long | 1.25 | .50 | .12 |
| Los Angeles Raiders |  |  |  |
| ☐ 13 Ronnie Lott | 1.25 | .50 | .12 |
| Los Angeles Raiders |  |  |  |
| ☐ 14 Nick Lowery | 1.00 | .40 | .10 |
| Kansas City Chiefs |  |  |  |
| ☐ 15 Charles Mann | 1.00 | .40 | .10 |
| Washington Redskins |  |  |  |
| ☐ 16 Dan Marino | 8.00 | 3.25 | .80 |
| Miami Dolphins |  |  |  |
| ☐ 17 Art Monk | 1.50 | .60 | .15 |
| Washington Redskins |  |  |  |
| ☐ 18 Joe Montana | 12.00 | 5.00 | 1.20 |
| San Francisco 49ers |  |  |  |
| ☐ 19 Warren Moon | 3.00 | 1.20 | .30 |
| Houston Oilers |  |  |  |
| ☐ 20 Christian Okoye | 1.25 | .50 | .12 |
| Kansas City Chiefs |  |  |  |
| ☐ 21 Leslie O'Neal | 1.00 | .40 | .10 |
| San Diego Chargers |  |  |  |
| ☐ 22 Andre Reed | 1.50 | .60 | .15 |
| Buffalo Bills |  |  |  |
| ☐ 23 Jerry Rice | 6.00 | 2.40 | .60 |
| San Francisco 49ers |  |  |  |
| ☐ 24 Andre Rison | 2.50 | 1.00 | .25 |
| Atlanta Falcons |  |  |  |
| ☐ 25 Deion Sanders | 4.00 | 1.60 | .40 |
| Atlanta Falcons |  |  |  |
| ☐ 26 Junior Seau | 2.00 | .80 | .20 |
| San Diego Chargers |  |  |  |
| ☐ 27 Mike Singletary | 1.50 | .60 | .15 |
| Chicago Bears |  |  |  |
| ☐ 28 Bruce Smith | 1.50 | .60 | .15 |
| Buffalo Bills |  |  |  |
| ☐ 29 Emmitt Smith | 12.00 | 5.00 | 1.20 |
| Dallas Cowboys |  |  |  |
| ☐ 30 Neil Smith | 1.25 | .50 | .12 |
| Kansas City Chiefs |  |  |  |
| ☐ 31 Pat Swilling | 1.25 | .50 | .12 |
| New Orleans Saints |  |  |  |
| ☐ 32 Lawrence Taylor | 2.00 | .80 | .20 |
| New York Giants |  |  |  |
| ☐ 33 Broderick Thomas | 1.00 | .40 | .10 |
| Tampa Bay Buccaneers |  |  |  |
| ☐ 34 Derrick Thomas | 2.00 | .80 | .20 |
| Kansas City Chiefs |  |  |  |
| ☐ 35 Thurman Thomas | 4.00 | 1.60 | .40 |
| Buffalo Bills |  |  |  |
| ☐ 36 Lorenzo White | 1.50 | .60 | .15 |
| Houston Oilers |  |  |  |

## 1986 Jeno's Pizza

The 1986 Jeno's Pizza football set contains 56 cards (two for each of the 28 teams). The two cards for each team typically represent a retired star and a current player. The cards are standard sized (2 1/2" by 3 1/2") and were printed horizontally (most of them) on thin card stock. The cards were distributed as a promotion with one card, sealed in plastic, contained in each special Jeno's box. Reportedly 10,000 sets were produced. There was also issued a Terry Bradshaw

Action Play Book; one had to send in a coupon to receive the book. The set price below includes the book.

|  | MINT | EXC | G-VG |
|---|---|---|---|
| COMPLETE SET (56) | 20.00 | 8.00 | 2.00 |
| COMMON PLAYER (1-56) | .40 | .16 | .04 |
| ☐ 1 Duane Thomas | .60 | .24 | .06 |
| Dallas Cowboys |  |  |  |
| ☐ 2 Butch Johnson | .40 | .16 | .04 |
| Dallas Cowboys |  |  |  |
| ☐ 3 Andy Headen | .40 | .16 | .04 |
| New York Giants |  |  |  |
| ☐ 4 Joe Morris | .50 | .20 | .05 |
| New York Giants |  |  |  |
| ☐ 5 Wilbert Montgomery | .50 | .20 | .05 |
| Philadelphia Eagles |  |  |  |
| ☐ 6 Harold Carmichael | .60 | .24 | .06 |
| Philadelphia Eagles |  |  |  |
| ☐ 7 Ottis Anderson | .60 | .24 | .06 |
| St. Louis Cardinals |  |  |  |
| ☐ 8 Roy Green | .50 | .20 | .05 |
| St. Louis Cardinals |  |  |  |
| ☐ 9 Mark Murphy | .40 | .16 | .04 |
| Washington Redskins |  |  |  |
| ☐ 10 Joe Theismann | 1.00 | .40 | .10 |
| Washington Redskins |  |  |  |
| ☐ 11 Jim McMahon | 1.00 | .40 | .10 |
| Chicago Bears |  |  |  |
| ☐ 12 Walter Payton | 2.50 | 1.00 | .25 |
| Chicago Bears |  |  |  |
| ☐ 13 Billy Sims | .75 | .30 | .07 |
| Detroit Lions |  |  |  |
| ☐ 14 James Jones | .40 | .16 | .04 |
| Detroit Lions |  |  |  |
| ☐ 15 Willie Davis | .75 | .30 | .07 |
| Green Bay Packers |  |  |  |
| ☐ 16 Eddie Lee Ivery | .40 | .16 | .04 |
| Green Bay Packers |  |  |  |
| ☐ 17 Fran Tarkenton | 1.50 | .60 | .15 |
| Minnesota Vikings |  |  |  |
| ☐ 18 Alan Page | .75 | .30 | .07 |
| Minnesota Vikings |  |  |  |
| ☐ 19 Ricky Bell | .60 | .24 | .06 |
| Tampa Bay Buccaneers |  |  |  |
| ☐ 20 Cecil Johnson | .40 | .16 | .04 |
| Tampa Bay Buccaneers |  |  |  |
| ☐ 21 Bubba Bean | .40 | .16 | .04 |
| Atlanta Falcons |  |  |  |
| ☐ 22 Gerald Riggs | .50 | .20 | .05 |
| Atlanta Falcons |  |  |  |
| ☐ 23 Eric Dickerson and | .75 | .30 | .07 |
| Barry Redden |  |  |  |
| Los Angeles Rams |  |  |  |
| ☐ 24 Jack Reynolds | .50 | .20 | .05 |
| Los Angeles Rams |  |  |  |
| ☐ 25 Archie Manning | 1.00 | .40 | .10 |
| New Orleans Saints |  |  |  |
| ☐ 26 Wayne Wilson | .60 | .24 | .06 |
| New Orleans Saints |  |  |  |
| ☐ 27 Dan Bunz and | .40 | .16 | .04 |
| Pete Johnson |  |  |  |
| San Francisco 49ers and |  |  |  |
| Cincinnati Bengals |  |  |  |
| ☐ 28 Roger Craig | 1.00 | .40 | .10 |
| San Francisco 49ers |  |  |  |
| ☐ 29 O.J. Simpson | 4.00 | 1.60 | .40 |
| Buffalo Bills |  |  |  |
| ☐ 30 Joe Cribbs | .50 | .20 | .05 |
| Buffalo Bills |  |  |  |
| ☐ 31 Rick Volk and | .60 | .24 | .06 |
| Leroy Kelly |  |  |  |
| Baltimore Colts and |  |  |  |
| Cleveland Browns |  |  |  |
| ☐ 32 Earl Morrall | .60 | .24 | .06 |
| Baltimore Colts |  |  |  |
| ☐ 33 Jim Kiick | .50 | .20 | .05 |
| Miami Dolphins |  |  |  |

| | | | |
|---|---|---|---|
| ☐ 34 Dan Marino | 4.00 | 1.60 | .40 |
| Miami Dolphins | | | |
| ☐ 35 Craig James | .75 | .30 | .07 |
| New England Patriots | | | |
| ☐ 36 Julius Adams | .40 | .16 | .04 |
| New England Patriots | | | |
| ☐ 37 Joe Namath | 4.00 | 1.60 | .40 |
| New York Jets | | | |
| ☐ 38 Freeman McNeil | .60 | .24 | .06 |
| New York Jets | | | |
| ☐ 39 Pete Johnson | .40 | .16 | .04 |
| Cincinnati Bengals | | | |
| ☐ 40 Larry Kinnebrew | .40 | .16 | .04 |
| Cincinnati Bengals | | | |
| ☐ 41 Brian Sipe | .50 | .20 | .05 |
| Cleveland Browns | | | |
| ☐ 42 Kevin Mack and | .60 | .24 | .06 |
| Earnest Byner | | | |
| Cleveland Browns | | | |
| ☐ 43 Dan Pastorini | .60 | .24 | .06 |
| Houston Oilers | | | |
| ☐ 44 Elvin Bethea and | .40 | .16 | .04 |
| Carter Hartwig | | | |
| Houston Oilers | | | |
| ☐ 45 Fran Tarkenton and | 1.00 | .40 | .10 |
| Jack Lambert | | | |
| Minnesota Vikings and | | | |
| Pittsburgh Steelers | | | |
| ☐ 46 Terry Bradshaw | 2.50 | 1.00 | .25 |
| Pittsburgh Steelers | | | |
| ☐ 47 Randy Gradishar and | .50 | .20 | .05 |
| Steve Foley | | | |
| Denver Broncos | | | |
| ☐ 48 Sammy Winder | .40 | .16 | .04 |
| Denver Broncos | | | |
| ☐ 49 Robert Holmes | .40 | .16 | .04 |
| Kansas City Chiefs | | | |
| ☐ 50 Buck Buchanan and | .75 | .30 | .07 |
| Curley Culp | | | |
| Kansas City Chiefs | | | |
| ☐ 51 Willie Jones and | .40 | .16 | .04 |
| Cedrick Hardman | | | |
| Los Angeles Raiders | | | |
| ☐ 52 Marcus Allen | 1.00 | .40 | .10 |
| Los Angeles Raiders | | | |
| ☐ 53 Dan Fouts and | .75 | .30 | .07 |
| Don Macek | | | |
| San Diego Chargers | | | |
| ☐ 54 Dan Fouts | 1.50 | .60 | .15 |
| San Diego Chargers | | | |
| ☐ 55 Blair Bush | .40 | .16 | .04 |
| Seattle Seahawks | | | |
| ☐ 56 Steve Largent | 2.00 | .80 | .20 |
| Seattle Seahawks | | | |
| ☐ xx Play Book | 3.00 | 1.20 | .30 |
| (Terry Bradshaw) | | | |

| | | | |
|---|---|---|---|
| Cleveland Browns | | | |
| ☐ 5 Preston Carpenter | 35.00 | 14.00 | 3.50 |
| Cleveland Browns | | | |
| ☐ 6 Vince Costello | 35.00 | 14.00 | 3.50 |
| Cleveland Browns | | | |
| ☐ 7 Dale Dodrill | 35.00 | 14.00 | 3.50 |
| Pittsburgh Steelers | | | |
| ☐ 8 Bob Gain | 35.00 | 14.00 | 3.50 |
| Cleveland Browns | | | |
| ☐ 9 Gary Glick | 35.00 | 14.00 | 3.50 |
| Pittsburgh Steelers | | | |
| ☐ 10 Lou Groza | 75.00 | 30.00 | 7.50 |
| Cleveland Browns | | | |
| ☐ 11 Gene Hickerson | 35.00 | 14.00 | 3.50 |
| Cleveland Browns | | | |
| ☐ 12 Billy Howton | 40.00 | 16.00 | 4.00 |
| Cleveland Browns | | | |
| ☐ 13 Art Hunter | 35.00 | 14.00 | 3.50 |
| Cleveland Browns | | | |
| ☐ 14 Joe Krupa | 35.00 | 14.00 | 3.50 |
| Pittsburgh Steelers | | | |
| ☐ 15 Bobby Layne | 75.00 | 30.00 | 7.50 |
| Pittsburgh Steelers | | | |
| ☐ 16 Joe Lewis | 35.00 | 14.00 | 3.50 |
| Pittsburgh Steelers | | | |
| ☐ 17 Jack McClairen | 35.00 | 14.00 | 3.50 |
| Pittsburgh Steelers | | | |
| ☐ 18 Mike McCormack | 50.00 | 20.00 | 5.00 |
| Cleveland Browns | | | |
| ☐ 19 Walt Michaels | 40.00 | 16.00 | 4.00 |
| Cleveland Browns | | | |
| ☐ 20 Bobby Mitchell | 75.00 | 30.00 | 7.50 |
| Cleveland Browns | | | |
| ☐ 21 Jim Ninowski | 40.00 | 16.00 | 4.00 |
| Cleveland Browns | | | |
| ☐ 22 Chuck Noll | 90.00 | 36.00 | 9.00 |
| Cleveland Browns | | | |
| ☐ 23 Jimmy Orr | 40.00 | 16.00 | 4.00 |
| Pittsburgh Steelers | | | |
| ☐ 24 Milt Plum | 40.00 | 16.00 | 4.00 |
| Cleveland Browns | | | |
| ☐ 25 Ray Renfro | 40.00 | 16.00 | 4.00 |
| Cleveland Browns | | | |
| ☐ 26 Mike Sandusky | 35.00 | 14.00 | 3.50 |
| Pittsburgh Steelers | | | |
| ☐ 27 Billy Ray Smith | 35.00 | 14.00 | 3.50 |
| Pittsburgh Steelers | | | |
| ☐ 28 Jim Ray Smith | 35.00 | 14.00 | 3.50 |
| Cleveland Browns | | | |
| ☐ 29 Ernie Stautner | 60.00 | 24.00 | 6.00 |
| Pittsburgh Steelers | | | |
| ☐ 30 Tom Tracy | 40.00 | 16.00 | 4.00 |
| Pittsburgh Steelers | | | |
| ☐ 31 Frank Varrichione | 35.00 | 14.00 | 3.50 |
| Pittsburgh Steelers | | | |

## 1959 Kahn's

CLEVELAND BROWNS
WILLIAM HOWTON - End
Height: 6'2".
Weight: .
College: Rice Institute
8 years in National Professional
Football League
Hometown: Houston, Texas

Compliments of Kahn's
"THE WIENER THE WORLD AWAITED"

The 1959 Kahn's football set of 31 black and white cards features players from the Cleveland Browns and the Pittsburgh Steelers. The cards measure approximately 3 1/4" by 3 15/16". The backs contain height, weight and short football career data. The statistics on the back are single spaced. The cards are unnumbered and hence are listed below alphabetically for convenience.

| | NRMT | VG-E | GOOD |
|---|---|---|---|
| COMPLETE SET (31) | 1500.00 | 650.00 | 165.00 |
| COMMON PLAYER (1-31) | 35.00 | 14.00 | 3.50 |
| | | | |
| ☐ 1 Dick Alban | 35.00 | 14.00 | 3.50 |
| Pittsburgh Steelers | | | |
| ☐ 2 Jim Brown | 375.00 | 150.00 | 37.00 |
| Cleveland Browns | | | |
| ☐ 3 Jack Butler | 35.00 | 14.00 | 3.50 |
| Pittsburgh Steelers | | | |
| ☐ 4 Lew Carpenter | 35.00 | 14.00 | 3.50 |

## 1960 Kahn's

...SBURGH STEELERS
BOBBY LAYNE—Quarterback
Height: 6'1".
Weight: 210 lbs.
Age: 34.
College: Texas
13 years in National Professional
Football League
Hometown: Lubbock, Texas

FREE! Kahn's Professional Football
Photo Album and Instruction Booklet.
Tips on playing football for the boys
and tips on twirling a baton for the
girls. To obtain this free Booklet,
just send 2 labels from Kahn's All
Meat Wieners with your name and
address to Kahn's, Cincinnati 29, Ohio.

Compliments of Kahn's
"THE WIENER THE WORLD AWAITED"

The 1960 Kahn's football set of 38 cards features Cleveland Browns and Pittsburgh Steelers. The cards measure approximately 3 1/4" by 3 15/16". In addition to data similar to the backs of the 1959 Kahn's cards, the backs of the 1960 Kahn's cards contain an ad for a free professional album and instruction booklet, which could be obtained by sending two labels to Kahn's. The cards are unnumbered and hence are listed below alphabetically for convenience. Willie Davis' card predates his 1964 Philadelphia Rookie Card by four years.

| | NRMT | VG-E | GOOD |
|---|---|---|---|
| COMPLETE SET (38) | 1300.00 | 550.00 | 150.00 |
| COMMON PLAYER (1-38) | 25.00 | 10.00 | 2.50 |
| | | | |
| ☐ 1 Sam Baker | 25.00 | 10.00 | 2.50 |
| Cleveland Browns | | | |
| ☐ 2 Jim Brown | 250.00 | 100.00 | 25.00 |
| Cleveland Browns | | | |
| ☐ 3 Ray Campbell | 25.00 | 10.00 | 2.50 |
| Pittsburgh Steelers | | | |

| | | | |
|---|---|---|---|
| ☐ 4 Preston Carpenter ........... Cleveland Browns | 25.00 | 10.00 | 2.50 |
| ☐ 5 Vince Costello ................. Cleveland Browns | 25.00 | 10.00 | 2.50 |
| ☐ 6 Willie Davis .................... Cleveland Browns | 75.00 | 30.00 | 7.50 |
| ☐ 7 Galen Fiss ..................... Cleveland Browns | 25.00 | 10.00 | 2.50 |
| ☐ 8 Bob Gain ....................... Cleveland Browns | 25.00 | 10.00 | 2.50 |
| ☐ 9 Lou Groza ...................... Cleveland Browns | 60.00 | 24.00 | 6.00 |
| ☐ 10 Gene Hickerson ............ Cleveland Browns | 25.00 | 10.00 | 2.50 |
| ☐ 11 John Henry Johnson ....... Pittsburgh Steelers | 50.00 | 20.00 | 5.00 |
| ☐ 12 Rich Kreitling ................ Cleveland Browns | 25.00 | 10.00 | 2.50 |
| ☐ 13 Joe Krupa ..................... Pittsburgh Steelers | 25.00 | 10.00 | 2.50 |
| ☐ 14 Bobby Layne ................. Pittsburgh Steelers | 60.00 | 24.00 | 6.00 |
| ☐ 15 Jack McClairen .............. Pittsburgh Steelers | 25.00 | 10.00 | 2.50 |
| ☐ 16 Mike McCormack ........... Cleveland Browns | 40.00 | 16.00 | 4.00 |
| ☐ 17 Walt Michaels ............... Cleveland Browns | 30.00 | 12.00 | 3.00 |
| ☐ 18 Bobby Mitchell .............. Cleveland Browns | 50.00 | 20.00 | 5.00 |
| ☐ 19 Dick Moegle ................. Pittsburgh Steelers | 25.00 | 10.00 | 2.50 |
| ☐ 20 John Morrow ................. Cleveland Browns | 25.00 | 10.00 | 2.50 |
| ☐ 21 Gern Nagler .................. Cleveland Browns | 25.00 | 10.00 | 2.50 |
| ☐ 22 John Nisby ................... Pittsburgh Steelers | 25.00 | 10.00 | 2.50 |
| ☐ 23 Jimmy Orr .................... Pittsburgh Steelers | 30.00 | 12.00 | 3.00 |
| ☐ 24 Bernie Parrish ............... Cleveland Browns | 25.00 | 10.00 | 2.50 |
| ☐ 25 Milt Plum ..................... Cleveland Browns | 30.00 | 12.00 | 3.00 |
| ☐ 26 John Reger ................... Pittsburgh Steelers | 25.00 | 10.00 | 2.50 |
| ☐ 27 Ray Renfro ................... Cleveland Browns | 30.00 | 12.00 | 3.00 |
| ☐ 28 Will Renfro ................... Cleveland Browns | 25.00 | 10.00 | 2.50 |
| ☐ 29 Mike Sandusky ............. Pittsburgh Steelers | 25.00 | 10.00 | 2.50 |
| ☐ 30 Dick Schafrath .............. Cleveland Browns | 25.00 | 10.00 | 2.50 |
| ☐ 31 Jim Ray Smith .............. Cleveland Browns | 25.00 | 10.00 | 2.50 |
| ☐ 32 Billy Ray Smith ............. Pittsburgh Steelers | 25.00 | 10.00 | 2.50 |
| ☐ 33 Ernie Stautner .............. Pittsburgh Steelers | 45.00 | 18.00 | 4.50 |
| ☐ 34 George Tarasovic .......... Pittsburgh Steelers | 25.00 | 10.00 | 2.50 |
| ☐ 35 Tom Tracy ................... Pittsburgh Steelers | 30.00 | 12.00 | 3.00 |
| ☐ 36 Frank Varrichione .......... Pittsburgh Steelers | 25.00 | 10.00 | 2.50 |
| ☐ 37 John Wooten ................ Cleveland Browns | 25.00 | 10.00 | 2.50 |
| ☐ 38 Lowe W. Wren .............. Pittsburgh Steelers | 25.00 | 10.00 | 2.50 |

# 1961 Kahn's

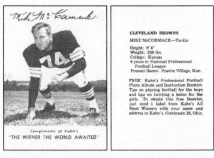

CLEVELAND BROWNS
MIKE McCORMACK—Tackle

Height: 6' 4"
Weight: 250 lbs.
College: Kansas
9 years in National Professional
Football League
Present Home: Prairie Village, Kan.

FREE! Kahn's Professional Football
Photo Album and Instruction Booklet.
Tips on playing football for the boys
and tips on twirling a baton for the
girls. To receive this free Booklet,
just send 1 label from Kahn's All
Meat Wieners with your name and
address to Kahn's, Cincinnati 25, Ohio.

Compliments of Kahn's
"THE WIENER THE WORLD AWAITED"

The 1961 Kahn's football set of 36 cards features Cleveland and Pittsburgh players as in the previous two years but adds players from teams not included in previous years, Baltimore Colts, Los Angeles

Rams, and Philadelphia Eagles. The cards measure approximately 3 1/4" by 4 1/16". The backs are the same as the 1960 Kahn's cards; however, the free booklet ad requires but one label to be sent in rather than the two labels required for the 1960 offer. Pictures of Larry Krutko and Tom Tracy are reversed. The cards are unnumbered and hence are listed below alphabetically for convenience.

| | NRMT | VG-E | GOOD |
|---|---|---|---|
| COMPLETE SET (36) ................. | 900.00 | 360.00 | 90.00 |
| COMMON PLAYER (1-36) ............ | 18.00 | 7.25 | 1.80 |
| ☐ 1 Sam Baker ..................... Cleveland Browns | 18.00 | 7.25 | 1.80 |
| ☐ 2 Jim Brown ...................... Cleveland Browns | 200.00 | 80.00 | 20.00 |
| ☐ 3 Preston Carpenter ........... Pittsburgh Steelers | 18.00 | 7.25 | 1.80 |
| ☐ 4 Vince Costello ................ Cleveland Browns | 18.00 | 7.25 | 1.80 |
| ☐ 5 Dean Derby .................... Pittsburgh Steelers | 18.00 | 7.25 | 1.80 |
| ☐ 6 Buddy Dial ..................... Pittsburgh Steelers | 22.00 | 9.00 | 2.20 |
| ☐ 7 Don Fleming ................... Cleveland Browns | 22.00 | 9.00 | 2.20 |
| ☐ 8 Bob Gain ....................... Cleveland Browns | 18.00 | 7.25 | 1.80 |
| ☐ 9 Bobby Joe Green ............ Pittsburgh Steelers | 18.00 | 7.25 | 1.80 |
| ☐ 10 Gene Hickerson ............ Cleveland Browns | 22.00 | 9.00 | 2.20 |
| ☐ 11 Jim Houston ................. Cleveland Browns | 22.00 | 9.00 | 2.20 |
| ☐ 12 Dan James .................. Pittsburgh Steelers | 18.00 | 7.25 | 1.80 |
| ☐ 13 John Henry Johnson ...... Pittsburgh Steelers | 35.00 | 14.00 | 3.50 |
| ☐ 14 Rich Kreitling ............... Cleveland Browns | 18.00 | 7.25 | 1.80 |
| ☐ 15 Joe Krupa .................... Pittsburgh Steelers | 18.00 | 7.25 | 1.80 |
| ☐ 16 Larry Krutko UER ......... Pittsburgh Steelers (Photo actually Tom Tracy) | 18.00 | 7.25 | 1.80 |
| ☐ 17 Bobby Layne ............... Pittsburgh Steelers | 50.00 | 20.00 | 5.00 |
| ☐ 18 Joe Lewis ................... Baltimore Colts | 18.00 | 7.25 | 1.80 |
| ☐ 19 Gene Lipscomb ........... Pittsburgh Steelers | 35.00 | 14.00 | 3.50 |
| ☐ 20 Mike McCormack ......... Cleveland Browns | 30.00 | 12.00 | 3.00 |
| ☐ 21 Bobby Mitchell ............ Cleveland Browns | 40.00 | 16.00 | 4.00 |
| ☐ 22 John Morrow ............... Cleveland Browns | 18.00 | 7.25 | 1.80 |
| ☐ 23 John Nisby ................. Pittsburgh Steelers | 18.00 | 7.25 | 1.80 |
| ☐ 24 Jimmy Orr .................. Baltimore Colts | 22.00 | 9.00 | 2.20 |
| ☐ 25 Milt Plum ................... Cleveland Browns | 22.00 | 10.00 | 2.50 |
| ☐ 26 John Reger ................. Pittsburgh Steelers | 18.00 | 7.25 | 1.80 |
| ☐ 27 Ray Renfro ................. Cleveland Browns | 25.00 | 10.00 | 2.50 |
| ☐ 28 Will Renfro ................. Cleveland Browns | 18.00 | 7.25 | 1.80 |
| ☐ 29 Mike Sandusky ........... Pittsburgh Steelers | 18.00 | 7.25 | 1.80 |
| ☐ 30 Dick Schafrath ............ Cleveland Browns | 18.00 | 7.25 | 1.80 |
| ☐ 31 Jim Ray Smith ............ Cleveland Browns | 18.00 | 7.25 | 1.80 |
| ☐ 32 Ernie Stautner ............ Pittsburgh Steelers | 40.00 | 16.00 | 4.00 |
| ☐ 33 George Tarasovic ........ Pittsburgh Steelers | 18.00 | 7.25 | 1.80 |
| ☐ 34 Tom Tracy UER ........... Pittsburgh Steelers (Photo actually Larry Krutko) | 22.00 | 9.00 | 2.20 |
| ☐ 35 Frank Varrichione ........ Los Angeles Rams | 18.00 | 7.25 | 1.80 |
| ☐ 36 John Wooten .............. Cleveland Browns | 18.00 | 7.25 | 1.80 |

# 1962 Kahn's

The 1962 Kahn's football card set contains 38 players from eight different teams. New teams added in this year's set are the Chicago Bears, Detroit Lions, and Minnesota Vikings. The cards measure approximately 3 1/4" by 4 3/16". The backs contain information comparable to the backs of previous years; however, the statistics are

MINNESOTA VIKINGS

**FRANCIS TARKENTON**
Quarterback

Height: 6' 1"
Weight: 190 lbs.
Age: 22
College: Georgia
2 years in National Professional
Football League
Present Home: Minneapolis

Broke into NFL by throwing four
touchdown passes and running
for fifth touchdown against Chicago Bears.

Compliments of Kahn's
"THE WIENER THE WORLD AWAITED"

double spaced, and the player's name on the back is in bold-faced type. The cards are unnumbered and hence are listed below alphabetically for convenience.

|  | NRMT | VG-E | GOOD |
|---|---|---|---|
| COMPLETE SET (38) | 1000.00 | 450.00 | 125.00 |
| COMMON PLAYER (1-38) | 18.00 | 7.25 | 1.80 |
| ☐ 1 Maxie Baughan | 22.00 | 9.00 | 2.20 |
| Philadelphia Eagles | | | |
| ☐ 2 Charley Britt | 18.00 | 7.25 | 1.80 |
| Los Angeles Rams | | | |
| ☐ 3 Jim Brown | 175.00 | 70.00 | 18.00 |
| Cleveland Browns | | | |
| ☐ 4 Preston Carpenter | 18.00 | 7.25 | 1.80 |
| Pittsburgh Steelers | | | |
| ☐ 5 Pete Case | 18.00 | 7.25 | 1.80 |
| Philadelphia Eagles | | | |
| ☐ 6 Howard Cassady | 22.00 | 9.00 | 2.20 |
| Cleveland Browns | | | |
| ☐ 7 Vince Costello | 18.00 | 7.25 | 1.80 |
| Cleveland Browns | | | |
| ☐ 8 Buddy Dial | 22.00 | 9.00 | 2.20 |
| Pittsburgh Steelers | | | |
| ☐ 9 Gene Hickerson | 18.00 | 7.25 | 1.80 |
| Cleveland Browns | | | |
| ☐ 10 Jim Houston | 22.00 | 9.00 | 2.20 |
| Cleveland Browns | | | |
| ☐ 11 Dan James | 18.00 | 7.25 | 1.80 |
| Pittsburgh Steelers | | | |
| ☐ 12 Rich Kreitling | 18.00 | 7.25 | 1.80 |
| Cleveland Browns | | | |
| ☐ 13 Joe Krupa | 18.00 | 7.25 | 1.80 |
| Pittsburgh Steelers | | | |
| ☐ 14 Bobby Layne | 45.00 | 18.00 | 4.50 |
| Pittsburgh Steelers | | | |
| ☐ 15 Ray Lemek | 18.00 | 7.25 | 1.80 |
| Pittsburgh Steelers | | | |
| ☐ 16 Gene Lipscomb | 30.00 | 12.00 | 3.00 |
| Pittsburgh Steelers | | | |
| ☐ 17 David Lloyd | 18.00 | 7.25 | 1.80 |
| Detroit Lions | | | |
| ☐ 18 Lou Michaels | 22.00 | 9.00 | 2.20 |
| Pittsburgh Steelers | | | |
| ☐ 19 Larry Morris | 18.00 | 7.25 | 1.80 |
| Chicago Bears | | | |
| ☐ 20 John Morrow | 18.00 | 7.25 | 1.80 |
| Cleveland Browns | | | |
| ☐ 21 Jim Ninowski | 22.00 | 9.00 | 2.20 |
| Cleveland Browns | | | |
| ☐ 22 Buzz Nutter | 18.00 | 7.25 | 1.80 |
| Pittsburgh Steelers | | | |
| ☐ 23 Jimmy Orr | 22.00 | 9.00 | 2.20 |
| Baltimore Colts | | | |
| ☐ 24 Bernie Parrish | 22.00 | 9.00 | 2.20 |
| Cleveland Browns | | | |
| ☐ 25 Milt Plum | 22.00 | 9.00 | 2.20 |
| Detroit Lions | | | |
| ☐ 26 Myron Pottios | 22.00 | 9.00 | 2.20 |
| Pittsburgh Steelers | | | |
| ☐ 27 John Reger | 18.00 | 7.25 | 1.80 |
| Pittsburgh Steelers | | | |
| ☐ 28 Ray Renfro | 22.00 | 9.00 | 2.20 |
| Cleveland Browns | | | |
| ☐ 29 Frank Ryan | 25.00 | 10.00 | 2.50 |
| Cleveland Browns | | | |
| ☐ 30 John Sample | 22.00 | 9.00 | 2.20 |
| Pittsburgh Steelers | | | |
| ☐ 31 Mike Sandusky | 18.00 | 7.25 | 1.80 |
| Pittsburgh Steelers | | | |
| ☐ 32 Dick Schafrath | 18.00 | 7.25 | 1.80 |
| Cleveland Browns | | | |
| ☐ 33 Jim Shofner | 22.00 | 9.00 | 2.20 |
| Cleveland Browns | | | |
| ☐ 34 Jim Ray Smith | 18.00 | 7.25 | 1.80 |
| Cleveland Browns | | | |
| ☐ 35 Ernie Stautner | 35.00 | 14.00 | 3.50 |
| Pittsburgh Steelers | | | |
| ☐ 36 Fran Tarkenton | 225.00 | 90.00 | 22.00 |

| Minnesota Vikings | | | |
|---|---|---|---|
| ☐ 37 Paul Wiggin | 22.00 | 9.00 | 2.20 |
| Cleveland Browns | | | |
| ☐ 38 John Wooten | 18.00 | 7.25 | 1.80 |
| Cleveland Browns | | | |

# 1963 Kahn's

GREEN BAY PACKERS

**JIM TAYLOR**
Fullback            Height: 6'0"
                    Weight: 215

Born:    September 20, 1935
         at Baton Rouge, La.
Hometown: Baton Rouge, La.
College or University Attended: L.S.U.

All-American, All-Star
Won S.E.C. Scoring Title 1956-57
Date Started in Pro's: 1958
All-Pro 1961, 1962:
Player of Year 1962; Jim Thorpe
Trophy
Records: Most Touchdowns, Season (19)
1962
       Mbr.    Western Champs - 1960,
World Champs - 1961, 1962

Compliments of Kahn's
"THE WIENER THE WORLD AWAITED"

The 1963 Kahn's football card set includes players from six new teams not appearing in previous Kahn sets. All 14 NFL teams are represented in this set. The new teams are Dallas Cowboys, Green Bay Packers, New York Giants, St. Louis Cardinals, San Francisco 49ers and Washington Redskins. The cards measure approximately 3 1/4" by 4 3/16". The backs contain player statistics comparable to previous years; however, this set may be distinguished from Kahn's sets of other years because it is the only Kahn's football card set that has a distinct white border surrounding the picture on the obverse. With a total of 92 different cards, this is the largest Kahn's football issue. The cards are unnumbered and hence are listed below alphabetically for convenience.

|  | NRMT | VG-E | GOOD |
|---|---|---|---|
| COMPLETE SET (92) | 2000.00 | 900.00 | 225.00 |
| COMMON PLAYER (1-92) | 15.00 | 6.00 | 1.50 |
| ☐ 1 Bill Barnes | 15.00 | 6.00 | 1.50 |
| Washington Redskins | | | |
| ☐ 2 Erich Barnes | 18.00 | 7.25 | 1.80 |
| New York Giants | | | |
| ☐ 3 Dick Bass | 18.00 | 7.25 | 1.80 |
| Los Angeles Rams | | | |
| ☐ 4 Don Bosseler | 15.00 | 6.00 | 1.50 |
| Washington Redskins | | | |
| ☐ 5 Jim Brown | 175.00 | 70.00 | 18.00 |
| Cleveland Browns | | | |
| ☐ 6 Roger Brown | 18.00 | 7.25 | 1.80 |
| Detroit Lions | | | |
| ☐ 7 Roosevelt Brown | 25.00 | 10.00 | 2.50 |
| New York Giants | | | |
| ☐ 8 Ron Bull | 18.00 | 7.25 | 1.80 |
| Chicago Bears | | | |
| ☐ 9 Preston Carpenter | 15.00 | 6.00 | 1.50 |
| Pittsburgh Steelers | | | |
| ☐ 10 Frank Clarke | 18.00 | 7.25 | 1.80 |
| Dallas Cowboys | | | |
| ☐ 11 Gail Cogdill | 18.00 | 7.25 | 1.80 |
| Detroit Lions | | | |
| ☐ 12 Bobby Joe Conrad | 18.00 | 7.25 | 1.80 |
| St. Louis Cardinals | | | |
| ☐ 13 John David Crow | 25.00 | 10.00 | 2.50 |
| St. Louis Cardinals | | | |
| ☐ 14 Dan Currie | 15.00 | 6.00 | 1.50 |
| Green Bay Packers | | | |
| ☐ 15 Buddy Dial | 18.00 | 7.25 | 1.80 |
| Pittsburgh Steelers | | | |
| ☐ 16 Mike Ditka | 60.00 | 24.00 | 6.00 |
| Chicago Bears | | | |
| ☐ 17 Fred Dugan | 15.00 | 6.00 | 1.50 |
| Washington Redskins | | | |
| ☐ 18 Galen Fiss | 15.00 | 6.00 | 1.50 |
| Cleveland Browns | | | |
| ☐ 19 Bill Forester | 18.00 | 7.25 | 1.80 |
| Green Bay Packers | | | |
| ☐ 20 Bob Gain | 15.00 | 6.00 | 1.50 |
| Cleveland Browns | | | |
| ☐ 21 Willie Galimore | 20.00 | 8.00 | 2.00 |
| Chicago Bears | | | |
| ☐ 22 Bill George | 25.00 | 10.00 | 2.50 |
| Chicago Bears | | | |
| ☐ 23 Frank Gifford | 100.00 | 40.00 | 10.00 |
| New York Giants | | | |
| ☐ 24 Bill Glass | 18.00 | 7.25 | 1.80 |
| Cleveland Browns | | | |
| ☐ 25 Forrest Gregg | 25.00 | 10.00 | 2.50 |
| Green Bay Packers | | | |
| ☐ 26 Fred Hageman | 15.00 | 6.00 | 1.50 |

| | | | | |
|---|---|---|---|---|
| Washington Redskins | | | | |
| ☐ 27 Jimmy Hill | | 15.00 | 6.00 | 1.50 |
| St. Louis Cardinals | | | | |
| ☐ 28 Sam Huff | | 30.00 | 12.00 | 3.00 |
| New York Giants | | | | |
| ☐ 29 Dan James | | 15.00 | 6.00 | 1.50 |
| Pittsburgh Steelers | | | | |
| ☐ 30 John Henry Johnson | | 25.00 | 10.00 | 2.50 |
| Pittsburgh Steelers | | | | |
| ☐ 31 Sonny Jurgensen | | 35.00 | 14.00 | 3.50 |
| Philadelphia Eagles | | | | |
| ☐ 32 Jim Katcavage | | 18.00 | 7.25 | 1.80 |
| New York Giants | | | | |
| ☐ 33 Ron Kostelnik | | 15.00 | 6.00 | 1.50 |
| Green Bay Packers | | | | |
| ☐ 34 Jerry Kramer | | 25.00 | 10.00 | 2.50 |
| Green Bay Packers | | | | |
| ☐ 35 Ron Kramer | | 18.00 | 7.25 | 1.80 |
| Green Bay Packers | | | | |
| ☐ 36 Dick Lane | | 25.00 | 10.00 | 2.50 |
| Detroit Lions | | | | |
| ☐ 37 Yale Lary | | 25.00 | 10.00 | 2.50 |
| Detroit Lions | | | | |
| ☐ 38 Eddie LeBaron | | 20.00 | 8.00 | 2.00 |
| Dallas Cowboys | | | | |
| ☐ 39 Dick Lynch | | 18.00 | 7.25 | 1.80 |
| New York Giants | | | | |
| ☐ 40 Tommy Mason | | 20.00 | 8.00 | 2.00 |
| Minnesota Vikings | | | | |
| ☐ 41 Tommy McDonald | | 20.00 | 8.00 | 2.00 |
| Philadelphia Eagles | | | | |
| ☐ 42 Lou Michaels | | 18.00 | 7.25 | 1.80 |
| Pittsburgh Steelers | | | | |
| ☐ 43 Bobby Mitchell | | 30.00 | 12.00 | 3.00 |
| Cleveland Browns | | | | |
| ☐ 44 Dick Modzelewski | | 18.00 | 7.25 | 1.80 |
| New York Giants | | | | |
| ☐ 45 Lenny Moore | | 30.00 | 12.00 | 3.00 |
| Baltimore Colts | | | | |
| ☐ 46 John Morrow | | 15.00 | 6.00 | 1.50 |
| Cleveland Browns | | | | |
| ☐ 47 John Nisby | | 15.00 | 6.00 | 1.50 |
| Washington Redskins | | | | |
| ☐ 48 Ray Nitschke | | 35.00 | 14.00 | 3.50 |
| Green Bay Packers | | | | |
| ☐ 49 Leo Nomellini | | 25.00 | 10.00 | 2.50 |
| San Francisco 49ers | | | | |
| ☐ 50 Jimmy Orr | | 18.00 | 7.25 | 1.80 |
| Baltimore Colts | | | | |
| ☐ 51 John Paluck | | 15.00 | 6.00 | 1.50 |
| Washington Redskins | | | | |
| ☐ 52 Jim Parker | | 25.00 | 10.00 | 2.50 |
| Baltimore Colts | | | | |
| ☐ 53 Bernie Parrish | | 18.00 | 7.25 | 1.80 |
| Cleveland Browns | | | | |
| ☐ 54 Jim Patton | | 18.00 | 7.25 | 1.80 |
| New York Giants | | | | |
| ☐ 55 Don Perkins | | 20.00 | 8.00 | 2.00 |
| Dallas Cowboys | | | | |
| ☐ 56 Richie Petitbon | | 18.00 | 7.25 | 1.80 |
| Chicago Bears | | | | |
| ☐ 57 Jim Phillips | | 15.00 | 6.00 | 1.50 |
| Los Angeles Rams | | | | |
| ☐ 58 Nick Pietrosante | | 18.00 | 7.25 | 1.80 |
| Detroit Lions | | | | |
| ☐ 59 Milt Plum | | 20.00 | 8.00 | 2.00 |
| Detroit Lions | | | | |
| ☐ 60 Myron Pottios | | 18.00 | 7.25 | 1.80 |
| Pittsburgh Steelers | | | | |
| ☐ 61 Sonny Randle | | 18.00 | 7.25 | 1.80 |
| St. Louis Cardinals | | | | |
| ☐ 62 John Reger | | 15.00 | 6.00 | 1.50 |
| Pittsburgh Steelers | | | | |
| ☐ 63 Ray Renfro | | 18.00 | 7.25 | 1.80 |
| Pittsburgh Steelers | | | | |
| ☐ 64 Pete Retzlaff | | 20.00 | 8.00 | 2.00 |
| Philadelphia Eagles | | | | |
| ☐ 65 Pat Richter | | 18.00 | 7.25 | 1.80 |
| Washington Redskins | | | | |
| ☐ 66 Jim Ringo | | 25.00 | 10.00 | 2.50 |
| Green Bay Packers | | | | |
| ☐ 67 Andy Robustelli | | 25.00 | 10.00 | 2.50 |
| New York Giants | | | | |
| ☐ 68 Joe Rutgens | | 15.00 | 6.00 | 1.50 |
| Washington Redskins | | | | |
| ☐ 69 Bob St. Clair | | 25.00 | 10.00 | 2.50 |
| San Francisco 49ers | | | | |
| ☐ 70 John Sample | | 18.00 | 7.25 | 1.80 |
| Washington Redskins | | | | |
| ☐ 71 Lonnie Sanders | | 15.00 | 6.00 | 1.50 |
| Washington Redskins | | | | |
| ☐ 72 Dick Schafrath | | 15.00 | 6.00 | 1.50 |
| Cleveland Browns | | | | |
| ☐ 73 Joe Schmidt | | 30.00 | 12.00 | 3.00 |
| Detroit Lions | | | | |
| ☐ 74 Del Shofner | | 20.00 | 8.00 | 2.00 |
| New York Giants | | | | |
| ☐ 75 J.D. Smith | | 15.00 | 6.00 | 1.50 |

| | | | | |
|---|---|---|---|---|
| San Francisco 49ers | | | | |
| ☐ 76 Norm Snead | | 20.00 | 8.00 | 2.00 |
| Washington Redskins | | | | |
| ☐ 77 Bill Stacy | | 15.00 | 6.00 | 1.50 |
| St. Louis Cardinals | | | | |
| ☐ 78 Bart Starr | | 50.00 | 20.00 | 5.00 |
| Green Bay Packers | | | | |
| ☐ 79 Ernie Stautner | | 30.00 | 12.00 | 3.00 |
| Pittsburgh Steelers | | | | |
| ☐ 80 Jim Steffen | | 15.00 | 6.00 | 1.50 |
| Washington Redskins | | | | |
| ☐ 81 Andy Stynchula | | 15.00 | 6.00 | 1.50 |
| Washington Redskins | | | | |
| ☐ 82 Fran Tarkenton | | 100.00 | 40.00 | 10.00 |
| Minnesota Vikings | | | | |
| ☐ 83 Jim Taylor | | 35.00 | 14.00 | 3.50 |
| Green Bay Packers | | | | |
| ☐ 84 Clendon Thomas | | 15.00 | 6.00 | 1.50 |
| Pittsburgh Steelers | | | | |
| ☐ 85 Fred(Fuzzy) Thurston | | 20.00 | 8.00 | 2.00 |
| Green Bay Packers | | | | |
| ☐ 86 Y.A. Tittle | | 50.00 | 20.00 | 5.00 |
| New York Giants | | | | |
| ☐ 87 Bob Toneff | | 15.00 | 6.00 | 1.50 |
| Washington Redskins | | | | |
| ☐ 88 Jerry Tubbs | | 18.00 | 7.25 | 1.80 |
| Dallas Cowboys | | | | |
| ☐ 89 John Unitas | | 100.00 | 40.00 | 10.00 |
| Baltimore Colts | | | | |
| ☐ 90 Billy Wade | | 18.00 | 7.25 | 1.80 |
| Chicago Bears | | | | |
| ☐ 91 Willie Wood | | 25.00 | 10.00 | 2.50 |
| Green Bay Packers | | | | |
| ☐ 92 Abe Woodson | | 18.00 | 7.25 | 1.80 |
| San Francisco 49ers | | | | |

## 1964 Kahn's

The 1964 Kahn's football card set of 53 is the only Kahn's football card set in full color. It is also the only set which does not contain the statement "Compliments of Kahn's, the Wiener the World Awaited" on the obverse. This slogan is contained on the back of the card which also contains player data similar to cards of other years. The cards measure approximately 3" by 3 5/8". The cards are unnumbered and hence are listed below alphabetically for convenience. Paul Warfield's card holds special interest in that it was issued very early in his career.

| | NRMT | VG-E | GOOD |
|---|---|---|---|
| COMPLETE SET (53) | 1350.00 | 600.00 | 150.00 |
| COMMON PLAYER (1-53) | 15.00 | 6.00 | 1.50 |
| | | | |
| ☐ 1 Doug Atkins | 25.00 | 10.00 | 2.50 |
| Chicago Bears | | | |
| ☐ 2 Terry Barr | 15.00 | 6.00 | 1.50 |
| Detroit Lions | | | |
| ☐ 3 Dick Bass | 18.00 | 7.25 | 1.80 |
| Los Angeles Rams | | | |
| ☐ 4 Ordell Braase | 15.00 | 6.00 | 1.50 |
| Baltimore Colts | | | |
| ☐ 5 Ed Brown | 18.00 | 7.25 | 1.80 |
| Pittsburgh Steelers | | | |
| ☐ 6 Jimmy Brown | 150.00 | 60.00 | 15.00 |
| Cleveland Browns | | | |
| ☐ 7 Gary Collins | 18.00 | 7.25 | 1.80 |
| Cleveland Browns | | | |
| ☐ 8 Bobby Joe Conrad | 18.00 | 7.25 | 1.80 |
| St. Louis Cardinals | | | |
| ☐ 9 Mike Ditka | 45.00 | 18.00 | 4.50 |
| Chicago Bears | | | |
| ☐ 10 Galen Fiss | 15.00 | 6.00 | 1.50 |
| Cleveland Browns | | | |
| ☐ 11 Paul Flatley | 18.00 | 7.25 | 1.80 |
| Minnesota Vikings | | | |
| ☐ 12 Joe Fortunato | 18.00 | 7.25 | 1.80 |
| Chicago Bears | | | |
| ☐ 13 Bill George | 25.00 | 10.00 | 2.50 |
| Chicago Bears | | | |

| | | | |
|---|---|---|---|
| ☐ 14 Bill Glass<br>Cleveland Browns | 18.00 | 7.25 | 1.80 |
| ☐ 15 Ernie Green<br>Cleveland Browns | 18.00 | 7.25 | 1.80 |
| ☐ 16 Dick Hoak<br>Pittsburgh Steelers | 15.00 | 6.00 | 1.50 |
| ☐ 17 Paul Hornung<br>Green Bay Packers | 45.00 | 18.00 | 4.50 |
| ☐ 18 Sam Huff<br>Washington Redskins | 30.00 | 12.00 | 3.00 |
| ☐ 19 Charlie Johnson<br>St. Louis Cardinals | 20.00 | 8.00 | 2.00 |
| ☐ 20 John Henry Johnson<br>Pittsburgh Steelers | 25.00 | 10.00 | 2.50 |
| ☐ 21 Alex Karras<br>Detroit Lions | 35.00 | 14.00 | 3.50 |
| ☐ 22 Jim Katcavage<br>New York Giants | 18.00 | 7.25 | 1.80 |
| ☐ 23 Joe Krupa<br>Pittsburgh Steelers | 15.00 | 6.00 | 1.50 |
| ☐ 24 Dick Lane<br>Detroit Lions | 25.00 | 10.00 | 2.50 |
| ☐ 25 Tommy Mason<br>Minnesota Vikings | 18.00 | 7.25 | 1.80 |
| ☐ 26 Don Meredith<br>Dallas Cowboys | 60.00 | 24.00 | 6.00 |
| ☐ 27 Bobby Mitchell<br>Washington Redskins | 30.00 | 12.00 | 3.00 |
| ☐ 28 Larry Morris<br>Chicago Bears | 15.00 | 6.00 | 1.50 |
| ☐ 29 Jimmy Orr<br>Baltimore Colts | 18.00 | 7.25 | 1.80 |
| ☐ 30 Jim Parker<br>Baltimore Colts | 25.00 | 10.00 | 2.50 |
| ☐ 31 Bernie Parrish<br>Cleveland Browns | 18.00 | 7.25 | 1.80 |
| ☐ 32 Don Perkins<br>Dallas Cowboys | 18.00 | 7.25 | 1.80 |
| ☐ 33 Jim Phillips<br>Los Angeles Rams | 15.00 | 6.00 | 1.50 |
| ☐ 34 Sonny Randle<br>St. Louis Cardinals | 18.00 | 7.25 | 1.80 |
| ☐ 35 Pete Retzlaff<br>Philadelphia Eagles | 18.00 | 7.25 | 1.80 |
| ☐ 36 Jim Ringo<br>Philadelphia Eagles | 25.00 | 10.00 | 2.50 |
| ☐ 37 Frank Ryan<br>Cleveland Browns | 20.00 | 8.00 | 2.00 |
| ☐ 38 Dick Schafrath<br>Cleveland Browns | 18.00 | 7.25 | 1.80 |
| ☐ 39 Joe Schmidt<br>Detroit Lions | 25.00 | 10.00 | 2.50 |
| ☐ 40 Del Shofner<br>New York Giants | 18.00 | 7.25 | 1.80 |
| ☐ 41 J.D. Smith<br>San Francisco 49ers | 15.00 | 6.00 | 1.50 |
| ☐ 42 Norm Snead<br>Philadelphia Eagles | 18.00 | 7.25 | 1.80 |
| ☐ 43 Bart Starr<br>Green Bay Packers | 45.00 | 18.00 | 4.50 |
| ☐ 44 Fran Tarkenton<br>Minnesota Vikings | 75.00 | 30.00 | 7.50 |
| ☐ 45 Jim Taylor<br>Green Bay Packers | 30.00 | 12.00 | 3.00 |
| ☐ 46 Clendon Thomas<br>Pittsburgh Steelers | 15.00 | 6.00 | 1.50 |
| ☐ 47 Y.A. Tittle<br>New York Giants | 45.00 | 18.00 | 4.50 |
| ☐ 48 Jerry Tubbs<br>Dallas Cowboys | 18.00 | 7.25 | 1.80 |
| ☐ 49 John Unitas<br>Baltimore Colts | 75.00 | 30.00 | 7.50 |
| ☐ 50 Billy Wade<br>Chicago Bears | 18.00 | 7.25 | 1.80 |
| ☐ 51 Paul Warfield<br>Cleveland Browns | 60.00 | 24.00 | 6.00 |
| ☐ 52 Alex Webster<br>New York Giants | 18.00 | 7.25 | 1.80 |
| ☐ 53 Abe Woodson<br>San Francisco 49ers | 15.00 | 6.00 | 1.50 |

## 1970 Kellogg's

The 1970 Kellogg's football set of 60 cards was Kellogg's first football issue. The cards have a 3D effect and are approximately 2 1/4" by 3 1/2". The cards could be obtained from boxes of cereal or as a set from a box top offer. The 1970 Kellogg's set can easily be distinguished from the 1971 Kellogg's set by recognizing the color of the helmet logo on the front of each card. In the 1970 set this helmet logo is blue, whereas with the 1971 set the helmet logo is red. The 1971 set also is distinguished by its thick blue (with white spots) border on each card front as well as by the small inset photo in the upper left corner of each reverse. The key card in the set is O.J. Simpson as 1970 was O.J.'s rookie year for cards.

| | NRMT | VG-E | GOOD |
|---|---|---|---|
| COMPLETE SET (60) | 75.00 | 30.00 | 7.50 |
| COMMON PLAYER (1-60) | .50 | .20 | .05 |
| ☐ 1 Carl Eller<br>Minnesota Vikings | 1.50 | .60 | .15 |
| ☐ 2 Jim Otto<br>Oakland Raiders | 1.50 | .60 | .15 |
| ☐ 3 Tom Matte<br>Baltimore Colts | .75 | .30 | .07 |
| ☐ 4 Bill Nelsen<br>Cleveland Browns | .60 | .24 | .06 |
| ☐ 5 Travis Williams<br>Green Bay Packers | .50 | .20 | .05 |
| ☐ 6 Len Dawson<br>Kansas City Chiefs | 2.50 | 1.00 | .25 |
| ☐ 7 Gene Washington<br>Minnesota Vikings | .75 | .30 | .07 |
| ☐ 8 Jim Nance<br>Boston Patriots | .60 | .24 | .06 |
| ☐ 9 Norm Snead<br>Philadelphia Eagles | .75 | .30 | .07 |
| ☐ 10 Dick Butkus<br>Chicago Bears | 5.00 | 2.00 | .50 |
| ☐ 11 George Sauer Jr.<br>New York Jets | .60 | .24 | .06 |
| ☐ 12 Bill Kilmer<br>New Orleans Saints | .75 | .30 | .07 |
| ☐ 13 Alex Karras<br>Detroit Lions | 2.00 | .80 | .20 |
| ☐ 14 Larry Wilson<br>St. Louis Cardinals | 1.50 | .60 | .15 |
| ☐ 15 Dave Robinson<br>Green Bay Packers | .60 | .24 | .06 |
| ☐ 16 Bill Brown<br>Minnesota Vikings | .60 | .24 | .06 |
| ☐ 17 Bob Griese<br>Miami Dolphins | 5.00 | 2.00 | .50 |
| ☐ 18 Al Denson<br>Denver Broncos | .50 | .20 | .05 |
| ☐ 19 Dick Post<br>San Diego Chargers | .50 | .20 | .05 |
| ☐ 20 Jan Stenerud<br>Kansas City Chiefs | 1.50 | .60 | .15 |
| ☐ 21 Paul Warfield<br>Miami Dolphins | 2.50 | 1.00 | .25 |
| ☐ 22 Mel Farr<br>Detroit Lions | .60 | .24 | .06 |
| ☐ 23 Mel Renfro<br>Dallas Cowboys | .75 | .30 | .07 |
| ☐ 24 Roy Jefferson<br>Pittsburgh Steelers | .60 | .24 | .06 |
| ☐ 25 Mike Garrett<br>Kansas City Chiefs | .60 | .24 | .06 |
| ☐ 26 Harry Jacobs<br>Buffalo Bills | .50 | .20 | .05 |
| ☐ 27 Carl Garrett<br>Boston Patriots | .50 | .20 | .05 |
| ☐ 28 Dave Wilcox<br>San Francisco 49ers | .60 | .24 | .06 |
| ☐ 29 Matt Snell<br>New York Jets | .75 | .30 | .07 |
| ☐ 30 Tom Woodeshick<br>Philadelphia Eagles | .50 | .20 | .05 |
| ☐ 31 Leroy Kelly<br>Cleveland Browns | 1.50 | .60 | .15 |
| ☐ 32 Floyd Little<br>Denver Broncos | 1.00 | .40 | .10 |
| ☐ 33 Ken Willard<br>San Francisco 49ers | .75 | .30 | .07 |
| ☐ 34 John Mackey<br>Baltimore Colts | 1.50 | .60 | .15 |
| ☐ 35 Merlin Olsen<br>Los Angeles Rams | 4.00 | 1.60 | .40 |
| ☐ 36 Dave Grayson<br>Oakland Raiders | .50 | .20 | .05 |
| ☐ 37 Lem Barney<br>Detroit Lions | 2.50 | 1.00 | .25 |

| | | NRMT | VG-E | GOOD |
|---|---|---|---|---|
| ☐ 38 | Deacon Jones | 1.50 | .60 | .15 |
| | Los Angeles Rams | | | |
| ☐ 39 | Bob Hayes | 1.00 | .40 | .10 |
| | Dallas Cowboys | | | |
| ☐ 40 | Lance Alworth | 2.50 | 1.00 | .25 |
| | San Diego Chargers | | | |
| ☐ 41 | Larry Csonka | 4.00 | 1.60 | .40 |
| | Miami Dolphins | | | |
| ☐ 42 | Bobby Bell | 1.50 | .60 | .15 |
| | Kansas City Chiefs | | | |
| ☐ 43 | George Webster | .60 | .24 | .06 |
| | Houston Oilers | | | |
| ☐ 44 | Johnny Roland | .60 | .24 | .06 |
| | St. Louis Cardinals | | | |
| ☐ 45 | Dick Shiner | .50 | .20 | .05 |
| | Pittsburgh Steelers | | | |
| ☐ 46 | Bubba Smith | 2.50 | 1.00 | .25 |
| | Baltimore Colts | | | |
| ☐ 47 | Daryle Lamonica | 1.00 | .40 | .10 |
| | Oakland Raiders | | | |
| ☐ 48 | O.J. Simpson | 40.00 | 16.00 | 4.00 |
| | Buffalo Bills | | | |
| ☐ 49 | Calvin Hill | 1.25 | .50 | .12 |
| | Dallas Cowboys | | | |
| ☐ 50 | Fred Biletnikoff | 2.00 | .80 | .20 |
| | Oakland Raiders | | | |
| ☐ 51 | Gale Sayers | 6.00 | 2.40 | .60 |
| | Chicago Bears | | | |
| ☐ 52 | Homer Jones | .50 | .20 | .05 |
| | Cleveland Browns | | | |
| ☐ 53 | Sonny Jurgensen | 3.00 | 1.20 | .30 |
| | Washington Redskins | | | |
| ☐ 54 | Bob Lilly | 2.50 | 1.00 | .25 |
| | Dallas Cowboys | | | |
| ☐ 55 | John Unitas | 7.50 | 3.00 | .75 |
| | Baltimore Colts | | | |
| ☐ 56 | Tommy Nobis | 1.25 | .50 | .12 |
| | Atlanta Falcons | | | |
| ☐ 57 | Ed Meador | .50 | .20 | .05 |
| | Los Angeles Rams | | | |
| ☐ 58 | Spider Lockhart | .60 | .24 | .06 |
| | New York Giants | | | |
| ☐ 59 | Don Maynard | 1.50 | .60 | .15 |
| | New York Jets | | | |
| ☐ 60 | Greg Cook | .60 | .24 | .06 |
| | Cincinnati Bengals | | | |

# 1971 Kellogg's

The 1971 Kellogg's set of 60 cards could be obtained only from boxes of cereal. One card was inserted in each specially marked box of Kellogg's Corn Flakes and Kellogg's Raisin Bran cereals. The cards measure approximately 2 1/4" by 3 1/2". This set is much more difficult to obtain than the previous Kellogg's set since no box top offer was available. The 1971 Kellogg's set can easily be distinguished from the 1970 Kellogg's set by recognizing the color of the helmet logo on the front of each card. In the 1970 set this helmet logo is blue, whereas with the 1971 set the helmet logo is red. The 1971 set also is distinguished by its thick blue (with white spots) border on each card front as well as by the small inset photo in the uppper left corner of each reverse. Among the key cards in the set is Joe Greene as 1971 was "Mean" Joe's rookie year for cards.

| | | NRMT | VG-E | GOOD |
|---|---|---|---|---|
| | COMPLETE SET (60) | 350.00 | 140.00 | 35.00 |
| | COMMON PLAYER (1-60) | 5.00 | 2.00 | .50 |
| ☐ 1 | Tom Barrington | 5.00 | 2.00 | .50 |
| | New Orleans Saints | | | |
| ☐ 2 | Chris Hanburger | 6.00 | 2.40 | .60 |
| | Washington Redskins | | | |
| ☐ 3 | Frank Nunley | 5.00 | 2.00 | .50 |
| | San Francisco 49ers | | | |
| ☐ 4 | Houston Antwine | 5.00 | 2.00 | .50 |
| | Boston Patriots | | | |

| | | NRMT | VG-E | GOOD |
|---|---|---|---|---|
| ☐ 5 | Ron Johnson | 6.00 | 2.40 | .60 |
| | New York Giants | | | |
| ☐ 6 | Craig Morton | 7.50 | 3.00 | .75 |
| | Dallas Cowboys | | | |
| ☐ 7 | Jack Snow | 6.00 | 2.40 | .60 |
| | Los Angeles Rams | | | |
| ☐ 8 | Mel Renfro | 7.50 | 3.00 | .75 |
| | Dallas Cowboys | | | |
| ☐ 9 | Les Josephson | 5.00 | 2.00 | .50 |
| | Los Angeles Rams | | | |
| ☐ 10 | Gary Garrison | 5.00 | 2.00 | .50 |
| | San Diego Chargers | | | |
| ☐ 11 | Dave Herman | 5.00 | 2.00 | .50 |
| | New York Jets | | | |
| ☐ 12 | Fred Dryer | 7.50 | 3.00 | .75 |
| | New York Giants | | | |
| ☐ 13 | Larry Brown | 7.50 | 3.00 | .75 |
| | Washington Redskins | | | |
| ☐ 14 | Gene Washington | 6.00 | 2.40 | .60 |
| | San Francisco 49ers | | | |
| ☐ 15 | Joe Greene | 30.00 | 12.00 | 3.00 |
| | Pittsburgh Steelers | | | |
| ☐ 16 | Marlin Briscoe | 6.00 | 2.40 | .60 |
| | Buffalo Bills | | | |
| ☐ 17 | Bob Grant | 5.00 | 2.00 | .50 |
| | Baltimore Colts | | | |
| ☐ 18 | Dan Conners | 5.00 | 2.00 | .50 |
| | Oakland Raiders | | | |
| ☐ 19 | Mike Curtis | 6.00 | 2.40 | .60 |
| | Baltimore Colts | | | |
| ☐ 20 | Harry Schuh | 5.00 | 2.00 | .50 |
| | Dallas Cowboys | | | |
| ☐ 21 | Rich Jackson | 5.00 | 2.00 | .50 |
| | Denver Broncos | | | |
| ☐ 22 | Clint Jones | 5.00 | 2.00 | .50 |
| | Minnesota Vikings | | | |
| ☐ 23 | Hewritt Dixon | 5.00 | 2.00 | .50 |
| | Oakland Raiders | | | |
| ☐ 24 | Jess Phillips | 5.00 | 2.00 | .50 |
| | Cincinnati Bengals | | | |
| ☐ 25 | Gary Cuozzo | 5.00 | 2.00 | .50 |
| | Minnesota Vikings | | | |
| ☐ 26 | Bo Scott | 5.00 | 2.00 | .50 |
| | Cleveland Browns | | | |
| ☐ 27 | Glen Ray Hines | 5.00 | 2.00 | .50 |
| | Houston Oilers | | | |
| ☐ 28 | John Unitas | 30.00 | 12.00 | 3.00 |
| | Baltimore Colts | | | |
| ☐ 29 | John Gilliam | 5.00 | 2.00 | .50 |
| | St. Louis Cardinals | | | |
| ☐ 30 | Harmon Wages | 5.00 | 2.00 | .50 |
| | Atlanta Falcons | | | |
| ☐ 31 | Walt Sweeney | 5.00 | 2.00 | .50 |
| | San Diego Chargers | | | |
| ☐ 32 | Bruce Taylor | 6.00 | 2.40 | .60 |
| | San Francisco 49ers | | | |
| ☐ 33 | George Blanda | 20.00 | 8.00 | 2.00 |
| | Oakland Raiders | | | |
| ☐ 34 | Ken Bowman | 5.00 | 2.00 | .50 |
| | Green Bay Packers | | | |
| ☐ 35 | Johnny Robinson | 6.00 | 2.40 | .60 |
| | Kansas City Chiefs | | | |
| ☐ 36 | Ed Podolak | 6.00 | 2.40 | .60 |
| | Kansas City Chiefs | | | |
| ☐ 37 | Curley Culp | 6.00 | 2.40 | .60 |
| | Kansas City Chiefs | | | |
| ☐ 38 | Jim Hart | 7.50 | 3.00 | .75 |
| | St. Louis Cardinals | | | |
| ☐ 39 | Dick Butkus | 20.00 | 8.00 | 2.00 |
| | Chicago Bears | | | |
| ☐ 40 | Floyd Little | 7.50 | 3.00 | .75 |
| | Denver Broncos | | | |
| ☐ 41 | Nick Buoniconti | 9.00 | 3.75 | .90 |
| | Miami Dolphins | | | |
| ☐ 42 | Larry Smith | 5.00 | 2.00 | .50 |
| | Los Angeles Rams | | | |
| ☐ 43 | Wayne Walker | 6.00 | 2.40 | .60 |
| | Detroit Lions | | | |
| ☐ 44 | MacArthur Lane | 6.00 | 2.40 | .60 |
| | St. Louis Cardinals | | | |
| ☐ 45 | John Brodie | 15.00 | 6.00 | 1.50 |
| | San Francisco 49ers | | | |
| ☐ 46 | Dick LeBeau | 5.00 | 2.00 | .50 |
| | Detroit Lions | | | |
| ☐ 47 | Claude Humphrey | 5.00 | 2.00 | .50 |
| | Atlanta Falcons | | | |
| ☐ 48 | Jerry LeVias | 5.00 | 2.00 | .50 |
| | Houston Oilers | | | |
| ☐ 49 | Erich Barnes | 5.00 | 2.00 | .50 |
| | Cleveland Browns | | | |
| ☐ 50 | Andy Russell | 6.00 | 2.40 | .60 |
| | Pittsburgh Steelers | | | |
| ☐ 51 | Donny Anderson | 6.00 | 2.40 | .60 |
| | Green Bay Packers | | | |
| ☐ 52 | Mike Reid | 7.50 | 3.00 | .75 |
| | Cincinnati Bengals | | | |
| ☐ 53 | Al Atkinson | 5.00 | 2.00 | .50 |
| | New York Jets | | | |

| | | | | |
|---|---|---|---|---|
| ☐ 54 Tom Dempsey | | 6.00 | 2.40 | .60 |
| New Orleans Saints | | | | |
| ☐ 55 Bob Griese | | 20.00 | 8.00 | 2.00 |
| Miami Dolphins | | | | |
| ☐ 56 Dick Gordon | | 5.00 | 2.00 | .50 |
| Chicago Bears | | | | |
| ☐ 57 Charlie Sanders | | 6.00 | 2.40 | .60 |
| Detroit Lions | | | | |
| ☐ 58 Doug Cunningham | | 5.00 | 2.00 | .50 |
| San Francisco 49ers | | | | |
| ☐ 59 Cyril Pinder | | 5.00 | 2.00 | .50 |
| Philadelphia Eagles | | | | |
| ☐ 60 Dave Osborn | | 6.00 | 2.40 | .60 |
| Minnesota Vikings | | | | |

| | | | | |
|---|---|---|---|---|
| ☐ 7 Harvey Martin UER | | 1.00 | .40 | .10 |
| Dallas Cowboys | | | | |
| (Photo actually | | | | |
| Billy Joe DuPree) | | | | |
| Mike Pruitt | | | | |
| Cleveland Browns | | | | |
| Joe Senser | | | | |
| Minnesota Vikings | | | | |
| ☐ 8 Art Still | | 1.00 | .40 | .10 |
| Kansas City Chiefs | | | | |
| Mel Gray | | | | |
| St. Louis Cardinals | | | | |
| Tommy Kramer | | | | |
| Minnesota Vikings | | | | |

## 1982 Kellogg's Panels

 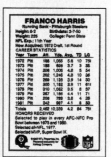

The 1982 Kellogg's National Football League set of 24 cards was issued in eight panels of three cards each. The cards measure 2 1/2" by 3 1/2" and the panels are approximately 4 1/8" by 7 1/2". The cards came with Kellogg's Raisin Bran cereal and contain statistics on the back. Cards are in color and contain the Kellogg's logo in the lower right corner of the front of the card. While not numbered, the cards have been listed in the checklist below alphabetically according to the left hand side player, when the panel is viewed from the front. Prices below are for full panels of three. It is possible (but not recommended) to separate the cards at the perforation marks. No value for individual cards is given. Sharp-eyed Cowboy fans will notice that the photos for Harvey Martin and Billy Joe DuPree were erroneously switched.

| | MINT | EXC | G-VG |
|---|---|---|---|
| COMPLETE SET (8) | 7.50 | 3.00 | .75 |
| COMMON PANEL (1-8) | 1.00 | .40 | .10 |
| | | | |
| ☐ 1 Ken Anderson | 1.25 | .50 | .12 |
| Cincinnati Bengals | | | |
| Frank Lewis | | | |
| Buffalo Bills | | | |
| Gifford Nielsen | | | |
| Houston Oilers | | | |
| ☐ 2 Ottis Anderson | 2.50 | 1.00 | .25 |
| St. Louis Cardinals | | | |
| Cris Collinsworth | | | |
| Cincinnati Bengals | | | |
| Franco Harris | | | |
| Pittsburgh Steelers | | | |
| ☐ 3 William Andrews | 1.00 | .40 | .10 |
| Atlanta Falcons | | | |
| Brian Sipe | | | |
| Cleveland Browns | | | |
| Fred Smerlas | | | |
| Buffalo Bills | | | |
| ☐ 4 Steve Bartkowski | 1.00 | .40 | .10 |
| Atlanta Falcons | | | |
| Robert Brazile | | | |
| Houston Oilers | | | |
| Jack Rudnay | | | |
| Kansas City Chiefs | | | |
| ☐ 5 Tony Dorsett | 1.50 | .60 | .15 |
| Dallas Cowboys | | | |
| Eric Hipple | | | |
| Detroit Lions | | | |
| Pat McInally | | | |
| Cincinnati Bengals | | | |
| ☐ 6 Billy Joe DuPree UER | 1.25 | .50 | .12 |
| Dallas Cowboys | | | |
| (Photo actually | | | |
| Harvey Martin) | | | |
| David Hill | | | |
| Detroit Lions | | | |
| John Stallworth | | | |
| Pittsburgh Steelers | | | |

## 1982 Kellogg's Teams

These 28 NFL team posters were inserted in specially marked boxes of Kellogg's Raisin Bran cereal. Each poster measures approximately 8" by 10 1/2" and is printed on thin paper stock. Inside a thin black border, the fronts feature a color painting of an action scene, with a smaller painting of another scene placed over to the side. The team name appears inside a bar at the bottom of the picture. The back carries the official contest rules and an entry form for the Kellogg's "Raisin Bran Super Bowl Sweepstakes". If the team pictured on the poster was the winning team in the 1983 Super Bowl, the collector was to print his name and address on the entry form and mail in the entire poster so that it would be received between January 30 and March 19, 1983. From the entries, the winners would be selected in a random drawing to receive one of four trips for two to the 1984 Super Bowl (1st prize) or one of 500 Spalding leather footballs (2nd prize). The posters are unnumbered and checklisted below alphabetically according to the team's city name. The NFL properties logo is prominently displayed on the card front. The posters are typically found with fold marks as they were folded into three parts both horizontally and vertically. The posters are copyrighted 1982 on the front. No players are explicitly identified on the cards. The poster backs are printed in light blue ink.

| | MINT | EXC | G-VG |
|---|---|---|---|
| COMPLETE SET (28) | 75.00 | 30.00 | 7.50 |
| COMMON TEAM (1-28) | 4.00 | 1.60 | .40 |
| | | | |
| ☐ 1 Atlanta Falcons | 4.00 | 1.60 | .40 |
| ☐ 2 Buffalo Bills | 4.00 | 1.60 | .40 |
| ☐ 3 Chicago Bears | 4.00 | 1.60 | .40 |
| ☐ 4 Cincinnati Bengals | 4.00 | 1.60 | .40 |
| ☐ 5 Cleveland Browns | 4.00 | 1.60 | .40 |
| ☐ 6 Dallas Cowboys | 5.00 | 2.00 | .50 |
| ☐ 7 Denver Broncos | 4.00 | 1.60 | .40 |
| ☐ 8 Detroit Lions | 4.00 | 1.60 | .40 |
| ☐ 9 Green Bay Packers | 4.00 | 1.60 | .40 |
| ☐ 10 Houston Oilers | 4.00 | 1.60 | .40 |
| ☐ 11 Indianapolis Colts | 4.00 | 1.60 | .40 |
| ☐ 12 Kansas City Chiefs | 4.00 | 1.60 | .40 |
| ☐ 13 Los Angeles Raiders | 5.00 | 2.00 | .50 |
| ☐ 14 Los Angeles Rams | 4.00 | 1.60 | .40 |
| ☐ 15 Miami Dolphins | 4.00 | 1.60 | .40 |
| ☐ 16 Minnesota Vikings | 4.00 | 1.60 | .40 |
| ☐ 17 New England Patriots | 4.00 | 1.60 | .40 |
| ☐ 18 New Orleans Saints | 4.00 | 1.60 | .40 |
| ☐ 19 New York Giants | 4.00 | 1.60 | .40 |
| ☐ 20 New York Jets | 4.00 | 1.60 | .40 |
| ☐ 21 Philadelphia Eagles | 4.00 | 1.60 | .40 |
| ☐ 22 Pittsburgh Steelers | 4.00 | 1.60 | .40 |
| ☐ 23 St. Louis Cardinals | 4.00 | 1.60 | .40 |
| ☐ 24 San Diego Chargers | 4.00 | 1.60 | .40 |
| ☐ 25 San Francisco 49ers | 4.00 | 1.60 | .40 |
| ☐ 26 Seattle Seahawks | 4.00 | 1.60 | .40 |
| ☐ 27 Tampa Bay Buccaneers | 4.00 | 1.60 | .40 |
| ☐ 28 Washington Redskins | 4.00 | 1.60 | .40 |

## 1989 King B Discs

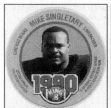 

The 1989 King B Football Discs set has 24 red-bordered 2 3/8″ diameter round discs. The fronts have helmetless color mug shots; the backs are white and have sparse bio and stats. One disc was included in each specially marked can of King B beef jerky. The discs are numbered on the back. The set is arranged alphabetically by teams, one player per team, with only 24 of the 28 NFL teams represented. The set, which was produced by Michael Schechter Associates, was apparently endorsed only by the NFLPA. There are many quarterbacks included in the set. The discs are referred to as "1st Annual Collectors Edition."

|  | MINT | EXC | G-VG |
|---|---|---|---|
| COMPLETE SET (24) | 45.00 | 18.00 | 4.50 |
| COMMON PLAYER (1-24) | 1.25 | .50 | .12 |
| ☐ 1 Chris Miller | 3.00 | 1.20 | .30 |
| Atlanta Falcons |  |  |  |
| ☐ 2 Shane Conlan | 1.50 | .60 | .15 |
| Buffalo Bills |  |  |  |
| ☐ 3 Richard Dent | 1.50 | .60 | .15 |
| Chicago Bears |  |  |  |
| ☐ 4 Boomer Esiason | 2.00 | .80 | .20 |
| Cincinnati Bengals |  |  |  |
| ☐ 5 Frank Minnifield | 1.25 | .50 | .12 |
| Cleveland Browns |  |  |  |
| ☐ 6 Herschel Walker | 2.00 | .80 | .20 |
| Dallas Cowboys |  |  |  |
| ☐ 7 Karl Mecklenburg | 1.50 | .60 | .15 |
| Denver Broncos |  |  |  |
| ☐ 8 Mike Cofer | 1.25 | .50 | .12 |
| Detroit Lions |  |  |  |
| ☐ 9 Warren Moon | 3.00 | 1.20 | .30 |
| Houston Oilers |  |  |  |
| ☐ 10 Chris Chandler | 1.50 | .60 | .15 |
| Indianapolis Colts |  |  |  |
| ☐ 11 Deron Cherry | 1.25 | .50 | .12 |
| Kansas City Chiefs |  |  |  |
| ☐ 12 Bo Jackson | 2.50 | 1.00 | .25 |
| Los Angeles Raiders |  |  |  |
| ☐ 13 Jim Everett | 1.50 | .60 | .15 |
| Los Angeles Rams |  |  |  |
| ☐ 14 Dan Marino | 9.00 | 3.75 | .90 |
| Miami Dolphins |  |  |  |
| ☐ 15 Anthony Carter | 1.50 | .60 | .15 |
| Minnesota Vikings |  |  |  |
| ☐ 16 Andre Tippett | 1.50 | .60 | .15 |
| New England Patriots |  |  |  |
| ☐ 17 Bobby Hebert | 1.50 | .60 | .15 |
| New Orleans Saints |  |  |  |
| ☐ 18 Phil Simms | 2.00 | .80 | .20 |
| New York Giants |  |  |  |
| ☐ 19 Al Toon | 1.50 | .60 | .15 |
| New York Jets |  |  |  |
| ☐ 20 Gary Anderson | 1.50 | .60 | .15 |
| San Diego Chargers |  |  |  |
| ☐ 21 Joe Montana | 12.00 | 5.00 | 1.20 |
| San Francisco 49ers |  |  |  |
| ☐ 22 Dave Krieg | 1.50 | .60 | .15 |
| Seattle Seahawks |  |  |  |
| ☐ 23 Randall Cunningham | 3.00 | 1.20 | .30 |
| Philadelphia Eagles |  |  |  |
| ☐ 24 Bubby Brister | 1.25 | .50 | .12 |
| Pittsburgh Steelers |  |  |  |

## 1990 King B Discs

The 1990 King B Discs set contains 24 discs each measuring approximately 2 3/8″ in diameter. The fronts have color head shots of the players (without helmets), encircled by a red border on a yellow background. The year "1990" in green block lettering and a King B football icon overlay the bottom of the picture. On the backs, the biographical and statistical information is encircled by a ring of stars. The discs are numbered on the back. The style of the set is very similar to the previous year.

|  | MINT | EXC | G-VG |
|---|---|---|---|
| COMPLETE SET (24) | 40.00 | 16.00 | 4.00 |
| COMMON PLAYER (1-24) | 1.25 | .50 | .12 |
| ☐ 1 Jim Everett | 1.50 | .60 | .15 |
| Los Angeles Rams |  |  |  |
| ☐ 2 Marcus Allen | 2.00 | .80 | .20 |
| Los Angeles Raiders |  |  |  |
| ☐ 3 Brian Blades | 1.50 | .60 | .15 |
| Seattle Seahawks |  |  |  |
| ☐ 4 Bubby Brister | 1.25 | .50 | .12 |
| Pittsburgh Steelers |  |  |  |
| ☐ 5 Mark Carrier | 1.50 | .60 | .15 |
| Tampa Bay Buccaneers |  |  |  |
| ☐ 6 Steve Jordan | 1.25 | .50 | .12 |
| Minnesota Vikings |  |  |  |
| ☐ 7 Barry Sanders | 6.00 | 2.40 | .60 |
| Detroit Lions |  |  |  |
| ☐ 8 Ronnie Lott | 2.00 | .80 | .20 |
| San Francisco 49ers |  |  |  |
| ☐ 9 Howie Long | 1.50 | .60 | .15 |
| Los Angeles Raiders |  |  |  |
| ☐ 10 Steve Atwater | 1.50 | .60 | .15 |
| Denver Broncos |  |  |  |
| ☐ 11 Dan Marino | 6.00 | 2.40 | .60 |
| Miami Dolphins |  |  |  |
| ☐ 12 Boomer Esiason | 2.00 | .80 | .20 |
| Cincinnati Bengals |  |  |  |
| ☐ 13 Dalton Hilliard | 1.25 | .50 | .12 |
| New Orleans Saints |  |  |  |
| ☐ 14 Phil Simms | 2.00 | .80 | .20 |
| New York Giants |  |  |  |
| ☐ 15 Jim Kelly | 3.00 | 1.20 | .30 |
| Buffalo Bills |  |  |  |
| ☐ 16 Mike Singletary | 1.50 | .60 | .15 |
| Chicago Bears |  |  |  |
| ☐ 17 John Stephens | 2.00 | .80 | .20 |
| New England Patriots |  |  |  |
| ☐ 18 Christian Okoye | 1.50 | .60 | .15 |
| Kansas City Chiefs |  |  |  |
| ☐ 19 Art Monk | 2.00 | .80 | .20 |
| Washington Redskins |  |  |  |
| ☐ 20 Chris Miller | 2.00 | .80 | .20 |
| Atlanta Falcons |  |  |  |
| ☐ 21 Roger Craig | 2.00 | .80 | .20 |
| San Francisco 49ers |  |  |  |
| ☐ 22 Duane Bickett | 1.25 | .50 | .12 |
| Indianapolis Colts |  |  |  |
| ☐ 23 Don Majkowski | 1.25 | .50 | .12 |
| Green Bay Packers |  |  |  |
| ☐ 24 Eric Metcalf | 2.00 | .80 | .20 |
| Cleveland Browns |  |  |  |

## 1991 King B Discs

This set of 24 discs was produced by Michael Schechter Associates, and each one measures approximately 2 5/8″ in diameter. One disc was included in each specially marked can of King B beef jerky. The front features a head shot of the player, his name, position, and team name printed in gold in the magenta border. The year and the King B logo are printed at the base of each picture. The circular backs are printed in scarlet and carry biographical and statistical information encircled by stars. Discs are numbered on the back.

|                          | MINT  | EXC   | G-VG |
|--------------------------|-------|-------|------|
| COMPLETE SET (24)        | 30.00 | 12.00 | 3.00 |
| COMMON PLAYER (1-24)     | 1.00  | .40   | .10  |
| ☐ 1 Mark Rypien          | 1.25  | .50   | .12  |
| Washington Redskins      |       |       |      |
| ☐ 2 Art Monk             | 1.50  | .60   | .15  |
| Washington Redskins      |       |       |      |
| ☐ 3 Sean Jones           | 1.00  | .40   | .10  |
| Houston Oilers           |       |       |      |
| ☐ 4 Bubby Brister        | 1.00  | .40   | .10  |
| Pittsburgh Steelers      |       |       |      |
| ☐ 5 Warren Moon          | 2.50  | 1.00  | .25  |
| Houston Oilers           |       |       |      |
| ☐ 6 Andre Rison          | 2.00  | .80   | .20  |
| Atlanta Falcons          |       |       |      |
| ☐ 7 Emmitt Smith         | 7.50  | 3.00  | .75  |
| Dallas Cowboys           |       |       |      |
| ☐ 8 Mervyn Fernandez     | 1.00  | .40   | .10  |
| Los Angeles Raiders      |       |       |      |
| ☐ 9 Rickey Jackson       | 1.00  | .40   | .10  |
| New Orleans Saints       |       |       |      |
| ☐ 10 Bruce Armstrong     | 1.00  | .40   | .10  |
| New England Patriots     |       |       |      |
| ☐ 11 Neal Anderson       | 1.25  | .50   | .12  |
| Chicago Bears            |       |       |      |
| ☐ 12 Christian Okoye     | 1.00  | .40   | .10  |
| Kansas City Chiefs       |       |       |      |
| ☐ 13 Thurman Thomas      | 2.50  | 1.00  | .25  |
| Buffalo Bills            |       |       |      |
| ☐ 14 Bruce Smith         | 1.25  | .50   | .12  |
| Buffalo Bills            |       |       |      |
| ☐ 15 Jeff Hostetler      | 1.50  | .60   | .15  |
| New York Giants          |       |       |      |
| ☐ 16 Barry Sanders       | 5.00  | 2.00  | .50  |
| Detroit Lions            |       |       |      |
| ☐ 17 Andre Reed          | 1.25  | .50   | .12  |
| Buffalo Bills            |       |       |      |
| ☐ 18 Derrick Thomas      | 2.00  | .80   | .20  |
| Kansas City Chiefs       |       |       |      |
| ☐ 19 Jim Everett         | 1.25  | .50   | .12  |
| Los Angeles Rams         |       |       |      |
| ☐ 20 Boomer Esiason      | 1.50  | .60   | .15  |
| Cincinnati Bengals       |       |       |      |
| ☐ 21 Merril Hoge         | 1.00  | .40   | .10  |
| Pittsburgh Steelers      |       |       |      |
| ☐ 22 Steve Atwater       | 1.25  | .50   | .12  |
| Denver Broncos           |       |       |      |
| ☐ 23 Dan Marino          | 6.00  | 2.40  | .60  |
| Miami Dolphins           |       |       |      |
| ☐ 24 Mark Collins        | 1.00  | .40   | .10  |
| New York Giants          |       |       |      |

| Washington Redskins      |       |       |      |
|--------------------------|-------|-------|------|
| ☐ 3 Andre Rison          | 2.00  | .80   | .20  |
| Atlanta Falcons          |       |       |      |
| ☐ 4 Thurman Thomas       | 2.50  | 1.00  | .25  |
| Buffalo Bills            |       |       |      |
| ☐ 5 Emmitt Smith         | 7.50  | 3.00  | .75  |
| Dallas Cowboys           |       |       |      |
| ☐ 6 Charles Mann         | 1.00  | .40   | .10  |
| Washington Redskins      |       |       |      |
| ☐ 7 Michael Irvin        | 3.00  | 1.20  | .30  |
| Dallas Cowboys           |       |       |      |
| ☐ 8 Jim Everett          | 1.25  | .50   | .12  |
| Los Angeles Rams         |       |       |      |
| ☐ 9 Gary Anderson        | 1.25  | .50   | .12  |
| Tampa Bay Buccaneers     |       |       |      |
| ☐ 10 Trace Armstrong     | 1.00  | .40   | .10  |
| Chicago Bears            |       |       |      |
| ☐ 11 John Elway          | 3.50  | 1.40  | .35  |
| Denver Broncos           |       |       |      |
| ☐ 12 Chip Lohmiller      | 1.00  | .40   | .10  |
| Washington Redskins      |       |       |      |
| ☐ 13 Bobby Hebert        | 1.25  | .50   | .12  |
| New Orleans Saints       |       |       |      |
| ☐ 14 Cornelius Bennett   | 1.25  | .50   | .12  |
| Buffalo Bills            |       |       |      |
| ☐ 15 Chris Miller        | 1.50  | .60   | .15  |
| Atlanta Falcons          |       |       |      |
| ☐ 16 Warren Moon         | 2.00  | .80   | .20  |
| Houston Oilers           |       |       |      |
| ☐ 17 Charles Haley       | 1.25  | .50   | .12  |
| San Francisco 49ers      |       |       |      |
| ☐ 18 Mark Rypien         | 1.25  | .50   | .12  |
| Washington Redskins      |       |       |      |
| ☐ 19 Darrell Green       | 1.25  | .50   | .12  |
| Washington Redskins      |       |       |      |
| ☐ 20 Barry Sanders       | 5.00  | 2.00  | .50  |
| Detroit Lions            |       |       |      |
| ☐ 21 Rodney Hampton      | 2.50  | 1.00  | .25  |
| New York Giants          |       |       |      |
| ☐ 22 Shane Conlan        | 1.25  | .50   | .12  |
| Buffalo Bills            |       |       |      |
| ☐ 23 Jerry Ball          | 1.00  | .40   | .10  |
| Detroit Lions            |       |       |      |
| ☐ 24 Morten Andersen     | 1.25  | .50   | .12  |
| New Orleans Saints       |       |       |      |

## 1993 King B Discs

This Fifth Annual Collectors Edition of the King B Discs set was produced by Michael Schechter Associates. One disc was included in each specially marked can of King B beef jerky. Each disc measures approximately 2 3/8" in diameter and features on its front a posed color player head shot bordered on the sides by a green gridiron design. The player's name, position, and team appear in orange and white lettering within the black margin above the photo. The year of the set, 1993, and a blue football helmet icon bearing the King B logo rest in the black margin at the bottom. The backs are white with black print, and they carry the player's name, team, position, biography, statistics (or highlights), and the King B helmet icon. The left and right edges are detailed with solid black and black outline stars. This set was also issued in an uncut sheet measuring 17 1/4" by 12 3/4". Each disc is numbered on the back.

|                          | MINT  | EXC   | G-VG |
|--------------------------|-------|-------|------|
| COMPLETE SET (24)        | 25.00 | 10.00 | 2.50 |
| COMMON PLAYER (1-24)     | 1.00  | .40   | .10  |
| ☐ 1 Luis Sharpe          | 1.00  | .40   | .10  |
| Phoenix Cardinals        |       |       |      |
| ☐ 2 Erik McMillan        | 1.00  | .40   | .10  |
| Philadelphia Eagles      |       |       |      |
| ☐ 3 Chris Doleman        | 1.00  | .40   | .10  |
| Minnesota Vikings        |       |       |      |
| ☐ 4 Cortez Kennedy       | 1.50  | .60   | .15  |
| Seattle Seahawks         |       |       |      |
| ☐ 5 Howie Long           | 1.25  | .50   | .12  |
| Los Angeles Raiders      |       |       |      |
| ☐ 6 Bill Romanowski      | 1.00  | .40   | .10  |
| San Francisco 49ers      |       |       |      |

## 1992 King B Discs

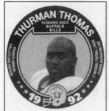

For the fourth consecutive year, Mike Schechter Associates has produced a 24-disc set for King B. One disc was included in each specially marked can of King B beef jerky. The discs measure approximately 2 3/8" in diameter. The fronts feature posed color player photos edged by a bright yellow border on a black face. The player's name appears in white at the top with his position and team name immediately below. The year in white block lettering and a bright yellow King B helmet icon are at the base of the picture. The backs are white with black print, and they carry biography, statistics, the player's name, and the King B helmet icon. The left and right edges are detailed with solid black and black outline stars. The discs are numbered on the back.

|                          | MINT  | EXC   | G-VG |
|--------------------------|-------|-------|------|
| COMPLETE SET (24)        | 25.00 | 10.00 | 2.50 |
| COMMON PLAYER (1-24)     | 1.00  | .40   | .10  |
| ☐ 1 Derrick Thomas       | 2.00  | .80   | .20  |
| Kansas City Chiefs       |       |       |      |
| ☐ 2 Wilber Marshall      | 1.25  | .50   | .12  |

| | | | |
|---|---|---|---|
| ☐ 7 Andre Tippett .......................... New England Patriots | 1.25 | .50 | .12 |
| ☐ 8 Simon Fletcher ....................... Denver Broncos | 1.00 | .40 | .10 |
| ☐ 9 Derrick Thomas...................... Kansas City Chiefs | 2.00 | .80 | .20 |
| ☐ 10 Rodney Peete ...................... Detroit Lions | 1.25 | .50 | .12 |
| ☐ 11 Ronnie Lott ........................... New York Jets | 1.50 | .60 | .15 |
| ☐ 12 Duane Bickett....................... Indianapolis Colts | 1.00 | .40 | .10 |
| ☐ 13 Steve Walsh ......................... New Orleans Saints | 1.25 | .50 | .12 |
| ☐ 14 Stan Humphries.................... San Diego Chargers | 1.50 | .60 | .15 |
| ☐ 15 Jeff George .......................... Indianapolis Colts | 2.50 | 1.00 | .25 |
| ☐ 16 Jay Novacek......................... Dallas Cowboys | 1.50 | .60 | .15 |
| ☐ 17 Andre Reed .......................... Buffalo Bills | 2.00 | .80 | .20 |
| ☐ 18 Andre Rison ......................... Atlanta Falcons | 2.00 | .80 | .20 |
| ☐ 19 Emmitt Smith ....................... Dallas Cowboys | 6.00 | 2.40 | .60 |
| ☐ 20 Neal Anderson...................... Chicago Bears | 1.25 | .50 | .12 |
| ☐ 21 Ricky Sanders ...................... Washington Redskins | 1.25 | .50 | .12 |
| ☐ 22 Thurman Thomas................... Buffalo Bills | 2.50 | 1.00 | .25 |
| ☐ 23 Lorenzo White....................... Houston Oilers | 1.25 | .50 | .12 |
| ☐ 24 Barry Foster .......................... Pittsburgh Steelers | 2.00 | .80 | .20 |

### 1989 Knudsen Raiders

This unnumbered 12-card set (of bookmarks) issued by Knudsen's Dairy in California measures approximately 2" by 8" and features members of the 1989 Los Angeles Raiders. These sets were distributed during the football season to those youngsters who checked out a book a week during the 1989 season from the Los Angeles Public Library. The backs of these bookmarks feature various reading tips for the youth to follow. The set is checklisted below by player's uniform number. The Shanahan card was apparently undistributed or withdrawn after he left the team.

| | MINT | EXC | G-VG |
|---|---|---|---|
| COMPLETE SET (14)........................ | 30.00 | 12.00 | 3.00 |
| COMMON CARD ............................. | 1.50 | .60 | .15 |
| | | | |
| ☐ 6 Jeff Gossett............................. | 1.50 | .60 | .15 |
| ☐ 13 Jay Schroeder....................... | 2.50 | 1.00 | .25 |
| ☐ 26 Vann McElroy........................ | 1.50 | .60 | .15 |
| ☐ 35 Steve Smith........................... | 2.00 | .80 | .20 |
| ☐ 36 Terry McDaniel...................... | 1.50 | .60 | .15 |
| ☐ 70 Scott Davis ........................... | 1.50 | .60 | .15 |
| ☐ 72 Don Mosebar ........................ | 1.50 | .60 | .15 |
| ☐ 75 Howie Long ........................... | 2.50 | 1.00 | .25 |
| ☐ 76 Steve Wisniewski................... | 1.50 | .60 | .15 |
| ☐ 81 Tim Brown ............................. | 5.00 | 2.00 | .50 |
| ☐ 83 Willie Gault............................. | 2.50 | 1.00 | .25 |
| ☐ xx Mike Shanahan SP CO............ | 15.00 | 6.00 | 1.50 |
| ☐ xx Raiders/Super Bowl ............... | 1.50 | .60 | .15 |
| ☐ xx Raiderettes SP...................... | 3.00 | 1.20 | .30 |

### 1990 Knudsen Chargers

This six-card set (of bookmarks) which measures approximately 2" by 8" was produced by Knudsen's to help promote readership by people under 15 years old in the San Diego area. They were given out in San Diego libraries on a weekly basis. The set was sponsored by Knudsen, American Library Association, and the San Diego Public Library. Between the Knudsen company name, the front features a color action photo of the player superimposed on a football stadium. The field is green, the bleachers are yellow with gray print, and the scoreboard above the player reads "The Reading Team". The box below the player gives brief biographical information and player highlights. The back has logos of the sponsors and describes two books that are available at the public library. We have checklisted this set in alphabetical order because they are otherwise unnumbered except for the player's uniform number displayed on the card front.

| | MINT | EXC | G-VG |
|---|---|---|---|
| COMPLETE SET (6).......................... | 12.00 | 5.00 | 1.20 |
| COMMON PLAYER (1-6).................. | 1.50 | .60 | .15 |
| | | | |
| ☐ 1 Marion Butts ........................... | 3.00 | 1.20 | .30 |
| ☐ 2 Anthony Miller.......................... | 3.00 | 1.20 | .30 |
| ☐ 3 Leslie O'Neal .......................... | 2.00 | .80 | .20 |
| ☐ 4 Gary Plummer .......................... | 1.50 | .60 | .15 |
| ☐ 5 Billy Ray Smith......................... | 1.50 | .60 | .15 |
| ☐ 6 Billy Joe Tolliver....................... | 2.00 | .80 | .20 |

### 1990 Knudsen 49ers

This six-card set (of bookmarks) which measures approximately 2" by 8" was produced by Knudsen's to help promote readership by people under 15 years old in the San Francisco area. They were given out in San Francisco libraries on a weekly basis. Between the Knudsen company name, the front features a color action photo of the player superimposed on a football stadium. The field is green, the bleachers are yellow with gray print, and the scoreboard above the player reads "The Reading Team". The box below the player gives brief biographical information and player highlights. The back has logos of the sponsors and describes two books that are available at the public library. We have checklisted this set in alphabetical order because they are otherwise unnumbered except for the player's uniform number displayed on the card front.

|  | MINT | EXC | G-VG |
|---|---|---|---|
| COMPLETE SET (6) | 20.00 | 8.00 | 2.00 |
| COMMON CARD (1-6) | 1.50 | .60 | .15 |
| ☐ 1 Roger Craig | 2.50 | 1.00 | .25 |
| ☐ 2 Ronnie Lott | 3.00 | 1.20 | .30 |
| ☐ 3 Joe Montana | 10.00 | 4.00 | 1.00 |
| ☐ 4 Jerry Rice | 6.00 | 2.40 | .60 |
| ☐ 5 George Siefert CO | 1.50 | .60 | .15 |
| ☐ 6 Michael Walter | 1.50 | .60 | .15 |

## 1990 Knudsen/Sealtest Patriots

This six-card set (of bookmarks) which measures approximately 2" by 8" was produced by Knudsen's and Sealtest to help promote readership by people under 15 years old in the New England area. Between the Knudsen or Sealtest company name, the front features a color action photo of the player superimposed on a football stadium. The field is green, the bleachers are yellow with gray print, and the scoreboard above the player reads "The Reading Team". The box below the player gives brief biographical information and player highlights. The back has logos of the sponsors and describes two books that are available at the public library. We have checklisted this set in alphabetical order because they are otherwise unnumbered except for the player's uniform number displayed on the card front.

|  | MINT | EXC | G-VG |
|---|---|---|---|
| COMPLETE SET (6) | 25.00 | 10.00 | 2.50 |
| COMMON PLAYER (1-6) | 4.00 | 1.60 | .40 |
| ☐ 1 Steve Grogan | 6.00 | 2.40 | .60 |
| ☐ 2 Ronnie Lippett | 5.00 | 2.00 | .50 |
| ☐ 3 Eric Sievers | 4.00 | 1.60 | .40 |
| ☐ 4 Mosi Tatupu | 5.00 | 2.00 | .50 |
| ☐ 5 Andre Tippett | 6.00 | 2.40 | .60 |
| ☐ 6 Garin Veris | 4.00 | 1.60 | .40 |

## 1990 Knudsen Rams

This six-card set (of bookmarks) which measures approximately 2" by 8" was produced by Knudsen's to help promote readership by people under 15 years old in the Los Angeles area. Between the Knudsen company name, the front features a color action photo of the player superimposed on a football stadium. The field is green, the bleachers are yellow with gray print, and the scoreboard above the player reads "The Reading Team". The box below the player gives brief biographical information and player highlights. The back has logos of the sponsors and describes two books that are available at the public library. We have checklisted this set in alphabetical order because they are otherwise unnumbered except for the player's uniform number displayed on the card front.

|  | MINT | EXC | G-VG |
|---|---|---|---|
| COMPLETE SET (6) | 25.00 | 10.00 | 2.50 |
| COMMON PLAYER (1-6) | 4.00 | 1.60 | .40 |

| | | | |
|---|---|---|---|
| ☐ 1 Henry Ellard | 6.00 | 2.40 | .60 |
| ☐ 2 Jim Everett | 6.00 | 2.40 | .60 |
| ☐ 3 Jerry Gray | 4.00 | 1.60 | .40 |
| ☐ 4 Pete Holohan | 4.00 | 1.60 | .40 |
| ☐ 5 Mike Lansford | 4.00 | 1.60 | .40 |
| ☐ 6 Irv Pankey | 4.00 | 1.60 | .40 |

## 1991 Knudsen

This 18-card set (of bookmarks) produced by Knudsen's Dairy in California measures approximately 2" by 8". They were presented to youngsters who checked out library books during the 1991 football season in order to promote reading. The fronts feature a player photo superimposed on the page of a book, with biography and career summary below. Card numbers appear in circles in the lower right corner of each card. The backs have logos of the sponsors and describe two books that are available at the public library. The bookmarks were distributed in the team's respective areas, San Diego Chargers (1-6), Los Angeles Rams (7-12), and San Francisco 49ers (13-18).

|  | MINT | EXC | G-VG |
|---|---|---|---|
| COMPLETE SET (18) | 35.00 | 14.00 | 3.50 |
| COMPLETE CHARGERS (6) | 11.00 | 4.50 | 1.10 |
| COMPLETE RAMS (6) | 9.00 | 3.75 | .90 |
| COMPLETE 49ERS (6) | 15.00 | 6.00 | 1.50 |
| COMMON PLAYER (1-6) | 1.50 | .60 | .15 |
| COMMON PLAYER (7-12) | 1.50 | .60 | .15 |
| COMMON PLAYER (13-18) | 1.50 | .60 | .15 |
| ☐ 1 Gill Byrd | 2.00 | .80 | .20 |
| ☐ 2 Courtney Hall | 1.50 | .60 | .15 |
| ☐ 3 Ronnie Harmon | 2.00 | .80 | .20 |
| ☐ 4 Anthony Miller | 2.50 | 1.00 | .25 |
| ☐ 5 Joe Phillips | 1.50 | .60 | .15 |
| ☐ 6 Junior Seau | 3.00 | 1.20 | .30 |
| ☐ 7 Jim Everett | 2.00 | .80 | .20 |
| ☐ 8 Kevin Greene | 2.00 | .80 | .20 |
| ☐ 9 Damone Johnson | 1.50 | .60 | .15 |
| ☐ 10 Tom Newberry | 1.50 | .60 | .15 |

| | | NRMT | VG-E | GOOD |
|---|---|---|---|---|
| ☐ 11 | John Robinson CO | 2.00 | .80 | .20 |
| ☐ 12 | Michael Stewart | 1.50 | .60 | .15 |
| ☐ 13 | Michael Carter | 2.00 | .80 | .20 |
| ☐ 14 | Charles Haley | 2.00 | .80 | .20 |
| ☐ 15 | Joe Montana | 7.50 | 3.00 | .75 |
| ☐ 16 | Tom Rathman | 2.00 | .80 | .20 |
| ☐ 17 | Jerry Rice | 5.00 | 2.00 | .50 |
| ☐ 18 | George Seifert CO | 1.50 | .60 | .15 |

# 1975 Laughlin Flaky Football

This 26-card set measures approximately 2 1/2" by 3 3/8". The title card indicates that the set was copyrighted in 1975 by noted artist, R.G. Laughlin. The typical orientation of the cards is that the city name is printed on the top of the card, with the mock team name running from top to bottom down the left side. The cartoon pictures are oriented horizontally inside the right angle formed by these two lines of text. The cards are numbered in the lower right hand corner (usually) and the backs of the cards are blank.

| | NRMT | VG-E | GOOD |
|---|---|---|---|
| COMPLETE SET (27) | 60.00 | 24.00 | 6.00 |
| COMMON PLAYER (1-26) | 4.00 | 1.60 | .40 |

| | | NRMT | VG-E | GOOD |
|---|---|---|---|---|
| ☐ 1 | Pittsburgh Stealers | 5.00 | 2.00 | .50 |
| ☐ 2 | Minnesota Spikings | 4.00 | 1.60 | .40 |
| ☐ 3 | Cincinnati Bungles | 4.00 | 1.60 | .40 |
| ☐ 4 | Chicago Bares | 5.00 | 2.00 | .50 |
| ☐ 5 | Miami Dullfins | 5.00 | 2.00 | .50 |
| ☐ 6 | Philadelphia Eggles | 4.00 | 1.60 | .40 |
| ☐ 7 | Cleveland Brawns | 4.00 | 1.60 | .40 |
| ☐ 8 | New York Gianuts | 5.00 | 2.00 | .50 |
| ☐ 9 | Buffalo Bulls | 4.00 | 1.60 | .40 |
| ☐ 10 | Dallas Plowboys | 5.00 | 2.00 | .50 |
| ☐ 11 | New England Pastry Nuts | 4.00 | 1.60 | .40 |
| ☐ 12 | Green Bay Porkers | 4.00 | 1.60 | .40 |
| ☐ 13 | Denver Bongos | 4.00 | 1.60 | .40 |
| ☐ 14 | St. Louis Cigardinals | 4.00 | 1.60 | .40 |
| ☐ 15 | New York Jests | 4.00 | 1.60 | .40 |
| ☐ 16 | Washington Redshins | 4.00 | 1.60 | .40 |
| ☐ 17 | Oakland Waders | 5.00 | 2.00 | .50 |
| ☐ 18 | Los Angeles Yams | 4.00 | 1.60 | .40 |
| ☐ 19 | Baltimore Kilts | 4.00 | 1.60 | .40 |
| ☐ 20 | New Orleans Scents | 4.00 | 1.60 | .40 |
| ☐ 21 | San Diego Charges | 4.00 | 1.60 | .40 |
| ☐ 22 | Detroit Loins | 4.00 | 1.60 | .40 |
| ☐ 23 | Kansas City Chefs | 4.00 | 1.60 | .40 |
| ☐ 24 | Atlanta Fakin's | 4.00 | 1.60 | .40 |
| ☐ 25 | Houston Owlers | 4.00 | 1.60 | .40 |
| ☐ 26 | San Francisco 40 Miners | 5.00 | 2.00 | .50 |
| ☐ NNO | Title Card | 6.00 | 2.40 | .60 |
| | Flaky Football | | | |

# 1948 Leaf

**56 --- BOB FOLSOM**

End – So. Methodist U.

| Weight–185 lbs. | Age–21 |
|---|---|
| Height–6' | Year–senior |

Is the only letterman now at SMU participating in four sports (football, basketball and track). Played with Army in 1945 and 1946 catching TD pass vs. Michigan in '46. Is very fast and tricky. Will be top receiver for his All-American teammate, Doak Walker.

**ALL-STAR FOOTBALL GUM**

Collect this series of Gridiron Greats.

Send 5 All Star Wrappers and 10c for big 12" x 6" felt pennant of any team listed on any All Star card.

| Colorado | Tennessee |
|---|---|
| Kansas | Texas Christian |
| Holy Cross | Florida |

Send Wrappers and Coins to
LEAF GUM CO., Box 9807   CHICAGO 80, ILL.
Copyright 1948

The 1948 Leaf set of 98 cards features black and white flesh areas and solid color backgrounds. The cards measure approximately 2 3/8" by 2 7/8". The cards can be found on either gray or cream colored card stock. The second 49 cards of this set are much more difficult to obtain than the first 49 cards. This set features the Rookie Cards of

many football stars since it was, along with the 1948 Bowman set, the first major post-war set of football cards. Such Rookie Cards include Sammy Baugh, Chuck Bednarik, Charley Conerly, Leon Hart, Jackie Jensen, Bobby Layne, Sid Luckman, Johnny Lujack, Leo Nomellini, Steve Van Buren, Doak Walker, and Bob Waterfield, among others, are featured in this set. The card backs say "Copyright 1948".

| | | NRMT | VG-E | GOOD |
|---|---|---|---|---|
| COMPLETE SET (98) | | 6000.00 | 2700.00 | 750.00 |
| COMMON PLAYER (1-49) | | 22.00 | 10.00 | 2.80 |
| COMMON PLAYER (50-98) | | 90.00 | 40.00 | 11.50 |
| ☐ 1 | Sid Luckman | 275.00 | 85.00 | 28.00 |
| | Chicago Bears | | | |
| ☐ 2 | Steve Suhey | 24.00 | 11.00 | 3.00 |
| | Pittsburgh Steelers | | | |
| ☐ 3A | Bulldog Turner | 90.00 | 40.00 | 11.50 |
| | Chicago Bears (Reddish background) | | | |
| ☐ 3B | Bulldog Turner | 90.00 | 40.00 | 11.50 |
| | Chicago Bears (White background) | | | |
| ☐ 4 | Doak Walker | 125.00 | 57.50 | 15.50 |
| | SMU | | | |
| ☐ 5 | Levi Jackson | 24.00 | 11.00 | 3.00 |
| | Yale | | | |
| ☐ 6 | Bobby Layne | 275.00 | 125.00 | 34.00 |
| | Chicago Bears | | | |
| ☐ 7 | Bill Fischer | 22.00 | 10.00 | 2.80 |
| | Notre Dame | | | |
| ☐ 8A | Vince Banonis | 25.00 | 11.50 | 3.10 |
| | Chicago Cardinals (White name on front) | | | |
| ☐ 8B | Vince Banonis | 24.00 | 11.00 | 3.00 |
| | Chicago Cardinals (Black name on front) | | | |
| ☐ 9 | Tommy Thompson | 35.00 | 16.00 | 4.40 |
| | Philadelphia Eagles | | | |
| ☐ 10 | Perry Moss | 22.00 | 10.00 | 2.80 |
| | Green Bay Packers | | | |
| ☐ 11 | Terry Brennan | 25.00 | 11.50 | 3.10 |
| | Notre Dame | | | |
| ☐ 12A | William Swiacki | 30.00 | 13.50 | 3.80 |
| | New York Giants (White name on front) | | | |
| ☐ 12B | William Swiacki | 25.00 | 11.50 | 3.10 |
| | New York Giants (Black name on front) | | | |
| ☐ 13 | Johnny Lujack | 125.00 | 57.50 | 15.50 |
| | Chicago Bears | | | |
| ☐ 14A | Mal Kutner | 25.00 | 11.50 | 3.10 |
| | Chicago Cardinals (White name on front) | | | |
| ☐ 14B | Mal Kutner | 24.00 | 11.00 | 3.00 |
| | Chicago Cardinals (Black name on front) | | | |
| ☐ 15 | Charlie Justice | 60.00 | 27.00 | 7.50 |
| | North Carolina | | | |
| ☐ 16 | Pete Pihos | 80.00 | 36.00 | 10.00 |
| | Philadelphia Eagles | | | |
| ☐ 17A | Kenny Washington | 45.00 | 20.00 | 5.75 |
| | Los Angeles Rams (White name on front) | | | |
| ☐ 17B | Kenny Washington | 38.00 | 17.00 | 4.70 |
| | Los Angeles Rams (Black name on front) | | | |
| ☐ 18 | Harry Gilmer | 35.00 | 16.00 | 4.40 |
| | Washington Redskins | | | |
| ☐ 19A | George McAfee ERR | 125.00 | 57.50 | 15.50 |
| | (Listed as Gorgeous George on front) Chicago Bears | | | |
| ☐ 19B | George McAfee COR | 85.00 | 38.00 | 10.50 |
| | Chicago Bears | | | |
| ☐ 20 | George Taliaferro | 25.00 | 11.50 | 3.10 |
| | Indiana | | | |
| ☐ 21 | Paul Christman | 38.00 | 17.00 | 4.70 |
| | Chicago Cardinals | | | |
| ☐ 22 | Steve Van Buren | 125.00 | 57.50 | 15.50 |
| | Philadelphia Eagles | | | |
| ☐ 23 | Ken Kavanaugh | 35.00 | 16.00 | 4.40 |
| | Chicago Bears | | | |
| ☐ 24 | Jim Martin | 25.00 | 11.50 | 3.10 |
| | Notre Dame | | | |
| ☐ 25 | Bud Angsman | 22.00 | 10.00 | 2.80 |
| | Chicago Cardinals | | | |
| ☐ 26 | Bob Waterfield | 175.00 | 80.00 | 22.00 |
| | Los Angeles Rams | | | |
| ☐ 27A | Fred Davis | 24.00 | 11.00 | 3.00 |
| | Chicago Bears (Yellow background) | | | |
| ☐ 27B | Fred Davis | 24.00 | 11.00 | 3.00 |
| | Chicago Bears (White background) | | | |
| ☐ 28 | Whitey Wistert | 27.00 | 12.00 | 3.40 |
| | Philadelphia Eagles | | | |
| ☐ 29 | Charley Trippi | 90.00 | 40.00 | 11.50 |

|  | | | |
|---|---|---|---|
| Chicago Cardinals | | | |
| ☐ 30 Paul Governali | 22.00 | 10.00 | 2.80 |
| New York Giants | | | |
| ☐ 31 Tom McWilliams | 22.00 | 10.00 | 2.80 |
| Mississippi State | | | |
| ☐ 32 Larry Zimmerman | 22.00 | 10.00 | 2.80 |
| Boston Yanks | | | |
| ☐ 33 Pat Harder UER | 35.00 | 16.00 | 4.40 |
| (Misspelled Harber) | | | |
| Chicago Cardinals | | | |
| ☐ 34 Sammy Baugh | 325.00 | 145.00 | 40.00 |
| Washington Redskins | | | |
| ☐ 35 Ted Fritsch Sr | 24.00 | 11.00 | 3.00 |
| Green Bay Packers | | | |
| ☐ 36 Bill Dudley | 80.00 | 36.00 | 10.00 |
| Detroit Lions | | | |
| ☐ 37 George Connor | 75.00 | 34.00 | 9.50 |
| Chicago Bears | | | |
| ☐ 38 Frank Dancewicz | 22.00 | 10.00 | 2.80 |
| Boston Yanks | | | |
| ☐ 39 Billy Dewell | 22.00 | 10.00 | 2.80 |
| Chicago Cardinals | | | |
| ☐ 40 John Nolan | 22.00 | 10.00 | 2.80 |
| Boston Yanks | | | |
| ☐ 41A Harry Szulborski | 24.00 | 11.00 | 3.00 |
| Purdue | | | |
| (Yellow jersey) | | | |
| ☐ 41B Harry Szulborski | 24.00 | 11.00 | 3.00 |
| Purdue | | | |
| (Orange jersey) | | | |
| ☐ 42 Tex Coulter | 24.00 | 11.00 | 3.00 |
| New York Giants | | | |
| ☐ 43 Robert Nussbaumer | 22.00 | 10.00 | 2.80 |
| Washington Redskins | | | |
| ☐ 44 Bob Mann | 22.00 | 10.00 | 2.80 |
| Detroit Lions | | | |
| ☐ 45 Jim White | 22.00 | 10.00 | 2.80 |
| New York Giants | | | |
| ☐ 46 Jack Jacobs | 22.00 | 10.00 | 2.80 |
| Green Bay Packers | | | |
| ☐ 47 John Clement | 22.00 | 10.00 | 2.80 |
| Pittsburgh Steelers | | | |
| ☐ 48 Frank Reagan | 22.00 | 10.00 | 2.80 |
| New York Giants | | | |
| ☐ 49 Frank Tripucka | 40.00 | 18.00 | 5.00 |
| Notre Dame | | | |
| ☐ 50 John Rauch | 100.00 | 45.00 | 12.50 |
| Georgia | | | |
| ☐ 51 Mike Dimitro | 90.00 | 40.00 | 11.50 |
| UCLA | | | |
| ☐ 52 Leo Nomellini | 240.00 | 110.00 | 30.00 |
| Minnesota | | | |
| ☐ 53 Charley Conerly | 250.00 | 115.00 | 31.00 |
| New York Giants | | | |
| ☐ 54 Chuck Bednarik | 250.00 | 115.00 | 31.00 |
| Pennsylvania | | | |
| ☐ 55 Chick Jagade | 90.00 | 40.00 | 11.50 |
| Indiana | | | |
| ☐ 56 Bob Folsom | 100.00 | 45.00 | 12.50 |
| SMU | | | |
| ☐ 57 Eugene Rossides | 100.00 | 45.00 | 12.50 |
| Columbia | | | |
| ☐ 58 Art Weiner | 90.00 | 40.00 | 11.50 |
| No. Carolina | | | |
| ☐ 59 Alex Sarkisian | 90.00 | 40.00 | 11.50 |
| Northwestern | | | |
| ☐ 60 Dick Harris | 90.00 | 40.00 | 11.50 |
| University of Texas | | | |
| ☐ 61 Len Younce | 90.00 | 40.00 | 11.50 |
| New York Giants | | | |
| ☐ 62 Gene Derricotte | 90.00 | 40.00 | 11.50 |
| Michigan | | | |
| ☐ 63 Roy Steiner | 90.00 | 40.00 | 11.50 |
| Alabama | | | |
| ☐ 64 Frank Seno | 90.00 | 40.00 | 11.50 |
| Boston Yanks | | | |
| ☐ 65 Bob Hendren | 90.00 | 40.00 | 11.50 |
| USC | | | |
| ☐ 66 Jack Cloud | 90.00 | 40.00 | 11.50 |
| William and Mary | | | |
| ☐ 67 Harrell Collins | 90.00 | 40.00 | 11.50 |
| LSU | | | |
| ☐ 68 Clyde LeForce | 90.00 | 40.00 | 11.50 |
| Detroit Lions | | | |
| ☐ 69 Larry Joe | 90.00 | 40.00 | 11.50 |
| Penn State | | | |
| ☐ 70 Phil O'Reilly | 90.00 | 40.00 | 11.50 |
| Purdue | | | |
| ☐ 71 Paul Campbell | 90.00 | 40.00 | 11.50 |
| Texas | | | |
| ☐ 72 Ray Evans | 90.00 | 40.00 | 11.50 |
| Pittsburgh Steelers | | | |
| ☐ 73 Jackie Jensen UER | 275.00 | 125.00 | 34.00 |
| (Misspelled Jackey | | | |
| on card front) | | | |
| California | | | |
| ☐ 74 Russ Steger | 90.00 | 40.00 | 11.50 |
| Illinois | | | |

|  | | | |
|---|---|---|---|
| ☐ 75 Tony Minisi | 90.00 | 40.00 | 11.50 |
| New York Giants | | | |
| ☐ 76 Clayton Tonnemaker | 90.00 | 40.00 | 11.50 |
| Minnesota | | | |
| ☐ 77 George Savitsky | 90.00 | 40.00 | 11.50 |
| Philadelphia Eagles | | | |
| ☐ 78 Clarence Self | 90.00 | 40.00 | 11.50 |
| Wisconsin | | | |
| ☐ 79 Rod Franz | 90.00 | 40.00 | 11.50 |
| California | | | |
| ☐ 80 Jim Youle | 90.00 | 40.00 | 11.50 |
| Boston Yanks | | | |
| ☐ 81 Billy Bye | 90.00 | 40.00 | 11.50 |
| Minnesota | | | |
| ☐ 82 Fred Enke | 90.00 | 40.00 | 11.50 |
| Detroit Lions | | | |
| ☐ 83 Fred Folger | 90.00 | 40.00 | 11.50 |
| Duke | | | |
| ☐ 84 Jug Girard | 90.00 | 40.00 | 11.50 |
| Green Bay Packers | | | |
| ☐ 85 Joe Scott | 90.00 | 40.00 | 11.50 |
| New York Giants | | | |
| ☐ 86 Bob Demoss | 90.00 | 40.00 | 11.50 |
| Purdue | | | |
| ☐ 87 Dave Templeton | 90.00 | 40.00 | 11.50 |
| Ohio State | | | |
| ☐ 88 Herb Siegert | 90.00 | 40.00 | 11.50 |
| Illinois | | | |
| ☐ 89 Bucky O'Conner | 90.00 | 40.00 | 11.50 |
| Los Angeles Rams | | | |
| ☐ 90 Joe Whisler | 90.00 | 40.00 | 11.50 |
| Ohio State | | | |
| ☐ 91 Leon Hart | 135.00 | 60.00 | 17.00 |
| Notre Dame | | | |
| ☐ 92 Earl Banks | 90.00 | 40.00 | 11.50 |
| Iowa | | | |
| ☐ 93 Frank Aschenbrenner | 90.00 | 40.00 | 11.50 |
| Northwestern | | | |
| ☐ 94 John Goldsberry | 90.00 | 40.00 | 11.50 |
| Indiana | | | |
| ☐ 95 Porter Payne | 90.00 | 40.00 | 11.50 |
| Georgia | | | |
| ☐ 96 Pete Perini | 90.00 | 40.00 | 11.50 |
| Ohio State | | | |
| ☐ 97 Jay Rhodemyre | 90.00 | 40.00 | 11.50 |
| Green Bay Packers | | | |
| ☐ 98 Al DiMarco | 135.00 | 34.00 | 11.00 |
| Iowa | | | |

# 1949 Leaf

The 1949 Leaf set is skip-numbered from number 1 to number 150. The set contains 49 cards. The set is styled very similarly to the other Leaf sets of the 1948-49 era. The cards measure approximately 2 3/8" by 2 7/8". The cards can be found on either gray or cream colored card stock. The card backs detail an offer to send in five wrappers and a dime for a 12" by 6" felt pennant of one of the teams listed on the different card backs including college and pro teams. There are no key Rookie Cards in this set as virtually all of the players in the 1949 set were also in the 1948 Leaf set as well. The card backs say "Copyright 1949".

|  | NRMT | VG-E | GOOD |
|---|---|---|---|
| COMPLETE SET (49) | 1500.00 | 700.00 | 190.00 |
| COMMON PLAYER (1-150) | 20.00 | 9.00 | 2.50 |
| | | | |
| ☐ 1 Bob Hendren | 60.00 | 12.00 | 3.60 |
| Washington Redskins | | | |
| ☐ 2 Joe Scott | 20.00 | 9.00 | 2.50 |
| New York Giants | | | |
| ☐ 3 Frank Reagan | 20.00 | 9.00 | 2.50 |
| Philadelphia Eagles | | | |
| ☐ 4 John Rauch | 20.00 | 9.00 | 2.50 |
| New York Bulldogs | | | |
| ☐ 7 Bill Fischer | 20.00 | 9.00 | 2.50 |
| Chicago Cardinals | | | |

| | | | |
|---|---|---|---|
| ☐ 9 Bud Angsman ....................... | 20.00 | 9.00 | 2.50 |
| Chicago Cardinals | | | |
| ☐ 10 Billy Dewell ...................... | 20.00 | 9.00 | 2.50 |
| Chicago Cardinals | | | |
| ☐ 13 Tommy Thompson............ | 24.00 | 11.00 | 3.00 |
| Philadelphia Eagles | | | |
| ☐ 15 Sid Luckman.................... | 110.00 | 50.00 | 14.00 |
| Chicago Bears | | | |
| ☐ 16 Charley Trippi................. | 40.00 | 18.00 | 5.00 |
| Chicago Cardinals | | | |
| ☐ 17 Bob Mann...................... | 20.00 | 9.00 | 2.50 |
| Detroit Lions | | | |
| ☐ 19 Paul Christman ............... | 24.00 | 11.00 | 3.00 |
| Chicago Cardinals | | | |
| ☐ 22 Bill Dudley ..................... | 35.00 | 16.00 | 4.40 |
| Detroit Lions | | | |
| ☐ 23 Clyde LeForce ................. | 20.00 | 9.00 | 2.50 |
| Detroit Lions | | | |
| ☐ 26 Sammy Baugh.................. | 200.00 | 90.00 | 25.00 |
| Washington Redskins | | | |
| ☐ 28 Pete Pihos ..................... | 35.00 | 16.00 | 4.40 |
| Philadelphia Eagles | | | |
| ☐ 31 Tex Coulter..................... | 20.00 | 9.00 | 2.50 |
| New York Giants | | | |
| ☐ 32 Mal Kutner...................... | 20.00 | 9.00 | 2.50 |
| Chicago Cardinals | | | |
| ☐ 35 Whitey Wistert ................ | 22.00 | 10.00 | 2.80 |
| Philadelphia Eagles | | | |
| ☐ 37 Ted Fritsch Sr.................. | 22.00 | 10.00 | 2.80 |
| Green Bay Packers | | | |
| ☐ 38 Vince Banonis ................. | 20.00 | 9.00 | 2.50 |
| Chicago Cardinals | | | |
| ☐ 39 Jim White....................... | 20.00 | 9.00 | 2.50 |
| New York Giants | | | |
| ☐ 40 George Connor................. | 35.00 | 16.00 | 4.40 |
| Chicago Bears | | | |
| ☐ 41 George McAfee ................ | 35.00 | 16.00 | 4.40 |
| Chicago Bears | | | |
| ☐ 43 Frank Tripucka ................ | 25.00 | 11.50 | 3.10 |
| Philadelphia Eagles | | | |
| ☐ 47 Fred Enke ...................... | 20.00 | 9.00 | 2.50 |
| Detroit Lions | | | |
| ☐ 49 Charley Conerly ............... | 80.00 | 36.00 | 10.00 |
| New York Giants | | | |
| ☐ 51 Ken Kavanaugh ................ | 24.00 | 11.00 | 3.00 |
| Chicago Bears | | | |
| ☐ 52 Bob DeMoss ................... | 20.00 | 9.00 | 2.50 |
| New York Bulldogs | | | |
| ☐ 56 John Lujack .................... | 80.00 | 36.00 | 10.00 |
| Chicago Bears | | | |
| ☐ 57 Jim Youle ...................... | 20.00 | 9.00 | 2.50 |
| Detroit Lions | | | |
| ☐ 62 Harry Gilmer ................... | 24.00 | 11.00 | 3.00 |
| Washington Redskins | | | |
| ☐ 65 Robert Nussbaumer............ | 20.00 | 9.00 | 2.50 |
| Chicago Cardinals | | | |
| ☐ 67 Bobby Layne ................... | 125.00 | 57.50 | 15.50 |
| New York Bulldogs | | | |
| ☐ 70 Herb Siegert ................... | 20.00 | 9.00 | 2.50 |
| Washington Redskins | | | |
| ☐ 74 Tony Minisi .................... | 20.00 | 9.00 | 2.50 |
| New York Giants | | | |
| ☐ 79 Steve Van Buren................ | 80.00 | 36.00 | 10.00 |
| Philadelphia Eagles | | | |
| ☐ 81 Perry Moss .................... | 20.00 | 9.00 | 2.50 |
| Green Bay Packers | | | |
| ☐ 89 Bob Waterfield................. | 90.00 | 40.00 | 11.50 |
| Los Angeles Rams | | | |
| ☐ 90 Jack Jacobs ................... | 20.00 | 9.00 | 2.50 |
| Green Bay Packers | | | |
| ☐ 95 Kenny Washington.............. | 27.00 | 12.00 | 3.40 |
| Los Angeles Rams | | | |
| ☐ 101 Pat Harder UER............... | 24.00 | 11.00 | 3.00 |
| (Misspelled Harber | | | |
| on card front) | | | |
| Chicago Cardinals | | | |
| ☐ 110 William Swiacki................ | 22.00 | 10.00 | 2.80 |
| New York Giants | | | |
| ☐ 118 Fred Davis .................... | 20.00 | 9.00 | 2.50 |
| Chicago Bears | | | |
| ☐ 126 Jay Rhodemyre ............... | 20.00 | 9.00 | 2.50 |
| Green Bay Packers | | | |
| ☐ 127 Frank Seno ................... | 20.00 | 9.00 | 2.50 |
| New York Bulldogs | | | |
| ☐ 134 Chuck Bednarik .............. | 80.00 | 36.00 | 10.00 |
| Philadelphia Eagles | | | |
| ☐ 144 George Savitsky .............. | 20.00 | 9.00 | 2.50 |
| Philadelphia Eagles | | | |
| ☐ 150 Bulldog Turner ............... | 100.00 | 25.00 | 8.00 |
| Chicago Bears | | | |

## 1961 Lions Jay Publishing

This 12-card set features (approximately) 5" by 7" black-and-white player photos. The photos show players in traditional poses with the quarterback preparing to throw, the runner heading downfield, and the defenseman ready for the tackle. These cards were packaged 12 to a packet and originally sold for 25 cents. The backs are blank. The cards are unnumbered and checklisted below in alphabetical order.

| | NRMT | VG-E | GOOD |
|---|---|---|---|
| COMPLETE SET (12)................... | 60.00 | 24.00 | 6.00 |
| COMMON PLAYER (1-12)............... | 5.00 | 2.00 | .50 |
| | | | |
| ☐ 1 Carl Brettschneider .................. | 5.00 | 2.00 | .50 |
| ☐ 2 Howard Cassady ................... | 6.00 | 2.40 | .60 |
| ☐ 3 Gail Cogdill........................ | 5.00 | 2.00 | .50 |
| ☐ 4 Jim Gibbons...................... | 6.00 | 2.40 | .60 |
| ☐ 5 Alex Karras........................ | 10.00 | 4.00 | 1.00 |
| ☐ 6 Yale Lary .......................... | 9.00 | 3.75 | .90 |
| ☐ 7 Jim Martin......................... | 5.00 | 2.00 | .50 |
| ☐ 8 Earl Morrall........................ | 7.50 | 3.00 | .75 |
| ☐ 9 Jim Ninowski...................... | 6.00 | 2.40 | .60 |
| ☐ 10 Nick Pietrosante ................. | 6.00 | 2.40 | .60 |
| ☐ 11 Joe Schmidt...................... | 10.00 | 4.00 | 1.00 |
| ☐ 12 George Wilson CO................. | 5.00 | 2.00 | .50 |

## 1964 Lions White Border

This 24-card team issue set consists of glossy black and white 7 3/8" by 9 3/8" posed action photos enclosed in a white border. Player's name and position are printed on one line with the team name in black ink along the bottom portion of the white border. The set is unnumbered and thus the cards are listed below alphabetically. Some of the players may have been reissued in later years as some of the cards can be found with a stamp on the back showing either Oct. 1964 or Sept. 1965.

| | NRMT | VG-E | GOOD |
|---|---|---|---|
| COMPLETE SET (24).................. | 75.00 | 30.00 | 7.50 |
| COMMON PLAYER (1-24)............... | 3.00 | 1.20 | .30 |
| | | | |
| ☐ 1 Dick Compton .................... | 3.00 | 1.20 | .30 |
| ☐ 2 Larry Ferguson ................... | 3.00 | 1.20 | .30 |
| ☐ 3 Dennis Gaubatz .................. | 3.00 | 1.20 | .30 |
| ☐ 4 Jim Gibbons...................... | 4.00 | 1.60 | .40 |
| ☐ 5 John Gonzaga .................... | 3.00 | 1.20 | .30 |
| ☐ 6 John Gordy ....................... | 4.00 | 1.60 | .40 |
| ☐ 7 Tom Hall .......................... | 3.00 | 1.20 | .30 |
| ☐ 8 Roger LaLonde ................... | 3.00 | 1.20 | .30 |
| ☐ 9 Dan LaRose....................... | 3.00 | 1.20 | .30 |
| ☐ 10 Yale Lary ........................ | 9.00 | 3.75 | .90 |
| ☐ 11 Dan Lewis ....................... | 4.00 | 1.60 | .40 |
| ☐ 12 Gary Lowe ....................... | 3.00 | 1.20 | .30 |
| ☐ 13 Bruce Maher .................... | 4.00 | 1.60 | .40 |
| ☐ 14 Hugh McInnis ................... | 3.00 | 1.20 | .30 |
| ☐ 15 Max Messner .................... | 3.00 | 1.20 | .30 |
| ☐ 16 Floyd Peters ..................... | 5.00 | 2.00 | .50 |
| ☐ 17 Daryl Sanders ................... | 3.00 | 1.20 | .30 |
| ☐ 18 Joe Schmidt..................... | 10.00 | 4.00 | 1.00 |
| ☐ 19 Bob Scholtz ..................... | 3.00 | 1.20 | .30 |
| ☐ 20 James Simon .................... | 3.00 | 1.20 | .30 |
| ☐ 21 J.D. Smith....................... | 4.00 | 1.60 | .40 |
| ☐ 22 Bill Quinlan ...................... | 3.00 | 1.20 | .30 |
| ☐ 23 Bob Whitlow ..................... | 3.00 | 1.20 | .30 |
| ☐ 24 Sam Williams ................... | 3.00 | 1.20 | .30 |

## 1966 Lions Marathon Oil

This set consists of seven (approximately) 5" by 7" photos. The fronts feature black-and-white photos with white borders. The player's name, position, and team name are printed in the bottom border. The backs are blank. The cards are unnumbered and checklisted below in alphabetical order.

| | NRMT | VG-E | GOOD |
|---|---|---|---|
| COMPLETE SET (7)..................... | 35.00 | 14.00 | 3.50 |
| COMMON PLAYER (1-7).................. | 5.00 | 2.00 | .50 |

| | | | |
|---|---|---|---|
| ☐ 1 Gail Cogdill | 6.00 | 2.40 | .60 |
| ☐ 2 John Gordy | 5.00 | 2.00 | .50 |
| ☐ 3 Alex Karras | 12.00 | 5.00 | 1.20 |
| ☐ 4 Ron Kramer | 6.00 | 2.40 | .60 |
| ☐ 5 Milt Plum | 7.50 | 3.00 | .75 |
| ☐ 6 Wayne Rasmussen | 5.00 | 2.00 | .50 |
| ☐ 7 Daryl Sanders | 5.00 | 2.00 | .50 |

## 1993 Lions 60th Season Commemorative

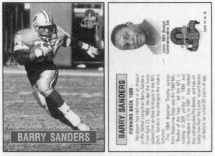

These 16 standard-size (2 1/2" by 3 1/2") 60th-season commemorative cards feature borderless player photos on their fronts. Some photos are color, others are black-and-white; some are action shots, others are posed. The player's name (or the card's title), the rectangle it appears in, and the 60th season logo, all appear in team colors. The white backs carry black-and-white head shots of the players. Also appearing are the players' names, the years they played for the Lions, position, and career highlights. The team color-coded 60th season logo reappears in a lower corner. The cards are numbered on the back. The cards came with their own approximately 6" by 8" four-page black vinyl card holder emblazoned with the Lions' 60th season logo.

| | MINT | EXC | G-VG |
|---|---|---|---|
| COMPLETE SET (16) | 10.00 | 4.00 | 1.00 |
| COMMON PLAYER (1-16) | .50 | .20 | .05 |
| | | | |
| ☐ 1 Barry Sanders | 3.00 | 1.20 | .30 |
| ☐ 2 Joe Schmidt | 1.00 | .40 | .10 |
| ☐ 3 The Fearsome Foursome | .75 | .30 | .07 |
|    Sam Williams | | | |
|    Roger Brown | | | |
|    Alex Karras | | | |
|    Darris McCord | | | |
| ☐ 4 Chris Spielman | .75 | .30 | .07 |
| ☐ 5 Billy Sims | .75 | .30 | .07 |
| ☐ 6 '40s Phenoms | .75 | .30 | .07 |
|    Alex Wojciechowicz | | | |
|    Byron(Whizzer) White | | | |
| ☐ 7 Thunder and Lightning | .50 | .20 | .05 |
|    Bennie Blades | | | |
|    Mel Gray | | | |
| ☐ 8 Bobby Layne | 1.50 | .60 | .15 |
| ☐ 9 Dutch Clark | .75 | .30 | .07 |
| ☐ 10 Great Games | .50 | .20 | .05 |
|    Thanksgiving 1962 | | | |
| ☐ 11 Charlie Sanders | .75 | .30 | .07 |
| ☐ 12 Lomas Brown | .50 | .20 | .05 |
| ☐ 13 Doug English | .50 | .20 | .05 |
| ☐ 14 Doak Walker | 1.50 | .60 | .15 |
| ☐ 15 Roaring '20s | 1.50 | .60 | .15 |
|    Lem Barney | | | |
|    Billy Sims | | | |
|    Barry Sanders | | | |
| ☐ 16 Anniversary Card | .50 | .20 | .05 |

## 1990 Little Big Leaguers

This 95-page book/album was published by Simon and Schuster and includes boyhood stories of today's pro football players. Moreover, five 8 1/2" by 11" sheets of cards (nine cards per sheet) are inserted at the end of the album; after perforation, the cards measure the standard size (2 1/2" by 3 1/2"). The fronts feature black and white photos of these players as kids. The cards have blue and white borders, and in the thicker blue borders above and below the picture, one finds the player's name and the words "Little Football Big Leaguers" respectively. The backs have the same design, only with biography and career summary in place of the picture. The cards are unnumbered and checklisted below in alphabetical order.

| | MINT | EXC | G-VG |
|---|---|---|---|
| COMPLETE SET (45) | 12.00 | 5.00 | 1.20 |
| COMMON PLAYER (1-45) | .25 | .10 | .02 |
| | | | |
| ☐ 1 Troy Aikman | 3.00 | 1.20 | .30 |
| ☐ 2 Morten Andersen | .35 | .14 | .03 |
| ☐ 3 Jerry Ball | .25 | .10 | .02 |
| ☐ 4 Carl Banks | .35 | .14 | .03 |
| ☐ 5 Bennie Blades | .25 | .10 | .02 |
| ☐ 6 Brian Blades | .35 | .14 | .03 |
| ☐ 7 Joey Browner | .35 | .14 | .03 |
| ☐ 8 Keith Byars | .35 | .14 | .03 |
| ☐ 9 Anthony Carter | .35 | .14 | .03 |
| ☐ 10 Deron Cherry | .25 | .10 | .02 |
| ☐ 11 Roger Craig | .50 | .20 | .05 |
| ☐ 12 John Elway | 1.50 | .60 | .15 |
| ☐ 13 Doug Flutie | .75 | .30 | .07 |
| ☐ 14 Tim Goad | .25 | .10 | .02 |
| ☐ 15 Bob Golic | .25 | .10 | .02 |
| ☐ 16 Dino Hackett | .25 | .10 | .02 |
| ☐ 17 Dan Hampton | .50 | .20 | .05 |
| ☐ 18 Bobby Hebert | .35 | .14 | .03 |
| ☐ 19 Darryl Henley | .25 | .10 | .02 |
| ☐ 20 Wes Hopkins | .25 | .10 | .02 |
| ☐ 21 Hank Ilesic | .25 | .10 | .02 |
| ☐ 22 Tunch Ilkin | .25 | .10 | .02 |
| ☐ 23 Perry Kemp | .25 | .10 | .02 |
| ☐ 24 Bernie Kosar | .50 | .20 | .05 |
| ☐ 25 Mike Lansford | .25 | .10 | .02 |
| ☐ 26 Shawn Lee | .25 | .10 | .02 |
| ☐ 27 Charles Mann | .35 | .14 | .03 |
| ☐ 28 Dan Marino | 2.50 | 1.00 | .25 |
| ☐ 29 Bruce Matthews | .25 | .10 | .02 |
| ☐ 30 Clay Matthews | .35 | .14 | .03 |
| ☐ 31 Freeman McNeil | .35 | .14 | .03 |
| ☐ 32 Warren Moon | .75 | .30 | .07 |
| ☐ 33 Anthony Munoz | .50 | .20 | .05 |
| ☐ 34 Andre Reed | .50 | .20 | .05 |
| ☐ 35 Andre Rison | .75 | .30 | .07 |
| ☐ 36 Phil Simms | .50 | .20 | .05 |
| ☐ 37 Mike Singletary | .50 | .20 | .05 |
| ☐ 38 Rohn Stark | .25 | .10 | .02 |
| ☐ 39 Kelly Stouffer | .25 | .10 | .02 |
| ☐ 40 Vinny Testaverde | .35 | .14 | .03 |
| ☐ 41 Doug Williams | .25 | .10 | .02 |
| ☐ 42 Marc Wilson | .25 | .10 | .02 |
| ☐ 43 Craig Wolfley | .25 | .10 | .02 |
| ☐ 44 Ron Wolfley | .25 | .10 | .02 |
| ☐ 45 Steve Young | 1.00 | .40 | .10 |

## 1978-79 Marketcom Test

The 1979 Marketcom NFL Football Superstars set includes 29 mini-posters measuring approximately 5 1/2" by 8 1/2". They are printed on paper-thin stock and are virtually always found with fold creases. Marketcom is credited at the bottom of each poster. The posters have blank backs. These posters are unnumbered so they are listed below in alphabetical order. The set may have been issued over two years

Franco Harris

# 1980 Marketcom

Jack Ham

Jack Ham

MINI-POSTER 11 of 50

since there have been reported variations involving statistics on the card backs for Otis Armstrong and Randy Gradishar. In addition Earl Campbell's rookie year was 1978 making a card for him in an Oilers uniform in 1978 unlikely.

| | NRMT | VG-E | GOOD |
|---|---|---|---|
| COMPLETE SET (32) | 250.00 | 100.00 | 25.00 |
| COMMON PLAYER (1-32) | 3.50 | 1.40 | .35 |

| | | | |
|---|---|---|---|
| ☐ 1 Otis Armstrong SP<br>Denver Broncos | 7.00 | 2.80 | .70 |
| ☐ 2 Steve Bartkowski SP<br>Atlanta Falcons | 10.00 | 4.00 | 1.00 |
| ☐ 3 Terry Bradshaw SP<br>Pittsburgh Steelers | 25.00 | 10.00 | 2.50 |
| ☐ 4 Earl Campbell<br>Houston Oilers | 25.00 | 10.00 | 2.50 |
| ☐ 5 Dave Casper<br>Oakland Raiders | 5.00 | 2.00 | .50 |
| ☐ 6 Dan Dierdorf SP<br>St. Louis Cardinals | 8.00 | 3.25 | .80 |
| ☐ 7 Dan Fouts SP<br>San Diego Chargers | 15.00 | 6.00 | 1.50 |
| ☐ 8 Tony Galbreath<br>New Orleans Saints | 3.50 | 1.40 | .35 |
| ☐ 9 Randy Gradishar SP<br>Denver Broncos | 7.00 | 2.80 | .70 |
| ☐ 10 Bob Griese SP<br>Miami Dolphins | 15.00 | 6.00 | 1.50 |
| ☐ 11 Steve Grogan<br>New England Patriots | 5.00 | 2.00 | .50 |
| ☐ 12 Ray Guy<br>Oakland Raiders | 6.00 | 2.40 | .60 |
| ☐ 13 Pat Haden SP<br>Los Angeles Rams | 10.00 | 4.00 | 1.00 |
| ☐ 14 Jack Ham<br>Pittsburgh Steelers | 7.00 | 2.80 | .70 |
| ☐ 15 Cliff Harris SP<br>Dallas Cowboys | 7.00 | 2.80 | .70 |
| ☐ 16 Franco Harris SP<br>Pittsburgh Steelers | 10.00 | 4.00 | 1.00 |
| ☐ 17 Jim Hart<br>St. Louis Cardinals | 5.00 | 2.00 | .50 |
| ☐ 18 Ron Jaworski<br>Philadelphia Eagles | 5.00 | 2.00 | .50 |
| ☐ 19 Bert Jones SP<br>Baltimore Colts | 12.00 | 5.00 | 1.20 |
| ☐ 20 Jack Lambert SP<br>Pittsburgh Steelers | 12.00 | 5.00 | 1.20 |
| ☐ 21 Reggie McKenzie<br>Buffalo Bills | 3.50 | 1.40 | .35 |
| ☐ 22 Karl Mecklenberg SP<br>Denver Broncos | 7.00 | 2.80 | .70 |
| ☐ 23 Craig Morton<br>Denver Broncos | 5.00 | 2.00 | .50 |
| ☐ 24 Dan Pastorini<br>Houston Oilers | 3.50 | 1.40 | .35 |
| ☐ 25 Walter Payton SP<br>Chicago Bears | 25.00 | 10.00 | 2.50 |
| ☐ 26 Lee Roy Selmon<br>Tampa Bay Buccaneers | 5.00 | 2.00 | .50 |
| ☐ 27 Roger Staubach SP<br>Dallas Cowboys | 30.00 | 12.00 | 3.00 |
| ☐ 28 Joe Theismann UER<br>(Misspelled Theisman<br>on card)<br>Washington Redskins | 9.00 | 3.75 | .90 |
| ☐ 29 Wesley Walker SP<br>New York Jets | 7.00 | 2.80 | .70 |
| ☐ 30 Randy White<br>Dallas Cowboys | 7.00 | 2.80 | .70 |
| ☐ 32 Jack Youngblood SP<br>Los Angeles Rams | 12.00 | 5.00 | 1.20 |
| ☐ 32 Jim Zorn<br>Seattle Seahawks | 5.00 | 2.00 | .50 |

In 1980, Marketcom issued a set of 50 Football Mini-Posters. These 5 1/2" by 8 1/2" cards are very attractive, featuring a large full color (action scene) picture of each player with a white border. The cards have the player's name on front at top and have a facsimile autograph on the picture as well; cards are numbered on the back at the bottom as "x of 50". There reportedly also exists a Rocky Bleier card numbered 51.

| | MINT | EXC | G-VG |
|---|---|---|---|
| COMPLETE SET (50) | 35.00 | 14.00 | 3.50 |
| COMMON PLAYER (1-50) | .50 | .20 | .05 |

| | | | |
|---|---|---|---|
| ☐ 1 Ottis Anderson<br>St. Louis Cardinals | 1.50 | .60 | .15 |
| ☐ 2 Brian Sipe<br>Cleveland Browns | .60 | .24 | .06 |
| ☐ 3 Lawrence McCutcheon<br>Los Angeles Rams | .60 | .24 | .06 |
| ☐ 4 Ken Anderson<br>Cincinnati Bengals | 1.25 | .50 | .12 |
| ☐ 5 Roland Harper<br>Chicago Bears | .50 | .20 | .05 |
| ☐ 6 Chuck Foreman<br>Minnesota Vikings | .75 | .30 | .07 |
| ☐ 7 Gary Danielson<br>Detroit Lions | .50 | .20 | .05 |
| ☐ 8 Wallace Francis<br>Atlanta Falcons | .50 | .20 | .05 |
| ☐ 9 John Jefferson<br>San Diego Chargers | .75 | .30 | .07 |
| ☐ 10 Charlie Waters<br>Dallas Cowboys | .75 | .30 | .07 |
| ☐ 11 Jack Ham<br>Pittsburgh Steelers | 1.00 | .40 | .10 |
| ☐ 12 Jack Lambert<br>Pittsburgh Steelers | 1.25 | .50 | .12 |
| ☐ 13 Walter Payton<br>Chicago Bears | 6.00 | 2.40 | .60 |
| ☐ 14 Bert Jones<br>Baltimore Colts | 1.00 | .40 | .10 |
| ☐ 15 Harvey Martin<br>Dallas Cowboys | .75 | .30 | .07 |
| ☐ 16 Jim Hart<br>St. Louis Cardinals | .60 | .24 | .06 |
| ☐ 17 Craig Morton<br>Denver Broncos | .75 | .30 | .07 |
| ☐ 18 Reggie McKenzie<br>Buffalo Bills | .50 | .20 | .05 |
| ☐ 19 Keith Wortman<br>St. Louis Cardinals | .50 | .20 | .05 |
| ☐ 20 Otis Armstrong<br>Denver Broncos | .75 | .30 | .07 |
| ☐ 21 Steve Grogan<br>New England Patriots | .75 | .30 | .07 |
| ☐ 22 Jim Zorn<br>Seattle Seahawks | .75 | .30 | .07 |
| ☐ 23 Bob Griese<br>Miami Dolphins | 2.00 | .80 | .20 |
| ☐ 24 Tony Dorsett<br>Dallas Cowboys | 3.00 | 1.20 | .30 |
| ☐ 25 Wesley Walker<br>New York Jets | .75 | .30 | .07 |
| ☐ 26 Dan Fouts<br>San Diego Chargers | 2.00 | .80 | .20 |
| ☐ 27 Dan Dierdorf<br>St. Louis Cardinals | 1.00 | .40 | .10 |
| ☐ 28 Steve Bartkowski<br>Atlanta Falcons | .75 | .30 | .07 |
| ☐ 29 Archie Manning<br>New Orleans Saints | 1.00 | .40 | .10 |
| ☐ 30 Randy Gradishar<br>Denver Broncos | .75 | .30 | .07 |
| ☐ 31 Randy White<br>Dallas Cowboys | 1.25 | .50 | .12 |

| | | | |
|---|---|---|---|
| ☐ 32 Joe Theismann<br>Washington Redskins | 2.00 | .80 | .20 |
| ☐ 33 Tony Galbreath<br>New Orleans Saints | .50 | .20 | .05 |
| ☐ 34 Cliff Harris<br>Dallas Cowboys | .75 | .30 | .07 |
| ☐ 35 Ray Guy<br>Oakland Raiders | 1.00 | .40 | .10 |
| ☐ 36 Dave Casper<br>Oakland Raiders | .75 | .30 | .07 |
| ☐ 37 Ron Jaworski<br>Philadelphia Eagles | .75 | .30 | .07 |
| ☐ 38 Greg Pruitt<br>Cleveland Browns | .75 | .30 | .07 |
| ☐ 39 Ken Burrough<br>Houston Oilers | .60 | .24 | .06 |
| ☐ 40 Robert Brazile<br>Houston Oilers | .60 | .24 | .06 |
| ☐ 41 Pat Haden<br>Los Angeles Rams | 1.00 | .40 | .10 |
| ☐ 42 Dan Pastorini<br>Houston Oilers | .60 | .24 | .06 |
| ☐ 43 Lee Roy Selmon<br>Tampa Bay Buccaneers | .75 | .30 | .07 |
| ☐ 44 Franco Harris<br>Pittsburgh Steelers | 2.00 | .80 | .20 |
| ☐ 45 Jack Youngblood<br>Los Angeles Rams | 1.25 | .50 | .12 |
| ☐ 46 Terry Bradshaw<br>Pittsburgh Steelers | 6.00 | 2.40 | .60 |
| ☐ 47 Roger Staubach<br>Dallas Cowboys | 7.50 | 3.00 | .75 |
| ☐ 48 Earl Campbell<br>Houston Oilers | 6.00 | 2.40 | .60 |
| ☐ 49 Phil Simms<br>New York Giants | 3.50 | 1.40 | .35 |
| ☐ 50 Delvin Williams<br>Miami Dolphins | .50 | .20 | .05 |

## 1981 Marketcom

Bob Griese

MINI-POSTER 23 of 50

In 1981, Marketcom issued a set of 50 Football Mini-Posters. These 5 1/2" by 8 1/2" cards are very attractive, featuring a large full color (action scene) picture of each player with a white border. The cards have player's name on front at top and have a facsimile autograph on the picture as well; cards are numbered on the back at the bottom. This set can be distinguished from the set of the previous year by the presence of statistics and text on the backs of this issue.

| | MINT | EXC | G-VG |
|---|---|---|---|
| COMPLETE SET (50) | 30.00 | 12.00 | 3.00 |
| COMMON PLAYER (1-50) | .50 | .20 | .05 |
| | | | |
| ☐ 1 Ottis Anderson<br>St. Louis Cardinals | .75 | .30 | .07 |
| ☐ 2 Brian Sipe<br>Cleveland Browns | .60 | .24 | .06 |
| ☐ 3 Rocky Bleier<br>Pittsburgh Steelers | 1.00 | .40 | .10 |
| ☐ 4 Ken Anderson<br>Cincinnati Bengals | 1.25 | .50 | .12 |
| ☐ 5 Roland Harper<br>Chicago Bears | .50 | .20 | .05 |
| ☐ 6 Steve Furness<br>Pittsburgh Steelers | .50 | .20 | .05 |
| ☐ 7 Gary Danielson<br>Detroit Lions | .50 | .20 | .05 |
| ☐ 8 Wallace Francis<br>Atlanta Falcons | .60 | .24 | .06 |
| ☐ 9 John Jefferson<br>San Diego Chargers | .60 | .24 | .06 |
| ☐ 10 Charlie Waters<br>Dallas Cowboys | .75 | .30 | .07 |
| ☐ 11 Jack Ham<br>Pittsburgh Steelers | 1.00 | .40 | .10 |

| | | | |
|---|---|---|---|
| ☐ 12 Jack Lambert<br>Pittsburgh Steelers | 1.25 | .50 | .12 |
| ☐ 13 Walter Payton<br>Chicago Bears | 6.00 | 2.40 | .60 |
| ☐ 14 Bert Jones<br>Baltimore Colts | 1.00 | .40 | .10 |
| ☐ 15 Harvey Martin<br>Dallas Cowboys | .75 | .30 | .07 |
| ☐ 16 Jim Hart<br>St. Louis Cardinals | .75 | .30 | .07 |
| ☐ 17 Craig Morton<br>Denver Broncos | .75 | .30 | .07 |
| ☐ 18 Reggie McKenzie<br>Buffalo Bills | .50 | .20 | .05 |
| ☐ 19 Keith Wortman<br>St. Louis Cardinals | .50 | .20 | .05 |
| ☐ 20 Joe Greene<br>Pittsburgh Steelers | 1.50 | .60 | .15 |
| ☐ 21 Steve Grogan<br>New England Patriots | .75 | .30 | .07 |
| ☐ 22 Jim Zorn<br>Seattle Seahawks | .75 | .30 | .07 |
| ☐ 23 Bob Griese<br>Miami Dolphins | 2.00 | .80 | .20 |
| ☐ 24 Tony Dorsett<br>Dallas Cowboys | 3.00 | 1.20 | .30 |
| ☐ 25 Wesley Walker<br>New York Jets | .75 | .30 | .07 |
| ☐ 26 Dan Fouts<br>San Diego Chargers | 2.00 | .80 | .20 |
| ☐ 27 Dan Dierdorf<br>St. Louis Cardinals | 1.00 | .40 | .10 |
| ☐ 28 Steve Bartkowski<br>Atlanta Falcons | .75 | .30 | .07 |
| ☐ 29 Archie Manning<br>New Orleans Saints | 1.00 | .40 | .10 |
| ☐ 30 Randy Gradishar<br>Denver Broncos | .75 | .30 | .07 |
| ☐ 31 Randy White<br>Dallas Cowboys | 1.25 | .50 | .12 |
| ☐ 32 Joe Theismann<br>Washington Redskins | 2.00 | .80 | .20 |
| ☐ 33 Tony Galbreath<br>New Orleans Saints | .50 | .20 | .05 |
| ☐ 34 Cliff Harris<br>Dallas Cowboys | .75 | .30 | .07 |
| ☐ 35 Ray Guy<br>Oakland Raiders | 1.00 | .40 | .10 |
| ☐ 36 Joe Ferguson<br>Buffalo Bills | .75 | .30 | .07 |
| ☐ 37 Ron Jaworski<br>Philadelphia Eagles | .75 | .30 | .07 |
| ☐ 38 Greg Pruitt<br>Cleveland Browns | .75 | .30 | .07 |
| ☐ 39 Ken Burrough<br>Houston Oilers | .60 | .24 | .06 |
| ☐ 40 Robert Brazile<br>Houston Oilers | .50 | .20 | .05 |
| ☐ 41 Pat Haden<br>Los Angeles Rams | 1.00 | .40 | .10 |
| ☐ 42 Ken Stabler<br>Oakland Raiders | 1.50 | .60 | .15 |
| ☐ 43 Lee Roy Selmon<br>Tampa Bay Buccaneers | .75 | .30 | .07 |
| ☐ 44 Franco Harris<br>Pittsburgh Steelers | 2.00 | .80 | .20 |
| ☐ 45 Jack Youngblood<br>Los Angeles Rams | 1.25 | .50 | .12 |
| ☐ 46 Terry Bradshaw<br>Pittsburgh Steelers | 5.00 | 2.00 | .50 |
| ☐ 47 Roger Staubach<br>Dallas Cowboys | 6.00 | 2.40 | .60 |
| ☐ 48 Earl Campbell<br>Houston Oilers | 5.00 | 2.00 | .50 |
| ☐ 49 Phil Simms<br>New York Giants | 1.50 | .60 | .15 |
| ☐ 50 Delvin Williams<br>Miami Dolphins | .50 | .20 | .05 |

## 1982 Marketcom

In 1982, Marketcom issued a set of 50 Football Mini-Posters. These 5 1/2" by 8 1/2" cards are very attractive, featuring a large full color (action scene) picture of each player with a white border. The cards have player's name on front at top and have a facsimile autograph on the picture as well; cards are numbered on the back at the bottom. The back carries biographical information, player profile, and statistics. The lower right corner of the card back indicates "St. Louis - Marketcom - Series C". There are no licensing logos or credits on the front which may be a clue as to why this particular year of Marketcom is much tougher to find than the others.

| | MINT | EXC | G-VG |
|---|---|---|---|
| COMPLETE SET (48) | 200.00 | 80.00 | 20.00 |
| COMMON PLAYER (1-48) | 2.00 | .80 | .20 |

| | NRMT | VG-E | GOOD |
|---|---|---|---|
| Cleveland Browns | | | |
| ☐ 40 Ken Anderson | 5.00 | 2.00 | .50 |
| Cincinnati Bengals | | | |
| ☐ 41 Richard Todd | 3.00 | 1.20 | .30 |
| New York Jets | | | |
| ☐ 42 Jack Youngblood | 5.00 | 2.00 | .50 |
| Los Angeles Rams | | | |
| ☐ 43 Ottis Anderson | 4.00 | 1.60 | .40 |
| St. Louis Cardinals | | | |
| ☐ 44 Brian Sipe | 3.00 | 1.20 | .30 |
| Cleveland Browns | | | |
| ☐ 45 Mark Gastineau | 3.00 | 1.20 | .30 |
| New York Jets | | | |
| ☐ 46 Mike Pruitt | 2.00 | .80 | .20 |
| Cleveland Browns | | | |
| ☐ 47 Cris Collinsworth | 3.00 | 1.20 | .30 |
| Cincinnati Bengals | | | |
| ☐ 48 Dan Fouts | 6.00 | 2.40 | .60 |
| San Diego Chargers | | | |

# 1971 Mattel Mini-Records

This 17-disc set was designed to be played on a special Mattel mini-record player, which is not included in the complete set price. One four-pack contained Butkus, Lamonica, Mackey, and Simpson, while another four-pack contained Brodie, Hayes, Olsen, and Sayers. These eight discs are easier to find than the others and are marked by DP in the checklist below. Packaging also included eight discs with a booklet featuring either Bart Starr or Joe Namath. Each black plastic disc, approximately 2 1/2" in diameter, features a recording on one side and a color drawing of the player on the other. The picture appears on a paper disk that is glued onto the smooth unrecorded side of the mini-record. On the recorded side, the player's name and the set's subtitle, "Instant Replay," appear in arcs stamped in the central portion of the mini-record. The hand-engraved player's name appears again along with a production number, copyright symbol, and the Mattel name and year of production in the central portion of the record and the grooves. Bart Starr exists as a two-sided white plastic disc. The discs are unnumbered and checklisted below in alphabetical order.

| | NRMT | VG-E | GOOD |
|---|---|---|---|
| COMPLETE SET (17) | 175.00 | 70.00 | 18.00 |
| COMMON PLAYER (1-17) | 4.00 | 1.60 | .40 |
| ☐ 1 Donny Anderson | 4.00 | 1.60 | .40 |
| Green Bay Packers | | | |
| ☐ 2 Lem Barney | 8.00 | 3.25 | .80 |
| Detroit Lions | | | |
| ☐ 3 John Brodie DP | 6.00 | 2.40 | .60 |
| San Francisco 49ers | | | |
| ☐ 4 Dick Butkus DP | 8.00 | 3.25 | .80 |
| Chicago Bears | | | |
| ☐ 5 Bob Hayes DP | 4.00 | 1.60 | .40 |
| Dallas Cowboys | | | |
| ☐ 6 Sonny Jurgensen | 10.00 | 4.00 | 1.00 |
| Washington Redskins | | | |
| ☐ 7 Alex Karras | 10.00 | 4.00 | 1.00 |
| Detroit Lions | | | |
| ☐ 8 Leroy Kelly | 8.00 | 3.25 | .80 |
| Cleveland Browns | | | |
| ☐ 9 Daryle Lamonica DP | 4.00 | 1.60 | .40 |
| Oakland Raiders | | | |
| ☐ 10 John Mackey DP | 6.00 | 2.40 | .60 |
| Baltimore Colts | | | |
| ☐ 11 Earl Morrall | 4.00 | 1.60 | .40 |
| Baltimore Colts | | | |
| ☐ 12 Joe Namath | 45.00 | 18.00 | 4.50 |
| New York Jets | | | |
| ☐ 13 Merlin Olsen DP | 6.00 | 2.40 | .60 |
| Los Angeles Rams | | | |
| ☐ 14 Alan Page | 8.00 | 3.25 | .80 |
| Minnesota Vikings | | | |
| ☐ 15 Gale Sayers DP | 12.00 | 5.00 | 1.20 |
| Chicago Bears | | | |
| ☐ 16 O.J. Simpson DP | 25.00 | 10.00 | 2.50 |
| Buffalo Bills | | | |

| | | | |
|---|---|---|---|
| ☐ 1 Joe Ferguson | 3.00 | 1.20 | .30 |
| Buffalo Bills | | | |
| ☐ 2 Kellen Winslow | 4.00 | 1.60 | .40 |
| San Diego Chargers | | | |
| ☐ 3 Jim Hart | 3.00 | 1.20 | .30 |
| St. Louis Cardinals | | | |
| ☐ 4 Archie Manning | 5.00 | 2.00 | .50 |
| New Orleans Saints | | | |
| ☐ 5 Earl Campbell | 20.00 | 8.00 | 2.00 |
| Houston Oilers | | | |
| ☐ 6 Wallace Francis | 2.00 | .80 | .20 |
| Atlanta Falcons | | | |
| ☐ 7 Randy Gradishar | 3.00 | 1.20 | .30 |
| Denver Broncos | | | |
| ☐ 8 Ken Stabler | 6.00 | 2.40 | .60 |
| Oakland Raiders | | | |
| ☐ 9 Danny White | 4.00 | 1.60 | .40 |
| Dallas Cowboys | | | |
| ☐ 10 Jack Ham | 5.00 | 2.00 | .50 |
| Pittsburgh Steelers | | | |
| ☐ 11 Lawrence Taylor | 20.00 | 8.00 | 2.00 |
| New York Giants | | | |
| ☐ 12 Eric Hipple | 2.00 | .80 | .20 |
| Detroit Lions | | | |
| ☐ 13 Ron Jaworski | 3.00 | 1.20 | .30 |
| Philadelphia Eagles | | | |
| ☐ 14 George Rogers | 3.00 | 1.20 | .30 |
| New Orleans Saints | | | |
| ☐ 15 Jack Lambert | 6.00 | 2.40 | .60 |
| Pittsburgh Steelers | | | |
| ☐ 16 Randy White | 6.00 | 2.40 | .60 |
| Dallas Cowboys | | | |
| ☐ 17 Terry Bradshaw | 15.00 | 6.00 | 1.50 |
| Pittsburgh Steelers | | | |
| ☐ 18 Ray Guy | 5.00 | 2.00 | .50 |
| Oakland Raiders | | | |
| ☐ 19 Rob Carpenter | 2.00 | .80 | .20 |
| New York Giants | | | |
| ☐ 20 Reggie McKenzie | 2.00 | .80 | .20 |
| Buffalo Bills | | | |
| ☐ 21 Tony Dorsett | 8.00 | 3.25 | .80 |
| Dallas Cowboys | | | |
| ☐ 22 Wesley Walker | 3.00 | 1.20 | .30 |
| New York Jets | | | |
| ☐ 23 Tommy Kramer | 3.00 | 1.20 | .30 |
| Minnesota Vikings | | | |
| ☐ 24 Dwight Clark | 4.00 | 1.60 | .40 |
| San Francisco 49ers | | | |
| ☐ 25 Franco Harris | 6.00 | 2.40 | .60 |
| Pittsburgh Steelers | | | |
| ☐ 26 Craig Morton | 3.00 | 1.20 | .30 |
| Denver Broncos | | | |
| ☐ 27 Harvey Martin | 3.00 | 1.20 | .30 |
| Dallas Cowboys | | | |
| ☐ 28 Jim Zorn | 3.00 | 1.20 | .30 |
| Seattle Seahawks | | | |
| ☐ 29 Steve Bartkowski | 3.00 | 1.20 | .30 |
| Atlanta Falcons | | | |
| ☐ 30 Joe Theismann | 6.00 | 2.40 | .60 |
| Washington Redskins | | | |
| ☐ 31 Dan Dierdorf | 4.00 | 1.60 | .40 |
| St. Louis Cardinals | | | |
| ☐ 32 Walter Payton | 20.00 | 8.00 | 2.00 |
| Chicago Bears | | | |
| ☐ 33 John Jefferson | 3.00 | 1.20 | .30 |
| San Diego Chargers | | | |
| ☐ 34 Phil Simms | 6.00 | 2.40 | .60 |
| New York Giants | | | |
| ☐ 35 Lee Roy Selmon | 3.00 | 1.20 | .30 |
| Tampa Bay Buccaneers | | | |
| ☐ 36 Joe Montana | 40.00 | 16.00 | 4.00 |
| San Francisco 49ers | | | |
| ☐ 37 Robert Brazile | 2.00 | .80 | .20 |
| Houston Oilers | | | |
| ☐ 38 Steve Grogan | 3.00 | 1.20 | .30 |
| New England Patriots | | | |
| ☐ 39 Dave Logan | 2.00 | .80 | .20 |

| | | EX-MT | VG-E | GOOD |
|---|---|---|---|---|
| ☐ 17 | Bart Starr | 30.00 | 12.00 | 3.00 |
| | Green Bay Packers | | | |
| ☐ XX | Record Player | 100.00 | 40.00 | 10.00 |

## 1894 Mayo N302

The 1894 Mayo College Football series contains 35 cards of college players from the Ivy League. The ACC designation is N302. The cards are sepia photos of the player surrounded with a black border, in which the player's name, his college, and a Mayo Cut Plug ad appears. The cards have black backs and measure approximately 1 5/8" by 2 7/8". The cards are unnumbered, but have been alphabetically numbered in the checklist below for your convenience. One of the cards has no identification of the player and is listed below as being anonymous. Those players who were All-American selections are listed below with the last two digits of their year(s) of selection. The Poe in the set is a direct descendant of the famous writer Edgar Allan Poe.

| | EX-MT | VG-E | GOOD |
|---|---|---|---|
| COMPLETE SET (35) | 18000. | 8000. | 2000. |
| COMMON PLAYER (1-35) | 450.00 | 180.00 | 45.00 |

| | | | | |
|---|---|---|---|---|
| ☐ 1 | R. Acton | 450.00 | 180.00 | 45.00 |
| | Harvard | | | |
| ☐ 2 | G.T. Adee | 500.00 | 200.00 | 50.00 |
| | Yale AA94 | | | |
| ☐ 3 | Armstrong | 450.00 | 180.00 | 45.00 |
| | Yale | | | |
| ☐ 4 | Barnett | 450.00 | 180.00 | 45.00 |
| | Princeton | | | |
| ☐ 5 | Beale | 450.00 | 180.00 | 45.00 |
| | Harvard | | | |
| ☐ 6 | A.M. Beard | 600.00 | 240.00 | 60.00 |
| | Yale | | | |
| ☐ 7 | C. Brewer | 600.00 | 240.00 | 60.00 |
| | Harvard AA92/93/95 | | | |
| ☐ 8 | Brown | 450.00 | 180.00 | 45.00 |
| | Princeton | | | |
| ☐ 9 | Burt | 450.00 | 180.00 | 45.00 |
| | Princeton | | | |
| ☐ 10 | Frank S. Butterworth | 600.00 | 240.00 | 60.00 |
| | Yale AA93/94 | | | |
| ☐ 11 | I.G. Crowdis | 450.00 | 180.00 | 45.00 |
| | Princeton | | | |
| ☐ 12 | R.W. Emmons | 450.00 | 180.00 | 45.00 |
| | Harvard | | | |
| ☐ 13 | Gonterman UER | 450.00 | 180.00 | 45.00 |
| | Harvard | | | |
| | (Misspelled Gouterman) | | | |
| ☐ 14 | Grey | 450.00 | 180.00 | 45.00 |
| | Harvard | | | |
| ☐ 15 | John C. Greenway | 450.00 | 180.00 | 45.00 |
| | Yale | | | |
| ☐ 16 | W.O. Hickok | 600.00 | 240.00 | 60.00 |
| | Yale AA93/94 | | | |
| ☐ 17 | Frank Hinkey | 700.00 | 280.00 | 70.00 |
| | Yale AA91/92/93/94 | | | |
| ☐ 18 | A.F. Holly | 450.00 | 180.00 | 45.00 |
| | Harvard | | | |
| ☐ 19 | Langdon Lea | 600.00 | 240.00 | 60.00 |
| | Princeton AA93/94/95 | | | |
| ☐ 20 | W.C. Mackie | 450.00 | 180.00 | 45.00 |
| | Harvard | | | |
| ☐ 21 | Manahan | 450.00 | 180.00 | 45.00 |
| | Harvard | | | |
| ☐ 22 | J.A. McCrea | 450.00 | 180.00 | 45.00 |
| | Yale | | | |
| ☐ 23 | F.B. Morse | 500.00 | 200.00 | 50.00 |
| | Princeton AA93 | | | |
| ☐ 24 | F.T. Murphy | 600.00 | 240.00 | 60.00 |
| | Yale AA95/96 | | | |
| ☐ 25 | Poe | 700.00 | 280.00 | 70.00 |
| | Princeton AA89 | | | |
| ☐ 26 | D. Riggs | 600.00 | 240.00 | 60.00 |
| | Princeton AA90/91 | | | |
| ☐ 27 | Phillip T. Stillman | 500.00 | 200.00 | 50.00 |
| | Yale AA94 | | | |
| ☐ 28 | K. Taylor | 450.00 | 180.00 | 45.00 |
| | Princeton | | | |
| ☐ 29 | S.B. Thorne | 500.00 | 200.00 | 50.00 |
| | Yale AA95 | | | |
| ☐ 30 | T.G. Trenchard | 600.00 | 240.00 | 60.00 |
| | Princeton AA93 | | | |
| ☐ 31 | W.D. Ward | 450.00 | 180.00 | 45.00 |
| | Princeton | | | |
| ☐ 32 | Bert G. Waters | 600.00 | 240.00 | 60.00 |
| | Harvard AA92/94 | | | |
| ☐ 33 | Arthur Wheeler | 600.00 | 240.00 | 60.00 |
| | Princeton AA92/93/94 | | | |
| ☐ 34 | Edgar N. Wrightington | 500.00 | 200.00 | 50.00 |
| | Harvard AA96 | | | |
| ☐ 35 | Anonymous | 1000.00 | 450.00 | 125.00 |

## 1975 McDonald's Quarterbacks

The 1975 McDonald's Quarterbacks set contains four cards, each of which was used as a promotion for McDonald's hamburger restaurants. The cards measure 2 1/2" by 3 7/16". One might get a quarter back if the coupon at the bottom of the card were presented at one of McDonald's retail establishments. Each coupon was valid for only one week, that particular week clearly marked on the coupon. The cards themselves are in color with yellow borders on the front and statistics on the back. The back of each card is a different color. Statistics are given for each of the quarterback's previous seasons record passing and rushing. The prices below are for the cards with coupons intact as that is the way they are usually found.

| | NRMT | VG-E | GOOD |
|---|---|---|---|
| COMPLETE SET (4) | 9.00 | 3.75 | .90 |
| COMMON PLAYER (1-4) | .60 | .24 | .06 |

| | | | | |
|---|---|---|---|---|
| ☐ 1 | Terry Bradshaw | 6.50 | 2.60 | .65 |
| | Pittsburgh Steelers | | | |
| ☐ 2 | Joe Ferguson | .90 | .36 | .09 |
| | Buffalo Bills | | | |
| ☐ 3 | Ken Stabler | 3.50 | 1.40 | .35 |
| | Oakland Raiders | | | |
| ☐ 4 | Al Woodall | .60 | .24 | .06 |
| | New York Jets | | | |

## 1985 McDonald's Bears

This set of 32 cards featuring the Chicago Bears was available with three different tab colors. Yellow tabs referenced the Super Bowl. Orange tabs referenced the NFC Championship Game. Blue tabs referenced the Divisional Playoff game. All three sets contain the same 32 players. The cards measure approximately 4 1/2" by 5 7/8" with the tab intact and 4 1/2" by 4 3/8" without the tab, noticeably larger than the McDonald's cards of 1986. Apparently this set was a test market which evidently was successful enough for McDonald's to distribute all 28 teams (plus All-Stars) in 1986. Apparently, this promotion was intended to last until the Bears were eliminated from the playoffs, but they never were; they won the Super Bowl in convincing fashion. Individual player card prices below refer to that player's value in the least expensive color tab. For individual prices on the more expensive color tabs, merely apply the ratio of that color's set price to the base

(cheapest) color set price and use the resulting multiple on the individual prices for that color. Prices listed are for cards with tabs intact.

|  | MINT | EXC | G-VG |
|---|---|---|---|
| COMPLETE SET (BLUE) | 40.00 | 16.00 | 4.00 |
| COMPLETE SET (ORANGE) | 25.00 | 10.00 | 2.50 |
| COMPLETE SET (YELLOW) | 20.00 | 8.00 | 2.00 |
| COMMON PLAYER | .50 | .20 | .05 |
| ☐ 4 Steve Fuller | .60 | .24 | .06 |
| ☐ 6 Kevin Butler | .75 | .30 | .07 |
| ☐ 8 Maury Buford | .50 | .20 | .05 |
| ☐ 9 Jim McMahon | 2.00 | .80 | .20 |
| ☐ 21 Leslie Frazier | .50 | .20 | .05 |
| ☐ 22 Dave Duerson | .60 | .24 | .06 |
| ☐ 26 Matt Suhey | .60 | .24 | .06 |
| ☐ 27 Mike Richardson | .50 | .20 | .05 |
| ☐ 29 Dennis Gentry | .60 | .24 | .06 |
| ☐ 33 Calvin Thomas | .50 | .20 | .05 |
| ☐ 34 Walter Payton | 6.00 | 2.40 | .60 |
| ☐ 45 Gary Fencik | .75 | .30 | .07 |
| ☐ 50 Mike Singletary | 2.00 | .80 | .20 |
| ☐ 55 Otis Wilson | .75 | .30 | .07 |
| ☐ 58 Wilber Marshall | 1.25 | .50 | .12 |
| ☐ 62 Mark Bortz | .50 | .20 | .05 |
| ☐ 63 Jay Hilgenberg | .90 | .36 | .09 |
| ☐ 72 William Perry | 1.00 | .40 | .10 |
| ☐ 73 Mike Hartenstine | .50 | .20 | .05 |
| ☐ 74 Jim Covert | .75 | .30 | .07 |
| ☐ 75 Stefan Humphries | .50 | .20 | .05 |
| ☐ 76 Steve McMichael | .90 | .36 | .09 |
| ☐ 78 Keith Van Horne | .60 | .24 | .06 |
| ☐ 80 Tim Wrightman | .50 | .20 | .05 |
| ☐ 82 Ken Margerum | .50 | .20 | .05 |
| ☐ 83 Willie Gault | 1.25 | .50 | .12 |
| ☐ 85 Dennis McKinnon | .50 | .20 | .05 |
| ☐ 87 Emery Moorehead | .50 | .20 | .05 |
| ☐ 95 Richard Dent | 1.50 | .60 | .15 |
| ☐ 99 Dan Hampton | 2.00 | .80 | .20 |
| ☐ xx Mike Ditka CO | 2.00 | .80 | .20 |
| ☐ xx Buddy Ryan ACO | 1.50 | .60 | .15 |

## 1986 McDonald's All-Stars

This 30-card set was issued in all of the cities that were not near NFL cities and hence is the easiest of the McDonald's subsets to find. The set was issued over a four-week period with blue tabs the first week, black (or gray) tabs the second week, gold (or orange) tabs the third week, and green tabs the fourth week. The cards measure approximately 3 1/16" by 4 11/16" with the tab intact and 3 1/16" by 3 5/8" without the tab. The value of cards without tabs or tabs scratched off is F-G at best. All-Stars were printed on a 30-card sheet; hence, there are no DP cards, unlike the situation with the team subsets,

where six cards were double printed. Since the cards are unnumbered, they are listed below by uniform number; in several instances, players on different teams have the same number.

|  | MINT | EXC | G-VG |
|---|---|---|---|
| COMPLETE SET (BLUE) | 6.00 | 2.40 | .60 |
| COMPLETE SET (BLACK) | 6.00 | 2.40 | .60 |
| COMPLETE SET (GOLD) | 6.00 | 2.40 | .60 |
| COMPLETE SET (GREEN) | 6.00 | 2.40 | .60 |
| COMMON PLAYER | .15 | .06 | .01 |
| ☐ 9 Jim McMahon | .25 | .10 | .02 |
| ☐ 11 Phil Simms | .25 | .10 | .02 |
| ☐ 13 Dan Marino | 2.00 | .80 | .20 |
| ☐ 14 Dan Fouts | .35 | .14 | .03 |
| ☐ 16 Joe Montana | 3.00 | 1.20 | .30 |
| ☐ 20A Deron Cherry | .15 | .06 | .01 |
| ☐ 20B Joe Morris | .15 | .06 | .01 |
| ☐ 32 Marcus Allen | .35 | .14 | .03 |
| ☐ 33 Roger Craig | .25 | .10 | .02 |
| ☐ 34A Kevin Mack | .15 | .06 | .01 |
| ☐ 34B Walter Payton | 1.50 | .60 | .15 |
| ☐ 42 Gerald Riggs | .15 | .06 | .01 |
| ☐ 45 Kenny Easley | .15 | .06 | .01 |
| ☐ 47A Joey Browner | .15 | .06 | .01 |
| ☐ 47B LeRoy Irvin | .15 | .06 | .01 |
| ☐ 52 Mike Webster | .25 | .10 | .02 |
| ☐ 54A E.J. Junior | .15 | .06 | .01 |
| ☐ 54B Randy White | .25 | .10 | .02 |
| ☐ 56 Lawrence Taylor | .35 | .14 | .03 |
| ☐ 63 Mike Munchak | .15 | .06 | .01 |
| ☐ 66 Joe Jacoby | .15 | .06 | .01 |
| ☐ 73 John Hannah | .25 | .10 | .02 |
| ☐ 75A Chris Hinton | .15 | .06 | .01 |
| ☐ 75B Rulon Jones | .15 | .06 | .01 |
| ☐ 75C Howie Long | .25 | .10 | .02 |
| ☐ 78 Anthony Munoz | .25 | .10 | .02 |
| ☐ 81 Art Monk | .35 | .14 | .03 |
| ☐ 82A Ozzie Newsome | .35 | .14 | .03 |
| ☐ 82B Mike Quick | .15 | .06 | .01 |
| ☐ 99 Mark Gastineau | .15 | .06 | .01 |

## 1986 McDonald's Bears

This 24-card set was issued in McDonald's Hamburger restaurants around Chicago. The set was issued over a four-week period with blue tabs the first week, black (or gray) tabs the second week, gold or orange tabs the third week, and green tabs the fourth week. The cards measure approximately 3 1/16" by 4 11/16" with the tab intact and 3 1/16" by 3 5/8" without the tab. The cards are numbered below by uniform number. The value of cards without tabs or tabs scratched off is F-G at best. The cards were printed on a 30-card sheet; hence, there are six double-printed cards listed DP in the checklist below. For individual prices on the more expensive color tabs, merely apply the ratio of that color's set price to the base (cheapest) color set price and use the resulting multiple on the individual prices for that color.

|  | MINT | EXC | G-VG |
|---|---|---|---|
| COMPLETE SET (BLUE) | 15.00 | 6.00 | 1.50 |
| COMPLETE SET (BLACK) | 7.50 | 3.00 | .75 |
| COMPLETE SET (GOLD) | 7.50 | 3.00 | .75 |
| COMPLETE SET (GREEN) | 7.50 | 3.00 | .75 |
| COMMON PLAYER | .30 | .12 | .03 |
| ☐ 6 Kevin Butler DP | .30 | .12 | .03 |
| ☐ 8 Maury Buford | .30 | .12 | .03 |
| ☐ 9 Jim McMahon DP | 1.00 | .40 | .10 |
| ☐ 22 Dave Duerson | .40 | .16 | .04 |
| ☐ 26 Matt Suhey | .40 | .16 | .04 |
| ☐ 27 Mike Richardson | .30 | .12 | .03 |
| ☐ 34 Walter Payton DP | 1.50 | .60 | .15 |
| ☐ 45 Gary Fencik | .40 | .16 | .04 |
| ☐ 50 Mike Singletary DP | .90 | .36 | .09 |

| | | | |
|---|---|---|---|
| ☐ 55 Otis Wilson | .40 | .16 | .04 |
| ☐ 57 Tom Thayer | .30 | .12 | .03 |
| ☐ 58 Wilber Marshall | .75 | .30 | .07 |
| ☐ 62 Mark Bortz DP | .30 | .12 | .03 |
| ☐ 63 Jay Hilgenberg | .50 | .20 | .05 |
| ☐ 72 William Perry DP | .50 | .20 | .05 |
| ☐ 74 Jim Covert | .40 | .16 | .04 |
| ☐ 76 Steve McMichael | .50 | .20 | .05 |
| ☐ 78 Keith Van Horne | .40 | .16 | .04 |
| ☐ 80 Tim Wrightman | .30 | .12 | .03 |
| ☐ 82 Ken Margerum | .30 | .12 | .03 |
| ☐ 83 Willie Gault | .75 | .30 | .07 |
| ☐ 87 Emery Moorehead | .30 | .12 | .03 |
| ☐ 95 Richard Dent | .90 | .36 | .09 |
| ☐ 99 Dan Hampton | 1.00 | .40 | .10 |

## 1986 McDonald's Bengals

This 24-card set was issued in McDonald's Hamburger restaurants around Cincinnati. The set was issued over a four-week period with blue tabs the first week, black (or gray) tabs the second week, gold (or orange) tabs the third week, and green tabs the fourth week. The cards measure approximately 3 1/16" by 4 11/16" with the tab intact and 3 1/16" by 3 5/8" without the tab. The cards are numbered below by uniform number. The value of cards without tabs or tabs scratched off is F-G at best. The cards were printed on a 30-card sheet; hence, there are six double-printed cards listed DP in the checklist below. For individual prices on the more expensive color tabs, merely apply the ratio of that color's set price to the base (cheapest) color set price and use the resulting multiple on the individual prices for that color.

| | MINT | EXC | G-VG |
|---|---|---|---|
| COMPLETE SET (BLUE) | 25.00 | 10.00 | 2.50 |
| COMPLETE SET (BLACK) | 12.50 | 5.00 | 1.25 |
| COMPLETE SET (GOLD) | 12.50 | 5.00 | 1.25 |
| COMPLETE SET (GREEN) | 12.50 | 5.00 | 1.25 |
| COMMON PLAYER | .50 | .20 | .05 |
| | | | |
| ☐ 7 Boomer Esiason | 3.00 | 1.20 | .30 |
| ☐ 14 Ken Anderson DP | 1.25 | .50 | .12 |
| ☐ 20 Ray Horton | .60 | .24 | .06 |
| ☐ 21 James Brooks DP | 1.00 | .40 | .10 |
| ☐ 22 James Griffin | .50 | .20 | .05 |
| ☐ 28 Larry Kinnebrew | .60 | .24 | .06 |
| ☐ 34 Louis Breeden DP | .50 | .20 | .05 |
| ☐ 37 Robert Jackson | .50 | .20 | .05 |
| ☐ 40 Charles Alexander DP | .50 | .20 | .05 |
| ☐ 52 Dave Rimington | .60 | .24 | .06 |
| ☐ 57 Reggie Williams | .75 | .30 | .07 |
| ☐ 65 Max Montoya | .75 | .30 | .07 |
| ☐ 69 Tim Krumrie | .60 | .24 | .06 |
| ☐ 73 Eddie Edwards | .60 | .24 | .06 |
| ☐ 74 Brian Blados DP | .50 | .20 | .05 |
| ☐ 77 Mike Wilson | .50 | .20 | .05 |
| ☐ 78 Anthony Munoz | 1.50 | .60 | .15 |
| ☐ 79 Ross Browner | .60 | .24 | .06 |
| ☐ 80 Cris Collinsworth | 1.00 | .40 | .10 |
| ☐ 81 Eddie Brown DP | .75 | .30 | .07 |
| ☐ 82 Rodney Holman | .60 | .24 | .06 |
| ☐ 83 M.L. Harris | .50 | .20 | .05 |
| ☐ 90 Emanuel King | .50 | .20 | .05 |
| ☐ 91 Carl Zander | .50 | .20 | .05 |

## 1986 McDonald's Bills

This 24-card set was issued in McDonald's Hamburger restaurants around Buffalo. The set was issued over a four-week period with blue tabs the first week, black (or gray) tabs the second week, gold (or orange) tabs the third week, and green tabs the fourth week. The cards measure approximately 3 1/16" by 4 11/16" with the tab intact and 3 1/16" by 3 5/8" without the tab. The cards are numbered below by

uniform number. The value of cards without tabs or tabs scratched off is F-G at best. The cards were printed on a 30-card sheet; hence, there are six double-printed cards listed DP in the checklist below. For individual prices on the more expensive color tabs, merely apply the ratio of that color's set price to the base (cheapest) color set price and use the resulting multiple on the individual prices for that color. Andre Reed and Bruce Smith appear in their Rookie Card year.

| | MINT | EXC | G-VG |
|---|---|---|---|
| COMPLETE SET (BLUE) | 150.00 | 60.00 | 15.00 |
| COMPLETE SET (BLACK) | 25.00 | 10.00 | 2.50 |
| COMPLETE SET (GOLD) | 20.00 | 8.00 | 2.00 |
| COMPLETE SET (GREEN) | 20.00 | 8.00 | 2.00 |
| COMMON PLAYER | .75 | .30 | .07 |
| | | | |
| ☐ 4 John Kidd | .75 | .30 | .07 |
| ☐ 7 Bruce Mathison | 1.00 | .40 | .10 |
| ☐ 11 Scott Norwood | 1.00 | .40 | .10 |
| ☐ 22 Steve Freeman | .75 | .30 | .07 |
| ☐ 26 Charles Romes | .75 | .30 | .07 |
| ☐ 28 Greg Bell DP | 1.25 | .50 | .12 |
| ☐ 29 Derrick Burroughs DP | .75 | .30 | .07 |
| ☐ 43 Martin Bayless DP | 1.00 | .40 | .10 |
| ☐ 51 Jim Ritcher | 1.00 | .40 | .10 |
| ☐ 54 Eugene Marve | .75 | .30 | .07 |
| ☐ 55 Jim Haslett | .75 | .30 | .07 |
| ☐ 57 Lucius Sanford | .75 | .30 | .07 |
| ☐ 63 Justin Cross DP | .75 | .30 | .07 |
| ☐ 65 Tim Vogler | .75 | .30 | .07 |
| ☐ 70 Joe Devlin | 1.00 | .40 | .10 |
| ☐ 72 Ken Jones | .75 | .30 | .07 |
| ☐ 76 Fred Smerlas | 1.25 | .50 | .12 |
| ☐ 77 Ben Williams | 1.00 | .40 | .10 |
| ☐ 78 Bruce Smith | 4.00 | 1.60 | .40 |
| ☐ 80 Jerry Butler DP | 1.00 | .40 | .10 |
| ☐ 83 Andre Reed | 4.00 | 1.60 | .40 |
| ☐ 85 Chris Burkett DP | 1.00 | .40 | .10 |
| ☐ 87 Eason Ramson | .75 | .30 | .07 |
| ☐ 95 Sean McNanie | .75 | .30 | .07 |

## 1986 McDonald's Broncos

This 24-card set was issued in McDonald's Hamburger restaurants around Denver. The set was issued over a four-week period with blue tabs the first week, black (or gray) tabs the second week, gold (or orange) tabs the third week, and green tabs the fourth week. The cards measure approximately 3 1/16" by 4 11/16" with the tab intact and 3 1/16" by 3 5/8" without the tab. The cards are numbered below by uniform number. The value of cards without tabs or tabs scratched off is F-G at best. The cards were printed on a 30-card sheet; hence, there are six double-printed cards listed DP in the checklist below. For individual prices on the more expensive color tabs, merely apply the ratio of that color's set price to the base (cheapest) color set price and use the resulting multiple on the individual prices for that color.

| | MINT | EXC | G-VG |
|---|---|---|---|
| COMPLETE SET (BLUE) | 25.00 | 10.00 | 2.50 |
| COMPLETE SET (BLACK) | 7.50 | 3.00 | .75 |
| COMPLETE SET (GOLD) | 7.50 | 3.00 | .75 |
| COMPLETE SET (GREEN) | 7.50 | 3.00 | .75 |
| COMMON PLAYER | .30 | .12 | .03 |
| ☐ 3 Rich Karlis | .30 | .12 | .03 |
| ☐ 7 John Elway DP | 2.50 | 1.00 | .25 |
| ☐ 20 Louis Wright | .50 | .20 | .05 |
| ☐ 22 Tony Lilly | .30 | .12 | .03 |
| ☐ 23 Sammy Winder | .40 | .16 | .04 |
| ☐ 30 Steve Sewell | .50 | .20 | .05 |
| ☐ 31 Mike Harden | .40 | .16 | .04 |
| ☐ 43 Steve Foley | .40 | .16 | .04 |
| ☐ 47 Gerald Willhite | .40 | .16 | .04 |
| ☐ 49 Dennis Smith | .50 | .20 | .05 |
| ☐ 50 Jim Ryan | .30 | .12 | .03 |
| ☐ 54 Keith Bishop DP | .30 | .12 | .03 |
| ☐ 55 Rick Dennison DP | .30 | .12 | .03 |
| ☐ 57 Tom Jackson | 1.00 | .40 | .10 |
| ☐ 60 Paul Howard | .30 | .12 | .03 |
| ☐ 64 Billy Bryan DP | .30 | .12 | .03 |
| ☐ 68 Rubin Carter DP | .30 | .12 | .03 |
| ☐ 70 Dave Studdard | .30 | .12 | .03 |
| ☐ 75 Rulon Jones | .40 | .16 | .04 |
| ☐ 77 Karl Mecklenburg | .60 | .24 | .06 |
| ☐ 79 Barney Chavous DP | .30 | .12 | .03 |
| ☐ 81 Steve Watson | .40 | .16 | .04 |
| ☐ 82 Vance Johnson | .60 | .24 | .06 |
| ☐ 84 Clint Sampson | .30 | .12 | .03 |

## 1986 McDonald's Browns

This 24-card set was issued in McDonald's Hamburger restaurants around Cleveland. The set was issued over a four-week period with blue tabs the first week, black (or gray) tabs the second week, gold (or orange) tabs the third week, and green tabs the fourth week. The cards measure approximately 3 1/16" by 4 11/16" with the tab intact and 3 1/16" by 3 5/8" without the tab. The cards are numbered below by uniform number. The value of cards without tabs or tabs scratched off is F-G at best. The cards were printed on a 30-card sheet; hence, there are six double-printed cards listed DP in the checklist below. For individual prices on the more expensive color tabs, merely apply the ratio of that color's set price to the base (cheapest) color set price and use the resulting multiple on the individual prices for that color. Bernie Kosar appears in his Rookie Card year.

| | MINT | EXC | G-VG |
|---|---|---|---|
| COMPLETE SET (BLUE) | 10.00 | 4.00 | 1.00 |
| COMPLETE SET (BLACK) | 6.00 | 2.40 | .60 |
| COMPLETE SET (GOLD) | 6.00 | 2.40 | .60 |
| COMPLETE SET (GREEN) | 6.00 | 2.40 | .60 |
| COMMON PLAYER | .25 | .10 | .02 |
| ☐ 9 Matt Bahr DP | .25 | .10 | .02 |
| ☐ 18 Gary Danielson | .35 | .14 | .03 |
| ☐ 19 Bernie Kosar DP | 2.00 | .80 | .20 |
| ☐ 27 Al Gross | .25 | .10 | .02 |
| ☐ 29 Hanford Dixon | .35 | .14 | .03 |
| ☐ 31 Frank Minnifield | .35 | .14 | .03 |
| ☐ 34 Kevin Mack | .75 | .30 | .07 |
| ☐ 37 Chris Rockins | .25 | .10 | .02 |
| ☐ 44 Earnest Byner | 1.00 | .40 | .10 |
| ☐ 51 Eddie Johnson | .25 | .10 | .02 |
| ☐ 55 Curtis Weathers | .25 | .10 | .02 |
| ☐ 56 Chip Banks DP | .35 | .14 | .03 |
| ☐ 57 Clay Matthews | .75 | .30 | .07 |
| ☐ 60 Tom Cousineau | .35 | .14 | .03 |
| ☐ 61 Mike Baab DP | .25 | .10 | .02 |
| ☐ 63 Cody Risien | .35 | .14 | .03 |
| ☐ 77 Rickey Bolden DP | .25 | .10 | .02 |
| ☐ 78 Carl Hairston | .35 | .14 | .03 |

| | MINT | EXC | G-VG |
|---|---|---|---|
| ☐ 79 Bob Golic | .50 | .20 | .05 |
| ☐ 82 Ozzie Newsome | 1.00 | .40 | .10 |
| ☐ 84 Glen Young | .25 | .10 | .02 |
| ☐ 85 Clarence Weathers | .25 | .10 | .02 |
| ☐ 86 Brian Brennan DP | .25 | .10 | .02 |
| ☐ 96 Reggie Camp | .25 | .10 | .02 |

## 1986 McDonald's Buccaneers

This 24-card set was issued in McDonald's Hamburger restaurants in the Tampa Bay area. The set was issued over a four-week period with blue tabs the first week, black (or gray) tabs the second week, gold (or orange) tabs the third week, and green tabs the fourth week. The cards measure approximately 3 1/16" by 4 11/16" with the tab intact and 3 1/16" by 3 5/8" without the tab. The cards are numbered below by uniform number. The value of cards without tabs or tabs scratched off is F-G at best. The cards were printed on a 30-card sheet; hence, there are six double-printed cards listed DP in the checklist below. For individual prices on the more expensive color tabs, merely apply the ratio of that color's set price to the base (cheapest) color set price and use the resulting multiple on the individual prices for that color.

| | MINT | EXC | G-VG |
|---|---|---|---|
| COMPLETE SET (BLUE) | 9.00 | 3.75 | .90 |
| COMPLETE SET (BLACK) | 9.00 | 3.75 | .90 |
| COMPLETE SET (GOLD) | 9.00 | 3.75 | .90 |
| COMPLETE SET (GREEN) | 9.00 | 3.75 | .90 |
| COMMON PLAYER | .25 | .10 | .02 |
| ☐ 1 Donald Igwebuike | .25 | .10 | .02 |
| ☐ 8 Steve Young | 4.50 | 1.80 | .45 |
| ☐ 17 Steve DeBerg | .75 | .30 | .07 |
| ☐ 21 John Holt | .25 | .10 | .02 |
| ☐ 23 Jeremiah Castille DP | .35 | .14 | .03 |
| ☐ 30 David Greenwood | .25 | .10 | .02 |
| ☐ 32 James Wilder | .50 | .20 | .05 |
| ☐ 44 Ivory Sully | .25 | .10 | .02 |
| ☐ 51 Chris Washington | .25 | .10 | .02 |
| ☐ 52 Scott Brantley DP | .25 | .10 | .02 |
| ☐ 54 Ervin Randle | .25 | .10 | .02 |
| ☐ 58 Jeff Davis DP | .25 | .10 | .02 |
| ☐ 60 Randy Grimes | .25 | .10 | .02 |
| ☐ 62 Sean Farrell | .35 | .14 | .03 |
| ☐ 66 George Yarno | .25 | .10 | .02 |
| ☐ 73 Ron Heller | .35 | .14 | .03 |
| ☐ 76 David Logan | .25 | .10 | .02 |
| ☐ 78 John Cannon DP | .25 | .10 | .02 |
| ☐ 82 Jerry Bell DP | .25 | .10 | .02 |
| ☐ 86 Calvin Magee | .25 | .10 | .02 |
| ☐ 87 Gerald Carter DP | .25 | .10 | .02 |
| ☐ 88 Jimmie Giles | .35 | .14 | .03 |
| ☐ 89 Kevin House | .35 | .14 | .03 |
| ☐ 90 Ron Holmes | .35 | .14 | .03 |

## 1986 McDonald's Cardinals

This 24-card set was issued in McDonald's Hamburger restaurants around St. Louis. The set was issued over a four-week period with blue tabs the first week, black (or gray) tabs the second week, gold (or orange) tabs the third week, and green tabs the fourth week. The cards measure approximately 3 1/16" by 4 11/16" with the tab intact and 3 1/16" by 3 5/8" without the tab. The cards are numbered below by uniform number. The value of cards without tabs or tabs scratched off is F-G at best. The cards were printed on a 30-card sheet; hence, there are six double-printed cards listed DP in the checklist below. For individual prices on the more expensive color tabs, merely apply the ratio of that color's set price to the base (cheapest) color set price and use the resulting multiple on the individual prices for that color.

| | MINT | EXC | G-VG |
|---|---|---|---|
| COMPLETE SET (BLUE) | 10.00 | 4.00 | 1.00 |
| COMPLETE SET (BLACK) | 6.00 | 2.40 | .60 |
| COMPLETE SET (GOLD) | 6.00 | 2.40 | .60 |
| COMPLETE SET (GREEN) | 6.00 | 2.40 | .60 |
| COMMON PLAYER | .25 | .10 | .02 |

| | | MINT | EXC | G-VG |
|---|---|---|---|---|
| ☐ 15 | Neil Lomax | .75 | .30 | .07 |
| ☐ 18 | Carl Birdsong DP | .25 | .10 | .02 |
| ☐ 30 | Stump Mitchell | .50 | .20 | .05 |
| ☐ 32 | Ottis Anderson DP | .75 | .30 | .07 |
| ☐ 43 | Lonnie Young | .35 | .14 | .03 |
| ☐ 45 | Leonard Smith | .35 | .14 | .03 |
| ☐ 47 | Cedric Mack | .35 | .14 | .03 |
| ☐ 48 | Lionel Washington | .35 | .14 | .03 |
| ☐ 53 | Freddie Joe Nunn | .35 | .14 | .03 |
| ☐ 54 | E.J. Junior | .35 | .14 | .03 |
| ☐ 57 | Niko Noga | .35 | .14 | .03 |
| ☐ 60 | Al "Bubba" Baker DP | .35 | .14 | .03 |
| ☐ 63 | Tootie Robbins | .35 | .14 | .03 |
| ☐ 65 | David Galloway | .25 | .10 | .02 |
| ☐ 66 | Doug Dawson DP | .25 | .10 | .02 |
| ☐ 67 | Luis Sharpe | .35 | .14 | .03 |
| ☐ 71 | Joe Bostic DP | .25 | .10 | .02 |
| ☐ 73 | Mark Duda DP | .25 | .10 | .02 |
| ☐ 75 | Curtis Greer | .35 | .14 | .03 |
| ☐ 80 | Doug Marsh | .25 | .10 | .02 |
| ☐ 81 | Roy Green | .75 | .30 | .07 |
| ☐ 83 | Pat Tilley | .35 | .14 | .03 |
| ☐ 84 | J.T. Smith | .50 | .20 | .05 |
| ☐ 89 | Greg Lafleur | .25 | .10 | .02 |

## 1986 McDonald's Chargers

This 24-card set was issued in McDonald's Hamburger restaurants around San Diego. The set was issued over a four-week period with blue tabs the first week, black (or gray) tabs the second week, gold (or orange) tabs the third week, and green tabs the fourth week. The cards measure approximately 3 1/16" by 4 11/16" with the tab intact and 3 1/16" by 3 5/8" without the tab. The cards are numbered below by uniform number. The value of cards without tabs or tabs scratched off is F-G at best. The cards were printed on a 30-card sheet; hence, there are six double-printed cards listed DP in the checklist below. For individual prices on the more expensive color tabs, merely apply the ratio of that color's set price to the base (cheapest) color set price and use the resulting multiple on the individual prices for that color.

| | MINT | EXC | G-VG |
|---|---|---|---|
| COMPLETE SET (BLUE) | 20.00 | 8.00 | 2.00 |
| COMPLETE SET (BLACK) | 15.00 | 6.00 | 1.50 |
| COMPLETE SET (GOLD) | 10.00 | 4.00 | 1.00 |
| COMPLETE SET (GREEN) | 10.00 | 4.00 | 1.00 |
| COMMON PLAYER | .40 | .16 | .04 |

| | | MINT | EXC | G-VG |
|---|---|---|---|---|
| ☐ 9 | Mark Herrmann | .60 | .24 | .06 |
| ☐ 14 | Dan Fouts DP | 1.50 | .60 | .15 |
| ☐ 18 | Charlie Joiner | 1.25 | .50 | .12 |
| ☐ 21 | Buford McGee | .50 | .20 | .05 |
| ☐ 22 | Gill Byrd DP | .60 | .24 | .06 |
| ☐ 26 | Lionel James | .50 | .20 | .05 |
| ☐ 29 | John Hendy | .40 | .16 | .04 |
| ☐ 37 | Jeff Dale DP | .40 | .16 | .04 |
| ☐ 40 | Gary Anderson DP | .75 | .30 | .07 |
| ☐ 43 | Tim Spencer | .50 | .20 | .05 |
| ☐ 51 | Woodrow Lowe | .50 | .20 | .05 |
| ☐ 54 | Billy Ray Smith | .75 | .30 | .07 |
| ☐ 60 | Dennis McKnight | .40 | .16 | .04 |
| ☐ 62 | Don Macek | .40 | .16 | .04 |
| ☐ 67 | Ed White | .60 | .24 | .06 |
| ☐ 74 | Jim Lachey | 1.25 | .50 | .12 |
| ☐ 78 | Chuck Ehin DP | .40 | .16 | .04 |
| ☐ 80 | Kellen Winslow | 1.25 | .50 | .12 |
| ☐ 83 | Trumaine Johnson | .50 | .20 | .05 |
| ☐ 85 | Eric Sievers | .75 | .30 | .07 |
| ☐ 88 | Pete Holohan | .50 | .20 | .05 |
| ☐ 89 | Wes Chandler DP | .75 | .30 | .07 |
| ☐ 93 | Earl Wilson | .40 | .16 | .04 |
| ☐ 99 | Lee Williams | 1.00 | .40 | .10 |

## 1986 McDonald's Chiefs

This 24-card set was issued in McDonald's Hamburger restaurants around Kansas City. The set was issued over a four-week period with blue tabs the first week, black (or gray) tabs the second week, gold (or orange) tabs the third week, and green tabs the fourth week. The cards measure approximately 3 1/16" by 4 11/16" with the tab intact and 3 1/16" by 3 5/8" without the tab. The cards are numbered below by uniform number. The value of cards without tabs or tabs scratched off is F-G at best. The cards were printed on a 30-card sheet; hence, there are six double-printed cards listed DP in the checklist below. For individual prices on the more expensive color tabs, merely apply the ratio of that color's set price to the base (cheapest) color set price and use the resulting multiple on the individual prices for that color.

| | MINT | EXC | G-VG |
|---|---|---|---|
| COMPLETE SET (BLUE) | 25.00 | 10.00 | 2.50 |
| COMPLETE SET (BLACK) | 40.00 | 16.00 | 4.00 |
| COMPLETE SET (GOLD) | 20.00 | 8.00 | 2.00 |
| COMPLETE SET (GREEN) | 20.00 | 8.00 | 2.00 |
| COMMON PLAYER | .75 | .30 | .07 |

| | | MINT | EXC | G-VG |
|---|---|---|---|---|
| ☐ 6 | Jim Arnold DP | .75 | .30 | .07 |
| ☐ 8 | Nick Lowery | 1.25 | .50 | .12 |
| ☐ 9 | Bill Kenney | 1.00 | .40 | .10 |
| ☐ 14 | Todd Blackledge DP | 1.00 | .40 | .10 |
| ☐ 20 | Deron Cherry DP | 1.25 | .50 | .12 |
| ☐ 29 | Albert Lewis | 2.00 | .80 | .20 |
| ☐ 31 | Kevin Ross | 1.25 | .50 | .12 |
| ☐ 34 | Lloyd Burruss DP | .75 | .30 | .07 |
| ☐ 41 | Garcia Lane | .75 | .30 | .07 |
| ☐ 42 | Jeff Smith | 1.00 | .40 | .10 |
| ☐ 43 | Mike Pruitt | 1.25 | .50 | .12 |
| ☐ 44 | Herman Heard | 1.25 | .50 | .12 |
| ☐ 50 | Calvin Daniels | .75 | .30 | .07 |
| ☐ 59 | Gary Spani | .75 | .30 | .07 |
| ☐ 63 | Bill Maas | 1.25 | .50 | .12 |
| ☐ 64 | Bob Olderman | .75 | .30 | .07 |
| ☐ 66 | Brad Budde DP | .75 | .30 | .07 |
| ☐ 67 | Art Still | 1.25 | .50 | .12 |
| ☐ 72 | David Lutz | .75 | .30 | .07 |
| ☐ 83 | Stephone Paige | 2.00 | .80 | .20 |
| ☐ 85 | Jonathan Hayes | 1.25 | .50 | .12 |
| ☐ 88 | Carlos Carson DP | 1.00 | .40 | .10 |
| ☐ 89 | Henry Marshall | 1.00 | .40 | .10 |
| ☐ 97 | Scott Radecic | .75 | .30 | .07 |

## 1986 McDonald's Colts

This 24-card set was issued in McDonald's Hamburger restaurants around Indianapolis. The set was issued over a four-week period with blue tabs the first week, black (or gray) tabs the second week, gold (or orange) tabs the third week, and green tabs the fourth week. The cards measure approximately 3 1/16" by 4 11/16" with the tab intact and 3 1/16" by 3 5/8" without the tab. The cards are numbered below by uniform number. The value of cards without tabs or tabs scratched off is F-G at best. The cards were printed on a 30-card sheet; hence, there are six double-printed cards listed DP in the checklist below. For individual prices on the more expensive color tabs, merely apply the ratio of that color's set price to the base (cheapest) color set price and use the resulting multiple on the individual prices for that color.

|  | MINT | EXC | G-VG |
|---|---|---|---|
| COMPLETE SET (BLUE) | 100.00 | 40.00 | 10.00 |
| COMPLETE SET (BLACK) | 25.00 | 10.00 | 2.50 |
| COMPLETE SET (GOLD) | 15.00 | 6.00 | 1.50 |
| COMPLETE SET (GREEN) | 15.00 | 6.00 | 1.50 |
| COMMON PLAYER | .60 | .24 | .06 |
| ☐ 2 Raul Allegre DP | .60 | .24 | .06 |
| ☐ 3 Rohn Stark | .75 | .30 | .07 |
| ☐ 25 Nesby Glasgow | .60 | .24 | .06 |
| ☐ 27 Preston Davis | .60 | .24 | .06 |
| ☐ 32 Randy McMillan | .75 | .30 | .07 |
| ☐ 34 George Wonsley | .75 | .30 | .07 |
| ☐ 38 Eugene Daniel | .60 | .24 | .06 |
| ☐ 44 Owen Gill | .60 | .24 | .06 |
| ☐ 47 Leonard Coleman | .60 | .24 | .06 |
| ☐ 50 Duane Bickett DP | 1.25 | .50 | .12 |
| ☐ 53 Ray Donaldson | .60 | .24 | .06 |
| ☐ 55 Barry Krauss | 1.00 | .40 | .10 |
| ☐ 64 Ben Utt | .60 | .24 | .06 |
| ☐ 66 Ron Solt | .75 | .30 | .07 |
| ☐ 72 Karl Baldischwiler DP | .60 | .24 | .06 |
| ☐ 75 Chris Hinton | 1.25 | .50 | .12 |
| ☐ 81 Pat Beach DP | .60 | .24 | .06 |
| ☐ 85 Matt Bouza DP | .60 | .24 | .06 |
| ☐ 87 Wayne Capers DP | .60 | .24 | .06 |
| ☐ 88 Robbie Martin | .75 | .30 | .07 |
| ☐ 92 Brad White | .60 | .24 | .06 |
| ☐ 93 Cliff Odom | .60 | .24 | .06 |
| ☐ 96 Blaise Winter | .90 | .36 | .09 |
| ☐ 98 Johnie Cooks | .75 | .30 | .07 |

## 1986 McDonald's Cowboys

This 25-card set was issued in McDonald's Hamburger restaurants around Dallas. The set was issued over a four-week period with blue tabs the first week, black (or gray) tabs the second week, gold (or

orange) tabs the third week, and green tabs the fourth week. The cards measure approximately 3 1/16" by 4 11/16" with the tab intact and 3 1/16" by 3 5/8" without the tab. The cards are numbered below by uniform number. The Herschel Walker card was produced later due to his popularity. Walker's card was produced only with a green tab without any coating on the tab to be scratched off; hence his cards are typically found in nice condition. The value of cards without tabs or tabs scratched off is F-G at best. The cards (other than Herschel Walker) were printed on a 30-card sheet; hence, there are six double-printed cards listed DP in the checklist below. For individual prices on the more expensive color tabs, merely apply the ratio of that color's set price to the base (cheapest) color set price and use the resulting multiple on the individual prices for that color.

|  | MINT | EXC | G-VG |
|---|---|---|---|
| COMPLETE SET (BLUE) | 8.00 | 3.25 | .80 |
| COMPLETE SET (BLACK) | 8.00 | 3.25 | .80 |
| COMPLETE SET (GOLD) | 8.00 | 3.25 | .80 |
| COMPLETE SET (GREEN) | 8.00 | 3.25 | .80 |
| COMMON PLAYER | .25 | .10 | .02 |
| ☐ 1 Rafael Septien | .25 | .10 | .02 |
| ☐ 11 Danny White | .50 | .20 | .05 |
| ☐ 24 Everson Walls | .50 | .20 | .05 |
| ☐ 26 Michael Downs DP | .25 | .10 | .02 |
| ☐ 27 Ron Fellows | .35 | .14 | .03 |
| ☐ 30 Timmy Newsome | .35 | .14 | .03 |
| ☐ 33 Tony Dorsett DP | 1.00 | .40 | .10 |
| ☐ 34 Herschel Walker | 2.00 | .80 | .20 |
| ☐ 40 Bill Bates DP | .50 | .20 | .05 |
| ☐ 47 Dextor Clinkscale DP | .25 | .10 | .02 |
| ☐ 50 Jeff Rohrer | .25 | .10 | .02 |
| ☐ 54 Randy White | .75 | .30 | .07 |
| ☐ 56 Eugene Lockhart | .35 | .14 | .03 |
| ☐ 58 Mike Hegman | .25 | .10 | .02 |
| ☐ 61 Jim Cooper DP | .25 | .10 | .02 |
| ☐ 63 Glen Titensor | .25 | .10 | .02 |
| ☐ 64 Tom Rafferty | .35 | .14 | .03 |
| ☐ 65 Kurt Peterson | .25 | .10 | .02 |
| ☐ 72 Ed Too Tall Jones | .75 | .30 | .07 |
| ☐ 75 Phil Pozderac | .25 | .10 | .02 |
| ☐ 77 Jim Jeffcoat | .50 | .20 | .05 |
| ☐ 78 John Dutton | .35 | .14 | .03 |
| ☐ 80 Tony Hill | .50 | .20 | .05 |
| ☐ 82 Mike Renfro | .35 | .14 | .03 |
| ☐ 84 Doug Cosbie DP | .35 | .14 | .03 |

## 1986 McDonald's Dolphins

This 25-card set was issued in McDonald's Hamburger restaurants around Miami. The set was issued over a four-week period with blue tabs the first week, black (or gray) tabs the second week, gold (or orange) tabs the third week, and green tabs the fourth week. The cards measure approximately 3 1/16" by 4 11/16" with the tab intact and 3 1/16" by 3 5/8" without the tab. The cards are numbered below by uniform number. Joe Carter and Tony Nathan have photos reversed so that there are 25 different cards, but since this error happened on a double-printed player, no additional value is assigned. The value of cards without tabs or tabs scratched off is F-G at best. The cards were printed on a 30-card sheet; hence, there are five double-printed cards listed DP in the checklist below. For individual prices on the more expensive color tabs, merely apply the ratio of that color's set price to the base (cheapest) color set price and use the resulting multiple on the individual prices for that color.

|  | MINT | EXC | G-VG |
|---|---|---|---|
| COMPLETE SET (BLUE) | 30.00 | 12.00 | 3.00 |
| COMPLETE SET (BLACK) | 15.00 | 6.00 | 1.50 |
| COMPLETE SET (GOLD) | 15.00 | 6.00 | 1.50 |
| COMPLETE SET (GREEN) | 15.00 | 6.00 | 1.50 |
| COMMON PLAYER | .50 | .20 | .05 |

| | MINT | EXC | G-VG |
|---|---|---|---|
| ☐ 4 Reggie Roby | 1.00 | .40 | .10 |
| ☐ 7 Fuad Reveiz | .75 | .30 | .07 |
| ☐ 10 Don Strock | .75 | .30 | .07 |
| ☐ 13 Dan Marino | 6.00 | 2.40 | .60 |
| ☐ 22 Tony Nathan | 1.00 | .40 | .10 |
| ☐ 23A Joe Carter ERR | 1.00 | .40 | .10 |
| (Photo actually | | | |
| Tony Nathan 22) | | | |
| ☐ 23B Joe Carter COR | .75 | .30 | .07 |
| ☐ 27 Lorenzo Hampton | .60 | .24 | .06 |
| ☐ 30 Ron Davenport | .60 | .24 | .06 |
| ☐ 43 Bud Brown DP | .50 | .20 | .05 |
| ☐ 47 Glenn Blackwood DP | .60 | .24 | .06 |
| ☐ 49 William Judson | .50 | .20 | .05 |
| ☐ 55 Hugh Green | .75 | .30 | .07 |
| ☐ 57 Dwight Stephenson | .75 | .30 | .07 |
| ☐ 58 Kim Bokamper DP | .50 | .20 | .05 |
| ☐ 59 Bob Brudzinski DP | .60 | .24 | .06 |
| ☐ 61 Roy Foster | .50 | .20 | .05 |
| ☐ 71 Mike Charles | .50 | .20 | .05 |
| ☐ 75 Doug Betters DP | .50 | .20 | .05 |
| ☐ 79 Jon Giesler | .50 | .20 | .05 |
| ☐ 83 Mark Clayton | 2.00 | .80 | .20 |
| ☐ 84 Bruce Hardy | .50 | .20 | .05 |
| ☐ 85 Mark Duper | 1.00 | .40 | .10 |
| ☐ 89 Nat Moore | .75 | .30 | .07 |
| ☐ 91 Mack Moore | .50 | .20 | .05 |

## 1986 McDonald's Eagles

This 24-card set was issued in McDonald's Hamburger restaurants around Philadelphia. The set was issued over a four-week period with blue tabs the first week, black (or gray) tabs the second week, gold (or orange) tabs the third week, and green tabs the fourth week. The cards measure approximately 3 1/16" by 4 11/16" with the tab intact and 3 1/16" by 3 5/8" without the tab. The cards are numbered below by uniform number. The value of cards without tabs or tabs scratched off is F-G at best. The cards were printed on a 30-card sheet; hence, there are six double-printed cards listed DP in the checklist below. For individual prices on the more expensive color tabs, merely apply the ratio of that color's set price to the base (cheapest) color set price and use the resulting multiple on the individual prices for that color. Randall Cunningham appears in this set, a year before his Topps Rookie Card.

| | MINT | EXC | G-VG |
|---|---|---|---|
| COMPLETE SET (BLUE) | 50.00 | 20.00 | 5.00 |
| COMPLETE SET (BLACK) | 15.00 | 6.00 | 1.50 |
| COMPLETE SET (GOLD) | 7.50 | 3.00 | .75 |
| COMPLETE SET (GREEN) | 7.50 | 3.00 | .75 |
| COMMON PLAYER | .25 | .10 | .02 |
| ☐ 7 Ron Jaworski | .50 | .20 | .05 |
| ☐ 8 Paul McFadden | .25 | .10 | .02 |
| ☐ 12 Randall Cunningham DP | 3.00 | 1.20 | .30 |
| ☐ 22 Brenard Wilson | .25 | .10 | .02 |
| ☐ 24 Ray Ellis | .25 | .10 | .02 |
| ☐ 29 Elbert Foules | .25 | .10 | .02 |
| ☐ 36 Herman Hunter | .25 | .10 | .02 |
| ☐ 41 Earnest Jackson | .50 | .20 | .05 |
| ☐ 43 Roynell Young | .35 | .14 | .03 |
| ☐ 48 Wes Hopkins | .50 | .20 | .05 |
| ☐ 50 Garry Cobb DP | .25 | .10 | .02 |
| ☐ 63 Ron Baker DP | .25 | .10 | .02 |
| ☐ 66 Ken Reeves | .25 | .10 | .02 |
| ☐ 71 Ken Clarke DP | .25 | .10 | .02 |
| ☐ 73 Steve Kenney | .25 | .10 | .02 |
| ☐ 74 Leonard Mitchell | .35 | .14 | .03 |
| ☐ 81 Kenny Jackson | .35 | .14 | .03 |
| ☐ 82 Mike Quick | .50 | .20 | .05 |
| ☐ 85 Ron Johnson | .25 | .10 | .02 |
| ☐ 88 John Spagnola | .25 | .10 | .02 |
| ☐ 91 Reggie White | 2.50 | 1.00 | .25 |

| | | | |
|---|---|---|---|
| ☐ 93 Thomas Strauthers | .25 | .10 | .02 |
| ☐ 94 Byron Darby DP | .25 | .10 | .02 |
| ☐ 98 Greg Brown DP | .25 | .10 | .02 |

## 1986 McDonald's Falcons

This 24-card set was issued in McDonald's Hamburger restaurants around Atlanta. The set was issued over a four-week period with blue tabs the first week, black (or gray) tabs the second week, gold (or orange) tabs the third week, and green tabs the fourth week. The cards measure approximately 3 1/16" by 4 11/16" with the tab intact and 3 1/16" by 3 5/8" without the tab. The cards are numbered below by uniform number. The value of cards without tabs or tabs scratched off is F-G at best. The cards were printed on a 30-card sheet; hence, there are six double-printed cards listed DP in the checklist below. For individual prices on the more expensive color tabs, merely apply the ratio of that color's set price to the base (cheapest) color set price and use the resulting multiple on the individual prices for that color.

| | MINT | EXC | G-VG |
|---|---|---|---|
| COMPLETE SET (BLUE) | 60.00 | 24.00 | 6.00 |
| COMPLETE SET (BLACK) | 225.00 | 90.00 | 22.00 |
| COMPLETE SET (GOLD) | 60.00 | 24.00 | 6.00 |
| COMPLETE SET (GREEN) | 15.00 | 6.00 | 1.50 |
| COMMON PLAYER | .60 | .24 | .06 |
| ☐ 3 Rick Donnelly | .60 | .24 | .06 |
| ☐ 16 Dave Archer DP | 1.00 | .40 | .10 |
| ☐ 18 Mick Luckhurst | .75 | .30 | .07 |
| ☐ 23 Bobby Butler | .60 | .24 | .06 |
| ☐ 26 James Britt DP | .60 | .24 | .06 |
| ☐ 37 Kenny Johnson | .60 | .24 | .06 |
| ☐ 39 Cliff Austin DP | .75 | .30 | .07 |
| ☐ 42 Gerald Riggs | 1.25 | .50 | .12 |
| ☐ 50 Buddy Curry | .60 | .24 | .06 |
| ☐ 56 Al Richardson | .60 | .24 | .06 |
| ☐ 57 Jeff Van Note | 1.00 | .40 | .10 |
| ☐ 58 David Frye | .60 | .24 | .06 |
| ☐ 61 John Scully | .60 | .24 | .06 |
| ☐ 62 Brett Miller | .60 | .24 | .06 |
| ☐ 74 Mike Pitts | 1.00 | .40 | .10 |
| ☐ 76 Mike Gann | .75 | .30 | .07 |
| ☐ 77 Rick Bryan | 1.00 | .40 | .10 |
| ☐ 78 Mike Kenn | 1.00 | .40 | .10 |
| ☐ 79 Bill Fralic | 1.25 | .50 | .12 |
| ☐ 81 Billy Johnson | 1.25 | .50 | .12 |
| ☐ 82 Stacey Bailey DP | .75 | .30 | .07 |
| ☐ 87 Cliff Benson DP | .60 | .24 | .06 |
| ☐ 88 Arthur Cox | .60 | .24 | .06 |
| ☐ 89 Charlie Brown DP | .75 | .30 | .07 |

## 1986 McDonald's 49ers

This 24-card set was issued in McDonald's Hamburger restaurants around San Francisco. The set was issued over a four-week period with blue tabs the first week, black (or gray) tabs the second week, gold (or orange) tabs the third week, and green tabs the fourth week. The cards measure approximately 3 1/16" by 4 11/16" with the tab intact and 3 1/16" by 3 5/8" without the tab. The cards are numbered below by uniform number. The value of cards without tabs or tabs scratched off is F-G at best. The cards were printed on a 30-card sheet; hence, there are six double-printed cards listed DP in the checklist below. For individual prices on the more expensive color tabs, merely apply the ratio of that color's set price to the base (cheapest) color set price and use the resulting multiple on the individual prices for that color. Jerry Rice appears in his Rookie Card year.

|  | MINT | EXC | G-VG |
|---|---|---|---|
| COMPLETE SET (BLUE) | 40.00 | 16.00 | 4.00 |
| COMPLETE SET (BLACK) | 20.00 | 8.00 | 2.00 |
| COMPLETE SET (GOLD) | 20.00 | 8.00 | 2.00 |
| COMPLETE SET (GREEN) | 20.00 | 8.00 | 2.00 |
| COMMON PLAYER | .75 | .30 | .07 |
| ☐ 16 Joe Montana | 8.00 | 3.25 | .80 |
| ☐ 21 Eric Wright | .75 | .30 | .07 |
| ☐ 26 Wendell Tyler | 1.00 | .40 | .10 |
| ☐ 27 Carlton Williamson | .75 | .30 | .07 |
| ☐ 33 Roger Craig DP | 1.25 | .50 | .12 |
| ☐ 42 Ronnie Lott | 2.00 | .80 | .20 |
| ☐ 49 Jeff Fuller | .75 | .30 | .07 |
| ☐ 50 Riki Ellison | .75 | .30 | .07 |
| ☐ 51 Randy Cross DP | 1.00 | .40 | .10 |
| ☐ 56 Fred Quillan | .75 | .30 | .07 |
| ☐ 58 Keena Turner | 1.00 | .40 | .10 |
| ☐ 62 Guy McIntyre | 1.00 | .40 | .10 |
| ☐ 68 John Ayers DP | .75 | .30 | .07 |
| ☐ 71 Keith Fahnhorst | .75 | .30 | .07 |
| ☐ 72 Jeff Stover | .75 | .30 | .07 |
| ☐ 76 Dwaine Board DP | .75 | .30 | .07 |
| ☐ 77 Bubba Paris | .75 | .30 | .07 |
| ☐ 78 Manu Tuiasosopo | .75 | .30 | .07 |
| ☐ 80 Jerry Rice | 8.00 | 3.25 | .80 |
| ☐ 81 Russ Francis | 1.00 | .40 | .10 |
| ☐ 86 John Frank | .75 | .30 | .07 |
| ☐ 87 Dwight Clark DP | 1.25 | .50 | .12 |
| ☐ 90 Todd Shell | .75 | .30 | .07 |
| ☐ 95 Michael Carter DP | 1.25 | .50 | .12 |

# 1986 McDonald's Giants

This 24-card set was issued in McDonald's Hamburger restaurants around New York. The set was issued over a four-week period with blue tabs the first week, black (or gray) tabs the second week, gold (or orange) tabs the third week, and green tabs the fourth week. The cards measure approximately 3 1/16" by 4 11/16" with the tab intact and 3 1/16" by 3 5/8" without the tab. The cards are numbered below by uniform number. The value of cards without tabs or tabs scratched off is F-G at best. The cards were printed on a 30-card sheet; hence, there are six double-printed cards listed DP in the checklist below. For individual prices on the more expensive color tabs, merely apply the ratio of that color's set price to the base (cheapest) color set price and use the resulting multiple on the individual prices for that color.

|  | MINT | EXC | G-VG |
|---|---|---|---|
| COMPLETE SET (BLUE) | 12.00 | 5.00 | 1.20 |
| COMPLETE SET (BLACK) | 9.00 | 3.75 | .90 |
| COMPLETE SET (GOLD) | 6.00 | 2.40 | .60 |

| COMPLETE SET (GREEN) | 6.00 | 2.40 | .60 |
|---|---|---|---|
| COMMON PLAYER | .25 | .10 | .02 |
| ☐ 5 Sean Landeta | .35 | .14 | .03 |
| ☐ 11 Phil Simms | 1.25 | .50 | .12 |
| ☐ 20 Joe Morris | .50 | .20 | .05 |
| ☐ 23 Perry Williams | .25 | .10 | .02 |
| ☐ 26 Rob Carpenter DP | .25 | .10 | .02 |
| ☐ 33 George Adams DP | .25 | .10 | .02 |
| ☐ 34 Elvis Patterson | .35 | .14 | .03 |
| ☐ 43 Terry Kinard | .35 | .14 | .03 |
| ☐ 44 Maurice Carthon | .35 | .14 | .03 |
| ☐ 48 Kenny Hill | .25 | .10 | .02 |
| ☐ 53 Harry Carson | .50 | .20 | .05 |
| ☐ 54 Andy Headen | .25 | .10 | .02 |
| ☐ 56 Lawrence Taylor | 1.50 | .60 | .15 |
| ☐ 60 Brad Benson DP | .25 | .10 | .02 |
| ☐ 63 Karl Nelson | .35 | .14 | .03 |
| ☐ 64 Jim Burt DP | .25 | .10 | .02 |
| ☐ 67 Billy Ard DP | .25 | .10 | .02 |
| ☐ 70 Leonard Marshall | .35 | .14 | .03 |
| ☐ 75 George Martin | .35 | .14 | .03 |
| ☐ 80 Phil McConkey | .35 | .14 | .03 |
| ☐ 84 Zeke Mowatt | .35 | .14 | .03 |
| ☐ 85 Don Hasselbeck | .25 | .10 | .02 |
| ☐ 86 Lionel Manuel | .35 | .14 | .03 |
| ☐ 89 Mark Bavaro DP | .50 | .20 | .05 |

# 1986 McDonald's Jets

This 24-card set was issued in McDonald's Hamburger restaurants around New York. The set was issued over a four-week period with blue tabs the first week, black (or gray) tabs the second week, gold (or orange) tabs the third week, and green tabs the fourth week. The cards measure approximately 3 1/16" by 4 11/16" with the tab intact and 3 1/16" by 3 5/8" without the tab. The cards are numbered below by uniform number. The value of cards without tabs or tabs scratched off is F-G at best. The cards were printed on a 30-card sheet; hence, there are six double-printed cards listed DP in the checklist below. For individual prices on the more expensive color tabs, merely apply the ratio of that color's set price to the base (cheapest) color set price and use the resulting multiple on the individual prices for that color.

|  | MINT | EXC | G-VG |
|---|---|---|---|
| COMPLETE SET (BLUE) | 150.00 | 60.00 | 15.00 |
| COMPLETE SET (BLACK) | 150.00 | 60.00 | 15.00 |
| COMPLETE SET (GOLD) | 25.00 | 10.00 | 2.50 |
| COMPLETE SET (GREEN) | 25.00 | 10.00 | 2.50 |
| COMMON PLAYER | 1.00 | .40 | .10 |
| ☐ 5 Pat Leahy | 1.50 | .60 | .15 |
| ☐ 7 Ken O'Brien | 2.00 | .80 | .20 |
| ☐ 21 Kirk Springs | 1.00 | .40 | .10 |
| ☐ 24 Freeman McNeil | 3.00 | 1.20 | .30 |
| ☐ 27 Russell Carter DP | 1.00 | .40 | .10 |
| ☐ 29 Johnny Lynn | 1.00 | .40 | .10 |
| ☐ 34 Johnny Hector | 1.50 | .60 | .15 |
| ☐ 39 Harry Hamilton | 1.50 | .60 | .15 |
| ☐ 49 Tony Paige | 2.00 | .80 | .20 |
| ☐ 53 Jim Sweeney | 1.25 | .50 | .12 |
| ☐ 56 Lance Mehl | 1.25 | .50 | .12 |
| ☐ 59 Kyle Clifton DP | 1.25 | .50 | .12 |
| ☐ 60 Dan Alexander DP | 1.00 | .40 | .10 |
| ☐ 65 Joe Fields DP | 1.25 | .50 | .12 |
| ☐ 73 Joe Klecko | 1.50 | .60 | .15 |
| ☐ 78 Barry Bennett DP | 1.00 | .40 | .10 |
| ☐ 80 Johnny(Lam) Jones | 1.25 | .50 | .12 |
| ☐ 82 Mickey Shuler | 1.25 | .50 | .12 |
| ☐ 85 Wesley Walker | 2.00 | .80 | .20 |
| ☐ 87 Kurt Sohn | 1.00 | .40 | .10 |
| ☐ 88 Al Toon | 3.00 | 1.20 | .30 |
| ☐ 89 Rocky Klever | 1.00 | .40 | .10 |
| ☐ 93 Marty Lyons | 1.50 | .60 | .15 |
| ☐ 99 Mark Gastineau DP | 1.00 | .40 | .10 |

# 1986 McDonald's Lions

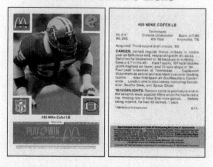

This 24-card set was issued in McDonald's Hamburger restaurants around Detroit. The set was issued over a four-week period with blue tabs the first week, black (or gray) tabs the second week, gold (or orange) tabs the third week, and green tabs the fourth week. The cards measure approximately 3 1/16" by 4 11/16" with the tab intact and 3 1/16" by 3 5/8" without the tab. The cards are numbered below by uniform number. The value of cards without tabs or tabs scratched off is F-G at best. The cards were printed on a 30-card sheet; hence, there are six double-printed cards listed DP in the checklist below. For individual prices on the more expensive color tabs, merely apply the ratio of that color's set price to the base (cheapest) color set price and use the resulting multiple on the individual prices for that color.

|                          | MINT | EXC  | G-VG |
|--------------------------|------|------|------|
| COMPLETE SET (BLUE)      | 6.00 | 2.40 | .60  |
| COMPLETE SET (BLACK)     | 6.00 | 2.40 | .60  |
| COMPLETE SET (GOLD)      | 6.00 | 2.40 | .60  |
| COMPLETE SET (GREEN)     | 6.00 | 2.40 | .60  |
| COMMON PLAYER            | .25  | .10  | .02  |
| ☐ 3 Eddie Murray         | .35  | .14  | .03  |
| ☐ 11 Michael Black DP    | .25  | .10  | .02  |
| ☐ 17 Eric Hipple         | .35  | .14  | .03  |
| ☐ 20 Billy Sims          | .75  | .30  | .07  |
| ☐ 21 Demetrious Johnson  | .25  | .10  | .02  |
| ☐ 27 Bobby Watkins       | .25  | .10  | .02  |
| ☐ 29 Bruce McNorton      | .25  | .10  | .02  |
| ☐ 30 James Jones         | .35  | .14  | .03  |
| ☐ 33 William Graham      | .25  | .10  | .02  |
| ☐ 35 Alvin Hall          | .25  | .10  | .02  |
| ☐ 39 Leonard Thompson    | .35  | .14  | .03  |
| ☐ 50 August Curley DP    | .25  | .10  | .02  |
| ☐ 52 Steve Mott          | .25  | .10  | .02  |
| ☐ 55 Mike Cofer DP       | .25  | .10  | .02  |
| ☐ 59 Jimmy Williams      | .25  | .10  | .02  |
| ☐ 70 Keith Dorney DP     | .25  | .10  | .02  |
| ☐ 71 Rich Strenger       | .25  | .10  | .02  |
| ☐ 75 Lomas Brown DP      | .35  | .14  | .03  |
| ☐ 76 Eric Williams       | .25  | .10  | .02  |
| ☐ 79 William Gay         | .25  | .10  | .02  |
| ☐ 82 Pete Mandley        | .25  | .10  | .02  |
| ☐ 86 Mark Nichols        | .25  | .10  | .02  |
| ☐ 87 David Lewis         | .25  | .10  | .02  |
| ☐ 89 Jeff Chadwick DP    | .35  | .14  | .03  |

# 1986 McDonald's Oilers

This 24-card set was issued in McDonald's Hamburger restaurants around Houston. The set was issued over a four-week period with blue tabs the first week, black (or gray) tabs the second week, gold (or orange) tabs the third week, and green tabs the fourth week. The cards measure approximately 3 1/16" by 4 11/16" with the tab intact and 3 1/16" by 3 5/8" without the tab. The cards are numbered below by uniform number. The value of cards without tabs or tabs scratched off is F-G at best. The cards were printed on a 30-card sheet; hence, there are six double-printed cards listed DP in the checklist below. For individual prices on the more expensive color tabs, merely apply the ratio of that color's set price to the base (cheapest) color set price and use the resulting multiple on the individual prices for that color.

|                          | MINT  | EXC  | G-VG |
|--------------------------|-------|------|------|
| COMPLETE SET (BLUE)      | 12.00 | 5.00 | 1.20 |
| COMPLETE SET (BLACK)     | 8.00  | 3.25 | .80  |
| COMPLETE SET (GOLD)      | 8.00  | 3.25 | .80  |
| COMPLETE SET (GREEN)     | 8.00  | 3.25 | .80  |
| COMMON PLAYER            | .30   | .12  | .03  |
| ☐ 1 Warren Moon          | 4.00  | 1.60 | .40  |
| ☐ 7 Tony Zendejas        | .40   | .16  | .04  |
| ☐ 10 Oliver Luck         | .40   | .16  | .04  |
| ☐ 21 Bo Eason            | .30   | .12  | .03  |
| ☐ 23 Richard Johnson     | .40   | .16  | .04  |
| ☐ 24 Steve Brown DP      | .30   | .12  | .03  |
| ☐ 25 Keith Bostic DP     | .30   | .12  | .03  |
| ☐ 29 Patrick Allen DP    | .30   | .12  | .03  |
| ☐ 33 Mike Rozier         | .75   | .30  | .07  |
| ☐ 40 Butch Woolfolk      | .40   | .16  | .04  |
| ☐ 53 Avon Riley          | .30   | .12  | .03  |
| ☐ 56 Robert Abraham DP   | .30   | .12  | .03  |
| ☐ 63 Mike Munchak        | .75   | .30  | .07  |
| ☐ 67 Mike Stensrud       | .40   | .16  | .04  |
| ☐ 70 Dean Steinkuhler    | .60   | .24  | .06  |
| ☐ 71 Richard Byrd DP     | .30   | .12  | .03  |
| ☐ 73 Harvey Salem        | .40   | .16  | .04  |
| ☐ 74 Bruce Matthews      | .75   | .30  | .07  |
| ☐ 79 Ray Childress       | 1.25  | .50  | .12  |
| ☐ 83 Tim Smith           | .40   | .16  | .04  |
| ☐ 85 Drew Hill           | 1.00  | .40  | .10  |
| ☐ 87 Jamie Williams      | .30   | .12  | .03  |
| ☐ 91 Johnny Meads        | .40   | .16  | .04  |
| ☐ 94 Frank Bush DP       | .30   | .12  | .03  |

# 1986 McDonald's Packers

This 24-card set was issued in McDonald's Hamburger restaurants around Green Bay and Milwaukee. The set was issued over a four-week period with blue tabs the first week, black (or gray) tabs the second week, gold (or orange) tabs the third week, and green tabs the fourth week. The cards measure approximately 3 1/16" by 4 11/16" with the tab intact and 3 1/16" by 3 5/8" without the tab. The cards are numbered below by uniform number. The value of cards without tabs or tabs scratched off is F-G at best. The cards were printed on a 30-card sheet; hence, there are six double-printed cards listed DP in the checklist below. For individual prices on the more expensive color tabs, merely apply the ratio of that color's set price to the base (cheapest) color set price and use the resulting multiple on the individual prices for that color.

|                          | MINT  | EXC  | G-VG |
|--------------------------|-------|------|------|
| COMPLETE SET (BLUE)      | 6.00  | 2.40 | .60  |
| COMPLETE SET (BLACK)     | 6.00  | 2.40 | .60  |
| COMPLETE SET (GOLD)      | 6.00  | 2.40 | .60  |
| COMPLETE SET (GREEN)     | 6.00  | 2.40 | .60  |
| COMMON PLAYER            | .25   | .10  | .02  |
| ☐ 10 Al Del Greco DP     | .25   | .10  | .02  |
| ☐ 12 Lynn Dickey         | .50   | .20  | .05  |
| ☐ 16 Randy Wright        | .35   | .14  | .03  |
| ☐ 18 Jim Zorn            | .50   | .20  | .05  |
| ☐ 22 Mark Lee            | .35   | .14  | .03  |
| ☐ 26 Tim Lewis           | .35   | .14  | .03  |
| ☐ 31 Gerry Ellis         | .25   | .10  | .02  |

| | MINT | EXC | G-VG |
|---|---|---|---|
| ☐ 33 Jessie Clark DP | .25 | .10 | .02 |
| ☐ 37 Mark Murphy | .35 | .14 | .03 |
| ☐ 41 Tom Flynn | .35 | .14 | .03 |
| ☐ 42 Gary Ellerson | .25 | .10 | .02 |
| ☐ 53 Mike Douglass | .25 | .10 | .02 |
| ☐ 55 Randy Scott | .25 | .10 | .02 |
| ☐ 59 John Anderson DP | .35 | .14 | .03 |
| ☐ 67 Karl Swanke | .25 | .10 | .02 |
| ☐ 75 Ken Ruettgers | .50 | .20 | .05 |
| ☐ 76 Alphonso Carreker DP | .25 | .10 | .02 |
| ☐ 77 Mike Butler DP | .25 | .10 | .02 |
| ☐ 79 Donnie Humphrey | .25 | .10 | .02 |
| ☐ 82 Paul Coffman DP | .35 | .14 | .03 |
| ☐ 85 Phillip Epps | .35 | .14 | .03 |
| ☐ 90 Ezra Johnson | .25 | .10 | .02 |
| ☐ 91 Brian Noble | .35 | .14 | .03 |
| ☐ 94 Charles Martin | .25 | .10 | .02 |

## 1986 McDonald's Patriots

This 24-card set was issued in McDonald's Hamburger restaurants around New England. The set was issued over a four-week period with blue tabs the first week, black (or gray) tabs the second week, gold (or orange) tabs the third week, and green tabs the fourth week. The cards measure approximately 3 1/16" by 4 11/16" with the tab intact and 3 1/16" by 3 5/8" without the tab. The cards are numbered below by uniform number. The value of cards without tabs or tabs scratched off is F-G at best. The cards were printed on a 30-card sheet; hence, there are six double-printed cards listed DP in the checklist below. For individual prices on the more expensive color tabs, merely apply the ratio of that color's set price to the base (cheapest) color set price and use the resulting multiple on the individual prices for that color.

| | MINT | EXC | G-VG |
|---|---|---|---|
| COMPLETE SET (BLUE) | 6.00 | 2.40 | .60 |
| COMPLETE SET (BLACK) | 6.00 | 2.40 | .60 |
| COMPLETE SET (GOLD) | 6.00 | 2.40 | .60 |
| COMPLETE SET (GREEN) | 6.00 | 2.40 | .60 |
| COMMON PLAYER | .25 | .10 | .02 |
| | | | |
| ☐ 3 Rich Camarillo DP | .25 | .10 | .02 |
| ☐ 11 Tony Eason DP | .50 | .20 | .05 |
| ☐ 14 Steve Grogan | .60 | .24 | .06 |
| ☐ 24 Robert Weathers | .25 | .10 | .02 |
| ☐ 26 Raymond Clayborn DP | .35 | .14 | .03 |
| ☐ 30 Mosi Tatupu | .35 | .14 | .03 |
| ☐ 31 Fred Marion | .25 | .10 | .02 |
| ☐ 32 Craig James | .60 | .24 | .06 |
| ☐ 33 Tony Collins DP | .35 | .14 | .03 |
| ☐ 38 Roland James | .25 | .10 | .02 |
| ☐ 42 Ronnie Lippett | .35 | .14 | .03 |
| ☐ 50 Larry McGrew | .25 | .10 | .02 |
| ☐ 55 Don Blackmon DP | .25 | .10 | .02 |
| ☐ 56 Andre Tippett | .60 | .24 | .06 |
| ☐ 57 Steve Nelson | .35 | .14 | .03 |
| ☐ 58 Pete Brock DP | .25 | .10 | .02 |
| ☐ 60 Garin Veris | .25 | .10 | .02 |
| ☐ 61 Ron Wooten | .25 | .10 | .02 |
| ☐ 73 John Hannah | .75 | .30 | .07 |
| ☐ 77 Kenneth Sims | .35 | .14 | .03 |
| ☐ 80 Irving Fryar | 1.00 | .40 | .10 |
| ☐ 81 Stephen Starring | .35 | .14 | .03 |
| ☐ 83 Cedric Jones | .35 | .14 | .03 |
| ☐ 86 Stanley Morgan | .75 | .30 | .07 |

## 1986 McDonald's Raiders

This 24-card set was issued in McDonald's Hamburger restaurants around Los Angeles. The set was issued over a four-week period with blue tabs the first week, black (or gray) tabs the second week, gold (or orange) tabs the third week, and green tabs the fourth week. The cards

---

measure approximately 3 1/16" by 4 11/16" with the tab intact and 3 1/16" by 3 5/8" without the tab. The cards are numbered below by uniform number. The value of cards without tabs or tabs scratched off is F-G at best. The cards were printed on a 30-card sheet; hence, there are six double-printed cards listed DP in the checklist below. For individual prices on the more expensive color tabs, merely apply the ratio of that color's set price to the base (cheapest) color set price and use the resulting multiple on the individual prices for that color.

| | MINT | EXC | G-VG |
|---|---|---|---|
| COMPLETE SET (BLUE) | 18.00 | 7.25 | 1.80 |
| COMPLETE SET (BLACK) | 12.00 | 5.00 | 1.20 |
| COMPLETE SET (GOLD) | 6.00 | 2.40 | .60 |
| COMPLETE SET (GREEN) | 6.00 | 2.40 | .60 |
| COMMON PLAYER | .25 | .10 | .02 |
| | | | |
| ☐ 1 Marc Wilson | .35 | .14 | .03 |
| ☐ 8 Ray Guy DP | .60 | .24 | .06 |
| ☐ 10 Chris Bahr DP | .25 | .10 | .02 |
| ☐ 16 Jim Plunkett | .75 | .30 | .07 |
| ☐ 22 Mike Haynes | .75 | .30 | .07 |
| ☐ 26 Vann McElroy | .35 | .14 | .03 |
| ☐ 27 Frank Hawkins | .25 | .10 | .02 |
| ☐ 32 Marcus Allen DP | 1.25 | .50 | .12 |
| ☐ 36 Mike Davis DP | .25 | .10 | .02 |
| ☐ 37 Lester Hayes | .50 | .20 | .05 |
| ☐ 46 Todd Christensen DP | .50 | .20 | .05 |
| ☐ 53 Rod Martin | .35 | .14 | .03 |
| ☐ 54 Reggie McKenzie | .35 | .14 | .03 |
| ☐ 55 Matt Millen | .50 | .20 | .05 |
| ☐ 70 Henry Lawrence | .25 | .10 | .02 |
| ☐ 71 Bill Pickel | .25 | .10 | .02 |
| ☐ 72 Don Mosebar | .35 | .14 | .03 |
| ☐ 73 Charley Hannah | .25 | .10 | .02 |
| ☐ 75 Howie Long | .75 | .30 | .07 |
| ☐ 79 Bruce Davis DP | .25 | .10 | .02 |
| ☐ 84 Jessie Hester | .50 | .20 | .05 |
| ☐ 85 Dokie Williams | .35 | .14 | .03 |
| ☐ 91 Brad Van Pelt | .35 | .14 | .03 |
| ☐ 99 Sean Jones | .75 | .30 | .07 |

## 1986 McDonald's Rams

This 24-card set was issued in McDonald's Hamburger restaurants around Los Angeles. The set was issued over a four-week period with blue tabs the first week, black (or gray) tabs the second week, gold (or orange) tabs the third week, and green tabs the fourth week. The cards measure approximately 3 1/16" by 4 11/16" with the tab intact and 3 1/16" by 3 5/8" without the tab. The cards are numbered below by uniform number. The value of cards without tabs or tabs scratched off is F-G at best. The cards were printed on a 30-card sheet; hence, there are six double-printed cards listed DP in the checklist below. For individual prices on the more expensive color tabs, merely apply the ratio of that color's set price to the base (cheapest) color set price and use the resulting multiple on the individual prices for that color.

| | MINT | EXC | G-VG |
|---|---|---|---|
| COMPLETE SET (BLUE) | 9.00 | 3.75 | .90 |
| COMPLETE SET (BLACK) | 6.00 | 2.40 | .60 |
| COMPLETE SET (GOLD) | 6.00 | 2.40 | .60 |
| COMPLETE SET (GREEN) | 6.00 | 2.40 | .60 |
| COMMON PLAYER | .25 | .10 | .02 |
| ☐ 1 Mike Lansford | .25 | .10 | .02 |
| ☐ 3 Dale Hatcher | .25 | .10 | .02 |
| ☐ 5 Dieter Brock DP | .35 | .14 | .03 |
| ☐ 20 Johnnie Johnson | .35 | .14 | .03 |
| ☐ 21 Nolan Cromwell DP | .50 | .20 | .05 |
| ☐ 22 Vince Newsome | .25 | .10 | .02 |
| ☐ 27 Gary Green | .25 | .10 | .02 |
| ☐ 29 Eric Dickerson DP | 1.50 | .60 | .15 |
| ☐ 44 Mike Guman | .25 | .10 | .02 |
| ☐ 47 LeRoy Irvin | .35 | .14 | .03 |
| ☐ 50 Jim Collins DP | .25 | .10 | .02 |
| ☐ 54 Mike Wilcher | .25 | .10 | .02 |
| ☐ 55 Carl Ekern | .25 | .10 | .02 |
| ☐ 56 Doug Smith | .35 | .14 | .03 |
| ☐ 58 Mel Owens | .35 | .14 | .03 |
| ☐ 60 Dennis Harrah | .25 | .10 | .02 |
| ☐ 71 Reggie Doss DP | .25 | .10 | .02 |
| ☐ 72 Kent Hill | .35 | .14 | .03 |
| ☐ 75 Irv Pankey | .25 | .10 | .02 |
| ☐ 78 Jackie Slater | .50 | .20 | .05 |
| ☐ 80 Henry Ellard | 1.00 | .40 | .10 |
| ☐ 81 David Hill | .25 | .10 | .02 |
| ☐ 87 Tony Hunter | .35 | .14 | .03 |
| ☐ 89 Ron Brown DP | .35 | .14 | .03 |

# 1986 McDonald's Redskins

This 24-card set was issued in McDonald's Hamburger restaurants around Washington. The set was issued over a four-week period with blue tabs the first week, black (or gray) tabs the second week, gold (or orange) tabs the third week, and green tabs the fourth week. The cards measure approximately 3 1/16" by 4 11/16" with the tab intact and 3 1/16" by 3 5/8" without the tab. The cards are numbered below by uniform number. The value of cards without tabs or tabs scratched off is F-G at best. The cards were printed on a 30-card sheet; hence, there are six double-printed cards listed DP in the checklist below. For individual prices on the more expensive color tabs, merely apply the ratio of that color's set price to the base (cheapest) color set price and use the resulting multiple on the individual prices for that color.

| | MINT | EXC | G-VG |
|---|---|---|---|
| COMPLETE SET (BLUE) | 6.00 | 2.40 | .60 |
| COMPLETE SET (BLACK) | 6.00 | 2.40 | .60 |
| COMPLETE SET (GOLD) | 6.00 | 2.40 | .60 |
| COMPLETE SET (GREEN) | 6.00 | 2.40 | .60 |
| COMMON PLAYER | .25 | .10 | .02 |
| ☐ 3 Mark Moseley | .50 | .20 | .05 |
| ☐ 10 Jay Schroeder | 1.00 | .40 | .10 |
| ☐ 22 Curtis Jordan | .25 | .10 | .02 |
| ☐ 28 Darrell Green | .75 | .30 | .07 |
| ☐ 32 Vernon Dean DP | .25 | .10 | .02 |
| ☐ 35 Keith Griffin | .25 | .10 | .02 |
| ☐ 37 Raphel Cherry DP | .35 | .14 | .03 |
| ☐ 38 George Rogers | .50 | .20 | .05 |
| ☐ 51 Monte Coleman DP | .35 | .14 | .03 |
| ☐ 52 Neal Olkewicz | .25 | .10 | .02 |
| ☐ 53 Jeff Bostic DP | .25 | .10 | .02 |
| ☐ 55 Mel Kaufman | .25 | .10 | .02 |
| ☐ 57 Rich Milot | .25 | .10 | .02 |
| ☐ 65 Dave Butz DP | .35 | .14 | .03 |
| ☐ 66 Joe Jacoby | .35 | .14 | .03 |

| | | | |
|---|---|---|---|
| ☐ 68 Russ Grimm | .35 | .14 | .03 |
| ☐ 71 Charles Mann | .50 | .20 | .05 |
| ☐ 72 Dexter Manley | .35 | .14 | .03 |
| ☐ 73 Mark May | .35 | .14 | .03 |
| ☐ 77 Darryl Grant | .25 | .10 | .02 |
| ☐ 81 Art Monk | 1.50 | .60 | .15 |
| ☐ 84 Gary Clark DP | 1.50 | .60 | .15 |
| ☐ 85 Don Warren | .35 | .14 | .03 |
| ☐ 86 Clint Didier | .25 | .10 | .02 |

# 1986 McDonald's Saints

This 24-card set was issued in McDonald's Hamburger restaurants around New Orleans. The set was issued over a four-week period with blue tabs the first week, black (or gray) tabs the second week, gold (or orange) tabs the third week, and green tabs the fourth week. The cards measure approximately 3 1/16" by 4 11/16" with the tab intact and 3 1/16" by 3 5/8" without the tab. The cards are numbered below by uniform number. The value of cards without tabs or tabs scratched off is F-G at best. The cards were printed on a 30-card sheet; hence, there are six double-printed cards listed DP in the checklist below. For individual prices on the more expensive color tabs, merely apply the ratio of that color's set price to the base (cheapest) color set price and use the resulting multiple on the individual prices for that color.

| | MINT | EXC | G-VG |
|---|---|---|---|
| COMPLETE SET (BLUE) | 150.00 | 60.00 | 15.00 |
| COMPLETE SET (BLACK) | 40.00 | 16.00 | 4.00 |
| COMPLETE SET (GOLD) | 20.00 | 8.00 | 2.00 |
| COMPLETE SET (GREEN) | 20.00 | 8.00 | 2.00 |
| COMMON PLAYER | .75 | .30 | .07 |
| ☐ 3 Bobby Hebert | 2.50 | 1.00 | .25 |
| ☐ 7 Morten Andersen DP | 1.25 | .50 | .12 |
| ☐ 10 Brian Hansen | 1.00 | .40 | .10 |
| ☐ 18 Dave Wilson | 1.00 | .40 | .10 |
| ☐ 20 Russell Gary | .75 | .30 | .07 |
| ☐ 25 Johnnie Poe | .75 | .30 | .07 |
| ☐ 30 Wayne Wilson | 1.00 | .40 | .10 |
| ☐ 44 Dave Waymer | 1.00 | .40 | .10 |
| ☐ 46 Hokie Gajan | 1.00 | .40 | .10 |
| ☐ 49 Frank Wattelett | .75 | .30 | .07 |
| ☐ 50 Jack Del Rio DP | 1.25 | .50 | .12 |
| ☐ 57 Rickey Jackson | 1.50 | .60 | .15 |
| ☐ 60 Steve Korte | 1.00 | .40 | .10 |
| ☐ 61 Joel Hilgenberg | .75 | .30 | .07 |
| ☐ 63 Brad Edelman DP | .75 | .30 | .07 |
| ☐ 64 Dave Lafary | .75 | .30 | .07 |
| ☐ 67 Stan Brock DP | .75 | .30 | .07 |
| ☐ 73 Frank Warren | .75 | .30 | .07 |
| ☐ 75 Bruce Clark DP | 1.00 | .40 | .10 |
| ☐ 84 Eric Martin | 2.00 | .80 | .20 |
| ☐ 85 Hoby Brenner DP | .75 | .30 | .07 |
| ☐ 88 Eugene Goodlow | .75 | .30 | .07 |
| ☐ 89 Tyrone Young | 1.00 | .40 | .10 |
| ☐ 99 Tony Elliott | .75 | .30 | .07 |

# 1986 McDonald's Seahawks

This 24-card set was issued in McDonald's Hamburger restaurants around Seattle. The set was issued over a four-week period with blue tabs the first week, black (or gray) tabs the second week, gold (or orange) tabs the third week, and green tabs the fourth week. The cards measure approximately 3 1/16" by 4 11/16" with the tab intact and 3 1/16" by 3 5/8" without the tab. The cards are numbered below by uniform number. The value of cards without tabs or tabs scratched off is F-G at best. The cards were printed on a 30-card sheet; hence, there are six double-printed cards listed DP in the checklist below. For individual prices on the more expensive color tabs, merely apply the ratio of that color's set price to the base (cheapest) color set price and use the resulting multiple on the individual prices for that color.

|                          | MINT | EXC  | G-VG |
|--------------------------|------|------|------|
| COMPLETE SET (BLUE)      | 7.00 | 2.80 | .70  |
| COMPLETE SET (BLACK)     | 7.00 | 2.80 | .70  |
| COMPLETE SET (GOLD)      | 7.00 | 2.80 | .70  |
| COMPLETE SET (GREEN)     | 7.00 | 2.80 | .70  |
| COMMON PLAYER            | .25  | .10  | .02  |

| | | | |
|---|---|---|---|
| ☐ 9 Norm Johnson | .50 | .20 | .05 |
| ☐ 17 Dave Krieg | 1.00 | .40 | .10 |
| ☐ 20 Terry Taylor | .35 | .14 | .03 |
| ☐ 22 Dave Brown DP | .35 | .14 | .03 |
| ☐ 28 Curt Warner | .60 | .24 | .06 |
| ☐ 33 Dan Doornink | .25 | .10 | .02 |
| ☐ 44 John Harris | .25 | .10 | .02 |
| ☐ 45 Kenny Easley | .50 | .20 | .05 |
| ☐ 46 David Hughes | .25 | .10 | .02 |
| ☐ 50 Fredd Young | .35 | .14 | .03 |
| ☐ 53 Keith Butler DP | .25 | .10 | .02 |
| ☐ 55 Michael Jackson | .25 | .10 | .02 |
| ☐ 58 Bruce Scholtz | .25 | .10 | .02 |
| ☐ 59 Blair Bush DP | .35 | .14 | .03 |
| ☐ 61 Robert Pratt | .25 | .10 | .02 |
| ☐ 64 Ron Essink | .25 | .10 | .02 |
| ☐ 65 Edwin Bailey DP | .25 | .10 | .02 |
| ☐ 72 Joe Nash | .35 | .14 | .03 |
| ☐ 77 Jeff Bryant DP | .25 | .10 | .02 |
| ☐ 78 Bob Cryder DP | .25 | .10 | .02 |
| ☐ 79 Jacob Green | .50 | .20 | .05 |
| ☐ 80 Steve Largent | 3.50 | 1.40 | .35 |
| ☐ 81 Daryl Turner | .50 | .20 | .05 |
| ☐ 82 Paul Skansi | .35 | .14 | .03 |

## 1986 McDonald's Steelers

This 24-card set was issued in McDonald's Hamburger restaurants around Pittsburgh. The set was issued over a four-week period with blue tabs the first week, black (or gray) tabs the second week, gold (or orange) tabs the third week, and green tabs the fourth week. The cards measure approximately 3 1/16" by 4 11/16" with the tab intact and 3 1/16" by 3 5/8" without the tab. The cards are numbered below by uniform number. The value of cards without tabs or tabs scratched off is F-G at best. The cards were printed on a 30-card sheet; hence, there are six double-printed cards listed DP in the checklist below. For individual prices on the more expensive color tabs, merely apply the ratio of that color's set price to the base (cheapest) color set price and use the resulting multiple on the individual prices for that color.

|                          | MINT  | EXC   | G-VG |
|--------------------------|-------|-------|------|
| COMPLETE SET (BLUE)      | 50.00 | 20.00 | 5.00 |
| COMPLETE SET (BLACK)     | 25.00 | 10.00 | 2.50 |

|                          | MINT  | EXC   | G-VG |
|--------------------------|-------|-------|------|
| COMPLETE SET (GOLD)      | 10.00 | 4.00  | 1.00 |
| COMPLETE SET (GREEN)     | 10.00 | 4.00  | 1.00 |
| COMMON PLAYER            | .40   | .16   | .04  |

| | | | |
|---|---|---|---|
| ☐ 1 Gary Anderson DP | .50 | .20 | .05 |
| ☐ 16 Mark Malone | .50 | .20 | .05 |
| ☐ 21 Eric Williams | .40 | .16 | .04 |
| ☐ 24 Rich Erenberg DP | .40 | .16 | .04 |
| ☐ 30 Frank Pollard | .50 | .20 | .05 |
| ☐ 31 Donnie Shell | .60 | .24 | .06 |
| ☐ 34 Walter Abercrombie DP | .50 | .20 | .05 |
| ☐ 49 Dwayne Woodruff | .40 | .16 | .04 |
| ☐ 50 David Little | .50 | .20 | .05 |
| ☐ 52 Mike Webster | .75 | .30 | .07 |
| ☐ 53 Bryan Hinkle | .40 | .16 | .04 |
| ☐ 56 Robin Cole DP | .40 | .16 | .04 |
| ☐ 57 Mike Merriweather | .75 | .30 | .07 |
| ☐ 62 Tunch Ilkin | .50 | .20 | .05 |
| ☐ 65 Ray Pinney | .50 | .20 | .05 |
| ☐ 67 Gary Dunn DP | .40 | .16 | .04 |
| ☐ 73 Craig Wolfley | .40 | .16 | .04 |
| ☐ 74 Terry Long | .40 | .16 | .04 |
| ☐ 82 John Stallworth | 1.00 | .40 | .10 |
| ☐ 83 Louis Lipps | 1.00 | .40 | .10 |
| ☐ 87 Weegie Thompson | .50 | .20 | .05 |
| ☐ 92 Keith Gary DP | .40 | .16 | .04 |
| ☐ 93 Keith Willis | .50 | .20 | .05 |
| ☐ 99 Darryl Sims | .50 | .20 | .05 |

## 1986 McDonald's Vikings

This 24-card set was issued in McDonald's Hamburger restaurants around Minneapolis and St. Paul. The set was issued over a four-week period with blue tabs the first week, black (or gray) tabs the second week, gold (or orange) tabs the third week, and green tabs the fourth week. The cards measure approximately 3 1/16" by 4 11/16" with the tab intact and 3 1/16" by 3 5/8" without the tab. The cards are numbered below by uniform number. The value of cards without tabs or tabs scratched off is F-G at best. The cards were printed on a 30-card sheet; hence, there are six double-printed cards listed DP in the checklist below. For individual prices on the more expensive color tabs, merely apply the ratio of that color's set price to the base (cheapest) color set price and use the resulting multiple on the individual prices for that color.

|                          | MINT  | EXC   | G-VG |
|--------------------------|-------|-------|------|
| COMPLETE SET (BLUE)      | 45.00 | 18.00 | 4.50 |
| COMPLETE SET (BLACK)     | 30.00 | 12.00 | 3.00 |
| COMPLETE SET (GOLD)      | 15.00 | 6.00  | 1.50 |
| COMPLETE SET (GREEN)     | 15.00 | 6.00  | 1.50 |
| COMMON PLAYER            | .60   | .24   | .06  |

| | | | |
|---|---|---|---|
| ☐ 8 Greg Coleman DP | .60 | .24 | .06 |
| ☐ 9 Tommy Kramer | 1.00 | .40 | .10 |
| ☐ 11 Wade Wilson | 1.50 | .60 | .15 |
| ☐ 20 Darrin Nelson | 1.00 | .40 | .10 |
| ☐ 23 Ted Brown DP | .75 | .30 | .07 |
| ☐ 37 Willie Teal | .60 | .24 | .06 |
| ☐ 39 Carl Lee | 1.00 | .40 | .10 |
| ☐ 46 Alfred Anderson DP | 1.00 | .40 | .10 |
| ☐ 47 Joey Browner DP | 1.00 | .40 | .10 |
| ☐ 55 Scott Studwell | 1.00 | .40 | .10 |
| ☐ 56 Chris Doleman | 1.25 | .50 | .12 |
| ☐ 59 Matt Blair DP | 1.00 | .40 | .10 |
| ☐ 67 Dennis Swilley | .75 | .30 | .07 |
| ☐ 68 Curtis Rouse | .60 | .24 | .06 |
| ☐ 75 Keith Millard | 1.25 | .50 | .12 |
| ☐ 76 Tim Irwin | .75 | .30 | .07 |
| ☐ 77 Mark Mullaney | .75 | .30 | .07 |
| ☐ 79 Doug Martin | .60 | .24 | .06 |
| ☐ 81 Anthony Carter DP | 1.50 | .60 | .15 |

| | | | |
|---|---|---|---|
| ☐ 83 Steve Jordan | 1.50 | .60 | .15 |
| ☐ 87 Leo Lewis | .75 | .30 | .07 |
| ☐ 89 Mike Jones | .60 | .24 | .06 |
| ☐ 96 Tim Newton | .60 | .24 | .06 |
| ☐ 99 David Howard | .60 | .24 | .06 |

# 1993 McDonald's GameDay

As part of the "McDonald's/NFL Kickoff Payoff" promotion, customers could win NFL Fantasy prizes, such as trips to Super Bowl XXVII, and McDonald's/GameDay trading cards featuring local NFL teams. Customers received a pull-tab gamepiece on packages of large and extra-large french fries, hash browns, 21- and 32-oz. soft drinks, and 16-oz. coffee. Every gamepiece won free food, an instant-win NFL Fantasy prize, or NFL Point Values of six (touchdown), three (field goal), or one (extra point). The Point Values could be collected and redeemed for trading cards or special discounts on merchandise. For ten points, customers received a six-card sheet at participating McDonald's restaurants while supplies lasted. Measuring approximately 2 1/2" by 4 3/4", the GameDay cards are identical to the regular issues, except that they have McDonald's logos on both sides, and on the backs they are renumbered with a "McD" prefix. Three sheets make a complete team set. Most McDonald's restaurants in a region offered cards of the local NFL team(s). In addition, many restaurants offered an All-Star set of 18 NFL superstars. Each NFL team has 18 cards in total on three different sheets (A, B, and C), and the cards are listed below in alphabetical team order, preceded by the All-Star set. One sheet was distributed per week for three weeks during the promotion.

| | MINT | EXC | G-VG |
|---|---|---|---|
| COMPLETE SET (87) | 60.00 | 24.00 | 6.00 |
| COMMON PANEL (1-87) | 1.00 | .40 | .10 |
| | | | |
| ☐ 1 All-Stars A | 2.50 | 1.00 | .25 |
| Deion Sanders | | | |
| Atlanta Falcons | | | |
| Thurman Thomas | | | |
| Buffalo Bills | | | |
| Troy Aikman | | | |
| Dallas Cowboys | | | |
| John Elway | | | |
| Denver Broncos | | | |
| Barry Sanders | | | |
| Detroit Lions | | | |
| Sterling Sharpe | | | |
| Green Bay Packers | | | |
| ☐ 2 All-Stars B | 1.50 | .60 | .15 |
| Derrick Thomas | | | |
| Kansas City Chiefs | | | |
| Howie Long | | | |
| Los Angeles Raiders | | | |
| Dan Marino | | | |
| Miami Dolphins | | | |
| Chris Doleman | | | |
| Minnesota Vikings | | | |
| Vaughan Johnson | | | |
| New Orleans Saints | | | |
| Phil Simms | | | |
| New York Giants | | | |
| ☐ 3 All-Stars C | 1.50 | .60 | .15 |
| Randall Cunningham | | | |
| Philadelphia Eagles | | | |

| | | | |
|---|---|---|---|
| Barry Foster | | | |
| Pittsburgh Steelers | | | |
| Jerry Rice | | | |
| San Francisco 49ers | | | |
| Junior Seau | | | |
| San Diego Chargers | | | |
| Cortez Kennedy | | | |
| Seattle Seahawks | | | |
| Mark Rypien | | | |
| Washington Redskins | | | |
| ☐ 4 Atlanta Falcons A | 1.50 | .60 | .15 |
| Deion Sanders | | | |
| Moe Gardner | | | |
| Tim Green | | | |
| Michael Haynes | | | |
| Chris Hinton | | | |
| Tim McKyer | | | |
| ☐ 5 Atlanta Falcons B | 1.50 | .60 | .15 |
| Chris Miller | | | |
| Bruce Pickens | | | |
| Mike Pritchard | | | |
| Andre Rison | | | |
| Darion Conner | | | |
| Jessie Tuggle | | | |
| ☐ 6 Atlanta Falcons C | 1.00 | .40 | .10 |
| Drew Hill | | | |
| Pierce Holt | | | |
| Elbert Shelley | | | |
| Jesse Solomon | | | |
| Bobby Hebert | | | |
| Lincoln Kennedy | | | |
| ☐ 7 Buffalo Bills A | 1.50 | .60 | .15 |
| Howard Ballard | | | |
| Don Beebe | | | |
| Cornelius Bennett | | | |
| Phil Hansen | | | |
| Henry Jones | | | |
| Jim Kelly | | | |
| ☐ 8 Buffalo Bills B | 1.50 | .60 | .15 |
| Nate Odomes | | | |
| Andre Reed | | | |
| Frank Reich | | | |
| Bruce Smith | | | |
| Darryl Talley | | | |
| Steve Tasker | | | |
| ☐ 9 Buffalo Bills C | 1.50 | .60 | .15 |
| Bill Brooks | | | |
| Jim Ritcher | | | |
| Thurman Thomas | | | |
| Kenneth Davis | | | |
| Jeff Wright | | | |
| Thomas Smith | | | |
| ☐ 10 Chicago Bears A | 1.50 | .60 | .15 |
| Neal Anderson | | | |
| Trace Armstrong | | | |
| Mark Carrier | | | |
| Wendell Davis | | | |
| Richard Dent | | | |
| Shaun Gayle | | | |
| ☐ 11 Chicago Bears B | 1.00 | .40 | .10 |
| Jim Harbaugh | | | |
| Darren Lewis | | | |
| Jim Morrissey | | | |
| William Perry | | | |
| Alonzo Spellman | | | |
| Tom Waddle | | | |
| ☐ 12 Chicago Bears C | 1.50 | .60 | .15 |
| Steve McMichael | | | |
| Craig Heyward | | | |
| Lemuel Stinson | | | |
| Keith Van Horne | | | |
| Donnell Woolford | | | |
| Curtis Conway | | | |
| ☐ 13 Cincinnati Bengals A | 1.50 | .60 | .15 |
| Derrick Fenner | | | |
| James Francis | | | |
| David Fulcher | | | |
| Harold Green | | | |
| Rod Jones | | | |
| David Klingler | | | |
| ☐ 14 Cincinnati Bengals B | 1.25 | .50 | .12 |
| Bruce Kozerski | | | |
| Tim Krumrie | | | |
| Ricardo McDonald | | | |
| Carl Pickens | | | |
| Reggie Rembert | | | |
| Daniel Stubbs | | | |
| ☐ 15 Cincinnati Bengals C | 1.00 | .40 | .10 |
| Eddie Brown | | | |
| Gary Reasons | | | |
| Lamar Rogers | | | |
| Alfred Williams | | | |
| Darryl Williams | | | |
| John Copeland | | | |
| ☐ 16 Cleveland Browns A | 1.50 | .60 | .15 |
| Rob Burnett | | | |
| Jay Hilgenberg | | | |
| Leroy Hoard | | | |

Michael Jackson
Mike Johnson
Bernie Kosar
☐ 17 Cleveland Browns B ............... 1.50 .60 .15
Eric Metcalf
Michael Dean Perry
Clay Matthews
Lawyer Tillman
Eric Turner
Tommy Vardell
☐ 18 Cleveland Browns C ............... 1.25 .50 .12
David Brandon
Tony Jones
Scott Galbraith
James Jones
Vinny Testaverde
Steve Everitt
☐ 19 Dallas Cowboys A .................. 2.00 .80 .20
Troy Aikman
Tony Casillas
Thomas Everett
Charles Haley
Alvin Harper
Michael Irvin
☐ 20 Dallas Cowboys B .................. 1.50 .60 .15
Jim Jeffcoat
Daryl Johnston
Robert Jones
Nate Newton
Ken Norton Jr.
Jay Novacek
☐ 21 Dallas Cowboys C .................. 2.00 .80 .20
Russell Maryland
Emmitt Smith
Kevin Smith
Mark Stepnoski
Tony Tolbert
Larry Brown
☐ 22 Denver Broncos A .................. 1.50 .60 .15
Steve Atwater
Mike Croel
Shane Dronett
John Elway
Simon Fletcher
Reggie Rivers
☐ 23 Denver Broncos B .................. 1.50 .60 .15
Vance Johnson
Greg Lewis
Tommy Maddox
Arthur Marshall
Shannon Sharpe
Dennis Smith
☐ 24 Denver Broncos C .................. 1.00 .40 .10
Rod Bernstine
Michael Brooks
Wymon Henderson
Greg Kragen
Karl Mecklenburg
Dan Williams
☐ 25 Detroit Lions A ...................... 1.00 .40 .10
Bennie Blades
Michael Cofer
Ray Crockett
Mel Gray
Willie Green
Jason Hanson
☐ 26 Detroit Lions B ...................... 2.00 .80 .20
Herman Moore
Rodney Peete
Brett Perriman
Kelvin Pritchett
Barry Sanders
Tracy Scroggins
☐ 27 Detroit Lions C ...................... 1.50 .60 .15
Pat Swilling
Lomas Brown
Erik Kramer
Chris Spielman
Andre Ware
William White
☐ 28 Green Bay Packers A ............... 2.00 .80 .20
Tony Bennett
Matt Brock
Terrell Buckley
LeRoy Butler
Chris Jacke
Brett Favre
☐ 29 Green Bay Packers B ............... 1.50 .60 .15
Jackie Harris
Brian Noble
Bryce Paup
Sterling Sharpe
Ed West
Johnny Holland
☐ 30 Green Bay Packers C ............... 1.50 .60 .15
Tunch Ilkin
George Teague
Reggie White

Ken O'Brien
John Stephens
Wayne Simmons
☐ 31 Houston Oilers A .................... 1.25 .50 .12
Cody Carlson
Ray Childress
Curtis Duncan
William Fuller
Haywood Jeffires
Lamar Lathon
☐ 32 Houston Oilers B .................... 1.50 .60 .15
Bruce Matthews
Bubba McDowell
Warren Moon
Mike Munchak
Eddie Robinson
Webster Slaughter
☐ 33 Houston Oilers C .................... 1.00 .40 .10
Ernest Givins
Cris Dishman
Al Smith
Lorenzo White
Lee Williams
Brad Hopkins
☐ 34 Indianapolis Colts A ............... 1.50 .60 .15
Chip Banks
Kerry Cash
Quentin Coryatt
Rodney Culver
Steve Emtman
Reggie Langhorne
☐ 35 Indianapolis Colts B ............... 1.25 .50 .12
Jeff Herrod
Anthony Johnson
Jeff George
Rohn Stark
Jack Trudeau
Clarence Verdin
☐ 36 Indianapolis Colts C ............... 1.25 .50 .12
Duane Bickett
Eugene Daniel
Jessie Hester
Chris Goode
Kirk Lowdermilk
Sean Dawkins
☐ 37 Kansas City Chiefs A ............... 1.25 .50 .12
Dale Carter
Willie Davis
Dave Krieg
Albert Lewis
Nick Lowery
J.J. Birden
☐ 38 Kansas City Chiefs B ............... 1.25 .50 .12
Charles Mincy
Christian Okoye
Kevin Ross
Dan Saleaumua
Tracy Simien
Harvey Williams
☐ 39 Kansas City Chiefs C ............... 3.00 1.20 .30
Todd McNair
Neil Smith
Derrick Thomas
Leonard Griffin
Barry Word
Joe Montana
☐ 40 Los Angeles Raiders A ............ 1.00 .40 .10
Eddie Anderson
Jeff Gossett
Ethan Horton
Jeff Jaeger
Howie Long
Todd Marinovich
☐ 41 Los Angeles Raiders B ............ 1.00 .40 .10
Terry McDaniel
Don Mosebar
Anthony Smith
Greg Townsend
Aaron Wallace
Steve Wisniewski
☐ 42 Los Angeles Raiders C ............ 1.50 .60 .15
Nick Bell
Tim Brown
Eric Dickerson
James Lofton
Jeff Hostetler
Patrick Bates
☐ 43 Los Angeles Rams A ............... 1.00 .40 .10
Flipper Anderson
Marc Boutte
Henry Ellard
Bill Hawkins
Cleveland Gary
David Lang
☐ 44 Los Angeles Rams B ............... 1.25 .50 .12
Jim Everett
Darryl Henley
Todd Lyght

Anthony Newman
Roman Phifer
Jim Price

☐ 45 Los Angeles Rams C.............. 2.00 .80 .20
Shane Conlan
Henry Rolling
Larry Kelm
Jackie Slater
Fred Stokes
Jerome Bettis

☐ 46 Miami Dolphins A.................. 1.25 .50 .12
Marco Coleman
Bryan Cox
Jeff Cross
Mark Duper
Keith Sims
Mark Higgs

☐ 47 Miami Dolphins B.................. 2.00 .80 .20
Keith Jackson
Dan Marino
John Offerdahl
Louis Oliver
Tony Paige
Pete Stoyanovich

☐ 48 Miami Dolphins C.................. 1.50 .60 .15
Tony Martin
Irving Fryar
Troy Vincent
Richmond Webb
Jarvis Williams
O.J. McDuffie

☐ 49 Minnesota Vikings A .............. 1.50 .60 .15
Terry Allen
Anthony Carter
Cris Carter
Jack Del Rio
Chris Doleman
Rich Gannon

☐ 50 Minnesota Vikings B .............. 1.00 .40 .10
Steve Jordan
Carl Lee
Randall McDaniel
John Randle
Sean Salisbury
Todd Scott

☐ 51 Minnesota Vikings C .............. 1.25 .50 .12
Jim McMahon
Audray McMillian
Mike Merriweather
Henry Thomas
Gary Zimmerman
Robert Smith

☐ 52 New England Patriots A.......... 1.00 .40 .10
Ray Agnew
Bruce Armstrong
Vincent Brown
Eugene Chung
Marv Cook
Maurice Hurst

☐ 53 New England Patriots B.......... 1.25 .50 .12
Pat Harlow
Eugene Lockhart
Greg McMurtry
Scott Zolak
Leonard Russell
Andre Tippett

☐ 54 New England Patriots C.......... 2.00 .80 .20
David Howard
Johnny Rembert
Jon Vaughn
Brent Williams
Scott Secules
Drew Bledsoe

☐ 55 New Orleans Saints A.............. 1.00 .40 .10
Morten Andersen
Gene Atkins
Toi Cook
Richard Cooper
Jim Dombrowski
Vaughn Dunbar

☐ 56 New Orleans Saints B.............. 1.00 .40 .10
Joel Hilgenberg
Rickey Jackson
Vaughan Johnson
Wayne Martin
Renaldo Turnbull
Frank Warren

☐ 57 New Orleans Saints C.............. 1.00 .40 .10
Irv Smith
Brad Muster
Dalton Hilliard
Eric Martin
Sam Mills
Willie Roaf

☐ 58 New York Giants A .................. 1.25 .50 .12
Jarrod Bunch
Mark Collins
Howard Cross

Rodney Hampton
Erik Howard
Greg Jackson

☐ 59 New York Giants B .................. 1.25 .50 .12
Pepper Johnson
Sean Landeta
Ed McCaffrey
Dave Meggett
Bart Oates
Phil Simms

☐ 60 New York Giants C .................. 1.25 .50 .12
Carlton Bailey
Carl Banks
John Elliott
Eric Dorsey
Lawrence Taylor
Mike Sherrard

☐ 61 New York Jets A.................... 1.00 .40 .10
Brad Baxter
Scott Mersereau
Chris Burkett
Kyle Clifton
Jeff Lageman
Mo Lewis

☐ 62 New York Jets B.................... 1.25 .50 .12
Johnny Mitchell
Rob Moore
Browning Nagle
Blair Thomas
Brian Washington
Marvin Washington

☐ 63 New York Jets C.................... 1.50 .60 .15
Boomer Esiason
James Hasty
Ronnie Lott
Leonard Marshall
Terance Mathis
Marvin Jones

☐ 64 Philadelphia Eagles A.............. 1.50 .60 .15
Eric Allen
Fred Barnett
Randall Cunningham
Byron Evans
Andy Harmon
Seth Joyner

☐ 65 Philadelphia Eagles B.............. 1.25 .50 .12
Heath Sherman
Vai Sikahema
Clyde Simmons
Herschel Walker
Andre Waters
Calvin Williams

☐ 66 Philadelphia Eagles C.............. 1.00 .40 .10
Keith Byars
Mike Golic
Leonard Renfro
William Thomas
Antone Davis
Lester Holmes

☐ 67 Phoenix Cardinals A................ 1.25 .50 .12
Johnny Bailey
Rich Camarillo
Larry Centers
Chris Chandler
Ken Harvey
Randal Hill

☐ 68 Phoenix Cardinals B ................ 1.00 .40 .10
Mark May
Robert Massey
Freddie Joe Nunn
Ricky Proehl
Eric Hill
Eric Swann

☐ 69 Phoenix Cardinals C ................ 1.50 .60 .15
Gary Clark
John Booty
Chuck Cecil
Steve Beuerlein
Ernest Dye
Garrison Hearst

☐ 70 Pittsburgh Steelers A .............. 1.25 .50 .12
Dermontti Dawson
Barry Foster
Jeff Graham
Eric Green
Carlton Haselrig
Bryan Hinkle

☐ 71 Pittsburgh Steelers B .............. 1.50 .60 .15
Merril Hoge
D.J. Johnson
Carnell Lake
David Little
Neil O'Donnell
Darren Perry

☐ 72 Pittsburgh Steelers C .............. 1.25 .50 .12
Bubby Brister
Kevin Greene
Greg Lloyd

Leon Searcy
Rod Woodson
Deon Figures
☐ 73 San Diego Chargers A ............ 1.25 .50 .12
Eric Bieniemy
Marion Butts
Burt Grossman
Ronnie Harmon
Stan Humphries
Nate Lewis
☐ 74 San Diego Chargers B ............ 1.25 .50 .12
Chris Mims
Leslie O'Neal
Stanley Richard
Junior Seau
Harry Swayne
Derrick Walker
☐ 75 San Diego Chargers C ............ 1.25 .50 .12
Jerrol Williams
Gill Byrd
John Friesz
Anthony Miller
Gary Plummer
Darrien Gordon
☐ 76 San Francisco 49ers A ............ 1.50 .60 .15
Ricky Watters
Michael Carter
Don Griffin
Dana Hall
Brent Jones
Harris Barton
☐ 77 San Francisco 49ers B ............ 1.50 .60 .15
Tom Rathman
Jerry Rice
Bill Romanowski
John Taylor
Steve Wallace
Mike Walter
☐ 78 San Francisco 49ers C ............ 1.50 .60 .15
Kevin Fagan
Todd Kelly
Guy McIntyre
Tim McDonald
Steve Young
Dana Stubblefield
☐ 79 Seattle Seahawks A ................ 1.00 .40 .10
Robert Blackmon
Brian Blades
Jeff Bryant
Dwayne Harper
Andy Heck
Tommy Kane
☐ 80 Seattle Seahawks B ................ 1.25 .50 .12
Cortez Kennedy
Dan McGwire
Rufus Porter
Ray Roberts
Eugene Robinson
Chris Warren
☐ 81 Seattle Seahawks C ................ 2.00 .80 .20
Ferrell Edmunds
Kelvin Martin
John L. Williams
Tony Woods
David Wyman
Rick Mirer
☐ 82 Tampa Bay Buccaneers A ........ 1.25 .50 .12
Gary Anderson
Tyji Armstrong
Reggie Cobb
Lawrence Dawsey
Steve DeBerg
Santana Dotson
☐ 83 Tampa Bay Buccaneers B ........ 1.00 .40 .10
Ron Hall
Courtney Hawkins
Keith McCants
Charles McRae
Ricky Reynolds
Broderick Thomas
☐ 84 Tampa Bay Buccaneers C ........ 1.00 .40 .10
Vince Workman
Paul Gruber
Hardy Nickerson
Marty Carter
Mark Wheeler
Eric Curry
☐ 85 Washington Redskins A .......... 1.50 .60 .15
Earnest Byner
Andre Collins
Brad Edwards
Ricky Ervins
Darrell Green
Desmond Howard
☐ 86 Washington Redskins B .......... 1.25 .50 .12
Tim Johnson
Jim Lachey
Chip Lohmiller

Mark Rypien
Ricky Sanders
Mark Schlereth
☐ 87 Washington Redskins C .......... 1.50 .60 .15
Al Noga
Kurt Gouveia
Charles Mann
Wilber Marshall
Art Monk
Tom Carter

## 1992 Metallic Images Tins

Developed by Metallic Images Inc. and sold through participating 7-Eleven stores, these four collectors tins each contain two decks of specially designed playing cards. A portion of the proceeds were donated to benefit the Children's Miracle Network, the official charity of the NFL Quarterback Club. Each edition depicts two quarterback legends and two current NFL quarterbacks. Representing the quarterback legends in the first edition are Y.A. Tittle and Johnny Unitas, while Warren Moon and Dan Marino are the current NFL quarterbacks. The fronts of playing cards in the Moon and Marino tins have the Quarterback Club logo, while those of the legends have a "Quarterback Legend" emblem. The tins are unnumbered.

|  | MINT | EXC | G-VG |
| --- | --- | --- | --- |
| COMPLETE SET (4) ........................... | 20.00 | 8.00 | 2.00 |
| COMMON PLAYER (1-4) ................... | 4.00 | 1.60 | .40 |
| ☐ 1 Dan Marino ............................... | 10.00 | 4.00 | 1.00 |
| Miami Dolphins |  |  |  |
| ☐ 2 Warren Moon ............................. | 5.00 | 2.00 | .50 |
| Houston Oilers |  |  |  |
| ☐ 3 Y.A. Tittle ................................. | 4.00 | 1.60 | .40 |
| New York Giants |  |  |  |
| ☐ 4 Johnny Unitas ............................ | 6.00 | 2.40 | .60 |
| Baltimore Colts |  |  |  |

## 1993 Metallic Images QB Legends

An offshoot of CUI, a Wilmington-based maker of collectible ceramic and glassware products, Metallic Images Inc. produced these 20 metal cards to honor outstanding NFL quarterbacks. Only 49,000 numbered sets were produced, each accompanied by a certificate of authenticity and packaged in a collectors tin featuring graphics on the sides and lid. These metallic cards measure approximately 2 9/16" by 3 9/16" and have rolled metal edges. The fronts display a color action shot cutout and superimposed on a team color-coded background with gold pinstripes. A black-and-white headshot appears in an oval at the upper left corner, while the team logo and uniform number are below. On a pinstripe panel inside a team color-coded border, the backs present career summary. The cards are numbered on the back.

| | MINT | EXC | G-VG |
|---|---|---|---|
| COMPLETE SET (20)...................... | 40.00 | 16.00 | 4.00 |
| COMMON PLAYER (1-20)............... | 1.50 | .60 | .15 |
| ☐ 1 Steve Bartkowski.................... Atlanta Falcons | 2.00 | .80 | .20 |
| ☐ 2 John Brodie............................ San Francisco 49ers | 2.50 | 1.00 | .25 |
| ☐ 3 Charley Conerly...................... New York Giants | 2.50 | 1.00 | .25 |
| ☐ 4 Lynn Dickey........................... Green Bay Packers | 1.50 | .60 | .15 |
| ☐ 5 Tom Flores............................. Oakland Raiders | 3.00 | 1.20 | .30 |
| ☐ 6 Roman Gabriel........................ Los Angeles Rams | 2.00 | .80 | .20 |
| ☐ 7 Bob Griese............................. Miami Dolphins | 6.00 | 2.40 | .60 |
| ☐ 8 Steve Grogan.......................... New England Patriots | 1.50 | .60 | .15 |
| ☐ 9 James Harris.......................... Los Angeles Rams | 1.50 | .60 | .15 |
| ☐ 10 Jim Hart.............................. St. Louis Cardinals | 1.50 | .60 | .15 |
| ☐ 11 Sonny Jurgensen................... Washington Redskins | 3.00 | 1.20 | .30 |
| ☐ 12 Billy Kilmer.......................... Washington Redskins | 2.00 | .80 | .20 |
| ☐ 13 Daryle Lamonica.................... Oakland Raiders | 2.50 | 1.00 | .25 |
| ☐ 14 Archie Manning...................... New Orleans Saints | 3.00 | 1.20 | .30 |
| ☐ 15 Craig Morton........................ Denver Broncos | 1.50 | .60 | .15 |
| ☐ 16 Dan Pastorini........................ Houston Oilers | 1.50 | .60 | .15 |
| ☐ 17 Jim Plunkett......................... Oakland Raiders | 2.50 | 1.00 | .25 |
| ☐ 18 Y.A. Tittle............................ New York Giants | 6.00 | 2.40 | .60 |
| ☐ 19 Johnny Unitas....................... Baltimore Colts | 7.50 | 3.00 | .75 |
| ☐ 20 Danny White.......................... Dallas Cowboys | 2.00 | .80 | .20 |

# 1985 Miller Lite Beer

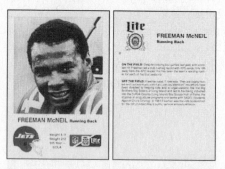

These oversized cards measure approximately 4 3/4" by 7" and feature on their fronts white-bordered posed player photos. The player's name and position, along with logos for his team and Miller Lite appear within the wide bottom margin. The logos reappear on the white backs, along with the player's career highlights. The cards are unnumbered and checklisted below in alphabetical order.

| | MINT | EXC | G-VG |
|---|---|---|---|
| COMPLETE SET (5)...................... | 100.00 | 40.00 | 10.00 |
| COMMON CARD (1-5)...................... | 12.50 | 5.00 | 1.25 |
| ☐ 1 John Hadl CO.......................... | 12.50 | 5.00 | 1.25 |
| ☐ 2 Freeman McNeil....................... New York Jets NFL Man of the Year | 20.00 | 8.00 | 2.00 |
| ☐ 3 Jack Reynolds......................... Lite Beer All-Stars | 12.50 | 5.00 | 1.25 |
| ☐ 4 Steve Young........................... Los Angeles Express | 60.00 | 24.00 | 6.00 |
| ☐ 5 1985 LA Express...................... Cheerleaders USFL Man of the Year | 12.50 | 5.00 | 1.25 |

# 1988 Monte Gum

This 100-card set was made in Europe by Monte Gum. The cards measure approximately 1 15/16" by 2 3/4" and contain thick yellow borders around a color photo. There was also an album issued with the set. The cards do not feature specific players, only generic team action scenes; hence they are not very popular with collectors. The cards have blank backs. The cards are numbered and subtitled at the bottom inside a black box.

| | MINT | EXC | G-VG |
|---|---|---|---|
| COMPLETE SET (100)...................... | 75.00 | 30.00 | 7.50 |
| COMMON TEAM (1-79)...................... | 1.00 | .40 | .10 |
| COMMON CARD (80-100)............... | .75 | .30 | .07 |
| ☐ 1 Atlanta Falcons....................... Atlanta Stadium | 1.25 | .50 | .12 |
| ☐ 2 Atlanta Falcons....................... Defense | 1.00 | .40 | .10 |
| ☐ 3 Atlanta Falcons....................... Offense | 1.00 | .40 | .10 |
| ☐ 4 Buffalo Bills........................... Blocked Punt | 1.00 | .40 | .10 |
| ☐ 5 Chicago Bears......................... At the Scrimmage Line | 1.00 | .40 | .10 |
| ☐ 6 Chicago Bears......................... (Action shot) | 1.00 | .40 | .10 |
| ☐ 7 Cincinnati Bengals................... Riverfront Stadium | 1.00 | .40 | .10 |
| ☐ 8 Cincinnati Bengals................... Inside the Stadium | 1.00 | .40 | .10 |
| ☐ 9 Cincinnati Bengals................... Goal Line Stand (Walter Payton diving) | 4.00 | 1.60 | .40 |
| ☐ 10 Cincinnati Bengals.................. (Action shot) | 1.00 | .40 | .10 |
| ☐ 11 Cincinnati Bengals.................. Cheerleader | 1.25 | .50 | .12 |
| ☐ 12 Cleveland Browns................... Cleveland Stadium | 1.00 | .40 | .10 |
| ☐ 13 Cleveland Browns................... QB Rollout (Bernie Kosar) | 2.00 | .80 | .20 |
| ☐ 14 Cleveland Browns................... Head Coach | 1.00 | .40 | .10 |
| ☐ 15 Cleveland Browns................... Fans | 1.00 | .40 | .10 |
| ☐ 16 Dallas Cowboys..................... Texas Stadium | 1.00 | .40 | .10 |
| ☐ 17 Dallas Cowboys..................... Touchdown Reception | 1.25 | .50 | .12 |
| ☐ 18 Dallas Cowboys..................... Cheerleader | 1.25 | .50 | .12 |
| ☐ 19 Denver Broncos..................... Mile High Stadium | 1.00 | .40 | .10 |
| ☐ 20 Denver Broncos..................... Swarming Defense | 1.00 | .40 | .10 |
| ☐ 21 Denver Broncos..................... (Randy Gradishar) | 1.50 | .60 | .15 |
| ☐ 22 Detroit Lions......................... QB Sack Celebration | 1.00 | .40 | .10 |
| ☐ 23 Green Bay Packers.................. On the Run | 1.00 | .40 | .10 |
| ☐ 24 Green Bay Packers.................. (Action shot) | 1.00 | .40 | .10 |
| ☐ 25 Houston Oilers....................... Houston Astrodome | 1.00 | .40 | .10 |
| ☐ 26 Houston Oilers....................... Tackled from behind | 1.00 | .40 | .10 |

| | | | |
|---|---|---|---|
| ☐ 27 Indianapolis Colts | 1.00 | .40 | .10 |
| Field Goal Attempt | | | |
| ☐ 28 Kansas City Chiefs | 1.00 | .40 | .10 |
| Up the Middle | | | |
| ☐ 29 Kansas City Chiefs | 1.00 | .40 | .10 |
| (Action shot) | | | |
| ☐ 30 Kansas City Chiefs | 1.25 | .50 | .12 |
| Cheerleader | | | |
| ☐ 31 Los Angeles Raiders | 1.00 | .40 | .10 |
| L.A. Memorial Coliseum | | | |
| ☐ 32 Los Angeles Raiders | 1.00 | .40 | .10 |
| Inside the Stadium | | | |
| ☐ 33 Los Angeles Raiders | 1.00 | .40 | .10 |
| In the Pocket | | | |
| ☐ 34 Los Angeles Raiders | 2.00 | .80 | .20 |
| (Marcus Allen; Super Bowl shot) | | | |
| ☐ 35 Los Angeles Rams | 1.00 | .40 | .10 |
| Anaheim Stadium | | | |
| ☐ 36 Los Angeles Rams | 2.00 | .80 | .20 |
| Power Blocking (Eric Dickerson running) | | | |
| ☐ 37 Los Angeles Rams | 1.00 | .40 | .10 |
| (Action shot) | | | |
| ☐ 38 Miami Dolphins | 1.25 | .50 | .12 |
| Attacking the Zone | | | |
| ☐ 39 Miami Dolphins | 1.25 | .50 | .12 |
| (Action shot) | | | |
| ☐ 40 Minnesota Vikings | 1.00 | .40 | .10 |
| (Metrodome) | | | |
| ☐ 41 Minnesota Vikings | 1.00 | .40 | .10 |
| Halfback Handoff | | | |
| ☐ 42 New England Patriots | 1.00 | .40 | .10 |
| Sullivan Stadium | | | |
| ☐ 43 New England Patriots | 1.25 | .50 | .12 |
| Throwing Deep (Steve Grogan) | | | |
| ☐ 44 New England Patriots | 2.50 | 1.00 | .25 |
| (Earl Campbell running) | | | |
| ☐ 45 New Orleans Saints | 1.50 | .60 | .15 |
| Swarming Linebackers (Roger Craig running) | | | |
| ☐ 46 New Orleans Saints UER | 1.25 | .50 | .12 |
| (Photo actually shows Washington and Michigan in '81 Rose Bowl game) | | | |
| ☐ 47 New York Giants | 1.25 | .50 | .12 |
| Turning the Corner | | | |
| ☐ 48 New York Giants | 1.00 | .40 | .10 |
| (Action shot) | | | |
| ☐ 49 New York Jets | 1.00 | .40 | .10 |
| Breaking Loose | | | |
| ☐ 50 New York Jets | 1.00 | .40 | .10 |
| (Line photo) | | | |
| ☐ 51 Philadelphia Eagles | 1.00 | .40 | .10 |
| Veterans Stadium | | | |
| ☐ 52 Philadelphia Eagles | 1.00 | .40 | .10 |
| Power Right | | | |
| ☐ 53 Philadelphia Eagles | 1.00 | .40 | .10 |
| (Action shot) | | | |
| ☐ 54 Philadelphia Eagles | 1.00 | .40 | .10 |
| Fans | | | |
| ☐ 55 Pittsburgh Steelers | 1.00 | .40 | .10 |
| Three Rivers Stadium | | | |
| ☐ 56 Pittsburgh Steelers | 1.25 | .50 | .12 |
| Swarming to the Ball | | | |
| ☐ 57 Pittsburgh Steelers | 1.00 | .40 | .10 |
| (Action shot) | | | |
| ☐ 58 St.Louis Cardinals | 1.00 | .40 | .10 |
| Busch Stadium | | | |
| ☐ 59 St.Louis Cardinals | 1.00 | .40 | .10 |
| Setting Up | | | |
| ☐ 60 St.Louis Cardinals | 1.00 | .40 | .10 |
| (Action shot) | | | |
| ☐ 61 St.Louis Cardinals UER | 1.00 | .40 | .10 |
| (Photo actually shows Saints vs. Browns game) | | | |
| ☐ 62 San Diego Chargers | 1.00 | .40 | .10 |
| Jack Murphy Stadium (Outside of stadium) | | | |
| ☐ 63 San Diego Chargers | 1.00 | .40 | .10 |
| Jack Murphy Stadium (Inside of stadium) | | | |
| ☐ 64 San Diego Chargers | 1.25 | .50 | .12 |
| Going for the Bomb | | | |
| ☐ 65 San Diego Chargers | 1.00 | .40 | .10 |
| Fans | | | |
| ☐ 66 San Francisco 49ers | 1.00 | .40 | .10 |
| Candlestick Park | | | |
| ☐ 67 San Francisco 49ers | 1.25 | .50 | .12 |
| Nose Guard on Attack | | | |
| ☐ 68 San Francisco 49ers | 8.00 | 3.25 | .80 |
| (Joe Montana) | | | |
| ☐ 69 San Francisco 49ers | 1.25 | .50 | .12 |
| ☐ 70 Seattle Seahawks | 1.00 | .40 | .10 |
| Shutting down the run | | | |
| ☐ 71 Seattle Seahawks | 1.00 | .40 | .10 |

| | | | |
|---|---|---|---|
| (Action shot) | | | |
| ☐ 72 Tampa Bay Buccaneers | 1.00 | .40 | .10 |
| Tampa Stadium | | | |
| ☐ 73 Tampa Bay Buccaneers | 1.00 | .40 | .10 |
| Tampa Stadium | | | |
| ☐ 74 Tampa Bay Buccaneers | 1.00 | .40 | .10 |
| Breaking Free | | | |
| ☐ 75 Tampa Bay Buccaneers | 1.00 | .40 | .10 |
| Defense | | | |
| ☐ 76 Washington Redskins | 1.00 | .40 | .10 |
| R.F.Kennedy Stadium | | | |
| ☐ 77 Washington Redskins | 1.00 | .40 | .10 |
| Redskins at the 50 | | | |
| ☐ 78 Washington Redskins | 1.00 | .40 | .10 |
| (Action shot) | | | |
| ☐ 79 Washington Redskins | 1.00 | .40 | .10 |
| Fans | | | |
| ☐ 80 Official NFL Football | .75 | .30 | .07 |
| ☐ 81 Helmets:Falcons/Bills | .75 | .30 | .07 |
| ☐ 82 Helmets:Bears/Bengals | .75 | .30 | .07 |
| ☐ 83 Helmets:Browns/ | .75 | .30 | .07 |
| Cowboys | | | |
| ☐ 84 Helmets:Broncos/Lions | .75 | .30 | .07 |
| ☐ 85 Helmets:Packers/ | .75 | .30 | .07 |
| Oilers | | | |
| ☐ 86 Helmets:Colts/Chiefs | .75 | .30 | .07 |
| ☐ 87 Helmets:Raiders/Rams | .75 | .30 | .07 |
| ☐ 88 Helmets:Dolphins/ | .75 | .30 | .07 |
| Vikings | | | |
| ☐ 89 Helmets:Patriots/ | .75 | .30 | .07 |
| Saints | | | |
| ☐ 90 Helmets:Giants/Jets | .75 | .30 | .07 |
| ☐ 91 Philadelphia Eagles | .75 | .30 | .07 |
| Helmet | | | |
| ☐ 92 Pittsburgh Steelers | .75 | .30 | .07 |
| Helmet | | | |
| ☐ 93 St. Louis Cardinals | .75 | .30 | .07 |
| Helmet | | | |
| ☐ 94 San Diego Chargers | .75 | .30 | .07 |
| Helmet | | | |
| ☐ 95 San Francisco 49ers | .75 | .30 | .07 |
| Helmet | | | |
| ☐ 96 Seattle Seahawks | .75 | .30 | .07 |
| Helmet | | | |
| ☐ 97 Tampa Bay Buccaneers | .75 | .30 | .07 |
| Helmet | | | |
| ☐ 98 Washington Redskins | .75 | .30 | .07 |
| Helmet | | | |
| ☐ 99 National Football | .75 | .30 | .07 |
| League Logo | | | |
| ☐ 100 American Football Fans | 1.00 | .40 | .10 |

## 1981 MSA Holsum Discs

This 32-disc set was apparently not widely distributed. Sponsor identification is impossible from the cards themselves. Several brands of bread (including Holsum and Gardner's in Wisconsin) carried one football card per specially marked loaf during the promotion. The discs are blank backed and are approximately 2 3/4" in diameter. Since they are unnumbered, they are listed below in alphabetical order. The discs were produced by Michael Schechter Associates and are licensed only by the NFL Players Association. There were also two different posters (Holsum and Gardner's) produced for holding and displaying the set. The key card in the set depicts Joe Montana in his rookie year for cards. The set is considered by some to be a 1980 issue, but it is more likely 1981 since Joe Montana did not distinguish himself with the 49ers until the 1980 season. Joe Montana only attempted 23 passes during the 1979 season. In addition Joe Cribbs' and Vagas Ferguson's first year in the NFL was 1980.

| | MINT | EXC | G-VG |
|---|---|---|---|
| COMPLETE SET (32) | 150.00 | 60.00 | 15.00 |
| COMMON PLAYER (1-32) | 2.00 | .80 | .20 |

| | | | |
|---|---|---|---|
| ☐ 1 Ken Anderson | 4.00 | 1.60 | .40 |
| Cincinnati Bengals | | | |
| ☐ 2 Ottis Anderson | 5.00 | 2.00 | .50 |
| St. Louis Cardinals | | | |
| ☐ 3 Steve Bartkowski | 3.00 | 1.20 | .30 |
| Atlanta Falcons | | | |
| ☐ 4 Ricky Bell | 3.00 | 1.20 | .30 |
| Tampa Bay Buccaneers | | | |
| ☐ 5 Terry Bradshaw | 15.00 | 6.00 | 1.50 |
| Pittsburgh Steelers | | | |
| ☐ 6 Harold Carmichael | 3.00 | 1.20 | .30 |
| Philadelphia Eagles | | | |
| ☐ 7 Joe Cribbs | 2.00 | .80 | .20 |
| Buffalo Bills | | | |
| ☐ 8 Gary Danielson | 2.00 | .80 | .20 |
| Detroit Lions | | | |
| ☐ 9 Lynn Dickey | 2.00 | .80 | .20 |
| Green Bay Packers | | | |
| ☐ 10 Dan Doornink | 2.00 | .80 | .20 |
| Seattle Seahawks | | | |
| ☐ 11 Vince Evans | 3.00 | 1.20 | .30 |
| Chicago Bears | | | |
| ☐ 12 Joe Ferguson | 3.00 | 1.20 | .30 |
| Buffalo Bills | | | |
| ☐ 13 Vagas Ferguson | 2.00 | .80 | .20 |
| New England Patriots | | | |
| ☐ 14 Dan Fouts | 8.00 | 3.25 | .80 |
| San Diego Chargers | | | |
| ☐ 15 Steve Fuller | 2.00 | .80 | .20 |
| Kansas City Chiefs | | | |
| ☐ 16 Archie Griffin | 3.00 | 1.20 | .30 |
| Cincinnati Bengals | | | |
| ☐ 17 Steve Grogan | 3.00 | 1.20 | .30 |
| New England Patriots | | | |
| ☐ 18 Bruce Harper | 2.00 | .80 | .20 |
| New York Jets | | | |
| ☐ 19 Jim Hart | 3.00 | 1.20 | .30 |
| St. Louis Cardinals | | | |
| ☐ 20 Jim Jensen | 2.00 | .80 | .20 |
| Denver Broncos | | | |
| ☐ 21 Bert Jones | 3.00 | 1.20 | .30 |
| Baltimore Colts | | | |
| ☐ 22 Archie Manning | 4.00 | 1.60 | .40 |
| New Orleans Saints | | | |
| ☐ 23 Ted McKnight | 2.00 | .80 | .20 |
| Kansas City Chiefs | | | |
| ☐ 24 Joe Montana | 75.00 | 30.00 | 7.50 |
| San Francisco 49ers | | | |
| ☐ 25 Craig Morton | 3.00 | 1.20 | .30 |
| Denver Broncos | | | |
| ☐ 26 Robert Newhouse | 3.00 | 1.20 | .30 |
| Dallas Cowboys | | | |
| ☐ 27 Phil Simms | 8.00 | 3.25 | .80 |
| New York Giants | | | |
| ☐ 28 Billy Taylor | 2.00 | .80 | .20 |
| New York Giants | | | |
| ☐ 29 Joe Theismann | 5.00 | 2.00 | .50 |
| Washington Redskins | | | |
| ☐ 30 Mark Van Eeghen | 2.00 | .80 | .20 |
| Oakland Raiders | | | |
| ☐ 31 Delvin Williams | 2.00 | .80 | .20 |
| Miami Dolphins | | | |
| ☐ 32 Tim Wilson | 2.00 | .80 | .20 |
| Houston Oilers | | | |

## 1990 MSA Superstars

HERSCHEL WALKER
MINNESOTA VIKINGS

This 12-card, 2 1/2" by 3 3/8", set was issued in boxes of (Ralston Purina) Staff and Food Club Frosted Flakes cereal. The cards were released as two cards in every box and a coupon was also inserted that enabled collectors to mail away and receive the set for 2 UPC symbol codes and postage and handling. These cards are unnumbered

so we have checklisted them alphabetically. The fronts of the cards have the word "Superstars" on top of the players photo and his name and team underneath. The back of the card features personal information about the player and statistical information in a textual style. There are no team logos on the card as the cards apparently were issued with only the permission of the National Football League Players Association. There is no mention of MSA on the cards, but they are very similar to the Mike Schechter baseball issue for Ralston Purina so they have been cataloged as such.

| | MINT | EXC | G-VG |
|---|---|---|---|
| COMPLETE SET (12) | 12.00 | 5.00 | 1.20 |
| COMMON PLAYER (1-12) | .60 | .24 | .06 |
| ☐ 1 Carl Banks | .75 | .30 | .07 |
| ☐ 2 Cornelius Bennett | .75 | .30 | .07 |
| ☐ 3 Roger Craig | 1.00 | .40 | .10 |
| ☐ 4 Jim Everett | 1.00 | .40 | .10 |
| ☐ 5 Bo Jackson | 2.00 | .80 | .20 |
| ☐ 6 Ronnie Lott | 1.25 | .50 | .12 |
| ☐ 7 Don Majkowski | .60 | .24 | .06 |
| ☐ 8 Dan Marino | 6.00 | 2.40 | .60 |
| ☐ 9 Karl Mecklenburg | .60 | .24 | .06 |
| ☐ 10 Christian Okoye | .60 | .24 | .06 |
| ☐ 11 Mike Singletary | .75 | .30 | .07 |
| ☐ 12 Herschel Walker | 1.00 | .40 | .10 |

## 1935 National Chicle

FOOTBALL STARS, No. 34

Bronko Nagurski, former Minnesota fullback now with the Chicago Bears, is perhaps the best known professional football player still active in the game. Twice All-American in college, he has since won All-National pro honors five times in succession. A product of the wheat farm country, he still works the soil between action on the football field and professional wrestling mat. He is one of the few players versatile enough to play any position on the team without losing his effectiveness. He is as much a traction to Minnesota football today as Red Grange is to Illinois.

Eddie Casey

BRONKO NAGURSKI, Fullback, University of Minnesota, All-American and five times All-National Star. 27 years old, 6 ft. 2 inches, 226 pounds. Home, International Falls, Minn. One of 240 football players with playing tips © 1935 National Chicle Co. Cambridge, Mass. U.S.A.

BRONKO NAGURSKI

The 1935 National Chicle set was the first nationally distributed bubble gum set dedicated exclusively to football players. The cards measure 2 3/8" by 2 7/8". Card numbers 25 to 36 are more difficult to obtain than other cards in this set. The Rockne and Nagurski cards are two of the most valuable football cards in existence. The set features professional (National Football League) players except for the Rockne card. There are minor variations on the back of nearly every card with respect to the presence of Eddie Casey's name or some other coach's.

| | EX-MT | VG-E | GOOD |
|---|---|---|---|
| COMPLETE SET (36) | 15000. | 6000. | 1650. |
| COMMON PLAYER (1-24) | 100.00 | 40.00 | 10.00 |
| COMMON PLAYER (25-36) | 400.00 | 160.00 | 40.00 |
| ☐ 1 Earl(Dutch) Clark | 500.00 | 150.00 | 30.00 |
| Detroit Lions | | | |
| ☐ 2 Bo Molenda | 100.00 | 40.00 | 10.00 |
| New York Giants | | | |
| ☐ 3 George Kenneally | 100.00 | 40.00 | 10.00 |
| Philadelphia Eagles | | | |
| ☐ 4 Ed Matesic | 100.00 | 40.00 | 10.00 |
| Philadelphia Eagles | | | |
| ☐ 5 Glenn Presnell | 100.00 | 40.00 | 10.00 |
| Detroit Lions | | | |
| ☐ 6 Pug Rentner | 100.00 | 40.00 | 10.00 |
| Boston Redskins | | | |
| ☐ 7 Ken Strong | 300.00 | 120.00 | 30.00 |
| New York Giants | | | |
| ☐ 8 Jim Zyntell | 100.00 | 40.00 | 10.00 |
| Philadelphia Eagles | | | |
| ☐ 9 Knute Rockne | 1500.00 | 600.00 | 150.00 |
| Notre Dame CO | | | |
| ☐ 10 Cliff Battles | 300.00 | 120.00 | 30.00 |
| Boston Redskins | | | |
| ☐ 11 Glen(Turk) Edwards | 300.00 | 120.00 | 30.00 |
| Boston Redskins | | | |
| ☐ 12 Tom Hupke | 100.00 | 40.00 | 10.00 |
| Detroit Lions | | | |
| ☐ 13 Homer Griffiths | 100.00 | 40.00 | 10.00 |
| Chicago Cardinals | | | |
| ☐ 14 Phil Sarboe UER | 100.00 | 40.00 | 10.00 |
| Chicago Cardinals | | | |
| (Misspelled Sorboe | | | |

| | | MINT | EXC | G-VG |
|---|---|---|---|---|
| | on both sides of card) | | | |
| ☐ 15 | Ben Ciccone | 100.00 | 40.00 | 10.00 |
| | Pittsburgh Pirates | | | |
| ☐ 16 | Ben Smith | 100.00 | 40.00 | 10.00 |
| | Pittsburgh Pirates | | | |
| ☐ 17 | Tom Jones | 100.00 | 40.00 | 10.00 |
| | New York Giants | | | |
| ☐ 18 | Mike Mikulak | 100.00 | 40.00 | 10.00 |
| | Chicago Cardinals | | | |
| ☐ 19 | Ralph G. Kercheval | 100.00 | 40.00 | 10.00 |
| | Brooklyn Dodgers | | | |
| ☐ 20 | Warren Heller | 100.00 | 40.00 | 10.00 |
| | Pittsburgh Pirates | | | |
| ☐ 21 | Cliff Montgomery | 100.00 | 40.00 | 10.00 |
| | Brooklyn Dodgers | | | |
| ☐ 22 | Shipwreck Kelley | 150.00 | 60.00 | 15.00 |
| | Brooklyn Dodgers | | | |
| ☐ 23 | Beattie Feathers | 200.00 | 80.00 | 20.00 |
| | Chicago Bears | | | |
| ☐ 24 | Clarke Hinkle | 300.00 | 120.00 | 30.00 |
| | Green Bay Packers | | | |
| ☐ 25 | Dale Burnett | 400.00 | 160.00 | 40.00 |
| | New York Giants | | | |
| ☐ 26 | John Dell Isola | 400.00 | 160.00 | 40.00 |
| | New York Giants | | | |
| | (Dell omitted from | | | |
| | name on card front) | | | |
| ☐ 27 | Bull Tosi | 400.00 | 160.00 | 40.00 |
| | Boston Redskins | | | |
| ☐ 28 | Stan Kosta | 400.00 | 160.00 | 40.00 |
| | Brooklyn Dodgers | | | |
| ☐ 29 | Jim MacMurdo | 400.00 | 160.00 | 40.00 |
| | Philadelphia Eagles | | | |
| ☐ 30 | Ernie Caddel | 400.00 | 160.00 | 40.00 |
| | Detroit Lions | | | |
| ☐ 31 | Nic Niccola | 400.00 | 160.00 | 40.00 |
| | Pittsburgh Pirates | | | |
| ☐ 32 | Swede Johnston | 400.00 | 160.00 | 40.00 |
| | Green Bay Packers | | | |
| ☐ 33 | Ernie Smith | 400.00 | 160.00 | 40.00 |
| | Green Bay Packers | | | |
| ☐ 34 | Bronko Nagurski | 6000.00 | 2500.00 | 600.00 |
| | Chicago Bears | | | |
| ☐ 35 | Luke Johnsos | 400.00 | 160.00 | 40.00 |
| | Chicago Bears | | | |
| ☐ 36 | Bernie Masterson | 750.00 | 250.00 | 50.00 |
| | Chicago Bears | | | |

## 1992 NewSport

This set of 32 glossy player photos was sponsored by NewSport and issued in France. It is reported that three photos were issued per month, and athletes from other sports were also featured. The set was also available in four-card uncut strips. The cards measure approximately 4" by 6" and display glossy color player photos with white borders. The player's name and position appear in the top border, while the NewSport and NFL logos adorn the bottom of the card face. In French, the backs present biography, complete statistics, and career summary. The cards are unnumbered and checklisted below in alphabetical order.

| | | MINT | EXC | G-VG |
|---|---|---|---|---|
| | COMPLETE SET (32) | 200.00 | 80.00 | 20.00 |
| | COMMON PLAYER (1-32) | 6.00 | 2.40 | .60 |
| ☐ 1 | Bubby Brister | 6.00 | 2.40 | .60 |
| | Pittsburgh Steelers | | | |
| ☐ 2 | James Brooks | 7.50 | 3.00 | .75 |
| | Cincinnati Bengals | | | |
| ☐ 3 | Joey Browner | 6.00 | 2.40 | .60 |
| | Minnesota Vikings | | | |

| | | MINT | EXC | G-VG |
|---|---|---|---|---|
| ☐ 4 | Gill Byrd | 6.00 | 2.40 | .60 |
| | San Diego Chargers | | | |
| ☐ 5 | Eric Dickerson | 10.00 | 4.00 | 1.00 |
| | Indianapolis Colts | | | |
| ☐ 6 | Henry Ellard | 6.00 | 2.40 | .60 |
| | Los Angeles Rams | | | |
| ☐ 7 | John Elway | 20.00 | 8.00 | 2.00 |
| | Denver Broncos | | | |
| ☐ 8 | Mervyn Fernandez | 7.50 | 3.00 | .75 |
| | Los Angeles Raiders | | | |
| ☐ 9 | David Fulcher | 6.00 | 2.40 | .60 |
| | Cincinnati Bengals | | | |
| ☐ 10 | Ernest Givins | 7.50 | 3.00 | .75 |
| | Houston Oilers | | | |
| ☐ 11 | Jay Hilgenberg | 6.00 | 2.40 | .60 |
| | Chicago Bears | | | |
| ☐ 12 | Michael Irvin | 20.00 | 8.00 | 2.00 |
| | Dallas Cowboys | | | |
| ☐ 13 | Dave Krieg | 7.50 | 3.00 | .75 |
| | Seattle Seahawks | | | |
| ☐ 14 | Albert Lewis | 6.00 | 2.40 | .60 |
| | Kansas City Chiefs | | | |
| ☐ 15 | James Lofton | 10.00 | 4.00 | 1.00 |
| | Buffalo Bills | | | |
| ☐ 16 | Dan Marino | 30.00 | 12.00 | 3.00 |
| | Miami Dolphins | | | |
| ☐ 17 | Wilber Marshall | 6.00 | 2.40 | .60 |
| | Washington Redskins | | | |
| ☐ 18 | Freeman McNeil | 7.50 | 3.00 | .75 |
| | New York Jets | | | |
| ☐ 19 | Karl Mecklenberg | 6.00 | 2.40 | .60 |
| | Denver Broncos | | | |
| ☐ 20 | Joe Montana | 40.00 | 16.00 | 4.00 |
| | San Francisco 49ers | | | |
| ☐ 21 | Christian Okoye | 7.50 | 3.00 | .75 |
| | Kansas City Chiefs | | | |
| ☐ 22 | Michael Dean Perry | 7.50 | 3.00 | .75 |
| | Cleveland Browns | | | |
| ☐ 23 | Tom Rathman | 7.50 | 3.00 | .75 |
| | San Francisco 49ers | | | |
| ☐ 24 | Mark Rypien | 7.50 | 3.00 | .75 |
| | Washington Redskins | | | |
| ☐ 25 | Barry Sanders | 30.00 | 12.00 | 3.00 |
| | Detroit Lions | | | |
| ☐ 26 | Deion Sanders | 12.00 | 5.00 | 1.20 |
| | Atlanta Falcons | | | |
| ☐ 27 | Sterling Sharpe | 20.00 | 8.00 | 2.00 |
| | Green Bay Packers | | | |
| ☐ 28 | Pat Swilling | 7.50 | 3.00 | .75 |
| | New Orleans Saints | | | |
| ☐ 29 | Lawrence Taylor | 12.00 | 5.00 | 1.20 |
| | New York Giants | | | |
| ☐ 30 | Vinny Testaverde | 7.50 | 3.00 | .75 |
| | Tampa Bay Buccaneers | | | |
| ☐ 31 | Andre Tippett | 6.00 | 2.40 | .60 |
| | New England Patriots | | | |
| ☐ 32 | Reggie White | 10.00 | 4.00 | 1.00 |
| | Green Bay Packers | | | |

## 1991-92 NFL Experience

This 28-card set measures approximately 2 1/2" by 4 3/4" and has black borders around each picture. Produced by the NFL, this stylized card set highlights Super Bowl players and scenes. Card fronts run either horizontally or vertically and carry the NFL Experience logo at the bottom center. The backs are printed horizontally with the words "The NFL Experience" and card number appearing in black in a light pink bar at the top. The bottom pink bar carries a description of front artwork, while the center portion describes some aspect of NFL life. Sponsors' logos appear on the right portion of each back.

Bob Hayes

|  | MINT | EXC | G-VG |
|---|---|---|---|
| COMPLETE SET (28)...................... | 10.00 | 4.00 | 1.00 |
| COMMON PLAYER (1-28)................. | .50 | .20 | .05 |
| ☐ 1 NFL Experience ......................... Theme Art | .75 | .30 | .07 |
| ☐ 2 Super Bowl I ............................ Max McGee | .50 | .20 | .05 |
| ☐ 3 Super Bowl II ........................... Vince Lombardi Bart Starr | 1.00 | .40 | .10 |
| ☐ 4 Super Bowl III .......................... Don Shula Joe Namath | 1.50 | .60 | .15 |
| ☐ 5 Super Bowl IV .......................... Kansas City Chiefs | .50 | .20 | .05 |
| ☐ 6 Super Bowl V ........................... Colts/Cowboys | .50 | .20 | .05 |
| ☐ 7 Super Bowl VI .......................... Duane Thomas Bob Lilly Roger Staubach Tom Landry Tex Schramm | 1.00 | .40 | .10 |
| ☐ 8 Super Bowl VII ......................... Miami Dolphins | .50 | .20 | .05 |
| ☐ 9 Super Bowl VIII ........................ Larry Csonka | .75 | .30 | .07 |
| ☐ 10 Super Bowl IX ......................... Pittsburgh Steelers | .50 | .20 | .05 |
| ☐ 11 Super Bowl X .......................... Lynn Swann Jack Lambert | .75 | .30 | .07 |
| ☐ 12 Super Bowl XI ......................... John Madden Raiders/Vikings | .75 | .30 | .07 |
| ☐ 13 Super Bowl XIII ....................... Randy White Harvey Martin Craig Morton | .60 | .24 | .06 |
| ☐ 14 Super Bowl XIII ....................... Steelers/Cowboys | .50 | .20 | .05 |
| ☐ 15 Super Bowl XIV ....................... Terry Bradshaw | 1.00 | .40 | .10 |
| ☐ 16 Super Bowl XV ........................ Raiders/Eagles | .50 | .20 | .05 |
| ☐ 17 Super Bowl XVI ....................... 49ers/Bengals | .50 | .20 | .05 |
| ☐ 18 Super Bowl XVII ...................... John Riggins | .75 | .30 | .07 |
| ☐ 19 Super Bowl XVIII ..................... Marcus Allen | .75 | .30 | .07 |
| ☐ 20 Super Bowl XIX ....................... 49ers/Dolphins | .50 | .20 | .05 |
| ☐ 21 Super Bowl XX ........................ Richard Dent | .60 | .24 | .06 |
| ☐ 22 Super Bowl XXI........................ New York Giants | .50 | .20 | .05 |
| ☐ 23 Super Bowl XXII....................... John Elway Doug Williams | .75 | .30 | .07 |
| ☐ 24 Super Bowl XXIII...................... 49ers/Bengals | .50 | .20 | .05 |
| ☐ 25 Super Bowl XXIV...................... Joe Montana | 3.00 | 1.20 | .30 |
| ☐ 26 Super Bowl XXV....................... Collage of 25 Super Bowls | .50 | .20 | .05 |
| ☐ 27 Super Bowl XXVI...................... Lombardi Trophy | .50 | .20 | .05 |
| ☐ 28 Joe Theismann........................ | .75 | .30 | .07 |

## 1972 NFLPA Vinyl Stickers

The 1972 NFLPA Vinyl Stickers set contains 20 stand-up type stickers depicting the players in a caricature-like style with big heads. These irregularly shaped stickers are approximately 2 3/4" by 4 3/4". Below the player's name at the bottom of the card is indicated copyright by the NFL Players Association in 1972. The set is sometimes offered as a short set excluding the shorter-printed cards, i.e., those listed by SP in the checklist below. Since they are unnumbered, they are listed below in alphabetical order according to the player's name. The Roger Staubach card holds special interest in that 1972 represents Roger's rookie year for cards. These stickers were originally available in vending machines at retail stores and other outlets. The Dick Butkus and Joe Namath stickers exist as reverse negatives.

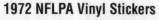

|  | NRMT | VG-E | GOOD |
|---|---|---|---|
| COMPLETE SET (20)........................ | 100.00 | 40.00 | 10.00 |
| COMMON PLAYER (1-20)................. | 2.00 | .80 | .20 |
| COMMON PLAYER SP ...................... | 10.00 | 4.00 | 1.00 |

| | | | |
|---|---|---|---|
| ☐ 1 Donny Anderson ...................... St. Louis Cardinals | 2.00 | .80 | .20 |
| ☐ 2 George Blanda.......................... Oakland Raiders | 6.00 | 2.40 | .60 |
| ☐ 3 Terry Bradshaw......................... Pittsburgh Steelers | 20.00 | 8.00 | 2.00 |
| ☐ 4 John Brockington...................... Green Bay Packers | 2.00 | .80 | .20 |
| ☐ 5 John Brodie.............................. San Francisco 49ers | 4.00 | 1.60 | .40 |
| ☐ 6 Dick Butkus.............................. Chicago Bears | 8.00 | 3.25 | .80 |
| ☐ 7 Dick Gordon.............................. Chicago Bears | 2.00 | .80 | .20 |
| ☐ 8 Joe Greene............................... Pittsburgh Steelers | 5.00 | 2.00 | .50 |
| ☐ 9 John Hadl................................. San Diego Chargers | 2.00 | .80 | .20 |
| ☐ 10 Bob Hayes.............................. Dallas Cowboys | 3.00 | 1.20 | .30 |
| ☐ 11 Ron Johnson SP ...................... New York Giants | 10.00 | 4.00 | 1.00 |
| ☐ 12 Floyd Little............................. Denver Broncos | 3.00 | 1.20 | .30 |
| ☐ 13 Joe Namath............................. New York Jets | 25.00 | 10.00 | 2.50 |
| ☐ 14 Tommy Nobis .......................... Atlanta Falcons | 3.00 | 1.20 | .30 |
| ☐ 15 Alan Page SP .......................... Minnesota Vikings | 15.00 | 6.00 | 1.50 |
| ☐ 16 Jim Plunkett............................ New England Patriots | 5.00 | 2.00 | .50 |
| ☐ 17 Gale Sayers............................ Chicago Bears | 10.00 | 4.00 | 1.00 |
| ☐ 18 Roger Staubach ...................... Dallas Cowboys | 25.00 | 10.00 | 2.50 |
| ☐ 19 Johnny Unitas.......................... Baltimore Colts | 20.00 | 8.00 | 2.00 |
| ☐ 20 Paul Warfield........................... Miami Dolphins | 4.00 | 1.60 | .40 |

## 1972 NFLPA Fabric Cards

Kansas City Chiefs

Len Dawson

The 1972 NFLPA Fabric Cards set includes 35 cards printed on cloth. These thin fabric cards measure approximately 2 1/4" by 3 1/2" and are blank backed. The cards are sometimes referred to as "Iron Ons" as they were intended to be semi-permanently ironed on to clothes. The full color portrait of the player is surrounded by a black border. Below the player's name at the bottom of the card is indicated copyright by the NFL Players Association in 1972. The cards may have been illegally reprinted. There is some additional interest in the Staubach card due to the fact that his 1972 Topps card (that same year) is considered his Rookie Card. Since they are unnumbered, they are listed below in alphabetical order according to the player's name. These fabric cards were originally available in vending machines at retail stores and other outlets.

201
Bob Griese
Miami Dolphins

(A full biography of this player will be found in the appropriate space in the album.)

| | NRMT | VG-E | GOOD |
|---|---|---|---|
| COMPLETE SET (35) | 150.00 | 60.00 | 15.00 |
| COMMON PLAYER (1-35) | 1.50 | .60 | .15 |
| ☐ 1 Donny Anderson | 1.50 | .60 | .15 |
| Green Bay Packers | | | |
| ☐ 2 George Blanda | 7.50 | 3.00 | .75 |
| Oakland Raiders | | | |
| ☐ 3 Terry Bradshaw | 20.00 | 8.00 | 2.00 |
| Pittsburgh Steelers | | | |
| ☐ 4 John Brockington | 1.50 | .60 | .15 |
| Green Bay Packers | | | |
| ☐ 5 John Brodie | 5.00 | 2.00 | .50 |
| San Francisco 49ers | | | |
| ☐ 6 Dick Butkus | 9.00 | 3.75 | .90 |
| Chicago Bears | | | |
| ☐ 7 Larry Csonka | 9.00 | 3.75 | .90 |
| Miami Dolphins | | | |
| ☐ 8 Mike Curtis | 1.50 | .60 | .15 |
| Baltimore Colts | | | |
| ☐ 9 Len Dawson | 6.00 | 2.40 | .60 |
| Kansas City Chiefs | | | |
| ☐ 10 Carl Eller | 3.00 | 1.20 | .30 |
| Minnesota Vikings | | | |
| ☐ 11 Mike Garrett | 1.50 | .60 | .15 |
| San Diego Chargers | | | |
| ☐ 12 Joe Greene | 7.50 | 3.00 | .75 |
| Pittsburgh Steelers | | | |
| ☐ 13 Bob Griese | 9.00 | 3.75 | .90 |
| Miami Dolphins | | | |
| ☐ 14 Dick Gordon | 1.50 | .60 | .15 |
| Chicago Bears | | | |
| ☐ 15 John Hadl | 2.00 | .80 | .20 |
| San Diego Chargers | | | |
| ☐ 16 Bob Hayes | 2.00 | .80 | .20 |
| Dallas Cowboys | | | |
| ☐ 17 Ron Johnson | 1.50 | .60 | .15 |
| New York Giants | | | |
| ☐ 18 Deacon Jones | 3.00 | 1.20 | .30 |
| San Diego Chargers | | | |
| ☐ 19 Sonny Jurgensen | 6.00 | 2.40 | .60 |
| Washington Redskins | | | |
| ☐ 20 Leroy Kelly | 3.00 | 1.20 | .30 |
| Cleveland Browns | | | |
| ☐ 21 Jim Kiick | 2.00 | .80 | .20 |
| Miami Dolphins | | | |
| ☐ 22 Greg Landry | 1.50 | .60 | .15 |
| Detroit Lions | | | |
| ☐ 23 Floyd Little | 2.50 | 1.00 | .25 |
| Denver Broncos | | | |
| ☐ 24 Mike Lucci | 1.50 | .60 | .15 |
| Detroit Lions | | | |
| ☐ 25 Archie Manning | 5.00 | 2.00 | .50 |
| New Orleans Saints | | | |
| ☐ 26 Joe Namath | 30.00 | 12.00 | 3.00 |
| New York Jets | | | |
| ☐ 27 Tommy Nobis | 3.00 | 1.20 | .30 |
| Atlanta Falcons | | | |
| ☐ 28 Alan Page | 3.00 | 1.20 | .30 |
| Minnesota Vikings | | | |
| ☐ 29 Jim Plunkett | 4.00 | 1.60 | .40 |
| New England Patriots | | | |
| ☐ 30 Gale Sayers | 10.00 | 4.00 | 1.00 |
| Chicago Bears | | | |
| ☐ 31 O.J. Simpson | 30.00 | 12.00 | 3.00 |
| Buffalo Bills | | | |
| ☐ 32 Roger Staubach | 30.00 | 12.00 | 3.00 |
| Dallas Cowboys | | | |
| ☐ 33 Duane Thomas | 2.00 | .80 | .20 |
| San Diego Chargers | | | |
| ☐ 34 Johnny Unitas | 20.00 | 8.00 | 2.00 |
| Baltimore Colts | | | |
| ☐ 35 Paul Warfield | 5.00 | 2.00 | .50 |
| Miami Dolphins | | | |

# 1971-72 NFLPA Wonderful World Stamps

This set of 390 stamps was issued under the auspices of the NFL Players Association in conjunction with an album entitled "The Wonderful World of Pro Football USA". The stamps are numbered and are approximately 1 15/16" by 2 7/8". The team order of the album is arranged alphabetically according to the city name (and then alphabetically by player name within each team), i.e., Atlanta Falcons (1-15), Baltimore Colts (16-30), Buffalo Bills (31-45), Chicago Bears (46-60), Cincinnati Bengals (61-75), Cleveland Browns (76-90), Dallas Cowboys (91-105), Denver Broncos (106-120), Detroit Lions (121-135), Green Bay Packers (136-150), Houston Oilers (151-165), Kansas City Chiefs (166-180), Los Angeles Rams (181-195), Miami Dolphins (196-210), Minnesota Vikings (211-225), New England Patriots (226-240), New Orleans Saints (241-255), New York Giants (256-270), New York Jets (271-285), Oakland Raiders (286-300), Philadelphia Eagles (301-315), Pittsburgh Steelers (316-330), St. Louis Cardinals (331-345), San Diego Chargers (346-360), San Francisco 49ers (361-375), and Washington Redskins (376-390). The picture stamp album contains 30 pages measuring approximately 9 1/2" by 13 1/4". The text narrates the story of pro football in the United States. The album includes spaces for 390 color player stamps. The checklist and stamp numbering below is according to the album; there are some discrepancies when compared to the actual stamps. The set was also issued in 1971 with slightly different numbers; the A variations listed below are 1971 stamps.

| | NRMT | VG-E | GOOD |
|---|---|---|---|
| COMPLETE SET (390) | 250.00 | 100.00 | 25.00 |
| COMMON PLAYER (1-390) | .35 | .14 | .03 |
| ☐ 1 Bob Berry | .50 | .20 | .05 |
| ☐ 2 Greg Brezina | .35 | .14 | .03 |
| ☐ 3 Ken Burrow | .35 | .14 | .03 |
| ☐ 4 Jim Butler | .35 | .14 | .03 |
| ☐ 5 Wes Chesson | .35 | .14 | .03 |
| ☐ 6 Claude Humphrey | .50 | .20 | .05 |
| ☐ 7 George Kunz | .75 | .30 | .07 |
| ☐ 8 Tom McCauley | .35 | .14 | .03 |
| ☐ 9 Jim Mitchell | .50 | .20 | .05 |
| ☐ 10 Tommy Nobis | 2.00 | .80 | .20 |
| ☐ 11 Ken Reaves | .35 | .14 | .03 |
| ☐ 12 Bill Sandeman | .35 | .14 | .03 |
| ☐ 13 John Small | .35 | .14 | .03 |
| ☐ 14 Harmon Wages | .35 | .14 | .03 |
| ☐ 15 John Zook | .50 | .20 | .05 |
| ☐ 16 Norm Bulaich | .50 | .20 | .05 |
| ☐ 17 Bill Curry | .75 | .30 | .07 |
| ☐ 18 Mike Curtis | .75 | .30 | .07 |
| ☐ 19 Ted Hendricks | 2.00 | .80 | .20 |
| ☐ 20 Roy Hilton | .35 | .14 | .03 |
| ☐ 21 Eddie Hinton | .35 | .14 | .03 |
| ☐ 22 David Lee | .35 | .14 | .03 |
| ☐ 23 Jerry Logan | .35 | .14 | .03 |
| ☐ 24 John Mackey | 2.00 | .80 | .20 |
| ☐ 25 Tom Matte | .75 | .30 | .07 |
| ☐ 26 Jim O'Brien | .50 | .20 | .05 |
| ☐ 27 Glenn Ressler | .35 | .14 | .03 |
| ☐ 28 Johnny Unitas | 12.00 | 5.00 | 1.20 |
| ☐ 29 Bob Vogel | .50 | .20 | .05 |
| ☐ 30 Rick Volk | .50 | .20 | .05 |
| ☐ 31 Paul Costa | .35 | .14 | .03 |
| ☐ 32 Jim Dunaway | .50 | .20 | .05 |
| ☐ 33 Paul Guidry | .35 | .14 | .03 |
| ☐ 34 Jim Harris | .35 | .14 | .03 |
| ☐ 35 Robert James | .35 | .14 | .03 |
| ☐ 36 Mike McBath | .35 | .14 | .03 |
| ☐ 37 Haven Moses | .75 | .30 | .07 |
| ☐ 38 Wayne Patrick | .35 | .14 | .03 |
| ☐ 39 John Pitts | .35 | .14 | .03 |
| ☐ 40 Jim Reilly | .35 | .14 | .03 |
| ☐ 41 Pete Richardson | .35 | .14 | .03 |
| ☐ 42 Dennis Shaw | .50 | .20 | .05 |
| ☐ 43 O.J. Simpson | 20.00 | 8.00 | 2.00 |
| ☐ 44 Mike Stratton | .50 | .20 | .05 |
| ☐ 45 Bob Tatarek | .35 | .14 | .03 |
| ☐ 46 Dick Butkus | 6.00 | 2.40 | .60 |
| ☐ 47 Jim Cadile | .35 | .14 | .03 |

| | | | | | | | |
|---|---|---|---|---|---|---|---|
| ☐ 48 Jack Concannon | .50 | .20 | .05 | ☐ 141 Gale Gillingham | .50 | .20 | .05 |
| ☐ 49 Bobby Douglass | .75 | .30 | .07 | ☐ 142 Dave Hampton | .50 | .20 | .05 |
| ☐ 50 George Farmer | .50 | .20 | .05 | ☐ 143 Doug Hart | .35 | .14 | .03 |
| ☐ 51 Dick Gordon | .50 | .20 | .05 | ☐ 144A John Hilton | .35 | .14 | .03 |
| ☐ 52 Bobby Joe Green | .35 | .14 | .03 | ☐ 144B MacArthur Lane | .75 | .30 | .07 |
| ☐ 53 Ed O'Bradovich | .35 | .14 | .03 | ☐ 145 Mike McCoy | .50 | .20 | .05 |
| ☐ 54A Bob Hyland | .35 | .14 | .03 | ☐ 146 Ray Nitschke | 2.50 | 1.00 | .25 |
| ☐ 54B Mac Percival | .35 | .14 | .03 | ☐ 147 Frank Patrick | .35 | .14 | .03 |
| ☐ 55A Ed O'Bradovich | .35 | .14 | .03 | ☐ 148 Francis Peay | .35 | .14 | .03 |
| ☐ 55B Gale Sayers | 7.50 | 3.00 | .75 | ☐ 149 Dave Robinson | .75 | .30 | .07 |
| ☐ 56A Mac Percival | .35 | .14 | .03 | ☐ 150 Bart Starr | 7.50 | 3.00 | .75 |
| ☐ 56B George Seals | .35 | .14 | .03 | ☐ 151 Bob Atkins | .35 | .14 | .03 |
| ☐ 57 Jim Seymour | .35 | .14 | .03 | ☐ 152 Elvin Bethea | .75 | .30 | .07 |
| ☐ 58A George Seals | .35 | .14 | .03 | ☐ 153 Garland Boyette | .35 | .14 | .03 |
| ☐ 58B Ron Smith | .50 | .20 | .05 | ☐ 154 Ken Burrough | .75 | .30 | .07 |
| ☐ 59 Bill Staley | .35 | .14 | .03 | ☐ 155 Woody Campbell | .35 | .14 | .03 |
| ☐ 60 Cecil Turner | .35 | .14 | .03 | ☐ 156 John Charles | .35 | .14 | .03 |
| ☐ 61 Al Beauchamp | .35 | .14 | .03 | ☐ 157 Lynn Dickey | .75 | .30 | .07 |
| ☐ 62 Virgil Carter | .50 | .20 | .05 | ☐ 158 Elbert Drungo | .35 | .14 | .03 |
| ☐ 63 Vernon Holland | .35 | .14 | .03 | ☐ 159 Gene Ferguson | .35 | .14 | .03 |
| ☐ 64 Bob Johnson | .50 | .20 | .05 | ☐ 160 Charlie Johnson | .75 | .30 | .07 |
| ☐ 65 Ron Lamb | .35 | .14 | .03 | ☐ 161 Charlie Joiner | 2.00 | .80 | .20 |
| ☐ 66 Dave Lewis | .35 | .14 | .03 | ☐ 162 Dan Pastorini | .75 | .30 | .07 |
| ☐ 67 Rufus Mayes | .50 | .20 | .05 | ☐ 163 Ron Pritchard | .35 | .14 | .03 |
| ☐ 68 Horst Muhlmann | .35 | .14 | .03 | ☐ 164 Walt Suggs | .35 | .14 | .03 |
| ☐ 69 Lemar Parrish | .75 | .30 | .07 | ☐ 165 Mike Tilleman | .35 | .14 | .03 |
| ☐ 70 Jess Phillips | .35 | .14 | .03 | ☐ 166 Bobby Bell | 2.00 | .80 | .20 |
| ☐ 71 Mike Reid | 1.50 | .60 | .15 | ☐ 167 Aaron Brown | .50 | .20 | .05 |
| ☐ 72 Ken Riley | .75 | .30 | .07 | ☐ 168 Buck Buchanan | 2.00 | .80 | .20 |
| ☐ 73 Paul Robinson | .50 | .20 | .05 | ☐ 169 Ed Budde | .75 | .30 | .07 |
| ☐ 74 Bob Trumpy | 1.50 | .60 | .15 | ☐ 170 Curley Culp | .75 | .30 | .07 |
| ☐ 75 Fred Willis | .35 | .14 | .03 | ☐ 171 Len Dawson | 5.00 | 2.00 | .50 |
| ☐ 76 Don Cockroft | .50 | .20 | .05 | ☐ 172 Willie Lanier | 2.50 | 1.00 | .25 |
| ☐ 77 Gary Collins | .50 | .20 | .05 | ☐ 173 Jim Lynch | .50 | .20 | .05 |
| ☐ 78 Gene Hickerson | .50 | .20 | .05 | ☐ 174 Jim Marsalis | .50 | .20 | .05 |
| ☐ 79 Fair Hooker | .50 | .20 | .05 | ☐ 175 Mo Moorman | .35 | .14 | .03 |
| ☐ 80 Jim Houston | .50 | .20 | .05 | ☐ 176 Ed Podolak | .50 | .20 | .05 |
| ☐ 81 Walter Johnson | .50 | .20 | .05 | ☐ 177 Johnny Robinson | .75 | .30 | .07 |
| ☐ 82 Joe Jones | .35 | .14 | .03 | ☐ 178 Jan Stenerud | 2.00 | .80 | .20 |
| ☐ 83 Leroy Kelly | 2.00 | .80 | .20 | ☐ 179 Otis Taylor | 1.00 | .40 | .10 |
| ☐ 84 Milt Morin | .50 | .20 | .05 | ☐ 180 Jim Tyrer | .50 | .20 | .05 |
| ☐ 85 Reece Morrison | .35 | .14 | .03 | ☐ 181 Kermit Alexander | .50 | .20 | .05 |
| ☐ 86 Bill Nelsen | .50 | .20 | .05 | ☐ 182 Coy Bacon | .35 | .14 | .03 |
| ☐ 87 Mike Phipps | .75 | .30 | .07 | ☐ 183 Dick Buzin | .35 | .14 | .03 |
| ☐ 88 Bo Scott | .50 | .20 | .05 | ☐ 184 Roman Gabriel | 1.00 | .40 | .10 |
| ☐ 89 Jerry Sherk | .50 | .20 | .05 | ☐ 185 Gene Howard | .35 | .14 | .03 |
| ☐ 90 Ron Snidow | .35 | .14 | .03 | ☐ 186 Ken Iman | .35 | .14 | .03 |
| ☐ 91 Herb Adderley | 2.00 | .80 | .20 | ☐ 187 Les Josephson | .50 | .20 | .05 |
| ☐ 92 George Andrie | .75 | .30 | .07 | ☐ 188 Marlin McKeever | .50 | .20 | .05 |
| ☐ 93 Mike Clark | .35 | .14 | .03 | ☐ 189 Merlin Olsen | 4.00 | 1.60 | .40 |
| ☐ 94 Dave Edwards | .50 | .20 | .05 | ☐ 190A Richie Petitbon | .75 | .30 | .07 |
| ☐ 95 Walt Garrison | 1.00 | .40 | .10 | ☐ 190B Phil Olsen | .35 | .14 | .03 |
| ☐ 96 Cornell Green | .75 | .30 | .07 | ☐ 191 David Ray | .35 | .14 | .03 |
| ☐ 97 Bob Hayes | 1.50 | .60 | .15 | ☐ 192 Lance Rentzel | .75 | .30 | .07 |
| ☐ 98 Calvin Hill | 1.50 | .60 | .15 | ☐ 193 Isiah Robertson | .50 | .20 | .05 |
| ☐ 99 Chuck Howley | .75 | .30 | .07 | ☐ 194 Larry Smith | .35 | .14 | .03 |
| ☐ 100 Lee Roy Jordan | 2.00 | .80 | .20 | ☐ 195 Jack Snow | .75 | .30 | .07 |
| ☐ 101 Dave Manders | .50 | .20 | .05 | ☐ 196 Nick Buoniconti | 2.00 | .80 | .20 |
| ☐ 102 Craig Morton | 1.25 | .50 | .12 | ☐ 197 Doug Crusan | .35 | .14 | .03 |
| ☐ 103 Ralph Neely | .50 | .20 | .05 | ☐ 198 Larry Csonka | 6.00 | 2.40 | .60 |
| ☐ 104 Mel Renfro | 1.00 | .40 | .10 | ☐ 199 Bob DeMarco | .50 | .20 | .05 |
| ☐ 105 Roger Staubach | 25.00 | 10.00 | 2.50 | ☐ 200 Marv Fleming | .50 | .20 | .05 |
| ☐ 106 Bobby Anderson | .75 | .30 | .07 | ☐ 201 Bob Griese | 7.50 | 3.00 | .75 |
| ☐ 107 Sam Brunelli | .35 | .14 | .03 | ☐ 202 Jim Kiick | 1.00 | .40 | .10 |
| ☐ 108 Dave Costa | .35 | .14 | .03 | ☐ 203 Bob Kuechenberg | 1.00 | .40 | .10 |
| ☐ 109 Mike Current | .35 | .14 | .03 | ☐ 204 Mercury Morris | 1.25 | .50 | .12 |
| ☐ 110 Pete Duranko | .35 | .14 | .03 | ☐ 205A Jim Riley | .35 | .14 | .03 |
| ☐ 111 George Goeddeke | .35 | .14 | .03 | ☐ 205B John Richardson | .35 | .14 | .03 |
| ☐ 112 Cornell Gordon | .35 | .14 | .03 | ☐ 206 Jim Riley | .35 | .14 | .03 |
| ☐ 113 Don Horn | .50 | .20 | .05 | ☐ 207 Jake Scott | .75 | .30 | .07 |
| ☐ 114 Rich Jackson | .35 | .14 | .03 | ☐ 208 Howard Twilley | .75 | .30 | .07 |
| ☐ 115 Larry Kaminski | .35 | .14 | .03 | ☐ 209 Paul Warfield | 4.00 | 1.60 | .40 |
| ☐ 116 Floyd Little | 1.50 | .60 | .15 | ☐ 210 Garo Yepremian | .75 | .30 | .07 |
| ☐ 117 Marv Montgomery | .35 | .14 | .03 | ☐ 211 Grady Alderman | .50 | .20 | .05 |
| ☐ 118 Steve Ramsey | .50 | .20 | .05 | ☐ 212 John Beasley | .35 | .14 | .03 |
| ☐ 119 Paul Smith | .50 | .20 | .05 | ☐ 213 John Henderson | .35 | .14 | .03 |
| ☐ 120 Billy Thompson | .75 | .30 | .07 | ☐ 214 Wally Hilgenberg | .35 | .14 | .03 |
| ☐ 121 Lem Barney | 2.50 | 1.00 | .25 | ☐ 215 Clinton Jones | .50 | .20 | .05 |
| ☐ 122 Nick Eddy | .50 | .20 | .05 | ☐ 216 Karl Kassulke | .35 | .14 | .03 |
| ☐ 123 Mel Farr | .75 | .30 | .07 | ☐ 217 Paul Krause | 1.25 | .50 | .12 |
| ☐ 124 Ed Flanagan | .35 | .14 | .03 | ☐ 218 Dave Osborn | .50 | .20 | .05 |
| ☐ 125 Larry Hand | .35 | .14 | .03 | ☐ 219 Alan Page | 2.00 | .80 | .20 |
| ☐ 126 Greg Landry | .75 | .30 | .07 | ☐ 220 Ed Sharockman | .35 | .14 | .03 |
| ☐ 127 Dick LeBeau | .50 | .20 | .05 | ☐ 221 Fran Tarkenton | 9.00 | 3.75 | .90 |
| ☐ 128 Mike Lucci | .50 | .20 | .05 | ☐ 222 Mick Tingelhoff | .75 | .30 | .07 |
| ☐ 129 Earl McCullouch | .50 | .20 | .05 | ☐ 223 Charlie West | .35 | .14 | .03 |
| ☐ 130 Bill Munson | .50 | .20 | .05 | ☐ 224 Lonnie Warwick | .35 | .14 | .03 |
| ☐ 131 Wayne Rasmussen | .35 | .14 | .03 | ☐ 225 Gene Washington | .50 | .20 | .05 |
| ☐ 132 Joe Robb | .35 | .14 | .03 | ☐ 226 Hank Barton | .35 | .14 | .03 |
| ☐ 133 Jerry Rush | .35 | .14 | .03 | ☐ 227A Larry Carwell | .35 | .14 | .03 |
| ☐ 134 Altie Taylor | .50 | .20 | .05 | ☐ 227B Ron Berger | .35 | .14 | .03 |
| ☐ 135 Wayne Walker | .50 | .20 | .05 | ☐ 228 Larry Carwell | .35 | .14 | .03 |
| ☐ 136 Ken Bowman | .35 | .14 | .03 | ☐ 229A Carl Garrett | .50 | .20 | .05 |
| ☐ 137 John Brockington | .75 | .30 | .07 | ☐ 229B Jim Cheyunski | .35 | .14 | .03 |
| ☐ 138 Fred Carr | .50 | .20 | .05 | ☐ 230A Jim Hunt | .35 | .14 | .03 |
| ☐ 139 Carroll Dale | .50 | .20 | .05 | ☐ 230B Carl Garrett | .50 | .20 | .05 |
| ☐ 140 Ken Ellis | .35 | .14 | .03 | ☐ 231 Rickie Harris | .35 | .14 | .03 |

| | | | |
|---|---|---|---|
| ☐ 232 Daryl Johnson | .35 | .14 | .03 |
| ☐ 233 Steve Kiner | .35 | .14 | .03 |
| ☐ 234 Jon Morris | .35 | .14 | .03 |
| ☐ 235 Jim Nance | .75 | .30 | .07 |
| ☐ 236 Tom Neville | .35 | .14 | .03 |
| ☐ 237 Jim Plunkett | 3.00 | 1.20 | .30 |
| ☐ 238 Ron Sellers | .50 | .20 | .05 |
| ☐ 239 Len St. Jean | .35 | .14 | .03 |
| ☐ 240A Gerald Warren | .35 | .14 | .03 |
| ☐ 240B Don Webb | .35 | .14 | .03 |
| ☐ 241 Dan Abramowicz | .75 | .30 | .07 |
| ☐ 242A Tony Baker | .35 | .14 | .03 |
| ☐ 242B Dick Absher | .35 | .14 | .03 |
| ☐ 243 Leo Carroll | .35 | .14 | .03 |
| ☐ 244 Jim Duncan | .35 | .14 | .03 |
| ☐ 245 Al Dodd | .35 | .14 | .03 |
| ☐ 246 Jim Flanigan | .35 | .14 | .03 |
| ☐ 247 Hoyle Granger | .35 | .14 | .03 |
| ☐ 248 Edd Hargett | .75 | .30 | .07 |
| ☐ 249 Glen Ray Hines | .35 | .14 | .03 |
| ☐ 250 Hugo Hollas | .35 | .14 | .03 |
| ☐ 251 Jake Kupp | .35 | .14 | .03 |
| ☐ 252 Dave Long | .35 | .14 | .03 |
| ☐ 253 Mike Morgan | .35 | .14 | .03 |
| ☐ 254 Tom Roussel | .35 | .14 | .03 |
| ☐ 255 Del Williams | .35 | .14 | .03 |
| ☐ 256 Otto Brown | .35 | .14 | .03 |
| ☐ 257 Bobby Duhon | .50 | .20 | .05 |
| ☐ 258 Scott Eaton | .35 | .14 | .03 |
| ☐ 259 Jim Files | .35 | .14 | .03 |
| ☐ 260 Tucker Frederickson | .75 | .30 | .07 |
| ☐ 261A Don Herrmann | .35 | .14 | .03 |
| ☐ 261B Pete Gogolak | .50 | .20 | .05 |
| ☐ 262 Bob Grim | .50 | .20 | .05 |
| ☐ 263 Don Herrmann | .35 | .14 | .03 |
| ☐ 264A Ernie Koy | .75 | .30 | .07 |
| ☐ 264B Ron Johnson | .75 | .30 | .07 |
| ☐ 265A Spider Lockhart | .50 | .20 | .05 |
| ☐ 265B Jim Kanicki | .35 | .14 | .03 |
| ☐ 266 Spider Lockhart | .50 | .20 | .05 |
| ☐ 267 Joe Morrison | .75 | .30 | .07 |
| ☐ 268 Bob Tucker | 1.00 | .40 | .10 |
| ☐ 269 Willie Williams | .35 | .14 | .03 |
| ☐ 270 Willie Young | .35 | .14 | .03 |
| ☐ 271 Al Atkinson | .35 | .14 | .03 |
| ☐ 272 Ralph Baker | .35 | .14 | .03 |
| ☐ 273 Emerson Boozer | .75 | .30 | .07 |
| ☐ 274 John Elliott | .35 | .14 | .03 |
| ☐ 275 Dave Herman | .35 | .14 | .03 |
| ☐ 276A Dave Herman | .35 | .14 | .03 |
| ☐ 276B Winston Hill | .50 | .20 | .05 |
| ☐ 277 Gus Hollomon | .35 | .14 | .03 |
| ☐ 278 Bob Howfield | .35 | .14 | .03 |
| ☐ 279 Pete Lammons | .50 | .20 | .05 |
| ☐ 280 Joe Namath UER | 20.00 | 8.00 | 2.00 |
| (Numbered 281) | | | |
| ☐ 281 Gerry Philbin | .50 | .20 | .05 |
| ☐ 282 Matt Snell | .75 | .30 | .07 |
| ☐ 283 Steve Tannen | .35 | .14 | .03 |
| ☐ 284 Earlie Thomas | .35 | .14 | .03 |
| ☐ 285 Al Woodall | .50 | .20 | .05 |
| ☐ 286 Fred Biletnikoff | 3.00 | 1.20 | .30 |
| ☐ 287 George Blanda | 5.00 | 2.00 | .50 |
| ☐ 288 Willie Brown | 2.00 | .80 | .20 |
| ☐ 289 Ray Chester | 1.00 | .40 | .10 |
| ☐ 290 Tony Cline | .35 | .14 | .03 |
| ☐ 291 Dan Conners | .35 | .14 | .03 |
| ☐ 292 Ben Davidson | 1.00 | .40 | .10 |
| ☐ 293 Hewritt Dixon | .50 | .20 | .05 |
| ☐ 294 Tom Keating | .50 | .20 | .05 |
| ☐ 295 Daryle Lamonica | 1.50 | .60 | .15 |
| ☐ 296 Gus Otto | .35 | .14 | .03 |
| ☐ 297 Jim Otto | 2.00 | .80 | .20 |
| ☐ 298 Rod Sherman | .35 | .14 | .03 |
| ☐ 299 Charles Smith | .35 | .14 | .03 |
| ☐ 300A Warren Wells | .50 | .20 | .05 |
| ☐ 300B Gene Upshaw | 2.50 | 1.00 | .25 |
| ☐ 301 Rick Arrington | .35 | .14 | .03 |
| ☐ 302 Gary Ballman | .50 | .20 | .05 |
| ☐ 303 Lee Bouggess | .35 | .14 | .03 |
| ☐ 304 Bill Bradley | .75 | .30 | .07 |
| ☐ 305A Richard Harris | .35 | .14 | .03 |
| ☐ 305B Happy Feller | .50 | .20 | .05 |
| ☐ 306A Ben Hawkins | .35 | .14 | .03 |
| ☐ 306B Richard Harris | .35 | .14 | .03 |
| ☐ 307 Ben Hawkins | .35 | .14 | .03 |
| ☐ 308 Harold Jackson | 1.25 | .50 | .12 |
| ☐ 309 Pete Liske | .75 | .30 | .07 |
| ☐ 310 Al Nelson | .35 | .14 | .03 |
| ☐ 311 Gary Pettigrew | .35 | .14 | .03 |
| ☐ 312 Tim Rossovich | .75 | .30 | .07 |
| ☐ 313 Tom Woodeshick | .50 | .20 | .05 |
| ☐ 314 Adrian Young | .35 | .14 | .03 |
| ☐ 315 Steve Zabel | .50 | .20 | .05 |
| ☐ 316 Chuck Allen | .35 | .14 | .03 |
| ☐ 317 Warren Bankston | .50 | .20 | .05 |
| ☐ 318 Chuck Beatty | .35 | .14 | .03 |
| ☐ 319 Terry Bradshaw | 15.00 | 6.00 | 1.50 |
| ☐ 320 John Fuqua | .50 | .20 | .05 |
| ☐ 321 Terry Hanratty | 1.00 | .40 | .10 |
| ☐ 322 Ray Mansfield | .35 | .14 | .03 |
| ☐ 323 Ben McGee | .35 | .14 | .03 |
| ☐ 324 John Rowser | .35 | .14 | .03 |
| ☐ 325 Andy Russell | .75 | .30 | .07 |
| ☐ 326 Ron Shanklin | .50 | .20 | .05 |
| ☐ 327 Dave Smith | .35 | .14 | .03 |
| ☐ 328 Bruce Van Dyke | .35 | .14 | .03 |
| ☐ 329 Lloyd Voss | .35 | .14 | .03 |
| ☐ 330 Bobby Walden | .35 | .14 | .03 |
| ☐ 331 Donny Anderson | .75 | .30 | .07 |
| ☐ 332 Jim Bakken | .75 | .30 | .07 |
| ☐ 333 Pete Beathard | .75 | .30 | .07 |
| ☐ 334A Mel Gray | 1.00 | .40 | .10 |
| ☐ 334B Miller Farr | .50 | .20 | .05 |
| ☐ 335A Jim Hart | 1.00 | .40 | .10 |
| ☐ 335B Mel Gray | 1.00 | .40 | .10 |
| ☐ 336 Jim Hart | 1.00 | .40 | .10 |
| ☐ 337A Chuck Latourette | .35 | .14 | .03 |
| ☐ 337B Rolf Krueger | .50 | .20 | .05 |
| ☐ 338 Chuck Latourette | .35 | .14 | .03 |
| ☐ 339A Bob Reynolds | .35 | .14 | .03 |
| ☐ 339B Ernie McMillan | .50 | .20 | .05 |
| ☐ 340 Bob Reynolds | .35 | .14 | .03 |
| ☐ 341 Jackie Smith | 2.00 | .80 | .20 |
| ☐ 342 Larry Stallings | .50 | .20 | .05 |
| ☐ 343 Chuck Walker | .35 | .14 | .03 |
| ☐ 344 Roger Wehrli | .75 | .30 | .07 |
| ☐ 345 Larry Wilson | 2.00 | .80 | .20 |
| ☐ 346 Bob Babich | .35 | .14 | .03 |
| ☐ 347 Pete Barnes | .35 | .14 | .03 |
| ☐ 348A Marty Domres | .50 | .20 | .05 |
| ☐ 348B Steve DeLong | .50 | .20 | .05 |
| ☐ 349 Marty Domres | .50 | .20 | .05 |
| ☐ 350 Gary Garrison | .50 | .20 | .05 |
| ☐ 351A Walker Gillette | .35 | .14 | .03 |
| ☐ 351B John Hadl | 1.25 | .50 | .12 |
| ☐ 352 Kevin Hardy | .35 | .14 | .03 |
| ☐ 353 Bob Howard | .35 | .14 | .03 |
| ☐ 354A Jim Hill | .35 | .14 | .03 |
| ☐ 354B Deacon Jones | 2.00 | .80 | .20 |
| ☐ 355 Terry Owens | .75 | .30 | .07 |
| ☐ 356 Dennis Partee | .35 | .14 | .03 |
| ☐ 357A Dennis Partee | .35 | .14 | .03 |
| ☐ 357B Jeff Queen | .35 | .14 | .03 |
| ☐ 358 Jim Tolbert | .35 | .14 | .03 |
| ☐ 359 Russ Washington | .35 | .14 | .03 |
| ☐ 360 Doug Wilkerson | .35 | .14 | .03 |
| ☐ 361 John Brodie | 3.00 | 1.20 | .30 |
| ☐ 362 Doug Cunningham | .35 | .14 | .03 |
| ☐ 363 Bruce Gossett | .35 | .14 | .03 |
| ☐ 364 Stan Hindman | .35 | .14 | .03 |
| ☐ 365 John Isenbarger | .50 | .20 | .05 |
| ☐ 366 Charlie Krueger | .50 | .20 | .05 |
| ☐ 367 Frank Nunley | .35 | .14 | .03 |
| ☐ 368 Woody Peoples | .35 | .14 | .03 |
| ☐ 369 Len Rohde | .35 | .14 | .03 |
| ☐ 370 Steve Spurrier | 5.00 | 2.00 | .50 |
| ☐ 371 Gene Washington | 1.00 | .40 | .10 |
| ☐ 372 Dave Wilcox | .75 | .30 | .07 |
| ☐ 373 Ken Willard | .75 | .30 | .07 |
| ☐ 374 Bob Windsor | .50 | .20 | .05 |
| ☐ 375 Dick Witcher | .50 | .20 | .05 |
| ☐ 376 Verlon Biggs | .75 | .30 | .07 |
| ☐ 377 Larry Brown | 2.50 | 1.00 | .25 |
| ☐ 378 Speedy Duncan | .50 | .20 | .05 |
| ☐ 379 Chris Hanburger | 1.00 | .40 | .10 |
| ☐ 380 Charlie Harraway | .50 | .20 | .05 |
| ☐ 381 Sonny Jurgensen | 4.00 | 1.60 | .40 |
| ☐ 382 Bill Kilmer | 1.50 | .60 | .15 |
| ☐ 383 Tommy Mason | .50 | .20 | .05 |
| ☐ 384 Ron McDole | .50 | .20 | .05 |
| ☐ 385 Brig Owens | .35 | .14 | .03 |
| ☐ 386 Jack Pardee | 1.50 | .60 | .15 |
| ☐ 387 Myron Pottios | .50 | .20 | .05 |
| ☐ 388 Jerry Smith | .50 | .20 | .05 |
| ☐ 389 Diron Talbert | .50 | .20 | .05 |
| ☐ 390 Charley Taylor | 3.00 | 1.20 | .30 |
| ☐ XX Wonderful World Album | 20.00 | 8.00 | 2.00 |

## 1979 NFLPA Pennant Stickers

The 1979 NFL Football Pennant Stickers set contains 50 stickers measuring approximately 2 1/2" by 5". The pennant-shaped stickers show a circular (black and white) photo of the player next to the NFL Players Association football logo. The set was apparently not approved by the NFL as the team logos are not shown on the cards. The player's name, position, and team are given at the bottom of the card. Not much is known about this set as there is no information on the card as to who sponsored the set. The back is blank as it is a peel-off backing only. Some of the stickers can be found with more than one color background.

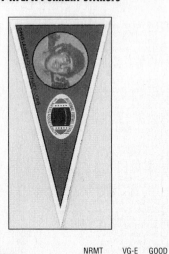

| | NRMT | VG-E | GOOD |
|---|---|---|---|
| COMPLETE SET (50) | 400.00 | 160.00 | 40.00 |
| COMMON PLAYER (1-50) | 3.00 | 1.20 | .30 |
| COMMON SP (10/36/44/47/49) | 10.00 | 4.00 | 1.00 |
| ☐ 1 Lyle Alzado | 5.00 | 2.00 | .50 |
| (Red) | | | |
| Cleveland Browns | | | |
| ☐ 2 Ken Anderson | 7.50 | 3.00 | .75 |
| (Blue) | | | |
| Cincinnati Bengals | | | |
| ☐ 3 Steve Bartkowski SP | 12.00 | 5.00 | 1.20 |
| (Yellow) | | | |
| Atlanta Falcons | | | |
| ☐ 4 Ricky Bell | 4.00 | 1.60 | .40 |
| (Red) | | | |
| Tampa Bay Buccaneers | | | |
| ☐ 5 Elvin Bethea | 3.00 | 1.20 | .30 |
| (Blue) | | | |
| Houston Oilers | | | |
| ☐ 6 Tom Blanchard | 3.00 | 1.20 | .30 |
| (Blue, red, or yellow) | | | |
| New Orleans Saints | | | |
| ☐ 7 Terry Bradshaw | 25.00 | 10.00 | 2.50 |
| (Yellow) | | | |
| Pittsburgh Steelers | | | |
| ☐ 8 Bob Breunig | 4.00 | 1.60 | .40 |
| (Red or yellow) | | | |
| Dallas Cowboys | | | |
| ☐ 9 Greg Brezina | 5.00 | 2.00 | .50 |
| (Purple) | | | |
| Atlanta Falcons | | | |
| ☐ 10 Doug Buffone SP | 10.00 | 4.00 | 1.00 |
| (Green) | | | |
| Chicago Bears | | | |
| ☐ 11 Earl Campbell SP | 50.00 | 20.00 | 5.00 |
| (Yellow) | | | |
| Houston Oilers | | | |
| ☐ 12 John Cappelletti | 3.00 | 1.20 | .30 |
| (Green) | | | |
| Los Angeles Rams | | | |
| ☐ 13 Harold Carmichael | 4.00 | 1.60 | .40 |
| (Blue) | | | |
| Philadelphia Eagles | | | |
| ☐ 14 Chuck Crist SP | 15.00 | 6.00 | 1.50 |
| (Green) | | | |
| San Francisco 49ers | | | |
| ☐ 15 Sam Cunningham | 4.00 | 1.60 | .40 |
| (Green) | | | |
| New England Patriots | | | |
| ☐ 16 Joe DeLamielleure | 3.00 | 1.20 | .30 |
| (Blue) | | | |
| Buffalo Bills | | | |
| ☐ 17 Tom Dempsey | 4.00 | 1.60 | .40 |
| (Blue, red, or yellow) | | | |
| Buffalo Bills | | | |
| ☐ 18 Tony Dorsett | 15.00 | 6.00 | 1.50 |
| (Yellow) | | | |
| Dallas Cowboys | | | |
| ☐ 19 Dan Fouts SP | 20.00 | 8.00 | 2.00 |
| (Green) | | | |
| San Diego Chargers | | | |
| ☐ 20 Roy Gerela | 4.00 | 1.60 | .40 |
| (Red or yellow) | | | |
| Pittsburgh Steelers | | | |
| ☐ 21 Bob Griese UER | 12.00 | 5.00 | 1.20 |
| (Purple; Griese) | | | |
| Miami Dolphins | | | |
| ☐ 22 Franco Harris | 15.00 | 6.00 | 1.50 |
| (Yellow) | | | |
| Pittsburgh Steelers | | | |
| ☐ 23 Jim Hart SP | 12.00 | 5.00 | 1.20 |
| St. Louis Cardinals | | | |
| ☐ 24 Charlie Joiner | 6.00 | 2.40 | .60 |
| (Green) | | | |
| San Diego Chargers | | | |
| ☐ 25 Paul Krause | 4.00 | 1.60 | .40 |
| (Green) | | | |
| Minnesota Vikings | | | |
| ☐ 26 Bob Kuechenberg | 4.00 | 1.60 | .40 |
| (Purple) | | | |
| Miami Dolphins | | | |
| ☐ 27 Greg Landry | 3.00 | 1.20 | .30 |
| (Purple) | | | |
| Detroit Lions | | | |
| ☐ 28 Archie Manning | 6.00 | 2.40 | .60 |
| (Blue) | | | |
| New Orleans Saints | | | |
| ☐ 29 Chester Marcol | 3.00 | 1.20 | .30 |
| (Purple) | | | |
| Green Bay Packers | | | |
| ☐ 30 Harvey Martin | 4.00 | 1.60 | .40 |
| (Red) | | | |
| Dallas Cowboys | | | |
| ☐ 31 Lawrence McCutcheon SP | 12.00 | 5.00 | 1.20 |
| (Yellow) | | | |
| Los Angeles Rams | | | |
| ☐ 32 Craig Morton | 4.00 | 1.60 | .40 |
| (Green) | | | |
| Denver Broncos | | | |
| ☐ 33 Haven Moses | 3.00 | 1.20 | .30 |
| (Green) | | | |
| Denver Broncos | | | |
| ☐ 34 Steve Odom | 3.00 | 1.20 | .30 |
| (Purple) | | | |
| Green Bay Packers | | | |
| ☐ 35 Morris Owens | 3.00 | 1.20 | .30 |
| (Green) | | | |
| Tampa Bay Buccaneers | | | |
| ☐ 36 Dan Pastorini SP | 10.00 | 4.00 | 1.00 |
| Houston Oilers | | | |
| ☐ 37 Walter Payton | 35.00 | 14.00 | 3.50 |
| (Green) | | | |
| Chicago Bears | | | |
| ☐ 38 Greg Pruitt SP | 12.00 | 5.00 | 1.20 |
| (Green) | | | |
| Cleveland Browns | | | |
| ☐ 39 John Riggins | 10.00 | 4.00 | 1.00 |
| (Purple) | | | |
| Washington Redskins | | | |
| ☐ 40 Jake Scott | 3.00 | 1.20 | .30 |
| (Red) | | | |
| Washington Redskins | | | |
| ☐ 41 Ken Stabler SP | 20.00 | 8.00 | 2.00 |
| (Blue) | | | |
| Oakland Raiders | | | |
| ☐ 42 Roger Staubach | 30.00 | 12.00 | 3.00 |
| (Yellow) | | | |
| Dallas Cowboys | | | |
| ☐ 43 Jan Stenerud | 6.00 | 2.40 | .60 |
| (Purple) | | | |
| Kansas City Chiefs | | | |
| ☐ 44 Art Still SP | 10.00 | 4.00 | 1.00 |
| Kansas City Chiefs | | | |
| ☐ 45 Mick Tingelhoff | 4.00 | 1.60 | .40 |
| (Blue) | | | |
| Minnesota Vikings | | | |
| ☐ 46 Richard Todd | 3.00 | 1.20 | .30 |
| (Yellow) | | | |
| New York Jets | | | |
| ☐ 47 Phil Villapiano SP | 10.00 | 4.00 | 1.00 |
| (Purple) | | | |
| Oakland Raiders | | | |
| ☐ 48 Wesley Walker | 5.00 | 2.00 | .50 |
| (Red or yellow) | | | |
| New York Jets | | | |
| ☐ 49 Roger Werhli SP | 10.00 | 4.00 | 1.00 |
| (Purple) | | | |
| St. Louis Cardinals | | | |
| ☐ 50 Jim Zorn SP | 12.00 | 5.00 | 1.20 |
| (Red) | | | |
| Seattle Seahawks | | | |

## 1993 NFL Properties Santa Claus

The first Santa Claus card produced by an NFL trading card licensee was in 1989. In 1993, each of the 12 trading card licensees produced an NFL Santa Claus Card, and the entire set, which included a checklist card issued by NFL Properties, was offered through a special mail-away offer for any 30 1993 NFL trading card wrappers and 1.50 for postage and handling. The cards were sent out to dealers along with a season's greeting card. All the cards measure the standard size (2 1/2"

by 3 1/2") and feature different artistic renderings of Santa Claus on their fronts and season's greetings on their backs. Although some cards are numbered while others are not, the cards are checklisted below alphabetically according to the licensee's name.

| | MINT | EXC | G-VG |
|---|---|---|---|
| COMPLETE SET (13) | 20.00 | 8.00 | 2.00 |
| COMMON PLAYER (1-13) | 2.00 | .80 | .20 |
| ☐ 1 Santa Claus Action Packed | 2.00 | .80 | .20 |
| ☐ 2 Santa Claus Classic | 2.00 | .80 | .20 |
| ☐ 3 Santa Claus Collector's Edge | 2.00 | .80 | .20 |
| ☐ 4 Santa Claus Fleer | 2.00 | .80 | .20 |
| ☐ 5 Santa Claus Pacific | 2.00 | .80 | .20 |
| ☐ 6 Santa Claus Pinnacle | 2.00 | .80 | .20 |
| ☐ 7 Santa Claus Playoff | 2.00 | .80 | .20 |
| ☐ 8 Santa Claus Pro Set | 2.00 | .80 | .20 |
| ☐ 9 Santa Claus SkyBox | 2.00 | .80 | .20 |
| ☐ 10 Santa Claus Topps | 2.00 | .80 | .20 |
| ☐ 11 Santa Claus Upper Deck | 2.00 | .80 | .20 |
| ☐ 12 Santa Claus Wild Card | 2.00 | .80 | .20 |
| ☐ 13 Checklist Card NFL Properties | 2.00 | .80 | .20 |

## 1993 NFL Properties Show Redemption Cards

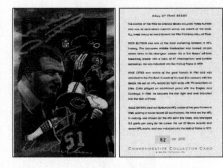

Produced by NFL Properties and handed out to attendees at card shows, these five oversized cards measure approximately 3 1/2" by 5" and feature on their fronts collages of player portraits and/or photos. A banner at the top of each card carries the city and dates that the show was held. On the card given out at the National in Chicago, listed below as card number 1 (the only unnumbered card), each of the honored players has signed the card in silver ink. Only 200 of these were produced and autographed, making it the rarest of the five cards. The card given out in St. Louis, listed below as 4B, replaced 4A, which

was done to commemorate the St. Louis Stallions NFL franchise that never materialized and so was not released. One thousand of 4B were distributed each of the three days of the show, making a total of 3,000. The white back of each card carries text about the players depicted on the front (except card number 2, the back of which carries the 49ers 1993 schedule) and the individual serial number out of the total produced. Card 4B also carries the date that the card was distributed next to the "X of 1000" production figure. Except for the first card, the cards are numbered on the back in Roman numerals. The 49ers card was available at the Team NFL booth at the 1993 San Francisco Labor Day Sports Collector's Convention in exchange for ten wrappers from any licensed 1993 NFL card product.

| | MINT | EXC | G-VG |
|---|---|---|---|
| COMPLETE SET (5) | 150.00 | 60.00 | 15.00 |
| COMMON CARD (1-5) | 10.00 | 4.00 | 1.00 |
| ☐ 1 Chicago Saluting Hall of Famers 7/24/93 (200) Dick Butkus Mike Ditka Gale Sayers (Signed in silver ink) | 100.00 | 40.00 | 10.00 |
| ☐ 2 San Francisco Labor Day Weekend 9/93 (1,000) NFL Kickoff '93 Ricky Watters Steve Young Keith DeLong Jerry Rice John Taylor Tim McDonald (1993 49er schedule on card back) | 25.00 | 10.00 | 2.50 |
| ☐ 3 San Francisco Labor Day Weekend 9/93 (1,000) Saluting Bay Area Legends Y.A. Tittle Ken Stabler (Career summaries on back) | 15.00 | 6.00 | 1.50 |
| ☐ 4B St. Louis Saluting Three Decades of Gateway City QBs 10/29-31/93 (3,000) Jim Hart Charley Johnson Neil Lomax | 10.00 | 4.00 | 1.00 |
| ☐ 5 Dallas Saluting The Super Bowl Champions 11/19-21/93 (3,000) Michael Irvin Troy Aikman Emmitt Smith Jay Novacek Russell Maryland Ken Norton Jr. | 20.00 | 8.00 | 2.00 |

## 1961 Nu-Card

The 1961 Nu-Card set of 80 cards features college players. The cards measure 2 1/2" by 3 1/2". One odd feature of the set is that the card numbers start with the number 101. The set features the first nationally distributed cards of Ernie Davis, Roman Gabriel, and John Hadl.

|  | NRMT | VG-E | GOOD |
|---|---|---|---|
| COMPLETE SET (80) | 200.00 | 80.00 | 20.00 |
| COMMON PLAYER (101-180) | 2.25 | .90 | .22 |
| ☐ 101 Bob Ferguson | 5.00 | 2.00 | .40 |
| Ohio State |  |  |  |
| ☐ 102 Ron Snidow | 3.00 | 1.20 | .30 |
| Oregon |  |  |  |
| ☐ 103 Steve Barnett | 2.25 | .90 | .22 |
| Oregon |  |  |  |
| ☐ 104 Greg Mather | 2.25 | .90 | .22 |
| Navy |  |  |  |
| ☐ 105 Vern Von Sydow | 2.25 | .90 | .22 |
| Navy |  |  |  |
| ☐ 106 John Hewitt | 2.25 | .90 | .22 |
| Navy |  |  |  |
| ☐ 107 Eddie Johns | 2.25 | .90 | .22 |
| Miami |  |  |  |
| ☐ 108 Walt Rappold | 2.25 | .90 | .22 |
| Duke |  |  |  |
| ☐ 109 Roy Winston | 4.00 | 1.60 | .40 |
| LSU |  |  |  |
| ☐ 110 Bob Boyda | 2.25 | .90 | .22 |
| Harvard |  |  |  |
| ☐ 111 Bill Neighbors | 4.00 | 1.60 | .40 |
| Alabama |  |  |  |
| ☐ 112 Don Purcell | 2.25 | .90 | .22 |
| Nebraska |  |  |  |
| ☐ 113 Ken Byers | 2.25 | .90 | .22 |
| Cincinnati |  |  |  |
| ☐ 114 Ed Pine | 2.25 | .90 | .22 |
| Utah |  |  |  |
| ☐ 115 Fred Oblak | 2.25 | .90 | .22 |
| Cincinnati |  |  |  |
| ☐ 116 Bobby Iles | 2.25 | .90 | .22 |
| TCU |  |  |  |
| ☐ 117 John Hadl | 10.00 | 4.00 | 1.00 |
| Kansas |  |  |  |
| ☐ 118 Charlie Mitchell | 2.25 | .90 | .22 |
| Washington |  |  |  |
| ☐ 119 Bill Swinford | 2.25 | .90 | .22 |
| Harvard |  |  |  |
| ☐ 120 Bill King | 2.25 | .90 | .22 |
| Dartmouth |  |  |  |
| ☐ 121 Mike Lucci | 5.00 | 2.00 | .50 |
| Tennessee |  |  |  |
| ☐ 122 Dave Sarette | 2.25 | .90 | .22 |
| Syracuse |  |  |  |
| ☐ 123 Alex Kroll | 3.00 | 1.20 | .30 |
| Rutgers |  |  |  |
| ☐ 124 Steve Bauwens | 2.25 | .90 | .22 |
| UCLA |  |  |  |
| ☐ 125 Jimmy Saxton | 3.50 | 1.40 | .35 |
| Texas |  |  |  |
| ☐ 126 Steve Simms | 2.25 | .90 | .22 |
| Rutgers |  |  |  |
| ☐ 127 Andy Timura | 2.25 | .90 | .22 |
| Univ. of Dayton |  |  |  |
| ☐ 128 Gary Collins | 5.00 | 2.00 | .50 |
| Maryland |  |  |  |
| ☐ 129 Ron Taylor | 2.25 | .90 | .22 |
| Missouri |  |  |  |
| ☐ 130 Bobby Dodd | 4.00 | 1.60 | .40 |
| Florida |  |  |  |
| ☐ 131 Curtis McClinton | 5.00 | 2.00 | .50 |
| Kansas |  |  |  |
| ☐ 132 Ray Poage | 3.50 | 1.40 | .35 |
| Univ. of Texas |  |  |  |
| ☐ 133 Gus Gonzales | 2.25 | .90 | .22 |
| Tulane |  |  |  |
| ☐ 134 Dick Locke | 2.25 | .90 | .22 |
| Arizona State |  |  |  |
| ☐ 135 Larry Libertore | 2.25 | .90 | .22 |
| Florida |  |  |  |
| ☐ 136 Stan Sczurek | 2.25 | .90 | .22 |
| Purdue |  |  |  |
| ☐ 137 Pete Case | 3.50 | 1.40 | .35 |
| Georgia |  |  |  |
| ☐ 138 Jesse Bradford | 2.25 | .90 | .22 |
| Arizona State |  |  |  |
| ☐ 139 Coolidge Hunt | 2.25 | .90 | .22 |
| Texas Tech |  |  |  |
| ☐ 140 Walter Doleschal | 2.25 | .90 | .22 |
| Lafayette |  |  |  |
| ☐ 141 Bill Williamson | 2.25 | .90 | .22 |
| Georgia Tech |  |  |  |
| ☐ 142 Pat Trammell | 6.00 | 2.40 | .60 |
| Alabama |  |  |  |
| ☐ 143 Ernie Davis | 60.00 | 24.00 | 6.00 |
| Syracuse |  |  |  |
| ☐ 144 Chuck Lamson | 2.25 | .90 | .22 |
| Wyoming |  |  |  |
| ☐ 145 Bobby Plummer | 2.25 | .90 | .22 |
| TCU |  |  |  |
| ☐ 146 Sonny Gibbs | 3.50 | 1.40 | .35 |
| TCU |  |  |  |
| ☐ 147 Joe Eilers | 2.25 | .90 | .22 |
| Texas A and M |  |  |  |

| ☐ 148 Roger Kochman | 2.25 | .90 | .22 |
|---|---|---|---|
| Penn State |  |  |  |
| ☐ 149 Norman Beal | 2.25 | .90 | .22 |
| Missouri |  |  |  |
| ☐ 150 Sherwyn Torson | 2.25 | .90 | .22 |
| Iowa |  |  |  |
| ☐ 151 Russ Hepner | 2.25 | .90 | .22 |
| Bowling Green |  |  |  |
| ☐ 152 Joe Romig | 3.50 | 1.40 | .35 |
| Colorado |  |  |  |
| ☐ 153 Larry Thompson | 2.25 | .90 | .22 |
| Tulane |  |  |  |
| ☐ 154 Tom Perdue | 2.25 | .90 | .22 |
| Ohio State |  |  |  |
| ☐ 155 Ken Bolin | 2.25 | .90 | .22 |
| Houston |  |  |  |
| ☐ 156 Art Perkins | 2.25 | .90 | .22 |
| North Texas State |  |  |  |
| ☐ 157 Jim Sanderson | 2.25 | .90 | .22 |
| Fresno State |  |  |  |
| ☐ 158 Bob Asack | 2.25 | .90 | .22 |
| Columbia |  |  |  |
| ☐ 159 Dan Celoni | 2.25 | .90 | .22 |
| Iowa State |  |  |  |
| ☐ 160 Bill McGuirt | 2.25 | .90 | .22 |
| Clemson |  |  |  |
| ☐ 161 Dave Hoppman | 2.25 | .90 | .22 |
| Iowa State |  |  |  |
| ☐ 162 Gary Barnes | 2.25 | .90 | .22 |
| Clemson |  |  |  |
| ☐ 163 Don Lisbon | 3.50 | 1.40 | .35 |
| Bowling Green |  |  |  |
| ☐ 164 Jerry Cross | 2.25 | .90 | .22 |
| Detroit |  |  |  |
| ☐ 165 George Pierovich | 2.25 | .90 | .22 |
| California |  |  |  |
| ☐ 166 Roman Gabriel | 18.00 | 7.25 | 1.80 |
| NC State |  |  |  |
| ☐ 167 Billy White | 2.25 | .90 | .22 |
| Oklahoma |  |  |  |
| ☐ 168 Gale Weidner | 2.25 | .90 | .22 |
| Colorado |  |  |  |
| ☐ 169 Charles Rieves | 2.25 | .90 | .22 |
| Houston |  |  |  |
| ☐ 170 Jim Furlong | 2.25 | .90 | .22 |
| Tulsa |  |  |  |
| ☐ 171 Tom Hutchinson | 2.25 | .90 | .22 |
| Kentucky |  |  |  |
| ☐ 172 Galen Hall | 5.00 | 2.00 | .50 |
| Penn State |  |  |  |
| ☐ 173 Wilburn Hollis | 3.50 | 1.40 | .35 |
| Iowa |  |  |  |
| ☐ 174 Don Kasso | 2.25 | .90 | .22 |
| Oregon State |  |  |  |
| ☐ 175 Bill Miller | 3.00 | 1.20 | .30 |
| University of Miami |  |  |  |
| ☐ 176 Ron Miller | 2.25 | .90 | .22 |
| Wisconsin |  |  |  |
| ☐ 177 Joe Williams | 2.25 | .90 | .22 |
| Iowa |  |  |  |
| ☐ 178 Mel Mellin | 2.25 | .90 | .22 |
| Washington State |  |  |  |
| ☐ 179 Tom Vassell | 2.25 | .90 | .22 |
| Columbia |  |  |  |
| ☐ 180 Mike Cotton | 3.50 | 1.40 | .35 |
| Texas |  |  |  |

## 1961 Nu-Card Pennant Inserts

This set of 258 pennant sticker pairs was inserted with the 1961 Nu-Card regular issue college football set. These inserts are actually 1 1/2" by 3 7/16" and one pair was to be inserted in each wax pack. The pennant pairs were printed with several different ink colors (orange, light blue, navy blue, purple, green, black, and red) on several different paper stock colors (white, red, gray, orange, and yellow). The pennant pairs are unnumbered and are ordered below alphabetically according to the lowest alphabetical member of the pair. Many of the teams are available paired with several different other colleges. Any additions to this list below would be welcome.

| | NRMT | VG-E | GOOD |
|---|---|---|---|
| COMPLETE SET (258) | 750.00 | 300.00 | 75.00 |
| COMMON PLAYER (1-258) | 3.00 | 1.20 | .30 |
| ☐ 1 Air Force/Georgetown | 3.00 | 1.20 | .30 |
| ☐ 2 Air Force/Queens | 3.00 | 1.20 | .30 |
| ☐ 3 Air Force/Upsala | 3.00 | 1.20 | .30 |
| ☐ 4 Alabama/Boston U. | 4.00 | 1.60 | .40 |
| ☐ 5 Alabama/Cornell | 4.00 | 1.60 | .40 |
| ☐ 6 Alabama/Detroit | 4.00 | 1.60 | .40 |
| ☐ 7 Alabama/Harvard | 4.00 | 1.60 | .40 |
| ☐ 8 Alabama/Wisconsin | 4.00 | 1.60 | .40 |
| ☐ 9 Allegheny/Colorado St. | 3.00 | 1.20 | .30 |
| ☐ 10 Allegheny/Oregon | 3.00 | 1.20 | .30 |
| ☐ 11 Allegheny/Piedmont | 3.00 | 1.20 | .30 |
| ☐ 12 Allegheny/Wm.and Mary | 3.00 | 1.20 | .30 |
| ☐ 13 Arizona/Kansas | 4.00 | 1.60 | .40 |
| ☐ 14 Arizona/Mississippi | 4.00 | 1.60 | .40 |
| ☐ 15 Arizona/Pennsylvania | 3.00 | 1.20 | .30 |
| ☐ 16 Arizona/S.M.U. | 3.00 | 1.20 | .30 |
| ☐ 17 Army/Ga.Tech | 4.00 | 1.60 | .40 |
| ☐ 18 Army/Iowa | 4.00 | 1.60 | .40 |
| ☐ 19 Army/Johns Hopkins | 3.00 | 1.20 | .30 |
| ☐ 20 Army/Maryland | 4.00 | 1.60 | .40 |
| ☐ 21 Army/Missouri | 4.00 | 1.60 | .40 |
| ☐ 22 Army/Pratt | 3.00 | 1.20 | .30 |
| ☐ 23 Army/Purdue | 4.00 | 1.60 | .40 |
| ☐ 24 Auburn/Florida | 4.00 | 1.60 | .40 |
| ☐ 25 Auburn/Gettysburg | 3.00 | 1.20 | .30 |
| ☐ 26 Auburn/Illinois | 4.00 | 1.60 | .40 |
| ☐ 27 Auburn/Syracuse | 4.00 | 1.60 | .40 |
| ☐ 28 Auburn/Virginia | 4.00 | 1.60 | .40 |
| ☐ 29 Barnard/Columbia | 3.00 | 1.20 | .30 |
| ☐ 30 Barnard/Maine | 3.00 | 1.20 | .30 |
| ☐ 31 Barnard/N.Carolina | 3.00 | 1.20 | .30 |
| ☐ 32 Baylor/Colorado St. | 3.00 | 1.20 | .30 |
| ☐ 33 Baylor/Drew | 3.00 | 1.20 | .30 |
| ☐ 34 Baylor/Oregon | 3.00 | 1.20 | .30 |
| ☐ 35 Baylor/Piedmont | 3.00 | 1.20 | .30 |
| ☐ 36 Boston Coll./Minnesota | 3.00 | 1.20 | .30 |
| ☐ 37 Boston Coll./Norwich | 3.00 | 1.20 | .30 |
| ☐ 38 Boston Coll./Winthrop | 3.00 | 1.20 | .30 |
| ☐ 39 Boston U./Cornell | 3.00 | 1.20 | .30 |
| ☐ 40 Boston U./Rensselaer | 3.00 | 1.20 | .30 |
| ☐ 41 Boston U./Stanford | 3.00 | 1.20 | .30 |
| ☐ 42 Boston U./Temple | 3.00 | 1.20 | .30 |
| ☐ 43 Boston U./Utah State | 3.00 | 1.20 | .30 |
| ☐ 44 Bridgeport/Holy Cross | 3.00 | 1.20 | .30 |
| ☐ 45 Bridgeport/N.Y.U. | 3.00 | 1.20 | .30 |
| ☐ 46 Bridgeport/Northwestrn | 3.00 | 1.20 | .30 |
| ☐ 47 Bucknell/Illinois | 3.00 | 1.20 | .30 |
| ☐ 48 Bucknell/Syracuse | 3.00 | 1.20 | .30 |
| ☐ 49 Bucknell/Virginia | 3.00 | 1.20 | .30 |
| ☐ 50 California/Delaware | 3.00 | 1.20 | .30 |
| ☐ 51 California/Hofstra | 3.00 | 1.20 | .30 |
| ☐ 52 California/Kentucky | 4.00 | 1.60 | .40 |
| ☐ 53 California/Marquette | 3.00 | 1.20 | .30 |
| ☐ 54 California/Michigan | 4.00 | 1.60 | .40 |
| ☐ 55 California/Notre Dame | 7.50 | 3.00 | .75 |
| ☐ 56 California/Wingate | 3.00 | 1.20 | .30 |
| ☐ 57 Charleston/Dickinson | 3.00 | 1.20 | .30 |
| ☐ 58 Charleston/Lafayette | 3.00 | 1.20 | .30 |
| ☐ 59 Charleston/U.of Mass. | 3.00 | 1.20 | .30 |
| ☐ 60 Cincinnati/Maine | 3.00 | 1.20 | .30 |
| ☐ 61 Cincinnati/Ohio Wesl. | 3.00 | 1.20 | .30 |
| ☐ 62 Citadel/Columbia | 3.00 | 1.20 | .30 |
| ☐ 63 Citadel/Maine | 3.00 | 1.20 | .30 |
| ☐ 64 Citadel/N.Carolina | 3.00 | 1.20 | .30 |
| ☐ 65 Coast Guard/Drake | 3.00 | 1.20 | .30 |
| ☐ 66 Coast Guard/Penn St. | 3.00 | 1.20 | .30 |
| ☐ 67 Coast Guard/Yale | 3.00 | 1.20 | .30 |
| ☐ 68 Coker/UCLA | 3.00 | 1.20 | .30 |
| ☐ 69 Coker/Wingate | 3.00 | 1.20 | .30 |
| ☐ 70 Colby/Kings Point | 3.00 | 1.20 | .30 |
| ☐ 71 Colby/Queens | 3.00 | 1.20 | .30 |
| ☐ 72 Colby/Rice | 3.00 | 1.20 | .30 |
| ☐ 73 Colby/Upsala | 3.00 | 1.20 | .30 |
| ☐ 74 Colgate/Dickinson | 3.00 | 1.20 | .30 |
| ☐ 75 Colgate/Lafayette | 3.00 | 1.20 | .30 |
| ☐ 76 Colgate/U.of Mass. | 3.00 | 1.20 | .30 |
| ☐ 77 Colgate/Springfield | 3.00 | 1.20 | .30 |
| ☐ 78 Colgate/Texas AM | 3.00 | 1.20 | .30 |
| ☐ 79 C.O.P./Princeton | 3.00 | 1.20 | .30 |
| ☐ 80 C.O.P./Oklahoma St. | 3.00 | 1.20 | .30 |
| ☐ 81 C.O.P./Oregon St. | 3.00 | 1.20 | .30 |
| ☐ 82 Colo.St./Drew | 3.00 | 1.20 | .30 |
| ☐ 83 Colo.St./Oregon | 3.00 | 1.20 | .30 |
| ☐ 84 Colo.St./Piedmont | 3.00 | 1.20 | .30 |
| ☐ 85 Colo.St./Wm.and Mary | 3.00 | 1.20 | .30 |
| ☐ 86 Columbia/Dominican | 3.00 | 1.20 | .30 |
| ☐ 87 Columbia/Maine | 3.00 | 1.20 | .30 |
| ☐ 88 Columbia/N.Carolina | 4.00 | 1.60 | .40 |
| ☐ 89 Cornell/Harvard | 3.00 | 1.20 | .30 |
| ☐ 90 Cornell/Rensselaer | 3.00 | 1.20 | .30 |
| ☐ 91 Cornell/Stanford | 4.00 | 1.60 | .40 |
| ☐ 92 Cornell/Wisconsin | 3.00 | 1.20 | .30 |
| ☐ 93 Dartmouth/Mich.St. | 3.00 | 1.20 | .30 |
| ☐ 94 Dartmouth/Ohio U. | 3.00 | 1.20 | .30 |
| ☐ 95 Dartmouth/Wagner | 3.00 | 1.20 | .30 |
| ☐ 96 Davidson/Ohio Wesl. | 3.00 | 1.20 | .30 |
| ☐ 97 Davidson/S.Carolina | 3.00 | 1.20 | .30 |
| ☐ 98 Davidson/Texas Tech | 3.00 | 1.20 | .30 |
| ☐ 99 Delaware/Marquette | 3.00 | 1.20 | .30 |
| ☐ 100 Delaware/Michigan | 4.00 | 1.60 | .40 |
| ☐ 101 Delaware/Notre Dame | 6.00 | 2.40 | .60 |
| ☐ 102 Delaware/UCLA | 3.00 | 1.20 | .30 |
| ☐ 103 Denver/Florida State | 4.00 | 1.60 | .40 |
| ☐ 104 Denver/Indiana | 3.00 | 1.20 | .30 |
| ☐ 105 Denver/Iowa State | 3.00 | 1.20 | .30 |
| ☐ 106 Denver/USC | 3.00 | 1.20 | .30 |
| ☐ 107 Detroit/Harvard | 3.00 | 1.20 | .30 |
| ☐ 108 Detroit/Rensselaer | 3.00 | 1.20 | .30 |
| ☐ 109 Detroit/Stanford | 3.00 | 1.20 | .30 |
| ☐ 110 Dickinson/U.of Mass. | 3.00 | 1.20 | .30 |
| ☐ 111 Dickinson/Regis | 3.00 | 1.20 | .30 |
| ☐ 112 Dickinson/Springfield | 3.00 | 1.20 | .30 |
| ☐ 113 Dickinson/Texas AM | 3.00 | 1.20 | .30 |
| ☐ 114 Dominican/North Car. | 3.00 | 1.20 | .30 |
| ☐ 115 Drake/Duke | 3.00 | 1.20 | .30 |
| ☐ 116 Drake/Kentucky | 3.00 | 1.20 | .30 |
| ☐ 117 Drake/Middlebury | 3.00 | 1.20 | .30 |
| ☐ 118 Drake/Penn St. | 3.00 | 1.20 | .30 |
| ☐ 119 Drake/St. Peters | 3.00 | 1.20 | .30 |
| ☐ 120 Drake/Yale | 3.00 | 1.20 | .30 |
| ☐ 121 Drew/Middlebury | 3.00 | 1.20 | .30 |
| ☐ 122 Drew/Oregon | 3.00 | 1.20 | .30 |
| ☐ 123 Drew/Piedmont | 3.00 | 1.20 | .30 |
| ☐ 124 Drew/Wm. and Mary | 3.00 | 1.20 | .30 |
| ☐ 125 Duke/Middlebury | 3.00 | 1.20 | .30 |
| ☐ 126 Duke/Rhode Island | 3.00 | 1.20 | .30 |
| ☐ 127 Duke/Seton Hall | 3.00 | 1.20 | .30 |
| ☐ 128 Duke/Yale | 4.00 | 1.60 | .40 |
| ☐ 129 Finch/Long Island AT | 3.00 | 1.20 | .30 |
| ☐ 130 Finch/Michigan St. | 3.00 | 1.20 | .30 |
| ☐ 131 Finch/Ohio U. | 3.00 | 1.20 | .30 |
| ☐ 132 Finch/Wagner | 3.00 | 1.20 | .30 |
| ☐ 133 Florida/Gettysburg | 3.00 | 1.20 | .30 |
| ☐ 134 Florida/Illinois | 4.00 | 1.60 | .40 |
| ☐ 135 Florida/Syracuse | 4.00 | 1.60 | .40 |
| ☐ 136 Florida/Virginia | 4.00 | 1.60 | .40 |
| ☐ 137 Florida St./Indiana | 4.00 | 1.60 | .40 |
| ☐ 138 Florida St./Iowa St. | 4.00 | 1.60 | .40 |
| ☐ 139 Florida St./So.Cal. | 4.00 | 1.60 | .40 |
| ☐ 140 Florida St./VMI | 4.00 | 1.60 | .40 |
| ☐ 141 Georgetown/Kings Point | 3.00 | 1.20 | .30 |
| ☐ 142 Georgetown/Rice | 3.00 | 1.20 | .30 |
| ☐ 143 Georgia/Missouri | 4.00 | 1.60 | .40 |
| ☐ 144 Georgia/Ohio Wesleyan | 3.00 | 1.20 | .30 |
| ☐ 145 Georgia/Rutgers | 3.00 | 1.20 | .30 |
| ☐ 146 Georgia/So.Carolina | 4.00 | 1.60 | .40 |
| ☐ 147 Ga.Tech/Johns Hopkins | 3.00 | 1.20 | .30 |
| ☐ 148 Ga.Tech/Maryland | 4.00 | 1.60 | .40 |
| ☐ 149 Ga.Tech/Missouri | 4.00 | 1.60 | .40 |
| ☐ 150 Gettysburg/Syracuse | 3.00 | 1.20 | .30 |
| ☐ 151 Harvard/Miami | 4.00 | 1.60 | .40 |
| ☐ 152 Harvard/NC State | 4.00 | 1.60 | .40 |
| ☐ 153 Harvard/Stanford | 4.00 | 1.60 | .40 |
| ☐ 154 Harvard/Utah State | 3.00 | 1.20 | .30 |
| ☐ 155 Harvard/Wisconsin | 4.00 | 1.60 | .40 |
| ☐ 156 Hofstra/Marquette | 3.00 | 1.20 | .30 |
| ☐ 157 Hofstra/Michigan | 4.00 | 1.60 | .40 |
| ☐ 158 Hofstra/Navy | 3.00 | 1.20 | .30 |
| ☐ 159 Hofstra/UCLA | 3.00 | 1.20 | .30 |
| ☐ 160 Holy Cross/Navy | 3.00 | 1.20 | .30 |
| ☐ 161 Holy Cross/New York | 3.00 | 1.20 | .30 |
| ☐ 162 Holy Cross/N'western | 3.00 | 1.20 | .30 |
| ☐ 163 Holy Cross/Nyack | 3.00 | 1.20 | .30 |
| ☐ 164 Howard/Kentucky | 3.00 | 1.20 | .30 |
| ☐ 165 Howard/Villanova | 3.00 | 1.20 | .30 |
| ☐ 166 Illinois/Syracuse | 4.00 | 1.60 | .40 |
| ☐ 167 Indiana/Iowa State | 3.00 | 1.20 | .30 |
| ☐ 168 Indiana/V.M.I. | 3.00 | 1.20 | .30 |
| ☐ 169 Iowa/Maryland | 4.00 | 1.60 | .40 |
| ☐ 170 Iowa/Missouri | 4.00 | 1.60 | .40 |
| ☐ 171 Iowa/Pratt | 3.00 | 1.20 | .30 |
| ☐ 172 Iowa State/So.Cal. | 4.00 | 1.60 | .40 |
| ☐ 173 Johns Hopkins/Pratt | 3.00 | 1.20 | .30 |
| ☐ 174 Johns Hopkins/Purdue | 3.00 | 1.20 | .30 |
| ☐ 175 Kansas/St.Francis | 3.00 | 1.20 | .30 |
| ☐ 176 Kansas/S.M.U. | 3.00 | 1.20 | .30 |
| ☐ 177 Kansas State/N.Y.U. | 3.00 | 1.20 | .30 |
| ☐ 178 Kansas State/T.C.U. | 3.00 | 1.20 | .30 |

| | | | |
|---|---|---|---|
| ☐ 179 Kentucky/Maryland | 4.00 | 1.60 | .40 |
| ☐ 180 Kentucky/Middlebury | 3.00 | 1.20 | .30 |
| ☐ 181 Kentucky/New Hampsh. | 3.00 | 1.20 | .30 |
| ☐ 182 Kentucky/Penn State | 4.00 | 1.60 | .40 |
| ☐ 183 Kentucky/Seton Hall | 3.00 | 1.20 | .30 |
| ☐ 184 Kentucky/Villanova | 3.00 | 1.20 | .30 |
| ☐ 185 Kings Point/Queens | 3.00 | 1.20 | .30 |
| ☐ 186 Kings Point/Rice | 3.00 | 1.20 | .30 |
| ☐ 187 Kings Point/Upsala | 3.00 | 1.20 | .30 |
| ☐ 188 Lafayette/U.of Mass. | 3.00 | 1.20 | .30 |
| ☐ 189 Lafayette/Regis | 3.00 | 1.20 | .30 |
| ☐ 190 Long Isl. AT/Mich.St. | 4.00 | 1.60 | .40 |
| ☐ 191 Long Isl. AT/Ohio U. | 3.00 | 1.20 | .30 |
| ☐ 192 Long Isl. AT/Wagner | 3.00 | 1.20 | .30 |
| ☐ 193 Loyola/Minnesota | 3.00 | 1.20 | .30 |
| ☐ 194 Loyola/Norwich | 3.00 | 1.20 | .30 |
| ☐ 195 Marquette/Michigan | 4.00 | 1.60 | .40 |
| ☐ 196 Marquette/Navy | 3.00 | 1.20 | .30 |
| ☐ 197 Marquette/New Platz | 3.00 | 1.20 | .30 |
| ☐ 198 Marquette/Notre Dame | 6.00 | 2.40 | .60 |
| ☐ 199 Marquette/UCLA | 3.00 | 1.20 | .30 |
| ☐ 200 Maryland/Missouri | 4.00 | 1.60 | .40 |
| ☐ 201 Mass./Regis | 3.00 | 1.20 | .30 |
| ☐ 202 Mass./Springfield | 3.00 | 1.20 | .30 |
| ☐ 203 Mass./Texas AM | 3.00 | 1.20 | .30 |
| ☐ 204 Michigan/Navy | 5.00 | 2.00 | .50 |
| ☐ 205 Michigan/New Platz | 4.00 | 1.60 | .40 |
| ☐ 206 Michigan/UCLA | 5.00 | 2.00 | .50 |
| ☐ 207 Michigan St./Ohio U. | 4.00 | 1.60 | .40 |
| ☐ 208 Michigan St./Wagner | 4.00 | 1.60 | .40 |
| ☐ 209 Middlebury/Penn St. | 3.00 | 1.20 | .30 |
| ☐ 210 Middlebury/Yale | 3.00 | 1.20 | .30 |
| ☐ 211 Minnesota/Norwich | 3.00 | 1.20 | .30 |
| ☐ 212 Minnesota/Winthrop | 3.00 | 1.20 | .30 |
| ☐ 213 Mississippi/Penn | 3.00 | 1.20 | .30 |
| ☐ 214 Mississippi/St.Francis | 3.00 | 1.20 | .30 |
| ☐ 215 Missouri/Purdue | 4.00 | 1.60 | .40 |
| ☐ 216 Navy/Notre Dame | 7.50 | 3.00 | .75 |
| ☐ 217 Navy/UCLA | 5.00 | 2.00 | .50 |
| ☐ 218 Navy/Wingate | 3.00 | 1.20 | .30 |
| ☐ 219 New Hamp./Villanova | 3.00 | 1.20 | .30 |
| ☐ 220 N.Y.U./Northwestern | 3.00 | 1.20 | .30 |
| ☐ 221 NCE/Temple | 3.00 | 1.20 | .30 |
| ☐ 222 NC State/Temple | 3.00 | 1.20 | .30 |
| ☐ 223 Northwestern/TCU | 3.00 | 1.20 | .30 |
| ☐ 224 Norwich/Winthrop | 3.00 | 1.20 | .30 |
| ☐ 225 Notre Dame/UCLA | 7.50 | 3.00 | .75 |
| ☐ 226 Notre Dame/Wingate | 5.00 | 2.00 | .50 |
| ☐ 227 Ohio U./Wagner | 3.00 | 1.20 | .30 |
| ☐ 228 Ohio Wesl./Roberts | 3.00 | 1.20 | .30 |
| ☐ 229 Ohio Wesl./S.Carolina | 3.00 | 1.20 | .30 |
| ☐ 230 Okla.St./Oregon St. | 4.00 | 1.60 | .40 |
| ☐ 231 Okla.St./Princeton | 4.00 | 1.60 | .40 |
| ☐ 232 Oregon/Piedmont | 3.00 | 1.20 | .30 |
| ☐ 233 Oregon/Wm.and Mary | 3.00 | 1.20 | .30 |
| ☐ 234 Oregon St./Princeton | 4.00 | 1.60 | .40 |
| ☐ 235 Penn State/St.Peter's | 3.00 | 1.20 | .30 |
| ☐ 236 Penn State/Seton Hall | 3.00 | 1.20 | .30 |
| ☐ 237 Penn State/Yale | 4.00 | 1.60 | .40 |
| ☐ 238 Penn/S.M.U. | 3.00 | 1.20 | .30 |
| ☐ 239 Penn/St.Francis | 3.00 | 1.20 | .30 |
| ☐ 240 Queens/Upsala | 3.00 | 1.20 | .30 |
| ☐ 241 Rensselaer/Stanford | 3.00 | 1.20 | .30 |
| ☐ 242 Rensselaer/Temple | 3.00 | 1.20 | .30 |
| ☐ 243 Rensselaer/Utah State | 3.00 | 1.20 | .30 |
| ☐ 244 Rhode Island/Yale | 3.00 | 1.20 | .30 |
| ☐ 245 Rice/Upsala | 3.00 | 1.20 | .30 |
| ☐ 246 Roberts/So.Carolina | 3.00 | 1.20 | .30 |
| ☐ 247 Roberts/Texas Tech | 3.00 | 1.20 | .30 |
| ☐ 248 Rutgers/So.Carolina | 3.00 | 1.20 | .30 |
| ☐ 249 St.Francis/S.M.U. | 3.00 | 1.20 | .30 |
| ☐ 250 St.Peter's/Villanova | 3.00 | 1.20 | .30 |
| ☐ 251 St.Peter's/Yale | 3.00 | 1.20 | .30 |
| ☐ 252 So.California/VMI | 4.00 | 1.60 | .40 |
| ☐ 253 So.Carolina/Texas Tech | 3.00 | 1.20 | .30 |
| ☐ 254 Syracuse/Virginia | 4.00 | 1.60 | .40 |
| ☐ 255 Temple/Wisconsin | 3.00 | 1.20 | .30 |
| ☐ 256 UCLA/Wingate | 4.00 | 1.60 | .40 |
| ☐ 257 Utah State/Wisconsin | 3.00 | 1.20 | .30 |
| ☐ 258 Villanova/Yale | 3.00 | 1.20 | .30 |

| | NRMT | VG-E | GOOD |
|---|---|---|---|
| COMPLETE SET (24) | 100.00 | 40.00 | 10.00 |
| COMMON PLAYER (1-24) | 5.00 | 2.00 | .50 |
| | | | |
| ☐ 1 Dalva Allen | 5.00 | 2.00 | .50 |
| ☐ 2 Tony Banfield | 5.00 | 2.00 | .50 |
| ☐ 3 George Blanda | 15.00 | 6.00 | 1.50 |
| ☐ 4 Billy Cannon | 7.50 | 3.00 | .75 |
| ☐ 5 Doug Cline | 5.00 | 2.00 | .50 |
| ☐ 6 Willard Dewveall | 6.00 | 2.40 | .60 |
| ☐ 7 Mike Dukes | 5.00 | 2.00 | .50 |
| ☐ 8 Don Floyd | 6.00 | 2.40 | .60 |
| ☐ 9 Fred Glick | 6.00 | 2.40 | .60 |
| ☐ 10 Bill Groman | 6.00 | 2.40 | .60 |
| ☐ 11 Charlie Hennigan | 7.50 | 3.00 | .75 |
| ☐ 12 Ed Husmann | 5.00 | 2.00 | .50 |
| ☐ 13 Al Jamison | 5.00 | 2.00 | .50 |
| ☐ 14 Mark Johnston | 5.00 | 2.00 | .50 |
| ☐ 15 Jacky Lee | 6.00 | 2.40 | .60 |
| ☐ 16 Bob McLeod | 5.00 | 2.00 | .50 |
| ☐ 17 Rich Michael | 5.00 | 2.00 | .50 |
| ☐ 18 Dennit Morris | 5.00 | 2.00 | .50 |
| ☐ 19 Jim Norton | 6.00 | 2.40 | .60 |
| ☐ 20 Bob Schmidt | 5.00 | 2.00 | .50 |
| ☐ 21 Dave Smith | 6.00 | 2.40 | .60 |
| ☐ 22 Bob Talamini | 6.00 | 2.40 | .60 |
| ☐ 23 Charles Tolar | 6.00 | 2.40 | .60 |
| ☐ 24 Hogan Wharton | 5.00 | 2.00 | .50 |

## 1964-65 Oilers Color Team Issue

This team-issued set of 16 player photos measures approximately 7 3/4" by 9 3/4" and features color posed shots of players in uniform. Eight photos were grouped together as a set and packaged in plastic bags; set 1 and 2 each originally sold for 50 cents. The year 1964 was Scott Appleton, Ode Burrell, and Don Trull's first year with the Oilers. In addition, the year of issue is determined by the fact that the last year with the Oilers for Tony Banfield and Ed Husmann was 1965. The photos are printed on thin paper stock, and white borders frame each picture. A facsimile autograph is inscribed across the pictures in black ink. The backs are blank. The photos are unnumbered and checklisted below in alphabetical order.

| | NRMT | VG-E | GOOD |
|---|---|---|---|
| COMPLETE SET (16) | 75.00 | 30.00 | 7.50 |
| COMMON PLAYER (1-16) | 5.00 | 2.00 | .50 |
| | | | |
| ☐ 1 Scott Appleton | 6.00 | 2.40 | .60 |
| ☐ 2 Tony Banfield | 6.00 | 2.40 | .60 |
| ☐ 3 Sonny Bishop | 6.00 | 2.40 | .60 |

## 1961 Oilers Jay Publishing

This 24-card set features (approximately) 5" by 7" black-and-white player photos. The photos show players in traditional poses with the quarterback preparing to throw, the runner heading downfield, and the defenseman ready for the tackle. Bob McLeod's first year with the Oilers was 1961 and Dennit Morris' last year with the Oilers was 1961. These cards were packaged 12 to a packet and originally sold for 25 cents. The backs are blank. The cards are unnumbered and checklisted below in alphabetical order.

| | | | |
|---|---|---|---|
| ☐ 4 George Blanda | 15.00 | 6.00 | 1.50 |
| ☐ 5 Sid Blanks | 6.00 | 2.40 | .60 |
| ☐ 6 Danny Brabham | 5.00 | 2.00 | .50 |
| ☐ 7 Ode Burrell | 6.00 | 2.40 | .60 |
| ☐ 8 Doug Cline | 5.00 | 2.00 | .50 |
| ☐ 9 Don Floyd | 6.00 | 2.40 | .60 |
| ☐ 10 Freddy Glick | 6.00 | 2.40 | .60 |
| ☐ 11 Charlie Hennigan | 7.50 | 3.00 | .75 |
| ☐ 12 Ed Husmann | 5.00 | 2.00 | .50 |
| ☐ 13 Walt Suggs | 6.00 | 2.40 | .60 |
| ☐ 14 Bob Talamini | 5.00 | 2.00 | .50 |
| ☐ 15 Charley Tolar | 7.50 | 3.00 | .75 |
| ☐ 16 Don Trull | 7.50 | 3.00 | .75 |

## 1969 Oilers

These approximately 8" by 10" black-and-white photos have white borders. Most of the photos feature posed action shots. The player's name, position, and team are printed in the bottom white border. The backs are blank. The photos are unnumbered and checklisted below in alphabetical order. The set is dated by the fact that Ed Carrington's only active year with the Houston Oilers was 1969. Also Charlie Joiner's rookie season was 1969, this photo predates his Rookie Card by three seasons.

| | NRMT | VG-E | GOOD |
|---|---|---|---|
| COMPLETE SET (39) | 100.00 | 40.00 | 10.00 |
| COMMON PLAYER (1-39) | 3.00 | 1.20 | .30 |
| | | | |
| ☐ 1 Jim Beirne | 4.00 | 1.60 | .40 |
| (Wide receiver) | | | |
| ☐ 2 Jim Beirne | 4.00 | 1.60 | .40 |
| (Split end) | | | |
| ☐ 3 Elvin Bethea | 5.00 | 2.00 | .50 |
| ☐ 4 Sonny Bishop | 3.00 | 1.20 | .30 |
| ☐ 5 Garland Boyette | 4.00 | 1.60 | .40 |
| ☐ 6 Ode Burrell | 4.00 | 1.60 | .40 |
| ☐ 7 Ed Carrington | 3.00 | 1.20 | .30 |
| ☐ 8 Joe Childress CO | 3.00 | 1.20 | .30 |
| ☐ 9 Bob Davis | 3.00 | 1.20 | .30 |
| ☐ 10 Hugh Devore CO | 3.00 | 1.20 | .30 |
| ☐ 11 Tom Domres | 3.00 | 1.20 | .30 |
| ☐ 12 F.A. Dry | 3.00 | 1.20 | .30 |
| ☐ 13 Miller Farr | 4.00 | 1.60 | .40 |
| ☐ 14 Mac Haik | 3.00 | 1.20 | .30 |
| (Action shot) | | | |
| ☐ 15 Mac Haik | 3.00 | 1.20 | .30 |
| (Portrait) | | | |
| ☐ 16 W.K. Hicks | 3.00 | 1.20 | .30 |
| ☐ 17 Glen Ray Hines | 4.00 | 1.60 | .40 |
| ☐ 18 Pat Holmes | 3.00 | 1.20 | .30 |
| ☐ 19 Roy Hopkins | 3.00 | 1.20 | .30 |
| ☐ 20 Charlie Joiner | 12.00 | 5.00 | 1.20 |
| ☐ 21 Jim LeMoine | 3.00 | 1.20 | .30 |
| ☐ 22 Bobby Maples | 4.00 | 1.60 | .40 |
| ☐ 23 Richard Marshall | 3.00 | 1.20 | .30 |
| ☐ 24 Zeke Moore | 4.00 | 1.60 | .40 |
| ☐ 25 Willie Parker | 3.00 | 1.20 | .30 |
| ☐ 26 Johnny Peacock | 4.00 | 1.60 | .40 |
| ☐ 27 Ron Pritchard | 3.00 | 1.20 | .30 |
| (Back peddling) | | | |
| ☐ 28 Ron Pritchard | 3.00 | 1.20 | .30 |
| (Cutting left) | | | |
| ☐ 29 Ron Pritchard | 3.00 | 1.20 | .30 |
| (Preparing to fend | | | |
| off blocker) | | | |
| ☐ 30 Tom Regner | 3.00 | 1.20 | .30 |
| ☐ 31 George Rice | 3.00 | 1.20 | .30 |
| ☐ 32 George Rice | 3.00 | 1.20 | .30 |
| ☐ 33 Bob Robertson | 3.00 | 1.20 | .30 |
| ☐ 34 Walt Suggs | 3.00 | 1.20 | .30 |
| ☐ 35 Don Trull | 5.00 | 2.00 | .50 |
| ☐ 36 Olen Underwood | 3.00 | 1.20 | .30 |
| ☐ 37 Loyd Wainscott | 3.00 | 1.20 | .30 |
| ☐ 38 Wayne Walker | 3.00 | 1.20 | .30 |
| ☐ 39 Glenn Woods | 3.00 | 1.20 | .30 |

## 1971 Oilers

This 23-card set measures approximately 4" by 5 1/2" and features black-and-white, close-up, player photos, bordered in white and printed on a textured paper stock. The team name appears at the top between an Oilers helmet and the NFL logo, while the player's name and position are printed in the bottom border. The cards are unnumbered and checklisted below in alphabetical order. The set's date is defined by the fact that Willie Alexander, Ron Billingsley, Ken

Burrough, Lynn Dickey, Robert Holmes, Dan Pastorini, Floyd Rice, Mike Tilleman's first year with the Houston Oilers was 1971, and Charlie Johnson's last year with the Oilers was 1971.

| | MINT | EXC | G-VG |
|---|---|---|---|
| COMPLETE SET (23) | 50.00 | 20.00 | 5.00 |
| COMMON PLAYER (1-23) | 1.50 | .60 | .15 |
| | | | |
| ☐ 1 Willie Alexander | 2.00 | .80 | .20 |
| ☐ 2 Jim Beirne | 2.00 | .80 | .20 |
| ☐ 3 Elvin Bethea | 4.00 | 1.60 | .40 |
| ☐ 4 Ron Billingsley | 1.50 | .60 | .15 |
| ☐ 5 Garland Boyette | 2.00 | .80 | .20 |
| ☐ 6 Leo Brooks | 1.50 | .60 | .15 |
| ☐ 7 Ken Burrough | 3.00 | 1.20 | .30 |
| ☐ 8 Woody Campbell | 2.00 | .80 | .20 |
| ☐ 9 Lynn Dickey | 3.00 | 1.20 | .30 |
| ☐ 10 Elbert Drungo | 1.50 | .60 | .15 |
| ☐ 11 Pat Holmes | 1.50 | .60 | .15 |
| ☐ 12 Robert Holmes | 2.00 | .80 | .20 |
| ☐ 13 Ken Houston | 9.00 | 3.75 | .90 |
| ☐ 14 Charley Johnson | 3.00 | 1.20 | .30 |
| ☐ 15 Charlie Joiner | 9.00 | 3.75 | .90 |
| ☐ 16 Zeke Moore | 1.50 | .60 | .15 |
| ☐ 17 Mark Moseley | 3.00 | 1.20 | .30 |
| ☐ 18 Dan Pastorini | 3.00 | 1.20 | .30 |
| ☐ 19 Alvin Reed | 2.00 | .80 | .20 |
| ☐ 20 Tom Regner | 1.50 | .60 | .15 |
| ☐ 21 Floyd Rice | 1.50 | .60 | .15 |
| ☐ 22 Mike Tilleman | 1.50 | .60 | .15 |
| ☐ 23 George Webster | 2.50 | 1.00 | .25 |

## 1973 Oilers McDonald's

This set of three photos was sponsored by McDonald's. Each photo measures approximately 8" by 10" and features a posed color close-up photo bordered in white. The player's name and team name are printed in black in the bottom white border. The top portion of the back has biographical information, career summary, and career statistics. The bottom portion carries the Oilers 1973 game schedule. The photos are unnumbered and are checklisted below alphabetically.

| | NRMT | VG-E | GOOD |
|---|---|---|---|
| COMPLETE SET (3) | 20.00 | 8.00 | 2.00 |
| COMMON PLAYER (1-3) | 6.00 | 2.40 | .60 |
| | | | |
| ☐ 1 John Matuszak | 8.00 | 3.25 | .80 |
| ☐ 2 Zeke Moore | 6.00 | 2.40 | .60 |
| ☐ 3 Dan Pastorini | 10.00 | 4.00 | 1.00 |

# 1984 Pacific Legends

This 30-card set (produced by Pacific Trading Cards in 1984) has a yellowish tone to the front of the cards, similar to Cramer's Baseball Legends, but is entitled "Football Legends." The cards measure approximately 2 1/2" by 3 1/2" and are numbered on the back. The set features prominent individuals who played football at universities in the Pac 10 conference (and its predecessors).

|  | MINT | EXC | G-VG |
|---|---|---|---|
| COMPLETE SET (30) | 18.00 | 7.25 | 1.80 |
| COMMON PLAYER (1-30) | .35 | .14 | .03 |
| ☐ 1 O.J. Simpson | 5.00 | 2.00 | .50 |
| ☐ 2 Mike Garrett | .75 | .30 | .07 |
| ☐ 3 Pop Warner | .50 | .20 | .05 |
| ☐ 4 Bob Schloredt | .35 | .14 | .03 |
| ☐ 5 Pat Haden | .75 | .30 | .07 |
| ☐ 6 Ernie Nevers | .60 | .24 | .06 |
| ☐ 7 Jackie Robinson | 2.00 | .80 | .20 |
| ☐ 8 Arnie Weinmeister | .50 | .20 | .05 |
| ☐ 9 Gary Beban | .75 | .30 | .07 |
| ☐ 10 Jim Plunkett | .75 | .30 | .07 |
| ☐ 11 Bobby Grayson | .35 | .14 | .03 |
| ☐ 12 Craig Morton | .50 | .20 | .05 |
| ☐ 13 Ben Davidson | .60 | .24 | .06 |
| ☐ 14 Jim Hardy | .35 | .14 | .03 |
| ☐ 15 Vern Burke | .35 | .14 | .03 |
| ☐ 16 Hugh McElhenny | .75 | .30 | .07 |
| ☐ 17 John Wayne | 5.00 | 2.00 | .50 |
| ☐ 18 Ricky Bell | .50 | .20 | .05 |
| ☐ 19 George Wilson | .35 | .14 | .03 |
| ☐ 20 Bob Waterfield | .75 | .30 | .07 |
| ☐ 21 Charlie Mitchell | .35 | .14 | .03 |
| ☐ 22 Donn Moomaw | .35 | .14 | .03 |
| ☐ 23 Don Heinrich | .35 | .14 | .03 |
| ☐ 24 Terry Baker | .50 | .20 | .05 |
| ☐ 25 Jack Thompson | .35 | .14 | .03 |
| ☐ 26 Charles White | .50 | .20 | .05 |
| ☐ 27 Frank Gifford | 1.50 | .60 | .15 |
| ☐ 28 Lynn Swann | 1.00 | .40 | .10 |
| ☐ 29 Brick Muller | .35 | .14 | .03 |
| ☐ 30 Ron Yary | .50 | .20 | .05 |

# 1989 Pacific Steve Largent

The 1989 Pacific Trading Cards Steve Largent set contains 110 standard-size (2 1/2" by 3 1/2") cards, 85 of which are numbered. The numbered cards have silver borders on the fronts with photos of various career highlights; some are horizontally oriented, others are vertically oriented. The backs all are horizontally oriented and have light blue borders with information about the highlight shown on the front. The other 25 unnumbered cards are actually puzzle pieces which

form a 12 1/2" by 17 1/2" poster of Largent in action. The cards were distributed as factory sets and in ten-card wax packs.

|  | MINT | EXC | G-VG |
|---|---|---|---|
| COMPLETE SET (110) | 30.00 | 12.00 | 3.00 |
| COMMON PLAYER (1-85) | .35 | .14 | .03 |
| COMMON PUZZLE PIECE | .15 | .06 | .01 |
| ☐ 1 Title Card | 1.50 | .60 | .15 |
| (checklist 1-42 on back) |  |  |  |
| ☐ 2 Santa, Can You Please | .35 | .14 | .03 |
| ☐ 3 Age 9 | .35 | .14 | .03 |
| ☐ 4 Junior High 1968 | .35 | .14 | .03 |
| ☐ 5 High School 1971 | .35 | .14 | .03 |
| ☐ 6 Baseball or Football | .35 | .14 | .03 |
| ☐ 7 Tulsa, Senior Bowl | .35 | .14 | .03 |
| ☐ 8 Led Nation in TD's | .35 | .14 | .03 |
| ☐ 9 Coach Patera and | .50 | .20 | .05 |
| Coach Jerry Rhome |  |  |  |
| ☐ 10 Rookie 1976 | .75 | .30 | .07 |
| ☐ 11 First NFL TD | .35 | .14 | .03 |
| ☐ 12 Seahawks' First Win | .35 | .14 | .03 |
| ☐ 13 First Team All-Rookie | .50 | .20 | .05 |
| ☐ 14 Beats Buffalo 56-7 | .35 | .14 | .03 |
| ☐ 15 The Huddle | .35 | .14 | .03 |
| ☐ 16 Captains Largent and | .50 | .20 | .05 |
| Norm Evans |  |  |  |
| ☐ 17 First Win Against | .35 | .14 | .03 |
| Raiders |  |  |  |
| ☐ 18 3000 Yards Receiving | .35 | .14 | .03 |
| ☐ 19 Jerry Rhome and Largent | .75 | .30 | .07 |
| ☐ 20 Great Hands | .35 | .14 | .03 |
| ☐ 21 Climbs Mt. Rainier | .35 | .14 | .03 |
| ☐ 22 Zorn Connection | .50 | .20 | .05 |
| ☐ 23 Steve Largent and | .50 | .20 | .05 |
| Jim Zorn (in jeans) |  |  |  |
| ☐ 24 First Team All-AFC | .35 | .14 | .03 |
| ☐ 25 Seahawks MVP 1981 | .50 | .20 | .05 |
| ☐ 26 Strike Season 1982 | .35 | .14 | .03 |
| ☐ 27 Training Camp 1983 | .35 | .14 | .03 |
| ☐ 28 Chuck Knox Head Coach | .50 | .20 | .05 |
| ☐ 29 50 Career TD's | .35 | .14 | .03 |
| ☐ 30 7000 Yards Receiving | .35 | .14 | .03 |
| ☐ 31 Tilley and Largent UER | .75 | .30 | .07 |
| Two Greats From Tulsa |  |  |  |
| (card back refers to |  |  |  |
| Howard Twilley) |  |  |  |
| ☐ 32 Cold Day in Cincy | .35 | .14 | .03 |
| ☐ 33 Catches 3 TD Passes | .35 | .14 | .03 |
| ☐ 34 Seahawks 12-4 in 1984 | .35 | .14 | .03 |
| ☐ 35 Defeated in AFC | .35 | .14 | .03 |
| Championships |  |  |  |
| ☐ 36 Preparing for 1985 | .35 | .14 | .03 |
| Season |  |  |  |
| ☐ 37 Career High 79 Catches | .35 | .14 | .03 |
| ☐ 38 Career High 1287 Yards | .35 | .14 | .03 |
| ☐ 39 10000 Yards Receiving | .35 | .14 | .03 |
| ☐ 40 Throws a Pass | .35 | .14 | .03 |
| ☐ 41 Game Day 1985 | .35 | .14 | .03 |
| ☐ 42 Seattle Sports Star | .50 | .20 | .05 |
| of the Year |  |  |  |
| ☐ 43 A Very Sore Elbow | .35 | .14 | .03 |
| ☐ 44 The Concentration | .35 | .14 | .03 |
| ☐ 45 Steve and Eugene | .50 | .20 | .05 |
| Robinson |  |  |  |
| ☐ 46 Breaks Carmichael's | .35 | .14 | .03 |
| Record |  |  |  |
| ☐ 47 Seahawks 37, Raiders 0 | .35 | .14 | .03 |
| ☐ 48 11000 Yards Receiving | .35 | .14 | .03 |
| ☐ 49 Rough Game | .35 | .14 | .03 |
| ☐ 50 Streak Continues | .35 | .14 | .03 |
| ☐ 51 Captains Lane, Brown, | .50 | .20 | .05 |
| and Largent |  |  |  |
| ☐ 52 Steve and Kyle Catch | .35 | .14 | .03 |
| a Big One |  |  |  |
| ☐ 53 Krieg Connection | .50 | .20 | .05 |
| ☐ 54 Steve and Kyle at | .35 | .14 | .03 |
| Seahawk Camp |  |  |  |
| ☐ 55 NFL All-Time Leading | .50 | .20 | .05 |
| Receiver |  |  |  |
| ☐ 56 Hall of Fame Ball | .35 | .14 | .03 |
| ☐ 57 Steve and Coach Knox | .50 | .20 | .05 |
| ☐ 58 1987 Seahawks MVP | .50 | .20 | .05 |
| ☐ 59 Largent at Quarterback | .75 | .30 | .07 |
| ☐ 60 NFL All-Time Great | .50 | .20 | .05 |
| ☐ 61 Travelers' NFL Man of | .50 | .20 | .05 |
| the Year 1988 |  |  |  |
| ☐ 62 Steve and Terry | .35 | .14 | .03 |
| Largent (exercising) |  |  |  |
| ☐ 63 Holding for Norm | .50 | .20 | .05 |
| Johnson |  |  |  |
| ☐ 64 Great Moves | .35 | .14 | .03 |
| ☐ 65 Great Hands | .35 | .14 | .03 |
| ☐ 66 Seven-Time Pro Bowl | .35 | .14 | .03 |
| Selection |  |  |  |
| ☐ 67 Agee, Largent, and | .50 | .20 | .05 |
| Paul Skansi |  |  |  |
| ☐ 68 Signing for Fans | .35 | .14 | .03 |

| | | | |
|---|---|---|---|
| ☐ 69 Miller, Joe Nash, | .35 | .14 | .03 |
| Largent, and | | | |
| Bryan Millard | | | |
| ☐ 70 Pro Bowl Greats, | 1.50 | .60 | .15 |
| Largent and John Elway | | | |
| ☐ 71 Hanging onto the Ball | .35 | .14 | .03 |
| ☐ 72 1618 Career Yards vs. | .35 | .14 | .03 |
| Denver | | | |
| ☐ 73 17 Pro Bowl Receptions | .35 | .14 | .03 |
| ☐ 74 Jim Zorn and Largent | .50 | .20 | .05 |
| in Hawaii | | | |
| ☐ 75 Mr. Seahawk | .50 | .20 | .05 |
| ☐ 76 Sets NFL Career | .50 | .20 | .05 |
| Yardage Record | | | |
| ☐ 77 Two of the Greatest | .75 | .30 | .07 |
| (with Charlie Joiner) | | | |
| ☐ 78 Steve Largent, | .75 | .30 | .07 |
| Jerry Rhome, and | | | |
| Charlie Joiner | | | |
| ☐ 79 NFL All-Time Leader | .50 | .20 | .05 |
| in Receptions | | | |
| ☐ 80 NFL All-Time Leader | .50 | .20 | .05 |
| in Consecutive | | | |
| Game Receptions | | | |
| ☐ 81 NFL All-Time Leader | .35 | .14 | .03 |
| 12686 Receiving Yards | | | |
| ☐ 82 NFL All-Time Leader | .50 | .20 | .05 |
| 1000 Yard Seasons | | | |
| ☐ 83 First Recipient of the | .75 | .30 | .07 |
| Bart Starr Trophy | | | |
| ☐ 84 Steve Largent, | .50 | .20 | .05 |
| Wide Receiver | | | |
| ☐ 85 Future Hall of Famer | 1.00 | .40 | .10 |

## 1991 Pacific Prototypes

This five-card set was sent out by Pacific Trading Cards to prospective dealers prior to the general release of their debut set of NFL football cards. The cards are standard size, 2 1/2" by 3 1/2" and are styled almost exactly like the regular issue Pacific cards that followed shortly thereafter. These prototype cards are distinguished from the regular issue cards by their different card numbers and the presence of zeroes for the stat totals on the prototype card backs. The cards are numbered on the back. The production run reportedly was approximately 5,000 sets, and these sets were distributed to dealers in the Pacific network with the rest being used as sales samples.

| | MINT | EXC | G-VG |
|---|---|---|---|
| COMPLETE SET (5) | 225.00 | 90.00 | 22.00 |
| COMMON PLAYER (1-5) | 15.00 | 6.00 | 1.50 |
| | | | |
| ☐ 1 Joe Montana | 90.00 | 36.00 | 9.00 |
| San Francisco 49ers | | | |
| (Different border | | | |
| from regular card) | | | |
| ☐ 32 Bo Jackson | 25.00 | 10.00 | 2.50 |
| Los Angeles Raiders | | | |
| ☐ 66 Eric Metcalf | 15.00 | 6.00 | 1.50 |
| Cleveland Browns | | | |
| ☐ 100 Barry Sanders | 50.00 | 20.00 | 5.00 |
| Detroit Lions | | | |
| (Different photo | | | |
| from regular card) | | | |
| ☐ 232 Troy Aikman | 90.00 | 36.00 | 9.00 |
| Dallas Cowboys | | | |

## 1991 Pacific

This 660-card standard size (2 1/2" by 3 1/2") set was the first full football set issued by Pacific Trading Cards. The cards were issued in two series of 550 and 110 cards, respectively. The cards in the first series were issued in alphabetical order by teams, which were also in

alphabetical order. There were a few exceptions with regard to players Pacific could not get permission from the National Football League Players Association to print. The cards feature a full-color glossy front with the name on the left hand side of the card. The left border of the card is in the same colors as the teams helmet. In the lower left hand corner of the card there is a Pacific pennant. The team identity and player's position is under the player's picture. The back of the card has an approximate 45 degree tilt to it and includes a full-color portrait of the player, complete biographical information, and interesting facts about the players. The order in which the cards appear are Atlanta Falcons (1-19), Buffalo Bills (20-37), Chicago Bears (38-56), Cincinnati Bengals (57-74), Cleveland Browns (75-91), Dallas Cowboys (92-110), Denver Broncos (111-129), Detroit Lions (130-148), Green Bay Packers (149-168), Houston Oilers (169-186), Indianapolis Colts (187-204), Kansas City Chiefs (205-224), Los Angeles Raiders (225-244), Los Angeles Rams (245-262), Miami Dolphins (263-282), Minnesota Vikings (283-302), New England Patriots (303-319), New Orleans Saints (320-339), New York Giants (340-342 and 344-360), New York Jets (361-380), Philadelphia Eagles (381-399), Phoenix Cardinals (400-418), Pittsburgh Steelers (419-436), San Diego Chargers (437 and 439-455), San Francisco 49ers (456-474), Seattle Seahawks (475-494), Tampa Bay Buccaneers (495-514), Washington Redskins (515-518 and 520-533), Rookie Cards (534-546 and 548-550), Atlanta Falcons (551-557), Buffalo Bills (558-560), Chicago Bears (561-565), Cincinnati Bengals (566-568), Cleveland Browns (569-571), Dallas Cowboys (572-575), Denver Broncos (576-579), Detroit Lions (580-582), Green Bay Packers (583-586), Houston Oilers (587-590), Indianapolis Colts (591-595), Kansas City Chiefs (596-598), Los Angeles Raiders (599-603), Los Angeles Rams (604-606), Miami Dolphins (607-609), Minnesota Vikings (610), New England Patriots (611-616), New Orleans Saints (617-619), New York Giants (620-622), New York Jets (623-625), Philadelphia Eagles (626-630), Phoenix Cardinals (631-637), Pittsburgh Steelers (638-640), San Diego Chargers (641-644), San Francisco 49ers (645-646), Seattle Seahawks (647-651), Tampa Bay Buccaneers (652-657), and Washington Redskins (658-660). Rookie Cards include Nick Bell, Mike Croel, Lawrence Dawsey, Craig Erickson, Ricky Ervins, Brett Favre, Jeff Graham, Mark Higgs, Randal Hill, Michael Jackson, Todd Marinovich, Dan McGwire, Herman Moore, Browning Nagle, Erric Pegram, Mike Pritchard, Leonard Russell, Jon Vaughn, and Harvey Williams. Pacific reported that their production run for this second series was limited to 5,894 foil cases. The cards were released in foil packs, jumbo packs, and factory sets. Some cards from the 1991 Pacific set were also sold in single-card retail blister repacks from Ace Novelty Co. Each card was accompanied by a metal pin of the same player. Most of the Ace Novelty cards either have different spacing than the regular issue Pacific cards or have changes in the card numbers. For example, Barry Sanders is card number 1 instead of card number 144 as he is in the regular Pacific set.

| | MINT | EXC | G-VG |
|---|---|---|---|
| COMPLETE SET (660) | 18.00 | 8.00 | 2.30 |
| COMPLETE SERIES 1 (550) | 10.00 | 4.50 | 1.25 |
| COMP.FACT.SERIES 1 (550) | 10.00 | 4.50 | 1.25 |
| COMPLETE SERIES 2 (110) | 8.00 | 3.60 | 1.00 |
| COMP.FACT.SERIES 2 (110) | 10.00 | 4.50 | 1.25 |
| COMMON PLAYER (1-550) | .04 | .02 | .01 |
| COMMON PLAYER (551-660) | .05 | .02 | .01 |
| | | | |
| ☐ 1 Deion Sanders | .25 | .11 | .03 |
| ☐ 2 Steve Broussard | .07 | .03 | .01 |
| ☐ 3 Aundray Bruce | .04 | .02 | .01 |
| ☐ 4 Rick Bryan | .04 | .02 | .01 |
| ☐ 5 John Rade | .04 | .02 | .01 |
| ☐ 6 Scott Case | .04 | .02 | .01 |
| ☐ 7 Tony Casillas | .04 | .02 | .01 |
| ☐ 8 Shawn Collins | .04 | .02 | .01 |
| ☐ 9 Darion Conner | .04 | .02 | .01 |
| ☐ 10 Tory Epps | .04 | .02 | .01 |

| | | | |
|---|---|---|---|
| ☐ 11 Bill Fralic | .04 | .02 | .01 |
| ☐ 12 Mike Gann | .04 | .02 | .01 |
| ☐ 13 Tim Green UER | .04 | .02 | .01 |
| (Listed as DT, should say DE) | | | |
| ☐ 14 Chris Hinton | .04 | .02 | .01 |
| ☐ 15 Houston Hoover UER | .04 | .02 | .01 |
| (Deion misspelled as Deon on card back) | | | |
| ☐ 16 Chris Miller | .10 | .05 | .01 |
| ☐ 17 Andre Rison | .25 | .11 | .03 |
| ☐ 18 Mike Rozier | .07 | .03 | .01 |
| ☐ 19 Jessie Tuggle | .04 | .02 | .01 |
| ☐ 20 Don Beebe | .10 | .05 | .01 |
| ☐ 21 Ray Bentley | .04 | .02 | .01 |
| ☐ 22 Shane Conlan | .07 | .03 | .01 |
| ☐ 23 Kent Hull | .04 | .02 | .01 |
| ☐ 24 Mark Kelso | .04 | .02 | .01 |
| ☐ 25 James Lofton UER | .10 | .05 | .01 |
| (Photo on front actually Flip Johnson) | | | |
| ☐ 26 Scott Norwood | .04 | .02 | .01 |
| ☐ 27 Andre Reed | .10 | .05 | .01 |
| ☐ 28 Leonard Smith | .04 | .02 | .01 |
| ☐ 29 Bruce Smith | .10 | .05 | .01 |
| ☐ 30 Leon Seals | .04 | .02 | .01 |
| ☐ 31 Darryl Talley | .07 | .03 | .01 |
| ☐ 32 Steve Tasker | .07 | .03 | .01 |
| ☐ 33 Thurman Thomas | .40 | .18 | .05 |
| ☐ 34 James Williams | .04 | .02 | .01 |
| ☐ 35 Will Wolford | .04 | .02 | .01 |
| ☐ 36 Frank Reich | .10 | .05 | .01 |
| ☐ 37 Jeff Wright | .10 | .05 | .01 |
| ☐ 38 Neal Anderson | .07 | .03 | .01 |
| ☐ 39 Trace Armstrong | .04 | .02 | .01 |
| ☐ 40 Johnny Bailey UER | .07 | .03 | .01 |
| (Gained 5320 yards in college, should be 6320) | | | |
| ☐ 41 Mark Bortz UER | .04 | .02 | .01 |
| (Johnny Bailey misspelled as Johhny on card back) | | | |
| ☐ 42 Cap Boso | .04 | .02 | .01 |
| ☐ 43 Kevin Butler | .04 | .02 | .01 |
| ☐ 44 Mark Carrier | .07 | .03 | .01 |
| ☐ 45 Jim Covert | .04 | .02 | .01 |
| ☐ 46 Wendell Davis | .04 | .02 | .01 |
| ☐ 47 Richard Dent | .07 | .03 | .01 |
| ☐ 48 Shaun Gayle | .04 | .02 | .01 |
| ☐ 49 Jim Harbaugh | .07 | .03 | .01 |
| ☐ 50 Jay Hilgenberg | .07 | .03 | .01 |
| ☐ 51 Brad Muster | .07 | .03 | .01 |
| ☐ 52 William Perry | .07 | .03 | .01 |
| ☐ 53 Mike Singletary UER | .10 | .05 | .01 |
| (No College listed, should say Baylor) | | | |
| ☐ 54 Peter Tom Willis | .04 | .02 | .01 |
| ☐ 55 Donnell Woolford | .04 | .02 | .01 |
| ☐ 56 Steve McMichael | .07 | .03 | .01 |
| ☐ 57 Eric Ball | .04 | .02 | .01 |
| ☐ 58 Lewis Billups | .04 | .02 | .01 |
| ☐ 59 Jim Breech | .04 | .02 | .01 |
| ☐ 60 James Brooks | .07 | .03 | .01 |
| ☐ 61 Eddie Brown | .04 | .02 | .01 |
| ☐ 62 Rickey Dixon | .04 | .02 | .01 |
| ☐ 63 Boomer Esiason | .15 | .07 | .02 |
| ☐ 64 James Francis | .07 | .03 | .01 |
| ☐ 65 David Fulcher | .04 | .02 | .01 |
| ☐ 66 David Grant | .04 | .02 | .01 |
| ☐ 67 Harold Green UER | .10 | .05 | .01 |
| (Misplaced apostrophe in Gamecocks) | | | |
| ☐ 68 Rodney Holman | .04 | .02 | .01 |
| ☐ 69 Stanford Jennings | .04 | .02 | .01 |
| ☐ 70A Tim Krumrie ERR | .10 | .05 | .01 |
| (Misspelled Krumprie on card front) | | | |
| ☐ 70B Tim Krumrie COR | .10 | .05 | .01 |
| ☐ 71 Tim McGee | .04 | .02 | .01 |
| ☐ 72 Anthony Munoz | .07 | .03 | .01 |
| ☐ 73 Mitchell Price | .04 | .02 | .01 |
| ☐ 74 Eric Thomas | .04 | .02 | .01 |
| ☐ 75 Ickey Woods | .04 | .02 | .01 |
| ☐ 76 Mike Baab | .04 | .02 | .01 |
| ☐ 77 Thane Gash | .04 | .02 | .01 |
| ☐ 78 David Grayson | .04 | .02 | .01 |
| ☐ 79 Mike Johnson | .04 | .02 | .01 |
| ☐ 80 Reggie Langhorne | .07 | .03 | .01 |
| ☐ 81 Kevin Mack | .07 | .03 | .01 |
| ☐ 82 Clay Matthews | .07 | .03 | .01 |
| ☐ 83A Eric Metcalf ERR | .15 | .07 | .02 |
| ("Terry is the son of Terry") | | | |
| ☐ 83B Eric Metcalf COR | .15 | .07 | .02 |
| ("Eric is the son of Terry") | | | |
| ☐ 84 Frank Minnifield | .04 | .02 | .01 |

| | | | |
|---|---|---|---|
| ☐ 85 Mike Oliphant | .04 | .02 | .01 |
| ☐ 86 Mike Pagel | .04 | .02 | .01 |
| ☐ 87 John Talley | .04 | .02 | .01 |
| ☐ 88 Lawyer Tillman | .04 | .02 | .01 |
| ☐ 89 Gregg Rakoczy UER | .04 | .02 | .01 |
| (Misspelled Greg on both sides of card) | | | |
| ☐ 90 Bryan Wagner | .04 | .02 | .01 |
| ☐ 91 Rob Burnett | .15 | .07 | .02 |
| ☐ 92 Tommie Agee | .04 | .02 | .01 |
| ☐ 93 Troy Aikman UER | 1.25 | .55 | .16 |
| (4328 yards is career total not season; text has him breaking passing record which is not true) | | | |
| ☐ 94A Bill Bates ERR | .10 | .05 | .01 |
| (Black line on card front) | | | |
| ☐ 94B Bill Bates COR | .10 | .05 | .01 |
| (No black line on card front) | | | |
| ☐ 95 Jack Del Rio | .04 | .02 | .01 |
| ☐ 96 Issiac Holt UER | .04 | .02 | .01 |
| (Photo on back actually Timmy Newsome) | | | |
| ☐ 97 Michael Irvin | .50 | .23 | .06 |
| ☐ 98 Jim Jeffcoat UER | .04 | .02 | .01 |
| (On back, red line has Jeff not Jim) | | | |
| ☐ 99 Jimmy Jones | .04 | .02 | .01 |
| ☐ 100 Kelvin Martin | .07 | .03 | .01 |
| ☐ 101 Nate Newton | .04 | .02 | .01 |
| ☐ 102 Danny Noonan | .04 | .02 | .01 |
| ☐ 103 Ken Norton | .10 | .05 | .01 |
| ☐ 104 Jay Novacek | .15 | .07 | .02 |
| ☐ 105 Mike Saxon | .04 | .02 | .01 |
| ☐ 106 Derrick Sheppard | .04 | .02 | .01 |
| ☐ 107 Emmitt Smith | 2.00 | .90 | .25 |
| ☐ 108 Daniel Stubbs | .04 | .02 | .01 |
| ☐ 109 Tony Tolbert | .04 | .02 | .01 |
| ☐ 110 Alexander Wright | .07 | .03 | .01 |
| ☐ 111 Steve Atwater | .10 | .05 | .01 |
| ☐ 112 Melvin Bratton | .04 | .02 | .01 |
| ☐ 113 Tyrone Braxton UER | .04 | .02 | .01 |
| (Went to North Dakota State, not South Dakota) | | | |
| ☐ 114 Alphonso Carreker | .04 | .02 | .01 |
| ☐ 115 John Elway | .35 | .16 | .04 |
| ☐ 116 Simon Fletcher | .07 | .03 | .01 |
| ☐ 117 Bobby Humphrey | .07 | .03 | .01 |
| ☐ 118 Mark Jackson | .07 | .03 | .01 |
| ☐ 119 Vance Johnson | .07 | .03 | .01 |
| ☐ 120 Greg Kragen UER | .04 | .02 | .01 |
| (Recovered 20 fumbles in '89, yet 11 in career) | | | |
| ☐ 121 Karl Mecklenburg UER | .07 | .03 | .01 |
| (Misspelled Mecklenberg on card front) | | | |
| ☐ 122A Orson Mobley ERR | .50 | .23 | .06 |
| (Misspelled Orsen) | | | |
| ☐ 122B Orson Mobley COR | .10 | .05 | .01 |
| ☐ 123 Alton Montgomery | .04 | .02 | .01 |
| ☐ 124 Ricky Nattiel | .04 | .02 | .01 |
| ☐ 125 Steve Sewell | .04 | .02 | .01 |
| ☐ 126 Shannon Sharpe | .60 | .25 | .08 |
| ☐ 127 Dennis Smith | .07 | .03 | .01 |
| ☐ 128A Andre Townsend ERR | .60 | .25 | .08 |
| (Misspelled Andie on card front) | | | |
| ☐ 128B Andre Townsend COR | .10 | .05 | .01 |
| ☐ 129 Mike Horan | .04 | .02 | .01 |
| ☐ 130 Jerry Ball | .07 | .03 | .01 |
| ☐ 131 Bennie Blades | .04 | .02 | .01 |
| ☐ 132 Lomas Brown | .04 | .02 | .01 |
| ☐ 133 Jeff Campbell UER | .04 | .02 | .01 |
| (No NFL totals line) | | | |
| ☐ 134 Robert Clark | .04 | .02 | .01 |
| ☐ 135 Michael Cofer | .04 | .02 | .01 |
| ☐ 136 Dennis Gibson | .04 | .02 | .01 |
| ☐ 137 Mel Gray | .07 | .03 | .01 |
| ☐ 138 LeRoy Irvin UER | .04 | .02 | .01 |
| (Misspelled LEROY; spent 10 years with Rams, not 11) | | | |
| ☐ 139 George Jamison | .04 | .02 | .01 |
| ☐ 140 Richard Johnson | .04 | .02 | .01 |
| ☐ 141 Eddie Murray | .07 | .03 | .01 |
| ☐ 142 Dan Owens | .04 | .02 | .01 |
| ☐ 143 Rodney Peete | .07 | .03 | .01 |
| ☐ 144 Barry Sanders | .75 | .35 | .09 |
| ☐ 145 Chris Spielman | .07 | .03 | .01 |
| ☐ 146 Mark Spindler | .04 | .02 | .01 |
| ☐ 147 Andre Ware | .10 | .05 | .01 |
| ☐ 148 William White | .04 | .02 | .01 |
| ☐ 149 Tony Bennett | .07 | .03 | .01 |
| ☐ 150 Robert Brown | .04 | .02 | .01 |
| ☐ 151 LeRoy Butler | .04 | .02 | .01 |

| | | | |
|---|---|---|---|
| ☐ 152 Anthony Dilweg | .07 | .03 | .01 |
| ☐ 153 Michael Haddix | .04 | .02 | .01 |
| ☐ 154 Ron Hallstrom | .04 | .02 | .01 |
| ☐ 155 Tim Harris | .07 | .03 | .01 |
| ☐ 156 Johnny Holland | .04 | .02 | .01 |
| ☐ 157 Chris Jacke | .04 | .02 | .01 |
| ☐ 158 Perry Kemp | .04 | .02 | .01 |
| ☐ 159 Mark Lee | .04 | .02 | .01 |
| ☐ 160 Don Majkowski | .07 | .03 | .01 |
| ☐ 161 Tony Mandarich UER | .04 | .02 | .01 |
| (United Stated) | | | |
| ☐ 162 Mark Murphy | .04 | .02 | .01 |
| ☐ 163 Brian Noble | .04 | .02 | .01 |
| ☐ 164 Shawn Patterson | .04 | .02 | .01 |
| ☐ 165 Jeff Query | .04 | .02 | .01 |
| ☐ 166 Sterling Sharpe | .50 | .23 | .06 |
| ☐ 167 Darrell Thompson | .07 | .03 | .01 |
| ☐ 168 Ed West | .04 | .02 | .01 |
| ☐ 169 Ray Childress UER | .07 | .03 | .01 |
| (Front DE, back DT) | | | |
| ☐ 170A Cris Dishman ERR | .30 | .14 | .04 |
| (Misspelled Chris on both sides) | | | |
| ☐ 170B Cris Dishman COR/ERR | 1.00 | .45 | .13 |
| (Misspelled Chris on back only) | | | |
| ☐ 170C Cris Dishman COR | .15 | .07 | .02 |
| ☐ 171 Curtis Duncan | .07 | .03 | .01 |
| ☐ 172 William Fuller | .07 | .03 | .01 |
| ☐ 173 Ernest Givins UER | .07 | .03 | .01 |
| (Missing a highlight line on back) | | | |
| ☐ 174 Drew Hill | .07 | .03 | .01 |
| ☐ 175A Haywood Jeffires ERR | .20 | .09 | .03 |
| (Misspelled Jeffries on both sides of card) | | | |
| ☐ 175B Haywood Jeffires COR | .20 | .09 | .03 |
| ☐ 176 Sean Jones | .07 | .03 | .01 |
| ☐ 177 Lamar Lathon | .04 | .02 | .01 |
| ☐ 178 Bruce Matthews | .07 | .03 | .01 |
| ☐ 179 Bubba McDowell | .04 | .02 | .01 |
| ☐ 180 Johnny Meads | .04 | .02 | .01 |
| ☐ 181 Warren Moon UER | .15 | .07 | .02 |
| (Birth listed as '65, should be '56) | | | |
| ☐ 182 Mike Munchak | .07 | .03 | .01 |
| ☐ 183 Allen Pinkett | .04 | .02 | .01 |
| ☐ 184 Dean Steinkuhler UER | .04 | .02 | .01 |
| (Oakland, should be Outland) | | | |
| ☐ 185 Lorenzo White UER | .07 | .03 | .01 |
| (Rout misspelled as route on card back) | | | |
| ☐ 186A John Grimsley ERR | .10 | .05 | .01 |
| (Misspelled Grimsby) | | | |
| ☐ 186B John Grimsley COR | .10 | .05 | .01 |
| ☐ 187 Pat Beach | .04 | .02 | .01 |
| ☐ 188 Albert Bentley | .04 | .02 | .01 |
| ☐ 189 Dean Biasucci | .04 | .02 | .01 |
| ☐ 190 Duane Bickett | .04 | .02 | .01 |
| ☐ 191 Bill Brooks | .07 | .03 | .01 |
| ☐ 192 Eugene Daniel | .04 | .02 | .01 |
| ☐ 193 Jeff George | .25 | .11 | .03 |
| ☐ 194 Jon Hand | .04 | .02 | .01 |
| ☐ 195 Jeff Herrod | .04 | .02 | .01 |
| ☐ 196A Jessie Hester ERR | .50 | .23 | .06 |
| (Misspelled Jesse) | | | |
| ☐ 196B Jessie Hester ERR | .10 | .05 | .01 |
| (Name corrected; 6-year player, not 7; no NFL total line) | | | |
| ☐ 197 Mike Prior | .04 | .02 | .01 |
| ☐ 198 Stacey Simmons | .04 | .02 | .01 |
| ☐ 199 Rohn Stark | .04 | .02 | .01 |
| ☐ 200 Pat Tomberlin | .04 | .02 | .01 |
| ☐ 201 Clarence Verdin | .04 | .02 | .01 |
| ☐ 202 Keith Taylor | .04 | .02 | .01 |
| ☐ 203 Jack Trudeau | .04 | .02 | .01 |
| ☐ 204 Chip Banks | .04 | .02 | .01 |
| ☐ 205 John Alt | .04 | .02 | .01 |
| ☐ 206 Deron Cherry | .04 | .02 | .01 |
| ☐ 207 Steve DeBerg | .07 | .03 | .01 |
| ☐ 208 Tim Grunhard | .04 | .02 | .01 |
| ☐ 209 Albert Lewis | .07 | .03 | .01 |
| ☐ 210 Nick Lowery UER | .07 | .03 | .01 |
| (12 years NFL exp., should be 13) | | | |
| ☐ 211 Bill Maas | .04 | .02 | .01 |
| ☐ 212 Chris Martin | .04 | .02 | .01 |
| ☐ 213 Todd McNair | .04 | .02 | .01 |
| ☐ 214 Christian Okoye | .07 | .03 | .01 |
| ☐ 215 Stephone Paige | .07 | .03 | .01 |
| ☐ 216 Steve Pelluer | .04 | .02 | .01 |
| ☐ 217 Kevin Porter | .04 | .02 | .01 |
| ☐ 218 Kevin Ross | .07 | .03 | .01 |
| ☐ 219 Dan Saleaumua | .04 | .02 | .01 |
| ☐ 220 Neil Smith | .10 | .05 | .01 |

| | | | |
|---|---|---|---|
| ☐ 221 David Szott UER | .04 | .02 | .01 |
| (Listed as Off. Guard) | | | |
| ☐ 222 Derrick Thomas | .25 | .11 | .03 |
| ☐ 223 Barry Word | .10 | .05 | .01 |
| ☐ 224 Percy Snow | .04 | .02 | .01 |
| ☐ 225 Marcus Allen | .15 | .07 | .02 |
| ☐ 226 Eddie Anderson UER | .04 | .02 | .01 |
| (Began career with Seahawks, not Raiders) | | | |
| ☐ 227 Steve Beuerlein UER | .20 | .09 | .03 |
| (Not injured during '90 season, but was inactive) | | | |
| ☐ 228A Tim Brown ERR | .35 | .16 | .04 |
| (No position on card) | | | |
| ☐ 228B Tim Brown COR | .25 | .11 | .03 |
| ☐ 229 Scott Davis | .04 | .02 | .01 |
| ☐ 230 Mike Dyal | .04 | .02 | .01 |
| ☐ 231 Mervyn Fernandez UER | .04 | .02 | .01 |
| (Card says free agent in '87, but was drafted in '83) | | | |
| ☐ 232 Willie Gault UER | .07 | .03 | .01 |
| (Text says 60 catches in '90, stats say 50) | | | |
| ☐ 233 Ethan Horton UER | .04 | .02 | .01 |
| (No height and weight listings) | | | |
| ☐ 234 Bo Jackson UER | .35 | .16 | .04 |
| (Drafted in '87, not '86) | | | |
| ☐ 235 Howie Long | .07 | .03 | .01 |
| ☐ 236 Terry McDaniel | .04 | .02 | .01 |
| ☐ 237 Max Montoya | .04 | .02 | .01 |
| ☐ 238 Don Mosebar | .04 | .02 | .01 |
| ☐ 239 Jay Schroeder | .07 | .03 | .01 |
| ☐ 240 Steve Smith | .07 | .03 | .01 |
| ☐ 241 Greg Townsend | .04 | .02 | .01 |
| ☐ 242 Aaron Wallace | .04 | .02 | .01 |
| ☐ 243 Lionel Washington | .04 | .02 | .01 |
| ☐ 244A Steve Wisniewski ERR | .10 | .05 | .01 |
| (Misspelled Winsniewski on both sides; Drafted, should say traded to) | | | |
| ☐ 244B Steve Wisniewski ERR | 1.00 | .45 | .13 |
| (Misspelled Winsniewski on card back) | | | |
| ☐ 244C Steve Wisniewski COR | .10 | .05 | .01 |
| ☐ 245 Flipper Anderson | .07 | .03 | .01 |
| ☐ 246 Latin Berry | .04 | .02 | .01 |
| ☐ 247 Robert Delpino | .07 | .03 | .01 |
| ☐ 248 Marcus Dupree | .07 | .03 | .01 |
| ☐ 249 Henry Ellard | .07 | .03 | .01 |
| ☐ 250 Jim Everett | .07 | .03 | .01 |
| ☐ 251 Cleveland Gary | .07 | .03 | .01 |
| ☐ 252 Jerry Gray | .04 | .02 | .01 |
| ☐ 253 Kevin Greene | .07 | .03 | .01 |
| ☐ 254 Pete Holohan UER | .04 | .02 | .01 |
| (Photo on back actually Kevin Greene) | | | |
| ☐ 255 Buford McGee | .04 | .02 | .01 |
| ☐ 256 Tom Newberry | .04 | .02 | .01 |
| ☐ 257A Irv Pankey ERR | .10 | .05 | .01 |
| (Misspelled as Panky on both sides of card) | | | |
| ☐ 257B Irv Pankey COR | .10 | .05 | .01 |
| ☐ 258 Jackie Slater | .07 | .03 | .01 |
| ☐ 259 Doug Smith | .04 | .02 | .01 |
| ☐ 260 Frank Stams | .04 | .02 | .01 |
| ☐ 261 Michael Stewart | .04 | .02 | .01 |
| ☐ 262 Fred Strickland | .04 | .02 | .01 |
| ☐ 263 J.B. Brown UER | .04 | .02 | .01 |
| (No periods after initials on card front) | | | |
| ☐ 264 Mark Clayton | .07 | .03 | .01 |
| ☐ 265 Jeff Cross | .04 | .02 | .01 |
| ☐ 266 Mark Dennis | .04 | .02 | .01 |
| ☐ 267 Mark Duper | .07 | .03 | .01 |
| ☐ 268 Ferrell Edmunds | .04 | .02 | .01 |
| ☐ 269 Dan Marino | .75 | .35 | .09 |
| ☐ 270 John Offerdahl | .07 | .03 | .01 |
| ☐ 271 Louis Oliver | .07 | .03 | .01 |
| ☐ 272 Tony Paige | .04 | .02 | .01 |
| ☐ 273 Reggie Roby | .04 | .02 | .01 |
| ☐ 274 Sammie Smith | .04 | .02 | .01 |
| (Picture is sideways on the card) | | | |
| ☐ 275 Keith Sims | .04 | .02 | .01 |
| ☐ 276 Brian Sochia | .04 | .02 | .01 |
| ☐ 277 Pete Stoyanovich | .07 | .03 | .01 |
| ☐ 278 Richmond Webb | .07 | .03 | .01 |
| ☐ 279 Jarvis Williams | .04 | .02 | .01 |
| ☐ 280 Tim McKyer | .07 | .03 | .01 |
| ☐ 281A Jim C. Jensen ERR | .10 | .05 | .01 |
| (Misspelled Jenson on card back) | | | |
| ☐ 281B Jim C. Jensen COR | .10 | .05 | .01 |

(Plays a skill position,
not skilled)

| | | | |
|---|---|---|---|
| ☐ 282 Scott Secules | .15 | .07 | .02 |
| ☐ 283 Ray Berry | .04 | .02 | .01 |
| ☐ 284 Joey Browner UER | .04 | .02 | .01 |
| (Safetys, sic) | | | |
| ☐ 285 Anthony Carter | .07 | .03 | .01 |
| ☐ 286A Cris Carter ERR | .25 | .11 | .03 |
| (Misspelled Chris on both sides) | | | |
| ☐ 286B Cris Carter COR/ERR | 1.25 | .55 | .16 |
| (Misspelled Chris on card back) | | | |
| ☐ 286C Cris Carter COR | .25 | .11 | .03 |
| ☐ 287 Chris Doleman | .07 | .03 | .01 |
| ☐ 288 Mark Dusbabek UER | .04 | .02 | .01 |
| (Front DT, back LB) | | | |
| ☐ 289 Hassan Jones | .04 | .02 | .01 |
| ☐ 290 Steve Jordan | .07 | .03 | .01 |
| ☐ 291 Carl Lee | .04 | .02 | .01 |
| ☐ 292 Kirk Lowdermilk | .04 | .02 | .01 |
| ☐ 293 Randall McDaniel | .04 | .02 | .01 |
| ☐ 294 Mike Merriweather | .04 | .02 | .01 |
| ☐ 295A Keith Millard UER | .10 | .05 | .01 |
| (No position on card) | | | |
| ☐ 295B Keith Millard COR | .10 | .05 | .01 |
| ☐ 296 Al Noga UER | .04 | .02 | .01 |
| (Card says DT, should say DE) | | | |
| ☐ 297 Scott Studwell UER | .04 | .02 | .01 |
| (83 career tackles, but bio says 156 tackles in '81 season) | | | |
| ☐ 298 Henry Thomas | .04 | .02 | .01 |
| ☐ 299 Herschel Walker | .10 | .05 | .01 |
| ☐ 300 Gary Zimmerman | .04 | .02 | .01 |
| ☐ 301 Rick Gannon | .07 | .03 | .01 |
| ☐ 302 Wade Wilson UER | .07 | .03 | .01 |
| (Led AFC, should say led NFC) | | | |
| ☐ 303 Vincent Brown | .04 | .02 | .01 |
| ☐ 304 Marv Cook | .07 | .03 | .01 |
| ☐ 305 Hart Lee Dykes | .04 | .02 | .01 |
| ☐ 306 Irving Fryar | .07 | .03 | .01 |
| ☐ 307 Tommy Hodson UER | .04 | .02 | .01 |
| (No NFL totals line) | | | |
| ☐ 308 Maurice Hurst | .04 | .02 | .01 |
| ☐ 309 Ronnie Lippett UER | .04 | .02 | .01 |
| (On back, reserves should be reserve) | | | |
| ☐ 310 Fred Marion | .04 | .02 | .01 |
| ☐ 311 Greg McMurtry | .04 | .02 | .01 |
| ☐ 312 Johnny Rembert | .04 | .02 | .01 |
| ☐ 313 Chris Singleton | .04 | .02 | .01 |
| ☐ 314 Ed Reynolds | .04 | .02 | .01 |
| ☐ 315 Andre Tippett | .07 | .03 | .01 |
| ☐ 316 Garin Veris | .04 | .02 | .01 |
| ☐ 317 Brent Williams | .04 | .02 | .01 |
| ☐ 318A John Stephens ERR | .10 | .05 | .01 |
| (Misspelled Stevens on both sides of card) | | | |
| ☐ 318B John Stephens COR/ERR | 1.00 | .45 | .13 |
| (Misspelled Stevens on card back) | | | |
| ☐ 318C John Stephens COR | .10 | .05 | .01 |
| ☐ 319 Sammy Martin | .04 | .02 | .01 |
| ☐ 320 Bruce Armstrong | .04 | .02 | .01 |
| ☐ 321A Morten Andersen ERR | .50 | .23 | .06 |
| (Misspelled Anderson on both sides of card) | | | |
| ☐ 321B Morten Andersen COR/ERR | 1.00 | .45 | .13 |
| (Misspelled Anderson on card back) | | | |
| ☐ 321C Morten Andersen COR | .10 | .05 | .01 |
| ☐ 322 Gene Atkins UER | .04 | .02 | .01 |
| (No NFL Exp. line) | | | |
| ☐ 323 Vince Buck | .04 | .02 | .01 |
| ☐ 324 John Fourcade | .04 | .02 | .01 |
| ☐ 325 Kevin Haverdink | .04 | .02 | .01 |
| ☐ 326 Bobby Hebert | .10 | .05 | .01 |
| ☐ 327 Craig Heyward | .04 | .02 | .01 |
| ☐ 328 Dalton Hilliard | .04 | .02 | .01 |
| ☐ 329 Rickey Jackson | .07 | .03 | .01 |
| ☐ 330A Vaughan Johnson ERR | .10 | .05 | .01 |
| (Misspelled Vaughn) | | | |
| ☐ 330B Vaughan Johnson COR | .10 | .05 | .01 |
| ☐ 331 Eric Martin | .07 | .03 | .01 |
| ☐ 332 Wayne Martin | .04 | .02 | .01 |
| ☐ 333 Rueben Mayes UER | .04 | .02 | .01 |
| (Misspelled Reuben on card back) | | | |
| ☐ 334 Sam Mills | .07 | .03 | .01 |
| ☐ 335 Brett Perriman | .10 | .05 | .01 |
| ☐ 336 Pat Swilling | .07 | .03 | .01 |
| ☐ 337 Renaldo Turnbull | .07 | .03 | .01 |
| ☐ 338 Lonzell Hill | .04 | .02 | .01 |

| | | | |
|---|---|---|---|
| ☐ 339 Steve Walsh UER | .04 | .02 | .01 |
| (19 of 20 for 70.3, should be 95 percent) | | | |
| ☐ 340 Carl Banks UER | .07 | .03 | .01 |
| (Led defensive in tackles, should say defense) | | | |
| ☐ 341 Mark Bavaro UER | .07 | .03 | .01 |
| (Weight on back 145, should say 245) | | | |
| ☐ 342 Maurice Carthon | .04 | .02 | .01 |
| ☐ 343 Pat Harlow | .10 | .05 | .01 |
| ☐ 344 Eric Dorsey | .04 | .02 | .01 |
| ☐ 345 John Elliott | .04 | .02 | .01 |
| ☐ 346 Rodney Hampton | .75 | .35 | .09 |
| ☐ 347 Jeff Hostetler | .25 | .11 | .03 |
| ☐ 348 Erik Howard UER | .04 | .02 | .01 |
| (Listed as DT, should be NT) | | | |
| ☐ 349 Pepper Johnson | .07 | .03 | .01 |
| ☐ 350A Sean Landeta ERR | .10 | .05 | .01 |
| (Misspelled Landetta on both sides of card) | | | |
| ☐ 350B Sean Landeta COR | .50 | .23 | .06 |
| ☐ 351 Leonard Marshall | .07 | .03 | .01 |
| ☐ 352 David Meggett | .10 | .05 | .01 |
| ☐ 353A Bart Oates ERR | .10 | .05 | .01 |
| (Misspelled Oats on both sides; misspelled Megget in Did You Know) | | | |
| ☐ 353B Bart Oates COR/ERR | 1.00 | .45 | .13 |
| (Misspelled Oats on card back; misspelled Megget in Did You Know) | | | |
| ☐ 353C Bart Oates COR | .10 | .05 | .01 |
| (Dave Meggett still misspelled as Megget) | | | |
| ☐ 354 Gary Reasons | .04 | .02 | .01 |
| ☐ 355 Phil Simms | .10 | .05 | .01 |
| ☐ 356 Lawrence Taylor | .10 | .05 | .01 |
| ☐ 357 Reyna Thompson | .04 | .02 | .01 |
| ☐ 358 Brian Williams UER | .04 | .02 | .01 |
| (Front C-G, back G) | | | |
| ☐ 359 Matt Bahr | .04 | .02 | .01 |
| ☐ 360 Mark Ingram | .07 | .03 | .01 |
| ☐ 361 Brad Baxter | .07 | .03 | .01 |
| ☐ 362 Mark Boyer | .04 | .02 | .01 |
| ☐ 363 Dennis Byrd | .07 | .03 | .01 |
| ☐ 364 Dave Cadigan UER | .04 | .02 | .01 |
| (Terance misspelled as Terrance on back) | | | |
| ☐ 365 Kyle Clifton | .04 | .02 | .01 |
| ☐ 366 James Hasty | .04 | .02 | .01 |
| ☐ 367 Joe Kelly UER | .04 | .02 | .01 |
| (Front 50, back 58) | | | |
| ☐ 368 Jeff Lageman | .04 | .02 | .01 |
| ☐ 369 Pat Leahy UER | .07 | .03 | .01 |
| (Career-best FG in '65, should say '85) | | | |
| ☐ 370 Terance Mathis | .04 | .02 | .01 |
| ☐ 371 Erik McMillan | .04 | .02 | .01 |
| ☐ 372 Rob Moore | .10 | .05 | .01 |
| ☐ 373 Ken O'Brien | .07 | .03 | .01 |
| ☐ 374 Tony Stargell | .04 | .02 | .01 |
| ☐ 375 Jim Sweeney UER | .04 | .02 | .01 |
| (Landetta, sic) | | | |
| ☐ 376 Al Toon | .07 | .03 | .01 |
| ☐ 377 Johnny Hector | .04 | .02 | .01 |
| ☐ 378 Jeff Criswell | .04 | .02 | .01 |
| ☐ 379 Mike Haight | .04 | .02 | .01 |
| ☐ 380 Troy Benson | .04 | .02 | .01 |
| ☐ 381 Eric Allen | .07 | .03 | .01 |
| ☐ 382 Fred Barnett | .15 | .07 | .02 |
| ☐ 383 Jerome Brown | .07 | .03 | .01 |
| ☐ 384 Keith Byars | .07 | .03 | .01 |
| ☐ 385 Randall Cunningham | .10 | .05 | .01 |
| ☐ 386 Byron Evans | .07 | .03 | .01 |
| ☐ 387 Wes Hopkins | .04 | .02 | .01 |
| ☐ 388 Keith Jackson | .15 | .07 | .02 |
| ☐ 389 Seth Joyner UER | .07 | .03 | .01 |
| (Fumble recovery line not aligned) | | | |
| ☐ 390 Bobby Wilson | .10 | .05 | .01 |
| ☐ 391 Heath Sherman | .07 | .03 | .01 |
| ☐ 392 Clyde Simmons UER | .07 | .03 | .01 |
| (Listed as DT, should say DE) | | | |
| ☐ 393 Ben Smith | .04 | .02 | .01 |
| ☐ 394 Andre Waters | .04 | .02 | .01 |
| ☐ 395 Reggie White UER | .15 | .07 | .02 |
| (Derrick Thomas holds NFL record with 7 sacks) | | | |
| ☐ 396 Calvin Williams | .20 | .09 | .03 |
| ☐ 397 Al Harris | .04 | .02 | .01 |
| ☐ 398 Anthony Toney | .04 | .02 | .01 |

| | | | |
|---|---|---|---|
| ☐ 399 Mike Quick | .07 | .03 | .01 |
| ☐ 400 Anthony Bell | .04 | .02 | .01 |
| ☐ 401 Rich Camarillo | .04 | .02 | .01 |
| ☐ 402 Roy Green | .07 | .03 | .01 |
| ☐ 403 Ken Harvey | .04 | .02 | .01 |
| ☐ 404 Eric Hill | .04 | .02 | .01 |
| ☐ 405 Garth Jax UER | .04 | .02 | .01 |
| (Should have comma before "the" and after "Cowboys" on card back) | | | |
| ☐ 406 Ernie Jones | .04 | .02 | .01 |
| ☐ 407A Cedric Mack ERR | .10 | .05 | .01 |
| (Misspelled Cedrick on card front) | | | |
| ☐ 407B Cedric Mack COR | .10 | .05 | .01 |
| (NFL Exp. line is red instead of black) | | | |
| ☐ 408 Dexter Manley | .04 | .02 | .01 |
| ☐ 409 Tim McDonald | .07 | .03 | .01 |
| ☐ 410 Freddie Joe Nunn | .04 | .02 | .01 |
| ☐ 411 Ricky Proehl | .10 | .05 | .01 |
| ☐ 412 Moe Gardner | .10 | .05 | .01 |
| ☐ 413 Timm Rosenbach | .07 | .03 | .01 |
| ☐ 414 Luis Sharpe UER | .04 | .02 | .01 |
| (Lomiller, sic) | | | |
| ☐ 415 Vai Sikahema UER | .07 | .03 | .01 |
| (Front RB, back PR) | | | |
| ☐ 416 Anthony Thompson | .04 | .02 | .01 |
| ☐ 417 Ron Wolfley UER | .04 | .02 | .01 |
| (Missing NFL fact line under vital stats) | | | |
| ☐ 418 Lonnie Young | .04 | .02 | .01 |
| ☐ 419 Gary Anderson | .04 | .02 | .01 |
| ☐ 420 Bubby Brister | .07 | .03 | .01 |
| ☐ 421 Thomas Everett | .04 | .02 | .01 |
| ☐ 422 Eric Green | .15 | .07 | .02 |
| ☐ 423 Delton Hall | .04 | .02 | .01 |
| ☐ 424 Bryan Hinkle | .04 | .02 | .01 |
| ☐ 425 Merril Hoge | .07 | .03 | .01 |
| ☐ 426 Carnell Lake | .04 | .02 | .01 |
| ☐ 427 Louis Lipps | .07 | .03 | .01 |
| ☐ 428 David Little | .04 | .02 | .01 |
| ☐ 429 Greg Lloyd | .04 | .02 | .01 |
| ☐ 430 Mike Mularkey | .04 | .02 | .01 |
| ☐ 431 Keith Willis UER | .04 | .02 | .01 |
| (No period after C in L.C. Greenwood on back) | | | |
| ☐ 432 Dwayne Woodruff | .04 | .02 | .01 |
| ☐ 433 Rod Woodson UER | .10 | .05 | .01 |
| (No NFL experience listed on card) | | | |
| ☐ 434 Tim Worley | .07 | .03 | .01 |
| ☐ 435 Warren Williams | .04 | .02 | .01 |
| ☐ 436 Terry Long UER | .04 | .02 | .01 |
| (Not 5th NFL team, tied for 7th) | | | |
| ☐ 437 Martin Bayless | .04 | .02 | .01 |
| ☐ 438 Jarrod Bunch | .15 | .07 | .02 |
| ☐ 439 Marion Butts | .10 | .05 | .01 |
| ☐ 440 Gill Byrd UER | .07 | .03 | .01 |
| (Pickoffs misspelled as two words) | | | |
| ☐ 441 Arthur Cox | .04 | .02 | .01 |
| ☐ 442 John Friesz | .10 | .05 | .01 |
| ☐ 443 Leo Goeas | .04 | .02 | .01 |
| ☐ 444 Burt Grossman | .04 | .02 | .01 |
| ☐ 445 Courtney Hall UER | .04 | .02 | .01 |
| (In DYK section, is should be in) | | | |
| ☐ 446 Ronnie Harmon | .04 | .02 | .01 |
| ☐ 447 Nate Lewis | .25 | .11 | .03 |
| ☐ 448 Anthony Miller | .20 | .09 | .03 |
| ☐ 449 Leslie O'Neal | .07 | .03 | .01 |
| ☐ 450 Gary Plummer | .04 | .02 | .01 |
| ☐ 451 Junior Seau | .25 | .11 | .03 |
| ☐ 452 Billy Ray Smith | .04 | .02 | .01 |
| ☐ 453 Billy Joe Tolliver | .07 | .03 | .01 |
| ☐ 454 Broderick Thompson | .04 | .02 | .01 |
| ☐ 455 Lee Williams | .07 | .03 | .01 |
| ☐ 456 Michael Carter | .04 | .02 | .01 |
| ☐ 457 Mike Cofer | .04 | .02 | .01 |
| ☐ 458 Kevin Fagan | .04 | .02 | .01 |
| ☐ 459 Charles Haley | .07 | .03 | .01 |
| ☐ 460 Pierce Holt | .04 | .02 | .01 |
| ☐ 461 Johnny Jackson | .04 | .02 | .01 |
| ☐ 462 Brent Jones | .10 | .05 | .01 |
| ☐ 463 Guy McIntyre | .07 | .03 | .01 |
| ☐ 464 Joe Montana | 1.00 | .45 | .13 |
| ☐ 465A Bubba Paris ERR | .10 | .05 | .01 |
| (Misspelled Parris; reversed negative) | | | |
| ☐ 465B Bubba Paris ERR | 1.00 | .45 | .13 |
| (Misspelled Parris) | | | |
| ☐ 465C Bubba Paris COR | .10 | .05 | .01 |
| ☐ 466 Tom Rathman UER | .07 | .03 | .01 |
| (Born 10/7/62, not 11/7/62) | | | |
| ☐ 467 Jerry Rice UER | .75 | .35 | .09 |
| (4th to catch 100, should say 2nd) | | | |
| ☐ 468 Mike Sherrard | .07 | .03 | .01 |
| ☐ 469 John Taylor UER | .10 | .05 | .01 |
| (AL1-Time, sic) | | | |
| ☐ 470 Steve Young | .50 | .23 | .06 |
| ☐ 471 Dennis Brown | .04 | .02 | .01 |
| ☐ 472 Dexter Carter | .07 | .03 | .01 |
| ☐ 473 Bill Romanowski | .04 | .02 | .01 |
| ☐ 474 Dave Waymer | .04 | .02 | .01 |
| ☐ 475 Robert Blackmon | .04 | .02 | .01 |
| ☐ 476 Derrick Fenner | .07 | .03 | .01 |
| ☐ 477 Nesby Glasgow UER | .04 | .02 | .01 |
| (Missing total line for fumbles) | | | |
| ☐ 478 Jacob Green | .04 | .02 | .01 |
| ☐ 479 Andy Heck | .04 | .02 | .01 |
| ☐ 480 Norm Johnson UER | .04 | .02 | .01 |
| (They own and operate card store, not run) | | | |
| ☐ 481 Tommy Kane | .04 | .02 | .01 |
| ☐ 482 Cortez Kennedy | .25 | .11 | .03 |
| ☐ 483A Dave Krieg ERR | .13 | .06 | .02 |
| (Misspelled Kreig on both sides) | | | |
| ☐ 483B Dave Krieg COR | .13 | .06 | .02 |
| ☐ 484 Bryan Millard | .04 | .02 | .01 |
| ☐ 485 Joe Nash | .04 | .02 | .01 |
| ☐ 486 Rufus Porter | .04 | .02 | .01 |
| ☐ 487 Eugene Robinson | .04 | .02 | .01 |
| ☐ 488 Mike Tice | .10 | .05 | .01 |
| ☐ 489 Chris Warren | .30 | .14 | .04 |
| ☐ 490 John L. Williams UER | .07 | .03 | .01 |
| (No period after L on card front) | | | |
| ☐ 491 Terry Wooden | .04 | .02 | .01 |
| ☐ 492 Tony Woods | .04 | .02 | .01 |
| ☐ 493 Brian Blades | .10 | .05 | .01 |
| ☐ 494 Paul Skansi | .04 | .02 | .01 |
| ☐ 495 Gary Anderson | .07 | .03 | .01 |
| ☐ 496 Mark Carrier | .07 | .03 | .01 |
| ☐ 497 Chris Chandler | .04 | .02 | .01 |
| ☐ 498 Steve Christie | .04 | .02 | .01 |
| ☐ 499 Reggie Cobb | .25 | .11 | .03 |
| ☐ 500 Reuben Davis | .04 | .02 | .01 |
| ☐ 501 Willie Drewrey UER | .04 | .02 | .01 |
| (Misspelled Drewery on both sides of card) | | | |
| ☐ 502 Randy Grimes | .04 | .02 | .01 |
| ☐ 503 Paul Gruber | .07 | .03 | .01 |
| ☐ 504 Wayne Haddix | .04 | .02 | .01 |
| ☐ 505 Ron Hall | .04 | .02 | .01 |
| ☐ 506 Harry Hamilton | .04 | .02 | .01 |
| ☐ 507 Bruce Hill | .04 | .02 | .01 |
| ☐ 508 Eugene Marve | .04 | .02 | .01 |
| ☐ 509 Keith McCants | .04 | .02 | .01 |
| ☐ 510 Winston Moss | .04 | .02 | .01 |
| ☐ 511 Kevin Murphy | .04 | .02 | .01 |
| ☐ 512 Mark Robinson | .04 | .02 | .01 |
| ☐ 513 Vinny Testaverde | .10 | .05 | .01 |
| ☐ 514 Broderick Thomas | .07 | .03 | .01 |
| ☐ 515A Jeff Bostic UER | .08 | .04 | .01 |
| (Lomiller, sic; on back, word "goal" touches lower border) | | | |
| ☐ 515B Jeff Bostic UER | .08 | .04 | .01 |
| (Lomiller, sic; on back, word "goal" is away from border) | | | |
| ☐ 516 Todd Bowles | .04 | .02 | .01 |
| ☐ 517 Earnest Byner | .07 | .03 | .01 |
| ☐ 518 Gary Clark | .07 | .03 | .01 |
| ☐ 519 Craig Erickson | 1.00 | .45 | .13 |
| (Philadelphia Eagles) | | | |
| ☐ 520 Darryl Grant | .04 | .02 | .01 |
| ☐ 521 Darrell Green | .07 | .03 | .01 |
| ☐ 522 Russ Grimm | .04 | .02 | .01 |
| ☐ 523 Stan Humphries | .20 | .09 | .03 |
| ☐ 524 Joe Jacoby UER | .04 | .02 | .01 |
| (Lomiller, sic) | | | |
| ☐ 525 Jim Lachey | .04 | .02 | .01 |
| ☐ 526 Chip Lohmiller | .07 | .03 | .01 |
| ☐ 527 Charles Mann | .07 | .03 | .01 |
| ☐ 528 Wilber Marshall | .07 | .03 | .01 |
| ☐ 529A Art Monk | .16 | .07 | .02 |
| (On back, "y" in history touches copyright symbol) | | | |
| ☐ 529B Art Monk | .16 | .07 | .02 |
| (On back, "y" in history is away from symbol) | | | |
| ☐ 530 Tracy Rocker | .04 | .02 | .01 |
| ☐ 531 Mark Rypien | .10 | .05 | .01 |
| ☐ 532 Ricky Sanders UER | .07 | .03 | .01 |
| (Stats say caught 56, text says 57) | | | |
| ☐ 533 Alvin Walton UER | .04 | .02 | .01 |

(Listed as WR,
should be S)
- [ ] 534 Todd Marinovich UER .......... .08 .04 .01
  (17 percent, should
  be 71 percent)
  Los Angeles Raiders
- [ ] 535 Mike Dumas ......................... .05 .02 .01
  Houston Oilers
- [ ] 536A Russell Maryland ERR ........ .40 .18 .05
  (No highlight line)
  Dallas Cowboys
- [ ] 536B Russell Maryland COR ........ .40 .18 .05
  (Highlight line added)
  Dallas Cowboys
- [ ] 537 Eric Turner UER ................... .20 .09 .03
  (Don Rogers misspelled
  as Rodgers)
  Cleveland Browns
- [ ] 538 Ernie Mills .......................... .10 .05 .01
  Pittsburgh Steelers
- [ ] 539 Ed King .............................. .05 .02 .01
  Cleveland Browns
- [ ] 540 Michael Stonebreaker .......... .05 .02 .01
  Chicago Bears
- [ ] 541 Chris Zorich ....................... .25 .11 .03
  Chicago Bears
- [ ] 542A Mike Croel UER .................. .20 .09 .03
  (Missing highlight line
  under bio notes; front
  photo reversed negative;
  on back, "y" in weekly
  inside copyright)
  Denver Broncos
- [ ] 542B Mike Croel UER .................. .20 .09 .03
  (Missing highlight line
  under bio notes; front
  photo reversed negative;
  on back, "y" in weekly
  barely touches copyright)
  Denver Broncos
- [ ] 543 Eric Moten .......................... .05 .02 .01
  San Diego Chargers
- [ ] 544 Dan McGwire ...................... .10 .05 .01
  Seattle Seahawks
- [ ] 545 Keith Cash .......................... .25 .11 .03
  Washington Redskins
- [ ] 546 Kenny Walker UER ............... .05 .02 .01
  (Drafted 8th round,
  not 7th)
  Denver Broncos
- [ ] 547 Leroy Hoard UER ................. .07 .03 .01
  (LeROY on card;
  not a draft pick)
  Cleveland Browns
- [ ] 548 Luis Chrisobol UER .............. .05 .02 .01
  (Should should be
  showed; front LB,
  back G)
  New York Giants
- [ ] 549 Stacy Danley ...................... .05 .02 .01
  Seattle Seahawks
- [ ] 550 Todd Lyght .......................... .10 .05 .01
  Los Angeles Rams
- [ ] 551 Brett Favre .......................... 2.00 .90 .25
- [ ] 552 Mike Pritchard ..................... .75 .35 .09
- [ ] 553 Moe Gardner ....................... .05 .02 .01
- [ ] 554 Tim McKyer ......................... .08 .04 .01
- [ ] 555 Erric Pegram ....................... 1.25 .55 .16
- [ ] 556 Norm Johnson ..................... .05 .02 .01
- [ ] 557 Bruce Pickens ..................... .10 .05 .01
- [ ] 558 Henry Jones ........................ .25 .11 .03
- [ ] 559 Phil Hansen ......................... .15 .07 .02
- [ ] 560 Cornelius Bennett ................. .10 .05 .01
- [ ] 561 Stan Thomas ....................... .05 .02 .01
- [ ] 562 Chris Zorich ........................ .12 .05 .02
- [ ] 563 Anthony Morgan ................... .10 .05 .01
- [ ] 564 Darren Lewis ....................... .20 .09 .03
- [ ] 565 Mike Stonebreaker ............... .05 .02 .01
- [ ] 566 Alfred Williams ..................... .15 .07 .02
- [ ] 567 Lamar Rogers ...................... .05 .02 .01
- [ ] 568 Erik Wilhelm UER .................. .30 .14 .04
  (No NFL Experience
  line on card back)
- [ ] 569 Ed King .............................. .05 .02 .01
- [ ] 570 Michael Jackson ................... .75 .35 .09
- [ ] 571 James Jones ........................ .15 .07 .02
- [ ] 572 Russell Maryland ................... .15 .07 .02
- [ ] 573 Dixon Edwards ..................... .05 .02 .01
- [ ] 574 Darrick Brownlow .................. .05 .02 .01
- [ ] 575 Larry Brown ......................... .25 .11 .03
- [ ] 576 Mike Croel .......................... .10 .05 .01
- [ ] 577 Keith Traylor ........................ .05 .02 .01
- [ ] 578 Kenny Walker ....................... .05 .02 .01
- [ ] 579 Reggie Johnson .................... .15 .07 .02
- [ ] 580 Herman Moore ..................... 1.00 .45 .13
- [ ] 581 Kelvin Pritchett ..................... .05 .02 .01
- [ ] 582 Kevin Scott .......................... .15 .07 .02
- [ ] 583 Vinnie Clark ......................... .05 .02 .01

- [ ] 584 Esera Tuaolo ....................... .05 .02 .01
- [ ] 585 Don Davey ........................... .05 .02 .01
- [ ] 586 Blair Kiel ............................. .15 .07 .02
- [ ] 587 Mike Dumas ......................... .05 .02 .01
- [ ] 588 Darryll Lewis ........................ .10 .05 .01
- [ ] 589 John Flannery ...................... .05 .02 .01
- [ ] 590 Kevin Donnalley .................... .05 .02 .01
- [ ] 591 Shane Curry ......................... .05 .02 .01
- [ ] 592 Mark Vander Poel .................. .05 .02 .01
- [ ] 593 Dave McCloughan ................. .05 .02 .01
- [ ] 594 Mel Agee ............................ .05 .02 .01
- [ ] 595 Kerry Cash .......................... .25 .11 .03
- [ ] 596 Harvey Williams .................... .20 .09 .03
- [ ] 597 Joe Valerio .......................... .05 .02 .01
- [ ] 598 Tim Barnett UER ................... .20 .09 .03
  (Harvey Williams
  pictured on front)
- [ ] 599 Todd Marinovich ................... .08 .04 .01
- [ ] 600 Nick Bell ............................ .20 .09 .03
- [ ] 601 Roger Craig ......................... .08 .04 .01
- [ ] 602 Ronnie Lott .......................... .10 .05 .01
- [ ] 603 Mike Jones .......................... .15 .07 .02
- [ ] 604 Todd Lyght .......................... .05 .02 .01
- [ ] 605 Roman Phifer ....................... .10 .05 .01
- [ ] 606 David Lang .......................... .15 .07 .02
- [ ] 607 Aaron Craver ........................ .05 .02 .01
- [ ] 608 Mark Higgs .......................... .60 .25 .08
- [ ] 609 Chris Green ......................... .05 .02 .01
- [ ] 610 Randy Baldwin ...................... .10 .05 .01
- [ ] 611 Pat Harlow .......................... .05 .02 .01
- [ ] 612 Leonard Russell .................... 1.00 .45 .13
- [ ] 613 Jerome Henderson ................ .05 .02 .01
- [ ] 614 Scott Zolak UER .................... .15 .07 .02
  (Bio says drafted in
  1984, should be 1991)
- [ ] 615 Jon Vaughn .......................... .20 .09 .03
- [ ] 616 Harry Colon ......................... .05 .02 .01
- [ ] 617 Wesley Carroll ...................... .10 .05 .01
- [ ] 618 Quinn Early .......................... .08 .04 .01
- [ ] 619 Reggie Jones ....................... .15 .07 .02
- [ ] 620 Jarrod Bunch ........................ .05 .02 .01
- [ ] 621 Kanavis McGhee ................... .10 .05 .01
- [ ] 622 Ed McCaffrey ....................... .15 .07 .02
- [ ] 623 Browning Nagle ..................... .20 .09 .03
- [ ] 624 Mo Lewis ............................ .10 .05 .01
- [ ] 625 Blair Thomas ........................ .08 .04 .01
- [ ] 626 Antone Davis ........................ .05 .02 .01
- [ ] 627 Jim McMahon ....................... .10 .05 .01
- [ ] 628 Scott Kowalkowski ................. .05 .02 .01
- [ ] 629 Brad Goebel ........................ .10 .05 .01
- [ ] 630 William Thomas ..................... .05 .02 .01
- [ ] 631 Eric Swann .......................... .20 .09 .03
- [ ] 632 Mike Jones .......................... .10 .05 .01
- [ ] 633 Aeneas Williams .................... .15 .07 .02
- [ ] 634 Dexter Davis ........................ .05 .02 .01
- [ ] 635 Tom Tupa UER ..................... .08 .04 .01
  (Did play in 1990,
  but not as QB)
- [ ] 636 Johnny Johnson .................... .25 .11 .03
- [ ] 637 Randal Hill .......................... .25 .11 .03
- [ ] 638 Jeff Graham ......................... .40 .18 .05
- [ ] 639 Ernie Mills ........................... .05 .02 .01
- [ ] 640 Adrian Cooper ...................... .20 .09 .03
- [ ] 641 Stanley Richard ..................... .10 .05 .01
- [ ] 642 Eric Bieniemy ....................... .15 .07 .02
- [ ] 643 Eric Moten ........................... .05 .02 .01
- [ ] 644 Shawn Jefferson .................... .10 .05 .01
- [ ] 645 Ted Washington ..................... .05 .02 .01
- [ ] 646 John Johnson ....................... .05 .02 .01
- [ ] 647 Dan McGwire ....................... .05 .02 .01
- [ ] 648 Doug Thomas ....................... .05 .02 .01
- [ ] 649 David Daniels ....................... .05 .02 .01
- [ ] 650 John Kasay .......................... .15 .07 .02
- [ ] 651 Jeff Kemp ........................... .05 .02 .01
- [ ] 652 Charles McRae ..................... .05 .02 .01
- [ ] 653 Lawrence Dawsey .................. .20 .09 .03
- [ ] 654 Robert Wilson ....................... .05 .02 .01
- [ ] 655 Dexter Manley ...................... .05 .02 .01
- [ ] 656 Chuck Weatherspoon ............. .05 .02 .01
- [ ] 657 Tim Ryan ............................ .05 .02 .01
- [ ] 658 Bobby Wilson ....................... .05 .02 .01
- [ ] 659 Ricky Ervins ......................... .20 .09 .03
- [ ] 660 Matt Millen .......................... .08 .04 .01

# 1991 Pacific Checklists

Upon request from collectors, Pacific produced checklist cards for their 1991 regular issue first series cards. These checklist cards were numbered 1-5 and were randomly inserted into the late-run foil and wax packs. The cards are standard size, 2 1/2" by 3 1/2". According to Pacific, only 10,000 checklist sets were produced.

|  | MINT | EXC | G-VG |
|---|---|---|---|
| COMPLETE SET (5) .......................... | 10.00 | 4.50 | 1.25 |
| COMMON CARD SP (1-5) ................ | 2.50 | 1.15 | .30 |

| | MINT | EXC | G-VG |
|---|---|---|---|
| ☐ 1 Checklist 1 UER ....................... (Misspells 89 Greg Rakoczy 99 Jimmie Jones 106 Derrick Shepard) | 2.50 | 1.15 | .30 |
| ☐ 2 Checklist 2 ............................. | 2.50 | 1.15 | .30 |
| ☐ 3 Checklist 3 ............................. | 2.50 | 1.15 | .30 |
| ☐ 4 Checklist 4 ............................. | 2.50 | 1.15 | .30 |
| ☐ 5 Checklist 5 UER ....................... (Misspells 501 Willie Drewrey) | 2.50 | 1.15 | .30 |

| | | | |
|---|---|---|---|
| ☐ 11 Barry Sanders ....................... Detroit Lions | 14.00 | 6.25 | 1.75 |
| ☐ 12 Thurman Thomas..................... Buffalo Bills | 8.00 | 3.60 | 1.00 |
| ☐ 13 Morten Andersen ..................... New Orleans Saints | 2.25 | 1.00 | .30 |
| ☐ 14 Jerry Ball............................... Detroit Lions | 2.25 | 1.00 | .30 |
| ☐ 15 Jerome Brown......................... Philadelphia Eagles | 3.00 | 1.35 | .40 |
| ☐ 16 Reggie White.......................... Philadelphia Eagles | 4.00 | 1.80 | .50 |
| ☐ 17 Bruce Smith ........................... Buffalo Bills | 2.25 | 1.00 | .30 |
| ☐ 18 Derrick Thomas....................... Kansas City Chiefs | 5.00 | 2.30 | .60 |
| ☐ 19 Lawrence Taylor....................... New York Giants | 4.00 | 1.80 | .50 |
| ☐ 20 Charles Haley ......................... San Francisco 49ers | 2.25 | 1.00 | .30 |
| ☐ 21 Albert Lewis........................... Kansas City Chiefs | 2.25 | 1.00 | .30 |
| ☐ 22 Rod Woodson.......................... Pittsburgh Steelers | 3.00 | 1.35 | .40 |
| ☐ 23 David Fulcher ......................... Cincinnati Bengals | 2.25 | 1.00 | .30 |
| ☐ 24 Joey Browner .......................... Minnesota Vikings | 2.25 | 1.00 | .30 |
| ☐ 25 Sean Landeta .......................... New York Giants | 2.25 | 1.00 | .30 |

## 1991 Pacific Picks The Pros

This 25-card Pacific bonus set features the best player for each position, offensive and defensive (and rookie first pick Russell Maryland). The standard-size (2 1/2" by 3 1/2") cards have color action player photos on the fronts, with either gold or silver foil borders. The words "Pacific Picks the Pros" are printed vertically in a blue and red colored stripe on the left side of the picture. The horizontally oriented backs present career summaries in a diagonal direction on a red and blue background. There were 10,000 cards produced with a gold foil border, and an equal number with a silver foil border. The silver foil bonus cards were randomly inserted into jumbo 99-cent cello packs, while the gold foil bonus cards were randomly inserted into the wax and foil packs. The cards are numbered on the back. Price differences between silver and gold seem to be negligible at this time.

| | MINT | EXC | G-VG |
|---|---|---|---|
| COMPLETE SET (25)....................... | 90.00 | 40.00 | 11.50 |
| COMMON PLAYER (1-25)................. | 2.25 | 1.00 | .30 |
| *GOLD/SILVER: SAME PRICE ......... | | | |
| ☐ 1 Russell Maryland ...................... Dallas Cowboys | 5.00 | 2.30 | .60 |
| ☐ 2 Andre Reed ............................. Buffalo Bills | 3.00 | 1.35 | .40 |
| ☐ 3 Jerry Rice................................ San Francisco 49ers | 14.00 | 6.25 | 1.75 |
| ☐ 4 Keith Jackson........................... Philadelphia Eagles | 4.00 | 1.80 | .50 |
| ☐ 5 Jim Lachey.............................. Washington Redskins | 2.25 | 1.00 | .30 |
| ☐ 6 Anthony Munoz......................... Cincinnati Bengals | 3.00 | 1.35 | .40 |
| ☐ 7 Randall McDaniel ..................... Minnesota Vikings | 2.25 | 1.00 | .30 |
| ☐ 8 Bruce Matthews ....................... Houston Oilers | 2.25 | 1.00 | .30 |
| ☐ 9 Kent Hull ............................... Buffalo Bills | 2.25 | 1.00 | .30 |
| ☐ 10 Joe Montana .......................... San Francisco 49ers | 20.00 | 9.00 | 2.50 |

## 1991 Pacific Flash Cards

The 1991 Pacific Flash Cards football set contains 110 cards measuring the standard size (2 1/2" by 3 1/2"). The front design has brightly colored triangles on a white card face and a math problem involving addition, subtraction, multiplication, or division. By performing one of these operations on the two numbers, one arrives at the uniform number of the player featured on the backs. The back design is similar to the front but has a glossy color game shot of the player, with either career summary or last year's highlights below the picture. The cards are numbered on the back.

| | MINT | EXC | G-VG |
|---|---|---|---|
| COMPLETE SET (110)...................... | 7.00 | 2.80 | .70 |
| COMMON PLAYER (1-110)............... | .05 | .02 | .00 |
| ☐ 1 Steve Young............................. San Francisco 49ers | .35 | .14 | .03 |
| ☐ 2 Hart Lee Dykes......................... New England Patriots | .05 | .02 | .00 |
| ☐ 3 Timm Rosenbach ...................... Phoenix Cardinals | .05 | .02 | .00 |
| ☐ 4 Andre Collins .......................... Washington Redskins | .05 | .02 | .00 |
| ☐ 5 Johnny Johnson ....................... Phoenix Cardinals | .25 | .10 | .02 |
| ☐ 6 Nick Lowery ............................ Kansas City Chiefs | .05 | .02 | .00 |
| ☐ 7 John Stephens ......................... New England Patriots | .10 | .04 | .01 |
| ☐ 8 Jim Arnold ............................. Detroit Lions | .05 | .02 | .00 |
| ☐ 9 Steve DeBerg .......................... Kansas City Chiefs | .10 | .04 | .01 |
| ☐ 10 Christian Okoye ...................... Kansas City Chiefs | .05 | .02 | .00 |
| ☐ 11 Eric Swann ............................ Phoenix Cardinals | .10 | .04 | .01 |
| ☐ 12 Jerry Robinson ....................... Los Angeles Raiders | .05 | .02 | .00 |
| ☐ 13 Steve Wisniewski .................... Los Angeles Raiders | .05 | .02 | .00 |
| ☐ 14 Jim Harbaugh ......................... | .10 | .04 | .01 |

Chicago Bears
☐ 15 Steve Broussard .05 .02 .00
Atlanta Falcons
☐ 16 Mike Singletary UER .15 .06 .01
Chicago Bears
(Joined Bears in '80,
should say '81)
☐ 17 Tim Green .05 .02 .00
Atlanta Falcons
☐ 18 Roger Craig .15 .06 .01
Los Angeles Raiders
☐ 19 Maury Buford .05 .02 .00
Chicago Bears
☐ 20 Marcus Allen .25 .10 .02
Los Angeles Raiders
☐ 21 Deion Sanders .35 .14 .03
Atlanta Falcons
☐ 22 Chris Miller .25 .10 .02
Atlanta Falcons
☐ 23 Joey Browner .05 .02 .00
Minnesota Vikings
☐ 24 Bubby Brister .05 .02 .00
Pittsburgh Steelers
☐ 25 Buford McGee .05 .02 .00
Los Angeles Rams
☐ 26 Ed West .05 .02 .00
Green Bay Packers
☐ 27 Mark Murphy .05 .02 .00
Green Bay Packers
☐ 28 Tim Worley .10 .04 .01
Pittsburgh Steelers
☐ 29 Keith Willis .05 .02 .00
Pittsburgh Steelers
☐ 30 Rich Gannon .05 .02 .00
Minnesota Vikings
☐ 31 Jim Everett .10 .04 .01
Los Angeles Rams
☐ 32 Duval Love .05 .02 .00
Los Angeles Rams
☐ 33 Bob Nelson .05 .02 .00
Green Bay Packers
☐ 34 Anthony Munoz .15 .06 .01
Cincinnati Bengals
☐ 35 Boomer Esiason .20 .08 .02
Cincinnati Bengals
☐ 36 Kenny Walker .10 .04 .01
Denver Broncos
☐ 37 Mike Horan .05 .02 .00
Denver Broncos
☐ 38 Gary Kubiak .10 .04 .01
Denver Broncos
☐ 39 David Treadwell .05 .02 .00
Denver Broncos
☐ 40 Robert Wilson .10 .04 .01
Tampa Bay Buccaneers
☐ 41 Lewis Billups .05 .02 .00
Cincinnati Bengals
☐ 42 Kevin Mack .05 .02 .00
Cleveland Browns
☐ 43 John Elway .75 .30 .07
Denver Broncos
☐ 44 Lee Johnson .05 .02 .00
Cincinnati Bengals
☐ 45 Ken Willis .05 .02 .00
Dallas Cowboys
☐ 46 Herman Moore .40 .16 .04
Detroit Lions
☐ 47 Eddie Murray .05 .02 .00
Detroit Lions
☐ 48 Mike Saxon .05 .02 .00
Dallas Cowboys
☐ 49 John L. Williams .10 .04 .01
Seattle Seahawks
☐ 50 Barry Sanders .75 .30 .07
Detroit Lions
☐ 51 Andre Ware .20 .08 .02
Detroit Lions
☐ 52 Dave Krieg .10 .04 .01
Seattle Seahawks
☐ 53 Cortez Kennedy .25 .10 .02
Seattle Seahawks
☐ 54 Bo Jackson .50 .20 .05
Los Angeles Raiders
☐ 55 Derrick Fenner .10 .04 .01
Seattle Seahawks
☐ 56 Steve Walsh .10 .04 .01
New Orleans Saints
☐ 57 Brett Maxie .05 .02 .00
New Orleans Saints
☐ 58 Stan Brock .05 .02 .00
New Orleans Saints
☐ 59 DeMond Winston .05 .02 .00
New Orleans Saints
☐ 60 Sam Mills .05 .02 .00
New Orleans Saints
☐ 61 Eric Martin .10 .04 .01
New Orleans Saints
☐ 62 Michael Carter .10 .04 .01

San Francisco 49ers
☐ 63 Steve Wallace .05 .02 .00
San Francisco 49ers
☐ 64 Jesse Sapolu .05 .02 .00
San Francisco 49ers
☐ 65 Bill Romanowski .05 .02 .00
San Francisco 49ers
☐ 66 Joe Montana 1.50 .60 .15
San Francisco 49ers
☐ 67 Sean Landeta .05 .02 .00
New York Giants
☐ 68 Doug Riesenberg .05 .02 .00
New York Giants
☐ 69 Myron Guyton .05 .02 .00
New York Giants
☐ 70 Andre Reed .15 .06 .01
Buffalo Bills
☐ 71 John Elliott .05 .02 .00
New York Giants
☐ 72 Jeff Hostetler .15 .06 .01
New York Giants
☐ 73 Rohn Stark .05 .02 .00
Indianapolis Colts
☐ 74 Jeff George .20 .08 .02
Indianapolis Colts
☐ 75 Duane Bickett .05 .02 .00
Indianapolis Colts
☐ 76 Emmitt Smith 1.50 .60 .15
Dallas Cowboys
☐ 77 Michael Irvin .50 .20 .05
Dallas Cowboys
☐ 78 Tony Stargell .05 .02 .00
New York Jets
☐ 79 Kyle Clifton .05 .02 .00
New York Jets
☐ 80 John Booty .05 .02 .00
New York Jets
☐ 81 Fred Barnett .20 .08 .02
New York Jets
☐ 82 Blair Thomas .15 .06 .01
New York Jets
☐ 83 Erik McMillan .05 .02 .00
New York Jets
☐ 84 Broderick Thomas .10 .04 .01
Tampa Bay Buccaneers
☐ 85 Jim Skow .05 .02 .00
Tampa Bay Buccaneers
☐ 86 Gary Anderson .10 .04 .01
Tampa Bay Buccaneers
☐ 87 Mark Robinson .05 .02 .00
Tampa Bay Buccaneers
☐ 88 Steve Christie .05 .02 .00
Tampa Bay Buccaneers
☐ 89 Cody Carlson .25 .10 .02
Houston Oilers
☐ 90 Warren Moon .30 .12 .03
Houston Oilers
☐ 91 Lorenzo White .10 .04 .01
Houston Oilers
☐ 92 Reggie Roby .05 .02 .00
Miami Dolphins
☐ 93 Jim C. Jensen .05 .02 .00
Miami Dolphins
☐ 94 Mark Clayton .15 .06 .01
Miami Dolphins
☐ 95 Willie Gault .10 .04 .01
Los Angeles Raiders
☐ 96 Don Mosebar .05 .02 .00
Los Angeles Raiders
☐ 97 Gary Plummer .05 .02 .00
San Diego Chargers
☐ 98 Leslie O'Neal .10 .04 .01
San Diego Chargers
☐ 99 Neal Anderson .15 .06 .01
Chicago Bears
☐ 100 Derrick Thomas .25 .10 .02
Kansas City Chiefs
☐ 101 Luis Sharpe .05 .02 .00
Phoenix Cardinals
☐ 102 D.J. Dozier .05 .02 .00
Minnesota Vikings
☐ 103 Jarrod Bunch .10 .04 .01
New York Giants
☐ 104 Mark Ingram .05 .02 .00
New York Giants
☐ 105 James Lofton .15 .06 .01
Buffalo Bills
☐ 106 Jay Schroeder .10 .04 .01
Los Angeles Raiders
☐ 107 Ronnie Lott .15 .06 .01
Los Angeles Raiders
☐ 108 Todd Marinovich .10 .04 .01
Los Angeles Raiders
☐ 109 Chris Zorich .20 .08 .02
Chicago Bears
☐ 110 Charles McRae .05 .02 .00
Tampa Bay Buccaneers

## 1992 Pacific Prototypes

The 1992 Pacific prototypes were given away at the Super Bowl card show in Minneapolis and used as sales samples. The cards measure the standard size (2 1/2" by 3 1/2"). The cards were intended to be a preview for the upcoming 1992 Pacific set since they used the new card design. The production run was approximately 5,000 sets. The fronts feature glossy color action player photos enclosed by white borders. The player's name is printed vertically in a color stripe running down the left side of the picture, with the team helmet in the lower left corner. In a horizontal format, the backs have a second color photo and player profile. The cards are numbered on the back.

|  | MINT | EXC | G-VG |
|---|---|---|---|
| COMPLETE SET (6) | 45.00 | 18.00 | 4.50 |
| COMMON PLAYER (1-6) | 5.00 | 2.00 | .50 |
| ☐ 1 Warren Moon | 10.00 | 4.00 | 1.00 |
|    Houston Oilers | | | |
| ☐ 2 Pat Swilling | 5.00 | 2.00 | .50 |
|    New Orleans Saints | | | |
| ☐ 3 Michael Irvin | 12.00 | 5.00 | 1.20 |
|    Dallas Cowboys | | | |
| ☐ 4 Haywood Jeffires | 7.50 | 3.00 | .75 |
|    Houston Oilers | | | |
| ☐ 5 Thurman Thomas | 12.00 | 5.00 | 1.20 |
|    Buffalo Bills | | | |
| ☐ 6 Leonard Russell | 7.50 | 3.00 | .75 |
|    New England Patriots | | | |

## 1992 Pacific

The 1992 Pacific Plus set consists of 660 cards measuring the standard size (2 1/2" by 3 1/2"). The cards were issued in two series of 330 cards each. The fronts feature glossy color action player photos enclosed by white borders. The player's name is printed vertically in a color stripe running down the left side of the picture, with the team helmet in the lower left corner. In a horizontal format, the backs have a second color photo and player profile. The cards are numbered on the back and checklisted below alphabetically according to teams as follows: Atlanta Falcons (1-13), Buffalo Bills (14-26), Chicago Bears (27-39), Cincinnati Bengals (40-51), Cleveland Browns (52-61), Dallas Cowboys (62-72), Denver Broncos (73-86), Detroit Lions (87-97), Green Bay Packers (98-108), Houston Oilers (109-119), Indianapolis Colts (120-130), Kansas City Chiefs (131-143), Los Angeles Raiders (144-154), Los Angeles Rams (155-165), Miami Dolphins (166-176), Minnesota Vikings (177-187), New England Patriots (188-198), New Orleans Saints (199-209), New York Giants (210-220), New York Jets (221-231), Philadelphia Eagles (232-242), Phoenix Cardinals (243-253), Pittsburgh Steelers (254-264), San Diego Chargers (265-275), San Francisco 49ers (276-286), Seattle Seahawks (287-297), Tampa

Bay Buccaneers (298-308), Washington Redskins (309-319), Draft Picks (320-330), Atlanta Falcons (331-341), Buffalo Bills (342-352), Chicago Bears (353-363), Cincinnati Bengals (364-374), Cleveland Browns (375-385), Dallas Cowboys (386-396), Denver Broncos (397-407), Detroit Lions (408-418), Green Bay Packers (419-429), Houston Oilers (430-440), Indianapolis Colts (441-451), Kansas City Chiefs (452-463), Los Angeles Raiders (464-474), Los Angeles Rams (475-487), Miami Dolphins (488-498), Minnesota Vikings (499-509), New England Patriots (510-522), New Orleans Saints (523-535), New York Giants (536-547), New York Jets (548-558), Philadelphia Eagles (559-570), Phoenix Cardinals (571-582), Pittsburgh Steelers (583-593), San Diego Chargers (594-604), San Francisco 49ers (605-615), Seattle Seahawks (616-626), Tampa Bay Buccaneers (627-637), Washington Redskins (638-648), and Rookies (649-660). Second series highlights include a nine-card Legends of the Game subset featuring Hall of Famer Bob Griese, with 1,000 numbered cards bearing his autograph. In addition, "Pacific Picks the Pros" gold-foil cards were randomly inserted in 14-card foil packs, while silver-foil versions of the same subset were inserted in 24-card foil packs. The cards were available in foil packs, jumbo packs, five-card change-maker packs (25 cents), and factory sets. The factory sets included the Stat Leaders insert set. The key Rookie Cards in this set are Steve Bono, Terrell Buckley, Amp Lee, Tony Smith, and Tommy Vardell.

|  | MINT | EXC | G-VG |
|---|---|---|---|
| COMPLETE SET (660) | 20.00 | 9.00 | 2.50 |
| COMPLETE FACT.SET (690) | 25.00 | 11.50 | 3.10 |
| COMPLETE SERIES 1 (330) | 10.00 | 4.50 | 1.25 |
| COMPLETE SERIES 2 (330) | 10.00 | 4.50 | 1.25 |
| COMMON PLAYER (1-330) | .04 | .02 | .01 |
| COMMON PLAYER (331-660) | .04 | .02 | .01 |
| ☐ 1 Steve Broussard | .08 | .04 | .01 |
| ☐ 2 Darion Conner | .04 | .02 | .01 |
| ☐ 3 Tory Epps | .04 | .02 | .01 |
| ☐ 4 Michael Haynes | .30 | .14 | .04 |
| ☐ 5 Chris Hinton | .04 | .02 | .01 |
| ☐ 6 Mike Kenn | .08 | .04 | .01 |
| ☐ 7 Tim McKyer | .08 | .04 | .01 |
| ☐ 8 Chris Miller | .10 | .05 | .01 |
| ☐ 9 Erric Pegram | .40 | .18 | .05 |
| ☐ 10 Mike Pritchard | .25 | .11 | .03 |
| ☐ 11 Moe Gardner | .04 | .02 | .01 |
| ☐ 12 Tim Green | .04 | .02 | .01 |
| ☐ 13 Norm Johnson | .04 | .02 | .01 |
| ☐ 14 Don Beebe | .10 | .05 | .01 |
| ☐ 15 Cornelius Bennett | .10 | .05 | .01 |
| ☐ 16 Al Edwards | .04 | .02 | .01 |
| ☐ 17 Mark Kelso | .04 | .02 | .01 |
| ☐ 18 James Lofton | .10 | .05 | .01 |
| ☐ 19 Frank Reich | .08 | .04 | .01 |
| ☐ 20 Leon Seals | .04 | .02 | .01 |
| ☐ 21 Darryl Talley | .08 | .04 | .01 |
| ☐ 22 Thurman Thomas | .40 | .18 | .05 |
| ☐ 23 Kent Hull | .04 | .02 | .01 |
| ☐ 24 Jeff Wright | .04 | .02 | .01 |
| ☐ 25 Nate Odomes | .08 | .04 | .01 |
| ☐ 26 Carwell Gardner | .04 | .02 | .01 |
| ☐ 27 Neal Anderson | .08 | .04 | .01 |
| ☐ 28 Mark Carrier | .08 | .04 | .01 |
| ☐ 29 Johnny Bailey | .04 | .02 | .01 |
| ☐ 30 Jim Harbaugh | .08 | .04 | .01 |
| ☐ 31 Jay Hilgenberg | .08 | .04 | .01 |
| ☐ 32 William Perry | .08 | .04 | .01 |
| ☐ 33 Wendell Davis | .04 | .02 | .01 |
| ☐ 34 Donnell Woolford | .04 | .02 | .01 |
| ☐ 35 Keith Van Horne | .04 | .02 | .01 |
| ☐ 36 Shaun Gayle | .04 | .02 | .01 |
| ☐ 37 Tom Waddle | .10 | .05 | .01 |
| ☐ 38 Chris Zorich | .08 | .04 | .01 |
| ☐ 39 Tom Thayer | .04 | .02 | .01 |
| ☐ 40 Rickey Dixon | .04 | .02 | .01 |
| ☐ 41 James Francis | .08 | .04 | .01 |
| ☐ 42 David Fulcher | .04 | .02 | .01 |
| ☐ 43 Reggie Rembert | .04 | .02 | .01 |
| ☐ 44 Anthony Munoz | .08 | .04 | .01 |
| ☐ 45 Harold Green | .08 | .04 | .01 |
| ☐ 46 Mitchell Price | .04 | .02 | .01 |
| ☐ 47 Rodney Holman | .04 | .02 | .01 |
| ☐ 48 Bruce Kozerski | .04 | .02 | .01 |
| ☐ 49 Bruce Reimers | .04 | .02 | .01 |
| ☐ 50 Erik Wilhelm | .04 | .02 | .01 |
| ☐ 51 Harlon Barnett | .04 | .02 | .01 |
| ☐ 52 Mike Johnson | .04 | .02 | .01 |
| ☐ 53 Brian Brennan | .04 | .02 | .01 |
| ☐ 54 Ed King | .04 | .02 | .01 |
| ☐ 55 Reggie Langhorne | .08 | .04 | .01 |
| ☐ 56 James Jones | .04 | .02 | .01 |
| ☐ 57 Mike Baab | .04 | .02 | .01 |
| ☐ 58 Dan Fike | .04 | .02 | .01 |
| ☐ 59 Frank Minnifield | .04 | .02 | .01 |
| ☐ 60 Clay Matthews | .08 | .04 | .01 |
| ☐ 61 Kevin Mack | .08 | .04 | .01 |
| ☐ 62 Tony Casillas | .04 | .02 | .01 |

| | | | |
|---|---|---|---|
| ☐ 63 Jay Novacek | .15 | .07 | .02 |
| ☐ 64 Larry Brown | .04 | .02 | .01 |
| ☐ 65 Michael Irvin | .50 | .23 | .06 |
| ☐ 66 Jack Del Rio | .04 | .02 | .01 |
| ☐ 67 Ken Willis | .04 | .02 | .01 |
| ☐ 68 Emmitt Smith | 2.00 | .90 | .25 |
| ☐ 69 Alan Veingrad | .04 | .02 | .01 |
| ☐ 70 John Gesek | .04 | .02 | .01 |
| ☐ 71 Steve Beuerlein | .20 | .09 | .03 |
| ☐ 72 Vinson Smith | .10 | .05 | .01 |
| ☐ 73 Steve Atwater | .08 | .04 | .01 |
| ☐ 74 Mike Croel | .08 | .04 | .01 |
| ☐ 75 John Elway | .40 | .18 | .05 |
| ☐ 76 Gaston Green | .08 | .04 | .01 |
| ☐ 77 Mike Horan | .04 | .02 | .01 |
| ☐ 78 Vance Johnson | .08 | .04 | .01 |
| ☐ 79 Karl Mecklenburg | .08 | .04 | .01 |
| ☐ 80 Shannon Sharpe | .25 | .11 | .03 |
| ☐ 81 David Treadwell | .04 | .02 | .01 |
| ☐ 82 Kenny Walker | .04 | .02 | .01 |
| ☐ 83 Greg Lewis | .04 | .02 | .01 |
| ☐ 84 Shawn Moore | .04 | .02 | .01 |
| ☐ 85 Alton Montgomery | .04 | .02 | .01 |
| ☐ 86 Michael Young | .04 | .02 | .01 |
| ☐ 87 Jerry Ball | .08 | .04 | .01 |
| ☐ 88 Bennie Blades | .04 | .02 | .01 |
| ☐ 89 Mel Gray | .08 | .04 | .01 |
| ☐ 90 Herman Moore | .30 | .14 | .04 |
| ☐ 91 Erik Kramer | .15 | .07 | .02 |
| ☐ 92 Willie Green | .04 | .02 | .01 |
| ☐ 93 George Jamison | .04 | .02 | .01 |
| ☐ 94 Chris Spielman | .08 | .04 | .01 |
| ☐ 95 Kelvin Pritchett | .04 | .02 | .01 |
| ☐ 96 William White | .04 | .02 | .01 |
| ☐ 97 Mike Utley | .20 | .09 | .03 |
| ☐ 98 Tony Bennett | .08 | .04 | .01 |
| ☐ 99 LeRoy Butler | .04 | .02 | .01 |
| ☐ 100 Vinnie Clark | .04 | .02 | .01 |
| ☐ 101 Ron Hallstrom | .04 | .02 | .01 |
| ☐ 102 Chris Jacke | .04 | .02 | .01 |
| ☐ 103 Tony Mandarich | .04 | .02 | .01 |
| ☐ 104 Sterling Sharpe | .50 | .23 | .06 |
| ☐ 105 Don Majkowski | .08 | .04 | .01 |
| ☐ 106 Johnny Holland | .04 | .02 | .01 |
| ☐ 107 Esera Tuaolo | .04 | .02 | .01 |
| ☐ 108 Darrell Thompson | .08 | .04 | .01 |
| ☐ 109 Bubba McDowell | .04 | .02 | .01 |
| ☐ 110 Curtis Duncan | .08 | .04 | .01 |
| ☐ 111 Lamar Lathon | .04 | .02 | .01 |
| ☐ 112 Drew Hill | .08 | .04 | .01 |
| ☐ 113 Bruce Matthews | .08 | .04 | .01 |
| ☐ 114 Bo Orlando | .15 | .07 | .02 |
| ☐ 115 Don Maggs | .04 | .02 | .01 |
| ☐ 116 Lorenzo White | .08 | .04 | .01 |
| ☐ 117 Ernest Givins | .08 | .04 | .01 |
| ☐ 118 Tony Jones | .04 | .02 | .01 |
| ☐ 119 Dean Steinkuhler | .04 | .02 | .01 |
| ☐ 120 Dean Biasucci | .04 | .02 | .01 |
| ☐ 121 Duane Bickett | .04 | .02 | .01 |
| ☐ 122 Bill Brooks | .08 | .04 | .01 |
| ☐ 123 Ken Clark | .04 | .02 | .01 |
| ☐ 124 Jessie Hester | .04 | .02 | .01 |
| ☐ 125 Anthony Johnson | .04 | .02 | .01 |
| ☐ 126 Chip Banks | .04 | .02 | .01 |
| ☐ 127 Mike Prior | .04 | .02 | .01 |
| ☐ 128 Rohn Stark | .04 | .02 | .01 |
| ☐ 129 Jeff Herrod | .04 | .02 | .01 |
| ☐ 130 Clarence Verdin | .04 | .02 | .01 |
| ☐ 131 Tim Manoa | .04 | .02 | .01 |
| ☐ 132 Brian Baldinger | .04 | .02 | .01 |
| ☐ 133 Tim Barnett | .08 | .04 | .01 |
| ☐ 134 J.J. Birden | .08 | .04 | .01 |
| ☐ 135 Deron Cherry | .04 | .02 | .01 |
| ☐ 136 Steve DeBerg | .08 | .04 | .01 |
| ☐ 137 Nick Lowery | .08 | .04 | .01 |
| ☐ 138 Todd McNair | .04 | .02 | .01 |
| ☐ 139 Christian Okoye | .08 | .04 | .01 |
| ☐ 140 Mark Vlasic | .08 | .04 | .01 |
| ☐ 141 Dan Saleaumua | .04 | .02 | .01 |
| ☐ 142 Neil Smith | .10 | .05 | .01 |
| ☐ 143 Robb Thomas | .04 | .02 | .01 |
| ☐ 144 Eddie Anderson | .04 | .02 | .01 |
| ☐ 145 Nick Bell | .08 | .04 | .01 |
| ☐ 146 Tim Brown | .25 | .11 | .03 |
| ☐ 147 Roger Craig | .08 | .04 | .01 |
| ☐ 148 Jeff Gossett | .04 | .02 | .01 |
| ☐ 149 Ethan Horton | .04 | .02 | .01 |
| ☐ 150 Jamie Holland | .04 | .02 | .01 |
| ☐ 151 Jeff Jaeger | .04 | .02 | .01 |
| ☐ 152 Todd Marinovich | .04 | .02 | .01 |
| ☐ 153 Marcus Allen | .08 | .04 | .01 |
| ☐ 154 Steve Smith | .08 | .04 | .01 |
| ☐ 155 Flipper Anderson | .08 | .04 | .01 |
| ☐ 156 Robert Delpino | .08 | .04 | .01 |
| ☐ 157 Cleveland Gary | .08 | .04 | .01 |
| ☐ 158 Kevin Greene | .08 | .04 | .01 |
| ☐ 159 Dale Hatcher | .04 | .02 | .01 |

| | | | |
|---|---|---|---|
| ☐ 160 Duval Love | .04 | .02 | .01 |
| ☐ 161 Ron Brown | .04 | .02 | .01 |
| ☐ 162 Jackie Slater | .08 | .04 | .01 |
| ☐ 163 Doug Smith | .04 | .02 | .01 |
| ☐ 164 Aaron Cox | .04 | .02 | .01 |
| ☐ 165 Larry Kelm | .04 | .02 | .01 |
| ☐ 166 Mark Clayton | .08 | .04 | .01 |
| ☐ 167 Louis Oliver | .08 | .04 | .01 |
| ☐ 168 Mark Higgs | .10 | .05 | .01 |
| ☐ 169 Aaron Craver | .04 | .02 | .01 |
| ☐ 170 Sammie Smith | .04 | .02 | .01 |
| ☐ 171 Tony Paige | .04 | .02 | .01 |
| ☐ 172 Jeff Cross | .04 | .02 | .01 |
| ☐ 173 David Griggs | .04 | .02 | .01 |
| ☐ 174 Richmond Webb | .08 | .04 | .01 |
| ☐ 175 Vestee Jackson | .04 | .02 | .01 |
| ☐ 176 Jim C. Jensen | .04 | .02 | .01 |
| ☐ 177 Anthony Carter | .08 | .04 | .01 |
| ☐ 178 Cris Carter | .10 | .05 | .01 |
| ☐ 179 Chris Doleman | .08 | .04 | .01 |
| ☐ 180 Rich Gannon | .04 | .02 | .01 |
| ☐ 181 Al Noga | .04 | .02 | .01 |
| ☐ 182 Randall McDaniel | .04 | .02 | .01 |
| ☐ 183 Todd Scott | .04 | .02 | .01 |
| ☐ 184 Henry Thomas | .04 | .02 | .01 |
| ☐ 185 Felix Wright | .04 | .02 | .01 |
| ☐ 186 Gary Zimmerman | .04 | .02 | .01 |
| ☐ 187 Herschel Walker | .10 | .05 | .01 |
| ☐ 188 Vincent Brown | .04 | .02 | .01 |
| ☐ 189 Harry Colon | .04 | .02 | .01 |
| ☐ 190 Irving Fryar | .08 | .04 | .01 |
| ☐ 191 Marv Cook | .08 | .04 | .01 |
| ☐ 192 Leonard Russell | .30 | .14 | .04 |
| ☐ 193 Hugh Millen | .04 | .02 | .01 |
| ☐ 194 Pat Harlow | .04 | .02 | .01 |
| ☐ 195 Jon Vaughn | .04 | .02 | .01 |
| ☐ 196 Ben Coates | .35 | .16 | .04 |
| ☐ 197 Johnny Rembert | .04 | .02 | .01 |
| ☐ 198 Greg McMurtry | .04 | .02 | .01 |
| ☐ 199 Morten Andersen | .08 | .04 | .01 |
| ☐ 200 Tommy Barnhardt | .04 | .02 | .01 |
| ☐ 201 Bobby Hebert | .10 | .05 | .01 |
| ☐ 202 Dalton Hilliard | .08 | .04 | .01 |
| ☐ 203 Sam Mills | .08 | .04 | .01 |
| ☐ 204 Pat Swilling | .08 | .04 | .01 |
| ☐ 205 Rickey Jackson | .08 | .04 | .01 |
| ☐ 206 Stan Brock | .04 | .02 | .01 |
| ☐ 207 Reggie Jones | .04 | .02 | .01 |
| ☐ 208 Gill Fenerty | .04 | .02 | .01 |
| ☐ 209 Eric Martin | .08 | .04 | .01 |
| ☐ 210 Matt Bahr | .04 | .02 | .01 |
| ☐ 211 Rodney Hampton | .40 | .18 | .05 |
| ☐ 212 Jeff Hostetler | .15 | .07 | .02 |
| ☐ 213 Pepper Johnson | .08 | .04 | .01 |
| ☐ 214 Leonard Marshall | .08 | .04 | .01 |
| ☐ 215 Doug Riesenberg | .04 | .02 | .01 |
| ☐ 216 Stephen Baker | .04 | .02 | .01 |
| ☐ 217 Mike Fox | .04 | .02 | .01 |
| ☐ 218 Bart Oates | .04 | .02 | .01 |
| ☐ 219 Everson Walls | .04 | .02 | .01 |
| ☐ 220 Gary Reasons | .04 | .02 | .01 |
| ☐ 221 Jeff Lageman | .04 | .02 | .01 |
| ☐ 222 Joe Kelly | .04 | .02 | .01 |
| ☐ 223 Mo Lewis | .04 | .02 | .01 |
| ☐ 224 Tony Stargell | .04 | .02 | .01 |
| ☐ 225 Jim Sweeney | .04 | .02 | .01 |
| ☐ 226 Freeman McNeil | .04 | .02 | .01 |
| ☐ 227 Brian Washington | .04 | .02 | .01 |
| ☐ 228 Johnny Hector | .04 | .02 | .01 |
| ☐ 229 Terance Mathis | .04 | .02 | .01 |
| ☐ 230 Rob Moore | .10 | .05 | .01 |
| ☐ 231 Brad Baxter | .08 | .04 | .01 |
| ☐ 232 Eric Allen | .08 | .04 | .01 |
| ☐ 233 Fred Barnett | .10 | .05 | .01 |
| ☐ 234 Jerome Brown | .08 | .04 | .01 |
| ☐ 235 Keith Byars | .08 | .04 | .01 |
| ☐ 236 William Thomas | .04 | .02 | .01 |
| ☐ 237 Jessie Small | .04 | .02 | .01 |
| ☐ 238 Robert Drummond | .04 | .02 | .01 |
| ☐ 239 Reggie White | .15 | .07 | .02 |
| ☐ 240 James Joseph | .04 | .02 | .01 |
| ☐ 241 Brad Goebel | .10 | .05 | .01 |
| ☐ 242 Clyde Simmons | .08 | .04 | .01 |
| ☐ 243 Rich Camarillo | .04 | .02 | .01 |
| ☐ 244 Ken Harvey | .04 | .02 | .01 |
| ☐ 245 Garth Jax | .04 | .02 | .01 |
| ☐ 246 Johnny Johnson UER | .10 | .05 | .01 |
| (Photo on back not him) | | | |
| ☐ 247 Mike Jones | .04 | .02 | .01 |
| ☐ 248 Ernie Jones | .04 | .02 | .01 |
| ☐ 249 Tom Tupa | .08 | .04 | .01 |
| ☐ 250 Ron Wolfley | .04 | .02 | .01 |
| ☐ 251 Luis Sharpe | .04 | .02 | .01 |
| ☐ 252 Eric Swann | .08 | .04 | .01 |
| ☐ 253 Anthony Thompson | .04 | .02 | .01 |
| ☐ 254 Gary Anderson | .04 | .02 | .01 |
| ☐ 255 Dermontti Dawson | .04 | .02 | .01 |

|  |  | | | |
|---|---|---|---|---|
| ☐ 256 | Jeff Graham | .08 | .04 | .01 |
| ☐ 257 | Eric Green | .10 | .05 | .01 |
| ☐ 258 | Louis Lipps | .08 | .04 | .01 |
| ☐ 259 | Neil O'Donnell | .50 | .23 | .06 |
| ☐ 260 | Rod Woodson | .10 | .05 | .01 |
| ☐ 261 | Dwight Stone | .04 | .02 | .01 |
| ☐ 262 | Aaron Jones | .04 | .02 | .01 |
| ☐ 263 | Keith Willis | .04 | .02 | .01 |
| ☐ 264 | Ernie Mills | .04 | .02 | .01 |
| ☐ 265 | Martin Bayless | .04 | .02 | .01 |
| ☐ 266 | Rod Bernstine | .08 | .04 | .01 |
| ☐ 267 | John Carney | .04 | .02 | .01 |
| ☐ 268 | John Friesz | .08 | .04 | .01 |
| ☐ 269 | Nate Lewis | .08 | .04 | .01 |
| ☐ 270 | Shawn Jefferson | .04 | .02 | .01 |
| ☐ 271 | Burt Grossman | .04 | .02 | .01 |
| ☐ 272 | Eric Moten | .04 | .02 | .01 |
| ☐ 273 | Gary Plummer | .04 | .02 | .01 |
| ☐ 274 | Henry Rolling | .04 | .02 | .01 |
| ☐ 275 | Steve Hendrickson | .04 | .02 | .01 |
| ☐ 276 | Michael Carter | .04 | .02 | .01 |
| ☐ 277 | Steve Bono | .50 | .23 | .06 |
| ☐ 278 | Dexter Carter | .08 | .04 | .01 |
| ☐ 279 | Mike Cofer | .04 | .02 | .01 |
| ☐ 280 | Charles Haley | .08 | .04 | .01 |
| ☐ 281 | Tom Rathman | .08 | .04 | .01 |
| ☐ 282 | Guy McIntyre | .08 | .04 | .01 |
| ☐ 283 | John Taylor | .10 | .05 | .01 |
| ☐ 284 | Dave Waymer | .04 | .02 | .01 |
| ☐ 285 | Steve Wallace | .04 | .02 | .01 |
| ☐ 286 | Jamie Williams | .04 | .02 | .01 |
| ☐ 287 | Brian Blades | .08 | .04 | .01 |
| ☐ 288 | Jeff Bryant | .04 | .02 | .01 |
| ☐ 289 | Grant Feasel | .04 | .02 | .01 |
| ☐ 290 | Jacob Green | .04 | .02 | .01 |
| ☐ 291 | Andy Heck | .04 | .02 | .01 |
| ☐ 292 | Kelly Stouffer | .04 | .02 | .01 |
| ☐ 293 | John Kasay | .04 | .02 | .01 |
| ☐ 294 | Cortez Kennedy | .10 | .05 | .01 |
| ☐ 295 | Bryan Millard | .04 | .02 | .01 |
| ☐ 296 | Eugene Robinson | .04 | .02 | .01 |
| ☐ 297 | Tony Woods | .04 | .02 | .01 |
| ☐ 298 | Jesse Anderson UER (Should have Tight End, not TIGHT END) | .04 | .02 | .01 |
| ☐ 299 | Gary Anderson | .08 | .04 | .01 |
| ☐ 300 | Mark Carrier | .08 | .04 | .01 |
| ☐ 301 | Reggie Cobb | .10 | .05 | .01 |
| ☐ 302 | Robert Wilson | .04 | .02 | .01 |
| ☐ 303 | Jesse Solomon | .04 | .02 | .01 |
| ☐ 304 | Broderick Thomas | .04 | .02 | .01 |
| ☐ 305 | Lawrence Dawsey | .10 | .05 | .01 |
| ☐ 306 | Charles McRae | .04 | .02 | .01 |
| ☐ 307 | Paul Gruber | .04 | .02 | .01 |
| ☐ 308 | Vinny Testaverde | .10 | .05 | .01 |
| ☐ 309 | Brian Mitchell | .08 | .04 | .01 |
| ☐ 310 | Darrell Green | .08 | .04 | .01 |
| ☐ 311 | Art Monk | .10 | .05 | .01 |
| ☐ 312 | Russ Grimm | .04 | .02 | .01 |
| ☐ 313 | Mark Rypien | .10 | .05 | .01 |
| ☐ 314 | Bobby Wilson | .04 | .02 | .01 |
| ☐ 315 | Wilber Marshall | .08 | .04 | .01 |
| ☐ 316 | Gerald Riggs | .08 | .04 | .01 |
| ☐ 317 | Chip Lohmiller | .08 | .04 | .01 |
| ☐ 318 | Joe Jacoby | .04 | .02 | .01 |
| ☐ 319 | Martin Mayhew | .04 | .02 | .01 |
| ☐ 320 | Amp Lee San Francisco 49ers | .25 | .11 | .03 |
| ☐ 321 | Terrell Buckley Green Bay Packers | .25 | .11 | .03 |
| ☐ 322 | Tommy Vardell Cleveland Browns | .30 | .14 | .04 |
| ☐ 323 | Ricardo McDonald Cincinnati Bengals | .10 | .05 | .01 |
| ☐ 324 | Joe Bowden Houston Oilers | .05 | .02 | .01 |
| ☐ 325 | Darryl Williams Cincinnati Bengals | .20 | .09 | .03 |
| ☐ 326 | Carlos Huerta San Diego Chargers | .05 | .02 | .01 |
| ☐ 327 | Patrick Rowe Cleveland Browns | .10 | .05 | .01 |
| ☐ 328 | Siran Stacy Philadelphia Eagles | .10 | .05 | .01 |
| ☐ 329 | Dexter McNabb Green Bay Packers | .05 | .02 | .01 |
| ☐ 330 | Willie Clay Detroit Lions | .05 | .02 | .01 |
| ☐ 331 | Oliver Barnett | .04 | .02 | .01 |
| ☐ 332 | Aundray Bruce | .04 | .02 | .01 |
| ☐ 333 | Ken Tippins | .10 | .05 | .01 |
| ☐ 334 | Jessie Tuggle | .04 | .02 | .01 |
| ☐ 335 | Brian Jordan | .08 | .04 | .01 |
| ☐ 336 | Andre Rison | .25 | .11 | .03 |
| ☐ 337 | Houston Hoover | .04 | .02 | .01 |
| ☐ 338 | Bill Fralic | .04 | .02 | .01 |
| ☐ 339 | Pat Chaffey | .15 | .07 | .02 |
| ☐ 340 | Keith Jones | .04 | .02 | .01 |
| ☐ 341 | Jamie Dukes | .04 | .02 | .01 |
| ☐ 342 | Chris Mohr | .04 | .02 | .01 |
| ☐ 343 | John Davis | .04 | .02 | .01 |
| ☐ 344 | Ray Bentley | .04 | .02 | .01 |
| ☐ 345 | Scott Norwood | .04 | .02 | .01 |
| ☐ 346 | Shane Conlan | .08 | .04 | .01 |
| ☐ 347 | Steve Tasker | .08 | .04 | .01 |
| ☐ 348 | Will Wolford | .04 | .02 | .01 |
| ☐ 349 | Gary Baldinger | .04 | .02 | .01 |
| ☐ 350 | Kirby Jackson | .04 | .02 | .01 |
| ☐ 351 | Jamie Mueller | .04 | .02 | .01 |
| ☐ 352 | Pete Metzelaars | .04 | .02 | .01 |
| ☐ 353 | Richard Dent | .08 | .04 | .01 |
| ☐ 354 | Ron Rivera | .04 | .02 | .01 |
| ☐ 355 | Jim Morrissey | .04 | .02 | .01 |
| ☐ 356 | John Roper | .04 | .02 | .01 |
| ☐ 357 | Steve McMichael | .08 | .04 | .01 |
| ☐ 358 | Ron Morris | .04 | .02 | .01 |
| ☐ 359 | Darren Lewis | .04 | .02 | .01 |
| ☐ 360 | Anthony Morgan | .04 | .02 | .01 |
| ☐ 361 | Stan Thomas | .04 | .02 | .01 |
| ☐ 362 | James Thornton | .04 | .02 | .01 |
| ☐ 363 | Brad Muster | .08 | .04 | .01 |
| ☐ 364 | Tim Krumrie | .04 | .02 | .01 |
| ☐ 365 | Lee Johnson | .04 | .02 | .01 |
| ☐ 366 | Eric Ball | .04 | .02 | .01 |
| ☐ 367 | Alonzo Mitz | .04 | .02 | .01 |
| ☐ 368 | David Grant | .04 | .02 | .01 |
| ☐ 369 | Lynn James | .04 | .02 | .01 |
| ☐ 370 | Lewis Billups | .04 | .02 | .01 |
| ☐ 371 | Jim Breech | .04 | .02 | .01 |
| ☐ 372 | Alfred Williams | .04 | .02 | .01 |
| ☐ 373 | Wayne Haddix | .04 | .02 | .01 |
| ☐ 374 | Tim McGee | .04 | .02 | .01 |
| ☐ 375 | Michael Jackson | .10 | .05 | .01 |
| ☐ 376 | Leroy Hoard | .08 | .04 | .01 |
| ☐ 377 | Tony Jones | .04 | .02 | .01 |
| ☐ 378 | Vince Newsome | .04 | .02 | .01 |
| ☐ 379 | Todd Philcox | .25 | .11 | .03 |
| ☐ 380 | Eric Metcalf | .10 | .05 | .01 |
| ☐ 381 | John Rienstra | .04 | .02 | .01 |
| ☐ 382 | Matt Stover | .04 | .02 | .01 |
| ☐ 383 | Brian Hansen | .04 | .02 | .01 |
| ☐ 384 | Joe Morris | .08 | .04 | .01 |
| ☐ 385 | Anthony Pleasant | .04 | .02 | .01 |
| ☐ 386 | Mark Stepnoski | .04 | .02 | .01 |
| ☐ 387 | Erik Williams | .04 | .02 | .01 |
| ☐ 388 | Jimmie Jones | .04 | .02 | .01 |
| ☐ 389 | Kevin Gogan | .04 | .02 | .01 |
| ☐ 390 | Manny Hendrix | .04 | .02 | .01 |
| ☐ 391 | Issiac Holt | .04 | .02 | .01 |
| ☐ 392 | Ken Norton | .08 | .04 | .01 |
| ☐ 393 | Tommie Agee | .04 | .02 | .01 |
| ☐ 394 | Alvin Harper | .40 | .18 | .05 |
| ☐ 395 | Alexander Wright | .08 | .04 | .01 |
| ☐ 396 | Mike Saxon | .04 | .02 | .01 |
| ☐ 397 | Michael Brooks | .04 | .02 | .01 |
| ☐ 398 | Bobby Humphrey | .08 | .04 | .01 |
| ☐ 399 | Ken Lanier | .04 | .02 | .01 |
| ☐ 400 | Steve Sewell | .04 | .02 | .01 |
| ☐ 401 | Robert Perryman | .04 | .02 | .01 |
| ☐ 402 | Wymon Henderson | .04 | .02 | .01 |
| ☐ 403 | Keith Kartz | .04 | .02 | .01 |
| ☐ 404 | Clarence Kay | .04 | .02 | .01 |
| ☐ 405 | Keith Traylor | .04 | .02 | .01 |
| ☐ 406 | Doug Widell | .04 | .02 | .01 |
| ☐ 407 | Dennis Smith | .08 | .04 | .01 |
| ☐ 408 | Marc Spindler | .04 | .02 | .01 |
| ☐ 409 | Lomas Brown | .04 | .02 | .01 |
| ☐ 410 | Robert Clark | .04 | .02 | .01 |
| ☐ 411 | Eric Andolsek | .04 | .02 | .01 |
| ☐ 412 | Mike Farr | .04 | .02 | .01 |
| ☐ 413 | Ray Crockett | .04 | .02 | .01 |
| ☐ 414 | Jeff Campbell | .04 | .02 | .01 |
| ☐ 415 | Dan Owens | .04 | .02 | .01 |
| ☐ 416 | Jim Arnold | .04 | .02 | .01 |
| ☐ 417 | Barry Sanders | .75 | .35 | .09 |
| ☐ 418 | Eddie Murray | .08 | .04 | .01 |
| ☐ 419 | Vince Workman | .08 | .04 | .01 |
| ☐ 420 | Ed West | .04 | .02 | .01 |
| ☐ 421 | Charles Wilson | .04 | .02 | .01 |
| ☐ 422 | Perry Kemp | .04 | .02 | .01 |
| ☐ 423 | Chuck Cecil | .04 | .02 | .01 |
| ☐ 424 | James Campen | .04 | .02 | .01 |
| ☐ 425 | Robert Brown | .04 | .02 | .01 |
| ☐ 426 | Brian Noble | .04 | .02 | .01 |
| ☐ 427 | Rich Moran | .04 | .02 | .01 |
| ☐ 428 | Vai Sikahema | .08 | .04 | .01 |
| ☐ 429 | Allen Rice | .04 | .02 | .01 |
| ☐ 430 | Haywood Jeffires | .10 | .05 | .01 |
| ☐ 431 | Warren Moon | .20 | .09 | .03 |
| ☐ 432 | Greg Montgomery | .04 | .02 | .01 |
| ☐ 433 | Sean Jones | .04 | .02 | .01 |
| ☐ 434 | Richard Johnson | .04 | .02 | .01 |
| ☐ 435 | Al Smith | .04 | .02 | .01 |
| ☐ 436 | Johnny Meads | .04 | .02 | .01 |

| | | | | | | | |
|---|---|---|---|---|---|---|---|
| 437 William Fuller | .04 | .02 | .01 | 534 Jim Dombrowski | .04 | .02 | .01 |
| 438 Mike Munchak | .08 | .04 | .01 | 535 Fred McAfee | .15 | .07 | .02 |
| 439 Ray Childress | .08 | .04 | .01 | 536 Phil Simms | .10 | .05 | .01 |
| 440 Cody Carlson | .20 | .09 | .03 | 537 Lewis Tillman | .08 | .04 | .01 |
| 441 Scott Radecic | .04 | .02 | .01 | 538 John Elliott | .04 | .02 | .01 |
| 442 Quintus McDonald | .10 | .05 | .01 | 539 Dave Meggett | .08 | .04 | .01 |
| 443 Eugene Daniel | .04 | .02 | .01 | 540 Mark Collins | .04 | .02 | .01 |
| 444 Mark Herrmann | .12 | .05 | .02 | 541 Ottis Anderson | .08 | .04 | .01 |
| 445 John Baylor | .04 | .02 | .01 | 542 Bobby Abrams | .04 | .02 | .01 |
| 446 Dave McCloughan | .04 | .02 | .01 | 543 Sean Landeta | .04 | .02 | .01 |
| 447 Mark Vander Poel | .04 | .02 | .01 | 544 Brian Williams | .04 | .02 | .01 |
| 448 Randy Dixon | .04 | .02 | .01 | 545 Erik Howard | .04 | .02 | .01 |
| 449 Keith Taylor | .04 | .02 | .01 | 546 Mark Ingram | .08 | .04 | .01 |
| 450 Alan Grant | .04 | .02 | .01 | 547 Kanavis McGhee | .04 | .02 | .01 |
| 451 Tony Siragusa | .04 | .02 | .01 | 548 Kyle Clifton | .04 | .02 | .01 |
| 452 Rich Baldinger | .04 | .02 | .01 | 549 Marvin Washington | .04 | .02 | .01 |
| 453 Derrick Thomas | .15 | .07 | .02 | 550 Jeff Criswell | .04 | .02 | .01 |
| 454 Bill Jones | .04 | .02 | .01 | 551 Dave Cadigan | .04 | .02 | .01 |
| 455 Troy Stradford | .04 | .02 | .01 | 552 Chris Burkett | .04 | .02 | .01 |
| 456 Barry Word | .10 | .05 | .01 | 553 Erik McMillan | .04 | .02 | .01 |
| 457 Tim Grunhard | .04 | .02 | .01 | 554 James Hasty | .04 | .02 | .01 |
| 458 Chris Martin | .04 | .02 | .01 | 555 Louie Aguiar | .04 | .02 | .01 |
| 459 Jayice Pearson | .04 | .02 | .01 | 556 Troy Johnson | .04 | .02 | .01 |
| 460 Dino Hackett | .04 | .02 | .01 | 557 Troy Taylor | .12 | .05 | .02 |
| 461 David Lutz | .04 | .02 | .01 | 558 Pat Kelly | .04 | .02 | .01 |
| 462 Albert Lewis | .08 | .04 | .01 | 559 Heath Sherman | .08 | .04 | .01 |
| 463 Fred Jones | .15 | .07 | .02 | 560 Roger Ruzek | .04 | .02 | .01 |
| 464 Winston Moss | .04 | .02 | .01 | 561 Andre Waters | .04 | .02 | .01 |
| 465 Sam Graddy | .20 | .09 | .03 | 562 Izel Jenkins | .04 | .02 | .01 |
| 466 Steve Wisniewski | .04 | .02 | .01 | 563 Keith Jackson | .10 | .05 | .01 |
| 467 Jay Schroeder | .08 | .04 | .01 | 564 Byron Evans | .04 | .02 | .01 |
| 468 Ronnie Lott | .10 | .05 | .01 | 565 Wes Hopkins | .04 | .02 | .01 |
| 469 Willie Gault | .08 | .04 | .01 | 566 Rich Miano | .04 | .02 | .01 |
| 470 Greg Townsend | .04 | .02 | .01 | 567 Seth Joyner | .08 | .04 | .01 |
| 471 Max Montoya | .04 | .02 | .01 | 568 Thomas Sanders | .04 | .02 | .01 |
| 472 Howie Long | .08 | .04 | .01 | 569 David Alexander | .04 | .02 | .01 |
| 473 Lionel Washington | .04 | .02 | .01 | 570 Jeff Kemp | .04 | .02 | .01 |
| 474 Riki Ellison | .04 | .02 | .01 | 571 Jock Jones | .10 | .05 | .01 |
| 475 Tom Newberry | .04 | .02 | .01 | 572 Craig Patterson | .04 | .02 | .01 |
| 476 Damone Johnson | .04 | .02 | .01 | 573 Robert Massey | .04 | .02 | .01 |
| 477 Pat Terrell | .04 | .02 | .01 | 574 Bill Lewis | .04 | .02 | .01 |
| 478 Marcus Dupree | .08 | .04 | .01 | 575 Freddie Joe Nunn | .04 | .02 | .01 |
| 479 Todd Lyght | .04 | .02 | .01 | 576 Aeneas Williams | .04 | .02 | .01 |
| 480 Buford McGee | .04 | .02 | .01 | 577 John Jackson | .04 | .02 | .01 |
| 481 Bern Brostek | .04 | .02 | .01 | 578 Tim McDonald | .08 | .04 | .01 |
| 482 Jim Price | .04 | .02 | .01 | 579 Michael Zordich | .04 | .02 | .01 |
| 483 Robert Young | .08 | .04 | .01 | 580 Eric Hill | .04 | .02 | .01 |
| 484 Tony Zendejas | .04 | .02 | .01 | 581 Lorenzo Lynch | .04 | .02 | .01 |
| 485 Robert Bailey | .10 | .05 | .01 | 582 Vernice Smith | .04 | .02 | .01 |
| 486 Alvin Wright | .04 | .02 | .01 | 583 Greg Lloyd | .04 | .02 | .01 |
| 487 Pat Carter | .04 | .02 | .01 | 584 Carnell Lake | .04 | .02 | .01 |
| 488 Pete Stoyanovich | .08 | .04 | .01 | 585 Hardy Nickerson | .04 | .02 | .01 |
| 489 Reggie Roby | .04 | .02 | .01 | 586 Delton Hall | .04 | .02 | .01 |
| 490 Harry Galbreath | .04 | .02 | .01 | 587 Gerald Williams | .04 | .02 | .01 |
| 491 Michael McGruder | .12 | .05 | .02 | 588 Bryan Hinkle | .04 | .02 | .01 |
| 492 J.B. Brown | .04 | .02 | .01 | 589 Barry Foster | .35 | .16 | .04 |
| 493 E.J. Junior | .04 | .02 | .01 | 590 Bubby Brister | .08 | .04 | .01 |
| 494 Ferrell Edmunds | .04 | .02 | .01 | 591 Rick Strom | .35 | .16 | .04 |
| 495 Scott Secules | .04 | .02 | .01 | 592 David Little | .04 | .02 | .01 |
| 496 Greg Baty | .15 | .07 | .02 | 593 Leroy Thompson | .40 | .18 | .05 |
| 497 Mike Iaquaniello | .04 | .02 | .01 | 594 Eric Bieniemy | .08 | .04 | .01 |
| 498 Keith Sims | .04 | .02 | .01 | 595 Courtney Hall | .04 | .02 | .01 |
| 499 John Randle | .04 | .02 | .01 | 596 George Thornton | .04 | .02 | .01 |
| 500 Joey Browner | .04 | .02 | .01 | 597 Donnie Elder | .04 | .02 | .01 |
| 501 Steve Jordan | .08 | .04 | .01 | 598 Billy Ray Smith | .04 | .02 | .01 |
| 502 Darrin Nelson | .04 | .02 | .01 | 599 Gill Byrd | .08 | .04 | .01 |
| 503 Audray McMillian | .04 | .02 | .01 | 600 Marion Butts | .10 | .05 | .01 |
| 504 Harry Newsome | .04 | .02 | .01 | 601 Ronnie Harmon | .04 | .02 | .01 |
| 505 Hassan Jones | .04 | .02 | .01 | 602 Anthony Shelton | .04 | .02 | .01 |
| 506 Ray Berry | .04 | .02 | .01 | 603 Mark May | .04 | .02 | .01 |
| 507 Mike Merriweather | .04 | .02 | .01 | 604 Craig McEwen | .04 | .02 | .01 |
| 508 Leo Lewis | .04 | .02 | .01 | 605 Steve Young | .35 | .16 | .04 |
| 509 Tim Irwin | .04 | .02 | .01 | 606 Keith Henderson | .04 | .02 | .01 |
| 510 Kirk Lowdermilk | .04 | .02 | .01 | 607 Pierce Holt | .04 | .02 | .01 |
| 511 Alfred Anderson | .04 | .02 | .01 | 608 Roy Foster | .04 | .02 | .01 |
| 512 Michael Timpson | .20 | .09 | .03 | 609 Don Griffin | .04 | .02 | .01 |
| 513 Jerome Henderson | .04 | .02 | .01 | 610 Harry Sydney | .04 | .02 | .01 |
| 514 Andre Tippett | .08 | .04 | .01 | 611 Todd Bowles | .04 | .02 | .01 |
| 515 Chris Singleton | .04 | .02 | .01 | 612 Ted Washington | .04 | .02 | .01 |
| 516 John Stephens | .08 | .04 | .01 | 613 Johnny Jackson | .04 | .02 | .01 |
| 517 Ronnie Lippett | .04 | .02 | .01 | 614 Jesse Sapolu | .04 | .02 | .01 |
| 518 Bruce Armstrong | .04 | .02 | .01 | 615 Brent Jones | .10 | .05 | .01 |
| 519 Marion Hobby | .04 | .02 | .01 | 616 Travis McNeal | .04 | .02 | .01 |
| 520 Tim Goad | .04 | .02 | .01 | 617 Darrick Brilz | .04 | .02 | .01 |
| 521 Mickey Washington | .04 | .02 | .01 | 618 Terry Wooden | .04 | .02 | .01 |
| 522 Fred Smerlas | .04 | .02 | .01 | 619 Tommy Kane | .04 | .02 | .01 |
| 523 Wayne Martin | .04 | .02 | .01 | 620 Nesby Glasgow | .04 | .02 | .01 |
| 524 Frank Warren | .04 | .02 | .01 | 621 Dwayne Harper | .04 | .02 | .01 |
| 525 Floyd Turner | .04 | .02 | .01 | 622 Rick Tuten | .04 | .02 | .01 |
| 526 Wesley Carroll | .08 | .04 | .01 | 623 Chris Warren | .25 | .11 | .03 |
| 527 Gene Atkins | .04 | .02 | .01 | 624 John L. Williams | .08 | .04 | .01 |
| 528 Vaughan Johnson | .08 | .04 | .01 | 625 Rufus Porter | .04 | .02 | .01 |
| 529 Hoby Brenner | .04 | .02 | .01 | 626 David Daniels | .04 | .02 | .01 |
| 530 Renaldo Turnbull | .08 | .04 | .01 | 627 Keith McCants | .04 | .02 | .01 |
| 531 Joel Hilgenberg | .04 | .02 | .01 | 628 Reuben Davis | .04 | .02 | .01 |
| 532 Craig Heyward | .04 | .02 | .01 | 629 Mark Royals | .04 | .02 | .01 |
| 533 Vince Buck | .04 | .02 | .01 | 630 Marty Carter | .20 | .09 | .03 |

| | MINT | EXC | G-VG |
|---|---|---|---|
| ☐ 631 Ian Beckles | .04 | .02 | .01 |
| ☐ 632 Ron Hall | .04 | .02 | .01 |
| ☐ 633 Eugene Marve | .04 | .02 | .01 |
| ☐ 634 Willie Drewrey | .04 | .02 | .01 |
| ☐ 635 Tom McHale | .04 | .02 | .01 |
| ☐ 636 Kevin Murphy | .04 | .02 | .01 |
| ☐ 637 Robert Hardy | .04 | .02 | .01 |
| ☐ 638 Ricky Sanders | .08 | .04 | .01 |
| ☐ 639 Gary Clark | .08 | .04 | .01 |
| ☐ 640 Andre Collins | .04 | .02 | .01 |
| ☐ 641 Brad Edwards | .04 | .02 | .01 |
| ☐ 642 Monte Coleman | .04 | .02 | .01 |
| ☐ 643 Clarence Vaughn | .10 | .05 | .01 |
| ☐ 644 Fred Stokes | .04 | .02 | .01 |
| ☐ 645 Charles Mann | .08 | .04 | .01 |
| ☐ 646 Earnest Byner | .08 | .04 | .01 |
| ☐ 647 Jim Lachey | .04 | .02 | .01 |
| ☐ 648 Jeff Bostic | .04 | .02 | .01 |
| ☐ 649 Chris Mims | .25 | .11 | .03 |
| ☐ 650 George Williams | .08 | .04 | .01 |
| ☐ 651 Ed Cunningham | .08 | .04 | .01 |
| ☐ 652 Tony Smith | .10 | .05 | .01 |
| ☐ 653 Will Furrer | .15 | .07 | .02 |
| ☐ 654 Matt Elliott | .08 | .04 | .01 |
| ☐ 655 Mike Mooney | .10 | .05 | .01 |
| ☐ 656 Eddie Blake | .08 | .04 | .01 |
| ☐ 657 Leon Searcy | .08 | .04 | .01 |
| ☐ 658 Kevin Turner | .15 | .07 | .02 |
| ☐ 659 Keith Hamilton | .15 | .07 | .02 |
| ☐ 660 Alan Haller | .10 | .05 | .01 |

## 1992 Pacific Checklists

These checklist cards were randomly inserted in both series foil, jumbo packs, and change maker (25 cents) packs. They are numbered on the back "X of 8". The first four cards were issued with the first series and the second four cards were released in second series products. The cards are standard size, 2 1/2" by 3 1/2".

| | MINT | EXC | G-VG |
|---|---|---|---|
| COMPLETE SET (8) | 3.00 | 1.35 | .40 |
| COMMON CARD (1-4) | .50 | .23 | .06 |
| COMMON CARD (5-8) | .50 | .23 | .06 |
| ☐ 1 Checklist 1 (1-110) | .50 | .23 | .06 |
| ☐ 2 Checklist 2 (111-220) | .50 | .23 | .06 |
| ☐ 3 Checklist 3 (221-330) | .50 | .23 | .06 |
| ☐ 4 Checklist 4 | .50 | .23 | .06 |
| (Highlight Cards) | | | |
| ☐ 5 Checklist 5 (1-110) | .50 | .23 | .06 |
| ☐ 6 Checklist 6 (111-220) | .50 | .23 | .06 |
| ☐ 7 Checklist 7 (221-330) | .50 | .23 | .06 |
| ☐ 8 Checklist 8 | .50 | .23 | .06 |
| (Highlight Cards) | | | |

## 1992 Pacific Bob Griese

This nine-card set captures highlights from the career of Hall of Famer Bob Griese and is subtitled "Legends of the Game." The standard-size (2 1/2" by 3 1/2") cards were randomly inserted in second series foil and jumbo packs; Griese personally autographed 1,000 cards. The color action player photos on the fronts have white borders, with the player's name and a caption in a multicolored stripe cutting across the bottom of the picture. In a horizontal format, the backs carry another color photo and career summary. The cards are numbered on the back continuing the numbering of the Legends of the Game Largent series. The Griese cards were also available as random inserts in triple folder card packs and five-card change-maker packs.

| | MINT | EXC | G-VG |
|---|---|---|---|
| COMPLETE SET (9) | 4.00 | 1.80 | .50 |
| COMMON GRIESE (10-18) | .50 | .23 | .06 |

| | MINT | EXC | G-VG |
|---|---|---|---|
| ☐ 10 Purdue Star | .50 | .23 | .06 |
| ☐ 11 AFL Star | .50 | .23 | .06 |
| ☐ 12 Super Bowl Star | .50 | .23 | .06 |
| ☐ 13 Thinking Man's QB | .50 | .23 | .06 |
| ☐ 14 349 Yards | .50 | .23 | .06 |
| ☐ 15 All-Star | .50 | .23 | .06 |
| ☐ 16 The 25,000 Yard Club | .50 | .23 | .06 |
| ☐ 17 Number 12 Retired | .50 | .23 | .06 |
| ☐ 18 Hall of Fame | .50 | .23 | .06 |
| ☐ AU Bob Griese AU | 100.00 | 45.00 | 12.50 |
| (Certified autograph) | | | |

## 1992 Pacific Steve Largent

This nine-card set captures highlights from the career of future Hall of Famer Steve Largent and is subtitled "Legends of the Game." The standard-size (2 1/2" by 3 1/2") cards were randomly inserted in first series foil packs, jumbo packs, triple folder card packs, and change maker (25 cents) packs; Largent personally autographed 1,000 cards. The color action photos on the fronts have white borders, with the player's name and a caption in a multicolored stripe cutting across the bottom of the picture. In a horizontal format, the backs carry another color photo and career summary. The cards are numbered on the back.

| | MINT | EXC | G-VG |
|---|---|---|---|
| COMPLETE SET (9) | 4.00 | 1.80 | .50 |
| COMMON LARGENT (1-9) | .50 | .23 | .06 |
| ☐ 1 Great Rookie Start | .50 | .23 | .06 |
| ☐ 2 Largent Leads NFL | .50 | .23 | .06 |
| ☐ 3 Hi-Steppin' | .50 | .23 | .06 |
| ☐ 4 NFL Leader | .50 | .23 | .06 |
| ☐ 5 Team Captain | .50 | .23 | .06 |
| ☐ 6 Pro Bowl | .50 | .23 | .06 |
| ☐ 7 Man of the Year | .50 | .23 | .06 |
| ☐ 8 The Final Season | .50 | .23 | .06 |
| ☐ 9 Retirement Celebration | .50 | .23 | .06 |
| ☐ AU Steve Largent AU | 100.00 | 45.00 | 12.50 |
| (Certified autograph) | | | |

## 1992 Pacific Picks The Pros

This 25-card standard-size (2 1/2" by 3 1/2") set features Pacific's pick at each position. The card design is strikingly similar to the 1991 Pacific Picks The Pros inserts set. The color action player photos on the fronts have either gold or silver foil borders, with the words "Pacific Picks the Pros" in corresponding foil lettering in a multicolored stripe running down the left side of the picture. The gold foil cards were randomly inserted in first series foil packs, while the silver foil cards were found in first series jumbo packs. Both were also

available as random inserts in change maker packs (suggested retail 25 cents) and in triple folder card packs. On a background of different shades of red and yellow, the diagonally oriented backs present career summary. The cards are numbered on the back.

|  | MINT | EXC | G-VG |
|---|---|---|---|
| COMPLETE SET (25) | 80.00 | 36.00 | 10.00 |
| COMMON PLAYER (1-25) | 2.25 | 1.00 | .30 |
| *GOLD/SILVER: SAME PRICE | | | |

| | MINT | EXC | G-VG |
|---|---|---|---|
| ☐ 1 Mark Rypien | 3.00 | 1.35 | .40 |
| Washington Redskins | | | |
| ☐ 2 Marv Cook | 2.25 | 1.00 | .30 |
| New England Patriots | | | |
| ☐ 3 Jim Lachey | 2.25 | 1.00 | .30 |
| Washington Redskins | | | |
| ☐ 4 Darrell Green | 2.25 | 1.00 | .30 |
| Washington Redskins | | | |
| ☐ 5 Derrick Thomas | 4.00 | 1.80 | .50 |
| Kansas City Chiefs | | | |
| ☐ 6 Thurman Thomas | 7.00 | 3.10 | .85 |
| Buffalo Bills | | | |
| ☐ 7 Kent Hull | 2.25 | 1.00 | .30 |
| Buffalo Bills | | | |
| ☐ 8 Tim McDonald | 2.25 | 1.00 | .30 |
| Phoenix Cardinals | | | |
| ☐ 9 Mike Croel | 2.25 | 1.00 | .30 |
| Denver Broncos | | | |
| ☐ 10 Anthony Munoz | 3.00 | 1.35 | .40 |
| Cincinnati Bengals | | | |
| ☐ 11 Jerome Brown | 3.00 | 1.35 | .40 |
| Philadelphia Eagles | | | |
| ☐ 12 Reggie White | 4.00 | 1.80 | .50 |
| Philadelphia Eagles | | | |
| ☐ 13 Gill Byrd | 2.25 | 1.00 | .30 |
| San Diego Chargers | | | |
| ☐ 14 Jessie Tuggle | 2.25 | 1.00 | .30 |
| Atlanta Falcons | | | |
| ☐ 15 Randall McDaniel | 2.25 | 1.00 | .30 |
| Minnesota Vikings | | | |
| ☐ 16 Sam Mills | 2.25 | 1.00 | .30 |
| New Orleans Saints | | | |
| ☐ 17 Pat Swilling | 2.25 | 1.00 | .30 |
| New Orleans Saints | | | |
| ☐ 18 Eugene Robinson | 2.25 | 1.00 | .30 |
| Seattle Seahawks | | | |
| ☐ 19 Michael Irvin | 10.00 | 4.50 | 1.25 |
| Dallas Cowboys | | | |
| ☐ 20 Emmitt Smith | 25.00 | 11.50 | 3.10 |
| Dallas Cowboys | | | |
| ☐ 21 Jeff Gossett | 2.25 | 1.00 | .30 |
| Los Angeles Raiders | | | |
| ☐ 22 Jeff Jaeger | 2.25 | 1.00 | .30 |
| Los Angeles Raiders | | | |
| ☐ 23 William Fuller | 2.25 | 1.00 | .30 |
| Houston Oilers | | | |
| ☐ 24 Mike Munchak | 2.25 | 1.00 | .30 |
| Houston Oilers | | | |
| ☐ 25 Andre Rison | 4.00 | 1.80 | .50 |
| Atlanta Falcons | | | |

## 1992 Pacific Prism Inserts

This ten-card set features the top running backs from the AFC and the NFC. According to Pacific, only 10,000 of each card were produced, and they were randomly inserted into series II foil packs and triple folder card packs. The cards are standard size, 2 1/2" by 3 1/2". The fronts display color action player photos cut out and superimposed on a prism-patterned background. The player's name appears in a colored streak toward the bottom of the front. On a background consisting of a pastel green football field, the backs use team-color coded bar graphs to present the player's yardage for each game of the 1991 season. The cards are numbered on the back.

|  | MINT | EXC | G-VG |
|---|---|---|---|
| COMPLETE SET (10) | 30.00 | 13.50 | 3.80 |
| COMMON PLAYER (1-10) | 1.50 | .65 | .19 |

| | MINT | EXC | G-VG |
|---|---|---|---|
| ☐ 1 Thurman Thomas | 4.00 | 1.80 | .50 |
| Buffalo Bills | | | |
| ☐ 2 Gaston Green | 1.50 | .65 | .19 |
| Denver Broncos | | | |
| ☐ 3 Christian Okoye | 1.50 | .65 | .19 |
| Kansas City Chiefs | | | |
| ☐ 4 Leonard Russell | 2.50 | 1.15 | .30 |
| New England Patriots | | | |
| ☐ 5 Mark Higgs | 2.00 | .90 | .25 |
| Miami Dolphins | | | |
| ☐ 6 Emmitt Smith | 10.00 | 4.50 | 1.25 |
| Dallas Cowboys | | | |
| ☐ 7 Barry Sanders | 6.00 | 2.70 | .75 |
| Detroit Lions | | | |
| ☐ 8 Rodney Hampton | 4.00 | 1.80 | .50 |
| New York Giants | | | |
| ☐ 9 Earnest Byner | 1.50 | .65 | .19 |
| Washington Redskins | | | |
| ☐ 10 Herschel Walker | 2.00 | .90 | .25 |
| Minnesota Vikings | | | |

## 1992 Pacific Statistical Leaders

This 30-card standard-size (2 1/2" by 3 1/2") set features the team statistical leaders from the 28 NFL teams, plus two cards devoted to the AFC and NFC rushing leaders. The cards were randomly inserted into both series foil packs, triple folder card packs, and change-maker (25 cents) packs. The whole set of these Stat Leaders was included as an insert with 1992 Pacific factory sets. The fronts display glossy color action photos bordered in white. At the bottom of the picture, the player's name and accomplishment appear in a multi-colored stripe. The backs reflect the team's colors and have mini-photos of three other team leaders. The cards are numbered on the back and the team leader cards are checklisted alphabetically according to team name.

|  | MINT | EXC | G-VG |
|---|---|---|---|
| COMPLETE SET (30) | 10.00 | 4.50 | 1.25 |
| COMMON PLAYER (1-30) | .30 | .14 | .04 |

| | MINT | EXC | G-VG |
|---|---|---|---|
| ☐ 1 Chris Miller | .35 | .16 | .04 |
| Atlanta Falcons | | | |
| ☐ 2 Thurman Thomas | 1.00 | .45 | .13 |
| Buffalo Bills | | | |
| ☐ 3 Jim Harbaugh | .35 | .16 | .04 |
| Chicago Bears | | | |
| ☐ 4 Jim Breech | .30 | .14 | .04 |
| Cincinnati Bengals | | | |
| ☐ 5 Kevin Mack | .30 | .14 | .04 |
| Cleveland Browns | | | |

| | MINT | EXC | G-VG |
|---|---|---|---|
| ☐ 6 Emmitt Smith ........................... | 4.00 | 1.80 | .50 |
|    Dallas Cowboys | | | |
| ☐ 7 Gaston Green ........................... | .30 | .14 | .04 |
|    Denver Broncos | | | |
| ☐ 8 Barry Sanders ......................... | 2.00 | .90 | .25 |
|    Detroit Lions | | | |
| ☐ 9 Tony Bennett ........................... | .30 | .14 | .04 |
|    Green Bay Packers | | | |
| ☐ 10 Warren Moon ........................ | .50 | .23 | .06 |
|    Houston Oilers | | | |
| ☐ 11 Bill Brooks ............................ | .30 | .14 | .04 |
|    Indianapolis Colts | | | |
| ☐ 12 Christian Okoye ..................... | .30 | .14 | .04 |
|    Kansas City Chiefs | | | |
| ☐ 13 Jay Schroeder ....................... | .30 | .14 | .04 |
|    Los Angeles Raiders | | | |
| ☐ 14 Robert Delpino ...................... | .30 | .14 | .04 |
|    Los Angeles Rams | | | |
| ☐ 15 Mark Higgs ........................... | .40 | .18 | .05 |
|    Miami Dolphins | | | |
| ☐ 16 John Randle .......................... | .30 | .14 | .04 |
|    Minnesota Vikings | | | |
| ☐ 17 Leonard Russell ..................... | .50 | .23 | .06 |
|    New England Patriots | | | |
| ☐ 18 Pat Swilling .......................... | .30 | .14 | .04 |
|    New Orleans Saints | | | |
| ☐ 19 Rodney Hampton ................... | 1.00 | .45 | .13 |
|    New York Giants | | | |
| ☐ 20 Terance Mathis ...................... | .30 | .14 | .04 |
|    New York Jets | | | |
| ☐ 21 Fred Barnett ......................... | .35 | .16 | .04 |
|    Philadelphia Eagles | | | |
| ☐ 22 Aeneas Williams ..................... | .30 | .14 | .04 |
|    Phoenix Cardinals | | | |
| ☐ 23 Neil O'Donnell ....................... | .75 | .35 | .09 |
|    Pittsburgh Steelers | | | |
| ☐ 24 Marion Butts ......................... | .35 | .16 | .04 |
|    San Diego Chargers | | | |
| ☐ 25 Steve Young .......................... | .75 | .35 | .09 |
|    San Francisco 49ers | | | |
| ☐ 26 John L. Williams ..................... | .30 | .14 | .04 |
|    Seattle Seahawks | | | |
| ☐ 27 Reggie Cobb ......................... | .35 | .16 | .04 |
|    Tampa Bay Buccaneers | | | |
| ☐ 28 Mark Rypien .......................... | .35 | .16 | .04 |
|    Washington Redskins | | | |
| ☐ 29 Thurman Thomas ................... | .50 | .23 | .06 |
|    Buffalo Bills | | | |
|    AFC Rushing Leaders | | | |
| ☐ 30 Emmitt Smith ......................... | 2.00 | .90 | .25 |
|    Dallas Cowboys | | | |
|    NFC Rushing Leaders | | | |

## 1992 Pacific Triple Folders

The 28 cards in this set measure 3 1/2" by 5" when folded and display a glossy action color player photo on the front. The player's name and position are printed in block letters. The two panels that make up the front photo are split down the center and can be opened to reveal three separate photos on the inside. The center panel carries an action color player photo and the player's name in block letters. The left inside panel has an action player photo while the right inside panel has a posed close-up shot. The backs carry career highlights and statistics. The background and lettering are team color-coded. The players chosen represent each of the 28 NFL teams, and the cards are arranged alphabetically according to team name. The cards are numbered on the back. Each triple folder card pack contained a bonus card from one of the following insert sets: Steve Largent subset, Bob Griese subset, team Statistical Leader subset, gold and silver foil subset, Rushing Leader Prism subset, or Checklist Card subset.

| | MINT | EXC | G-VG |
|---|---|---|---|
| COMPLETE SET (28) ........................ | 20.00 | 8.00 | 2.00 |
| COMMON PLAYER (1-28) ................ | .75 | .30 | .07 |

| | MINT | EXC | G-VG |
|---|---|---|---|
| ☐ 1 Chris Miller ............................ | 1.00 | .40 | .10 |
|    Atlanta Falcons | | | |
| ☐ 2 Thurman Thomas..................... | 1.50 | .60 | .15 |
|    Buffalo Bills | | | |
| ☐ 3 Neal Anderson........................ | .75 | .30 | .07 |
|    Chicago Bears | | | |
| ☐ 4 Tim McGee............................ | .75 | .30 | .07 |
|    Cincinnati Bengals | | | |
| ☐ 5 Kevin Mack............................ | .75 | .30 | .07 |
|    Cleveland Browns | | | |
| ☐ 6 Emmitt Smith ......................... | 5.00 | 2.00 | .50 |
|    Dallas Cowboys | | | |
| ☐ 7 John Elway............................ | 2.50 | 1.00 | .25 |
|    Denver Broncos | | | |
| ☐ 8 Barry Sanders ......................... | 3.00 | 1.20 | .30 |
|    Detroit Lions | | | |
| ☐ 9 Sterling Sharpe ....................... | 2.00 | .80 | .20 |
|    Green Bay Packers | | | |
| ☐ 10 Warren Moon ........................ | 1.25 | .50 | .12 |
|    Houston Oilers | | | |
| ☐ 11 Bill Brooks ............................ | .75 | .30 | .07 |
|    Indianapolis Colts | | | |
| ☐ 12 Christian Okoye ..................... | .75 | .30 | .07 |
|    Kansas City Chiefs | | | |
| ☐ 13 Nick Bell ............................. | 1.00 | .40 | .10 |
|    Los Angeles Raiders | | | |
| ☐ 14 Robert Delpino ...................... | .75 | .30 | .07 |
|    Los Angeles Rams | | | |
| ☐ 15 Mark Higgs ........................... | 1.25 | .50 | .12 |
|    Miami Dolphins | | | |
| ☐ 16 Rich Gannon .......................... | .75 | .30 | .07 |
|    Minnesota Vikings | | | |
| ☐ 17 Leonard Russell ..................... | 1.25 | .50 | .12 |
|    New England Patriots | | | |
| ☐ 18 Pat Swilling .......................... | .75 | .30 | .07 |
|    New Orleans Saints | | | |
| ☐ 19 Rodney Hampton ................... | 1.50 | .60 | .15 |
|    New York Giants | | | |
| ☐ 20 Rob Moore ........................... | 1.25 | .50 | .12 |
|    New York Jets | | | |
| ☐ 21 Reggie White.......................... | 1.25 | .50 | .12 |
|    Philadelphia Eagles | | | |
| ☐ 22 Johnny Johnson .................... | 1.25 | .50 | .12 |
|    Phoenix Cardinals | | | |
| ☐ 23 Neil O'Donnell ....................... | 1.50 | .60 | .15 |
|    Pittsburgh Steelers | | | |
| ☐ 24 Marion Butts ......................... | 1.00 | .40 | .10 |
|    San Diego Chargers | | | |
| ☐ 25 Steve Young .......................... | 2.00 | .80 | .20 |
|    San Francisco 49ers | | | |
| ☐ 26 John L. Williams ..................... | .75 | .30 | .07 |
|    Seattle Seahawks | | | |
| ☐ 27 Reggie Cobb ......................... | 1.25 | .50 | .12 |
|    Tampa Bay Buccaneers | | | |
| ☐ 28 Mark Rypien .......................... | 1.00 | .40 | .10 |
|    Washington Redskins | | | |

## 1993 Pacific Prototypes

These five standard-size (2 1/2" by 3 1/2") cards were issued to preview the design of the 1993 Pacific Plus football series. Each card was packed in a cello pack with an ad card. The color action photos on the fronts are tilted slightly to the left and set on a two-color marbleized card face reflecting the team's colors. The player's name appears in script at the bottom of the picture, with the team helmet in the lower left corner. On two-toned marbleized background, the horizontal backs carry a color close-up shot, biography, statistics, and career highlights. Running across the text portion are the words "1993 Prototypes." The cards are numbered on the back. The cards were given away at the July 1993 National Sports Collectors Convention in Chicago and used as sales samples. The production run was reportedly 5,000 sets.

|  | MINT | EXC | G-VG |
|---|---|---|---|
| COMPLETE SET (5) | 20.00 | 8.00 | 2.00 |
| COMMON PLAYER (1-5) | 1.50 | .60 | .15 |
| ☐ 1 Emmitt Smith | 10.00 | 4.00 | 1.00 |
| Dallas Cowboys |  |  |  |
| ☐ 2 Barry Sanders | 6.00 | 2.40 | .60 |
| Detroit Lions |  |  |  |
| ☐ 3 Derrick Thomas | 2.50 | 1.00 | .25 |
| Kansas City Chiefs |  |  |  |
| ☐ 4 Jim Everett | 1.50 | .60 | .15 |
| Los Angeles Rams |  |  |  |
| ☐ 5 Steve Young | 4.00 | 1.60 | .40 |
| San Francisco 49ers |  |  |  |

# 1993 Pacific

The 1993 Pacific football set consists of 440 standard-size (2 1/2" by 3 1/2") cards. Just 5,000 cases or 99,000 of each card were reportedly producd. Randomly inserted throughout the 12-card foil packs were a 25-card Pacific Picks the Pros gold foil set and a 20-card Prism set. The production run on the insert sets was 8,000 each. The color action photos on the fronts are tilted slightly to the left and set on a two-color marbleized card face reflecting the team's colors. The player's name appears in script at the bottom of the picture, with the team helmet in the lower left corner. On two-toned marbelized background, the horizontal backs carry a color close-up shot, biography, statistics, and career highlights. The cards are numbered on the back and checklisted below according to NFC Divisions (East, Central, and West) and AFC Divisions as follows: Dallas Cowboys (1-14), Philadelphia Eagles (15-28), Washington Redskins (29-42), New York Giants (43-56), Phoenix Cardinals (57-70), Minnesota Vikings (71-84), Green Bay Packers (85-98), Detroit Lions (99-112), Tampa Bay Buccaneers (113-126), Chicago Bears (127-140), San Francisco 49ers (141-154), New Orleans Saints (155-168), Atlanta Falcons (169-182), Los Angeles Rams (183-196), Buffalo Bills (197-210), Miami Dolphins (211-224), Indianapolis Colts (225-238), New York Jets (239-252), New England Patriots (253-266), Pittsburgh Steelers (267-280), Houston Oilers (281-294), Cleveland Browns (295-308), Cincinnati Bengals (309-322), San Diego Chargers (323-336), Kansas City Chiefs (337-350), Denver Broncos (351-364), Los Angeles Raiders (365-378), and Seattle Seahawks (379-392). The set closes with the following topical subsets: NFL Stars (393-417) and Rookies (418-440). Rookie Cards include Jerome Bettis, Drew Bledsoe, Reggie Brooks, Garrison Hearst, O.J. McDuffie, Natrone Means, Glyn Milburn, Rick Mirer, Robert Smith and Kevin Williams.

|  | MINT | EXC | G-VG |
|---|---|---|---|
| COMPLETE SET (440) | 30.00 | 13.50 | 3.80 |
| COMMON PLAYER (1-440) | .05 | .02 | .01 |
| ☐ 1 Emmitt Smith | 2.00 | .90 | .25 |
| ☐ 2 Troy Aikman | 1.25 | .55 | .16 |
| ☐ 3 Larry Brown | .05 | .02 | .01 |
| ☐ 4 Tony Casillas | .05 | .02 | .01 |
| ☐ 5 Thomas Everett | .05 | .02 | .01 |
| ☐ 6 Alvin Harper | .25 | .11 | .03 |
| ☐ 7 Michael Irvin | .40 | .18 | .05 |
| ☐ 8 Charles Haley | .08 | .04 | .01 |
| ☐ 9 Leon Lett | .35 | .16 | .04 |
| ☐ 10 Kevin Smith | .08 | .04 | .01 |
| ☐ 11 Robert Jones | .05 | .02 | .01 |
| ☐ 12 Jimmy Smith | .05 | .02 | .01 |
| ☐ 13 Derrick Gainer | .10 | .05 | .01 |
| ☐ 14 Lin Elliott | .05 | .02 | .01 |
| ☐ 15 William Thomas | .05 | .02 | .01 |
| ☐ 16 Clyde Simmons | .08 | .04 | .01 |
| ☐ 17 Seth Joyner | .08 | .04 | .01 |
| ☐ 18 Randall Cunningham | .10 | .05 | .01 |
| ☐ 19 Byron Evans | .05 | .02 | .01 |
| ☐ 20 Fred Barnett | .10 | .05 | .01 |

| ☐ 21 Calvin Williams | .10 | .05 | .01 |
|---|---|---|---|
| ☐ 22 James Joseph | .05 | .02 | .01 |
| ☐ 23 Heath Sherman | .05 | .02 | .01 |
| ☐ 24 Siran Stacy | .05 | .02 | .01 |
| ☐ 25 Andy Harmon | .05 | .02 | .01 |
| ☐ 26 Eric Allen | .08 | .04 | .01 |
| ☐ 27 Herschel Walker | .10 | .05 | .01 |
| ☐ 28 Vai Sikahema | .05 | .02 | .01 |
| ☐ 29 Earnest Byner | .08 | .04 | .01 |
| ☐ 30 Jeff Bostic | .05 | .02 | .01 |
| ☐ 31 Monte Coleman | .05 | .02 | .01 |
| ☐ 32 Ricky Ervins | .08 | .04 | .01 |
| ☐ 33 Darrell Green | .08 | .04 | .01 |
| ☐ 34 Mark Schlereth | .05 | .02 | .01 |
| ☐ 35 Mark Rypien | .08 | .04 | .01 |
| ☐ 36 Art Monk | .10 | .05 | .01 |
| ☐ 37 Brian Mitchell | .08 | .04 | .01 |
| ☐ 38 Chip Lohmiller | .05 | .02 | .01 |
| ☐ 39 Charles Mann | .05 | .02 | .01 |
| ☐ 40 Shane Collins | .05 | .02 | .01 |
| ☐ 41 Jim Lachey | .05 | .02 | .01 |
| ☐ 42 Desmond Howard | .05 | .02 | .01 |
| ☐ 43 Rodney Hampton | .30 | .14 | .04 |
| ☐ 44 Dave Brown | .75 | .35 | .09 |
| ☐ 45 Mark Collins | .05 | .02 | .01 |
| ☐ 46 Jarrod Bunch | .05 | .02 | .01 |
| ☐ 47 William Roberts | .05 | .02 | .01 |
| ☐ 48 Sean Landeta | .05 | .02 | .01 |
| ☐ 49 Lawrence Taylor | .10 | .05 | .01 |
| ☐ 50 Ed McCaffrey | .05 | .02 | .01 |
| ☐ 51 Bart Oates | .05 | .02 | .01 |
| ☐ 52 Pepper Johnson | .05 | .02 | .01 |
| ☐ 53 Eric Dorsey | .05 | .02 | .01 |
| ☐ 54 Erik Howard | .05 | .02 | .01 |
| ☐ 55 Phil Simms | .10 | .05 | .01 |
| ☐ 56 Derek Brown | .08 | .04 | .01 |
| ☐ 57 Johnny Bailey | .05 | .02 | .01 |
| ☐ 58 Rich Camarillo | .05 | .02 | .01 |
| ☐ 59 Larry Centers | .25 | .11 | .03 |
| ☐ 60 Chris Chandler | .08 | .04 | .01 |
| ☐ 61 Randal Hill | .10 | .05 | .01 |
| ☐ 62 Ricky Proehl | .08 | .04 | .01 |
| ☐ 63 Freddie Joe Nunn | .05 | .02 | .01 |
| ☐ 64 Robert Massey | .05 | .02 | .01 |
| ☐ 65 Aeneas Williams | .05 | .02 | .01 |
| ☐ 66 Luis Sharpe | .05 | .02 | .01 |
| ☐ 67 Eric Swann | .08 | .04 | .01 |
| ☐ 68 Timm Rosenbach | .05 | .02 | .01 |
| ☐ 69 Anthony Edwards | .25 | .11 | .03 |
| ☐ 70 Greg Davis | .05 | .02 | .01 |
| ☐ 71 Terry Allen | .10 | .05 | .01 |
| ☐ 72 Anthony Carter | .08 | .04 | .01 |
| ☐ 73 Cris Carter | .10 | .05 | .01 |
| ☐ 74 Roger Craig | .08 | .04 | .01 |
| ☐ 75 Jack Del Rio | .05 | .02 | .01 |
| ☐ 76 Chris Doleman | .08 | .04 | .01 |
| ☐ 77 Rich Gannon | .08 | .04 | .01 |
| ☐ 78 Hassan Jones | .05 | .02 | .01 |
| ☐ 79 Steve Jordan | .08 | .04 | .01 |
| ☐ 80 Randall McDaniel | .05 | .02 | .01 |
| ☐ 81 Sean Salisbury | .08 | .04 | .01 |
| ☐ 82 Harry Newsome | .05 | .02 | .01 |
| ☐ 83 Carlos Jenkins | .05 | .02 | .01 |
| ☐ 84 Jake Reed | .05 | .02 | .01 |
| ☐ 85 Edgar Bennett | .10 | .05 | .01 |
| ☐ 86 Tony Bennett | .05 | .02 | .01 |
| ☐ 87 Terrell Buckley | .10 | .05 | .01 |
| ☐ 88 Ty Detmer | .08 | .04 | .01 |
| ☐ 89 Brett Favre | .75 | .35 | .09 |
| ☐ 90 Chris Jacke | .05 | .02 | .01 |
| ☐ 91 Sterling Sharpe | .40 | .18 | .05 |
| ☐ 92 James Campen | .05 | .02 | .01 |
| ☐ 93 Brian Noble | .05 | .02 | .01 |
| ☐ 94 Lester Archambeau | .10 | .05 | .01 |
| ☐ 95 Harry Sydney | .05 | .02 | .01 |
| ☐ 96 Corey Harris | .05 | .02 | .01 |
| ☐ 97 Don Majkowski | .08 | .04 | .01 |
| ☐ 98 Ken Ruettgers | .05 | .02 | .01 |
| ☐ 99 Lomas Brown | .05 | .02 | .01 |
| ☐ 100 Jason Hanson | .05 | .02 | .01 |
| ☐ 101 Robert Porcher | .08 | .04 | .01 |
| ☐ 102 Chris Spielman | .05 | .02 | .01 |
| ☐ 103 Erik Kramer | .15 | .07 | .02 |
| ☐ 104 Tracy Scroggins | .08 | .04 | .01 |
| ☐ 105 Rodney Peete | .08 | .04 | .01 |
| ☐ 106 Barry Sanders | .75 | .35 | .09 |
| ☐ 107 Herman Moore | .35 | .16 | .04 |
| ☐ 108 Brett Perriman | .08 | .04 | .01 |
| ☐ 109 Mel Gray | .05 | .02 | .01 |
| ☐ 110 Dennis Gibson | .05 | .02 | .01 |
| ☐ 111 Bennie Blades | .05 | .02 | .01 |
| ☐ 112 Andre Ware | .08 | .04 | .01 |
| ☐ 113 Gary Anderson | .05 | .02 | .01 |
| ☐ 114 Tyji Armstrong | .05 | .02 | .01 |
| ☐ 115 Reggie Cobb | .10 | .05 | .01 |
| ☐ 116 Marty Carter | .05 | .02 | .01 |
| ☐ 117 Lawrence Dawsey | .10 | .05 | .01 |

|  |  | | | |
|---|------|---|---|---|
| ☐ 118 | Steve DeBerg | .08 | .04 | .01 |
| ☐ 119 | Ron Hall | .05 | .02 | .01 |
| ☐ 120 | Courtney Hawkins | .08 | .04 | .01 |
| ☐ 121 | Broderick Thomas | .05 | .02 | .01 |
| ☐ 122 | Keith McCants | .05 | .02 | .01 |
| ☐ 123 | Bruce Reimers | .05 | .02 | .01 |
| ☐ 124 | Darrick Brownlow | .05 | .02 | .01 |
| ☐ 125 | Mark Wheeler | .05 | .02 | .01 |
| ☐ 126 | Ricky Reynolds | .05 | .02 | .01 |
| ☐ 127 | Neal Anderson | .08 | .04 | .01 |
| ☐ 128 | Trace Armstrong | .05 | .02 | .01 |
| ☐ 129 | Mark (USC) Carrier | .05 | .02 | .01 |
| ☐ 130 | Richard Dent | .08 | .04 | .01 |
| ☐ 131 | Wendell Davis | .05 | .02 | .01 |
| ☐ 132 | Darren Lewis | .05 | .02 | .01 |
| ☐ 133 | Tom Waddle | .10 | .05 | .01 |
| ☐ 134 | Jim Harbaugh | .08 | .04 | .01 |
| ☐ 135 | Steve McMichael | .05 | .02 | .01 |
| ☐ 136 | William Perry | .05 | .02 | .01 |
| ☐ 137 | Alonzo Spellman | .08 | .04 | .01 |
| ☐ 138 | John Roper | .05 | .02 | .01 |
| ☐ 139 | Peter Tom Willis | .05 | .02 | .01 |
| ☐ 140 | Dante Jones | .05 | .02 | .01 |
| ☐ 141 | Harris Barton | .05 | .02 | .01 |
| ☐ 142 | Michael Carter | .05 | .02 | .01 |
| ☐ 143 | Eric Davis | .05 | .02 | .01 |
| ☐ 144 | Dana Hall | .05 | .02 | .01 |
| ☐ 145 | Amp Lee | .08 | .04 | .01 |
| ☐ 146 | Don Griffin | .05 | .02 | .01 |
| ☐ 147 | Jerry Rice | .60 | .25 | .08 |
| ☐ 148 | Ricky Watters | .30 | .14 | .04 |
| ☐ 149 | Steve Young | .30 | .14 | .04 |
| ☐ 150 | Bill Romanowski | .05 | .02 | .01 |
| ☐ 151 | Klaus Wilmsmeyer | .05 | .02 | .01 |
| ☐ 152 | Steve Bono | .15 | .07 | .02 |
| ☐ 153 | Tom Rathman | .08 | .04 | .01 |
| ☐ 154 | Odessa Turner | .05 | .02 | .01 |
| ☐ 155 | Morten Andersen | .08 | .04 | .01 |
| ☐ 156 | Richard Cooper | .05 | .02 | .01 |
| ☐ 157 | Toi Cook | .05 | .02 | .01 |
| ☐ 158 | Quinn Early | .08 | .04 | .01 |
| ☐ 159 | Vaughn Dunbar | .08 | .04 | .01 |
| ☐ 160 | Rickey Jackson | .08 | .04 | .01 |
| ☐ 161 | Wayne Martin | .05 | .02 | .01 |
| ☐ 162 | Hoby Brenner | .05 | .02 | .01 |
| ☐ 163 | Joel Hilgenberg | .05 | .02 | .01 |
| ☐ 164 | Mike Buck | .05 | .02 | .01 |
| ☐ 165 | Torrance Small | .05 | .02 | .01 |
| ☐ 166 | Eric Martin | .08 | .04 | .01 |
| ☐ 167 | Vaughan Johnson | .05 | .02 | .01 |
| ☐ 168 | Sam Mills | .08 | .04 | .01 |
| ☐ 169 | Steve Broussard | .05 | .02 | .01 |
| ☐ 170 | Darion Conner | .05 | .02 | .01 |
| ☐ 171 | Drew Hill | .08 | .04 | .01 |
| ☐ 172 | Chris Hinton | .05 | .02 | .01 |
| ☐ 173 | Chris Miller | .10 | .05 | .01 |
| ☐ 174 | Tim McKyer | .08 | .04 | .01 |
| ☐ 175 | Norm Johnson | .05 | .02 | .01 |
| ☐ 176 | Mike Pritchard | .10 | .05 | .01 |
| ☐ 177 | Andre Rison | .25 | .11 | .03 |
| ☐ 178 | Deion Sanders | .15 | .07 | .02 |
| ☐ 179 | Tony Smith | .05 | .02 | .01 |
| ☐ 180 | Bruce Pickens | .05 | .02 | .01 |
| ☐ 181 | Michael Haynes | .20 | .09 | .03 |
| ☐ 182 | Jessie Tuggle | .05 | .02 | .01 |
| ☐ 183 | Marc Boutte | .05 | .02 | .01 |
| ☐ 184 | Don Bracken | .05 | .02 | .01 |
| ☐ 185 | Bern Brostek | .05 | .02 | .01 |
| ☐ 186 | Henry Ellard | .08 | .04 | .01 |
| ☐ 187 | Jim Everett | .05 | .02 | .01 |
| ☐ 188 | Sean Gilbert | .08 | .04 | .01 |
| ☐ 189 | Cleveland Gary | .08 | .04 | .01 |
| ☐ 190 | Todd Kinchen | .08 | .04 | .01 |
| ☐ 191 | Pat Terrell | .05 | .02 | .01 |
| ☐ 192 | Jackie Slater | .05 | .02 | .01 |
| ☐ 193 | David Lang | .05 | .02 | .01 |
| ☐ 194 | Flipper Anderson | .08 | .04 | .01 |
| ☐ 195 | Tony Zendejas | .05 | .02 | .01 |
| ☐ 196 | Roman Phifer | .05 | .02 | .01 |
| ☐ 197 | Steve Christie | .05 | .02 | .01 |
| ☐ 198 | Cornelius Bennett | .10 | .05 | .01 |
| ☐ 199 | Phil Hansen | .05 | .02 | .01 |
| ☐ 200 | Don Beebe | .10 | .05 | .01 |
| ☐ 201 | Mark Kelso | .05 | .02 | .01 |
| ☐ 202 | Bruce Smith | .10 | .05 | .01 |
| ☐ 203 | Darryl Talley | .05 | .02 | .01 |
| ☐ 204 | Andre Reed | .10 | .05 | .01 |
| ☐ 205 | Mike Lodish | .05 | .02 | .01 |
| ☐ 206 | Jim Kelly | .25 | .11 | .03 |
| ☐ 207 | Thurman Thomas | .35 | .16 | .04 |
| ☐ 208 | Kenneth Davis | .05 | .02 | .01 |
| ☐ 209 | Frank Reich | .08 | .04 | .01 |
| ☐ 210 | Kent Hull | .05 | .02 | .01 |
| ☐ 211 | Marco Coleman | .08 | .04 | .01 |
| ☐ 212 | Bryan Cox | .08 | .04 | .01 |
| ☐ 213 | Jeff Cross | .05 | .02 | .01 |
| ☐ 214 | Mark Higgs | .10 | .05 | .01 |
| ☐ 215 | Keith Jackson | .10 | .05 | .01 |
| ☐ 216 | Scott Miller | .05 | .02 | .01 |
| ☐ 217 | John Offerdahl | .05 | .02 | .01 |
| ☐ 218 | Dan Marino | .75 | .35 | .09 |
| ☐ 219 | Keith Sims | .05 | .02 | .01 |
| ☐ 220 | Chuck Klingbeil | .05 | .02 | .01 |
| ☐ 221 | Troy Vincent | .08 | .04 | .01 |
| ☐ 222 | Mike Williams | .10 | .05 | .01 |
| ☐ 223 | Pete Stoyanovich | .05 | .02 | .01 |
| ☐ 224 | J.B. Brown | .05 | .02 | .01 |
| ☐ 225 | Ashley Ambrose | .05 | .02 | .01 |
| ☐ 226 | Jason Belser | .10 | .05 | .01 |
| ☐ 227 | Jeff George | .15 | .07 | .02 |
| ☐ 228 | Quentin Coryatt | .10 | .05 | .01 |
| ☐ 229 | Duane Bickett | .05 | .02 | .01 |
| ☐ 230 | Steve Emtman | .08 | .04 | .01 |
| ☐ 231 | Anthony Johnson | .05 | .02 | .01 |
| ☐ 232 | Rohn Stark | .05 | .02 | .01 |
| ☐ 233 | Jessie Hester | .05 | .02 | .01 |
| ☐ 234 | Reggie Langhorne | .08 | .04 | .01 |
| ☐ 235 | Clarence Verdin | .05 | .02 | .01 |
| ☐ 236 | Dean Biasucci | .05 | .02 | .01 |
| ☐ 237 | Jack Trudeau | .05 | .02 | .01 |
| ☐ 238 | Tony Siragusa | .05 | .02 | .01 |
| ☐ 239 | Chris Burkett | .05 | .02 | .01 |
| ☐ 240 | Brad Baxter | .08 | .04 | .01 |
| ☐ 241 | Rob Moore | .10 | .05 | .01 |
| ☐ 242 | Browning Nagle | .08 | .04 | .01 |
| ☐ 243 | Jim Sweeney | .05 | .02 | .01 |
| ☐ 244 | Kurt Barber | .05 | .02 | .01 |
| ☐ 245 | Siupeli Malamala | .10 | .05 | .01 |
| ☐ 246 | Mike Brim | .05 | .02 | .01 |
| ☐ 247 | Mo Lewis | .05 | .02 | .01 |
| ☐ 248 | Johnny Mitchell | .25 | .11 | .03 |
| ☐ 249 | Ken Whisenhunt | .10 | .05 | .01 |
| ☐ 250 | James Hasty | .05 | .02 | .01 |
| ☐ 251 | Kyle Clifton | .05 | .02 | .01 |
| ☐ 252 | Terance Mathis | .05 | .02 | .01 |
| ☐ 253 | Ray Agnew | .05 | .02 | .01 |
| ☐ 254 | Eugene Chung | .05 | .02 | .01 |
| ☐ 255 | Marv Cook | .05 | .02 | .01 |
| ☐ 256 | Johnny Rembert | .05 | .02 | .01 |
| ☐ 257 | Maurice Hurst | .05 | .02 | .01 |
| ☐ 258 | Jon Vaughn | .05 | .02 | .01 |
| ☐ 259 | Leonard Russell | .08 | .04 | .01 |
| ☐ 260 | Pat Harlow | .05 | .02 | .01 |
| ☐ 261 | Andre Tippett | .05 | .02 | .01 |
| ☐ 262 | Michael Timpson | .05 | .02 | .01 |
| ☐ 263 | Greg McMurtry | .05 | .02 | .01 |
| ☐ 264 | Chris Singleton | .05 | .02 | .01 |
| ☐ 265 | Reggie Redding | .10 | .05 | .01 |
| ☐ 266 | Walter Stanley | .05 | .02 | .01 |
| ☐ 267 | Gary Anderson (K) | .05 | .02 | .01 |
| ☐ 268 | Merril Hoge | .05 | .02 | .01 |
| ☐ 269 | Barry Foster | .25 | .11 | .03 |
| ☐ 270 | Charles Davenport | .05 | .02 | .01 |
| ☐ 271 | Jeff Graham | .08 | .04 | .01 |
| ☐ 272 | Adrian Cooper | .05 | .02 | .01 |
| ☐ 273 | David Little | .05 | .02 | .01 |
| ☐ 274 | Neil O'Donnell | .25 | .11 | .03 |
| ☐ 275 | Rod Woodson | .10 | .05 | .01 |
| ☐ 276 | Ernie Mills | .05 | .02 | .01 |
| ☐ 277 | Dwight Stone | .05 | .02 | .01 |
| ☐ 278 | Darren Perry | .05 | .02 | .01 |
| ☐ 279 | Dermontti Dawson | .05 | .02 | .01 |
| ☐ 280 | Carlton Haselrig | .05 | .02 | .01 |
| ☐ 281 | Pat Coleman | .05 | .02 | .01 |
| ☐ 282 | Ernest Givins | .08 | .04 | .01 |
| ☐ 283 | Warren Moon | .20 | .09 | .03 |
| ☐ 284 | Haywood Jeffires | .10 | .05 | .01 |
| ☐ 285 | Cody Carlson | .20 | .09 | .03 |
| ☐ 286 | Ray Childress | .05 | .02 | .01 |
| ☐ 287 | Bruce Matthews | .08 | .04 | .01 |
| ☐ 288 | Webster Slaughter | .08 | .04 | .01 |
| ☐ 289 | Bo Orlando | .05 | .02 | .01 |
| ☐ 290 | Lorenzo White | .08 | .04 | .01 |
| ☐ 291 | Eddie Robinson | .05 | .02 | .01 |
| ☐ 292 | Bubba McDowell | .05 | .02 | .01 |
| ☐ 293 | Bucky Richardson | .05 | .02 | .01 |
| ☐ 294 | Sean Jones | .05 | .02 | .01 |
| ☐ 295 | David Brandon | .05 | .02 | .01 |
| ☐ 296 | Shawn Collins | .05 | .02 | .01 |
| ☐ 297 | Lawyer Tillman | .05 | .02 | .01 |
| ☐ 298 | Bob Dahl | .05 | .02 | .01 |
| ☐ 299 | Kevin Mack | .05 | .02 | .01 |
| ☐ 300 | Bernie Kosar | .10 | .05 | .01 |
| ☐ 301 | Tommy Vardell | .05 | .02 | .01 |
| ☐ 302 | Jay Hilgenberg | .05 | .02 | .01 |
| ☐ 303 | Michael Dean Perry | .10 | .05 | .01 |
| ☐ 304 | Michael Jackson | .10 | .05 | .01 |
| ☐ 305 | Eric Metcalf | .10 | .05 | .01 |
| ☐ 306 | Rico Smith | .10 | .05 | .01 |
| ☐ 307 | Stevon Moore | .10 | .05 | .01 |
| ☐ 308 | Leroy Hoard | .08 | .04 | .01 |
| ☐ 309 | Eric Ball | .05 | .02 | .01 |
| ☐ 310 | Derrick Fenner | .05 | .02 | .01 |
| ☐ 311 | James Francis | .05 | .02 | .01 |

|  |  | | | |
|---|--------|---|---|---|
| 312 | Ricardo McDonald | .05 | .02 | .01 |
| 313 | Tim Krumrie | .05 | .02 | .01 |
| 314 | Carl Pickens | .10 | .05 | .01 |
| 315 | David Klingler | .15 | .07 | .02 |
| 316 | Donald Hollas | .05 | .02 | .01 |
| 317 | Harold Green | .08 | .04 | .01 |
| 318 | Daniel Stubbs | .05 | .02 | .01 |
| 319 | Alfred Williams | .05 | .02 | .01 |
| 320 | Darryl Williams | .08 | .04 | .01 |
| 321 | Mike Arthur | .10 | .05 | .01 |
| 322 | Leonard Wheeler | .05 | .02 | .01 |
| 323 | Gill Byrd | .05 | .02 | .01 |
| 324 | Eric Bieniemy | .08 | .04 | .01 |
| 325 | Marion Butts | .10 | .05 | .01 |
| 326 | John Carney | .05 | .02 | .01 |
| 327 | Stan Humphries | .10 | .05 | .01 |
| 328 | Ronnie Harmon | .05 | .02 | .01 |
| 329 | Junior Seau | .10 | .05 | .01 |
| 330 | Nate Lewis | .08 | .04 | .01 |
| 331 | Harry Swayne | .05 | .02 | .01 |
| 332 | Leslie O'Neal | .08 | .04 | .01 |
| 333 | Eric Moten | .05 | .02 | .01 |
| 334 | Blaise Winter | .10 | .05 | .01 |
| 335 | Anthony Miller | .15 | .07 | .02 |
| 336 | Gary Plummer | .05 | .02 | .01 |
| 337 | Willie Davis | .10 | .05 | .01 |
| 338 | J.J. Birden | .08 | .04 | .01 |
| 339 | Tim Barnett | .08 | .04 | .01 |
| 340 | Dave Krieg | .08 | .04 | .01 |
| 341 | Barry Word | .10 | .05 | .01 |
| 342 | Tracy Simien | .05 | .02 | .01 |
| 343 | Christian Okoye | .08 | .04 | .01 |
| 344 | Todd McNair | .05 | .02 | .01 |
| 345 | Dan Saleaumua | .05 | .02 | .01 |
| 346 | Derrick Thomas | .15 | .07 | .02 |
| 347 | Harvey Williams | .10 | .05 | .01 |
| 348 | Kimble Anders | .40 | .18 | .05 |
| 349 | Tim Grunhard | .05 | .02 | .01 |
| 350 | Tony Hargain UER | .10 | .05 | .01 |
| | (Hargrain on front) | | | |
| 351 | Simon Fletcher | .08 | .04 | .01 |
| 352 | John Elway | .35 | .16 | .04 |
| 353 | Mike Croel | .08 | .04 | .01 |
| 354 | Steve Atwater | .08 | .04 | .01 |
| 355 | Tommy Maddox | .15 | .07 | .02 |
| 356 | Karl Mecklenburg | .05 | .02 | .01 |
| 357 | Shane Dronett | .05 | .02 | .01 |
| 358 | Kenny Walker | .05 | .02 | .01 |
| 359 | Reggie Rivers | .20 | .09 | .03 |
| 360 | Cedric Tillman | .15 | .07 | .02 |
| 361 | Arthur Marshall | .25 | .11 | .03 |
| 362 | Greg Lewis | .05 | .02 | .01 |
| 363 | Shannon Sharpe | .25 | .11 | .03 |
| 364 | Doug Widell | .05 | .02 | .01 |
| 365 | Todd Marinovich | .05 | .02 | .01 |
| 366 | Nick Bell | .08 | .04 | .01 |
| 367 | Eric Dickerson | .10 | .05 | .01 |
| 368 | Max Montoya | .05 | .02 | .01 |
| 369 | Winston Moss | .05 | .02 | .01 |
| 370 | Howie Long | .08 | .04 | .01 |
| 371 | Willie Gault | .08 | .04 | .01 |
| 372 | Tim Brown | .25 | .11 | .03 |
| 373 | Steve Smith | .08 | .04 | .01 |
| 374 | Steve Wisniewski | .05 | .02 | .01 |
| 375 | Alexander Wright | .08 | .04 | .01 |
| 376 | Ethan Horton | .05 | .02 | .01 |
| 377 | Napoleon McCallum | .05 | .02 | .01 |
| 378 | Terry McDaniel | .05 | .02 | .01 |
| 379 | Patrick Hunter | .05 | .02 | .01 |
| 380 | Robert Blackmon | .05 | .02 | .01 |
| 381 | John Kasay | .05 | .02 | .01 |
| 382 | Cortez Kennedy | .10 | .05 | .01 |
| 383 | Andy Heck | .05 | .02 | .01 |
| 384 | Bill Hitchcock | .10 | .05 | .01 |
| 385 | Rick Mirer | 3.00 | 1.35 | .40 |
| 386 | Jeff Bryant | .05 | .02 | .01 |
| 387 | Eugene Robinson | .05 | .02 | .01 |
| 388 | John L. Williams | .08 | .04 | .01 |
| 389 | Chris Warren | .20 | .09 | .03 |
| 390 | Rufus Porter | .05 | .02 | .01 |
| 391 | Joe Tofflemire | .10 | .05 | .01 |
| 392 | Dan McGwire | .08 | .04 | .01 |
| 393 | Boomer Esiason | .12 | .05 | .02 |
| | Cincinnati Bengals | | | |
| 394 | Brad Muster | .08 | .04 | .01 |
| | Chicago Bears | | | |
| 395 | James Lofton | .10 | .05 | .01 |
| | Buffalo Bills | | | |
| 396 | Tim McGee | .05 | .02 | .01 |
| | Cincinnati Bengals | | | |
| 397 | Steve Beuerlein | .15 | .07 | .02 |
| | Dallas Cowboys | | | |
| 398 | Gaston Green | .08 | .04 | .01 |
| | Denver Broncos | | | |
| 399 | Bill Brooks | .05 | .02 | .01 |
| | Indianapolis Colts | | | |
| 400 | Ronnie Lott | .10 | .05 | .01 |
| | Los Angeles Raiders | | | |
| 401 | Jay Schroeder | .05 | .02 | .01 |
| | Los Angeles Raiders | | | |
| 402 | Marcus Allen | .08 | .04 | .01 |
| | Los Angeles Raiders | | | |
| 403 | Kevin Greene | .05 | .02 | .01 |
| | Los Angeles Rams | | | |
| 404 | Kirk Lowdermilk | .05 | .02 | .01 |
| | Minnesota Vikings | | | |
| 405 | Hugh Millen | .05 | .02 | .01 |
| | New England Patriots | | | |
| 406 | Pat Swilling | .08 | .04 | .01 |
| | New Orleans Saints | | | |
| 407 | Bobby Hebert | .10 | .05 | .01 |
| | New Orleans Saints | | | |
| 408 | Carl Banks | .05 | .02 | .01 |
| | New York Giants | | | |
| 409 | Jeff Hostetler | .10 | .05 | .01 |
| | New York Giants | | | |
| 410 | Leonard Marshall | .05 | .02 | .01 |
| | New York Giants | | | |
| 411 | Ken O'Brien | .08 | .04 | .01 |
| | New York Jets | | | |
| 412 | Joe Montana | 1.00 | .45 | .13 |
| | San Francisco 49ers | | | |
| 413 | Reggie White | .15 | .07 | .02 |
| | Philadelphia Eagles | | | |
| 414 | Gary Clark | .08 | .04 | .01 |
| | Washington Redskins | | | |
| 415 | Johnny Johnson | .10 | .05 | .01 |
| | Phoenix Cardinals | | | |
| 416 | Tim McDonald | .05 | .02 | .01 |
| | Phoenix Cardinals | | | |
| 417 | Pierce Holt | .05 | .02 | .01 |
| | San Francisco 49ers | | | |
| 418 | Gino Torretta | .30 | .14 | .04 |
| | Minnesota Vikings | | | |
| 419 | Glyn Milburn | .75 | .35 | .09 |
| | Denver Broncos | | | |
| 420 | O.J. McDuffie | 1.25 | .55 | .16 |
| | Miami Dolphins | | | |
| 421 | Coleman Rudolph | .10 | .05 | .01 |
| | New York Jets | | | |
| 422 | Reggie Brooks | 2.00 | .90 | .25 |
| | Washington Redskins | | | |
| 423 | Garrison Hearst | .60 | .25 | .08 |
| | Phoenix Cardinals | | | |
| 424 | Leonard Renfro | .10 | .05 | .01 |
| | Philadelphia Eagles | | | |
| 425 | Kevin Williams | .50 | .23 | .06 |
| | Dallas Cowboys | | | |
| 426 | Demetrius DuBose | .20 | .09 | .03 |
| | Tampa Bay Buccaneers | | | |
| 427 | Elvis Grbac | .50 | .23 | .06 |
| | San Francisco 49ers | | | |
| 428 | Lincoln Kennedy | .15 | .07 | .02 |
| | Atlanta Falcons | | | |
| 429 | Carlton Gray | .20 | .09 | .03 |
| | Seattle Seahawks | | | |
| 430 | Micheal Barrow | .10 | .05 | .01 |
| | Houston Oilers | | | |
| 431 | George Teague | .20 | .09 | .03 |
| | Green Bay Packers | | | |
| 432 | Curtis Conway | .50 | .23 | .06 |
| | Chicago Bears | | | |
| 433 | Natrone Means | 1.50 | .65 | .19 |
| | San Diego Chargers | | | |
| 434 | Jerome Bettis | 3.00 | 1.35 | .40 |
| | Los Angeles Rams | | | |
| 435 | Drew Bledsoe | 3.00 | 1.35 | .40 |
| | New England Patriots | | | |
| 436 | Robert Smith | .35 | .16 | .04 |
| | Minnesota Vikings | | | |
| 437 | Deon Figures | .15 | .07 | .02 |
| | Pittsburgh Steelers | | | |
| 438 | Qadry Ismail | .50 | .23 | .06 |
| | Minnesota Vikings | | | |
| 439 | Chris Slade | .35 | .16 | .04 |
| | New England Patriots | | | |
| 440 | Dana Stubblefield | .50 | .23 | .06 |
| | San Francisco 49ers | | | |

# 1993 Pacific Checklists

These four standard-size (2 1/2" by 3 1/2") checklist cards were randomly inserted in foil packs. The players' names are printed on a gray marbleized panel tilted slightly to the left. The cards are numbered on their fronts at the lower right corner.

| | MINT | EXC | G-VG |
|---|---|---|---|
| COMPLETE SET (4) | 2.00 | .80 | .20 |
| COMMON CARD (1-4) | .50 | .20 | .05 |
| | | | |
| ☐ 1 Checklist 1 UER | .50 | .20 | .05 |
| (42 Joe Jacoby replaced | | | |
| by Desmond Howard) | | | |

| | MINT | EXC | G-VG |
|---|---|---|---|
| ☐ 2 Checklist 2 | .50 | .20 | .05 |
| ☐ 3 Checklist 3 | .50 | .20 | .05 |
| ☐ 4 Checklist 4 | .50 | .20 | .05 |

# 1993 Pacific Picks the Pros Gold

These 25 standard size (2 1/2" by 3 1/2") cards showcasing Pacific's picks at each position were random inserts in '93 Pacific packs. Cards from the parallel silver version of this set were randomly inserted in packs of '93 Pacific Triple Folders. The fronts feature gold foil-bordered color player action shots. The player's name and position appear in white lettering in the gold-foil margin beneath the photo. The horizontal white-bordered back carries the player's name, position, team name, and season highlights in diagonal black lettering set on a gray and blue background. The cards are numbered on the back.

| | MINT | EXC | G-VG |
|---|---|---|---|
| COMPLETE SET (25) | 100.00 | 45.00 | 12.50 |
| COMMON PLAYER (1-25) | 3.00 | 1.35 | .40 |
| ☐ 1 Jerry Rice | 12.00 | 5.50 | 1.50 |
| San Francisco 49ers | | | |
| ☐ 2 Sterling Sharpe | 12.00 | 5.50 | 1.50 |
| Green Bay Packers | | | |
| ☐ 3 Richmond Webb | 3.00 | 1.35 | .40 |
| Miami Dolphins | | | |
| ☐ 4 Harris Barton | 3.00 | 1.35 | .40 |
| San Francisco 49ers | | | |
| ☐ 5 Randall McDaniel | 3.00 | 1.35 | .40 |
| Minnesota Vikings | | | |
| ☐ 6 Steve Wisniewski | 3.00 | 1.35 | .40 |
| Los Angeles Raiders | | | |
| ☐ 7 Mark Stepnoski | 3.00 | 1.35 | .40 |
| Dallas Cowboys | | | |
| ☐ 8 Steve Young | 8.00 | 3.60 | 1.00 |
| San Francisco 49ers | | | |
| ☐ 9 Emmitt Smith | 27.00 | 12.00 | 3.40 |
| Dallas Cowboys | | | |
| ☐ 10 Barry Foster | 8.00 | 3.60 | 1.00 |
| Pittsburgh Steelers | | | |
| ☐ 11 Nick Lowery | 3.00 | 1.35 | .40 |
| Kansas City Chiefs | | | |
| ☐ 12 Reggie White | 5.00 | 2.30 | .60 |
| Green Bay Packers | | | |
| ☐ 13 Leslie O'Neal | 3.00 | 1.35 | .40 |
| San Diego Chargers | | | |
| ☐ 14 Cortez Kennedy | 4.00 | 1.80 | .50 |
| Seattle Seahawks | | | |
| ☐ 15 Ray Childress | 3.00 | 1.35 | .40 |
| Houston Oilers | | | |
| ☐ 16 Vaughan Johnson | 3.00 | 1.35 | .40 |
| New Orleans Saints | | | |
| ☐ 17 Wilber Marshall | 3.00 | 1.35 | .40 |
| Houston Oilers | | | |
| ☐ 18 Junior Seau | 4.00 | 1.80 | .50 |
| San Diego Chargers | | | |
| ☐ 19 Sam Mills | 3.00 | 1.35 | .40 |
| New Orleans Saints | | | |
| ☐ 20 Rod Woodson | 4.00 | 1.80 | .50 |
| Pittsburgh Steelers | | | |
| ☐ 21 Ricky Reynolds | 3.00 | 1.35 | .40 |
| Tampa Bay Buccaneers | | | |
| ☐ 22 Steve Atwater | 3.00 | 1.35 | .40 |
| Denver Broncos | | | |
| ☐ 23 Chuck Cecil | 3.00 | 1.35 | .40 |
| Phoenix Cardinals | | | |
| ☐ 24 Rich Camarillo | 3.00 | 1.35 | .40 |
| Phoenix Cardinals | | | |
| ☐ 25 Dale Carter | 3.00 | 1.35 | .40 |
| Kansas City Chiefs | | | |

# 1993 Pacific Silver Prism Inserts

There are three slightly different versions of this 20-card standard-size (2 1/2" by 3 1/2") set, and that difference involves the prismatic backgrounds. The standard 1993 Pacific Prism Inserts were produced with triangular prismatic backgrounds in quantities of 8,000 cards each, and were randomly inserted in regular (maroon-colored) 1993 Pacific, as well as 1993 Pacific Triple Folder packs. The circular versions of the prismatic background cards were inserted one per special (gold-colored) retail packs, and were apparently easier to get, since they're currently selling for considerably less than the triangular background versions. The third version uses a gold triangular prismatic background. The production of these cards was reportedly limited to 1,000 each, and they were randomly inserted in 1993 Pacific Triple Folder packs. The fronts feature color player action cut-outs over borderless prismatic foil backgrounds. The player's name appears in team-colored block lettering at the bottom. The borderless back carries the same player photo, but this time with its original on-field background. The player's name appears in white cursive lettering near a lower corner. The cards are numbered on the back. Randomly inserted in 12-card foil packs, this 20-card standard-size (2 1/2" by 3 1/2") insert set features 20 of the NFL's top players on a "Prism" background that makes the player contrast sharply with the background. The backs display a full-bleed color action player photo with the player's name and position in script. The cards are numbered on the back at the lower right "X of 20."

| | MINT | EXC | G-VG |
|---|---|---|---|
| COMPLETE SET (20) | 175.00 | 80.00 | 22.00 |
| COMMON PLAYER (1-20) | 5.00 | 2.30 | .60 |
| *CIRCULAR: .25X to .50X | | | |
| *GOLD: 1.5X to 2.5X VALUE | | | |
| ☐ 1 Troy Aikman | 24.00 | 11.00 | 3.00 |
| Dallas Cowboys | | | |
| ☐ 2 Jerome Bettis | 18.00 | 8.00 | 2.30 |
| Los Angeles Rams | | | |
| ☐ 3 Drew Bledsoe | 18.00 | 8.00 | 2.30 |
| New England Patriots | | | |
| ☐ 4 Reggie Brooks | 10.00 | 4.50 | 1.25 |
| Washington Redskins | | | |
| ☐ 5 Brett Favre | 12.00 | 5.50 | 1.50 |
| Green Bay Packers | | | |
| ☐ 6 Barry Foster | 8.00 | 3.60 | 1.00 |
| Pittsburgh Steelers | | | |
| ☐ 7 Garrison Hearst | 7.00 | 3.10 | .85 |
| Phoenix Cardinals | | | |
| ☐ 8 Michael Irvin | 10.00 | 4.50 | 1.25 |
| Dallas Cowboys | | | |
| ☐ 9 Cortez Kennedy | 5.00 | 2.30 | .60 |
| Seattle Seahawks | | | |
| ☐ 10 David Klingler | 6.00 | 2.70 | .75 |
| Cincinnati Bengals | | | |
| ☐ 11 Dan Marino | 16.00 | 7.25 | 2.00 |
| Miami Dolphins | | | |

| | | | |
|---|---|---|---|
| ☐ 12 Rick Mirer | 18.00 | 8.00 | 2.30 |
| Seattle Seahawks | | | |
| ☐ 13 Joe Montana | 20.00 | 9.00 | 2.50 |
| Kansas City Chiefs | | | |
| ☐ 14 Jay Novacek | 5.00 | 2.30 | .60 |
| Dallas Cowboys | | | |
| ☐ 15 Jerry Rice | 12.00 | 5.50 | 1.50 |
| San Francisco 49ers | | | |
| ☐ 16 Barry Sanders | 12.00 | 5.50 | 1.50 |
| Detroit Lions | | | |
| ☐ 17 Sterling Sharpe | 10.00 | 4.50 | 1.25 |
| Green Bay Packers | | | |
| ☐ 18 Emmitt Smith | 30.00 | 13.50 | 3.80 |
| Dallas Cowboys | | | |
| ☐ 19 Thurman Thomas | 8.00 | 3.60 | 1.00 |
| Buffalo Bills | | | |
| ☐ 20 Steve Young | 7.00 | 3.10 | .85 |
| San Francisco 49ers | | | |

## 1993 Pacific Prism Promos

These two standard-size (2 1/2" by 3 1/2") cards were given out and used as sales samples at the July 1993 Chicago National Sports Collectors Convention to preview Pacific's soon to be released 108-card prism set. The card design appears to be identical with that of the regular series of 1993 Pacific Prism football cards. In contrast to the regular prism cards, the players on the back are touching the helmets and the helmets are smaller. Moreover, the players are very close to the border on the left hand side of the card. Reportedly 5,550 promo sets were produced. The card fronts feature a color player cut out on a prismatic background, with the player's name at the bottom. On a marbleized background with the team helmet, the horizontal backs features two player cut outs and season summary. The cards are numbered on the back.

| | MINT | EXC | G-VG |
|---|---|---|---|
| COMPLETE SET (2) | 30.00 | 12.00 | 3.00 |
| COMMON PLAYER | 20.00 | 8.00 | 2.00 |
| | | | |
| ☐ 22 Emmitt Smith | 20.00 | 8.00 | 2.00 |
| Dallas Cowboys | | | |
| ☐ 61 Drew Bledsoe | 20.00 | 8.00 | 2.00 |
| New England Patriots | | | |

## 1993 Pacific Prisms

After debuting as an insert set in the 1992 Pacific NFL series, Pacific decided to release a 108-card set of Prism cards. The standard-size (2 1/2" by 3 1/2") cards comprising this set were issued in one-card packs and feature on their fronts color player action cut-outs over borderless triangular prismatic foil backgrounds. The player's name,

the characters of which resemble hand-printed upper case lettering, appears in team colors at the bottom. The horizontal back carries two color player photos, a helmet bearing his team's logo, and player profile, all superposed upon a grayish background. Just 17,000 of each card (or 2,500 cases) were produced. The cards are numbered on the back and checklisted below alphabetically according to teams as follows: Atlanta Falcons (1-5), Buffalo Bills (6-8), Chicago Bears (9-11), Cincinnati Bengals (12-14), Cleveland Browns (15-17), Dallas Cowboys (18-22), Denver Broncos (23-25), Detroit Lions (26-29), Green Bay Packers (30-33), Houston Oilers (34-37), Indianapolis Colts (38-40), Kansas City Chiefs (41-44), Los Angeles Raiders (45-47), Los Angeles Rams (48-51), Miami Dolphins (52-56), Minnesota Vikings (57-60), New England Patriots (61-65), New Orleans Saints (66-68), New York Giants (69-72), New York Jets (73-76), Philadelphia Eagles (77-79), Phoenix Cardinals (80-83), Pittsburgh Steelers (84-86), San Diego Chargers (87-89), San Francisco 49ers (90-93), Seattle Seahawks (94-98), Tampa Bay Buccaneers (99-102), and Washington Redskins (103-108). Rookie Cards include Jerome Bettis, Drew Bledsoe, Reggie Brooks and Rick Mirer.

| | MINT | EXC | G-VG |
|---|---|---|---|
| COMPLETE SET (108) | 200.00 | 90.00 | 25.00 |
| COMMON PLAYER (1-108) | 1.25 | .55 | .16 |
| | | | |
| ☐ 1 Chris Miller | 1.75 | .80 | .22 |
| ☐ 2 Mike Pritchard | 1.75 | .80 | .22 |
| ☐ 3 Andre Rison | 2.25 | 1.00 | .30 |
| ☐ 4 Deion Sanders | 2.25 | 1.00 | .30 |
| ☐ 5 Tony Smith | 1.25 | .55 | .16 |
| ☐ 6 Jim Kelly | 2.50 | 1.15 | .30 |
| ☐ 7 Andre Reed | 1.75 | .80 | .22 |
| ☐ 8 Thurman Thomas | 5.00 | 2.30 | .60 |
| ☐ 9 Neal Anderson | 1.25 | .55 | .16 |
| ☐ 10 Jim Harbaugh | 1.50 | .65 | .19 |
| ☐ 11 Donnell Woolford | 1.25 | .55 | .16 |
| ☐ 12 David Klingler | 3.00 | 1.35 | .40 |
| ☐ 13 Carl Pickens | 1.50 | .65 | .19 |
| ☐ 14 Alfred Williams | 1.25 | .55 | .16 |
| ☐ 15 Michael Jackson | 1.75 | .80 | .22 |
| ☐ 16 Bernie Kosar | 1.75 | .80 | .22 |
| ☐ 17 Tommy Vardell | 1.50 | .65 | .19 |
| ☐ 18 Troy Aikman | 16.00 | 7.25 | 2.00 |
| ☐ 19 Alvin Harper | 4.00 | 1.80 | .50 |
| ☐ 20 Michael Irvin | 7.00 | 3.10 | .85 |
| ☐ 21 Russell Maryland | 1.75 | .80 | .22 |
| ☐ 22 Emmitt Smith | 20.00 | 9.00 | 2.50 |
| ☐ 23 John Elway | 7.00 | 3.10 | .85 |
| ☐ 24 Tommy Maddox | 2.00 | .90 | .25 |
| ☐ 25 Shannon Sharpe | 2.50 | 1.15 | .30 |
| ☐ 26 Herman Moore | 4.00 | 1.80 | .50 |
| ☐ 27 Rodney Peete | 1.50 | .65 | .19 |
| ☐ 28 Barry Sanders | 10.00 | 4.50 | 1.25 |
| ☐ 29 Pat Swilling | 1.50 | .65 | .19 |
| ☐ 30 Terrell Buckley | 1.75 | .80 | .22 |
| ☐ 31 Brett Favre | 10.00 | 4.50 | 1.25 |
| ☐ 32 Sterling Sharpe | 7.00 | 3.10 | .85 |
| ☐ 33 Reggie White | 2.00 | .90 | .25 |
| ☐ 34 Ernest Givins | 1.25 | .55 | .16 |
| ☐ 35 Haywood Jeffires | 1.75 | .80 | .22 |
| ☐ 36 Warren Moon | 2.00 | .90 | .25 |
| ☐ 37 Lorenzo White | 1.50 | .65 | .19 |
| ☐ 38 Steve Emtman | 1.50 | .65 | .19 |
| ☐ 39 Jeff George | 2.25 | 1.00 | .30 |
| ☐ 40 Reggie Langhorne | 1.50 | .65 | .19 |
| ☐ 41 Dale Carter | 1.25 | .55 | .16 |
| ☐ 42 Joe Montana | 16.00 | 7.25 | 2.00 |
| ☐ 43 Derrick Thomas | 2.00 | .90 | .25 |
| ☐ 44 Barry Word | 1.75 | .80 | .22 |
| ☐ 45 Nick Bell | 1.50 | .65 | .19 |
| ☐ 46 Eric Dickerson | 1.75 | .80 | .22 |
| ☐ 47 Jeff Jaeger | 1.25 | .55 | .16 |
| ☐ 48 Jerome Bettis | 20.00 | 9.00 | 2.50 |
| ☐ 49 Henry Ellard | 1.50 | .65 | .19 |
| ☐ 50 Jim Everett | 1.25 | .55 | .16 |
| ☐ 51 Cleveland Gary | 1.50 | .65 | .19 |
| ☐ 52 Marco Coleman | 1.25 | .55 | .16 |
| ☐ 53 Mark Higgs | 1.75 | .80 | .22 |
| ☐ 54 Keith Jackson | 1.75 | .80 | .22 |
| ☐ 55 Dan Marino | 12.00 | 5.50 | 1.50 |
| ☐ 56 Troy Vincent | 1.50 | .65 | .19 |
| ☐ 57 Terry Allen | 1.75 | .80 | .22 |
| ☐ 58 Jack Del Rio | 1.25 | .55 | .16 |
| ☐ 59 Sean Salisbury | 1.50 | .65 | .19 |
| ☐ 60 Robert Smith | 4.00 | 1.80 | .50 |
| ☐ 61 Drew Bledsoe | 20.00 | 9.00 | 2.50 |
| ☐ 62 Marv Cook | 1.25 | .55 | .16 |
| ☐ 63 Irving Fryar | 1.25 | .55 | .16 |
| ☐ 64 Leonard Russell | 1.50 | .65 | .19 |
| ☐ 65 Andre Tippett | 1.25 | .55 | .16 |
| ☐ 66 Morten Andersen | 1.50 | .65 | .19 |
| ☐ 67 Vaughn Dunbar | 1.50 | .65 | .19 |
| ☐ 68 Eric Martin | 1.50 | .65 | .19 |
| ☐ 69 David Brown | 4.00 | 1.80 | .50 |
| ☐ 70 Rodney Hampton | 3.00 | 1.35 | .40 |
| ☐ 71 Phil Simms | 1.75 | .80 | .22 |

| | | | |
|---|---|---|---|
| ☐ 72 Lawrence Taylor | 2.00 | .90 | .25 |
| ☐ 73 Ronnie Lott | 1.75 | .80 | .22 |
| ☐ 74 Johnny Mitchell | 2.00 | .90 | .25 |
| ☐ 75 Rob Moore | 1.75 | .80 | .22 |
| ☐ 76 Browning Nagle | 1.50 | .65 | .19 |
| ☐ 77 Fred Barnett | 1.75 | .80 | .22 |
| ☐ 78 Randall Cunningham | 1.75 | .80 | .22 |
| ☐ 79 Herschel Walker | 1.75 | .80 | .22 |
| ☐ 80 Gary Clark | 1.50 | .65 | .19 |
| ☐ 81 Ken Harvey | 1.25 | .55 | .16 |
| ☐ 82 Garrison Hearst | 4.00 | 1.80 | .50 |
| ☐ 83 Ricky Proehl | 1.50 | .65 | .19 |
| ☐ 84 Barry Foster | 4.00 | 1.80 | .50 |
| ☐ 85 Ernie Mills | 1.25 | .55 | .16 |
| ☐ 86 Neil O'Donnell | 3.00 | 1.35 | .40 |
| ☐ 87 Stan Humphries | 1.75 | .80 | .22 |
| ☐ 88 Leslie O'Neal | 1.50 | .65 | .19 |
| ☐ 89 Junior Seau | 1.75 | .80 | .22 |
| ☐ 90 Amp Lee | 1.50 | .65 | .19 |
| ☐ 91 Jerry Rice | 8.00 | 3.60 | 1.00 |
| ☐ 92 Ricky Watters | 4.00 | 1.80 | .50 |
| ☐ 93 Steve Young | 4.00 | 1.80 | .50 |
| ☐ 94 Cortez Kennedy | 1.75 | .80 | .22 |
| ☐ 95 Rick Mirer | 20.00 | 9.00 | 2.50 |
| ☐ 96 Eugene Robinson | 1.25 | .55 | .16 |
| ☐ 97 Chris Warren | 2.00 | .90 | .25 |
| ☐ 98 John L. Williams | 1.25 | .55 | .16 |
| ☐ 99 Reggie Cobb | 1.75 | .80 | .22 |
| ☐ 100 Lawrence Dawsey | 1.75 | .80 | .22 |
| ☐ 101 Santana Dotson | 1.75 | .80 | .22 |
| ☐ 102 Courtney Hawkins | 1.25 | .55 | .16 |
| ☐ 103 Reggie Brooks | 14.00 | 6.25 | 1.75 |
| ☐ 104 Ricky Ervins | 1.50 | .65 | .19 |
| ☐ 105 Desmond Howard | 2.00 | .90 | .25 |
| ☐ 106 Art Monk | 1.75 | .80 | .22 |
| ☐ 107 Mark Rypien | 1.50 | .65 | .19 |
| ☐ 108 Ricky Sanders | 1.50 | .65 | .19 |

| | | | |
|---|---|---|---|
| New England Patriots | | | |
| ☐ 11 Rob Moore | .75 | .30 | .07 |
| New York Jets | | | |
| ☐ 12 Barry Foster | .75 | .30 | .07 |
| Pittsburgh Steelers | | | |
| ☐ 13 Stan Humphries | .75 | .30 | .07 |
| San Diego Chargers | | | |
| ☐ 14 Cortez Kennedy | .75 | .30 | .07 |
| Seattle Seahawks | | | |
| ☐ 15 Rick Mirer | 3.00 | 1.20 | .30 |
| Seattle Seahawks | | | |
| ☐ 16 Deion Sanders | 1.25 | .50 | .12 |
| Atlanta Falcons | | | |
| ☐ 17 Curtis Conway | 1.00 | .40 | .10 |
| Chicago Bears | | | |
| ☐ 18 Tommy Vardell | .75 | .30 | .07 |
| Cleveland Browns | | | |
| ☐ 19 Emmitt Smith | 4.00 | 1.60 | .40 |
| Dallas Cowboys | | | |
| ☐ 20 Barry Sanders | 2.00 | .80 | .20 |
| Detroit Lions | | | |
| ☐ 21 Brett Favre | 1.50 | .60 | .15 |
| Green Bay Packers | | | |
| ☐ 22 Cleveland Gary | .50 | .20 | .05 |
| Los Angeles Rams | | | |
| ☐ 23 Morten Andersen | .50 | .20 | .05 |
| New Orleans Saints | | | |
| ☐ 24 Marcus Buckley | .50 | .20 | .05 |
| New York Giants | | | |
| ☐ 25 Rodney Hampton | 1.00 | .40 | .10 |
| New York Giants | | | |
| ☐ 26 Herschel Walker | .75 | .30 | .07 |
| Philadelphia Eagles | | | |
| ☐ 27 Garrison Hearst | 1.00 | .40 | .10 |
| Phoenix Cardinals | | | |
| ☐ 28 Jerry Rice | 2.00 | .80 | .20 |
| San Francisco 49ers | | | |
| ☐ 29 Lawrence Dawsey | .50 | .20 | .05 |
| Tampa Bay Buccaneers | | | |
| ☐ 30 Desmond Howard | 1.00 | .40 | .10 |
| Washington Redskins | | | |

## 1993 Pacific Triple Folders

These 30 cards measure approximately 3 1/2" by 10 1/8" when folded out and feature gray-bordered color action shots on all of their panels, except the backs. When the front panels are closed they merge into a single color player action photo, with the player's name and position printed in team color-coded marbleized lettering down the left side and along the bottom. On a team color-coded marbleized background, the back carries the player's name, position, team, career highlights, and 1992 stats. The cards are numbered on the back. There were reportedly only 2,500 cases of Triple Folders produced by Pacific.

| | MINT | EXC | G-VG |
|---|---|---|---|
| COMPLETE SET (30) | 20.00 | 8.00 | 2.00 |
| COMMON PLAYER (1-30) | .50 | .20 | .05 |
| | | | |
| ☐ 1 Thurman Thomas | 1.25 | .50 | .12 |
| Buffalo Bills | | | |
| ☐ 2 Carl Pickens | .75 | .30 | .07 |
| Cincinnati Bengals | | | |
| ☐ 3 Glyn Milburn | .75 | .30 | .07 |
| Denver Broncos | | | |
| ☐ 4 Lorenzo White | .50 | .20 | .05 |
| Houston Oilers | | | |
| ☐ 5 Anthony Johnson | .50 | .20 | .05 |
| Indianapolis Colts | | | |
| ☐ 6 Joe Montana | 4.00 | 1.60 | .40 |
| Kansas City Chiefs | | | |
| ☐ 7 Nick Bell | .50 | .20 | .05 |
| Los Angeles Raiders | | | |
| ☐ 8 Dan Marino | 2.50 | 1.00 | .25 |
| Miami Dolphins | | | |
| ☐ 9 Anthony Carter | .50 | .20 | .05 |
| Minnesota Vikings | | | |
| ☐ 10 Drew Bledsoe | 3.00 | 1.20 | .30 |

## 1993 Pacific Triple Folder Rookies/Superstars

Randomly inserted in Triple Folder packs, these 20 standard-size (2 1/2" by 3 1/2") cards feature borderless color player action shots on their fronts. The player's name and position appears in white cursive lettering in a lower corner. On a team-colored background consisting of football icons, the back carries the player's name, position, team name and helmet, and 1992 season highlights. Card numbers 2-8, 11, 13, and 19 are rookies; the remainder are superstars. The cards are numbered on the back.

| | MINT | EXC | G-VG |
|---|---|---|---|
| COMPLETE SET (20) | 25.00 | 10.00 | 2.50 |
| COMMON PLAYER (1-20) | .35 | .14 | .03 |
| | | | |
| ☐ 1 Troy Aikman | 4.00 | 1.60 | .40 |
| Dallas Cowboys | | | |
| ☐ 2 Victor Bailey | .50 | .20 | .05 |
| Philadelphia Eagles | | | |
| ☐ 3 Jerome Bettis | 4.00 | 1.60 | .40 |
| Los Angeles Rams | | | |
| ☐ 4 Drew Bledsoe | 4.00 | 1.60 | .40 |
| New England Patriots | | | |
| ☐ 5 Reggie Brooks | 2.00 | .80 | .20 |
| Washington Redskins | | | |
| ☐ 6 Derek Brown | 1.00 | .40 | .10 |
| New Orleans Saints | | | |
| ☐ 7 Marcus Buckley | .35 | .14 | .03 |
| New York Giants | | | |
| ☐ 8 Curtis Conway | .75 | .30 | .07 |

| | MINT | EXC | G-VG |
|---|---|---|---|
| Chicago Bears | | | |
| ☐ 9 Brett Favre | 1.50 | .60 | .15 |
| Green Bay Packers | | | |
| ☐ 10 Barry Foster | .75 | .30 | .07 |
| Pittsburgh Steelers | | | |
| ☐ 11 Garrison Hearst | .75 | .30 | .07 |
| Phoenix Cardinals | | | |
| ☐ 12 Cortez Kennedy | .50 | .20 | .05 |
| Seattle Seahawks | | | |
| ☐ 13 Rick Mirer | 4.00 | 1.60 | .40 |
| Seattle Seahawks | | | |
| ☐ 14 Joe Montana | 4.00 | 1.60 | .40 |
| Kansas City Chiefs | | | |
| ☐ 15 Jerry Rice | 2.50 | 1.00 | .25 |
| San Francisco 49ers | | | |
| ☐ 16 Barry Sanders | 2.50 | 1.00 | .25 |
| Detroit Lions | | | |
| ☐ 17 Sterling Sharpe | 1.50 | .60 | .15 |
| Green Bay Packers | | | |
| ☐ 18 Emmitt Smith | 4.00 | 1.60 | .40 |
| Dallas Cowboys | | | |
| ☐ 19 Robert Smith | .50 | .20 | .05 |
| Minnesota Vikings | | | |
| ☐ 20 Thurman Thomas | 1.00 | .40 | .10 |
| Buffalo Bills | | | |

## 1994 Pacific Prisms

These 128 standard-size (2 1/2" by 3 1/2") cards feature borderless fronts with color action player photos cut out and superimposed on a prism-patterned background. The player's name appears at the bottom beneath the action cutout. The back contains the same color action player photo with a blurred background. The player's name and position appear at lower left.

| | MINT | EXC | G-VG |
|---|---|---|---|
| COMPLETE SET (128) | 200.00 | 90.00 | 25.00 |
| COMMON PLAYER (1-126) | 1.00 | .45 | .13 |
| *GOLD CARDS: 4X TO 7X VALUE | | | |
| ☐ 1 Troy Aikman | 12.00 | 5.50 | 1.50 |
| Dallas Cowboys | | | |
| ☐ 2 Marcus Allen | 1.25 | .55 | .16 |
| Kansas City Chiefs | | | |
| ☐ 3 Morten Andersen | 1.00 | .45 | .13 |
| New Orleans Saints | | | |
| ☐ 4 Fred Barnett | 1.00 | .45 | .13 |
| Philadelphia Eagles | | | |
| ☐ 5 Mario Bates | 3.00 | 1.35 | .40 |
| New Orleans Saints | | | |
| ☐ 6 Edgar Bennett | 1.00 | .45 | .13 |
| Green Bay Packers | | | |
| ☐ 7 Rod Bernstine | 1.00 | .45 | .13 |
| Denver Broncos | | | |
| ☐ 8 Jerome Bettis | 12.00 | 5.50 | 1.50 |
| Los Angeles Rams | | | |
| ☐ 9 Steve Beuerlein | 1.00 | .45 | .13 |
| Arizona Cardinals | | | |
| ☐ 10 Brian Blades | 1.00 | .45 | .13 |
| Seattle Seahawks | | | |
| ☐ 11 Drew Bledsoe | 12.00 | 5.50 | 1.50 |
| New England Patriots | | | |
| ☐ 12 Vincent Brisby | 2.00 | .90 | .25 |
| New England Patriots | | | |
| ☐ 13 Reggie Brooks | 6.00 | 2.70 | .75 |
| Washington Redskins | | | |
| ☐ 14 Derek Brown RB | 1.50 | .65 | .19 |
| New Orleans Saints | | | |
| ☐ 15 Gary Brown | 2.25 | 1.00 | .30 |
| Houston Oilers | | | |
| ☐ 16 Tim Brown | 1.50 | .65 | .19 |
| Los Angeles Rams | | | |
| ☐ 17 Marion Butts | 1.00 | .45 | .13 |
| San Diego Chargers | | | |
| ☐ 18 Keith Byars | 1.00 | .45 | .13 |

| | MINT | EXC | G-VG |
|---|---|---|---|
| Miami Dolphins | | | |
| ☐ 19 Cody Carlson | 1.00 | .45 | .13 |
| Houston Oilers | | | |
| ☐ 20 Anthony Carter | 1.25 | .55 | .16 |
| Minnesota Vikings | | | |
| ☐ 21 Tom Carter | 1.00 | .45 | .13 |
| Washington Redskins | | | |
| ☐ 22 Gary Clark | 1.25 | .55 | .16 |
| Arizona Cardinals | | | |
| ☐ 23 Ben Coates | 1.00 | .45 | .13 |
| New England Patriots | | | |
| ☐ 24 Reggie Cobb | 1.00 | .45 | .13 |
| Tampa Bay Buccaneers | | | |
| ☐ 25 Curtis Conway | 1.50 | .65 | .19 |
| Chicago Bears | | | |
| ☐ 26 John Copeland | 1.00 | .45 | .13 |
| Cincinnati Bengals | | | |
| ☐ 27 Randall Cunningham | 1.25 | .55 | .16 |
| Philadelphia Eagles | | | |
| ☐ 28 Willie Davis | 1.00 | .45 | .13 |
| Kansas City Chiefs | | | |
| ☐ 29 Sean Dawkins | 4.00 | 1.80 | .50 |
| Indianapolis Colts | | | |
| ☐ 30 Lawrence Dawsey | 1.00 | .45 | .13 |
| Tampa Bay Buccaneers | | | |
| ☐ 31 Richard Dent | 1.00 | .45 | .13 |
| Chicago Bears | | | |
| ☐ 32 Trent Dilfer | 12.00 | 5.50 | 1.50 |
| Tampa Bay Buccaneers | | | |
| ☐ 33 Troy Drayton | 1.00 | .45 | .13 |
| Los Angeles Rams | | | |
| ☐ 34 Vaughn Dunbar | 1.00 | .45 | .13 |
| New Orleans Saints | | | |
| ☐ 35 Henry Ellard | 1.00 | .45 | .13 |
| Los Angeles Rams | | | |
| ☐ 36 John Elway | 4.00 | 1.80 | .50 |
| Denver Broncos | | | |
| ☐ 37 Craig Erickson | 1.00 | .45 | .13 |
| Tampa Bay Buccaneers | | | |
| ☐ 38 Boomer Esiason | 1.25 | .55 | .16 |
| New York Jets | | | |
| ☐ 39 Marshall Faulk | 14.00 | 6.25 | 1.75 |
| Indianapolis Colts | | | |
| ☐ 40 Brett Favre | 7.00 | 3.10 | .85 |
| Green Bay Packers | | | |
| ☐ 41 William Floyd | 4.00 | 1.80 | .50 |
| San Francisco 49ers | | | |
| ☐ 42 Glenn Foley | 3.00 | 1.35 | .40 |
| New York Jets | | | |
| ☐ 43 Barry Foster | 2.25 | 1.00 | .30 |
| Pittsburgh Steelers | | | |
| ☐ 44 Irving Fryar | 1.00 | .45 | .13 |
| Miami Dolphins | | | |
| ☐ 45 Jeff George | 1.25 | .55 | .16 |
| Indianapolis Colts | | | |
| ☐ 46 Scottie Graham | 3.00 | 1.35 | .40 |
| Minnesota Vikings | | | |
| ☐ 47 Rodney Hampton | 2.25 | 1.00 | .30 |
| New York Giants | | | |
| ☐ 48 Jim Harbaugh | 1.00 | .45 | .13 |
| Chicago Bears | | | |
| ☐ 49 Alvin Harper | 1.25 | .55 | .16 |
| Dallas Cowboys | | | |
| ☐ 50 Courtney Hawkins | 1.00 | .45 | .13 |
| Tampa Bay Buccaneers | | | |
| ☐ 51 Garrison Hearst | 2.00 | .90 | .25 |
| Arizona Cardinals | | | |
| ☐ 52 Vaughn Hebron | 1.00 | .45 | .13 |
| Philadelphia Eagles | | | |
| ☐ 53 Greg Hill | 6.00 | 2.70 | .75 |
| Kansas City Chiefs | | | |
| ☐ 54 Jeff Hostetler | 1.25 | .55 | .16 |
| Los Angeles Raiders | | | |
| ☐ 55 Michael Irvin | 4.00 | 1.80 | .50 |
| Dallas Cowboys | | | |
| ☐ 56 Qadry Ismail | 1.50 | .65 | .19 |
| Minnesota Vikings | | | |
| ☐ 57 Raghib Ismail | 1.25 | .55 | .16 |
| Los Angeles Raiders | | | |
| ☐ 58 Anthony Johnson | 1.00 | .45 | .13 |
| Indianapolis Colts | | | |
| ☐ 59 Charles Johnson | 6.00 | 2.70 | .75 |
| Pittsburgh Steelers | | | |
| ☐ 60 Johnny Johnson | 1.25 | .55 | .16 |
| New York Jets | | | |
| ☐ 61 Brent Jones | 1.00 | .45 | .13 |
| San Francisco 49ers | | | |
| ☐ 62 Kyle Clifton | 1.00 | .45 | .13 |
| New York Jets | | | |
| ☐ 63 Jim Kelly | 2.25 | 1.00 | .30 |
| Buffalo Bills | | | |
| ☐ 64 Cortez Kennedy | 1.00 | .45 | .13 |
| Seattle Seahawks | | | |
| ☐ 65 Terry Kirby | 4.00 | 1.80 | .50 |
| Miami Dolphins | | | |
| ☐ 66 David Klingler | 1.25 | .55 | .16 |
| Cincinnati Bengals | | | |
| ☐ 67 Erik Kramer | 1.25 | .55 | .16 |

| | | | |
|---|---|---|---|
| Detroit Lions | | | |
| ☐ 68 Reggie Langhorne | 1.00 | .45 | .13 |
| Indianapolis Colts | | | |
| ☐ 69 Chuck Levy | 5.00 | 2.30 | .60 |
| Arizona Cardinals | | | |
| ☐ 70 Dan Marino | 8.00 | 3.60 | 1.00 |
| Miami Dolphins | | | |
| ☐ 71 O.J. McDuffie | 2.00 | .90 | .25 |
| Miami Dolphins | | | |
| ☐ 72 Natrone Means | 2.00 | .90 | .25 |
| San Diego Chargers | | | |
| ☐ 73 Eric Metcalf | 1.00 | .45 | .13 |
| Cleveland Browns | | | |
| ☐ 74 Glyn Milburn | 2.00 | .90 | .25 |
| Denver Broncos | | | |
| ☐ 75 Anthony Miller | 1.50 | .65 | .19 |
| San Diego Chargers | | | |
| ☐ 76 Rick Mirer | 12.00 | 5.50 | 1.50 |
| Seattle Seahawks | | | |
| ☐ 77 Johnny Mitchell | 1.25 | .55 | .16 |
| New York Jets | | | |
| ☐ 78 Scott Mitchell | 2.50 | 1.15 | .30 |
| Miami Dolphins | | | |
| ☐ 79 Joe Montana | 12.00 | 5.50 | 1.50 |
| Kansas City Chiefs | | | |
| ☐ 80 Warren Moon | 1.25 | .55 | .16 |
| Houston Oilers | | | |
| ☐ 81 Derrick Moore | 1.00 | .45 | .13 |
| Detroit Lions | | | |
| ☐ 82 Herman Moore | 1.50 | .65 | .19 |
| Detroit Lions | | | |
| ☐ 83 Rob Moore | 1.00 | .45 | .13 |
| New York Jets | | | |
| ☐ 84 Ron Moore | 4.00 | 1.80 | .50 |
| Arizona Cardinals | | | |
| ☐ 85 Johnnie Morton | 6.00 | 2.70 | .75 |
| Detroit Lions | | | |
| ☐ 86 Neil O'Donnell | 1.25 | .55 | .16 |
| Pittsburgh Steelers | | | |
| ☐ 87 David Palmer | 7.00 | 3.10 | .85 |
| Minnesota Vikings | | | |
| ☐ 88 Erric Pegram | 1.75 | .80 | .22 |
| Atlanta Falcons | | | |
| ☐ 89 Carl Pickens | 1.00 | .45 | .13 |
| Cincinnati Bengals | | | |
| ☐ 90 Anthony Pleasant | 1.00 | .45 | .13 |
| Cleveland Browns | | | |
| ☐ 91 Roosevelt Potts | 1.00 | .45 | .13 |
| Indianapolis Colts | | | |
| ☐ 92 Mike Pritchard | 1.00 | .45 | .13 |
| Atlanta Falcons | | | |
| ☐ 93 Andre Reed | 1.25 | .55 | .16 |
| Buffalo Bills | | | |
| ☐ 94 Errict Rhett | 8.00 | 3.60 | 1.00 |
| Tampa Bay Buccaneers | | | |
| ☐ 95 Jerry Rice | 6.00 | 2.70 | .75 |
| San Francisco 49ers | | | |
| ☐ 96 Andre Rison | 1.50 | .65 | .19 |
| Atlanta Falcons | | | |
| ☐ 97 Greg Robinson | 1.25 | .55 | .16 |
| Los Angeles Raiders | | | |
| ☐ 98 T.J. Rubley | 1.50 | .65 | .19 |
| Los Angeles Rams | | | |
| ☐ 99 Leonard Russell | 1.00 | .45 | .13 |
| New England Patriots | | | |
| ☐ 100 Barry Sanders | 7.00 | 3.10 | .85 |
| Detroit Lions | | | |
| ☐ 101 Deion Sanders | 1.50 | .65 | .19 |
| Atlanta Falcons | | | |
| ☐ 102 Ricky Sanders | 1.00 | .45 | .13 |
| Washington Redskins | | | |
| ☐ 103 Junior Seau | 1.00 | .45 | .13 |
| San Diego Chargers | | | |
| ☐ 104 Shannon Sharpe | 1.50 | .65 | .19 |
| Denver Broncos | | | |
| ☐ 105 Sterling Sharpe | 4.00 | 1.80 | .50 |
| Green Bay Packers | | | |
| ☐ 106 Heath Shuler | 20.00 | 9.00 | 2.50 |
| Washington Redskins | | | |
| ☐ 107 Phil Simms | 1.25 | .55 | .16 |
| New York Giants | | | |
| ☐ 108 Webster Slaughter | 1.00 | .45 | .13 |
| Houston Oilers | | | |
| ☐ 109 Bruce Smith | 1.25 | .55 | .16 |
| Buffalo Bills | | | |
| ☐ 110 Emmitt Smith | 16.00 | 7.25 | 2.00 |
| Dallas Cowboys | | | |
| ☐ 111 Irv Smith | 1.00 | .45 | .13 |
| New Orleans Saints | | | |
| ☐ 112 Robert Smith | 1.25 | .55 | .16 |
| Minnesota Vikings | | | |
| ☐ 113 Vinny Testaverde | 1.00 | .45 | .13 |
| Cleveland Browns | | | |
| ☐ 114 Derrick Thomas | 1.50 | .65 | .19 |
| Kansas City Chiefs | | | |
| ☐ 115 Thurman Thomas | 2.50 | 1.15 | .30 |
| Buffalo Bills | | | |
| ☐ 116 Leroy Thompson | 1.00 | .45 | .13 |

| | | | |
|---|---|---|---|
| Pittsburgh Steelers | | | |
| ☐ 117 Lewis Tillmen | 1.00 | .45 | .13 |
| New York Giants | | | |
| ☐ 118 Michael Timpson | 1.00 | .45 | .13 |
| New England Patriots | | | |
| ☐ 119 Herschel Walker | 1.25 | .55 | .16 |
| Philadelphia Eagles | | | |
| ☐ 120 Chris Warren | 1.25 | .55 | .16 |
| Seattle Seahawks | | | |
| ☐ 121 Ricky Watters | 2.00 | .90 | .25 |
| San Francisco 49ers | | | |
| ☐ 122 Lorenzo White | 1.00 | .45 | .13 |
| Houston Oilers | | | |
| ☐ 123 Reggie White | 1.25 | .55 | .16 |
| Green Bay Packers | | | |
| ☐ 124 Dan Wilkinson | 4.00 | 1.80 | .50 |
| Cincinnati Bengals | | | |
| ☐ 125 Kevin Williams | 1.25 | .55 | .16 |
| Dallas Cowboys | | | |
| ☐ 126 Steve Young | 1.50 | .65 | .19 |
| San Francisco 49ers | | | |
| ☐ CL1 Checklist 1 | .50 | .23 | .06 |
| ☐ CL2 Checklist 2 | .50 | .23 | .06 |

## 1994 Pacific Prisms Team Helmets

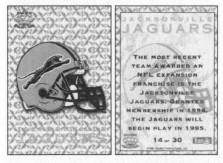

Randomly inserted in foil packs, this 30-card standard size (2 1/2" by 3 1/2") set features a borderless front with a colored picture of a team helmet set against a prismatic background. The team's name appears at the bottom. The back features a brief history of the team on a background consisting of a ghosted version of the team helmet. The cards are numbered on the back by "X of 30".

| | MINT | EXC | G-VG |
|---|---|---|---|
| COMPLETE SET (30) | 3.00 | 1.35 | .40 |
| COMMON LOGO (1-30) | .15 | .07 | .02 |
| | | | |
| ☐ 1 Arizona Cardinals | .15 | .07 | .02 |
| ☐ 2 Atlanta Falcons | .15 | .07 | .02 |
| ☐ 3 Buffalo Bills | .15 | .07 | .02 |
| ☐ 4 Carolina Panthers | .15 | .07 | .02 |
| ☐ 5 Chicago Bears | .15 | .07 | .02 |
| ☐ 6 Cincinnati Bengals | .15 | .07 | .02 |
| ☐ 7 Cleveland Browns | .15 | .07 | .02 |
| ☐ 8 Dallas Cowboys | .15 | .07 | .02 |
| ☐ 9 Denver Broncos | .15 | .07 | .02 |
| ☐ 10 Detroit Lions | .15 | .07 | .02 |
| ☐ 11 Green Bay Packers | .15 | .07 | .02 |
| ☐ 12 Houston Oilers | .15 | .07 | .02 |
| ☐ 13 Indianapolis Colts | .15 | .07 | .02 |
| ☐ 14 Jacksonville Jaguars | .15 | .07 | .02 |
| ☐ 15 Kansas City Chiefs | .15 | .07 | .02 |
| ☐ 16 Los Angeles Raiders | .15 | .07 | .02 |
| ☐ 17 Los Angeles Rams | .15 | .07 | .02 |
| ☐ 18 Miami Dolphins | .15 | .07 | .02 |
| ☐ 19 Minnesota Vikings | .15 | .07 | .02 |
| ☐ 20 New England Patriots | .15 | .07 | .02 |
| ☐ 21 New Orleans Saints | .15 | .07 | .02 |
| ☐ 22 New York Giants | .15 | .07 | .02 |
| ☐ 23 New York Jets | .15 | .07 | .02 |
| ☐ 24 Philadelphia Eagles | .15 | .07 | .02 |
| ☐ 25 Pittsburgh Steelers | .15 | .07 | .02 |
| ☐ 26 San Diego Chargers | .15 | .07 | .02 |
| ☐ 27 San Francisco 49ers | .15 | .07 | .02 |
| ☐ 28 Seattle Seahawks | .15 | .07 | .02 |
| ☐ 29 Tampa Bay Buccaneers | .15 | .07 | .02 |
| ☐ 30 Washington Redskins | .15 | .07 | .02 |

## 1961 Packers Lake to Lake

The 1961 Lake to Lake Green Bay Packers set consists of 36 unnumbered, green and white cards each measuring approximately 2 1/2" by 3 1/4". The obverse contains the card number, the player's

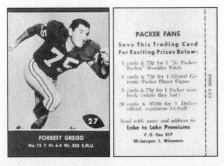

FORREST GREGG
No. 75 T. Ht. 6-4 Wr. 250 S.M.U.

PACKER FANS

Save This Trading Card
For Exciting Prizes Below:

5 cards & 75c for 1 "Jr. Packer-
backer" Shoulder Patch

5 cards & 75c for 1 Glazed Ceramic Packer Player Figure

5 cards & 75c for 1 Packer year-
book (while they last)

20 cards & $3.00 for 1 Delov
official, regulation football.

Send with name and address to:

Lake to Lake Premiums
P. O. Box 217
Sheboygan 1, Wisconsin

uniform number, his position, and his height, weight, and college. The
backs contain advertisements for the Packer fans to obtain Lake to
Lake premiums. Card numbers 1-8 and 17-24 are more difficult to
obtain than other cards in the set. Lineman Ken Iman's card was
issued ten years before his Rookie Card; Defensive back Herb
Adderley's card was issued three years before his Rookie Card.

|  | NRMT | VG-E | GOOD |
|---|---|---|---|
| COMPLETE SET (36) | 600.00 | 240.00 | 60.00 |
| COMMON CARD (1-8/17-24) | 25.00 | 10.00 | 2.50 |
| COMMON CARD (9-16/25-32) | 2.50 | 1.00 | .25 |
| COMMON CARD (33-36) | 5.00 | 2.00 | .50 |
| ☐ 1 Jerry Kramer SP | 40.00 | 16.00 | 4.00 |
| ☐ 2 Norm Masters SP | 25.00 | 10.00 | 2.50 |
| ☐ 3 Willie Davis SP | 50.00 | 20.00 | 5.00 |
| ☐ 4 Bill Quinlan SP | 25.00 | 10.00 | 2.50 |
| ☐ 5 Jim Temp SP | 25.00 | 10.00 | 2.50 |
| ☐ 6 Emlen Tunnell SP | 40.00 | 16.00 | 4.00 |
| ☐ 7 Gary Knafelc SP | 25.00 | 10.00 | 2.50 |
| ☐ 8 Henry Jordan SP | 30.00 | 12.00 | 3.00 |
| ☐ 9 Bill Forester | 3.00 | 1.20 | .30 |
| ☐ 10 Paul Hornung | 12.00 | 5.00 | 1.20 |
| ☐ 11 Jesse Whittenton | 2.50 | 1.00 | .25 |
| ☐ 12 Andy Cvercko | 2.50 | 1.00 | .25 |
| ☐ 13 Jim Taylor | 9.00 | 3.75 | .90 |
| ☐ 14 Hank Gremminger | 2.50 | 1.00 | .25 |
| ☐ 15 Tom Moore | 3.00 | 1.20 | .30 |
| ☐ 16 John Symank | 2.50 | 1.00 | .25 |
| ☐ 17 Max McGee SP | 35.00 | 14.00 | 3.50 |
| ☐ 18 Bart Starr SP | 80.00 | 32.00 | 8.00 |
| ☐ 19 Ray Nitschke SP | 60.00 | 24.00 | 6.00 |
| ☐ 20 Dave Hanner SP | 25.00 | 10.00 | 2.50 |
| ☐ 21 Tom Bettis SP | 25.00 | 10.00 | 2.50 |
| ☐ 22 Fuzzy Thurston SP | 30.00 | 12.00 | 3.00 |
| ☐ 23 Lew Carpenter SP | 25.00 | 10.00 | 2.50 |
| ☐ 24 Boyd Dowler SP | 30.00 | 12.00 | 3.00 |
| ☐ 25 Ken Iman | 2.50 | 1.00 | .25 |
| ☐ 26 Bob Skoronski | 2.50 | 1.00 | .25 |
| ☐ 27 Forrest Gregg | 7.50 | 3.00 | .75 |
| ☐ 28 Jim Ringo | 7.50 | 3.00 | .75 |
| ☐ 29 Ron Kramer | 3.00 | 1.20 | .30 |
| ☐ 30 Herb Adderley | 10.00 | 4.00 | 1.00 |
| ☐ 31 Dan Currie | 2.50 | 1.00 | .25 |
| ☐ 32 John Roach | 2.50 | 1.00 | .25 |
| ☐ 33 Dale Hackbart | 5.00 | 2.00 | .50 |
| ☐ 34 Larry Hickman | 5.00 | 2.00 | .50 |
| ☐ 35 Nelson Toburen | 5.00 | 2.00 | .50 |
| ☐ 36 Willie Wood | 10.00 | 4.00 | 1.00 |

# 1969 Packers Drenks Potato Chip Pins

The 1969 Packers Drenks Potato Chip set contains 20 pins, each
measuring approximately 1 1/8" in diameter. The fronts have a green
and white background, with a black and white headshot in the center
of the white football-shaped area. The team name at the top and player
information at the bottom follow the curve of the pin. The pins are
unnumbered and checklisted below in alphabetical order.

|  | NRMT | VG-E | GOOD |
|---|---|---|---|
| COMPLETE SET (20) | 60.00 | 24.00 | 6.00 |
| COMMON PLAYER (1-20) | 1.50 | .60 | .15 |
| ☐ 1 Herb Adderley | 6.00 | 2.40 | .60 |
| ☐ 2 Lionel Aldridge | 2.00 | .80 | .20 |
| ☐ 3 Donny Anderson | 2.50 | 1.00 | .25 |
| ☐ 4 Ken Bowman | 1.50 | .60 | .15 |
| ☐ 5 Carroll Dale | 2.00 | .80 | .20 |
| ☐ 6 Willie Davis | 6.00 | 2.40 | .60 |
| ☐ 7 Boyd Dowler | 2.50 | 1.00 | .25 |
| ☐ 8 Marv Fleming | 2.50 | 1.00 | .25 |
| ☐ 9 Gale Gillingham | 2.00 | .80 | .20 |
| ☐ 10 Jim Grabowski | 2.50 | 1.00 | .25 |
| ☐ 11 Forrest Gregg | 6.00 | 2.40 | .60 |
| ☐ 12 Don Horn | 1.50 | .60 | .15 |
| ☐ 13 Bob Jeter | 2.00 | .80 | .20 |
| ☐ 14 Henry Jordan | 2.50 | 1.00 | .25 |
| ☐ 15 Ray Nitschke | 7.50 | 3.00 | .75 |
| ☐ 16 Elijah Pitts | 2.00 | .80 | .20 |
| ☐ 17 Dave Robinson | 2.50 | 1.00 | .25 |
| ☐ 18 Bart Starr | 12.00 | 5.00 | 1.20 |
| ☐ 19 Travis Williams | 2.00 | .80 | .20 |
| ☐ 20 Willie Wood | 6.00 | 2.40 | .60 |

# 1972 Packers Team Issue

This team-issued set consists of 45 black-and-white photos, each
measuring approximately 8" by 10" and printed on thin glossy paper.
The fronts feature either posed action shots or kneeling poses of the
players inside white borders. The player's name, position, and team
name are printed in black in the bottom white border. The backs are
blank. Several players have two photos in the set: Dale, Hudson,
Thomas, Snider, and Widby. For the last two, one of the photos
pictures them in their former team's uniform. Furthermore, Napper
never played in the NFL, and Pittman never played for the Packers,
suggesting that these photos may have been taken during training
camp or preseason. The photos are unnumbered and checklisted
below in alphabetical order.

|  | NRMT | VG-E | GOOD |
|---|---|---|---|
| COMPLETE SET (45) | 80.00 | 32.00 | 8.00 |
| COMMON PLAYER (1-45) | 1.50 | .60 | .15 |
| ☐ 1 Ken Bowman | 2.00 | .80 | .20 |
| ☐ 2 John Brockington | 3.50 | 1.40 | .35 |
| ☐ 3 Bob Brown | 2.00 | .80 | .20 |
| ☐ 4 Willie Buchanon | 2.50 | 1.00 | .25 |
| ☐ 5 Fred Carr | 2.50 | 1.00 | .25 |
| ☐ 6 Jim Carter | 1.50 | .60 | .15 |
| ☐ 7 Carroll Dale | 2.50 | 1.00 | .25 |
| ☐ 8 Carroll Dale | 2.50 | 1.00 | .25 |
| (Action pose) |  |  |  |
| ☐ 9 Dan Devine CO/GM | 2.00 | .80 | .20 |
| ☐ 10 Ken Ellis | 1.50 | .60 | .15 |
| ☐ 11 Len Garrett | 1.50 | .60 | .15 |
| ☐ 12 Gale Gillingham | 2.00 | .80 | .20 |
| ☐ 13 Leland Glass | 1.50 | .60 | .15 |
| ☐ 14 Charlie Hall | 1.50 | .60 | .15 |
| ☐ 15 Jim Hill | 2.00 | .80 | .20 |
| ☐ 16 Dick Himes | 1.50 | .60 | .15 |
| ☐ 17 Bob Hudson | 1.50 | .60 | .15 |
| (Head shot) |  |  |  |
| ☐ 18 Bob Hudson | 1.50 | .60 | .15 |
| (Kneeling pose) |  |  |  |
| ☐ 19 Kevin Hunt | 1.50 | .60 | .15 |
| ☐ 20 Scott Hunter | 2.50 | 1.00 | .25 |
| ☐ 21 Dave Kopay | 2.00 | .80 | .20 |
| ☐ 22 Bob Kroll | 1.50 | .60 | .15 |
| ☐ 23 Pete Lammons | 2.00 | .80 | .20 |
| ☐ 24 MacArthur Lane | 3.00 | 1.20 | .30 |
| ☐ 25 Bill Lueck | 1.50 | .60 | .15 |
| ☐ 26 Al Matthews | 1.50 | .60 | .15 |
| ☐ 27 Mike McCoy | 2.00 | .80 | .20 |
| ☐ 28 Rich McGeorge | 2.00 | .80 | .20 |

---

| | MINT | EXC | G-VG |
|---|---|---|---|
| ☐ 29 Charlie Napper | 1.50 | .60 | .15 |
| ☐ 30 Ray Nitschke | 7.50 | 3.00 | .75 |
| ☐ 31 Charlie Pittman | 2.00 | .80 | .20 |
| ☐ 32 Malcolm Snider (Action pose; Falcons' uniform) | 1.50 | .60 | .15 |
| ☐ 33 Malcolm Snider (Kneeling pose) | 1.50 | .60 | .15 |
| ☐ 34 Jon Staggers | 2.50 | 1.00 | .25 |
| ☐ 35 Bart Starr | 9.00 | 3.75 | .90 |
| ☐ 36 Jerry Tagge | 2.50 | 1.00 | .25 |
| ☐ 37 Isaac Thomas (Action pose) | 1.50 | .60 | .15 |
| ☐ 38 Isaac Thomas (Kneeling pose) | 1.50 | .60 | .15 |
| ☐ 39 Vern Vanoy | 1.50 | .60 | .15 |
| ☐ 40 Ron Widby (Action pose; Cowboys' uniform) | 2.00 | .80 | .20 |
| ☐ 41 Ron Widby (Kneeling pose) | 2.00 | .80 | .20 |
| ☐ 42 Clarence Williams | 1.50 | .60 | .15 |
| ☐ 43 Perry Williams | 1.50 | .60 | .15 |
| ☐ 44 Keith Wortman | 2.00 | .80 | .20 |
| ☐ 45 Coaching Staff | 7.50 | 3.00 | .75 |

Bart Starr
Hank Kuhlmann
Dave Hanner
Burt Gustafson
John Polonchek
Don Doll
Red Cochran
Dan Devine
Rollie Dotsch

## 1990 Packers 25th Anniversary

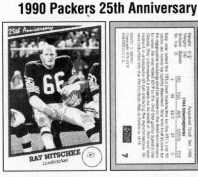

RAY NITSCHKE
Linebacker

This 45-card standard size (2 1/2" by 3 1/2") set was issued by Champion Cards of Owosso, Michigan and produced by Pacific Trading Cards, Inc. This set celebrated the 25th anniversary of the 1966 Green Bay Packers, the first team to win the Super Bowl. This set has a mix of color and sepia-toned photos and a mix of action and portrait shots on the front with a biography of the player on the back of the card. The only member of the 1966 Packers not featured in this set is Paul Hornung.

| | MINT | EXC | G-VG |
|---|---|---|---|
| COMPLETE SET (45) | 10.00 | 4.00 | 1.00 |
| COMMON CARD (1-45) | .25 | .10 | .02 |
| ☐ 1 Introduction Card | .50 | .20 | .05 |
| ☐ 2 Bart Starr | 2.00 | .80 | .20 |
| ☐ 3 Herb Adderley | .75 | .30 | .07 |
| ☐ 4 Bob Skoronski | .25 | .10 | .02 |
| ☐ 5 Tom Brown | .35 | .14 | .03 |
| ☐ 6 Lee Roy Caffey | .35 | .14 | .03 |
| ☐ 7 Ray Nitschke | 1.00 | .40 | .10 |
| ☐ 8 Carroll Dale | .35 | .14 | .03 |
| ☐ 9 Jim Taylor | 1.25 | .50 | .12 |
| ☐ 10 Ken Bowman | .25 | .10 | .02 |
| ☐ 11 Gale Gillingham | .35 | .14 | .03 |
| ☐ 12 Jim Grabowski | .50 | .20 | .05 |
| ☐ 13 Dave Robinson | .50 | .20 | .05 |
| ☐ 14 Donny Anderson | .50 | .20 | .05 |
| ☐ 15 Willie Wood | .75 | .30 | .07 |
| ☐ 16 Zeke Bratkowski | .50 | .20 | .05 |
| ☐ 17 Doug Hart | .25 | .10 | .02 |
| ☐ 18 Jerry Kramer | .75 | .30 | .07 |
| ☐ 19 Marv Fleming | .35 | .14 | .03 |
| ☐ 20 Lionel Aldridge | .25 | .10 | .02 |
| ☐ 21 Red Mack UER (Text reads returned to football before the following season, should be retired) | .25 | .10 | .02 |

| | MINT | EXC | G-VG |
|---|---|---|---|
| ☐ 22 Ron Kostelnik | .25 | .10 | .02 |
| ☐ 23 Boyd Dowler | .50 | .20 | .05 |
| ☐ 24 Vince Lombardi CO | 1.25 | .50 | .12 |
| ☐ 25 Forrest Gregg | .75 | .30 | .07 |
| ☐ 26 Max McGee Superstar | .35 | .14 | .03 |
| ☐ 27 Fuzzy Thurston | .50 | .20 | .05 |
| ☐ 28 Bob Brown | .35 | .14 | .03 |
| ☐ 29 Willie Davis | .75 | .30 | .07 |
| ☐ 30 Elijah Pitts | .50 | .20 | .05 |
| ☐ 31 Henry Jordan | .50 | .20 | .05 |
| ☐ 32 Bart Starr | 2.00 | .80 | .20 |
| ☐ 33 Super Bowl I (Jim Taylor) | .75 | .30 | .07 |
| ☐ 34 1966 Packers | .50 | .20 | .05 |
| ☐ 35 Max McGee | .50 | .20 | .05 |
| ☐ 36 Jim Weatherwax | .25 | .10 | .02 |
| ☐ 37 Bob Long | .25 | .10 | .02 |
| ☐ 38 Don Chandler | .35 | .14 | .03 |
| ☐ 39 Bill Anderson | .25 | .10 | .02 |
| ☐ 40 Tommy Joe Crutcher | .35 | .14 | .03 |
| ☐ 41 Dave Hathcock | .25 | .10 | .02 |
| ☐ 42 Steve Wright | .25 | .10 | .02 |
| ☐ 43 Phil Vandersea | .25 | .10 | .02 |
| ☐ 44 Bill Curry | .50 | .20 | .05 |
| ☐ 45 Bob Jeter | .35 | .14 | .03 |

## 1991 Packers Super Bowl II

Herb ADDERLEY

This 50-card Green Bay Packers set was released by Sportscards of Michigan and commemorates the 25th anniversary of the team's win in Super Bowl II. The cards are printed on thin card stock and measure the standard size (2 1/2" by 3 1/2"). The fronts feature either black and white or color player photos with dark green borders. The player's name, team logo, and "Super Bowl II" appear in a yellow stripe below the picture. The backs have biography and career highlights. The cards are numbered on the back.

| | MINT | EXC | G-VG |
|---|---|---|---|
| COMPLETE SET (50) | 10.00 | 4.00 | 1.00 |
| COMMON CARD (1-49) | .25 | .10 | .02 |
| ☐ 1 Intro Card Super Bowl Trophy | .50 | .20 | .05 |
| ☐ 2 Steve Wright | .25 | .10 | .02 |
| ☐ 3 Jim Flanigan | .25 | .10 | .02 |
| ☐ 4 Tom Brown | .35 | .14 | .03 |
| ☐ 5 Tommy Joe Crutcher | .35 | .14 | .03 |
| ☐ 6 Doug Hart | .35 | .14 | .03 |
| ☐ 7 Bob Hyland | .25 | .10 | .02 |
| ☐ 8 John Rowser | .25 | .10 | .02 |
| ☐ 9 Bob Skoronski | .25 | .10 | .02 |
| ☐ 10 Jim Weatherwax | .25 | .10 | .02 |
| ☐ 11 Ben Wilson | .25 | .10 | .02 |
| ☐ 12 Don Horn | .35 | .14 | .03 |
| ☐ 13 Allen Brown | .25 | .10 | .02 |
| ☐ 14 Dick Capp | .25 | .10 | .02 |
| ☐ 15 Super Bowl II Action Donny Anderson | .50 | .20 | .05 |
| ☐ 16 Ice Bowl: The Play Bart Starr | 1.25 | .50 | .12 |
| ☐ 17 Chuck Mercein | .35 | .14 | .03 |
| ☐ 18 Herb Adderley | .75 | .30 | .07 |
| ☐ 19 Ken Bowman | .25 | .10 | .02 |
| ☐ 20 Lee Roy Caffey | .35 | .14 | .03 |
| ☐ 21 Carroll Dale | .35 | .14 | .03 |
| ☐ 22 Marv Fleming | .35 | .14 | .03 |
| ☐ 23 Jim Grabowski | .50 | .20 | .05 |
| ☐ 24 Bob Jeter | .35 | .14 | .03 |
| ☐ 25 Jerry Kramer | .75 | .30 | .07 |
| ☐ 26 Max McGee | .50 | .20 | .05 |
| ☐ 27 Elijah Pitts | .50 | .20 | .05 |
| ☐ 28 Bart Starr | 1.50 | .60 | .15 |
| ☐ 29 Fuzzy Thurston | .50 | .20 | .05 |
| ☐ 30 Willie Wood | .75 | .30 | .07 |

| | | | |
|---|---|---|---|
| ☐ 31 Lionel Aldridge | .35 | .14 | .03 |
| ☐ 32 Donny Anderson | .50 | .20 | .05 |
| ☐ 33 Zeke Bratkowski | .50 | .20 | .05 |
| ☐ 34 Bob Brown | .35 | .14 | .03 |
| ☐ 35 Don Chandler | .35 | .14 | .03 |
| ☐ 36 Willie Davis | .75 | .30 | .07 |
| ☐ 37 Boyd Dowler | .50 | .20 | .05 |
| ☐ 38 Gale Gillingham | .35 | .14 | .03 |
| ☐ 39 Henry Jordan | .50 | .20 | .05 |
| ☐ 40 Ron Kostelnik | .25 | .10 | .02 |
| ☐ 41 Vince Lombardi CO | 1.25 | .50 | .12 |
| ☐ 42 Bob Long | .25 | .10 | .02 |
| ☐ 43 Ray Nitschke | 1.00 | .40 | .10 |
| ☐ 44 Dave Robinson | .50 | .20 | .05 |
| ☐ 45 Bart Starr MVP | 1.25 | .50 | .12 |
| ☐ 46 Travis Williams | .35 | .14 | .03 |
| ☐ 47 1967 Packers Team | .50 | .20 | .05 |
| ☐ 48 Ice Bowl Game Summary | .25 | .10 | .02 |
| ☐ 49 Ice Bowl | .25 | .10 | .02 |
| ☐ NNO Packer Pro Shop | .25 | .10 | .02 |

## 1992 Packers Hall of Fame

FORREST GREGG
OFFENSIVE TACKLE #75

This 110-card set features all 106 Packer Hall of Fame inductees. It was available to collectors exclusively at the Packer Hall of Fame gift shop, and yearly updates will be issued as new members are selected for induction to the Hall of Fame. The cards measure the standard size (2 1/2" by 3 1/2") and are printed on thin cardboard stock. The fronts display black and white or color player photos enclosed by an oval gold border on a dark green card face. The player's name, position, and jersey number are in a gold band beneath the picture. The horizontally oriented backs carry biography and career highlights. The player's name appears in green in a gold banner at the top, while the card number is printed on a small helmet at the bottom center. There is no number 1 card, but there are two number 45's.

| | MINT | EXC | G-VG |
|---|---|---|---|
| COMPLETE SET (110) | 12.50 | 5.00 | 1.25 |
| COMMON CARD (1-108) | .10 | .04 | .01 |
| | | | |
| ☐ 2 Red Dunn | .20 | .08 | .02 |
| ☐ 3 Mike Michalske | .50 | .20 | .05 |
| ☐ 4 Cal Hubbard | .50 | .20 | .05 |
| ☐ 5 Johnny(Blood) McNally | .50 | .20 | .05 |
| ☐ 6 Verne Lewellen | .10 | .04 | .01 |
| ☐ 7 Cub Buck | .10 | .04 | .01 |
| ☐ 8 Whitey Woodin | .10 | .04 | .01 |
| ☐ 9 Jug Earp | .10 | .04 | .01 |
| ☐ 10 Charlie Mathys | .10 | .04 | .01 |
| ☐ 11 Andrew Turnbull PRES | .10 | .04 | .01 |
| ☐ 12 Curly Lambeau | .50 | .20 | .05 |
| Founder/Coach | | | |
| ☐ 13 George Calhoun PUB | .10 | .04 | .01 |
| ☐ 14 Boob Darling | .10 | .04 | .01 |
| ☐ 15 Eddie Jankowski | .10 | .04 | .01 |
| ☐ 16 Swede Johnston | .10 | .04 | .01 |
| ☐ 17 George Svendsen | .10 | .04 | .01 |
| ☐ 18 Bobby Monnett | .10 | .04 | .01 |
| ☐ 19 Joe Laws | .10 | .04 | .01 |
| ☐ 20 Tiny Engebretsen | .10 | .04 | .01 |
| ☐ 21 Milt Gantenbein | .10 | .04 | .01 |
| ☐ 22 Hank Bruder | .10 | .04 | .01 |
| ☐ 23 Clarke Hinkle | .50 | .20 | .05 |
| ☐ 24 Lon Evans | .10 | .04 | .01 |
| ☐ 25 Buckets Goldenberg | .10 | .04 | .01 |
| ☐ 26 Nate Barrager | .10 | .04 | .01 |
| ☐ 27 Arnie Herber | .30 | .12 | .03 |
| ☐ 28 Lee Joannes PRES | .10 | .04 | .01 |
| ☐ 29 Jerry Clifford VP | .10 | .04 | .01 |
| ☐ 30 Pete Tinsley | .10 | .04 | .01 |
| ☐ 31 Baby Ray | .10 | .04 | .01 |
| ☐ 32 Andy Uram | .10 | .04 | .01 |
| ☐ 33 Larry Craig | .10 | .04 | .01 |
| ☐ 34 Charlie Brock | .10 | .04 | .01 |

| | | | |
|---|---|---|---|
| ☐ 35 Ted Fritsch Sr. | .20 | .08 | .02 |
| ☐ 36 Lou Brock | .10 | .04 | .01 |
| ☐ 37 Carl Mulleneaux | .10 | .04 | .01 |
| ☐ 38 Harry Jacunski | .10 | .04 | .01 |
| ☐ 39 Cecil Isbell | .20 | .08 | .02 |
| ☐ 40 Bud Svendsen | .10 | .04 | .01 |
| ☐ 41 Russ Letlow | .10 | .04 | .01 |
| ☐ 42 Don Hutson | .75 | .30 | .07 |
| ☐ 43 Irv Comp | .10 | .04 | .01 |
| ☐ 44 John Martinkovic | .10 | .04 | .01 |
| ☐ 45A Bobby Dillon | .20 | .08 | .02 |
| ☐ 45B Lavern Dilweg UER | .50 | .20 | .05 |
| (Back is that of card 45 card, Bobby Dillon) | | | |
| ☐ 46 Wilner Burke | .10 | .04 | .01 |
| Band Director | | | |
| ☐ 47 Dick Wildung | .10 | .04 | .01 |
| ☐ 48 Billy Howton | .20 | .08 | .02 |
| ☐ 49 Tobin Rote | .20 | .08 | .02 |
| ☐ 50 Jim Ringo | .50 | .20 | .05 |
| ☐ 51 Deral Teteak | .10 | .04 | .01 |
| ☐ 52 Bob Forte | .10 | .04 | .01 |
| ☐ 53 Tony Canadeo | .50 | .20 | .05 |
| ☐ 54 Al Carmichael | .10 | .04 | .01 |
| ☐ 55 Bob Mann | .10 | .04 | .01 |
| ☐ 56 Jack Vainisi | .10 | .04 | .01 |
| Scout | | | |
| ☐ 57 Ken Bowman | .10 | .04 | .01 |
| ☐ 58 Bob Skoronski | .10 | .04 | .01 |
| ☐ 59 Dave Hanner | .10 | .04 | .01 |
| ☐ 60 Bill Forester | .20 | .08 | .02 |
| ☐ 61 Fred Cone | .10 | .04 | .01 |
| ☐ 62 Lionel Aldridge | .20 | .08 | .02 |
| ☐ 63 Carroll Dale | .20 | .08 | .02 |
| ☐ 64 Howie Ferguson | .10 | .04 | .01 |
| ☐ 65 Gary Knafelc | .10 | .04 | .01 |
| ☐ 66 Ron Kramer | .20 | .08 | .02 |
| ☐ 67 Forrest Gregg | .50 | .20 | .05 |
| ☐ 68 Phil Bengtson CO | .10 | .04 | .01 |
| ☐ 69 Dan Currie | .10 | .04 | .01 |
| ☐ 70 Al Schneider | .10 | .04 | .01 |
| Contributor | | | |
| ☐ 71 Bob Jeter | .20 | .08 | .02 |
| ☐ 72 Jesse Whittenton | .10 | .04 | .01 |
| ☐ 73 Hank Gremminger | .10 | .04 | .01 |
| ☐ 74 Ron Kostelnik | .10 | .04 | .01 |
| ☐ 75 Gale Gillingham | .20 | .08 | .02 |
| ☐ 76 Lee Roy Caffey | .20 | .08 | .02 |
| ☐ 77 Henry Jordan | .20 | .08 | .02 |
| ☐ 78 Boyd Dowler | .20 | .08 | .02 |
| ☐ 79 Fred Carr | .20 | .08 | .02 |
| ☐ 80 Bud Jorgensen TR | .10 | .04 | .01 |
| ☐ 81 Eugene Brusky | .10 | .04 | .01 |
| Team Physician | | | |
| ☐ 82 Fred Trowbridge | .10 | .04 | .01 |
| Executive Committee | | | |
| ☐ 83 Jan Stenerud | .50 | .20 | .05 |
| ☐ 84 Jerry Atkinson | .10 | .04 | .01 |
| Contributor | | | |
| ☐ 85 Larry McCarren | .10 | .04 | .01 |
| ☐ 86 Fred Leicht | .10 | .04 | .01 |
| Executive Committee | | | |
| ☐ 87 Max McGee | .20 | .08 | .02 |
| ☐ 88 Zeke Bratkowski | .20 | .08 | .02 |
| ☐ 89 Dave Robinson | .20 | .08 | .02 |
| ☐ 90 Herb Adderley | .50 | .20 | .05 |
| ☐ 91 Dominic Olejniczak | .20 | .08 | .02 |
| President | | | |
| ☐ 92 Jerry Kramer | .50 | .20 | .05 |
| ☐ 93 Super Bowl I | .10 | .04 | .01 |
| ☐ 94 Don Chandler | .10 | .04 | .01 |
| ☐ 95 John Brockington | .30 | .12 | .03 |
| ☐ 96 Lynn Dickey | .20 | .08 | .02 |
| ☐ 97 Bart Starr | 1.00 | .40 | .10 |
| ☐ 98 Willie Wood | .50 | .20 | .05 |
| ☐ 99 Packer Hall of Fame | .20 | .08 | .02 |
| ☐ 100 Donny Anderson | .20 | .08 | .02 |
| ☐ 101 Chester Marcol | .10 | .04 | .01 |
| ☐ 102 Fuzzy Thurston | .20 | .08 | .02 |
| ☐ 103 Paul Hornung | .75 | .30 | .07 |
| ☐ 104 Jim Taylor | .75 | .30 | .07 |
| ☐ 105 Vince Lombardi CO | .75 | .30 | .07 |
| ☐ 106 Willie Davis | .50 | .20 | .05 |
| ☐ 107 Ray Nitschke | .50 | .20 | .05 |
| ☐ 108 Elijah Pitts | .20 | .08 | .02 |
| ☐ xx Honor Roll | .20 | .08 | .02 |
| Checklist Card | | | |
| ☐ xx Packer Hall of Fame | .20 | .08 | .02 |
| Catalog Order Form | | | |

## 1993 Packers Archives Postcards

These 40 postcards were made by Champion Cards of Green Bay to commemorate the Packers' 75th anniversary and, except for the unnumbered title card, measure approximately 3 1/2" by 5 1/2". The

white-bordered postcards are framed by team color-coded lines and feature mostly black-and-white archival photos of Packer players and teams of yesteryear. Most of the cards display the Packers' 75th anniversary logo in the lower left. The horizontal white backs carry on their left sides information about the subject depicted on the front. On the right side is a ghosted Champion Cards logo. The postcards are numbered on the back within a football icon that appears at the bottom.

| | MINT | EXC | G-VG |
|---|---|---|---|
| COMPLETE SET (40) | 15.00 | 6.00 | 1.50 |
| COMMON PLAYER (1-39) | .50 | .20 | .05 |
| ☐ 1 The First Team 1919 | .75 | .30 | .07 |
| ☐ 2 The 1920s | .50 | .20 | .05 |
| ☐ 3 The 1930s | .50 | .20 | .05 |
| ☐ 4 The 1940s | .50 | .20 | .05 |
| ☐ 5 The 1950s | .50 | .20 | .05 |
| ☐ 6 The 1960s | .50 | .20 | .05 |
| ☐ 7 The 1970s | .50 | .20 | .05 |
| ☐ 8 The 1980s | .50 | .20 | .05 |
| ☐ 9 The 1990s | .50 | .20 | .05 |
| ☐ 10 Curly Lambeau 1919 | .75 | .30 | .07 |
| ☐ 11 Jim Ringo 1953 | .75 | .30 | .07 |
| ☐ 12 Ice Bowl 1967 | .75 | .30 | .07 |
| ☐ 13 Jerry Kramer 1958 | .75 | .30 | .07 |
| ☐ 14 Ray Nitschke 1958 | 1.00 | .40 | .10 |
| ☐ 15 Fuzzy Thurston 1959 | .75 | .30 | .07 |
| ☐ 16 James Lofton 1978-86 | 1.00 | .40 | .10 |
| ☐ 17 Super Bowl I Action | .75 | .30 | .07 |
| ☐ 18 Don Hutson 1935-45 | 1.00 | .40 | .10 |
| ☐ 19 Tony Canadeo 1941-43, 46-52 | .75 | .30 | .07 |
| ☐ 20 Bobby Dillon 1952-59 | .50 | .20 | .05 |
| ☐ 21 The Quarterback | .75 | .30 | .07 |
| ☐ 22 Willie Wood 1960-71 | .75 | .30 | .07 |
| ☐ 23 David Beverly 1975-80 | .50 | .20 | .05 |
| ☐ 24 James Lofton 1978 | 1.00 | .40 | .10 |
| ☐ 25 Tim Harris 1986-90 | .75 | .30 | .07 |
| ☐ 26 1929 Championship Team | .50 | .20 | .05 |
| ☐ 27 1930 Championship Team | .50 | .20 | .05 |
| ☐ 28 1931 Championship Team | .50 | .20 | .05 |
| ☐ 29 1936 Championship Team | .50 | .20 | .05 |
| ☐ 30 1939 Championship Team | .50 | .20 | .05 |
| ☐ 31 1944 Championship Team | .50 | .20 | .05 |
| ☐ 32 1961 Championship Team | .75 | .30 | .07 |
| ☐ 33 1962 Championship Team | .75 | .30 | .07 |
| ☐ 34 1965 Championship Team | .75 | .30 | .07 |
| ☐ 35 1966 Championship Team | .75 | .30 | .07 |
| ☐ 36 1967 Championship Team | .75 | .30 | .07 |
| ☐ 37 Old City Stadium | .50 | .20 | .05 |
| ☐ 38 New City Stadium | .50 | .20 | .05 |
| ☐ 39 Lambeau Field - 1992 | .50 | .20 | .05 |
| ☐ NNO Title card | .50 | .20 | .05 |

(3 3/4" by 5 3/4")

# 1988 Panini Stickers

This set of 433 different stickers (457 different subjects including half stickers) was issued in 1988 by Panini. Panini had been producing stickers under Topps license but, beginning with this set, Panini established its own trade name in this country separate from Topps. The stickers measure approximately 2 1/8" by 2 3/4", are numbered on both the front and the back, and are in alphabetical order by team. The album for the set is easily obtainable. It is organized in team order like the sticker numbering. On the inside back cover of the sticker album the company offered (via direct mail-order) up to 30 different stickers of your choice for either ten cents each (only in Canada) or in trade one-for-one for your unwanted extra stickers (only in the United States) plus 1.00 for postage and handling; this is one reason why the values of the most popular players in these sticker sets are somewhat depressed compared to traditional card set prices. Each sticker pack included one foil sticker. Team name foils were produced in pairs; the other member of the pair is listed parenthetically. The team name foils contain a referee signal on the sticker back, the helmet foils have the team's stadium on the back, and the uniform foils include a team "Huddles" cartoon card on the back. The album for the set features John Elway on the cover. Bo Jackson appears in his Rookie Football Card year and Simon Fletcher appears one year prior to his Rookie Cards.

| | MINT | EXC | G-VG |
|---|---|---|---|
| COMPLETE SET (447) | 30.00 | 12.00 | 3.00 |
| COMMON PLAYER (1-447) | .05 | .02 | .00 |
| ☐ 1 Super Bowl XXII Program Cover | .15 | .06 | .01 |
| ☐ 2 Bills Helmet FOIL | .05 | .02 | .00 |
| ☐ 3 Bills Action | .05 | .02 | .00 |
| ☐ 4 Cornelius Bennett | .50 | .20 | .05 |
| ☐ 5 Chris Burkett | .05 | .02 | .00 |
| ☐ 6 Derrick Burroughs | .05 | .02 | .00 |
| ☐ 7 Shane Conlan | .25 | .10 | .02 |
| ☐ 8 Ronnie Harmon | .25 | .10 | .02 |
| ☐ 9 Jim Kelly | .75 | .30 | .07 |
| ☐ 10 Bills FOIL (240) | .05 | .02 | .00 |
| ☐ 11 Mark Kelso | .05 | .02 | .00 |
| ☐ 12 Nate Odomes | .05 | .02 | .00 |
| ☐ 13 Andre Reed | .25 | .10 | .02 |
| ☐ 14 Fred Smerlas | .05 | .02 | .00 |
| ☐ 15 Bruce Smith | .25 | .10 | .02 |
| ☐ 16 Bills Uniform FOIL | .05 | .02 | .00 |
| ☐ 17 Bengals Helmet FOIL | .05 | .02 | .00 |
| ☐ 18 Bengals Action | .05 | .02 | .00 |
| ☐ 19 Jim Breech | .05 | .02 | .00 |
| ☐ 20 James Brooks | .10 | .04 | .01 |
| ☐ 21 Eddie Brown | .10 | .04 | .01 |
| ☐ 22 Cris Collinsworth | .10 | .04 | .01 |
| ☐ 23 Boomer Esiason | .25 | .10 | .02 |
| ☐ 24 Rodney Holman | .10 | .04 | .01 |
| ☐ 25 Bengals FOIL (255) | .05 | .02 | .00 |
| ☐ 26 Larry Kinnebrew | .05 | .02 | .00 |
| ☐ 27 Tim Krumrie | .05 | .02 | .00 |
| ☐ 28 Anthony Munoz | .15 | .06 | .01 |
| ☐ 29 Reggie Williams | .10 | .04 | .01 |
| ☐ 30 Carl Zander | .05 | .02 | .00 |
| ☐ 31 Bengals Uniform FOIL | .05 | .02 | .00 |
| ☐ 32 Browns Helmet FOIL | .05 | .02 | .00 |
| ☐ 33 Browns Action (Bernie Kosar) | .15 | .06 | .01 |
| ☐ 34 Earnest Byner | .10 | .04 | .01 |
| ☐ 35 Hanford Dixon | .05 | .02 | .00 |
| ☐ 36 Bob Golic | .10 | .04 | .01 |
| ☐ 37 Mike Johnson | .05 | .02 | .00 |
| ☐ 38 Bernie Kosar | .35 | .14 | .03 |
| ☐ 39 Kevin Mack | .10 | .04 | .01 |
| ☐ 40 Browns FOIL (270) | .05 | .02 | .00 |
| ☐ 41 Clay Matthews | .15 | .06 | .01 |
| ☐ 42 Gerald McNeil | .05 | .02 | .00 |
| ☐ 43 Frank Minnifield | .05 | .02 | .00 |
| ☐ 44 Ozzie Newsome | .15 | .06 | .01 |
| ☐ 45 Cody Risien | .05 | .02 | .00 |
| ☐ 46 Browns Uniform FOIL | .05 | .02 | .00 |
| ☐ 47 Broncos Helmet FOIL | .05 | .02 | .00 |
| ☐ 48 Broncos Action | .05 | .02 | .00 |
| ☐ 49 Keith Bishop | .05 | .02 | .00 |
| ☐ 50 Tony Dorsett | .35 | .14 | .03 |
| ☐ 51 John Elway | 1.00 | .40 | .10 |
| ☐ 52 Simon Fletcher | .25 | .10 | .02 |
| ☐ 53 Mark Jackson | .10 | .04 | .01 |
| ☐ 54 Vance Johnson | .10 | .04 | .01 |
| ☐ 55 Broncos FOIL (285) | .05 | .02 | .00 |
| ☐ 56 Rulon Jones | .05 | .02 | .00 |
| ☐ 57 Rich Karlis | .05 | .02 | .00 |
| ☐ 58 Karl Mecklenburg | .10 | .04 | .01 |
| ☐ 59 Ricky Nattiel | .10 | .04 | .01 |
| ☐ 60 Sammy Winder | .05 | .02 | .00 |
| ☐ 61 Broncos Uniform FOIL | .05 | .02 | .00 |
| ☐ 62 Oilers Helmet FOIL | .05 | .02 | .00 |

|  |  | | | |
|---|---|---|---|---|
| ☐ 63 | Oilers Action (Warren Moon) | .25 | .10 | .02 |
| ☐ 64 | Keith Bostic | .05 | .02 | .00 |
| ☐ 65 | Steve Brown | .05 | .02 | .00 |
| ☐ 66 | Ray Childress | .15 | .06 | .01 |
| ☐ 67 | Jeff Donaldson | .05 | .02 | .00 |
| ☐ 68 | John Grimsley | .05 | .02 | .00 |
| ☐ 69 | Robert Lyles | .05 | .02 | .00 |
| ☐ 70 | Oilers FOIL (300) | .05 | .02 | .00 |
| ☐ 71 | Drew Hill | .10 | .04 | .01 |
| ☐ 72 | Warren Moon | .75 | .30 | .07 |
| ☐ 73 | Mike Munchak | .15 | .06 | .01 |
| ☐ 74 | Mike Rozier | .10 | .04 | .01 |
| ☐ 75 | Johnny Meads | .05 | .02 | .00 |
| ☐ 76 | Oilers Uniform FOIL | .05 | .02 | .00 |
| ☐ 77 | Colts Helmet FOIL | .05 | .02 | .00 |
| ☐ 78 | Colts Action (Eric Dickerson) | .15 | .06 | .01 |
| ☐ 79 | Albert Bentley | .10 | .04 | .01 |
| ☐ 80 | Dean Biasucci | .05 | .02 | .00 |
| ☐ 81 | Duane Bickett | .15 | .06 | .01 |
| ☐ 82 | Bill Brooks | .15 | .06 | .01 |
| ☐ 83 | Johnie Cooks | .05 | .02 | .00 |
| ☐ 84 | Eric Dickerson | .50 | .20 | .05 |
| ☐ 85 | Colts FOIL (315) | .05 | .02 | .00 |
| ☐ 86 | Ray Donaldson | .05 | .02 | .00 |
| ☐ 87 | Chris Hinton | .10 | .04 | .01 |
| ☐ 88 | Cliff Odom | .05 | .02 | .00 |
| ☐ 89 | Barry Krauss | .10 | .04 | .01 |
| ☐ 90 | Jack Trudeau | .15 | .06 | .01 |
| ☐ 91 | Colts Uniform FOIL | .05 | .02 | .00 |
| ☐ 92 | Chiefs Helmet FOIL | .05 | .02 | .00 |
| ☐ 93 | Chiefs Action | .05 | .02 | .00 |
| ☐ 94 | Carlos Carson | .05 | .02 | .00 |
| ☐ 95 | Deron Cherry | .10 | .04 | .01 |
| ☐ 96 | Dino Hackett | .05 | .02 | .00 |
| ☐ 97 | Bill Kenney | .05 | .02 | .00 |
| ☐ 98 | Albert Lewis | .10 | .04 | .01 |
| ☐ 99 | Nick Lowery | .10 | .04 | .01 |
| ☐ 100 | Chiefs FOIL (330) | .05 | .02 | .00 |
| ☐ 101 | Bill Maas | .05 | .02 | .00 |
| ☐ 102 | Christian Okoye | .15 | .06 | .01 |
| ☐ 103 | Stephone Paige | .10 | .04 | .01 |
| ☐ 104 | Paul Palmer | .05 | .02 | .00 |
| ☐ 105 | Kevin Ross | .05 | .02 | .00 |
| ☐ 106 | Chiefs Uniform FOIL | .05 | .02 | .00 |
| ☐ 107 | Raiders Helmet FOIL | .05 | .02 | .00 |
| ☐ 108 | Raiders Action (Bo Jackson) | .25 | .10 | .02 |
| ☐ 109 | Marcus Allen | .35 | .14 | .03 |
| ☐ 110 | Todd Christensen | .15 | .06 | .01 |
| ☐ 111 | Mike Haynes | .15 | .06 | .01 |
| ☐ 112 | Bo Jackson | 1.00 | .40 | .10 |
| ☐ 113 | James Lofton | .20 | .08 | .02 |
| ☐ 114 | Howie Long | .15 | .06 | .01 |
| ☐ 115 | Raiders FOIL (345) | .05 | .02 | .00 |
| ☐ 116 | Rod Martin | .05 | .02 | .00 |
| ☐ 117 | Vann McElroy | .05 | .02 | .00 |
| ☐ 118 | Bill Pickel | .05 | .02 | .00 |
| ☐ 119 | Don Mosebar | .05 | .02 | .00 |
| ☐ 120 | Stacey Toran | .05 | .02 | .00 |
| ☐ 121 | Raiders Uniform FOIL | .05 | .02 | .00 |
| ☐ 122 | Dolphins Helmet FOIL | .05 | .02 | .00 |
| ☐ 123 | Dolphins Action | .05 | .02 | .00 |
| ☐ 124 | John Bosa | .05 | .02 | .00 |
| ☐ 125 | Mark Clayton | .15 | .06 | .01 |
| ☐ 126 | Mark Duper | .10 | .04 | .01 |
| ☐ 127 | Lorenzo Hampton | .05 | .02 | .00 |
| ☐ 128 | William Judson | .05 | .02 | .00 |
| ☐ 129 | Dan Marino | 2.00 | .80 | .20 |
| ☐ 130 | Dolphins FOIL (360) | .05 | .02 | .00 |
| ☐ 131 | John Offerdahl | .10 | .04 | .01 |
| ☐ 132 | Reggie Roby | .05 | .02 | .00 |
| ☐ 133 | Jackie Shipp | .05 | .02 | .00 |
| ☐ 134 | Dwight Stephenson | .10 | .04 | .01 |
| ☐ 135 | Troy Stradford | .10 | .04 | .01 |
| ☐ 136 | Dolphins Uniform FOIL | .05 | .02 | .00 |
| ☐ 137 | Patriots Helmet FOIL | .05 | .02 | .00 |
| ☐ 138 | Patriots Action | .05 | .02 | .00 |
| ☐ 139 | Bruce Armstrong | .05 | .02 | .00 |
| ☐ 140 | Raymond Clayborn | .05 | .02 | .00 |
| ☐ 141 | Reggie Dupard | .05 | .02 | .00 |
| ☐ 142 | Steve Grogan | .10 | .04 | .01 |
| ☐ 143 | Craig James | .15 | .06 | .01 |
| ☐ 144 | Ronnie Lippett | .05 | .02 | .00 |
| ☐ 145 | Patriots FOIL (375) | .05 | .02 | .00 |
| ☐ 146 | Fred Marion | .05 | .02 | .00 |
| ☐ 147 | Stanley Morgan | .15 | .06 | .01 |
| ☐ 148 | Mosi Tatupu | .05 | .02 | .00 |
| ☐ 149 | Andre Tippett | .10 | .04 | .01 |
| ☐ 150 | Garin Veris | .05 | .02 | .00 |
| ☐ 151 | Patriots Uniform FOIL | .05 | .02 | .00 |
| ☐ 152 | Jets Helmet FOIL | .05 | .02 | .00 |
| ☐ 153 | Jets Action (Ken O'Brien) | .05 | .02 | .00 |
| ☐ 154 | Bob Crable | .05 | .02 | .00 |
| ☐ 155 | Mark Gastineau | .10 | .04 | .01 |
| ☐ 156 | Pat Leahy | .05 | .02 | .00 |
| ☐ 157 | Johnny Hector | .10 | .04 | .01 |
| ☐ 158 | Marty Lyons | .10 | .04 | .01 |
| ☐ 159 | Freeman McNeil | .15 | .06 | .01 |
| ☐ 160 | Jets FOIL (390) | .05 | .02 | .00 |
| ☐ 161 | Ken O'Brien | .10 | .04 | .01 |
| ☐ 162 | Mickey Shuler | .05 | .02 | .00 |
| ☐ 163 | Al Toon | .10 | .04 | .01 |
| ☐ 164 | Roger Vick | .05 | .02 | .00 |
| ☐ 165 | Wesley Walker | .10 | .04 | .01 |
| ☐ 166 | Jets Uniform FOIL | .05 | .02 | .00 |
| ☐ 167 | Steelers Helmet FOIL | .05 | .02 | .00 |
| ☐ 168 | Steelers Action | .05 | .02 | .00 |
| ☐ 169 | Walter Abercrombie | .05 | .02 | .00 |
| ☐ 170 | Gary Anderson | .05 | .02 | .00 |
| ☐ 171 | Todd Blackledge | .05 | .02 | .00 |
| ☐ 172 | Thomas Everett | .15 | .06 | .01 |
| ☐ 173 | Delton Hall | .05 | .02 | .00 |
| ☐ 174 | Bryan Hinkle | .05 | .02 | .00 |
| ☐ 175 | Steelers FOIL (405) | .05 | .02 | .00 |
| ☐ 176 | Earnest Jackson | .10 | .04 | .01 |
| ☐ 177 | Louis Lipps | .10 | .04 | .01 |
| ☐ 178 | David Little | .05 | .02 | .00 |
| ☐ 179 | Mike Merriweather | .10 | .04 | .01 |
| ☐ 180 | Mike Webster | .15 | .06 | .01 |
| ☐ 181 | Steelers Uniform FOIL | .05 | .02 | .00 |
| ☐ 182 | Chargers Helmet FOIL | .05 | .02 | .00 |
| ☐ 183 | Chargers Action | .05 | .02 | .00 |
| ☐ 184 | Gary Anderson | .15 | .06 | .01 |
| ☐ 185 | Chip Banks | .10 | .04 | .01 |
| ☐ 186 | Martin Bayless | .05 | .02 | .00 |
| ☐ 187 | Chuck Ehin | .05 | .02 | .00 |
| ☐ 188 | Vencie Glenn | .05 | .02 | .00 |
| ☐ 189 | Lionel James | .05 | .02 | .00 |
| ☐ 190 | Chargers FOIL (420) | .05 | .02 | .00 |
| ☐ 191 | Mark Malone | .05 | .02 | .00 |
| ☐ 192 | Ralf Mojsiejenko | .05 | .02 | .00 |
| ☐ 193 | Billy Ray Smith | .10 | .04 | .01 |
| ☐ 194 | Lee Williams | .15 | .06 | .01 |
| ☐ 195 | Kellen Winslow | .15 | .06 | .01 |
| ☐ 196 | Chargers Uniform FOIL | .05 | .02 | .00 |
| ☐ 197 | Seahawks Helmet FOIL | .05 | .02 | .00 |
| ☐ 198 | Seahawks Action (Dave Krieg) | .10 | .04 | .01 |
| ☐ 199 | Eugene Robinson | .05 | .02 | .00 |
| ☐ 200 | Jeff Bryant | .05 | .02 | .00 |
| ☐ 201 | Ray Butler | .05 | .02 | .00 |
| ☐ 202 | Jacob Green | .10 | .04 | .01 |
| ☐ 203 | Norm Johnson | .10 | .04 | .01 |
| ☐ 204 | Dave Krieg | .10 | .04 | .01 |
| ☐ 205 | Seahawks FOIL (435) | .05 | .02 | .00 |
| ☐ 206 | Steve Largent | .75 | .30 | .07 |
| ☐ 207 | Joe Nash | .05 | .02 | .00 |
| ☐ 208 | Curt Warner | .10 | .04 | .01 |
| ☐ 209 | Bobby Joe Edmonds | .10 | .04 | .01 |
| ☐ 210 | Daryl Turner | .05 | .02 | .00 |
| ☐ 211 | Seahawks Uniform FOIL | .05 | .02 | .00 |
| ☐ 212 | AFC Logo | .05 | .02 | .00 |
| ☐ 213 | Bernie Kosar | .35 | .14 | .03 |
| ☐ 214 | Curt Warner | .10 | .04 | .01 |
| ☐ 215 | Jerry Rice and Steve Largent | 1.00 | .40 | .10 |
| ☐ 216 | Mark Bavaro and Anthony Munoz | .15 | .06 | .01 |
| ☐ 217 | Gary Zimmerman and Bill Fralic | .10 | .04 | .01 |
| ☐ 218 | Dwight Stephenson and Mike Munchak | .10 | .04 | .01 |
| ☐ 219 | Joe Montana | 2.50 | 1.00 | .25 |
| ☐ 220 | Charles White and Eric Dickerson | .40 | .16 | .04 |
| ☐ 221 | Morten Andersen and Vai Sikahema | .10 | .04 | .01 |
| ☐ 222 | Bruce Smith and Reggie White | .30 | .12 | .03 |
| ☐ 223 | Michael Carter and Steve McMichael | .10 | .04 | .01 |
| ☐ 224 | Jim Arnold | .05 | .02 | .00 |
| ☐ 225 | Carl Banks and Andre Tippett | .10 | .04 | .01 |
| ☐ 226 | Barry Wilburn and Mike Singletary | .10 | .04 | .01 |
| ☐ 227 | Hanford Dixon and Frank Minnifield | .05 | .02 | .00 |
| ☐ 228 | Ronnie Lott and Joey Browner | .15 | .06 | .01 |
| ☐ 229 | NFC Logo | .05 | .02 | .00 |
| ☐ 230 | Gary Clark | .15 | .06 | .01 |
| ☐ 231 | Richard Dent | .15 | .06 | .01 |
| ☐ 232 | Falcons Helmet FOIL | .05 | .02 | .00 |
| ☐ 233 | Falcons Action | .05 | .02 | .00 |
| ☐ 234 | Rick Bryan | .05 | .02 | .00 |
| ☐ 235 | Bobby Butler | .05 | .02 | .00 |
| ☐ 236 | Tony Casillas | .15 | .06 | .01 |
| ☐ 237 | Floyd Dixon | .05 | .02 | .00 |
| ☐ 238 | Rick Donnelly | .05 | .02 | .00 |
| ☐ 239 | Bill Fralic | .10 | .04 | .01 |

|  | | | |
|---|---|---|---|
| ☐ 240 Falcons FOIL (10) | .05 | .02 | .00 |
| ☐ 241 Mike Gann | .05 | .02 | .00 |
| ☐ 242 Chris Miller | .50 | .20 | .05 |
| ☐ 243 Robert Moore | .05 | .02 | .00 |
| ☐ 244 John Rade | .05 | .02 | .00 |
| ☐ 245 Gerald Riggs | .10 | .04 | .01 |
| ☐ 246 Falcons Uniform FOIL | .05 | .02 | .00 |
| ☐ 247 Bears Helmet FOIL | .05 | .02 | .00 |
| ☐ 248 Bears Action | .15 | .06 | .01 |
| (Jim McMahon) | | | |
| ☐ 249 Neal Anderson | .50 | .20 | .05 |
| ☐ 250 Jim Covert | .10 | .04 | .01 |
| ☐ 251 Richard Dent | .15 | .06 | .01 |
| ☐ 252 Dave Duerson | .05 | .02 | .00 |
| ☐ 253 Dennis Gentry | .05 | .02 | .00 |
| ☐ 254 Jay Hilgenberg | .10 | .04 | .01 |
| ☐ 255 Bears FOIL (25) | .05 | .02 | .00 |
| ☐ 256 Jim McMahon | .25 | .10 | .02 |
| ☐ 257 Steve McMichael | .10 | .04 | .01 |
| ☐ 258 Matt Suhey | .05 | .02 | .00 |
| ☐ 259 Mike Singletary | .20 | .08 | .02 |
| ☐ 260 Otis Wilson | .10 | .04 | .01 |
| ☐ 261 Bears Uniform FOIL | .05 | .02 | .00 |
| ☐ 262 Cowboys Helmet FOIL | .05 | .02 | .00 |
| ☐ 263 Cowboys Action | .15 | .06 | .01 |
| (Herschel Walker) | | | |
| ☐ 264 Bill Bates | .10 | .04 | .01 |
| ☐ 265 Doug Cosbie | .05 | .02 | .00 |
| ☐ 266 Ron Francis | .05 | .02 | .00 |
| ☐ 267 Jim Jeffcoat | .15 | .06 | .01 |
| ☐ 268 Ed Too Tall Jones | .20 | .08 | .02 |
| ☐ 269 Eugene Lockhart | .05 | .02 | .00 |
| ☐ 270 Cowboys FOIL (40) | .05 | .02 | .00 |
| ☐ 271 Danny Noonan | .05 | .02 | .00 |
| ☐ 272 Steve Pelluer | .10 | .04 | .01 |
| ☐ 273 Herschel Walker | .35 | .14 | .03 |
| ☐ 274 Everson Walls | .10 | .04 | .01 |
| ☐ 275 Randy White | .20 | .08 | .02 |
| ☐ 276 Cowboys Uniform FOIL | .05 | .02 | .00 |
| ☐ 277 Lions Helmet FOIL | .05 | .02 | .00 |
| ☐ 278 Lions Action | .05 | .02 | .00 |
| ☐ 279 Jim Arnold | .05 | .02 | .00 |
| ☐ 280 Jerry Ball | .10 | .04 | .01 |
| ☐ 281 Michael Cofer | .05 | .02 | .00 |
| ☐ 282 Keith Ferguson | .05 | .02 | .00 |
| ☐ 283 Dennis Gibson | .05 | .02 | .00 |
| ☐ 284 James Griffin | .05 | .02 | .00 |
| ☐ 285 Lions FOIL (55) | .05 | .02 | .00 |
| ☐ 286 James Jones | .10 | .04 | .01 |
| ☐ 287 Chuck Long | .10 | .04 | .01 |
| ☐ 288 Pete Mandley | .05 | .02 | .00 |
| ☐ 289 Eddie Murray | .05 | .02 | .00 |
| ☐ 290 Garry James | .05 | .02 | .00 |
| ☐ 291 Lions Uniform FOIL | .05 | .02 | .00 |
| ☐ 292 Packers Helmet FOIL | .05 | .02 | .00 |
| ☐ 293 Packers Action | .05 | .02 | .00 |
| ☐ 294 John Anderson | .05 | .02 | .00 |
| ☐ 295 Dave Brown | .05 | .02 | .00 |
| ☐ 296 Alphonso Carreker | .05 | .02 | .00 |
| ☐ 297 Kenneth Davis | .20 | .08 | .02 |
| ☐ 298 Phillip Epps | .05 | .02 | .00 |
| ☐ 299 Brent Fullwood | .05 | .02 | .00 |
| ☐ 300 Packers FOIL (70) | .05 | .02 | .00 |
| ☐ 301 Tim Harris | .15 | .06 | .01 |
| ☐ 302 Johnny Holland | .10 | .04 | .01 |
| ☐ 303 Mark Murphy | .05 | .02 | .00 |
| ☐ 304 Brian Noble | .05 | .02 | .00 |
| ☐ 305 Walter Stanley | .10 | .04 | .01 |
| ☐ 306 Packers Uniform FOIL | .05 | .02 | .00 |
| ☐ 307 Rams Helmet FOIL | .05 | .02 | .00 |
| ☐ 308 Rams Action | .05 | .02 | .00 |
| ☐ 309 Jim Collins | .05 | .02 | .00 |
| ☐ 310 Henry Ellard | .15 | .06 | .01 |
| ☐ 311 Jim Everett | .25 | .10 | .02 |
| ☐ 312 Jerry Gray | .05 | .02 | .00 |
| ☐ 313 LeRoy Irvin | .05 | .02 | .00 |
| ☐ 314 Mike Lansford | .05 | .02 | .00 |
| ☐ 315 Rams FOIL (85) | .05 | .02 | .00 |
| ☐ 316 Mel Owens | .05 | .02 | .00 |
| ☐ 317 Jackie Slater | .10 | .04 | .01 |
| ☐ 318 Doug Smith | .05 | .02 | .00 |
| ☐ 319 Charles White | .10 | .04 | .01 |
| ☐ 320 Mike Wilcher | .05 | .02 | .00 |
| ☐ 321 Rams Uniform FOIL | .05 | .02 | .00 |
| ☐ 322 Vikings Helmet FOIL | .05 | .02 | .00 |
| ☐ 323 Vikings Action | .05 | .02 | .00 |
| ☐ 324 Joey Browner | .10 | .04 | .01 |
| ☐ 325 Anthony Carter | .15 | .06 | .01 |
| ☐ 326 Chris Doleman | .15 | .06 | .01 |
| ☐ 327 D.J. Dozier | .10 | .04 | .01 |
| ☐ 328 Steve Jordan | .10 | .04 | .01 |
| ☐ 329 Tommy Kramer | .10 | .04 | .01 |
| ☐ 330 Vikings FOIL (100) | .05 | .02 | .00 |
| ☐ 331 Darrin Nelson | .10 | .04 | .01 |
| ☐ 332 Jesse Solomon | .10 | .04 | .01 |
| ☐ 333 Scott Studwell | .10 | .04 | .01 |
| ☐ 334 Wade Wilson | .35 | .14 | .03 |
| ☐ 335 Gary Zimmerman | .05 | .02 | .00 |
| ☐ 336 Vikings Uniform FOIL | .05 | .02 | .00 |
| ☐ 337 Saints Helmet FOIL | .05 | .02 | .00 |
| ☐ 338 Saints Action | .15 | .06 | .01 |
| (Bobby Hebert) | | | |
| ☐ 339 Morten Andersen | .10 | .04 | .01 |
| ☐ 340 Bruce Clark | .05 | .02 | .00 |
| ☐ 341 Brad Edelman | .05 | .02 | .00 |
| ☐ 342 Bobby Hebert | .15 | .06 | .01 |
| ☐ 343 Dalton Hilliard | .10 | .04 | .01 |
| ☐ 344 Rickey Jackson | .15 | .06 | .01 |
| ☐ 345 Saints FOIL (115) | .05 | .02 | .00 |
| ☐ 346 Vaughan Johnson | .10 | .04 | .01 |
| ☐ 347 Rueben Mayes | .10 | .04 | .01 |
| ☐ 348 Sam Mills | .10 | .04 | .01 |
| ☐ 349 Pat Swilling | .35 | .14 | .03 |
| ☐ 350 Dave Waymer | .05 | .02 | .00 |
| ☐ 351 Saints Uniform FOIL | .05 | .02 | .00 |
| ☐ 352 Giants Helmet FOIL | .05 | .02 | .00 |
| ☐ 353 Giants Action | .05 | .02 | .00 |
| ☐ 354 Carl Banks | .15 | .06 | .01 |
| ☐ 355 Mark Bavaro | .15 | .06 | .01 |
| ☐ 356 Jim Burt | .05 | .02 | .00 |
| ☐ 357 Harry Carson | .10 | .04 | .01 |
| ☐ 358 Terry Kinard | .05 | .02 | .00 |
| ☐ 359 Lionel Manuel | .05 | .02 | .00 |
| ☐ 360 Giants FOIL (130) | .10 | .04 | .01 |
| ☐ 361 Leonard Marshall | .05 | .02 | .00 |
| ☐ 362 George Martin | .05 | .02 | .00 |
| ☐ 363 Joe Morris | .10 | .04 | .01 |
| ☐ 364 Phil Simms | .35 | .14 | .03 |
| ☐ 365 George Adams | .05 | .02 | .00 |
| ☐ 366 Giants Uniform FOIL | .05 | .02 | .00 |
| ☐ 367 Eagles Helmet FOIL | .25 | .10 | .02 |
| ☐ 368 Eagles Action | .25 | .10 | .02 |
| (Randall Cunningham) | | | |
| ☐ 369 Jerome Brown | .25 | .10 | .02 |
| ☐ 370 Keith Byars | .15 | .06 | .01 |
| ☐ 371 Randall Cunningham | .50 | .20 | .05 |
| ☐ 372 Terry Hoage | .05 | .02 | .00 |
| ☐ 373 Seth Joyner | .20 | .08 | .02 |
| ☐ 374 Mike Quick | .15 | .06 | .01 |
| ☐ 375 Eagles FOIL (145) | .05 | .02 | .00 |
| ☐ 376 Clyde Simmons | .20 | .08 | .02 |
| ☐ 377 Anthony Toney | .05 | .02 | .00 |
| ☐ 378 Andre Waters | .10 | .04 | .01 |
| ☐ 379 Reggie White | .35 | .14 | .03 |
| ☐ 380 Roynell Young | .05 | .02 | .00 |
| ☐ 381 Eagles Uniform FOIL | .05 | .02 | .00 |
| ☐ 382 Cardinals Helmet FOIL | .05 | .02 | .00 |
| ☐ 383 Cardinals Action | .05 | .02 | .00 |
| ☐ 384 Robert Awalt | .05 | .02 | .00 |
| ☐ 385 Roy Green | .15 | .06 | .01 |
| ☐ 386 Neil Lomax | .10 | .04 | .01 |
| ☐ 387 Stump Mitchell | .10 | .04 | .01 |
| ☐ 388 Niko Noga | .05 | .02 | .00 |
| ☐ 389 Freddie Joe Nunn | .05 | .02 | .00 |
| ☐ 390 Cardinals FOIL (160) | .05 | .02 | .00 |
| ☐ 391 Luis Sharpe | .10 | .04 | .01 |
| ☐ 392 Vai Sikahema | .10 | .04 | .01 |
| ☐ 393 J.T. Smith | .10 | .04 | .01 |
| ☐ 394 Leonard Smith | .05 | .02 | .00 |
| ☐ 395 Lonnie Young | .05 | .02 | .00 |
| ☐ 396 Cardinals Uniform FOIL | .05 | .02 | .00 |
| ☐ 397 49ers Helmet FOIL | .05 | .02 | .00 |
| ☐ 398 49ers Action | .75 | .30 | .07 |
| (Joe Montana) | | | |
| ☐ 399 Dwaine Board | .05 | .02 | .00 |
| ☐ 400 Michael Carter | .10 | .04 | .01 |
| ☐ 401 Roger Craig | .25 | .10 | .02 |
| ☐ 402 Jeff Fuller | .05 | .02 | .00 |
| ☐ 403 Don Griffin | .05 | .02 | .00 |
| ☐ 404 Ronnie Lott | .20 | .08 | .02 |
| ☐ 405 49ers FOIL (175) | .05 | .02 | .00 |
| ☐ 406 Joe Montana | 2.50 | 1.00 | .25 |
| ☐ 407 Tom Rathman | .25 | .10 | .02 |
| ☐ 408 Jerry Rice | 1.25 | .50 | .12 |
| ☐ 409 Keena Turner | .05 | .02 | .00 |
| ☐ 410 Michael Walter | .05 | .02 | .00 |
| ☐ 411 49ers Uniform FOIL | .05 | .02 | .00 |
| ☐ 412 Bucs Helmet FOIL | .05 | .02 | .00 |
| ☐ 413 Bucs Action | .05 | .02 | .00 |
| ☐ 414 Mark Carrier | .35 | .14 | .03 |
| ☐ 415 Gerald Carter | .05 | .02 | .00 |
| ☐ 416 Ron Holmes | .10 | .04 | .01 |
| ☐ 417 Rod Jones | .05 | .02 | .00 |
| ☐ 418 Calvin Magee | .05 | .02 | .00 |
| ☐ 419 Ervin Randle | .05 | .02 | .00 |
| ☐ 420 Buccaneers FOIL (190) | .05 | .02 | .00 |
| ☐ 421 Donald Igwebuike | .25 | .10 | .02 |
| ☐ 422 Vinny Testaverde | .25 | .10 | .02 |
| ☐ 423 Jackie Walker | .05 | .02 | .00 |
| ☐ 424 Chris Washington | .05 | .02 | .00 |
| ☐ 425 James Wilder | .10 | .04 | .01 |
| ☐ 426 Bucs Uniform FOIL | .05 | .02 | .00 |
| ☐ 427 Redskins Helmet FOIL | .05 | .02 | .00 |
| ☐ 428 Redskins Action | .10 | .04 | .01 |

(Doug Williams)

| | MINT | EXC | G-VG |
|---|---|---|---|
| ☐ 429 Gary Clark | .15 | .06 | .01 |
| ☐ 430 Monte Coleman | .05 | .02 | .00 |
| ☐ 431 Darrell Green | .10 | .04 | .01 |
| ☐ 432 Charles Mann | .10 | .04 | .01 |
| ☐ 433 Kelvin Bryant | .10 | .04 | .01 |
| ☐ 434 Art Monk | .25 | .10 | .02 |
| ☐ 435 Redskins FOIL (205) | .05 | .02 | .00 |
| ☐ 436 Ricky Sanders | .15 | .06 | .01 |
| ☐ 437 Jay Schroeder | .15 | .06 | .01 |
| ☐ 438 Alvin Walton | .05 | .02 | .00 |
| ☐ 439 Barry Wilburn | .10 | .04 | .01 |
| ☐ 440 Doug Williams | .10 | .04 | .01 |
| ☐ 441 Redskins Uniform FOIL | .05 | .02 | .00 |
| ☐ 442 Super Bowl action (Left half) | .05 | .02 | .00 |
| ☐ 443 Super Bowl action (Right half) | .05 | .02 | .00 |
| ☐ 444 Doug Williams (Super Bowl MVP) | .15 | .06 | .01 |
| ☐ 445 Super Bowl action | .05 | .02 | .00 |
| ☐ 446 Super Bowl action (Left half) | .05 | .02 | .00 |
| ☐ 447 Super Bowl action (Right half) | .05 | .02 | .00 |
| ☐ xx Panini Album (John Elway on cover) | 2.50 | 1.00 | .25 |

# 1989 Panini Stickers

NEW YORK JETS™

PAT LEAHY

Football '89

359

Look for Panini's Football '89 Sticker Album in your local store.

PANINI

Made in Italy by EDIZIONI PANINI S.p.A. - Modena - 1989

BEND AND PEEL

This set of 416 stickers was issued in 1989 by Panini. The stickers measure approximately 1 15/16" by 3" and are numbered on the front and on the back. The album for the set is easily obtainable. It is organized in team order like the sticker numbering. On the inside back cover of the sticker album the company offered (via direct mail-order) up to 30 different stickers of your choice for either ten cents each (only in Canada) or in trade one-for-one for your unwanted extra stickers (only in the United States) plus 1.00 for postage and handling; this is one reason why the values of the most popular players in these sticker sets are somewhat depressed compared to traditional card set prices. The album for the set features Joe Montana on the cover. Tim Brown, Cris Carter, Michael Irvin, Keith Jackson, Jay Novacek, Sterling Sharpe, Thurman Thomas, Rod Woodson appear in their Rookie Card year. The stickers were also issued in a UK version which is distinguished by the presence of stats printed on the sticker backs.

| | MINT | EXC | G-VG |
|---|---|---|---|
| COMPLETE SET (416) | 25.00 | 10.00 | 2.50 |
| COMMON PLAYER (1-416) | .05 | .02 | .00 |
| ☐ 1 SB XXIII Program | .10 | .04 | .01 |
| ☐ 2 SB XXIII Program | .05 | .02 | .00 |
| ☐ 3 Floyd Dixon | .05 | .02 | .00 |
| ☐ 4 Tony Casillas | .10 | .04 | .01 |
| ☐ 5 Bill Fralic | .10 | .04 | .01 |
| ☐ 6 Aundray Bruce | .05 | .02 | .00 |
| ☐ 7 Scott Case | .05 | .02 | .00 |
| ☐ 8 Rick Donnelly | .05 | .02 | .00 |
| ☐ 9 Falcons Logo FOIL | .05 | .02 | .00 |
| ☐ 10 Falcons Helmet FOIL | .05 | .02 | .00 |
| ☐ 11 Marcus Cotton | .05 | .02 | .00 |
| ☐ 12 Chris Miller | .25 | .10 | .02 |
| ☐ 13 Robert Moore | .05 | .02 | .00 |
| ☐ 14 Bobby Butler | .05 | .02 | .00 |
| ☐ 15 Rick Bryan | .05 | .02 | .00 |
| ☐ 16 John Settle | .10 | .04 | .01 |
| ☐ 17 Jim McMahon | .15 | .06 | .01 |
| ☐ 18 Neal Anderson | .15 | .06 | .01 |
| ☐ 19 Dave Duerson | .05 | .02 | .00 |
| ☐ 20 Steve McMichael | .05 | .02 | .00 |
| ☐ 21 Jay Hilgenberg | .05 | .02 | .00 |
| ☐ 22 Dennis McKinnon | .05 | .02 | .00 |
| ☐ 23 Bears Logo FOIL | .05 | .02 | .00 |
| ☐ 24 Bears Helmet FOIL | .05 | .02 | .00 |

| | MINT | EXC | G-VG |
|---|---|---|---|
| ☐ 25 Richard Dent | .15 | .06 | .01 |
| ☐ 26 Dennis Gentry | .05 | .02 | .00 |
| ☐ 27 Mike Singletary | .15 | .06 | .01 |
| ☐ 28 Vestee Jackson | .05 | .02 | .00 |
| ☐ 29 Mike Tomczak | .15 | .06 | .01 |
| ☐ 30 Dan Hampton | .15 | .06 | .01 |
| ☐ 31 Michael Irvin | 1.25 | .50 | .12 |
| ☐ 32 Eugene Lockhart | .10 | .04 | .01 |
| ☐ 33 Herschel Walker | .30 | .12 | .03 |
| ☐ 34 Kelvin Martin | .15 | .06 | .01 |
| ☐ 35 Jim Jeffcoat | .10 | .04 | .01 |
| ☐ 36 Everson Walls | .10 | .04 | .01 |
| ☐ 37 Cowboys Logo FOIL | .05 | .02 | .00 |
| ☐ 38 Cowboys Helmet FOIL | .05 | .02 | .00 |
| ☐ 39 Danny Noonan | .05 | .02 | .00 |
| ☐ 40 Ray Alexander | .05 | .02 | .00 |
| ☐ 41 Garry Cobb | .05 | .02 | .00 |
| ☐ 42 Ed Too Tall Jones | .15 | .06 | .01 |
| ☐ 43 Kevin Brooks | .05 | .02 | .00 |
| ☐ 44 Bill Bates | .10 | .04 | .01 |
| ☐ 45 Lions Logo FOIL | .05 | .02 | .00 |
| ☐ 46 Chuck Long | .10 | .04 | .01 |
| ☐ 47 Jim Arnold | .05 | .02 | .00 |
| ☐ 48 Michael Cofer | .05 | .02 | .00 |
| ☐ 49 Eddie Murray | .05 | .02 | .00 |
| ☐ 50 Keith Ferguson | .05 | .02 | .00 |
| ☐ 51 Pete Mandley | .05 | .02 | .00 |
| ☐ 52 Lions Helmet FOIL | .05 | .02 | .00 |
| ☐ 53 Jerry Ball | .05 | .02 | .00 |
| ☐ 54 Bennie Blades | .15 | .06 | .01 |
| ☐ 55 Dennis Gibson | .05 | .02 | .00 |
| ☐ 56 Chris Spielman | .15 | .06 | .01 |
| ☐ 57 Eric Williams | .05 | .02 | .00 |
| ☐ 58 Lomas Brown | .05 | .02 | .00 |
| ☐ 59 Johnny Holland | .10 | .04 | .01 |
| ☐ 60 Tim Harris | .15 | .06 | .01 |
| ☐ 61 Mark Murphy | .05 | .02 | .00 |
| ☐ 62 Walter Stanley | .10 | .04 | .01 |
| ☐ 63 Brent Fullwood | .05 | .02 | .00 |
| ☐ 64 Ken Ruettgers | .10 | .04 | .01 |
| ☐ 65 Packers Logo FOIL | .05 | .02 | .00 |
| ☐ 66 Packers Helmet FOIL | .05 | .02 | .00 |
| ☐ 67 John Anderson | .05 | .02 | .00 |
| ☐ 68 Brian Noble | .05 | .02 | .00 |
| ☐ 69 Sterling Sharpe | 1.25 | .50 | .12 |
| ☐ 70 Keith Woodside | .10 | .04 | .01 |
| ☐ 71 Mark Lee | .05 | .02 | .00 |
| ☐ 72 Don Majkowski | .15 | .06 | .01 |
| ☐ 73 Aaron Cox | .10 | .04 | .01 |
| ☐ 74 LeRoy Irvin | .05 | .02 | .00 |
| ☐ 75 Jim Everett | .15 | .06 | .01 |
| ☐ 76 Mike Lansford | .05 | .02 | .00 |
| ☐ 77 Mike Wilcher | .05 | .02 | .00 |
| ☐ 78 Henry Ellard | .10 | .04 | .01 |
| ☐ 79 Rams Helmet FOIL | .05 | .02 | .00 |
| ☐ 80 Jerry Gray | .05 | .02 | .00 |
| ☐ 81 Doug Smith | .05 | .02 | .00 |
| ☐ 82 Tom Newberry | .10 | .04 | .01 |
| ☐ 83 Jackie Slater | .10 | .04 | .01 |
| ☐ 84 Greg Bell | .10 | .04 | .01 |
| ☐ 85 Kevin Greene | .10 | .04 | .01 |
| ☐ 86 Chris Doleman | .10 | .04 | .01 |
| ☐ 87 Steve Jordan | .10 | .04 | .01 |
| ☐ 88 Jesse Solomon | .05 | .02 | .00 |
| ☐ 89 Randall McDaniel | .05 | .02 | .00 |
| ☐ 90 Hassan Jones | .10 | .04 | .01 |
| ☐ 91 Joey Browner | .10 | .04 | .01 |
| ☐ 92 Vikings Logo FOIL | .05 | .02 | .00 |
| ☐ 93 Vikings Helmet FOIL | .05 | .02 | .00 |
| ☐ 94 Anthony Carter | .10 | .04 | .01 |
| ☐ 95 Gary Zimmerman | .05 | .02 | .00 |
| ☐ 96 Wade Wilson | .15 | .06 | .01 |
| ☐ 97 Scott Studwell | .10 | .04 | .01 |
| ☐ 98 Keith Millard | .10 | .04 | .01 |
| ☐ 99 Carl Lee | .10 | .04 | .01 |
| ☐ 100 Morten Andersen | .10 | .04 | .01 |
| ☐ 101 Bobby Hebert | .15 | .06 | .01 |
| ☐ 102 Rueben Mayes | .10 | .04 | .01 |
| ☐ 103 Sam Mills | .10 | .04 | .01 |
| ☐ 104 Vaughan Johnson | .10 | .04 | .01 |
| ☐ 105 Pat Swilling | .15 | .06 | .01 |
| ☐ 106 Saints Logo FOIL | .05 | .02 | .00 |
| ☐ 107 Saints Helmet FOIL | .05 | .02 | .00 |
| ☐ 108 Brad Edelman | .05 | .02 | .00 |
| ☐ 109 Craig Heyward | .15 | .06 | .01 |
| ☐ 110 Eric Martin | .10 | .04 | .01 |
| ☐ 111 Dalton Hilliard | .10 | .04 | .01 |
| ☐ 112 Lonzell Hill | .05 | .02 | .00 |
| ☐ 113 Rickey Jackson | .10 | .04 | .01 |
| ☐ 114 Erik Howard | .05 | .02 | .00 |
| ☐ 115 Phil Simms | .25 | .10 | .02 |
| ☐ 116 Leonard Marshall | .10 | .04 | .01 |
| ☐ 117 Joe Morris | .10 | .04 | .01 |
| ☐ 118 Bart Oates | .10 | .04 | .01 |
| ☐ 119 Mark Bavaro | .10 | .04 | .01 |
| ☐ 120 Giants Logo FOIL | .05 | .02 | .00 |
| ☐ 121 Giants Helmet FOIL | .05 | .02 | .00 |

| | | | |
|---|---|---|---|
| ☐ 122 Terry Kinard | .05 | .02 | .00 |
| ☐ 123 Carl Banks | .10 | .04 | .01 |
| ☐ 124 Lionel Manuel | .05 | .02 | .00 |
| ☐ 125 Stephen Baker | .15 | .06 | .01 |
| ☐ 126 Pepper Johnson | .10 | .04 | .01 |
| ☐ 127 Jim Burt | .05 | .02 | .00 |
| ☐ 128 Cris Carter | .35 | .14 | .03 |
| ☐ 129 Mike Quick | .10 | .04 | .01 |
| ☐ 130 Terry Hoage | .05 | .02 | .00 |
| ☐ 131 Keith Jackson | .75 | .30 | .07 |
| ☐ 132 Clyde Simmons | .15 | .06 | .01 |
| ☐ 133 Eric Allen | .05 | .02 | .00 |
| ☐ 134 Eagles Logo FOIL | .05 | .02 | .00 |
| ☐ 135 Eagles Helmet FOIL | .05 | .02 | .00 |
| ☐ 136 Randall Cunningham | .50 | .20 | .05 |
| ☐ 137 Mike Pitts | .05 | .02 | .00 |
| ☐ 138 Keith Byars | .10 | .04 | .01 |
| ☐ 139 Seth Joyner | .15 | .06 | .01 |
| ☐ 140 Jerome Brown | .15 | .06 | .01 |
| ☐ 141 Reggie White | .30 | .12 | .03 |
| ☐ 142 Jay Novacek | .30 | .12 | .03 |
| ☐ 143 Neil Lomax | .10 | .04 | .01 |
| ☐ 144 Ken Harvey | .10 | .04 | .01 |
| ☐ 145 Freddie Joe Nunn | .05 | .02 | .00 |
| ☐ 146 Robert Awalt | .05 | .02 | .00 |
| ☐ 147 Niko Noga | .05 | .02 | .00 |
| ☐ 148 Cardinals Logo FOIL | .05 | .02 | .00 |
| ☐ 149 Cardinals Helmet FOIL | .05 | .02 | .00 |
| ☐ 150 Tim McDonald | .25 | .10 | .02 |
| ☐ 151 Roy Green | .10 | .04 | .01 |
| ☐ 152 Stump Mitchell | .10 | .04 | .01 |
| ☐ 153 J.T. Smith | .10 | .04 | .01 |
| ☐ 154 Luis Sharpe | .05 | .02 | .00 |
| ☐ 155 Vai Sikahema | .10 | .04 | .01 |
| ☐ 156 Jeff Fuller | .05 | .02 | .00 |
| ☐ 157 Joe Montana | 2.00 | .80 | .20 |
| ☐ 158 Harris Barton | .05 | .02 | .00 |
| ☐ 159 Michael Carter | .10 | .04 | .01 |
| ☐ 160 Jeff Fuller | .05 | .02 | .00 |
| ☐ 161 Jerry Rice | 1.25 | .50 | .12 |
| ☐ 162 49ers Logo FOIL | .05 | .02 | .00 |
| ☐ 163 49ers Helmet FOIL | .05 | .02 | .00 |
| ☐ 164 Tom Rathman | .15 | .06 | .01 |
| ☐ 165 Roger Craig | .20 | .08 | .02 |
| ☐ 166 Ronnie Lott | .20 | .08 | .02 |
| ☐ 167 Charles Haley | .15 | .06 | .01 |
| ☐ 168 John Taylor | .50 | .20 | .05 |
| ☐ 169 Michael Walter | .05 | .02 | .00 |
| ☐ 170 Ron Hall | .05 | .02 | .00 |
| ☐ 171 Ervin Randle | .05 | .02 | .00 |
| ☐ 172 James Wilder | .10 | .04 | .01 |
| ☐ 173 Ron Holmes | .05 | .02 | .00 |
| ☐ 174 Mark Carrier | .20 | .08 | .02 |
| ☐ 175 William Howard | .05 | .02 | .00 |
| ☐ 176 Bucs Logo FOIL | .05 | .02 | .00 |
| ☐ 177 Bucs Helmet FOIL | .05 | .02 | .00 |
| ☐ 178 Lars Tate | .05 | .02 | .00 |
| ☐ 179 Vinny Testaverde | .20 | .08 | .02 |
| ☐ 180 Paul Gruber | .15 | .06 | .01 |
| ☐ 181 Bruce Hill | .10 | .04 | .01 |
| ☐ 182 Reuben Davis | .05 | .02 | .00 |
| ☐ 183 Ricky Reynolds | .05 | .02 | .00 |
| ☐ 184 Ricky Sanders | .15 | .06 | .01 |
| ☐ 185 Gary Clark | .15 | .06 | .01 |
| ☐ 186 Mark May | .05 | .02 | .00 |
| ☐ 187 Darrell Green | .10 | .04 | .01 |
| ☐ 188 Jim Lachey | .10 | .04 | .01 |
| ☐ 189 Doug Williams | .10 | .04 | .01 |
| ☐ 190 Redskins Helmet FOIL | .05 | .02 | .00 |
| ☐ 191 Redskins Logo FOIL | .05 | .02 | .00 |
| ☐ 192 Kelvin Bryant | .05 | .02 | .00 |
| ☐ 193 Charles Mann | .05 | .02 | .00 |
| ☐ 194 Alvin Walton | .05 | .02 | .00 |
| ☐ 195 Art Monk | .20 | .08 | .02 |
| ☐ 196 Barry Wilburn | .05 | .02 | .00 |
| ☐ 197 Mark Rypien | .25 | .10 | .02 |
| ☐ 198 NFC Logo | .05 | .02 | .00 |
| ☐ 199 Scott Case | .05 | .02 | .00 |
| ☐ 200 Herschel Walker | .30 | .12 | .03 |
| ☐ 201 Herschel Walker and Roger Craig | .25 | .10 | .02 |
| ☐ 202 Henry Ellard and Jerry Rice | .35 | .14 | .03 |
| ☐ 203 Bruce Matthews and Tom Newberry | .05 | .02 | .00 |
| ☐ 204 Gary Zimmerman and Anthony Munoz | .10 | .04 | .01 |
| ☐ 205 Boomer Esiason | .15 | .06 | .01 |
| ☐ 206 Jay Hilgenberg | .10 | .04 | .01 |
| ☐ 207 Keith Jackson | .25 | .10 | .02 |
| ☐ 208 Reggie White and Bruce Smith | .25 | .10 | .02 |
| ☐ 209 Keith Millard and Tim Krumrie | .10 | .04 | .01 |
| ☐ 210 Carl Lee and Frank Minnifield | .05 | .02 | .00 |
| ☐ 211 Joey Browner | .10 | .04 | .01 |

| | | | |
|---|---|---|---|
| and Deron Cherry | | | |
| ☐ 212 Shane Conlan | .10 | .04 | .01 |
| ☐ 213 Mike Singletary | .15 | .06 | .01 |
| ☐ 214 Cornelius Bennett | .15 | .06 | .01 |
| ☐ 215 AFC Logo | .05 | .02 | .00 |
| ☐ 216 Boomer Esiason | .25 | .10 | .02 |
| ☐ 217 Erik McMillan | .10 | .04 | .01 |
| ☐ 218 Jim Kelly | .50 | .20 | .05 |
| ☐ 219 Cornelius Bennett | .15 | .06 | .01 |
| ☐ 220 Fred Smerlas | .10 | .04 | .01 |
| ☐ 221 Shane Conlan | .10 | .04 | .01 |
| ☐ 222 Scott Norwood | .05 | .02 | .00 |
| ☐ 223 Mark Kelso | .05 | .02 | .00 |
| ☐ 224 Bills Logo FOIL | .05 | .02 | .00 |
| ☐ 225 Bills Helmet FOIL | .05 | .02 | .00 |
| ☐ 226 Thurman Thomas | 1.25 | .50 | .12 |
| ☐ 227 Pete Metzelaars | .05 | .02 | .00 |
| ☐ 228 Bruce Smith | .25 | .10 | .02 |
| ☐ 229 Art Still | .10 | .04 | .01 |
| ☐ 230 Kent Hull | .10 | .04 | .01 |
| ☐ 231 Andre Reed | .25 | .10 | .02 |
| ☐ 232 Tim Krumrie | .05 | .02 | .00 |
| ☐ 233 Boomer Esiason | .25 | .10 | .02 |
| ☐ 234 Ickey Woods | .10 | .04 | .01 |
| ☐ 235 Eric Thomas | .10 | .04 | .01 |
| ☐ 236 Rodney Holman | .10 | .04 | .01 |
| ☐ 237 Jim Skow | .05 | .02 | .00 |
| ☐ 238 Bengals Helmet FOIL | .05 | .02 | .00 |
| ☐ 239 James Brooks | .10 | .04 | .01 |
| ☐ 240 David Fulcher | .10 | .04 | .01 |
| ☐ 241 Carl Zander | .05 | .02 | .00 |
| ☐ 242 Eddie Brown | .10 | .04 | .01 |
| ☐ 243 Max Montoya | .05 | .02 | .00 |
| ☐ 244 Anthony Munoz | .15 | .06 | .01 |
| ☐ 245 Felix Wright | .05 | .02 | .00 |
| ☐ 246 Clay Matthews | .15 | .06 | .01 |
| ☐ 247 Hanford Dixon | .05 | .02 | .00 |
| ☐ 248 Ozzie Newsome | .15 | .06 | .01 |
| ☐ 249 Bernie Kosar | .25 | .10 | .02 |
| ☐ 250 Kevin Mack | .10 | .04 | .01 |
| ☐ 251 Bengals Helmet FOIL | .05 | .02 | .00 |
| ☐ 252 Brian Brennan | .05 | .02 | .00 |
| ☐ 253 Reggie Langhorne | .05 | .02 | .00 |
| ☐ 254 Cody Risien | .05 | .02 | .00 |
| ☐ 255 Webster Slaughter | .15 | .06 | .01 |
| ☐ 256 Mike Johnson | .05 | .02 | .00 |
| ☐ 257 Frank Minnifield | .05 | .02 | .00 |
| ☐ 258 Mike Horan | .05 | .02 | .00 |
| ☐ 259 Dennis Smith | .10 | .04 | .01 |
| ☐ 260 Ricky Nattiel | .05 | .02 | .00 |
| ☐ 261 Karl Mecklenburg | .10 | .04 | .01 |
| ☐ 262 Keith Bishop | .05 | .02 | .00 |
| ☐ 263 John Elway | 1.00 | .40 | .10 |
| ☐ 264 Broncos Helmet FOIL | .05 | .02 | .00 |
| ☐ 265 Broncos Logo FOIL | .05 | .02 | .00 |
| ☐ 266 Simon Fletcher | .15 | .06 | .01 |
| ☐ 267 Vance Johnson | .10 | .04 | .01 |
| ☐ 268 Tony Dorsett | .35 | .14 | .03 |
| ☐ 269 Greg Kragen | .10 | .04 | .01 |
| ☐ 270 Mike Harden | .05 | .02 | .00 |
| ☐ 271 Mark Jackson | .05 | .02 | .00 |
| ☐ 272 Warren Moon | .50 | .20 | .05 |
| ☐ 273 Mike Rozier | .10 | .04 | .01 |
| ☐ 274 Oilers Logo FOIL | .05 | .02 | .00 |
| ☐ 275 Allen Pinkett | .10 | .04 | .01 |
| ☐ 276 Tony Zendejas | .05 | .02 | .00 |
| ☐ 277 Alonzo Highsmith | .10 | .04 | .01 |
| ☐ 278 Johnny Meads | .05 | .02 | .00 |
| ☐ 279 Oilers Helmet FOIL | .05 | .02 | .00 |
| ☐ 280 Mike Munchak | .10 | .04 | .01 |
| ☐ 281 John Grimsley | .05 | .02 | .00 |
| ☐ 282 Ernest Givins | .15 | .06 | .01 |
| ☐ 283 Drew Hill | .10 | .04 | .01 |
| ☐ 284 Bruce Matthews | .10 | .04 | .01 |
| ☐ 285 Ray Childress | .10 | .04 | .01 |
| ☐ 286 Colts Logo FOIL | .05 | .02 | .00 |
| ☐ 287 Chris Hinton | .10 | .04 | .01 |
| ☐ 288 Clarence Verdin | .10 | .04 | .01 |
| ☐ 289 Jon Hand | .15 | .06 | .01 |
| ☐ 290 Chris Chandler | .15 | .06 | .01 |
| ☐ 291 Eugene Daniel | .05 | .02 | .00 |
| ☐ 292 Dean Biasucci | .05 | .02 | .00 |
| ☐ 293 Colts Helmet FOIL | .05 | .02 | .00 |
| ☐ 294 Duane Bickett | .10 | .04 | .01 |
| ☐ 295 Rohn Stark | .05 | .02 | .00 |
| ☐ 296 Albert Bentley | .10 | .04 | .01 |
| ☐ 297 Bill Brooks | .10 | .04 | .01 |
| ☐ 298 O'Brien Alston | .05 | .02 | .00 |
| ☐ 299 Ray Donaldson | .05 | .02 | .00 |
| ☐ 300 Carlos Carson | .05 | .02 | .00 |
| ☐ 301 Lloyd Burruss | .05 | .02 | .00 |
| ☐ 302 Steve DeBerg | .15 | .06 | .01 |
| ☐ 303 Irv Eatman | .05 | .02 | .00 |
| ☐ 304 Dino Hackett | .05 | .02 | .00 |
| ☐ 305 Albert Lewis | .10 | .04 | .01 |
| ☐ 306 Chiefs Helmet FOIL | .05 | .02 | .00 |
| ☐ 307 Chiefs Logo FOIL | .05 | .02 | .00 |
| ☐ 308 Deron Cherry | .10 | .04 | .01 |

| | | | |
|---|---|---|---|
| ☐ 309 Paul Palmer | .05 | .02 | .00 |
| ☐ 310 Neil Smith | .35 | .14 | .03 |
| ☐ 311 Christian Okoye | .10 | .04 | .01 |
| ☐ 312 Stephone Paige | .10 | .04 | .01 |
| ☐ 313 Bill Maas | .05 | .02 | .00 |
| ☐ 314 Marcus Allen | .25 | .10 | .02 |
| ☐ 315 Vann McElroy | .05 | .02 | .00 |
| ☐ 316 Mervyn Fernandez | .10 | .04 | .01 |
| ☐ 317 Bill Pickel | .05 | .02 | .00 |
| ☐ 318 Greg Townsend | .10 | .04 | .01 |
| ☐ 319 Tim Brown | 1.00 | .40 | .10 |
| ☐ 320 Raiders Logo FOIL | .05 | .02 | .00 |
| ☐ 321 Raiders Helmet FOIL | .05 | .02 | .00 |
| ☐ 322 James Lofton | .15 | .06 | .01 |
| ☐ 323 Willie Gault | .10 | .04 | .01 |
| ☐ 324 Jay Schroeder | .10 | .04 | .01 |
| ☐ 325 Matt Millen | .05 | .02 | .00 |
| ☐ 326 Howie Long | .10 | .04 | .01 |
| ☐ 327 Bo Jackson | .50 | .20 | .05 |
| ☐ 328 Lorenzo Hampton | .05 | .02 | .00 |
| ☐ 329 Jarvis Williams | .05 | .02 | .00 |
| ☐ 330 Jim C. Jensen | .05 | .02 | .00 |
| ☐ 331 Dan Marino | 1.50 | .60 | .15 |
| ☐ 332 John Offerdahl | .10 | .04 | .01 |
| ☐ 333 Brian Sochia | .05 | .02 | .00 |
| ☐ 334 Dolphins Logo FOIL | .05 | .02 | .00 |
| ☐ 335 Dolphins Helmet FOIL | .05 | .02 | .00 |
| ☐ 336 Ferrell Edmunds | .05 | .02 | .00 |
| ☐ 337 Mark Brown | .05 | .02 | .00 |
| ☐ 338 Mark Duper | .10 | .04 | .01 |
| ☐ 339 Troy Stradford | .05 | .02 | .00 |
| ☐ 340 T.J. Turner | .05 | .02 | .00 |
| ☐ 341 Mark Clayton | .15 | .06 | .01 |
| ☐ 342 Patriots Logo FOIL | .05 | .02 | .00 |
| ☐ 343 Johnny Rembert | .05 | .02 | .00 |
| ☐ 344 Garin Veris | .05 | .02 | .00 |
| ☐ 345 Stanley Morgan | .10 | .04 | .01 |
| ☐ 346 John Stephens | .25 | .10 | .02 |
| ☐ 347 Fred Marion | .05 | .02 | .00 |
| ☐ 348 Irving Fryar | .15 | .06 | .01 |
| ☐ 349 Patriots Helmet FOIL | .05 | .02 | .00 |
| ☐ 350 Andre Tippett | .10 | .04 | .01 |
| ☐ 351 Roland James | .05 | .02 | .00 |
| ☐ 352 Brent Williams | .05 | .02 | .00 |
| ☐ 353 Raymond Clayborn | .05 | .02 | .00 |
| ☐ 354 Tony Eason | .10 | .04 | .01 |
| ☐ 355 Bruce Armstrong | .05 | .02 | .00 |
| ☐ 356 Jets Logo FOIL | .05 | .02 | .00 |
| ☐ 357 Marty Lyons | .10 | .04 | .01 |
| ☐ 358 Bobby Humphery | .05 | .02 | .00 |
| ☐ 359 Pat Leahy | .05 | .02 | .00 |
| ☐ 360 Mickey Shuler | .10 | .04 | .01 |
| ☐ 361 James Hasty | .05 | .02 | .00 |
| ☐ 362 Ken O'Brien | .10 | .04 | .01 |
| ☐ 363 Jets Helmet FOIL | .05 | .02 | .00 |
| ☐ 364 Alex Gordon | .05 | .02 | .00 |
| ☐ 365 Al Toon | .10 | .04 | .01 |
| ☐ 366 Erik McMillan | .10 | .04 | .01 |
| ☐ 367 Johnny Hector | .10 | .04 | .01 |
| ☐ 368 Wesley Walker | .10 | .04 | .01 |
| ☐ 369 Freeman McNeil | .10 | .04 | .01 |
| ☐ 370 Steelers Logo FOIL | .05 | .02 | .00 |
| ☐ 371 Gary Anderson | .05 | .02 | .00 |
| ☐ 372 Rodney Carter | .05 | .02 | .00 |
| ☐ 373 Merril Hoge | .10 | .04 | .01 |
| ☐ 374 David Little | .05 | .02 | .00 |
| ☐ 375 Bubby Brister | .15 | .06 | .01 |
| ☐ 376 Thomas Everett | .10 | .04 | .01 |
| ☐ 377 Steelers Helmet FOIL | .05 | .02 | .00 |
| ☐ 378 Rod Woodson | .50 | .20 | .05 |
| ☐ 379 Bryan Hinkle | .05 | .02 | .00 |
| ☐ 380 Tunch Ilkin | .05 | .02 | .00 |
| ☐ 381 Aaron Jones | .05 | .02 | .00 |
| ☐ 382 Louis Lipps | .10 | .04 | .01 |
| ☐ 383 Warren Williams | .05 | .02 | .00 |
| ☐ 384 Anthony Miller | .50 | .20 | .05 |
| ☐ 385 Gary Anderson | .15 | .06 | .01 |
| ☐ 386 Lee Williams | .10 | .04 | .01 |
| ☐ 387 Lionel James | .10 | .04 | .01 |
| ☐ 388 Gary Plummer | .05 | .02 | .00 |
| ☐ 389 Gill Byrd | .10 | .04 | .01 |
| ☐ 390 Chargers Helmet FOIL | .05 | .02 | .00 |
| ☐ 391 Ralf Mojsiejenko | .05 | .02 | .00 |
| ☐ 392 Rod Bernstine | .35 | .14 | .03 |
| ☐ 393 Keith Browner | .05 | .02 | .00 |
| ☐ 394 Billy Ray Smith | .10 | .04 | .01 |
| ☐ 395 Leslie O'Neal | .15 | .06 | .01 |
| ☐ 396 Jamie Holland | .05 | .02 | .00 |
| ☐ 397 Tony Woods | .10 | .04 | .01 |
| ☐ 398 Bruce Scholtz | .05 | .02 | .00 |
| ☐ 399 Joe Nash | .05 | .02 | .00 |
| ☐ 400 Curt Warner | .10 | .04 | .01 |
| ☐ 401 John L. Williams | .10 | .04 | .01 |
| ☐ 402 Bryan Millard | .05 | .02 | .00 |
| ☐ 403 Seahawks Logo FOIL | .05 | .02 | .00 |
| ☐ 404 Seahawks Helmet FOIL | .05 | .02 | .00 |
| ☐ 405 Steve Largent | .50 | .20 | .05 |
| ☐ 406 Norm Johnson | .10 | .04 | .01 |
| ☐ 407 Jacob Green | .10 | .04 | .01 |
| ☐ 408 Dave Krieg | .10 | .04 | .01 |
| ☐ 409 Paul Moyer | .05 | .02 | .00 |
| ☐ 410 Brian Blades | .50 | .20 | .05 |
| ☐ 411 SB XXIII | .05 | .02 | .00 |
| ☐ 412 Jerry Rice | 1.00 | .40 | .10 |
| ☐ 413 SB XXIII | .10 | .04 | .01 |
| ☐ 414 SB XXIII | .10 | .04 | .01 |
| ☐ 415 SB XXIII | .10 | .04 | .01 |
| ☐ 416 SB XXIII | .10 | .04 | .01 |
| ☐ xx Panini Album | 3.00 | 1.20 | .30 |

(Joe Montana on cover)

# 1990 Panini Stickers

This set contains 396 colorful stickers. The stickers are numbered in team order, i.e., Buffalo Bills (3-15), Cincinnati Bengals (16-28), Cleveland Browns (29-41), Denver Broncos (42-54), Houston Oilers (55-67), Indianapolis Colts (68-80), Kansas City Chiefs (81-93), Los Angeles Raiders (94-106), Miami Dolphins (107-119), New England Patriots (120-132), New York Jets (133-145), Pittsburgh Steelers (146-158), San Diego Chargers (159-171), Seattle Seahawks (172-184), Atlanta Falcons (209-221), Chicago Bears (222-234), Dallas Cowboys (235-247), Detroit Lions (248-260), Green Bay Packers (261-273), Los Angeles Rams (274-286), Minnesota Vikings (287-299), New Orleans Saints (300-312), New York Giants (313-325), Philadelphia Eagles (326-338), Phoenix Cardinals (339-351), San Francisco 49ers (352-364), Tampa Bay Buccaneers (365-377), and Washington Redskins (378-390). Each sticker measures approximately 1 7/8" by 2 15/16". The cover of the album contains pictures of Mike Singletary, Ronnie Lott, and Lawrence Taylor as the theme is "The Hitters." The stickers were also issued in a UK version which is distinguished by the presence of stats printed on the sticker backs.

| | MINT | EXC | G-VG |
|---|---|---|---|
| COMPLETE SET (396) | 20.00 | 8.00 | 2.00 |
| COMMON PLAYER (1-396) | .05 | .02 | .00 |
| | | | |
| ☐ 1 Super Bowl XXIV FOIL Program Cover (top) | .15 | .06 | .01 |
| ☐ 2 Super Bowl XXIV FOIL Program Cover (bottom) | .10 | .04 | .01 |
| ☐ 3 Bills Crest FOIL | .05 | .02 | .00 |
| ☐ 4 Thurman Thomas | .35 | .14 | .03 |
| ☐ 5 Nate Odomes | .05 | .02 | .00 |
| ☐ 6 Jim Kelly | .35 | .14 | .03 |
| ☐ 7 Cornelius Bennett | .15 | .06 | .01 |
| ☐ 8 Scott Norwood | .05 | .02 | .00 |
| ☐ 9 Mark Kelso | .05 | .02 | .00 |
| ☐ 10 Kent Hull | .05 | .02 | .00 |
| ☐ 11 Jim Ritcher | .05 | .02 | .00 |
| ☐ 12 Darryl Talley | .10 | .04 | .01 |
| ☐ 13 Bruce Smith | .15 | .06 | .01 |
| ☐ 14 Shane Conlan | .10 | .04 | .01 |
| ☐ 15 Andre Reed | .15 | .06 | .01 |
| ☐ 16 Jason Buck | .05 | .02 | .00 |
| ☐ 17 David Fulcher | .10 | .04 | .01 |
| ☐ 18 Jim Skow | .05 | .02 | .00 |
| ☐ 19 Anthony Munoz | .15 | .06 | .01 |
| ☐ 20 Eric Thomas | .05 | .02 | .00 |
| ☐ 21 Eric Ball | .05 | .02 | .00 |
| ☐ 22 Tim Krumrie | .05 | .02 | .00 |
| ☐ 23 James Brooks | .10 | .04 | .01 |
| ☐ 24 Bengals Crest FOIL | .05 | .02 | .00 |
| ☐ 25 Rodney Holman | .05 | .02 | .00 |
| ☐ 26 Boomer Esiason | .20 | .08 | .02 |
| ☐ 27 Eddie Brown | .10 | .04 | .01 |
| ☐ 28 Tim McGee | .10 | .04 | .01 |
| ☐ 29 Browns Crest FOIL | .05 | .02 | .00 |
| ☐ 30 Mike Johnson | .05 | .02 | .00 |

|  |  | | | |
|---|--------|---|---|---|
| ☐ 31 | David Grayson | .05 | .02 | .00 |
| ☐ 32 | Thane Gash | .05 | .02 | .00 |
| ☐ 33 | Robert Banks | .05 | .02 | .00 |
| ☐ 34 | Eric Metcalf | .20 | .08 | .02 |
| ☐ 35 | Kevin Mack | .10 | .04 | .01 |
| ☐ 36 | Reggie Langhorne | .05 | .02 | .00 |
| ☐ 37 | Webster Slaughter | .10 | .04 | .01 |
| ☐ 38 | Felix Wright | .05 | .02 | .00 |
| ☐ 39 | Bernie Kosar | .25 | .10 | .02 |
| ☐ 40 | Frank Minnifield | .05 | .02 | .00 |
| ☐ 41 | Clay Matthews | .15 | .06 | .01 |
| ☐ 42 | Vance Johnson | .10 | .04 | .01 |
| ☐ 43 | Ron Holmes | .05 | .02 | .00 |
| ☐ 44 | Melvin Bratton | .10 | .04 | .01 |
| ☐ 45 | Greg Kragen | .05 | .02 | .00 |
| ☐ 46 | Karl Mecklenburg | .10 | .04 | .01 |
| ☐ 47 | Dennis Smith | .10 | .04 | .01 |
| ☐ 48 | Bobby Humphrey | .10 | .04 | .01 |
| ☐ 49 | Simon Fletcher | .10 | .04 | .01 |
| ☐ 50 | Broncos Crest FOIL | .05 | .02 | .00 |
| ☐ 51 | Michael Brooks | .05 | .02 | .00 |
| ☐ 52 | Steve Atwater | .10 | .04 | .01 |
| ☐ 53 | John Elway | .75 | .30 | .07 |
| ☐ 54 | David Treadwell | .05 | .02 | .00 |
| ☐ 55 | Oilers Crest FOIL | .05 | .02 | .00 |
| ☐ 56 | Bubba McDowell | .05 | .02 | .00 |
| ☐ 57 | Ray Childress | .10 | .04 | .01 |
| ☐ 58 | Bruce Matthews | .05 | .02 | .00 |
| ☐ 59 | Allen Pinkett | .10 | .04 | .01 |
| ☐ 60 | Warren Moon | .40 | .16 | .04 |
| ☐ 61 | John Grimsley | .05 | .02 | .00 |
| ☐ 62 | Alonzo Highsmith | .10 | .04 | .01 |
| ☐ 63 | Mike Munchak | .10 | .04 | .01 |
| ☐ 64 | Ernest Givins | .10 | .04 | .01 |
| ☐ 65 | Johnny Meads | .05 | .02 | .00 |
| ☐ 66 | Drew Hill | .10 | .04 | .01 |
| ☐ 67 | William Fuller | .05 | .02 | .00 |
| ☐ 68 | Duane Bickett | .10 | .04 | .01 |
| ☐ 69 | Jack Trudeau | .10 | .04 | .01 |
| ☐ 70 | Jon Hand | .10 | .04 | .01 |
| ☐ 71 | Chris Hinton | .10 | .04 | .01 |
| ☐ 72 | Bill Brooks | .10 | .04 | .01 |
| ☐ 73 | Donnell Thompson | .05 | .02 | .00 |
| ☐ 74 | Jeff Herrod | .05 | .02 | .00 |
| ☐ 75 | Andre Rison | .25 | .10 | .02 |
| ☐ 76 | Colts Crest FOIL | .05 | .02 | .00 |
| ☐ 77 | Chris Chandler | .10 | .04 | .01 |
| ☐ 78 | Ray Donaldson | .05 | .02 | .00 |
| ☐ 79 | Albert Bentley | .10 | .04 | .01 |
| ☐ 80 | Keith Taylor | .05 | .02 | .00 |
| ☐ 81 | Chiefs Crest FOIL | .05 | .02 | .00 |
| ☐ 82 | Leonard Griffin | .05 | .02 | .00 |
| ☐ 83 | Dino Hackett | .05 | .02 | .00 |
| ☐ 84 | Christian Okoye | .10 | .04 | .01 |
| ☐ 85 | Chris Martin | .10 | .04 | .01 |
| ☐ 86 | John Alt | .05 | .02 | .00 |
| ☐ 87 | Kevin Ross | .05 | .02 | .00 |
| ☐ 88 | Steve DeBerg | .10 | .04 | .01 |
| ☐ 89 | Albert Lewis | .10 | .04 | .01 |
| ☐ 90 | Stephone Paige | .10 | .04 | .01 |
| ☐ 91 | Derrick Thomas | .30 | .12 | .03 |
| ☐ 92 | Neil Smith | .15 | .06 | .01 |
| ☐ 93 | Pete Mandley | .05 | .02 | .00 |
| ☐ 94 | Howie Long | .10 | .04 | .01 |
| ☐ 95 | Greg Townsend | .05 | .02 | .00 |
| ☐ 96 | Mervyn Fernandez | .10 | .04 | .01 |
| ☐ 97 | Scott Davis | .05 | .02 | .00 |
| ☐ 98 | Steve Beuerlein | .35 | .14 | .03 |
| ☐ 99 | Mike Dyal | .05 | .02 | .00 |
| ☐ 100 | Willie Gault | .10 | .04 | .01 |
| ☐ 101 | Eddie Anderson | .05 | .02 | .00 |
| ☐ 102 | Raiders Crest FOIL | .05 | .02 | .00 |
| ☐ 103 | Terry McDaniel | .05 | .02 | .00 |
| ☐ 104 | Bo Jackson | .50 | .20 | .05 |
| ☐ 105 | Steve Wisniewski | .05 | .02 | .00 |
| ☐ 106 | Steve Smith | .10 | .04 | .01 |
| ☐ 107 | Dolphins Crest FOIL | .05 | .02 | .00 |
| ☐ 108 | Mark Clayton | .15 | .06 | .01 |
| ☐ 109 | Louis Oliver | .10 | .04 | .01 |
| ☐ 110 | Jarvis Williams | .05 | .02 | .00 |
| ☐ 111 | Ferrell Edmunds | .05 | .02 | .00 |
| ☐ 112 | Jeff Cross | .05 | .02 | .00 |
| ☐ 113 | John Offerdahl | .10 | .04 | .01 |
| ☐ 114 | Brian Sochia | .05 | .02 | .00 |
| ☐ 115 | Dan Marino | 1.50 | .60 | .15 |
| ☐ 116 | Jim C. Jensen | .05 | .02 | .00 |
| ☐ 117 | Sammie Smith | .05 | .02 | .00 |
| ☐ 118 | Reggie Roby | .05 | .02 | .00 |
| ☐ 119 | Roy Foster | .05 | .02 | .00 |
| ☐ 120 | Bruce Armstrong | .05 | .02 | .00 |
| ☐ 121 | Steve Grogan | .10 | .04 | .01 |
| ☐ 122 | Hart Lee Dykes | .05 | .02 | .00 |
| ☐ 123 | Andre Tippett | .10 | .04 | .01 |
| ☐ 124 | Johnny Rembert | .05 | .02 | .00 |
| ☐ 125 | Ed Reynolds | .05 | .02 | .00 |
| ☐ 126 | Cedric Jones | .05 | .02 | .00 |
| ☐ 127 | Vincent Brown | .05 | .02 | .00 |
| ☐ 128 | Patriots Crest FOIL | .05 | .02 | .00 |
| ☐ 129 | Brent Williams | .05 | .02 | .00 |
| ☐ 130 | John Stephens | .10 | .04 | .01 |
| ☐ 131 | Eric Sievers | .05 | .02 | .00 |
| ☐ 132 | Maurice Hurst | .05 | .02 | .00 |
| ☐ 133 | Jets Crest FOIL | .05 | .02 | .00 |
| ☐ 134 | Johnny Hector | .10 | .04 | .01 |
| ☐ 135 | Eric McMillan | .05 | .02 | .00 |
| ☐ 136 | Jeff Lageman | .05 | .02 | .00 |
| ☐ 137 | Al Toon | .10 | .04 | .01 |
| ☐ 138 | James Hasty | .05 | .02 | .00 |
| ☐ 139 | Kyle Clifton | .05 | .02 | .00 |
| ☐ 140 | Ken O'Brien | .10 | .04 | .01 |
| ☐ 141 | Jim Sweeney | .05 | .02 | .00 |
| ☐ 142 | Jo Jo Townsell | .10 | .04 | .01 |
| ☐ 143 | Dennis Byrd | .25 | .10 | .02 |
| ☐ 144 | Mickey Shuler | .10 | .04 | .01 |
| ☐ 145 | Alex Gordon | .05 | .02 | .00 |
| ☐ 146 | Keith Willis | .05 | .02 | .00 |
| ☐ 147 | Louis Lipps | .10 | .04 | .01 |
| ☐ 148 | David Little | .05 | .02 | .00 |
| ☐ 149 | Greg Lloyd | .10 | .04 | .01 |
| ☐ 150 | Carnell Lake | .05 | .02 | .00 |
| ☐ 151 | Tim Worley | .10 | .04 | .01 |
| ☐ 152 | Dwayne Woodruff | .05 | .02 | .00 |
| ☐ 153 | Gerald Williams | .05 | .02 | .00 |
| ☐ 154 | Steelers Crest FOIL | .05 | .02 | .00 |
| ☐ 155 | Merril Hoge | .10 | .04 | .01 |
| ☐ 156 | Bubby Brister | .10 | .04 | .01 |
| ☐ 157 | Tunch Ilkin | .05 | .02 | .00 |
| ☐ 158 | Rod Woodson | .15 | .06 | .01 |
| ☐ 159 | Chargers Crest FOIL | .05 | .02 | .00 |
| ☐ 160 | Leslie O'Neal | .10 | .04 | .01 |
| ☐ 161 | Billy Ray Smith | .05 | .02 | .00 |
| ☐ 162 | Marion Butts | .15 | .06 | .01 |
| ☐ 163 | Lee Williams | .10 | .04 | .01 |
| ☐ 164 | Gill Byrd | .10 | .04 | .01 |
| ☐ 165 | Jim McMahon | .15 | .06 | .01 |
| ☐ 166 | Courtney Hall | .05 | .02 | .00 |
| ☐ 167 | Burt Grossman | .15 | .06 | .01 |
| ☐ 168 | Gary Plummer | .05 | .02 | .00 |
| ☐ 169 | Anthony Miller | .20 | .08 | .02 |
| ☐ 170 | Billy Joe Tolliver | .15 | .06 | .01 |
| ☐ 171 | Vencie Glenn | .05 | .02 | .00 |
| ☐ 172 | Andy Heck | .05 | .02 | .00 |
| ☐ 173 | Brian Blades | .15 | .06 | .01 |
| ☐ 174 | Bryan Millard | .05 | .02 | .00 |
| ☐ 175 | Tony Woods | .05 | .02 | .00 |
| ☐ 176 | Rufus Porter | .05 | .02 | .00 |
| ☐ 177 | Dave Wyman | .05 | .02 | .00 |
| ☐ 178 | John L. Williams | .10 | .04 | .01 |
| ☐ 179 | Jacob Green | .05 | .02 | .00 |
| ☐ 180 | Seahawks Crest FOIL | .05 | .02 | .00 |
| ☐ 181 | Eugene Robinson | .05 | .02 | .00 |
| ☐ 182 | Jeff Bryant | .05 | .02 | .00 |
| ☐ 183 | Dave Krieg | .10 | .04 | .01 |
| ☐ 184 | Joe Nash | .05 | .02 | .00 |
| ☐ 185 | Christian Okoye LL | .05 | .02 | .00 |
| ☐ 186 | Felix Wright LL | .05 | .02 | .00 |
| ☐ 187 | Rod Woodson LL | .10 | .04 | .01 |
| ☐ 188 | Barry Sanders AP and Christian Okoye AP | .40 | .16 | .04 |
| ☐ 189 | Jerry Rice AP and Sterling Sharpe AP | .50 | .20 | .05 |
| ☐ 190 | Bruce Matthews AP | .05 | .02 | .00 |
| ☐ 191 | Jay Hilgenberg AP | .05 | .02 | .00 |
| ☐ 192 | Tom Newberry AP | .05 | .02 | .00 |
| ☐ 193 | Anthony Munoz AP | .10 | .04 | .01 |
| ☐ 194 | Jim Lachey AP | .05 | .02 | .00 |
| ☐ 195 | Keith Jackson AP | .15 | .06 | .01 |
| ☐ 196 | Joe Montana AP | 1.00 | .40 | .10 |
| ☐ 197 | David Fulcher AP and Ronnie Lott AP | .10 | .04 | .01 |
| ☐ 198 | Albert Lewis AP and Eric Allen AP | .05 | .02 | .00 |
| ☐ 199 | Reggie White AP | .20 | .08 | .02 |
| ☐ 200 | Keith Millard AP | .05 | .02 | .00 |
| ☐ 201 | Chris Doleman AP | .05 | .02 | .00 |
| ☐ 202 | Mike Singletary AP | .15 | .06 | .01 |
| ☐ 203 | Tim Harris AP | .05 | .02 | .00 |
| ☐ 204 | Lawrence Taylor AP | .20 | .08 | .02 |
| ☐ 205 | Rich Camarillo AP | .05 | .02 | .00 |
| ☐ 206 | Sterling Sharpe LL | .25 | .10 | .02 |
| ☐ 207 | Chris Doleman LL | .05 | .02 | .00 |
| ☐ 208 | Barry Sanders LL | .40 | .16 | .04 |
| ☐ 209 | Falcons Crest FOIL | .05 | .02 | .00 |
| ☐ 210 | Michael Haynes | .35 | .14 | .03 |
| ☐ 211 | Scott Case | .05 | .02 | .00 |
| ☐ 212 | Marcus Cotton | .05 | .02 | .00 |
| ☐ 213 | Chris Miller | .15 | .06 | .01 |
| ☐ 214 | Keith Jones | .05 | .02 | .00 |
| ☐ 215 | Tim Green | .05 | .02 | .00 |
| ☐ 216 | Deion Sanders | .35 | .14 | .03 |
| ☐ 217 | Shawn Collins | .10 | .04 | .01 |
| ☐ 218 | John Settle | .05 | .02 | .00 |
| ☐ 219 | Bill Fralic | .05 | .02 | .00 |
| ☐ 220 | Aundray Bruce | .05 | .02 | .00 |

| | | | |
|---|---|---|---|
| ☐ 221 Jessie Tuggle | .05 | .02 | .00 |
| ☐ 222 James Thornton | .05 | .02 | .00 |
| ☐ 223 Dennis Gentry | .05 | .02 | .00 |
| ☐ 224 Richard Dent | .15 | .06 | .01 |
| ☐ 225 Jay Hilgenberg | .05 | .02 | .00 |
| ☐ 226 Steve McMichael | .05 | .02 | .00 |
| ☐ 227 Brad Muster | .10 | .04 | .01 |
| ☐ 228 Donnell Woodford | .05 | .02 | .00 |
| ☐ 229 Mike Singletary | .15 | .06 | .01 |
| ☐ 230 Bears Crest FOIL | .05 | .02 | .00 |
| ☐ 231 Mark Bortz | .05 | .02 | .00 |
| ☐ 232 Kevin Butler | .05 | .02 | .00 |
| ☐ 233 Neal Anderson | .10 | .04 | .01 |
| ☐ 234 Trace Armstrong | .05 | .02 | .00 |
| ☐ 235 Cowboys Crest FOIL | .05 | .02 | .00 |
| ☐ 236 Mark Tuinei | .10 | .04 | .01 |
| ☐ 237 Tony Tolbert | .05 | .02 | .00 |
| ☐ 238 Eugene Lockhart | .10 | .04 | .01 |
| ☐ 239 Daryl Johnston | .25 | .10 | .02 |
| ☐ 240 Troy Aikman | 2.00 | .80 | .20 |
| ☐ 241 Jim Jeffcoat | .10 | .04 | .01 |
| ☐ 242 James Dixon | .05 | .02 | .00 |
| ☐ 243 Jesse Solomon | .05 | .02 | .00 |
| ☐ 244 Ken Norton Jr. | .25 | .10 | .02 |
| ☐ 245 Kelvin Martin | .05 | .02 | .00 |
| ☐ 246 Danny Noonan | .05 | .02 | .00 |
| ☐ 247 Michael Irvin | .50 | .20 | .05 |
| ☐ 248 Eric Williams | .05 | .02 | .00 |
| ☐ 249 Richard Johnson | .05 | .02 | .00 |
| ☐ 250 Michael Cofer | .05 | .02 | .00 |
| ☐ 251 Chris Spielman | .10 | .04 | .01 |
| ☐ 252 Rodney Peete | .20 | .08 | .02 |
| ☐ 253 Bennie Blades | .10 | .04 | .01 |
| ☐ 254 Jerry Ball | .05 | .02 | .00 |
| ☐ 255 Eddie Murray | .08 | .03 | .01 |
| ☐ 256 Lions Crest FOIL | .05 | .02 | .00 |
| ☐ 257 Barry Sanders | 1.25 | .50 | .12 |
| ☐ 258 Jerry Holmes | .05 | .02 | .00 |
| ☐ 259 Dennis Gibson | .05 | .02 | .00 |
| ☐ 260 Lomas Brown | .05 | .02 | .00 |
| ☐ 261 Packers Crest FOIL | .05 | .02 | .00 |
| ☐ 262 Dave Brown | .05 | .02 | .00 |
| ☐ 263 Mark Murphy | .05 | .02 | .00 |
| ☐ 264 Perry Kemp | .05 | .02 | .00 |
| ☐ 265 Don Majkowski | .10 | .04 | .01 |
| ☐ 266 Chris Jacke | .05 | .02 | .00 |
| ☐ 267 Keith Woodside | .10 | .04 | .01 |
| ☐ 268 Tony Mandarich | .05 | .02 | .00 |
| ☐ 269 Robert Brown | .05 | .02 | .00 |
| ☐ 270 Sterling Sharpe | .50 | .20 | .05 |
| ☐ 271 Tim Harris | .10 | .04 | .01 |
| ☐ 272 Brent Fullwood | .05 | .02 | .00 |
| ☐ 273 Brian Noble | .05 | .02 | .00 |
| ☐ 274 Alvin Wright | .05 | .02 | .00 |
| ☐ 275 Flipper Anderson | .10 | .04 | .01 |
| ☐ 276 Jackie Slater | .10 | .04 | .01 |
| ☐ 277 Kevin Greene | .10 | .04 | .01 |
| ☐ 278 Pete Holohan | .05 | .02 | .00 |
| ☐ 279 Tom Newberry | .05 | .02 | .00 |
| ☐ 280 Jerry Gray | .05 | .02 | .00 |
| ☐ 281 Henry Ellard | .10 | .04 | .01 |
| ☐ 282 Rams Crest FOIL | .05 | .02 | .00 |
| ☐ 283 LeRoy Irvin | .05 | .02 | .00 |
| ☐ 284 Jim Everett | .15 | .06 | .01 |
| ☐ 285 Greg Bell | .10 | .04 | .01 |
| ☐ 286 Doug Smith | .05 | .02 | .00 |
| ☐ 287 Vikings Crest FOIL | .05 | .02 | .00 |
| ☐ 288 Joey Browner | .10 | .04 | .01 |
| ☐ 289 Wade Wilson | .15 | .06 | .01 |
| ☐ 290 Chris Doleman | .10 | .04 | .01 |
| ☐ 291 Al Noga | .05 | .02 | .00 |
| ☐ 292 Herschel Walker | .20 | .08 | .02 |
| ☐ 293 Henry Thomas | .10 | .04 | .01 |
| ☐ 294 Steve Jordan | .10 | .04 | .01 |
| ☐ 295 Anthony Carter | .10 | .04 | .01 |
| ☐ 296 Keith Millard | .10 | .04 | .01 |
| ☐ 297 Carl Lee | .05 | .02 | .00 |
| ☐ 298 Randall McDaniel | .05 | .02 | .00 |
| ☐ 299 Gary Zimmerman | .05 | .02 | .00 |
| ☐ 300 Morten Andersen | .05 | .02 | .00 |
| ☐ 301 Rickey Jackson | .10 | .04 | .01 |
| ☐ 302 Sam Mills | .05 | .02 | .00 |
| ☐ 303 Hoby Brenner | .05 | .02 | .00 |
| ☐ 304 Dalton Hilliard | .05 | .02 | .00 |
| ☐ 305 Robert Massey | .05 | .02 | .00 |
| ☐ 306 John Fourcade | .10 | .04 | .01 |
| ☐ 307 Lonzell Hill | .05 | .02 | .00 |
| ☐ 308 Saints Crest FOIL | .05 | .02 | .00 |
| ☐ 309 Jim Dombrowski | .05 | .02 | .00 |
| ☐ 310 Pat Swilling | .15 | .06 | .01 |
| ☐ 311 Vaughan Johnson | .05 | .02 | .00 |
| ☐ 312 Eric Martin | .10 | .04 | .01 |
| ☐ 313 Giants Crest FOIL | .05 | .02 | .00 |
| ☐ 314 Ottis Anderson | .10 | .04 | .01 |
| ☐ 315 Myron Guyton | .05 | .02 | .00 |
| ☐ 316 Terry Kinard | .05 | .02 | .00 |
| ☐ 317 Mark Bavaro | .10 | .04 | .01 |
| ☐ 318 Phil Simms | .25 | .10 | .02 |
| ☐ 319 Lawrence Taylor | .30 | .12 | .03 |
| ☐ 320 Odessa Turner | .05 | .02 | .00 |
| ☐ 321 Erik Howard | .05 | .02 | .00 |
| ☐ 322 Mark Collins | .05 | .02 | .00 |
| ☐ 323 Dave Meggett | .15 | .06 | .01 |
| ☐ 324 Leonard Marshall | .05 | .02 | .00 |
| ☐ 325 Carl Banks | .10 | .04 | .01 |
| ☐ 326 Anthony Toney | .05 | .02 | .00 |
| ☐ 327 Seth Joyner | .15 | .06 | .01 |
| ☐ 328 Cris Carter | .20 | .08 | .02 |
| ☐ 329 Eric Allen | .05 | .02 | .00 |
| ☐ 330 Keith Jackson | .20 | .08 | .02 |
| ☐ 331 Clyde Simmons | .10 | .04 | .01 |
| ☐ 332 Byron Evans | .05 | .02 | .00 |
| ☐ 333 Keith Byars | .10 | .04 | .01 |
| ☐ 334 Eagles Crest FOIL | .05 | .02 | .00 |
| ☐ 335 Reggie White | .25 | .10 | .02 |
| ☐ 336 Izel Jenkins | .05 | .02 | .00 |
| ☐ 337 Jerome Brown | .15 | .06 | .01 |
| ☐ 338 David Alexander | .05 | .02 | .00 |
| ☐ 339 Cardinals Crest FOIL | .05 | .02 | .00 |
| ☐ 340 Rich Camarillo | .05 | .02 | .00 |
| ☐ 341 Ken Harvey | .05 | .02 | .00 |
| ☐ 342 Luis Sharpe | .05 | .02 | .00 |
| ☐ 343 Timm Rosenbach | .10 | .04 | .01 |
| ☐ 344 Tim McDonald | .15 | .06 | .01 |
| ☐ 345 Vai Sikahema | .05 | .02 | .00 |
| ☐ 346 Freddie Joe Nunn | .05 | .02 | .00 |
| ☐ 347 Ernie Jones | .05 | .02 | .00 |
| ☐ 348 J.T. Smith | .10 | .04 | .01 |
| ☐ 349 Eric Hill | .05 | .02 | .00 |
| ☐ 350 Roy Green | .10 | .04 | .01 |
| ☐ 351 Anthony Bell | .05 | .02 | .00 |
| ☐ 352 Kevin Fagan | .05 | .02 | .00 |
| ☐ 353 Roger Craig | .15 | .06 | .01 |
| ☐ 354 Ronnie Lott | .20 | .08 | .02 |
| ☐ 355 Mike Cofer | .05 | .02 | .00 |
| ☐ 356 John Taylor | .20 | .08 | .02 |
| ☐ 357 Joe Montana | 2.00 | .80 | .20 |
| ☐ 358 Charles Haley | .10 | .04 | .01 |
| ☐ 359 Guy McIntyre | .05 | .02 | .00 |
| ☐ 360 49ers Crest FOIL | .05 | .02 | .00 |
| ☐ 361 Pierce Holt | .15 | .06 | .01 |
| ☐ 362 Tom Rathman | .15 | .06 | .01 |
| ☐ 363 Jerry Rice | 1.00 | .40 | .10 |
| ☐ 364 Michael Carter | .10 | .04 | .01 |
| ☐ 365 Buccaneers Crest FOIL | .05 | .02 | .00 |
| ☐ 366 Lars Tate | .05 | .02 | .00 |
| ☐ 367 Paul Gruber | .10 | .04 | .01 |
| ☐ 368 Winston Moss | .05 | .02 | .00 |
| ☐ 369 Reuben Davis | .05 | .02 | .00 |
| ☐ 370 Mark Robinson | .05 | .02 | .00 |
| ☐ 371 Bruce Hill | .05 | .02 | .00 |
| ☐ 372 Kevin Murphy | .05 | .02 | .00 |
| ☐ 373 Ricky Reynolds | .05 | .02 | .00 |
| ☐ 374 Harry Hamilton | .05 | .02 | .00 |
| ☐ 375 Vinny Testaverde | .15 | .06 | .01 |
| ☐ 376 Mark Carrier | .15 | .06 | .01 |
| ☐ 377 Ervin Randle | .05 | .02 | .00 |
| ☐ 378 Ricky Sanders | .10 | .04 | .01 |
| ☐ 379 Charles Mann | .10 | .04 | .01 |
| ☐ 380 Jim Lachey | .10 | .04 | .01 |
| ☐ 381 Wilber Marshall | .10 | .04 | .01 |
| ☐ 382 A.J. Johnson | .05 | .02 | .00 |
| ☐ 383 Darrell Green | .10 | .04 | .01 |
| ☐ 384 Mark Rypien | .15 | .06 | .01 |
| ☐ 385 Gerald Riggs | .10 | .04 | .01 |
| ☐ 386 Redskins Crest FOIL | .05 | .02 | .00 |
| ☐ 387 Alvin Walton | .05 | .02 | .00 |
| ☐ 388 Art Monk | .15 | .06 | .01 |
| ☐ 389 Gary Clark | .15 | .06 | .01 |
| ☐ 390 Earnest Byner | .10 | .04 | .01 |
| ☐ 391 SB XXIV Action FOIL (Jerry Rice) | .50 | .20 | .05 |
| ☐ 392 SB XXIV Action FOIL (49er Offensive Line) | .15 | .06 | .01 |
| ☐ 393 SB XXIV Action FOIL (Tom Rathman) | .25 | .10 | .02 |
| ☐ 394 SB XXIV Action FOIL (Chet Brooks) | .10 | .04 | .01 |
| ☐ 395 SB XXIV Action FOIL (John Elway) | .75 | .30 | .07 |
| ☐ 396 Joe Montana FOIL SB XXIV MVP | 2.50 | 1.00 | .25 |
| ☐ xx Panini Album | 2.00 | .80 | .20 |

## 1974 Parker Brothers Pro Draft

This 50-card set was printed by Topps for distribution by Parker Brothers in early 1974 as part of a football board game. The only players in this set (game) are offensive players (with an emphasis on the skill positions) and all come from the first 132 cards in the 1974 Topps football card set. The cards are very similar and often confused with the 1974 Topps regular issue football cards. There are several

| | NRMT | VG-E | GOOD |
|---|---|---|---|
| ☐ 119 Roy Jefferson * | 3.00 | 1.20 | .30 |
| ☐ 124 Forrest Blue * | 6.00 | 2.40 | .60 |
| (Not All-Pro on card; Topps card is All-Pro) | | | |
| ☐ 126 Tom Mack * | 7.50 | 3.00 | .75 |
| (Not All-Pro on card; Topps card is All-Pro) | | | |
| ☐ 127 Bob Tucker * | 6.00 | 2.40 | .60 |
| (Not All-Pro on card; Topps card is All-Pro) | | | |

## 1989 Parker Brothers Talking Football

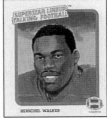

notable differences between these cards and the 1974 Topps regular issue; those cards with 1972 statistics on the back (unlike the 1974 Topps regular issue) are indicated in the checklist below with an asterisk. Those cards with pose variations (different from the 1974 Topps) are noted as well parenthetically; these six pose variations are numbers 23, 49, 116, 124, 126, and 127. Parker Brothers game cards can also be distinguished by the presence of two asterisks rather than one on the copyright line. However, there are certain cards in the regular 1974 Topps set that do have two asterisks but are not Parker Brothers Pro Draft cards. Cards in the 1974 Topps regular set with two asterisks include 26, 129, 130, 156, 162, 219, 265-364, 367-422, and 424-528; the rest have only one asterisk. The Parker Brothers cards are skip-numbered with the number on the back corresponding to that player's number in the Topps regular issue. The cards measure 2 1/2" by 3 1/2".

| | NRMT | VG-E | GOOD |
|---|---|---|---|
| COMPLETE SET (50) | 75.00 | 30.00 | 7.50 |
| COMMON PLAYER | 1.00 | .40 | .10 |
| COMMON PLAYER (WITH *) | 2.00 | .80 | .20 |
| | | | |
| ☐ 4 Ken Bowman | 1.00 | .40 | .10 |
| ☐ 6 Jerry Smith * | 2.50 | 1.00 | .25 |
| ☐ 7 Ed Podolak * | 2.50 | 1.00 | .25 |
| ☐ 9 Pat Matson * | 1.00 | .40 | .10 |
| ☐ 11 Frank Pitts * | 2.00 | .80 | .20 |
| ☐ 15 Winston Hill * | 1.00 | .40 | .10 |
| ☐ 18 Rich Coady * | 2.00 | .80 | .20 |
| ☐ 19 Ken Willard * | 3.50 | 1.40 | .35 |
| ☐ 21 Ben Hawkins * | 2.00 | .80 | .20 |
| ☐ 23 Norm Snead * | 8.00 | 3.25 | .80 |
| (Vertical pose; Topps has horizontal pose) | | | |
| ☐ 24 Jim Yarborough * | 2.00 | .80 | .20 |
| ☐ 28 Bob Hayes * | 5.00 | 2.00 | .50 |
| ☐ 32 Dan Dierdorf * | 6.00 | 2.40 | .60 |
| ☐ 35 Essex Johnson * | 2.00 | .80 | .20 |
| ☐ 39 Mike Siani * | 1.00 | .40 | .10 |
| ☐ 42 Del Williams | 1.00 | .40 | .10 |
| ☐ 43 Don McCauley * | 2.00 | .80 | .20 |
| ☐ 44 Randy Jackson * | 2.00 | .80 | .20 |
| ☐ 46 Gene Washington * | 3.50 | 1.40 | .35 |
| San Francisco 49ers | | | |
| ☐ 49 Bob Windsor * | 5.00 | 2.00 | .50 |
| (Vertical pose; Topps has horizontal pose) | | | |
| ☐ 50 John Hadl * | 4.00 | 1.60 | .40 |
| ☐ 52 Steve Owens * | 4.00 | 1.60 | .40 |
| ☐ 54 Rayfield Wright * | 2.00 | .80 | .20 |
| ☐ 57 Milt Sunde * | 2.00 | .80 | .20 |
| ☐ 58 Bill Kilmer * | 5.00 | 2.00 | .50 |
| ☐ 61 Rufus Mayes * | 2.00 | .80 | .20 |
| ☐ 63 Gene Washington * | 2.50 | 1.00 | .25 |
| Denver Broncos | | | |
| ☐ 65 Gene Upshaw * | 4.00 | 1.60 | .40 |
| ☐ 75 Fred Willis * | 2.00 | .80 | .20 |
| ☐ 77 Tom Neville * | 1.00 | .40 | .10 |
| ☐ 78 Ted Kwalick * | 3.00 | 1.20 | .30 |
| ☐ 80 John Niland * | 2.00 | .80 | .20 |
| ☐ 81 Ted Fritsch Jr. * | 1.00 | .40 | .10 |
| ☐ 83 Jack Snow * | 3.00 | 1.20 | .30 |
| ☐ 87 Mike Phipps * | 3.00 | 1.20 | .30 |
| ☐ 90 MacArthur Lane * | 3.00 | 1.20 | .30 |
| ☐ 95 Calvin Hill * | 3.50 | 1.40 | .35 |
| ☐ 98 Len Rohde | 1.00 | .40 | .10 |
| ☐ 101 Gary Garrison * | 2.50 | 1.00 | .25 |
| ☐ 103 Len St. Jean | 1.00 | .40 | .10 |
| ☐ 107 Jim Mitchell * | 2.00 | .80 | .20 |
| ☐ 109 Harry Schuh * | 1.00 | .40 | .10 |
| ☐ 110 Greg Pruitt * | 4.00 | 1.60 | .40 |
| ☐ 111 Ed Flanagan * | 1.00 | .40 | .10 |
| ☐ 113 Chuck Foreman * | 5.00 | 2.00 | .50 |
| ☐ 116 Charlie Johnson * | 6.00 | 2.40 | .60 |
| (Vertical pose; Topps has horizontal pose) | | | |

Measuring approximately 2 5/8" by 3", this 34-card set was licensed only by the NFL Players Association. When players are shown together on a card, it relates to their respective position(s). The cards are unnumbered so they are listed below in alphabetical order according to the AFC (1-17) and the NFC (18-34). For cards with more than one subject, those players are in turn alphabetically listed so that they can be alphabetized consistently along with the single player cards.

| | MINT | EXC | G-VG |
|---|---|---|---|
| COMPLETE SET (34) | 75.00 | 30.00 | 7.50 |
| COMMON CARD (1-34) | 1.50 | .60 | .15 |
| | | | |
| ☐ 1 AFC Team Roster | 1.50 | .60 | .15 |
| ☐ 2 Marcus Allen | 4.00 | 1.60 | .40 |
| Los Angeles Raiders | | | |
| ☐ 3 Cornelius Bennett | 3.00 | 1.20 | .30 |
| Buffalo Bills | | | |
| John Offerdahl | | | |
| Miami Dolphins | | | |
| ☐ 4 Keith Bishop | 1.50 | .60 | .15 |
| Denver Broncos | | | |
| Mike Munchak | | | |
| Houston Oilers | | | |
| ☐ 5 Keith Bostic | 1.50 | .60 | .15 |
| Houston Oilers | | | |
| Deron Cherry | | | |
| Kansas City Chiefs | | | |
| Hanford Dixon | | | |
| Cleveland Browns | | | |
| ☐ 6 Carlos Carson | 2.00 | .80 | .20 |
| Kansas City Chiefs | | | |
| Stanley Morgan | | | |
| New England Patriots | | | |
| ☐ 7 Todd Christensen | 2.00 | .80 | .20 |
| Los Angeles Raiders | | | |
| Mickey Shuler | | | |
| New York Jets | | | |
| ☐ 8 Eric Dickerson | 5.00 | 2.00 | .50 |
| Indianapolis Colts | | | |
| ☐ 9 Ray Donaldson | 2.00 | .80 | .20 |
| Indianapolis Colts | | | |
| Irving Fryar | | | |
| New England Patriots | | | |
| ☐ 10 Jacob Green | 2.00 | .80 | .20 |
| Seattle Seahawks | | | |
| Bruce Smith | | | |
| Buffalo Bills | | | |
| ☐ 11 Mark Haynes | 1.50 | .60 | .15 |
| Denver Broncos | | | |
| Frank Minnifield | | | |
| Cleveland Browns | | | |
| Dennis Smith | | | |
| Denver Broncos | | | |
| ☐ 12 Chris Hinton | 2.50 | 1.00 | .25 |
| Indianapolis Colts | | | |
| Anthony Munoz | | | |
| Cincinnati Bengals | | | |
| ☐ 13 Steve Largent | 5.00 | 2.00 | .50 |
| Seattle Seahawks | | | |
| Al Toon | | | |
| New York Jets | | | |

| | | MINT | EXC | G-VG |
|---|---|---|---|---|
| ☐ 14 | Howie Long ..................... | 2.00 | .80 | .20 |
| | Los Angeles Raiders | | | |
| | Bill Maas | | | |
| | Kansas City Chiefs | | | |
| ☐ 15 | Nick Lowery ..................... | 2.00 | .80 | .20 |
| | Kansas City Chiefs | | | |
| | Reggie Roby | | | |
| | Miami Dolphins | | | |
| ☐ 16 | Dan Marino ..................... | 15.00 | 6.00 | 1.50 |
| | Miami Dolphins | | | |
| ☐ 17 | Karl Mecklenburg ............ | 2.50 | 1.00 | .25 |
| | Denver Broncos | | | |
| | Andre Tippett | | | |
| | New England Patriots | | | |
| ☐ 18 | NFC Team Roster ........... | 1.50 | .60 | .15 |
| ☐ 19 | Morten Andersen ............ | 1.50 | .60 | .15 |
| | New Orleans Saints | | | |
| | Jim Arnold | | | |
| | Detroit Lions | | | |
| ☐ 20 | Carl Banks ..................... | 3.00 | 1.20 | .30 |
| | New York Giants | | | |
| | Mike Singletary | | | |
| | Chicago Bears | | | |
| ☐ 21 | Mark Bavaro ..................... | 2.00 | .80 | .20 |
| | New York Giants | | | |
| | Doug Cosbie | | | |
| | Dallas Cowboys | | | |
| ☐ 22 | Joey Browner ..................... | 2.00 | .80 | .20 |
| | Minnesota Vikings | | | |
| | Darrell Green | | | |
| | Washington Redskins | | | |
| | Leonard Smith | | | |
| | Phoenix Cardinals | | | |
| ☐ 23 | Anthony Carter ............... | 10.00 | 4.00 | 1.00 |
| | Minnesota Vikings | | | |
| | Jerry Rice | | | |
| | San Francisco 49ers | | | |
| ☐ 24 | Gary Clark ..................... | 3.00 | 1.20 | .30 |
| | Washington Redskins | | | |
| | Mike Quick | | | |
| | Philadelphia Eagles | | | |
| ☐ 25 | Richard Dent ..................... | 2.50 | 1.00 | .25 |
| | Chicago Bears | | | |
| | Chris Doleman | | | |
| | Minnesota Vikings | | | |
| ☐ 26 | Brad Edelman ..................... | 1.50 | .60 | .15 |
| | New Orleans Saints | | | |
| | Bill Fralic | | | |
| | Atlanta Falcons | | | |
| ☐ 27 | Carl Ekern ..................... | 1.50 | .60 | .15 |
| | Los Angeles Rams | | | |
| | Rickey Jackson | | | |
| | New Orleans Saints | | | |
| ☐ 28 | Jerry Gray ..................... | 2.50 | 1.00 | .25 |
| | Los Angeles Rams | | | |
| | LeRoy Irvin | | | |
| | Los Angeles Rams | | | |
| | Ronnie Lott | | | |
| | San Francisco 49ers | | | |
| ☐ 29 | Mel Gray ..................... | 1.50 | .60 | .15 |
| | New Orleans Saints | | | |
| | Jay Hilgenberg | | | |
| | Chicago Bears | | | |
| ☐ 30 | Dexter Manley ..................... | 3.50 | 1.40 | .35 |
| | Washington Redskins | | | |
| | Reggie White | | | |
| | Philadelphia Eagles | | | |
| ☐ 31 | Rueben Mayes ..................... | 1.50 | .60 | .15 |
| | New Orleans Saints | | | |
| ☐ 32 | Joe Montana ..................... | 20.00 | 8.00 | 2.00 |
| | San Francisco 49ers | | | |
| ☐ 33 | Jackie Slater ..................... | 1.50 | .60 | .15 |
| | Los Angeles Rams | | | |
| | Gary Zimmerman | | | |
| | Minnesota Vikings | | | |
| ☐ 34 | Herschel Walker ............ | 2.50 | 1.00 | .25 |
| | Dallas Cowboys | | | |

# 1988 Walter Payton Commemorative

Each of the 132 cards in this set pictures and features Walter Payton in some aspect of his great career. Cards listed below are generally listed by the title on the card back. Cards are standard size, 2 1/2" by 3 1/2". Each set was packaged inside its own numbered dark blue plastic box. Card fronts carry the NFL logo in the upper left corner and the Bears logo in the lower right corner. The set was issued in conjunction with a soft-cover book (not his autobiography) "Sweetness."

| | MINT | EXC | G-VG |
|---|---|---|---|
| COMPLETE SET (132) .................... | 45.00 | 18.00 | 4.50 |
| COMMON CARD (1-132) ................ | .50 | .20 | .05 |

| | | | |
|---|---|---|---|
| ☐ 1 Leading Scorer in ..................... | 1.00 | .40 | .10 |
| NCAA History | | | |
| ☐ 2 1975 Game-by-Game ............... | .50 | .20 | .05 |

| | | | |
|---|---|---|---|
| ☐ 3 Vs. New York Jets ................... | .50 | .20 | .05 |
| ☐ 4 Vs. Miami Dolphins ................. | .50 | .20 | .05 |
| ☐ 5 Vs. Baltimore/ ..................... | .50 | .20 | .05 |
| Indianapolis Colts | | | |
| ☐ 6 Vs. Buffalo Bills ..................... | .50 | .20 | .05 |
| ☐ 7 Vs. New England ..................... | .50 | .20 | .05 |
| Patriots | | | |
| ☐ 8 Vs. Houston Oilers ................. | .50 | .20 | .05 |
| ☐ 9 Vs. Pittsburgh ..................... | .50 | .20 | .05 |
| Steelers | | | |
| ☐ 10 Vs. Cincinnati ..................... | .50 | .20 | .05 |
| Bengals | | | |
| ☐ 11 Vs. Cleveland Browns ............ | .50 | .20 | .05 |
| ☐ 12 Vs. Kansas City ..................... | .50 | .20 | .05 |
| Chiefs | | | |
| ☐ 13 Vs. Oakland/ ..................... | .50 | .20 | .05 |
| Los Angeles Raiders | | | |
| ☐ 14 Vs. San Diego ..................... | .50 | .20 | .05 |
| Chargers | | | |
| ☐ 15 Vs. Denver Broncos ............... | .50 | .20 | .05 |
| ☐ 16 Vs. Seattle Seahawks ............ | .50 | .20 | .05 |
| ☐ 17 Vs. Washington ..................... | .50 | .20 | .05 |
| Redskins | | | |
| ☐ 18 Vs. New York Giants ............... | .50 | .20 | .05 |
| ☐ 19 Vs. Dallas Cowboys ............... | .50 | .20 | .05 |
| ☐ 20 Vs. St. Louis ..................... | .50 | .20 | .05 |
| Cardinals | | | |
| ☐ 21 Vs. Philadelphia ..................... | .50 | .20 | .05 |
| Eagles | | | |
| ☐ 22 Vs. New Orleans ..................... | .50 | .20 | .05 |
| Saints | | | |
| ☐ 23 Vs. Atlanta Falcons ............... | .50 | .20 | .05 |
| ☐ 24 Vs. Los Angeles Rams ............ | .50 | .20 | .05 |
| ☐ 25 Vs. San Francisco ................. | .50 | .20 | .05 |
| 49ers | | | |
| ☐ 26 Vs. Detroit Lions ................... | .50 | .20 | .05 |
| ☐ 27 Vs. Minnesota Vikings ............ | .50 | .20 | .05 |
| ☐ 28 Vs. Tampa Bay ..................... | .50 | .20 | .05 |
| Buccaneers | | | |
| ☐ 29 Vs. Green Bay Packers ............ | .50 | .20 | .05 |
| ☐ 30 1976 Game-By-Game ............... | .50 | .20 | .05 |
| ☐ 31 Appears in Nine Pro ............... | .50 | .20 | .05 |
| Bowls | | | |
| ☐ 32 Post-Season Stats ................. | .50 | .20 | .05 |
| ☐ 33 Owns 23 Bear Records ............ | .50 | .20 | .05 |
| ☐ 34 Season-by-Season ................. | .50 | .20 | .05 |
| Statistics | | | |
| ☐ 35 1977 Game-By-Game ............... | .50 | .20 | .05 |
| ☐ 36 NFL Record for Most ............... | .50 | .20 | .05 |
| Yards Gained, | | | |
| Rushing | | | |
| ☐ 37 NFL Record for Most ............... | .50 | .20 | .05 |
| Combined Yards, | | | |
| Career | | | |
| ☐ 38 NFL Record for Most ............... | .50 | .20 | .05 |
| Rushing Touchdowns | | | |
| ☐ 39 NFL Record for Most ............... | .50 | .20 | .05 |
| Games, 100 Yards | | | |
| Rushing, Career | | | |
| ☐ 40 NFL Record for Most ............... | .50 | .20 | .05 |
| Consecutive Combined | | | |
| 2000-Yard Seasons (3) | | | |
| ☐ 41 NFL Record for Most ............... | .50 | .20 | .05 |
| Yards Gained, | | | |
| Rushing, Game (275) | | | |
| ☐ 42 NFL Record for Most ............... | .50 | .20 | .05 |
| Rushing Attempts, | | | |
| Career (3838) | | | |
| ☐ 43 NFL Record for Most ............... | .50 | .20 | .05 |
| Combined Attempts, | | | |
| Career (4347) | | | |
| ☐ 44 NFL Record for Most ............... | .50 | .20 | .05 |
| Seasons, 1000 Yards | | | |
| Rushing (10) | | | |
| ☐ 45 1978 Game-By-Game ............... | .50 | .20 | .05 |
| ☐ 46 The Top 10 Average ............... | .50 | .20 | .05 |
| Per Carry Days 1 | | | |

| | | | |
|---|---|---|---|
| vs. Saints 12/14/80 | | | |
| ☐ 47 The Top 10 Average | .50 | .20 | .05 |
| Per Carry Days 2 | | | |
| vs. Broncos 9/9/84 | | | |
| ☐ 48 The Top 10 Average | .50 | .20 | .05 |
| Per Carry Days 3 | | | |
| at Green Bay | | | |
| 10/30/77 | | | |
| ☐ 49 The Top 10 Average | .50 | .20 | .05 |
| Per Carry Days 4 | | | |
| vs. Vikings 9/9/79 | | | |
| ☐ 50 The Top 10 Average | .50 | .20 | .05 |
| Per Carry Days 5 | | | |
| vs. Minnesota | | | |
| 10/10/76 | | | |
| ☐ 51 The Top 10 Average | .50 | .20 | .05 |
| Per Carry Days 6 | | | |
| vs. Saints 10/2/76 | | | |
| ☐ 52 The Top 10 Average | .50 | .20 | .05 |
| Per Carry Days 7 | | | |
| at Denver 10/16/78 | | | |
| ☐ 53 The Top 10 Average | .50 | .20 | .05 |
| Per Carry Days 8 | | | |
| at San Francisco | | | |
| 10/28/79 | | | |
| ☐ 54 The Top 10 Average | .50 | .20 | .05 |
| Per Carry Days 9 | | | |
| vs. Lions 9/18/77 | | | |
| ☐ 55 The Top 10 Average | .50 | .20 | .05 |
| Per Carry Days 10 | | | |
| at Tampa Bay | | | |
| 11/9/86 | | | |
| ☐ 56 1979 Game-By-Game | .50 | .20 | .05 |
| ☐ 57 In Training | .50 | .20 | .05 |
| Didn't Play Until | | | |
| 11th Grade | | | |
| ☐ 58 In Training | .50 | .20 | .05 |
| Running the Hill | | | |
| ☐ 59 In Training | .50 | .20 | .05 |
| Jumping Rope | | | |
| ☐ 60 In Training | .50 | .20 | .05 |
| ☐ 61 Personal Life | .50 | .20 | .05 |
| Interests include ... | | | |
| ☐ 62 Personal Life | .50 | .20 | .05 |
| Corporate Spokesman | | | |
| ☐ 63 Personal Life | .50 | .20 | .05 |
| Family Man | | | |
| ☐ 64 Personal Life | .50 | .20 | .05 |
| Relatives in NFL | | | |
| ☐ 65 Personal Life | .50 | .20 | .05 |
| "Sweetness" autobi- | | | |
| ography written, 1978 | | | |
| ☐ 66 Personal Life | .50 | .20 | .05 |
| National Committee | | | |
| for Prevention of | | | |
| Child Abuse | | | |
| ☐ 67 Personal Life | .50 | .20 | .05 |
| Chicago 1986 Sports | | | |
| Father of the Year | | | |
| ☐ 68 Personal Life | .50 | .20 | .05 |
| Active in | | | |
| Many Charities | | | |
| ☐ 69 Personal Life | .50 | .20 | .05 |
| Parade Grand Marshall | | | |
| ☐ 70 1980 Game-By-Game | .50 | .20 | .05 |
| ☐ 71 Nobody Did It Better | .50 | .20 | .05 |
| 1976 TSN NFC | | | |
| Player of the Year | | | |
| ☐ 72 Nobody Did It Better | .50 | | .05 |
| 1976 Chicago | | | |
| Red Cloud | | | |
| Athlete of the Year | | | |
| ☐ 73 Nobody Did It Better | .50 | .20 | .05 |
| 1977 UPI Athlete | | | |
| of the Year | | | |
| ☐ 74 Nobody Did It Better | .50 | .20 | .05 |
| 1977 PFWA NFL MVP | | | |
| ☐ 75 Nobody Did It Better | .50 | .20 | .05 |
| 1977 UPI and TSN NFC | | | |
| Player of the Year | | | |
| ☐ 76 Nobody Did It Better | .50 | .20 | .05 |
| 1977 All Pro Pick | | | |
| AP, UPI, and NEA | | | |
| ☐ 77 Nobody Did It Better | .50 | .20 | .05 |
| 1977 PFWA, NEA, | | | |
| Mutual Radio, AP, | | | |
| FB Digest, Sport | | | |
| Magazine NFL | | | |
| Player of the Year | | | |
| ☐ 78 Nobody Did It Better | .50 | .20 | .05 |
| TSN NFC All-Star | | | |
| 1976-79 | | | |
| ☐ 79 Nobody Did It Better | .50 | .20 | .05 |
| TSN NFL All-Star | | | |
| 1980, 1984, and 1985 | | | |
| ☐ 80 1981 Game-By-Game | .50 | .20 | .05 |
| ☐ 81 As Quarterback | .50 | .20 | .05 |
| ☐ 82 Kickoff Return | .50 | .20 | .05 |

| | | | |
|---|---|---|---|
| ☐ 83 Complete Player | .50 | .20 | .05 |
| ☐ 84 Touchdown | .50 | .20 | .05 |
| ☐ 85 1982 Game-By-Game | .50 | .20 | .05 |
| ☐ 86 Most Consecutive | .50 | .20 | .05 |
| Games, Career (176) | | | |
| ☐ 87 Five Longest Runs | .50 | .20 | .05 |
| ☐ 88 Pass Receiving | .50 | .20 | .05 |
| ☐ 89 Ditka On Payton | 1.00 | .40 | .10 |
| ☐ 90 1983 Game-By-Game | .50 | .20 | .05 |
| ☐ 91 Breaks Career Rushing | .50 | .20 | .05 |
| Record 10/7/84 | | | |
| ☐ 92 Breaks Career Rushing | .50 | .20 | .05 |
| ☐ 93 Breaks Career Rushing | .50 | .20 | .05 |
| ☐ 94 Breaks Career Rushing | .50 | .20 | .05 |
| ☐ 95 1984 Game-By-Game | .50 | .20 | .05 |
| ☐ 96 Bears Win 1985 NFC | .50 | .20 | .05 |
| Championship | | | |
| over Rams | | | |
| ☐ 97 Super Bowl XX | .50 | .20 | .05 |
| ☐ 98 Super Bowl XX | .50 | .20 | .05 |
| ☐ 99 Super Bowl XX | .50 | .20 | .05 |
| ☐ 100 Super Bowl XX | .50 | .20 | .05 |
| ☐ 101 1985 Game-By-Game | .50 | .20 | .05 |
| ☐ 102 Sweetness | .50 | .20 | .05 |
| ☐ 103 Sweetness | .50 | .20 | .05 |
| Unanimous Choice to | | | |
| Pro Bowl Squad 1977 | | | |
| ☐ 104 Sweetness | .50 | .20 | .05 |
| ☐ 105 Sweetness | .50 | .20 | .05 |
| 1979 Pro Bowl Starter, | | | |
| AP All-NFC | | | |
| ☐ 106 Sweetness | .50 | .20 | .05 |
| ☐ 107 Sweetness | .50 | .20 | .05 |
| ☐ 108 Sweetness | .50 | .20 | .05 |
| ☐ 109 Sweetness | .50 | .20 | .05 |
| ☐ 110 1986 Game-By-Game | .50 | .20 | .05 |
| ☐ 111 Final Season | .50 | .20 | .05 |
| Goodbye to Green Bay | | | |
| ☐ 112 Final Season | .50 | .20 | .05 |
| ☐ 113 Last Regular Season | .50 | .20 | .05 |
| Home Game | | | |
| ☐ 114 Last Regular Season | .50 | .20 | .05 |
| Home Game | | | |
| Number Retired | | | |
| ☐ 115 Last Regular Season | .50 | .20 | .05 |
| Home Game | | | |
| Presented with Portrait | | | |
| ☐ 116 Last Regular Season | .50 | .20 | .05 |
| Home Game | | | |
| ☐ 117 Last Regular Season | .50 | .20 | .05 |
| Home Game | | | |
| Soldier Field Has | | | |
| Been Known as | | | |
| Payton's Place | | | |
| ☐ 118 Last Regular Season | .50 | .20 | .05 |
| Home Game | | | |
| ☐ 119 Last Regular Season | .50 | .20 | .05 |
| Game vs. Raiders | | | |
| ☐ 120 Last Regular Season | .50 | .20 | .05 |
| Game | | | |
| ☐ 121 Last Regular Season | .50 | .20 | .05 |
| Game, Catches | | | |
| Two Passes | | | |
| ☐ 122 Last Regular Season | .50 | .20 | .05 |
| Game | | | |
| ☐ 123 Last Regular Season | .50 | .20 | .05 |
| Game | | | |
| ☐ 124 Last Regular Season | .50 | .20 | .05 |
| Game, Plays 190th | | | |
| Game, Bears' | | | |
| All-Time Record | | | |
| ☐ 125 Last Regular Season | .50 | .20 | .05 |
| Game | | | |
| ☐ 126 Last Regular Season | .50 | .20 | .05 |
| Game, Ends Career | | | |
| with 21,803 | | | |
| Combined Yards | | | |
| ☐ 127 Last Regular Season | .50 | .20 | .05 |
| Game, Finishes With | | | |
| 4542 Career | | | |
| Receiving Yards | | | |
| ☐ 128 Last Regular Season | .50 | .20 | .05 |
| Game, 16,726 Career | | | |
| Rushing Yards | | | |
| ☐ 129 1987 Game-By-Game | .50 | .20 | .05 |
| ☐ 130 The End Of An Era | .50 | .20 | .05 |
| ☐ 131 Thanks For The | .50 | .20 | .05 |
| Memories | | | |
| ☐ 132 Last Few Moments | 1.00 | .40 | .10 |

# 1976 Pepsi Discs

The 1976 Pepsi Discs set contains 40 numbered discs, each measuring approximately 3 1/2" in diameter. Each disc has a player photo, biographical information, and 1975 statistics. Disc numbers 1-

20 are from many different teams and are known as "All-Stars." Numbers 21-40 feature Cincinnati Bengals, since this set was a regional issue produced in the Cincinnati area. Numbers 1, 5, 7, 8, and 14 are much scarcer than the other 35 and are marked SP in the checklist below. Ed Marinaro also exists as a New York Jet, which is very difficult to find. It has been reported that Ed Marinaro may be a sixth SP. The checklist for the set is printed on the tab; the checklist below values the discs with the tabs intact as that is the way they are most commonly found.

| | NRMT | VG-E | GOOD |
|---|---|---|---|
| COMPLETE SET (40) | 100.00 | 40.00 | 10.00 |
| COMMON PLAYER (1-20) | .50 | .20 | .05 |
| COMMON PLAYER (21-40) | .50 | .20 | .05 |
| COMMON PLAYER SP | 20.00 | 8.00 | 2.00 |
| ☐ 1 Steve Bartkowski SP | 25.00 | 10.00 | 2.50 |
|    Atlanta Falcons | | | |
| ☐ 2 Lydell Mitchell | .75 | .30 | .07 |
|    Baltimore Colts | | | |
| ☐ 3 Wally Chambers | .50 | .20 | .05 |
|    Chicago Bears | | | |
| ☐ 4 Doug Buffone | .50 | .20 | .05 |
|    Chicago Bears | | | |
| ☐ 5 Jerry Sherk SP | 20.00 | 8.00 | 2.00 |
|    Cleveland Browns | | | |
| ☐ 6 Drew Pearson | 1.00 | .40 | .10 |
|    Dalllas Cowboys | | | |
| ☐ 7 Otis Armstrong SP | 25.00 | 10.00 | 2.50 |
|    Denver Broncos | | | |
| ☐ 8 Charlie Sanders SP | 20.00 | 8.00 | 2.00 |
|    Detroit Lions | | | |
| ☐ 9 John Brockington | .75 | .30 | .07 |
|    Green Bay Packers | | | |
| ☐ 10 Curley Culp | .75 | .30 | .07 |
|    Houston Oilers | | | |
| ☐ 11 Jan Stenerud | 1.25 | .50 | .12 |
|    Kansas City Chiefs | | | |
| ☐ 12 Lawrence McCutcheon | .75 | .30 | .07 |
|    Los Angeles Rams | | | |
| ☐ 13 Chuck Foreman | 1.00 | .40 | .10 |
|    Minnesota Vikings | | | |
| ☐ 14 Bob Pollard SP | 20.00 | 8.00 | 2.00 |
|    New Orleans Saints | | | |
| ☐ 15 Ed Marinaro | 10.00 | 4.00 | 1.00 |
|    Minnesota Vikings | | | |
| ☐ 16 Jack Lambert | 3.00 | 1.20 | .30 |
|    Pittsburgh Steelers | | | |
| ☐ 17 Terry Metcalf | .75 | .30 | .07 |
|    St. Louis Cardinals | | | |
| ☐ 18 Mel Gray | .75 | .30 | .07 |
|    St. Louis Cardinals | | | |
| ☐ 19 Russ Washington | .50 | .20 | .05 |
|    San Diego Chargers | | | |
| ☐ 20 Charley Taylor | 1.50 | .60 | .15 |
|    Washington Redskins | | | |
| ☐ 21 Ken Anderson | 2.00 | .80 | .20 |
| ☐ 22 Bob Brown | .50 | .20 | .05 |
| ☐ 23 Ron Carpenter | .50 | .20 | .05 |
| ☐ 24 Tom Casanova | 1.00 | .40 | .10 |
| ☐ 25 Boobie Clark | .75 | .30 | .07 |
| ☐ 26 Isaac Curtis | 1.00 | .40 | .10 |
| ☐ 27 Lenvil Elliott | .50 | .20 | .05 |
| ☐ 28 Stan Fritts | .50 | .20 | .05 |
| ☐ 29 Vernon Holland | .50 | .20 | .05 |
| ☐ 30 Bob Johnson | .75 | .30 | .07 |
| ☐ 31 Ken Johnson | .50 | .20 | .05 |
| ☐ 32 Bill Kollar | .50 | .20 | .05 |
| ☐ 33 Jim LeClair | .50 | .20 | .05 |
| ☐ 34 Chip Myers | .50 | .20 | .05 |
| ☐ 35 Lemar Parrish | .75 | .30 | .07 |
| ☐ 36 Ron Pritchard | .50 | .20 | .05 |

| | | | |
|---|---|---|---|
| ☐ 37 Bob Trumpy | 1.25 | .50 | .12 |
| ☐ 38 Sherman White | .50 | .20 | .05 |
| ☐ 39 Archie Griffin | 1.25 | .50 | .12 |
| ☐ 40 John Shinners | .50 | .20 | .05 |

# 1964 Philadelphia

The 1964 Philadelphia Gum set of 198 football cards, featuring National Football League players, is the first of four annual issues released by the company. The cards measure 2 1/2" by 3 1/2". Each player card has a question about that player in a cartoon at the bottom of the reverse; the answer is given upside down in blue ink. Each team has a team picture card as well as a card diagramming one of the team's plays; this "play card" shows a small black and white picture of the team's coach on the front of the card. The card backs are printed in blue and black on a gray card stock. The cards are numbered within team, i.e., Baltimore Colts (1-14), Chicago Bears (15-28), Cleveland Browns (29-42), Dallas Cowboys (43-56), Detroit Lions (57-70), Green Bay Packers (71-84), Los Angeles Rams (85-98), Minnesota Vikings (99-112), New York Giants (113-126), Philadelphia Eagles (127-140), Pittsburgh Steelers (141-154), San Francisco 49ers (155-168), St. Louis Cardinals (169-182), Washington Redskins (183-196), and Checklists (197-198). Within each team group the players are arranged alphabetically by last name. The two checklist cards erroneously say "Official 1963 Checklist" at the top. The key Rookie Cards in this set are Herb Adderley, Willie Davis, John Mackey, Merlin Olsen, and Jack Pardee.

| | NRMT | VG-E | GOOD |
|---|---|---|---|
| COMPLETE SET (198) | 900.00 | 400.00 | 115.00 |
| COMMON PLAYER (1-198) | 2.00 | .90 | .25 |
| ☐ 1 Raymond Berry | 20.00 | 4.00 | 1.20 |
| ☐ 2 Tom Gilburg | 2.00 | .90 | .25 |
| ☐ 3 John Mackey | 25.00 | 11.50 | 3.10 |
| ☐ 4 Gino Marchetti | 4.50 | 2.00 | .55 |
| ☐ 5 Jim Martin | 2.25 | 1.00 | .30 |
| ☐ 6 Tom Matte | 6.50 | 2.90 | .80 |
| ☐ 7 Jimmy Orr | 2.25 | 1.00 | .30 |
| ☐ 8 Jim Parker | 4.00 | 1.80 | .50 |
| ☐ 9 Bill Pellington | 2.00 | .90 | .25 |
| ☐ 10 Alex Sandusky | 2.00 | .90 | .25 |
| ☐ 11 Dick Szymanski | 2.00 | .90 | .25 |
| ☐ 12 John Unitas | 40.00 | 18.00 | 5.00 |
| ☐ 13 Baltimore Colts | 4.00 | 1.80 | .50 |
|    Team Card | | | |
| ☐ 14 Baltimore Colts | 28.00 | 12.50 | 3.50 |
|    Play Card | | | |
|    (Don Shula) | | | |
| ☐ 15 Doug Atkins | 4.00 | 1.80 | .50 |
| ☐ 16 Ron Bull | 2.25 | 1.00 | .30 |
| ☐ 17 Mike Ditka | 30.00 | 13.50 | 3.80 |
| ☐ 18 Joe Fortunato | 2.25 | 1.00 | .30 |
| ☐ 19 Willie Galimore | 2.25 | 1.00 | .30 |
| ☐ 20 Joe Marconi | 2.00 | .90 | .25 |
| ☐ 21 Bennie McRae | 2.50 | 1.15 | .30 |
| ☐ 22 Johnny Morris | 2.25 | 1.00 | .30 |
| ☐ 23 Richie Petitbon | 2.25 | 1.00 | .30 |
| ☐ 24 Mike Pyle | 2.00 | .90 | .25 |
| ☐ 25 Roosevelt Taylor | 4.50 | 2.00 | .55 |
| ☐ 26 Bill Wade | 2.25 | 1.00 | .30 |
| ☐ 27 Chicago Bears | 4.00 | 1.80 | .50 |
|    Team Card | | | |
| ☐ 28 Chicago Bears | 10.00 | 4.50 | 1.25 |
|    Play Card | | | |
|    (George Halas) | | | |
| ☐ 29 Johnny Brewer | 2.00 | .90 | .25 |
| ☐ 30 Jim Brown | 65.00 | 29.00 | 8.25 |
| ☐ 31 Gary Collins | 6.50 | 2.90 | .80 |
| ☐ 32 Vince Costello | 2.00 | .90 | .25 |
| ☐ 33 Galen Fiss | 2.00 | .90 | .25 |
| ☐ 34 Bill Glass | 2.00 | .90 | .25 |
| ☐ 35 Ernie Green | 3.00 | 1.35 | .40 |

| | | | |
|---|---|---|---|
| ☐ 36 Rich Kreitling | 2.00 | .90 | .25 |
| ☐ 37 John Morrow | 2.00 | .90 | .25 |
| ☐ 38 Frank Ryan | 2.50 | 1.15 | .30 |
| ☐ 39 Charlie Scales | 2.50 | 1.15 | .30 |
| ☐ 40 Dick Schafrath | 2.50 | 1.15 | .30 |
| ☐ 41 Cleveland Browns Team Card | 4.00 | 1.80 | .50 |
| ☐ 42 Cleveland Browns Play Card (Blanton Collier) | 2.00 | .90 | .25 |
| ☐ 43 Don Bishop | 2.25 | 1.00 | .30 |
| ☐ 44 Frank Clarke | 4.00 | 1.80 | .50 |
| ☐ 45 Mike Connelly | 2.00 | .90 | .25 |
| ☐ 46 Lee Folkins | 2.00 | .90 | .25 |
| ☐ 47 Cornell Green | 5.00 | 2.30 | .60 |
| ☐ 48 Bob Lilly | 30.00 | 13.50 | 3.80 |
| ☐ 49 Amos Marsh | 2.00 | .90 | .25 |
| ☐ 50 Tommy McDonald | 2.25 | 1.00 | .30 |
| ☐ 51 Don Meredith | 30.00 | 13.50 | 3.80 |
| ☐ 52 Pettis Norman | 2.50 | 1.15 | .30 |
| ☐ 53 Don Perkins | 3.00 | 1.35 | .40 |
| ☐ 54 Guy Reese | 2.25 | 1.00 | .30 |
| ☐ 55 Dallas Cowboys Team Card | 4.00 | 1.80 | .50 |
| ☐ 56 Dallas Cowboys Play Card (Tom Landry) | 12.00 | 5.50 | 1.50 |
| ☐ 57 Terry Barr | 2.00 | .90 | .25 |
| ☐ 58 Roger Brown | 2.25 | 1.00 | .30 |
| ☐ 59 Gail Cogdill | 2.00 | .90 | .25 |
| ☐ 60 John Gordy | 2.00 | .90 | .25 |
| ☐ 61 Dick Lane | 4.00 | 1.80 | .50 |
| ☐ 62 Yale Lary | 4.00 | 1.80 | .50 |
| ☐ 63 Dan Lewis | 2.00 | .90 | .25 |
| ☐ 64 Darris McCord | 2.00 | .90 | .25 |
| ☐ 65 Earl Morrall | 4.00 | 1.80 | .50 |
| ☐ 66 Joe Schmidt | 4.50 | 2.00 | .55 |
| ☐ 67 Pat Studstill | 4.00 | 1.80 | .50 |
| ☐ 68 Wayne Walker | 4.00 | 1.80 | .50 |
| ☐ 69 Detroit Lions Team Card | 4.00 | 1.80 | .50 |
| ☐ 70 Detroit Lions Play Card (George Wilson) | 2.00 | .90 | .25 |
| ☐ 71 Herb Adderley | 30.00 | 13.50 | 3.80 |
| ☐ 72 Willie Davis | 30.00 | 13.50 | 3.80 |
| ☐ 73 Forrest Gregg | 4.00 | 1.80 | .50 |
| ☐ 74 Paul Hornung | 25.00 | 11.50 | 3.10 |
| ☐ 75 Henry Jordan | 2.25 | 1.00 | .30 |
| ☐ 76 Jerry Kramer | 5.00 | 2.30 | .60 |
| ☐ 77 Tom Moore | 2.25 | 1.00 | .30 |
| ☐ 78 Jim Ringo UER (Green Bay on front, Philadelphia on back) | 4.00 | 1.80 | .50 |
| ☐ 79 Bart Starr | 27.00 | 12.00 | 3.40 |
| ☐ 80 Jim Taylor | 15.00 | 6.75 | 1.90 |
| ☐ 81 Jesse Whittenton | 2.50 | 1.15 | .30 |
| ☐ 82 Willie Wood | 8.00 | 3.60 | 1.00 |
| ☐ 83 Green Bay Packers Team Card | 4.00 | 1.80 | .50 |
| ☐ 84 Green Bay Packers Play Card (Vince Lombardi) | 24.00 | 11.00 | 3.00 |
| ☐ 85 Jon Arnett | 2.25 | 1.00 | .30 |
| ☐ 86 Pervis Atkins | 2.50 | 1.15 | .30 |
| ☐ 87 Dick Bass | 2.25 | 1.00 | .30 |
| ☐ 88 Carroll Dale | 2.25 | 1.00 | .30 |
| ☐ 89 Roman Gabriel | 6.00 | 2.70 | .75 |
| ☐ 90 Ed Meador | 2.25 | 1.00 | .30 |
| ☐ 91 Merlin Olsen | 50.00 | 23.00 | 6.25 |
| ☐ 92 Jack Pardee | 10.00 | 4.50 | 1.25 |
| ☐ 93 Jim Phillips | 2.00 | .90 | .25 |
| ☐ 94 Carver Shannon | 2.00 | .90 | .25 |
| ☐ 95 Frank Varrichione | 2.00 | .90 | .25 |
| ☐ 96 Danny Villanueva | 2.25 | 1.00 | .30 |
| ☐ 97 Los Angeles Rams Team Card | 4.00 | 1.80 | .50 |
| ☐ 98 Los Angeles Rams Play Card (Harland Svare) | 2.00 | .90 | .25 |
| ☐ 99 Grady Alderman | 3.00 | 1.35 | .40 |
| ☐ 100 Larry Bowie | 2.00 | .90 | .25 |
| ☐ 101 Bill Brown | 6.00 | 2.70 | .75 |
| ☐ 102 Paul Flatley | 2.50 | 1.15 | .30 |
| ☐ 103 Rip Hawkins | 2.00 | .90 | .25 |
| ☐ 104 Jim Marshall | 8.00 | 3.60 | 1.00 |
| ☐ 105 Tommy Mason | 2.25 | 1.00 | .30 |
| ☐ 106 Jim Prestel | 2.00 | .90 | .25 |
| ☐ 107 Jerry Reichow | 2.00 | .90 | .25 |
| ☐ 108 Ed Sharockman | 2.00 | .90 | .25 |
| ☐ 109 Fran Tarkenton | 40.00 | 18.00 | 5.00 |
| ☐ 110 Mick Tingelhoff | 8.00 | 3.60 | 1.00 |
| ☐ 111 Minnesota Vikings Team Card | 4.00 | 1.80 | .50 |
| ☐ 112 Minnesota Vikings Play Card (Norm Van Brocklin) | 5.00 | 2.30 | .60 |
| ☐ 113 Erich Barnes | 2.25 | 1.00 | .30 |
| ☐ 114 Roosevelt Brown | 4.00 | 1.80 | .50 |
| ☐ 115 Don Chandler | 2.25 | 1.00 | .30 |
| ☐ 116 Darrell Dess | 2.00 | .90 | .25 |
| ☐ 117 Frank Gifford | 45.00 | 20.00 | 5.75 |
| ☐ 118 Dick James | 2.00 | .90 | .25 |
| ☐ 119 Jim Katcavage | 2.25 | 1.00 | .30 |
| ☐ 120 John Lovetere | 2.00 | .90 | .25 |
| ☐ 121 Dick Lynch | 3.00 | 1.35 | .40 |
| ☐ 122 Jim Patton | 2.25 | 1.00 | .30 |
| ☐ 123 Del Shofner | 2.25 | 1.00 | .30 |
| ☐ 124 Y.A. Tittle | 18.00 | 8.00 | 2.30 |
| ☐ 125 New York Giants Team Card | 4.00 | 1.80 | .50 |
| ☐ 126 New York Giants Play Card (Allie Sherman) | 2.00 | .90 | .25 |
| ☐ 127 Sam Baker | 2.25 | 1.00 | .30 |
| ☐ 128 Maxie Baughan | 2.25 | 1.00 | .30 |
| ☐ 129 Timmy Brown | 2.25 | 1.00 | .30 |
| ☐ 130 Mike Clark | 2.00 | .90 | .25 |
| ☐ 131 Irv Cross | 7.00 | 3.10 | .85 |
| ☐ 132 Ted Dean | 2.00 | .90 | .25 |
| ☐ 133 Ron Goodwin | 2.00 | .90 | .25 |
| ☐ 134 King Hill | 2.25 | 1.00 | .30 |
| ☐ 135 Clarence Peaks | 2.00 | .90 | .25 |
| ☐ 136 Pete Retzlaff | 2.25 | 1.00 | .30 |
| ☐ 137 Jim Schrader | 2.00 | .90 | .25 |
| ☐ 138 Norm Snead | 4.00 | 1.80 | .50 |
| ☐ 139 Philadelphia Eagles Team Card | 4.00 | 1.80 | .50 |
| ☐ 140 Philadelphia Eagles Play Card (Nick Skorich) | 2.00 | .90 | .25 |
| ☐ 141 Gary Ballman | 2.50 | 1.15 | .30 |
| ☐ 142 Charley Bradshaw | 2.00 | .90 | .25 |
| ☐ 143 Ed Brown | 2.25 | 1.00 | .30 |
| ☐ 144 John Henry Johnson | 4.50 | 2.00 | .55 |
| ☐ 145 Joe Krupa | 2.00 | .90 | .25 |
| ☐ 146 Bill Mack | 2.00 | .90 | .25 |
| ☐ 147 Lou Michaels | 2.00 | .90 | .25 |
| ☐ 148 Buzz Nutter | 2.00 | .90 | .25 |
| ☐ 149 Myron Pottios | 2.00 | .90 | .25 |
| ☐ 150 John Reger | 2.00 | .90 | .25 |
| ☐ 151 Mike Sandusky | 2.00 | .90 | .25 |
| ☐ 152 Clendon Thomas | 2.00 | .90 | .25 |
| ☐ 153 Pittsburgh Steelers Team Card | 4.00 | 1.80 | .50 |
| ☐ 154 Pittsburgh Steelers Play Card (Buddy Parker) | 2.00 | .90 | .25 |
| ☐ 155 Kermit Alexander | 4.00 | 1.80 | .50 |
| ☐ 156 Bernie Casey | 2.25 | 1.00 | .30 |
| ☐ 157 Dan Colchico | 2.00 | .90 | .25 |
| ☐ 158 Clyde Conner | 2.00 | .90 | .25 |
| ☐ 159 Tommy Davis | 2.00 | .90 | .25 |
| ☐ 160 Matt Hazeltine | 2.00 | .90 | .25 |
| ☐ 161 Jim Johnson | 12.00 | 5.50 | 1.50 |
| ☐ 162 Don Lisbon | 2.50 | 1.15 | .30 |
| ☐ 163 Lamar McHan | 2.25 | 1.00 | .30 |
| ☐ 164 Bob St. Clair | 4.00 | 1.80 | .50 |
| ☐ 165 J.D. Smith | 2.25 | 1.00 | .30 |
| ☐ 166 Abe Woodson | 2.25 | 1.00 | .30 |
| ☐ 167 San Francisco 49ers Team Card | 4.00 | 1.80 | .50 |
| ☐ 168 San Francisco 49ers Play Card (Red Hickey) | 2.00 | .90 | .25 |
| ☐ 169 Garland Boyette UER (Photo on front is not Boyette) | 2.00 | .90 | .25 |
| ☐ 170 Bobby Joe Conrad | 2.25 | 1.00 | .30 |
| ☐ 171 Bob DeMarco | 2.50 | 1.15 | .30 |
| ☐ 172 Ken Gray | 2.50 | 1.15 | .30 |
| ☐ 173 Jimmy Hill | 2.00 | .90 | .25 |
| ☐ 174 Charlie Johnson UER (Misspelled Charley on both sides) | 3.00 | 1.35 | .40 |
| ☐ 175 Ernie McMillan | 2.25 | 1.00 | .30 |
| ☐ 176 Dale Meinert | 2.00 | .90 | .25 |
| ☐ 177 Luke Owens | 2.00 | .90 | .25 |
| ☐ 178 Sonny Randle | 2.25 | 1.00 | .30 |
| ☐ 179 Joe Robb | 2.00 | .90 | .25 |
| ☐ 180 Bill Stacy | 2.00 | .90 | .25 |
| ☐ 181 St. Louis Cardinals Team Card | 4.00 | 1.80 | .50 |
| ☐ 182 St. Louis Cardinals Play Card (Wally Lemm) | 2.00 | .90 | .25 |
| ☐ 183 Bill Barnes | 2.00 | .90 | .25 |
| ☐ 184 Don Bosseler | 2.00 | .90 | .25 |
| ☐ 185 Sam Huff | 5.50 | 2.50 | .70 |
| ☐ 186 Sonny Jurgensen | 18.00 | 8.00 | 2.30 |
| ☐ 187 Bob Khayat | 2.00 | .90 | .25 |
| ☐ 188 Riley Mattson | 2.00 | .90 | .25 |
| ☐ 189 Bobby Mitchell | 6.00 | 2.70 | .75 |
| ☐ 190 John Nisby | 2.00 | .90 | .25 |

| | | | |
|---|---|---|---|
| ☐ 191 Vince Promuto | 2.00 | .90 | .25 |
| ☐ 192 Joe Rutgens | 2.00 | .90 | .25 |
| ☐ 193 Lonnie Sanders | 2.00 | .90 | .25 |
| ☐ 194 Jim Steffen | 2.00 | .90 | .25 |
| ☐ 195 Washington Redskins Team Card | 4.00 | 1.80 | .50 |
| ☐ 196 Washington Redskins Play Card (Bill McPeak) | 2.00 | .90 | .25 |
| ☐ 197 Checklist 1 UER (Dated 1963) | 30.00 | 6.00 | 1.80 |
| ☐ 198 Checklist 2 UER (Dated 1963, 174 Charley Johnson should be Charlie) | 55.00 | 11.00 | 3.30 |

## 1965 Philadelphia

The 1965 Philadelphia Gum set of NFL players is complete at 198 cards. The cards measure the standard 2 1/2" by 3 1/2". The card backs show (when rubbed with a coin) a question and answer interrelated to other cards. Each team has a team picture card as well as a card featuring a diagram of one of the team's plays; this play card shows a small coach's picture in black and white on the front of the card. The card backs are printed in maroon on a gray card stock. The cards are numbered within team, i.e., Baltimore Colts (1-14), Chicago Bears (15-28), Cleveland Browns (29-42), Dallas Cowboys (43-56), Detroit Lions (57-70), Green Bay Packers (71-84), Los Angeles Rams (85-98), Minnesota Vikings (99-112), New York Giants (113-126), Philadelphia Eagles (127-140), Pittsburgh Steelers (141-154), St. Louis Cardinals (155-168), San Francisco 49ers (169-182), Washington Redskins (183-196), and Checklists (197-198). Within each team group the players are arranged alphabetically by last name. The key Rookie Cards in this set are Carl Eller, Paul Krause, Mel Renfro, Charley Taylor, and Paul Warfield.

| | NRMT | VG-E | GOOD |
|---|---|---|---|
| COMPLETE SET (198) | 800.00 | 350.00 | 100.00 |
| COMMON PLAYER (1-198) | 1.75 | .80 | .22 |
| | | | |
| ☐ 1 Baltimore Colts Team Card | 10.00 | 2.00 | .60 |
| ☐ 2 Raymond Berry | 6.50 | 2.90 | .80 |
| ☐ 3 Bob Boyd | 1.75 | .80 | .22 |
| ☐ 4 Wendell Harris | 1.75 | .80 | .22 |
| ☐ 5 Jerry Logan | 1.75 | .80 | .22 |
| ☐ 6 Tony Lorick | 1.75 | .80 | .22 |
| ☐ 7 Lou Michaels | 1.75 | .80 | .22 |
| ☐ 8 Lenny Moore | 6.00 | 2.70 | .75 |
| ☐ 9 Jimmy Orr | 2.00 | .90 | .25 |
| ☐ 10 Jim Parker | 3.50 | 1.55 | .45 |
| ☐ 11 Dick Szymanski | 1.75 | .80 | .22 |
| ☐ 12 John Unitas | 40.00 | 18.00 | 5.00 |
| ☐ 13 Bob Vogel | 2.25 | 1.00 | .30 |
| ☐ 14 Baltimore Colts Play Card (Don Shula) | 15.00 | 6.75 | 1.90 |
| ☐ 15 Chicago Bears Team Card | 3.50 | 1.55 | .45 |
| ☐ 16 Jon Arnett | 2.00 | .90 | .25 |
| ☐ 17 Doug Atkins | 3.50 | 1.55 | .45 |
| ☐ 18 Rudy Bukich | 2.50 | 1.15 | .30 |
| ☐ 19 Mike Ditka | 25.00 | 11.50 | 3.10 |
| ☐ 20 Dick Evey | 1.75 | .80 | .22 |
| ☐ 21 Joe Fortunato | 2.00 | .90 | .25 |
| ☐ 22 Bobby Joe Green | 2.25 | 1.00 | .30 |
| ☐ 23 Johnny Morris | 2.00 | .90 | .25 |
| ☐ 24 Mike Pyle | 1.75 | .80 | .22 |
| ☐ 25 Roosevelt Taylor | 2.00 | .90 | .25 |
| ☐ 26 Bill Wade | 2.00 | .90 | .25 |
| ☐ 27 Bob Wetoska | 1.75 | .80 | .22 |
| ☐ 28 Chicago Bears Play Card (George Halas) | 6.00 | 2.70 | .75 |

| | | | |
|---|---|---|---|
| ☐ 29 Cleveland Browns Team Card | 3.50 | 1.55 | .45 |
| ☐ 30 Walter Beach | 1.75 | .80 | .22 |
| ☐ 31 Jim Brown | 60.00 | 27.00 | 7.50 |
| ☐ 32 Gary Collins | 1.75 | .80 | .22 |
| ☐ 33 Bill Glass | 1.75 | .80 | .22 |
| ☐ 34 Ernie Green | 2.00 | .90 | .25 |
| ☐ 35 Jim Houston | 3.00 | 1.35 | .40 |
| ☐ 36 Dick Modzelewski | 2.00 | .90 | .25 |
| ☐ 37 Bernie Parrish | 2.00 | .90 | .25 |
| ☐ 38 Walter Roberts | 1.75 | .80 | .22 |
| ☐ 39 Frank Ryan | 2.25 | 1.00 | .30 |
| ☐ 40 Dick Schafrath | 1.75 | .80 | .22 |
| ☐ 41 Paul Warfield | 80.00 | 36.00 | 10.00 |
| ☐ 42 Cleveland Browns Play Card (Blanton Collier) | 2.00 | .90 | .25 |
| ☐ 43 Dallas Cowboys Team Card UER (Cowboys Dallas on back) | 3.50 | 1.55 | .45 |
| ☐ 44 Frank Clarke | 2.00 | .90 | .25 |
| ☐ 45 Mike Connelly | 1.75 | .80 | .22 |
| ☐ 46 Buddy Dial | 2.00 | .90 | .25 |
| ☐ 47 Bob Lilly | 15.00 | 6.75 | 1.90 |
| ☐ 48 Tony Liscio | 2.50 | 1.15 | .30 |
| ☐ 49 Tommy McDonald | 2.00 | .90 | .25 |
| ☐ 50 Don Meredith | 25.00 | 11.50 | 3.10 |
| ☐ 51 Pettis Norman | 2.00 | .90 | .25 |
| ☐ 52 Don Perkins | 2.00 | .90 | .25 |
| ☐ 53 Mel Renfro | 15.00 | 6.75 | 1.90 |
| ☐ 54 Jim Ridlon | 1.75 | .80 | .22 |
| ☐ 55 Jerry Tubbs | 2.00 | .90 | .25 |
| ☐ 56 Dallas Cowboys Play Card (Tom Landry) | 8.00 | 3.60 | 1.00 |
| ☐ 57 Detroit Lions Team Card | 3.50 | 1.55 | .45 |
| ☐ 58 Terry Barr | 1.75 | .80 | .22 |
| ☐ 59 Roger Brown | 2.00 | .90 | .22 |
| ☐ 60 Gail Cogdill | 1.75 | .80 | .22 |
| ☐ 61 Jim Gibbons | 1.75 | .80 | .22 |
| ☐ 62 John Gordy | 1.75 | .80 | .22 |
| ☐ 63 Yale Lary | 3.50 | 1.55 | .45 |
| ☐ 64 Dick LeBeau | 3.50 | 1.55 | .45 |
| ☐ 65 Earl Morrall | 3.50 | 1.55 | .45 |
| ☐ 66 Nick Pietrosante | 1.75 | .80 | .22 |
| ☐ 67 Pat Studstill | 2.00 | .90 | .25 |
| ☐ 68 Wayne Walker | 2.00 | .90 | .25 |
| ☐ 69 Tom Watkins | 1.75 | .80 | .22 |
| ☐ 70 Detroit Lions Play Card (George Wilson) | 2.00 | .90 | .25 |
| ☐ 71 Green Bay Packers Team Card | 3.50 | 1.55 | .45 |
| ☐ 72 Herb Adderley | 8.00 | 3.60 | 1.00 |
| ☐ 73 Willie Davis | 8.00 | 3.60 | 1.00 |
| ☐ 74 Boyd Dowler | 2.00 | .90 | .25 |
| ☐ 75 Forrest Gregg | 4.00 | 1.80 | .50 |
| ☐ 76 Paul Hornung | 24.00 | 11.00 | 3.00 |
| ☐ 77 Henry Jordan | 2.00 | .90 | .25 |
| ☐ 78 Tom Moore | 2.00 | .90 | .25 |
| ☐ 79 Ray Nitschke | 12.00 | 5.50 | 1.50 |
| ☐ 80 Elijah Pitts | 4.00 | 1.80 | .50 |
| ☐ 81 Bart Starr | 25.00 | 11.50 | 3.10 |
| ☐ 82 Jim Taylor | 13.00 | 5.75 | 1.65 |
| ☐ 83 Willie Wood | 7.00 | 3.10 | .85 |
| ☐ 84 Green Bay Packers Play Card (Vince Lombardi) | 11.00 | 4.90 | 1.40 |
| ☐ 85 Los Angeles Rams Team Card | 3.50 | 1.55 | .45 |
| ☐ 86 Dick Bass | 2.00 | .90 | .25 |
| ☐ 87 Roman Gabriel | 5.50 | 2.50 | .70 |
| ☐ 88 Roosevelt Grier | 4.00 | 1.80 | .50 |
| ☐ 89 Deacon Jones | 8.00 | 3.60 | 1.00 |
| ☐ 90 Lamar Lundy | 4.00 | 1.80 | .50 |
| ☐ 91 Marlin McKeever | 1.75 | .80 | .22 |
| ☐ 92 Ed Meador | 2.00 | .90 | .25 |
| ☐ 93 Bill Munson | 4.00 | 1.80 | .50 |
| ☐ 94 Merlin Olsen | 18.00 | 8.00 | 2.30 |
| ☐ 95 Bobby Smith | 1.75 | .80 | .22 |
| ☐ 96 Frank Varrichione | 1.75 | .80 | .22 |
| ☐ 97 Ben Wilson | 1.75 | .80 | .22 |
| ☐ 98 Los Angeles Rams Play Card (Harland Svare) | 2.00 | .90 | .25 |
| ☐ 99 Minnesota Vikings Team Card | 3.50 | 1.55 | .45 |
| ☐ 100 Grady Alderman | 1.75 | .80 | .22 |
| ☐ 101 Hal Bedsole | 2.25 | 1.00 | .30 |
| ☐ 102 Bill Brown | 1.75 | .80 | .22 |
| ☐ 103 Bill Butler | 1.75 | .80 | .22 |
| ☐ 104 Fred Cox | 4.00 | 1.80 | .50 |
| ☐ 105 Carl Eller | 25.00 | 11.50 | 3.10 |
| ☐ 106 Paul Flatley | 2.00 | .90 | .25 |
| ☐ 107 Jim Marshall | 6.50 | 2.90 | .80 |
| ☐ 108 Tommy Mason | 2.00 | .90 | .25 |

| | | | |
|---|---|---|---|
| ☐ 109 George Rose | 1.75 | .80 | .22 |
| ☐ 110 Fran Tarkenton | 35.00 | 16.00 | 4.40 |
| ☐ 111 Mick Tingelhoff | 2.50 | 1.15 | .30 |
| ☐ 112 Minnesota Vikings | 3.00 | 1.35 | .40 |
| Play Card | | | |
| (Norm Van Brocklin) | | | |
| ☐ 113 New York Giants | 3.50 | 1.55 | .45 |
| Team Card | | | |
| ☐ 114 Erich Barnes | 2.00 | .90 | .25 |
| ☐ 115 Roosevelt Brown | 3.50 | 1.55 | .45 |
| ☐ 116 Clarence Childs | 1.75 | .80 | .22 |
| ☐ 117 Jerry Hillebrand | 1.75 | .80 | .22 |
| ☐ 118 Greg Larson | 3.00 | 1.35 | .40 |
| ☐ 119 Dick Lynch | 2.00 | .90 | .25 |
| ☐ 120 Joe Morrison | 3.50 | 1.55 | .45 |
| ☐ 121 Lou Slaby | 1.75 | .80 | .22 |
| ☐ 122 Aaron Thomas | 3.00 | 1.35 | .40 |
| ☐ 123 Steve Thurlow | 1.75 | .80 | .22 |
| ☐ 124 Ernie Wheelwright | 1.75 | .80 | .22 |
| ☐ 125 Gary Wood | 2.25 | 1.00 | .30 |
| ☐ 126 New York Giants | 2.00 | .90 | .25 |
| Play Card | | | |
| (Allie Sherman) | | | |
| ☐ 127 Philadelphia Eagles | 3.50 | 1.55 | .45 |
| Team Card | | | |
| ☐ 128 Sam Baker | 2.00 | .90 | .25 |
| ☐ 129 Maxie Baughan | 2.00 | .90 | .25 |
| ☐ 130 Timmy Brown | 2.00 | .90 | .25 |
| ☐ 131 Jack Concannon | 3.00 | 1.35 | .40 |
| ☐ 132 Irv Cross | 2.50 | 1.15 | .30 |
| ☐ 133 Earl Gros | 1.75 | .80 | .22 |
| ☐ 134 Dave Lloyd | 1.75 | .80 | .22 |
| ☐ 135 Floyd Peters | 3.50 | 1.55 | .45 |
| ☐ 136 Nate Ramsey | 1.75 | .80 | .22 |
| ☐ 137 Pete Retzlaff | 2.00 | .90 | .25 |
| ☐ 138 Jim Ringo | 3.50 | 1.55 | .45 |
| ☐ 139 Norm Snead | 2.50 | 1.15 | .30 |
| ☐ 140 Philadelphia Eagles | 2.25 | 1.00 | .30 |
| Play Card | | | |
| (Joe Kuharich) | | | |
| ☐ 141 Pittsburgh Steelers | 3.50 | 1.55 | .45 |
| Team Card | | | |
| ☐ 142 John Baker | 1.75 | .80 | .22 |
| ☐ 143 Gary Ballman | 2.00 | .90 | .25 |
| ☐ 144 Charley Bradshaw | 1.75 | .80 | .22 |
| ☐ 145 Ed Brown | 2.00 | .90 | .25 |
| ☐ 146 Dick Haley | 1.75 | .80 | .22 |
| ☐ 147 John Henry Johnson | 4.50 | 2.00 | .55 |
| ☐ 148 Brady Keys | 1.75 | .80 | .22 |
| ☐ 149 Ray Lemek | 1.75 | .80 | .22 |
| ☐ 150 Ben McGee | 1.75 | .80 | .22 |
| ☐ 151 Clarence Peaks | 1.75 | .80 | .22 |
| ☐ 152 Myron Pottios | 1.75 | .80 | .22 |
| ☐ 153 Clendon Thomas | 1.75 | .80 | .22 |
| ☐ 154 Pittsburgh Steelers | 2.00 | .90 | .25 |
| Play Card | | | |
| (Buddy Parker) | | | |
| ☐ 155 St. Louis Cardinals | 3.50 | 1.55 | .45 |
| Team Card | | | |
| ☐ 156 Jim Bakken | 4.00 | 1.80 | .50 |
| ☐ 157 Joe Childress | 1.75 | .80 | .22 |
| ☐ 158 Bobby Joe Conrad | 2.00 | .90 | .25 |
| ☐ 159 Bob DeMarco | 1.75 | .80 | .22 |
| ☐ 160 Pat Fischer | 4.00 | 1.80 | .50 |
| ☐ 161 Irv Goode | 1.75 | .80 | .22 |
| ☐ 162 Ken Gray | 2.00 | .90 | .25 |
| ☐ 163 Charlie Johnson UER | 2.50 | 1.15 | .30 |
| (Misspelled Charley | | | |
| on both sides) | | | |
| ☐ 164 Bill Koman | 1.75 | .80 | .22 |
| ☐ 165 Dale Meinert | 1.75 | .80 | .22 |
| ☐ 166 Jerry Stovall | 2.50 | 1.15 | .30 |
| ☐ 167 Abe Woodson | 2.00 | .90 | .25 |
| ☐ 168 St. Louis Cardinals | 2.00 | .90 | .25 |
| Play Card | | | |
| (Wally Lemm) | | | |
| ☐ 169 San Francisco 49ers | 3.50 | 1.55 | .45 |
| Team Card | | | |
| ☐ 170 Kermit Alexander | 1.75 | .80 | .22 |
| ☐ 171 John Brodie | 12.00 | 5.50 | 1.50 |
| ☐ 172 Bernie Casey | 2.00 | .90 | .25 |
| ☐ 173 John David Crow | 2.00 | .90 | .25 |
| ☐ 174 Tommy Davis | 1.75 | .80 | .22 |
| ☐ 175 Matt Hazeltine | 1.75 | .80 | .22 |
| ☐ 176 Jim Johnson | 4.00 | 1.80 | .50 |
| ☐ 177 Charlie Krueger | 2.50 | 1.15 | .30 |
| ☐ 178 Roland Lakes | 1.75 | .80 | .22 |
| ☐ 179 George Mira | 4.00 | 1.80 | .50 |
| ☐ 180 Dave Parks | 4.00 | 1.80 | .50 |
| ☐ 181 John Thomas | 1.75 | .80 | .22 |
| ☐ 182 San Francisco 49ers | 2.50 | 1.15 | .30 |
| Play Card | | | |
| (Jack Christiansen) | | | |
| ☐ 183 Washington Redskins | 3.50 | 1.55 | .45 |
| Team Card | | | |
| ☐ 184 Pervis Atkins | 1.75 | .80 | .22 |
| ☐ 185 Preston Carpenter | 1.75 | .80 | .22 |

| | | | |
|---|---|---|---|
| ☐ 186 Angelo Coia | 1.75 | .80 | .22 |
| ☐ 187 Sam Huff | 5.00 | 2.30 | .60 |
| ☐ 188 Sonny Jurgensen | 15.00 | 6.75 | 1.90 |
| ☐ 189 Paul Krause | 16.00 | 7.25 | 2.00 |
| ☐ 190 Jim Martin | 2.00 | .90 | .25 |
| ☐ 191 Bobby Mitchell | 5.00 | 2.30 | .60 |
| ☐ 192 John Nisby | 1.75 | .80 | .22 |
| ☐ 193 John Paluck | 1.75 | .80 | .22 |
| ☐ 194 Vince Promuto | 1.75 | .80 | .22 |
| ☐ 195 Charley Taylor | 60.00 | 27.00 | 7.50 |
| ☐ 196 Washington Redskins | 2.00 | .90 | .25 |
| Play Card | | | |
| (Bill McPeak) | | | |
| ☐ 197 Checklist 1 | 30.00 | 6.00 | 1.80 |
| ☐ 198 Checklist 2 UER | 50.00 | 10.00 | 3.00 |
| (163 Charley Johnson | | | |
| should be Charlie) | | | |

# 1966 Philadelphia

The 1966 Philadelphia Gum football card set contains 198 cards featuring NFL players. The cards measure the standard 2 1/2" by 3 1/2". The backs contain the player's name, a card number, a short biography, and a "Guess Who" quiz. The quiz answer is found on another card. The last two cards in the set are checklist cards. Each team's "play card" shows a color photo of actual game action, described on the back. The card backs are printed in green and black on a white card stock. The cards are numbered within team, i.e., Atlanta Falcons (1-13), Baltimore Colts (14-26), Chicago Bears (27-39), Cleveland Browns (40-52), Dallas Cowboys (53-65), Detroit Lions (66-78), Green Bay Packers (79-91), Los Angeles Rams (92-104), Minnesota Vikings (105-117), New York Giants (118-130), Philadelphia Eagles (131-143), Pittsburgh Steelers (144-156), St. Louis Cardinals (157-169), San Francisco 49ers (170-182), Washington Redskins (183-195), Referee Signals (196), and Checklists (197-198). Within each team group the players are arranged alphabetically by last name. The set features the debut of Chicago Bears' greats, Dick Butkus and Gale Sayers.

| | NRMT | VG-E | GOOD |
|---|---|---|---|
| COMPLETE SET (198) | 900.00 | 400.00 | 115.00 |
| COMMON PLAYER (1-198) | 1.75 | .80 | .22 |
| | | | |
| ☐ 1 Atlanta Falcons | 8.50 | 1.25 | .45 |
| Insignia | | | |
| ☐ 2 Larry Benz | 1.75 | .80 | .22 |
| ☐ 3 Dennis Claridge | 1.75 | .80 | .22 |
| ☐ 4 Perry Lee Dunn | 1.75 | .80 | .22 |
| ☐ 5 Dan Grimm | 1.75 | .80 | .22 |
| ☐ 6 Alex Hawkins | 2.00 | .90 | .25 |
| ☐ 7 Ralph Heck | 1.75 | .80 | .22 |
| ☐ 8 Frank Lasky | 1.75 | .80 | .22 |
| ☐ 9 Guy Reese | 1.75 | .80 | .22 |
| ☐ 10 Bob Richards | 1.75 | .80 | .22 |
| ☐ 11 Ron Smith | 2.50 | 1.15 | .30 |
| ☐ 12 Ernie Wheelwright | 1.75 | .80 | .22 |
| ☐ 13 Atlanta Falcons | 2.50 | 1.15 | .30 |
| Roster | | | |
| ☐ 14 Baltimore Colts | 3.00 | 1.35 | .40 |
| Team Card | | | |
| ☐ 15 Raymond Berry | 6.50 | 2.90 | .80 |
| ☐ 16 Bob Boyd | 1.75 | .80 | .22 |
| ☐ 17 Jerry Logan | 1.75 | .80 | .22 |
| ☐ 18 John Mackey | 7.00 | 3.10 | .85 |
| ☐ 19 Tom Matte | 2.25 | 1.00 | .30 |
| ☐ 20 Lou Michaels | 1.75 | .80 | .22 |
| ☐ 21 Lenny Moore | 6.00 | 2.70 | .75 |
| ☐ 22 Jimmy Orr | 2.00 | .90 | .25 |
| ☐ 23 Jim Parker | 3.50 | 1.55 | .45 |
| ☐ 24 John Unitas | 30.00 | 13.50 | 3.80 |
| ☐ 25 Bob Vogel | 1.75 | .80 | .22 |
| ☐ 26 Baltimore Colts | 3.00 | 1.35 | .40 |
| Play Card | | | |

| | | | |
|---|---|---|---|
| (Moore/Parker) | | | |
| ☐ 27 Chicago Bears | 3.00 | 1.35 | .40 |
| Team Card | | | |
| ☐ 28 Doug Atkins | 3.50 | 1.55 | .45 |
| ☐ 29 Rudy Bukich | 1.75 | .80 | .22 |
| ☐ 30 Ron Bull | 1.75 | .80 | .22 |
| ☐ 31 Dick Butkus | 175.00 | 80.00 | 22.00 |
| ☐ 32 Mike Ditka | 16.00 | 7.25 | 2.00 |
| ☐ 33 Joe Fortunato | 2.00 | .90 | .25 |
| ☐ 34 Bobby Joe Green | 1.75 | .80 | .22 |
| ☐ 35 Roger LeClerc | 1.75 | .80 | .22 |
| ☐ 36 Johnny Morris | 2.00 | .90 | .25 |
| ☐ 37 Mike Pyle | 1.75 | .80 | .22 |
| ☐ 38 Gale Sayers | 225.00 | 100.00 | 28.00 |
| ☐ 39 Chicago Bears | 20.00 | 9.00 | 2.50 |
| Play Card | | | |
| (Gale Sayers) | | | |
| ☐ 40 Cleveland Browns | 3.00 | 1.35 | .40 |
| Team Card | | | |
| ☐ 41 Jim Brown | 55.00 | 25.00 | 7.00 |
| ☐ 42 Gary Collins | 1.75 | .80 | .22 |
| ☐ 43 Ross Fichtner | 1.75 | .80 | .22 |
| ☐ 44 Ernie Green | 2.00 | .90 | .25 |
| ☐ 45 Gene Hickerson | 2.50 | 1.15 | .30 |
| ☐ 46 Jim Houston | 2.00 | .90 | .25 |
| ☐ 47 John Morrow | 1.75 | .80 | .22 |
| ☐ 48 Walter Roberts | 1.75 | .80 | .22 |
| ☐ 49 Frank Ryan | 2.25 | 1.00 | .30 |
| ☐ 50 Dick Schafrath | 1.75 | .80 | .22 |
| ☐ 51 Paul Wiggin | 2.50 | 1.15 | .30 |
| ☐ 52 Cleveland Browns | 2.00 | .90 | .25 |
| Play Card | | | |
| (Ernie Green sweep) | | | |
| ☐ 53 Dallas Cowboys | 3.00 | 1.35 | .40 |
| Team Card | | | |
| ☐ 54 George Andrie UER | 2.50 | 1.15 | .30 |
| (Text says startling, | | | |
| should be starting) | | | |
| ☐ 55 Frank Clarke | 2.00 | .90 | .25 |
| ☐ 56 Mike Connelly | 1.75 | .80 | .22 |
| ☐ 57 Cornell Green | 2.25 | 1.00 | .30 |
| ☐ 58 Bob Hayes | 16.00 | 7.25 | 2.00 |
| ☐ 59 Chuck Howley | 10.00 | 4.50 | 1.25 |
| ☐ 60 Bob Lilly | 10.00 | 4.50 | 1.25 |
| ☐ 61 Don Meredith | 25.00 | 11.50 | 3.10 |
| ☐ 62 Don Perkins | 2.00 | .90 | .25 |
| ☐ 63 Mel Renfro | 5.00 | 2.30 | .60 |
| ☐ 64 Danny Villanueva | 2.00 | .90 | .25 |
| ☐ 65 Dallas Cowboys | 2.00 | .90 | .25 |
| Play Card | | | |
| (Danny Villanueva | | | |
| kicking field goal) | | | |
| ☐ 66 Detroit Lions | 3.00 | 1.35 | .40 |
| Team Card | | | |
| ☐ 67 Roger Brown | 2.00 | .90 | .25 |
| ☐ 68 John Gordy | 1.75 | .80 | .22 |
| ☐ 69 Alex Karras | 10.00 | 4.50 | 1.25 |
| ☐ 70 Dick LeBeau | 2.00 | .90 | .25 |
| ☐ 71 Amos Marsh | 1.75 | .80 | .22 |
| ☐ 72 Milt Plum | 2.00 | .90 | .25 |
| ☐ 73 Bobby Smith | 1.75 | .80 | .22 |
| ☐ 74 Wayne Rasmussen | 1.75 | .80 | .22 |
| ☐ 75 Pat Studstill | 2.00 | .90 | .25 |
| ☐ 76 Wayne Walker | 2.00 | .90 | .25 |
| ☐ 77 Tom Watkins | 1.75 | .80 | .22 |
| ☐ 78 Detroit Lions | 2.00 | .90 | .25 |
| Play Card | | | |
| (George Izo pass) | | | |
| ☐ 79 Green Bay Packers | 3.00 | 1.35 | .40 |
| Team Card | | | |
| ☐ 80 Herb Adderley UER | 5.00 | 2.30 | .60 |
| (Adderly on back) | | | |
| ☐ 81 Lee Roy Caffey | 2.50 | 1.15 | .30 |
| ☐ 82 Don Chandler | 2.00 | .90 | .25 |
| ☐ 83 Willie Davis | 5.00 | 2.30 | .60 |
| ☐ 84 Boyd Dowler | 2.00 | .90 | .25 |
| ☐ 85 Forrest Gregg | 3.50 | 1.55 | .45 |
| ☐ 86 Tom Moore | 1.75 | .80 | .22 |
| ☐ 87 Ray Nitschke | 8.00 | 3.60 | 1.00 |
| ☐ 88 Bart Starr | 25.00 | 11.50 | 3.10 |
| ☐ 89 Jim Taylor | 14.00 | 6.25 | 1.75 |
| ☐ 90 Willie Wood | 4.50 | 2.00 | .55 |
| ☐ 91 Green Bay Packers | 2.00 | .90 | .25 |
| Play Card | | | |
| (Don Chandler FG) | | | |
| ☐ 92 Los Angeles Rams | 3.00 | 1.35 | .40 |
| Team Card | | | |
| ☐ 93 Willie Brown | 1.75 | .80 | .22 |
| (Flanker) | | | |
| ☐ 94 Dick Bass and | 3.50 | 1.55 | .45 |
| Roman Gabriel | | | |
| ☐ 95 Bruce Gossett | 2.25 | 1.00 | .30 |
| (Tom Landry small | | | |
| photo on back) | | | |
| ☐ 96 Deacon Jones | 6.00 | 2.70 | .75 |
| ☐ 97 Tommy McDonald | 2.00 | .90 | .25 |
| ☐ 98 Marlin McKeever | 1.75 | .80 | .22 |
| ☐ 99 Aaron Martin | 1.75 | .80 | .22 |

| | | | |
|---|---|---|---|
| ☐ 100 Ed Meador | 2.00 | .90 | .25 |
| ☐ 101 Bill Munson | 2.25 | 1.00 | .30 |
| ☐ 102 Merlin Olsen | 8.00 | 3.60 | 1.00 |
| ☐ 103 Jim Stiger | 1.75 | .80 | .22 |
| ☐ 104 Los Angeles Rams | 2.25 | 1.00 | .30 |
| Play Card | | | |
| (Willie Brown run) | | | |
| ☐ 105 Minnesota Vikings | 3.00 | 1.35 | .40 |
| Team Card | | | |
| ☐ 106 Grady Alderman | 1.75 | .80 | .22 |
| ☐ 107 Bill Brown | 2.00 | .90 | .25 |
| ☐ 108 Fred Cox | 2.00 | .90 | .25 |
| ☐ 109 Paul Flatley | 2.00 | .90 | .25 |
| ☐ 110 Rip Hawkins | 1.75 | .80 | .22 |
| ☐ 111 Tommy Mason | 2.00 | .90 | .25 |
| ☐ 112 Ed Sharockman | 1.75 | .80 | .22 |
| ☐ 113 Gordon Smith | 1.75 | .80 | .22 |
| ☐ 114 Fran Tarkenton | 30.00 | 13.50 | 3.80 |
| ☐ 115 Mick Tingelhoff | 2.25 | 1.00 | .30 |
| ☐ 116 Bobby Walden | 2.50 | 1.15 | .30 |
| ☐ 117 Minnesota Vikings | 2.25 | 1.00 | .30 |
| Play Card | | | |
| (Bill Brown run) | | | |
| ☐ 118 New York Giants | 3.00 | 1.35 | .40 |
| Team Card | | | |
| ☐ 119 Roosevelt Brown | 3.00 | 1.35 | .40 |
| ☐ 120 Henry Carr | 2.50 | 1.15 | .30 |
| ☐ 121 Clarence Childs | 1.75 | .80 | .22 |
| ☐ 122 Tucker Frederickson | 3.00 | 1.35 | .40 |
| ☐ 123 Jerry Hillebrand | 1.75 | .80 | .22 |
| ☐ 124 Greg Larson | 1.75 | .80 | .22 |
| ☐ 125 Spider Lockhart | 3.00 | 1.35 | .40 |
| ☐ 126 Dick Lynch | 2.00 | .90 | .25 |
| ☐ 127 Earl Morrall and | 2.50 | 1.15 | .30 |
| Bob Scholtz | | | |
| ☐ 128 Joe Morrison | 1.75 | .80 | .22 |
| ☐ 129 Steve Thurlow | 1.75 | .80 | .22 |
| ☐ 130 New York Giants | 2.00 | .90 | .25 |
| Play Card | | | |
| (Chuck Mercein over) | | | |
| ☐ 131 Philadelphia Eagles | 3.00 | 1.35 | .40 |
| Team Card | | | |
| ☐ 132 Sam Baker | 2.00 | .90 | .25 |
| ☐ 133 Maxie Baughan | 2.00 | .90 | .25 |
| ☐ 134 Bob Brown | 6.00 | 2.70 | .75 |
| ☐ 135 Timmy Brown | 2.00 | .90 | .25 |
| (Lou Groza small | | | |
| photo on back) | | | |
| ☐ 136 Irv Cross | 2.50 | 1.15 | .30 |
| ☐ 137 Earl Gros | 1.75 | .80 | .22 |
| ☐ 138 Ray Poage | 1.75 | .80 | .22 |
| ☐ 139 Nate Ramsey | 1.75 | .80 | .22 |
| ☐ 140 Pete Retzlaff | 2.00 | .90 | .25 |
| ☐ 141 Jim Ringo | 3.00 | 1.35 | .40 |
| (Joe Schmidt small | | | |
| photo on back) | | | |
| ☐ 142 Norm Snead | 2.25 | 1.00 | .30 |
| (Norm Van Brocklin | | | |
| small photo on back) | | | |
| ☐ 143 Philadelphia Eagles | 2.00 | .90 | .25 |
| Play Card | | | |
| (Earl Gros tackled) | | | |
| ☐ 144 Pittsburgh Steelers | 3.00 | 1.35 | .40 |
| Team Card | | | |
| (Lee Roy Jordan small | | | |
| photo on back) | | | |
| ☐ 145 Gary Ballman | 2.00 | .90 | .25 |
| ☐ 146 Charley Bradshaw | 1.75 | .80 | .22 |
| ☐ 147 Jim Butler | 1.75 | .80 | .22 |
| ☐ 148 Mike Clark | 1.75 | .80 | .22 |
| ☐ 149 Dick Hoak | 2.50 | 1.15 | .30 |
| ☐ 150 Roy Jefferson | 3.00 | 1.35 | .40 |
| ☐ 151 Frank Lambert | 1.75 | .80 | .22 |
| ☐ 152 Mike Lind | 1.75 | .80 | .22 |
| ☐ 153 Bill Nelsen | 4.00 | 1.80 | .50 |
| ☐ 154 Clarence Peaks | 1.75 | .80 | .22 |
| ☐ 155 Clendon Thomas | 1.75 | .80 | .22 |
| ☐ 156 Pittsburgh Steelers | 2.00 | .90 | .25 |
| Play Card | | | |
| (Gary Ballman scores) | | | |
| ☐ 157 St. Louis Cardinals | 3.00 | 1.35 | .40 |
| Team Card | | | |
| ☐ 158 Jim Bakken | 2.00 | .90 | .25 |
| ☐ 159 Bobby Joe Conrad | 2.00 | .90 | .25 |
| ☐ 160 Willis Crenshaw | 2.25 | 1.00 | .30 |
| ☐ 161 Bob DeMarco | 1.75 | .80 | .22 |
| ☐ 162 Pat Fischer | 2.25 | 1.00 | .30 |
| ☐ 163 Charlie Johnson UER | 2.25 | 1.00 | .30 |
| (Misspelled Charley | | | |
| on both sides) | | | |
| ☐ 164 Dale Meinert | 1.75 | .80 | .22 |
| ☐ 165 Sonny Randle | 2.00 | .90 | .25 |
| ☐ 166 Sam Silas | 2.25 | 1.00 | .30 |
| ☐ 167 Bill Triplett | 1.75 | .80 | .22 |
| ☐ 168 Larry Wilson | 3.50 | 1.55 | .45 |
| ☐ 169 St. Louis Cardinals | 2.00 | .90 | .25 |
| Play Card | | | |

| | | NRMT | VG-E | GOOD |
|---|---|---|---|---|
| ☐ 170 | San Francisco 49ers | 3.00 | 1.35 | .40 |
| | Team Card | | | |
| | (Vince Lombardi small | | | |
| | photo on back) | | | |
| ☐ 171 | Kermit Alexander | 1.75 | .80 | .22 |
| ☐ 172 | Bruce Bosley | 1.75 | .80 | .22 |
| ☐ 173 | John Brodie | 10.00 | 4.50 | 1.25 |
| ☐ 174 | Bernie Casey | 2.00 | .90 | .25 |
| ☐ 175 | John David Crow | 2.00 | .90 | .25 |
| | (Don Shula small | | | |
| | photo on back) | | | |
| ☐ 176 | Tommy Davis | 1.75 | .80 | .22 |
| ☐ 177 | Jim Johnson | 3.00 | 1.35 | .40 |
| ☐ 178 | Gary Lewis | 1.75 | .80 | .22 |
| ☐ 179 | Dave Parks | 2.00 | .90 | .25 |
| ☐ 180 | Walter Rock | 1.75 | .80 | .22 |
| | (Paul Hornung small | | | |
| | photo on back) | | | |
| ☐ 181 | Ken Willard | 4.00 | 1.80 | .50 |
| | (George Halas small | | | |
| | photo on back) | | | |
| ☐ 182 | San Francisco 49ers | 2.00 | .90 | .25 |
| | Play Card | | | |
| | (Tommy Davis FG) | | | |
| ☐ 183 | Washington Redskins | 3.00 | 1.35 | .40 |
| | Team Card | | | |
| ☐ 184 | Rickie Harris | 1.75 | .80 | .22 |
| ☐ 185 | Sonny Jurgensen | 9.00 | 4.00 | 1.15 |
| ☐ 186 | Paul Krause | 5.00 | 2.30 | .60 |
| ☐ 187 | Bobby Mitchell | 5.00 | 2.30 | .60 |
| ☐ 188 | Vince Promuto | 1.75 | .80 | .22 |
| ☐ 189 | Pat Richter | 2.50 | 1.15 | .30 |
| | (Craig Morton small | | | |
| | photo on back) | | | |
| ☐ 190 | Joe Rutgens | 1.75 | .80 | .22 |
| ☐ 191 | John Sample | 2.00 | .90 | .25 |
| ☐ 192 | Lonnie Sanders | 1.75 | .80 | .22 |
| ☐ 193 | Jim Steffen | 1.75 | .80 | .22 |
| ☐ 194 | Charley Taylor UER | 18.00 | 8.00 | 2.30 |
| | (Called Charley and | | | |
| | Charlie on card back | | | |
| ☐ 195 | Washington Redskins | 2.00 | .90 | .25 |
| | Play Card | | | |
| ☐ 196 | Referee Signals | 3.00 | 1.35 | .40 |
| ☐ 197 | Checklist 1 | 22.00 | 4.40 | 1.30 |
| ☐ 198 | Checklist 2 UER | 45.00 | 9.00 | 2.70 |
| | (163 Charley Johnson | | | |
| | should be Charlie) | | | |

## 1967 Philadelphia

The 1967 Philadelphia Gum set of NFL players is complete at 198 cards and was Philadelphia Gum's last issue. This set is easily distinguished from the other Philadelphia football sets by its yellow border on the fronts of the cards. The card backs are printed in brown on a white card stock. The cards are numbered within team, i.e., Atlanta Falcons (1-12), Baltimore Colts (13-24), Chicago Bears (25-36), Cleveland Browns (37-48), Dallas Cowboys (49-60), Detroit Lions (61-72), Green Bay Packers (73-84), Los Angeles Rams (85-96), Minnesota Vikings (97-108), New York Giants (109-120), New Orleans Saints (121-132), Philadelphia Eagles (133-144), Pittsburgh Steelers (145-156), St. Louis Cardinals (157-168), San Francisco 49ers (169-180), Washington Redskins (181-192), Play Cards (193-195), Referee Signals (196), and Checklists (197-198). Within each team group the players are arranged alphabetically by last name. The key Rookie Cards in this set are Lee Roy Jordan, Leroy Kelly, Tommy Nobis, Dan Reeves. The cards measure standard size, 2 1/2" by 3 1/2".

| | NRMT | VG-E | GOOD |
|---|---|---|---|
| COMPLETE SET (198) | 650.00 | 300.00 | 80.00 |
| COMMON PLAYER (1-198) | 1.75 | .80 | .22 |
| | | | |
| ☐ 1 Atlanta Falcons | 6.00 | .90 | .30 |
| Team Card | | | |

| | | | | |
|---|---|---|---|---|
| ☐ 2 | Junior Coffey | 2.50 | 1.15 | .30 |
| ☐ 3 | Alex Hawkins | 2.00 | .90 | .25 |
| ☐ 4 | Randy Johnson | 2.50 | 1.15 | .30 |
| ☐ 5 | Lou Kirouac | 1.75 | .80 | .22 |
| ☐ 6 | Billy Martin | 1.75 | .80 | .22 |
| ☐ 7 | Tommy Nobis | 16.00 | 7.25 | 2.00 |
| ☐ 8 | Jerry Richardson | 6.00 | 2.70 | .75 |
| ☐ 9 | Marion Rushing | 1.75 | .80 | .22 |
| ☐ 10 | Ron Smith | 1.75 | .80 | .22 |
| ☐ 11 | Ernie Wheelwright UER | 1.75 | .80 | .22 |
| | (Misspelled Wheelright | | | |
| | on both sides) | | | |
| ☐ 12 | Atlanta Falcons | 2.00 | .90 | .25 |
| | Insignia | | | |
| ☐ 13 | Baltimore Colts | 3.00 | 1.35 | .40 |
| | Team Card | | | |
| ☐ 14 | Raymond Berry UER | 5.00 | 2.30 | .60 |
| | (Photo actually | | | |
| | Bob Boyd) | | | |
| ☐ 15 | Bob Boyd | 1.75 | .80 | .22 |
| ☐ 16 | Ordell Braase | 1.75 | .80 | .22 |
| ☐ 17 | Alvin Haymond | 1.75 | .80 | .22 |
| ☐ 18 | Tony Lorick | 1.75 | .80 | .22 |
| ☐ 19 | Lenny Lyles | 1.75 | .80 | .22 |
| ☐ 20 | John Mackey | 6.00 | 2.70 | .75 |
| ☐ 21 | Tom Matte | 2.25 | 1.00 | .30 |
| ☐ 22 | Lou Michaels | 1.75 | .80 | .22 |
| ☐ 23 | John Unitas | 28.00 | 12.50 | 3.50 |
| ☐ 24 | Baltimore Colts | 2.00 | .90 | .25 |
| | Insignia | | | |
| ☐ 25 | Chicago Bears | 3.00 | 1.35 | .40 |
| | Team Card | | | |
| ☐ 26 | Rudy Bukich UER | 1.75 | .80 | .22 |
| | (Misspelled Buckich | | | |
| | on card back) | | | |
| ☐ 27 | Ron Bull | 1.75 | .80 | .22 |
| ☐ 28 | Dick Butkus | 50.00 | 23.00 | 6.25 |
| ☐ 29 | Mike Ditka | 14.00 | 6.25 | 1.75 |
| ☐ 30 | Dick Gordon | 2.50 | 1.15 | .30 |
| ☐ 31 | Roger LeClerc | 1.75 | .80 | .22 |
| ☐ 32 | Bennie McRae | 1.75 | .80 | .22 |
| ☐ 33 | Richie Petitbon | 2.00 | .90 | .25 |
| ☐ 34 | Mike Pyle | 1.75 | .80 | .22 |
| ☐ 35 | Gale Sayers | 75.00 | 34.00 | 9.50 |
| ☐ 36 | Chicago Bears | 2.00 | .90 | .25 |
| | Insignia | | | |
| ☐ 37 | Cleveland Browns | 3.00 | 1.35 | .40 |
| | Team Card | | | |
| ☐ 38 | Johnny Brewer | 1.75 | .80 | .22 |
| ☐ 39 | Gary Collins | 2.00 | .90 | .25 |
| ☐ 40 | Ross Fichtner | 1.75 | .80 | .22 |
| ☐ 41 | Ernie Green | 2.00 | .90 | .25 |
| ☐ 42 | Gene Hickerson | 1.75 | .80 | .22 |
| ☐ 43 | Leroy Kelly | 28.00 | 12.50 | 3.50 |
| ☐ 44 | Frank Ryan | 2.25 | 1.00 | .30 |
| ☐ 45 | Dick Schafrath | 1.75 | .80 | .22 |
| ☐ 46 | Paul Warfield | 20.00 | 9.00 | 2.50 |
| ☐ 47 | John Wooten | 1.75 | .80 | .22 |
| ☐ 48 | Cleveland Browns | 2.00 | .90 | .25 |
| | Insignia | | | |
| ☐ 49 | Dallas Cowboys | 3.00 | 1.35 | .40 |
| | Team Card | | | |
| ☐ 50 | George Andrie | 2.00 | .90 | .25 |
| ☐ 51 | Cornell Green | 2.00 | .90 | .25 |
| ☐ 52 | Bob Hayes | 5.00 | 2.30 | .60 |
| ☐ 53 | Chuck Howley | 2.50 | 1.15 | .30 |
| ☐ 54 | Lee Roy Jordan | 22.00 | 10.00 | 2.80 |
| ☐ 55 | Bob Lilly | 7.50 | 3.40 | .95 |
| ☐ 56 | Dave Manders | 2.50 | 1.15 | .30 |
| ☐ 57 | Don Meredith | 22.00 | 10.00 | 2.80 |
| ☐ 58 | Dan Reeves | 32.00 | 14.50 | 4.00 |
| ☐ 59 | Mel Renfro | 2.50 | 1.15 | .30 |
| ☐ 60 | Dallas Cowboys | 2.00 | .90 | .25 |
| | Insignia | | | |
| ☐ 61 | Detroit Lions | 3.00 | 1.35 | .40 |
| | Team Card | | | |
| ☐ 62 | Roger Brown | 2.00 | .90 | .25 |
| ☐ 63 | Gail Cogdill | 1.75 | .80 | .22 |
| ☐ 64 | John Gordy | 1.75 | .80 | .22 |
| ☐ 65 | Ron Kramer | 2.00 | .90 | .25 |
| ☐ 66 | Dick LeBeau | 2.00 | .90 | .25 |
| ☐ 67 | Mike Lucci | 5.00 | 2.30 | .60 |
| ☐ 68 | Amos Marsh | 1.75 | .80 | .22 |
| ☐ 69 | Tom Nowatzke | 1.75 | .80 | .22 |
| ☐ 70 | Pat Studstill | 2.00 | .90 | .25 |
| ☐ 71 | Karl Sweetan | 2.00 | .90 | .25 |
| ☐ 72 | Detroit Lions | 2.00 | .90 | .25 |
| | Insignia | | | |
| ☐ 73 | Green Bay Packers | 3.00 | 1.35 | .40 |
| | Team Card | | | |
| ☐ 74 | Herb Adderley UER | 4.00 | 1.80 | .50 |
| | (Adderly on back) | | | |
| ☐ 75 | Lee Roy Caffey | 2.00 | .90 | .25 |
| ☐ 76 | Willie Davis | 4.00 | 1.80 | .50 |
| ☐ 77 | Forrest Gregg | 3.50 | 1.55 | .45 |
| ☐ 78 | Henry Jordan | 2.00 | .90 | .25 |
| ☐ 79 | Ray Nitschke | 5.00 | 2.30 | .60 |

| | | MINT | EXC | G-VG |
|---|---|---|---|---|
| ☐ 80 | Dave Robinson | 5.00 | 2.30 | .60 |
| ☐ 81 | Bob Skoronski | 1.75 | .80 | .22 |
| ☐ 82 | Bart Starr | 22.00 | 10.00 | 2.80 |
| ☐ 83 | Willie Wood | 4.00 | 1.80 | .50 |
| ☐ 84 | Green Bay Packers Insignia | 2.00 | .90 | .25 |
| ☐ 85 | Los Angeles Rams Team Card | 3.00 | 1.35 | .40 |
| ☐ 86 | Dick Bass | 2.00 | .90 | .25 |
| ☐ 87 | Maxie Baughan | 2.00 | .90 | .25 |
| ☐ 88 | Roman Gabriel | 4.00 | 1.80 | .50 |
| ☐ 89 | Bruce Gossett | 1.75 | .80 | .22 |
| ☐ 90 | Deacon Jones | 5.00 | 2.30 | .60 |
| ☐ 91 | Tommy McDonald | 2.00 | .90 | .25 |
| ☐ 92 | Marlin McKeever | 1.75 | .80 | .22 |
| ☐ 93 | Tom Moore | 1.75 | .80 | .22 |
| ☐ 94 | Merlin Olsen | 6.00 | 2.70 | .75 |
| ☐ 95 | Clancy Williams | 1.75 | .80 | .22 |
| ☐ 96 | Los Angeles Rams Insignia | 2.00 | .90 | .25 |
| ☐ 97 | Minnesota Vikings Team Card | 3.00 | 1.35 | .40 |
| ☐ 98 | Grady Alderman | 1.75 | .80 | .22 |
| ☐ 99 | Bill Brown | 2.00 | .90 | .25 |
| ☐ 100 | Fred Cox | 2.00 | .90 | .25 |
| ☐ 101 | Paul Flatley | 2.00 | .90 | .25 |
| ☐ 102 | Dale Hackbart | 1.75 | .80 | .22 |
| ☐ 103 | Jim Marshall | 4.00 | 1.80 | .50 |
| ☐ 104 | Tommy Mason | 2.00 | .90 | .25 |
| ☐ 105 | Milt Sunde | 1.75 | .80 | .22 |
| ☐ 106 | Fran Tarkenton | 25.00 | 11.50 | 3.10 |
| ☐ 107 | Mick Tingelhoff | 2.00 | .90 | .25 |
| ☐ 108 | Minnesota Vikings Insignia | 2.00 | .90 | .25 |
| ☐ 109 | New York Giants Team Card | 3.00 | 1.35 | .40 |
| ☐ 110 | Henry Carr | 2.00 | .90 | .25 |
| ☐ 111 | Clarence Childs | 1.75 | .80 | .22 |
| ☐ 112 | Allen Jacobs | 1.75 | .80 | .22 |
| ☐ 113 | Homer Jones | 3.00 | 1.35 | .40 |
| ☐ 114 | Tom Kennedy | 1.75 | .80 | .22 |
| ☐ 115 | Spider Lockhart | 2.00 | .90 | .25 |
| ☐ 116 | Joe Morrison | 2.00 | .90 | .25 |
| ☐ 117 | Francis Peay | 2.00 | .90 | .25 |
| ☐ 118 | Jeff Smith | 1.75 | .80 | .22 |
| ☐ 119 | Aaron Thomas | 2.00 | .90 | .25 |
| ☐ 120 | New York Giants Insignia | 2.00 | .90 | .25 |
| ☐ 121 | New Orleans Saints Insignia (See also card 132) | 3.00 | 1.35 | .40 |
| ☐ 122 | Charley Bradshaw | 1.75 | .80 | .22 |
| ☐ 123 | Paul Hornung | 18.00 | 8.00 | 2.30 |
| ☐ 124 | Elbert Kimbrough | 1.75 | .80 | .22 |
| ☐ 125 | Earl Leggett | 1.75 | .80 | .22 |
| ☐ 126 | Obert Logan | 1.75 | .80 | .22 |
| ☐ 127 | Riley Mattson | 1.75 | .80 | .22 |
| ☐ 128 | John Morrow | 1.75 | .80 | .22 |
| ☐ 129 | Bob Scholtz | 1.75 | .80 | .22 |
| ☐ 130 | Dave Whitsell | 2.50 | 1.15 | .30 |
| ☐ 131 | Gary Wood | 2.00 | .90 | .25 |
| ☐ 132 | New Orleans Saints Roster UER (121 on back) | 2.50 | 1.15 | .30 |
| ☐ 133 | Philadelphia Eagles Team Card | 3.00 | 1.35 | .40 |
| ☐ 134 | Sam Baker | 2.00 | .90 | .25 |
| ☐ 135 | Bob Brown | 1.75 | .80 | .22 |
| ☐ 136 | Timmy Brown | 2.00 | .90 | .25 |
| ☐ 137 | Earl Gros | 1.75 | .80 | .22 |
| ☐ 138 | Dave Lloyd | 1.75 | .80 | .22 |
| ☐ 139 | Floyd Peters | 2.00 | .90 | .25 |
| ☐ 140 | Pete Retzlaff | 2.00 | .90 | .25 |
| ☐ 141 | Joe Scarpati | 1.75 | .80 | .22 |
| ☐ 142 | Norm Snead | 2.25 | 1.00 | .30 |
| ☐ 143 | Jim Skaggs | 1.75 | .80 | .22 |
| ☐ 144 | Philadelphia Eagles Insignia | 2.00 | .90 | .25 |
| ☐ 145 | Pittsburgh Steelers Team Card | 3.00 | 1.35 | .40 |
| ☐ 146 | Bill Asbury | 1.75 | .80 | .22 |
| ☐ 147 | John Baker | 1.75 | .80 | .22 |
| ☐ 148 | Gary Ballman | 2.00 | .90 | .25 |
| ☐ 149 | Mike Clark | 1.75 | .80 | .22 |
| ☐ 150 | Riley Gunnels | 1.75 | .80 | .22 |
| ☐ 151 | John Hilton | 1.75 | .80 | .22 |
| ☐ 152 | Roy Jefferson | 2.00 | .90 | .25 |
| ☐ 153 | Brady Keys | 1.75 | .80 | .22 |
| ☐ 154 | Ben McGee | 1.75 | .80 | .22 |
| ☐ 155 | Bill Nelsen | 2.25 | 1.00 | .30 |
| ☐ 156 | Pittsburgh Steelers Insignia | 2.00 | .90 | .25 |
| ☐ 157 | St. Louis Cardinals Team Card | 3.00 | 1.35 | .40 |
| ☐ 158 | Jim Bakken | 2.00 | .90 | .25 |
| ☐ 159 | Bobby Joe Conrad | 2.00 | .90 | .25 |
| ☐ 160 | Ken Gray | 2.00 | .90 | .25 |
| ☐ 161 | Charlie Johnson UER (Misspelled Charley on both sides) | 2.25 | 1.00 | .30 |
| ☐ 162 | Joe Robb | 1.75 | .80 | .22 |
| ☐ 163 | Johnny Roland | 4.00 | 1.80 | .50 |
| ☐ 164 | Roy Shivers | 2.00 | .90 | .25 |
| ☐ 165 | Jackie Smith | 15.00 | 6.75 | 1.90 |
| ☐ 166 | Jerry Stovall | 2.00 | .90 | .25 |
| ☐ 167 | Larry Wilson | 3.50 | 1.55 | .45 |
| ☐ 168 | St. Louis Cardinals Insignia | 2.00 | .90 | .25 |
| ☐ 169 | San Francisco 49ers Team Card | 3.00 | 1.35 | .40 |
| ☐ 170 | Kermit Alexander | 1.75 | .80 | .22 |
| ☐ 171 | Bruce Bosley | 1.75 | .80 | .22 |
| ☐ 172 | John Brodie | 8.00 | 3.60 | 1.00 |
| ☐ 173 | Bernie Casey | 2.00 | .90 | .25 |
| ☐ 174 | Tommy Davis | 1.75 | .80 | .22 |
| ☐ 175 | Howard Mudd | 1.75 | .80 | .22 |
| ☐ 176 | Dave Parks | 2.00 | .90 | .25 |
| ☐ 177 | John Thomas | 1.75 | .80 | .22 |
| ☐ 178 | Dave Wilcox | 5.50 | 2.50 | .70 |
| ☐ 179 | Ken Willard | 1.75 | .80 | .22 |
| ☐ 180 | San Francisco 49ers Insignia | 2.00 | .90 | .25 |
| ☐ 181 | Washington Redskins Team Card | 3.00 | 1.35 | .40 |
| ☐ 182 | Charlie Gogolak | 2.50 | 1.15 | .30 |
| ☐ 183 | Chris Hanburger | 8.00 | 3.60 | 1.00 |
| ☐ 184 | Len Hauss | 3.50 | 1.55 | .45 |
| ☐ 185 | Sonny Jurgensen | 9.00 | 4.00 | 1.15 |
| ☐ 186 | Bobby Mitchell | 5.00 | 2.30 | .60 |
| ☐ 187 | Brig Owens | 1.75 | .80 | .22 |
| ☐ 188 | Jim Shorter | 1.75 | .80 | .22 |
| ☐ 189 | Jerry Smith | 2.50 | 1.15 | .30 |
| ☐ 190 | Charley Taylor | 8.00 | 3.60 | 1.00 |
| ☐ 191 | A.D. Whitfield | 1.75 | .80 | .22 |
| ☐ 192 | Washington Redskins Insignia | 2.00 | .90 | .25 |
| ☐ 193 | Cleveland Browns Play Card (Leroy Kelly) | 5.00 | 2.30 | .60 |
| ☐ 194 | New York Giants Play Card (Joe Morrison) | 2.00 | .90 | .25 |
| ☐ 195 | Atlanta Falcons Play Card (Ernie Wheelright) | 2.00 | .90 | .25 |
| ☐ 196 | Referee Signals | 2.50 | 1.15 | .30 |
| ☐ 197 | Checklist 1 | 20.00 | 4.00 | 1.20 |
| ☐ 198 | Checklist 2 UER (161 Charley Johnson should be Charlie) | 40.00 | 8.00 | 2.40 |

# 1991 Pinnacle Promo Emmitt Smith

This promo card measures the standard size, 2 1/2" by 3 1/2". The promo card back is slightly different from the regular card back; the helmet on the card back is not centered and the text of the promo mentions Emmitt's holdout.

| | MINT | EXC | G-VG |
|---|---|---|---|
| COMPLETE SET (1) | 7.50 | 3.00 | .75 |
| COMMON CARD | 7.50 | 3.00 | .75 |
| ☐ 1 Emmitt Smith Dallas Cowboys | 7.50 | 3.00 | .75 |

# 1991 Pinnacle Promo Panels

These (approximately) 5" by 7" promo panels each feature four cards to show the design of the 1991 Pinnacle series cards. They were introduced and initially distributed at the Super Bowl XXVI Card Show.

The cards, which would measure the standard size (2 1/2" by 3 1/2") if cut, display two color photos on a black panel with white borders. The backs carry a color cut-out action shot, biography, player profile, and statistics. The cards are numbered on the back as in the regular series; the panels themselves, however, are unnumbered. The panels are listed below alphabetically according to the player's name on the card featured at upper left corner of each panel.

|  | MINT | EXC | G-VG |
|---|---|---|---|
| COMPLETE SET (12) | 40.00 | 16.00 | 4.00 |
| COMMON PANEL (1-12) | 2.50 | 1.00 | .25 |
| ☐ 1 John Alt | 2.50 | 1.00 | .25 |
| Kansas City Chiefs | | | |
| Eric Green | | | |
| Pittsburgh Steelers | | | |
| Don Mosebar | | | |
| Los Angeles Raiders | | | |
| Greg Townsend | | | |
| Los Angeles Raiders | | | |
| ☐ 2 Bruce Armstrong | 8.00 | 3.25 | .80 |
| New England Patriots | | | |
| Joe Montana | | | |
| San Francisco 49ers | | | |
| Jim Lachey | | | |
| Washington Redskins | | | |
| Bruce Matthews | | | |
| Houston Oilers | | | |
| ☐ 3 Don Beebe | 2.50 | 1.00 | .25 |
| Buffalo Bills | | | |
| Irving Fryar | | | |
| New England Patriots | | | |
| Ricky Proehl | | | |
| Phoenix Cardinals | | | |
| Vinny Testaverde | | | |
| Tampa Bay Buccaneers | | | |
| ☐ 4 Duane Bickett | 2.50 | 1.00 | .25 |
| Indianapolis Colts | | | |
| Tony Bennett | | | |
| Green Bay Packers | | | |
| John Friesz | | | |
| San Diego Chargers | | | |
| Rob Burnett | | | |
| Cleveland Browns | | | |
| ☐ 5 Mark Bortz | 3.00 | 1.20 | .30 |
| Chicago Bears | | | |
| Warren Moon | | | |
| Houston Oilers | | | |
| Jim Breech | | | |
| Cincinnati Bengals | | | |
| Eric Metcalf | | | |
| Cleveland Browns | | | |
| ☐ 6 Dermontti Dawson | 2.50 | 1.00 | .25 |
| Pittsburgh Steelers | | | |
| Jerry Gray | | | |
| Los Angeles Rams | | | |
| Nick Lowery | | | |
| Kansas City Chiefs | | | |
| Scott Case | | | |
| Atlanta Falcons | | | |
| ☐ 7 Chris Doleman | 8.00 | 3.25 | .80 |
| Minnesota Vikings | | | |
| Troy Aikman | | | |
| Dallas Cowboys | | | |
| Sterling Sharpe | | | |
| Green Bay Packers | | | |
| Sean Landeta | | | |
| New York Giants | | | |
| ☐ 8 Darryl Henley | 3.00 | 1.20 | .30 |
| Los Angeles Rams | | | |
| Karl Mecklenburg | | | |
| Denver Broncos | | | |
| Sam Mills | | | |
| New Orleans Saints | | | |
| Rod Woodson | | | |
| Pittsburgh Steelers | | | |
| ☐ 9 Mark Higgs | 3.00 | 1.20 | .30 |

| | | | |
|---|---|---|---|
| Miami Dolphins | | | |
| Jay Schroeder | | | |
| Los Angeles Raiders | | | |
| Mark Carrier | | | |
| Chicago Bears | | | |
| Jim Everett | | | |
| Los Angeles Rams | | | |
| ☐ 10 Louis Lipps | 3.00 | 1.20 | .30 |
| Pittsburgh Steelers | | | |
| John Offerdahl | | | |
| Miami Dolphins | | | |
| Herschel Walker | | | |
| Minnesota Vikings | | | |
| Jeff George | | | |
| Indianapolis Colts | | | |
| ☐ 11 Greg McMurtry | 2.50 | 1.00 | .25 |
| New England Patriots | | | |
| Henry Ellard | | | |
| Los Angeles Rams | | | |
| Brian Mitchell | | | |
| Washington Redskins | | | |
| Mark Clayton | | | |
| Miami Dolphins | | | |
| ☐ 12 Andre Rison | 3.00 | 1.20 | .30 |
| Atlanta Falcons | | | |
| Jeff Hostetler | | | |
| New York Giants | | | |
| Hugh Millen | | | |
| New England Patriots | | | |
| Jack Del Rio | | | |
| Dallas Cowboys | | | |

# 1991 Pinnacle

The premier edition of the 1991 Score Pinnacle set contains 415 cards measuring the standard size (2 1/2" by 3 1/2"). The front design of the veteran player cards features two color photos, an action photo and a head shot, on a black background with white borders. The card backs have a color action shot superimposed on a black background. The rookie cards have the same design, except with a green background on the front, and head shots rather than action shots on the back. The backs also include a biography, player profile, and statistics (where appropriate). The set includes 58 rookies (253, 281-336, 393) and four special cards. Special subsets featured are Head to Head (351-355), Technicians (356-362), Gamewinners (363-371), Idols (372-386), and Sideline (394-415). A patented anti-counterfeit device appears on the bottom border of each card back. The cards are numbered on the back. Rookie Cards in this set include Nick Bell, Bryan Cox, Lawrence Dawsey, Ricky Ervins, Jeff Graham, Mark Higgs, Randal Hill, Todd Marinovich, Russell Maryland, Dan McGwire, Erric Pegram, Mike Pritchard, Leonard Russell, and Harvey Williams.

|  | MINT | EXC | G-VG |
|---|---|---|---|
| COMPLETE SET (415) | 35.00 | 16.00 | 4.40 |
| COMMON PLAYER (1-415) | .08 | .04 | .01 |
| ☐ 1 Warren Moon | .40 | .18 | .05 |
| Houston Oilers | | | |
| ☐ 2 Morten Andersen | .12 | .05 | .02 |
| New Orleans Saints | | | |
| ☐ 3 Rohn Stark | .08 | .04 | .01 |
| Indianapolis Colts | | | |
| ☐ 4 Mark Bortz | .08 | .04 | .01 |
| Chicago Bears | | | |
| ☐ 5 Mark Higgs | 1.25 | .55 | .16 |
| Miami Dolphins | | | |
| ☐ 6 Troy Aikman | 5.00 | 2.30 | .60 |
| Dallas Cowboys | | | |
| ☐ 7 John Elway | 1.50 | .65 | .19 |
| Denver Broncos | | | |
| ☐ 8 Neal Anderson | .12 | .05 | .02 |
| Chicago Bears | | | |
| ☐ 9 Chris Doleman | .12 | .05 | .02 |
| Minnesota Vikings | | | |

| | | | |
|---|---|---|---|
| ☐ 10 Jay Schroeder | .12 | .05 | .02 |
| Los Angeles Raiders | | | |
| ☐ 11 Sterling Sharpe | 1.75 | .80 | .22 |
| Green Bay Packers | | | |
| ☐ 12 Steve DeBerg | .12 | .05 | .02 |
| Kansas City Chiefs | | | |
| ☐ 13 Ronnie Lott | .15 | .07 | .02 |
| Los Angeles Raiders | | | |
| ☐ 14 Sean Landeta | .08 | .04 | .01 |
| New York Giants | | | |
| ☐ 15 Jim Everett | .12 | .05 | .02 |
| Los Angeles Rams | | | |
| ☐ 16 Jim Breech | .08 | .04 | .01 |
| Cincinnati Bengals | | | |
| ☐ 17 Barry Foster | 1.00 | .45 | .13 |
| Pittsburgh Steelers | | | |
| ☐ 18 Mike Merriweather | .08 | .04 | .01 |
| Minnesota Vikings | | | |
| ☐ 19 Eric Metcalf | .15 | .07 | .02 |
| Cleveland Browns | | | |
| ☐ 20 Mark Carrier | .12 | .05 | .02 |
| Chicago Bears | | | |
| ☐ 21 James Brooks | .12 | .05 | .02 |
| Cincinnati Bengals | | | |
| ☐ 22 Nate Odomes | .15 | .07 | .02 |
| Buffalo Bills | | | |
| ☐ 23 Rodney Hampton | 1.50 | .65 | .19 |
| New York Giants | | | |
| ☐ 24 Chris Miller | .15 | .07 | .02 |
| Atlanta Falcons | | | |
| ☐ 25 Roger Craig | .15 | .07 | .02 |
| Los Angeles Raiders | | | |
| ☐ 26 Louis Oliver | .12 | .05 | .02 |
| Miami Dolphins | | | |
| ☐ 27 Allen Pinkett | .08 | .04 | .01 |
| Houston Oilers | | | |
| ☐ 28 Bubby Brister | .15 | .07 | .02 |
| Pittsburgh Steelers | | | |
| ☐ 29 Reyna Thompson | .08 | .04 | .01 |
| New York Giants | | | |
| ☐ 30 Issiac Holt | .08 | .04 | .01 |
| Dallas Cowboys | | | |
| ☐ 31 Steve Broussard | .12 | .05 | .02 |
| Atlanta Falcons | | | |
| ☐ 32 Christian Okoye | .12 | .05 | .02 |
| Kansas City Chiefs | | | |
| ☐ 33 Dave Meggett | .15 | .07 | .02 |
| New York Jets | | | |
| ☐ 34 Andre Reed | .25 | .11 | .03 |
| Buffalo Bills | | | |
| ☐ 35 Shane Conlan | .12 | .05 | .02 |
| Buffalo Bills | | | |
| ☐ 36 Eric Ball | .08 | .04 | .01 |
| Cincinnati Bengals | | | |
| ☐ 37 Johnny Bailey | .12 | .05 | .02 |
| Chicago Bears | | | |
| ☐ 38 Don Majkowski | .12 | .05 | .02 |
| Green Bay Packers | | | |
| ☐ 39 Gerald Williams | .08 | .04 | .01 |
| Pittsburgh Steelers | | | |
| ☐ 40 Kevin Mack | .12 | .05 | .02 |
| Cleveland Browns | | | |
| ☐ 41 Jeff Herrod | .08 | .04 | .01 |
| Indianapolis Colts | | | |
| ☐ 42 Emmitt Smith | 8.00 | 3.60 | 1.00 |
| Dallas Cowboys | | | |
| ☐ 43 Wendell Davis | .08 | .04 | .01 |
| Chicago Bears | | | |
| ☐ 44 Lorenzo White | .15 | .07 | .02 |
| Houston Oilers | | | |
| ☐ 45 Andre Rison | .50 | .23 | .06 |
| Atlanta Falcons | | | |
| ☐ 46 Jerry Gray | .08 | .04 | .01 |
| Los Angeles Rams | | | |
| ☐ 47 Dennis Smith | .12 | .05 | .02 |
| Denver Broncos | | | |
| ☐ 48 Gaston Green | .12 | .05 | .02 |
| Denver Broncos | | | |
| ☐ 49 Dermontti Dawson | .08 | .04 | .01 |
| Pittsburgh Steelers | | | |
| ☐ 50 Jeff Hostetler | .50 | .23 | .06 |
| New York Giants | | | |
| ☐ 51 Nick Lowery | .12 | .05 | .02 |
| Kansas City Chiefs | | | |
| ☐ 52 Merril Hoge | .12 | .05 | .02 |
| Pittsburgh Steelers | | | |
| ☐ 53 Bobby Hebert | .15 | .07 | .02 |
| New Orleans Saints | | | |
| ☐ 54 Scott Case | .08 | .04 | .01 |
| Atlanta Falcons | | | |
| ☐ 55 Jack Del Rio | .08 | .04 | .01 |
| Dallas Cowboys | | | |
| ☐ 56 Cornelius Bennett | .15 | .07 | .02 |
| Buffalo Bills | | | |
| ☐ 57 Tony Mandarich | .08 | .04 | .01 |
| Green Bay Packers | | | |
| ☐ 58 Bill Brooks | .12 | .05 | .02 |
| Indianapolis Colts | | | |
| ☐ 59 Jessie Tuggle | .08 | .04 | .01 |
| Atlanta Falcons | | | |
| ☐ 60 Hugh Millen | .25 | .11 | .03 |
| New England Patriots | | | |
| ☐ 61 Tony Bennett | .12 | .05 | .02 |
| Green Bay Packers | | | |
| ☐ 62 Cris Dishman | .30 | .14 | .04 |
| Houston Oilers | | | |
| ☐ 63 Darryl Henley | .08 | .04 | .01 |
| Los Angeles Rams | | | |
| ☐ 64 Duane Bickett | .08 | .04 | .01 |
| Indianapolis Colts | | | |
| ☐ 65 Jay Hilgenberg | .12 | .05 | .02 |
| Chicago Bears | | | |
| ☐ 66 Joe Montana | 3.00 | 1.35 | .40 |
| San Francisco 49ers | | | |
| ☐ 67 Bill Fralic | .08 | .04 | .01 |
| Atlanta Falcons | | | |
| ☐ 68 Sam Mills | .12 | .05 | .02 |
| New Orleans Saints | | | |
| ☐ 69 Bruce Armstrong | .08 | .04 | .01 |
| New England Patriots | | | |
| ☐ 70 Dan Marino | 3.00 | 1.35 | .40 |
| Miami Dolphins | | | |
| ☐ 71 Jim Lachey | .08 | .04 | .01 |
| Washington Redskins | | | |
| ☐ 72 Rod Woodson | .15 | .07 | .02 |
| Pittsburgh Steelers | | | |
| ☐ 73 Simon Fletcher | .12 | .05 | .02 |
| Denver Broncos | | | |
| ☐ 74 Bruce Matthews | .12 | .05 | .02 |
| Houston Oilers | | | |
| ☐ 75 Howie Long | .12 | .05 | .02 |
| Los Angeles Raiders | | | |
| ☐ 76 John Friesz | .25 | .11 | .03 |
| San Diego Chargers | | | |
| ☐ 77 Karl Mecklenburg | .12 | .05 | .02 |
| Denver Broncos | | | |
| ☐ 78 John L. Williams UER | .12 | .05 | .02 |
| Seattle Seahawks (Two photos show 42 Chris Warren) | | | |
| ☐ 79 Rob Burnett | .30 | .14 | .04 |
| Cleveland Browns | | | |
| ☐ 80 Anthony Carter | .12 | .05 | .02 |
| Minnesota Vikings | | | |
| ☐ 81 Henry Ellard | .12 | .05 | .02 |
| Los Angeles Rams | | | |
| ☐ 82 Don Beebe | .15 | .07 | .02 |
| Buffalo Bills | | | |
| ☐ 83 Louis Lipps | .12 | .05 | .02 |
| Pittsburgh Steelers | | | |
| ☐ 84 Greg McMurtry | .08 | .04 | .01 |
| New England Patriots | | | |
| ☐ 85 Will Wolford | .08 | .04 | .01 |
| Buffalo Bills | | | |
| ☐ 86 Eric Green | .40 | .18 | .05 |
| Pittsburgh Steelers | | | |
| ☐ 87 Irving Fryar | .12 | .05 | .02 |
| New England Patriots | | | |
| ☐ 88 John Offerdahl | .12 | .05 | .02 |
| Miami Dolphins | | | |
| ☐ 89 John Alt | .08 | .04 | .01 |
| Kansas City Chiefs | | | |
| ☐ 90 Tom Tupa | .12 | .05 | .02 |
| Phoenix Cardinals | | | |
| ☐ 91 Don Mosebar | .08 | .04 | .01 |
| Los Angeles Raiders | | | |
| ☐ 92 Jeff George | .75 | .35 | .09 |
| Indianapolis Colts | | | |
| ☐ 93 Vinny Testaverde | .25 | .11 | .03 |
| Tampa Bay Buccaneers | | | |
| ☐ 94 Greg Townsend | .08 | .04 | .01 |
| Los Angeles Raiders | | | |
| ☐ 95 Derrick Fenner | .12 | .05 | .02 |
| Seattle Seahawks | | | |
| ☐ 96 Brian Mitchell | .35 | .16 | .04 |
| Washington Redskins | | | |
| ☐ 97 Herschel Walker | .15 | .07 | .02 |
| Minnesota Vikings | | | |
| ☐ 98 Ricky Proehl | .25 | .11 | .03 |
| Phoenix Cardinals | | | |
| ☐ 99 Mark Clayton | .12 | .05 | .02 |
| Miami Dolphins | | | |
| ☐ 100 Derrick Thomas | .50 | .23 | .06 |
| Kansas City Chiefs | | | |
| ☐ 101 Jim Harbaugh | .15 | .07 | .02 |
| Chicago Bears | | | |
| ☐ 102 Barry Word | .15 | .07 | .02 |
| Kansas City Chiefs | | | |
| ☐ 103 Jerry Rice | 2.00 | .90 | .25 |
| San Francisco 49ers | | | |
| ☐ 104 Keith Byars | .12 | .05 | .02 |
| Philadelphia Eagles | | | |
| ☐ 105 Marion Butts | .15 | .07 | .02 |
| San Diego Chargers | | | |
| ☐ 106 Rich Moran | .08 | .04 | .01 |

Green Bay Packers
| | | | |
|---|---|---|---|
| ☐ 107 Thurman Thomas | 1.00 | .45 | .13 |

Buffalo Bills
| | | | |
|---|---|---|---|
| ☐ 108 Stephone Paige | .12 | .05 | .02 |

Kansas City Chiefs
| | | | |
|---|---|---|---|
| ☐ 109 David Johnson | .08 | .04 | .01 |

Pittsburgh Steelers
| | | | |
|---|---|---|---|
| ☐ 110 William Perry | .12 | .05 | .02 |

Chicago Bears
| | | | |
|---|---|---|---|
| ☐ 111 Haywood Jeffires | .30 | .14 | .04 |

Houston Oilers
| | | | |
|---|---|---|---|
| ☐ 112 Rodney Peete | .12 | .05 | .02 |

Detroit Lions
| | | | |
|---|---|---|---|
| ☐ 113 Andy Heck | .08 | .04 | .01 |

Seattle Seahawks
| | | | |
|---|---|---|---|
| ☐ 114 Kevin Ross | .12 | .05 | .02 |

Kansas City Chiefs
| | | | |
|---|---|---|---|
| ☐ 115 Michael Carter | .08 | .04 | .01 |

San Francisco 49ers
| | | | |
|---|---|---|---|
| ☐ 116 Tim McKyer | .12 | .05 | .02 |

Atlanta Falcons
| | | | |
|---|---|---|---|
| ☐ 117 Kenneth Davis | .12 | .05 | .02 |

Buffalo Bills
| | | | |
|---|---|---|---|
| ☐ 118 Richmond Webb | .12 | .05 | .02 |

Miami Dolphins
| | | | |
|---|---|---|---|
| ☐ 119 Rich Camarillo | .08 | .04 | .01 |

Phoenix Cardinals
| | | | |
|---|---|---|---|
| ☐ 120 James Francis | .12 | .05 | .02 |

Cincinnati Bengals
| | | | |
|---|---|---|---|
| ☐ 121 Craig Heyward | .08 | .04 | .01 |

New Orleans Saints
| | | | |
|---|---|---|---|
| ☐ 122 Hardy Nickerson | .08 | .04 | .01 |

Pittsburgh Steelers
| | | | |
|---|---|---|---|
| ☐ 123 Michael Brooks | .08 | .04 | .01 |

Denver Broncos
| | | | |
|---|---|---|---|
| ☐ 124 Fred Barnett | .40 | .18 | .05 |

Philadelphia Eagles
| | | | |
|---|---|---|---|
| ☐ 125 Cris Carter | .15 | .07 | .02 |

Minnesota Vikings
| | | | |
|---|---|---|---|
| ☐ 126 Brian Jordan | .20 | .09 | .03 |

Atlanta Falcons
| | | | |
|---|---|---|---|
| ☐ 127 Pat Leahy | .08 | .04 | .01 |

New York Jets
| | | | |
|---|---|---|---|
| ☐ 128 Kevin Greene | .12 | .05 | .02 |

Los Angeles Rams
| | | | |
|---|---|---|---|
| ☐ 129 Trace Armstrong | .08 | .04 | .01 |

Chicago Bears
| | | | |
|---|---|---|---|
| ☐ 130 Eugene Lockhart | .08 | .04 | .01 |

New England Patriots
| | | | |
|---|---|---|---|
| ☐ 131 Albert Lewis | .12 | .05 | .02 |

Kansas City Chiefs
| | | | |
|---|---|---|---|
| ☐ 132 Ernie Jones | .08 | .04 | .01 |

Phoenix Cardinals
| | | | |
|---|---|---|---|
| ☐ 133 Eric Martin | .12 | .05 | .02 |

New Orleans Saints
| | | | |
|---|---|---|---|
| ☐ 134 Anthony Thompson | .08 | .04 | .01 |

Phoenix Cardinals
| | | | |
|---|---|---|---|
| ☐ 135 Tim Krumrie | .08 | .04 | .01 |

Cincinnati Bengals
| | | | |
|---|---|---|---|
| ☐ 136 James Lofton | .15 | .07 | .02 |

Buffalo Bills
| | | | |
|---|---|---|---|
| ☐ 137 John Taylor | .15 | .07 | .02 |

San Francisco 49ers
| | | | |
|---|---|---|---|
| ☐ 138 Jeff Cross | .08 | .04 | .01 |

Miami Dolphins
| | | | |
|---|---|---|---|
| ☐ 139 Tommy Kane | .08 | .04 | .01 |

Seattle Seahawks
| | | | |
|---|---|---|---|
| ☐ 140 Robb Thomas | .08 | .04 | .01 |

Kansas City Chiefs
| | | | |
|---|---|---|---|
| ☐ 141 Gary Anderson | .08 | .04 | .01 |

Pittsburgh Steelers
| | | | |
|---|---|---|---|
| ☐ 142 Mark Murphy | .08 | .04 | .01 |

Green Bay Packers
| | | | |
|---|---|---|---|
| ☐ 143 Rickey Jackson | .12 | .05 | .02 |

New Orleans Saints
| | | | |
|---|---|---|---|
| ☐ 144 Ken O'Brien | .12 | .05 | .02 |

New York Jets
| | | | |
|---|---|---|---|
| ☐ 145 Ernest Givins | .12 | .05 | .02 |

Houston Oilers
| | | | |
|---|---|---|---|
| ☐ 146 Jessie Hester | .12 | .05 | .02 |

Indianapolis Colts
| | | | |
|---|---|---|---|
| ☐ 147 Deion Sanders | .50 | .23 | .06 |

Atlanta Falcons
| | | | |
|---|---|---|---|
| ☐ 148 Keith Henderson | .25 | .11 | .03 |

San Francisco 49ers
| | | | |
|---|---|---|---|
| ☐ 149 Chris Singleton | .08 | .04 | .01 |

New England Patriots
| | | | |
|---|---|---|---|
| ☐ 150 Rod Bernstine | .15 | .07 | .02 |

San Diego Chargers
| | | | |
|---|---|---|---|
| ☐ 151 Quinn Early | .12 | .05 | .02 |

New Orleans Saints
| | | | |
|---|---|---|---|
| ☐ 152 Boomer Esiason | .30 | .14 | .04 |

Cincinnati Bengals
| | | | |
|---|---|---|---|
| ☐ 153 Mike Gann | .08 | .04 | .01 |

Atlanta Falcons
| | | | |
|---|---|---|---|
| ☐ 154 Dino Hackett | .08 | .04 | .01 |

Kansas City Chiefs
| | | | |
|---|---|---|---|
| ☐ 155 Perry Kemp | .08 | .04 | .01 |

Green Bay Packers
| | | | |
|---|---|---|---|
| ☐ 156 Mark Ingram | .12 | .05 | .02 |

New York Giants
| | | | |
|---|---|---|---|
| ☐ 157 Daryl Johnston | .50 | .23 | .06 |

Dallas Cowboys
| | | | |
|---|---|---|---|
| ☐ 158 Eugene Daniel | .08 | .04 | .01 |

Indianapolis Colts
| | | | |
|---|---|---|---|
| ☐ 159 Dalton Hilliard | .08 | .04 | .01 |

New Orleans Saints
| | | | |
|---|---|---|---|
| ☐ 160 Rufus Porter | .08 | .04 | .01 |

Seattle Seahawks
| | | | |
|---|---|---|---|
| ☐ 161 Tunch Ilkin | .08 | .04 | .01 |

Pittsburgh Steelers
| | | | |
|---|---|---|---|
| ☐ 162 James Hasty | .08 | .04 | .01 |

New York Jets
| | | | |
|---|---|---|---|
| ☐ 163 Keith McKeller | .08 | .04 | .01 |

Buffalo Bills
| | | | |
|---|---|---|---|
| ☐ 164 Heath Sherman | .12 | .05 | .02 |

Philadelphia Eagles
| | | | |
|---|---|---|---|
| ☐ 165 Vai Sikahema | .12 | .05 | .02 |

Green Bay Packers
| | | | |
|---|---|---|---|
| ☐ 166 Pat Terrell | .08 | .04 | .01 |

Los Angeles Rams
| | | | |
|---|---|---|---|
| ☐ 167 Anthony Munoz | .12 | .05 | .02 |

Cincinnati Bengals
| | | | |
|---|---|---|---|
| ☐ 168 Brad Edwards | .08 | .04 | .01 |

Washington Redskins
| | | | |
|---|---|---|---|
| ☐ 169 Tom Rathman | .12 | .05 | .02 |

San Francisco 49ers
| | | | |
|---|---|---|---|
| ☐ 170 Steve McMichael | .12 | .05 | .02 |

Chicago Bears
| | | | |
|---|---|---|---|
| ☐ 171 Vaughan Johnson | .12 | .05 | .02 |

New Orleans Saints
| | | | |
|---|---|---|---|
| ☐ 172 Nate Lewis | .50 | .23 | .06 |

San Diego Chargers
| | | | |
|---|---|---|---|
| ☐ 173 Mark Rypien | .15 | .07 | .02 |

Washington Redskins
| | | | |
|---|---|---|---|
| ☐ 174 Rob Moore | .15 | .07 | .02 |

New York Jets
| | | | |
|---|---|---|---|
| ☐ 175 Tim Green | .08 | .04 | .01 |

Atlanta Falcons
| | | | |
|---|---|---|---|
| ☐ 176 Tony Casillas | .08 | .04 | .01 |

Dallas Cowboys
| | | | |
|---|---|---|---|
| ☐ 177 Jon Hand | .08 | .04 | .01 |

Indianapolis Colts
| | | | |
|---|---|---|---|
| ☐ 178 Todd McNair | .08 | .04 | .01 |

Kansas City Chiefs
| | | | |
|---|---|---|---|
| ☐ 179 Toi Cook | .08 | .04 | .01 |

New Orleans Saints
| | | | |
|---|---|---|---|
| ☐ 180 Eddie Brown | .08 | .04 | .01 |

Cincinnati Bengals
| | | | |
|---|---|---|---|
| ☐ 181 Mark Jackson | .12 | .05 | .02 |

Denver Broncos
| | | | |
|---|---|---|---|
| ☐ 182 Pete Stoyanovich | .12 | .05 | .02 |

Miami Dolphins
| | | | |
|---|---|---|---|
| ☐ 183 Bryce Paup | .50 | .23 | .06 |

Green Bay Packers
| | | | |
|---|---|---|---|
| ☐ 184 Anthony Miller | .50 | .23 | .06 |

San Diego Chargers
| | | | |
|---|---|---|---|
| ☐ 185 Dan Saleaumua | .08 | .04 | .01 |

Kansas City Chiefs
| | | | |
|---|---|---|---|
| ☐ 186 Guy McIntyre | .12 | .05 | .02 |

San Francisco
| | | | |
|---|---|---|---|
| ☐ 187 Broderick Thomas | .12 | .05 | .02 |

Tampa Bay Buccaneers
| | | | |
|---|---|---|---|
| ☐ 188 Frank Warren | .08 | .04 | .01 |

New Orleans Saints
| | | | |
|---|---|---|---|
| ☐ 189 Drew Hill | .12 | .05 | .02 |

Houston Oilers
| | | | |
|---|---|---|---|
| ☐ 190 Reggie White | .40 | .18 | .05 |

Philadelphia Eagles
| | | | |
|---|---|---|---|
| ☐ 191 Chris Hinton | .08 | .04 | .01 |

Atlanta Falcons
| | | | |
|---|---|---|---|
| ☐ 192 David Little | .08 | .04 | .01 |

Pittsburgh Steelers
| | | | |
|---|---|---|---|
| ☐ 193 David Fulcher | .08 | .04 | .01 |

Cincinnati Bengals
| | | | |
|---|---|---|---|
| ☐ 194 Clarence Verdin | .08 | .04 | .01 |

Indianapolis Colts
| | | | |
|---|---|---|---|
| ☐ 195 Junior Seau | .75 | .35 | .09 |

San Diego Chargers
| | | | |
|---|---|---|---|
| ☐ 196 Blair Thomas | .12 | .05 | .02 |

New York Jets
| | | | |
|---|---|---|---|
| ☐ 197 Stan Brock | .08 | .04 | .01 |

New Orleans Saints
| | | | |
|---|---|---|---|
| ☐ 198 Gary Clark | .15 | .07 | .02 |

Washington Redskins
| | | | |
|---|---|---|---|
| ☐ 199 Michael Irvin | 2.00 | .90 | .25 |

Dallas Cowboys
| | | | |
|---|---|---|---|
| ☐ 200 Ronnie Harmon | .08 | .04 | .01 |

San Diego Chargers
| | | | |
|---|---|---|---|
| ☐ 201 Steve Young | 1.00 | .45 | .13 |

San Francisco 49ers
| | | | |
|---|---|---|---|
| ☐ 202 Brian Noble | .08 | .04 | .01 |

Green Bay Packers
| | | | |
|---|---|---|---|
| ☐ 203 Dan Stryzinski | .08 | .04 | .01 |

Pittsburgh Steelers
| | | | |
|---|---|---|---|
| ☐ 204 Darryl Talley | .12 | .05 | .02 |

| |  |  |  | | | |
|---|---|---|---|---|---|---|
| | | | Buffalo Bills | | | |
| ☐ | 205 | David Alexander | | .08 | .04 | .01 |
| | | | Philadelphia Eagles | | | |
| ☐ | 206 | Pat Swilling | | .15 | .07 | .02 |
| | | | New Orleans Saints | | | |
| ☐ | 207 | Gary Plummer | | .08 | .04 | .01 |
| | | | San Diego Chargers | | | |
| ☐ | 208 | Robert Delpino | | .12 | .05 | .02 |
| | | | Los Angeles Rams | | | |
| ☐ | 209 | Norm Johnson | | .08 | .04 | .01 |
| | | | Atlanta Falcons | | | |
| ☐ | 210 | Mike Singletary | | .15 | .07 | .02 |
| | | | Chicago Bears | | | |
| ☐ | 211 | Anthony Johnson | | .08 | .04 | .01 |
| | | | Indianapolis Colts | | | |
| ☐ | 212 | Eric Allen | | .12 | .05 | .02 |
| | | | Philadelphia Eagles | | | |
| ☐ | 213 | Gill Fenerty | | .12 | .05 | .02 |
| | | | New Orleans Saints | | | |
| ☐ | 214 | Neil Smith | | .15 | .07 | .02 |
| | | | Kansas City Chiefs | | | |
| ☐ | 215 | Joe Phillips | | .08 | .04 | .01 |
| | | | San Diego Chargers | | | |
| ☐ | 216 | Ottis Anderson | | .12 | .05 | .02 |
| | | | New York Giants | | | |
| ☐ | 217 | LeRoy Butler | | .08 | .04 | .01 |
| | | | Green Bay Packers | | | |
| ☐ | 218 | Ray Childress | | .12 | .05 | .02 |
| | | | Houston Oilers | | | |
| ☐ | 219 | Rodney Holman | | .08 | .04 | .01 |
| | | | Cincinnati Bengals | | | |
| ☐ | 220 | Kevin Fagan | | .08 | .04 | .01 |
| | | | San Francisco 49ers | | | |
| ☐ | 221 | Bruce Smith | | .15 | .07 | .02 |
| | | | Buffalo Bills | | | |
| ☐ | 222 | Brad Muster | | .12 | .05 | .02 |
| | | | Chicago Bears | | | |
| ☐ | 223 | Mike Horan | | .08 | .04 | .01 |
| | | | Denver Broncos | | | |
| ☐ | 224 | Steve Atwater | | .15 | .07 | .02 |
| | | | Denver Broncos | | | |
| ☐ | 225 | Rich Gannon | | .12 | .05 | .02 |
| | | | Minnesota Vikings | | | |
| ☐ | 226 | Anthony Pleasant | | .08 | .04 | .01 |
| | | | Cleveland Browns | | | |
| ☐ | 227 | Steve Jordan | | .12 | .05 | .02 |
| | | | Minnesota Vikings | | | |
| ☐ | 228 | Lomas Brown | | .08 | .04 | .01 |
| | | | Detroit Lions | | | |
| ☐ | 229 | Jackie Slater | | .12 | .05 | .02 |
| | | | Los Angeles Rams | | | |
| ☐ | 230 | Brad Baxter | | .12 | .05 | .02 |
| | | | New York Jets | | | |
| ☐ | 231 | Joe Morris | | .12 | .05 | .02 |
| | | | Cleveland Browns | | | |
| ☐ | 232 | Marcus Allen | | .50 | .23 | .06 |
| | | | Los Angeles Raiders | | | |
| ☐ | 233 | Chris Warren | | .75 | .35 | .09 |
| | | | Seattle Seahawks | | | |
| ☐ | 234 | Johnny Johnson | | .75 | .35 | .09 |
| | | | Phoenix Cardinals | | | |
| ☐ | 235 | Phil Simms | | .15 | .07 | .02 |
| | | | New York Giants | | | |
| ☐ | 236 | Dave Krieg | | .12 | .05 | .02 |
| | | | Seattle Seahawks | | | |
| ☐ | 237 | Jim McMahon | | .15 | .07 | .02 |
| | | | Philadelphia Eagles | | | |
| ☐ | 238 | Richard Dent | | .12 | .05 | .02 |
| | | | Chicago Bears | | | |
| ☐ | 239 | John Washington | | .15 | .07 | .02 |
| | | | New York Giants | | | |
| ☐ | 240 | Sammie Smith | | .08 | .04 | .01 |
| | | | Miami Dolphins | | | |
| ☐ | 241 | Brian Brennan | | .08 | .04 | .01 |
| | | | Cleveland Browns | | | |
| ☐ | 242 | Cortez Kennedy | | .75 | .35 | .09 |
| | | | Seattle Seahawks | | | |
| ☐ | 243 | Tim McDonald | | .08 | .04 | .01 |
| | | | Phoenix Cardinals | | | |
| ☐ | 244 | Charles Haley | | .12 | .05 | .02 |
| | | | San Francisco 49ers | | | |
| ☐ | 245 | Joey Browner | | .08 | .04 | .01 |
| | | | Minnesota Vikings | | | |
| ☐ | 246 | Eddie Murray | | .12 | .05 | .02 |
| | | | Detroit Lions | | | |
| ☐ | 247 | Bob Golic | | .08 | .04 | .01 |
| | | | Los Angeles Raiders | | | |
| ☐ | 248 | Myron Guyton | | .08 | .04 | .01 |
| | | | New York Giants | | | |
| ☐ | 249 | Dennis Byrd | | .12 | .05 | .02 |
| | | | New York Jets | | | |
| ☐ | 250 | Barry Sanders | | 2.50 | 1.15 | .30 |
| | | | Detroit Lions | | | |
| ☐ | 251 | Clay Matthews | | .12 | .05 | .02 |
| | | | Cleveland Browns | | | |
| ☐ | 252 | Pepper Johnson | | .12 | .05 | .02 |
| | | | New York Giants | | | |
| ☐ | 253 | Eric Swann | | .50 | .23 | .06 |
| | | | Phoenix Cardinals | | | |
| ☐ | 254 | Lamar Lathon | | .08 | .04 | .01 |
| | | | Houston Oilers | | | |
| ☐ | 255 | Andre Tippett | | .12 | .05 | .02 |
| | | | New England Patriots | | | |
| ☐ | 256 | Tom Newberry | | .08 | .04 | .01 |
| | | | Los Angeles Rams | | | |
| ☐ | 257 | Kyle Clifton | | .08 | .04 | .01 |
| | | | New York Jets | | | |
| ☐ | 258 | Leslie O'Neal | | .12 | .05 | .02 |
| | | | San Diego Chargers | | | |
| ☐ | 259 | Bubba McDowell | | .08 | .04 | .01 |
| | | | Houston Oilers | | | |
| ☐ | 260 | Scott Davis | | .08 | .04 | .01 |
| | | | Los Angeles Raiders | | | |
| ☐ | 261 | Wilber Marshall | | .12 | .05 | .02 |
| | | | Washington Redskins | | | |
| ☐ | 262 | Marv Cook | | .08 | .04 | .01 |
| | | | New England Patriots | | | |
| ☐ | 263 | Jeff Lageman | | .08 | .04 | .01 |
| | | | New York Jets | | | |
| ☐ | 264 | Mike Young | | .08 | .04 | .01 |
| | | | Denver Broncos | | | |
| ☐ | 265 | Gary Zimmerman | | .08 | .04 | .01 |
| | | | Minnesota Vikings | | | |
| ☐ | 266 | Mike Munchak | | .12 | .05 | .02 |
| | | | Houston Oilers | | | |
| ☐ | 267 | David Treadwell | | .08 | .04 | .01 |
| | | | Denver Broncos | | | |
| ☐ | 268 | Steve Wisniewski | | .08 | .04 | .01 |
| | | | Los Angeles Raiders | | | |
| ☐ | 269 | Mark Duper | | .12 | .05 | .02 |
| | | | Miami Dolphins | | | |
| ☐ | 270 | Chris Spielman | | .12 | .05 | .02 |
| | | | Detroit Lions | | | |
| ☐ | 271 | Brett Perriman | | .15 | .07 | .02 |
| | | | Detroit Lions | | | |
| ☐ | 272 | Lionel Washington | | .08 | .04 | .01 |
| | | | Los Angeles Raiders | | | |
| ☐ | 273 | Lawrence Taylor | | .40 | .18 | .05 |
| | | | New York Giants | | | |
| ☐ | 274 | Mark Collins | | .08 | .04 | .01 |
| | | | New York Giants | | | |
| ☐ | 275 | Mark Carrier | | .12 | .05 | .02 |
| | | | Tampa Bay Buccaneers | | | |
| ☐ | 276 | Paul Gruber | | .12 | .05 | .02 |
| | | | Tampa Bay Buccaneers | | | |
| ☐ | 277 | Earnest Byner | | .15 | .07 | .02 |
| | | | Washington Redskins | | | |
| ☐ | 278 | Andre Collins | | .08 | .04 | .01 |
| | | | Washington Redskins | | | |
| ☐ | 279 | Reggie Cobb | | .75 | .35 | .09 |
| | | | Tampa Bay Buccaneers | | | |
| ☐ | 280 | Art Monk | | .15 | .07 | .02 |
| | | | Washington Redskins | | | |
| ☐ | 281 | Henry Jones | | .50 | .23 | .06 |
| | | | Buffalo Bills | | | |
| ☐ | 282 | Mike Pritchard | | 2.00 | .90 | .25 |
| | | | Atlanta Falcons | | | |
| ☐ | 283 | Moe Gardner | | .25 | .11 | .03 |
| | | | Atlanta Falcons | | | |
| ☐ | 284 | Chris Zorich | | .60 | .25 | .08 |
| | | | Chicago Bears | | | |
| ☐ | 285 | Keith Traylor | | .08 | .04 | .01 |
| | | | Denver Broncos | | | |
| ☐ | 286 | Mike Dumas | | .10 | .05 | .01 |
| | | | Houston Oilers | | | |
| ☐ | 287 | Ed King | | .08 | .04 | .01 |
| | | | Cleveland Browns | | | |
| ☐ | 288 | Russell Maryland | | 1.00 | .45 | .13 |
| | | | Dallas Cowboys | | | |
| ☐ | 289 | Alfred Williams | | .30 | .14 | .04 |
| | | | Cincinnati Bengals | | | |
| ☐ | 290 | Derek Russell | | .50 | .23 | .06 |
| | | | Denver Broncos | | | |
| ☐ | 291 | Vinnie Clark | | .08 | .04 | .01 |
| | | | Green Bay Packers | | | |
| ☐ | 292 | Mike Croel | | .40 | .18 | .05 |
| | | | Denver Broncos | | | |
| ☐ | 293 | Todd Marinovich | | .12 | .05 | .02 |
| | | | Los Angeles Raiders | | | |
| ☐ | 294 | Phil Hansen | | .30 | .14 | .04 |
| | | | Buffalo Bills | | | |
| ☐ | 295 | Aaron Craver | | .08 | .04 | .01 |
| | | | Miami Dolphins | | | |
| ☐ | 296 | Nick Bell | | .40 | .18 | .05 |
| | | | Los Angeles Raiders | | | |
| ☐ | 297 | Kenny Walker | | .08 | .04 | .01 |
| | | | Denver Broncos | | | |
| ☐ | 298 | Roman Phifer | | .20 | .09 | .03 |
| | | | Los Angeles Rams | | | |
| ☐ | 299 | Kanavis McGhee | | .25 | .11 | .03 |
| | | | New York Giants | | | |
| ☐ | 300 | Ricky Ervins | | .40 | .18 | .05 |
| | | | Washington Redskins | | | |
| ☐ | 301 | Jim Price | | .15 | .07 | .02 |
| | | | Los Angeles Rams | | | |
| ☐ | 302 | John Johnson | | .08 | .04 | .01 |

| | | | |
|---|---|---|---|
| San Francisco 49ers | | | |
| ☐ 303 George Thornton | .08 | .04 | .01 |
| San Diego Chargers | | | |
| ☐ 304 Huey Richardson | .08 | .04 | .01 |
| Pittsburgh Steelers | | | |
| ☐ 305 Harry Colon | .08 | .04 | .01 |
| New England Patriots | | | |
| ☐ 306 Antone Davis | .08 | .04 | .01 |
| Philadelphia Eagles | | | |
| ☐ 307 Todd Lyght | .25 | .11 | .03 |
| Los Angeles Rams | | | |
| ☐ 308 Bryan Cox | 1.00 | .45 | .13 |
| Miami Dolphins | | | |
| ☐ 309 Brad Goebel | .25 | .11 | .03 |
| Philadelphia Eagles | | | |
| ☐ 310 Eric Moten | .08 | .04 | .01 |
| San Diego Chargers | | | |
| ☐ 311 John Kasay | .25 | .11 | .03 |
| Atlanta Falcons | | | |
| ☐ 312 Esera Tuaolo | .08 | .04 | .01 |
| Green Bay Packers | | | |
| ☐ 313 Bobby Wilson | .15 | .07 | .02 |
| Washington Redskins | | | |
| ☐ 314 Mo Lewis | .20 | .09 | .03 |
| New York Jets | | | |
| ☐ 315 Harvey Williams | .40 | .18 | .05 |
| Kansas City Chiefs | | | |
| ☐ 316 Mike Stonebreaker | .08 | .04 | .01 |
| Chicago Bears | | | |
| ☐ 317 Charles McRae | .08 | .04 | .01 |
| Tampa Bay Buccaneers | | | |
| ☐ 318 John Flannery | .08 | .04 | .01 |
| Houston Oilers | | | |
| ☐ 319 Ted Washington | .08 | .04 | .01 |
| San Francisco 49ers | | | |
| ☐ 320 Stanley Richard | .20 | .09 | .03 |
| San Diego Chargers | | | |
| ☐ 321 Browning Nagle | .40 | .18 | .05 |
| New York Jets | | | |
| ☐ 322 Ed McCaffery | .30 | .14 | .04 |
| New York Giants | | | |
| ☐ 323 Jeff Graham | .75 | .35 | .09 |
| Pittsburgh Steelers | | | |
| ☐ 324 Stan Thomas | .08 | .04 | .01 |
| Chicago Bears | | | |
| ☐ 325 Lawrence Dawsey | .40 | .18 | .05 |
| Tampa Bay Buccaneers | | | |
| ☐ 326 Eric Bieniemy | .25 | .11 | .03 |
| San Diego Chargers | | | |
| ☐ 327 Tim Barnett | .40 | .18 | .05 |
| Kansas City Chiefs | | | |
| ☐ 328 Erric Pegram | 3.00 | 1.35 | .40 |
| Atlanta Falcons | | | |
| ☐ 329 Lamar Rogers | .08 | .04 | .01 |
| Cincinnati Bengals | | | |
| ☐ 330 Ernie Mills | .30 | .14 | .04 |
| Pittsburgh Steelers | | | |
| ☐ 331 Pat Harlow | .15 | .07 | .02 |
| New England Patriots | | | |
| ☐ 332 Greg Lewis | .08 | .04 | .01 |
| Denver Broncos | | | |
| ☐ 333 Jarrod Bunch | .35 | .16 | .04 |
| New York Giants | | | |
| ☐ 334 Dan McGwire | .20 | .09 | .03 |
| Seattle Seahawks | | | |
| ☐ 335 Randal Hill | .75 | .35 | .09 |
| Phoenix Cardinals | | | |
| ☐ 336 Leonard Russell | 2.00 | .90 | .25 |
| New England Patriots | | | |
| ☐ 337 Carnell Lake | .08 | .04 | .01 |
| Pittsburgh Steelers | | | |
| ☐ 338 Brian Blades | .15 | .07 | .02 |
| Seattle Seahawks | | | |
| ☐ 339 Darrell Green | .12 | .05 | .02 |
| Washington Redskins | | | |
| ☐ 340 Bobby Humphrey | .12 | .05 | .02 |
| Denver Broncos | | | |
| ☐ 341 Mervyn Fernandez | .08 | .04 | .01 |
| Los Angeles Raiders | | | |
| ☐ 342 Ricky Sanders | .12 | .05 | .02 |
| Washington Redskins | | | |
| ☐ 343 Keith Jackson | .30 | .14 | .04 |
| Philadelphia Eagles | | | |
| ☐ 344 Carl Banks | .12 | .05 | .02 |
| New York Giants | | | |
| ☐ 345 Gill Byrd | .12 | .05 | .02 |
| San Diego Chargers | | | |
| ☐ 346 Al Toon | .12 | .05 | .02 |
| New York Jets | | | |
| ☐ 347 Stephen Baker | .08 | .04 | .01 |
| New York Giants | | | |
| ☐ 348 Randall Cunningham | .30 | .14 | .04 |
| Philadelphia Eagles | | | |
| ☐ 349 Flipper Anderson | .12 | .05 | .02 |
| Los Angeles Rams | | | |
| ☐ 350 Jay Novacek | .30 | .14 | .04 |
| Dallas Cowboys | | | |
| ☐ 351 Steve Young HH | .20 | .09 | .03 |
| vs. Bruce Smith | | | |
| ☐ 352 Barry Sanders HH | .60 | .25 | .08 |
| vs. Joey Browner | | | |
| ☐ 353 Joe Montana HH | .60 | .25 | .08 |
| vs. Mark Carrier | | | |
| ☐ 354 Thurman Thomas HH | .50 | .23 | .06 |
| vs. Lawrence Taylor | | | |
| ☐ 355 Jerry Rice HH | .50 | .23 | .06 |
| vs. Darrell Green | | | |
| ☐ 356 Warren Moon TECH | .25 | .11 | .03 |
| Houston Oilers | | | |
| ☐ 357 Anthony Munoz TECH | .17 | .08 | .02 |
| Cincinnati Bengals | | | |
| ☐ 358 Barry Sanders TECH | 1.00 | .45 | .13 |
| Detroit Lions | | | |
| ☐ 359 Jerry Rice TECH | .75 | .35 | .09 |
| San Francisco 49ers | | | |
| ☐ 360 Joey Browner TECH | .10 | .05 | .01 |
| Minnesota Vikings | | | |
| ☐ 361 Morten Andersen TECH | .10 | .05 | .01 |
| New Orleans Saints | | | |
| ☐ 362 Sean Landeta TECH | .10 | .05 | .01 |
| New York Giants | | | |
| ☐ 363 Thurman Thomas GW | .50 | .23 | .06 |
| Buffalo Bills | | | |
| ☐ 364 Emmitt Smith GW | 3.00 | 1.35 | .40 |
| Dallas Cowboys | | | |
| ☐ 365 Gaston Green GW | .10 | .05 | .01 |
| Denver Broncos | | | |
| ☐ 366 Barry Sanders GW | 1.00 | .45 | .13 |
| Detroit Lions | | | |
| ☐ 367 Christian Okoye GW | .10 | .05 | .01 |
| Kansas City Chiefs | | | |
| ☐ 368 Earnest Byner GW | .15 | .07 | .02 |
| Washington Redskins | | | |
| ☐ 369 Neal Anderson GW | .10 | .05 | .01 |
| Chicago Bears | | | |
| ☐ 370 Herschel Walker GW | .15 | .07 | .02 |
| Minnesota Vikings | | | |
| ☐ 371 Rodney Hampton GW | .75 | .35 | .09 |
| New York Giants | | | |
| ☐ 372 Darryl Talley IDOL | .10 | .05 | .01 |
| Ted Hendricks | | | |
| ☐ 373 Mark Carrier IDOL | .10 | .05 | .01 |
| Ronnie Lott | | | |
| ☐ 374 Jim Breech IDOL | .10 | .05 | .01 |
| Jan Stenerud | | | |
| ☐ 375 Rodney Hampton IDOL | .35 | .16 | .04 |
| Ottis Anderson | | | |
| ☐ 376 Kevin Mack IDOL | .10 | .05 | .01 |
| Earnest Byner | | | |
| ☐ 377 Steve Jordan IDOL | .15 | .07 | .02 |
| Oscar Robertson | | | |
| ☐ 378 Boomer Esiason IDOL | .15 | .07 | .02 |
| Bert Jones | | | |
| ☐ 379 Steve DeBerg IDOL | .15 | .07 | .02 |
| Roman Gabriel | | | |
| ☐ 380 Al Toon IDOL | .10 | .05 | .01 |
| Wesley Walker | | | |
| ☐ 381 Ronnie Lott IDOL | .15 | .07 | .02 |
| Charley Taylor | | | |
| ☐ 382 Henry Ellard IDOL | .10 | .05 | .01 |
| Bob Hayes | | | |
| ☐ 383 Troy Aikman IDOL | 1.25 | .55 | .16 |
| Roger Staubach | | | |
| ☐ 384 Thurman Thomas IDOL | .50 | .23 | .06 |
| Earl Campbell | | | |
| ☐ 385 Dan Marino IDOL | .75 | .35 | .09 |
| Terry Bradshaw | | | |
| ☐ 386 Howie Long IDOL | .25 | .11 | .03 |
| Joe Green | | | |
| ☐ 387 Franco Harris | .15 | .07 | .02 |
| Pittsburgh Steelers | | | |
| Immaculate Reception | | | |
| ☐ 388 Esera Tuaolo | .08 | .04 | .01 |
| Green Bay Packers | | | |
| ☐ 389 Super Bowl XXVI | .08 | .04 | .01 |
| (Super Bowl Records) | | | |
| ☐ 390 Charles Mann | .13 | .06 | .02 |
| Washington Redskins | | | |
| ☐ 391 Kenny Walker | .08 | .04 | .01 |
| Denver Broncos | | | |
| ☐ 392 Reggie Roby | .08 | .04 | .01 |
| Miami Dolphins | | | |
| ☐ 393 Bruce Pickens | .20 | .09 | .03 |
| Atlanta Falcons | | | |
| ☐ 394 Ray Childress SL | .10 | .05 | .01 |
| Houston Oilers | | | |
| ☐ 395 Karl Mecklenburg SL | .10 | .05 | .01 |
| Denver Broncos | | | |
| ☐ 396 Dean Biasucci SL | .10 | .05 | .01 |
| Indianapolis Colts | | | |
| ☐ 397 John Alt SL | .10 | .05 | .01 |
| Kansas City Chiefs | | | |
| ☐ 398 Marcus Allen SL | .25 | .11 | .03 |
| Los Angeles Raiders | | | |
| ☐ 399 John Offerdahl SL | .10 | .05 | .01 |
| Miami Dolphins | | | |

| | | | | |
|---|---|---|---|---|
| ☐ 400 | Richard Tardits SL | .10 | .05 | .01 |
| | New England Patriots | | | |
| ☐ 401 | Al Toon SL | .10 | .05 | .01 |
| | New York Jets | | | |
| ☐ 402 | Joey Browner SL | .10 | .05 | .01 |
| | Minnesota Vikings | | | |
| ☐ 403 | Spencer Tillman SL | .20 | .09 | .03 |
| | New York Giants | | | |
| ☐ 404 | Jay Novacek SL | .15 | .07 | .02 |
| | Dallas Cowboys | | | |
| ☐ 405 | Stephen Braggs SL | .10 | .05 | .01 |
| | Cleveland Browns | | | |
| ☐ 406 | Mike Tice SL | .20 | .09 | .03 |
| | Seattle Seahawks | | | |
| ☐ 407 | Kevin Greene SL | .10 | .05 | .01 |
| | Los Angeles Rams | | | |
| ☐ 408 | Reggie White SL | .25 | .11 | .03 |
| | Philadelphia Eagles | | | |
| ☐ 409 | Brian Noble SL | .10 | .05 | .01 |
| | Green Bay Packers | | | |
| ☐ 410 | Bart Oates SL | .10 | .05 | .01 |
| | New York Giants | | | |
| ☐ 411 | Art Monk SL | .15 | .07 | .02 |
| | Washington Redskins | | | |
| ☐ 412 | Ron Wolfley SL | .10 | .05 | .01 |
| | Phoenix Cardinals | | | |
| ☐ 413 | Louis Lipps SL | .10 | .05 | .01 |
| | Pittsburgh Steelers | | | |
| ☐ 414 | Dante Jones SL | .60 | .25 | .08 |
| | Chicago Bears | | | |
| ☐ 415 | Kenneth Davis SL | .10 | .05 | .01 |
| | Buffalo Bills | | | |

## 1992 Pinnacle Samples

This six-card sample set measures the standard size (2 1/2" by 3 1/2"), and features action color player photos on a black card face. The image of the player is partially cut out and extends beyond the photo background. A thin white line forms a frame near the card edge. The player's name appears at the bottom in a gradated bar that reflects the team's color. The horizontally oriented backs have white borders and black backgrounds. A gradated purple bar at the top contains the player's name, the word "sample," and the card number. A close-up player photo appears in the center. The back is rounded out with biography, statistics (1991 and career), player profile, and a picture of the team helmet in a circular format.

| | MINT | EXC | G-VG |
|---|---|---|---|
| COMPLETE SET (6) | 6.00 | 2.40 | .60 |
| COMMON PLAYER | 1.00 | .40 | .10 |
| | | | |
| ☐ 1 Reggie White | 1.50 | .60 | .15 |
| Philadelphia Eagles | | | |
| ☐ 5 Pepper Johnson | 1.00 | .40 | .10 |
| New York Giants | | | |
| ☐ 19 Chris Spielman | 1.00 | .40 | .10 |
| Detroit Lions | | | |
| ☐ 59 Mike Croel | 1.25 | .50 | .12 |
| Denver Broncos | | | |
| ☐ 100 Bobby Hebert | 1.00 | .40 | .10 |
| New Orleans Saints | | | |
| ☐ 102 Rodney Hampton | 2.00 | .80 | .20 |
| New York Giants | | | |

## 1992 Pinnacle SB XXVII Promo Panel

This panel measures approximately 7" by 10" and features two rows of four cards each. If cut, the cards would measure the standard size (2 1/2" by 3 1/2"). The fronts display color action player photos on a black card face accented by thin white border stripes. The backs are white and carry the Super Bowl XXVII emblem, the player's name, and various logos. Since neither the sheet nor the individual cards are

numbered, the cards are listed below beginning in the upper left corner and ending in the lower right corner.

| | MINT | EXC | G-VG |
|---|---|---|---|
| COMPLETE SET (1) | 5.00 | 2.00 | .50 |
| COMMON PANEL | 5.00 | 2.00 | .50 |
| | | | |
| ☐ 1 SB XXVII Promo Panel | 5.00 | 2.00 | .50 |
| John Elway | | | |
| Denver Broncos | | | |
| Sterling Sharpe | | | |
| Green Bay Packers | | | |
| Warren Moon | | | |
| Houston Oilers | | | |
| Tommy Vardell | | | |
| Cleveland Browns | | | |
| Derrick Thomas | | | |
| Kansas City Chiefs | | | |
| Pat Swilling | | | |
| New Orleans Saints | | | |
| Neil Smith | | | |
| Kansas City Chiefs | | | |
| Cortez Kennedy | | | |
| Seattle Seahawks | | | |

## 1992 Pinnacle

The 1992 Score Pinnacle set consists of 360 cards measuring the standard size (2 1/2" by 3 1/2"). Thirteen Team Pinnacle cards were randomly inserted throughout the 16-card packs, and a 30-card Team 2000 insert set was included only in the 27-card super packs. The fronts feature action color player photos on a black card face. The image of the player is partially cut out and extends beyond the photo background. A thin white line forms a frame near the card edge. The player's name appears at the bottom in a gradated bar that matches the player's uniform. The horizontally oriented backs have white borders and black backgrounds. A gradated purple bar at the top contains the player's name. A close-up player photo appears in the center. The back is rounded out with biographical and statistical information, and a player profile. The set closes with the following subsets: Rookies (314-330), Sidelines (331-334), Gamewinners (335-344), Hall of Famers (345-347), and Idols (348-357). The cards are numbered on the back. Rookie Cards include Steve Bono, Edgar Bennett, Amp Lee, and Tommy Vardell.

| | MINT | EXC | G-VG |
|---|---|---|---|
| COMPLETE SET (360) | 25.00 | 11.50 | 3.10 |
| COMMON PLAYER (1-360) | .08 | .04 | .01 |
| | | | |
| ☐ 1 Reggie White | .30 | .14 | .04 |
| Philadelphia Eagles | | | |
| ☐ 2 Eric Green | .12 | .05 | .02 |
| Pittsburgh Steelers | | | |

| | | | |
|---|---|---|---|
| ☐ 3 Craig Heyward | .08 | .04 | .01 |
| New Orleans Saints | | | |
| ☐ 4 Phil Simms | .12 | .05 | .02 |
| New York Giants | | | |
| ☐ 5 Pepper Johnson | .10 | .05 | .01 |
| New York Giants | | | |
| ☐ 6 Sean Landeta | .08 | .04 | .01 |
| New York Giants | | | |
| ☐ 7 Dino Hackett | .08 | .04 | .01 |
| Kansas City Chiefs | | | |
| ☐ 8 Andre Ware | .10 | .05 | .01 |
| Detroit Lions | | | |
| ☐ 9 Ricky Nattiel | .08 | .04 | .01 |
| Denver Broncos | | | |
| ☐ 10 Jim Price | .08 | .04 | .01 |
| Los Angeles Rams | | | |
| ☐ 11 Jim Ritcher | .08 | .04 | .01 |
| Buffalo Bills | | | |
| ☐ 12 Kelly Stouffer | .08 | .04 | .01 |
| Seattle Seahawks | | | |
| ☐ 13 Ray Crockett | .08 | .04 | .01 |
| Detroit Lions | | | |
| ☐ 14 Steve Tasker | .10 | .05 | .01 |
| Buffalo Bills | | | |
| ☐ 15 Barry Sanders | 2.00 | .90 | .25 |
| Detroit Lions | | | |
| ☐ 16 Pat Swilling | .10 | .05 | .01 |
| New Orleans Saints | | | |
| ☐ 17 Moe Gardner | .08 | .04 | .01 |
| Atlanta Falcons | | | |
| ☐ 18 Steve Young | .75 | .35 | .09 |
| San Francisco 49ers | | | |
| ☐ 19 Chris Spielman | .10 | .05 | .01 |
| Detroit Lions | | | |
| ☐ 20 Richard Dent | .10 | .05 | .01 |
| Chicago Bears | | | |
| ☐ 21 Anthony Munoz | .10 | .05 | .01 |
| Cincinnati Bengals | | | |
| ☐ 22 Thurman Thomas | .75 | .35 | .09 |
| Buffalo Bills | | | |
| ☐ 23 Ricky Sanders | .10 | .05 | .01 |
| Washington Redskins | | | |
| ☐ 24 Steve Atwater | .10 | .05 | .01 |
| Denver Broncos | | | |
| ☐ 25 Tony Tolbert | .08 | .04 | .01 |
| Dallas Cowboys | | | |
| ☐ 26 Haywood Jeffires | .12 | .05 | .02 |
| Houston Oilers | | | |
| ☐ 27 Duane Bickett | .08 | .04 | .01 |
| Indianapolis Colts | | | |
| ☐ 28 Tim McDonald | .08 | .04 | .01 |
| Phoenix Cardinals | | | |
| ☐ 29 Cris Carter | .12 | .05 | .02 |
| Minnesota Vikings | | | |
| ☐ 30 Derrick Thomas | .30 | .14 | .04 |
| Kansas City Chiefs | | | |
| ☐ 31 Hugh Millen | .10 | .05 | .01 |
| New England Patriots | | | |
| ☐ 32 Bart Oates | .08 | .04 | .01 |
| New York Giants | | | |
| ☐ 33 Darryl Talley | .10 | .05 | .01 |
| Buffalo Bills | | | |
| ☐ 34 Marion Butts | .12 | .05 | .02 |
| San Diego Chargers | | | |
| ☐ 35 Pete Stoyanovich | .10 | .05 | .01 |
| Miami Dolphins | | | |
| ☐ 36 Ronnie Lott | .12 | .05 | .02 |
| Los Angeles Raiders | | | |
| ☐ 37 Simon Fletcher | .10 | .05 | .01 |
| Denver Broncos | | | |
| ☐ 38 Morten Andersen | .10 | .05 | .01 |
| New Orleans Saints | | | |
| ☐ 39 Clyde Simmons | .10 | .05 | .01 |
| Philadelphia Eagles | | | |
| ☐ 40 Mark Rypien | .12 | .05 | .02 |
| Washington Redskins | | | |
| ☐ 41 Henry Ellard | .10 | .05 | .01 |
| Los Angeles Rams | | | |
| ☐ 42 Michael Irvin | 1.25 | .55 | .16 |
| Dallas Cowboys | | | |
| ☐ 43 Louis Lipps | .10 | .05 | .01 |
| Pittsburgh Steelers | | | |
| ☐ 44 John L. Williams | .10 | .05 | .01 |
| Seattle Seahawks | | | |
| ☐ 45 Broderick Thomas | .08 | .04 | .01 |
| Tampa Bay Buccaneers | | | |
| ☐ 46 Don Majkowski | .10 | .05 | .01 |
| Green Bay Packers | | | |
| ☐ 47 William Perry | .10 | .05 | .01 |
| Chicago Bears | | | |
| ☐ 48 David Fulcher | .08 | .04 | .01 |
| Cincinnati Bengals | | | |
| ☐ 49 Tony Bennett | .10 | .05 | .01 |
| Green Bay Packers | | | |
| ☐ 50 Clay Matthews | .10 | .05 | .01 |
| Cleveland Browns | | | |
| ☐ 51 Warren Moon | .35 | .16 | .04 |

| | | | |
|---|---|---|---|
| Houston Oilers | | | |
| ☐ 52 Bruce Armstrong | .08 | .04 | .01 |
| New England Patriots | | | |
| ☐ 53 Bill Brooks | .10 | .05 | .01 |
| Indianapolis Colts | | | |
| ☐ 54 Greg Townsend | .08 | .04 | .01 |
| Los Angeles Raiders | | | |
| ☐ 55 Steve Broussard | .10 | .05 | .01 |
| Atlanta Falcons | | | |
| ☐ 56 Mel Gray | .10 | .05 | .01 |
| Detroit Lions | | | |
| ☐ 57 Kevin Mack | .10 | .05 | .01 |
| Cleveland Browns | | | |
| ☐ 58 Emmitt Smith | 4.00 | 1.80 | .50 |
| Dallas Cowboys | | | |
| ☐ 59 Mike Croel | .10 | .05 | .01 |
| Denver Broncos | | | |
| ☐ 60 Brian Mitchell | .12 | .05 | .02 |
| Washington Redskins | | | |
| ☐ 61 Bennie Blades | .08 | .04 | .01 |
| Detroit Lions | | | |
| ☐ 62 Carnell Lake | .08 | .04 | .01 |
| Pittsburgh Steelers | | | |
| ☐ 63 Cornelius Bennett | .12 | .05 | .02 |
| Buffalo Bills | | | |
| ☐ 64 Darrell Thompson | .10 | .05 | .01 |
| Green Bay Packers | | | |
| ☐ 65 Jessie Hester | .08 | .04 | .01 |
| Indianapolis Colts | | | |
| ☐ 66 Marv Cook | .10 | .05 | .01 |
| New England Patriots | | | |
| ☐ 67 Tim Brown | .40 | .18 | .05 |
| Los Angeles Raiders | | | |
| ☐ 68 Mark Duper | .10 | .05 | .01 |
| Miami Dolphins | | | |
| ☐ 69 Robert Delpino | .10 | .05 | .01 |
| Los Angeles Rams | | | |
| ☐ 70 Eric Martin | .10 | .05 | .01 |
| New Orleans Saints | | | |
| ☐ 71 Wendell Davis | .08 | .04 | .01 |
| Chicago Bears | | | |
| ☐ 72 Vaughan Johnson | .10 | .05 | .01 |
| New Orleans Saints | | | |
| ☐ 73 Brian Blades | .10 | .05 | .01 |
| Seattle Seahawks | | | |
| ☐ 74 Ed King | .08 | .04 | .01 |
| Cleveland Browns | | | |
| ☐ 75 Gaston Green | .10 | .05 | .01 |
| Denver Broncos | | | |
| ☐ 76 Christian Okoye | .10 | .05 | .01 |
| Kansas City Chiefs | | | |
| ☐ 77 Rohn Stark | .08 | .04 | .01 |
| Indianapolis Colts | | | |
| ☐ 78 Kevin Greene | .10 | .05 | .01 |
| Los Angeles Rams | | | |
| ☐ 79 Jay Novacek | .25 | .11 | .03 |
| Dallas Cowboys | | | |
| ☐ 80 Chip Lohmiller | .10 | .05 | .01 |
| Washington Redskins | | | |
| ☐ 81 Cris Dishman | .10 | .05 | .01 |
| Houston Oilers | | | |
| ☐ 82 Ethan Horton | .08 | .04 | .01 |
| Los Angeles Raiders | | | |
| ☐ 83 Pat Harlow | .08 | .04 | .01 |
| New England Patriots | | | |
| ☐ 84 Mark Ingram | .10 | .05 | .01 |
| New York Giants | | | |
| ☐ 85 Mark Carrier | .10 | .05 | .01 |
| Chicago Bears | | | |
| ☐ 86 Sam Mills | .10 | .05 | .01 |
| New Orleans Saints | | | |
| ☐ 87 Mark Higgs | .15 | .07 | .02 |
| Miami Dolphins | | | |
| ☐ 88 Keith Jackson | .12 | .05 | .02 |
| Philadelphia Eagles | | | |
| ☐ 89 Gary Anderson | .08 | .04 | .01 |
| Pittsburgh Steelers | | | |
| ☐ 90 Ken Harvey | .08 | .04 | .01 |
| Phoenix Cardinals | | | |
| ☐ 91 Anthony Carter | .10 | .05 | .01 |
| Minnesota Vikings | | | |
| ☐ 92 Randall McDaniel | .08 | .04 | .01 |
| Minnesota Vikings | | | |
| ☐ 93 Johnny Johnson | .20 | .09 | .03 |
| Phoenix Cardinals | | | |
| ☐ 94 Shane Conlan | .10 | .05 | .01 |
| Buffalo Bills | | | |
| ☐ 95 Sterling Sharpe | 1.25 | .55 | .16 |
| Green Bay Packers | | | |
| ☐ 96 Guy McIntyre | .10 | .05 | .01 |
| San Francisco 49ers | | | |
| ☐ 97 Albert Lewis | .10 | .05 | .01 |
| Kansas City Chiefs | | | |
| ☐ 98 Chris Doleman | .10 | .05 | .01 |
| Minnesota Vikings | | | |
| ☐ 99 Andre Rison | .40 | .18 | .05 |
| Atlanta Falcons | | | |
| ☐ 100 Bobby Hebert | .12 | .05 | .02 |

| | | | |
|---|---|---|---|
| New Orleans Saints | | | |
| ☐ 101 Dan Owens | .08 | .04 | .01 |
| Detroit Lions | | | |
| ☐ 102 Rodney Hampton | .75 | .35 | .09 |
| New York Giants | | | |
| ☐ 103 Ernie Jones | .08 | .04 | .01 |
| Phoenix Cardinals | | | |
| ☐ 104 Reggie Cobb | .12 | .05 | .02 |
| Tampa Bay Buccaneers | | | |
| ☐ 105 Wilber Marshall | .10 | .05 | .01 |
| Washington Redskins | | | |
| ☐ 106 Mike Munchak | .10 | .05 | .01 |
| Houston Oilers | | | |
| ☐ 107 Cortez Kennedy | .20 | .09 | .03 |
| Seattle Seahawks | | | |
| ☐ 108 Todd Lyght | .08 | .04 | .01 |
| Los Angeles Rams | | | |
| ☐ 109 Burt Grossman | .08 | .04 | .01 |
| San Diego Chargers | | | |
| ☐ 110 Ferrell Edmunds | .08 | .04 | .01 |
| Miami Dolphins | | | |
| ☐ 111 Jim Everett | .10 | .05 | .01 |
| Los Angeles Rams | | | |
| ☐ 112 Hardy Nickerson | .08 | .04 | .01 |
| Pittsburgh Steelers | | | |
| ☐ 113 Andre Tippett | .10 | .05 | .01 |
| New England Patriots | | | |
| ☐ 114 Ronnie Harmon | .08 | .04 | .01 |
| San Diego Chargers | | | |
| ☐ 115 Andre Waters | .08 | .04 | .01 |
| Philadelphia Eagles | | | |
| ☐ 116 Ernest Givins | .10 | .05 | .01 |
| Houston Oilers | | | |
| ☐ 117 Eric Hill | .08 | .04 | .01 |
| Phoenix Cardinals | | | |
| ☐ 118 Erric Pegram | .75 | .35 | .09 |
| Atlanta Falcons | | | |
| ☐ 119 Jarrod Bunch | .08 | .04 | .01 |
| New York Giants | | | |
| ☐ 120 Marcus Allen | .10 | .05 | .01 |
| Los Angeles Raiders | | | |
| ☐ 121 Barry Foster | .75 | .35 | .09 |
| Pittsburgh Steelers | | | |
| ☐ 122 Kent Hull | .08 | .04 | .01 |
| Buffalo Bills | | | |
| ☐ 123 Neal Anderson | .10 | .05 | .01 |
| Chicago Bears | | | |
| ☐ 124 Stephen Braggs | .08 | .04 | .01 |
| Cleveland Browns | | | |
| ☐ 125 Nick Lowery | .10 | .05 | .01 |
| Kansas City Chiefs | | | |
| ☐ 126 Jeff Hostetler | .30 | .14 | .04 |
| New York Giants | | | |
| ☐ 127 Michael Carter | .08 | .04 | .01 |
| San Francisco 49ers | | | |
| ☐ 128 Don Warren | .08 | .04 | .01 |
| Washington Redskins | | | |
| ☐ 129 Brad Baxter | .10 | .05 | .01 |
| New York Jets | | | |
| ☐ 130 John Taylor | .12 | .05 | .02 |
| San Francisco 49ers | | | |
| ☐ 131 Harold Green | .10 | .05 | .01 |
| Cincinnati Bengals | | | |
| ☐ 132 Mike Merriweather | .08 | .04 | .01 |
| Minnesota Vikings | | | |
| ☐ 133 Gary Clark | .10 | .05 | .01 |
| Washington Redskins | | | |
| ☐ 134 Vince Buck | .08 | .04 | .01 |
| New Orleans Saints | | | |
| ☐ 135 Dan Saleaumua | .08 | .04 | .01 |
| Kansas City Chiefs | | | |
| ☐ 136 Gary Zimmerman | .08 | .04 | .01 |
| Minnesota Vikings | | | |
| ☐ 137 Richmond Webb | .10 | .05 | .01 |
| Miami Dolphins | | | |
| ☐ 138 Art Monk | .12 | .05 | .02 |
| Washington Redskins | | | |
| ☐ 139 Mervyn Fernandez | .08 | .04 | .01 |
| Los Angeles Raiders | | | |
| ☐ 140 Mark Jackson | .10 | .05 | .01 |
| Denver Broncos | | | |
| ☐ 141 Freddie Joe Nunn | .08 | .04 | .01 |
| Phoenix Cardinals | | | |
| ☐ 142 Jeff Lageman | .08 | .04 | .01 |
| New York Jets | | | |
| ☐ 143 Kenny Walker | .08 | .04 | .01 |
| Denver Broncos | | | |
| ☐ 144 Mark Carrier | .10 | .05 | .01 |
| Tampa Bay Buccaneers | | | |
| ☐ 145 Jon Vaughn | .08 | .04 | .01 |
| New England Patriots | | | |
| ☐ 146 Greg Davis | .08 | .04 | .01 |
| Phoenix Cardinals | | | |
| ☐ 147 Bubby Brister | .10 | .05 | .01 |
| Pittsburgh Steelers | | | |
| ☐ 148 Mo Lewis | .08 | .04 | .01 |
| New York Jets | | | |
| ☐ 149 Howie Long | .10 | .05 | .01 |
| Los Angeles Raiders | | | |
| ☐ 150 Rod Bernstine | .10 | .05 | .01 |
| San Diego Chargers | | | |
| ☐ 151 Nick Bell | .10 | .05 | .01 |
| Los Angeles Raiders | | | |
| ☐ 152 Terry Allen | .35 | .16 | .04 |
| Minnesota Vikings | | | |
| ☐ 153 William Fuller | .08 | .04 | .01 |
| Houston Oilers | | | |
| ☐ 154 Dexter Carter | .10 | .05 | .01 |
| San Francisco 49ers | | | |
| ☐ 155 Gene Atkins | .08 | .04 | .01 |
| New Orleans Saints | | | |
| ☐ 156 Don Beebe | .12 | .05 | .02 |
| Buffalo Bills | | | |
| ☐ 157 Mark Collins | .08 | .04 | .01 |
| New York Giants | | | |
| ☐ 158 Jerry Ball | .10 | .05 | .01 |
| Detroit Lions | | | |
| ☐ 159 Fred Barnett | .12 | .05 | .02 |
| Philadelphia Eagles | | | |
| ☐ 160 Rodney Holman | .08 | .04 | .01 |
| Cincinnati Bengals | | | |
| ☐ 161 Stephen Baker | .08 | .04 | .01 |
| New York Giants | | | |
| ☐ 162 Jeff Graham | .10 | .05 | .01 |
| Pittsburgh Steelers | | | |
| ☐ 163 Leonard Russell | .60 | .25 | .08 |
| New England Patriots | | | |
| ☐ 164 Jeff Gossett | .08 | .04 | .01 |
| Los Angeles Raiders | | | |
| ☐ 165 Vinny Testaverde | .12 | .05 | .02 |
| Tampa Bay Buccaneers | | | |
| ☐ 166 Maurice Hurst | .08 | .04 | .01 |
| New England Patriots | | | |
| ☐ 167 Louis Oliver | .10 | .05 | .01 |
| Miami Dolphins | | | |
| ☐ 168 Jim Morrissey | .08 | .04 | .01 |
| Chicago Bears | | | |
| ☐ 169 Greg Kragen | .08 | .04 | .01 |
| Denver Broncos | | | |
| ☐ 170 Andre Collins | .08 | .04 | .01 |
| Washington Redskins | | | |
| ☐ 171 Dave Meggett | .10 | .05 | .01 |
| New York Giants | | | |
| ☐ 172 Keith Henderson | .08 | .04 | .01 |
| San Francisco 49ers | | | |
| ☐ 173 Vince Newsome | .08 | .04 | .01 |
| Cleveland Browns | | | |
| ☐ 174 Chris Hinton | .08 | .04 | .01 |
| Atlanta Falcons | | | |
| ☐ 175 James Hasty | .08 | .04 | .01 |
| New York Jets | | | |
| ☐ 176 John Offerdahl | .10 | .05 | .01 |
| Miami Dolphins | | | |
| ☐ 177 Lomas Brown | .08 | .04 | .01 |
| Detroit Lions | | | |
| ☐ 178 Neil O'Donnell | 1.00 | .45 | .13 |
| Pittsburgh Steelers | | | |
| ☐ 179 Leonard Marshall | .10 | .05 | .01 |
| New York Giants | | | |
| ☐ 180 Bubba McDowell | .08 | .04 | .01 |
| Houston Oilers | | | |
| ☐ 181 Herman Moore | .60 | .25 | .08 |
| Detroit Lions | | | |
| ☐ 182 Rob Moore | .12 | .05 | .02 |
| New York Jets | | | |
| ☐ 183 Earnest Byner | .10 | .05 | .01 |
| Washington Redskins | | | |
| ☐ 184 Keith McCants | .08 | .04 | .01 |
| Tampa Bay Buccaneers | | | |
| ☐ 185 Floyd Turner | .08 | .04 | .01 |
| New Orleans Saints | | | |
| ☐ 186 Steve Jordan | .10 | .05 | .01 |
| Minnesota Vikings | | | |
| ☐ 187 Nate Odomes | .10 | .05 | .01 |
| Buffalo Bills | | | |
| ☐ 188 Jeff Herrod | .08 | .04 | .01 |
| Indianapolis Colts | | | |
| ☐ 189 Jim Harbaugh | .10 | .05 | .01 |
| Chicago Bears | | | |
| ☐ 190 Jessie Tuggle | .08 | .04 | .01 |
| Atlanta Falcons | | | |
| ☐ 191 Al Smith | .08 | .04 | .01 |
| Houston Oilers | | | |
| ☐ 192 Lawrence Dawsey | .12 | .05 | .02 |
| Tampa Bay Buccaneers | | | |
| ☐ 193 Steve Bono | 1.00 | .45 | .13 |
| San Francisco 49ers | | | |
| ☐ 194 Greg Lloyd | .08 | .04 | .01 |
| Pittsburgh Steelers | | | |
| ☐ 195 Steve Wisniewski | .08 | .04 | .01 |
| Los Angeles Raiders | | | |
| ☐ 196 Larry Kelm | .08 | .04 | .01 |
| Los Angeles Rams | | | |
| ☐ 197 Tommy Kane | .08 | .04 | .01 |
| Seattle Seahawks | | | |
| ☐ 198 Mark Schlereth | .15 | .07 | .02 |

| | | | | | | | | |
|---|---|---|---|---|---|---|---|---|
| Washington Redskins | | | | | Philadelphia Eagles | | | |
| ☐ 199 Ray Childress | .10 | .05 | .01 | ☐ 248 | Bennie Thompson | .20 | .09 | .03 |
| Houston Oilers | | | | | New Orleans Saints | | | |
| ☐ 200 Vincent Brown | .08 | .04 | .01 | ☐ 249 | Tunch Ilkin | .08 | .04 | .01 |
| New England Patriots | | | | | Pittsburgh Steelers | | | |
| ☐ 201 Rodney Peete | .10 | .05 | .01 | ☐ 250 | Brad Edwards | .08 | .04 | .01 |
| Detroit Lions | | | | | Washington Redskins | | | |
| ☐ 202 Dennis Smith | .10 | .05 | .01 | ☐ 251 | Jeff Jaeger | .08 | .04 | .01 |
| Denver Broncos | | | | | Los Angeles Raiders | | | |
| ☐ 203 Bruce Matthews | .10 | .05 | .01 | ☐ 252 | Gill Byrd | .10 | .05 | .01 |
| Houston Oilers | | | | | San Diego Chargers | | | |
| ☐ 204 Rickey Jackson | .10 | .05 | .01 | ☐ 253 | Jeff Feagles | .08 | .04 | .01 |
| New Orleans Saints | | | | | Philadelphia Eagles | | | |
| ☐ 205 Eric Allen | .10 | .05 | .01 | ☐ 254 | Jamie Dukes | .08 | .04 | .01 |
| Philadelphia Eagles | | | | | Atlanta Falcons | | | |
| ☐ 206 Rich Camarillo | .08 | .04 | .01 | ☐ 255 | Greg McMurtry | .08 | .04 | .01 |
| Phoenix Cardinals | | | | | New England Patriots | | | |
| ☐ 207 Jim Lachey | .08 | .04 | .01 | ☐ 256 | Anthony Johnson | .08 | .04 | .01 |
| Washington Redskins | | | | | Indianapolis Colts | | | |
| ☐ 208 Kevin Ross | .10 | .05 | .01 | ☐ 257 | Lamar Lathon | .08 | .04 | .01 |
| Kansas City Chiefs | | | | | Houston Oilers | | | |
| ☐ 209 Irving Fryar | .10 | .05 | .01 | ☐ 258 | John Roper | .08 | .04 | .01 |
| New England Patriots | | | | | Chicago Bears | | | |
| ☐ 210 Mark Clayton | .10 | .05 | .01 | ☐ 259 | Lorenzo White | .10 | .05 | .01 |
| Miami Dolphins | | | | | Houston Oilers | | | |
| ☐ 211 Keith Byars | .10 | .05 | .01 | ☐ 260 | Brian Noble | .08 | .04 | .01 |
| Philadelphia Eagles | | | | | Green Bay Packers | | | |
| ☐ 212 John Elway | 1.00 | .45 | .13 | ☐ 261 | Chris Singleton | .08 | .04 | .01 |
| Denver Broncos | | | | | New England Patriots | | | |
| ☐ 213 Harris Barton | .08 | .04 | .01 | ☐ 262 | Todd Marinovich | .08 | .04 | .01 |
| San Francisco 49ers | | | | | Los Angeles Raiders | | | |
| ☐ 214 Aeneas Williams | .08 | .04 | .01 | ☐ 263 | Jay Hilgenberg | .10 | .05 | .01 |
| Phoenix Cardinals | | | | | Chicago Bears | | | |
| ☐ 215 Rich Gannon | .10 | .05 | .01 | ☐ 264 | Kyle Clifton | .08 | .04 | .01 |
| Minnesota Vikings | | | | | New York Jets | | | |
| ☐ 216 Toi Cook | .08 | .04 | .01 | ☐ 265 | Tony Casillas | .08 | .04 | .01 |
| New Orleans Saints | | | | | Dallas Cowboys | | | |
| ☐ 217 Rod Woodson | .12 | .05 | .02 | ☐ 266 | James Francis | .10 | .05 | .01 |
| Pittsburgh Steelers | | | | | Cincinnati Bengals | | | |
| ☐ 218 Gary Anderson | .10 | .05 | .01 | ☐ 267 | Eddie Anderson | .08 | .04 | .01 |
| Tampa Bay Buccaneers | | | | | Los Angeles Raiders | | | |
| ☐ 219 Reggie Roby | .08 | .04 | .01 | ☐ 268 | Tim Harris | .10 | .05 | .01 |
| Miami Dolphins | | | | | San Francisco 49ers | | | |
| ☐ 220 Karl Mecklenburg | .10 | .05 | .01 | ☐ 269 | James Lofton | .12 | .05 | .02 |
| Denver Broncos | | | | | Buffalo Bills | | | |
| ☐ 221 Rufus Porter | .08 | .04 | .01 | ☐ 270 | Jay Schroeder | .10 | .05 | .01 |
| Seattle Seahawks | | | | | Los Angeles Raiders | | | |
| ☐ 222 Jon Hand | .08 | .04 | .01 | ☐ 271 | Ed West | .08 | .04 | .01 |
| Indianapolis Colts | | | | | Green Bay Packers | | | |
| ☐ 223 Tim Barnett | .10 | .05 | .01 | ☐ 272 | Don Mosebar | .08 | .04 | .01 |
| Kansas City Chiefs | | | | | Los Angeles Raiders | | | |
| ☐ 224 Eric Swann | .10 | .05 | .01 | ☐ 273 | Jackie Slater | .10 | .05 | .01 |
| Phoenix Cardinals | | | | | Los Angeles Rams | | | |
| ☐ 225 Eugene Robinson | .08 | .04 | .01 | ☐ 274 | Fred McAfee | .25 | .11 | .03 |
| Seattle Seahawks | | | | | New Orleans Saints | | | |
| ☐ 226 Mike Young | .08 | .04 | .01 | ☐ 275 | Steve Sewell | .08 | .04 | .01 |
| Denver Broncos | | | | | Denver Broncos | | | |
| ☐ 227 Frank Warren | .08 | .04 | .01 | ☐ 276 | Charles Mann | .10 | .05 | .01 |
| New Orleans Saints | | | | | Washington Redskins | | | |
| ☐ 228 Mike Kenn | .10 | .05 | .01 | ☐ 277 | Ron Hall | .08 | .04 | .01 |
| Atlanta Falcons | | | | | Tampa Bay Buccaneers | | | |
| ☐ 229 Tim Green | .08 | .04 | .01 | ☐ 278 | Darrell Green | .10 | .05 | .01 |
| Atlanta Falcons | | | | | Washington Redskins | | | |
| ☐ 230 Barry Word | .12 | .05 | .02 | ☐ 279 | Jeff Cross | .08 | .04 | .01 |
| Kansas City Chiefs | | | | | Miami Dolphins | | | |
| ☐ 231 Mike Pritchard | .50 | .23 | .06 | ☐ 280 | Jeff Wright | .08 | .04 | .01 |
| Atlanta Falcons | | | | | Buffalo Bills | | | |
| ☐ 232 John Kasay | .08 | .04 | .01 | ☐ 281 | Issiac Holt | .08 | .04 | .01 |
| Seattle Seahawks | | | | | Dallas Cowboys | | | |
| ☐ 233 Derek Russell | .10 | .05 | .01 | ☐ 282 | Dermontti Dawson | .08 | .04 | .01 |
| Denver Broncos | | | | | Pittsburgh Steelers | | | |
| ☐ 234 Jim Breech | .08 | .04 | .01 | ☐ 283 | Michael Haynes | .60 | .25 | .08 |
| Cincinnati Bengals | | | | | Atlanta Falcons | | | |
| ☐ 235 Pierce Holt | .08 | .04 | .01 | ☐ 284 | Tony Mandarich | .08 | .04 | .01 |
| San Francisco 49ers | | | | | Green Bay Packers | | | |
| ☐ 236 Tim Krumrie | .08 | .04 | .01 | ☐ 285 | Leroy Hoard | .10 | .05 | .01 |
| Cincinnati Bengals | | | | | Cleveland Browns | | | |
| ☐ 237 William Roberts | .08 | .04 | .01 | ☐ 286 | Darryl Henley | .08 | .04 | .01 |
| New York Giants | | | | | Los Angeles Rams | | | |
| ☐ 238 Erik Kramer | .20 | .09 | .03 | ☐ 287 | Tim McGee | .08 | .04 | .01 |
| Detroit Lions | | | | | Cincinnati Bengals | | | |
| ☐ 239 Brett Perriman | .10 | .05 | .01 | ☐ 288 | Willie Gault | .10 | .05 | .01 |
| Detroit Lions | | | | | Los Angeles Raiders | | | |
| ☐ 240 Reyna Thompson | .08 | .04 | .01 | ☐ 289 | Dalton Hilliard | .08 | .04 | .01 |
| New York Giants | | | | | New Orleans Saints | | | |
| ☐ 241 Chris Miller | .12 | .05 | .02 | ☐ 290 | Tim McKyer | .10 | .05 | .01 |
| Atlanta Falcons | | | | | Atlanta Falcons | | | |
| ☐ 242 Drew Hill | .10 | .05 | .01 | ☐ 291 | Tom Waddle | .12 | .05 | .02 |
| Atlanta Falcons | | | | | Chicago Bears | | | |
| ☐ 243 Curtis Duncan | .10 | .05 | .01 | ☐ 292 | Eric Thomas | .08 | .04 | .01 |
| Houston Oilers | | | | | Cincinnati Bengals | | | |
| ☐ 244 Seth Joyner | .10 | .05 | .01 | ☐ 293 | Herschel Walker | .08 | .04 | .01 |
| Philadelphia Eagles | | | | | Philadelphia Eagles | | | |
| ☐ 245 Ken Norton Jr. | .12 | .05 | .02 | ☐ 294 | Donnell Woolford | .08 | .04 | .01 |
| Dallas Cowboys | | | | | Chicago Bears | | | |
| ☐ 246 Calvin Williams | .12 | .05 | .02 | ☐ 295 | James Brooks | .10 | .05 | .01 |
| Philadelphia Eagles | | | | | Cleveland Browns | | | |
| ☐ 247 James Joseph | .08 | .04 | .01 | ☐ 296 | Brad Muster | .10 | .05 | .01 |

|  |  |  |  |
|---|---|---|---|
| Chicago Bears | | | |
| ☐ 297 Brent Jones | .12 | .05 | .02 |
| San Francisco 49ers | | | |
| ☐ 298 Erik Howard | .08 | .04 | .01 |
| New York Giants | | | |
| ☐ 299 Alvin Harper UER | .60 | .25 | .08 |
| (Born in Frostproof, | | | |
| not Frostfree) | | | |
| Dallas Cowboys | | | |
| ☐ 300 Joey Browner | .08 | .04 | .01 |
| Minnesota Vikings | | | |
| ☐ 301 Jack Del Rio | .08 | .04 | .01 |
| Minnesota Vikings | | | |
| ☐ 302 Cleveland Gary | .10 | .05 | .01 |
| Los Angeles Rams | | | |
| ☐ 303 Brett Favre | 2.00 | .90 | .25 |
| Green Bay Packers | | | |
| ☐ 304 Freeman McNeil | .08 | .04 | .01 |
| New York Jets | | | |
| ☐ 305 Willie Green | .08 | .04 | .01 |
| Detroit Lions | | | |
| ☐ 306 Percy Snow | .08 | .04 | .01 |
| Kansas City Chiefs | | | |
| ☐ 307 Neil Smith | .12 | .05 | .02 |
| Kansas City Chiefs | | | |
| ☐ 308 Eric Bieniemy | .10 | .05 | .01 |
| San Diego Chargers | | | |
| ☐ 309 Keith Traylor | .08 | .04 | .01 |
| Denver Broncos | | | |
| ☐ 310 Ernie Mills | .08 | .04 | .01 |
| Pittsburgh Steelers | | | |
| ☐ 311 Will Wolford | .08 | .04 | .01 |
| Buffalo Bills | | | |
| ☐ 312 Robert Young | .10 | .05 | .01 |
| Los Angeles Rams | | | |
| ☐ 313 Anthony Smith | .10 | .05 | .01 |
| Los Angeles Raiders | | | |
| ☐ 314 Robert Porcher | .40 | .18 | .05 |
| Detroit Lions | | | |
| ☐ 315 Leon Searcy | .12 | .05 | .02 |
| Pittsburgh Steelers | | | |
| ☐ 316 Amp Lee | .50 | .23 | .06 |
| San Francisco 49ers | | | |
| ☐ 317 Siran Stacy | .20 | .09 | .03 |
| Philadelphia Eagles | | | |
| ☐ 318 Patrick Rowe | .20 | .09 | .03 |
| Cleveland Browns | | | |
| ☐ 319 Chris Mims | .40 | .18 | .05 |
| San Diego Chargers | | | |
| ☐ 320 Matt Elliott | .12 | .05 | .02 |
| Washington Redskins | | | |
| ☐ 321 Ricardo McDonald | .15 | .07 | .02 |
| Cincinnati Bengals | | | |
| ☐ 322 Keith Hamilton | .25 | .11 | .03 |
| New York Giants | | | |
| ☐ 323 Edgar Bennett | .60 | .25 | .08 |
| Green Bay Packers | | | |
| ☐ 324 Chris Hakel | .15 | .07 | .02 |
| Washington Redskins | | | |
| ☐ 325 Dexter McNabb | .12 | .05 | .02 |
| Green Bay Packers | | | |
| ☐ 326 Roderick Milstead | .15 | .07 | .02 |
| Dallas Cowboys | | | |
| ☐ 327 Joe Bowden | .12 | .05 | .02 |
| Houston Oilers | | | |
| ☐ 328 Brian Bollinger | .12 | .05 | .02 |
| San Francisco 49ers | | | |
| ☐ 329 Darryl Williams | .35 | .16 | .04 |
| Cincinnati Bengals | | | |
| ☐ 330 Tommy Vardell | .50 | .23 | .06 |
| Cleveland Browns | | | |
| ☐ 331 Glenn Parker SL | .08 | .04 | .01 |
| Mitch Frerotte | | | |
| Buffalo Bills | | | |
| ☐ 332 Herschel Walker SL | .10 | .05 | .01 |
| Phiadelphia Eagles | | | |
| ☐ 333 Mike Cofer SL | .08 | .04 | .01 |
| San Francisco 49ers | | | |
| ☐ 334 Mark Rypien SL | .10 | .05 | .01 |
| Washington Redskins | | | |
| ☐ 335 Andre Rison GW | .15 | .07 | .02 |
| Atlanta Falcons | | | |
| ☐ 336 Henry Ellard GW | .08 | .04 | .01 |
| Los Angeles Rams | | | |
| ☐ 337 Rob Moore GW | .10 | .05 | .01 |
| New York Jets | | | |
| ☐ 338 Fred Barnett GW | .10 | .05 | .01 |
| Philadelphia Eagles | | | |
| ☐ 339 Mark Clayton GW | .08 | .04 | .01 |
| Miami Dolphins | | | |
| ☐ 340 Eric Martin GW | .08 | .04 | .01 |
| New Orleans Saints | | | |
| ☐ 341 Irving Fryar GW | .08 | .04 | .01 |
| New England Patriots | | | |
| ☐ 342 Tim Brown GW | .20 | .09 | .03 |
| Los Angeles Raiders | | | |
| ☐ 343 Sterling Sharpe GW | .35 | .16 | .04 |
| Green Bay Packers | | | |

|  |  |  |  |
|---|---|---|---|
| ☐ 344 Gary Clark GW | .10 | .05 | .01 |
| Washington Redskins | | | |
| ☐ 345 John Mackey HOF | .08 | .04 | .01 |
| Baltimore Colts | | | |
| ☐ 346 Lem Barney HOF | .08 | .04 | .01 |
| Detroit Lions | | | |
| ☐ 347 John Riggins HOF | .08 | .04 | .01 |
| Washington Redskins | | | |
| ☐ 348 Marion Butts IDOL | .10 | .05 | .01 |
| William Andrews | | | |
| ☐ 349 Jeff Lageman IDOL | .08 | .04 | .01 |
| Jack Lambert | | | |
| ☐ 350 Eric Green IDOL | .10 | .05 | .01 |
| Sam Rutigliano | | | |
| ☐ 351 Reggie White IDOL | .20 | .09 | .03 |
| Bobby Jones | | | |
| ☐ 352 Marv Cook IDOL | .08 | .04 | .01 |
| Dan Gable | | | |
| ☐ 353 John Elway IDOL | .60 | .25 | .08 |
| Roger Staubach | | | |
| ☐ 354 Steve Tasker IDOL | .08 | .04 | .01 |
| Ed Podolak | | | |
| ☐ 355 Nick Lowery IDOL | .08 | .04 | .01 |
| Jan Stenerud | | | |
| ☐ 356 Mark Clayton IDOL | .08 | .04 | .01 |
| Paul Warfield | | | |
| ☐ 357 Warren Moon IDOL | .15 | .07 | .02 |
| Roman Gabriel | | | |
| ☐ 358 Eric Metcalf | .12 | .05 | .02 |
| Cleveland Browns | | | |
| ☐ 359 Charles Haley | .10 | .05 | .01 |
| Dallas Cowboys | | | |
| ☐ 360 Terrell Buckley | .50 | .23 | .06 |
| Green Bay Packers | | | |

## 1992 Pinnacle Team Pinnacle

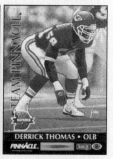

2 of 13

These 13 double-sided cards feature paintings by sports artist Christopher Greco. The cards, which measure the standard size (2 1/2" by 3 1/2"), were randomly inserted into 1992 Score Pinnacle packs. Score estimates the odds of finding a team pinnacle card to be at least one in 36. One side showcases the best offensive player by position while the other side has his defensive counterpart. On both sides, a gold foil stripe carrying the player's name and position and a black stripe appear beneath the portrait. The card number is printed on the back in the black stripe.

|  | MINT | EXC | G-VG |
|---|---|---|---|
| COMPLETE SET (13) | 140.00 | 65.00 | 17.50 |
| COMMON PLAYER (1-13) | 10.00 | 4.50 | 1.25 |
| ☐ 1 Mark Rypien | 12.00 | 5.50 | 1.50 |
| Washington Redskins | | | |
| Ronnie Lott | | | |
| Los Angeles Raiders | | | |
| ☐ 2 Barry Sanders | 30.00 | 13.50 | 3.80 |
| Detroit Lions | | | |
| Derrick Thomas | | | |
| Kansas City Chiefs | | | |
| ☐ 3 Thurman Thomas | 18.00 | 8.00 | 2.30 |
| Buffalo Bills | | | |
| Pat Swilling | | | |
| New Orleans Saints | | | |
| ☐ 4 Eric Green | 10.00 | 4.50 | 1.25 |
| Pittsburgh Steelers | | | |
| Steve Atwater | | | |
| Denver Broncos | | | |
| ☐ 5 Haywood Jeffires | 10.00 | 4.50 | 1.25 |
| Houston Oilers | | | |
| Darrell Green | | | |
| Washington Redskins | | | |
| ☐ 6 Michael Irvin | 18.00 | 8.00 | 2.30 |
| Dallas Cowboys | | | |
| Eric Allen | | | |
| Philadelphia Eagles | | | |

☐ 7 Bruce Matthews ........................ 10.00 4.50 1.25
   Houston Oilers
   Jerry Ball
   Detroit Lions
☐ 8 Steve Wisniewski ..................... 10.00 4.50 1.25
   Los Angeles Raiders
   Pepper Johnson
   New York Giants
☐ 9 William Roberts ...................... 10.00 4.50 1.25
   New York Giants
   Karl Mecklenburg
   Denver Broncos
☐ 10 Jim Lachey ........................... 10.00 4.50 1.25
   Washington Redskins
   William Fuller
   Houston Oilers
☐ 11 Anthony Munoz ..................... 12.00 5.50 1.50
   Cincinnati Bengals
   Reggie White
   Philadelphia Eagles
☐ 12 Mel Gray ............................... 10.00 4.50 1.25
   Detroit Lions
   Steve Tasker
   Buffalo Bills
☐ 13 Jeff Jaeger ........................... 10.00 4.50 1.25
   Los Angeles Raiders
   Jeff Gossett
   Los Angeles Raiders

## 1992 Pinnacle Team 2000

This 30-card standard-size (2 1/2" by 3 1/2") set focuses on young players who are expected to be the NFL's major stars in the year 2000. The cards were inserted two per 27-card jumbo pack. The cards are bordered by a 1/2" black stripe that runs along the left edge and bottom forming a right angle. The two ends of the black stripe are sloped. The words "Team 2000" and the player's name appear in gold foil in the stripe. The team helmet is displayed in the lower left corner. The horizontally oriented backs show a close-up color player photo and a career summary on a black background. The cards are numbered on the back.

|  | MINT | EXC | G-VG |
|---|---|---|---|
| COMPLETE SET (30) | 15.00 | 6.75 | 1.90 |
| COMMON PLAYER (1-30) | .25 | .11 | .03 |

☐ 1 Todd Marinovich ...................... .25 .11 .03
   Los Angeles Raiders
☐ 2 Rodney Hampton ..................... 1.50 .65 .19
   New York Giants
☐ 3 Mike Croel ............................. .30 .14 .04
   Denver Broncos
☐ 4 Leonard Russell ...................... .75 .35 .09
   New England Patriots
☐ 5 Herman Moore ........................ .75 .35 .09
   Detroit Lions
☐ 6 Rob Moore ............................. .30 .14 .04
   New York Jets
☐ 7 Jon Vaughn ............................ .25 .11 .03
   New England Patriots
☐ 8 Lamar Lathon .......................... .25 .11 .03
   Houston Oilers
☐ 9 Ed King ................................. .25 .11 .03
   Cleveland Browns
☐ 10 Moe Gardner ......................... .25 .11 .03
   Atlanta Falcons
☐ 11 Barry Foster .......................... 1.00 .45 .13
   Pittsburgh Steelers
☐ 12 Eric Green ............................ .30 .14 .04
   Pittsburgh Steelers
☐ 13 Kenny Walker ........................ .25 .11 .03
   Denver Broncos
☐ 14 Tim Barnett ........................... .30 .14 .04
   Kansas City Chiefs

☐ 15 Derrick Thomas ...................... .40 .18 .05
   Kansas City Chiefs
☐ 16 Steve Atwater ........................ .25 .11 .03
   Denver Broncos
☐ 17 Nick Bell .............................. .25 .11 .03
   Los Angeles Raiders
☐ 18 John Friesz ........................... .30 .14 .04
   San Diego Chargers
☐ 19 Emmitt Smith ......................... 5.00 2.30 .60
   Dallas Cowboys
☐ 20 Eric Swann ........................... .30 .14 .04
   Phoenix Cardinals
☐ 21 Barry Sanders ....................... 2.50 1.15 .30
   Detroit Lions
☐ 22 Mark Carrier .......................... .25 .11 .03
   Chicago Bears
☐ 23 Brett Favre ............................ 3.00 1.35 .40
   Atlanta Falcons
☐ 24 James Francis ........................ .25 .11 .03
   Cincinnati Bengals
☐ 25 Lawrence Dawsey ................... .30 .14 .04
   Tampa Bay Buccaneers
☐ 26 Keith McCants ........................ .25 .11 .03
   Tampa Bay Buccaneers
☐ 27 Broderick Thomas ................... .25 .11 .03
   Tampa Bay Buccaneers
☐ 28 Mike Pritchard ........................ .50 .23 .06
   Atlanta Falcons
☐ 29 Bruce Pickens ....................... .25 .11 .03
☐ 30 Todd Lyght ............................ .30 .14 .04
   Los Angeles Rams

## 1993 Pinnacle Samples

This sample panel measures approximately 7 1/2" by 7" and features two rows of three cards each. If cut, the cards would measure the standard size (2 1/2" by 3 1/2"). The fronts display color action player photos on a black card face accented by thin white picture frames. The team name and the player's name are printed above and below the picture respectively; the gold-foil stamped Pinnacle logo at the lower right corner rounds out the card face. On a black background, the horizontal backs carry a color close-up photo, biography, career summary, and 1992 season statistics. The cards are numbered at the upper left corner, and the word "Sample" is printed just below Score's anti-counterfeiting device.

|  | MINT | EXC | G-VG |
|---|---|---|---|
| COMPLETE SET (6) | 7.50 | 3.00 | .75 |
| COMMON PLAYER (1-6) | 1.00 | .40 | .10 |

☐ 1 Brett Favre ............................. 3.00 1.20 .30
   Green Bay Packers
☐ 2 Tommy Vardell ........................ 1.50 .60 .15
   Cleveland Browns
☐ 3 Jarrod Bunch ........................... 1.00 .40 .10
   New York Giants
☐ 4 Mike Croel .............................. 1.25 .50 .12
   Denver Broncos
☐ 5 Morten Andersen ..................... 1.00 .40 .10
   New Orleans Saints
☐ 6 Barry Foster ........................... 2.50 1.00 .25
   Pittsburgh Steelers

## 1993 Pinnacle

The 1993 Score Pinnacle set consists of 360 standard-size (2 1/2" by 3 1/2") cards, including a four-card subset saluting the 1993 Hall of Fame inductees, and a four-card Hometown Heroes subset featuring four players who played for their hometown NFL teams. For each order of 20 boxes, Pinnacle would send one of 3,000 autographed cards by their 1993 spokesman, Franco Harris. The black-bordered

Leonard Russell

fronts display color action player photos framed by a thin white line. The team name and the player's name are printed above and below the picture, respectively. On a black background, the horizontal backs carry a color close-up player portrait, biography, career summary, team logo, and 1992 season and career statistics. The set closes with the Hall of Fame (352-355) and Hometown Hero (356-360) subsets. The cards are numbered on the back.

|  | MINT | EXC | G-VG |
|---|---|---|---|
| COMPLETE SET (360) | 30.00 | 13.50 | 3.80 |
| COMMON PLAYER (1-360) | .10 | .05 | .01 |
| ☐ 1 Brett Favre | 1.50 | .65 | .19 |
| Green Bay Packers |  |  |  |
| ☐ 2 Tommy Vardell | .12 | .05 | .02 |
| Cleveland Browns |  |  |  |
| ☐ 3 Jarrod Bunch | .10 | .05 | .01 |
| New York Giants |  |  |  |
| ☐ 4 Mike Croel | .12 | .05 | .02 |
| Denver Broncos |  |  |  |
| ☐ 5 Morten Andersen | .12 | .05 | .02 |
| New Orleans Saints |  |  |  |
| ☐ 6 Barry Foster | .50 | .23 | .06 |
| Pittsburgh Steelers |  |  |  |
| ☐ 7 Chris Spielman | .10 | .05 | .01 |
| Detroit Lions |  |  |  |
| ☐ 8 Jim Jeffcoat | .10 | .05 | .01 |
| Dallas Cowboys |  |  |  |
| ☐ 9 Ken Ruettgers | .10 | .05 | .01 |
| Green Bay Packers |  |  |  |
| ☐ 10 Cris Dishman | .10 | .05 | .01 |
| Houston Oilers |  |  |  |
| ☐ 11 Ricky Watters | .75 | .35 | .09 |
| San Francisco 49ers |  |  |  |
| ☐ 12 Alfred Williams | .10 | .05 | .01 |
| Cincinnati Bengals |  |  |  |
| ☐ 13 Mark Kelso | .10 | .05 | .01 |
| Buffalo Bills |  |  |  |
| ☐ 14 Moe Gardner | .10 | .05 | .01 |
| Atlanta Falcons |  |  |  |
| ☐ 15 Terry Allen | .15 | .07 | .02 |
| Minnesota Vikings |  |  |  |
| ☐ 16 Willie Gault | .12 | .05 | .02 |
| Los Angeles Raiders |  |  |  |
| ☐ 17 Bubba McDowell | .10 | .05 | .01 |
| Houston Oilers |  |  |  |
| ☐ 18 Brian Mitchell | .12 | .05 | .02 |
| Washington Redskins |  |  |  |
| ☐ 19 Karl Mecklenburg | .10 | .05 | .01 |
| Denver Broncos |  |  |  |
| ☐ 20 Jim Everett | .10 | .05 | .01 |
| Los Angeles Rams |  |  |  |
| ☐ 21 Bobby Humphrey | .10 | .05 | .01 |
| Miami Dolphins |  |  |  |
| ☐ 22 Tim Krumrie | .10 | .05 | .01 |
| Cincinnati Bengals |  |  |  |
| ☐ 23 Ken Norton Jr | .12 | .05 | .02 |
| Dallas Cowboys |  |  |  |
| ☐ 24 Wendell Davis | .10 | .05 | .01 |
| Chicago Bears |  |  |  |
| ☐ 25 Brad Baxter | .12 | .05 | .02 |
| New York Jets |  |  |  |
| ☐ 26 Mel Gray | .10 | .05 | .01 |
| Detroit Lions |  |  |  |
| ☐ 27 Jon Vaughn | .10 | .05 | .01 |
| Seattle Seahawks |  |  |  |
| ☐ 28 James Hasty | .10 | .05 | .01 |
| New York Jets |  |  |  |
| ☐ 29 Chris Warren | .30 | .14 | .04 |
| Seattle Seahawks |  |  |  |
| ☐ 30 Tim Harris | .10 | .05 | .01 |
| Philadelphia Eagles |  |  |  |
| ☐ 31 Eric Metcalf | .15 | .07 | .02 |
| Cleveland Browns |  |  |  |
| ☐ 32 Rob Moore | .15 | .07 | .02 |
| New York Jets |  |  |  |

| ☐ 33 Charles Haley | .12 | .05 | .02 |
|---|---|---|---|
| Dallas Cowboys |  |  |  |
| ☐ 34 Leonard Marshall | .10 | .05 | .01 |
| New York Jets |  |  |  |
| ☐ 35 Jeff Graham | .12 | .05 | .02 |
| Pittsburgh Steelers |  |  |  |
| ☐ 36 Eugene Robinson | .10 | .05 | .01 |
| Seattle Seahawks |  |  |  |
| ☐ 37 Darryl Talley | .10 | .05 | .01 |
| Buffalo Bills |  |  |  |
| ☐ 38 Brent Jones | .15 | .07 | .02 |
| San Francisco 49ers |  |  |  |
| ☐ 39 Reggie Roby | .10 | .05 | .01 |
| Miami Dolphins |  |  |  |
| ☐ 40 Bruce Armstrong | .10 | .05 | .01 |
| New England Patriots |  |  |  |
| ☐ 41 Audray McMillian | .10 | .05 | .01 |
| Minnesota Vikings |  |  |  |
| ☐ 42 Bern Brostek | .10 | .05 | .01 |
| Los Angeles Rams |  |  |  |
| ☐ 43 Tony Bennett | .10 | .05 | .01 |
| Green Bay Packers |  |  |  |
| ☐ 44 Albert Lewis | .10 | .05 | .01 |
| Kansas City Chiefs |  |  |  |
| ☐ 45 Derrick Thomas | .30 | .14 | .04 |
| Kansas City Chiefs |  |  |  |
| ☐ 46 Cris Carter | .15 | .07 | .02 |
| Minnesota Vikings |  |  |  |
| ☐ 47 Richmond Webb | .10 | .05 | .01 |
| Miami Dolphins |  |  |  |
| ☐ 48 Sean Landeta | .10 | .05 | .01 |
| New York Giants |  |  |  |
| ☐ 49 Cleveland Gary | .12 | .05 | .02 |
| Los Angeles Rams |  |  |  |
| ☐ 50 Mark Carrier | .12 | .05 | .02 |
| Chicago Bears |  |  |  |
| ☐ 51 Lawrence Dawsey | .15 | .07 | .02 |
| Tampa Bay Buccaneers |  |  |  |
| ☐ 52 Lamar Lathon | .10 | .05 | .01 |
| Houston Oilers |  |  |  |
| ☐ 53 Nick Bell | .12 | .05 | .02 |
| Los Angeles Rams |  |  |  |
| ☐ 54 Curtis Duncan | .10 | .05 | .01 |
| Houston Oilers |  |  |  |
| ☐ 55 Irving Fryar | .10 | .05 | .01 |
| Miami Dolphins |  |  |  |
| ☐ 56 Seth Joyner | .12 | .05 | .02 |
| Philadelphia Eagles |  |  |  |
| ☐ 57 Jay Novacek | .15 | .07 | .02 |
| Dallas Cowboys |  |  |  |
| ☐ 58 John L. Williams | .12 | .05 | .02 |
| Seattle Seahawks |  |  |  |
| ☐ 59 Amp Lee | .12 | .05 | .02 |
| San Francisco 49ers |  |  |  |
| ☐ 60 Marion Butts | .15 | .07 | .02 |
| San Diego Chargers |  |  |  |
| ☐ 61 Clyde Simmons | .12 | .05 | .02 |
| Philadelphia Eagles |  |  |  |
| ☐ 62 Rich Gannon | .12 | .05 | .02 |
| Washington Redskins |  |  |  |
| ☐ 63 Anthony Johnson | .10 | .05 | .01 |
| Indianapolis Colts |  |  |  |
| ☐ 64 Dave Meggett | .12 | .05 | .02 |
| New York Giants |  |  |  |
| ☐ 65 James Francis | .10 | .05 | .01 |
| Cincinnati Bengals |  |  |  |
| ☐ 66 Trace Armstrong | .10 | .05 | .01 |
| Chicago Bears |  |  |  |
| ☐ 67 Mo Lewis | .10 | .05 | .01 |
| New York Jets |  |  |  |
| ☐ 68 Cornelius Bennett | .15 | .07 | .02 |
| Buffalo Bills |  |  |  |
| ☐ 69 Mark Duper | .12 | .05 | .02 |
| Miami Dolphins |  |  |  |
| ☐ 70 Frank Reich | .12 | .05 | .02 |
| Buffalo Bills |  |  |  |
| ☐ 71 Eric Green | .15 | .07 | .02 |
| Pittsburgh Steelers |  |  |  |
| ☐ 72 Bruce Matthews | .12 | .05 | .02 |
| Houston Oilers |  |  |  |
| ☐ 73 Steve Broussard | .10 | .05 | .01 |
| Atlanta Falcons |  |  |  |
| ☐ 74 Anthony Carter | .12 | .05 | .02 |
| Minnesota Vikings |  |  |  |
| ☐ 75 Sterling Sharpe | 1.00 | .45 | .13 |
| Green Bay Packers |  |  |  |
| ☐ 76 Mike Kenn | .10 | .05 | .01 |
| Atlanta Falcons |  |  |  |
| ☐ 77 Andre Rison | .40 | .18 | .05 |
| Atlanta Falcons |  |  |  |
| ☐ 78 Todd Marinovich | .10 | .05 | .01 |
| Los Angeles Rams |  |  |  |
| ☐ 79 Vincent Brown | .10 | .05 | .01 |
| New England Patriots |  |  |  |
| ☐ 80 Harold Green | .12 | .05 | .02 |
| Cincinnati Bengals |  |  |  |
| ☐ 81 Art Monk | .15 | .07 | .02 |

| | | | | | | | | |
|---|---|---|---|---|---|---|---|---|
| | Washington Redskins | | | | | Houston Oilers | | |
| ☐ 82 | Reggie Cobb | .15 | .07 | .02 | ☐ 131 | Richard Dent | .12 | .05 | .02 |
| | Tampa Bay Buccaneers | | | | | Chicago Bears | | |
| ☐ 83 | Johnny Johnson | .15 | .07 | .02 | ☐ 132 | Herman Moore | .75 | .35 | .09 |
| | New York Jets | | | | | Detroit Lions | | |
| ☐ 84 | Tommy Kane | .10 | .05 | .01 | ☐ 133 | Michael Irvin | 1.00 | .45 | .13 |
| | Seattle Seahawks | | | | | Dallas Cowboys | | |
| ☐ 85 | Rohn Stark | .10 | .05 | .01 | ☐ 134 | Ernest Givins | .12 | .05 | .02 |
| | Indianapolis Colts | | | | | Houston Oilers | | |
| ☐ 86 | Steve Tasker | .10 | .05 | .01 | ☐ 135 | Mark Rypien | .12 | .05 | .02 |
| | Buffalo Bills | | | | | Washington Redskins | | |
| ☐ 87 | Ronnie Harmon | .10 | .05 | .01 | ☐ 136 | Leonard Russell | .12 | .05 | .02 |
| | San Diego Chargers | | | | | New England Patriots | | |
| ☐ 88 | Pepper Johnson | .10 | .05 | .01 | ☐ 137 | Reggie White | .25 | .11 | .03 |
| | Cleveland Browns | | | | | Green Bay Packers | | |
| ☐ 89 | Hardy Nickerson | .10 | .05 | .01 | ☐ 138 | Thurman Thomas | .75 | .35 | .09 |
| | Tampa Bay Buccaneers | | | | | Buffalo Bills | | |
| ☐ 90 | Alvin Harper | .50 | .23 | .06 | ☐ 139 | Nick Lowery | .10 | .05 | .01 |
| | Dallas Cowboys | | | | | Kansas City Chiefs | | |
| ☐ 91 | Louis Oliver | .10 | .05 | .01 | ☐ 140 | Al Smith | .10 | .05 | .01 |
| | Miami Dolphins | | | | | Houston Oilers | | |
| ☐ 92 | Rod Woodson | .15 | .07 | .02 | ☐ 141 | Jackie Harris | .50 | .23 | .06 |
| | Pittsburgh Steelers | | | | | Green Bay Packers | | |
| ☐ 93 | Sam Mills | .12 | .05 | .02 | ☐ 142 | Duane Bickett | .10 | .05 | .01 |
| | New Orleans Saints | | | | | Indianapolis Colts | | |
| ☐ 94 | Randall McDaniel | .10 | .05 | .01 | ☐ 143 | Lawyer Tillman | .10 | .05 | .01 |
| | Minnesota Vikings | | | | | Cleveland Browns | | |
| ☐ 95 | Johnny Holland | .10 | .05 | .01 | ☐ 144 | Steve Wisniewski | .10 | .05 | .01 |
| | Green Bay Packers | | | | | Los Angeles Raiders | | |
| ☐ 96 | Jackie Slater | .10 | .05 | .01 | ☐ 145 | Derrick Fenner | .10 | .05 | .01 |
| | Los Angeles Rams | | | | | Cincinnati Bengals | | |
| ☐ 97 | Don Mosebar | .10 | .05 | .01 | ☐ 146 | Harris Barton | .10 | .05 | .01 |
| | Los Angeles Raiders | | | | | San Francisco 49ers | | |
| ☐ 98 | Andre Ware | .12 | .05 | .02 | ☐ 147 | Rich Camarillo | .10 | .05 | .01 |
| | Detroit Lions | | | | | Phoenix Cardinals | | |
| ☐ 99 | Kelvin Martin | .10 | .05 | .01 | ☐ 148 | John Offerdahl | .10 | .05 | .01 |
| | Seattle Seahawks | | | | | Miami Dolphins | | |
| ☐ 100 | Emmitt Smith | 4.00 | 1.80 | .50 | ☐ 149 | Mike Johnson | .10 | .05 | .01 |
| | Dallas Cowboys | | | | | Cleveland Browns | | |
| ☐ 101 | Michael Brooks | .10 | .05 | .01 | ☐ 150 | Ricky Reynolds | .10 | .05 | .01 |
| | New York Giants | | | | | Tampa Bay Buccaneers | | |
| ☐ 102 | Dan Saleaumua | .10 | .05 | .01 | ☐ 151 | Fred Barnett | .15 | .07 | .02 |
| | Kansas City Chiefs | | | | | Philadelphia Eagles | | |
| ☐ 103 | John Elway | .90 | .40 | .11 | ☐ 152 | Nate Newton | .10 | .05 | .01 |
| | Denver Broncos | | | | | Dallas Cowboys | | |
| ☐ 104 | Henry Jones | .10 | .05 | .01 | ☐ 153 | Chris Doleman | .12 | .05 | .02 |
| | Buffalo Bills | | | | | Minnesota Vikings | | |
| ☐ 105 | William Perry | .10 | .05 | .01 | ☐ 154 | Todd Scott | .10 | .05 | .01 |
| | Chicago Bears | | | | | Minnesota Vikings | | |
| ☐ 106 | James Lofton | .15 | .07 | .02 | ☐ 155 | Tim McKyer | .12 | .05 | .02 |
| | Los Angeles Raiders | | | | | Atlanta Falcons | | |
| ☐ 107 | Carnell Lake | .10 | .05 | .01 | ☐ 156 | Ken Harvey | .10 | .05 | .01 |
| | Pittsburgh Steelers | | | | | Phoenix Cardinals | | |
| ☐ 108 | Chip Lohmiller | .10 | .05 | .01 | ☐ 157 | Jeff Feagles | .10 | .05 | .01 |
| | Washington Redskins | | | | | Philadelphia Eagles | | |
| ☐ 109 | Andre Tippett | .10 | .05 | .01 | ☐ 158 | Vince Workman | .10 | .05 | .01 |
| | New England Patriots | | | | | Tampa Bay Buccaneers | | |
| ☐ 110 | Barry Word | .15 | .07 | .02 | ☐ 159 | Bart Oates | .10 | .05 | .01 |
| | Minnesota Vikings | | | | | New York Giants | | |
| ☐ 111 | Haywood Jeffires | .15 | .07 | .02 | ☐ 160 | Chris Miller | .15 | .07 | .02 |
| | Houston Oilers | | | | | Atlanta Falcons | | |
| ☐ 112 | Kenny Walker | .10 | .05 | .01 | ☐ 161 | Pete Stoyanovich | .10 | .05 | .01 |
| | Denver Broncos | | | | | Miami Dolphins | | |
| ☐ 113 | John Randle | .10 | .05 | .01 | ☐ 162 | Steve Wallace | .10 | .05 | .01 |
| | Minnesota Vikings | | | | | San Francisco 49ers | | |
| ☐ 114 | Donnell Woolford | .10 | .05 | .01 | ☐ 163 | Dermontti Dawson | .10 | .05 | .01 |
| | Chicago Bears | | | | | Pittsburgh Steelers | | |
| ☐ 115 | Johnny Bailey | .10 | .05 | .01 | ☐ 164 | Kenneth Davis | .10 | .05 | .01 |
| | Phoenix Cardinals | | | | | Buffalo Bills | | |
| ☐ 116 | Marcus Allen | .12 | .05 | .02 | ☐ 165 | Mike Munchak | .12 | .05 | .02 |
| | Kansas City Chiefs | | | | | Houston Oilers | | |
| ☐ 117 | Mark Jackson | .12 | .05 | .02 | ☐ 166 | George Jamison | .10 | .05 | .01 |
| | New York Giants | | | | | Detroit Lions | | |
| ☐ 118 | Ray Agnew | .10 | .05 | .01 | ☐ 167 | Christian Okoye | .12 | .05 | .02 |
| | New England Patriots | | | | | Kansas City Chiefs | | |
| ☐ 119 | Gill Byrd | .10 | .05 | .01 | ☐ 168 | Chris Hinton | .10 | .05 | .01 |
| | San Diego Chargers | | | | | Atlanta Falcons | | |
| ☐ 120 | Kyle Clifton | .10 | .05 | .01 | ☐ 169 | Vaughan Johnson | .10 | .05 | .01 |
| | New York Jets | | | | | New Orleans Saints | | |
| ☐ 121 | Marv Cook | .10 | .05 | .01 | ☐ 170 | Gaston Green | .12 | .05 | .02 |
| | New England Patriots | | | | | Los Angeles Raiders | | |
| ☐ 122 | Jerry Ball | .10 | .05 | .01 | ☐ 171 | Kevin Greene | .10 | .05 | .01 |
| | Cleveland Browns | | | | | Pittsburgh Steelers | | |
| ☐ 123 | Steve Jordan | .12 | .05 | .02 | ☐ 172 | Rob Burnett | .10 | .05 | .01 |
| | Minnesota Vikings | | | | | Cleveland Browns | | |
| ☐ 124 | Shannon Sharpe | .35 | .16 | .04 | ☐ 173 | Norm Johnson | .10 | .05 | .01 |
| | Denver Broncos | | | | | Atlanta Falcons | | |
| ☐ 125 | Brian Blades | .12 | .05 | .02 | ☐ 174 | Eric Hill | .10 | .05 | .01 |
| | Seattle Seahawks | | | | | Phoenix Cardinals | | |
| ☐ 126 | Rodney Hampton | .75 | .35 | .09 | ☐ 175 | Lomas Brown | .10 | .05 | .01 |
| | New York Giants | | | | | Detroit Lions | | |
| ☐ 127 | Bobby Hebert | .15 | .07 | .02 | ☐ 176 | Chip Banks | .10 | .05 | .01 |
| | Atlanta Falcons | | | | | Indianapolis Colts | | |
| ☐ 128 | Jessie Tuggle | .10 | .05 | .01 | ☐ 177 | Greg Townsend | .10 | .05 | .01 |
| | Atlanta Falcons | | | | | Los Angeles Raiders | | |
| ☐ 129 | Tom Newberry | .10 | .05 | .01 | ☐ 178 | David Fulcher | .10 | .05 | .01 |
| | Los Angeles Rams | | | | | Cincinnati Bengals | | |
| ☐ 130 | Keith McCants | .10 | .05 | .01 | ☐ 179 | Gary Anderson | .12 | .05 | .02 |

| Tampa Bay Buccaneers | | | |
|---|---|---|---|
| ☐ 180 Brian Washington | .10 | .05 | .01 |
| New York Jets | | | |
| ☐ 181 Brett Perriman | .12 | .05 | .02 |
| Detroit Lions | | | |
| ☐ 182 Chris Chandler | .12 | .05 | .02 |
| Phoenix Cardinals | | | |
| ☐ 183 Phil Hansen | .10 | .05 | .01 |
| Buffalo Bills | | | |
| ☐ 184 Mark Clayton | .10 | .05 | .01 |
| Miami Dolphins | | | |
| ☐ 185 Frank Warren | .10 | .05 | .01 |
| New Orleans Saints | | | |
| ☐ 186 Tim Brown | .40 | .18 | .05 |
| Los Angeles Raiders | | | |
| ☐ 187 Mark Stepnoski | .10 | .05 | .01 |
| Dallas Cowboys | | | |
| ☐ 188 Bryan Cox | .12 | .05 | .02 |
| Miami Dolphins | | | |
| ☐ 189 Gary Zimmerman | .10 | .05 | .01 |
| Denver Broncos | | | |
| ☐ 190 Neil O'Donnell | .50 | .23 | .06 |
| Pittsburgh Steelers | | | |
| ☐ 191 Anthony Smith | .10 | .05 | .01 |
| Los Angeles Raiders | | | |
| ☐ 192 Craig Heyward | .10 | .05 | .01 |
| Chicago Bears | | | |
| ☐ 193 Keith Byars | .12 | .05 | .02 |
| Miami Dolphins | | | |
| ☐ 194 Sean Salisbury | .12 | .05 | .02 |
| Minnesota Vikings | | | |
| ☐ 195 Todd Lyght | .10 | .05 | .01 |
| Los Angeles Rams | | | |
| ☐ 196 Jessie Hester | .10 | .05 | .01 |
| Indianapolis Colts | | | |
| ☐ 197 Rufus Porter | .10 | .05 | .01 |
| Seattle Seahawks | | | |
| ☐ 198 Steve Christie | .10 | .05 | .01 |
| Buffalo Bills | | | |
| ☐ 199 Nate Lewis | .12 | .05 | .02 |
| San Diego Chargers | | | |
| ☐ 200 Barry Sanders | 1.50 | .65 | .19 |
| Detroit Lions | | | |
| ☐ 201 Michael Haynes | .40 | .18 | .05 |
| Atlanta Falcons | | | |
| ☐ 202 John Taylor | .15 | .07 | .02 |
| San Francisco 49ers | | | |
| ☐ 203 John Friesz | .12 | .05 | .02 |
| San Diego Chargers | | | |
| ☐ 204 William Fuller | .10 | .05 | .01 |
| Houston Oilers | | | |
| ☐ 205 Dennis Smith | .10 | .05 | .01 |
| Denver Broncos | | | |
| ☐ 206 Adrian Cooper | .10 | .05 | .01 |
| Pittsburgh Steelers | | | |
| ☐ 207 Henry Thomas | .10 | .05 | .01 |
| Minnesota Vikings | | | |
| ☐ 208 Gerald Williams | .10 | .05 | .01 |
| Pittsburgh Steelers | | | |
| ☐ 209 Chris Burkett | .10 | .05 | .01 |
| New York Jets | | | |
| ☐ 210 Broderick Thomas | .10 | .05 | .01 |
| Tampa Bay Buccaneers | | | |
| ☐ 211 Marvin Washington | .10 | .05 | .01 |
| New York Jets | | | |
| ☐ 212 Bennie Blades | .10 | .05 | .01 |
| Detroit Lions | | | |
| ☐ 213 Tony Casillas | .10 | .05 | .01 |
| Dallas Cowboys | | | |
| ☐ 214 Bubby Brister | .10 | .05 | .01 |
| Pittsburgh Steelers | | | |
| ☐ 215 Don Griffin | .10 | .05 | .01 |
| San Francisco 49ers | | | |
| ☐ 216 Jeff Cross | .10 | .05 | .01 |
| Miami Dolphins | | | |
| ☐ 217 Derrick Walker | .10 | .05 | .01 |
| San Diego Chargers | | | |
| ☐ 218 Lorenzo White | .12 | .05 | .02 |
| Houston Oilers | | | |
| ☐ 219 Ricky Sanders | .12 | .05 | .02 |
| Washington Redskins | | | |
| ☐ 220 Rickey Jackson | .12 | .05 | .02 |
| New Orleans Saints | | | |
| ☐ 221 Simon Fletcher | .12 | .05 | .02 |
| Denver Broncos | | | |
| ☐ 222 Troy Vincent | .12 | .05 | .02 |
| Miami Dolphins | | | |
| ☐ 223 Gary Clark | .12 | .05 | .02 |
| Phoenix Cardinals | | | |
| ☐ 224 Stanley Richard | .10 | .05 | .01 |
| San Diego Chargers | | | |
| ☐ 225 Dave Krieg | .12 | .05 | .02 |
| Kansas City Chiefs | | | |
| ☐ 226 Warren Moon | .35 | .16 | .04 |
| Houston Oilers | | | |
| ☐ 227 Reggie Langhorne | .12 | .05 | .02 |
| Indianapolis Colts | | | |
| ☐ 228 Kent Hull | .10 | .05 | .01 |

| Buffalo Bills | | | |
|---|---|---|---|
| ☐ 229 Ferrell Edmunds | .10 | .05 | .01 |
| Seattle Seahawks | | | |
| ☐ 230 Cortez Kennedy | .15 | .07 | .02 |
| Seattle Seahawks | | | |
| ☐ 231 Hugh Millen | .10 | .05 | .01 |
| Dallas Cowboys | | | |
| ☐ 232 Eugene Chung | .10 | .05 | .01 |
| New England Patriots | | | |
| ☐ 233 Rodney Peete | .12 | .05 | .02 |
| Detroit Lions | | | |
| ☐ 234 Tom Waddle | .15 | .07 | .02 |
| Chicago Bears | | | |
| ☐ 235 David Klingler | .30 | .14 | .04 |
| Cincinnati Bengals | | | |
| ☐ 236 Mark Carrier | .12 | .05 | .02 |
| Cleveland Browns | | | |
| ☐ 237 Jay Schroeder | .10 | .05 | .01 |
| Cincinnati Bengals | | | |
| ☐ 238 James Jones | .10 | .05 | .01 |
| Cleveland Browns | | | |
| ☐ 239 Phil Simms | .15 | .07 | .02 |
| New York Giants | | | |
| ☐ 240 Steve Atwater | .12 | .05 | .02 |
| Denver Broncos | | | |
| ☐ 241 Jeff Herrod | .10 | .05 | .01 |
| Indianapolis Colts | | | |
| ☐ 242 Dale Carter | .15 | .07 | .02 |
| Kansas City Chiefs | | | |
| ☐ 243 Glenn Cadrez | .15 | .07 | .02 |
| New York Jets | | | |
| ☐ 244 Wayne Martin | .10 | .05 | .01 |
| New Orleans Saints | | | |
| ☐ 245 Willie Davis | .20 | .09 | .03 |
| Kansas City Chiefs | | | |
| ☐ 246 Lawrence Taylor | .15 | .07 | .02 |
| New York Giants | | | |
| ☐ 247 Stan Humphries | .15 | .07 | .02 |
| San Diego Chargers | | | |
| ☐ 248 Byron Evans | .10 | .05 | .01 |
| Philadelphia Eagles | | | |
| ☐ 249 Wilber Marshall | .12 | .05 | .02 |
| Houston Oilers | | | |
| ☐ 250 Michael Bankston | .15 | .07 | .02 |
| Phoenix Cardinals | | | |
| ☐ 251 Steve McMichael | .10 | .05 | .01 |
| Chicago Bears | | | |
| ☐ 252 Brad Edwards | .10 | .05 | .01 |
| Washington Redskins | | | |
| ☐ 253 Will Wolford | .10 | .05 | .01 |
| Indianapolis Colts | | | |
| ☐ 254 Paul Gruber | .10 | .05 | .01 |
| Tampa Bay Buccaneers | | | |
| ☐ 255 Steve Young | .50 | .23 | .06 |
| San Francisco 49ers | | | |
| ☐ 256 Chuck Cecil | .10 | .05 | .01 |
| Phoenix Cardinals | | | |
| ☐ 257 Pierce Holt | .10 | .05 | .01 |
| Atlanta Falcons | | | |
| ☐ 258 Anthony Miller | .30 | .14 | .04 |
| San Diego Chargers | | | |
| ☐ 259 Carl Banks | .10 | .05 | .01 |
| Washington Redskins | | | |
| ☐ 260 Brad Muster | .12 | .05 | .02 |
| New Orleans Saints | | | |
| ☐ 261 Clay Matthews | .12 | .05 | .02 |
| Cleveland Browns | | | |
| ☐ 262 Rod Bernstine | .12 | .05 | .02 |
| Denver Broncos | | | |
| ☐ 263 Tim Barnett | .12 | .05 | .02 |
| Kansas City Chiefs | | | |
| ☐ 264 Greg Lloyd | .10 | .05 | .01 |
| Philadelphia Eagles | | | |
| ☐ 265 Sean Jones | .10 | .05 | .01 |
| Houston Oilers | | | |
| ☐ 266 J.J. Birden | .12 | .05 | .02 |
| Kansas City Chiefs | | | |
| ☐ 267 Tim McDonald | .10 | .05 | .01 |
| San Francisco 49ers | | | |
| ☐ 268 Charles Mann | .10 | .05 | .01 |
| Washington Redskins | | | |
| ☐ 269 Bruce Smith | .15 | .07 | .02 |
| Buffalo Bills | | | |
| ☐ 270 Sean Gilbert | .12 | .05 | .02 |
| Los Angeles Rams | | | |
| ☐ 271 Ricardo McDonald | .10 | .05 | .01 |
| Cincinnati Bengals | | | |
| ☐ 272 Jeff Hostetler | .15 | .07 | .02 |
| Los Angeles Raiders | | | |
| ☐ 273 Russell Maryland | .15 | .07 | .02 |
| Dallas Cowboys | | | |
| ☐ 274 Dave Brown | 1.50 | .65 | .19 |
| New York Giants | | | |
| ☐ 275 Ronnie Lott | .15 | .07 | .02 |
| New York Jets | | | |
| ☐ 276 Jim Kelly | .40 | .18 | .05 |
| Buffalo Bills | | | |
| ☐ 277 Joe Montana | 3.00 | 1.35 | .40 |

Kansas City Chiefs
| | | | | |
|---|---|---|---|---|
| ☐ 278 | Eric Allen | .12 | .05 | .02 |

Philadelphia Eagles
| | | | | |
|---|---|---|---|---|
| ☐ 279 | Browning Nagle | .12 | .05 | .02 |

New York Jets
| | | | | |
|---|---|---|---|---|
| ☐ 280 | Neal Anderson | .12 | .05 | .02 |

Chicago Bears
| | | | | |
|---|---|---|---|---|
| ☐ 281 | Troy Aikman | 3.00 | 1.35 | .40 |

Dallas Cowboys
| | | | | |
|---|---|---|---|---|
| ☐ 282 | Ed McCaffrey | .10 | .05 | .01 |

New York Giants
| | | | | |
|---|---|---|---|---|
| ☐ 283 | Robert Jones | .10 | .05 | .01 |

Dallas Cowboys
| | | | | |
|---|---|---|---|---|
| ☐ 284 | Dalton Hilliard | .10 | .05 | .01 |

New Orleans Saints
| | | | | |
|---|---|---|---|---|
| ☐ 285 | Johnny Mitchell | .50 | .23 | .06 |

New York Jets
| | | | | |
|---|---|---|---|---|
| ☐ 286 | Jay Hilgenberg | .10 | .05 | .01 |

Cleveland Browns
| | | | | |
|---|---|---|---|---|
| ☐ 287 | Eric Martin | .12 | .05 | .02 |

New Orleans Saints
| | | | | |
|---|---|---|---|---|
| ☐ 288 | Steve Emtman | .12 | .05 | .02 |

Indianapolis Colts
| | | | | |
|---|---|---|---|---|
| ☐ 289 | Vaughn Dunbar | .12 | .05 | .02 |

New Orleans Saints
| | | | | |
|---|---|---|---|---|
| ☐ 290 | Mark Wheeler | .10 | .05 | .01 |

Tampa Bay Buccaneers
| | | | | |
|---|---|---|---|---|
| ☐ 291 | Leslie O'Neal | .12 | .05 | .02 |

San Diego Chargers
| | | | | |
|---|---|---|---|---|
| ☐ 292 | Jerry Rice | 1.25 | .55 | .16 |

San Francisco 49ers
| | | | | |
|---|---|---|---|---|
| ☐ 293 | Neil Smith | .15 | .07 | .02 |

Kansas City Chiefs
| | | | | |
|---|---|---|---|---|
| ☐ 294 | Kerry Cash | .10 | .05 | .01 |

Indianapolis Colts
| | | | | |
|---|---|---|---|---|
| ☐ 295 | Dan McGwire | .12 | .05 | .02 |

Seattle Seahawks
| | | | | |
|---|---|---|---|---|
| ☐ 296 | Carl Pickens | .15 | .07 | .02 |

Cincinnati Bengals
| | | | | |
|---|---|---|---|---|
| ☐ 297 | Terrell Buckley | .15 | .07 | .02 |

Green Bay Packers
| | | | | |
|---|---|---|---|---|
| ☐ 298 | Randall Cunningham | .20 | .09 | .03 |

Philadelphia Eagles
| | | | | |
|---|---|---|---|---|
| ☐ 299 | Santana Dotson | .15 | .07 | .02 |

Tampa Bay Buccaneers
| | | | | |
|---|---|---|---|---|
| ☐ 300 | Keith Jackson | .15 | .07 | .02 |

Miami Dolphins
| | | | | |
|---|---|---|---|---|
| ☐ 301 | Jim Lachey | .10 | .05 | .01 |

Washington Redskins
| | | | | |
|---|---|---|---|---|
| ☐ 302 | Dan Marino | 1.50 | .65 | .19 |

Miami Dolphins
| | | | | |
|---|---|---|---|---|
| ☐ 303 | Lee Williams | .10 | .05 | .01 |

Houston Oilers
| | | | | |
|---|---|---|---|---|
| ☐ 304 | Burt Grossman | .10 | .05 | .01 |

San Diego Chargers
| | | | | |
|---|---|---|---|---|
| ☐ 305 | Kevin Mack | .10 | .05 | .01 |

Cleveland Browns
| | | | | |
|---|---|---|---|---|
| ☐ 306 | Pat Swilling | .12 | .05 | .02 |

Detroit Lions
| | | | | |
|---|---|---|---|---|
| ☐ 307 | Arthur Marshall | .40 | .18 | .05 |

Denver Broncos
| | | | | |
|---|---|---|---|---|
| ☐ 308 | Jim Harbaugh | .12 | .05 | .02 |

Chicago Bears
| | | | | |
|---|---|---|---|---|
| ☐ 309 | Kurt Barber | .10 | .05 | .01 |

New York Jets
| | | | | |
|---|---|---|---|---|
| ☐ 310 | Harvey Williams | .15 | .07 | .02 |

Kansas City Chiefs
| | | | | |
|---|---|---|---|---|
| ☐ 311 | Ricky Ervins | .12 | .05 | .02 |

Washington Redskins
| | | | | |
|---|---|---|---|---|
| ☐ 312 | Flipper Anderson | .12 | .05 | .02 |

Los Angeles Rams
| | | | | |
|---|---|---|---|---|
| ☐ 313 | Bernie Kosar | .15 | .07 | .02 |

Cleveland Browns
| | | | | |
|---|---|---|---|---|
| ☐ 314 | Boomer Esiason | .25 | .11 | .03 |

New York Jets
| | | | | |
|---|---|---|---|---|
| ☐ 315 | Deion Sanders | .30 | .14 | .04 |

Atlanta Falcons
| | | | | |
|---|---|---|---|---|
| ☐ 316 | Ray Childress | .10 | .05 | .01 |

Houston Oilers
| | | | | |
|---|---|---|---|---|
| ☐ 317 | Howie Long | .12 | .05 | .02 |

Los Angeles Raiders
| | | | | |
|---|---|---|---|---|
| ☐ 318 | Henry Ellard | .12 | .05 | .02 |

Los Angeles Rams
| | | | | |
|---|---|---|---|---|
| ☐ 319 | Marco Coleman | .12 | .05 | .02 |

Miami Dolphins
| | | | | |
|---|---|---|---|---|
| ☐ 320 | Chris Mims | .12 | .05 | .02 |

San Diego Chargers
| | | | | |
|---|---|---|---|---|
| ☐ 321 | Quentin Coryatt | .15 | .07 | .02 |

Indianapolis Colts
| | | | | |
|---|---|---|---|---|
| ☐ 322 | Jason Hanson | .10 | .05 | .01 |

Detroit Lions
| | | | | |
|---|---|---|---|---|
| ☐ 323 | Ricky Proehl | .12 | .05 | .02 |

Phoenix Cardinals
| | | | | |
|---|---|---|---|---|
| ☐ 324 | Randal Hill | .15 | .07 | .02 |

Phoenix Cardinals
| | | | | |
|---|---|---|---|---|
| ☐ 325 | Vinny Testaverde | .10 | .05 | .01 |

Cleveland Browns
| | | | | |
|---|---|---|---|---|
| ☐ 326 | Jeff George | .25 | .11 | .03 |

Indianapolis Colts
| | | | | |
|---|---|---|---|---|
| ☐ 327 | Junior Seau | .15 | .07 | .02 |

San Diego Chargers
| | | | | |
|---|---|---|---|---|
| ☐ 328 | Earnest Byner | .12 | .05 | .02 |

Washington Redskins
| | | | | |
|---|---|---|---|---|
| ☐ 329 | Andre Reed | .15 | .07 | .02 |

Buffalo Bills
| | | | | |
|---|---|---|---|---|
| ☐ 330 | Phillippi Sparks | .10 | .05 | .01 |

New York Giants
| | | | | |
|---|---|---|---|---|
| ☐ 331 | Kevin Ross | .10 | .05 | .01 |

Kansas City Chiefs
| | | | | |
|---|---|---|---|---|
| ☐ 332 | Clarence Verdin | .10 | .05 | .01 |

Indianapolis Colts
| | | | | |
|---|---|---|---|---|
| ☐ 333 | Darryl Henley | .10 | .05 | .01 |

Los Angeles Rams
| | | | | |
|---|---|---|---|---|
| ☐ 334 | Dana Hall | .10 | .05 | .01 |

San Francisco 49ers
| | | | | |
|---|---|---|---|---|
| ☐ 335 | Greg McMurtry | .10 | .05 | .01 |

New England Patriots
| | | | | |
|---|---|---|---|---|
| ☐ 336 | Ron Hall | .10 | .05 | .01 |

Tampa Bay Buccaneers
| | | | | |
|---|---|---|---|---|
| ☐ 337 | Darrell Green | .12 | .05 | .02 |

Washington Redskins
| | | | | |
|---|---|---|---|---|
| ☐ 338 | Carlton Bailey | .10 | .05 | .01 |

New York Giants
| | | | | |
|---|---|---|---|---|
| ☐ 339 | Irv Eatman | .10 | .05 | .01 |

Los Angeles Rams
| | | | | |
|---|---|---|---|---|
| ☐ 340 | Greg Kragen | .10 | .05 | .01 |

Denver Broncos
| | | | | |
|---|---|---|---|---|
| ☐ 341 | Wade Wilson | .12 | .05 | .02 |

New Orleans Saints
| | | | | |
|---|---|---|---|---|
| ☐ 342 | Klaus Wilmsmeyer | .10 | .05 | .01 |

San Francisco 49ers
| | | | | |
|---|---|---|---|---|
| ☐ 343 | Derek Brown | .12 | .05 | .02 |

New York Giants
| | | | | |
|---|---|---|---|---|
| ☐ 344 | Erik Williams | .10 | .05 | .01 |

Dallas Cowboys
| | | | | |
|---|---|---|---|---|
| ☐ 345 | Jim McMahon | .15 | .07 | .02 |

Minnesota Vikings
| | | | | |
|---|---|---|---|---|
| ☐ 346 | Mike Sherrard | .10 | .05 | .01 |

New York Giants
| | | | | |
|---|---|---|---|---|
| ☐ 347 | Mark Bavaro | .10 | .05 | .01 |

Philadelphia Eagles
| | | | | |
|---|---|---|---|---|
| ☐ 348 | Anthony Munoz | .12 | .05 | .02 |

Tampa Bay Buccaneers
| | | | | |
|---|---|---|---|---|
| ☐ 349 | Eric Dickerson | .15 | .07 | .02 |

Atlanta Falcons
| | | | | |
|---|---|---|---|---|
| ☐ 350 | Steve Beuerlein | .25 | .11 | .03 |

Phoenix Cardinals
| | | | | |
|---|---|---|---|---|
| ☐ 351 | Tim McGee | .10 | .05 | .01 |

Washington Redskins
| | | | | |
|---|---|---|---|---|
| ☐ 352 | Terry McDaniel | .10 | .05 | .01 |

Los Angeles Raiders
| | | | | |
|---|---|---|---|---|
| ☐ 353 | Dan Fouts HOF | .10 | .05 | .01 |

San Diego Chargers
| | | | | |
|---|---|---|---|---|
| ☐ 354 | Chuck Noll HOF | .10 | .05 | .01 |

Pittsburgh Steelers
| | | | | |
|---|---|---|---|---|
| ☐ 355 | Bill Walsh HOF | .20 | .09 | .03 |

San Francisco 49ers
| | | | | |
|---|---|---|---|---|
| ☐ 356 | Larry Little HOF | .10 | .05 | .01 |

Miami Dolphins
| | | | | |
|---|---|---|---|---|
| ☐ 357 | Todd Marinovich HH | .10 | .05 | .01 |

Los Angeles Raiders
| | | | | |
|---|---|---|---|---|
| ☐ 358 | Jeff George HH | .10 | .05 | .01 |

Indianapolis Colts
| | | | | |
|---|---|---|---|---|
| ☐ 359 | Bernie Kosar HH | .12 | .05 | .02 |

Cleveland Browns
| | | | | |
|---|---|---|---|---|
| ☐ 360 | Rob Moore HH | .12 | .05 | .02 |

New York Jets
| | | | | |
|---|---|---|---|---|
| ☐ NNO | Franco Harris AU/3000 | 35.00 | 16.00 | 4.40 |

# 1993 Pinnacle Men of Autumn

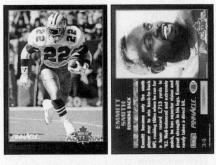

The 1993 Pinnacle Men of Autumn set consists of 55 standard-size (2 1/2" by 3 1/2") cards. Not available in regular Pinnacle packs, one of these cards was inserted into each 16-card 1993 Score football foil pack. The fronts feature color on-field action shots on a glossy black laminate. The photos are edged with a red line and the borders are of the glossy black backing. The player's name and position appears in gold foil in the bottom margin, and the Men of Autumn logo rests at the bottom of the photo. The horizontal backs display a red-edged, black-bordered player close-up on the right half, while a brief review of the player's performance appears on the left half. The cards are numbered on the back.

|  | MINT | EXC | G-VG |
|---|---|---|---|
| COMPLETE SET (55) | 14.00 | 6.25 | 1.75 |
| COMMON PLAYER (1-55) | .25 | .11 | .03 |
| ☐ 1 Andre Rison | .50 | .23 | .06 |
| Atlanta Falcons | | | |
| ☐ 2 Thurman Thomas | 1.00 | .45 | .13 |
| Buffalo Bills | | | |
| ☐ 3 Wendell Davis | .25 | .11 | .03 |
| Chicago Bears | | | |
| ☐ 4 Harold Green | .25 | .11 | .03 |
| Cincinnati Bengals | | | |
| ☐ 5 Eric Metcalf | .25 | .11 | .03 |
| Cleveland Browns | | | |
| ☐ 6 Michael Irvin | 1.25 | .55 | .16 |
| Dallas Cowboys | | | |
| ☐ 7 John Elway | 1.50 | .65 | .19 |
| Denver Broncos | | | |
| ☐ 8 Barry Sanders | 2.00 | .90 | .25 |
| Detroit Lions | | | |
| ☐ 9 Sterling Sharpe | 1.25 | .55 | .16 |
| Green Bay Packers | | | |
| ☐ 10 Warren Moon | .40 | .18 | .05 |
| Houston Oilers | | | |
| ☐ 11 Rohn Stark | .25 | .11 | .03 |
| Indianapolis Colts | | | |
| ☐ 12 Derrick Thomas | .35 | .16 | .04 |
| Kansas City Chiefs | | | |
| ☐ 13 Terry McDaniel | .25 | .11 | .03 |
| Los Angeles Raiders | | | |
| ☐ 14 Cleveland Gary | .25 | .11 | .03 |
| Los Angeles Rams | | | |
| ☐ 15 Dan Marino | 2.00 | .90 | .25 |
| Miami Dolphins | | | |
| ☐ 16 Terry Allen | .35 | .16 | .04 |
| Minnesota Vikings | | | |
| ☐ 17 Marv Cook | .25 | .11 | .03 |
| New England Patriots | | | |
| ☐ 18 Bobby Hebert | .25 | .11 | .03 |
| New Orleans Saints | | | |
| ☐ 19 Rodney Hampton | 1.00 | .45 | .13 |
| New York Giants | | | |
| ☐ 20 Brad Baxter | .25 | .11 | .03 |
| New York Jets | | | |
| ☐ 21 Reggie White | .40 | .18 | .05 |
| Philadelphia Eagles | | | |
| ☐ 22 Ricky Proehl | .25 | .11 | .03 |
| Phoenix Cardinals | | | |
| ☐ 23 Barry Foster | 1.00 | .45 | .13 |
| Pittsburgh Steelers | | | |
| ☐ 24 Junior Seau | .35 | .16 | .04 |
| San Diego Chargers | | | |
| ☐ 25 Steve Young | .75 | .35 | .09 |
| San Francisco 49ers | | | |
| ☐ 26 Cortez Kennedy | .35 | .16 | .04 |
| Seattle Seahawks | | | |
| ☐ 27 Reggie Cobb | .35 | .16 | .04 |
| Tampa Bay Buccaneers | | | |
| ☐ 28 Mark Rypien | .35 | .16 | .04 |
| Washington Redskins | | | |
| ☐ 29 Deion Sanders | .50 | .23 | .06 |
| Atlanta Falcons | | | |
| ☐ 30 Bruce Smith | .35 | .16 | .04 |
| Buffalo Bills | | | |
| ☐ 31 Richard Dent | .25 | .11 | .03 |
| Chicago Bears | | | |
| ☐ 32 Alfred Williams | .25 | .11 | .03 |
| Cincinnati Bengals | | | |
| ☐ 33 Clay Matthews | .25 | .11 | .03 |
| Cleveland Browns | | | |
| ☐ 34 Emmitt Smith | 5.00 | 2.30 | .60 |
| Dallas Cowboys | | | |
| ☐ 35 Simon Fletcher | .25 | .11 | .03 |
| Denver Broncos | | | |
| ☐ 36 Chris Spielman | .25 | .11 | .03 |
| Detroit Lions | | | |
| ☐ 37 Brett Favre | 2.00 | .90 | .25 |
| Green Bay Packers | | | |
| ☐ 38 Bruce Matthews | .25 | .11 | .03 |
| Houston Oilers | | | |
| ☐ 39 Jeff Herrod | .25 | .11 | .03 |
| Indianapolis Colts | | | |
| ☐ 40 Nick Lowery | .25 | .11 | .03 |
| Kansas City Chiefs | | | |
| ☐ 41 Steve Wisniewski | .25 | .11 | .03 |
| Los Angeles Raiders | | | |
| ☐ 42 Jim Everett | .35 | .16 | .04 |
| Los Angeles Rams | | | |
| ☐ 43 Keith Jackson | .35 | .16 | .04 |
| Miami Dolphins | | | |
| ☐ 44 Chris Doleman | .25 | .11 | .03 |
| Minnesota Vikings | | | |
| ☐ 45 Irving Fryar | .25 | .11 | .03 |
| New England Patriots | | | |
| ☐ 46 Rickey Jackson | .25 | .11 | .03 |
| New Orleans Saints | | | |
| ☐ 47 Pepper Johnson | .25 | .11 | .03 |
| New York Giants | | | |
| ☐ 48 Randall Cunningham | .35 | .16 | .04 |
| Philadelphia Eagles | | | |
| ☐ 49 Rich Camarillo | .25 | .11 | .03 |
| Phoenix Cardinals | | | |
| ☐ 50 Rod Woodson | .35 | .16 | .04 |
| Pittsburgh Steelers | | | |
| ☐ 51 Ronnie Harmon | .25 | .11 | .03 |
| San Diego Chargers | | | |
| ☐ 52 Ricky Watters | 1.00 | .45 | .13 |
| San Francisco 49ers | | | |
| ☐ 53 Chris Warren | .40 | .18 | .05 |
| Seattle Seahawks | | | |
| ☐ 54 Lawrence Dawsey | .35 | .16 | .04 |
| Tampa Bay Buccaneers | | | |
| ☐ 55 Wilber Marshall | .25 | .11 | .03 |
| Washington Redskins | | | |

# 1993 Pinnacle Rookies

The 1993 Pinnacle Rookies set consists of 25 standard-size (2 1/2" by 3 1/2") cards, which were random inserted reportedly in one of approximately every 36 1993 Pinnacle foil packs. The black fronts feature a color action player cut-out emerging from a diamond-shaped "FX" metallic design in the center of the card. The set title and the Pinnacle logo are stamped in copper-foil above and below the picture, respectively. The player's name appears on a team color-coded metallic bar below the picture, with the team name below. The black backs carry a copper-colored panel containing career highlights with the copper-colored player's name at the top of the card. The cards are numbered on the back "X of 25."

|  | MINT | EXC | G-VG |
|---|---|---|---|
| COMPLETE SET (25) | 400.00 | 180.00 | 50.00 |
| COMMON PLAYER (1-25) | 10.00 | 4.50 | 1.25 |
| ☐ 1 Drew Bledsoe | 100.00 | 45.00 | 12.50 |
| New England Patriots | | | |
| ☐ 2 Garrison Hearst | 25.00 | 11.50 | 3.10 |
| Phoenix Cardinals | | | |
| ☐ 3 John Copeland | 10.00 | 4.50 | 1.25 |
| Cincinnati Bengals | | | |
| ☐ 4 Eric Curry | 10.00 | 4.50 | 1.25 |
| Tampa Bay Buccaneers | | | |
| ☐ 5 Curtis Conway | 16.00 | 7.25 | 2.00 |
| Chicago Bears | | | |
| ☐ 6 Lincoln Kennedy | 10.00 | 4.50 | 1.25 |
| Atlanta Falcons | | | |
| ☐ 7 Jerome Bettis | 100.00 | 45.00 | 12.50 |
| Los Angeles Rams | | | |
| ☐ 8 Dan Williams | 10.00 | 4.50 | 1.25 |
| Denver Broncos | | | |
| ☐ 9 Patrick Bates | 10.00 | 4.50 | 1.25 |
| Los Angeles Raiders | | | |
| ☐ 10 Brad Hopkins | 10.00 | 4.50 | 1.25 |
| Houston Oilers | | | |
| ☐ 11 Wayne Simmons | 10.00 | 4.50 | 1.25 |
| Green Bay Packers | | | |
| ☐ 12 Rick Mirer | 100.00 | 45.00 | 12.50 |
| Seattle Seahawks | | | |
| ☐ 13 Tom Carter | 10.00 | 4.50 | 1.25 |
| Washington Redskins | | | |
| ☐ 14 Irv Smith | 10.00 | 4.50 | 1.25 |
| New Orleans Saints | | | |
| ☐ 15 Marvin Jones | 10.00 | 4.50 | 1.25 |

New York Jets

| | | | |
|---|---|---|---|
| ☐ 16 Deon Figures | 10.00 | 4.50 | 1.25 |
| Pittsburgh Steelers | | | |
| ☐ 17 Leonard Renfro | 10.00 | 4.50 | 1.25 |
| Philadelphia Eagles | | | |
| ☐ 18 O.J.McDuffie | 25.00 | 11.50 | 3.10 |
| Miami Dolphins | | | |
| ☐ 19 Dana Stubblefield | 14.00 | 6.25 | 1.75 |
| San Francisco 49ers | | | |
| ☐ 20 Carlton Gray | 10.00 | 4.50 | 1.25 |
| Seattle Seahawks | | | |
| ☐ 21 Demetrius DuBose | 10.00 | 4.50 | 1.25 |
| Tampa Bay Buccaneers | | | |
| ☐ 22 Troy Drayton | 10.00 | 4.50 | 1.25 |
| Los Angeles Rams | | | |
| ☐ 23 Natrone Means | 30.00 | 13.50 | 3.80 |
| San Diego Chargers | | | |
| ☐ 24 Reggie Brooks | 50.00 | 23.00 | 6.25 |
| Washington Redskins | | | |
| ☐ 25 Glyn Milburn | 30.00 | 13.50 | 3.80 |
| Denver Broncos | | | |

## 1993 Pinnacle Super Bowl XXVII

The 1993 Pinnacle Super Bowl XXVII set consists of ten standard-size (2 1/2" by 3 1/2") cards commemorating the 1993 Super Bowl Champion Dallas Cowboys. The cards were randomly inserted in foil packs of 1993 Pinnacle (one per hobby box). The horizontal front features a color action player shot that is borderless, except on the left, where a dark blue stripe carries the set title in blue-foil. Within a black panel, the horizontal back carries the player's name, game highlights, SB XXVII logo, and helmets of the Bills and the Cowboys. The cards are numbered on the back "X of 10."

| | MINT | EXC | G-VG |
|---|---|---|---|
| COMPLETE SET (10) | 60.00 | 27.00 | 7.50 |
| COMMON PLAYER (1-10) | 4.00 | 1.80 | .50 |
| | | | |
| ☐ 1 Rose Bowl | 4.00 | 1.80 | .50 |
| ☐ 2 Thomas Everett | 4.00 | 1.80 | .50 |
| ☐ 3 Emmitt Smith | 35.00 | 16.00 | 4.40 |
| ☐ 4 Ken Norton Jr. | 4.00 | 1.80 | .50 |
| ☐ 5 Michael Irvin | 10.00 | 4.50 | 1.25 |
| ☐ 6 Jay Novacek | 4.00 | 1.80 | .50 |
| ☐ 7 Charles Haley | 4.00 | 1.80 | .50 |
| ☐ 8 Leon Lett | 4.00 | 1.80 | .50 |
| ☐ 9 Alvin Harper | 6.00 | 2.70 | .75 |
| ☐ 10 Tony Casillas | 4.00 | 1.80 | .50 |

## 1993 Pinnacle Team Pinnacle

The 1993 Pinnacle Team Pinnacle set consists of 13 two-player standard-size (2 1/2" by 3 1/2") cards. One side showcases the best

player by position for the AFC, while the flip side carries his defensive counterpart for the NFC. The cards were randomly inserted in 1993 Pinnacle foil packs at an insertion rate of at least one in 90 packs. Both sides display black-bordered color action player paintings framed by a thin white line. The player's name, position, and conference designation appear on a gray stripe along the bottom of the portrait. Both sides of the card are numbered "X of 13."

| | MINT | EXC | G-VG |
|---|---|---|---|
| COMPLETE SET (13) | 250.00 | 115.00 | 31.00 |
| COMMON PLAYER (1-13) | 10.00 | 4.50 | 1.25 |
| | | | |
| ☐ 1 Troy Aikman | 100.00 | 45.00 | 12.50 |
| Dallas Cowboys | | | |
| Joe Montana | | | |
| Kansas City Chiefs | | | |
| ☐ 2 Thurman Thomas | 75.00 | 34.00 | 9.50 |
| Buffalo Bills | | | |
| Emmitt Smith | | | |
| Dallas Cowboys | | | |
| ☐ 3 Rodney Hampton | 25.00 | 11.50 | 3.10 |
| New York Giants | | | |
| Barry Foster | | | |
| Pittsburgh Steelers | | | |
| ☐ 4 Sterling Sharpe | 35.00 | 16.00 | 4.40 |
| Green Bay Packers | | | |
| Anthony Miller | | | |
| San Diego Chargers | | | |
| ☐ 5 Haywood Jeffires | 30.00 | 13.50 | 3.80 |
| Houston Oilers | | | |
| Michael Irvin | | | |
| Dallas Cowboys | | | |
| ☐ 6 Jay Novacek | 15.00 | 6.75 | 1.90 |
| Dallas Cowboys | | | |
| Keith Jackson | | | |
| Miami Dolphins | | | |
| ☐ 7 Richmond Webb | 10.00 | 4.50 | 1.25 |
| Miami Dolphins | | | |
| Steve Wallace | | | |
| San Francisco 49ers | | | |
| ☐ 8 Reggie White | 15.00 | 6.75 | 1.90 |
| Green Bay Packers | | | |
| Leslie O'Neal | | | |
| San Diego Chargers | | | |
| ☐ 9 Cortez Kennedy | 12.00 | 5.50 | 1.50 |
| Seattle Seahawks | | | |
| Sean Gilbert | | | |
| Los Angeles Rams | | | |
| ☐ 10 Derrick Thomas | 15.00 | 6.75 | 1.90 |
| Kansas City Chiefs | | | |
| Wilber Marshall | | | |
| Houston Oilers | | | |
| ☐ 11 Sam Mills | 12.00 | 5.50 | 1.50 |
| New Orleans Saints | | | |
| Junior Seau | | | |
| San Diego Chargers | | | |
| ☐ 12 Rod Woodson | 15.00 | 6.75 | 1.90 |
| Pittsburgh Steelers | | | |
| Deion Sanders | | | |
| Atlanta Falcons | | | |
| ☐ 13 Steve Atwater | 10.00 | 4.50 | 1.25 |
| Denver Broncos | | | |
| Tim McDonald | | | |
| San Francisco 49ers | | | |

## 1993 Pinnacle Team 2001

The 1993 Pinnacle Team 2001 set consists of 30 standard-size (2 1/2" by 3 1/2") cards showcasing the league's young players who are expected to be the NFL's major stars in the year 2001. The cards were inserted one per 27-card super pack of 1993 Pinnacle. The front features a color action player photo bordered by a wide black stripe that runs along the left and bottom edges. The gold-foil set title appears along the left border; the player's name is gold-foil stamped within the lower border. The team logo appears at the lower left. The horizontal back displays a close-up player shot on one side, and a black panel on the other containing the gold-foil player's name, team name, position, and 1992 season highlights. The cards are numbered on the back "X of 30."

|  | MINT | EXC | G-VG |
|---|---|---|---|
| COMPLETE SET (30).......................... | 16.00 | 7.25 | 2.00 |
| COMMON PLAYER (1-30)................. | .25 | .11 | .03 |
| ☐ 1 Junior Seau................................ | .30 | .14 | .04 |
| San Diego Chargers |  |  |  |
| ☐ 2 Cortez Kennedy......................... | .30 | .14 | .04 |
| Seattle Seahawks |  |  |  |
| ☐ 3 Carl Pickens ............................. | .30 | .14 | .04 |
| Cincinnati Bengals |  |  |  |
| ☐ 4 David Klingler........................... | .50 | .23 | .06 |
| Cincinnati Bengals |  |  |  |
| ☐ 5 Santana Dotson......................... | .25 | .11 | .03 |
| Tampa Bay Buccaneers |  |  |  |
| ☐ 6 Sean Gilbert ............................. | .25 | .11 | .03 |
| Los Angeles Rams |  |  |  |
| ☐ 7 Brett Favre................................ | 3.00 | 1.35 | .40 |
| Green Bay Packers |  |  |  |
| ☐ 8 Steve Emtman........................... | .25 | .11 | .03 |
| Indianapolis Colts |  |  |  |
| ☐ 9 Rodney Hampton ...................... | 1.25 | .55 | .16 |
| New York Giants |  |  |  |
| ☐ 10 Browning Nagle......................... | .25 | .11 | .03 |
| New York Jets |  |  |  |
| ☐ 11 Amp Lee .................................. | .30 | .14 | .04 |
| San Francisco 49ers |  |  |  |
| ☐ 12 Vaughn Dunbar ......................... | .25 | .11 | .03 |
| New Orleans Saints |  |  |  |
| ☐ 13 Quentin Coryatt ........................ | .30 | .14 | .04 |
| Indianapolis Colts |  |  |  |
| ☐ 14 Marco Coleman ......................... | .25 | .11 | .03 |
| Miami Dolphins |  |  |  |
| ☐ 15 Johnny Mitchell........................ | .60 | .25 | .08 |
| New York Jets |  |  |  |
| ☐ 16 Arthur Marshall ........................ | .30 | .14 | .04 |
| Denver Broncos |  |  |  |
| ☐ 17 Dale Carter .............................. | .30 | .14 | .04 |
| Kansas City Chiefs |  |  |  |
| ☐ 18 Henry Jones ............................. | .25 | .11 | .03 |
| Buffalo Bills |  |  |  |
| ☐ 19 Terrell Buckley ......................... | .30 | .14 | .04 |
| Green Bay Packers |  |  |  |
| ☐ 20 Tommy Vardell.......................... | .30 | .14 | .04 |
| Cleveland Browns |  |  |  |
| ☐ 21 Tommy Maddox ......................... | .25 | .11 | .03 |
| Denver Broncos |  |  |  |
| ☐ 22 Barry Foster ............................ | 1.50 | .65 | .19 |
| Pittsburgh Steelers |  |  |  |
| ☐ 23 Herman Moore .......................... | 1.00 | .45 | .13 |
| Detroit Lions |  |  |  |
| ☐ 24 Ricky Watters............................ | 1.75 | .80 | .22 |
| San Francisco 49ers |  |  |  |
| ☐ 25 Mike Croel ............................... | .25 | .11 | .03 |
| Denver Broncos |  |  |  |
| ☐ 26 Russell Maryland ...................... | .25 | .11 | .03 |
| Dallas Cowboys |  |  |  |
| ☐ 27 Terry Allen............................... | .30 | .14 | .04 |
| Minnesota Vikings |  |  |  |
| ☐ 28 Jon Vaughn .............................. | .25 | .11 | .03 |
| Seattle Seahawks |  |  |  |
| ☐ 29 Todd Marinovich ....................... | .25 | .11 | .03 |
| Los Angeles Raiders |  |  |  |
| ☐ 30 Jeff Graham .............................. | .25 | .11 | .03 |
| Pittsburgh Steelers |  |  |  |

## 1994 Pinnacle/Sportflics Super Bowl

This seven-card 1994 Magic Motion set was issued by Pinnacle Brands, Inc. (Score) at the 1994 Super Bowl Card Show in Atlanta. Cards were distributed individually by exchanging three Pinnacle Brands wrappers from foil packs. The cards were produced and distributed in the following quantities: 3,000 for Gary Brown and Emmitt Smith; 2,000 for Sterling Sharpe, Jerome Bettis/Reggie Brooks, and Drew Bledsoe/Rick Mirer; and 1,000 for Jerry Rice and Deion Sanders. The "Magic Motion" process is an improved version of the old Sportflics. The cards measure standard size (2 1/2" by 3 1/2"). The full-bleed fronts when tilted can show two different action pictures of the same player, with footballs moving over the goal posts under the photo. The player's last name appears in a blue rectangle which also changes from bold size lettering to reduced size lettering. The horizontal backs have a player portrait on the left side with a ghosted action shot on the right. Season highlights for the player are superimposed over the ghosted photo. An "S" prefix and a "B" suffix appear on either side of the card number printed on a yellow oval on the card back.

|  | MINT | EXC | G-VG |
|---|---|---|---|
| COMPLETE SET (7).......................... | 150.00 | 60.00 | 15.00 |
| COMMON PLAYER (1-7).................. | 20.00 | 8.00 | 2.00 |
| ☐ 1 Gary Brown .............................. | 20.00 | 8.00 | 2.00 |
| Houston Oilers |  |  |  |
| ☐ 2 Emmitt Smith............................ | 40.00 | 16.00 | 4.00 |
| Dallas Cowboys |  |  |  |
| ☐ 3 Sterling Sharpe ......................... | 30.00 | 12.00 | 3.00 |
| Green Bay Packers |  |  |  |
| ☐ 4 Jerome Bettis............................ | 30.00 | 12.00 | 3.00 |
| Los Angeles Rams |  |  |  |
| Reggie Brooks |  |  |  |
| Washington Redskins |  |  |  |
| ☐ 5 Drew Bledsoe............................ | 30.00 | 12.00 | 3.00 |
| New England Patriots |  |  |  |
| Rick Mirer |  |  |  |
| Seattle Seahawks |  |  |  |
| ☐ 6 Jerry Rice................................. | 40.00 | 16.00 | 4.00 |
| San Francisco 49ers |  |  |  |
| ☐ 7 Deion Sanders........................... | 40.00 | 16.00 | 4.00 |
| Atlanta Falcons |  |  |  |

## 1994 Pinnacle Canton Bound Promo

Measuring the standard size (2 1/2" by 3 1/2"), this promo was issued to promote the September 1994 release of Pinnacle's 25-card Canton Bound set. The front features a color action shot of Ronnie Lott that is borderless, except for the colorful bottom border that carries the set's title in neon-type lettering. The player's name appears near the right edge in vertical gold-foil lettering. On a borderless back composed of multiple player photos, the back carries the player's biography, career highlights, and statistics. The "Sample" disclaimer appears diagonally across the front and back. The card is numbered on the back.

|  | MINT | EXC | G-VG |
|---|---|---|---|
| COMPLETE SET (1)........................... | 2.00 | .80 | .20 |
| COMMON PLAYER............................ | 2.00 | .80 | .20 |
| ☐ 1 Ronnie Lott .............................. | 2.00 | .80 | .20 |
| New York Jets |  |  |  |

## 1994 Pinnacle Canton Bound

These 25 standard-size (2 1/2" by 3 1/2") cards feature Pinnacle's picks for future Hall of Fame inductees. Production was limited to 100,000 sets, and each set contained a numbered certificate of authenticity. The fronts feature color player action shots that are borderless, and carry the player's name in vertical gold-foil lettering near the right edge. On a borderless back composed of multiple player photos, the back carries the player's biography, career highlights, and statistics. The cards are numbered on the back.

|  | MINT | EXC | G-VG |
|---|---|---|---|
| COMPLETE SET (25)......................... | 12.50 | 5.00 | 1.25 |
| COMMON PLAYER (1-25)................. | .25 | .10 | .02 |

| | | | |
|---|---|---|---|
| ☐ 1 Troy Aikman | 2.00 | .80 | .20 |
| Dallas Cowboys | | | |
| ☐ 2 Emmitt Smith | 2.50 | 1.00 | .25 |
| Dallas Cowboys | | | |
| ☐ 3 Barry Sanders | 1.25 | .50 | .12 |
| Detroit Lions | | | |
| ☐ 4 Jerry Rice | 1.25 | .50 | .12 |
| San Francisco 49ers | | | |
| ☐ 5 Sterling Sharpe | 1.00 | .40 | .10 |
| Green Bay Packers | | | |
| ☐ 6 Ronnie Lott | .35 | .14 | .03 |
| New York Jets | | | |
| ☐ 7 John Elway | 1.00 | .40 | .10 |
| Denver Broncos | | | |
| ☐ 8 Joe Montana | 2.50 | 1.00 | .25 |
| Kansas City Chiefs | | | |
| ☐ 9 Reggie White | .50 | .20 | .05 |
| Green Bay Packers | | | |
| ☐ 10 Thurman Thomas | .75 | .30 | .07 |
| Buffalo Bills | | | |
| ☐ 11 Bruce Smith | .35 | .14 | .03 |
| Buffalo Bills | | | |
| ☐ 12 Cortez Kennedy | .35 | .14 | .03 |
| Seattle Seahawks | | | |
| ☐ 13 Dan Marino | 1.50 | .60 | .15 |
| Miami Dolphins | | | |
| ☐ 14 James Lofton | .35 | .14 | .03 |
| Buffalo Bills | | | |
| ☐ 15 Art Monk | .50 | .20 | .05 |
| Washington Redskins | | | |
| ☐ 16 Warren Moon | .75 | .30 | .07 |
| Minnesota Vikings | | | |
| ☐ 17 Barry Foster | .60 | .24 | .06 |
| Pittsburgh Steelers | | | |
| ☐ 18 Steve Young | .75 | .30 | .07 |
| San Francisco 49ers | | | |
| ☐ 19 Phil Simms | .50 | .20 | .05 |
| New York Giants | | | |
| ☐ 20 Richard Dent | .35 | .14 | .03 |
| Chicago Bears | | | |
| ☐ 21 Marcus Allen | .75 | .30 | .07 |
| Kansas City Chiefs | | | |
| ☐ 22 Junior Seau | .35 | .14 | .03 |
| San Diego Chargers | | | |
| ☐ 23 Michael Irvin | 1.00 | .40 | .10 |
| Dallas Cowboys | | | |
| ☐ 24 Deion Sanders | .75 | .30 | .07 |
| Atlanta Falcons | | | |
| ☐ 25 Jerome Bettis | 2.00 | .80 | .20 |
| Los Angeles Rams | | | |

## 1992 Playoff Promos

These seven cards were issued to give collectors a preview of the forthcoming 1993 Playoff series. The cards measure the standard size (2 1/2" by 3 1/2"). These cards are distinguished from other cards by the Tekchrome printing process, which enhances the action photography and gives the cards a three-dimensional appearance, and by their thicker (22 point) card stock. The fronts feature glossy full-bleed color player photos that exhibit a metallic-like sheen. The player's name appears in silver lettering in a black bar toward the bottom of the photo. The backs have a full-bleed color close-up photo with the player's name in a team color-coded vertical bar that descends from the top edge. The usual statistical information that is featured on the regular issue cards is replaced here by a detailed look at the player's performance in a key game in 1992. The cards are numbered on the back "X of 6 Promo".

| | MINT | EXC | G-VG |
|---|---|---|---|
| COMPLETE SET (7) | 30.00 | 12.00 | 3.00 |
| COMMON PLAYER (1-6) | 1.50 | .60 | .15 |
| ☐ 1 Calvin Williams | 2.50 | 1.00 | .25 |
| Philadelphia Eagles | | | |
| ☐ 2 John Elway | 7.50 | 3.00 | .75 |
| Denver Broncos | | | |
| ☐ 3 Dalton Hilliard | 1.50 | .60 | .15 |
| New Orleans Saints | | | |
| ☐ 4 Steve Young | 6.00 | 2.40 | .60 |
| San Francisco 49ers | | | |
| ☐ 5 Emmitt Smith | 15.00 | 6.00 | 1.50 |
| Dallas Cowboys | | | |
| ☐ 6 Mike Golic | 1.50 | .60 | .15 |
| Philadelphia Eagles | | | |
| ☐ NNO Header/Intro Card | 1.50 | .60 | .15 |

## 1992 Playoff

Distributed by Cardz Distribution, Inc., the 150 cards in this set measure the standard size (2 1/2" by 3 1/2") and are printed on a 22-point card stock. The fronts displays full-bleed player photos accented by the player's name in a black bar near the bottom. The pictures show the featured player in color. Other players may be color or black and white. Most of the backgrounds are black and white, but a few are color. On account of the TEKCHROME printing process, the cards have a metallic sheen that gives depth to the pictures. The backs have a full-bleed color close-up photo with the player's name in a team color-coded vertical bar that descends from the top edge. A black box centered at the bottom presents a detailed look at the player's performance during a key game in the 1992 season. The cards are numbered on the back. Twelve different versions of the display box were produced, each featuring a different football player. The key Rookie Cards in this set are Steve Bono, Terrell Buckley, Willie Davis, Amp Lee, and Darryl Williams.

| | MINT | EXC | G-VG |
|---|---|---|---|
| COMPLETE SET (150) | 45.00 | 20.00 | 5.75 |
| COMMON PLAYER (1-150) | .25 | .11 | .03 |
| ☐ 1 Emmitt Smith | 10.00 | 4.50 | 1.25 |
| Dallas Cowboys | | | |
| ☐ 2 Steve Young | 1.50 | .65 | .19 |
| San Francisco 49ers | | | |
| ☐ 3 Jack Del Rio | .25 | .11 | .03 |
| Minnesota Vikings | | | |
| ☐ 4 Bobby Hebert | .35 | .16 | .04 |
| New Orleans Saints | | | |
| ☐ 5 Shannon Sharpe | .60 | .25 | .08 |
| Denver Broncos | | | |
| ☐ 6 Gary Clark | .30 | .14 | .04 |
| Washington Redskins | | | |
| ☐ 7 Christian Okoye | .30 | .14 | .04 |
| Kansas City Chiefs | | | |
| ☐ 8 Ernest Givins | .30 | .14 | .04 |
| Houston Oilers | | | |
| ☐ 9 Mike Horan | .25 | .11 | .03 |

| | | | |
|---|---|---|---|
| Denver Broncos | | | |
| ☐ 10 Dennis Gentry | .25 | .11 | .03 |
| Chicago Bears | | | |
| ☐ 11 Michael Irvin | 3.00 | 1.35 | .40 |
| Dallas Cowboys | | | |
| ☐ 12 Eric Floyd | .25 | .11 | .03 |
| Philadelphia Eagles | | | |
| ☐ 13 Brent Jones | .35 | .16 | .04 |
| San Francisco 49ers | | | |
| ☐ 14 Anthony Carter | .30 | .14 | .04 |
| Minnesota Vikings | | | |
| ☐ 15 Tony Martin | .25 | .11 | .03 |
| Miami Dolphins | | | |
| ☐ 16 Greg Lewis UER | .25 | .11 | .03 |
| Denver Broncos | | | |
| ("Returning" should be | | | |
| "returned" on back) | | | |
| ☐ 17 Todd McNair | .25 | .11 | .03 |
| Kansas City Chiefs | | | |
| ☐ 18 Earnest Byner | .30 | .14 | .04 |
| Washington Redskins | | | |
| ☐ 19 Steve Beuerlein | .50 | .23 | .06 |
| Dallas Cowboys | | | |
| ☐ 20 Roger Craig | .30 | .14 | .04 |
| Minnesota Vikings | | | |
| ☐ 21 Mark Higgs | .50 | .23 | .06 |
| Miami Dolphins | | | |
| ☐ 22 Guy McIntyre | .30 | .14 | .04 |
| San Francisco 49ers | | | |
| ☐ 23 Don Warren | .25 | .11 | .03 |
| Washington Redskins | | | |
| ☐ 24 Alvin Harper | 1.50 | .65 | .19 |
| Dallas Cowboys | | | |
| ☐ 25 Mark Jackson | .30 | .14 | .04 |
| Denver Broncos | | | |
| ☐ 26 Chris Doleman | .30 | .14 | .04 |
| Minnesota Vikings | | | |
| ☐ 27 Jesse Sapolu | .25 | .11 | .03 |
| San Francisco 49ers | | | |
| ☐ 28 Tony Tolbert | .25 | .11 | .03 |
| Dallas Cowboys | | | |
| ☐ 29 Wendell Davis | .25 | .11 | .03 |
| Chicago Bears | | | |
| ☐ 30 Dan Saleaumua | .25 | .11 | .03 |
| Kansas City Chiefs | | | |
| ☐ 31 Jeff Bostic | .25 | .11 | .03 |
| Washington Redskins | | | |
| ☐ 32 Jay Novacek | .50 | .23 | .06 |
| Dallas Cowboys | | | |
| ☐ 33 Cris Carter | .35 | .16 | .04 |
| Minnesota Vikings | | | |
| ☐ 34 Tony Paige | .25 | .11 | .03 |
| Miami Dolphins | | | |
| ☐ 35 Greg Kragen | .25 | .11 | .03 |
| Denver Broncos | | | |
| ☐ 36 Jeff Dellenbach | .25 | .11 | .03 |
| Miami Dolphins | | | |
| ☐ 37 Keith DeLong | .25 | .11 | .03 |
| San Francisco 49ers | | | |
| ☐ 38 Todd Scott | .25 | .11 | .03 |
| Minnesota Vikings | | | |
| ☐ 39 Jeff Feagles | .25 | .11 | .03 |
| Philadelphia Eagles | | | |
| ☐ 40 Mike Saxon | .25 | .11 | .03 |
| Dallas Cowboys | | | |
| ☐ 41 Martin Mayhew | .25 | .11 | .03 |
| Washington Redskins | | | |
| ☐ 42 Steve Bono | 1.50 | .65 | .19 |
| San Francisco 49ers | | | |
| ☐ 43 Willie Davis | 1.00 | .45 | .13 |
| Kansas City Chiefs | | | |
| ☐ 44 Mark Stepnoski | .25 | .11 | .03 |
| Dallas Cowboys | | | |
| ☐ 45 Harry Newsome | .25 | .11 | .03 |
| Minnesota Vikings | | | |
| ☐ 46 Thane Gash | .25 | .11 | .03 |
| San Francisco 49ers | | | |
| ☐ 47 Gaston Green | .30 | .14 | .04 |
| Denver Broncos | | | |
| ☐ 48 James Washington | .25 | .11 | .03 |
| Dallas Cowboys | | | |
| ☐ 49 Kenny Walker | .25 | .11 | .03 |
| Denver Broncos | | | |
| ☐ 50 Jeff Davidson | .25 | .11 | .03 |
| Denver Broncos | | | |
| ☐ 51 Shane Conlan | .30 | .14 | .04 |
| Buffalo Bills | | | |
| ☐ 52 Richard Dent | .30 | .14 | .04 |
| Chicago Bears | | | |
| ☐ 53 Haywood Jeffires | .35 | .16 | .04 |
| Houston Oilers | | | |
| ☐ 54 Harry Galbreath | .25 | .11 | .03 |
| Miami Dolphins | | | |
| ☐ 55 Terry Allen | 1.00 | .45 | .13 |
| Minnesota Vikings | | | |
| ☐ 56 Tommy Barnhardt | .25 | .11 | .03 |
| New Orleans Saints | | | |
| ☐ 57 Mike Golic | .25 | .11 | .03 |
| Philadelphia Eagles | | | |
| ☐ 58 Dalton Hilliard | .25 | .11 | .03 |
| New Orleans Saints | | | |
| ☐ 59 Danny Copeland | .25 | .11 | .03 |
| Washington Redskins | | | |
| ☐ 60 Jerry Fontenot | .30 | .14 | .04 |
| Chicago Bears | | | |
| ☐ 61 Kelvin Martin | .30 | .14 | .04 |
| Dallas Cowboys | | | |
| ☐ 62 Mark Kelso | .25 | .11 | .03 |
| Buffalo Bills | | | |
| ☐ 63 Wymon Henderson | .25 | .11 | .03 |
| Denver Broncos | | | |
| ☐ 64 Mark Rypien | .35 | .16 | .04 |
| Washington Redskins | | | |
| ☐ 65 Bobby Humphrey | .30 | .14 | .04 |
| Miami Dolphins | | | |
| ☐ 66 Rich Gannon UER | .30 | .14 | .04 |
| Minnesota Vikings | | | |
| (Tarkington misspelled; | | | |
| Minneapolis instead | | | |
| of Minnesota on back) | | | |
| ☐ 67 Darren Lewis | .25 | .11 | .03 |
| Chicago Bears | | | |
| ☐ 68 Barry Foster | 2.50 | 1.15 | .30 |
| Pittsburgh Steelers | | | |
| ☐ 69 Ken Norton | .30 | .14 | .04 |
| Dallas Cowboys | | | |
| ☐ 70 James Lofton | .35 | .16 | .04 |
| Buffalo Bills | | | |
| ☐ 71 Trace Armstrong | .25 | .11 | .03 |
| Chicago Bears | | | |
| ☐ 72 Vestee Jackson | .25 | .11 | .03 |
| Miami Dolphins | | | |
| ☐ 73 Clyde Simmons | .30 | .14 | .04 |
| Philadelphia Eagles | | | |
| ☐ 74 Brad Muster | .30 | .14 | .04 |
| Chicago Bears | | | |
| ☐ 75 Cornelius Bennett | .35 | .16 | .04 |
| Buffalo Bills | | | |
| ☐ 76 Mike Merriweather | .25 | .11 | .03 |
| Minnesota Vikings | | | |
| ☐ 77 John Elway | 2.25 | 1.00 | .30 |
| Denver Broncos | | | |
| ☐ 78 Herschel Walker | .35 | .16 | .04 |
| Philadelphia Eagles | | | |
| ☐ 79 Hassan Jones UER | .25 | .11 | .03 |
| Minnesota Vikings | | | |
| (Minneapolis instead | | | |
| of Minnesota on back) | | | |
| ☐ 80 Jim Harbaugh | .30 | .14 | .04 |
| Chicago Bears | | | |
| ☐ 81 Issiac Holt | .25 | .11 | .03 |
| Dallas Cowboys | | | |
| ☐ 82 David Alexander | .25 | .11 | .03 |
| Philadelphia Eagles | | | |
| ☐ 83 Brian Mitchell | .30 | .14 | .04 |
| Washington Redskins | | | |
| ☐ 84 Mark Tuinei | .25 | .11 | .03 |
| Dallas Cowboys | | | |
| ☐ 85 Tom Rathman | .30 | .14 | .04 |
| San Francisco 49ers | | | |
| ☐ 86 Reggie White | .60 | .25 | .08 |
| Philadelphia Eagles | | | |
| ☐ 87 William Perry | .30 | .14 | .04 |
| Chicago Bears | | | |
| ☐ 88 Jeff Wright | .25 | .11 | .03 |
| Buffalo Bills | | | |
| ☐ 89 Keith Kartz | .25 | .11 | .03 |
| Denver Broncos | | | |
| ☐ 90 Andre Waters | .25 | .11 | .03 |
| Philadelphia Eagles | | | |
| ☐ 91 Darryl Talley | .30 | .14 | .04 |
| Buffalo Bills | | | |
| ☐ 92 Morten Andersen | .30 | .14 | .04 |
| New Orleans Saints | | | |
| ☐ 93 Tom Waddle | .35 | .16 | .04 |
| Chicago Bears | | | |
| ☐ 94 Felix Wright UER | .25 | .11 | .03 |
| Minnesota Vikings | | | |
| (Minneapolis instead | | | |
| of Minnesota on back) | | | |
| ☐ 95 Keith Jackson | .35 | .16 | .04 |
| Miami Dolphins | | | |
| ☐ 96 Art Monk | .35 | .16 | .04 |
| Washington Redskins | | | |
| ☐ 97 Seth Joyner | .30 | .14 | .04 |
| Philadelphia Eagles | | | |
| ☐ 98 Steve McMichael | .30 | .14 | .04 |
| Chicago Bears | | | |
| ☐ 99 Thurman Thomas | 2.25 | 1.00 | .30 |
| Buffalo Bills | | | |
| ☐ 100 Warren Moon | 1.00 | .45 | .13 |
| Houston Oilers | | | |
| ☐ 101 Tony Casillas | .25 | .11 | .03 |
| Dallas Cowboys | | | |
| ☐ 102 Vance Johnson | .30 | .14 | .04 |
| Denver Broncos | | | |

| | | | |
|---|---|---|---|
| ☐ 103 Doug Dawson | .30 | .14 | .04 |
| Houston Oilers | | | |
| ☐ 104 Bill Maas | .25 | .11 | .03 |
| Kansas City Chiefs | | | |
| ☐ 105 Mark Clayton | .30 | .14 | .04 |
| Miami Dolphins | | | |
| ☐ 106 Hoby Brenner | .25 | .11 | .03 |
| New Orleans Saints | | | |
| ☐ 107 Gary Anderson | .25 | .11 | .03 |
| Pittsburgh Steelers | | | |
| ☐ 108 Marc Logan | .25 | .11 | .03 |
| San Francisco 49ers | | | |
| ☐ 109 Ricky Sanders | .30 | .14 | .04 |
| Washington Redskins | | | |
| ☐ 110 Vai Sikahema | .30 | .14 | .04 |
| Philadelphia Eagles | | | |
| ☐ 111 Neil Smith | .35 | .16 | .04 |
| Kansas City Chiefs | | | |
| ☐ 112 Cody Carlson | .50 | .23 | .06 |
| Houston Oilers | | | |
| ☐ 113 Jimmie Jones | .25 | .11 | .03 |
| Dallas Cowboys | | | |
| ☐ 114 Pat Swilling | .30 | .14 | .04 |
| New Orleans Saints | | | |
| ☐ 115 Neil O'Donnell | 1.75 | .80 | .22 |
| Pittsburgh Steelers | | | |
| ☐ 116 Chip Lohmiller | .30 | .14 | .04 |
| Washington Redskins | | | |
| ☐ 117 Mike Croel | .30 | .14 | .04 |
| Denver Broncos | | | |
| ☐ 118 Pete Metzelaars | .25 | .11 | .03 |
| Buffalo Bills | | | |
| ☐ 119 Ray Childress | .30 | .14 | .04 |
| Houston Oilers | | | |
| ☐ 120 Fred Banks | .25 | .11 | .03 |
| Miami Dolphins | | | |
| ☐ 121 Derek Kennard | .25 | .11 | .03 |
| New Orleans Saints | | | |
| ☐ 122 Daryl Johnston | .35 | .16 | .04 |
| Dallas Cowboys | | | |
| ☐ 123 Lorenzo White UER | .30 | .14 | .04 |
| Houston Oilers | | | |
| (Minneapolis instead | | | |
| of Minnesota on back) | | | |
| ☐ 124 Hardy Nickerson | .25 | .11 | .03 |
| Pittsburgh Steelers | | | |
| ☐ 125 Derrick Thomas | .75 | .35 | .09 |
| Kansas City Chiefs | | | |
| ☐ 126 Steve Walsh | .25 | .11 | .03 |
| New Orleans Saints | | | |
| ☐ 127 Doug Widell | .25 | .11 | .03 |
| Denver Broncos | | | |
| ☐ 128 Calvin Williams | .35 | .16 | .04 |
| Philadelphia Eagles | | | |
| ☐ 129 Tim Harris | .30 | .14 | .04 |
| San Francisco 49ers | | | |
| ☐ 130 Rod Woodson | .35 | .16 | .04 |
| Pittsburgh Steelers | | | |
| ☐ 131 Craig Heyward | .25 | .11 | .03 |
| New Orleans Saints | | | |
| ☐ 132 Barry Word | .35 | .16 | .04 |
| Kansas City Chiefs | | | |
| ☐ 133 Mark Duper | .30 | .14 | .04 |
| Miami Dolphins | | | |
| ☐ 134 Tim Johnson | .25 | .11 | .03 |
| Washington Redskins | | | |
| ☐ 135 John Gesek | .25 | .11 | .03 |
| Dallas Cowboys | | | |
| ☐ 136 Steve Jackson | .25 | .11 | .03 |
| Houston Oilers | | | |
| ☐ 137 Dave Krieg | .30 | .14 | .04 |
| Kansas City Chiefs | | | |
| ☐ 138 Barry Sanders UER | 4.50 | 2.00 | .55 |
| (Won Heisman in | | | |
| 1988, not 1986) | | | |
| Detroit Lions | | | |
| ☐ 139 Michael Haynes | 1.50 | .65 | .19 |
| Atlanta Falcons | | | |
| ☐ 140 Eric Metcalf | .35 | .16 | .04 |
| Cleveland Browns | | | |
| ☐ 141 Stan Humphries | .50 | .23 | .06 |
| San Diego Chargers | | | |
| ☐ 142 Sterling Sharpe | 3.00 | 1.35 | .40 |
| Green Bay Packers | | | |
| ☐ 143 Todd Marinovich | .25 | .11 | .03 |
| Los Angeles Raiders | | | |
| ☐ 144 Rodney Hampton | 2.50 | 1.15 | .30 |
| New York Giants | | | |
| ☐ 145 Rodney Peete | .30 | .14 | .04 |
| Detroit Lions | | | |
| ☐ 146 Darryl Williams | .75 | .35 | .09 |
| Cincinnati Bengals | | | |
| ☐ 147 Darren Perry | .50 | .23 | .06 |
| Pittsburgh Steelers | | | |
| ☐ 148 Terrell Buckley | .75 | .35 | .09 |
| Green Bay Packers | | | |
| ☐ 149 Amp Lee | 1.00 | .45 | .13 |

| | | | |
|---|---|---|---|
| San Francisco 49ers | | | |
| ☐ 150 Ricky Watters | 2.50 | 1.15 | .30 |
| San Francisco 49ers | | | |

## 1993 Playoff Promos

Measuring the standard-size (2 1/2" by 3 1/2"), these six cards were issued to preview the design of the 1993 Playoff Collectors Edition football set. Printed on a thicker (22 point) card using the Tekchrome printing process, the action player photos on the fronts are full-bleed and have a metallic sheen to them. The player's name appears in silver lettering on a short black bar that overlays the bottom of the picture. On a full-bleed color close-up photo, the backs have the player's name on a brick-red vertical bar and a brief player profile on a black panel. The cards are numbered "X of 6 Promo."

| | MINT | EXC | G-VG |
|---|---|---|---|
| COMPLETE SET (6) | 20.00 | 8.00 | 2.00 |
| COMMON PLAYER (1-6) | 1.50 | .60 | .15 |
| ☐ 1 Emmitt Smith | 10.00 | 4.00 | 1.00 |
| Dallas Cowboys | | | |
| ☐ 2 Barry Foster | 4.00 | 1.60 | .40 |
| Pittsburgh Steelers | | | |
| ☐ 3 Quinn Early | 1.50 | .60 | .15 |
| New Orleans Saints | | | |
| ☐ 4 Tim Brown | 2.50 | 1.00 | .25 |
| Los Angeles Raiders | | | |
| ☐ 5 Steve Young | 4.00 | 1.60 | .40 |
| San Francisco 49ers | | | |
| ☐ 6 Sterling Sharpe | 5.00 | 2.00 | .50 |
| Green Bay Packers | | | |

## 1993 Playoff

The 1993 Playoff Collectors Edition football set consists of 315 standard-size (2 1/2" by 3 1/2") cards. A special insert card known as "The Trading Card" was randomly inserted in hobby foil packs and redeemable for a ten-card Rookie Round Up set; the same card in retail foil packs was redeemable for a six-card The Headliners set. A five-card Brett Favre subset was randomly inserted in hobby display boxes, while a five-card Ricky Watters subset was found in retail dispaly boxes. Finally, a seven-card The Playoff Card Club subset was available in both hobby and retail display cases. A Rookie card or special insert card was found in every pack. Topical subsets featured include The Backs (277-282), Connections (283-292), and Rookies (293-315). Rookie Cards include Jerome Bettis, Drew Bledsoe, Reggie Brooks, O.J. McDuffie, Rick Mirer and Ron Moore.

| | MINT | EXC | G-VG |
|---|---|---|---|
| COMPLETE SET (315) | 55.00 | 25.00 | 7.00 |
| COMMON PLAYER (1-315) | .15 | .07 | .02 |

| | | | |
|---|---|---|---|
| ☐ 1 Troy Aikman | 5.00 | 2.30 | .60 |
| Dallas Cowboys | | | |
| ☐ 2 Jerry Rice | 2.00 | .90 | .25 |
| San Francisco 49ers | | | |
| ☐ 3 Keith Jackson | .25 | .11 | .03 |
| Miami Dolphins | | | |
| ☐ 4 Sean Gilbert | .20 | .09 | .03 |
| Los Angeles Rams | | | |
| ☐ 5 Jim Kelly | .75 | .35 | .09 |
| Buffalo Bills | | | |
| ☐ 6 Junior Seau | .25 | .11 | .03 |
| San Diego Chargers | | | |
| ☐ 7 Deion Sanders | .50 | .23 | .06 |
| Atlanta Falcons | | | |
| ☐ 8 Joe Montana | 3.50 | 1.55 | .45 |
| San Francisco 49ers | | | |
| ☐ 9 Terrell Buckley | .25 | .11 | .03 |
| Green Bay Packers | | | |
| ☐ 10 Emmitt Smith | 7.00 | 3.10 | .85 |
| Dallas Cowboys | | | |
| ☐ 11 Pete Stoyanovich | .15 | .07 | .02 |
| Miami Dolphins | | | |
| ☐ 12 Randall Cunningham | .35 | .16 | .04 |
| Philadelphia Eagles | | | |
| ☐ 13 Boomer Esiason | .35 | .16 | .04 |
| Cincinnati Bengals | | | |
| ☐ 14 Mike Saxon | .15 | .07 | .02 |
| Dallas Cowboys | | | |
| ☐ 15 Chuck Cecil | .15 | .07 | .02 |
| Green Bay Packers | | | |
| ☐ 16 Vinny Testaverde | .25 | .11 | .03 |
| Tampa Bay Buccaneers | | | |
| ☐ 17 Jeff Hostetler | .25 | .11 | .03 |
| New York Giants | | | |
| ☐ 18 Mark Clayton | .20 | .09 | .03 |
| Green Bay Packers | | | |
| ☐ 19 Nick Bell | .20 | .09 | .03 |
| Los Angeles Raiders | | | |
| ☐ 20 Frank Reich | .20 | .09 | .03 |
| Buffalo Bills | | | |
| ☐ 21 Henry Ellard | .20 | .09 | .03 |
| Los Angeles Rams | | | |
| ☐ 22 Andre Reed | .25 | .11 | .03 |
| Buffalo Bills | | | |
| ☐ 23 Mark Ingram | .20 | .09 | .03 |
| New York Giants | | | |
| ☐ 24 Mike Brim | .15 | .07 | .02 |
| New York Jets | | | |
| ☐ 25A Bernie Kosar UER | .25 | .11 | .03 |
| Cleveland Browns | | | |
| (Name spelled Kozar on | | | |
| both sides) | | | |
| ☐ 25B Bernie Kosar COR | .50 | .23 | .06 |
| Cleveland Browns | | | |
| ☐ 26 Jeff George | .50 | .23 | .06 |
| Indianapolis Colts | | | |
| ☐ 27 Tommy Maddox | .50 | .23 | .06 |
| Denver Broncos | | | |
| ☐ 28 Kent Graham | 1.25 | .55 | .16 |
| New York Giants | | | |
| ☐ 29 David Klingler | .60 | .25 | .08 |
| Cincinnati Bengals | | | |
| ☐ 30 Robert Delpino | .20 | .09 | .03 |
| Los Angeles Rams | | | |
| ☐ 31 Kevin Fagan | .15 | .07 | .02 |
| San Francisco 49ers | | | |
| ☐ 32 Mark Bavaro | .20 | .09 | .03 |
| Cleveland Browns | | | |
| ☐ 33 Harold Green | .20 | .09 | .03 |
| Cincinnati Bengals | | | |
| ☐ 34 Shawn McCarthy | .15 | .07 | .02 |
| New England Patriots | | | |
| ☐ 35 Ricky Proehl | .20 | .09 | .03 |
| Phoenix Cardinals | | | |
| ☐ 36 Eugene Robinson | .15 | .07 | .02 |
| Seattle Seahawks | | | |
| ☐ 37 Phil Simms | .25 | .11 | .03 |
| New York Giants | | | |
| ☐ 38 David Lang | .15 | .07 | .02 |
| Los Angeles Rams | | | |
| ☐ 39 Santana Dotson | .25 | .11 | .03 |
| Tampa Bay Buccaneers | | | |
| ☐ 40 Brett Perriman | .20 | .09 | .03 |
| Detroit Lions | | | |
| ☐ 41 Jim Harbaugh | .20 | .09 | .03 |
| Chicago Bears | | | |
| ☐ 42 Keith Byars | .20 | .09 | .03 |
| Philadelphia Eagles | | | |
| ☐ 43 Quentin Coryatt | .25 | .11 | .03 |
| Indianapolis Colts | | | |
| ☐ 44 Louis Oliver | .15 | .07 | .02 |
| Miami Dolphins | | | |
| ☐ 45 Howie Long | .20 | .09 | .03 |
| Los Angeles Raiders | | | |
| ☐ 46 Mike Sherrard | .15 | .07 | .02 |
| San Francisco 49ers | | | |
| ☐ 47 Earnest Byner | .20 | .09 | .03 |

| | | | |
|---|---|---|---|
| Washington Redskins | | | |
| ☐ 48 Neil Smith | .25 | .11 | .03 |
| Kansas City Chiefs | | | |
| ☐ 49 Audray McMillan | .15 | .07 | .02 |
| Minnesota Vikings | | | |
| ☐ 50 Vaughn Dunbar | .20 | .09 | .03 |
| New Orleans Saints | | | |
| ☐ 51 Ronnie Lott | .25 | .11 | .03 |
| Los Angeles Raiders | | | |
| ☐ 52 Clyde Simmons | .20 | .09 | .03 |
| Philadelphia Eagles | | | |
| ☐ 53 Kevin Scott | .15 | .07 | .02 |
| Detroit Lions | | | |
| ☐ 54 Bubby Brister | .15 | .07 | .02 |
| Pittsburgh Steelers | | | |
| ☐ 55 Randal Hill | .25 | .11 | .03 |
| Phoenix Cardinals | | | |
| ☐ 56 Pat Swilling | .20 | .09 | .03 |
| New Orleans Saints | | | |
| ☐ 57 Steve Beuerlein | .30 | .14 | .04 |
| Dallas Cowboys | | | |
| ☐ 58 Gary Clark | .20 | .09 | .03 |
| Washington Redskins | | | |
| ☐ 59 Brian Noble | .15 | .07 | .02 |
| Green Bay Packers | | | |
| ☐ 60 Leslie O'Neal | .20 | .09 | .03 |
| San Diego Chargers | | | |
| ☐ 61 Vincent Brown | .15 | .07 | .02 |
| New England Patriots | | | |
| ☐ 62 Edgar Bennett | .25 | .11 | .03 |
| Green Bay Packers | | | |
| ☐ 63 Anthony Carter | .20 | .09 | .03 |
| Minnesota Vikings | | | |
| ☐ 64 Glenn Cadrez UER | .25 | .11 | .03 |
| New York Jets | | | |
| (Name misspelled Cadez on front) | | | |
| ☐ 65 Dalton Hilliard | .15 | .07 | .02 |
| New Orleans Saints | | | |
| ☐ 66 James Lofton | .25 | .11 | .03 |
| Buffalo Bills | | | |
| ☐ 67 Walter Stanley | .15 | .07 | .02 |
| New England Patriots | | | |
| ☐ 68 Tim Harris | .15 | .07 | .02 |
| San Francisco 49ers | | | |
| ☐ 69 Carl Banks | .20 | .09 | .03 |
| New York Giants | | | |
| ☐ 70 Andre Ware | .20 | .09 | .03 |
| Detroit Lions | | | |
| ☐ 71 Karl Mecklenburg | .20 | .09 | .03 |
| Denver Broncos | | | |
| ☐ 72 Russell Maryland | .25 | .11 | .03 |
| Dallas Cowboys | | | |
| ☐ 73 Leroy Thompson | .20 | .09 | .03 |
| Pittsburgh Steelers | | | |
| ☐ 74 Tommy Kane | .15 | .07 | .02 |
| Seattle Seahawks | | | |
| ☐ 75 Dan Marino | 2.00 | .90 | .25 |
| Miami Dolphins | | | |
| ☐ 76 Darrell Fullington | .15 | .07 | .02 |
| Tampa Bay Buccaneers | | | |
| ☐ 77 Jessie Tuggle | .15 | .07 | .02 |
| Atlanta Falcons | | | |
| ☐ 78 Bruce Smith | .25 | .11 | .03 |
| Buffalo Bills | | | |
| ☐ 79 Neal Anderson | .20 | .09 | .03 |
| Chicago Bears | | | |
| ☐ 80 Kevin Mack | .20 | .09 | .03 |
| Cleveland Browns | | | |
| ☐ 81 Shane Dronett | .15 | .07 | .02 |
| Denver Broncos | | | |
| ☐ 82 Nick Lowery | .15 | .07 | .02 |
| Kansas City Chiefs | | | |
| ☐ 83 Sheldon White | .15 | .07 | .02 |
| Detroit Lions | | | |
| ☐ 84 Flipper Anderson | .20 | .09 | .03 |
| Los Angeles Rams | | | |
| ☐ 85 Jeff Herrod | .15 | .07 | .02 |
| Indianapolis Colts | | | |
| ☐ 86 Dwight Stone | .15 | .07 | .02 |
| Pittsburgh Steelers | | | |
| ☐ 87 Dave Krieg | .20 | .09 | .03 |
| Kansas City Chiefs | | | |
| ☐ 88 Bryan Cox | .20 | .09 | .03 |
| Miami Dolphins | | | |
| ☐ 89 Greg McMurtry | .15 | .07 | .02 |
| New England Patriots | | | |
| ☐ 90 Rickey Jackson | .20 | .09 | .03 |
| New Orleans Saints | | | |
| ☐ 91 Ernie Mills | .15 | .07 | .02 |
| Pittsburgh Steelers | | | |
| ☐ 92 Browning Nagle | .20 | .09 | .03 |
| New York Jets | | | |
| ☐ 93 John Taylor | .25 | .11 | .03 |
| San Francisco 49ers | | | |
| ☐ 94 Eric Dickerson | .25 | .11 | .03 |
| Los Angeles Raiders | | | |
| ☐ 95 Johnny Holland | .15 | .07 | .02 |
| Green Bay Packers | | | |

| | | | |
|---|---|---|---|
| ☐ 96 Anthony Miller........................ | .40 | .18 | .05 |
| San Diego Chargers | | | |
| ☐ 97 Fred Barnett......................... | .25 | .11 | .03 |
| Philadelphia Eagles | | | |
| ☐ 98 Ricky Ervins UER ................... | .20 | .09 | .03 |
| Washington Redskins | | | |
| (Name misspelled | | | |
| Rickey on back) | | | |
| ☐ 99 Leonard Russell ..................... | .20 | .09 | .03 |
| New England Patriots | | | |
| ☐ 100 Lawrence Taylor.................... | .35 | .16 | .04 |
| New York Giants | | | |
| ☐ 101 Tony Casillas...................... | .15 | .07 | .02 |
| Dallas Cowboys | | | |
| ☐ 102 John Elway.......................... | 1.25 | .55 | .16 |
| Denver Broncos | | | |
| ☐ 103 Bennie Blades...................... | .15 | .07 | .02 |
| Detroit Lions | | | |
| ☐ 104 Harry Sydney ...................... | .15 | .07 | .02 |
| Green Bay Packers | | | |
| ☐ 105 Bubba McDowell .................... | .15 | .07 | .02 |
| Houston Oilers | | | |
| ☐ 106 Todd McNair ....................... | .15 | .07 | .02 |
| Kansas City Chiefs | | | |
| ☐ 107 Steve Smith........................ | .20 | .09 | .03 |
| Los Angeles Raiders | | | |
| ☐ 108 Jim Everett........................ | .15 | .07 | .02 |
| Los Angeles Rams | | | |
| ☐ 109 Bobby Humphrey .................... | .20 | .09 | .03 |
| Miami Dolphins | | | |
| ☐ 110 Rich Gannon........................ | .20 | .09 | .03 |
| Minnesota Vikings | | | |
| ☐ 111 Marv Cook.......................... | .15 | .07 | .02 |
| New England Patriots | | | |
| ☐ 112 Wayne Martin ...................... | .15 | .07 | .02 |
| New Orleans Saints | | | |
| ☐ 113 Sean Landeta ...................... | .15 | .07 | .02 |
| New York Giants | | | |
| ☐ 114 Brad Baxter UER ................... | .20 | .09 | .03 |
| New York Jets | | | |
| (Reversed negative on front) | | | |
| ☐ 115 Reggie White....................... | .40 | .18 | .05 |
| Philadelphia Eagles | | | |
| ☐ 116 Johnny Johnson .................... | .25 | .11 | .03 |
| Phoenix Cardinals | | | |
| ☐ 117 Jeff Graham ....................... | .20 | .09 | .03 |
| Pittsburgh Steelers | | | |
| ☐ 118 Darren Carrington ................. | .35 | .16 | .04 |
| San Diego Chargers | | | |
| ☐ 119 Ricky Watters ..................... | 1.00 | .45 | .13 |
| San Francisco 49ers | | | |
| ☐ 120 Art Monk UER ...................... | .25 | .11 | .03 |
| Washington Redskins | | | |
| (Reversed negative on back) | | | |
| ☐ 121 Cornelius Bennett ................. | .25 | .11 | .03 |
| Buffalo Bills | | | |
| ☐ 122 Wade Wilson........................ | .20 | .09 | .03 |
| Atlanta Falcons | | | |
| ☐ 123 Daniel Stubbs...................... | .15 | .07 | .02 |
| Cincinnati Bengals | | | |
| ☐ 124 Brad Muster ....................... | .20 | .09 | .03 |
| Chicago Bears | | | |
| ☐ 125 Mike Tomczak ...................... | .15 | .07 | .02 |
| Cleveland Browns | | | |
| ☐ 126 Jay Novacek........................ | .25 | .11 | .03 |
| Dallas Cowboys | | | |
| ☐ 127 Shannon Sharpe .................... | .50 | .23 | .06 |
| Denver Broncos | | | |
| ☐ 128 Rodney Peete....................... | .20 | .09 | .03 |
| Detroit Lions | | | |
| ☐ 129 Daryl Johnston .................... | .25 | .11 | .03 |
| Dallas Cowboys | | | |
| ☐ 130 Warren Moon ....................... | .50 | .23 | .06 |
| Houston Oilers | | | |
| ☐ 131 Willie Gault....................... | .20 | .09 | .03 |
| Los Angeles Raiders | | | |
| ☐ 132 Tony Martin ....................... | .15 | .07 | .02 |
| Miami Dolphins | | | |
| ☐ 133 Terry Allen........................ | .25 | .11 | .03 |
| Minnesota Vikings | | | |
| ☐ 134 Hugh Millen........................ | .15 | .07 | .02 |
| New England Patriots | | | |
| ☐ 135 Rob Moore ......................... | .25 | .11 | .03 |
| New York Jets | | | |
| ☐ 136 Andy Harmon ....................... | .15 | .07 | .02 |
| Philadelphia Eagles | | | |
| ☐ 137 Kelvin Martin ..................... | .20 | .09 | .03 |
| Dallas Cowboys | | | |
| ☐ 138 Rod Woodson ....................... | .25 | .11 | .03 |
| Pittsburgh Steelers | | | |
| ☐ 139 Nate Lewis ........................ | .20 | .09 | .03 |
| San Diego Chargers | | | |
| ☐ 140 Darryl Talley ..................... | .15 | .07 | .02 |
| Buffalo Bills | | | |
| ☐ 141 Guy McIntyre ...................... | .15 | .07 | .02 |
| San Francisco 49ers | | | |
| ☐ 142 John L. Williams .................. | .20 | .09 | .03 |

| | | | |
|---|---|---|---|
| Seattle Seahawks | | | |
| ☐ 143 Brad Edwards....................... | .15 | .07 | .02 |
| Washington Redskins | | | |
| ☐ 144 Trace Armstrong .................... | .15 | .07 | .02 |
| Chicago Bears | | | |
| ☐ 145 Kenneth Davis ...................... | .20 | .09 | .03 |
| Buffalo Bills | | | |
| ☐ 146 Clay Matthews...................... | .20 | .09 | .03 |
| Cleveland Browns | | | |
| ☐ 147 Gaston Green ....................... | .20 | .09 | .03 |
| Denver Broncos | | | |
| ☐ 148 Chris Spielman .................... | .15 | .07 | .02 |
| Detroit Lions | | | |
| ☐ 149 Cody Carlson....................... | .50 | .23 | .06 |
| Houston Oilers | | | |
| ☐ 150 Derrick Thomas..................... | .40 | .18 | .05 |
| Kansas City Chiefs | | | |
| ☐ 151 Terry McDaniel..................... | .15 | .07 | .02 |
| Los Angeles Raiders | | | |
| ☐ 152 Kevin Greene....................... | .15 | .07 | .02 |
| Los Angeles Rams | | | |
| ☐ 153 Roger Craig ....................... | .20 | .09 | .03 |
| Minnesota Vikings | | | |
| ☐ 154 Craig Heyward...................... | .15 | .07 | .02 |
| New Orleans Saints | | | |
| ☐ 155 Rodney Hampton ................... | 1.00 | .45 | .13 |
| New York Giants | | | |
| ☐ 156 Heath Sherman ..................... | .15 | .07 | .02 |
| Philadelphia Eagles | | | |
| ☐ 157 Mark Stepnoski .................... | .15 | .07 | .02 |
| Dallas Cowboys | | | |
| ☐ 158 Chris Chandler .................... | .20 | .09 | .03 |
| Phoenix Cardinals | | | |
| ☐ 159 Rod Bernstine ..................... | .20 | .09 | .03 |
| San Diego Chargers | | | |
| ☐ 160 Pierce Holt ....................... | .15 | .07 | .02 |
| San Francisco 49ers | | | |
| ☐ 161 Wilber Marshall ................... | .20 | .09 | .03 |
| Washington Redskins | | | |
| ☐ 162 Reggie Cobb ....................... | .25 | .11 | .03 |
| Tampa Bay Buccaneers | | | |
| ☐ 163 Tom Rathman ....................... | .20 | .09 | .03 |
| San Francisco 49ers | | | |
| ☐ 164 Michael Haynes..................... | .60 | .25 | .08 |
| Atlanta Falcons | | | |
| ☐ 165 Nate Odomes ....................... | .20 | .09 | .03 |
| Buffalo Bills | | | |
| ☐ 166 Tom Waddle......................... | .25 | .11 | .03 |
| Chicago Bears | | | |
| ☐ 167 Eric Ball ......................... | .15 | .07 | .02 |
| Cincinnati Bengals | | | |
| ☐ 168 Brett Favre........................ | 2.00 | .90 | .25 |
| Green Bay Packers | | | |
| ☐ 169 Michael Jackson ................... | .25 | .11 | .03 |
| Cleveland Browns | | | |
| ☐ 170 Lorenzo White...................... | .20 | .09 | .03 |
| Houston Oilers | | | |
| ☐ 171 Cleveland Gary .................... | .20 | .09 | .03 |
| Los Angeles Rams | | | |
| ☐ 172 Jay Schroeder ..................... | .15 | .07 | .02 |
| Los Angeles Raiders | | | |
| ☐ 173 Tony Paige ........................ | .15 | .07 | .02 |
| Miami Dolphins | | | |
| ☐ 174 Jack Del Rio ...................... | .15 | .07 | .02 |
| Minnesota Vikings | | | |
| ☐ 175 Jon Vaughn......................... | .15 | .07 | .02 |
| New England Patriots | | | |
| ☐ 176 Morten Andersen UER ............... | .20 | .09 | .03 |
| New Orleans Saints | | | |
| (Misspelled Morton) | | | |
| ☐ 177 Chris Burkett...................... | .15 | .07 | .02 |
| New York Jets | | | |
| ☐ 178 Vai Sikahema ...................... | .15 | .07 | .02 |
| Philadelphia Eagles | | | |
| ☐ 179 Ronnie Harmon ..................... | .20 | .09 | .03 |
| San Diego Chargers | | | |
| ☐ 180 Amp Lee ........................... | .20 | .09 | .03 |
| San Francisco 49ers | | | |
| ☐ 181 Chip Lohmiller..................... | .15 | .07 | .02 |
| Washington Redskins | | | |
| ☐ 182 Steve Broussard.................... | .15 | .07 | .02 |
| Atlanta Falcons | | | |
| ☐ 183 Don Beebe.......................... | .25 | .11 | .03 |
| Buffalo Bills | | | |
| ☐ 184 Tommy Vardell...................... | .20 | .09 | .03 |
| Cleveland Browns | | | |
| ☐ 185 Keith Jennings .................... | .15 | .07 | .02 |
| Chicago Bears | | | |
| ☐ 186 Simon Fletcher .................... | .20 | .09 | .03 |
| Denver Broncos | | | |
| ☐ 187 Mel Gray .......................... | .20 | .09 | .03 |
| Detroit Lions | | | |
| ☐ 188 Vince Workman...................... | .15 | .07 | .02 |
| Green Bay Packers | | | |
| ☐ 189 Haywood Jeffires .................. | .25 | .11 | .03 |
| Houston Oilers | | | |
| ☐ 190 Barry Word ........................ | .25 | .11 | .03 |
| Kansas City Chiefs | | | |

| | | | | |
|---|---|---:|---:|---:|
| ☐ 191 | Ethan Horton<br>Los Angeles Raiders | .15 | .07 | .02 |
| ☐ 192 | Mark Higgs<br>Miami Dolphins | .25 | .11 | .03 |
| ☐ 193 | Irving Fryar<br>New England Patriots | .20 | .09 | .03 |
| ☐ 194 | Charles Haley<br>Dallas Cowboys | .20 | .09 | .03 |
| ☐ 195 | Steve Bono<br>San Francisco 49ers | .40 | .18 | .05 |
| ☐ 196 | Mike Golic<br>Philadelphia Eagles | .15 | .07 | .02 |
| ☐ 197 | Gary Anderson<br>Pittsburgh Steelers | .15 | .07 | .02 |
| ☐ 198 | Sterling Sharpe<br>Green Bay Packers | 1.50 | .65 | .19 |
| ☐ 199 | Andre Tippett<br>New England Patriots | .15 | .07 | .02 |
| ☐ 200 | Thurman Thomas<br>Buffalo Bills | 1.00 | .45 | .13 |
| ☐ 201 | Chris Miller<br>Atlanta Falcons | .25 | .11 | .03 |
| ☐ 202 | Henry Jones<br>Buffalo Bills | .15 | .07 | .02 |
| ☐ 203 | Mo Lewis<br>New York Jets | .15 | .07 | .02 |
| ☐ 204 | Marion Butts<br>San Diego Chargers | .25 | .11 | .03 |
| ☐ 205 | Mike Johnson<br>Cleveland Browns | .15 | .07 | .02 |
| ☐ 206 | Alvin Harper<br>Dallas Cowboys | 1.00 | .45 | .13 |
| ☐ 207 | Ray Childress<br>Houston Oilers | .15 | .07 | .02 |
| ☐ 208 | Anthony Johnson<br>Indianapolis Colts | .15 | .07 | .02 |
| ☐ 209 | Tony Bennett<br>Green Bay Packers | .15 | .07 | .02 |
| ☐ 210 | Anthony Newman<br>Los Angeles Rams | .15 | .07 | .02 |
| ☐ 211 | Christian Okoye<br>Kansas City Chiefs | .20 | .09 | .03 |
| ☐ 212 | Marcus Allen<br>Los Angeles Raiders | .20 | .09 | .03 |
| ☐ 213 | Jackie Harris<br>Green Bay Packers | .75 | .35 | .09 |
| ☐ 214 | Mark Duper<br>Miami Dolphins | .20 | .09 | .03 |
| ☐ 215 | Cris Carter<br>Minnesota Vikings | .25 | .11 | .03 |
| ☐ 216 | John Stephens<br>New England Patriots | .15 | .07 | .02 |
| ☐ 217 | Barry Sanders<br>Detroit Lions | 2.50 | 1.15 | .30 |
| ☐ 218A | Herman Moore UER<br>Detroit Lions<br>(First name misspelled Sherman) | 1.00 | .45 | .13 |
| ☐ 218B | Herman Moore COR<br>Detroit Lions | 1.25 | .55 | .16 |
| ☐ 219 | Marvin Washington<br>New England Patriots | .15 | .07 | .02 |
| ☐ 220 | Calvin Williams<br>Philadelphia Eagles | .25 | .11 | .03 |
| ☐ 221 | John Randle<br>Minnesota Vikings | .15 | .07 | .02 |
| ☐ 222 | Marco Coleman<br>Miami Dolphins | .20 | .09 | .03 |
| ☐ 223 | Eric Martin<br>New Orleans Saints | .20 | .09 | .03 |
| ☐ 224 | David Meggett<br>New York Giants | .20 | .09 | .03 |
| ☐ 225 | Brian Washington<br>New York Jets | .15 | .07 | .02 |
| ☐ 226 | Barry Foster<br>Pittsburgh Steelers | .75 | .35 | .09 |
| ☐ 227 | Michael Zordich<br>Phoenix Cardinals | .15 | .07 | .02 |
| ☐ 228 | Stan Humphries<br>San Diego Chargers | .25 | .11 | .03 |
| ☐ 229 | Mike Cofer<br>San Francisco 49ers | .15 | .07 | .02 |
| ☐ 230 | Chris Warren<br>Seattle Seahawks | .40 | .18 | .05 |
| ☐ 231 | Keith McCants<br>Tampa Bay Buccaneers | .15 | .07 | .02 |
| ☐ 232 | Mark Rypien<br>Washington Redskins | .20 | .09 | .03 |
| ☐ 233 | James Francis<br>Cincinnati Bengals | .15 | .07 | .02 |
| ☐ 234 | Andre Rison<br>Atlanta Falcons | .60 | .25 | .08 |
| ☐ 235 | William Perry<br>Chicago Bears | .20 | .09 | .03 |
| ☐ 236 | Chip Banks<br>Indianapolis Colts | .15 | .07 | .02 |
| ☐ 237 | Willie Davis<br>Kansas City Chiefs | .30 | .14 | .04 |
| ☐ 238 | Chris Doleman<br>Minnesota Vikings | .20 | .09 | .03 |
| ☐ 239 | Tim Brown<br>Los Angeles Raiders | .50 | .23 | .06 |
| ☐ 240 | Darren Perry<br>Pittsburgh Steelers | .15 | .07 | .02 |
| ☐ 241 | Johnny Bailey<br>Phoenix Cardinals | .15 | .07 | .02 |
| ☐ 242 | Ernest Givins UER<br>Houston Oilers<br>(Spelled Givens on back) | .20 | .09 | .03 |
| ☐ 243 | John Carney<br>San Diego Chargers | .15 | .07 | .02 |
| ☐ 244 | Cortez Kennedy<br>Seattle Seahawks | .25 | .11 | .03 |
| ☐ 245 | Lawrence Dawsey<br>Tampa Bay Buccaneers | .25 | .11 | .03 |
| ☐ 246 | Martin Mayhew<br>Washington Redskins | .15 | .07 | .02 |
| ☐ 247 | Shane Conlan<br>Buffalo Bills | .15 | .07 | .02 |
| ☐ 248 | J.J. Birden<br>Kansas City Chiefs | .20 | .09 | .03 |
| ☐ 249 | Quinn Early<br>New Orleans Saints | .20 | .09 | .03 |
| ☐ 250 | Michael Irvin<br>Dallas Cowboys | 1.50 | .65 | .19 |
| ☐ 251 | Neil O'Donnell<br>Pittsburgh Steelers | .75 | .35 | .09 |
| ☐ 252 | Stan Gelbaugh<br>Seattle Seahawks | .15 | .07 | .02 |
| ☐ 253 | Drew Hill<br>Atlanta Falcons | .20 | .09 | .03 |
| ☐ 254 | Wendell Davis<br>Chicago Bears | .20 | .09 | .03 |
| ☐ 255 | Tim Johnson<br>Washington Redskins | .15 | .07 | .02 |
| ☐ 256 | Seth Joyner<br>Philadelphia Eagles | .20 | .09 | .03 |
| ☐ 257 | Derrick Fenner<br>Cincinnati Bengals | .15 | .07 | .02 |
| ☐ 258 | Steve Young<br>San Francisco 49ers | 1.00 | .45 | .13 |
| ☐ 259 | Jackie Slater<br>Los Angeles Rams | .15 | .07 | .02 |
| ☐ 260 | Eric Metcalf<br>Cleveland Browns | .25 | .11 | .03 |
| ☐ 261 | Rufus Porter<br>Seattle Seahawks | .15 | .07 | .02 |
| ☐ 262 | Ken Norton Jr.<br>Dallas Cowboys | .20 | .09 | .03 |
| ☐ 263 | Tim McDonald<br>Phoenix Cardinals | .15 | .07 | .02 |
| ☐ 264 | Mark Jackson<br>Denver Broncos | .20 | .09 | .03 |
| ☐ 265 | Hardy Nickerson<br>Pittsburgh Steelers | .15 | .07 | .02 |
| ☐ 266 | Anthony Munoz<br>Cincinnati Bengals | .20 | .09 | .03 |
| ☐ 267 | Mark Carrier<br>Tampa Bay Buccaneers | .20 | .09 | .03 |
| ☐ 268 | Mike Pritchard<br>Atlanta Falcons | .25 | .11 | .03 |
| ☐ 269 | Steve Emtman<br>Indianapolis Colts | .20 | .09 | .03 |
| ☐ 270 | Ricky Sanders<br>Washington Redskins | .20 | .09 | .03 |
| ☐ 271 | Robert Massey<br>Phoenix Cardinals | .15 | .07 | .02 |
| ☐ 272 | Pete Metzelaars<br>Buffalo Bills | .15 | .07 | .02 |
| ☐ 273 | Reggie Langhorne<br>Indianapolis Colts | .20 | .09 | .03 |
| ☐ 274 | Tim McGee<br>Washington Redskins | .15 | .07 | .02 |
| ☐ 275 | Reggie Rivers<br>Denver Broncos | .50 | .23 | .06 |
| ☐ 276 | Jimmie Jones<br>Dallas Cowboys | .15 | .07 | .02 |
| ☐ 277 | Lorenzo White TB<br>Houston Oilers | .15 | .07 | .02 |
| ☐ 278 | Emmitt Smith TB<br>Dallas Cowboys | 4.00 | 1.80 | .50 |
| ☐ 279 | Thurman Thomas TB<br>Buffalo Bills | .60 | .25 | .08 |
| ☐ 280 | Barry Sanders TB<br>Detroit Lions | 1.00 | .45 | .13 |
| ☐ 281 | Rodney Hampton TB<br>New York Giants | .40 | .18 | .05 |
| ☐ 282 | Barry Foster TB<br>Pittsburgh Steelers | .35 | .16 | .04 |
| ☐ 283 | Troy Aikman PC<br>Dallas Cowboys | 2.50 | 1.15 | .30 |
| ☐ 284 | Michael Irvin PC<br>Dallas Cowboys | .60 | .25 | .08 |
| ☐ 285 | Brett Favre PC<br>Green Bay Packers | 1.00 | .45 | .13 |

| | | | |
|---|---|---|---|
| ☐ 286 Sterling Sharpe PC | .60 | .25 | .08 |
| Green Bay Packers | | | |
| ☐ 287 Steve Young PC | .40 | .18 | .05 |
| San Francisco 49ers | | | |
| ☐ 288 Jerry Rice PC | .75 | .35 | .09 |
| San Francisco 49ers | | | |
| ☐ 289 Stan Humphries PC | .20 | .09 | .03 |
| San Diego Chargers | | | |
| ☐ 290 Anthony Miller PC | .20 | .09 | .03 |
| San Diego Chargers | | | |
| ☐ 291 Dan Marino PC | 1.00 | .45 | .13 |
| Miami Dolphins | | | |
| ☐ 292 Keith Jackson PC | .20 | .09 | .03 |
| Miami Dolphins | | | |
| ☐ 293 Patick Bates | .40 | .18 | .05 |
| Los Angeles Raiders | | | |
| ☐ 294 Jerome Bettis | 8.00 | 3.60 | 1.00 |
| Los Angeles Rams | | | |
| ☐ 295 Drew Bledsoe | 8.00 | 3.60 | 1.00 |
| New England Patriots | | | |
| ☐ 296 Tom Carter | .60 | .25 | .08 |
| Washington Redskins | | | |
| ☐ 297 Curtis Conway | 1.50 | .65 | .19 |
| Chicago Bears | | | |
| ☐ 298 John Copeland | .75 | .35 | .09 |
| Cincinnati Bengals | | | |
| ☐ 299 Eric Curry | .75 | .35 | .09 |
| Tampa Bay Buccaneers | | | |
| ☐ 300 Reggie Brooks | 5.00 | 2.30 | .60 |
| Washington Redskins | | | |
| ☐ 301 Steve Everitt | .30 | .14 | .04 |
| Cleveland Browns | | | |
| ☐ 302 Deon Figures | .50 | .23 | .06 |
| Pittsburgh Steelers | | | |
| ☐ 303 Garrison Hearst | 2.00 | .90 | .25 |
| Phoenix Cardinals | | | |
| ☐ 304 Qadry Ismail UER | 1.50 | .65 | .19 |
| Minnesota Vikings | | | |
| (Misspelled Quadry | | | |
| on both sides) | | | |
| ☐ 305 Marvin Jones | .60 | .25 | .08 |
| New York Jets | | | |
| ☐ 306 Lincoln Kennedy | .50 | .23 | .06 |
| Atlanta Falcons | | | |
| ☐ 307 O.J. McDuffie | 4.00 | 1.80 | .50 |
| Miami Dolphins | | | |
| ☐ 308 Rick Mirer | 8.00 | 3.60 | 1.00 |
| Seattle Seahawks | | | |
| ☐ 309 Wayne Simmons | .35 | .16 | .04 |
| Green Bay Packers | | | |
| ☐ 310 Irv Smith | .60 | .25 | .08 |
| New Orleans Saints | | | |
| ☐ 311 Robert Smith | 1.00 | .45 | .13 |
| Minnesota Vikings | | | |
| ☐ 312 Dana Stubblefield | 1.25 | .55 | .16 |
| San Francisco 49ers | | | |
| ☐ 313 George Teague | .50 | .23 | .06 |
| Green Bay Packers | | | |
| ☐ 314 Dan Williams | .40 | .18 | .05 |
| Denver Broncos | | | |
| ☐ 315 Kevin Williams | 1.75 | .80 | .22 |
| Dallas Cowboys | | | |

## 1993 Playoff Checklists

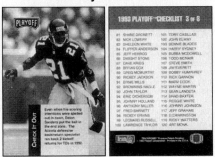

These eight standard-size (2 1/2" by 3 1/2") cards feature full-bleed color action player photos on the fronts. Overlaying the picture at the bottom is a silver box edged on its left by a black stripe carrying the words "Check It Out." The silver box carries statistical highlights on the featured player(s). The checklist on the backs is printed on a white panel bordered on the top by a red stripe and on the bottom by a black stripe. The checklist cards are numbered on the back.

| | MINT | EXC | G-VG |
|---|---|---|---|
| COMPLETE SET (8) | 6.00 | 2.70 | .75 |

| | | | |
|---|---|---|---|
| COMMON PLAYER (1-8) | .50 | .23 | .06 |
| ☐ 1A Warren Moon UER | 1.00 | .45 | .13 |
| Houston Oilers | | | |
| (Kosar misspelled Kozar) | | | |
| ☐ 1B Warren Moon COR | 1.00 | .45 | .13 |
| Houston Oilers | | | |
| ☐ 2 Barry Sanders | 2.00 | .90 | .25 |
| Detroit Lions | | | |
| ☐ 3 Deion Sanders | .75 | .35 | .09 |
| Atlanta Falcons | | | |
| ☐ 4 Ron Woodson | .50 | .23 | .06 |
| Pittsburgh Steelers | | | |
| ☐ 5 Junior Seau | .50 | .23 | .06 |
| San Diego Chargers | | | |
| ☐ 6 Mark Rypien | .50 | .23 | .06 |
| Washington Redskins | | | |
| ☐ 7 Derrick Thomas | .50 | .23 | .06 |
| Kansas City Chiefs | | | |
| ☐ 8 Dallas Players UER | 1.25 | .55 | .16 |
| Daryl Johnston | | | |
| Alvin Harper | | | |
| Michael Irvin | | | |
| (Stan Humphries listed as 299; | | | |
| should be 289) | | | |

## 1993 Playoff Club

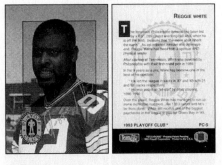

Featuring all-time great, still active football players, this seven-card, standard-size (2 1/2" by 3 1/2") set was available in both hobby and retail display boxes. On the fronts, the color head shots inside a picture frame contrast with the black-and-white surrounding photo. The gold Playoff Club emblem appears at the lower left corner, and the player's signature is inscribed in gold ink across the picture. On the backs, a career summary is overprinted on a white panel with a gray Playoff Club emblem. The cards are numbered on the back with a "PC" prefix.

| | MINT | EXC | G-VG |
|---|---|---|---|
| COMPLETE SET (7) | 30.00 | 13.50 | 3.80 |
| COMMON PLAYER (PC1-PC7) | 2.00 | .90 | .25 |
| ☐ PC1 Joe Montana | 25.00 | 11.50 | 3.10 |
| Kansas City Chiefs | | | |
| ☐ PC2 Art Monk | 2.00 | .90 | .25 |
| Washington Redskins | | | |
| ☐ PC3 Lawrence Taylor | 3.00 | 1.35 | .40 |
| New York Giants | | | |
| ☐ PC4 Ronnie Lott | 2.00 | .90 | .25 |
| Los Angeles Raiders | | | |
| ☐ PC5 Reggie White | 4.00 | 1.80 | .50 |
| Green Bay Packers | | | |
| ☐ PC6 Anthony Munoz | 2.00 | .90 | .25 |
| Tampa Bay Buccaneers | | | |
| ☐ PC7 Jackie Slater | 2.00 | .90 | .25 |
| Los Angeles Rams | | | |

## 1993 Playoff Brett Favre

Randomly inserted in hobby display boxes, these five standard-size (2 1/2" by 3 1/2") cards trace the career of Brett Favre, quarterback of the Green Bay Packers. The fronts display full-bleed color action player photos with a metallic sheen to them. The player's name appears in a black box at the bottom. On a green panel displaying a ghosted silhouette of Favre preparing to pass, the backs present season highlights. The cards are numbered on the back as "X of 5."

| | MINT | EXC | G-VG |
|---|---|---|---|
| COMPLETE SET (5) | 90.00 | 40.00 | 11.50 |
| COMMON FAVRE (1-5) | 20.00 | 9.00 | 2.50 |
| ☐ 1 Brett Favre | 20.00 | 9.00 | 2.50 |
| The Early Years | | | |

| | | | |
|---|---|---|---|
| ☐ 2 Brett Favre...................................<br>The College Years | 20.00 | 9.00 | 2.50 |
| ☐ 3 Brett Favre...................................<br>Turning Pro | 20.00 | 9.00 | 2.50 |
| ☐ 4 Brett Favre...................................<br>Green Bay Star | 20.00 | 9.00 | 2.50 |
| ☐ 5 Brett Favre...................................<br>1992: The Storybook<br>Season | 20.00 | 9.00 | 2.50 |

## 1993 Playoff Ricky Watters

Randomly inserted in retail display boxes, these five standard-size (2 1/2" by 3 1/2") cards trace the career of San Francisco running back Ricky Watters. The fronts display full-bleed color action player photos with a metallic sheen to them. The player's name appears in a black box at the bottom. On a tan panel displaying a ghosted silhouette of Watters running, the backs present season highlights. The cards are numbered on the back as "X of 5."

| | MINT | EXC | G-VG |
|---|---|---|---|
| COMPLETE SET (5)........................... | 80.00 | 36.00 | 10.00 |
| COMMON WATTERS (1-5)................ | 16.00 | 7.25 | 2.00 |
| ☐ 1 Ricky Watters...........................<br>The Early Years | 16.00 | 7.25 | 2.00 |
| ☐ 2 Ricky Watters...........................<br>Irish Eyes Were Smiling | 16.00 | 7.25 | 2.00 |
| ☐ 3 Ricky Watters...........................<br>The Bay Watters | 16.00 | 7.25 | 2.00 |
| ☐ 4 Ricky Watters...........................<br>A Second-Year Rookie | 16.00 | 7.25 | 2.00 |
| ☐ 5 Ricky Watters...........................<br>Rookie of the Year | 16.00 | 7.25 | 2.00 |

## 1993 Playoff Headliners Redemption

The Trading Card, a special card randomly inserted in retail foil packs, entitled the collector to receive these six standard-size (2 1/2" by 3 1/2") cards. A similar card randomly inserted in hobby foil packs entitled the collector to receive a ten-card Rookie Roundup set. According to the card back, 48,475 Trading Cards were produced for random insertion. The borderless fronts feature metallic color player action shots that are cut out and superposed upon a grayish background with oblique silvery newspaper type. The player's name appears in silver-colored lettering within a black rectangle at the top. The set's logo is shown at the upper right. The borderless back carries a color player headshot superposed upon a whiteish background with oblique beige-colored logos of the player's team. The player's name and 1992 season highlights appear in white lettering within the black

rectangle at the top. The cards are numbered on the back with an "H" prefix.

| | MINT | EXC | G-VG |
|---|---|---|---|
| COMPLETE SET (6)........................... | 35.00 | 16.00 | 4.40 |
| COMMON PLAYER (H1-H6)............... | 1.25 | .55 | .16 |
| ☐ H1 Brett Favre ............................<br>Green Bay Packers | 8.00 | 3.60 | 1.00 |
| ☐ H2 Sterling Sharpe......................<br>Green Bay Packers | 5.00 | 2.30 | .60 |
| ☐ H3 Emmitt Smith .........................<br>Dallas Cowboys | 18.00 | 8.00 | 2.30 |
| ☐ H4 Jerry Rice ..............................<br>San Francisco 49ers | 6.00 | 2.70 | .75 |
| ☐ H5 Thurman Thomas ...................<br>Buffalo Bills | 4.00 | 1.80 | .50 |
| ☐ H6 David Klingler ........................<br>Cincinnati Bengals | 1.25 | .55 | .16 |
| ☐ NNO Headliner Redemption ......... | 20.00 | 9.00 | 2.50 |

## 1993 Playoff Promo Inserts

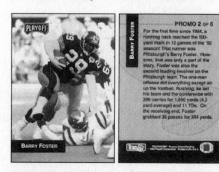

One Playoff Promo Insert (or Playoff Ricky Watters card) was inserted in every special retail pack of 1993 Playoff. The six standard-size (2 1/2" by 3 1/2") promos feature borderless player action shots on their fronts. The featured player is in color, but the background is black-and-white. The player's name appears in silver-colored lettering within a black bar at the lower left. The back carries the player's career highlights on a colored panel. His name appears vertically in white lettering within a black bar at the upper left. The cards are numbered on the back as "Promo X of 6."

| | MINT | EXC | G-VG |
|---|---|---|---|
| COMPLETE SET (6)........................... | 10.00 | 4.50 | 1.25 |
| COMMON PLAYER (1-6)................... | 1.00 | .45 | .13 |
| ☐ 1 Michael Irvin ...........................<br>Dallas Cowboys | 3.50 | 1.55 | .45 |
| ☐ 2 Barry Foster ............................<br>Pittsburgh Steelers | 2.50 | 1.15 | .30 |
| ☐ 3 Quinn Early .............................<br>New Orleans Saints | 1.00 | .45 | .13 |
| ☐ 4 Tim Brown ...............................<br>Los Angeles Raiders | 1.50 | .65 | .19 |
| ☐ 5 Reggie White............................<br>Philadelphia Eagles | 1.25 | .55 | .16 |
| ☐ 6 Sterling Sharpe ........................<br>Green Bay Packers | 3.50 | 1.55 | .45 |

# 1993 Playoff Rookie Roundup Redemption

The Trading Card, a special insert card (1993 Playoff Rookie Roundup Redemption) found in hobby foil packs, could be redeemed through a mail-in offer by the collector for this ten-card, standard-size (2 1/2" by 3 1/2") set. A similar card randomly inserted in retail foil packs entitled the collector to receive a six-card The Headliners set. These cards showcase the ten hottest rookies of the 1993 NFL season; according to the card back, 15,683 Trading Cards were produced for random insertion. The borderless fronts feature metallic color player action shots that are cut out and superimposed on a grayish background with oblique silvery newspaper type. The player's name appears in the silver-colored lower right corner in silver metallic lettering. The Rookie Roundup logo is printed on the right edge. The borderless back carries a color player headshot superimposed on a white background with oblique gray-colored logos of the player's team. The player's name and 1993 season highlights appear in white lettering within the black rectangle at the bottom. The cards are numbered on the back with an "R" prefix.

|  | MINT | EXC | G-VG |
|---|---|---|---|
| COMPLETE SET (10) | 50.00 | 23.00 | 6.25 |
| COMMON PLAYER (R1-R10) | 2.00 | .90 | .25 |
| ☐ NNO Rookie Roundup Redemption Card | 30.00 | 13.50 | 3.80 |
| ☐ R1 Jerome Bettis Los Angeles Rams | 12.00 | 5.50 | 1.50 |
| ☐ R2 Drew Bledsoe New England Patriots | 12.00 | 5.50 | 1.50 |
| ☐ R3 Reggie Brooks Washington Redskins | 8.00 | 3.60 | 1.00 |
| ☐ R4 Derek Brown New Orleans Saints | 3.00 | 1.35 | .40 |
| ☐ R5 Garrison Hearst Phoenix Cardinals | 4.00 | 1.80 | .50 |
| ☐ R6 Terry Kirby Miami Dolphins | 5.00 | 2.30 | .60 |
| ☐ R7 Glyn Milburn Denver Broncos | 4.00 | 1.80 | .50 |
| ☐ R8 Rick Mirer Seattle Seahawks | 12.00 | 5.50 | 1.50 |
| ☐ R9 Roosevelt Potts Indianapolis Colts | 2.00 | .90 | .25 |
| ☐ R10 Dana Stubblefield San Francisco 49ers | 2.00 | .90 | .25 |

# 1993 Playoff Contenders Promos

This six-card standard-size (2 1/2" by 3 1/2") set was issued to herald the release of the 150-card 1993 Playoff Contenders set. The fronts display borderless color action shots that have a metallic sheen. The player's name appears below the Playoff logo, both within a silver-colored box in a lower corner. The horizontal back carries a color player close-up on the left, and a broad team color-coded stripe on the right, in which appears the player's name, his team's helmet, and season highlights. The cards are numbered on the back by Roman numerals.

|  | MINT | EXC | G-VG |
|---|---|---|---|
| COMPLETE SET (6) | 12.00 | 5.00 | 1.20 |
| COMMON PLAYER (1-6) | .50 | .20 | .05 |
| ☐ 1 Drew Bledsoe New England Patriots | 4.00 | 1.60 | .40 |
| ☐ 2 Neil Smith Kansas City Chiefs | .50 | .20 | .05 |
| ☐ 3 Rick Mirer | 4.00 | 1.60 | .40 |

|  | MINT | EXC | G-VG |
|---|---|---|---|
| Seattle Seahawks |  |  |  |
| ☐ 4 Rodney Hampton New York Giants | 1.00 | .40 | .10 |
| ☐ 5 Barry Sanders Detroit Lions | 2.50 | 1.00 | .25 |
| ☐ 6 Emmitt Smith Dallas Cowboys | 4.00 | 1.60 | .40 |

# 1993 Playoff Contenders

This 150-card standard-size (2 1/2" by 3 1/2") set has fronts that display borderless color action shots that have a metallic sheen. The player's name appears below the Playoff logo, both within a silver-colored box usually placed in a lower corner. The horizontal back carries a color player close-up on the left, and a broad team-colored stripe on the right, in which appears the player's name, his team's helmet, and season highlights. The cards are numbered on the back. Rookie Cards include Jerome Bettis, Drew Bledsoe, Reggie Brooks, Terry Kirby, O.J. McDuffie, Rick Mirer and Ron Moore.

|  | MINT | EXC | G-VG |
|---|---|---|---|
| COMPLETE SET (150) | 45.00 | 20.00 | 5.75 |
| COMMON PLAYER (1-150) | .10 | .05 | .01 |
| ☐ 1 Brett Favre Green Bay Packers | 1.50 | .65 | .19 |
| ☐ 2 Thurman Thomas Buffalo Bills | .75 | .35 | .09 |
| ☐ 3 Barry Word Minnesota Vikings | .15 | .07 | .02 |
| ☐ 4 Herman Moore Detroit Lions | .60 | .25 | .08 |
| ☐ 5 Reggie Langhorne Indianapolis Colts | .10 | .05 | .01 |
| ☐ 6 Wilber Marshall Houston Oilers | .10 | .05 | .01 |
| ☐ 7 Ricky Watters San Francisco 49ers | .75 | .35 | .09 |
| ☐ 8 Marcus Allen Kansas City Chiefs | .40 | .18 | .05 |
| ☐ 9 Jeff Hostetler Los Angeles Raiders | .15 | .07 | .02 |
| ☐ 10 Steve Young San Francisco 49ers | .50 | .23 | .06 |
| ☐ 11 Bobby Hebert Atlanta Falcons | .10 | .05 | .01 |
| ☐ 12 David Klingler Cleveland Browns | .50 | .23 | .06 |
| ☐ 13 Craig Heyward Chicago Bears | .10 | .05 | .01 |
| ☐ 14 Andre Reed Buffalo Bills | .15 | .07 | .02 |
| ☐ 15 Tommy Vardell Cleveland Browns | .12 | .05 | .02 |

| | | | |
|---|---|---|---|
| ☐ 16 Anthony Carter | .12 | .05 | .02 |
| Minnesota Vikings | | | |
| ☐ 17 Mel Gray | .10 | .05 | .01 |
| Detroit Lions | | | |
| ☐ 18 Dan Marino | 2.00 | .90 | .25 |
| Miami Dolphins | | | |
| ☐ 19 Haywood Jeffires | .15 | .07 | .02 |
| Houston Oilers | | | |
| ☐ 20 Joe Montana | 3.50 | 1.55 | .45 |
| Kansas City Chiefs | | | |
| ☐ 21 Tim Brown | .10 | .05 | .01 |
| Los Angeles Raiders | | | |
| ☐ 22 Jim McMahon | .15 | .07 | .02 |
| Minnesota Vikings | | | |
| ☐ 23 Scott Mitchell | 1.25 | .55 | .16 |
| Miami Dolphins | | | |
| ☐ 24 Rickey Jackson | .12 | .05 | .02 |
| New Orleans Saints | | | |
| ☐ 25 Troy Aikman | 3.00 | 1.35 | .40 |
| Dallas Cowboys | | | |
| ☐ 26 Rodney Hampton | .75 | .35 | .09 |
| New York Giants | | | |
| ☐ 27 Fred Barnett | .15 | .07 | .02 |
| Philadelphia Eagles | | | |
| ☐ 28 Gary Clark | .10 | .05 | .01 |
| Phoenix Cardinals | | | |
| ☐ 29 Barry Foster | .75 | .35 | .09 |
| Pittsburgh Steelers | | | |
| ☐ 30 Brian Blades | .12 | .05 | .02 |
| Seattle Seahawks | | | |
| ☐ 31 Tim McDonald | .10 | .05 | .01 |
| San Francisco 49ers | | | |
| ☐ 32 Kelvin Martin | .10 | .05 | .01 |
| Seattle Seahawks | | | |
| ☐ 33 Henry Jones | .10 | .05 | .01 |
| Buffalo Bills | | | |
| ☐ 34 Erric Pegram | .75 | .35 | .09 |
| Atlanta Falcons | | | |
| ☐ 35 Don Beebe | .15 | .07 | .02 |
| Buffalo Bills | | | |
| ☐ 36 Eric Metcalf | .10 | .05 | .01 |
| Cleveland Browns | | | |
| ☐ 37 Charles Haley | .12 | .05 | .02 |
| Dallas Cowboys | | | |
| ☐ 38 Robert Delpino | .12 | .05 | .02 |
| Denver Broncos | | | |
| ☐ 39 Leonard Russell UER | .12 | .05 | .02 |
| New England Patriots | | | |
| (Detroit Lions logo on back) | | | |
| ☐ 40 Jackie Harris | .50 | .23 | .06 |
| Green Bay Packers | | | |
| ☐ 41 Ernest Givins | .12 | .05 | .02 |
| Houston Oilers | | | |
| ☐ 42 Willie Davis | .20 | .09 | .03 |
| Kansas City Chiefs | | | |
| ☐ 43 Alexander Wright | .12 | .05 | .02 |
| Los Angeles Raiders | | | |
| ☐ 44 Keith Byars | .12 | .05 | .02 |
| Miami Dolphins | | | |
| ☐ 45 David Meggett | .12 | .05 | .02 |
| New York Giants | | | |
| ☐ 46 Johnny Johnson | .15 | .07 | .02 |
| New York Jets | | | |
| ☐ 47 Mark Bavaro | .10 | .05 | .01 |
| Philadelphia Eagles | | | |
| ☐ 48 Seth Joyner | .12 | .05 | .02 |
| Philadelphia Eagles | | | |
| ☐ 49 Junior Seau | .10 | .05 | .01 |
| San Diego Chargers | | | |
| ☐ 50 Emmitt Smith | 4.00 | 1.80 | .50 |
| Dallas Cowboys | | | |
| ☐ 51 Shannon Sharpe | .10 | .05 | .01 |
| Denver Broncos | | | |
| ☐ 52 Rodney Peete | .12 | .05 | .02 |
| Detroit Lions | | | |
| ☐ 53 Andre Rison | .25 | .11 | .03 |
| Atlanta Falcons | | | |
| ☐ 54 Cornelius Bennett | .10 | .05 | .01 |
| Buffalo Bills | | | |
| ☐ 55 Mark Carrier | .12 | .05 | .02 |
| Cleveland Browns | | | |
| ☐ 56 Mark Clayton | .10 | .05 | .01 |
| Green Bay Packers | | | |
| ☐ 57 Warren Moon | .30 | .14 | .04 |
| Houston Oilers | | | |
| ☐ 58 J.J. Birden | .12 | .05 | .02 |
| Kansas City Chiefs | | | |
| ☐ 59 Howie Long | .12 | .05 | .02 |
| Los Angeles Raiders | | | |
| ☐ 60 Irving Fryar | .10 | .05 | .01 |
| Miami Dolphins | | | |
| ☐ 61 Mark Jackson | .12 | .05 | .02 |
| New York Giants | | | |
| ☐ 62 Eric Martin | .12 | .05 | .02 |
| New Orleans Saints | | | |
| ☐ 63 Herschel Walker | .15 | .07 | .02 |
| Philadelphia Eagles | | | |

| | | | |
|---|---|---|---|
| ☐ 64 Cortez Kennedy | .15 | .07 | .02 |
| Seattle Seahawks | | | |
| ☐ 65 Steve Beuerlein | .25 | .11 | .03 |
| Phoenix Cardinals | | | |
| ☐ 66 Jim Kelly | .50 | .23 | .06 |
| Buffalo Bills | | | |
| ☐ 67 Bernie Kosar | .30 | .14 | .04 |
| Dallas Cowboys | | | |
| ☐ 68 Pat Swilling | .10 | .05 | .01 |
| Detroit Lions | | | |
| ☐ 69 Michael Irvin | 1.00 | .45 | .13 |
| Dallas Cowboys | | | |
| ☐ 70 Harvey Williams | .15 | .07 | .02 |
| Kansas City Chiefs | | | |
| ☐ 71 Steve Smith | .12 | .05 | .02 |
| Los Angeles Raiders | | | |
| ☐ 72 Wade Wilson | .10 | .05 | .01 |
| New Orleans Saints | | | |
| ☐ 73 Phil Simms | .15 | .07 | .02 |
| New York Giants | | | |
| ☐ 74 Vinny Testaverde | .10 | .05 | .01 |
| Cleveland Browns | | | |
| ☐ 75 Barry Sanders | 1.50 | .65 | .19 |
| Detroit Lions | | | |
| ☐ 76 Ken Norton Jr. | .10 | .05 | .01 |
| Dallas Cowboys | | | |
| ☐ 77 Rod Woodson | .10 | .05 | .01 |
| Pittsburgh Steelers | | | |
| ☐ 78 Webster Slaughter | .10 | .05 | .01 |
| Houston Oilers | | | |
| ☐ 79 Derrick Thomas | .30 | .14 | .04 |
| Kansas City Chiefs | | | |
| ☐ 80 Mike Sherrard | .10 | .05 | .01 |
| New York Giants | | | |
| ☐ 81 Calvin Williams | .15 | .07 | .02 |
| Philadelphia Eagles | | | |
| ☐ 82 Jay Novacek | .15 | .07 | .02 |
| Dallas Cowboys | | | |
| ☐ 83 Michael Brooks | .10 | .05 | .01 |
| New York Giants | | | |
| ☐ 84 Randall Cunningham | .20 | .09 | .03 |
| Philadelphia Eagles | | | |
| ☐ 85 Chris Warren | .30 | .14 | .04 |
| Seattle Seahawks | | | |
| ☐ 86 Johnny Mitchell | .40 | .18 | .05 |
| New York Jets | | | |
| ☐ 87 Jim Harbaugh | .12 | .05 | .02 |
| Cincinnati Bengals | | | |
| ☐ 88 Rod Bernstine | .12 | .05 | .02 |
| Denver Broncos | | | |
| ☐ 89 John Elway | 1.00 | .45 | .13 |
| Denver Broncos | | | |
| ☐ 90 Jerry Rice | 1.25 | .55 | .16 |
| San Francisco 49ers | | | |
| ☐ 91 Brent Jones | .15 | .07 | .02 |
| San Francisco 49ers | | | |
| ☐ 92 Cris Carter | .15 | .07 | .02 |
| Minnesota Vikings | | | |
| ☐ 93 Alvin Harper | .50 | .23 | .06 |
| Dallas Cowboys | | | |
| ☐ 94 Horace Copeland | .75 | .35 | .09 |
| Tampa Bay Buccaneers | | | |
| ☐ 95 Raghib Ismail | .75 | .35 | .09 |
| Los Angeles Raiders | | | |
| ☐ 96 Darrin Smith | .75 | .35 | .09 |
| Dallas Cowboys | | | |
| ☐ 97 Reggie Brooks | 4.00 | 1.80 | .50 |
| Washington Redskins | | | |
| ☐ 98 Demetrius DuBose | .35 | .16 | .04 |
| Tampa Bay Buccaneers | | | |
| ☐ 99 Eric Curry | .50 | .23 | .06 |
| Tampa Bay Buccaneers | | | |
| ☐ 100 Rick Mirer | 6.00 | 2.70 | .75 |
| Seattle Seahawks | | | |
| ☐ 101 Carlton Gray UER | .30 | .14 | .04 |
| Seattle Seahawks | | | |
| (Name spelled Grey on front) | | | |
| ☐ 102 Dana Stubblefield | 1.00 | .45 | .13 |
| San Francisco 49ers | | | |
| ☐ 103 Todd Kelly | .20 | .09 | .03 |
| San Francisco 49ers | | | |
| ☐ 104 Natrone Means | 2.50 | 1.15 | .30 |
| San Diego Chargers | | | |
| ☐ 105 Darrien Gordon | .40 | .18 | .05 |
| San Diego Chargers | | | |
| ☐ 106 Deon Figures | .30 | .14 | .04 |
| Pittsburgh Steelers | | | |
| ☐ 107 Garrison Hearst | 1.00 | .45 | .13 |
| Phoenix Cardinals | | | |
| ☐ 108 Ron Moore | 4.00 | 1.80 | .50 |
| Phoenix Cardinals | | | |
| ☐ 109 Leonard Renfro | .20 | .09 | .03 |
| Philadelphia Eagles | | | |
| ☐ 110 Lester Holmes | .15 | .07 | .02 |
| Philadelphia Eagles | | | |
| ☐ 111 Vaughn Hebron | .75 | .35 | .09 |
| Philadelphia Eagles | | | |

| | | | |
|---|---|---|---|
| ☐ 112 Marvin Jones | .40 | .18 | .05 |
| New York Jets | | | |
| ☐ 113 Irv Smith | .50 | .23 | .06 |
| New Orleans Saints | | | |
| ☐ 114 Willie Roaf | .25 | .11 | .03 |
| New Orleans Saints | | | |
| ☐ 115 Derek Brown | 1.75 | .80 | .22 |
| New Orleans Saints | | | |
| ☐ 116 Vincent Brisby | 1.25 | .55 | .16 |
| New England Patriots | | | |
| ☐ 117 Drew Bledsoe | 6.00 | 2.70 | .75 |
| New England Patriots | | | |
| ☐ 118 Gino Torretta | .50 | .23 | .06 |
| Minnesota Vikings | | | |
| ☐ 119 Robert Smith | 1.00 | .45 | .13 |
| Minnesota Vikings | | | |
| ☐ 120 Qadry Ismail | 1.00 | .45 | .13 |
| Minnesota Vikings | | | |
| ☐ 121 O.J. McDuffie | 2.50 | 1.15 | .30 |
| Miami Dolphins | | | |
| ☐ 122 Terry Kirby | 2.50 | 1.15 | .30 |
| Miami Dolphins | | | |
| ☐ 123 Troy Drayton | .40 | .18 | .05 |
| Los Angeles Rams | | | |
| ☐ 124 Jerome Bettis | 6.00 | 2.70 | .75 |
| Los Angeles Rams | | | |
| ☐ 125 Patrick Bates | .25 | .11 | .03 |
| Los Angeles Raiders | | | |
| ☐ 126 Roosevelt Potts | .50 | .23 | .06 |
| Indianapolis Colts | | | |
| ☐ 127 Tom Carter | .40 | .18 | .05 |
| Washington Redskins | | | |
| ☐ 128 Patrick Robinson | .25 | .11 | .03 |
| Los Angeles Raiders | | | |
| ☐ 129 Brad Hopkins | .20 | .09 | .03 |
| Houston Oilers | | | |
| ☐ 130 George Teague | .40 | .18 | .05 |
| Green Bay Packers | | | |
| ☐ 131 Wayne Simmons | .25 | .11 | .03 |
| Green Bay Packers | | | |
| ☐ 132 Mark Brunell | .40 | .18 | .05 |
| Green Bay Packers | | | |
| ☐ 133 Ryan McNeil | .20 | .09 | .03 |
| Detroit Lions | | | |
| ☐ 134 Dan Williams | .35 | .16 | .04 |
| Denver Broncos | | | |
| ☐ 135 Glyn Milburn | 1.50 | .65 | .19 |
| Denver Broncos | | | |
| ☐ 136 Kevin Williams | 1.00 | .45 | .13 |
| Dallas Cowboys | | | |
| ☐ 137 Derrick Lassic | .40 | .18 | .05 |
| Dallas Cowboys | | | |
| ☐ 138 Steve Everitt | .15 | .07 | .02 |
| Cleveland Browns | | | |
| ☐ 139 Lance Gunn | .30 | .14 | .04 |
| Cincinnati Bengals | | | |
| ☐ 140 John Copeland | .50 | .23 | .06 |
| Cincinnati Bengals | | | |
| ☐ 141 Curtis Conway | 1.25 | .55 | .16 |
| Cincinnati Bengals | | | |
| ☐ 142 Thomas Smith | .30 | .14 | .04 |
| Buffalo Bills | | | |
| ☐ 143 Russell Copeland | .30 | .14 | .04 |
| Buffalo Bills | | | |
| ☐ 144 Lincoln Kennedy | .30 | .14 | .04 |
| Atlanta Falcons | | | |
| ☐ 145 Boomer Esiason CL | .10 | .05 | .01 |
| New York Jets | | | |
| ☐ 146 Neil Smith CL | .10 | .05 | .01 |
| Kansas City Chiefs | | | |
| ☐ 147 Jack Del Rio CL | .10 | .05 | .01 |
| Minnesota Vikings | | | |
| ☐ 148 Morten Andersen CL | .12 | .05 | .02 |
| New Orleans Saints | | | |
| ☐ 149 Sterling Sharpe CL | .20 | .09 | .03 |
| Green Bay Packers | | | |
| ☐ 150 Reggie White CL | .10 | .05 | .01 |
| Green Bay Packers | | | |

## 1993 Playoff Contenders Rick Mirer

Randomly inserted in 1993 Playoff Contenders packs, these five standard-size (2 1/2" by 3 1/2") cards feature on their fronts borderless color player action shots that have a metallic sheen. The player's name appears in a black box at the bottom. On a blue panel displaying a ghosted version of Mirer's photo on card number 3, the back presents career highlights. The cards are numbered on the back as "X of 5.".

| | MINT | EXC | G-VG |
|---|---|---|---|
| COMPLETE SET (5) | 100.00 | 45.00 | 12.50 |
| COMMON MIRER (1-5) | 20.00 | 9.00 | 2.50 |
| ☐ 1 Rick Mirer | 20.00 | 9.00 | 2.50 |
| This Kid Can Play | | | |

| | | | |
|---|---|---|---|
| ☐ 2 Rick Mirer | 20.00 | 9.00 | 2.50 |
| Notre Dame All-American | | | |
| ☐ 3 Rick Mirer | 20.00 | 9.00 | 2.50 |
| First-Round Draft Pick | | | |
| ☐ 4 Rick Mirer | 20.00 | 9.00 | 2.50 |
| Seattle in the Hunt | | | |
| ☐ 5 Rick Mirer | 20.00 | 9.00 | 2.50 |
| A Tough Guy | | | |

## 1993 Playoff Contenders Rookie Contenders

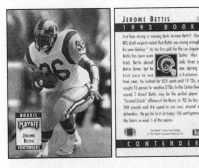

Randomly inserted in packs of 1993 Playoff Contenders, these ten standard-size (2 1/2" by 3 1/2") cards feature on their fronts borderless color player action shots that have a metallic sheen and blurred backgrounds, which serves to focus attention on the rookie. The player's name, along with the Playoff logo, appears within a gold-colored box in a lower corner. The white back carries the player's name at the top, with the set's title shown in white lettering within black stripes across the top and bottom. The player's career highlights round out the card. The cards are numbered on the back as "X of 10."

| | MINT | EXC | G-VG |
|---|---|---|---|
| COMPLETE SET (10) | 110.00 | 50.00 | 14.00 |
| COMMON PLAYER (1-10) | 3.00 | 1.35 | .40 |
| ☐ 1 Jerome Bettis | 35.00 | 16.00 | 4.40 |
| Los Angeles Rams | | | |
| ☐ 2 Drew Bledsoe UER | 35.00 | 16.00 | 4.40 |
| New England Patriots | | | |
| (Text states he played for | | | |
| Washington; he played for Washington St.) | | | |
| ☐ 3 Reggie Brooks | 20.00 | 9.00 | 2.50 |
| Washington Redskins | | | |
| ☐ 4 Derek Brown | 10.00 | 4.50 | 1.25 |
| New Orleans Saints | | | |
| ☐ 5 Garrison Hearst | 7.00 | 3.10 | .85 |
| Phoenix Cardinals | | | |
| ☐ 6 Vaughn Hebron | 3.00 | 1.35 | .40 |
| Philadelphia Eagles | | | |
| ☐ 7 Qadry Ismail | 6.00 | 2.70 | .75 |
| Minnesota Vikings | | | |
| ☐ 8 Derrick Lassic | 3.00 | 1.35 | .40 |
| Dallas Cowboys | | | |
| ☐ 9 Glyn Milburn | 8.00 | 3.60 | 1.00 |
| Denver Broncos | | | |
| ☐ 10 Dana Stubblefield | 3.00 | 1.35 | .40 |
| San Francisco 49ers | | | |

## 1994 Playoff Super Bowl Promos

## 1994 Playoff

This six-card standard size (2 1/2" by 3 1/2") set was issued by Playoff to commemorate the 1994 Super Bowl. The fronts display borderless color action shots that have a metallic sheen. The player's name appears above and below the Playoff logo, both within a silver-colored oval in a lower corner. The white backs carry the 1994 Super Bowl logo in the center. The cards are numbered in the upper right corner with the word "Promo" printed below the number.

|  | MINT | EXC | G-VG |
|---|---|---|---|
| COMPLETE SET (6) | 12.00 | 5.00 | 1.20 |
| COMMON PLAYER (1-6) | 1.50 | .60 | .15 |
| ☐ 1 Jerry Rice | 5.00 | 2.00 | .50 |
| San Francisco 49ers | | | |
| ☐ 2 Daryl Johnston | 1.50 | .60 | .15 |
| Dallas Cowboys | | | |
| ☐ 3 Herschel Walker | 1.50 | .60 | .15 |
| Philadelphia Eagles | | | |
| ☐ 4 Reggie White | 2.50 | 1.00 | .25 |
| Green Bay Packers | | | |
| ☐ 5 Scott Mitchell | 2.50 | 1.00 | .25 |
| Miami Dolphins | | | |
| ☐ 6 Thurman Thomas | 2.50 | 1.00 | .25 |
| Buffalo Bills | | | |

## 1994 Playoff Prototypes

These six standard-size (2 1/2" by 3 1/2") prototypes feature on their fronts borderless metallic color player action shots. The player's name appears within an oval emblem in one corner. The borderless back carries a color closeup with the player's name, team helmet, and career highlights. The cards are unnumbered and checklisted below in alphabetical order.

|  | MINT | EXC | G-VG |
|---|---|---|---|
| COMPLETE SET (6) | 10.00 | 4.00 | 1.00 |
| COMMON PLAYER (1-6) | 1.00 | .40 | .10 |
| ☐ 1 Marcus Allen | 1.50 | .60 | .15 |
| Kansas City Chiefs | | | |
| ☐ 2 Rick Mirer | 3.00 | 1.20 | .30 |
| Seattle Seahawks | | | |
| ☐ 3 Barry Sanders | 2.50 | 1.00 | .25 |
| Detroit Lions | | | |
| ☐ 4 Junior Seau | 1.00 | .40 | .10 |
| San Diego Chargers | | | |
| ☐ 5 Sterling Sharpe | 2.00 | .80 | .20 |
| Green Bay Packers | | | |
| ☐ 6 Emmitt Smith | 4.00 | 1.60 | .40 |
| Dallas Cowboys | | | |

These 336 standard-size (2 1/2" by 3 1/2") feature borderless card fronts with metallic color player action shots. The player's name appears within an oval emblem in one corner. The borderless backs carry a color closeup with the player's name, team helmet, and career highlights. Topical subsets featured are Sack Pack (226-232), Ground Attack (233-262), Summerall's Best (263-290), and Rookies (291-336).

|  | MINT | EXC | G-VG |
|---|---|---|---|
| COMPLETE SET (336) | 50.00 | 23.00 | 6.25 |
| COMMON PLAYER (1-336) | .15 | .07 | .02 |
| ☐ 1 Joe Montana | 2.50 | 1.15 | .30 |
| Kansas City Chiefs | | | |
| ☐ 2 Derrick Thomas | .30 | .14 | .04 |
| Kansas City Chiefs | | | |
| ☐ 3 Dan Marino | 1.50 | .65 | .19 |
| Miami Dolphins | | | |
| ☐ 4 Cris Carter | .20 | .09 | .03 |
| Minnesota Vikings | | | |
| ☐ 5 Boomer Esiason | .25 | .11 | .03 |
| New York Jets | | | |
| ☐ 6 Bruce Smith | .25 | .11 | .03 |
| Buffalo Bills | | | |
| ☐ 7 Andre Rison | .30 | .14 | .04 |
| Atlanta Falcons | | | |
| ☐ 8 Curtis Conway | .30 | .14 | .04 |
| Chicago Bears | | | |
| ☐ 9 Michael Irvin | .60 | .25 | .08 |
| Dallas Cowboys | | | |
| ☐ 10 Shannon Sharpe | .30 | .14 | .04 |
| Denver Broncos | | | |
| ☐ 11 Pat Swilling | .15 | .07 | .02 |
| Detroit Lions | | | |
| ☐ 12 John Parrella | .15 | .07 | .02 |
| Buffalo Bills | | | |
| ☐ 13 Mel Gray | .15 | .07 | .02 |
| Detroit Lions | | | |
| ☐ 14 Ray Childress | .15 | .07 | .02 |
| Houston Oilers | | | |
| ☐ 15 Willie Davis | .20 | .09 | .03 |
| Kansas City Chiefs | | | |
| ☐ 16 Raghib Ismail | .30 | .14 | .04 |
| Los Angeles Raiders | | | |
| ☐ 17 Jim Everett | .20 | .09 | .03 |
| Los Angeles Rams | | | |
| ☐ 18 Mark Higgs | .15 | .07 | .02 |
| Miami Dolphins | | | |
| ☐ 19 Trace Armstrong | .15 | .07 | .02 |
| Chicago Bears | | | |
| ☐ 20 Jim Kelly | .40 | .18 | .05 |
| Buffalo Bills | | | |
| ☐ 21 Rob Burnett | .15 | .07 | .02 |
| Cleveland Browns | | | |
| ☐ 22 Jay Novacek | .20 | .09 | .03 |
| Dallas Cowboys | | | |
| ☐ 23 Robert Delpino | .15 | .07 | .02 |
| Denver Broncos | | | |
| ☐ 24 Brett Perriman | .15 | .07 | .02 |
| Detroit Lions | | | |
| ☐ 25 Troy Aikman | 2.50 | 1.15 | .30 |
| Dallas Cowboys | | | |
| ☐ 26 Reggie White | .30 | .14 | .04 |
| Green Bay Packers | | | |
| ☐ 27 Lorenzo White | .15 | .07 | .02 |
| Houston Oilers | | | |
| ☐ 28 Bubba McDowell | .15 | .07 | .02 |
| Houston Oilers | | | |
| ☐ 29 Steve Emtman | .15 | .07 | .02 |
| Indianapolis Colts | | | |
| ☐ 30 Brett Favre | 1.00 | .45 | .13 |
| Green Bay Packers | | | |
| ☐ 31 Derek Russell | .15 | .07 | .02 |
| Denver Broncos | | | |

| | | | |
|---|---|---|---|
| ☐ 32 Jeff Hostetler | .20 | .09 | .03 |
| Los Angeles Raiders | | | |
| ☐ 33 Henry Ellard | .15 | .07 | .02 |
| Los Angeles Rams | | | |
| ☐ 34 Jack Del Rio | .15 | .07 | .02 |
| Minnesota Vikings | | | |
| ☐ 35 Mike Saxon | .15 | .07 | .02 |
| New England Patriots | | | |
| ☐ 36 Rickey Jackson | .15 | .07 | .02 |
| New Orleans Saints | | | |
| ☐ 37 Phil Simms | .25 | .11 | .03 |
| New York Giants | | | |
| ☐ 38 Quinn Early | .15 | .07 | .02 |
| New Orleans Saints | | | |
| ☐ 39 Russell Copeland | .15 | .07 | .02 |
| Buffalo Bills | | | |
| ☐ 40 Carl Pickens | .15 | .07 | .02 |
| Cincinnati Bengals | | | |
| ☐ 41 Lance Gunn | .15 | .07 | .02 |
| Cincinnati Bengals | | | |
| ☐ 42 Bernie Kosar | .20 | .09 | .03 |
| Miami Dolphins | | | |
| ☐ 43 John Elway | .75 | .35 | .09 |
| Denver Broncos | | | |
| ☐ 44 George Teague | .15 | .07 | .02 |
| Green Bay Packers | | | |
| ☐ 45 Nick Lowery | .15 | .07 | .02 |
| Kansas City Chiefs | | | |
| ☐ 46 Haywood Jeffires | .25 | .11 | .03 |
| Houston Oilers | | | |
| ☐ 47 Will Shields | .15 | .07 | .02 |
| Kansas City Chiefs | | | |
| ☐ 48 Daryl Johnston | .20 | .09 | .03 |
| Dallas Cowboys | | | |
| ☐ 49 Pete Metzelaars | .15 | .07 | .02 |
| Buffalo Bills | | | |
| ☐ 50 Warren Moon | .20 | .09 | .03 |
| Minnesota Vikings | | | |
| ☐ 51 Cornelius Bennett | .20 | .09 | .03 |
| Buffalo Bills | | | |
| ☐ 52 Vinny Testaverde | .20 | .09 | .03 |
| Cleveland Browns | | | |
| ☐ 53 John Mangun | .20 | .09 | .03 |
| Chicago Bears | | | |
| ☐ 54 Tommy Vardell | .15 | .07 | .02 |
| Cleveland Browns | | | |
| ☐ 55 Lincoln Coleman | .50 | .23 | .06 |
| Dallas Cowboys | | | |
| ☐ 56 Karl Mecklenburg | .15 | .07 | .02 |
| Denver Broncos | | | |
| ☐ 57 Jackie Harris | .30 | .14 | .04 |
| Green Bay Packers | | | |
| ☐ 58 Curtis Duncan | .15 | .07 | .02 |
| Houston Oilers | | | |
| ☐ 59 Quentin Coryatt | .15 | .07 | .02 |
| Indianapolis Colts | | | |
| ☐ 60 Tim Brown | .30 | .14 | .04 |
| Los Angeles Raiders | | | |
| ☐ 61 Irving Fryar | .20 | .09 | .03 |
| Miami Dolphins | | | |
| ☐ 62 Sean Gilbert | .15 | .07 | .02 |
| Los Angeles Rams | | | |
| ☐ 63 Qadry Ismail | .30 | .14 | .04 |
| Minnesota Vikings | | | |
| ☐ 64 Irv Smith | .15 | .07 | .02 |
| New Orleans Saints | | | |
| ☐ 65 Mark Jackson | .15 | .07 | .02 |
| New York Giants | | | |
| ☐ 66 Ronnie Lott | .25 | .11 | .03 |
| New York Jets | | | |
| ☐ 67 Henry Jones | .15 | .07 | .02 |
| Buffalo Bills | | | |
| ☐ 68 Horace Copeland | .15 | .07 | .02 |
| Buffalo Bills | | | |
| ☐ 69 John Copeland | .15 | .07 | .02 |
| Cincinnati Bengals | | | |
| ☐ 70 Mark Carrier | .15 | .07 | .02 |
| Cleveland Browns | | | |
| ☐ 71 Michael Jackson | .15 | .07 | .02 |
| Cleveland Browns | | | |
| ☐ 72 Jason Elam | .15 | .07 | .02 |
| Denver Broncos | | | |
| ☐ 73 Rod Bernstine | .15 | .07 | .02 |
| Denver Broncos | | | |
| ☐ 74 Wayne Simmons | .15 | .07 | .02 |
| Green Bay Packers | | | |
| ☐ 75 Cody Carlson | .15 | .07 | .02 |
| Houston Oilers | | | |
| ☐ 76 Alexander Wright | .15 | .07 | .02 |
| Los Angeles Raiders | | | |
| ☐ 77 Shane Conlan | .15 | .07 | .02 |
| Los Angeles Rams | | | |
| ☐ 78 Keith Jackson | .25 | .11 | .03 |
| Miami Dolphins | | | |
| ☐ 79 Sean Salisbury | .15 | .07 | .02 |
| Minnesota Vikings | | | |
| ☐ 80 Vaughan Johnson | .15 | .07 | .02 |

| | | | |
|---|---|---|---|
| New Orleans Saints | | | |
| ☐ 81 Rob Moore | .20 | .09 | .03 |
| New York Jets | | | |
| ☐ 82 Andre Reed | .25 | .11 | .03 |
| Buffalo Bills | | | |
| ☐ 83 David Klinger | .30 | .14 | .04 |
| Cincinnati Bengals | | | |
| ☐ 84 Jim Harbaugh | .15 | .07 | .02 |
| Indianapolis Colts | | | |
| ☐ 85 John Jett | .30 | .14 | .04 |
| Dallas Cowboys | | | |
| ☐ 86 Sterling Sharpe | .60 | .25 | .08 |
| Green Bay Packers | | | |
| ☐ 87 Webster Slaughter | .15 | .07 | .02 |
| Houston Oilers | | | |
| ☐ 88 J.J. Birden | .15 | .07 | .02 |
| Kansas City Chiefs | | | |
| ☐ 89 O.J. McDuffie | .50 | .23 | .06 |
| Miami Dolphins | | | |
| ☐ 90 Andre Tippett | .15 | .07 | .02 |
| New England Patriots | | | |
| ☐ 91 Don Beebe | .15 | .07 | .02 |
| Buffalo Bills | | | |
| ☐ 92 Mark Stepnoski | .15 | .07 | .02 |
| Dallas Cowboys | | | |
| ☐ 93 Neil Smith | .15 | .07 | .02 |
| Kansas City Chiefs | | | |
| ☐ 94 Terry Kirby | 1.00 | .45 | .13 |
| Miami Dolphins | | | |
| ☐ 95 Wade Wilson | .15 | .07 | .02 |
| New Orleans Saints | | | |
| ☐ 96 Darryl Talley | .15 | .07 | .02 |
| Buffalo Bills | | | |
| ☐ 97 Anthony Smith | .15 | .07 | .02 |
| Los Angeles Raiders | | | |
| ☐ 98 Willie Roaf | .15 | .07 | .02 |
| New Orleans Saints | | | |
| ☐ 99 Mo Lewis | .15 | .07 | .02 |
| New York Giants | | | |
| ☐ 100 James Washington | .15 | .07 | .02 |
| Dallas Cowboys | | | |
| ☐ 101 Nate Odomes | .15 | .07 | .02 |
| Buffalo Bills | | | |
| ☐ 102 Chris Gedney | .15 | .07 | .02 |
| Chicago Bears | | | |
| ☐ 103 Joe Walter | .15 | .07 | .02 |
| Cincinnati Bengals | | | |
| ☐ 104 Alvin Harper | .15 | .07 | .02 |
| Dallas Cowboys | | | |
| ☐ 105 Simon Fletcher | .15 | .07 | .02 |
| Denver Broncos | | | |
| ☐ 106 Rodney Peete | .15 | .07 | .02 |
| Dallas Cowboys | | | |
| ☐ 107 Terrell Buckley | .15 | .07 | .02 |
| Green Bay Packers | | | |
| ☐ 108 Jeff George | .20 | .09 | .03 |
| Atlanta Falcons | | | |
| ☐ 109 James Jett | .60 | .25 | .08 |
| Los Angeles Raiders | | | |
| ☐ 110 Tony Casillas | .15 | .07 | .02 |
| Kansas City Chiefs | | | |
| ☐ 111 Marco Coleman | .15 | .07 | .02 |
| Miami Dolphins | | | |
| ☐ 112 Anthony Carter | .15 | .07 | .02 |
| Minnesota Vikings | | | |
| ☐ 113 Lincoln Kennedy | .15 | .07 | .02 |
| Atlanta Falcons | | | |
| ☐ 114 Chris Calloway | .15 | .07 | .02 |
| New York Giants | | | |
| ☐ 115 Randall Cunningham | .20 | .09 | .03 |
| Philadelphia Eagles | | | |
| ☐ 116 Steve Beuerlein | .15 | .07 | .02 |
| Arizona Cardinals | | | |
| ☐ 117 Neil O'Donnell | .25 | .11 | .03 |
| Pittsburgh Steelers | | | |
| ☐ 118 Stan Humphries | .15 | .07 | .02 |
| San Diego Chargers | | | |
| ☐ 119 John Taylor | .15 | .07 | .02 |
| San Francisco 49ers | | | |
| ☐ 120 Cortez Kennedy | .15 | .07 | .02 |
| Seattle Seahawks | | | |
| ☐ 121 Santana Dotson | .15 | .07 | .02 |
| Tampa Bay Buccaneers | | | |
| ☐ 122 Thomas Smith | .15 | .07 | .02 |
| Buffalo Bills | | | |
| ☐ 123 Kevin Williams | .30 | .14 | .04 |
| Dallas Cowboys | | | |
| ☐ 124 Andre Ware | .15 | .07 | .02 |
| Minnesota Vikings | | | |
| ☐ 125 Ethan Horton | .15 | .07 | .02 |
| Washington Redskins | | | |
| ☐ 126 Mike Sherrard | .15 | .07 | .02 |
| New York Giants | | | |
| ☐ 127 Fred Barnett | .20 | .09 | .03 |
| Philadelphia Eagles | | | |
| ☐ 128 Ricky Proehl | .20 | .09 | .03 |
| Arizona Cardinals | | | |
| ☐ 129 Kevin Greene | .15 | .07 | .02 |

| | | | |
|---|---|---|---|
| Pittsburgh Steelers | | | |
| ☐ 130 John Carney | .15 | .07 | .02 |
| San Diego Chargers | | | |
| ☐ 131 Tim McDonald | .15 | .07 | .02 |
| San Francisco 49ers | | | |
| ☐ 132 Rick Mirer | 3.50 | 1.55 | .45 |
| Seattle Seahawks | | | |
| ☐ 133 Blair Thomas | .15 | .07 | .02 |
| New York Jets | | | |
| ☐ 134 Hardy Nickerson | .15 | .07 | .02 |
| Tampa Bay Buccaneers | | | |
| ☐ 135 Heath Sherman | .15 | .07 | .02 |
| Philadelphia Eagles | | | |
| ☐ 136 Andre Hastings | .15 | .07 | .02 |
| Pittsburgh Steelers | | | |
| ☐ 137 Randal Hill | .15 | .07 | .02 |
| Arizona Cardinals | | | |
| ☐ 138 Mike Cofer | .15 | .07 | .02 |
| San Francisco 49ers | | | |
| ☐ 139 Brian Blades | .15 | .07 | .02 |
| Seattle Seahawks | | | |
| ☐ 140 Earnest Byner | .15 | .07 | .02 |
| Washington Redskins | | | |
| ☐ 141 Bill Bates | .15 | .07 | .02 |
| Dallas Cowboys | | | |
| ☐ 142 Junior Seau | .25 | .11 | .03 |
| San Diego Chargers | | | |
| ☐ 143 Johnny Bailey | .15 | .07 | .02 |
| Arizona Cardinals | | | |
| ☐ 144 Dwight Stone | .15 | .07 | .02 |
| Pittsburgh Steelers | | | |
| ☐ 145 Todd Kelly | .15 | .07 | .02 |
| San Francisco 49ers | | | |
| ☐ 146 Tyrone Montgomery | .15 | .07 | .02 |
| Los Angeles Raiders | | | |
| ☐ 147 Herschel Walker | .25 | .11 | .03 |
| Philadelphia Eagles | | | |
| ☐ 148 Gary Clark | .25 | .11 | .03 |
| Arizona Cardinals | | | |
| ☐ 149 Eric Green | .20 | .09 | .03 |
| Pittsburgh Steelers | | | |
| ☐ 150 Steve Young | .30 | .14 | .04 |
| San Francisco 49ers | | | |
| ☐ 151 Anthony Miller | .30 | .14 | .04 |
| Denver Broncos | | | |
| ☐ 152 Dana Stubblefield | .30 | .14 | .04 |
| San Francisco 49ers | | | |
| ☐ 153 Dean Wells | .20 | .09 | .03 |
| Seattle Seahawks | | | |
| ☐ 154 Vincent Brisby | .60 | .25 | .08 |
| New England Patriots | | | |
| ☐ 155 Chris Chandler | .15 | .07 | .02 |
| Arizona Cardinals | | | |
| ☐ 156 Clyde Simmons | .15 | .07 | .02 |
| Arizona Cardinals | | | |
| ☐ 157 Rod Woodson | .15 | .07 | .02 |
| Pittsburgh Steelers | | | |
| ☐ 158 Nate Lewis | .20 | .09 | .03 |
| Los Angeles Rams | | | |
| ☐ 159 Martin Harrison | .15 | .07 | .02 |
| San Francisco 49ers | | | |
| ☐ 160 Kelvin Martin | .15 | .07 | .02 |
| Seattle Seahawks | | | |
| ☐ 161 Craig Erickson | .15 | .07 | .02 |
| Tampa Bay Buccaneers | | | |
| ☐ 162 Johnny Mitchell | .20 | .09 | .03 |
| New York Jets | | | |
| ☐ 163 Calvin Williams | .15 | .07 | .02 |
| Philadelphia Eagles | | | |
| ☐ 164 Deon Figures | .15 | .07 | .02 |
| Pittsburgh Steelers | | | |
| ☐ 165 Tom Rathman | .15 | .07 | .02 |
| San Francisco 49ers | | | |
| ☐ 166 Rick Hamilton | .15 | .07 | .02 |
| Washington Redskins | | | |
| ☐ 167 John L. Williams | .15 | .07 | .02 |
| Pittsburgh Steelers | | | |
| ☐ 168 Demetrius DuBose | .15 | .07 | .02 |
| Tampa Bay Buccaneers | | | |
| ☐ 169 Michael Brooks | .15 | .07 | .02 |
| New York Giants | | | |
| ☐ 170 Marion Butts | .15 | .07 | .02 |
| New England Patriots | | | |
| ☐ 171 Brent Jones | .15 | .07 | .02 |
| San Francisco 49ers | | | |
| ☐ 172 Bobby Hebert | .20 | .09 | .03 |
| Atlanta Falcons | | | |
| ☐ 173 Brad Edwards | .15 | .07 | .02 |
| Washington Redskins | | | |
| ☐ 174 Dave Wyman | .15 | .07 | .02 |
| Denver Broncos | | | |
| ☐ 175 Herman Moore | .30 | .14 | .04 |
| Detroit Lions | | | |
| ☐ 176 LeRoy Butler | .15 | .07 | .02 |
| Green Bay Packers | | | |
| ☐ 177 Reggie Langhorne | .15 | .07 | .02 |
| Indianapolis Colts | | | |
| ☐ 178 Dave Krieg | .15 | .07 | .02 |

| | | | |
|---|---|---|---|
| Detroit Lions | | | |
| ☐ 179 Patrick Bates | .15 | .07 | .02 |
| Los Angeles Raiders | | | |
| ☐ 180 Erik Kramer | .30 | .14 | .04 |
| Chicago Bears | | | |
| ☐ 181 Troy Drayton | .15 | .07 | .02 |
| Los Angeles Rams | | | |
| ☐ 182 David Meggett | .15 | .07 | .02 |
| New York Giants | | | |
| ☐ 183 Eric Allen | .15 | .07 | .02 |
| Philadelphia Eagles | | | |
| ☐ 184 Mark Bavaro | .15 | .07 | .02 |
| Philadelphia Eagles | | | |
| ☐ 185 Leslie O'Neal | .15 | .07 | .02 |
| San Diego Chargers | | | |
| ☐ 186 Jerry Rice | 1.00 | .45 | .13 |
| San Francisco 49ers | | | |
| ☐ 187 Desmond Howard | .30 | .14 | .04 |
| Washington Redskins | | | |
| ☐ 188 Deion Sanders | .30 | .14 | .04 |
| Atlanta Falcons | | | |
| ☐ 189 Bill Maas | .15 | .07 | .02 |
| Green Bay Packers | | | |
| ☐ 190 Frank Wycheck | .40 | .18 | .05 |
| Washington Redskins | | | |
| ☐ 191 Ernest Givins | .25 | .11 | .03 |
| Houston Oilers | | | |
| ☐ 192 Terry McDaniel | .15 | .07 | .02 |
| Los Angeles Raiders | | | |
| ☐ 193 Bryan Cox | .15 | .07 | .02 |
| Miami Dolphins | | | |
| ☐ 194 Guy McIntyre | .15 | .07 | .02 |
| San Francisco 49ers | | | |
| ☐ 195 Pierce Holt | .15 | .07 | .02 |
| Atlanta Falcons | | | |
| ☐ 196 Fred Stokes | .15 | .07 | .02 |
| Los Angeles Rams | | | |
| ☐ 197 Mike Pritchard | .15 | .07 | .02 |
| Atlanta Falcons | | | |
| ☐ 198 Terry Obee | .30 | .14 | .04 |
| Chicago Bears | | | |
| ☐ 199 Mark Collins | .15 | .07 | .02 |
| Kansas City Chiefs | | | |
| ☐ 200 Drew Bledsoe | 3.50 | 1.55 | .45 |
| New England Patriots | | | |
| ☐ 201 Barry Word | .15 | .07 | .02 |
| Minnesota Vikings | | | |
| ☐ 202 Derrick Lassic | .15 | .07 | .02 |
| Dallas Cowboys | | | |
| ☐ 203 Chris Spielman | .15 | .07 | .02 |
| Detroit Lions | | | |
| ☐ 204 John Jurkovic | .30 | .14 | .04 |
| Green Bay Packers | | | |
| ☐ 205 Ken Norton Jr. | .20 | .09 | .03 |
| San Francisco 49ers | | | |
| ☐ 206 Dale Carter | .15 | .07 | .02 |
| Kansas City Chiefs | | | |
| ☐ 207 Chris Doleman | .15 | .07 | .02 |
| Atlanta Falcons | | | |
| ☐ 208 Keith Hamilton | .15 | .07 | .02 |
| New York Giants | | | |
| ☐ 209 Andy Harmon | .15 | .07 | .02 |
| Philadelphia Eagles | | | |
| ☐ 210 John Friesz | .20 | .09 | .03 |
| Washington Redskins | | | |
| ☐ 211 Steve Bono | .20 | .09 | .03 |
| San Francisco 49ers | | | |
| ☐ 212 Mark Rypien | .20 | .09 | .03 |
| Washington Redskins | | | |
| ☐ 213 Ricky Sanders | .15 | .07 | .02 |
| Washington Redskins | | | |
| ☐ 214 Michael Haynes | .30 | .14 | .04 |
| New Orleans Saints | | | |
| ☐ 215 Todd McNair | .15 | .07 | .02 |
| Kansas City Chiefs | | | |
| ☐ 216 Leon Lett | .15 | .07 | .02 |
| Dallas Cowboys | | | |
| ☐ 217 Scott Mitchell | .60 | .25 | .08 |
| Detroit Lions | | | |
| ☐ 218 Mike Morris | .20 | .09 | .03 |
| Minnesota Vikings | | | |
| ☐ 219 Darrin Smith | .15 | .07 | .02 |
| Dallas Cowboys | | | |
| ☐ 220 Jim McMahon | .20 | .09 | .03 |
| Arizona Cardinals | | | |
| ☐ 221 Garrison Hearst | .40 | .18 | .05 |
| Arizona Cardinals | | | |
| ☐ 222 Leroy Thompson | .15 | .07 | .02 |
| Pittsburgh Steelers | | | |
| ☐ 223 Darren Carrington | .15 | .07 | .02 |
| San Diego Chargers | | | |
| ☐ 224 Pete Stoyanovich | .15 | .07 | .02 |
| Miami Dolphins | | | |
| ☐ 225 Chris Miller | .20 | .09 | .03 |
| Los Angeles Rams | | | |
| ☐ 226 Bruce Smith SP | .20 | .09 | .03 |
| Buffalo Bills | | | |
| ☐ 227 Simon Fletcher SP | .15 | .07 | .02 |

|  |  |  | | | |
|---|---|---|---|---|---|
| ☐ 228 | Reggie White SP | Green Bay Packers | .15 | .07 | .02 |
| ☐ 229 | Neil Smith SP | Kansas City Chiefs | .15 | .07 | .02 |
| ☐ 230 | Chris Doleman SP | Minnesota Vikings | .15 | .07 | .02 |
| ☐ 231 | Keith Hamilton SP | New York Giants | .15 | .07 | .02 |
| ☐ 232 | Dana Stubblefield SP | San Francisco 49ers | .15 | .07 | .02 |
| ☐ 233 | Erric Pegram GA | Atlanta Falcons | .40 | .18 | .05 |
| ☐ 234 | Thurman Thomas GA | Buffalo Bills | .50 | .23 | .06 |
| ☐ 235 | Lewis Tillman GA | Chicago Bears | .15 | .07 | .02 |
| ☐ 236 | Harold Green GA | Cincinnati Bengals | .15 | .07 | .02 |
| ☐ 237 | Eric Metcalf GA | Cleveland Browns | .20 | .09 | .03 |
| ☐ 238 | Emmitt Smith GA | Dallas Cowboys | 3.00 | 1.35 | .40 |
| ☐ 239 | Glyn Milburn GA | Denver Broncos | .40 | .18 | .05 |
| ☐ 240 | Barry Sanders GA | Detroit Lions | 1.25 | .55 | .16 |
| ☐ 241 | Edgar Bennett GA | Green Bay Packers | .15 | .07 | .02 |
| ☐ 242 | Gary Brown GA | Houston Oilers | .60 | .25 | .08 |
| ☐ 243 | Roosevelt Potts GA | Indianapolis Colts | .15 | .07 | .02 |
| ☐ 244 | Marcus Allen GA | Kansas City Chiefs | .20 | .09 | .03 |
| ☐ 245 | Greg Robinson GA | Los Angeles Raiders | .20 | .09 | .03 |
| ☐ 246 | Jerome Bettis GA | Los Angeles Rams | 3.50 | 1.55 | .45 |
| ☐ 247 | Keith Byars GA | Miami Dolphins | .15 | .07 | .02 |
| ☐ 248 | Robert Smith GA | Minnesota Vikings | .20 | .09 | .03 |
| ☐ 249 | Leonard Russell GA | New England Patriots | .15 | .07 | .02 |
| ☐ 250 | Derek Brown GA | New Orleans Saints | .60 | .25 | .08 |
| ☐ 251 | Rodney Hampton GA | New York Giants | .50 | .23 | .06 |
| ☐ 252 | Johnny Johnson GA | New York Jets | .20 | .09 | .03 |
| ☐ 253 | Vaughn Hebron GA | Philadelphia Eagles | .15 | .07 | .02 |
| ☐ 254 | Ron Moore GA | Arizona Cardinals | 1.00 | .45 | .13 |
| ☐ 255 | Barry Foster GA | Pittsburgh Steelers | .30 | .14 | .04 |
| ☐ 256 | Natrone Means GA | San Diego Chargers | .50 | .23 | .06 |
| ☐ 257 | Ricky Watters GA | San Francisco 49ers | .40 | .18 | .05 |
| ☐ 258 | Chris Warren GA | Seattle Seahawks | .15 | .07 | .02 |
| ☐ 259 | Vince Workman GA | Tampa Bay Buccaneers | .15 | .07 | .02 |
| ☐ 260 | Reggie Brooks GA | Washington Redskins | 1.50 | .65 | .19 |
| ☐ 261 | Carolina Panthers | Logo | .30 | .14 | .04 |
| ☐ 262 | Jacksonville Jaguars | Logo | .30 | .14 | .04 |
| ☐ 263 | Troy Aikman SB | Dallas Cowboys | 1.50 | .65 | .19 |
| ☐ 264 | Barry Sanders SB | Detroit Lions | .75 | .35 | .09 |
| ☐ 265 | Emmitt Smith SB | Dallas Cowboys | 2.00 | .90 | .25 |
| ☐ 266 | Michael Irvin SB | Dallas Cowboys | .30 | .14 | .04 |
| ☐ 267 | Jerry Rice SB | San Francisco 49ers | .50 | .23 | .06 |
| ☐ 268 | Shannon Sharpe SB | Denver Broncos | .20 | .09 | .03 |
| ☐ 269 | Bob Kratch SB | New York Giants | .15 | .07 | .02 |
| ☐ 270 | Howard Ballard SB | Seattle Seahawks | .15 | .07 | .02 |
| ☐ 271 | Erik Williams SB | Dallas Cowboys | .15 | .07 | .02 |
| ☐ 272 | Guy McIntyre SB | San Francisco 49ers | .15 | .07 | .02 |
| ☐ 273 | Kelvin Williams SB | Dallas Cowboys | .20 | .09 | .03 |
| ☐ 274 | Mel Gray SB | Detroit Lions | .15 | .07 | .02 |
| ☐ 275 | Eddie Murray SB | Dallas Cowboys | .15 | .07 | .02 |
| ☐ 276 | Mark Stepnoski SB | Dallas Cowboys | .15 | .07 | .02 |
| ☐ 277 | Tommy Barnhardt SB | New Orleans Saints | .15 | .07 | .02 |
| ☐ 278 | Derrick Thomas SB | Kansas City Chiefs | .20 | .09 | .03 |
| ☐ 279 | Ken Norton Jr. SB | San Francisco 49ers | .20 | .09 | .03 |
| ☐ 280 | Chris Spielman SB | Detroit Lions | .15 | .07 | .02 |
| ☐ 281 | Deion Sanders SB | Atlanta Falcons | .20 | .09 | .03 |
| ☐ 282 | Mark Collins SB | New York Giants | .15 | .07 | .02 |
| ☐ 283 | Bruce Smith SB | Buffalo Bills | .15 | .07 | .02 |
| ☐ 284 | Reggie White SB | Green Bay Packers | .20 | .09 | .03 |
| ☐ 285 | Sean Gilbert SB | Los Angeles Rams | .15 | .07 | .02 |
| ☐ 286 | Cortez Kennedy SB | Seattle Seahawks | .20 | .09 | .03 |
| ☐ 287 | Steve Atwater SB | Denver Broncos | .15 | .07 | .02 |
| ☐ 288 | Tim McDonald SB | San Francisco 49ers | .15 | .07 | .02 |
| ☐ 289 | Jerome Bettis SB | Los Angeles Rams | 2.00 | .90 | .25 |
| ☐ 290 | Dana Stubblefield SB | San Francisco 49ers | .15 | .07 | .02 |
| ☐ 291 | Bert Emanuel | Atlanta Falcons | .50 | .23 | .06 |
| ☐ 292 | Jeff Burris | Buffalo Bills | .30 | .14 | .04 |
| ☐ 293 | Bucky Brooks | Buffalo Bills | .40 | .18 | .05 |
| ☐ 294 | Dan Wilkinson | Cincinnati Bengals | 1.00 | .45 | .13 |
| ☐ 295 | Darnay Scott | Cincinnati Bengals | .75 | .35 | .09 |
| ☐ 296 | Derrick Alexander | Cleveland Browns | 1.00 | .45 | .13 |
| ☐ 297 | Antonio Langham | Cleveland Browns | .60 | .25 | .08 |
| ☐ 298 | Shante Carver | Dallas Cowboys | .30 | .14 | .04 |
| ☐ 299 | Shelby Hill | Dallas Cowboys | .30 | .14 | .04 |
| ☐ 300 | Larry Allen | Dallas Cowboys | .25 | .11 | .03 |
| ☐ 301 | Johnnie Morton | Detroit Lions | 1.50 | .65 | .19 |
| ☐ 302 | Van Malone | Detroit Lions | .25 | .11 | .03 |
| ☐ 303 | Aaron Taylor | Green Bay Packers | .25 | .11 | .03 |
| ☐ 304 | Marshall Faulk | Indianapolis Colts | 6.00 | 2.70 | .75 |
| ☐ 305 | Eric Mahlum | Indianapolis Colts | .25 | .11 | .03 |
| ☐ 306 | Trev Alberts | Indianapolis Colts | 1.00 | .45 | .13 |
| ☐ 307 | Greg Hill | Kansas City Chiefs | 1.50 | .65 | .19 |
| ☐ 308 | Donnell Bennett | Kansas City Chiefs | .40 | .18 | .05 |
| ☐ 309 | Rob Fredrickson | Los Angeles Raiders | .25 | .11 | .03 |
| ☐ 310 | James Folston | Los Angeles Raiders | .25 | .11 | .03 |
| ☐ 311 | Isaac Bruce | Los Angeles Rams | .40 | .18 | .05 |
| ☐ 312 | Tim Ruddy | Miami Dolphins | .25 | .11 | .03 |
| ☐ 313 | Aubrey Beavers | Miami Dolphins | .30 | .14 | .04 |
| ☐ 314 | David Palmer | Minnesota Vikings | 2.25 | 1.00 | .30 |
| ☐ 315 | DeWayne Washington | Minnesota Vikings | .25 | .11 | .03 |
| ☐ 316 | Willie McGinest | New England Patriots | 1.00 | .45 | .13 |
| ☐ 317 | Mario Bates | New Orleans Saints | .75 | .35 | .09 |
| ☐ 318 | Kevin Lee | New England Patriots | .60 | .25 | .08 |
| ☐ 319 | Jason Sehorn | New York Giants | .25 | .11 | .03 |
| ☐ 320 | Thomas Randolph | New York Giants | .25 | .11 | .03 |
| ☐ 321 | Ryan Yarborough | New York Giants | .50 | .23 | .06 |
| ☐ 322 | Bernard Williams | Philadelphia Eagles | .25 | .11 | .03 |
| ☐ 323 | Chuck Levy | Arizona Cardinals | 1.25 | .55 | .16 |
| ☐ 324 | Jamir Miller | Arizona Cardinals | .60 | .25 | .08 |
| ☐ 325 | Charles Johnson | | 2.00 | .90 | .25 |

| | | MINT | EXC | G-VG |
|---|---|---|---|---|
| | Pittsburgh Steelers | | | |
| ☐ 326 | Bryant Young | .50 | .23 | .06 |
| | San Francisco 49ers | | | |
| ☐ 327 | William Floyd | 1.00 | .45 | .13 |
| | San Francisco 49ers | | | |
| ☐ 328 | Kevin Mitchell | .25 | .11 | .03 |
| | San Francisco 49ers | | | |
| ☐ 329 | Sam Adams | .50 | .23 | .06 |
| | Seattle Seahawks | | | |
| ☐ 330 | Kevin Mawae | .25 | .11 | .03 |
| | Seattle Seahawks | | | |
| ☐ 331 | Errict Rhett | 2.25 | 1.00 | .30 |
| | Tampa Bay Buccaneers | | | |
| ☐ 332 | Trent Dilfer | 4.00 | 1.80 | .50 |
| | Tampa Bay Buccaneers | | | |
| ☐ 333 | Heath Shuler | 10.00 | 4.50 | 1.25 |
| | Washington Redskins | | | |
| ☐ 334 | Aaron Glenn | .30 | .14 | .04 |
| | New York Jets | | | |
| ☐ 335 | Todd Steussie | .25 | .11 | .03 |
| | Minnesota Vikings | | | |
| ☐ 336 | Toby Wright | .25 | .11 | .03 |
| | Los Angeles Rams | | | |
| ☐ NNO | Rookie Roundup Redemption | 40.00 | 18.00 | 5.00 |
| ☐ NNO | Gale Sayers Playoff Club | 30.00 | 13.50 | 3.80 |
| ☐ NNO | Gale Sayers Autograph | 250.00 | 115.00 | 31.00 |

## 1994 Playoff Jerome Bettis

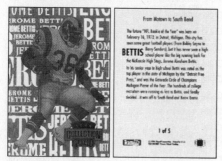

Randomly inserted in regular issue packs, this standard-size (2 1/2" by 3 1/2") five-card set highlights Jerome Bettis. The cards were printed on thick card stock. On a silver foil background carrying his name in different white fonts, the fronts feature color action player photos with the "1994 Playoff Collection" logo in a lower corner. On a bright yellow background, the backs carry biographical information. The cards are numbered on the back with "x of 5".

| | MINT | EXC | G-VG |
|---|---|---|---|
| COMPLETE SET (5) | 125.00 | 57.50 | 15.50 |
| COMMON BETTIS (1-5) | 25.00 | 11.50 | 3.10 |
| ☐ 1 Jerome Bettis | 25.00 | 11.50 | 3.10 |
| From Motown to South Bend | | | |
| ☐ 2 Jerome Bettis | 25.00 | 11.50 | 3.10 |
| The Luck of the Irish | | | |
| ☐ 3 Jerome Bettis | 25.00 | 11.50 | 3.10 |
| I Love LA | | | |
| ☐ 4 Jerome Bettis | 25.00 | 11.50 | 3.10 |
| Welcome to the NFL | | | |
| ☐ 5 Jerome Bettis | 25.00 | 11.50 | 3.10 |
| The Rookie of the Year | | | |

## 1994 Playoff Checklists

Randomly inserted in regular issue packs, these ten standard-size (2 1/2" by 3 1/2") cards feature on their fronts borderless metallic color action shots with player information in a silver foil box at the bottom. The backs carry the set's checklists. The cards are numbered on the back as "X of 10".

| | MINT | EXC | G-VG |
|---|---|---|---|
| COMPLETE SET (10) | 5.00 | 2.30 | .60 |
| COMMON PLAYER (1-10) | .50 | .23 | .06 |
| ☐ 1 Checklist | .50 | .23 | .06 |
| Keith Cash | | | |
| Kansas City Chiefs | | | |
| ☐ 2 Checklist | .50 | .23 | .06 |

| | | MINT | EXC | G-VG |
|---|---|---|---|---|
| | Kerry Cash | | | |
| | Indianapolis Colts | | | |
| ☐ 3 | Checklist | .75 | .35 | .09 |
| | Qadry Ismail | | | |
| | Minnesota Vikings | | | |
| ☐ 4 | Checklist | .75 | .35 | .09 |
| | Raghib Ismail | | | |
| | Los Angeles Raiders | | | |
| ☐ 5 | Checklist | .50 | .23 | .06 |
| | Bruce Matthews | | | |
| | Houston Oilers | | | |
| ☐ 6 | Checklist | .60 | .25 | .08 |
| | Clay Matthews | | | |
| | Cleveland Browns | | | |
| ☐ 7 | Checklist | .75 | .35 | .09 |
| | Shannon Sharpe | | | |
| | Denver Broncos | | | |
| ☐ 8 | Checklist | 1.00 | .45 | .13 |
| | Sterling Sharpe | | | |
| | Green Bay Packers | | | |
| ☐ 9 | Checklist | .60 | .25 | .08 |
| | John Taylor | | | |
| | San Francisco 49ers | | | |
| ☐ 10 | Checklist | .50 | .23 | .06 |
| | Keith Taylor | | | |
| | New Orleans Saints | | | |

## 1994 Playoff Club

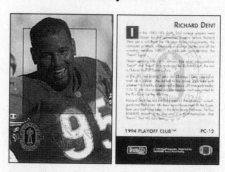

Randomly inserted in packs, these six standard-size (2 1/2" by 3 1/2") feature borderless card fronts with metallic color action shots. The words "Playoff Club" appear within an oval emblem in one corner, while the player's facsimile signature appears in the other corner. On a white background, the backs carry the player's name and career highlights. The cards are numbered on the back with a "PC" prefix.

| | MINT | EXC | G-VG |
|---|---|---|---|
| COMPLETE SET (6) | 30.00 | 13.50 | 3.80 |
| COMMON PLAYER (PC8-PC13) | 2.50 | 1.15 | .30 |
| ☐ PC8 Jerry Rice | 20.00 | 9.00 | 2.50 |
| San Francisco 49ers | | | |
| ☐ PC9 Marcus Allen | 4.00 | 1.80 | .50 |
| Kansas City Chiefs | | | |
| ☐ PC10 Howie Long | 4.00 | 1.80 | .50 |
| Los Angeles Raiders | | | |
| ☐ PC11 Clay Matthews | 2.50 | 1.15 | .30 |
| Cleveland Browns | | | |
| ☐ PC12 Richard Dent | 2.50 | 1.15 | .30 |
| Chicago Bears | | | |
| ☐ PC13 Morten Andersen | 2.50 | 1.15 | .30 |
| New Orleans Saints | | | |

## 1979 Police Chiefs

The 1979 Kansas City Chiefs Police set consists of ten cards co-sponsored by Hardee's Restaurants and the Kansas City (Missouri) Police Department, in addition to the Chiefs' football club. The cards measure approximately 2 5/8" by 4 1/8". The card backs discuss a football term and related legal/safety issue in a section entitled "Chief's Tips". The set is unnumbered but the player's uniform number appears on the front of the cards; the cards are numbered and ordered below by uniform number. The Chiefs' helmet logo is found on both the fronts and backs of the cards.

|  | NRMT | VG-E | GOOD |
|---|---|---|---|
| COMPLETE SET (10) | 12.00 | 5.00 | 1.20 |
| COMMON PLAYER | 1.25 | .50 | .12 |
| ☐ 1 Bob Grupp | 1.25 | .50 | .12 |
| ☐ 4 Steve Fuller | 1.50 | .60 | .15 |
| ☐ 22 Ted McKnight | 1.25 | .50 | .12 |
| ☐ 24 Gary Green | 1.50 | .60 | .15 |
| ☐ 26 Gary Barbaro | 1.75 | .70 | .17 |
| ☐ 32 Tony Reed | 1.50 | .60 | .15 |
| ☐ 58 Jack Rudnay | 1.25 | .50 | .12 |
| ☐ 67 Art Still | 2.00 | .80 | .20 |
| ☐ 73 Bob Simmons | 1.25 | .50 | .12 |
| ☐ xx Marv Levy CO | 2.00 | .80 | .20 |

## 1979 Police Cowboys

The 1979 Dallas Cowboy Police set consists of 15 cards sponsored by the Kiwanis Clubs, the Dallas Cowboys Weekly (the official fan newspaper), and the local law enforcement agency. The cards measure approximately 2 5/8" by 4 1/8". The cards are unnumbered but have been numbered in the checklist below by the player's uniform number which appears on the fronts of the cards. The backs contain "Cowboys Tips" which draw analogies between action on the football field and law abiding action in real life. D.D. Lewis replaced Thomas (Hollywood) Henderson midway through the season; hence, both of these cards are available in lesser quantities than the other cards in this set.

|  | NRMT | VG-E | GOOD |
|---|---|---|---|
| COMPLETE SET (15) | 20.00 | 8.00 | 2.00 |
| COMMON PLAYER | .60 | .24 | .06 |

| | | | |
|---|---|---|---|
| ☐ 12 Roger Staubach | 6.00 | 2.40 | .60 |
| ☐ 33 Tony Dorsett | 3.00 | 1.20 | .30 |
| ☐ 41 Charlie Waters | 1.00 | .40 | .10 |
| ☐ 43 Cliff Harris | 1.00 | .40 | .10 |
| ☐ 44 Robert Newhouse | 1.00 | .40 | .10 |
| ☐ 50 D.D. Lewis SP | 3.00 | 1.20 | .30 |
| ☐ 53 Bob Breunig | 1.00 | .40 | .10 |
| ☐ 54 Randy White | 1.50 | .60 | .15 |
| ☐ 56 Thomas Henderson SP | 3.00 | 1.20 | .30 |
| ☐ 67 Pat Donovan | .60 | .24 | .06 |
| ☐ 79 Harvey Martin | 1.00 | .40 | .10 |
| ☐ 80 Tony Hill | 1.00 | .40 | .10 |
| ☐ 88 Drew Pearson | 1.25 | .50 | .12 |
| ☐ 89 Billy Joe DuPree | 1.00 | .40 | .10 |
| ☐ xx Tom Landry CO | 2.50 | 1.00 | .25 |

## 1979 Police Seahawks

The 1979 Seattle Seahawks Police set consists of 16 cards each measuring approximately 2 5/8" by 4 1/8". In addition to the local law enforcement agency, the set was sponsored by the Washington State Crime Prevention Association, the Kiwanis Club, and Coca-Cola, the logos of which all appear on the back of the cards. In addition to the 13 player cards, cards for the mascot, coach, and Sea Gal were issued. The set is unnumbered but has been listed below in alphabetical order by subject. The backs contain "Tips from the Seahawks". A 1979 copyright date can be found on the back of the cards.

|  | NRMT | VG-E | GOOD |
|---|---|---|---|
| COMPLETE SET (16) | 15.00 | 6.00 | 1.50 |
| COMMON PLAYER (1-16) | .75 | .30 | .07 |
| ☐ 1 Steve August | .75 | .30 | .07 |
| ☐ 2 Autry Beamon | .75 | .30 | .07 |
| ☐ 3 Terry Beeson | .75 | .30 | .07 |
| ☐ 4 Dennis Boyd | .75 | .30 | .07 |
| ☐ 5 Dave Brown | 1.00 | .40 | .10 |
| ☐ 6 Efren Herrera | .75 | .30 | .07 |
| ☐ 7 Steve Largent | 7.50 | 3.00 | .75 |
| ☐ 8 Tom Lynch | .75 | .30 | .07 |
| ☐ 9 Bob Newton | .75 | .30 | .07 |
| ☐ 10 Jack Patera CO | 1.00 | .40 | .10 |
| ☐ 11 Sea Gal (Keri Truscan) | 1.00 | .40 | .10 |
| ☐ 12 Seahawk (Mascot) | .75 | .30 | .07 |
| ☐ 13 David Sims | .75 | .30 | .07 |
| ☐ 14 Sherman Smith | 1.00 | .40 | .10 |
| ☐ 15 John Yarno | .75 | .30 | .07 |
| ☐ 16 Jim Zorn | 2.00 | .80 | .20 |

## 1980 Police Broncos Stamps

The 1980 Denver Broncos set are not cards but stamps each measuring approximately 3" by 3". Each stamp actually contains three smaller stamps, two player stamps and the Denver Broncos logo stamp. The set is co-sponsored by Albertson's, the Kiwanis Club, and the local law enforcement agency. A different stamp pair was given away each week during the football season by Albertson's food stores in the Denver Metro area. The set is unnumbered, although player uniform numbers appear on each small stamp. The set has been listed below in alphabetical order based on the player stamp on the left side. The back of each pair states "Support your local Law Enforcement Agency" and gives instructions on how to reach the police by phone. The backs of the stamps contain 1980 NFL and NFL Player's Association copyright dates. There was also a poster (to hold the stamps) issued which originally was priced at 99 cents. It was a color action picture of four Broncos tackling a Chargers running back measuring approximately 21" by 29"; the poster is much more difficult to find now than the set of stamps.

|  | MINT | EXC | G-VG |
|---|---|---|---|
| COMPLETE SET (9) | 7.50 | 3.00 | .75 |
| COMMON PAIR (1-9) | .75 | .30 | .07 |
| ☐ 1 Barney Chavous and Rubin Carter | 1.00 | .40 | .10 |
| ☐ 2 Bernard Jackson and Haven Moses | 1.00 | .40 | .10 |
| ☐ 3 Tom Jackson and Riley Odoms | 1.50 | .60 | .15 |
| ☐ 4 Brison Manor and Steve Foley | .75 | .30 | .07 |
| ☐ 5 Claudie Minor and Randy Gradishar | 1.00 | .40 | .10 |
| ☐ 6 Craig Morton and Tom Glassic | 1.25 | .50 | .12 |
| ☐ 7 Jim Turner and Bob Swenson | 1.00 | .40 | .10 |
| ☐ 8 Rick Upchurch and Billy Thompson | 1.25 | .50 | .12 |
| ☐ 9 Louis Wright and Joe Rizzo | .75 | .30 | .07 |

# 1980 Police Buccaneers

GENE SANDERS
Offensive Line
6' 3"  260 lbs.
Texas A & M

KIDS & KOPS
TIPS from the BUCCANEERS

PICK:
A screen by a receiver on a defensive back to take him out of coverage.

★ ☐ ★

Pick your playground carefully. Don't play where it is not safe.

Enjoy Coca-Cola

GREATER TAMPA
CHAMBER OF COMMERCE
LAW ENFORCEMENT COUNCIL
And Your Local Law Enforcement Agencies

This set is complete at 56 cards measuring approximately 2 5/8" by 4 1/8". Since there are no numbers on the cards, the set has been listed in alphabetical order by player. In addition to player cards, an assortment of coaches, mascots, and Swash-Buc-Lers (cheerleaders) are included. The set was sponsored by the Greater Tampa Chamber of Commerce Law Enforcement Council, the local law enforcement agencies, and Coca-Cola. Tips from the Buccaneers are written on the backs. The fronts contain the Tampa Bay helmet logo. Cards are also available with a Paradyne (Corporation) back; these scarce back variations are worth two to three times the values below.

|  | MINT | EXC | G-VG |
|---|---|---|---|
| COMPLETE SET (56) | 125.00 | 50.00 | 12.50 |
| COMMON CARD (1-56) | 2.50 | 1.00 | .25 |
| ☐ 1 Ricky Bell | 6.00 | 2.40 | .60 |
| ☐ 2 Rick Berns | 3.50 | 1.40 | .35 |
| ☐ 3 Tom Blanchard | 2.50 | 1.00 | .25 |
| ☐ 4 Scott Brantley | 2.50 | 1.00 | .25 |
| ☐ 5 Aaron Brown | 2.50 | 1.00 | .25 |
| ☐ 6 Cedric Brown | 2.50 | 1.00 | .25 |
| ☐ 7 Mark Cotney | 2.50 | 1.00 | .25 |
| ☐ 8 Randy Crowder | 2.50 | 1.00 | .25 |
| ☐ 9 Gary Davis | 2.50 | 1.00 | .25 |
| ☐ 10 Johnny Davis | 3.50 | 1.40 | .35 |
| ☐ 11 Tony Davis | 2.50 | 1.00 | .25 |
| ☐ 12 Jerry Eckwood | 4.50 | 1.80 | .45 |
| ☐ 13 Chuck Fusina | 3.50 | 1.40 | .35 |

| ☐ 14 Jimmie Giles | 4.50 | 1.80 | .45 |
|---|---|---|---|
| ☐ 15 Isaac Hagins | 2.50 | 1.00 | .25 |
| ☐ 16 Charley Hannah | 2.50 | 1.00 | .25 |
| ☐ 17 Andy Hawkins | 2.50 | 1.00 | .25 |
| ☐ 18 Kevin House | 4.50 | 1.80 | .45 |
| ☐ 19 Cecil Johnson | 2.50 | 1.00 | .25 |
| ☐ 20 Gordon Jones | 3.50 | 1.40 | .35 |
| ☐ 21 Curtis Jordan | 2.50 | 1.00 | .25 |
| ☐ 22 Bill Kollar | 2.50 | 1.00 | .25 |
| ☐ 23 Jim Leonard | 2.50 | 1.00 | .25 |
| ☐ 24 David Lewis | 3.50 | 1.40 | .35 |
| ☐ 25 Reggie Lewis | 2.50 | 1.00 | .25 |
| ☐ 26 David Logan | 3.50 | 1.40 | .35 |
| ☐ 27 Larry Mucker | 2.50 | 1.00 | .25 |
| ☐ 28 Jim O'Bradovich | 3.50 | 1.40 | .35 |
| ☐ 29 Mike Rae | 3.50 | 1.40 | .35 |
| ☐ 30 Dave Reavis | 2.50 | 1.00 | .25 |
| ☐ 31 Danny Reece | 2.50 | 1.00 | .25 |
| ☐ 32 Greg Roberts | 2.50 | 1.00 | .25 |
| ☐ 33 Gene Sanders | 2.50 | 1.00 | .25 |
| ☐ 34 Dewey Selmon | 3.50 | 1.40 | .35 |
| ☐ 35 Lee Roy Selmon | 6.00 | 2.40 | .60 |
| ☐ 36 Ray Snell | 2.50 | 1.00 | .25 |
| ☐ 37 Dave Stalls | 2.50 | 1.00 | .25 |
| ☐ 38 Norris Thomas | 2.50 | 1.00 | .25 |
| ☐ 39 Mike Washington | 2.50 | 1.00 | .25 |
| ☐ 40 Doug Williams | 6.00 | 2.40 | .60 |
| ☐ 41 Steve Wilson | 2.50 | 1.00 | .25 |
| ☐ 42 Richard Wood | 3.50 | 1.40 | .35 |
| ☐ 43 George Yarno | 2.50 | 1.00 | .25 |
| ☐ 44 Garo Yepremian | 4.50 | 1.80 | .45 |
| ☐ 45 Logo Card | 2.50 | 1.00 | .25 |
| ☐ 46 Team Photo | 4.50 | 1.80 | .45 |
| ☐ 47 Hugh Culverhouse OWN | 3.50 | 1.40 | .35 |
| ☐ 48 John McKay CO | 3.50 | 1.40 | .35 |
| ☐ 49 Mascot Capt. Crush | 2.50 | 1.00 | .25 |
| ☐ 50 Cheerleaders: Swash-Buc-Lers | 3.50 | 1.40 | .35 |
| ☐ 51 Swash-Buc-Lers (Buzz) | 3.50 | 1.40 | .35 |
| ☐ 52 Swash-Buc-Lers (Check with me) | 3.50 | 1.40 | .35 |
| ☐ 53 Swash-Buc-Lers (Gap Two) | 3.50 | 1.40 | .35 |
| ☐ 54 Swash-Buc-Lers (Gas) | 3.50 | 1.40 | .35 |
| ☐ 55 Swash-Buc-Lers (Pass Protection) | 3.50 | 1.40 | .35 |
| ☐ 56 Swash-Buc-Lers (Post Pattern) | 3.50 | 1.40 | .35 |

# 1980 Police Cardinals

32 • OTTIS ANDERSON
Running Back: Ht: 6-2 Wt: 215
st. louis cardinals

Cardinal Tips
SPLIT-SECOND DECISIONS

From the moment he takes the handoff, a good running back has to make several split-second decisions while he weaves through the defense on a long run.

Quick thinking can keep you on your feet. You can't think quickly or clearly if you use drugs or alcohol. Don't give in to the temptation.

Courtesy of your area
Law Enforcement
Agency,
St. Louis Cardinals,
KMOX Radio and
Community Federal
Savings and Loan
If you need a police officer dial "911" (Except Pageland).

The 15-card 1980 St. Louis Cardinals set was sponsored by the local law enforcement agency, the St. Louis Cardinals, KMOX Radio (which broadcasts the Cardinals' games), and Community Federal Savings and Loan: the last three of which have their logos on the backs of the cards. The cards measure approximately 2 5/8" by 4 1/8". The set is unnumbered but has been listed by player uniform number in the checklist below. The backs present "Cardinal Tips" and information on how to contact a police officer by telephone. Card backs feature black print with red trim on white card stock. Ottis Anderson appears in his Rookie Card year.

|  | MINT | EXC | G-VG |
|---|---|---|---|
| COMPLETE SET (15) | 12.00 | 5.00 | 1.20 |
| COMMON PLAYER | .75 | .30 | .07 |
| ☐ 17 Jim Hart | 2.00 | .80 | .20 |
| ☐ 22 Roger Wehrli | 1.25 | .50 | .12 |
| ☐ 24 Wayne Morris | 1.00 | .40 | .10 |

| | | | |
|---|---|---|---|
| ☐ 32 Ottis Anderson | 3.00 | 1.20 | .30 |
| ☐ 33 Theotis Brown | 1.00 | .40 | .10 |
| ☐ 37 Ken Green | .75 | .30 | .07 |
| ☐ 55 Eric Williams | .75 | .30 | .07 |
| ☐ 56 Tim Kearney | .75 | .30 | .07 |
| ☐ 59 Calvin Favron | .75 | .30 | .07 |
| ☐ 68 Terry Stieve | .75 | .30 | .07 |
| ☐ 72 Dan Dierdorf | 2.00 | .80 | .20 |
| ☐ 73 Mike Dawson | .75 | .30 | .07 |
| ☐ 82 Bob Pollard | .75 | .30 | .07 |
| ☐ 83 Pat Tilley | 1.25 | .50 | .12 |
| ☐ 85 Mel Gray | 1.50 | .60 | .15 |

## 1980 Police Chiefs

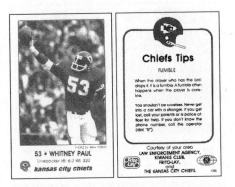

The unnumbered, ten-card, 1980 Kansas City Chiefs Police set has been listed by the player's uniform number in the checklist below. The cards measure approximately 2 5/8 by 4 1/8". The Stenerud card was supposedly distributed on a limited basis and is thus more difficult to obtain. In addition to the Chiefs and the local law enforcement agencies, the set is sponsored by the Kiwanis Club and Frito-Lay, whose logos appear on the backs of the cards. The 1980 date can be found on the back of the cards as can "Chiefs Tips".

| | MINT | EXC | G-VG |
|---|---|---|---|
| COMPLETE SET (10) | 10.00 | 4.00 | 1.00 |
| COMMON PLAYER | 1.00 | .40 | .10 |
| | | | |
| ☐ 1 Bob Grupp | 1.00 | .40 | .10 |
| ☐ 3 Jan Stenerud SP | 3.00 | 1.20 | .30 |
| ☐ 32 Tony Reed | 1.25 | .50 | .12 |
| ☐ 53 Whitney Paul | 1.00 | .40 | .10 |
| ☐ 59 Gary Spani | 1.00 | .40 | .10 |
| ☐ 67 Art Still | 1.50 | .60 | .15 |
| ☐ 86 J.T. Smith | 1.50 | .60 | .15 |
| ☐ 99 Mike Bell | 1.00 | .40 | .10 |
| ☐ xx Defensive Team | 1.25 | .50 | .12 |
| ☐ xx Offensive Team | 1.25 | .50 | .12 |

## 1980 Police Cowboys

Quite similar to the 1979 set, the 1980 Dallas Cowboys police set is unnumbered other than the player's uniform number (as is listed in the checklist below). The cards in this 14-card set measure approximately 2 5/8 by 4 1/8". The sponsors are the same as those of

the 1979 issue and the section entitled "Cowboys Tips" is contained on the back. The Kiwanis and Cowboys helmet logos appear on the fronts of the cards.

| | MINT | EXC | G-VG |
|---|---|---|---|
| COMPLETE SET (14) | 12.00 | 5.00 | 1.20 |
| COMMON PLAYER | .75 | .30 | .07 |
| | | | |
| ☐ 1 Rafael Septien | 1.00 | .40 | .10 |
| ☐ 11 Danny White | 2.50 | 1.00 | .25 |
| ☐ 25 Aaron Kyle | .75 | .30 | .07 |
| ☐ 26 Preston Pearson | 1.25 | .50 | .12 |
| ☐ 31 Benny Barnes | .75 | .30 | .07 |
| ☐ 35 Scott Laidlaw | .75 | .30 | .07 |
| ☐ 42 Randy Hughes | .75 | .30 | .07 |
| ☐ 62 John Fitzgerald | .75 | .30 | .07 |
| ☐ 63 Larry Cole | 1.00 | .40 | .10 |
| ☐ 64 Tom Rafferty | 1.00 | .40 | .10 |
| ☐ 68 Herb Scott | .75 | .30 | .07 |
| ☐ 70 Rayfield Wright | .75 | .30 | .07 |
| ☐ 78 John Dutton | 1.00 | .40 | .10 |
| ☐ 87 Jay Saldi | .75 | .30 | .07 |

## 1980 Police Dolphins

The 1980 Miami Dolphins set contains 16 unnumbered cards, which have been listed by player uniform number in the checklist below. The cards measure approximately 2 5/8 by 4 1/8". The set was sponsored by the Kiwanis Club, the local law enforcement agency, and the Miami Dolphins logo. The backs contain "Dolphins Tips" and the Miami Dolphins logo. The backs are printed in black with blue accent on white card stock. The fronts contain the Kiwanis logo, but not the Dolphins logo as in the following year. The card of Larry Little is reportedly more difficult to obtain than other cards in this set.

| | MINT | EXC | G-VG |
|---|---|---|---|
| COMPLETE SET (16) | 75.00 | 30.00 | 7.50 |
| COMMON PLAYER | 3.00 | 1.20 | .30 |
| | | | |
| ☐ 5 Uwe Von Schamann | 3.00 | 1.20 | .30 |
| ☐ 10 Don Strock | 5.00 | 2.00 | .50 |
| ☐ 12 Bob Griese | 15.00 | 6.00 | 1.50 |
| ☐ 22 Tony Nathan | 7.50 | 3.00 | .75 |
| ☐ 24 Delvin Williams | 6.00 | 2.40 | .60 |
| ☐ 25 Tim Foley | 4.00 | 1.60 | .40 |
| ☐ 50 Larry Gordon | 3.00 | 1.20 | .30 |
| ☐ 58 Kim Bokamper | 3.00 | 1.20 | .30 |
| ☐ 64 Ed Newman | 3.00 | 1.20 | .30 |
| ☐ 66 Larry Little SP | 15.00 | 6.00 | 1.50 |
| ☐ 67 Bob Kuechenberg | 6.00 | 2.40 | .60 |
| ☐ 73 Bob Baumhower | 4.00 | 1.60 | .40 |
| ☐ 77 A.J. Duhe | 5.00 | 2.00 | .50 |
| ☐ 82 Duriel Harris | 4.00 | 1.60 | .40 |
| ☐ 89 Nat Moore | 6.00 | 2.40 | .60 |
| ☐ xx Don Shula CO | 10.00 | 4.00 | 1.00 |

## 1980 Police Falcons

The 1980 Atlanta Falcons set contains 30 unnumbered cards each measuring approximately 2 5/8 by 4 1/8". Although uniform numbers can be found on the front of the cards, the cards have been listed alphabetically on the checklist below for convenience. Logos of the three sponsors, the Atlanta Police Athletic League, the Northside Atlanta Jaycees, and Coca-Cola, can be found on the back of the cards with short "Tips from the Falcons". Card backs have black printing with red accent. The Falcon helmet and stylized logo appear on the front of the cards with the player's name, uniform number, position, height, weight and college.

|  | MINT | EXC | G-VG |
|---|---|---|---|
| COMPLETE SET (30) | 50.00 | 20.00 | 5.00 |
| COMMON PLAYER (1-30) | 1.50 | .60 | .15 |
| ☐ 1 William Andrews | 5.00 | 2.00 | .50 |
| ☐ 2 Steve Bartkowski | 10.00 | 4.00 | 1.00 |
| ☐ 3 Bubba Bean | 2.50 | 1.00 | .25 |
| ☐ 4 Warren Bryant | 1.50 | .60 | .15 |
| ☐ 5 Rick Byas | 1.50 | .60 | .15 |
| ☐ 6 Lynn Cain | 3.00 | 1.20 | .30 |
| ☐ 7 Buddy Curry | 1.50 | .60 | .15 |
| ☐ 8 Edgar Fields | 1.50 | .60 | .15 |
| ☐ 9 Wallace Francis | 3.50 | 1.40 | .35 |
| ☐ 10 Alfred Jackson | 3.00 | 1.20 | .30 |
| ☐ 11 John James | 1.50 | .60 | .15 |
| ☐ 12 Alfred Jenkins | 4.00 | 1.60 | .40 |
| ☐ 13 Kenny Johnson | 1.50 | .60 | .15 |
| ☐ 14 Mike Kenn | 3.50 | 1.40 | .35 |
| ☐ 15 Fulton Kuykendall | 1.50 | .60 | .15 |
| ☐ 16 Rolland Lawrence | 2.50 | 1.00 | .25 |
| ☐ 17 Tim Mazzetti | 1.50 | .60 | .15 |
| ☐ 18 Dewey McLean | 1.50 | .60 | .15 |
| ☐ 19 Jeff Merrow | 2.00 | .80 | .20 |
| ☐ 20 Junior Miller | 3.50 | 1.40 | .35 |
| ☐ 21 Tom Pridemore | 1.50 | .60 | .15 |
| ☐ 22 Frank Reed | 1.50 | .60 | .15 |
| ☐ 23 Al Richardson | 1.50 | .60 | .15 |
| ☐ 24 Dave Scott | 1.50 | .60 | .15 |
| ☐ 25 Don Smith | 1.50 | .60 | .15 |
| ☐ 26 Reggie Smith | 1.50 | .60 | .15 |
| ☐ 27 R.C. Thielemann | 2.00 | .80 | .20 |
| ☐ 28 Jeff Van Note | 3.50 | 1.40 | .35 |
| ☐ 29 Joel Williams | 1.50 | .60 | .15 |
| ☐ 30 Jeff Yeates | 1.50 | .60 | .15 |

## 1980 Police Oilers

The 14-card set of the 1980 Houston Oilers is unnumbered other than uniform numbers, which are used in the checklist below. The cards measure approximately 2 5/8" by 4 1/8". The Kiwanis Club, the local law enforcement agency, and the Houston Oilers sponsored this set. The backs feature "Oilers Tips" and a Kiwanis logo. The fronts feature logos of the Kiwanis and the City of Houston.

|  | MINT | EXC | G-VG |
|---|---|---|---|
| COMPLETE SET (14) | 15.00 | 6.00 | 1.50 |
| COMMON PLAYER | .90 | .36 | .09 |
| ☐ 0 Ken Burrough | 1.50 | .60 | .15 |
| ☐ 12 Ken Stabler | 5.00 | 2.00 | .50 |

|  |  |  |  |
|---|---|---|---|
| ☐ 14 Gifford Nielsen | 1.25 | .50 | .12 |
| ☐ 18 Cliff Parsley | .90 | .36 | .09 |
| ☐ 26 Rob Carpenter | 1.25 | .50 | .12 |
| ☐ 36 Carter Hartwig | .90 | .36 | .09 |
| ☐ 47 Ronnie Coleman | .90 | .36 | .09 |
| ☐ 52 Robert Brazile | 1.50 | .60 | .15 |
| ☐ 54 Gregg Bingham | .90 | .36 | .09 |
| ☐ 55 Carl Mauck | .90 | .36 | .09 |
| ☐ 78 Curley Culp | 1.25 | .50 | .12 |
| ☐ 82 Mike Renfro | 1.25 | .50 | .12 |
| ☐ 84 Billy Johnson | 1.50 | .60 | .15 |
| ☐ NNO Bum Phillips CO | 1.50 | .60 | .15 |

## 1980 Police Rams

This unnumbered, 14-card set has been listed in the checklist below by uniform number, which appears on the fronts of the cards. The cards measure approximately 2 5/8" by 4 1/8". The Kiwanis Club, who sponsored this set along with the local law enforcement agency and the Rams, has their logo on the fronts of the cards. These cards, which contain "Rams Tips" on the backs, were distributed by police officers, one per week over a 14-week period.

|  | MINT | EXC | G-VG |
|---|---|---|---|
| COMPLETE SET (14) | 18.00 | 7.25 | 1.80 |
| COMMON PLAYER | 1.00 | .40 | .10 |
| ☐ 11 Pat Haden | 3.00 | 1.20 | .30 |
| ☐ 15 Vince Ferragamo | 2.50 | 1.00 | .25 |
| ☐ 21 Nolan Cromwell | 2.00 | .80 | .20 |
| ☐ 26 Wendell Tyler | 2.00 | .80 | .20 |
| ☐ 32 Cullen Bryant | 1.25 | .50 | .12 |
| ☐ 53 Jim Youngblood | 1.25 | .50 | .12 |
| ☐ 59 Bob Brudzinski | 1.00 | .40 | .10 |
| ☐ 61 Rich Saul | 1.00 | .40 | .10 |
| ☐ 77 Doug France | 1.00 | .40 | .10 |
| ☐ 82 Willie Miller | 1.00 | .40 | .10 |
| ☐ 85 Jack Youngblood | 3.50 | 1.40 | .35 |
| ☐ 88 Preston Dennard | 1.00 | .40 | .10 |
| ☐ 90 Larry Brooks | 1.00 | .40 | .10 |
| ☐ xx Ray Malavasi CO | 1.00 | .40 | .10 |

## 1980 Police Seahawks

The 1980 Seattle Seahawks set of 16 cards is numbered and contains the 1980 date on the back. The cards measure approximately 2 5/8" by 4 1/8". In addition to the local law enforcement agency, the set is sponsored by the Washington State Crime Prevention Association, the Kiwanis Club, Coca-Cola, and the Ernst Home Centers, each of which has their logo appearing on the back. Also appearing on the backs of the cards are "Tips from the Seahawks". The card backs have blue printing with red accent on white card stock. A stylized Seahawks helmet logo appears on the front.

|  | MINT | EXC | G-VG |
|---|---|---|---|
| COMPLETE SET (16) | 12.00 | 5.00 | 1.20 |
| COMMON PLAYER (1-16) | .60 | .24 | .06 |
| ☐ 1 Sam McCullum | 1.00 | .40 | .10 |
| ☐ 2 Dan Doornink | .60 | .24 | .06 |
| ☐ 3 Sherman Smith | 1.00 | .40 | .10 |
| ☐ 4 Efren Herrera | .60 | .24 | .06 |
| ☐ 5 Bill Gregory | .60 | .24 | .06 |
| ☐ 6 Keith Simpson | .60 | .24 | .06 |
| ☐ 7 Manu Tuiasosopo | .75 | .30 | .07 |
| ☐ 8 Michael Jackson | .60 | .24 | .06 |
| ☐ 9 Steve Raible | .60 | .24 | .06 |
| ☐ 10 Steve Largent | 6.00 | 2.40 | .60 |
| ☐ 11 Jim Zorn | 2.00 | .80 | .20 |
| ☐ 12 Nick Bebout | .60 | .24 | .06 |
| ☐ 13 The Seahawk (mascot) | .75 | .30 | .07 |
| ☐ 14 Jack Patera CO | .75 | .30 | .07 |
| ☐ 15 Robert Hardy | .60 | .24 | .06 |
| ☐ 16 Keith Butler | .60 | .24 | .06 |

## 1981 Police Bears

The 1981 Chicago Bears police set contains 24 unnumbered cards. The cards measure approximately 2 5/8" by 4 1/8". Although uniform numbers appear on the fronts of the cards, they have been listed alphabetically in the checklist below. The set is sponsored by the Kiwanis Club, the local law enforcement agency and the Chicago Bears. Appearing on the backs along with a Chicago Bears helmet are "Chicago Bears Tips". The card backs have blue print with orange accent. The Kiwanis logo and Chicago Bears helmet appear on the fronts of the cards.

|  | MINT | EXC | G-VG |
|---|---|---|---|
| COMPLETE SET (24) | 20.00 | 8.00 | 2.00 |
| COMMON PLAYER (1-24) | .50 | .20 | .05 |
| ☐ 1 Ted Albrecht | .50 | .20 | .05 |
| ☐ 2 Neill Armstrong CO | .75 | .30 | .07 |
| ☐ 3 Brian Baschnagel | .75 | .30 | .07 |
| ☐ 4 Gary Campbell | .50 | .20 | .05 |
| ☐ 5 Robin Earl | .50 | .20 | .05 |
| ☐ 6 Allan Ellis | .50 | .20 | .05 |
| ☐ 7 Vince Evans | 1.00 | .40 | .10 |
| ☐ 8 Gary Fencik | 1.00 | .40 | .10 |
| ☐ 9 Dan Hampton | 4.00 | 1.60 | .40 |
| ☐ 10 Roland Harper | .75 | .30 | .07 |
| ☐ 11 Mike Hartenstine | .50 | .20 | .05 |
| ☐ 12 Tom Hicks | .50 | .20 | .05 |
| ☐ 13 Noah Jackson | .75 | .30 | .07 |
| ☐ 14 Dennis Lick | .50 | .20 | .05 |
| ☐ 15 Jerry Muckensturm | .50 | .20 | .05 |
| ☐ 16 Dan Neal | .50 | .20 | .05 |
| ☐ 17 Jim Osborne | .50 | .20 | .05 |
| ☐ 18 Alan Page | 4.00 | 1.60 | .40 |
| ☐ 19 Walter Payton | 12.00 | 5.00 | 1.20 |
| ☐ 20 Doug Plank | .75 | .30 | .07 |
| ☐ 21 Terry Schmidt | .50 | .20 | .05 |
| ☐ 22 James Scott | .75 | .30 | .07 |
| ☐ 23 Revie Sorey | .75 | .30 | .07 |
| ☐ 24 Rickey Watts | .75 | .30 | .07 |

## 1981 Police Chargers

The 1981 San Diego Chargers set contains 24 unnumbered cards of 22 subjects. The cards measure approximately 2 5/8" by 4 1/8". The cards are listed in the checklist below by the uniform number which appears on the fronts of the cards. The set is sponsored by the Kiwanis Club, the local law enforcement agency, and Pepsi-Cola. A Chargers helmet logo and "Chargers Tips" appear on the card backs. The card backs have black print with blue trim on white card stock. The Kiwanis and Chargers helmet logos appear on the fronts. Fouts and Winslow each exist with two different safety tips on the backs; the variations are distinguished below by the first few words of the safety tip. The complete set price below includes the variation cards.

|  | MINT | EXC | G-VG |
|---|---|---|---|
| COMPLETE SET (24) | 50.00 | 20.00 | 5.00 |
| COMMON CARD | 1.25 | .50 | .12 |
| ☐ 6 Rolf Benirschke | 2.00 | .80 | .20 |
| ☐ 14A Dan Fouts | 18.00 | 7.25 | 1.80 |
| (After a team ...) | | | |
| ☐ 14B Dan Fouts | 9.00 | 3.75 | .90 |
| (Once you've ...) | | | |
| ☐ 18 Charlie Joiner | 5.00 | 2.00 | .50 |
| ☐ 25 John Cappelletti | 2.50 | 1.00 | .25 |
| ☐ 28 Willie Buchanon | 1.50 | .60 | .15 |
| ☐ 29 Mike Williams | 1.25 | .50 | .12 |
| ☐ 43 Bob Gregor | 1.25 | .50 | .12 |
| ☐ 44 Pete Shaw | 1.25 | .50 | .12 |
| ☐ 46 Chuck Muncie | 2.00 | .80 | .20 |
| ☐ 51 Woodrow Lowe | 2.00 | .80 | .20 |
| ☐ 57 Linden King | 1.25 | .50 | .12 |
| ☐ 59 Cliff Thrift | 1.25 | .50 | .12 |
| ☐ 62 Don Macek | 1.25 | .50 | .12 |
| ☐ 63 Doug Wilkerson | 1.50 | .60 | .15 |
| ☐ 66 Billy Shields | 1.25 | .50 | .12 |
| ☐ 67 Ed White | 1.50 | .60 | .15 |
| ☐ 68 Leroy Jones | 1.25 | .50 | .12 |
| ☐ 70 Russ Washington | 1.50 | .60 | .15 |
| ☐ 74 Louie Kelcher | 1.50 | .60 | .15 |
| ☐ 79 Gary Johnson | 1.50 | .60 | .15 |
| ☐ 80A Kellen Winslow | 10.00 | 4.00 | 1.00 |
| (Go all out ...) | | | |
| ☐ 80B Kellen Winslow | 5.00 | 2.00 | .50 |
| (The length of ...) | | | |
| ☐ xx Don Coryell CO | 2.00 | .80 | .20 |

## 1981 Police Chiefs

The 1981 Kansas City Chiefs Police set consists of ten cards, some of which have more than one player pictured. The cards are numbered on the back as well as prominently displaying the player's uniform number on the fronts of the cards. The cards measure approximately 2 5/8" by 4 1/8". The set is sponsored by the area law enforcement agency, the Kiwanis Club, Frito-Lay, and the Kansas City Chiefs. The Kiwanis Club and Frito-Lay logos, in addition to the Chiefs helmet logo, appear on the backs of the cards. Also "Chiefs Tips" are featured on the card backs. The card backs have black print with red accent on white card stock.

|  | MINT | EXC | G-VG |
|---|---|---|---|
| COMPLETE SET (10) | 5.00 | 2.00 | .50 |
| COMMON CARD (1-10) | .50 | .20 | .05 |
| ☐ 1 Warpaint and Carla | .75 | .30 | .07 |
| (Mascots) | | | |
| ☐ 2 Art Still | .90 | .36 | .09 |
| ☐ 3 Steve Fuller and | .75 | .30 | .07 |
| Jack Rudnay | | | |

86 • J.T. SMITH
Wide Receiver Ht: 6'2" Wt: 185
kansas city chiefs

**Chiefs Tips**

CATCH

A "catch" is when a player grabs and holds on to a forward pass.

You can help your neighborhood policeman "catch" criminals by finding a policeman or telling your parents when you see someone breaking the law.

Six in a Series of Ten

Courtesy of your area
LAW ENFORCEMENT AGENCY,
KIWANIS CLUB,
FRITO-LAY,
and
THE KANSAS CITY CHIEFS. 1981

| | | | |
|---|---|---|---|
| ☐ 4 Gary Green | .75 | .30 | .07 |
| ☐ 5 Tom Condon and Marv Levy CO | .75 | .30 | .07 |
| ☐ 6 J.T. Smith | .90 | .36 | .09 |
| ☐ 7 Gary Spani and Whitney Paul | .50 | .20 | .05 |
| ☐ 8 Nick Lowery and Steve Fuller | .90 | .36 | .09 |
| ☐ 9 Gary Barbaro | .75 | .30 | .07 |
| ☐ 10 Henry Marshall | .60 | .24 | .06 |

## 1981 Police Cowboys

26 • Michael Downs
Safety
DALLAS COWBOYS

**Cowboys Tips**

FOUL

Any violation of a playing rule.

Play by the rules and be a winner.

Courtesy of your area
Kiwanis Club, Law Enforcement Agency
and the
Dallas Cowboys Weekly,
the official Cowboys fan newspaper.

The 1981 Dallas Cowboys set of 14 cards is quite similar to sets of the previous two years. Since the cards are unnumbered, except for uniform number, the players have been listed by uniform number in the checklist below. The cards measure approximately 2 5/8" by 4 1/8". The set is sponsored by the Kiwanis Club, the local law enforcement agency, and the Dallas Cowboys Weekly. Appearing on the back along with a Cowboys helmet logo are "Cowboys Tips". A Kiwanis logo and Cowboys helmet logo appear on the front.

| | MINT | EXC | G-VG |
|---|---|---|---|
| COMPLETE SET (14) | 12.00 | 5.00 | 1.20 |
| COMMON PLAYER | .80 | .32 | .08 |
| | | | |
| ☐ 18 Glenn Carano | 1.00 | .40 | .10 |
| ☐ 20 Ron Springs | .80 | .32 | .08 |
| ☐ 23 James Jones | .80 | .32 | .08 |
| ☐ 26 Michael Downs | 1.00 | .40 | .10 |
| ☐ 32 Dennis Thurman | 1.25 | .50 | .12 |
| ☐ 45 Steve Wilson | .80 | .32 | .08 |
| ☐ 51 Anthony Dickerson | .80 | .32 | .08 |
| ☐ 52 Robert Shaw | 1.00 | .40 | .10 |
| ☐ 58 Mike Hegman | .80 | .32 | .08 |
| ☐ 59 Guy Brown | .80 | .32 | .08 |
| ☐ 61 Jim Cooper | .80 | .32 | .08 |
| ☐ 72 Ed Too Tall Jones | 2.50 | 1.00 | .25 |
| ☐ 84 Doug Cosbie | 1.50 | .60 | .15 |
| ☐ 86 Butch Johnson | 1.25 | .50 | .12 |

## 1981 Police Cowboys Thousand Oaks

This 14-card set was issued in Thousand Oaks, California, where the Cowboys conduct their summer pre-season workouts. These unnumbered cards measure approximately 2 5/8" by 4 1/8". Similar to other Cowboys sets, the distinguishing factors of this set are the

88 • Drew Pearson
Wide Receiver
DALLAS COWBOYS

**Cowboys Tips**

SHOTGUN FORMATION

In the shotgun formation the quarterback lines up seven yards behind the center to receive the snap. This allows the quarterback to set up quickly and see the defense better on passing plays.

A team that uses the shotgun is not afraid to be different. If a friend asks you to do something you know is wrong, don't you be afraid to be different.

Courtesy of the
Thousand Oaks Kiwanis Club and
Thousand Oaks Police Dept.
and
Dallas Cowboys Weekly,
the official Cowboys fan newspaper.

Thousand Oaks Kiwanis Club and Thousand Oaks Police Department names printed on the backs in the place where other sets had the Kiwanis Club and law enforcement agency printed. The 14 players in this set are different from those in the regular set above. The cards are listed below by uniform number.

| | MINT | EXC | G-VG |
|---|---|---|---|
| COMPLETE SET (14) | 25.00 | 10.00 | 2.50 |
| COMMON PLAYER | 1.25 | .50 | .12 |
| | | | |
| ☐ 11 Danny White | 3.00 | 1.20 | .30 |
| ☐ 31 Benny Barnes | 1.25 | .50 | .12 |
| ☐ 33 Tony Dorsett | 6.00 | 2.40 | .60 |
| ☐ 41 Charlie Waters | 2.50 | 1.00 | .25 |
| ☐ 42 Randy Hughes | 1.25 | .50 | .12 |
| ☐ 44 Robert Newhouse | 2.00 | .80 | .20 |
| ☐ 54 Randy White | 4.00 | 1.60 | .40 |
| ☐ 55 D.D. Lewis | 1.50 | .60 | .15 |
| ☐ 78 John Dutton | 1.50 | .60 | .15 |
| ☐ 79 Harvey Martin | 2.00 | .80 | .20 |
| ☐ 80 Tony Hill | 2.00 | .80 | .20 |
| ☐ 88 Drew Pearson | 3.00 | 1.20 | .30 |
| ☐ 89 Billy Joe DuPree | 2.50 | 1.00 | .25 |
| ☐ xx Tom Landry CO | 4.00 | 1.60 | .40 |

## 1981 Police Dolphins

10 • DON STROCK
6'5" – 220 lbs
Quarterback
Virginia Tech

**DOLPHINS TIPS**

PLAYBOOK

All football players are given playbooks, which contain all the offensive and defensive plays they must know.

To be successful, football players must put in long hours studying their playbooks. Studying your schoolbooks will help you get a good education and a good job.

Courtesy of your local
Kiwanis Club,
Law Enforcement Agency,
and the Miami Dolphins.
In case of emergency dial "911"

The 1981 Miami Dolphins police set consists of 16 numbered cards. The cards measure approximately 2 5/8" by 4 1/8". Player uniform numbers also appear on the fronts of the cards, as does a Kiwanis and blue Dolphins logo. The set is sponsored by the local Kiwanis Club, the local law enforcement agency, and the Dolphins. The backs feature the Dolphins logo and "Dolphins Tips". Card backs are printed in black with gold and blue accent on thin white card stock.

| | MINT | EXC | G-VG |
|---|---|---|---|
| COMPLETE SET (16) | 20.00 | 8.00 | 2.00 |
| COMMON PLAYER (1-16) | 1.00 | .40 | .10 |
| | | | |
| ☐ 1 Duriel Harris | 1.25 | .50 | .12 |
| ☐ 2 Bob Kuechenberg | 1.50 | .60 | .15 |
| ☐ 3 Don Bessillieu | 1.00 | .40 | .10 |
| ☐ 4 Gerald Small | 1.00 | .40 | .10 |
| ☐ 5 David Woodley | 1.50 | .60 | .15 |
| ☐ 6 Don McNeal | 1.25 | .50 | .12 |
| ☐ 7 Nat Moore | 2.00 | .80 | .20 |
| ☐ 8 A.J. Duhe | 1.50 | .60 | .15 |
| ☐ 9 Glenn Blackwood | 1.25 | .50 | .12 |

| | MINT | EXC | G-VG |
|---|---|---|---|
| ☐ 10 Don Strock | 2.00 | .80 | .20 |
| ☐ 11 Doug Betters | 1.00 | .40 | .10 |
| ☐ 12 George Roberts | 1.00 | .40 | .10 |
| ☐ 13 Bob Baumhower | 1.50 | .60 | .15 |
| ☐ 14 Kim Bokamper | 1.00 | .40 | .10 |
| ☐ 15 Tony Nathan | 2.00 | .80 | .20 |
| ☐ 16 Don Shula CO | 4.00 | 1.60 | .40 |

## 1981 Police Falcons

The 1981 Atlanta Falcons 30-card police set is unnumbered but has been listed in the checklist below by player uniform number. The cards measure approximately 2 5/8" by 4 1/8". The set is sponsored by the Atlanta Police Athletic League, whose logo appears on the front, and Coca-Cola and Chevron, whose logos appear on the back. The player's name and brief biographical data, in addition to "Tips from the Falcons," are contained on the backs of the cards. Card backs have black printing with red and blue accent on thin white card stock. The fronts inform the public that the Atlanta Falcons were the NFC Western Division Champions of 1980.

| | MINT | EXC | G-VG |
|---|---|---|---|
| COMPLETE SET (30) | 15.00 | 6.00 | 1.50 |
| COMMON PLAYER | .40 | .16 | .04 |
| | | | |
| ☐ 6 John James | .40 | .16 | .04 |
| ☐ 10 Steve Bartkowski | 3.50 | 1.40 | .35 |
| ☐ 16 Reggie Smith | .40 | .16 | .04 |
| ☐ 18 Mick Luckhurst | .50 | .20 | .05 |
| ☐ 21 Lynn Cain | 1.00 | .40 | .10 |
| ☐ 23 Bobby Butler | .40 | .16 | .04 |
| ☐ 27 Tom Pridemore | .40 | .16 | .04 |
| ☐ 30 Scott Woerner | .40 | .16 | .04 |
| ☐ 31 William Andrews | 1.50 | .60 | .15 |
| ☐ 36 Bob Glazebrook | .40 | .16 | .04 |
| ☐ 37 Kenny Johnson | .40 | .16 | .04 |
| ☐ 50 Buddy Curry | .40 | .16 | .04 |
| ☐ 51 Jim Laughlin | .40 | .16 | .04 |
| ☐ 54 Fulton Kuykendall | .50 | .20 | .05 |
| ☐ 56 Al Richardson | .40 | .16 | .04 |
| ☐ 57 Jeff Van Note | 1.00 | .40 | .10 |
| ☐ 58 Joel Williams | .40 | .16 | .04 |
| ☐ 65 Don Smith | .40 | .16 | .04 |
| ☐ 66 Warren Bryant | .50 | .20 | .05 |
| ☐ 68 R.C. Thielemann | .50 | .20 | .05 |
| ☐ 70 Dave Scott | .40 | .16 | .04 |
| ☐ 74 Wilson Faumuina | .40 | .16 | .04 |
| ☐ 75 Jeff Merrow | .50 | .20 | .05 |
| ☐ 78 Mike Kenn | 1.00 | .40 | .10 |
| ☐ 79 Jeff Yeates | .40 | .16 | .04 |
| ☐ 80 Junior Miller | .75 | .30 | .07 |
| ☐ 84 Alfred Jenkins | 1.00 | .40 | .10 |
| ☐ 85 Alfred Jackson | .75 | .30 | .07 |
| ☐ 89 Wallace Francis | 1.25 | .50 | .12 |
| ☐ xx Leeman Bennett CO | .40 | .16 | .04 |

## 1981 Police Jets

This unnumbered Police issue is complete at ten cards. Cards measure approximately 2 5/8" by 4 1/8" and have a green border around the photo on the front of the cards. The set was sponsored by New York City Crime Prevention Section, Frito-Lay, Kiwanis Club, and the New York Jets. The backs each contain a safety tip printed in red ink. The 1981 date is printed on the card backs. Apparently these Jets Police cards were printed on a sheet such that six of the cards were double printed and four of the cards were single printed. The single-printed cards, which are more difficult to find, are indicated below by SP.

| | MINT | EXC | G-VG |
|---|---|---|---|
| COMPLETE SET (10) | 20.00 | 8.00 | 2.00 |
| COMMON PLAYER | 1.25 | .50 | .12 |
| COMMON PLAYER SP | 2.50 | 1.00 | .25 |
| | | | |
| ☐ 14 Richard Todd SP | 4.00 | 1.60 | .40 |
| ☐ 42 Bruce Harper | 1.25 | .50 | .12 |
| ☐ 51 Greg Buttle | 2.00 | .80 | .20 |
| ☐ 73 Joe Klecko | 3.00 | 1.20 | .30 |
| ☐ 79 Marvin Powell | 1.50 | .60 | .15 |
| ☐ 80 Johnny Lam Jones SP | 3.50 | 1.40 | .35 |
| ☐ 85 Wesley Walker SP | 6.00 | 2.40 | .60 |
| ☐ 93 Marty Lyons | 2.00 | .80 | .20 |
| ☐ 99 Mark Gastineau | 2.50 | 1.00 | .25 |
| ☐ xx Team Effort SP | 2.50 | 1.00 | .25 |

## 1981 Police Steelers

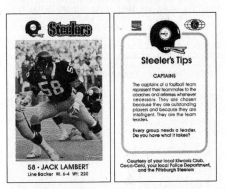

The 1981 Pittsburgh Steelers police set consists of 16 unnumbered cards which have been listed in the checklist below by the uniform number appearing on the fronts of the cards. The cards measure approximately 2 5/8" by 4 1/8". The set is sponsored by the local police department, the Pittsburgh Steelers, the Kiwanis Club, and Coca-Cola, the last three of which have their logos appearing on the backs of the cards. In addition, "Steelers' Tips" are featured on the back. Card backs have black printing with gold accent on white card stock. This set is very similar to the 1982 Police Steelers set; differences are noted parenthetically in the list below.

| | MINT | EXC | G-VG |
|---|---|---|---|
| COMPLETE SET (16) | 20.00 | 8.00 | 2.00 |
| COMMON PLAYER | .75 | .30 | .07 |
| | | | |
| ☐ 9 Matt Bahr | 1.00 | .40 | .10 |
| ☐ 12 Terry Bradshaw (Passing) | 7.50 | 3.00 | .75 |
| ☐ 31 Donnie Shell (Referee back) | 1.25 | .50 | .12 |
| ☐ 32 Franco Harris (Running with ball) | 4.00 | 1.60 | .40 |
| ☐ 47 Mel Blount (Running without ball) | 2.50 | 1.00 | .25 |
| ☐ 52 Mike Webster (Standing) | 1.50 | .60 | .15 |
| ☐ 57 Sam Davis | .75 | .30 | .07 |
| ☐ 58 Jack Lambert (Facing left) | 2.50 | 1.00 | .25 |
| ☐ 59 Jack Ham | 2.50 | 1.00 | .25 |

|  | | | |
|---|---|---|---|
| (Sportsmanship back) | | | |
| ☐ 64 Steve Furness | .75 | .30 | .07 |
| ☐ 68 L.C. Greenwood | 1.50 | .60 | .15 |
| ☐ 75 Joe Greene | 3.50 | 1.40 | .35 |
| ☐ 76 John Banaszak | .75 | .30 | .07 |
| ☐ 79 Larry Brown | .75 | .30 | .07 |
| (Chin 7/16" from bottom) | | | |
| ☐ 82 John Stallworth | 2.50 | 1.00 | .25 |
| (Running with ball) | | | |
| ☐ 88 Lynn Swann | 4.50 | 1.80 | .45 |
| (Double coverage back) | | | |

## 1982 Police Broncos

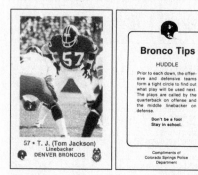

57 • T. J. (Tom Jackson)
Linebacker
DENVER BRONCOS

**Bronco Tips**

HUDDLE

Prior to each down, the offensive and defensive teams form a tight circle to find out what play will be used next. The plays are called by the quarterback on offense and the middle linebacker on defense.

**Don't be a fool
Stay in school.**

Compliments of
Colorado Springs Police
Department

The 1982 Denver Broncos set contains 15 unnumbered cards. The cards measure approximately 2 5/8" by 4 1/8". The uniform numbers, which appear on the fronts of the cards, are used in the checklist below. The set was sponsored by the Colorado Springs Police Department and features "Broncos Tips" and the Broncos helmet logo on the back. Card backs feature black print on white card stock. The fronts contain both the Denver helmet logo and the logo of the Colorado Springs Police Department. The cards of Barney Chavous and Randy Gradishar are supposedly harder to find than the other cards in the set, with Chavous considered the more difficult of the two. In addition Riley Odoms and Dave Preston seem to be harder to find.

|  | MINT | EXC | G-VG |
|---|---|---|---|
| COMPLETE SET (15) | 125.00 | 50.00 | 12.50 |
| COMMON PLAYER | 2.00 | .80 | .20 |
| ☐ 7 Craig Morton | 7.50 | 3.00 | .75 |
| ☐ 11 Luke Prestridge | 2.00 | .80 | .20 |
| ☐ 20 Louis Wright | 4.00 | 1.60 | .40 |
| ☐ 24 Rick Parros | 2.00 | .80 | .20 |
| ☐ 36 Bill Thompson | 4.00 | 1.60 | .40 |
| ☐ 41 Rob Lytle | 3.00 | 1.20 | .30 |
| ☐ 46 Dave Preston SP | 6.00 | 2.40 | .60 |
| ☐ 51 Bob Swenson | 3.00 | 1.20 | .30 |
| ☐ 53 Randy Gradishar SP | 50.00 | 20.00 | 5.00 |
| ☐ 57 Tom Jackson | 10.00 | 4.00 | 1.00 |
| ☐ 60 Paul Howard | 2.00 | .80 | .20 |
| ☐ 68 Rubin Carter | 2.00 | .80 | .20 |
| ☐ 79 Barney Chavous SP | 50.00 | 20.00 | 5.00 |
| ☐ 80 Rick Upchurch | 6.00 | 2.40 | .60 |
| ☐ 88 Riley Odoms SP | 10.00 | 4.00 | 1.00 |

## 1982 Police Chargers

The 1982 San Diego Chargers Police set contains 16 unnumbered cards. The cards measure approximately 2 5/8" by 4 1/8". Although uniform numbers appear on the fronts of the cards, the set has been listed below in alphabetical order. The set is sponsored by the Kiwanis Club, the local law enforcement agency, and Pepsi-Cola. Chargers Tips, in addition to the helmet logo of the Chargers, the Pepsi-Cola logo and a police logo appear on the backs. Card backs have black printing with blue accent on white backs. The Kiwanis logo and Chargers helmet appear on the fronts of the cards.

|  | MINT | EXC | G-VG |
|---|---|---|---|
| COMPLETE SET (16) | 45.00 | 18.00 | 4.50 |
| COMMON CARD (1-16) | 2.00 | .80 | .20 |
| ☐ 1 Rolf Benirschke | 2.50 | 1.00 | .25 |
| ☐ 2 James Brooks | 6.00 | 2.40 | .60 |
| ☐ 3 Wes Chandler | 5.00 | 2.00 | .50 |
| ☐ 4 Dan Fouts | 10.00 | 4.00 | 1.00 |
| ☐ 5 Tim Fox | 2.00 | .80 | .20 |
| ☐ 6 Gary Johnson | 3.00 | 1.20 | .30 |

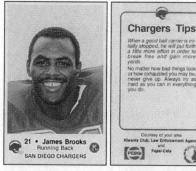

**Chargers Tips**

When a good ball carrier is initially stopped, he will put forth a little more effort in order to break free and gain more yards.

No matter how bad things look or how exhausted you may be, never give up. Always try as hard as you can in everything you do.

Courtesy of your area
Kiwanis Club, Law Enforcement Agency
and
Pepsi-Cola

21 • James Brooks
Running Back
SAN DIEGO CHARGERS

| ☐ 7 Charlie Joiner | 6.00 | 2.40 | .60 |
|---|---|---|---|
| ☐ 8 Louie Kelcher | 3.00 | 1.20 | .30 |
| ☐ 9 Linden King | 2.00 | .80 | .20 |
| ☐ 10 Bruce Laird | 2.00 | .80 | .20 |
| ☐ 11 David Lewis | 2.00 | .80 | .20 |
| ☐ 12 Don Macek | 2.00 | .80 | .20 |
| ☐ 13 Billy Shields | 2.00 | .80 | .20 |
| ☐ 14 Eric Sievers | 3.00 | 1.20 | .30 |
| ☐ 15 Russ Washington | 2.00 | .80 | .20 |
| ☐ 16 Kellen Winslow | 6.00 | 2.40 | .60 |

## 1982 Police Chiefs

37 • JOE DELANEY
Running Back
Ht: 5'10" Wt: 184
kansas city chiefs

**Chiefs Tips**
Ten in a Series of Ten
Coach

The coach prepares his team for each game. He helps them learn to play their best.

Your teacher is like a coach. Your teacher wants to help you do your best.

Courtesy of your area
LAW ENFORCEMENT AGENCY
and
FRITO-LAY

The 1982 Kansas City Chiefs Police set features ten numbered (on back) cards, some of which portray more than one player. The cards measure approximately 2 5/8" by 4 1/8". The backs deviate somewhat from a standard police set in that a cartoon is utilized to drive home the sage "Chiefs Tips". This set is sponsored by the local law enforcement agency, Frito-Lay, and the Kiwanis Club. The backs contain a 1982 date and logos of the Kiwanis, Frito-Lay, and the Chiefs. Card backs have black print with red accent on white card stock. Each player's uniform number is given on the front of the card.

|  | MINT | EXC | G-VG |
|---|---|---|---|
| COMPLETE SET (10) | 5.00 | 2.00 | .50 |
| COMMON CARD (1-10) | .50 | .20 | .05 |
| ☐ 1 Bill Kenney and Jack Rudnay | .60 | .24 | .06 |
| ☐ 2 Steve Fuller and Nick Lowery | .90 | .36 | .09 |
| ☐ 3 Matt Herkenhoff | .50 | .20 | .05 |
| ☐ 4 Art Still | .75 | .30 | .07 |
| ☐ 5 Gary Spani | .50 | .20 | .05 |
| ☐ 6 James Hadnot | .60 | .24 | .06 |
| ☐ 7 Mike Bell | .60 | .24 | .06 |
| ☐ 8 Carol Canfield (Chiefette) | .60 | .24 | .06 |
| ☐ 9 Gary Green | .60 | .24 | .06 |
| ☐ 10 Joe Delaney | .90 | .36 | .09 |

## 1982 Police Dolphins

The 1982 Miami Dolphins set of 16 numbered cards is one of the most attractive of the police sets. The cards measure approximately 2 5/8" by 4 1/8". The orange and greenish-blue frame line on the front contains the player's number and name. The Kiwanis logo is also

contained on the front. The backs are printed in black, orange, greenish-blue, and blue ink and feature "Dolphins Tips," the Dolphins logo, and the Kiwanis logo. The set is sponsored by the Kiwanis Club, the local law enforcement agency, and the Dolphins. Shula and Von Schamann are supposedly a little tougher to find than the other cards in the set.

|  | MINT | EXC | G-VG |
|---|---|---|---|
| COMPLETE SET (16) | 25.00 | 10.00 | 2.50 |
| COMMON PLAYER (1-16) | 1.00 | .40 | .10 |
| ☐ 1 Don Shula CO SP | 8.00 | 3.25 | .80 |
| ☐ 2 Uwe Von Schamann SP | 4.00 | 1.60 | .40 |
| ☐ 3 Jimmy Cefalo | 1.50 | .60 | .15 |
| ☐ 4 Andra Franklin | 1.50 | .60 | .15 |
| ☐ 5 Larry Gordon | 1.00 | .40 | .10 |
| ☐ 6 Nat Moore | 2.00 | .80 | .20 |
| ☐ 7 Bob Baumhower | 1.25 | .50 | .12 |
| ☐ 8 A.J. Duhe | 1.50 | .60 | .15 |
| ☐ 9 Tony Nathan | 2.00 | .80 | .20 |
| ☐ 10 Glenn Blackwood | 1.25 | .50 | .12 |
| ☐ 11 Don Strock | 2.00 | .80 | .20 |
| ☐ 12 David Woodley | 1.50 | .60 | .15 |
| ☐ 13 Kim Bokamper | 1.00 | .40 | .10 |
| ☐ 14 Bob Kuechenberg | 1.50 | .60 | .15 |
| ☐ 15 Duriel Harris | 1.25 | .50 | .12 |
| ☐ 16 Ed Newman | 1.00 | .40 | .10 |

## 1982 Police Redskins

The 1982 Washington Redskins set contains 15 numbered (in very small print on the card backs) full-color cards. The cards measure approximately 2 5/8" by 4 1/8". The set is sponsored by Frito-Lay, the local law enforcement agency, the Washington Redskins, and an organization known as PACT (Police and Citizens Together). Logos of Frito-Lay and PACT appear on the backs of the cards as do "Redskins PACT Tips". A Redskins helmet appears on the fronts of the cards.

|  | MINT | EXC | G-VG |
|---|---|---|---|
| COMPLETE SET (15) | 10.00 | 4.00 | 1.00 |
| COMMON CARD (1-15) | .50 | .20 | .05 |
| ☐ 1 Dave Butz | .75 | .30 | .07 |
| ☐ 2 Art Monk | 2.50 | 1.00 | .25 |
| ☐ 3 Mark Murphy | .50 | .20 | .05 |
| ☐ 4 Monte Coleman | .60 | .24 | .06 |
| ☐ 5 Mark Moseley | .75 | .30 | .07 |
| ☐ 6 George Starke | .50 | .20 | .05 |

| ☐ 7 Perry Brooks | .50 | .20 | .05 |
|---|---|---|---|
| ☐ 8 Joe Washington | .75 | .30 | .07 |
| ☐ 9 Don Warren | .60 | .24 | .06 |
| ☐ 10 Joe Lavender | .50 | .20 | .05 |
| ☐ 11 Joe Theismann | 2.50 | 1.00 | .25 |
| ☐ 12 Tony Peters | .50 | .20 | .05 |
| ☐ 13 Neal Olkewicz | .50 | .20 | .05 |
| ☐ 14 Mike Nelms | .60 | .24 | .06 |
| ☐ 15 John Riggins | 2.00 | .80 | .20 |

## 1982 Police Seahawks

Similar to the 1980 set in design, this 16-card, numbered set is sponsored by the Washington State Crime Prevention Association, the Kiwanis Club, Coca-Cola, and Ernst Home Centers in addition to the local law enforcement agency. The cards measure approximately 2 5/8" by 4 1/8". A 1982 date and short "Tips from the Seahawks" appear on the backs. Card backs have blue print with red trim on white card stock. Cards of Jack Patera and Sam McCullum are reported to be more difficult to obtain than other cards in this set.

|  | MINT | EXC | G-VG |
|---|---|---|---|
| COMPLETE SET (16) | 10.00 | 4.00 | 1.00 |
| COMMON PLAYER (1-16) | .40 | .16 | .04 |
| ☐ 1 Sam McCullum SP | 1.25 | .50 | .12 |
| ☐ 2 Manu Tuiasosopo | .50 | .20 | .05 |
| ☐ 3 Sherman Smith | .60 | .24 | .06 |
| ☐ 4 Karen Godwin (Sea Gal) | .60 | .24 | .06 |
| ☐ 5 Dave Brown | .60 | .24 | .06 |
| ☐ 6 Keith Simpson | .40 | .16 | .04 |
| ☐ 7 Steve Largent | 4.50 | 1.80 | .45 |
| ☐ 8 Michael Jackson | .50 | .20 | .05 |
| ☐ 9 Kenny Easley | .75 | .30 | .07 |
| ☐ 10 Dan Doornick | .40 | .16 | .04 |
| ☐ 11 Jim Zorn | 1.25 | .50 | .12 |
| ☐ 12 Jack Patera CO SP | 1.25 | .50 | .12 |
| ☐ 13 Jacob Green | .60 | .24 | .06 |
| ☐ 14 Dave Krieg | 2.00 | .80 | .20 |
| ☐ 15 Steve August | .40 | .16 | .04 |
| ☐ 16 Keith Butler | .40 | .16 | .04 |

## 1982 Police Steelers

The 16-card, 1982 Pittsburgh Steelers set is unnumbered, but has been listed in the checklist below by the player's uniform number which appears on the fronts of the cards. The cards measure 2 5/8" by 4 1/8". The backs of the cards feature Steelers' Tips, the Kiwanis logo, the Coca-Cola logo, and a Steelers helmet logo. The local police department sponsored this set, in addition to the organizations whose logos appear on the back. Card backs feature black print with gold trim. This set is very similar to the 1981 Police Steelers set; differences are noted parenthetically in the list below.

| | MINT | EXC | G-VG |
|---|---|---|---|
| COMPLETE SET (16) | 10.00 | 4.00 | 1.00 |
| COMMON PLAYER | .40 | .16 | .04 |
| ☐ 12 Terry Bradshaw (Portrait) | 4.00 | 1.60 | .40 |
| ☐ 31 Donnie Shell (Double Coverage back) | .60 | .24 | .06 |
| ☐ 32 Franco Harris (Portrait) | 2.00 | .80 | .20 |
| ☐ 44 Frank Pollard | .40 | .16 | .04 |
| ☐ 47 Mel Blount (Running with ball) | 1.25 | .50 | .12 |
| ☐ 52 Mike Webster (Portrait) | .75 | .30 | .07 |
| ☐ 58 Jack Lambert (Facing forward) | 2.00 | .80 | .20 |
| ☐ 59 Jack Ham (Teamwork back) | 1.50 | .60 | .15 |
| ☐ 65 Tom Beasley | .40 | .16 | .04 |
| ☐ 67 Gary Dunn | .40 | .16 | .04 |
| ☐ 74 Ray Pinney | .40 | .16 | .04 |
| ☐ 79 Larry Brown (Chin 5/16" from bottom) | .40 | .16 | .04 |
| ☐ 82 John Stallworth (Posed shot) | 1.25 | .50 | .12 |
| ☐ 88 Lynn Swann (Sportsmanship back) | 2.50 | 1.00 | .25 |
| ☐ 89 Bennie Cunningham | .50 | .20 | .05 |
| ☐ 90 Bob Kohrs | .40 | .16 | .04 |

# 1983 Police Chiefs

34 • LLOYD BURRUSS
Safety Ht: 6-0 Wt: 202
kansas city chiefs

The 1983 Kansas City Chiefs set contains ten numbered cards. The cards measure approximately 2 5/8" by 4 1/8". Sponsored by Frito-Lay, the local law enforcement agency, the Kiwanis Club, and KCTV-5, the set features cartoon "Chiefs Tips" and Crime Tips on the backs. A 1983 date plus logos of the Chiefs, Frito-Lay, the Kiwanis, and KCTV-5 also appear on the backs. Uniform numbers are given on the front of the player's card.

| | MINT | EXC | G-VG |
|---|---|---|---|
| COMPLETE SET (10) | 5.00 | 2.00 | .50 |
| COMMON CARD (1-10) | .50 | .20 | .05 |
| ☐ 1 John Mackovic CO | .75 | .30 | .07 |
| ☐ 2 Tom Condon | .50 | .20 | .05 |
| ☐ 3 Gary Spani | .50 | .20 | .05 |
| ☐ 4 Carlos Carson | .75 | .30 | .07 |
| ☐ 5 Brad Budde | .60 | .24 | .06 |
| ☐ 6 Lloyd Burruss | .50 | .20 | .05 |
| ☐ 7 Gary Green | .60 | .24 | .06 |
| ☐ 8 Mike Bell | .60 | .24 | .06 |
| ☐ 9 Nick Lowery | .90 | .36 | .09 |
| ☐ 10 Sandi Byrd (Chiefette) | .60 | .24 | .06 |

# 1983 Police Cowboys

This unnumbered set of 28 cards was sponsored by the Kiwannis Club, Law Enforcement Agency, and the Dallas Cowboys Weekly.

Cowboys Tips

DOUBLE COVERAGE
The best receivers are often covered by two defenders instead of one. This tactic is known as "double coverage" and is used to make it more difficult for the receiver to catch the ball.

Bicycles are the most commonly stolen items and should have the protection of "double coverage." Safeguard your bicycle by making sure you have engraved your family's drivers license number on the frame and remembering to lock it up when you aren't using it.

Supports Crimestoppers

Courtesy of your area Kiwanis Club, Law Enforcement Agency and the Dallas Cowboys Weekly, the official Cowboys fan newspaper.

72 • Ed Jones
Defensive End
DALLAS COWBOYS

Cards are approximately 2 5/8" by 4 1/8" and have a white border around the photo on the front of the cards. The backs each contain a safety tip. Cards are listed in the checklist below in uniform number order. Four cheerleaders are included in the set and are so indicated by CHEER.

| | MINT | EXC | G-VG |
|---|---|---|---|
| COMPLETE SET (28) | 18.00 | 7.25 | 1.80 |
| COMMON CARD | .50 | .20 | .05 |
| ☐ 1 Rafael Septien | .60 | .24 | .06 |
| ☐ 11 Danny White | 2.00 | .80 | .20 |
| ☐ 20 Ron Springs | .50 | .20 | .05 |
| ☐ 24 Everson Walls | 1.00 | .40 | .10 |
| ☐ 26 Michael Downs | .50 | .20 | .05 |
| ☐ 30 Timmy Newsome | .50 | .20 | .05 |
| ☐ 32 Dennis Thurman | .60 | .24 | .06 |
| ☐ 33 Tony Dorsett | 3.00 | 1.20 | .30 |
| ☐ 47 Dextor Clinkscale | .50 | .20 | .05 |
| ☐ 53 Bob Breunig | .75 | .30 | .07 |
| ☐ 54 Randy White | 2.50 | 1.00 | .25 |
| ☐ 65 Kurt Petersen | .50 | .20 | .05 |
| ☐ 67 Pat Donovan | .50 | .20 | .05 |
| ☐ 70 Howard Richards | .50 | .20 | .05 |
| ☐ 72 Ed Too Tall Jones | 2.00 | .80 | .20 |
| ☐ 78 John Dutton | .75 | .30 | .07 |
| ☐ 79 Harvey Martin | 1.00 | .40 | .10 |
| ☐ 80 Tony Hill | .75 | .30 | .07 |
| ☐ 83 Doug Donley | .50 | .20 | .05 |
| ☐ 84 Doug Cosbie | .60 | .24 | .06 |
| ☐ 86 Butch Johnson | .60 | .24 | .06 |
| ☐ 88 Drew Pearson | 1.50 | .60 | .15 |
| ☐ 89 Billy Joe DuPree | .75 | .30 | .07 |
| ☐ xx Tom Landry CO | 2.00 | .80 | .20 |
| ☐ xx Dana Presley CHEER | .75 | .30 | .07 |
| ☐ xx Toni Washington CHEER | .75 | .30 | .07 |
| ☐ xx Melinda May CHEER | .75 | .30 | .07 |
| ☐ xx Judy Trammell CHEER | .75 | .30 | .07 |

# 1983 Police Dolphins

DON SHULA

DOLPHINS TIPS

■ COACH:
The coach is responsible for preparing his team to play their best each game. For the players to have a chance to win the game, they must be on time for meetings and attend practices.

Your parents are responsible for preparing you to face life. They help you overcome problems. The police will assist you and help you plan for the future. Feel free to ask for assistance.

Courtesy of your local Kiwanis Club, Law Enforcement Agency, BURGER KING®, and the Miami Dolphins.

In case of emergency dial "911".

This numbered set of 16 cards features the Miami Dolphins. Cards measure approximately 2 5/8" by 4 1/8". The cards are numbered on the back in the bottom right corner. The cards look very similar to the 1982 Police Dolphins set. Card backs feature black print with orange and aquamarine accent on white card stock. The cards were sponsored by Kiwanis, Law Enforcement Agencies, Burger King, and the Miami Dolphins. The Burger King and Kiwanis logos both appear on the fronts of the cards.

| | MINT | EXC | G-VG |
|---|---|---|---|
| COMPLETE SET (16)......................... | 12.00 | 5.00 | 1.20 |
| COMMON CARD (1-16) ................... | .60 | .24 | .06 |
| ☐ 1 Earnest Rhone............................ | .60 | .24 | .06 |
| ☐ 2 Andra Franklin............................ | .90 | .36 | .09 |
| ☐ 3 Eric Laakso ................................ | .60 | .24 | .06 |
| ☐ 4 Joe Rose .................................... | .60 | .24 | .06 |
| ☐ 5 David Woodley............................ | 1.00 | .40 | .10 |
| ☐ 6 Uwe Von Schamann.................... | .90 | .36 | .09 |
| ☐ 7 Eddie Hill .................................. | .60 | .24 | .06 |
| ☐ 8 Bruce Hardy ............................... | .60 | .24 | .06 |
| ☐ 9 Woody Bennett ........................... | .60 | .24 | .06 |
| ☐ 10 Fulton Walker ........................... | .75 | .30 | .07 |
| ☐ 11 Lyle Blackwood......................... | .90 | .36 | .09 |
| ☐ 12 A.J. Duhe ................................. | 1.00 | .40 | .10 |
| ☐ 13 Bob Baumhower ........................ | .90 | .36 | .09 |
| ☐ 14 Duriel Harris ............................ | .90 | .36 | .09 |
| ☐ 15 Bob Brudzinski ......................... | .90 | .36 | .09 |
| ☐ 16 Don Shula CO........................... | 2.50 | 1.00 | .25 |

## 1983 Police Latrobe

This 30-card set is subtitled "The Birth of Professional Football" in Latrobe, Pennsylvania. Cards measure 2 1/2" by 3 1/2" and are numbered. Cards were not printed in full color, rather either sepia or black and white. The set is not attractive and, hence, has never been very aggressively pursued by collectors. The set is available with two kinds of backs. There is no difference in value between the two sets of backs although the set with safety tips on the back seems to be more in demand due to the many collectors of police issues.

| | MINT | EXC | G-VG |
|---|---|---|---|
| COMPLETE SET (30)......................... | 8.00 | 3.25 | .80 |
| COMMON CARD (1-30) ................... | .35 | .14 | .03 |
| ☐ 1 John Kinport Brallier ............... | 1.25 | .50 | .12 |
| ☐ 2 John K. Brallier ........................ | 1.00 | .40 | .10 |
| ☐ 3 Latrobe YMCA Team 1895 ........ | .35 | .14 | .03 |
| ☐ 4 Brallier and Team ..................... | .35 | .14 | .03 |
|    at W and J 1895 | | | |
| ☐ 5 Latrobe A.A. Team 1896 .......... | .35 | .14 | .03 |
| ☐ 6 Latrobe A.A. 1897 .................... | .35 | .14 | .03 |
| ☐ 7 1st All Pro Team 1897 .............. | .35 | .14 | .03 |
| ☐ 8 David J. Berry Mgr. ................... | .50 | .20 | .05 |
| ☐ 9 Harry Cap Ryan RT .................. | .35 | .14 | .03 |
| ☐ 10 Walter Okeson LE .................... | .35 | .14 | .03 |
| ☐ 11 Edward Wood RE ..................... | .35 | .14 | .03 |
| ☐ 12 E.Big Bill Hammer C................. | .35 | .14 | .03 |
| ☐ 13 Marcus Saxman LH................... | .35 | .14 | .03 |
| ☐ 14 Charles Shumaker SUB ............ | .35 | .14 | .03 |
| ☐ 15 Charles McDyre LE................... | .35 | .14 | .03 |
| ☐ 16 Edward Abbatticchio FB ........... | .50 | .20 | .05 |
| ☐ 17 George Flickinger C/LT............. | .35 | .14 | .03 |
| ☐ 18 Walter Howard RH ................... | .35 | .14 | .03 |
| ☐ 19 Thomas Doggie ........................ | .35 | .14 | .03 |
|    Trenchard RE | | | |
| ☐ 20 John Kinport Brallier ............... | .75 | .30 | .07 |
|    QB | | | |
| ☐ 21 Jack Gass LH ........................... | .35 | .14 | .03 |
| ☐ 22 Dave Campbell LT..................... | .35 | .14 | .03 |
| ☐ 23 Edward Blair RH ...................... | .35 | .14 | .03 |
| ☐ 24 John Johnston RG ..................... | .35 | .14 | .03 |
| ☐ 25 Sam Johnston LG ...................... | .35 | .14 | .03 |
| ☐ 26 Alex Laird SUB ........................ | .35 | .14 | .03 |
| ☐ 27 Latrobe A.A. 1897 Team ......... | .35 | .14 | .03 |
| ☐ 28 Pro Football............................ | .35 | .14 | .03 |
|    Memorial Plaque | | | |
| ☐ 29 Commemorative...................... | .35 | .14 | .03 |
|    Medallion | | | |
| ☐ 30 Birth of Pro Football............... | 1.00 | .40 | .10 |
|    Checklist Card | | | |

## 1983 Police Packers

This 19-card set is somewhat more difficult to find than the other Packers Police sets. There are three different types of backs: First Wisconsin Banks, without First Wisconsin Banks, and Waukesha P.D. The hardest to get of these three is the set without First Wisconsin Banks. All cards are approximately 2 5/8" by 4 1/8". Card backs are printed in green ink on white card stock. A safety tip ("Packer Tips") is given on the back. Cards are unnumbered except for uniform number.

| | MINT | EXC | G-VG |
|---|---|---|---|
| COMPLETE SET (19)......................... | 25.00 | 10.00 | 2.50 |
| COMMON CARD .............................. | 1.00 | .40 | .10 |
| ☐ 10 Jan Stenerud.......................... | 3.00 | 1.20 | .30 |
| ☐ 12 Lynn Dickey ........................... | 2.00 | .80 | .20 |
| ☐ 24 Johnnie Gray........................... | 1.00 | .40 | .10 |
| ☐ 29 Mike McCoy ........................... | 1.50 | .60 | .15 |
| ☐ 31 Gerry Ellis ............................. | 1.00 | .40 | .10 |
| ☐ 40 Eddie Lee Ivery....................... | 2.00 | .80 | .20 |
| ☐ 52 George Cumby ........................ | 1.25 | .50 | .12 |
| ☐ 53 Mike Douglass ........................ | 1.25 | .50 | .12 |
| ☐ 54 Larry McCarren ....................... | 1.00 | .40 | .10 |
| ☐ 59 John Anderson......................... | 1.50 | .60 | .15 |
| ☐ 63 Terry Jones ............................ | 1.00 | .40 | .10 |
| ☐ 64 Sid Kitson .............................. | 1.00 | .40 | .10 |
| ☐ 68 Greg Koch .............................. | 1.00 | .40 | .10 |
| ☐ 80 James Lofton .......................... | 4.00 | 1.60 | .40 |
| ☐ 82 Paul Coffman .......................... | 2.00 | .80 | .20 |
| ☐ 83 John Jefferson ........................ | 2.50 | 1.00 | .25 |
| ☐ 85 Phillip Epps ............................ | 2.00 | .80 | .20 |
| ☐ 90 Ezra Johnson .......................... | 1.00 | .40 | .10 |
| ☐ xx Bart Starr CO .......................... | 4.00 | 1.60 | .40 |

## 1983 Police Redskins

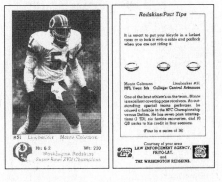

The 1983 Washington Redskins Police set consists of 16 numbered cards sponsored by Frito-Lay, the local law enforcement agency, PACT, and the Redskins. The cards measure 2 5/8" by 4 1/8" and were given out one per week (and are numbered according to that order) by the police department, except for week number 10, whose card featured Jeris White. White sat out the season and his card was not distributed; hence, it is available in lesser quantity than other cards in the set. Interestingly enough, the seventh week featured the issuance of Joe Theisman's card, who coincidentally, wears uniform number 7. The final card in this set, issued the 16th week, featured John Riggins.

Logos of Frito-Lay and PACT appear on the back along with "Redskins/PACT Tips". The backs are printed in black with red accent on white card stock. There were some cards produced with a maroon color back. Although these maroon backs are more difficult to find, they are valued essentially the same.

| | MINT | EXC | G-VG |
|---|---|---|---|
| COMPLETE SET (16) | 10.00 | 4.00 | 1.00 |
| COMMON CARD (1-16) | .50 | .20 | .05 |
| ☐ 1 Joe Washington | 1.00 | .40 | .10 |
| ☐ 2 The Hogs | .75 | .30 | .07 |
|   (Offensive Line) | | | |
| ☐ 3 Mark Moseley | 1.00 | .40 | .10 |
| ☐ 4 Monte Coleman | .60 | .24 | .06 |
| ☐ 5 Mike Nelms | .60 | .24 | .06 |
| ☐ 6 Neal Olkewicz | .50 | .20 | .05 |
| ☐ 7 Joe Theismann | 2.50 | 1.00 | .25 |
| ☐ 8 Charlie Brown | .60 | .24 | .06 |
| ☐ 9 Dave Butz | .75 | .30 | .07 |
| ☐ 10 Jeris White SP | 1.50 | .60 | .15 |
| ☐ 11 Mark Murphy | .50 | .20 | .05 |
| ☐ 12 Dexter Manley | .75 | .30 | .07 |
| ☐ 13 Art Monk | 2.50 | 1.00 | .25 |
| ☐ 14 Rich Milot | .50 | .20 | .05 |
| ☐ 15 Vernon Dean | .50 | .20 | .05 |
| ☐ 16 John Riggins | 2.00 | .80 | .20 |

## 1983 Police Steelers

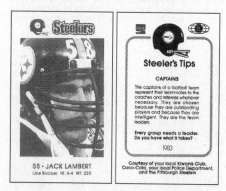

This 17-card set features the Pittsburgh Steelers. Cards measure approximately 2 5/8" by 4 1/8" and read "1983" on the card backs. There was an error on the Chuck Noll ("Knoll") card, which was corrected. The set is considered complete with either one of the Noll variations. The set is unnumbered and hence is listed below ordered (and numbered) alphabetically by subject.

| | MINT | EXC | G-VG |
|---|---|---|---|
| COMPLETE SET (16) | 7.50 | 3.00 | .75 |
| COMMON CARD (1-16) | .25 | .10 | .02 |
| ☐ 1 Walter Abercrombie | .35 | .14 | .03 |
| ☐ 2 Gary Anderson | .35 | .14 | .03 |
| ☐ 3 Mel Blount | .75 | .30 | .07 |
| ☐ 4 Terry Bradshaw | 2.50 | 1.00 | .25 |
| ☐ 5 Robin Cole | .25 | .10 | .02 |
| ☐ 6 Steve Courson | .25 | .10 | .02 |
| ☐ 7 Bennie Cunningham | .35 | .14 | .03 |
| ☐ 8 Franco Harris | 1.50 | .60 | .15 |
| ☐ 9 Greg Hawthorne | .25 | .10 | .02 |
| ☐ 10 Jack Lambert | 1.00 | .40 | .10 |
| ☐ 11A Chuck Noll CO ERR | 4.00 | 1.60 | .40 |
|   (Misspelled Knoll) | | | |
| ☐ 11B Chuck Noll CO COR | 1.00 | .40 | .10 |
| ☐ 12 Donnie Shell | .35 | .14 | .03 |
| ☐ 13 John Stallworth | 1.00 | .40 | .10 |
| ☐ 14 Mike Webster | .75 | .30 | .07 |
| ☐ 15 Dwayne Woodruff | .25 | .10 | .02 |
| ☐ 16 Rick Woods | .25 | .10 | .02 |

## 1983 Police Vikings

The 1983 Minnesota Vikings set contains 17 numbered cards. The cards measure approximately 2 5/8" by 4 1/8". This first Viking police set is sponsored by Pillsbury, Minnesota Crime Prevention Officers Association, Green Giant, and Burger King. In addition to the Vikings' logo, logos of all five organizations appear on the backs. The fronts contain a Vikings logo.

| | MINT | EXC | G-VG |
|---|---|---|---|
| COMPLETE SET (17) | 10.00 | 4.00 | 1.00 |
| COMMON PLAYER (1-17) | .50 | .20 | .05 |
| ☐ 1 Checklist Card | .75 | .30 | .07 |
| ☐ 2 Tommy Kramer | 1.00 | .40 | .10 |
| ☐ 3 Ted Brown | .60 | .24 | .06 |
| ☐ 4 Joe Senser | .60 | .24 | .06 |
| ☐ 5 Sammie White | 1.00 | .40 | .10 |
| ☐ 6 Doug Martin | .60 | .24 | .06 |
| ☐ 7 Matt Blair | 1.00 | .40 | .10 |
| ☐ 8 Bud Grant CO | 1.50 | .60 | .15 |
| ☐ 9 Scott Studwell | .60 | .24 | .06 |
| ☐ 10 Greg Coleman | .50 | .20 | .05 |
| ☐ 11 John Turner | .50 | .20 | .05 |
| ☐ 12 Jim Hough | .50 | .20 | .05 |
| ☐ 13 Joey Browner | 2.00 | .80 | .20 |
| ☐ 14 Dennis Swilley | .60 | .24 | .06 |
| ☐ 15 Darrin Nelson | .75 | .30 | .07 |
| ☐ 16 Mark Mullaney | .60 | .24 | .06 |
| ☐ 17 Fran Tarkenton | 3.00 | 1.20 | .30 |
|   (All-Time Great) | | | |

## 1984 Police Buccaneers

This unnumbered 56-card set features the Tampa Bay Buccaneers players, cheerleaders, and other personnel. Cards measure approximately 2 5/8" by 4 1/8". Backs are printed in red ink on white card stock and feature "Kids and Kops Tips from the Buccaneers". Cards were sponsored by the Greater Tampa Chamber of Commerce Community Security Council, Coca Cola, and the local law enforcement agencies. In action (IA) cards were issued as an additional card for three players. The cards are essentially ordered below alphabetically according to the player's name with the exception of the non-player cards who are listed first.

| | MINT | EXC | G-VG |
|---|---|---|---|
| COMPLETE SET (56) | 50.00 | 20.00 | 5.00 |
| COMMON CARD (1-56) | .80 | .32 | .08 |
| ☐ 1 Swash-Buc-Lers | 1.50 | .60 | .15 |
| ☐ 2 Hugh Culverhouse OWN | 1.00 | .40 | .10 |
| ☐ 3 John McKay (25 Years | 1.25 | .50 | .12 |
|   as Head Coach) | | | |
| ☐ 4 John McKay CO | 1.25 | .50 | .12 |
| ☐ 5 Defensive Action | 1.00 | .40 | .10 |
| ☐ 6 Fred Acorn | .80 | .32 | .08 |
| ☐ 7 Obed Ariri | .80 | .32 | .08 |

| | | | |
|---|---|---|---|
| ☐ 8 Adger Armstrong | .80 | .32 | .08 |
| ☐ 9 Jerry Bell | 1.00 | .40 | .10 |
| ☐ 10 Theo Bell | 1.50 | .60 | .15 |
| ☐ 11 Byron Braggs | .80 | .32 | .08 |
| ☐ 12 Scott Brantley | .80 | .32 | .08 |
| ☐ 13 Cedric Brown | .80 | .32 | .08 |
| ☐ 14 Keith Browner | 1.50 | .60 | .15 |
| ☐ 15 John Cannon | .80 | .32 | .08 |
| ☐ 16 Jay Carroll | .80 | .32 | .08 |
| ☐ 17 Gerald Carter | 1.00 | .40 | .10 |
| ☐ 18 Melvin Carter | .80 | .32 | .08 |
| ☐ 19 Jeremiah Castille | 1.25 | .50 | .12 |
| ☐ 20 Mark Cotney | .80 | .32 | .08 |
| ☐ 21 Steve Courson | 1.00 | .40 | .10 |
| ☐ 22 Jeff Davis | .80 | .32 | .08 |
| ☐ 23 Steve DeBerg | 4.00 | 1.60 | .40 |
| ☐ 24 Sean Farrell | 1.00 | .40 | .10 |
| ☐ 25 Frank Garcia | .80 | .32 | .08 |
| ☐ 26 Jimmie Giles | 1.50 | .60 | .15 |
| ☐ 27 Hugh Green | 2.00 | .80 | .20 |
| ☐ 28 Hugh Green IA | 1.50 | .60 | .15 |
| ☐ 29 Randy Grimes | .80 | .32 | .08 |
| ☐ 30 Ron Heller | 1.25 | .50 | .12 |
| ☐ 31 John Holt | .80 | .32 | .08 |
| ☐ 32 Kevin House | 1.50 | .60 | .15 |
| ☐ 33 Noah Jackson | 1.00 | .40 | .10 |
| ☐ 34 Cecil Johnson | .80 | .32 | .08 |
| ☐ 35 Ken Kaplan | .80 | .32 | .08 |
| ☐ 36 Blair Kiel | 2.00 | .80 | .20 |
| ☐ 37 David Logan | 1.00 | .40 | .10 |
| ☐ 38 Brison Manor | .80 | .32 | .08 |
| ☐ 39 Michael Morton | .80 | .32 | .08 |
| ☐ 40 James Owens | 1.00 | .40 | .10 |
| ☐ 41 Beasley Reece | 1.00 | .40 | .10 |
| ☐ 42 Gene Sanders | .80 | .32 | .08 |
| ☐ 43 Lee Roy Selmon | 3.00 | 1.20 | .30 |
| ☐ 44 Lee Roy Selmon IA | 2.00 | .80 | .20 |
| ☐ 45 Danny Spradlin | 1.00 | .40 | .10 |
| ☐ 46 Kelly Thomas | .80 | .32 | .08 |
| ☐ 47 Norris Thomas | .80 | .32 | .08 |
| ☐ 48 Jack Thompson | 1.50 | .60 | .15 |
| ☐ 49 Perry Tuttle | 1.50 | .60 | .15 |
| ☐ 50 Chris Washington | .80 | .32 | .08 |
| ☐ 51 Mike Washington | .80 | .32 | .08 |
| ☐ 52 James Wilder | 2.00 | .80 | .20 |
| ☐ 53 James Wilder IA | 1.50 | .60 | .15 |
| ☐ 54 Steve Wilson | .80 | .32 | .08 |
| ☐ 55 Mark White | .80 | .32 | .08 |
| ☐ 56 Richard Wood | 1.50 | .60 | .15 |

## 1984 Police Chiefs

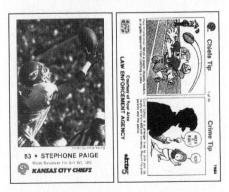

This numbered (on back) ten-card set features the Kansas City Chiefs. Backs contain a "Chiefs Tip" and a "Crime Tip," each with an accompanying cartoon. Cards measure approximately 2 5/8" by 4 1/8". Cards were also sponsored by Frito-Lay and KCTV.

| | MINT | EXC | G-VG |
|---|---|---|---|
| COMPLETE SET (10) | 5.00 | 2.00 | .50 |
| COMMON CARD (1-10) | .50 | .20 | .05 |
| | | | |
| ☐ 1 John Mackovic CO | .75 | .30 | .07 |
| ☐ 2 Deron Cherry | 1.00 | .40 | .10 |
| ☐ 3 Bill Kenney | .60 | .24 | .06 |
| ☐ 4 Henry Marshall | .50 | .20 | .05 |
| ☐ 5 Nick Lowery | .75 | .30 | .07 |
| ☐ 6 Theotis Brown | .60 | .24 | .06 |
| ☐ 7 Stephone Paige | 1.25 | .50 | .12 |
| ☐ 8 Gary Spani and Art Still | .75 | .30 | .07 |
| ☐ 9 Albert Lewis | 1.00 | .40 | .10 |
| ☐ 10 Carlos Carson | .60 | .24 | .06 |

## 1984 Police Dolphins

This unnumbered 17-card set features the Miami Dolphins. The Mark Clayton card was added to the set after the first sixteen cards had been distributed. Cards measure approximately 2 5/8" by 4 1/8". Cards are listed below alphabetically by player's name. The Dan Marino card is noteworthy in that it features Marino during his rookie year for cards.

| | MINT | EXC | G-VG |
|---|---|---|---|
| COMPLETE SET (17) | 20.00 | 8.00 | 2.00 |
| COMMON CARD (1-17) | .50 | .20 | .05 |
| | | | |
| ☐ 1 Bob Baumhower | .75 | .30 | .07 |
| ☐ 2 Doug Betters | .60 | .24 | .06 |
| ☐ 3 Glenn Blackwood | .75 | .30 | .07 |
| ☐ 4 Kim Bokamper | .50 | .20 | .05 |
| ☐ 5 Dolfan Denny (Mascot) | .50 | .20 | .05 |
| ☐ 6 A.J. Duhe | .75 | .30 | .07 |
| ☐ 7 Mark Duper | 2.00 | .80 | .20 |
| ☐ 8 Jim Jensen | .60 | .24 | .06 |
| ☐ 9 Dan Marino | 12.00 | 5.00 | 1.20 |
| ☐ 10 Don McNeal | .50 | .20 | .05 |
| ☐ 11 Nat Moore | 1.00 | .40 | .10 |
| ☐ 12 Tony Nathan | 1.00 | .40 | .10 |
| ☐ 13 Ed Newman | .50 | .20 | .05 |
| ☐ 14 Don Shula CO | 1.50 | .60 | .15 |
| ☐ 15 Dwight Stephenson | .75 | .30 | .07 |
| ☐ 16 Fulton Walker | .50 | .20 | .05 |
| ☐ 17 Mark Clayton SP | 3.00 | 1.20 | .30 |

## 1984 Police Eagles

This numbered eight-card set features the Philadelphia Eagles. Backs are printed in black ink with red accent. Cards measure approximately 2 5/8" by 4 1/8". The set was sponsored by Frito-Lay, the local police department, and the Philadelphia Eagles.

| | MINT | EXC | G-VG |
|---|---|---|---|
| COMPLETE SET (8) | 5.00 | 2.00 | .50 |
| COMMON CARD (1-8) | .50 | .20 | .05 |
| | | | |
| ☐ 1 Mike Quick | 1.25 | .50 | .12 |
| ☐ 2 Dennis Harrison | .50 | .20 | .05 |
| ☐ 3 Jerry Robinson | .75 | .30 | .07 |
| ☐ 4 Wilbert Montgomery | 1.25 | .50 | .12 |

| | MINT | EXC | G-VG |
|---|---|---|---|
| ☐ 5 Herman Edwards | .50 | .20 | .05 |
| ☐ 6 Kenny Jackson | .75 | .30 | .07 |
| ☐ 7 Anthony Griggs | .50 | .20 | .05 |
| ☐ 8 Ron Jaworski | 1.50 | .60 | .15 |

## 1984 Police 49ers

This set of 12 cards was issued in three panels of four cards each. Individual cards measure approximately 2 1/2" by 4 1/16" and feature the San Francisco 49ers. Since the cards are unnumbered, they are ordered and numbered below alphabetically by the subject's name. The set is sponsored by 7-Eleven, Dr. Pepper, and KCBS.

| | MINT | EXC | G-VG |
|---|---|---|---|
| COMPLETE SET (12) | 18.00 | 7.25 | 1.80 |
| COMMON CARD (1-12) | .75 | .30 | .07 |
| | | | |
| ☐ 1 Dwaine Board | .75 | .30 | .07 |
| ☐ 2 Roger Craig | 4.00 | 1.60 | .40 |
| ☐ 3 Riki Ellison | .75 | .30 | .07 |
| ☐ 4 Keith Fahnhorst | .75 | .30 | .07 |
| ☐ 5 Joe Montana and | 10.00 | 4.00 | 1.00 |
|     Dwight Clark | | | |
| ☐ 6 Jack Reynolds | 1.00 | .40 | .10 |
| ☐ 7 Freddie Solomon | 1.00 | .40 | .10 |
| ☐ 8 Keena Turner | 1.00 | .40 | .10 |
| ☐ 9 Wendell Tyler | 1.00 | .40 | .10 |
| ☐ 10 Bill Walsh CO | 3.00 | 1.20 | .30 |
| ☐ 11 Ray Wersching | .75 | .30 | .07 |
| ☐ 12 Eric Wright | .75 | .30 | .07 |

## 1984 Police Packers

This 25-card set is numbered on the back. The card backs were printed in green ink. Cards were sponsored by First Wisconsin Banks, the local law enforcement agency, and the Green Bay Packers. The cards measure approximately 2 5/8" by 4".

| | MINT | EXC | G-VG |
|---|---|---|---|
| COMPLETE SET (25) | 12.00 | 5.00 | 1.20 |
| COMMON CARD (1-25) | .40 | .16 | .04 |
| | | | |
| ☐ 1 John Jefferson | .75 | .30 | .07 |
| ☐ 2 Forrest Gregg CO | 2.00 | .80 | .20 |
| ☐ 3 John Anderson | .60 | .24 | .06 |
| ☐ 4 Eddie Garcia | .40 | .16 | .04 |
| ☐ 5 Tim Lewis | .50 | .20 | .05 |
| ☐ 6 Jessie Clark | .50 | .20 | .05 |
| ☐ 7 Karl Swanke | .40 | .16 | .04 |

| | MINT | EXC | G-VG |
|---|---|---|---|
| ☐ 8 Lynn Dickey | 1.25 | .50 | .12 |
| ☐ 9 Eddie Lee Ivery | .75 | .30 | .07 |
| ☐ 10 Dick Modzelewski CO | .40 | .16 | .04 |
|     (Defensive Coord.) | | | |
| ☐ 11 Mark Murphy | .40 | .16 | .04 |
| ☐ 12 Dave Drechsler | .40 | .16 | .04 |
| ☐ 13 Mike Douglass | .40 | .16 | .04 |
| ☐ 14 James Lofton | 3.00 | 1.20 | .30 |
| ☐ 15 Bucky Scribner | .40 | .16 | .04 |
| ☐ 16 Randy Scott | .40 | .16 | .04 |
| ☐ 17 Mark Lee | .60 | .24 | .06 |
| ☐ 18 Gerry Ellis | .40 | .16 | .04 |
| ☐ 19 Terry Jones | .40 | .16 | .04 |
| ☐ 20 Greg Koch | .40 | .16 | .04 |
| ☐ 21 Bob Schnelker CO | .40 | .16 | .04 |
|     (Offensive Coord.) | | | |
| ☐ 22 George Cumby | .50 | .20 | .05 |
| ☐ 23 Larry McCarren | .40 | .16 | .04 |
| ☐ 24 Syd Kitson | .40 | .16 | .04 |
| ☐ 25 Paul Coffman | .60 | .24 | .06 |

## 1984 Police Redskins

This numbered (on back) set of 16 cards features the Washington Redskins. Cards measure approximately 2 5/8" by 4 1/8". Backs are printed in black ink with a maroon accent. The set was sponsored by Frito-Lay, the local law enforcement agency, and the Washington Redskins.

| | MINT | EXC | G-VG |
|---|---|---|---|
| COMPLETE SET (16) | 7.50 | 3.00 | .75 |
| COMMON CARD (1-16) | .40 | .16 | .04 |
| | | | |
| ☐ 1 John Riggins | 1.50 | .60 | .15 |
| ☐ 2 Darryl Grant | .40 | .16 | .04 |
| ☐ 3 Art Monk | 2.00 | .80 | .20 |
| ☐ 4 Neal Olkewicz | .40 | .16 | .04 |
| ☐ 5 The Hogs | .60 | .24 | .06 |
|     (Offensive Line) | | | |
| ☐ 6 Jeff Hayes | .40 | .16 | .04 |
| ☐ 7 Joe Theismann | 2.00 | .80 | .20 |
| ☐ 8 Clint Didier | .50 | .20 | .05 |
| ☐ 9 Mark Murphy | .40 | .16 | .04 |
| ☐ 10 Don Warren | .50 | .20 | .05 |
| ☐ 11 Darrell Green | 1.50 | .60 | .15 |
| ☐ 12 Dave Butz | .60 | .24 | .06 |
| ☐ 13 Ken Coffey | .40 | .16 | .04 |
| ☐ 14 Rich Milot | .40 | .16 | .04 |
| ☐ 15 Charlie Brown | .50 | .20 | .05 |
| ☐ 16 Joe Washington | .60 | .24 | .06 |

## 1984 Police Steelers

This unnumbered set of 16 cards features players from the Pittsburgh Steelers. Cards measure 2 5/8" by 4 1/8". Card backs feature black printing on thin white card stock. The set was sponsored by McDonald's, Kiwanis, and local police departments. The players are listed below by uniform number. The set can be differentiated from other similar Steelers police sets by the presence of the Kiwanis logo on the card fronts.

| | MINT | EXC | G-VG |
|---|---|---|---|
| COMPLETE SET (16) | 7.00 | 2.80 | .70 |
| COMMON CARD | .40 | .16 | .04 |
| | | | |
| ☐ 1 Gary Anderson | .50 | .20 | .05 |
| ☐ 16 Mark Malone | .50 | .20 | .05 |
| ☐ 19 David Woodley | .60 | .24 | .06 |
| ☐ 30 Frank Pollard | .40 | .16 | .04 |
| ☐ 32 Franco Harris | 1.50 | .60 | .15 |

32 • FRANCO HARRIS
Running Back Ht: 6-2 Wt: 225

| | | | |
|---|---|---|---|
| ☐ 34 Walter Abercrombie | .50 | .20 | .05 |
| ☐ 49 Dwayne Woodruff | .40 | .16 | .04 |
| ☐ 52 Mike Webster | .75 | .30 | .07 |
| ☐ 57 Mike Merriweather | .60 | .24 | .06 |
| ☐ 58 Jack Lambert | 1.25 | .50 | .12 |
| ☐ 67 Gary Dunn | .40 | .16 | .04 |
| ☐ 73 Craig Wolfley | .40 | .16 | .04 |
| ☐ 82 John Stallworth | 1.00 | .40 | .10 |
| ☐ 83 Louis Lipps | 1.00 | .40 | .10 |
| ☐ 92 Keith Gary | .40 | .16 | .04 |
| ☐ 92 Keith Willis | .50 | .20 | .05 |

## 1984 Police Vikings

This numbered 18-card set features the Minnesota Vikings. Cards measure approximately 2 5/8" by 4 1/8" and are dated in the lower right corner of the reverse. The set was printed on thick card stock. Logos on the card backs are printed in color. The set was sponsored by Pillsbury, Burger King, and the Minnesota Crime Prevention Officers Association.

| | MINT | EXC | G-VG |
|---|---|---|---|
| COMPLETE SET (18) | 7.00 | 2.80 | .70 |
| COMMON CARD (1-18) | .40 | .16 | .04 |
| | | | |
| ☐ 1 Checklist Card | .60 | .24 | .06 |
| ☐ 2 Keith Nord | .40 | .16 | .04 |
| ☐ 3 Joe Senser | .50 | .20 | .05 |
| ☐ 4 Tommy Kramer | 1.00 | .40 | .10 |
| ☐ 5 Darrin Nelson | .60 | .24 | .06 |
| ☐ 6 Tim Irwin | .40 | .16 | .04 |
| ☐ 7 Mark Mullaney | .50 | .20 | .05 |
| ☐ 8 Les Steckel CO | .40 | .16 | .04 |
| ☐ 9 Greg Coleman | .40 | .16 | .04 |
| ☐ 10 Tommy Hannon | .40 | .16 | .04 |
| ☐ 11 Curtis Rouse | .40 | .16 | .04 |
| ☐ 12 Scott Studwell | .50 | .20 | .05 |
| ☐ 13 Steve Jordan | 1.25 | .50 | .12 |
| ☐ 14 Willie Teal | .40 | .16 | .04 |
| ☐ 15 Ted Brown | .50 | .20 | .05 |
| ☐ 16 Sammie White | .75 | .30 | .07 |
| ☐ 17 Matt Blair | .60 | .24 | .06 |
| ☐ 18 Jim Marshall | 1.50 | .60 | .15 |
| (All Time Great) | | | |

## 1985 Police Chiefs

This ten-card set features the Kansas City Chiefs. Cards in the set measure approximately 2 5/8" by 4 1/8". The card back gives the card number and the year of issue; printing is in black and red on white

67 • ART STILL
Defensive End Ht: 6-7 Wt: 257
**KANSAS CITY CHIEFS**

card stock. The set was sponsored by Frito-Lay, KCTV-5, and area law enforcement agencies. Two cartoons are featured on the back of each card picturing a Chiefs Tip and a Crime Tip.

| | MINT | EXC | G-VG |
|---|---|---|---|
| COMPLETE SET (10) | 5.00 | 2.00 | .50 |
| COMMON PLAYER (1-10) | .50 | .20 | .05 |
| | | | |
| ☐ 1 John Mackovic CO | .75 | .30 | .07 |
| ☐ 2 Herman Heard | .60 | .24 | .06 |
| ☐ 3 Bill Kenney | .75 | .30 | .07 |
| ☐ 4 Deron Cherry and | .90 | .36 | .09 |
| Lloyd Burruss | | | |
| ☐ 5 Jim Arnold | .50 | .20 | .05 |
| ☐ 6 Kevin Ross | .60 | .24 | .06 |
| ☐ 7 David Lutz | .50 | .20 | .05 |
| ☐ 8 Chieftettes Cheerleaders | .75 | .30 | .07 |
| ☐ 9 Bill Maas | .75 | .30 | .07 |
| ☐ 10 Art Still | .90 | .36 | .09 |

## 1985 Police Dolphins

58
Kim Bokamper
Defensive End

This 16-card set is numbered on the back. The card backs are printed in black ink on white card stock. Cards measure 2 5/8" by 4 1/8". The set was sponsored by Kiwanis, Hospital Corporation of America, the Dolphins, and area law enforcement agencies. Uniform numbers are printed on the card front above the player's name.

| | MINT | EXC | G-VG |
|---|---|---|---|
| COMPLETE SET (16) | 12.00 | 5.00 | 1.20 |
| COMMON PLAYER (1-16) | .40 | .16 | .04 |
| | | | |
| ☐ 1 William Judson | .40 | .16 | .04 |
| ☐ 2 Fulton Walker | .50 | .20 | .05 |
| ☐ 3 Mark Clayton | 1.50 | .60 | .15 |
| ☐ 4 Lyle Blackwood and | 1.00 | .40 | .10 |
| Glenn Blackwood | | | |
| (Bruise Brothers) | | | |
| ☐ 5 Dan Marino | 7.00 | 2.80 | .70 |
| ☐ 6 Reggie Roby | .60 | .24 | .06 |
| ☐ 7 Doug Betters | .50 | .20 | .05 |
| ☐ 8 Jay Brophy | .40 | .16 | .04 |
| ☐ 9 Dolfan Denny (Mascot) | .40 | .16 | .04 |
| ☐ 10 Kim Bokamper | .40 | .16 | .04 |
| ☐ 11 Mark Duper | 1.00 | .40 | .10 |
| ☐ 12 Nat Moore | .75 | .30 | .07 |
| ☐ 13 Mike Kozlowski | .40 | .16 | .04 |
| ☐ 14 Don Shula CO | 1.25 | .50 | .12 |
| ☐ 15 Don McNeal | .40 | .16 | .04 |
| ☐ 16 Tony Nathan | .75 | .30 | .07 |

## 1985 Police Eagles

This 16-card set is numbered on the back. The card backs are printed in black and red ink on white card stock. Cards measure 2 5/8" by 4 1/8". The set was sponsored by Frito-Lay, local Police Departments, and the Eagles. Uniform numbers are printed on the card front before the player's name.

|  | MINT | EXC | G-VG |
|---|---|---|---|
| COMPLETE SET (16) | 6.00 | 2.40 | .60 |
| COMMON PLAYER (1-16) | .40 | .16 | .04 |
| ☐ 1 Ken Clarke | .40 | .16 | .04 |
| ☐ 2 Roynell Young | .60 | .24 | .06 |
| ☐ 3 Ray Ellis | .40 | .16 | .04 |
| ☐ 4 Ron Baker | .40 | .16 | .04 |
| ☐ 5 John Spagnola | .50 | .20 | .05 |
| ☐ 6 Reggie Wilkes | .50 | .20 | .05 |
| ☐ 7 Ron Jaworski | 1.25 | .50 | .12 |
| ☐ 8 Steve Kenney | .40 | .16 | .04 |
| ☐ 9 Paul McFadden | .40 | .16 | .04 |
| ☐ 10 Mike Quick | 1.00 | .40 | .10 |
| ☐ 11 Hubie Oliver | .40 | .16 | .04 |
| ☐ 12 Greg Brown | .50 | .20 | .05 |
| ☐ 13 Anthony Griggs | .40 | .16 | .04 |
| ☐ 14 Michael Haddix | .50 | .20 | .05 |
| ☐ 15 Kenny Jackson | .50 | .20 | .05 |
| ☐ 16 Vyto Kab | .40 | .16 | .04 |

## 1985 Police 49ers

This set of 16 cards was issued in four panels of four cards each. Individual cards measure approximately 2 1/2" by 4" and feature the San Francisco 49ers. Since the cards are unnumbered, they are ordered and numbered below alphabetically by the subject's name. The set is differentiated from the similar 1984 Police 49ers set since this 1985 set is only sponsored by 7-Eleven and Dr. Pepper.

|  | MINT | EXC | G-VG |
|---|---|---|---|
| COMPLETE SET (16) | 15.00 | 6.00 | 1.50 |
| COMMON PLAYER (1-16) | .40 | .16 | .04 |
| ☐ 1 John Ayers | .40 | .16 | .04 |
| ☐ 2 Roger Craig | 2.00 | .80 | .20 |
| ☐ 3 Fred Dean | .75 | .30 | .07 |
| ☐ 4 Riki Ellison | .50 | .20 | .05 |
| ☐ 5 Keith Fahnhorst | .40 | .16 | .04 |
| ☐ 6 Russ Francis | .75 | .30 | .07 |
| ☐ 7 Dwight Hicks | .60 | .24 | .06 |

|  | MINT | EXC | G-VG |
|---|---|---|---|
| ☐ 8 Ronnie Lott | 1.50 | .60 | .15 |
| ☐ 9 Dana McLemore | .40 | .16 | .04 |
| ☐ 10 Joe Montana | 8.00 | 3.25 | .80 |
| ☐ 11 Todd Shell | .50 | .20 | .05 |
| ☐ 12 Freddie Solomon | .50 | .20 | .05 |
| ☐ 13 Keena Turner | .50 | .20 | .05 |
| ☐ 14 Bill Walsh CO | 1.25 | .50 | .12 |
| ☐ 15 Ray Wersching | .40 | .16 | .04 |
| ☐ 16 Eric Wright | .50 | .20 | .05 |

## 1985 Police Packers

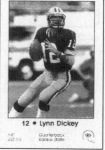

This 25-card set of Green Bay Packers is numbered on the back. Cards measure approximately 2 3/4" by 4". The backs contain a "1985 Packer Tip". Each player's uniform number is given on the card front.

|  | MINT | EXC | G-VG |
|---|---|---|---|
| COMPLETE SET (25) | 8.00 | 3.25 | .80 |
| COMMON PLAYER (1-25) | .40 | .16 | .04 |
| ☐ 1 Forrest Gregg CO | 1.50 | .60 | .15 |
| ☐ 2 Paul Coffman | .60 | .24 | .06 |
| ☐ 3 Terry Jones | .40 | .16 | .04 |
| ☐ 4 Ron Hallstrom | .40 | .16 | .04 |
| ☐ 5 Eddie Lee Ivery | 1.00 | .40 | .10 |
| ☐ 6 John Anderson | .60 | .24 | .06 |
| ☐ 7 Tim Lewis | .50 | .20 | .05 |
| ☐ 8 Bob Schnelker CO (Offensive Coord.) | .40 | .16 | .04 |
| ☐ 9 Al Del Greco | .40 | .16 | .04 |
| ☐ 10 Mark Murphy | .40 | .16 | .04 |
| ☐ 11 Tim Huffman | .40 | .16 | .04 |
| ☐ 12 Del Rodgers | .40 | .16 | .04 |
| ☐ 13 Mark Lee | .60 | .24 | .06 |
| ☐ 14 Tom Flynn | .50 | .20 | .05 |
| ☐ 15 Dick Modzelewski CO (Defensive Coord.) | .40 | .16 | .04 |
| ☐ 16 Randy Scott | .40 | .16 | .04 |
| ☐ 17 Bucky Scribner | .40 | .16 | .04 |
| ☐ 18 George Cumby | .50 | .20 | .05 |
| ☐ 19 James Lofton | 2.50 | 1.00 | .25 |
| ☐ 20 Mike Douglass | .50 | .20 | .05 |
| ☐ 21 Alphonso Carreker | .40 | .16 | .04 |
| ☐ 22 Greg Koch | .40 | .16 | .04 |
| ☐ 23 Gerry Ellis | .40 | .16 | .04 |
| ☐ 24 Ezra Johnson | .40 | .16 | .04 |
| ☐ 25 Lynn Dickey | 1.00 | .40 | .10 |

## 1985 Police Raiders/Rams

This 30-card set is actually two subsets, 15 cards featuring Los Angeles Rams and 15 cards featuring Los Angeles Raiders. The set was actually sponsored by the Sheriff's Department of Los Angeles County, KIIS Radio, and the Rams/Raiders, so technically it is a safety set but not a "police" set. The cards are unnumbered except for the uniform number listed on the card back. The list below is organized alphabetically within each team. Card backs are printed in black ink on white card stock. Cards measure approximately 2 13/16" by 4 1/8".

|  | MINT | EXC | G-VG |
|---|---|---|---|
| COMPLETE SET (30) | 20.00 | 8.00 | 2.00 |
| COMMON RAIDERS (1-15) | .50 | .20 | .05 |
| COMMON RAMS (16-30) | .50 | .20 | .05 |
| ☐ 1 Marcus Allen | 4.00 | 1.60 | .40 |
| ☐ 2 Lyle Alzado | 1.25 | .50 | .12 |
| ☐ 3 Todd Christensen | 1.00 | .40 | .10 |
| ☐ 4 Dave Dalby | .75 | .30 | .07 |
| ☐ 5 Mike Davis | .50 | .20 | .05 |
| ☐ 6 Ray Guy | 1.00 | .40 | .10 |
| ☐ 7 Frank Hawkins | .50 | .20 | .05 |
| ☐ 8 Lester Hayes | .75 | .30 | .07 |

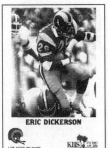

ERIC DICKERSON

LOS ANGELES RAMS

| | | | |
|---|---|---|---|
| ☐ 9 Mike Haynes | 1.00 | .40 | .10 |
| ☐ 10 Howie Long | 1.25 | .50 | .12 |
| ☐ 11 Rod Martin | .75 | .30 | .07 |
| ☐ 12 Mickey Marvin | .50 | .20 | .05 |
| ☐ 13 Jim Plunkett | 1.25 | .50 | .12 |
| ☐ 14 Brad Van Pelt | .75 | .30 | .07 |
| ☐ 15 Dokie Williams | .75 | .30 | .07 |
| ☐ 16 Bill Bain | .50 | .20 | .05 |
| ☐ 17 Mike Barber | .50 | .20 | .05 |
| ☐ 18 Dieter Brock | .75 | .30 | .07 |
| ☐ 19 Nolan Cromwell | 1.00 | .40 | .10 |
| ☐ 20 Eric Dickerson | 4.00 | 1.60 | .40 |
| ☐ 21 Reggie Doss | .50 | .20 | .05 |
| ☐ 22 Carl Ekern | .60 | .24 | .06 |
| ☐ 23 Kent Hill | .60 | .24 | .06 |
| ☐ 24 LeRoy Irvin | .75 | .30 | .07 |
| ☐ 25 Johnnie Johnson | .75 | .30 | .07 |
| ☐ 26 Jeff Kemp | .75 | .30 | .07 |
| ☐ 27 Mike Lansford | .50 | .20 | .05 |
| ☐ 28 Mel Owens | .60 | .24 | .06 |
| ☐ 29 Barry Redden | .60 | .24 | .06 |
| ☐ 30 Mike Wilcher | .50 | .20 | .05 |

## 1985 Police Redskins

#71    Defensive End    Charles Mann

This 16-card set of Washington Redskins is numbered on the back. Cards measure approximately 2 5/8" by 4 1/8" and the backs contain a "McGruff Says". Each player's uniform number is given on the card front. The set was sponsored by Frito-Lay, the Redskins, and local law enforcement agencies. Card backs are written in maroon and black on white card stock.

| | MINT | EXC | G-VG |
|---|---|---|---|
| COMPLETE SET (16) | 7.00 | 2.80 | .70 |
| COMMON PLAYER (1-16) | .40 | .16 | .04 |
| | | | |
| ☐ 1 Darrell Green | 1.00 | .40 | .10 |
| ☐ 2 Clint Didier | .50 | .20 | .05 |
| ☐ 3 Neal Olkewicz | .40 | .16 | .04 |
| ☐ 4 Darryl Grant | .40 | .16 | .04 |
| ☐ 5 Joe Jacoby | .50 | .20 | .05 |
| ☐ 6 Vernon Dean | .40 | .16 | .04 |
| ☐ 7 Joe Theismann | 1.50 | .60 | .15 |
| ☐ 8 Mel Kaufman | .40 | .16 | .04 |
| ☐ 9 Calvin Muhammad | .40 | .16 | .04 |
| ☐ 10 Dexter Manley | .60 | .24 | .06 |
| ☐ 11 John Riggins | 1.25 | .50 | .12 |
| ☐ 12 Mark May | .40 | .16 | .04 |
| ☐ 13 Dave Butz | .60 | .24 | .06 |
| ☐ 14 Art Monk | 1.50 | .60 | .15 |
| ☐ 15 Russ Grimm | .50 | .20 | .05 |
| ☐ 16 Charles Mann | .60 | .24 | .06 |

## 1985 Police Seahawks

Kenny Easley

6 3    206 lbs.    Safety    UCLA

This 16-card set of Seattle Seahawks is unnumbered; not even the uniform number is given. Cards measure approximately 2 5/8" by 4 1/8" and the backs contain "Tips from the Seahawks". The set was sponsored by Coca-Cola, McDonald's, KOMO-TV4, Kiwanis, the Washington State Crime Prevention Association, and local law enforcement agencies. Card backs are written in red and blue on white card stock. The year of issue is printed in the bottom right corner of the reverse.

| | MINT | EXC | G-VG |
|---|---|---|---|
| COMPLETE SET (16) | 7.00 | 2.80 | .70 |
| COMMON PLAYER (1-16) | .40 | .16 | .04 |
| | | | |
| ☐ 1 Dave Brown | .60 | .24 | .06 |
| ☐ 2 Jeff Bryant | .50 | .20 | .05 |
| ☐ 3 Blair Bush | .50 | .20 | .05 |
| ☐ 4 Keith Butler | .40 | .16 | .04 |
| ☐ 5 Dan Doornink | .40 | .16 | .04 |
| ☐ 6 Kenny Easley | .75 | .30 | .07 |
| ☐ 7 Jacob Green | .60 | .24 | .06 |
| ☐ 8 John Harris | .40 | .16 | .04 |
| ☐ 9 Norm Johnson | .60 | .24 | .06 |
| ☐ 10 Chuck Knox CO | .75 | .30 | .07 |
| ☐ 11 Dave Krieg | 1.50 | .60 | .15 |
| ☐ 12 Steve Largent | 3.50 | 1.40 | .35 |
| ☐ 13 Joe Nash | .50 | .20 | .05 |
| ☐ 14 Bruce Scholtz | .40 | .16 | .04 |
| ☐ 15 Curt Warner | .75 | .30 | .07 |
| ☐ 16 Fredd Young | .60 | .24 | .06 |

## 1985 Police Steelers

49 • DWAYNE WOODRUFF
Cornerback  Ht: 6-0  Wt: 198

This 16-card set of Pittsburgh Steelers is unnumbered except for uniform number. Cards measure approximately 2 5/8" by 4 1/8". The backs contain "Steeler Tips". The set was sponsored by Kiwanis, Giant Eagle, local Police Departments, and the Steelers. Card backs are written in black on white card stock. The 1985, 1986, and 1987 Police Steelers sets are identical except for the individual card differences noted parenthetically below.

| | MINT | EXC | G-VG |
|---|---|---|---|
| COMPLETE SET (16) | 6.00 | 2.40 | .60 |
| COMMON PLAYER | .40 | .16 | .04 |
| | | | |
| ☐ 1 Gary Anderson | .50 | .20 | .05 |
| (Kickoff back) | | | |
| ☐ 16 Mark Malone | .50 | .20 | .05 |
| (Playbook back) | | | |

| | MINT | EXC | G-VG |
|---|---|---|---|
| ☐ 21 Eric Williams | .40 | .16 | .04 |
| ☐ 30 Frank Pollard | .40 | .16 | .04 |
| (Second Effort back) | | | |
| ☐ 31 Donnie Shell | .60 | .24 | .06 |
| (Zone back) | | | |
| ☐ 34 Walter Abercrombie | .50 | .20 | .05 |
| (Teamwork back) | | | |
| ☐ 49 Dwayne Woodruff | .40 | .16 | .04 |
| (Turnover back) | | | |
| ☐ 50 David Little | .50 | .20 | .05 |
| ☐ 52 Mike Webster | .75 | .30 | .07 |
| (Offside back) | | | |
| ☐ 53 Bryan Hinkle | .40 | .16 | .04 |
| (Blindside back) | | | |
| ☐ 56 Robin Cole | .40 | .16 | .04 |
| (Timeout back) | | | |
| ☐ 57 Mike Merriweather | .60 | .24 | .06 |
| (Blitz back) | | | |
| ☐ 82 John Stallworth | 1.25 | .50 | .12 |
| (Captains back) | | | |
| ☐ 83 Louis Lipps | .75 | .30 | .07 |
| (Pride back) | | | |
| ☐ 93 Keith Willis | .40 | .16 | .04 |
| (QB Sack back) | | | |
| ☐ xx Chuck Noll CO | 1.00 | .40 | .10 |
| (Coach back) | | | |

# 1985 Police Vikings

This 16-card set of Minnesota Vikings is numbered on the back. Cards measure approximately 2 5/8" by 4 1/8" and the backs contain a "Crime Prevention Tip". The set was sponsored by Frito-Lay, Pepsi-Cola, KS95-FM, and local area law enforcement agencies. Card backs are written in red and blue on white card stock. The set commemorates the 25th (Silver) Anniversary Season for the Vikings. The checklist card tells which week each card was available.

| | MINT | EXC | G-VG |
|---|---|---|---|
| COMPLETE SET (16) | 7.00 | 2.80 | .70 |
| COMMON PLAYER (1-16) | .40 | .16 | .04 |
| ☐ 1 Checklist Card | .60 | .24 | .06 |
| ☐ 2 Bud Grant CO | 1.25 | .50 | .12 |
| ☐ 3 Matt Blair | .60 | .24 | .06 |
| ☐ 4 Alfred Anderson | .60 | .24 | .06 |
| ☐ 5 Fred McNeill | .40 | .16 | .04 |
| ☐ 6 Tommy Kramer | 1.00 | .40 | .10 |
| ☐ 7 Jan Stenerud | 1.25 | .50 | .12 |
| ☐ 8 Sammie White | .75 | .30 | .07 |
| ☐ 9 Doug Martin | .50 | .20 | .05 |
| ☐ 10 Greg Coleman | .40 | .16 | .04 |
| ☐ 11 Steve Riley | .40 | .16 | .04 |
| ☐ 12 Walker Lee Ashley | .40 | .16 | .04 |
| ☐ 13 Tim Irwin | .40 | .16 | .04 |
| ☐ 14 Scott Studwell | .50 | .20 | .05 |
| ☐ 15 Darrin Nelson | .60 | .24 | .06 |
| ☐ 16 Mick Tingelhoff | .75 | .30 | .07 |
| (All-Time Great) | | | |

# 1986 Police Bears/Patriots

This set was supposedly not an authorized police issue as it is unclear which police department(s) truly sponsored the set. The 17 cards feature members of the Chicago Bears and New England Patriots who were in the Super Bowl in early 1986. The cards measure approximately 2 5/8" by 4 1/4". The card fronts give the player's name and uniform number under his red/blue bordered color photo. The card backs are printed in black ink on white card stock. Cards are numbered on the back in the lower right corner: the Bears (2-9) and the Patriots (10-17).

32 Craig James
RUNNING BACK

| | MINT | EXC | G-VG |
|---|---|---|---|
| COMPLETE SET (17) | 15.00 | 6.00 | 1.50 |
| COMMON PLAYER (1-17) | .50 | .20 | .05 |
| ☐ 1 Title Card | .75 | .30 | .07 |
| (Checklist on back of card) | | | |
| ☐ 2 Richard Dent | 2.00 | .80 | .20 |
| ☐ 3 Walter Payton | 6.00 | 2.40 | .60 |
| ☐ 4 William Perry | 1.25 | .50 | .12 |
| ☐ 5 Jim McMahon | 1.50 | .60 | .15 |
| ☐ 6 Dave Duerson | .75 | .30 | .07 |
| ☐ 7 Gary Fencik | .75 | .30 | .07 |
| ☐ 8 Otis Wilson | .75 | .30 | .07 |
| ☐ 9 Willie Gault | 1.50 | .60 | .15 |
| ☐ 10 Craig James | 1.25 | .50 | .12 |
| ☐ 11 Fred Marion | .50 | .20 | .05 |
| ☐ 12 Ronnie Lippett | .75 | .30 | .07 |
| ☐ 13 Stanley Morgan | 1.50 | .60 | .15 |
| ☐ 14 John Hannah | 2.00 | .80 | .20 |
| ☐ 15 Andre Tippett | 1.25 | .50 | .12 |
| ☐ 16 Tony Franklin | .50 | .20 | .05 |
| ☐ 17 Tony Eason | 1.00 | .40 | .10 |

# 1986 Police Chiefs

63 • WILLIE LANIER
Linebacker 1967-77
"Pro Football Hall of Fame"
KANSAS CITY CHIEFS

This ten-card set features the Kansas City Chiefs. Cards in the set measure approximately 2 5/8" by 4 1/8" and the card back gives the card number and the year of issue. Printing is in black and red on white card stock. The set was sponsored by Frito-Lay, KCTV-5, and area law enforcement agencies. Two cartoons are featured on the back of each card picturing a "Chiefs Tip" and a "Crime Tip".

| | MINT | EXC | G-VG |
|---|---|---|---|
| COMPLETE SET (10) | 5.00 | 2.00 | .50 |
| COMMON PLAYER (1-10) | .50 | .20 | .05 |
| ☐ 1 John Mackovic CO | .75 | .30 | .07 |
| ☐ 2 Willie Lanier | 1.25 | .50 | .12 |
| (Hall of Fame) | | | |
| ☐ 3 Stephone Paige | 1.00 | .40 | .10 |
| ☐ 4 Brad Budde | .50 | .20 | .05 |
| ☐ 5 Nick Lowery | .90 | .36 | .09 |
| ☐ 6 Scott Radecic | .50 | .20 | .05 |
| ☐ 7 Mike Pruitt | .60 | .24 | .06 |
| ☐ 8 Albert Lewis | .90 | .36 | .09 |
| ☐ 9 Todd Blackledge | .75 | .30 | .07 |
| ☐ 10 Deron Cherry | .90 | .36 | .09 |

## 1986 Police Dolphins

This 16-card set is numbered on the card backs, which are printed in black ink on white card stock. Cards measure approximately 2 5/8" by 4 1/8". The set was sponsored by Kiwanis, Anon Anew, the Dolphins, and area law enforcement agencies. Uniform numbers are printed on the front of the card.

|  | MINT | EXC | G-VG |
|---|---|---|---|
| COMPLETE SET (16) | 10.00 | 4.00 | 1.00 |
| COMMON PLAYER (1-16) | .40 | .16 | .04 |
| ☐ 1 Dwight Stephenson | .60 | .24 | .06 |
| ☐ 2 Bob Baumhower | .50 | .20 | .05 |
| ☐ 3 Dolfan Denny (Mascot) | .40 | .16 | .04 |
| ☐ 4 Don Shula CO | 1.25 | .50 | .12 |
| ☐ 5 Dan Marino | 5.00 | 2.00 | .50 |
| ☐ 6 Tony Nathan | .75 | .30 | .07 |
| ☐ 7 Mark Duper | 1.00 | .40 | .10 |
| ☐ 8 John Offerdahl | 1.00 | .40 | .10 |
| ☐ 9 Fuad Reveiz | .40 | .16 | .04 |
| ☐ 10 Hugh Green | .60 | .24 | .06 |
| ☐ 11 Lorenzo Hampton | .50 | .20 | .05 |
| ☐ 12 Mark Clayton | 1.50 | .60 | .15 |
| ☐ 13 Nat Moore | .75 | .30 | .07 |
| ☐ 14 Bob Brudzinski | .40 | .16 | .04 |
| ☐ 15 Reggie Roby | .50 | .20 | .05 |
| ☐ 16 T.J. Turner | .50 | .20 | .05 |

## 1986 Police Eagles

This 16-card set is numbered on the card backs, which are printed in black and red ink on white card stock. Cards measure approximately 2 5/8" by 4 1/8". The set was sponsored by Frito-Lay, local Police Departments, and the Eagles. Uniform numbers are printed on the card front before the player's name. Randall Cunningham's card predates his 1987 Topps Rookie Card by one year.

|  | MINT | EXC | G-VG |
|---|---|---|---|
| COMPLETE SET (16) | 8.00 | 3.25 | .80 |
| COMMON PLAYER (1-16) | .40 | .16 | .04 |
| ☐ 1 Greg Brown | .50 | .20 | .05 |
| ☐ 2 Reggie White | 3.00 | 1.20 | .30 |
| ☐ 3 John Spagnola | .50 | .20 | .05 |
| ☐ 4 Mike Quick | .75 | .30 | .07 |
| ☐ 5 Ken Clarke | .40 | .16 | .04 |
| ☐ 6 Ken Reeves | .40 | .16 | .04 |
| ☐ 7 Mike Reichenbach | .40 | .16 | .04 |
| ☐ 8 Wes Hopkins | .60 | .24 | .06 |
| ☐ 9 Roynell Young | .60 | .24 | .06 |
| ☐ 10 Randall Cunningham | 4.50 | 1.80 | .45 |
| ☐ 11 Paul McFadden | .40 | .16 | .04 |
| ☐ 12 Matt Cavanaugh | .60 | .24 | .06 |
| ☐ 13 Ron Jaworski | 1.00 | .40 | .10 |
| ☐ 14 Byron Darby | .40 | .16 | .04 |
| ☐ 15 Andre Waters | .60 | .24 | .06 |
| ☐ 16 Buddy Ryan CO | .75 | .30 | .07 |

## 1986 Police Lions

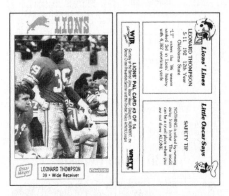

This 14-card set of Detroit Lions is numbered on the card backs, which are printed in black ink on white card stock. Cards measure approximately 2 5/8" by 4 1/8". The set was sponsored by the Detroit Lions, Oscar Mayer, Claussen, WJR/WHYT, the Detroit Crime Prevention Section, and the Pontiac Police Athletic League. Uniform numbers are printed on the card front along with the player's name and position.

|  | MINT | EXC | G-VG |
|---|---|---|---|
| COMPLETE SET (14) | 6.00 | 2.40 | .60 |
| COMMON PLAYER (1-14) | .50 | .20 | .05 |
| ☐ 1 William Gay | .50 | .20 | .05 |
| ☐ 2 Pontiac Silverdome | .60 | .24 | .06 |
| ☐ 3 Leonard Thompson | .60 | .24 | .06 |
| ☐ 4 Eddie Murray | .75 | .30 | .07 |
| ☐ 5 Eric Hipple | .75 | .30 | .07 |
| ☐ 6 James Jones | .75 | .30 | .07 |
| ☐ 7 Darryl Rogers CO | .50 | .20 | .05 |
| ☐ 8 Chuck Long | .75 | .30 | .07 |
| ☐ 9 Garry James | .60 | .24 | .06 |
| ☐ 10 Michael Cofer | .60 | .24 | .06 |
| ☐ 11 Jeff Chadwick | .75 | .30 | .07 |
| ☐ 12 Jimmy Williams | .50 | .20 | .05 |
| ☐ 13 Keith Dorney | .50 | .20 | .05 |
| ☐ 14 Bobby Watkins | .50 | .20 | .05 |

## 1986 Police Packers

This 25-card set of Green Bay Packers is unnumbered except for uniform number. Cards measure approximately 2 3/4" by 4" and the backs contain a "Safety Tip". The obverse features the prominent heading "1986 Packers". Card backs are written in green ink on white card stock.

|  | MINT | EXC | G-VG |
|---|---|---|---|
| COMPLETE SET (25) | 7.00 | 2.80 | .70 |
| COMMON PLAYER | .35 | .14 | .03 |
| ☐ 10 Al Del Greco | .35 | .14 | .03 |
| ☐ 12 Lynn Dickey | 1.00 | .40 | .10 |
| ☐ 16 Randy Wright | .50 | .20 | .05 |
| ☐ 26 Tim Lewis | .50 | .20 | .05 |
| ☐ 31 Gerry Ellis | .35 | .14 | .03 |
| ☐ 33 Jessie Clark | .35 | .14 | .03 |
| ☐ 37 Mark Murphy | .35 | .14 | .03 |
| ☐ 40 Eddie Lee Ivery | .75 | .30 | .07 |
| ☐ 41 Tom Flynn | .50 | .20 | .05 |
| ☐ 42 Gary Ellerson | .35 | .14 | .03 |
| ☐ 55 Randy Scott | .35 | .14 | .03 |
| ☐ 58 Mark Cannon | .50 | .20 | .05 |
| ☐ 59 John Anderson | .50 | .20 | .05 |
| ☐ 65 Ron Hallstrom | .35 | .14 | .03 |

| | | | |
|---|---|---|---|
| ☐ 67 Karl Swanke | .35 | .14 | .03 |
| ☐ 76 Alphonso Carreker | .35 | .14 | .03 |
| ☐ 80 James Lofton | 1.50 | .60 | .15 |
| ☐ 82 Paul Coffman | .60 | .24 | .06 |
| ☐ 85 Phillip Epps | .50 | .20 | .05 |
| ☐ 90 Ezra Johnson | .35 | .14 | .03 |
| ☐ 91 Brian Noble | .50 | .20 | .05 |
| ☐ 93 Robert Brown | .35 | .14 | .03 |
| ☐ 94 Charles Martin | .35 | .14 | .03 |
| ☐ 99 John Dorsey | .35 | .14 | .03 |
| ☐ xx Forrest Gregg CO | 1.25 | .50 | .12 |

# 1986 Police Redskins

This 16-card set of Washington Redskins is numbered on the back. Cards measure approximately 2 5/8" by 4 1/8" and the backs contain a "Crime Prevention Tip". Each player's uniform number is given on the card front. The set was sponsored by Frito-Lay, the Redskins, WMAL-AM63, and local law enforcement agencies. Card backs are printed in maroon and black on white card stock. The set commemorates the Redskins 50th Anniversary as a team.

| | MINT | EXC | G-VG |
|---|---|---|---|
| COMPLETE SET (16) | 6.00 | 2.40 | .60 |
| COMMON PLAYER (1-16) | .35 | .14 | .03 |
| | | | |
| ☐ 1 Darrell Green | .75 | .30 | .07 |
| ☐ 2 Joe Jacoby | .50 | .20 | .05 |
| ☐ 3 Charles Mann | .50 | .20 | .05 |
| ☐ 4 Jay Schroeder | 1.00 | .40 | .10 |
| ☐ 5 Raphel Cherry | .35 | .14 | .03 |
| ☐ 6 Russ Grimm | .50 | .20 | .05 |
| ☐ 7 Mel Kaufman | .35 | .14 | .03 |
| ☐ 8 Gary Clark | 1.50 | .60 | .15 |
| ☐ 9 Vernon Dean | .35 | .14 | .03 |
| ☐ 10 Mark May | .50 | .20 | .05 |
| ☐ 11 Dave Butz | .50 | .20 | .05 |
| ☐ 12 Jeff Bostic | .50 | .20 | .05 |
| ☐ 13 Dean Hamel | .35 | .14 | .03 |
| ☐ 14 Dexter Manley | .50 | .20 | .05 |
| ☐ 15 George Rogers | .60 | .24 | .06 |
| ☐ 16 Art Monk | 1.25 | .50 | .12 |

# 1986 Police Seahawks

This 16-card set of Seattle Seahawks is unnumbered; not even the uniform number is given explicitly on the front of the card. Cards

measure approximately 2 5/8" by 4 1/8" and the backs contain "Tips from the Seahawks". The year of issue is not printed anywhere on the cards. The cards are unnumbered so they are ordered below alphabetically.

| | MINT | EXC | G-VG |
|---|---|---|---|
| COMPLETE SET (16) | 7.00 | 2.80 | .70 |
| COMMON PLAYER (1-16) | .40 | .16 | .04 |
| | | | |
| ☐ 1 Edwin Bailey | .40 | .16 | .04 |
| ☐ 2 Dave Brown | .60 | .24 | .06 |
| ☐ 3 Jeff Bryant | .50 | .20 | .05 |
| ☐ 4 Blair Bush | .50 | .20 | .05 |
| ☐ 5 Keith Butler | .40 | .16 | .04 |
| ☐ 6 Kenny Easley | .75 | .30 | .07 |
| ☐ 7 Jacob Green | .60 | .24 | .06 |
| ☐ 8 Michael Jackson | .40 | .16 | .04 |
| ☐ 9 Chuck Knox CO | .60 | .24 | .06 |
| ☐ 10 Dave Krieg | 1.25 | .50 | .12 |
| ☐ 11 Steve Largent | 3.00 | 1.20 | .30 |
| ☐ 12 Joe Nash | .50 | .20 | .05 |
| ☐ 13 Bruce Scholtz | .40 | .16 | .04 |
| ☐ 14 Terry Taylor | .50 | .20 | .05 |
| ☐ 15 Curt Warner | .75 | .30 | .07 |
| ☐ 16 Fredd Young | .60 | .24 | .06 |

# 1986 Police Steelers

This 15-card set of Pittsburgh Steelers is unnumbered except for uniform number. Cards measure approximately 2 5/8" by 4 1/8". The backs contain "Steeler Tips". The set was sponsored by Kiwanis, Giant Eagle, local Police Departments, and the Steelers. Card backs are written in black on white card stock. The 1985, 1986, and 1987 Police Steelers sets are identical except for the individual card differences noted parenthetically below.

| | MINT | EXC | G-VG |
|---|---|---|---|
| COMPLETE SET (15) | 5.00 | 2.00 | .50 |
| COMMON PLAYER | .35 | .14 | .03 |
| | | | |
| ☐ 1 Gary Anderson | .50 | .20 | .05 |
| (Field Goal back) | | | |
| ☐ 16 Mark Malone | .50 | .20 | .05 |
| (Quarterback back) | | | |
| ☐ 24 Rich Erenberg | .50 | .20 | .05 |
| ☐ 30 Frank Pollard | .50 | .20 | .05 |
| (Running Back back) | | | |
| ☐ 31 Donnie Shell | .50 | .20 | .05 |
| (Interception back) | | | |

| | MINT | EXC | G-VG |
|---|---|---|---|
| ☐ 34 Walter Abercrombie (Penalty back) | .50 | .20 | .05 |
| ☐ 49 Dwayne Woodruff (Practice back) | .35 | .14 | .03 |
| ☐ 52 Mike Webster (Possession back) | .75 | .30 | .07 |
| ☐ 53 Bryan Hinkle (Prevent back) | .35 | .14 | .03 |
| ☐ 56 Robin Cole (Equipment back) | .35 | .14 | .03 |
| ☐ 57 Mike Merriweather (Linebacker back) | .50 | .20 | .05 |
| ☐ 62 Tunch Ilkin | .50 | .20 | .05 |
| ☐ 64 Edmund Nelson | .35 | .14 | .03 |
| ☐ 67 Gary Dunn (Defensive Holding back) | .35 | .14 | .03 |
| ☐ 82 John Stallworth (Victory back) | 1.00 | .40 | .10 |
| ☐ 83 Louis Lipps (Receiver back) | .75 | .30 | .07 |

## 1986 Police Vikings

This 14-card set of Minnesota Vikings is numbered on the back. Cards measure approximately 2 5/8" by 4 1/8" and the backs contain a "Crime Prevention Tip". The checklist for the set is on the back of the head coach card.

| | MINT | EXC | G-VG |
|---|---|---|---|
| COMPLETE SET (14) | 6.00 | 2.40 | .60 |
| COMMON PLAYER (1-14) | .40 | .16 | .04 |
| ☐ 1 Jerry Burns CO (Checklist back) | .50 | .20 | .05 |
| ☐ 2 Darrin Nelson | .60 | .24 | .06 |
| ☐ 3 Tommy Kramer | .75 | .30 | .07 |
| ☐ 4 Anthony Carter | 1.50 | .60 | .15 |
| ☐ 5 Scott Studwell | .50 | .20 | .05 |
| ☐ 6 Chris Doleman | 1.50 | .60 | .15 |
| ☐ 7 Joey Browner | 1.00 | .40 | .10 |
| ☐ 8 Steve Jordan | .60 | .24 | .06 |
| ☐ 9 David Howard | .40 | .16 | .04 |
| ☐ 10 Tim Newton | .40 | .16 | .04 |
| ☐ 11 Leo Lewis | .50 | .20 | .05 |
| ☐ 12 Keith Millard | 1.25 | .50 | .12 |
| ☐ 13 Doug Martin | .40 | .16 | .04 |
| ☐ 14 Bill Brown (All-Time Great) | .60 | .24 | .06 |

## 1987 Police Bills

This eight-card set of Buffalo Bills is numbered on the back. The card backs are printed in gray and black ink on white card stock. Cards measure approximately 2 5/8" by 4 1/8". The set was sponsored by the Buffalo Bills, Erie and Niagara County Sheriff's Departments, Louis Rich Turkey Products, Claussen Pickles, and WBEN Radio. Uniform numbers are printed on the card front along with the player's name and position. The photos in the set were taken by Robert L. Smith, the Bills' official team photographer.

| | MINT | EXC | G-VG |
|---|---|---|---|
| COMPLETE SET (8) | 10.00 | 4.00 | 1.00 |
| COMMON PLAYER (1-8) | .75 | .30 | .07 |
| ☐ 1 Marv Levy CO | 1.50 | .60 | .15 |
| ☐ 2 Bruce Smith | 3.00 | 1.20 | .30 |
| ☐ 3 Joe Devlin | .75 | .30 | .07 |
| ☐ 4 Jim Kelly | 5.00 | 2.00 | .50 |

| | MINT | EXC | G-VG |
|---|---|---|---|
| ☐ 5 Eugene Marve | .75 | .30 | .07 |
| ☐ 6 Andre Reed | 3.00 | 1.20 | .30 |
| ☐ 7 Pete Metzelaars | .75 | .30 | .07 |
| ☐ 8 John Kidd | .75 | .30 | .07 |

## 1987 Police Chargers

The 1987 San Diego Chargers Police set contains 21 numbered cards. The cards measure approximately 2 5/8" by 4 1/8". Uniform numbers appear on the fronts of the cards. The set is sponsored by the San Diego Chargers, Oscar Mayer, and local law enforcement agencies. The Chargers helmet logo, "Chargers Tips," and the Oscar Mayer logo appear on the backs. Card backs have black printing on white backs. The Chargers helmet along with height, weight, age, and experience statistics appear on the fronts of the cards. Card 13 was never issued apparently for superstitious reasons. Cards 3 (Benirschke released) and 17 (Walters arrested) were distributed in lesser quantities and hence are a little tougher to find, especially Benirschke. Chip Banks (22) was the player substituted in the set for Rolf Benirschke.

| | MINT | EXC | G-VG |
|---|---|---|---|
| COMPLETE SET (21) | 25.00 | 10.00 | 2.50 |
| COMMON PLAYER (1-22) | .75 | .30 | .07 |
| ☐ 1 Alex Spanos OWN | .75 | .30 | .07 |
| ☐ 2 Gary Anderson | 1.50 | .60 | .15 |
| ☐ 3 Rolf Benirschke SP | 7.50 | 3.00 | .75 |
| ☐ 4 Gill Byrd | 1.50 | .60 | .15 |
| ☐ 5 Wes Chandler | 1.50 | .60 | .15 |
| ☐ 6 Sam Claphan | .75 | .30 | .07 |
| ☐ 7 Jeff Dale | .75 | .30 | .07 |
| ☐ 8 Pete Holohan | 1.00 | .40 | .10 |
| ☐ 9 Lionel James | 1.25 | .50 | .12 |
| ☐ 10 Jim Lachey | 1.50 | .60 | .15 |
| ☐ 11 Woodrow Lowe | 1.00 | .40 | .10 |
| ☐ 12 Don Macek | .75 | .30 | .07 |
| ☐ 14 Dan Fouts | 4.00 | 1.60 | .40 |
| ☐ 15 Eric Sievers | 1.00 | .40 | .10 |
| ☐ 16 Billy Ray Smith | 1.50 | .60 | .15 |
| ☐ 17 Danny Walters SP | 4.00 | 1.60 | .40 |
| ☐ 18 Lee Williams | 2.00 | .80 | .20 |
| ☐ 19 Kellen Winslow | 2.50 | 1.00 | .25 |
| ☐ 20 Al Saunders CO | 1.00 | .40 | .10 |
| ☐ 21 Dennis McKnight | .75 | .30 | .07 |
| ☐ 22 Chip Banks | 1.50 | .60 | .15 |

## 1987 Police Chiefs

This ten-card set features the Kansas City Chiefs. Cards in the set measure approximately 2 5/8" by 4 1/8". The card back gives the card number and the year of issue; printing is in black and red on white card stock. The set was sponsored by Frito-Lay, US Sprint, KCTV-5, and area law enforcement agencies. Two cartoons are featured on the back of each card picturing a "Chiefs Tip" and a "Crime Tip". Reportedly more than 4.5 million cards were given out by over 275 different police departments.

|  | MINT | EXC | G-VG |
|---|---|---|---|
| COMPLETE SET (10) | 4.00 | 1.60 | .40 |
| COMMON PLAYER (1-10) | .40 | .16 | .04 |
| ☐ 1 Frank Gansz CO | .50 | .20 | .05 |
| ☐ 2 Tim Cofield | .40 | .16 | .04 |
| ☐ 3 Deron Cherry | .90 | .36 | .09 |
| and Albert Lewis |  |  |  |
| ☐ 4 Chiefs Cheerleaders | .60 | .24 | .06 |
| ☐ 5 Jeff Smith | .50 | .20 | .05 |
| ☐ 6 Rick Donnalley | .40 | .16 | .04 |
| ☐ 7 Lloyd Burruss | .60 | .24 | .06 |
| and Kevin Ross |  |  |  |
| ☐ 8 Dino Hackett | .50 | .20 | .05 |
| ☐ 9 Bill Maas | .50 | .20 | .05 |
| ☐ 10 Carlos Carson | .60 | .24 | .06 |

## 1987 Police Dolphins

This 16-card set is numbered on the back and measures approximately 2 5/8" by 4 1/8". The set was sponsored by Kiwanis, Children's Center of Fair Oaks Hospital at Boca/Delray, the Dolphins, and area law enforcement agencies. Uniform numbers are printed on the front of the card. Reportedly approximately three million cards were produced for this promotion. The Dwight Stephenson card is considered more difficult to find than the other cards in the set.

|  | MINT | EXC | G-VG |
|---|---|---|---|
| COMPLETE SET (16) | 15.00 | 6.00 | 1.50 |
| COMMON PLAYER (1-16) | .60 | .24 | .06 |
| ☐ 1 Joe Robbie OWN | .75 | .30 | .07 |
| ☐ 2 Glenn Blackwood | .75 | .30 | .07 |
| ☐ 3 Mark Duper | 1.00 | .40 | .10 |
| ☐ 4 Fuad Reveiz | .60 | .24 | .06 |

| ☐ 5 Dolfan Denny (Mascot) | .60 | .24 | .06 |
|---|---|---|---|
| ☐ 6 Dwight Stephenson SP | 4.00 | 1.60 | .40 |
| ☐ 7 Hugh Green | 1.00 | .40 | .10 |
| ☐ 8 Larry Csonka | 2.00 | .80 | .20 |
| (All-Time Great) |  |  |  |
| ☐ 9 Bud Brown | .60 | .24 | .06 |
| ☐ 10 Don Shula CO | 1.50 | .60 | .15 |
| ☐ 11 T.J. Turner | .60 | .24 | .06 |
| ☐ 12 Reggie Roby | .75 | .30 | .07 |
| ☐ 13 Dan Marino | 6.00 | 2.40 | .60 |
| ☐ 14 John Offerdahl | 1.25 | .50 | .12 |
| ☐ 15 Bruce Hardy | .60 | .24 | .06 |
| ☐ 16 Lorenzo Hampton | .75 | .30 | .07 |

## 1987 Police Eagles

Ron Baker

This set of 12 cards featuring Philadelphia Eagles was issued very late in the year and was not widely distributed. Reportedly 10,000 sets were distributed by officers of the New Jersey police force. Cards measure approximately 2 3/4" by 4 1/8" and feature a crime prevention tip on the back. The set was sponsored by the New Jersey State Police Crime Prevention Resource Center. The cards are unnumbered and are listed alphabetically below for reference.

|  | MINT | EXC | G-VG |
|---|---|---|---|
| COMPLETE SET (12) | 50.00 | 20.00 | 5.00 |
| COMMON PLAYER (1-12) | 3.00 | 1.20 | .30 |
| ☐ 1 Ron Baker | 3.00 | 1.20 | .30 |
| ☐ 2 Keith Byars | 6.00 | 2.40 | .60 |
| ☐ 3 Ken Clarke | 3.00 | 1.20 | .30 |
| ☐ 4 Randall Cunningham | 15.00 | 6.00 | 1.50 |
| ☐ 5 Paul McFadden | 3.00 | 1.20 | .30 |
| ☐ 6 Mike Quick | 5.00 | 2.00 | .50 |
| ☐ 7 Mike Reidenbach | 3.00 | 1.20 | .30 |
| ☐ 8 Buddy Ryan CO | 5.00 | 2.00 | .50 |
| ☐ 9 John Spagnola | 3.00 | 1.20 | .30 |
| ☐ 10 Anthony Toney | 4.00 | 1.60 | .40 |
| ☐ 11 Andre Waters | 4.00 | 1.60 | .40 |
| ☐ 12 Reggie White | 12.00 | 5.00 | 1.20 |

## 1987 Police Giants

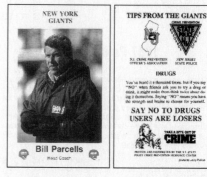

Bill Parcells
Head Coach

This set of 12 cards featuring New York Giants was issued very late in the year and was not widely distributed. Reportedly 10,000 sets were distributed by officers of the New Jersey police force. Cards measure approximately 2 3/4" by 4 1/8" and feature a crime prevention tip on the back. The set was sponsored by the New Jersey State Police Crime Prevention Resource Center. The Giants helmet appears below the player photo which differentiates this set from the very similar 1988 Police Giants set. These unnumbered cards are listed alphabetically in the checklist below.

|  | MINT | EXC | G-VG |
|---|---|---|---|
| COMPLETE SET (12) | 60.00 | 24.00 | 6.00 |
| COMMON CARD (1-12) | 3.00 | 1.20 | .30 |
| ☐ 1 Carl Banks | 7.50 | 3.00 | .75 |
| ☐ 2 Mark Bavaro | 6.00 | 2.40 | .60 |
| ☐ 3 Brad Benson | 3.00 | 1.20 | .30 |
| ☐ 4 Jim Burt | 4.00 | 1.60 | .40 |
| ☐ 5 Harry Carson | 6.00 | 2.40 | .60 |
| ☐ 6 Maurice Carthon | 4.00 | 1.60 | .40 |
| ☐ 7 Sean Landeta | 4.00 | 1.60 | .40 |
| ☐ 8 Leonard Marshall | 6.00 | 2.40 | .60 |
| ☐ 9 George Martin | 4.00 | 1.60 | .40 |
| ☐ 10 Joe Morris | 6.00 | 2.40 | .60 |
| ☐ 11 Bill Parcells CO | 6.00 | 2.40 | .60 |
| ☐ 12 Phil Simms | 15.00 | 6.00 | 1.50 |

## 1987 Police Lions

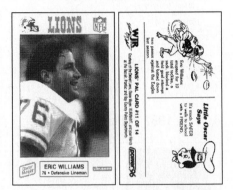

This 14-card set of Detroit Lions is numbered on the back. The card backs are printed in blue ink on white card stock and contain a safety tip entitled "Little Oscar Says". Cards measure approximately 2 5/8" by 4 1/8". The set was sponsored by the Detroit Lions, Oscar Mayer, Claussen Pickles, WJR/WHYT, the Detroit Crime Prevention Section, and the Pontiac Police Athletic League. Uniform numbers are printed on the card front along with the player's name and position. Reportedly, nearly three million cards were distributed through the participating police agencies. The Lions team name appears above the player photo which differentiates this set from the 1988 Police Lions set.

|  | MINT | EXC | G-VG |
|---|---|---|---|
| COMPLETE SET (14) | 5.00 | 2.00 | .50 |
| COMMON PLAYER (1-14) | .40 | .16 | .04 |
| ☐ 1 Michael Cofer<br>Vernon Maxwell<br>William Gay | .50 | .20 | .05 |
| ☐ 2 Rich Strenger | .40 | .16 | .04 |
| ☐ 3 Keith Ferguson | .40 | .16 | .04 |
| ☐ 4 James Jones | .60 | .24 | .06 |
| ☐ 5 Jeff Chadwick | .50 | .20 | .05 |
| ☐ 6 Devon Mitchell | .40 | .16 | .04 |
| ☐ 7 Eddie Murray | .60 | .24 | .06 |
| ☐ 8 Reggie Rogers | .50 | .20 | .05 |
| ☐ 9 Chuck Long | .75 | .30 | .07 |
| ☐ 10 Jimmie Giles | .60 | .24 | .06 |
| ☐ 11 Eric Williams | .40 | .16 | .04 |
| ☐ 12 Lomas Brown | .50 | .20 | .05 |
| ☐ 13 Jimmy Williams | .40 | .16 | .04 |
| ☐ 14 Garry James | .50 | .20 | .05 |

## 1987 Police Packers

This 22-card set of Green Bay Packers is numbered on the front in the lower right corner below the photo. Sponsors were the Employers Health Insurance Company, Arson Task Force, local law enforcement agencies, and the Green Bay Packers. Cards measure 2 3/4" by 4". The backs contain a "Safety Tip". The obverse features the prominent heading "1987 Packers". Card backs are written in green ink on white card stock. Cards 5, 6, and 20 were never issued as apparently they

were scheduled to be players who were later cut and released from the team. Reportedly 35,000 sets were distributed.

|  | MINT | EXC | G-VG |
|---|---|---|---|
| COMPLETE SET (22) | 8.00 | 3.25 | .80 |
| COMMON PLAYER (1-25) | .40 | .16 | .04 |
| ☐ 1 Forrest Gregg CO | 1.00 | .40 | .10 |
| ☐ 2 George Greene | .40 | .16 | .04 |
| ☐ 3 Ron Hallstrom | .40 | .16 | .04 |
| ☐ 4 Ezra Johnson | .40 | .16 | .04 |
| ☐ 7 Robert Brown | .40 | .16 | .04 |
| ☐ 8 Tom Neville | .40 | .16 | .04 |
| ☐ 9 Rich Moran | .40 | .16 | .04 |
| ☐ 10 Ken Ruettgers | .60 | .24 | .06 |
| ☐ 11 Alan Veingrad | .40 | .16 | .04 |
| ☐ 12 Mark Lee | .60 | .24 | .06 |
| ☐ 13 John Dorsey | .40 | .16 | .04 |
| ☐ 14 Paul Ott Carruth | .40 | .16 | .04 |
| ☐ 15 Randy Wright | .50 | .20 | .05 |
| ☐ 16 Phillip Epps | .60 | .24 | .06 |
| ☐ 17 Al Del Greco | .40 | .16 | .04 |
| ☐ 18 Tim Harris | 1.50 | .60 | .15 |
| ☐ 19 Kenneth Davis | 1.25 | .50 | .12 |
| ☐ 21 John Anderson | .60 | .24 | .06 |
| ☐ 22 Mark Murphy | .50 | .20 | .05 |
| ☐ 23 Ken Stills | .40 | .16 | .04 |
| ☐ 24 Brian Noble | .50 | .20 | .05 |
| ☐ 25 Mark Cannon | .50 | .20 | .05 |

## 1987 Police Redskins

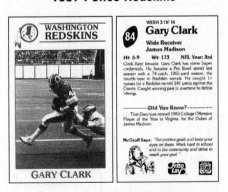

This 16-card set of Washington Redskins is numbered on the back. The cards measure approximately 2 5/8" by 4 1/8" and the backs contain a "McGruff Says" crime prevention tip. The set was sponsored by Frito-Lay and PACT (Police and Citizens Together). Card backs are written in red and black on white card stock. The cards were given out one per week in the greater Washington metropolitan area.

|  | MINT | EXC | G-VG |
|---|---|---|---|
| COMPLETE SET (16) | 5.00 | 2.00 | .50 |
| COMMON PLAYER (1-16) | .35 | .14 | .03 |
| ☐ 1 Joe Jacoby | .50 | .20 | .05 |
| ☐ 2 Gary Clark | 1.00 | .40 | .10 |
| ☐ 3 Dexter Manley | .60 | .24 | .06 |
| ☐ 4 Darrell Green | .75 | .30 | .07 |
| ☐ 5 Alvin Walton | .35 | .14 | .03 |
| ☐ 6 Clint Didier | .50 | .20 | .05 |
| ☐ 7 Art Monk | 1.25 | .50 | .12 |
| ☐ 8 Darryl Grant | .35 | .14 | .03 |

| | MINT | EXC | G-VG |
|---|---|---|---|
| ☐ 9 Kelvin Bryant | .50 | .20 | .05 |
| ☐ 10 Jay Schroeder | .75 | .30 | .07 |
| ☐ 11 Don Warren | .50 | .20 | .05 |
| ☐ 12 Steve Cox | .35 | .14 | .03 |
| ☐ 13 Mark May | .35 | .14 | .03 |
| ☐ 14 Jeff Bostic | .50 | .20 | .05 |
| ☐ 15 Charles Mann | .50 | .20 | .05 |
| ☐ 16 Dave Butz | .50 | .20 | .05 |

## 1987 Police Seahawks

This 16-card set of Seattle Seahawks is unnumbered; not even the uniform number is given explicitly on the front of the card. Cards measure approximately 2 5/8" by 4 1/8". The backs contain a safety tip. The year of issue is not printed anywhere on the cards. The card fronts have a silver border and feature a blue and green Seahawks logo. The cards are listed below alphabetically for convenience.

| | MINT | EXC | G-VG |
|---|---|---|---|
| COMPLETE SET (16) | 5.00 | 2.00 | .50 |
| COMMON PLAYER (1-16) | .35 | .14 | .03 |
| ☐ 1 Jeff Bryant | .50 | .20 | .05 |
| ☐ 2 Kenny Easley | .60 | .24 | .06 |
| ☐ 3 Bobby Joe Edmonds | .50 | .20 | .05 |
| ☐ 4 Jacob Green | .60 | .24 | .06 |
| ☐ 5 Chuck Knox CO | .60 | .24 | .06 |
| ☐ 6 Dave Krieg | 1.00 | .40 | .10 |
| ☐ 7 Steve Largent | 2.50 | 1.00 | .25 |
| ☐ 8 Ron Mattes | .35 | .14 | .03 |
| ☐ 9 Bryan Millard | .35 | .14 | .03 |
| ☐ 10 Eugene Robinson | .60 | .24 | .06 |
| ☐ 11 Bruce Scholtz | .35 | .14 | .03 |
| ☐ 12 Paul Skansi | .50 | .20 | .05 |
| ☐ 13 Curt Warner | .75 | .30 | .07 |
| ☐ 14 John L. Williams | 1.50 | .60 | .15 |
| ☐ 15 Mike Wilson | .35 | .14 | .03 |
| ☐ 16 Fredd Young | .50 | .20 | .05 |

## 1987 Police Steelers

This 16-card set of Pittsburgh Steelers is unnumbered except for uniform number. Cards measure approximately 2 5/8" by 4 1/8". The backs contain "Steeler Tips". The set was sponsored by Kiwanis, Giant

Eagle, local Police Departments, and the Steelers. The cards were given out by Pittsburgh area police officers one card per week. Card backs are written in black on white card stock. The 1985, 1986, 1987 Police Steelers sets are identical except for the individual card differences noted parenthetically below.

| | MINT | EXC | G-VG |
|---|---|---|---|
| COMPLETE SET (16) | 5.00 | 2.00 | .50 |
| COMMON PLAYER (1-16) | .35 | .14 | .03 |
| ☐ 1 Walter Abercrombie (Option Pass back) | .50 | .20 | .05 |
| ☐ 2 Gary Anderson (Extra Point back) | .50 | .20 | .05 |
| ☐ 3 Bubby Brister | .90 | .36 | .09 |
| ☐ 4 Gary Dunn (Neutral Zone back) | .35 | .14 | .03 |
| ☐ 5 Preston Gothard | .35 | .14 | .03 |
| ☐ 6 Bryan Hinkle (Outside Linebackers back) | .50 | .20 | .05 |
| ☐ 7 Earnest Jackson | .50 | .20 | .05 |
| ☐ 8 Louis Lipps (Corner Pattern back) | .75 | .30 | .07 |
| ☐ 9 Mark Malone (Adverse Conditions back) | .50 | .20 | .05 |
| ☐ 10 Mike Merriweather (Instant Replay back) | .50 | .20 | .05 |
| ☐ 11 Chuck Noll CO (Referee back) | .75 | .30 | .07 |
| ☐ 12 John Rienstra | .35 | .14 | .03 |
| ☐ 13 Donnie Shell (Defense back) | .50 | .20 | .05 |
| ☐ 14 John Stallworth (Crackback Block back) | 1.00 | .40 | .10 |
| ☐ 15 Mike Webster (Sportsmanship back) | .75 | .30 | .07 |
| ☐ 16 Keith Willis (Down back) | .35 | .14 | .03 |

## 1987 Police Vikings

This 14-card set of Minnesota Vikings is numbered on the back. Cards measure approximately 2 5/8" by 4 1/8" and are in full color on the front. The backs contain a "Crime Prevention Tip". The checklist for the set is on the back of the first card. Purple Power '87 is actually an action montage by artist Cliff Spohn. Reportedly 2.1 million cards were distributed during the 14-week promotion. The set was sponsored by the Vikings, Frito-Lay, Campbell's Soup, and KSTP-FM in cooperation with the Minnesota Crime Prevention Officers Association.

| | MINT | EXC | G-VG |
|---|---|---|---|
| COMPLETE SET (14) | 6.00 | 2.40 | .60 |
| COMMON PLAYER (1-14) | .40 | .16 | .04 |
| ☐ 1 Purple Power '87 (checklist back) | .60 | .24 | .06 |
| ☐ 2 Jerry Burns CO | .50 | .20 | .05 |
| ☐ 3 Scott Studwell | .50 | .20 | .05 |
| ☐ 4 Tommy Kramer | .75 | .30 | .07 |
| ☐ 5 Gerald Robinson | .40 | .16 | .04 |
| ☐ 6 Wade Wilson | 1.50 | .60 | .15 |
| ☐ 7 Anthony Carter | 1.25 | .50 | .12 |
| ☐ 8 Terry Tausch | .40 | .16 | .04 |
| ☐ 9 Leo Lewis | .50 | .20 | .05 |
| ☐ 10 Keith Millard | .75 | .30 | .07 |
| ☐ 11 Carl Lee | .60 | .24 | .06 |
| ☐ 12 Steve Jordan | .75 | .30 | .07 |
| ☐ 13 D.J. Dozier | .75 | .30 | .07 |
| ☐ 14 Alan Page ATG | 1.50 | .60 | .15 |

## 1988 Police Bills

This eight-card set of Buffalo Bills is numbered in the upper right corner of each reverse. Cards measure approximately 2 5/8" by 4 1/8". The set was sponsored by the Buffalo Bills, Erie and Niagara County Sheriff's Departments, Louis Rich Turkey Products, and WBEN Radio. Uniform numbers are printed on the card front along with the player's name and position. The photos in the set were taken by several photographers, each of whom is credited on the lower right front beside the respective photo.

|  | MINT | EXC | G-VG |
|---|---|---|---|
| COMPLETE SET (8) | 6.00 | 2.40 | .60 |
| COMMON PLAYER (1-8) | .75 | .30 | .07 |
| ☐ 1 Steve Tasker | 1.00 | .40 | .10 |
| ☐ 2 Cornelius Bennett | 2.50 | 1.00 | .25 |
| ☐ 3 Shane Conlan | 1.50 | .60 | .15 |
| ☐ 4 Mark Kelso | .75 | .30 | .07 |
| ☐ 5 Will Wolford | 1.00 | .40 | .10 |
| ☐ 6 Chris Burkett | 1.00 | .40 | .10 |
| ☐ 7 Kent Hull | 1.00 | .40 | .10 |
| ☐ 8 Art Still | 1.00 | .40 | .10 |

## 1988 Police Chargers

The 1988 Police San Diego Chargers set contains 12 cards each measuring approximately 2 5/8" by 4". The fronts are white and navy blue with color photos, and the backs feature career highlights and safety tips.

|  | MINT | EXC | G-VG |
|---|---|---|---|
| COMPLETE SET (12) | 8.00 | 3.25 | .80 |
| COMMON PLAYER (1-12) | .60 | .24 | .06 |
| ☐ 1 Gary Anderson | 1.50 | .60 | .15 |
| ☐ 2 Rod Bernstine | 2.00 | .80 | .20 |
| ☐ 3 Gill Byrd | 1.00 | .40 | .10 |
| ☐ 4 Vencie Glenn | .60 | .24 | .06 |
| ☐ 5 Lionel James | 1.00 | .40 | .10 |
| ☐ 6 Babe Laufenberg | .75 | .30 | .07 |
| ☐ 7 Don Macek | .60 | .24 | .06 |
| ☐ 8 Mark Malone | .75 | .30 | .07 |
| ☐ 9 Dennis McKnight | .60 | .24 | .06 |
| ☐ 10 Anthony Miller | 3.00 | 1.20 | .30 |
| ☐ 11 Billy Ray Smith | 1.25 | .50 | .12 |
| ☐ 12 Lee Williams | 1.25 | .50 | .12 |

## 1988 Police Chiefs

The 1988 Police Kansas City Chiefs set contains ten numbered cards each measuring approximately 2 5/8" by 4 1/8". There are nine player cards and one coach card. The backs have one "Chiefs Tip" and one "Crime Tip."

|  | MINT | EXC | G-VG |
|---|---|---|---|
| COMPLETE SET (10) | 5.00 | 2.00 | .50 |
| COMMON PLAYER (1-10) | .50 | .20 | .05 |
| ☐ 1 Frank Gansz CO | .60 | .24 | .06 |
| ☐ 2 Bill Kenney | .75 | .30 | .07 |
| ☐ 3 Carlos Carson | .60 | .24 | .06 |
| ☐ 4 Paul Palmer | .60 | .24 | .06 |
| ☐ 5 Christian Okoye | 1.50 | .60 | .15 |
| ☐ 6 Mark Adickes | .50 | .20 | .05 |
| ☐ 7 Bill Maas | .60 | .24 | .06 |
| ☐ 8 Albert Lewis | .75 | .30 | .07 |
| ☐ 9 Deron Cherry | .75 | .30 | .07 |
| ☐ 10 Stephone Paige | .75 | .30 | .07 |

## 1988 Police Colts

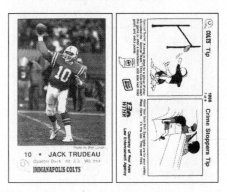

The 1988 Police Indianapolis Colts set contains eight numbered cards measuring approximately 2 5/8" by 4 1/8". There are seven player cards and one coach card. The backs have one "Colts Tip" and one "Crime Tip."

|  | MINT | EXC | G-VG |
|---|---|---|---|
| COMPLETE SET (8) | 6.00 | 2.40 | .60 |
| COMMON PLAYER (1-8) | .60 | .24 | .06 |
| ☐ 1 Eric Dickerson | 2.50 | 1.00 | .25 |
| ☐ 2 Barry Krauss | .75 | .30 | .07 |
| ☐ 3 Bill Brooks | 1.00 | .40 | .10 |
| ☐ 4 Duane Bickett | 1.00 | .40 | .10 |
| ☐ 5 Chris Hinton | 1.00 | .40 | .10 |
| ☐ 6 Eugene Daniel | .60 | .24 | .06 |
| ☐ 7 Jack Trudeau | 1.00 | .40 | .10 |
| ☐ 8 Ron Meyer CO | .75 | .30 | .07 |

## 1988 Police Eagles

The 1988 Police Philadelphia Eagles set contains 12 unnumbered cards measuring approximately 2 3/4" by 4 1/8". There are 11 player cards and one coach card. The backs have safety tips. The cards are listed below in alphabetical order by subject's name.

|  | MINT | EXC | G-VG |
|---|---|---|---|
| COMPLETE SET (12) | 50.00 | 20.00 | 5.00 |
| COMMON PLAYER (1-12) | 3.00 | 1.20 | .30 |
| ☐ 1 Jerome Brown | 5.00 | 2.00 | .50 |
| ☐ 2 Keith Byars | 5.00 | 2.00 | .50 |
| ☐ 3 Randall Cunningham | 10.00 | 4.00 | 1.00 |
| ☐ 4 Matt Darwin | 3.00 | 1.20 | .30 |
| ☐ 5 Keith Jackson | 10.00 | 4.00 | 1.00 |
| ☐ 6 Seth Joyner | 5.00 | 2.00 | .50 |
| ☐ 7 Mike Quick | 4.00 | 1.60 | .40 |
| ☐ 8 Buddy Ryan CO | 5.00 | 2.00 | .50 |
| ☐ 9 Clyde Simmons | 5.00 | 2.00 | .50 |
| ☐ 10 John Teltschik | 3.00 | 1.20 | .30 |
| ☐ 11 Anthony Toney | 4.00 | 1.60 | .40 |
| ☐ 12 Reggie White | 7.50 | 3.00 | .75 |

## 1988 Police 49ers

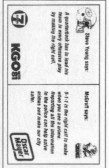

The 1988 Police San Francisco 49ers set contains 20 unnumbered cards measuring approximately 2 1/2" by 4". There are 19 player cards and one coach card. The fronts are basically "pure" with white borders. The backs have a football tip and a McGruff crime tip. The cards are listed below in alphabetical order by subject's name. The set is sponsored by 7-Eleven and Oscar Mayer, which differentiates this set from the similar-looking 1985 Police 49ers set.

|  | MINT | EXC | G-VG |
|---|---|---|---|
| COMPLETE SET (20) | 20.00 | 8.00 | 2.00 |
| COMMON PLAYER (1-20) | .50 | .20 | .05 |
| ☐ 1 Harris Barton | .60 | .24 | .06 |
| ☐ 2 Dwaine Board | .50 | .20 | .05 |
| ☐ 3 Michael Carter | 1.25 | .50 | .12 |
| ☐ 4 Roger Craig | 1.50 | .60 | .15 |
| ☐ 5 Randy Cross | .75 | .30 | .07 |
| ☐ 6 Riki Ellison | .50 | .20 | .05 |
| ☐ 7 John Frank | .60 | .24 | .06 |
| ☐ 8 Jeff Fuller | .50 | .20 | .05 |
| ☐ 9 Pete Kugler | .50 | .20 | .05 |

| ☐ 10 Ronnie Lott | 2.00 | .80 | .20 |
|---|---|---|---|
| ☐ 11 Joe Montana | 9.00 | 3.75 | .90 |
| ☐ 12 Tom Rathman | 2.00 | .80 | .20 |
| ☐ 13 Jerry Rice | 7.50 | 3.00 | .75 |
| ☐ 14 Jeff Stover | .50 | .20 | .05 |
| ☐ 15 Keena Turner | .60 | .24 | .06 |
| ☐ 16 Bill Walsh CO | 1.25 | .50 | .12 |
| ☐ 17 Michael Walter | .50 | .20 | .05 |
| ☐ 18 Mike Wilson | .50 | .20 | .05 |
| ☐ 19 Eric Wright | .60 | .24 | .06 |
| ☐ 20 Steve Young | 4.00 | 1.60 | .40 |

## 1988 Police Giants

The 1988 Police New York Giants set contains 12 unnumbered cards measuring approximately 2 3/4" by 4 1/8". There are 11 player cards and one coach card. The backs have safety tips. The cards are listed below in alphabetical order by subject's name. The Giants team name and helmets appear above the player photo which differentiates this set from the very similar 1987 Police Giants set.

|  | MINT | EXC | G-VG |
|---|---|---|---|
| COMPLETE SET (12) | 50.00 | 20.00 | 5.00 |
| COMMON PLAYER (1-12) | 3.00 | 1.20 | .30 |
| ☐ 1 Bill Ard | 3.00 | 1.20 | .30 |
| ☐ 2 Jim Burt | 3.00 | 1.20 | .30 |
| ☐ 3 Harry Carson | 6.00 | 2.40 | .60 |
| ☐ 4 Maurice Carthon | 4.00 | 1.60 | .40 |
| ☐ 5 Leonard Marshall | 5.00 | 2.00 | .50 |
| ☐ 6 George Martin | 4.00 | 1.60 | .40 |
| ☐ 7 Phil McConkey | 4.00 | 1.60 | .40 |
| ☐ 8 Joe Morris | 5.00 | 2.00 | .50 |
| ☐ 9 Karl Nelson | 3.00 | 1.20 | .30 |
| ☐ 10 Bart Oates | 4.00 | 1.60 | .40 |
| ☐ 11 Bill Parcells CO | 6.00 | 2.40 | .60 |
| ☐ 12 Phil Simms | 10.00 | 4.00 | 1.00 |

## 1988 Police Lions

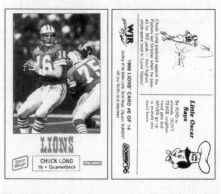

The 1988 Police Detroit Lions set contains 14 numbered cards measuring approximately 2 5/8" by 4 1/8". There are 13 single player cards plus one for Detroit's top three 1988 draft picks. The backs have career highlights and safety tips. The Lions team name appears below the player photo which differentiates this set from the similar-looking 1987 Police Lions set.

| | MINT | EXC | G-VG |
|---|---|---|---|
| COMPLETE SET (14)........................ | 5.00 | 2.00 | .50 |
| COMMON PLAYER (1-14)................ | .50 | .20 | .05 |
| ☐ 1 Rob Rubick ................................ | .50 | .20 | .05 |
| ☐ 2 Paul Butcher ............................. | .50 | .20 | .05 |
| ☐ 3 Pete Mandley ............................ | .60 | .24 | .06 |
| ☐ 4 Jimmy Williams ......................... | .50 | .20 | .05 |
| ☐ 5 Harvey Salem ........................... | .60 | .24 | .06 |
| ☐ 6 Chuck Long .............................. | .75 | .30 | .07 |
| ☐ 7 Pat Carter ................................ | 1.00 | .40 | .10 |
| Bennie Blades | | | |
| Chris Spielman | | | |
| ☐ 8 Jerry Ball ................................. | .75 | .30 | .07 |
| ☐ 9 Lomas Brown............................ | .60 | .24 | .06 |
| ☐ 10 Dennis Gibson ........................ | .50 | .20 | .05 |
| ☐ 11 Jim Arnold ............................. | .50 | .20 | .05 |
| ☐ 12 Michael Cofer .......................... | .50 | .20 | .05 |
| ☐ 13 James Jones ........................... | .60 | .24 | .06 |
| ☐ 14 Steve Mott.............................. | .50 | .20 | .05 |

## 1988 Police Packers

87 • Walter Stanley

The 1988 Police Green Bay Packers set contains 25 cards measuring approximately 2 3/4" by 4". There are 24 player cards and one coach card. The backs have football tips and safety tips. The cards are unnumbered so they are listed below in alphabetical order.

| | MINT | EXC | G-VG |
|---|---|---|---|
| COMPLETE SET (25)........................ | 10.00 | 4.00 | 1.00 |
| COMMON PLAYER (1-25)................ | .40 | .16 | .04 |
| ☐ 1 John Anderson........................... | .60 | .24 | .06 |
| ☐ 2 Jerry Boyarsky.......................... | .40 | .16 | .04 |
| ☐ 3 Don Bracken ............................ | .40 | .16 | .04 |
| ☐ 4 Dave Brown .............................. | .50 | .20 | .05 |
| ☐ 5 Mark Cannon............................ | .50 | .20 | .05 |
| ☐ 6 Alphonso Carreker ..................... | .40 | .16 | .04 |
| ☐ 7 Paul Ott Carruth ....................... | .40 | .16 | .04 |
| ☐ 8 Kenneth Davis .......................... | 1.00 | .40 | .10 |
| ☐ 9 John Dorsey ............................. | .40 | .16 | .04 |
| ☐ 10 Brent Fullwood ........................ | .60 | .24 | .06 |
| ☐ 11 Tiger Greene ........................... | .40 | .16 | .04 |
| ☐ 12 Ron Hallstrom .......................... | .40 | .16 | .04 |
| ☐ 13 Tim Harris ............................... | 1.00 | .40 | .10 |
| ☐ 14 Johnny Holland ........................ | .60 | .24 | .06 |
| ☐ 15 Lindy Infante CO ...................... | .75 | .30 | .07 |
| ☐ 16 Mark Lee................................. | .60 | .24 | .06 |
| ☐ 17 Don Majkowski ........................ | 1.25 | .50 | .12 |
| ☐ 18 Rich Moran .............................. | .40 | .16 | .04 |
| ☐ 19 Mark Murphy ........................... | .50 | .20 | .05 |
| ☐ 20 Ken Ruettgers ......................... | .60 | .24 | .06 |
| ☐ 21 Walter Stanley ......................... | .75 | .30 | .07 |
| ☐ 22 Keith Uecker ........................... | .40 | .16 | .04 |
| ☐ 23 Ed West.................................. | .60 | .24 | .06 |
| ☐ 24 Randy Wright ........................... | .50 | .20 | .05 |
| ☐ 25 Max Zendejas .......................... | .40 | .16 | .04 |

## 1988 Police Raiders

The 1988 Police Los Angeles Raiders set contains 12 numbered cards measuring approximately 2 3/4" by 4 1/8". There are 11 player cards and one coach card. The backs have biographical information and safety tips. The set was sponsored by Texaco and the Los Angeles Raiders.

| | MINT | EXC | G-VG |
|---|---|---|---|
| COMPLETE SET (12)........................ | 8.00 | 3.25 | .80 |
| COMMON PLAYER (1-12)................ | .40 | .16 | .04 |
| ☐ 1 Vann McElroy ........................... | .40 | .16 | .04 |
| ☐ 2 Bill Pickel ................................ | .40 | .16 | .04 |

34 BO JACKSON, RB

| | MINT | EXC | G-VG |
|---|---|---|---|
| ☐ 3 Marcus Allen ............................ | 1.50 | .60 | .15 |
| ☐ 4 Rod Martin............................... | .50 | .20 | .05 |
| ☐ 5 Lionel Washington ..................... | .40 | .16 | .04 |
| ☐ 6 Don Mosebar............................ | .50 | .20 | .05 |
| ☐ 7 Reggie McKenzie....................... | .40 | .16 | .04 |
| ☐ 8 Todd Christensen ...................... | .75 | .30 | .07 |
| ☐ 9 Bo Jackson .............................. | 4.00 | 1.60 | .40 |
| ☐ 10 James Lofton ........................... | 1.50 | .60 | .15 |
| ☐ 11 Howie Long............................. | .75 | .30 | .07 |
| ☐ 12 Mike Shanahan CO................. | .50 | .20 | .05 |

## 1988 Police Redskins

The 1988 Police Washington Redskins set contains 16 player cards measuring approximately 2 5/8" by 4 1/8". The fronts feature color action photos. The backs feature career highlights and safety tips. The Redskins team name appearing above the photo on the card front differentiates this set from other similar-looking Police Redskins sets.

| | MINT | EXC | G-VG |
|---|---|---|---|
| COMPLETE SET (16)........................ | 5.00 | 2.00 | .50 |
| COMMON PLAYER (1-16)................ | .35 | .14 | .03 |
| ☐ 1 Jeff Bostic .............................. | .50 | .20 | .05 |
| ☐ 2 Dave Butz ............................... | .50 | .20 | .05 |
| ☐ 3 Gary Clark............................... | .75 | .30 | .07 |
| ☐ 4 Brian Davis.............................. | .50 | .20 | .05 |
| ☐ 5 Joe Jacoby.............................. | .50 | .20 | .05 |
| ☐ 6 Markus Koch............................ | .35 | .14 | .03 |
| ☐ 7 Charles Mann........................... | .50 | .20 | .05 |
| ☐ 8 Wilber Marshall ........................ | .60 | .24 | .06 |
| ☐ 9 Mark May ................................ | .35 | .14 | .03 |
| ☐ 10 Raleigh McKenzie..................... | .35 | .14 | .03 |
| ☐ 11 Art Monk................................. | 1.00 | .40 | .10 |
| ☐ 12 Ricky Sanders.......................... | .75 | .30 | .07 |
| ☐ 13 Alvin Walton ............................ | .35 | .14 | .03 |
| ☐ 14 Don Warren............................. | .50 | .20 | .05 |
| ☐ 15 Barry Wilburn........................... | .50 | .20 | .05 |
| ☐ 16 Doug Williams.......................... | .75 | .30 | .07 |

## 1988 Police Seahawks

The 1988 Police Seattle Seahawks set contains 16 cards measuring approximately 2 5/8" by 4 1/8". There are 15 player cards and one coach card. The fronts have gray borders and color photos. The backs have safety tips. Terry Taylor's card was pulled from distribution after his suspension from the team. This unnumbered set is listed alphabetically below for convenience.

|                            | MINT  | EXC  | G-VG |
|----------------------------|-------|------|------|
| COMPLETE SET (15)          | 15.00 | 6.00 | 1.50 |
| COMMON PLAYER (1-15)       | .50   | .20  | .05  |
| ☐ 1 Brian Bosworth         | 1.00  | .40  | .10  |
| ☐ 2 Jeff Bryant            | .60   | .24  | .06  |
| ☐ 3 Ray Butler             | .60   | .24  | .06  |
| ☐ 4 Jacob Green            | .75   | .30  | .07  |
| ☐ 5 Patrick Hunter         | .60   | .24  | .06  |
| ☐ 6 Norm Johnson           | .60   | .24  | .06  |
| ☐ 7 Chuck Knox CO          | .75   | .30  | .07  |
| ☐ 8 Dave Krieg             | 1.25  | .50  | .12  |
| ☐ 9 Steve Largent          | 2.50  | 1.00 | .25  |
| ☐ 10 Ron Mattes            | .50   | .20  | .05  |
| ☐ 11 Bryan Millard         | .50   | .20  | .05  |
| ☐ 12 Paul Moyer            | .50   | .20  | .05  |
| ☐ 13 Terry Taylor SP       | 2.50  | 1.00 | .25  |
| ☐ 14 Curt Warner           | .75   | .30  | .07  |
| ☐ 15 John L. Williams      | 1.25  | .50  | .12  |
| ☐ 16 Fredd Young SP        | 6.00  | 2.40 | .60  |

## 1988 Police Steelers

The 1988 Police Pittsburgh Steelers set contains 16 player cards measuring approximately 2 5/8" by 4 1/8". The fronts show the players in uniform but not wearing helmets. The backs have definitions of football terms and safety tips. This unnumbered set is listed alphabetically below for convenience. The 1988 Police Steelers set is distinguishable from the 1985-87 Police Steelers sets by the Steelers helmet on back having three white diamonds instead of one white and two black diamonds.

|                            | MINT | EXC  | G-VG |
|----------------------------|------|------|------|
| COMPLETE SET (16)          | 5.00 | 2.00 | .50  |
| COMMON PLAYER (1-16)       | .35  | .14  | .03  |
| ☐ 1 Gary Anderson          | .50  | .20  | .05  |
| ☐ 2 Bubby Brister          | .75  | .30  | .07  |
| ☐ 3 Thomas Everett         | .60  | .24  | .06  |
| ☐ 4 Delton Hall            | .35  | .14  | .03  |
| ☐ 5 Bryan Hinkle           | .50  | .20  | .05  |
| ☐ 6 Tunch Ilkin            | .35  | .14  | .03  |
| ☐ 7 Earnest Jackson        | .50  | .20  | .05  |
| ☐ 8 Louis Lipps            | .60  | .24  | .06  |
| ☐ 9 David Little           | .35  | .14  | .03  |
| ☐ 10 Mike Merriweather     | .50  | .20  | .05  |
| ☐ 11 Frank Pollard         | .35  | .14  | .03  |
| ☐ 12 John Rienstra         | .35  | .14  | .03  |
| ☐ 13 Mike Webster          | .75  | .30  | .07  |

| ☐ 14 Keith Willis          | .35  | .14  | .03  |
| ☐ 15 Craig Wolfley         | .35  | .14  | .03  |
| ☐ 16 Rod Woodson           | 1.25 | .50  | .12  |

## 1988 Police Vikings

The 1988 Police Minnesota Vikings set contains 12 numbered cards measuring approximately 2 5/8" by 4 1/8". There are nine cards of current players, plus one checklist card, one "Vikings Defense" card, and one of "All-Time Great" Paul Krause.

|                            | MINT | EXC  | G-VG |
|----------------------------|------|------|------|
| COMPLETE SET (12)          | 5.00 | 2.00 | .50  |
| COMMON PLAYER (1-12)       | .40  | .16  | .04  |
| ☐ 1 Vikings Offense        | .60  | .24  | .06  |
| (Checklist on back)        |      |      |      |
| ☐ 2 Jesse Solomon          | .50  | .20  | .05  |
| ☐ 3 Kirk Lowdermilk        | .40  | .16  | .04  |
| ☐ 4 Darrin Nelson          | .60  | .24  | .06  |
| ☐ 5 Chris Doleman          | 1.00 | .40  | .10  |
| ☐ 6 D.J. Dozier            | .50  | .20  | .05  |
| ☐ 7 Gary Zimmerman         | .75  | .30  | .07  |
| ☐ 8 Allen Rice             | .40  | .16  | .04  |
| ☐ 9 Joey Browner           | .75  | .30  | .07  |
| ☐ 10 Anthony Carter        | 1.25 | .50  | .12  |
| ☐ 11 Vikings Defense       | .40  | .16  | .04  |
| ☐ 12 Paul Krause           | 1.00 | .40  | .10  |
| (All-Time Great)           |      |      |      |

## 1989 Police Bills

This eight-card set of Buffalo Bills is numbered in the upper right corner of each reverse. Cards measure approximately 2 1/2" by 3 1/2". The set was sponsored by the Buffalo Bills, Erie County Sheriff's Department, Louis Rich Turkey Products, and WBEN Radio. Uniform numbers are printed on the card front along with the player's name and position. The photos in the set were taken by several photographers, each of whom is credited on the lower right front beside the respective photo.

|                            | MINT | EXC  | G-VG |
|----------------------------|------|------|------|
| COMPLETE SET (8)           | 9.00 | 3.75 | .90  |
| COMMON PLAYER (1-8)        | .60  | .24  | .06  |
| ☐ 1 Leon Seals             | .75  | .30  | .07  |
| ☐ 2 Thurman Thomas         | 6.00 | 2.40 | .60  |

|                          | MINT  | EXC  | G-VG |
|--------------------------|-------|------|------|
| ☐ 3 Jim Ritcher          | .75   | .30  | .07  |
| ☐ 4 Scott Norwood        | .60   | .24  | .06  |
| ☐ 5 Darryl Talley        | 1.25  | .50  | .12  |
| ☐ 6 Nate Odomes          | .75   | .30  | .07  |
| ☐ 7 Leonard Smith        | .60   | .24  | .06  |
| ☐ 8 Ray Bentley          | .75   | .30  | .07  |

## 1989 Police Buccaneers

This ten-card set measures 2 5/8" by 4 1/8" and features members of the Tampa Bay Buccaneers. The fronts of the cards feature an action color shot along with the identification of the player and his position and uniform number. The back of the card features biographical information, some text, one line of career statistics, and the card number. This set was sponsored by IMC Fertilizer, Inc. and the Polk County Law Enforcement Office.

|                          | MINT  | EXC  | G-VG |
|--------------------------|-------|------|------|
| COMPLETE SET (10)        | 15.00 | 6.00 | 1.50 |
| COMMON PLAYER (1-10)     | 1.25  | .50  | .12  |
| ☐ 1 Vinny Testaverde     | 5.00  | 2.00 | .50  |
| ☐ 2 Mark Carrier         | 4.00  | 1.60 | .40  |
| ☐ 3 Randy Grimes         | 1.25  | .50  | .12  |
| ☐ 4 Paul Gruber          | 2.00  | .80  | .20  |
| ☐ 5 Ron Hall             | 2.00  | .80  | .20  |
| ☐ 6 William Howard       | 1.25  | .50  | .12  |
| ☐ 7 Curt Jarvis          | 1.25  | .50  | .12  |
| ☐ 8 Ervin Randle         | 1.25  | .50  | .12  |
| ☐ 9 Ricky Reynolds       | 2.00  | .80  | .20  |
| ☐ 10 Rob Taylor          | 1.25  | .50  | .12  |

## 1989 Police Cardinals

The 1989 Police Phoenix Cardinals set contains 15 cards measuring approximately 2 5/8" by 4 3/16". The fronts have white borders and color action photos; the vertically oriented backs have brief bios, career highlights, and safety messages. The set features members of the Phoenix Cardinals. The set was also sponsored by Louis Rich Meats and KTSP-TV. The cards are unnumbered except for uniform number which is prominently displayed on both sides of the card. Two cards were given out every two weeks during the season. It has been reported that 1.6 million cards were produced; 100,000 of each player. Derek Kennard's card was supposedly withdrawn at some time during the promotion after he was arrested. Reportedly, Freddie Joe Nunn was also planned for inclusion in this set but was withdrawn as well.

|                          | MINT  | EXC  | G-VG |
|--------------------------|-------|------|------|
| COMPLETE SET (15)        | 20.00 | 8.00 | 2.00 |
| COMMON PLAYER            | .75   | .30  | .07  |
| ☐ 5 Gary Hogeboom        | 1.25  | .50  | .12  |
| ☐ 24 Ron Wolfley         | 1.00  | .40  | .10  |
| ☐ 30 Stump Mitchell      | 1.25  | .50  | .12  |
| ☐ 31 Earl Ferrell        | .75   | .30  | .07  |
| ☐ 36 Vai Sikahema        | 1.25  | .50  | .12  |
| ☐ 43 Lonnie Young        | 1.00  | .40  | .10  |
| ☐ 46 Tim McDonald        | 2.00  | .80  | .20  |
| ☐ 65 David Galloway      | .75   | .30  | .07  |
| ☐ 67 Luis Sharpe         | 1.00  | .40  | .10  |
| ☐ 70 Derek Kennard SP    | 7.50  | 3.00 | .75  |
| ☐ 79 Bob Clasby          | .75   | .30  | .07  |
| ☐ 80 Robert Awalt        | 1.00  | .40  | .10  |
| ☐ 81 Roy Green           | 2.00  | .80  | .20  |
| ☐ 84 J.T. Smith          | 1.50  | .60  | .15  |
| ☐ 85 Jay Novacek         | 4.00  | 1.60 | .40  |

## 1989 Police Chargers

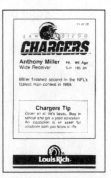

The 1989 Police San Diego Chargers set contains 12 cards measuring approximately 2 5/8" by 4 3/16". The fronts have white borders and color action photos; the vertically oriented backs have brief bios, career highlights, and safety messages. The set was sponsored by Louis Rich Co. The set was given away in two six-card panels; the first group at the Chargers' October 22nd home game and the other at the November 5th game. The cards are numbered on the back.

|                          | MINT  | EXC  | G-VG |
|--------------------------|-------|------|------|
| COMPLETE SET (12)        | 8.00  | 3.25 | .80  |
| COMMON PLAYER (1-12)     | .60   | .24  | .06  |
| ☐ 1 Tim Spencer          | .75   | .30  | .07  |
| ☐ 2 Vencie Glenn         | .60   | .24  | .06  |
| ☐ 3 Gill Byrd            | .75   | .30  | .07  |
| ☐ 4 Jim McMahon          | 1.50  | .60  | .15  |
| ☐ 5 David Richards       | .75   | .30  | .07  |
| ☐ 6 Don Macek            | .60   | .24  | .06  |
| ☐ 7 Billy Ray Smith      | .75   | .30  | .07  |
| ☐ 8 Gary Plummer         | .60   | .24  | .06  |
| ☐ 9 Lee Williams         | 1.00  | .40  | .10  |
| ☐ 10 Leslie O'Neal       | 1.25  | .50  | .12  |
| ☐ 11 Anthony Miller      | 2.50  | 1.00 | .25  |
| ☐ 12 Broderick Thompson  | .60   | .24  | .06  |

## 1989 Police Chiefs

The 1989 Police Kansas City Chiefs set contains ten cards measuring approximately 2 5/8" by 4 1/8". The fronts have white borders and color action photos; the horizontally-oriented backs have safety tips. The set was sponsored by Western Auto and KCTV Channel 5. These cards were printed on very thin stock. The cards are numbered on the back.

| | MINT | EXC | G-VG |
|---|---|---|---|
| COMPLETE SET (10) | 5.00 | 2.00 | .50 |
| COMMON PLAYER (1-10) | .50 | .20 | .05 |
| | | | |
| ☐ 1 Marty Schottenheimer CO | .75 | .30 | .07 |
| ☐ 2 Irv Eatman | .50 | .20 | .05 |
| ☐ 3 Kevin Ross | .60 | .24 | .06 |
| ☐ 4 Bill Maas | .60 | .24 | .06 |
| ☐ 5 Chiefs Cheerleaders | .60 | .24 | .06 |
| ☐ 6 Carlos Carson | .60 | .24 | .06 |
| ☐ 7 Steve DeBerg | 1.00 | .40 | .10 |
| ☐ 8 Jonathan Hayes | .60 | .24 | .06 |
| ☐ 9 Deron Cherry | .75 | .30 | .07 |
| ☐ 10 Dino Hackett | .60 | .24 | .06 |

# 1989 Police Colts

The 1989 Police Indianapolis Colts set contains nine numbered cards measuring approximately 2 5/8" by 4 1/8". The fronts have white borders and color action photos; the horizontally-oriented backs have safety tips. These cards were printed on very thin stock. The set was also sponsored by Louis Rich Co. and WTHR-TV-13. According to sources, at least 50,000 sets were given away. One card was given to young persons each week during the season.

| | MINT | EXC | G-VG |
|---|---|---|---|
| COMPLETE SET (9) | 7.00 | 2.80 | .70 |
| COMMON PLAYER (1-9) | .60 | .24 | .06 |
| | | | |
| ☐ 1 Colts Team Card | 1.00 | .40 | .10 |
| ☐ 2 Dean Biasucci | .60 | .24 | .06 |
| ☐ 3 Andre Rison | 3.00 | 1.20 | .30 |
| ☐ 4 Chris Chandler | 1.25 | .50 | .12 |
| ☐ 5 O'Brien Alston | .75 | .30 | .07 |
| ☐ 6 Ray Donaldson | .60 | .24 | .06 |
| ☐ 7 Donnell Thompson | .75 | .30 | .07 |
| ☐ 8 Fredd Young | .75 | .30 | .07 |
| ☐ 9 Eric Dickerson | 2.00 | .80 | .20 |

# 1989 Police Eagles

This nine-card set was distributed by the New Jersey State Police in Trenton, New Jersey. These unnumbered cards measure approximately 8 1/2" by 11" and feature action player photos of members of the Philadelphia Eagles inside white borders. Player information is centered beneath the picture between the New Jersey State Police Crime Prevention Resource Center emblem and Security Savings Bank logo. The back carries the title "Alcohol and Other Drugs: Facts and Myths" and features five questions and answers on this topic. Sponsor and team logo at the bottom round out the back. The cards are unnumbered and checklisted below alphabetically. The set is tough to find because, reportedly, it was issued after the season.

| | MINT | EXC | G-VG |
|---|---|---|---|
| COMPLETE SET (9) | 40.00 | 16.00 | 4.00 |
| COMMON PLAYER (1-9) | 3.00 | 1.20 | .30 |
| | | | |
| ☐ 1 Cris Carter | 10.00 | 4.00 | 1.00 |
| ☐ 2 Gregg Garrity | 3.00 | 1.20 | .30 |

| | | | |
|---|---|---|---|
| ☐ 3 Mike Golic | 4.00 | 1.60 | .40 |
| ☐ 4 Keith Jackson | 9.00 | 3.75 | .90 |
| ☐ 5 Clyde Simmons | 6.00 | 2.40 | .60 |
| ☐ 6 John Teltschik | 3.00 | 1.20 | .30 |
| ☐ 7 Anthony Toney | 4.00 | 1.60 | .40 |
| ☐ 8 Andre Waters | 4.00 | 1.60 | .40 |
| ☐ 9 Luis Zendejas | 3.00 | 1.20 | .30 |

# 1989 Police Lions

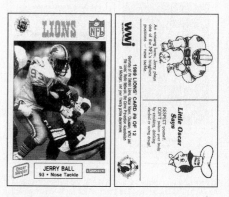

The 1989 Police Detroit Lions set contains 12 numbered cards measuring approximately 2 5/8" by 4 1/8". The set was also sponsored by Oscar Meyer. The fronts have white borders and color action photos; some are horizontally oriented, others are vertically oriented. The horizontally oriented backs have safety tips and brief career highlights. These cards were printed on very thin stock. The set is notable for a card of Barry Sanders, showing a photo of him at his postdraft press conference. It has been reported that three million cards were given away during this program by police officers in Michigan and Ontario.

| | MINT | EXC | G-VG |
|---|---|---|---|
| COMPLETE SET (12) | 10.00 | 4.00 | 1.00 |
| COMMON PLAYER (1-12) | .35 | .14 | .03 |
| | | | |
| ☐ 1 George Jamison | .35 | .14 | .03 |
| ☐ 2 Wayne Fontes CO | .50 | .20 | .05 |
| ☐ 3 Kevin Glover | .35 | .14 | .03 |
| ☐ 4 Chris Spielman | .75 | .30 | .07 |
| ☐ 5 Eddie Murray | .50 | .20 | .05 |
| ☐ 6 Bennie Blades | .75 | .30 | .07 |
| ☐ 7 Joe Milinchik | .35 | .14 | .03 |
| ☐ 8 Michael Cofer | .50 | .20 | .05 |
| ☐ 9 Jerry Ball | .60 | .24 | .06 |
| ☐ 10 Dennis Gibson | .35 | .14 | .03 |
| ☐ 11 Barry Sanders | 7.50 | 3.00 | .75 |
| ☐ 12 Jim Arnold | .35 | .14 | .03 |

# 1989 Police Packers

The 1989 Police Green Bay Packers set contains 15 numbered cards measuring approximately 2 3/4" by 4". The fronts have white borders and color action photos bordered in Packers yellow; the vertically oriented backs have safety tips. These cards were printed on very thin stock. Sterling Sharpe appears in his Rookie Card year.

| | MINT | EXC | G-VG |
|---|---|---|---|
| COMPLETE SET (15)........................ | 6.00 | 2.40 | .60 |
| COMMON PLAYER (1-15)................ | .35 | .14 | .03 |

| | | MINT | EXC | G-VG |
|---|---|---|---|---|
| ☐ 1 | Lindy Infante CO ............... | .50 | .20 | .05 |
| ☐ 2 | Don Majkowski.................. | .75 | .30 | .07 |
| ☐ 3 | Brent Fullwood................. | .50 | .20 | .05 |
| ☐ 4 | Mark Lee........................... | .50 | .20 | .05 |
| ☐ 5 | Dave Brown...................... | .50 | .20 | .05 |
| ☐ 6 | Mark Murphy..................... | .50 | .20 | .05 |
| ☐ 7 | Johnny Holland................. | .50 | .20 | .05 |
| ☐ 8 | John Anderson.................. | .50 | .20 | .05 |
| ☐ 9 | Ken Ruettgers................... | .50 | .20 | .05 |
| ☐ 10 | Sterling Sharpe................ | 3.00 | 1.20 | .30 |
| ☐ 11 | Ed West........................... | .50 | .20 | .05 |
| ☐ 12 | Walter Stanley.................. | .50 | .20 | .05 |
| ☐ 13 | Brian Noble...................... | .50 | .20 | .05 |
| ☐ 14 | Shawn Patterson.............. | .35 | .14 | .03 |
| ☐ 15 | Tim Harris........................ | .75 | .30 | .07 |

## 1989 Police Rams

John Robinson Coach
1 of 16

This 16-card standard size (2 1/2" by 3 1/2") set was issued in an uncut (perforated) sheet of 16 numbered cards which feature an action photo of various members of the 1989 Rams on the front and a football tip along with a safety tip on the back of the card. The safety tip features the popular anti-crime mascot McGruff. There was also a coupon for Frito-Lay products on the bottom of the sheet. The set was also sponsored by 7-Eleven stores.

| | MINT | EXC | G-VG |
|---|---|---|---|
| COMPLETE SET (16)........................ | 15.00 | 6.00 | 1.50 |
| COMMON PLAYER (1-16)................ | 1.00 | .40 | .10 |

| | | MINT | EXC | G-VG |
|---|---|---|---|---|
| ☐ 1 | John Robinson CO .............. | 2.00 | .80 | .20 |
| ☐ 2 | Jim Everett....................... | 2.50 | 1.00 | .25 |
| ☐ 3 | Doug Smith....................... | 1.25 | .50 | .12 |
| ☐ 4 | Duval Love........................ | 1.00 | .40 | .10 |
| ☐ 5 | Henry Ellard...................... | 2.00 | .80 | .20 |
| ☐ 6 | Mel Owens........................ | 1.25 | .50 | .12 |
| ☐ 7 | Jerry Gray......................... | 1.25 | .50 | .12 |
| ☐ 8 | Kevin Greene..................... | 1.50 | .60 | .15 |
| ☐ 9 | Vince Newsome.................. | 1.00 | .40 | .10 |
| ☐ 10 | Irv Pankey........................ | 1.00 | .40 | .10 |
| ☐ 11 | Tom Newberry................... | 1.50 | .60 | .15 |
| ☐ 12 | Pete Holohan.................... | 1.00 | .40 | .10 |
| ☐ 13 | Mike Lansford.................... | 1.00 | .40 | .10 |
| ☐ 14 | Greg Bell.......................... | 1.50 | .60 | .15 |
| ☐ 15 | Jackie Slater..................... | 1.50 | .60 | .15 |
| ☐ 16 | Dale Hatcher..................... | 1.00 | .40 | .10 |

## 1989 Police Redskins

The 1989 Police Washington Redskins set contains 16 cards measuring approximately 2 5/8" by 4 1/8". The fronts have maroon borders and color action photos; the vertically oriented backs have safety tips, bios, and career highlights. These cards were printed on very thin stock. The cards are unnumbered, so therefore are listed below according to uniform number.

| | MINT | EXC | G-VG |
|---|---|---|---|
| COMPLETE SET (16)........................ | 5.00 | 2.00 | .50 |
| COMMON PLAYER........................ | .35 | .14 | .03 |

| | | MINT | EXC | G-VG |
|---|---|---|---|---|
| ☐ 11 | Mark Rypien...................... | 1.00 | .40 | .10 |
| ☐ 17 | Doug Williams................... | .50 | .20 | .05 |
| ☐ 21 | Earnest Byner................... | .60 | .24 | .06 |

### 83 RICKY SANDERS

HT: 5-11    Pos: Wide Receiver    Wt: 180
NFL Exp: 4th Yr
College: SW Texas St.

Selected as the Redskins' 1988 Most Valuable Player by his peers, Ricky enjoyed an outstanding season last year. He led the team with 73 receptions for 1,148 yards, and his 12 touchdown receptions tied the club record for most touchdowns in a season. Ricky caught five passes for 143 yards against Pittsburgh, including a 55-yarder for a touchdown. In Week 5 against the Giants, he caught seven passes for 141 yards and two touchdowns.

*Ricky Sanders Says: "Friends who pressure you into breaking the law are not really friends. Choose your friends with care. It's your future."*

DID YOU KNOW: That in high school in Belton, Tx, Ricky qualified for the state meet in the pole vault, hurdles, and long jump!

Mobil®        5

| | | MINT | EXC | G-VG |
|---|---|---|---|---|
| ☐ 22 | Jamie Morris..................... | .35 | .14 | .03 |
| ☐ 28 | Darrell Green..................... | .75 | .30 | .07 |
| ☐ 34 | Brian Davis........................ | .50 | .20 | .05 |
| ☐ 37 | Gerald Riggs..................... | .60 | .24 | .06 |
| ☐ 50 | Ravin Caldwell................... | .50 | .20 | .05 |
| ☐ 52 | Neal Olkewicz.................... | .35 | .14 | .03 |
| ☐ 58 | Wilber Marshall................. | .60 | .24 | .06 |
| ☐ 73 | Mark May.......................... | .35 | .14 | .03 |
| ☐ 74 | Markus Koch...................... | .35 | .14 | .03 |
| ☐ 81 | Art Monk........................... | 1.00 | .40 | .10 |
| ☐ 83 | Ricky Sanders................... | .75 | .30 | .07 |
| ☐ 84 | Gary Clark........................ | .75 | .30 | .07 |
| ☐ 85 | Don Warren....................... | .50 | .20 | .05 |

## 1989 Police Seahawks

Kelly Stouffer
Quarterback

TIPS from the SEAHAWKS

Washington State Crime Prevention Association

SUNRICH

Policemen are your friends. Let's join them and take a bite out of crime.

Kodak    1989    Coke

COURTESY OF THE ABOVE SPONSORS AND YOUR LOCAL LAW ENFORCEMENT AGENCY

The 1989 Police Seattle Seahawks set contains 16 cards measuring approximately 2 5/8" by 4 1/8". The fronts have light blue borders and color action photos; the vertically-oriented backs have safety tips. These cards were printed on very thin stock. The cards are unnumbered, so therefore are listed alphabetically by subject's name. The Largent card contains a list of Steve's records on the back instead of the typical safety tip found on all the other cards in the set.

| | MINT | EXC | G-VG |
|---|---|---|---|
| COMPLETE SET (16)........................ | 7.00 | 2.80 | .70 |
| COMMON PLAYER (1-16)................ | .40 | .16 | .04 |

| | | MINT | EXC | G-VG |
|---|---|---|---|---|
| ☐ 1 | Brian Blades..................... | 1.25 | .50 | .12 |
| ☐ 2 | Brian Bosworth.................. | .60 | .24 | .06 |
| ☐ 3 | Jeff Bryant........................ | .50 | .20 | .05 |
| ☐ 4 | Jacob Green...................... | .60 | .24 | .06 |
| ☐ 5 | Chuck Knox CO.................. | .60 | .24 | .06 |
| ☐ 6 | Dave Krieg........................ | 1.00 | .40 | .10 |
| ☐ 7 | Steve Largent.................... | 2.50 | 1.00 | .25 |
| ☐ 8 | Bryan Millard..................... | .40 | .16 | .04 |
| ☐ 9 | Rufus Porter...................... | .60 | .24 | .06 |
| ☐ 10 | Paul Moyer........................ | .40 | .16 | .04 |
| ☐ 11 | Eugene Robinson .............. | .50 | .20 | .05 |
| ☐ 12 | Ruben Rodriguez .............. | .40 | .16 | .04 |
| ☐ 13 | Kelly Stouffer.................... | .60 | .24 | .06 |
| ☐ 14 | Curt Warner...................... | .60 | .24 | .06 |
| ☐ 15 | John L. Williams................ | .75 | .30 | .07 |
| ☐ 16 | Tony Woods...................... | .60 | .24 | .06 |

## 1989 Police Steelers

The 1989 Police Pittsburgh Steelers set contains 16 cards measuring approximately 2 5/8" by 4 1/8". The fronts have white borders and color action photos; the vertically-oriented backs have safety tips. These cards were printed on very thin stock. The cards are unnumbered, so therefore are listed below according to uniform number. The card backs are subtitled "Steelers Tips '89". It has been reported that 175,000 cards of each player were given away by police officers in Western Pennsylvania.

|  | MINT | EXC | G-VG |
|---|---|---|---|
| COMPLETE SET (16) | 5.00 | 2.00 | .50 |
| COMMON PLAYER | .40 | .16 | .04 |
|  |  |  |  |
| ☐ 1 Gary Anderson | .50 | .20 | .05 |
| ☐ 6 Bubby Brister | .60 | .24 | .06 |
| ☐ 18 Harry Newsome | .40 | .16 | .04 |
| ☐ 24 Rodney Carter | .50 | .20 | .05 |
| ☐ 26 Rod Woodson | .75 | .30 | .07 |
| ☐ 27 Thomas Everett | .60 | .24 | .06 |
| ☐ 33 Merril Hoge | .60 | .24 | .06 |
| ☐ 53 Bryan Hinkle | .40 | .16 | .04 |
| ☐ 54 Hardy Nickerson | .50 | .20 | .05 |
| ☐ 62 Tunch Ilkin | .40 | .16 | .04 |
| ☐ 63 Dermontti Dawson | .50 | .20 | .05 |
| ☐ 74 Terry Long | .40 | .16 | .04 |
| ☐ 78 Tim Johnson | .40 | .16 | .04 |
| ☐ 83 Louis Lipps | .75 | .30 | .07 |
| ☐ 97 Aaron Jones | .40 | .16 | .04 |
| ☐ 98 Gerald Williams | .40 | .16 | .04 |

## 1989 Police Vikings

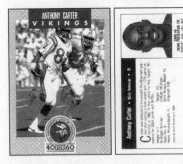

The 1989 Police Minnesota Vikings set contains ten standard-size (2 1/2" by 3 1/2") cards. The fronts have gray borders and color action photos; the horizontally oriented backs have safety tips, bios, and career highlights. It has been reported that 175,000 cards of each player were given away by the police officers in the state of Minnesota. The cards are numbered on the back.

|  | MINT | EXC | G-VG |
|---|---|---|---|
| COMPLETE SET (10) | 5.00 | 2.00 | .50 |
| COMMON PLAYER (1-10) | .50 | .20 | .05 |
|  |  |  |  |
| ☐ 1 Team Card | .60 | .24 | .06 |
| (schedule on back) |  |  |  |
| ☐ 2 Henry Thomas | .75 | .30 | .07 |
| ☐ 3 Rick Fenney | .60 | .24 | .06 |

| ☐ 4 Chuck Nelson | .50 | .20 | .05 |
|---|---|---|---|
| ☐ 5 Jim Gustafson | .50 | .20 | .05 |
| ☐ 6 Wade Wilson | 1.00 | .40 | .10 |
| ☐ 7 Randall McDaniel | .75 | .30 | .07 |
| ☐ 8 Jesse Solomon | .50 | .20 | .05 |
| ☐ 9 Anthony Carter | 1.00 | .40 | .10 |
| ☐ 10 Joe Kapp | 1.00 | .40 | .10 |
| (All-Time Great) |  |  |  |

## 1990 Police Bills

This eight-card set was sponsored by Blue Shield of Western New York, and its company logo graces both sides of the card. The oversized cards measure approximately 4" by 6". The color action player photos on the fronts have red borders on a white card face. The Bills' helmet and player identification appear above the picture, while biography is given below the picture. In black print, the back has career summary, statistics, and "Tips from the Sheriff" in the form of anti-drug and alcohol messages. The cards are unnumbered and checklisted below in alphabetical order.

|  | MINT | EXC | G-VG |
|---|---|---|---|
| COMPLETE SET (8) | 6.00 | 2.40 | .60 |
| COMMON PLAYER (1-8) | .50 | .20 | .05 |
|  |  |  |  |
| ☐ 1 Carlton Bailey | .75 | .30 | .07 |
| ☐ 2 Kirby Jackson | .50 | .20 | .05 |
| ☐ 3 Jim Kelly | 3.00 | 1.20 | .30 |
| ☐ 4 James Lofton | 1.25 | .50 | .12 |
| ☐ 5 Keith McKeller | .75 | .30 | .07 |
| ☐ 6 Mark Pike | .50 | .20 | .05 |
| ☐ 7 Andre Reed | 1.50 | .60 | .15 |
| ☐ 8 Jeff Wright | .75 | .30 | .07 |

## 1990 Police Cardinals

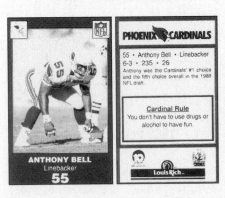

This 16-card police set was sponsored by Louis Rich Meats and KTSP-TV. The cards measure approximately 2 5/8" by 4 1/4". The color action player photos on the fronts have maroon borders, with player information below the pictures in the bottom border. The team and NFL logos overlay the upper corners of the pictures. The backs have biography, a "Cardinal Rule" in the form of a safety tip, and sponsor logos. The cards are unnumbered (except for the prominent display of the player's uniform number) and checklisted below in alphabetical order.

| | MINT | EXC | G-VG |
|---|---|---|---|
| COMPLETE SET (16)...................... | 15.00 | 6.00 | 1.50 |
| COMMON PLAYER (1-16)................ | .75 | .30 | .07 |
| ☐ 1 Anthony Bell......................... | 1.00 | .40 | .10 |
| ☐ 2 Joe Bugel CO....................... | 1.00 | .40 | .10 |
| ☐ 3 Rich Camarillo...................... | .75 | .30 | .07 |
| ☐ 4 Roy Green............................ | 2.00 | .80 | .20 |
| ☐ 5 Ken Harvey.......................... | 1.25 | .50 | .12 |
| ☐ 6 Eric Hill.............................. | 1.00 | .40 | .10 |
| ☐ 7 Tim McDonald...................... | 2.00 | .80 | .20 |
| ☐ 8 Tootie Robbins..................... | .75 | .30 | .07 |
| ☐ 9 Timm Rosenbach................... | 1.25 | .50 | .12 |
| ☐ 10 Luis Sharpe....................... | 1.00 | .40 | .10 |
| ☐ 11 Vai Sikahema..................... | 1.25 | .50 | .12 |
| ☐ 12 J.T. Smith......................... | 1.25 | .50 | .12 |
| ☐ 13 Lance Smith....................... | 1.00 | .40 | .10 |
| ☐ 14 Jim Wahler........................ | .75 | .30 | .07 |
| ☐ 15 Ron Wolfley....................... | 1.00 | .40 | .10 |
| ☐ 16 Lonnie Young..................... | 1.00 | .40 | .10 |

## 1990 Police Chargers

 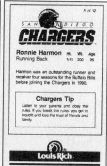

This 12-card set measures approximately 2 5/8" by 4 1/8" and features members of the 1990 San Diego Chargers. The set was sponsored by Louis Rich Meats. The card fronts have full-color photos framed by solid blue borders while the backs have brief biographies of the players and limited personal information. There is also a safety tip on the back of the card. The set was issued in two six-card panels or sheets (but is also found as individual cards). The cards are numbered on the back.

| | MINT | EXC | G-VG |
|---|---|---|---|
| COMPLETE SET (12)........................ | 7.00 | 2.80 | .70 |
| COMMON PLAYER (1-12)................. | .50 | .20 | .05 |
| ☐ 1 Martin Bayless ....................... | .50 | .20 | .05 |
| ☐ 2 Marion Butts .......................... | 1.25 | .50 | .12 |
| ☐ 3 Gill Byrd ............................... | .75 | .30 | .07 |
| ☐ 4 Burt Grossman........................ | .75 | .30 | .07 |
| ☐ 5 Ronnie Harmon....................... | 1.00 | .40 | .10 |
| ☐ 6 Anthony Miller........................ | 1.50 | .60 | .15 |
| ☐ 7 Leslie O'Neal ........................ | 1.00 | .40 | .10 |
| ☐ 8 Joe Phillips ........................... | .60 | .24 | .06 |
| ☐ 9 Gary Plummer........................ | .50 | .20 | .05 |
| ☐ 10 Billy Ray Smith..................... | .75 | .30 | .07 |
| ☐ 11 Billy Joe Tolliver.................... | 1.00 | .40 | .10 |
| ☐ 12 Lee Williams........................ | 1.00 | .40 | .10 |

## 1990 Police Colts

This eight-card set features members of the 1990 Indianapolis Colts. The cards in the set measure approximately 2 5/8" by 4 1/8" and have full-color action shots of the featured players on the front along with safety and crime-prevention tips on the back. The set was sponsored by Region Central Indiana Crime Stoppers, Louis Rich, and Station 13 WTHR. The cards are numbered on the back.

| | MINT | EXC | G-VG |
|---|---|---|---|
| COMPLETE SET (8)......................... | 5.00 | 2.00 | .50 |
| COMMON PLAYER (1-8).................. | .60 | .24 | .06 |
| ☐ 1 Harvey Armstrong.................... | .75 | .30 | .07 |
| ☐ 2 Pat Beach ............................. | .60 | .24 | .06 |
| ☐ 3 Albert Bentley ........................ | 1.00 | .40 | .10 |
| ☐ 4 Kevin Call ............................. | .60 | .24 | .06 |
| ☐ 5 Jeff George ........................... | 2.00 | .80 | .20 |

81 • PAT BEACH
Tight End  Ht: 6-4  Wt: 249
**INDIANAPOLIS COLTS**

| | | | |
|---|---|---|---|
| ☐ 6 Mike Prior ............................. | .60 | .24 | .06 |
| ☐ 7 Rohn Stark ............................ | .75 | .30 | .07 |
| ☐ 8 Clarence Verdin...................... | .75 | .30 | .07 |

## 1990 Police Eagles

Sponsored by the N.J. Crime Prevention Officer's Association and the New Jersey State Police Crime Prevention Resource Center, this 12-card set measures approximately 2 5/8" by 4 1/8" and features action player photos on a white card face. The team name appears above the photo between two helmet icons, and the player's name, position, and personal information appear below. The backs contains sponsor logos, safety tips, and the slogan "Take a bite out of crime" by McGruff the crime dog. The cards are unnumbered and checklisted below in alphabetical order.

| | MINT | EXC | G-VG |
|---|---|---|---|
| COMPLETE SET (12)........................ | 30.00 | 12.00 | 3.00 |
| COMMON CARD (1-12) ................... | 2.00 | .80 | .20 |
| ☐ 1 David Alexander...................... | 2.00 | .80 | .20 |
| ☐ 2 Eric Allen.............................. | 2.50 | 1.00 | .25 |
| ☐ 3 Randall Cunningham................ | 7.50 | 3.00 | .75 |
| ☐ 4 Keith Byars........................... | 4.00 | 1.60 | .40 |
| ☐ 5 James Feagles....................... | 2.00 | .80 | .20 |
| ☐ 6 Mike Golic............................ | 2.50 | 1.00 | .25 |
| ☐ 7 Keith Jackson........................ | 5.00 | 2.00 | .50 |
| ☐ 8 Rich Kotite CO....................... | 2.50 | 1.00 | .25 |
| ☐ 9 Roger Ruzek ......................... | 2.00 | .80 | .20 |
| ☐ 10 Mickey Shuler...................... | 2.50 | 1.00 | .25 |
| ☐ 11 Clyde Simmons..................... | 4.00 | 1.60 | .40 |
| ☐ 12 Reggie White........................ | 7.50 | 3.00 | .75 |

## 1990 Police Giants

This 12-card set was printed and distributed by the New Jersey State Police Crime Prevention Resource Center. The cards measure approximtely 2 3/4" by 4 1/8". The fronts display color action player photos bordered in white. The team name appears at the top between two representations of the team helmet, while player information is printed beneath the picture. In dark blue print on white, the backs carry logos, "Tips from the Giants" in the form of public service announcements, and the McGruff the Crime Dog "Take a Bite out of Crime" slogan. The cards are unnumbered and checklisted below in alphabetical order.

**Ottis Anderson**

|  | MINT | EXC | G-VG |
|---|---|---|---|
| COMPLETE SET (12) | 30.00 | 12.00 | 3.00 |
| COMMON CARD (1-12) | 2.00 | .80 | .20 |
| ☐ 1 Ottis Anderson | 4.00 | 1.60 | .40 |
| ☐ 2 Matt Bahr | 2.50 | 1.00 | .25 |
| ☐ 3 Eric Dorsey | 2.00 | .80 | .20 |
| ☐ 4 John Elliott | 2.00 | .80 | .20 |
| ☐ 5 Ray Handley CO | 2.50 | 1.00 | .25 |
| ☐ 6 Jeff Hostetler | 5.00 | 2.00 | .50 |
| ☐ 7 Erik Howard | 2.00 | .80 | .20 |
| ☐ 8 Pepper Johnson | 2.50 | 1.00 | .25 |
| ☐ 9 Leonard Marshall | 2.50 | 1.00 | .25 |
| ☐ 10 Bart Oates | 2.50 | 1.00 | .25 |
| ☐ 11 Gary Reasons | 2.00 | .80 | .20 |
| ☐ 12 Phil Simms | 7.50 | 3.00 | .75 |

## 1990 Police Lions

This 12-card set was issued by Oscar Mayer in conjunction with the Detroit Lions, Claussen, WWJ radio station, the Detroit Crime Prevention Society, and the Crime Prevention Association of Michigan. The fronts of the cards feature an action photo of the player on the front and a drawing of the player along with a brief note about the player on the back. In addition there is a safety tip from Little Oscar (the symbol for Oscar Mayer) on the back. The cards measure approximately 2 5/8" by 4 1/8". The cards are numbered on the back.

|  | MINT | EXC | G-VG |
|---|---|---|---|
| COMPLETE SET (12) | 5.00 | 2.00 | .50 |
| COMMON PLAYER (1-12) | .35 | .14 | .03 |
| ☐ 1 William White | .35 | .14 | .03 |
| ☐ 2 Chris Spielman | .60 | .24 | .06 |
| ☐ 3 Rodney Peete | 1.00 | .40 | .10 |
| ☐ 4 Jimmy Williams | .50 | .20 | .05 |
| ☐ 5 Bennie Blades | .60 | .24 | .06 |
| ☐ 6 Barry Sanders | 2.50 | 1.00 | .25 |
| ☐ 7 Jerry Ball | .60 | .24 | .06 |
| ☐ 8 Richard Johnson | .50 | .20 | .05 |
| ☐ 9 Michael Cofer | .35 | .14 | .03 |
| ☐ 10 Lomas Brown | .50 | .20 | .05 |
| ☐ 11 Joe Schmidt GM, Andre Ware, and Wayne Fontes CO | .75 | .30 | .07 |
| ☐ 12 Eddie Murray | .50 | .20 | .05 |

## 1990 Police Packers

This 20-card set, which measures approximately 2 3/4" by 4", was issued by police departments in Wisconsin and featured members of the 1990 Green Bay Packers. The fronts have white borders with a "Packers '90" title on the front and the name of the subject along with their position and NFL experience. The backs of the card feature a safety tip and small ads for the sponsors of the set.

|  | MINT | EXC | G-VG |
|---|---|---|---|
| COMPLETE SET (20) | 6.00 | 2.40 | .60 |
| COMMON PLAYER (1-20) | .25 | .10 | .02 |
| ☐ 1 Lindy Infante CO | .35 | .14 | .03 |
| ☐ 2 Keith Woodside | .35 | .14 | .03 |
| ☐ 3 Chris Jacke | .35 | .14 | .03 |
| ☐ 4 Chuck Cecil | .35 | .14 | .03 |
| ☐ 5 Tony Mandarich | .35 | .14 | .03 |
| ☐ 6 Brent Fullwood | .35 | .14 | .03 |
| ☐ 7 Robert Brown | .35 | .14 | .03 |
| ☐ 8 Scott Stephen | .35 | .14 | .03 |
| ☐ 9 Anthony Dilweg | .35 | .14 | .03 |
| ☐ 10 Mark Murphy | .25 | .10 | .02 |
| ☐ 11 Johnny Holland | .35 | .14 | .03 |
| ☐ 12 Sterling Sharpe | 2.00 | .80 | .20 |
| ☐ 13 Tim Harris | .50 | .20 | .05 |
| ☐ 14 Ed West | .35 | .14 | .03 |
| ☐ 15 Jeff Query | .35 | .14 | .03 |
| ☐ 16 Mark Lee | .35 | .14 | .03 |
| ☐ 17 Rich Moran | .25 | .10 | .02 |
| ☐ 18 Perry Kemp | .35 | .14 | .03 |
| ☐ 19 Brian Noble | .35 | .14 | .03 |
| ☐ 20 Dan Majkowksi | .50 | .20 | .05 |

## 1990 Police Redskins

This 16-card set, which measures approximately 2 5/8" by 4 1/8", features members of the 1990 Washington Redskins. This set features white borders surrounding full-color photos on the front and biographical information on the back along with a safety tip. The set was sponsored by Mobil Oil, PACT (Police and Citizens Together), and Fox-5 of Washington WTIC. We have checklisted this set alphabetically.

|  | MINT | EXC | G-VG |
|---|---|---|---|
| COMPLETE SET (16) | 4.00 | 1.60 | .40 |
| COMMON PLAYER (1-16) | .25 | .10 | .02 |

| | MINT | EXC | G-VG |
|---|---|---|---|
| ☐ 1 Todd Bowles | .35 | .14 | .03 |
| ☐ 2 Earnest Byner | .50 | .20 | .05 |
| ☐ 3 Ravin Caldwell | .25 | .10 | .02 |
| ☐ 4 Gary Clark | .60 | .24 | .06 |
| ☐ 5 Darrell Green | .50 | .20 | .05 |
| ☐ 6 Jimmie Johnson | .25 | .10 | .02 |
| ☐ 7 Jim Lachey | .50 | .20 | .05 |
| ☐ 8 Chip Lohmiller | .25 | .10 | .02 |
| ☐ 9 Charles Mann | .50 | .20 | .05 |
| ☐ 10 Greg Manusky | .25 | .10 | .02 |
| ☐ 11 Wilber Marshall | .50 | .20 | .05 |
| ☐ 12 Art Monk | .75 | .30 | .07 |
| ☐ 13 Gerald Riggs | .50 | .20 | .05 |
| ☐ 14 Mark Rypien | .60 | .24 | .06 |
| ☐ 15 Alvin Walton | .25 | .10 | .02 |
| ☐ 16 Don Warren | .35 | .14 | .03 |

## 1990 Police Seahawks

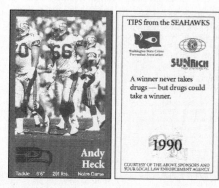

Tackle  6'6"  291 lbs.  Notre Dame
Andy Heck

TIPS from the SEAHAWKS

A winner never takes drugs — but drugs could take a winner.

1990

COURTESY OF THE ABOVE SPONSORS AND YOUR LOCAL LAW ENFORCEMENT AGENCY

This 16-card set was issued in the Seattle area to promote the various safety tips using members of the 1990 Seattle Seahawks. The cards measure approximately 2 5/8" by 4 1/8" and have solid green borders which frame a full-color photo of the player pictured. On the back is a safety tip. Since the cards are unnumbered, we have checklisted this set in alphabetical order.

| | MINT | EXC | G-VG |
|---|---|---|---|
| COMPLETE SET (16) | 5.00 | 2.00 | .50 |
| COMMON PLAYER (1-16) | .35 | .14 | .03 |
| | | | |
| ☐ 1 Brian Blades | .75 | .30 | .07 |
| ☐ 2 Grant Feasel | .35 | .14 | .03 |
| ☐ 3 Jacob Green | .60 | .24 | .06 |
| ☐ 4 Andy Heck | .50 | .20 | .05 |
| ☐ 5 James Jefferson | .50 | .20 | .05 |
| ☐ 6 Norm Johnson | .50 | .20 | .05 |
| ☐ 7 Cortez Kennedy | 1.50 | .60 | .15 |
| ☐ 8 Chuck Knox CO | .60 | .24 | .06 |
| ☐ 9 Dave Krieg | .75 | .30 | .07 |
| ☐ 10 Travis McNeal | .50 | .20 | .05 |
| ☐ 11 Bryan Millard | .35 | .14 | .03 |
| ☐ 12 Rufus Porter | .50 | .20 | .05 |
| ☐ 13 Paul Skansi | .50 | .20 | .05 |
| ☐ 14 John L. Williams | .75 | .30 | .07 |
| ☐ 15 Tony Woods | .50 | .20 | .05 |
| ☐ 16 David Wyman | .35 | .14 | .03 |

## 1990 Police Steelers

This 16-card set, which measures approximately 2 5/8" by 4 1/8", was issued to promote safety in the Pittsburgh Area using members of the Pittsburgh Steelers to make safety tips. The fronts of the cards feature color portrait shots of the players surrounded by white borders. There are advertisements for the Giant Eagle shopping chain and the Kiwanis Club on the front along with the Steelers name on top of the photo and underneath the photo is the player's name and position. The back of the card features a safety tip. The back says the cards were sponsored by the local Kiwanis club, Giant Eagle, the local police departments, and the Pittsburgh Steelers. The set is checklisted below alphabetically.

| | MINT | EXC | G-VG |
|---|---|---|---|
| COMPLETE SET (16) | 5.00 | 2.00 | .50 |
| COMMON PLAYER (1-16) | .35 | .14 | .03 |
| | | | |
| ☐ 1 Gary Anderson | .50 | .20 | .05 |
| ☐ 2 Bubby Brister | .60 | .24 | .06 |
| ☐ 3 Thomas Everett | .60 | .24 | .06 |

GIANT EAGLE  Steelers

33 • MERRIL HOGE
Running Back  Ht: 6-2  Wt: 230

**Steelers 90 Tips**

A touchdown is awarded when the ball is carried or caught on, above or behind the opponent's goal line.

Don't get caught trespassing on other people's property.

GIANT EAGLE

Courtesy of your local Kiwanis Club, Giant Eagle, your local Police Department, and the Pittsburgh Steelers

| | MINT | EXC | G-VG |
|---|---|---|---|
| ☐ 4 Merril Hoge | .50 | .20 | .05 |
| ☐ 5 Tunch Ilkin | .35 | .14 | .03 |
| ☐ 6 Carnell Lake | .35 | .14 | .03 |
| ☐ 7 Louis Lipps | .75 | .30 | .07 |
| ☐ 8 David Little | .50 | .20 | .05 |
| ☐ 9 Greg Lloyd | .50 | .20 | .05 |
| ☐ 10 Mike Mularkey | .35 | .14 | .03 |
| ☐ 11 Hardy Nickerson | .50 | .20 | .05 |
| ☐ 12 Chuck Noll CO | .75 | .30 | .07 |
| ☐ 13 John Rienstra | .35 | .14 | .03 |
| ☐ 14 Keith Willis | .35 | .14 | .03 |
| ☐ 15 Rod Woodson | .75 | .30 | .07 |
| ☐ 16 Tim Worley | .60 | .24 | .06 |

## 1990 Police Vikings

WADE WILSON
VIKINGS

WCCO RADIO 830

Gatorade
THIRST QUENCHER

He's known crime prevention

This ten-card set was issued to promote safety in the Minneapolis area by using members of the 1990 Minnesota Vikings. The card photos have posed action shots on the front along with an advertisement for Gatorade on the front and a crime prevention tip on the back. We have checklisted the cards in this set in alphabetical order. The cards measure approximately 2 1/2" by 3 1/2".

| | MINT | EXC | G-VG |
|---|---|---|---|
| COMPLETE SET (10) | 5.00 | 2.00 | .50 |
| COMMON PLAYER (1-10) | .50 | .20 | .05 |
| | | | |
| ☐ 1 Ray Berry | .50 | .20 | .05 |
| ☐ 2 Anthony Carter | 1.00 | .40 | .10 |
| ☐ 3 Chris Doleman | .75 | .30 | .07 |
| ☐ 4 Rick Fenney | .60 | .24 | .06 |
| ☐ 5 Hassan Jones | .60 | .24 | .06 |
| ☐ 6 Carl Lee | .60 | .24 | .06 |
| ☐ 7 Mike Merriweather | .60 | .24 | .06 |
| ☐ 8 Scott Studwell | .60 | .24 | .06 |
| ☐ 9 Herschel Walker | 1.25 | .50 | .12 |
| ☐ 10 Wade Wilson | 1.00 | .40 | .10 |

## 1991 Police Bills

This eight-card Police set was sponsored by Blue Shield of Western New York. The cards measure the standard size (2 1/2" by 3 1/2") and are printed on white card stock. The top portion of the front features the player's name centered above the team name, with the team helmet and Blue Shield logo on either side. The center features an action player photo while biographical information is printed below. The three-sectioned front is separated by red borders. The backs have player profile, career statistics, and safety tips sponsored by the Erie County Sheriff's Department. The cards are unnumbered and checklisted below alphabetically.

| | MINT | EXC | G-VG |
|---|---|---|---|
| COMPLETE SET (8) | 7.00 | 2.80 | .70 |
| COMMON PLAYER (1-8) | .75 | .30 | .07 |
| ☐ 1 Howard Ballard | .75 | .30 | .07 |
| ☐ 2 Don Beebe | 2.00 | .80 | .20 |
| ☐ 3 John Davis | 1.00 | .40 | .10 |
| ☐ 4 Kenneth Davis | 1.25 | .50 | .12 |
| ☐ 5 Mark Kelso | .75 | .30 | .07 |
| ☐ 6 Frank Reich | 2.00 | .80 | .20 |
| ☐ 7 Butch Rolle | 1.00 | .40 | .10 |
| ☐ 8 J.D. Williams | .75 | .30 | .07 |

# 1991 Police Lions

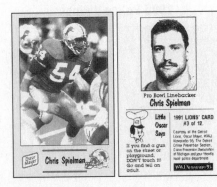

This 12-card Police Lions set was distributed during the season by participating Michigan police departments. The cards measure approximately 2 5/8" by 4 1/8" and feature color action shots of each player enclosed in a yellow border on thin card stock. Oscar Mayer's logo, player's name, and team helmet appearing at the bottom of each card are highlighted by blue lines above and below. Card backs, printed vertically, carry a black and white head shot of the player, player information, while a safety tip from the main sponsor appears at the bottom left half of card. The bottom right half lists card numbers and other sponsor names.

| | MINT | EXC | G-VG |
|---|---|---|---|
| COMPLETE SET (12) | 5.00 | 2.00 | .50 |
| COMMON PLAYER (1-12) | .35 | .14 | .03 |
| ☐ 1 Mel Gray | .60 | .24 | .06 |
| ☐ 2 Ken Dallafior | .35 | .14 | .03 |
| ☐ 3 Chris Spielman | .60 | .24 | .06 |
| ☐ 4 Bennie Blades | .60 | .24 | .06 |
| ☐ 5 Robert Clark | .50 | .20 | .05 |
| ☐ 6 Eric Andolsek | .50 | .20 | .05 |
| ☐ 7 Rodney Peete | .75 | .30 | .07 |
| ☐ 8 William White | .35 | .14 | .03 |
| ☐ 9 Lomas Brown | .50 | .20 | .05 |
| ☐ 10 Jerry Ball | .50 | .20 | .05 |
| ☐ 11 Michael Cofer | .50 | .20 | .05 |
| ☐ 12 Barry Sanders | 2.50 | 1.00 | .25 |

# 1991 Police Packers

This 20-card set was printed on white card stock. These standard-size cards (2 1/2" by 3 1/2") feature player action shots on the fronts enclosed by yellow and green borders. A yellow banner design in the

top left corner has "1991 Packers" printed in black. Player's name and position appear in gold in the top right green border. College team and years played with Packers are noted in a gold band at bottom. The backs are printed in green ink and have Packer (safety) tips based on the player's position. Sponsor names appear at the bottom of card. Only card number 1 is printed horizontally front and back. The cards are numbered on the back.

| | MINT | EXC | G-VG |
|---|---|---|---|
| COMPLETE SET (20) | 6.00 | 2.40 | .60 |
| COMMON PLAYER (1-20) | .30 | .12 | .03 |
| ☐ 1 Lambeau Field | .30 | .12 | .03 |
| ☐ 2 Sterling Sharpe | 1.50 | .60 | .15 |
| ☐ 3 James Campen | .40 | .16 | .04 |
| ☐ 4 Chuck Cecil | .40 | .16 | .04 |
| ☐ 5 Lindy Infante CO | .40 | .16 | .04 |
| ☐ 6 Keith Woodside | .40 | .16 | .04 |
| ☐ 7 Perry Kemp | .40 | .16 | .04 |
| ☐ 8 Johnny Holland | .50 | .20 | .05 |
| ☐ 9 Don Majkowski | .60 | .24 | .06 |
| ☐ 10 Tony Bennett | .60 | .24 | .06 |
| ☐ 11 LeRoy Butler | .30 | .12 | .03 |
| ☐ 12 Tony Mandarich | .40 | .16 | .04 |
| ☐ 13 Darrell Thompson | .75 | .30 | .07 |
| ☐ 14 Matt Brock | .40 | .16 | .04 |
| ☐ 15 Charles Wilson | .30 | .12 | .03 |
| ☐ 16 Brian Noble | .40 | .16 | .04 |
| ☐ 17 Ed West | .40 | .16 | .04 |
| ☐ 18 Chris Jacke | .40 | .16 | .04 |
| ☐ 19 Blair Kiel | .50 | .20 | .05 |
| ☐ 20 Mark Murphy | .40 | .16 | .04 |

# 1991 Police Raiders

This 12-card set was sponsored by Clovis Police Department, REHCO Heating and Air Conditioning, and the Los Angeles Raiders. Five thousand sets were distributed throughout the Fresno/Clovis area as part of a sixth grade DARE (Drug Awareness Resistance Education) program. The cards measure the standard size (2 1/2" by 3 1/2"). Card fronts feature color action player photos with white borders. The player's name appears in a gray stripe above the picture, while sponsor logos overlay another gray stripe at the bottom of the card face. The backs have biographical information and a safety tip printed in black lettering on a white background. The cards are numbered on the back.

| | MINT | EXC | G-VG |
|---|---|---|---|
| COMPLETE SET (12) | 15.00 | 6.00 | 1.50 |
| COMMON PLAYER (1-12) | .75 | .30 | .07 |
| ☐ 1 Art Shell CO | 2.50 | 1.00 | .25 |
| ☐ 2 Marcus Allen | 3.00 | 1.20 | .30 |

| | | | |
|---|---|---|---|
| ☐ 3 Mervyn Fernandez | 1.50 | .60 | .15 |
| ☐ 4 Willie Gault | 1.50 | .60 | .15 |
| ☐ 5 Howie Long | 1.50 | .60 | .15 |
| ☐ 6 Don Mosebar | 1.00 | .40 | .10 |
| ☐ 7 Winston Moss | .75 | .30 | .07 |
| ☐ 8 Jay Schroeder | 1.25 | .50 | .12 |
| ☐ 9 Steve Wisniewski | 1.00 | .40 | .10 |
| ☐ 10 Ethan Horton | 1.00 | .40 | .10 |
| ☐ 11 Lionel Washington | 1.00 | .40 | .10 |
| ☐ 12 Greg Townsend | 1.25 | .50 | .12 |

## 1991 Police Redskins

This 16-card set was jointly sponsored by Mobil, PACT (Police and Citizens Together), and WTTG Channel 5 TV. The set was released in the Washington area during the 1991 season. The cards measure approximately 2 5/8" by 4 1/8" and are printed on thin card stock. Card fronts carry a full-color player action shot on a white background. The word "Washington" is printed in black in a gold bar up the left side while the team name appears in large red print up the left side. Player's name is reversed out in a black stripe at bottom, while player's number appears in a gold circle to the left. Vertically printed backs present biographical information, player profile, an anti-drug message, and trivia question. Sponsors' logos appear at bottom. The cards are unnumbered and checklisted below in alphabetical order.

| | MINT | EXC | G-VG |
|---|---|---|---|
| COMPLETE SET (16) | 5.00 | 2.00 | .50 |
| COMMON PLAYER (1-16) | .25 | .10 | .02 |
| ☐ 1 John Brandes | .25 | .10 | .02 |
| ☐ 2 Earnest Byner | .50 | .20 | .05 |
| ☐ 3 Gary Clark | .75 | .30 | .07 |
| ☐ 4 Andre Collins | .50 | .20 | .05 |
| ☐ 5 Darrell Green | .60 | .24 | .06 |
| ☐ 6 Joe Howard | .35 | .14 | .03 |
| ☐ 7 Tim Johnson | .35 | .14 | .03 |
| ☐ 8 Jim Lachey | .50 | .20 | .05 |
| ☐ 9 Chip Lohmiller | .35 | .14 | .03 |
| ☐ 10 Charles Mann | .50 | .20 | .05 |
| ☐ 11 Art Monk | 1.00 | .40 | .10 |
| ☐ 12 Mark Rypien | .75 | .30 | .07 |
| ☐ 13 Mark Schlereth | .35 | .14 | .03 |
| ☐ 14 Fred Stokes | .25 | .10 | .02 |
| ☐ 15 Don Warren | .35 | .14 | .03 |
| ☐ 16 Eric Williams | .25 | .10 | .02 |

## 1991 Police Steelers

This 16-card set was sponsored by the Kiwanis and Giant Eagle. The cards measure approximately 2 5/8" by 4 1/8". They were distributed by participating Pennsylvania police departments. The fronts feature color action player photos, with the team name at the top sandwiched between the two sponsor logos. Player information appears below the picture. On the card backs below a Steelers helmet, the backs have "Steelers Tips '91," which consist of anti-crime or anti-drug messages. The cards are unnumbered and checklisted below in alphabetical order.

| | MINT | EXC | G-VG |
|---|---|---|---|
| COMPLETE SET (16) | 5.00 | 2.00 | .50 |
| COMMON PLAYER (1-16) | .35 | .14 | .03 |
| ☐ 1 Gary Anderson | .50 | .20 | .05 |
| ☐ 2 Bubby Brister | .60 | .24 | .06 |
| ☐ 3 Dermontti Dawson | .50 | .20 | .05 |
| ☐ 4 Eric Green | .75 | .30 | .07 |

| | | | |
|---|---|---|---|
| ☐ 5 Bryan Hinkle | .50 | .20 | .05 |
| ☐ 6 Merril Hoge | .50 | .20 | .05 |
| ☐ 7 John Jackson | .50 | .20 | .05 |
| ☐ 8 David Johnson | .35 | .14 | .03 |
| ☐ 9 Carnell Lake | .35 | .14 | .03 |
| ☐ 10 Louis Lipps | .60 | .24 | .06 |
| ☐ 11 Greg Lloyd | .50 | .20 | .05 |
| ☐ 12 Mike Mularkey | .35 | .14 | .03 |
| ☐ 13 Chuck Noll CO | .75 | .30 | .07 |
| ☐ 14 Dan Stryzinski | .35 | .14 | .03 |
| ☐ 15 Gerald Williams | .35 | .14 | .03 |
| ☐ 16 Rod Woodson | .75 | .30 | .07 |

## 1991 Police Surge WLAF

This 39-card set was sponsored by American Airlines and presents players of the WLAF Sacramento Surge. The cards measure approximately 2 3/8" by 3 1/2". The fronts feature a color posed photo of the player, with a drawing of the Sacramento helmet inside a triangle at the lower right hand corner. The backs have the Sacramento and WLAF logos at the top, biographical information, and a player quote consisting of an anti-drug message. The set was issued in the Summer of 1991. The cards are unnumbered and hence are listed alphabetically below for convenience.

| | MINT | EXC | G-VG |
|---|---|---|---|
| COMPLETE SET (39) | 15.00 | 6.00 | 1.50 |
| COMMON PLAYER (1-39) | .50 | .20 | .05 |
| ☐ 1 Mike Adams | .60 | .24 | .06 |
| ☐ 2 Sam Archer | .50 | .20 | .05 |
| ☐ 3 John Buddenberg | .50 | .20 | .05 |
| ☐ 4 Jon Burman | .50 | .20 | .05 |
| ☐ 5 Tony Burse | .75 | .30 | .07 |
| ☐ 6 Ricardo Cartwright | .50 | .20 | .05 |
| ☐ 7 Greg Coauette | .50 | .20 | .05 |
| ☐ 8 Paco Craig | .50 | .20 | .05 |
| ☐ 9 John Dominic | .50 | .20 | .05 |
| ☐ 10 Mike Elkins | 1.00 | .40 | .10 |
| ☐ 11 Oliver Erhorn | .50 | .20 | .05 |
| ☐ 12 Mel Farr Jr. | 1.00 | .40 | .10 |
| ☐ 13 Victor Floyd | .50 | .20 | .05 |
| ☐ 14 Byron Forsythe | .50 | .20 | .05 |
| ☐ 15 Paul Frazier | .50 | .20 | .05 |
| ☐ 16 Tom Gerhart | .50 | .20 | .05 |
| ☐ 17 Mike Hall | .50 | .20 | .05 |
| ☐ 18 Anthony Henton | .50 | .20 | .05 |
| ☐ 19 Nate Hill | .50 | .20 | .05 |
| ☐ 20 Kubanai Kalombo | .50 | .20 | .05 |

| | | MINT | EXC | G-VG |
|---|---|---|---|---|
| ☐ | 21 Shawn Knight | .75 | .30 | .07 |
| ☐ | 22 Sean Kugler | .50 | .20 | .05 |
| ☐ | 23 Matti Lindholm | .50 | .20 | .05 |
| ☐ | 24 Art Malone | .75 | .30 | .07 |
| ☐ | 25 Robert McWright | .50 | .20 | .05 |
| ☐ | 26 Tim Moore | .50 | .20 | .05 |
| ☐ | 27 Pete Najarian | .50 | .20 | .05 |
| ☐ | 28 Mark Nua | .50 | .20 | .05 |
| ☐ | 29 Carl Parker | .50 | .20 | .05 |
| ☐ | 30 Leon Perry | .50 | .20 | .05 |
| ☐ | 31 Juha Salo | .50 | .20 | .05 |
| ☐ | 32 Saute Sapolu | .50 | .20 | .05 |
| ☐ | 33 Paul Soltis | .50 | .20 | .05 |
| ☐ | 34 Richard Stephens | .50 | .20 | .05 |
| ☐ | 35 Kay Stephenson CO | .75 | .30 | .07 |
| ☐ | 36 Kendall Trainor | .75 | .30 | .07 |
| ☐ | 37 Mike Wallace | .50 | .20 | .05 |
| ☐ | 38 Curtis Wilson | .50 | .20 | .05 |
| ☐ | 39 Rick Zumwalt | .75 | .30 | .07 |

## 1991 Police Vikings

This ten-card standard-size (2 1/2" by 3 1/2") set was sponsored by Gatorade. The cards were distributed by participating Minnesota police departments, one per week, beginning on Aug. 23 with Rick Fenney, and concluding on Oct. 27 with Chris Doleman. Card fronts display an action player photo enclosed in a purple border, while player's name is printed at the top in a gray rectangle. Gatorade's logo appears at the bottom of the picture. The first card's back lists the Vikings' game schedule. The horizontally oriented backs of the remaining cards feature a black and white close-up of the player and a biographical sketch on the left portion. Player's name, position, and jersey number appear in a black box at the top right, while the Vikadontis Rex mascot appears below. A crime prevention tip appears under the card number, while sponsor logos of Super Bowl XXVI, KFAN Sports Radio, and K102 Radio round out the back design.

| | MINT | EXC | G-VG |
|---|---|---|---|
| COMPLETE SET (10) | 5.00 | 2.00 | .50 |
| COMMON PLAYER (1-10) | .40 | .16 | .04 |

| | | MINT | EXC | G-VG |
|---|---|---|---|---|
| ☐ | 1 Rick Fenney | .50 | .20 | .05 |
| ☐ | 2 Wade Wilson | 1.00 | .40 | .10 |
| ☐ | 3 Mike Merriweather | .50 | .20 | .05 |
| ☐ | 4 Hassan Jones | .50 | .20 | .05 |
| ☐ | 5 Rich Gannon | .60 | .24 | .06 |
| ☐ | 6 Mark Dusbabek | .50 | .20 | .05 |
| ☐ | 7 Sean Salisbury | .75 | .30 | .07 |
| ☐ | 8 Reggie Rutland | .40 | .16 | .04 |
| ☐ | 9 Tim Irwin | .40 | .16 | .04 |
| ☐ | 10 Chris Doleman | .75 | .30 | .07 |

## 1992 Police Bills

This seven-card set was sponsored by Blue Shield of Western New York. The oversized cards measure approximately 4" by 6" and are printed on white card stock. The top portion of the front features the player's name centered above the team name, with the team helmet and Blue Shield logo on either side. The center features an action color player photo while biographical information is printed below. The three-section front is separated by red borders. The backs have player profile, career statistics, and safety tips sponsored by the Erie County Sheriff's Department. The cards are unnumbered and checklisted below alphabetically.

| | MINT | EXC | G-VG |
|---|---|---|---|
| COMPLETE SET (7) | 5.00 | 2.00 | .50 |
| COMMON PLAYER (1-7) | .60 | .24 | .06 |

| | | MINT | EXC | G-VG |
|---|---|---|---|---|
| ☐ | 1 Carlton Bailey | .75 | .30 | .07 |
| ☐ | 2 Steve Christie | .75 | .30 | .07 |
| ☐ | 3 Shane Conlan | 1.00 | .40 | .10 |
| ☐ | 4 Phil Hansen | .75 | .30 | .07 |
| ☐ | 5 Henry Jones | 1.00 | .40 | .10 |
| ☐ | 6 Chris Mohr | .60 | .24 | .06 |
| ☐ | 7 Thurman Thomas | 2.50 | 1.00 | .25 |

## 1992 Police Cardinals

Sponsored by KTVK-TV (Channel 3) and the Arizona Public Service Co., this 16-card set measures the standard-size (2 1/2" by 3 1/2"). The fronts display color player photos bordered above and partially on the left by stripes that fade from red to yellow. In the lower left corner, an electronic scoreboard gives the player's jersey number and position. Beneath the team name and logo, the player's name and jersey number are printed between two red stripes toward the bottom of the card. The horizontal backs present biographical information and, on a red panel, recycling and conservation tips. The cards are unnumbered and checklisted below in alphabetical order.

| | MINT | EXC | G-VG |
|---|---|---|---|
| COMPLETE SET (16) | 9.00 | 3.75 | .90 |
| COMMON CARD (1-16) | .50 | .20 | .05 |

| | | MINT | EXC | G-VG |
|---|---|---|---|---|
| ☐ | 1 Joe Bugel CO | .60 | .24 | .06 |
| ☐ | 2 Rich Camarillo | .50 | .20 | .05 |
| ☐ | 3 Ed Cunningham | .50 | .20 | .05 |
| ☐ | 4 Greg Davis | .50 | .20 | .05 |
| ☐ | 5 Ken Harvey | .75 | .30 | .07 |
| ☐ | 6 Randal Hill | 1.50 | .60 | .15 |
| ☐ | 7 Ernie Jones | .75 | .30 | .07 |
| ☐ | 8 Mike Jones | .50 | .20 | .05 |
| ☐ | 9 Tim McDonald | 1.00 | .40 | .10 |
| ☐ | 10 Freddie Joe Nunn | .60 | .24 | .06 |
| ☐ | 11 Ricky Proehl | 1.00 | .40 | .10 |
| ☐ | 12 Timm Rosenbach | .75 | .30 | .07 |
| ☐ | 13 Tony Sacca | 1.00 | .40 | .10 |
| ☐ | 14 Lance Smith | .75 | .30 | .07 |
| ☐ | 15 Eric Swann | 1.00 | .40 | .10 |
| ☐ | 16 Aeneas Williams | .75 | .30 | .07 |

## 1992 Police Giants

This 12-card police set was printed and distributed by the New Jersey State Police Crime Prevention Resource Center. The cards measure approximately 2 3/4" by 4 1/8". The fronts feature color action player photos bordered in white. The team name appears above the picture, while the player's name and brief biographical information are printed below it. The backs carry sponsor logos, "Tips from the Giants" in the form of public service announcements, and the McGruff crime dog slogan "Take a Bite Out of Crime." The cards are unnumbered and checklisted below in alphabetical order.

| | MINT | EXC | G-VG |
|---|---|---|---|
| COMPLETE SET (12) | 15.00 | 6.00 | 1.50 |
| COMMON PLAYER (1-12) | 1.00 | .40 | .10 |
| ☐ 1 Ottis Anderson | 2.00 | .80 | .20 |
| ☐ 2 Matt Bahr | 1.25 | .50 | .12 |
| ☐ 3 Eric Dorsey | 1.00 | .40 | .10 |
| ☐ 4 John Elliott | 1.00 | .40 | .10 |
| ☐ 5 Ray Handley CO | 1.50 | .60 | .15 |
| ☐ 6 Jeff Hostetler | 3.00 | 1.20 | .30 |
| ☐ 7 Erik Howard | 1.00 | .40 | .10 |
| ☐ 8 Pepper Johnson | 1.25 | .50 | .12 |
| ☐ 9 Leonard Marshall | 1.50 | .60 | .15 |
| ☐ 10 Bart Oates | 1.25 | .50 | .12 |
| ☐ 11 Gary Reasons | 1.00 | .40 | .10 |
| ☐ 12 Phil Simms | 4.00 | 1.60 | .40 |

# 1992 Police Redskins

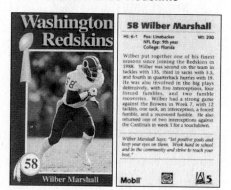

This 16-card set was jointly sponsored by Mobil, PACT (Police and Citizens Together), and Fox WTTG Channel 5. The cards measure approximately 2 1/2" by 4 1/8" and features action color player photos on a brick-red background. The pictures are offset, bleeding off the right edge of the card, and are framed on the other three sides in white. At the upper left corner of the picture is the Vince Lombardi trophy, and at the lower left corner is the uniform number in a circle. The team name appears at the top in mustard. The white backs carry biographical information, career highlights, and anti-drug and crime prevention tips in the form of player quotes. The cards are unnumbered and checklisted below in alphabetical order.

| | MINT | EXC | G-VG |
|---|---|---|---|
| COMPLETE SET (16) | 5.00 | 2.00 | .50 |
| COMMON PLAYER (1-16) | .35 | .14 | .03 |
| ☐ 1 Jeff Bostic | .50 | .20 | .05 |
| ☐ 2 Earnest Byner | .60 | .24 | .06 |
| ☐ 3 Gary Clark | .75 | .30 | .07 |
| ☐ 4 Monte Coleman | .35 | .14 | .03 |
| ☐ 5 Andre Collins | .50 | .20 | .05 |
| ☐ 6 Danny Copeland | .35 | .14 | .03 |
| ☐ 7 Kurt Gouveia | .35 | .14 | .03 |
| ☐ 8 Darrell Green | .60 | .24 | .06 |
| ☐ 9 Jim Lachey | .50 | .20 | .05 |
| ☐ 10 Charles Mann | .50 | .20 | .05 |
| ☐ 11 Wilber Marshall | .60 | .24 | .06 |
| ☐ 12 Raleigh McKenzie | .35 | .14 | .03 |
| ☐ 13 Art Monk | 1.00 | .40 | .10 |
| ☐ 14 Mark Rypien | .60 | .24 | .06 |
| ☐ 15 Mark Schlereth | .35 | .14 | .03 |
| ☐ 16 Eric Williams | .35 | .14 | .03 |

# 1992 Police Steelers

This 16-card set was sponsored by the Kiwanis Club and Giant Eagle, and it was distributed by local police departments. The cards measure approximately 2 5/8" by 4 3/16" and feature still color player photos on white card stock. Beneath the picture are the player's name, number, position, height, and weight. The team name and sponsor logos appear at the top. The backs are plain white with public service "Steelers Tips '92" printed within a black outline. The cards are unnumbered and checklisted below in alphabetical order.

| | MINT | EXC | G-VG |
|---|---|---|---|
| COMPLETE SET (16) | 5.00 | 2.00 | .50 |
| COMMON CARD (1-16) | .35 | .14 | .03 |
| ☐ 1 Gary Anderson | .50 | .20 | .05 |
| ☐ 2 Bubby Brister | .50 | .20 | .05 |
| ☐ 3 Bill Cowher CO | .60 | .24 | .06 |
| ☐ 4 Dermontti Dawson | .50 | .20 | .05 |
| ☐ 5 Eric Green | .60 | .24 | .06 |
| ☐ 6 Carlton Haselrig | .35 | .14 | .03 |
| ☐ 7 Merril Hoge | .50 | .20 | .05 |
| ☐ 8 John Jackson | .50 | .20 | .05 |
| ☐ 9 Carnell Lake | .35 | .14 | .03 |
| ☐ 10 Louis Lipps | .60 | .24 | .06 |
| ☐ 11 Greg Lloyd | .35 | .14 | .03 |
| ☐ 12 Neil O'Donnell | 2.00 | .80 | .20 |
| ☐ 13 Tom Ricketts | .35 | .14 | .03 |
| ☐ 14 Gerald Williams | .35 | .14 | .03 |
| ☐ 15 Jerrol Williams | .35 | .14 | .03 |
| ☐ 16 Rod Woodson | .75 | .30 | .07 |

# 1992 Police Vikings

This ten-card standard size (2 1/2" by 3 1/2") set was primarily sponsored by Gatorade. The card fronts display an action color player photo framed by a purple border, while the player's name and team name appear in a gray rectangle at the top. The Gatorade logo appears at the bottom of the picture. The horizontally oriented backs carry a black-and-white close-up of the player and biographical information within a black outline box on the left side of the card. The player's name and position appear in a black bar at the top. Below are Vikadontis Rex (the team mascot), a crime prevention tip, and other sponsor logos (KFAN Sports Radio AM 1130 and K102). The cards are numbered on the back.

| | MINT | EXC | G-VG |
|---|---|---|---|
| COMPLETE SET (10) | 5.00 | 2.00 | .50 |
| COMMON CARD (1-10) | .40 | .16 | .04 |
| ☐ 1 Dennis Green CO<br>(Schedule on back) | .60 | .24 | .06 |
| ☐ 2 John Randle | .40 | .16 | .04 |
| ☐ 3 Todd Scott | .50 | .20 | .05 |
| ☐ 4 Anthony Carter | 1.00 | .40 | .10 |
| ☐ 5 Steve Jordan | .60 | .24 | .06 |
| ☐ 6 Terry Allen | 2.00 | .80 | .20 |
| ☐ 7 Brian Habib | .40 | .16 | .04 |
| ☐ 8 Fuad Reveiz | .40 | .16 | .04 |
| ☐ 9 Roger Craig | .75 | .30 | .07 |
| ☐ 10 Cris Carter | .75 | .30 | .07 |

# 1993 Police Packers

These 20 standard-size (2 1/2" by 3 1/2") cards were issued to commemorate the Packers' 75th anniversary and feature on their fronts white-bordered color player photos. Two team color-coded stripes edge the pictures at the bottom. The 75th anniversary logo appears at the upper left, and the words "Celebrating 75 Years of Pro Football 1919-1993" appear below the photo. The white back carries the player's name, position, years in the NFL, alma mater, and Packers helmet at the upper left. Below are safety messages written by area grade schoolers. The cards are numbered on the back.

|  | MINT | EXC | G-VG |
|---|---|---|---|
| COMPLETE SET (20) | 6.00 | 2.40 | .60 |
| COMMON PLAYER (1-20) | .25 | .10 | .02 |
| ☐ 1 Ron Wolf GM | .25 | .10 | .02 |
| ☐ 2 Wayne Simmons | .35 | .14 | .03 |
| ☐ 3 James Campen | .25 | .10 | .02 |
| ☐ 4 Matt Brock | .25 | .10 | .02 |
| ☐ 5 Mike Holmgren CO | .35 | .14 | .03 |
| ☐ 6 Brian Noble | .35 | .14 | .03 |
| ☐ 7 Ken O'Brien | .35 | .14 | .03 |
| ☐ 8 George Teague | .50 | .20 | .05 |
| ☐ 9 Brett Favre | 1.50 | .60 | .15 |
| ☐ 10 LeRoy Butler | .25 | .10 | .02 |
| ☐ 11 Harry Galbreath | .25 | .10 | .02 |
| ☐ 12 Chris Jacke | .35 | .14 | .03 |
| ☐ 13 Sterling Sharpe | 1.25 | .50 | .12 |
| ☐ 14 Terrell Buckley | .50 | .20 | .05 |
| ☐ 15 Ken Ruettgers | .50 | .20 | .05 |
| ☐ 16 Johnny Holland | .35 | .14 | .03 |
| ☐ 17 Edgar Bennett | .75 | .30 | .07 |
| ☐ 18 Jackie Harris | .75 | .30 | .07 |
| ☐ 19 Tony Bennett | .50 | .20 | .05 |
| ☐ 20 Reggie White | 1.00 | .40 | .10 |

# 1993 Police Redskins

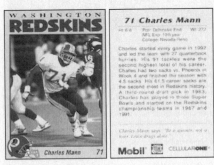

These 16 cards measure approximately 2 3/4" by 4 1/8" and feature on their fronts yellow-bordered color player action shots. The player's name, team helmet, and uniform number rest within the bottom yellow margin. The white back carries the player's name and uniform number at the top, followed below by biography, career highlights, and safety message. The logos for Mobil, Cellular One, and Police and Citizens Together (PACT) at the bottom round out the card. The cards are unnumbered and checklisted below in alphabetical order.

|  | MINT | EXC | G-VG |
|---|---|---|---|
| COMPLETE SET (16) | 5.00 | 2.00 | .50 |
| COMMON PLAYER (1-16) | .30 | .12 | .03 |

| ☐ 1 Ray Brown | .30 | .12 | .03 |
|---|---|---|---|
| ☐ 2 Andre Collins | .40 | .16 | .04 |
| ☐ 3 Brad Edwards | .30 | .12 | .03 |
| ☐ 4 Matt Elliott | .30 | .12 | .03 |
| ☐ 5 Ricky Ervins | .50 | .20 | .05 |
| ☐ 6 Darrell Green | .50 | .20 | .05 |
| ☐ 7 Desmond Howard | .75 | .30 | .07 |
| ☐ 8 Joe Jacoby | .40 | .16 | .04 |
| ☐ 9 Tim Johnson | .30 | .12 | .03 |
| ☐ 10 Jim Lachey | .40 | .16 | .04 |
| ☐ 11 Chip Lohmiller | .40 | .16 | .04 |
| ☐ 12 Charles Mann | .40 | .16 | .04 |
| ☐ 13 Raleigh McKenzie | .30 | .12 | .03 |
| ☐ 14 Brian Mitchell | .50 | .20 | .05 |
| ☐ 15 Terry Orr | .30 | .12 | .03 |
| ☐ 16 Mark Rypien | .50 | .20 | .05 |

# 1993 Police Steelers

Sponsored by the Pittsburgh Police Department, Kiwanis Club, and Giant Eagle, these 16 cards, when cut from the sheet, measure approximately 2 1/2" by 4". The fronts feature white-bordered color player action shots, with the player's name, uniform number, position, height, and weight appearing in black lettering within the bottom white margin. The team name appears in team color-coded lettering within the white margin above the photo, along with the Kiwanis and Giant Eagle logos. The white back has a large Steeler helmet logo at the upper left, followed below by the words "Steelers Tips '93," then the player's name, position, and highlight. The tip then appears, which contains a stay-in-school, anti-drug, or safety message. The Giant Eagle and Kiwanis logos at the bottom round out the card. The cards are unnumbered and checklisted below in alphabetical order.

|  | MINT | EXC | G-VG |
|---|---|---|---|
| COMPLETE SET (16) | 5.00 | 2.00 | .50 |
| COMMON PLAYER (1-16) | .30 | .12 | .03 |
| ☐ 1 Gary Anderson | .40 | .16 | .04 |
| ☐ 2 Adrian Cooper | .40 | .16 | .04 |
| ☐ 3 Bill Cowher CO | .40 | .16 | .04 |
| ☐ 4 Dermontti Dawson | .30 | .12 | .03 |
| ☐ 5 Donald Evans | .30 | .12 | .03 |
| ☐ 6 Eric Green | .50 | .20 | .05 |
| ☐ 7 Bryan Hinkle | .30 | .12 | .03 |
| ☐ 8 Merril Hoge | .40 | .16 | .04 |
| ☐ 9 Garry Howe | .30 | .12 | .03 |
| ☐ 10 Greg Lloyd | .40 | .16 | .04 |
| ☐ 11 Neil O'Donnell | 1.00 | .40 | .10 |
| ☐ 12 Jerry Olsavsky | .30 | .12 | .03 |
| ☐ 13 Leon Searcy | .40 | .16 | .04 |
| ☐ 14 Dwight Stone | .40 | .16 | .04 |
| ☐ 15 Gerald Williams | .30 | .12 | .03 |
| ☐ 16 Rod Woodson | .60 | .24 | .06 |

# 1993 Police Vikings

This set was primarily sponsored by Gatorade, and the ten standard-size (2 1/2" by 3 1/2") cards feature on their fronts purple-bordered color player photos. The player's name and team name appear within a gray rectangle at the top, and the Gatorade logo is displayed at the bottom. The white and horizontal back carries a black-and-white player headshot in the upper left, with his biography shown below. His name, position, and uniform number appear in the black stripe at the bottom. Below are Vikadontis Rex (the team mascot), a crime prevention tip, and other sponsor logos (KFAN Sports Radio and K102). The cards are numbered on the back.

|  | MINT | EXC | G-VG |
|---|---|---|---|
| COMPLETE SET (10) | 5.00 | 2.00 | .50 |
| COMMON PLAYER (1-10) | .40 | .16 | .04 |

| | | | |
|---|---|---|---|
| ☐ 1 Dennis Green CO | .50 | .20 | .05 |
| (CL/schedule on back) | | | |
| ☐ 2 Henry Thomas | .50 | .20 | .05 |
| ☐ 3 Todd Scott | .40 | .16 | .04 |
| ☐ 4 Jack Del Rio | .40 | .16 | .04 |
| ☐ 5 Vencie Glenn | .40 | .16 | .04 |
| ☐ 6 Fuad Reveiz | .40 | .16 | .04 |
| ☐ 7 Cris Carter | .75 | .30 | .07 |
| ☐ 8 Terry Allen | 1.25 | .50 | .12 |
| ☐ 9 Roger Craig | .75 | .30 | .07 |
| ☐ 10 Carlos Jenkins | .40 | .16 | .04 |

## 1976 Popsicle Teams

This set of 28 teams is printed on plastic material similar to that found on thin credit cards. There is a variation on the New York Giants card; one version shows the helmet logo as Giants and the other shows it as New York. The first version was apparently issued in error and the correction was issued but it is now unclear as to which version is more difficult to find. The title card reads, "Pro Quarterback, Pro Football's Leading Magazine". The cards measure approximately 3 3/8" by 2 1/8", have rounded corners, and are slightly thinner than a credit card. Below the NFL logo and the team, the front features a color helmet shot and a color action photo. The back contains a brief team history. Some consider the new expansion teams, Tampa Bay and Seattle, to be somewhat tougher to find. The cards are unnumbered and are ordered below alphabetically by team location name. The set is considered complete with just the 28 team cards.

|  | NRMT | VG-E | GOOD |
|---|---|---|---|
| COMPLETE SET (28) | 35.00 | 14.00 | 3.50 |
| COMMON TEAM (1-28) | 2.00 | .80 | .20 |

| | | | |
|---|---|---|---|
| ☐ 1 Atlanta Falcons | 2.00 | .80 | .20 |
| ☐ 2 Baltimore Colts | 2.00 | .80 | .20 |
| ☐ 3 Buffalo Bills | 2.00 | .80 | .20 |
| ☐ 4 Chicago Bears | 2.00 | .80 | .20 |
| ☐ 5 Cincinnati Bengals | 2.00 | .80 | .20 |
| ☐ 6 Cleveland Browns | 2.00 | .80 | .20 |
| ☐ 7 Dallas Cowboys | 3.00 | 1.20 | .30 |
| ☐ 8 Denver Broncos | 2.00 | .80 | .20 |
| ☐ 9 Detroit Lions | 2.00 | .80 | .20 |
| ☐ 10 Green Bay Packers | 2.00 | .80 | .20 |
| ☐ 11 Houston Oilers | 2.00 | .80 | .20 |
| ☐ 12 Kansas City Chiefs | 2.00 | .80 | .20 |
| ☐ 13 Los Angeles Rams | 2.00 | .80 | .20 |

| | | | |
|---|---|---|---|
| ☐ 14 Miami Dolphins | 3.00 | 1.20 | .30 |
| ☐ 15 Minnesota Vikings | 2.00 | .80 | .20 |
| ☐ 16 New England Patriots | 2.00 | .80 | .20 |
| ☐ 17 New Orleans Saints | 2.00 | .80 | .20 |
| ☐ 18A New York Giants | 3.00 | 1.20 | .30 |
| (Giants on helmet) | | | |
| ☐ 18B New York Giants | 4.00 | 1.60 | .40 |
| (New York on helmet) | | | |
| ☐ 19 New York Jets | 2.00 | .80 | .20 |
| ☐ 20 Oakland Raiders | 3.00 | 1.20 | .30 |
| ☐ 21 Philadelphia Eagles | 2.00 | .80 | .20 |
| ☐ 22 Pittsburgh Steelers | 3.00 | 1.20 | .30 |
| ☐ 23 St. Louis Cardinals | 2.00 | .80 | .20 |
| ☐ 24 San Diego Chargers | 2.00 | .80 | .20 |
| ☐ 25 San Francisco 49ers | 3.00 | 1.20 | .30 |
| ☐ 26 Seattle Seahawks | 2.00 | .80 | .20 |
| ☐ 27 Tampa Bay Buccaneers | 2.00 | .80 | .20 |
| ☐ 28 Washington Redskins | 3.00 | 1.20 | .30 |
| ☐ xx Title Card SP | 25.00 | 10.00 | 2.50 |
| Pro Quarterback, Pro Football's Leading Magazine | | | |

## 1962 Post Cereal

The 1962 Post Cereal set of 200 cards is Post's only American football issue. The cards were distributed on the back panels of various flavors of Post Cereals. As is typical of the Post package-back issues, the cards are blank-backed and are typically found poorly cut from the cereal box. The cards (when properly trimmed) measure 2 1/2" by 3 1/2". The cards are grouped in order of the team's 1961 season finish, i.e., Green Bay Packers (1-15), New York Giants (16-30), Philadelphia Eagles (31-45), Detroit Lions (46-60), Cleveland Browns (61-75), Baltimore Colts (76-90), San Francisco 49ers (91-105), Chicago Bears (106-120), Pittsburgh Steelers (121-133), Dallas Cowboys (134-146), St. Louis Cardinals (147-159), Los Angeles Rams (160-173), Minnesota Vikings (174-186), and Washington Redskins (187-200). The players within each team are also grouped in alphabetical order with the exception of 135 Frank Clarke of the Cowboys. Certain cards printed only on ,unpopular types of cereal are relatively difficult to obtain. Thirty-one such cards are known and are indicated by an SP (short printed) in the checklist. Some players who had been traded had asterisks after their positions. Jim Ninowski (57) and Sam Baker (74) can be found with either a red or black (traded) asterisk. The set price below does not include both variations. The cards of Jim Johnson, Bob Lilly, and Larry Wilson predate their Rookie Cards. Also noteworthy is the card of Fran Tarkenton, whose rookie year for cards is 1962.

|  | NRMT | VG-E | GOOD |
|---|---|---|---|
| COMPLETE SET (200) | 4500.00 | 2000.00 | 500.00 |
| COMMON PLAYER (1-200) | 4.00 | 1.60 | .40 |

| | | | |
|---|---|---|---|
| ☐ 1 Dan Currie | 4.00 | 1.60 | .40 |
| ☐ 2 Boyd Dowler | 5.00 | 2.00 | .50 |
| ☐ 3 Bill Forester | 4.00 | 1.60 | .40 |
| ☐ 4 Forrest Gregg | 6.00 | 2.40 | .60 |
| ☐ 5 Dave Hanner | 4.00 | 1.60 | .40 |
| ☐ 6 Paul Hornung | 12.00 | 5.00 | 1.20 |
| ☐ 7 Henry Jordan | 4.00 | 1.60 | .40 |
| ☐ 8 Jerry Kramer SP | 25.00 | 10.00 | 2.50 |
| ☐ 9 Max McGee | 5.00 | 2.00 | .50 |
| ☐ 10 Tom Moore SP | 250.00 | 100.00 | 25.00 |
| ☐ 11 Jim Ringo | 6.00 | 2.40 | .60 |
| ☐ 12 Bart Starr | 20.00 | 8.00 | 2.00 |
| ☐ 13 Jim Taylor | 10.00 | 4.00 | 1.00 |
| ☐ 14 Fuzzy Thurston | 5.00 | 2.00 | .50 |
| ☐ 15 Jesse Whittenton | 4.00 | 1.60 | .40 |
| ☐ 16 Erich Barnes | 4.00 | 1.60 | .40 |
| ☐ 17 Roosevelt Brown | 6.00 | 2.40 | .60 |
| ☐ 18 Bob Gaiters | 4.00 | 1.60 | .40 |
| ☐ 19 Roosevelt Grier | 6.00 | 2.40 | .60 |
| ☐ 20 Sam Huff | 8.00 | 3.25 | .80 |
| ☐ 21 Jim Katcavage | 4.00 | 1.60 | .40 |
| ☐ 22 Cliff Livingston | 4.00 | 1.60 | .40 |
| ☐ 23 Dick Lynch | 4.00 | 1.60 | .40 |

| | | | |
|---|---|---|---|
| ☐ 24 Joe Morrison SP | 75.00 | 30.00 | 7.50 |
| ☐ 25 Dick Nolan SP | 50.00 | 20.00 | 5.00 |
| ☐ 26 Andy Robustelli | 6.00 | 2.40 | .60 |
| ☐ 27 Kyle Rote | 6.00 | 2.40 | .60 |
| ☐ 28 Del Shofner SP | 100.00 | 40.00 | 10.00 |
| ☐ 29 Y.A. Tittle SP | 100.00 | 40.00 | 10.00 |
| (Only player in set shown with helmet on) | | | |
| ☐ 30 Alex Webster | 5.00 | 2.00 | .50 |
| ☐ 31 Bill Barnes | 4.00 | 1.60 | .40 |
| ☐ 32 Maxie Baughan | 6.00 | 2.40 | .60 |
| ☐ 33 Chuck Bednarik | 8.00 | 3.25 | .80 |
| ☐ 34 Tom Brookshier | 10.00 | 4.00 | 1.00 |
| ☐ 35 Jimmy Carr | 4.00 | 1.60 | .40 |
| ☐ 36 Ted Dean SP | 60.00 | 24.00 | 6.00 |
| ☐ 37 Sonny Jurgensen | 10.00 | 4.00 | 1.00 |
| ☐ 38 Tommy McDonald | 5.00 | 2.00 | .50 |
| ☐ 39 Clarence Peaks | 4.00 | 1.60 | .40 |
| ☐ 40 Pete Retzlaff | 5.00 | 2.00 | .50 |
| ☐ 41 Jesse Richardson SP | 125.00 | 50.00 | 12.50 |
| ☐ 42 Leo Sugar | 4.00 | 1.60 | .40 |
| ☐ 43 Bobby Walston SP | 50.00 | 20.00 | 5.00 |
| ☐ 44 Chuck Weber | 10.00 | 4.00 | 1.00 |
| ☐ 45 Ed Khayat | 4.00 | 1.60 | .40 |
| ☐ 46 Howard Cassady | 5.00 | 2.00 | .50 |
| ☐ 47 Gail Cogdill | 4.00 | 1.60 | .40 |
| ☐ 48 Jim Gibbons SP | 60.00 | 24.00 | 6.00 |
| ☐ 49 Bill Glass | 5.00 | 2.00 | .50 |
| ☐ 50 Alex Karras | 10.00 | 4.00 | 1.00 |
| ☐ 51 Dick Lane | 6.00 | 2.40 | .60 |
| ☐ 52 Yale Lary | 6.00 | 2.40 | .60 |
| ☐ 53 Dan Lewis | 4.00 | 1.60 | .40 |
| ☐ 54 Darris McCord SP | 100.00 | 40.00 | 10.00 |
| ☐ 55 Jim Martin | 4.00 | 1.60 | .40 |
| ☐ 56 Earl Morrall | 5.00 | 2.00 | .50 |
| ☐ 57A Jim Ninowski (red asterisk) | 5.00 | 2.00 | .50 |
| ☐ 57B Jim Ninowski (black asterisk) | 5.00 | 2.00 | .50 |
| ☐ 58 Nick Pietrosante | 6.00 | 2.40 | .60 |
| ☐ 59 Joe Schmidt SP | 125.00 | 50.00 | 12.50 |
| ☐ 60 Harley Sewell | 4.00 | 1.60 | .40 |
| ☐ 61 Jim Brown | 50.00 | 20.00 | 5.00 |
| ☐ 62 Galen Fiss SP | 50.00 | 20.00 | 5.00 |
| ☐ 63 Bob Gain | 4.00 | 1.60 | .40 |
| ☐ 64 Jim Houston | 4.00 | 1.60 | .40 |
| ☐ 65 Mike McCormack | 6.00 | 2.40 | .60 |
| ☐ 66 Gene Hickerson | 4.00 | 1.60 | .40 |
| ☐ 67 Bobby Mitchell | 8.00 | 3.25 | .80 |
| ☐ 68 John Morrow | 4.00 | 1.60 | .40 |
| ☐ 69 Bernie Parrish | 4.00 | 1.60 | .40 |
| ☐ 70 Milt Plum | 5.00 | 2.00 | .50 |
| ☐ 71 Ray Renfro | 4.00 | 1.60 | .40 |
| ☐ 72 Dick Schafrath | 4.00 | 1.60 | .40 |
| ☐ 73 Jim Ray Smith | 4.00 | 1.60 | .40 |
| ☐ 74A Sam Baker SP (red asterisk) | 350.00 | 140.00 | 35.00 |
| ☐ 74B Sam Baker SP (black asterisk) | 300.00 | 120.00 | 30.00 |
| ☐ 75 Paul Wiggin | 25.00 | 10.00 | 2.50 |
| ☐ 76 Raymond Berry | 7.50 | 3.00 | .75 |
| ☐ 77 Bob Boyd | 4.00 | 1.60 | .40 |
| ☐ 78 Ordell Braase | 4.00 | 1.60 | .40 |
| ☐ 79 Art Donovan | 6.00 | 2.40 | .60 |
| ☐ 80 Dee Mackey | 4.00 | 1.60 | .40 |
| ☐ 81 Gino Marchetti | 8.00 | 3.25 | .80 |
| ☐ 82 Lenny Moore | 10.00 | 4.00 | 1.00 |
| ☐ 83 Jim Mutscheller | 4.00 | 1.60 | .40 |
| ☐ 84 Steve Myhra | 4.00 | 1.60 | .40 |
| ☐ 85 Jimmy Orr | 5.00 | 2.00 | .50 |
| ☐ 86 Jim Parker | 6.00 | 2.40 | .60 |
| ☐ 87 Bill Pellington | 4.00 | 1.60 | .40 |
| ☐ 88 Alex Sandusky | 4.00 | 1.60 | .40 |
| ☐ 89 Dick Szymanski | 4.00 | 1.60 | .40 |
| ☐ 90 John Unitas | 25.00 | 10.00 | 2.50 |
| ☐ 91 Bruce Bosley | 4.00 | 1.60 | .40 |
| ☐ 92 John Brodie | 10.00 | 4.00 | 1.00 |
| ☐ 93 Dave Baker SP | 350.00 | 140.00 | 35.00 |
| ☐ 94 Tommy Davis | 4.00 | 1.60 | .40 |
| ☐ 95 Bob Harrison | 4.00 | 1.60 | .40 |
| ☐ 96 Matt Hazeltine | 4.00 | 1.60 | .40 |
| ☐ 97 Jim Johnson SP | 75.00 | 30.00 | 7.50 |
| ☐ 98 Bill Kilmer | 6.00 | 2.40 | .60 |
| ☐ 99 Jerry Mertens | 4.00 | 1.60 | .40 |
| ☐ 100 Frank Morze | 4.00 | 1.60 | .40 |
| ☐ 101 R.C. Owens | 4.00 | 1.60 | .40 |
| ☐ 102 J.D. Smith | 4.00 | 1.60 | .40 |
| ☐ 103 Bob St. Clair SP | 125.00 | 50.00 | 12.50 |
| ☐ 104 Monty Stickles | 4.00 | 1.60 | .40 |
| ☐ 105 Abe Woodson | 5.00 | 2.00 | .50 |
| ☐ 106 Doug Atkins | 6.00 | 2.40 | .60 |
| ☐ 107 Ed Brown | 5.00 | 2.00 | .50 |
| ☐ 108 J.C. Caroline | 4.00 | 1.60 | .40 |
| ☐ 109 Rick Casares | 5.00 | 2.00 | .50 |
| ☐ 110 Angelo Coia SP | 250.00 | 100.00 | 25.00 |
| ☐ 111 Mike Ditka SP | 75.00 | 30.00 | 7.50 |
| ☐ 112 Joe Fortunato | 4.00 | 1.60 | .40 |
| ☐ 113 Willie Galimore | 5.00 | 2.00 | .50 |

| | | | |
|---|---|---|---|
| ☐ 114 Bill George | 6.00 | 2.40 | .60 |
| ☐ 115 Stan Jones | 6.00 | 2.40 | .60 |
| ☐ 116 Johnny Morris | 5.00 | 2.00 | .50 |
| ☐ 117 Larry Morris SP | 50.00 | 20.00 | 5.00 |
| ☐ 118 Richie Petitbon | 5.00 | 2.00 | .50 |
| ☐ 119 Bill Wade | 5.00 | 2.00 | .50 |
| ☐ 120 Maury Youmans | 4.00 | 1.60 | .40 |
| ☐ 121 Preston Carpenter | 4.00 | 1.60 | .40 |
| ☐ 122 Buddy Dial | 5.00 | 2.00 | .50 |
| ☐ 123 Bobby Joe Green | 4.00 | 1.60 | .40 |
| ☐ 124 Mike Henry | 5.00 | 2.00 | .50 |
| ☐ 125 John Henry Johnson | 6.00 | 2.40 | .60 |
| ☐ 126 Bobby Layne | 15.00 | 6.00 | 1.50 |
| ☐ 127 Gene Lipscomb | 5.00 | 2.00 | .50 |
| ☐ 128 Lou Michaels | 4.00 | 1.60 | .40 |
| ☐ 129 John Nisby | 4.00 | 1.60 | .40 |
| ☐ 130 John Reger | 4.00 | 1.60 | .40 |
| ☐ 131 Mike Sandusky | 4.00 | 1.60 | .40 |
| ☐ 132 George Tarasovic | 4.00 | 1.60 | .40 |
| ☐ 133 Tom Tracy SP | 100.00 | 40.00 | 10.00 |
| ☐ 134 Glynn Gregory | 4.00 | 1.60 | .40 |
| ☐ 135 Frank Clarke SP | 75.00 | 30.00 | 7.50 |
| ☐ 136 Mike Connelly SP | 50.00 | 20.00 | 5.00 |
| ☐ 137 L.G. Dupre | 4.00 | 1.60 | .40 |
| ☐ 138 Bob Fry | 4.00 | 1.60 | .40 |
| ☐ 139 Allen Green SP | 125.00 | 50.00 | 12.50 |
| ☐ 140 Bill Howton | 5.00 | 2.00 | .50 |
| ☐ 141 Bob Lilly | 25.00 | 10.00 | 2.50 |
| ☐ 142 Don Meredith | 15.00 | 6.00 | 1.50 |
| ☐ 143 Dick Moegle | 4.00 | 1.60 | .40 |
| ☐ 144 Don Perkins | 5.00 | 2.00 | .50 |
| ☐ 145 Jerry Tubbs SP | 100.00 | 40.00 | 10.00 |
| ☐ 146 J.W. Lockett | 4.00 | 1.60 | .40 |
| ☐ 147 Ed Cook | 4.00 | 1.60 | .40 |
| ☐ 148 John David Crow | 5.00 | 2.00 | .50 |
| ☐ 149 Sam Etcheverry | 5.00 | 2.00 | .50 |
| ☐ 150 Frank Fuller | 4.00 | 1.60 | .40 |
| ☐ 151 Prentice Gautt | 4.00 | 1.60 | .40 |
| ☐ 152 Jimmy Hill | 4.00 | 1.60 | .40 |
| ☐ 153 Bill Koman SP | 50.00 | 20.00 | 5.00 |
| ☐ 154 Larry Wilson | 20.00 | 8.00 | 2.00 |
| ☐ 155 Dale Meinert | 4.00 | 1.60 | .40 |
| ☐ 156 Ed Henke | 4.00 | 1.60 | .40 |
| ☐ 157 Sonny Randle | 5.00 | 2.00 | .50 |
| ☐ 158 Ralph Guglielmi SP | 50.00 | 20.00 | 5.00 |
| ☐ 159 Joe Childress | 4.00 | 1.60 | .40 |
| ☐ 160 Jon Arnett | 5.00 | 2.00 | .50 |
| ☐ 161 Dick Bass | 4.00 | 1.60 | .40 |
| ☐ 162 Zeke Bratkowski | 5.00 | 2.00 | .50 |
| ☐ 163 Carroll Dale | 25.00 | 10.00 | 2.50 |
| ☐ 164 Art Hunter | 4.00 | 1.60 | .40 |
| ☐ 165 John Lovetere | 4.00 | 1.60 | .40 |
| ☐ 166 Lamar Lundy | 5.00 | 2.00 | .50 |
| ☐ 167 Ollie Matson | 8.00 | 3.25 | .80 |
| ☐ 168 Ed Meador | 4.00 | 1.60 | .40 |
| ☐ 169 Jack Pardee SP | 100.00 | 40.00 | 10.00 |
| ☐ 170 Jim Phillips | 4.00 | 1.60 | .40 |
| ☐ 171 Les Richter | 4.00 | 1.60 | .40 |
| ☐ 172 Frank Ryan | 5.00 | 2.00 | .50 |
| ☐ 173 Frank Varrichione | 4.00 | 1.60 | .40 |
| ☐ 174 Grady Alderman | 4.00 | 1.60 | .40 |
| ☐ 175 Rip Hawkins | 4.00 | 1.60 | .40 |
| ☐ 176 Don Joyce SP | 125.00 | 50.00 | 12.50 |
| ☐ 177 Bill Lapham | 4.00 | 1.60 | .40 |
| ☐ 178 Tommy Mason | 5.00 | 2.00 | .50 |
| ☐ 179 Hugh McElhenny | 6.00 | 2.40 | .60 |
| ☐ 180 Dave Middleton | 4.00 | 1.60 | .40 |
| ☐ 181 Dick Pesonen | 25.00 | 10.00 | 2.50 |
| ☐ 182 Karl Rubke | 4.00 | 1.60 | .40 |
| ☐ 183 George Shaw | 4.00 | 1.60 | .40 |
| ☐ 184 Fran Tarkenton | 50.00 | 20.00 | 5.00 |
| ☐ 185 Mel Triplett | 4.00 | 1.60 | .40 |
| ☐ 186 Frank Youso SP | 100.00 | 40.00 | 10.00 |
| ☐ 187 Bill Bishop | 4.00 | 1.60 | .40 |
| ☐ 188 Bill Anderson SP | 75.00 | 30.00 | 7.50 |
| ☐ 189 Don Bosseler | 4.00 | 1.60 | .40 |
| ☐ 190 Fred Hageman | 4.00 | 1.60 | .40 |
| ☐ 191 Sam Horner | 4.00 | 1.60 | .40 |
| ☐ 192 Jim Kerr | 4.00 | 1.60 | .40 |
| ☐ 193 Joe Krakoski SP | 250.00 | 100.00 | 25.00 |
| ☐ 194 Fred Dugan | 4.00 | 1.60 | .40 |
| ☐ 195 John Paluck | 4.00 | 1.60 | .40 |
| ☐ 196 Vince Promuto | 4.00 | 1.60 | .40 |
| ☐ 197 Joe Rutgens | 4.00 | 1.60 | .40 |
| ☐ 198 Norm Snead | 5.00 | 2.00 | .50 |
| ☐ 199 Andy Stynchula | 4.00 | 1.60 | .40 |
| ☐ 200 Bob Toneff | 4.00 | 1.60 | .40 |

# 1962 Post Booklets

Each of these booklets measures approximately 5" by 3" and contained fifteen pages. The front cover carries the title of each booklet and a color cartoon headshot of the player inside a circle. While the first page presents biography and career summary, the remainder of each booklet consists of various tips, diagrams of basic formations and

plays, officials' signals, football lingo, statistics, or team standings. The booklets are illustrated throughout by crude color drawings. These booklets are numbered on the front page in the upper right corner.

|  | NRMT | VG-E | GOOD |
|---|---|---|---|
| COMPLETE SET (4) | 50.00 | 20.00 | 5.00 |
| COMMON PLAYER (1-4) | 8.00 | 3.25 | .80 |
| ☐ 1 Jon Arnett | 8.00 | 3.25 | .80 |
| Football Formations To Watch (Important Rules of the Game) | | | |
| ☐ 2 Paul Hornung | 25.00 | 10.00 | 2.50 |
| Fundamentals of Football | | | |
| ☐ 3 Sonny Jurgensen | 15.00 | 6.00 | 1.50 |
| How To Play On Offense (How To Call Signals And Key Plays) | | | |
| ☐ 4 Sam Huff | 12.00 | 5.00 | 1.20 |
| How To Play Defense | | | |

## 1977 Pottsville Maroons

Reportedly issued in 1977, this standard-size (2 1/2" by 3 1/2") 17-card set features helmetless player photos of the disputed 1925 NFL champion Pottsville Maroons on the card fronts. The pictures are white-bordered and red-screened, with the player's name, card number, and team name in red beneath each photo. The player's name, team, and card number appear again at the top of the card back, along with the name of the college (if any) attended previous to playing for the Maroons and brief biographical information, all in red. The set producer's name, Joseph C. Zacko Sr., appears at the bottom, along with the copyright date, 1977. The cards are numbered on the back.

|  | NRMT | VG-E | GOOD |
|---|---|---|---|
| COMPLETE SET (17) | 20.00 | 8.00 | 2.00 |
| COMMON PLAYER (1-17) | 1.50 | .60 | .15 |
| ☐ 1 Team History | 2.00 | .80 | .20 |
| ☐ 2 The Symbolic Shoe | 1.50 | .60 | .15 |
| ☐ 3 Jack Ernst | 1.50 | .60 | .15 |
| ☐ 4 Tony Latone | 1.50 | .60 | .15 |
| ☐ 5 Duke Osborn | 1.50 | .60 | .15 |
| ☐ 6 Frank Bucher | 1.50 | .60 | .15 |
| ☐ 7 Frankie Racis | 1.50 | .60 | .15 |
| ☐ 8 Russ Hathaway | 1.50 | .60 | .15 |
| ☐ 9 W.H.(Hoot) Flanagan | 1.50 | .60 | .15 |
| ☐ 10 Charlie Berry | 2.50 | 1.00 | .25 |
| ☐ 11 Russ Stein | 1.50 | .60 | .15 |

| | | | |
|---|---|---|---|
| Herb Stein | | | |
| ☐ 12 Howard Lebengood | 1.50 | .60 | .15 |
| ☐ 13 Denny Hughes | 1.50 | .60 | .15 |
| ☐ 14 Barney Wentz | 1.50 | .60 | .15 |
| ☐ 15 Eddie Doyle UER | 1.50 | .60 | .15 |
| (Bio says American troops landed in Africa 1943; should be 1942) | | | |
| ☐ 16 Walter French | 1.50 | .60 | .15 |
| ☐ 17 Dick Rauch | 2.00 | .80 | .20 |

## 1992 Power

CHRIS MILLER

The 1992 Pro Set Power football set consists of 330 cards, each measuring the standard size (2 1/2" by 3 1/2"). Production was limited to 10,000 numbered 20-box wax cases. The fronts feature action player photos with the featured player in color against a semi-ghosted background. The player's name appears in brick-red lettering at the bottom. The horizontal backs have a second color player photo with a shadow border. The player's name and team name are printed in the team's colors, and a brief player profile fills out the back. The cards are numbered on the back. The numbering of card numbers 1-199 corresponds to the player's uniform number. A ten-card insert set of gold foil-stamped "Power Combos" were randomly inserted in foil packs. Rookie Cards include Edgar Bennett, Steve Bono, Terrell Buckley, Dale Carter, Quentin Coryatt, Vaughn Dunbar, Steve Emtman, David Klingler, Amp Lee, Johnny Mitchell, Carl Pickens, Tony Smith, and Tommy Vardell.

|  | MINT | EXC | G-VG |
|---|---|---|---|
| COMPLETE SET (330) | 30.00 | 13.50 | 3.80 |
| COMMON PLAYER (1-330) | .10 | .05 | .01 |
| ☐ 1 Warren Moon | .35 | .16 | .04 |
| Houston Oilers | | | |
| ☐ 2 Mike Horan | .10 | .05 | .01 |
| Denver Broncos | | | |
| ☐ 3 Bobby Hebert | .15 | .07 | .02 |
| New Orleans Saints | | | |
| ☐ 4 Jim Harbaugh | .12 | .05 | .02 |
| Chicago Bears | | | |
| ☐ 5 Sean Landeta | .10 | .05 | .01 |
| New York Giants | | | |
| ☐ 6 Bubby Brister | .12 | .05 | .02 |
| Pittsburgh Steelers | | | |
| ☐ 7 John Elway | 1.00 | .45 | .13 |
| Denver Broncos | | | |
| ☐ 8 Troy Aikman | 3.00 | 1.35 | .40 |
| Dallas Cowboys | | | |
| ☐ 9 Rodney Peete | .12 | .05 | .02 |
| Detroit Lions | | | |
| ☐ 10 Dan McGwire | .12 | .05 | .02 |
| Seattle Seahawks | | | |
| ☐ 11 Mark Rypien | .15 | .07 | .02 |
| Washington Redskins | | | |
| ☐ 12 Randall Cunningham | .20 | .09 | .03 |
| Philadelphia Eagles | | | |
| ☐ 13 Dan Marino | 1.50 | .65 | .19 |
| Miami Dolphins | | | |
| ☐ 14 Vinny Testaverde | .15 | .07 | .02 |
| Tampa Bay Buccaneers | | | |
| ☐ 15 Jeff Hostetler | .30 | .14 | .04 |
| New York Giants | | | |
| ☐ 16 Joe Montana | 2.00 | .90 | .25 |
| San Francisco 49ers | | | |
| ☐ 17 Dave Krieg | .12 | .05 | .02 |
| Kansas City Chiefs | | | |
| ☐ 18 Jeff Jaeger | .10 | .05 | .01 |
| Los Angeles Raiders | | | |
| ☐ 19 Bernie Kosar | .15 | .07 | .02 |
| Cleveland Browns | | | |
| ☐ 20 Barry Sanders | 2.00 | .90 | .25 |
| Detroit Lions | | | |

| | | | |
|---|---|---|---|
| ☐ 21 Deion Sanders | .40 | .18 | .05 |
| Atlanta Falcons | | | |
| ☐ 22 Emmitt Smith | 5.00 | 2.30 | .60 |
| Dallas Cowboys | | | |
| ☐ 23 Mel Gray | .12 | .05 | .02 |
| Detroit Lions | | | |
| ☐ 24 Stanley Richard | .10 | .05 | .01 |
| San Diego Chargers | | | |
| ☐ 25 Brad Muster | .12 | .05 | .02 |
| Chicago Bears | | | |
| ☐ 26 Rod Woodson | .15 | .07 | .02 |
| Pittsburgh Steelers | | | |
| ☐ 27 Rodney Hampton | .75 | .35 | .09 |
| New York Giants | | | |
| ☐ 28 Darrell Green | .12 | .05 | .02 |
| Washington Redskins | | | |
| ☐ 29 Barry Foster | .75 | .35 | .09 |
| Pittsburgh Steelers | | | |
| ☐ 30 Dave Meggett | .12 | .05 | .02 |
| New York Giants | | | |
| ☐ 31 Lonnie Young | .10 | .05 | .01 |
| New York Jets | | | |
| ☐ 32 Marcus Allen | .12 | .05 | .02 |
| Los Angeles Raiders | | | |
| ☐ 33 Merril Hoge | .12 | .05 | .02 |
| Pittsburgh Steelers | | | |
| ☐ 34 Thurman Thomas | .75 | .35 | .09 |
| Buffalo Bills | | | |
| ☐ 35 Neal Anderson | .12 | .05 | .02 |
| Chicago Bears | | | |
| ☐ 36 Bennie Blades | .10 | .05 | .01 |
| Detroit Lions | | | |
| ☐ 37 Pat Terrell | .10 | .05 | .01 |
| Los Angeles Rams | | | |
| ☐ 38 Nick Bell | .12 | .05 | .02 |
| Los Angeles Raiders | | | |
| ☐ 39 Johnny Johnson | .20 | .09 | .03 |
| Phoenix Cardinals | | | |
| ☐ 40 Bill Bates | .10 | .05 | .01 |
| Dallas Cowboys | | | |
| ☐ 41 Keith Byars | .12 | .05 | .02 |
| Philadelphia Eagles | | | |
| ☐ 42 Ronnie Lott | .15 | .07 | .02 |
| Los Angeles Raiders | | | |
| ☐ 43 Elvis Patterson | .10 | .05 | .01 |
| Los Angeles Raiders | | | |
| ☐ 44 Lorenzo White | .12 | .05 | .02 |
| Houston Oilers | | | |
| ☐ 45 Tony Stargell | .10 | .05 | .01 |
| Indianapolis Colts | | | |
| ☐ 46 Tim McDonald | .12 | .05 | .02 |
| Phoenix Cardinals | | | |
| ☐ 47 Kirby Jackson | .10 | .05 | .01 |
| Buffalo Bills | | | |
| ☐ 48 Lionel Washington | .10 | .05 | .01 |
| Los Angeles Raiders | | | |
| ☐ 49 Dennis Smith | .12 | .05 | .02 |
| Denver Broncos | | | |
| ☐ 50 Mike Singletary | .15 | .07 | .02 |
| Chicago Bears | | | |
| ☐ 51 Mike Croel | .12 | .05 | .02 |
| Denver Broncos | | | |
| ☐ 52 Pepper Johnson | .12 | .05 | .02 |
| New York Giants | | | |
| ☐ 53 Vaughan Johnson | .12 | .05 | .02 |
| New Orleans Saints | | | |
| ☐ 54 Chris Spielman | .12 | .05 | .02 |
| Detroit Lions | | | |
| ☐ 55 Junior Seau | .10 | .05 | .01 |
| San Diego Chargers | | | |
| ☐ 56 Lawrence Taylor | .20 | .09 | .03 |
| New York Giants | | | |
| ☐ 57 Clay Matthews | .12 | .05 | .02 |
| Cleveland Browns | | | |
| ☐ 58 Derrick Thomas | .30 | .14 | .04 |
| Kansas City Chiefs | | | |
| ☐ 59 Seth Joyner | .12 | .05 | .02 |
| Philadelphia Eagles | | | |
| ☐ 60 Stan Thomas | .10 | .05 | .01 |
| Chicago Bears | | | |
| ☐ 61 Nate Newton | .10 | .05 | .01 |
| Dallas Cowboys | | | |
| ☐ 62 Matt Brock | .10 | .05 | .01 |
| Green Bay Packers | | | |
| ☐ 63 Gene Chilton | .10 | .05 | .01 |
| New England Patriots | | | |
| ☐ 64 Randall McDaniel | .10 | .05 | .01 |
| Minnesota Vikings | | | |
| ☐ 65 Max Montoya | .10 | .05 | .01 |
| Los Angeles Raiders | | | |
| ☐ 66 Joe Jacoby | .10 | .05 | .01 |
| Washington Redskins | | | |
| ☐ 67 Russell Maryland | .25 | .11 | .03 |
| Dallas Cowboys | | | |
| ☐ 68 Ed King | .10 | .05 | .01 |
| Cleveland Browns | | | |
| ☐ 69 Mark Schlereth | .15 | .07 | .02 |

| | | | |
|---|---|---|---|
| Washington Redskins | | | |
| ☐ 70 Charles McRae | .10 | .05 | .01 |
| Tampa Bay Buccaneers | | | |
| ☐ 71 Charles Mann | .12 | .05 | .02 |
| Washington Redskins | | | |
| ☐ 72 William Perry | .12 | .05 | .02 |
| Chicago Bears | | | |
| ☐ 73 Simon Fletcher | .12 | .05 | .02 |
| Denver Broncos | | | |
| ☐ 74 Paul Gruber | .10 | .05 | .01 |
| Tampa Bay Buccaneers | | | |
| ☐ 75 Howie Long | .12 | .05 | .02 |
| Los Angeles Raiders | | | |
| ☐ 76 Steve McMichael | .12 | .05 | .02 |
| Chicago Bears | | | |
| ☐ 77 Karl Mecklenburg | .12 | .05 | .02 |
| Denver Broncos | | | |
| ☐ 78 Anthony Munoz | .12 | .05 | .02 |
| Cincinnati Bengals | | | |
| ☐ 79 Ray Childress | .12 | .05 | .02 |
| Houston Oilers | | | |
| ☐ 80 Jerry Rice | 1.25 | .55 | .16 |
| San Francisco 49ers | | | |
| ☐ 81 Art Monk | .15 | .07 | .02 |
| Washington Redskins | | | |
| ☐ 82 John Taylor | .15 | .07 | .02 |
| San Francisco 49ers | | | |
| ☐ 83 Andre Reed | .15 | .07 | .02 |
| Buffalo Bills | | | |
| ☐ 84 Haywood Jeffires | .15 | .07 | .02 |
| Houston Oilers | | | |
| ☐ 85 Mark Duper | .12 | .05 | .02 |
| Miami Dolphins | | | |
| ☐ 86 Fred Barnett | .15 | .07 | .02 |
| Philadelphia Eagles | | | |
| ☐ 87 Tom Waddle | .15 | .07 | .02 |
| Chicago Bears | | | |
| ☐ 88 Michael Irvin | 1.25 | .55 | .16 |
| Dallas Cowboys | | | |
| ☐ 89 Brian Blades | .12 | .05 | .02 |
| Seattle Seahawks | | | |
| ☐ 90 Neil Smith | .15 | .07 | .02 |
| Kansas City Chiefs | | | |
| ☐ 91 Kevin Greene | .12 | .05 | .02 |
| Los Angeles Rams | | | |
| ☐ 92 Reggie White | .30 | .14 | .04 |
| Philadelphia Eagles | | | |
| ☐ 93 Jerry Ball | .12 | .05 | .02 |
| Detroit Lions | | | |
| ☐ 94 Charles Haley | .12 | .05 | .02 |
| Dallas Cowboys | | | |
| ☐ 95 Richard Dent | .12 | .05 | .02 |
| Chicago Bears | | | |
| ☐ 96 Clyde Simmons | .12 | .05 | .02 |
| Philadelphia Eagles | | | |
| ☐ 97 Cornelius Bennett | .15 | .07 | .02 |
| Buffalo Bills | | | |
| ☐ 98 Eric Swann | .12 | .05 | .02 |
| Phoenix Cardinals | | | |
| ☐ 99 Doug Smith | .10 | .05 | .01 |
| Houston Oilers | | | |
| ☐ 100 Jim Kelly | .50 | .23 | .06 |
| Buffalo Bills | | | |
| ☐ 101 Michael Jackson | .25 | .11 | .03 |
| Cleveland Browns | | | |
| ☐ 102 Steve Christie | .10 | .05 | .01 |
| Buffalo Bills | | | |
| ☐ 103 Timm Rosenbach | .10 | .05 | .01 |
| Phoenix Cardinals | | | |
| ☐ 104 Brett Favre | 2.00 | .90 | .25 |
| Green Bay Packers | | | |
| ☐ 105 Jeff Feagles | .10 | .05 | .01 |
| Philadelphia Eagles | | | |
| ☐ 106 Kevin Butler | .10 | .05 | .01 |
| Chicago Bears | | | |
| ☐ 107 Boomer Esiason | .20 | .09 | .03 |
| Cincinnati Bengals | | | |
| ☐ 108 Steve Young | .75 | .35 | .09 |
| San Francisco 49ers | | | |
| ☐ 109 Norm Johnson | .10 | .05 | .01 |
| Atlanta Falcons | | | |
| ☐ 110 Jay Schroeder | .12 | .05 | .02 |
| Los Angeles Raiders | | | |
| ☐ 111 Jeff George | .40 | .18 | .05 |
| Indianapolis Colts | | | |
| ☐ 112 Chris Miller | .15 | .07 | .02 |
| Atlanta Falcons | | | |
| ☐ 113 Steve Bono | 1.00 | .45 | .13 |
| San Francisco 49ers | | | |
| ☐ 114 Neil O'Donnell | .75 | .35 | .09 |
| Pittsburgh Steelers | | | |
| ☐ 115 David Klingler | 1.00 | .45 | .13 |
| Cincinnati Bengals | | | |
| ☐ 116 Rich Gannon | .12 | .05 | .02 |
| Minnesota Vikings | | | |
| ☐ 117 Chris Chandler | .12 | .05 | .02 |
| Phoenix Cardinals | | | |
| ☐ 118 Stan Gelbaugh | .10 | .05 | .01 |

|  |  |  | | | |
|---|---|---|---|---|---|
| | | Seattle Seahawks | | | |
| ☐ 119 | Scott Mitchell | Miami Dolphins | 1.25 | .55 | .16 |
| ☐ 120 | Mark Carrier | Chicago Bears | .12 | .05 | .02 |
| ☐ 121 | Terry Allen | Minnesota Vikings | .35 | .16 | .04 |
| ☐ 122 | Tim McKyer | Atlanta Falcons | .12 | .05 | .02 |
| ☐ 123 | Barry Word | Kansas City Chiefs | .10 | .05 | .01 |
| ☐ 124 | Freeman McNeil | New York Jets | .10 | .05 | .01 |
| ☐ 125 | Louis Oliver | Miami Dolphins | .12 | .05 | .02 |
| ☐ 126 | Jarvis Williams | Miami Dolphins | .10 | .05 | .01 |
| ☐ 127 | Steve Atwater | Denver Broncos | .12 | .05 | .02 |
| ☐ 128 | Cris Dishman | Houston Oilers | .12 | .05 | .02 |
| ☐ 129 | Eric Dickerson | Los Angeles Raiders | .15 | .07 | .02 |
| ☐ 130 | Brad Baxter | New York Jets | .12 | .05 | .02 |
| ☐ 131 | Frank Minnifield | Cleveland Browns | .10 | .05 | .01 |
| ☐ 132 | Ricky Watters | San Francisco 49ers | 1.00 | .45 | .13 |
| ☐ 133 | David Fulcher | Cincinnati Bengals | .10 | .05 | .01 |
| ☐ 134 | Herschel Walker | Philadelphia Eagles | .15 | .07 | .02 |
| ☐ 135 | Christian Okoye | Kansas City Chiefs | .12 | .05 | .02 |
| ☐ 136 | Jerome Henderson | New England Patriots | .10 | .05 | .01 |
| ☐ 137 | Nate Odomes | Buffalo Bills | .12 | .05 | .02 |
| ☐ 138 | Todd Scott | Minnesota Vikings | .10 | .05 | .01 |
| ☐ 139 | Robert Delpino | Los Angeles Rams | .12 | .05 | .02 |
| ☐ 140 | Gary Anderson | Tampa Bay Buccaneers | .12 | .05 | .02 |
| ☐ 141 | Todd Lyght | Los Angeles Rams | .10 | .05 | .01 |
| ☐ 142 | Chris Warren | Seattle Seahawks | .40 | .18 | .05 |
| ☐ 143 | Mike Brim | New York Jets | .10 | .05 | .01 |
| ☐ 144 | Tom Rathman | San Francisco 49ers | .12 | .05 | .02 |
| ☐ 145 | Dexter McNabb | Green Bay Packers | .10 | .05 | .01 |
| ☐ 146 | Vince Workman | Green Bay Packers | .12 | .05 | .02 |
| ☐ 147 | Anthony Johnson | Washington Redskins | .10 | .05 | .01 |
| ☐ 148 | Brian Washington | New York Jets | .10 | .05 | .01 |
| ☐ 149 | David Tate | Chicago Bears | .10 | .05 | .01 |
| ☐ 150 | Johnny Holland | Green Bay Packers | .10 | .05 | .01 |
| ☐ 151 | Monte Coleman | Washington Redskins | .10 | .05 | .01 |
| ☐ 152 | Keith McCants | Tampa Bay Buccaneers | .10 | .05 | .01 |
| ☐ 153 | Eugene Seale | Houston Oilers | .10 | .05 | .01 |
| ☐ 154 | Al Smith | Houston Oilers | .10 | .05 | .01 |
| ☐ 155 | Andre Collins | Washington Redskins | .10 | .05 | .01 |
| ☐ 156 | Pat Swilling | New Orleans Saints | .12 | .05 | .02 |
| ☐ 157 | Rickey Jackson | New Orleans Saints | .12 | .05 | .02 |
| ☐ 158 | Wilber Marshall | Washington Redskins | .12 | .05 | .02 |
| ☐ 159 | Kyle Clifton | New York Jets | .10 | .05 | .01 |
| ☐ 160 | Fred Stokes | Washington Redskins | .10 | .05 | .01 |
| ☐ 161 | Lance Smith | Phoenix Cardinals | .10 | .05 | .01 |
| ☐ 162 | Guy McIntyre | San Francisco 49ers | .12 | .05 | .02 |
| ☐ 163 | Bill Maas | Kansas City Chiefs | .10 | .05 | .01 |
| ☐ 164 | Gerald Perry | Los Angeles Rams | .10 | .05 | .01 |
| ☐ 165 | Bart Oates | New York Giants | .10 | .05 | .01 |
| ☐ 166 | Tony Jones | Cleveland Browns | .10 | .05 | .01 |
| ☐ 167 | Moe Gardner | Atlanta Falcons | .10 | .05 | .01 |
| ☐ 168 | Joe Wolf | Phoenix Cardinals | .10 | .05 | .01 |
| ☐ 169 | Tim Krumrie | Cincinnati Bengals | .10 | .05 | .01 |
| ☐ 170 | Leonard Marshall | New York Giants | .12 | .05 | .02 |
| ☐ 171 | Kevin Call | Indianapolis Colts | .10 | .05 | .01 |
| ☐ 172 | Keith Kartz | Denver Broncos | .10 | .05 | .01 |
| ☐ 173 | Ron Heller | Philadelphia Eagles | .10 | .05 | .01 |
| ☐ 174 | Steve Wallace | San Francisco 49ers | .10 | .05 | .01 |
| ☐ 175 | Tony Casillas | Dallas Cowboys | .10 | .05 | .01 |
| ☐ 176 | Tim Irwin | Minnesota Vikings | .10 | .05 | .01 |
| ☐ 177 | Pat Harlow | New England Patriots | .10 | .05 | .01 |
| ☐ 178 | Bruce Smith | Buffalo Bills | .15 | .07 | .02 |
| ☐ 179 | Jim Lachey | Washington Redskins | .10 | .05 | .01 |
| ☐ 180 | Andre Rison | Atlanta Falcons | .40 | .18 | .05 |
| ☐ 181 | Michael Haynes | Atlanta Falcons | .60 | .25 | .08 |
| ☐ 182 | Rod Bernstine | San Diego Chargers | .12 | .05 | .02 |
| ☐ 183 | Mark Clayton | Miami Dolphins | .12 | .05 | .02 |
| ☐ 184 | Jay Novacek | Dallas Cowboys | .25 | .11 | .03 |
| ☐ 185 | Rob Moore | New York Jets | .15 | .07 | .02 |
| ☐ 186 | Willie Green | Detroit Lions | .10 | .05 | .01 |
| ☐ 187 | Ricky Proehl | Phoenix Cardinals | .15 | .07 | .02 |
| ☐ 188 | Al Toon | New York Jets | .12 | .05 | .02 |
| ☐ 189 | Webster Slaughter | Houston Oilers | .12 | .05 | .02 |
| ☐ 190 | Tony Bennett | Green Bay Packers | .12 | .05 | .02 |
| ☐ 191 | Jeff Cross | Miami Dolphins | .10 | .05 | .01 |
| ☐ 192 | Michael Dean Perry | Cleveland Browns | .15 | .07 | .02 |
| ☐ 193 | Greg Townsend | Los Angeles Raiders | .10 | .05 | .01 |
| ☐ 194 | Alfred Williams | Cincinnati Bengals | .10 | .05 | .01 |
| ☐ 195 | William Fuller | Houston Oilers | .10 | .05 | .01 |
| ☐ 196 | Cortez Kennedy | Seattle Seahawks | .10 | .05 | .01 |
| ☐ 197 | Henry Thomas | Minnesota Vikings | .10 | .05 | .01 |
| ☐ 198 | Esera Tuaolo | Green Bay Packers | .10 | .05 | .01 |
| ☐ 199 | Tim Green | Atlanta Falcons | .10 | .05 | .01 |
| ☐ 200 | Keith Jackson | Miami Dolphins | .15 | .07 | .02 |
| ☐ 201 | Don Majkowski | Green Bay Packers | .12 | .05 | .02 |
| ☐ 202 | Steve Beuerlein | Dallas Cowboys | .35 | .16 | .04 |
| ☐ 203 | Hugh Millen | New England Patriots | .12 | .05 | .02 |
| ☐ 204 | Browning Nagle | New York Jets | .12 | .05 | .02 |
| ☐ 205 | Chip Lohmiller | Washington Redskins | .12 | .05 | .02 |
| ☐ 206 | Phil Simms | New York Giants | .15 | .07 | .02 |
| ☐ 207 | Jim Everett | Los Angeles Rams | .10 | .05 | .01 |
| ☐ 208 | Erik Kramer | Detroit Lions | .20 | .09 | .03 |
| ☐ 209 | Todd Marinovich | Los Angeles Raiders | .10 | .05 | .01 |
| ☐ 210 | Henry Jones | Buffalo Bills | .10 | .05 | .01 |
| ☐ 211 | Dwight Stone | Pittsburgh Steelers | .10 | .05 | .01 |
| ☐ 212 | Andre Waters | Philadelphia Eagles | .10 | .05 | .01 |
| ☐ 213 | Darryl Henley | Los Angeles Rams | .10 | .05 | .01 |
| ☐ 214 | Mark Higgs | Miami Dolphins | .15 | .07 | .02 |
| ☐ 215 | Dalton Hilliard | New Orleans Saints | .10 | .05 | .01 |
| ☐ 216 | Earnest Byner | Dallas Cowboys | .12 | .05 | .02 |

| | | | |
|---|---|---|---|
| Washington Redskins | | | |
| ☐ 217 Eric Metcalf | .15 | .07 | .02 |
| Cleveland Browns | | | |
| ☐ 218 Gill Byrd | .12 | .05 | .02 |
| San Diego Chargers | | | |
| ☐ 219 Robert Williams | .15 | .07 | .02 |
| Dallas Cowboys | | | |
| ☐ 220 Kenneth Davis | .12 | .05 | .02 |
| Buffalo Bills | | | |
| ☐ 221 Larry Brown | .10 | .05 | .01 |
| Dallas Cowboys | | | |
| ☐ 222 Mark Collins | .10 | .05 | .01 |
| New York Giants | | | |
| ☐ 223 Vinnie Clark | .10 | .05 | .01 |
| Green Bay Packers | | | |
| ☐ 224 Patrick Hunter | .10 | .05 | .01 |
| Seattle Seahawks | | | |
| ☐ 225 Gaston Green | .12 | .05 | .02 |
| Denver Broncos | | | |
| ☐ 226 Everson Walls | .10 | .05 | .01 |
| Cleveland Browns | | | |
| ☐ 227 Harold Green | .12 | .05 | .02 |
| Cincinnati Bengals | | | |
| ☐ 228 Albert Lewis | .12 | .05 | .02 |
| Kansas City Chiefs | | | |
| ☐ 229 Don Griffin | .10 | .05 | .01 |
| San Francisco 49ers | | | |
| ☐ 230 Lorenzo Lynch | .10 | .05 | .01 |
| Phoenix Cardinals | | | |
| ☐ 231 Brian Mitchell | .12 | .05 | .02 |
| Washington Redskins | | | |
| ☐ 232 Thomas Everett | .10 | .05 | .01 |
| Dallas Cowboys | | | |
| ☐ 233 Leonard Russell | .60 | .25 | .08 |
| New England Patriots | | | |
| ☐ 234 Eric Bieniemy | .12 | .05 | .02 |
| San Diego Chargers | | | |
| ☐ 235 John L. Williams | .12 | .05 | .02 |
| Seattle Seahawks | | | |
| ☐ 236 Leroy Hoard | .12 | .05 | .02 |
| Cleveland Browns | | | |
| ☐ 237 Darren Lewis | .10 | .05 | .01 |
| Chicago Bears | | | |
| ☐ 238 Reggie Cobb | .15 | .07 | .02 |
| Tampa Bay Buccaneers | | | |
| ☐ 239 Steve Broussard | .12 | .05 | .02 |
| Atlanta Falcons | | | |
| ☐ 240 Marion Butts | .15 | .07 | .02 |
| San Diego Chargers | | | |
| ☐ 241 Mike Pritchard | .50 | .23 | .06 |
| Atlanta Falcons | | | |
| ☐ 242 Dexter Carter | .12 | .05 | .02 |
| San Francisco 49ers | | | |
| ☐ 243 Aeneas Williams | .10 | .05 | .01 |
| Phoenix Cardinals | | | |
| ☐ 244 Bruce Pickens | .10 | .05 | .01 |
| Atlanta Falcons | | | |
| ☐ 245 Harvey Williams | .15 | .07 | .02 |
| Kansas City Chiefs | | | |
| ☐ 246 Bobby Humphrey | .12 | .05 | .02 |
| Miami Dolphins | | | |
| ☐ 247 Duane Bickett | .10 | .05 | .01 |
| Indianapolis Colts | | | |
| ☐ 248 James Francis | .12 | .05 | .02 |
| Cincinnati Bengals | | | |
| ☐ 249 Broderick Thomas | .10 | .05 | .01 |
| Tampa Bay Buccaneers | | | |
| ☐ 250 Chip Banks | .10 | .05 | .01 |
| Indianapolis Colts | | | |
| ☐ 251 Bryan Cox | .12 | .05 | .02 |
| Miami Dolphins | | | |
| ☐ 252 Sam Mills | .12 | .05 | .02 |
| New Orleans Saints | | | |
| ☐ 253 Ken Norton Jr. | .12 | .05 | .02 |
| Dallas Cowboys | | | |
| ☐ 254 Jeff Herrod | .10 | .05 | .01 |
| Indianapolis Colts | | | |
| ☐ 255 John Roper | .10 | .05 | .01 |
| Chicago Bears | | | |
| ☐ 256 Darryl Talley | .12 | .05 | .02 |
| Buffalo Bills | | | |
| ☐ 257 Andre Tippett | .12 | .05 | .02 |
| New England Patriots | | | |
| ☐ 258 Jeff Lageman | .10 | .05 | .01 |
| New York Jets | | | |
| ☐ 259 Chris Doleman | .12 | .05 | .02 |
| Minnesota Vikings | | | |
| ☐ 260 Shane Conlan | .12 | .05 | .02 |
| Buffalo Bills | | | |
| ☐ 261 Jessie Tuggle | .10 | .05 | .01 |
| Atlanta Falcons | | | |
| ☐ 262 Eric Hill | .10 | .05 | .01 |
| Phoenix Cardinals | | | |
| ☐ 263 Bruce Armstrong | .10 | .05 | .01 |
| New England Patriots | | | |
| ☐ 264 Bill Fralic | .10 | .05 | .01 |
| Atlanta Falcons | | | |
| ☐ 265 Alvin Harper | .60 | .25 | .08 |
| Dallas Cowboys | | | |
| ☐ 266 Bill Brooks | .12 | .05 | .02 |
| Indianapolis Colts | | | |
| ☐ 267 Henry Ellard | .12 | .05 | .02 |
| Los Angeles Rams | | | |
| ☐ 268 Cris Carter | .15 | .07 | .02 |
| Minnesota Vikings | | | |
| ☐ 269 Irving Fryar | .12 | .05 | .02 |
| New England Patriots | | | |
| ☐ 270 Lawrence Dawsey | .15 | .07 | .02 |
| Tampa Bay Buccaneers | | | |
| ☐ 271 James Lofton | .15 | .07 | .02 |
| Buffalo Bills | | | |
| ☐ 272 Ernest Givins | .12 | .05 | .02 |
| Houston Oilers | | | |
| ☐ 273 Terance Mathis | .10 | .05 | .01 |
| New York Jets | | | |
| ☐ 274 Randal Hill | .15 | .07 | .02 |
| Phoenix Cardinals | | | |
| ☐ 275 Eddie Brown | .10 | .05 | .01 |
| Cincinnati Bengals | | | |
| ☐ 276 Tim Brown | .40 | .18 | .05 |
| Los Angeles Raiders | | | |
| ☐ 277 Anthony Carter | .12 | .05 | .02 |
| Minnesota Vikings | | | |
| ☐ 278 Wendell Davis | .10 | .05 | .01 |
| Chicago Bears | | | |
| ☐ 279 Mark Ingram | .12 | .05 | .02 |
| New York Giants | | | |
| ☐ 280 Anthony Miller | .30 | .14 | .04 |
| San Diego Chargers | | | |
| ☐ 281 Clarence Verdin | .10 | .05 | .01 |
| Indianapolis Colts | | | |
| ☐ 282 Flipper Anderson | .12 | .05 | .02 |
| Los Angeles Rams | | | |
| ☐ 283 Ricky Sanders | .12 | .05 | .02 |
| Washington Redskins | | | |
| ☐ 284 Steve Jordan | .12 | .05 | .02 |
| Minnesota Vikings | | | |
| ☐ 285 Gary Clark | .12 | .05 | .02 |
| Washington Redskins | | | |
| ☐ 286 Sterling Sharpe | 1.25 | .55 | .16 |
| Green Bay Packers | | | |
| ☐ 287 Herman Moore | .60 | .25 | .08 |
| Detroit Lions | | | |
| ☐ 288 Stephen Baker | .10 | .05 | .01 |
| New York Giants | | | |
| ☐ 289 Marv Cook | .12 | .05 | .02 |
| New England Patriots | | | |
| ☐ 290 Ernie Jones | .10 | .05 | .01 |
| Phoenix Cardinals | | | |
| ☐ 291 Eric Green | .15 | .07 | .02 |
| Pittsburgh Steelers | | | |
| ☐ 292 Mervyn Fernandez | .10 | .05 | .01 |
| Los Angeles Raiders | | | |
| ☐ 293 Greg McMurtry | .10 | .05 | .01 |
| New England Patriots | | | |
| ☐ 294 Quinn Early | .12 | .05 | .02 |
| New Orleans Saints | | | |
| ☐ 295 Tim Harris | .12 | .05 | .02 |
| San Francisco 49ers | | | |
| ☐ 296 Will Furrer | .30 | .14 | .04 |
| Chicago Bears | | | |
| ☐ 297 Jason Hanson | .25 | .11 | .03 |
| Detroit Lions | | | |
| ☐ 298 Chris Hakel | .15 | .07 | .02 |
| Washington Redskins | | | |
| ☐ 299 Ty Detmer | .15 | .07 | .02 |
| Green Bay Packers | | | |
| ☐ 300 David Klingler | .75 | .35 | .09 |
| Cincinnati Bengals | | | |
| ☐ 301 Amp Lee | .50 | .23 | .06 |
| San Francisco 49ers | | | |
| ☐ 302 Troy Vincent | .20 | .09 | .03 |
| Miami Dolphins | | | |
| ☐ 303 Kevin Smith | .50 | .23 | .06 |
| Dallas Cowboys | | | |
| ☐ 304 Terrell Buckley | .50 | .23 | .06 |
| Green Bay Packers | | | |
| ☐ 305 Dana Hall | .25 | .11 | .03 |
| San Francisco 49ers | | | |
| ☐ 306 Tony Smith | .35 | .16 | .04 |
| Atlanta Falcons | | | |
| ☐ 307 Steve Israel | .12 | .05 | .02 |
| Los Angeles Rams | | | |
| ☐ 308 Vaughn Dunbar | .40 | .18 | .05 |
| New Orleans Saints | | | |
| ☐ 309 Ashley Ambrose | .15 | .07 | .02 |
| Indianapolis Colts | | | |
| ☐ 310 Edgar Bennett | .60 | .25 | .08 |
| Green Bay Packers | | | |
| ☐ 311 Dale Carter | .50 | .23 | .06 |
| Kansas City Chiefs | | | |
| ☐ 312 Rodney Culver | .20 | .09 | .03 |
| Indianapolis Colts | | | |
| ☐ 313 Matt Darby | .12 | .05 | .02 |
| Buffalo Bills | | | |
| ☐ 314 Tommy Vardell | .50 | .23 | .06 |

Cleveland Browns

| | MINT | EXC | G-VG |
|---|---|---|---|
| ☐ 315 Quentin Coryatt | .50 | .23 | .06 |
| Indianapolis Colts | | | |
| ☐ 316 Robert Jones | .20 | .09 | .03 |
| Dallas Cowboys | | | |
| ☐ 317 Joe Bowden | .12 | .05 | .02 |
| Houston Oilers | | | |
| ☐ 318 Eugene Chung | .12 | .05 | .02 |
| New England Patriots | | | |
| ☐ 319 Troy Auzenne | .12 | .05 | .02 |
| Chicago Bears | | | |
| ☐ 320 Santana Dotson | .50 | .23 | .06 |
| Tampa Bay Buccaneers | | | |
| ☐ 321 Greg Skrepenak | .15 | .07 | .02 |
| Los Angeles Raiders | | | |
| ☐ 322 Steve Emtman | .20 | .09 | .03 |
| Indianapolis Colts | | | |
| ☐ 323 Carl Pickens | .75 | .35 | .09 |
| Cincinnati Bengals | | | |
| ☐ 324 Johnny Mitchell | 1.00 | .45 | .13 |
| New York Jets | | | |
| ☐ 325 Patrick Rowe | .20 | .09 | .03 |
| Cleveland Browns | | | |
| ☐ 326 Alonzo Spellman | .40 | .18 | .05 |
| Chicago Bears | | | |
| ☐ 327 Robert Porcher | .40 | .18 | .05 |
| Detroit Lions | | | |
| ☐ 328 Chris Mims | .40 | .18 | .05 |
| San Diego Chargers | | | |
| ☐ 329 Marc Boutte | .12 | .05 | .02 |
| Los Angeles Rams | | | |
| ☐ 330 Shane Dronett | .30 | .14 | .04 |
| Denver Broncos | | | |

## 1992 Power Combos

Randomly inserted into foil packs, this ten-card, standard-size (2 1/2" by 3 1/2") set spotlights powerful offensive and defensive player combinations. The horizontal fronts feature a full-bleed color photo of both players with the background ghosted. The words "Combos" and "Power" are printed across the top in holographic lettering. On a purple panel inside marbleized borders, the backs present biography on both players and summarize their contribution to the team. The cards are numbered on the back at the bottom center.

| | MINT | EXC | G-VG |
|---|---|---|---|
| COMPLETE SET (10) | 50.00 | 23.00 | 6.25 |
| COMMON PLAYER (1-10) | 4.00 | 1.80 | .50 |
| ☐ 1 Steve Emtman | 5.00 | 2.30 | .60 |
| Quentin Coryatt | | | |
| Indianapolis Colts | | | |
| ☐ 2 Barry Word | 4.00 | 1.80 | .50 |
| Christian Okoye | | | |
| Kansas City Chiefs | | | |
| ☐ 3 Sam Mills | 4.00 | 1.80 | .50 |
| Vaughan Johnson | | | |
| New Orleans Saints | | | |
| ☐ 4 Broderick Thomas | 4.00 | 1.80 | .50 |
| Keith McCants | | | |
| Tampa Bay Buccaneers | | | |
| ☐ 5 Michael Irvin | 35.00 | 16.00 | 4.40 |
| Emmitt Smith | | | |
| Dallas Cowboys | | | |
| ☐ 6 Jerry Ball | 4.00 | 1.80 | .50 |
| Chris Spielman | | | |
| Detroit Lions | | | |
| ☐ 7 Ricky Sanders | 4.00 | 1.80 | .50 |
| Gary Clark | | | |
| Art Monk | | | |
| Washington Redskins | | | |
| ☐ 8 Dave Johnson | 4.00 | 1.80 | .50 |
| Rod Woodson | | | |
| Pittsburgh Steelers | | | |

| | MINT | EXC | G-VG |
|---|---|---|---|
| ☐ 9 Bill Fralic | 4.00 | 1.80 | .50 |
| Chris Hinton | | | |
| Atlanta Falcons | | | |
| ☐ 10 Irving Fryar | 4.00 | 1.80 | .50 |
| Marv Cook | | | |
| New England Patriots | | | |

## 1992-93 Power Emmitt Smith

This ten-card standard size (2 1/2" by 3 1/2") set features Emmitt Smith's career highlights. The production run was 25,000 sets. The offer for this set was found on the back of a Pro Set Emmitt Smith special card, which was randomly inserted in second series foil packs. To order the ten-card set, the collector had to mail in ten 1992 NFL Pro Set (first or second series) wrappers and ten 1992 Pro Set Power wrappers along with 7.50 for each set ordered (limit four sets per person). For an additional 20.00, the first 7,500 orders received a personally autographed and hand numbered uncut sheet set with a limit of one per person. The fronts display full-bleed color action player photos in which the featured player is enhanced by ghosting of the background. The words "Pro Set Power" appear in holographic lettering at one of the upper corners, while a blue stripe toward the bottom carries the player's name and card subtitle. A special Emmitt Smith Commemorative emblem at the lower left corner rounds out the front. The team color-coded backs summarize Smith's career and feature a "Report Card" at the bottom. The cards are numbered on the back and have a "PS" prefix.

| | MINT | EXC | G-VG |
|---|---|---|---|
| COMPLETE SET (10) | 20.00 | 8.00 | 2.00 |
| COMMON PLAYER (1-10) | 2.50 | 1.00 | .25 |
| ☐ 1 Emmitt Smith | 2.50 | 1.00 | .25 |
| (Title card) | | | |
| ☐ 2 Emmitt Smith | 2.50 | 1.00 | .25 |
| Drafted by the | | | |
| Dallas Cowboys | | | |
| ☐ 3 Emmitt Smith | 2.50 | 1.00 | .25 |
| Emmitt Scores Four | | | |
| Touchdowns | | | |
| ☐ 4 Emmitt Smith | 2.50 | 1.00 | .25 |
| Pro Set Offensive | | | |
| Rookie of the Year | | | |
| ☐ 5 Emmitt Smith | 2.50 | 1.00 | .25 |
| Cowboys Beat | | | |
| Undefeated Redskins | | | |
| ☐ 6 Emmitt Smith | 2.50 | 1.00 | .25 |
| Cowboys Beat Chicago | | | |
| In Playoffs | | | |
| ☐ 7 Emmitt Smith | 2.50 | 1.00 | .25 |
| Back-to-Back | | | |
| Rushing Titles | | | |
| ☐ 8 Emmitt Smith | 2.50 | 1.00 | .25 |
| Emmitt's Three | | | |
| Pro Bowls | | | |
| ☐ 9 Emmitt Smith | 2.50 | 1.00 | .25 |
| Emmitt's Super Day | | | |
| ☐ 10 Emmitt Smith | 2.50 | 1.00 | .25 |
| Running Back of | | | |
| the '90s | | | |

## 1993 Power Prototypes

This ten-card standard-size (2 1/2" by 3 1/2") set was issued to preview the style of the 1993 Pro Set Power football series. Pro Set sent one of these prototype cards to each dealer or wholesaler. The cards were also packaged in a cello pack with an ad card and given away at the 1993 National Sports Collectors Convention. The full-bleed color action photos on the fronts have a shadow-border effect that gives the appearance of depth to the pictures. The player's name and

team name are printed in a red, gray, and blue-striped box at the lower left corner. The Pro Set Power logo is silver foil stamped on the fronts. The horizontal backs carry a color close-up photo, career summary, and a rating of players (from 1 to 10). The cards are numbered on the back at the upper left corner.

|  | MINT | EXC | G-VG |
|---|---|---|---|
| COMPLETE SET (10) | 10.00 | 4.00 | 1.00 |
| COMMON PLAYER | .50 | .20 | .05 |
|  |  |  |  |
| ☐ 20 Barry Sanders | 2.50 | 1.00 | .25 |
| Detroit Lions |  |  |  |
| ☐ 22 Emmitt Smith | 5.00 | 2.00 | .50 |
| Dallas Cowboys |  |  |  |
| ☐ 26 Rod Woodson | .75 | .30 | .07 |
| Pittsburgh Steelers |  |  |  |
| ☐ 32 Ricky Watters | 1.50 | .60 | .15 |
| San Francisco 49ers |  |  |  |
| ☐ 37 Larry Centers | .50 | .20 | .05 |
| Phoenix Cardinals |  |  |  |
| ☐ 71 Santana Dotson | .60 | .24 | .06 |
| Tampa Bay Buccaneers |  |  |  |
| ☐ 80 Jerry Rice | 2.50 | 1.00 | .25 |
| San Francisco 49ers |  |  |  |
| ☐ 138 Reggie Rivers | .50 | .20 | .05 |
| Denver Broncos |  |  |  |
| ☐ 193 Trace Armstrong | .50 | .20 | .05 |
| Chicago Bears |  |  |  |
| ☐ xx Title/Ad Card | .50 | .20 | .05 |

## 1993 Power

The 1993 Pro Set Power football set consists of 200 standard-size (2 1/2" by 3 1/2") cards. Including foil and jumbo cases, a total of 8,000 cases were produced. Randomly inserted throughout the foil packs were a 40-card Power Moves subset and a 30-card Power Draft Picks subset. Also one gold Star Power card was inserted in every pack. The vignetted fronts feature borderless color player action shots, with the player's name within a red, white, and blue rectangle at the lower left. The horizontal back carries a color player action shot, which is flanked on the left by a rating scale, and on the right by 1992 stats. The player's name appears above the photo, and his position and team appear below. 1992 season highlights at the bottom round out the card. The cards are numbered on the back. Also randomly inserted in 1993 Pro Set Power foil packs were two redemption cards entitling the collector to receive an Emmitt Smith hologram card through a mail-in offer. Randomly inserted in 1993 Pro Set Power jumbo packs, were seven update cards depicting traded players in their new teams' uniforms. Except for the new player photos and "UD" suffixes to the numbers on the backs, the design is identical to the players' regular 1993 Pro Set Power cards.

|  | MINT | EXC | G-VG |
|---|---|---|---|
| COMPLETE SET (200) | 8.00 | 3.60 | 1.00 |
| COMMON PLAYER (1-200) | .05 | .02 | .01 |
| *GOLD CARDS: 1.25X TO 2X VALUE |  |  |  |
|  |  |  |  |
| ☐ 1 Warren Moon | .15 | .07 | .02 |
| Houston Oilers |  |  |  |
| ☐ 2 Steve Christie | .05 | .02 | .01 |
| Buffalo Bills |  |  |  |
| ☐ 3 Jim Breech | .05 | .02 | .01 |
| Cincinnati Bengals |  |  |  |
| ☐ 4 Brett Favre | .75 | .35 | .09 |
| Green Bay Packers |  |  |  |
| ☐ 5 Sean Landeta | .05 | .02 | .01 |
| New York Giants |  |  |  |
| ☐ 6 Jim Arnold | .05 | .02 | .01 |
| Detroit Lions |  |  |  |
| ☐ 7 John Elway | .35 | .16 | .04 |
| Denver Broncos |  |  |  |
| ☐ 8 Troy Aikman | 1.25 | .55 | .16 |
| Dallas Cowboys |  |  |  |
| ☐ 9 Rodney Peete | .08 | .04 | .01 |
| Detroit Lions |  |  |  |
| ☐ 10 Pete Stoyanovich | .05 | .02 | .01 |
| Miami Dolphins |  |  |  |
| ☐ 11 Mark Rypien | .08 | .04 | .01 |
| Washington Redskins |  |  |  |
| ☐ 12 Jim Kelly | .25 | .11 | .03 |
| Buffalo Bills |  |  |  |
| ☐ 13 Dan Marino | .75 | .35 | .09 |
| Miami Dolphins |  |  |  |
| ☐ 14 Neil O'Donnell | .25 | .11 | .03 |
| Pittsburgh Steelers |  |  |  |
| ☐ 15 David Klingler | .15 | .07 | .02 |
| Cincinnati Bengals |  |  |  |
| ☐ 16 Rich Gannon | .08 | .04 | .01 |
| Minnesota Vikings |  |  |  |
| ☐ 16UD Rich Gannon | .18 | .08 | .02 |
| Washington Redskins |  |  |  |
| ☐ 17 Dave Krieg | .05 | .02 | .01 |
| Kansas City Chiefs |  |  |  |
| ☐ 18 Jeff Jaeger | .05 | .02 | .01 |
| Los Angeles Raiders |  |  |  |
| ☐ 19 Bernie Kosar | .10 | .05 | .01 |
| Cleveland Browns |  |  |  |
| ☐ 20 Barry Sanders | .75 | .35 | .09 |
| Detroit Lions |  |  |  |
| ☐ 21 Deion Sanders | .15 | .07 | .02 |
| Atlanta Falcons |  |  |  |
| ☐ 22 Emmitt Smith | 2.00 | .90 | .25 |
| Dallas Cowboys |  |  |  |
| ☐ 23 Barry Word | .10 | .05 | .01 |
| Kansas City Chiefs |  |  |  |
| ☐ 23UD Barry Word | .20 | .09 | .03 |
| Minnesota Vikings |  |  |  |
| ☐ 24 Stanley Richard | .05 | .02 | .01 |
| San Diego Chargers |  |  |  |
| ☐ 25 Louis Oliver | .05 | .02 | .01 |
| Miami Dolphins |  |  |  |
| ☐ 26 Rod Woodson | .10 | .05 | .01 |
| Pittsburgh Steelers |  |  |  |
| ☐ 27 Rodney Hampton | .30 | .14 | .04 |
| New York Giants |  |  |  |
| ☐ 28 Cris Dishman | .05 | .02 | .01 |
| Houston Oilers |  |  |  |
| ☐ 29 Barry Foster | .25 | .11 | .03 |
| Pittsburgh Steelers |  |  |  |
| ☐ 30 Dave Meggett | .08 | .04 | .01 |
| New York Giants |  |  |  |
| ☐ 31 Kevin Ross | .05 | .02 | .01 |
| Kansas City Chiefs |  |  |  |
| ☐ 32 Ricky Watters | .30 | .14 | .04 |
| San Francisco 49ers |  |  |  |
| ☐ 33 Darren Lewis | .05 | .02 | .01 |
| Chicago Bears |  |  |  |
| ☐ 34 Thurman Thomas | .35 | .16 | .04 |
| Buffalo Bills |  |  |  |
| ☐ 35 Rodney Culver | .05 | .02 | .01 |
| Indianapolis Colts |  |  |  |
| ☐ 36 Bennie Blades | .05 | .02 | .01 |
| Detroit Lions |  |  |  |
| ☐ 37 Larry Centers | .20 | .09 | .03 |
| Phoenix Cardinals |  |  |  |
| ☐ 38 Todd Scott | .05 | .02 | .01 |
| Minnesota Vikings |  |  |  |
| ☐ 39 Darren Perry | .05 | .02 | .01 |
| Pittsburgh Steelers |  |  |  |
| ☐ 40 Robert Massey | .05 | .02 | .01 |
| Phoenix Cardinals |  |  |  |
| ☐ 41 Keith Byars | .08 | .04 | .01 |
| Philadelphia Eagles |  |  |  |
| ☐ 41UD Keith Byars UER | .20 | .09 | .03 |
| Miami Dolphins |  |  |  |
| (Misspelled Mimai |  |  |  |
| on back) |  |  |  |
| ☐ 42 Chris Warren | .15 | .07 | .02 |
| Seattle Seahawks |  |  |  |
| ☐ 43 Cleveland Gary | .08 | .04 | .01 |

| | | | |
|---|---|---|---|
| Los Angeles Rams | | | |
| ☐ 44 Lorenzo White | .08 | .04 | .01 |
| Houston Oilers | | | |
| ☐ 45 Tony Stargell | .05 | .02 | .01 |
| Indianapolis Colts | | | |
| ☐ 46 Bennie Thompson | .05 | .02 | .01 |
| Kansas City Chiefs | | | |
| ☐ 47 A.J. Johnson | .05 | .02 | .01 |
| Washington Redskins | | | |
| ☐ 48 Daryl Johnston | .10 | .05 | .01 |
| Dallas Cowboys | | | |
| ☐ 49 Dennis Smith | .05 | .02 | .01 |
| Denver Broncos | | | |
| ☐ 50 Johnny Holland | .05 | .02 | .01 |
| Green Bay Packers | | | |
| ☐ 51 Ken Norton Jr. | .10 | .05 | .01 |
| Dallas Cowboys | | | |
| ☐ 52 Pepper Johnson | .05 | .02 | .01 |
| New York Giants | | | |
| ☐ 52UD Pepper Johnson | .15 | .07 | .02 |
| Cleveland Browns | | | |
| ☐ 53 Vaughan Johnson | .05 | .02 | .01 |
| New Orleans Saints | | | |
| ☐ 54 Chris Spielman | .05 | .02 | .01 |
| Detroit Lions | | | |
| ☐ 55 Junior Seau | .10 | .05 | .01 |
| San Diego Chargers | | | |
| ☐ 56 Chris Doleman | .08 | .04 | .01 |
| Minnesota Vikings | | | |
| ☐ 57 Rickey Jackson | .08 | .04 | .01 |
| New Orleans Saints | | | |
| ☐ 58 Derrick Thomas | .15 | .07 | .02 |
| Kansas City Chiefs | | | |
| ☐ 59 Seth Joyner | .05 | .02 | .01 |
| Philadelphia Eagles | | | |
| ☐ 60 Stan Thomas | .05 | .02 | .01 |
| Chicago Bears | | | |
| ☐ 61 Nate Newton | .05 | .02 | .01 |
| Dallas Cowboys | | | |
| ☐ 62 Matt Brock | .05 | .02 | .01 |
| Green Bay Packers | | | |
| ☐ 63 Mike Munchak | .08 | .04 | .01 |
| Houston Oilers | | | |
| ☐ 64 Randall McDaniel | .05 | .02 | .01 |
| Minnesota Vikings | | | |
| ☐ 65 Ron Hallstrom | .05 | .02 | .01 |
| Green Bay Packers | | | |
| ☐ 66 Andy Heck | .05 | .02 | .01 |
| Seattle Seahawks | | | |
| ☐ 67 Russell Maryland | .10 | .05 | .01 |
| Dallas Cowboys | | | |
| ☐ 68 Bruce Wilkerson | .05 | .02 | .01 |
| Los Angeles Raiders | | | |
| ☐ 69 Mark Schlereth | .05 | .02 | .01 |
| Washington Redskins | | | |
| ☐ 70 John Fina | .05 | .02 | .01 |
| Buffalo Bills | | | |
| ☐ 71 Santana Dotson | .10 | .05 | .01 |
| Tampa Bay Buccaneers | | | |
| ☐ 72 Don Mosebar UER | .05 | .02 | .01 |
| Los Angeles Raiders | | | |
| (Listed as tackle; | | | |
| should be center) | | | |
| ☐ 73 Simon Fletcher | .08 | .04 | .01 |
| Denver Broncos | | | |
| ☐ 74 Paul Gruber | .05 | .02 | .01 |
| Tampa Bay Buccaneers | | | |
| ☐ 75 Howard Ballard | .05 | .02 | .01 |
| Buffalo Bills | | | |
| ☐ 76 John Alt | .05 | .02 | .01 |
| Kansas City Chiefs | | | |
| ☐ 77 Carlton Haselrig | .05 | .02 | .01 |
| Pittsburgh Steelers | | | |
| ☐ 78 Bruce Smith | .10 | .05 | .01 |
| Buffalo Bills | | | |
| ☐ 79 Ray Childress | .05 | .02 | .01 |
| Houston Oilers | | | |
| ☐ 80 Jerry Rice | .50 | .23 | .06 |
| San Francisco 49ers | | | |
| ☐ 81 Art Monk | .10 | .05 | .01 |
| Washington Redskins | | | |
| ☐ 82 John Taylor | .10 | .05 | .01 |
| San Francisco 49ers | | | |
| ☐ 83 Andre Reed | .10 | .05 | .01 |
| Buffalo Bills | | | |
| ☐ 84 Sterling Sharpe | .40 | .18 | .05 |
| Green Bay Packers | | | |
| ☐ 85 Sam Graddy | .05 | .02 | .01 |
| Los Angeles Raiders | | | |
| ☐ 86 Fred Barnett | .10 | .05 | .01 |
| Philadelphia Eagels | | | |
| ☐ 87 Ricky Proehl | .08 | .04 | .01 |
| Phoenix Cardinals | | | |
| ☐ 88 Michael Irvin | .40 | .18 | .05 |
| Dallas Cowboys | | | |
| ☐ 89 Webster Slaughter | .08 | .04 | .01 |
| Houston Oilers | | | |
| ☐ 90 Tony Bennett | .05 | .02 | .01 |
| Green Bay Packers | | | |
| ☐ 91 Leslie O'Neal | .08 | .04 | .01 |
| San Diego Chargers | | | |
| ☐ 92 Michael Dean Perry | .05 | .02 | .01 |
| Cleveland Browns | | | |
| ☐ 93 Greg Townsend | .05 | .02 | .01 |
| Los Angeles Raiders | | | |
| ☐ 94 Anthony Smith | .05 | .02 | .01 |
| Los Angeles Raiders | | | |
| ☐ 95 Richard Dent | .08 | .04 | .01 |
| Chicago Bears | | | |
| ☐ 96 Clyde Simmons | .08 | .04 | .01 |
| Philadelphia Eagles | | | |
| ☐ 97 Cornelius Bennett | .08 | .04 | .01 |
| Buffalo Bills | | | |
| ☐ 98 Eric Swann | .05 | .02 | .01 |
| Phoenix Cardinals | | | |
| ☐ 99 Cortez Kennedy | .10 | .05 | .01 |
| Seattle Seahawks | | | |
| ☐ 100 Emmitt Smith | .75 | .35 | .09 |
| Dallas Cowboys | | | |
| ☐ 101 Michael Jackson | .10 | .05 | .01 |
| Cleveland Browns | | | |
| ☐ 102 Lin Elliott | .05 | .02 | .01 |
| Dallas Cowboys | | | |
| ☐ 103 Rohn Stark | .05 | .02 | .01 |
| Indianapolis Colts | | | |
| ☐ 104 Jim Harbaugh | .08 | .04 | .01 |
| Chicago Bears | | | |
| ☐ 105 Greg Davis | .05 | .02 | .01 |
| Phoenix Cardinals | | | |
| ☐ 106 Mike Cofer | .05 | .02 | .01 |
| San Francisco 49ers | | | |
| ☐ 107 Morten Andersen | .08 | .04 | .01 |
| New Orleans Saints | | | |
| ☐ 108 Steve Young | .25 | .11 | .03 |
| San Francisco 49ers | | | |
| ☐ 109 Norm Johnson | .05 | .02 | .01 |
| Atlanta Falcons | | | |
| ☐ 110 Dan McGwire | .08 | .04 | .01 |
| Seattle Seahawks | | | |
| ☐ 111 Jim Everett | .05 | .02 | .01 |
| Los Angeles Rams | | | |
| ☐ 112 Randall Cunningham | .10 | .05 | .01 |
| Philadelphia Eagles | | | |
| ☐ 113 Steve Bono | .15 | .07 | .02 |
| San Francisco 49ers | | | |
| ☐ 114 Cody Carlson | .10 | .05 | .01 |
| Houston Oilers | | | |
| ☐ 115 Jeff Hostetler | .10 | .05 | .01 |
| Los Angeles Raiders | | | |
| ☐ 116 Rich Camarillo | .05 | .02 | .01 |
| Phoenix Cardinals | | | |
| ☐ 117 Chris Chandler | .08 | .04 | .01 |
| Phoenix Cardinals | | | |
| ☐ 118 Stan Gelbaugh | .05 | .02 | .01 |
| Seattle Seahawks | | | |
| ☐ 119 Tony Sacca | .08 | .04 | .01 |
| Phoenix Cardinals | | | |
| ☐ 120 Henry Jones | .05 | .02 | .01 |
| Buffalo Bills | | | |
| ☐ 121 Terry Allen | .10 | .05 | .01 |
| Minnesota Vikings | | | |
| ☐ 122 Amp Lee | .08 | .04 | .01 |
| San Francisco 49ers | | | |
| ☐ 123 Mel Gray | .05 | .02 | .01 |
| Detroit Lions | | | |
| ☐ 124 Jon Vaughn | .05 | .02 | .01 |
| New England Patriots | | | |
| ☐ 124UD Jon Vaughn UER | .15 | .07 | .02 |
| Seattle Seahawks | | | |
| (Misspelled Saehawks | | | |
| on front) | | | |
| ☐ 125 Bubba McDowell | .05 | .02 | .01 |
| Houston Oilers | | | |
| ☐ 126 Aundray McMillan | .05 | .02 | .01 |
| Minnesota Vikings | | | |
| ☐ 127 Terrell Buckley | .10 | .05 | .01 |
| Green Bay Packers | | | |
| ☐ 128 Dana Hall | .05 | .02 | .01 |
| San Francisco 49ers | | | |
| ☐ 129 Eric Dickerson | .10 | .05 | .01 |
| Los Angeles Raiders | | | |
| ☐ 130 Martin Bayless | .05 | .02 | .01 |
| Kansas City Chiefs | | | |
| ☐ 131 Steve Israel | .05 | .02 | .01 |
| Los Angeles Rams | | | |
| ☐ 132 Vaughn Dunbar | .08 | .04 | .01 |
| New Orleans Saints | | | |
| ☐ 133 Ronnie Harmon | .05 | .02 | .01 |
| San Diego Chargers | | | |
| ☐ 134 Dale Carter | .10 | .05 | .01 |
| Kansas City Chiefs | | | |
| ☐ 135 Neal Anderson | .08 | .04 | .01 |
| Chicago Bears | | | |
| ☐ 136 Merton Hanks | .05 | .02 | .01 |
| San Francisco 49ers | | | |
| ☐ 137 James Washington | .05 | .02 | .01 |

Dallas Cowboys
☐ 138 Reggie Rivers ........................ .20 .09 .03
    Denver Broncos
☐ 139 Bruce Pickens ...................... .05 .02 .01
    Atlanta Falcons
☐ 140 Gary Anderson ...................... .08 .04 .01
    Tampa Bay Buccaneers
☐ 141 Eugene Robinson .................... .05 .02 .01
    Seattle Seahawks
☐ 142 Charles Mincy UER .............. .20 .09 .03
    Kansas City Chiefs
    (Listed as running back;
    he is a defensive back)
☐ 143 Matt Darby ........................... .05 .02 .01
    Buffalo Bills
☐ 144 Tom Rathman ........................ .08 .04 .01
    San Francisco 49ers
☐ 145 Mike Prior ............................ .05 .02 .01
    Green Bay Packers
☐ 146 Sean Lumpkin ....................... .05 .02 .01
    New Orleans Saints
☐ 147 Greg Jackson ........................ .05 .02 .01
    New York Giants
☐ 148 Wes Hopkins ......................... .05 .02 .01
    Philadelphia Eagles
☐ 149 David Tate UER ..................... .05 .02 .01
    New York Jets
    (Listed as linebacker;
    should be safety)
☐ 150 James Francis ....................... .05 .02 .01
    Cincinnati Bengals
☐ 151 Bryan Cox ............................ .08 .04 .01
    Miami Dolphins
☐ 152 Keith McCants ....................... .05 .02 .01
    Tampa Bay Buccaneers
☐ 152UD Keith McCants .................. .15 .07 .02
    Houston Oilers
☐ 153 Mark Stepnoski ..................... .05 .02 .01
    Dallas Cowboys
☐ 154 Al Smith .............................. .05 .02 .01
    Houston Oilers
☐ 155 Robert Jones ........................ .05 .02 .01
    Dallas Cowboys
☐ 156 Lawrence Taylor ................... .10 .05 .01
    New York Giants
☐ 157 Clay Matthews ...................... .08 .04 .01
    Cleveland Browns
☐ 158 Wilber Marshall ..................... .10 .05 .01
    Washington Redskins
☐ 158UD Wilber Marshall UER ........ .18 .08 .02
    Houston Oilers
    (Misspelled Marshal
    on front)
☐ 159 Mike Johnson ....................... .05 .02 .01
    Cleveland Browns
☐ 160 Adam Schreiber .................... .10 .05 .01
    Minnesota Vikings
☐ 161 Tim Grunhard ....................... .05 .02 .01
    Kansas City Chiefs
☐ 162 Mark Bortz ........................... .05 .02 .01
    Chicago Bears
☐ 163 Gene Chilton ........................ .05 .02 .01
    New England Patriots
☐ 164 Jamie Dukes ........................ .05 .02 .01
    Atlanta Falcons
☐ 165 Bart Oates ........................... .05 .02 .01
    New York Giants
☐ 166 Kevin Gogan ......................... .05 .02 .01
    Dallas Cowboys
☐ 167 Kent Hull ............................. .05 .02 .01
    Buffalo Bills
☐ 168 Ed King ............................... .05 .02 .01
    Cleveland Browns
☐ 169 Eugene Chung ...................... .05 .02 .01
    New England Patriots
☐ 170 Troy Auzenne ....................... .05 .02 .01
    Chicago Bears
☐ 171 Charles Mann ....................... .05 .02 .01
    Washington Redskins
☐ 172 William Perry ........................ .05 .02 .01
    Chicago Bears
☐ 173 Mike Lodish .......................... .05 .02 .01
    Buffalo Bills
☐ 174 Bruce Matthews .................... .08 .04 .01
    Houston Oilers
☐ 175 Tony Casillas ........................ .05 .02 .01
    Dallas Cowboys
☐ 176 Steve Wisniewski ................... .05 .02 .01
    Los Angeles Raiders
☐ 177 Karl Mecklenburg ................. .05 .02 .01
    Denver Broncos
☐ 178 Richmond Webb .................... .05 .02 .01
    Miami Dolphins
☐ 179 Erik Williams ........................ .05 .02 .01
    Dallas Cowboys
☐ 180 Andre Rison ......................... .25 .11 .03
    Atlanta Falcons
☐ 181 Michael Haynes ..................... .20 .09 .03

Atlanta Falcons
☐ 182 Don Beebe ........................... .10 .05 .01
    Buffalo Bills
☐ 183 Anthony Miller ...................... .15 .07 .02
    San Diego Chargers
☐ 184 Jay Novacek ......................... .10 .05 .01
    Dallas Cowboys
☐ 185 Rob Moore ........................... .10 .05 .01
    New York Jets
☐ 186 Willie Green .......................... .08 .04 .01
    Detroit Lions
☐ 187 Tom Waddle .......................... .10 .05 .01
    Chicago Bears
☐ 188 Keith Jackson ....................... .10 .05 .01
    Miami Dolphins
☐ 189 Steve Tasker ........................ .05 .02 .01
    Buffalo Bills
☐ 190 Marco Coleman ..................... .08 .04 .01
    Miami Dolphins
☐ 191 Jeff Wright ........................... .05 .02 .01
    Buffalo Bills
☐ 192 Burt Grossman ..................... .05 .02 .01
    San Diego Chargers
☐ 193 Trace Armstrong .................... .05 .02 .01
    Chicago Bears
☐ 194 Charles Haley ....................... .08 .04 .01
    Dallas Cowboys
☐ 195 Greg Lloyd ........................... .05 .02 .01
    Pittsburgh Steelers
☐ 196 Marc Boutte ......................... .05 .02 .01
    Los Angeles Rams
☐ 197 Rufus Porter ........................ .05 .02 .01
    Seattle Seahawks
☐ 198 Dennis Gibson ...................... .05 .02 .01
    Detroit Lions
☐ 199 Shane Dronett ...................... .05 .02 .01
    Denver Broncos
☐ 200 Joe Montana ......................... 1.25 .55 .16
    Kansas City Chiefs
☐ H1 Emmitt Smith ....................... 50.00 23.00 6.25
    Hologram Redemption
    Dallas Cowboys
    Back to Back
☐ H2 Emmitt Smith ....................... 50.00 23.00 6.25
    Hologram Redemption
    Dallas Cowboys
    Super Bowl XXVII

# 1993 Power All-Power Defense

Randomly inserted at a rate of 2 per jumbo pack, these 25 standard-size (2 1/2" by 3 1/2") cards feature on their fronts borderless color player photos with textured brown backgrounds. The player's name appears in yellow lettering within a black rectangle near the bottom. The textured brown background continues on the back, which carries the player's name, team, position, and biography in a yellow box at the upper left. Career highlights in red lettering follow alongside and below. The cards are numbered on the back with an "APD" prefix.

|  | MINT | EXC | G-VG |
|---|---|---|---|
| COMPLETE SET (25) .................... | 4.00 | 1.80 | .50 |
| COMMON PLAYER (1-25) .............. | .20 | .09 | .03 |
| *GOLD CARDS: 1.25X TO 2X VALUE | | | |

☐ 1 Clyde Simmons ........................ .30 .14 .04
    Philadelphia Eagles
☐ 2 Anthony Smith ......................... .20 .09 .03
    Los Angeles Raiders
☐ 3 Ray Childress .......................... .20 .09 .03
    Houston Oilers
☐ 4 Michael Dean Perry .................. .20 .09 .03
    Cleveland Browns
☐ 5 Bruce Smith ............................ .30 .14 .04
    Buffalo Bills

| | | | |
|---|---|---|---|
| ☐ 6 Cortez Kennedy | .30 | .14 | .04 |
| Seattle Seahawks | | | |
| ☐ 7 Charles Haley | .20 | .09 | .03 |
| Dallas Cowboys | | | |
| ☐ 8 Marco Coleman | .20 | .09 | .03 |
| Miami Dolphins | | | |
| ☐ 9 Alonzo Spellman | .30 | .14 | .04 |
| Chicago Bears | | | |
| ☐ 10 Junior Seau | .30 | .14 | .04 |
| San Diego Chargers | | | |
| ☐ 11 Ken Norton Jr. | .30 | .14 | .04 |
| Dallas Cowboys | | | |
| ☐ 12 Derrick Thomas | .20 | .09 | .03 |
| Kansas City Chiefs | | | |
| ☐ 13 Wilber Marshall | .20 | .09 | .03 |
| Washington Redskins | | | |
| ☐ 14 Chris Doleman | .20 | .09 | .03 |
| Minnesota Vikings | | | |
| ☐ 15 Seth Joyner | .30 | .14 | .04 |
| Philadelphia Eagles | | | |
| ☐ 16 Al Smith | .20 | .09 | .03 |
| Houston Oilers | | | |
| ☐ 17 Deion Sanders | .50 | .23 | .06 |
| Atlanta Falcons | | | |
| ☐ 18 Rod Woodson | .30 | .14 | .04 |
| Pittsburgh Steelers | | | |
| ☐ 19 Aundray McMillan | .20 | .09 | .03 |
| Minnesota Vikings | | | |
| ☐ 20 Dale Carter | .20 | .09 | .03 |
| Kansas City Chiefs | | | |
| ☐ 21 Terell Buckley | .30 | .14 | .04 |
| Green Bay Packers | | | |
| ☐ 22 Bennie Thompson | .20 | .09 | .03 |
| Kansas City Chiefs | | | |
| ☐ 23 Chris Spielman | .20 | .09 | .03 |
| Detroit Lions | | | |
| ☐ 24 Lawrence Taylor | .40 | .18 | .05 |
| New York Giants | | | |
| ☐ 25 Tony Bennett | .20 | .09 | .03 |
| Green Bay Packers | | | |

## 1993 Power Combos

Randomly inserted in foil packs, these ten standard-size (2 1/2" by 3 1/2") cards feature on their horizontal fronts two-player photos that are bordered in black, blue, and purple. The players' names appear in red lettering within a black bar near the bottom. The horizontal back carries the team name of the two players in yellow lettering within a purple rectangle at the top. The players' names, uniform numbers, positions, biography, and career highlights follow below. All this is on a green, grassy background bordered in the same colors as the front. The cards are numbered on the back.

| | MINT | EXC | G-VG |
|---|---|---|---|
| COMPLETE SET (10) | 6.00 | 2.70 | .75 |
| COMMON PAIR (1-10) | .50 | .23 | .06 |
| *GOLD CARDS: 1.25X to 2X VALUE | | | |
| *PRISM CARDS: 2X to 3X VALUE | | | |
| | | | |
| ☐ 1 Emmitt Smith | 4.00 | 1.80 | .50 |
| Dallas Cowboys | | | |
| Barry Sanders | | | |
| Detroit Lions | | | |
| ☐ 2 Terrell Buckley | 1.25 | .55 | .16 |
| Green Bay Packers | | | |
| Sterling Sharpe | | | |
| Green Bay Packers | | | |
| ☐ 3 Junior Seau | .50 | .23 | .06 |
| San Diego Chargers | | | |
| Gary Plummer | | | |
| San Diego Chargers | | | |
| ☐ 4 Deion Sanders | .75 | .35 | .09 |
| Atlanta Falcons | | | |
| Tim McKyer | | | |

| | | | |
|---|---|---|---|
| Atlanta Falcons | | | |
| ☐ 5 Bruce Smith | .60 | .25 | .08 |
| Buffalo Bills | | | |
| Darryl Talley | | | |
| Buffalo Bills | | | |
| ☐ 6 Warren Moon | .75 | .35 | .09 |
| Houston Oilers | | | |
| Webster Slaughter | | | |
| Houston Oilers | | | |
| ☐ 7 Chris Doleman | .50 | .23 | .06 |
| Minnesota Vikings | | | |
| Henry Thomas | | | |
| Minnesota Vikings | | | |
| ☐ 8 Karl Mecklenburg | .50 | .23 | .06 |
| Denver Broncos | | | |
| Michael Brooks | | | |
| Denver Broncos | | | |
| ☐ 9 Ken Norton Jr. | .60 | .25 | .08 |
| Dallas Cowboys | | | |
| Robert Jones | | | |
| Dallas Cowboys | | | |
| ☐ 10 Marco Coleman | .50 | .23 | .06 |
| Miami Dolphins | | | |
| Bryan Cox | | | |
| Miami Dolphins | | | |

## 1993 Power Draft Picks

Randomly inserted in 1993 Pro Set Power packs, these 30 standard-size (2 1/2" by 3 1/2") cards feature on their fronts borderless color player photos with black-and-white backgrounds. The player's name appears in red lettering near the bottom. The black and horizontal back carries the player's name in red lettering near the top, followed below by his team and career highlights. The cards are numbered on the back with a "PDP" prefix.

| | MINT | EXC | G-VG |
|---|---|---|---|
| COMPLETE SET (30) | 8.00 | 3.60 | 1.00 |
| COMMON PLAYER (1-30) | .15 | .07 | .02 |
| *GOLD CARDS: 1.25X TO 2X VALUE | | | |
| | | | |
| ☐ 1 Lincoln Kennedy UER | .15 | .07 | .02 |
| (Misnumbered 10) | | | |
| Atlanta Falcons | | | |
| ☐ 2 Thomas Smith UER | .20 | .09 | .03 |
| (Misnumbered 20) | | | |
| Buffalo Bills | | | |
| ☐ 3 Robert Smith UER | .50 | .23 | .06 |
| (Misnumbered 30) | | | |
| Minnesota Vikings | | | |
| ☐ 4 John Copeland UER | .30 | .14 | .04 |
| (Misnumbered 40) | | | |
| Cincinnati Bengals | | | |
| ☐ 5 Dan Footman UER | .15 | .07 | .02 |
| (Misnumbered 50) | | | |
| Cleveland Browns | | | |
| ☐ 6 Darrin Smith UER | .30 | .14 | .04 |
| (Misnumbered 60) | | | |
| Dallas Cowboys | | | |
| ☐ 7 Qadry Ismail UER | .50 | .23 | .06 |
| (Misnumbered 70) | | | |
| Minnesota Vikings | | | |
| ☐ 8 Ryan McNeil UER | .20 | .09 | .03 |
| (Misnumbered 80) | | | |
| Detroit Lions | | | |
| ☐ 9 George Teague UER | .25 | .11 | .03 |
| (Misnumbered 90) | | | |
| Green Bay Packers | | | |
| ☐ 10 Brad Hopkins | .15 | .07 | .02 |
| Houston Oilers | | | |
| ☐ 11 Ernest Dye | .15 | .07 | .02 |
| Phoenix Cardinals | | | |
| ☐ 12 Jaime Fields | .15 | .07 | .02 |
| Kansas City Chiefs | | | |
| ☐ 13 Patrick Bates | .20 | .09 | .03 |

Los Angeles Raiders
| | | MINT | EXC | G-VG |
|---|---|---|---|---|
| ☐ 14 Jerome Bettis | | 2.00 | .90 | .25 |

Los Angeles Rams
☐ 15 O.J. McDuffie ... 1.00 .45 .13
Miami Dolphins
☐ 16 Gino Torretta ... .30 .14 .04
Minnesota Vikings
☐ 17 Drew Bledsoe ... 2.00 .90 .25
New England Patriots
☐ 18 Irv Smith ... .25 .11 .03
New Orleans Saints
☐ 19 Marcus Buckley ... .20 .09 .03
New York Giants
☐ 20 Coleman Rudolph ... .15 .07 .02
New York Jets
☐ 21 Leonard Renfro ... .15 .07 .02
Philadelphia Eagles
☐ 22 Garrison Hearst ... 1.00 .45 .13
Phoenix Cardinals
☐ 23 Deon Figures ... .15 .07 .02
Pittsburgh Steelers
☐ 24 Natrone Means ... 1.00 .45 .13
San Diego Chargers
☐ 25 Todd Kelly ... .20 .09 .03
San Francisco 49ers
☐ 26 Carlton Gray ... .20 .09 .03
Seattle Seahawks
☐ 27 Eric Curry ... .25 .11 .03
Tampa Bay Buccaneers
☐ 28 Tom Carter ... .20 .09 .03
Washington Redskins
☐ 29 AFC Logo CL ... .15 .07 .02
☐ 30 NFC Logo CL ... .15 .07 .02

## 1993 Power Moves

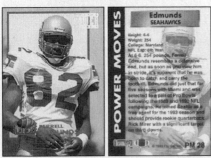

The first 30 cards of this 40-card standard-size (2 1/2" by 3 1/2") were randomly inserted in 1993 Pro Set Power packs, the last ten were random inserts in 1993 Pro Set Power jumbo packs. The cards feature on their fronts borderless color player photos framed by a red line. The player's name appears in red lettering near the bottom. The back carries a ghosted version of the photo on the front, with the player's last name and team printing in black lettering within a grayish plaque at the top. Biography and career highlights follow below. The set's title appears in vertical white lettering within a black stripe that edges the left side. The cards are numbered on the back with a "PM" prefix.

| | MINT | EXC | G-VG |
|---|---|---|---|
| COMPLETE SET (40) | 6.00 | 2.70 | .75 |
| COMPLETE SERIES 1 (30) | 4.00 | 1.80 | .50 |
| COMPLETE SERIES 2 (10) | 2.00 | .90 | .25 |
| COMMON CARD (PM1-PM30) | .20 | .09 | .03 |
| COMMON CARD (PM31-PM40) | .20 | .09 | .03 |
| *GOLD CARDS: 1.25X TO 2X VALUE | | | |

☐ PM1 Bobby Hebert ... .20 .09 .03
Atlanta Falcons
☐ PM2 Billy Brooks ... .20 .09 .03
Buffalo Bills
☐ PM3 Vinny Testaverde ... .25 .11 .03
Cleveland Browns
☐ PM4 Hugh Millen ... .20 .09 .03
Dallas Cowboys
☐ PM5 Rod Bernstine ... .20 .09 .03
Denver Broncos
☐ PM6 Robert Delpino ... .20 .09 .03
Denver Broncos
☐ PM7 Pat Swilling ... .20 .09 .03
Detroit Lions
☐ PM8 Reggie White ... .50 .23 .06
Green Bay Packers
☐ PM9 Aaron Cox ... .20 .09 .03
Indianapolis Colts
☐ PM10 Joe Montana ... 2.50 1.15 .30

Kansas City Chiefs
☐ PM11 Gaston Green ... .20 .09 .03
Los Angeles Raiders
☐ PM12 Jeff Hostetler ... .25 .11 .03
Los Angeles Raiders
☐ PM13 Shane Conlan ... .20 .09 .03
Los Angeles Rams
☐ PM14 Irv Eatman ... .20 .09 .03
Los Angeles Rams
☐ PM15 Mark Ingram ... .20 .09 .03
Miami Dolphins
☐ PM16 Irving Fryar ... .25 .11 .03
Miami Dolphins
☐ PM17 Don Majkowski ... .20 .09 .03
Indianapolis Colts
☐ PM18 Will Wolford ... .20 .09 .03
Indianapolis Colts
☐ PM19 Boomer Esiason ... .30 .14 .04
New York Jets
☐ PM20 Ronnie Lott ... .25 .11 .03
New York Jets
☐ PM21 Johnny Johnson ... .25 .11 .03
New York Jets
☐ PM22 Steve Beuerlein ... .30 .14 .04
Phoenix Cardinals
☐ PM23 Chuck Cecil ... .20 .09 .03
Phoenix Cardinals
☐ PM24 Gary Clark ... .25 .11 .03
Phoenix Cardinals
☐ PM25 Kevin Greene ... .20 .09 .03
Pittsburgh Steelers
☐ PM26 Jerrol Williams ... .20 .09 .03
San Diego Chargers
☐ PM27 Tim McDonald ... .20 .09 .03
San Francisco 49ers
☐ PM28 Ferrell Edmunds ... .20 .09 .03
Seattle Seahawks
☐ PM29 Kelvin Martin ... .20 .09 .03
Seattle Seahawks
☐ PM30 Hardy Nickerson ... .20 .09 .03
Tampa Bay Buccaneers
☐ PM31 Jerry Ball ... .20 .09 .03
Cleveland Browns
☐ PM32 Jim McMahon ... .25 .11 .03
Minnesota Vikings
☐ PM33 Marcus Allen ... .60 .25 .08
Kansas City Chiefs
☐ PM34 John Stephens ... .20 .09 .03
Atlanta Falcons
☐ PM35 John Booty ... .20 .09 .03
Phoenix Cardinals
☐ PM36 Wade Wilson ... .20 .09 .03
New Orleans Saints
☐ PM37 Mark Bavaro ... .25 .11 .03
Philadelphia Eagles
☐ PM38 Bill Fralic ... .20 .09 .03
Detroit Lions
☐ PM39 Mark Clayton ... .20 .09 .03
Green Bay Packers
☐ PM40 Mike Sherrard ... .20 .09 .03
New York Giants

## 1993 Power Update Combos

Randomly inserted in 1993 Power Update packs, these 10 standard-size (2 1/2" by 3 1/2") multiplayer cards feature on their horizontal fronts multicolor-bordered color player action shots. The players' names appear in red lettering at the bottom. The horizontal back carries each player's name at the top, followed below by combo highlights, all on a simulated turf background. The cards are numbered on the back with a "PC" prefix.

| | MINT | EXC | G-VG |
|---|---|---|---|
| COMPLETE SET (10) | 15.00 | 6.75 | 1.90 |
| COMMON PLAYER (PC1-PC10) | 1.00 | .45 | .13 |

*GOLD CARDS: 1.25X TO 2X VALUE
*PRISM CARDS: 2X to 3X HI VALUE

| | | | |
|---|---|---|---|
| ☐ PC1 Andre Rison | 1.50 | .65 | .19 |
| Michael Haynes | | | |
| Mike Pritchard | | | |
| Drew Hill | | | |
| Atlanta Falcons | | | |
| ☐ PC2 Steve Young | 3.00 | 1.35 | .40 |
| Jerry Rice UER | | | |
| San Francisco 49ers | | | |
| (Young's uniform number on | | | |
| back is 7) | | | |
| ☐ PC3 Jim Kelly | 2.00 | .90 | .25 |
| Frank Reich | | | |
| Buffalo Bills | | | |
| ☐ PC4 Alvin Harper | 2.50 | 1.15 | .30 |
| Michael Irvin | | | |
| Dallas Cowboys | | | |
| ☐ PC5 Rod Woodson | 1.00 | .45 | .13 |
| Deon Figures | | | |
| Pittsburgh Steelers | | | |
| ☐ PC6 Bruce Smith | 1.00 | .45 | .13 |
| Cornelius Bennett | | | |
| Buffalo Bills | | | |
| ☐ PC7 Bryan Cox | 1.00 | .45 | .13 |
| Marco Coleman | | | |
| Miami Dolphins | | | |
| ☐ PC8 Troy Aikman | 8.00 | 3.60 | 1.00 |
| Emmitt Smith | | | |
| Dallas Cowboys | | | |
| ☐ PC9 Tim Brown | 2.00 | .90 | .25 |
| Raghib Ismail | | | |
| Los Angeles Raiders | | | |
| ☐ PC10 Art Monk | 1.00 | .45 | .13 |
| Desmond Howard | | | |
| Ricky Sanders UER | | | |
| Washington Redskins | | | |
| (Atlanta Falcons on back | | | |

## 1993 Power Update Impact Rookies

Randomly inserted in 1993 Power Update packs, these 15 standard-size (2 1/2" by 3 1/2") cards feature gray-bordered color player action shots on their fronts. The player's name appears in yellow lettering at the bottom right. The gray back carries the player's team name and helmet at the top, followed by college, position, and career highlights. The cards are numbered on the back with an "IR" prefix.

| | MINT | EXC | G-VG |
|---|---|---|---|
| COMPLETE SET (15) | 14.00 | 6.25 | 1.75 |
| COMMON PLAYER (IR1-IR15) | .40 | .18 | .05 |
| | | | |
| ☐ IR1 Rick Mirer | 4.00 | 1.80 | .50 |
| Seattle Seahawks | | | |
| ☐ IR2 Drew Bledsoe | 4.00 | 1.80 | .50 |
| New England Patriots | | | |
| ☐ IR3 Jerome Bettis | 4.00 | 1.80 | .50 |
| Los Angeles Rams | | | |
| ☐ IR4 Derek Brown | 1.00 | .45 | .13 |
| New Orleans Saints | | | |
| ☐ IR5 Roosevelt Potts | .50 | .23 | .06 |
| Indianapolis Colts | | | |
| ☐ IR6 Glyn Milburn | 1.50 | .65 | .19 |
| Denver Broncos | | | |
| ☐ IR7 Adrian Murrell | .60 | .25 | .08 |
| Pittsburgh Steelers | | | |
| ☐ IR8 Victor Bailey | .60 | .25 | .08 |
| Philadelphia Eagles | | | |
| ☐ IR9 Vincent Brisby | .75 | .35 | .09 |
| New England Patriots | | | |
| ☐ IR10 O.J. McDuffie | 1.50 | .65 | .19 |
| Miami Dolphins | | | |
| ☐ IR11 James Jett | 1.25 | .55 | .16 |
| Los Angeles Raiders | | | |
| ☐ IR12 Eric Curry | .50 | .23 | .06 |
| New England Patriots | | | |
| ☐ IR13 Dana Stubblefield | .75 | .35 | .09 |
| San Francisco 49ers | | | |
| ☐ IR14 William Roaf | .40 | .18 | .05 |
| New Orleans Saints | | | |
| ☐ IR15 Patrick Bates | .40 | .18 | .05 |
| Los Angeles Raiders | | | |

## 1993 Power Update Moves

These 50 standard-size (2 1/2" by 3 1/2") cards shared packs with 1993 Pro Set Power Update Power Prospects cards. The fronts feature color player action shots with purplish borders and framed with red and blue lines. The player's name appears in yellow lettering within the lower margin. The back carries the player's team name and helmet from before his trade at the upper right, and the name and helmet of his new team at the upper left. Below are the date of the trade, followed by a brief biography and season highlights. The background blends from the purplish lithic at the top to a white striated design near the bottom. The cards are numbered on the back with a "PMUD" prefix.

| | MINT | EXC | G-VG |
|---|---|---|---|
| COMPLETE SET (50) | 4.00 | 1.80 | .50 |
| COMMON PLAYER (1-50) | .10 | .05 | .01 |
| *GOLD CARDS: 1.25X TO 2X VALUE | | | |
| | | | |
| ☐ 1 Bobby Hebert | .10 | .05 | .01 |
| Atlanta Falcons | | | |
| ☐ 2 Bill Brooks | .10 | .05 | .01 |
| Buffalo Bills | | | |
| ☐ 3 Vinny Testaverde | .15 | .07 | .02 |
| Cleveland Browns | | | |
| ☐ 4 Hugh Millen | .10 | .05 | .01 |
| Dallas Cowboys | | | |
| ☐ 5 Rod Bernstine | .10 | .05 | .01 |
| Denver Broncos | | | |
| ☐ 6 Robert Delpino | .10 | .05 | .01 |
| Denver Broncos | | | |
| ☐ 7 Pat Swilling | .10 | .05 | .01 |
| Detroit Lions | | | |
| ☐ 8 Reggie White | .35 | .16 | .04 |
| Green Bay Packers | | | |
| ☐ 9 Aaron Cox | .10 | .05 | .01 |
| Indianapolis Colts | | | |
| ☐ 10 Joe Montana | 2.25 | 1.00 | .30 |
| Kansas City Chiefs | | | |
| ☐ 11 Vinnie Clark UER | .10 | .05 | .01 |
| Atlanta Falcons | | | |
| (Name misspelled | | | |
| Vinny on card) | | | |
| ☐ 12 Jeff Hostetler | .15 | .07 | .02 |
| Los Angeles Raiders | | | |
| ☐ 13 Shane Conlan | .10 | .05 | .01 |
| Los Angeles Rams | | | |
| ☐ 14 Irv Eatman | .10 | .05 | .01 |
| Los Angeles Rams | | | |
| ☐ 15 Mark Ingram | .10 | .05 | .01 |
| Miami Dolphins | | | |
| ☐ 16 Irving Fryar | .15 | .07 | .02 |
| Miami Dolphins | | | |
| ☐ 17 Don Majkowski | .10 | .05 | .01 |
| Indianapolis Colts | | | |
| ☐ 18 Will Wolford | .10 | .05 | .01 |
| Indianapolis Colts | | | |
| ☐ 19 Boomer Esiason | .20 | .09 | .03 |
| New York Jets | | | |
| ☐ 20 Ronnie Lott | .15 | .07 | .02 |
| New York Jets | | | |
| ☐ 21 Johnny Johnson | .15 | .07 | .02 |
| New York Jets | | | |
| ☐ 22 Steve Beuerlein | .20 | .09 | .03 |
| Phoenix Cardinals | | | |

| | | | |
|---|---|---|---|
| ☐ 23 Chuck Cecil | .10 | .05 | .01 |
| Phoenix Cardinals | | | |
| ☐ 24 Gary Clark | .15 | .07 | .02 |
| Phoenix Cardinals | | | |
| ☐ 25 Kevin Greene | .10 | .05 | .01 |
| Pittsburgh Steelers | | | |
| ☐ 26 Jerrol Williams | .10 | .05 | .01 |
| San Diego Chargers | | | |
| ☐ 27 Tim McDonald | .10 | .05 | .01 |
| San Francisco 49ers | | | |
| ☐ 28 Ferrell Edmunds | .10 | .05 | .01 |
| Seattle Seahawks | | | |
| ☐ 29 Kelvin Martin | .10 | .05 | .01 |
| Seattle Seahawks | | | |
| ☐ 30 Hardy Nickerson | .10 | .05 | .01 |
| Tampa Bay Buccaneers | | | |
| ☐ 31 Jumpy Geathers | .10 | .05 | .01 |
| Atlanta Falcons | | | |
| ☐ 32 Craig Heyward | .10 | .05 | .01 |
| Chicago Bears | | | |
| ☐ 33 Tim McKyer | .10 | .05 | .01 |
| Detroit Lions | | | |
| ☐ 34 Mark Carrier WR | .15 | .07 | .02 |
| Cleveland Browns | | | |
| ☐ 35 Gary Zimmerman | .10 | .05 | .01 |
| Denver Broncos | | | |
| ☐ 36 Jay Schroeder | .10 | .05 | .01 |
| Cincinnati Bengals | | | |
| ☐ 37 Keith Millard | .10 | .05 | .01 |
| Philadelphia Eagles | | | |
| ☐ 38 Vince Workman | .10 | .05 | .01 |
| Tampa Bay Buccaneers | | | |
| ☐ 39 Kirk Lowdermilk | .10 | .05 | .01 |
| Indianapolis Colts | | | |
| ☐ 40 Fred Stokes | .10 | .05 | .01 |
| Los Angeles Rams | | | |
| ☐ 41 Ernie Jones | .10 | .05 | .01 |
| Los Angeles Rams | | | |
| ☐ 42 Keith Byars | .15 | .07 | .02 |
| Miami Dolphins | | | |
| ☐ 43 Carlton Bailey | .10 | .05 | .01 |
| New York Giants | | | |
| ☐ 44 Michael Brooks | .10 | .05 | .01 |
| New York Giants | | | |
| ☐ 45 Tim McGee | .10 | .05 | .01 |
| Washington Redskins | | | |
| ☐ 46 Leonard Marshall | .10 | .05 | .01 |
| New York Jets | | | |
| ☐ 47 Bubby Brister | .10 | .05 | .01 |
| Philadelphia Eagles | | | |
| ☐ 48 Mike Tomczak | .10 | .05 | .01 |
| Pittsburgh Steelers | | | |
| ☐ 49 Mark Jackson | .10 | .05 | .01 |
| New York Giants | | | |
| ☐ 50 Wade Wilson | .10 | .05 | .01 |
| New Orleans Saints | | | |

## 1993 Power Update Prospects

These 60 standard-size (2 1/2" by 3 1/2") cards shared packs with 1993 Pro Set Power Update Power Moves cards. The fronts feature gray-bordered color player action shots with horizontally interrupted backgrounds. The player's name appears in yellow lettering within the lower margin. The grayish back carries the player's name and team helmet in the upper panel followed in the lower panel by career highlights. The cards are numbered on the back with a "PP" prefix. Rookie Cards include Jerome Bettis, Drew Bledsoe, Reggie Brooks and Rick Mirer and Ron Moore

| | MINT | EXC | G-VG |
|---|---|---|---|
| COMPLETE SET (60) | 15.00 | 6.75 | 1.90 |
| COMMON PLAYER (1-60) | .10 | .05 | .01 |
| *GOLD CARDS: 1.25X TO 2X VALUE | | | |

| | | | |
|---|---|---|---|
| ☐ 1 Drew Bledsoe | 2.50 | 1.15 | .30 |
| New England Patriots | | | |
| ☐ 2 Rick Mirer | 2.50 | 1.15 | .30 |
| Seattle Seahawks | | | |
| ☐ 3 Trent Green | .50 | .23 | .06 |
| San Diego Chargers | | | |
| ☐ 4 Mark Brunell | .25 | .11 | .03 |
| Green Bay Packers | | | |
| ☐ 5 Billy Joe Hobert | .50 | .23 | .06 |
| Los Angeles Raiders | | | |
| ☐ 6 Ron Moore | 1.50 | .65 | .19 |
| Phoenix Cardinals | | | |
| ☐ 7 Elvis Grbac UER | .50 | .23 | .06 |
| San Francisco 49ers | | | |
| (Spelled Grback on both sides) | | | |
| ☐ 8 Garrison Hearst | 1.00 | .45 | .13 |
| Phoenix Cardinals | | | |
| ☐ 9 Jerome Bettis | 2.50 | 1.15 | .30 |
| Los Angeles Rams | | | |
| ☐ 10 Reggie Brooks | 1.50 | .65 | .19 |
| Washington Redskins | | | |
| ☐ 11 Robert Smith | .50 | .23 | .06 |
| Minnesota Vikings | | | |
| ☐ 12 Vaughn Hebron | .30 | .14 | .04 |
| Philadelphia Eagles | | | |
| ☐ 13 Derek Brown | .75 | .35 | .09 |
| New Orleans Saints | | | |
| ☐ 14 Roosevelt Potts | .30 | .14 | .04 |
| Indianapolis Colts | | | |
| ☐ 15 Terry Kirby UER | 1.25 | .55 | .16 |
| Miami Dolphins | | | |
| (Card says wide receiver; he is a running back) | | | |
| ☐ 16 Glyn Milburn | 1.00 | .45 | .13 |
| Denver Broncos | | | |
| ☐ 17 Greg Robinson | .50 | .23 | .06 |
| Los Angeles Raiders | | | |
| ☐ 18 Natrone Means | 1.00 | .45 | .13 |
| San Diego Chargers | | | |
| ☐ 19 Curtis Conway | .60 | .25 | .08 |
| Chicago Bears | | | |
| ☐ 20 James Jett | 1.00 | .45 | .13 |
| Los Angeles Raiders | | | |
| ☐ 21 O.J. McDuffie | 1.25 | .55 | .16 |
| Miami Dolphins | | | |
| ☐ 22 Raghib Ismail | .40 | .18 | .05 |
| Los Angeles Raiders | | | |
| ☐ 23 Qadry Ismail | .75 | .35 | .09 |
| Minnesota Vikings | | | |
| ☐ 24 Kevin Williams | .75 | .35 | .09 |
| Dallas Cowboys | | | |
| ☐ 25 Victor Bailey UER | .40 | .18 | .05 |
| Philadelphia Eagles | | | |
| (Name spelled Baily on front) | | | |
| ☐ 26 Vincent Brisby | .50 | .23 | .06 |
| New England Patriots | | | |
| ☐ 27 Irv Smith | .20 | .09 | .03 |
| New Orleans Saints | | | |
| ☐ 28 Troy Drayton | .25 | .11 | .03 |
| Los Angeles Rams | | | |
| ☐ 29 Wayne Simmons | .12 | .05 | .02 |
| Green Bay Packers | | | |
| ☐ 30 Marvin Jones | .20 | .09 | .03 |
| New York Jets | | | |
| ☐ 31 Demetrius DuBose | .20 | .09 | .03 |
| Tampa Bay Buccaneers | | | |
| ☐ 32 Chad Brown | .15 | .07 | .02 |
| Pittsburgh Steelers | | | |
| ☐ 33 Micheal Barrow | .10 | .05 | .01 |
| Houston Oilers | | | |
| ☐ 34 Darrin Smith | .40 | .18 | .05 |
| Dallas Cowboys | | | |
| ☐ 35 Deon Figures | .20 | .09 | .03 |
| Pittsburgh Steelers | | | |
| ☐ 36 Darrien Gordon | .15 | .07 | .02 |
| San Diego Chargers | | | |
| ☐ 37 Patrick Bates | .12 | .05 | .02 |
| Los Angeles Raiders | | | |
| ☐ 38 George Teague | .15 | .07 | .02 |
| Green Bay Packers | | | |
| ☐ 39 Lance Gunn | .15 | .07 | .02 |
| Cincinnati Bengals | | | |
| ☐ 40 Tom Carter | .20 | .09 | .03 |
| Washington Redskins | | | |
| ☐ 41 Carlton Gray | .20 | .09 | .03 |
| Seattle Seahawks | | | |
| ☐ 42 John Copeland | .35 | .16 | .04 |
| Cincinnati Bengals | | | |
| ☐ 43 Eric Curry | .40 | .18 | .05 |
| Tampa Bay Buccaneers | | | |
| ☐ 44 Dana Stubblefield | .40 | .18 | .05 |
| San Francisco 49ers | | | |
| ☐ 45 Leonard Renfro | .10 | .05 | .01 |
| Philadelphia Eagles | | | |
| ☐ 46 Dan Williams | .12 | .05 | .02 |
| Denver Broncos | | | |
| ☐ 47 Todd Kelly | .12 | .05 | .02 |
| San Francisco 49ers | | | |

| | | | |
|---|---|---|---|
| ☐ 48 Chris Slade............................. | .30 | .14 | .04 |
| New England Patriots | | | |
| ☐ 49 Carl Simpson UER ................. | .10 | .05 | .01 |
| Chicago Bears | | | |
| (Defensive Back spelled Dfensive on back) | | | |
| ☐ 50 Coleman Rudolph ................... | .10 | .05 | .01 |
| New York Jets | | | |
| ☐ 51 Mike Strahan......................... | .10 | .05 | .01 |
| New York Giants | | | |
| ☐ 52 Dan Footman......................... | .12 | .05 | .02 |
| Cleveland Browns | | | |
| ☐ 53 Steve Everitt.......................... | .10 | .05 | .01 |
| Cleveland Browns | | | |
| ☐ 54 Will Shields........................... | .10 | .05 | .01 |
| Kansas City Chiefs | | | |
| ☐ 55 Ben Coleman ......................... | .10 | .05 | .01 |
| Phoenix Cardinals | | | |
| ☐ 56 William Roaf......................... | .12 | .05 | .02 |
| New Orleans Saints | | | |
| ☐ 57 Lincoln Kennedy .................... | .15 | .07 | .02 |
| Atlanta Falcons | | | |
| ☐ 58 Brad Hopkins ........................ | .10 | .05 | .01 |
| Houston Oilers | | | |
| ☐ 59 Ernest Dye............................. | .10 | .05 | .01 |
| Phoenix Cardinals | | | |
| ☐ 60 Jason Elam ........................... | .10 | .05 | .01 |
| Denver Broncos | | | |

## 1994 Press Pass SB Photo Board

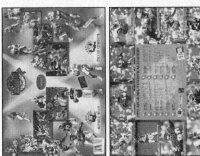

Press Pass, a Dallas-based collectibles firm, shipped 50,000 individually numbered (approximately) 10" by 14" Photo Boards to hobby and retail outlets Jan. 24, the day after both Buffalo and Dallas earned their Super Bowl berths. The Photo Board was also available at the NFL Experience and the Super Bowl Card Show V in Atlanta. The front visually describes each team's road to the Super Bowl with color photos from NFL playoff action. The Super Bowl logo is featured on the front of each board etched in gold foil. The back carries color action photos of AFC and NFC statistical leaders and an outstanding 1993 rookie from each conference, as well as accompanying statistics. The sheet is unnumbered, and the AFC and NFC statistical leaders honored on its back are listed below.

| | MINT | EXC | G-VG |
|---|---|---|---|
| COMPLETE SET (1).......................... | 10.00 | 4.00 | 1.00 |
| COMMON PANEL............................. | 10.00 | 4.00 | 1.00 |
| | | | |
| ☐ 1 SB XXVIII Photo Board ............. | 10.00 | 4.00 | 1.00 |
| John Elway | | | |
| Rick Mirer | | | |
| Reggie Langhorne | | | |
| Neil Smith | | | |
| Nate Odomes | | | |
| Thurman Thomas | | | |
| Steve Young | | | |
| Jerome Bettis | | | |
| Sterling Sharpe | | | |
| Reggie White | | | |
| Deion Sanders | | | |
| Emmitt Smith | | | |

## 1993-94 Pro Athletes Outreach

This 12-card set was issued by Pro Athletes Outreach, a Christian leadership training ministry for pro athletes and their families. The tri-fold cards measure approximately 7 1/8" by 4 1/8". The right portion of the tri-fold carries a color player photo bordered in white on a light gray background. Below the picture are the player's name, position, and the PAO logo. The remainder of the card front and back contains the player's personal Christian testimony followed by an invitation to write them in care of the PAO address, for more information. With the exception of the Gill Byrd card, a second black-and-white player photo

appears on the left portion of the tri-fold card. A brief career summary rounds out the card. The cards are unnumbered and checklisted below in alphabetical order.

| | MINT | EXC | G-VG |
|---|---|---|---|
| COMPLETE SET (12).......................... | 6.00 | 2.40 | .60 |
| COMMON PLAYER (1-12)................. | .50 | .20 | .05 |
| | | | |
| ☐ 1 Mark Boyer ............................... | .50 | .20 | .05 |
| New York Jets | | | |
| ☐ 2 Gill Byrd ................................... | .60 | .24 | .06 |
| San Diego Chargers | | | |
| ☐ 3 Darren Carrington ..................... | .50 | .20 | .05 |
| San Diego Chargers | | | |
| ☐ 4 Paul Coffman ............................ | .60 | .24 | .06 |
| Green Bay Packers | | | |
| ☐ 5 Burnell Dent ............................. | .50 | .20 | .05 |
| Green Bay Packers | | | |
| ☐ 6 Johnny Holland ......................... | .50 | .20 | .05 |
| Green Bay Packers | | | |
| ☐ 7 Jeff Kemp................................. | .60 | .24 | .06 |
| Philadelphia Eagles | | | |
| ☐ 8 Steve Largent............................ | 1.50 | .60 | .15 |
| Seattle Seahawks | | | |
| ☐ 9 John Offerdahl .......................... | .60 | .24 | .06 |
| Miami Dolphins | | | |
| ☐ 10 Stephone Paige........................ | .60 | .24 | .06 |
| Kansas City Chiefs | | | |
| ☐ 11 Doug Smith ............................. | .50 | .20 | .05 |
| Los Angeles Rams | | | |
| ☐ 12 Rob Taylor .............................. | .50 | .20 | .05 |
| Tampa Bay Buccaneers | | | |

## 1990-91 ProLine Samples

Unlike the borderless regular set, the fronts of these standard-size (2 1/2" by 3 1/2") cards have silver borders. Many photos (both front and back) are different or are cropped differently than the corresponding regular-issue cards, and many of the quotes on the back also are different than the regular issue cards. The word "SAMPLE" is printed in small type next to the mugshots on the backs. The cards are skipnumbered on the back by odd numbers except that sample card number 15 was apparently not issued.

| | MINT | EXC | G-VG |
|---|---|---|---|
| COMPLETE SET (18)....................... | 125.00 | 50.00 | 12.50 |
| COMMON PLAYER............................ | 6.00 | 2.40 | .60 |
| | | | |
| ☐ 1 Charles Mann........................... | 6.00 | 2.40 | .60 |
| Washington Redskins | | | |
| ☐ 3 Troy Aikman............................. | 35.00 | 14.00 | 3.50 |
| Dallas Cowboys | | | |

| | MINT | EXC | G-VG |
|---|---|---|---|
| ☐ 5 Boomer Esiason | 9.00 | 3.75 | .90 |
| Cincinnati Bengals | | | |
| ☐ 7 Warren Moon | 12.00 | 5.00 | 1.20 |
| Houston Oilers | | | |
| ☐ 9 Bill Fralic | 6.00 | 2.40 | .60 |
| Atlanta Falcons | | | |
| ☐ 11 Lawrence Taylor | 9.00 | 3.75 | .90 |
| New York Giants | | | |
| ☐ 13 George Seifert CO | 6.00 | 2.40 | .60 |
| San Francisco 49ers | | | |
| ☐ 17 Dan Marino | 30.00 | 12.00 | 3.00 |
| Miami Dolphins | | | |
| ☐ 19 Jim Everett | 7.50 | 3.00 | .75 |
| Los Angeles Rams | | | |
| ☐ 21 John Elway | 15.00 | 6.00 | 1.50 |
| Denver Broncos | | | |
| ☐ 23 Jeff George | 9.00 | 3.75 | .90 |
| Indianapolis Colts | | | |
| ☐ 25 Lindy Infante CO | 6.00 | 2.40 | .60 |
| Green Bay Packers | | | |
| ☐ 27 Dan Reeves CO | 6.00 | 2.40 | .60 |
| Denver Broncos | | | |
| ☐ 29 Steve Largent | 12.00 | 5.00 | 1.20 |
| Seattle Seahawks | | | |
| ☐ 31 Roger Craig | 9.00 | 3.75 | .90 |
| San Francisco 49ers | | | |
| ☐ 33 Marty Schottenheimer CO | 6.00 | 2.40 | .60 |
| Kansas City Chiefs | | | |
| ☐ 35 Mike Ditka CO | 9.00 | 3.75 | .90 |
| Chicago Bears | | | |
| ☐ 37 Sam Wyche CO | 6.00 | 2.40 | .60 |
| Cincinnati Bengals | | | |

# 1991 ProLine Portraits

This 300-card standard-size (2 1/2" by 3 1/2") set features some of the NFL's most popular players in non-game shots. The players and coaches are posed wearing their team's colors. The fronts are beautiful full-color borderless shots of the players, while the backs feature a quote from the player and a portrait pose of the player. The cards were available in wax packs. Essentially the whole set was available individually autographed; these certified autographed cards randomly included in packs were unnumbered cards. The key Rookie Cards in this set are Nick Bell, Randal Hill, Dan McGwire, Herman Moore, Browning Nagle, and Mike Pritchard. The cards are numbered on the back. The Santa Claus card could be obtained through a mail-in offer in exchange for ten 1991 Pro Line Portraits foil pack wrappers. The card features on the front a portrait of Santa Claus running toward the end zone, with a stuffed toy bag over his right shoulder. The horizontally oriented back carries a quote from Santa. The card is numbered on the back by its year of issue.

| | MINT | EXC | G-VG |
|---|---|---|---|
| COMPLETE SET (300) | 6.00 | 2.70 | .75 |
| COMMON PLAYER (1-300) | .04 | .02 | .01 |
| | | | |
| ☐ 1 Jim Kelly | .30 | .14 | .04 |
| Buffalo Bills | | | |
| ☐ 2 Carl Banks | .08 | .04 | .01 |
| New York Giants | | | |
| ☐ 3 Neal Anderson | .08 | .04 | .01 |
| Chicago Bears | | | |
| ☐ 4 James Brooks | .08 | .04 | .01 |
| Cincinnati Bengals | | | |
| ☐ 5 Reggie Langhorne | .08 | .04 | .01 |
| Cleveland Browns | | | |
| ☐ 6 Robert Awalt | .04 | .02 | .01 |
| Dallas Cowboys | | | |
| ☐ 7 Greg Kragen | .04 | .02 | .01 |
| Denver Broncos | | | |
| ☐ 8 Steve Young | .50 | .23 | .06 |
| San Francisco 49ers | | | |

| | | | |
|---|---|---|---|
| ☐ 9 Nick Bell | .20 | .09 | .03 |
| Los Angeles Raiders | | | |
| ☐ 10 Ray Childress | .08 | .04 | .01 |
| Houston Oilers | | | |
| ☐ 11 Albert Bentley | .04 | .02 | .01 |
| Indianapolis Colts | | | |
| ☐ 12 Albert Lewis | .04 | .02 | .01 |
| Kansas City Chiefs | | | |
| ☐ 13 Howie Long | .08 | .04 | .01 |
| Los Angeles Raiders | | | |
| ☐ 14 Flipper Anderson | .08 | .04 | .01 |
| Los Angeles Rams | | | |
| ☐ 15 Mark Clayton | .08 | .04 | .01 |
| Miami Dolphins | | | |
| ☐ 16 Jarrod Bunch | .15 | .07 | .02 |
| New York Giants | | | |
| ☐ 17 Bruce Armstrong | .04 | .02 | .01 |
| New England Patriots | | | |
| ☐ 18 Vinnie Clark | .04 | .02 | .01 |
| Green Bay Packers | | | |
| ☐ 19 Rob Moore | .10 | .05 | .01 |
| New York Jets | | | |
| ☐ 20 Eric Allen | .08 | .04 | .01 |
| Philadelphia Eagles | | | |
| ☐ 21 Timm Rosenbach | .08 | .04 | .01 |
| Phoenix Cardinals | | | |
| ☐ 22 Gary Anderson | .04 | .02 | .01 |
| Pittsburgh Steelers | | | |
| ☐ 23 Martin Bayless | .04 | .02 | .01 |
| San Diego Chargers | | | |
| ☐ 24 Kevin Fagan | .04 | .02 | .01 |
| San Francisco 49ers | | | |
| ☐ 25 Brian Blades | .10 | .05 | .01 |
| Seattle Seahawks | | | |
| ☐ 26 Gary Anderson | .08 | .04 | .01 |
| Tampa Bay Buccaneers | | | |
| ☐ 27 Earnest Byner | .08 | .04 | .01 |
| Washington Redskins | | | |
| ☐ 28 O.J. Simpson RET | 1.00 | .45 | .13 |
| Buffalo Bills | | | |
| ☐ 29 Dan Henning CO | .04 | .02 | .01 |
| San Diego Chargers | | | |
| ☐ 30 Sean Landeta | .04 | .02 | .01 |
| New York Giants | | | |
| ☐ 31 James Lofton | .10 | .05 | .01 |
| Buffalo Bills | | | |
| ☐ 32 Mike Singletary | .10 | .05 | .01 |
| Chicago Bears | | | |
| ☐ 33 David Fulcher | .04 | .02 | .01 |
| Cincinnati Bengals | | | |
| ☐ 34 Mark Murphy | .04 | .02 | .01 |
| Green Bay Packers | | | |
| ☐ 35 Issiac Holt | .04 | .02 | .01 |
| Dallas Cowboys | | | |
| ☐ 36 Dennis Smith | .08 | .04 | .01 |
| Denver Broncos | | | |
| ☐ 37 Lomas Brown | .04 | .02 | .01 |
| Detroit Lions | | | |
| ☐ 38 Ernest Givins | .08 | .04 | .01 |
| Houston Oilers | | | |
| ☐ 39 Duane Bickett | .04 | .02 | .01 |
| Indianapolis Colts | | | |
| ☐ 40 Barry Word | .10 | .05 | .01 |
| Kansas City Chiefs | | | |
| ☐ 41 Tony Mandarich | .04 | .02 | .01 |
| Green Bay Packers | | | |
| ☐ 42 Cleveland Gary | .08 | .04 | .01 |
| Los Angeles Rams | | | |
| ☐ 43 Ferrell Edmunds | .04 | .02 | .01 |
| Miami Dolphins | | | |
| ☐ 44 Randal Hill | .30 | .14 | .04 |
| Miami Dolphins | | | |
| ☐ 45 Irving Fryar | .08 | .04 | .01 |
| New England Patriots | | | |
| ☐ 46 Henry Jones | .25 | .11 | .03 |
| Buffalo Bills | | | |
| ☐ 47 Blair Thomas | .08 | .04 | .01 |
| New York Jets | | | |
| ☐ 48 Andre Waters | .04 | .02 | .01 |
| Philadelphia Eagles | | | |
| ☐ 49 J.T. Smith | .04 | .02 | .01 |
| Phoenix Cardinals | | | |
| ☐ 50 Thomas Everett | .04 | .02 | .01 |
| Pittsburgh Steelers | | | |
| ☐ 51 Marion Butts | .10 | .05 | .01 |
| San Diego Chargers | | | |
| ☐ 52 Tom Rathman | .08 | .04 | .01 |
| San Francisco 49ers | | | |
| ☐ 53 Vann McElroy | .04 | .02 | .01 |
| Seattle Seahawks | | | |
| ☐ 54 Mark Carrier | .08 | .04 | .01 |
| Tampa Bay Buccaneers | | | |
| ☐ 55 Jim Lachey | .04 | .02 | .01 |
| Washington Redskins | | | |
| ☐ 56 Joe Theismann RET | .08 | .04 | .01 |
| Washington Redskins | | | |
| ☐ 57 Jerry Glanville CO | .04 | .02 | .01 |

|  |  | | | |
|---|---|---|---|---|
| | Atlanta Falcons | | | |
| ☐ 58 | Doug Riesenberg | .04 | .02 | .01 |
| | New York Giants | | | |
| ☐ 59 | Cornelius Bennett | .10 | .05 | .01 |
| | Buffalo Bills | | | |
| ☐ 60 | Mark Carrier | .08 | .04 | .01 |
| | Chicago Bears | | | |
| ☐ 61 | Rodney Holman | .04 | .02 | .01 |
| | Cincinnati Bengals | | | |
| ☐ 62 | Leroy Hoard | .08 | .04 | .01 |
| | Cleveland Browns | | | |
| ☐ 63 | Michael Irvin | .50 | .23 | .06 |
| | Dallas Cowboys | | | |
| ☐ 64 | Bobby Humphrey | .08 | .04 | .01 |
| | Denver Broncos | | | |
| ☐ 65 | Mel Gray | .08 | .04 | .01 |
| | Detroit Lions | | | |
| ☐ 66 | Brian Noble | .04 | .02 | .01 |
| | Green Bay Packers | | | |
| ☐ 67 | Al Smith | .04 | .02 | .01 |
| | Houston Oilers | | | |
| ☐ 68 | Eric Dickerson | .10 | .05 | .01 |
| | Indianapolis Colts | | | |
| ☐ 69 | Steve DeBerg | .08 | .04 | .01 |
| | Kansas City Chiefs | | | |
| ☐ 70 | Jay Schroeder | .08 | .04 | .01 |
| | Los Angeles Raiders | | | |
| ☐ 71 | Irv Pankey | .04 | .02 | .01 |
| | Los Angeles Rams | | | |
| ☐ 72 | Reggie Roby | .04 | .02 | .01 |
| | Miami Dolphins | | | |
| ☐ 73 | Wade Wilson | .08 | .04 | .01 |
| | Minnesota Vikings | | | |
| ☐ 74 | Johnny Rembert | .04 | .02 | .01 |
| | New England Patriots | | | |
| ☐ 75 | Russell Maryland | .40 | .18 | .05 |
| | Dallas Cowboys | | | |
| ☐ 76 | Al Toon | .08 | .04 | .01 |
| | New York Jets | | | |
| ☐ 77 | Randall Cunningham | .10 | .05 | .01 |
| | Philadelphia Eagles | | | |
| ☐ 78 | Lonnie Young | .04 | .02 | .01 |
| | New York Jets | | | |
| ☐ 79 | Carnell Lake | .04 | .02 | .01 |
| | Pittsburgh Steelers | | | |
| ☐ 80 | Burt Grossman | .04 | .02 | .01 |
| | San Diego Chargers | | | |
| ☐ 81 | Jim Mora CO | .04 | .02 | .01 |
| | New Orleans Saints | | | |
| ☐ 82 | Dave Krieg | .08 | .04 | .01 |
| | Seattle Seahawks | | | |
| ☐ 83 | Bruce Hill | .04 | .02 | .01 |
| | Tampa Bay Buccaneers | | | |
| ☐ 84 | Ricky Sanders | .08 | .04 | .01 |
| | Washington Redskins | | | |
| ☐ 85 | Roger Staubach RET | .15 | .07 | .02 |
| | Dallas Cowboys | | | |
| ☐ 86 | Richard Williamson CO | .04 | .02 | .01 |
| | Tampa Bay Buccaneers | | | |
| ☐ 87 | Everson Walls | .04 | .02 | .01 |
| | New York Giants | | | |
| ☐ 88 | Shane Conlan | .04 | .02 | .01 |
| | Buffalo Bills | | | |
| ☐ 89 | Mike Ditka CO | .10 | .05 | .01 |
| | Chicago Bears | | | |
| ☐ 90 | Mark Bortz | .04 | .02 | .01 |
| | Chicago Bears | | | |
| ☐ 91 | Tim McGee | .04 | .02 | .01 |
| | Cincinnati Bengals | | | |
| ☐ 92 | Michael Dean Perry | .20 | .09 | .03 |
| | Cleveland Browns | | | |
| ☐ 93 | Danny Noonan | .04 | .02 | .01 |
| | Dallas Cowboys | | | |
| ☐ 94 | Mark Jackson | .08 | .04 | .01 |
| | Denver Broncos | | | |
| ☐ 95 | Chris Miller | .10 | .05 | .01 |
| | Atlanta Falcons | | | |
| ☐ 96 | Ed McCaffrey | .15 | .07 | .02 |
| | New York Giants | | | |
| ☐ 97 | Lorenzo White | .08 | .04 | .01 |
| | Houston Oilers | | | |
| ☐ 98 | Ray Donaldson | .04 | .02 | .01 |
| | Indianapolis Colts | | | |
| ☐ 99 | Nick Lowery | .08 | .04 | .01 |
| | Kansas City Chiefs | | | |
| ☐ 100 | Steve Smith | .08 | .04 | .01 |
| | Los Angeles Raiders | | | |
| ☐ 101 | Jackie Slater | .08 | .04 | .01 |
| | Los Angeles Rams | | | |
| ☐ 102 | Louis Oliver | .08 | .04 | .01 |
| | Miami Dolphins | | | |
| ☐ 103 | Kanavis McGhee | .10 | .05 | .01 |
| | New York Giants | | | |
| ☐ 104 | Ray Agnew | .04 | .02 | .01 |
| | New England Patriots | | | |
| ☐ 105 | Sam Mills | .08 | .04 | .01 |
| | New Orleans Saints | | | |
| ☐ 106 | Bill Pickel | .04 | .02 | .01 |
| | New York Jets | | | |
| ☐ 107 | Keith Byars | .08 | .04 | .01 |
| | Philadelphia Eagles | | | |
| ☐ 108 | Ricky Proehl | .10 | .05 | .01 |
| | Phoenix Cardinals | | | |
| ☐ 109 | Merril Hoge | .08 | .04 | .01 |
| | Pittsburgh Steelers | | | |
| ☐ 110 | Rod Bernstine | .10 | .05 | .01 |
| | San Diego Chargers | | | |
| ☐ 111 | Andy Heck | .04 | .02 | .01 |
| | Seattle Seahawks | | | |
| ☐ 112 | Broderick Thomas | .08 | .04 | .01 |
| | Tampa Bay Buccaneers | | | |
| ☐ 113 | Andre Collins | .04 | .02 | .01 |
| | Washington Redskins | | | |
| ☐ 114 | Paul Warfield RET | .08 | .04 | .01 |
| | Cleveland Browns | | | |
| ☐ 115 | Bill Belichick CO | .04 | .02 | .01 |
| | Cleveland Browns | | | |
| ☐ 116 | Ottis Anderson | .08 | .04 | .01 |
| | New York Giants | | | |
| ☐ 117 | Andre Reed | .10 | .05 | .01 |
| | Buffalo Bills | | | |
| ☐ 118 | Andre Rison | .25 | .11 | .03 |
| | Atlanta Falcons | | | |
| ☐ 119 | Dexter Carter | .08 | .04 | .01 |
| | San Francisco 49ers | | | |
| ☐ 120 | Anthony Munoz | .08 | .04 | .01 |
| | Cincinnati Bengals | | | |
| ☐ 121 | Bernie Kosar | .10 | .05 | .01 |
| | Cleveland Browns | | | |
| ☐ 122 | Alonzo Highsmith | .04 | .02 | .01 |
| | Dallas Cowboys | | | |
| ☐ 123 | David Treadwell | .04 | .02 | .01 |
| | Denver Broncos | | | |
| ☐ 124 | Rodney Peete | .08 | .04 | .01 |
| | Detroit Lions | | | |
| ☐ 125 | Haywood Jeffires | .15 | .07 | .02 |
| | Houston Oilers | | | |
| ☐ 126 | Clarence Verdin | .04 | .02 | .01 |
| | Indianapolis Colts | | | |
| ☐ 127 | Christian Okoye | .08 | .04 | .01 |
| | Kansas City Chiefs | | | |
| ☐ 128 | Greg Townsend | .04 | .02 | .01 |
| | Los Angeles Raiders | | | |
| ☐ 129 | Tom Newberry | .04 | .02 | .01 |
| | Los Angeles Rams | | | |
| ☐ 130 | Keith Sims | .04 | .02 | .01 |
| | Miami Dolphins | | | |
| ☐ 131 | Myron Guyton | .04 | .02 | .01 |
| | New York Giants | | | |
| ☐ 132 | Andre Tippett | .08 | .04 | .01 |
| | New England Patriots | | | |
| ☐ 133 | Steve Walsh | .04 | .02 | .01 |
| | New Orleans Saints | | | |
| ☐ 134 | Erik McMillan | .04 | .02 | .01 |
| | New York Jets | | | |
| ☐ 135 | Jim McMahon | .10 | .05 | .01 |
| | Philadelphia Eagles | | | |
| ☐ 136 | Derek Hill | .04 | .02 | .01 |
| | Phoenix Cardinals | | | |
| ☐ 137 | David Johnson | .04 | .02 | .01 |
| | Pittsburgh Steelers | | | |
| ☐ 138 | Leslie O'Neal | .08 | .04 | .01 |
| | San Diego Chargers | | | |
| ☐ 139 | Pierce Holt | .04 | .02 | .01 |
| | San Francisco 49ers | | | |
| ☐ 140 | Cortez Kennedy | .25 | .11 | .03 |
| | Seattle Seahawks | | | |
| ☐ 141 | Danny Peebles | .04 | .02 | .01 |
| | Tampa Bay Buccaneers | | | |
| ☐ 142 | Alvin Walton | .04 | .02 | .01 |
| | Washington Redskins | | | |
| ☐ 143 | Drew Pearson RET | .08 | .04 | .01 |
| | Dallas Cowboys | | | |
| ☐ 144 | Dick MacPherson CO | .04 | .02 | .01 |
| | New England Patriots | | | |
| ☐ 145 | Erik Howard | .04 | .02 | .01 |
| | New York Giants | | | |
| ☐ 146 | Steve Tasker | .08 | .04 | .01 |
| | Buffalo Bills | | | |
| ☐ 147 | Bill Fralic | .08 | .04 | .01 |
| | Atlanta Falcons | | | |
| ☐ 148 | Don Warren | .04 | .02 | .01 |
| | Washington Redskins | | | |
| ☐ 149 | Eric Thomas | .04 | .02 | .01 |
| | Cincinnati Bengals | | | |
| ☐ 150 | Jack Pardee CO | .04 | .02 | .01 |
| | Houston Oilers | | | |
| ☐ 151 | Gary Zimmerman | .04 | .02 | .01 |
| | Minnesota Vikings | | | |
| ☐ 152 | Leonard Marshall | .08 | .04 | .01 |
| | New York Giants | | | |
| ☐ 153 | Chris Spielman | .04 | .02 | .01 |
| | Detroit Lions | | | |
| ☐ 154 | Sam Wyche CO | .04 | .02 | .01 |
| | Cincinnati Bengals | | | |
| ☐ 155 | Rohn Stark | .04 | .02 | .01 |

Indianapolis Colts
| | | | |
|---|---|---|---|
| ☐ 156 Stephone Paige | .08 | .04 | .01 |

Kansas City Chiefs
| | | | |
|---|---|---|---|
| ☐ 157 Lionel Washington | .04 | .02 | .01 |

Los Angeles Raiders
| | | | |
|---|---|---|---|
| ☐ 158 Henry Ellard | .08 | .04 | .01 |

Los Angeles Rams
| | | | |
|---|---|---|---|
| ☐ 159 Dan Marino | .75 | .35 | .09 |

Miami Dolphins
| | | | |
|---|---|---|---|
| ☐ 160 Lindy Infante CO | .04 | .02 | .01 |

Green Bay Packers
| | | | |
|---|---|---|---|
| ☐ 161 Dan McGwire | .10 | .05 | .01 |

Seattle Seahawks
| | | | |
|---|---|---|---|
| ☐ 162 Ken O'Brien | .08 | .04 | .01 |

New York Jets
| | | | |
|---|---|---|---|
| ☐ 163 Tim McDonald | .08 | .04 | .01 |

Phoenix Cardinals
| | | | |
|---|---|---|---|
| ☐ 164 Louis Lipps | .08 | .04 | .01 |

Pittsburgh Steelers
| | | | |
|---|---|---|---|
| ☐ 165 Billy Joe Tolliver | .08 | .04 | .01 |

San Diego Chargers
| | | | |
|---|---|---|---|
| ☐ 166 Harris Barton | .04 | .02 | .01 |

San Francisco 49ers
| | | | |
|---|---|---|---|
| ☐ 167 Tony Woods | .04 | .02 | .01 |

Seattle Seahawks
| | | | |
|---|---|---|---|
| ☐ 168 Matt Millen | .08 | .04 | .01 |

Washington Redskins
| | | | |
|---|---|---|---|
| ☐ 169 Gale Sayers RET | .10 | .05 | .01 |

Chicago Bears
| | | | |
|---|---|---|---|
| ☐ 170 Ron Meyer CO | .04 | .02 | .01 |

Indianapolis Colts
| | | | |
|---|---|---|---|
| ☐ 171 William Roberts | .04 | .02 | .01 |

New York Giants
| | | | |
|---|---|---|---|
| ☐ 172 Thurman Thomas | .40 | .18 | .05 |

Buffalo Bills
| | | | |
|---|---|---|---|
| ☐ 173 Steve McMichael | .08 | .04 | .01 |

Chicago Bears
| | | | |
|---|---|---|---|
| ☐ 174 Ickey Woods | .04 | .02 | .01 |

Cincinnati Bengals
| | | | |
|---|---|---|---|
| ☐ 175 Eugene Lockhart | .04 | .02 | .01 |

New England Patriots
| | | | |
|---|---|---|---|
| ☐ 176 George Seifert CO | .08 | .04 | .01 |

San Francisco 49ers
| | | | |
|---|---|---|---|
| ☐ 177 Keith Jones | .04 | .02 | .01 |

Atlanta Falcons
| | | | |
|---|---|---|---|
| ☐ 178 Jack Trudeau | .04 | .02 | .01 |

Indianapolis Colts
| | | | |
|---|---|---|---|
| ☐ 179 Kevin Porter | .04 | .02 | .01 |

Kansas City Chiefs
| | | | |
|---|---|---|---|
| ☐ 180 Ronnie Lott | .10 | .05 | .01 |

Los Angeles Raiders
| | | | |
|---|---|---|---|
| ☐ 181 M. Schottenheimer CO | .04 | .02 | .01 |

Kansas City Chiefs
| | | | |
|---|---|---|---|
| ☐ 182 Morten Andersen | .08 | .04 | .01 |

New Orleans Saints
| | | | |
|---|---|---|---|
| ☐ 183 Anthony Thompson | .04 | .02 | .01 |

Phoenix Cardinals
| | | | |
|---|---|---|---|
| ☐ 184 Tim Worley | .08 | .04 | .01 |

Pittsburgh Steelers
| | | | |
|---|---|---|---|
| ☐ 185 Billy Ray Smith | .04 | .02 | .01 |

San Diego Chargers
| | | | |
|---|---|---|---|
| ☐ 186 David Whitmore | .04 | .02 | .01 |

San Francisco 49ers
| | | | |
|---|---|---|---|
| ☐ 187 Jacob Green | .04 | .02 | .01 |

Seattle Seahawks
| | | | |
|---|---|---|---|
| ☐ 188 Browning Nagle | .20 | .09 | .03 |

New York Jets
| | | | |
|---|---|---|---|
| ☐ 189 Franco Harris RET | .10 | .05 | .01 |

Pittsburgh Steelers
| | | | |
|---|---|---|---|
| ☐ 190 Art Shell CO | .08 | .04 | .01 |

Los Angeles Raiders
| | | | |
|---|---|---|---|
| ☐ 191 Bart Oates | .04 | .02 | .01 |

New York Giants
| | | | |
|---|---|---|---|
| ☐ 192 William Perry | .08 | .04 | .01 |

Chicago Bears
| | | | |
|---|---|---|---|
| ☐ 193 Chuck Noll CO | .08 | .04 | .01 |

Pittsburgh Steelers
| | | | |
|---|---|---|---|
| ☐ 194 Troy Aikman | 1.25 | .55 | .16 |

Dallas Cowboys
| | | | |
|---|---|---|---|
| ☐ 195 Jeff George | .25 | .11 | .03 |

Indianapolis Colts
| | | | |
|---|---|---|---|
| ☐ 196 Derrick Thomas | .25 | .11 | .03 |

Kansas City Chiefs
| | | | |
|---|---|---|---|
| ☐ 197 Roger Craig | .08 | .04 | .01 |

Los Angeles Raiders
| | | | |
|---|---|---|---|
| ☐ 198 John Fourcade | .04 | .02 | .01 |

New Orleans Saints
| | | | |
|---|---|---|---|
| ☐ 199 Rod Woodson | .10 | .05 | .01 |

Pittsburgh Steelers
| | | | |
|---|---|---|---|
| ☐ 200 Anthony Miller | .20 | .09 | .03 |

San Diego Chargers
| | | | |
|---|---|---|---|
| ☐ 201 Jerry Rice | .75 | .35 | .09 |

San Francisco 49ers
| | | | |
|---|---|---|---|
| ☐ 202 Eugene Robinson | .04 | .02 | .01 |

Seattle Seahawks
| | | | |
|---|---|---|---|
| ☐ 203 Charles Mann | .08 | .04 | .01 |

Washington Redskins
| | | | |
|---|---|---|---|
| ☐ 204 Mel Blount RET | .08 | .04 | .01 |

Pittsburgh Steelers
| | | | |
|---|---|---|---|
| ☐ 205 Don Shula CO | .08 | .04 | .01 |

Miami Dolphins
| | | | |
|---|---|---|---|
| ☐ 206 Jumbo Elliott | .04 | .02 | .01 |

New York Giants
| | | | |
|---|---|---|---|
| ☐ 207 Jay Hilgenberg | .08 | .04 | .01 |

Chicago Bears
| | | | |
|---|---|---|---|
| ☐ 208 Deron Cherry | .04 | .02 | .01 |

Kansas City Chiefs
| | | | |
|---|---|---|---|
| ☐ 209 Dan Reeves CO | .08 | .04 | .01 |

Denver Broncos
| | | | |
|---|---|---|---|
| ☐ 210 Roman Phifer | .10 | .05 | .01 |

Los Angeles Rams
| | | | |
|---|---|---|---|
| ☐ 211 David Little | .04 | .02 | .01 |

Pittsburgh Steelers
| | | | |
|---|---|---|---|
| ☐ 212 Lee Williams | .08 | .04 | .01 |

San Diego Chargers
| | | | |
|---|---|---|---|
| ☐ 213 John Taylor | .10 | .05 | .01 |

San Francisco 49ers
| | | | |
|---|---|---|---|
| ☐ 214 Monte Coleman | .04 | .02 | .01 |

Washington Redskins
| | | | |
|---|---|---|---|
| ☐ 215 Walter Payton RET | .15 | .07 | .02 |

Chicago Bears
| | | | |
|---|---|---|---|
| ☐ 216 John Robinson CO | .04 | .02 | .01 |

Los Angeles Rams
| | | | |
|---|---|---|---|
| ☐ 217 Pepper Johnson | .08 | .04 | .01 |

New York Giants
| | | | |
|---|---|---|---|
| ☐ 218 Tom Thayer | .04 | .02 | .01 |

Chicago Bears
| | | | |
|---|---|---|---|
| ☐ 219 Dan Saleaumua | .04 | .02 | .01 |

Kansas City Chiefs
| | | | |
|---|---|---|---|
| ☐ 220 Ernest Spears | .04 | .02 | .01 |

New Orleans Saints
| | | | |
|---|---|---|---|
| ☐ 221 Bubby Brister | .08 | .04 | .01 |

Pittsburgh Steelers
| | | | |
|---|---|---|---|
| ☐ 222 Junior Seau | .25 | .11 | .03 |

San Diego Chargers
| | | | |
|---|---|---|---|
| ☐ 223 Brent Jones | .10 | .05 | .01 |

San Francisco 49ers
| | | | |
|---|---|---|---|
| ☐ 224 Rufus Porter | .04 | .02 | .01 |

Seattle Seahawks
| | | | |
|---|---|---|---|
| ☐ 225 Jack Kemp RET | .15 | .07 | .02 |

Buffalo Bills
| | | | |
|---|---|---|---|
| ☐ 226 Wayne Fontes CO | .04 | .02 | .01 |

Detroit Lions
| | | | |
|---|---|---|---|
| ☐ 227 Phil Simms | .10 | .05 | .01 |

New York Giants
| | | | |
|---|---|---|---|
| ☐ 228 Shaun Gayle | .04 | .02 | .01 |

Chicago Bears
| | | | |
|---|---|---|---|
| ☐ 229 Bill Maas | .04 | .02 | .01 |

Kansas City Chiefs
| | | | |
|---|---|---|---|
| ☐ 230 Renaldo Turnbull | .08 | .04 | .01 |

New Orleans Saints
| | | | |
|---|---|---|---|
| ☐ 231 Bryan Hinkle | .04 | .02 | .01 |

Pittsburgh Steelers
| | | | |
|---|---|---|---|
| ☐ 232 Gary Plummer | .04 | .02 | .01 |

San Diego Chargers
| | | | |
|---|---|---|---|
| ☐ 233 Jerry Burns CO | .04 | .02 | .01 |

Minnesota Vikings
| | | | |
|---|---|---|---|
| ☐ 234 Lawrence Taylor | .10 | .05 | .01 |

New York Giants
| | | | |
|---|---|---|---|
| ☐ 235 Joe Gibbs CO | .04 | .02 | .01 |

Washington Redskins
| | | | |
|---|---|---|---|
| ☐ 236 Neil Smith | .10 | .05 | .01 |

Kansas City Chiefs
| | | | |
|---|---|---|---|
| ☐ 237 Rich Kotite CO | .04 | .02 | .01 |

Philadelphia Eagles
| | | | |
|---|---|---|---|
| ☐ 238 Jim Covert | .04 | .02 | .01 |

Chicago Bears
| | | | |
|---|---|---|---|
| ☐ 239 Tim Grunhard | .04 | .02 | .01 |

Kansas City Chiefs
| | | | |
|---|---|---|---|
| ☐ 240 Joe Bugel CO | .04 | .02 | .01 |

Phoenix Cardinals
| | | | |
|---|---|---|---|
| ☐ 241 Dave Wyman | .04 | .02 | .01 |

Seattle Seahawks
| | | | |
|---|---|---|---|
| ☐ 242 Maury Buford | .04 | .02 | .01 |

Chicago Bears
| | | | |
|---|---|---|---|
| ☐ 243 Kevin Ross | .04 | .02 | .01 |

Kansas City Chiefs
| | | | |
|---|---|---|---|
| ☐ 244 Jimmy Johnson CO | .08 | .04 | .01 |

Dallas Cowboys
| | | | |
|---|---|---|---|
| ☐ 245 Jim Morrissey | .15 | .07 | .02 |

Chicago Bears
| | | | |
|---|---|---|---|
| ☐ 246 Jeff Hostetler | .25 | .11 | .03 |

New York Giants
| | | | |
|---|---|---|---|
| ☐ 247 Andre Ware | .10 | .05 | .01 |

Houston Oilers
| | | | |
|---|---|---|---|
| ☐ 248 Steve Largent RET | .10 | .05 | .01 |

Seattle Seahawks
| | | | |
|---|---|---|---|
| ☐ 249 Chuck Knox CO | .04 | .02 | .01 |

Seattle Seahawks
| | | | |
|---|---|---|---|
| ☐ 250 Boomer Esiason | .15 | .07 | .02 |

Cincinnati Bengals
| | | | |
|---|---|---|---|
| ☐ 251 Kevin Butler | .04 | .02 | .01 |

Chicago Bears
| | | | |
|---|---|---|---|
| ☐ 252 Bruce Smith | .10 | .05 | .01 |

Buffalo Bills
| | | | |
|---|---|---|---|
| ☐ 253 Webster Slaughter | .08 | .04 | .01 |

| | | | |
|---|---|---|---|
| Cleveland Browns | | | |
| ☐ 254 Mike Sherrard | .08 | .04 | .01 |
| San Francisco 49ers | | | |
| ☐ 255 Steve Broussard | .08 | .04 | .01 |
| Atlanta Falcons | | | |
| ☐ 256 Warren Moon | .20 | .09 | .03 |
| Houston Oilers | | | |
| ☐ 257 John Elway | .35 | .16 | .04 |
| Denver Broncos | | | |
| ☐ 258 Bob Golic | .04 | .02 | .01 |
| Los Angeles Raiders | | | |
| ☐ 259 Jim Everett | .08 | .04 | .01 |
| Los Angeles Rams | | | |
| ☐ 260 Bruce Coslet CO | .04 | .02 | .01 |
| New York Jets | | | |
| ☐ 261 James Francis | .08 | .04 | .01 |
| Cincinnati Bengals | | | |
| ☐ 262 Eric Dorsey | .04 | .02 | .01 |
| New York Giants | | | |
| ☐ 263 Marcus Dupree | .08 | .04 | .01 |
| Los Angeles Rams | | | |
| ☐ 264 Hart Lee Dykes | .04 | .02 | .01 |
| New England Patriots | | | |
| ☐ 265 Vinny Testaverde | .10 | .05 | .01 |
| Tampa Bay Buccaneers | | | |
| ☐ 266 Chip Lohmiller | .08 | .04 | .01 |
| Washington Redskins | | | |
| ☐ 267 John Riggins RET | .08 | .04 | .01 |
| Washington Redskins | | | |
| ☐ 268 Mike Schad | .04 | .02 | .01 |
| Philadelphia Eagles | | | |
| ☐ 269 Kevin Greene | .04 | .02 | .01 |
| Los Angeles Rams | | | |
| ☐ 270 Dean Biasucci | .04 | .02 | .01 |
| Indianapolis Colts | | | |
| ☐ 271 Mike Pritchard | .75 | .35 | .09 |
| Atlanta Falcons | | | |
| ☐ 272 Ted Washington | .04 | .02 | .01 |
| San Francisco 49ers | | | |
| ☐ 273 Alfred Williams | .15 | .07 | .02 |
| Cincinnati Bengals | | | |
| ☐ 274 Chris Zorich | .25 | .11 | .03 |
| Chicago Bears | | | |
| ☐ 275 Reggie Barrett | .04 | .02 | .01 |
| Detroit Lions | | | |
| ☐ 276 Chris Hinton | .04 | .02 | .01 |
| Atlanta Falcons | | | |
| ☐ 277 Tracy Johnson | .10 | .05 | .01 |
| Atlanta Falcons | | | |
| ☐ 278 Jim Harbaugh | .08 | .04 | .01 |
| Chicago Bears | | | |
| ☐ 279 John Roper | .04 | .02 | .01 |
| Chicago Bears | | | |
| ☐ 280 Mike Dumas | .04 | .02 | .01 |
| Houston Oilers | | | |
| ☐ 281 Herman Moore | 1.00 | .45 | .13 |
| Detroit Lions | | | |
| ☐ 282 Eric Turner | .20 | .09 | .03 |
| Cleveland Browns | | | |
| ☐ 283 Steve Atwater | .10 | .05 | .01 |
| Denver Broncos | | | |
| ☐ 284 Michael Cofer | .04 | .02 | .01 |
| Detroit Lions | | | |
| ☐ 285 Darion Conner | .04 | .02 | .01 |
| Atlanta Falcons | | | |
| ☐ 286 Darryl Talley | .08 | .04 | .01 |
| Buffalo Bills | | | |
| ☐ 287 Donnell Woolford | .04 | .02 | .01 |
| Chicago Bears | | | |
| ☐ 288 Keith McCants | .04 | .02 | .01 |
| Tampa Bay Buccaneers | | | |
| ☐ 289 Ray Handley CO | .04 | .02 | .01 |
| New York Giants | | | |
| ☐ 290 Ahmad Rashad RET | .08 | .04 | .01 |
| Minnesota Vikings | | | |
| ☐ 291 Eric Swann | .20 | .09 | .03 |
| Phoenix Cardinals | | | |
| ☐ 292 Dalton Hilliard | .04 | .02 | .01 |
| New Orleans Saints | | | |
| ☐ 293 Rickey Jackson | .08 | .04 | .01 |
| New Orleans Saints | | | |
| ☐ 294 Vaughan Johnson | .08 | .04 | .01 |
| New Orleans Saints | | | |
| ☐ 295 Eric Martin | .08 | .04 | .01 |
| New Orleans Saints | | | |
| ☐ 296 Pat Swilling | .08 | .04 | .01 |
| New Orleans Saints | | | |
| ☐ 297 Anthony Carter | .08 | .04 | .01 |
| Minnesota Vikings | | | |
| ☐ 298 Guy McIntyre | .08 | .04 | .01 |
| San Francisco 49ers | | | |
| ☐ 299 Bennie Blades | .04 | .02 | .01 |
| Detroit Lions | | | |
| ☐ 300 Paul Farren | .04 | .02 | .01 |
| Cleveland Browns | | | |
| ☐ NNO Santa Claus 1991 | 5.00 | 2.30 | .60 |

# 1991 ProLine Portraits Autographs

This 300-card standard-size (2 1/2" by 3 1/2") set features some of the NFL's most popular players in non-game shots. The players and coaches are posed wearing their team's colors. The fronts are beautiful full-color borderless shots of the players, while the backs feature a quote from the player and a portrait pose of the player. The cards were available in wax packs. Essentially the whole set was available individually autographed; these certified autographed cards randomly included in packs were unnumbered cards. They are listed below according to the numbers assigned to them in the regular series. It has been reported by collectors that an autographed card is found with a frequency of about one per three boxes of 1991 ProLine. The Tim McDonald card (163) is not included in the set price as only one card is known to exist. Cards with signatures cut in half are considered to have major defects. The autographed Santa card is not considered part of the this set.

| | MINT | EXC | G-VG |
|---|---|---|---|
| COMPLETE SET (299) | 6000.00 | 2700.00 | 600.00 |
| COMMON PLAYER (1-300) | 8.00 | 3.25 | .80 |
| ☐ 1A Jim Kelly | 50.00 | 20.00 | 5.00 |
| (Autopenned) | | | |
| ☐ 1B Jim Kelly | 125.00 | 50.00 | 12.50 |
| (Real signature) | | | |
| ☐ 2 Carl Banks | 15.00 | 6.00 | 1.50 |
| ☐ 3 Neal Anderson | 20.00 | 8.00 | 2.00 |
| ☐ 4 James Brooks | 15.00 | 6.00 | 1.50 |
| ☐ 5 Reggie Langhorne | 75.00 | 30.00 | 7.50 |
| ☐ 6 Robert Awalt | 8.00 | 3.25 | .80 |
| ☐ 7 Greg Kragen | 8.00 | 3.25 | .80 |
| ☐ 8 Steve Young | 75.00 | 30.00 | 7.50 |
| ☐ 9 Nick Bell | 15.00 | 6.00 | 1.50 |
| ☐ 10 Ray Childress | 12.00 | 5.00 | 1.20 |
| ☐ 11 Albert Bentley | 10.00 | 4.00 | 1.00 |
| ☐ 12 Albert Lewis | 75.00 | 30.00 | 7.50 |
| ☐ 13 Howie Long | 30.00 | 12.00 | 3.00 |
| ☐ 14 Flipper Anderson | 15.00 | 6.00 | 1.50 |
| ☐ 15 Mark Clayton | 25.00 | 10.00 | 2.50 |
| ☐ 16 Jarrod Bunch | 12.00 | 5.00 | 1.20 |
| ☐ 17 Bruce Armstrong | 8.00 | 3.25 | .80 |
| ☐ 18 Vinnie Clark | 8.00 | 3.25 | .80 |
| ☐ 19 Rob Moore | 18.00 | 7.25 | 1.80 |
| ☐ 20 Eric Allen | 15.00 | 6.00 | 1.50 |
| ☐ 21 Timm Rosenbach | 12.00 | 5.00 | 1.20 |
| ☐ 22 Gary Anderson | 8.00 | 3.25 | .80 |
| ☐ 23 Martin Bayless | 8.00 | 3.25 | .80 |
| ☐ 24 Kevin Fagan | 10.00 | 4.00 | 1.00 |
| ☐ 25 Brian Blades | 15.00 | 6.00 | 1.50 |
| ☐ 26 Gary Anderson | 12.00 | 5.00 | 1.20 |
| ☐ 27 Earnest Byner | 15.00 | 6.00 | 1.50 |
| ☐ 28 O.J. Simpson RET | 300.00 | 120.00 | 30.00 |
| ☐ 29 Dan Henning CO | 8.00 | 3.25 | .80 |
| ☐ 30 Sean Landeta | 8.00 | 3.25 | .80 |
| ☐ 31 James Lofton | 30.00 | 12.00 | 3.00 |
| ☐ 32 Mike Singletary | 75.00 | 30.00 | 7.50 |
| ☐ 33 David Fulcher | 8.00 | 3.25 | .80 |
| ☐ 34 Mark Murphy | 8.00 | 3.25 | .80 |
| ☐ 35 Issiac Holt | 18.00 | 7.25 | 1.80 |
| ☐ 36 Dennis Smith | 12.00 | 5.00 | 1.20 |
| ☐ 37 Lomas Brown | 12.00 | 5.00 | 1.20 |
| ☐ 38 Ernest Givins | 15.00 | 6.00 | 1.50 |
| ☐ 39 Duane Bickett | 8.00 | 3.25 | .80 |
| ☐ 40 Barry Word | 15.00 | 6.00 | 1.50 |
| ☐ 41 Tony Mandarich | 8.00 | 3.25 | .80 |
| ☐ 42 Cleveland Gary | 18.00 | 7.25 | 1.80 |
| ☐ 43 Ferrell Edmunds | 15.00 | 6.00 | 1.50 |
| ☐ 44 Randal Hill | 20.00 | 8.00 | 2.00 |
| ☐ 45 Irving Fryar | 15.00 | 6.00 | 1.50 |
| ☐ 46 Henry Jones | 18.00 | 7.25 | 1.80 |
| ☐ 47 Blair Thomas | 15.00 | 6.00 | 1.50 |
| ☐ 48 Andre Waters | 8.00 | 3.25 | .80 |
| ☐ 49 J.T. Smith | 12.00 | 5.00 | 1.20 |
| ☐ 50 Thomas Everett | 12.00 | 5.00 | 1.20 |

| | | | | |
|---|---|---|---|---|
| ☐ 51 Marion Butts | 20.00 | 8.00 | 2.00 |
| ☐ 52 Tom Rathman | 20.00 | 8.00 | 2.00 |
| ☐ 53 Vann McElroy | 8.00 | 3.25 | .80 |
| ☐ 54 Mark Carrier | 15.00 | 6.00 | 1.50 |
| ☐ 55 Jim Lachey | 15.00 | 6.00 | 1.50 |
| ☐ 56 Joe Theismann RET | 40.00 | 16.00 | 4.00 |
| ☐ 57 Jerry Glanville CO | 15.00 | 6.00 | 1.50 |
| ☐ 58 Doug Riesenberg | 8.00 | 3.25 | .80 |
| ☐ 59 Cornelius Bennett | 25.00 | 10.00 | 2.50 |
| ☐ 60 Mark Carrier | 100.00 | 40.00 | 10.00 |
| ☐ 61 Rodney Holman | 250.00 | 100.00 | 25.00 |
| ☐ 62 Leroy Hoard | 12.00 | 5.00 | 1.20 |
| ☐ 63 Michael Irvin | 85.00 | 34.00 | 8.50 |
| ☐ 64 Bobby Humphrey | 12.00 | 5.00 | 1.20 |
| ☐ 65 Mel Gray | 12.00 | 5.00 | 1.20 |
| ☐ 66 Brian Noble | 8.00 | 3.25 | .80 |
| ☐ 67 Al Smith | 8.00 | 3.25 | .80 |
| ☐ 68 Eric Dickerson | 40.00 | 16.00 | 4.00 |
| ☐ 69 Steve DeBerg | 20.00 | 8.00 | 2.00 |
| ☐ 70 Jay Schroeder | 20.00 | 8.00 | 2.00 |
| ☐ 71 Irv Pankey | 8.00 | 3.25 | .80 |
| ☐ 72 Reggie Roby | 12.00 | 5.00 | 1.20 |
| ☐ 73 Wade Wilson | 15.00 | 6.00 | 1.50 |
| ☐ 74 Johnny Rembert | 8.00 | 3.25 | .80 |
| ☐ 75 Russell Maryland | 25.00 | 10.00 | 2.50 |
| ☐ 76 Al Toon | 20.00 | 8.00 | 2.00 |
| ☐ 77 Randall Cunningham | 75.00 | 30.00 | 7.50 |
| ☐ 78 Lonnie Young | 10.00 | 4.00 | 1.00 |
| ☐ 79 Carnell Lake | 12.00 | 5.00 | 1.20 |
| ☐ 80 Burt Grossman | 8.00 | 3.25 | .80 |
| ☐ 81 Jim Mora CO | 8.00 | 3.25 | .80 |
| ☐ 82 Dave Krieg | 20.00 | 8.00 | 2.00 |
| ☐ 83 Bruce Hill | 8.00 | 3.25 | .80 |
| ☐ 84 Ricky Sanders | 20.00 | 8.00 | 2.00 |
| ☐ 85 Roger Staubach RET | 150.00 | 60.00 | 15.00 |
| ☐ 86 Richard Williamson CO | 8.00 | 3.25 | .80 |
| ☐ 87 Everson Walls | 12.00 | 5.00 | 1.20 |
| ☐ 88 Shane Conlan | 20.00 | 8.00 | 2.00 |
| ☐ 89 Mike Ditka CO | 40.00 | 16.00 | 4.00 |
| ☐ 90 Mark Bortz | 8.00 | 3.25 | .80 |
| ☐ 91 Tim McGee | 12.00 | 5.00 | 1.20 |
| ☐ 92 Michael Dean Perry | 25.00 | 10.00 | 2.50 |
| ☐ 93 Danny Noonan | 10.00 | 4.00 | 1.00 |
| ☐ 94 Mark Jackson | 20.00 | 8.00 | 2.00 |
| ☐ 95 Chris Miller | 20.00 | 8.00 | 2.00 |
| ☐ 96 Ed McCaffrey | 12.00 | 5.00 | 1.20 |
| ☐ 97 Lorenzo White | 12.00 | 5.00 | 1.20 |
| ☐ 98 Ray Donaldson | 10.00 | 4.00 | 1.00 |
| ☐ 99 Nick Lowery | 8.00 | 3.25 | .80 |
| (May be autopenned) | | | |
| ☐ 100 Steve Smith | 12.00 | 5.00 | 1.20 |
| ☐ 101 Jackie Slater | 12.00 | 5.00 | 1.20 |
| ☐ 102 Louis Oliver | 12.00 | 5.00 | 1.20 |
| ☐ 103 Kanavis McGhee | 12.00 | 5.00 | 1.20 |
| ☐ 104 Ray Agnew | 8.00 | 3.25 | .80 |
| ☐ 105 Sam Mills | 12.00 | 5.00 | 1.20 |
| ☐ 106 Bill Pickel | 8.00 | 3.25 | .80 |
| ☐ 107 Keith Byars | 18.00 | 7.25 | 1.80 |
| ☐ 108 Ricky Proehl | 12.00 | 5.00 | 1.20 |
| ☐ 109 Merril Hoge | 20.00 | 8.00 | 2.00 |
| ☐ 110 Rod Bernstine | 20.00 | 8.00 | 2.00 |
| ☐ 111 Andy Heck | 8.00 | 3.25 | .80 |
| ☐ 112 Broderick Thomas | 8.00 | 3.25 | .80 |
| ☐ 113 Andre Collins | 12.00 | 5.00 | 1.20 |
| ☐ 114 Paul Warfield RET | 30.00 | 12.00 | 3.00 |
| ☐ 115 Bill Belichick CO | 8.00 | 3.25 | .80 |
| ☐ 116 Ottis Anderson | 25.00 | 10.00 | 2.50 |
| ☐ 117 Andre Reed | 30.00 | 12.00 | 3.00 |
| ☐ 118A Andre Rison | 30.00 | 12.00 | 3.00 |
| (Ball-point pen) | | | |
| ☐ 118B Andre Rison | 50.00 | 20.00 | 5.00 |
| (Signed in Sharpie) | | | |
| ☐ 119 Dexter Carter | 12.00 | 5.00 | 1.20 |
| ☐ 120 Anthony Munoz | 20.00 | 8.00 | 2.00 |
| ☐ 121 Bernie Kosar | 40.00 | 16.00 | 4.00 |
| ☐ 122 Alonzo Highsmith | 75.00 | 30.00 | 7.50 |
| ☐ 123 David Treadwell | 10.00 | 4.00 | 1.00 |
| ☐ 124 Rodney Peete | 20.00 | 8.00 | 2.00 |
| ☐ 125 Haywood Jeffires | 25.00 | 10.00 | 2.50 |
| ☐ 126 Clarence Verdin | 8.00 | 3.25 | .80 |
| ☐ 127 Christian Okoye | 15.00 | 6.00 | 1.50 |
| ☐ 128 Greg Townsend | 100.00 | 40.00 | 10.00 |
| ☐ 129 Tom Newberry | 8.00 | 3.25 | .80 |
| ☐ 130 Keith Sims | 8.00 | 3.25 | .80 |
| ☐ 131 Myron Guyton | 10.00 | 4.00 | 1.00 |
| ☐ 132 Andre Tippett | 15.00 | 6.00 | 1.50 |
| ☐ 133 Steve Walsh | 12.00 | 5.00 | 1.20 |
| ☐ 134 Erik McMillan | 8.00 | 3.25 | .80 |
| ☐ 135 Jim McMahon | 250.00 | 100.00 | 25.00 |
| ☐ 136 Derek Hill | 10.00 | 4.00 | 1.00 |
| ☐ 137 David Johnson | 8.00 | 3.25 | .80 |
| ☐ 138 Leslie O'Neal | 12.00 | 5.00 | 1.20 |
| ☐ 139 Pierce Holt | 12.00 | 5.00 | 1.20 |
| ☐ 140 Cortez Kennedy | 25.00 | 10.00 | 2.50 |
| ☐ 141 Danny Peebles | 8.00 | 3.25 | .80 |
| ☐ 142 Alvin Walton | 12.00 | 5.00 | 1.20 |
| ☐ 143 Drew Pearson RET | 30.00 | 12.00 | 3.00 |
| ☐ 144 Dick MacPherson CO | 8.00 | 3.25 | .80 |
| ☐ 145 Erik Howard | 10.00 | 4.00 | 1.00 |
| ☐ 146 Steve Tasker | 15.00 | 6.00 | 1.50 |
| ☐ 147 Bill Fralic | 12.00 | 5.00 | 1.20 |
| ☐ 148 Don Warren | 8.00 | 3.25 | .80 |
| ☐ 149 Eric Thomas | 8.00 | 3.25 | .80 |
| ☐ 150 Jack Pardee CO | 8.00 | 3.25 | .80 |
| ☐ 151 Gary Zimmerman | 8.00 | 3.25 | .80 |
| ☐ 152 Leonard Marshall | 20.00 | 8.00 | 2.00 |
| (Frequently miscut) | | | |
| ☐ 153 Chris Spielman | 12.00 | 5.00 | 1.20 |
| ☐ 154 Sam Wyche CO | 8.00 | 3.25 | .80 |
| ☐ 155 Rohn Stark | 12.00 | 5.00 | 1.20 |
| ☐ 156 Stephone Paige | 12.00 | 5.00 | 1.20 |
| ☐ 157 Lionel Washington | 100.00 | 40.00 | 10.00 |
| ☐ 158 Henry Ellard | 15.00 | 6.00 | 1.50 |
| ☐ 159 Dan Marino | 150.00 | 60.00 | 15.00 |
| ☐ 160 Lindy Infante CO | 8.00 | 3.25 | .80 |
| ☐ 161 Dan McGwire | 20.00 | 8.00 | 2.00 |
| ☐ 162 Ken O'Brien | 20.00 | 8.00 | 2.00 |
| ☐ 164 Louis Lipps | 20.00 | 8.00 | 2.00 |
| ☐ 165 Billy Joe Tolliver | 12.00 | 5.00 | 1.20 |
| ☐ 166 Harris Barton | 8.00 | 3.25 | .80 |
| ☐ 167 Tony Woods | 8.00 | 3.25 | .80 |
| ☐ 168 Matt Millen | 8.00 | 3.25 | .80 |
| ☐ 169 Gale Sayers RET | 75.00 | 30.00 | 7.50 |
| ☐ 170 Ron Meyer CO | 8.00 | 3.25 | .80 |
| ☐ 171 William Roberts | 10.00 | 4.00 | 1.00 |
| ☐ 172 Thurman Thomas | 75.00 | 30.00 | 7.50 |
| ☐ 173 Steve McMichael | 8.00 | 3.25 | .80 |
| ☐ 174 Ickey Woods | 12.00 | 5.00 | 1.20 |
| ☐ 175 Eugene Lockhart | 8.00 | 3.25 | .80 |
| ☐ 176 George Seifert CO | 15.00 | 6.00 | 1.50 |
| ☐ 177 Keith Jones | 12.00 | 5.00 | 1.20 |
| ☐ 178 Jack Trudeau | 12.00 | 5.00 | 1.20 |
| ☐ 179 Kevin Porter | 8.00 | 3.25 | .80 |
| ☐ 180 Ronnie Lott | 30.00 | 12.00 | 3.00 |
| ☐ 181 M. Schottenheimer CO | 12.00 | 5.00 | 1.20 |
| ☐ 182 Morten Andersen | 12.00 | 5.00 | 1.20 |
| ☐ 183 Anthony Thompson | 12.00 | 5.00 | 1.20 |
| ☐ 184 Tim Worley | 15.00 | 6.00 | 1.50 |
| ☐ 185 Billy Ray Smith | 8.00 | 3.25 | .80 |
| ☐ 186 David Whitmore | 8.00 | 3.25 | .80 |
| ☐ 187 Jacob Green | 12.00 | 5.00 | 1.20 |
| ☐ 188 Browning Nagle | 25.00 | 10.00 | 2.50 |
| ☐ 189 Franco Harris RET | 75.00 | 30.00 | 7.50 |
| ☐ 190 Art Shell CO | 30.00 | 12.00 | 3.00 |
| ☐ 191 Bart Oates | 8.00 | 3.25 | .80 |
| ☐ 192 William Perry | 25.00 | 10.00 | 2.50 |
| ☐ 193 Chuck Noll CO | 30.00 | 12.00 | 3.00 |
| ☐ 194 Troy Aikman | 150.00 | 60.00 | 15.00 |
| ☐ 195 Jeff George | 35.00 | 14.00 | 3.50 |
| ☐ 196 Derrick Thomas | 35.00 | 14.00 | 3.50 |
| ☐ 197 Roger Craig | 25.00 | 10.00 | 2.50 |
| ☐ 198 John Fourcade | 8.00 | 3.25 | .80 |
| ☐ 199 Rod Woodson | 25.00 | 10.00 | 2.50 |
| ☐ 200 Anthony Miller | 15.00 | 6.00 | 1.50 |
| ☐ 201 Jerry Rice | 175.00 | 70.00 | 18.00 |
| ☐ 202 Eugene Robinson | 8.00 | 3.25 | .80 |
| ☐ 203 Charles Mann | 12.00 | 5.00 | 1.20 |
| ☐ 204 Mel Blount RET | 30.00 | 12.00 | 3.00 |
| ☐ 205 Don Shula CO | 50.00 | 20.00 | 5.00 |
| ☐ 206 Jumbo Elliott | 10.00 | 4.00 | 1.00 |
| ☐ 207 Jay Hilgenberg | 10.00 | 4.00 | 1.00 |
| ☐ 208 Deron Cherry | 15.00 | 6.00 | 1.50 |
| ☐ 209 Dan Reeves CO | 15.00 | 6.00 | 1.50 |
| ☐ 210 Roman Phifer | 8.00 | 3.25 | .80 |
| ☐ 211 David Little | 8.00 | 3.25 | .80 |
| ☐ 212 Lee Williams | 8.00 | 3.25 | .80 |
| ☐ 213 John Taylor | 25.00 | 10.00 | 2.50 |
| ☐ 214 Monte Coleman | 15.00 | 6.00 | 1.50 |
| ☐ 215 Walter Payton RET | 100.00 | 40.00 | 10.00 |
| ☐ 216 John Robinson CO | 12.00 | 5.00 | 1.20 |
| ☐ 217 Pepper Johnson | 15.00 | 6.00 | 1.50 |
| ☐ 218 Tom Thayer | 8.00 | 3.25 | .80 |
| ☐ 219 Dan Saleaumua | 8.00 | 3.25 | .80 |
| ☐ 220 Ernest Spears | 8.00 | 3.25 | .80 |
| ☐ 221 Bubby Brister | 15.00 | 6.00 | 1.50 |
| (Signed Bubby 6) | | | |
| ☐ 222 Junior Seau | 20.00 | 8.00 | 2.00 |
| ☐ 223 Brent Jones | 15.00 | 6.00 | 1.50 |
| ☐ 224 Rufus Porter | 8.00 | 3.25 | .80 |
| ☐ 225 Jack Kemp RET | 75.00 | 30.00 | 7.50 |
| (Autopenned) | | | |
| ☐ 226 Wayne Fontes CO | 8.00 | 3.25 | .80 |
| ☐ 227 Phil Simms | 40.00 | 16.00 | 4.00 |
| ☐ 228 Shaun Gayle | 8.00 | 3.25 | .80 |
| ☐ 229 Bill Maas | 8.00 | 3.25 | .80 |
| ☐ 230 Renaldo Turnbull | 12.00 | 5.00 | 1.20 |
| ☐ 231 Bryan Hinkle | 8.00 | 3.25 | .80 |
| ☐ 232 Gary Plummer | 8.00 | 3.25 | .80 |
| ☐ 233 Jerry Burns CO | 8.00 | 3.25 | .80 |
| ☐ 234 Lawrence Taylor | 75.00 | 30.00 | 7.50 |
| ☐ 235 Joe Gibbs CO | 20.00 | 8.00 | 2.00 |
| ☐ 236 Neil Smith | 100.00 | 40.00 | 10.00 |
| (Most signatures are cut off) | | | |

| | | | |
|---|---|---|---|
| ☐ 237 Rich Kotite CO | 8.00 | 3.25 | .80 |
| ☐ 238 Jim Covert | 8.00 | 3.25 | .80 |
| ☐ 239 Tim Grunhard | 8.00 | 3.25 | .80 |
| (Two different signatures known for this card) | | | |
| ☐ 240 Joe Bugel CO | 8.00 | 3.25 | .80 |
| ☐ 241 Dave Wyman | 20.00 | 8.00 | 2.00 |
| ☐ 242 Maury Buford | 8.00 | 3.25 | .80 |
| ☐ 243 Kevin Ross | 8.00 | 3.25 | .80 |
| ☐ 244 Jimmy Johnson CO | 40.00 | 16.00 | 4.00 |
| ☐ 245 Jim Morrissey | 8.00 | 3.25 | .80 |
| ☐ 246 Jeff Hostetler | 25.00 | 10.00 | 2.50 |
| ☐ 247 Andre Ware | 20.00 | 8.00 | 2.00 |
| ☐ 248 Steve Largent RET | 60.00 | 24.00 | 6.00 |
| ☐ 249 Chuck Knox CO | 15.00 | 6.00 | 1.50 |
| ☐ 250 Boomer Esiason | 25.00 | 10.00 | 2.50 |
| ☐ 251 Kevin Butler | 12.00 | 5.00 | 1.20 |
| ☐ 252 Bruce Smith | 30.00 | 12.00 | 3.00 |
| ☐ 253 Webster Slaughter | 15.00 | 6.00 | 1.50 |
| ☐ 254 Mike Sherrard | 12.00 | 5.00 | 1.20 |
| ☐ 255 Steve Broussard | 12.00 | 5.00 | 1.20 |
| ☐ 256 Warren Moon | 60.00 | 24.00 | 6.00 |
| ☐ 257 John Elway | 75.00 | 30.00 | 7.50 |
| ☐ 258 Bob Golic | 15.00 | 6.00 | 1.50 |
| ☐ 259 Jim Everett | 25.00 | 10.00 | 2.50 |
| ☐ 260 Bruce Coslet CO | 8.00 | 3.25 | .80 |
| ☐ 261 James Francis | 250.00 | 100.00 | 25.00 |
| ☐ 262 Eric Dorsey | 12.00 | 5.00 | 1.20 |
| ☐ 263 Marcus Dupree | 15.00 | 6.00 | 1.50 |
| ☐ 264 Hart Lee Dykes | 8.00 | 3.25 | .80 |
| ☐ 265 Vinny Testaverde | 20.00 | 8.00 | 2.00 |
| ☐ 266 Chip Lohmiller | 12.00 | 5.00 | 1.20 |
| ☐ 267 John Riggins RET | 30.00 | 12.00 | 3.00 |
| ☐ 268 Mike Schad | 10.00 | 4.00 | 1.00 |
| ☐ 269 Kevin Greene | 12.00 | 5.00 | 1.20 |
| ☐ 270 Dean Biasucci | 8.00 | 3.25 | .80 |
| ☐ 271 Mike Pritchard | 25.00 | 10.00 | 2.50 |
| ☐ 272 Ted Washington | 12.00 | 5.00 | 1.20 |
| ☐ 273 Alfred Williams | 8.00 | 3.25 | .80 |
| ☐ 274 Chris Zorich | 18.00 | 7.25 | 1.80 |
| ☐ 275 Reggie Barrett | 15.00 | 6.00 | 1.50 |
| ☐ 276 Chris Hinton | 12.00 | 5.00 | 1.20 |
| ☐ 277 Tracy Johnson | 10.00 | 4.00 | 1.00 |
| ☐ 278 Jim Harbaugh | 25.00 | 10.00 | 2.50 |
| ☐ 279 John Roper | 10.00 | 4.00 | 1.00 |
| ☐ 280 Mike Dumas | 15.00 | 6.00 | 1.50 |
| ☐ 281 Herman Moore | 25.00 | 10.00 | 2.50 |
| ☐ 282 Eric Turner | 15.00 | 6.00 | 1.50 |
| ☐ 283 Steve Atwater | 15.00 | 6.00 | 1.50 |
| ☐ 284 Michael Cofer | 8.00 | 3.25 | .80 |
| ☐ 285 Darion Conner | 8.00 | 3.25 | .80 |
| ☐ 286 Darryl Talley | 18.00 | 7.25 | 1.80 |
| ☐ 287 Donnell Woolford | 8.00 | 3.25 | .80 |
| ☐ 288 Keith McCants | 8.00 | 3.25 | .80 |
| ☐ 289 Ray Handley CO | 8.00 | 3.25 | .80 |
| ☐ 290 Ahmad Rashad RET | 175.00 | 70.00 | 18.00 |
| ☐ 291 Eric Swann | 15.00 | 6.00 | 1.50 |
| ☐ 292 Dalton Hilliard | 25.00 | 10.00 | 2.50 |
| (Signatures usually miscut) | | | |
| ☐ 293 Rickey Jackson | 15.00 | 6.00 | 1.50 |
| ☐ 294 Vaughan Johnson | 12.00 | 5.00 | 1.20 |
| ☐ 295 Eric Martin | 12.00 | 5.00 | 1.20 |
| ☐ 296 Pat Swilling | 30.00 | 12.00 | 3.00 |
| ☐ 297 Anthony Carter | 25.00 | 10.00 | 2.50 |
| (Signatures usually miscut) | | | |
| ☐ 298 Guy McIntyre | 75.00 | 30.00 | 7.50 |
| ☐ 299 Bennie Blades | 15.00 | 6.00 | 1.50 |
| ☐ 300 Paul Farren | 8.00 | 3.25 | .80 |
| ☐ NNO Santa Claus Sendaway (Signed) | 40.00 | 16.00 | 4.00 |
| ☐ NNO Santa Claus Sendaway (Signed and numbered) | 80.00 | 32.00 | 8.00 |

## 1991 ProLine Portraits Collectibles

These two standard-size (2 1/2" by 3 1/2") cards were inserted in 1991 Pro Line foil packs. The Rashad family card features one of the most visible families in football. Ahmad is a commentator for NBC Sports while wife Phylicia is a television star as well as the sister of Debbie Allen, the singer-actress. The Rashad card features them with their daughter posed against a nature background. The horizontally oriented back carries a quote by Ahmad on the importance of family life. The Stewart card pictures him kissing a golf trophy. The back carries his advice to youngsters on how to approach the game. The cards are numbered on the back. In small print to the left of the card number, it reads "Pro Line Portraits Collectible".

| | MINT | EXC | G-VG |
|---|---|---|---|
| COMPLETE SET (2) | 20.00 | 9.00 | 2.50 |
| COMMON CARD (PLC1-PLC2) | 10.00 | 4.50 | 1.25 |
| ☐ 1 Rashad Family (Ahmad, Phylicia, and daughter) | 10.00 | 4.50 | 1.25 |
| ☐ 2 Payne Stewart (Golfer) | 10.00 | 4.50 | 1.25 |

## 1991 ProLine Portraits Collectible Autograph

This standard-size (2 1/2" by 3 1/2") cards was inserted in 1991 Pro Line foil packs. The Stewart card pictures him kissing a golf trophy. The back carries his advice to youngsters on how to approach the game. The card is unnumbered.

| | MINT | EXC | G-VG |
|---|---|---|---|
| COMPLETE SET | 100.00 | 40.00 | 10.00 |
| COMMON CARD | 100.00 | 40.00 | 10.00 |
| ☐ 1 Payne Stewart (Golfer) | 100.00 | 40.00 | 10.00 |

## 1991 ProLine Portraits Wives

This seven-card standard size (2 1/2" by 3 1/2") set was included in the 1991 Pro Line Portraits set as inserts in the regular foil packs. These seven cards feature wives of some of the NFL's most popular personalities, including former television actress Jennifer Montana and star of the Cosby show, Phylicia Rashad. The cards are numbered on the back with an "SC" prefix.

| | MINT | EXC | G-VG |
|---|---|---|---|
| COMPLETE SET (7) | .75 | .35 | .09 |
| COMMON WIVES (SC1-SC7) | .10 | .05 | .01 |
| ☐ SC1 Jennifer Montana | .30 | .14 | .04 |
| ☐ SC2 Babette Kosar | .10 | .05 | .01 |

|  | | | |
|---|---|---|---|
| ☐ SC3 Janet Elway | .10 | .05 | .01 |
| ☐ SC4 Michelle Oates | .10 | .05 | .01 |
| ☐ SC5 Toni Lipps | .10 | .05 | .01 |
| ☐ SC6 Stacey O'Brien | .10 | .05 | .01 |
| ☐ SC7 Phylicia Rashad | .20 | .09 | .03 |

## 1991 ProLine Portraits Wives Autographs

This seven-card standard-size (2 1/2" by 3 1/2") set was included in the 1991 Pro Line Portraits set as inserts in the regular foil packs. These cards feature wives of some of the NFL's most popular personalities, including former television actress Jennifer Montana and star of the Cosby show, Phylicia Rashad. Less than 15 of Rashad's cards are currently known to exist. The cards are unnumbered but are listed below according to the numbers assigned to them in the regular series.

|  | MINT | EXC | G-VG |
|---|---|---|---|
| COMPLETE SET (7) | 600.00 | 240.00 | 60.00 |
| COMMON WIFE (1-7) | 15.00 | 6.00 | 1.50 |
| ☐ 1 Jennifer Montana | 75.00 | 30.00 | 7.50 |
| ☐ 2 Babette Kosar | 15.00 | 6.00 | 1.50 |
| ☐ 3 Janet Elway | 15.00 | 6.00 | 1.50 |
| ☐ 4 Michelle Oates | 15.00 | 6.00 | 1.50 |
| ☐ 5 Toni Lipps | 15.00 | 6.00 | 1.50 |
| ☐ 6 Stacey O'Brien | 15.00 | 6.00 | 1.50 |
| ☐ 7 Phylicia Rashad | 500.00 | 200.00 | 50.00 |

## 1991 ProLine Punt, Pass, and Kick

This 12-card standard-size (2 1/2" by 3 1/2") set was issued to honor 1991 NFL quarterbacks in conjunction with the long-standing Punt, Pass, and Kick program. Cards 1-11 show each quarterback in various still-life poses. Card fronts also feature an embossed Punt, Pass, and Kick logo in the lower right corner and the NFL ProLine Portraits logo at the bottom center. Horizontally oriented card backs have player's name printed in reverse-out fashion in a team color. The team's name in black appears in the upper right corner. A close-up head shot is centered on the lower middle section of the back, and a quote from the quarterback about being successful in the NFL is printed on a silver background. The cards are numbered on the back.

|  | MINT | EXC | G-VG |
|---|---|---|---|
| COMPLETE SET (12) | 75.00 | 30.00 | 7.50 |
| COMMON CARD (PPK1-PPK11) | 3.00 | 1.20 | .30 |
| ☐ PPK1 Troy Aikman | 25.00 | 10.00 | 2.50 |
| Dallas Cowboys | | | |

| ☐ PPK2 Bubby Brister | 3.00 | 1.20 | .30 |
|---|---|---|---|
| Pittsburgh Steelers | | | |
| ☐ PPK3 Randall Cunningham | 6.00 | 2.40 | .60 |
| Philadelphia Eagles | | | |
| ☐ PPK4 John Elway | 10.00 | 4.00 | 1.00 |
| Denver Broncos | | | |
| ☐ PPK5 Boomer Esiason | 6.00 | 2.40 | .60 |
| Cincinnati Bengals | | | |
| ☐ PPK6 Jim Everett | 4.00 | 1.60 | .40 |
| Los Angeles Rams | | | |
| ☐ PPK7 Jim Kelly | 8.00 | 3.25 | .80 |
| Buffalo Bills | | | |
| ☐ PPK8 Bernie Kosar | 6.00 | 2.40 | .60 |
| Cleveland Browns | | | |
| ☐ PPK9 Dan Marino | 20.00 | 8.00 | 2.00 |
| Miami Dolphins | | | |
| ☐ PPK10 Warren Moon | 8.00 | 3.25 | .80 |
| Houston Oilers | | | |
| ☐ PPK11 Phil Simms | 6.00 | 2.40 | .60 |
| New York Giants | | | |
| ☐ SC3 Punt, Pass, and Kick | 3.00 | 1.20 | .30 |
| Checklist | | | |

## 1991-92 ProLine Profiles Anthony Munoz

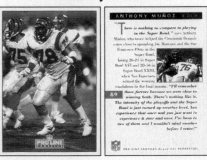

This nine-card set was inserted into the Super Bowl XXVI game program. The standard-size (2 1/2" by 3 1/2") slick four-color cards depict different phases of the career of Munoz, and the ProLine Profile logo is centered at the bottom of each perforated card. The back features a black bar with the player's name reversed out in white lettering, while the card numbers appear in burnt orange in the right corner of the black bar. The backs present career highlights, family life, and community service projects that Munoz promotes.

|  | MINT | EXC | G-VG |
|---|---|---|---|
| COMPLETE SET (9) | 4.00 | 1.60 | .40 |
| COMMON PLAYER (1-9) | .50 | .20 | .05 |
| ☐ 1 Anthony Munoz | .50 | .20 | .05 |
| 1991 NFL Man of Year | | | |
| ☐ 2 Anthony Munoz | .50 | .20 | .05 |
| Little League Player | | | |
| ☐ 3 Anthony Munoz | .50 | .20 | .05 |
| 1980 Rose Bowl | | | |
| ☐ 4 Anthony Munoz | .50 | .20 | .05 |
| Community Service | | | |
| ☐ 5 Anthony Munoz | .50 | .20 | .05 |
| Portrait | | | |
| ☐ 6 Anthony Munoz | .50 | .20 | .05 |
| 1981 AFC | | | |
| Championship Game | | | |
| ☐ 7 Anthony Munoz | .50 | .20 | .05 |
| 1992 Pro Bowl | | | |
| ☐ 8 Anthony Munoz | .50 | .20 | .05 |
| Super Bowl XVI | | | |
| and XXIII | | | |
| ☐ 9 Anthony Munoz | .50 | .20 | .05 |
| Physical Fitness Photo | | | |

## 1992 ProLine Draft Day

Each of these draft day collectible cards measures the standard size (2 1/2" by 3 1/2"). The fronts feature full-bleed color photos, while the horizontally oriented backs have an head shot surrounded by an extended quote. Emtman is pictured sitting on a boat holding a fishing rod, with a "stringer" of NFL helmets dangling from the bow. The other card features a group picture of NFL coaches on the front, while the head shot and extended quote on the back are by Chris Berman, an ESPN commentator. The cards are numbered on the back.

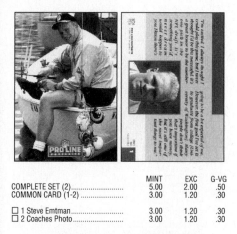

|  | MINT | EXC | G-VG |
|---|---|---|---|
| COMPLETE SET (2) | 5.00 | 2.00 | .50 |
| COMMON CARD (1-2) | 3.00 | 1.20 | .30 |
| ☐ 1 Steve Emtman | 3.00 | 1.20 | .30 |
| ☐ 2 Coaches Photo | 3.00 | 1.20 | .30 |

## 1992 ProLine Prototypes

This 13-card sample set was distributed by ProLine to show the design of their 1992 ProLine football card series. The cards measure the standard size (2 1/2" by 3 1/2") and were distributed as a complete set in a cello pack. The fronts feature full-bleed color photos, while the backs carry a color close-up photo, extended quote, or statistics. The set includes samples of the following ProLine series: Profiles (28-36), Spirit (12), and Portraits (379, 386). The cards are numbered on the back, and their numbering is the same as in the regular series. These cards were also distributed by Classic at major card and trade shows. These prototypes can be distinguished from the regular issue cards in that they are vertically marked "prototype" in the lower left corner of the Profiles reverse and or "sample" next to the picture on the Portraits reverse.

|  | MINT | EXC | G-VG |
|---|---|---|---|
| COMPLETE SET (13) | 10.00 | 4.00 | 1.00 |
| COMMON PLAYER | .50 | .20 | .05 |
| ☐ 12 Kathie Lee Gifford | 1.00 | .40 | .10 |
| ☐ 28 Thurman Thomas (Bills' uniform, action shot) | 1.00 | .40 | .10 |
| ☐ 29 Thurman Thomas (With his mother) | 1.00 | .40 | .10 |
| ☐ 30 Thurman Thomas (OSU Cowboy uniform, action shot) | 1.00 | .40 | .10 |
| ☐ 31 Thurman Thomas (With family) | 1.00 | .40 | .10 |
| ☐ 32 Thurman Thomas (Color portrait) | 1.00 | .40 | .10 |
| ☐ 33 Thurman Thomas (Action shot, Super Bowl XXV) | 1.00 | .40 | .10 |
| ☐ 34 Thurman Thomas (Fishing) | 1.00 | .40 | .10 |
| ☐ 35 Thurman Thomas (Stretching on track) | 1.00 | .40 | .10 |
| ☐ 36 Thurman Thomas (Close-up photo) | 1.00 | .40 | .10 |
| ☐ 379 Jessie Tuggle | .50 | .20 | .05 |
| ☐ 386 Neil O'Donnell | 1.50 | .60 | .15 |
| ☐ NNO Advertisement Card | .50 | .20 | .05 |

## 1992 ProLine Portraits

Together with the 1992 Pro Line Profiles, this 167-card standard-size (2 1/2" by 3 1/2") set constitutes the bulk of the 1992 Pro Line Collection. The set is numbered in continuation of the 1991 Pro Line Portraits set. Only 35,000 ten-box cases were produced. Each Pro Line Collection pack contained nine Profiles and three Portraits cards. Pro Line's goal was to have an autographed card in each box and, as a bonus, some autographed cards from last year were included. Also autograph cards could be obtained through a mail-in offer in exchange for 12 1991 Pro Line Portraits wrappers (black) and 12 1992 Pro Line Collection wrappers (white). In addition, Quarterback Gold cards were randomly inserted throughout the packs. The fronts display full-bleed color photos in non-game shots while the backs carry personal information. The cards are numbered on the back. A special boxed set, with the cards displayed in two notebooks, was distributed at the National, and the Portrait series differs from the regular series in two respects, the cards are unnumbered and are stamped with a "The National, 1992" seal. The key Rookie Cards in this set are Edgar Bennett, Terrell Buckley, Dale Carter, Marco Coleman, Quentin Coryatt, Vaughn Dunbar, Steve Emtman, David Klingler, Tommy Maddox, Johnny Mitchell and Tommy Vardell. The 1992 Pro Line Santa Claus card could be obtained through a mail-in offer advertised in various national sports and collecting publications in exchange for ten 1991 Pro Line Portraits wrappers (black) and ten 1992 Pro Line Collection wrappers (white). A 52-cent self-addressed stamped envelope was also required. The front features a color portrait of Santa standing before his locker, wearing a white Super Bowl XXVI jacket, and balancing a football on his left index finger. The horizontal back is predominantly silver and features a color head shot surrounded by a quote. The first 10,000 to respond to the offer received as a bonus the newest addition to the NFL Spirit series, a Mrs. Claus card picturing her sewing the laces on last year's Pro Line Santa card framed at her left elbow. The back carries a head shot of the couple and a quote from Mrs. Claus. Where one might expect the card number, the backs have "Special Collectible 1992."

|  | MINT | EXC | G-VG |
|---|---|---|---|
| COMPLETE SET (167) | 6.00 | 2.70 | .75 |
| COMMON PLAYER (301-467) | .04 | .02 | .01 |
| ☐ 301 Steve Emtman Indianapolis Colts | .15 | .07 | .02 |
| ☐ 302 Al Edwards Buffalo Bills | .04 | .02 | .01 |
| ☐ 303 Wendell Davis Chicago Bears | .04 | .02 | .01 |
| ☐ 304 Lewis Billups Green Bay Packers | .04 | .02 | .01 |
| ☐ 305 Brian Brennan Cleveland Browns | .04 | .02 | .01 |
| ☐ 306 John Gesek Dallas Cowboys | .04 | .02 | .01 |
| ☐ 307 Terrell Buckley Green Bay Packers | .25 | .11 | .03 |
| ☐ 308 Johnny Mitchell New York Jets | .50 | .23 | .06 |
| ☐ 309 LeRoy Butler Green Bay Packers | .04 | .02 | .01 |
| ☐ 310 William Fuller Houston Oilers | .04 | .02 | .01 |
| ☐ 311 Bill Brooks Indianapolis Colts | .06 | .03 | .01 |
| ☐ 312 Dino Hackett Kansas City Chiefs | .04 | .02 | .01 |
| ☐ 313 Willie Gault Los Angeles Raiders | .06 | .03 | .01 |
| ☐ 314 Aaron Cox Los Angeles Rams | .04 | .02 | .01 |
| ☐ 315 Jeff Cross San Francisco 49ers | .04 | .02 | .01 |

| | | | |
|---|---|---|---|
| ☐ 316 Emmitt Smith | 2.00 | .90 | .25 |
| Dallas Cowboys | | | |
| ☐ 317 Marv Cook | .06 | .03 | .01 |
| New England Patriots | | | |
| ☐ 318 Gill Fenerty | .04 | .02 | .01 |
| New Orleans Saints | | | |
| ☐ 319 Jeff Carlson | .15 | .07 | .02 |
| New York Giants | | | |
| ☐ 320 Brad Baxter | .06 | .03 | .01 |
| New York Jets | | | |
| ☐ 321 Fred Barnett | .08 | .04 | .01 |
| Philadelphia Eagles | | | |
| ☐ 322 Kurt Barber | .10 | .05 | .01 |
| New York Jets | | | |
| ☐ 323 Eric Green | .08 | .04 | .01 |
| Pittsburgh Steelers | | | |
| ☐ 324 Greg Clark | .04 | .02 | .01 |
| San Diego Chargers | | | |
| ☐ 325 Keith DeLong | .04 | .02 | .01 |
| San Francisco 49ers | | | |
| ☐ 326 Patrick Hunter | .04 | .02 | .01 |
| Seattle Seahawks | | | |
| ☐ 327 Troy Vincent | .10 | .05 | .01 |
| Miami Dolphins | | | |
| ☐ 328 Gary Clark | .06 | .03 | .01 |
| Washington Redskins | | | |
| ☐ 329 Joe Montana | 1.50 | .65 | .19 |
| San Francisco 49ers | | | |
| ☐ 330 Michael Haynes | .30 | .14 | .04 |
| Atlanta Falcons | | | |
| ☐ 331 Edgar Bennett | .30 | .14 | .04 |
| Green Bay Packers | | | |
| ☐ 332 Darren Lewis | .04 | .02 | .01 |
| Chicago Bears | | | |
| ☐ 333 Derrick Fenner | .06 | .03 | .01 |
| Cincinnati Bengals | | | |
| ☐ 334 Rob Burnett | .04 | .02 | .01 |
| Cleveland Browns | | | |
| ☐ 335 Alvin Harper | .40 | .18 | .05 |
| Dallas Cowboys | | | |
| ☐ 336 Vance Johnson | .06 | .03 | .01 |
| Denver Broncos | | | |
| ☐ 337 William White | .04 | .02 | .01 |
| Houston Oilers | | | |
| ☐ 338 Sterling Sharpe | .50 | .23 | .06 |
| Green Bay Packers | | | |
| ☐ 339 Sean Jones | .04 | .02 | .01 |
| Houston Oilers | | | |
| ☐ 340 Jeff Herrod | .04 | .02 | .01 |
| Indianapolis Colts | | | |
| ☐ 341 Chris Martin | .04 | .02 | .01 |
| Kansas City Chiefs | | | |
| ☐ 342 Ethan Horton | .04 | .02 | .01 |
| Los Angeles Raiders | | | |
| ☐ 343 Robert Delpino | .06 | .03 | .01 |
| Los Angeles Rams | | | |
| ☐ 344 Mark Higgs | .10 | .05 | .01 |
| Miami Dolphins | | | |
| ☐ 345 Chris Doleman | .06 | .03 | .01 |
| Minnesota Vikings | | | |
| ☐ 346 Tom Hodson | .04 | .02 | .01 |
| New England Patriots | | | |
| ☐ 347 Craig Heyward | .04 | .02 | .01 |
| New Orleans Saints | | | |
| ☐ 348 Cary Conklin | .10 | .05 | .01 |
| Washington Redskins | | | |
| ☐ 349 James Hasty | .04 | .02 | .01 |
| New York Jets | | | |
| ☐ 350 Antone Davis | .04 | .02 | .01 |
| Philadelphia Eagles | | | |
| ☐ 351 Ernie Jones | .04 | .02 | .01 |
| Phoenix Cardinals | | | |
| ☐ 352 Greg Lloyd | .04 | .02 | .01 |
| Pittsburgh Steelers | | | |
| ☐ 353 John Friesz | .06 | .03 | .01 |
| San Diego Chargers | | | |
| ☐ 354 Charles Haley | .06 | .03 | .01 |
| San Francisco 49ers | | | |
| ☐ 355 Tracy Scroggins | .20 | .09 | .03 |
| Detroit Lions | | | |
| ☐ 356 Paul Gruber | .04 | .02 | .01 |
| Tampa Bay Buccaneers | | | |
| ☐ 357 Ricky Ervins | .06 | .03 | .01 |
| Washington Redskins | | | |
| ☐ 358 Brad Muster | .06 | .03 | .01 |
| Chicago Bears | | | |
| ☐ 359 Deion Sanders | .20 | .09 | .03 |
| Atlanta Falcons | | | |
| ☐ 360 Mitch Frerotte | .10 | .05 | .01 |
| Buffalo Bills | | | |
| ☐ 361 Stan Thomas | .04 | .02 | .01 |
| Chicago Bears | | | |
| ☐ 362 Harold Green | .06 | .03 | .01 |
| Cincinnati Bengals | | | |
| ☐ 363 Eric Metcalf | .08 | .04 | .01 |
| Cleveland Browns | | | |
| ☐ 364 Ken Norton Jr | .06 | .03 | .01 |
| Dallas Cowboys | | | |
| ☐ 365 Dave Widell | .04 | .02 | .01 |
| Doug Widell | | | |
| Denver Broncos | | | |
| ☐ 366 Mike Tomczak | .04 | .02 | .01 |
| Green Bay Packers | | | |
| ☐ 367 Bubba McDowell | .04 | .02 | .01 |
| Houston Oilers | | | |
| ☐ 368 Jessie Hester | .04 | .02 | .01 |
| Indianapolis Colts | | | |
| ☐ 369 Ervin Randle | .04 | .02 | .01 |
| Tampa Bay Buccaneers | | | |
| ☐ 370 Tony Smith | .04 | .02 | .01 |
| Los Angeles Raiders | | | |
| ☐ 371 Pat Terrell | .04 | .02 | .01 |
| Los Angeles Rams | | | |
| ☐ 372 Jim C. Jensen | .04 | .02 | .01 |
| Miami Dolphins | | | |
| ☐ 373 Mike Merriweather | .04 | .02 | .01 |
| Minnesota Vikings | | | |
| ☐ 374 Chris Singleton | .04 | .02 | .01 |
| New England Patriots | | | |
| ☐ 375 Floyd Turner | .04 | .02 | .01 |
| New Orleans Saints | | | |
| ☐ 376 Jim Sweeney | .04 | .02 | .01 |
| New York Jets | | | |
| ☐ 377 Keith Jackson | .08 | .04 | .01 |
| Philadelphia Eagles | | | |
| ☐ 378 Walter Reeves | .04 | .02 | .01 |
| Phoenix Cardinals | | | |
| ☐ 379 Neil O'Donnell | .50 | .23 | .06 |
| Pittsburgh Steelers | | | |
| ☐ 380 Nate Lewis | .06 | .03 | .01 |
| San Diego Chargers | | | |
| ☐ 381 Keith Henderson | .04 | .02 | .01 |
| San Francisco 49ers | | | |
| ☐ 382 Kelly Stouffer | .04 | .02 | .01 |
| Seattle Seahawks | | | |
| ☐ 383 Ricky Reynolds | .04 | .02 | .01 |
| Tampa Bay Buccaneers | | | |
| ☐ 384 Joe Jacoby | .04 | .02 | .01 |
| Washington Redskins | | | |
| ☐ 385 Fred Biletnikoff RET | .04 | .02 | .01 |
| Oakland Raiders | | | |
| ☐ 386 Jessie Tuggle | .04 | .02 | .01 |
| Atlanta Falcons | | | |
| ☐ 387 Tom Waddle | .08 | .04 | .01 |
| Chicago Bears | | | |
| ☐ 388 Dave Shula CO | .04 | .02 | .01 |
| Cincinnati Bengals | | | |
| ☐ 389 Van Waiters | .04 | .02 | .01 |
| Cleveland Browns | | | |
| ☐ 390 Jay Novacek | .15 | .07 | .02 |
| Dallas Cowboys | | | |
| ☐ 391 Michael Young | .04 | .02 | .01 |
| Denver Broncos | | | |
| ☐ 392 Mike Holmgren CO | .04 | .02 | .01 |
| Green Bay Packers | | | |
| ☐ 393 Doug Smith | .04 | .02 | .01 |
| Houston Oilers | | | |
| ☐ 394 Mike Prior | .04 | .02 | .01 |
| Indianapolis Colts | | | |
| ☐ 395 Harvey Williams | .08 | .04 | .01 |
| Kansas City Chiefs | | | |
| ☐ 396 Aaron Wallace | .04 | .02 | .01 |
| Los Angeles Raiders | | | |
| ☐ 397 Tony Zendejas | .04 | .02 | .01 |
| Los Angeles Rams | | | |
| ☐ 398 Sammie Smith | .04 | .02 | .01 |
| Denver Broncos | | | |
| ☐ 399 Henry Thomas | .04 | .02 | .01 |
| Minnesota Vikings | | | |
| ☐ 400 Jon Vaughn | .04 | .02 | .01 |
| New England Patriots | | | |
| ☐ 401 Brian Washington | .04 | .02 | .01 |
| New York Jets | | | |
| ☐ 402 Leon Searcy | .04 | .02 | .01 |
| Pittsburgh Steelers | | | |
| ☐ 403 Lance Smith | .04 | .02 | .01 |
| Phoenix Cardinals | | | |
| ☐ 404 Warren Williams | .04 | .02 | .01 |
| Pittsburgh Steelers | | | |
| ☐ 405 Bobby Ross CO | .04 | .02 | .01 |
| San Diego Chargers | | | |
| ☐ 406 Harry Sydney | .04 | .02 | .01 |
| San Francisco 49ers | | | |
| ☐ 407 John L. Williams | .06 | .03 | .01 |
| Seattle Seahawks | | | |
| ☐ 408 Ken Willis | .04 | .02 | .01 |
| Tampa Bay Buccaneers | | | |
| ☐ 409 Brian Mitchell | .06 | .03 | .01 |
| Washington Redskins | | | |
| ☐ 410 Dick Butkus RET | .10 | .05 | .01 |
| Chicago Bears | | | |
| ☐ 411 Chuck Knox CO | .04 | .02 | .01 |
| Los Angeles Rams | | | |
| ☐ 412 Robert Porcher | .20 | .09 | .03 |
| Detroit Lions | | | |

☐ 413 Calvin Williams ..................... .08 .04 .01
    Philadelphia Eagles
☐ 414 Bill Cowher CO ..................... .04 .02 .01
    Pittsburgh Steelers
☐ 415 Eric Moore .......................... .04 .02 .01
    New York Giants
☐ 416 Derek Brown ........................ .10 .05 .01
    New York Giants
☐ 417 Dennis Green CO .................. .04 .02 .01
    Minnesota Vikings
☐ 418 Tom Flores CO ..................... .04 .02 .01
    Seattle Seahawks
☐ 419 Dale Carter .......................... .25 .11 .03
    Kansas City Chiefs
☐ 420 Tony Dorsett RET ................. .06 .03 .01
    Dallas Cowboys
☐ 421 Marco Coleman..................... .30 .14 .04
    Miami Dolphins
☐ 422 Sam Wyche CO ..................... .04 .02 .01
    Tampa Bay Buccaneers
☐ 423 Ray Crockett ........................ .04 .02 .01
    Detroit Lions
☐ 424 Dan Fouts RET ..................... .04 .02 .01
    San Diego Chargers
☐ 425 Hugh Millen.......................... .06 .03 .01
    New England Patriots
☐ 426 Quentin Coryatt .................... .30 .14 .04
    Indianapolis Colts
☐ 427 Brian Jordan ........................ .06 .03 .01
    Atlanta Falcons
☐ 428 Frank Gifford RET.................. .10 .05 .01
    New York Giants
☐ 429 Toby Caston ......................... .04 .02 .01
    Detroit Lions
☐ 430 Ted Marchibroda CO ............. .04 .02 .01
    Indianapolis Colts
☐ 431 Cris Carter ........................... .08 .04 .01
    Minnesota Vikings
☐ 432 Tim Krumrie.......................... .04 .02 .01
    Cincinnati Bengals
☐ 433 Otto Graham RET .................. .04 .02 .01
    Cleveland Browns
☐ 434 Vaughn Dunbar ..................... .20 .09 .03
    New Orleans Saints
☐ 435 John Fina ............................. .04 .02 .01
    Buffalo Bills
☐ 436 Sonny Jurgensen RET............ .04 .02 .01
    Washington Redskins
☐ 437 Robert Jones......................... .12 .05 .02
    Dallas Cowboys
☐ 438 Steve DeOssie ...................... .04 .02 .01
    New York Giants
☐ 439 Eddie LeBaron RET ............... .04 .02 .01
    Washington Redskins
☐ 440 Chester McGlockton.............. .20 .09 .03
    Los Angeles Raiders
☐ 441 Ken Stabler RET .................... .10 .05 .01
    Oakland Raiders
☐ 442 Joe DeLamielleure RET ......... .04 .02 .01
    Buffalo Bills
☐ 443 Charley Taylor RET................ .06 .03 .01
    Washington Redskins
☐ 444 Greg Skrepenak .................... .10 .05 .01
    Los Angeles Raiders
☐ 445 Y.A. Tittle RET...................... .06 .03 .01
    New York Giants
☐ 446 Chuck Smith ........................ .10 .05 .01
    Atlanta Falcons
☐ 447 Kellen Winslow RET .............. .06 .03 .01
    San Diego Chargers
☐ 448 Kevin Smith.......................... .25 .11 .03
    Dallas Cowboys
☐ 449 Phillippi Sparks .................... .04 .02 .01
    New York Giants
☐ 450 Alonzo Spellman ................... .20 .09 .03
    Chicago Bears
☐ 451 Mark Rypien ......................... .08 .04 .01
    Washington Redskins
☐ 452 Darryl Williams ..................... .20 .09 .03
    Cincinnati Bengals
☐ 453 Tommy Vardell....................... .25 .11 .03
    Cleveland Browns
☐ 454 Tommy Maddox...................... .40 .18 .05
    Denver Broncos
☐ 455 Steve Israel .......................... .04 .02 .01
    Los Angeles Rams
☐ 456 Marquez Pope ....................... .10 .05 .01
    San Diego Chargers
☐ 457 Eugene Chung ....................... .04 .02 .01
    New England Patriots
☐ 458 Lynn Swann RET ................... .06 .03 .01
    Pittsburgh Steelers
☐ 459 Sean Gilbert ......................... .30 .14 .04
    Los Angeles Rams
☐ 460 Chris Mims ........................... .25 .11 .03
    San Diego Chargers
☐ 461 Al Davis OWN....................... .06 .03 .01

    Los Angeles Raiders
☐ 462 Richard Todd RET................. .04 .02 .01
    New York Jets
☐ 463 Mike Fox ............................. .04 .02 .01
    New York Giants
☐ 464 David Klingler........................ .50 .23 .06
    Cincinnati Bengals
☐ 465 Darren Woodson.................... .20 .09 .03
    Dallas Cowboys
☐ 466 Jason Hanson ....................... .15 .07 .02
    Detroit Lions
☐ 467 Lem Barney RET ................... .06 .03 .01
    Detroit Lions
☐ NNO Santa Claus Sendaway........ 8.00 3.60 1.00
☐ NNO Mrs. Claus Sendaway .......... 6.00 2.70 .75

## 1992 ProLine Portraits Autographs

This 167-card standard-size (2 1/2" by 3 1/2") set continues the numbering of the 1991 Pro Line Portraits set. Reportedly 35,000 ten-box cases were produced. Pro Line's goal was to have an autographed card in each box. Also autograph cards could be obtained through a mail-in offer in exchange for 12 1991 Pro Line Portraits wrappers (black) and 12 1992 Pro Line Collection wrappers (white). The fronts display full-bleed color photos in non-game shots while the backs carry personal information. The cards are unnumbered but are listed below according to the numbers assigned to them in the regular series. The following cards were not signed: 349 James Hasty, 370 Anthony Smith, 417 Dennis Green, 428 Frank Gifford, 451 Mark Rypien, 462 Richard Todd. The Santa and Mrs. Claus autographed cards are not considered part of the complete set.

|  | MINT | EXC | G-VG |
|---|---|---|---|
| COMPLETE SET (161)..................... | 1600.00 | 700.00 | 200.00 |
| COMMON PLAYER (301-467).......... | 6.00 | 2.40 | .60 |
| ☐ 301 Steve Emtman..................... | 15.00 | 6.00 | 1.50 |
| ☐ 302 Al Edwards ......................... | 6.00 | 2.40 | .60 |
| ☐ 303 Wendell Davis ..................... | 6.00 | 2.40 | .60 |
| ☐ 304 Lewis Billups....................... | 30.00 | 12.00 | 3.00 |
| ☐ 305 Brian Brennan ..................... | 6.00 | 2.40 | .60 |
| ☐ 306 John Gesek ......................... | 10.00 | 4.00 | 1.00 |
| ☐ 307 Terrell Buckley ..................... | 15.00 | 6.00 | 1.50 |
| ☐ 308 Johnny Mitchell.................... | 20.00 | 8.00 | 2.00 |
| ☐ 309 LeRoy Butler ....................... | 6.00 | 2.40 | .60 |
| ☐ 310 William Fuller ...................... | 6.00 | 2.40 | .60 |
| ☐ 311 Bill Brooks........................... | 6.00 | 2.40 | .60 |
| ☐ 312 Dino Hackett ....................... | 6.00 | 2.40 | .60 |
| ☐ 313 Willie Gault ......................... | 12.00 | 5.00 | 1.20 |
| ☐ 314 Aaron Cox .......................... | 6.00 | 2.40 | .60 |
| ☐ 315 Jeff Cross........................... | 6.00 | 2.40 | .60 |
| ☐ 316 Emmitt Smith....................... | 100.00 | 40.00 | 10.00 |
| ☐ 317 Marv Cook........................... | 6.00 | 2.40 | .60 |
| ☐ 318 Gill Fenerty ......................... | 6.00 | 2.40 | .60 |
| ☐ 319 Jeff Carlson ........................ | 12.00 | 5.00 | 1.20 |
| ☐ 320 Brad Baxter ........................ | 6.00 | 2.40 | .60 |
| ☐ 321 Fred Barnett ........................ | 10.00 | 4.00 | 1.00 |
| ☐ 322 Kurt Barber ......................... | 8.00 | 3.25 | .80 |
| ☐ 323 Eric Green ........................... | 12.00 | 5.00 | 1.20 |
| ☐ 324 Greg Clark .......................... | 6.00 | 2.40 | .60 |
| ☐ 325 Keith DeLong ...................... | 6.00 | 2.40 | .60 |
| ☐ 326 Patrick Hunter ..................... | 6.00 | 2.40 | .60 |
| ☐ 327 Troy Vincent........................ | 10.00 | 4.00 | 1.00 |
| ☐ 328 Gary Clark........................... | 15.00 | 6.00 | 1.50 |
| ☐ 329 Joe Montana........................ | 150.00 | 60.00 | 15.00 |
| ☐ 330 Michael Haynes.................... | 15.00 | 6.00 | 1.50 |
| ☐ 331 Edgar Bennett ..................... | 20.00 | 8.00 | 2.00 |
| ☐ 332 Darren Lewis ....................... | 6.00 | 2.40 | .60 |
| ☐ 333 Derrick Fenner..................... | 6.00 | 2.40 | .60 |
| ☐ 334 Rob Burnett......................... | 6.00 | 2.40 | .60 |
| ☐ 335 Alvin Harper ........................ | 18.00 | 7.25 | 1.80 |
| ☐ 336 Vance Johnson .................... | 6.00 | 2.40 | .60 |
| ☐ 337 William White....................... | 6.00 | 2.40 | .60 |
| ☐ 338 Sterling Sharpe .................... | 30.00 | 12.00 | 3.00 |

| | | | |
|---|---|---|---|
| ☐ 339 Sean Jones | 6.00 | 2.40 | .60 |
| ☐ 340 Jeff Herrod | 6.00 | 2.40 | .60 |
| ☐ 341 Chris Martin | 6.00 | 2.40 | .60 |
| ☐ 342 Ethan Horton | 6.00 | 2.40 | .60 |
| ☐ 343 Robert Delpino | 6.00 | 2.40 | .60 |
| ☐ 344 Mark Higgs | 6.00 | 2.40 | .60 |
| ☐ 345 Chris Doleman | 12.00 | 5.00 | 1.20 |
| ☐ 346 Tom Hodson | 10.00 | 4.00 | 1.00 |
| ☐ 347 Craig Heyward | 10.00 | 4.00 | 1.00 |
| ☐ 348 Cary Conklin | 12.00 | 5.00 | 1.20 |
| ☐ 350 Antone Davis | 6.00 | 2.40 | .60 |
| ☐ 351 Ernie Jones | 6.00 | 2.40 | .60 |
| ☐ 352 Greg Lloyd | 6.00 | 2.40 | .60 |
| ☐ 353 John Friesz | 12.00 | 5.00 | 1.20 |
| ☐ 354 Charles Haley | 10.00 | 4.00 | 1.00 |
| ☐ 355 Tracy Scroggins | 6.00 | 2.40 | .60 |
| ☐ 356 Paul Gruber | 6.00 | 2.40 | .60 |
| ☐ 357 Ricky Ervins | 15.00 | 6.00 | 1.50 |
| ☐ 358 Brad Muster | 10.00 | 4.00 | 1.00 |
| ☐ 359 Deion Sanders | 40.00 | 16.00 | 4.00 |
| (Deion also signed and numbered 200 cards from his personal stock; these are worth double) | | | |
| ☐ 360 Mitch Frerotte | 10.00 | 4.00 | 1.00 |
| ☐ 361 Stan Thomas | 6.00 | 2.40 | .60 |
| ☐ 362 Harold Green | 8.00 | 3.25 | .80 |
| ☐ 363 Eric Metcalf | 15.00 | 6.00 | 1.50 |
| ☐ 364 Ken Norton Jr. | 15.00 | 6.00 | 1.50 |
| ☐ 365 Dave Widell / Doug Widell | 18.00 | 7.25 | 1.80 |
| ☐ 366 Mike Tomczak | 10.00 | 4.00 | 1.00 |
| ☐ 367 Bubba McDowell | 6.00 | 2.40 | .60 |
| ☐ 368 Jessie Hester | 6.00 | 2.40 | .60 |
| (Signed in ball-point pen) | | | |
| ☐ 369 Ervin Randle | 6.00 | 2.40 | .60 |
| ☐ 371 Pat Terrell | 6.00 | 2.40 | .60 |
| ☐ 372 Jim C. Jensen | 6.00 | 2.40 | .60 |
| ☐ 373 Mike Merriweather | 6.00 | 2.40 | .60 |
| ☐ 374 Chris Singleton | 6.00 | 2.40 | .60 |
| ☐ 375 Floyd Turner | 6.00 | 2.40 | .60 |
| ☐ 376 Jim Sweeney | 6.00 | 2.40 | .60 |
| ☐ 377 Keith Jackson | 20.00 | 8.00 | 2.00 |
| ☐ 378 Walter Reeves | 6.00 | 2.40 | .60 |
| ☐ 379 Neil O'Donnell | 20.00 | 8.00 | 2.00 |
| ☐ 380 Nate Lewis | 6.00 | 2.40 | .60 |
| ☐ 381 Keith Henderson | 6.00 | 2.40 | .60 |
| ☐ 382 Kelly Stouffer | 10.00 | 4.00 | 1.00 |
| ☐ 383 Ricky Reynolds | 6.00 | 2.40 | .60 |
| ☐ 384 Joe Jacoby | 10.00 | 4.00 | 1.00 |
| ☐ 385 Fred Biletnikoff RET | 100.00 | 40.00 | 10.00 |
| ☐ 386 Jessie Tuggle | 6.00 | 2.40 | .60 |
| ☐ 387 Tom Waddle | 10.00 | 4.00 | 1.00 |
| ☐ 388 Dave Shula CO | 10.00 | 4.00 | 1.00 |
| ☐ 389 Van Waiters | 6.00 | 2.40 | .60 |
| ☐ 390 Jay Novacek | 18.00 | 7.25 | 1.80 |
| ☐ 391 Michael Young | 6.00 | 2.40 | .60 |
| ☐ 392 Mike Holmgren CO | 6.00 | 2.40 | .60 |
| ☐ 393 Doug Smith | 6.00 | 2.40 | .60 |
| ☐ 394 Mike Prior | 6.00 | 2.40 | .60 |
| ☐ 395 Harvey Williams | 12.00 | 5.00 | 1.20 |
| ☐ 396 Aaron Wallace | 15.00 | 6.00 | 1.50 |
| ☐ 397 Tony Zendejas | 6.00 | 2.40 | .60 |
| ☐ 398 Sammie Smith | 8.00 | 3.25 | .80 |
| ☐ 399 Henry Thomas | 6.00 | 2.40 | .60 |
| ☐ 400 Jon Vaughn | 8.00 | 3.25 | .80 |
| ☐ 401 Brian Washington | 6.00 | 2.40 | .60 |
| ☐ 402 Leon Searcy | 6.00 | 2.40 | .60 |
| ☐ 403 Lance Smith | 8.00 | 3.25 | .80 |
| ☐ 404 Warren Williams | 6.00 | 2.40 | .60 |
| ☐ 405 Bobby Ross CO | 6.00 | 2.40 | .60 |
| ☐ 406 Harry Sydney | 6.00 | 2.40 | .60 |
| ☐ 407 John L. Williams | 12.00 | 5.00 | 1.20 |
| ☐ 408 Ken Willis | 6.00 | 2.40 | .60 |
| ☐ 409 Brian Mitchell | 8.00 | 3.25 | .80 |
| ☐ 410 Dick Butkus RET | 30.00 | 12.00 | 3.00 |
| ☐ 411 Chuck Knox CO | 8.00 | 3.25 | .80 |
| ☐ 412 Robert Porcher | 10.00 | 4.00 | 1.00 |
| ☐ 413 Calvin Williams | 8.00 | 3.25 | .80 |
| ☐ 414 Bill Cowher CO | 6.00 | 2.40 | .60 |
| ☐ 415 Eric Moore | 6.00 | 2.40 | .60 |
| ☐ 416 Derek Brown | 12.00 | 5.00 | 1.20 |
| ☐ 418 Tom Flores CO | 6.00 | 2.40 | .60 |
| ☐ 419 Dale Carter | 15.00 | 6.00 | 1.50 |
| ☐ 420 Tony Dorsett RET | 40.00 | 16.00 | 4.00 |
| ☐ 421 Marco Coleman | 18.00 | 7.25 | 1.80 |
| ☐ 422 Sam Wyche CO | 6.00 | 2.40 | .60 |
| ☐ 423 Ray Crockett | 6.00 | 2.40 | .60 |
| ☐ 424 Dan Fouts RET | 30.00 | 12.00 | 3.00 |
| ☐ 425 Hugh Millen | 8.00 | 3.25 | .80 |
| ☐ 426 Quentin Coryatt | 20.00 | 8.00 | 2.00 |
| ☐ 427 Brian Jordan | 12.00 | 5.00 | 1.20 |
| ☐ 429 Toby Caston | 6.00 | 2.40 | .60 |
| ☐ 430 Ted Marchibroda CO | 6.00 | 2.40 | .60 |
| ☐ 431 Cris Carter | 10.00 | 4.00 | 1.00 |
| ☐ 432 Tim Krumrie | 6.00 | 2.40 | .60 |
| ☐ 433 Otto Graham RET | 30.00 | 12.00 | 3.00 |
| ☐ 434 Vaughn Dunbar | 15.00 | 6.00 | 1.50 |
| ☐ 435 John Fina | 6.00 | 2.40 | .60 |
| ☐ 436 Sonny Jurgensen RET | 30.00 | 12.00 | 3.00 |
| ☐ 437 Robert Jones | 12.00 | 5.00 | 1.20 |
| ☐ 438 Steve DeOssie | 6.00 | 2.40 | .60 |
| ☐ 439 Eddie LeBaron RET | 20.00 | 8.00 | 2.00 |
| ☐ 440 Chester McGlockton | 10.00 | 4.00 | 1.00 |
| ☐ 441 Ken Stabler RET | 30.00 | 12.00 | 3.00 |
| ☐ 442 Joe DeLamielleure RET | 10.00 | 4.00 | 1.00 |
| ☐ 443 Charley Taylor RET | 30.00 | 12.00 | 3.00 |
| ☐ 444 Greg Skrepenak | 10.00 | 4.00 | 1.00 |
| ☐ 445 Y.A. Tittle RET | 30.00 | 12.00 | 3.00 |
| ☐ 446 Chuck Smith | 10.00 | 4.00 | 1.00 |
| ☐ 447 Kellen Winslow RET | 18.00 | 7.25 | 1.80 |
| ☐ 448 Kevin Smith | 12.00 | 5.00 | 1.20 |
| ☐ 449 Phillippi Sparks | 6.00 | 2.40 | .60 |
| ☐ 450 Alonzo Spellman | 12.00 | 5.00 | 1.20 |
| ☐ 452 Darryl Williams | 8.00 | 3.25 | .80 |
| ☐ 453 Tommy Vardell | 15.00 | 6.00 | 1.50 |
| ☐ 454 Tommy Maddox | 25.00 | 10.00 | 2.50 |
| ☐ 455 Steve Israel | 6.00 | 2.40 | .60 |
| ☐ 456 Marquez Pope | 8.00 | 3.25 | .80 |
| ☐ 457 Eugene Chung | 8.00 | 3.25 | .80 |
| ☐ 458 Lynn Swann RET | 75.00 | 30.00 | 7.50 |
| ☐ 459 Sean Gilbert | 15.00 | 6.00 | 1.50 |
| ☐ 460 Chris Mims | 10.00 | 4.00 | 1.00 |
| ☐ 461 Al Davis OWN | 150.00 | 60.00 | 15.00 |
| ☐ 463 Mike Fox | 6.00 | 2.40 | .60 |
| ☐ 464 David Klingler | 30.00 | 12.00 | 3.00 |
| ☐ 465 Darren Woodson | 15.00 | 6.00 | 1.50 |
| ☐ 466 Jason Hanson | 8.00 | 3.25 | .80 |
| ☐ 467 Lem Barney RET | 20.00 | 8.00 | 2.00 |
| ☐ NNO Santa Claus | 20.00 | 8.00 | 2.00 |
| ☐ NNO Mrs. Santa Claus | 20.00 | 8.00 | 2.00 |

## 1992 ProLine Portraits Checklists

Nine lettered checklist cards were randomly inserted in foil packs of the 1992 Pro Line Portraits. The fronts of all the checklist cards combine to form a three by three-card composite of the Pro Line Collection emblem on a screened background of NFL logos. The backs present an introduction to Pro Line Collection (card A) and checklists for 1991-92 Portrait series, collectible series, and 1992 Profiles series (cards B-I). The cards are standard size (2 1/2" by 3 1/2").

| | MINT | EXC | G-VG |
|---|---|---|---|
| COMPLETE SET (9) | .75 | .35 | .09 |
| COMMON CHECKLISTS (A-I) | .15 | .07 | .02 |
| | | | |
| ☐ A Introduction Card | .15 | .07 | .02 |
| ☐ B Checklist 1-75 | .15 | .07 | .02 |
| ☐ C Checklist 76-150 | .15 | .07 | .02 |
| ☐ D Checklist 151-225 | .15 | .07 | .02 |
| ☐ E Checklist 226-300 | .15 | .07 | .02 |
| ☐ F Checklist 301-375 | .15 | .07 | .02 |
| ☐ G Checklist 376-450 | .15 | .07 | .02 |
| ☐ H Checklist 451-467 and Inserts | .15 | .07 | .02 |
| ☐ I Checklist Profiles | .15 | .07 | .02 |

## 1992 ProLine Portraits Collectibles

These standard-size (2 1/2" by 3 1/2") cards were inserted in 1992 Pro Line foil packs. Their numbering picks up after the two special collectible cards issued the previous year. The fronts display full-bleed color photos, while the backs carry extended quotes on a silver panel. In small print to the left of the card number, it reads "Pro Line Portraits Collectible".

|  | MINT | EXC | G-VG |
|---|---|---|---|
| COMPLETE SET (6)............................ | 12.00 | 5.50 | 1.50 |
| COMMON CARD (PLC3-PLC8)......... | 2.00 | .90 | .25 |
| ☐ PLC3 Coaches Photo ................... | 2.00 | .90 | .25 |
|     Chris Berman | | | |
| ☐ PLC4 Joe Gibbs CO..................... | 2.00 | .90 | .25 |
|     (Racing) | | | |
| ☐ PLC5 Gifford Family .................... | 2.00 | .90 | .25 |
|     Frank Gifford | | | |
|     Kathie Lee Gifford | | | |
|     Cody Gifford | | | |
| ☐ PLC6 Dale Jarrett ....................... | 4.00 | 1.80 | .50 |
|     (NASCAR driver) | | | |
| ☐ PLC7 Paul Tagliabue COM .......... | 2.00 | .90 | .25 |
| ☐ PLC8 Don Shula CO and .............. | 3.00 | 1.35 | .40 |
|     Dave Shula CO | | | |

## 1992 ProLine Portraits Collectibles Autographs

These standard-size (2 1/2" by 3 1/2") cards were inserted in 1992 ProLine foil packs. The fronts display full-bleed color photos, while the backs carry extended quotes on a silver panel. The cards are unnumbered but are listed below according to the numbers assigned to them in the regular series.

|  | MINT | EXC | G-VG |
|---|---|---|---|
| COMPLETE SET (4)........................... | 125.00 | 50.00 | 12.50 |
| COMMON PLAYER............................. | 6.00 | 2.40 | .60 |
| ☐ 3 Coaches Photo ......................... | 25.00 | 10.00 | 2.50 |
|     Chris Berman | | | |
| ☐ 6 Dale Jarrett .............................. | 25.00 | 10.00 | 2.50 |
|     (NASCAR driver) | | | |
| ☐ 7 Paul Tagliabue COM.................. | 6.00 | 2.40 | .60 |
|     (Autopenned) | | | |
| ☐ 8 Don Shula CO and..................... | 75.00 | 30.00 | 7.50 |
|     Dave Shula CO | | | |

## 1992 ProLine Portraits QB Gold

Featuring the top NFL quarterbacks, this 18-card set was randomly inserted into 1992 Pro Line Collection foil packs. Pro Line estimates that an average of 3 Quarterback Gold cards would be found in each box. Also dealers were sent a complete set with each hobby case purchased. The cards measure the standard size (2 1/2" by 3 1/2") and feature posed color player photos of NFL quarterbacks of the fronts. The pictures are bordered on two sides by gold foil stripes that run the length of the card. The player's name and the words "Quarterback Gold" are printed in black on the stripes. The backs are bordered by

gold stripes at the top and bottom. The background is off-white and displays passing and rushing statistics in black print. The cards are numbered on the back.

|  | MINT | EXC | G-VG |
|---|---|---|---|
| COMPLETE SET (18)......................... | 12.00 | 5.50 | 1.50 |
| COMMON PLAYER (1-18)................. | .40 | .18 | .05 |
| ☐ 1 Troy Aikman............................. | 4.00 | 1.80 | .50 |
|     Dallas Cowboys | | | |
| ☐ 2 Bubby Brister ........................... | .40 | .18 | .05 |
|     Pittsburgh Steelers | | | |
| ☐ 3 Randall Cunningham................. | .60 | .25 | .08 |
|     Philadelphia Eagles | | | |
| ☐ 4 John Elway............................... | 2.00 | .90 | .25 |
|     Denver Broncos | | | |
| ☐ 5 Boomer Esiason........................ | .60 | .25 | .08 |
|     Cincinnati Bengals | | | |
| ☐ 6 Jim Everett.............................. | .60 | .25 | .08 |
|     Los Angeles Rams | | | |
| ☐ 7 Jeff George ............................. | .40 | .18 | .05 |
|     Indianapolis Colts | | | |
| ☐ 8 Jim Harbaugh ........................... | .60 | .25 | .08 |
|     Chicago Bears | | | |
| ☐ 9 Jeff Hostetler ........................... | .60 | .25 | .08 |
|     New York Giants | | | |
| ☐ 10 Jim Kelly ............................... | 1.50 | .65 | .19 |
|     Buffalo Bills | | | |
| ☐ 11 Bernie Kosar .......................... | .60 | .25 | .08 |
|     Cleveland Browns | | | |
| ☐ 12 Dan Marino ............................ | 3.00 | 1.35 | .40 |
|     Miami Dolphins | | | |
| ☐ 13 Chris Miller UER...................... | .60 | .25 | .08 |
|     (Birthdate incorrectly | | | |
|     listed as 8-91-65) | | | |
|     Atlanta Falcons | | | |
| ☐ 14 Joe Montana .......................... | 4.00 | 1.80 | .50 |
|     San Francisco 49ers | | | |
| ☐ 15 Warren Moon .......................... | 1.00 | .45 | .13 |
|     Houston Oilers | | | |
| ☐ 16 Mark Rypien ........................... | .60 | .25 | .08 |
|     Washington Redskins | | | |
| ☐ 17 Phil Simms ............................ | .60 | .25 | .08 |
|     New York Giants | | | |
| ☐ 18 Steve Young........................... | 1.50 | .65 | .19 |
|     San Francisco 49ers | | | |

## 1992 ProLine Portraits Rookie Gold

Featuring the top NFL rookies, one card of this 28-card set was randomly inserted into each 1992 Pro Line Collection jumbo pack. Also dealers were sent a complete set with each hobby case purchased. The cards measure the standard size (2 1/2" by 3 1/2") and feature posed color player photos on the fronts. The pictures are bordered on two sides by gold foil stripes that run the length of the card. The player's name and the words "Rookie Gold" are printed in black on the stripes. The backs are bordered by gold stripes at the top and bottom. The background is white and displays complete college statistics in black print. The cards are numbered on the back. Production was limited to 4,000 cases of the jumbo packs.

| | MINT | EXC | G-VG |
|---|---|---|---|
| COMPLETE SET (28) | 12.00 | 5.50 | 1.50 |
| COMMON PLAYER (1-28) | .30 | .14 | .04 |
| ☐ 1 Tony Smith | .50 | .23 | .06 |
| Atlanta Falcons | | | |
| ☐ 2 John Fina | .30 | .14 | .04 |
| Buffalo Bills | | | |
| ☐ 3 Alonzo Spellman | .50 | .23 | .06 |
| Chicago Bears | | | |
| ☐ 4 David Klinger | 1.75 | .80 | .22 |
| Cincinnati Bengals | | | |
| ☐ 5 Tommy Vardell | .60 | .25 | .08 |
| Cleveland Browns | | | |
| ☐ 6 Kevin Smith | .60 | .25 | .08 |
| Dallas Cowboys | | | |
| ☐ 7 Tommy Maddox | 1.25 | .55 | .16 |
| Denver Broncos | | | |
| ☐ 8 Robert Porcher | .50 | .23 | .06 |
| Detroit Lions | | | |
| ☐ 9 Terrell Buckley | .60 | .25 | .08 |
| Green Bay Packers | | | |
| ☐ 10 Eddie Robinson | .30 | .14 | .04 |
| Houston Oilers | | | |
| ☐ 11 Steve Emtman | .30 | .14 | .04 |
| Indianapolis Colts | | | |
| ☐ 12 Quentin Coryatt | .75 | .35 | .09 |
| Indianapolis Colts | | | |
| ☐ 13 Dale Carter | .50 | .23 | .06 |
| Kansas City Chiefs | | | |
| ☐ 14 Chester McGlockton | .30 | .14 | .04 |
| Los Angeles Raiders | | | |
| ☐ 15 Sean Gilbert | .75 | .35 | .09 |
| Los Angeles Rams | | | |
| ☐ 16 Troy Vincent | .50 | .23 | .06 |
| Miami Dolphins | | | |
| ☐ 17 Robert Harris | .30 | .14 | .04 |
| Minnesota Vikings | | | |
| ☐ 18 Eugene Chung | .30 | .14 | .04 |
| New England Patriots | | | |
| ☐ 19 Vaughn Dunbar | .60 | .25 | .08 |
| New Orleans Saints | | | |
| ☐ 20 Derek Brown | .50 | .23 | .06 |
| New York Giants | | | |
| ☐ 21 Johnny Mitchell | 1.50 | .65 | .19 |
| New York Jets | | | |
| ☐ 22 Siran Stacy | .50 | .23 | .06 |
| Philadelphia Eagles | | | |
| ☐ 23 Tony Sacca | .50 | .23 | .06 |
| Phoenix Cardinals | | | |
| ☐ 24 Leon Searcy | .30 | .14 | .04 |
| Pittsburgh Steelers | | | |
| ☐ 25 Chris Mims | .60 | .25 | .08 |
| San Diego Chargers | | | |
| ☐ 26 Dana Hall | .50 | .23 | .06 |
| San Francisco 49ers | | | |
| ☐ 27 Courtney Hawkins | .75 | .35 | .09 |
| Tampa Bay Buccaneers | | | |
| ☐ 28 Shane Collins | .30 | .14 | .04 |
| Washington Redskins | | | |

# 1992 ProLine Portraits Team NFL

This five-card standard-size (2 1/2" by 3 1/2") set marks the debut of Pro Line's Team NFL Collectible cards, which features stars from other sports as well as celebrities from the entertainment world. On the fronts, each personality is pictured wearing attire of their favorite NFL team. The horizontal backs have team color-coded stripes at the top and an extended quote on a silver panel. In small print to the left of the card number, it reads "Team NFL."

| | MINT | EXC | G-VG |
|---|---|---|---|
| COMPLETE SET (5) | 10.00 | 4.50 | 1.25 |
| COMMON CARD (TNC1-TNC5) | 1.50 | .65 | .19 |
| ☐ TNC1 Muhammad Ali | 4.00 | 1.80 | .50 |
| ☐ TNC2 Milton Berle | 1.50 | .65 | .19 |
| ☐ TNC3 Don Mattingly | 3.00 | 1.35 | .40 |
| ☐ TNC4 Martin Mull | 1.50 | .65 | .19 |
| ☐ TNC5 Isiah Thomas | 2.00 | .90 | .25 |

# 1992 ProLine Portraits Team NFL Autographs

This five-card standard-size (2 1/2" by 3 1/2") set marks the debut of ProLine's Team NFL Collectible cards, which features stars from other sports as well as celebrities from the entertainment world. On the fronts, each personality is pictured wearing attire of their favorite NFL team. The horizontal backs have team color-coded stripes at the top and an extended quote on a silver panel. The cards are unnumbered but are listed below according to the numbers assigned to them in the regular series.

| | MINT | EXC | G-VG |
|---|---|---|---|
| COMPLETE SET (5) | 225.00 | 90.00 | 22.00 |
| COMMON PLAYER (1-5) | 20.00 | 8.00 | 2.00 |
| ☐ 1A Muhammad Ali | 100.00 | 40.00 | 10.00 |
| ☐ 1B Muhammad Ali | 300.00 | 120.00 | 30.00 |
| (Signed Cassius Clay) | | | |
| ☐ 2 Milton Berle | 35.00 | 14.00 | 3.50 |
| ☐ 3 Don Mattingly | 50.00 | 20.00 | 5.00 |
| ☐ 4 Martin Mull | 20.00 | 8.00 | 2.00 |
| ☐ 5 Isiah Thomas | 25.00 | 10.00 | 2.50 |
| (Card is signed Isiah) | | | |

# 1992 ProLine Portraits Wives

This 16-card standard-size (2 1/2" by 3 1/2") set was included in the 1992 Pro Line Portraits set, and its numbering is in continuation of the 1991 Pro Line Wives set. The set features full-bleed photos of wives of star NFL players and coaches. The cards are numbered on the back with an "SC" prefix.

| | MINT | EXC | G-VG |
|---|---|---|---|
| COMPLETE SET (16) | 1.50 | .65 | .19 |
| COMMON WIVES (SC8-SC23) | .15 | .07 | .02 |
| ☐ SC8 Ortancis Carter | .15 | .07 | .02 |
| ☐ SC9 Faith Cherry | .15 | .07 | .02 |

| | | | |
|---|---|---|---|
| ☐ SC10 Kaye Cowher | .15 | .07 | .02 |
| ☐ SC11 Dainnese Gault | .15 | .07 | .02 |
| ☐ SC12 Kathie Lee Gifford | .25 | .11 | .03 |
| ☐ SC13 Carole Hinton | .15 | .07 | .02 |
| ☐ SC14 Diane Long | .15 | .07 | .02 |
| ☐ SC15 Karen Lott | .15 | .07 | .02 |
| ☐ SC16 Felicia Moon | .15 | .07 | .02 |
| ☐ SC17 Cindy Noble | .15 | .07 | .02 |
| ☐ SC18 Linda Seifert | .15 | .07 | .02 |
| ☐ SC19 Mitzi Testaverde | .15 | .07 | .02 |
| ☐ SC20 Robin Swilling | .15 | .07 | .02 |
| ☐ SC21 Lesley Visser ANN | .20 | .09 | .03 |
| ☐ SC22 Toni Doleman | .15 | .07 | .02 |
| ☐ SC23 Diana Ditka | .15 | .07 | .02 |
| (With Mike Ditka) | | | |

# 1992 ProLine Portraits Wives Autographs

This 16-card standard-size (2 1/2" by 3 1/2") set was included in the 1992 ProLine Portraits set, and its numbering is in continuation of the 1991 ProLine Wives set. The set features full-bleed photos of wives of star NFL players and coaches. The cards are unnumbered but are listed below according to the numbers assigned to them in the regular series. Kathie Lee Gifford (12) did not sign her cards.

| | MINT | EXC | G-VG |
|---|---|---|---|
| COMMON PLAYER (8-23) | 10.00 | 4.00 | 1.00 |
| | | | |
| ☐ 8 Ortancis Carter | 10.00 | 4.00 | 1.00 |
| ☐ 9 Faith Cherry | 10.00 | 4.00 | 1.00 |
| ☐ 10 Kaye Cowher | 10.00 | 4.00 | 1.00 |
| ☐ 11 Dainnese Gault | 10.00 | 4.00 | 1.00 |
| ☐ 13 Carole Hinton | 10.00 | 4.00 | 1.00 |
| ☐ 14 Diane Long | 10.00 | 4.00 | 1.00 |
| ☐ 15 Karen Lott | 10.00 | 4.00 | 1.00 |
| ☐ 16 Felicia Moon | 10.00 | 4.00 | 1.00 |
| ☐ 17 Cindy Noble | 10.00 | 4.00 | 1.00 |
| ☐ 18 Linda Seifert | 10.00 | 4.00 | 1.00 |
| ☐ 19 Mitzi Testaverde | 10.00 | 4.00 | 1.00 |
| ☐ 20 Robin Swilling | 10.00 | 4.00 | 1.00 |
| ☐ 21 Lesley Visser ANN | 20.00 | 8.00 | 2.00 |
| ☐ 22 Toni Doleman | 10.00 | 4.00 | 1.00 |
| ☐ 23 Diana Ditka | 10.00 | 4.00 | 1.00 |
| (With Mike Ditka) | | | |

# 1992 ProLine Profiles

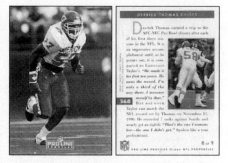

Together with the 1992 Pro Line Portraits, this 495-card standard-size (2 1/2" by 3 1/2") set constitutes the bulk of the 1992 Pro Line Collection. This year's all new Profiles set consists of nine-card mini-biographies on 55 of the NFL's most well-known personalities. Only

35,000 ten-box cases were produced. Each set chronicles the player's career from his days in college to the present day, including his life off of the football field. Each Pro Line Collection pack contained nine Profiles and three Portraits cards, and Quarterback Gold cards were randomly inserted throughout the packs. The fronts display full-bleed color photos, and the fifth card in each subset features a color portrait by a noted sports artist. The text on the backs captures moments from the player's career or life, including quotes from the player himself. The set concludes with a ten-card Art Monk bonus set, which was offered through a mail-in offer in exchange for ten 1991 Pro Line Portraits wrappers (black) and ten 1992 Pro Line Collection wrappers (white). The cards in each subset are numbered "X of 9." A special boxed set, with the cards displayed in two notebooks, was distributed at the National, and the Profiles series differs from the regular series in two respects, the cards are unnumbered (except within nine-card subsets) and are stamped with a "The National, 1992" seal. Players from the following teams are featured in the set (the teams are listed alphabetically): Atlanta Falcons (262-270, 334-342, 451-459), Buffalo Bills (28-36, 154-162, 352-360, 424-432), Chicago Bears (163-171, 397-405, 487-495), Cincinnati Bengals (82-90, 235-243), Cleveland Browns (100-108, 325-333), Dallas Cowboys (37-45, 181-189, 289-297), Denver Broncos (226-234), Detroit Lions (10-18), Green Bay Packers (73-81), Houston Oilers (280-288, 442-450), Kansas City Chiefs (316-324, 361-369), Los Angeles Raiders (1-9, 109-117, 379-387, 388-396), Los Angeles Rams (244-252), Miami Dolphins (118-126), Minnesota Vikings (64-72, 217-225), New England Patriots (415-423), New Orleans Saints (370-378), New York Giants (19-27, 271-279, 343-351, 460-468), New York Jets (145-153, 307-315), Philadelphia Eagles (190-198, 469-477), Phoenix Cardinals (199-207), Pittsburgh Steelers (91-99, 253-261), San Diego Chargers (136-144), San Francisco 49ers (46-54, 406-414), Seattle Seahawks (172-180, 298-306), Tampa Bay Buccaneers (55-63), and Washington Redskins (127-135, 208-216, 433-441, 478-486).

| | MINT | EXC | G-VG |
|---|---|---|---|
| COMPLETE SET (495) | 10.00 | 4.50 | 1.25 |
| COMMON PLAYER (1-495) | .04 | .02 | .01 |
| | | | |
| ☐ 1 Ronnie Lott | .10 | .05 | .01 |
| (Tackling opponent) | | | |
| ☐ 2 Ronnie Lott | .10 | .05 | .01 |
| (As youth, in baseball uniform) | | | |
| ☐ 3 Ronnie Lott | .10 | .05 | .01 |
| (Playing for USC) | | | |
| ☐ 4 Ronnie Lott | .10 | .05 | .01 |
| (Arms raised in triumph) | | | |
| ☐ 5 Ronnie Lott | .10 | .05 | .01 |
| (Portrait by Chris Hopkins) | | | |
| ☐ 6 Ronnie Lott | .10 | .05 | .01 |
| (At the Sports City Cafe) | | | |
| ☐ 7 Ronnie Lott | .10 | .05 | .01 |
| (With family) | | | |
| ☐ 8 Ronnie Lott | .10 | .05 | .01 |
| (Catching) | | | |
| ☐ 9 Ronnie Lott | .10 | .05 | .01 |
| (In tuxedo) | | | |
| ☐ 10 Rodney Peete | .04 | .02 | .01 |
| (Right arm raised) | | | |
| ☐ 11 Rodney Peete | .04 | .02 | .01 |
| (As youth, in football uniform) | | | |
| ☐ 12 Rodney Peete | .04 | .02 | .01 |
| (Playing baseball) | | | |
| ☐ 13 Rodney Peete | .04 | .02 | .01 |
| (In sweats with ball) | | | |
| ☐ 14 Rodney Peete | .04 | .02 | .01 |
| (Portrait by Merv Corning) | | | |
| ☐ 15 Rodney Peete | .04 | .02 | .01 |
| (Looking for receiver) | | | |
| ☐ 16 Rodney Peete | .04 | .02 | .01 |
| (Playing pool) | | | |
| ☐ 17 Rodney Peete | .04 | .02 | .01 |
| (Passing) | | | |
| ☐ 18 Rodney Peete | .04 | .02 | .01 |
| (Injured) | | | |
| ☐ 19 Carl Banks | .04 | .02 | .01 |
| (In action on field) | | | |
| ☐ 20 Carl Banks | .04 | .02 | .01 |
| (Playing basketball at Beecher High School) | | | |
| ☐ 21 Carl Banks | .04 | .02 | .01 |
| (In Michigan State uniform) | | | |
| ☐ 22 Carl Banks | .04 | .02 | .01 |
| (With family) | | | |
| ☐ 23 Carl Banks | .04 | .02 | .01 |

(Portrait by
Merv Corning)

☐ 24 Carl Banks......................... .04 .02 .01
(Talking, wearing
suit)

☐ 25 Carl Banks......................... .04 .02 .01
(Tackling opponent)

☐ 26 Carl Banks......................... .04 .02 .01
(On the air)

☐ 27 Carl Banks......................... .04 .02 .01
(Close-up)

☐ 28 Thurman Thomas.................. .20 .09 .03
(Running with ball,
blue jersey)

☐ 29 Thurman Thomas.................. .20 .09 .03
(With mother,
Terlisha Cockrell)

☐ 30 Thurman Thomas.................. .20 .09 .03
(At Oklahoma State)

☐ 31 Thurman Thomas.................. .20 .09 .03
(With family)

☐ 32 Thurman Thomas.................. .20 .09 .03
(Portrait by
Gary Kelley)

☐ 33 Thurman Thomas.................. .20 .09 .03
(Running with ball,
white jersey)

☐ 34 Thurman Thomas.................. .20 .09 .03
(Fishing)

☐ 35 Thurman Thomas.................. .20 .09 .03
(Stretching)

☐ 36 Thurman Thomas.................. .20 .09 .03
(Close-up)

☐ 37 Roger Staubach RET.............. .15 .07 .02
(With Heisman Trophy)

☐ 38 Roger Staubach RET.............. .15 .07 .02
(At Naval Academy)

☐ 39 Roger Staubach RET.............. .15 .07 .02
(In Navy dress whites)

☐ 40 Roger Staubach RET.............. .15 .07 .02
(Front view,
running with ball)

☐ 41 Roger Staubach RET.............. .15 .07 .02
(Portrait by
John Collier)

☐ 42 Roger Staubach RET.............. .15 .07 .02
(Passing, side view)

☐ 43 Roger Staubach RET.............. .15 .07 .02
(With family)

☐ 44 Roger Staubach RET.............. .15 .07 .02
(With young person
at Daytop, substance
abuse recovery facility)

☐ 45 Roger Staubach RET.............. .15 .07 .02
(Calling the play)

☐ 46 Jerry Rice........................... .30 .14 .04
(With MVP trophy)

☐ 47 Jerry Rice........................... .30 .14 .04
(At Mississippi
Valley State)

☐ 48 Jerry Rice........................... .30 .14 .04
(Running with ball)

☐ 49 Jerry Rice........................... .30 .14 .04
(With family)

☐ 50 Jerry Rice........................... .30 .14 .04
(Portrait by
Gary Kelley)

☐ 51 Jerry Rice........................... .30 .14 .04
(With March of Dimes
Ambassador, Ashley
Johnson)

☐ 52 Jerry Rice........................... .30 .14 .04
(Playing tennis)

☐ 53 Jerry Rice........................... .30 .14 .04
(Arms raised in
triumph)

☐ 54 Jerry Rice........................... .30 .14 .04
(Close-up)

☐ 55 Vinny Testaverde.................. .08 .04 .01
(Posed with Heisman)

☐ 56 Vinny Testaverde.................. .08 .04 .01
(At Fork Union
Military Academy)

☐ 57 Vinny Testaverde.................. .08 .04 .01
(Playing for the
University of Miami)

☐ 58 Vinny Testaverde.................. .08 .04 .01
(Passing)

☐ 59 Vinny Testaverde.................. .08 .04 .01
(Portrait by
Merv Corning)

☐ 60 Vinny Testaverde.................. .08 .04 .01
(Running with ball)

☐ 61 Vinny Testaverde.................. .08 .04 .01
(With family)

☐ 62 Vinny Testaverde.................. .08 .04 .01
(View from hips up,
fist raised in triumph)

☐ 63 Vinny Testaverde.................. .08 .04 .01
(With Vince Hanley)

☐ 64 Anthony Carter...................... .08 .04 .01
(Maneuvering around
opponent, with ball)

☐ 65 Anthony Carter...................... .08 .04 .01
(In high school
football game,
black-and-white)

☐ 66 Anthony Carter...................... .08 .04 .01
(At Michigan,
running with ball)

☐ 67 Anthony Carter...................... .08 .04 .01
(Fishing)

☐ 68 Anthony Carter...................... .08 .04 .01
(Portrait by
John Collier)

☐ 69 Anthony Carter...................... .08 .04 .01
(Running, looking
over shoulder)

☐ 70 Anthony Carter...................... .08 .04 .01
(With family)

☐ 71 Anthony Carter...................... .08 .04 .01
(Catching pass)

☐ 72 Anthony Carter...................... .08 .04 .01
(Close-up)

☐ 73 Sterling Sharpe ................... .25 .11 .03
(Catching)

☐ 74 Sterling Sharpe ................... .25 .11 .03
(Passing, in high
school)

☐ 75 Sterling Sharpe ................... .25 .11 .03
(Walking on field
at South Carolina)

☐ 76 Sterling Sharpe ................... .25 .11 .03
(With books on
SC campus)

☐ 77 Sterling Sharpe ................... .25 .11 .03
(Portrait by
Chris Hopkins)

☐ 78 Sterling Sharpe ................... .25 .11 .03
(Running with ball
against Rams)

☐ 79 Sterling Sharpe ................... .25 .11 .03
(At the piano)

☐ 80 Sterling Sharpe ................... .25 .11 .03
(Running with ball
against Lions)

☐ 81 Sterling Sharpe ................... .25 .11 .03
(In brick arch
with football)

☐ 82 Anthony Munoz..................... .08 .04 .01
(With NFL Man of
the Year award)

☐ 83 Anthony Munoz..................... .08 .04 .01
(As youth, batting)

☐ 84 Anthony Munoz..................... .08 .04 .01
(Playing for USC)

☐ 85 Anthony Munoz..................... .08 .04 .01
(With child at
Children's Hospital)

☐ 86 Anthony Munoz..................... .08 .04 .01
(Portrait by
Merv Corning)

☐ 87 Anthony Munoz..................... .08 .04 .01
(Blocking opponent)

☐ 88 Anthony Munoz..................... .08 .04 .01
(Holding baby, with
fellow players and
children)

☐ 89 Anthony Munoz..................... .08 .04 .01
(In action for
Bengals)

☐ 90 Anthony Munoz..................... .08 .04 .01
(Close-up)

☐ 91 Bubby Brister ...................... .04 .02 .01
(Passing, white
jersey)

☐ 92 Bubby Brister ...................... .04 .02 .01
(NLU uniform)

☐ 93 Bubby Brister ...................... .04 .02 .01
(Baseball uniform)

☐ 94 Bubby Brister ...................... .04 .02 .01
(With kids at
Ronald McDonald House)

☐ 95 Bubby Brister ...................... .04 .02 .01
(Portrait by
Greg Spalenka)

☐ 96 Bubby Brister ...................... .04 .02 .01
(Wearing western
attire)

☐ 97 Bubby Brister ...................... .04 .02 .01
(Running with ball,
white jersey)

☐ 98 Bubby Brister ...................... .04 .02 .01
(Passing, black
jersey)

| | | | |
|---|---|---|---|
| ☐ 99 Bubby Brister | .04 | .02 | .01 |
| (Close-up) | | | |
| ☐ 100 Bernie Kosar | .10 | .05 | .01 |
| (Passing, white jersey) | | | |
| ☐ 101 Bernie Kosar | .10 | .05 | .01 |
| (In high school) | | | |
| ☐ 102 Bernie Kosar | .10 | .05 | .01 |
| (Playing for Miami) | | | |
| ☐ 103 Bernie Kosar | .10 | .05 | .01 |
| (Being tackled) | | | |
| ☐ 104 Bernie Kosar | .10 | .05 | .01 |
| (Portrait by Greg Spalenka) | | | |
| ☐ 105 Bernie Kosar | .10 | .05 | .01 |
| (With family) | | | |
| ☐ 106 Bernie Kosar | .10 | .05 | .01 |
| (Playing golf) | | | |
| ☐ 107 Bernie Kosar | .10 | .05 | .01 |
| (Looking for receiver) | | | |
| ☐ 108 Bernie Kosar | .10 | .05 | .01 |
| (Close-up) | | | |
| ☐ 109 Art Shell CO | .08 | .04 | .01 |
| (On sidelines) | | | |
| ☐ 110 Art Shell CO | .08 | .04 | .01 |
| (At Maryland State) | | | |
| ☐ 111 Art Shell CO | .08 | .04 | .01 |
| (Playing for Raiders) | | | |
| ☐ 112 Art Shell CO | .08 | .04 | .01 |
| (Playing basketball with sons) | | | |
| ☐ 113 Art Shell CO | .08 | .04 | .01 |
| (Portrait by Chris Hopkins) | | | |
| ☐ 114 Art Shell CO | .08 | .04 | .01 |
| (Talking to player on sidelines) | | | |
| ☐ 115 Art Shell CO | .08 | .04 | .01 |
| (In front of big screen TV) | | | |
| ☐ 116 Art Shell CO | .08 | .04 | .01 |
| (In line of scrimmage) | | | |
| ☐ 117 Art Shell CO | .08 | .04 | .01 |
| (With teddy bear) | | | |
| ☐ 118 Don Shula CO | .08 | .04 | .01 |
| (With players) | | | |
| ☐ 119 Don Shula CO | .08 | .04 | .01 |
| (At John Carroll University) | | | |
| ☐ 120 Don Shula CO | .08 | .04 | .01 |
| (Coaching Baltimore Colts) | | | |
| ☐ 121 Don Shula CO | .08 | .04 | .01 |
| (With son, Mike) | | | |
| ☐ 122 Don Shula CO | .08 | .04 | .01 |
| (Portrait by Merv Corning) | | | |
| ☐ 123 Don Shula CO | .08 | .04 | .01 |
| (With daughters) | | | |
| ☐ 124 Don Shula CO | .08 | .04 | .01 |
| (With Dan Marino) | | | |
| ☐ 125 Don Shula CO | .08 | .04 | .01 |
| (With doctor at The Don Shula Foundation) | | | |
| ☐ 126 Don Shula CO | .08 | .04 | .01 |
| (With Super Bowl Trophies) | | | |
| ☐ 127 Joe Gibbs CO | .08 | .04 | .01 |
| (Writing out play) | | | |
| ☐ 128 Joe Gibbs CO | .08 | .04 | .01 |
| (Playing for San Diego State) | | | |
| ☐ 129 Joe Gibbs CO | .08 | .04 | .01 |
| (Coaching on sidelines) | | | |
| ☐ 130 Joe Gibbs CO | .08 | .04 | .01 |
| (With sons) | | | |
| ☐ 131 Joe Gibbs CO | .08 | .04 | .01 |
| (Portrait by John Collier) | | | |
| ☐ 132 Joe Gibbs CO | .08 | .04 | .01 |
| (Reading in office) | | | |
| ☐ 133 Joe Gibbs CO | .08 | .04 | .01 |
| (With Youth For Tomorrow group) | | | |
| ☐ 134 Joe Gibbs CO | .08 | .04 | .01 |
| (In front of race car) | | | |
| ☐ 135 Joe Gibbs CO | .08 | .04 | .01 |
| (In front of Church) | | | |
| ☐ 136 Junior Seau | .10 | .05 | .01 |
| (Holding ball) | | | |
| ☐ 137 Junior Seau | .10 | .05 | .01 |
| (As youth, in football uniform) | | | |
| ☐ 138 Junior Seau | .10 | .05 | .01 |
| (At USC) | | | |
| ☐ 139 Junior Seau | .10 | .05 | .01 |
| (Finger pointing up) | | | |
| ☐ 140 Junior Seau | .10 | .05 | .01 |
| (Portrait by Merv Corning) | | | |
| ☐ 141 Junior Seau | .10 | .05 | .01 |
| (With wife, Gina) | | | |
| ☐ 142 Junior Seau | .10 | .05 | .01 |
| (Running on beach) | | | |
| ☐ 143 Junior Seau | .10 | .05 | .01 |
| (Lifting weights) | | | |
| ☐ 144 Junior Seau | .10 | .05 | .01 |
| (In swim trunks with seaweed) | | | |
| ☐ 145 Al Toon | .04 | .02 | .01 |
| (Running with ball, white jersey) | | | |
| ☐ 146 Al Toon | .04 | .02 | .01 |
| (During Pee-Wee football days) | | | |
| ☐ 147 Al Toon | .04 | .02 | .01 |
| (On the field at Wisconsin) | | | |
| ☐ 148 Al Toon | .04 | .02 | .01 |
| (With family) | | | |
| ☐ 149 Al Toon | .04 | .02 | .01 |
| (Portrait by Gary Kelley) | | | |
| ☐ 150 Al Toon | .04 | .02 | .01 |
| (Catching) | | | |
| ☐ 151 Al Toon | .04 | .02 | .01 |
| (Working out) | | | |
| ☐ 152 Al Toon | .04 | .02 | .01 |
| (Running with ball, green jersey) | | | |
| ☐ 153 Al Toon | .04 | .02 | .01 |
| (Close-up) | | | |
| ☐ 154 Jack Kemp RET | .10 | .05 | .01 |
| (In office) | | | |
| ☐ 155 Jack Kemp RET | .10 | .05 | .01 |
| (Portrait from Occidental College) | | | |
| ☐ 156 Jack Kemp RET | .10 | .05 | .01 |
| (Playing for Chargers) | | | |
| ☐ 157 Jack Kemp RET | .10 | .05 | .01 |
| (With family) | | | |
| ☐ 158 Jack Kemp RET | .10 | .05 | .01 |
| (Portrait by Merv Corning) | | | |
| ☐ 159 Jack Kemp RET | .10 | .05 | .01 |
| (Playing for Buffalo) | | | |
| ☐ 160 Jack Kemp RET | .10 | .05 | .01 |
| (Passing) | | | |
| ☐ 161 Jack Kemp RET | .10 | .05 | .01 |
| (With son, Jeff) | | | |
| ☐ 162 Jack Kemp RET | .10 | .05 | .01 |
| (In Washington) | | | |
| ☐ 163 Jim Harbaugh | .08 | .04 | .01 |
| (Passing, blue jersey) | | | |
| ☐ 164 Jim Harbaugh | .08 | .04 | .01 |
| (Playing in high school) | | | |
| ☐ 165 Jim Harbaugh | .08 | .04 | .01 |
| (Playing for Michigan) | | | |
| ☐ 166 Jim Harbaugh | .08 | .04 | .01 |
| (Passing, white jersey) | | | |
| ☐ 167 Jim Harbaugh | .08 | .04 | .01 |
| (Portrait by Gary Kelley) | | | |
| ☐ 168 Jim Harbaugh | .08 | .04 | .01 |
| (With children in children's home) | | | |
| ☐ 169 Jim Harbaugh | .08 | .04 | .01 |
| (Working out) | | | |
| ☐ 170 Jim Harbaugh | .08 | .04 | .01 |
| (Calling play) | | | |
| ☐ 171 Jim Harbaugh | .08 | .04 | .01 |
| (Close-up) | | | |
| ☐ 172 Dan McGwire | .08 | .04 | .01 |
| (From waist up) | | | |
| ☐ 173 Dan McGwire | .08 | .04 | .01 |
| (At Purdue) | | | |
| ☐ 174 Dan McGwire | .08 | .04 | .01 |
| (At San Diego) | | | |
| ☐ 175 Dan McGwire | .08 | .04 | .01 |
| (From waist down) | | | |
| ☐ 176 Dan McGwire | .08 | .04 | .01 |
| (Portrait by Chris Hopkins) | | | |
| ☐ 177 Dan McGwire | .08 | .04 | .01 |
| (Passing, blue jersey) | | | |
| ☐ 178 Dan McGwire | .08 | .04 | .01 |
| (Passing, white jersey) | | | |
| ☐ 179 Dan McGwire | .08 | .04 | .01 |
| (Working out) | | | |

| | | | | |
|---|---|---|---|---|
| ☐ 180 Dan McGwire | .08 | .04 | .01 |
| (With wife, Dana) | | | |
| ☐ 181 Troy Aikman | .60 | .25 | .08 |
| (Passing, wearing blue jersey) | | | |
| ☐ 182 Troy Aikman | .60 | .25 | .08 |
| (As youth) | | | |
| ☐ 183 Troy Aikman | .60 | .25 | .08 |
| (Passing, at UCLA) | | | |
| ☐ 184 Troy Aikman | .60 | .25 | .08 |
| (Preparing to pass, with Cowboys) | | | |
| ☐ 185 Troy Aikman | .60 | .25 | .08 |
| (Portrait by Greg Spalenka) | | | |
| ☐ 186 Troy Aikman | .60 | .25 | .08 |
| (Golfing) | | | |
| ☐ 187 Troy Aikman | .60 | .25 | .08 |
| (Looking for opening, front view) | | | |
| ☐ 188 Troy Aikman | .60 | .25 | .08 |
| (In sweats, passing) | | | |
| ☐ 189 Troy Aikman | .60 | .25 | .08 |
| (In cowboy hat) | | | |
| ☐ 190 Keith Byars | .08 | .04 | .01 |
| (With little brother) | | | |
| ☐ 191 Keith Byars | .08 | .04 | .01 |
| (Childhood picture) | | | |
| ☐ 192 Keith Byars | .08 | .04 | .01 |
| (High School football photo) | | | |
| ☐ 193 Keith Byars | .08 | .04 | .01 |
| (Ohio State photo, red jersey) | | | |
| ☐ 194 Keith Byars | .08 | .04 | .01 |
| (Portrait by Chris Hopkins) | | | |
| ☐ 195 Keith Byars | .08 | .04 | .01 |
| (Working out) | | | |
| ☐ 196 Keith Byars | .08 | .04 | .01 |
| (Running, green jersey) | | | |
| ☐ 197 Keith Byars | .08 | .04 | .01 |
| (Running, white jersey) | | | |
| ☐ 198 Keith Byars | .08 | .04 | .01 |
| (Close-up) | | | |
| ☐ 199 Timm Rosenbach | .04 | .02 | .01 |
| (Running with ball, red jersey) | | | |
| ☐ 200 Timm Rosenbach | .04 | .02 | .01 |
| (In high school football uniform) | | | |
| ☐ 201 Timm Rosenbach | .04 | .02 | .01 |
| (At Washington State) | | | |
| ☐ 202 Timm Rosenbach | .04 | .02 | .01 |
| (With wife, Kerry) | | | |
| ☐ 203 Timm Rosenbach | .04 | .02 | .01 |
| (Portrait by John Collier) | | | |
| ☐ 204 Timm Rosenbach | .04 | .02 | .01 |
| (Passing, white jersey) | | | |
| ☐ 205 Timm Rosenbach | .04 | .02 | .01 |
| (Roping a calf) | | | |
| ☐ 206 Timm Rosenbach | .04 | .02 | .01 |
| (Working out) | | | |
| ☐ 207 Timm Rosenbach | .04 | .02 | .01 |
| (Seated on hay, in western attire) | | | |
| ☐ 208 Gary Clark | .08 | .04 | .01 |
| (In the end zone) | | | |
| ☐ 209 Gary Clark | .08 | .04 | .01 |
| (Playing for James Madison Univ.) | | | |
| ☐ 210 Gary Clark | .08 | .04 | .01 |
| (Catching ball in end zone) | | | |
| ☐ 211 Gary Clark | .08 | .04 | .01 |
| (With daughter) | | | |
| ☐ 212 Gary Clark | .08 | .04 | .01 |
| (Portrait by John Collier) | | | |
| ☐ 213 Gary Clark | .08 | .04 | .01 |
| (Running, slouched position) | | | |
| ☐ 214 Gary Clark | .08 | .04 | .01 |
| (Playing basketball) | | | |
| ☐ 215 Gary Clark | .08 | .04 | .01 |
| (Lifted by teammates) | | | |
| ☐ 216 Gary Clark | .08 | .04 | .01 |
| (Close-up) | | | |
| ☐ 217 Chris Doleman | .04 | .02 | .01 |
| (Playing for Vikings, white jersey) | | | |

| | | | | |
|---|---|---|---|---|
| ☐ 218 Chris Doleman | .04 | .02 | .01 |
| (In Pittsburgh uniform) | | | |
| ☐ 219 Chris Doleman | .04 | .02 | .01 |
| (With wife, Toni, and dog) | | | |
| ☐ 220 Chris Doleman | .04 | .02 | .01 |
| (Playing for Vikings, blue jersey) | | | |
| ☐ 221 Chris Doleman | .04 | .02 | .01 |
| (Portrait by John Collier) | | | |
| ☐ 222 Chris Doleman | .04 | .02 | .01 |
| (Working out) | | | |
| ☐ 223 Chris Doleman | .04 | .02 | .01 |
| (Leaping over opponent) | | | |
| ☐ 224 Chris Doleman | .04 | .02 | .01 |
| (Playing golf) | | | |
| ☐ 225 Chris Doleman | .04 | .02 | .01 |
| (Close-up) | | | |
| ☐ 226 John Elway | .30 | .14 | .04 |
| (Passing, orange jersey) | | | |
| ☐ 227 John Elway | .30 | .14 | .04 |
| (Playing for Stanford) | | | |
| ☐ 228 John Elway | .30 | .14 | .04 |
| (Passing, white jersey) | | | |
| ☐ 229 John Elway | .30 | .14 | .04 |
| (With family) | | | |
| ☐ 230 John Elway | .30 | .14 | .04 |
| (Portrait by Greg Spalenka) | | | |
| ☐ 231 John Elway | .30 | .14 | .04 |
| (Working out) | | | |
| ☐ 232 John Elway | .30 | .14 | .04 |
| (Sitting on car) | | | |
| ☐ 233 John Elway | .30 | .14 | .04 |
| (Running with ball) | | | |
| ☐ 234 John Elway | .30 | .14 | .04 |
| (Close-up) | | | |
| ☐ 235 Boomer Esiason | .10 | .05 | .01 |
| (Calling play) | | | |
| ☐ 236 Boomer Esiason | .10 | .05 | .01 |
| (In high school) | | | |
| ☐ 237 Boomer Esiason | .10 | .05 | .01 |
| (In Terps uniform) | | | |
| ☐ 238 Boomer Esiason | .10 | .05 | .01 |
| (Passing) | | | |
| ☐ 239 Boomer Esiason | .10 | .05 | .01 |
| (Portrait by Greg Spalenka) | | | |
| ☐ 240 Boomer Esiason | .10 | .05 | .01 |
| (With dogs) | | | |
| ☐ 241 Boomer Esiason | .10 | .05 | .01 |
| (With Kinny McQuade) | | | |
| ☐ 242 Boomer Esiason | .10 | .05 | .01 |
| (Looking for pass receiver) | | | |
| ☐ 243 Boomer Esiason | .10 | .05 | .01 |
| (Close-up) | | | |
| ☐ 244 Jim Everett | .08 | .04 | .01 |
| (Passing, white jersey) | | | |
| ☐ 245 Jim Everett | .08 | .04 | .01 |
| (In high school uniform) | | | |
| ☐ 246 Jim Everett | .08 | .04 | .01 |
| (Playing for Purdue) | | | |
| ☐ 247 Jim Everett | .08 | .04 | .01 |
| (With family) | | | |
| ☐ 248 Jim Everett | .08 | .04 | .01 |
| (Portrait by Greg Spalenka) | | | |
| ☐ 249 Jim Everett | .08 | .04 | .01 |
| (Running with ball, blue jersey) | | | |
| ☐ 250 Jim Everett | .08 | .04 | .01 |
| (Fishing) | | | |
| ☐ 251 Jim Everett | .08 | .04 | .01 |
| (Handing off ball) | | | |
| ☐ 252 Jim Everett | .08 | .04 | .01 |
| (Close-up) | | | |
| ☐ 253 Eric Green | .08 | .04 | .01 |
| (Running with ball) | | | |
| ☐ 254 Eric Green | .08 | .04 | .01 |
| (With coach Sam Rutigliano) | | | |
| ☐ 255 Eric Green | .08 | .04 | .01 |
| (Being blocked by opponent) | | | |
| ☐ 256 Eric Green | .08 | .04 | .01 |
| (Playing basketball) | | | |
| ☐ 257 Eric Green | .08 | .04 | .01 |
| (Portrait by Merv Corning) | | | |
| ☐ 258 Eric Green | .08 | .04 | .01 |

(In locker room)
| | | | | |
|---|---|---|---|---|
| ☐ 259 Eric Green | .08 | .04 | .01 |
| (Blocking opponent) | | | | |
| ☐ 260 Eric Green | .08 | .04 | .01 |
| (Catching) | | | | |
| ☐ 261 Eric Green | .08 | .04 | .01 |
| (Close-up) | | | | |
| ☐ 262 Jerry Glanville CO | .04 | .02 | .01 |
| (On motorcycle) | | | | |
| ☐ 263 Jerry Glanville CO | .04 | .02 | .01 |
| (With Lions coaching staff) | | | | |
| ☐ 264 Jerry Glanville CO | .04 | .02 | .01 |
| (Coaching, clapping) | | | | |
| ☐ 265 Jerry Glanville CO | .04 | .02 | .01 |
| (With family) | | | | |
| ☐ 266 Jerry Glanville CO | .04 | .02 | .01 |
| (Portrait by Gary Kelley) | | | | |
| ☐ 267 Jerry Glanville CO | .04 | .02 | .01 |
| (Coaching, with players) | | | | |
| ☐ 268 Jerry Glanville CO | .04 | .02 | .01 |
| (In race car) | | | | |
| ☐ 269 Jerry Glanville CO | .04 | .02 | .01 |
| (With country music stars) | | | | |
| ☐ 270 Jerry Glanville CO | .04 | .02 | .01 |
| (In black western attire) | | | | |
| ☐ 271 Jeff Hostetler | .10 | .05 | .01 |
| (Passing, blue jersey) | | | | |
| ☐ 272 Jeff Hostetler | .10 | .05 | .01 |
| (Playing for West Virginia) | | | | |
| ☐ 273 Jeff Hostetler | .10 | .05 | .01 |
| (Lifting weights) | | | | |
| ☐ 274 Jeff Hostetler | .10 | .05 | .01 |
| (With family) | | | | |
| ☐ 275 Jeff Hostetler | .10 | .05 | .01 |
| (Portrait by John Collier) | | | | |
| ☐ 276 Jeff Hostetler | .10 | .05 | .01 |
| (Passing, white jersey) | | | | |
| ☐ 277 Jeff Hostetler | .10 | .05 | .01 |
| (At Ronald McDonald house) | | | | |
| ☐ 278 Jeff Hostetler | .10 | .05 | .01 |
| (With father-in-law) | | | | |
| ☐ 279 Jeff Hostetler | .10 | .05 | .01 |
| (Close-up) | | | | |
| ☐ 280 Haywood Jeffires | .10 | .05 | .01 |
| (Catching, Houston uniform) | | | | |
| ☐ 281 Haywood Jeffires | .10 | .05 | .01 |
| (Playing for North Carolina) | | | | |
| ☐ 282 Haywood Jeffires | .10 | .05 | .01 |
| (With wife, Robin) | | | | |
| ☐ 283 Haywood Jeffires | .10 | .05 | .01 |
| (Pushing past opponent) | | | | |
| ☐ 284 Haywood Jeffires | .10 | .05 | .01 |
| (Portrait by John Collier) | | | | |
| ☐ 285 Haywood Jeffires | .10 | .05 | .01 |
| (With car) | | | | |
| ☐ 286 Haywood Jeffires | .10 | .05 | .01 |
| (With Boy and Girls Club members) | | | | |
| ☐ 287 Haywood Jeffires | .10 | .05 | .01 |
| (Being tackled) | | | | |
| ☐ 288 Haywood Jeffires | .10 | .05 | .01 |
| (Close-up) | | | | |
| ☐ 289 Michael Irvin | .25 | .11 | .03 |
| (Running with ball) | | | | |
| ☐ 290 Michael Irvin | .25 | .11 | .03 |
| (Playing basketball) | | | | |
| ☐ 291 Michael Irvin | .25 | .11 | .03 |
| (In Miami uniform) | | | | |
| ☐ 292 Michael Irvin | .25 | .11 | .03 |
| (With wife, Sandy) | | | | |
| ☐ 293 Michael Irvin | .25 | .11 | .03 |
| (Portrait by Gary Kelley) | | | | |
| ☐ 294 Michael Irvin | .25 | .11 | .03 |
| (Catching) | | | | |
| ☐ 295 Michael Irvin | .25 | .11 | .03 |
| (With student, Nyna Sherte) | | | | |
| ☐ 296 Michael Irvin | .25 | .11 | .03 |
| (Playing in Pro Bowl) | | | | |
| ☐ 297 Michael Irvin | .25 | .11 | .03 |
| (Close-up) | | | | |
| ☐ 298 Steve Largent RET | .10 | .05 | .01 |
| (Catching, blue jersey) | | | | |
| ☐ 299 Steve Largent RET | .10 | .05 | .01 |
| (Playing for Tulsa) | | | | |
| ☐ 300 Steve Largent RET | .10 | .05 | .01 |
| (With family) | | | | |
| ☐ 301 Steve Largent RET | .10 | .05 | .01 |
| (At school for disabled children) | | | | |
| ☐ 302 Steve Largent RET | .10 | .05 | .01 |
| (Portrait by Chris Hopkins) | | | | |
| ☐ 303 Steve Largent RET | .10 | .05 | .01 |
| (Catching, white jersey) | | | | |
| ☐ 304 Steve Largent RET | .10 | .05 | .01 |
| (In dress attire) | | | | |
| ☐ 305 Steve Largent RET | .10 | .05 | .01 |
| (Running, white jersey) | | | | |
| ☐ 306 Steve Largent RET | .10 | .05 | .01 |
| (Close-up) | | | | |
| ☐ 307 Ken O'Brien | .04 | .02 | .01 |
| (Passing, side view) | | | | |
| ☐ 308 Ken O'Brien | .04 | .02 | .01 |
| (With University of California-Davis) | | | | |
| ☐ 309 Ken O'Brien | .04 | .02 | .01 |
| (With family) | | | | |
| ☐ 310 Ken O'Brien | .04 | .02 | .01 |
| (Passing, front view) | | | | |
| ☐ 311 Ken O'Brien | .04 | .02 | .01 |
| (Portrait by Chris Hopkins) | | | | |
| ☐ 312 Ken O'Brien | .04 | .02 | .01 |
| (Shaking hands with Tony Eason) | | | | |
| ☐ 313 Ken O'Brien | .04 | .02 | .01 |
| (Playing golf) | | | | |
| ☐ 314 Ken O'Brien | .04 | .02 | .01 |
| (Handing off the ball) | | | | |
| ☐ 315 Ken O'Brien | .04 | .02 | .01 |
| (Close-up) | | | | |
| ☐ 316 Christian Okoye | .04 | .02 | .01 |
| (Running with ball, red jersey) | | | | |
| ☐ 317 Christian Okoye | .04 | .02 | .01 |
| (Close-up at Asuza Pacific Univ.) | | | | |
| ☐ 318 Christian Okoye | .04 | .02 | .01 |
| (Cooking) | | | | |
| ☐ 319 Christian Okoye | .04 | .02 | .01 |
| (Running with ball, white jersey) | | | | |
| ☐ 320 Christian Okoye | .04 | .02 | .01 |
| (Portrait by Chris Hopkins) | | | | |
| ☐ 321 Christian Okoye | .04 | .02 | .01 |
| (In Nigerian attire) | | | | |
| ☐ 322 Christian Okoye | .04 | .02 | .01 |
| (With daughter, Christiana) | | | | |
| ☐ 323 Christian Okoye | .04 | .02 | .01 |
| (Withstanding an opponent) | | | | |
| ☐ 324 Christian Okoye | .04 | .02 | .01 |
| (In casual attire) | | | | |
| ☐ 325 Michael Dean Perry | .08 | .04 | .01 |
| (Blocking opponent, white jersey) | | | | |
| ☐ 326 Michael Dean Perry | .08 | .04 | .01 |
| (Playing for Clemson) | | | | |
| ☐ 327 Michael Dean Perry | .08 | .04 | .01 |
| (Blocking opponent, brown jersey) | | | | |
| ☐ 328 Michael Dean Perry | .08 | .04 | .01 |
| (With family) | | | | |
| ☐ 329 Michael Dean Perry | .08 | .04 | .01 |
| (Portrait by Merv Corning) | | | | |
| ☐ 330 Michael Dean Perry | .08 | .04 | .01 |
| (At Children's Hospital) | | | | |
| ☐ 331 Michael Dean Perry | .08 | .04 | .01 |
| (Playing basketball) | | | | |
| ☐ 332 Michael Dean Perry | .08 | .04 | .01 |
| (Blocking opponent, horizontal shot) | | | | |
| ☐ 333 Michael Dean Perry | .08 | .04 | .01 |
| (With AFC Player of the Year trophy) | | | | |
| ☐ 334 Chris Miller | .10 | .05 | .01 |
| (Passing, black jersey) | | | | |
| ☐ 335 Chris Miller | .10 | .05 | .01 |
| (As youth, fishing) | | | | |
| ☐ 336 Chris Miller | .10 | .05 | .01 |
| (Playing for Oregon) | | | | |
| ☐ 337 Chris Miller | .10 | .05 | .01 |

(In baseball uniform)

| | | | |
|---|---|---|---|
| ☐ 338 Chris Miller | .10 | .05 | .01 |
| (Portrait by Greg Spalenka) | | | |
| ☐ 339 Chris Miller | .10 | .05 | .01 |
| (Running with ball) | | | |
| ☐ 340 Chris Miller | .10 | .05 | .01 |
| (With wife, Jennifer) | | | |
| ☐ 341 Chris Miller | .10 | .05 | .01 |
| (In the Pro Bowl) | | | |
| ☐ 342 Chris Miller | .10 | .05 | .01 |
| (Close-up) | | | |
| ☐ 343 Phil Simms | .10 | .05 | .01 |
| (Passing, blue jersey) | | | |
| ☐ 344 Phil Simms | .10 | .05 | .01 |
| (Calling the play) | | | |
| ☐ 345 Phil Simms | .10 | .05 | .01 |
| (With family) | | | |
| ☐ 346 Phil Simms | .10 | .05 | .01 |
| (Playing pool) | | | |
| ☐ 347 Phil Simms | .10 | .05 | .01 |
| (Portrait by Greg Spalenka) | | | |
| ☐ 348 Phil Simms | .10 | .05 | .01 |
| (Running with ball) | | | |
| ☐ 349 Phil Simms | .10 | .05 | .01 |
| (With young man from the Eastern Christian School for handicapped children) | | | |
| ☐ 350 Phil Simms | .10 | .05 | .01 |
| (Passing, white jersey) | | | |
| ☐ 351 Phil Simms | .10 | .05 | .01 |
| (Close-up) | | | |
| ☐ 352 Bruce Smith | .08 | .04 | .01 |
| (Tackling opponent, white jersey) | | | |
| ☐ 353 Bruce Smith | .08 | .04 | .01 |
| (At Virginia Tech) | | | |
| ☐ 354 Bruce Smith | .08 | .04 | .01 |
| (Close-up in game) | | | |
| ☐ 355 Bruce Smith | .08 | .04 | .01 |
| (With wife, Carmen) | | | |
| ☐ 356 Bruce Smith | .08 | .04 | .01 |
| (Portrait by John Collier) | | | |
| ☐ 357 Bruce Smith | .08 | .04 | .01 |
| (In Pro Bowl) | | | |
| ☐ 358 Bruce Smith | .08 | .04 | .01 |
| (Working out) | | | |
| ☐ 359 Bruce Smith | .08 | .04 | .01 |
| (Blocking, blue jersey) | | | |
| ☐ 360 Bruce Smith | .08 | .04 | .01 |
| (Close-up) | | | |
| ☐ 361 Derrick Thomas | .10 | .05 | .01 |
| (Running, red jersey) | | | |
| ☐ 362 Derrick Thomas | .10 | .05 | .01 |
| (At the University of Alabama) | | | |
| ☐ 363 Derrick Thomas | .10 | .05 | .01 |
| (With his father's Air Force momentos) | | | |
| ☐ 364 Derrick Thomas | .10 | .05 | .01 |
| (Seated on helmet) | | | |
| ☐ 365 Derrick Thomas | .10 | .05 | .01 |
| (Portrait by Merv Corning) | | | |
| ☐ 366 Derrick Thomas | .10 | .05 | .01 |
| (With motivational program participants) | | | |
| ☐ 367 Derrick Thomas | .10 | .05 | .01 |
| (Posed with Limo) | | | |
| ☐ 368 Derrick Thomas | .10 | .05 | .01 |
| (In Pro Bowl) | | | |
| ☐ 369 Derrick Thomas | .10 | .05 | .01 |
| (Close-up) | | | |
| ☐ 370 Pat Swilling | .08 | .04 | .01 |
| (Relaxed against tree) | | | |
| ☐ 371 Pat Swilling | .08 | .04 | .01 |
| (At Georgia Tech) | | | |
| ☐ 372 Pat Swilling | .08 | .04 | .01 |
| (With family) | | | |
| ☐ 373 Pat Swilling | .08 | .04 | .01 |
| (Running on field) | | | |
| ☐ 374 Pat Swilling | .08 | .04 | .01 |
| (Portrait by John Collier) | | | |
| ☐ 375 Pat Swilling | .08 | .04 | .01 |
| (Working out) | | | |
| ☐ 376 Pat Swilling | .08 | .04 | .01 |
| (Tackling opponent on icy field) | | | |
| ☐ 377 Pat Swilling | .08 | .04 | .01 |

(With underprivileged children)

| | | | |
|---|---|---|---|
| ☐ 378 Pat Swilling | .08 | .04 | .01 |
| (Relaxed at home) | | | |
| ☐ 379 Eric Dickerson | .10 | .05 | .01 |
| (Close-up in Rams football gear) | | | |
| ☐ 380 Eric Dickerson | .10 | .05 | .01 |
| (Playing for SMU) | | | |
| ☐ 381 Eric Dickerson | .10 | .05 | .01 |
| (With great aunt Viola) | | | |
| ☐ 382 Eric Dickerson | .10 | .05 | .01 |
| (Running with ball, Rams uniform) | | | |
| ☐ 383 Eric Dickerson | .10 | .05 | .01 |
| (Portrait by Merv Corning) | | | |
| ☐ 384 Eric Dickerson | .10 | .05 | .01 |
| (Running with ball, Colts uniform) | | | |
| ☐ 385 Eric Dickerson | .10 | .05 | .01 |
| (Working out) | | | |
| ☐ 386 Eric Dickerson | .10 | .05 | .01 |
| (Leaping over other players, Colts uniform) | | | |
| ☐ 387 Eric Dickerson | .10 | .05 | .01 |
| (Close-up) | | | |
| ☐ 388 Howie Long | .08 | .04 | .01 |
| (Being blocked by opponent) | | | |
| ☐ 389 Howie Long | .08 | .04 | .01 |
| (At Villanova) | | | |
| ☐ 390 Howie Long | .08 | .04 | .01 |
| (Rushing Quarterback) | | | |
| ☐ 391 Howie Long | .08 | .04 | .01 |
| (With family) | | | |
| ☐ 392 Howie Long | .08 | .04 | .01 |
| (Portrait by Chris Hopkins) | | | |
| ☐ 393 Howie Long | .08 | .04 | .01 |
| (On sidelines) | | | |
| ☐ 394 Howie Long | .08 | .04 | .01 |
| (Boxing) | | | |
| ☐ 395 Howie Long | .08 | .04 | .01 |
| (Blocking pass) | | | |
| ☐ 396 Howie Long | .08 | .04 | .01 |
| (Close-up) | | | |
| ☐ 397 Mike Singletary | .10 | .05 | .01 |
| (Crouched, ready for play) | | | |
| ☐ 398 Mike Singletary | .10 | .05 | .01 |
| (At Baylor) | | | |
| ☐ 399 Mike Singletary | .10 | .05 | .01 |
| (With children) | | | |
| ☐ 400 Mike Singletary | .10 | .05 | .01 |
| (In the gym) | | | |
| ☐ 401 Mike Singletary | .10 | .05 | .01 |
| (Portrait by Gary Kelley) | | | |
| ☐ 402 Mike Singletary | .10 | .05 | .01 |
| (Rushing, white jersey) | | | |
| ☐ 403 Mike Singletary | .10 | .05 | .01 |
| (With Man of the Year Award) | | | |
| ☐ 404 Mike Singletary | .10 | .05 | .01 |
| (Tackling, blue jersey) | | | |
| ☐ 405 Mike Singletary | .10 | .05 | .01 |
| (In sweatshirt) | | | |
| ☐ 406 John Taylor | .08 | .04 | .01 |
| (Celebrating on the field) | | | |
| ☐ 407 John Taylor | .08 | .04 | .01 |
| (In high school) | | | |
| ☐ 408 John Taylor | .08 | .04 | .01 |
| (Playing for Delaware State) | | | |
| ☐ 409 John Taylor | .08 | .04 | .01 |
| (Posed with bowling ball and pins) | | | |
| ☐ 410 John Taylor | .08 | .04 | .01 |
| (Portrait by John Collier) | | | |
| ☐ 411 John Taylor | .08 | .04 | .01 |
| (With family) | | | |
| ☐ 412 John Taylor | .08 | .04 | .01 |
| (With kids from Northern Light School) | | | |
| ☐ 413 John Taylor | .08 | .04 | .01 |
| (Catching) | | | |
| ☐ 414 John Taylor | .08 | .04 | .01 |
| (Close-up) | | | |
| ☐ 415 Andre Tippett | .04 | .02 | .01 |
| (Blocking opponent, arms outspred) | | | |

| | | | |
|---|---|---|---|
| ☐ 416 Andre Tippett | .04 | .02 | .01 |
| (At Iowa State) | | | |
| ☐ 417 Andre Tippett | .04 | .02 | .01 |
| (With daughter, Janea Lynn) | | | |
| ☐ 418 Andre Tippett | .04 | .02 | .01 |
| (In Okinawa with karate masters) | | | |
| ☐ 419 Andre Tippett | .04 | .02 | .01 |
| (Portrait by Gary Kelley) | | | |
| ☐ 420 Andre Tippett | .04 | .02 | .01 |
| (Running on the field) | | | |
| ☐ 421 Andre Tippett | .04 | .02 | .01 |
| (Performing karate move) | | | |
| ☐ 422 Andre Tippett | .04 | .02 | .01 |
| (In action, from knees up) | | | |
| ☐ 423 Andre Tippett | .04 | .02 | .01 |
| (Close-up) | | | |
| ☐ 424 Jim Kelly | .20 | .09 | .03 |
| (Passing, white jersey) | | | |
| ☐ 425 Jim Kelly | .20 | .09 | .03 |
| (With Punt, Pass, and Kick trophy) | | | |
| ☐ 426 Jim Kelly | .20 | .09 | .03 |
| (Passing for Miami) | | | |
| ☐ 427 Jim Kelly | .20 | .09 | .03 |
| (With family) | | | |
| ☐ 428 Jim Kelly | .20 | .09 | .03 |
| (Portrait by Greg Spalenka) | | | |
| ☐ 429 Jim Kelly | .20 | .09 | .03 |
| (With sports jersey collection) | | | |
| ☐ 430 Jim Kelly | .20 | .09 | .03 |
| (With young cancer patients) | | | |
| ☐ 431 Jim Kelly | .20 | .09 | .03 |
| (Calling play) | | | |
| ☐ 432 Jim Kelly | .20 | .09 | .03 |
| (Close-up) | | | |
| ☐ 433 Mark Rypien | .08 | .04 | .01 |
| (Passing, horizontal shot) | | | |
| ☐ 434 Mark Rypien | .08 | .04 | .01 |
| (In high school football uniform) | | | |
| ☐ 435 Mark Rypien | .08 | .04 | .01 |
| (At Washington State) | | | |
| ☐ 436 Mark Rypien | .08 | .04 | .01 |
| (Playing golf) | | | |
| ☐ 437 Mark Rypien | .08 | .04 | .01 |
| (Portrait by Merv Corning) | | | |
| ☐ 438 Mark Rypien | .08 | .04 | .01 |
| (With family) | | | |
| ☐ 439 Mark Rypien | .08 | .04 | .01 |
| (Passing, vertical shot) | | | |
| ☐ 440 Mark Rypien | .08 | .04 | .01 |
| (With young cystic fibrosis patients) | | | |
| ☐ 441 Mark Rypien | .08 | .04 | .01 |
| (Close-up) | | | |
| ☐ 442 Warren Moon | .15 | .07 | .02 |
| (Passing, white jersey) | | | |
| ☐ 443 Warren Moon | .15 | .07 | .02 |
| (As youth, in football uniform) | | | |
| ☐ 444 Warren Moon | .15 | .07 | .02 |
| (Playing for Washington) | | | |
| ☐ 445 Warren Moon | .15 | .07 | .02 |
| (With Edmonton Eskimos) | | | |
| ☐ 446 Warren Moon | .15 | .07 | .02 |
| (Portrait by Greg Spalenka) | | | |
| ☐ 447 Warren Moon | .15 | .07 | .02 |
| (With family) | | | |
| ☐ 448 Warren Moon | .15 | .07 | .02 |
| (Calling the play) | | | |
| ☐ 449 Warren Moon | .15 | .07 | .02 |
| (In his office) | | | |
| ☐ 450 Warren Moon | .15 | .07 | .02 |
| (Posed with football and helmet) | | | |
| ☐ 451 Deion Sanders | .10 | .05 | .01 |
| (In position for a play) | | | |
| ☐ 452 Deion Sanders | .10 | .05 | .01 |
| (As youth, in football uniform) | | | |
| ☐ 453 Deion Sanders | .10 | .05 | .01 |
| (With Florida State) | | | |
| ☐ 454 Deion Sanders | .10 | .05 | .01 |
| (Playing baseball) | | | |
| ☐ 455 Deion Sanders | .10 | .05 | .01 |
| (Portrait by Gary Kelley) | | | |
| ☐ 456 Deion Sanders | .10 | .05 | .01 |
| (Running with ball) | | | |
| ☐ 457 Deion Sanders | .10 | .05 | .01 |
| (With family) | | | |
| ☐ 458 Deion Sanders | .10 | .05 | .01 |
| (Walking on field) | | | |
| ☐ 459 Deion Sanders | .10 | .05 | .01 |
| (Close-up) | | | |
| ☐ 460 Lawrence Taylor | .10 | .05 | .01 |
| (Facing opponent, blue jersey) | | | |
| ☐ 461 Lawrence Taylor | .10 | .05 | .01 |
| (At North Carolina State) | | | |
| ☐ 462 Lawrence Taylor | .10 | .05 | .01 |
| (Side view, white jersey) | | | |
| ☐ 463 Lawrence Taylor | .10 | .05 | .01 |
| (Playing golf on football field) | | | |
| ☐ 464 Lawrence Taylor | .10 | .05 | .01 |
| (Portrait by Chris Hopkins) | | | |
| ☐ 465 Lawrence Taylor | .10 | .05 | .01 |
| (In Honolulu) | | | |
| ☐ 466 Lawrence Taylor | .10 | .05 | .01 |
| (In front of his restaurant) | | | |
| ☐ 467 Lawrence Taylor | .10 | .05 | .01 |
| (Stepping over Jets player) | | | |
| ☐ 468 Lawrence Taylor | .10 | .05 | .01 |
| (Close-up) | | | |
| ☐ 469 Randall Cunningham | .10 | .05 | .01 |
| (Looking for receiver) | | | |
| ☐ 470 Randall Cunningham | .10 | .05 | .01 |
| (In Pop Warner team uniform) | | | |
| ☐ 471 Randall Cunningham | .10 | .05 | .01 |
| (Playing for UNLV) | | | |
| ☐ 472 Randall Cunningham | .10 | .05 | .01 |
| (Running with ball) | | | |
| ☐ 473 Randall Cunningham | .10 | .05 | .01 |
| (Portrait by Greg Spalenka) | | | |
| ☐ 474 Randall Cunningham | .10 | .05 | .01 |
| (Playing golf) | | | |
| ☐ 475 Randall Cunningham | .10 | .05 | .01 |
| (Passing) | | | |
| ☐ 476 Randall Cunningham | .10 | .05 | .01 |
| (Working out) | | | |
| ☐ 477 Randall Cunningham | .10 | .05 | .01 |
| (In dress attire) | | | |
| ☐ 478 Earnest Byner | .08 | .04 | .01 |
| (Redskins uniform, running, side view) | | | |
| ☐ 479 Earnest Byner | .08 | .04 | .01 |
| (At East Carolina, black and white) | | | |
| ☐ 480 Earnest Byner | .08 | .04 | .01 |
| (Browns, brown jersey) | | | |
| ☐ 481 Earnest Byner | .08 | .04 | .01 |
| (With family) | | | |
| ☐ 482 Earnest Byner | .08 | .04 | .01 |
| (Portrait by Chris Hopkins) | | | |
| ☐ 483 Earnest Byner | .08 | .04 | .01 |
| (Browns, white jersey) | | | |
| ☐ 484 Earnest Byner | .08 | .04 | .01 |
| (Fishing) | | | |
| ☐ 485 Earnest Byner | .08 | .04 | .01 |
| (Redskins uniform, running, front view) | | | |
| ☐ 486 Earnest Byner | .08 | .04 | .01 |
| (In workout attire) | | | |
| ☐ 487 Mike Ditka CO | .10 | .05 | .01 |
| (On sideline, in shirt and tie) | | | |
| ☐ 488 Mike Ditka CO | .10 | .05 | .01 |
| (Playing for Bears) | | | |
| ☐ 489 Mike Ditka CO | .10 | .05 | .01 |
| (With family) | | | |
| ☐ 490 Mike Ditka CO | .10 | .05 | .01 |
| (Playing for Cowboys) | | | |
| ☐ 491 Mike Ditka CO | .10 | .05 | .01 |
| (Portrait by | | | |

Garry Kelley)

| | MINT | EXC | G-VG |
|---|---|---|---|
| ☐ 492 Mike Ditka CO | .10 | .05 | .01 |
| (With antique car) | | | |
| ☐ 493 Mike Ditka CO | .10 | .05 | .01 |
| (Playing golf) | | | |
| ☐ 494 Mike Ditka CO | .10 | .05 | .01 |
| (Eating) | | | |
| ☐ 495 Mike Ditka CO | .10 | .05 | .01 |
| (Close-up) | | | |
| ☐ 496 Art Monk | .75 | .35 | .09 |
| (Catching, close-up) | | | |
| ☐ 497 Art Monk | .75 | .35 | .09 |
| (Running hurdles in high school) | | | |
| ☐ 498 Art Monk | .75 | .35 | .09 |
| (Running with ball, front view) | | | |
| ☐ 499 Art Monk | .75 | .35 | .09 |
| (With family) | | | |
| ☐ 500 Art Monk | .75 | .35 | .09 |
| (Portrait by Gary Kelley) | | | |
| ☐ 501 Art Monk | .75 | .35 | .09 |
| (With youth at his football camp) | | | |
| ☐ 502 Art Monk | .75 | .35 | .09 |
| (Running with ball, side view) | | | |
| ☐ 503 Art Monk | .75 | .35 | .09 |
| (Working out) | | | |
| ☐ 504 Art Monk | .75 | .35 | .09 |
| (Ready to catch ball, hands extended) | | | |
| ☐ NNO Art Monk Pro Line Collection Bonus Set (Title Card) | .75 | .35 | .09 |

## 1992 ProLine Profile Autographs

These inserts parallel the regular Profiles set. The 1992 ProLine autographs were randomly inserted in 1992 ProLine foil (not jumbo) packs at the rate of approximately one per box. Like the Portrait autographs, these cards are signed in black Sharpie, embossed with an NFL,seal and are missing the card number to distinguish them from regular cards. The Art Monk autographs (496-504) were sent to the earliest respondents to the wrapper mail-in offer. They are not considered part of the complete set. The card numbers were not removed from the Art Monk autographs. The prices below refer to all autograph cards from the subset. However, certain types of Profile autographs are more popular than others. Cards showing the player in NFL action or in the uniform of a popular college sometimes bring a 25 to 50 percent premium above the prices listed below. The following cards are not known to exist in signed form: 46-49, 56, 58, 76, 154-162, 334-342, 356, 376, 383, 433-441, 457-459, 504. Card 2 was not signed by Ronnie Lott but by his wife Karen.

| | MINT | EXC | G-VG |
|---|---|---|---|
| COMPLETE SET (457) | 4000.00 | 1800.00 | 500.00 |
| RONNIE LOTT (1-9) | 10.00 | 4.50 | 1.25 |
| RODNEY PEETE (10-18) | 6.00 | 2.70 | .75 |
| CARL BANKS (19-27) | 6.00 | 2.70 | .75 |
| THURMAN THOMAS (28-36) | 25.00 | 11.50 | 3.10 |
| ROGER STAUBACH (37-45) | 25.00 | 11.50 | 3.10 |
| JERRY RICE (46-54) | 40.00 | 18.00 | 5.00 |
| VINNY TESTAVERDE (55-63) | 6.00 | 2.70 | .75 |
| ANTHONY CARTER (64-72) | 6.00 | 2.70 | .75 |
| STERLING SHARPE (73-81) | 20.00 | 9.00 | 2.50 |
| ANTHONY MUNOZ (82-90) | 8.00 | 3.60 | 1.00 |
| BUBBY BRISTER (91-99) | 6.00 | 2.70 | .75 |
| BERNIE KOSAR (100-108) | 10.00 | 4.50 | 1.25 |
| ART SHELL (109-117) | 10.00 | 4.50 | 1.25 |
| DON SHULA (118-126) | 25.00 | 11.50 | 3.10 |
| JOE GIBBS (127-135) | 8.00 | 3.60 | 1.00 |
| JUNIOR SEAU (136-144) | 8.00 | 3.60 | 1.00 |
| AL TOON (145-153) | 6.00 | 2.70 | .75 |
| JACK KEMP (154-162) | .00 | .00 | .00 |
| JIM HARBAUGH (163-171) | 8.00 | 3.60 | 1.00 |
| DAN MCGWIRE (172-180) | 8.00 | 3.60 | 1.00 |
| TROY AIKMAN (181-189) | 50.00 | 23.00 | 6.25 |
| KEITH BYARS (190-198) | 6.00 | 2.70 | .75 |
| TIMM ROSENBACH (199-207) | 10.00 | 4.50 | 1.25 |
| GARY CLARK (208-216) | 8.00 | 3.60 | 1.00 |
| CHRIS DOLEMAN (217-225) | 6.00 | 2.70 | .75 |
| JOHN ELWAY (226-234) | 25.00 | 11.50 | 3.10 |
| BOOMER ESIASON (235-243) | 10.00 | 4.50 | 1.25 |
| JIM EVERETT (244-252) | 30.00 | 13.50 | 3.80 |
| ERIC GREEN (253-261) | 8.00 | 3.60 | 1.00 |
| JERRY GLANVILLE (262-270) | 6.00 | 2.70 | .75 |
| JEFF HOSTETLER (271-279) | 8.00 | 3.60 | 1.00 |
| HAYWOOD JEFFIRES (280-288) | 10.00 | 4.50 | 1.25 |
| MICHAEL IRVIN (289-297) | 40.00 | 18.00 | 5.00 |
| STEVE LARGENT (298-306) | 20.00 | 9.00 | 2.50 |
| KEN O'BRIEN (307-315) | 6.00 | 2.70 | .75 |
| CHRISTIAN OKOYE (316-324) | 6.00 | 2.70 | .75 |
| MICHAEL D. PERRY (325-333) | 6.00 | 2.70 | .75 |
| CHRIS MILLER (334-342) | .00 | .00 | .00 |
| PHIL SIMMS (343-351) | 20.00 | 9.00 | 2.50 |
| BRUCE SMITH (352-360) | 15.00 | 6.75 | 1.90 |
| DERRICK THOMAS (361-369) | 15.00 | 6.75 | 1.90 |
| PAT SWILLING (370-378) | 8.00 | 3.60 | 1.00 |
| ERIC DICKERSON (379-387) | 20.00 | 9.00 | 2.50 |
| HOWIE LONG (388-396) | 8.00 | 3.60 | 1.00 |
| MIKE SINGLETARY (397-405) | 12.00 | 5.50 | 1.50 |
| JOHN TAYLOR (406-414) | 10.00 | 4.50 | 1.25 |
| ANDRE TIPPETT (415-423) | 6.00 | 2.70 | .75 |
| JIM KELLY (424-432) | 25.00 | 11.50 | 3.10 |
| MARK RYPIEN (433-441) | .00 | .00 | .00 |
| WARREN MOON (442-450) | 20.00 | 9.00 | 2.50 |
| DEION SANDERS (451-459) | 75.00 | 34.00 | 9.50 |
| LAWRENCE TAYLOR (460-468) | 15.00 | 6.75 | 1.90 |
| RANDALL CUNNING. (469-477) | 20.00 | 9.00 | 2.50 |
| EARNEST BYNER (478-486) | 6.00 | 2.70 | .75 |
| MIKE DITKA (487-495) | 12.00 | 5.50 | 1.50 |
| ART MONK (496-504) | 50.00 | 23.00 | 6.25 |

## 1992 ProLine Mobil

Produced by NFL Properties, this 72-card regionally distributed set consists of 1991 Portraits (1-9) and 1992 Profiles (10-72) cards. The set was part of an eight-week promotion in Southern California. Each week a nine-card pack could be obtained by purchasing at least eight gallons of Mobil Super Unleaded Plus. The nine cards available the first week were a title card, a checklist, and seven Portrait cards which have printed on their fronts the dates that nine-card packs of that player would be available. During the following seven weeks, one player was featured per week in the packs. All the cards measure the standard size (2 1/2" by 3 1/2") and carry full-bleed posed and action color player/family photos. The ProLine logo is at the bottom. The backs feature player information with the Mobil logo at the bottom. Card number 9 picturing Eric Dickerson in a Raiders' uniform is exclusive to the set. The cards are numbered on the back "X of 9" and arranged below chronologically according to the eight-week promotion. The week the cards were available is listed under the first card of the nine-card cello pack. Each nine-card cello pack included an unperforated sheet with four coupon offers.

| | MINT | EXC | G-VG |
|---|---|---|---|
| COMPLETE SET (72) | 8.00 | 3.25 | .80 |
| COMMON PLAYER (1-72) | .10 | .04 | .01 |
| ☐ 1 Title Card | .10 | .04 | .01 |
| (October 3-9) | | | |
| ☐ 2 Checklist | .10 | .04 | .01 |
| ☐ 3 Ronnie Lott | .20 | .08 | .02 |
| Los Angeles Raiders | | | |
| ☐ 4 Junior Seau | .30 | .12 | .03 |
| San Diego Chargers | | | |
| ☐ 5 Jim Everett | .15 | .06 | .01 |
| Los Angeles Rams | | | |
| ☐ 6 Howie Long | .15 | .06 | .01 |
| Los Angeles Raiders | | | |
| ☐ 7 Jerry Rice | .75 | .30 | .07 |
| San Francisco 49ers | | | |
| ☐ 8 Art Shell CO | .15 | .06 | .01 |
| Los Angeles Raiders | | | |
| ☐ 9 Eric Dickerson | .50 | .20 | .05 |
| Los Angeles Raiders | | | |
| ☐ 10 Ronnie Lott | .15 | .06 | .01 |
| (October 10-16) | | | |
| (Making Hit) | | | |
| ☐ 11 Ronnie Lott | .15 | .06 | .01 |
| (Little Leaguer) | | | |
| ☐ 12 Ronnie Lott | .15 | .06 | .01 |
| (Playing for USC) | | | |
| ☐ 13 Ronnie Lott | .15 | .06 | .01 |
| (Exultation) | | | |
| ☐ 14 Ronnie Lott | .15 | .06 | .01 |

| | | | |
|---|---|---|---|
| (Portrait) | | | |
| ☐ 15 Ronnie Lott | .15 | .06 | .01 |
| (Behind Bar) | | | |
| ☐ 16 Ronnie Lott | .15 | .06 | .01 |
| (With Family) | | | |
| ☐ 17 Ronnie Lott | .15 | .06 | .01 |
| (Catching Ball) | | | |
| ☐ 18 Ronnie Lott | .15 | .06 | .01 |
| (Tuxedo) | | | |
| ☐ 19 Junior Seau | .15 | .06 | .01 |
| (October 17-23) | | | |
| (With Ball) | | | |
| ☐ 20 Junior Seau | .15 | .06 | .01 |
| (Young Junior) | | | |
| ☐ 21 Junior Seau | .15 | .06 | .01 |
| (Pointing) | | | |
| ☐ 22 Junior Seau | .15 | .06 | .01 |
| (Over Fallen Opponent) | | | |
| ☐ 23 Junior Seau | .15 | .06 | .01 |
| (Portrait) | | | |
| ☐ 24 Junior Seau | .15 | .06 | .01 |
| (With Wife) | | | |
| ☐ 25 Junior Seau | .15 | .06 | .01 |
| (Running in Surf) | | | |
| ☐ 26 Junior Seau | .15 | .06 | .01 |
| (Weightlifting) | | | |
| ☐ 27 Junior Seau | .15 | .06 | .01 |
| (Seaweed Boa) | | | |
| ☐ 28 Jim Everett | .10 | .04 | .01 |
| (October 24-30) | | | |
| (Looking for Receiver) | | | |
| ☐ 29 Jim Everett | .10 | .04 | .01 |
| (Young Jim) | | | |
| ☐ 30 Jim Everett | .10 | .04 | .01 |
| (Playing for Purdue) | | | |
| ☐ 31 Jim Everett | .10 | .04 | .01 |
| (With Parents, Sister) | | | |
| ☐ 32 Jim Everett | .10 | .04 | .01 |
| (Portrait) | | | |
| ☐ 33 Jim Everett | .10 | .04 | .01 |
| (Eluding Rush) | | | |
| ☐ 34 Jim Everett | .10 | .04 | .01 |
| (Fishing) | | | |
| ☐ 35 Jim Everett | .10 | .04 | .01 |
| (Handing Off) | | | |
| ☐ 36 Jim Everett | .10 | .04 | .01 |
| (Studio Photo) | | | |
| ☐ 37 Howie Long | .10 | .04 | .01 |
| (October 31-November 6) | | | |
| (Hand Up to Block Pass) | | | |
| ☐ 38 Howie Long | .10 | .04 | .01 |
| (High School Footballer) | | | |
| ☐ 39 Howie Long | .10 | .04 | .01 |
| (Closing in for Sack) | | | |
| ☐ 40 Howie Long | .10 | .04 | .01 |
| (With Family) | | | |
| ☐ 41 Howie Long | .10 | .04 | .01 |
| (Portrait) | | | |
| ☐ 42 Howie Long | .10 | .04 | .01 |
| (Fundraising for Kids) | | | |
| ☐ 43 Howie Long | .10 | .04 | .01 |
| (Hitting the Heavy Bag) | | | |
| ☐ 44 Howie Long | .10 | .04 | .01 |
| (Taking Swipe at Ball) | | | |
| ☐ 45 Howie Long | .10 | .04 | .01 |
| (Studio Photo) | | | |
| ☐ 46 Jerry Rice | .40 | .16 | .04 |
| (November 7-13) | | | |
| (With Trophy) | | | |
| ☐ 47 Jerry Rice | .40 | .16 | .04 |
| (Avoiding Block) | | | |
| ☐ 48 Jerry Rice | .40 | .16 | .04 |
| (Eluding Steeler) | | | |
| ☐ 49 Jerry Rice | .40 | .16 | .04 |
| (With Family) | | | |
| ☐ 50 Jerry Rice | .40 | .16 | .04 |
| (Portrait) | | | |
| ☐ 51 Jerry Rice | .40 | .16 | .04 |
| (With Toddler) | | | |
| ☐ 52 Jerry Rice | .40 | .16 | .04 |
| (Playing Tennis) | | | |
| ☐ 53 Jerry Rice | .40 | .16 | .04 |
| (Scoring TD) | | | |
| ☐ 54 Jerry Rice | .40 | .16 | .04 |
| (Studio Photo) | | | |
| ☐ 55 Art Shell CO | .15 | .06 | .01 |
| (November 14-20) | | | |
| (In Front of His Team) | | | |
| ☐ 56 Art Shell CO | .15 | .06 | .01 |
| (At Maryland State) | | | |
| ☐ 57 Art Shell CO | .15 | .06 | .01 |
| (Blocking Viking) | | | |
| ☐ 58 Art Shell CO | .15 | .06 | .01 |
| (Playing Basketball) | | | |
| ☐ 59 Art Shell CO | .15 | .06 | .01 |
| (Portrait) | | | |
| ☐ 60 Art Shell CO | .15 | .06 | .01 |
| (Talking to Player) | | | |
| ☐ 61 Art Shell CO | .15 | .06 | .01 |
| (In Front of TV) | | | |
| ☐ 62 Art Shell CO | .15 | .06 | .01 |
| (Blocking for Raiders) | | | |
| ☐ 63 Art Shell CO | .15 | .06 | .01 |
| (With Teddy Bear) | | | |
| ☐ 64 Eric Dickerson | .20 | .08 | .02 |
| (November 21-30) | | | |
| (Studio Suit Up) | | | |
| ☐ 65 Eric Dickerson | .20 | .08 | .02 |
| (Running for SMU) | | | |
| ☐ 66 Eric Dickerson | .20 | .08 | .02 |
| (With Mom) | | | |
| ☐ 67 Eric Dickerson | .20 | .08 | .02 |
| (49ers in Pursuit) | | | |
| ☐ 68 Eric Dickerson | .20 | .08 | .02 |
| (Portrait) | | | |
| ☐ 69 Eric Dickerson | .20 | .08 | .02 |
| (Running for Colts) | | | |
| ☐ 70 Eric Dickerson | .20 | .08 | .02 |
| (On Training Ramp) | | | |
| ☐ 71 Eric Dickerson | .20 | .08 | .02 |
| (Running Against Rams) | | | |
| ☐ 72 Eric Dickerson | .20 | .08 | .02 |
| (Posed With Football) | | | |

## 1992-93 ProLine SB Program

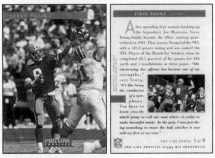

This nine-card standard-size (2 1/2" by 3 1/2") set features Steve Young. One Steve Young promo card was inserted in each copy of the 1993 Super Bowl program. The fronts display full-bleed glossy color photos that capture Young both on and off the field. In text printed around a small color picture, the backs discuss chapters in Young's career and life and carry Young's comments as well. The cards are numbered on the back "X of 9."

| | MINT | EXC | G-VG |
|---|---|---|---|
| COMPLETE SET (9) | 7.50 | 3.00 | .75 |
| COMMON PLAYER (1-9) | 1.25 | .50 | .12 |
| ☐ 1 Steve Young | 1.25 | .50 | .12 |
| (Just after release of ball) | | | |
| ☐ 2 Steve Young | 1.25 | .50 | .12 |
| (Posed beside statute of Brigham Young) | | | |
| ☐ 3 Steve Young | 1.25 | .50 | .12 |
| (In BYU uniform) | | | |
| ☐ 4 Steve Young | 1.25 | .50 | .12 |
| (In Los Angeles Express uniform USFL) | | | |
| ☐ 5 Steve Young | 1.25 | .50 | .12 |
| (Portrait) | | | |
| ☐ 6 Steve Young | 1.25 | .50 | .12 |
| (In Tampa Bay Buccaneers uniform) | | | |
| ☐ 7 Steve Young | 1.25 | .50 | .12 |
| (Posed with children for the Children's Miracle Network) | | | |
| ☐ 8 Steve Young | 1.25 | .50 | .12 |
| (In San Francisco 49ers uniform) | | | |
| ☐ 9 Steve Young | 1.25 | .50 | .12 |
| (Close-up shot; posed in law library) | | | |

## 1993 ProLine Live Draft Day NYC

Packaged in a cello pack, this set of ten cards was passed out at the NFL Draft held April 25th in New York. The standard-size (2 1/2" by 3 1/2") cards were created in anticipation of the draft, thus portraying the featured players with several possible teams, and to preview the

1993 Classic NFL ProLine card design. The full-bleed color player photos on the fronts are accented on the right by a team color-coded stripe that carries the player's name and team name. The "Classic ProLine Live" and "NFL Draft 1993" logos at the lower corners round out the card face. Above a team color-coded panel presenting biography, statistics, and career highlights, the backs display a full-bleed color close-up photo. All the cards are numbered "1" on the back and are checklisted below alphabetically according to player's last name. Suffixes have been added in order to differentiate specific cards. Reportedly about 1,000 sets were distributed at the NFL Draft in New York City.

| | MINT | EXC | G-VG |
|---|---|---|---|
| COMPLETE SET (10)........................ | 120.00 | 50.00 | 12.00 |
| COMMON PLAYER (1A-1J)............... | 5.00 | 2.00 | .50 |
| ☐ 1A Drew Bledsoe.......................... | 20.00 | 8.00 | 2.00 |
|    New England Patriots | | | |
| ☐ 1B Drew Bledsoe.......................... | 20.00 | 8.00 | 2.00 |
|    Kansas City Chiefs | | | |
| ☐ 1C Drew Bledsoe.......................... | 20.00 | 8.00 | 2.00 |
|    Seattle Seahawks | | | |
| ☐ 1D Eric Curry.............................. | 5.00 | 2.00 | .50 |
|    Phoenix Cardinals | | | |
| ☐ 1E Eric Curry.............................. | 5.00 | 2.00 | .50 |
|    New England Patriots | | | |
| ☐ 1F Marvin Jones.......................... | 5.00 | 2.00 | .50 |
|    New York Jets | | | |
| ☐ 1G Marvin Jones.......................... | 5.00 | 2.00 | .50 |
|    New England Patriots | | | |
| ☐ 1H Rick Mirer.............................. | 20.00 | 8.00 | 2.00 |
|    Seattle Seahawks | | | |
| ☐ 1I Rick Mirer.............................. | 20.00 | 8.00 | 2.00 |
|    New England Patriots | | | |
| ☐ 1J Rick Mirer.............................. | 20.00 | 8.00 | 2.00 |
|    San Francisco 49ers | | | |

## 1993 ProLine Live Draft Day QVC

Packaged in a cello pack, this set of ten cards has the same fronts as the set passed out at the NFL Draft held April 25th in New York. The standard-size (2 1/2" by 3 1/2") cards were created in anticipation of the draft, thus portraying the featured players with several possible teams, and to preview the 1993 Classic NFL ProLine card design. The full-bleed color player photos on the fronts are accented on the right by a team color-coded stripe that carries the player's name and team name. The "Classic ProLine Live" and "NFL Draft 1993" logos at the lower corners round out the card face. On a white, screened back with "1993 Draft Day" in gray lettering, the QVC-version's back has an oversized version of the Classic ProLine Live logo with black lettering immediately below. Reportedly only 9,300 sets with this special back were produced for sale through QVC.

| | MINT | EXC | G-VG |
|---|---|---|---|
| COMPLETE SET (10)........................ | 20.00 | 8.00 | 2.00 |
| COMMON PLAYER (1A-1J)............... | 1.00 | .40 | .10 |
| ☐ 1A Drew Bledsoe.......................... | 3.50 | 1.40 | .35 |
|    New England Patriots | | | |
| ☐ 1B Drew Bledsoe.......................... | 3.50 | 1.40 | .35 |
|    Kansas City Chiefs | | | |
| ☐ 1C Drew Bledsoe.......................... | 3.50 | 1.40 | .35 |
|    Seattle Seahawks | | | |
| ☐ 1D Eric Curry.............................. | 1.00 | .40 | .10 |
|    Phoenix Cardinals | | | |
| ☐ 1E Eric Curry.............................. | 1.00 | .40 | .10 |
|    New England Patriots | | | |
| ☐ 1F Marvin Jones.......................... | 1.00 | .40 | .10 |
|    New York Jets | | | |
| ☐ 1G Marvin Jones.......................... | 1.00 | .40 | .10 |
|    New England Patriots | | | |
| ☐ 1H Rick Mirer.............................. | 3.50 | 1.40 | .35 |
|    Seattle Seahawks | | | |
| ☐ 1I Rick Mirer.............................. | 3.50 | 1.40 | .35 |
|    New England Patriots | | | |
| ☐ 1J Rick Mirer.............................. | 3.50 | 1.40 | .35 |
|    San Francisco 49ers | | | |

## 1993 ProLine Live Promo

This standard-size (2 1/2" by 3 1/2") card was issued to preview the design of Classic's 1993 Pro Line Live series. The front features a full-bleed color action photo that are bordered on the right by a silver stripe that carries the player's name and team name. The top portion of the back has a second color action photo, while the bottom portion consists of a silver panel overprinted with player information. This promo card can be distinguished from the regular card by the disclaimer "For Promotional Purposes Only" printed on the back.

| | MINT | EXC | G-VG |
|---|---|---|---|
| COMPLETE SET (1)........................ | 5.00 | 2.00 | .50 |
| COMMON PLAYER........................ | 5.00 | 2.00 | .50 |
| ☐ 1 Troy Aikman.............................. | 5.00 | 2.00 | .50 |
|    Dallas Cowboys | | | |

## 1993 ProLine Live

The 1993 premier edition of the Classic Pro Line Collection consists of 285 Classic Pro Line Live cards, 48 Portraits, and thirteen nine-card Profiles. Just 20,000 sequentially numbered ten-box cases were produced. Randomly inserted on an average of two per case were over 40,000 autograph cards, signed by Troy Aikman, Thurman Thomas, Sterling Sharpe, Ronnie Lott, Derrick Thomas, Rodney Hampton, and more. Also randomly inserted were '93 classic basketball draft pick preview cards and a 20-card limited printed foil-stamped insert set. The fronts feature full-bleed color action photos that are bordered on the right by a team color-coded stripe that carries the player's name and team name. The top portion of the back has a second color action photo, while the bottom portion consists of a team color-coded panel overprinted with player information. The cards are numbered on the back and checklisted below alphabetically according to teams as follows: Atlanta Falcons (1-10), Buffalo Bills (11-22), Chicago Bears (23-31), Cincinnati Bengals (32-40), Cleveland Browns (41-50), Dallas Cowboys (51-65), Denver Broncos (66-75), Detroit Lions (76-85), Green Bay Packers (86-95), Houston Oilers (96-105), Indianapolis Colts (106-115), Kansas City Chiefs (116-124), Los Angeles Raiders (125-135), Los Angeles Rams (136-144), Miami Dolphins (145-156), Minnesota Vikings (157-166), New England Patriots (167-175), New Orleans Saints (176-185), New York Giants (186-195), New York Jets (196-205), Philadelphia Eagles (206-215), Phoenix Cardinals (216-224), Pittsburgh Steelers (225-234), San Diego Chargers (235-244), San Francisco 49ers (245-254), Seattle Seahawks (255-264), Tampa Bay Buccaneers (265-274), and Washington Redskins (275-285). Rookie Cards include Jerome Bettis, Drew Bledsoe, Reggie Brooks, Garrison Hearst, Billy Joe Hobert, Terry Kirby, O.J. McDuffie, Natrone Means, Glyn Milburn, Rick Mirer, Robert Smith and Kevin Williams.

| | MINT | EXC | G-VG |
|---|---|---|---|
| COMPLETE SET (285) | 15.00 | 6.75 | 1.90 |
| COMMON PLAYER (1-285) | .04 | .02 | .01 |
| ☐ 1 Michael Haynes | .20 | .09 | .03 |
| ☐ 2 Chris Hinton | .04 | .02 | .01 |
| ☐ 3 Pierce Holt | .04 | .02 | .01 |
| ☐ 4 Chris Miller | .08 | .04 | .01 |
| ☐ 5 Mike Pritchard | .08 | .04 | .01 |
| ☐ 6 Andre Rison | .25 | .11 | .03 |
| ☐ 7 Deion Sanders | .15 | .07 | .02 |
| ☐ 8 Jessie Tuggle | .04 | .02 | .01 |
| ☐ 9 Lincoln Kennedy | .15 | .07 | .02 |
| ☐ 10 Roger Harper | .15 | .07 | .02 |
| ☐ 11 Cornelius Bennett | .08 | .04 | .01 |
| ☐ 12 Henry Jones | .04 | .02 | .01 |
| ☐ 13 Jim Kelly | .25 | .11 | .03 |
| ☐ 14 Bill Brooks | .06 | .03 | .01 |
| ☐ 15 Nate Odomes | .06 | .03 | .01 |
| ☐ 16 Andre Reed | .08 | .04 | .01 |
| ☐ 17 Frank Reich | .06 | .03 | .01 |
| ☐ 18 Bruce Smith | .08 | .04 | .01 |
| ☐ 19 Steve Tasker | .04 | .02 | .01 |
| ☐ 20 Thurman Thomas | .35 | .16 | .04 |
| ☐ 21 Thomas Smith | .10 | .05 | .01 |
| ☐ 22 John Parrella | .10 | .05 | .01 |
| ☐ 23 Neal Anderson | .06 | .03 | .01 |
| ☐ 24 Mark Carrier USC | .06 | .03 | .01 |
| ☐ 25 Jim Harbaugh | .06 | .03 | .01 |
| ☐ 26 Darren Lewis | .06 | .03 | .01 |
| ☐ 27 Steve McMichael | .04 | .02 | .01 |
| ☐ 28 Alonzo Spellman | .06 | .03 | .01 |
| ☐ 29 Tom Waddle | .08 | .04 | .01 |
| ☐ 30 Curtis Conway | .50 | .23 | .06 |
| ☐ 31 Carl Simpson | .10 | .05 | .01 |
| ☐ 32 David Fulcher | .04 | .02 | .01 |
| ☐ 33 Harold Green | .06 | .03 | .01 |
| ☐ 34 David Klingler | .15 | .07 | .02 |
| ☐ 35 Tim Krumrie | .04 | .02 | .01 |
| ☐ 36 Carl Pickens | .10 | .05 | .01 |
| ☐ 37 Alfred Williams | .04 | .02 | .01 |
| ☐ 38 Darryl Williams | .06 | .03 | .01 |
| ☐ 39 John Copeland | .25 | .11 | .03 |
| ☐ 40 Tony McGee | .20 | .09 | .03 |
| ☐ 41 Bernie Kosar | .08 | .04 | .01 |
| ☐ 42 Kevin Mack | .06 | .03 | .01 |
| ☐ 43 Clay Matthews | .06 | .03 | .01 |
| ☐ 44 Eric Metcalf | .08 | .04 | .01 |
| ☐ 45 Michael Dean Perry | .08 | .04 | .01 |
| ☐ 46 Vinny Testaverde | .08 | .04 | .01 |
| ☐ 47 Jerry Ball | .04 | .02 | .01 |
| ☐ 48 Tommy Vardell | .06 | .03 | .01 |
| ☐ 49 Steve Everitt | .10 | .05 | .01 |
| ☐ 50 Dan Footman | .15 | .07 | .02 |
| ☐ 51 Troy Aikman | 1.25 | .55 | .16 |
| ☐ 52 Daryl Johnston | .08 | .04 | .01 |
| ☐ 53 Tony Casillas | .04 | .02 | .01 |
| ☐ 54 Charles Haley | .06 | .03 | .01 |
| ☐ 55 Alvin Harper | .25 | .11 | .03 |
| ☐ 56 Michael Irvin | .40 | .18 | .05 |
| ☐ 57 Robert Jones | .04 | .02 | .01 |
| ☐ 58 Russell Maryland | .08 | .04 | .01 |
| ☐ 59 Nate Newton | .04 | .02 | .01 |
| ☐ 60 Ken Norton Jr. | .06 | .03 | .01 |
| ☐ 61 Jay Novacek | .08 | .04 | .01 |
| ☐ 62 Emmitt Smith | 2.00 | .90 | .25 |
| ☐ 63 Kevin Smith | .06 | .03 | .01 |
| ☐ 64 Kevin Williams | .50 | .23 | .06 |
| ☐ 65 Darrin Smith | .30 | .14 | .04 |
| ☐ 66 Steve Atwater | .06 | .03 | .01 |
| ☐ 67 Rod Bernstine | .06 | .03 | .01 |
| ☐ 68 Mike Croel | .06 | .03 | .01 |
| ☐ 69 John Elway | .35 | .16 | .04 |
| ☐ 70 Tommy Maddox | .10 | .05 | .01 |
| ☐ 71 Karl Mecklenburg | .06 | .03 | .01 |
| ☐ 72 Shannon Sharpe | .20 | .09 | .03 |
| ☐ 73 Dennis Smith | .04 | .02 | .01 |
| ☐ 74 Dan Williams | .10 | .05 | .01 |
| ☐ 75 Glyn Milburn | .60 | .25 | .08 |
| ☐ 76 Pat Swilling | .06 | .03 | .01 |
| ☐ 77 Bennie Blades | .04 | .02 | .01 |
| ☐ 78 Herman Moore | .35 | .16 | .04 |
| ☐ 79 Rodney Peete | .06 | .03 | .01 |
| ☐ 80 Brett Perriman | .06 | .03 | .01 |
| ☐ 81 Barry Sanders | .75 | .35 | .09 |
| ☐ 82 Chris Spielman | .04 | .02 | .01 |
| ☐ 83 Andre Ware | .06 | .03 | .01 |
| ☐ 84 Ryan McNeil | .10 | .05 | .01 |
| ☐ 85 Antonio London | .10 | .05 | .01 |
| ☐ 86 Tony Bennett | .04 | .02 | .01 |
| ☐ 87 Terrell Buckley | .08 | .04 | .01 |
| ☐ 88 Brett Favre | .75 | .35 | .09 |
| ☐ 89 Brian Noble | .04 | .02 | .01 |
| ☐ 90 Ken O'Brien | .06 | .03 | .01 |
| ☐ 91 Sterling Sharpe | .40 | .18 | .05 |
| ☐ 92 Reggie White | .15 | .07 | .02 |
| ☐ 93 John Stephens | .04 | .02 | .01 |
| ☐ 94 Wayne Simmons | .12 | .05 | .02 |
| ☐ 95 George Teague | .20 | .09 | .03 |
| ☐ 96 Ray Childress | .04 | .02 | .01 |
| ☐ 97 Curtis Duncan | .06 | .03 | .01 |
| ☐ 98 Ernest Givins | .06 | .03 | .01 |
| ☐ 99 Haywood Jeffires | .08 | .04 | .01 |
| ☐ 100 Bubba McDowell | .04 | .02 | .01 |
| ☐ 101 Warren Moon | .15 | .07 | .02 |
| ☐ 102 Al Smith | .04 | .02 | .01 |
| ☐ 103 Lorenzo White | .06 | .03 | .01 |
| ☐ 104 Brad Hopkins | .10 | .05 | .01 |
| ☐ 105 Micheal Barrow | .04 | .02 | .01 |
| ☐ 106 Duane Bickett | .04 | .02 | .01 |
| ☐ 107 Quentin Coryatt | .08 | .04 | .01 |
| ☐ 108 Steve Emtman | .06 | .03 | .01 |
| ☐ 109 Jeff George | .15 | .07 | .02 |
| ☐ 110 Anthony Johnson | .04 | .02 | .01 |
| ☐ 111 Reggie Langhorne | .06 | .03 | .01 |
| ☐ 112 Jack Trudeau | .04 | .02 | .01 |
| ☐ 113 Clarence Verdin | .04 | .02 | .01 |
| ☐ 114 Jessie Hester | .04 | .02 | .01 |
| ☐ 115 Roosevelt Potts | .25 | .11 | .03 |
| ☐ 116 Dale Carter | .08 | .04 | .01 |
| ☐ 117 Dave Krieg | .06 | .03 | .01 |
| ☐ 118 Nick Lowery | .04 | .02 | .01 |
| ☐ 119 Christian Okoye | .06 | .03 | .01 |
| ☐ 120 Neil Smith | .08 | .04 | .01 |
| ☐ 121 Derrick Thomas | .15 | .07 | .02 |
| ☐ 122 Harvey Williams | .08 | .04 | .01 |
| ☐ 123 Barry Word | .08 | .04 | .01 |
| ☐ 124 Joe Montana | 1.00 | .45 | .13 |
| ☐ 125 Marcus Allen | .06 | .03 | .01 |
| ☐ 126 James Lofton | .08 | .04 | .01 |
| ☐ 127 Nick Bell | .06 | .03 | .01 |
| ☐ 128 Tim Brown | .25 | .11 | .03 |
| ☐ 129 Eric Dickerson | .08 | .04 | .01 |
| ☐ 130 Jeff Hostetler | .08 | .04 | .01 |
| ☐ 131 Howie Long | .06 | .03 | .01 |
| ☐ 132 Todd Marinovich | .04 | .02 | .01 |
| ☐ 133 Greg Townsend | .04 | .02 | .01 |
| ☐ 134 Patrick Bates | .10 | .05 | .01 |
| ☐ 135 Billy Joe Hobert | .25 | .11 | .03 |
| ☐ 136 Flipper Anderson | .06 | .03 | .01 |
| ☐ 137 Shane Conlan | .04 | .02 | .01 |
| ☐ 138 Henry Ellard | .06 | .03 | .01 |
| ☐ 139 Jim Everett | .04 | .02 | .01 |
| ☐ 140 Cleveland Gary | .06 | .03 | .01 |
| ☐ 141 Sean Gilbert | .06 | .03 | .01 |
| ☐ 142 Todd Lyght | .04 | .02 | .01 |
| ☐ 143 Jerome Bettis | 3.00 | 1.35 | .40 |
| ☐ 144 Troy Drayton | .25 | .11 | .03 |
| ☐ 145 Louis Oliver | .04 | .02 | .01 |
| ☐ 146 Marco Coleman | .06 | .03 | .01 |
| ☐ 147 Bryan Cox | .06 | .03 | .01 |
| ☐ 148 Mark Duper | .06 | .03 | .01 |
| ☐ 149 Irving Fryar | .06 | .03 | .01 |
| ☐ 150 Mark Higgs | .08 | .04 | .01 |
| ☐ 151 Keith Jackson | .08 | .04 | .01 |
| ☐ 152 Dan Marino | .75 | .35 | .09 |
| ☐ 153 Troy Vincent | .06 | .03 | .01 |
| ☐ 154 Richmond Webb | .04 | .02 | .01 |
| ☐ 155 O.J. McDuffie | 1.25 | .55 | .16 |
| ☐ 156 Terry Kirby | 1.50 | .65 | .19 |
| ☐ 157 Terry Allen | .08 | .04 | .01 |
| ☐ 158 Anthony Carter | .06 | .03 | .01 |
| ☐ 159 Cris Carter | .08 | .04 | .01 |
| ☐ 160 Chris Doleman | .06 | .03 | .01 |
| ☐ 161 Randall McDaniel | .04 | .02 | .01 |
| ☐ 162 Audray McMillian | .04 | .02 | .01 |
| ☐ 163 Henry Thomas | .04 | .02 | .01 |
| ☐ 164 Gary Zimmerman | .04 | .02 | .01 |

| | | | |
|---|---|---|---|
| ☐ 165 Robert Smith | .35 | .16 | .04 |
| ☐ 166 Qadry Ismail | .50 | .23 | .06 |
| ☐ 167 Vincent Brown | .04 | .02 | .01 |
| ☐ 168 Marv Cook | .04 | .02 | .01 |
| ☐ 169 Greg McMurtry | .04 | .02 | .01 |
| ☐ 170 Jon Vaughn | .04 | .02 | .01 |
| ☐ 171 Leonard Russell | .06 | .03 | .01 |
| ☐ 172 Andre Tippett | .04 | .02 | .01 |
| ☐ 173 Scott Zolak | .04 | .02 | .01 |
| ☐ 174 Drew Bledsoe | 3.00 | 1.35 | .40 |
| ☐ 175 Chris Slade | .30 | .14 | .04 |
| ☐ 176 Morten Andersen | .06 | .03 | .01 |
| ☐ 177 Vaughn Dunbar | .06 | .03 | .01 |
| ☐ 178 Rickey Jackson | .06 | .03 | .01 |
| ☐ 179 Vaughan Johnson | .04 | .02 | .01 |
| ☐ 180 Eric Martin | .06 | .03 | .01 |
| ☐ 181 Sam Mills | .06 | .03 | .01 |
| ☐ 182 Brad Muster | .06 | .03 | .01 |
| ☐ 183 Willie Roaf | .10 | .05 | .01 |
| ☐ 184 Irv Smith | .20 | .09 | .03 |
| ☐ 185 Reggie Freeman | .10 | .05 | .01 |
| ☐ 186 Michael Brooks | .06 | .03 | .01 |
| ☐ 187 Dave Brown | .75 | .35 | .09 |
| ☐ 188 Rodney Hampton | .30 | .14 | .04 |
| ☐ 189 Pepper Johnson | .04 | .02 | .01 |
| ☐ 190 Ed McCaffrey | .04 | .02 | .01 |
| ☐ 191 David Meggett | .06 | .03 | .01 |
| ☐ 192 Bart Oates | .04 | .02 | .01 |
| ☐ 193 Phil Simms | .08 | .04 | .01 |
| ☐ 194 Lawrence Taylor | .10 | .05 | .01 |
| ☐ 195 Michael Strahan | .10 | .05 | .01 |
| ☐ 196 Brad Baxter | .06 | .03 | .01 |
| ☐ 197 Johnny Johnson | .08 | .04 | .01 |
| ☐ 198 Boomer Esiason | .12 | .05 | .02 |
| ☐ 199 Ronnie Lott | .08 | .04 | .01 |
| ☐ 200 Johnny Mitchell | .25 | .11 | .03 |
| ☐ 201 Rob Moore | .08 | .04 | .01 |
| ☐ 202 Browning Nagle | .06 | .03 | .01 |
| ☐ 203 Blair Thomas | .06 | .03 | .01 |
| ☐ 204 Marvin Jones | .15 | .07 | .02 |
| ☐ 205 Coleman Rudolph | .10 | .05 | .01 |
| ☐ 206 Eric Allen | .06 | .03 | .01 |
| ☐ 207 Fred Barnett | .08 | .04 | .01 |
| ☐ 208 Tim Harris | .04 | .02 | .01 |
| ☐ 209 Randall Cunningham | .10 | .05 | .01 |
| ☐ 210 Seth Joyner | .06 | .03 | .01 |
| ☐ 211 Clyde Simmons | .06 | .03 | .01 |
| ☐ 212 Herschel Walker | .08 | .04 | .01 |
| ☐ 213 Calvin Williams | .08 | .04 | .01 |
| ☐ 214 Lester Holmes | .04 | .02 | .01 |
| ☐ 215 Leonard Renfro | .10 | .05 | .01 |
| ☐ 216 Chris Chandler | .06 | .03 | .01 |
| ☐ 217 Gary Clark | .06 | .03 | .01 |
| ☐ 218 Ken Harvey | .04 | .02 | .01 |
| ☐ 219 Randal Hill | .08 | .04 | .01 |
| ☐ 220 Steve Beuerlein | .15 | .07 | .02 |
| ☐ 221 Ricky Proehl | .06 | .03 | .01 |
| ☐ 222 Timm Rosenbach | .04 | .02 | .01 |
| ☐ 223 Garrison Hearst | .60 | .25 | .08 |
| ☐ 224 Ernest Dye | .10 | .05 | .01 |
| ☐ 225 Bubby Brister | .04 | .02 | .01 |
| ☐ 226 Dermontti Dawson | .04 | .02 | .01 |
| ☐ 227 Barry Foster | .25 | .11 | .03 |
| ☐ 228 Kevin Greene | .04 | .02 | .01 |
| ☐ 229 Merril Hoge | .04 | .02 | .01 |
| ☐ 230 Greg Lloyd | .04 | .02 | .01 |
| ☐ 231 Neil O'Donnell | .25 | .11 | .03 |
| ☐ 232 Rod Woodson | .08 | .04 | .01 |
| ☐ 233 Deon Figures | .15 | .07 | .02 |
| ☐ 234 Chad Brown | .10 | .05 | .01 |
| ☐ 235 Marion Butts | .08 | .04 | .01 |
| ☐ 236 Gill Byrd | .06 | .03 | .01 |
| ☐ 237 Ronnie Harmon | .06 | .03 | .01 |
| ☐ 238 Stan Humphries | .08 | .04 | .01 |
| ☐ 239 Anthony Miller | .15 | .07 | .02 |
| ☐ 240 Leslie O'Neal | .06 | .03 | .01 |
| ☐ 241 Stanley Richard | .04 | .02 | .01 |
| ☐ 242 Junior Seau | .08 | .04 | .01 |
| ☐ 243 Darrien Gordon | .20 | .09 | .03 |
| ☐ 244 Natrone Means | 1.25 | .55 | .16 |
| ☐ 245 Dana Hall | .06 | .03 | .01 |
| ☐ 246 Brent Jones | .08 | .04 | .01 |
| ☐ 247 Tim McDonald | .04 | .02 | .01 |
| ☐ 248 Steve Bono | .15 | .07 | .02 |
| ☐ 249 Jerry Rice | .50 | .23 | .06 |
| ☐ 250 John Taylor | .08 | .04 | .01 |
| ☐ 251 Ricky Watters | .30 | .14 | .04 |
| ☐ 252 Steve Young | .25 | .11 | .03 |
| ☐ 253 Dana Stubblefield | .40 | .18 | .05 |
| ☐ 254 Todd Kelly | .10 | .05 | .01 |
| ☐ 255 Brian Blades | .06 | .03 | .01 |
| ☐ 256 Ferrell Edmunds | .04 | .02 | .01 |
| ☐ 257 Stan Gelbaugh | .04 | .02 | .01 |
| ☐ 258 Cortez Kennedy | .08 | .04 | .01 |
| ☐ 259 Dan McGwire | .06 | .03 | .01 |
| ☐ 260 Chris Warren | .15 | .07 | .02 |
| ☐ 261 John L. Williams | .06 | .03 | .01 |

| | | | |
|---|---|---|---|
| ☐ 262 David Wyman | .04 | .02 | .01 |
| ☐ 263 Rick Mirer | 3.00 | 1.35 | .40 |
| ☐ 264 Carlton Gray | .20 | .09 | .03 |
| ☐ 265 Marty Carter | .04 | .02 | .01 |
| ☐ 266 Reggie Cobb | .08 | .04 | .01 |
| ☐ 267 Lawrence Dawsey | .08 | .04 | .01 |
| ☐ 268 Santana Dotson | .08 | .04 | .01 |
| ☐ 269 Craig Erickson | .08 | .04 | .01 |
| ☐ 270 Paul Gruber | .04 | .02 | .01 |
| ☐ 271 Keith McCants | .04 | .02 | .01 |
| ☐ 272 Broderick Thomas | .04 | .02 | .01 |
| ☐ 273 Eric Curry | .25 | .11 | .03 |
| ☐ 274 Demetrius DuBose | .15 | .07 | .02 |
| ☐ 275 Earnest Byner | .06 | .03 | .01 |
| ☐ 276 Ricky Ervins | .06 | .03 | .01 |
| ☐ 277 Brad Edwards | .04 | .02 | .01 |
| ☐ 278 Jim Lachey | .04 | .02 | .01 |
| ☐ 279 Charles Mann | .06 | .03 | .01 |
| ☐ 280 Carl Banks | .04 | .02 | .01 |
| ☐ 281 Art Monk | .08 | .04 | .01 |
| ☐ 282 Mark Rypien | .06 | .03 | .01 |
| ☐ 283 Ricky Sanders | .06 | .03 | .01 |
| ☐ 284 Tom Carter | .25 | .11 | .03 |
| ☐ 285 Reggie Brooks | 1.75 | .80 | .22 |

## 1993 ProLine Live Autographs

The 1993 ProLine Live Autographs set comprises 35 standard-size (2 1/2" by 3 1/2") cards. Randomly inserted reportedly at an average of two per 1993 ProLine Live case, the cards are similar in design to that issue. The fronts sport color player action photos that are bordered on the right by a team color-coded stripe that carries the player's name and team name. The player's autograph across the photo and the limited edition number round out the card front. The white backs carry a congratulatory message. The cards are numbered and are checklisted below according to the numbers assigned them in the regular series.

| | MINT | EXC | G-VG |
|---|---|---|---|
| COMPLETE SET (35) | 1500.00 | 700.00 | 190.00 |
| COMMON 1050 (23/87/120/217) | 18.00 | 8.00 | 2.30 |
| COMMON 1000 (67/146/160) | 20.00 | 9.00 | 2.50 |
| COMMON 950 (96/119/131/158) | 20.00 | 9.00 | 2.50 |
| COMMON 900 (46/107/129/201) | 20.00 | 9.00 | 2.50 |
| | | | |
| ☐ 7 Deion Sanders | 100.00 | 45.00 | 12.50 |
| Atlanta Falcons (900 signed) | | | |
| ☐ 16 Andre Reed | 25.00 | 11.50 | 3.10 |
| Buffalo Bills (1050 signed) | | | |
| ☐ 23 Neal Anderson | 18.00 | 8.00 | 2.30 |
| Chicago Bears (1050 signed) | | | |
| ☐ 34 David Klingler | 25.00 | 11.50 | 3.10 |
| Cincinnati Bengals (1200 signed) | | | |
| ☐ 46 Vinny Testaverde | 20.00 | 9.00 | 2.50 |
| Cleveland Browns (900) | | | |
| ☐ 51 Troy Aikman | 175.00 | 80.00 | 22.00 |
| Dallas Cowboys (700) | | | |
| ☐ 67 Rod Bernstine | 20.00 | 9.00 | 2.50 |
| Denver Broncos (1000) | | | |
| ☐ 70 Tommy Maddox | 25.00 | 11.50 | 3.10 |
| Denver Broncos (1050) | | | |
| ☐ 76 Pat Swilling | 30.00 | 13.50 | 3.80 |
| Detroit Lions (950) | | | |
| ☐ 79 Rodney Peete | 40.00 | 18.00 | 5.00 |
| Detroit Lions (1000) | | | |

| | | MINT | EXC | G-VG |
|---|---|---|---|---|
| ☐ 87 | Terrell Buckley | 18.00 | 8.00 | 2.30 |
| | Green Bay Packers (1050) | | | |
| ☐ 88 | Brett Favre | 150.00 | 70.00 | 19.00 |
| | Green Bay Packers (650) | | | |
| ☐ 91 | Sterling Sharpe | 80.00 | 36.00 | 10.00 |
| | Green Bay Packers (1050) | | | |
| ☐ 96 | Ray Childress | 20.00 | 9.00 | 2.50 |
| | Houston Oilers (950) | | | |
| ☐ 99 | Haywood Jeffires | 40.00 | 18.00 | 5.00 |
| | Houston Oilers (950) | | | |
| ☐ 107 | Quentin Coryatt | 20.00 | 9.00 | 2.50 |
| | Indianapolis Colts (900) | | | |
| ☐ 108 | Steve Emtman | 20.00 | 9.00 | 2.50 |
| | Indianapolis Colts (800) | | | |
| ☐ 109 | Jeff George | 35.00 | 16.00 | 4.40 |
| | Indianapolis Colts (1050) | | | |
| ☐ 119 | Christian Okoye | 20.00 | 9.00 | 2.50 |
| | Kansas City Chiefs (900) | | | |
| ☐ 120 | Neil Smith | 18.00 | 8.00 | 2.30 |
| | Kansas City Chiefs (1050) | | | |
| ☐ 121 | Derrick Thomas | 80.00 | 36.00 | 10.00 |
| | Kansas City Chiefs (550) | | | |
| ☐ 124 | Joe Montana | 250.00 | 115.00 | 31.00 |
| | Kansas City Chiefs (600) | | | |
| ☐ 129 | Eric Dickerson | 20.00 | 9.00 | 2.50 |
| | Los Angeles Raiders (900) | | | |
| ☐ 131 | Howie Long | 20.00 | 9.00 | 2.50 |
| | Los Angeles Raiders (950) | | | |
| ☐ 146 | Marco Coleman | 20.00 | 9.00 | 2.50 |
| | Miami Dolphins (1000) | | | |
| ☐ 151 | Keith Jackson | 40.00 | 18.00 | 5.00 |
| | Miami Dolphins (650) | | | |
| ☐ 158 | Anthony Carter | 20.00 | 9.00 | 2.50 |
| | Minnesota Vikings (950) | | | |
| ☐ 160 | Chris Doleman | 20.00 | 9.00 | 2.50 |
| | Minnesota Vikings (1000) | | | |
| ☐ 188 | Rodney Hampton | 50.00 | 23.00 | 6.25 |
| | New York Giants (650) | | | |
| ☐ 199 | Ronnie Lott | 25.00 | 11.50 | 3.10 |
| | New York Jets (1050) | | | |
| ☐ 201 | Rob Moore | 20.00 | 9.00 | 2.50 |
| | New York Jets (950) | | | |
| ☐ 217 | Gary Clark | 18.00 | 8.00 | 2.30 |
| | Arizona Cardinals (1050) | | | |
| ☐ 227 | Barry Foster | 90.00 | 40.00 | 11.50 |
| | Pittsburgh Steelers (750) | | | |
| ☐ 231 | Neil O'Donnell | 30.00 | 13.50 | 3.80 |
| | Pittsburgh Steelers (1050) | | | |
| ☐ 242 | Junior Seau | 25.00 | 11.50 | 3.10 |
| | San Diego Chargers (900) | | | |

## 1993 ProLine Live Future Stars

The 1993 ProLine Live Future Stars set comprises 28 standard-size (2 1/2" by 3 1/2") cards. The insertion rate was one per 1993 ProLine Live jumbo pack. The fronts sport color player action shots with black-and-white backgrounds that are borderless, except on the right, where a gold foil-stamped stripe carries the player's name and team name. The gold foil-stamped production number, "1 of 22,000," also appears along the right side. Above a team color-coded panel presenting biography, statistics, and career highlights, the backs carry a full-bleed color action player shot. The cards are numbered on the back with an "FS" prefix.

| | MINT | EXC | G-VG |
|---|---|---|---|
| COMPLETE SET (28) | 15.00 | 6.75 | 1.90 |
| COMMON PLAYER (1-28) | .25 | .11 | .03 |
| ☐ 1 Patrick Bates | .25 | .11 | .03 |
| Los Angeles Raiders | | | |

| | | MINT | EXC | G-VG |
|---|---|---|---|---|
| ☐ 2 | Jerome Bettis | 4.00 | 1.80 | .50 |
| | Los Angeles Rams | | | |
| ☐ 3 | Drew Bledsoe | 4.00 | 1.80 | .50 |
| | New England Patriots | | | |
| ☐ 4 | Tom Carter | .25 | .11 | .03 |
| | Washington Redskins | | | |
| ☐ 5 | Curtis Conway | .75 | .35 | .09 |
| | Chicago Bears | | | |
| ☐ 6 | Steve Everitt | .25 | .11 | .03 |
| | Cleveland Browns | | | |
| ☐ 7 | Deon Figures | .30 | .14 | .04 |
| | Pittsburgh Steelers | | | |
| ☐ 8 | Darrien Gordon | .30 | .14 | .04 |
| | San Diego Chargers | | | |
| ☐ 9 | Lester Holmes | .25 | .11 | .03 |
| | Philadelphia Eagles | | | |
| ☐ 10 | Brad Hopkins | .25 | .11 | .03 |
| | Houston Oilers | | | |
| ☐ 11 | Marvin Jones | .40 | .18 | .05 |
| | New York Jets | | | |
| ☐ 12 | Lincoln Kennedy | .30 | .14 | .04 |
| | Atlanta Falcons | | | |
| ☐ 13 | O.J. McDuffie | 1.25 | .55 | .16 |
| | Miami Dolphins | | | |
| ☐ 14 | Rick Mirer | 4.00 | 1.80 | .50 |
| | Seattle Seahawks | | | |
| ☐ 15 | Willie Roaf | .25 | .11 | .03 |
| | New Orleans Saints | | | |
| ☐ 16 | Will Shields | .25 | .11 | .03 |
| | Kansas City Chiefs | | | |
| ☐ 17 | Wayne Simmons | .25 | .11 | .03 |
| | Green Bay Packers | | | |
| ☐ 18 | Robert Smith | .50 | .23 | .06 |
| | Minnesota Vikings | | | |
| ☐ 19 | Thomas Smith | .25 | .11 | .03 |
| | Buffalo Bills | | | |
| ☐ 20 | Michael Strahan | .25 | .11 | .03 |
| | New York Giants | | | |
| ☐ 21 | Dana Stubblefield | .50 | .23 | .06 |
| | San Francisco 49ers | | | |
| ☐ 22 | Dan Williams | .25 | .11 | .03 |
| | Denver Broncos | | | |
| ☐ 23 | Kevin Williams (WR) | .75 | .35 | .09 |
| | Dallas Cowboys | | | |
| ☐ 24 | Garrison Hearst | 1.00 | .45 | .13 |
| | Phoenix Cardinals | | | |
| ☐ 25 | John Copeland | .50 | .23 | .06 |
| | Cleveland Browns | | | |
| ☐ 26 | Ryan McNeil | .25 | .11 | .03 |
| | Detroit Lions | | | |
| ☐ 27 | Eric Curry | .50 | .23 | .06 |
| | Tampa Bay Buccaneers | | | |
| ☐ 28 | Roosevelt Potts | .40 | .18 | .05 |
| | Indianapolis Colts | | | |

## 1993 ProLine Live Illustrated

Illustrated by comic artist Neal Adams, this six-card set was randomly inserted on an average of three per case in 1993 Classic Pro Line Collection packs. Reportedly only 10,000 of each card were produced. The front of each card features Adams' colorful player action illustration, which is borderless on three sides. The right side is edged by a team-colored stripe that carries the player's name and team name. In its top half, the back carries a portion of the same player action drawing, followed below by career highlights in a team-colored area at the bottom. The cards are standard size (2 1/2" by 3 1/2"). The cards are numbered on the back with an "SP" prefix.

| | MINT | EXC | G-VG |
|---|---|---|---|
| COMPLETE SET (6) | 20.00 | 9.00 | 2.50 |
| COMMON PLAYER (SP1-SP6) | 2.00 | .90 | .25 |
| ☐ SP1 Troy Aikman | 10.00 | 4.50 | 1.25 |
| Dallas Cowboys | | | |

| | MINT | EXC | G-VG |
|---|---|---|---|
| ☐ SP2 Jerry Rice .............................. | 4.00 | 1.80 | .50 |
| San Francisco 49ers | | | |
| ☐ SP3 Michael Irvin....................... | 4.00 | 1.80 | .50 |
| Dallas Cowboys | | | |
| ☐ SP4 Thurman Thomas ................ | 3.00 | 1.35 | .40 |
| Buffalo Bills | | | |
| ☐ SP5 Lawrence Taylor .................. | 2.00 | .90 | .25 |
| New York Giants | | | |
| ☐ SP6 Deion Sanders ..................... | 2.00 | .90 | .25 |
| Atlanta Falcons | | | |

## 1993 ProLine Live LPs

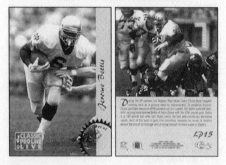

These 20 limited-print, foil-stamped cards spotlight top young NFL talent. The standard-size (2 1/2" by 3 1/2") cards were randomly inserted throughout 1993 Classic Pro Line Collection packs on an average of four per point of purchase. Each card front features a color player action shot that is borderless on three sides. The right side is edged by a team-colored stripe that carries the player's name in gold foil. The gold-foil limited print seal, which carries the words "One of 40,000," appears at the lower right. In its top half, the back carries another player action shot, followed below by career highlights in a team-colored area at the bottom. The cards are numbered on the back with an "LP" prefix.

| | MINT | EXC | G-VG |
|---|---|---|---|
| COMPLETE SET (20)........................ | 40.00 | 18.00 | 5.00 |
| COMMON PLAYER (LP1-LP20) ........ | 1.00 | .45 | .13 |
| ☐ LP1 Chris Webber ....................... | 8.00 | 3.60 | 1.00 |
| (Dunking football) | | | |
| ☐ LP2 Shaquille O'Neal................... | 8.00 | 3.60 | 1.00 |
| (Wearing street clothes) | | | |
| ☐ LP3 Jamal Mashburn................... | 6.00 | 2.70 | .75 |
| (Wearing ProLine apparel) | | | |
| ☐ LP4 Marcus Allen ....................... | 1.25 | .55 | .16 |
| Kansas City Chiefs | | | |
| ☐ LP5 Neal Anderson ..................... | 1.00 | .45 | .13 |
| Chicago Bears | | | |
| ☐ LP6 Reggie Cobb ....................... | 1.25 | .55 | .16 |
| Tampa Bay Buccaneers | | | |
| ☐ LP7 Rod Bernstine ...................... | 1.00 | .45 | .13 |
| Denver Broncos | | | |
| ☐ LP8 Barry Word .......................... | 1.00 | .45 | .13 |
| Kansas City Chiefs | | | |
| ☐ LP9 Troy Aikman ........................ | 6.00 | 2.70 | .75 |
| Dallas Cowboys | | | |
| ☐ LP10 Brett Favre ........................ | 3.00 | 1.35 | .40 |
| Green Bay Packers | | | |
| ☐ LP11 Ricky Watters ..................... | 2.00 | .90 | .25 |
| San Francisco 49ers | | | |
| ☐ LP12 Terry Allen ......................... | 1.25 | .55 | .16 |
| Minnesota Vikings | | | |

| | MINT | EXC | G-VG |
|---|---|---|---|
| ☐ LP13 Rodney Hampton.............. | 2.00 | .90 | .25 |
| New York Giants | | | |
| ☐ LP14 Garrison Hearst................. | 1.50 | .65 | .19 |
| Arizona Cardinals | | | |
| ☐ LP15 Jerome Bettis...................... | 7.00 | 3.10 | .85 |
| Los Angeles Rams | | | |
| ☐ LP16 Barry Foster ....................... | 2.00 | .90 | .25 |
| Pittsburgh Steelers | | | |
| ☐ LP17 Harold Green...................... | 1.00 | .45 | .13 |
| Cincinnati Bengals | | | |
| ☐ LP18 Tommy Vardell................... | 1.00 | .45 | .13 |
| Cleveland Browns | | | |
| ☐ LP19 Lorenzo White..................... | 1.00 | .45 | .13 |
| Houston Oilers | | | |
| ☐ LP20 Marion Butts ...................... | 1.00 | .45 | .13 |
| San Diego Chargers | | | |

## 1993 ProLine Live Tonx

Issued to herald the release of 1993 Classic NFL Tonx in the fall, these six milk cap game cards were random inserts in packs of 1993 ProLine Live. The circular cards measure about 1 5/8" in diameter and could be popped out of their standard-size (2 1/2" by 3 1/2") promotional holders. The front of each disc features a borderless color player action shot. The black back carries the player's team helmet at the top, followed below by his position, and name within a blue stripe. The cards are unnumbered and checklisted below in alphabetical order.

| | MINT | EXC | G-VG |
|---|---|---|---|
| COMPLETE SET (6)........................... | 7.00 | 3.10 | .85 |
| COMMON PLAYER (1-6)................... | .50 | .23 | .06 |
| ☐ 1 Troy Aikman............................. | 2.50 | 1.15 | .30 |
| Dallas Cowboys | | | |
| ☐ 2 Michael Irvin ............................ | 1.25 | .55 | .16 |
| Dallas Cowboys | | | |
| ☐ 3 Jerry Rice................................. | 1.50 | .65 | .19 |
| San Francisco 49ers | | | |
| ☐ 4 Deion Sanders.......................... | .75 | .35 | .09 |
| Atlanta Falcons | | | |
| ☐ 5 Lawrence Taylor....................... | .50 | .23 | .06 |
| New York Giants | | | |
| ☐ 6 Thurman Thomas...................... | 1.00 | .45 | .13 |
| Buffalo Bills | | | |

## 1993 ProLine Portraits

As part of the 1993 Classic Pro Line Collection, this 44-card standard-size (2 1/2" by 3 1/2") set features full-bleed non-game photos on the front. The bottom center of the back has a color head shot, and a player quote on a silver panel wraps around the picture. The set closes with a Throwbacks (507-511) subset. The cards are numbered on the back in continuation of the 1992 Pro Line Portraits set. Rookie Cards include Jerome Bettis, Drew Bledsoe and Rock Mirer.

| | MINT | EXC | G-VG |
|---|---|---|---|
| COMPLETE SET (44)........................ | 6.00 | 2.70 | .75 |
| COMMON PLAYER (468-511).......... | .04 | .02 | .01 |
| ☐ 468 Willie Roaf............................ | .10 | .05 | .01 |
| New Orleans Saints | | | |
| ☐ 469 Terry Allen............................ | .08 | .04 | .01 |
| Minnesota Vikings | | | |
| ☐ 470 Jerry Ball.............................. | .04 | .02 | .01 |
| Cleveland Browns | | | |
| ☐ 471 Patrick Bates........................ | .10 | .05 | .01 |
| Los Angeles Raiders | | | |
| ☐ 472 Ray Bentley........................... | .04 | .02 | .01 |
| Cincinnati Bengals | | | |
| ☐ 473 Jerome Bettis........................ | 2.00 | .90 | .25 |

| | | | |
|---|---|---|---|
| Los Angeles Rams | | | |
| ☐ 474 Steve Beuerlein | .10 | .05 | .01 |
| Phoenix Cardinals | | | |
| ☐ 475 Drew Bledsoe | 2.00 | .90 | .25 |
| New England Patriots | | | |
| ☐ 476 Dave Brown | .75 | .35 | .09 |
| New York Giants | | | |
| ☐ 477 Gill Byrd | .04 | .02 | .01 |
| San Diego Chargers | | | |
| ☐ 478 Tony Casillas | .04 | .02 | .01 |
| Dallas Cowboys | | | |
| ☐ 479 Chuck Cecil | .04 | .02 | .01 |
| Green Bay Packers | | | |
| ☐ 480 Reggie Cobb | .08 | .04 | .01 |
| Tampa Bay Buccaneers | | | |
| ☐ 481 Pat Harlow | .04 | .02 | .01 |
| New England Patriots | | | |
| ☐ 482 John Copeland | .25 | .11 | .03 |
| Cincinnati Bengals | | | |
| ☐ 483 Bryan Cox | .06 | .03 | .01 |
| Miami Dolphins | | | |
| ☐ 484 Eric Curry | .25 | .11 | .03 |
| Tampa Bay Buccaneers | | | |
| ☐ 485 Jeff Lageman | .04 | .02 | .01 |
| New York Jets | | | |
| ☐ 486 Brett Favre | .60 | .25 | .08 |
| Green Bay Packers | | | |
| ☐ 487 Barry Foster | .25 | .11 | .03 |
| Pittsburgh Steelers | | | |
| ☐ 488 Gaston Green | .06 | .03 | .01 |
| Los Angeles Raiders | | | |
| ☐ 489 Rodney Hampton | .30 | .14 | .04 |
| New York Giants | | | |
| ☐ 490 Tim Harris | .04 | .02 | .01 |
| Philadelphia Eagles | | | |
| ☐ 491 Garrison Hearst | .60 | .25 | .08 |
| Phoenix Cardinals | | | |
| ☐ 492 Tony Smith | .04 | .02 | .01 |
| Atlanta Falcons | | | |
| ☐ 493 Marvin Jones | .15 | .07 | .02 |
| New York Jets | | | |
| ☐ 494 Lincoln Kennedy | .15 | .07 | .02 |
| Atlanta Falcons | | | |
| ☐ 495 Wilber Marshall | .06 | .03 | .01 |
| Washington Redskins | | | |
| ☐ 496 Terry McDaniel | .04 | .02 | .01 |
| Los Angeles Raiders | | | |
| ☐ 497 Rick Mirer | 2.00 | .90 | .25 |
| Seattle Seahawks | | | |
| ☐ 498 Art Monk | .08 | .04 | .01 |
| Washington Redskins | | | |
| ☐ 499 Mike Munchak | .06 | .03 | .01 |
| Houston Oilers | | | |
| ☐ 500 Frank Reich | .06 | .03 | .01 |
| Buffalo Bills | | | |
| ☐ 501 Barry Sanders | .75 | .35 | .09 |
| Detroit Lions | | | |
| ☐ 502 Shannon Sharpe | .20 | .09 | .03 |
| Denver Broncos | | | |
| ☐ 503 Gino Torretta | .30 | .14 | .04 |
| Minnesota Vikings | | | |
| ☐ 504 Ricky Watters | .30 | .14 | .04 |
| San Francisco 49ers | | | |
| ☐ 505 Richmond Webb | .04 | .02 | .01 |
| Miami Dolphins | | | |
| ☐ 506 Reggie White | .15 | .07 | .02 |
| Green Bay Packers | | | |
| ☐ 507 Bert Jones TB | .04 | .02 | .01 |
| Baltimore Colts | | | |
| ☐ 508 Billy Kilmer TB | .04 | .02 | .01 |
| Washington Redskins | | | |
| ☐ 509 John Mackey TB | .04 | .02 | .01 |
| Baltimore Colts | | | |
| ☐ 510 Archie Manning TB | .04 | .02 | .01 |
| New Orleans Saints | | | |
| ☐ 511 Harvey Martin | .04 | .02 | .01 |
| Dallas Cowboys | | | |

## 1993 ProLine Portraits Wives

Randomly inserted in 1993 Pro Line packs, this four-card standard-size (2 1/2" by 3 1/2") set features wives of NFL stars. The fronts feature full-bleed color action photos, while the horizontal backs carry a quote and a color close-up shot. The cards are numbered on the back in continuation of the 1992 Pro Line Wives ("Spirit") subset.

| | MINT | EXC | G-VG |
|---|---|---|---|
| COMPLETE SET (4) | .50 | .23 | .06 |
| COMMON PLAYER (SC25-SC28) | .15 | .07 | .02 |
| ☐ 25 Annette Rypien | .15 | .07 | .02 |
| ☐ 26 Ann Stark | .15 | .07 | .02 |
| ☐ 27 Cindy Walker | .15 | .07 | .02 |
| ☐ 28 Cindy Reed | .15 | .07 | .02 |

## 1993 ProLine Profiles

As part of the 1993 Classic Pro Line Collection, this 117-card standard-size (2 1/2" by 3 1/2") set features thirteen nine-card subsets devoted to outstanding NFL players. The fronts display full-bleed color action player photos. The lettering and the stripe carrying the player's name are team color-coded. The backs have a second color action shot, career highlights in the form of an expanded caption, and a player quote. The cards are numbered on the back with each subset ("X of 9") and for the entire Profiles set.

| | MINT | EXC | G-VG |
|---|---|---|---|
| COMPLETE SET (117) | 6.00 | 2.70 | .75 |
| COMMON PLAYER (496-612) | .04 | .02 | .01 |
| ☐ 496 Ray Childress | .04 | .02 | .01 |
| (Versus Steelers) | | | |
| ☐ 497 Ray Childress | .04 | .02 | .01 |
| (Young Ray in YMCA jersey) | | | |
| ☐ 498 Ray Childress | .04 | .02 | .01 |
| (With Aggie trophies) | | | |
| ☐ 499 Ray Childress | .04 | .02 | .01 |
| (Versus Rams) | | | |
| ☐ 500 Ray Childress | .04 | .02 | .01 |
| (Portrait) | | | |
| ☐ 501 Ray Childress | .04 | .02 | .01 |
| (With family) | | | |
| ☐ 502 Ray Childress | .04 | .02 | .01 |
| ☐ 503 Ray Childress | .04 | .02 | .01 |
| (During Pro Bowl) | | | |
| ☐ 504 Ray Childress | .04 | .02 | .01 |
| (Holding calf) | | | |
| ☐ 505 Jeff George | .10 | .05 | .01 |
| ☐ 506 Jeff George | .10 | .05 | .01 |
| (Young Jeff suited up) | | | |

| | | | | | | | | |
|---|---|---|---|---|---|---|---|---|
| ☐ 507 | Jeff George (Playing billiards) | .10 | .05 | .01 | ☐ 558 | Dan Marino (Studio closeup) | .40 | .18 | .05 |

| | | | | |
|---|---|---|---|---|
| ☐ 507 Jeff George (Playing billiards) | .10 | .05 | .01 |
| ☐ 508 Jeff George (In varsity jacket) | .10 | .05 | .01 |
| ☐ 509 Jeff George (Portrait) | .10 | .05 | .01 |
| ☐ 510 Jeff George | .10 | .05 | .01 |
| ☐ 511 Jeff George (With handicapped boy) | .10 | .05 | .01 |
| ☐ 512 Jeff George (Versus Buccaneers) | .10 | .05 | .01 |
| ☐ 513 Jeff George (Studio with football) | .10 | .05 | .01 |
| ☐ 514 Franco Harris (Bust) | .08 | .04 | .01 |
| ☐ 515 Franco Harris (Versus Raiders) | .08 | .04 | .01 |
| ☐ 516 Franco Harris (With son) | .08 | .04 | .01 |
| ☐ 517 Franco Harris (Versus Vikings) | .08 | .04 | .01 |
| ☐ 518 Franco Harris (Portrait) | .08 | .04 | .01 |
| ☐ 519 Franco Harris (Carrying ball) | .08 | .04 | .01 |
| ☐ 520 Franco Harris (With Salvation Army kids) | .08 | .04 | .01 |
| ☐ 521 Franco Harris (With ball held aloft) | .08 | .04 | .01 |
| ☐ 522 Franco Harris (With bicycle) | .08 | .04 | .01 |
| ☐ 523 Keith Jackson (Carrying football) | .08 | .04 | .01 |
| ☐ 524 Keith Jackson (With family) | .08 | .04 | .01 |
| ☐ 525 Keith Jackson (On Sooner sideline) | .08 | .04 | .01 |
| ☐ 526 Keith Jackson (In recording studio) | .08 | .04 | .01 |
| ☐ 527 Keith Jackson | .08 | .04 | .01 |
| ☐ 528 Keith Jackson | .08 | .04 | .01 |
| ☐ 529 Keith Jackson | .08 | .04 | .01 |
| ☐ 530 Keith Jackson | .08 | .04 | .01 |
| ☐ 531 Keith Jackson | .08 | .04 | .01 |
| ☐ 532 Jimmy Johnson (With SB XXVII trophy) | .04 | .02 | .01 |
| ☐ 533 Jimmy Johnson (In Arkansas uniform) | .04 | .02 | .01 |
| ☐ 534 Jimmy Johnson (Smiling) | .04 | .02 | .01 |
| ☐ 535 Jimmy Johnson (With sons) | .04 | .02 | .01 |
| ☐ 535A Jimmy Johnson (Name spelled Johnny on back of card) | .10 | .05 | .01 |
| ☐ 535B Jimmy Johnson (Name spelled Jimmy on back of card) | .10 | .05 | .01 |
| ☐ 536 Jimmy Johnson (Portrait) | .04 | .02 | .01 |
| ☐ 537 Jimmy Johnson (On telephone) | .04 | .02 | .01 |
| ☐ 538 Jimmy Johnson | .04 | .02 | .01 |
| ☐ 539 Jimmy Johnson | .04 | .02 | .01 |
| ☐ 540 Jimmy Johnson | .04 | .02 | .01 |
| ☐ 541 James Lofton (Catching ball) | .08 | .04 | .01 |
| ☐ 542 James Lofton | .08 | .04 | .01 |
| ☐ 543 James Lofton | .08 | .04 | .01 |
| ☐ 544 James Lofton (Versus Dolphins) | .08 | .04 | .01 |
| ☐ 545 James Lofton (Portrait) | .08 | .04 | .01 |
| ☐ 546 James Lofton (On track) | .08 | .04 | .01 |
| ☐ 547 James Lofton (In Bills uniform) | .08 | .04 | .01 |
| ☐ 548 James Lofton (With family) | .08 | .04 | .01 |
| ☐ 549 James Lofton | .08 | .04 | .01 |
| ☐ 550 Dan Marino (Versus Jets) | .40 | .18 | .05 |
| ☐ 551 Dan Marino (U.of Pitt.) | .40 | .18 | .05 |
| ☐ 552 Dan Marino (Spinning football) | .40 | .18 | .05 |
| ☐ 553 Dan Marino (With son) | .40 | .18 | .05 |
| ☐ 554 Dan Marino (Portrait) | .40 | .18 | .05 |
| ☐ 555 Dan Marino (Dropping back) | .40 | .18 | .05 |
| ☐ 556 Dan Marino (Playing golf) | .40 | .18 | .05 |
| ☐ 557 Dan Marino (By goal post) | .40 | .18 | .05 |

| | | | |
|---|---|---|---|
| ☐ 558 Dan Marino (Studio closeup) | .40 | .18 | .05 |
| ☐ 559 Joe Montana (Helmetless, with ball, horizontal card) | .50 | .23 | .06 |
| ☐ 560 Joe Montana (In high school jersey) | .50 | .23 | .06 |
| ☐ 561 Joe Montana (Handing off) | .50 | .23 | .06 |
| ☐ 562 Joe Montana | .50 | .23 | .06 |
| ☐ 563 Joe Montana | .50 | .23 | .06 |
| ☐ 564 Joe Montana (Making TD gesture) | .50 | .23 | .06 |
| ☐ 565 Joe Montana (High-fiving Rice) | .50 | .23 | .06 |
| ☐ 566 Joe Montana (With wife) | .50 | .23 | .06 |
| ☐ 567 Joe Montana (Studio pose) | .50 | .23 | .06 |
| ☐ 568 Jay Novacek | .08 | .04 | .01 |
| ☐ 569 Jay Novacek (Young Jay with pooch) | .08 | .04 | .01 |
| ☐ 570 Jay Novacek (Hurling javelin) | .08 | .04 | .01 |
| ☐ 571 Jay Novacek (In Cardinal uniform) | .08 | .04 | .01 |
| ☐ 572 Jay Novacek (Portrait) | .08 | .04 | .01 |
| ☐ 573 Jay Novacek (With wife) | .08 | .04 | .01 |
| ☐ 574 Jay Novacek (Rodeoing, horizontal card) | .08 | .04 | .01 |
| ☐ 575 Jay Novacek (Doing pushups) | .08 | .04 | .01 |
| ☐ 576 Jay Novacek (Riding horse, horizontal card) | .08 | .04 | .01 |
| ☐ 577 Gale Sayers | .08 | .04 | .01 |
| ☐ 578 Gale Sayers (In Kansas jersey) | .08 | .04 | .01 |
| ☐ 579 Gale Sayers (Versus Lions) | .08 | .04 | .01 |
| ☐ 580 Gale Sayers (Carrying ball) | .08 | .04 | .01 |
| ☐ 581 Gale Sayers (Portrait) | .08 | .04 | .01 |
| ☐ 582 Gale Sayers (Versus Redskins) | .08 | .04 | .01 |
| ☐ 583 Gale Sayers (With wife) | .08 | .04 | .01 |
| ☐ 584 Gale Sayers (With disabled kids) | .08 | .04 | .01 |
| ☐ 585 Gale Sayers | .08 | .04 | .01 |
| ☐ 586 Emmitt Smith | .75 | .35 | .09 |
| ☐ 587 Emmitt Smith | .75 | .35 | .09 |
| ☐ 588 Emmitt Smith (Playing for Gators) | .75 | .35 | .09 |
| ☐ 589 Emmitt Smith | .75 | .35 | .09 |
| ☐ 590 Emmitt Smith | .75 | .35 | .09 |
| ☐ 591 Emmitt Smith | .75 | .35 | .09 |
| ☐ 592 Emmitt Smith | .75 | .35 | .09 |
| ☐ 593 Emmitt Smith (Running toward camera) | .75 | .35 | .09 |
| ☐ 594 Emmitt Smith (Close-up shot, chin resting on hands; SB ring displayed) | .75 | .35 | .09 |
| ☐ 595 Herschel Walker | .08 | .04 | .01 |
| ☐ 596 Herschel Walker | .08 | .04 | .01 |
| ☐ 597 Herschel Walker (Jumping rope) | .08 | .04 | .01 |
| ☐ 598 Herschel Walker (Practicing Twae Kwon-Do) | .08 | .04 | .01 |
| ☐ 599 Herschel Walker (Portrait) | .08 | .04 | .01 |
| ☐ 600 Herschel Walker (Action shot in Cowboy uniform) | .08 | .04 | .01 |
| ☐ 601 Herschel Walker | .08 | .04 | .01 |
| ☐ 602 Herschel Walker (Competing in bobsled at '92 Winter Olympics) | .08 | .04 | .01 |
| ☐ 603 Herschel Walker (Side shot of shoulders, without shirt) | .08 | .04 | .01 |
| ☐ 604 Steve Young (Just after release of ball) | .20 | .09 | .03 |
| ☐ 605 Steve Young (Standing beside statute of Brigham Young) | .20 | .09 | .03 |
| ☐ 606 Steve Young (Action shot in | .20 | .09 | .03 |

| | MINT | EXC | G-VG |
|---|---|---|---|
| ☐ 607 Steve Young (BYU uniform) | .20 | .09 | .03 |
| ☐ 608 Steve Young (Taking snap in LA Express uniform) | .20 | .09 | .03 |
| ☐ 609 Steve Young (Portrait) | .20 | .09 | .03 |
| (Action shot in Buccanneer uniform) | | | |
| ☐ 610 Steve Young (With kids) | .20 | .09 | .03 |
| ☐ 611 Steve Young | .20 | .09 | .03 |
| ☐ 612 Steve Young (Studio closeup) | .20 | .09 | .03 |

## 1994 ProLine Live Draft Day Prototypes

This 13-card standard-size (2 1/2" by 3 1/2") set previews the 1994 NFL Draft by portraying the featured players with several possible teams (with the exception of Troy Aikman). The fronts feature full-bleed color action player photos. At the bottom the player's name is printed in team color-coded letters, which in turn are underscored by a team color-coded stripe. The backs have a full-bleed ghosted photo except for a square at the player's head. The set name, draft date (April 24, 1994), and production figures (1 of 19,940) are stenciled over the ghosted photo. The cards are numbered on the back.

| | MINT | EXC | G-VG |
|---|---|---|---|
| COMPLETE SET (13) | 30.00 | 12.00 | 3.00 |
| COMMON PLAYER (1-13) | 2.00 | .80 | .20 |
| ☐ FD1 Dan Wilkinson Cincinnati Bengals | 3.00 | 1.20 | .30 |
| ☐ FD2 Dan Wilkinson New England Patriots | 3.00 | 1.20 | .30 |
| ☐ FD3 Marshall Faulk Cincinnati Bengals | 5.00 | 2.00 | .50 |
| ☐ FD4 Marshall Faulk Indianapolis Colts | 5.00 | 2.00 | .50 |
| ☐ FD5 Marshall Faulk Tampa Bay Buccaneers | 5.00 | 2.00 | .50 |
| ☐ FD6 Troy Aikman Dallas Cowboys 1989 First Pick | 5.00 | 2.00 | .50 |
| ☐ FD7 Trent Dilfer Washingtonedskins | 4.00 | 1.60 | .40 |
| ☐ FD8 Trent Dilfer Indianapolis Colts | 4.00 | 1.60 | .40 |
| ☐ FD9 Heath Shuler Washington Redskins | 7.50 | 3.00 | .75 |
| ☐ FD10 Heath Shuler Indianapolis Colts | 7.50 | 3.00 | .75 |
| ☐ FD11 Aaron Glenn Tampa Bay Buccaneers | 2.00 | .80 | .20 |
| ☐ FD12 Aaron Glenn Los Angeles Rams | 2.00 | .80 | .20 |
| ☐ FD13 Dan Wilkinson Arizona Cardinals | 3.00 | 1.20 | .30 |

## 1994 ProLine Live

These 405 standard-size (2 1/2" by 3 1/2") cards feature borderless fronts and color action shots. The player's name appears in uppercase lettering at the bottom along with his team name within a team color-coded stripe. The backs carry another color player action shot with statistics appearing within a ghosted stripe near the bottom of the photo. Career highlights and biography appear within a team color-coded band down the left side.

| | MINT | EXC | G-VG |
|---|---|---|---|
| COMPLETE SET (405) | 22.00 | 10.00 | 2.80 |
| COMMON PLAYER (1-405) | .05 | .02 | .01 |
| ☐ 1 Emmitt Smith Dallas Cowboys | 1.75 | .80 | .22 |
| ☐ 2 Andre Rison Atlanta Falcons | .15 | .07 | .02 |
| ☐ 3 Deion Sanders Atlanta Falcons | .15 | .07 | .02 |
| ☐ 4 Jeff George Atlanta Falcons | .08 | .04 | .01 |
| ☐ 5 Cornelius Bennett Buffalo Bills | .08 | .04 | .01 |
| ☐ 6 Jim Kelly Buffalo Bills | .20 | .09 | .03 |
| ☐ 7 Andre Reed Buffalo Bills | .10 | .05 | .01 |
| ☐ 8 Bruce Smith Buffalo Bills | .10 | .05 | .01 |
| ☐ 9 Thurman Thomas Buffalo Bills | .25 | .11 | .03 |
| ☐ 10 Mark Carrier Chicago Bears | .05 | .02 | .01 |
| ☐ 11 Curtis Conway Chicago Bears | .15 | .07 | .02 |
| ☐ 12 Donnell Woolford Chicago Bears | .05 | .02 | .01 |
| ☐ 13 Chris Zorich Chicago Bears | .05 | .02 | .01 |
| ☐ 14 Erik Kramer Chicago Bears | .15 | .07 | .02 |
| ☐ 15 John Copeland Cincinnati Bengals | .05 | .02 | .01 |
| ☐ 16 Harold Green Cincinnati Bengals | .05 | .02 | .01 |
| ☐ 17 David Klingler Cincinnati Bengals | .15 | .07 | .02 |
| ☐ 18 Tony McGee Cincinnati Bengals | .05 | .02 | .01 |
| ☐ 19 Carl Pickens Cincinnati Bengals | .08 | .04 | .01 |
| ☐ 20 Michael Jackson Cleveland Browns | .08 | .04 | .01 |
| ☐ 21 Eric Metcalf Cleveland Browns | .08 | .04 | .01 |
| ☐ 22 Michael Dean Perry Cleveland Browns | .05 | .02 | .01 |
| ☐ 23 Vinny Testaverde Cleveland Browns | .08 | .04 | .01 |
| ☐ 24 Eric Turner Cleveland Browns | .05 | .02 | .01 |
| ☐ 25 Tommy Vardell Cleveland Browns | .08 | .04 | .01 |
| ☐ 26 Troy Aikman Dallas Cowboys | 1.25 | .55 | .16 |
| ☐ 27 Charles Haley Dallas Cowboys | .05 | .02 | .01 |
| ☐ 28 Michael Irvin Dallas Cowboys | .30 | .14 | .04 |
| ☐ 29 Pierce Holt Atlanta Falcons | .05 | .02 | .01 |
| ☐ 30 Russell Maryland Dallas Cowboys | .05 | .02 | .01 |
| ☐ 31 Erik Williams Dallas Cowboys | .05 | .02 | .01 |
| ☐ 32 Thomas Everett Tampa Bay Buccaneers | .05 | .02 | .01 |
| ☐ 33 Steve Atwater Denver Broncos | .05 | .02 | .01 |
| ☐ 34 John Elway Denver Broncos | .40 | .18 | .05 |
| ☐ 35 Glyn Milburn Denver Broncos | .20 | .09 | .03 |
| ☐ 36 Shannon Sharpe Denver Broncos | .15 | .07 | .02 |
| ☐ 37 Anthony Miller Denver Broncos | .15 | .07 | .02 |

| | | | |
|---|---|---|---|
| ☐ 38 Barry Sanders | .60 | .25 | .08 |
| Detroit Lions | | | |
| ☐ 39 Chris Spielman | .05 | .02 | .01 |
| Detroit Lions | | | |
| ☐ 40 Pat Swilling | .05 | .02 | .01 |
| Detroit Lions | | | |
| ☐ 41 Brett Perriman | .05 | .02 | .01 |
| Detroit Lions | | | |
| ☐ 42 Herman Moore | .15 | .07 | .02 |
| Detroit Lions | | | |
| ☐ 43 Scott Mitchell | .30 | .14 | .04 |
| Detroit Lions | | | |
| ☐ 44 Edgar Bennett | .05 | .02 | .01 |
| Green Bay Packers | | | |
| ☐ 45 Terrell Buckley | .05 | .02 | .01 |
| Green Bay Packers | | | |
| ☐ 46 LeRoy Butler | .05 | .02 | .01 |
| Green Bay Packers | | | |
| ☐ 47 Brett Favre | .50 | .23 | .06 |
| Green Bay Packers | | | |
| ☐ 48 Jackie Harris | .15 | .07 | .02 |
| Green Bay Packers | | | |
| ☐ 49 Sterling Sharpe | .30 | .14 | .04 |
| Green Bay Packers | | | |
| ☐ 50 Reggie White | .15 | .07 | .02 |
| Green Bay Packers | | | |
| ☐ 51 Gary Brown | .30 | .14 | .04 |
| Houston Oilers | | | |
| ☐ 52 Cody Carlson | .05 | .02 | .01 |
| Houston Oilers | | | |
| ☐ 53 Ray Childress | .05 | .02 | .01 |
| Houston Oilers | | | |
| ☐ 54 Ernest Givins | .10 | .05 | .01 |
| Houston Oilers | | | |
| ☐ 55 Bruce Matthews | .05 | .02 | .01 |
| Houston Oilers | | | |
| ☐ 56 Quentin Coryatt | .05 | .02 | .01 |
| Indianapolis Colts | | | |
| ☐ 57 Steve Emtman | .05 | .02 | .01 |
| Indianapolis Colts | | | |
| ☐ 58 Roosevelt Potts | .08 | .04 | .01 |
| Indianapolis Colts | | | |
| ☐ 59 Tony Bennett | .05 | .02 | .01 |
| Indianapolis Colts | | | |
| ☐ 60 Marcus Allen | .05 | .02 | .01 |
| Kansas City Chiefs | | | |
| ☐ 61 Joe Montana | 1.25 | .55 | .16 |
| Kansas City Chiefs | | | |
| ☐ 62 Neil Smith | .08 | .04 | .01 |
| Kansas City Chiefs | | | |
| ☐ 63 Derrick Thomas | .15 | .07 | .02 |
| Kansas City Chiefs | | | |
| ☐ 64 Dale Carter | .05 | .02 | .01 |
| Kansas City Chiefs | | | |
| ☐ 65 Tim Brown | .15 | .07 | .02 |
| Los Angeles Raiders | | | |
| ☐ 66 Jeff Hostetler | .08 | .04 | .01 |
| Los Angeles Raiders | | | |
| ☐ 67 Terry McDaniel | .05 | .02 | .01 |
| Los Angeles Raiders | | | |
| ☐ 68 Chester McGlockton | .05 | .02 | .01 |
| Los Angeles Raiders | | | |
| ☐ 69 Anthony Smith | .05 | .02 | .01 |
| Los Angeles Raiders | | | |
| ☐ 70 Albert Lewis | .05 | .02 | .01 |
| Los Angeles Raiders | | | |
| ☐ 71 Jerome Bettis | 2.00 | .90 | .25 |
| Los Angeles Rams | | | |
| ☐ 72 Shane Conlan | .05 | .02 | .01 |
| Los Angeles Rams | | | |
| ☐ 73 Troy Drayton | .08 | .04 | .01 |
| Los Angeles Rams | | | |
| ☐ 74 Sean Gilbert | .05 | .02 | .01 |
| Los Angeles Rams | | | |
| ☐ 75 Chris Miller | .05 | .02 | .01 |
| Los Angeles Rams | | | |
| ☐ 76 Bryan Cox | .05 | .02 | .01 |
| Miami Dolphins | | | |
| ☐ 77 Irving Fryar | .08 | .04 | .01 |
| Miami Dolphins | | | |
| ☐ 78 Keith Jackson | .10 | .05 | .01 |
| Miami Dolphins | | | |
| ☐ 79 Terry Kirby | .50 | .23 | .06 |
| Miami Dolphins | | | |
| ☐ 80 Dan Marino | .75 | .35 | .09 |
| Miami Dolphins | | | |
| ☐ 81 O.J. McDuffie | .25 | .11 | .03 |
| Miami Dolphins | | | |
| ☐ 82 Terry Allen | .05 | .02 | .01 |
| Minnesota Vikings | | | |
| ☐ 83 Cris Carter | .05 | .02 | .01 |
| Minnesota Vikings | | | |
| ☐ 84 Chris Doleman | .05 | .02 | .01 |
| Atlanta Falcons | | | |
| ☐ 85 Randall McDaniel | .05 | .02 | .01 |
| Minnesota Vikings | | | |
| ☐ 86 John Randle | .05 | .02 | .01 |
| Minnesota Vikings | | | |

| | | | |
|---|---|---|---|
| ☐ 87 Robert Smith | .10 | .05 | .01 |
| Minnesota Vikings | | | |
| ☐ 88 Jason Belser | .05 | .02 | .01 |
| Indianapolis Colts | | | |
| ☐ 89 Jack Del Rio | .05 | .02 | .01 |
| Minnesota Vikings | | | |
| ☐ 90 Vincent Brown | .05 | .02 | .01 |
| New England Patriots | | | |
| ☐ 91 Ben Coates | .05 | .02 | .01 |
| New England Patriots | | | |
| ☐ 92 Chris Slade | .05 | .02 | .01 |
| New England Patriots | | | |
| ☐ 93 Derek Brown | .30 | .14 | .04 |
| New Orleans Saints | | | |
| ☐ 94 Morten Andersen | .05 | .02 | .01 |
| New Orleans Saints | | | |
| ☐ 95 Willie Roaf | .05 | .02 | .01 |
| New Orleans Saints | | | |
| ☐ 96 Irv Smith | .05 | .02 | .01 |
| New Orleans Saints | | | |
| ☐ 97 Tyrone Hughes | .05 | .02 | .01 |
| New Orleans Saints | | | |
| ☐ 98 Michael Haynes | .15 | .07 | .02 |
| New Orleans Saints | | | |
| ☐ 99 Jim Everett | .10 | .05 | .01 |
| New Orleans Saints | | | |
| ☐ 100 Michael Brooks | .05 | .02 | .01 |
| New York Giants | | | |
| ☐ 101 Leroy Thompson | .05 | .02 | .01 |
| Pittsburgh Steelers | | | |
| ☐ 102 Rodney Hampton | .25 | .11 | .03 |
| New York Giants | | | |
| ☐ 103 David Meggett | .05 | .02 | .01 |
| New York Giants | | | |
| ☐ 104 Phil Simms | .10 | .05 | .01 |
| New York Giants | | | |
| ☐ 105 Boomer Esiason | .10 | .05 | .01 |
| New York Jets | | | |
| ☐ 106 Johnny Johnson | .08 | .04 | .01 |
| New York Jets | | | |
| ☐ 107 Gary Anderson | .05 | .02 | .01 |
| Pittsburgh Steelers | | | |
| ☐ 108 Mo Lewis | .05 | .02 | .01 |
| New York Jets | | | |
| ☐ 109 Ronnie Lott | .10 | .05 | .01 |
| New York Jets | | | |
| ☐ 110 Johnny Mitchell | .10 | .05 | .01 |
| New York Jets | | | |
| ☐ 111 Howard Cross | .05 | .02 | .01 |
| New York Giants | | | |
| ☐ 112 Victor Bailey | .05 | .02 | .01 |
| Philadelphia Eagles | | | |
| ☐ 113 Fred Barnett | .08 | .04 | .01 |
| Philadelphia Eagles | | | |
| ☐ 114 Randall Cunningham | .10 | .05 | .01 |
| Philadelphia Eagles | | | |
| ☐ 115 Calvin Williams | .05 | .02 | .01 |
| Philadelphia Eagles | | | |
| ☐ 116 Steve Beuerlein | .08 | .04 | .01 |
| Arizona Cardinals | | | |
| ☐ 117 Gary Clark | .10 | .05 | .01 |
| Arizona Cardinals | | | |
| ☐ 118 Ron Moore | .40 | .18 | .05 |
| Arizona Cardinals | | | |
| ☐ 119 Ricky Proehl | .08 | .04 | .01 |
| Arizona Cardinals | | | |
| ☐ 120 Eric Swann | .05 | .02 | .01 |
| Arizona Cardinals | | | |
| ☐ 121 Barry Foster | .15 | .07 | .02 |
| Pittsburgh Steelers | | | |
| ☐ 122 Kevin Greene | .05 | .02 | .01 |
| Pittsburgh Steelers | | | |
| ☐ 123 Greg Lloyd | .05 | .02 | .01 |
| Pittsburgh Steelers | | | |
| ☐ 124 Neil O'Donnell | .12 | .05 | .02 |
| Pittsburgh Steelers | | | |
| ☐ 125 Rod Woodson | .10 | .05 | .01 |
| Pittsburgh Steelers | | | |
| ☐ 126 Ronnie Harmon | .05 | .02 | .01 |
| San Diego Chargers | | | |
| ☐ 127 Mark Higgs | .05 | .02 | .01 |
| Miami Dolphins | | | |
| ☐ 128 Stan Humphries | .05 | .02 | .01 |
| San Diego Chargers | | | |
| ☐ 129 Leslie O'Neal | .05 | .02 | .01 |
| San Diego Chargers | | | |
| ☐ 130 Chris Mims | .05 | .02 | .01 |
| San Diego Chargers | | | |
| ☐ 131 Stanley Richard | .05 | .02 | .01 |
| San Diego Chargers | | | |
| ☐ 132 Junior Seau | .10 | .05 | .01 |
| San Diego Chargers | | | |
| ☐ 133 Brent Jones | .08 | .04 | .01 |
| San Francisco 49ers | | | |
| ☐ 134 Tim McDonald | .05 | .02 | .01 |
| San Francisco 49ers | | | |
| ☐ 135 Jerry Rice | .50 | .23 | .06 |

| | | | |
|---|---|---|---|
| San Francisco 49ers | | | |
| ☐ 136 Dana Stubblefield | .15 | .07 | .02 |
| San Francisco 49ers | | | |
| ☐ 137 Ricky Watters | .20 | .09 | .03 |
| San Francisco 49ers | | | |
| ☐ 138 Steve Young | .15 | .07 | .02 |
| San Francisco 49ers | | | |
| ☐ 139 Cortez Kennedy | .08 | .04 | .01 |
| Seattle Seahawks | | | |
| ☐ 140 Rick Mirer | 2.00 | .90 | .25 |
| Seattle Seahawks | | | |
| ☐ 141 Eugene Robinson | .05 | .02 | .01 |
| Seattle Seahawks | | | |
| ☐ 142 Chris Warren | .10 | .05 | .01 |
| Seattle Seahawks | | | |
| ☐ 143 Nate Odomes | .05 | .02 | .01 |
| Seattle Seahawks | | | |
| ☐ 144 Howard Ballard | .05 | .02 | .01 |
| Seattle Seahawks | | | |
| ☐ 145 Flipper Anderson | .05 | .02 | .01 |
| Los Angeles Rams | | | |
| ☐ 146 Chris Jacke | .05 | .02 | .01 |
| Green Bay Packers | | | |
| ☐ 147 Santana Dotson | .08 | .04 | .01 |
| Tampa Bay Buccaneers | | | |
| ☐ 148 Craig Erickson | .08 | .04 | .01 |
| Tampa Bay Buccaneers | | | |
| ☐ 149 Hardy Nickerson | .05 | .02 | .01 |
| Tampa Bay Buccaneers | | | |
| ☐ 150 Lawrence Dawsey | .05 | .02 | .01 |
| Tampa Bay Buccaneers | | | |
| ☐ 151 Terry Wooden | .05 | .02 | .01 |
| Seattle Seahawks | | | |
| ☐ 152 Ethan Horton | .05 | .02 | .01 |
| Washington Redskins | | | |
| ☐ 153 John Kasay | .05 | .02 | .01 |
| Seattle Seahawks | | | |
| ☐ 154 Desmond Howard | .15 | .07 | .02 |
| Washington Redskins | | | |
| ☐ 155 Ken Harvey | .05 | .02 | .01 |
| Washington Redskins | | | |
| ☐ 156 William Fuller | .05 | .02 | .01 |
| Philadelphia Eagles | | | |
| ☐ 157 Clyde Simmons | .08 | .04 | .01 |
| Arizona Cardinals | | | |
| ☐ 158 Randal Hill | .08 | .04 | .01 |
| Arizona Cardinals | | | |
| ☐ 159 Garrison Hearst | .20 | .09 | .03 |
| Arizona Cardinals | | | |
| ☐ 160 Mike Pritchard | .08 | .04 | .01 |
| Denver Broncos | | | |
| ☐ 161 Jessie Tuggie | .05 | .02 | .01 |
| Atlanta Falcons | | | |
| ☐ 162 Erric Pegram | .20 | .09 | .03 |
| Atlanta Falcons | | | |
| ☐ 163 Kevin Ross | .05 | .02 | .01 |
| Atlanta Falcons | | | |
| ☐ 164 Bill Brooks | .08 | .04 | .01 |
| Buffalo Bills | | | |
| ☐ 165 Darryl Talley | .05 | .02 | .01 |
| Buffalo Bills | | | |
| ☐ 166 Steve Tasker | .05 | .02 | .01 |
| Buffalo Bills | | | |
| ☐ 167 Pete Stoyanovich | .05 | .02 | .01 |
| Miami Dolphins | | | |
| ☐ 168 Dante Jones | .05 | .02 | .01 |
| Chicago Bears | | | |
| ☐ 169 Vencie Glenn | .05 | .02 | .01 |
| Minnesota Vikings | | | |
| ☐ 170 Tom Waddle | .05 | .02 | .01 |
| Chicago Bears | | | |
| ☐ 171 Harlon Barnett | .05 | .02 | .01 |
| New England Patriots | | | |
| ☐ 172 Trace Armstrong | .05 | .02 | .01 |
| Chicago Bears | | | |
| ☐ 173 Tim Worley | .05 | .02 | .01 |
| Chicago Bears | | | |
| ☐ 174 Alfred Williams | .05 | .02 | .01 |
| Cincinnati Bengals | | | |
| ☐ 175 Louis Oliver | .05 | .02 | .01 |
| Cincinnati Bengals | | | |
| ☐ 176 Darryl Williams | .05 | .02 | .01 |
| Cincinnati Bengals | | | |
| ☐ 177 Clay Matthews | .08 | .04 | .01 |
| Atlanta Falcons | | | |
| ☐ 178 Kyle Clifton | .05 | .02 | .01 |
| New York Jets | | | |
| ☐ 179 Alvin Harper | .08 | .04 | .01 |
| Dallas Cowboys | | | |
| ☐ 180 Jay Novacek | .08 | .04 | .01 |
| Dallas Cowboys | | | |
| ☐ 181 Ken Norton Jr. | .08 | .04 | .01 |
| San Francisco 49ers | | | |
| ☐ 182 Kevin Williams | .15 | .07 | .02 |
| Dallas Cowboys | | | |
| ☐ 183 Daryl Johnston | .05 | .02 | .01 |
| Dallas Cowboys | | | |
| ☐ 184 Rod Bernstine | .05 | .02 | .01 |
| Denver Broncos | | | |
| ☐ 185 Karl Mecklenburg | .05 | .02 | .01 |
| Denver Broncos | | | |
| ☐ 186 Dennis Smith | .05 | .02 | .01 |
| Denver Broncos | | | |
| ☐ 187 Robert Delpino | .05 | .02 | .01 |
| Denver Broncos | | | |
| ☐ 188 Bennie Blades | .05 | .02 | .01 |
| Detroit Lions | | | |
| ☐ 189 Jason Hanson | .05 | .02 | .01 |
| Detroit Lions | | | |
| ☐ 190 Derrick Moore | .08 | .04 | .01 |
| Detroit Lions | | | |
| ☐ 191 Mark Clayton | .05 | .02 | .01 |
| Green Bay Packers | | | |
| ☐ 192 Webster Slaughter | .05 | .02 | .01 |
| Houston Oilers | | | |
| ☐ 193 Haywood Jeffires | .10 | .05 | .01 |
| Houston Oilers | | | |
| ☐ 194 Bubba McDowell | .05 | .02 | .01 |
| Houston Oilers | | | |
| ☐ 195 Warren Moon | .10 | .05 | .01 |
| Minnesota Vikings | | | |
| ☐ 196 Al Smith | .05 | .02 | .01 |
| Houston Oilers | | | |
| ☐ 197 Bill Romanowski | .05 | .02 | .01 |
| Philadelphia Eagles | | | |
| ☐ 198 John Carney | .05 | .02 | .01 |
| San Diego Chargers | | | |
| ☐ 199 Kerry Cash | .05 | .02 | .01 |
| Indianapolis Colts | | | |
| ☐ 200 Darren Carrington | .05 | .02 | .01 |
| San Diego Chargers | | | |
| ☐ 201 Jeff Lageman | .05 | .02 | .01 |
| New York Jets | | | |
| ☐ 202 Tracy Simien | .05 | .02 | .01 |
| Kansas City Chiefs | | | |
| ☐ 203 Willie Davis | .08 | .04 | .01 |
| Kansas City Chiefs | | | |
| ☐ 204 Dan Saleaumua | .05 | .02 | .01 |
| Kansas City Chiefs | | | |
| ☐ 205 Raghib Ismail | .15 | .07 | .02 |
| Los Angeles Raiders | | | |
| ☐ 206 James Jett | .30 | .14 | .04 |
| Los Angeles Raiders | | | |
| ☐ 207 Todd Lyght | .05 | .02 | .01 |
| Los Angeles Rams | | | |
| ☐ 208 Roman Phifer | .05 | .02 | .01 |
| Los Angeles Rams | | | |
| ☐ 209 Jimmie Jones | .05 | .02 | .01 |
| Los Angeles Rams | | | |
| ☐ 210 Jeff Cross | .05 | .02 | .01 |
| Miami Dolphins | | | |
| ☐ 211 Eric Davis | .05 | .02 | .01 |
| San Francisco 49ers | | | |
| ☐ 212 Keith Byars | .08 | .04 | .01 |
| Miami Dolphins | | | |
| ☐ 213 Richmond Webb | .05 | .02 | .01 |
| Miami Dolphins | | | |
| ☐ 214 Anthony Carter | .05 | .02 | .01 |
| Detroit Lions | | | |
| ☐ 215 Henry Thomas | .05 | .02 | .01 |
| Minnesota Vikings | | | |
| ☐ 216 Andre Tippett | .05 | .02 | .01 |
| New England Patriots | | | |
| ☐ 217 Rickey Jackson | .05 | .02 | .01 |
| New Orleans Saints | | | |
| ☐ 218 Vaughan Johnson | .05 | .02 | .01 |
| New Orleans Saints | | | |
| ☐ 219 Eric Martin | .05 | .02 | .01 |
| New Orleans Saints | | | |
| ☐ 220 Sam Mills | .05 | .02 | .01 |
| New Orleans Saints | | | |
| ☐ 221 Renaldo Turnbull | .05 | .02 | .01 |
| New Orleans Saints | | | |
| ☐ 222 Mark Collins | .05 | .02 | .01 |
| Kansas City Chiefs | | | |
| ☐ 223 Mike Johnson | .05 | .02 | .01 |
| Detroit Lions | | | |
| ☐ 224 Rob Moore | .08 | .04 | .01 |
| New York Jets | | | |
| ☐ 225 Seth Joyner | .05 | .02 | .01 |
| Arizona Cardinals | | | |
| ☐ 226 Herschel Walker | .10 | .05 | .01 |
| Philadelphia Eagles | | | |
| ☐ 227 Eric Green | .08 | .04 | .01 |
| Pittsburgh Steelers | | | |
| ☐ 228 Marion Butts | .08 | .04 | .01 |
| New England Patriots | | | |
| ☐ 229 John Friesz | .08 | .04 | .01 |
| Washington Redskins | | | |
| ☐ 230 John Taylor | .08 | .04 | .01 |
| San Francisco 49ers | | | |
| ☐ 231 Dexter Carter | .05 | .02 | .01 |
| San Francisco 49ers | | | |
| ☐ 232 Brian Blades | .05 | .02 | .01 |
| Seattle Seahawks | | | |
| ☐ 233 Reggie Cobb | .05 | .02 | .01 |

| | | | | |
|---|---|---|---|---|
| Green Bay Packers | | | | |
| ☐ 234 Paul Gruber | .05 | .02 | .01 |
| Tampa Bay Buccaneers | | | |
| ☐ 235 Ricky Reynolds | .05 | .02 | .01 |
| New England Patriots | | | |
| ☐ 236 Vince Workman | .05 | .02 | .01 |
| Tampa Bay Buccaneers | | | |
| ☐ 237 Darrell Green | .05 | .02 | .01 |
| Washington Redskins | | | |
| ☐ 238 Jim Lachey | .05 | .02 | .01 |
| Washington Redskins | | | |
| ☐ 239 James Hasty | .05 | .02 | .01 |
| New York Jets | | | |
| ☐ 240 Howie Long | .10 | .05 | .01 |
| Los Angeles Raiders | | | |
| ☐ 241 Aeneas Williams | .05 | .02 | .01 |
| Arizona Cardinals | | | |
| ☐ 242 Mike Kenn | .05 | .02 | .01 |
| Atlanta Falcons | | | |
| ☐ 243 Henry Jones | .05 | .02 | .01 |
| Buffalo Bills | | | |
| ☐ 244 Kenneth Davis | .05 | .02 | .01 |
| Buffalo Bills | | | |
| ☐ 245 Tim Krumrie | .05 | .02 | .01 |
| Cincinnati Bengals | | | |
| ☐ 246 Derrick Fenner | .05 | .02 | .01 |
| Cincinnati Bengals | | | |
| ☐ 247 Mark Carrier | .05 | .02 | .01 |
| Cleveland Browns | | | |
| ☐ 248 Robert Porcher | .05 | .02 | .01 |
| Detroit Lions | | | |
| ☐ 249 Darren Woodson | .05 | .02 | .01 |
| Dallas Cowboys | | | |
| ☐ 250 Kevin Smith | .05 | .02 | .01 |
| Dallas Cowboys | | | |
| ☐ 251 Mark Stepnoski | .05 | .02 | .01 |
| Dallas Cowboys | | | |
| ☐ 252 Simon Fletcher | .05 | .02 | .01 |
| Denver Broncos | | | |
| ☐ 253 Derek Russell | .05 | .02 | .01 |
| Denver Broncos | | | |
| ☐ 254 Mike Croel | .05 | .02 | .01 |
| Denver Broncos | | | |
| ☐ 255 Johnny Holland | .05 | .02 | .01 |
| Green Bay Packers | | | |
| ☐ 256 Bryce Paup | .05 | .02 | .01 |
| Green Bay Packers | | | |
| ☐ 257 Cris Dishman | .05 | .02 | .01 |
| Houston Oilers | | | |
| ☐ 258 Sean Jones | .05 | .02 | .01 |
| Green Bay Packers | | | |
| ☐ 259 Marcus Robertson | .05 | .02 | .01 |
| Houston Oilers | | | |
| ☐ 260 Steve Jackson | .05 | .02 | .01 |
| Houston Oilers | | | |
| ☐ 261 Jeff Herrod | .05 | .02 | .01 |
| Indianapolis Colts | | | |
| ☐ 262 John Alt | .05 | .02 | .01 |
| Kansas City Chiefs | | | |
| ☐ 263 Nick Lowery | .05 | .02 | .01 |
| Kansas City Chiefs | | | |
| ☐ 264 Greg Robinson | .10 | .05 | .01 |
| Los Angeles Raiders | | | |
| ☐ 265 Alexander Wright | .05 | .02 | .01 |
| Los Angeles Raiders | | | |
| ☐ 266 Steve Wisniewski | .05 | .02 | .01 |
| Los Angeles Raiders | | | |
| ☐ 267 Henry Ellard | .05 | .02 | .01 |
| Washington Redskins | | | |
| ☐ 268 Tracy Scroggins | .05 | .02 | .01 |
| Detroit Lions | | | |
| ☐ 269 Jackie Slater | .05 | .02 | .01 |
| Los Angeles Rams | | | |
| ☐ 270 Troy Vincent | .05 | .02 | .01 |
| Miami Dolphins | | | |
| ☐ 271 Qadry Ismail | .15 | .07 | .02 |
| Minnesota Vikings | | | |
| ☐ 272 Steve Jordan | .05 | .02 | .01 |
| Minnesota Vikings | | | |
| ☐ 273 Leonard Russell | .08 | .04 | .01 |
| New England Patriots | | | |
| ☐ 274 Maurice Hurst | .05 | .02 | .01 |
| New England Patriots | | | |
| ☐ 275 Scottie Graham | .40 | .18 | .05 |
| Minnesota Vikings | | | |
| ☐ 276 Carlton Bailey | .05 | .02 | .01 |
| New York Giants | | | |
| ☐ 277 John Elliott | .05 | .02 | .01 |
| New York Giants | | | |
| ☐ 278 Corey Miller | .05 | .02 | .01 |
| New York Giants | | | |
| ☐ 279 Brad Baxter | .05 | .02 | .01 |
| New York Jets | | | |
| ☐ 280 Brian Washington | .05 | .02 | .01 |
| New York Jets | | | |
| ☐ 281 Tim Harris | .05 | .02 | .01 |
| Philadelphia Eagles | | | |
| ☐ 282 Byron Evans | .05 | .02 | .01 |

| | | | | |
|---|---|---|---|---|
| Philadelphia Eagles | | | | |
| ☐ 283 Dermontti Dawson | .05 | .02 | .01 |
| Pittsburgh Steelers | | | |
| ☐ 284 Carnell Lake | .05 | .02 | .01 |
| Pittsburgh Steelers | | | |
| ☐ 285 Jeff Graham | .05 | .02 | .01 |
| Pittsburgh Steelers | | | |
| ☐ 286 Merton Hanks | .05 | .02 | .01 |
| San Francisco 49ers | | | |
| ☐ 287 Harris Barton | .05 | .02 | .01 |
| San Francisco 49ers | | | |
| ☐ 288 Guy McIntyre | .05 | .02 | .01 |
| San Francisco 49ers | | | |
| ☐ 289 Kelvin Martin | .05 | .02 | .01 |
| Seattle Seahawks | | | |
| ☐ 290 John L. Williams | .05 | .02 | .01 |
| Pittsburgh Steelers | | | |
| ☐ 291 Courtney Hawkins | .05 | .02 | .01 |
| Tampa Bay Buccaneers | | | |
| ☐ 292 Vaughn Hebron | .05 | .02 | .01 |
| Philadelphia Eagles | | | |
| ☐ 293 Brian Mitchell | .05 | .02 | .01 |
| Washington Redskins | | | |
| ☐ 294 Andre Collins | .05 | .02 | .01 |
| Washington Redskins | | | |
| ☐ 295 Art Monk | .10 | .05 | .01 |
| New York Jets | | | |
| ☐ 296 Mark Rypien | .08 | .04 | .01 |
| Cleveland Browns | | | |
| ☐ 297 Ricky Sanders | .05 | .02 | .01 |
| Washington Redskins | | | |
| ☐ 298 Eric Hill | .05 | .02 | .01 |
| Arizona Cardinals | | | |
| ☐ 299 Larry Centers | .05 | .02 | .01 |
| Arizona Cardinals | | | |
| ☐ 300 Norm Johnson | .05 | .02 | .01 |
| Atlanta Falcons | | | |
| ☐ 301 Pete Metzelaars | .05 | .02 | .01 |
| Buffalo Bills | | | |
| ☐ 302 Ricardo McDonald | .05 | .02 | .01 |
| Cincinnati Bengals | | | |
| ☐ 303 Stevon Moore | .05 | .02 | .01 |
| Cleveland Browns | | | |
| ☐ 304 Mike Sherrard | .05 | .02 | .01 |
| New York Giants | | | |
| ☐ 305 Andy Harmon | .05 | .02 | .01 |
| Philadelphia Eagles | | | |
| ☐ 306 Anthony Johnson | .05 | .02 | .01 |
| N ew York Jets | | | |
| ☐ 307 J.J. Birden | .05 | .02 | .01 |
| Kansas City Chiefs | | | |
| ☐ 308 Neal Anderson | .05 | .02 | .01 |
| Chicago Bears | | | |
| ☐ 309 Lewis Tillman | .05 | .02 | .01 |
| Chicago Bears | | | |
| ☐ 310 Richard Dent | .10 | .05 | .01 |
| San Francisco 49ers | | | |
| ☐ 311 Nate Newton | .05 | .02 | .01 |
| Dallas Cowboys | | | |
| ☐ 312 Sean Dawkins | .50 | .23 | .06 |
| Indianapolis Colts | | | |
| ☐ 313 Lawrence Taylor | .05 | .02 | .01 |
| New York Giants | | | |
| ☐ 314 Wilber Marshall | .08 | .04 | .01 |
| Houston Oilers | | | |
| ☐ 315 Tom Carter | .05 | .02 | .01 |
| Washington Redskins | | | |
| ☐ 316 Reggie Brooks | .75 | .35 | .09 |
| Washington Redskins | | | |
| ☐ 317 Eric Curry | .05 | .02 | .01 |
| Tampa Bay Buccaneers | | | |
| ☐ 318 Horace Copeland | .05 | .02 | .01 |
| Tampa Bay Buccaneers | | | |
| ☐ 319 Natrone Means | .25 | .11 | .03 |
| San Diego Chargers | | | |
| ☐ 320 Eric Allen | .08 | .04 | .01 |
| Philadelphia Eagles | | | |
| ☐ 321 Marvin Jones | .05 | .02 | .01 |
| New York Jets | | | |
| ☐ 322 Keith Hamilton | .05 | .02 | .01 |
| New York Giants | | | |
| ☐ 323 Vincent Brisby | .30 | .14 | .04 |
| New England Patriots | | | |
| ☐ 324 Drew Bledsoe | 2.00 | .90 | .25 |
| New England Patriots | | | |
| ☐ 325 Tom Rathman | .05 | .02 | .01 |
| San Francisco 49ers | | | |
| ☐ 326 Ed McCaffrey | .05 | .02 | .01 |
| New York Giants | | | |
| ☐ 327 Steve Israel | .05 | .02 | .01 |
| Los Angeles Rams | | | |
| ☐ 328 Dan Wilkinson | .50 | .23 | .06 |
| Cincinnati Bengals | | | |
| ☐ 329 Marshall Faulk | 3.00 | 1.35 | .40 |
| Indianapolis Colts | | | |
| ☐ 330 Heath Shuler | 5.00 | 2.30 | .60 |
| Washington Redskins | | | |
| ☐ 331 Willie McGinest | .50 | .23 | .06 |

| | | | |
|---|---|---|---|
| New England Patriots | | | |
| ☐ 332 Trev Alberts | .50 | .23 | .06 |
| Indianapolis Colts | | | |
| ☐ 333 Trent Dilfer | 2.25 | 1.00 | .30 |
| Tampa Bay Buccaneers | | | |
| ☐ 334 Bryant Young | .25 | .11 | .03 |
| San Francisco 49ers | | | |
| ☐ 335 Sam Adams | .25 | .11 | .03 |
| Seattle Seahawks | | | |
| ☐ 336 Antonio Langham | .30 | .14 | .04 |
| Cleveland Browns | | | |
| ☐ 337 Jamir Miller | .30 | .14 | .04 |
| Arizona Cardinals | | | |
| ☐ 338 John Thierry | .30 | .14 | .04 |
| Chicago Bears | | | |
| ☐ 339 Aaron Glenn | .15 | .07 | .02 |
| New York Jets | | | |
| ☐ 340 Joe Johnson | .10 | .05 | .01 |
| New Orleans Saints | | | |
| ☐ 341 Bernard Williams | .10 | .05 | .01 |
| Philadelphia Eagles | | | |
| ☐ 342 Wayne Gandy | .10 | .05 | .01 |
| Los Angeles Rams | | | |
| ☐ 343 Aaron Taylor | .10 | .05 | .01 |
| Green Bay Packers | | | |
| ☐ 344 Charles Johnson | 1.00 | .45 | .13 |
| Pittsburgh Steelers | | | |
| ☐ 345 DeWayne Washington | .10 | .05 | .01 |
| Minnesota Vikings | | | |
| ☐ 346 Todd Steussie | .10 | .05 | .01 |
| Minnesota Vikings | | | |
| ☐ 347 Tim Bowens | .15 | .07 | .02 |
| Miami Dolphins | | | |
| ☐ 348 Johnnie Morton | .75 | .35 | .09 |
| Detroit Lions | | | |
| ☐ 349 Rob Fredrickson | .10 | .05 | .01 |
| Los Angeles Raiders | | | |
| ☐ 350 Shante Carver | .15 | .07 | .02 |
| Dallas Cowboys | | | |
| ☐ 351 Thomas Lewis | .40 | .18 | .05 |
| New York Giants | | | |
| ☐ 352 Greg Hill | .75 | .35 | .09 |
| Kansas City Chiefs | | | |
| ☐ 353 Henry Ford | .10 | .05 | .01 |
| Houston Oilers | | | |
| ☐ 354 Jeff Burris | .15 | .07 | .02 |
| Buffalo Bills | | | |
| ☐ 355 William Floyd | .50 | .23 | .06 |
| San Francisco 49ers | | | |
| ☐ 356 Derrick Alexander | .50 | .23 | .06 |
| Cleveland Browns | | | |
| ☐ 357 Darnay Scott | .40 | .18 | .05 |
| Cincinnati Bengals | | | |
| ☐ 358 Isaac Bruce | .20 | .09 | .03 |
| Los Angeles Rams | | | |
| ☐ 359 Errict Rhett | 1.00 | .45 | .13 |
| Tampa Bay Buccaneers | | | |
| ☐ 360 Kevin Lee | .30 | .14 | .04 |
| New England Patriots | | | |
| ☐ 361 Chuck Levy | .60 | .25 | .08 |
| Arizona Cardinals | | | |
| ☐ 362 David Palmer | 1.00 | .45 | .13 |
| Minnesota Vikings | | | |
| ☐ 363 Ryan Yarborough | .25 | .11 | .03 |
| New York Jets | | | |
| ☐ 364 Charlie Garner | .60 | .25 | .08 |
| Philadelphia Eagles | | | |
| ☐ 365 Isaac Davis | .15 | .07 | .02 |
| San Diego Chargers | | | |
| ☐ 366 Mario Bates | .40 | .18 | .05 |
| New Orleans Saints | | | |
| ☐ 367 Bert Emanuel | .25 | .11 | .03 |
| Atlanta Falcons | | | |
| ☐ 368 Thomas Randolph | .15 | .07 | .02 |
| New York Giants | | | |
| ☐ 369 Bucky Brooks | .20 | .09 | .03 |
| Buffalo Bills | | | |
| ☐ 370 Allen Aldridge | .10 | .05 | .01 |
| Denver Broncos | | | |
| ☐ 371 Charlie Ward | 1.00 | .45 | .13 |
| 1993 Heisman Trophy Winner | | | |
| ☐ 372 Aubrey Beavers | .15 | .07 | .02 |
| Miami Dolphins | | | |
| ☐ 373 Donnell Bennett | .20 | .09 | .03 |
| Kansas City Chiefs | | | |
| ☐ 374 Jason Sehorn | .15 | .07 | .02 |
| New York Giants | | | |
| ☐ 375 Lonnie Johnson | .15 | .07 | .02 |
| Buffalo Bills | | | |
| ☐ 376 Tyronne Drakeford | .10 | .05 | .01 |
| San Francisco 49ers | | | |
| ☐ 377 Andre Coleman | .30 | .14 | .04 |
| San Diego Chargers | | | |
| ☐ 378 Lamar Smith | .25 | .11 | .03 |
| Seattle Seahawks | | | |
| ☐ 379 Calvin Jones | .60 | .25 | .08 |
| Los Angeles Raiders | | | |
| ☐ 380 LeShon Johnson | .50 | .23 | .06 |

| | | | |
|---|---|---|---|
| Green Bay Packers | | | |
| ☐ 381 Byron Morris | .40 | .18 | .05 |
| Pittsburgh Steelers | | | |
| ☐ 382 Lake Dawson | .60 | .25 | .08 |
| Kansas City Chiefs | | | |
| ☐ 383 Corey Sawyer | .15 | .07 | .02 |
| Cincinnati Bengals | | | |
| ☐ 384 Willie Jackson | .30 | .14 | .04 |
| Dallas Cowboys | | | |
| ☐ 385 Perry Klein | .50 | .23 | .06 |
| Atlanta Falcons | | | |
| ☐ 386 Ronnie Woolfork | .10 | .05 | .01 |
| Miami Dolphins | | | |
| ☐ 387 Doug Nussmeier | .40 | .18 | .05 |
| New Orleans Saints | | | |
| ☐ 388 Rob Waldrop | .10 | .05 | .01 |
| Kansas City Chiefs | | | |
| ☐ 389 Glenn Foley | .40 | .18 | .05 |
| New York Jets | | | |
| ☐ 390 Troy Aikman CC | .50 | .23 | .06 |
| Michael Irvin | | | |
| Dallas Cowboys | | | |
| ☐ 391 Steve Young CC | .25 | .11 | .03 |
| Jerry Rice | | | |
| San Francisco 49ers | | | |
| ☐ 392 Brett Favre CC | .35 | .16 | .04 |
| Sterling Sharpe | | | |
| Green Bay Packers | | | |
| ☐ 393 Jim Kelly CC | .15 | .07 | .02 |
| Andre Reed | | | |
| Buffalo Bills | | | |
| ☐ 394 John Elway CC | .20 | .09 | .03 |
| Shannon Sharpe | | | |
| Denver Broncos | | | |
| ☐ 395 Carolina Panthers | .10 | .05 | .01 |
| ☐ 396 Jacksonville Jaguars | .10 | .05 | .01 |
| ☐ 397 Checklist 1 | .05 | .02 | .01 |
| ☐ 398 Checklist 2 | .05 | .02 | .01 |
| ☐ 399 Checklist 3 | .05 | .02 | .01 |
| ☐ 400 Checklist 4 | .05 | .02 | .01 |
| ☐ 401 Sterling Sharpe III | .15 | .07 | .02 |
| Green Bay Packers | | | |
| ☐ 402 Derrick Thomas III | .05 | .02 | .01 |
| Kansas City Chiefs | | | |
| ☐ 403 Joe Montana III | .60 | .25 | .08 |
| Kansas City Chiefs | | | |
| ☐ 404 Emmitt Smith III | .75 | .35 | .09 |
| Dallas Cowboys | | | |
| ☐ 405 Barry Sanders III | .30 | .14 | .04 |
| Detroit Lions | | | |
| ☐ ES1 Emmitt Smith | 50.00 | 23.00 | 6.25 |
| Super Bowl MVP | | | |
| Dallas Cowboys | | | |

# 1994 ProLine Live Classic Basketball Previews

Issued two per case, these five standard-size (2 1/2" by 3 1/2") basketball cards have color action shots on borderless fronts. The player's name and position appear in a black box at the bottom, along with the word "Preview" above his name. The backs carry another color action shot with biography and statistics appearing on the faded bottom part of the photo. The cards are numbered on back with a "BP" prefix.

| | MINT | EXC | G-VG |
|---|---|---|---|
| COMPLETE SET (5) | 90.00 | 40.00 | 11.50 |
| COMMON PLAYER (BP1-BP5) | 10.00 | 4.50 | 1.25 |
| | | | |
| ☐ BP1 Eric Montross | 15.00 | 6.75 | 1.90 |
| ☐ BP2 Jason Kidd | 25.00 | 11.50 | 3.10 |
| ☐ BP3 Yinka Dare | 10.00 | 4.50 | 1.25 |
| ☐ BP4 Glenn Robinson | 40.00 | 18.00 | 5.00 |
| ☐ BP5 Clifford Rozier | 10.00 | 4.50 | 1.25 |

# 1988 Pro Set Test Designs

These five Randall Cunningham cards are the test designs for the 1989 Pro Set football cards. As tests, they were produced in very small quantities. The cards are standard size, 2 1/2" by 3 1/2". It seems that all cards in this five-card set were printed at the same time and in the same (small) quantities. The five variations are basically experiments with and without borders and different color combinations. Horizontally oriented backs have a close-up photograph of player, statistical and biographical information, card number, and the Pro Set logo in a box enclosed in a white border. Player's name and personal statistics appear in reverse-out lettering in a colored band across the top of the card. The cards are numbered on the back. Only the most avid master set collector would feel that these cards are part of the 1989 Pro Set master set.

|  | MINT | EXC | G-VG |
|---|---|---|---|
| COMPLETE SET (5) | 175.00 | 70.00 | 18.00 |
| COMMON PLAYER | 45.00 | 18.00 | 4.50 |
| ☐ 315A Randall Cunningham Philadelphia Eagles (No name or team designated on card front; borderless; vertical logo) | 45.00 | 18.00 | 4.50 |
| ☐ 315B Randall Cunningham Philadelphia Eagles (No name or team designated on card front; silver border; vertical logo) | 45.00 | 18.00 | 4.50 |
| ☐ 315C Randall Cunningham Philadelphia Eagles (Name and team designated on card front; borderless; horizontal logo) | 45.00 | 18.00 | 4.50 |
| ☐ 315D Randall Cunningham Philadelphia Eagles (Name and team designated on card front; black border; horizontal logo) | 45.00 | 18.00 | 4.50 |
| ☐ 315E Randall Cunningham Philadelphia Eagles (Name and team designated on card front; gray border; horizontal logo) | 45.00 | 18.00 | 4.50 |

# 1988 Pro Set Test

This eight-card set was supposedly produced as a give-away to show interested parties what the new "Pro Set" cards were going to be like. They were produced in limited quantities and merely given away primarily at the National Candy show in Phoenix. They are standard size, 2 1/2" by 3 1/2". The only front photo that was the same in the actual set was Jerry Rice. This set is also distinguishable in that the backs are oriented vertically rather than horizontally as the regular set.

|  | MINT | EXC | G-VG |
|---|---|---|---|
| COMPLETE SET (8) | 225.00 | 90.00 | 22.00 |
| COMMON PLAYER (1-8) | 10.00 | 4.00 | 1.00 |
| ☐ 1 Dan Marino Miami Dolphins | 90.00 | 36.00 | 9.00 |
| ☐ 2 Jerry Rice San Francisco 49ers | 75.00 | 30.00 | 7.50 |
| ☐ 3 Eric Dickerson Indianapolis Colts | 25.00 | 10.00 | 2.50 |
| ☐ 4 Reggie White | 25.00 | 10.00 | 2.50 |

| | | | |
|---|---|---|---|
| Philadelphia Eagles | | | |
| ☐ 5 Mike Singletary | 20.00 | 8.00 | 2.00 |
| Chicago Bears | | | |
| ☐ 6 Frank Minnifield | 10.00 | 4.00 | 1.00 |
| Cleveland Browns | | | |
| ☐ 7 Phil Simms | 25.00 | 10.00 | 2.50 |
| New York Giants | | | |
| ☐ 8 Jim Kelly | 45.00 | 18.00 | 4.50 |
| Buffalo Bills | | | |

# 1989 Pro Set

Pro Set's 1989 football set was produced in three series. The cards are standard size, 2 1/2" by 3 1/2", and feature full-color photos on both the card front and back. The first series of 440 cards is ordered numerically by teams and alphabetically within teams, e.g., Atlanta Falcons (1-16), Buffalo Bills (17-34), Chicago Bears (35-53), Cincinnati Bengals (54-72), Cleveland Browns (73-86), Dallas Cowboys (87-98), Denver Broncos (99-114), Detroit Lions (115-127), Green Bay Packers (128-139), Houston Oilers (140-154), Indianapolis Colts (155-166), Kansas City Chiefs (167-181), Los Angeles Raiders (182-194), Los Angeles Rams (195-210), Miami Dolphins (211-225), Minnesota Vikings (226-243), New England Patriots (244-260), New Orleans Saints (261-278), New York Giants (279-293), New York Jets (294-311), Philadelphia Eagles (312-327), Phoenix Cardinals (328-341), Pittsburgh Steelers (342-355), San Diego Chargers (356-368), San Francisco 49ers (369-389), Seattle Seahawks (390-408), Tampa Bay Buccaneers (409-421), Washington Redskins (422-440). The William Perry card number 47 was supposedly a mistake in that it was apparently printed and released briefly before appropriate permissions had been granted. The Pete Rozelle commemorative card was expressly intended to be scarce as it was supposed to be placed randomly in one out of every 200 first series wax packs. The set is considered complete without either the Perry or the Rozelle cards. The second series contains 100 cards. The fronts of the second series cards have color action photos bordered in red; otherwise, they are similar in appearance to the first series. Cards numbered 485-515 feature the 1989 first-round draft picks from the previous spring's college draft and cards numbered 516-540 are "Pro Set Prospects". These cards were distributed only in Series II packs, usually three to five per pack. The 1989 Pro Set Final Update contains 21 standard-size (2 1/2" by 3 1/2") cards. The fronts have color action photos which are similar in appearance to the regular 1989 Pro Set cards. Cards numbered 542-549 are Pro Set Prospects, 550-555 have no special stripe, and cards 556-561 are designated as "Traded". These cards were distributed in Final Series II packs as well as being offered direct from Pro Set as a shrink-wrapped set for 2.00 plus 50 Pro Set Play Book points. Rookie Cards include Troy Aikman, Flipper Anderson, Don Beebe, Brian Blades, Bubby Brister, Tim Brown, Marion Butts, Mark Carrier, Cris Carter, Bobby Humphrey, Michael Irvin, Keith

Jackson, Reggie Langhorne, Don Majkowski, Dave Meggett, Eric Metcalf, Anthony Miller, Chris Miller, Jay Novacek, Rodney Peete, Andre Rison, Mark Rypien, Barry Sanders, Deion Sanders, Sterling Sharpe, Neil Smith, John Stephens, John Taylor, Broderick Thomas, Derrick Thomas, Thurman Thomas, and Rod Woodson.

| | MINT | EXC | G-VG |
|---|---|---|---|
| COMPLETE SET (561) | 24.00 | 11.00 | 3.00 |
| COMPLETE SERIES 1 (440) | 8.00 | 3.60 | 1.00 |
| COMPLETE SERIES 2 (100) | 12.00 | 5.50 | 1.50 |
| COMPLETE FINAL SERIES (21) | 4.00 | 1.80 | .50 |
| COMPLETE FINAL FACT. (21) | 5.00 | 2.30 | .60 |
| COMMON PLAYER (1-440) | .04 | .02 | .01 |
| COMMON PLAYER (441-540) | .04 | .02 | .01 |
| COMMON PLAYER (541-561) | .04 | .02 | .01 |

| | | | |
|---|---|---|---|
| ☐ 1 Stacey Bailey | .04 | .02 | .01 |
| ☐ 2 Aundray Bruce | .10 | .05 | .01 |
| ☐ 3 Rick Bryan | .04 | .02 | .01 |
| ☐ 4 Bobby Butler | .04 | .02 | .01 |
| ☐ 5 Scott Case | .10 | .05 | .01 |
| ☐ 6 Tony Casillas | .04 | .02 | .01 |
| ☐ 7 Floyd Dixon | .04 | .02 | .01 |
| ☐ 8 Rick Donnelly | .04 | .02 | .01 |
| ☐ 9 Bill Fralic | .06 | .03 | .01 |
| ☐ 10 Mike Gann | .04 | .02 | .01 |
| ☐ 11 Mike Kenn | .06 | .03 | .01 |
| ☐ 12 Chris Miller | .75 | .35 | .09 |
| ☐ 13 John Rade | .04 | .02 | .01 |
| ☐ 14 Gerald Riggs UER | .06 | .03 | .01 |
| (Uniform number is 42 but 43 on back) | | | |
| ☐ 15 John Settle | .04 | .02 | .01 |
| ☐ 16 Marion Campbell CO | .04 | .02 | .01 |
| ☐ 17 Cornelius Bennett | .20 | .09 | .03 |
| ☐ 18 Derrick Burroughs | .04 | .02 | .01 |
| ☐ 19 Shane Conlan | .04 | .02 | .01 |
| ☐ 20 Ronnie Harmon | .20 | .09 | .03 |
| ☐ 21 Kent Hull | .10 | .05 | .01 |
| ☐ 22 Jim Kelly | .50 | .23 | .06 |
| ☐ 23 Mark Kelso | .06 | .03 | .01 |
| ☐ 24 Pete Metzelaars | .04 | .02 | .01 |
| ☐ 25 Scott Norwood | .04 | .02 | .01 |
| ☐ 26 Andre Reed | .25 | .11 | .03 |
| ☐ 27 Fred Smerlas | .06 | .03 | .01 |
| ☐ 28 Bruce Smith | .20 | .09 | .03 |
| ☐ 29 Leonard Smith | .04 | .02 | .01 |
| ☐ 30 Art Still | .06 | .03 | .01 |
| ☐ 31 Darryl Talley | .06 | .03 | .01 |
| ☐ 32 Thurman Thomas | 2.25 | 1.00 | .30 |
| ☐ 33 Will Wolford | .15 | .07 | .02 |
| ☐ 34 Marv Levy CO | .06 | .03 | .01 |
| ☐ 35 Neal Anderson | .10 | .05 | .01 |
| ☐ 36 Kevin Butler | .04 | .02 | .01 |
| ☐ 37 Jim Covert | .04 | .02 | .01 |
| ☐ 38 Richard Dent | .06 | .03 | .01 |
| ☐ 39 Dave Duerson | .04 | .02 | .01 |
| ☐ 40 Dennis Gentry | .04 | .02 | .01 |
| ☐ 41 Dan Hampton | .06 | .03 | .01 |
| ☐ 42 Jay Hilgenberg | .06 | .03 | .01 |
| ☐ 43 Dennis McKinnon UER | .04 | .02 | .01 |
| (Caught 20 or 21 passes as a rookie) | | | |
| ☐ 44 Jim McMahon | .08 | .04 | .01 |
| ☐ 45 Steve McMichael | .06 | .03 | .01 |
| ☐ 46 Brad Muster | .20 | .09 | .03 |
| ☐ 47A William Perry SP | 5.00 | 2.30 | .60 |
| ☐ 47B Ron Morris | .10 | .05 | .01 |
| ☐ 48 Ron Rivera | .04 | .02 | .01 |
| ☐ 49 Vestee Jackson | .10 | .05 | .01 |
| ☐ 50 Mike Singletary | .08 | .04 | .01 |
| ☐ 51 Mike Tomczak | .06 | .03 | .01 |
| ☐ 52 Keith Van Horne | .04 | .02 | .01 |
| ☐ 53A Mike Ditka CO | .10 | .05 | .01 |
| (No HOF mention on card front) | | | |
| ☐ 53B Mike Ditka CO | .40 | .18 | .05 |
| (HOF banner on front) | | | |
| ☐ 54 Lewis Billups | .06 | .03 | .01 |
| ☐ 55 James Brooks | .06 | .03 | .01 |
| ☐ 56 Eddie Brown | .06 | .03 | .01 |
| ☐ 57 Jason Buck | .10 | .05 | .01 |
| ☐ 58 Boomer Esiason | .25 | .11 | .03 |
| ☐ 59 David Fulcher | .06 | .03 | .01 |
| ☐ 60A Rodney Holman | .25 | .11 | .03 |
| (BENGALS on front) | | | |
| ☐ 60B Rodney Holman | 2.00 | .90 | .25 |
| (Bengals on front) | | | |
| ☐ 61 Reggie Williams | .06 | .03 | .01 |
| ☐ 62 Joe Kelly | .10 | .05 | .01 |
| ☐ 63 Tim Krumrie | .04 | .02 | .01 |
| ☐ 64 Tim McGee | .06 | .03 | .01 |
| ☐ 65 Max Montoya | .04 | .02 | .01 |
| ☐ 66 Anthony Munoz | .06 | .03 | .01 |
| ☐ 67 Jim Skow | .04 | .02 | .01 |
| ☐ 68 Eric Thomas | .15 | .07 | .02 |
| ☐ 69 Leon White | .04 | .02 | .01 |
| ☐ 70 Ickey Woods | .06 | .03 | .01 |
| ☐ 71 Carl Zander | .04 | .02 | .01 |
| ☐ 72 Sam Wyche CO | .06 | .03 | .01 |
| ☐ 73 Brian Brennan | .04 | .02 | .01 |
| ☐ 74 Earnest Byner | .06 | .03 | .01 |
| ☐ 75 Hanford Dixon | .04 | .02 | .01 |
| ☐ 76 Mike Pagel | .06 | .03 | .01 |
| ☐ 77 Bernie Kosar | .08 | .04 | .01 |
| ☐ 78 Reggie Langhorne | .25 | .11 | .03 |
| ☐ 79 Kevin Mack | .06 | .03 | .01 |
| ☐ 80 Clay Matthews | .06 | .03 | .01 |
| ☐ 81 Gerald McNeil | .04 | .02 | .01 |
| ☐ 82 Frank Minnifield | .04 | .02 | .01 |
| ☐ 83 Cody Risien | .06 | .03 | .01 |
| ☐ 84 Webster Slaughter | .20 | .09 | .03 |
| ☐ 85 Felix Wright | .04 | .02 | .01 |
| ☐ 86 Bud Carson CO UER | .04 | .02 | .01 |
| (NFLPA logo on back) | | | |
| ☐ 87 Bill Bates | .04 | .02 | .01 |
| ☐ 88 Kevin Brooks | .04 | .02 | .01 |
| ☐ 89 Michael Irvin | 3.00 | 1.35 | .40 |
| ☐ 90 Jim Jeffcoat | .06 | .03 | .01 |
| ☐ 91 Ed Too Tall Jones | .08 | .04 | .01 |
| ☐ 92 Eugene Lockhart | .04 | .02 | .01 |
| ☐ 93 Nate Newton | .25 | .11 | .03 |
| ☐ 94 Danny Noonan | .06 | .03 | .01 |
| ☐ 95 Steve Pelluer | .06 | .03 | .01 |
| ☐ 96 Herschel Walker | .15 | .07 | .02 |
| ☐ 97 Everson Walls | .04 | .02 | .01 |
| ☐ 98 Jimmy Johnson CO | .15 | .07 | .02 |
| ☐ 99 Keith Bishop | .04 | .02 | .01 |
| ☐ 100A John Elway ERR | 3.00 | 1.35 | .40 |
| (Drafted 1st Round) | | | |
| ☐ 100B John Elway COR | .50 | .23 | .06 |
| (Acquired Trade) | | | |
| ☐ 101 Simon Fletcher | .25 | .11 | .03 |
| ☐ 102 Mike Harden | .04 | .02 | .01 |
| ☐ 103 Mike Horan | .04 | .02 | .01 |
| ☐ 104 Mark Jackson | .06 | .03 | .01 |
| ☐ 105 Vance Johnson | .06 | .03 | .01 |
| ☐ 106 Rulon Jones | .04 | .02 | .01 |
| ☐ 107 Clarence Kay | .04 | .02 | .01 |
| ☐ 108 Karl Mecklenburg | .06 | .03 | .01 |
| ☐ 109 Ricky Nattiel | .04 | .02 | .01 |
| ☐ 110 Steve Sewell | .04 | .02 | .01 |
| ☐ 111 Dennis Smith | .06 | .03 | .01 |
| ☐ 112 Gerald Willhite | .04 | .02 | .01 |
| ☐ 113 Sammy Winder | .04 | .02 | .01 |
| ☐ 114 Dan Reeves CO | .06 | .03 | .01 |
| ☐ 115 Jim Arnold | .04 | .02 | .01 |
| ☐ 116 Jerry Ball | .15 | .07 | .02 |
| ☐ 117 Bennie Blades | .10 | .05 | .01 |
| ☐ 118 Lomas Brown | .04 | .02 | .01 |
| ☐ 119 Mark Cofer | .04 | .02 | .01 |
| ☐ 120 Garry James | .04 | .02 | .01 |
| ☐ 121 James Jones | .04 | .02 | .01 |
| ☐ 122 Chuck Long | .06 | .03 | .01 |
| ☐ 123 Pete Mandley | .04 | .02 | .01 |
| ☐ 124 Ed Murray | .06 | .03 | .01 |
| ☐ 125 Chris Spielman | .25 | .11 | .03 |
| ☐ 126 Dennis Gibson | .04 | .02 | .01 |
| ☐ 127 Wayne Fontes CO | .04 | .02 | .01 |
| ☐ 128 John Anderson | .04 | .02 | .01 |
| ☐ 129 Brent Fullwood | .04 | .02 | .01 |
| ☐ 130 Mark Cannon | .04 | .02 | .01 |
| ☐ 131 Tim Harris | .06 | .03 | .01 |
| ☐ 132 Mark Lee | .04 | .02 | .01 |
| ☐ 133 Don Majkowski | .15 | .07 | .02 |
| ☐ 134 Mark Murphy | .04 | .02 | .01 |
| ☐ 135 Brian Noble | .04 | .02 | .01 |
| ☐ 136 Ken Ruettgers | .10 | .05 | .01 |
| ☐ 137 Johnny Holland | .04 | .02 | .01 |
| ☐ 138 Randy Wright | .06 | .03 | .01 |
| ☐ 139 Lindy Infante CO | .04 | .02 | .01 |
| ☐ 140 Steve Brown | .04 | .02 | .01 |
| ☐ 141 Ray Childress | .06 | .03 | .01 |
| (Sacking Joe Montana) | | | |
| ☐ 142 Jeff Donaldson | .04 | .02 | .01 |
| ☐ 143 Ernest Givins | .06 | .03 | .01 |
| ☐ 144 John Grimsley | .04 | .02 | .01 |
| ☐ 145 Alonzo Highsmith | .04 | .02 | .01 |
| ☐ 146 Drew Hill | .06 | .03 | .01 |
| ☐ 147 Robert Lyles | .04 | .02 | .01 |
| ☐ 148 Bruce Matthews | .25 | .11 | .03 |
| ☐ 149 Warren Moon | .30 | .14 | .04 |
| ☐ 150 Mike Munchak | .06 | .03 | .01 |
| ☐ 151 Allen Pinkett | .06 | .03 | .01 |
| ☐ 152 Mike Rozier | .06 | .03 | .01 |
| ☐ 153 Tony Zendejas | .04 | .02 | .01 |
| ☐ 154 Jerry Glanville CO | .06 | .03 | .01 |
| ☐ 155 Albert Bentley | .04 | .02 | .01 |
| ☐ 156 Dean Biasucci | .04 | .02 | .01 |
| ☐ 157 Duane Bickett | .04 | .02 | .01 |
| ☐ 158 Bill Brooks | .06 | .03 | .01 |
| ☐ 159 Chris Chandler | .20 | .09 | .03 |
| ☐ 160 Pat Beach | .04 | .02 | .01 |
| ☐ 161 Ray Donaldson | .04 | .02 | .01 |

| | | | |
|---|---|---|---|
| ☐ 162 Jon Hand | .04 | .02 | .01 |
| ☐ 163 Chris Hinton | .06 | .03 | .01 |
| ☐ 164 Rohn Stark | .06 | .03 | .01 |
| ☐ 165 Fredd Young | .04 | .02 | .01 |
| ☐ 166 Ron Meyer CO | .04 | .02 | .01 |
| ☐ 167 Lloyd Burruss | .04 | .02 | .01 |
| ☐ 168 Carlos Carson | .06 | .03 | .01 |
| ☐ 169 Deron Cherry | .06 | .03 | .01 |
| ☐ 170 Irv Eatman | .04 | .02 | .01 |
| ☐ 171 Dino Hackett | .04 | .02 | .01 |
| ☐ 172 Steve DeBerg | .06 | .03 | .01 |
| ☐ 173 Albert Lewis | .06 | .03 | .01 |
| ☐ 174 Nick Lowery | .06 | .03 | .01 |
| ☐ 175 Bill Maas | .06 | .03 | .01 |
| ☐ 176 Christian Okoye | .06 | .03 | .01 |
| ☐ 177 Stephone Paige | .06 | .03 | .01 |
| ☐ 178 Mark Adickes | .04 | .02 | .01 |
| (Out of alphabetical sequence for his team) | | | |
| ☐ 179 Kevin Ross | .15 | .07 | .02 |
| ☐ 180 Neil Smith | 1.00 | .45 | .13 |
| ☐ 181 Marty Schottenheimer CO | .06 | .03 | .01 |
| ☐ 182 Marcus Allen | .25 | .11 | .03 |
| ☐ 183 Tim Brown | 1.50 | .65 | .19 |
| ☐ 184 Willie Gault | .06 | .03 | .01 |
| ☐ 185 Bo Jackson | .75 | .35 | .09 |
| ☐ 186 Howie Long | .08 | .04 | .01 |
| ☐ 187 Vann McElroy | .04 | .02 | .01 |
| ☐ 188 Matt Millen | .06 | .03 | .01 |
| ☐ 189 Don Mosebar | .10 | .05 | .01 |
| ☐ 190 Bill Pickel | .04 | .02 | .01 |
| ☐ 191 Jerry Robinson UER | .06 | .03 | .01 |
| (Stats show 1 TD, but text says 2 TD's) | | | |
| ☐ 192 Jay Schroeder | .06 | .03 | .01 |
| ☐ 193A Stacey Toran | .04 | .02 | .01 |
| (No mention of death on card front) | | | |
| ☐ 193B Stacey Toran | .50 | .23 | .06 |
| (1961-1989 banner on card front) | | | |
| ☐ 194 Mike Shanahan CO | .04 | .02 | .01 |
| ☐ 195 Greg Bell | .06 | .03 | .01 |
| ☐ 196 Ron Brown | .04 | .02 | .01 |
| ☐ 197 Aaron Cox | .10 | .05 | .01 |
| ☐ 198 Henry Ellard | .06 | .03 | .01 |
| ☐ 199 Jim Everett | .15 | .07 | .02 |
| ☐ 200 Jerry Gray | .04 | .02 | .01 |
| ☐ 201 Kevin Greene | .06 | .03 | .01 |
| ☐ 202 Pete Holohan | .04 | .02 | .01 |
| ☐ 203 LeRoy Irvin | .04 | .02 | .01 |
| ☐ 204 Mike Lansford | .04 | .02 | .01 |
| ☐ 205 Tom Newberry | .15 | .07 | .02 |
| ☐ 206 Mel Owens | .04 | .02 | .01 |
| ☐ 207 Jackie Slater | .06 | .03 | .01 |
| ☐ 208 Doug Smith | .06 | .03 | .01 |
| ☐ 209 Mike Wilcher | .04 | .02 | .01 |
| ☐ 210 John Robinson CO | .06 | .03 | .01 |
| ☐ 211 John Bosa | .04 | .02 | .01 |
| ☐ 212 Mark Brown | .04 | .02 | .01 |
| ☐ 213 Mark Clayton | .06 | .03 | .01 |
| ☐ 214A Ferrell Edmunds ERR | .50 | .23 | .06 |
| (Misspelled Edmonds on front and back) | | | |
| ☐ 214B Ferrell Edmunds COR | .15 | .07 | .02 |
| ☐ 215 Roy Foster | .04 | .02 | .01 |
| ☐ 216 Lorenzo Hampton | .04 | .02 | .01 |
| ☐ 217 Jim C. Jensen UER | .04 | .02 | .01 |
| (Born Albington, should be Abington) | | | |
| ☐ 218 William Judson | .04 | .02 | .01 |
| ☐ 219 Eric Kumerow | .04 | .02 | .01 |
| ☐ 220 Dan Marino | 1.25 | .55 | .16 |
| ☐ 221 John Offerdahl | .06 | .03 | .01 |
| ☐ 222 Fuad Reveiz | .04 | .02 | .01 |
| ☐ 223 Reggie Roby | .06 | .03 | .01 |
| ☐ 224 Brian Sochia | .06 | .03 | .01 |
| ☐ 225 Don Shula CO | .20 | .09 | .03 |
| ☐ 226 Alfred Anderson | .04 | .02 | .01 |
| ☐ 227 Joey Browner | .06 | .03 | .01 |
| ☐ 228 Anthony Carter | .08 | .04 | .01 |
| ☐ 229 Chris Doleman | .15 | .07 | .02 |
| ☐ 230 Hassan Jones | .10 | .05 | .01 |
| ☐ 231 Steve Jordan | .06 | .03 | .01 |
| ☐ 232 Tommy Kramer | .06 | .03 | .01 |
| ☐ 233 Carl Lee | .10 | .05 | .01 |
| ☐ 234 Kirk Lowdermilk | .15 | .07 | .02 |
| ☐ 235 Randall McDaniel | .20 | .09 | .03 |
| ☐ 236 Doug Martin | .04 | .02 | .01 |
| ☐ 237 Keith Millard | .06 | .03 | .01 |
| ☐ 238 Darrin Nelson | .06 | .03 | .01 |
| ☐ 239 Jesse Solomon | .04 | .02 | .01 |
| ☐ 240 Scott Studwell | .04 | .02 | .01 |
| ☐ 241 Wade Wilson | .06 | .03 | .01 |
| ☐ 242 Gary Zimmerman | .06 | .03 | .01 |
| ☐ 243 Jerry Burns CO | .04 | .02 | .01 |
| ☐ 244 Bruce Armstrong | .10 | .05 | .01 |
| ☐ 245 Raymond Clayborn | .06 | .03 | .01 |
| ☐ 246 Reggie Dupard | .04 | .02 | .01 |
| ☐ 247 Tony Eason | .06 | .03 | .01 |
| ☐ 248 Sean Farrell | .04 | .02 | .01 |
| ☐ 249 Doug Flutie | .30 | .14 | .04 |
| ☐ 250 Brent Williams | .15 | .07 | .02 |
| ☐ 251 Roland James | .04 | .02 | .01 |
| ☐ 252 Ronnie Lippett | .04 | .02 | .01 |
| ☐ 253 Fred Marion | .04 | .02 | .01 |
| ☐ 254 Larry McGrew | .04 | .02 | .01 |
| ☐ 255 Stanley Morgan | .06 | .03 | .01 |
| ☐ 256 Johnny Rembert | .04 | .02 | .01 |
| ☐ 257 John Stephens | .20 | .09 | .03 |
| ☐ 258 Andre Tippett | .06 | .03 | .01 |
| ☐ 259 Garin Veris | .04 | .02 | .01 |
| ☐ 260A Raymond Berry CO | .10 | .05 | .01 |
| (No HOF mention on card front) | | | |
| ☐ 260B Raymond Berry CO | .20 | .09 | .03 |
| (HOF banner on card front) | | | |
| ☐ 261 Morten Andersen | .06 | .03 | .01 |
| ☐ 262 Hoby Brenner | .04 | .02 | .01 |
| ☐ 263 Stan Brock | .04 | .02 | .01 |
| ☐ 264 Brad Edelman | .04 | .02 | .01 |
| ☐ 265 James Geathers | .04 | .02 | .01 |
| ☐ 266A Bobby Hebert ERR | .75 | .35 | .09 |
| ("passers" in 42-0) | | | |
| ☐ 266B Bobby Hebert COR | .20 | .09 | .03 |
| ("passes" in 42-0) | | | |
| ☐ 267 Craig Heyward | .20 | .09 | .03 |
| ☐ 268 Lonzell Hill | .04 | .02 | .01 |
| ☐ 269 Dalton Hilliard | .06 | .03 | .01 |
| ☐ 270 Rickey Jackson | .06 | .03 | .01 |
| ☐ 271 Steve Korte | .04 | .02 | .01 |
| ☐ 272 Eric Martin | .06 | .03 | .01 |
| ☐ 273 Rueben Mayes | .06 | .03 | .01 |
| ☐ 274 Sam Mills | .06 | .03 | .01 |
| ☐ 275 Brett Perriman | .30 | .14 | .04 |
| ☐ 276 Pat Swilling | .20 | .09 | .03 |
| ☐ 277 John Tice | .04 | .02 | .01 |
| ☐ 278 Jim Mora CO | .06 | .03 | .01 |
| ☐ 279 Eric Moore | .06 | .03 | .01 |
| ☐ 280 Carl Banks | .06 | .03 | .01 |
| ☐ 281 Mark Bavaro | .06 | .03 | .01 |
| ☐ 282 Maurice Carthon | .04 | .02 | .01 |
| ☐ 283 Mark Collins | .15 | .07 | .02 |
| ☐ 284 Erik Howard | .04 | .02 | .01 |
| ☐ 285 Terry Kinard | .04 | .02 | .01 |
| ☐ 286 Sean Landeta | .06 | .03 | .01 |
| ☐ 287 Lionel Manuel | .04 | .02 | .01 |
| ☐ 288 Leonard Marshall | .06 | .03 | .01 |
| ☐ 289 Joe Morris | .06 | .03 | .01 |
| ☐ 290 Bart Oates | .04 | .02 | .01 |
| ☐ 291 Phil Simms | .15 | .07 | .02 |
| ☐ 292 Lawrence Taylor | .15 | .07 | .02 |
| ☐ 293 Bill Parcells CO | .10 | .05 | .01 |
| ☐ 294 Dave Cadigan | .04 | .02 | .01 |
| ☐ 295 Kyle Clifton | .15 | .07 | .02 |
| ☐ 296 Alex Gordon | .04 | .02 | .01 |
| ☐ 297 James Hasty | .04 | .02 | .01 |
| ☐ 298 Johnny Hector | .04 | .02 | .01 |
| ☐ 299 Bobby Humphery | .04 | .02 | .01 |
| ☐ 300 Pat Leahy | .06 | .03 | .01 |
| ☐ 301 Marty Lyons | .06 | .03 | .01 |
| ☐ 302 Reggie McElroy | .04 | .02 | .01 |
| ☐ 303 Erik McMillan | .10 | .05 | .01 |
| ☐ 304 Freeman McNeil | .06 | .03 | .01 |
| ☐ 305 Ken O'Brien | .06 | .03 | .01 |
| ☐ 306 Pat Ryan | .04 | .02 | .01 |
| ☐ 307 Mickey Shuler | .04 | .02 | .01 |
| ☐ 308 Al Toon | .06 | .03 | .01 |
| ☐ 309 Jo Jo Townsell | .04 | .02 | .01 |
| ☐ 310 Roger Vick | .04 | .02 | .01 |
| ☐ 311 Joe Walton CO | .04 | .02 | .01 |
| ☐ 312 Jerome Brown | .06 | .03 | .01 |
| ☐ 313 Keith Byars | .06 | .03 | .01 |
| ☐ 314 Cris Carter | 1.00 | .45 | .13 |
| ☐ 315 Randall Cunningham | .30 | .14 | .04 |
| ☐ 316 Terry Hoage | .04 | .02 | .01 |
| ☐ 317 Wes Hopkins | .04 | .02 | .01 |
| ☐ 318 Keith Jackson | 1.25 | .55 | .16 |
| ☐ 319 Mike Quick | .06 | .03 | .01 |
| ☐ 320 Mike Reichenbach | .04 | .02 | .01 |
| ☐ 321 Dave Rimington | .06 | .03 | .01 |
| ☐ 322 John Teltschik | .04 | .02 | .01 |
| ☐ 323 Anthony Toney | .04 | .02 | .01 |
| ☐ 324 Andre Waters | .06 | .03 | .01 |
| ☐ 325 Reggie White | .20 | .09 | .03 |
| ☐ 326 Luis Zendejas | .04 | .02 | .01 |
| ☐ 327 Buddy Ryan CO | .06 | .03 | .01 |
| ☐ 328 Robert Awalt | .04 | .02 | .01 |
| ☐ 329 Tim McDonald | .30 | .14 | .04 |
| ☐ 330 Roy Green | .06 | .03 | .01 |
| ☐ 331 Neil Lomax | .06 | .03 | .01 |
| ☐ 332 Cedric Mack | .04 | .02 | .01 |

|  |  | | | |
|---|---|---|---|---|
| 333 | Stump Mitchell | .06 | .03 | .01 |
| 334 | Niko Noga | .04 | .02 | .01 |
| 335 | Jay Novacek | 1.00 | .45 | .13 |
| 336 | Freddie Joe Nunn | .06 | .03 | .01 |
| 337 | Luis Sharpe | .04 | .02 | .01 |
| 338 | Vai Sikahema | .06 | .03 | .01 |
| 339 | J.T. Smith | .04 | .02 | .01 |
| 340 | Ron Wolfley | .04 | .02 | .01 |
| 341 | Gene Stallings CO | .10 | .05 | .01 |
| 342 | Gary Anderson | .04 | .02 | .01 |
| 343 | Bubby Brister | .25 | .11 | .03 |
| 344 | Dermontti Dawson | .10 | .05 | .01 |
| 345 | Thomas Everett | .25 | .11 | .03 |
| 346 | Delton Hall | .04 | .02 | .01 |
| 347 | Bryan Hinkle | .04 | .02 | .01 |
| 348 | Merril Hoge | .20 | .09 | .03 |
| 349 | Tunch Ilkin | .04 | .02 | .01 |
| 350 | Aaron Jones | .10 | .05 | .01 |
| 351 | Louis Lipps | .06 | .03 | .01 |
| 352 | David Little | .04 | .02 | .01 |
| 353 | Hardy Nickerson | .30 | .14 | .04 |
| 354 | Rod Woodson | 1.00 | .45 | .13 |
| 355A | Chuck Noll CO ERR | .15 | .07 | .02 |
| | ("one of only three") | | | |
| 355B | Chuck Noll CO COR | .15 | .07 | .02 |
| | ("one of only two") | | | |
| 356 | Gary Anderson | .06 | .03 | .01 |
| 357 | Rod Bernstine | .40 | .18 | .05 |
| 358 | Gill Byrd | .06 | .03 | .01 |
| 359 | Vencie Glenn | .04 | .02 | .01 |
| 360 | Dennis McKnight | .04 | .02 | .01 |
| 361 | Lionel James | .06 | .03 | .01 |
| 362 | Mark Malone | .06 | .03 | .01 |
| 363A | Anthony Miller ERR | 2.00 | .90 | .25 |
| | (TD total 14.8) | | | |
| 363B | Anthony Miller COR | 2.00 | .90 | .25 |
| | (TD total 3) | | | |
| 364 | Ralf Mojsiejenko | .04 | .02 | .01 |
| 365 | Leslie O'Neal | .08 | .04 | .01 |
| 366 | Jamie Holland | .04 | .02 | .01 |
| 367 | Lee Williams | .06 | .03 | .01 |
| 368 | Dan Henning CO | .04 | .02 | .01 |
| 369 | Harris Barton | .15 | .07 | .02 |
| 370 | Michael Carter | .04 | .02 | .01 |
| 371 | Mike Cofer | .10 | .05 | .01 |
| | (Joe Montana holding) | | | |
| 372 | Roger Craig | .08 | .04 | .01 |
| 373 | Riki Ellison | .04 | .02 | .01 |
| 374 | Jim Fahnhorst | .04 | .02 | .01 |
| 375 | John Frank | .06 | .03 | .01 |
| 376 | Jeff Fuller | .04 | .02 | .01 |
| 377 | Don Griffin | .06 | .03 | .01 |
| 378 | Charles Haley | .06 | .03 | .01 |
| 379 | Ronnie Lott | .15 | .07 | .02 |
| 380 | Tim McKyer | .06 | .03 | .01 |
| 381 | Joe Montana | 1.25 | .55 | .16 |
| 382 | Tom Rathman | .06 | .03 | .01 |
| 383 | Jerry Rice | 1.00 | .45 | .13 |
| 384 | John Taylor | .75 | .35 | .09 |
| 385 | Keena Turner | .06 | .03 | .01 |
| 386 | Michael Walter | .04 | .02 | .01 |
| 387 | Bubba Paris | .06 | .03 | .01 |
| 388 | Steve Young | .60 | .25 | .08 |
| 389 | George Seifert CO UER | .10 | .05 | .01 |
| | (NFLPA logo on back) | | | |
| 390 | Brian Blades | .75 | .35 | .09 |
| 391A | Brian Bosworth ERR | .30 | .14 | .04 |
| | (Seattle on front) | | | |
| 391B | Brian Bosworth COR | .10 | .05 | .01 |
| | (Listed by team nick-name on front) | | | |
| 392 | Jeff Bryant | .04 | .02 | .01 |
| 393 | Jacob Green | .06 | .03 | .01 |
| 394 | Norm Johnson | .04 | .02 | .01 |
| 395 | Dave Krieg | .06 | .03 | .01 |
| 396 | Steve Largent | .25 | .11 | .03 |
| 397 | Bryan Millard | .04 | .02 | .01 |
| 398 | Paul Moyer | .04 | .02 | .01 |
| 399 | Joe Nash | .04 | .02 | .01 |
| 400 | Rufus Porter | .10 | .05 | .01 |
| 401 | Eugene Robinson | .25 | .11 | .03 |
| 402 | Bruce Scholtz | .04 | .02 | .01 |
| 403 | Kelly Stouffer | .12 | .05 | .02 |
| 404A | Curt Warner ERR | 1.25 | .55 | .16 |
| | ("yards (1,455) ...") | | | |
| 404B | Curt Warner COR | .10 | .05 | .01 |
| | ("yards (6,074) ...") | | | |
| 405 | John L. Williams | .06 | .03 | .01 |
| 406 | Tony Woods | .04 | .02 | .01 |
| 407 | David Wyman | .06 | .03 | .01 |
| 408 | Chuck Knox CO | .06 | .03 | .01 |
| 409 | Mark Carrier | .75 | .35 | .09 |
| 410 | Randy Grimes | .04 | .02 | .01 |
| 411 | Paul Gruber | .10 | .05 | .01 |
| 412 | Harry Hamilton | .04 | .02 | .01 |
| 413 | Ron Holmes | .04 | .02 | .01 |
| 414 | Donald Igwebuike | .04 | .02 | .01 |
| 415 | Dan Turk | .04 | .02 | .01 |
| 416 | Ricky Reynolds | .06 | .03 | .01 |
| 417 | Bruce Hill | .04 | .02 | .01 |
| 418 | Lars Tate | .06 | .03 | .01 |
| 419 | Vinny Testaverde | .25 | .11 | .03 |
| 420 | James Wilder | .06 | .03 | .01 |
| 421 | Ray Perkins CO | .04 | .02 | .01 |
| 422 | Jeff Bostic | .04 | .02 | .01 |
| 423 | Kelvin Bryant | .06 | .03 | .01 |
| 424 | Gary Clark | .10 | .05 | .01 |
| 425 | Monte Coleman | .04 | .02 | .01 |
| 426 | Darrell Green | .06 | .03 | .01 |
| 427 | Joe Jacoby | .06 | .03 | .01 |
| 428 | Jim Lachey | .06 | .03 | .01 |
| 429 | Charles Mann | .06 | .03 | .01 |
| 430 | Dexter Manley | .06 | .03 | .01 |
| 431 | Darryl Grant | .04 | .02 | .01 |
| 432 | Mark May | .06 | .03 | .01 |
| 433 | Art Monk | .15 | .07 | .02 |
| 434 | Mark Rypien | .40 | .18 | .05 |
| 435 | Ricky Sanders | .06 | .03 | .01 |
| 436 | Alvin Walton | .04 | .02 | .01 |
| 437 | Don Warren | .04 | .02 | .01 |
| 438 | Jamie Morris | .06 | .03 | .01 |
| 439 | Doug Williams | .06 | .03 | .01 |
| 440 | Joe Gibbs CO | .10 | .05 | .01 |
| 441 | Marcus Cotton | .04 | .02 | .01 |
| | Atlanta Falcons | | | |
| 442 | Joel Williams | .04 | .02 | .01 |
| | Atlanta Falcons | | | |
| 443 | Joe Devlin | .06 | .03 | .01 |
| | Buffalo Bills | | | |
| 444 | Robb Riddick | .04 | .02 | .01 |
| | Buffalo Bills | | | |
| 445 | William Perry | .06 | .03 | .01 |
| | Chicago Bears | | | |
| 446 | Thomas Sanders | .04 | .02 | .01 |
| | Chicago Bears | | | |
| 447 | Brian Blados | .04 | .02 | .01 |
| | Cincinnati Bengals | | | |
| 448 | Cris Collinsworth | .04 | .02 | .01 |
| | Cincinnati Bengals | | | |
| 449 | Stanford Jennings | .04 | .02 | .01 |
| | Cincinnati Bengals | | | |
| 450 | Barry Krauss UER | .04 | .02 | .01 |
| | (Listed as playing for Indianapolis 1979-88) | | | |
| | Cleveland Browns | | | |
| 451 | Ozzie Newsome | .15 | .07 | .02 |
| | Cleveland Browns | | | |
| 452 | Mike Oliphant | .15 | .07 | .02 |
| | Cleveland Browns | | | |
| 453 | Tony Dorsett | .20 | .09 | .03 |
| | Denver Broncos | | | |
| 454 | Bruce McNorton | .04 | .02 | .01 |
| | Detroit Lions | | | |
| 455 | Eric Dickerson | .20 | .09 | .03 |
| | Indianapolis Colts | | | |
| 456 | Keith Bostic | .04 | .02 | .01 |
| | Indianapolis Colts | | | |
| 457 | Sam Clancy | .15 | .07 | .02 |
| | Indianapolis Colts | | | |
| 458 | Jack Del Rio | .25 | .11 | .03 |
| | Kansas City Chiefs | | | |
| 459 | Mike Webster | .06 | .03 | .01 |
| | Kansas City Chiefs | | | |
| 460 | Bob Golic | .04 | .02 | .01 |
| | Los Angeles Raiders | | | |
| 461 | Otis Wilson | .04 | .02 | .01 |
| | Los Angeles Raiders | | | |
| 462 | Mike Haynes | .06 | .03 | .01 |
| | Los Angeles Raiders | | | |
| 463 | Greg Townsend | .06 | .03 | .01 |
| | Los Angeles Raiders | | | |
| 464 | Mark Duper | .06 | .03 | .01 |
| | Miami Dolphins | | | |
| 465 | E.J. Junior | .06 | .03 | .01 |
| | Miami Dolphins | | | |
| 466 | Troy Stradford | .04 | .02 | .01 |
| | Miami Dolphins | | | |
| 467 | Mike Merriweather | .06 | .03 | .01 |
| | Minnesota Vikings | | | |
| 468 | Irving Fryar | .06 | .03 | .01 |
| | New England Patriots | | | |
| 469 | Vaughan Johnson | .25 | .11 | .03 |
| | New Orleans Saints | | | |
| 470 | Pepper Johnson | .06 | .03 | .01 |
| | New York Giants | | | |
| 471 | Gary Reasons | .04 | .02 | .01 |
| | New York Giants | | | |
| 472 | Perry Williams | .04 | .02 | .01 |
| | New York Giants | | | |
| 473 | Wesley Walker | .06 | .03 | .01 |
| | New York Jets | | | |
| 474 | Anthony Bell | .04 | .02 | .01 |
| | Phoenix Cardinals | | | |
| 475 | Earl Ferrell | .04 | .02 | .01 |

| | | | | |
|---|---|---|---|---|
| Phoenix Cardinals | | | | |
| ☐ 476 Craig Wolfley | .06 | .03 | .01 |
| Pittsburgh Steelers | | | |
| ☐ 477 Billy Ray Smith | .06 | .03 | .01 |
| San Diego Chargers | | | |
| ☐ 478A Jim McMahon | .10 | .05 | .01 |
| (No mention of trade on card front) | | | |
| San Diego Chargers | | | |
| ☐ 478B Jim McMahon | .40 | .18 | .05 |
| (Traded banner on card front) | | | |
| San Diego Chargers | | | |
| ☐ 478C Jim McMahon | 40.00 | 18.00 | 5.00 |
| (Traded banner on card front but no line on back saying also see card 44) | | | |
| San Diego Chargers | | | |
| ☐ 479 Eric Wright | .04 | .02 | .01 |
| San Francisco 49ers | | | |
| ☐ 480A Earnest Byner | .12 | .05 | .02 |
| (No mention of trade on card front) | | | |
| Washington Redskins | | | |
| ☐ 480B Earnest Byner | .40 | .18 | .05 |
| (Traded banner on card front) | | | |
| Washington Redskins | | | |
| ☐ 480C Earnest Byner | 40.00 | 18.00 | 5.00 |
| (Traded banner on card front but no line on back saying also see card 74) | | | |
| Washington Redskins | | | |
| ☐ 481 Russ Grimm | .04 | .02 | .01 |
| Washington Redskins | | | |
| ☐ 482 Wilber Marshall | .06 | .03 | .01 |
| Washington Redskins | | | |
| ☐ 483A Gerald Riggs | .06 | .03 | .01 |
| (No mention of trade on card front) | | | |
| Washington Redskins | | | |
| ☐ 483B Gerald Riggs | .50 | .23 | .06 |
| (Traded banner on card front) | | | |
| Washington Redskins | | | |
| ☐ 483C Gerald Riggs | 40.00 | 18.00 | 5.00 |
| (Traded banner on card front but no line on back saying also see card 14) | | | |
| Washington Redskins | | | |
| ☐ 484 Brian Davis | .04 | .02 | .01 |
| Washington Redskins | | | |
| ☐ 485 Shawn Collins | .10 | .05 | .01 |
| Atlanta Falcons | | | |
| ☐ 486 Deion Sanders | 1.50 | .65 | .19 |
| Atlanta Falcons | | | |
| ☐ 487 Trace Armstrong | .25 | .11 | .03 |
| Chicago Bears | | | |
| ☐ 488 Donnell Woolford | .20 | .09 | .03 |
| Chicago Bears | | | |
| ☐ 489 Eric Metcalf | .75 | .35 | .09 |
| Cleveland Browns | | | |
| ☐ 490 Troy Aikman | 6.00 | 2.70 | .75 |
| Dallas Cowboys | | | |
| ☐ 491 Steve Walsh | .10 | .05 | .01 |
| Dallas Cowboys | | | |
| ☐ 492 Steve Atwater | .25 | .11 | .03 |
| Denver Broncos | | | |
| ☐ 493 Bobby Humphrey UER | .10 | .05 | .01 |
| Denver Broncos | | | |
| (Jersey 41 on back, should be 26) | | | |
| ☐ 494 Barry Sanders | 4.00 | 1.80 | .50 |
| Detroit Lions | | | |
| ☐ 495 Tony Mandarich | .06 | .03 | .01 |
| Green Bay Packers | | | |
| ☐ 496 David Williams | .10 | .05 | .01 |
| Houston Oilers | | | |
| ☐ 497 Andre Rison UER | 1.50 | .65 | .19 |
| (Jersey number not listed on back) | | | |
| Indianapolis Colts | | | |
| ☐ 498 Derrick Thomas | 1.50 | .65 | .19 |
| Kansas City Chiefs | | | |
| ☐ 499 Cleveland Gary | .25 | .11 | .03 |
| Los Angeles Rams | | | |
| ☐ 500 Bill Hawkins | .04 | .02 | .01 |
| Los Angeles Rams | | | |
| ☐ 501 Louis Oliver | .15 | .07 | .02 |
| Miami Dolphins | | | |
| ☐ 502 Sammie Smith | .06 | .03 | .01 |
| Miami Dolphins | | | |
| ☐ 503 Hart Lee Dykes | .04 | .02 | .01 |
| New England Patriots | | | |
| ☐ 504 Wayne Martin | .20 | .09 | .03 |

| | | | | |
|---|---|---|---|---|
| New Orleans Saints | | | | |
| ☐ 505 Brian Williams | .04 | .02 | .01 |
| New York Giants | | | |
| ☐ 506 Jeff Lageman | .15 | .07 | .02 |
| New York Jets | | | |
| ☐ 507 Eric Hill | .10 | .05 | .01 |
| Phoenix Cardinals | | | |
| ☐ 508 Joe Wolf | .04 | .02 | .01 |
| Phoenix Cardinals | | | |
| ☐ 509 Timm Rosenbach | .20 | .09 | .03 |
| Phoenix Cardinals | | | |
| ☐ 510 Tom Ricketts | .04 | .02 | .01 |
| Pittsburgh Steelers | | | |
| ☐ 511 Tim Worley | .25 | .11 | .03 |
| Pittsburgh Steelers | | | |
| ☐ 512 Burt Grossman | .15 | .07 | .02 |
| San Diego Chargers | | | |
| ☐ 513 Keith DeLong | .10 | .05 | .01 |
| San Francisco 49ers | | | |
| ☐ 514 Andy Heck | .10 | .05 | .01 |
| Seattle Seahawks | | | |
| ☐ 515 Broderick Thomas | .25 | .11 | .03 |
| Tampa Bay Buccaneers | | | |
| ☐ 516 Don Beebe | .75 | .35 | .09 |
| Buffalo Bills | | | |
| ☐ 517 James Thornton | .10 | .05 | .01 |
| Chicago Bears | | | |
| ☐ 518 Eric Kattus | .04 | .02 | .01 |
| Cincinnati Bengals | | | |
| ☐ 519 Bruce Kozerski | .10 | .05 | .01 |
| Cincinnati Bengals | | | |
| ☐ 520 Brian Washington | .15 | .07 | .02 |
| Cleveland Browns | | | |
| ☐ 521 Rodney Peete UER | .35 | .16 | .04 |
| Detroit Lions | | | |
| (Jersey 19 on back, should be 9) | | | |
| ☐ 522 Erik Affholter | .04 | .02 | .01 |
| Green Bay Packers | | | |
| ☐ 523 Anthony Dilweg | .10 | .05 | .01 |
| Green Bay Packers | | | |
| ☐ 524 O'Brien Alston | .04 | .02 | .01 |
| Indianapolis Colts | | | |
| ☐ 525 Mike Elkins | .04 | .02 | .01 |
| Kansas City Chiefs | | | |
| ☐ 526 Jonathan Hayes | .10 | .05 | .01 |
| Kansas City Chiefs | | | |
| ☐ 527 Terry McDaniel | .15 | .07 | .02 |
| Los Angeles Raiders | | | |
| ☐ 528 Frank Stams | .04 | .02 | .01 |
| Los Angeles Rams | | | |
| ☐ 529 Darryl Ingram | .04 | .02 | .01 |
| Minnesota Vikings | | | |
| ☐ 530 Henry Thomas | .06 | .03 | .01 |
| Minnesota Vikings | | | |
| ☐ 531 Eric Coleman | .04 | .02 | .01 |
| New England Patriots | | | |
| ☐ 532 Sheldon White | .04 | .02 | .01 |
| New York Giants | | | |
| ☐ 533 Eric Allen | .30 | .14 | .04 |
| Philadelphia Eagles | | | |
| ☐ 534 Robert Drummond | .04 | .02 | .01 |
| Philadelphia Eagles | | | |
| ☐ 535A Gizmo Williams | 20.00 | 9.00 | 2.50 |
| (Without Scouting Photo on front and "Footbal" misspelled on back) | | | |
| Philadelphia Eagles | | | |
| ☐ 535B Gizmo Williams | .20 | .09 | .03 |
| (Without Scouting Photo on front but "Canadian Football" on back) | | | |
| Philadelphia Eagles | | | |
| ☐ 535C Gizmo Williams | .10 | .05 | .01 |
| (With Scouting Photo on card front) | | | |
| Philadelphia Eagles | | | |
| ☐ 536 Billy Joe Tolliver | .15 | .07 | .02 |
| San Diego Chargers | | | |
| ☐ 537 Danny Stubbs | .04 | .02 | .01 |
| San Francisco 49ers | | | |
| ☐ 538 Wesley Walls | .04 | .02 | .01 |
| San Francisco 49ers | | | |
| ☐ 539A James Jefferson ERR | .40 | .18 | .05 |
| (No Prospect banner on card front) | | | |
| Seattle Seahawks | | | |
| ☐ 539B James Jefferson COR | .10 | .05 | .01 |
| (Prospect banner on card front) | | | |
| Seattle Seahawks | | | |
| ☐ 540 Tracy Rocker | .04 | .02 | .01 |
| Washington Redskins | | | |
| ☐ 541 Art Shell CO | .10 | .05 | .01 |
| Los Angeles Raiders | | | |
| ☐ 542 Lemuel Stinson | .10 | .05 | .01 |
| Chicago Bears | | | |
| ☐ 543 Tyrone Braxton UER | .10 | .05 | .01 |

Denver Broncos
(back photo actually
Ken Bell)

| | | | | |
|---|---|---|---|---|
| ☐ 544 David Treadwell | .10 | .05 | .01 |
| Denver Broncos | | | |
| ☐ 545 Flipper Anderson | .40 | .18 | .05 |
| Los Angeles Rams | | | |
| ☐ 546 Dave Meggett | .35 | .16 | .04 |
| New York Giants | | | |
| ☐ 547 Lewis Tillman | .30 | .14 | .04 |
| New York Giants | | | |
| ☐ 548 Carnell Lake | .15 | .07 | .02 |
| Pittsburgh Steelers | | | |
| ☐ 549 Marion Butts | .50 | .23 | .06 |
| San Diego Chargers | | | |
| ☐ 550 Sterling Sharpe | 3.00 | 1.35 | .40 |
| Green Bay Packers | | | |
| ☐ 551 Ezra Johnson | .04 | .02 | .01 |
| Indianapolis Colts | | | |
| ☐ 552 Clarence Verdin | .15 | .07 | .02 |
| Indianapolis Colts | | | |
| ☐ 553 Mervyn Fernandez | .04 | .02 | .01 |
| Los Angeles Raiders | | | |
| ☐ 554 Ottis Anderson | .06 | .03 | .01 |
| New York Giants | | | |
| ☐ 555 Gary Hogeboom | .06 | .03 | .01 |
| Kansas City Chiefs | | | |
| ☐ 556 Paul Palmer TR | .04 | .02 | .01 |
| Dallas Cowboys | | | |
| ☐ 557 Jesse Solomon TR | .04 | .02 | .01 |
| Dallas Cowboys | | | |
| ☐ 558 Chip Banks TR | .06 | .03 | .01 |
| Indianapolis Colts | | | |
| ☐ 559 Steve Pelluer TR | .06 | .03 | .01 |
| Kansas City Chiefs | | | |
| ☐ 560 Darrin Nelson TR | .06 | .03 | .01 |
| San Diego Chargers | | | |
| ☐ 561 Herschel Walker TR | .15 | .07 | .02 |
| Minnesota Vikings | | | |
| ☐ CC1 Pete Rozelle SP | .75 | .35 | .09 |
| (Commissioner) | | | |

## 1989 Pro Set Super Bowl Logos

This 23-card set contains a card for each Super Bowl played up through the production of the 1989 Pro Set regular set. These cards were inserted with the regular player cards in the wax packs of the 1989 Pro Set. The cards are standard size, 2 1/2" by 3 1/2", and are unnumbered. In future years the company says that it intends to add an additional card for each future Super Bowl after it is played along with that year's Pro Set cards.

| | MINT | EXC | G-VG |
|---|---|---|---|
| COMPLETE SET (23) | 4.00 | 1.60 | .40 |
| COMMON CARD (1-23) | .30 | .12 | .03 |
| | | | |
| ☐ 1 Super Bowl I | .30 | .12 | .03 |
| ☐ 2 Super Bowl II | .30 | .12 | .03 |
| ☐ 3 Super Bowl III | .30 | .12 | .03 |
| ☐ 4 Super Bowl IV | .30 | .12 | .03 |
| ☐ 5 Super Bowl V | .30 | .12 | .03 |
| ☐ 6 Super Bowl VI | .30 | .12 | .03 |
| ☐ 7 Super Bowl VII | .30 | .12 | .03 |
| ☐ 8 Super Bowl VIII | .30 | .12 | .03 |
| ☐ 9 Super Bowl IX | .30 | .12 | .03 |
| ☐ 10 Super Bowl X | .30 | .12 | .03 |
| ☐ 11 Super Bowl XI | .30 | .12 | .03 |
| ☐ 12 Super Bowl XII | .30 | .12 | .03 |
| ☐ 13 Super Bowl XIII | .30 | .12 | .03 |
| ☐ 14 Super Bowl XIV | .30 | .12 | .03 |
| ☐ 15 Super Bowl XV | .30 | .12 | .03 |
| ☐ 16 Super Bowl XVI | .30 | .12 | .03 |
| ☐ 17 Super Bowl XVII | .30 | .12 | .03 |
| ☐ 18 Super Bowl XVIII | .30 | .12 | .03 |
| ☐ 19 Super Bowl XIX | .30 | .12 | .03 |
| ☐ 20 Super Bowl XX | .30 | .12 | .03 |
| ☐ 21 Super Bowl XXI | .30 | .12 | .03 |
| ☐ 22 Super Bowl XXII | .30 | .12 | .03 |
| ☐ 23 Super Bowl XXIII | .30 | .12 | .03 |

## 1989 Pro Set Announcers

The 1989 Pro Set Announcers set contains 30 standard-size (2 1/2" by 3 1/2") cards. The fronts have color photos bordered in red with TV network logos; otherwise, they are similar in appearance to the regular 1989 Pro Set cards. One announcer card was included in each Series II pack. Although Dan Jiggetts was listed as card number 21 on early checklists, he was replaced by Verne Lundquist when the cards were actually released. Those announcers who had previously played in the NFL were depicted with a photo from their active playing career.

| | MINT | EXC | G-VG |
|---|---|---|---|
| COMPLETE SET (30) | 5.00 | 2.00 | .50 |
| COMMON ANNOUNCER (1-30) | .10 | .04 | .01 |
| | | | |
| ☐ 1 Dan Dierdorf | .20 | .08 | .02 |
| ABC | | | |
| ☐ 2 Frank Gifford | .50 | .20 | .05 |
| ABC | | | |
| ☐ 3 Al Michaels | .15 | .06 | .01 |
| ABC | | | |
| ☐ 4 Pete Axthelm | .10 | .04 | .01 |
| ESPN | | | |
| ☐ 5 Chris Berman | .25 | .10 | .02 |
| ESPN | | | |
| ☐ 6 Tom Jackson | .15 | .06 | .01 |
| ESPN | | | |
| ☐ 7 Mike Patrick | .10 | .04 | .01 |
| ESPN | | | |
| ☐ 8 John Saunders | .10 | .04 | .01 |
| ESPN | | | |
| ☐ 9 Joe Theismann | .30 | .12 | .03 |
| ESPN | | | |
| ☐ 10 Steve Sabol | .10 | .04 | .01 |
| NFL Films | | | |
| ☐ 11 Jack Buck | .10 | .04 | .01 |
| CBS | | | |
| ☐ 12 Terry Bradshaw | .50 | .20 | .05 |
| CBS | | | |
| ☐ 13 James Brown | .10 | .04 | .01 |
| CBS | | | |
| ☐ 14 Dan Fouts | .30 | .12 | .03 |
| CBS | | | |
| ☐ 15 Dick Butkus | .40 | .16 | .04 |
| CBS | | | |
| ☐ 16 Irv Cross | .10 | .04 | .01 |
| CBS | | | |
| ☐ 17 Brent Musburger | .15 | .06 | .01 |
| CBS | | | |
| ☐ 18 Ken Stabler | .25 | .10 | .02 |
| CBS | | | |
| ☐ 19 Dick Stockton | .10 | .04 | .01 |
| CBS | | | |
| ☐ 20 Hank Stram | .10 | .04 | .01 |
| CBS | | | |
| ☐ 21 Verne Lundquist | .10 | .04 | .01 |
| CBS | | | |
| ☐ 22 Will McDonough | .10 | .04 | .01 |
| CBS | | | |
| ☐ 23 Bob Costas | .25 | .10 | .02 |
| NBC | | | |
| ☐ 24 Dick Enberg | .15 | .06 | .01 |
| NBC | | | |
| ☐ 25 Joe Namath | .60 | .24 | .06 |
| NBC | | | |
| ☐ 26 Bob Trumpy | .10 | .04 | .01 |
| NBC | | | |
| ☐ 27 Merlin Olsen | .25 | .10 | .02 |
| NBC | | | |
| ☐ 28 Ahmad Rashad | .30 | .12 | .03 |

| | MINT | EXC | G-VG |
|---|---|---|---|
| NBC | | | |
| ☐ 29 O.J. Simpson | 1.50 | .60 | .15 |
| NBC | | | |
| ☐ 30 Bill Walsh | .30 | .12 | .03 |
| NBC | | | |

## 1989 Pro Set Promos

Cards 445, 455, and 463 were planned for inclusion in the Pro Set second series but were withdrawn before mass production began. Note, however, that Thomas Sanders was included in the set but as number 446. The Santa Claus card was mailed out to dealers and NFL dignitaries in December 1989. The Super Bowl Show card was given out to attendees at the show in New Orleans in late January 1990. All of these cards are standard size (2 1/2" by 3 1/2") and utilize the 1989 Pro Set design.

| | MINT | EXC | G-VG |
|---|---|---|---|
| COMPLETE SET (5) | 100.00 | 40.00 | 10.00 |
| COMMON CARD | 5.00 | 2.00 | .50 |
| | | | |
| ☐ 445 Thomas Sanders | 20.00 | 8.00 | 2.00 |
| Chicago Bears | | | |
| ☐ 455 Blair Bush | 20.00 | 8.00 | 2.00 |
| Green Bay Packers | | | |
| ☐ 463 James Lofton | 25.00 | 10.00 | 2.50 |
| Los Angeles Raiders | | | |
| ☐ 1989 Santa Claus | 50.00 | 20.00 | 5.00 |
| ☐ xx Super Bowl Show I | 5.00 | 2.00 | .50 |
| New Orleans | | | |
| (Super Bowl XXIV) | | | |

## 1989-90 Pro Set GTE SB Album

This set was produced by Pro Set for GTE and issued in a special folder inside plastic sheets. Each ticket holder at the Super Bowl game in New Orleans received a set. Later Pro Set offered their surplus of these sets to the public at 20.00 per set, one to a customer; they apparently ran out quickly. The cards are standard size (2 1/2" by 3 1/2") and feature solely members of the San Francisco 49ers and Denver Broncos. The cards are distinguished from the regular issue Pro Set cards (even though they have the same card numbers) by their silver and gold top and bottom borders on each obverse.

| | MINT | EXC | G-VG |
|---|---|---|---|
| COMPLETE SET (40) | 25.00 | 10.00 | 2.50 |
| COMMON PLAYER | .40 | .16 | .04 |
| | | | |
| ☐ 99 Keith Bishop | .40 | .16 | .04 |
| Denver Broncos | | | |
| ☐ 100 John Elway | 5.00 | 2.00 | .50 |
| Denver Broncos | | | |

| | | | |
|---|---|---|---|
| ☐ 101 Simon Fletcher | .60 | .24 | .06 |
| Denver Broncos | | | |
| ☐ 103 Mike Horan | .40 | .16 | .04 |
| Denver Broncos | | | |
| ☐ 104 Mark Jackson | .60 | .24 | .06 |
| Denver Broncos | | | |
| ☐ 105 Vance Johnson | .60 | .24 | .06 |
| Denver Broncos | | | |
| ☐ 107 Clarence Kay | .40 | .16 | .04 |
| Denver Broncos | | | |
| ☐ 108 Karl Mecklenburg | .60 | .24 | .06 |
| Denver Broncos | | | |
| ☐ 109 Ricky Nattiel | .60 | .24 | .06 |
| Denver Broncos | | | |
| ☐ 110 Steve Sewell | .60 | .24 | .06 |
| Denver Broncos | | | |
| ☐ 111 Dennis Smith | .50 | .20 | .05 |
| Denver Broncos | | | |
| ☐ 113 Sammy Winder | .50 | .20 | .05 |
| Denver Broncos | | | |
| ☐ 114 Dan Reeves CO | .60 | .24 | .06 |
| Denver Broncos | | | |
| ☐ 369 Harris Barton | .40 | .16 | .04 |
| San Francisco 49ers | | | |
| ☐ 370 Michael Carter | .60 | .24 | .06 |
| San Francisco 49ers | | | |
| ☐ 371 Mike Cofer | .40 | .16 | .04 |
| San Francisco 49ers | | | |
| ☐ 372 Roger Craig | 2.00 | .80 | .20 |
| San Francisco 49ers | | | |
| ☐ 374 Jim Fahnhorst | .40 | .16 | .04 |
| San Francisco 49ers | | | |
| ☐ 377 Don Griffin | .50 | .20 | .05 |
| San Francisco 49ers | | | |
| ☐ 378 Charles Haley | .60 | .24 | .06 |
| San Francisco 49ers | | | |
| ☐ 379 Ronnie Lott | 2.00 | .80 | .20 |
| San Francisco 49ers | | | |
| ☐ 380 Tim McKyer | .50 | .20 | .05 |
| San Francisco 49ers | | | |
| ☐ 381 Joe Montana | 10.00 | 4.00 | 1.00 |
| San Francisco 49ers | | | |
| ☐ 382 Tom Rathman | .75 | .30 | .07 |
| San Francisco 49ers | | | |
| ☐ 383 Jerry Rice | 6.00 | 2.40 | .60 |
| San Francisco 49ers | | | |
| ☐ 384 John Taylor | 2.00 | .80 | .20 |
| San Francisco 49ers | | | |
| ☐ 385 Keena Turner | .50 | .20 | .05 |
| San Francisco 49ers | | | |
| ☐ 386 Michael Walter | .40 | .16 | .04 |
| San Francisco 49ers | | | |
| ☐ 387 Bubba Paris | .40 | .16 | .04 |
| San Francisco 49ers | | | |
| ☐ 388 Steve Young | 3.00 | 1.20 | .30 |
| San Francisco 49ers | | | |
| ☐ 389 George Seifert CO | .50 | .20 | .05 |
| San Francisco 49ers | | | |
| ☐ 479 Eric Wright | .60 | .24 | .06 |
| San Francisco 49ers | | | |
| ☐ 492 Steve Atwater | 1.00 | .40 | .10 |
| Denver Broncos | | | |
| ☐ 493 Bobby Humphrey | .75 | .30 | .07 |
| Denver Broncos | | | |
| ☐ 537 Danny Stubbs | .40 | .16 | .04 |
| San Francisco 49ers | | | |
| ☐ 543 Tyrone Braxton | .50 | .20 | .05 |
| Denver Broncos | | | |
| ☐ 544 David Treadwell | .40 | .16 | .04 |
| Denver Broncos | | | |
| ☐ xx AFC Logo | .60 | .24 | .06 |
| XXIV Collectible | | | |
| ☐ xx NFC Logo | .60 | .24 | .06 |
| XXIV Collectible | | | |
| ☐ xx Superdome | .60 | .24 | .06 |
| XXIV Collectible | | | |

## 1990 Pro Set Draft Day

This four-card standard size (2 1/2" by 3 1/2") set was issued by Pro Set on the date of the 1990 NFL draft. The cards, which are all numbered 669, feature action shots in the 1990 Pro Set design of all potential number one draft picks according to Pro Set's crystal ball. The backs of the cards have a horizontal format with one half of the card being a full-color portrait of the player and the other half consisting of biographical information. The set is checklisted below in alphabetical order by subject. The fourth card in the set, not listed below but listed in with the 1990 Pro Set regular issue cards, Jeff George Colts card, was actually later issued unchanged in selected first series Pro Set packs accounting for its much lesser value.

| | MINT | EXC | G-VG |
|---|---|---|---|
| COMPLETE SET (3) | 30.00 | 12.00 | 3.00 |
| COMMON PLAYER (669A-669C) | 4.00 | 1.60 | .40 |

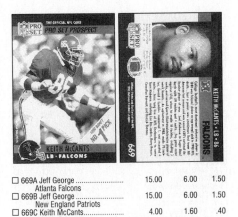

| | | | |
|---|---|---|---|
| ☐ 669A Jeff George ....................... Atlanta Falcons | 15.00 | 6.00 | 1.50 |
| ☐ 669B Jeff George ....................... New England Patriots | 15.00 | 6.00 | 1.50 |
| ☐ 669C Keith McCants.................. Atlanta Falcons | 4.00 | 1.60 | .40 |

## 1990 Pro Set

The 1990 Pro Set first series contains 377 standard-size (2 1/2" by 3 1/2") cards. The fronts have striking color action photos and team colored borders on the top and bottom edges; there are no borders on the sides. The horizontally oriented backs have stats and color mug shots. Cards 1-29 are special selections from Pro Set commemorating events or leaders from the previous year. The cards in the set are numbered by teams, Atlanta Falcons (30-38), Buffalo Bills (39-48), Chicago Bears (49-59), Cincinnati Bengals (60-68), Cleveland Browns (69-77), Dallas Cowboys (78-85), Denver Broncos (86-94), Detroit Lions (95-106), Green Bay Packers (107-116), Houston Oilers (117-127), Indianapolis Colts (128-139), Kansas City Chiefs (140-148), Los Angeles Raiders (149-161), Los Angeles Rams (162-176), Miami Dolphins (177-185), Minnesota Vikings (186-200), New England Patriots (201-209), New Orleans Saints (210-221), New York Giants (222-232), New York Jets (233-242), Philadelphia Eagles (243-253), Phoenix Cardinals (254-265), Pittsburgh Steelers (266-275), San Diego Chargers (276-283), San Francisco 49ers (284-299), Seattle Seahawks (300-308), Tampa Bay Buccaneers (309-319), Washington Redskins (320-333), and Pro Bowl Selections (334-378). Pro Set also produced and randomly inserted 10,000 Lombardi Trophy hologram cards; speculation is that there is one special Lombardi card in every tenth case. These attractive "Lombardi" cards are hand numbered "x" of 10,000. The withdrawn card of Eric Dickerson is not included in the complete set price below. Similarly, the set price below does not include any of the tougher variation cards, e.g., 1A Barry Sanders, 75A Cody Risien, etc. The second series of Pro Set football features cards in the same style and size as the first series. The second series is somewhat skip-numbered in that some numbers were saved for inclusion in Pro Set's Final Update. Cards 796-798 are black and white photos. Pro Set issued their AFC Pro Bowl series at the end of Series I and their NFC Pro Bowl series to open Series II. AFC Pro Bowlers have their regular cards in Series II and the NFC Pro bowlers in Series I. The only exceptions to this rule are AFC coach Bud Carson (all coaches are in Series I) and Chris Hinton, who doesn't have a regular card. Draft cards found near the end of the second series are sequenced by draft order. The 1990 Pro Set Final Update series was issued in a special mail-away offer. The series includes only players either not issued by Pro Set in their first two series or players who were traded during the season. The series also includes a special Ronnie Lott stay in school card and the 1990 Pro Set Rookie of the

Year card which introduced the 1991 Pro Set design. The notable Rookie Cards in the set are Fred Barnett, Reggie Cobb, Derrick Fenner, Jeff George, Harold Green, Rodney Hampton, Michael Haynes, Jeff Hostetler, Stan Humphries, Haywood Jeffires, Johnny Johnson, Cortez Kennedy, Brian Mitchell, Rob Moore, Ricky Proehl, Junior Seau, Emmitt Smith, Blair Thomas, Renaldo Turnbull, Andre Ware, and Barry Word.

| | MINT | EXC | G-VG |
|---|---|---|---|
| COMPLETE SET (801)...................... | 20.00 | 9.00 | 2.50 |
| COMPLETE SERIES 1 (377)............. | 8.00 | 3.60 | 1.00 |
| COMPLETE SERIES 2 (392)............. | 8.00 | 3.60 | 1.00 |
| COMPLETE FINAL SERIES (32) ........ | 4.00 | 1.80 | .50 |
| COMPLETE FINAL FACT. (32)........ | 4.00 | 1.80 | .50 |
| COMMON PLAYER (1-378)............. | .04 | .02 | .01 |
| COMMON (379-752/781-798)...... | .04 | .02 | .01 |
| COMMON (753-780/799-800/SC4)... | .04 | .02 | .01 |
| ☐ 1A Barry Sanders ROY .............. (Distributed to dealers at the Hawaii trade show in February 1990; distinguished from the regular card by profile head shot photo without ROY trophy on on card back) | 100.00 | 45.00 | 12.50 |
| ☐ 1B Barry Sanders UER .............. Rookie of the Year (TD total says 14, but adds up to 11) | .50 | .23 | .06 |
| ☐ 2A Joe Montana ERR .................. Player of the Year (Jim Kelly's stats in text) | .50 | .23 | .06 |
| ☐ 2B Joe Montana COR.................. Player of the Year (Corrected from 3521 yards to 3130) | .50 | .23 | .06 |
| ☐ 3 Lindy Infante UER .................. Coach of the Year (missing Coach next to Packers) | .04 | .02 | .01 |
| ☐ 4 Warren Moon UER .................. Man of the Year (missing R symbol) | .12 | .05 | .02 |
| ☐ 5 Keith Millard........................ Defensive Player of the Year | .04 | .02 | .01 |
| ☐ 6 Derrick Thomas UER .............. Defensive Rookie of the Year (no 1989 on front banner of card) | .15 | .07 | .02 |
| ☐ 7 Ottis Anderson ...................... Comeback Player of the Year | .04 | .02 | .01 |
| ☐ 8 Joe Montana ......................... Passing Leader | .50 | .23 | .06 |
| ☐ 9 Christian Okoye...................... Rushing Leader | .04 | .02 | .01 |
| ☐ 10 Thurman Thomas................... Total Yardage Leader | .20 | .09 | .03 |
| ☐ 11 Mike Cofer............................ Kick Scoring Leader | .04 | .02 | .01 |
| ☐ 12 Dalton Hilliard UER ............... TD Scoring Leader (O.J. Simpson not listed in stats, but is mentioned in text) | .04 | .02 | .01 |
| ☐ 13 Sterling Sharpe ...................... Receiving Leader | .25 | .11 | .03 |
| ☐ 14 Rich Camarillo....................... Punting Leader | .04 | .02 | .01 |
| ☐ 15A Walter Stanley ERR.............. Punt Return Leader (jersey on front reads 87, back says 8 or 86) | .50 | .23 | .06 |
| ☐ 15B Walter Stanley COR ............. Punt Return Leader | .04 | .02 | .01 |
| ☐ 16 Rod Woodson ....................... Kickoff Return Leader | .08 | .04 | .01 |
| ☐ 17 Felix Wright.......................... Interception Leader | .04 | .02 | .01 |
| ☐ 18A Chris Doleman ERR ............. Sack Leader (Townsent, Jeffcoact) | .08 | .04 | .01 |
| ☐ 18B Chris Doleman COR ............. Sack Leader (Townsend, Jeffcoat) | .08 | .04 | .01 |
| ☐ 19A Andre Ware.......................... Heisman Trophy (No drafted stripe on card front) | .15 | .07 | .02 |
| ☐ 19B Andre Ware.......................... Heisman Trophy (Drafted stripe | .15 | .07 | .02 |

on card front)
| □ 20A Mohammed Elewonibi | .04 | .02 | .01 |
| Outland Trophy | | | |
| (No drafted stripe | | | |
| on card front) | | | |
| □ 20B Mohammed Elewonibi | .04 | .02 | .01 |
| Outland Trophy | | | |
| (Drafted stripe | | | |
| on card front) | | | |
| □ 21A Percy Snow | .05 | .02 | .01 |
| Lombardi Award | | | |
| (No drafted stripe | | | |
| on card front) | | | |
| □ 21B Percy Snow | .05 | .02 | .01 |
| Lombardi Award | | | |
| (Drafted stripe | | | |
| on card front) | | | |
| □ 22A Anthony Thompson | .10 | .05 | .01 |
| Maxwell Award | | | |
| (No drafted stripe | | | |
| on card front) | | | |
| □ 22B Anthony Thompson | .10 | .05 | .01 |
| Maxwell Award | | | |
| (Drafted stripe | | | |
| on card front) | | | |
| □ 23 Buck Buchanan | .04 | .02 | .01 |
| (Sacking Bart Starr) | | | |
| 1990 HOF Selection | | | |
| □ 24 Bob Griese | .04 | .02 | .01 |
| 1990 HOF Selection | | | |
| □ 25A Franco Harris ERR | .05 | .02 | .01 |
| 1990 HOF Selection | | | |
| (Born 2/7/50) | | | |
| □ 25B Franco Harris COR | .05 | .02 | .01 |
| 1990 HOF Selection | | | |
| (Born 3/7/50) | | | |
| □ 26 Ted Hendricks | .04 | .02 | .01 |
| 1990 HOF Selection | | | |
| □ 27A Jack Lambert ERR | .05 | .02 | .01 |
| 1990 HOF Selection | | | |
| (Born 7/2/52) | | | |
| □ 27B Jack Lambert COR | .05 | .02 | .01 |
| 1990 HOF Selection | | | |
| (Born 7/8/52) | | | |
| □ 28 Tom Landry | .08 | .04 | .01 |
| 1990 HOF Selection | | | |
| □ 29 Bob St.Clair | .04 | .02 | .01 |
| 1990 HOF Selection | | | |
| □ 30 Aundray Bruce UER | .04 | .02 | .01 |
| (Stats say Falcons) | | | |
| □ 31 Tony Casillas UER | .04 | .02 | .01 |
| (Stats say Falcons) | | | |
| □ 32 Shawn Collins | .04 | .02 | .01 |
| □ 33 Marcus Cotton | .04 | .02 | .01 |
| □ 34 Bill Fralic | .08 | .04 | .01 |
| □ 35 Chris Miller | .15 | .07 | .02 |
| □ 36 Deion Sanders UER | .25 | .11 | .03 |
| (Stats say Falcons) | | | |
| □ 37 John Settle | .04 | .02 | .01 |
| □ 38 Jerry Glanville CO | .04 | .02 | .01 |
| □ 39 Cornelius Bennett | .10 | .05 | .01 |
| □ 40 Jim Kelly | .30 | .14 | .04 |
| □ 41 Mark Kelso UER | .04 | .02 | .01 |
| (No fumble rec. in '88; | | | |
| mentioned in '89) | | | |
| □ 42 Scott Norwood | .04 | .02 | .01 |
| □ 43 Nate Odomes | .25 | .11 | .03 |
| □ 44 Scott Radecic | .04 | .02 | .01 |
| □ 45 Jim Ritcher | .10 | .05 | .01 |
| □ 46 Leonard Smith | .04 | .02 | .01 |
| □ 47 Darryl Talley | .08 | .04 | .01 |
| □ 48 Marv Levy CO | .08 | .04 | .01 |
| □ 49 Neal Anderson | .08 | .04 | .01 |
| □ 50 Kevin Butler | .04 | .02 | .01 |
| □ 51 Jim Covert | .04 | .02 | .01 |
| □ 52 Richard Dent | .08 | .04 | .01 |
| □ 53 Jay Hilgenberg | .08 | .04 | .01 |
| □ 54 Steve McMichael | .08 | .04 | .01 |
| □ 55 Ron Morris | .04 | .02 | .01 |
| □ 56 John Roper | .04 | .02 | .01 |
| □ 57 Mike Singletary | .10 | .05 | .01 |
| □ 58 Keith Van Horne | .04 | .02 | .01 |
| □ 59 Mike Ditka CO | .10 | .05 | .01 |
| □ 60 Lewis Billups | .04 | .02 | .01 |
| □ 61 Eddie Brown | .04 | .02 | .01 |
| □ 62 Jason Buck | .04 | .02 | .01 |
| □ 63A Rickey Dixon ERR | .50 | .23 | .06 |
| (Info missing under | | | |
| bio notes) | | | |
| □ 63B Rickey Dixon COR | .10 | .05 | .01 |
| □ 64 Tim McGee | .08 | .04 | .01 |
| □ 65 Eric Thomas | .04 | .02 | .01 |
| □ 66 Ickey Woods | .04 | .02 | .01 |
| □ 67 Carl Zander | .04 | .02 | .01 |
| □ 68A Sam Wyche CO ERR | .50 | .23 | .06 |
| (Info missing under | | | |
| bio notes) | | | |
| □ 68B Sam Wyche CO COR | .08 | .04 | .01 |

| □ 69 Paul Farren | .04 | .02 | .01 |
| □ 70 Thane Gash | .04 | .02 | .01 |
| □ 71 David Grayson | .04 | .02 | .01 |
| □ 72 Bernie Kosar | .10 | .05 | .01 |
| □ 73 Reggie Langhorne | .08 | .04 | .01 |
| □ 74 Eric Metcalf | .15 | .07 | .02 |
| □ 75A Ozzie Newsome ERR | .10 | .05 | .01 |
| Born Muscle Shoals | | | |
| □ 75B Ozzie Newsome COR | .10 | .05 | .01 |
| (Born Little Rock) | | | |
| □ 75C Cody Risien SP | 5.00 | 2.30 | .60 |
| (withdrawn) | | | |
| □ 76 Felix Wright | .04 | .02 | .01 |
| □ 77 Bud Carson CO | .04 | .02 | .01 |
| □ 78 Troy Aikman | 1.25 | .55 | .16 |
| □ 79 Michael Irvin | .75 | .35 | .09 |
| □ 80 Jim Jeffcoat | .04 | .02 | .01 |
| □ 81 Crawford Ker | .04 | .02 | .01 |
| □ 82 Eugene Lockhart | .04 | .02 | .01 |
| □ 83 Kelvin Martin | .25 | .11 | .03 |
| □ 84 Ken Norton | .50 | .23 | .06 |
| □ 85 Jimmy Johnson CO | .08 | .04 | .01 |
| □ 86 Steve Atwater | .10 | .05 | .01 |
| □ 87 Tyrone Braxton | .04 | .02 | .01 |
| □ 88 John Elway | .40 | .18 | .05 |
| □ 89 Simon Fletcher | .08 | .04 | .01 |
| □ 90 Ron Holmes | .04 | .02 | .01 |
| □ 91 Bobby Humphrey | .08 | .04 | .01 |
| □ 92 Vance Johnson | .08 | .04 | .01 |
| □ 93 Ricky Nattiel | .04 | .02 | .01 |
| □ 94 Dan Reeves CO | .04 | .02 | .01 |
| □ 95 Jim Arnold | .04 | .02 | .01 |
| □ 96 Jerry Ball | .08 | .04 | .01 |
| □ 97 Bennie Blades | .04 | .02 | .01 |
| □ 98 Lomas Brown | .04 | .02 | .01 |
| □ 99 Michael Cofer | .04 | .02 | .01 |
| □ 100 Richard Johnson | .04 | .02 | .01 |
| □ 101 Eddie Murray | .08 | .04 | .01 |
| □ 102 Barry Sanders | 1.00 | .45 | .13 |
| □ 103 Chris Spielman | .08 | .04 | .01 |
| □ 104 William White | .10 | .05 | .01 |
| □ 105 Eric Williams | .10 | .05 | .01 |
| □ 106 Wayne Fontes CO UER | .04 | .02 | .01 |
| (Says born in MO, | | | |
| actually born in MA) | | | |
| □ 107 Brent Fullwood | .04 | .02 | .01 |
| □ 108 Ron Hallstrom | .04 | .02 | .01 |
| □ 109 Tim Harris | .08 | .04 | .01 |
| □ 110A Johnny Holland ERR | 1.00 | .45 | .13 |
| (No name or position | | | |
| at top of reverse) | | | |
| □ 110B Johnny Holland COR | .05 | .02 | .01 |
| □ 111A Perry Kemp ERR | .50 | .23 | .06 |
| (Photo on back is | | | |
| actually Ken Stiles, | | | |
| wearing gray shirt) | | | |
| □ 111B Perry Kemp COR | .05 | .02 | .01 |
| (Wearing green shirt) | | | |
| □ 112 Don Majkowski | .08 | .04 | .01 |
| □ 113 Mark Murphy | .04 | .02 | .01 |
| □ 114A Sterling Sharpe ERR | .75 | .35 | .09 |
| (Born Glenville, Ga.) | | | |
| □ 114B Sterling Sharpe COR | 2.00 | .90 | .25 |
| (Born Chicago) | | | |
| □ 115 Ed West | .10 | .05 | .01 |
| □ 116 Lindy Infante CO | .04 | .02 | .01 |
| □ 117 Steve Brown | .04 | .02 | .01 |
| □ 118 Ray Childress | .08 | .04 | .01 |
| □ 119 Ernest Givins | .08 | .04 | .01 |
| □ 120 John Grimsley | .04 | .02 | .01 |
| □ 121 Alonzo Highsmith | .04 | .02 | .01 |
| □ 122 Drew Hill | .08 | .04 | .01 |
| □ 123 Bubba McDowell | .04 | .02 | .01 |
| □ 124 Dean Steinkuhler | .04 | .02 | .01 |
| □ 125 Lorenzo White | .15 | .07 | .02 |
| □ 126 Tony Zendejas | .04 | .02 | .01 |
| □ 127 Jack Pardee CO | .04 | .02 | .01 |
| □ 128 Albert Bentley | .04 | .02 | .01 |
| □ 129 Dean Biasucci | .04 | .02 | .01 |
| □ 130 Duane Bickett | .04 | .02 | .01 |
| □ 131 Bill Brooks | .08 | .04 | .01 |
| □ 132 Jon Hand | .04 | .02 | .01 |
| □ 133 Mike Prior | .04 | .02 | .01 |
| □ 134A Andre Rison | .30 | .14 | .04 |
| (No mention of trade | | | |
| on card front) | | | |
| □ 134B Andre Rison | .75 | .35 | .09 |
| (Traded banner on card | | | |
| front; also reissued | | | |
| with Final Update) | | | |
| □ 134C Andre Rison | .50 | .23 | .06 |
| (Traded banner on card | | | |
| front; message from | | | |
| Lud Denny on back) | | | |
| □ 135 Rohn Stark | .08 | .04 | .01 |
| □ 136 Donnell Thompson | .04 | .02 | .01 |
| □ 137 Clarence Verdin | .04 | .02 | .01 |

| | | | |
|---|---|---|---|
| ☐ 138 Fredd Young | .04 | .02 | .01 |
| ☐ 139 Ron Meyer CO | .04 | .02 | .01 |
| ☐ 140 John Alt | .10 | .05 | .01 |
| ☐ 141 Steve DeBerg | .08 | .04 | .01 |
| ☐ 142 Irv Eatman | .04 | .02 | .01 |
| ☐ 143 Dino Hackett | .04 | .02 | .01 |
| ☐ 144 Nick Lowery | .08 | .04 | .01 |
| ☐ 145 Bill Maas | .08 | .04 | .01 |
| ☐ 146 Stephone Paige | .08 | .04 | .01 |
| ☐ 147 Neil Smith | .20 | .09 | .03 |
| ☐ 148 Marty Schottenheimer CO | .04 | .02 | .01 |
| ☐ 149 Steve Beuerlein | .25 | .11 | .03 |
| ☐ 150 Tim Brown | .30 | .14 | .04 |
| ☐ 151 Mike Dyal | .04 | .02 | .01 |
| ☐ 152A Mervyn Fernandez ERR (Acquired: Free Agent '87) | .08 | .04 | .01 |
| ☐ 152B Mervyn Fernandez COR (Acquired: Drafted 10th Round, 1983) | .08 | .04 | .01 |
| ☐ 153 Willie Gault | .08 | .04 | .01 |
| ☐ 154 Bob Golic | .04 | .02 | .01 |
| ☐ 155 Bo Jackson | .40 | .18 | .05 |
| ☐ 156 Don Mosebar | .04 | .02 | .01 |
| ☐ 157 Steve Smith | .08 | .04 | .01 |
| ☐ 158 Greg Townsend | .08 | .04 | .01 |
| ☐ 159 Bruce Wilkerson | .04 | .02 | .01 |
| ☐ 160 Steve Wisniewski (Blocking for Bo Jackson) | .04 | .02 | .01 |
| ☐ 161A Art Shell CO ERR (Born 11/25/46) | .05 | .02 | .01 |
| ☐ 161B Art Shell CO COR (Born 11/26/46; large HOF print on front) | .50 | .23 | .06 |
| ☐ 161C Art Shell CO COR (Born 11/26/46; small HOF print on front) | .04 | .02 | .01 |
| ☐ 162 Flipper Anderson | .08 | .04 | .01 |
| ☐ 163 Greg Bell UER (Stats have 5 catches, should be 9) | .08 | .04 | .01 |
| ☐ 164 Henry Ellard | .08 | .04 | .01 |
| ☐ 165 Jim Everett | .08 | .04 | .01 |
| ☐ 166 Jerry Gray | .04 | .02 | .01 |
| ☐ 167 Kevin Greene | .08 | .04 | .01 |
| ☐ 168 Pete Holohan | .04 | .02 | .01 |
| ☐ 169 Larry Kelm | .04 | .02 | .01 |
| ☐ 170 Tom Newberry | .04 | .02 | .01 |
| ☐ 171 Vince Newsome | .04 | .02 | .01 |
| ☐ 172 Irv Pankey | .04 | .02 | .01 |
| ☐ 173 Jackie Slater | .08 | .04 | .01 |
| ☐ 174 Fred Strickland | .04 | .02 | .01 |
| ☐ 175 Mike Wilcher UER (Fumble rec. number different from 1989 Pro Set card) | .04 | .02 | .01 |
| ☐ 176 John Robinson CO UER (Stats say Rams, should say L.A. Rams) | .04 | .02 | .01 |
| ☐ 177 Mark Clayton | .08 | .04 | .01 |
| ☐ 178 Roy Foster | .04 | .02 | .01 |
| ☐ 179 Harry Galbreath | .15 | .07 | .02 |
| ☐ 180 Jim C. Jensen | .04 | .02 | .01 |
| ☐ 181 Dan Marino | .75 | .35 | .09 |
| ☐ 182 Louis Oliver | .08 | .04 | .01 |
| ☐ 183 Sammie Smith | .04 | .02 | .01 |
| ☐ 184 Brian Sochia | .04 | .02 | .01 |
| ☐ 185 Don Shula CO | .08 | .04 | .01 |
| ☐ 186 Joey Browner | .08 | .04 | .01 |
| ☐ 187 Anthony Carter | .08 | .04 | .01 |
| ☐ 188 Chris Doleman | .08 | .04 | .01 |
| ☐ 189 Steve Jordan | .08 | .04 | .01 |
| ☐ 190 Carl Lee | .04 | .02 | .01 |
| ☐ 191 Randall McDaniel | .04 | .02 | .01 |
| ☐ 192 Mike Merriweather | .08 | .04 | .01 |
| ☐ 193 Keith Millard | .08 | .04 | .01 |
| ☐ 194 Al Noga | .04 | .02 | .01 |
| ☐ 195 Scott Studwell | .04 | .02 | .01 |
| ☐ 196 Henry Thomas | .04 | .02 | .01 |
| ☐ 197 Herschel Walker | .10 | .05 | .01 |
| ☐ 198 Wade Wilson | .08 | .04 | .01 |
| ☐ 199 Gary Zimmerman | .08 | .04 | .01 |
| ☐ 200 Jerry Burns CO | .04 | .02 | .01 |
| ☐ 201 Vincent Brown | .15 | .07 | .02 |
| ☐ 202 Hart Lee Dykes | .04 | .02 | .01 |
| ☐ 203 Sean Farrell | .04 | .02 | .01 |
| ☐ 204A Fred Marion (Belt visible on John Taylor) | | | |
| ☐ 204B Fred Marion (Belt not visible) | .04 | .02 | .01 |
| ☐ 205 Stanley Morgan UER (Text says he reached 10,000 yards fastest; 3 players did it in 10 seasons) | .08 | .04 | .01 |

| | | | |
|---|---|---|---|
| ☐ 206 Eric Sievers | .04 | .02 | .01 |
| ☐ 207 John Stephens | .08 | .04 | .01 |
| ☐ 208 Andre Tippett | .08 | .04 | .01 |
| ☐ 209 Rod Rust CO | .04 | .02 | .01 |
| ☐ 210A Morten Andersen ERR (Card number and name on back in white) | .50 | .23 | .06 |
| ☐ 210B Morten Andersen COR (Card number and name on back in black) | .08 | .04 | .01 |
| ☐ 211 Brad Edelman | .04 | .02 | .01 |
| ☐ 212 John Fourcade | .04 | .02 | .01 |
| ☐ 213 Dalton Hilliard | .08 | .04 | .01 |
| ☐ 214 Rickey Jackson (Forcing Jim Kelly fumble) | .08 | .04 | .01 |
| ☐ 215 Vaughan Johnson | .08 | .04 | .01 |
| ☐ 216A Eric Martin ERR (Card number and name on back in white) | .50 | .23 | .06 |
| ☐ 216B Eric Martin COR (Card number and name on back in black) | .08 | .04 | .01 |
| ☐ 217 Sam Mills | .08 | .04 | .01 |
| ☐ 218 Pat Swilling UER (Total fumble recoveries listed as 4, should be 5) | .10 | .05 | .01 |
| ☐ 219 Frank Warren | .10 | .05 | .01 |
| ☐ 220 Jim Wilks | .04 | .02 | .01 |
| ☐ 221A Jim Mora CO ERR (Card number and name on back in white) | .50 | .23 | .06 |
| ☐ 221B Jim Mora CO COR (Card number and name on back in black) | .05 | .02 | .01 |
| ☐ 222 Raul Allegre | .04 | .02 | .01 |
| ☐ 223 Carl Banks | .08 | .04 | .01 |
| ☐ 224 John Elliott | .04 | .02 | .01 |
| ☐ 225 Erik Howard | .04 | .02 | .01 |
| ☐ 226 Pepper Johnson | .08 | .04 | .01 |
| ☐ 227 Leonard Marshall UER (In Super Bowl XXI, George Martin had the safety) | .08 | .04 | .01 |
| ☐ 228 David Meggett | .10 | .05 | .01 |
| ☐ 229 Bart Oates | .04 | .02 | .01 |
| ☐ 230 Phil Simms | .10 | .05 | .01 |
| ☐ 231 Lawrence Taylor | .10 | .05 | .01 |
| ☐ 232 Bill Parcells CO | .08 | .04 | .01 |
| ☐ 233 Troy Benson | .04 | .02 | .01 |
| ☐ 234 Kyle Clifton UER (Born: Onley, should be Olney) | .04 | .02 | .01 |
| ☐ 235 Johnny Hector | .04 | .02 | .01 |
| ☐ 236 Jeff Lageman | .04 | .02 | .01 |
| ☐ 237 Pat Leahy | .08 | .04 | .01 |
| ☐ 238 Freeman McNeil | .08 | .04 | .01 |
| ☐ 239 Ken O'Brien | .08 | .04 | .01 |
| ☐ 240 Al Toon | .08 | .04 | .01 |
| ☐ 241 Jo Jo Townsell | .04 | .02 | .01 |
| ☐ 242 Bruce Coslet CO | .04 | .02 | .01 |
| ☐ 243 Eric Allen | .08 | .04 | .01 |
| ☐ 244 Jerome Brown | .08 | .04 | .01 |
| ☐ 245 Keith Byars | .08 | .04 | .01 |
| ☐ 246 Cris Carter | .20 | .09 | .03 |
| ☐ 247 Randall Cunningham | .15 | .07 | .02 |
| ☐ 248 Keith Jackson | .25 | .11 | .03 |
| ☐ 249 Mike Quick (Darrell Green also in photo) | .08 | .04 | .01 |
| ☐ 250 Clyde Simmons | .08 | .04 | .01 |
| ☐ 251 Andre Waters | .08 | .04 | .01 |
| ☐ 252 Reggie White | .15 | .07 | .02 |
| ☐ 253 Buddy Ryan CO | .04 | .02 | .01 |
| ☐ 254 Rich Camarillo | .04 | .02 | .01 |
| ☐ 255 Earl Ferrell (No mention of retirement on card front) | .04 | .02 | .01 |
| ☐ 256 Roy Green | .08 | .04 | .01 |
| ☐ 257 Ken Harvey | .12 | .05 | .02 |
| ☐ 258 Ernie Jones | .15 | .07 | .02 |
| ☐ 259 Tim McDonald | .08 | .04 | .01 |
| ☐ 260 Timm Rosenbach UER (Born '67, should be '66) | .04 | .02 | .01 |
| ☐ 261 Luis Sharpe | .04 | .02 | .01 |
| ☐ 262 Vai Sikahema | .08 | .04 | .01 |
| ☐ 263 J.T. Smith | .04 | .02 | .01 |
| ☐ 264 Ron Wolfley UER (Born Blaisdel, should be Blasdel) | .04 | .02 | .01 |
| ☐ 265 Joe Bugel CO | .04 | .02 | .01 |
| ☐ 266 Gary Anderson | .04 | .02 | .01 |
| ☐ 267 Bubby Brister | .10 | .05 | .01 |
| ☐ 268 Merril Hoge | .08 | .04 | .01 |
| ☐ 269 Carnell Lake | .04 | .02 | .01 |
| ☐ 270 Louis Lipps | .08 | .04 | .01 |
| ☐ 271 David Little | .04 | .02 | .01 |
| ☐ 272 Greg Lloyd | .04 | .02 | .01 |

| | | | |
|---|---|---|---|
| ☐ 273 Keith Willis | .04 | .02 | .01 |
| ☐ 274 Tim Worley | .08 | .04 | .01 |
| ☐ 275 Chuck Noll CO | .04 | .02 | .01 |
| ☐ 276 Marion Butts | .10 | .05 | .01 |
| ☐ 277 Gill Byrd | .08 | .04 | .01 |
| ☐ 278 Vencie Glenn UER | .04 | .02 | .01 |
| (Sack total should | | | |
| be 2, not 2.5) | | | |
| ☐ 279 Burt Grossman | .04 | .02 | .01 |
| ☐ 280 Gary Plummer | .04 | .02 | .01 |
| ☐ 281 Billy Ray Smith | .08 | .04 | .01 |
| ☐ 282 Billy Joe Tolliver | .04 | .02 | .01 |
| ☐ 283 Dan Henning CO | .04 | .02 | .01 |
| ☐ 284 Harris Barton | .04 | .02 | .01 |
| ☐ 285 Michael Carter | .04 | .02 | .01 |
| ☐ 286 Mike Cofer | .04 | .02 | .01 |
| ☐ 287 Roger Craig | .08 | .04 | .01 |
| ☐ 288 Don Griffin | .04 | .02 | .01 |
| ☐ 289A Charles Haley ERR | .08 | .04 | .01 |
| (Fumble recoveries 1 | | | |
| in '86 and 4 total) | | | |
| ☐ 289B Charles Haley COR | .75 | .35 | .09 |
| (Fumble recoveries 2 | | | |
| in '86 and 5 total) | | | |
| ☐ 290 Pierce Holt | .15 | .07 | .02 |
| ☐ 291 Ronnie Lott | .10 | .05 | .01 |
| ☐ 292 Guy McIntyre | .08 | .04 | .01 |
| ☐ 293 Joe Montana | 1.00 | .45 | .13 |
| ☐ 294 Tom Rathman | .08 | .04 | .01 |
| ☐ 295 Jerry Rice | .75 | .35 | .09 |
| ☐ 296 Jesse Sapolu | .04 | .02 | .01 |
| ☐ 297 John Taylor | .20 | .09 | .03 |
| ☐ 298 Michael Walter | .04 | .02 | .01 |
| ☐ 299 George Seifert CO | .04 | .02 | .01 |
| ☐ 300 Jeff Bryant | .04 | .02 | .01 |
| ☐ 301 Jacob Green | .04 | .02 | .01 |
| ☐ 302 Norm Johnson UER | .04 | .02 | .01 |
| (Card shop not in | | | |
| Garden Grove, should | | | |
| say Fullerton) | | | |
| ☐ 303 Bryan Millard | .04 | .02 | .01 |
| ☐ 304 Joe Nash | .04 | .02 | .01 |
| ☐ 305 Eugene Robinson | .04 | .02 | .01 |
| ☐ 306 John L. Williams | .08 | .04 | .01 |
| ☐ 307 Dave Wyman | .04 | .02 | .01 |
| (NFL EXP is in caps, | | | |
| inconsistent with rest | | | |
| of the set) | | | |
| ☐ 308 Chuck Knox CO | .04 | .02 | .01 |
| ☐ 309 Mark Carrier | .10 | .05 | .01 |
| ☐ 310 Paul Gruber | .08 | .04 | .01 |
| ☐ 311 Harry Hamilton | .04 | .02 | .01 |
| ☐ 312 Bruce Hill | .04 | .02 | .01 |
| ☐ 313 Donald Igwebuike | .04 | .02 | .01 |
| ☐ 314 Kevin Murphy | .04 | .02 | .01 |
| ☐ 315 Ervin Randle | .04 | .02 | .01 |
| ☐ 316 Mark Robinson | .04 | .02 | .01 |
| ☐ 317 Lars Tate | .04 | .02 | .01 |
| ☐ 318 Vinny Testaverde | .15 | .07 | .02 |
| ☐ 319A Ray Perkins CO ERR | .75 | .35 | .09 |
| (No name or title | | | |
| at top of reverse) | | | |
| ☐ 319B Ray Perkins CO COR | .04 | .02 | .01 |
| ☐ 320 Earnest Byner | .08 | .04 | .01 |
| ☐ 321 Gary Clark | .10 | .05 | .01 |
| (Randall Cunningham look- | | | |
| ing on from sidelines) | | | |
| ☐ 322 Darryl Grant | .04 | .02 | .01 |
| ☐ 323 Darrell Green | .08 | .04 | .01 |
| ☐ 324 Jim Lachey | .08 | .04 | .01 |
| ☐ 325 Charles Mann | .08 | .04 | .01 |
| ☐ 326 Wilber Marshall | .08 | .04 | .01 |
| ☐ 327 Ralf Mojsiejenko | .04 | .02 | .01 |
| ☐ 328 Art Monk | .10 | .05 | .01 |
| ☐ 329 Gerald Riggs | .08 | .04 | .01 |
| ☐ 330 Mark Rypien | .10 | .05 | .01 |
| ☐ 331 Ricky Sanders | .08 | .04 | .01 |
| ☐ 332 Alvin Walton | .04 | .02 | .01 |
| ☐ 333 Joe Gibbs CO | .04 | .02 | .01 |
| ☐ 334 Aloha Stadium | .04 | .02 | .01 |
| Site of Pro Bowl | | | |
| ☐ 335 Brian Blades PB | .08 | .04 | .01 |
| ☐ 336 James Brooks PB | .04 | .02 | .01 |
| ☐ 337 Shane Conlan PB | .04 | .02 | .01 |
| ☐ 338 Eric Dickerson PB SP | 5.00 | 2.30 | .60 |
| (Card withdrawn) | | | |
| ☐ 339 Ray Donaldson PB | .04 | .02 | .01 |
| ☐ 340 Ferrell Edmunds PB | .04 | .02 | .01 |
| ☐ 341 Boomer Esiason PB | .08 | .04 | .01 |
| ☐ 342 David Fulcher PB | .04 | .02 | .01 |
| ☐ 343A Chris Hinton PB | .50 | .23 | .06 |
| (No mention of trade | | | |
| on card front) | | | |
| ☐ 343B Chris Hinton PB | .04 | .02 | .01 |
| (Traded banner | | | |
| on card front) | | | |
| ☐ 344 Rodney Holman PB | .04 | .02 | .01 |
| ☐ 345 Kent Hull PB | .04 | .02 | .01 |
| ☐ 346 Tunch Ilkin PB | .04 | .02 | .01 |
| ☐ 347 Mike Johnson PB | .04 | .02 | .01 |
| ☐ 348 Greg Kragen PB | .04 | .02 | .01 |
| ☐ 349 Dave Krieg PB | .04 | .02 | .01 |
| ☐ 350 Albert Lewis PB | .08 | .04 | .01 |
| ☐ 351 Howie Long PB | .08 | .04 | .01 |
| ☐ 352 Bruce Matthews PB | .04 | .02 | .01 |
| ☐ 353 Clay Matthews PB | .08 | .04 | .01 |
| ☐ 354 Erik McMillan PB | .04 | .02 | .01 |
| ☐ 355 Karl Mecklenburg PB | .04 | .02 | .01 |
| ☐ 356 Anthony Miller PB | .08 | .04 | .01 |
| ☐ 357 Frank Minnifield PB | .04 | .02 | .01 |
| ☐ 358 Max Montoya PB | .04 | .02 | .01 |
| ☐ 359 Warren Moon PB | .10 | .05 | .01 |
| ☐ 360 Mike Munchak PB | .04 | .02 | .01 |
| ☐ 361 Anthony Munoz PB | .08 | .04 | .01 |
| ☐ 362 John Offerdahl PB | .04 | .02 | .01 |
| ☐ 363 Christian Okoye PB | .04 | .02 | .01 |
| ☐ 364 Leslie O'Neal PB | .04 | .02 | .01 |
| ☐ 365 Rufus Porter PB UER | .04 | .02 | .01 |
| (TM logo missing) | | | |
| ☐ 366 Andre Reed PB | .04 | .02 | .01 |
| ☐ 367 Johnny Rembert PB | .04 | .02 | .01 |
| ☐ 368 Reggie Roby PB | .04 | .02 | .01 |
| ☐ 369 Kevin Ross PB | .04 | .02 | .01 |
| ☐ 370 Webster Slaughter PB | .04 | .02 | .01 |
| ☐ 371 Bruce Smith PB | .08 | .04 | .01 |
| ☐ 372 Dennis Smith PB | .04 | .02 | .01 |
| ☐ 373 Derrick Thomas PB | .20 | .09 | .03 |
| ☐ 374 Thurman Thomas PB | .25 | .11 | .03 |
| ☐ 375 David Treadwell PB | .04 | .02 | .01 |
| ☐ 376 Lee Williams PB | .04 | .02 | .01 |
| ☐ 377 Rod Woodson PB | .08 | .04 | .01 |
| ☐ 378 Bud Carson CO PB | .04 | .02 | .01 |
| ☐ 379 Eric Allen PB | .04 | .02 | .01 |
| Philadelphia Eagles | | | |
| ☐ 380 Neal Anderson PB | .04 | .02 | .01 |
| Chicago Bears | | | |
| ☐ 381 Jerry Ball PB | .04 | .02 | .01 |
| Detroit Lions | | | |
| ☐ 382 Joey Browner PB | .04 | .02 | .01 |
| Minnesota Vikings | | | |
| ☐ 383 Rich Camarillo PB | .04 | .02 | .01 |
| Phoenix Cardinals | | | |
| ☐ 384 Mark Carrier PB | .04 | .02 | .01 |
| Tampa Bay Buccaneers | | | |
| ☐ 385 Roger Craig PB | .08 | .04 | .01 |
| San Francisco 49ers | | | |
| ☐ 386A Randall Cunningham PB | .10 | .05 | .01 |
| (Small print on front) | | | |
| Philadelphia Eagles | | | |
| ☐ 386B Randall Cunningham PB | .10 | .05 | .01 |
| (Large print on front) | | | |
| Philadelphia Eagles | | | |
| ☐ 387 Chris Doleman PB | .04 | .02 | .01 |
| Minnesota Vikings | | | |
| ☐ 388 Henry Ellard PB | .04 | .02 | .01 |
| Los Angeles Rams | | | |
| ☐ 389 Bill Fralic PB | .04 | .02 | .01 |
| Atlanta Falcons | | | |
| ☐ 390 Brent Fullwood PB | .04 | .02 | .01 |
| Green Bay Packers | | | |
| ☐ 391 Jerry Gray PB | .04 | .02 | .01 |
| Los Angeles Rams | | | |
| ☐ 392 Kevin Greene PB | .04 | .02 | .01 |
| Los Angeles Rams | | | |
| ☐ 393 Tim Harris PB | .04 | .02 | .01 |
| Green Bay Packers | | | |
| ☐ 394 Jay Hilgenberg PB | .04 | .02 | .01 |
| Chicago Bears | | | |
| ☐ 395 Dalton Hilliard PB | .04 | .02 | .01 |
| New Orleans Saints | | | |
| ☐ 396 Keith Jackson PB | .12 | .05 | .02 |
| Philadelphia Eagles | | | |
| ☐ 397 Vaughan Johnson PB | .04 | .02 | .01 |
| New Orleans Saints | | | |
| ☐ 398 Steve Jordan PB | .04 | .02 | .01 |
| Minnesota Vikings | | | |
| ☐ 399 Carl Lee PB | .04 | .02 | .01 |
| Minnesota Vikings | | | |
| ☐ 400 Ronnie Lott PB | .08 | .04 | .01 |
| San Francisco 49ers | | | |
| ☐ 401 Don Majkowski PB | .04 | .02 | .01 |
| Green Bay Packers | | | |
| (Not pictured in Pro | | | |
| Bowl uniform) | | | |
| ☐ 402 Charles Mann PB | .04 | .02 | .01 |
| Washington Redskins | | | |
| ☐ 403 Randall McDaniel PB | .04 | .02 | .01 |
| Minnesota Vikings | | | |
| ☐ 404 Tim McDonald PB | .04 | .02 | .01 |
| Phoenix Cardinals | | | |
| ☐ 405 Guy McIntyre PB | .04 | .02 | .01 |
| San Francisco 49ers | | | |
| ☐ 406 David Meggett PB | .08 | .04 | .01 |
| New York Giants | | | |

| | | | |
|---|---|---|---|
| ☐ 407 Keith Millard PB .................... | .04 | .02 | .01 |
| Minnesota Vikings | | | |
| ☐ 408 Joe Montana PB .................... | .50 | .23 | .06 |
| San Francisco 49ers | | | |
| (not pictured in Pro | | | |
| Bowl uniform) | | | |
| ☐ 409 Eddie Murray PB .................... | .04 | .02 | .01 |
| Detroit Lions | | | |
| ☐ 410 Tom Newberry PB ................. | .04 | .02 | .01 |
| Los Angeles Rams | | | |
| ☐ 411 Jerry Rice PB ....................... | .35 | .16 | .04 |
| San Francisco 49ers | | | |
| ☐ 412 Mark Rypien PB .................... | .08 | .04 | .01 |
| Washington Redskins | | | |
| ☐ 413 Barry Sanders PB ................. | .50 | .23 | .06 |
| Detroit Lions | | | |
| ☐ 414 Luis Sharpe PB .................... | .04 | .02 | .01 |
| Phoenix Cardinals | | | |
| ☐ 415 Sterling Sharpe PB ............... | .25 | .11 | .03 |
| Green Bay Packers | | | |
| ☐ 416 Mike Singletary PB ................ | .04 | .02 | .01 |
| Chicago Bears | | | |
| ☐ 417 Jackie Slater PB ................... | .04 | .02 | .01 |
| Los Angeles Rams | | | |
| ☐ 418 Doug Smith PB ..................... | .04 | .02 | .01 |
| Los Angeles Rams | | | |
| ☐ 419 Chris Spielman PB ................ | .04 | .02 | .01 |
| Detroit Lions | | | |
| ☐ 420 Pat Swilling PB ..................... | .08 | .04 | .01 |
| New Orleans Saints | | | |
| ☐ 421 John Taylor PB ..................... | .04 | .02 | .01 |
| San Francisco 49ers | | | |
| ☐ 422 Lawrence Taylor PB .............. | .08 | .04 | .01 |
| (Mike Singletary assist- | | | |
| ing in tackle of | | | |
| Christian Okoye) | | | |
| New York Giants | | | |
| ☐ 423 Reggie White PB ................... | .08 | .04 | .01 |
| Philadelphia Eagles | | | |
| ☐ 424 Ron Wolfley PB ..................... | .04 | .02 | .01 |
| Phoenix Cardinals | | | |
| ☐ 425 Gary Zimmerman PB.............. | .04 | .02 | .01 |
| Minnesota Vikings | | | |
| ☐ 426 John Robinson CO PB............ | .04 | .02 | .01 |
| Los Angeles Rams | | | |
| ☐ 427 Scott Case UER .................... | .04 | .02 | .01 |
| Atlanta Falcons | | | |
| (front CB, back S) | | | |
| ☐ 428 Mike Kenn ........................... | .08 | .04 | .01 |
| Atlanta Falcons | | | |
| ☐ 429 Mike Gann ........................... | .04 | .02 | .01 |
| Atlanta Falcons | | | |
| ☐ 430 Tim Green ............................ | .04 | .02 | .01 |
| Atlanta Falcons | | | |
| ☐ 431 Michael Haynes..................... | 1.25 | .55 | .16 |
| Atlanta Falcons | | | |
| ☐ 432 Jessie Tuggle UER ............... | .25 | .11 | .03 |
| Atlanta Falcons | | | |
| (Front Jesse, | | | |
| back Jessie) | | | |
| ☐ 433 John Rade............................ | .04 | .02 | .01 |
| Atlanta Falcons | | | |
| ☐ 434 Andre Rison ......................... | .25 | .11 | .03 |
| Atlanta Falcons | | | |
| ☐ 435 Don Beebe............................ | .10 | .05 | .01 |
| Buffalo Bills | | | |
| ☐ 436 Ray Bentley ......................... | .04 | .02 | .01 |
| Buffalo Bills | | | |
| ☐ 437 Shane Conlan ...................... | .08 | .04 | .01 |
| Buffalo Bills | | | |
| ☐ 438 Kent Hull ............................. | .04 | .02 | .01 |
| Buffalo Bills | | | |
| ☐ 439 Pete Metzelaars.................... | .04 | .02 | .01 |
| Buffalo Bills | | | |
| ☐ 440 Andre Reed UER ................... | .15 | .07 | .02 |
| Buffalo Bills | | | |
| (Vance Johnson also had | | | |
| more catches in '85) | | | |
| ☐ 441 Frank Reich .......................... | .20 | .09 | .03 |
| Buffalo Bills | | | |
| ☐ 442 Leon Seals ........................... | .10 | .05 | .01 |
| Buffalo Bills | | | |
| ☐ 443 Bruce Smith ........................ | .10 | .05 | .01 |
| Buffalo Bills | | | |
| ☐ 444 Thurman Thomas.................. | .40 | .18 | .05 |
| Buffalo Bills | | | |
| ☐ 445 Will Wolford ......................... | .04 | .02 | .01 |
| Buffalo Bills | | | |
| ☐ 446 Trace Armstrong................... | .04 | .02 | .01 |
| Chicago Bears | | | |
| ☐ 447 Mark Bortz........................... | .10 | .05 | .01 |
| Chicago Bears | | | |
| ☐ 448 Tom Thayer.......................... | .10 | .05 | .01 |
| Chicago Bears | | | |
| ☐ 449A Dan Hampton ERR............. | .50 | .23 | .06 |
| Chicago Bears | | | |
| (Card back says DE) | | | |

| | | | |
|---|---|---|---|
| ☐ 449B Dan Hampton COR............. | .08 | .04 | .01 |
| Chicago Bears | | | |
| (Card back says DT) | | | |
| ☐ 450 Shaun Gayle.......................... | .10 | .05 | .01 |
| Chicago Bears | | | |
| ☐ 451 Dennis Gentry ...................... | .04 | .02 | .01 |
| Chicago Bears | | | |
| ☐ 452 Jim Harbaugh........................ | .15 | .07 | .02 |
| Chicago Bears | | | |
| ☐ 453 Vestee Jackson ..................... | .04 | .02 | .01 |
| Chicago Bears | | | |
| ☐ 454 Brad Muster .......................... | .08 | .04 | .01 |
| Chicago Bears | | | |
| ☐ 455 William Perry ........................ | .08 | .04 | .01 |
| Chicago Bears | | | |
| ☐ 456 Ron Rivera ........................... | .04 | .02 | .01 |
| Chicago Bears | | | |
| ☐ 457 James Thornton ..................... | .04 | .02 | .01 |
| Chicago Bears | | | |
| ☐ 458 Mike Tomczak........................ | .08 | .04 | .01 |
| Chicago Bears | | | |
| ☐ 459 Donnell Woolford .................. | .04 | .02 | .01 |
| Chicago Bears | | | |
| ☐ 460 Eric Ball .............................. | .04 | .02 | .01 |
| Cincinnati Bengals | | | |
| ☐ 461 James Brooks ....................... | .08 | .04 | .01 |
| Cincinnati Bengals | | | |
| ☐ 462 David Fulcher........................ | .08 | .04 | .01 |
| Cincinnati Bengals | | | |
| ☐ 463 Boomer Esiason..................... | .20 | .09 | .03 |
| Cincinnati Bengals | | | |
| ☐ 464 Rodney Holman ..................... | .04 | .02 | .01 |
| Cincinnati Bengals | | | |
| ☐ 465 Bruce Kozerski ..................... | .04 | .02 | .01 |
| Cincinnati Bengals | | | |
| ☐ 466 Tim Krumrie .......................... | .04 | .02 | .01 |
| (Tackling Eric Dickerson) | | | |
| Cincinnati Bengals | | | |
| ☐ 467 Anthony Munoz...................... | .08 | .04 | .01 |
| Cincinnati Bengals | | | |
| (Type on front smaller | | | |
| compared to other cards) | | | |
| ☐ 468 Brian Blados ......................... | .04 | .02 | .01 |
| Cincinnati Bengals | | | |
| ☐ 469 Mike Baab ........................... | .04 | .02 | .01 |
| Cleveland Browns | | | |
| ☐ 470 Brian Brennan ...................... | .04 | .02 | .01 |
| Cleveland Browns | | | |
| ☐ 471 Raymond Clayborn ............... | .08 | .04 | .01 |
| Cleveland Browns | | | |
| ☐ 472 Mike Johnson ....................... | .04 | .02 | .01 |
| Cleveland Browns | | | |
| ☐ 473 Kevin Mack .......................... | .08 | .04 | .01 |
| Cleveland Browns | | | |
| ☐ 474 Clay Matthews....................... | .08 | .04 | .01 |
| Cleveland Browns | | | |
| ☐ 475 Frank Minnifield .................... | .04 | .02 | .01 |
| Cleveland Browns | | | |
| ☐ 476 Gregg Rakoczy ..................... | .04 | .02 | .01 |
| Cleveland Browns | | | |
| ☐ 477 Webster Slaughter ............... | .08 | .04 | .01 |
| Cleveland Browns | | | |
| ☐ 478 James Dixon ......................... | .04 | .02 | .01 |
| Dallas Cowboys | | | |
| ☐ 479 Robert Awalt UER ................. | .04 | .02 | .01 |
| Dallas Cowboys | | | |
| (front 89, back 46) | | | |
| ☐ 480 Dennis McKinnon UER.......... | .04 | .02 | .01 |
| Dallas Cowboys | | | |
| (front 81, back 85) | | | |
| ☐ 481 Danny Noonan ...................... | .04 | .02 | .01 |
| Dallas Cowboys | | | |
| ☐ 482 Jesse Solomon ..................... | .04 | .02 | .01 |
| Dallas Cowboys | | | |
| ☐ 483 Danny Stubbs UER................ | .04 | .02 | .01 |
| Dallas Cowboys | | | |
| (front 66, back 96) | | | |
| ☐ 484 Steve Walsh .......................... | .04 | .02 | .01 |
| Dallas Cowboys | | | |
| ☐ 485 Michael Brooks ..................... | .20 | .09 | .03 |
| Denver Broncos | | | |
| ☐ 486 Mark Jackson........................ | .08 | .04 | .01 |
| Denver Broncos | | | |
| ☐ 487 Greg Kragen ........................ | .04 | .02 | .01 |
| Denver Broncos | | | |
| ☐ 488 Ken Lanier............................ | .04 | .02 | .01 |
| Denver Broncos | | | |
| ☐ 489 Karl Mecklenburg.................. | .08 | .04 | .01 |
| Denver Broncos | | | |
| ☐ 490 Steve Sewell ......................... | .04 | .02 | .01 |
| Denver Broncos | | | |
| ☐ 491 Dennis Smith ........................ | .08 | .04 | .01 |
| Denver Broncos | | | |
| ☐ 492 David Treadwell ..................... | .04 | .02 | .01 |
| Denver Broncos | | | |
| ☐ 493 Michael Young ...................... | .10 | .05 | .01 |
| Denver Broncos | | | |

| | | | |
|---|---|---|---|
| ☐ 494 Robert Clark.................... Detroit Lions | .08 | .04 | .01 |
| ☐ 495 Dennis Gibson.................... Detroit Lions | .04 | .02 | .01 |
| ☐ 496A Kevin Glover ERR............. Detroit Lions (Card back says C/G) | .15 | .07 | .02 |
| ☐ 496B Kevin Glover COR ............ Detroit Lions (Card back says C) | .08 | .04 | .01 |
| ☐ 497 Mel Gray ......................... Detroit Lions | .08 | .04 | .01 |
| ☐ 498 Rodney Peete.................... Detroit Lions | .08 | .04 | .01 |
| ☐ 499 Dave Brown..................... Green Bay Packers | .04 | .02 | .01 |
| ☐ 500 Jerry Holmes.................... Green Bay Packers | .04 | .02 | .01 |
| ☐ 501 Chris Jacke ..................... Green Bay Packers | .04 | .02 | .01 |
| ☐ 502 Alan Veingrad................... Green Bay Packers | .04 | .02 | .01 |
| ☐ 503 Mark Lee ........................ Green Bay Packers | .04 | .02 | .01 |
| ☐ 504 Tony Mandarich ................ Green Bay Packers | .04 | .02 | .01 |
| ☐ 505 Brian Noble ..................... Green Bay Packers | .04 | .02 | .01 |
| ☐ 506 Jeff Query ....................... Green Bay Packers | .04 | .02 | .01 |
| ☐ 507 Ken Ruettgers .................. Green Bay Packers | .04 | .02 | .01 |
| ☐ 508 Patrick Allen .................... Houston Oilers | .04 | .02 | .01 |
| ☐ 509 Curtis Duncan .................. Houston Oilers | .08 | .04 | .01 |
| ☐ 510 William Fuller ................... Houston Oilers | .08 | .04 | .01 |
| ☐ 511 Haywood Jeffires .............. Houston Oilers | 1.00 | .45 | .13 |
| ☐ 512 Sean Jones ..................... Houston Oilers | .08 | .04 | .01 |
| ☐ 513 Terry Kinard ..................... Houston Oilers | .04 | .02 | .01 |
| ☐ 514 Bruce Matthews ................ Houston Oilers | .08 | .04 | .01 |
| ☐ 515 Gerald McNeil .................. Houston Oilers | .04 | .02 | .01 |
| ☐ 516 Greg Montgomery.............. Houston Oilers | .10 | .05 | .01 |
| ☐ 517 Warren Moon .................... Houston Oilers | .25 | .11 | .03 |
| ☐ 518 Mike Munchak.................... Houston Oilers | .08 | .04 | .01 |
| ☐ 519 Allen Pinkett..................... Houston Oilers | .04 | .02 | .01 |
| ☐ 520 Pat Beach........................ Indianapolis Colts | .04 | .02 | .01 |
| ☐ 521 Eugene Daniel .................. Indianapolis Colts | .04 | .02 | .01 |
| ☐ 522 Kevin Call ....................... Indianapolis Colts | .04 | .02 | .01 |
| ☐ 523 Ray Donaldson.................. Indianapolis Colts | .04 | .02 | .01 |
| ☐ 524 Jeff Herrod ...................... Indianapolis Colts | .10 | .05 | .01 |
| ☐ 525 Keith Taylor...................... Indianapolis Colts | .04 | .02 | .01 |
| ☐ 526 Jack Trudeau.................... Indianapolis Colts | .08 | .04 | .01 |
| ☐ 527 Deron Cherry.................... Kansas City Chiefs | .08 | .04 | .01 |
| ☐ 528 Jeff Donaldson ................. Kansas City Chiefs | .04 | .02 | .01 |
| ☐ 529 Albert Lewis ..................... Kansas City Chiefs | .04 | .02 | .01 |
| ☐ 530 Pete Mandley ................... Kansas City Chiefs | .04 | .02 | .01 |
| ☐ 531 Chris Martin ..................... Kansas City Chiefs | .10 | .05 | .01 |
| ☐ 532 Christian Okoye.................. Kansas City Chiefs | .08 | .04 | .01 |
| ☐ 533 Steve Pelluer ................... Kansas City Chiefs | .04 | .02 | .01 |
| ☐ 534 Kevin Ross ...................... Kansas City Chiefs | .08 | .04 | .01 |
| ☐ 535 Dan Saleaumua................. Kansas City Chiefs | .04 | .02 | .01 |
| ☐ 536 Derrick Thomas.................. Kansas City Chiefs | .25 | .11 | .03 |
| ☐ 537 Mike Webster.................... Kansas City Chiefs | .08 | .04 | .01 |
| ☐ 538 Marcus Allen .................... Los Angeles Raiders | .15 | .07 | .02 |
| ☐ 539 Greg Bell ........................ Los Angeles Raiders | .04 | .02 | .01 |
| ☐ 540 Thomas Benson .................. Los Angeles Raiders | .04 | .02 | .01 |

| | | | |
|---|---|---|---|
| ☐ 541 Ron Brown...................... Los Angeles Raiders | .04 | .02 | .01 |
| ☐ 542 Scott Davis...................... Los Angeles Raiders | .04 | .02 | .01 |
| ☐ 543 Riki Ellison ..................... Los Angeles Raiders | .04 | .02 | .01 |
| ☐ 544 Jamie Holland ................. Los Angeles Raiders | .04 | .02 | .01 |
| ☐ 545 Howie Long ..................... Los Angeles Raiders | .08 | .04 | .01 |
| ☐ 546 Terry McDaniel.................. Los Angeles Raiders | .04 | .02 | .01 |
| ☐ 547 Max Montoya ................... Los Angeles Raiders | .04 | .02 | .01 |
| ☐ 548 Jay Schroeder .................. Los Angeles Raiders | .08 | .04 | .01 |
| ☐ 549 Lionel Washington .............. Los Angeles Raiders | .04 | .02 | .01 |
| ☐ 550 Robert Delpino .................. Los Angeles Rams | .08 | .04 | .01 |
| ☐ 551 Bobby Humphery ............... Los Angeles Rams | .04 | .02 | .01 |
| ☐ 552 Mike Lansford ................... Los Angeles Rams | .04 | .02 | .01 |
| ☐ 553 Michael Stewart ................ Los Angeles Rams | .04 | .02 | .01 |
| ☐ 554 Doug Smith ..................... Los Angeles Rams | .08 | .04 | .01 |
| ☐ 555 Curt Warner ..................... Los Angeles Rams | .08 | .04 | .01 |
| ☐ 556 Alvin Wright ..................... Los Angeles Rams | .04 | .02 | .01 |
| ☐ 557 Jeff Cross........................ Miami Dolphins | .04 | .02 | .01 |
| ☐ 558 Jeff Dellenbach ................ Miami Dolphins | .04 | .02 | .01 |
| ☐ 559 Mark Duper ..................... Miami Dolphins | .08 | .04 | .01 |
| ☐ 560 Ferrell Edmunds................. Miami Dolphins | .04 | .02 | .01 |
| ☐ 561 Tim McKyer...................... Miami Dolphins | .08 | .04 | .01 |
| ☐ 562 John Offerdahl .................. Miami Dolphins | .08 | .04 | .01 |
| ☐ 563 Reggie Roby .................... Miami Dolphins | .08 | .04 | .01 |
| ☐ 564 Pete Stoyanovich ............... Miami Dolphins | .08 | .04 | .01 |
| ☐ 565 Alfred Anderson ................ Minnesota Vikings | .04 | .02 | .01 |
| ☐ 566 Ray Berry ........................ Minnesota Vikings | .04 | .02 | .01 |
| ☐ 567 Rick Fenney...................... Minnesota Vikings | .04 | .02 | .01 |
| ☐ 568 Rich Gannon..................... Minnesota Vikings | .25 | .11 | .03 |
| ☐ 569 Tim Irwin........................ Minnesota Vikings | .04 | .02 | .01 |
| ☐ 570 Hassan Jones.................... Minnesota Vikings | .04 | .02 | .01 |
| ☐ 571 Cris Carter ...................... Minnesota Vikings | .20 | .09 | .03 |
| ☐ 572 Kirk Lowdermilk................. Minnesota Vikings | .04 | .02 | .01 |
| ☐ 573 Reggie Rutland .................. Minnesota Vikings | .10 | .05 | .01 |
| ☐ 574 Ken Stills........................ Minnesota Vikings | .04 | .02 | .01 |
| ☐ 575 Bruce Armstrong................. New England Patriots | .04 | .02 | .01 |
| ☐ 576 Irving Fryar ...................... New England Patriots | .08 | .04 | .01 |
| ☐ 577 Roland James ................... New England Patriots | .04 | .02 | .01 |
| ☐ 578 Robert Perryman................. New England Patriots | .04 | .02 | .01 |
| ☐ 579 Cedric Jones .................... New England Patriots | .04 | .02 | .01 |
| ☐ 580 Steve Grogan ................... New England Patriots | .08 | .04 | .01 |
| ☐ 581 Johnny Rembert ................. New England Patriots | .04 | .02 | .01 |
| ☐ 582 Ed Reynolds ..................... New England Patriots | .04 | .02 | .01 |
| ☐ 583 Brent Williams................... New England Patriots | .04 | .02 | .01 |
| ☐ 584 Marc Wilson...................... New England Patriots | .08 | .04 | .01 |
| ☐ 585 Hoby Brenner.................... New Orleans Saints | .04 | .02 | .01 |
| ☐ 586 Stan Brock ...................... New Orleans Saints | .04 | .02 | .01 |
| ☐ 587 Jim Dombrowski ................ New Orleans Saints | .10 | .05 | .01 |
| ☐ 588 Joel Hilgenberg ................. New Orleans Saints | .10 | .05 | .01 |
| ☐ 589 Robert Massey ................... | .04 | .02 | .01 |

New Orleans Saints
| | | | |
|---|---|---|---|
| ☐ 590 Floyd Turner.......................... | .04 | .02 | .01 |

New Orleans Saints
| | | | |
|---|---|---|---|
| ☐ 591 Ottis Anderson...................... | .08 | .04 | .01 |

New York Giants
| | | | |
|---|---|---|---|
| ☐ 592 Mark Bavaro.......................... | .08 | .04 | .01 |

New York Giants
| | | | |
|---|---|---|---|
| ☐ 593 Maurice Carthon ................... | .04 | .02 | .01 |

New York Giants
| | | | |
|---|---|---|---|
| ☐ 594 Eric Dorsey ........................... | .04 | .02 | .01 |

New York Giants
| | | | |
|---|---|---|---|
| ☐ 595 Myron Guyton ....................... | .04 | .02 | .01 |

New York Giants
| | | | |
|---|---|---|---|
| ☐ 596 Jeff Hostetler........................ | .50 | .23 | .06 |

New York Giants
| | | | |
|---|---|---|---|
| ☐ 597 Sean Landeta ........................ | .08 | .04 | .01 |

New York Giants
| | | | |
|---|---|---|---|
| ☐ 598 Lionel Manuel ....................... | .04 | .02 | .01 |

New York Giants
| | | | |
|---|---|---|---|
| ☐ 599 Odessa Turner ...................... | .15 | .07 | .02 |

New York Giants
| | | | |
|---|---|---|---|
| ☐ 600 Perry Williams....................... | .04 | .02 | .01 |

New York Giants
| | | | |
|---|---|---|---|
| ☐ 601 James Hasty .......................... | .04 | .02 | .01 |

New York Jets
| | | | |
|---|---|---|---|
| ☐ 602 Erik McMillan ........................ | .04 | .02 | .01 |

New York Jets
| | | | |
|---|---|---|---|
| ☐ 603 Alex Gordon UER ................... | .04 | .02 | .01 |

New York Jets
(reversed photo on back)
| | | | |
|---|---|---|---|
| ☐ 604 Ron Stallworth ....................... | .04 | .02 | .01 |

New York Jets
| | | | |
|---|---|---|---|
| ☐ 605 Byron Evans.......................... | .10 | .05 | .01 |

Philadelphia Eagles
| | | | |
|---|---|---|---|
| ☐ 606 Ron Heller............................. | .08 | .04 | .01 |

Philadelphia Eagles
| | | | |
|---|---|---|---|
| ☐ 607 Wes Hopkins.......................... | .04 | .02 | .01 |

(Hitting Ottis Anderson)
Philadelphia Eagles
| | | | |
|---|---|---|---|
| ☐ 608 Mickey Shuler UER .............. | .04 | .02 | .01 |

Philadelphia Eagles
(Reversed photo on back)
| | | | |
|---|---|---|---|
| ☐ 609 Seth Joyner............................ | .08 | .04 | .01 |

Philadelphia Eagles
| | | | |
|---|---|---|---|
| ☐ 610 Jim McMahon ........................ | .10 | .05 | .01 |

Philadelphia Eagles
| | | | |
|---|---|---|---|
| ☐ 611 Mike Pitts ............................. | .04 | .02 | .01 |

(Riding Ottis Anderson)
Philadelphia Eagles
| | | | |
|---|---|---|---|
| ☐ 612 Izel Jenkins .......................... | .04 | .02 | .01 |

Philadelphia Eagles
| | | | |
|---|---|---|---|
| ☐ 613 Anthony Bell........................... | .04 | .02 | .01 |

Phoenix Cardinals
| | | | |
|---|---|---|---|
| ☐ 614 David Galloway ...................... | .04 | .02 | .01 |

Phoenix Cardinals
| | | | |
|---|---|---|---|
| ☐ 615 Eric Hill ................................ | .04 | .02 | .01 |

Phoenix Cardinals
| | | | |
|---|---|---|---|
| ☐ 616 Cedric Mack .......................... | .04 | .02 | .01 |

Phoenix Cardinals
| | | | |
|---|---|---|---|
| ☐ 617 Freddie Joe Nunn ................. | .08 | .04 | .01 |

Phoenix Cardinals
| | | | |
|---|---|---|---|
| ☐ 618 Tootie Robbins ...................... | .04 | .02 | .01 |

Phoenix Cardinals
| | | | |
|---|---|---|---|
| ☐ 619 Tom Tupa............................. | .10 | .05 | .01 |

Phoenix Cardinals
| | | | |
|---|---|---|---|
| ☐ 620 Joe Wolf............................... | .04 | .02 | .01 |

Phoenix Cardinals
| | | | |
|---|---|---|---|
| ☐ 621 Dermontti Dawson ............... | .04 | .02 | .01 |

Pittsburgh Steelers
| | | | |
|---|---|---|---|
| ☐ 622 Thomas Everett...................... | .04 | .02 | .01 |

Pittsburgh Steelers
| | | | |
|---|---|---|---|
| ☐ 623 Tunch Ilkin ........................... | .04 | .02 | .01 |

Pittsburgh Steelers
| | | | |
|---|---|---|---|
| ☐ 624 Hardy Nickerson .................... | .08 | .04 | .01 |

Pittsburgh Steelers
| | | | |
|---|---|---|---|
| ☐ 625 Gerald Williams...................... | .04 | .02 | .01 |

Pittsburgh Steelers
| | | | |
|---|---|---|---|
| ☐ 626 Rod Woodson......................... | .20 | .09 | .03 |

Pittsburgh Steelers
| | | | |
|---|---|---|---|
| ☐ 627A Rod Bernstine TE ERR ........ | .40 | .18 | .05 |

San Diego Chargers
| | | | |
|---|---|---|---|
| ☐ 627B Rod Bernstine RB COR ....... | .15 | .07 | .02 |

San Diego Chargers
| | | | |
|---|---|---|---|
| ☐ 628 Courtney Hall ........................ | .04 | .02 | .01 |

San Diego Chargers
| | | | |
|---|---|---|---|
| ☐ 629 Ronnie Harmon...................... | .08 | .04 | .01 |

San Diego Chargers
| | | | |
|---|---|---|---|
| ☐ 630A Anthony Miller ERR ........... | .35 | .16 | .04 |

San Diego Chargers
(Back says WR)
| | | | |
|---|---|---|---|
| ☐ 630B Anthony Miller COR ........... | .30 | .14 | .04 |

San Diego Chargers
(Back says WR-KR)
| | | | |
|---|---|---|---|
| ☐ 631 Joe Phillips............................ | .04 | .02 | .01 |

San Diego Chargers
| | | | |
|---|---|---|---|
| ☐ 632A Leslie O'Neal ERR .............. | .50 | .23 | .06 |

San Diego Chargers
(Listed as LB-DE on
front and back)
| | | | |
|---|---|---|---|
| ☐ 632B Leslie O'Neal ERR .............. | .12 | .05 | .02 |

San Diego Chargers
(Listed as LB-DE on
front and LB on back)
| | | | |
|---|---|---|---|
| ☐ 632C Leslie O'Neal COR............... | .08 | .04 | .01 |

San Diego Chargers
(Listed as LB on
front and back)
| | | | |
|---|---|---|---|
| ☐ 633A David Richards ERR........... | .12 | .05 | .02 |

San Diego Chargers
(Back says G-T)
| | | | |
|---|---|---|---|
| ☐ 633B David Richards COR .......... | .12 | .05 | .02 |

San Diego Chargers
(Back says G)
| | | | |
|---|---|---|---|
| ☐ 634 Mark Vlasic .......................... | .04 | .02 | .01 |

San Diego Chargers
| | | | |
|---|---|---|---|
| ☐ 635 Lee Williams ......................... | .08 | .04 | .01 |

San Diego Chargers
| | | | |
|---|---|---|---|
| ☐ 636 Chet Brooks ......................... | .04 | .02 | .01 |

San Francisco 49ers
| | | | |
|---|---|---|---|
| ☐ 637 Keena Turner......................... | .08 | .04 | .01 |

San Francisco 49ers
| | | | |
|---|---|---|---|
| ☐ 638 Kevin Fagan........................... | .04 | .02 | .01 |

San Francisco 49ers
| | | | |
|---|---|---|---|
| ☐ 639 Brent Jones........................... | .40 | .18 | .05 |

(Making catch in front
of Lawrence Taylor)
San Francisco 49ers
| | | | |
|---|---|---|---|
| ☐ 640 Matt Millen........................... | .08 | .04 | .01 |

(Hitting Herschel Walker)
San Francisco 49ers
| | | | |
|---|---|---|---|
| ☐ 641 Bubba Paris.......................... | .08 | .04 | .01 |

San Francisco 49ers
| | | | |
|---|---|---|---|
| ☐ 642 Bill Romanowski .................... | .10 | .05 | .01 |

San Francisco 49ers
| | | | |
|---|---|---|---|
| ☐ 643 Fred Smerlas UER ................ | .08 | .04 | .01 |

San Francisco 49ers
(Front 67, back 76)
| | | | |
|---|---|---|---|
| ☐ 644 Dave Waymer......................... | .04 | .02 | .01 |

San Francisco 49ers
| | | | |
|---|---|---|---|
| ☐ 645 Steve Young........................... | .40 | .18 | .05 |

San Francisco 49ers
| | | | |
|---|---|---|---|
| ☐ 646 Brian Blades.......................... | .15 | .07 | .02 |

Seattle Seahawks
| | | | |
|---|---|---|---|
| ☐ 647 Andy Heck ............................ | .04 | .02 | .01 |

Seattle Seahawks
| | | | |
|---|---|---|---|
| ☐ 648 Dave Krieg............................ | .08 | .04 | .01 |

Seattle Seahawks
| | | | |
|---|---|---|---|
| ☐ 649 Rufus Porter ......................... | .04 | .02 | .01 |

Seattle Seahawks
| | | | |
|---|---|---|---|
| ☐ 650 Kelly Stouffer ........................ | .04 | .02 | .01 |

Seattle Seahawks
| | | | |
|---|---|---|---|
| ☐ 651 Tony Woods........................... | .04 | .02 | .01 |

Seattle Seahawks
| | | | |
|---|---|---|---|
| ☐ 652 Gary Anderson....................... | .08 | .04 | .01 |

Tampa Bay Buccaneers
| | | | |
|---|---|---|---|
| ☐ 653 Reuben Davis......................... | .04 | .02 | .01 |

Tampa Bay Buccaneers
| | | | |
|---|---|---|---|
| ☐ 654 Randy Grimes......................... | .04 | .02 | .01 |

Tampa Bay Buccaneers
| | | | |
|---|---|---|---|
| ☐ 655 Ron Hall............................... | .04 | .02 | .01 |

Tampa Bay Buccaneers
| | | | |
|---|---|---|---|
| ☐ 656 Eugene Marve ....................... | .04 | .02 | .01 |

Tampa Bay Buccaneers
| | | | |
|---|---|---|---|
| ☐ 657A Curt Jarvis ERR .................. | .50 | .23 | .06 |

Tampa Bay Buccaneers
(No NFL logo on
front of card)
| | | | |
|---|---|---|---|
| ☐ 657B Curt Jarvis COR .................. | .05 | .02 | .01 |

Tampa Bay Buccaneers
| | | | |
|---|---|---|---|
| ☐ 658 Ricky Reynolds ..................... | .04 | .02 | .01 |

Tampa Bay Buccaneers
| | | | |
|---|---|---|---|
| ☐ 659 Broderick Thomas................. | .04 | .02 | .01 |

Tampa Bay Buccaneers
| | | | |
|---|---|---|---|
| ☐ 660 Jeff Bostic ............................ | .04 | .02 | .01 |

Washington Redskins
| | | | |
|---|---|---|---|
| ☐ 661 Todd Bowles .......................... | .10 | .05 | .01 |

Washington Redskins
| | | | |
|---|---|---|---|
| ☐ 662 Ravin Caldwell....................... | .04 | .02 | .01 |

Washington Redskins
| | | | |
|---|---|---|---|
| ☐ 663 Russ Grimm UER................... | .04 | .02 | .01 |

Washington Redskins
(Back photo is act-
ually Jeff Bostic)
| | | | |
|---|---|---|---|
| ☐ 664 Joe Jacoby ........................... | .08 | .04 | .01 |

Washington Redskins
| | | | |
|---|---|---|---|
| ☐ 665 Mark May .............................. | .04 | .02 | .01 |

Washington Redskins
(Front G, back G/T)
| | | | |
|---|---|---|---|
| ☐ 666 Walter Stanley ...................... | .04 | .02 | .01 |

Washington Redskins
| | | | |
|---|---|---|---|
| ☐ 667 Don Warren........................... | .04 | .02 | .01 |

Washington Redskins
| | | | |
|---|---|---|---|
| ☐ 668 Stan Humphries .................... | .50 | .23 | .06 |

Washington Redskins
| | | | |
|---|---|---|---|
| ☐ 669A Jeff George SP..................... | 2.00 | .90 | .25 |

(Illinois uniform;

| | | | |
|---|---|---|---|
| issued in first series) Indianapolis Colts | | | |
| ☐ 669B Jeff George ......................... (Colts uniform; issued in second series) Indianapolis Colts | .75 | .35 | .09 |
| ☐ 670 Blair Thomas......................... New York Jets (No color stripe along line with AFC symbol and Jets logo) | .10 | .05 | .01 |
| ☐ 671 Cortez Kennedy UER ............. Seattle Seahawks (No scouting photo line on back) | .75 | .35 | .09 |
| ☐ 672 Keith McCants...................... Tampa Bay Buccaneers | .10 | .05 | .01 |
| ☐ 673 Junior Seau .......................... San Diego Chargers | .75 | .35 | .09 |
| ☐ 674 Mark Carrier ......................... Chicago Bears | .20 | .09 | .03 |
| ☐ 675 Andre Ware ........................... Detroit Lions | .10 | .05 | .01 |
| ☐ 676 Chris Singleton UER............. New England Patriots (Parsippany High, should be Parsippany Hills High) | .10 | .05 | .01 |
| ☐ 677 Richmond Webb ..................... Miami Dolphins | .20 | .09 | .03 |
| ☐ 678 Ray Agnew............................ New England Patriots | .04 | .02 | .01 |
| ☐ 679 Anthony Smith ...................... Los Angeles Raiders | .40 | .18 | .05 |
| ☐ 680 James Francis ....................... Cincinnati Bengals | .15 | .07 | .02 |
| ☐ 681 Percy Snow........................... Kansas City Chiefs | .04 | .02 | .01 |
| ☐ 682 Renaldo Turnbull................... New Orleans Saints | .40 | .18 | .05 |
| ☐ 683 Lamar Lathon ....................... Houston Oilers | .15 | .07 | .02 |
| ☐ 684 James Williams ..................... Buffalo Bills | .10 | .05 | .01 |
| ☐ 685 Emmitt Smith ........................ Dallas Cowboys | 2.50 | 1.15 | .30 |
| ☐ 686 Tony Bennett......................... Green Bay Packers | .30 | .14 | .04 |
| ☐ 687 Darrell Thompson ................. Green Bay Packers | .15 | .07 | .02 |
| ☐ 688 Steve Broussard..................... Atlanta Falcons | .10 | .05 | .01 |
| ☐ 689 Eric Green ............................ Pittsburgh Steelers | .40 | .18 | .05 |
| ☐ 690 Ben Smith ............................ Philadelphia Eagles | .10 | .05 | .01 |
| ☐ 691 Bern Brostek UER ................. Los Angeles Rams (Listed as Center but is playing Guard) | .04 | .02 | .01 |
| ☐ 692 Rodney Hampton ................... New York Giants | 1.50 | .65 | .19 |
| ☐ 693 Dexter Carter........................ San Francisco 49ers | .15 | .07 | .02 |
| ☐ 694 Rob Moore............................ New York Jets | .40 | .18 | .05 |
| ☐ 695 Alexander Wright ................... Dallas Cowboys | .10 | .05 | .01 |
| ☐ 696 Darion Conner....................... Atlanta Falcons | .10 | .05 | .01 |
| ☐ 697 Reggie Rembert UER ............ Cincinnati Bengals (Missing Scouting Line credit on the front) | .04 | .02 | .01 |
| ☐ 698A Terry Wooden ERR ............. Seattle Seahawks (Number on back is 51) | .15 | .07 | .02 |
| ☐ 698B Terry Wooden COR............. Seattle Seahawks (Number on back is 90) | .10 | .05 | .01 |
| ☐ 699 Reggie Cobb ......................... Tampa Bay Buccaneers | .75 | .35 | .09 |
| ☐ 700 Anthony Thompson................ Phoenix Cardinals | .04 | .02 | .01 |
| ☐ 701 Fred Washington .................... Chicago Bears (Final Update version mentions his death; this card does not) | .04 | .02 | .01 |
| ☐ 702 Ron Cox............................... Chicago Bears | .04 | .02 | .01 |
| ☐ 703 Robert Blackmon ................... Seattle Seahawks | .10 | .05 | .01 |
| ☐ 704 Dan Owens........................... Detroit Lions | .10 | .05 | .01 |
| ☐ 705 Anthony Johnson .................... Indianapolis Colts | .12 | .05 | .02 |
| ☐ 706 Aaron Wallace....................... | .15 | .07 | .02 |

| | | | |
|---|---|---|---|
| Los Angeles Raiders | | | |
| ☐ 707 Harold Green......................... Cincinnati Bengals | .30 | .14 | .04 |
| ☐ 708 Keith Sims............................ Miami Dolphins | .10 | .05 | .01 |
| ☐ 709 Tim Grunhard......................... Kansas City Chiefs | .04 | .02 | .01 |
| ☐ 710 Jeff Alm............................... Houston Oilers | .04 | .02 | .01 |
| ☐ 711 Carwell Gardner .................... Buffalo Bills | .12 | .05 | .02 |
| ☐ 712 Kenny Davidson ..................... Pittsburgh Steelers | .10 | .05 | .01 |
| ☐ 713 Vince Buck ........................... New Orleans Saints | .10 | .05 | .01 |
| ☐ 714 Leroy Hoard .......................... Cleveland Browns | .15 | .07 | .02 |
| ☐ 715 Andre Collins......................... Washington Redskins | .15 | .07 | .02 |
| ☐ 716 Dennis Brown ........................ San Francisco 49ers | .10 | .05 | .01 |
| ☐ 717 LeRoy Butler.......................... Green Bay Packers | .20 | .09 | .03 |
| ☐ 718A Pat Terrell 41 ERR ............... Los Angeles Rams | .20 | .09 | .03 |
| ☐ 718B Pat Terrell 37 COR ............... Los Angeles Rams | .10 | .05 | .01 |
| ☐ 719 Mike Bellamy......................... Philadelphia Eagles | .04 | .02 | .01 |
| ☐ 720 Mike Fox ............................. New York Giants | .04 | .02 | .01 |
| ☐ 721 Alton Montgomery ................. Denver Broncos | .10 | .05 | .01 |
| ☐ 722 Eric Davis ............................ San Francisco 49ers | .15 | .07 | .02 |
| ☐ 723A Oliver Barnett ERR ............. Atlanta Falcons (Front says DT) | .40 | .18 | .05 |
| ☐ 723B Oliver Barnett COR............. Atlanta Falcons (Front says NT) | .10 | .05 | .01 |
| ☐ 724 Thomas Hoover ..................... Atlanta Falcons | .04 | .02 | .01 |
| ☐ 725 Howard Ballard ..................... Buffalo Bills | .10 | .05 | .01 |
| ☐ 726 Keith McKeller....................... Buffalo Bills | .15 | .07 | .02 |
| ☐ 727 Wendell Davis ....................... Chicago Bears (Pro Set Prospect in white, not black) | .15 | .07 | .02 |
| ☐ 728 Peter Tom Willis..................... Chicago Bears | .10 | .05 | .01 |
| ☐ 729 Bernard Clark ....................... Cincinnati Bengals | .04 | .02 | .01 |
| ☐ 730 Doug Widell .......................... Denver Broncos | .10 | .05 | .01 |
| ☐ 731 Eric Andolsek ....................... Detroit Lions | .04 | .02 | .01 |
| ☐ 732 Jeff Campbell ........................ Detroit Lions | .10 | .05 | .01 |
| ☐ 733 Marc Spindler ....................... Detroit Lions | .04 | .02 | .01 |
| ☐ 734 Keith Woodside...................... Green Bay Packers | .04 | .02 | .01 |
| ☐ 735 Willis Peguese....................... Houston Oilers | .04 | .02 | .01 |
| ☐ 736 Frank Stams .......................... Los Angeles Rams | .04 | .02 | .01 |
| ☐ 737 Jeff Uhlenhake ...................... Miami Dolphins | .04 | .02 | .01 |
| ☐ 738 Todd Kalis ............................ Minnesota Vikings | .04 | .02 | .01 |
| ☐ 739 Tommy Hodson UER ............. New England Patriots (Born Matthews, should be Mathews) | .15 | .07 | .02 |
| ☐ 740 Greg McMurtry ...................... New England Patriots | .12 | .05 | .02 |
| ☐ 741 Mike Buck ............................ New Orleans Saints | .20 | .09 | .03 |
| ☐ 742 Kevin Haverdink UER ............ New Orleans Saints (Jersey says 70, back says 74) | .04 | .02 | .01 |
| ☐ 743A Johnny Bailey ...................... Chicago Bears (Back says 46) | .50 | .23 | .06 |
| ☐ 743B Johnny Bailey ...................... Chicago Bears (Back says 22) | .25 | .11 | .03 |
| ☐ 744A Eric Moore .......................... New York Giants (No Pro Set Prospect on front of card) | .12 | .05 | .02 |
| ☐ 744B Eric Moore .......................... New York Giants (Pro Set Prospect | .05 | .02 | .01 |

| | | | |
|---|---|---|---|
| ☐ 745 Tony Stargell (on front of card) New York Jets | .10 | .05 | .01 |
| ☐ 746 Fred Barnett Philadelphia Eagles | .50 | .23 | .06 |
| ☐ 747 Walter Reeves Phoenix Cardinals | .04 | .02 | .01 |
| ☐ 748 Derek Hill Pittsburgh Steelers | .04 | .02 | .01 |
| ☐ 749 Quinn Early San Diego Chargers | .08 | .04 | .01 |
| ☐ 750 Ronald Lewis San Francisco 49ers | .04 | .02 | .01 |
| ☐ 751 Ken Clark Indianapolis Colts | .10 | .05 | .01 |
| ☐ 752 Garry Lewis Los Angeles Raiders | .04 | .02 | .01 |
| ☐ 753 James Lofton Buffalo Bills | .10 | .05 | .01 |
| ☐ 754 Steve Tasker UER Buffalo Bills (Back says photo is against Raiders, but front shows a Steeler) | .04 | .02 | .01 |
| ☐ 755 Jim Shofner CO Cleveland Browns | .04 | .02 | .01 |
| ☐ 756 Jimmie Jones Dallas Cowboys | .15 | .07 | .02 |
| ☐ 757 Jay Novacek Dallas Cowboys | .30 | .14 | .04 |
| ☐ 758 Jessie Hester Indianapolis Colts | .25 | .11 | .03 |
| ☐ 759 Barry Word Kansas City Chiefs | .30 | .14 | .04 |
| ☐ 760 Eddie Anderson Los Angeles Raiders | .10 | .05 | .01 |
| ☐ 761 Cleveland Gary Los Angeles Rams | .08 | .04 | .01 |
| ☐ 762 Marcus Dupree Los Angeles Rams | .04 | .02 | .01 |
| ☐ 763 David Griggs Miami Dolphins | .15 | .07 | .02 |
| ☐ 764 Rueben Mayes New Orleans Saints | .08 | .04 | .01 |
| ☐ 765 Stephen Baker New York Giants | .04 | .02 | .01 |
| ☐ 766 Reyna Thompson UER New York Giants (Front CB, back ST-CB) | .10 | .05 | .01 |
| ☐ 767 Everson Walls New York Giants | .04 | .02 | .01 |
| ☐ 768 Brad Baxter New York Jets | .20 | .09 | .03 |
| ☐ 769 Steve Walsh New Orleans Saints | .04 | .02 | .01 |
| ☐ 770 Heath Sherman Philadelphia Eagles | .15 | .07 | .02 |
| ☐ 771 Johnny Johnson Phoenix Cardinals | .75 | .35 | .09 |
| ☐ 772A Dexter Manley Phoenix Cardinals (Back mentions substance abuse violation) | 30.00 | 13.50 | 3.80 |
| ☐ 772B Dexter Manley Phoenix Cardinals (Bio on back changed; doesn't mention substance abuse violation) | .08 | .04 | .01 |
| ☐ 773 Ricky Proehl Phoenix Cardinals | .50 | .23 | .06 |
| ☐ 774 Frank Cornish San Diego Chargers | .04 | .02 | .01 |
| ☐ 775 Tommy Kane Seattle Seahawks | .10 | .05 | .01 |
| ☐ 776 Derrick Fenner Seattle Seahawks | .15 | .07 | .02 |
| ☐ 777 Steve Christie Tampa Bay Buccaneers | .15 | .07 | .02 |
| ☐ 778 Wayne Haddix Tampa Bay Buccaneers | .04 | .02 | .01 |
| ☐ 779 Richard Williamson UER Tampa Bay Buccaneers (Experience is misspelled as esperience) | .04 | .02 | .01 |
| ☐ 780 Brian Mitchell Washington Redskins | .40 | .18 | .05 |
| ☐ 781 American Bowl/London Raiders vs. Saints | .04 | .02 | .01 |
| ☐ 782 American Bowl/Berlin Rams vs. Chiefs | .04 | .02 | .01 |
| ☐ 783 American Bowl/Tokyo Broncos vs. Seahawks | .04 | .02 | .01 |
| ☐ 784 American Bowl/Montreal Steelers vs. Patriots | .04 | .02 | .01 |
| ☐ 785A Berlin Wall Paul Tagliabue ("Peered through the Berlin Wall") | .08 | .04 | .01 |

| | | | |
|---|---|---|---|
| ☐ 785B Berlin Wall Paul Tagliabue ("Posed at the Berlin Wall") | .08 | .04 | .01 |
| ☐ 786 Raiders Stay in LA (Al Davis) | .10 | .05 | .01 |
| ☐ 787 Falcons Back in Black (Jerry Glanville) | .04 | .02 | .01 |
| ☐ 788 NFL Goes International World League Spring Debut (Number on back is black, Newsreel cards are otherwise white; only Newsreel card with silver borders) | .04 | .02 | .01 |
| ☐ 789 Overseas Appeal (Cheerleaders) | .04 | .02 | .01 |
| ☐ 790 Photo Contest (Mike Mularkey awash) | .04 | .02 | .01 |
| ☐ 791 Photo Contest (Gary Reasons hitting Bobby Humphrey) | .04 | .02 | .01 |
| ☐ 792 Photo Contest (Maurice Hurst covering Drew Hill) | .04 | .02 | .01 |
| ☐ 793 Photo Contest (Ronnie Lott celebrating) | .04 | .02 | .01 |
| ☐ 794 Photo Contest (Felix Wright grabbing Barry Sanders' jersey) | .50 | .23 | .06 |
| ☐ 795 Photo Contest (George Seifert in Gatorade Shower) | .04 | .02 | .01 |
| ☐ 796 Photo Contest (Doug Smith praying) | .04 | .02 | .01 |
| ☐ 797 Photo Contest (Doug Widell keeping cool) | .04 | .02 | .01 |
| ☐ 798 Photo Contest (Todd Bowles covering Cris Carter) | .04 | .02 | .01 |
| ☐ 799 Ronnie Lott School | .08 | .04 | .01 |
| ☐ 800D Mark Carrier D-ROY Chicago Bears | .04 | .02 | .01 |
| ☐ 800O Emmitt Smith O-ROY Dallas Cowboys | 1.00 | .45 | .13 |
| ☐ SC4 Fred Washington UER Chicago Bears (Memorial to his death; word patches repeated in fourth line of text) | .04 | .02 | .01 |

## 1990 Pro Set Theme Art

The 1990 Pro Set Super Bowl Theme Art set contains 25 standard-size (2 1/2" by 3 1/2") cards. The fronts have full color theme art from the Super Bowls; both sides have attractive silver borders. The horizontally-oriented backs have photos of the winning teams' rings and miscellaneous info about the games. These cards were distributed one per 1990 Pro Set Series I pack.

| | MINT | EXC | G-VG |
|---|---|---|---|
| COMPLETE SET (24) | 3.00 | 1.20 | .30 |
| COMMON PLAYER (1-24) | .15 | .06 | .01 |
| | | | |
| ☐ 1 Super Bowl I | .15 | .06 | .01 |
| ☐ 2 Super Bowl II | .15 | .06 | .01 |
| ☐ 3 Super Bowl III | .15 | .06 | .01 |
| ☐ 4 Super Bowl IV | .15 | .06 | .01 |
| ☐ 5 Super Bowl V | .15 | .06 | .01 |
| ☐ 6 Super Bowl VI | .15 | .06 | .01 |
| ☐ 7 Super Bowl VII | .15 | .06 | .01 |
| ☐ 8 Super Bowl VIII | .15 | .06 | .01 |
| ☐ 9 Super Bowl IX | .15 | .06 | .01 |
| ☐ 10 Super Bowl X | .15 | .06 | .01 |
| ☐ 11 Super Bowl XI | .15 | .06 | .01 |
| ☐ 12 Super Bowl XII | .15 | .06 | .01 |

| | | | |
|---|---|---|---|
| ☐ 13 Super Bowl XIII UER | .15 | .06 | .01 |
| (Colgate University 7, | | | |
| should be Colgate 13) | | | |
| ☐ 14 Super Bowl XIV | .15 | .06 | .01 |
| ☐ 15 Super Bowl XV | .15 | .06 | .01 |
| ☐ 16 Super Bowl XVI | .15 | .06 | .01 |
| ☐ 17 Super Bowl XVII | .15 | .06 | .01 |
| ☐ 18 Super Bowl XVIII | .15 | .06 | .01 |
| ☐ 19 Super Bowl XIX | .15 | .06 | .01 |
| ☐ 20 Super Bowl XX | .15 | .06 | .01 |
| ☐ 21 Super Bowl XXI | .15 | .06 | .01 |
| ☐ 22A Super Bowl XXII ERR | 1.00 | .40 | .10 |
| (Jan. 31, 1989 on back) | | | |
| ☐ 22B Super Bowl XXII COR | .25 | .10 | .02 |
| (Jan. 31, 1988 on back) | | | |
| ☐ 23 Super Bowl XXIII | .15 | .06 | .01 |
| ☐ 24 Super Bowl XXIV | .25 | .10 | .02 |
| Theme Art | | | |

## 1990 Pro Set Inserts

These special cards were inserted in the 1990 Pro Set football card packs. They are all standard size, 2 1/2" by 3 1/2". Super Pro introduces a new comic book character. The Lombardi Trophy Hologram was a major marketing breakthrough as it virtually single-handedly introduced a wave of purposely limited, high quality inserts to the card collecting hobby as most of the other major companies followed Pro Set's success.

| | MINT | EXC | G-VG |
|---|---|---|---|
| COMPLETE SET (7) | 65.00 | 29.00 | 8.25 |
| COMMON CARD | .40 | .18 | .05 |
| | | | |
| ☐ CC2 Paul Tagliabue SP | 1.00 | .45 | .13 |
| NFL Commissioner | | | |
| (First series only) | | | |
| ☐ NNO Lombardi Trophy SP | 60.00 | 27.00 | 7.50 |
| (Hologram; limited | | | |
| edition numbered | | | |
| out of 10,000) | | | |
| ☐ NNO Super Bowl XXIV Logo | .40 | .18 | .05 |
| ☐ SC Super Pro SP | 1.00 | .45 | .13 |
| (Second series only) | | | |
| ☐ SC2 Santa Claus SP | 1.00 | .45 | .13 |
| (Second series only; | | | |
| No quote mark | | | |
| after Andre Ware) | | | |
| ☐ SC3 Joe Robbie Mem SP | 1.00 | .45 | .13 |
| (Second series only) | | | |
| ☐ SP1 Payne Stewart SP | 1.00 | .45 | .13 |
| (First series only) | | | |

## 1990 Pro Set Super Bowl MVP's

This 24-card standard size (2 1/2" by 3 1/2") set displays color portraits of Super Bowl MVP's by noted sports artist Merv Corning. The portraits bleed to the sides of the card, and they are bordered above by a silver stripe and below by two stripes in the team's colors as well as another silver stripe. The horizontally oriented backs present a color action photo on the left portion and summary of the player's Super Bowl performance on the right portion. The cards are numbered on the back; the set numbering is in chronological order by Super Bowl number. These cards were included as an insert with Pro Set's second series football card packs.

| | MINT | EXC | G-VG |
|---|---|---|---|
| COMPLETE SET (24) | 4.00 | 1.60 | .40 |
| COMMON PLAYER (1-24) | .10 | .04 | .01 |
| | | | |
| ☐ 1 Bart Starr | .25 | .10 | .02 |
| Green Bay Packers | | | |
| Super Bowl I | | | |

| | | | |
|---|---|---|---|
| ☐ 2 Bart Starr | .25 | .10 | .02 |
| Green Bay Packers | | | |
| Super Bowl II | | | |
| ☐ 3 Joe Namath | .60 | .24 | .06 |
| New York Jets | | | |
| Super Bowl III | | | |
| ☐ 4 Len Dawson | .15 | .06 | .01 |
| Kansas City Chiefs | | | |
| Super Bowl IV | | | |
| ☐ 5 Chuck Howley | .10 | .04 | .01 |
| Dallas Cowboys | | | |
| Super Bowl V | | | |
| ☐ 6 Roger Staubach | .60 | .24 | .06 |
| Dallas Cowboys | | | |
| Super Bowl VI | | | |
| ☐ 7 Jake Scott | .10 | .04 | .01 |
| Miami Dolphins | | | |
| Super Bowl VII | | | |
| ☐ 8 Larry Csonka | .25 | .10 | .02 |
| Miami Dolphins | | | |
| Super Bowl VIII | | | |
| ☐ 9 Franco Harris | .25 | .10 | .02 |
| Pittsburgh Steelers | | | |
| Super Bowl IX | | | |
| ☐ 10 Lynn Swann | .20 | .08 | .02 |
| Pittsburgh Steelers | | | |
| Super Bowl X | | | |
| ☐ 11 Fred Biletnikoff | .20 | .08 | .02 |
| Oakland Raiders | | | |
| Super Bowl XI | | | |
| ☐ 12 Harvey Martin | .10 | .04 | .01 |
| Randy White | | | |
| Dallas Cowboys | | | |
| Super Bowl XII | | | |
| ☐ 13 Terry Bradshaw | .50 | .20 | .05 |
| Pittsburgh Steelers | | | |
| Super Bowl XIII | | | |
| ☐ 14 Terry Bradshaw | .50 | .20 | .05 |
| Pittsburgh Steelers | | | |
| Super Bowl XIV | | | |
| ☐ 15 Jim Plunkett | .15 | .06 | .01 |
| Los Angeles Raiders | | | |
| Super Bowl XV | | | |
| ☐ 16 Joe Montana | 1.00 | .40 | .10 |
| San Francisco 49ers | | | |
| Super Bowl XVI | | | |
| ☐ 17 John Riggins | .20 | .08 | .02 |
| Washington Redskins | | | |
| Super Bowl XVII | | | |
| ☐ 18 Marcus Allen | .20 | .08 | .02 |
| Los Angeles Raiders | | | |
| Super Bowl XVIII | | | |
| ☐ 19 Joe Montana | 1.00 | .40 | .10 |
| San Francisco 49ers | | | |
| Super Bowl XIX | | | |
| ☐ 20 Richard Dent | .10 | .04 | .01 |
| Chicago Bears | | | |
| Super Bowl XX | | | |
| ☐ 21 Phil Simms | .20 | .08 | .02 |
| New York Giants | | | |
| Super Bowl XXI | | | |
| ☐ 22 Doug Williams | .10 | .04 | .01 |
| Washington Redskins | | | |
| Super Bowl XXII | | | |
| ☐ 23 Jerry Rice | .50 | .20 | .05 |
| San Francisco 49ers | | | |
| Super Bowl XXIII | | | |
| ☐ 24 Joe Montana | 1.00 | .40 | .10 |
| San Francisco 49ers | | | |
| Super Bowl XXIV | | | |

## 1990 Pro Set Collect-A-Books

This 36-card (booklet) set, which measures the standard 2 1/2" by 3 1/2", features some of the leading stars of the National Football League. The set features action photos of the players on the front of

| | | | |
|---|---|---|---|
| ☐ 29 Shane Conlan | .15 | .06 | .01 |
| Buffalo Bills | | | |
| ☐ 30 Carl Banks | .15 | .06 | .01 |
| New York Giants | | | |
| ☐ 31 Charles Mann | .15 | .06 | .01 |
| Washington Redskins | | | |
| ☐ 32 Anthony Munoz | .25 | .10 | .02 |
| Cincinnati Bengals | | | |
| ☐ 33 Dan Hampton | .25 | .10 | .02 |
| Chicago Bears | | | |
| ☐ 34 Michael Dean Perry | .25 | .10 | .02 |
| Cleveland Browns | | | |
| ☐ 35 Joey Browner | .15 | .06 | .01 |
| Minnesota Vikings | | | |
| ☐ 36 Ken O'Brien | .15 | .06 | .01 |
| New York Jets | | | |
| ☐ SB Super Bowl Story | 1.00 | .40 | .10 |
| 24 Years of Champions | | | |

the card along with their name on the top of the front and the NFL Pro Set logo on the lower left hand corner. The cards have six pages including the outer cover photos and is interesting in that both Michael Dean Perry and Eric Dickerson have cards in this set but do not have cards in the regular Pro Set series. The set was released in three series of 12 cards each, with there being one rookie in each of the subsets. Not included in the complete set price below is a 1990-91 Pro Set Collect-A-Book Super Bowl XXV, numbered "SB" in the checklist below which presents color pictures with captions summarizing Super Bowls I-XXIV. The front and back cover form one painting of a wall and table covered with football memorabilia. This single item was apparently only available as part of the Super Bowl XXV Commemorative Tin.

| | MINT | EXC | G-VG |
|---|---|---|---|
| COMPLETE SET (36) | 6.00 | 2.40 | .60 |
| COMMON PLAYER (1-12) | .15 | .06 | .01 |
| COMMON PLAYER (13-24) | .15 | .06 | .01 |
| COMMON PLAYER (25-36) | .15 | .06 | .01 |

| | | | |
|---|---|---|---|
| ☐ 1 Jim Kelly | .50 | .20 | .05 |
| Buffalo Bills | | | |
| ☐ 2 Andre Ware | .25 | .10 | .02 |
| Detroit Lions | | | |
| ☐ 3 Phil Simms | .25 | .10 | .02 |
| New York Giants | | | |
| ☐ 4 Bubby Brister | .15 | .06 | .01 |
| Pittsburgh Steelers | | | |
| ☐ 5 Bernie Kosar | .25 | .10 | .02 |
| Cleveland Browns | | | |
| ☐ 6 Eric Dickerson | .25 | .10 | .02 |
| Indianapolis Colts | | | |
| ☐ 7 Barry Sanders | .75 | .30 | .07 |
| Detroit Lions | | | |
| ☐ 8 Jerry Rice | .75 | .30 | .07 |
| San Francisco 49ers | | | |
| ☐ 9 Keith Millard | .15 | .06 | .01 |
| Minnesota Vikings | | | |
| ☐ 10 Erik McMillan | .15 | .06 | .01 |
| New York Jets | | | |
| ☐ 11 Ickey Woods | .15 | .06 | .01 |
| Cincinnati Bengals | | | |
| ☐ 12 Mike Singletary | .25 | .10 | .02 |
| Chicago Bears | | | |
| ☐ 13 Randall Cunningham | .35 | .14 | .03 |
| Philadelphia Eagles | | | |
| ☐ 14 Boomer Esiason | .25 | .10 | .02 |
| Cincinnati Bengals | | | |
| ☐ 15 John Elway | .60 | .24 | .06 |
| Denver Broncos | | | |
| ☐ 16 Wade Wilson | .25 | .10 | .02 |
| Minnesota Vikings | | | |
| ☐ 17 Troy Aikman | 1.50 | .60 | .15 |
| Dallas Cowboys | | | |
| ☐ 18 Dan Marino | 1.25 | .50 | .12 |
| Miami Dolphins | | | |
| ☐ 19 Lawrence Taylor | .35 | .14 | .03 |
| New York Giants | | | |
| ☐ 20 Roger Craig | .25 | .10 | .02 |
| San Francisco 49ers | | | |
| ☐ 21 Merril Hoge | .15 | .06 | .01 |
| Pittsburgh Steelers | | | |
| ☐ 22 Christian Okoye | .15 | .06 | .01 |
| Kansas City Chiefs | | | |
| ☐ 23 Blair Thomas | .15 | .06 | .01 |
| New York Jets | | | |
| ☐ 24 William Perry | .15 | .06 | .01 |
| Chicago Bears | | | |
| ☐ 25 Bill Fralic | .15 | .06 | .01 |
| Atlanta Falcons | | | |
| ☐ 26 Warren Moon | .35 | .14 | .03 |
| Houston Oilers | | | |
| ☐ 27 Jim Everett | .15 | .06 | .01 |
| Los Angeles Rams | | | |
| ☐ 28 Jeff George | .50 | .20 | .05 |
| Indianapolis Colts | | | |

# 1990-91 Pro Set Super Bowl 160

This 160-card set measures the now standard, 2 1/2 by 3 1/2 and was issued by Pro Set as a complete set in a special commemorative box. Cards were also issued in eight-card wax packs along with six pieces of gum. The cards were introduced at the first Dallas Cowboys Pro Set Sports Collectors Show at Texas Stadium. The set features the highlights of the first 24 Super Bowls with the set being divided into the following sub-sets: Super Bowl Tickets (1-24), Super Bowl Supermen (25-135), Super Bowl Super Moments (136-151), and nine puzzle cards depicting the twenty-fifth Super Bowl Art (152-160).

| | MINT | EXC | G-VG |
|---|---|---|---|
| COMPLETE SET (160) | 4.00 | 1.60 | .40 |
| COMMON TICKET (1-24) | .05 | .02 | .00 |
| COMMON COACH (25-31) | .05 | .02 | .00 |
| COMMON PLAYER (32-135) | .05 | .02 | .00 |
| COMMON MOMENT (136-151) | .05 | .02 | .00 |
| COMMON PUZZLE (152-160) | .03 | .01 | .00 |

| | | | |
|---|---|---|---|
| ☐ 1 SB I Ticket | .10 | .04 | .01 |
| ☐ 2 SB II Ticket | .05 | .02 | .00 |
| ☐ 3 SB III Ticket | .05 | .02 | .00 |
| ☐ 4 SB IV Ticket | .05 | .02 | .00 |
| ☐ 5 SB V Ticket | .05 | .02 | .00 |
| ☐ 6 SB VI Ticket | .05 | .02 | .00 |
| ☐ 7 SB VII Ticket | .05 | .02 | .00 |
| ☐ 8 SB VIII Ticket | .05 | .02 | .00 |
| ☐ 9 SB IX Ticket | .05 | .02 | .00 |
| ☐ 10 SB X Ticket | .05 | .02 | .00 |
| ☐ 11 SB XI Ticket | .05 | .02 | .00 |
| ☐ 12 SB XII Ticket | .05 | .02 | .00 |
| ☐ 13 SB XIII Ticket | .05 | .02 | .00 |
| ☐ 14 SB XIV Ticket | .05 | .02 | .00 |
| ☐ 15 SB XV Ticket | .05 | .02 | .00 |
| ☐ 16 SB XVI Ticket | .05 | .02 | .00 |
| ☐ 17 SB XVII Ticket | .05 | .02 | .00 |
| ☐ 18 SB XVIII Ticket | .05 | .02 | .00 |
| ☐ 19 SB XIX Ticket | .05 | .02 | .00 |
| ☐ 20 SB XX Ticket | .05 | .02 | .00 |
| ☐ 21 SB XXI Ticket | .05 | .02 | .00 |
| ☐ 22 SB XXII Ticket | .05 | .02 | .00 |
| ☐ 23 SB XXIII Ticket | .05 | .02 | .00 |
| ☐ 24 SB XXIV Ticket | .05 | .02 | .00 |
| ☐ 25 Tom Flores CO | .05 | .02 | .00 |
| ☐ 26 Joe Gibbs CO | .05 | .02 | .00 |
| ☐ 27 Tom Landry CO | .15 | .06 | .01 |
| ☐ 28 Vince Lombardi CO | .15 | .06 | .01 |
| ☐ 29 Chuck Noll CO | .10 | .04 | .01 |
| ☐ 30 Don Shula CO | .15 | .06 | .01 |
| ☐ 31 Bill Walsh CO | .15 | .06 | .01 |
| ☐ 32 Terry Bradshaw | .25 | .10 | .02 |
| ☐ 33 Joe Montana | .50 | .20 | .05 |
| ☐ 34 Joe Namath | .50 | .20 | .05 |
| ☐ 35 Jim Plunkett | .10 | .04 | .01 |
| ☐ 36 Bart Starr | .20 | .08 | .02 |

| | | | |
|---|---|---|---|
| ☐ 37 Roger Staubach | .35 | .14 | .03 |
| ☐ 38 Marcus Allen | .15 | .06 | .01 |
| ☐ 39 Roger Craig | .10 | .04 | .01 |
| ☐ 40 Larry Csonka | .15 | .06 | .01 |
| ☐ 41 Franco Harris | .10 | .04 | .01 |
| ☐ 42 John Riggins | .10 | .04 | .01 |
| ☐ 43 Timmy Smith | .05 | .02 | .00 |
| ☐ 44 Matt Snell | .05 | .02 | .00 |
| ☐ 45 Fred Biletnikoff | .10 | .04 | .01 |
| ☐ 46 Cliff Branch | .05 | .02 | .00 |
| ☐ 47 Max McGee | .05 | .02 | .00 |
| ☐ 48 Jerry Rice | .35 | .14 | .03 |
| ☐ 49 Ricky Sanders | .05 | .02 | .00 |
| ☐ 50 George Sauer Jr. | .05 | .02 | .00 |
| ☐ 51 John Stallworth | .10 | .04 | .01 |
| ☐ 52 Lynn Swann | .15 | .06 | .01 |
| ☐ 53 Dave Casper | .05 | .02 | .00 |
| ☐ 54 Marv Fleming | .05 | .02 | .00 |
| ☐ 55 Dan Ross | .05 | .02 | .00 |
| ☐ 56 Forrest Gregg | .10 | .04 | .01 |
| ☐ 57 Winston Hill | .05 | .02 | .00 |
| ☐ 58 Joe Jacoby | .05 | .02 | .00 |
| ☐ 59 Anthony Munoz | .10 | .04 | .01 |
| ☐ 60 Art Shell | .10 | .04 | .01 |
| ☐ 61 Rayfield Wright | .05 | .02 | .00 |
| ☐ 62 Ron Yary | .05 | .02 | .00 |
| ☐ 63 Randy Cross | .05 | .02 | .00 |
| ☐ 64 Jerry Kramer | .10 | .04 | .01 |
| ☐ 65 Bob Kuechenberg | .05 | .02 | .00 |
| ☐ 66 Larry Little | .05 | .02 | .00 |
| ☐ 67 Gerry Mullins | .05 | .02 | .00 |
| ☐ 68 John Niland | .05 | .02 | .00 |
| ☐ 69 Gene Upshaw | .10 | .04 | .01 |
| ☐ 70 Dave Dalby | .05 | .02 | .00 |
| ☐ 71 Jim Langer | .05 | .02 | .00 |
| ☐ 72 Dwight Stephenson | .05 | .02 | .00 |
| ☐ 73 Mike Webster | .10 | .04 | .01 |
| ☐ 74 Ross Browner | .05 | .02 | .00 |
| ☐ 75 Willie Davis | .10 | .04 | .01 |
| ☐ 76 Richard Dent | .10 | .04 | .01 |
| ☐ 77 L.C. Greenwood | .10 | .04 | .01 |
| ☐ 78 Ed Too Tall Jones | .15 | .06 | .01 |
| ☐ 79 Harvey Martin | .05 | .02 | .00 |
| ☐ 80 Dwight White | .05 | .02 | .00 |
| ☐ 81 Buck Buchanan | .10 | .04 | .01 |
| ☐ 82 Curley Culp | .05 | .02 | .00 |
| ☐ 83 Manny Fernandez | .05 | .02 | .00 |
| ☐ 84 Joe Greene | .15 | .06 | .01 |
| ☐ 85 Bob Lilly | .15 | .06 | .01 |
| ☐ 86 Alan Page | .10 | .04 | .01 |
| ☐ 87 Randy White | .15 | .06 | .01 |
| ☐ 88 Nick Buoniconti | .10 | .04 | .01 |
| ☐ 89 Lee Roy Jordan | .10 | .04 | .01 |
| ☐ 90 Jack Lambert | .15 | .06 | .01 |
| ☐ 91 Willie Lanier | .10 | .04 | .01 |
| ☐ 92 Ray Nitschke | .15 | .06 | .01 |
| ☐ 93 Mike Singletary | .15 | .06 | .01 |
| ☐ 94 Carl Banks | .05 | .02 | .00 |
| ☐ 95 Charles Haley | .05 | .02 | .00 |
| ☐ 96 Jack Ham | .10 | .04 | .01 |
| ☐ 97 Ted Hendricks | .10 | .04 | .01 |
| ☐ 98 Chuck Howley | .05 | .02 | .00 |
| ☐ 99 Rod Martin | .05 | .02 | .00 |
| ☐ 100 Herb Adderley | .10 | .04 | .01 |
| ☐ 101 Mel Blount | .10 | .04 | .01 |
| ☐ 102 Willie Brown | .10 | .04 | .01 |
| ☐ 103 Lester Hayes | .05 | .02 | .00 |
| ☐ 104 Mike Haynes | .10 | .04 | .01 |
| ☐ 105 Ronnie Lott | .15 | .06 | .01 |
| ☐ 106 Mel Renfro | .10 | .04 | .01 |
| ☐ 107 Eric Wright | .05 | .02 | .00 |
| ☐ 108 Dick Anderson | .05 | .02 | .00 |
| ☐ 109 David Fulcher | .05 | .02 | .00 |
| ☐ 110 Cliff Harris | .05 | .02 | .00 |
| ☐ 111 Johnny Robinson | .05 | .02 | .00 |
| ☐ 112 Jake Scott | .05 | .02 | .00 |
| ☐ 113 Donnie Shell | .05 | .02 | .00 |
| ☐ 114 Mike Wagner | .05 | .02 | .00 |
| ☐ 115 Willie Wood | .10 | .04 | .01 |
| ☐ 116 Ray Guy | .10 | .04 | .01 |
| ☐ 117 Lee Johnson | .05 | .02 | .00 |
| ☐ 118 Larry Seiple | .05 | .02 | .00 |
| ☐ 119 Jerrel Wilson | .05 | .02 | .00 |
| ☐ 120 Kevin Butler | .05 | .02 | .00 |
| ☐ 121 Don Chandler | .05 | .02 | .00 |
| ☐ 122 Jan Stenerud | .10 | .04 | .01 |
| ☐ 123 Jim Turner | .05 | .02 | .00 |
| ☐ 124 Ray Wersching | .05 | .02 | .00 |
| ☐ 125 Larry Anderson | .05 | .02 | .00 |
| ☐ 126 Stanford Jennings | .05 | .02 | .00 |
| ☐ 127 Mike Nelms | .05 | .02 | .00 |
| ☐ 128 John Taylor | .10 | .04 | .01 |
| ☐ 129 Fulton Walker | .05 | .02 | .00 |
| ☐ 130 E.J. Holub | .05 | .02 | .00 |
| ☐ 131 George Siefert CO | .05 | .02 | .00 |
| ☐ 132 Jim Taylor | .15 | .06 | .01 |
| ☐ 133 Joe Theismann | .15 | .06 | .01 |

| | | | |
|---|---|---|---|
| ☐ 134 Johnny Unitas | .30 | .12 | .03 |
| ☐ 135 Reggie Williams | .05 | .02 | .00 |
| ☐ 136 Two Networks (Paul Christman and Frank Gifford) | .10 | .04 | .01 |
| ☐ 137 First Fly-Over (Military jets) | .05 | .02 | .00 |
| ☐ 138 Weeb Ewbank (Super Bowl Super Moment) | .05 | .02 | .00 |
| ☐ 139 Otis Taylor (Super Bowl Super Moment) | .05 | .02 | .00 |
| ☐ 140 Jim O'Brien (Super Bowl Super Moment) | .05 | .02 | .00 |
| ☐ 141 Garo Yepremian (Super Bowl Super Moment) | .05 | .02 | .00 |
| ☐ 142 Pete Rozelle and Art Rooney | .05 | .02 | .00 |
| ☐ 143 Percy Howard (Super Bowl Super Moment) | .05 | .02 | .00 |
| ☐ 144 Jackie Smith (Super Bowl Super Moment) | .10 | .04 | .01 |
| ☐ 145 Record Crowd (Super Bowl Super Moment) | .05 | .02 | .00 |
| ☐ 146 Yellow Ribbon UER (Fourth line says more than year, should say more than a year) | .05 | .02 | .00 |
| ☐ 147 Dan Bunz and Charles Alexander (Super Bowl Super Moment) | .05 | .02 | .00 |
| ☐ 148 Smurfs (Redskins) (Super Bowl Super Moment) | .05 | .02 | .00 |
| ☐ 149 The Fridge William Perry Scores (Super Bowl Super Moment) | .10 | .04 | .01 |
| ☐ 150 Phil McConkey (Super Bowl Super Moment) | .05 | .02 | .00 |
| ☐ 151 Doug Williams (Super Bowl Super Moment) | .05 | .02 | .00 |
| ☐ 152 Top row left XXV Theme Art Puzzle | .03 | .01 | .00 |
| ☐ 153 Top row middle XXV Theme Art Puzzle | .03 | .01 | .00 |
| ☐ 154 Top row right XXV Theme Art Puzzle | .03 | .01 | .00 |
| ☐ 155 Center row left XXV Theme Art Puzzle | .03 | .01 | .00 |
| ☐ 156 Center row middle XXV Theme Art Puzzle | .03 | .01 | .00 |
| ☐ 157 Center row right XXV Theme Art Puzzle | .03 | .01 | .00 |
| ☐ 158 Bottom row left XXV Theme Art Puzzle | .03 | .01 | .00 |
| ☐ 159 Bottom row middle XXV Theme Art Puzzle | .03 | .01 | .00 |
| ☐ 160 Bottom row right XXV Theme Art Puzzle | .05 | .02 | .00 |
| ☐ xx Special Offer Card (SB Game Program direct from Pro Set) | .10 | .04 | .01 |

## 1990-91 Pro Set Super Bowl Binder

This standard size (2 1/2" by 3 1/2") set of 56 cards features members of the all-time Super Bowl team and members of the teams which competed in the 25th Super Bowl, New York Giants and Buffalo Bills. This set also included card number 799 from the 1990 Pro Set Football set: the Ronnie Lott Stay in School Card. Published reports indicated that Pro Set made 125,000 of these sets, 90,000 for distribution at the Super Bowl and 35,000 for a special mail-away offer at 30.00 per set. The set is housed in an attractive binder with special plastic pages holding four cards per. The cards of the players playing in the Super Bowl have the same number on the back as their regular issue set but the fronts acknowledge their teams as champions of their conferences.

| | MINT | EXC | G-VG |
|---|---|---|---|
| COMPLETE SET (56) | 20.00 | 8.00 | 2.00 |
| COMMON CARD | .25 | .10 | .02 |
| ☐ 1 Vince Lombardi CO Green Bay Packers | .35 | .14 | .03 |

| | | | |
|---|---|---|---|
| ☐ 2 Joe Montana | 3.50 | 1.40 | .35 |
| San Francisco 49ers | | | |
| ☐ 3 Larry Csonka | .50 | .20 | .05 |
| Miami Dolphins | | | |
| ☐ 4 Franco Harris | .50 | .20 | .05 |
| Pittsburgh Steelers | | | |
| ☐ 5 Jerry Rice | 2.00 | .80 | .20 |
| San Francisco 49ers | | | |
| ☐ 6 Lynn Swann | .50 | .20 | .05 |
| Pittsburgh Steelers | | | |
| ☐ 7 Forrest Gregg | .35 | .14 | .03 |
| Green Bay Packers | | | |
| ☐ 8 Art Shell | .35 | .14 | .03 |
| Oakland Raiders | | | |
| ☐ 9 Jerry Kramer | .25 | .10 | .02 |
| Green Bay Packers | | | |
| ☐ 10 Gene Upshaw | .35 | .14 | .03 |
| Oakland Raiders | | | |
| ☐ 11 Mike Webster | .35 | .14 | .03 |
| Pittsburgh Steelers | | | |
| ☐ 12 Dave Casper | .25 | .10 | .02 |
| Oakland Raiders | | | |
| ☐ 13 Jan Stenerud | .35 | .14 | .03 |
| Kansas City Chiefs | | | |
| ☐ 14 John Taylor | .35 | .14 | .03 |
| San Francisco 49ers | | | |
| ☐ 15 L.C. Greenwood | .25 | .10 | .02 |
| Pittsburgh Steelers | | | |
| ☐ 16 Ed Too Tall Jones | .35 | .14 | .03 |
| Dallas Cowboys | | | |
| ☐ 17 Joe Greene | .50 | .20 | .05 |
| Pittsburgh Steelers | | | |
| ☐ 18 Randy White | .50 | .20 | .05 |
| Dallas Cowboys | | | |
| ☐ 19 Jack Lambert | .50 | .20 | .05 |
| Pittsburgh Steelers | | | |
| ☐ 20 Mike Singletary | .35 | .14 | .03 |
| Chicago Bears | | | |
| ☐ 21 Jack Ham | .35 | .14 | .03 |
| Pittsburgh Steelers | | | |
| ☐ 22 Ted Hendricks | .35 | .14 | .03 |
| Oakland Raiders | | | |
| ☐ 23 Mel Blount | .35 | .14 | .03 |
| Pittsburgh Steelers | | | |
| ☐ 24 Ronnie Lott | .50 | .20 | .05 |
| San Francisco 49ers | | | |
| ☐ 25 Donnie Shell | .25 | .10 | .02 |
| Pittsburgh Steelers | | | |
| ☐ 26 Willie Wood | .35 | .14 | .03 |
| Green Bay Packers | | | |
| ☐ 27 Ray Guy | .35 | .14 | .03 |
| Oakland Raiders | | | |
| ☐ 39 Cornelius Bennett | .50 | .20 | .05 |
| Buffalo Bills | | | |
| ☐ 40 Jim Kelly | 1.50 | .60 | .15 |
| Buffalo Bills | | | |
| ☐ 47 Darryl Talley | .35 | .14 | .03 |
| Buffalo Bills | | | |
| ☐ 48 Marv Levy CO | .35 | .14 | .03 |
| Buffalo Bills | | | |
| ☐ 223 Carl Banks | .35 | .14 | .03 |
| New York Giants | | | |
| ☐ 226 Pepper Johnson | .35 | .14 | .03 |
| New York Giants | | | |
| ☐ 228 Dave Meggett | .35 | .14 | .03 |
| New York Giants | | | |
| ☐ 230 Phil Simms | .50 | .20 | .05 |
| New York Giants | | | |
| ☐ 231 Lawrence Taylor | .75 | .30 | .07 |
| New York Giants | | | |
| ☐ 232 Bill Parcells CO | .35 | .14 | .03 |
| New York Giants | | | |
| ☐ 437 Shane Conlan | .35 | .14 | .03 |
| Buffalo Bills | | | |
| ☐ 438 Kent Hull | .25 | .10 | .02 |
| Buffalo Bills | | | |
| ☐ 440 Andre Reed | .75 | .30 | .07 |

| | | | |
|---|---|---|---|
| Buffalo Bills | | | |
| ☐ 443 Bruce Smith | .75 | .30 | .07 |
| Buffalo Bills | | | |
| ☐ 444 Thurman Thomas | 1.50 | .60 | .15 |
| Buffalo Bills | | | |
| ☐ 591 Ottis Anderson | .50 | .20 | .05 |
| New York Giants | | | |
| ☐ 592 Mark Bavaro | .35 | .14 | .03 |
| New York Giants | | | |
| ☐ 596 Jeff Hostetler | .75 | .30 | .07 |
| New York Giants | | | |
| ☐ 692 Rodney Hampton | 1.00 | .40 | .10 |
| New York Giants | | | |
| ☐ 725 Howard Ballard | .25 | .10 | .02 |
| Buffalo Bills | | | |
| ☐ 753 James Lofton | .50 | .20 | .05 |
| Buffalo Bills | | | |
| ☐ 754 Steve Tasker | .25 | .10 | .02 |
| Buffalo Bills | | | |
| ☐ 765 Stephen Baker | .50 | .20 | .05 |
| New York Giants | | | |
| ☐ 766 Reyna Thompson | .25 | .10 | .02 |
| New York Giants | | | |
| ☐ 799 Ronnie Lott Education | .35 | .14 | .03 |
| ☐ SC1 2,000,000th Fan | .50 | .20 | .05 |
| ☐ SC2 Buick Checklist Card | .50 | .20 | .05 |
| ☐ SC3 Lamar Hunt Trophy | .50 | .20 | .05 |
| ☐ SC4 George Halas Trophy | .50 | .20 | .05 |

## 1990-91 Pro Set Pro Bowl 106

This standard size (2 1/2" by 3 1/2") set of 106 cards honored the members of the Pro Bowl teams for each conference in the annual Pro Bowl game. This set features regular cards already issued by Pro Set with no identification that these cards are for the Pro Bowl game. The only exceptions are the four players who were in Pro Set's Final Update. These Pro Bowl cards show "1990 Final Update" on the front of the card; this notation was not used on the regular issue Final Update cards. These are obviously the key cards in the set as they are distinguishable from regular Pro Set's issue whereas the other Pro Bowl cards are not. Therefore, the set is skip-numbered as seen below. In addition to the player cards, the 1990 Super Bowl Theme Art insert set was also issued in this set. This set is housed in an attractive white binder with the identification of the Pro Bowl game on the front of the binder.

| | MINT | EXC | G-VG |
|---|---|---|---|
| COMPLETE SET (106) | 40.00 | 16.00 | 4.00 |
| COMMON CARD | .04 | .02 | .00 |
| | | | |
| ☐ 39 Cornelius Bennett | .07 | .03 | .01 |
| Buffalo Bills | | | |
| ☐ 40 Jim Kelly | .25 | .10 | .02 |
| Buffalo Bills | | | |
| ☐ 49 Neal Anderson | .07 | .03 | .01 |
| Chicago Bears | | | |
| ☐ 52 Richard Dent | .07 | .03 | .01 |
| Chicago Bears | | | |
| ☐ 53 Jay Hilgenberg | .04 | .02 | .00 |
| Chicago Bears | | | |
| ☐ 57 Mike Singletary | .07 | .03 | .01 |
| Chicago Bears | | | |
| ☐ 86 Steve Atwater | .07 | .03 | .01 |
| Denver Broncos | | | |
| ☐ 91 Bobby Humphrey | .07 | .03 | .01 |
| Denver Broncos | | | |
| ☐ 96 Jerry Ball | .04 | .02 | .00 |
| Detroit Lions | | | |
| ☐ 98 Lomas Brown | .04 | .02 | .00 |
| Detroit Lions | | | |
| ☐ 102 Barry Sanders | 1.00 | .40 | .10 |
| Detroit Lions | | | |

| | | | |
|---|---|---|---|
| ☐ 114 Sterling Sharpe | .75 | .30 | .07 |
| Green Bay Packers | | | |
| ☐ 118 Ray Childress | .07 | .03 | .01 |
| Houston Oilers | | | |
| ☐ 119 Ernest Givins | .07 | .03 | .01 |
| Houston Oilers | | | |
| ☐ 122 Drew Hill | .07 | .03 | .01 |
| Houston Oilers | | | |
| ☐ 135 Rohn Stark | .04 | .02 | .00 |
| Indianapolis Colts | | | |
| ☐ 137 Clarence Verdin | .04 | .02 | .00 |
| Indianapolis Colts | | | |
| ☐ 144 Nick Lowery | .04 | .02 | .00 |
| Kansas City Chiefs | | | |
| ☐ 155 Bo Jackson | .40 | .16 | .04 |
| Los Angeles Raiders | | | |
| ☐ 156 Don Mosebar | .04 | .02 | .00 |
| Los Angeles Raiders | | | |
| ☐ 158 Greg Townsend | .07 | .03 | .01 |
| Los Angeles Raiders | | | |
| ☐ 160 Steve Wisniewski | .04 | .02 | .00 |
| Los Angeles Raiders | | | |
| ☐ 173 Jackie Slater | .07 | .03 | .01 |
| Los Angeles Rams | | | |
| ☐ 186 Joey Browner | .07 | .03 | .01 |
| Minnesota Vikings | | | |
| ☐ 188 Chris Doleman | .07 | .03 | .01 |
| Minnesota Vikings | | | |
| ☐ 189 Steve Jordan | .07 | .03 | .01 |
| Minnesota Vikings | | | |
| ☐ 190 Carl Lee | .04 | .02 | .00 |
| Minnesota Vikings | | | |
| ☐ 191 Randall McDaniel | .04 | .02 | .00 |
| Minnesota Vikings | | | |
| ☐ 210 Morten Andersen | .07 | .03 | .01 |
| New Orleans Saints | | | |
| ☐ 215 Vaughan Johnson | .07 | .03 | .01 |
| New Orleans Saints | | | |
| ☐ 218 Pat Swilling | .10 | .04 | .01 |
| New Orleans Saints | | | |
| ☐ 226 Pepper Johnson | .04 | .02 | .00 |
| New York Giants | | | |
| ☐ 229 Bart Oates | .04 | .02 | .00 |
| New York Giants | | | |
| ☐ 231 Lawrence Taylor | .10 | .04 | .01 |
| New York Giants | | | |
| ☐ 244 Jerome Brown | .07 | .03 | .01 |
| Philadelphia Eagles | | | |
| ☐ 247 Randall Cunningham | .15 | .06 | .01 |
| Philadelphia Eagles | | | |
| ☐ 248 Keith Jackson | .25 | .10 | .02 |
| Philadelphia Eagles | | | |
| ☐ 252 Reggie White | .15 | .06 | .01 |
| Philadelphia Eagles | | | |
| ☐ 271 David Little | .04 | .02 | .00 |
| Pittsburgh Steelers | | | |
| ☐ 276 Marion Butts | .10 | .04 | .01 |
| San Diego Chargers | | | |
| ☐ 289 Charles Haley | .07 | .03 | .01 |
| San Francisco 49ers | | | |
| ☐ 291 Ronnie Lott | .10 | .04 | .01 |
| San Francisco 49ers | | | |
| ☐ 292 Guy McIntyre | .04 | .02 | .00 |
| San Francisco 49ers | | | |
| ☐ 293 Joe Montana | 1.00 | .40 | .10 |
| San Francisco 49ers | | | |
| ☐ 295 Jerry Rice | .75 | .30 | .07 |
| San Francisco 49ers | | | |
| ☐ 320 Earnest Byner | .07 | .03 | .01 |
| Washington Redskins | | | |
| ☐ 321 Gary Clark | .10 | .04 | .01 |
| Washington Redskins | | | |
| ☐ 323 Darrell Green | .07 | .03 | .01 |
| Washington Redskins | | | |
| ☐ 324 Jim Lachey | .07 | .03 | .01 |
| Washington Redskins | | | |
| ☐ 334 Pro Bowl | .04 | .02 | .00 |
| Aloha Stadium | | | |
| ☐ 434 Andre Rison | .25 | .10 | .02 |
| Atlanta Falcons | | | |
| ☐ 438 Kent Hull | .04 | .02 | .00 |
| Buffalo Bills | | | |
| ☐ 440 Andre Reed | .15 | .06 | .01 |
| Buffalo Bills | | | |
| ☐ 443 Bruce Smith | .10 | .04 | .01 |
| Buffalo Bills | | | |
| ☐ 444 Thurman Thomas | .40 | .16 | .04 |
| Buffalo Bills | | | |
| ☐ 447 Mark Bortz | .04 | .02 | .00 |
| Chicago Bears | | | |
| ☐ 462 David Fulcher | .04 | .02 | .00 |
| Cincinnati Bengals | | | |
| ☐ 464 Rodney Holman | .04 | .02 | .00 |
| Cincinnati Bengals | | | |
| ☐ 467 Anthony Munoz | .10 | .04 | .01 |
| Cincinnati Bengals | | | |
| ☐ 491 Dennis Smith | .04 | .02 | .00 |

| | | | |
|---|---|---|---|
| Denver Broncos | | | |
| ☐ 497 Mel Gray | .04 | .02 | .00 |
| Detroit Lions | | | |
| ☐ 514 Bruce Matthews | .04 | .02 | .00 |
| Houston Oilers | | | |
| ☐ 517 Warren Moon | .25 | .10 | .02 |
| Houston Oilers | | | |
| ☐ 529 Albert Lewis | .07 | .03 | .01 |
| Kansas City Chiefs | | | |
| ☐ 534 Kevin Ross | .04 | .02 | .00 |
| Kansas City Chiefs | | | |
| ☐ 536 Derrick Thomas | .30 | .12 | .03 |
| Kansas City Chiefs | | | |
| ☐ 557 Jeff Cross | .04 | .02 | .00 |
| Miami Dolphins | | | |
| ☐ 560 Ferrell Edmunds | .04 | .02 | .00 |
| Miami Dolphins | | | |
| ☐ 562 John Offerdahl | .07 | .03 | .01 |
| Miami Dolphins | | | |
| ☐ 575 Bruce Armstrong | .04 | .02 | .00 |
| New England Patriots | | | |
| ☐ 597 Sean Landeta | .04 | .02 | .00 |
| New York Giants | | | |
| ☐ 626 Rod Woodson | .20 | .08 | .02 |
| Pittsburgh Steelers | | | |
| ☐ 630 Anthony Miller | .25 | .10 | .02 |
| San Diego Chargers | | | |
| ☐ 632 Leslie O'Neal | .10 | .04 | .01 |
| San Diego Chargers | | | |
| ☐ 677 Richmond Webb | .20 | .08 | .02 |
| Miami Dolphins | | | |
| ☐ 754 Steve Tasker SP | 9.00 | 3.75 | .90 |
| (1990 Final Update | | | |
| on card front) | | | |
| Buffalo Bills | | | |
| ☐ 766 Reyna Thompson SP | 9.00 | 3.75 | .90 |
| (1990 Final Update | | | |
| on card front) | | | |
| New York Giants | | | |
| ☐ 771 Johnny Johnson SP | 15.00 | 6.00 | 1.50 |
| (1990 Final Update | | | |
| on card front) | | | |
| Phoenix Cardinals | | | |
| ☐ 778 Wayne Haddix SP | 9.00 | 3.75 | .90 |
| (1990 Final Update | | | |
| on card front) | | | |
| Tampa Bay Buccaneers | | | |
| ☐ 800 Mark Carrier | .10 | .04 | .01 |
| Defensive ROY | | | |
| Chicago Bears | | | |
| ☐ SB1 Super Bowl I | .15 | .06 | .01 |
| Theme Art | | | |
| ☐ SB2 Super Bowl II | .15 | .06 | .01 |
| Theme Art | | | |
| ☐ SB3 Super Bowl III | .15 | .06 | .01 |
| Theme Art | | | |
| ☐ SB4 Super Bowl IV | .15 | .06 | .01 |
| Theme Art | | | |
| ☐ SB5 Super Bowl V | .15 | .06 | .01 |
| Theme Art | | | |
| ☐ SB6 Super Bowl VI | .15 | .06 | .01 |
| Theme Art | | | |
| ☐ SB7 Super Bowl VII | .15 | .06 | .01 |
| Theme Art | | | |
| ☐ SB8 Super Bowl VIII | .15 | .06 | .01 |
| Theme Art | | | |
| ☐ SB9 Super Bowl IX | .15 | .06 | .01 |
| Theme Art | | | |
| ☐ SB10 Super Bowl X | .15 | .06 | .01 |
| Theme Art | | | |
| ☐ SB11 Super Bowl XI | .15 | .06 | .01 |
| Theme Art | | | |
| ☐ SB12 Super Bowl XII | .20 | .08 | .02 |
| Theme Art | | | |
| (Top of the back is | | | |
| white, regular issue | | | |
| card is black) | | | |
| ☐ SB13 Super Bowl XIII | .15 | .06 | .01 |
| Theme Art | | | |
| ☐ SB14 Super Bowl XIV | .15 | .06 | .01 |
| Theme Art | | | |
| ☐ SB15 Super Bowl XV | .15 | .06 | .01 |
| Theme Art | | | |
| ☐ SB16 Super Bowl XVI | .15 | .06 | .01 |
| Theme Art | | | |
| ☐ SB17 Super Bowl XVII | .15 | .06 | .01 |
| Theme Art | | | |
| ☐ SB18 Super Bowl XVIII | .15 | .06 | .01 |
| Theme Art | | | |
| ☐ SB19 Super Bowl XIX | .15 | .06 | .01 |
| Theme Art | | | |
| ☐ SB20 Super Bowl XX | .15 | .06 | .01 |
| Theme Art | | | |
| ☐ SB21 Super Bowl XXI | .15 | .06 | .01 |
| Theme Art | | | |
| ☐ SB22 Super Bowl XXII | .25 | .10 | .02 |
| Theme Art | | | |
| ☐ SB23 Super Bowl XXIII | .15 | .06 | .01 |

Theme Art
☐ SB24 Super Bowl XXIV ............... .15 .06 .01
Theme Art

## 1991 Pro Set Draft Day

This eight-card standard size (2 1/2" by 3 1/2") set was issued by Pro Set on April 21, 1991 the date of the NFL draft. The cards, which are all numbered 694, feature action shots in the 1991 Pro Set design of all the potential number one draft picks. The backs of the cards have a horizontal format, with one half of the card being a full-color portrait of the player and the other half consisting of biographical information. The set is checklisted below in alphabetical order. The Russell Maryland card was eventually released (on a somewhat limited basis) with the first series of 1991 Pro Set cards and is listed there rather than here.

| | MINT | EXC | G-VG |
|---|---|---|---|
| COMPLETE SET (7) ........................ | 300.00 | 120.00 | 30.00 |
| COMMON PLAYER (694A-694G) ...... | 20.00 | 8.00 | 2.00 |
| ☐ 694A Nick Bell .............................. | 30.00 | 12.00 | 3.00 |
| San Francisco 49ers | | | |
| ☐ 694B Mike Croel ........................... | 30.00 | 12.00 | 3.00 |
| New England Patriots | | | |
| ☐ 694C Raghib(Rocket) Ismail ........ | 60.00 | 24.00 | 6.00 |
| Atlanta Falcons | | | |
| ☐ 694D Raghib(Rocket) Ismail ........ | 90.00 | 36.00 | 9.00 |
| Dallas Cowboys | | | |
| ☐ 694E Raghib(Rocket) Ismail ........ | 60.00 | 24.00 | 6.00 |
| New England Patriots | | | |
| ☐ 694F Todd Lyght .......................... | 20.00 | 8.00 | 2.00 |
| Atlanta Falcons | | | |
| ☐ 694G Dan McGwire ....................... | 30.00 | 12.00 | 3.00 |
| New England Patriots | | | |

## 1991 Pro Set National Banquet

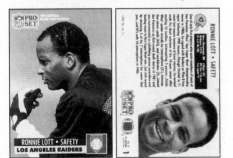

This five-card set was given away by Pro Set, one of the sponsors of the 1991 12th National Sports Collectors Convention in Anaheim, California. The standard-size (2 1/2" by 3 1/2") player cards have full-bleed color photos on the fronts. The horizontally oriented backs have other color photos and career summaries. The back of the ProFiles card has a picture of TV announcers Tim Brant and Craig James. The cards are numbered on the back.

| | MINT | EXC | G-VG |
|---|---|---|---|
| COMPLETE SET (5) ........................... | 4.00 | 1.60 | .40 |
| COMMON PLAYER (1-5) ................... | 1.00 | .40 | .10 |
| ☐ 1 Ronnie Lott .............................. | 1.25 | .50 | .12 |
| ☐ 2 Roy Firestone ........................... | 1.25 | .50 | .12 |

(Television celebrity)
| ☐ 3 Roger Craig ............................... | 1.25 | .50 | .12 |
| ☐ 4 ProFiles .................................... | 1.25 | .50 | .12 |
| Television show | | | |
| (Craig James and | | | |
| Tim Brant) | | | |
| ☐ 5 Title card ................................. | 1.00 | .40 | .10 |

## 1991 Pro Set Promos

The Tele-Clinic card was given away as a promotion at Super Bowl XXV and was co-sponsored by NFL Pro Set, The Learning Channel, and Sports Illustrated for Kids. The card features a color photo on the front of an NFL player giving some football tips to a young kid. This card promotes the annual Super Bowl football clinic, in which current and former NFL stars talk to kids about football and life. The Super Bowl Card Show II card was issued in conjunction with the second annual Super Bowl show which was held in Tampa, Florida across the street from Tampa Stadium. The card is in the design on the Pro Set Super Bowl insert set from 1989 with a little inset on the bottom right hand corner of the card which states "Super Bowl Card Show II, January 24-27, 1991". The back of the card has information about the show and the other promotional activities which accompanied Super Bowl week. The Perry and Roberts cards were apparently planned but pulled from the Pro Bowl albums just prior to distribution. All of the above cards measure the standard card size, 2 1/2" by 3 1/2".

| | MINT | EXC | G-VG |
|---|---|---|---|
| COMPLETE SET (6) ........................... | 150.00 | 60.00 | 15.00 |
| COMMON CARD .............................. | 2.00 | .80 | .20 |
| ☐ NNO NFL Kids on the Block .......... | 2.00 | .80 | .20 |
| (Tele-Clinic) | | | |
| ☐ NNO Super Bowl XXV .................... | 6.00 | 2.40 | .60 |
| Card Show II | | | |
| ☐ NNO Michael Dean Perry .............. | 50.00 | 20.00 | 5.00 |
| Pro Bowl Special | | | |
| (unnumbered; without | | | |
| Pro Set logo) | | | |
| ☐ NNO Michael Dean Perry .............. | 75.00 | 30.00 | 7.50 |
| Pro Bowl Special | | | |
| (unnumbered; with | | | |
| Pro Set logo) | | | |
| ☐ NNO William Roberts ................... | 50.00 | 20.00 | 5.00 |
| Pro Bowl Special | | | |
| (unnumbered) | | | |
| ☐ NNO Emmitt Smith Gazette .......... | 3.00 | 1.20 | .30 |
| (Given away with Pro | | | |
| Set Gazette mail-out) | | | |

## 1991 Pro Set

The first series of 1991 Pro Set football cards contains 405 standard size (2 1/2" by 3 1/2") cards. The first series includes 54 various special cards to start the set in subsets which include the Pro Set Rookies of the Year (both of whom are numbered 1, therefore there is no card 2 in the set). Cards numbered 3 through 19 are various NFL leaders, while cards 20-26 celebrate various milestones reached during the 1990 season. Cards numbered 27 through 31 feature the 1991 inductees into the Hall of Fame with original art drawings by Merv Corning, while cards number 32 through 36 feature various college award winners. Cards number 37 through 45 honor various past winners of the Heisman trophy, while cards number 46 through 54 relate to Super Bowl XXV. From card number 55 through 324 the cards are sequenced in alphabetical order by team, which are also in alphabetical order (except for the two participants in the Super Bowl). The only card for each team which is not in alphabetical order is the coach card, which is always the final card in a team's sequence. The team lists are as follows, New York Giants (55-72), Buffalo Bills (73-

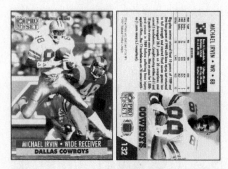

90), Atlanta Falcons (91-99), Chicago Bears (100-108), Cincinnati Bengals (109-117), Cleveland Browns (118-126), Dallas Cowboys (127-135), Denver Broncos (136-144), Detroit Lions (145-153), Green Bay Packers (154-162), Houston Oilers (163-171), Indianapolis Colts (172-180), Kansas City Chiefs (181-189), Los Angeles Raiders (190-198), Los Angeles Rams (199-207), Miami Dolphins (208-216), Minnesota Vikings (217-225), New England Patriots (226-234), New Orleans Saints (235-243), New York Jets (244-252), Philadelphia Eagles (253-261), Phoenix Cardinals (262-270), Pittsburgh Steelers (271-279), San Diego Chargers (280-288), San Francisco 49ers (289-297), Seattle Seahawks (298-306), Tampa Bay Buccaneers (307-315), Washington Redskins (316-324). There are also 18 cards which highlight some of the special games of the 1990 season (325-342). In addition, similar to the 1990 second series there is a newsreel subset. Other special features include an 18-card subset about NFL officals (352-369), nine cards in the mode begun by Ronnie Lott's (90PS-799) Stay in School Card (370-378), and 27 All-NFC drawings again drawn by artist Merv Corning. The second series of the 1991 Pro Set football set contains 407 cards measuring the standard size (2 1/2" by 3 1/2"). The front design features full-bleed glossy color action photos, with player identification and team name at the bottom in two colored stripes reflecting the team's colors. The horizontally oriented backs have a color head shot on the right side, with player profile and/or statistics on the right. The cards are numbered on the back. The second series begins with original artwork by Merv Corning of the All-AFC team (406-432). The player cards are then checklisted alphabetically within and according to teams as follows: Atlanta Falcons (433-441), Buffalo Bills (442-450), Chicago Bears (451-459), Cincinnati Bengals (460-468), Cleveland Browns (469-477), Dallas Cowboys (478-486), Denver Broncos (487-495), Detroit Lions (496-504), Green Bay Packers (505-513), Houston Oilers (514-522), Indianapolis Colts (523-531), Kansas City Chiefs (532-540), Los Angeles Raiders (541-549), Los Angeles Rams (550-558), Miami Dolphins (559-567), Minnesota Vikings (568-576), New England Patriots (577-585), New Orleans Saints (586-594), New York Giants (595-603), New York Jets (604-612), Philadelphia Eagles (613-621), Phoenix Cardinals (622-630), Pittsburgh Steelers (631-639), San Diego Chargers (640-648), San Francisco 49ers (649-657), Seattle Seahawks (658-666), Tampa Bay Buccaneers (667-675), and Washington Redskins (676-684). Additional subsets featured in the second series are NFL Newsreel (685-692), Legends (694-702), World League Leaders (703-711), Hall of Fame Photo Contest (712-720), Think About It (721-729), First-Round Draft Choices (730-756), Second-Round Draft Choices (757-772), and Third-Round Draft Choices (785-812). The 1991 Pro Set Final Update set features hot rookies, traded players, NFL Newsreel cards (813-815), and a Super Bowl XXV Theme Art card. Rookie Cards include Terry Allen, Ty Detmer, Ricky Ervins, Brett Favre, Jeff Graham, Alvin Harper, Mark Higgs, Raghib (Rocket) Ismail, Michael Jackson, Erik Kramer, Todd Marinovich, Russell Maryland, Dan McGwire, Herman Moore, Browning Nagle, Neil O'Donnell, Mike Pritchard, Leonard Russell, Tom Waddle, Ricky Watters, and Harvey Williams.

|  | MINT | EXC | G-VG |
|---|---|---|---|
| COMPLETE SET (850) | 18.00 | 8.00 | 2.30 |
| COMPLETE SERIES 1 (405) | 7.00 | 3.10 | .85 |
| COMPLETE SERIES 2 (407) | 7.00 | 3.10 | .85 |
| COMPLETE FINAL FACT. (38) | 4.00 | 1.80 | .50 |
| COMMON PLAYER (1-405) | .04 | .02 | .01 |
| COMMON PLAYER (406-812) | .04 | .02 | .01 |
| COMMON PLAYER (813-850) | .05 | .02 | .01 |
| ☐ 1D Mark Carrier | .04 | .02 | .01 |
| Defensive ROY |  |  |  |
| ☐ 10 Emmitt Smith | 1.00 | .45 | .13 |
| Offensive ROY |  |  |  |
| ☐ 2 Does Not Exist | .00 | .00 | .00 |
| ☐ 3 Joe Montana | .50 | .23 | .06 |
| NFL Player of the Year |  |  |  |

| ☐ 4 Art Shell | .08 | .04 | .01 |
|---|---|---|---|
| NFL Coach of the Year |  |  |  |
| ☐ 5 Mike Singletary | .08 | .04 | .01 |
| NFL Man of the Year |  |  |  |
| ☐ 6 Bruce Smith | .08 | .04 | .01 |
| NFL Defensive Player of the Year |  |  |  |
| ☐ 7 Barry Word | .08 | .04 | .01 |
| NFL Comeback Player of the Year |  |  |  |
| ☐ 8A Jim Kelly | .20 | .09 | .03 |
| NFL Passing Leader (NFLPA logo on back) |  |  |  |
| ☐ 8B Jim Kelly | .15 | .07 | .02 |
| NFL Passing Leader (No NFLPA logo on back) |  |  |  |
| ☐ 8C Jim Kelly | 10.00 | 4.50 | 1.25 |
| NFL Passing Leader (No NFLPA logo on back but the registered symbol remains) |  |  |  |
| ☐ 9 Warren Moon | .10 | .05 | .01 |
| NFL Passing Yardage and TD Leader |  |  |  |
| ☐ 10 Barry Sanders | .35 | .16 | .04 |
| NFL Rushing and TD Leader |  |  |  |
| ☐ 11 Jerry Rice | .35 | .16 | .04 |
| NFL Receiving and Receiving Yardage Leader |  |  |  |
| ☐ 12 Jay Novacek | .08 | .04 | .01 |
| Tight End Leader |  |  |  |
| ☐ 13 Thurman Thomas | .20 | .09 | .03 |
| NFL Total Yardage Leader |  |  |  |
| ☐ 14 Nick Lowery | .04 | .02 | .01 |
| NFL Scoring Leader, Kickers |  |  |  |
| ☐ 15 Mike Horan | .04 | .02 | .01 |
| NFL Punting Leader |  |  |  |
| ☐ 16 Clarence Verdin | .04 | .02 | .01 |
| NFL Punt Return Leader |  |  |  |
| ☐ 17 Kevin Clark | .04 | .02 | .01 |
| NFL Kickoff Return Leader |  |  |  |
| ☐ 18 Mark Carrier | .04 | .02 | .01 |
| NFL Interception Leader |  |  |  |
| ☐ 19A Derrick Thomas ERR | 18.00 | 8.00 | 2.30 |
| NFL Sack Leader (Bills helmet on front) |  |  |  |
| ☐ 19B Derrick Thomas COR | .15 | .07 | .02 |
| NFL Sack Leader (Chiefs helmet on front) |  |  |  |
| ☐ 20 Ottis Anderson ML | .08 | .04 | .01 |
| 10000 Career Rushing Yards |  |  |  |
| ☐ 21 Roger Craig ML | .08 | .04 | .01 |
| Most Career Receptions by RB |  |  |  |
| ☐ 22 Art Monk ML | .08 | .04 | .01 |
| 700 Career Receptions |  |  |  |
| ☐ 23 Chuck Noll ML | .08 | .04 | .01 |
| 200 Victories |  |  |  |
| ☐ 24 Randall Cunningham ML | .08 | .04 | .01 |
| Leads team in rushing, fourth straight year UER (586 rushes, should be 486; average 5.9, should be 7.1) |  |  |  |
| ☐ 25 Dan Marino ML | .35 | .16 | .04 |
| 7th Straight 3000 yard season |  |  |  |
| ☐ 26 49ers Road Record ML | .04 | .02 | .01 |
| 18 victories in row, still alive |  |  |  |
| ☐ 27 Earl Campbell HOF | .10 | .05 | .01 |
| ☐ 28 John Hannah HOF | .04 | .02 | .01 |
| ☐ 29 Stan Jones HOF | .04 | .02 | .01 |
| ☐ 30 Tex Schramm HOF | .04 | .02 | .01 |
| ☐ 31 Jan Stenerud HOF | .04 | .02 | .01 |
| ☐ 32 Russell Maryland | .40 | .18 | .05 |
| Outland Winner |  |  |  |
| ☐ 33 Chris Zorich | .25 | .11 | .03 |
| Lombardi Winner |  |  |  |
| ☐ 34 Darryll Lewis UER | .10 | .05 | .01 |
| Thorpe Winner (Name misspelled Darryl on card) |  |  |  |
| ☐ 35 Alfred Williams | .15 | .07 | .02 |
| Butkus Winner |  |  |  |
| ☐ 36 Raghib(Rocket) Ismail | 2.00 | .90 | .25 |
| Walter Camp POY |  |  |  |
| ☐ 37 Ty Detmer HH | .75 | .35 | .09 |
| ☐ 38 Andre Ware HH | .10 | .05 | .01 |
| ☐ 39 Barry Sanders HH | .35 | .16 | .04 |

| | | | |
|---|---|---|---|
| ☐ 40 Tim Brown HH UER | .15 | .07 | .02 |
| (No "Official Photo and Stat Card of the NFL" on card back) | | | |
| ☐ 41 Vinny Testaverde HH | .04 | .02 | .01 |
| ☐ 42 Bo Jackson HH | .15 | .07 | .02 |
| ☐ 43 Mike Rozier HH | .04 | .02 | .01 |
| ☐ 44 Herschel Walker HH | .08 | .04 | .01 |
| ☐ 45 Marcus Allen HH | .08 | .04 | .01 |
| ☐ 46A James Lofton SB | .12 | .05 | .02 |
| (NFLPA logo on back) | | | |
| ☐ 46B James Lofton SB | .09 | .04 | .01 |
| (No NFLPA logo on back) | | | |
| ☐ 47A Bruce Smith SB | .15 | .07 | .02 |
| (Official NFL Card in black letters) | | | |
| ☐ 47B Bruce Smith SB | .10 | .05 | .01 |
| (Official NFL Card in white letters) | | | |
| ☐ 48 Myron Guyton SB | .04 | .02 | .01 |
| ☐ 49 Stephen Baker SB | .04 | .02 | .01 |
| ☐ 50 Mark Ingram SB UER | .04 | .02 | .01 |
| (First repeated twice on back title) | | | |
| ☐ 51 Ottis Anderson SB | .08 | .04 | .01 |
| ☐ 52 Thurman Thomas SB | .20 | .09 | .03 |
| ☐ 53 Matt Bahr SB | .04 | .02 | .01 |
| ☐ 54 Scott Norwood SB | .04 | .02 | .01 |
| ☐ 55 Stephen Baker | .04 | .02 | .01 |
| ☐ 56 Carl Banks | .08 | .04 | .01 |
| ☐ 57 Mark Collins | .04 | .02 | .01 |
| ☐ 58 Steve DeOssie | .04 | .02 | .01 |
| ☐ 59 Eric Dorsey | .04 | .02 | .01 |
| ☐ 60 John Elliott | .04 | .02 | .01 |
| ☐ 61 Myron Guyton | .04 | .02 | .01 |
| ☐ 62 Rodney Hampton | .75 | .35 | .09 |
| ☐ 63 Jeff Hostetler | .25 | .11 | .03 |
| ☐ 64 Erik Howard | .04 | .02 | .01 |
| ☐ 65 Mark Ingram | .08 | .04 | .01 |
| ☐ 66 Greg Jackson | .10 | .05 | .01 |
| ☐ 67 Leonard Marshall | .08 | .04 | .01 |
| ☐ 68 David Meggett | .10 | .05 | .01 |
| ☐ 69 Eric Moore | .04 | .02 | .01 |
| ☐ 70 Bart Oates | .04 | .02 | .01 |
| ☐ 71 Gary Reasons | .04 | .02 | .01 |
| ☐ 72 Bill Parcells CO | .08 | .04 | .01 |
| ☐ 73 Howard Ballard | .04 | .02 | .01 |
| ☐ 74A Cornelius Bennett | .30 | .14 | .04 |
| (NFLPA logo on back) | | | |
| ☐ 74B Cornelius Bennett | .10 | .05 | .01 |
| (No NFLPA logo on back) | | | |
| ☐ 75 Shane Conlan | .08 | .04 | .01 |
| ☐ 76 Kent Hull | .04 | .02 | .01 |
| ☐ 77 Kirby Jackson | .04 | .02 | .01 |
| ☐ 78A Jim Kelly | .60 | .25 | .08 |
| (NFLPA logo on back) | | | |
| ☐ 78B Jim Kelly | .30 | .14 | .04 |
| (No NFLPA logo on back) | | | |
| ☐ 79 Mark Kelso | .04 | .02 | .01 |
| ☐ 80 Nate Odomes | .10 | .05 | .01 |
| ☐ 81 Andre Reed | .10 | .05 | .01 |
| ☐ 82 Jim Ritcher | .04 | .02 | .01 |
| ☐ 83 Bruce Smith | .10 | .05 | .01 |
| ☐ 84 Darryl Talley | .08 | .04 | .01 |
| ☐ 85 Steve Tasker | .08 | .04 | .01 |
| ☐ 86 Thurman Thomas | .40 | .18 | .05 |
| ☐ 87 James Williams | .04 | .02 | .01 |
| ☐ 88 Will Wolford | .04 | .02 | .01 |
| ☐ 89 Jeff Wright UER | .10 | .05 | .01 |
| (Went to Central Missouri State, not Central Missouri) | | | |
| ☐ 90 Marv Levy CO | .08 | .04 | .01 |
| ☐ 91 Steve Broussard | .08 | .04 | .01 |
| ☐ 92A Darion Conner ERR | 10.00 | 4.50 | 1.25 |
| (Drafted 1st round, '99) | | | |
| ☐ 92B Darion Conner COR | .10 | .05 | .01 |
| (Drafted 2nd round, '90) | | | |
| ☐ 93 Bill Fralic | .04 | .02 | .01 |
| ☐ 94 Tim Green | .04 | .02 | .01 |
| ☐ 95 Michael Haynes | .04 | .02 | .01 |
| ☐ 96 Chris Hinton | .04 | .02 | .01 |
| ☐ 97 Chris Miller UER | .10 | .05 | .01 |
| (Two commas after city in his birth info) | | | |
| ☐ 98 Deion Sanders UER | .25 | .11 | .03 |
| (Career TD's 3, but only 2 in yearly stats) | | | |
| ☐ 99 Jerry Glanville CO | .04 | .02 | .01 |
| ☐ 100 Kevin Butler | .04 | .02 | .01 |
| ☐ 101 Mark Carrier | .08 | .04 | .01 |
| ☐ 102 Jim Covert | .04 | .02 | .01 |
| ☐ 103 Richard Dent | .08 | .04 | .01 |
| ☐ 104 Jim Harbaugh | .08 | .04 | .01 |
| ☐ 105 Brad Muster | .08 | .04 | .01 |
| ☐ 106 Lemuel Stinson | .04 | .02 | .01 |
| ☐ 107 Keith Van Horne | .04 | .02 | .01 |
| ☐ 108 Mike Ditka CO UER | .10 | .05 | .01 |
| (Winning percent in '87 was .733, not .753) | | | |
| ☐ 109 Lewis Billups | .04 | .02 | .01 |
| ☐ 110 James Brooks | .08 | .04 | .01 |
| ☐ 111 Boomer Esiason | .15 | .07 | .02 |
| ☐ 112 James Francis | .08 | .04 | .01 |
| ☐ 113 David Fulcher | .04 | .02 | .01 |
| ☐ 114 Rodney Holman | .04 | .02 | .01 |
| ☐ 115 Tim McGee | .04 | .02 | .01 |
| ☐ 116 Anthony Munoz | .08 | .04 | .01 |
| ☐ 117 Sam Wyche CO | .04 | .02 | .01 |
| ☐ 118 Paul Farren | .04 | .02 | .01 |
| ☐ 119 Thane Gash | .04 | .02 | .01 |
| ☐ 120 Mike Johnson | .04 | .02 | .01 |
| ☐ 121A Bernie Kosar | .14 | .06 | .02 |
| (NFLPA logo on back) | | | |
| ☐ 121B Bernie Kosar | .14 | .06 | .02 |
| (No NFLPA logo on back) | | | |
| ☐ 122 Clay Matthews | .08 | .04 | .01 |
| ☐ 123 Eric Metcalf | .10 | .05 | .01 |
| ☐ 124 Frank Minnifield | .04 | .02 | .01 |
| ☐ 125A Webster Slaughter | .08 | .04 | .01 |
| (NFLPA logo on back) | | | |
| ☐ 125B Webster Slaughter | .09 | .04 | .01 |
| (No NFLPA logo on back) | | | |
| ☐ 126 Bill Belichick CO | .04 | .02 | .01 |
| ☐ 127 Tommie Agee | .04 | .02 | .01 |
| ☐ 128 Troy Aikman | 1.25 | .55 | .16 |
| ☐ 129 Jack Del Rio | .04 | .02 | .01 |
| ☐ 130 John Gesek | .08 | .04 | .01 |
| ☐ 131 Issiac Holt | .04 | .02 | .01 |
| ☐ 132 Michael Irvin | .50 | .23 | .06 |
| ☐ 133 Ken Norton | .10 | .05 | .01 |
| ☐ 134 Daniel Stubbs | .04 | .02 | .01 |
| ☐ 135 Jimmy Johnson CO | .08 | .04 | .01 |
| ☐ 136 Steve Atwater | .10 | .05 | .01 |
| ☐ 137 Michael Brooks | .04 | .02 | .01 |
| ☐ 138 John Elway | .35 | .16 | .04 |
| ☐ 139 Wymon Henderson | .04 | .02 | .01 |
| ☐ 140 Bobby Humphrey | .08 | .04 | .01 |
| ☐ 141 Mark Jackson | .08 | .04 | .01 |
| ☐ 142 Karl Mecklenburg | .08 | .04 | .01 |
| ☐ 143 Doug Widell | .04 | .02 | .01 |
| ☐ 144 Dan Reeves CO | .08 | .04 | .01 |
| ☐ 145 Eric Andolsek | .04 | .02 | .01 |
| ☐ 146 Jerry Ball | .04 | .02 | .01 |
| ☐ 147 Bennie Blades | .04 | .02 | .01 |
| ☐ 148 Lomas Brown | .04 | .02 | .01 |
| ☐ 149 Robert Clark | .04 | .02 | .01 |
| ☐ 150 Michael Cofer | .04 | .02 | .01 |
| ☐ 151 Dan Owens | .04 | .02 | .01 |
| ☐ 152 Rodney Peete | .08 | .04 | .01 |
| ☐ 153 Wayne Fontes CO | .04 | .02 | .01 |
| ☐ 154 Tim Harris | .08 | .04 | .01 |
| ☐ 155 Johnny Holland | .04 | .02 | .01 |
| ☐ 156 Don Majkowski | .08 | .04 | .01 |
| ☐ 157 Tony Mandarich | .04 | .02 | .01 |
| ☐ 158 Mark Murphy | .04 | .02 | .01 |
| ☐ 159 Brian Noble | .04 | .02 | .01 |
| ☐ 160 Jeff Query | .04 | .02 | .01 |
| ☐ 161 Sterling Sharpe | .50 | .23 | .06 |
| ☐ 162 Lindy Infante CO | .04 | .02 | .01 |
| ☐ 163 Ray Childress | .08 | .04 | .01 |
| ☐ 164 Ernest Givins | .08 | .04 | .01 |
| ☐ 165 Richard Johnson | .04 | .02 | .01 |
| ☐ 166 Bruce Matthews | .08 | .04 | .01 |
| ☐ 167 Warren Moon | .20 | .09 | .03 |
| ☐ 168 Mike Munchak | .08 | .04 | .01 |
| ☐ 169 Al Smith | .04 | .02 | .01 |
| ☐ 170 Lorenzo White | .08 | .04 | .01 |
| ☐ 171 Jack Pardee CO | .04 | .02 | .01 |
| ☐ 172 Albert Bentley | .04 | .02 | .01 |
| ☐ 173 Duane Bickett | .04 | .02 | .01 |
| ☐ 174 Bill Brooks | .08 | .04 | .01 |
| ☐ 175A Eric Dickerson | .40 | .18 | .05 |
| (NFLPA logo on back) | | | |
| ☐ 175B Eric Dickerson | 1.25 | .55 | .16 |
| (No NFLPA logo on back and 667 yards rushing for 1990 in text) | | | |
| ☐ 175C Eric Dickerson | .25 | .11 | .03 |
| (No NFLPA logo on back and 677 yards rushing for 1990 in text) | | | |
| ☐ 176 Ray Donaldson | .04 | .02 | .01 |
| ☐ 177 Jeff George | .25 | .11 | .03 |
| ☐ 178 Jeff Herrod | .04 | .02 | .01 |
| ☐ 179 Clarence Verdin | .04 | .02 | .01 |
| ☐ 180 Ron Meyer CO | .04 | .02 | .01 |
| ☐ 181 John Alt | .04 | .02 | .01 |
| ☐ 182 Steve DeBerg | .08 | .04 | .01 |
| ☐ 183 Albert Lewis | .08 | .04 | .01 |
| ☐ 184 Nick Lowery UER | .08 | .04 | .01 |
| (In his 13th year, not 12th) | | | |
| ☐ 185 Christian Okoye | .08 | .04 | .01 |

| | | | |
|---|---|---|---|
| ☐ 186 Stephone Paige | .08 | .04 | .01 |
| ☐ 187 Kevin Porter | .04 | .02 | .01 |
| ☐ 188 Derrick Thomas | .25 | .11 | .03 |
| ☐ 189 Marty Schottenheimer CO | .04 | .02 | .01 |
| ☐ 190 Willie Gault | .08 | .04 | .01 |
| ☐ 191 Howie Long | .08 | .04 | .01 |
| ☐ 192 Terry McDaniel | .04 | .02 | .01 |
| ☐ 193 Jay Schroeder UER | .08 | .04 | .01 |
| (Passing total yards 13863, should be 13683) | | | |
| ☐ 194 Steve Smith | .08 | .04 | .01 |
| ☐ 195 Greg Townsend | .04 | .02 | .01 |
| ☐ 196 Lionel Washington | .04 | .02 | .01 |
| ☐ 197 Steve Wisniewski UER | .04 | .02 | .01 |
| (Back says drafted, should say traded to) | | | |
| ☐ 198 Art Shell CO | .08 | .04 | .01 |
| ☐ 199 Henry Ellard | .08 | .04 | .01 |
| ☐ 200 Jim Everett | .08 | .04 | .01 |
| ☐ 201 Jerry Gray | .04 | .02 | .01 |
| ☐ 202 Kevin Greene | .08 | .04 | .01 |
| ☐ 203 Buford McGee | .04 | .02 | .01 |
| ☐ 204 Tom Newberry | .04 | .02 | .01 |
| ☐ 205 Frank Stams | .04 | .02 | .01 |
| ☐ 206 Alvin Wright | .04 | .02 | .01 |
| ☐ 207 John Robinson CO | .04 | .02 | .01 |
| ☐ 208 Jeff Cross | .04 | .02 | .01 |
| ☐ 209 Mark Duper | .08 | .04 | .01 |
| ☐ 210 Dan Marino | .75 | .35 | .09 |
| ☐ 211A Tim McKyer | .25 | .11 | .03 |
| (No Traded box on front) | | | |
| ☐ 211B Tim McKyer | .10 | .05 | .01 |
| (Traded box on front) | | | |
| ☐ 212 John Offerdahl | .08 | .04 | .01 |
| ☐ 213 Sammie Smith | .04 | .02 | .01 |
| ☐ 214 Richmond Webb | .08 | .04 | .01 |
| ☐ 215 Jarvis Williams | .04 | .02 | .01 |
| ☐ 216 Don Shula CO | .08 | .04 | .01 |
| ☐ 217A Darrell Fullington | .08 | .04 | .01 |
| ERR (No registered symbol on card back) | | | |
| ☐ 217B Darrell Fullington | .08 | .04 | .01 |
| COR (Registered symbol on card back) | | | |
| ☐ 218 Tim Irwin | .04 | .02 | .01 |
| ☐ 219 Mike Merriweather | .04 | .02 | .01 |
| ☐ 220 Keith Millard | .08 | .04 | .01 |
| ☐ 221 Al Noga | .04 | .02 | .01 |
| ☐ 222 Henry Thomas | .04 | .02 | .01 |
| ☐ 223 Wade Wilson | .08 | .04 | .01 |
| ☐ 224 Gary Zimmerman | .04 | .02 | .01 |
| ☐ 225 Jerry Burns CO | .04 | .02 | .01 |
| ☐ 226 Bruce Armstrong | .04 | .02 | .01 |
| ☐ 227 Marv Cook | .04 | .02 | .01 |
| ☐ 228 Hart Lee Dykes | .04 | .02 | .01 |
| ☐ 229 Tommy Hodson | .04 | .02 | .01 |
| ☐ 230 Ronnie Lippett | .04 | .02 | .01 |
| ☐ 231 Ed Reynolds | .04 | .02 | .01 |
| ☐ 232 Chris Singleton | .04 | .02 | .01 |
| ☐ 233 John Stephens | .08 | .04 | .01 |
| ☐ 234 Dick MacPherson CO | .04 | .02 | .01 |
| ☐ 235 Stan Brock | .04 | .02 | .01 |
| ☐ 236 Craig Heyward | .04 | .02 | .01 |
| ☐ 237 Vaughan Johnson | .08 | .04 | .01 |
| ☐ 238 Robert Massey | .04 | .02 | .01 |
| ☐ 239 Brett Maxie | .04 | .02 | .01 |
| ☐ 240 Rueben Mayes | .04 | .02 | .01 |
| ☐ 241 Pat Swilling | .08 | .04 | .01 |
| ☐ 242 Renaldo Turnbull | .08 | .04 | .01 |
| ☐ 243 Jim Mora CO | .04 | .02 | .01 |
| ☐ 244 Kyle Clifton | .04 | .02 | .01 |
| ☐ 245 Jeff Criswell | .04 | .02 | .01 |
| ☐ 246 James Hasty | .04 | .02 | .01 |
| ☐ 247 Erik McMillan | .04 | .02 | .01 |
| ☐ 248 Scott Mersereau | .04 | .02 | .01 |
| ☐ 249 Ken O'Brien | .08 | .04 | .01 |
| ☐ 250A Blair Thomas | .35 | .16 | .04 |
| (NFLPA logo on back) | | | |
| ☐ 250B Blair Thomas | .15 | .07 | .02 |
| (No NFLPA logo on back) | | | |
| ☐ 251 Al Toon | .08 | .04 | .01 |
| ☐ 252 Bruce Coslet CO | .04 | .02 | .01 |
| ☐ 253 Eric Allen | .08 | .04 | .01 |
| ☐ 254 Fred Barnett | .15 | .07 | .02 |
| ☐ 255 Keith Byars | .08 | .04 | .01 |
| ☐ 256 Randall Cunningham | .10 | .05 | .01 |
| ☐ 257 Seth Joyner | .08 | .04 | .01 |
| ☐ 258 Clyde Simmons | .08 | .04 | .01 |
| ☐ 259 Jessie Small | .04 | .02 | .01 |
| ☐ 260 Andre Waters | .04 | .02 | .01 |
| ☐ 261 Rich Kotite CO | .04 | .02 | .01 |
| ☐ 262 Roy Green | .08 | .04 | .01 |
| ☐ 263 Ernie Jones | .04 | .02 | .01 |
| ☐ 264 Tim McDonald | .08 | .04 | .01 |
| ☐ 265 Timm Rosenbach | .08 | .04 | .01 |
| ☐ 266 Rod Saddler | .04 | .02 | .01 |

| | | | |
|---|---|---|---|
| ☐ 267 Luis Sharpe | .04 | .02 | .01 |
| ☐ 268 Anthony Thompson UER | .04 | .02 | .01 |
| (Terra Haute should be Terre Haute) | | | |
| ☐ 269 Marcus Turner | .10 | .05 | .01 |
| ☐ 270 Joe Bugel CO | .04 | .02 | .01 |
| ☐ 271 Gary Anderson | .04 | .02 | .01 |
| ☐ 272 Dermontti Dawson | .04 | .02 | .01 |
| ☐ 273 Eric Green | .15 | .07 | .02 |
| ☐ 274 Merril Hoge | .08 | .04 | .01 |
| ☐ 275 Tunch Ilkin | .04 | .02 | .01 |
| ☐ 276 David Johnson | .04 | .02 | .01 |
| ☐ 277 Louis Lipps | .08 | .04 | .01 |
| ☐ 278 Rod Woodson | .10 | .05 | .01 |
| ☐ 279 Chuck Noll CO | .08 | .04 | .01 |
| ☐ 280 Martin Bayless | .04 | .02 | .01 |
| ☐ 281 Marion Butts UER | .10 | .05 | .01 |
| (2 years exp., should be 3) | | | |
| ☐ 282 Gill Byrd | .08 | .04 | .01 |
| ☐ 283 Burt Grossman | .04 | .02 | .01 |
| ☐ 284 Courtney Hall | .04 | .02 | .01 |
| ☐ 285 Anthony Miller | .20 | .09 | .03 |
| ☐ 286 Leslie O'Neal | .08 | .04 | .01 |
| ☐ 287 Billy Joe Tolliver | .08 | .04 | .01 |
| ☐ 288 Dan Henning CO | .04 | .02 | .01 |
| ☐ 289 Dexter Carter | .08 | .04 | .01 |
| ☐ 290 Michael Carter | .04 | .02 | .01 |
| ☐ 291 Kevin Fagan | .04 | .02 | .01 |
| ☐ 292 Pierce Holt | .04 | .02 | .01 |
| ☐ 293 Guy McIntyre | .08 | .04 | .01 |
| (Joe Montana also in photo) | | | |
| ☐ 294 Tom Rathman | .04 | .04 | .01 |
| ☐ 295 John Taylor | .10 | .05 | .01 |
| ☐ 296 Steve Young | .50 | .23 | .06 |
| ☐ 297 George Seifert CO | .08 | .04 | .01 |
| ☐ 298 Brian Blades | .10 | .05 | .01 |
| ☐ 299 Jeff Bryant | .04 | .02 | .01 |
| ☐ 300 Norm Johnson | .04 | .02 | .01 |
| ☐ 301 Tommy Kane | .04 | .02 | .01 |
| ☐ 302 Cortez Kennedy UER | .25 | .11 | .03 |
| (Played for Seattle in '90, not Miami) | | | |
| ☐ 303 Bryan Millard | .04 | .02 | .01 |
| ☐ 304 John L. Williams | .08 | .04 | .01 |
| ☐ 305 David Wyman | .04 | .02 | .01 |
| ☐ 306A Chuck Knox CO ERR | .08 | .04 | .01 |
| (Has NFLPA logo, but should not) | | | |
| ☐ 306B Chuck Knox CO COR | .50 | .23 | .06 |
| (No NFLPA logo on back) | | | |
| ☐ 307 Gary Anderson | .08 | .04 | .01 |
| ☐ 308 Reggie Cobb | .25 | .11 | .03 |
| ☐ 309 Randy Grimes | .04 | .02 | .01 |
| ☐ 310 Harry Hamilton | .04 | .02 | .01 |
| ☐ 311 Bruce Hill | .04 | .02 | .01 |
| ☐ 312 Eugene Marve | .04 | .02 | .01 |
| ☐ 313 Ervin Randle | .04 | .02 | .01 |
| ☐ 314 Vinny Testaverde | .10 | .05 | .01 |
| ☐ 315 Richard Williamson CO UER (Coach: 1st year, should be 2nd year) | .04 | .02 | .01 |
| ☐ 316 Earnest Byner | .08 | .04 | .01 |
| ☐ 317 Gary Clark | .08 | .04 | .01 |
| ☐ 318A Andre Collins | .08 | .04 | .01 |
| (NFLPA logo on back) | | | |
| ☐ 318B Andre Collins | .05 | .02 | .01 |
| (No NFLPA logo on back) | | | |
| ☐ 319 Darryl Grant | .04 | .02 | .01 |
| ☐ 320 Chip Lohmiller | .08 | .04 | .01 |
| ☐ 321 Martin Mayhew | .04 | .02 | .01 |
| ☐ 322 Mark Rypien | .10 | .05 | .01 |
| ☐ 323 Alvin Walton | .04 | .02 | .01 |
| ☐ 324 Joe Gibbs CO UER | .08 | .04 | .01 |
| (Has registered symbol but should not) | | | |
| ☐ 325 Jerry Glanville REP | .04 | .02 | .01 |
| ☐ 326A John Elway REP | .08 | .04 | .01 |
| (NFLPA logo on back) | | | |
| ☐ 326B John Elway REP | .05 | .02 | .01 |
| (No NFLPA logo on back) | | | |
| ☐ 327 Boomer Esiason REP | .08 | .04 | .01 |
| ☐ 328A Steve Tasker REP | .08 | .04 | .01 |
| (NFLPA logo on back) | | | |
| ☐ 328B Steve Tasker REP | .05 | .02 | .01 |
| (No NFLPA logo on back) | | | |
| ☐ 329 Jerry Rice REP | .35 | .16 | .04 |
| ☐ 330 Jeff Rutledge REP | .04 | .02 | .01 |
| ☐ 331 K.C. Defense REP | .04 | .02 | .01 |
| ☐ 332 49ers Streak REP (Cleveland Gary) | .04 | .02 | .01 |
| ☐ 333 Monday Meeting REP (John Taylor) | .04 | .02 | .01 |
| ☐ 334A Randall Cunningham REP (NFLPA logo on back) | .15 | .07 | .02 |
| ☐ 334B Randall Cunningham | .15 | .07 | .02 |

| | | | |
|---|---|---|---|
| REP | | | |
| (No NFLPA logo on back) | | | |
| ☐ 335A Bo Jackson and ... | .50 | .23 | .06 |
| Barry Sanders REP | | | |
| (NFLPA logo on back) | | | |
| ☐ 335B Bo Jackson and ... | .35 | .16 | .04 |
| Barry Sanders REP | | | |
| (No NFLPA logo on back) | | | |
| ☐ 336 Lawrence Taylor REP | .04 | .02 | .01 |
| ☐ 337 Warren Moon REP | .10 | .05 | .01 |
| ☐ 338 Alan Grant REP | .04 | .02 | .01 |
| ☐ 339 Todd McNair REP | .04 | .02 | .01 |
| ☐ 340A Miami Dolphins REP | .04 | .02 | .01 |
| (Mark Clayton; | | | |
| TM symbol on Chiefs | | | |
| player's shoulder) | | | |
| ☐ 340B Miami Dolphins REP | .04 | .02 | .01 |
| (Mark Clayton; | | | |
| TM symbol off Chiefs | | | |
| player's shoulder) | | | |
| ☐ 341A Highest Scoring REP | .08 | .04 | .01 |
| Jim Kelly Passing | | | |
| (NFLPA logo on back) | | | |
| ☐ 341B Highest Scoring REP | .05 | .02 | .01 |
| Jim Kelly Passing | | | |
| (No NFLPA logo on back) | | | |
| ☐ 342 Matt Bahr REP | .04 | .02 | .01 |
| ☐ 343 Robert Tisch NEW | .04 | .02 | .01 |
| (With Wellington Mara) | | | |
| ☐ 344 Sam Jankovich NEW | .04 | .02 | .01 |
| ☐ 345 In-the-Grasp NEW | .08 | .04 | .01 |
| (John Elway) | | | |
| ☐ 346 Bo Jackson NEW | .15 | .07 | .02 |
| (Career in Jeopardy) | | | |
| ☐ 347 NFL Teacher of the | .04 | .02 | .01 |
| Year Jack Williams | | | |
| with Paul Tagliabue | | | |
| ☐ 348 Ronnie Lott NEW | .08 | .04 | .01 |
| (Plan B Free Agent) | | | |
| ☐ 349 Super Bowl XXV | .04 | .02 | .01 |
| Teleclinic NEW (Greg | | | |
| Gumbel with Warren | | | |
| Moon, Derrick Thomas, | | | |
| and Wade Wilson) | | | |
| ☐ 350 Whitney Houston NEW | .15 | .07 | .02 |
| ☐ 351 U.S. Troops in | .04 | .02 | .01 |
| Saudia Arabia NEW | | | |
| (Troops watching TV | | | |
| with gas masks) | | | |
| ☐ 352 Art McNally OFF | .04 | .02 | .01 |
| ☐ 353 Dick Jorgensen OFF | .04 | .02 | .01 |
| ☐ 354 Jerry Seeman OFF | .04 | .02 | .01 |
| ☐ 355 Jim Tunney OFF | .04 | .02 | .01 |
| ☐ 356 Gerry Austin OFF | .04 | .02 | .01 |
| ☐ 357 Gene Barth OFF | .04 | .02 | .01 |
| ☐ 358 Red Cashion OFF | .04 | .02 | .01 |
| ☐ 359 Tom Dooley OFF | .04 | .02 | .01 |
| ☐ 360 Johnny Grier OFF | .04 | .02 | .01 |
| ☐ 361 Pat Haggerty OFF | .04 | .02 | .01 |
| ☐ 362 Dale Hamer OFF | .04 | .02 | .01 |
| ☐ 363 Dick Hantak OFF | .04 | .02 | .01 |
| ☐ 364 Jerry Markbreit OFF | .04 | .02 | .01 |
| ☐ 365 Gordon McCarter OFF | .04 | .02 | .01 |
| ☐ 366 Bob McElwee OFF | .04 | .02 | .01 |
| ☐ 367 Howard Roe OFF | .04 | .02 | .01 |
| (Illustrations on back | | | |
| smaller than other | | | |
| officials' cards) | | | |
| ☐ 368 Tom White OFF | .04 | .02 | .01 |
| ☐ 369 Norm Schachter OFF | .04 | .02 | .01 |
| ☐ 370A Warren Moon | .15 | .07 | .02 |
| Crack Kills | | | |
| (Small type on back) | | | |
| ☐ 370B Warren Moon | .10 | .05 | .01 |
| Crack Kills | | | |
| (Large type on back) | | | |
| ☐ 371A Boomer Esiason | .06 | .03 | .01 |
| Don't Drink | | | |
| (Small type on back) | | | |
| ☐ 371B Boomer Esiason | .08 | .04 | .01 |
| Don't Drink | | | |
| (Large type on back) | | | |
| ☐ 372A Troy Aikman | .60 | .25 | .08 |
| Play It Straight | | | |
| (Small type on back) | | | |
| ☐ 372B Troy Aikman | .60 | .25 | .08 |
| Play It Straight | | | |
| (Large type on back) | | | |
| ☐ 373A Carl Banks | .06 | .03 | .01 |
| Read | | | |
| (Small type on back) | | | |
| ☐ 373B Carl Banks | .04 | .02 | .01 |
| Read | | | |
| (Large type on back) | | | |
| ☐ 374A Jim Everett | .06 | .03 | .01 |
| Study | | | |
| (Small type on back) | | | |
| ☐ 374B Jim Everett | .04 | .02 | .01 |

| | | | |
|---|---|---|---|
| Study | | | |
| (Large type on back) | | | |
| ☐ 375A Anthony Munoz | .25 | .11 | .03 |
| Quadante en la Escuela | | | |
| (Dificul; small type) | | | |
| ☐ 375B Anthony Munoz | .25 | .11 | .03 |
| Quadante en la Escuela | | | |
| (Dificil; small type) | | | |
| ☐ 375C Anthony Munoz | .25 | .11 | .03 |
| Quadante en la Escuela | | | |
| (Dificil; large type) | | | |
| ☐ 375D Anthony Munoz | .10 | .05 | .01 |
| Quedate en la Escuela | | | |
| (Large type) | | | |
| ☐ 376A Ray Childress | .06 | .03 | .01 |
| Don't Pollute | | | |
| (Small type on back) | | | |
| ☐ 376B Ray Childress | .04 | .02 | .01 |
| Don't Pollute | | | |
| (Large type on back) | | | |
| ☐ 377A Charles Mann | .06 | .03 | .01 |
| Steroids Destroy | | | |
| (Small type on back) | | | |
| ☐ 377B Charles Mann | .04 | .02 | .01 |
| Steroids Destroy | | | |
| (Large type on back) | | | |
| ☐ 378A Jackie Slater | .06 | .03 | .01 |
| Keep the Peace | | | |
| (Small type on back) | | | |
| ☐ 378B Jackie Slater | .04 | .02 | .01 |
| Keep the Peace | | | |
| (Large type on back) | | | |
| ☐ 379 Jerry Rice NFC | .35 | .16 | .04 |
| ☐ 380 Andre Rison NFC | .12 | .05 | .02 |
| ☐ 381 Jim Lachey NFC | .04 | .02 | .01 |
| ☐ 382 Jackie Slater NFC | .04 | .02 | .01 |
| ☐ 383 Randall McDaniel NFC | .04 | .02 | .01 |
| ☐ 384 Mark Bortz NFC | .04 | .02 | .01 |
| ☐ 385 Jay Hilgenberg NFC | .04 | .02 | .01 |
| ☐ 386 Keith Jackson NFC | .08 | .04 | .01 |
| ☐ 387 Joe Montana NFC | .50 | .23 | .06 |
| ☐ 388 Barry Sanders NFC | .35 | .16 | .04 |
| ☐ 389 Neal Anderson NFC | .04 | .02 | .01 |
| ☐ 390 Reggie White NFC | .08 | .04 | .01 |
| ☐ 391 Chris Doleman NFC | .04 | .02 | .01 |
| ☐ 392 Jerome Brown NFC | .08 | .04 | .01 |
| ☐ 393 Charles Haley NFC | .04 | .02 | .01 |
| ☐ 394 Lawrence Taylor NFC | .08 | .04 | .01 |
| ☐ 395 Pepper Johnson NFC | .04 | .02 | .01 |
| ☐ 396 Mike Singletary NFC | .08 | .04 | .01 |
| ☐ 397 Darrell Green NFC | .04 | .02 | .01 |
| ☐ 398 Carl Lee NFC | .04 | .02 | .01 |
| ☐ 399 Joey Browner NFC | .04 | .02 | .01 |
| ☐ 400 Ronnie Lott NFC | .08 | .04 | .01 |
| ☐ 401 Sean Landeta NFC | .04 | .02 | .01 |
| ☐ 402 Morten Andersen NFC | .04 | .02 | .01 |
| ☐ 403 Mel Gray NFC | .04 | .02 | .01 |
| ☐ 404 Reyna Thompson NFC | .04 | .02 | .01 |
| ☐ 405 Jimmy Johnson CO NFC | .08 | .04 | .01 |
| ☐ 406 Andre Reed AFC | .08 | .04 | .01 |
| Buffalo Bills | | | |
| ☐ 407 Anthony Miller AFC | .08 | .04 | .01 |
| San Diego Chargers | | | |
| ☐ 408 Anthony Munoz AFC | .08 | .04 | .01 |
| Cincinnati Bengals | | | |
| ☐ 409 Bruce Armstrong AFC | .04 | .02 | .01 |
| New England Patriots | | | |
| ☐ 410 Bruce Matthews AFC | .04 | .02 | .01 |
| Houston Oilers | | | |
| ☐ 411 Mike Munchak AFC | .04 | .02 | .01 |
| Houston Oilers | | | |
| ☐ 412 Kent Hull AFC | .04 | .02 | .01 |
| Buffalo Bills | | | |
| ☐ 413 Rodney Holman AFC | .04 | .02 | .01 |
| Cincinnati Bengals | | | |
| ☐ 414 Warren Moon AFC | .10 | .05 | .01 |
| Houston Oilers | | | |
| ☐ 415 Thurman Thomas AFC | .20 | .09 | .03 |
| Buffalo Bills | | | |
| ☐ 416 Marion Butts AFC | .08 | .04 | .01 |
| San Diego Chargers | | | |
| ☐ 417 Bruce Smith AFC | .08 | .04 | .01 |
| Buffalo Bills | | | |
| ☐ 418 Greg Townsend AFC | .04 | .02 | .01 |
| Los Angeles Raiders | | | |
| ☐ 419 Ray Childress AFC | .04 | .02 | .01 |
| Houston Oilers | | | |
| ☐ 420 Derrick Thomas AFC | .10 | .05 | .01 |
| Kansas City Chiefs | | | |
| ☐ 421 Leslie O'Neal AFC | .04 | .02 | .01 |
| San Diego Chargers | | | |
| ☐ 422 John Offerdahl AFC | .04 | .02 | .01 |
| Miami Dolphins | | | |
| ☐ 423 Shane Conlan AFC | .04 | .02 | .01 |
| Buffalo Bills | | | |
| ☐ 424 Rod Woodson AFC | .08 | .04 | .01 |
| Pittsburgh Steelers | | | |
| ☐ 425 Albert Lewis AFC | .04 | .02 | .01 |

|  |  | | | |
|---|---|---|---|---|
| | Kansas City Chiefs | | | |
| ☐ 426 | Steve Atwater AFC | .08 | .04 | .01 |
| | Denver Broncos | | | |
| ☐ 427 | David Fulcher AFC | .04 | .02 | .01 |
| | Cincinnati Bengals | | | |
| ☐ 428 | Rohn Stark AFC | .04 | .02 | .01 |
| | Indianapolis Colts | | | |
| ☐ 429 | Nick Lowery AFC | .04 | .02 | .01 |
| | Kansas City Chiefs | | | |
| ☐ 430 | Clarence Verdin AFC | .04 | .02 | .01 |
| | Indianapolis Colts | | | |
| ☐ 431 | Steve Tasker AFC | .04 | .02 | .01 |
| | Buffalo Bills | | | |
| ☐ 432 | Art Shell CO AFC | .08 | .04 | .01 |
| | Los Angeles Raiders | | | |
| ☐ 433 | Scott Case | .04 | .02 | .01 |
| ☐ 434 | Tory Epps UER | .04 | .02 | .01 |
| | (No TM next to Pro Set on card back) | | | |
| ☐ 435 | Mike Gann UER | .04 | .02 | .01 |
| | (Text has 2 fumble recoveries, stats say 3) | | | |
| ☐ 436 | Brian Jordan UER | .10 | .05 | .01 |
| | (No TM next to Pro Set on card back) | | | |
| ☐ 437 | Mike Kenn | .08 | .04 | .01 |
| ☐ 438 | John Rade | .04 | .02 | .01 |
| ☐ 439 | Andre Rison | .25 | .11 | .03 |
| ☐ 440 | Mike Rozier | .08 | .04 | .01 |
| ☐ 441 | Jessie Tuggle | .15 | .07 | .02 |
| ☐ 442 | Don Beebe | .10 | .05 | .01 |
| ☐ 443 | John Davis | .04 | .02 | .01 |
| ☐ 444 | James Lofton | .10 | .05 | .01 |
| ☐ 445 | Keith McKeller | .04 | .02 | .01 |
| ☐ 446 | Jamie Mueller | .04 | .02 | .01 |
| ☐ 447 | Scott Norwood | .04 | .02 | .01 |
| ☐ 448 | Frank Reich | .10 | .05 | .01 |
| ☐ 449 | Leon Seals | .04 | .02 | .01 |
| ☐ 450 | Leonard Smith | .04 | .02 | .01 |
| ☐ 451 | Neal Anderson | .08 | .04 | .01 |
| ☐ 452 | Trace Armstrong | .04 | .02 | .01 |
| ☐ 453 | Mark Bortz | .04 | .02 | .01 |
| ☐ 454 | Wendell Davis | .04 | .02 | .01 |
| ☐ 455 | Shaun Gayle | .04 | .02 | .01 |
| ☐ 456 | Jay Hilgenberg | .08 | .04 | .01 |
| ☐ 457 | Steve McMichael | .08 | .04 | .01 |
| ☐ 458 | Mike Singletary | .10 | .05 | .01 |
| ☐ 459 | Donnell Woolford | .04 | .02 | .01 |
| ☐ 460 | Jim Breech | .04 | .02 | .01 |
| ☐ 461 | Eddie Brown | .04 | .02 | .01 |
| ☐ 462 | Barney Bussey | .04 | .02 | .01 |
| ☐ 463 | Bruce Kozerski | .04 | .02 | .01 |
| ☐ 464 | Tim Krumrie | .04 | .02 | .01 |
| ☐ 465 | Bruce Reimers | .04 | .02 | .01 |
| ☐ 466 | Kevin Walker | .04 | .02 | .01 |
| ☐ 467 | Ickey Woods | .04 | .02 | .01 |
| ☐ 468 | Carl Zander UER | .04 | .02 | .01 |
| | (DOB: 4/12/63, should be 3/23/63) | | | |
| ☐ 469 | Mike Baab | .04 | .02 | .01 |
| ☐ 470 | Brian Brennan | .04 | .02 | .01 |
| ☐ 471 | Rob Burnett | .15 | .07 | .02 |
| ☐ 472 | Raymond Clayborn | .08 | .04 | .01 |
| ☐ 473 | Reggie Langhorne | .08 | .04 | .01 |
| ☐ 474 | Kevin Mack | .08 | .04 | .01 |
| ☐ 475 | Anthony Pleasant | .04 | .02 | .01 |
| ☐ 476 | Joe Morris | .08 | .04 | .01 |
| ☐ 477 | Dan Fike | .04 | .02 | .01 |
| ☐ 478 | Ray Horton | .04 | .02 | .01 |
| ☐ 479 | Jim Jeffcoat | .04 | .02 | .01 |
| ☐ 480 | Jimmie Jones | .04 | .02 | .01 |
| | (Randall Cunningham also in photo) | | | |
| ☐ 481 | Kelvin Martin | .08 | .04 | .01 |
| ☐ 482 | Nate Newton | .04 | .02 | .01 |
| ☐ 483 | Danny Noonan | .04 | .02 | .01 |
| ☐ 484 | Jay Novacek | .15 | .07 | .02 |
| ☐ 485 | Emmitt Smith | 2.00 | .90 | .25 |
| ☐ 486 | James Washington | .20 | .09 | .03 |
| ☐ 487 | Simon Fletcher | .08 | .04 | .01 |
| ☐ 488 | Ron Holmes | .04 | .02 | .01 |
| ☐ 489 | Mike Horan | .04 | .02 | .01 |
| ☐ 490 | Vance Johnson | .08 | .04 | .01 |
| ☐ 491 | Keith Kartz | .04 | .02 | .01 |
| ☐ 492 | Greg Kragen | .04 | .02 | .01 |
| ☐ 493 | Ken Lanier | .04 | .02 | .01 |
| ☐ 494 | Warren Powers | .04 | .02 | .01 |
| ☐ 495 | Dennis Smith | .08 | .04 | .01 |
| ☐ 496 | Jeff Campbell | .04 | .02 | .01 |
| ☐ 497 | Ken Dallafior | .04 | .02 | .01 |
| ☐ 498 | Dennis Gibson | .04 | .02 | .01 |
| ☐ 499 | Kevin Glover | .04 | .02 | .01 |
| ☐ 500 | Mel Gray | .08 | .04 | .01 |
| ☐ 501 | Eddie Murray | .08 | .04 | .01 |
| ☐ 502 | Barry Sanders | .75 | .35 | .09 |
| ☐ 503 | Chris Spielman | .08 | .04 | .01 |
| ☐ 504 | William White | .04 | .02 | .01 |
| ☐ 505 | Matt Brock | .04 | .02 | .01 |
| ☐ 506 | Robert Brown | .04 | .02 | .01 |
| ☐ 507 | LeRoy Butler | .04 | .02 | .01 |
| ☐ 508 | James Campen | .04 | .02 | .01 |
| ☐ 509 | Jerry Holmes | .04 | .02 | .01 |
| ☐ 510 | Perry Kemp | .04 | .02 | .01 |
| ☐ 511 | Ken Ruettgers | .04 | .02 | .01 |
| ☐ 512 | Scott Stephen | .04 | .02 | .01 |
| ☐ 513 | Ed West | .04 | .02 | .01 |
| ☐ 514 | Cris Dishman | .15 | .07 | .02 |
| ☐ 515 | Curtis Duncan | .08 | .04 | .01 |
| ☐ 516 | Drew Hill UER | .08 | .04 | .01 |
| | (Text says 390 catches and 6368 yards, stats say 450 and 7715) | | | |
| ☐ 517 | Haywood Jeffires | .15 | .07 | .02 |
| ☐ 518 | Sean Jones | .08 | .04 | .01 |
| ☐ 519 | Lamar Lathon | .04 | .02 | .01 |
| ☐ 520 | Don Maggs | .04 | .02 | .01 |
| ☐ 521 | Bubba McDowell | .04 | .02 | .01 |
| ☐ 522 | Johnny Meads | .04 | .02 | .01 |
| ☐ 523A | Chip Banks ERR | .50 | .23 | .06 |
| | (No text) | | | |
| ☐ 523B | Chip Banks COR | .08 | .04 | .01 |
| ☐ 524 | Pat Beach | .04 | .02 | .01 |
| ☐ 525 | Sam Clancy | .04 | .02 | .01 |
| ☐ 526 | Eugene Daniel | .04 | .02 | .01 |
| ☐ 527 | Jon Hand | .04 | .02 | .01 |
| ☐ 528 | Jessie Hester | .08 | .04 | .01 |
| ☐ 529A | Mike Prior ERR | .50 | .23 | .06 |
| | (No textual information) | | | |
| ☐ 529B | Mike Prior COR | .08 | .04 | .01 |
| ☐ 530 | Keith Taylor | .04 | .02 | .01 |
| ☐ 531 | Donnell Thompson | .04 | .02 | .01 |
| ☐ 532 | Dino Hackett | .04 | .02 | .01 |
| ☐ 533 | David Lutz | .04 | .02 | .01 |
| ☐ 534 | Chris Martin | .04 | .02 | .01 |
| ☐ 535 | Kevin Ross | .08 | .04 | .01 |
| ☐ 536 | Dan Saleaumua | .04 | .02 | .01 |
| ☐ 537 | Neil Smith | .10 | .05 | .01 |
| ☐ 538 | Percy Snow | .04 | .02 | .01 |
| ☐ 539 | Robb Thomas | .04 | .02 | .01 |
| ☐ 540 | Barry Word | .10 | .05 | .01 |
| ☐ 541 | Marcus Allen | .08 | .04 | .01 |
| ☐ 542 | Eddie Anderson | .04 | .02 | .01 |
| ☐ 543 | Scott Davis | .04 | .02 | .01 |
| ☐ 544 | Mervyn Fernandez | .04 | .02 | .01 |
| ☐ 545 | Ethan Horton | .04 | .02 | .01 |
| ☐ 546 | Ronnie Lott | .10 | .05 | .01 |
| ☐ 547 | Don Mosebar | .04 | .02 | .01 |
| ☐ 548 | Jerry Robinson | .04 | .02 | .01 |
| ☐ 549 | Aaron Wallace | .04 | .02 | .01 |
| ☐ 550 | Flipper Anderson | .08 | .04 | .01 |
| ☐ 551 | Cleveland Gary | .08 | .04 | .01 |
| ☐ 552 | Damone Johnson | .04 | .02 | .01 |
| ☐ 553 | Duval Love | .04 | .02 | .01 |
| ☐ 554 | Irv Pankey | .04 | .02 | .01 |
| ☐ 555 | Mike Piel | .04 | .02 | .01 |
| ☐ 556 | Jackie Slater | .08 | .04 | .01 |
| ☐ 557 | Michael Stewart | .04 | .02 | .01 |
| ☐ 558 | Pat Terrell | .04 | .02 | .01 |
| ☐ 559 | J.B. Brown | .04 | .02 | .01 |
| ☐ 560 | Mark Clayton | .08 | .04 | .01 |
| ☐ 561 | Ferrell Edmunds | .04 | .02 | .01 |
| ☐ 562 | Harry Galbreath | .04 | .02 | .01 |
| ☐ 563 | David Griggs | .04 | .02 | .01 |
| ☐ 564 | Jim C. Jensen | .04 | .02 | .01 |
| ☐ 565 | Louis Oliver | .08 | .04 | .01 |
| ☐ 566 | Tony Paige | .04 | .02 | .01 |
| ☐ 567 | Keith Sims | .04 | .02 | .01 |
| ☐ 568 | Joey Browner | .04 | .02 | .01 |
| ☐ 569 | Anthony Carter | .08 | .04 | .01 |
| ☐ 570 | Chris Doleman | .08 | .04 | .01 |
| ☐ 571 | Rich Gannon UER | .08 | .04 | .01 |
| | (Acquired in '87, not '88 as in text) | | | |
| ☐ 572 | Hassan Jones | .04 | .02 | .01 |
| ☐ 573 | Steve Jordan | .08 | .04 | .01 |
| ☐ 574 | Carl Lee | .04 | .02 | .01 |
| ☐ 575 | Randall McDaniel | .04 | .02 | .01 |
| ☐ 576 | Herschel Walker | .10 | .05 | .01 |
| ☐ 577 | Ray Agnew | .04 | .02 | .01 |
| ☐ 578 | Vincent Brown | .04 | .02 | .01 |
| ☐ 579 | Irving Fryar | .08 | .04 | .01 |
| ☐ 580 | Tim Goad | .04 | .02 | .01 |
| ☐ 581 | Maurice Hurst | .04 | .02 | .01 |
| ☐ 582 | Fred Marion | .04 | .02 | .01 |
| ☐ 583 | Johnny Rembert | .04 | .02 | .01 |
| ☐ 584 | Andre Tippett | .08 | .04 | .01 |
| ☐ 585 | Brent Williams | .04 | .02 | .01 |
| ☐ 586 | Morten Andersen | .08 | .04 | .01 |
| ☐ 587 | Toi Cook | .04 | .02 | .01 |
| ☐ 588 | Jim Dombrowski | .04 | .02 | .01 |
| ☐ 589 | Dalton Hilliard | .04 | .02 | .01 |
| ☐ 590 | Rickey Jackson | .08 | .04 | .01 |
| ☐ 591 | Eric Martin | .08 | .04 | .01 |
| ☐ 592 | Sam Mills | .08 | .04 | .01 |
| ☐ 593 | Bobby Hebert | .10 | .05 | .01 |

| | | | |
|---|---|---|---|
| ☐ 594 Steve Walsh | .04 | .02 | .01 |
| ☐ 595 Ottis Anderson | .08 | .04 | .01 |
| ☐ 596 Pepper Johnson | .08 | .04 | .01 |
| ☐ 597 Bob Kratch | .10 | .05 | .01 |
| ☐ 598 Sean Landeta | .04 | .02 | .01 |
| ☐ 599 Doug Riesenberg | .04 | .02 | .01 |
| ☐ 600 William Roberts | .04 | .02 | .01 |
| ☐ 601 Phil Simms | .10 | .05 | .01 |
| ☐ 602 Lawrence Taylor | .10 | .05 | .01 |
| ☐ 603 Everson Walls | .04 | .02 | .01 |
| ☐ 604 Brad Baxter | .08 | .04 | .01 |
| ☐ 605 Dennis Byrd | .04 | .02 | .01 |
| ☐ 606 Jeff Lageman | .04 | .02 | .01 |
| ☐ 607 Pat Leahy | .08 | .04 | .01 |
| ☐ 608 Rob Moore | .10 | .05 | .01 |
| ☐ 609 Joe Mott | .04 | .02 | .01 |
| ☐ 610 Tony Stargell | .04 | .02 | .01 |
| ☐ 611 Brian Washington | .04 | .02 | .01 |
| ☐ 612 Marvin Washington | .20 | .09 | .03 |
| ☐ 613 David Alexander | .04 | .02 | .01 |
| ☐ 614 Jerome Brown | .08 | .04 | .01 |
| ☐ 615 Byron Evans | .08 | .04 | .01 |
| ☐ 616 Ron Heller | .04 | .02 | .01 |
| ☐ 617 Wes Hopkins | .04 | .02 | .01 |
| ☐ 618 Keith Jackson | .15 | .07 | .02 |
| ☐ 619 Heath Sherman | .08 | .04 | .01 |
| ☐ 620 Reggie White | .15 | .07 | .02 |
| ☐ 621 Calvin Williams | .20 | .09 | .03 |
| ☐ 622 Ken Harvey | .04 | .02 | .01 |
| ☐ 623 Eric Hill | .04 | .02 | .01 |
| ☐ 624 Johnny Johnson | .25 | .11 | .03 |
| ☐ 625 Freddie Joe Nunn | .04 | .02 | .01 |
| ☐ 626 Ricky Proehl | .10 | .05 | .01 |
| ☐ 627 Tootie Robbins | .04 | .02 | .01 |
| ☐ 628 Jay Taylor | .04 | .02 | .01 |
| ☐ 629 Tom Tupa | .08 | .04 | .01 |
| ☐ 630 Jim Wahler | .10 | .05 | .01 |
| ☐ 631 Bubby Brister | .08 | .04 | .01 |
| ☐ 632 Thomas Everett | .04 | .02 | .01 |
| ☐ 633 Bryan Hinkle | .04 | .02 | .01 |
| ☐ 634 Carnell Lake | .04 | .02 | .01 |
| ☐ 635 David Little | .04 | .02 | .01 |
| ☐ 636 Hardy Nickerson | .04 | .02 | .01 |
| ☐ 637 Gerald Williams | .04 | .02 | .01 |
| ☐ 638 Keith Willis | .04 | .02 | .01 |
| ☐ 639 Tim Worley | .08 | .04 | .01 |
| ☐ 640 Rod Bernstine | .10 | .05 | .01 |
| ☐ 641 Frank Cornish | .04 | .02 | .01 |
| ☐ 642 Gary Plummer | .04 | .02 | .01 |
| ☐ 643 Henry Rolling | .04 | .02 | .01 |
| ☐ 644 Sam Seale | .04 | .02 | .01 |
| ☐ 645 Junior Seau | .25 | .11 | .03 |
| ☐ 646 Billy Ray Smith | .04 | .02 | .01 |
| ☐ 647 Broderick Thompson | .04 | .02 | .01 |
| ☐ 648 Derrick Walker | .04 | .02 | .01 |
| ☐ 649 Todd Bowles | .04 | .02 | .01 |
| ☐ 650 Don Griffin | .04 | .02 | .01 |
| ☐ 651 Charles Haley | .08 | .04 | .01 |
| ☐ 652 Brent Jones UER | .10 | .05 | .01 |
| (Born in Santa Clara, not San Jose) | | | |
| ☐ 653 Joe Montana | 1.00 | .45 | .13 |
| ☐ 654 Jerry Rice | .75 | .35 | .09 |
| ☐ 655 Bill Romanowski | .04 | .02 | .01 |
| ☐ 656 Michael Walter | .04 | .02 | .01 |
| ☐ 657 Dave Waymer | .04 | .02 | .01 |
| ☐ 658 Jeff Chadwick | .04 | .02 | .01 |
| ☐ 659 Derrick Fenner | .08 | .04 | .01 |
| ☐ 660 Nesby Glasgow | .04 | .02 | .01 |
| ☐ 661 Jacob Green | .04 | .02 | .01 |
| ☐ 662 Dwayne Harper | .15 | .07 | .02 |
| ☐ 663 Andy Heck | .04 | .02 | .01 |
| ☐ 664 Dave Krieg | .08 | .04 | .01 |
| ☐ 665 Rufus Porter | .04 | .02 | .01 |
| ☐ 666 Eugene Robinson | .04 | .02 | .01 |
| ☐ 667 Mark Carrier | .08 | .04 | .01 |
| ☐ 668 Steve Christie | .04 | .02 | .01 |
| ☐ 669 Reuben Davis | .04 | .02 | .01 |
| ☐ 670 Paul Gruber | .08 | .04 | .01 |
| ☐ 671 Wayne Haddix | .04 | .02 | .01 |
| ☐ 672 Ron Hall | .04 | .02 | .01 |
| ☐ 673 Keith McCants UER | .04 | .02 | .01 |
| (Senior All-American, sic, left school after junior year) | | | |
| ☐ 674 Ricky Reynolds | .04 | .02 | .01 |
| ☐ 675 Mark Robinson | .04 | .02 | .01 |
| ☐ 676 Jeff Bostic | .04 | .02 | .01 |
| ☐ 677 Darrell Green | .08 | .04 | .01 |
| ☐ 678 Markus Koch | .04 | .02 | .01 |
| ☐ 679 Jim Lachey | .04 | .02 | .01 |
| ☐ 680 Charles Mann | .08 | .04 | .01 |
| ☐ 681 Wilber Marshall | .08 | .04 | .01 |
| ☐ 682 Art Monk | .10 | .05 | .01 |
| ☐ 683 Gerald Riggs | .08 | .04 | .01 |
| ☐ 684 Ricky Sanders | .08 | .04 | .01 |
| ☐ 685 Ray Handley NEW | .04 | .02 | .01 |

| | | | |
|---|---|---|---|
| replaces Bill Parcells as Giants head coach | | | |
| ☐ 686 NFL announces NEW expansion | .04 | .02 | .01 |
| ☐ 687 Miami gets NEW Super Bowl XXIX | .04 | .02 | .01 |
| ☐ 688 Giants' George Young NEW .. is named NFL Executive of the Year by The Sporting News | .04 | .02 | .01 |
| ☐ 689 Five-millionth fan NEW visits Pro Football Hall of Fame | .04 | .02 | .01 |
| ☐ 690 Sports Illustrated NEW. poll finds pro football is America's Number 1 spectator sport | .04 | .02 | .01 |
| ☐ 691 American Bowl NEW London Theme Art | .04 | .02 | .01 |
| ☐ 692 American Bowl NEW Berlin Theme Art | .04 | .02 | .01 |
| ☐ 693 American Bowl NEW Tokyo Theme Art | .04 | .02 | .01 |
| ☐ 694A Russell Maryland Dallas Cowboys (Says he runs a 4.91 40, card 32 has 4.8) | 1.25 | .55 | .16 |
| ☐ 694B Joe Ferguson LEG | .08 | .04 | .01 |
| ☐ 695 Carl Hairston LEG | .04 | .02 | .01 |
| ☐ 696 Dan Hampton LEG | .08 | .04 | .01 |
| ☐ 697 Mike Haynes LEG | .04 | .02 | .01 |
| ☐ 698 Marty Lyons LEG | .04 | .02 | .01 |
| ☐ 699 Ozzie Newsome LEG | .08 | .04 | .01 |
| ☐ 700 Scott Studwell LEG | .04 | .02 | .01 |
| ☐ 701 Mike Webster LEG | .08 | .04 | .01 |
| ☐ 702 Dwayne Woodruff LEG | .04 | .02 | .01 |
| ☐ 703 Larry Kennan CO London Monarchs | .04 | .02 | .01 |
| ☐ 704 Stan Gelbaugh LL London Monarchs | .20 | .09 | .03 |
| ☐ 705 John Brantley LL Birmingham Fire | .04 | .02 | .01 |
| ☐ 706 Danny Lockett LL London Monarchs | .04 | .02 | .01 |
| ☐ 707 Anthony Parker LL NY/NJ Knights | .10 | .05 | .01 |
| ☐ 708 Dan Crossman LL London Monarchs | .04 | .02 | .01 |
| ☐ 709 Eric Wilkerson LL NY/NJ Knights | .04 | .02 | .01 |
| ☐ 710 Judd Garrett LL London Monarchs | .10 | .05 | .01 |
| ☐ 711 Tony Baker LL Frankfurt Galaxy | .04 | .02 | .01 |
| ☐ 712 1st Place BW PHOTO Randall Cunningham | .08 | .04 | .01 |
| ☐ 713 2nd Place BW PHOTO Mark Ingram | .04 | .02 | .01 |
| ☐ 714 3rd Place BW PHOTO Pete Holohan Barney Bussey Carl Carter | .04 | .02 | .01 |
| ☐ 715 1st Place Color PHOTO Action Sterling Sharpe | .10 | .05 | .01 |
| ☐ 716 2nd Place Color PHOTO Action Jim Harbaugh | .04 | .02 | .01 |
| ☐ 717 3rd Place Color PHOTO Action Anthony Miller David Fulcher | .04 | .02 | .01 |
| ☐ 718 1st Place Color PHOTO Feature Bill Parcells CO Lawrence Taylor | .08 | .04 | .01 |
| ☐ 719 2nd Place Color PHOTO Feature Patriotic Crowd | .04 | .02 | .01 |
| ☐ 720 3rd Place Color PHOTO Feature Alfredo Roberts | .04 | .02 | .01 |
| ☐ 721 Ray Bentley Read And Study Buffalo Bills | .04 | .02 | .01 |
| ☐ 722 Earnest Byner Never Give Up Washington Redskins | .08 | .04 | .01 |
| ☐ 723 Bill Fralic Steroids Destroy Atlanta Falcons | .04 | .02 | .01 |
| ☐ 724 Joe Jacoby Don't Pollute Washington Redskins | .04 | .02 | .01 |
| ☐ 725 Howie Long Aids Kills Los Angeles Raiders | .08 | .04 | .01 |
| ☐ 726 Dan Marino School's The Ticket | .35 | .16 | .04 |

|  |  | | | |
|---|---|---|---|---|
| | Miami Dolphins | | | |
| ☐ 727 | Ron Rivera | .04 | .02 | .01 |
| | Leer Y Estudiar | | | |
| | Chicago Bears | | | |
| ☐ 728 | Mike Singletary | .08 | .04 | .01 |
| | Be The Best | | | |
| | Chicago Bears | | | |
| ☐ 729 | Cornelius Bennett | .08 | .04 | .01 |
| | Chill | | | |
| | Buffalo Bills | | | |
| ☐ 730 | Russell Maryland | .15 | .07 | .02 |
| | Dallas Cowboys | | | |
| ☐ 731 | Eric Turner | .20 | .09 | .03 |
| | Cleveland Browns | | | |
| ☐ 732 | Bruce Pickens UER | .10 | .05 | .01 |
| | Atlanta Falcons | | | |
| | (Wearing 38, but card back lists 39) | | | |
| ☐ 733 | Mike Croel | .20 | .09 | .03 |
| | Denver Broncos | | | |
| ☐ 734 | Todd Lyght | .10 | .05 | .01 |
| | Los Angeles Rams | | | |
| ☐ 735 | Eric Swann | .20 | .09 | .03 |
| | Phoenix Cardinals | | | |
| ☐ 736 | Charles McRae | .04 | .02 | .01 |
| | Tampa Bay Buccaneers | | | |
| ☐ 737 | Antone Davis | .04 | .02 | .01 |
| | Philadelphia Eagles | | | |
| ☐ 738 | Stanley Richard | .10 | .05 | .01 |
| | San Diego Chargers | | | |
| ☐ 739 | Herman Moore | 1.00 | .45 | .13 |
| | Detroit Lions | | | |
| ☐ 740 | Pat Harlow | .10 | .05 | .01 |
| | New England Patriots | | | |
| ☐ 741 | Alvin Harper | 1.00 | .45 | .13 |
| | Dallas Cowboys | | | |
| ☐ 742 | Mike Pritchard | .75 | .35 | .09 |
| | Atlanta Falcons | | | |
| ☐ 743 | Leonard Russell | 1.00 | .45 | .13 |
| | New England Patriots | | | |
| ☐ 744 | Huey Richardson | .04 | .02 | .01 |
| | Pittsburgh Steelers | | | |
| ☐ 745 | Dan McGwire | .10 | .05 | .01 |
| | Seattle Seahawks | | | |
| ☐ 746 | Bobby Wilson | .10 | .05 | .01 |
| | Washington Redskins | | | |
| ☐ 747 | Alfred Williams | .10 | .05 | .01 |
| | Cincinnati Bengals | | | |
| ☐ 748 | Vinnie Clark | .04 | .02 | .01 |
| | Green Bay Packers | | | |
| ☐ 749 | Kelvin Pritchett | .04 | .02 | .01 |
| | Detroit Lions | | | |
| ☐ 750 | Harvey Williams | .20 | .09 | .03 |
| | Kansas City Chiefs | | | |
| ☐ 751 | Stan Thomas | .04 | .02 | .01 |
| | Chicago Bears | | | |
| ☐ 752 | Randal Hill | .30 | .14 | .04 |
| | Phoenix Cardinals | | | |
| ☐ 753 | Todd Marinovich | .08 | .04 | .01 |
| | Los Angeles Raiders | | | |
| ☐ 754 | Ted Washington | .04 | .02 | .01 |
| | San Francisco 49ers | | | |
| ☐ 755 | Henry Jones | .25 | .11 | .03 |
| | Buffalo Bills | | | |
| ☐ 756 | Jarrod Bunch | .15 | .07 | .02 |
| | New York Giants | | | |
| ☐ 757 | Mike Dumas | .04 | .02 | .01 |
| | Houston Oilers | | | |
| ☐ 758 | Ed King | .04 | .02 | .01 |
| | Cleveland Browns | | | |
| ☐ 759 | Reggie Johnson | .15 | .07 | .02 |
| | Denver Broncos | | | |
| ☐ 760 | Roman Phifer | .10 | .05 | .01 |
| | Los Angeles Rams | | | |
| ☐ 761 | Mike Jones | .10 | .05 | .01 |
| | Phoenix Cardinals | | | |
| ☐ 762 | Brett Favre | 2.00 | .90 | .25 |
| | Atlanta Falcons | | | |
| ☐ 763 | Browning Nagle | .20 | .09 | .03 |
| | New York Jets | | | |
| ☐ 764 | Esera Tuaolo | .04 | .02 | .01 |
| | Green Bay Packers | | | |
| ☐ 765 | George Thornton | .04 | .02 | .01 |
| | San Diego Chargers | | | |
| ☐ 766 | Dixon Edwards | .04 | .02 | .01 |
| | Dallas Cowboys | | | |
| ☐ 767 | Darryll Lewis | .04 | .02 | .01 |
| | Houston Oilers | | | |
| ☐ 768 | Eric Bieniemy | .15 | .07 | .02 |
| | San Diego Chargers | | | |
| ☐ 769 | Shane Curry | .04 | .02 | .01 |
| | Indianapolis Colts | | | |
| ☐ 770 | Jerome Henderson | .04 | .02 | .01 |
| | New England Patriots | | | |
| ☐ 771 | Wesley Carroll | .10 | .05 | .01 |
| | New Orleans Saints | | | |
| ☐ 772 | Nick Bell | .20 | .09 | .03 |
| | Los Angeles Raiders | | | |
| ☐ 773 | John Flannery | .04 | .02 | .01 |
| | Houston Oilers | | | |
| ☐ 774 | Ricky Watters | 1.25 | .55 | .16 |
| | San Francisco 49ers | | | |
| ☐ 775 | Jeff Graham | .40 | .18 | .05 |
| | Pittsburgh Steelers | | | |
| ☐ 776 | Eric Moten | .04 | .02 | .01 |
| | San Diego Chargers | | | |
| ☐ 777 | Jesse Campbell | .10 | .05 | .01 |
| | Philadelphia Eagles | | | |
| ☐ 778 | Chris Zorich | .12 | .05 | .02 |
| | Chicago Bears | | | |
| ☐ 779 | Joe Valerio | .04 | .02 | .01 |
| | Kansas City Chiefs | | | |
| ☐ 780 | Doug Thomas | .04 | .02 | .01 |
| | Seattle Seahawks | | | |
| ☐ 781 | Lamar Rogers UER | .04 | .02 | .01 |
| | Cincinnati Bengals | | | |
| | (No "Official Card of NFL" and TM on card front) | | | |
| ☐ 782 | John Johnson | .04 | .02 | .01 |
| | San Francisco 49ers | | | |
| ☐ 783 | Phil Hansen | .15 | .07 | .02 |
| | Buffalo Bills | | | |
| ☐ 784 | Kanavis McGhee | .10 | .05 | .01 |
| | New York Giants | | | |
| ☐ 785 | Calvin Stephens UER | .10 | .05 | .01 |
| | New England Patriots | | | |
| | (Card says New England, others say New England Patriots) | | | |
| ☐ 786 | James Jones | .15 | .07 | .02 |
| | Cleveland Browns | | | |
| ☐ 787 | Reggie Barrett | .04 | .02 | .01 |
| | Detroit Lions | | | |
| ☐ 788 | Aeneas Williams | .15 | .07 | .02 |
| | Phoenix Cardinals | | | |
| ☐ 789 | Aaron Craver | .04 | .02 | .01 |
| | Miami Dolphins | | | |
| ☐ 790 | Keith Traylor | .04 | .02 | .01 |
| | Denver Broncos | | | |
| ☐ 791 | Godfrey Myles | .10 | .05 | .01 |
| | Dallas Cowboys | | | |
| ☐ 792 | Mo Lewis | .10 | .05 | .01 |
| | New York Jets | | | |
| ☐ 793 | James Richards | .04 | .02 | .01 |
| | Dallas Cowboys | | | |
| ☐ 794 | Carlos Jenkins | .15 | .07 | .02 |
| | Minnesota Vikings | | | |
| ☐ 795 | Lawrence Dawsey | .20 | .09 | .03 |
| | Tampa Bay Buccaneers | | | |
| ☐ 796 | Don Davey | .04 | .02 | .01 |
| | Green Bay Packers | | | |
| ☐ 797 | Jake Reed | .15 | .07 | .02 |
| | Minnesota Vikings | | | |
| ☐ 798 | Dave McCloughan | .04 | .02 | .01 |
| | Indianapolis Colts | | | |
| ☐ 799 | Eric Williams | .20 | .09 | .03 |
| | Dallas Cowboys | | | |
| ☐ 800 | Steve Jackson | .15 | .07 | .02 |
| | Houston Oilers | | | |
| ☐ 801 | Bob Dahl | .04 | .02 | .01 |
| | Cincinnati Bengals | | | |
| ☐ 802 | Ernie Mills | .10 | .05 | .01 |
| | Pittsburgh Steelers | | | |
| ☐ 803 | David Daniels | .04 | .02 | .01 |
| | Seattle Seahawks | | | |
| ☐ 804 | Rob Selby | .04 | .02 | .01 |
| | Philadelphia Eagles | | | |
| ☐ 805 | Ricky Ervins | .20 | .09 | .03 |
| | Washington Redskins | | | |
| ☐ 806 | Tim Barnett | .20 | .09 | .03 |
| | Kansas City Chiefs | | | |
| ☐ 807 | Chris Gardocki | .04 | .02 | .01 |
| | Chicago Bears | | | |
| ☐ 808 | Kevin Donnalley | .04 | .02 | .01 |
| | Houston Oilers | | | |
| ☐ 809 | Robert Wilson | .04 | .02 | .01 |
| | Tampa Bay Buccaneers | | | |
| ☐ 810 | Chuck Webb | .04 | .02 | .01 |
| | Green Bay Packers | | | |
| ☐ 811 | Darryl Wren | .10 | .05 | .01 |
| | Buffalo Bills | | | |
| ☐ 812 | Ed McCaffrey | .15 | .07 | .02 |
| | New York Giants | | | |
| ☐ 813 | Shula's 300th Victory NEW | .09 | .04 | .01 |
| ☐ 814 | Raiders-49ers sell out Coliseum NEW | .05 | .02 | .01 |
| ☐ 815 | NFL International NEW | .05 | .02 | .01 |
| ☐ 816 | Moe Gardner | .10 | .05 | .01 |
| | Atlanta Falcons | | | |
| ☐ 817 | Tim McKyer | .08 | .04 | .01 |
| | Atlanta Falcons | | | |
| ☐ 818 | Tom Waddle | .60 | .25 | .08 |
| | Chicago Bears | | | |

| | | | |
|---|---|---|---|
| ☐ 819 Michael Jackson | .75 | .35 | .09 |
| Cleveland Browns | | | |
| ☐ 820 Tony Casillas | .05 | .02 | .01 |
| Dallas Cowboys | | | |
| ☐ 821 Gaston Green | .08 | .04 | .01 |
| Denver Broncos | | | |
| ☐ 822 Kenny Walker | .05 | .02 | .01 |
| Denver Broncos | | | |
| ☐ 823 Willie Green | .50 | .23 | .06 |
| Detroit Lions | | | |
| ☐ 824 Erik Kramer | .60 | .25 | .08 |
| Detroit Lions | | | |
| ☐ 825 William Fuller | .08 | .04 | .01 |
| Houston Oilers | | | |
| ☐ 826 Allen Pinkett | .05 | .02 | .01 |
| Houston Oilers | | | |
| ☐ 827 Rick Venturi CO | .05 | .02 | .01 |
| Indianapolis Colts | | | |
| ☐ 828 Bill Maas | .05 | .02 | .01 |
| Kansas City Chiefs | | | |
| ☐ 829 Jeff Jaeger | .05 | .02 | .01 |
| Los Angeles Raiders | | | |
| ☐ 830 Robert Delpino | .08 | .04 | .01 |
| Los Angeles Rams | | | |
| ☐ 831 Mark Higgs | .60 | .25 | .08 |
| Miami Dolphins | | | |
| ☐ 832 Reggie Roby | .05 | .02 | .01 |
| Miami Dolphins | | | |
| ☐ 833 Terry Allen | .75 | .35 | .09 |
| Minnesota Vikings | | | |
| ☐ 834 Cris Carter | .10 | .05 | .01 |
| Minnesota Vikings | | | |
| (No indication when | | | |
| acquired on waivers) | | | |
| ☐ 835 John Randle | .35 | .16 | .04 |
| Minnesota Vikings | | | |
| ☐ 836 Hugh Millen | .10 | .05 | .01 |
| New England Patriots | | | |
| ☐ 837 Jon Vaughn | .20 | .09 | .03 |
| New England Patriots | | | |
| ☐ 838 Gill Fenerty | .08 | .04 | .01 |
| New Orleans Saints | | | |
| ☐ 839 Floyd Turner | .05 | .02 | .01 |
| New Orleans Saints | | | |
| ☐ 840 Irv Eatman | .05 | .02 | .01 |
| New York Jets | | | |
| ☐ 841 Lonnie Young | .05 | .02 | .01 |
| New York Jets | | | |
| ☐ 842 Jim McMahon | .10 | .05 | .01 |
| Philadelphia Eagles | | | |
| ☐ 843 Randal Hill UER | .15 | .07 | .02 |
| Phoenix Cardinals | | | |
| (Traded to Phoenix, | | | |
| not drafted) | | | |
| ☐ 844 Barry Foster | .50 | .23 | .06 |
| Pittsburgh Steelers | | | |
| ☐ 845 Neil O'Donnell | 1.50 | .65 | .19 |
| Pittsburgh Steelers | | | |
| ☐ 846 John Friesz UER | .10 | .05 | .01 |
| San Diego Chargers | | | |
| (Wears 17, not 7) | | | |
| ☐ 847 Broderick Thomas | .08 | .04 | .01 |
| Tampa Bay Buccaneers | | | |
| ☐ 848 Brian Mitchell | .15 | .07 | .02 |
| Washington Redskins | | | |
| ☐ 849 Mike Utley | .30 | .14 | .04 |
| Detroit Lions | | | |
| ☐ 850 Mike Croel ROY | .10 | .05 | .01 |
| Denver Broncos | | | |

## 1991 Pro Set Inserts

These special insert cards were inserted into packs of the 1991 Pro Set regular issue and are standard size, 2 1/2" by 3 1/2". The Pro Set XXV logo card is a continuation of the Super Bowl series began in the 1989 Pro Set set. The Walter Payton special insert card features the recently retired all-time great running back of the Chicago Bears with his racing stripes; the card provides information about his post football career as a race car driver. The Pro Set Gazette card features some of the specials and highlights of the 1991 Pro Set series. The Grange card honors Red Grange, Illinois' Galloping Ghost of the 1920's, who passed away early in 1991. The front of the card features a sepia-toned photo of Grange while the back has a biography of Grange. The first series inserts were 336AU, 396AU, PSS1, PSS2, and Super Bowl Logo XXV. The Mini Pro Set Gazette was issued with both series. Six additional distinct insert cards were issued with the second series; they were SC1, SC3, SC4, SC5, MVPC25, and Santa Claus. The Lawrence Taylor autographed cards are personally autographed on the card front in black ink with his uniform number written underneath the signature.

| | MINT | EXC | G-VG |
|---|---|---|---|
| COMPLETE SET (16) | 450.00 | 200.00 | 57.50 |
| COMMON CARD | .15 | .07 | .02 |
| ☐ AU336 Lawrence Taylor | 200.00 | 90.00 | 25.00 |
| REP (autographed/500) | | | |
| ☐ AU394 Lawrence Taylor | 200.00 | 90.00 | 25.00 |
| PB (autographed/500) | | | |
| ☐ AU699 Ozzie Newsome | 30.00 | 13.50 | 3.80 |
| (Certified autograph) | | | |
| ☐ AU824 Erik Kramer | 30.00 | 13.50 | 3.80 |
| (Certified autograph) | | | |
| ☐ MVPC25 Ottis Anderson | .50 | .23 | .06 |
| MVP Super Bowl XXV | | | |
| ☐ NNO Mini Pro Set Gazette | .50 | .23 | .06 |
| ☐ NNO Pro Set Gazette | .50 | .23 | .06 |
| ☐ NNO Santa Claus | 1.00 | .45 | .13 |
| ☐ NNO Super Bowl XXV Art | .15 | .07 | .02 |
| ☐ NNO Super Bowl XXV Logo | .50 | .23 | .06 |
| ☐ PSS1 Walter Payton | 1.50 | .65 | .19 |
| and Team 34 | | | |
| ☐ PSS2 Red Grange | 1.00 | .45 | .13 |
| ☐ SC1 Super Bowl XXVI | .40 | .18 | .05 |
| Theme Art UER | | | |
| (Card says SB 26, | | | |
| should be 25) | | | |
| ☐ SC3 Jim Thorpe | 1.25 | .55 | .16 |
| Pioneers of the Game | | | |
| ☐ SC4 Otto Graham | 1.25 | .55 | .16 |
| Pioneers of the Game | | | |
| ☐ SC5 Paul Brown | 1.00 | .45 | .13 |
| Pioneers of the Game | | | |

## 1991 Pro Set UK Sheets

This set of five (approximately) 5 1/8" by 11 3/4" six-card strips was issued by Pro Set in England as an advertisement in Today, a newspaper in Middlesex, England. The unperforated strips are numbered 1-5, and each presents a "collection" of six player cards that measure the standard size (2 1/2" by 3 1/2"). The sheets were issued one per week in consecutive Sunday editions of the paper during the Fall of 1991. The cards and their numbering are identical to the 1991 regular issues. They are checklisted below by strips, and within strips listed beginning from the top left card and moving to the bottom right card.

| | MINT | EXC | G-VG |
|---|---|---|---|
| COMPLETE SET (5) | 25.00 | 10.00 | 2.50 |
| COMMON SHEET (1-5) | 2.50 | 1.00 | .25 |
| ☐ 1 Quarterbacks | 12.00 | 5.00 | 1.20 |
| 200 Jim Everett | | | |
| Los Angeles Rams | | | |
| 167 Warren Moon | | | |
| Houston Oilers | | | |
| 111 Boomer Esiason | | | |

Cincinnati Bengals
128 Troy Aikman
Dallas Cowboys
726 Dan Marino
Miami Dolphins
Think About It
138 John Elway
Denver Broncos

| | MINT | EXC | G-VG |
|---|---|---|---|
| ☐ 2 Running Backs | 10.00 | 4.00 | 1.00 |

576 Herschel Walker
Minnesota Vikings
86 Thurman Thomas
Buffalo Bills
213 Sammie Smith
Miami Dolphins
722 Earnest Byner
Cleveland Browns
Think About It
123 Eric Metcalf
Cleveland Browns
485 Emmitt Smith
Dallas Cowboys

| | | | |
|---|---|---|---|
| ☐ 3 Receivers | 8.00 | 3.25 | .80 |

209 Mark Duper
Miami Dolphins
654 Jerry Rice
San Francisco 49ers
251 Al Toon
New York Jets
161 Sterling Sharpe
Green Bay Packers
618 Keith Jackson
Philadelphia Eagles
115 Tim McGee
Cincinnati Bengals

| | | | |
|---|---|---|---|
| ☐ 4 Kickers | 2.50 | 1.00 | .25 |

460 Jim Breech
Cincinnati Bengals
447 Scott Norwood
Buffalo Bills
489 Mike Horan
Denver Broncos
300 Norm Johnson
Seattle Seahawks
184 Nick Lowery
Kansas City Chiefs
401 Sean Landeta
New York Giants

| | | | |
|---|---|---|---|
| ☐ 5 Defensive | 3.50 | 1.40 | .35 |

728 Mike Singletary
Think About It
Chicago Bears
56 Carl Banks
New York Giants
98 Deion Sanders
Atlanta Falcons
191 Howie Long
Los Angeles Raiders
131 Issiac Holt
Dallas Cowboys
241 Pat Swilling
New Orleans Saints

## 1991 Pro Set WLAF Helmets

This set of ten standard size cards (2 1/2" by 3 1/2") features (on the front of each card) a helmet of the teams of the WLAF's first season. These cards were included in the 1991 Pro Set first series wax packs. The back has information about the teams.

| | MINT | EXC | G-VG |
|---|---|---|---|
| COMPLETE SET (10) | 2.00 | .80 | .20 |
| COMMON HELMETS (1-10) | .30 | .12 | .03 |
| | | | |
| ☐ 1 Barcelona Dragons Helmet | .30 | .12 | .03 |

| | MINT | EXC | G-VG |
|---|---|---|---|
| ☐ 2 Birmingham Fire Helmet | .30 | .12 | .03 |
| ☐ 3 Frankfurt Galaxy Helmet | .30 | .12 | .03 |
| ☐ 4 London Monarchs Helmet | .30 | .12 | .03 |
| ☐ 5 Montreal Machine Helmet | .30 | .12 | .03 |
| ☐ 6 NY-NJ Knights Helmet | .30 | .12 | .03 |
| ☐ 7 Orlando Thunder Helmet | .30 | .12 | .03 |
| ☐ 8 Ral.-Durham Skyhawks Helmet | .30 | .12 | .03 |
| ☐ 9 Sacramento Surge Helmet | .30 | .12 | .03 |
| ☐ 10 San Antonio Riders Helmet | .30 | .12 | .03 |

## 1991 Pro Set WLAF Inserts

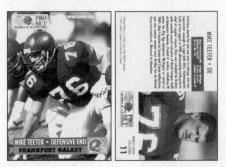

This 32-card standard size set was issued by Pro Set as an insert to the 1991 Pro Set Football first series. This set features the leading players from the WLAF. All ten WLAF teams are represented, and each team's head coach and quarterback are depicted on a card. Some of the more well-known athletes in this set include former Notre Dame quarterback Tony Rice and former star quarterback Roman Gabriel.

| | MINT | EXC | G-VG |
|---|---|---|---|
| COMPLETE SET (32) | 4.00 | 1.60 | .40 |
| COMMON CARD (WL1-WL32) | .10 | .04 | .01 |
| | | | |
| ☐ WL1 Mike Lynn (President/CEO) | .30 | .12 | .03 |
| ☐ WL2 London 24, Frankfurt 11; World League Opener Larry Kennan CO | .10 | .04 | .01 |
| ☐ WL3 Jack Bicknell CO Barcelona Dragons | .10 | .04 | .01 |
| ☐ WL4 Scott Erney Barcelona Dragons | .20 | .08 | .02 |
| ☐ WL5 A.J. Green (Anthony on card front) Barcelona Dragons | .20 | .08 | .02 |
| ☐ WL6 Chan Gailey CO Birmingham Fire | .10 | .04 | .01 |
| ☐ WL7 Paul McGowan Birmingham Fire | .10 | .04 | .01 |
| ☐ WL8 Brent Pease Birmingham Fire | .20 | .08 | .02 |
| ☐ WL9 Jack Elway CO Frankfurt Galaxy | .30 | .12 | .03 |
| ☐ WL10 Mike Perez Frankfurt Galaxy | .30 | .12 | .03 |
| ☐ WL11 Mike Tetter Frankfurt Galaxy | .10 | .04 | .01 |
| ☐ WL12 Larry Kennan CO UER London Monarchs (Coaching experience should say first year) | .10 | .04 | .01 |
| ☐ WL13 Corris Ervin London Monarchs | .10 | .04 | .01 |
| ☐ WL14 John Witkowski London Monarchs | .20 | .08 | .02 |
| ☐ WL15 Jacques Dussault CO Montreal Machine | .10 | .04 | .01 |
| ☐ WL16 Ray Savage Montreal Machine UER (Back should say DE, not Defensive End) | .10 | .04 | .01 |
| ☐ WL17 Kevin Sweeney Montreal Machine | .30 | .12 | .03 |
| ☐ WL18 Mouse Davis CO NY-NJ Knights | .30 | .12 | .03 |

| | MINT | EXC | G-VG |
|---|---|---|---|
| ☐ WL19 Todd Hammel UER ........... NY-NJ Knights (Missing TM on card front) | .20 | .08 | .02 |
| ☐ WL20 Anthony Parker ................. NY-NJ Knights | .20 | .08 | .02 |
| ☐ WL21 Don Mathews CO .............. Orlando Thunder | .10 | .04 | .01 |
| ☐ WL22 Kerwin Bell....................... Orlando Thunder | .30 | .12 | .03 |
| ☐ WL23 Wayne Davis ..................... Orlando Thunder | .10 | .04 | .01 |
| ☐ WL24 Roman Gabriel CO ............ Raleigh-Durham Skyhawks | .40 | .16 | .04 |
| ☐ WL25 John Carter ...................... Raleigh-Durham Skyhawks | .20 | .08 | .02 |
| ☐ WL26 Mark Maye ....................... Raleigh-Durham Skyhawks | .20 | .08 | .02 |
| ☐ WL27 Kay Stephenson CO .......... Sacramento Surge | .20 | .08 | .02 |
| ☐ WL28 Ben Bennett ..................... Sacramento Surge | .40 | .16 | .04 |
| ☐ WL29 Shawn Knight .................... Sacramento Surge UER (Back has NFL Exp., WLAF cards have Pro Exp.) | .20 | .08 | .02 |
| ☐ WL30 Mike Riley ........................ San Antonio Riders | .10 | .04 | .01 |
| ☐ WL31 Jason Garrett .................... San Antonio Riders | .40 | .16 | .04 |
| ☐ WL32 Greg Gilbert ..................... San Antonio Riders UER (6th round choice, should say 5th) | .20 | .08 | .02 |

## 1991 Pro Set WLAF World Bowl Combo 43

With a few subtle changes, this 43-card set is a reissue of the 1991 Pro Set WLAF Helmet and 1991 Pro Set WLAF sets. The cards have been renumbered on the back and measure the standard size (2 1/2" by 3 1/2"). As with the previous sets, the front designs have borderless color player photos, while the backs have color head and shoulders shots and player information in a horizontal format. The cards are checklisted below alphabetically according to teams as follows: Barcelona Dragons (3-5), Birmingham Fire (6-8), Frankfurt Galaxy (9-11), London Monarchs (12-14), Montreal Machine (15-17), New York-New Jersey Knights (18-20), Orlando Thunder (21-23), Raleigh-Durham Skyhawks (24-26), Sacramento Surge (27-29), and San Antonio Riders (30-32). The helmet cards can also be distinguished on the back by the presence of Chronology narrative instead of Schedule. The set was passed out to attendees of the World Bowl Game in Wembley Stadium, London, England. Ben Bennett and Tony Rice were not included in this set as they were in the 32-card insert set.

| | MINT | EXC | G-VG |
|---|---|---|---|
| COMPLETE SET (43)...................... | 20.00 | 8.00 | 2.00 |
| COMMON CARD (1-32) ................. | .35 | .14 | .03 |
| COMMON HELMET (34-43) ............. | .75 | .30 | .07 |
| ☐ 1 Mike Lynn PRES .................... | .75 | .30 | .07 |
| ☐ 2 World League Opener .............. London 24, Frankfurt 11 | .50 | .20 | .05 |
| ☐ 3 Jack Bicknell CO .................... | .50 | .20 | .05 |
| ☐ 4 Scott Erney ........................... | .50 | .20 | .05 |
| ☐ 5 Anthony Greene ..................... | .50 | .20 | .05 |
| ☐ 6 Chan Gailey CO ..................... | .50 | .20 | .05 |
| ☐ 7 Paul McGowan ...................... | .35 | .14 | .03 |
| ☐ 8 Brent Pease........................... | .50 | .20 | .05 |
| ☐ 9 Jack Elway CO ....................... | .75 | .30 | .07 |

| | MINT | EXC | G-VG |
|---|---|---|---|
| ☐ 10 Mike Perez ......................... | .75 | .30 | .07 |
| ☐ 11 Mike Teeter ........................ | .35 | .14 | .03 |
| ☐ 12 Larry Kennan CO .................. | .35 | .14 | .03 |
| ☐ 13 Corris Ervin ........................ | .35 | .14 | .03 |
| ☐ 14 John Witkowski..................... | .50 | .20 | .05 |
| ☐ 15 Jacques Dussault CO ............. | .35 | .14 | .03 |
| ☐ 16 Ray Savage ......................... | .35 | .14 | .03 |
| ☐ 17 Kevin Sweeney ..................... | .75 | .30 | .07 |
| ☐ 18 Mouse Davis CO.................... | .75 | .30 | .07 |
| ☐ 19 Todd Hammel ....................... | .50 | .20 | .05 |
| ☐ 20 Anthony Parker ..................... | .50 | .20 | .05 |
| ☐ 21 Don Matthews CO .................. | .35 | .14 | .03 |
| ☐ 22 Kerwin Bell.......................... | .75 | .30 | .07 |
| ☐ 23 Wayne Davis ....................... | .35 | .14 | .03 |
| ☐ 24 Roman Gabriel CO ................ | .75 | .30 | .07 |
| ☐ 25 Jon Carter .......................... | .50 | .20 | .05 |
| ☐ 26 Bobby McAllister ................... | 1.00 | .40 | .10 |
| ☐ 27 Kay Stephenson CO ............... | .35 | .14 | .03 |
| ☐ 28 Mike Elkins ......................... | 1.00 | .40 | .10 |
| ☐ 29 Shawn Knight........................ | .50 | .20 | .05 |
| ☐ 30 Mike Riley CO....................... | .35 | .14 | .03 |
| ☐ 31 Jason Garrett ....................... | .75 | .30 | .07 |
| ☐ 32 Greg Gilbert......................... | .50 | .20 | .05 |
| ☐ 33 World Bowl Trophy ................. | 5.00 | 2.00 | .50 |
| ☐ 34 Barcelona Dragons................. Helmet | .75 | .30 | .07 |
| ☐ 35 Birmingham Fire .................... Helmet | .75 | .30 | .07 |
| ☐ 36 Frankfurt Galaxy.................... Helmet | .75 | .30 | .07 |
| ☐ 37 London Monarchs .................. Helmet | .75 | .30 | .07 |
| ☐ 38 Montreal Machine .................. Helmet | .75 | .30 | .07 |
| ☐ 39 NY-NJ Knights ...................... Helmet | .75 | .30 | .07 |
| ☐ 40 Orlando Thunder ................... Helmet | .75 | .30 | .07 |
| ☐ 41 Ral.-Durham Skyhawks........... Helmet | .75 | .30 | .07 |
| ☐ 42 Sacramento Surge ................. Helmet | .75 | .30 | .07 |
| ☐ 43 San Antonio Riders ................ Helmet | .75 | .30 | .07 |

## 1991 Pro Set WLAF 150

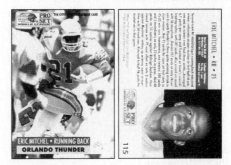

The premier edition of the 1991 Pro Set World League of American Football set contains 150 standard-size (2 1/2" by 3 1/2") cards. The front features a borderless color action player photo, with the player's name, position, and team appearing in various color stripes at the bottom of the card face. The horizontally oriented backs have a color head shot on the right portion, while the left portion has a biography and career summary. The first 29 cards of the set are subdivided as follows: League Overview (1-3), World Bowl (4-9), Helmet Collectibles (10-19), and 1991 Statistical Leaders (20-29). The player cards are numbered 30-150, and they are checklisted below alphabetically within and according to teams as follows: Barcelona Dragons (30-43), Birmingham Fire (44-57), Frankfurt Galaxy (58-68), London Monarchs (69-86), Montreal Machine (87-95), New York-New Jersey Knights (96-110), Orlando Thunder (111-22), Raleigh-Durham Skyhawks (123-31), Sacramento Surge (132-40), and San Antonio Riders (141-50). The cards are numbered on the back.

| | MINT | EXC | G-VG |
|---|---|---|---|
| COMPLETE SET (150)...................... | 4.00 | 1.60 | .40 |
| COMMON CARD (1-150) ................. | .05 | .02 | .00 |
| ☐ 1 World League Logo .................. | .15 | .06 | .01 |
| ☐ 2 Mike Lynn PRES .................... | .15 | .06 | .01 |
| ☐ 3 First Weekend ....................... | .15 | .06 | .01 |
| ☐ 4 World Bowl Trophy .................. | .25 | .10 | .02 |

| | | | |
|---|---|---|---|
| ☐ 5 Jon Horton | .05 | .02 | .00 |
| ☐ 6 Stan Gelbaugh | .50 | .20 | .05 |
| ☐ 7 Dan Crossman | .05 | .02 | .00 |
| ☐ 8 Marlon Brown | .05 | .02 | .00 |
| ☐ 9 Judd Garrett | .25 | .10 | .02 |
| ☐ 10 Barcelona Dragons Helmet | .05 | .02 | .00 |
| ☐ 11 Birmingham Fire Helmet | .05 | .02 | .00 |
| ☐ 12 Frankfurt Galaxy Helmet | .05 | .02 | .00 |
| ☐ 13 London Monarchs Helmet | .05 | .02 | .00 |
| ☐ 14 Montreal Machine Helmet | .05 | .02 | .00 |
| ☐ 15 NY-NJ Knights Helmet | .05 | .02 | .00 |
| ☐ 16 Orlando Thunder Helmet | .05 | .02 | .00 |
| ☐ 17 Raleigh-Durham Skyhawks Helmet | .05 | .02 | .00 |
| ☐ 18 Sacramento Surge Helmet | .05 | .02 | .00 |
| ☐ 19 San Antonio Riders Helmet | .05 | .02 | .00 |
| ☐ 20 Eric Wilkerson SL | .05 | .02 | .00 |
| ☐ 21 Stan Gelbaugh SL | .25 | .10 | .02 |
| ☐ 22 Judd Garrett SL | .15 | .06 | .01 |
| ☐ 23 Tony Baker SL | .05 | .02 | .00 |
| ☐ 24 Byron Williams SL | .05 | .02 | .00 |
| ☐ 25 Chris Mohr SL | .10 | .04 | .01 |
| ☐ 26 Errol Tucker SL | .05 | .02 | .00 |
| ☐ 27 Carl Painter SL | .05 | .02 | .00 |
| ☐ 28 Anthony Parker SL | .10 | .04 | .01 |
| ☐ 29 Danny Lockett SL | .10 | .04 | .01 |
| ☐ 30 Scott Adams | .05 | .02 | .00 |
| ☐ 31 Jim Bell | .05 | .02 | .00 |
| ☐ 32 Lydell Carr | .15 | .06 | .01 |
| ☐ 33 Bruce Clark | .15 | .06 | .01 |
| ☐ 34 Demetrius Davis | .10 | .04 | .01 |
| ☐ 35 Scott Erney | .10 | .04 | .01 |
| ☐ 36 Ron Goetz | .05 | .02 | .00 |
| ☐ 37 Xisco Marcos | .05 | .02 | .00 |
| ☐ 38 Paul Palmer | .15 | .06 | .01 |
| ☐ 39 Tony Rice | .30 | .12 | .03 |
| ☐ 40 Bobby Sign | .05 | .02 | .00 |
| ☐ 41 Gene Taylor | .05 | .02 | .00 |
| ☐ 42 Barry Voorhees | .05 | .02 | .00 |
| ☐ 43 Jack Bicknell CO | .10 | .04 | .01 |
| ☐ 44 Kenny Bell | .05 | .02 | .00 |
| ☐ 45 Willie Bouyer | .05 | .02 | .00 |
| ☐ 46 John Brantley | .10 | .04 | .01 |
| ☐ 47 Elroy Harris | .05 | .02 | .00 |
| ☐ 48 James Henry | .05 | .02 | .00 |
| ☐ 49 John Holland | .10 | .04 | .01 |
| ☐ 50 Arthur Hunter | .05 | .02 | .00 |
| ☐ 51 Eric Jones | .05 | .02 | .00 |
| ☐ 52 Kirk Maggio | .05 | .02 | .00 |
| ☐ 53 Paul McGowan | .05 | .02 | .00 |
| ☐ 54 John Miller | .05 | .02 | .00 |
| ☐ 55 Maurice Oliver | .05 | .02 | .00 |
| ☐ 56 Darrel Phillips | .05 | .02 | .00 |
| ☐ 57 Chan Gailey CO | .05 | .02 | .00 |
| ☐ 58 Tony Baker | .10 | .04 | .01 |
| ☐ 59 Tim Broady | .05 | .02 | .00 |
| ☐ 60 Garry Frank | .05 | .02 | .00 |
| ☐ 61 Jason Johnson | .05 | .02 | .00 |
| ☐ 62 Stefan Maslo | .05 | .02 | .00 |
| ☐ 63 Mark Mraz | .05 | .02 | .00 |
| ☐ 64 Yepi Pau'u | .05 | .02 | .00 |
| ☐ 65 Mike Perez | .20 | .08 | .02 |
| ☐ 66 Mike Teeter | .05 | .02 | .00 |
| ☐ 67 Chris Williams | .05 | .02 | .00 |
| ☐ 68 Jack Elway CO | .20 | .08 | .02 |
| ☐ 69 Theo Adams | .05 | .02 | .00 |
| ☐ 70 Jeff Alexander | .05 | .02 | .00 |
| ☐ 71 Philip Alexander | .05 | .02 | .00 |
| ☐ 72 Paul Berardelli | .05 | .02 | .00 |
| ☐ 73 Dana Brinson | .05 | .02 | .00 |
| ☐ 74 Marlon Brown | .05 | .02 | .00 |
| ☐ 75 Dedrick Dodge | .05 | .02 | .00 |
| ☐ 76 Victor Ebubedike | .05 | .02 | .00 |
| ☐ 77 Corris Ervin | .05 | .02 | .00 |
| ☐ 78 Steve Gabbard | .05 | .02 | .00 |
| ☐ 79 Judd Garrett | .15 | .06 | .01 |
| ☐ 80 Stan Gelbaugh | .50 | .20 | .05 |
| ☐ 81 Roy Hart | .05 | .02 | .00 |
| ☐ 82 Jon Horton | .05 | .02 | .00 |
| ☐ 83 Danny Lockett | .05 | .02 | .00 |
| ☐ 84 Doug Marrone | .05 | .02 | .00 |
| ☐ 85 Ken Sale | .05 | .02 | .00 |
| ☐ 86 Larry Kennan CO | .05 | .02 | .00 |
| ☐ 87 Mike Cadore | .05 | .02 | .00 |
| ☐ 88 K.D. Dunn | .05 | .02 | .00 |
| ☐ 89 Ricky Johnson | .05 | .02 | .00 |
| ☐ 90 Chris Mohr | .05 | .02 | .00 |
| ☐ 91 Bjorn Nittmo | .10 | .04 | .01 |

| | | | |
|---|---|---|---|
| ☐ 92 Michael Proctor | .05 | .02 | .00 |
| ☐ 93 Richard Shelton | .15 | .06 | .01 |
| ☐ 94 Tracy Simien | .25 | .10 | .02 |
| ☐ 95 Jacques Dussault CO | .05 | .02 | .00 |
| ☐ 96 Cornell Burbage | .10 | .04 | .01 |
| ☐ 97 Joe Campbell | .05 | .02 | .00 |
| ☐ 98 Monty Gilbreath | .05 | .02 | .00 |
| ☐ 99 Jeff Graham | .25 | .10 | .02 |
| ☐ 100 Kip Lewis | .05 | .02 | .00 |
| ☐ 101 Bob Lilljedahl | .05 | .02 | .00 |
| ☐ 102 Falanda Newton | .10 | .04 | .01 |
| ☐ 103 Anthony Parker | .10 | .04 | .01 |
| ☐ 104 Caesar Rentie | .05 | .02 | .00 |
| ☐ 105 Ron Sancho | .10 | .04 | .01 |
| ☐ 106 Craig Schlichting | .05 | .02 | .00 |
| ☐ 107 Lonnie Turner | .05 | .02 | .00 |
| ☐ 108 Eric Wilkerson | .05 | .02 | .00 |
| ☐ 109 Tony Woods | .10 | .04 | .01 |
| ☐ 110 Darrell(Mouse) Davis CO | .15 | .06 | .01 |
| ☐ 111 Kerwin Bell | .20 | .08 | .02 |
| ☐ 112 Wayne Davis | .05 | .02 | .00 |
| ☐ 113 John Guerrero | .05 | .02 | .00 |
| ☐ 114 Myron Jones | .05 | .02 | .00 |
| ☐ 115 Eric Mitchel | .20 | .08 | .02 |
| ☐ 116 Billy Owens | .05 | .02 | .00 |
| ☐ 117 Carl Painter | .10 | .04 | .01 |
| ☐ 118 Rob Sterling | .05 | .02 | .00 |
| ☐ 119 Errol Tucker | .05 | .02 | .00 |
| ☐ 120 Byron Williams | .05 | .02 | .00 |
| ☐ 121 Mike Withycombe | .05 | .02 | .00 |
| ☐ 122 Don Matthews CO | .05 | .02 | .00 |
| ☐ 123 Jon Carter | .05 | .02 | .00 |
| ☐ 124 Marvin Hargrove | .05 | .02 | .00 |
| ☐ 125 Clarkston Hines | .05 | .02 | .00 |
| ☐ 126 Ray Jackson | .05 | .02 | .00 |
| ☐ 127 Bobby McAllister | .25 | .10 | .02 |
| ☐ 128 Darryl McGill | .05 | .02 | .00 |
| ☐ 129 Pat McGuirk | .05 | .02 | .00 |
| ☐ 130 Shawn Woodson | .05 | .02 | .00 |
| ☐ 131 Roman Gabriel CO | .25 | .10 | .02 |
| ☐ 132 Greg Coauette | .05 | .02 | .00 |
| ☐ 133 Mike Elkins | .15 | .06 | .01 |
| ☐ 134 Victor Floyd | .05 | .02 | .00 |
| ☐ 135 Shawn Knight | .10 | .04 | .01 |
| ☐ 136 Pete Najarian | .05 | .02 | .00 |
| ☐ 137 Carl Parker | .05 | .02 | .00 |
| ☐ 138 Richard Stephens | .05 | .02 | .00 |
| ☐ 139 Curtis Wilson | .05 | .02 | .00 |
| ☐ 140 Kay Stephenson CO | .10 | .04 | .01 |
| ☐ 141 Ricky Blake | .25 | .10 | .02 |
| ☐ 142 Donnie Gardner | .05 | .02 | .00 |
| ☐ 143 Jason Garrett | .25 | .10 | .02 |
| ☐ 144 Mike Johnson | .05 | .02 | .00 |
| ☐ 145 Undra Johnson | .10 | .04 | .01 |
| ☐ 146 John Layfield | .05 | .02 | .00 |
| ☐ 147 Mark Ledbetter | .05 | .02 | .00 |
| ☐ 148 Gary Richard | .05 | .02 | .00 |
| ☐ 149 Tim Walton | .05 | .02 | .00 |
| ☐ 150 Mike Riley CO | .05 | .02 | .00 |

## 1991 Pro Set Cinderella Story

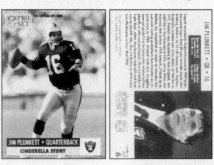

This nine-card set was issued as a perforated insert sheet in The Official NFL Pro Set Card Book, which chronicles the history of NFL Pro Set cards. The unifying theme of this set is summed up by the words "Cinderella Story" on the card fronts. The set highlights players or teams who overcame formidable obstacles to become winners. After perforation, the cards measure the standard size (2 1/2" by 3 1/2"). The front design is similar to the 1991 regular issue, with full-bleed player photos and player (or team) identification in colored stripes traversing the bottom of the card. All the cards feature color photos, with the exception of card numbers 4-6. The back has an extended caption for the card on the left portion, and a different photo on the right portion. The cards are numbered on the back.

| | MINT | EXC | G-VG |
|---|---|---|---|
| COMPLETE SET (9)............................ | 6.00 | 2.40 | .60 |
| COMMON PLAYER (1-9).................... | .50 | .20 | .05 |
| ☐ 1 Rocky Bleier.............................. | .75 | .30 | .07 |
|    Pittsburgh Steelers | | | |
| ☐ 2 Tom Dempsey........................... | .50 | .20 | .05 |
|    New Orleans Saints | | | |
| ☐ 3 Dan Hampton........................... | .75 | .30 | .07 |
|    Chicago Bears | | | |
| ☐ 4 Charlie Hennigan...................... | .50 | .20 | .05 |
|    Houston Oilers | | | |
| ☐ 5 Dante Lavelli........................... | .75 | .30 | .07 |
|    Cleveland Browns | | | |
| ☐ 6 Jim Plunkett............................ | .75 | .30 | .07 |
|    Oakland Raiders | | | |
| ☐ 7 1968 New York Jets.................. | 1.00 | .40 | .10 |
|    (Joe Namath handing off) | | | |
| ☐ 8 1981 San Francisco ................. | 2.50 | 1.00 | .25 |
|    49ers (Joe | | | |
|    Montana passing) | | | |
| ☐ 9 1979 Tampa Bay Bucs ............. | .50 | .20 | .05 |
|    (Ricky Bell running) | | | |

# 1991 Pro Set Platinum

The 1991 Pro Set Platinum football first series contains 150 cards measuring the standard size (2 1/2" by 3 1/2"). The front design has full-bleed glossy color player photos capturing game action. The Pro Set Platinum icon appears in the lower left corner. The horizontally oriented backs feature other glossy color action photos. In the black rectangle below the picture, the player's name, team, and position are given, along with a "Platinum Performer" feature that highlights the player's outstanding performance. The cards are numbered on the back in the lower right corner and checklisted below alphabetically according to teams as follows: Atlanta Falcons (1-4), Buffalo Bills (5-9), Chicago Bears (10-14), Cincinnati Bengals (15-19), Cleveland Browns (20-23), Dallas Cowboys (24-27), Denver Broncos (28-31), Detroit Lions (32-35), Green Bay Packers (36-39), Houston Oilers (40-44), Indianapolis Colts (45-47), Kansas City Chiefs (48-51), Los Angeles Raiders (52-56), Los Angeles Rams (57-61), Miami Dolphins (62-67), Minnesota Vikings (68-71), New England Patriots (72-74), New Orleans Saints (75-78), New York Giants (79-82), New York Jets (83-87), Philadelphia Eagles (88-91), Phoenix Cardinals (92-95), Pittsburgh Steelers (96-100), San Diego Chargers (101-105), San Francisco 49ers (106-110), Seattle Seahawks (111-115), Tampa Bay Buccaneers (116-122), and Washington Redskins (123-127). Other subsets included in the first series are Special Teams (128-135) and Platinum Performers (136-150). The second series contains 165 standard-size (2 1/2" by 3 1/2") cards. The front design has a full-bleed glossy color player photo, with the silver Pro Set Platinum logo in one of the lower corners of the card face. In a horizontal format, the upper portion of the back features another color action photo, with player identification and career summary in a black stripe below the picture. The cards are numbered on the back and checklisted below alphabetically according to teams as follows: Atlanta Falcons (151-155), Buffalo Bills (156-160), Chicago Bears (161-165), Cincinnati Bengals (166-170), Cleveland Browns (171-174), Dallas Cowboys (175-179), Denver Broncos (180-184), Detroit Lions (185-189), Green Bay Packers (190-194), Houston Oilers (195-199), Indianapolis Colts (200-203), Kansas City Chiefs (204-208), Los Angeles Raiders (209-213), Los Angeles Rams (214-218), Miami Dolphins (219-222), Minnesota Vikings (223-227), New England Patriots (228-232), New Orleans Saints (233-237), New York Giants (238-242), New York Jets (243-246), Philadelphia Eagles (247-251), Phoenix Cardinals (252-

256), Pittsburgh Steelers (257-261), San Diego Chargers (262-266), San Francisco 49ers (267-271), Seattle Seahawks (272-275), Tampa Bay Buccaneers (276-278), and Washington Redskins (279-284). A special subset features Platinum Prospects (286-315). Special Collectibles (PC1-PC10) cards were randomly distributed in 12-card foil packs. Also randomly inserted in the packs were bonus card certificates, which could be redeemed for a limited edition (1,500 made of each) platinum cards of Paul Brown (first series) or Emmitt Smith (second series). The key Rookie Cards in the second series are Nick Bell, Ricky Ervins, Brett Favre, Mark Higgs, Todd Marinovich, Dan McGwire, Browning Nagle, Mike Pritchard, Leonard Russell, and Harvey Williams.

| | MINT | EXC | G-VG |
|---|---|---|---|
| COMPLETE SET (315)...................... | 10.00 | 4.50 | 1.25 |
| COMPLETE SERIES 1 (150).............. | 5.00 | 2.30 | .60 |
| COMPLETE SERIES 2 (165).............. | 5.00 | 2.30 | .60 |
| COMMON PLAYER (1-150)............. | .05 | .02 | .01 |
| COMMON PLAYER (151-315)........... | .05 | .02 | .01 |
| ☐ 1 Chris Miller ............................. | .10 | .05 | .01 |
| ☐ 2 Andre Rison ............................ | .25 | .11 | .03 |
| ☐ 3 Tim Green .............................. | .05 | .02 | .01 |
| ☐ 4 Jessie Tuggle .......................... | .05 | .02 | .01 |
| ☐ 5 Thurman Thomas...................... | .40 | .18 | .05 |
|    (Jim Kelly also in photo) | | | |
| ☐ 6 Darryl Talley ........................... | .08 | .04 | .01 |
| ☐ 7 Kent Hull ............................... | .05 | .02 | .01 |
| ☐ 8 Bruce Smith ........................... | .10 | .05 | .01 |
| ☐ 9 Shane Conlan .......................... | .08 | .04 | .01 |
| ☐ 10 Jim Harbaugh ........................ | .08 | .04 | .01 |
| ☐ 11 Neal Anderson ....................... | .08 | .04 | .01 |
| ☐ 12 Mark Bortz ........................... | .05 | .02 | .01 |
| ☐ 13 Richard Dent .......................... | .08 | .04 | .01 |
| ☐ 14 Steve McMichael ..................... | .08 | .04 | .01 |
| ☐ 15 James Brooks ........................ | .08 | .04 | .01 |
| ☐ 16 Boomer Esiason...................... | .15 | .07 | .02 |
| ☐ 17 Tim Krumrie........................... | .05 | .02 | .01 |
| ☐ 18 James Francis ........................ | .08 | .04 | .01 |
| ☐ 19 Lewis Billups......................... | .05 | .02 | .01 |
| ☐ 20 Eric Metcalf........................... | .10 | .05 | .01 |
| ☐ 21 Kevin Mack ........................... | .05 | .02 | .01 |
| ☐ 22 Clay Matthews........................ | .08 | .04 | .01 |
| ☐ 23 Mike Johnson ........................ | .05 | .02 | .01 |
| ☐ 24 Troy Aikman........................... | 1.25 | .55 | .16 |
| ☐ 25 Emmitt Smith.......................... | 2.00 | .90 | .25 |
| ☐ 26 Daniel Stubbs......................... | .05 | .02 | .01 |
| ☐ 27 Ken Norton ............................ | .10 | .05 | .01 |
| ☐ 28 John Elway............................ | .35 | .16 | .04 |
| ☐ 29 Bobby Humphrey ..................... | .08 | .04 | .01 |
| ☐ 30 Simon Fletcher........................ | .08 | .04 | .01 |
| ☐ 31 Karl Mecklenburg ..................... | .08 | .04 | .01 |
| ☐ 32 Rodney Peete ........................ | .08 | .04 | .01 |
| ☐ 33 Barry Sanders ........................ | .75 | .35 | .09 |
| ☐ 34 Michael Cofer ......................... | .05 | .02 | .01 |
| ☐ 35 Jerry Ball ............................. | .08 | .04 | .01 |
| ☐ 36 Sterling Sharpe........................ | .50 | .23 | .06 |
| ☐ 37 Tony Mandarich ....................... | .05 | .02 | .01 |
| ☐ 38 Brian Noble ........................... | .05 | .02 | .01 |
| ☐ 39 Tim Harris ............................ | .08 | .04 | .01 |
| ☐ 40 Warren Moon .......................... | .20 | .09 | .03 |
| ☐ 41 Ernest Givens UER................... | .08 | .04 | .01 |
|    (Misspelled Givens | | | |
|    on card back) | | | |
| ☐ 42 Mike Munchak......................... | .08 | .04 | .01 |
| ☐ 43 Sean Jones ........................... | .08 | .04 | .01 |
| ☐ 44 Ray Childress ......................... | .08 | .04 | .01 |
| ☐ 45 Jeff George ........................... | .25 | .11 | .03 |
| ☐ 46 Albert Bentley......................... | .05 | .02 | .01 |
| ☐ 47 Duane Bickett ......................... | .05 | .02 | .01 |
| ☐ 48 Steve DeBerg ......................... | .08 | .04 | .01 |
| ☐ 49 Christian Okoye ....................... | .08 | .04 | .01 |
| ☐ 50 Neil Smith ............................ | .10 | .05 | .01 |
| ☐ 51 Derrick Thomas........................ | .25 | .11 | .03 |
| ☐ 52 Willie Gault ........................... | .08 | .04 | .01 |
| ☐ 53 Don Mosebar .......................... | .05 | .02 | .01 |
| ☐ 54 Howie Long ........................... | .08 | .04 | .01 |
| ☐ 55 Greg Townsend........................ | .05 | .02 | .01 |
| ☐ 56 Terry McDaniel......................... | .05 | .02 | .01 |
| ☐ 57 Jackie Slater........................... | .08 | .04 | .01 |
| ☐ 58 Jim Everett............................ | .08 | .04 | .01 |
| ☐ 59 Cleveland Gary ....................... | .08 | .04 | .01 |
| ☐ 60 Mike Piel ............................. | .05 | .02 | .01 |
| ☐ 61 Jerry Gray ............................ | .05 | .02 | .01 |
| ☐ 62 Dan Marino ........................... | .75 | .35 | .09 |
| ☐ 63 Sammie Smith ........................ | .05 | .02 | .01 |
| ☐ 64 Richmond Webb ...................... | .08 | .04 | .01 |
| ☐ 65 Louis Oliver .......................... | .08 | .04 | .01 |
| ☐ 66 Ferrell Edmunds ...................... | .05 | .02 | .01 |
| ☐ 67 Jeff Cross............................. | .05 | .02 | .01 |
| ☐ 68 Wade Wilson .......................... | .08 | .04 | .01 |
| ☐ 69 Chris Doleman ........................ | .08 | .04 | .01 |
| ☐ 70 Joey Browner ......................... | .05 | .02 | .01 |
| ☐ 71 Keith Millard .......................... | .08 | .04 | .01 |
| ☐ 72 John Stephens ........................ | .08 | .04 | .01 |
| ☐ 73 Andre Tippett ......................... | .08 | .04 | .01 |

| | | |
|---|---|---|
| ☐ 74 Brent Williams | .05 | .02 | .01 |
| ☐ 75 Craig Heyward | .05 | .02 | .01 |
| ☐ 76 Eric Martin | .08 | .04 | .01 |
| ☐ 77 Pat Swilling | .08 | .04 | .01 |
| ☐ 78 Sam Mills | .08 | .04 | .01 |
| ☐ 79 Jeff Hostetler | .25 | .11 | .03 |
| ☐ 80 Ottis Anderson | .08 | .04 | .01 |
| ☐ 81 Lawrence Taylor | .10 | .05 | .01 |
| ☐ 82 Pepper Johnson | .08 | .04 | .01 |
| ☐ 83 Blair Thomas | .08 | .04 | .01 |
| ☐ 84 Al Toon | .08 | .04 | .01 |
| ☐ 85 Ken O'Brien | .08 | .04 | .01 |
| ☐ 86 Erik McMillan | .05 | .02 | .01 |
| ☐ 87 Dennis Byrd | .08 | .04 | .01 |
| ☐ 88 Randall Cunningham | .10 | .05 | .01 |
| ☐ 89 Fred Barnett | .15 | .07 | .02 |
| ☐ 90 Seth Joyner | .08 | .04 | .01 |
| ☐ 91 Reggie White | .15 | .07 | .02 |
| ☐ 92 Timm Rosenbach | .08 | .04 | .01 |
| ☐ 93 Johnny Johnson | .25 | .11 | .03 |
| ☐ 94 Tim McDonald | .08 | .04 | .01 |
| ☐ 95 Freddie Joe Nunn | .05 | .02 | .01 |
| ☐ 96 Bubby Brister | .08 | .04 | .01 |
| ☐ 97 Gary Anderson UER | .05 | .02 | .01 |
| (Listed as RB) | | | |
| ☐ 98 Merril Hoge | .08 | .04 | .01 |
| ☐ 99 Keith Willis | .05 | .02 | .01 |
| ☐ 100 Rod Woodson | .10 | .05 | .01 |
| ☐ 101 Billy Joe Tolliver | .08 | .04 | .01 |
| ☐ 102 Marion Butts | .10 | .05 | .01 |
| ☐ 103 Rod Bernstine | .10 | .05 | .01 |
| ☐ 104 Lee Williams | .08 | .04 | .01 |
| ☐ 105 Burt Grossman UER | .05 | .02 | .01 |
| (Photo on back | | | |
| is reversed) | | | |
| ☐ 106 Tom Rathman | .08 | .04 | .01 |
| ☐ 107 John Taylor | .10 | .05 | .01 |
| ☐ 108 Michael Carter | .05 | .02 | .01 |
| ☐ 109 Guy McIntyre | .08 | .04 | .01 |
| ☐ 110 Pierce Holt | .05 | .02 | .01 |
| ☐ 111 John L. Williams | .08 | .04 | .01 |
| ☐ 112 Dave Krieg | .08 | .04 | .01 |
| ☐ 113 Bryan Millard | .05 | .02 | .01 |
| ☐ 114 Cortez Kennedy | .25 | .11 | .03 |
| ☐ 115 Derrick Fenner | .08 | .04 | .01 |
| ☐ 116 Vinny Testaverde | .10 | .05 | .01 |
| ☐ 117 Reggie Cobb | .25 | .11 | .03 |
| ☐ 118 Gary Anderson | .08 | .04 | .01 |
| ☐ 119 Bruce Hill | .05 | .02 | .01 |
| ☐ 120 Wayne Haddix | .05 | .02 | .01 |
| ☐ 121 Broderick Thomas | .05 | .02 | .01 |
| ☐ 122 Keith McCants | .05 | .02 | .01 |
| ☐ 123 Andre Collins | .05 | .02 | .01 |
| ☐ 124 Earnest Byner | .05 | .02 | .01 |
| ☐ 125 Jim Lachey | .05 | .02 | .01 |
| ☐ 126 Mark Rypien | .10 | .05 | .01 |
| ☐ 127 Charles Mann | .08 | .04 | .01 |
| ☐ 128 Nick Lowery | .08 | .04 | .01 |
| Kansas City Chiefs | | | |
| ☐ 129 Chip Lohmiller | .08 | .04 | .01 |
| Washington Redskins | | | |
| ☐ 130 Mike Horan | .05 | .02 | .01 |
| Denver Broncos | | | |
| ☐ 131 Rohn Stark | .05 | .02 | .01 |
| Indianapolis Colts | | | |
| ☐ 132 Sean Landeta | .05 | .02 | .01 |
| New York Giants | | | |
| ☐ 133 Clarence Verdin | .05 | .02 | .01 |
| Indianapolis Colts | | | |
| ☐ 134 Johnny Bailey | .08 | .04 | .01 |
| Chicago Bears | | | |
| ☐ 135 Herschel Walker | .10 | .05 | .01 |
| Minnesota Vikings | | | |
| ☐ 136 Bo Jackson PP | .35 | .16 | .04 |
| Los Angeles Raiders | | | |
| ☐ 137 Dexter Carter PP | .08 | .04 | .01 |
| San Francisco 49ers | | | |
| ☐ 138 Warren Moon PP | .15 | .07 | .02 |
| Houston Oilers | | | |
| ☐ 139 Joe Montana PP | 1.00 | .45 | .13 |
| San Francisco 49ers | | | |
| ☐ 140 Jerry Rice PP | .75 | .35 | .09 |
| San Francisco 49ers | | | |
| ☐ 141 Deion Sanders PP | .25 | .11 | .03 |
| Atlanta Falcons | | | |
| ☐ 142 Ronnie Lippett PP | .05 | .02 | .01 |
| New England Patriots | | | |
| ☐ 143 Terance Mathis PP | .05 | .02 | .01 |
| New York Jets | | | |
| ☐ 144 Gaston Green PP | .08 | .04 | .01 |
| Los Angeles Rams | | | |
| ☐ 145 Dean Biasucci PP | .05 | .02 | .01 |
| Indianapolis Colts | | | |
| ☐ 146 Charles Haley PP | .08 | .04 | .01 |
| San Francisco 49ers | | | |
| ☐ 147 Derrick Thomas PP | .25 | .11 | .03 |
| Kansas City Chiefs | | | |
| ☐ 148 Lawrence Taylor PP | .05 | .02 | .01 |
| New York Giants | | | |
| ☐ 149 Art Shell CO PP | .08 | .04 | .01 |
| Los Angeles Raiders | | | |
| ☐ 150 Bill Parcells CO PP | .08 | .04 | .01 |
| New York Giants | | | |
| ☐ 151 Steve Broussard | .08 | .04 | .01 |
| ☐ 152 Darion Conner | .05 | .02 | .01 |
| ☐ 153 Bill Fralic | .05 | .02 | .01 |
| ☐ 154 Mike Gann | .05 | .02 | .01 |
| ☐ 155 Tim McKyer | .08 | .04 | .01 |
| ☐ 156 Don Beebe UER | .10 | .05 | .01 |
| (4 TD's against | | | |
| Dolphins, should be | | | |
| against Steelers) | | | |
| ☐ 157 Cornelius Bennett | .10 | .05 | .01 |
| ☐ 158 Andre Reed | .10 | .05 | .01 |
| ☐ 159 Leonard Smith | .05 | .02 | .01 |
| ☐ 160 Will Wolford | .05 | .02 | .01 |
| ☐ 161 Mark Carrier | .08 | .04 | .01 |
| ☐ 162 Wendell Davis | .05 | .02 | .01 |
| ☐ 163 Jay Hilgenberg | .08 | .04 | .01 |
| ☐ 164 Brad Muster | .08 | .04 | .01 |
| ☐ 165 Mike Singletary | .10 | .05 | .01 |
| ☐ 166 Eddie Brown | .05 | .02 | .01 |
| ☐ 167 David Fulcher | .05 | .02 | .01 |
| ☐ 168 Rodney Holman | .05 | .02 | .01 |
| ☐ 169 Anthony Munoz | .08 | .04 | .01 |
| ☐ 170 Craig Taylor | .05 | .02 | .01 |
| ☐ 171 Mike Baab | .05 | .02 | .01 |
| ☐ 172 David Grayson | .05 | .02 | .01 |
| ☐ 173 Reggie Langhorne | .08 | .04 | .01 |
| ☐ 174 Joe Morris | .08 | .04 | .01 |
| ☐ 175 Kevin Gogan | .15 | .07 | .02 |
| ☐ 176 Jack Del Rio | .05 | .02 | .01 |
| ☐ 177 Issiac Holt | .05 | .02 | .01 |
| ☐ 178 Michael Irvin | .50 | .23 | .06 |
| ☐ 179 Jay Novacek | .15 | .07 | .02 |
| ☐ 180 Steve Atwater | .10 | .05 | .01 |
| ☐ 181 Mark Jackson | .08 | .04 | .01 |
| ☐ 182 Ricky Nattiel | .05 | .02 | .01 |
| ☐ 183 Warren Powers | .05 | .02 | .01 |
| ☐ 184 Dennis Smith | .08 | .04 | .01 |
| ☐ 185 Bennie Blades | .05 | .02 | .01 |
| ☐ 186 Lomas Brown UER | .05 | .02 | .01 |
| (Spent 6 seasons with | | | |
| Detroit, not 7) | | | |
| ☐ 187 Robert Clark UER | .05 | .02 | .01 |
| (Plan B acquisition | | | |
| in '89, not '90) | | | |
| ☐ 188 Mel Gray | .08 | .04 | .01 |
| ☐ 189 Chris Spielman | .08 | .04 | .01 |
| ☐ 190 Johnny Holland | .05 | .02 | .01 |
| ☐ 191 Don Majkowski | .08 | .04 | .01 |
| ☐ 192 Bryce Paup | .25 | .11 | .03 |
| ☐ 193 Darrell Thompson | .08 | .04 | .01 |
| ☐ 194 Ed West UER | .05 | .02 | .01 |
| (Photo on back | | | |
| is reversed) | | | |
| ☐ 195 Cris Dishman | .15 | .07 | .02 |
| ☐ 196 Drew Hill | .08 | .04 | .01 |
| ☐ 197 Bruce Matthews | .08 | .04 | .01 |
| ☐ 198 Bubba McDowell | .05 | .02 | .01 |
| ☐ 199 Allen Pinkett | .05 | .02 | .01 |
| ☐ 200 Bill Brooks | .08 | .04 | .01 |
| ☐ 201 Jeff Herrod | .05 | .02 | .01 |
| ☐ 202 Anthony Johnson | .05 | .02 | .01 |
| ☐ 203 Mike Prior | .05 | .02 | .01 |
| ☐ 204 John Alt | .05 | .02 | .01 |
| ☐ 205 Stephone Paige | .08 | .04 | .01 |
| ☐ 206 Kevin Ross | .08 | .04 | .01 |
| ☐ 207 Dan Saleaumua | .05 | .02 | .01 |
| ☐ 208 Barry Word | .10 | .05 | .01 |
| ☐ 209 Marcus Allen | .15 | .07 | .02 |
| ☐ 210 Roger Craig | .08 | .04 | .01 |
| ☐ 211 Ronnie Lott | .10 | .05 | .01 |
| ☐ 212 Winston Moss | .05 | .02 | .01 |
| ☐ 213 Jay Schroeder | .08 | .04 | .01 |
| ☐ 214 Robert Delpino | .08 | .04 | .01 |
| ☐ 215 Henry Ellard | .08 | .04 | .01 |
| ☐ 216 Kevin Greene | .08 | .04 | .01 |
| ☐ 217 Tom Newberry | .05 | .02 | .01 |
| ☐ 218 Michael Stewart | .05 | .02 | .01 |
| ☐ 219 Mark Duper | .08 | .04 | .01 |
| ☐ 220 Mark Higgs | .60 | .25 | .08 |
| ☐ 221 John Offerdahl UER | .08 | .04 | .01 |
| (2nd round pick in | | | |
| '86, not 6th) | | | |
| ☐ 222 Keith Sims | .05 | .02 | .01 |
| ☐ 223 Anthony Carter | .08 | .04 | .01 |
| ☐ 224 Cris Carter | .10 | .05 | .01 |
| ☐ 225 Steve Jordan | .08 | .04 | .01 |
| ☐ 226 Randall McDaniel | .05 | .02 | .01 |
| ☐ 227 Al Noga | .05 | .02 | .01 |
| ☐ 228 Ray Agnew | .05 | .02 | .01 |
| ☐ 229 Bruce Armstrong | .05 | .02 | .01 |
| ☐ 230 Irving Fryar | .08 | .04 | .01 |

| | | | |
|---|---|---|---|
| ☐ 231 Greg McMurtry | .05 | .02 | .01 |
| ☐ 232 Chris Singleton | .05 | .02 | .01 |
| ☐ 233 Morten Andersen | .08 | .04 | .01 |
| ☐ 234 Vince Buck | .05 | .02 | .01 |
| ☐ 235 Gill Fenerty | .08 | .04 | .01 |
| ☐ 236 Rickey Jackson | .08 | .04 | .01 |
| ☐ 237 Vaughan Johnson | .08 | .04 | .01 |
| ☐ 238 Carl Banks | .08 | .04 | .01 |
| ☐ 239 Mark Collins | .05 | .02 | .01 |
| ☐ 240 Rodney Hampton | .75 | .35 | .09 |
| ☐ 241 David Meggett | .10 | .05 | .01 |
| ☐ 242 Bart Oates | .05 | .02 | .01 |
| ☐ 243 Kyle Clifton | .05 | .02 | .01 |
| ☐ 244 Jeff Lageman | .05 | .02 | .01 |
| ☐ 245 Freeman McNeil UER | .05 | .02 | .01 |
| (Drafted in '81, | | | |
| not '80) | | | |
| ☐ 246 Rob Moore | .10 | .05 | .01 |
| ☐ 247 Eric Allen | .08 | .04 | .01 |
| ☐ 248 Keith Byars | .08 | .04 | .01 |
| ☐ 249 Keith Jackson | .15 | .07 | .02 |
| ☐ 250 Jim McMahon | .10 | .05 | .01 |
| ☐ 251 Andre Waters | .05 | .02 | .01 |
| ☐ 252 Ken Harvey | .05 | .02 | .01 |
| ☐ 253 Ernie Jones | .05 | .02 | .01 |
| ☐ 254 Luis Sharpe | .05 | .02 | .01 |
| ☐ 255 Anthony Thompson | .05 | .02 | .01 |
| ☐ 256 Tom Tupa | .08 | .04 | .01 |
| ☐ 257 Eric Green | .15 | .07 | .02 |
| ☐ 258 Barry Foster | .50 | .23 | .06 |
| ☐ 259 Bryan Hinkle | .05 | .02 | .01 |
| ☐ 260 Tunch Ilkin | .05 | .02 | .01 |
| ☐ 261 Louis Lipps | .08 | .04 | .01 |
| ☐ 262 Gill Byrd | .08 | .04 | .01 |
| ☐ 263 John Friesz | .10 | .05 | .01 |
| ☐ 264 Anthony Miller | .20 | .09 | .03 |
| ☐ 265 Junior Seau | .25 | .11 | .03 |
| ☐ 266 Ronnie Harmon | .05 | .02 | .01 |
| ☐ 267 Harris Barton | .05 | .02 | .01 |
| ☐ 268 Todd Bowles | .05 | .02 | .01 |
| ☐ 269 Don Griffin | .05 | .02 | .01 |
| ☐ 270 Bill Romanowski | .05 | .02 | .01 |
| ☐ 271 Steve Young | .50 | .23 | .06 |
| ☐ 272 Brian Blades | .10 | .05 | .01 |
| ☐ 273 Jacob Green | .05 | .02 | .01 |
| ☐ 274 Rufus Porter | .05 | .02 | .01 |
| ☐ 275 Eugene Robinson | .05 | .02 | .01 |
| ☐ 276 Mark Carrier | .08 | .04 | .01 |
| ☐ 277 Reuben Davis | .05 | .02 | .01 |
| ☐ 278 Paul Gruber | .08 | .04 | .01 |
| ☐ 279 Gary Clark | .08 | .04 | .01 |
| ☐ 280 Darrell Green | .08 | .04 | .01 |
| ☐ 281 Wilber Marshall | .08 | .04 | .01 |
| ☐ 282 Matt Millen | .08 | .04 | .01 |
| ☐ 283 Alvin Walton | .05 | .02 | .01 |
| ☐ 284 Joe Gibbs CO UER | .08 | .04 | .01 |
| (NFLPA logo on back) | | | |
| ☐ 285 Don Shula CO UER | .08 | .04 | .01 |
| Miami Dolphins | | | |
| (NFLPA logo on back) | | | |
| ☐ 286 Larry Brown | .25 | .11 | .03 |
| Dallas Cowboys | | | |
| ☐ 287 Mike Croel | .20 | .09 | .03 |
| Denver Broncos | | | |
| ☐ 288 Antone Davis | .10 | .05 | .01 |
| Philadelphia Eagles | | | |
| ☐ 289 Ricky Ervins UER | .20 | .09 | .03 |
| Washington Redskins | | | |
| (2nd round choice, | | | |
| should say 3rd) | | | |
| ☐ 290 Brett Favre | 2.00 | .90 | .25 |
| Atlanta Falcons | | | |
| ☐ 291 Pat Harlow | .10 | .05 | .01 |
| New England Patriots | | | |
| ☐ 292 Michael Jackson | .75 | .35 | .09 |
| Cleveland Browns | | | |
| ☐ 293 Henry Jones | .25 | .11 | .03 |
| Buffalo Bills | | | |
| ☐ 294 Aaron Craver | .06 | .03 | .01 |
| Miami Dolphins | | | |
| ☐ 295 Nick Bell | .20 | .09 | .03 |
| Los Angeles Raiders | | | |
| ☐ 296 Todd Lyght | .10 | .05 | .01 |
| Los Angeles Rams | | | |
| ☐ 297 Todd Marinovich | .10 | .05 | .01 |
| Los Angeles Raiders | | | |
| ☐ 298 Russell Maryland | .40 | .18 | .05 |
| Dallas Cowboys | | | |
| ☐ 299 Kanavis McGhee | .10 | .05 | .01 |
| New York Giants | | | |
| ☐ 300 Dan McGwire | .10 | .05 | .01 |
| Seattle Seahawks | | | |
| ☐ 301 Charles McRae | .06 | .03 | .01 |
| Tampa Bay Buccaneers | | | |
| ☐ 302 Eric Moten | .06 | .03 | .01 |
| San Diego Chargers | | | |
| ☐ 303 Jerome Henderson | .06 | .03 | .01 |

| | | | |
|---|---|---|---|
| New England Patriots | | | |
| ☐ 304 Browning Nagle | .20 | .09 | .03 |
| New York Jets | | | |
| ☐ 305 Mike Pritchard | .75 | .35 | .09 |
| Atlanta Falcons | | | |
| ☐ 306 Stanley Richard | .10 | .05 | .01 |
| San Diego Chargers | | | |
| ☐ 307 Randal Hill | .30 | .14 | .04 |
| Phoenix Cardinals | | | |
| ☐ 308 Leonard Russell | 1.00 | .45 | .13 |
| New England Patriots | | | |
| ☐ 309 Eric Swann | .20 | .09 | .03 |
| Phoenix Cardinals | | | |
| ☐ 310 Phil Hansen | .15 | .07 | .02 |
| Buffalo Bills | | | |
| ☐ 311 Moe Gardner | .10 | .05 | .01 |
| Atlanta Falcons | | | |
| ☐ 312 Jon Vaughn | .20 | .09 | .03 |
| New England Patriots | | | |
| ☐ 313 Aeneas Williams UER | .15 | .07 | .02 |
| Phoenix Cardinals | | | |
| (Misspelled Aaneas | | | |
| on card back) | | | |
| ☐ 314 Alfred Williams | .15 | .07 | .02 |
| Cincinnati Bengals | | | |
| ☐ 315 Harvey Williams | .20 | .09 | .03 |
| Kansas City Chiefs | | | |
| ☐ PM1 Emmitt Smith Platinum | 450.00 | 200.00 | 57.50 |
| NNO SP | | | |
| ☐ PM2 Paul Brown Platinum | 150.00 | 70.00 | 19.00 |
| NNO | | | |

# 1991 Pro Set Platinum PC

These ten Pro Set Platinum Collectible cards were inserted in 1991 Pro Set Platinum second series foil packs. The standard-size (2 1/2" by 3 1/2") cards feature full-bleed color player photos on the fronts, with a second color photo on the horizontally oriented backs. The set is subdivided as follows: Platinum Profile (1-3), Platinum Photo (4-5), and Platinum Game Breaker (6-10). The Platinum Game Breaker cards present in alphabetical order five standout NFL running backs. The cards are numbered on the back with a "PC" prefix.

| | MINT | EXC | G-VG |
|---|---|---|---|
| COMPLETE SET (10) | 10.00 | 4.50 | 1.25 |
| COMMON PLAYER (PC1-PC10) | .50 | .23 | .06 |
| ☐ PC1 Bobby Hebert | .50 | .23 | .06 |
| New Orleans Saints | | | |
| ☐ PC2 Art Monk | .75 | .35 | .09 |
| Washington Redskins | | | |
| ☐ PC3 Kenny Walker | .50 | .23 | .06 |
| Denver Broncos | | | |
| ☐ PC4 Low Fives | .50 | .23 | .06 |
| Houston Oilers | | | |
| ☐ PC5 Touchdown | .50 | .23 | .06 |
| Kevin Mack | | | |
| Cleveland Browns | | | |
| ☐ PC6 Neal Anderson | .50 | .23 | .06 |
| Chicago Bears | | | |
| ☐ PC7 Gaston Green | .50 | .23 | .06 |
| Denver Broncos | | | |
| ☐ PC8 Barry Sanders | 3.00 | 1.35 | .40 |
| Detroit Lions | | | |
| ☐ PC9 Emmitt Smith | 6.00 | 2.70 | .75 |
| Dallas Cowboys | | | |
| ☐ PC10 Thurman Thomas | 1.50 | .65 | .19 |
| Buffalo Bills | | | |

# 1991 Pro Set Spanish

The 1991 Pro Set Spanish football card set contains 300 cards selected from 1991 Pro Set Series I and II. In addition, the set also features five randomly-inserted special collectibles available only in the Spanish language edition. Though the standard-size (2 1/2" by 3 1/2") cards display the same player photos, the terminology has been translated into Spanish. The cards are numbered on the back and checklisted below alphabetically according to teams as follows: Atlanta Falcons (1-9), Buffalo Bills (10-18), Chicago Bears (19-27), Cincinnati Bengals (28-36), Cleveland Browns (37-45), Dallas Cowboys (46-54), Denver Broncos (55-63), Detroit Lions (64-72), Green Bay Packers (73-81), Houston Oilers (82-90), Indianapolis Colts (91-99), Kansas City Chiefs (100-108), Los Angeles Raiders (109-117), Los Angeles Rams (118-126), Miami Dolphins (127-135), Minnesota Vikings (136-144), New England Patriots (145-153), New Orleans Saints (154-162), New York Giants (163-171), New York Jets (172-180), Philadelphia Eagles (181-189), Phoenix Cardinals (190-198), Pittsburgh Steelers (199-207), San Diego Chargers (208-216), San Francisco 49ers (217-225), Seattle Seahawks (226-34), Tampa Bay Buccaneers (235-243), and Washington Redskins (244-252). Special subsets featured include Rookies (253-279), NFC Superstars (280-288), AFC Superstars (289-297), Think About It (298-300), and Special Cards (E1-E5). The cards are numbered on the back.

|  | MINT | EXC | G-VG |
|---|---|---|---|
| COMPLETE SET (300) | 12.00 | 5.00 | 1.20 |
| COMMON PLAYER (1-300) | .04 | .02 | .00 |

| | | MINT | EXC | G-VG |
|---|---|---|---|---|
| ☐ | 1 Steve Broussard | .07 | .03 | .01 |
| ☐ | 2 Darion Conner | .07 | .03 | .01 |
| ☐ | 3 Tory Epps | .04 | .02 | .00 |
| ☐ | 4 Bill Fralic | .04 | .02 | .00 |
| ☐ | 5 Mike Gann | .04 | .02 | .00 |
| ☐ | 6 Chris Miller | .15 | .06 | .01 |
| ☐ | 7 Andre Rison | .20 | .08 | .02 |
| ☐ | 8 Deion Sanders | .25 | .10 | .02 |
| ☐ | 9 Jessie Tuggle | .04 | .02 | .00 |
| ☐ | 10 Cornelius Bennett | .10 | .04 | .01 |
| ☐ | 11 Shane Conlan | .07 | .03 | .01 |
| ☐ | 12 Kent Hull | .04 | .02 | .00 |
| ☐ | 13 Kirby Jackson | .04 | .02 | .00 |
| ☐ | 14 James Lofton | .15 | .06 | .01 |
| ☐ | 15 Andre Reed | .15 | .06 | .01 |
| ☐ | 16 Bruce Smith | .15 | .06 | .01 |
| ☐ | 17 Darryl Talley | .10 | .04 | .01 |
| ☐ | 18 Thurman Thomas | .50 | .20 | .05 |
| ☐ | 19 Neal Anderson | .07 | .03 | .01 |
| ☐ | 20 Trace Armstrong | .04 | .02 | .00 |
| ☐ | 21 Mark Carrier USC | .07 | .03 | .01 |
| ☐ | 22 Wendell Davis | .10 | .04 | .01 |
| ☐ | 23 Richard Dent | .07 | .03 | .01 |
| ☐ | 24 Jim Harbaugh | .10 | .04 | .01 |
| ☐ | 25 Ron Rivera | .04 | .02 | .00 |
| ☐ | 26 Mike Singletary | .10 | .04 | .01 |
| ☐ | 27 Lemuel Stinson | .04 | .02 | .00 |
| ☐ | 28 James Brooks | .07 | .03 | .01 |
| ☐ | 29 Eddie Brown | .04 | .02 | .00 |
| ☐ | 30 Boomer Esiason | .15 | .06 | .01 |
| ☐ | 31 James Francis | .07 | .03 | .01 |
| ☐ | 32 David Fulcher | .04 | .02 | .00 |
| ☐ | 33 Rodney Holman | .04 | .02 | .00 |
| ☐ | 34 Anthony Munoz | .10 | .04 | .01 |
| ☐ | 35 Bruce Reimers | .04 | .02 | .00 |
| ☐ | 36 Ickey Woods | .04 | .02 | .00 |
| ☐ | 37 Mike Baab | .04 | .02 | .00 |
| ☐ | 38 Brian Brennan | .04 | .02 | .00 |
| ☐ | 39 Raymond Clayborn | .04 | .02 | .00 |
| ☐ | 40 Mike Johnson | .04 | .02 | .00 |
| ☐ | 41 Clay Matthews | .10 | .04 | .01 |
| ☐ | 42 Eric Metcalf | .15 | .06 | .01 |
| ☐ | 43 Frank Minnifield | .04 | .02 | .00 |
| ☐ | 44 Joe Morris | .07 | .03 | .01 |
| ☐ | 45 Anthony Pleasant | .04 | .02 | .00 |
| ☐ | 46 Troy Aikman | 1.25 | .50 | .12 |
| ☐ | 47 Jack Del Rio | .04 | .02 | .00 |
| ☐ | 48 Issiac Holt | .04 | .02 | .00 |
| ☐ | 49 Michael Irvin | .50 | .20 | .05 |
| ☐ | 50 Jimmie Jones | .04 | .02 | .00 |
| ☐ | 51 Nate Newton | .07 | .03 | .01 |
| ☐ | 52 Danny Noonan | .04 | .02 | .00 |
| ☐ | 53 Jay Novacek | .10 | .04 | .01 |
| ☐ | 54 Emmitt Smith | 2.00 | .80 | .20 |
| ☐ | 55 Steve Atwater | .04 | .02 | .00 |
| ☐ | 56 Michael Brooks | .04 | .02 | .00 |
| ☐ | 57 John Elway | .35 | .14 | .03 |
| ☐ | 58 Mike Horan | .04 | .02 | .00 |
| ☐ | 59 Mark Jackson | .04 | .02 | .00 |
| ☐ | 60 Karl Mecklenburg | .07 | .03 | .01 |
| ☐ | 61 Warren Powers | .04 | .02 | .00 |
| ☐ | 62 Dennis Smith | .04 | .02 | .00 |
| ☐ | 63 Doug Widell | .04 | .02 | .00 |
| ☐ | 64 Jerry Ball | .04 | .02 | .00 |
| ☐ | 65 Bennie Blades | .04 | .02 | .00 |
| ☐ | 66 Robert Clark | .04 | .02 | .00 |
| ☐ | 67 Ken Dallafior | .04 | .02 | .00 |
| ☐ | 68 Mel Gray | .04 | .02 | .00 |
| ☐ | 69 Eddie Murray | .04 | .02 | .00 |
| ☐ | 70 Rodney Peete | .10 | .04 | .01 |
| ☐ | 71 Barry Sanders | .75 | .30 | .07 |
| ☐ | 72 Chris Spielman | .07 | .03 | .01 |
| ☐ | 73 Robert Brown | .04 | .02 | .00 |
| ☐ | 74 LeRoy Butler | .04 | .02 | .00 |
| ☐ | 75 Perry Kemp | .04 | .02 | .00 |
| ☐ | 76 Don Majkowski | .04 | .02 | .00 |
| ☐ | 77 Tony Mandarich | .04 | .02 | .00 |
| ☐ | 78 Mark Murphy | .04 | .02 | .00 |
| ☐ | 79 Brian Noble | .04 | .02 | .00 |
| ☐ | 80 Sterling Sharpe | .50 | .20 | .05 |
| ☐ | 81 Ed West | .04 | .02 | .00 |
| ☐ | 82 Ray Childress | .07 | .03 | .01 |
| ☐ | 83 Cris Dishman | .07 | .03 | .01 |
| ☐ | 84 Ernest Givins | .07 | .03 | .01 |
| ☐ | 85 Drew Hill | .07 | .03 | .01 |
| ☐ | 86 Haywood Jeffires | .20 | .08 | .02 |
| ☐ | 87 Lamar Lathon | .04 | .02 | .00 |
| ☐ | 88 Bruce Matthews | .04 | .02 | .00 |
| ☐ | 89 Bubba McDowell | .04 | .02 | .00 |
| ☐ | 90 Warren Moon | .25 | .10 | .02 |
| ☐ | 91 Chip Banks | .04 | .02 | .00 |
| ☐ | 92 Albert Bentley | .07 | .03 | .01 |
| ☐ | 93 Duane Bickett | .07 | .03 | .01 |
| ☐ | 94 Bill Brooks | .07 | .03 | .01 |
| ☐ | 95 Sam Clancy | .04 | .02 | .00 |
| ☐ | 96 Ray Donaldson | .04 | .02 | .00 |
| ☐ | 97 Jeff George | .25 | .10 | .02 |
| ☐ | 98 Mike Prior | .04 | .02 | .00 |
| ☐ | 99 Clarence Verdin | .04 | .02 | .00 |
| ☐ | 100 Steve DeBerg | .07 | .03 | .01 |
| ☐ | 101 Albert Lewis | .07 | .03 | .01 |
| ☐ | 102 Christian Okoye | .07 | .03 | .01 |
| ☐ | 103 Kevin Ross | .04 | .02 | .00 |
| ☐ | 104 Stephone Paige | .07 | .03 | .01 |
| ☐ | 105 Kevin Porter | .04 | .02 | .00 |
| ☐ | 106 Percy Snow | .04 | .02 | .00 |
| ☐ | 107 Derrick Thomas | .25 | .10 | .02 |
| ☐ | 108 Barry Word | .15 | .06 | .01 |
| ☐ | 109 Marcus Allen | .15 | .06 | .01 |
| ☐ | 110 Mervyn Fernandez | .07 | .03 | .01 |
| ☐ | 111 Howie Long | .10 | .04 | .01 |
| ☐ | 112 Ronnie Lott | .15 | .06 | .01 |
| ☐ | 113 Terry McDaniel | .04 | .02 | .00 |
| ☐ | 114 Max Montoya | .04 | .02 | .00 |
| ☐ | 115 Don Mosebar | .04 | .02 | .00 |
| ☐ | 116 Jay Schroeder | .07 | .03 | .01 |
| ☐ | 117 Greg Townsend | .04 | .02 | .00 |
| ☐ | 118 Flipper Anderson | .07 | .03 | .01 |
| ☐ | 119 Henry Ellard | .07 | .03 | .01 |
| ☐ | 120 Jim Everett | .10 | .04 | .01 |
| ☐ | 121 Kevin Greene | .07 | .03 | .01 |
| ☐ | 122 Damone Johnson | .04 | .02 | .00 |
| ☐ | 123 Buford McGee | .04 | .02 | .00 |
| ☐ | 124 Tom Newberry | .04 | .02 | .00 |
| ☐ | 125 Michael Stewart | .04 | .02 | .00 |
| ☐ | 126 Alvin Wright | .04 | .02 | .00 |
| ☐ | 127 Mark Clayton | .07 | .03 | .01 |
| ☐ | 128 Jeff Cross | .04 | .02 | .00 |
| ☐ | 129 Mark Duper | .07 | .03 | .01 |
| ☐ | 130 Ferrell Edmunds | .04 | .02 | .00 |
| ☐ | 131 Dan Marino | .75 | .30 | .07 |
| ☐ | 132 Tim McKyer | .04 | .02 | .00 |
| ☐ | 133 John Offerdahl | .07 | .03 | .01 |
| ☐ | 134 Louis Oliver | .04 | .02 | .00 |
| ☐ | 135 Sammie Smith | .07 | .03 | .01 |
| ☐ | 136 Joey Browner | .07 | .03 | .01 |
| ☐ | 137 Anthony Carter | .10 | .04 | .01 |
| ☐ | 138 Chris Doleman | .07 | .03 | .01 |
| ☐ | 139 Hassan Jones | .04 | .02 | .00 |
| ☐ | 140 Steve Jordan | .07 | .03 | .01 |

|  |  | | | |
|---|---|---|---|---|
| ☐ 141 | Carl Lee | .04 | .02 | .00 |
| ☐ 142 | Al Noga | .04 | .02 | .00 |
| ☐ 143 | Henry Thomas | .04 | .02 | .00 |
| ☐ 144 | Herschel Walker | .15 | .06 | .01 |
| ☐ 145 | Ray Agnew | .04 | .02 | .00 |
| ☐ 146 | Bruce Armstrong | .04 | .02 | .00 |
| ☐ 147 | Marv Cook | .07 | .03 | .01 |
| ☐ 148 | Irving Fryar | .07 | .03 | .01 |
| ☐ 149 | Tommy Hodson | .07 | .03 | .01 |
| ☐ 150 | Fred Marion | .04 | .02 | .00 |
| ☐ 151 | Johnny Rembert | .04 | .02 | .00 |
| ☐ 152 | Chris Singleton | .04 | .02 | .00 |
| ☐ 153 | Andre Tippett | .07 | .03 | .01 |
| ☐ 154 | Morten Andersen | .04 | .02 | .00 |
| ☐ 155 | Toi Cook | .04 | .02 | .00 |
| ☐ 156 | Craig Heyward | .07 | .03 | .01 |
| ☐ 157 | Dalton Hilliard | .04 | .02 | .00 |
| ☐ 158 | Rickey Jackson | .07 | .03 | .01 |
| ☐ 159 | Vaughan Johnson | .04 | .02 | .00 |
| ☐ 160 | Rueben Mayes | .04 | .02 | .00 |
| ☐ 161 | Pat Swilling | .07 | .03 | .01 |
| ☐ 162 | Bobby Hebert | .07 | .03 | .01 |
| ☐ 163 | Ottis Anderson | .10 | .04 | .01 |
| ☐ 164 | Carl Banks | .07 | .03 | .01 |
| ☐ 165 | Rodney Hampton | .30 | .12 | .03 |
| ☐ 166 | Jeff Hostetler | .20 | .08 | .02 |
| ☐ 167 | Mark Ingram | .04 | .02 | .00 |
| ☐ 168 | Leonard Marshall | .04 | .02 | .00 |
| ☐ 169 | Dave Meggett | .10 | .04 | .01 |
| ☐ 170 | Lawrence Taylor | .15 | .06 | .01 |
| ☐ 171 | Everson Walls | .04 | .02 | .00 |
| ☐ 172 | Brad Baxter | .15 | .06 | .01 |
| ☐ 173 | Jeff Lageman | .07 | .03 | .01 |
| ☐ 174 | Pat Leahy | .04 | .02 | .00 |
| ☐ 175 | Erik McMillan | .04 | .02 | .00 |
| ☐ 176 | Scott Mersereau | .07 | .03 | .01 |
| ☐ 177 | Rob Moore | .15 | .06 | .01 |
| ☐ 178 | Ken O'Brien | .07 | .03 | .01 |
| ☐ 179 | Blair Thomas | .10 | .04 | .01 |
| ☐ 180 | Al Toon | .07 | .03 | .01 |
| ☐ 181 | Eric Allen | .04 | .02 | .00 |
| ☐ 182 | Jerome Brown | .07 | .03 | .01 |
| ☐ 183 | Keith Byars | .07 | .03 | .01 |
| ☐ 184 | Randall Cunningham | .20 | .08 | .02 |
| ☐ 185 | Byron Evans | .04 | .02 | .00 |
| ☐ 186 | Keith Jackson | .15 | .06 | .01 |
| ☐ 187 | Heath Sherman | .07 | .03 | .01 |
| ☐ 188 | Clyde Simmons | .07 | .03 | .01 |
| ☐ 189 | Reggie White | .15 | .06 | .01 |
| ☐ 190 | Rich Camarillo | .04 | .02 | .00 |
| ☐ 191 | Johnny Johnson | .25 | .10 | .02 |
| ☐ 192 | Ernie Jones | .07 | .03 | .01 |
| ☐ 193 | Tim McDonald | .07 | .03 | .01 |
| ☐ 194 | Freddie Joe Nunn | .04 | .02 | .00 |
| ☐ 195 | Luis Sharpe | .04 | .02 | .00 |
| ☐ 196 | Jay Taylor | .04 | .02 | .00 |
| ☐ 197 | Anthony Thompson | .07 | .03 | .01 |
| ☐ 198 | Tom Tupa | .04 | .02 | .00 |
| ☐ 199 | Gary Anderson | .04 | .02 | .00 |
| ☐ 200 | Bubby Brister | .04 | .02 | .00 |
| ☐ 201 | Eric Green | .07 | .03 | .01 |
| ☐ 202 | Bryan Hinkle | .04 | .02 | .00 |
| ☐ 203 | Merril Hoge | .04 | .02 | .00 |
| ☐ 204 | Carnell Lake | .04 | .02 | .00 |
| ☐ 205 | Louis Lipps | .07 | .03 | .01 |
| ☐ 206 | Keith Willis | .04 | .02 | .00 |
| ☐ 207 | Rod Woodson | .10 | .04 | .01 |
| ☐ 208 | Rod Bernstine | .07 | .03 | .01 |
| ☐ 209 | Marion Butts | .10 | .04 | .01 |
| ☐ 210 | Anthony Miller | .15 | .06 | .01 |
| ☐ 211 | Leslie O'Neal | .07 | .03 | .01 |
| ☐ 212 | Henry Rolling | .04 | .02 | .00 |
| ☐ 213 | Junior Seau | .15 | .06 | .01 |
| ☐ 214 | Billy Ray Smith | .04 | .02 | .00 |
| ☐ 215 | Broderick Thompson | .04 | .02 | .00 |
| ☐ 216 | Derrick Walker | .04 | .02 | .00 |
| ☐ 217 | Dexter Carter | .07 | .03 | .01 |
| ☐ 218 | Don Griffin | .04 | .02 | .00 |
| ☐ 219 | Charles Haley | .07 | .03 | .01 |
| ☐ 220 | Pierce Holt | .07 | .03 | .01 |
| ☐ 221 | Joe Montana | 1.25 | .50 | .12 |
| ☐ 222 | Jerry Rice | .75 | .30 | .07 |
| ☐ 223 | John Taylor | .07 | .03 | .01 |
| ☐ 224 | Michael Walter | .04 | .02 | .00 |
| ☐ 225 | Steve Young | .30 | .12 | .03 |
| ☐ 226 | Brian Blades | .07 | .03 | .01 |
| ☐ 227 | Jeff Bryant | .04 | .02 | .00 |
| ☐ 228 | Jacob Green | .07 | .03 | .01 |
| ☐ 229 | Tommy Kane | .07 | .03 | .01 |
| ☐ 230 | Dave Krieg | .07 | .03 | .01 |
| ☐ 231 | Bryan Millard | .04 | .02 | .00 |
| ☐ 232 | Rufus Porter | .04 | .02 | .00 |
| ☐ 233 | Eugene Robinson | .04 | .02 | .00 |
| ☐ 234 | John L. Williams | .07 | .03 | .01 |
| ☐ 235 | Gary Anderson | .07 | .03 | .01 |
| ☐ 236 | Mark Carrier | .07 | .03 | .01 |
| ☐ 237 | Reggie Cobb | .15 | .06 | .01 |
| ☐ 238 | Reuben Davis | .04 | .02 | .00 |
| ☐ 239 | Paul Gruber | .07 | .03 | .01 |
| ☐ 240 | Harry Hamilton | .04 | .02 | .00 |
| ☐ 241 | Keith McCants | .04 | .02 | .00 |
| ☐ 242 | Ricky Reynolds | .04 | .02 | .00 |
| ☐ 243 | Vinny Testaverde | .07 | .03 | .01 |
| ☐ 244 | Earnest Byner | .07 | .03 | .01 |
| ☐ 245 | Gary Clark | .10 | .04 | .01 |
| ☐ 246 | Andre Collins | .07 | .03 | .01 |
| ☐ 247 | Darrell Green | .07 | .03 | .01 |
| ☐ 248 | Jim Lachey | .07 | .03 | .01 |
| ☐ 249 | Charles Mann | .07 | .03 | .01 |
| ☐ 250 | Wilber Marshall | .07 | .03 | .01 |
| ☐ 251 | Art Monk | .15 | .06 | .01 |
| ☐ 252 | Mark Rypien | .10 | .04 | .01 |
| ☐ 253 | Russell Maryland <br> Dallas Cowboys | .20 | .08 | .02 |
| ☐ 254 | Mike Croel <br> Denver Broncos | .15 | .06 | .01 |
| ☐ 255 | Stanley Richard <br> San Diego Chargers | .10 | .04 | .01 |
| ☐ 256 | Leonard Russell <br> New England Patriots | .25 | .10 | .02 |
| ☐ 257 | Dan McGwire <br> Seattle Seahawks | .15 | .06 | .01 |
| ☐ 258 | Todd Marinovich <br> Los Angeles Raiders | .07 | .03 | .01 |
| ☐ 259 | Eric Swann <br> Phoenix Cardinals | .20 | .08 | .02 |
| ☐ 260 | Mike Pritchard <br> Atlanta Falcons | .30 | .12 | .03 |
| ☐ 261 | Alfred Williams <br> Cincinnati Bengals | .10 | .04 | .01 |
| ☐ 262 | Brett Favre <br> Atlanta Falcons | 1.50 | .60 | .15 |
| ☐ 263 | Browning Nagle <br> New York Jets | .20 | .08 | .02 |
| ☐ 264 | Darryll Lewis <br> Houston Oilers | .07 | .03 | .01 |
| ☐ 265 | Nick Bell <br> Los Angeles Raiders | .15 | .06 | .01 |
| ☐ 266 | Jeff Graham <br> Pittsburgh Steelers | .15 | .06 | .01 |
| ☐ 267 | Eric Moten <br> San Diego Chargers | .07 | .03 | .01 |
| ☐ 268 | Roman Phifer <br> Los Angeles Rams | .07 | .03 | .01 |
| ☐ 269 | Eric Bieniemy <br> San Diego Chargers | .10 | .04 | .01 |
| ☐ 270 | Phil Hansen <br> Buffalo Bills | .10 | .04 | .01 |
| ☐ 271 | Reggie Barrett <br> Detroit Lions | .07 | .03 | .01 |
| ☐ 272 | Aeneas Williams <br> Phoenix Cardinals | .10 | .04 | .01 |
| ☐ 273 | Aaron Craver <br> Miami Dolphins | .07 | .03 | .01 |
| ☐ 274 | Lawrence Dawsey <br> Tampa Bay Buccaneers | .15 | .06 | .01 |
| ☐ 275 | Ricky Ervins <br> Washington Redskins | .20 | .08 | .02 |
| ☐ 276 | Jake Reed <br> Minnesota Vikings | .10 | .04 | .01 |
| ☐ 277 | Eric Williams <br> Dallas Cowboys | .10 | .04 | .01 |
| ☐ 278 | Tim Barnett <br> Kansas City Chiefs | .10 | .04 | .01 |
| ☐ 279 | Keith Traylor <br> Denver Broncos | .07 | .03 | .01 |
| ☐ 280 | Jerry Rice PB UER <br> (Back color is AFC red, instead of NFC blue) <br> San Francisco 49ers | .30 | .12 | .03 |
| ☐ 281 | Jim Lachey <br> Washington Redskins | .04 | .02 | .00 |
| ☐ 282 | Barry Sanders <br> Detroit Lions | .60 | .24 | .06 |
| ☐ 283 | Neal Anderson <br> Chicago Bears | .07 | .03 | .01 |
| ☐ 284 | Reggie White <br> Philadelphia Eagles | .15 | .06 | .01 |
| ☐ 285 | Lawrence Taylor <br> New York Giants | .15 | .06 | .01 |
| ☐ 286 | Mike Singletary <br> Chicago Bears | .10 | .04 | .01 |
| ☐ 287 | Joey Browner <br> Minnesota Vikings | .04 | .02 | .00 |
| ☐ 288 | Morten Andersen SS <br> New Orleans Saints | .04 | .02 | .00 |
| ☐ 289 | Andre Reed SS <br> Buffalo Bills | .10 | .04 | .01 |
| ☐ 290 | Anthony Munoz SS <br> Cincinnati Bengals | .10 | .04 | .01 |
| ☐ 291 | Warren Moon SS <br> Houston Oilers | .20 | .08 | .02 |
| ☐ 292 | Thurman Thomas SS <br> Buffalo Bills | .30 | .12 | .03 |

| | | | |
|---|---|---|---|
| ☐ 293 Ray Childress SS | .04 | .02 | .00 |
| Houston Oilers | | | |
| ☐ 294 Derrick Thomas SS | .15 | .06 | .01 |
| Kansas City Chiefs | | | |
| ☐ 295 Rod Woodson SS | .10 | .04 | .01 |
| Pittsburgh Steelers | | | |
| ☐ 296 Steve Atwater SS | .04 | .02 | .00 |
| Denver Broncos | | | |
| ☐ 297 David Fulcher SS | .04 | .02 | .00 |
| Cincinnati Bengals | | | |
| ☐ 298 Anthony Munoz Think | .10 | .04 | .01 |
| Cincinnati Bengals | | | |
| ☐ 299 Ron Rivera Think | .04 | .02 | .00 |
| Chicago Bears | | | |
| ☐ 300 Cornelius Bennett | .10 | .04 | .01 |
| Think | | | |
| Buffalo Bills | | | |
| ☐ E1 Tom Flores | 2.50 | 1.00 | .25 |
| ☐ E2 Anthony Munoz | 2.50 | 1.00 | .25 |
| ☐ E3 Tony Casillas | 2.50 | 1.00 | .25 |
| ☐ E4 Super Bowl XXVI Logo | 2.50 | 1.00 | .25 |
| Minneapolis | | | |
| ☐ E5 Felicidades | 2.50 | 1.00 | .25 |

| | | | |
|---|---|---|---|
| ☐ 320 Chip Lohmiller | .35 | .14 | .03 |
| ☐ 321 Martin Mayhew | .35 | .14 | .03 |
| ☐ 322 Mark Rypien | .75 | .30 | .07 |
| ☐ 323 Alvin Walton | .35 | .14 | .03 |
| ☐ 324 Joe Gibbs CO | .50 | .20 | .05 |
| ☐ 370 Warren Moon | .75 | .30 | .07 |
| Think About It | | | |
| ☐ 444 James Lofton | .75 | .30 | .07 |
| ☐ 445 Keith McKeller | .50 | .20 | .05 |
| ☐ 449 Leon Seals | .35 | .14 | .03 |
| ☐ 450 Leonard Smith | .35 | .14 | .03 |
| ☐ 676 Jeff Bostic | .35 | .14 | .03 |
| ☐ 677 Darrell Green | .75 | .30 | .07 |
| ☐ 678 Markus Koch | .35 | .14 | .03 |
| ☐ 679 Jim Lachey | .50 | .20 | .05 |
| ☐ 680 Charles Mann | .50 | .20 | .05 |
| ☐ 681 Wilber Marshall | .50 | .20 | .05 |
| ☐ 682 Art Monk | .75 | .30 | .07 |
| ☐ 683 Gerald Riggs | .50 | .20 | .05 |
| ☐ 684 Ricky Sanders | .75 | .30 | .07 |
| ☐ 725 Howie Long | .75 | .30 | .07 |
| Think About It | | | |
| ☐ 726 Dan Marino | 1.50 | .60 | .15 |
| Think About It | | | |
| ☐ 746 Bobby Wilson | .50 | .20 | .05 |
| ☐ 805 Ricky Ervins | .75 | .30 | .07 |
| ☐ 848 Brian Mitchell | .75 | .30 | .07 |
| ☐ NNO Jim Kelly SP | 20.00 | 8.00 | 2.00 |

# 1991-92 Pro Set Super Bowl Binder

This 49-card standard-size (2 1/2" by 3 1/2") set was sponsored by American Express and produced by Pro Set to commemorate Super Bowl XXVI. The set was sold in a white binder that housed four cards per page. It includes five new cards (1-5), four Think About It cards (300, 370, 725-726), as well as player cards for the Buffalo Bills (73-77, 79-84, 86, 88-90, 444-445, 449-450) and Washington Redskins (316-318, 320-324, 676-684, 746, 805, 848). The player cards are the same as the regular issue (including numbering), except that the Bills' cards have a "1991 AFC Champs" logo on the front, while the Redskins' cards carry a "1991 NFC Champs" logo on their fronts. A Jim Kelly card was apparently produced separately (individually cellophane wrapped and unnumbered) and was only available at the Super Bowl with the seat-cushion sets. Kelly was not included in sets sent out as as part of the mail-away offer advertised after the Super Bowl. The Kelly card does not include the Pro Set logo on the back.

| | MINT | EXC | G-VG |
|---|---|---|---|
| COMPLETE SET (49) | 20.00 | 8.00 | 2.00 |
| COMMON CARD | .35 | .14 | .03 |
| | | | |
| ☐ 1 The NFL Experience | .75 | .30 | .07 |
| ☐ 2 Super Bowl XXVI | .50 | .20 | .05 |
| ☐ 3 AFC Standings | .50 | .20 | .05 |
| ☐ 4 NFC Standings | .50 | .20 | .05 |
| ☐ 5 The Metrodome | .50 | .20 | .05 |
| ☐ 73 Howard Ballard | .35 | .14 | .03 |
| ☐ 74 Cornelius Bennett | .75 | .30 | .07 |
| ☐ 75 Shane Conlan | .50 | .20 | .05 |
| ☐ 76 Kent Hull | .50 | .20 | .05 |
| ☐ 77 Kirby Jackson | .35 | .14 | .03 |
| ☐ 79 Mark Kelso | .35 | .14 | .03 |
| ☐ 80 Nate Odomes | .35 | .14 | .03 |
| ☐ 81 Andre Reed | .75 | .30 | .07 |
| ☐ 82 Jim Ritcher | .35 | .14 | .03 |
| ☐ 83 Bruce Smith | .75 | .30 | .07 |
| ☐ 84 Darryl Talley | .50 | .20 | .05 |
| ☐ 86 Thurman Thomas | 2.50 | 1.00 | .25 |
| ☐ 88 Will Wolford | .35 | .14 | .03 |
| ☐ 89 Jeff Wright | .35 | .14 | .03 |
| ☐ 90 Marv Levy CO | .35 | .14 | .03 |
| ☐ 300 Cornelius Bennett | .50 | .20 | .05 |
| Piensalo | | | |
| ☐ 316 Earnest Byner | .50 | .20 | .05 |
| ☐ 317 Gary Clark | .75 | .30 | .07 |
| ☐ 318 Andre Collins | .50 | .20 | .05 |

# 1992 Pro Set

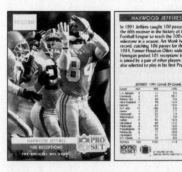

The 1992 Pro Set football card set contains two series featuring cards measuring the standard size (2 1/2" by 3 1/2"). The 400-card first series also features a four-card Emmitt Smith hologram subset, numbered ES1-ES4, which were randomly inserted into the foil packs. The ES1 card was the least difficult to find, while the ES4 card was the most difficult. Reportedly the numbered cases purchased directly from Pro Set by hobby dealers had a higher collation of the Smith holograms. The fronts feature full-bleed color player photos, with the player's name in a stripe at the card bottom and the NFL Pro Set logo in the lower right corner. In a horizontal format, the backs have a close-up color player photo, biography, career highlights, and complete statistical information. The first series opens with the following topical subsets: Statistical Leaders (1-18), Milestones (19-27), Draft Day (28-33), Innovators (34-36), 1991 Replays (37-63), and Super Bowl XXVI Replays (64-72). Super Bowl participants Washington Redskins (73-90) and Buffalo Bills (91-108) start the team listings followed alphabetically by the rest of the league. Player cards within each team are also alphabetical. The rest of the teams: Atlanta Falcons (109-117), Chicago Bears (118-126), Cincinnati Bengals (127-135), Cleveland Browns (136-144), Dallas Cowboys (145-153), Denver Broncos (154-162), Detroit Lions (163-171), Green Bay Packers (172-180), Houston Oilers (181-189), Indianapolis Colts (190-198), Kansas City Chiefs (199-207), Los Angeles Raiders (208-216), Los Angeles Rams (217-225), Miami Dolphins (226-234), Minnesota Vikings (235-243), New England Patriots (244-252), New Orleans Saints (253-261), New York Giants (262-270), New York Jets (271-279), Philadelphia Eagles (280-288), Phoenix Cardinals (289-297), Pittsburgh Steelers (298-306), San Diego Chargers (307-315), San Francisco 49ers (316-324), Seattle Seahawks (325-333), and Tampa Bay Buccaneers (334-342). The first series closes with the following special subsets: Pro Set Newsreel (343-346), Magic Numbers (347-351), Play Smart (352-360), NFC Spirit of the Game (361-374), AFC Pro Bowl Stars (375-400). The second series consists of 300 cards with a reported production run of 10,000 (6,000 foil, 4,000 jumbo) numbered cases. Randomly inserted throughout the second series packs were a ten-card "Hall of Fame 2000" subset, a 30-card gold-foil stamped "Team MVPs" set, as well as an unnumbered Santa Claus card and a Pro Set Emmitt Smith Power Preview special offer card. Santa Claus' card shows him standing in front of a wooden fence and wearing a cowboy hat, boots, and a duster with his red suit. Santa has a stuffed toy bag over his left shoulder and is holding Pro Set cards in his right hand; his foot rests on a Giants' helmet. The back displays Santa's name in red script above a red ribbon printed with the words "Spirit of the Season" and career highlights printed below. Santa's back is bordered by a thin red line within a wider green border. The regular issue card fronts feature color action player photos that are full-bleed except on their left side, where they are edged by a white stripe that shades to gray. The player's name and team name are printed vertically in this two-toned stripe, with the team logo on a gray block in the lower left corner. On a light gray screened background with white team logos, the backs have a color close-up photo, biography, career highlights, and statistics. The cards are numbered on the back. After opening with a NFC Pro Bowl (401-427) subset, the second series cards are checklisted below alphabetically according to teams as follows: Atlanta Falcons (428-436), Buffalo Bills (437-445), Chicago Bears (446-454), Cincinnati Bengals (455-463), Cleveland Browns (464-472), Dallas Cowboys (473-481), Denver Broncos (482-490), Detroit Lions (491-499), Green Bay Packers (500-508), Houston Oilers (509-517), Indianapolis Colts (518-526), Kansas City Chiefs (527-535), Los Angeles Raiders (536-544), Los Angeles Rams (545-553), Miami Dolphins (554-562), Minnesota Vikings (563-571), New England Patriots (572-580), New Orleans Saints (581-589), New York Giants (590-598), New York Jets (599-607), Philadelphia Eagles (608-616), Phoenix Cardinals (617-625), Pittsburgh Steelers (626-634), San Diego Chargers (635-643), San Francisco 49ers (644-652), Seattle Seahawks (653-661), Tampa Bay Buccaneers (662-670), and Washington Redskins (671-679). The set closes with Spirit of the Game (680-693) cards and some miscellaneous special cards (694-700). Production figures for the second series were reportedly 6,000 20-box wax cases and 4,000 18-box jumbo cases. The key Rookie Cards in the set are Edgar Bennett, Steve Bono, Terrell Buckley, Quentin Coryatt, Vaughn Dunbar, Steve Emtman, David Klingler, Amp Lee, Tommy Maddox, Johnny Mitchell and Carl Pickens.

| | MINT | EXC | G-VG |
|---|---|---|---|
| COMPLETE SET (700) | 22.00 | 10.00 | 2.80 |
| COMPLETE SERIES 1 (400) | 8.00 | 3.60 | 1.00 |
| COMPLETE SERIES 2 (300) | 14.00 | 6.25 | 1.75 |
| COMMON PLAYER (1-400) | .04 | .02 | .01 |
| COMMON PLAYER (401-700) | .05 | .02 | .01 |
| ☐ 1 Mike Croel LL | .04 | .02 | .01 |
| Rookie of the Year | | | |
| Denver Broncos | | | |
| ☐ 2 Thurman Thomas LL | .20 | .09 | .03 |
| Player of the Year | | | |
| Buffalo Bills | | | |
| ☐ 3 Wayne Fontes CO LL | .04 | .02 | .01 |
| Coach of the Year | | | |
| Detroit Lions | | | |
| ☐ 4 Anthony Munoz LL | .04 | .02 | .01 |
| Man of the Year | | | |
| Cincinnati Bengals | | | |
| ☐ 5 Steve Young LL | .08 | .04 | .01 |
| Passing Leader | | | |
| San Francisco 49ers | | | |
| ☐ 6 Warren Moon LL | .10 | .05 | .01 |
| Passing Yardage Leader | | | |
| Houston Oilers | | | |
| ☐ 7 Emmitt Smith LL | .75 | .35 | .09 |
| Rushing Leader | | | |
| Dallas Cowboys | | | |
| ☐ 8 Haywood Jeffires LL | .08 | .04 | .01 |
| Receiving Leader | | | |
| Houston Oilers | | | |
| ☐ 9 Marv Cook LL | .04 | .02 | .01 |
| Receiving Leader/TE | | | |
| New England Patriots | | | |
| ☐ 10 Michael Irvin LL | .25 | .11 | .03 |
| Receiving Yardage Leader | | | |
| Dallas Cowboys | | | |
| ☐ 11 Thurman Thomas LL UER | .20 | .09 | .03 |
| Total Yardage Leader | | | |
| (Total combined yards | | | |
| should be 2,038) | | | |
| Buffalo Bills | | | |
| ☐ 12 Chip Lohmiller LL UER | .04 | .02 | .01 |
| Scoring Leader | | | |
| (FG Attempt Totals | | | |
| are off by one) | | | |
| Washington Redskins | | | |
| ☐ 13 Barry Sanders LL | .30 | .14 | .04 |
| Scoring Leader TD's | | | |
| Detroit Lions | | | |
| ☐ 14 Reggie Roby LL | .04 | .02 | .01 |
| Punting Leader | | | |
| Miami Dolphins | | | |
| ☐ 15 Mel Gray LL | .04 | .02 | .01 |

| | | | |
|---|---|---|---|
| Kickoff/Punt Return | | | |
| Leader | | | |
| Detroit Lions | | | |
| ☐ 16 Ronnie Lott LL | .08 | .04 | .01 |
| Interception Leader | | | |
| Los Angeles Raiders | | | |
| ☐ 17 Pat Swilling LL | .08 | .04 | .01 |
| Sack Leader | | | |
| New Orleans Saints | | | |
| ☐ 18 Reggie White LL | .08 | .04 | .01 |
| Defensive MVP | | | |
| Philadelphia Eagles | | | |
| ☐ 19 Haywood Jeffires ML | .08 | .04 | .01 |
| 100 Receptions | | | |
| Houston Oilers | | | |
| ☐ 20 Pat Leahy ML | .08 | .04 | .01 |
| 300 Field Goals | | | |
| New York Jets | | | |
| ☐ 21 James Lofton ML | .08 | .04 | .01 |
| 13,000 Yards | | | |
| Buffalo Bills | | | |
| ☐ 22 Art Monk ML | .08 | .04 | .01 |
| 800 Receptions | | | |
| Washington Redskins | | | |
| ☐ 23 Don Shula ML | .08 | .04 | .01 |
| 300 Wins | | | |
| Miami Dolphins | | | |
| ☐ 24A Nick Lowery ML ERR | .04 | .02 | .01 |
| 9th 100-Point Season | | | |
| (Says he wears 9) | | | |
| Kansas City Chiefs | | | |
| ☐ 24B Nick Lowery ML COR | .04 | .02 | .01 |
| 9th 100-Point Season | | | |
| (Says he wears 8) | | | |
| Kansas City Chiefs | | | |
| ☐ 25 John Elway ML | .15 | .07 | .02 |
| 2,000 Completed Passes | | | |
| Denver Broncos | | | |
| ☐ 26 Chicago Bears ML | .04 | .02 | .01 |
| 8 Straight Opening Wins | | | |
| ☐ 27 Marcus Allen ML | .08 | .04 | .01 |
| 2,000 Rushing Attempts | | | |
| Los Angeles Raiders | | | |
| ☐ 28 Terrell Buckley DD | .25 | .11 | .03 |
| Green Bay Packers | | | |
| ☐ 29 Amp Lee DD | .25 | .11 | .03 |
| San Francisco 49ers | | | |
| ☐ 30 Chris Mims DD | .25 | .11 | .03 |
| San Diego Chargers | | | |
| ☐ 31 Leon Searcy DD | .05 | .02 | .01 |
| Pittsburgh Steelers | | | |
| ☐ 32 Jimmy Smith DD | .10 | .05 | .01 |
| Dallas Cowboys | | | |
| ☐ 33 Siran Stacy DD | .10 | .05 | .01 |
| Philadelphia Eagles | | | |
| ☐ 34 Pete Gogolak INN | .05 | .02 | .01 |
| ☐ 35 Cheerleaders INN | .05 | .02 | .01 |
| Dallas Cowboys | | | |
| ☐ 36 Houston Astrodome INN | .05 | .02 | .01 |
| ☐ 37 Week 1: REP | .04 | .02 | .01 |
| Chiefs 14, Falcons 3 | | | |
| (Christian Okoye) | | | |
| ☐ 38 Week 2: REP | .04 | .02 | .01 |
| Bills 52, Steelers 34 | | | |
| (Don Beebe) | | | |
| ☐ 39 Week 3: REP | .04 | .02 | .01 |
| Bears 20, Giants 17 | | | |
| (Wendell Davis) | | | |
| ☐ 40 Week 4: REP | .04 | .02 | .01 |
| Dolphins 16, Packers 13 | | | |
| (Don Shula CO) | | | |
| ☐ 41 Week 5: REP | .08 | .04 | .01 |
| Raiders 12, 49ers 6 | | | |
| (Ronnie Lott) | | | |
| ☐ 42 Week 6: REP | .08 | .04 | .01 |
| Redskins 20, Bears 7 | | | |
| (Art Monk) | | | |
| ☐ 43 Week 7: REP | .20 | .09 | .03 |
| Bills 42, Colts 6 | | | |
| (Thurman Thomas) | | | |
| ☐ 44 Week 8: REP | .04 | .02 | .01 |
| Patriots 26, Vikings 23 | | | |
| (John Stephens) | | | |
| ☐ 45 Week 9: REP UER | .04 | .02 | .01 |
| Vikings 28, Cardinals 0 | | | |
| (Herschel Walker; | | | |
| misspelled Hershel | | | |
| on card back) | | | |
| ☐ 46 Week 10: REP | .04 | .02 | .01 |
| Jets 19, Packers 16 | | | |
| (Chris Burkett) | | | |
| ☐ 47 Week 11: REP | .04 | .02 | .01 |
| Colts 28, Jets 27 | | | |
| (Line play) | | | |
| ☐ 48 Week 12: REP | .08 | .04 | .01 |
| Falcons 43, Buccaneers 7 | | | |
| (Andre Rison) | | | |
| ☐ 49 Week 13: REP | .10 | .05 | .01 |

Cowboys 24, Redskins 21
(Steve Beuerlein
and Michael Irvin)

| | | | |
|---|---|---|---|
| ☐ 50 Week 14: REP | .04 | .02 | .01 |
| Broncos 20, Patriots 3 | | | |
| (Irving Fryar) | | | |
| ☐ 51 Week 15: REP | .04 | .02 | .01 |
| Bills 30, Raiders 27 | | | |
| (Bills' Defense) | | | |
| ☐ 52 Week 16: REP | .04 | .02 | .01 |
| Cowboys 25, Eagles 13 | | | |
| (Kelvin Martin) | | | |
| ☐ 53 Week 17: REP | .04 | .02 | .01 |
| Jets 23, Dolphins 20 | | | |
| (Bruce Coslet CO) | | | |
| ☐ 54 AFC Wild Card REP | .04 | .02 | .01 |
| Chiefs 10, Raiders 6 | | | |
| (Fred Jones) | | | |
| ☐ 55 AFC Wild Card REP | .04 | .02 | .01 |
| Oilers 17, Jets 10 | | | |
| (Oilers' Run-and-Shoot) | | | |
| ☐ 56 NFC Wild Card REP | .04 | .02 | .01 |
| Cowboys 17, Bears 13 | | | |
| (Bill Bates) | | | |
| ☐ 57 NFC Wild Card REP | .08 | .04 | .01 |
| Falcons 27, Saints 20 | | | |
| (Michael Haynes) | | | |
| ☐ 58 AFC Divisional Playoff REP | .04 | .02 | .01 |
| Broncos 26, Oilers 24 | | | |
| (Bronco interception) | | | |
| ☐ 59 AFC Divisional Playoff REP | .20 | .09 | .03 |
| Bills 37, Chiefs 14 | | | |
| (Thurman Thomas) | | | |
| ☐ 60 NFC Divisional Playoff REP | .04 | .02 | .01 |
| Lions 38, Cowboys 6 | | | |
| (Eric Kramer) | | | |
| ☐ 61 NFC Divisional Playoff REP | .04 | .02 | .01 |
| Redskins 24, Falcons 7 | | | |
| (Darrell Green) | | | |
| ☐ 62 AFC Championship REP | .04 | .02 | .01 |
| Bills 10, Broncos 7 | | | |
| (Carlton Bailey) | | | |
| ☐ 63 NFC Championship REP | .04 | .02 | .01 |
| Redskins 41, Lions 10 | | | |
| (Mark Rypien) | | | |
| ☐ 64 TD Reversed, | .04 | .02 | .01 |
| FG Blocked SBREP | | | |
| ☐ 65 (Brad) Edwards Picks | .04 | .02 | .01 |
| Off First of Two SBREP | | | |
| ☐ 66 Rypien to Byner, 10-0 SBREP | .04 | .02 | .01 |
| ☐ 67 Riggs Puts Redskins | .04 | .02 | .01 |
| Up 17-10 SBREP | | | |
| ☐ 68 Gouveia Interception | .04 | .02 | .01 |
| Buries Bills SBREP | | | |
| ☐ 69 Thomas Scores Bills' | .20 | .09 | .03 |
| First TD SBREP | | | |
| ☐ 70 Clark Catches | .08 | .04 | .01 |
| Rypien's Second TD SBREP | | | |
| ☐ 71 Bills Convert Late | .04 | .02 | .01 |
| Break SBREP | | | |
| ☐ 72 Redskins Run Out | .04 | .02 | .01 |
| the Clock SBREP | | | |
| ☐ 73 Jeff Bostic | .04 | .02 | .01 |
| ☐ 74 Earnest Byner | .08 | .04 | .01 |
| ☐ 75 Gary Clark | .08 | .04 | .01 |
| ☐ 76 Andre Collins | .04 | .02 | .01 |
| ☐ 77 Darrell Green | .08 | .04 | .01 |
| ☐ 78 Joe Jacoby | .04 | .02 | .01 |
| ☐ 79 Jim Lachey | .04 | .02 | .01 |
| ☐ 80 Chip Lohmiller | .08 | .04 | .01 |
| ☐ 81 Charles Mann | .08 | .04 | .01 |
| ☐ 82 Martin Mayhew | .04 | .02 | .01 |
| ☐ 83 Matt Millen | .08 | .04 | .01 |
| ☐ 84 Brian Mitchell | .08 | .04 | .01 |
| ☐ 85 Art Monk | .10 | .05 | .01 |
| ☐ 86 Gerald Riggs | .08 | .04 | .01 |
| ☐ 87 Mark Rypien | .10 | .05 | .01 |
| ☐ 88 Fred Stokes | .04 | .02 | .01 |
| ☐ 89 Bobby Wilson | .04 | .02 | .01 |
| ☐ 90 Joe Gibbs CO | .08 | .04 | .01 |
| ☐ 91 Howard Ballard | .04 | .02 | .01 |
| ☐ 92 Cornelius Bennett UER | .10 | .05 | .01 |
| (Interception total reads 0; | | | |
| he had 4) | | | |
| ☐ 93 Kenneth Davis | .08 | .04 | .01 |
| ☐ 94 Al Edwards | .04 | .02 | .01 |
| ☐ 95 Kent Hull | .04 | .02 | .01 |
| ☐ 96 Kirby Jackson | .04 | .02 | .01 |
| ☐ 97 Mark Kelso | .04 | .02 | .01 |
| ☐ 98 James Lofton UER | .08 | .04 | .01 |
| (Says he played in '75 | | | |
| Pro Bowl, but he wasn't | | | |
| in NFL until 1978) | | | |
| ☐ 99 Keith McKeller | .04 | .02 | .01 |
| ☐ 100 Nate Odomes | .08 | .04 | .01 |
| ☐ 101 Jim Ritcher | .04 | .02 | .01 |
| ☐ 102 Leon Seals | .04 | .02 | .01 |
| ☐ 103 Steve Tasker | .08 | .04 | .01 |
| ☐ 104 Darryl Talley | .08 | .04 | .01 |
| ☐ 105 Thurman Thomas | .40 | .18 | .05 |
| ☐ 106 Will Wolford | .04 | .02 | .01 |
| ☐ 107 Jeff Wright | .04 | .02 | .01 |
| ☐ 108 Marv Levy CO | .08 | .04 | .01 |
| ☐ 109 Darion Conner | .04 | .02 | .01 |
| ☐ 110 Bill Fralic | .04 | .02 | .01 |
| ☐ 111 Moe Gardner | .04 | .02 | .01 |
| ☐ 112 Michael Haynes | .30 | .14 | .04 |
| ☐ 113 Chris Miller | .10 | .05 | .01 |
| ☐ 114 Erric Pegram | .40 | .18 | .05 |
| ☐ 115 Bruce Pickens | .04 | .02 | .01 |
| ☐ 116 Andre Rison | .25 | .11 | .03 |
| ☐ 117 Jerry Glanville CO | .04 | .02 | .01 |
| ☐ 118 Neal Anderson | .08 | .04 | .01 |
| ☐ 119 Trace Armstrong | .04 | .02 | .01 |
| ☐ 120 Wendell Davis | .04 | .02 | .01 |
| ☐ 121 Richard Dent | .08 | .04 | .01 |
| ☐ 122 Jay Hilgenberg | .08 | .04 | .01 |
| ☐ 123 Lemuel Stinson | .04 | .02 | .01 |
| ☐ 124 Stan Thomas | .04 | .02 | .01 |
| ☐ 125 Tom Waddle | .10 | .05 | .01 |
| ☐ 126 Mike Ditka CO | .10 | .05 | .01 |
| ☐ 127 James Brooks | .08 | .04 | .01 |
| ☐ 128 Eddie Brown | .04 | .02 | .01 |
| ☐ 129 David Fulcher | .04 | .02 | .01 |
| ☐ 130 Harold Green | .08 | .04 | .01 |
| ☐ 131 Tim Krumrie UER | .04 | .02 | .01 |
| (Misspelled Krumerie | | | |
| on card front) | | | |
| ☐ 132 Anthony Munoz | .08 | .04 | .01 |
| ☐ 133 Craig Taylor | .04 | .02 | .01 |
| ☐ 134 Eric Thomas | .04 | .02 | .01 |
| ☐ 135 David Shula CO | .04 | .02 | .01 |
| ☐ 136 Mike Baab | .04 | .02 | .01 |
| ☐ 137 Brian Brennan | .04 | .02 | .01 |
| ☐ 138 Michael Jackson | .10 | .05 | .01 |
| ☐ 139 James Jones UER | .04 | .02 | .01 |
| (DL on front, DT on back) | | | |
| ☐ 140 Ed King | .04 | .02 | .01 |
| ☐ 141 Clay Matthews | .08 | .04 | .01 |
| ☐ 142 Eric Metcalf | .10 | .05 | .01 |
| ☐ 143 Joe Morris | .08 | .04 | .01 |
| ☐ 144A Bill Belichick CO ERR | .12 | .05 | .02 |
| (No HC next to name | | | |
| on back) | | | |
| ☐ 144B Bill Belichick CO COR | .12 | .05 | .02 |
| (HC next to | | | |
| name on back) | | | |
| ☐ 145 Steve Beuerlein | .20 | .09 | .03 |
| ☐ 146 Larry Brown | .04 | .02 | .01 |
| ☐ 147 Ray Horton | .04 | .02 | .01 |
| ☐ 148 Ken Norton | .08 | .04 | .01 |
| ☐ 149 Mike Saxon | .04 | .02 | .01 |
| ☐ 150 Emmitt Smith | 2.00 | .90 | .25 |
| ☐ 151 Mark Stepnoski | .04 | .02 | .01 |
| ☐ 152 Alexander Wright | .08 | .04 | .01 |
| ☐ 153 Jimmy Johnson CO | .08 | .04 | .01 |
| ☐ 154 Mike Croel | .08 | .04 | .01 |
| ☐ 155 John Elway | .40 | .18 | .05 |
| ☐ 156 Gaston Green UER | .08 | .04 | .01 |
| (Lists 1991 team as | | | |
| Rams, but was Broncos) | | | |
| ☐ 157 Wymon Henderson | .04 | .02 | .01 |
| ☐ 158 Karl Mecklenburg UER | .08 | .04 | .01 |
| (Card back repeats | | | |
| Super Bowl XXI) | | | |
| ☐ 159 Warren Powers | .04 | .02 | .01 |
| ☐ 160 Steve Sewell UER | .04 | .02 | .01 |
| (Card back repeats | | | |
| Super Bowl XXI) | | | |
| ☐ 161 Doug Widell | .04 | .02 | .01 |
| ☐ 162 Dan Reeves CO | .08 | .04 | .01 |
| ☐ 163 Eric Andolsek | .04 | .02 | .01 |
| ☐ 164 Jerry Ball | .08 | .04 | .01 |
| ☐ 165 Bennie Blades | .04 | .02 | .01 |
| ☐ 166 Ray Crockett | .04 | .02 | .01 |
| ☐ 167 Willie Green UER | .04 | .02 | .01 |
| (Card back repeats | | | |
| and in last sentence) | | | |
| ☐ 168 Erik Kramer | .15 | .07 | .02 |
| ☐ 169 Barry Sanders | .75 | .35 | .09 |
| ☐ 170 Chris Spielman UER | .08 | .04 | .01 |
| (Card says named to | | | |
| Pro Bowl 1989-90, | | | |
| should say 1989-91) | | | |
| ☐ 171 Wayne Fontes CO | .04 | .02 | .01 |
| ☐ 172 Vinnie Clark | .04 | .02 | .01 |
| ☐ 173 Tony Mandarich | .04 | .02 | .01 |
| ☐ 174 Brian Noble | .04 | .02 | .01 |
| ☐ 175 Bryce Paup | .04 | .02 | .01 |
| ☐ 176 Sterling Sharpe | .50 | .23 | .06 |
| ☐ 177 Darrell Thompson | .08 | .04 | .01 |
| ☐ 178 Esera Tuaolo UER | .04 | .02 | .01 |
| (Text has 1 TD via inter- | | | |
| ception, stats do not) | | | |
| ☐ 179 Ed West | .04 | .02 | .01 |

|  | | | |
|---|---|---|---|
| ☐ 180 Mike Holmgren CO | .04 | .02 | .01 |
| ☐ 181 Ray Childress | .08 | .04 | .01 |
| ☐ 182 Cris Dishman | .08 | .04 | .01 |
| ☐ 183 Curtis Duncan | .08 | .04 | .01 |
| ☐ 184 William Fuller | .04 | .02 | .01 |
| ☐ 185 Lamar Lathon | .04 | .02 | .01 |
| ☐ 186 Warren Moon | .20 | .09 | .03 |
| ☐ 187 Bo Orlando | .15 | .07 | .02 |
| ☐ 188 Lorenzo White | .08 | .04 | .01 |
| ☐ 189 Jack Pardee CO | .04 | .02 | .01 |
| ☐ 190 Chip Banks | .04 | .02 | .01 |
| ☐ 191 Dean Biasucci UER | .04 | .02 | .01 |
| (PK on front, K on back) | | | |
| ☐ 192 Bill Brooks | .08 | .04 | .01 |
| ☐ 193 Ray Donaldson | .04 | .02 | .01 |
| ☐ 194 Jeff Herrod | .04 | .02 | .01 |
| ☐ 195 Mike Prior | .04 | .02 | .01 |
| ☐ 196 Mark Vander Poel | .04 | .02 | .01 |
| ☐ 197 Clarence Verdin | .04 | .02 | .01 |
| ☐ 198 Ted Marchibroda CO | .04 | .02 | .01 |
| ☐ 199 John Alt | .04 | .02 | .01 |
| ☐ 200 Deron Cherry | .04 | .02 | .01 |
| ☐ 201 Steve DeBerg | .08 | .04 | .01 |
| ☐ 202 Nick Lowery | .08 | .04 | .01 |
| ☐ 203 Neil Smith | .10 | .05 | .01 |
| ☐ 204 Derrick Thomas | .15 | .07 | .02 |
| ☐ 205 Joe Valerio | .04 | .02 | .01 |
| ☐ 206 Barry Word | .10 | .05 | .01 |
| ☐ 207 M. Schottenheimer CO | .04 | .02 | .01 |
| ☐ 208 Marcus Allen | .08 | .04 | .01 |
| ☐ 209 Nick Bell | .08 | .04 | .01 |
| ☐ 210 Tim Brown | .25 | .11 | .03 |
| ☐ 211 Howie Long | .08 | .04 | .01 |
| ☐ 212 Ronnie Lott | .10 | .05 | .01 |
| ☐ 213 Todd Marinovich | .04 | .02 | .01 |
| ☐ 214 Greg Townsend | .04 | .02 | .01 |
| ☐ 215 Steve Wright | .04 | .02 | .01 |
| ☐ 216 Art Shell CO | .08 | .04 | .01 |
| ☐ 217 Flipper Anderson | .08 | .04 | .01 |
| ☐ 218 Robert Delpino | .08 | .04 | .01 |
| ☐ 219 Henry Ellard | .08 | .04 | .01 |
| ☐ 220 Kevin Greene | .08 | .04 | .01 |
| ☐ 221 Todd Lyght | .04 | .02 | .01 |
| ☐ 222 Tom Newberry | .04 | .02 | .01 |
| ☐ 223 Roman Phifer | .04 | .02 | .01 |
| ☐ 224 Michael Stewart | .04 | .02 | .01 |
| ☐ 225 Chuck Knox CO | .04 | .02 | .01 |
| ☐ 226 Aaron Craver | .04 | .02 | .01 |
| ☐ 227 Jeff Cross | .04 | .02 | .01 |
| ☐ 228 Mark Duper | .08 | .04 | .01 |
| ☐ 229 Ferrell Edmunds | .04 | .02 | .01 |
| ☐ 230 Jim C. Jensen | .04 | .02 | .01 |
| ☐ 231 Louis Oliver UER | .08 | .04 | .01 |
| (Card has 215 tackles, but he only had 88) | | | |
| ☐ 232 Reggie Roby | .04 | .02 | .01 |
| ☐ 233 Sammie Smith | .04 | .02 | .01 |
| ☐ 234 Don Shula CO | .08 | .04 | .01 |
| ☐ 235 Joey Browner | .04 | .02 | .01 |
| ☐ 236 Anthony Carter | .08 | .04 | .01 |
| ☐ 237 Chris Doleman | .08 | .04 | .01 |
| ☐ 238 Steve Jordan | .08 | .04 | .01 |
| ☐ 239 Kirk Lowdermilk | .04 | .02 | .01 |
| ☐ 240 Henry Thomas | .04 | .02 | .01 |
| ☐ 241 Herschel Walker | .10 | .05 | .01 |
| ☐ 242 Felix Wright | .04 | .02 | .01 |
| ☐ 243 Dennis Green CO | .08 | .04 | .01 |
| ☐ 244 Ray Agnew | .04 | .02 | .01 |
| ☐ 245 Marv Cook | .08 | .04 | .01 |
| ☐ 246 Irving Fryar UER | .08 | .04 | .01 |
| (WR/KR on front, WR on back) | | | |
| ☐ 247 Pat Harlow | .04 | .02 | .01 |
| ☐ 248 Hugh Millen | .08 | .04 | .01 |
| ☐ 249 Leonard Russell | .30 | .14 | .04 |
| ☐ 250 Andre Tippett | .08 | .04 | .01 |
| ☐ 251 Jon Vaughn | .04 | .02 | .01 |
| ☐ 252 Dick MacPherson CO | .04 | .02 | .01 |
| ☐ 253 Morten Andersen | .08 | .04 | .01 |
| ☐ 254 Bobby Hebert | .10 | .05 | .01 |
| ☐ 255 Joel Hilgenberg | .04 | .02 | .01 |
| ☐ 256 Vaughan Johnson | .08 | .04 | .01 |
| ☐ 257 Sam Mills | .08 | .04 | .01 |
| ☐ 258 Pat Swilling | .08 | .04 | .01 |
| ☐ 259 Floyd Turner | .04 | .02 | .01 |
| ☐ 260 Steve Walsh | .04 | .02 | .01 |
| ☐ 261 Jim Mora CO UER | .04 | .02 | .01 |
| (No TM by Pro Set logo) | | | |
| ☐ 262 Stephen Baker | .04 | .02 | .01 |
| ☐ 263 Mark Collins | .04 | .02 | .01 |
| ☐ 264 Rodney Hampton | .40 | .18 | .05 |
| ☐ 265 Jeff Hostetler | .15 | .07 | .02 |
| ☐ 266 Erik Howard | .04 | .02 | .01 |
| ☐ 267 Sean Landeta | .04 | .02 | .01 |
| ☐ 268 Gary Reasons UER | .04 | .02 | .01 |
| (Fumble recovery noted on card, but not in stats) | | | |
| ☐ 269 Everson Walls | .04 | .02 | .01 |
| ☐ 270 Ray Handley CO | .04 | .02 | .01 |
| ☐ 271 Louis Aguiar | .04 | .02 | .01 |
| ☐ 272 Brad Baxter | .08 | .04 | .01 |
| ☐ 273 Chris Burkett | .04 | .02 | .01 |
| ☐ 274 Irv Eatman | .04 | .02 | .01 |
| ☐ 275 Jeff Lageman | .04 | .02 | .01 |
| ☐ 276 Freeman McNeil | .04 | .02 | .01 |
| ☐ 277 Rob Moore | .10 | .05 | .01 |
| ☐ 278 Lonnie Young | .04 | .02 | .01 |
| ☐ 279 Bruce Coslet CO | .04 | .02 | .01 |
| ☐ 280 Jerome Brown | .08 | .04 | .01 |
| ☐ 281 Keith Byars | .08 | .04 | .01 |
| ☐ 282 Bruce Collie UER | .04 | .02 | .01 |
| (No stats on back) | | | |
| ☐ 283 Keith Jackson | .10 | .05 | .01 |
| ☐ 284 James Joseph | .04 | .02 | .01 |
| ☐ 285 Seth Joyner | .08 | .04 | .01 |
| ☐ 286 Andre Waters | .04 | .02 | .01 |
| ☐ 287 Reggie White | .15 | .07 | .02 |
| ☐ 288 Rich Kotite CO | .04 | .02 | .01 |
| ☐ 289 Rich Camarillo | .04 | .02 | .01 |
| ☐ 290 Garth Jax | .04 | .02 | .01 |
| ☐ 291 Ernie Jones | .04 | .02 | .01 |
| ☐ 292 Tim McDonald | .08 | .04 | .01 |
| ☐ 293 Rod Saddler | .04 | .02 | .01 |
| ☐ 294 Anthony Thompson UER | .04 | .02 | .01 |
| (NO TD stats for 1991 receiving) | | | |
| ☐ 295 Tom Tupa UER | .08 | .04 | .01 |
| (QB/P on front, QB on back) | | | |
| ☐ 296 Ron Wolfley | .04 | .02 | .01 |
| ☐ 297 Joe Bugel CO | .04 | .02 | .01 |
| ☐ 298 Gary Anderson | .04 | .02 | .01 |
| ☐ 299 Jeff Graham | .08 | .04 | .01 |
| ☐ 300 Eric Green | .10 | .05 | .01 |
| ☐ 301 Bryan Hinkle | .04 | .02 | .01 |
| ☐ 302 Tunch Ilkin | .04 | .02 | .01 |
| ☐ 303 Louis Lipps | .08 | .04 | .01 |
| ☐ 304 Neil O'Donnell | .50 | .23 | .06 |
| ☐ 305 Rod Woodson | .10 | .05 | .01 |
| ☐ 306 Bill Cowher CO | .04 | .02 | .01 |
| ☐ 307 Eric Bieniemy | .08 | .04 | .01 |
| ☐ 308 Marion Butts | .10 | .05 | .01 |
| ☐ 309 John Friesz | .08 | .04 | .01 |
| ☐ 310 Courtney Hall | .04 | .02 | .01 |
| ☐ 311 Ronnie Harmon | .04 | .02 | .01 |
| ☐ 312 Henry Rolling | .04 | .02 | .01 |
| ☐ 313 Billy Ray Smith | .04 | .02 | .01 |
| ☐ 314 George Thornton | .04 | .02 | .01 |
| ☐ 315 Bobby Ross CO | .04 | .02 | .01 |
| ☐ 316 Todd Bowles | .04 | .02 | .01 |
| ☐ 317 Michael Carter | .04 | .02 | .01 |
| ☐ 318 Don Griffin | .04 | .02 | .01 |
| ☐ 319 Charles Haley | .08 | .04 | .01 |
| ☐ 320 Brent Jones | .10 | .05 | .01 |
| ☐ 321 John Taylor | .10 | .05 | .01 |
| ☐ 322 Ted Washington | .04 | .02 | .01 |
| ☐ 323 Steve Young | .35 | .16 | .04 |
| ☐ 324 George Seifert CO | .08 | .04 | .01 |
| ☐ 325 Brian Blades | .08 | .04 | .01 |
| ☐ 326 Jacob Green | .04 | .02 | .01 |
| ☐ 327 Patrick Hunter | .04 | .02 | .01 |
| ☐ 328 Tommy Kane | .04 | .02 | .01 |
| ☐ 329 Cortez Kennedy | .10 | .05 | .01 |
| ☐ 330 Dave Krieg | .08 | .04 | .01 |
| ☐ 331 Rufus Porter | .04 | .02 | .01 |
| ☐ 332 John L. Williams | .08 | .04 | .01 |
| ☐ 333 Tom Flores CO | .04 | .02 | .01 |
| ☐ 334 Gary Anderson | .08 | .04 | .01 |
| ☐ 335 Mark Carrier | .08 | .04 | .01 |
| ☐ 336 Reuben Davis | .04 | .02 | .01 |
| ☐ 337 Lawrence Dawsey | .10 | .05 | .01 |
| ☐ 338 Keith McCants UER | .04 | .02 | .01 |
| (LB on front, DE on back) | | | |
| ☐ 339 Vinny Testaverde | .10 | .05 | .01 |
| ☐ 340 Broderick Thomas | .04 | .02 | .01 |
| ☐ 341 Robert Wilson | .04 | .02 | .01 |
| ☐ 342 Sam Wyche CO | .04 | .02 | .01 |
| ☐ 343 1991 Teacher of the Year NEW | .04 | .02 | .01 |
| ☐ 344 Owners Reject Instant Replay NEW | .04 | .02 | .01 |
| ☐ 345 NFL Experience Unveiled NEW | .04 | .02 | .01 |
| ☐ 346 Noll Retires Tosses Coin NEW | .04 | .02 | .01 |
| ☐ 347 Isaac Curtis and Tim McGee MN UER (Birthdates switched) Cincinnati Bengals | .04 | .02 | .01 |
| ☐ 348 Drew Pearson Michael Irvin MN Dallas Cowboys | .25 | .11 | .03 |
| ☐ 349 Billy Sims Barry Sanders MN | .25 | .11 | .03 |

Detroit Lions
| | | | | |
|---|---|---|---|---|
| ☐ 350 Kenny Stabler | .10 | .05 | .01 |
| Todd Marinovich MN | | | |
| Los Angeles Raiders | | | |
| ☐ 351 Craig James | .10 | .05 | .01 |
| Leonard Russell MN | | | |
| New England Patriots | | | |
| ☐ 352 Bob Golic | .04 | .02 | .01 |
| Graffiti | | | |
| It's a Sign of | | | |
| Ignorance | | | |
| ☐ 353 Pat Harlow | .04 | .02 | .01 |
| Vote, Let | | | |
| Your Choice Be Heard | | | |
| ☐ 354 Esera Tuaolo | .04 | .02 | .01 |
| Stand Tall, Be Proud | | | |
| of Your Heritage | | | |
| ☐ 355 Mark Schlereth | .10 | .05 | .01 |
| Save The Environment | | | |
| Be a Team Player | | | |
| ☐ 356 Trace Armstrong | .04 | .02 | .01 |
| Drug Abuse | | | |
| Stay in Control | | | |
| ☐ 357 Eric Bieniemy | .04 | .02 | .01 |
| Save a Life | | | |
| Buckle Up | | | |
| ☐ 358 Bill Romanowski | .04 | .02 | .01 |
| Education | | | |
| Stay In School | | | |
| ☐ 359 Irv Eatman | .04 | .02 | .01 |
| Exercise | | | |
| Be Active | | | |
| ☐ 360 Jonathan Hayes | .04 | .02 | .01 |
| Diabetes | | | |
| Be Your Best | | | |
| ☐ 361 Atlanta Falcons | .04 | .02 | .01 |
| Spirit of the Game | | | |
| (Helmet) | | | |
| ☐ 362 Chicago Bears | .04 | .02 | .01 |
| Spirit of the Game | | | |
| (Vintage game photo) | | | |
| ☐ 363 Dallas Cowboys | .04 | .02 | .01 |
| Spirit of the Game | | | |
| (Mascot) | | | |
| ☐ 364 Detroit Lions | .04 | .02 | .01 |
| Spirit of the Game | | | |
| (Overhead game photo) | | | |
| ☐ 365 Green Bay Packers | .04 | .02 | .01 |
| Spirit of the Game | | | |
| (60's huddle) | | | |
| ☐ 366 Los Angeles Rams | .04 | .02 | .01 |
| Spirit of the Game | | | |
| (Fans) | | | |
| ☐ 367 Minnesota Vikings | .04 | .02 | .01 |
| Spirit of the Game | | | |
| (Vintage game photo) | | | |
| ☐ 368 New Orleans Saints UER | .04 | .02 | .01 |
| Spirit of the Game | | | |
| (Fans; Post-season record | | | |
| was 0-3, not 0-2) | | | |
| ☐ 369 New York Giants | .04 | .02 | .01 |
| Spirit of the Game | | | |
| (Fan's banner) | | | |
| ☐ 370 Philadelphia Eagles | .04 | .02 | .01 |
| Spirit of the Game | | | |
| (Eric Allen) | | | |
| ☐ 371 Phoenix Cardinals | .04 | .02 | .01 |
| Spirit of the Game | | | |
| (Fan) | | | |
| ☐ 372 San Francisco 49ers | .04 | .02 | .01 |
| Spirit of the Game | | | |
| (Tom Rathman) | | | |
| ☐ 373 Tampa Bay Buccaneers | .04 | .02 | .01 |
| Spirit of the Game | | | |
| (Mascot) | | | |
| ☐ 374 Washington Redskins | .04 | .02 | .01 |
| Spirit of the Game | | | |
| (Fans) | | | |
| ☐ 375 Steve Atwater PB UER | .04 | .02 | .01 |
| (Photo shows regular | | | |
| game instead of Pro Bowl) | | | |
| Denver Broncos | | | |
| ☐ 376 Cornelius Bennett PB | .08 | .04 | .01 |
| Buffalo Bills | | | |
| ☐ 377 Tim Brown PB | .15 | .07 | .02 |
| Los Angeles Raiders | | | |
| ☐ 378 Marion Butts PB | .04 | .02 | .01 |
| San Diego Chargers | | | |
| ☐ 379 Ray Childress PB | .04 | .02 | .01 |
| (Photo shows regular | | | |
| game instead of Pro Bowl) | | | |
| Houston Oilers | | | |
| ☐ 380 Mark Clayton PB | .08 | .04 | .01 |
| Miami Dolphins | | | |
| ☐ 381 Marv Cook PB | .04 | .02 | .01 |
| New England Patriots | | | |
| ☐ 382 Cris Dishman PB | .04 | .02 | .01 |
| Houston Oilers | | | |

| | | | | |
|---|---|---|---|---|
| ☐ 383 William Fuller PB | .04 | .02 | .01 |
| Houston Oilers | | | |
| ☐ 384 Gaston Green PB | .04 | .02 | .01 |
| Denver Broncos | | | |
| ☐ 385 Jeff Jaeger PB | .04 | .02 | .01 |
| Los Angeles Raiders | | | |
| ☐ 386 Haywood Jeffires PB | .08 | .04 | .01 |
| Houston Oilers | | | |
| ☐ 387 James Lofton PB | .10 | .05 | .01 |
| Buffalo Bills | | | |
| ☐ 388 Ronnie Lott PB | .08 | .04 | .01 |
| Los Angeles Raiders | | | |
| ☐ 389 Karl Mecklenburg PB | .04 | .02 | .01 |
| Denver Broncos | | | |
| ☐ 390 Warren Moon PB | .10 | .05 | .01 |
| Houston Oilers | | | |
| ☐ 391 Anthony Munoz PB | .04 | .02 | .01 |
| Cincinnati Bengals | | | |
| ☐ 392 Dennis Smith PB | .04 | .02 | .01 |
| Denver Broncos | | | |
| ☐ 393 Neil Smith PB | .04 | .02 | .01 |
| Kansas City Chiefs | | | |
| ☐ 394 Darryl Talley PB | .04 | .02 | .01 |
| Buffalo Bills | | | |
| ☐ 395 Derrick Thomas PB | .10 | .05 | .01 |
| Kansas City Chiefs | | | |
| ☐ 396 Thurman Thomas PB | .20 | .09 | .03 |
| Buffalo Bills | | | |
| ☐ 397 Greg Townsend PB | .04 | .02 | .01 |
| Los Angeles Raiders | | | |
| ☐ 398 Richmond Webb PB | .04 | .02 | .01 |
| Miami Dolphins | | | |
| ☐ 399 Rod Woodson PB | .08 | .04 | .01 |
| Pittsburgh Steelers | | | |
| ☐ 400 Dan Reeves CO PB | .04 | .02 | .01 |
| Denver Broncos | | | |
| ☐ 401 Troy Aikman PB | .60 | .25 | .08 |
| Dallas Cowboys | | | |
| ☐ 402 Eric Allen PB | .05 | .02 | .01 |
| Philadelphia Eagles | | | |
| ☐ 403 Bennie Blades PB | .05 | .02 | .01 |
| Detroit Lions | | | |
| ☐ 404 Lomas Brown PB | .05 | .02 | .01 |
| Detroit Lions | | | |
| ☐ 405 Mark Carrier PB | .05 | .02 | .01 |
| Chicago Bears | | | |
| ☐ 406 Gary Clark PB | .08 | .04 | .01 |
| Washington Redskins | | | |
| ☐ 407 Mel Gray PB | .05 | .02 | .01 |
| Detroit Lions | | | |
| ☐ 408 Darrell Green PB | .05 | .02 | .01 |
| Washington Redskins | | | |
| ☐ 409 Michael Irvin PB | .25 | .11 | .03 |
| Dallas Cowboys | | | |
| ☐ 410 Vaughan Johnson PB | .05 | .02 | .01 |
| New Orleans Saints | | | |
| ☐ 411 Seth Joyner PB | .05 | .02 | .01 |
| Philadelphia Eagles | | | |
| ☐ 412 Jim Lachey PB | .05 | .02 | .01 |
| Washington Redskins | | | |
| ☐ 413 Chip Lohmiller PB | .05 | .02 | .01 |
| Washington Redskins | | | |
| ☐ 414 Charles Mann PB | .05 | .02 | .01 |
| Washington Redskins | | | |
| ☐ 415 Chris Miller PB | .08 | .04 | .01 |
| Atlanta Falcons | | | |
| ☐ 416 Sam Mills PB | .05 | .02 | .01 |
| New Orleans Saints | | | |
| ☐ 417 Bart Oates PB | .05 | .02 | .01 |
| New York Giants | | | |
| ☐ 418 Jerry Rice PB | .25 | .11 | .03 |
| San Francisco 49ers | | | |
| ☐ 419 Andre Rison PB | .10 | .05 | .01 |
| Atlanta Falcons | | | |
| ☐ 420 Mark Rypien PB | .08 | .04 | .01 |
| Washington Redskins | | | |
| ☐ 421 Barry Sanders PB | .35 | .16 | .04 |
| Detroit Lions | | | |
| ☐ 422 Deion Sanders PB | .08 | .04 | .01 |
| Atlanta Falcons | | | |
| ☐ 423 Mark Schlereth PB | .05 | .02 | .01 |
| Washington Redskins | | | |
| ☐ 424 Mike Singletary PB | .08 | .04 | .01 |
| Chicago Bears | | | |
| ☐ 425 Emmitt Smith PB | .75 | .35 | .09 |
| Dallas Cowboys | | | |
| ☐ 426 Pat Swilling PB | .08 | .04 | .01 |
| New Orleans Saints | | | |
| ☐ 427 Reggie White PB | .08 | .04 | .01 |
| Philadelphia Eagles | | | |
| ☐ 428 Rick Bryan | .05 | .02 | .01 |
| ☐ 429 Tim Green | .05 | .02 | .01 |
| ☐ 430 Drew Hill | .08 | .04 | .01 |
| ☐ 431 Norm Johnson | .05 | .02 | .01 |
| ☐ 432 Keith Jones | .05 | .02 | .01 |
| ☐ 433 Mike Pritchard | .25 | .11 | .03 |
| ☐ 434 Deion Sanders | .20 | .09 | .03 |

| | | | |
|---|---|---|---|
| ☐ 435 Tony Smith | .20 | .09 | .03 |
| ☐ 436 Jessie Tuggle | .05 | .02 | .01 |
| ☐ 437 Steve Christie | .05 | .02 | .01 |
| ☐ 438 Shane Conlan | .08 | .04 | .01 |
| ☐ 439 Matt Darby | .05 | .02 | .01 |
| ☐ 440 John Fina | .05 | .02 | .01 |
| ☐ 441 Henry Jones | .05 | .02 | .01 |
| ☐ 442 Jim Kelly | .25 | .11 | .03 |
| ☐ 443 Pete Metzelaars | .05 | .02 | .01 |
| ☐ 444 Andre Reed | .10 | .05 | .01 |
| ☐ 445 Bruce Smith | .10 | .05 | .01 |
| ☐ 446 Troy Auzenne | .05 | .02 | .01 |
| ☐ 447 Mark Carrier | .08 | .04 | .01 |
| ☐ 448 Will Furrer | .10 | .05 | .01 |
| ☐ 449 Jim Harbaugh | .08 | .04 | .01 |
| ☐ 450 Brad Muster | .08 | .04 | .01 |
| ☐ 451 Darren Lewis | .05 | .02 | .01 |
| ☐ 452 Mike Singletary | .08 | .04 | .01 |
| ☐ 453 Alonzo Spellman | .20 | .09 | .03 |
| ☐ 454 Chris Zorich | .08 | .04 | .01 |
| ☐ 455 Jim Breech | .05 | .02 | .01 |
| ☐ 456 Boomer Esiason | .15 | .07 | .02 |
| ☐ 457 Derrick Fenner | .08 | .04 | .01 |
| ☐ 458 James Francis | .08 | .04 | .01 |
| ☐ 459 David Klingler | .50 | .23 | .06 |
| ☐ 460 Tim McGee | .05 | .02 | .01 |
| ☐ 461 Carl Pickens | .35 | .16 | .04 |
| ☐ 462 Alfred Williams | .05 | .02 | .01 |
| ☐ 463 Darryl Williams | .20 | .09 | .03 |
| ☐ 464 Mark Bavaro | .08 | .04 | .01 |
| ☐ 465 Jay Hilgenberg | .08 | .04 | .01 |
| ☐ 466 Leroy Hoard | .08 | .04 | .01 |
| ☐ 467 Bernie Kosar | .10 | .05 | .01 |
| ☐ 468 Michael Dean Perry | .10 | .05 | .01 |
| ☐ 469 Todd Philcox | .25 | .11 | .03 |
| ☐ 470 Patrick Rowe | .10 | .05 | .01 |
| ☐ 471 Tommy Vardell | .25 | .11 | .03 |
| ☐ 472 Everson Walls | .05 | .02 | .01 |
| ☐ 473 Troy Aikman | 1.25 | .55 | .16 |
| ☐ 474 Kenneth Gant | .25 | .11 | .03 |
| ☐ 475 Charles Haley | .08 | .04 | .01 |
| ☐ 476 Michael Irvin | .50 | .23 | .06 |
| ☐ 477 Robert Jones | .12 | .05 | .02 |
| ☐ 478 Russell Maryland | .15 | .07 | .02 |
| ☐ 479 Jay Novacek | .15 | .07 | .02 |
| ☐ 480 Kevin Smith | .25 | .11 | .03 |
| ☐ 481 Tony Tolbert | .05 | .02 | .01 |
| ☐ 482 Steve Atwater | .08 | .04 | .01 |
| ☐ 483 Shane Dronett | .20 | .09 | .03 |
| ☐ 484 Simon Fletcher | .08 | .04 | .01 |
| ☐ 485 Greg Lewis | .05 | .02 | .01 |
| ☐ 486 Tommy Maddox | .35 | .16 | .04 |
| ☐ 487 Shannon Sharpe | .25 | .11 | .03 |
| ☐ 488 Dennis Smith | .08 | .04 | .01 |
| ☐ 489 Sammie Smith | .05 | .02 | .01 |
| ☐ 490 Kenny Walker | .05 | .02 | .01 |
| ☐ 491 Lomas Brown | .05 | .02 | .01 |
| ☐ 492 Mike Farr | .05 | .02 | .01 |
| ☐ 493 Mel Gray | .08 | .04 | .01 |
| ☐ 494 Jason Hanson | .15 | .07 | .02 |
| ☐ 495 Herman Moore | .30 | .14 | .04 |
| ☐ 496 Rodney Peete | .08 | .04 | .01 |
| ☐ 497 Robert Porcher | .20 | .09 | .03 |
| ☐ 498 Kelvin Pritchett | .05 | .02 | .01 |
| ☐ 499 Andre Ware | .08 | .04 | .01 |
| ☐ 500 Sanjay Beach | .10 | .05 | .01 |
| ☐ 501 Edgar Bennett | .30 | .14 | .04 |
| ☐ 502 Lewis Billups | .05 | .02 | .01 |
| ☐ 503 Terrell Buckley | .10 | .05 | .01 |
| ☐ 504 Ty Detmer | .08 | .04 | .01 |
| ☐ 505 Brett Favre | 1.00 | .45 | .13 |
| ☐ 506 Johnny Holland | .05 | .02 | .01 |
| ☐ 507 Dexter McNabb | .05 | .02 | .01 |
| ☐ 508 Vince Workman | .08 | .04 | .01 |
| ☐ 509 Cody Carlson | .20 | .09 | .03 |
| ☐ 510 Ernest Givins | .08 | .04 | .01 |
| ☐ 511 Jerry Gray | .05 | .02 | .01 |
| ☐ 512 Haywood Jeffires | .10 | .05 | .01 |
| ☐ 513 Bruce Matthews | .08 | .04 | .01 |
| ☐ 514 Bubba McDowell | .05 | .02 | .01 |
| ☐ 515 Bucky Richardson | .20 | .09 | .03 |
| ☐ 516 Webster Slaughter | .08 | .04 | .01 |
| ☐ 517 Al Smith | .05 | .02 | .01 |
| ☐ 518 Mel Agee | .05 | .02 | .01 |
| ☐ 519 Ashley Ambrose | .10 | .05 | .01 |
| ☐ 520 Kevin Call | .05 | .02 | .01 |
| ☐ 521 Ken Clark | .05 | .02 | .01 |
| ☐ 522 Quentin Coryatt | .30 | .14 | .04 |
| ☐ 523 Steve Emtman | .15 | .07 | .02 |
| ☐ 524 Jeff George | .20 | .09 | .03 |
| ☐ 525 Jessie Hester | .05 | .02 | .01 |
| ☐ 526 Anthony Johnson | .05 | .02 | .01 |
| ☐ 527 Tim Barnett | .08 | .04 | .01 |
| ☐ 528 Martin Bayless | .05 | .02 | .01 |
| ☐ 529 J.J. Birden | .08 | .04 | .01 |
| ☐ 530 Dale Carter | .25 | .11 | .03 |
| ☐ 531 Dave Krieg | .08 | .04 | .01 |

| | | | |
|---|---|---|---|
| ☐ 532 Albert Lewis | .08 | .04 | .01 |
| ☐ 533 Nick Lowery | .08 | .04 | .01 |
| ☐ 534 Christian Okoye | .08 | .04 | .01 |
| ☐ 535 Harvey Williams | .10 | .05 | .01 |
| ☐ 536 Aundray Bruce | .05 | .02 | .01 |
| ☐ 537 Eric Dickerson | .10 | .05 | .01 |
| ☐ 538 Willie Gault | .08 | .04 | .01 |
| ☐ 539 Ethan Horton | .05 | .02 | .01 |
| ☐ 540 Jeff Jaeger | .05 | .02 | .01 |
| ☐ 541 Napoleon McCallum | .05 | .02 | .01 |
| ☐ 542 Chester McGlockton | .20 | .09 | .03 |
| ☐ 543 Steve Smith | .08 | .04 | .01 |
| ☐ 544 Steve Wisniewski | .05 | .02 | .01 |
| ☐ 545 Marc Boutte | .05 | .02 | .01 |
| ☐ 546 Pat Carter | .05 | .02 | .01 |
| ☐ 547 Jim Everett | .10 | .05 | .01 |
| ☐ 548 Cleveland Gary | .08 | .04 | .01 |
| ☐ 549 Sean Gilbert | .30 | .14 | .04 |
| ☐ 550 Steve Israel | .05 | .02 | .01 |
| ☐ 551 Todd Kinchen | .20 | .09 | .03 |
| ☐ 552 Jackie Slater | .08 | .04 | .01 |
| ☐ 553 Tony Zendejas | .05 | .02 | .01 |
| ☐ 554 Robert Clark | .05 | .02 | .01 |
| ☐ 555 Mark Clayton | .08 | .04 | .01 |
| ☐ 556 Marco Coleman | .30 | .14 | .04 |
| ☐ 557 Bryan Cox | .08 | .04 | .01 |
| ☐ 558 Keith Jackson UER | .10 | .05 | .01 |
| (Card says drafted in | | | |
| '88, but acquired as | | | |
| free agent in '92) | | | |
| ☐ 559 Dan Marino | .75 | .35 | .09 |
| ☐ 560 John Offerdahl | .08 | .04 | .01 |
| ☐ 561 Troy Vincent | .10 | .05 | .01 |
| ☐ 562 Richmond Webb | .08 | .04 | .01 |
| ☐ 563 Terry Allen | .15 | .07 | .02 |
| ☐ 564 Cris Carter | .10 | .05 | .01 |
| ☐ 565 Roger Craig | .08 | .04 | .01 |
| ☐ 566 Rich Gannon | .08 | .04 | .01 |
| ☐ 567 Hassan Jones | .05 | .02 | .01 |
| ☐ 568 Randall McDaniel | .05 | .02 | .01 |
| ☐ 569 Al Noga | .05 | .02 | .01 |
| ☐ 570 Todd Scott | .05 | .02 | .01 |
| ☐ 571 Van Waiters | .05 | .02 | .01 |
| ☐ 572 Bruce Armstrong | .05 | .02 | .01 |
| ☐ 573 Gene Chilton | .05 | .02 | .01 |
| ☐ 574 Eugene Chung | .05 | .02 | .01 |
| ☐ 575 Todd Collins | .15 | .07 | .02 |
| ☐ 576 Hart Lee Dykes | .05 | .02 | .01 |
| ☐ 577 David Howard | .05 | .02 | .01 |
| ☐ 578 Eugene Lockhart | .05 | .02 | .01 |
| ☐ 579 Greg McMurtry | .05 | .02 | .01 |
| ☐ 580 Rodney Smith | .10 | .05 | .01 |
| ☐ 581 Gene Atkins | .05 | .02 | .01 |
| ☐ 582 Vince Buck | .05 | .02 | .01 |
| ☐ 583 Wesley Carroll | .08 | .04 | .01 |
| ☐ 584 Jim Dombrowski | .05 | .02 | .01 |
| ☐ 585 Vaughn Dunbar | .20 | .09 | .03 |
| ☐ 586 Craig Heyward | .05 | .02 | .01 |
| ☐ 587 Dalton Hilliard | .05 | .02 | .01 |
| ☐ 588 Wayne Martin | .05 | .02 | .01 |
| ☐ 589 Renaldo Turnbull | .08 | .04 | .01 |
| ☐ 590 Carl Banks | .08 | .04 | .01 |
| ☐ 591 Derek Brown | .10 | .05 | .01 |
| ☐ 592 Jarrod Bunch | .05 | .02 | .01 |
| ☐ 593 Mark Ingram | .08 | .04 | .01 |
| ☐ 594 Ed McCaffrey | .08 | .04 | .01 |
| ☐ 595 Phil Simms | .10 | .05 | .01 |
| ☐ 596 Phillippi Sparks | .05 | .02 | .01 |
| ☐ 597 Lawrence Taylor | .10 | .05 | .01 |
| ☐ 598 Lewis Tillman | .08 | .04 | .01 |
| ☐ 599 Kyle Clifton | .05 | .02 | .01 |
| ☐ 600 Mo Lewis | .05 | .02 | .01 |
| ☐ 601 Terance Mathis | .05 | .02 | .01 |
| ☐ 602 Scott Mersereau | .05 | .02 | .01 |
| ☐ 603 Johnny Mitchell | .50 | .23 | .06 |
| ☐ 604 Browning Nagle | .08 | .04 | .01 |
| ☐ 605 Ken O'Brien | .08 | .04 | .01 |
| ☐ 606 Al Toon | .08 | .04 | .01 |
| ☐ 607 Marvin Washington | .05 | .02 | .01 |
| ☐ 608 Eric Allen | .08 | .04 | .01 |
| ☐ 609 Fred Barnett | .10 | .05 | .01 |
| ☐ 610 John Booty | .05 | .02 | .01 |
| ☐ 611 Randall Cunningham | .10 | .05 | .01 |
| ☐ 612 Rich Miano | .05 | .02 | .01 |
| ☐ 613 Clyde Simmons | .08 | .04 | .01 |
| ☐ 614 Siran Stacy | .05 | .02 | .01 |
| ☐ 615 Herschel Walker | .10 | .05 | .01 |
| ☐ 616 Calvin Williams | .10 | .05 | .01 |
| ☐ 617 Chris Chandler | .08 | .04 | .01 |
| ☐ 618 Randal Hill | .10 | .05 | .01 |
| ☐ 619 Johnny Johnson | .10 | .05 | .01 |
| ☐ 620 Lorenzo Lynch | .05 | .02 | .01 |
| ☐ 621 Robert Massey | .05 | .02 | .01 |
| ☐ 622 Ricky Proehl | .10 | .05 | .01 |
| ☐ 623 Timm Rosenbach | .05 | .02 | .01 |
| ☐ 624 Tony Sacca | .12 | .05 | .02 |
| ☐ 625 Aeneas Williams UER | .05 | .02 | .01 |

(Name misspelled
Aaneas)
| | | | | |
|---|---|---|---|---|
| ☐ 626 Bubby Brister | .08 | .04 | .01 |
| ☐ 627 Barry Foster | .35 | .16 | .04 |
| ☐ 628 Merrill Hoge | .08 | .04 | .01 |
| ☐ 629 David Johnson | .05 | .02 | .01 |
| ☐ 630 David Little | .05 | .02 | .01 |
| ☐ 631 Greg Lloyd | .05 | .02 | .01 |
| ☐ 632 Ernie Mills | .05 | .02 | .01 |
| ☐ 633 Leon Searcy | .05 | .02 | .01 |
| ☐ 634 Dwight Stone | .05 | .02 | .01 |
| ☐ 635 Sam Anno | .10 | .05 | .01 |
| ☐ 636 Burt Grossman | .05 | .02 | .01 |
| ☐ 637 Stan Humphries | .20 | .09 | .03 |
| ☐ 638 Nate Lewis | .08 | .04 | .01 |
| ☐ 639 Anthony Miller | .15 | .07 | .02 |
| ☐ 640 Chris Mims | .15 | .07 | .02 |
| ☐ 641 Marquez Pope | .10 | .05 | .01 |
| ☐ 642 Stanley Richard | .05 | .02 | .01 |
| ☐ 643 Junior Seau | .15 | .07 | .02 |
| ☐ 644 Brian Bollinger | .05 | .02 | .01 |
| ☐ 645 Steve Bono | .50 | .23 | .06 |
| ☐ 646 Dexter Carter | .08 | .04 | .01 |
| ☐ 647 Dana Hall | .15 | .07 | .02 |
| ☐ 648 Amp Lee | .10 | .05 | .01 |
| ☐ 649 Joe Montana | 1.00 | .45 | .13 |
| ☐ 650 Tom Rathman | .08 | .04 | .01 |
| ☐ 651 Jerry Rice | .50 | .23 | .06 |
| ☐ 652 Ricky Watters | .50 | .23 | .06 |
| ☐ 653 Robert Blackmon | .05 | .02 | .01 |
| ☐ 654 John Kasay | .05 | .02 | .01 |
| ☐ 655 Ronnie Lee | .10 | .05 | .01 |
| ☐ 656 Dan McGwire | .08 | .04 | .01 |
| ☐ 657 Ray Roberts | .05 | .02 | .01 |
| ☐ 658 Kelly Stouffer | .05 | .02 | .01 |
| ☐ 659 Chris Warren | .25 | .11 | .03 |
| ☐ 660 Tony Woods | .05 | .02 | .01 |
| ☐ 661 David Wyman | .05 | .02 | .01 |
| ☐ 662 Reggie Cobb | .10 | .05 | .01 |
| ☐ 663A Steve DeBerg ERR | .08 | .04 | .01 |

(Career yardage 1,455;
found in foil packs)

| | | | | |
|---|---|---|---|---|
| ☐ 663B Steve DeBerg COR | .08 | .04 | .01 |

(Career yardage 31,455;
found in jumbo packs)

| | | | | |
|---|---|---|---|---|
| ☐ 664 Santana Dotson | .25 | .11 | .03 |
| ☐ 665 Willie Drewery | .05 | .02 | .01 |
| ☐ 666 Paul Gruber | .05 | .02 | .01 |
| ☐ 667 Ron Hall | .05 | .02 | .01 |
| ☐ 668 Courtney Hawkins | .25 | .11 | .03 |
| ☐ 669 Charles McRae | .05 | .02 | .01 |
| ☐ 670 Ricky Reynolds | .05 | .02 | .01 |
| ☐ 671 Monte Coleman | .05 | .02 | .01 |
| ☐ 672 Brad Edwards | .05 | .02 | .01 |
| ☐ 673 James Geathers UER | .05 | .02 | .01 |

(Card says played in
New Orleans in '89;
should say Washington)

| | | | | |
|---|---|---|---|---|
| ☐ 674 Kelly Goodburn | .05 | .02 | .01 |
| ☐ 675 Kurt Gouveia | .05 | .02 | .01 |
| ☐ 676 Chris Hakel | .10 | .05 | .01 |
| ☐ 677 Wilber Marshall | .08 | .04 | .01 |
| ☐ 678 Ricky Sanders | .08 | .04 | .01 |
| ☐ 679 Mark Schlereth | .05 | .02 | .01 |
| ☐ 680 Buffalo Bills | .05 | .02 | .01 |

Spirit of the Game
Rich Stadium
| | | | | |
|---|---|---|---|---|
| ☐ 681 Cincinnati Bengals | .05 | .02 | .01 |

Spirit of the Game
Boomer Esiason
(with tiger cub)
| | | | | |
|---|---|---|---|---|
| ☐ 682 Cleveland Browns | .05 | .02 | .01 |

Spirit of the Game
The Dog Pound
| | | | | |
|---|---|---|---|---|
| ☐ 683 Denver Broncos | .05 | .02 | .01 |

Spirit of the Game
Bronco Statue
| | | | | |
|---|---|---|---|---|
| ☐ 684 Houston Oilers | .05 | .02 | .01 |

Spirit of the Game
"Luv Ya Blue"
| | | | | |
|---|---|---|---|---|
| ☐ 685 Indianapolis Colts | .05 | .02 | .01 |

Spirit of the Game
Hoosier Dome
| | | | | |
|---|---|---|---|---|
| ☐ 686 Kansas City Chiefs | .05 | .02 | .01 |

Spirit of the Game
Mack Lee Hill Award
Mack Lee Hill
Tracy Simien
| | | | | |
|---|---|---|---|---|
| ☐ 687 Los Angeles Raiders | .05 | .02 | .01 |

Spirit of the Game
The Team of the Decades
| | | | | |
|---|---|---|---|---|
| ☐ 688 Miami Dolphins | .05 | .02 | .01 |

Spirit of the Game
Dolphins' helmet
| | | | | |
|---|---|---|---|---|
| ☐ 689 New England Patriots | .05 | .02 | .01 |

Spirit of the Game
Francis J. Kilroy VP
| | | | | |
|---|---|---|---|---|
| ☐ 690 New York Jets | .05 | .02 | .01 |

Spirit of the Game
Team mascot
| | | | | |
|---|---|---|---|---|
| ☐ 691 Pittsburgh Steelers | .05 | .02 | .01 |

Spirit of the Game
Steelers' helmet
| | | | | |
|---|---|---|---|---|
| ☐ 692 San Diego Chargers | .05 | .02 | .01 |

Spirit of the Game
Charger in parachute
| | | | | |
|---|---|---|---|---|
| ☐ 693 Seattle Seahawks | .05 | .02 | .01 |

Spirit of the Game
Kingdome
| | | | | |
|---|---|---|---|---|
| ☐ 694 Play Smart | .05 | .02 | .01 |

Stephen Baker
New York Giants
| | | | | |
|---|---|---|---|---|
| ☐ 695 Hank Williams Jr. NEW | .20 | .09 | .03 |
| ☐ 696 3 Brothers in NFL NEW | .05 | .02 | .01 |

Brian Baldinger
Gary Baldinger
Rich Baldinger
| | | | | |
|---|---|---|---|---|
| ☐ 697 Japan Bowl NEW | .05 | .02 | .01 |

August 2, 1992
| | | | | |
|---|---|---|---|---|
| ☐ 698 Georgia Dome NEW | .05 | .02 | .01 |
| ☐ 699 Theme Art NEW | .05 | .02 | .01 |

Super Bowl XXVII
| | | | | |
|---|---|---|---|---|
| ☐ 700 Mark Rypien | .08 | .04 | .01 |

Super Bowl XXVI MVP
| | | | | |
|---|---|---|---|---|
| ☐ AU150 Emmitt Smith AU | 200.00 | 90.00 | 25.00 |

(Certified autograph)
| | | | | |
|---|---|---|---|---|
| ☐ AU168 Erik Kramer AU | 30.00 | 13.50 | 3.80 |

(Certified autograph)
| | | | | |
|---|---|---|---|---|
| ☐ NNO Santa Claus | 1.25 | .55 | .16 |

Spirit of the Season
| | | | | |
|---|---|---|---|---|
| ☐ NNO Emmitt Smith | .50 | .23 | .06 |

Power Preview
| | | | | |
|---|---|---|---|---|
| ☐ SC5 Super Bowl XXVI | .50 | .23 | .06 |

## 1992 Pro Set HOF Inductees

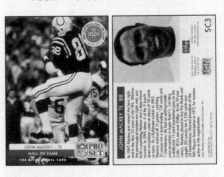

This "Special Collectibles" subset was issued as a random insert with 1992 Pro Set packs. These standard-size (2 1/2" by 3 1/2") cards are numbered with an "SC" prefix and feature the 1992 Pro Football Hall of Fame induction class.

| | MINT | EXC | G-VG |
|---|---|---|---|
| COMPLETE SET (4) | 1.50 | .65 | .19 |
| COMMON CARD (SC1-SC4) | .40 | .18 | .05 |
| | | | |
| ☐ SC1 Lem Barney | .40 | .18 | .05 |
| ☐ SC2 Al Davis | .40 | .18 | .05 |
| ☐ SC3 John Mackey | .40 | .18 | .05 |
| ☐ SC4 John Riggins | .50 | .23 | .06 |

## 1992 Pro Set Gold MVPs

This 30-card standard-size (2 1/2" by 3 1/2" inches) insert set features the most valuable player for each of the 28 NFL teams plus two outstanding coaches. Card numbers 1-15 were offered one per series I jumbo pack, while card numbers 16-30 were inserted one per series II jumbo pack. Series II jumbo pack production was limited to 4,000 numbered cases. The cards differ in design according to series. Series I inserts have full-bleed color action player photos. A diamond-shaped "'92 MVP" emblem appears at the upper right corner, while a gold-foil stamped bar (carrying the player's name) and NFL/Pro Set logo cuts across the bottom. The horizontal backs have career summary, statistics, biography, and a color head shot. Series II inserts have full-bleed color action photos edged on the left by a two-toned stripe. A gray block at the lower left corner carries "MVP" in gold foil. On a screened background, the backs have a color close-up shot and career

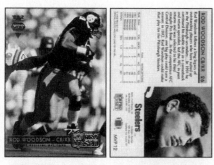

summary. The set is arranged as follows: AFC "Team MVPs" (1-14), a coach card of Don Shula (15), 14 NFC "Team MVPs" (16-29), and a coach card of Jimmy Johnson (30). All cards are numbered on the back with an "MVP" prefix.

| | MINT | EXC | G-VG |
|---|---|---|---|
| COMPLETE SET (30)...................... | 24.00 | 11.00 | 3.00 |
| COMPLETE SERIES 1 (15)............... | 6.00 | 2.70 | .75 |
| COMPLETE SERIES 2 (15)............... | 18.00 | 8.00 | 2.30 |
| COMMON PLAYER (1-15)................. | .25 | .11 | .03 |
| COMMON PLAYER (16-30)............... | .35 | .16 | .04 |
| ☐ 1 Thurman Thomas...................... Buffalo Bills | 2.00 | .90 | .25 |
| ☐ 2 Anthony Munoz......................... Cincinnati Bengals | .30 | .14 | .04 |
| ☐ 3 Clay Matthews......................... Cleveland Browns | .30 | .14 | .04 |
| ☐ 4 John Elway............................. Denver Broncos | 1.50 | .65 | .19 |
| ☐ 5 Warren Moon............................ Houston Oilers | .60 | .25 | .08 |
| ☐ 6 Bill Brooks.............................. Indianapolis Colts | .25 | .11 | .03 |
| ☐ 7 Derrick Thomas......................... Kansas City Chiefs | .50 | .23 | .06 |
| ☐ 8 Todd Marinovich........................ Los Angeles Raiders | .25 | .11 | .03 |
| ☐ 9 Mark Higgs.............................. Miami Dolphins | .50 | .23 | .06 |
| ☐ 10 Leonard Russell...................... New England Patriots | .75 | .35 | .09 |
| ☐ 11 Rob Moore............................. New York Jets | .30 | .14 | .04 |
| ☐ 12 Rod Woodson......................... Pittsburgh Steelers | .40 | .18 | .05 |
| ☐ 13 Marion Butts.......................... San Diego Chargers | .30 | .14 | .04 |
| ☐ 14 Brian Blades.......................... Seattle Seahawks | .25 | .11 | .03 |
| ☐ 15 Don Shula CO........................ Miami Dolphins | .30 | .14 | .04 |
| ☐ 16 Deion Sanders........................ Atlanta Falcons | .75 | .35 | .09 |
| ☐ 17 Neal Anderson........................ Chicago Bears | .45 | .20 | .06 |
| ☐ 18 Emmitt Smith.......................... Dallas Cowboys | 8.00 | 3.60 | 1.00 |
| ☐ 19 Barry Sanders......................... Detroit Lions | 4.00 | 1.80 | .50 |
| ☐ 20 Brett Favre............................. Green Bay Packers | 3.00 | 1.35 | .40 |
| ☐ 21 Kevin Greene.......................... Los Angeles Rams | .35 | .16 | .04 |
| ☐ 22 Terry Allen............................ Minnesota Vikings | 1.00 | .45 | .13 |
| ☐ 23 Pat Swilling........................... New Orleans Saints | .35 | .16 | .04 |
| ☐ 24 Rodney Hampton..................... New York Giants | 2.00 | .90 | .25 |
| ☐ 25 Randall Cunningham................. Philadelphia Eagles | .50 | .23 | .06 |
| ☐ 26 Randal Hill............................ Phoenix Cardinals | .45 | .20 | .06 |
| ☐ 27 Jerry Rice............................. San Francisco 49ers | 2.50 | 1.15 | .30 |
| ☐ 28 Vinny Testaverde...................... Tampa Bay Buccaneers | .45 | .20 | .06 |
| ☐ 29 Mark Rypien........................... Washington Redskins | .45 | .20 | .06 |
| ☐ 30 Jimmy Johnson CO................... Dallas Cowboys | .45 | .20 | .06 |

## 1992 Pro Set Ground Force

These six standard-size (2 1/2 by 3 1/2") cards were inserted only in foil packs of numbered hobby cases. They are identical in design and numbering to their regular issue counterparts, except that these insert cards are stamped with a gold foil "Ground Force" logo.

| | MINT | EXC | G-VG |
|---|---|---|---|
| COMPLETE SET (6)......................... | 30.00 | 13.50 | 3.80 |
| COMMON CARD.............................. | 2.00 | .90 | .25 |
| ☐ 86 Gerald Riggs.......................... Washington Redskins | 2.00 | .90 | .25 |
| ☐ 105 Thurman Thomas................... Buffalo Bills | 6.00 | 2.70 | .75 |
| ☐ 118 Neal Anderson...................... Chicago Bears | 2.00 | .90 | .25 |
| ☐ 150 Emmitt Smith........................ Dallas Cowboys | 20.00 | 9.00 | 2.50 |
| ☐ 206 Barry Word........................... Kansas City Chiefs | 2.00 | .90 | .25 |
| ☐ 249 Leonard Russell..................... New England Patriots | 4.00 | 1.80 | .50 |

## 1992 Pro Set HOF 2000

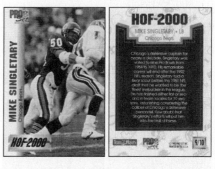

This ten-card standard size (2 1/2 by 3 1/2") set features ten of the NFL's all-time top players whom Pro Set predicts are worthy candidates for the Hall of Fame in the beginning of the next century. The cards were randomly inserted in series II foil packs. The fronts are like the regular issue Pro Set series, with full-bleed color action photos edged on the left a two-toned stripe, except that "HOF-2000" is gold-foil stamped on two horizontal bars at the lower left corner. On the backs, a purple panel on a screened background summarizes the player's career. The cards are numbered on the back "X/10."

| | MINT | EXC | G-VG |
|---|---|---|---|
| COMPLETE SET (10)........................ | 20.00 | 9.00 | 2.50 |
| COMMON PLAYER (1-10)................. | 2.00 | .90 | .25 |
| ☐ 1 Marcus Allen........................... Los Angeles Raiders | 2.00 | .90 | .25 |
| ☐ 2 Richard Dent............................ Chicago Bears | 2.00 | .90 | .25 |
| ☐ 3 Eric Dickerson......................... Los Angeles Raiders | 2.00 | .90 | .25 |
| ☐ 4 Ronnie Lott............................. Los Angeles Raiders | 2.00 | .90 | .25 |
| ☐ 5 Art Monk................................ Washington Redskins | 2.00 | .90 | .25 |
| ☐ 6 Joe Montana........................... | 8.00 | 3.60 | 1.00 |

| | | MINT | EXC | G-VG |
|---|---|---|---|---|
| | San Francisco 49ers | | | |
| ☐ 7 | Warren Moon | 3.00 | 1.35 | .40 |
| | Houston Oilers | | | |
| ☐ 8 | Anthony Munoz | 2.00 | .90 | .25 |
| | Cincinnati Bengals | | | |
| ☐ 9 | Mike Singletary | 2.00 | .90 | .25 |
| | Chicago Bears | | | |
| ☐ 10 | Lawrence Taylor | 2.50 | 1.15 | .30 |
| | New York Giants | | | |

## 1992 Pro Set Emmitt Smith Holograms

This four-card hologram set was randomly inserted into 1992 Pro Set I foil packs. The ES1 card was the least difficult to find, while the ES4 card was the most difficult. The holograms on the fronts capture different moments in Smith's career, while the red, white, and blue backs present player profile, statistics (1991 and projected), or career summary. The cards are numbered on the back.

| | MINT | EXC | G-VG |
|---|---|---|---|
| COMPLETE SET (4) | 150.00 | 70.00 | 19.00 |
| COMMON SMITH (ES1-ES4) | 25.00 | 11.50 | 3.10 |
| ☐ ES1 Emmitt Smith Stats 1990-1999 | 25.00 | 11.50 | 3.10 |
| ☐ ES2 Emmitt Smith Drafted by Cowboys | 30.00 | 13.50 | 3.80 |
| ☐ ES3 Emmitt Smith '90 Pro Set Offensive Rookie of the Year | 45.00 | 20.00 | 5.75 |
| ☐ ES4 Emmitt Smith '91 NFL Rushing Leader | 70.00 | 32.00 | 8.75 |

## 1992 Pro Set Club

The theme of the 1992 Pro Set Club set is "Football Practice." Each of the nine cards measures the standard-size, 2 1/2" by 3 1/2". The full-bleed color photos on the fronts illustrate various aspects of the game. The card subtitle appears in a pastel purple bar superimposed over the picture toward the bottom. At the left end of the bar is the Pro Set Club logo. On a yellow panel inside a turquoise bordered speckled with green, the backs discuss how to play football and challenge the reader to "do it yourself," "think about it," "check it out," or "take a look." The cards are numbered on the back in a pastel purple circle.

| | MINT | EXC | G-VG |
|---|---|---|---|
| COMPLETE SET (9) | 7.00 | 2.80 | .70 |
| COMMON PLAYER (1-9) | 1.00 | .40 | .10 |

| | | MINT | EXC | G-VG |
|---|---|---|---|---|
| ☐ 1 | Quarterback Throwing Pass | 1.25 | .50 | .12 |
| ☐ 2 | Coach Reviewing Play Strategy | 1.00 | .40 | .10 |
| ☐ 3 | Team Stretching | 1.00 | .40 | .10 |
| ☐ 4 | Offensive Play | 1.00 | .40 | .10 |
| ☐ 5 | Kickoff | 1.00 | .40 | .10 |
| ☐ 6 | Player's Stance | 1.00 | .40 | .10 |
| ☐ 7 | Football Is a Spectator Sport | 1.00 | .40 | .10 |
| ☐ 8 | Defensive Practice | 1.00 | .40 | .10 |
| ☐ 9 | Play in Motion | 1.00 | .40 | .10 |

## 1992-93 Pro Set Super Bowl XXVII

Produced by Pro Set to commemorate Super Bowl XXVII, this 38-card standard-size (2 1/2" by 3 1/2") set was packaged in two cello packs. For those who paid admission to Super Bowl XXVII, January 31, 1993, in Pasadena, a set was inserted into the GTE seat cushion. The set was also available through mail-order for 22.00 plus either a Dallas Cowboys or Buffalo Bills mini-binder. Just 7,000 sets were produced for the mail-away offer. The cards have the same design as the regular issue except for the following differences: 1) all cards have a Super Bowl XXVII emblem on their fronts; 2) the Bills' and the Cowboys' cards have AFC Champion and NFC Champion respectively printed beneath the player's name; and 3) all the backs have a screened background of Super Bowl XXVII emblems. The set includes an AFL Conference logo card (1), Buffalo Bills (2-18), an NFL Conference logo card (19), Dallas Cowboys (20-36), a Newsreel card (37), and a card of Marco Coleman (701), the 1992 Pro Set Rookie of the Year. With the exception of the Coleman, all the cards are numbered on the back "XXVII" and checklisted below in alphabetical order within teams.

| | MINT | EXC | G-VG |
|---|---|---|---|
| COMPLETE SET (38) | 20.00 | 8.00 | 2.00 |
| COMMON PLAYER (1-38) | .25 | .10 | .02 |

| | MINT | EXC | G-VG |
|---|---|---|---|
| ☐ 1 AFC Logo | .35 | .14 | .03 |
| ☐ 2 Cornelius Bennett | .35 | .14 | .03 |
| ☐ 3 Steve Christie | .25 | .10 | .02 |
| ☐ 4 Shane Conlan | .35 | .14 | .03 |
| ☐ 5 Matt Darby | .25 | .10 | .02 |
| ☐ 6 Kenneth Davis | .50 | .20 | .05 |
| ☐ 7 John Fina | .25 | .10 | .02 |
| ☐ 8 Henry Jones | .35 | .14 | .03 |
| ☐ 9 Jim Kelly | 1.50 | .60 | .15 |
| ☐ 10 Marv Levy CO | .35 | .14 | .03 |
| ☐ 11 James Lofton | .50 | .20 | .05 |
| ☐ 12 Pete Metzelaars | .25 | .10 | .02 |
| ☐ 13 Nate Odomes | .25 | .10 | .02 |
| ☐ 14 Andre Reed | .50 | .20 | .05 |
| ☐ 15 Bruce Smith | .50 | .20 | .05 |
| ☐ 16 Darryl Talley | .35 | .14 | .03 |
| ☐ 17 Steve Tasker | .35 | .14 | .03 |
| ☐ 18 Thurman Thomas | 2.00 | .80 | .20 |
| ☐ 19 NFC Logo | .35 | .14 | .03 |
| ☐ 20 Troy Aikman | 5.00 | 2.00 | .50 |
| ☐ 21 Steve Beuerlein | .75 | .30 | .07 |
| ☐ 22 Tony Casillas | .35 | .14 | .03 |
| ☐ 23 Kenneth Gant | .25 | .10 | .02 |
| ☐ 24 Charles Haley | .35 | .14 | .03 |
| ☐ 25 Alvin Harper | 1.25 | .50 | .12 |
| ☐ 26 Michael Irvin | 2.50 | 1.00 | .25 |
| ☐ 27 Jimmy Johnson CO | .35 | .14 | .03 |
| ☐ 28 Robert Jones | .50 | .20 | .05 |
| ☐ 29 Russell Maryland | .50 | .20 | .05 |
| ☐ 30 Nate Newton | .35 | .14 | .03 |
| ☐ 31 Ken Norton Jr. | .35 | .14 | .03 |
| ☐ 32 Jay Novacek | .50 | .20 | .05 |
| ☐ 33 Emmitt Smith | 7.50 | 3.00 | .75 |
| ☐ 34 Kevin Smith | .50 | .20 | .05 |
| ☐ 35 Mark Stepnoski | .25 | .10 | .02 |

| | | | |
|---|---|---|---|
| ☐ 36 Tony Tolbert | .25 | .10 | .02 |
| ☐ 37 Newsreel Art | .50 | .20 | .05 |
| Super Bowl XXVII | | | |
| ☐ 701 Marco Coleman PS-ROY | .75 | .30 | .07 |
| Miami Dolphins | | | |

## 1993 Pro Set Promos

These six standard-size (2 1/2" by 3 1/2") cards were distributed to dealers, promoters, and card show attendees to promote the release of the 1993 Pro Set issue. The six cards were also issued in an uncut ten-card 8" by 13 1/2" sheet, the bottom row of which consisted of five copies of the Emmitt Smith card. The fronts feature color player action shots that are borderless, except at the bottom, where the photo appears to be torn away, revealing an irregular gray stripe that carries the player's name in team color-coded lettering. On the regular series cards, the color of this stripe varies, reflecting the team's primary color. The back appears to be torn away on the left edge, revealing a gray stripe that carries the player's name in vertical team color-coded lettering, and his position and team in black lettering. A color player action photo is displayed at the top, which blends into a grayish background that carries the player's biography, career highlights, and stats. On the regular cards, the stat box has a white background rather than a grayish one. The cards are unnumbered and checklisted below in alphabetical order.

| | MINT | EXC | G-VG |
|---|---|---|---|
| COMPLETE SET (6) | 9.00 | 3.75 | .90 |
| COMMON PLAYER (1-6) | 1.00 | .40 | .10 |
| | | | |
| ☐ 1 Jerome Bettis | 3.00 | 1.20 | .30 |
| Los Angeles Rams | | | |
| ☐ 2 Reggie Brooks | 1.75 | .70 | .17 |
| Washington Redskins | | | |
| ☐ 3 Cortez Kennedy | 1.25 | .50 | .12 |
| Seattle Seahawks | | | |
| ☐ 4 Junior Seau | 1.25 | .50 | .12 |
| San Diego Chargers | | | |
| ☐ 5 Emmitt Smith | 3.00 | 1.20 | .30 |
| Dallas Cowboys | | | |
| ☐ 6 Wade Wilson | 1.00 | .40 | .10 |
| New Orleans Saints | | | |

## 1993 Pro Set

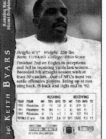

The 1993 Pro Set football set was issued in one series of 449 standard-size (2 1/2" by 3 1/2") cards. Including foil and jumbo cases, a total of 15,000 cases were reportedly produced. Randomly inserted throughout the foil packs was a Draft Day '93 insert set. The fronts

feature color player action shots that are borderless, except at the bottom, where the photo appears to be torn away, revealing an irregular team color-coded stripe that carries the player's name in white lettering. The back appears to be torn away on the left edge, revealing a team color-coded stripe that carries the player's name, position, and team in vertical white lettering. A color player action photo is displayed at the top, which blends into a grayish background that carries his biography, career highlights, and stats. The cards are numbered on the back. After an 18-card Stat Leader subset (1-18) and an 11-card Replay 1992 subset (19-29), the cards are checklisted below according to teams as follows: Dallas Cowboys (30-44), Buffalo Bills (45-59), Atlanta Falcons (60-74), Chicago Bears (75-89), Cincinnati Bengals (90-104), Cleveland Browns (105-119), Denver Broncos (120-134), Detroit Lions (135-149), Green Bay Packers (150-164), Houston Oilers (165-179), Indianapolis Colts (180-194), Kansas City Chiefs (195-209), Los Angeles Raiders (210-224), Los Angeles Rams (225-238), Miami Dolphins (240-254), Minnesota Vikings (255-269), New England Patriots (270-284), New Orleans Saints (285-299), New York Giants (300-314), New York Jets (315-329), Philadelphia Eagles (330-344), Phoenix Cardinals (345-359), Pittsburgh Steelers (360-374), San Diego Chargers (375-389), San Francisco 49ers (390-404), Seattle Seahawks (405-419), Tampa Bay Buccaneers (420-434), and Washington Redskins (435-449). Other insert sets included in the packs were 27-card All-Rookies Forecast, 14-card Rookie Running Backs, ten-card College Connections (jumbo only), and six-card Rookie Quarterbacks (jumbo only). Rookie Cards include Jerome Bettis, Drew Bledsoe, Vincent Brisby, Reggie Brooks, Derek Brown, Curtis Conway, Garrison Hearst, Billy Jo Hebert, Qadry Ismail, Terry Kirby, O.J. McDuffie, Rick Mirer, Natrone Means, Glyn Milburn, Ron Moore, Roosevelt Potts, Greg Robinson, Robert Smith and Dana Stubblefield.

| | MINT | EXC | G-VG |
|---|---|---|---|
| COMPLETE SET (449) | 20.00 | 9.00 | 2.50 |
| COMMON PLAYER (1-449) | .05 | .02 | .01 |
| | | | |
| ☐ 1 Marco Coleman | .08 | .04 | .01 |
| Miami Dolphins | | | |
| Rookie of the Year | | | |
| ☐ 2 Steve Young | .12 | .05 | .02 |
| Player of the Year | | | |
| ☐ 3 Mike Holmgren | .05 | .02 | .01 |
| Coach of the Year | | | |
| ☐ 4 John Elway | .15 | .07 | .02 |
| Man of the Year | | | |
| ☐ 5 Steve Young | .12 | .05 | .02 |
| Passing Leader | | | |
| ☐ 6 Dan Marino | .25 | .11 | .03 |
| Passing Yardage | | | |
| ☐ 7 Emmitt Smith | .75 | .35 | .09 |
| Rushing Leader | | | |
| ☐ 8 Sterling Sharpe | .20 | .09 | .03 |
| Receiving Leader | | | |
| ☐ 9 Jay Novacek | .08 | .04 | .01 |
| Receiving TE | | | |
| ☐ 10 Sterling Sharpe | .20 | .09 | .03 |
| Receiving Yardage | | | |
| ☐ 11 Thurman Thomas | .15 | .07 | .02 |
| Total Yardage | | | |
| ☐ 12 Pete Stoyanovich | .05 | .02 | .01 |
| Scoring Leader | | | |
| ☐ 13 Greg Montgomery | .05 | .02 | .01 |
| Punting Leader | | | |
| ☐ 14 Johnny Bailey | .05 | .02 | .01 |
| Punt Return | | | |
| ☐ 15 Jon Vaughn | .05 | .02 | .01 |
| Kickoff Return | | | |
| ☐ 16 Audray McMillian | .05 | .02 | .01 |
| Henry Jones UER | | | |
| Interception | | | |
| (Name spelled McMillan on back) | | | |
| ☐ 17 Clyde Simmons | .05 | .02 | .01 |
| Sack Leader | | | |
| ☐ 18 Cortez Kennedy | .08 | .04 | .01 |
| Defensive MVP | | | |
| ☐ 19 AFC Wildcard | .05 | .02 | .01 |
| (Stan Humphries) | | | |
| ☐ 20 AFC Wildcard | .05 | .02 | .01 |
| (Don Beebe) | | | |
| ☐ 21 NFC Wildcard | .05 | .02 | .01 |
| (Eric Allen) | | | |
| ☐ 22 NFC Wildcard | .05 | .02 | .01 |
| (Brian Mitchell) | | | |
| ☐ 23 AFC Divisional | .05 | .02 | .01 |
| (Frank Reich) | | | |
| ☐ 24 AFC Divisional | .30 | .14 | .04 |
| (Dan Marino) | | | |
| ☐ 25 NFC Divisional | .50 | .23 | .06 |
| (Troy Aikman) | | | |
| ☐ 26 NFC Divisional | .15 | .07 | .02 |
| (Ricky Watters) | | | |
| ☐ 27 AFC Championship | .05 | .02 | .01 |
| (Bruce Smith sacking | | | |

| | | | |
|---|---|---|---|
| (Dan Marino) | | | |
| ☐ 28 NFC Championship | .05 | .02 | .01 |
| (Tony Casillas sacking | | | |
| Steve Young) | | | |
| ☐ 29 Super Bowl 28 Logo | .05 | .02 | .01 |
| ☐ 30 Troy Aikman | 1.25 | .55 | .16 |
| ☐ 31 Thomas Everett | .05 | .02 | .01 |
| ☐ 32 Charles Haley | .08 | .04 | .01 |
| ☐ 33 Alvin Harper | .25 | .11 | .03 |
| ☐ 34 Michael Irvin | .40 | .18 | .05 |
| ☐ 35 Robert Jones | .05 | .02 | .01 |
| ☐ 36 Russell Maryland | .10 | .05 | .01 |
| ☐ 37 Ken Norton | .08 | .04 | .01 |
| ☐ 38 Jay Novacek | .10 | .05 | .01 |
| ☐ 39 Emmitt Smith | 2.00 | .90 | .25 |
| ☐ 40 Darrin Smith | .30 | .14 | .04 |
| ☐ 41 Mark Stepnoski | .05 | .02 | .01 |
| ☐ 42 Kevin Williams | .50 | .23 | .06 |
| ☐ 43 Daryl Johnston | .10 | .05 | .01 |
| ☐ 44 Derrick Lassic | .20 | .09 | .03 |
| ☐ 45 Don Beebe | .10 | .05 | .01 |
| ☐ 46 Cornelius Bennett | .10 | .05 | .01 |
| ☐ 47 Bill Brooks | .05 | .02 | .01 |
| ☐ 48 Kenneth Davis | .05 | .02 | .01 |
| ☐ 49 Jim Kelly | .25 | .11 | .03 |
| ☐ 50 Andre Reed | .10 | .05 | .01 |
| ☐ 51 Bruce Smith | .10 | .05 | .01 |
| ☐ 52 Thomas Smith | .10 | .05 | .01 |
| ☐ 53 Darryl Talley | .05 | .02 | .01 |
| ☐ 54 Thurman Thomas | .35 | .16 | .04 |
| ☐ 55 Russell Copeland | .15 | .07 | .02 |
| ☐ 56 Steve Christie | .05 | .02 | .01 |
| ☐ 57 Pete Metzelaars | .05 | .02 | .01 |
| ☐ 58 Frank Reich | .08 | .04 | .01 |
| ☐ 59 Henry Jones | .05 | .02 | .01 |
| ☐ 60 Vinnie Clark | .05 | .02 | .01 |
| ☐ 61 Eric Dickerson | .10 | .05 | .01 |
| ☐ 62 Jumpy Geathers | .05 | .02 | .01 |
| ☐ 63 Roger Harper | .15 | .07 | .02 |
| ☐ 64 Michael Haynes | .20 | .09 | .03 |
| ☐ 65 Bobby Hebert | .10 | .05 | .01 |
| ☐ 66 Lincoln Kennedy | .15 | .07 | .02 |
| ☐ 67 Chris Miller | .10 | .05 | .01 |
| ☐ 68 Andre Rison | .25 | .11 | .03 |
| ☐ 69 Deion Sanders | .15 | .07 | .02 |
| ☐ 70 Jessie Tuggle | .05 | .02 | .01 |
| ☐ 71 Ron George | .05 | .02 | .01 |
| ☐ 72 Erric Pegram | .25 | .11 | .03 |
| ☐ 73 Melvin Jenkins | .05 | .02 | .01 |
| ☐ 74 Pierce Holt | .05 | .02 | .01 |
| ☐ 75 Neal Anderson | .08 | .04 | .01 |
| ☐ 76 Mark Carrier | .08 | .04 | .01 |
| ☐ 77 Curtis Conway | .50 | .23 | .06 |
| ☐ 78 Richard Dent | .08 | .04 | .01 |
| ☐ 79 Jim Harbaugh | .08 | .04 | .01 |
| ☐ 80 Craig Heyward | .05 | .02 | .01 |
| ☐ 81 Darren Lewis | .05 | .02 | .01 |
| ☐ 82 Alonzo Spellman | .08 | .04 | .01 |
| ☐ 83 Tom Waddle | .10 | .05 | .01 |
| ☐ 84 Wendell Davis | .05 | .02 | .01 |
| ☐ 85 Chris Zorich | .08 | .04 | .01 |
| ☐ 86 Carl Simpson | .10 | .05 | .01 |
| ☐ 87 Chris Gedney | .10 | .05 | .01 |
| ☐ 88 Trace Armstrong | .05 | .02 | .01 |
| ☐ 89 Peter Tom Willis | .05 | .02 | .01 |
| ☐ 90 John Copeland | .25 | .11 | .03 |
| ☐ 91 Derrick Fenner | .05 | .02 | .01 |
| ☐ 92 James Francis | .05 | .02 | .01 |
| ☐ 93 Harold Green | .08 | .04 | .01 |
| ☐ 94 David Klingler | .15 | .07 | .02 |
| ☐ 95 Tim Krumrie | .05 | .02 | .01 |
| ☐ 96 Tony McGee | .20 | .09 | .03 |
| ☐ 97 Carl Pickens | .10 | .05 | .01 |
| ☐ 98 Alfred Williams | .05 | .02 | .01 |
| ☐ 99 Doug Pelfrey | .10 | .05 | .01 |
| ☐ 100 Lance Gunn | .15 | .07 | .02 |
| ☐ 101 Jay Schroeder | .05 | .02 | .01 |
| ☐ 102 Steve Tovar | .10 | .05 | .01 |
| ☐ 103 Jeff Query | .05 | .02 | .01 |
| ☐ 104 Ty Parten | .10 | .05 | .01 |
| ☐ 105 Jerry Ball | .05 | .02 | .01 |
| ☐ 106 Mark Carrier | .08 | .04 | .01 |
| ☐ 107 Rob Burnett | .05 | .02 | .01 |
| ☐ 108 Michael Jackson | .10 | .05 | .01 |
| ☐ 109 Mike Johnson | .05 | .02 | .01 |
| ☐ 110 Bernie Kosar Cowboys | .10 | .05 | .01 |
| ☐ 111 Clay Matthews | .08 | .04 | .01 |
| ☐ 112 Eric Metcalf | .10 | .05 | .01 |
| ☐ 113 Michael Dean Perry | .10 | .05 | .01 |
| ☐ 114 Vinny Testaverde | .10 | .05 | .01 |
| ☐ 115 Eric Turner | .08 | .04 | .01 |
| ☐ 116 Tommy Vardell | .08 | .04 | .01 |
| ☐ 117 Leroy Hoard | .08 | .04 | .01 |
| ☐ 118 Steve Everitt | .10 | .05 | .01 |
| ☐ 119 Everson Walls | .05 | .02 | .01 |
| ☐ 120 Steve Atwater | .08 | .04 | .01 |
| ☐ 121 Rod Bernstine | .08 | .04 | .01 |
| ☐ 122 Mike Croel | .08 | .04 | .01 |
| ☐ 123 John Elway | .35 | .16 | .04 |
| ☐ 124 Simon Fletcher | .08 | .04 | .01 |
| ☐ 125 Glyn Milburn | .75 | .35 | .09 |
| ☐ 126 Reggie Rivers | .20 | .09 | .03 |
| ☐ 127 Shannon Sharpe | .10 | .05 | .01 |
| ☐ 128 Dennis Smith | .05 | .02 | .01 |
| ☐ 129 Dan Williams | .10 | .05 | .01 |
| ☐ 130 Rondell Jones | .10 | .05 | .01 |
| ☐ 131 Jason Elam | .10 | .05 | .01 |
| ☐ 132 Arthur Marshall | .25 | .11 | .03 |
| ☐ 133 Gary Zimmerman | .05 | .02 | .01 |
| ☐ 134 Karl Mecklenberg | .05 | .02 | .01 |
| ☐ 135 Bennie Blades | .05 | .02 | .01 |
| ☐ 136 Lomas Brown | .05 | .02 | .01 |
| ☐ 137 Bill Fralic | .05 | .02 | .01 |
| ☐ 138 Mel Gray | .05 | .02 | .01 |
| ☐ 139 Willie Green | .08 | .04 | .01 |
| ☐ 140 Ryan McNeil | .10 | .05 | .01 |
| ☐ 141 Rodney Peete | .08 | .04 | .01 |
| ☐ 142 Barry Sanders | .75 | .35 | .09 |
| ☐ 143 Chris Spielman | .05 | .02 | .01 |
| ☐ 144 Pat Swilling | .08 | .04 | .01 |
| ☐ 145 Andre Ware | .08 | .04 | .01 |
| ☐ 146 Herman Moore | .35 | .16 | .04 |
| ☐ 147 Tim McKyer | .08 | .04 | .01 |
| ☐ 148 Brett Perriman | .08 | .04 | .01 |
| ☐ 149 Antonio London | .10 | .05 | .01 |
| ☐ 150 Edgar Bennett | .10 | .05 | .01 |
| ☐ 151 Terrell Buckley | .10 | .05 | .01 |
| ☐ 152 Brett Favre | .75 | .35 | .09 |
| ☐ 153 Jackie Harris | .30 | .14 | .04 |
| ☐ 154 Johnny Holland | .05 | .02 | .01 |
| ☐ 155 Sterling Sharpe | .40 | .18 | .05 |
| ☐ 156 Tim Hauck | .05 | .02 | .01 |
| ☐ 157 George Teague | .20 | .09 | .03 |
| ☐ 158 Reggie White | .15 | .07 | .02 |
| ☐ 159 Mark Clayton | .05 | .02 | .01 |
| ☐ 160 Ty Detmer | .08 | .04 | .01 |
| ☐ 161 Wayne Simmons | .12 | .05 | .02 |
| ☐ 162 Mark Brunell | .25 | .11 | .03 |
| ☐ 163 Tony Bennett | .05 | .02 | .01 |
| ☐ 164 Brian Noble | .05 | .02 | .01 |
| ☐ 165 Cody Carlson | .20 | .09 | .03 |
| ☐ 166 Ray Childress | .05 | .02 | .01 |
| ☐ 167 Cris Dishman | .05 | .02 | .01 |
| ☐ 168 Curtis Duncan | .05 | .02 | .01 |
| ☐ 169 Brad Hopkins | .10 | .05 | .01 |
| ☐ 170 Haywood Jeffires | .10 | .05 | .01 |
| ☐ 171 Wilber Marshall | .08 | .04 | .01 |
| ☐ 172 Micheal Barrow UER | .05 | .02 | .01 |
| (Name spelled Michael on | | | |
| both sided) | | | |
| ☐ 173 Bubba McDowell | .05 | .02 | .01 |
| ☐ 174 Warren Moon | .15 | .07 | .02 |
| ☐ 175 Webster Slaughter | .08 | .04 | .01 |
| ☐ 176 Travis Hannah | .20 | .09 | .03 |
| ☐ 177 Lorenzo White | .08 | .04 | .01 |
| ☐ 178 Ernest Givins UER | .08 | .04 | .01 |
| (Name spelled Givens on front) | | | |
| ☐ 179 Keith McCants | .05 | .02 | .01 |
| ☐ 180 Kerry Cash | .05 | .02 | .01 |
| ☐ 181 Quentin Coryatt | .10 | .05 | .01 |
| ☐ 182 Kirk Lowdermilk | .05 | .02 | .01 |
| ☐ 183 Rodney Culver | .05 | .02 | .01 |
| ☐ 184 Rohn Stark | .05 | .02 | .01 |
| ☐ 185 Steve Emtman | .08 | .04 | .01 |
| ☐ 186 Jeff George | .15 | .07 | .02 |
| ☐ 187 Jeff Herrod | .05 | .02 | .01 |
| ☐ 188 Reggie Langhorne | .08 | .04 | .01 |
| ☐ 189 Roosevelt Potts | .25 | .11 | .03 |
| ☐ 190 Jack Trudeau | .05 | .02 | .01 |
| ☐ 191 Will Wolford | .05 | .02 | .01 |
| ☐ 192 Jessie Hester | .05 | .02 | .01 |
| ☐ 193 Anthony Johnson | .05 | .02 | .01 |
| ☐ 194 Ray Buchanan | .10 | .05 | .01 |
| ☐ 195 Dale Carter | .10 | .05 | .01 |
| ☐ 196 Willie Davis | .10 | .05 | .01 |
| ☐ 197 John Alt | .05 | .02 | .01 |
| ☐ 198 Joe Montana | 1.25 | .55 | .16 |
| ☐ 199 Will Shields | .10 | .05 | .01 |
| ☐ 200 Neil Smith | .10 | .05 | .01 |
| ☐ 201 Derrick Thomas | .15 | .07 | .02 |
| ☐ 202 Harvey Williams | .10 | .05 | .01 |
| ☐ 203 Marcus Allen | .15 | .07 | .02 |
| ☐ 204 J.J. Birden | .08 | .04 | .01 |
| ☐ 205 Tim Barnett | .08 | .04 | .01 |
| ☐ 206 Albert Lewis | .08 | .04 | .01 |
| ☐ 207 Nick Lowery | .05 | .02 | .01 |
| ☐ 208 Dave Krieg | .08 | .04 | .01 |
| ☐ 209 Keith Cash | .05 | .02 | .01 |
| ☐ 210 Patrick Bates | .10 | .05 | .01 |
| ☐ 211 Nick Bell | .08 | .04 | .01 |
| ☐ 212 Tim Brown | .08 | .04 | .01 |
| ☐ 213 Willie Gault | .08 | .04 | .01 |
| ☐ 214 Ethan Horton | .05 | .02 | .01 |
| ☐ 215 Jeff Hostetler | .10 | .05 | .01 |
| ☐ 216 Howie Long | .08 | .04 | .01 |

|  |  | | | |
|---|--------|---|---|---|
| ☐ 217 | Greg Townsend | .05 | .02 | .01 |
| ☐ 218 | Raghib Ismail | .40 | .18 | .05 |
| ☐ 219 | Alexander Wright | .08 | .04 | .01 |
| ☐ 220 | Greg Robinson | .60 | .25 | .08 |
| ☐ 221 | Billy Joe Hobert | .25 | .11 | .03 |
| ☐ 222 | Steve Wisniewski | .05 | .02 | .01 |
| ☐ 223 | Steve Smith | .08 | .04 | .01 |
| ☐ 224 | Vince Evans | .05 | .02 | .01 |
| ☐ 225 | Flipper Anderson | .08 | .04 | .01 |
| ☐ 226 | Jerome Bettis | 3.00 | 1.35 | .40 |
| ☐ 227 | Troy Drayton | .25 | .11 | .03 |
| ☐ 228 | Henry Ellard | .08 | .04 | .01 |
| ☐ 229 | Jim Everett | .10 | .05 | .01 |
| ☐ 230 | Tony Zendejas | .05 | .02 | .01 |
| ☐ 231 | Todd Lyght | .05 | .02 | .01 |
| ☐ 232 | Todd Kinchen | .08 | .04 | .01 |
| ☐ 233 | Jackie Slater | .05 | .02 | .01 |
| ☐ 234 | Fred Stokes | .05 | .02 | .01 |
| ☐ 235 | Russell White | .20 | .09 | .03 |
| ☐ 236 | Cleveland Gary | .08 | .04 | .01 |
| ☐ 237 | Sean LaChapelle | .15 | .07 | .02 |
| ☐ 238 | Steve Israel | .05 | .02 | .01 |
| ☐ 239 | Shane Conlan | .05 | .02 | .01 |
| ☐ 240 | Keith Byars | .08 | .04 | .01 |
| ☐ 241 | Marco Coleman | .08 | .04 | .01 |
| ☐ 242 | Bryan Cox | .08 | .04 | .01 |
| ☐ 243 | Irving Fryar | .05 | .02 | .01 |
| ☐ 244 | Richmond Webb | .05 | .02 | .01 |
| ☐ 245 | Mark Higgs | .10 | .05 | .01 |
| ☐ 246 | Terry Kirby | 1.50 | .65 | .19 |
| ☐ 247 | Mark Ingram | .08 | .04 | .01 |
| ☐ 248 | John Offerdahl | .05 | .02 | .01 |
| ☐ 249 | Keith Jackson | .10 | .05 | .01 |
| ☐ 250 | Dan Marino | .75 | .35 | .09 |
| ☐ 251 | O.J. McDuffie | 1.25 | .55 | .16 |
| ☐ 252 | Louis Oliver | .05 | .02 | .01 |
| ☐ 253 | Pete Stoyanovich | .05 | .02 | .01 |
| ☐ 254 | Troy Vincent | .08 | .04 | .01 |
| ☐ 255 | Anthony Carter | .08 | .04 | .01 |
| ☐ 256 | Cris Carter | .10 | .05 | .01 |
| ☐ 257 | Roger Craig | .08 | .04 | .01 |
| ☐ 258 | Jack Del Rio | .05 | .02 | .01 |
| ☐ 259 | Chris Doleman | .08 | .04 | .01 |
| ☐ 260 | Barry Ward | .05 | .02 | .01 |
| ☐ 261 | Qadry Ismail | .50 | .23 | .06 |
| ☐ 262 | Jim McMahon | .10 | .05 | .01 |
| ☐ 263 | Robert Smith | .35 | .16 | .04 |
| ☐ 264 | Fred Strickland | .05 | .02 | .01 |
| ☐ 265 | Randall McDaniel | .05 | .02 | .01 |
| ☐ 266 | Carl Lee | .05 | .02 | .01 |
| ☐ 267 | Orlanda Truitt UER | .10 | .05 | .01 |
| | (Name spelled Olanda on front) | | | |
| ☐ 268 | Terry Allen | .10 | .05 | .01 |
| ☐ 269 | Audray McMillian | .05 | .02 | .01 |
| ☐ 270 | Drew Bledsoe | 3.00 | 1.35 | .40 |
| ☐ 271 | Eugene Chung | .05 | .02 | .01 |
| ☐ 272 | Marv Cook | .05 | .02 | .01 |
| ☐ 273 | Pat Harlow | .05 | .02 | .01 |
| ☐ 274 | Greg McMurtry | .05 | .02 | .01 |
| ☐ 275 | Leonard Russell | .08 | .04 | .01 |
| ☐ 276 | Chris Slade | .30 | .14 | .04 |
| ☐ 277 | Andre Tippett | .05 | .02 | .01 |
| ☐ 278 | Vincent Brisby | .50 | .23 | .06 |
| ☐ 279 | Ben Coates | .08 | .04 | .01 |
| ☐ 280 | Sam Gash | .10 | .05 | .01 |
| ☐ 281 | Bruce Armstrong | .05 | .02 | .01 |
| ☐ 282 | Rod Smith | .05 | .02 | .01 |
| ☐ 283 | Michael Timpson | .05 | .02 | .01 |
| ☐ 284 | Scott Sisson | .10 | .05 | .01 |
| ☐ 285 | Morten Andersen | .08 | .04 | .01 |
| ☐ 286 | Reggie Freeman | .10 | .05 | .01 |
| ☐ 287 | Dalton Hilliard | .05 | .02 | .01 |
| ☐ 288 | Rickey Jackson | .08 | .04 | .01 |
| ☐ 289 | Vaughan Johnson | .05 | .02 | .01 |
| ☐ 290 | Eric Martin | .08 | .04 | .01 |
| ☐ 291 | Sam Mills | .08 | .04 | .01 |
| ☐ 292 | Brad Muster | .08 | .04 | .01 |
| ☐ 293 | William Roaf | .10 | .05 | .01 |
| ☐ 294 | Irv Smith | .20 | .09 | .03 |
| ☐ 295 | Wade Wilson | .08 | .04 | .01 |
| ☐ 296 | Derek Brown | .75 | .35 | .09 |
| ☐ 297 | Quinn Early | .08 | .04 | .01 |
| ☐ 298 | Steve Walsh | .05 | .02 | .01 |
| ☐ 299 | Renaldo Turnbull | .08 | .04 | .01 |
| ☐ 300 | Jessie Armstead | .15 | .07 | .02 |
| ☐ 301 | Carlton Bailey | .05 | .02 | .01 |
| ☐ 302 | Michael Brooks | .05 | .02 | .01 |
| ☐ 303 | Rodney Hampton | .30 | .14 | .04 |
| ☐ 304 | Ed McCaffrey | .05 | .02 | .01 |
| ☐ 305 | Dave Meggett | .08 | .04 | .01 |
| ☐ 306 | Bart Oates | .05 | .02 | .01 |
| ☐ 307 | Mike Sherrard | .05 | .02 | .01 |
| ☐ 308 | Phil Simms | .10 | .05 | .01 |
| ☐ 309 | Lawrence Taylor | .10 | .05 | .01 |
| ☐ 310 | Mark Jackson | .08 | .04 | .01 |
| ☐ 311 | Jarrod Bunch | .05 | .02 | .01 |
| ☐ 312 | Howard Cross | .05 | .02 | .01 |
| ☐ 313 | Michael Strahan | .10 | .05 | .01 |
| ☐ 314 | Marcus Buckley | .10 | .05 | .01 |
| ☐ 315 | Brad Baxter | .08 | .04 | .01 |
| ☐ 316 | Adrian Murrell | .12 | .05 | .02 |
| ☐ 317 | Boomer Esiason | .12 | .05 | .02 |
| ☐ 318 | Johnny Johnson | .10 | .05 | .01 |
| ☐ 319 | Marvin Jones | .15 | .07 | .02 |
| ☐ 320 | Jeff Lageman | .05 | .02 | .01 |
| ☐ 321 | Ronnie Lott | .10 | .05 | .01 |
| ☐ 322 | Leonard Marshall | .05 | .02 | .01 |
| ☐ 323 | Johnny Mitchell | .25 | .11 | .03 |
| ☐ 324 | Rob Moore | .10 | .05 | .01 |
| ☐ 325 | Browning Nagle | .08 | .04 | .01 |
| ☐ 326 | Blair Thomas | .08 | .04 | .01 |
| ☐ 327 | Brian Washington | .05 | .02 | .01 |
| ☐ 328 | Terance Mathis | .05 | .02 | .01 |
| ☐ 329 | Kyle Clifton | .05 | .02 | .01 |
| ☐ 330 | Eric Allen | .08 | .04 | .01 |
| ☐ 331 | Victor Bailey | .35 | .16 | .04 |
| ☐ 332 | Fred Barnett | .10 | .05 | .01 |
| ☐ 333 | Mark Bavaro | .05 | .02 | .01 |
| ☐ 334 | Randall Cunningham | .10 | .05 | .01 |
| ☐ 335 | Ken O'Brien | .08 | .04 | .01 |
| ☐ 336 | Seth Joyner | .08 | .04 | .01 |
| ☐ 337 | Leonard Renfro | .10 | .05 | .01 |
| ☐ 338 | Heath Sherman | .05 | .02 | .01 |
| ☐ 339 | Clyde Simmons | .08 | .04 | .01 |
| ☐ 340 | Herschel Walker | .10 | .05 | .01 |
| ☐ 341 | Calvin Williams | .10 | .05 | .01 |
| ☐ 342 | Bubby Brister | .05 | .02 | .01 |
| ☐ 343 | Vaughn Hebron | .30 | .14 | .04 |
| ☐ 344 | Keith Millard | .05 | .02 | .01 |
| ☐ 345 | Johnny Bailey | .05 | .02 | .01 |
| ☐ 346 | Steve Beuerlein | .15 | .07 | .02 |
| ☐ 347 | Chuck Cecil | .05 | .02 | .01 |
| ☐ 348 | Larry Centers | .15 | .07 | .02 |
| ☐ 349 | Chris Chandler | .08 | .04 | .01 |
| ☐ 350 | Ernest Dye | .10 | .05 | .01 |
| ☐ 351 | Garrison Hearst | .60 | .25 | .08 |
| ☐ 352 | Randal Hill | .10 | .05 | .01 |
| ☐ 353 | John Booty | .05 | .02 | .01 |
| ☐ 354 | Gary Clark | .08 | .04 | .01 |
| ☐ 355 | Ron Moore | 2.00 | .90 | .25 |
| ☐ 356 | Ricky Proehl | .08 | .04 | .01 |
| ☐ 357 | Eric Swann | .08 | .04 | .01 |
| ☐ 358 | Ken Harvey | .05 | .02 | .01 |
| ☐ 359 | Ben Coleman | .10 | .05 | .01 |
| ☐ 360 | Deon Figures | .15 | .07 | .02 |
| ☐ 361 | Barry Foster | .25 | .11 | .03 |
| ☐ 362 | Jeff Graham | .08 | .04 | .01 |
| ☐ 363 | Eric Green | .10 | .05 | .01 |
| ☐ 364 | Kevin Greene | .05 | .02 | .01 |
| ☐ 365 | Andre Hastings | .20 | .09 | .03 |
| ☐ 366 | Greg Lloyd | .05 | .02 | .01 |
| ☐ 367 | Neil O'Donnell | .25 | .11 | .03 |
| ☐ 368 | Dwight Stone | .05 | .02 | .01 |
| ☐ 369 | Mike Tomczak | .05 | .02 | .01 |
| ☐ 370 | Rod Woodson | .10 | .05 | .01 |
| ☐ 371 | Chad Brown | .10 | .05 | .01 |
| ☐ 372 | Ernie Mills | .05 | .02 | .01 |
| ☐ 373 | Darren Perry | .05 | .02 | .01 |
| ☐ 374 | Leon Searcy | .05 | .02 | .01 |
| ☐ 375 | Marion Butts | .10 | .05 | .01 |
| ☐ 376 | John Carney | .05 | .02 | .01 |
| ☐ 377 | Ronnie Harmon | .05 | .02 | .01 |
| ☐ 378 | Stan Humphries | .10 | .05 | .01 |
| ☐ 379 | Nate Lewis | .08 | .04 | .01 |
| ☐ 380 | Natrone Means | 1.25 | .55 | .16 |
| ☐ 381 | Anthony Miller | .15 | .07 | .02 |
| ☐ 382 | Chris Mims | .08 | .04 | .01 |
| ☐ 383 | Leslie O'Neal | .08 | .04 | .01 |
| ☐ 384 | Joe Cocozzo | .15 | .07 | .02 |
| ☐ 385 | Junior Seau | .10 | .05 | .01 |
| ☐ 386 | Jerrol Williams | .05 | .02 | .01 |
| ☐ 387 | John Friesz | .08 | .04 | .01 |
| ☐ 388 | Darrien Gordon | .20 | .09 | .03 |
| ☐ 389 | Derrick Walker | .05 | .02 | .01 |
| ☐ 390 | Dana Hall | .05 | .02 | .01 |
| ☐ 391 | Brent Jones | .10 | .05 | .01 |
| ☐ 392 | Todd Kelly | .10 | .05 | .01 |
| ☐ 393 | Amp Lee | .08 | .04 | .01 |
| ☐ 394 | Tim McDonald | .05 | .02 | .01 |
| ☐ 395 | Jerry Rice | .60 | .25 | .08 |
| ☐ 396 | Dana Stubblefield | .50 | .23 | .06 |
| ☐ 397 | John Taylor | .10 | .05 | .01 |
| ☐ 398 | Ricky Watters | .30 | .14 | .04 |
| ☐ 399 | Steve Young | .25 | .11 | .03 |
| ☐ 400 | Steve Bono | .15 | .07 | .02 |
| ☐ 401 | Adrian Hardy | .05 | .02 | .01 |
| ☐ 402 | Tom Rathman | .08 | .04 | .01 |
| ☐ 403 | Elvis Grbac UER | .50 | .23 | .06 |
| | (Name spelled Grabac on front) | | | |
| ☐ 404 | Bill Romanowski | .05 | .02 | .01 |
| ☐ 405 | Brian Blades | .08 | .04 | .01 |
| ☐ 406 | Ferrell Edmunds | .05 | .02 | .01 |
| ☐ 407 | Carlton Gray | .20 | .09 | .03 |
| ☐ 408 | Cortez Kennedy | .10 | .05 | .01 |

| | | | |
|---|---|---|---|
| ☐ 409 Kelvin Martin | .05 | .02 | .01 |
| ☐ 410 Dan McGwire | .08 | .04 | .01 |
| ☐ 411 Rick Mirer | 3.00 | 1.35 | .40 |
| ☐ 412 Rufus Porter | .05 | .02 | .01 |
| ☐ 413 Chris Warren | .15 | .07 | .02 |
| ☐ 414 Jon Vaughn | .05 | .02 | .01 |
| ☐ 415 John L. Williams | .08 | .04 | .01 |
| ☐ 416 Eugene Robinson | .05 | .02 | .01 |
| ☐ 417 Michael McCrary | .12 | .05 | .02 |
| ☐ 418 Michael Bates | .25 | .11 | .03 |
| ☐ 419 Stan Gelbaugh | .05 | .02 | .01 |
| ☐ 420 Reggie Cobb | .10 | .05 | .01 |
| ☐ 421 Eric Curry | .25 | .11 | .03 |
| ☐ 422 Lawrence Dawsey | .10 | .05 | .01 |
| ☐ 423 Santana Dotson | .10 | .05 | .01 |
| ☐ 424 Craig Erickson | .10 | .05 | .01 |
| ☐ 425 Ron Hall | .05 | .02 | .01 |
| ☐ 426 Courtney Hawkins | .08 | .04 | .01 |
| ☐ 427 Broderick Thomas | .05 | .02 | .01 |
| ☐ 428 Vince Workman | .05 | .02 | .01 |
| ☐ 429 Demetrius DuBose | .15 | .07 | .02 |
| ☐ 430 Lamar Thomas | .25 | .11 | .03 |
| ☐ 431 John Lynch | .10 | .05 | .01 |
| ☐ 432 Hardy Nickerson | .05 | .02 | .01 |
| ☐ 433 Horace Copeland | .50 | .23 | .06 |
| ☐ 434 Steve DeBerg | .08 | .04 | .01 |
| ☐ 435 Joe Jacoby | .05 | .02 | .01 |
| ☐ 436 Tom Carter | .25 | .11 | .03 |
| ☐ 437 Andre Collins | .05 | .02 | .01 |
| ☐ 438 Darrell Green | .08 | .04 | .01 |
| ☐ 439 Desmond Howard | .20 | .09 | .03 |
| ☐ 440 Chip Lohmiller | .05 | .02 | .01 |
| ☐ 441 Charles Mann | .05 | .02 | .01 |
| ☐ 442 Tim McGee | .05 | .02 | .01 |
| ☐ 443 Art Monk | .10 | .05 | .01 |
| ☐ 444 Mark Rypien | .08 | .04 | .01 |
| ☐ 445 Ricky Sanders | .05 | .02 | .01 |
| ☐ 446 Brian Mitchell | .08 | .04 | .01 |
| ☐ 447 Reggie Brooks | 1.75 | .80 | .22 |
| ☐ 448 Carl Banks | .05 | .02 | .01 |
| ☐ 449 Cary Conklin | .08 | .04 | .01 |
| ☐ NNO Santa Card | 3.00 | 1.35 | .40 |

| | | | |
|---|---|---|---|
| ☐ 8 Steve Everitt | .40 | .18 | .05 |
| Cleveland Browns | | | |
| ☐ 9 Ernest Dye | .40 | .18 | .05 |
| Phoenix Cardinals | | | |
| ☐ 10 Todd Rucci | .40 | .18 | .05 |
| New England Patriots | | | |
| ☐ 11 William Roaf | .40 | .18 | .05 |
| New Orleans Saints | | | |
| ☐ 12 Lincoln Kennedy | .50 | .23 | .06 |
| Atlanta Falcons | | | |
| ☐ 13 Irv Smith | .50 | .23 | .06 |
| New Orleans Saints | | | |
| ☐ 14 Jason Elam | .40 | .18 | .05 |
| Denver Broncos | | | |
| ☐ 15 Harold Alexander | .40 | .18 | .05 |
| Atlanta Falcons | | | |
| ☐ 16 John Copeland | .75 | .35 | .09 |
| Cincinnati Bengals | | | |
| ☐ 17 Eric Curry | .75 | .35 | .09 |
| Tampa Bay Buccaneers | | | |
| ☐ 18 Dana Stubblefield | 1.00 | .45 | .13 |
| San Francisco 49ers | | | |
| ☐ 19 Leonard Renfro | .40 | .18 | .05 |
| Philadelphia Eagles | | | |
| ☐ 20 Marvin Jones | .50 | .23 | .06 |
| New York Jets | | | |
| ☐ 21 Demetrius DuBose | .50 | .23 | .06 |
| Tampa Bay Buccaneers | | | |
| ☐ 22 Chris Slade | .50 | .23 | .06 |
| New England Patriots | | | |
| ☐ 23 Darrin Smith | .75 | .35 | .09 |
| Dallas Cowboys | | | |
| ☐ 24 Deon Figures | .50 | .23 | .06 |
| Pittsburgh Steelers | | | |
| ☐ 25 Darrien Gordon | .50 | .23 | .06 |
| San Diego Chargers | | | |
| ☐ 26 Patrick Bates | .40 | .18 | .05 |
| Los Angeles Raiders | | | |
| ☐ 27 George Teague | .50 | .23 | .06 |
| Green Bay Packers | | | |

## 1993 Pro Set College Connections

Randomly inserted in jumbo packs, this ten-card standard-size (2 1/2" by 3 1/2") set spotlights NFL stars who come from the same college. The horizontal fronts feature two color action player cutouts alongside one another, each on a silver prismatic background. The set title is displayed on a gray stripe at the bottom. On two granite panels, the back presents biographical information and player comparisons. The cards are numbered on the back with a "CC" prefix.

| | MINT | EXC | G-VG |
|---|---|---|---|
| COMPLETE SET (10) | 35.00 | 16.00 | 4.40 |
| COMMON PLAYER (CC1-CC10) | 1.00 | .45 | .13 |
| ☐ CC1 Barry Sanders | 3.00 | 1.35 | .40 |
| Thurman Thomas | | | |
| ☐ CC2 Jerome Bettis | 8.00 | 3.60 | 1.00 |
| Reggie Brooks | | | |
| ☐ CC3 Neal Anderson | 7.00 | 3.10 | .85 |
| Emmitt Smith | | | |
| ☐ CC4 Raghib Ismail | 2.00 | .90 | .25 |
| Tim Brown | | | |
| ☐ CC5 Rodney Hampton | 2.00 | .90 | .25 |
| Garrison Hearst | | | |
| ☐ CC6 Derrick Thomas | 1.00 | .45 | .13 |
| Cornelius Bennett | | | |
| ☐ CC7 Jim McMahon | 1.50 | .65 | .19 |
| Steve Young | | | |
| ☐ CC8 Rick Mirer | 12.00 | 5.50 | 1.50 |
| Joe Montana | | | |
| ☐ CC9 Terrell Buckley | 1.00 | .45 | .13 |
| Deion Sanders | | | |

## 1993 Pro Set All-Rookies

The 1993 Pro Set All-Rookies set comprises 27 standard-size (2 1/2" by 3 1/2") cards, randomly inserted in 1993 Pro Set foil packs. The fronts display color action player cut-outs on prismatic backgrounds. The player's name appears at the bottom of the picture, and the set title appears within a brown lithic stripe edging the right side. The green back has a ghosted football field design with player profile and team logo. An irregular gray stripe along the left side carries the player's name and the card's number.

| | MINT | EXC | G-VG |
|---|---|---|---|
| COMPLETE SET (27) | 25.00 | 11.50 | 3.10 |
| COMMON PLAYER (1-27) | .40 | .18 | .05 |
| ☐ 1 Rick Mirer | 12.00 | 5.50 | 1.50 |
| Seattle Seahawks | | | |
| ☐ 2 Garrison Hearst | 1.25 | .55 | .16 |
| Phoenix Cardinals | | | |
| ☐ 3 Jerome Bettis | 12.00 | 5.50 | 1.50 |
| Los Angeles Rams | | | |
| ☐ 4 Vincent Brisby | 1.00 | .45 | .13 |
| New England Patriots | | | |
| ☐ 5 O.J. McDuffie | 3.00 | 1.35 | .40 |
| Miami Dolphins | | | |
| ☐ 6 Curtis Conway | 1.25 | .55 | .16 |
| Chicago Bears | | | |
| ☐ 7 Raghib Ismail | 1.00 | .45 | .13 |
| Los Angeles Raiders | | | |

| | | MINT | EXC | G-VG |
|---|---|---|---|---|
| ☐ CC10 Mark Rypien | | 5.00 | 2.30 | .60 |
| Drew Bledsoe | | | | |

## 1993 Pro Set Rookie Quarterbacks

The 1993 Pro Set Rookie Quarterbacks set comprises six standard-size (2 1/2" by 3 1/2") cards, randomly inserted in 1993 Pro Set jumbo packs. The fronts display color action player cut-outs on prismatic backgrounds. The player's name appears at the bottom of the picture, and the set title appears within a gray lithic stripe edging right side. The back sports a textured pinkish background that carries the player's career highlights and the team logo. The player's name appears on an irregular purple stripe edging the left side. The cards are numbered on the back with an "RQ" prefix.

| | MINT | EXC | G-VG |
|---|---|---|---|
| COMPLETE SET (6) | 16.00 | 7.25 | 2.00 |
| COMMON PLAYER (RQ1-RQ6) | 1.00 | .45 | .13 |
| | | | |
| ☐ RQ1 Drew Bledsoe | 8.00 | 3.60 | 1.00 |
| New England Patriots | | | |
| ☐ RQ2 Rick Mirer | 8.00 | 3.60 | 1.00 |
| Seattle Seahawks | | | |
| ☐ RQ3 Mark Brunell | 1.00 | .45 | .13 |
| Green Bay Packers | | | |
| ☐ RQ4 Billy Joe Hobert | 1.00 | .45 | .13 |
| Los Angeles Raiders | | | |
| ☐ RQ5 Trent Green | 1.25 | .55 | .16 |
| San Diego Chargers | | | |
| ☐ RQ6 Elvis Grbac | 1.00 | .45 | .13 |
| San Francisco 49ers | | | |

## 1993 Pro Set Rookie Running Backs

The 1993 Pro Set Rookie Running Backs set comprises 14 standard-size (2 1/2" by 3 1/2") cards, randomly inserted in 1993 Pro Set foil packs. The fronts display color action player cut-outs on prismatic backgrounds. The player's name appears at the bottom of the picture, and the set's title appears within a brown lithic stripe edging right side. The back sports a textured gray background that carries the player's position, team, biography, and career highlights. The player's name appears within an irregular light brown stripe edging the left side. The cards are numbered on the back with an "RRB" prefix.

| | MINT | EXC | G-VG |
|---|---|---|---|
| COMPLETE SET (14) | 20.00 | 9.00 | 2.50 |
| COMMON PLAYER (1-14) | .60 | .25 | .08 |

| | MINT | EXC | G-VG |
|---|---|---|---|
| ☐ 1 Derrick Lassic | .60 | .25 | .08 |
| Dallas Cowboys | | | |
| ☐ 2 Reggie Brooks | 3.50 | 1.55 | .45 |
| Washington Redskins | | | |
| ☐ 3 Garrison Hearst | 2.00 | .90 | .25 |
| Phoenix Cardinals | | | |
| ☐ 4 Ron Moore | 2.50 | 1.15 | .30 |
| Phoenix Cardinals | | | |
| ☐ 5 Robert Smith | 1.00 | .45 | .13 |
| Minnesota Vikings | | | |
| ☐ 6 Jerome Bettis | 6.00 | 2.70 | .75 |
| Los Angeles Rams | | | |
| ☐ 7 Russell White | .60 | .25 | .08 |
| Los Angeles Rams | | | |
| ☐ 8 Derek Brown | 1.50 | .65 | .19 |
| New Orleans Saints | | | |
| ☐ 9 Roosevelt Potts | .75 | .35 | .09 |
| Indianapolis Colts | | | |
| ☐ 10 Terry Kirby | 2.25 | 1.00 | .30 |
| Miami Dolphins | | | |
| ☐ 11 Glyn Milburn | 2.00 | .90 | .25 |
| Denver Broncos | | | |
| ☐ 12 Greg Robinson | 1.25 | .55 | .16 |
| Los Angeles Raiders | | | |
| ☐ 13 Natrone Means | 2.25 | 1.00 | .30 |
| San Diego Chargers | | | |
| ☐ 14 Vaughn Hebron | .60 | .25 | .08 |
| Philadelphia Eagles | | | |

## 1994 Pro Set National Promos *

Distributed during the 1994 National Sports Collectors Convention, this eight-card standard-size (2 1/2" by 3 1/2") set features prototype cards from Pro Set football, power football, and power racing. The cards are identical to the regular issue except for a black diagonal "proto" stripe cutting across the lower right corner. The front of the title card has the convention logo on a blue screened background with the words Pro Set faintly detectible. The title card also carries the serial number "X" out of 10,000. The football cards are unnumbered and checklisted below in alphabetical order; the racing cards are numbered as listed below.

| | MINT | EXC | G-VG |
|---|---|---|---|
| COMPLETE SET (8) | 10.00 | 4.00 | 1.00 |
| COMMON PLAYER (1-8) | 1.00 | .40 | .10 |
| | | | |
| ☐ 1 Jerome Bettis | 3.00 | 1.20 | .30 |
| Los Angeles Rams | | | |
| Fire Power | | | |
| ☐ 2 Drew Bledsoe | 3.00 | 1.20 | .30 |
| New England Patriots | | | |
| ☐ 3 Brett Favre | 2.00 | .80 | .20 |
| Sterling Sharpe | | | |
| Green Bay Packers | | | |
| Air Power | | | |
| ☐ 4 Ron Moore | 2.00 | .80 | .20 |
| Arizona Cardinals | | | |
| ☐ 5 William Roaf | 1.00 | .40 | .10 |
| New Orleans Saints | | | |
| Power Line | | | |
| ☐ DB1 Dale Earnhardt | 3.00 | 1.20 | .30 |
| Twin 125 Winner | | | |
| (Racing) | | | |
| ☐ NNO Title Card | 1.00 | .40 | .10 |
| (1994 National) | | | |
| ☐ PW1 Ernie Irvan | 2.00 | .80 | .20 |
| Power Winners | | | |
| (Racing) | | | |

# 1991 Quarterback Legends

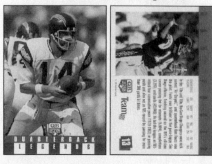

This 50-card set, measuring the standard size (2 1/2" by 3 1/2"), was produced by NFL Quarterback Legends and issued on high-quality card stock. The set is packaged in a red, white, and blue box. Card fronts feature a color action shot of the player. At the bottom of the card appears a red stripe and a blue and white checker board stripe, with the words "Quarterback Legends" reversed out in white and blue lettering. Card backs, printed horizontally, feature a full-bleed red stripe at the top with player's name in blue, another action photo, and statistical and biographical information. Sponsors' (QB Legends and Team NFL) logos and card number appear to the bottom right of card. The cards are numbered on the back. The first 46 cards in the set are ordered alphabetically by name. The last four cards depict legendary feats. The team name listed in the checklist below corresponds to uniform on front of cards; the photo on back of cards sometimes has player in a different team uniform. This set was introduced and distributed at the Quarterback Legends Show in Nashville, Tennessee in January, 1992.

|  | MINT | EXC | G-VG |
|---|---|---|---|
| COMPLETE SET (50) | 15.00 | 6.00 | 1.50 |
| COMMON PLAYER (1-50) | .25 | .10 | .02 |
| ☐ 1 Ken Anderson<br>Cincinnati Bengals | .75 | .30 | .07 |
| ☐ 2 Steve Bartkowski<br>Atlanta Falcons | .35 | .14 | .03 |
| ☐ 3 George Blanda<br>Oakland Raiders | 1.00 | .40 | .10 |
| ☐ 4 Terry Bradshaw<br>Pittsburgh Steelers | 1.50 | .60 | .15 |
| ☐ 5 Zeke Bratkowski<br>Green Bay Packers | .25 | .10 | .02 |
| ☐ 6 John Brodie<br>San Francisco 49ers | .50 | .20 | .05 |
| ☐ 7 Charley Conerly<br>New York Giants | .50 | .20 | .05 |
| ☐ 8 Len Dawson<br>Kansas City Chiefs | .50 | .20 | .05 |
| ☐ 9 Lynn Dickey<br>Green Bay Packers | .25 | .10 | .02 |
| ☐ 10 Joe Ferguson<br>Buffalo Bills | .25 | .10 | .02 |
| ☐ 11 Vince Ferragamo<br>Los Angeles Rams | .25 | .10 | .02 |
| ☐ 12 Tom Flores<br>Oakland Raiders | .35 | .14 | .03 |
| ☐ 13 Dan Fouts<br>San Diego Chargers | .75 | .30 | .07 |
| ☐ 14 Roman Gabriel<br>Los Angeles Rams | .35 | .14 | .03 |
| ☐ 15 Otto Graham<br>Cleveland Browns | .75 | .30 | .07 |
| ☐ 16 Bob Griese<br>Miami Dolphins | .75 | .30 | .07 |
| ☐ 17 Steve Grogan<br>New England Patriots | .35 | .14 | .03 |
| ☐ 18 John Hadl<br>Los Angeles Rams | .35 | .14 | .03 |
| ☐ 19 James Harris<br>Los Angeles Rams | .25 | .10 | .02 |
| ☐ 20 Jim Hart<br>St. Louis Cardinals | .25 | .10 | .02 |
| ☐ 21 Ron Jaworski<br>Philadelphia Eagles | .25 | .10 | .02 |
| ☐ 22 Charlie Johnson<br>Denver Broncos | .25 | .10 | .02 |
| ☐ 23 Bert Jones<br>Baltimore Colts | .35 | .14 | .03 |
| ☐ 24 Sonny Jurgensen<br>Washington Redskins | .50 | .20 | .05 |
| ☐ 25 Joe Kapp<br>Minnesota Vikings | .25 | .10 | .02 |
| ☐ 26 Billy Kilmer<br>Washington Redskins | .35 | .14 | .03 |
| ☐ 27 Daryle Lamonica<br>Oakland Raiders | .35 | .14 | .03 |
| ☐ 28 Greg Landry<br>Detroit Lions | .25 | .10 | .02 |
| ☐ 29 Neil Lomax<br>St. Louis Cardinals | .25 | .10 | .02 |
| ☐ 30 Archie Manning<br>New Orleans Saints | .50 | .20 | .05 |
| ☐ 31 Earl Morrall<br>Baltimore Colts | .35 | .14 | .03 |
| ☐ 32 Craig Morton<br>Denver Broncos | .35 | .14 | .03 |
| ☐ 33 Gifford Nielsen<br>Houston Oilers | .25 | .10 | .02 |
| ☐ 34 Dan Pastorini<br>Houston Oilers | .25 | .10 | .02 |
| ☐ 35 Jim Plunkett<br>Oakland Raiders | .35 | .14 | .03 |
| ☐ 36 Norm Snead<br>New York Giants | .25 | .10 | .02 |
| ☐ 37 Ken Stabler<br>Oakland Raiders | .75 | .30 | .07 |
| ☐ 38 Bart Starr<br>Green Bay Packers | 1.00 | .40 | .10 |
| ☐ 39 Roger Staubach<br>Dallas Cowboys | 2.00 | .80 | .20 |
| ☐ 40 Joe Theismann<br>Washington Redskins | .75 | .30 | .07 |
| ☐ 41 Y.A. Tittle<br>New York Giants | .75 | .30 | .07 |
| ☐ 42 Johnny Unitas<br>Baltimore Colts | 1.00 | .40 | .10 |
| ☐ 43 Bill Wade<br>Chicago Bears | .25 | .10 | .02 |
| ☐ 44 Danny White<br>Dallas Cowboys | .35 | .14 | .03 |
| ☐ 45 Doug Williams<br>Washington Redskins | .25 | .10 | .02 |
| ☐ 46 Jim Zorn<br>Seattle Seahawks | .35 | .14 | .03 |
| ☐ 47 Otto Graham<br>Cleveland Browns<br>Legendary Feats | .75 | .30 | .07 |
| ☐ 48 Johnny Unitas<br>Baltimore Colts<br>Legendary Feats | 1.00 | .40 | .10 |
| ☐ 49 Bart Starr<br>Green Bay Packers<br>Legendary Feats | 1.00 | .40 | .10 |
| ☐ 50 Terry Bradshaw<br>Pittsburgh Steelers<br>Legendary Feats | 1.25 | .50 | .12 |

# 1992 Quarterback Greats GE

Produced by NFL Properties, this 12-card set was prepared for General Electric Silicones and features members of the Quarterback Club. The cards measure the standard size (2 1/2" by 3 1/2") and could be obtained by sending in proofs of purchase. The fronts carry action color player photos on a red face. The player's name is printed in white lettering above the picture. A blue and red bar icon containing the words "Quarterback Greats" runs horizontally from the top right and overlaps the picture. The backs carry statistics and career highlights. The GE logo and NFL Team Players logo appear at the bottom. The Quarterback Club icon (a black box with a brightly colored football player outline) is in the upper left corner.

|  | MINT | EXC | G-VG |
|---|---|---|---|
| COMPLETE SET (12) | 12.00 | 5.00 | 1.20 |
| COMMON PLAYER (1-11) | .50 | .20 | .05 |
| ☐ 1 Troy Aikman<br>Dallas Cowboys | 6.00 | 2.40 | .60 |

| | MINT | EXC | G-VG |
|---|---|---|---|
| ☐ 2 Bubby Brister | .50 | .20 | .05 |
| Pittsburgh Steelers | | | |
| ☐ 3 Randall Cunningham | 1.00 | .40 | .10 |
| Philadelphia Eagles | | | |
| ☐ 4 John Elway | 2.00 | .80 | .20 |
| Denver Broncos | | | |
| ☐ 5 Boomer Esiason | .75 | .30 | .07 |
| Cincinnati Bengals | | | |
| ☐ 6 Jim Everett | .50 | .20 | .05 |
| Los Angeles Rams | | | |
| ☐ 7 Jim Kelly | 1.50 | .60 | .15 |
| Buffalo Bills | | | |
| ☐ 8 Bernie Kosar | .75 | .30 | .07 |
| Cleveland Browns | | | |
| ☐ 9 Dan Marino | 4.00 | 1.60 | .40 |
| Miami Dolphins | | | |
| ☐ 10 Warren Moon | 1.25 | .50 | .12 |
| Houston Oilers | | | |
| ☐ 11 Phil Simms | .75 | .30 | .07 |
| New York Giants | | | |
| ☐ NNO Title Card | .50 | .20 | .05 |
| (Checklist) | | | |

## 1993 Quarterback Legends

This 50-card set showcases outstanding quarterbacks throughout NFL history. The cards measure the standard size (2 1/2" by 3 1/2"). The fronts feature action player photos in which the player appears in color against a sepia-toned background. The borders shade from white to pastel yellow as one moves from left to right, and the set title "Quarterback Legends" is printed vertically on the left edge in bronze lettering. The horizontal backs carry a close-up color player photo and career summary. The set closes with a Legendary Feats (48-50) subset. The cards are numbered on the back.

| | MINT | EXC | G-VG |
|---|---|---|---|
| COMPLETE SET (50) | 15.00 | 6.00 | 1.50 |
| COMMON PLAYER (1-50) | .25 | .10 | .02 |
| ☐ 1 Checklist Card | .35 | .14 | .03 |
| ☐ 2 Ken Anderson | .75 | .30 | .07 |
| Cincinnati Bengals | | | |
| ☐ 3 Steve Bartkowski | .35 | .14 | .03 |
| Atlanta Falcons | | | |
| ☐ 4 George Blanda | 1.00 | .40 | .10 |
| Oakland Raiders | | | |
| ☐ 5 Terry Bradshaw | 1.50 | .60 | .15 |
| Pittsburgh Steelers | | | |
| ☐ 6 Zeke Bratkowski | .25 | .10 | .02 |
| Green Bay Packers | | | |
| ☐ 7 John Brodie | .50 | .20 | .05 |
| San Francisco 49ers | | | |
| ☐ 8 Charley Conerly | .50 | .20 | .05 |
| New York Giants | | | |
| ☐ 9 Len Dawson | .50 | .20 | .05 |
| Kansas City Chiefs | | | |
| ☐ 10 Lynn Dickey | .25 | .10 | .02 |
| Green Bay Packers | | | |
| ☐ 11 Joe Ferguson | .25 | .10 | .02 |
| Buffalo Bills | | | |
| ☐ 12 Vince Ferragamo | .25 | .10 | .02 |
| Los Angeles Rams | | | |
| ☐ 13 Tom Flores | .35 | .14 | .03 |
| Oakland Raiders | | | |
| ☐ 14 Dan Fouts | .75 | .30 | .07 |
| San Diego Chargers | | | |
| ☐ 15 Roman Gabriel | .35 | .14 | .03 |
| Los Angeles Rams | | | |
| ☐ 16 Otto Graham | .75 | .30 | .07 |
| Cleveland Browns | | | |
| ☐ 17 Bob Griese | 1.00 | .40 | .10 |
| Miami Dolphins | | | |
| ☐ 18 Steve Grogan | .35 | .14 | .03 |
| New England Patriots | | | |
| ☐ 19 John Hadl | .35 | .14 | .03 |
| San Diego Chargers | | | |
| ☐ 20 James Harris | .25 | .10 | .02 |
| San Diego Chargers | | | |
| ☐ 21 Jim Hart | .25 | .10 | .02 |
| St. Louis Cardinals | | | |
| ☐ 22 Ron Jaworski | .25 | .10 | .02 |
| Philadelphia Eagles | | | |
| ☐ 23 Charlie Johnson | .25 | .10 | .02 |
| St. Louis Cardinals | | | |
| ☐ 24 Bert Jones | .35 | .14 | .03 |
| Baltimore Colts | | | |
| ☐ 25 Sonny Jurgensen | .50 | .20 | .05 |
| Washington Redskins | | | |
| ☐ 26 Joe Kapp | .25 | .10 | .02 |
| Minnesota Vikings | | | |
| ☐ 27 Billy Kilmer | .35 | .14 | .03 |
| Washington Redskins | | | |
| ☐ 28 Daryle Lamonica | .35 | .14 | .03 |
| Oakland Raiders | | | |
| ☐ 29 Greg Landry | .25 | .10 | .02 |
| Detroit Lions | | | |
| ☐ 30 Neil Lomax | .25 | .10 | .02 |
| Phoenix Cardinals | | | |
| ☐ 31 Archie Manning | .50 | .20 | .05 |
| New Orleans Saints | | | |
| ☐ 32 Earl Morrall | .35 | .14 | .03 |
| Miami Dolphins | | | |
| ☐ 33 Craig Morton | .35 | .14 | .03 |
| Dallas Cowboys | | | |
| ☐ 34 Gifford Nielsen | .25 | .10 | .02 |
| Houston Oilers | | | |
| ☐ 35 Dan Pastorini | .25 | .10 | .02 |
| Houston Oilers | | | |
| ☐ 36 Jim Plunkett | .35 | .14 | .03 |
| Oakland Raiders | | | |
| ☐ 37 Norm Snead | .25 | .10 | .02 |
| Philadelphia Eagles | | | |
| ☐ 38 Ken Stabler | .75 | .30 | .07 |
| Oakland Raiders | | | |
| ☐ 39 Bart Starr | 1.00 | .40 | .10 |
| Green Bay Packers | | | |
| ☐ 40 Roger Staubach | 2.00 | .80 | .20 |
| Dallas Cowboys | | | |
| ☐ 41 Joe Theismann | .75 | .30 | .07 |
| Washington Redskins | | | |
| ☐ 42 Y.A. Tittle | .75 | .30 | .07 |
| New York Giants | | | |
| ☐ 43 Johnny Unitas | 1.00 | .40 | .10 |
| Baltimore Colts | | | |
| ☐ 44 Bill Wade | .25 | .10 | .02 |
| Chicago Bears | | | |
| ☐ 45 Danny White | .35 | .14 | .03 |
| Dallas Cowboys | | | |
| ☐ 46 Doug Williams | .25 | .10 | .02 |
| Tampa Bay Buccaneers | | | |
| ☐ 47 Jim Zorn | .25 | .10 | .02 |
| Seattle Seahawks | | | |
| ☐ 48 George Blanda | .75 | .30 | .07 |
| Oakland Raiders | | | |
| Miracle Streak | | | |
| ☐ 49 Bob Griese | .50 | .20 | .05 |
| Earl Morrall | | | |
| Miami Dolphins | | | |
| Perfect Season | | | |
| ☐ 50 Doug Williams | .35 | .14 | .03 |
| Washington Redskins | | | |
| Record-setting Super | | | |
| Bowl XXII | | | |

## 1935 R311-2 Premium Photos

The R311-2 (as referenced in the American Card Catalog) Football Stars and Scenes set consists of 17 glossy, unnumbered, 6" by 8" photos. Both professional and collegiate players are pictured on these photos. These blank-back photos have been numbered in the checklist below alphabetically by the player's name or title. These premium photos were available from National Chicle with one premium given for every 20 wrappers mailed in.

| | EX-MT | VG-E | GOOD |
|---|---|---|---|
| COMPLETE SET (17) | 2000.00 | 900.00 | 225.00 |
| COMMON PHOTO (1-17) | 100.00 | 40.00 | 10.00 |
| ☐ 1 Joe Bach | 100.00 | 40.00 | 10.00 |
| ☐ 2 Eddie Casey | 100.00 | 40.00 | 10.00 |
| ☐ 3 George Christensen | 100.00 | 40.00 | 10.00 |
| (Tarzan) | | | |
| ☐ 4 Red Grange | 300.00 | 120.00 | 30.00 |
| (The Galloping Ghost) | | | |
| ☐ 5 Stan Kostka; | 100.00 | 40.00 | 10.00 |
| TD Next stop | | | |
| ☐ 6 Joseph Maniaci; | 100.00 | 40.00 | 10.00 |
| Fordham Back | | | |
| (26 with ball, | | | |
| shown trying to gain | | | |
| around left end) | | | |
| ☐ 7 Harry Newman | 100.00 | 40.00 | 10.00 |
| ☐ 8 Walter Switzer | 100.00 | 40.00 | 10.00 |
| Cornell quarter- | | | |
| back (with ball) | | | |
| ☐ 9 Chicago Bears; 1934 | 200.00 | 80.00 | 20.00 |
| Western Champs | | | |
| ☐ 10 New York Giants | 200.00 | 80.00 | 20.00 |
| World's Football | | | |
| Champions 1934 | | | |
| ☐ 11 Notre Dame's Quick | 125.00 | 50.00 | 12.50 |
| Kick Against | | | |
| Army, 1934 | | | |
| ☐ 12 Pittsburgh in Rough | 100.00 | 40.00 | 10.00 |
| Going Against the | | | |
| Navy 1934 | | | |
| ☐ 13 Pittsburgh Pirates | 200.00 | 80.00 | 20.00 |
| Football Club 1935 | | | |
| ☐ 14 Touchdown: Morton | 100.00 | 40.00 | 10.00 |
| of Yale | | | |
| ☐ 15 A Tight Spot | 100.00 | 40.00 | 10.00 |
| ☐ 16 Cotton Goes Places | 100.00 | 40.00 | 10.00 |
| ☐ 17 The Greatest Tackle | 150.00 | 60.00 | 15.00 |
| Picture Ever Photo- | | | |
| graphed; Ace Gutkowsky | | | |
| Detroit Lions stopped | | | |
| in mid-air by Steve | | | |
| Hokuf Boston Redskins | | | |

## 1985 Raiders Shell Oil Posters

Available only at participating Southern California Shell stations during the 1985 season, these five posters measure approximately 11 5/8" by 18" and feature an artist's color renderings of the Raiders in action. The unnumbered posters are blank-backed, except for number 1 below, the back of which carries the Raiders and Shell logos along with the number in which each subsequent poster was released. The posters are listed below accordingly.

| | MINT | EXC | G-VG |
|---|---|---|---|
| COMPLETE SET (5) | 25.00 | 10.00 | 2.50 |
| COMMON POSTER (1-5) | 5.00 | 2.00 | .50 |
| ☐ 1 Pro Bowl | 6.00 | 2.40 | .60 |
| (No release date) | | | |
| ☐ 2 Defensive Front | 6.00 | 2.40 | .60 |
| (September) | | | |
| ☐ 3 Deep Secondary | 5.00 | 2.00 | .50 |
| (October) | | | |
| ☐ 4 Big Offensive Line | 5.00 | 2.00 | .50 |
| (November) | | | |

| | | | |
|---|---|---|---|
| ☐ 5 Scores | 5.00 | 2.00 | .50 |
| (December) | | | |

## 1989 Raiders Swanson

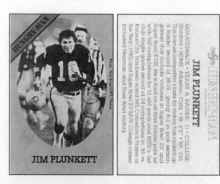

This three-card set was issued in a perforated strip containing five card slots; after perforation, the cards measure approximately 2 1/2" by 3 3/4". The first two slots consist of manufacturer's coupons to save 25 cents on the purchase of any variety of Swanson Hungry-Man dinners. The player cards feature an oval-shamped black and white player photo on a silver card face. A red diagonal with the words "Hungry-Man" cuts across the upper left corner, and the player's name appears in black lettering below the picture. The horizontal backs present biographical information and player profile. The cards are unnumbered and checklisted below in alphabetical order.

| | MINT | EXC | G-VG |
|---|---|---|---|
| COMPLETE SET (3) | 7.50 | 3.00 | .75 |
| COMMON PLAYER (1-3) | 2.50 | 1.00 | .25 |
| ☐ 1 Marcus Allen | 5.00 | 2.00 | .50 |
| ☐ 2 Howie Long | 2.50 | 1.00 | .25 |
| ☐ 3 Jim Plunkett | 2.50 | 1.00 | .25 |

## 1990-91 Raiders Main Street Dairy

This set of six half-pint milk cartons features the Raiders' team patch, a head shot of a player, and a safety tip to youngsters on one of its panels. When collapsed, the cartons measure approximately 4 1/2" by 6". The cartons were issued in the Los Angeles area and were printed in three colors, brown (chocolate lowfat), red (vitamin D), and blue (2 percent low fat). The primary color of the carton is given on the continuation line below.

| | MINT | EXC | G-VG |
|---|---|---|---|
| COMPLETE SET (6).......................... | 15.00 | 6.00 | 1.50 |
| COMMON PLAYER (1-6).................. | 2.50 | 1.00 | .25 |
| ☐ 1 Bob Golic .............................. | 3.50 | 1.40 | .35 |
| (Blue) | | | |
| ☐ 2 Terry McDaniel......................... | 2.50 | 1.00 | .25 |
| (Brown) | | | |
| ☐ 3 Don Mosebar ........................... | 2.50 | 1.00 | .25 |
| (Red) | | | |
| ☐ 4 Jay Schroeder.......................... | 3.50 | 1.40 | .35 |
| (Blue) | | | |
| ☐ 5 Art Shell CO ............................ | 3.50 | 1.40 | .35 |
| (Red) | | | |
| ☐ 6 Steve Wisniewski ..................... | 2.50 | 1.00 | .25 |
| (Brown) | | | |

## 1991-92 Raiders Adohr Farms Dairy

This set of ten half-pint milk cartons features the Raiders' team patch, a head shot of a player, and a safety message on one of its panels. When collapsed, the cartons measure approximately 4 1/2" by 6". The cartons were issued in the Los Angeles area and were printed in red (vitamin D) and blue (2 percent lowfat). Apparently only the Greg Townsend carton was issued in two varieties. The primary color of the carton is given on the continuation line. The cartons are unnumbered and checklisted below in alphabetical order. Apparently Adohr Farms Dairy bought out Main Street Dairy and with the buyout, obtained the rights to produce the selected Raiders.

| | MINT | EXC | G-VG |
|---|---|---|---|
| COMPLETE SET (10)......................... | 25.00 | 10.00 | 2.50 |
| COMMON PLAYER (1-10)................. | 2.50 | 1.00 | .25 |
| ☐ 1 Jeff Gossett.............................. | 2.50 | 1.00 | .25 |
| (Red) | | | |
| ☐ 2 Ethan Horton............................ | 2.50 | 1.00 | .25 |
| (Blue) | | | |
| ☐ 3 Jeff Jaeger .............................. | 2.50 | 1.00 | .25 |
| (Red) | | | |
| ☐ 4 Ronnie Lott .............................. | 5.00 | 2.00 | .50 |
| (Blue) | | | |
| ☐ 5 Terry McDaniel.......................... | 2.50 | 1.00 | .25 |
| (Red) | | | |
| ☐ 6 Don Mosebar ........................... | 2.50 | 1.00 | .25 |
| (Red) | | | |
| ☐ 7 Jay Schroeder.......................... | 3.50 | 1.40 | .35 |
| (Red) | | | |
| ☐ 8 Art Shell CO ............................ | 3.50 | 1.40 | .35 |
| (Red) | | | |
| ☐ 9 Greg Townsend......................... | 3.50 | 1.40 | .35 |
| (Red or blue) | | | |
| ☐ 10 Steve Wisniewski .................... | 2.50 | 1.00 | .25 |
| (Red) | | | |

## 1993-94 Raiders Adohr Farms Dairy

This set of six half-pint vitamin D milk cartons features the Raiders team patch, a head shot of a player, and a message about education or crime prevention, all printed in red. When collapsed, the cartons measure approximately 4 1/2" by 6". Two million milk cartons were distributed only to Los Angeles area schools and hospitals in a two-week period during the season. Reportedly only 1,400 were produced flat and undistributed. The cartons are unnumbered and checklisted below in alphabetical order.

| | MINT | EXC | G-VG |
|---|---|---|---|
| COMPLETE SET (6).......................... | 15.00 | 6.00 | 1.50 |
| COMMON PLAYER (1-6).................. | 2.50 | 1.00 | .25 |
| ☐ 1 Jeff Gossett.............................. | 2.50 | 1.00 | .25 |
| ☐ 2 Ethan Horton............................ | 2.50 | 1.00 | .25 |
| ☐ 3 Terry McDaniel......................... | 2.50 | 1.00 | .25 |
| ☐ 4 Don Mosebar ........................... | 2.50 | 1.00 | .25 |
| ☐ 5 Art Shell CO ............................ | 3.50 | 1.40 | .35 |
| ☐ 6 Steve Wisniewski ..................... | 2.50 | 1.00 | .25 |

## 1950 Rams Admiral

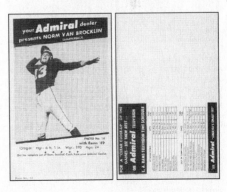

This 35-card set was sponsored by Admiral and features cards measuring approximately 3 1/2" by 5 1/2". The front design has a black and white action pose of the player, without borders on the sides of the picture. The words "Your Admiral dealer presents" followed by the player's name and position appear in the black stripe at the top of each card. A black border separates the bottom of the picture from the biographical information below. In a horizontal format, the backs are blank on the right half, and have a season schedule as well as Admiral advertisements on the left half. The cards are numbered on the front by the photos. Card numbers 26-35 are slightly smaller and have blank backs. Norm Van Brocklin appears in his Rookie Card year.

|  | NRMT | VG-E | GOOD |
|---|---|---|---|
| COMPLETE SET (35) | 350.00 | 140.00 | 35.00 |
| COMMON CARD (1-35) | 7.50 | 3.00 | .75 |

| | | NRMT | VG-E | GOOD |
|---|---|---|---|---|
| ☐ 1 | Joe Stydahar CO | 12.00 | 5.00 | 1.20 |
| ☐ 2 | Hampton Pool CO | 7.50 | 3.00 | .75 |
| ☐ 3 | Fred Naumetz | 7.50 | 3.00 | .75 |
| ☐ 4 | Jack Finlay | 7.50 | 3.00 | .75 |
| ☐ 5 | Gil Bouley | 7.50 | 3.00 | .75 |
| ☐ 6 | Bob Reinhard | 7.50 | 3.00 | .75 |
| ☐ 7 | Bob Boyd | 9.00 | 3.75 | .90 |
| ☐ 8 | Bob Waterfield | 35.00 | 14.00 | 3.50 |
| ☐ 9 | Mel Hein CO | 12.00 | 5.00 | 1.20 |
| ☐ 10 | Howard(Red) Hickey CO | 9.00 | 3.75 | .90 |
| ☐ 11 | Ralph Pasquariello | 7.50 | 3.00 | .75 |
| ☐ 12 | Jack Zilly | 7.50 | 3.00 | .75 |
| ☐ 13 | Tom Kalmanir | 7.50 | 3.00 | .75 |
| ☐ 14 | Norm Van Brocklin | 50.00 | 20.00 | 5.00 |
| ☐ 15 | Woodley Lewis | 9.00 | 3.75 | .90 |
| ☐ 16 | Glenn Davis | 25.00 | 10.00 | 2.50 |
| ☐ 17 | Dick Hoerner | 7.50 | 3.00 | .75 |
| ☐ 18 | Bob Kelley ANN | 7.50 | 3.00 | .75 |
| ☐ 19 | Paul(Tank) Younger | 12.00 | 5.00 | 1.20 |
| ☐ 20 | George Sims | 7.50 | 3.00 | .75 |
| ☐ 21 | Dick Huffman | 7.50 | 3.00 | .75 |
| ☐ 22 | Tom Fears | 25.00 | 10.00 | 2.50 |
| ☐ 23 | Vitamin T. Smith | 9.00 | 3.75 | .90 |
| ☐ 24 | Elroy Hirsch | 30.00 | 12.00 | 3.00 |
| ☐ 25 | Don Paul | 9.00 | 3.75 | .90 |
| ☐ 26 | Bill Lange | 7.50 | 3.00 | .75 |
| ☐ 27 | Paul Barry | 7.50 | 3.00 | .75 |
| ☐ 28 | Deacon Dan Towler | 9.00 | 3.75 | .90 |
| ☐ 29 | Vic Vasicek | 7.50 | 3.00 | .75 |
| ☐ 30 | Bill Smyth | 7.50 | 3.00 | .75 |
| ☐ 31 | Larry Brink | 7.50 | 3.00 | .75 |
| ☐ 32 | Jerry Williams | 7.50 | 3.00 | .75 |
| ☐ 33 | Stan West | 7.50 | 3.00 | .75 |
| ☐ 34 | Art Statuto | 7.50 | 3.00 | .75 |
| ☐ 35 | Ed Champagne | 7.50 | 3.00 | .75 |

# 1953 Rams Black Border

This 36-card unnumbered set measures approximately 4 1/4" by 6 3/8" and was issued by the Los Angeles Rams for their fans. This set has black borders on the front framing posed action shots with the player's signature across the bottom portion of the picture. Biographical information on the back relating to the player pictured listing the player's name, height, weight, age, and college is also included. Among the interesting cards in this set are early cards of Dick "Night-Train" Lane and Andy Robustelli. The cards were available directly from the team as a complete set. We have checklisted this set in alphabetical order. Many cards from the 1953-1955 and 1957 Rams Team Issue Black Border sets are identical except for text differences on the card backs. Player stat lines are also helpful in identifying year of issue; the year of issue is typically the next year after the last year on the stats. The first few words of the first line of text is listed for players without stat lines.

| | | NRMT | VG-E | GOOD |
|---|---|---|---|---|
| | COMPLETE SET (36) | 150.00 | 60.00 | 15.00 |
| | COMMON PLAYER (1-36) | 3.00 | 1.20 | .30 |
| ☐ 1 | Ben Agajanian | 5.00 | 2.00 | .50 |
| ☐ 2 | Bob Boyd | 4.00 | 1.60 | .40 |
| | (Born in Riverside ...) | | | |
| ☐ 3 | Larry Brink | 3.00 | 1.20 | .30 |

| | | NRMT | VG-E | GOOD |
|---|---|---|---|---|
| ☐ 4 | Rudy Bukich | 6.00 | 2.40 | .60 |
| ☐ 5 | Tom Dahms | 3.00 | 1.20 | .30 |
| | (4 text lines) | | | |
| ☐ 6 | Dick Daugherty | 3.00 | 1.20 | .30 |
| | (Regular Ram ...) | | | |
| ☐ 7 | Jack Dwyer | 3.00 | 1.20 | .30 |
| | (Played 1951 ...) | | | |
| ☐ 8 | Tom Fears | 12.00 | 5.00 | 1.20 |
| | (1952 stats) | | | |
| ☐ 9 | Bob Fry | 3.00 | 1.20 | .30 |
| | (Was sprinter ...) | | | |
| ☐ 10 | Frank Fuller | 3.00 | 1.20 | .30 |
| | (Attended ...) | | | |
| ☐ 11 | Norbert Hecker | 4.00 | 1.60 | .40 |
| ☐ 12 | Elroy Hirsch | 15.00 | 6.00 | 1.50 |
| | (1952 stats) | | | |
| ☐ 13 | John Hock | 3.00 | 1.20 | .30 |
| | (Just completed ...) | | | |
| ☐ 14 | Bob Kelley ANN | 3.00 | 1.20 | .30 |
| | (Signature in upper left of photo) | | | |
| ☐ 15 | Dick Lane | 18.00 | 7.25 | 1.80 |
| ☐ 16 | Woodley Lewis | 4.00 | 1.60 | .40 |
| | (Ram utility ...) | | | |
| ☐ 17 | Tom McCormick | 3.00 | 1.20 | .30 |
| | (Set three ...) | | | |
| ☐ 18 | Lewis(Bud) McFadin | 3.00 | 1.20 | .30 |
| | (Came to Rams ...) | | | |
| ☐ 19 | Leon McLaughlin | 3.00 | 1.20 | .30 |
| | (Played every ...) | | | |
| ☐ 20 | Brad Myers | 3.00 | 1.20 | .30 |
| ☐ 21 | Don Paul | 4.00 | 1.60 | .40 |
| | (A five year ...) | | | |
| ☐ 22 | Hampton Pool CO | 3.00 | 1.20 | .30 |
| | (Hampton Pool ...) | | | |
| ☐ 23 | Duane Putnam | 3.00 | 1.20 | .30 |
| | (As rookie ...) | | | |
| ☐ 24 | Volney Quinlan | 3.00 | 1.20 | .30 |
| | (Nickname ...) | | | |
| ☐ 25 | Herb Rich | 3.00 | 1.20 | .30 |
| ☐ 26 | Andy Robustelli | 12.00 | 5.00 | 1.20 |
| | (Rams' regular ...) | | | |
| ☐ 27 | Vitamin T. Smith | 4.00 | 1.60 | .40 |
| ☐ 28 | Harland Svare | 3.00 | 1.20 | .30 |
| | (Attended ...) | | | |
| ☐ 29 | Len Teeuws | 3.00 | 1.20 | .30 |
| ☐ 30 | Harry Thompson | 3.00 | 1.20 | .30 |
| | (Used at ...) | | | |
| ☐ 31 | Charley Toogood | 3.00 | 1.20 | .30 |
| | (Been defensive ...) | | | |
| ☐ 32 | Deacon Dan Towler | 4.00 | 1.60 | .40 |
| | (National football ...) | | | |
| ☐ 33 | Norm Van Brocklin | 20.00 | 8.00 | 2.00 |
| | (1952 stats) | | | |
| ☐ 34 | Stan West | 3.00 | 1.20 | .30 |
| | (Rams' regular ...) | | | |
| ☐ 35 | Paul(Tank) Younger | 6.00 | 2.40 | .60 |
| | (1952 stats) | | | |
| ☐ 36 | Coaches: John Sauer, William Battles, and Howard(Red) Hickey | 4.00 | 1.60 | .40 |

# 1954 Rams Black Border

This 36-card set measures approximately 4 1/4" by 6 3/8". The front features a black and white posed action photo enclosed by a black border, with the player's signature across the bottom portion of the picture. The back lists the player's name, height, weight, age, and college, along with basic biographical information. The set was available direct from the team as part of a package for their fans. The cards are listed alphabetically below since they are unnumbered. Many cards from the 1953-1955 and 1957 Rams Team Issue Black Border sets are identical except for text differences on the card backs. Player stat lines are also helpful in identifying year of issue; the year of issue is typically the next year after the last year on the stats. The first few words of the first line of text is listed for players without stat lines. The set features the first card appearance of Gene "Big Daddy" Lipscomb.

| | NRMT | VG-E | GOOD |
|---|---|---|---|
| COMPLETE SET (36) | 150.00 | 60.00 | 15.00 |
| COMMON PLAYER (1-36) | 3.00 | 1.20 | .30 |
| ☐ 1 Bob Boyd | 3.00 | 1.20 | .30 |
| (One of fastest ...) | | | |
| ☐ 2 Bob Carey | 3.00 | 1.20 | .30 |
| ☐ 3 Bobby Cross | 3.00 | 1.20 | .30 |
| ☐ 4 Tom Dahms | 3.00 | 1.20 | .30 |
| (5 text lines) | | | |
| ☐ 5 Don Doll | 3.00 | 1.20 | .30 |
| ☐ 6 Jack Dwyer | 3.00 | 1.20 | .30 |
| (Regular defensive ...) | | | |
| ☐ 7 Tom Fears | 12.00 | 5.00 | 1.20 |
| (1953 stats) | | | |
| ☐ 8 Bob Griffin | 3.00 | 1.20 | .30 |
| (All American ...) | | | |
| ☐ 9 Art Hauser | 3.00 | 1.20 | .30 |
| (Was fastest ...) | | | |
| ☐ 10 Hall Haynes | 3.00 | 1.20 | .30 |
| ☐ 11 Elroy Hirsch | 15.00 | 6.00 | 1.50 |
| (1953 stats) | | | |
| ☐ 12 Ed Hughes | 3.00 | 1.20 | .30 |
| ☐ 13 Bob Kelley ANN | 3.00 | 1.20 | .30 |
| (Signature across photo) | | | |
| ☐ 14 Woodley Lewis | 4.00 | 1.60 | .40 |
| (Established ...) | | | |
| ☐ 15 Gene Lipscomb | 12.00 | 5.00 | 1.20 |
| ☐ 16 Tom McCormick | 3.00 | 1.20 | .30 |
| (Rams' regular ...) | | | |
| ☐ 17 Bud McFadin | 3.00 | 1.20 | .30 |
| (Although ...) | | | |
| ☐ 18 Leon McLaughlin | 3.00 | 1.20 | .30 |
| (Started every ...) | | | |
| ☐ 19 Paul Miller | 3.00 | 1.20 | .30 |
| (Lettered at ...) | | | |
| ☐ 20 Don Paul | 4.00 | 1.60 | .40 |
| (One of two ...) | | | |
| ☐ 21 Hampton Pool CO | 3.00 | 1.20 | .30 |
| (Since taking ...) | | | |
| ☐ 22 Duane Putnam | 3.00 | 1.20 | .30 |
| (Offensive guard ...) | | | |
| ☐ 23 Volney Quinlan | 3.00 | 1.20 | .30 |
| (Had best ...) | | | |
| ☐ 24 Les Richter | 6.00 | 2.40 | .60 |
| (Rated one ...) | | | |
| ☐ 25 Andy Robustelli | 12.00 | 5.00 | 1.20 |
| (L.A.'s regular ...) | | | |
| ☐ 26 Will Sherman | 4.00 | 1.60 | .40 |
| (Played at ...) | | | |
| ☐ 27 Harland Svare | 3.00 | 1.20 | .30 |
| (An outside ...) | | | |
| ☐ 28 Harry Thompson | 3.00 | 1.20 | .30 |
| (Played offensive ...) | | | |
| ☐ 29 Charley Toogood | 3.00 | 1.20 | .30 |
| ☐ 30 Deacon Dan Towler | 4.00 | 1.60 | .40 |
| (Since becoming ...) | | | |
| ☐ 31 Norm Van Brocklin | 20.00 | 8.00 | 2.00 |
| (1953 stats) | | | |
| ☐ 32 Bill Wade | 6.00 | 2.40 | .60 |
| (Selected as ...) | | | |
| ☐ 33 Duane Wardlow | 3.00 | 1.20 | .30 |
| ☐ 34 Stan West | 3.00 | 1.20 | .30 |
| (Virtually ...) | | | |
| ☐ 35 Paul(Tank) Younger | 6.00 | 2.40 | .60 |
| (1953 stats) | | | |
| ☐ 36 Coaches Card | 4.00 | 1.60 | .40 |
| Bill Battles | | | |
| Howard(Red) Hickey | | | |
| John Sauer | | | |
| Dick Voris | | | |
| Buck Weaver | | | |
| Hampton Pool | | | |

## 1955 Rams Black Border

This 37-card set measures approximately 4 1/4" by 6 3/8". The front features a black and white posed action photo enclosed by a black border, with the player's signature across the bottom portion of the picture. The back lists the player's name, height, weight, age, and college, along with basic biographical information. The set was available direct from the team as part of a package for their fans. The cards are listed alphabetically below since they are unnumbered. Many cards from the 1953-1955 and 1957 Rams Team Issue Black Border sets are identical except for text differences on the card backs. Player stat lines are also helpful in identifying year of issue; the year of issue is typically the next year after the last year on the stats. The first few words of the first line of text is listed for players without stat lines.

| | NRMT | VG-E | GOOD |
|---|---|---|---|
| COMPLETE SET (37) | 150.00 | 60.00 | 15.00 |
| COMMON PLAYER (1-37) | 3.00 | 1.20 | .30 |
| ☐ 1 Jack Bighead | 3.00 | 1.20 | .30 |
| ☐ 2 Bob Boyd | 3.00 | 1.20 | .30 |
| ☐ 3 Don Burroughs | 3.00 | 1.20 | .30 |
| ☐ 4 Jim Cason | 3.00 | 1.20 | .30 |
| ☐ 5 Bob Cross | 3.00 | 1.20 | .30 |
| ☐ 6 Jack Ellena | 3.00 | 1.20 | .30 |
| ☐ 7 Tom Fears | 12.00 | 5.00 | 1.20 |
| ☐ 8 Sid Fournet | 3.00 | 1.20 | .30 |
| ☐ 9 Frank Fuller | 3.00 | 1.20 | .30 |
| ☐ 10 Sid Gillman and staff | 6.00 | 2.40 | .60 |
| ☐ 11 Bob Griffin | 3.00 | 1.20 | .30 |
| ☐ 12 Art Hauser | 3.00 | 1.20 | .30 |
| ☐ 13 Hall Haynes | 3.00 | 1.20 | .30 |
| ☐ 14 Elroy Hirsch | 15.00 | 6.00 | 1.50 |
| ☐ 15 John Hock | 3.00 | 1.20 | .30 |
| ☐ 16 Glenn Holtzman | 3.00 | 1.20 | .30 |
| ☐ 17 Ed Hughes | 3.00 | 1.20 | .30 |
| ☐ 18 Woodley Lewis | 4.00 | 1.60 | .40 |
| ☐ 19 Gene Lipscomb | 8.00 | 3.25 | .80 |
| ☐ 20 Tom McCormick | 3.00 | 1.20 | .30 |
| ☐ 21 Bud McFadin | 3.00 | 1.20 | .30 |
| ☐ 22 Leon McLaughlin | 3.00 | 1.20 | .30 |
| ☐ 23 Paul Miller | 3.00 | 1.20 | .30 |
| ☐ 24 Larry Morris | 3.00 | 1.20 | .30 |
| ☐ 25 Don Paul | 4.00 | 1.60 | .40 |
| ☐ 26 Duane Putnam | 3.00 | 1.20 | .30 |
| ☐ 27 Volney Quinlan | 3.00 | 1.20 | .30 |
| ☐ 28 Les Richter | 5.00 | 2.00 | .50 |
| ☐ 29 Andy Robustelli | 12.00 | 5.00 | 1.20 |
| ☐ 30 Bill Sherman | 4.00 | 1.60 | .40 |
| ☐ 31 Corky Taylor | 3.00 | 1.20 | .30 |
| ☐ 32 Charley Toogood | 3.00 | 1.20 | .30 |
| ☐ 33 Deacon Dan Towler | 4.00 | 1.60 | .40 |
| ☐ 34 Norm Van Brocklin | 20.00 | 8.00 | 2.00 |
| ☐ 35 Bill Wade | 6.00 | 2.40 | .60 |
| ☐ 36 Ron Waller | 3.00 | 1.20 | .30 |
| ☐ 37 Paul(Tank) Younger | 6.00 | 2.40 | .60 |

## 1956 Rams White Border

This 37-card team-issued set measures approximately 4 1/4" by 6 3/8" and features members of the Los Angeles Rams. The set has posed action shots on the front framed by a white border with the player's signature across the picture, while the back has biographical information about the player listing the player's name, height, weight, age, number of years in NFL, and college. We have checklisted this (unnumbered) set in alphabetical order. The set was available direct from the team as part of a package for their fans.

| | NRMT | VG-E | GOOD |
|---|---|---|---|
| COMPLETE SET (37) | 150.00 | 60.00 | 15.00 |
| COMMON PLAYER (1-37) | 3.00 | 1.20 | .30 |
| ☐ 1 Bob Boyd | 4.00 | 1.60 | .40 |
| ☐ 2 Rudy Bukich | 5.00 | 2.00 | .50 |
| ☐ 3 Don Burroughs | 3.00 | 1.20 | .30 |
| ☐ 4 Jim Cason | 3.00 | 1.20 | .30 |
| ☐ 5 Leon Clarke | 4.00 | 1.60 | .40 |
| ☐ 6 Dick Daugherty | 3.00 | 1.20 | .30 |
| ☐ 7 Jack Ellena | 3.00 | 1.20 | .30 |
| ☐ 8 Tom Fears | 12.00 | 5.00 | 1.20 |
| ☐ 9 Sid Fournet | 3.00 | 1.20 | .30 |
| ☐ 10 Bob Fry | 3.00 | 1.20 | .30 |
| ☐ 11 Sid Gillman and | 6.00 | 2.40 | .60 |
| Coaches: Joe Madro, | | | |
| Jack Faulkner, | | | |
| Joe Thomas, and | | | |
| Lowell Storm | | | |

| | | NRMT | VG-E | GOOD |
|---|---|---|---|---|
| ☐ 12 | Bob Griffin | 3.00 | 1.20 | .30 |
| ☐ 13 | Art Hauser | 3.00 | 1.20 | .30 |
| ☐ 14 | Elroy Hirsch | 15.00 | 6.00 | 1.50 |
| ☐ 15 | John Hock | 3.00 | 1.20 | .30 |
| ☐ 16 | Bob Holladay | 3.00 | 1.20 | .30 |
| ☐ 17 | Glenn Holtzman | 3.00 | 1.20 | .30 |
| ☐ 18 | Bob Kelley ANN | 3.00 | 1.20 | .30 |
| ☐ 19 | Joe Marconi | 4.00 | 1.60 | .40 |
| ☐ 20 | Bud McFadin | 3.00 | 1.20 | .30 |
| ☐ 21 | Paul Miller | 3.00 | 1.20 | .30 |
| ☐ 22 | Ron Miller | 3.00 | 1.20 | .30 |
| ☐ 23 | Larry Morris | 3.00 | 1.20 | .30 |
| ☐ 24 | John Morrow | 3.00 | 1.20 | .30 |
| ☐ 25 | Brad Myers | 3.00 | 1.20 | .30 |
| ☐ 26 | Hugh Pitts | 3.00 | 1.20 | .30 |
| ☐ 27 | Duane Putnam | 3.00 | 1.20 | .30 |
| ☐ 28 | Les Richter | 5.00 | 2.00 | .50 |
| ☐ 29 | Bill Sherman | 4.00 | 1.60 | .40 |
| ☐ 30 | Charley Toogood | 3.00 | 1.20 | .30 |
| ☐ 31 | Norm Van Brocklin | 20.00 | 8.00 | 2.00 |
| ☐ 32 | Bill Wade | 5.00 | 2.00 | .50 |
| ☐ 33 | Ron Waller | 4.00 | 1.60 | .40 |
| ☐ 34 | Duane Wardlow | 3.00 | 1.20 | .30 |
| ☐ 35 | Jesse Whittenton | 4.00 | 1.60 | .40 |
| ☐ 36 | Tom Wilson | 4.00 | 1.60 | .40 |
| ☐ 37 | Paul (Tank) Younger | 6.00 | 2.40 | .60 |

# 1957 Rams Black Border

This 38-card team-issued set measures approximately 4 1/4" by 6 3/8" and features posed action shots on the front surrounded by black borders with the player's signature across the picture. The card backs contain biographical information about the player listing the player's name, height, weight, age, number of years in NFL, and college. We have checklisted this (unnumbered) set in alphabetical order. The set was available direct from the team as part of a package for their fans. Many cards from the 1953-1955 and 1957 Rams Team Issue Black Border sets are identical except for text differences on the card backs. Player stat lines are also helpful in identifying year of issue; the year of issue is typically the next year after the last year on the stats. The first few words of the first line of text is listed for players without stat lines. The set features the first card appearance of Jack Pardee.

| | | NRMT | VG-E | GOOD |
|---|---|---|---|---|
| | COMPLETE SET (38) | 150.00 | 60.00 | 15.00 |
| | COMMON PLAYER (1-38) | 3.00 | 1.20 | .30 |
| ☐ 1 | Jon Arnett | 7.50 | 3.00 | .75 |
| ☐ 2 | Bob Boyd | 4.00 | 1.60 | .40 |
| | (Frequently called ...) | | | |
| ☐ 3 | Alex Bravo | 3.00 | 1.20 | .30 |
| ☐ 4 | Bill Brundige ANN | 3.00 | 1.20 | .30 |
| ☐ 5 | Don Burroughs | 3.00 | 1.20 | .30 |
| ☐ 6 | Jerry Castete | 3.00 | 1.20 | .30 |
| ☐ 7 | Leon Clarke | 4.00 | 1.60 | .40 |
| ☐ 8 | Paige Cothren | 3.00 | 1.20 | .30 |
| ☐ 9 | Dick Daugherty | 3.00 | 1.20 | .30 |
| | (Has the ...) | | | |
| ☐ 10 | Bob Dougherty | 3.00 | 1.20 | .30 |
| ☐ 11 | Bob Fry | 3.00 | 1.20 | .30 |
| | (One of the ...) | | | |
| ☐ 12 | Frank Fuller | 3.00 | 1.20 | .30 |
| | (One of the ...) | | | |
| ☐ 13 | Sid Gillman and | 12.00 | 5.00 | 1.20 |
| | Coaches: Joe Madro, George Allen, Jack Faulkner, and Lowell Storm | | | |
| ☐ 14 | Bob Griffin | 3.00 | 1.20 | .30 |
| | (After four ...) | | | |
| ☐ 15 | Art Hauser | 3.00 | 1.20 | .30 |

| | | NRMT | VG-E | GOOD |
|---|---|---|---|---|
| | (One of the ...) | | | |
| ☐ 16 | Elroy Hirsch | 15.00 | 6.00 | 1.50 |
| | (A legendary ...) | | | |
| ☐ 17 | John Hock | 3.00 | 1.20 | .30 |
| | (Teamed with ...) | | | |
| ☐ 18 | Glenn Holtzman | 3.00 | 1.20 | .30 |
| ☐ 19 | John Houser | 3.00 | 1.20 | .30 |
| ☐ 20 | Bob Kelley ANN | 3.00 | 1.20 | .30 |
| | (Signature near right border of photo) | | | |
| ☐ 21 | Lamar Lundy | 7.50 | 3.00 | .75 |
| ☐ 22 | Joe Marconi | 3.00 | 1.20 | .30 |
| ☐ 23 | Paul Miller | 3.00 | 1.20 | .30 |
| | (From a ...) | | | |
| ☐ 24 | Larry Morris | 3.00 | 1.20 | .30 |
| ☐ 25 | Ken Panfil | 3.00 | 1.20 | .30 |
| ☐ 26 | Jack Pardee | 15.00 | 6.00 | 1.50 |
| ☐ 27 | Duane Putnam | 3.00 | 1.20 | .30 |
| | (Named to a ...) | | | |
| ☐ 28 | Les Richter | 5.00 | 2.00 | .50 |
| | (One of the ...) | | | |
| ☐ 29 | Will Sherman | 4.00 | 1.60 | .40 |
| | (One of the ...) | | | |
| ☐ 30 | Del Shofner | 7.50 | 3.00 | .75 |
| ☐ 31 | Billy Ray Smith | 5.00 | 2.00 | .50 |
| ☐ 32 | George Strugar | 3.00 | 1.20 | .30 |
| ☐ 33 | Norm Van Brocklin | 20.00 | 8.00 | 2.00 |
| | (When Van Brocklin ...) | | | |
| ☐ 34 | Bill Wade | 5.00 | 2.00 | .50 |
| | (In the first ...) | | | |
| ☐ 35 | Ron Waller | 3.00 | 1.20 | .30 |
| ☐ 36 | Jesse Whittenton | 3.00 | 1.20 | .30 |
| ☐ 37 | Tom Wilson | 4.00 | 1.60 | .40 |
| ☐ 38 | Paul (Tank) Younger | 6.00 | 2.40 | .60 |
| | (One of a ...) | | | |

# 1959 Rams Bell Brand

Fullback — Ollie Matson — LA Rams

The 1959 Bell Brand Los Angeles Rams set contains 40 numbered cards each measuring 2 1/2" by 3 1/2". The catalog designation for this set is F387-1. The obverses contain white-bordered color photos of the player with a facsimile autograph. The backs contain the card number, a short biography and vital statistics of the player, a Bell Brand ad, and advertisements for Los Angeles Rams' merchandise. These cards were issued as inserts in potato chip and corn chip bags in the Los Angeles area and are frequently found with oil stains from the chips. The set features the first card appearance of Frank Ryan.

| | | NRMT | VG-E | GOOD |
|---|---|---|---|---|
| | COMPLETE SET (40) | 1200.00 | 500.00 | 135.00 |
| | COMMON PLAYER (1-40) | 30.00 | 12.00 | 3.00 |
| ☐ 1 | Bill Wade | 40.00 | 16.00 | 4.00 |
| ☐ 2 | Buddy Humphrey | 30.00 | 12.00 | 3.00 |
| ☐ 3 | Frank Ryan | 50.00 | 20.00 | 5.00 |
| ☐ 4 | Ed Meador | 35.00 | 14.00 | 3.50 |
| ☐ 5 | Tom Wilson | 30.00 | 12.00 | 3.00 |
| ☐ 6 | Don Burroughs | 30.00 | 12.00 | 3.00 |
| ☐ 7 | Jon Arnett | 40.00 | 16.00 | 4.00 |
| ☐ 8 | Del Shofner | 50.00 | 20.00 | 5.00 |
| ☐ 9 | Jack Pardee | 50.00 | 20.00 | 5.00 |
| ☐ 10 | Ollie Matson | 75.00 | 30.00 | 7.50 |
| ☐ 11 | Joe Marconi | 30.00 | 12.00 | 3.00 |
| ☐ 12 | Jim Jones | 30.00 | 12.00 | 3.00 |
| ☐ 13 | Jack Morris | 30.00 | 12.00 | 3.00 |
| ☐ 14 | Willard Sherman | 35.00 | 14.00 | 3.50 |
| ☐ 15 | Clendon Thomas | 35.00 | 14.00 | 3.50 |
| ☐ 16 | Les Richter | 35.00 | 14.00 | 3.50 |
| ☐ 17 | John Morrow | 30.00 | 12.00 | 3.00 |
| ☐ 18 | Lou Michaels | 35.00 | 14.00 | 3.50 |
| ☐ 19 | Bob Reifsnyder | 30.00 | 12.00 | 3.00 |
| ☐ 20 | John Guzik | 30.00 | 12.00 | 3.00 |
| ☐ 21 | Duane Putnam | 30.00 | 12.00 | 3.00 |
| ☐ 22 | John Houser | 30.00 | 12.00 | 3.00 |
| ☐ 23 | Alex Lansford | 30.00 | 12.00 | 3.00 |

| | | | |
|---|---|---|---|
| ☐ 24 Gene Selawski | 35.00 | 14.00 | 3.50 |
| ☐ 25 John Baker | 30.00 | 12.00 | 3.00 |
| ☐ 26 Bob Fry | 30.00 | 12.00 | 3.00 |
| ☐ 27 John Lovetere | 30.00 | 12.00 | 3.00 |
| ☐ 28 George Strugar | 30.00 | 12.00 | 3.00 |
| ☐ 29 Roy Wilkins | 30.00 | 12.00 | 3.00 |
| ☐ 30 Charley Bradshaw | 30.00 | 12.00 | 3.00 |
| ☐ 31 Gene Brito | 35.00 | 14.00 | 3.50 |
| ☐ 32 Jim Phillips | 35.00 | 14.00 | 3.50 |
| ☐ 33 Leon Clarke | 35.00 | 14.00 | 3.50 |
| ☐ 34 Lamar Lundy | 40.00 | 16.00 | 4.00 |
| ☐ 35 Sam Williams | 30.00 | 12.00 | 3.00 |
| ☐ 36 Sid Gillman CO | 50.00 | 20.00 | 5.00 |
| ☐ 37 Jack Faulkner CO | 30.00 | 12.00 | 3.00 |
| ☐ 38 Joe Madro CO | 30.00 | 12.00 | 3.00 |
| ☐ 39 Don Paul CO | 30.00 | 12.00 | 3.00 |
| ☐ 40 Lou Rymkus CO | 35.00 | 14.00 | 3.50 |

## 1960 Rams Bell Brand

End      DEL SHOFNER      L.A. Rams

The 1960 Bell Brand Los Angeles Rams Football set contains 39 cards in a format similar to the 1959 Bell Brand set. The cards again measure 2 1/2" by 3 1/2". The fronts of the cards have distinctive yellow borders. The catalog designation for this set is F387-2. Card numbers 1-18, except number 2, are repeated photos from the 1959 set and were available throughout the 1960 season. Numbers 19-39 were available later in the 1960 season. These cards were issued as inserts in potato chip and corn chip bags in the Los Angeles area and are frequently found with oil stains from the chips. Card number 2 Selawski was withdrawn early in the year (after he was cut from the team) and was available only upon request from the company; therefore he is not included in the complete set price below.

| | NRMT | VG-E | GOOD |
|---|---|---|---|
| COMPLETE SET (38) | 1500.00 | 650.00 | 160.00 |
| COMMON PLAYER (1-18) | 25.00 | 10.00 | 2.50 |
| COMMON PLAYER (19-39) | 50.00 | 20.00 | 5.00 |

| | | | |
|---|---|---|---|
| ☐ 1 Joe Marconi | 25.00 | 10.00 | 2.50 |
| ☐ 2 Gene Selawski SP | 1000.00 | 400.00 | 125.00 |
| ☐ 3 Frank Ryan | 40.00 | 16.00 | 4.00 |
| ☐ 4 Ed Meador | 30.00 | 12.00 | 3.00 |
| ☐ 5 Tom Wilson | 25.00 | 10.00 | 2.50 |
| ☐ 6 Gene Brito | 30.00 | 12.00 | 3.00 |
| ☐ 7 Jon Arnett | 35.00 | 14.00 | 3.50 |
| ☐ 8 Alex Lansford | 25.00 | 10.00 | 2.50 |
| ☐ 9 Jack Pardee | 45.00 | 18.00 | 4.50 |
| ☐ 10 Ollie Matson | 60.00 | 24.00 | 6.00 |
| ☐ 11 John Lovetere | 25.00 | 10.00 | 2.50 |
| ☐ 12 Bill Jolko | 25.00 | 10.00 | 2.50 |
| ☐ 13 Jim Phillips | 30.00 | 12.00 | 3.00 |
| ☐ 14 Lamar Lundy | 35.00 | 14.00 | 3.50 |
| ☐ 15 Del Shofner | 40.00 | 16.00 | 4.00 |
| ☐ 16 Les Richter | 30.00 | 12.00 | 3.00 |
| ☐ 17 Bill Wade | 35.00 | 14.00 | 3.50 |
| ☐ 18 Lou Michaels | 30.00 | 12.00 | 3.00 |
| ☐ 19 Dick Bass | 60.00 | 24.00 | 6.00 |
| ☐ 20 Charley Britt | 50.00 | 20.00 | 5.00 |
| ☐ 21 Willard Sherman | 60.00 | 24.00 | 6.00 |
| ☐ 22 George Strugar | 50.00 | 20.00 | 5.00 |
| ☐ 23 Bob Long | 50.00 | 20.00 | 5.00 |
| ☐ 24 Danny Villanueva | 60.00 | 24.00 | 6.00 |
| ☐ 25 Jim Boeke | 50.00 | 20.00 | 5.00 |
| ☐ 26 Clendon Thomas | 50.00 | 20.00 | 5.00 |
| ☐ 27 Art Hunter | 50.00 | 20.00 | 5.00 |
| ☐ 28 Carl Karldivacz | 50.00 | 20.00 | 5.00 |
| ☐ 29 John Baker | 50.00 | 20.00 | 5.00 |
| ☐ 30 Charley Bradshaw | 50.00 | 20.00 | 5.00 |
| ☐ 31 John Guzik | 50.00 | 20.00 | 5.00 |
| ☐ 32 Buddy Humphrey | 50.00 | 20.00 | 5.00 |
| ☐ 33 Carroll Dale | 60.00 | 24.00 | 6.00 |
| ☐ 34 Don Ellensick | 50.00 | 20.00 | 5.00 |
| ☐ 35 Ray Hord | 50.00 | 20.00 | 5.00 |

| | | | |
|---|---|---|---|
| ☐ 36 Charles Janerette | 50.00 | 20.00 | 5.00 |
| ☐ 37 John Kenerson | 50.00 | 20.00 | 5.00 |
| ☐ 38 Jerry Stalcup | 50.00 | 20.00 | 5.00 |
| ☐ 39 Bob Waterfield CO | 90.00 | 36.00 | 9.00 |

## 1987 Rams Jello/General Foods

This ten-card set was sponsored by Jello and Birds Eye and features players of the Los Angeles Rams. The cards measure the standard 2 1/2" by 3 1/2". The cards are numbered on the back; card backs are printed in black ink on heavy white card stock. The set comes as a perforated sheet including a coupon each for Birds Eye Cob Corn and any Jello product. This unnumbered set is listed below alphabetically.

| | MINT | EXC | G-VG |
|---|---|---|---|
| COMPLETE SET (10) | 7.50 | 3.00 | .75 |
| COMMON PLAYER (1-10) | .35 | .14 | .03 |

| | | | |
|---|---|---|---|
| ☐ 1 Ron Brown | .50 | .20 | .05 |
| ☐ 2 Nolan Cromwell | .60 | .24 | .06 |
| ☐ 3 Eric Dickerson | 3.00 | 1.20 | .30 |
| ☐ 4 Carl Ekern | .35 | .14 | .03 |
| ☐ 5 Jim Everett | 1.50 | .60 | .15 |
| ☐ 6 Dennis Harrah | .50 | .20 | .05 |
| ☐ 7 LeRoy Irvin | .50 | .20 | .05 |
| ☐ 8 Mike Lansford | .35 | .14 | .03 |
| ☐ 9 Jackie Slater | .60 | .24 | .06 |
| ☐ 10 Doug Smith | .50 | .20 | .05 |

## 1987 Rams Oscar Mayer

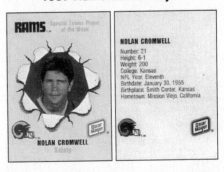

This 19-card standard-size (2 1/2" by 3 1/2") set was sponsored by Oscar Mayer to honor the Special Teams Player of the Week. On a light blue background, the front features a color head shot inside a bullet hole design, with the jagged edges of the paper turned out. The team helmet and sponsor logo appear below the head shot. In dark blue print on white, the backs have biographical information as well as the Rams' helmet and the sponsor logo. The cards are unnumbered and checklisted below in alphabetical order.

| | MINT | EXC | G-VG |
|---|---|---|---|
| COMPLETE SET (19) | 15.00 | 6.00 | 1.50 |
| COMMON PLAYER (1-19) | .75 | .30 | .07 |

| | | | |
|---|---|---|---|
| ☐ 1 Sam Anno | .75 | .30 | .07 |
| ☐ 2 Ron Brown | 1.00 | .40 | .10 |
| ☐ 3 Nolan Cromwell | 1.25 | .50 | .12 |
| ☐ 4 Henry Ellard | 1.50 | .60 | .15 |
| ☐ 5 Jerry Gray | 1.00 | .40 | .10 |
| ☐ 6 Kevin Greene | 1.50 | .60 | .15 |

| | | | |
|---|---|---|---|
| ☐ 7 Mike Guman | .75 | .30 | .07 |
| ☐ 8 Dale Hatcher | .75 | .30 | .07 |
| ☐ 9 Clifford Hicks | .75 | .30 | .07 |
| ☐ 10 Mark Jerue | .75 | .30 | .07 |
| ☐ 11 Johnnie Johnson | 1.00 | .40 | .10 |
| ☐ 12 Larry Kelm | 1.00 | .40 | .10 |
| ☐ 13 Mike Lansford | .75 | .30 | .07 |
| ☐ 14 Vince Newsome | .75 | .30 | .07 |
| ☐ 15 Michael Stewart | .75 | .30 | .07 |
| ☐ 16 Mickey Sutton | .75 | .30 | .07 |
| ☐ 17 Tim Tyrrell | .75 | .30 | .07 |
| ☐ 18 Norwood Vann | .75 | .30 | .07 |
| ☐ 19 Charles White | 1.25 | .50 | .12 |

## 1992 Rams Carl's Jr.

This 21-card safety set was sponsored by Carl's Jr. restaurants and distributed by the Orange County Sheriff's Department. The cards measure the standard size (2 1/2" by 3 1/2"). It was reported that 80,000 sets were produced. Eleven Rams players participated in the program with autograph sessions at six Carl's Junior restaurants in Southern California. The fronts feature color action player photos inside a blue picture frame on a white card face. Player information appears below the photo between a Rams' helmet and a "Drug Use is Life Abuse" warning. Printed in black on white, the horizontal backs have a black-and-white headshot, biography, player profile, and an anti-drug or alcohol slogan. The cards are numbered on the back.

| | MINT | EXC | G-VG |
|---|---|---|---|
| COMPLETE SET (21) | 15.00 | 6.00 | 1.50 |
| COMMON PLAYER (1-18) | .60 | .24 | .06 |
| ☐ 1 Carl Karcher | .75 | .30 | .07 |
| (Founder) | | | |
| ☐ 2 Happy Star | .75 | .30 | .07 |
| (Carl's Jr. symbol) | | | |
| ☐ 3 Tony Zendejas | .60 | .24 | .06 |
| ☐ 4 Henry Ellard | 1.25 | .50 | .12 |
| ☐ 5 Jackie Slater | .75 | .30 | .07 |
| ☐ 6 Bern Brostek | .60 | .24 | .06 |
| ☐ 7 Cleveland Gary | 1.00 | .40 | .10 |
| ☐ 8 Larry Kelm | .75 | .30 | .07 |
| ☐ 9 Roman Phifer | .75 | .30 | .07 |
| ☐ 10 Jim Everett | 1.25 | .50 | .12 |
| ☐ 11 Anthony Newman | .60 | .24 | .06 |
| ☐ 12 Steve Israel | .75 | .30 | .07 |
| ☐ 13 Marc Boutte | .75 | .30 | .07 |
| ☐ 14 Darryl Henley | .75 | .30 | .07 |
| ☐ 15 Michael Stewart | .60 | .24 | .06 |
| ☐ 16 Flipper Anderson | 1.00 | .40 | .10 |
| ☐ 17 Kevin Greene | 1.00 | .40 | .10 |
| ☐ 18 Sean Gilbert | 1.25 | .50 | .12 |
| ☐ NNO Skippy | 1.50 | .60 | .15 |
| Be Drug Free | | | |
| ☐ NNO Spike | 1.50 | .60 | .15 |
| Be Drug Free | | | |
| ☐ NNO Wise Owl Mike | 1.50 | .60 | .15 |
| Be Drug Free | | | |

## 1969 Redskins High's Dairy

This eight-card set was sponsored by High's Dairy Stores and measures approximately 8" by 10". The front has white borders and a full color painting of the player by Alex Fournier, with the player's signature near the bottom of the portrait. The plain white back gives biographical and statistical information on the player on its left side, and information about Fournier on the right. The High's logo rests in the lower right. The cards are unnumbered and checklisted below in alphabetical order.

| | NRMT | VG-E | GOOD |
|---|---|---|---|
| COMPLETE SET (8) | 75.00 | 30.00 | 7.50 |
| COMMON PLAYER (1-8) | 6.00 | 2.40 | .60 |
| ☐ 1 Chris Hanburger | 10.00 | 4.00 | 1.00 |
| ☐ 2 Len Hauss | 7.50 | 3.00 | .75 |
| ☐ 3 Sam Huff | 12.00 | 5.00 | 1.20 |
| ☐ 4 Sonny Jurgensen | 20.00 | 8.00 | 2.00 |
| ☐ 5 Carl Kammerer | 6.00 | 2.40 | .60 |
| ☐ 6 Brig Owens | 6.00 | 2.40 | .60 |
| ☐ 7 Pat Richter | 7.50 | 3.00 | .75 |
| ☐ 8 Charley Taylor | 15.00 | 6.00 | 1.50 |

## 1991 Redskins Mobil Schedules

Distributed at area Mobil stations, this 16-piece tri-fold paper schedule set measures 2 1/2" by 3 1/2" when folded and features a color action shot of Art Monk on the front with the Mobil logo on the back. When completely opened, the left panel contains the preseason and postseason schedule while the right panel presents the regular season schedule. The center panel features a full color action player shot. The player's name, biography, and profile appear on the following fold. The schedules are unnumbered and checklisted below in alphabetical order.

| | MINT | EXC | G-VG |
|---|---|---|---|
| COMPLETE SET (16) | 7.50 | 3.00 | .75 |
| COMMON PLAYER (1-16) | .40 | .16 | .04 |
| ☐ 1 Earnest Byner | .60 | .24 | .06 |
| ☐ 2 Gary Clark | 1.00 | .40 | .10 |
| ☐ 3 Andre Collins | .60 | .24 | .06 |
| ☐ 4 Kurt Gouveia | .40 | .16 | .04 |
| ☐ 5 Darrell Green | 1.00 | .40 | .10 |
| ☐ 6 Jimmie Johnson | .40 | .16 | .04 |
| ☐ 7 Markus Koch | .40 | .16 | .04 |
| ☐ 8 Jim Lachey | .60 | .24 | .06 |
| ☐ 9 Chip Lohmiller | .40 | .16 | .04 |
| ☐ 10 Charles Mann | .60 | .24 | .06 |
| ☐ 11 Martin Mayhew | .40 | .16 | .04 |
| ☐ 12 Art Monk | 1.25 | .50 | .12 |
| ☐ 13 Mark Rypien | 1.00 | .40 | .10 |
| ☐ 14 Mark Schlereth | .40 | .16 | .04 |
| ☐ 15 Ed Simmons | .40 | .16 | .04 |
| ☐ 16 Eric Williams | .40 | .16 | .04 |

## 1992 Redskins Mobil Schedules

Distributed at area Mobil stations, this 16-piece tri-fold paper schedule set measures 2 1/2" by 3 1/2" when folded and features a color action shot of Fred Stokes sacking Jim Kelly on the front with the Mobil logo on the back. When completely opened, the left panel contains the preseason and postseason schedule while the right panel contains the

| | MINT | EXC | G-VG |
|---|---|---|---|
| ☐ 12 Brian Mitchell | .75 | .30 | .07 |
| ☐ 13 Mark Rypien | .75 | .30 | .07 |
| ☐ 14 Ricky Sanders | 1.00 | .40 | .10 |
| ☐ 15 Mark Schlereth | .40 | .16 | .04 |
| ☐ 16 Ed Simmons | .40 | .16 | .04 |

## 1993 Rice Council *

Sponsored by the USA Rice Council (Houston, Texas), this ten-card set of recipe trading cards was issued to promote the consumption of rice. Measuring the standard size (2 1/2" by 3 1/2"), the fronts feature color photos with either blue or red borders. The player's name appears in black lettering in an orange stripe beneath the picture. The backs present biographical information, career summary, a favorite rice recipe, an up-close trivia fact, and the athlete's favorite charity to which the profits generated from the sale of the cards will be donated. The sports represented in this set are baseball (1, 3, 7), football (2, 5), tennis (4), swimming (6), and bobsledding (8). The cards are numbered on the back.

| | MINT | EXC | G-VG |
|---|---|---|---|
| COMPLETE SET (10) | 8.00 | 3.25 | .80 |
| COMMON PLAYER (1-10) | .35 | .14 | .03 |
| ☐ 1 Steve Sax | .50 | .20 | .05 |
| ☐ 2 Troy Aikman | 4.00 | 1.60 | .40 |
| ☐ 3 Roger Clemens | 2.00 | .80 | .20 |
| ☐ 4 Zina Garrison | .50 | .20 | .05 |
| ☐ 5 Warren Moon | 1.00 | .40 | .10 |
| ☐ 6 Summer Sanders | .75 | .30 | .07 |
| ☐ 7 Steve Sax | .50 | .20 | .05 |
| ☐ 8 Brian Shimer | .35 | .14 | .03 |
| ☐ 9 Food Guide Pyramid | .35 | .14 | .03 |
| ☐ 10 Ten Tips to Healthy  Eating for Kids | .35 | .14 | .03 |

regular season schedule. The center panel features a full color action player shot. The player's name, biography, and profile appear on the following fold. The schedules are unnumbered and checklisted below in alphabetical order.

| | MINT | EXC | G-VG |
|---|---|---|---|
| COMPLETE SET (16) | 7.50 | 3.00 | .75 |
| COMMON PLAYER (1-16) | .40 | .16 | .04 |
| ☐ 1 Gary Clark | 1.00 | .40 | .10 |
| ☐ 2 Brad Edwards | .40 | .16 | .04 |
| ☐ 3 Ricky Ervins | 1.00 | .40 | .10 |
| ☐ 4 Jumpy Geathers | .60 | .24 | .06 |
| ☐ 5 Darrell Green | 1.00 | .40 | .10 |
| ☐ 6 Joe Jacoby | .40 | .16 | .04 |
| ☐ 7 Tim Johnson | .40 | .16 | .04 |
| ☐ 8 Charles Mann | .60 | .24 | .06 |
| ☐ 9 Wilber Marshall | .75 | .30 | .07 |
| ☐ 10 Ron Middleton | .40 | .16 | .04 |
| ☐ 11 Brian Mitchell | .75 | .30 | .07 |
| ☐ 12 Art Monk | 1.25 | .50 | .12 |
| ☐ 13 Jim Lachey | .60 | .24 | .06 |
| ☐ 14 Chip Lohmiller | .40 | .16 | .04 |
| ☐ 15 Mark Rypien | .75 | .30 | .07 |
| ☐ 16 Fred Stokes | .40 | .16 | .04 |

## 1993 Redskins Mobil Schedules

Distributed at area Mobil stations, this 16-piece tri-fold paper schedule set measures 2 1/2" by 3 1/2" when folded and features a color action shot of Andre Collins tackling Emmitt Smith on the front with the Mobil logo on the back. When completely opened, the left panel contains the preseason and postseason schedule while the right panel contains the regular season schedule. The center panel features a full color action player shot. The player's name, biography, and profile appear on the following fold. The schedules are unnumbered and checklisted below in alphabetical order.

| | MINT | EXC | G-VG |
|---|---|---|---|
| COMPLETE SET (16) | 7.50 | 3.00 | .75 |
| COMMON PLAYER (1-16) | .40 | .16 | .04 |
| ☐ 1 Todd Bowles | .40 | .16 | .04 |
| ☐ 2 Ernest Byner | .60 | .24 | .06 |
| ☐ 3 Monte Coleman | .60 | .24 | .06 |
| ☐ 4 Andre Collins | .60 | .24 | .06 |
| ☐ 5 Shane Collins | .40 | .16 | .04 |
| ☐ 6 Danny Copeland | .40 | .16 | .04 |
| ☐ 7 Kurt Gouveia | .40 | .16 | .04 |
| ☐ 8 Darrell Green | 1.00 | .40 | .10 |
| ☐ 9 A.J. Johnson | .60 | .24 | .06 |
| ☐ 10 Jim Lachey | .60 | .24 | .06 |
| ☐ 11 Ron Middleton | .40 | .16 | .04 |

## 1974 Saints Circle Inset

Each of these 22 photos measures approximately 10" by 8". The fronts feature black-and-white action player photos with white borders. In one of the upper corners, a black-and-white headshot appears in a circle. The player's name, position, and team name are printed in the lower border. The backs are blank. The photos are unnumbered and checklisted below in alphabetical order. The year of issue for this set is clearly determined by the fact that Jack DeGrenier's only year with the Saints was 1974; in addition 1974 was the first year with the Saints for Tom Blanchard, Larry Cipa, Don Coleman, Phil LaPorta, Alvin Maxson, Rod McNeill, Rick Middleton, Joel Parker, Terry Schmidt, Paul Seal, and Dave Thompson and the last year with the Saints for John Beasley, Odell Lawson, Jerry Moore, and Jess Phillips.

|  | MINT | EXC | G-VG |
|---|---|---|---|
| COMPLETE SET (22) | 100.00 | 40.00 | 10.00 |
| COMMON PLAYER (1-22) | 5.00 | 2.00 | .50 |
| ☐ 1 John Beasley | 5.00 | 2.00 | .50 |
| ☐ 2 Tom Blanchard | 6.00 | 2.40 | .60 |
| ☐ 3 Larry Cipa | 5.00 | 2.00 | .50 |
| ☐ 4 Don Coleman | 5.00 | 2.00 | .50 |
| ☐ 5 Wayne Colman | 5.00 | 2.00 | .50 |
| ☐ 6 Jack DeGrenier | 5.00 | 2.00 | .50 |
| ☐ 7 Rick Kingrea | 5.00 | 2.00 | .50 |
| ☐ 8 Phil LaPorta | 5.00 | 2.00 | .50 |
| ☐ 9 Odell Lawson | 5.00 | 2.00 | .50 |
| ☐ 10 Archie Manning | 20.00 | 8.00 | 2.00 |
| ☐ 11 Alvin Maxson | 7.50 | 3.00 | .75 |
| ☐ 12 Bill McClard | 6.00 | 2.40 | .60 |
| ☐ 13 Rod McNeill | 5.00 | 2.00 | .50 |
| ☐ 14 Jim Merlo | 6.00 | 2.40 | .60 |
| ☐ 15 Rick Middleton | 5.00 | 2.00 | .50 |
| ☐ 16 Derland Moore | 6.00 | 2.40 | .60 |
| ☐ 17 Jerry Moore | 5.00 | 2.00 | .50 |
| ☐ 18 Joel Parker | 5.00 | 2.00 | .50 |
| ☐ 19 Jess Phillips | 5.00 | 2.00 | .50 |
| ☐ 20 Terry Schmidt | 5.00 | 2.00 | .50 |
| ☐ 21 Paul Seal | 5.00 | 2.00 | .50 |
| ☐ 22 Dave Thompson | 5.00 | 2.00 | .50 |

## 1979 Saints Coke

The 1979 Coca-Cola New Orleans Saints set contains 45 black and white cards with red borders. The cards measure 2 1/2" by 3 1/2". The Coca-Cola logo appears in the upper right hand corner while a New Orleans Saints helmet appears in the lower left. The backs of this gray stock card contain minimal biographical data, the card number and the Coke logo. The cards were produced in conjunction with Topps. There were also unnumbered ad cards for Coke, Mr. Pibb, and Sprite, one of which was included in each pack of cards.

|  | NRMT | VG-E | GOOD |
|---|---|---|---|
| COMPLETE SET (45) | 45.00 | 18.00 | 4.50 |
| COMMON PLAYER (1-45) | .75 | .30 | .07 |
| ☐ 1 Archie Manning | 7.50 | 3.00 | .75 |
| ☐ 2 Ed Burns | .75 | .30 | .07 |
| ☐ 3 Bobby Scott | 1.50 | .60 | .15 |
| ☐ 4 Russell Erxleben | 1.25 | .50 | .12 |
| ☐ 5 Eric Felton | .75 | .30 | .07 |
| ☐ 6 David Gray | .75 | .30 | .07 |
| ☐ 7 Ricky Ray | .75 | .30 | .07 |
| ☐ 8 Clarence Chapman | .75 | .30 | .07 |
| ☐ 9 Kim Jones | .75 | .30 | .07 |
| ☐ 10 Mike Strachan | 1.00 | .40 | .10 |
| ☐ 11 Tony Galbreath | 1.50 | .60 | .15 |
| ☐ 12 Tom Myers | 1.25 | .50 | .12 |
| ☐ 13 Chuck Muncie | 2.50 | 1.00 | .25 |
| ☐ 14 Jack Holmes | .75 | .30 | .07 |
| ☐ 15 Don Schwartz | .75 | .30 | .07 |
| ☐ 16 Ralph McGill | .75 | .30 | .07 |
| ☐ 17 Ken Bordelon | .75 | .30 | .07 |
| ☐ 18 Jim Kovach | 1.00 | .40 | .10 |
| ☐ 19 Pat Hughes | .75 | .30 | .07 |
| ☐ 20 Reggie Mathis | .75 | .30 | .07 |
| ☐ 21 Jim Merlo | 1.00 | .40 | .10 |
| ☐ 22 Joe Federspiel | 1.00 | .40 | .10 |
| ☐ 23 Don Reese | .75 | .30 | .07 |
| ☐ 24 Roger Finnie | .75 | .30 | .07 |
| ☐ 25 John Hill | .75 | .30 | .07 |
| ☐ 26 Barry Bennett | .75 | .30 | .07 |
| ☐ 27 Dave Lafary | .75 | .30 | .07 |
| ☐ 28 Robert Woods | .75 | .30 | .07 |
| ☐ 29 Conrad Dobler | 1.50 | .60 | .15 |
| ☐ 30 John Watson | .75 | .30 | .07 |
| ☐ 31 Fred Sturt | .75 | .30 | .07 |
| ☐ 32 J.T. Taylor | .75 | .30 | .07 |

| ☐ 33 Mike Fultz | .75 | .30 | .07 |
|---|---|---|---|
| ☐ 34 Joe Campbell | .75 | .30 | .07 |
| ☐ 35 Derland Moore | 1.00 | .40 | .10 |
| ☐ 36 Elex Price | .75 | .30 | .07 |
| ☐ 37 Elois Grooms | .75 | .30 | .07 |
| ☐ 38 Emanuel Zanders | .75 | .30 | .07 |
| ☐ 39 Ike Harris | 1.00 | .40 | .10 |
| ☐ 40 Tinker Owens | 1.25 | .50 | .12 |
| ☐ 41 Rich Mauti | .75 | .30 | .07 |
| ☐ 42 Henry Childs | 1.00 | .40 | .10 |
| ☐ 43 Larry Hardy | .75 | .30 | .07 |
| ☐ 44 Brooks Williams | .75 | .30 | .07 |
| ☐ 45 Wes Chandler | 5.00 | 2.00 | .50 |

## 1992 Saints McDag

This 32-card safety set was produced by McDag Productions Inc. for the New Orleans Saints and Behavioral Health Inc. The cards measure the standard size (2 1/2" by 3 1/2") and feature posed color player photos with white borders. The pictures are studio shots with a blue background. Running horizontally down the left is a wide brown stripe with the team name and year in yellow outline lettering. A mustard stripe at the bottom of the photo intersects the brown stripe and contains the player's name. The backs are white with black print and carry biographical information, career highlights, and "Tips from the Team" in the form of public service messages. There is also an address and phone number for obtaining free cards. The cards are unnumbered and checklisted below in alphabetical order.

|  | MINT | EXC | G-VG |
|---|---|---|---|
| COMPLETE SET (32) | 10.00 | 4.00 | 1.00 |
| COMMON CARD (1-32) | .25 | .10 | .02 |
| ☐ 1 Morten Andersen | .50 | .20 | .05 |
| ☐ 2 Gene Atkins | .35 | .14 | .03 |
| ☐ 3 Toi Cook | .35 | .14 | .03 |
| ☐ 4 Tommy Barnhardt | .25 | .10 | .02 |
| ☐ 5 Hoby Brenner | .35 | .14 | .03 |
| ☐ 6 Stan Brock | .25 | .10 | .02 |
| ☐ 7 Vince Buck | .50 | .20 | .05 |
| ☐ 8 Wesley Carroll | .35 | .14 | .03 |
| ☐ 9 Jim Dombrowski | .25 | .10 | .02 |
| ☐ 10 Vaughn Dunbar | 1.00 | .40 | .10 |
| ☐ 11 Quinn Early | .50 | .20 | .05 |
| ☐ 12 Bobby Hebert | 1.00 | .40 | .10 |
| ☐ 13 Craig Heyward | .50 | .20 | .05 |
| ☐ 14 Joel Hilgenberg | .25 | .10 | .02 |
| ☐ 15 Dalton Hilliard | .50 | .20 | .05 |
| ☐ 16 Rickey Jackson | .50 | .20 | .05 |
| ☐ 17 Vaughan Johnson | .35 | .14 | .03 |
| ☐ 18 Reginald Jones | .35 | .14 | .03 |
| ☐ 19 Eric Martin | .50 | .20 | .05 |
| ☐ 20 Wayne Martin | .50 | .20 | .05 |
| ☐ 21 Brett Maxie | .25 | .10 | .02 |
| ☐ 22 Fred McAfee | .35 | .14 | .03 |
| ☐ 23 Sam Mills | .50 | .20 | .05 |
| ☐ 24 Jim Mora CO | .50 | .20 | .05 |
| ☐ 25 Pat Swilling | .75 | .30 | .07 |
| ☐ 26 John Tice | .35 | .14 | .03 |
| ☐ 27 Renaldo Turnbull | .50 | .20 | .05 |
| ☐ 28 Floyd Turner | .35 | .14 | .03 |
| ☐ 29 Steve Walsh | .50 | .20 | .05 |
| ☐ 30 Frank Warren | .25 | .10 | .02 |
| ☐ 31 Jim Wilks | .25 | .10 | .02 |
| ☐ 32 Saints Cheerleaders | .50 | .20 | .05 |

## 1962-63 Salada Coins

This 154-coin set features popular NFL and AFL players from selected teams. Each team had a specific rim color. The numbering of the coins is essentially by teams, i.e., Colts (1-11 blue), Packers (12-22 green),

49ers (23-33 salmon), Bears (34-44 black), Rams (45-55 yellow), Browns (56-66 black), Steelers (67-77 black), Lions (78-88 blue), Redskins (89-99 yellow), Eagles (100-110 green), Giants (111-121 blue), Patriots (122-132 salmon), Titans (133-143 blue), and Bills (144-154 salmon). All players are pictured without their helmets. The coins measure approximately 1 1/2" in diameter. The coin backs give the player's name, position, pro team, college, height, and weight. The coins were originally produced on sheets measuring 31 1/2" by 25"; the 255 coins on the sheet included the complete set as well as duplicates and triplicates. Double prints (DP) and triple prints (TP) are listed below. The double-printed coins are generally from certain teams, i.e., Packers, Bears, Browns, Lions, Eagles, Giants, Patriots, Titans, and Bills. Those coins below not listed explicitly as to the frequency of printing are in fact single printed (SP) and hence more difficult to find. The set is sometimes found intact as a presentation set in its own custom box; such a set would be valued 25 percent higher than the complete set price below.

|  | NRMT | VG-E | GOOD |
|---|---|---|---|
| COMPLETE SET (154) | 2700.00 | 1250.00 | 300.00 |
| COMMON PLAYER DP | 6.00 | 2.40 | .60 |
| COMMON PLAYER SP | 25.00 | 10.00 | 2.50 |
| ☐ 1 Johnny Unitas | 150.00 | 60.00 | 15.00 |
| ☐ 2 Lenny Moore | 80.00 | 32.00 | 8.00 |
| ☐ 3 Jim Parker | 50.00 | 20.00 | 5.00 |
| ☐ 4 Gino Marchetti | 60.00 | 24.00 | 6.00 |
| ☐ 5 Dick Szymanski | 25.00 | 10.00 | 2.50 |
| ☐ 6 Alex Sandusky | 25.00 | 10.00 | 2.50 |
| ☐ 7 Raymond Berry | 80.00 | 32.00 | 8.00 |
| ☐ 8 Jimmy Orr | 30.00 | 12.00 | 3.00 |
| ☐ 9 Ordell Braase | 25.00 | 10.00 | 2.50 |
| ☐ 10 Bill Pellington | 25.00 | 10.00 | 2.50 |
| ☐ 11 Bob Boyd | 25.00 | 10.00 | 2.50 |
| ☐ 12 Paul Hornung DP | 25.00 | 10.00 | 2.50 |
| ☐ 13 Jim Taylor DP | 20.00 | 8.00 | 2.00 |
| ☐ 14 Henry Jordan DP | 6.00 | 2.40 | .60 |
| ☐ 15 Dan Currie DP | 6.00 | 2.40 | .60 |
| ☐ 16 Bill Forester DP | 6.00 | 2.40 | .60 |
| ☐ 17 Dave Hanner DP | 6.00 | 2.40 | .60 |
| ☐ 18 Bart Starr DP | 30.00 | 12.00 | 3.00 |
| ☐ 19 Max McGee DP | 7.50 | 3.00 | .75 |
| ☐ 20 Jerry Kramer DP | 9.00 | 3.75 | .90 |
| ☐ 21 Forrest Gregg DP | 12.00 | 5.00 | 1.20 |
| ☐ 22 Jim Ringo DP | 12.00 | 5.00 | 1.20 |
| ☐ 23 Billy Kilmer | 50.00 | 20.00 | 5.00 |
| ☐ 24 Charlie Krueger | 25.00 | 10.00 | 2.50 |
| ☐ 25 Bob St. Clair | 50.00 | 20.00 | 5.00 |
| ☐ 26 Abe Woodson | 25.00 | 10.00 | 2.50 |
| ☐ 27 Jimmy Johnson | 60.00 | 24.00 | 6.00 |
| ☐ 28 Matt Hazeltine | 25.00 | 10.00 | 2.50 |
| ☐ 29 Bruce Bosley | 25.00 | 10.00 | 2.50 |
| ☐ 30 Dan Conners | 25.00 | 10.00 | 2.50 |
| ☐ 31 John Brodie | 80.00 | 32.00 | 8.00 |
| ☐ 32 J.D. Smith | 25.00 | 10.00 | 2.50 |
| ☐ 33 Monty Stickles | 25.00 | 10.00 | 2.50 |
| ☐ 34 Johnny Morris DP | 9.00 | 3.75 | .90 |
| ☐ 35 Stan Jones DP | 12.00 | 5.00 | 1.20 |
| ☐ 36 J.C. Caroline DP | 6.00 | 2.40 | .60 |
| ☐ 37 Richie Petitbon DP | 9.00 | 3.75 | .90 |
| ☐ 38 Joe Fortunato DP | 9.00 | 3.75 | .90 |
| ☐ 39 Larry Morris DP | 6.00 | 2.40 | .60 |
| ☐ 40 Doug Atkins DP | 12.00 | 5.00 | 1.20 |
| ☐ 41 Billy Wade DP | 7.50 | 3.00 | .75 |
| ☐ 42 Rick Casares DP | 9.00 | 3.75 | .90 |
| ☐ 43 Willie Galimore DP | 9.00 | 3.75 | .90 |
| ☐ 44 Angelo Coia DP | 6.00 | 2.40 | .60 |
| ☐ 45 Ollie Matson | 60.00 | 24.00 | 6.00 |
| ☐ 46 Carroll Dale | 30.00 | 12.00 | 3.00 |
| ☐ 47 Ed Meador | 30.00 | 12.00 | 3.00 |
| ☐ 48 Jon Arnett | 35.00 | 14.00 | 3.50 |
| ☐ 49 Joe Marconi | 25.00 | 10.00 | 2.50 |
| ☐ 50 John LoVetere | 25.00 | 10.00 | 2.50 |
| ☐ 51 Red Phillips | 25.00 | 10.00 | 2.50 |
| ☐ 52 Zeke Bratkowski | 35.00 | 14.00 | 3.50 |
| ☐ 53 Dick Bass | 30.00 | 12.00 | 3.00 |
| ☐ 54 Les Richter | 30.00 | 12.00 | 3.00 |
| ☐ 55 Art Hunter DP | 6.00 | 2.40 | .60 |
| ☐ 56 Jim Brown TP | 60.00 | 24.00 | 6.00 |
| ☐ 57 Mike McCormack DP | 12.00 | 5.00 | 1.20 |
| ☐ 58 Bob Gain DP | 6.00 | 2.40 | .60 |
| ☐ 59 Paul Wiggin DP | 7.50 | 3.00 | .75 |
| ☐ 60 Jim Houston DP | 7.50 | 3.00 | .75 |
| ☐ 61 Ray Renfro DP | 7.50 | 3.00 | .75 |
| ☐ 62 Galen Fiss DP | 6.00 | 2.40 | .60 |
| ☐ 63 J.R. Smith DP | 6.00 | 2.40 | .60 |
| ☐ 64 John Morrow DP | 6.00 | 2.40 | .60 |
| ☐ 65 Gene Hickerson DP | 6.00 | 2.40 | .60 |
| ☐ 66 Jim Ninowski DP | 7.50 | 3.00 | .75 |
| ☐ 67 Tom Tracy | 30.00 | 12.00 | 3.00 |
| ☐ 68 Buddy Dial | 30.00 | 12.00 | 3.00 |
| ☐ 69 Mike Sandusky | 25.00 | 10.00 | 2.50 |
| ☐ 70 Lou Michaels | 30.00 | 12.00 | 3.00 |
| ☐ 71 Preston Carpenter | 25.00 | 10.00 | 2.50 |
| ☐ 72 John Reger | 25.00 | 10.00 | 2.50 |
| ☐ 73 John Henry Johnson | 60.00 | 24.00 | 6.00 |
| ☐ 74 Gene Lipscomb | 40.00 | 16.00 | 4.00 |
| ☐ 75 Mike Henry | 30.00 | 12.00 | 3.00 |
| ☐ 76 George Tarasovic | 25.00 | 10.00 | 2.50 |
| ☐ 77 Bobby Layne | 70.00 | 28.00 | 7.00 |
| ☐ 78 Harley Sewell DP | 6.00 | 2.40 | .60 |
| ☐ 79 Darris McCord DP | 6.00 | 2.40 | .60 |
| ☐ 80 Yale Lary DP | 12.00 | 5.00 | 1.20 |
| ☐ 81 Jim Gibbons DP | 6.00 | 2.40 | .60 |
| ☐ 82 Gail Cogdill DP | 6.00 | 2.40 | .60 |
| ☐ 83 Nick Pietrosante DP | 9.00 | 3.75 | .90 |
| ☐ 84 Alex Karras DP | 15.00 | 6.00 | 1.50 |
| ☐ 85 Dick Lane DP | 12.00 | 5.00 | 1.20 |
| ☐ 86 Joe Schmidt DP | 15.00 | 6.00 | 1.50 |
| ☐ 87 John Gordy DP | 6.00 | 2.40 | .60 |
| ☐ 88 Milt Plum DP | 7.50 | 3.00 | .75 |
| ☐ 89 Andy Stynchula | 25.00 | 10.00 | 2.50 |
| ☐ 90 Bob Toneff | 25.00 | 10.00 | 2.50 |
| ☐ 91 Bill Anderson | 25.00 | 10.00 | 2.50 |
| ☐ 92 Sam Horner | 25.00 | 10.00 | 2.50 |
| ☐ 93 Norm Snead | 30.00 | 12.00 | 3.00 |
| ☐ 94 Bobby Mitchell | 60.00 | 24.00 | 6.00 |
| ☐ 95 Billy Barnes | 25.00 | 10.00 | 2.50 |
| ☐ 96 Rod Breedlove | 25.00 | 10.00 | 2.50 |
| ☐ 97 Fred Hageman | 25.00 | 10.00 | 2.50 |
| ☐ 98 Vince Promuto | 25.00 | 10.00 | 2.50 |
| ☐ 99 Joe Rutgens | 25.00 | 10.00 | 2.50 |
| ☐ 100 Maxie Baughan DP | 9.00 | 3.75 | .90 |
| ☐ 101 Pete Retzlaff DP | 7.50 | 3.00 | .75 |
| ☐ 102 Tom Brookshier DP | 9.00 | 3.75 | .90 |
| ☐ 103 Sonny Jurgensen DP | 20.00 | 8.00 | 2.00 |
| ☐ 104 Ed Khayat DP | 6.00 | 2.40 | .60 |
| ☐ 105 Chuck Bednarik DP | 15.00 | 6.00 | 1.50 |
| ☐ 106 Tommy McDonald DP | 9.00 | 3.75 | .90 |
| ☐ 107 Bobby Walston DP | 6.00 | 2.40 | .60 |
| ☐ 108 Ted Dean DP | 6.00 | 2.40 | .60 |
| ☐ 109 Clarence Peaks DP | 6.00 | 2.40 | .60 |
| ☐ 110 Jimmy Carr DP | 6.00 | 2.40 | .60 |
| ☐ 111 Sam Huff DP | 15.00 | 6.00 | 1.50 |
| ☐ 112 Erich Barnes DP | 7.50 | 3.00 | .75 |
| ☐ 113 Del Shofner DP | 9.00 | 3.75 | .90 |
| ☐ 114 Bob Gaiters DP | 6.00 | 2.40 | .60 |
| ☐ 115 Alex Webster DP | 9.00 | 3.75 | .90 |
| ☐ 116 Dick Modzelewski DP | 7.50 | 3.00 | .75 |
| ☐ 117 Jim Katcavage DP | 7.50 | 3.00 | .75 |
| ☐ 118 Roosevelt Brown DP | 12.00 | 5.00 | 1.20 |
| ☐ 119 Y.A. Tittle DP | 25.00 | 10.00 | 2.50 |
| ☐ 120 Andy Robustelli DP | 12.00 | 5.00 | 1.20 |
| ☐ 121 Dick Lynch DP | 7.50 | 3.00 | .75 |
| ☐ 122 Don Webb DP | 6.00 | 2.40 | .60 |
| ☐ 123 Larry Eisenhauer DP | 6.00 | 2.40 | .60 |
| ☐ 124 Babe Parilli DP | 7.50 | 3.00 | .75 |
| ☐ 125 Charles Long DP | 6.00 | 2.40 | .60 |
| ☐ 126 Billy Lott DP | 6.00 | 2.40 | .60 |
| ☐ 127 Harry Jacobs DP | 6.00 | 2.40 | .60 |
| ☐ 128 Bob Dee DP | 6.00 | 2.40 | .60 |
| ☐ 129 Ron Burton DP | 7.50 | 3.00 | .75 |
| ☐ 130 Jim Colclough TP | 3.00 | 1.20 | .30 |
| ☐ 131 Gino Cappelletti DP | 9.00 | 3.75 | .90 |
| ☐ 132 Tommy Addison DP | 6.00 | 2.40 | .60 |
| ☐ 133 Larry Grantham DP | 7.50 | 3.00 | .75 |
| ☐ 134 Dick Christy DP | 6.00 | 2.40 | .60 |
| ☐ 135 Bill Mathis DP | 7.50 | 3.00 | .75 |
| ☐ 136 Butch Songin DP | 6.00 | 2.40 | .60 |
| ☐ 137 Dainard Paulson DP | 6.00 | 2.40 | .60 |
| ☐ 138 Roger Ellis DP | 6.00 | 2.40 | .60 |
| ☐ 139 Mike Hudock DP | 6.00 | 2.40 | .60 |
| ☐ 140 Don Maynard DP | 20.00 | 8.00 | 2.00 |
| ☐ 141 Al Dorow DP | 7.50 | 3.00 | .75 |
| ☐ 142 Jack Klotz DP | 6.00 | 2.40 | .60 |
| ☐ 143 Lee Riley DP | 6.00 | 2.40 | .60 |
| ☐ 144 Bill Atkins DP | 6.00 | 2.40 | .60 |
| ☐ 145 Art Baker DP | 6.00 | 2.40 | .60 |
| ☐ 146 Stew Barber DP | 6.00 | 2.40 | .60 |
| ☐ 147 Glen Bass DP | 6.00 | 2.40 | .60 |
| ☐ 148 Al Bemiller DP | 6.00 | 2.40 | .60 |
| ☐ 149 Richie Lucas DP | 7.50 | 3.00 | .75 |
| ☐ 150 Archie Matsos DP | 6.00 | 2.40 | .60 |
| ☐ 151 Warren Rabb DP | 6.00 | 2.40 | .60 |
| ☐ 152 Ken Rice DP | 6.00 | 2.40 | .60 |
| ☐ 153 Billy Shaw DP | 7.50 | 3.00 | .75 |
| ☐ 154 Laverne Torczon DP | 6.00 | 2.40 | .60 |

## 1959 San Giorgio Flipbooks

This 17-card set features members of the NFL in an action sequence. The set is sometimes referenced as the San Giorgio Macaroni Football Flipbooks. The set features only members of the Philadelphia Eagles, Pittsburgh Steelers, and Washington Redskins. When the flipbooks are still in the uncut form (which is most desirable), they measure approximately 5 3/4" by 3 9/16". The sheets are blank backed, in black and white, and provide 14 small numbered pages when cut apart.

| | NRMT | VG-E | GOOD |
|---|---|---|---|
| COMPLETE SET (17) | 1500.00 | 650.00 | 165.00 |
| COMMON PLAYER (1-17) | 100.00 | 40.00 | 10.00 |
| ☐ 1 Sam Baker | 125.00 | 50.00 | 12.50 |
| Washington Redskins | | | |
| ☐ 2 Billy Barnes | 100.00 | 40.00 | 10.00 |
| Philadelphia Eagles | | | |
| ☐ 3 Chuck Bednarik | 200.00 | 80.00 | 20.00 |
| Philadelphia Eagles | | | |
| ☐ 4 Don Bosseler | 100.00 | 40.00 | 10.00 |
| Washington Redskins | | | |
| ☐ 5 Pete Brewster | 100.00 | 40.00 | 10.00 |
| Pittsburgh Steelers | | | |
| ☐ 6 Jack Butler | 100.00 | 40.00 | 10.00 |
| Pittsburgh Steelers | | | |
| ☐ 7 Proverb Jacobs | 100.00 | 40.00 | 10.00 |
| Philadelphia Eagles | | | |
| ☐ 8 Eddie LeBaron | 150.00 | 60.00 | 15.00 |
| Washington Redskins | | | |
| ☐ 9 Tommy McDonald | 150.00 | 60.00 | 15.00 |
| Philadelphia Eagles | | | |
| ☐ 10 Ed Meadows | 100.00 | 40.00 | 10.00 |
| Philadelphia Eagles | | | |
| ☐ 11 Gern Nagler | 100.00 | 40.00 | 10.00 |
| Pittsburgh Steelers | | | |
| ☐ 12 Clarence Peaks | 100.00 | 40.00 | 10.00 |
| Philadelphia Eagles | | | |
| ☐ 13 Pete Retzlaff | 125.00 | 50.00 | 12.50 |
| Philadelphia Eagles | | | |
| ☐ 14 Mike Sommer | 100.00 | 40.00 | 10.00 |
| Washington Redskins | | | |
| ☐ 15 Tom Tracy | 125.00 | 50.00 | 12.50 |
| Pittsburgh Steelers | | | |
| ☐ 16 Bobby Walston | 100.00 | 40.00 | 10.00 |
| Philadelphia Eagles | | | |
| ☐ 17 Chuck Weber | 100.00 | 40.00 | 10.00 |
| Philadelphia Eagles | | | |

## 1989 Score Promos

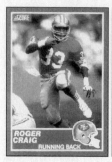

This set of six football cards was intended as a preview of Score's first football set, after two years of baseball card issues. The cards were sent out to prospective dealers along with the ordering forms for Score's debut football set. The cards are standard size, 2 1/2" by 3 1/2", and have full color on both sides. The cards are distinguishable

from the regular issue cards of the same numbers as indicated in the checklist below. One good way to recognize these promos is that the stats on the promo card backs are carried out to only one decimal place instead of two. In addition, the promo cards show a registered symbol (R with circle around it) rather than a trademark (TM) symbol.

| | MINT | EXC | G-VG |
|---|---|---|---|
| COMPLETE SET (6) | 75.00 | 30.00 | 7.50 |
| COMMON PLAYER (1-6) | 5.00 | 2.00 | .50 |
| ☐ 1 Joe Montana | 35.00 | 14.00 | 3.50 |
| San Francisco 49ers | | | |
| ☐ 2 Bo Jackson | 15.00 | 6.00 | 1.50 |
| Los Angeles Raiders | | | |
| ☐ 3 Boomer Esiason | 12.50 | 5.00 | 1.25 |
| Cincinnati Bengals | | | |
| ☐ 4 Roger Craig | 9.00 | 3.75 | .90 |
| San Francisco 49ers (Born: Preston, Mississippi, should be Davenport, Iowa) | | | |
| ☐ 5 Ed Too Tall Jones | 5.00 | 2.00 | .50 |
| Dallas Cowboys (Registered seven sacks, regular card issue has registered 7.0 sacks) | | | |
| ☐ 6 Phil Simms | 9.00 | 3.75 | .90 |
| New York Giants (Moorehead State, should say Morehead State; front photo cropped so that Score logo blocks part of the ball) | | | |

## 1989 Score

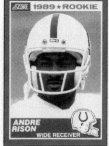
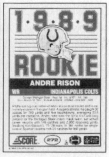

This set of 330 football cards was Score's first football set after two years of baseball card issues. The cards are very similar in design to the 1989 Score baseball cards. The cards are standard size, 2 1/2" by 3 1/2", and have full color on both sides. The front of the card shows the player in an action photo whereas the reverse photo of the player is a portrait. The first 244 cards in the set are regular player cards. Cards 245-272 are rookie cards of players drafted in the spring '89 NFL draft. Other creative subsets within this set are post-season action (273-275), "combo" cards showing related players like the Three Amigos (277-284), All-Pro selections (285-309), Speedburners (310-317), Predators (318-325), and Record Breakers (326-329). The last card in the set is a tribute to Tom Landry. The noteworthy Rookie Cards in this set are Troy Aikman, Steve Atwater, Don Beebe, Steve Beuerlein, Brian Blades, Bubby Brister, Tim Brown, Mark Carrier, Cris Carter, Gaston Green, Michael Irvin, Keith Jackson, Reggie Langhorne, Don Majkowski, Eric Metcalf, Anthony Miller, Chris Miller, Andre Rison, Mark Rypien, Barry Sanders, Deion Sanders, John Stephens, John Taylor, Broderick Thomas, Derrick Thomas, Thurman Thomas, and Rod Woodson.

| | MINT | EXC | G-VG |
|---|---|---|---|
| COMPLETE SET (330) | 140.00 | 65.00 | 17.50 |
| COMPLETE FACT.SET (330) | 150.00 | 70.00 | 19.00 |
| COMMON PLAYER (1-330) | .10 | .05 | .01 |
| ☐ 1 Joe Montana | 4.00 | 1.80 | .50 |
| San Francisco 49ers | | | |
| ☐ 2 Bo Jackson | 1.50 | .65 | .19 |
| Los Angeles Raiders | | | |
| ☐ 3 Boomer Esiason | .40 | .18 | .05 |
| Cincinnati Bengals | | | |
| ☐ 4 Roger Craig | .15 | .07 | .02 |
| San Francisco 49ers | | | |
| ☐ 5 Ed Too Tall Jones | .15 | .07 | .02 |
| Dallas Cowboys | | | |
| ☐ 6 Phil Simms | .35 | .16 | .04 |

New York Giants
☐ 7 Dan Hampton .......................... .12 .05 .02
Chicago Bears
☐ 8 John Settle ................................ .10 .05 .01
Atlanta Falcons
☐ 9 Bernie Kosar ........................... .15 .07 .02
Cleveland Browns
☐ 10 Al Toon ................................... .12 .05 .02
New York Jets
☐ 11 Bubby Brister ........................ .50 .23 .06
Pittsburgh Steelers
☐ 12 Mark Clayton ......................... .12 .05 .02
Miami Dolphins
☐ 13 Dan Marino ............................ 4.00 1.80 .50
Miami Dolphins
☐ 14 Joe Morris .............................. .12 .05 .02
New York Giants
☐ 15 Warren Moon ......................... 1.50 .65 .19
Houston Oilers
☐ 16 Chuck Long ............................ .12 .05 .02
Detroit Lions
☐ 17 Mark Jackson ........................ .12 .05 .02
Denver Broncos
☐ 18 Michael Irvin .......................... 20.00 9.00 2.50
Dallas Cowboys
☐ 19 Bruce Smith ........................... .50 .23 .06
Buffalo Bills
☐ 20 Anthony Carter ...................... .15 .07 .02
Minnesota Vikings
☐ 21 Charles Haley ........................ .12 .05 .02
San Francisco 49ers
☐ 22 Dave Duerson ........................ .10 .05 .01
Chicago Bears
☐ 23 Troy Stradford ....................... .10 .05 .01
Miami Dolphins
☐ 24 Freeman McNeil ..................... .12 .05 .02
New York Jets
☐ 25 Jerry Gray .............................. .10 .05 .01
Los Angeles Rams
☐ 26 Bill Maas ................................ .12 .05 .02
Kansas City Chiefs
☐ 27 Chris Chandler ....................... .50 .23 .06
Indianapolis Colts
☐ 28 Tom Newberry ........................ .30 .14 .04
Los Angeles Rams
☐ 29 Albert Lewis ........................... .12 .05 .02
Kansas City Chiefs
☐ 30 Jay Schroeder ........................ .12 .05 .02
Los Angeles Raiders
☐ 31 Dalton Hilliard ........................ .12 .05 .02
New Orleans Saints
☐ 32 Tony Eason ............................ .12 .05 .02
New England Patriots
☐ 33 Rick Donnelly UER ................. .10 .05 .01
(229.11 yards per punt)
Atlanta Falcons
☐ 34 Herschel Walker ..................... .40 .18 .05
Dallas Cowboys
☐ 35 Wesley Walker ....................... .12 .05 .02
New York Jets
☐ 36 Chris Doleman ....................... .50 .23 .06
Minnesota Vikings
☐ 37 Pat Swilling ............................ .40 .18 .05
New Orleans Saints
☐ 38 Joey Browner .......................... .12 .05 .02
Minnesota Vikings
☐ 39 Shane Conlan ......................... .10 .05 .01
Buffalo Bills
☐ 40 Mike Tomczak ........................ .12 .05 .02
Chicago Bears
☐ 41 Webster Slaughter .................. .40 .18 .05
Cleveland Browns
☐ 42 Ray Donaldson ....................... .10 .05 .01
Indianapolis Colts
☐ 43 Christian Okoye ...................... .12 .05 .02
Kansas City Chiefs
☐ 44 John Bosa ............................... .10 .05 .01
Miami Dolphins
☐ 45 Aaron Cox .............................. .20 .09 .03
Los Angeles Rams
☐ 46 Bobby Hebert ......................... .25 .11 .03
New Orleans Saints
☐ 47 Carl Banks ............................. .12 .05 .02
New York Giants
☐ 48 Jeff Fuller .............................. .10 .05 .01
San Francisco 49ers
☐ 49 Gerald Willhite ....................... .10 .05 .01
Denver Broncos
☐ 50 Mike Singletary ...................... .15 .07 .02
Chicago Bears
☐ 51 Stanley Morgan ...................... .12 .05 .02
New England Patriots
☐ 52 Mark Bavaro ........................... .12 .05 .02
New York Giants
☐ 53 Mickey Shuler ........................ .10 .05 .01
New York Jets
☐ 54 Keith Millard ........................... .12 .05 .02
Minnesota Vikings

☐ 55 Andre Tippett .......................... .12 .05 .02
New England Patriots
☐ 56 Vance Johnson ....................... .12 .05 .02
Denver Broncos
☐ 57 Bennie Blades ........................ .35 .16 .04
Detroit Lions
☐ 58 Tim Harris ............................... .12 .05 .02
Green Bay Packers
☐ 59 Hanford Dixon ......................... .10 .05 .01
Cleveland Browns
☐ 60 Chris Miller ............................. 3.00 1.35 .40
Atlanta Falcons
☐ 61 Cornelius Bennett .................... .75 .35 .09
Buffalo Bills
☐ 62 Neal Anderson ........................ .40 .18 .05
Chicago Bears
☐ 63 Ickey Woods UER ................... .12 .05 .02
(Jersey is 31 but
listed as 30
on card back)
Cincinnati Bengals
☐ 64 Gary Anderson ........................ .12 .05 .02
San Diego Chargers
☐ 65 Vaughan Johnson ................... 1.00 .45 .13
New Orleans Saints
☐ 66 Ronnie Lippett ........................ .10 .05 .01
New England Patriots
☐ 67 Mike Quick .............................. .12 .05 .02
Philadelphia Eagles
☐ 68 Roy Green ............................... .12 .05 .02
Phoenix Cardinals
☐ 69 Tim Krumrie ............................ .10 .05 .01
Cincinnati Bengals
☐ 70 Mark Malone ........................... .12 .05 .02
San Diego Chargers
☐ 71 James Jones ........................... .10 .05 .01
Detroit Lions
☐ 72 Cris Carter ............................. 4.00 1.80 .50
Philadelphia Eagles
☐ 73 Ricky Nattiel ........................... .10 .05 .01
Denver Broncos
☐ 74 Jim Arnold UER ...................... .10 .05 .01
(238.83 yards per punt)
Detroit Lions
☐ 75 Randall Cunningham ............... .75 .35 .09
Philadelphia Eagles
☐ 76 John L. Williams ..................... .12 .05 .02
Seattle Seahawks
☐ 77 Paul Gruber ............................ .25 .11 .03
Tampa Bay Buccaneers
☐ 78 Rod Woodson .......................... 3.50 1.55 .45
Pittsburgh Steelers
☐ 79 Ray Childress .......................... .12 .05 .02
Houston Oilers
☐ 80 Doug Williams ......................... .12 .05 .02
Washington Redskins
☐ 81 Deron Cherry .......................... .12 .05 .02
Kansas City Chiefs
☐ 82 John Offerdahl ........................ .12 .05 .02
Miami Dolphins
☐ 83 Louis Lipps ............................. .12 .05 .02
Pittsburgh Steelers
☐ 84 Neil Lomax .............................. .12 .05 .02
Phoenix Cardinals
☐ 85 Wade Wilson ........................... .12 .05 .02
Minnesota Vikings
☐ 86 Tim Brown ............................... 7.00 3.10 .85
Los Angeles Raiders
☐ 87 Chris Hinton ........................... .12 .05 .02
Indianapolis Colts
☐ 88 Stump Mitchell ........................ .12 .05 .02
Phoenix Cardinals
☐ 89 Tunch Ilkin ............................. .10 .05 .01
Pittsburgh Steelers
☐ 90 Steve Pelluer .......................... .12 .05 .02
Dallas Cowboys
☐ 91 Brian Noble ............................. .12 .05 .02
Green Bay Packers
☐ 92 Reggie White .......................... 1.00 .45 .13
Philadelphia Eagles
☐ 93 Aundray Bruce ........................ .25 .11 .03
Atlanta Falcons
☐ 94 Garry James ........................... .10 .05 .01
Detroit Lions
☐ 95 Drew Hill ................................. .15 .07 .02
Houston Oilers
☐ 96 Anthony Munoz ....................... .12 .05 .02
Cincinnati Bengals
☐ 97 James Wilder ........................... .12 .05 .02
Tampa Bay Buccaneers
☐ 98 Dexter Manley .......................... .12 .05 .02
Washington Redskins
☐ 99 Lee Williams ............................ .12 .05 .02
San Diego Chargers
☐ 100 Dave Krieg .............................. .12 .05 .02
Seattle Seahawks
☐ 101A Keith Jackson ERR ............... 5.00 2.30 .60

| | | | |
|---|---|---|---|
| (Listed as 84 on card back) Philadelphia Eagles | | | |
| ☐ 101B Keith Jackson COR | 5.00 | 2.30 | .60 |
| (Listed as 88 on card back) Philadelphia Eagles | | | |
| ☐ 102 Luis Sharpe | .10 | .05 | .01 |
| Phoenix Cardinals | | | |
| ☐ 103 Kevin Greene | .25 | .11 | .03 |
| Los Angeles Rams | | | |
| ☐ 104 Duane Bickett | .12 | .05 | .02 |
| Indianapolis Colts | | | |
| ☐ 105 Mark Rypien | 1.50 | .65 | .19 |
| Washington Redskins | | | |
| ☐ 106 Curt Warner | .12 | .05 | .02 |
| Seattle Seahawks | | | |
| ☐ 107 Jacob Green | .12 | .05 | .02 |
| Seattle Seahawks | | | |
| ☐ 108 Gary Clark | .40 | .18 | .05 |
| Washington Redskins | | | |
| ☐ 109 Bruce Matthews | .75 | .35 | .09 |
| Houston Oilers | | | |
| ☐ 110 Bill Fralic | .12 | .05 | .02 |
| Atlanta Falcons | | | |
| ☐ 111 Bill Bates | .10 | .05 | .01 |
| Dallas Cowboys | | | |
| ☐ 112 Jeff Bryant | .10 | .05 | .01 |
| Seattle Seahawks | | | |
| ☐ 113 Charles Mann | .12 | .05 | .02 |
| Washington Redskins | | | |
| ☐ 114 Richard Dent | .12 | .05 | .02 |
| Chicago Bears | | | |
| ☐ 115 Bruce Hill | .10 | .05 | .01 |
| Tampa Bay Buccaneers | | | |
| ☐ 116 Mark May | .12 | .05 | .02 |
| Washington Redskins | | | |
| ☐ 117 Mark Collins | .30 | .14 | .04 |
| New York Giants | | | |
| ☐ 118 Ron Holmes | .10 | .05 | .01 |
| Tampa Bay Buccaneers | | | |
| ☐ 119 Scott Case | .20 | .09 | .03 |
| Atlanta Falcons | | | |
| ☐ 120 Tom Rathman | .12 | .05 | .02 |
| San Francisco 49ers | | | |
| ☐ 121 Dennis McKinnon | .10 | .05 | .01 |
| Chicago Bears | | | |
| ☐ 122A Ricky Sanders ERR | .50 | .23 | .06 |
| (Listed as 46 on card back) Washington Redskins | | | |
| ☐ 122B Ricky Sanders COR | 1.25 | .55 | .16 |
| (Listed as 83 on card back) Washington Redskins | | | |
| ☐ 123 Michael Carter | .12 | .05 | .02 |
| San Francisco 49ers | | | |
| ☐ 124 Ozzie Newsome | .25 | .11 | .03 |
| Cleveland Browns | | | |
| ☐ 125 Irving Fryar UER | .12 | .05 | .02 |
| New England Patriots ("wide reveiver") | | | |
| ☐ 126A Ron Hall ERR | .25 | .11 | .03 |
| Tampa Bay Buccaneers (Both photos actually someone else, a black player, whereas Hall is white) | | | |
| ☐ 126B Ron Hall COR | .75 | .35 | .09 |
| Tampa Bay Buccaneers | | | |
| ☐ 127 Clay Matthews | .12 | .05 | .02 |
| Cleveland Browns | | | |
| ☐ 128 Leonard Marshall | .12 | .05 | .02 |
| New York Giants | | | |
| ☐ 129 Kevin Mack | .12 | .05 | .02 |
| Cleveland Browns | | | |
| ☐ 130 Art Monk | .30 | .14 | .04 |
| Washington Redskins | | | |
| ☐ 131 Garin Veris | .10 | .05 | .01 |
| New England Patriots | | | |
| ☐ 132 Steve Jordan | .12 | .05 | .02 |
| Minnesota Vikings | | | |
| ☐ 133 Frank Minnifield | .10 | .05 | .01 |
| Cleveland Browns | | | |
| ☐ 134 Eddie Brown | .12 | .05 | .02 |
| Cincinnati Bengals | | | |
| ☐ 135 Stacey Bailey | .10 | .05 | .01 |
| Atlanta Falcons | | | |
| ☐ 136 Rickey Jackson | .12 | .05 | .02 |
| New Orleans Saints | | | |
| ☐ 137 Henry Ellard | .12 | .05 | .02 |
| Los Angeles Rams | | | |
| ☐ 138 Jim Burt | .12 | .05 | .02 |
| New York Giants | | | |
| ☐ 139 Jerome Brown | .12 | .05 | .02 |
| Philadelphia Eagles | | | |
| ☐ 140 Rodney Holman | .50 | .23 | .06 |
| Cincinnati Bengals | | | |
| ☐ 141 Sammy Winder | .10 | .05 | .01 |
| Denver Broncos | | | |
| ☐ 142 Marcus Cotton | .10 | .05 | .01 |
| Atlanta Falcons | | | |
| ☐ 143 Jim Jeffcoat | .12 | .05 | .02 |
| Dallas Cowboys | | | |
| ☐ 144 Rueben Mayes | .12 | .05 | .02 |
| New Orleans Saints | | | |
| ☐ 145 Jim McMahon | .15 | .07 | .02 |
| Chicago Bears | | | |
| ☐ 146 Reggie Williams | .12 | .05 | .02 |
| Cincinnati Bengals | | | |
| ☐ 147 John Anderson | .10 | .05 | .01 |
| Green Bay Packers | | | |
| ☐ 148 Harris Barton | .30 | .14 | .04 |
| San Francisco 49ers | | | |
| ☐ 149 Phillip Epps | .10 | .05 | .01 |
| Green Bay Packers | | | |
| ☐ 150 Jay Hilgenberg | .12 | .05 | .02 |
| Chicago Bears | | | |
| ☐ 151 Earl Ferrell | .10 | .05 | .01 |
| Phoenix Cardinals | | | |
| ☐ 152 Andre Reed | .60 | .25 | .08 |
| Buffalo Bills | | | |
| ☐ 153 Dennis Gentry | .10 | .05 | .01 |
| Chicago Bears | | | |
| ☐ 154 Max Montoya | .10 | .05 | .01 |
| Cincinnati Bengals | | | |
| ☐ 155 Darrin Nelson | .12 | .05 | .02 |
| Minnesota Vikings | | | |
| ☐ 156 Jeff Chadwick | .12 | .05 | .02 |
| Detroit Lions | | | |
| ☐ 157 James Brooks | .12 | .05 | .02 |
| Cincinnati Bengals | | | |
| ☐ 158 Keith Bishop | .10 | .05 | .01 |
| Denver Broncos | | | |
| ☐ 159 Robert Awalt | .10 | .05 | .01 |
| Phoenix Cardinals | | | |
| ☐ 160 Marty Lyons | .12 | .05 | .02 |
| New York Jets | | | |
| ☐ 161 Johnny Hector | .12 | .05 | .02 |
| New York Jets | | | |
| ☐ 162 Tony Casillas | .10 | .05 | .01 |
| Atlanta Falcons | | | |
| ☐ 163 Kyle Clifton | .35 | .16 | .04 |
| New York Jets | | | |
| ☐ 164 Cody Risien | .12 | .05 | .02 |
| Cleveland Browns | | | |
| ☐ 165 Jamie Holland | .10 | .05 | .01 |
| San Diego Chargers | | | |
| ☐ 166 Merril Hoge | .50 | .23 | .06 |
| Pittsburgh Steelers | | | |
| ☐ 167 Chris Spielman | .75 | .35 | .09 |
| Detroit Lions | | | |
| ☐ 168 Carlos Carson | .12 | .05 | .02 |
| Kansas City Chiefs | | | |
| ☐ 169 Jerry Ball | .35 | .16 | .04 |
| Detroit Lions | | | |
| ☐ 170 Don Majkowski | .50 | .23 | .06 |
| Green Bay Packers | | | |
| ☐ 171 Everson Walls | .10 | .05 | .01 |
| Dallas Cowboys | | | |
| ☐ 172 Mike Rozier | .12 | .05 | .02 |
| Houston Oilers | | | |
| ☐ 173 Matt Millen | .12 | .05 | .02 |
| Los Angeles Raiders | | | |
| ☐ 174 Karl Mecklenburg | .12 | .05 | .02 |
| Denver Broncos | | | |
| ☐ 175 Paul Palmer | .10 | .05 | .01 |
| Kansas City Chiefs | | | |
| ☐ 176 Brian Blades UER | 2.00 | .90 | .25 |
| (Photo on back is reversed negative) Seattle Seahawks | | | |
| ☐ 177 Brent Fullwood | .10 | .05 | .01 |
| Green Bay Packers | | | |
| ☐ 178 Anthony Miller | 6.00 | 2.70 | .75 |
| San Diego Chargers | | | |
| ☐ 179 Brian Sochia | .12 | .05 | .02 |
| Miami Dolphins | | | |
| ☐ 180 Stephen Baker | .40 | .18 | .05 |
| New York Giants | | | |
| ☐ 181 Jesse Solomon | .10 | .05 | .01 |
| Minnesota Vikings | | | |
| ☐ 182 John Grimsley | .10 | .05 | .01 |
| Houston Oilers | | | |
| ☐ 183 Timmy Newsome | .10 | .05 | .01 |
| Dallas Cowboys | | | |
| ☐ 184 Steve Sewell | .10 | .05 | .01 |
| Denver Broncos | | | |
| ☐ 185 Dean Biasucci | .10 | .05 | .01 |
| Indianapolis Colts | | | |
| ☐ 186 Alonzo Highsmith | .10 | .05 | .01 |
| Houston Oilers | | | |
| ☐ 187 Randy Grimes | .10 | .05 | .01 |
| Tampa Bay Buccaneers | | | |
| ☐ 188A Mark Carrier ERR | 3.50 | 1.55 | .45 |

| | | | |
|---|---|---|---|
| (Photo on back is actually Bruce Hill) Tampa Bay Buccaneers | | | |
| ☐ 188B Mark Carrier COR............. (Wearing helmet in photo on back) Tampa Bay Buccaneers | 3.50 | 1.55 | .45 |
| ☐ 189 Vann McElroy.................... Los Angeles Raiders | .10 | .05 | .01 |
| ☐ 190 Greg Bell......................... Los Angeles Rams | .12 | .05 | .02 |
| ☐ 191 Quinn Early..................... San Diego Chargers | .75 | .35 | .09 |
| ☐ 192 Lawrence Taylor................ New York Giants | .60 | .25 | .08 |
| ☐ 193 Albert Bentley................. Indianapolis Colts | .10 | .05 | .01 |
| ☐ 194 Ernest Givins.................. Houston Oilers | .12 | .05 | .02 |
| ☐ 195 Jackie Slater.................. Los Angeles Rams | .12 | .05 | .02 |
| ☐ 196 Jim Sweeney................... New York Jets | .12 | .05 | .02 |
| ☐ 197 Freddie Joe Nunn.............. Phoenix Cardinals | .12 | .05 | .02 |
| ☐ 198 Keith Byars.................... Philadelphia Eagles | .15 | .07 | .02 |
| ☐ 199 Hardy Nickerson............... Pittsburgh Steelers | 1.00 | .45 | .13 |
| ☐ 200 Steve Beuerlein............... Los Angeles Raiders | 3.50 | 1.55 | .45 |
| ☐ 201 Bruce Armstrong............... New England Patriots | .20 | .09 | .03 |
| ☐ 202 Lionel Manuel.................. New York Giants | .10 | .05 | .01 |
| ☐ 203 J.T. Smith..................... Phoenix Cardinals | .10 | .05 | .01 |
| ☐ 204 Mark Ingram................... New York Giants | 1.00 | .45 | .13 |
| ☐ 205 Fred Smerlas.................. Buffalo Bills | .12 | .05 | .02 |
| ☐ 206 Bryan Hinkle................... Pittsburgh Steelers | .10 | .05 | .01 |
| ☐ 207 Steve McMichael............... Chicago Bears | .12 | .05 | .02 |
| ☐ 208 Nick Lowery................... Kansas City Chiefs | .12 | .05 | .02 |
| ☐ 209 Jack Trudeau.................. Indianapolis Colts | .12 | .05 | .02 |
| ☐ 210 Lorenzo Hampton............... Miami Dolphins | .10 | .05 | .01 |
| ☐ 211 Thurman Thomas................ Buffalo Bills | 20.00 | 9.00 | 2.50 |
| ☐ 212 Steve Young................... San Francisco 49ers | 2.50 | 1.15 | .30 |
| ☐ 213 James Lofton.................. Los Angeles Raiders | .30 | .14 | .04 |
| ☐ 214 Jim Covert.................... Chicago Bears | .10 | .05 | .01 |
| ☐ 215 Ronnie Lott................... San Francisco 49ers | .35 | .16 | .04 |
| ☐ 216 Stephone Paige................ Kansas City Chiefs | .12 | .05 | .02 |
| ☐ 217 Mark Duper.................... Miami Dolphins | .15 | .07 | .02 |
| ☐ 218A Willie Gault ERR.............. (Front photo actually 93 Greg Townsend) Los Angeles Raiders | .30 | .14 | .04 |
| ☐ 218B Willie Gault COR.............. (83 clearly visible) Los Angeles Raiders | .60 | .25 | .08 |
| ☐ 219 Ken Ruettgers................. Green Bay Packers | .20 | .09 | .03 |
| ☐ 220 Kevin Ross.................... Kansas City Chiefs | .40 | .18 | .05 |
| ☐ 221 Jerry Rice.................... San Francisco 49ers | 3.00 | 1.35 | .40 |
| ☐ 222 Billy Ray Smith................ San Diego Chargers | .12 | .05 | .02 |
| ☐ 223 Jim Kelly..................... Buffalo Bills | 1.50 | .65 | .19 |
| ☐ 224 Vinny Testaverde.............. Tampa Bay Buccaneers | .50 | .23 | .06 |
| ☐ 225 Steve Largent................. Seattle Seahawks | .75 | .35 | .09 |
| ☐ 226 Warren Williams............... Pittsburgh Steelers | .15 | .07 | .02 |
| ☐ 227 Morten Andersen.............. New Orleans Saints | .12 | .05 | .02 |
| ☐ 228 Bill Brooks................... Indianapolis Colts | .25 | .11 | .03 |
| ☐ 229 Reggie Langhorne.............. Cleveland Browns | 1.50 | .65 | .19 |
| ☐ 230 Pepper Johnson............... New York Giants | .12 | .05 | .02 |
| ☐ 231 Pat Leahy..................... New York Jets | .12 | .05 | .02 |

| | | | |
|---|---|---|---|
| ☐ 232 Fred Marion.................... New England Patriots | .10 | .05 | .01 |
| ☐ 233 Gary Zimmerman................ Minnesota Vikings | .12 | .05 | .02 |
| ☐ 234 Marcus Allen.................. Los Angeles Raiders | .75 | .35 | .09 |
| ☐ 235 Gaston Green.................. Los Angeles Rams | .50 | .23 | .06 |
| ☐ 236 John Stephens................. New England Patriots | 1.00 | .45 | .13 |
| ☐ 237 Terry Kinard.................. New York Giants | .12 | .05 | .02 |
| ☐ 238 John Taylor................... San Francisco 49ers | 3.00 | 1.35 | .40 |
| ☐ 239 Brian Bosworth................ Seattle Seahawks | .10 | .05 | .01 |
| ☐ 240 Anthony Toney................. Philadelphia Eagles | .10 | .05 | .01 |
| ☐ 241 Ken O'Brien................... New York Jets | .12 | .05 | .02 |
| ☐ 242 Howie Long.................... Los Angeles Raiders | .15 | .07 | .02 |
| ☐ 243 Doug Flutie................... New England Patriots | .75 | .35 | .09 |
| ☐ 244 Jim Everett................... Los Angeles Rams | .30 | .14 | .04 |
| ☐ 245 Broderick Thomas.............. Tampa Bay Buccaneers | 1.00 | .45 | .13 |
| ☐ 246 Deion Sanders................. Atlanta Falcons | 8.00 | 3.60 | 1.00 |
| ☐ 247 Donnell Woolford............... Chicago Bears | .75 | .35 | .09 |
| ☐ 248 Wayne Martin.................. New Orleans Saints | .60 | .25 | .08 |
| ☐ 249 David Williams................ Houston Oilers | .25 | .11 | .03 |
| ☐ 250 Bill Hawkins.................. Los Angeles Rams | .10 | .05 | .01 |
| ☐ 251 Eric Hill..................... Phoenix Cardinals | .25 | .11 | .03 |
| ☐ 252 Burt Grossman................. San Diego Chargers | .40 | .18 | .05 |
| ☐ 253 Tracy Rocker.................. Washington Redskins | .10 | .05 | .01 |
| ☐ 254 Steve Wisniewski.............. Los Angeles Raiders | .50 | .23 | .06 |
| ☐ 255 Jessie Small.................. Philadelphia Eagles | .10 | .05 | .01 |
| ☐ 256 David Braxton................. Minnesota Vikings | .10 | .05 | .01 |
| ☐ 257 Barry Sanders................. Detroit Lions | 35.00 | 16.00 | 4.40 |
| ☐ 258 Derrick Thomas................ Kansas City Chiefs | 7.00 | 3.10 | .85 |
| ☐ 259 Eric Metcalf.................. Cleveland Browns | 3.00 | 1.35 | .40 |
| ☐ 260 Keith DeLong.................. San Francisco 49ers | .25 | .11 | .03 |
| ☐ 261 Hart Lee Dykes................ New England Patriots | .10 | .05 | .01 |
| ☐ 262 Sammie Smith................. Miami Dolphins | .12 | .05 | .02 |
| ☐ 263 Steve Atwater................. Denver Broncos | 1.50 | .65 | .19 |
| ☐ 264 Eric Ball..................... Cincinnati Bengals | .30 | .14 | .04 |
| ☐ 265 Don Beebe..................... Buffalo Bills | 2.50 | 1.15 | .30 |
| ☐ 266 Brian Williams................ New York Giants | .10 | .05 | .01 |
| ☐ 267 Jeff Lageman.................. New York Jets | .35 | .16 | .04 |
| ☐ 268 Tim Worley.................... Pittsburgh Steelers | .75 | .35 | .09 |
| ☐ 269 Tony Mandarich............... Green Bay Packers | .12 | .05 | .02 |
| ☐ 270 Troy Aikman................... Dallas Cowboys | 55.00 | 25.00 | 7.00 |
| ☐ 271 Andy Heck..................... Seattle Seahawks | .25 | .11 | .03 |
| ☐ 272 Andre Rison................... Indianapolis Colts | 7.00 | 3.10 | .85 |
| ☐ 273 AFC Championship.............. Bengals over Bills (Ickey Woods and Boomer Esiason) | .20 | .09 | .03 |
| ☐ 274 NFC Championship.............. 49ers over Bears (Joe Montana) | .75 | .35 | .09 |
| ☐ 275 Super Bowl XXIII............... 49ers over Bengals (Joe Montana and Jerry Rice) | 1.75 | .80 | .22 |
| ☐ 276 Rodney Carter................. Pittsburgh Steelers | .10 | .05 | .01 |
| ☐ 277 Mark Jackson,................. Vance Johnson, | .12 | .05 | .02 |

and Ricky Nattiel
Denver Broncos
☐ 278 John L. Williams .12 .05 .02
and Curt Warner
Seattle Seahawks
☐ 279 Joe Montana and 1.75 .80 .22
Jerry Rice
San Francisco 49ers
☐ 280 Roy Green and .12 .05 .02
Neil Lomax
Phoenix Cardinals
☐ 281 Randall Cunningham .50 .23 .06
and Keith Jackson
Philadelphia Eagles
☐ 282 Chris Doleman and .12 .05 .02
Keith Millard
Minnesota Vikings
☐ 283 Mark Duper and .15 .07 .02
Mark Clayton
Miami Dolphins
☐ 284 Marcus Allen and 1.00 .45 .13
Bo Jackson
Los Angeles Raiders
☐ 285 Frank Minnifield AP .12 .05 .02
Cleveland Browns
☐ 286 Bruce Matthews AP .12 .05 .02
Houston Oilers
☐ 287 Joey Browner AP .12 .05 .02
Minnesota Vikings
☐ 288 Jay Hilgenberg AP .12 .05 .02
Chicago Bears
☐ 289 Carl Lee AP .20 .09 .03
Minnesota Vikings
☐ 290 Scott Norwood AP .12 .05 .02
Buffalo Bills
☐ 291 John Taylor AP .60 .25 .08
San Francisco 49ers
☐ 292 Jerry Rice AP 1.50 .65 .19
San Francisco 49ers
☐ 293A Keith Jackson AP ERR 2.50 1.15 .30
(Listed as 84
on card back)
Philadelphia Eagles
☐ 293B Keith Jackson AP COR 2.50 1.15 .30
(Listed as 88
on card back)
Philadelphia Eagles
☐ 294 Gary Zimmerman AP .12 .05 .02
Minnesota Vikings
☐ 295 Lawrence Taylor AP .30 .14 .04
New York Giants
☐ 296 Reggie White AP .50 .23 .06
Philadelphia Eagles
☐ 297 Roger Craig AP .15 .07 .02
San Francisco 49ers
☐ 298 Boomer Esiason AP .25 .11 .03
Cincinnati Bengals
☐ 299 Cornelius Bennett AP .30 .14 .04
Buffalo Bills
☐ 300 Mike Horan AP .12 .05 .02
Denver Broncos
☐ 301 Deron Cherry AP .12 .05 .02
Kansas City Chiefs
☐ 302 Tom Newberry AP .12 .05 .02
Los Angeles Rams
☐ 303 Mike Singletary AP .15 .07 .02
Chicago Bears
☐ 304 Shane Conlan AP .12 .05 .02
Buffalo Bills
☐ 305A Tim Brown ERR AP 2.50 1.15 .30
(Photo on front act-
ually 80 James Lofton)
Los Angeles Raiders
☐ 305B Tim Brown COR AP 2.50 1.15 .30
(Dark jersey 81)
Los Angeles Raiders
☐ 306 Henry Ellard AP .12 .05 .02
Los Angeles Rams
☐ 307 Bruce Smith AP .25 .11 .03
Buffalo Bills
☐ 308 Tim Krumrie AP .12 .05 .02
Cincinnati Bengals
☐ 309 Anthony Munoz AP .15 .07 .02
Cincinnati Bengals
☐ 310 Darrell Green SPD .15 .07 .02
Washington Redskins
☐ 311 Anthony Miller SPD 1.50 .65 .19
San Diego Chargers
☐ 312 Wesley Walker SPD .12 .05 .02
New York Jets
☐ 313 Ron Brown SPD .12 .05 .02
Los Angeles Rams
☐ 314 Bo Jackson SPD .75 .35 .09
Los Angeles Raiders
☐ 315 Philip Epps SPD .12 .05 .02
Green Bay Packers
☐ 316A Eric Thomas ERR SPD .30 .14 .04
(Listed as 31

on card back)
Cincinnati Bengals
☐ 316B Eric Thomas COR SPD .60 .25 .08
(Listed as 22
on card back)
Cincinnati Bengals
☐ 317 Herschel Walker SPD .20 .09 .03
Dallas Cowboys
☐ 318 Jacob Green PRED .12 .05 .02
Seattle Seahawks
☐ 319 Andre Tippett PRED .12 .05 .02
New England Patriots
☐ 320 Freddie Joe Nunn PRED .12 .05 .02
Phoenix Cardinals
☐ 321 Reggie White PRED .50 .23 .06
Philadelphia Eagles
☐ 322 Lawrence Taylor PRED .25 .11 .03
New York Giants
☐ 323 Greg Townsend PRED .12 .05 .02
Los Angeles Raiders
☐ 324 Tim Harris PRED .12 .05 .02
Green Bay Packers
☐ 325 Bruce Smith PRED .20 .09 .03
Buffalo Bills
☐ 326 Tony Dorsett RB .40 .18 .05
Denver Broncos
☐ 327 Steve Largent RB .50 .23 .06
Seattle Seahawks
☐ 328 Tim Brown RB 2.00 .90 .25
Los Angeles Raiders
☐ 329 Joe Montana RB 2.00 .90 .25
San Francisco 49ers
☐ 330 Tom Landry Tribute 1.00 .45 .13
Dallas Cowboys

# 1989 Score Supplemental

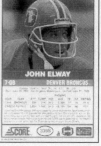

The 1989 Score Football Supplemental set contains 110 standard-size (2 1/2" by 3 1/2") cards, numbered with the suffix "S". The fronts have purple borders; otherwise, the cards are identical to the regular issue 1989 Score football cards. This set is notable for the popular Bo Jackson football/baseball card (number 384S), similar to card number 697 in the 1990 Score baseball set. These cards were distributed only as a complete boxed set. Rookie cards include Eric Allen, Simon Fletcher, Bobby Humphrey, Dave Meggett, Rodney Peete, Frank Reich, Sterling Sharpe, Neil Smith and Lorenzo White.

| | MINT | EXC | G-VG |
|---|---|---|---|
| COMPLETE FACT.SET (110) | 28.00 | 12.50 | 3.50 |
| COMMON PLAYER (331S-440S) | .06 | .03 | .01 |
| ☐ 331S Herschel Walker | .25 | .11 | .03 |
| Minnesota Vikings | | | |
| ☐ 332S Allen Pinkett | .08 | .04 | .01 |
| Houston Oilers | | | |
| ☐ 333S Sterling Sharpe | 20.00 | 9.00 | 2.50 |
| Green Bay Packers | | | |
| ☐ 334S Alvin Walton | .06 | .03 | .01 |
| Washington Redskins | | | |
| ☐ 335S Frank Reich | 2.50 | 1.15 | .30 |
| Buffalo Bills | | | |
| ☐ 336S Jim Thornton | .12 | .05 | .02 |
| Chicago Bears | | | |
| ☐ 337S David Fulcher | .08 | .04 | .01 |
| Cincinnati Bengals | | | |
| ☐ 338S Raul Allegre | .06 | .03 | .01 |
| New York Giants | | | |
| ☐ 339S John Elway | 2.00 | .90 | .25 |
| Denver Broncos | | | |
| ☐ 340S Michael Cofer | .08 | .04 | .01 |
| Detroit Lions | | | |
| ☐ 341S Jim Skow | .06 | .03 | .01 |
| Cincinnati Bengals | | | |
| ☐ 342S Steve DeBerg | .08 | .04 | .01 |

| | | | | |
|---|---|---|---|---|
| Kansas City Chiefs | | | | |
| ☐ 343S Mervyn Fernandez | .06 | .03 | .01 |
| Los Angeles Raiders | | | | |
| ☐ 344S Mike Lansford | .06 | .03 | .01 |
| Los Angeles Rams | | | | |
| ☐ 345S Reggie Roby | .08 | .04 | .01 |
| Miami Dolphins | | | | |
| ☐ 346S Raymond Clayborn | .08 | .04 | .01 |
| New England Patriots | | | | |
| ☐ 347S Lonzell Hill | .06 | .03 | .01 |
| New Orleans Saints | | | | |
| ☐ 348S Ottis Anderson | .06 | .03 | .01 |
| New York Giants | | | | |
| ☐ 349S Erik McMillan | .25 | .11 | .03 |
| New York Jets | | | | |
| ☐ 350S Al Harris | .06 | .03 | .01 |
| Philadelphia Eagles | | | | |
| ☐ 351S Jack Del Rio | .75 | .35 | .09 |
| Dallas Cowboys | | | | |
| ☐ 352S Gary Anderson | .06 | .03 | .01 |
| Pittsburgh Steelers | | | | |
| ☐ 353S Jim McMahon | .10 | .05 | .01 |
| San Diego Chargers | | | | |
| ☐ 354S Keena Turner | .06 | .03 | .01 |
| San Francisco 49ers | | | | |
| ☐ 355S Tony Woods | .06 | .03 | .01 |
| Seattle Seahawks | | | | |
| ☐ 356S Donald Igwebuike | .06 | .03 | .01 |
| Tampa Bay Buccaneers | | | | |
| ☐ 357S Gerald Riggs | .08 | .04 | .01 |
| Washington Redskins | | | | |
| ☐ 358S Eddie Murray | .08 | .04 | .01 |
| Detroit Lions | | | | |
| ☐ 359S Dino Hackett | .06 | .03 | .01 |
| Kansas City Chiefs | | | | |
| ☐ 360S Brad Muster | .50 | .23 | .06 |
| Chicago Bears | | | | |
| ☐ 361S Paul Palmer | .06 | .03 | .01 |
| Dallas Cowboys | | | | |
| ☐ 362S Jerry Robinson | .08 | .04 | .01 |
| Los Angeles Raiders | | | | |
| ☐ 363S Simon Fletcher | 1.00 | .45 | .13 |
| Denver Broncos | | | | |
| ☐ 364S Tommy Kramer | .08 | .04 | .01 |
| Minnesota Vikings | | | | |
| ☐ 365S Jim C. Jensen | .06 | .03 | .01 |
| Miami Dolphins | | | | |
| ☐ 366S Lorenzo White | .75 | .35 | .09 |
| Houston Oilers | | | | |
| ☐ 367S Fredd Young | .06 | .03 | .01 |
| Indianapolis Colts | | | | |
| ☐ 368S Ron Jaworski | .08 | .04 | .01 |
| Kansas City Chiefs | | | | |
| ☐ 369S Mel Owens | .06 | .03 | .01 |
| Los Angeles Rams | | | | |
| ☐ 370S Dave Waymer | .06 | .03 | .01 |
| New Orleans Saints | | | | |
| ☐ 371S Sean Landeta | .08 | .04 | .01 |
| New York Giants | | | | |
| ☐ 372S Sam Mills | .08 | .04 | .01 |
| New Orleans Saints | | | | |
| ☐ 373S Todd Blackledge | .08 | .04 | .01 |
| Pittsburgh Steelers | | | | |
| ☐ 374S Jo Jo Townsell | .06 | .03 | .01 |
| New York Jets | | | | |
| ☐ 375S Ron Wolfley | .06 | .03 | .01 |
| Phoenix Cardinals | | | | |
| ☐ 376S Ralf Mojsiejenko | .06 | .03 | .01 |
| Washington Redskins | | | | |
| ☐ 377S Eric Wright | .06 | .03 | .01 |
| San Francisco 49ers | | | | |
| ☐ 378S Nesby Glasgow | .06 | .03 | .01 |
| Seattle Seahawks | | | | |
| ☐ 379S Darryl Talley | .08 | .04 | .01 |
| Buffalo Bills | | | | |
| ☐ 380S Eric Allen | 1.00 | .45 | .13 |
| Philadelphia Eagles | | | | |
| ☐ 381S Dennis Smith | .08 | .04 | .01 |
| Denver Broncos | | | | |
| ☐ 382S John Tice | .06 | .03 | .01 |
| New Orleans Saints | | | | |
| ☐ 383S Jesse Solomon | .06 | .03 | .01 |
| Dallas Cowboys | | | | |
| ☐ 384S Bo Jackson | 3.50 | 1.55 | .45 |
| (FB/BB Pose) | | | | |
| Los Angeles Raiders | | | | |
| ☐ 385S Mike Merriweather | .08 | .04 | .01 |
| Minnesota Vikings | | | | |
| ☐ 386S Maurice Carthon | .06 | .03 | .01 |
| New York Giants | | | | |
| ☐ 387S Dave Grayson | .08 | .04 | .01 |
| Cleveland Browns | | | | |
| ☐ 388S Wilber Marshall | .08 | .04 | .01 |
| Washington Redskins | | | | |
| ☐ 389S David Wyman | .08 | .04 | .01 |
| Seattle Seahawks | | | | |
| ☐ 390S Thomas Everett | .40 | .18 | .05 |
| Pittsburgh Steelers | | | | |

| | | | | |
|---|---|---|---|---|
| ☐ 391S Alex Gordon | .06 | .03 | .01 |
| New York Giants | | | | |
| ☐ 392S D.J. Dozier | .06 | .03 | .01 |
| Minnesota Vikings | | | | |
| ☐ 393S Scott Radecic | .10 | .05 | .01 |
| Buffalo Bills | | | | |
| ☐ 394S Eric Thomas | .08 | .04 | .01 |
| Cincinnati Bengals | | | | |
| ☐ 395S Mike Gann | .06 | .03 | .01 |
| Atlanta Falcons | | | | |
| ☐ 396S William Perry | .08 | .04 | .01 |
| Chicago Bears | | | | |
| ☐ 397S Carl Hairston | .06 | .03 | .01 |
| Cleveland Browns | | | | |
| ☐ 398S Billy Ard | .06 | .03 | .01 |
| Green Bay Packers | | | | |
| ☐ 399S Donnell Thompson | .06 | .03 | .01 |
| Indianapolis Colts | | | | |
| ☐ 400S Mike Webster | .08 | .04 | .01 |
| Kansas City Chiefs | | | | |
| ☐ 401S Scott Davis | .06 | .03 | .01 |
| Los Angeles Raiders | | | | |
| ☐ 402S Sean Farrell | .06 | .03 | .01 |
| New England Patriots | | | | |
| ☐ 403S Mike Golic | .30 | .14 | .04 |
| Philadelphia Eagles | | | | |
| ☐ 404S Mike Kenn | .08 | .04 | .01 |
| Atlanta Falcons | | | | |
| ☐ 405S Keith Van Horne | .06 | .03 | .01 |
| Chicago Bears | | | | |
| ☐ 406S Bob Golic | .06 | .03 | .01 |
| Los Angeles Raiders | | | | |
| ☐ 407S Neil Smith | 2.50 | 1.15 | .30 |
| Kansas City Chiefs | | | | |
| ☐ 408S Dermontti Dawson | .15 | .07 | .02 |
| Pittsburgh Steelers | | | | |
| ☐ 409S Leslie O'Neal | .06 | .03 | .01 |
| San Diego Chargers | | | | |
| ☐ 410S Matt Bahr | .06 | .03 | .01 |
| Cleveland Browns | | | | |
| ☐ 411S Guy McIntyre | .30 | .14 | .04 |
| San Francisco 49ers | | | | |
| ☐ 412S Bryan Millard | .06 | .03 | .01 |
| Seattle Seahawks | | | | |
| ☐ 413S Joe Jacoby | .08 | .04 | .01 |
| Washington Redskins | | | | |
| ☐ 414S Rob Taylor | .06 | .03 | .01 |
| Tampa Bay Buccaneers | | | | |
| ☐ 415S Tony Zendejas | .06 | .03 | .01 |
| Houston Oilers | | | | |
| ☐ 416S Vai Sikahema | .08 | .04 | .01 |
| Phoenix Cardinals | | | | |
| ☐ 417S Gary Reasons | .06 | .03 | .01 |
| New York Giants | | | | |
| ☐ 418S Shawn Collins | .15 | .07 | .02 |
| Atlanta Falcons | | | | |
| ☐ 419S Mark Green | .06 | .03 | .01 |
| Chicago Bears | | | | |
| ☐ 420S Courtney Hall | .30 | .14 | .04 |
| San Diego Chargers | | | | |
| ☐ 421S Bobby Humphrey | .25 | .11 | .03 |
| Denver Broncos | | | | |
| ☐ 422S Myron Guyton | .15 | .07 | .02 |
| New York Giants | | | | |
| ☐ 423S Darryl Ingram | .06 | .03 | .01 |
| Minnesota Vikings | | | | |
| ☐ 424S Chris Jacke | .30 | .14 | .04 |
| Green Bay Packers | | | | |
| ☐ 425S Keith Jones | .06 | .03 | .01 |
| Atlanta Falcons | | | | |
| ☐ 426S Robert Massey | .20 | .09 | .03 |
| New Orleans Saints | | | | |
| ☐ 427S Bubba McDowell | .30 | .14 | .04 |
| Houston Oilers | | | | |
| ☐ 428S Dave Meggett | .75 | .35 | .09 |
| New York Giants | | | | |
| ☐ 429S Louis Oliver | .30 | .14 | .04 |
| Miami Dolphins | | | | |
| ☐ 430S Danny Peebles | .08 | .04 | .01 |
| Tampa Bay Buccaneers | | | | |
| ☐ 431S Rodney Peete | .75 | .35 | .09 |
| Detroit Lions | | | | |
| ☐ 432S Jeff Query | .20 | .09 | .03 |
| Green Bay Packers | | | | |
| ☐ 433S Timm Rosenbach UER | .30 | .14 | .04 |
| Phoenix Cardinals | | | | |
| (Photo actually | | | | |
| Gary Hogeboom) | | | | |
| ☐ 434S Frank Stams | .06 | .03 | .01 |
| Los Angeles Rams | | | | |
| ☐ 435S Lawyer Tillman | .30 | .14 | .04 |
| Cleveland Browns | | | | |
| ☐ 436S Billy Joe Tolliver | .20 | .09 | .03 |
| San Diego Chargers | | | | |
| ☐ 437S Floyd Turner | .25 | .11 | .03 |
| New Orleans Saints | | | | |
| ☐ 438S Steve Walsh | .25 | .11 | .03 |

Dallas Cowboys
| | | MINT | EXC | G-VG |
|---|---|---|---|---|
| ☐ 439S Joe Wolf | | .06 | .03 | .01 |

Phoenix Cardinals
☐ 440S Trace Armstrong .............. .50 .23 .06
Chicago Bears

Los Angeles Rams
☐ 256 Cornelius Bennett.................. 3.00 1.20 .30
Buffalo Bills

## 1989-90 Score Franco Harris

These 2 1/2" by 3 1/2" cards were given away to all persons at the Super Bowl Show I in New Orleans who acquired Franco Harris' autograph while at the show. However, there were two different backs prepared and distributed since Franco's "Sure-shot" election was announced during the course of the show, after which time the "Hall of Famer" variety was passed out. The cards are unnumbered. The card fronts are in the style of the popular 1989 Score regular issue football cards. Although both varieties were produced on a limited basis, it is thought that the "Sure-shot" variety is the tougher of the two.

| | MINT | EXC | G-VG |
|---|---|---|---|
| COMPLETE SET (2)........................... | 125.00 | 50.00 | 12.50 |
| COMMON PLAYER (1A-1B) .............. | 60.00 | 24.00 | 6.00 |
| | | | |
| ☐ 1A Franco Harris ........................... | 75.00 | 30.00 | 7.50 |
| (Sure-shot) | | | |
| ☐ 1B Franco Harris ........................... | 60.00 | 24.00 | 6.00 |
| (Hall of Famer) | | | |

## 1990 Score Promos

 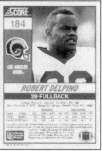

This set of three football cards was intended as a preview of Score's football set. The cards were sent out to prospective dealers along with the ordering forms for Score's 1990 football set. The cards are standard size, 2 1/2" by 3 1/2", and have full color on both sides. The cards are distinguishable from the regular issue cards of the same numbers as indicated in the checklist below. The promo cards show a registered symbol (R with circle around it) rather than a trademark (TM) symbol as on the regular cards. In addition, these promos are cropped tighter than the regular issue cards.

| | MINT | EXC | G-VG |
|---|---|---|---|
| COMPLETE SET (3)........................... | 15.00 | 6.00 | 1.50 |
| COMMON PLAYER ........................... | 2.00 | .80 | .20 |
| | | | |
| ☐ 20 Barry Sanders ........................... | 12.50 | 5.00 | 1.25 |
| Detroit Lions | | | |
| ☐ 184 Robert Delpino ........................... | 2.00 | .80 | .20 |

## 1990 Score

The 1990 Score football set was issued in two separate series each featuring 330 standard-size (2 1/2" by 3 1/2") cards. The fronts have sharp color action photos and multicolored borders; the vertically oriented backs have large color mug shots and brief stats. Cards numbered 289-310 are draft picks, 311-320 are Hot Guns (HG), and 321-330 are Ground Force (GF). The Hot Gun and Ground Force cards indicate that there are 12 in each of these attractive subsets; however, only ten of each were included in this first series as the last two were saved for inclusion in Score's second series. . The second series of 1990 Score football cards was very similar to the first series of 330. There are a number of special subsets, i.e., 551-555 are Crunch Crew (CC), 556-560 are Rocket Man (RM), 561-562 are Ground Force (GF), 563-564 are Hot Gun (HG), 565-590 are All-Pros, 591-594 are Record Breakers (RB), 595-601 are Hall of Famers (HOF), 606-617 are Class of '90, and 618-657 are Draft Picks. Rookie Cards include Barry Foster, Rodney Hampton, Blair Thomas, Andre Ware Mark Carrier, Barry Foster, Jeff George, Eric Green, Harold Green, Rodney Hampton, Haywood Jeffires, Cortez Kennedy and Junior Seau. The five-card "Final Five" set was a special insert in the 1990 Score Football Factory Sets. These cards, which measure the standard 2 1/2" by 3 1/2", honor the final five picks of the 1990 National Football League Draft and are numbered with a "B" prefix. These cards have a "Final Five" logo on the front along with the photo of the player, while the back has a brief biographical description of the player.

| | MINT | EXC | G-VG |
|---|---|---|---|
| COMPLETE SET (660)........................ | 8.00 | 3.60 | 1.00 |
| COMPLETE FACT.SET (665) ............. | 8.00 | 3.60 | 1.00 |
| COMMON PLAYER (1-330)............... | .04 | .02 | .01 |
| COMMON PLAYER (331-660)........... | .04 | .02 | .01 |
| COMMON PLAYER (B1-B5) ............. | .05 | .02 | .01 |
| | | | |
| ☐ 1 Joe Montana ........................... | 1.00 | .45 | .13 |
| San Francisco 49ers | | | |
| ☐ 2 Christian Okoye......................... | .08 | .04 | .01 |
| Kansas City Chiefs | | | |
| ☐ 3 Mike Singletary UER ................. | .10 | .05 | .01 |
| Chicago Bears | | | |
| (Text says 146 tackles | | | |
| in '89, should be 151) | | | |
| ☐ 4 Jim Everett UER ......................... | .08 | .04 | .01 |
| Los Angeles Rams | | | |
| (Text says 415 yards | | | |
| against Saints, should | | | |
| be 454) | | | |
| ☐ 5 Phil Simms ........................... | .10 | .05 | .01 |
| New York Giants | | | |
| ☐ 6 Brent Fullwood......................... | .04 | .02 | .01 |
| Green Bay Packers | | | |
| ☐ 7 Bill Fralic ........................... | .08 | .04 | .01 |
| Atlanta Falcons | | | |
| ☐ 8 Leslie O'Neal ........................... | .08 | .04 | .01 |
| San Diego Chargers | | | |
| ☐ 9 John Taylor ........................... | .15 | .07 | .02 |
| San Francisco 49ers | | | |
| ☐ 10 Bo Jackson ........................... | .40 | .18 | .05 |
| Los Angeles Raiders | | | |
| ☐ 11 John Stephens......................... | .08 | .04 | .01 |
| New England Patriots | | | |
| ☐ 12 Art Monk ........................... | .10 | .05 | .01 |
| Washington Redskins | | | |
| ☐ 13 Dan Marino ........................... | .75 | .35 | .09 |
| Miami Dolphins | | | |
| ☐ 14 John Settle ........................... | .04 | .02 | .01 |
| Atlanta Falcons | | | |
| ☐ 15 Don Majkowski ........................... | .08 | .04 | .01 |

| | | | |
|---|---|---|---|
| Green Bay Packers | | | |
| ☐ 16 Bruce Smith | .10 | .05 | .01 |
| Buffalo Bills | | | |
| ☐ 17 Brad Muster | .08 | .04 | .01 |
| Chicago Bears | | | |
| ☐ 18 Jason Buck | .04 | .02 | .01 |
| Cincinnati Bengals | | | |
| ☐ 19 James Brooks | .08 | .04 | .01 |
| Cincinnati Bengals | | | |
| ☐ 20 Barry Sanders | 1.00 | .45 | .13 |
| Detroit Lions | | | |
| ☐ 21 Troy Aikman | 1.25 | .55 | .16 |
| Dallas Cowboys | | | |
| ☐ 22 Allen Pinkett | .04 | .02 | .01 |
| Houston Oilers | | | |
| ☐ 23 Duane Bickett | .04 | .02 | .01 |
| Indianapolis Colts | | | |
| ☐ 24 Kevin Ross | .08 | .04 | .01 |
| Kansas City Chiefs | | | |
| ☐ 25 John Elway | .40 | .18 | .05 |
| Denver Broncos | | | |
| ☐ 26 Jeff Query | .04 | .02 | .01 |
| Green Bay Packers | | | |
| ☐ 27 Eddie Murray | .08 | .04 | .01 |
| Detroit Lions | | | |
| ☐ 28 Richard Dent | .08 | .04 | .01 |
| Chicago Bears | | | |
| ☐ 29 Lorenzo White | .15 | .07 | .02 |
| Houston Oilers | | | |
| ☐ 30 Eric Metcalf | .15 | .07 | .02 |
| Cleveland Browns | | | |
| ☐ 31 Jeff Dellenbach | .04 | .02 | .01 |
| Miami Dolphins | | | |
| ☐ 32 Leon White | .04 | .02 | .01 |
| Cincinnati Bengals | | | |
| ☐ 33 Jim Jeffcoat | .04 | .02 | .01 |
| Dallas Cowboys | | | |
| ☐ 34 Herschel Walker | .10 | .05 | .01 |
| Minnesota Vikings | | | |
| ☐ 35 Mike Johnson UER | .04 | .02 | .01 |
| Cleveland Browns | | | |
| (Front photo actually | | | |
| 51 Eddie Johnson) | | | |
| ☐ 36 Joe Phillips | .04 | .02 | .01 |
| San Diego Chargers | | | |
| ☐ 37 Willie Gault | .08 | .04 | .01 |
| Los Angeles Raiders | | | |
| ☐ 38 Keith Millard | .08 | .04 | .01 |
| Minnesota Vikings | | | |
| ☐ 39 Fred Marion | .04 | .02 | .01 |
| New England Patriots | | | |
| ☐ 40 Boomer Esiason | .20 | .09 | .03 |
| Cincinnati Bengals | | | |
| ☐ 41 Dermontti Dawson | .04 | .02 | .01 |
| Pittsburgh Steelers | | | |
| ☐ 42 Dino Hackett | .04 | .02 | .01 |
| Kansas City Chiefs | | | |
| ☐ 43 Reggie Roby | .08 | .04 | .01 |
| Miami Dolphins | | | |
| ☐ 44 Roger Vick | .04 | .02 | .01 |
| New York Jets | | | |
| ☐ 45 Bobby Hebert | .15 | .07 | .02 |
| New Orleans Saints | | | |
| ☐ 46 Don Beebe | .15 | .07 | .02 |
| Buffalo Bills | | | |
| ☐ 47 Neal Anderson | .08 | .04 | .01 |
| Chicago Bears | | | |
| ☐ 48 Johnny Holland | .04 | .02 | .01 |
| Green Bay Packers | | | |
| ☐ 49 Bobby Humphery | .04 | .02 | .01 |
| New York Jets | | | |
| ☐ 50 Lawrence Taylor | .10 | .05 | .01 |
| New York Giants | | | |
| ☐ 51 Billy Ray Smith | .08 | .04 | .01 |
| San Diego Chargers | | | |
| ☐ 52 Robert Perryman | .04 | .02 | .01 |
| New England Patriots | | | |
| ☐ 53 Gary Anderson | .04 | .02 | .01 |
| Pittsburgh Steelers | | | |
| ☐ 54 Raul Allegre | .04 | .02 | .01 |
| New York Giants | | | |
| ☐ 55 Pat Swilling | .10 | .05 | .01 |
| New Orleans Saints | | | |
| ☐ 56 Chris Doleman | .08 | .04 | .01 |
| Minnesota Vikings | | | |
| ☐ 57 Andre Reed | .15 | .07 | .02 |
| Buffalo Bills | | | |
| ☐ 58 Seth Joyner | .08 | .04 | .01 |
| Philadelphia Eagles | | | |
| ☐ 59 Bart Oates | .04 | .02 | .01 |
| New York Giants | | | |
| ☐ 60 Bernie Kosar | .10 | .05 | .01 |
| Cleveland Browns | | | |
| ☐ 61 Dave Krieg | .08 | .04 | .01 |
| Seattle Seahawks | | | |
| ☐ 62 Lars Tate | .04 | .02 | .01 |
| Tampa Bay Buccaneers | | | |
| ☐ 63 Scott Norwood | .04 | .02 | .01 |

| | | | |
|---|---|---|---|
| Buffalo Bills | | | |
| ☐ 64 Kyle Clifton | .04 | .02 | .01 |
| New York Jets | | | |
| ☐ 65 Alan Veingrad | .04 | .02 | .01 |
| Green Bay Packers | | | |
| ☐ 66 Gerald Riggs UER | .08 | .04 | .01 |
| Washington Redskins | | | |
| (Text begins Depite, | | | |
| should be Despite) | | | |
| ☐ 67 Tim Worley | .08 | .04 | .01 |
| Pittsburgh Steelers | | | |
| ☐ 68 Rodney Holman | .04 | .02 | .01 |
| Cincinnati Bengals | | | |
| ☐ 69 Tony Zendejas | .04 | .02 | .01 |
| Houston Oilers | | | |
| ☐ 70 Chris Miller | .15 | .07 | .02 |
| Atlanta Falcons | | | |
| ☐ 71 Wilber Marshall | .08 | .04 | .01 |
| Washington Redskins | | | |
| ☐ 72 Skip McClendon | .04 | .02 | .01 |
| Cincinnati Bengals | | | |
| ☐ 73 Jim Covert | .04 | .02 | .01 |
| Chicago Bears | | | |
| ☐ 74 Sam Mills | .08 | .04 | .01 |
| New Orleans Saints | | | |
| ☐ 75 Chris Hinton | .08 | .04 | .01 |
| Indianapolis Colts | | | |
| ☐ 76 Irv Eatman | .04 | .02 | .01 |
| Kansas City Chiefs | | | |
| ☐ 77 Bubba Paris UER | .08 | .04 | .01 |
| San Francisco 49ers | | | |
| (No team name on who | | | |
| drafted him) | | | |
| ☐ 78 John Elliott UER | .04 | .02 | .01 |
| New York Giants | | | |
| (No team name on who | | | |
| drafted him; missing | | | |
| Team/FA status) | | | |
| ☐ 79 Thomas Everett | .04 | .02 | .01 |
| Pittsburgh Steelers | | | |
| ☐ 80 Steve Smith | .08 | .04 | .01 |
| Los Angeles Raiders | | | |
| ☐ 81 Jackie Slater | .08 | .04 | .01 |
| Lost Angeles Rams | | | |
| ☐ 82 Kelvin Martin | .25 | .11 | .03 |
| Dallas Cowboys | | | |
| ☐ 83 Jo Jo Townsell | .04 | .02 | .01 |
| New York Jets | | | |
| ☐ 84 Jim C. Jensen | .04 | .02 | .01 |
| Miami Dolphins | | | |
| ☐ 85 Bobby Humphrey | .08 | .04 | .01 |
| Denver Broncos | | | |
| ☐ 86 Mike Dyal | .04 | .02 | .01 |
| Los Angeles Raiders | | | |
| ☐ 87 Andre Rison UER | .25 | .11 | .03 |
| Indianapolis Colts | | | |
| (Front 87, back 85) | | | |
| ☐ 88 Brian Sochia | .04 | .02 | .01 |
| Miami Dolphins | | | |
| ☐ 89 Greg Bell | .08 | .04 | .01 |
| Los Angeles Rams | | | |
| ☐ 90 Dalton Hilliard | .08 | .04 | .01 |
| New Orleans Saints | | | |
| ☐ 91 Carl Banks | .08 | .04 | .01 |
| New York Giants | | | |
| ☐ 92 Dennis Smith | .08 | .04 | .01 |
| Denver Broncos | | | |
| ☐ 93 Bruce Matthews | .08 | .04 | .01 |
| Houston Oilers | | | |
| ☐ 94 Charles Haley | .08 | .04 | .01 |
| San Francisco 49ers | | | |
| ☐ 95 Deion Sanders UER | .25 | .11 | .03 |
| Atlanta Falcons | | | |
| (Reversed photo on back) | | | |
| ☐ 96 Stephone Paige | .08 | .04 | .01 |
| Kansas City Chiefs | | | |
| ☐ 97 Marion Butts | .10 | .05 | .01 |
| San Diego Chargers | | | |
| ☐ 98 Howie Long | .08 | .04 | .01 |
| Los Angeles Raiders | | | |
| ☐ 99 Donald Igwebuike | .04 | .02 | .01 |
| Tampa Bay Buccaneers | | | |
| ☐ 100 Roger Craig UER | .08 | .04 | .01 |
| San Francisco 49ers | | | |
| (Text says 2 TD's in | | | |
| SB XXIV, should be 1; | | | |
| everything misspelled) | | | |
| ☐ 101 Charles Mann | .08 | .04 | .01 |
| Washington Redskins | | | |
| ☐ 102 Fredd Young | .04 | .02 | .01 |
| Indianapolis Colts | | | |
| ☐ 103 Chris Jacke | .04 | .02 | .01 |
| Green Bay Packers | | | |
| ☐ 104 Scott Case | .04 | .02 | .01 |
| Atlanta Falcons | | | |
| ☐ 105 Warren Moon | .25 | .11 | .03 |
| Houston Oilers | | | |
| ☐ 106 Clyde Simmons | .08 | .04 | .01 |

| | | | |
|---|---|---|---|
| Philadelphia Eagles | | | |
| ☐ 107 Steve Atwater | .10 | .05 | .01 |
| Denver Broncos | | | |
| ☐ 108 Morten Andersen | .08 | .04 | .01 |
| New Orleans Saints | | | |
| ☐ 109 Eugene Marve | .04 | .02 | .01 |
| Tampa Bay Buccaneers | | | |
| ☐ 110 Thurman Thomas | .40 | .18 | .05 |
| Buffalo Bills | | | |
| ☐ 111 Carnell Lake | .04 | .02 | .01 |
| Pittsburgh Steelers | | | |
| ☐ 112 Jim Kelly | .30 | .14 | .04 |
| Buffalo Bills | | | |
| ☐ 113 Stanford Jennings | .04 | .02 | .01 |
| Cincinnati Bengals | | | |
| ☐ 114 Jacob Green | .04 | .02 | .01 |
| Seattle Seahawks | | | |
| ☐ 115 Karl Mecklenburg | .08 | .04 | .01 |
| Denver Broncos | | | |
| ☐ 116 Ray Childress | .08 | .04 | .01 |
| Houston Oilers | | | |
| ☐ 117 Erik McMillan | .04 | .02 | .01 |
| New York Jets | | | |
| ☐ 118 Harry Newsome | .04 | .02 | .01 |
| Pittsburgh Steelers | | | |
| ☐ 119 James Dixon | .04 | .02 | .01 |
| Dallas Cowboys | | | |
| ☐ 120 Hassan Jones | .04 | .02 | .01 |
| Minnesoata Vikings | | | |
| ☐ 121 Eric Allen | .08 | .04 | .01 |
| Philadelphia Eagles | | | |
| ☐ 122 Felix Wright | .04 | .02 | .01 |
| Cleveland Browns | | | |
| ☐ 123 Merril Hoge | .08 | .04 | .01 |
| Pittsburgh Steelers | | | |
| ☐ 124 Eric Ball | .04 | .02 | .01 |
| Cincinnati Bengals | | | |
| ☐ 125 Flipper Anderson | .08 | .04 | .01 |
| Los Angeles Rams | | | |
| ☐ 126 James Jefferson | .04 | .02 | .01 |
| Seattle Seahawks | | | |
| ☐ 127 Tim McDonald | .08 | .04 | .01 |
| Phoenix Cardinals | | | |
| ☐ 128 Larry Kinnebrew | .04 | .02 | .01 |
| Buffalo Bills | | | |
| ☐ 129 Mark Collins | .04 | .02 | .01 |
| New York Giants | | | |
| ☐ 130 Ickey Woods | .04 | .02 | .01 |
| Cincinnati Bengals | | | |
| ☐ 131 Jeff Donaldson UER | .04 | .02 | .01 |
| Houston Oilers | | | |
| (Stats say 0 int. and | | | |
| 0 fumble rec., text | | | |
| says 4 and 1) | | | |
| ☐ 132 Rich Camarillo | .04 | .02 | .01 |
| Phoenix Cardinals | | | |
| ☐ 133 Melvin Bratton | .04 | .02 | .01 |
| Denver Broncos | | | |
| ☐ 134A Kevin Butler | .35 | .16 | .04 |
| Chicago Bears | | | |
| (Photo on back | | | |
| has helmet on) | | | |
| ☐ 134B Kevin Butler | .05 | .02 | .01 |
| Chicago Bears | | | |
| (Photo on back | | | |
| has no helmet on) | | | |
| ☐ 135 Albert Bentley | .04 | .02 | .01 |
| Indianapolis Colts | | | |
| ☐ 136A Vai Sikahema | .35 | .16 | .04 |
| Phoenix Cardinals | | | |
| (Photo on back | | | |
| has helmet on) | | | |
| ☐ 136B Vai Sikahema | .08 | .04 | .01 |
| Phoenix Cardinals | | | |
| (Photo on back | | | |
| has no helmet on) | | | |
| ☐ 137 Todd McNair | .15 | .07 | .02 |
| Kansas City Chiefs | | | |
| ☐ 138 Alonzo Highsmith | .04 | .02 | .01 |
| Houston Oilers | | | |
| ☐ 139 Brian Blades | .15 | .07 | .02 |
| Seattle Seahawks | | | |
| ☐ 140 Jeff Lageman | .04 | .02 | .01 |
| New York Jets | | | |
| ☐ 141 Eric Thomas | .04 | .02 | .01 |
| Cincinnati Bengals | | | |
| ☐ 142 Derek Hill | .04 | .02 | .01 |
| Pittsburgh Steelers | | | |
| ☐ 143 Rick Fenney | .04 | .02 | .01 |
| Minnesota Vikings | | | |
| ☐ 144 Herman Heard | .04 | .02 | .01 |
| Kansas City Chiefs | | | |
| ☐ 145 Steve Young | .50 | .23 | .06 |
| San Francisco 49ers | | | |
| ☐ 146 Kent Hull | .04 | .02 | .01 |
| Buffalo Bills | | | |
| ☐ 147A Joey Browner | .35 | .16 | .04 |
| Minnesota Vikings | | | |
| (Photo on back | | | |
| looking to side) | | | |
| ☐ 147B Joey Browner | .05 | .02 | .01 |
| Minnesota Vikings | | | |
| (Photo on back | | | |
| looking up) | | | |
| ☐ 148 Frank Minnifield | .04 | .02 | .01 |
| Cleveland Browns | | | |
| ☐ 149 Robert Massey | .04 | .02 | .01 |
| New Orleans Saints | | | |
| ☐ 150 Dave Meggett | .10 | .05 | .01 |
| New York Giants | | | |
| ☐ 151 Bubba McDowell | .04 | .02 | .01 |
| Houston Oilers | | | |
| ☐ 152 Rickey Dixon | .04 | .02 | .01 |
| Cincinnati Bengals | | | |
| ☐ 153 Ray Donaldson | .04 | .02 | .01 |
| Indianapolis Colts | | | |
| ☐ 154 Alvin Walton | .04 | .02 | .01 |
| Washington Redskins | | | |
| ☐ 155 Mike Cofer | .04 | .02 | .01 |
| San Francisco 49ers | | | |
| ☐ 156 Darryl Talley | .08 | .04 | .01 |
| Buffalo Bills | | | |
| ☐ 157 A.J. Johnson | .04 | .02 | .01 |
| Washington Redskins | | | |
| ☐ 158 Jerry Gray | .04 | .02 | .01 |
| Los Angeles Rams | | | |
| ☐ 159 Keith Byars | .08 | .04 | .01 |
| Philadelphia Eagles | | | |
| ☐ 160 Andy Heck | .04 | .02 | .01 |
| Seattle Seahawks | | | |
| ☐ 161 Mike Munchak | .08 | .04 | .01 |
| Houston Oilers | | | |
| ☐ 162 Dennis Gentry | .04 | .02 | .01 |
| Chicago Bears | | | |
| ☐ 163 Timm Rosenbach UER | .04 | .02 | .01 |
| Phoenix Cardinals | | | |
| (Born 1967 in Everett, | | | |
| Wa., should be 1966 | | | |
| in Missoula, Mont.) | | | |
| ☐ 164 Randall McDaniel | .04 | .02 | .01 |
| Minnesota Vikings | | | |
| ☐ 165 Pat Leahy | .08 | .04 | .01 |
| New York Jets | | | |
| ☐ 166 Bubby Brister | .10 | .05 | .01 |
| Pittsburgh Steelers | | | |
| ☐ 167 Aundray Bruce | .04 | .02 | .01 |
| Atlanta Falcons | | | |
| ☐ 168 Bill Brooks | .08 | .04 | .01 |
| Indianapolis Colts | | | |
| ☐ 169 Eddie Anderson | .10 | .05 | .01 |
| Los Angeles Raiders | | | |
| ☐ 170 Ronnie Lott | .10 | .05 | .01 |
| San Francisco 49ers | | | |
| ☐ 171 Jay Hilgenberg | .08 | .04 | .01 |
| Chicago Bears | | | |
| ☐ 172 Joe Nash | .04 | .02 | .01 |
| Seattle Seahawks | | | |
| ☐ 173 Simon Fletcher | .08 | .04 | .01 |
| Denver Broncos | | | |
| ☐ 174 Shane Conlan | .08 | .04 | .01 |
| Buffalo Bills | | | |
| ☐ 175 Sean Landeta | .08 | .04 | .01 |
| New York Giants | | | |
| ☐ 176 John Alt | .10 | .05 | .01 |
| Kansas City Chiefs | | | |
| ☐ 177 Clay Matthews | .08 | .04 | .01 |
| Cleveland Browns | | | |
| ☐ 178 Anthony Munoz | .08 | .04 | .01 |
| Cincinnati Bengals | | | |
| ☐ 179 Pete Holohan | .04 | .02 | .01 |
| Los Angeles Rams | | | |
| ☐ 180 Robert Awalt | .04 | .02 | .01 |
| Phoenix Cardinals | | | |
| ☐ 181 Rohn Stark | .08 | .04 | .01 |
| Indianapolis Colts | | | |
| ☐ 182 Vance Johnson | .08 | .04 | .01 |
| Denver Droncos | | | |
| ☐ 183 David Fulcher | .08 | .04 | .01 |
| Cincinnati Bengals | | | |
| ☐ 184 Robert Delpino | .08 | .04 | .01 |
| Los Angeles Rams | | | |
| ☐ 185 Drew Hill | .08 | .04 | .01 |
| Houston Oilers | | | |
| ☐ 186 Reggie Langhorne UER | .08 | .04 | .01 |
| Cleveland Browns | | | |
| (Stats read 1988, | | | |
| not 1989) | | | |
| ☐ 187 Lonzell Hill | .04 | .02 | .01 |
| New Orleans Saints | | | |
| ☐ 188 Tom Rathman UER | .08 | .04 | .01 |
| San Francisco 49ers | | | |
| (On back, blocker | | | |
| misspelled) | | | |
| ☐ 189 Greg Montgomery | .10 | .05 | .01 |
| Houston Oilers | | | |
| ☐ 190 Leonard Smith | .04 | .02 | .01 |

| | | | |
|---|---|---|---|
| ☐ 191 Chris Spielman | .08 | .04 | .01 |
| Buffalo Bills | | | |
| Detroit Lions | | | |
| ☐ 192 Tom Newberry | .04 | .02 | .01 |
| Los Angeles Rams | | | |
| ☐ 193 Cris Carter | .20 | .09 | .03 |
| Philadelphia Eagles | | | |
| ☐ 194 Kevin Porter | .04 | .02 | .01 |
| Kansas City Chiefs | | | |
| ☐ 195 Donnell Thompson | .04 | .02 | .01 |
| Indianapolis Colts | | | |
| ☐ 196 Vaughan Johnson | .08 | .04 | .01 |
| New Orleans Saints | | | |
| ☐ 197 Steve McMichael | .08 | .04 | .01 |
| Chicago Bears | | | |
| ☐ 198 Jim Sweeney | .04 | .02 | .01 |
| New York Jets | | | |
| ☐ 199 Rich Karlis UER | .04 | .02 | .01 |
| Minnesota Vikings | | | |
| (No comma between day | | | |
| and year in birth data) | | | |
| ☐ 200 Jerry Rice | .75 | .35 | .09 |
| San Francisco 49ers | | | |
| ☐ 201 Dan Hampton UER | .08 | .04 | .01 |
| Chicago Bears | | | |
| (Card says he's a DE, | | | |
| should be DT) | | | |
| ☐ 202 Jim Lachey | .08 | .04 | .01 |
| Washington Redskins | | | |
| ☐ 203 Reggie White | .15 | .07 | .02 |
| Philadelphia Eagles | | | |
| ☐ 204 Jerry Ball | .08 | .04 | .01 |
| Detroit Lions | | | |
| ☐ 205 Russ Grimm | .04 | .02 | .01 |
| Washington Redskins | | | |
| ☐ 206 Tim Green | .04 | .02 | .01 |
| Atlanta Falcons | | | |
| ☐ 207 Shawn Collins | .04 | .02 | .01 |
| Atlanta Falcons | | | |
| ☐ 208A Ralf Mojsiejenko ERR | .50 | .23 | .06 |
| Washington Redskins | | | |
| (Chargers stats) | | | |
| ☐ 208B Ralf Mojsiejenko COR | .08 | .04 | .01 |
| Washington Redskins | | | |
| (Redskins stats) | | | |
| ☐ 209 Trace Armstrong | .04 | .02 | .01 |
| Chicago Bears | | | |
| ☐ 210 Keith Jackson | .25 | .11 | .03 |
| Philadelphia Eagles | | | |
| ☐ 211 Jamie Holland | .04 | .02 | .01 |
| San Diego Chargers | | | |
| ☐ 212 Mark Clayton | .08 | .04 | .01 |
| Miami Dolphins | | | |
| ☐ 213 Jeff Cross | .04 | .02 | .01 |
| Miami Dolphins | | | |
| ☐ 214 Bob Gagliano | .04 | .02 | .01 |
| Detroit Lions | | | |
| ☐ 215 Louis Oliver UER | .08 | .04 | .01 |
| Miami Dolphins | | | |
| (Text says played at | | | |
| Miami, should be | | | |
| Florida as in bio) | | | |
| ☐ 216 Jim Arnold | .04 | .02 | .01 |
| Detroit Lions | | | |
| ☐ 217 Robert Clark | .08 | .04 | .01 |
| Detroit Lions | | | |
| ☐ 218 Gill Byrd | .08 | .04 | .01 |
| San Diego Chargers | | | |
| ☐ 219 Rodney Peete | .08 | .04 | .01 |
| Detroit Lions | | | |
| ☐ 220 Anthony Miller | .30 | .14 | .04 |
| San Diego Chargers | | | |
| ☐ 221 Steve Grogan | .08 | .04 | .01 |
| New England Patriots | | | |
| ☐ 222 Vince Newsome | .04 | .02 | .01 |
| Los Angeles Rams | | | |
| ☐ 223 Tom Benson | .04 | .02 | .01 |
| Los Angeles Raiders | | | |
| ☐ 224 Kevin Murphy | .04 | .02 | .01 |
| Tampa Bay Buccaneers | | | |
| ☐ 225 Henry Ellard | .08 | .04 | .01 |
| Los Angeles Rams | | | |
| ☐ 226 Richard Johnson | .04 | .02 | .01 |
| Detroit Lions | | | |
| ☐ 227 Jim Skow | .04 | .02 | .01 |
| Cincinnati Bengals | | | |
| ☐ 228 Keith Jones | .04 | .02 | .01 |
| Atlanta Falcons | | | |
| ☐ 229 Dave Brown | .04 | .02 | .01 |
| Green Bay Packers | | | |
| ☐ 230 Marcus Allen | .15 | .07 | .02 |
| Los Angeles Raiders | | | |
| ☐ 231 Steve Walsh | .04 | .02 | .01 |
| Dallas Cowboys | | | |
| ☐ 232 Jim Harbaugh | .12 | .05 | .02 |
| Chicago Bears | | | |
| ☐ 233 Mel Gray | .08 | .04 | .01 |
| Detroit Lions | | | |
| ☐ 234 David Treadwell | .04 | .02 | .01 |
| Denver Broncos | | | |
| ☐ 235 John Offerdahl | .08 | .04 | .01 |
| Miami Dolphins | | | |
| ☐ 236 Gary Reasons | .04 | .02 | .01 |
| New York Giants | | | |
| ☐ 237 Tim Krumrie | .04 | .02 | .01 |
| Cincinnati Bengals | | | |
| ☐ 238 Dave Duerson | .04 | .02 | .01 |
| Chicago Bears | | | |
| ☐ 239 Gary Clark UER | .10 | .05 | .01 |
| Washington Redskins | | | |
| (Stats read 1988, | | | |
| not 1989) | | | |
| ☐ 240 Mark Jackson | .08 | .04 | .01 |
| Denver Broncos | | | |
| ☐ 241 Mark Murphy | .04 | .02 | .01 |
| Green Bay Packers | | | |
| ☐ 242 Jerry Holmes | .04 | .02 | .01 |
| Detroit Lions | | | |
| ☐ 243 Tim McGee | .08 | .04 | .01 |
| Cincinnati Bengals | | | |
| ☐ 244 Mike Tomczak | .08 | .04 | .01 |
| Chicago Bears | | | |
| ☐ 245 Sterling Sharpe UER | .75 | .35 | .09 |
| Green Bay Packers | | | |
| (Broke 47-yard-old | | | |
| record, should be year) | | | |
| ☐ 246 Bennie Blades | .04 | .02 | .01 |
| Detroit Lions | | | |
| ☐ 247 Ken Harvey UER | .12 | .05 | .02 |
| Phoenix Cardinals | | | |
| (Sacks and fumble | | | |
| recovery listings | | | |
| are switched; dis- | | | |
| appointing misspelled) | | | |
| ☐ 248 Ron Heller | .04 | .02 | .01 |
| Philadelphia Eagles | | | |
| ☐ 249 Louis Lipps | .08 | .04 | .01 |
| Pittsburgh Steelers | | | |
| ☐ 250 Wade Wilson | .08 | .04 | .01 |
| Minnesota Vikings | | | |
| ☐ 251 Freddie Joe Nunn | .08 | .04 | .01 |
| Phoenix Cardinals | | | |
| ☐ 252 Jerome Brown UER | .08 | .04 | .01 |
| Philadelphia Eagles | | | |
| ('89 stats show 2 fum- | | | |
| ble rec., should be 1) | | | |
| ☐ 253 Myron Guyton | .04 | .02 | .01 |
| New York Giants | | | |
| ☐ 254 Nate Odomes | .25 | .11 | .03 |
| Buffalo Bills | | | |
| ☐ 255 Rod Woodson | .20 | .09 | .03 |
| Pittsburgh Steelers | | | |
| ☐ 256 Cornelius Bennett | .10 | .05 | .01 |
| Buffalo Bills | | | |
| ☐ 257 Keith Woodside | .04 | .02 | .01 |
| Green Bay Packers | | | |
| ☐ 258 Jeff Uhlenhake UER | .04 | .02 | .01 |
| Miami Dolphins | | | |
| (Text calls him Ron) | | | |
| ☐ 259 Harry Hamilton | .04 | .02 | .01 |
| Tampa Bay Buccaneers | | | |
| ☐ 260 Mark Bavaro | .08 | .04 | .01 |
| New York Giants | | | |
| ☐ 261 Vinny Testaverde | .15 | .07 | .02 |
| Tampa Bay Buccaneers | | | |
| ☐ 262 Steve DeBerg | .08 | .04 | .01 |
| Kansas City Chiefs | | | |
| ☐ 263 Steve Wisniewski UER | .04 | .02 | .01 |
| Los Angeles Raiders | | | |
| (Drafted by Dallas, | | | |
| not the Raiders) | | | |
| ☐ 264 Pete Mandley | .04 | .02 | .01 |
| Kansas City Chiefs | | | |
| ☐ 265 Tim Harris | .08 | .04 | .01 |
| Green Bay Packers | | | |
| ☐ 266 Jack Trudeau | .08 | .04 | .01 |
| Indianapolis Colts | | | |
| ☐ 267 Mark Kelso | .04 | .02 | .01 |
| Buffalo Bills | | | |
| ☐ 268 Brian Noble | .04 | .02 | .01 |
| Green Bay Packers | | | |
| ☐ 269 Jessie Tuggle | .25 | .11 | .03 |
| Atlanta Falcons | | | |
| ☐ 270 Ken O'Brien | .08 | .04 | .01 |
| New York Jets | | | |
| ☐ 271 David Little | .04 | .02 | .01 |
| Pittsburgh Steelers | | | |
| ☐ 272 Pete Stoyanovich | .08 | .04 | .01 |
| Miami Dolphins | | | |
| ☐ 273 Odessa Turner | .15 | .07 | .02 |
| New York Giants | | | |
| ☐ 274 Anthony Toney | .04 | .02 | .01 |
| Philadelphia Eagles | | | |
| ☐ 275 Tunch Ilkin | .04 | .02 | .01 |
| Pittsburgh Steelers | | | |

| | | | |
|---|---|---|---|
| ☐ 276 Carl Lee.................... | .04 | .02 | .01 |
| Minnesota Vikings | | | |
| ☐ 277 Hart Lee Dykes........... | .04 | .02 | .01 |
| New England Patriots | | | |
| ☐ 278 Al Noga.................... | .04 | .02 | .01 |
| Minnesota Vikings | | | |
| ☐ 279 Greg Lloyd................ | .04 | .02 | .01 |
| Pittsburgh Steelers | | | |
| ☐ 280 Billy Joe Tolliver......... | .04 | .02 | .01 |
| San Diego Chargers | | | |
| ☐ 281 Kirk Lowdermilk.......... | .04 | .02 | .01 |
| Minnesota Vikings | | | |
| ☐ 282 Earl Ferrell............... | .04 | .02 | .01 |
| Phoenix Cardinals | | | |
| ☐ 283 Eric Sievers.............. | .04 | .02 | .01 |
| New England Patriots | | | |
| ☐ 284 Steve Jordan............. | .08 | .04 | .01 |
| Minnesota Vikings | | | |
| ☐ 285 Burt Grossman........... | .04 | .02 | .01 |
| San Diego Chargers | | | |
| ☐ 286 Johnny Rembert.......... | .04 | .02 | .01 |
| New England Patriots | | | |
| ☐ 287 Jeff Jaeger............... | .04 | .02 | .01 |
| Los Angeles Raiders | | | |
| ☐ 288 James Hasty.............. | .04 | .02 | .01 |
| New York Jets | | | |
| ☐ 289 Tony Mandarich.......... | .04 | .02 | .01 |
| Draft Pick | | | |
| ☐ 290 Chris Singleton.......... | .10 | .05 | .01 |
| Draft Pick | | | |
| ☐ 291 Lynn James.............. | .04 | .02 | .01 |
| Draft Pick | | | |
| ☐ 292 Andre Ware.............. | .15 | .07 | .02 |
| Draft Pick | | | |
| ☐ 293 Ray Agnew............... | .04 | .02 | .01 |
| Draft Pick | | | |
| ☐ 294 Joel Smeenge............ | .04 | .02 | .01 |
| Draft Pick | | | |
| ☐ 295 Marc Spindler........... | .04 | .02 | .01 |
| Draft Pick | | | |
| ☐ 296 Renaldo Turnbull........ | .40 | .18 | .05 |
| Draft Pick | | | |
| ☐ 297 Reggie Rembert......... | .04 | .02 | .01 |
| Draft Pick | | | |
| ☐ 298 Jeff Alm................. | .04 | .02 | .01 |
| Draft Pick | | | |
| ☐ 299 Cortez Kennedy.......... | .75 | .35 | .09 |
| Draft Pick | | | |
| ☐ 300 Blair Thomas............ | .10 | .05 | .01 |
| Draft Pick | | | |
| ☐ 301 Pat Terrell.............. | .10 | .05 | .01 |
| Draft Pick | | | |
| ☐ 302 Junior Seau............. | .75 | .35 | .09 |
| Draft Pick | | | |
| ☐ 303 Mohammed Elewonibi...... | .04 | .02 | .01 |
| Draft Pick | | | |
| ☐ 304 Tony Bennett............ | .30 | .14 | .04 |
| Draft Pick | | | |
| ☐ 305 Percy Snow.............. | .04 | .02 | .01 |
| Draft Pick | | | |
| ☐ 306 Richmond Webb.......... | .20 | .09 | .03 |
| Draft Pick | | | |
| ☐ 307 Rodney Hampton......... | 1.50 | .65 | .19 |
| Draft Pick | | | |
| ☐ 308 Barry Foster............ | 1.00 | .45 | .13 |
| Draft Pick | | | |
| ☐ 309 John Friesz............. | .25 | .11 | .03 |
| Draft Pick | | | |
| ☐ 310 Ben Smith............... | .10 | .05 | .01 |
| Draft Pick | | | |
| ☐ 311 Joe Montana HG......... | .50 | .23 | .06 |
| San Francisco 49ers | | | |
| ☐ 312 Jim Everett HG.......... | .04 | .02 | .01 |
| Los Angeles Rams | | | |
| ☐ 313 Mark Rypien HG......... | .08 | .04 | .01 |
| Washington Redskins | | | |
| ☐ 314 Phil Simms HG UER...... | .08 | .04 | .01 |
| New York Giants | | | |
| (Lists him as playing | | | |
| in the AFC) | | | |
| ☐ 315 Don Majkowski HG....... | .04 | .02 | .01 |
| Green Bay Packers | | | |
| ☐ 316 Boomer Esiason HG...... | .08 | .04 | .01 |
| Cincinnati Bengals | | | |
| ☐ 317 Warren Moon HG........ | .12 | .05 | .02 |
| Houston Oilers | | | |
| (Moon on card) | | | |
| ☐ 318 Jim Kelly HG............ | .12 | .05 | .02 |
| Buffalo Bills | | | |
| ☐ 319 Bernie Kosar HG UER.... | .08 | .04 | .01 |
| Cleveland Browns | | | |
| (Word just is mis- | | | |
| spelled as justs) | | | |
| ☐ 320 Dan Marino HG UER...... | .35 | .16 | .04 |
| Miami Dolphins | | | |
| (Text says 378 com- | | | |
| pletions in 1984, | | | |

| | | | |
|---|---|---|---|
| should be 1986) | | | |
| ☐ 321 Christian Okoye GF........ | .04 | .02 | .01 |
| Kansas City Chiefs | | | |
| ☐ 322 Thurman Thomas GF...... | .20 | .09 | .03 |
| Buffalo Bills | | | |
| ☐ 323 James Brooks GF......... | .04 | .02 | .01 |
| Cincinnati Bengals | | | |
| ☐ 324 Bobby Humphrey GF...... | .04 | .02 | .01 |
| Denver Broncos | | | |
| ☐ 325 Barry Sanders GF........ | .50 | .23 | .06 |
| Detroit Lions | | | |
| ☐ 326 Neal Anderson GF........ | .04 | .02 | .01 |
| Chicago Bears | | | |
| ☐ 327 Dalton Hilliard GF........ | .04 | .02 | .01 |
| New Orleans Saints | | | |
| ☐ 328 Greg Bell GF............. | .04 | .02 | .01 |
| Los Angeles Rams | | | |
| ☐ 329 Roger Craig GF UER...... | .08 | .04 | .01 |
| San Francisco 49ers | | | |
| (Text says 2 TD's in | | | |
| SB XXIV, should be 1) | | | |
| ☐ 330 Bo Jackson GF........... | .20 | .09 | .03 |
| Los Angeles Raiders | | | |
| ☐ 331 Don Warren.............. | .04 | .02 | .01 |
| Washington Redskins | | | |
| ☐ 332 Rufus Porter............ | .04 | .02 | .01 |
| Seattle Seahawks | | | |
| ☐ 333 Sammie Smith........... | .04 | .02 | .01 |
| Miami Dolphins | | | |
| ☐ 334 Lewis Tillman UER....... | .08 | .04 | .01 |
| New York Giants | | | |
| (Born 4/16/67, should | | | |
| be 1966) | | | |
| ☐ 335 Michael Walter........... | .04 | .02 | .01 |
| San Francisco 49ers | | | |
| ☐ 336 Marc Logan............. | .04 | .02 | .01 |
| Miami Dolphins | | | |
| ☐ 337 Ron Hallstrom........... | .04 | .02 | .01 |
| Green Bay Packers | | | |
| ☐ 338 Stanley Morgan.......... | .08 | .04 | .01 |
| New England Patriots | | | |
| ☐ 339 Mark Robinson.......... | .04 | .02 | .01 |
| Tampa Bay Buccaneers | | | |
| ☐ 340 Frank Reich............. | .15 | .07 | .02 |
| Buffalo Bills | | | |
| ☐ 341 Chip Lohmiller.......... | .08 | .04 | .01 |
| Washington Redskins | | | |
| ☐ 342 Steve Beuerlein........ | .25 | .11 | .03 |
| Los Angeles Raiders | | | |
| ☐ 343 John L. Williams........ | .08 | .04 | .01 |
| Seattle Seahawks | | | |
| ☐ 344 Irving Fryar............. | .08 | .04 | .01 |
| New England Patriots | | | |
| ☐ 345 Anthony Carter.......... | .08 | .04 | .01 |
| Minnesota Vikings | | | |
| ☐ 346 Al Toon................. | .08 | .04 | .01 |
| New York Jets | | | |
| ☐ 347 J.T. Smith.............. | .04 | .02 | .01 |
| Phoenix Cardinals | | | |
| ☐ 348 Pierce Holt............. | .15 | .07 | .02 |
| San Francisco 49ers | | | |
| ☐ 349 Ferrell Edmunds........ | .04 | .02 | .01 |
| Miami Dolphins | | | |
| ☐ 350 Mark Rypien............ | .10 | .05 | .01 |
| Washington Redskins | | | |
| ☐ 351 Paul Gruber............ | .08 | .04 | .01 |
| Tampa Bay Buccaneers | | | |
| ☐ 352 Ernest Givins........... | .08 | .04 | .01 |
| Houston Oilers | | | |
| ☐ 353 Ervin Randle............ | .04 | .02 | .01 |
| Tampa Bay Buccaneers | | | |
| ☐ 354 Guy McIntyre........... | .08 | .04 | .01 |
| San Francisco 49ers | | | |
| ☐ 355 Webster Slaughter...... | .08 | .04 | .01 |
| Cleveland Browns | | | |
| ☐ 356 Reuben Davis........... | .04 | .02 | .01 |
| Tampa Bay Buccaneers | | | |
| ☐ 357 Rickey Jackson......... | .08 | .04 | .01 |
| New Orleans Saints | | | |
| ☐ 358 Earnest Byner.......... | .08 | .04 | .01 |
| Washington Redskins | | | |
| ☐ 359 Eddie Brown............ | .04 | .02 | .01 |
| Cincinnati Bengals | | | |
| ☐ 360 Troy Stradford......... | .04 | .02 | .01 |
| Miami Dolphins | | | |
| ☐ 361 Pepper Johnson........ | .08 | .04 | .01 |
| New York Giants | | | |
| ☐ 362 Ravin Caldwell......... | .04 | .02 | .01 |
| Washington Redskins | | | |
| ☐ 363 Chris Mohr............. | .10 | .05 | .01 |
| Tampa Bay Buccaneers | | | |
| ☐ 364 Jeff Bryant............. | .04 | .02 | .01 |
| Seattle Seahawks | | | |
| ☐ 365 Bruce Collie............ | .04 | .02 | .01 |
| San Francisco 49ers | | | |
| ☐ 366 Courtney Hall.......... | .04 | .02 | .01 |
| San Diego Chargers | | | |
| ☐ 367 Jerry Olsavsky......... | .04 | .02 | .01 |

Pittsburgh Steelers
| | | | |
|---|---|---|---|
| ☐ 368 David Galloway | .04 | .02 | .01 |

Phoenix Cardinals
| | | | |
|---|---|---|---|
| ☐ 369 Wes Hopkins | .04 | .02 | .01 |

Philadelphia Eagles
| | | | |
|---|---|---|---|
| ☐ 370 Johnny Hector | .04 | .02 | .01 |

New York Jets
| | | | |
|---|---|---|---|
| ☐ 371 Clarence Verdin | .04 | .02 | .01 |

Indiananpolis Colts
| | | | |
|---|---|---|---|
| ☐ 372 Nick Lowery | .08 | .04 | .01 |

Kansas City Chiefs
| | | | |
|---|---|---|---|
| ☐ 373 Tim Brown | .35 | .16 | .04 |

Los Angeles Raiders
| | | | |
|---|---|---|---|
| ☐ 374 Kevin Greene | .08 | .04 | .01 |

Los Angeles Rams
| | | | |
|---|---|---|---|
| ☐ 375 Leonard Marshall | .08 | .04 | .01 |

New York Giants
| | | | |
|---|---|---|---|
| ☐ 376 Roland James | .04 | .02 | .01 |

New England Patriots
| | | | |
|---|---|---|---|
| ☐ 377 Scott Studwell | .04 | .02 | .01 |

Minnesota Vikins
| | | | |
|---|---|---|---|
| ☐ 378 Jarvis Williams | .04 | .02 | .01 |

Miami Dolphins
| | | | |
|---|---|---|---|
| ☐ 379 Mike Saxon | .04 | .02 | .01 |

Dallas Cowboys
| | | | |
|---|---|---|---|
| ☐ 380 Kevin Mack | .08 | .04 | .01 |

Cleveland Browns
| | | | |
|---|---|---|---|
| ☐ 381 Joe Kelly | .04 | .02 | .01 |

Cincinnati Bengals
| | | | |
|---|---|---|---|
| ☐ 382 Tom Thayer | .10 | .05 | .01 |

Chicago Bears
| | | | |
|---|---|---|---|
| ☐ 383 Roy Green | .08 | .04 | .01 |

Phoenix Cardinals
| | | | |
|---|---|---|---|
| ☐ 384 Michael Brooks | .20 | .09 | .03 |

Denver Broncos
| | | | |
|---|---|---|---|
| ☐ 385 Michael Cofer | .04 | .02 | .01 |

Detroit Lions
| | | | |
|---|---|---|---|
| ☐ 386 Ken Ruettgers | .04 | .02 | .01 |

Green Bay Packers
| | | | |
|---|---|---|---|
| ☐ 387 Dean Steinkuhler | .04 | .02 | .01 |

Houston Oilers
| | | | |
|---|---|---|---|
| ☐ 388 Maurice Carthon | .04 | .02 | .01 |

New York Giants
| | | | |
|---|---|---|---|
| ☐ 389 Ricky Sanders | .08 | .04 | .01 |

Washington Redskins
| | | | |
|---|---|---|---|
| ☐ 390 Winston Moss | .04 | .02 | .01 |

Tampa Bay Buccaneers
| | | | |
|---|---|---|---|
| ☐ 391 Tony Woods | .04 | .02 | .01 |

Seattle Seahawks
| | | | |
|---|---|---|---|
| ☐ 392 Keith DeLong | .04 | .02 | .01 |

San Francisco 49ers
| | | | |
|---|---|---|---|
| ☐ 393 David Wyman | .04 | .02 | .01 |

Seattle Seahawks
| | | | |
|---|---|---|---|
| ☐ 394 Vencie Glenn | .04 | .02 | .01 |

San Diego Chargers
| | | | |
|---|---|---|---|
| ☐ 395 Harris Barton | .04 | .02 | .01 |

San Francisco 49ers
| | | | |
|---|---|---|---|
| ☐ 396 Bryan Hinkle | .04 | .02 | .01 |

Pittsburgh Steelers
| | | | |
|---|---|---|---|
| ☐ 397 Derek Kennard | .04 | .02 | .01 |

Phoenix Carinals
| | | | |
|---|---|---|---|
| ☐ 398 Heath Sherman | .15 | .07 | .02 |

Philadelphia Eagles
| | | | |
|---|---|---|---|
| ☐ 399 Troy Benson | .04 | .02 | .01 |

New York Jets
| | | | |
|---|---|---|---|
| ☐ 400 Gary Zimmerman | .08 | .04 | .01 |

Minnesota Vikings
| | | | |
|---|---|---|---|
| ☐ 401 Mark Duper | .08 | .04 | .01 |

Miami Dolphins
| | | | |
|---|---|---|---|
| ☐ 402 Eugene Lockhart | .04 | .02 | .01 |

Dallas Cowboys
| | | | |
|---|---|---|---|
| ☐ 403 Tim Manoa | .04 | .02 | .01 |

Cleveland Browns
| | | | |
|---|---|---|---|
| ☐ 404 Reggie Williams | .08 | .04 | .01 |

Cincinnati Bengals
| | | | |
|---|---|---|---|
| ☐ 405 Mark Bortz | .10 | .05 | .01 |

Chicago Bears
| | | | |
|---|---|---|---|
| ☐ 406 Mike Kenn | .08 | .04 | .01 |

Atlanta Falcons
| | | | |
|---|---|---|---|
| ☐ 407 John Grimsley | .04 | .02 | .01 |

Houston Oilers
| | | | |
|---|---|---|---|
| ☐ 408 Bill Romanowski | .10 | .05 | .01 |

San Francisco 49ers
| | | | |
|---|---|---|---|
| ☐ 409 Perry Kemp | .04 | .02 | .01 |

Green Bay Packers
| | | | |
|---|---|---|---|
| ☐ 410 Norm Johnson | .04 | .02 | .01 |

Seattle Seahawks
| | | | |
|---|---|---|---|
| ☐ 411 Broderick Thomas | .08 | .04 | .01 |

Tampa Bay Buccaneers
| | | | |
|---|---|---|---|
| ☐ 412 Joe Wolf | .04 | .02 | .01 |

Phoenix Cardinals
| | | | |
|---|---|---|---|
| ☐ 413 Andre Waters | .08 | .04 | .01 |

Philadelphia Eagles
| | | | |
|---|---|---|---|
| ☐ 414 Jason Staurovsky | .04 | .02 | .01 |

New England Patriots
| | | | |
|---|---|---|---|
| ☐ 415 Eric Martin | .08 | .04 | .01 |

New Orleans Saints
| | | | |
|---|---|---|---|
| ☐ 416 Joe Prokop | .04 | .02 | .01 |

New York Jets
| | | | |
|---|---|---|---|
| ☐ 417 Steve Sewell | .04 | .02 | .01 |

Denver Broncos
| | | | |
|---|---|---|---|
| ☐ 418 Cedric Jones | .04 | .02 | .01 |

New England Patriots
| | | | |
|---|---|---|---|
| ☐ 419 Alphonso Carreker | .04 | .02 | .01 |

Denver Broncos
| | | | |
|---|---|---|---|
| ☐ 420 Keith Willis | .04 | .02 | .01 |

Pittsburgh Steelers
| | | | |
|---|---|---|---|
| ☐ 421 Bobby Butler | .04 | .02 | .01 |

Atlanta Falcons
| | | | |
|---|---|---|---|
| ☐ 422 John Roper | .04 | .02 | .01 |

Chicago Bears
| | | | |
|---|---|---|---|
| ☐ 423 Tim Spencer | .04 | .02 | .01 |

San Diego Chargers
| | | | |
|---|---|---|---|
| ☐ 424 Jesse Sapolu | .04 | .02 | .01 |

San Francisco 49ers
| | | | |
|---|---|---|---|
| ☐ 425 Ron Wolfley | .04 | .02 | .01 |

Phoenix Cardinals
| | | | |
|---|---|---|---|
| ☐ 426 Doug Smith | .08 | .04 | .01 |

Los Angeles Rams
| | | | |
|---|---|---|---|
| ☐ 427 William Howard | .04 | .02 | .01 |

Tampa Bay Buccaneers
| | | | |
|---|---|---|---|
| ☐ 428 Keith Van Horne | .04 | .02 | .01 |

Chicago Bears
| | | | |
|---|---|---|---|
| ☐ 429 Tony Jordan | .04 | .02 | .01 |

Phoenix Cardinals
| | | | |
|---|---|---|---|
| ☐ 430 Mervyn Fernandez | .04 | .02 | .01 |

Los Angles Raiders
| | | | |
|---|---|---|---|
| ☐ 431 Shaun Gayle | .10 | .05 | .01 |

Chicago Bears
| | | | |
|---|---|---|---|
| ☐ 432 Ricky Nattiel | .04 | .02 | .01 |

Denver Broncos
| | | | |
|---|---|---|---|
| ☐ 433 Albert Lewis | .08 | .04 | .01 |

Kansas City Chiefs
| | | | |
|---|---|---|---|
| ☐ 434 Fred Banks | .15 | .07 | .02 |

Miami Dolphins
| | | | |
|---|---|---|---|
| ☐ 435 Henry Thomas | .04 | .02 | .01 |

Minnesota Vikings
| | | | |
|---|---|---|---|
| ☐ 436 Chet Brooks | .04 | .02 | .01 |

San Francisco 49ers
| | | | |
|---|---|---|---|
| ☐ 437 Mark Ingram | .08 | .04 | .01 |

New York Giants
| | | | |
|---|---|---|---|
| ☐ 438 Jeff Gossett | .04 | .02 | .01 |

Los Angeles Raiders
| | | | |
|---|---|---|---|
| ☐ 439 Mike Wilcher | .04 | .02 | .01 |

Los Angles Rams
| | | | |
|---|---|---|---|
| ☐ 440 Deron Cherry UER | .08 | .04 | .01 |

Kansas City Chiefs
(Text says 7 cons. Pro
Bowls, but he didn't
play in 1989 Pro Bowl)
| | | | |
|---|---|---|---|
| ☐ 441 Mike Rozier | .08 | .04 | .01 |

Houston Oilers
| | | | |
|---|---|---|---|
| ☐ 442 Jon Hand | .04 | .02 | .01 |

Indianapolis Colts
| | | | |
|---|---|---|---|
| ☐ 443 Ozzie Newsome | .10 | .05 | .01 |

Cleveland Browns
| | | | |
|---|---|---|---|
| ☐ 444 Sammy Martin | .04 | .02 | .01 |

New England Patriots
| | | | |
|---|---|---|---|
| ☐ 445 Luis Sharpe | .04 | .02 | .01 |

Phoenix Cardinals
| | | | |
|---|---|---|---|
| ☐ 446 Lee Williams | .08 | .04 | .01 |

San Diego Chargers
| | | | |
|---|---|---|---|
| ☐ 447 Chris Martin | .10 | .05 | .01 |

Kansas City Chiefs
| | | | |
|---|---|---|---|
| ☐ 448 Kevin Fagan | .04 | .02 | .01 |

San Francisco 49ers
| | | | |
|---|---|---|---|
| ☐ 449 Gene Lang | .04 | .02 | .01 |

Atlanta Falcons
| | | | |
|---|---|---|---|
| ☐ 450 Greg Townsend | .08 | .04 | .01 |

Los Angeles Raiders
| | | | |
|---|---|---|---|
| ☐ 451 Robert Lyles | .04 | .02 | .01 |

Houston Oilers
| | | | |
|---|---|---|---|
| ☐ 452 Eric Hill | .04 | .02 | .01 |

Phoenix Cardinals
| | | | |
|---|---|---|---|
| ☐ 453 John Teltschik | .04 | .02 | .01 |

Philadelphia Eagles
| | | | |
|---|---|---|---|
| ☐ 454 Vestee Jackson | .04 | .02 | .01 |

Chicago Bears
| | | | |
|---|---|---|---|
| ☐ 455 Bruce Reimers | .04 | .02 | .01 |

Cincinnati Bengals
| | | | |
|---|---|---|---|
| ☐ 456 Butch Rolle | .10 | .05 | .01 |

Buffalo Bills
| | | | |
|---|---|---|---|
| ☐ 457 Lawyer Tillman | .04 | .02 | .01 |

Cleveland Browns
| | | | |
|---|---|---|---|
| ☐ 458 Andre Tippett | .08 | .04 | .01 |

New England Patriots
| | | | |
|---|---|---|---|
| ☐ 459 James Thornton | .04 | .02 | .01 |

Chicago Bears
| | | | |
|---|---|---|---|
| ☐ 460 Randy Grimes | .04 | .02 | .01 |

Tampa Bay Buccaneers
| | | | |
|---|---|---|---|
| ☐ 461 Larry Roberts | .04 | .02 | .01 |

San Francisco 49ers
| | | | |
|---|---|---|---|
| ☐ 462 Ron Holmes | .04 | .02 | .01 |

Denver Broncos
| | | | |
|---|---|---|---|
| ☐ 463 Mike Wise | .04 | .02 | .01 |

Los Angles Rams

| | | | |
|---|---|---|---|
| ☐ 464 Danny Copeland | .04 | .02 | .01 |
| Kansas City Chiefs | | | |
| ☐ 465 Bruce Wilkerson | .04 | .02 | .01 |
| Los Angles Raiders | | | |
| ☐ 466 Mike Quick | .08 | .04 | .01 |
| Philadelphia Eagles | | | |
| ☐ 467 Mickey Shuler | .04 | .02 | .01 |
| New York Jets | | | |
| ☐ 468 Mike Prior | .04 | .02 | .01 |
| Indianapolis Colts | | | |
| ☐ 469 Ron Rivera | .04 | .02 | .01 |
| Chicago Bears | | | |
| ☐ 470 Dean Biasucci | .04 | .02 | .01 |
| Indianapolis Colts | | | |
| ☐ 471 Perry Williams | .04 | .02 | .01 |
| New York Giants | | | |
| ☐ 472 Darren Comeaux UER | .04 | .02 | .01 |
| Seattle Seahawks | | | |
| (Front 53, back 52) | | | |
| ☐ 473 Freeman McNeil | .08 | .04 | .01 |
| New York Jets | | | |
| ☐ 474 Tyrone Braxton | .04 | .02 | .01 |
| Denver Broncos | | | |
| ☐ 475 Jay Schroeder | .08 | .04 | .01 |
| Los Angeles Raiders | | | |
| ☐ 476 Naz Worthen | .04 | .02 | .01 |
| Kansas City Chiefs | | | |
| ☐ 477 Lionel Washington | .04 | .02 | .01 |
| Los Angeles Raiders | | | |
| ☐ 478 Carl Zander | .04 | .02 | .01 |
| Cincinnati Bengals | | | |
| ☐ 479 Al(Bubba) Baker | .08 | .04 | .01 |
| Cleveland Browns | | | |
| ☐ 480 Mike Merriweather | .08 | .04 | .01 |
| Minnesota Vikings | | | |
| ☐ 481 Mike Gann | .04 | .02 | .01 |
| Atlanta Falcons | | | |
| ☐ 482 Brent Williams | .04 | .02 | .01 |
| New England Patriots | | | |
| ☐ 483 Eugene Robinson | .04 | .02 | .01 |
| Seattle Seahawks | | | |
| ☐ 484 Ray Horton | .04 | .02 | .01 |
| Dallas Cowboys | | | |
| ☐ 485 Bruce Armstrong | .04 | .02 | .01 |
| New England Patriots | | | |
| ☐ 486 John Fourcade | .04 | .02 | .01 |
| New Orleans Saints | | | |
| ☐ 487 Lewis Billups | .04 | .02 | .01 |
| Cincinnati Bengals | | | |
| ☐ 488 Scott Davis | .04 | .02 | .01 |
| Los Angeles Raiders | | | |
| ☐ 489 Ken Sims | .04 | .02 | .01 |
| New England Patriots | | | |
| ☐ 490 Chris Chandler | .08 | .04 | .01 |
| Indianapolis Colts | | | |
| ☐ 491 Mark Lee | .04 | .02 | .01 |
| Green Bay Packers | | | |
| ☐ 492 Johnny Meads | .04 | .02 | .01 |
| Houston Oilers | | | |
| ☐ 493 Tim Irwin | .04 | .02 | .01 |
| Minnesota Vikings | | | |
| ☐ 494 E.J. Junior | .04 | .02 | .01 |
| Miami Dolphins | | | |
| ☐ 495 Hardy Nickerson | .08 | .04 | .01 |
| Pittsburgh Steelers | | | |
| ☐ 496 Rob McGovern | .04 | .02 | .01 |
| Kansas City Chiefs | | | |
| ☐ 497 Fred Strickland | .04 | .02 | .01 |
| Los Angeles Rams | | | |
| ☐ 498 Reggie Rutland | .10 | .05 | .01 |
| Minnesota Vikings | | | |
| ☐ 499 Mel Owens | .04 | .02 | .01 |
| Los Angeles Rams | | | |
| ☐ 500 Derrick Thomas | .25 | .11 | .03 |
| Kansas City Chiefs | | | |
| ☐ 501 Jerrol Williams | .04 | .02 | .01 |
| Pittsburgh Steelers | | | |
| ☐ 502 Maurice Hurst | .04 | .02 | .01 |
| New England Patriots | | | |
| ☐ 503 Larry Kelm | .04 | .02 | .01 |
| Los Angeles Rams | | | |
| ☐ 504 Herman Fontenot | .04 | .02 | .01 |
| Green Bay Packers | | | |
| ☐ 505 Pat Beach | .04 | .02 | .01 |
| Indianapolis Colts | | | |
| ☐ 506 Haywood Jeffires | 1.00 | .45 | .13 |
| Houston Oilers | | | |
| ☐ 507 Neil Smith | .20 | .09 | .03 |
| Kansas City Chiefs | | | |
| ☐ 508 Cleveland Gary | .08 | .04 | .01 |
| Los Angeles Rams | | | |
| ☐ 509 William Perry | .08 | .04 | .01 |
| Chicago Bears | | | |
| ☐ 510 Michael Carter | .04 | .02 | .01 |
| San Francisco 49ers | | | |
| ☐ 511 Walker Lee Ashley | .04 | .02 | .01 |
| Kansas City Chiefs | | | |
| ☐ 512 Bob Golic | .04 | .02 | .01 |
| Los Angeles Raiders | | | |
| ☐ 513 Danny Villa | .04 | .02 | .01 |
| New England Patriots | | | |
| ☐ 514 Matt Millen | .08 | .04 | .01 |
| San Francisco 49ers | | | |
| ☐ 515 Don Griffin | .04 | .02 | .01 |
| San Francisco 49ers | | | |
| ☐ 516 Jonathan Hayes | .04 | .02 | .01 |
| Kansas City Chiefs | | | |
| ☐ 517 Gerald Williams | .04 | .02 | .01 |
| Pittsburgh Steelers | | | |
| ☐ 518 Scott Fulhage | .04 | .02 | .01 |
| Atlanta Falcons | | | |
| ☐ 519 Irv Pankey | .04 | .02 | .01 |
| Los Angeles Rams | | | |
| ☐ 520 Randy Dixon | .04 | .02 | .01 |
| Indianapolis Colts | | | |
| ☐ 521 Terry McDaniel | .04 | .02 | .01 |
| Los Angeles Raiders | | | |
| ☐ 522 Dan Saleaumua | .04 | .02 | .01 |
| Kansas City Chiefs | | | |
| ☐ 523 Darrin Nelson | .08 | .04 | .01 |
| San Diego Chargers | | | |
| ☐ 524 Leonard Griffin | .04 | .02 | .01 |
| Kansas City Chiefs | | | |
| ☐ 525 Michael Ball | .04 | .02 | .01 |
| Indianapolis Colts | | | |
| ☐ 526 Ernie Jones | .15 | .07 | .02 |
| Phoenix Cardinals | | | |
| ☐ 527 Tony Eason UER | .08 | .04 | .01 |
| New York Jets | | | |
| (Drafted in 1963, | | | |
| should be 1983) | | | |
| ☐ 528 Ed Reynolds | .04 | .02 | .01 |
| New England Patriots | | | |
| ☐ 529 Gary Hogeboom | .08 | .04 | .01 |
| Phoenix Cardinals | | | |
| ☐ 530 Don Mosebar | .04 | .02 | .01 |
| Los Angeles Raiders | | | |
| ☐ 531 Ottis Anderson | .08 | .04 | .01 |
| New York Giants | | | |
| ☐ 532 Bucky Scribner | .04 | .02 | .01 |
| Minnesota Vikins | | | |
| ☐ 533 Aaron Cox | .04 | .02 | .01 |
| Los Angeles Rams | | | |
| ☐ 534 Sean Jones | .08 | .04 | .01 |
| Houston Oilers | | | |
| ☐ 535 Doug Flutie | .15 | .07 | .02 |
| New England Patriots | | | |
| ☐ 536 Leo Lewis | .04 | .02 | .01 |
| Minnesota Vikings | | | |
| ☐ 537 Art Still | .08 | .04 | .01 |
| Buffalo Bills | | | |
| ☐ 538 Matt Bahr | .04 | .02 | .01 |
| Cleveland Browns | | | |
| ☐ 539 Keena Turner | .08 | .04 | .01 |
| San Francisco 49ers | | | |
| ☐ 540 Sammy Winder | .04 | .02 | .01 |
| Denver Broncos | | | |
| ☐ 541 Mike Webster | .08 | .04 | .01 |
| Kansas City Chiefs | | | |
| ☐ 542 Doug Riesenberg | .04 | .02 | .01 |
| New York Giants | | | |
| ☐ 543 Dan Fike | .04 | .02 | .01 |
| Cleveland Browns | | | |
| ☐ 544 Clarence Kay | .04 | .02 | .01 |
| Denver Broncos | | | |
| ☐ 545 Jim Burt | .04 | .02 | .01 |
| San Francisco 49ers | | | |
| ☐ 546 Mike Horan | .04 | .02 | .01 |
| Denver Broncos | | | |
| ☐ 547 Al Harris | .04 | .02 | .01 |
| Philadelphia Eagles | | | |
| ☐ 548 Maury Buford | .04 | .02 | .01 |
| Chicago Bears | | | |
| ☐ 549 Jerry Robinson | .08 | .04 | .01 |
| Los Angeles Raiders | | | |
| ☐ 550 Tracy Rocker | .04 | .02 | .01 |
| Washington Redskins | | | |
| ☐ 551 Karl Mecklenburg CC | .04 | .02 | .01 |
| Denver Broncos | | | |
| ☐ 552 Lawrence Taylor CC | .08 | .04 | .01 |
| New York Giants | | | |
| ☐ 553 Derrick Thomas CC | .15 | .07 | .02 |
| Kansas City Chiefs | | | |
| ☐ 554 Mike Singletary CC | .08 | .04 | .01 |
| Chicago Bears | | | |
| ☐ 555 Tim Harris CC | .04 | .02 | .01 |
| Green Bay Packers | | | |
| ☐ 556 Jerry Rice RM | .35 | .16 | .04 |
| San Francisco 49ers | | | |
| ☐ 557 Art Monk RM | .08 | .04 | .01 |
| Washington Redskins | | | |
| ☐ 558 Mark Carrier RM | .04 | .02 | .01 |
| Tampa Bay Buccaneers | | | |
| ☐ 559 Andre Reed RM | .08 | .04 | .01 |

Buffalo Bills

| | | | | |
|---|---|---|---|---|
| ☐ 560 Sterling Sharpe RM | .25 | .11 | .03 |
| Green Bay Packers | | | |
| ☐ 561 Herschel Walker GF | .08 | .04 | .01 |
| Minnesota Vikings | | | |
| ☐ 562 Ottis Anderson GF | .08 | .04 | .01 |
| New York Giants | | | |
| ☐ 563 Randall Cunningham HG | .08 | .04 | .01 |
| Philadelphia Eagles | | | |
| ☐ 564 John Elway HG | .20 | .09 | .03 |
| Denver Broncos | | | |
| ☐ 565 David Fulcher AP | .04 | .02 | .01 |
| Cincinnati Bengals | | | |
| ☐ 566 Ronnie Lott AP | .08 | .04 | .01 |
| San Francisco 49ers | | | |
| ☐ 567 Jerry Gray AP | .04 | .02 | .01 |
| Los Angeles Rams | | | |
| ☐ 568 Albert Lewis AP | .04 | .02 | .01 |
| Kansas City Chiefs | | | |
| ☐ 569 Karl Mecklenburg AP | .04 | .02 | .01 |
| Denver Broncos | | | |
| ☐ 570 Mike Singletary AP | .08 | .04 | .01 |
| Chicago Bears | | | |
| ☐ 571 Lawrence Taylor AP | .08 | .04 | .01 |
| New York Giants | | | |
| ☐ 572 Tim Harris AP | .04 | .02 | .01 |
| Green Bay Packers | | | |
| ☐ 573 Keith Millard AP | .08 | .04 | .01 |
| Minnesota Vikings | | | |
| ☐ 574 Reggie White AP | .08 | .04 | .01 |
| Philadelphia Eagles | | | |
| ☐ 575 Chris Doleman AP | .04 | .02 | .01 |
| Minnesota Vikings | | | |
| ☐ 576 Dave Meggett AP | .08 | .04 | .01 |
| New York Giants | | | |
| ☐ 577 Rod Woodson AP | .08 | .04 | .01 |
| Pittsburgh Steelers | | | |
| ☐ 578 Sean Landeta AP | .04 | .02 | .01 |
| New York Giants | | | |
| ☐ 579 Eddie Murray AP | .04 | .02 | .01 |
| Detroit Lions | | | |
| ☐ 580 Barry Sanders AP | .50 | .23 | .06 |
| Detroit Lions | | | |
| ☐ 581 Christian Okoye AP | .04 | .02 | .01 |
| Kansas City Chiefs | | | |
| ☐ 582 Joe Montana AP | .50 | .23 | .06 |
| San Francisco 49ers | | | |
| ☐ 583 Jay Hilgenberg AP | .04 | .02 | .01 |
| Chicago Bears | | | |
| ☐ 584 Bruce Matthews AP | .04 | .02 | .01 |
| Houston Oilers | | | |
| ☐ 585 Tom Newberry AP | .04 | .02 | .01 |
| Los Angeles Rams | | | |
| ☐ 586 Gary Zimmerman AP | .04 | .02 | .01 |
| Minnesota Vikings | | | |
| ☐ 587 Anthony Munoz AP | .08 | .04 | .01 |
| Cincinnati Bengals | | | |
| ☐ 588 Keith Jackson AP | .12 | .05 | .02 |
| Philadelphia Eagles | | | |
| ☐ 589 Sterling Sharpe AP | .30 | .14 | .04 |
| Green Bay Packers | | | |
| ☐ 590 Jerry Rice AP | .35 | .16 | .04 |
| San Francisco 49ers | | | |
| ☐ 591 Bo Jackson RB | .20 | .09 | .03 |
| Los Angeles Raiders | | | |
| ☐ 592 Steve Largent RB | .12 | .05 | .02 |
| Seattle Seahawks | | | |
| ☐ 593 Flipper Anderson RB | .04 | .02 | .01 |
| Los Angeles Rams | | | |
| ☐ 594 Joe Montana RB | .50 | .23 | .06 |
| San Francisco 49ers | | | |
| ☐ 595 Franco Harris HOF | .08 | .04 | .01 |
| ☐ 596 Bob St. Clair HOF | .04 | .02 | .01 |
| ☐ 597 Tom Landry HOF | .08 | .04 | .01 |
| ☐ 598 Jack Lambert HOF | .04 | .02 | .01 |
| ☐ 599 Ted Hendricks HOF | .04 | .02 | .01 |
| UER | | | |
| (Int. avg. says 12.8, | | | |
| should be 8.9) | | | |
| ☐ 600A Buck Buchanan HOF | .08 | .04 | .01 |
| UER | | | |
| (Drafted in 1983) | | | |
| ☐ 600B Buck Buchanan HOF | .08 | .04 | .01 |
| COR | | | |
| (Drafted in 1963) | | | |
| ☐ 601 Bob Griese | .08 | .04 | .01 |
| HOF | | | |
| ☐ 602 Super Bowl Wrap | .04 | .02 | .01 |
| ☐ 603A Vince Lombardi UER | .15 | .07 | .02 |
| Lombardi Legend | | | |
| (Disciplinarian mis- | | | |
| spelled; no logo for | | | |
| Curtis Mgt. at bottom) | | | |
| ☐ 603B Vince Lombardi UER | .15 | .07 | .02 |
| Lombardi Legend | | | |
| (Disciplinarian mis- | | | |
| spelled; logo for | | | |
| Curtis Mgt. at bottom) | | | |

| | | | | |
|---|---|---|---|---|
| ☐ 604 Mark Carrier UER | .10 | .05 | .01 |
| Tampa Bay Buccaneers | | | |
| (Front 88, back 89) | | | |
| ☐ 605 Randall Cunningham | .15 | .07 | .02 |
| Philadelphia Eagles | | | |
| ☐ 606 Percy Snow | .04 | .02 | .01 |
| Kansas City Chiefs | | | |
| (Class of '90) | | | |
| ☐ 607 Andre Ware | .04 | .02 | .01 |
| Detroit Lions | | | |
| (Class of '90) | | | |
| ☐ 608 Blair Thomas | .04 | .02 | .01 |
| New York Jets | | | |
| (Class of '90) | | | |
| ☐ 609 Eric Green | .15 | .07 | .02 |
| Pittsburgh Steelers | | | |
| (Class of '90) | | | |
| ☐ 610 Reggie Rembert | .04 | .02 | .01 |
| New York Jets | | | |
| (Class of '90) | | | |
| ☐ 611 Richmond Webb | .10 | .05 | .01 |
| Miami Dolphins | | | |
| (Class of '90) | | | |
| ☐ 612 Bern Brostek | .04 | .02 | .01 |
| Los Angeles Rams | | | |
| (Class of '90) | | | |
| ☐ 613 James Williams | .04 | .02 | .01 |
| Buffalo Bills | | | |
| (Class of '90) | | | |
| ☐ 614 Mark Carrier | .08 | .04 | .01 |
| Chicago Bears | | | |
| (Class of '90) | | | |
| ☐ 615 Renaldo Turnbull | .20 | .09 | .03 |
| New Orleans Saints | | | |
| (Class of '90) | | | |
| ☐ 616 Cortez Kennedy | .35 | .16 | .04 |
| Seattle Seahawks | | | |
| (Class of '90) | | | |
| ☐ 617 Keith McCants | .04 | .02 | .01 |
| Tampa Bay Buccaneers | | | |
| (Class of '90) | | | |
| ☐ 618 Anthony Thompson | .10 | .05 | .01 |
| Draft Pick | | | |
| ☐ 619 LeRoy Butler | .20 | .09 | .03 |
| Draft Pick | | | |
| ☐ 620 Aaron Wallace | .15 | .07 | .02 |
| Draft Pick | | | |
| ☐ 621 Alexander Wright | .12 | .05 | .02 |
| Draft Pick | | | |
| ☐ 622 Keith McCants | .10 | .05 | .01 |
| Draft Pick | | | |
| ☐ 623 Jimmie Jones UER | .15 | .07 | .02 |
| Draft Pick | | | |
| (January misspelled) | | | |
| ☐ 624 Anthony Johnson | .10 | .05 | .01 |
| Draft Pick | | | |
| ☐ 625 Fred Washington | .04 | .02 | .01 |
| Draft Pick | | | |
| ☐ 626 Mike Bellamy | .04 | .02 | .01 |
| Draft Pick | | | |
| ☐ 627 Mark Carrier | .20 | .09 | .03 |
| Draft Pick | | | |
| ☐ 628 Harold Green | .25 | .11 | .03 |
| Draft Pick | | | |
| ☐ 629 Eric Green | .40 | .18 | .05 |
| Draft Pick | | | |
| ☐ 630 Andre Collins | .15 | .07 | .02 |
| Draft Pick | | | |
| ☐ 631 Lamar Lathon | .15 | .07 | .02 |
| Draft Pick | | | |
| ☐ 632 Terry Wooden | .10 | .05 | .01 |
| Draft Pick | | | |
| ☐ 633 Jesse Anderson | .04 | .02 | .01 |
| Draft Pick | | | |
| ☐ 634 Jeff George | .75 | .35 | .09 |
| Draft Pick | | | |
| ☐ 635 Carwell Gardner | .12 | .05 | .02 |
| Draft Pick | | | |
| ☐ 636 Darrell Thompson | .15 | .07 | .02 |
| Draft Pick | | | |
| ☐ 637 Vince Buck | .10 | .05 | .01 |
| Draft Pick | | | |
| ☐ 638 Mike Jones | .04 | .02 | .01 |
| Draft Pick | | | |
| ☐ 639 Charles Arbuckle | .10 | .05 | .01 |
| Draft Pick | | | |
| ☐ 640 Dennis Brown | .10 | .05 | .01 |
| Draft Pick | | | |
| ☐ 641 James Williams | .10 | .05 | .01 |
| Draft Pick | | | |
| ☐ 642 Bern Brostek | .04 | .02 | .01 |
| Draft Pick | | | |
| ☐ 643 Darion Conner | .10 | .05 | .01 |
| Draft Pick | | | |
| ☐ 644 Mike Fox | .04 | .02 | .01 |
| Draft Pick | | | |
| ☐ 645 Cary Conklin | .35 | .16 | .04 |

| | | MINT | EXC | G-VG |
|---|---|---|---|---|
| Draft Pick | | | | |
| ☐ 646 Tim Grunhard | .04 | .02 | .01 |
| Draft Pick | | | | |
| ☐ 647 Ron Cox | .04 | .02 | .01 |
| Draft Pick | | | | |
| ☐ 648 Keith Sims | .10 | .05 | .01 |
| Draft Pick | | | | |
| ☐ 649 Alton Montgomery | .10 | .05 | .01 |
| Draft Pick | | | | |
| ☐ 650 Greg McMurtry | .12 | .05 | .02 |
| Draft Pick | | | | |
| ☐ 651 Scott Mitchell | 1.25 | .55 | .16 |
| Draft Pick | | | | |
| ☐ 652 Tim Ryan | .04 | .02 | .01 |
| Draft Pick | | | | |
| ☐ 653 Jeff Mills | .04 | .02 | .01 |
| Draft Pick | | | | |
| ☐ 654 Ricky Proehl | .50 | .23 | .06 |
| Draft Pick | | | | |
| ☐ 655 Steve Broussard | .10 | .05 | .01 |
| Draft Pick | | | | |
| ☐ 656 Peter Tom Willis | .12 | .05 | .02 |
| Draft Pick | | | | |
| ☐ 657 Dexter Carter | .15 | .07 | .02 |
| Draft Pick | | | | |
| ☐ 658 Tony Casillas | .04 | .02 | .01 |
| Atlanta Falcons | | | | |
| ☐ 659 Joe Morris | .08 | .04 | .01 |
| New York Giants | | | | |
| ☐ 660 Greg Kragen | .04 | .02 | .01 |
| Denver Broncos | | | | |
| ☐ B1 Judd Garrett | .05 | .02 | .01 |
| Philadelphia Eagles | | | | |
| ☐ B2 Matt Stover | .15 | .07 | .02 |
| New York Giants | | | | |
| ☐ B3 Ken McMichael | .05 | .02 | .01 |
| Phoenix Cardinals | | | | |
| ☐ B4 Demetrius Davis | .05 | .02 | .01 |
| Los Angeles Raiders | | | | |
| ☐ B5 Elliott Searcy | .05 | .02 | .01 |
| San Diego Chargers | | | | |

## 1990 Score Hot Card

This ten-card standard size (2 1/2" by 3 1/2") set was issued by Score as an insert (one per) in their 100-card blister packs, which feature Score cards from both Series 1 and Series 2. The cards have black borders which surround the player's photo set against the sun. The back of the card features a large color photo of the player on the top 2/3 of the card and brief biographical identification on the bottom.

| | MINT | EXC | G-VG |
|---|---|---|---|
| COMPLETE SET (10) | 25.00 | 10.00 | 2.50 |
| COMMON PLAYER (1-10) | 1.50 | .60 | .15 |
| ☐ 1 Joe Montana | 10.00 | 4.00 | 1.00 |
| San Francisco 49ers | | | |
| ☐ 2 Bo Jackson | 3.00 | 1.20 | .30 |
| Los Angeles Raiders | | | |
| ☐ 3 Barry Sanders | 5.00 | 2.00 | .50 |
| Detroit Lions | | | |
| ☐ 4 Jerry Rice | 5.00 | 2.00 | .50 |
| San Francisco 49ers | | | |
| ☐ 5 Eric Metcalf | 1.50 | .60 | .15 |
| Cleveland Browns | | | |
| ☐ 6 Don Majkowski | 1.50 | .60 | .15 |
| Green Bay Packers | | | |
| ☐ 7 Christian Okoye | 1.50 | .60 | .15 |
| Kansas City Chiefs | | | |
| ☐ 8 Bobby Humphrey | 1.50 | .60 | .15 |
| Denver Broncos | | | |
| ☐ 9 Dan Marino | 6.00 | 2.40 | .60 |
| Miami Dolphins | | | |
| ☐ 10 Sterling Sharpe | 5.00 | 2.00 | .50 |
| Green Bay Packers | | | |

## 1990 Score Supplemental

This 110-card standard size set (2 1/2" by 3 1/2") was issued in the same design as the regular Score issue, but with blue and purple borders. The set included cards of rookies and cards of players who switched teams during the off-season. The set was released through Score's dealer outlets and was available only in complete set form from the company. The key Rookie Cards in the set are Reggie Cobb, Derrick Fenner, Stan Humphries, Johnny Johnson, Rob Moore, Emmitt Smith, and Barry Word. The cards are numbered on the back with a "T" suffix.

| | MINT | EXC | G-VG |
|---|---|---|---|
| COMPLETE FACT.SET (110) | 110.00 | 50.00 | 14.00 |
| COMMON PLAYER (1T-110T) | .10 | .05 | .01 |
| ☐ 1T Marcus Dupree | .10 | .05 | .01 |
| Los Angeles Rams | | | |
| ☐ 2T Jerry Kauric | .10 | .05 | .01 |
| Cleveland Browns | | | |
| ☐ 3T Everson Walls | .10 | .05 | .01 |
| New York Giants | | | |
| ☐ 4T Elliott Smith | .10 | .05 | .01 |
| Denver Broncos | | | |
| ☐ 5T Donald Evans UER | .15 | .07 | .02 |
| Pittsburgh Steelers | | | |
| (Misspelled Pittsburg | | | |
| on card back) | | | |
| ☐ 6T Jerry Holmes | .10 | .05 | .01 |
| Green Bay Packers | | | |
| ☐ 7T Dan Stryzinski | .10 | .05 | .01 |
| Pittsburgh Steelers | | | |
| ☐ 8T Gerald McNeil | .10 | .05 | .01 |
| Houston Oilers | | | |
| ☐ 9T Rick Tuten | .15 | .07 | .02 |
| Buffalo Bills | | | |
| ☐ 10T Mickey Shuler | .10 | .05 | .01 |
| Philadelphia Eagles | | | |
| ☐ 11T Jay Novacek | 2.00 | .90 | .25 |
| Dallas Cowboys | | | |
| ☐ 12T Eric Williams | .20 | .09 | .03 |
| Washington Redskins | | | |
| ☐ 13T Stanley Morgan | .15 | .07 | .02 |
| Indianapolis Colts | | | |
| ☐ 14T Wayne Haddix | .10 | .05 | .01 |
| Tampa Bay Buccaneers | | | |
| ☐ 15T Gary Anderson | .15 | .07 | .02 |
| Tampa Bay Buccaneers | | | |
| ☐ 16T Stan Humphries | 3.00 | 1.35 | .40 |
| Washington Redskins | | | |
| ☐ 17T Raymond Clayborn | .15 | .07 | .02 |
| Cleveland Browns | | | |
| ☐ 18T Mark Boyer | .15 | .07 | .02 |
| New York Jets | | | |
| ☐ 19T Dave Waymer | .10 | .05 | .01 |
| San Francisco 49ers | | | |
| ☐ 20T Andre Rison | 1.50 | .65 | .19 |
| Atlanta Falcons | | | |
| ☐ 21T Daniel Stubbs | .10 | .05 | .01 |
| Dallas Cowboys | | | |
| ☐ 22T Mike Rozier | .15 | .07 | .02 |
| Atlanta Falcons | | | |
| ☐ 23T Damian Johnson | .10 | .05 | .01 |
| New England Patriots | | | |
| ☐ 24T Don Smith | .10 | .05 | .01 |
| Buffalo Bills | | | |
| ☐ 25T Max Montoya | .10 | .05 | .01 |
| Los Angeles Raiders | | | |
| ☐ 26T Terry Kinard | .10 | .05 | .01 |
| Houston Oilers | | | |
| ☐ 27T Herb Welch | .10 | .05 | .01 |
| Detroit Lions | | | |
| ☐ 28T Cliff Odom | .10 | .05 | .01 |
| Miami Dolphins | | | |
| ☐ 29T John Kidd | .10 | .05 | .01 |

| | | | | |
|---|---|---|---|---|
| San Diego Chargers | | | | |
| □ 30T Barry Word | 1.25 | .55 | .16 | |
| Kansas City Chiefs | | | | |
| □ 31T Rich Karlis | .10 | .05 | .01 | |
| Detroit Lions | | | | |
| □ 32T Mike Baab | .10 | .05 | .01 | |
| Cleveland Browns | | | | |
| □ 33T Ronnie Harmon | .30 | .14 | .04 | |
| San Diego Chargers | | | | |
| □ 34T Jeff Donaldson | .10 | .05 | .01 | |
| Kansas City Chiefs | | | | |
| □ 35T Riki Ellison | .10 | .05 | .01 | |
| Los Angeles Raiders | | | | |
| □ 36T Steve Walsh | .10 | .05 | .01 | |
| New Orleans Saints | | | | |
| □ 37T Bill Lewis | .15 | .07 | .02 | |
| Phoenix Cardinals | | | | |
| □ 38T Tim McKyer | .15 | .07 | .02 | |
| Miami Dolphins | | | | |
| □ 39T James Wilder | .15 | .07 | .02 | |
| Detroit Lions | | | | |
| □ 40T Tony Paige | .10 | .05 | .01 | |
| Miami Dolphins | | | | |
| □ 41T Derrick Fenner | .50 | .23 | .06 | |
| Seattle Seahawks | | | | |
| □ 42T Thane Gash | .10 | .05 | .01 | |
| Cleveland Browns | | | | |
| □ 43T Dave Duerson | .10 | .05 | .01 | |
| New York Giants | | | | |
| □ 44T Clarence Weathers | .10 | .05 | .01 | |
| Green Bay Packers | | | | |
| □ 45T Matt Bahr | .10 | .05 | .01 | |
| New York Giants | | | | |
| □ 46T Alonzo Highsmith | .10 | .05 | .01 | |
| Dallas Cowboys | | | | |
| □ 47T Joe Kelly | .10 | .05 | .01 | |
| New York Jets | | | | |
| □ 48T Chris Hinton | .10 | .05 | .01 | |
| Atlanta Falcons | | | | |
| □ 49T Bobby Humphery | .10 | .05 | .01 | |
| Los Angeles Rams | | | | |
| □ 50T Greg Bell | .10 | .05 | .01 | |
| Los Angeles Raiders | | | | |
| □ 51T Fred Smerlas | .15 | .07 | .02 | |
| San Francisco 49ers | | | | |
| □ 52T Walter Stanley | .10 | .05 | .01 | |
| Washington Redskins | | | | |
| □ 53T Jim Skow | .10 | .05 | .01 | |
| Tampa Bay Buccaneers | | | | |
| □ 54T Renaldo Turnbull | 1.00 | .45 | .13 | |
| New Orleans Saints | | | | |
| □ 55T Bern Brostek | .10 | .05 | .01 | |
| Los Angeles Rams | | | | |
| □ 56T Charles Wilson | .15 | .07 | .02 | |
| Green Bay Packers | | | | |
| □ 57T Keith McCants | .25 | .11 | .03 | |
| Tampa Bay Buccaneers | | | | |
| □ 58T Alexander Wright | .30 | .14 | .04 | |
| Dallas Cowboys | | | | |
| □ 59T Ian Beckles | .10 | .05 | .01 | |
| Tampa Bay Buccaneers | | | | |
| □ 60T Eric Davis | .40 | .18 | .05 | |
| San Francisco 49ers | | | | |
| □ 61T Chris Singleton | .20 | .09 | .03 | |
| New England Patriots | | | | |
| □ 62T Rob Moore | 2.50 | 1.15 | .30 | |
| New York Jets | | | | |
| □ 63T Darion Conner | .10 | .05 | .01 | |
| Atlanta Falcons | | | | |
| □ 64T Tim Grunhard | .10 | .05 | .01 | |
| Kansas City Chiefs | | | | |
| □ 65T Junior Seau | 5.00 | 2.30 | .60 | |
| San Diego Chargers | | | | |
| □ 66T Tony Stargell | .30 | .14 | .04 | |
| New York Jets | | | | |
| □ 67T Anthony Thompson | .35 | .16 | .04 | |
| Phoenix Cardinals | | | | |
| □ 68T Cortez Kennedy | 4.00 | 1.80 | .50 | |
| Seattle Seahawks | | | | |
| □ 69T Darrell Thompson | .75 | .35 | .09 | |
| Green Bay Packers | | | | |
| □ 70T Calvin Williams | 3.00 | 1.35 | .40 | |
| Philadelphia Eagles | | | | |
| □ 71T Rodney Hampton | 8.00 | 3.60 | 1.00 | |
| New York Giants | | | | |
| □ 72T Terry Wooden | .10 | .05 | .01 | |
| Seattle Seahawks | | | | |
| □ 73T Leo Goeas | .15 | .07 | .02 | |
| San Diego Chargers | | | | |
| □ 74T Ken Willis | .10 | .05 | .01 | |
| Dallas Cowboys | | | | |
| □ 75T Ricky Proehl | 1.00 | .45 | .13 | |
| Phoenix Cardinals | | | | |
| □ 76T Steve Christie | .50 | .23 | .06 | |
| Tampa Bay Buccaneers | | | | |
| □ 77T Andre Ware | .75 | .35 | .09 | |
| Detroit Lions | | | | |
| □ 78T Jeff George | 5.00 | 2.30 | .60 | |

| | | | |
|---|---|---|---|
| Indianapolis Colts | | | |
| □ 79T Walter Wilson | .10 | .05 | .01 |
| San Diego Chargers | | | |
| □ 80T Johnny Bailey | 1.25 | .55 | .16 |
| Chicago Bears | | | |
| □ 81T Harold Green | 1.50 | .65 | .19 |
| Cincinnati Bengals | | | |
| □ 82T Mark Carrier | .60 | .25 | .08 |
| Chicago Bears | | | |
| □ 83T Frank Cornish | .10 | .05 | .01 |
| San Diego Chargers | | | |
| □ 84T James Williams | .10 | .05 | .01 |
| Buffalo Bills | | | |
| □ 85T James Francis | .60 | .25 | .08 |
| Cincinnati Bengals | | | |
| □ 86T Percy Snow | .10 | .05 | .01 |
| Kansas City Chiefs | | | |
| □ 87T Anthony Johnson | .20 | .09 | .03 |
| Indianapolis Colts | | | |
| □ 88T Tim Ryan | .10 | .05 | .01 |
| Chicago Bears | | | |
| □ 89T Dan Owens | .20 | .09 | .03 |
| Detroit Lions | | | |
| □ 90T Aaron Wallace | .25 | .11 | .03 |
| Los Angeles Raiders | | | |
| □ 91T Steve Broussard | .30 | .14 | .04 |
| Atlanta Falcons | | | |
| □ 92T Eric Green | 2.00 | .90 | .25 |
| Pittsburgh Steelers | | | |
| □ 93T Blair Thomas | .30 | .14 | .04 |
| New York Jets | | | |
| □ 94T Robert Blackmon | .30 | .14 | .04 |
| Seattle Seahawks | | | |
| □ 95T Alan Grant | .10 | .05 | .01 |
| Indianapolis Colts | | | |
| □ 96T Andre Collins | .50 | .23 | .06 |
| Washington Redskins | | | |
| □ 97T Dexter Carter | .50 | .23 | .06 |
| San Francisco 49ers | | | |
| □ 98T Reggie Cobb | 4.00 | 1.80 | .50 |
| Tampa Bay Buccaneers | | | |
| □ 99T Dennis Brown | .20 | .09 | .03 |
| San Francisco 49ers | | | |
| □ 100T Kenny Davidson | .25 | .11 | .03 |
| Pittsburgh Steelers | | | |
| □ 101T Emmitt Smith | 85.00 | 38.00 | 10.50 |
| Dallas Cowboys | | | |
| □ 102T Jeff Alm | .10 | .05 | .01 |
| Houston Oilers | | | |
| □ 103T Alton Montgomery | .10 | .05 | .01 |
| Denver Broncos | | | |
| □ 104T Tony Bennett | .75 | .35 | .09 |
| Green Bay Packers | | | |
| □ 105T Johnny Johnson | 4.50 | 2.00 | .55 |
| Phoenix Cardinals | | | |
| □ 106T Leroy Hoard | .50 | .23 | .06 |
| Cleveland Browns | | | |
| □ 107T Ray Agnew | .10 | .05 | .01 |
| New England Patriots | | | |
| □ 108T Richmond Webb | .60 | .25 | .08 |
| Miami Dolphins | | | |
| □ 109T Keith Sims | .10 | .05 | .01 |
| Miami Dolphins | | | |
| □ 110T Barry Foster | 8.00 | 3.60 | 1.00 |
| Pittsburgh Steelers | | | |

# 1990 Score Young Superstars

This 40-card standard size (2 1/2" by 3 1/2") set was issued by Score in 1990 (via a mail-in offer), featuring forty of the leading young football players. This set features a glossy front with the player's photo being surrounded by black borders on the front of the card. The back, meanwhile, features a full color photo of the player along with seasonal and career statistics about the player.

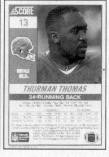

|  | MINT | EXC | G-VG |
|---|---|---|---|
| COMPLETE SET (40) | 6.00 | 2.40 | .60 |
| COMMON PLAYER (1-40) | .10 | .04 | .01 |
| ☐ 1 Barry Sanders | 1.25 | .50 | .12 |
| Detroit Lions |  |  |  |
| ☐ 2 Bobby Humphrey | .10 | .04 | .01 |
| Denver Broncos |  |  |  |
| ☐ 3 Ickey Woods | .10 | .04 | .01 |
| Cincinnati Bengals |  |  |  |
| ☐ 4 Shawn Collins | .10 | .04 | .01 |
| Atlanta Falcons |  |  |  |
| ☐ 5 Dave Meggett | .20 | .08 | .02 |
| New York Giants |  |  |  |
| ☐ 6 Keith Jackson | .30 | .12 | .03 |
| Philadelphia Eagles |  |  |  |
| ☐ 7 Sterling Sharpe | 1.00 | .40 | .10 |
| Green Bay Packers |  |  |  |
| ☐ 8 Troy Aikman | 2.00 | .80 | .20 |
| Dallas Cowboys |  |  |  |
| ☐ 9 Tim McDonald | .20 | .08 | .02 |
| Phoenix Cardinals |  |  |  |
| ☐ 10 Tim Brown | .50 | .20 | .05 |
| Los Angeles Raiders |  |  |  |
| ☐ 11 Trace Armstrong | .10 | .04 | .01 |
| Chicago Bears |  |  |  |
| ☐ 12 Eric Metcalf UER | .20 | .08 | .02 |
| Cleveland Browns |  |  |  |
| (Led Bears in rushing, |  |  |  |
| should be Browns) |  |  |  |
| ☐ 13 Derrick Thomas | .50 | .20 | .05 |
| Kansas City Chiefs |  |  |  |
| ☐ 14 Eric Hill | .10 | .04 | .01 |
| Phoenix Cardinals |  |  |  |
| ☐ 15 Deion Sanders | .50 | .20 | .05 |
| Atlanta Falcons |  |  |  |
| ☐ 16 Steve Atwater | .10 | .04 | .01 |
| Denver Broncos |  |  |  |
| ☐ 17 Carnell Lake | .10 | .04 | .01 |
| Pittsburgh Steelers |  |  |  |
| ☐ 18 Andre Reed | .30 | .12 | .03 |
| Buffalo Bills |  |  |  |
| ☐ 19 Chris Spielman | .10 | .04 | .01 |
| Detroit Lions |  |  |  |
| ☐ 20 Eric Allen | .10 | .04 | .01 |
| Philadelphia Eagles |  |  |  |
| ☐ 21 Erik McMillan | .10 | .04 | .01 |
| New York Jets |  |  |  |
| ☐ 22 Louis Oliver | .10 | .04 | .01 |
| Miami Dolphins |  |  |  |
| ☐ 23 Robert Massey | .10 | .04 | .01 |
| New Orleans Saints |  |  |  |
| ☐ 24 John Roper | .10 | .04 | .01 |
| Chicago Bears |  |  |  |
| ☐ 25 Burt Grossman | .10 | .04 | .01 |
| San Diego Chargers |  |  |  |
| ☐ 26 Chris Jacke | .10 | .04 | .01 |
| Green Bay Packers |  |  |  |
| ☐ 27 Steve Wisniewski | .10 | .04 | .01 |
| Los Angeles Raiders |  |  |  |
| ☐ 28 Alonzo Highsmith | .10 | .04 | .01 |
| Dallas Cowboys |  |  |  |
| ☐ 29 Mark Carrier | .30 | .12 | .03 |
| Tampa Bay Buccaneers |  |  |  |
| ☐ 30 Bruce Armstrong | .10 | .04 | .01 |
| New England Patriots |  |  |  |
| ☐ 31 Jerome Brown | .20 | .08 | .02 |
| Philadelphia Eagles |  |  |  |
| ☐ 32 Cornelius Bennett | .20 | .08 | .02 |
| Buffalo Bills |  |  |  |
| ☐ 33 Flipper Anderson | .10 | .04 | .01 |
| Los Angeles Rams |  |  |  |
| ☐ 34 Brian Blades | .30 | .12 | .03 |
| Seattle Seahawks |  |  |  |
| ☐ 35 Anthony Miller | .30 | .12 | .03 |
| San Diego Chargers |  |  |  |
| ☐ 36 Thurman Thomas | .75 | .30 | .07 |
| Buffalo Bills |  |  |  |
| ☐ 37 Chris Miller | .30 | .12 | .03 |
| Atlanta Falcons |  |  |  |
| ☐ 38 Aundray Bruce | .10 | .04 | .01 |
| Atlanta Falcons |  |  |  |
| ☐ 39 Robert Clark | .10 | .04 | .01 |
| Detroit Lions |  |  |  |
| ☐ 40 Robert Delpino | .10 | .04 | .01 |
| Los Angeles Rams |  |  |  |

## 1990 Score 100 Hottest

This 100-card standard size (2 1/2" by 3 1/2") set, featuring some of the most popular football stars of 1990, was issued by Score in conjunction with Publications International, which issued an attractive magazine-style publication giving more biographical information about the players featured on the front. These cards have the same photos on the front as the regular issue Score Football cards with the only difference being the numbering on the back of the card.

|  | MINT | EXC | G-VG |
|---|---|---|---|
| COMPLETE SET (100) | 10.00 | 4.00 | 1.00 |
| COMMON PLAYER (1-100) | .10 | .04 | .01 |
| ☐ 1 Bo Jackson | .30 | .12 | .03 |
| Los Angeles Raiders |  |  |  |
| ☐ 2 Joe Montana | 1.50 | .60 | .15 |
| San Francisco 49ers |  |  |  |
| ☐ 3 Deion Sanders | .30 | .12 | .03 |
| Atlanta Falcons |  |  |  |
| ☐ 4 Dan Marino | .75 | .30 | .07 |
| Miami Dolphins |  |  |  |
| ☐ 5 Barry Sanders | .75 | .30 | .07 |
| Detroit Lions |  |  |  |
| ☐ 6 Neal Anderson | .15 | .06 | .01 |
| Chicago Bears |  |  |  |
| ☐ 7 Phil Simms | .20 | .08 | .02 |
| New York Giants |  |  |  |
| ☐ 8 Bobby Humphrey | .10 | .04 | .01 |
| Denver Broncos |  |  |  |
| ☐ 9 Roger Craig | .20 | .08 | .02 |
| San Francisco 49ers |  |  |  |
| ☐ 10 John Elway | .50 | .20 | .05 |
| Denver Broncos |  |  |  |
| ☐ 11 James Brooks | .15 | .06 | .01 |
| Cincinnati Bengals |  |  |  |
| ☐ 12 Ken O'Brien | .10 | .04 | .01 |
| New York Jets |  |  |  |
| ☐ 13 Thurman Thomas | .50 | .20 | .05 |
| Buffalo Bills |  |  |  |
| ☐ 14 Troy Aikman | 1.50 | .60 | .15 |
| Dallas Cowboys |  |  |  |
| ☐ 15 Karl Mecklenburg | .10 | .04 | .01 |
| Denver Broncos |  |  |  |
| ☐ 16 Dave Krieg | .10 | .04 | .01 |
| Seattle Seahawks |  |  |  |
| ☐ 17 Chris Spielman | .10 | .04 | .01 |
| Detroit Lions |  |  |  |
| ☐ 18 Tim Harris | .15 | .06 | .01 |
| Green Bay Packers |  |  |  |
| ☐ 19 Tim Worley | .10 | .04 | .01 |
| Pittsburgh Steelers |  |  |  |
| ☐ 20 Clay Matthews | .15 | .06 | .01 |
| Cleveland Browns |  |  |  |
| ☐ 21 Lars Tate | .10 | .04 | .01 |
| Tampa Bay Buccaneers |  |  |  |
| ☐ 22 Hart Lee Dykes | .10 | .04 | .01 |
| New England Patriots |  |  |  |
| ☐ 23 Cornelius Bennett | .15 | .06 | .01 |
| Buffalo Bills |  |  |  |
| ☐ 24 Anthony Miller | .20 | .08 | .02 |
| San Diego Chargers |  |  |  |
| ☐ 25 Lawrence Taylor | .30 | .12 | .03 |
| New York Giants |  |  |  |
| ☐ 26 Jay Hilgenberg | .10 | .04 | .01 |
| Chicago Bears |  |  |  |
| ☐ 27 Tom Rathman | .15 | .06 | .01 |
| San Francisco 49ers |  |  |  |
| ☐ 28 Brian Blades | .25 | .10 | .02 |
| Seattle Seahawks |  |  |  |
| ☐ 29 David Fulcher | .10 | .04 | .01 |
| Cincinnati Bengals |  |  |  |
| ☐ 30 Cris Carter | .20 | .08 | .02 |
| Philadelphia Eagles |  |  |  |
| ☐ 31 Marcus Allen | .30 | .12 | .03 |
| Los Angeles Raiders |  |  |  |
| ☐ 32 Eric Metcalf | .15 | .06 | .01 |
| Cleveland Browns |  |  |  |
| ☐ 33 Bruce Smith | .15 | .06 | .01 |
| Buffalo Bills |  |  |  |
| ☐ 34 Jim Kelly | .50 | .20 | .05 |
| Buffalo Bills |  |  |  |
| ☐ 35 Wade Wilson | .15 | .06 | .01 |
| Minnesota Vikings |  |  |  |
| ☐ 36 Rich Camarillo | .10 | .04 | .01 |
| Phoenix Cardinals |  |  |  |
| ☐ 37 Boomer Esiason | .20 | .08 | .02 |

Cincinnati Bengals
| | | | | |
|---|---|---|---|---|
| ☐ 38 John Offerdahl | | .10 | .04 | .01 |

Miami Dolphins
| | | | | |
|---|---|---|---|---|
| ☐ 39 Vance Johnson | | .10 | .04 | .01 |

Denver Broncos
| | | | | |
|---|---|---|---|---|
| ☐ 40 Ronnie Lott | | .20 | .08 | .02 |

San Francisco 49ers
| | | | | |
|---|---|---|---|---|
| ☐ 41 Kevin Ross | | .10 | .04 | .01 |

Kansas City Chiefs
| | | | | |
|---|---|---|---|---|
| ☐ 42 Greg Bell | | .10 | .04 | .01 |

Los Angeles Raiders
| | | | | |
|---|---|---|---|---|
| ☐ 43 Erik McMillan | | .10 | .04 | .01 |

New York Jets
| | | | | |
|---|---|---|---|---|
| ☐ 44 Mike Singletary | | .20 | .08 | .02 |

Chicago Bears
| | | | | |
|---|---|---|---|---|
| ☐ 45 Roger Vick | | .10 | .04 | .01 |

New York Jets
| | | | | |
|---|---|---|---|---|
| ☐ 46 Keith Jackson | | .20 | .08 | .02 |

Philadelphia Eagles
| | | | | |
|---|---|---|---|---|
| ☐ 47 Henry Ellard | | .15 | .06 | .01 |

Los Angeles Rams
| | | | | |
|---|---|---|---|---|
| ☐ 48 Gary Anderson | | .15 | .06 | .01 |

Tampa Bay Buccaneers
| | | | | |
|---|---|---|---|---|
| ☐ 49 Art Monk | | .25 | .10 | .02 |

Washington Redskins
| | | | | |
|---|---|---|---|---|
| ☐ 50 Jim Everett | | .15 | .06 | .01 |

Los Angeles Rams
| | | | | |
|---|---|---|---|---|
| ☐ 51 Anthony Munoz | | .15 | .06 | .01 |

Cincinnati Bengals
| | | | | |
|---|---|---|---|---|
| ☐ 52 Ray Childress | | .15 | .06 | .01 |

Houston Oilers
| | | | | |
|---|---|---|---|---|
| ☐ 53 Howie Long | | .15 | .06 | .01 |

Los Angeles Raiders
| | | | | |
|---|---|---|---|---|
| ☐ 54 Chris Hinton | | .10 | .04 | .01 |

Atlanta Falcons
| | | | | |
|---|---|---|---|---|
| ☐ 55 John Stephens | | .20 | .08 | .02 |

New England Patriots
| | | | | |
|---|---|---|---|---|
| ☐ 56 Reggie White | | .25 | .10 | .02 |

Philadelphia Eagles
| | | | | |
|---|---|---|---|---|
| ☐ 57 Rodney Peete | | .15 | .06 | .01 |

Detroit Lions
| | | | | |
|---|---|---|---|---|
| ☐ 58 Don Majkowski | | .10 | .04 | .01 |

Green Bay Packers
| | | | | |
|---|---|---|---|---|
| ☐ 59 Michael Cofer | | .10 | .04 | .01 |

San Francisco 49ers
| | | | | |
|---|---|---|---|---|
| ☐ 60 Bubby Brister | | .10 | .04 | .01 |

Pittsburgh Steelers
| | | | | |
|---|---|---|---|---|
| ☐ 61 Jerry Gray | | .10 | .04 | .01 |

Los Angeles Rams
| | | | | |
|---|---|---|---|---|
| ☐ 62 Rodney Holman | | .10 | .04 | .01 |

Cincinnati Bengals
| | | | | |
|---|---|---|---|---|
| ☐ 63 Vinny Testaverde | | .15 | .06 | .01 |

Tampa Bay Buccaneers
| | | | | |
|---|---|---|---|---|
| ☐ 64 Sterling Sharpe | | .50 | .20 | .05 |

Green Bay Packers
| | | | | |
|---|---|---|---|---|
| ☐ 65 Keith Millard | | .10 | .04 | .01 |

Minnesota Vikings
| | | | | |
|---|---|---|---|---|
| ☐ 66 Jim Lachey | | .10 | .04 | .01 |

Washington Redskins
| | | | | |
|---|---|---|---|---|
| ☐ 67 Dave Meggett | | .15 | .06 | .01 |

New York Giants
| | | | | |
|---|---|---|---|---|
| ☐ 68 Brent Fullwood | | .10 | .04 | .01 |

Green Bay Packers
| | | | | |
|---|---|---|---|---|
| ☐ 69 Bobby Hebert | | .15 | .06 | .01 |

New Orleans Saints
| | | | | |
|---|---|---|---|---|
| ☐ 70 Joey Browner | | .10 | .04 | .01 |

Minnesota Vikings
| | | | | |
|---|---|---|---|---|
| ☐ 71 Flipper Anderson | | .15 | .06 | .01 |

Los Angeles Rams
| | | | | |
|---|---|---|---|---|
| ☐ 72 Tim McGee | | .10 | .04 | .01 |

Cincinnati Bengals
| | | | | |
|---|---|---|---|---|
| ☐ 73 Eric Allen | | .10 | .04 | .01 |

Philadelphia Eagles
| | | | | |
|---|---|---|---|---|
| ☐ 74 Charles Haley | | .15 | .06 | .01 |

San Francisco 49ers
| | | | | |
|---|---|---|---|---|
| ☐ 75 Christian Okoye | | .15 | .06 | .01 |

Kansas City Chiefs
| | | | | |
|---|---|---|---|---|
| ☐ 76 Herschel Walker | | .20 | .08 | .02 |

Minnesota Vikings
| | | | | |
|---|---|---|---|---|
| ☐ 77 Kelvin Martin | | .10 | .04 | .01 |

Dallas Cowboys
| | | | | |
|---|---|---|---|---|
| ☐ 78 Bill Fralic | | .10 | .04 | .01 |

Atlanta Falcons
| | | | | |
|---|---|---|---|---|
| ☐ 79 Leslie O'Neal | | .15 | .06 | .01 |

San Diego Chargers
| | | | | |
|---|---|---|---|---|
| ☐ 80 Bernie Kosar | | .20 | .08 | .02 |

Cleveland Browns
| | | | | |
|---|---|---|---|---|
| ☐ 81 Eric Sievers | | .10 | .04 | .01 |

New England Patriots
| | | | | |
|---|---|---|---|---|
| ☐ 82 Timm Rosenbach | | .10 | .04 | .01 |

Phoenix Cardinals
| | | | | |
|---|---|---|---|---|
| ☐ 83 Steve DeBerg | | .15 | .06 | .01 |

Kansas City Chiefs
| | | | | |
|---|---|---|---|---|
| ☐ 84 Duane Bickett | | .10 | .04 | .01 |

Indianapolis Colts
| | | | | |
|---|---|---|---|---|
| ☐ 85 Chris Doleman | | .15 | .06 | .01 |

Minnesota Vikings
| | | | | |
|---|---|---|---|---|
| ☐ 86 Carl Banks | | .15 | .06 | .01 |

New York Giants
| | | | | |
|---|---|---|---|---|
| ☐ 87 Vaughan Johnson | | .10 | .04 | .01 |

New Orleans Saints
| | | | | |
|---|---|---|---|---|
| ☐ 88 Dennis Smith | | .10 | .04 | .01 |

Denver Broncos
| | | | | |
|---|---|---|---|---|
| ☐ 89 Billy Joe Tolliver | | .15 | .06 | .01 |

San Diego Chargers
| | | | | |
|---|---|---|---|---|
| ☐ 90 Dalton Hilliard | | .10 | .04 | .01 |

New Orleans Saints
| | | | | |
|---|---|---|---|---|
| ☐ 91 John Taylor | | .20 | .08 | .02 |

San Francisco 49ers
| | | | | |
|---|---|---|---|---|
| ☐ 92 Mark Rypien | | .20 | .08 | .02 |

Washington Redskins
| | | | | |
|---|---|---|---|---|
| ☐ 93 Chris Miller | | .30 | .12 | .03 |

Atlanta Falcons
| | | | | |
|---|---|---|---|---|
| ☐ 94 Mark Clayton | | .20 | .08 | .02 |

Miami Dolphins
| | | | | |
|---|---|---|---|---|
| ☐ 95 Andre Reed | | .25 | .10 | .02 |

Buffalo Bills
| | | | | |
|---|---|---|---|---|
| ☐ 96 Warren Moon | | .50 | .20 | .05 |

Houston Oilers
| | | | | |
|---|---|---|---|---|
| ☐ 97 Bruce Matthews | | .10 | .04 | .01 |

Houston Oilers
| | | | | |
|---|---|---|---|---|
| ☐ 98 Rod Woodson | | .25 | .10 | .02 |

Pittsburgh Steelers
| | | | | |
|---|---|---|---|---|
| ☐ 99 Pat Swilling | | .15 | .06 | .01 |

New Orleans Saints
| | | | | |
|---|---|---|---|---|
| ☐ 100 Jerry Rice | | 1.00 | .40 | .10 |

San Francisco 49ers

## 1990-91 Score Franco Harris

This 2 1/2" by 3 1/2" card was given away to all persons at the Super Bowl Card Show II in Tampa who acquired Franco Harris' autograph while at the show. It was estimated that between 1500 and 5000 cards were printed. The card features a Leroy Nieman painting of Harris on the front which has the words "All-Time Super Bowl Silver Anniversary Team" on top of the portrait and Franco Harris' name and position underneath the drawing. The back of the card is split horizontally between a shot of Harris celebrating a Super Bowl victory and a brief Super Bowl history of Harris on the back. The card is unnumbered.

| | MINT | EXC | G-VG |
|---|---|---|---|
| COMPLETE SET (1) | 125.00 | 50.00 | 12.50 |
| COMMON CARD | 125.00 | 50.00 | 12.50 |
| | | | |
| ☐ 1 Franco Harris | 125.00 | 50.00 | 12.50 |
| (Leroy Nieman's artistic rendition) | | | |

## 1991 Score Prototypes

Measuring the standard size (2 1/2" by 3 1/2"), this six-card prototype set was issued to show the design of the 1991 Score regular series. As with the regular issue, the fronts display color action player photos with borders that shade from white to a solid color, while the horizontal backs carry biographical and statistical information on the left half and a color close-up photo on the right. The prototypes may be distinguished from the regular issues by noting the following minor differences: 1) the prototypes omit the tiny trademark symbol next to the Team NFL logo; 2) the shading of the borders on the front has been reversed on the Singletary and Cunningham cards; 3) statistics are printed in bluish-green on the prototypes rather than green as on the regular issues (except for Taylor, whose statistics are printed in red on his regular card); 4) on the Taylor prototype, his name appears in a blue (rather than a black) stripe on the back; and 5) the Montana, Esiason, and Thomas cards are cropped slightly differently. All cards are numbered on the back; the numbering of the prototype cards corresponds to their regular issue counterparts except for the Taylor card, who is card number 529 in the regular issue.

|  | MINT | EXC | G-VG |
|---|---|---|---|
| COMPLETE SET (6) | 10.00 | 4.00 | 1.00 |
| COMMON PLAYER | 1.00 | .40 | .10 |
| ☐ 1 Joe Montana<br>San Francisco 49ers | 6.00 | 2.40 | .60 |
| ☐ 4 Lawrence Taylor<br>New York Giants | 1.25 | .50 | .12 |
| ☐ 5 Derrick Thomas<br>Kansas City Chiefs | 1.50 | .60 | .15 |
| ☐ 6 Mike Singletary<br>Chicago Bears | 1.00 | .40 | .10 |
| ☐ 7 Boomer Esiason<br>Cincinnati Bengals | 1.25 | .50 | .12 |
| ☐ 12 Randall Cunningham<br>Philadelphia Eagles | 1.50 | .60 | .15 |

# 1991 Score

The 1991 Score set consists of two series. The cards feature brilliant full-color photographs on the front and the backs have an horizontal format with the left half containing biographical and statistical information, while the right side of the card has a player portrait. The cards are standard size (2 1/2" by 3 1/2"). Notable subsets in the first series include a Draft Pick subset (311-319), the players who had plays which resulted in 90 or more yards (320-328), two Top Leaders (329-330), and a Dream Team subset (331-345). The second series of the 1991 Score football set consists of 345 cards. As part of a promotion, the 11 offensive Dream Team members each signed 500 of their cards. Of this total, 5,478 were randomly inserted in Series II packs and 22 were given away in a mail-in sweepstakes. As with the first series, the fronts feature full-color photos with various color borders. The horizontally oriented backs have player information and the team helmet on the left half, while the right half has a color head shot. Topical subsets featured include 1991 Rookie Draft Picks (564-589, 591-596, 598-612, 614-616), Team MVP's (620-647), Crunch Crew (648-654), Sack Attack (655-661), Top Leaders (662-669), 1991 Hall of Fame (670-674), and Dream Team (676-686). The set closes with four bonus cards (B1-B4), which were available as part of each factory set. The key Rookie Cards in the set are Nick Bell, Mike Croel, Ricky Ervins, Brett Favre, Alvin Harper, Todd Marinovich, Dan McGwire, Herman Moore, Mike Pritchard, Ricky Watters, and Harvey Williams.

|  | MINT | EXC | G-VG |
|---|---|---|---|
| COMPLETE SET (686) | 8.00 | 3.60 | 1.00 |
| COMPLETE FACT.SET (690) | 8.00 | 3.60 | 1.00 |
| COMMON PLAYER (1-345) | .04 | .02 | .01 |
| COMMON PLAYER (346-686) | .04 | .02 | .01 |
| COMMON BONUS CARDS (B1-B4) | .06 | .03 | .01 |
| ☐ 1 Joe Montana<br>San Francisco 49ers | 1.00 | .45 | .13 |
| ☐ 2 Eric Allen<br>Philadelphia Eagles | .08 | .04 | .01 |
| ☐ 3 Rohn Stark<br>Indianapolis Colts | .04 | .02 | .01 |
| ☐ 4 Frank Reich<br>Buffalo Bills | .10 | .05 | .01 |
| ☐ 5 Derrick Thomas<br>Kansas City Chiefs | .25 | .11 | .03 |
| ☐ 6 Mike Singletary<br>Chicago Bears | .10 | .05 | .01 |
| ☐ 7 Boomer Esiason<br>Cincinnati Bengals | .15 | .07 | .02 |
| ☐ 8 Matt Millen<br>San Francisco 49ers | .08 | .04 | .01 |
| ☐ 9 Chris Spielman<br>Detroit Lions | .08 | .04 | .01 |

| ☐ 10 Gerald McNeil<br>Houston Oilers | .04 | .02 | .01 |
|---|---|---|---|
| ☐ 11 Nick Lowery<br>Kansas City Chiefs | .08 | .04 | .01 |
| ☐ 12 Randall Cunningham<br>Philadelphia Eagles | .10 | .05 | .01 |
| ☐ 13 Marion Butts<br>San Diego Chargers | .10 | .05 | .01 |
| ☐ 14 Tim Brown<br>Los Angeles Raiders | .20 | .09 | .03 |
| ☐ 15 Emmitt Smith<br>Dallas Cowboys | 2.00 | .90 | .25 |
| ☐ 16 Rich Camarillo<br>Phoenix Cardinals | .04 | .02 | .01 |
| ☐ 17 Mike Merriweather<br>Minnesota Vikings | .04 | .02 | .01 |
| ☐ 18 Derrick Fenner<br>Seattle Seahawks | .08 | .04 | .01 |
| ☐ 19 Clay Matthews<br>Cleveland Browns | .08 | .04 | .01 |
| ☐ 20 Barry Sanders<br>Detroit Lions | .75 | .35 | .09 |
| ☐ 21 James Brooks<br>Cincinnati Bengals | .08 | .04 | .01 |
| ☐ 22 Alton Montgomery<br>Denver Broncos | .04 | .02 | .01 |
| ☐ 23 Steve Atwater<br>Denver Broncos | .10 | .05 | .01 |
| ☐ 24 Ron Morris<br>Chicago Bears | .04 | .02 | .01 |
| ☐ 25 Brad Muster<br>Chicago Bears | .08 | .04 | .01 |
| ☐ 26 Andre Rison<br>Atlanta Falcons | .25 | .11 | .03 |
| ☐ 27 Brian Brennan<br>Cleveland Browns | .04 | .02 | .01 |
| ☐ 28 Leonard Smith<br>Buffalo Bills | .04 | .02 | .01 |
| ☐ 29 Kevin Butler<br>Chicago Bears | .04 | .02 | .01 |
| ☐ 30 Tim Harris<br>Green Bay Packers | .08 | .04 | .01 |
| ☐ 31 Jay Novacek<br>Dallas Cowboys | .15 | .07 | .02 |
| ☐ 32 Eddie Murray<br>Detroit Lions | .08 | .04 | .01 |
| ☐ 33 Keith Woodside<br>Green Bay Packers | .04 | .02 | .01 |
| ☐ 34 Ray Crockett<br>Detroit Lions | .10 | .05 | .01 |
| ☐ 35 Eugene Lockhart<br>Dallas Cowboys | .04 | .02 | .01 |
| ☐ 36 Bill Romanowski<br>San Francisco 49ers | .04 | .02 | .01 |
| ☐ 37 Eddie Brown<br>Cincinnati Bengals | .04 | .02 | .01 |
| ☐ 38 Eugene Daniel<br>Indianapolis Colts | .04 | .02 | .01 |
| ☐ 39 Scott Fulhage<br>Atlanta Falcons | .04 | .02 | .01 |
| ☐ 40 Harold Green<br>Cincinnati Bengals | .08 | .04 | .01 |
| ☐ 41 Mark Jackson<br>Denver Broncos | .08 | .04 | .01 |
| ☐ 42 Sterling Sharpe<br>Green Bay Packers | .50 | .23 | .06 |
| ☐ 43 Mel Gray<br>Detroit Lions | .08 | .04 | .01 |
| ☐ 44 Jerry Holmes<br>Green Bay Packers | .04 | .02 | .01 |
| ☐ 45 Allen Pinkett<br>Houston Oilers | .04 | .02 | .01 |
| ☐ 46 Warren Powers<br>Denver Broncos | .04 | .02 | .01 |
| ☐ 47 Rodney Peete<br>Detroit Lions | .08 | .04 | .01 |
| ☐ 48 Lorenzo White<br>Houston Oilers | .08 | .04 | .01 |
| ☐ 49 Dan Owens<br>Detroit Lions | .04 | .02 | .01 |
| ☐ 50 James Francis<br>Cincinnati Bengals | .08 | .04 | .01 |
| ☐ 51 Ken Norton<br>Dallas Cowboys | .10 | .05 | .01 |
| ☐ 52 Ed West<br>Green Bay Packers | .04 | .02 | .01 |
| ☐ 53 Andre Reed<br>Buffalo Bills | .10 | .05 | .01 |
| ☐ 54 John Grimsley<br>Houston Oilers | .04 | .02 | .01 |
| ☐ 55 Michael Cofer<br>Detroit Lions | .04 | .02 | .01 |
| ☐ 56 Chris Doleman<br>Minnesota Vikings | .08 | .04 | .01 |
| ☐ 57 Pat Swilling<br>New Orleans Saints | .08 | .04 | .01 |
| ☐ 58 Jessie Tuggle | .04 | .02 | .01 |

| | | | | |
|---|---|---|---|---|
| Atlanta Falcons | | | | |
| ☐ 59 Mike Johnson | .04 | .02 | .01 | |
| Cleveland Browns | | | | |
| ☐ 60 Steve Walsh | .04 | .02 | .01 | |
| New Orleans Saints | | | | |
| ☐ 61 Sam Mills | .08 | .04 | .01 | |
| New Orleans Saints | | | | |
| ☐ 62 Don Mosebar | .04 | .02 | .01 | |
| Los Angeles Raiders | | | | |
| ☐ 63 Jay Hilgenberg | .08 | .04 | .01 | |
| Chicago Bears | | | | |
| ☐ 64 Cleveland Gary | .08 | .04 | .01 | |
| Los Angeles Rams | | | | |
| ☐ 65 Andre Tippett | .08 | .04 | .01 | |
| New England Patriots | | | | |
| ☐ 66 Tom Newberry | .04 | .02 | .01 | |
| Los Angeles Rams | | | | |
| ☐ 67 Maurice Hurst | .04 | .02 | .01 | |
| New England Patriots | | | | |
| ☐ 68 Louis Oliver | .08 | .04 | .01 | |
| Miami Dolphins | | | | |
| ☐ 69 Fred Marion | .04 | .02 | .01 | |
| New England Patriots | | | | |
| ☐ 70 Christian Okoye | .08 | .04 | .01 | |
| Kansas City Chiefs | | | | |
| ☐ 71 Marv Cook | .04 | .02 | .01 | |
| New England Patriots | | | | |
| ☐ 72 Darryl Talley | .08 | .04 | .01 | |
| Buffalo Bills | | | | |
| ☐ 73 Rick Fenney | .04 | .02 | .01 | |
| Minnesota Vikings | | | | |
| ☐ 74 Kelvin Martin | .08 | .04 | .01 | |
| Dallas Cowboys | | | | |
| ☐ 75 Howie Long | .08 | .04 | .01 | |
| Los Angeles Raiders | | | | |
| ☐ 76 Steve Wisniewski | .04 | .02 | .01 | |
| Los Angeles Raiders | | | | |
| ☐ 77 Karl Mecklenburg | .08 | .04 | .01 | |
| Denver Broncos | | | | |
| ☐ 78 Dan Saleaumua | .04 | .02 | .01 | |
| Kansas City Chiefs | | | | |
| ☐ 79 Ray Childress | .08 | .04 | .01 | |
| Houston Oilers | | | | |
| ☐ 80 Henry Ellard | .08 | .04 | .01 | |
| Los Angeles Rams | | | | |
| ☐ 81 Ernest Givins UER | .08 | .04 | .01 | |
| Houston Oilers | | | | |
| (3rd on Oilers in | | | | |
| receiving, not 4th) | | | | |
| ☐ 82 Ferrell Edmunds | .04 | .02 | .01 | |
| Miami Dolphins | | | | |
| ☐ 83 Steve Jordan | .08 | .04 | .01 | |
| Minnesota Vikings | | | | |
| ☐ 84 Tony Mandarich | .04 | .02 | .01 | |
| Green Bay Packers | | | | |
| ☐ 85 Eric Martin | .08 | .04 | .01 | |
| New Orleans Saints | | | | |
| ☐ 86 Rich Gannon | .08 | .04 | .01 | |
| Minnesota Vikings | | | | |
| ☐ 87 Irving Fryar | .08 | .04 | .01 | |
| New England Patriots | | | | |
| ☐ 88 Tom Rathman | .08 | .04 | .01 | |
| San Francisco 49ers | | | | |
| ☐ 89 Dan Hampton | .08 | .04 | .01 | |
| Chicago Bears | | | | |
| ☐ 90 Barry Word | .10 | .05 | .01 | |
| Kansas City Chiefs | | | | |
| ☐ 91 Kevin Greene | .08 | .04 | .01 | |
| Los Angeles Rams | | | | |
| ☐ 92 Sean Landeta | .04 | .02 | .01 | |
| New York Giants | | | | |
| ☐ 93 Trace Armstrong | .04 | .02 | .01 | |
| Chicago Bears | | | | |
| ☐ 94 Dennis Byrd | .08 | .04 | .01 | |
| New York Jets | | | | |
| ☐ 95 Timm Rosenbach | .08 | .04 | .01 | |
| Phoenix Cardinals | | | | |
| ☐ 96 Anthony Toney | .04 | .02 | .01 | |
| Philadelphia Eagles | | | | |
| ☐ 97 Tim Krumrie | .04 | .02 | .01 | |
| Cincinnati Bengals | | | | |
| ☐ 98 Jerry Ball | .08 | .04 | .01 | |
| Detroit Lions | | | | |
| ☐ 99 Tim Green | .04 | .02 | .01 | |
| Atlanta Falcons | | | | |
| ☐ 100 Bo Jackson | .35 | .16 | .04 | |
| Los Angeles Raiders | | | | |
| ☐ 101 Myron Guyton | .04 | .02 | .01 | |
| New York Giants | | | | |
| ☐ 102 Mike Mularkey | .04 | .02 | .01 | |
| Pittsburgh Steelers | | | | |
| ☐ 103 Jerry Gray | .04 | .02 | .01 | |
| Los Angeles Rams | | | | |
| ☐ 104 Scott Stephen | .04 | .02 | .01 | |
| Green Bay Packers | | | | |
| ☐ 105 Anthony Bell | .04 | .02 | .01 | |
| Phoenix Cardinals | | | | |
| ☐ 106 Lomas Brown | .04 | .02 | .01 | |

| | | | | |
|---|---|---|---|---|
| Detroit Lions | | | | |
| ☐ 107 David Little | .04 | .02 | .01 | |
| Pittsburgh Steelers | | | | |
| ☐ 108 Brad Baxter | .08 | .04 | .01 | |
| New York Jets | | | | |
| ☐ 109 Freddie Joe Nunn | .04 | .02 | .01 | |
| Phoenix Cardinals | | | | |
| ☐ 110 Dave Meggett | .10 | .05 | .01 | |
| New York Giants | | | | |
| ☐ 111 Mark Rypien | .10 | .05 | .01 | |
| Washington Redskins | | | | |
| ☐ 112 Warren Williams | .04 | .02 | .01 | |
| Pittsburgh Steelers | | | | |
| ☐ 113 Ron Rivera | .04 | .02 | .01 | |
| Chicago Bears | | | | |
| ☐ 114 Terance Mathis | .04 | .02 | .01 | |
| New York Jets | | | | |
| ☐ 115 Anthony Munoz | .08 | .04 | .01 | |
| Cincinnati Bengals | | | | |
| ☐ 116 Jeff Bryant | .04 | .02 | .01 | |
| Seattle Seahawks | | | | |
| ☐ 117 Issiac Holt | .04 | .02 | .01 | |
| Dallas Cowboys | | | | |
| ☐ 118 Steve Sewell | .04 | .02 | .01 | |
| Denver Broncos | | | | |
| ☐ 119 Tim Newton | .04 | .02 | .01 | |
| Tampa Bay Buccaneers | | | | |
| ☐ 120 Emile Harry | .04 | .02 | .01 | |
| Kansas City Chiefs | | | | |
| ☐ 121 Gary Anderson | .04 | .02 | .01 | |
| Pittsburgh Steelers | | | | |
| ☐ 122 Mark Lee | .04 | .02 | .01 | |
| Green Bay Packers | | | | |
| ☐ 123 Alfred Anderson | .04 | .02 | .01 | |
| Minnesota Vikings | | | | |
| ☐ 124 Tony Blaylock | .04 | .02 | .01 | |
| Cleveland Browns | | | | |
| ☐ 125 Earnest Byner | .08 | .04 | .01 | |
| Washington Redskins | | | | |
| ☐ 126 Bill Maas | .04 | .02 | .01 | |
| Kansas City Chiefs | | | | |
| ☐ 127 Keith Taylor | .04 | .02 | .01 | |
| Indianapolis Colts | | | | |
| ☐ 128 Cliff Odom | .04 | .02 | .01 | |
| Miami Dolphins | | | | |
| ☐ 129 Bob Golic | .04 | .02 | .01 | |
| Los Angeles Raiders | | | | |
| ☐ 130 Bart Oates | .04 | .02 | .01 | |
| New York Giants | | | | |
| ☐ 131 Jim Arnold | .04 | .02 | .01 | |
| Detroit Lions | | | | |
| ☐ 132 Jeff Herrod | .04 | .02 | .01 | |
| Indianapolis Colts | | | | |
| ☐ 133 Bruce Armstrong | .04 | .02 | .01 | |
| New England Patriots | | | | |
| ☐ 134 Craig Heyward | .04 | .02 | .01 | |
| New Orleans Saints | | | | |
| ☐ 135 Joey Browner | .04 | .02 | .01 | |
| Minnesota Vikings | | | | |
| ☐ 136 Darren Comeaux | .04 | .02 | .01 | |
| Seattle Seahawks | | | | |
| ☐ 137 Pat Beach | .04 | .02 | .01 | |
| Indianapolis Colts | | | | |
| ☐ 138 Dalton Hilliard | .04 | .02 | .01 | |
| New Orleans Saints | | | | |
| ☐ 139 David Treadwell | .04 | .02 | .01 | |
| Denver Broncos | | | | |
| ☐ 140 Gary Anderson | .08 | .04 | .01 | |
| Tampa Bay Buccaneers | | | | |
| ☐ 141 Eugene Robinson | .04 | .02 | .01 | |
| Seattle Seahawks | | | | |
| ☐ 142 Scott Case | .04 | .02 | .01 | |
| Atlanta Falcons | | | | |
| ☐ 143 Paul Farren | .04 | .02 | .01 | |
| Cleveland Browns | | | | |
| ☐ 144 Gill Fenerty | .08 | .04 | .01 | |
| New Orleans Saints | | | | |
| ☐ 145 Tim Irwin | .04 | .02 | .01 | |
| Minnesota Vikings | | | | |
| ☐ 146 Norm Johnson | .04 | .02 | .01 | |
| Seattle Seahawks | | | | |
| ☐ 147 Willie Gault | .08 | .04 | .01 | |
| Los Angeles Raiders | | | | |
| ☐ 148 Clarence Verdin | .04 | .02 | .01 | |
| Indianapolis Colts | | | | |
| ☐ 149 Jeff Uhlenhake | .04 | .02 | .01 | |
| Miami Dolphins | | | | |
| ☐ 150 Erik McMillan | .04 | .02 | .01 | |
| New York Jets | | | | |
| ☐ 151 Kevin Ross | .08 | .04 | .01 | |
| Kansas City Chiefs | | | | |
| ☐ 152 Pepper Johnson | .08 | .04 | .01 | |
| New York Giants | | | | |
| ☐ 153 Bryan Hinkle | .04 | .02 | .01 | |
| Pittsburgh Steelers | | | | |
| ☐ 154 Gary Clark | .08 | .04 | .01 | |
| Washington Redskins | | | | |
| ☐ 155 Robert Delpino | .08 | .04 | .01 | |

| | | | |
|---|---|---|---|
| Los Angeles Rams | | | |
| ☐ 156 Doug Smith | .04 | .02 | .01 |
| Los Angeles Rams | | | |
| ☐ 157 Chris Martin | .04 | .02 | .01 |
| Kansas City Chiefs | | | |
| ☐ 158 Ray Berry | .04 | .02 | .01 |
| Minnesota Vikings | | | |
| ☐ 159 Steve Christie | .04 | .02 | .01 |
| Tampa Bay Buccaneers | | | |
| ☐ 160 Don Smith | .04 | .02 | .01 |
| Buffalo Bills | | | |
| ☐ 161 Greg McMurtry | .04 | .02 | .01 |
| New England Patriots | | | |
| ☐ 162 Jack Del Rio | .04 | .02 | .01 |
| Dallas Cowboys | | | |
| ☐ 163 Floyd Dixon | .04 | .02 | .01 |
| Atlanta Falcons | | | |
| ☐ 164 Buford McGee | .04 | .02 | .01 |
| Los Angeles Rams | | | |
| ☐ 165 Brett Maxie | .04 | .02 | .01 |
| New Orleans Saints | | | |
| ☐ 166 Morten Andersen | .08 | .04 | .01 |
| New Orleans Saints | | | |
| ☐ 167 Kent Hull | .04 | .02 | .01 |
| Buffalo Bills | | | |
| ☐ 168 Skip McClendon | .04 | .02 | .01 |
| Cincinnati Bengals | | | |
| ☐ 169 Keith Sims | .04 | .02 | .01 |
| Miami Dolphins | | | |
| ☐ 170 Leonard Marshall | .08 | .04 | .01 |
| New York Giants | | | |
| ☐ 171 Tony Woods | .04 | .02 | .01 |
| Seattle Seahawks | | | |
| ☐ 172 Byron Evans | .08 | .04 | .01 |
| Philadelphia Eagles | | | |
| ☐ 173 Rob Burnett | .15 | .07 | .02 |
| Cleveland Browns | | | |
| ☐ 174 Tory Epps | .04 | .02 | .01 |
| Atlanta Falcons | | | |
| ☐ 175 Toi Cook | .04 | .02 | .01 |
| New Orleans Saints | | | |
| ☐ 176 John Elliott | .04 | .02 | .01 |
| New York Giants | | | |
| ☐ 177 Tommie Agee | .04 | .02 | .01 |
| Dallas Cowboys | | | |
| ☐ 178 Keith Van Horne | .04 | .02 | .01 |
| Chicago Bears | | | |
| ☐ 179 Dennis Smith | .08 | .04 | .01 |
| Denver Broncos | | | |
| ☐ 180 James Lofton | .10 | .05 | .01 |
| Buffalo Bills | | | |
| ☐ 181 Art Monk | .10 | .05 | .01 |
| Washington Redskins | | | |
| ☐ 182 Anthony Carter | .08 | .04 | .01 |
| Minnesota Vikings | | | |
| ☐ 183 Louis Lipps | .08 | .04 | .01 |
| Pittsburgh Steelers | | | |
| ☐ 184 Bruce Hill | .04 | .02 | .01 |
| Tampa Bay Buccaneers | | | |
| ☐ 185 Mike Young | .04 | .02 | .01 |
| Denver Broncos | | | |
| ☐ 186 Eric Green | .15 | .07 | .02 |
| Pittsburgh Steelers | | | |
| ☐ 187 Barney Bussey | .04 | .02 | .01 |
| Cincinnati Bengals | | | |
| ☐ 188 Curtis Duncan | .08 | .04 | .01 |
| Houston Oilers | | | |
| ☐ 189 Robert Awalt | .04 | .02 | .01 |
| Dallas Cowboys | | | |
| ☐ 190 Johnny Johnson | .25 | .11 | .03 |
| Phoenix Cardinals | | | |
| ☐ 191 Jeff Cross | .04 | .02 | .01 |
| Miami Dolphins | | | |
| ☐ 192 Keith McKeller | .04 | .02 | .01 |
| Buffalo Bills | | | |
| ☐ 193 Robert Brown | .04 | .02 | .01 |
| Green Bay Packers | | | |
| ☐ 194 Vincent Brown | .04 | .02 | .01 |
| New England Patriots | | | |
| ☐ 195 Calvin Williams | .20 | .09 | .03 |
| Philadelphia Eagles | | | |
| ☐ 196 Sean Jones | .08 | .04 | .01 |
| Houston Oilers | | | |
| ☐ 197 Willie Drewrey | .04 | .02 | .01 |
| Tampa Bay Buccaneers | | | |
| ☐ 198 Bubba McDowell | .04 | .02 | .01 |
| Houston Oilers | | | |
| ☐ 199 Al Noga | .04 | .02 | .01 |
| Minnesota Vikings | | | |
| ☐ 200 Ronnie Lott | .10 | .05 | .01 |
| San Francisco 49ers | | | |
| ☐ 201 Warren Moon | .20 | .09 | .03 |
| Houston Oilers | | | |
| ☐ 202 Chris Hinton | .04 | .02 | .01 |
| Atlanta Falcons | | | |
| ☐ 203 Jim Sweeney | .04 | .02 | .01 |
| New York Jets | | | |
| ☐ 204 Wayne Haddix | .04 | .02 | .01 |

| | | | |
|---|---|---|---|
| Tampa Bay Buccaneers | | | |
| ☐ 205 Tim Jorden | .04 | .02 | .01 |
| Phoenix Cardinals | | | |
| ☐ 206 Marvin Allen | .04 | .02 | .01 |
| New England Patriots | | | |
| ☐ 207 Jim Morrissey | .15 | .07 | .02 |
| Chicago Bears | | | |
| ☐ 208 Ben Smith | .04 | .02 | .01 |
| Philadelphia Eagles | | | |
| ☐ 209 William White | .04 | .02 | .01 |
| Detroit Lions | | | |
| ☐ 210 Jim C. Jensen | .04 | .02 | .01 |
| Miami Dolphins | | | |
| ☐ 211 Doug Reed | .04 | .02 | .01 |
| Los Angeles Rams | | | |
| ☐ 212 Ethan Horton | .04 | .02 | .01 |
| Los Angeles Raiders | | | |
| ☐ 213 Chris Jacke | .04 | .02 | .01 |
| Green Bay Packers | | | |
| ☐ 214 Johnny Hector | .04 | .02 | .01 |
| New York Jets | | | |
| ☐ 215 Drew Hill UER | .08 | .04 | .01 |
| Houston Oilers | | | |
| (Tied for the NFC lead, | | | |
| should say AFC) | | | |
| ☐ 216 Roy Green | .08 | .04 | .01 |
| Phoenix Cardinals | | | |
| ☐ 217 Dean Steinkuhler | .04 | .02 | .01 |
| Houston Oilers | | | |
| ☐ 218 Cedric Mack | .04 | .02 | .01 |
| Phoenix Cardinals | | | |
| ☐ 219 Chris Miller | .10 | .05 | .01 |
| Atlanta Falcons | | | |
| ☐ 220 Keith Byars | .08 | .04 | .01 |
| Philadelphia Eagles | | | |
| ☐ 221 Lewis Billups | .04 | .02 | .01 |
| Cincinnati Bengals | | | |
| ☐ 222 Roger Craig | .08 | .04 | .01 |
| San Francisco 49ers | | | |
| ☐ 223 Shaun Gayle | .04 | .02 | .01 |
| Chicago Bears | | | |
| ☐ 224 Mike Rozier | .08 | .04 | .01 |
| Atlanta Falcons | | | |
| ☐ 225 Troy Aikman | 1.25 | .55 | .16 |
| Dallas Cowboys | | | |
| ☐ 226 Bobby Humphrey | .08 | .04 | .01 |
| Denver Broncos | | | |
| ☐ 227 Eugene Marve | .04 | .02 | .01 |
| Tampa Bay Buccaneers | | | |
| ☐ 228 Michael Carter | .04 | .02 | .01 |
| San Francisco 49ers | | | |
| ☐ 229 Richard Johnson | .04 | .02 | .01 |
| Houston Oilers | | | |
| ☐ 230 Billy Joe Tolliver | .08 | .04 | .01 |
| San Diego Chargers | | | |
| ☐ 231 Mark Murphy | .04 | .02 | .01 |
| Green Bay Packers | | | |
| ☐ 232 John L. Williams | .08 | .04 | .01 |
| Seattle Seahawks | | | |
| ☐ 233 Ronnie Harmon | .04 | .02 | .01 |
| San Diego Chargers | | | |
| ☐ 234 Thurman Thomas | .40 | .18 | .05 |
| Buffalo Bills | | | |
| ☐ 235 Martin Mayhew | .04 | .02 | .01 |
| Washington Redskins | | | |
| ☐ 236 Richmond Webb | .08 | .04 | .01 |
| Miami Dolphins | | | |
| ☐ 237 Gerald Riggs UER | .08 | .04 | .01 |
| Washington Redskins | | | |
| (Earnest Byner mis- | | | |
| spelled as Ernest) | | | |
| ☐ 238 Mike Prior | .04 | .02 | .01 |
| Indianapolis Colts | | | |
| ☐ 239 Mike Gann | .04 | .02 | .01 |
| Atlanta Falcons | | | |
| ☐ 240 Alvin Walton | .04 | .02 | .01 |
| Washington Redskins | | | |
| ☐ 241 Tim McGee | .04 | .02 | .01 |
| Cincinnati Bengals | | | |
| ☐ 242 Bruce Matthews | .08 | .04 | .01 |
| Houston Oilers | | | |
| ☐ 243 Johnny Holland | .04 | .02 | .01 |
| Green Bay Packers | | | |
| ☐ 244 Martin Bayless | .04 | .02 | .01 |
| San Diego Chargers | | | |
| ☐ 245 Eric Metcalf | .10 | .05 | .01 |
| Cleveland Browns | | | |
| ☐ 246 John Alt | .04 | .02 | .01 |
| Kansas City Chiefs | | | |
| ☐ 247 Max Montoya | .04 | .02 | .01 |
| Los Angeles Raiders | | | |
| ☐ 248 Rod Bernstine | .10 | .05 | .01 |
| San Diego Chargers | | | |
| ☐ 249 Paul Gruber | .08 | .04 | .01 |
| Tampa Bay Buccaneers | | | |
| ☐ 250 Charles Haley | .08 | .04 | .01 |
| San Francisco 49ers | | | |
| ☐ 251 Scott Norwood | .04 | .02 | .01 |

| | | | |
|---|---|---|---|
| Buffalo Bills | | | |
| ☐ 252 Michael Haddix | .04 | .02 | .01 |
| Green Bay Packers | | | |
| ☐ 253 Ricky Sanders | .08 | .04 | .01 |
| Washington Redskins | | | |
| ☐ 254 Ervin Randle | .04 | .02 | .01 |
| Tampa Bay Buccaneers | | | |
| ☐ 255 Duane Bickett | .04 | .02 | .01 |
| Indianapolis Colts | | | |
| ☐ 256 Mike Munchak | .08 | .04 | .01 |
| Houston Oilers | | | |
| ☐ 257 Keith Jones | .04 | .02 | .01 |
| Atlanta Falcons | | | |
| ☐ 258 Riki Ellison | .04 | .02 | .01 |
| Los Angeles Raiders | | | |
| ☐ 259 Vince Newsome | .04 | .02 | .01 |
| Los Angeles Rams | | | |
| ☐ 260 Lee Williams | .08 | .04 | .01 |
| San Diego Chargers | | | |
| ☐ 261 Steve Smith | .08 | .04 | .01 |
| Los Angeles Raiders | | | |
| ☐ 262 Sam Clancy | .04 | .02 | .01 |
| Indianapolis Colts | | | |
| ☐ 263 Pierce Holt | .04 | .02 | .01 |
| San Francisco 49ers | | | |
| ☐ 264 Jim Harbaugh | .08 | .04 | .01 |
| Chicago Bears | | | |
| ☐ 265 Dino Hackett | .04 | .02 | .01 |
| Kansas City Chiefs | | | |
| ☐ 266 Andy Heck | .04 | .02 | .01 |
| Seattle Seahawks | | | |
| ☐ 267 Leo Goeas | .04 | .02 | .01 |
| San Diego Chargers | | | |
| ☐ 268 Russ Grimm | .04 | .02 | .01 |
| Washington Redskins | | | |
| ☐ 269 Gill Byrd | .08 | .04 | .01 |
| San Diego Chargers | | | |
| ☐ 270 Neal Anderson | .08 | .04 | .01 |
| Chicago Bears | | | |
| ☐ 271 Jackie Slater | .08 | .04 | .01 |
| Los Angeles Rams | | | |
| ☐ 272 Joe Nash | .04 | .02 | .01 |
| Seattle Seahawks | | | |
| ☐ 273 Todd Bowles | .04 | .02 | .01 |
| Washington Redskins | | | |
| ☐ 274 D.J. Dozier | .08 | .04 | .01 |
| Minnesota Vikings | | | |
| ☐ 275 Kevin Fagan | .04 | .02 | .01 |
| San Francisco 49ers | | | |
| ☐ 276 Don Warren | .04 | .02 | .01 |
| Washington Redskins | | | |
| ☐ 277 Jim Jeffcoat | .04 | .02 | .01 |
| Dallas Cowboys | | | |
| ☐ 278 Bruce Smith | .10 | .05 | .01 |
| Buffalo Bills | | | |
| ☐ 279 Cortez Kennedy | .25 | .11 | .03 |
| Seattle Seahawks | | | |
| ☐ 280 Thane Gash | .04 | .02 | .01 |
| Cleveland Browns | | | |
| ☐ 281 Perry Kemp | .04 | .02 | .01 |
| Green Bay Packers | | | |
| ☐ 282 John Taylor | .10 | .05 | .01 |
| San Francisco 49ers | | | |
| ☐ 283 Stephone Paige | .08 | .04 | .01 |
| Kansas City Chiefs | | | |
| ☐ 284 Paul Skansi | .04 | .02 | .01 |
| Seattle Seahawks | | | |
| ☐ 285 Shawn Collins | .04 | .02 | .01 |
| Atlanta Falcons | | | |
| ☐ 286 Mervyn Fernandez | .04 | .02 | .01 |
| Los Angeles Raiders | | | |
| ☐ 287 Daniel Stubbs | .04 | .02 | .01 |
| Dallas Cowboys | | | |
| ☐ 288 Chip Lohmiller | .08 | .04 | .01 |
| Washington Redskins | | | |
| ☐ 289 Brian Blades | .10 | .05 | .01 |
| Seattle Seahawks | | | |
| ☐ 290 Mark Carrier | .08 | .04 | .01 |
| Tampa Bay Buccaneers | | | |
| ☐ 291 Carl Zander | .04 | .02 | .01 |
| Cincinnati Bengals | | | |
| ☐ 292 David Wyman | .04 | .02 | .01 |
| Seattle Seahawks | | | |
| ☐ 293 Jeff Bostic | .04 | .02 | .01 |
| Washington Redskins | | | |
| ☐ 294 Irv Pankey | .04 | .02 | .01 |
| Los Angeles Rams | | | |
| ☐ 295 Keith Millard | .08 | .04 | .01 |
| Minnesota Vikings | | | |
| ☐ 296 Jamie Mueller | .04 | .02 | .01 |
| Buffalo Bills | | | |
| ☐ 297 Bill Fralic | .04 | .02 | .01 |
| Atlanta Falcons | | | |
| ☐ 298 Wendell Davis | .04 | .02 | .01 |
| Chicago Bears | | | |
| ☐ 299 Ken Clarke | .04 | .02 | .01 |
| Minnesota Vikings | | | |
| ☐ 300 Wymon Henderson | .04 | .02 | .01 |

| | | | |
|---|---|---|---|
| Denver Broncos | | | |
| ☐ 301 Jeff Campbell | .04 | .02 | .01 |
| Detroit Lions | | | |
| ☐ 302 Cody Carlson | .75 | .35 | .09 |
| Houston Oilers | | | |
| ☐ 303 Matt Brock | .04 | .02 | .01 |
| Green Bay Packers | | | |
| ☐ 304 Maurice Carthon | .04 | .02 | .01 |
| New York Giants | | | |
| ☐ 305 Scott Mersereau | .04 | .02 | .01 |
| New York Jets | | | |
| ☐ 306 Steve Wright | .04 | .02 | .01 |
| Los Angeles Raiders | | | |
| ☐ 307 J.B. Brown | .04 | .02 | .01 |
| Miami Dolphins | | | |
| ☐ 308 Ricky Reynolds | .04 | .02 | .01 |
| Tampa Bay Buccaneers | | | |
| ☐ 309 Darryl Pollard | .04 | .02 | .01 |
| San Francisco 49ers | | | |
| ☐ 310 Donald Evans | .04 | .02 | .01 |
| Pittsburgh Steelers | | | |
| ☐ 311 Nick Bell | .20 | .09 | .03 |
| Los Angeles Raiders | | | |
| ☐ 312 Pat Harlow | .10 | .05 | .01 |
| New England Patriots | | | |
| ☐ 313 Dan McGwire | .10 | .05 | .01 |
| Seattle Seahawks | | | |
| ☐ 314 Mike Dumas | .05 | .02 | .01 |
| Houston Oilers | | | |
| ☐ 315 Mike Croel | .20 | .09 | .03 |
| Denver Broncos | | | |
| ☐ 316 Chris Smith | .05 | .02 | .01 |
| Cincinnati Bengals | | | |
| ☐ 317 Kenny Walker | .05 | .02 | .01 |
| Denver Broncos | | | |
| ☐ 318 Todd Lyght | .10 | .05 | .01 |
| Los Angeles Rams | | | |
| ☐ 319 Mike Stonebreaker | .05 | .02 | .01 |
| Chicago Bears | | | |
| ☐ 320 Randall Cunningham 90 | .08 | .04 | .01 |
| Philadelphia Eagles | | | |
| ☐ 321 Terance Mathis 90 | .04 | .02 | .01 |
| New York Jets | | | |
| ☐ 322 Gaston Green 90 | .04 | .02 | .01 |
| Los Angeles Rams | | | |
| ☐ 323 Johnny Bailey 90 | .04 | .02 | .01 |
| Chicago Bears | | | |
| ☐ 324 Donnie Elder 90 | .04 | .02 | .01 |
| San Diego Chargers | | | |
| ☐ 325 Dwight Stone 90 UER | .04 | .02 | .01 |
| Pittsburgh Steelers | | | |
| (No '91 copyright | | | |
| on card back) | | | |
| ☐ 326 J.J. Birden 90 | .30 | .14 | .04 |
| Kansas City Chiefs | | | |
| ☐ 327 Alexander Wright 90 | .08 | .04 | .01 |
| Dallas Cowboys | | | |
| ☐ 328 Eric Metcalf 90 | .08 | .04 | .01 |
| Cleveland Browns | | | |
| ☐ 329 Andre Rison TL | .12 | .05 | .02 |
| Atlanta Falcons | | | |
| ☐ 330 Warren Moon TL UER | .10 | .05 | .01 |
| Houston Oilers | | | |
| (Not Blanda's record, | | | |
| should be Van Brocklin) | | | |
| ☐ 331 Steve Tasker DT | .04 | .02 | .01 |
| Buffalo Bills | | | |
| ☐ 332 Mel Gray DT | .04 | .02 | .01 |
| Detroit Lions | | | |
| ☐ 333 Nick Lowery DT | .04 | .02 | .01 |
| Kansas City Chiefs | | | |
| ☐ 334 Sean Landeta DT | .04 | .02 | .01 |
| New York Giants | | | |
| ☐ 335 David Fulcher DT | .04 | .02 | .01 |
| Cincinnati Bengals | | | |
| ☐ 336 Joey Browner DT | .04 | .02 | .01 |
| Minnesota Vikings | | | |
| ☐ 337 Albert Lewis DT | .04 | .02 | .01 |
| Kansas City Chiefs | | | |
| ☐ 338 Rod Woodson DT | .08 | .04 | .01 |
| Pittsburgh Steelers | | | |
| ☐ 339 Shane Conlan DT | .04 | .02 | .01 |
| Buffalo Bills | | | |
| ☐ 340 Pepper Johnson DT | .04 | .02 | .01 |
| New York Giants | | | |
| ☐ 341 Chris Spielman DT | .04 | .02 | .01 |
| Detroit Lions | | | |
| ☐ 342 Derrick Thomas DT | .12 | .05 | .02 |
| Kansas City Chiefs | | | |
| ☐ 343 Ray Childress DT | .04 | .02 | .01 |
| Houston Oilers | | | |
| ☐ 344 Reggie White DT | .08 | .04 | .01 |
| Philadelphia Eagles | | | |
| ☐ 345 Bruce Smith DT | .08 | .04 | .01 |
| Buffalo Bills | | | |
| ☐ 346 Darrell Green | .08 | .04 | .01 |
| Washington Redskins | | | |
| ☐ 347 Ray Bentley | .04 | .02 | .01 |

| | | | |
|---|---|---|---|
| Buffalo Bills | | | |
| ☐ 348 Herschel Walker | .10 | .05 | .01 |
| Minnesota Vikings | | | |
| ☐ 349 Rodney Holman | .04 | .02 | .01 |
| Cincinnati Bengals | | | |
| ☐ 350 Al Toon | .08 | .04 | .01 |
| New York Jets | | | |
| ☐ 351 Harry Hamilton | .04 | .02 | .01 |
| Tampa Bay Buccaneers | | | |
| ☐ 352 Albert Lewis | .08 | .04 | .01 |
| Kansas City Chiefs | | | |
| ☐ 353 Renaldo Turnbull | .08 | .04 | .01 |
| New Orleans Saints | | | |
| ☐ 354 Junior Seau | .25 | .11 | .03 |
| San Diego Chargers | | | |
| ☐ 355 Merril Hoge | .08 | .04 | .01 |
| Pittsburgh Steelers | | | |
| ☐ 356 Shane Conlan | .08 | .04 | .01 |
| Buffalo Bills | | | |
| ☐ 357 Jay Schroeder | .08 | .04 | .01 |
| Los Angeles Raiders | | | |
| ☐ 358 Steve Broussard | .08 | .04 | .01 |
| Atlanta Falcons | | | |
| ☐ 359 Mark Bavaro | .08 | .04 | .01 |
| New York Giants | | | |
| ☐ 360 Jim Lachey | .04 | .02 | .01 |
| Washington Redskins | | | |
| ☐ 361 Greg Townsend | .04 | .02 | .01 |
| Los Angeles Raiders | | | |
| ☐ 362 Dave Krieg | .08 | .04 | .01 |
| Seattle Seahawks | | | |
| ☐ 363 Jessie Hester | .08 | .04 | .01 |
| Indianapolis Colts | | | |
| ☐ 364 Steve Tasker | .08 | .04 | .01 |
| Buffalo Bills | | | |
| ☐ 365 Ron Hall | .04 | .02 | .01 |
| Tampa Bay Buccaneers | | | |
| ☐ 366 Pat Leahy | .08 | .04 | .01 |
| New York Jets | | | |
| ☐ 367 Jim Everett | .08 | .04 | .01 |
| Los Angeles Rams | | | |
| ☐ 368 Felix Wright | .04 | .02 | .01 |
| Cleveland Browns | | | |
| ☐ 369 Ricky Proehl | .10 | .05 | .01 |
| Phoenix Cardinals | | | |
| ☐ 370 Anthony Miller | .20 | .09 | .03 |
| San Diego Chargers | | | |
| ☐ 371 Keith Jackson | .15 | .07 | .02 |
| Philadelphia Eagles | | | |
| ☐ 372 Pete Stoyanovich | .08 | .04 | .01 |
| Miami Dolphins | | | |
| ☐ 373 Tommy Kane | .04 | .02 | .01 |
| Seattle Seahawks | | | |
| ☐ 374 Richard Johnson | .04 | .02 | .01 |
| Detroit Lions | | | |
| ☐ 375 Randall McDaniel | .04 | .02 | .01 |
| Minnesota Vikings | | | |
| ☐ 376 John Stephens | .08 | .04 | .01 |
| New England Patriots | | | |
| ☐ 377 Haywood Jeffires | .15 | .07 | .02 |
| Houston Oilers | | | |
| ☐ 378 Rodney Hampton | .75 | .35 | .09 |
| New York Giants | | | |
| ☐ 379 Tim Grunhard | .04 | .02 | .01 |
| Kansas City Chiefs | | | |
| ☐ 380 Jerry Rice | .75 | .35 | .09 |
| San Francisco 49ers | | | |
| ☐ 381 Ken Harvey | .04 | .02 | .01 |
| Phoenix Cardinals | | | |
| ☐ 382 Vaughan Johnson | .08 | .04 | .01 |
| New Orleans Saints | | | |
| ☐ 383 J.T. Smith | .04 | .02 | .01 |
| Phoenix Cardinals | | | |
| ☐ 384 Carnell Lake | .04 | .02 | .01 |
| Pittsburgh Steelers | | | |
| ☐ 385 Dan Marino | .75 | .35 | .09 |
| Miami Dolphins | | | |
| ☐ 386 Kyle Clifton | .04 | .02 | .01 |
| New York Jets | | | |
| ☐ 387 Wilber Marshall | .08 | .04 | .01 |
| Washington Redskins | | | |
| ☐ 388 Pete Holohan | .04 | .02 | .01 |
| Los Angeles Rams | | | |
| ☐ 389 Gary Plummer | .04 | .02 | .01 |
| San Diego Chargers | | | |
| ☐ 390 William Perry | .08 | .04 | .01 |
| Chicago Bears | | | |
| ☐ 391 Mark Robinson | .04 | .02 | .01 |
| Buffalo Bills | | | |
| ☐ 392 Nate Odomes | .10 | .05 | .01 |
| Buffalo Bills | | | |
| ☐ 393 Ickey Woods | .04 | .02 | .01 |
| Cincinnati Bengals | | | |
| ☐ 394 Reyna Thompson | .04 | .02 | .01 |
| New York Giants | | | |
| ☐ 395 Deion Sanders | .25 | .11 | .03 |
| Atlanta Falcons | | | |
| ☐ 396 Harris Barton | .04 | .02 | .01 |
| San Francisco 49ers | | | |
| ☐ 397 Sammie Smith | .04 | .02 | .01 |
| Miami Dolphins | | | |
| ☐ 398 Vinny Testaverde | .10 | .05 | .01 |
| Tampa Bay Buccaneers | | | |
| ☐ 399 Ray Donaldson | .04 | .02 | .01 |
| Indianapolis Colts | | | |
| ☐ 400 Tim McKyer | .08 | .04 | .01 |
| Miami Dolphins | | | |
| ☐ 401 Nesby Glasgow | .04 | .02 | .01 |
| Seattle Seahawks | | | |
| ☐ 402 Brent Williams | .04 | .02 | .01 |
| New England Patriots | | | |
| ☐ 403 Rob Moore | .10 | .05 | .01 |
| New York Jets | | | |
| ☐ 404 Bubby Brister | .08 | .04 | .01 |
| Pittsburgh Steelers | | | |
| ☐ 405 David Fulcher | .04 | .02 | .01 |
| Cincinnati Bengals | | | |
| ☐ 406 Reggie Cobb | .25 | .11 | .03 |
| Tampa Bay Buccaneers | | | |
| ☐ 407 Jerome Brown | .08 | .04 | .01 |
| Philadelphia Eagles | | | |
| ☐ 408 Erik Howard | .04 | .02 | .01 |
| New York Giants | | | |
| ☐ 409 Tony Paige | .04 | .02 | .01 |
| Miami Dolphins | | | |
| ☐ 410 John Elway | .35 | .16 | .04 |
| Denver Broncos | | | |
| ☐ 411 Charles Mann | .08 | .04 | .01 |
| Washington Redskins | | | |
| ☐ 412 Luis Sharpe | .04 | .02 | .01 |
| Phoenix Cardinals | | | |
| ☐ 413 Hassan Jones | .04 | .02 | .01 |
| Minnesota Vikings | | | |
| ☐ 414 Frank Minnifield | .04 | .02 | .01 |
| Cleveland Browns | | | |
| ☐ 415 Steve DeBerg | .08 | .04 | .01 |
| Kansas City Chiefs | | | |
| ☐ 416 Mark Carrier | .08 | .04 | .01 |
| Chicago Bears | | | |
| ☐ 417 Brian Jordan | .10 | .05 | .01 |
| Atlanta Falcons | | | |
| ☐ 418 Reggie Langhorne | .08 | .04 | .01 |
| Cleveland Browns | | | |
| ☐ 419 Don Majkowski | .08 | .04 | .01 |
| Green Bay Packers | | | |
| ☐ 420 Marcus Allen | .15 | .07 | .02 |
| Los Angeles Raiders | | | |
| ☐ 421 Michael Brooks | .04 | .02 | .01 |
| Denver Broncos | | | |
| ☐ 422 Vai Sikahema | .08 | .04 | .01 |
| Phoenix Cardinals | | | |
| ☐ 423 Dermontti Dawson | .04 | .02 | .01 |
| Pittsburgh Steelers | | | |
| ☐ 424 Jacob Green | .04 | .02 | .01 |
| Seattle Seahawks | | | |
| ☐ 425 Flipper Anderson | .08 | .04 | .01 |
| Los Angeles Rams | | | |
| ☐ 426 Bill Brooks | .08 | .04 | .01 |
| Indianapolis Colts | | | |
| ☐ 427 Keith McCants | .04 | .02 | .01 |
| Tampa Bay Buccaneers | | | |
| ☐ 428 Ken O'Brien | .08 | .04 | .01 |
| New York Jets | | | |
| ☐ 429 Fred Barnett | .15 | .07 | .02 |
| Philadelphia Eagles | | | |
| ☐ 430 Mark Duper | .08 | .04 | .01 |
| Miami Dolphins | | | |
| ☐ 431 Mark Kelso | .04 | .02 | .01 |
| Buffalo Bills | | | |
| ☐ 432 Leslie O'Neal | .08 | .04 | .01 |
| San Diego Chargers | | | |
| ☐ 433 Ottis Anderson | .08 | .04 | .01 |
| New York Giants | | | |
| ☐ 434 Jesse Sapolu | .04 | .02 | .01 |
| San Francisco 49ers | | | |
| ☐ 435 Gary Zimmerman | .04 | .02 | .01 |
| Minnesota Vikings | | | |
| ☐ 436 Kevin Porter | .04 | .02 | .01 |
| Kansas City Chiefs | | | |
| ☐ 437 Anthony Thompson | .04 | .02 | .01 |
| Phoenix Cardinals | | | |
| ☐ 438 Robert Clark | .04 | .02 | .01 |
| Detroit Lions | | | |
| ☐ 439 Chris Warren | .30 | .14 | .04 |
| Seattle Seahawks | | | |
| ☐ 440 Gerald Williams | .04 | .02 | .01 |
| Pittsburgh Steelers | | | |
| ☐ 441 Jim Skow | .04 | .02 | .01 |
| Tampa Bay Buccaneers | | | |
| ☐ 442 Rick Donnelly | .04 | .02 | .01 |
| Seattle Seahawks | | | |
| ☐ 443 Guy McIntyre | .08 | .04 | .01 |
| San Francisco 49ers | | | |
| ☐ 444 Jeff Lageman | .04 | .02 | .01 |
| New York Jets | | | |
| ☐ 445 John Offerdahl | .08 | .04 | .01 |

| | | | |
|---|---|---|---|
| Miami Dolphins | | | |
| ☐ 446 Clyde Simmons.............. | .08 | .04 | .01 |
| Philadelphia Eagles | | | |
| ☐ 447 John Kidd...................... | .04 | .02 | .01 |
| San Diego Chargers | | | |
| ☐ 448 Chip Banks.................... | .04 | .02 | .01 |
| Indianapolis Colts | | | |
| ☐ 449 Johnny Meads................ | .04 | .02 | .01 |
| Houston Oilers | | | |
| ☐ 450 Rickey Jackson ............. | .08 | .04 | .01 |
| New Orleans Saints | | | |
| ☐ 451 Lee Johnson ................. | .04 | .02 | .01 |
| Cincinnati Bengals | | | |
| ☐ 452 Michael Irvin ................ | .50 | .23 | .06 |
| Dallas Cowboys | | | |
| ☐ 453 Leon Seals .................... | .04 | .02 | .01 |
| Buffalo Bills | | | |
| ☐ 454 Darrell Thompson ......... | .08 | .04 | .01 |
| Green Bay Packers | | | |
| ☐ 455 Everson Walls .............. | .04 | .02 | .01 |
| New York Giants | | | |
| ☐ 456 LeRoy Butler ................ | .04 | .02 | .01 |
| Green Bay Packers | | | |
| ☐ 457 Marcus Dupree ............. | .08 | .04 | .01 |
| Los Angeles Rams | | | |
| ☐ 458 Kirk Lowdermilk ........... | .04 | .02 | .01 |
| Minnesota Vikings | | | |
| ☐ 459 Chris Singleton ............ | .04 | .02 | .01 |
| New England Patriots | | | |
| ☐ 460 Seth Joyner .................. | .08 | .04 | .01 |
| Philadelphia Eagles | | | |
| ☐ 461 Rueben Mayes UER ....... | .04 | .02 | .01 |
| New Orleans Saints | | | |
| (Hayes in bio should | | | |
| be Heyward) | | | |
| ☐ 462 Ernie Jones .................. | .04 | .02 | .01 |
| Phoenix Cardinals | | | |
| ☐ 463 Greg Kragen ................. | .04 | .02 | .01 |
| Denver Broncos | | | |
| ☐ 464 Bennie Blades ............... | .04 | .02 | .01 |
| Detroit Lions | | | |
| ☐ 465 Mark Bortz ................... | .04 | .02 | .01 |
| Chicago Bears | | | |
| ☐ 466 Tony Stargell................ | .04 | .02 | .01 |
| New York Jets | | | |
| ☐ 467 Mike Cofer ................... | .04 | .02 | .01 |
| San Francisco 49ers | | | |
| ☐ 468 Randy Grimes ............... | .04 | .02 | .01 |
| Tampa Bay Buccaneers | | | |
| ☐ 469 Tim Worley ................... | .08 | .04 | .01 |
| Pittsburgh Steelers | | | |
| ☐ 470 Kevin Mack ................... | .08 | .04 | .01 |
| Cleveland Browns | | | |
| ☐ 471 Wes Hopkins ................ | .04 | .02 | .01 |
| Philadelphia Eagles | | | |
| ☐ 472 Will Wolford ................. | .04 | .02 | .01 |
| Buffalo Bills | | | |
| ☐ 473 Sam Seale .................... | .04 | .02 | .01 |
| San Diego Chargers | | | |
| ☐ 474 Jim Ritcher .................. | .04 | .02 | .01 |
| Buffalo Bills | | | |
| ☐ 475 Jeff Hostetler................ | .25 | .11 | .03 |
| New York Giants | | | |
| ☐ 476 Mitchell Price ............... | .04 | .02 | .01 |
| Cincinnati Bengals | | | |
| ☐ 477 Ken Lanier ................... | .04 | .02 | .01 |
| Denver Broncos | | | |
| ☐ 478 Naz Worthen ................ | .04 | .02 | .01 |
| Kansas City Chiefs | | | |
| ☐ 479 Ed Reynolds ................. | .04 | .02 | .01 |
| New England Patriots | | | |
| ☐ 480 Mark Clayton................ | .08 | .04 | .01 |
| Miami Dolphins | | | |
| ☐ 481 Matt Bahr .................... | .04 | .02 | .01 |
| New York Giants | | | |
| ☐ 482 Gary Reasons ............... | .04 | .02 | .01 |
| New York Giants | | | |
| ☐ 483 Dave Szott................... | .04 | .02 | .01 |
| Kansas City Chiefs | | | |
| ☐ 484 Barry Foster ................ | .50 | .23 | .06 |
| Pittsburgh Steelers | | | |
| ☐ 485 Bruce Reimers .............. | .04 | .02 | .01 |
| Cincinnati Bengals | | | |
| ☐ 486 Dean Biasucci ............... | .04 | .02 | .01 |
| Indianapolis Colts | | | |
| ☐ 487 Cris Carter ................... | .10 | .05 | .01 |
| Minnesota Vikings | | | |
| ☐ 488 Albert Bentley .............. | .04 | .02 | .01 |
| Indianapolis Colts | | | |
| ☐ 489 Robert Massey .............. | .04 | .02 | .01 |
| New Orleans Saints | | | |
| ☐ 490 Al Smith ...................... | .04 | .02 | .01 |
| Houston Oilers | | | |
| ☐ 491 Greg Lloyd ................... | .04 | .02 | .01 |
| Pittsburgh Steelers | | | |
| ☐ 492 Steve McMichael UER ........... | .08 | .04 | .01 |
| Chicago Bears | | | |
| (Photo on back act- | | | |

| | | | |
|---|---|---|---|
| ually Dan Hampton) | | | |
| ☐ 493 Jeff Wright ............................ | .10 | .05 | .01 |
| Buffalo Bills | | | |
| ☐ 494 Scott Davis.......................... | .04 | .02 | .01 |
| Los Angeles Raiders | | | |
| ☐ 495 Freeman McNeil .................. | .04 | .02 | .01 |
| New York Jets | | | |
| ☐ 496 Simon Fletcher..................... | .08 | .04 | .01 |
| Denver Broncos | | | |
| ☐ 497 Terry McDaniel..................... | .04 | .02 | .01 |
| Los Angeles Raiders | | | |
| ☐ 498 Heath Sherman .................... | .08 | .04 | .01 |
| Philadelphia Eagles | | | |
| ☐ 499 Jeff Jaeger .......................... | .04 | .02 | .01 |
| Los Angeles Raiders | | | |
| ☐ 500 Mark Collins ........................ | .04 | .02 | .01 |
| New York Giants | | | |
| ☐ 501 Tim Goad ............................ | .04 | .02 | .01 |
| New England Patriots | | | |
| ☐ 502 Jeff George .......................... | .25 | .11 | .03 |
| Indianapolis Colts | | | |
| ☐ 503 Jimmie Jones........................ | .04 | .02 | .01 |
| Dallas Cowboys | | | |
| ☐ 504 Henry Thomas ...................... | .04 | .02 | .01 |
| Minnesota Vikings | | | |
| ☐ 505 Steve Young ........................ | .50 | .23 | .06 |
| San Francisco 49ers | | | |
| ☐ 506 William Roberts .................... | .04 | .02 | .01 |
| New York Giants | | | |
| ☐ 507 Neil Smith ........................... | .10 | .05 | .01 |
| Kansas City Chiefs | | | |
| ☐ 508 Mike Saxon .......................... | .04 | .02 | .01 |
| Dallas Cowboys | | | |
| ☐ 509 Johnny Bailey....................... | .08 | .04 | .01 |
| Chicago Bears | | | |
| ☐ 510 Broderick Thomas................. | .08 | .04 | .01 |
| Tampa Bay Buccaneers | | | |
| ☐ 511 Wade Wilson ....................... | .08 | .04 | .01 |
| Minnesota Vikings | | | |
| ☐ 512 Hart Lee Dykes ................... | .04 | .02 | .01 |
| New England Patriots | | | |
| ☐ 513 Hardy Nickerson .................. | .04 | .02 | .01 |
| Pittsburgh Steelers | | | |
| ☐ 514 Tim McDonald...................... | .08 | .04 | .01 |
| Phoenix Cardinals | | | |
| ☐ 515 Frank Cornish....................... | .04 | .02 | .01 |
| San Diego Chargers | | | |
| ☐ 516 Jarvis Williams ..................... | .04 | .02 | .01 |
| Miami Dolphins | | | |
| ☐ 517 Carl Lee .............................. | .04 | .02 | .01 |
| Minnesota Vikings | | | |
| ☐ 518 Carl Banks ........................... | .08 | .04 | .01 |
| New York Giants | | | |
| ☐ 519 Mike Golic ........................... | .04 | .02 | .01 |
| Philadelphia Eagles | | | |
| ☐ 520 Brian Noble ......................... | .04 | .02 | .01 |
| Green Bay Packers | | | |
| ☐ 521 James Hasty ........................ | .04 | .02 | .01 |
| New York Jets | | | |
| ☐ 522 Bubba Paris ......................... | .04 | .02 | .01 |
| San Francisco 49ers | | | |
| ☐ 523 Kevin Walker ....................... | .04 | .02 | .01 |
| Cincinnati Bengals | | | |
| ☐ 524 William Fuller....................... | .08 | .04 | .01 |
| Houston Oilers | | | |
| ☐ 525 Eddie Anderson .................... | .04 | .02 | .01 |
| Los Angeles Raiders | | | |
| ☐ 526 Roger Ruzek ........................ | .04 | .02 | .01 |
| Philadelphia Eagles | | | |
| ☐ 527 Robert Blackmon .................. | .04 | .02 | .01 |
| Seattle Seahawks | | | |
| ☐ 528 Vince Buck .......................... | .04 | .02 | .01 |
| New Orleans Saints | | | |
| ☐ 529 Lawrence Taylor.................... | .10 | .05 | .01 |
| New York Giants | | | |
| ☐ 530 Reggie Roby ........................ | .04 | .02 | .01 |
| Miami Dolphins | | | |
| ☐ 531 Doug Riesenberg ................. | .04 | .02 | .01 |
| New York Giants | | | |
| ☐ 532 Joe Jacoby .......................... | .04 | .02 | .01 |
| Washington Redskins | | | |
| ☐ 533 Kirby Jackson ...................... | .04 | .02 | .01 |
| Buffalo Bills | | | |
| ☐ 534 Robb Thomas ...................... | .04 | .02 | .01 |
| Kansas City Chiefs | | | |
| ☐ 535 Don Griffin .......................... | .04 | .02 | .01 |
| San Francisco 49ers | | | |
| ☐ 536 Andre Waters ...................... | .04 | .02 | .01 |
| Philadelphia Eagles | | | |
| ☐ 537 Marc Logan ......................... | .04 | .02 | .01 |
| Miami Dolphins | | | |
| ☐ 538 James Thornton.................... | .04 | .02 | .01 |
| Chicago Bears | | | |
| ☐ 539 Ray Agnew .......................... | .04 | .02 | .01 |
| New England Patriots | | | |
| ☐ 540 Frank Stams ........................ | .04 | .02 | .01 |
| Los Angeles Rams | | | |
| ☐ 541 Brett Perriman...................... | .10 | .05 | .01 |

| | | | |
|---|---|---|---|
| New Orleans Saints | | | |
| ☐ 542 Andre Ware | .10 | .05 | .01 |
| Detroit Lions | | | |
| ☐ 543 Kevin Haverdink | .04 | .02 | .01 |
| New Orleans Saints | | | |
| ☐ 544 Greg Jackson | .10 | .05 | .01 |
| New York Giants | | | |
| ☐ 545 Tunch Ilkin | .04 | .02 | .01 |
| Pittsburgh Steelers | | | |
| ☐ 546 Dexter Carter | .08 | .04 | .01 |
| San Francisco 49ers | | | |
| ☐ 547 Rod Woodson | .10 | .05 | .01 |
| Pittsburgh Steelers | | | |
| ☐ 548 Donnell Woolford | .04 | .02 | .01 |
| Chicago Bears | | | |
| ☐ 549 Mark Boyer | .04 | .02 | .01 |
| New York Jets | | | |
| ☐ 550 Jeff Query | .04 | .02 | .01 |
| Green Bay Packers | | | |
| ☐ 551 Burt Grossman | .04 | .02 | .01 |
| San Diego Chargers | | | |
| ☐ 552 Mike Kenn | .08 | .04 | .01 |
| Atlanta Falcons | | | |
| ☐ 553 Richard Dent | .08 | .04 | .01 |
| Chicago Bears | | | |
| ☐ 554 Gaston Green | .08 | .04 | .01 |
| Los Angeles Rams | | | |
| ☐ 555 Phil Simms | .10 | .05 | .01 |
| New York Giants | | | |
| ☐ 556 Brent Jones | .10 | .05 | .01 |
| San Francisco 49ers | | | |
| ☐ 557 Ronnie Lippett | .04 | .02 | .01 |
| New England Patriots | | | |
| ☐ 558 Mike Horan | .04 | .02 | .01 |
| Denver Broncos | | | |
| ☐ 559 Danny Noonan | .04 | .02 | .01 |
| Dallas Cowboys | | | |
| ☐ 560 Reggie White | .15 | .07 | .02 |
| Philadelphia Eagles | | | |
| ☐ 561 Rufus Porter | .04 | .02 | .01 |
| Seattle Seahawks | | | |
| ☐ 562 Aaron Wallace | .04 | .02 | .01 |
| Los Angeles Raiders | | | |
| ☐ 563 Vance Johnson | .08 | .04 | .01 |
| Denver Broncos | | | |
| ☐ 564A Aaron Craver ERR | .05 | .02 | .01 |
| Miami Dolphins | | | |
| (No copyright line | | | |
| on back) | | | |
| ☐ 564B Aaron Craver COR | .05 | .02 | .01 |
| Miami Dolphins | | | |
| ☐ 565A Russell Maryland ERR | .40 | .18 | .05 |
| Dallas Cowboys | | | |
| (No copyright line | | | |
| on back) | | | |
| ☐ 565B Russell Maryland COR | .40 | .18 | .05 |
| Dallas Cowboys | | | |
| ☐ 566 Paul Justin | .05 | .02 | .01 |
| Chicago Bears | | | |
| ☐ 567 Walter Dean | .05 | .02 | .01 |
| Green Bay Packers | | | |
| ☐ 568 Herman Moore | 1.00 | .45 | .13 |
| Detroit Lions | | | |
| ☐ 569 Bill Musgrave | .30 | .14 | .04 |
| Dallas Cowboys | | | |
| ☐ 570 Rob Carpenter | .10 | .05 | .01 |
| Cincinnati Bengals | | | |
| ☐ 571 Greg Lewis | .05 | .02 | .01 |
| Denver Broncos | | | |
| ☐ 572 Ed King | .05 | .02 | .01 |
| Cleveland Browns | | | |
| ☐ 573 Ernie Mills | .10 | .05 | .01 |
| Pittsburgh Steelers | | | |
| ☐ 574 Jake Reed | .15 | .07 | .02 |
| Minnesota Vikings | | | |
| ☐ 575 Ricky Watters | 1.25 | .55 | .16 |
| San Francisco 49ers | | | |
| ☐ 576 Derek Russell | .25 | .11 | .03 |
| Denver Broncos | | | |
| ☐ 577 Shawn Moore | .15 | .07 | .02 |
| Denver Broncos | | | |
| ☐ 578 Eric Bieniemy | .15 | .07 | .02 |
| San Diego Chargers | | | |
| ☐ 579 Chris Zorich | .25 | .11 | .03 |
| Chicago Bears | | | |
| ☐ 580 Scott Miller | .05 | .02 | .01 |
| Miami Dolphins | | | |
| ☐ 581 Jarrod Bunch | .15 | .07 | .02 |
| New York Giants | | | |
| ☐ 582 Ricky Ervins | .20 | .09 | .03 |
| Washington Redskins | | | |
| ☐ 583 Browning Nagle | .20 | .09 | .03 |
| New York Jets | | | |
| ☐ 584 Eric Turner | .20 | .09 | .03 |
| Cleveland Browns | | | |
| ☐ 585 William Thomas | .05 | .02 | .01 |
| Philadelphia Eagles | | | |
| ☐ 586 Stanley Richard | .10 | .05 | .01 |
| San Diego Chargers | | | |
| ☐ 587 Adrian Cooper | .20 | .09 | .03 |
| Pittsburgh Steelers | | | |
| ☐ 588 Harvey Williams | .20 | .09 | .03 |
| Kansas City Chiefs | | | |
| ☐ 589 Alvin Harper | 1.00 | .45 | .13 |
| Dallas Cowboys | | | |
| ☐ 590 John Carney | .04 | .02 | .01 |
| San Diego Chargers | | | |
| ☐ 591 Mark Vander Poel | .05 | .02 | .01 |
| Indianapolis Colts | | | |
| ☐ 592 Mike Pritchard | .75 | .35 | .09 |
| Atlanta Falcons | | | |
| ☐ 593 Eric Moten | .05 | .02 | .01 |
| San Diego Chargers | | | |
| ☐ 594 Moe Gardner | .10 | .05 | .01 |
| Atlanta Falcons | | | |
| ☐ 595 Wesley Carroll | .10 | .05 | .01 |
| New Orleans Saints | | | |
| ☐ 596 Eric Swann | .20 | .09 | .03 |
| Phoenix Cardinals | | | |
| ☐ 597 Joe Kelly | .04 | .02 | .01 |
| New York Jets | | | |
| ☐ 598 Steve Jackson | .15 | .07 | .02 |
| Houston Oilers | | | |
| ☐ 599 Kelvin Pritchett | .05 | .02 | .01 |
| Dallas Cowboys | | | |
| ☐ 600 Jesse Campbell | .10 | .05 | .01 |
| Philadelphia Eagles | | | |
| ☐ 601 Darryll Lewis UER | .10 | .05 | .01 |
| Houston Oilers | | | |
| (Misspelled Darryl | | | |
| on card) | | | |
| ☐ 602 Howard Griffith | .05 | .02 | .01 |
| Indianapolis Colts | | | |
| ☐ 603 Blaise Bryant | .05 | .02 | .01 |
| New York Jets | | | |
| ☐ 604 Vinnie Clark | .05 | .02 | .01 |
| Green Bay Packers | | | |
| ☐ 605 Mel Agee | .05 | .02 | .01 |
| Indianapolis Colts | | | |
| ☐ 606 Bobby Wilson | .10 | .05 | .01 |
| Washington Redskins | | | |
| ☐ 607 Kevin Donnalley | .05 | .02 | .01 |
| Houston Oilers | | | |
| ☐ 608 Randal Hill | .30 | .14 | .04 |
| Miami Dolphins | | | |
| ☐ 609 Stan Thomas | .05 | .02 | .01 |
| Chicago Bears | | | |
| ☐ 610 Mike Heldt | .05 | .02 | .01 |
| San Diego Chargers | | | |
| ☐ 611 Brett Favre | 2.00 | .90 | .25 |
| Atlanta Falcons | | | |
| ☐ 612 Lawrence Dawsey UER | .20 | .09 | .03 |
| Tampa Bay Buccaneers | | | |
| (Went to Florida State, | | | |
| not Florida) | | | |
| ☐ 613 Dennis Gibson | .04 | .02 | .01 |
| Detroit Lions | | | |
| ☐ 614 Dean Dingman | .05 | .02 | .01 |
| Pittsburgh Steelers | | | |
| ☐ 615 Bruce Pickens | .10 | .05 | .01 |
| Atlanta Falcons | | | |
| ☐ 616 Todd Marinovich | .10 | .05 | .01 |
| Los Angeles Raiders | | | |
| ☐ 617 Gene Atkins | .04 | .02 | .01 |
| New Orleans Saints | | | |
| ☐ 618 Marcus Dupree | .04 | .02 | .01 |
| (Comeback Player) | | | |
| Los Angeles Rams | | | |
| ☐ 619 Warren Moon | .10 | .05 | .01 |
| (Man of the Year) | | | |
| Houston Oilers | | | |
| ☐ 620 Joe Montana | .50 | .23 | .06 |
| (Team MVP) | | | |
| San Francisco 49ers | | | |
| ☐ 621 Neal Anderson | .04 | .02 | .01 |
| (Team MVP) | | | |
| Chicago Bears | | | |
| ☐ 622 James Brooks | .04 | .02 | .01 |
| (Team MVP) | | | |
| Cincinnati Bengals | | | |
| ☐ 623 Thurman Thomas | .20 | .09 | .03 |
| (Team MVP) | | | |
| Buffalo Bills | | | |
| ☐ 624 Bobby Humphrey | .04 | .02 | .01 |
| (Team MVP) | | | |
| Denver Broncos | | | |
| ☐ 625 Kevin Mack | .04 | .02 | .01 |
| (Team MVP) | | | |
| Cleveland Browns | | | |
| ☐ 626 Mark Carrier | .04 | .02 | .01 |
| (Team MVP) | | | |
| Tampa Bay Buccaneers | | | |
| ☐ 627 Johnny Johnson | .12 | .05 | .02 |
| (Team MVP) | | | |
| Phoenix Cardinals | | | |
| ☐ 628 Marion Butts | .08 | .04 | .01 |

| | MINT | EXC | G-VG |
|---|---|---|---|
| (Team MVP) | | | |
| San Diego Chargers | | | |
| ☐ 629 Steve DeBerg | .08 | .04 | .01 |
| (Team MVP) | | | |
| Kansas City Chiefs | | | |
| ☐ 630 Jeff George | .10 | .05 | .01 |
| (Team MVP) | | | |
| Indianapolis Colts | | | |
| ☐ 631 Troy Aikman | .60 | .25 | .08 |
| (Team MVP) | | | |
| Dallas Cowboys | | | |
| ☐ 632 Dan Marino | .35 | .16 | .04 |
| (Team MVP) | | | |
| Miami Dolphins | | | |
| ☐ 633 Randall Cunningham | .08 | .04 | .01 |
| (Team MVP) | | | |
| Philadelphia Eagles | | | |
| ☐ 634 Andre Rison | .12 | .05 | .02 |
| (Team MVP) | | | |
| Atlanta Falcons | | | |
| ☐ 635 Pepper Johnson | .04 | .02 | .01 |
| (Team MVP) | | | |
| New York Giants | | | |
| ☐ 636 Pat Leahy | .04 | .02 | .01 |
| (Team MVP) | | | |
| New York Jets | | | |
| ☐ 637 Barry Sanders | .35 | .16 | .04 |
| (Team MVP) | | | |
| Detroit Lions | | | |
| ☐ 638 Warren Moon | .10 | .05 | .01 |
| (Team MVP) | | | |
| Houston Oilers | | | |
| ☐ 639 Sterling Sharpe | .25 | .11 | .03 |
| (Team MVP) | | | |
| Green Bay Packers | | | |
| ☐ 640 Bruce Armstrong | .04 | .02 | .01 |
| (Team MVP) | | | |
| New England Patriots | | | |
| ☐ 641 Bo Jackson | .15 | .07 | .02 |
| (Team MVP) | | | |
| Los Angeles Raiders | | | |
| ☐ 642 Henry Ellard | .04 | .02 | .01 |
| (Team MVP) | | | |
| Los Angeles Rams | | | |
| ☐ 643 Earnest Byner | .04 | .02 | .01 |
| (Team MVP) | | | |
| Washington Redskins | | | |
| ☐ 644 Pat Swilling | .08 | .04 | .01 |
| (Team MVP) | | | |
| New Orleans Saints | | | |
| ☐ 645 John L. Williams | .04 | .02 | .01 |
| (Team MVP) | | | |
| Seattle Seahawks | | | |
| ☐ 646 Rod Woodson | .08 | .04 | .01 |
| (Team MVP) | | | |
| Pittsburgh Steelers | | | |
| ☐ 647 Chris Doleman | .04 | .02 | .01 |
| (Team MVP) | | | |
| Minnesota Vikings | | | |
| ☐ 648 Joey Browner CC | .04 | .02 | .01 |
| Minnesota Vikings | | | |
| ☐ 649 Erik McMillan CC | .04 | .02 | .01 |
| New York Jets | | | |
| ☐ 650 David Fulcher CC | .04 | .02 | .01 |
| Cincinnati Bengals | | | |
| ☐ 651A Ronnie Lott CC ERR | .08 | .04 | .01 |
| San Francisco 49ers | | | |
| (Front 47, back 42) | | | |
| ☐ 651B Ronnie Lott CC COR | .08 | .04 | .01 |
| San Francisco 49ers | | | |
| (Front 47, back 42 | | | |
| is now blacked out) | | | |
| ☐ 652 Louis Oliver CC | .04 | .02 | .01 |
| Miami Dolphins | | | |
| ☐ 653 Mark Robinson CC | .04 | .02 | .01 |
| Tampa Bay Buccaneers | | | |
| ☐ 654 Dennis Smith CC | .04 | .02 | .01 |
| Denver Broncos | | | |
| ☐ 655 Reggie White | .08 | .04 | .01 |
| (Sack Attack) | | | |
| Philadelphia Eagles | | | |
| ☐ 656 Charles Haley | .04 | .02 | .01 |
| (Sack Attack) | | | |
| San Francisco 49ers | | | |
| ☐ 657 Leslie O'Neal | .04 | .02 | .01 |
| (Sack Attack) | | | |
| San Diego Chargers | | | |
| ☐ 658 Kevin Greene | .04 | .02 | .01 |
| (Sack Attack) | | | |
| Los Angeles Rams | | | |
| ☐ 659 Dennis Byrd | .04 | .02 | .01 |
| (Sack Attack) | | | |
| New York Jets | | | |
| ☐ 660 Bruce Smith | .08 | .04 | .01 |
| (Sack Attack) | | | |
| Buffalo Bills | | | |
| ☐ 661 Derrick Thomas | .12 | .05 | .02 |
| (Sack Attack) | | | |
| Kansas City Chiefs | | | |
| ☐ 662 Steve DeBerg | .08 | .04 | .01 |
| (Top Leader) | | | |
| Kansas City Chiefs | | | |
| ☐ 663 Barry Sanders | .35 | .16 | .04 |
| (Top Leader) | | | |
| Detroit Lions | | | |
| ☐ 664 Thurman Thomas | .20 | .09 | .03 |
| (Top Leader) | | | |
| Buffalo Bills | | | |
| ☐ 665 Jerry Rice | .35 | .16 | .04 |
| (Top Leader) | | | |
| San Francisco 49ers | | | |
| ☐ 666 Derrick Thomas | .12 | .05 | .02 |
| (Top Leader) | | | |
| Kansas City Chiefs | | | |
| ☐ 667 Bruce Smith | .08 | .04 | .01 |
| (Top Leader) | | | |
| Buffalo Bills | | | |
| ☐ 668 Mark Carrier | .04 | .02 | .01 |
| (Top Leader) | | | |
| Chicago Bears | | | |
| ☐ 669 Richard Johnson | .04 | .02 | .01 |
| (Top Leader) | | | |
| Houston Oilers | | | |
| ☐ 670 Jan Stenerud HOF | .04 | .02 | .01 |
| Kansas City Chiefs | | | |
| Green Bay Packers | | | |
| Minnesota Vikings | | | |
| ☐ 671 Stan Jones HOF | .04 | .02 | .01 |
| Chicago Bears | | | |
| Washington Redskins | | | |
| ☐ 672 John Hannah HOF | .04 | .02 | .01 |
| New England Patriots | | | |
| ☐ 673 Tex Schramm HOF | .04 | .02 | .01 |
| Dallas Cowboys | | | |
| ☐ 674 Earl Campbell HOF | .10 | .05 | .01 |
| Houston Oilers | | | |
| New Orleans Saints | | | |
| ☐ 675 Mark Carrier and | .30 | .14 | .04 |
| Emmitt Smith | | | |
| (Rookies of the Year) | | | |
| ☐ 676 Warren Moon DT | .10 | .05 | .01 |
| Houston Oilers | | | |
| ☐ 677 Barry Sanders DT | .35 | .16 | .04 |
| Detroit Lions | | | |
| ☐ 678 Thurman Thomas DT | .20 | .09 | .03 |
| Buffalo Bills | | | |
| ☐ 679 Andre Reed DT | .08 | .04 | .01 |
| Buffalo Bills | | | |
| ☐ 680 Andre Rison DT | .12 | .05 | .02 |
| Atlanta Falcons | | | |
| ☐ 681 Keith Jackson DT | .08 | .04 | .01 |
| Philadelphia Eagles | | | |
| ☐ 682 Bruce Armstrong DT | .04 | .02 | .01 |
| New England Patriots | | | |
| ☐ 683 Jim Lachey DT | .04 | .02 | .01 |
| Washington Redskins | | | |
| ☐ 684 Bruce Matthews DT | .04 | .02 | .01 |
| Houston Oilers | | | |
| ☐ 685 Mike Munchak DT | .04 | .02 | .01 |
| Houston Oilers | | | |
| ☐ 686 Don Mosebar DT | .04 | .02 | .01 |
| Los Angeles Raiders | | | |
| ☐ B1 Jeff Hostetler SB | .25 | .11 | .03 |
| New York Giants | | | |
| ☐ B2 Matt Bahr SB | .06 | .03 | .01 |
| New York Giants | | | |
| ☐ B3 Ottis Anderson SB | .06 | .03 | .01 |
| New York Giants | | | |
| ☐ B4 Ottis Anderson SB | .06 | .03 | .01 |
| New York Giants | | | |

# 1991 Score Hot Rookie

The 1991 Score Hot Rookie cards measure the standard size (2 1/2" by 3 1/2") and were inserted in blister packs. The front design has color action shots of the players (in college uniforms) lifted from their real-life background and superimposed on a hot pink and yellow geometric design. The black borders provide a sharp contrast. The back has a color head shot of the player and a brief player profile. The cards are numbered on the back.

| | MINT | EXC | G-VG |
|---|---|---|---|
| COMPLETE SET (10) | 9.00 | 3.75 | .90 |
| COMMON PLAYER (1-10) | 1.00 | .40 | .10 |
| ☐ 1 Dan McGwire | 1.25 | .50 | .12 |
| San Diego State | | | |
| ☐ 2 Todd Lyght | 1.25 | .50 | .12 |
| Notre Dame | | | |
| ☐ 3 Mike Dumas | 1.00 | .40 | .10 |
| Indiana | | | |
| ☐ 4 Pat Harlow | 1.00 | .40 | .10 |
| Southern California | | | |

| | MINT | EXC | G-VG |
|---|---|---|---|
| ☐ 5 Nick Bell | 1.50 | .60 | .15 |
|   Iowa | | | |
| ☐ 6 Chris Smith | 1.00 | .40 | .10 |
|   BYU | | | |
| ☐ 7 Mike Stonebreaker | 1.00 | .40 | .10 |
|   Notre Dame | | | |
| ☐ 8 Mike Croel | 1.50 | .60 | .15 |
|   Nebraska | | | |
| ☐ 9 Kenny Walker | 1.25 | .50 | .12 |
|   Nebraska | | | |
| ☐ 10 Rob Carpenter | 1.00 | .40 | .10 |
|   Syracuse | | | |

## 1991 Score Young Superstars

This 40-card set features some of the leading young players in football. The key player in the set is Emmitt Smith. The cards measure the standard size (2 1/2" by 3 1/2"). The front has a color action player photo, with a white border on a purple and black background. The player's name appears in yellow lettering above the picture, while the team name is given in the lower left corner. The back has a color head shot, a scouting report, career summary, biography, and statistics. The predominant color on the back is yellow, and the card number appears in a red triangle. This set was available from a mail-away offer on 1991 Score Football wax packs.

| | MINT | EXC | G-VG |
|---|---|---|---|
| COMPLETE SET (40) | 6.00 | 2.40 | .60 |
| COMMON PLAYER (1-40) | .10 | .04 | .01 |
| ☐ 1 Johnny Bailey | .15 | .06 | .01 |
|   Chicago Bears | | | |
| ☐ 2 Johnny Johnson | .30 | .12 | .03 |
|   Phoenix Cardinals | | | |
| ☐ 3 Fred Barnett | .20 | .08 | .02 |
|   Philadelphia Eagles | | | |
| ☐ 4 Keith McCants | .10 | .04 | .01 |
|   Tampa Bay Buccaneers | | | |
| ☐ 5 Brad Baxter | .20 | .08 | .02 |
|   New York Jets | | | |
| ☐ 6 Dan Owens | .10 | .04 | .01 |
|   Detroit Lions | | | |
| ☐ 7 Steve Broussard | .15 | .06 | .01 |
|   Atlanta Falcons | | | |
| ☐ 8 Ricky Proehl | .15 | .06 | .01 |
|   Phoenix Cardinals | | | |
| ☐ 9 Marion Butts | .15 | .06 | .01 |
|   San Diego Chargers | | | |
| ☐ 10 Reggie Cobb | .30 | .12 | .03 |
|   Tampa Bay Buccaneers | | | |
| ☐ 11 Dennis Byrd | .25 | .10 | .02 |
|   New York Jets | | | |

| | | | |
|---|---|---|---|
| ☐ 12 Emmitt Smith | 2.50 | 1.00 | .25 |
|   Dallas Cowboys | | | |
| ☐ 13 Mark Carrier | .15 | .06 | .01 |
|   Chicago Bears | | | |
| ☐ 14 Keith Sims | .10 | .04 | .01 |
|   Miami Dolphins | | | |
| ☐ 15 Dexter Carter | .15 | .06 | .01 |
|   San Francisco 49ers | | | |
| ☐ 16 Chris Singleton | .10 | .04 | .01 |
|   New England Patriots | | | |
| ☐ 17 Steve Christie | .10 | .04 | .01 |
|   Tampa Bay Buccaneers | | | |
| ☐ 18 Frank Cornish | .10 | .04 | .01 |
|   San Diego Chargers | | | |
| ☐ 19 Timm Rosenbach | .10 | .04 | .01 |
|   Phoenix Cardinals | | | |
| ☐ 20 Sammie Smith | .10 | .04 | .01 |
|   Miami Dolphins | | | |
| ☐ 21 Calvin Williams UER | .15 | .06 | .01 |
|   (Listed as WR on front, | | | |
|   but back says FB) | | | |
|   Philadelphia Eagles | | | |
| ☐ 22 Merril Hoge | .10 | .04 | .01 |
|   Pittsburgh Steelers | | | |
| ☐ 23 Hart Lee Dykes | .10 | .04 | .01 |
|   New England Patriots | | | |
| ☐ 24 Darrell Thompson | .15 | .06 | .01 |
|   Green Bay Packers | | | |
| ☐ 25 James Francis | .10 | .04 | .01 |
|   Cincinnati Bengals | | | |
| ☐ 26 John Elliott | .10 | .04 | .01 |
|   New York Giants | | | |
| ☐ 27 Jeff George | .30 | .12 | .03 |
|   Indianapolis Colts | | | |
| ☐ 28 Broderick Thomas | .15 | .06 | .01 |
|   Tampa Bay Buccaneers | | | |
| ☐ 29 Eric Green | .15 | .06 | .01 |
|   Pittsburgh Steelers | | | |
| ☐ 30 Steve Walsh | .15 | .06 | .01 |
|   New Orleans Saints | | | |
| ☐ 31 Harold Green | .30 | .12 | .03 |
|   Cincinnati Bengals | | | |
| ☐ 32 Andre Ware | .20 | .08 | .02 |
|   Detroit Lions | | | |
| ☐ 33 Richmond Webb | .10 | .04 | .01 |
|   Miami Dolphins | | | |
| ☐ 34 Junior Seau | .30 | .12 | .03 |
|   San Diego Chargers | | | |
| ☐ 35 Tim Grunhard | .10 | .04 | .01 |
|   Kansas City Chiefs | | | |
| ☐ 36 Tim Worley | .15 | .06 | .01 |
|   Pittsburgh Steelers | | | |
| ☐ 37 Haywood Jeffires | .30 | .12 | .03 |
|   Houston Oilers | | | |
| ☐ 38 Rod Woodson | .20 | .08 | .02 |
|   Pittsburgh Steelers | | | |
| ☐ 39 Rodney Hampton | .40 | .16 | .04 |
|   New York Giants | | | |
| ☐ 40 Dave Szott | .10 | .04 | .01 |
|   Kansas City Chiefs | | | |

## 1991 Score National 10

This set contains ten cards measuring the standard size (2 1/2" by 3 1/2"). The front design is distinctively colorful at the top and bottom of the obverse. In the middle of the back the cards are labeled as 12th National Sports Collectors Convention. The cards are numbered on the back. The cards were given away as a complete set wrapped in its own cello wrapper.

| | MINT | EXC | G-VG |
|---|---|---|---|
| COMPLETE SET (10) | 12.00 | 5.00 | 1.20 |
| COMMON PLAYER (1-10) | .75 | .30 | .07 |

| | MINT | EXC | G-VG |
|---|---|---|---|
| ☐ 1 Emmitt Smith ............... Dallas Cowboys | 6.00 | 2.40 | .60 |
| ☐ 2 Mark Carrier ............... Chicago Bears | 1.00 | .40 | .10 |
| ☐ 3 Steve Broussard ............... Atlanta Falcons | 1.00 | .40 | .10 |
| ☐ 4 Johnny Johnson ............... Phoenix Cardinals | 2.00 | .80 | .20 |
| ☐ 5 Steve Christie ............... Tampa Bay Buccaneers | .75 | .30 | .07 |
| ☐ 6 Richmond Webb ............... Miami Dolphins | .75 | .30 | .07 |
| ☐ 7 James Francis ............... Cincinnati Bengals | .75 | .30 | .07 |
| ☐ 8 Jeff George ............... Indianapolis Colts | 2.00 | .80 | .20 |
| ☐ 9 Rodney Hampton ............... New York Giants | 2.50 | 1.00 | .25 |
| ☐ 10 Calvin Williams ............... Philadelphia Eagles | 1.00 | .40 | .10 |

## 1991 Score Supplemental

This 110-card standard size (2 1/2" by 3 1/2") set features rookies and players who switched teams during the off-season. The front design is the same as the regular Score issue, but with borders that shade from blue-green to white. Within gold borders, the horizontally oriented backs have player information and a color head shot. The cards are numbered on the back with a "T" suffix. Rookie Cards include Bryan Cox, Michael Jackson, Erric Pegram and Leonard Russell.

| | MINT | EXC | G-VG |
|---|---|---|---|
| COMPLETE FACT.SET (110) ............ | 6.00 | 2.70 | .75 |
| COMMON PLAYER (1T-110T)............ | .04 | .02 | .01 |
| | | | |
| ☐ 1T Ronnie Lott ............... Los Angeles Raiders | .10 | .05 | .01 |
| ☐ 2T Matt Millen ............... Washington Redskins | .08 | .04 | .01 |
| ☐ 3T Tim McKyer ............... Atlanta Falcons | .08 | .04 | .01 |
| ☐ 4T Vince Newsome ............... Cleveland Browns | .04 | .02 | .01 |
| ☐ 5T Gaston Green ............... Denver Broncos | .08 | .04 | .01 |
| ☐ 6T Brett Perriman ............... Detroit Lions | .10 | .05 | .01 |
| ☐ 7T Roger Craig ............... Los Angeles Raiders | .08 | .04 | .01 |
| ☐ 8T Pete Holohan ............... Kansas City Chiefs | .04 | .02 | .01 |
| ☐ 9T Tony Zendejas ............... Los Angeles Rams | .04 | .02 | .01 |
| ☐ 10T Lee Williams ............... Houston Oilers | .08 | .04 | .01 |
| ☐ 11T Mike Stonebreaker ............... Chicago Bears | .04 | .02 | .01 |
| ☐ 12T Felix Wright ............... Minnesota Vikings | .04 | .02 | .01 |
| ☐ 13T Lonnie Young ............... New York Jets | .04 | .02 | .01 |
| ☐ 14T Hugh Millen ............... New England Patriots | .10 | .05 | .01 |
| ☐ 15T Roy Green ............... Philadelphia Eagles | .08 | .04 | .01 |
| ☐ 16T Greg Davis ............... Phoenix Cardinals | .10 | .05 | .01 |
| ☐ 17T Dexter Manley ............... Tampa Bay Buccaneers | .04 | .02 | .01 |
| ☐ 18T Ted Washington ............... San Francisco 49ers | .04 | .02 | .01 |
| ☐ 19T Norm Johnson ............... | .04 | .02 | .01 |

| | MINT | EXC | G-VG |
|---|---|---|---|
| Atlanta Falcons | | | |
| ☐ 20T Joe Morris ............... Cleveland Browns | .08 | .04 | .01 |
| ☐ 21T Robert Perryman ............... Denver Broncos | .04 | .02 | .01 |
| ☐ 22T Mike Iaquaniello UER ............ Miami Dolphins (Free agent in '91, not '87) | .04 | .02 | .01 |
| ☐ 23T Gerald Perry UER ............ Los Angeles Rams (School should be Southern University A and M) | .10 | .05 | .01 |
| ☐ 24T Zeke Mowatt ............... New York Giants | .04 | .02 | .01 |
| ☐ 25T Rich Miano ............... Philadelphia Eagles | .15 | .07 | .02 |
| ☐ 26T Nick Bell ............... Los Angeles Raiders | .10 | .05 | .01 |
| ☐ 27T Terry Orr ............... Washington Redskins | .15 | .07 | .02 |
| ☐ 28T Matt Stover ............... Cleveland Browns | .15 | .07 | .02 |
| ☐ 29T Bubba Paris ............... Indianapolis Colts | .04 | .02 | .01 |
| ☐ 30T Ron Brown ............... Los Angeles Rams | .04 | .02 | .01 |
| ☐ 31T Don Davey ............... Green Bay Packers | .04 | .02 | .01 |
| ☐ 32T Lee Rouson ............... Cleveland Browns | .04 | .02 | .01 |
| ☐ 33T Terry Hoage UER ............... Washington Redskins (Eaggles, sic) | .04 | .02 | .01 |
| ☐ 34T Tony Covington ............... Tampa Bay Buccaneers | .04 | .02 | .01 |
| ☐ 35T John Rienstra ............... Cleveland Browns | .04 | .02 | .01 |
| ☐ 36T Charles Dimry ............... Denver Broncos | .10 | .05 | .01 |
| ☐ 37T Todd Marinovich ............... Los Angeles Raiders | .08 | .04 | .01 |
| ☐ 38T Winston Moss ............... Los Angeles Raiders | .04 | .02 | .01 |
| ☐ 39T Vestee Jackson ............... Miami Dolphins | .04 | .02 | .01 |
| ☐ 40T Brian Hansen ............... Cleveland Browns | .04 | .02 | .01 |
| ☐ 41T Irv Eatman ............... New York Jets | .04 | .02 | .01 |
| ☐ 42T Jarrod Bunch ............... New York Giants | .04 | .02 | .01 |
| ☐ 43T Kanavis McGhee ............... New York Giants | .10 | .05 | .01 |
| ☐ 44T Vai Sikahema ............... Green Bay Packers | .08 | .04 | .01 |
| ☐ 45T Charles McRae ............... Tampa Bay Buccaneers | .04 | .02 | .01 |
| ☐ 46T Quinn Early ............... New Orleans Saints | .08 | .04 | .01 |
| ☐ 47T Jeff Faulkner ............... Phoenix Cardinals | .10 | .05 | .01 |
| ☐ 48T William Frizzell ............... Tampa Bay Buccaneers | .04 | .02 | .01 |
| ☐ 49T John Booty ............... Philadelphia Eagles | .04 | .02 | .01 |
| ☐ 50T Tim Harris ............... San Francisco 49ers | .08 | .04 | .01 |
| ☐ 51T Derek Russell ............... Denver Broncos | .10 | .05 | .01 |
| ☐ 52T John Flannery ............... Houston Oilers | .04 | .02 | .01 |
| ☐ 53T Tim Barnett ............... Kansas City Chiefs | .15 | .07 | .02 |
| ☐ 54T Alfred Williams ............... Cincinnati Bengals | .15 | .07 | .02 |
| ☐ 55T Dan McGwire ............... Seattle Seahawks | .04 | .02 | .01 |
| ☐ 56T Ernie Mills ............... Pittsburgh Steelers | .04 | .02 | .01 |
| ☐ 57T Stanley Richard ............... San Diego Chargers | .04 | .02 | .01 |
| ☐ 58T Huey Richardson ............... Pittsburgh Steelers | .04 | .02 | .01 |
| ☐ 59T Jerome Henderson ............... New England Patriots | .04 | .02 | .01 |
| ☐ 60T Bryan Cox ............... Miami Dolphins | .40 | .18 | .05 |
| ☐ 61T Russell Maryland ............... Dallas Cowboys | .15 | .07 | .02 |
| ☐ 62T Reggie Jones ............... New Orleans Saints | .15 | .07 | .02 |
| ☐ 63T Mo Lewis ............... New York Jets | .10 | .05 | .01 |
| ☐ 64T Moe Gardner ............... Atlanta Falcons | .04 | .02 | .01 |
| ☐ 65T Wesley Carroll ............... | .04 | .02 | .01 |

New Orleans Saints
☐ 66T Michael Jackson .................. .75 .35 .09
Cleveland Browns
☐ 67T Shawn Jefferson .................. .10 .05 .01
San Diego Chargers
☐ 68T Chris Zorich ..................... .12 .05 .02
Chicago Bears
☐ 69T Kenny Walker ..................... .04 .02 .01
Denver Broncos
☐ 70T Erric Pegram ..................... 1.25 .55 .16
Atlanta Falcons
☐ 71T Alvin Harper ..................... .50 .23 .06
Dallas Cowboys
☐ 72T Harry Colon ...................... .04 .02 .01
New England Patriots
☐ 73T Scott Miller ..................... .04 .02 .01
Miami Dolphins
☐ 74T Lawrence Dawsey ................. .10 .05 .01
Tampa Bay Buccaneers
☐ 75T Phil Hansen ..................... .15 .07 .02
Buffalo Bills
☐ 76T Roman Phifer .................... .10 .05 .01
Los Angeles Rams
☐ 77T Greg Lewis ...................... .04 .02 .01
Denver Broncos
☐ 78T Merton Hanks .................... .10 .05 .01
San Francisco 49ers
☐ 79T James Jones ..................... .15 .07 .02
Cleveland Browns
☐ 80T Vinnie Clark .................... .04 .02 .01
Green Bay Packers
☐ 81T R.J. Kors ....................... .04 .02 .01
New York Jets
☐ 82T Mike Pritchard .................. .40 .18 .05
Atlanta Falcons
☐ 83T Stan Thomas ..................... .04 .02 .01
Chicago Bears
☐ 84T Lamar Rogers .................... .04 .02 .01
Cincinnati Bengals
☐ 85T Eric Williams ................... .20 .09 .03
Dallas Cowboys
☐ 86T Keith Traylor ................... .04 .02 .01
Denver Broncos
☐ 87T Mike Dumas ...................... .04 .02 .01
Houston Oilers
☐ 88T Mel Agee ........................ .04 .02 .01
Indianapolis Colts
☐ 89T Harvey Williams ................. .10 .05 .01
Kansas City Chiefs
☐ 90T Todd Lyght ...................... .04 .02 .01
Los Angeles Rams
☐ 91T Jake Reed ....................... .04 .02 .01
Minnesota Vikings
☐ 92T Pat Harlow ...................... .04 .02 .01
New England Patriots
☐ 93T Antone Davis .................... .04 .02 .01
Philadelphia Eagles
☐ 94T Aeneas Williams ................. .15 .07 .02
Phoenix Cardinals
☐ 95T Eric Bieniemy ................... .04 .02 .01
San Diego Chargers
☐ 96T John Kasay ...................... .10 .05 .01
Seattle Seahawks
☐ 97T Robert Wilson ................... .04 .02 .01
Tampa Bay Buccaneers
☐ 98T Ricky Ervins .................... .15 .07 .02
Washington Redskins
☐ 99T Mike Croel ...................... .10 .05 .01
Denver Broncos
☐ 100T David Lang ...................... .15 .07 .02
Los Angeles Rams
☐ 101T Esera Tuaolo .................... .04 .02 .01
Green Bay Packers
☐ 102T Randal Hill ..................... .15 .07 .02
Phoenix Cardinals
☐ 103T Jon Vaughn ...................... .15 .07 .02
New England Patriots
☐ 104T Dave McCloughan ................. .04 .02 .01
Indianapolis Colts
☐ 105T David Daniels .................... .04 .02 .01
Seattle Seahawks
☐ 106T Eric Moten ...................... .04 .02 .01
San Diego Chargers
☐ 107T Anthony Morgan .................. .10 .05 .01
Chicago Bears
☐ 108T Ed King ......................... .04 .02 .01
Cleveland Browns
☐ 109T Leonard Russell ................. 1.00 .45 .13
New England Patriots
☐ 110T Aaron Craver .................... .04 .02 .01
Miami Dolphins

# 1992 Score

The 1992 Score football set contains 550 standard-size (2 1/2" by 3 1/2") cards. The fronts display color action player photos enclosed by a solid colored border. The player's name appears in a green stripe at the top, while his position is printed in the bottom dark blue border. The backs have a close-up photo (with goal posts serving as the borders) and player profile; biography and statistics (1991 and career) appear in a green box at the card bottom. Topical subsets featured include Draft Pick (476-514), Crunch Crew (515-519), Rookie of the Year (520-523), Little Big Men (524-528), Sack Attack (529-533), Hall of Fame (535-537), and 90 Plus Club (538-547). The cards are numbered on the back. A 25-card Dream Team subset was randomly inserted throughout the foil packs. The key Rookie Cards in this set are Edgar Bennett, Steve Bono, Terrell Buckley, Amp Lee, and Tommy Vardell.

|  | MINT | EXC | G-VG |
|---|---|---|---|
| COMPLETE SET (550) | 22.00 | 10.00 | 2.80 |
| COMMON PLAYER (1-550) | .05 | .02 | .01 |

☐ 1 Barry Sanders ...................... .75 .35 .09
Detroit Lions
☐ 2 Pat Swilling ....................... .08 .04 .01
New Orleans Saints
☐ 3 Moe Gardner ........................ .05 .02 .01
Atlanta Falcons
☐ 4 Steve Young ........................ .35 .16 .04
San Francisco 49ers
☐ 5 Chris Spielman ..................... .08 .04 .01
Detroit Lions
☐ 6 Richard Dent ....................... .08 .04 .01
Chicago Bears
☐ 7 Anthony Munoz ...................... .08 .04 .01
Cincinnati Bengals
☐ 8 Martin Mayhew ...................... .05 .02 .01
Washington Redskins
☐ 9 Terry McDaniel ..................... .05 .02 .01
Los Angeles Raiders
☐ 10 Thurman Thomas ................... .40 .18 .05
Buffalo Bills
☐ 11 Ricky Sanders ..................... .08 .04 .01
Washington Redskins
☐ 12 Steve Atwater ..................... .08 .04 .01
Denver Broncos
☐ 13 Tony Tolbert ...................... .05 .02 .01
Dallas Cowboys
☐ 14 Vince Workman ..................... .08 .04 .01
Green Bay Packers
☐ 15 Haywood Jeffires .................. .10 .05 .01
Houston Oilers
☐ 16 Duane Bickett ..................... .05 .02 .01
Indianapolis Colts
☐ 17 Jeff Uhlenhake .................... .05 .02 .01
Miami Dolphins
☐ 18 Tim McDonald ...................... .08 .04 .01
Phoenix Cardinals
☐ 19 Cris Carter ....................... .10 .05 .01
Minnesota Vikings
☐ 20 Derrick Thomas .................... .15 .07 .02
Kansas City Chiefs
☐ 21 Hugh Millen ....................... .08 .04 .01
New England Patriots
☐ 22 Bart Oates ........................ .05 .02 .01
New York Giants
☐ 23 Eugene Robinson ................... .05 .02 .01
Seattle Seahawks
☐ 24 Jerrol Williams ................... .05 .02 .01
Pittsburgh Steelers
☐ 25 Reggie White ...................... .15 .07 .02
Philadelphia Eagles
☐ 26 Marion Butts ...................... .10 .05 .01
San Diego Chargers
☐ 27 Jim Sweeney ....................... .05 .02 .01

New York Jets
☐ 28 Tom Newberry .05 .02 .01
Los Angeles Rams
☐ 29 Pete Stoyanovich .08 .04 .01
Miami Dolphins
☐ 30 Ronnie Lott .10 .05 .01
Los Angeles Raiders
☐ 31 Simon Fletcher .08 .04 .01
Denver Broncos
☐ 32 Dino Hackett .05 .02 .01
Kansas City Chiefs
☐ 33 Morten Andersen .08 .04 .01
New Orleans Saints
☐ 34 Clyde Simmons .08 .04 .01
Philadelphia Eagles
☐ 35 Mark Rypien .10 .05 .01
Washington Redskins
☐ 36 Greg Montgomery .05 .02 .01
Houston Oilers
☐ 37 Nate Lewis .08 .04 .01
San Diego Chargers
☐ 38 Henry Ellard .08 .04 .01
Los Angeles Rams
☐ 39 Luis Sharpe .05 .02 .01
Phoenix Cardinals
☐ 40 Michael Irvin .50 .23 .06
Dallas Cowboys
☐ 41 Louis Lipps .08 .04 .01
Pittsburgh Steelers
☐ 42 John L. Williams .08 .04 .01
Seattle Seahawks
☐ 43 Broderick Thomas .05 .02 .01
Tampa Bay Buccaneers
☐ 44 Michael Haynes .30 .14 .04
Atlanta Falcons
☐ 45 Don Majkowski .08 .04 .01
Green Bay Packers
☐ 46 William Perry .08 .04 .01
Chicago Bears
☐ 47 David Fulcher .05 .02 .01
Cincinnati Bengals
☐ 48 Tony Bennett .08 .04 .01
Green Bay Packers
☐ 49 Clay Matthews .08 .04 .01
Cleveland Browns
☐ 50 Warren Moon .20 .09 .03
Houston Oilers
☐ 51 Bruce Armstrong .05 .02 .01
New England Patriots
☐ 52 Harry Newsome .05 .02 .01
Minnesota Vikings
☐ 53 Bill Brooks .08 .04 .01
Indianapolis Colts
☐ 54 Greg Townsend .05 .02 .01
Los Angeles Raiders
☐ 55 Tom Rathman .08 .04 .01
San Francisco 49ers
☐ 56 Sean Landeta .05 .02 .01
New York Giants
☐ 57 Kyle Clifton .05 .02 .01
New York Jets
☐ 58 Steve Broussard .08 .04 .01
Atlanta Falcons
☐ 59 Mark Carrier .08 .04 .01
Tampa Bay Buccaneers
☐ 60 Mel Gray .08 .04 .01
Detroit Lions
☐ 61 Tim Krumrie .05 .02 .01
Cincinnati Bengals
☐ 62 Rufus Porter .05 .02 .01
Seattle Seahawks
☐ 63 Kevin Mack .08 .04 .01
Cleveland Browns
☐ 64 Todd Bowles .05 .02 .01
San Francisco 49ers
☐ 65 Emmitt Smith 2.00 .90 .25
Dallas Cowboys
☐ 66 Mike Croel .08 .04 .01
Denver Broncos
☐ 67 Brian Mitchell .08 .04 .01
Washington Redskins
☐ 68 Bennie Blades .05 .02 .01
Detroit Lions
☐ 69 Carnell Lake .05 .02 .01
Pittsburgh Steelers
☐ 70 Cornelius Bennett .10 .05 .01
Buffalo Bills
☐ 71 Darrell Thompson .08 .04 .01
Green Bay Packers
☐ 72 Wes Hopkins .05 .02 .01
Philadelphia Eagles
☐ 73 Jessie Hester .05 .02 .01
Indianapolis Colts
☐ 74 Irv Eatman .05 .02 .01
New York Jets
☐ 75 Marv Cook .08 .04 .01
New England Patriots
☐ 76 Tim Brown .25 .11 .03

Los Angeles Raiders
☐ 77 Pepper Johnson .08 .04 .01
New York Giants
☐ 78 Mark Duper .08 .04 .01
Miami Dolphins
☐ 79 Robert Delpino .08 .04 .01
Los Angeles Rams
☐ 80 Charles Mann .08 .04 .01
Washington Redskins
☐ 81 Brian Jordan .08 .04 .01
Atlanta Falcons
☐ 82 Wendell Davis .05 .02 .01
Chicago Bears
☐ 83 Lee Johnson .05 .02 .01
Cincinnati Bengals
☐ 84 Ricky Reynolds .05 .02 .01
Tampa Bay Buccaneers
☐ 85 Vaughan Johnson .08 .04 .01
New Orleans Saints
☐ 86 Brian Blades .08 .04 .01
Seattle Seahawks
☐ 87 Sam Seale .05 .02 .01
San Diego Chargers
☐ 88 Ed King .05 .02 .01
Cleveland Browns
☐ 89 Gaston Green .08 .04 .01
Denver Broncos
☐ 90 Christian Okoye .08 .04 .01
Kansas City Chiefs
☐ 91 Chris Jacke .05 .02 .01
Green Bay Packers
☐ 92 Rohn Stark .05 .02 .01
Indianapolis Colts
☐ 93 Kevin Greene .08 .04 .01
Los Angeles Rams
☐ 94 Jay Novacek .15 .07 .02
Dallas Cowboys
☐ 95 Chip Lohmiller .08 .04 .01
Washington Redskins
☐ 96 Cris Dishman .08 .04 .01
Houston Oilers
☐ 97 Ethan Horton .05 .02 .01
Los Angeles Raiders
☐ 98 Pat Harlow .05 .02 .01
New England Patriots
☐ 99 Mark Ingram .08 .04 .01
New York Giants
☐ 100 Mark Carrier .08 .04 .01
Chicago Bears
☐ 101 Deron Cherry .05 .02 .01
Kansas City Chiefs
☐ 102 Sam Mills .08 .04 .01
New Orleans Saints
☐ 103 Mark Higgs .10 .05 .01
Miami Dolphins
☐ 104 Keith Jackson .10 .05 .01
Philadelphia Eagles
☐ 105 Steve Tasker .08 .04 .01
Buffalo Bills
☐ 106 Ken Harvey .05 .02 .01
Phoenix Cardinals
☐ 107 Bryan Hinkle .05 .02 .01
Pittsburgh Steelers
☐ 108 Anthony Carter .08 .04 .01
Minnesota Vikings
☐ 109 Johnny Hector .05 .02 .01
New York Jets
☐ 110 Randall McDaniel .05 .02 .01
Minnesota Vikings
☐ 111 Johnny Johnson .10 .05 .01
Phoenix Cardinals
☐ 112 Shane Conlan .08 .04 .01
Buffalo Bills
☐ 113 Ray Horton .05 .02 .01
Dallas Cowboys
☐ 114 Sterling Sharpe .50 .23 .06
Green Bay Packers
☐ 115 Guy McIntyre .08 .04 .01
San Francisco 49ers
☐ 116 Tom Waddle .10 .05 .01
Chicago Bears
☐ 117 Albert Lewis .08 .04 .01
Kansas City Chiefs
☐ 118 Riki Ellison .05 .02 .01
Los Angeles Raiders
☐ 119 Chris Doleman .08 .04 .01
Minnesota Vikings
☐ 120 Andre Rison .25 .11 .03
Atlanta Falcons
☐ 121 Bobby Hebert .10 .05 .01
New Orleans Saints
☐ 122 Dan Owens .05 .02 .01
Detroit Lions
☐ 123 Rodney Hampton .40 .18 .05
New York Giants
☐ 124 Ron Holmes .05 .02 .01
Denver Broncos
☐ 125 Ernie Jones .05 .02 .01

Phoenix Cardinals
| | | | |
|---|---|---|---|
| ☐ 126 Michael Carter | .05 | .02 | .01 |

San Francisco 49ers
| | | | |
|---|---|---|---|
| ☐ 127 Reggie Cobb | .10 | .05 | .01 |

Tampa Bay Buccaneers
| | | | |
|---|---|---|---|
| ☐ 128 Esera Tuaolo | .05 | .02 | .01 |

Green Bay Packers
| | | | |
|---|---|---|---|
| ☐ 129 Wilber Marshall | .08 | .04 | .01 |

Washington Redskins
| | | | |
|---|---|---|---|
| ☐ 130 Mike Munchak | .08 | .04 | .01 |

Houston Oilers
| | | | |
|---|---|---|---|
| ☐ 131 Cortez Kennedy | .10 | .05 | .01 |

Seattle Seahawks
| | | | |
|---|---|---|---|
| ☐ 132 Lamar Lathon | .05 | .02 | .01 |

Houston Oilers
| | | | |
|---|---|---|---|
| ☐ 133 Todd Lyght | .05 | .02 | .01 |

Los Angeles Rams
| | | | |
|---|---|---|---|
| ☐ 134 Jeff Feagles | .05 | .02 | .01 |

Philadelphia Eagles
| | | | |
|---|---|---|---|
| ☐ 135 Burt Grossman | .05 | .02 | .01 |

San Diego Chargers
| | | | |
|---|---|---|---|
| ☐ 136 Mike Cofer | .05 | .02 | .01 |

San Francisco 49ers
| | | | |
|---|---|---|---|
| ☐ 137 Frank Warren | .05 | .02 | .01 |

New Orleans Saints
| | | | |
|---|---|---|---|
| ☐ 138 Jarvis Williams | .05 | .02 | .01 |

Miami Dolphins
| | | | |
|---|---|---|---|
| ☐ 139 Eddie Brown | .05 | .02 | .01 |

Cincinnati Bengals
| | | | |
|---|---|---|---|
| ☐ 140 John Elliott | .05 | .02 | .01 |

New York Giants
| | | | |
|---|---|---|---|
| ☐ 141 Jim Everett | .05 | .02 | .01 |

Los Angeles Rams
| | | | |
|---|---|---|---|
| ☐ 142 Hardy Nickerson | .05 | .02 | .01 |

Pittsburgh Steelers
| | | | |
|---|---|---|---|
| ☐ 143 Eddie Murray | .08 | .04 | .01 |

Detroit Lions
| | | | |
|---|---|---|---|
| ☐ 144 Andre Tippett | .08 | .04 | .01 |

New England Patriots
| | | | |
|---|---|---|---|
| ☐ 145 Heath Sherman | .08 | .04 | .01 |

Philadelphia Eagles
| | | | |
|---|---|---|---|
| ☐ 146 Ronnie Harmon | .05 | .02 | .01 |

San Diego Chargers
| | | | |
|---|---|---|---|
| ☐ 147 Eric Metcalf | .10 | .05 | .01 |

Cleveland Browns
| | | | |
|---|---|---|---|
| ☐ 148 Tony Martin | .05 | .02 | .01 |

Miami Dolphins
| | | | |
|---|---|---|---|
| ☐ 149 Chris Burkett | .05 | .02 | .01 |

New York Jets
| | | | |
|---|---|---|---|
| ☐ 150 Andre Waters | .05 | .02 | .01 |

Philadelphia Eagles
| | | | |
|---|---|---|---|
| ☐ 151 Ray Donaldson | .05 | .02 | .01 |

Indianapolis Colts
| | | | |
|---|---|---|---|
| ☐ 152 Paul Gruber | .05 | .02 | .01 |

Tampa Bay Buccaneers
| | | | |
|---|---|---|---|
| ☐ 153 Chris Singleton | .05 | .02 | .01 |

New England Patriots
| | | | |
|---|---|---|---|
| ☐ 154 Clarence Kay | .05 | .02 | .01 |

Denver Broncos
| | | | |
|---|---|---|---|
| ☐ 155 Ernest Givins | .08 | .04 | .01 |

Houston Oilers
| | | | |
|---|---|---|---|
| ☐ 156 Eric Hill | .05 | .02 | .01 |

Phoenix Cardinals
| | | | |
|---|---|---|---|
| ☐ 157 Jesse Sapolu | .05 | .02 | .01 |

San Francisco 49ers
| | | | |
|---|---|---|---|
| ☐ 158 Jack Del Rio | .05 | .02 | .01 |

Dallas Cowboys
| | | | |
|---|---|---|---|
| ☐ 159 Erric Pegram | .40 | .18 | .05 |

Atlanta Falcons
| | | | |
|---|---|---|---|
| ☐ 160 Joey Browner | .05 | .02 | .01 |

Minnesota Vikings
| | | | |
|---|---|---|---|
| ☐ 161 Marcus Allen | .08 | .04 | .01 |

Los Angeles Raiders
| | | | |
|---|---|---|---|
| ☐ 162 Eric Moten | .05 | .02 | .01 |

San Diego Chargers
| | | | |
|---|---|---|---|
| ☐ 163 Donnell Thompson | .05 | .02 | .01 |

Indianapolis Colts
| | | | |
|---|---|---|---|
| ☐ 164 Chuck Cecil | .05 | .02 | .01 |

Green Bay Packers
| | | | |
|---|---|---|---|
| ☐ 165 Matt Millen | .08 | .04 | .01 |

Washington Redskins
| | | | |
|---|---|---|---|
| ☐ 166 Barry Foster | .35 | .16 | .04 |

Pittsburgh Steelers
| | | | |
|---|---|---|---|
| ☐ 167 Kent Hull | .05 | .02 | .01 |

Buffalo Bills
| | | | |
|---|---|---|---|
| ☐ 168 Tony Jones | .05 | .02 | .01 |

Houston Oilers
| | | | |
|---|---|---|---|
| ☐ 169 Mike Prior | .05 | .02 | .01 |

Indianapolis Colts
| | | | |
|---|---|---|---|
| ☐ 170 Neal Anderson | .08 | .04 | .01 |

Chicago Bears
| | | | |
|---|---|---|---|
| ☐ 171 Roger Craig | .08 | .04 | .01 |

Los Angeles Raiders
| | | | |
|---|---|---|---|
| ☐ 172 Felix Wright | .05 | .02 | .01 |

Minnesota Vikings
| | | | |
|---|---|---|---|
| ☐ 173 James Francis | .08 | .04 | .01 |

Cincinnati Bengals
| | | | |
|---|---|---|---|
| ☐ 174 Eugene Lockhart | .05 | .02 | .01 |

New England Patriots
| | | | |
|---|---|---|---|
| ☐ 175 Dalton Hilliard | .05 | .02 | .01 |

New Orleans Saints
| | | | |
|---|---|---|---|
| ☐ 176 Nick Lowery | .08 | .04 | .01 |

Kansas City Chiefs
| | | | |
|---|---|---|---|
| ☐ 177 Tim McKyer | .08 | .04 | .01 |

Atlanta Falcons
| | | | |
|---|---|---|---|
| ☐ 178 Lorenzo White | .08 | .04 | .01 |

Houston Oilers
| | | | |
|---|---|---|---|
| ☐ 179 Jeff Hostetler | .15 | .07 | .02 |

New York Giants
| | | | |
|---|---|---|---|
| ☐ 180 Jackie Harris | .50 | .23 | .06 |

Green Bay Packers
| | | | |
|---|---|---|---|
| ☐ 181 Ken Norton | .08 | .04 | .01 |

Dallas Cowboys
| | | | |
|---|---|---|---|
| ☐ 182 Flipper Anderson | .08 | .04 | .01 |

Los Angeles Rams
| | | | |
|---|---|---|---|
| ☐ 183 Don Warren | .05 | .02 | .01 |

Washington Redskins
| | | | |
|---|---|---|---|
| ☐ 184 Brad Baxter | .08 | .04 | .01 |

New York Jets
| | | | |
|---|---|---|---|
| ☐ 185 John Taylor | .10 | .05 | .01 |

San Francisco 49ers
| | | | |
|---|---|---|---|
| ☐ 186 Harold Green | .08 | .04 | .01 |

Cincinnati Bengals
| | | | |
|---|---|---|---|
| ☐ 187 James Washington | .05 | .02 | .01 |

Dallas Cowboys
| | | | |
|---|---|---|---|
| ☐ 188 Aaron Craver | .05 | .02 | .01 |

Miami Dolphins
| | | | |
|---|---|---|---|
| ☐ 189 Mike Merriweather | .05 | .02 | .01 |

Minnesota Vikings
| | | | |
|---|---|---|---|
| ☐ 190 Gary Clark | .08 | .04 | .01 |

Washington Redskins
| | | | |
|---|---|---|---|
| ☐ 191 Vince Buck | .05 | .02 | .01 |

New Orleans Saints
| | | | |
|---|---|---|---|
| ☐ 192 Cleveland Gary | .08 | .04 | .01 |

Los Angeles Rams
| | | | |
|---|---|---|---|
| ☐ 193 Dan Saleaumua | .05 | .02 | .01 |

Kansas City Chiefs
| | | | |
|---|---|---|---|
| ☐ 194 Gary Zimmerman | .05 | .02 | .01 |

Minnesota Vikings
| | | | |
|---|---|---|---|
| ☐ 195 Richmond Webb | .08 | .04 | .01 |

Miami Dolphins
| | | | |
|---|---|---|---|
| ☐ 196 Gary Plummer | .05 | .02 | .01 |

San Diego Chargers
| | | | |
|---|---|---|---|
| ☐ 197 Willie Green | .05 | .02 | .01 |

Detroit Lions
| | | | |
|---|---|---|---|
| ☐ 198 Chris Warren | .25 | .11 | .03 |

Seattle Seahawks
| | | | |
|---|---|---|---|
| ☐ 199 Mike Pritchard | .25 | .11 | .03 |

Atlanta Falcons
| | | | |
|---|---|---|---|
| ☐ 200 Art Monk | .10 | .05 | .01 |

Washington Redskins
| | | | |
|---|---|---|---|
| ☐ 201 Matt Stover | .05 | .02 | .01 |

Cleveland Browns
| | | | |
|---|---|---|---|
| ☐ 202 Tim Grunhard | .05 | .02 | .01 |

Kansas City Chiefs
| | | | |
|---|---|---|---|
| ☐ 203 Mervyn Fernandez | .05 | .02 | .01 |

Los Angeles Raiders
| | | | |
|---|---|---|---|
| ☐ 204 Mark Jackson | .08 | .04 | .01 |

Denver Broncos
| | | | |
|---|---|---|---|
| ☐ 205 Freddie Joe Nunn | .05 | .02 | .01 |

Phoenix Cardinals
| | | | |
|---|---|---|---|
| ☐ 206 Stan Thomas | .05 | .02 | .01 |

Chicago Bears
| | | | |
|---|---|---|---|
| ☐ 207 Keith McKeller | .05 | .02 | .01 |

Buffalo Bills
| | | | |
|---|---|---|---|
| ☐ 208 Jeff Lageman | .05 | .02 | .01 |

New York Jets
| | | | |
|---|---|---|---|
| ☐ 209 Kenny Walker | .05 | .02 | .01 |

Denver Broncos
| | | | |
|---|---|---|---|
| ☐ 210 Dave Krieg | .08 | .04 | .01 |

Seattle Seahawks
| | | | |
|---|---|---|---|
| ☐ 211 Dean Biasucci | .05 | .02 | .01 |

Indianapolis Colts
| | | | |
|---|---|---|---|
| ☐ 212 Herman Moore | .30 | .14 | .04 |

Detroit Lions
| | | | |
|---|---|---|---|
| ☐ 213 Jon Vaughn | .05 | .02 | .01 |

New England Patriots
| | | | |
|---|---|---|---|
| ☐ 214 Howard Cross | .05 | .02 | .01 |

New York Giants
| | | | |
|---|---|---|---|
| ☐ 215 Greg Davis | .05 | .02 | .01 |

Phoenix Cardinals
| | | | |
|---|---|---|---|
| ☐ 216 Bubby Brister | .08 | .04 | .01 |

Pittsburgh Steelers
| | | | |
|---|---|---|---|
| ☐ 217 John Kasay | .05 | .02 | .01 |

Seattle Seahawks
| | | | |
|---|---|---|---|
| ☐ 218 Ron Hall | .05 | .02 | .01 |

Tampa Bay Buccaneers
| | | | |
|---|---|---|---|
| ☐ 219 Mo Lewis | .05 | .02 | .01 |

New York Jets
| | | | |
|---|---|---|---|
| ☐ 220 Eric Green | .10 | .05 | .01 |

Pittsburgh Steelers
| | | | |
|---|---|---|---|
| ☐ 221 Scott Case | .05 | .02 | .01 |

Atlanta Falcons
| | | | |
|---|---|---|---|
| ☐ 222 Sean Jones | .05 | .02 | .01 |

Houston Oilers
| | | | |
|---|---|---|---|
| ☐ 223 Winston Moss | .05 | .02 | .01 |

| | | | |
|---|---|---|---|
| Los Angeles Raiders | | | |
| ☐ 224 Reggie Langhorne | .08 | .04 | .01 |
| Cleveland Browns | | | |
| ☐ 225 Greg Lewis | .05 | .02 | .01 |
| Denver Broncos | | | |
| ☐ 226 Todd McNair | .05 | .02 | .01 |
| Kansas City Chiefs | | | |
| ☐ 227 Rod Bernstine | .08 | .04 | .01 |
| San Diego Chargers | | | |
| ☐ 228 Joe Jacoby | .05 | .02 | .01 |
| Washington Redskins | | | |
| ☐ 229 Brad Muster | .08 | .04 | .01 |
| Chicago Bears | | | |
| ☐ 230 Nick Bell | .08 | .04 | .01 |
| Los Angeles Raiders | | | |
| ☐ 231 Terry Allen | .20 | .09 | .03 |
| Minnesota Vikings | | | |
| ☐ 232 Cliff Odom | .05 | .02 | .01 |
| Miami Dolphins | | | |
| ☐ 233 Brian Hansen | .05 | .02 | .01 |
| Cleveland Browns | | | |
| ☐ 234 William Fuller | .05 | .02 | .01 |
| Houston Oilers | | | |
| ☐ 235 Issiac Holt | .05 | .02 | .01 |
| Dallas Cowboys | | | |
| ☐ 236 Dexter Carter | .08 | .04 | .01 |
| San Francisco 49ers | | | |
| ☐ 237 Gene Atkins | .05 | .02 | .01 |
| New Orleans Saints | | | |
| ☐ 238 Pat Beach | .05 | .02 | .01 |
| Indianapolis Colts | | | |
| ☐ 239 Tim McGee | .05 | .02 | .01 |
| Cincinnati Bengals | | | |
| ☐ 240 Dermontti Dawson | .05 | .02 | .01 |
| Pittsburgh Steelers | | | |
| ☐ 241 Dan Fike | .05 | .02 | .01 |
| Cleveland Browns | | | |
| ☐ 242 Don Beebe | .10 | .05 | .01 |
| Buffalo Bills | | | |
| ☐ 243 Jeff Bostic | .05 | .02 | .01 |
| Washington Redskins | | | |
| ☐ 244 Mark Collins | .05 | .02 | .01 |
| New York Giants | | | |
| ☐ 245 Steve Sewell | .05 | .02 | .01 |
| Denver Broncos | | | |
| ☐ 246 Steve Walsh | .05 | .02 | .01 |
| New Orleans Saints | | | |
| ☐ 247 Erik Kramer | .10 | .05 | .01 |
| Detroit Lions | | | |
| ☐ 248 Scott Norwood | .05 | .02 | .01 |
| Buffalo Bills | | | |
| ☐ 249 Jesse Solomon | .05 | .02 | .01 |
| Tampa Bay Buccaneers | | | |
| ☐ 250 Jerry Ball | .08 | .04 | .01 |
| Detroit Lions | | | |
| ☐ 251 Eugene Daniel | .05 | .02 | .01 |
| Indianapolis Colts | | | |
| ☐ 252 Michael Stewart | .05 | .02 | .01 |
| Los Angeles Rams | | | |
| ☐ 253 Fred Barnett | .10 | .05 | .01 |
| Philadelphia Eagles | | | |
| ☐ 254 Rodney Holman | .05 | .02 | .01 |
| Cincinnati Bengals | | | |
| ☐ 255 Stephen Baker | .05 | .02 | .01 |
| New York Giants | | | |
| ☐ 256 Don Griffin | .05 | .02 | .01 |
| San Francisco 49ers | | | |
| ☐ 257 Will Wolford | .05 | .02 | .01 |
| Buffalo Bills | | | |
| ☐ 258 Perry Kemp | .05 | .02 | .01 |
| Green Bay Packers | | | |
| ☐ 259 Leonard Russell | .30 | .14 | .04 |
| New England Patriots | | | |
| ☐ 260 Jeff Gossett | .05 | .02 | .01 |
| Los Angeles Raiders | | | |
| ☐ 261 Dwayne Harper | .05 | .02 | .01 |
| Seattle Seahawks | | | |
| ☐ 262 Vinny Testaverde | .10 | .05 | .01 |
| Tampa Bay Buccaneers | | | |
| ☐ 263 Maurice Hurst | .05 | .02 | .01 |
| New England Patriots | | | |
| ☐ 264 Tony Casillas | .05 | .02 | .01 |
| Dallas Cowboys | | | |
| ☐ 265 Louis Oliver | .08 | .04 | .01 |
| Miami Dolphins | | | |
| ☐ 266 Jim Morrissey | .05 | .02 | .01 |
| Chicago Bears | | | |
| ☐ 267 Kenneth Davis | .08 | .04 | .01 |
| Buffalo Bills | | | |
| ☐ 268 John Alt | .05 | .02 | .01 |
| Kansas City Chiefs | | | |
| ☐ 269 Michael Zordich | .05 | .02 | .01 |
| Phoenix Cardinals | | | |
| ☐ 270 Brian Brennan | .05 | .02 | .01 |
| Cleveland Browns | | | |
| ☐ 271 Greg Kragen | .05 | .02 | .01 |
| Denver Broncos | | | |
| ☐ 272 Andre Collins | .05 | .02 | .01 |
| Washington Redskins | | | |
| ☐ 273 Dave Meggett | .08 | .04 | .01 |
| New York Giants | | | |
| ☐ 274 Scott Fulhage | .05 | .02 | .01 |
| Atlanta Falcons | | | |
| ☐ 275 Tony Zendejas | .05 | .02 | .01 |
| Los Angeles Rams | | | |
| ☐ 276 Herschel Walker | .10 | .05 | .01 |
| Minnesota Vikings | | | |
| ☐ 277 Keith Henderson | .05 | .02 | .01 |
| San Francisco 49ers | | | |
| ☐ 278 Johnny Bailey | .05 | .02 | .01 |
| Chicago Bears | | | |
| ☐ 279 Vince Newsome | .05 | .02 | .01 |
| Cleveland Browns | | | |
| ☐ 280 Chris Hinton | .05 | .02 | .01 |
| Atlanta Falcons | | | |
| ☐ 281 Robert Blackmon | .05 | .02 | .01 |
| Seattle Seahawks | | | |
| ☐ 282 James Hasty | .05 | .02 | .01 |
| New York Jets | | | |
| ☐ 283 John Offerdahl | .08 | .04 | .01 |
| Miami Dolphins | | | |
| ☐ 284 Wesley Carroll | .08 | .04 | .01 |
| New Orleans Saints | | | |
| ☐ 285 Lomas Brown | .05 | .02 | .01 |
| Detroit Lions | | | |
| ☐ 286 Neil O'Donnell | .50 | .23 | .06 |
| Pittsburgh Steelers | | | |
| ☐ 287 Kevin Porter | .05 | .02 | .01 |
| Kansas City Chiefs | | | |
| ☐ 288 Lionel Washington | .05 | .02 | .01 |
| Los Angeles Raiders | | | |
| ☐ 289 Carlton Bailey | .20 | .09 | .03 |
| Buffalo Bills | | | |
| ☐ 290 Leonard Marshall | .08 | .04 | .01 |
| New York Giants | | | |
| ☐ 291 John Carney | .05 | .02 | .01 |
| San Diego Chargers | | | |
| ☐ 292 Bubba McDowell | .05 | .02 | .01 |
| Houston Oilers | | | |
| ☐ 293 Nate Newton | .05 | .02 | .01 |
| Dallas Cowboys | | | |
| ☐ 294 Dave Waymer | .05 | .02 | .01 |
| San Francisco 49ers | | | |
| ☐ 295 Rob Moore | .10 | .05 | .01 |
| New York Jets | | | |
| ☐ 296 Earnest Byner | .08 | .04 | .01 |
| Washington Redskins | | | |
| ☐ 297 Jason Staurovsky | .05 | .02 | .01 |
| New England Patriots | | | |
| ☐ 298 Keith McCants | .05 | .02 | .01 |
| Tampa Bay Buccaneers | | | |
| ☐ 299 Floyd Turner | .05 | .02 | .01 |
| New Orleans Saints | | | |
| ☐ 300 Steve Jordan | .08 | .04 | .01 |
| Minnesota Vikings | | | |
| ☐ 301 Nate Odomes | .08 | .04 | .01 |
| Buffalo Bills | | | |
| ☐ 302 Gerald Riggs | .08 | .04 | .01 |
| Washington Redskins | | | |
| ☐ 303 Marvin Washington | .05 | .02 | .01 |
| New York Jets | | | |
| ☐ 304 Anthony Thompson | .05 | .02 | .01 |
| Phoenix Cardinals | | | |
| ☐ 305 Steve DeBerg | .08 | .04 | .01 |
| Kansas City Chiefs | | | |
| ☐ 306 Jim Harbaugh | .08 | .04 | .01 |
| Chicago Bears | | | |
| ☐ 307 Larry Brown | .05 | .02 | .01 |
| Dallas Cowboys | | | |
| ☐ 308 Roger Ruzek | .05 | .02 | .01 |
| Philadelphia Eagles | | | |
| ☐ 309 Jessie Tuggle | .05 | .02 | .01 |
| Atlanta Falcons | | | |
| ☐ 310 Al Smith | .05 | .02 | .01 |
| Houston Oilers | | | |
| ☐ 311 Mark Kelso | .05 | .02 | .01 |
| Buffalo Bills | | | |
| ☐ 312 Lawrence Dawsey | .10 | .05 | .01 |
| Tampa Bay Buccaneers | | | |
| ☐ 313 Steve Bono | .50 | .23 | .06 |
| San Francisco 49ers | | | |
| ☐ 314 Greg Lloyd | .05 | .02 | .01 |
| Pittsburgh Steelers | | | |
| ☐ 315 Steve Wisniewski | .05 | .02 | .01 |
| Los Angeles Raiders | | | |
| ☐ 316 Gill Fenerty | .05 | .02 | .01 |
| New Orleans Saints | | | |
| ☐ 317 Mark Stepnoski | .05 | .02 | .01 |
| Dallas Cowboys | | | |
| ☐ 318 Derek Russell | .08 | .04 | .01 |
| Denver Broncos | | | |
| ☐ 319 Chris Martin | .05 | .02 | .01 |
| Kansas City Chiefs | | | |
| ☐ 320 Shaun Gayle | .05 | .02 | .01 |
| Chicago Bears | | | |
| ☐ 321 Bob Golic | .05 | .02 | .01 |

| | | | |
|---|---|---|---|
| Los Angeles Raiders | | | |
| ☐ 322 Larry Kelm | .05 | .02 | .01 |
| Los Angeles Rams | | | |
| ☐ 323 Mike Brim | .05 | .02 | .01 |
| New York Jets | | | |
| ☐ 324 Tommy Kane | .05 | .02 | .01 |
| Seattle Seahawks | | | |
| ☐ 325 Mark Schlereth | .10 | .05 | .01 |
| Washington Redskins | | | |
| ☐ 326 Ray Childress | .08 | .04 | .01 |
| Houston Oilers | | | |
| ☐ 327 Richard Brown | .05 | .02 | .01 |
| Cleveland Browns | | | |
| ☐ 328 Vincent Brown | .05 | .02 | .01 |
| New England Patriots | | | |
| ☐ 329 Mike Farr UER | .05 | .02 | .01 |
| (Back of card refers | | | |
| to him as Mel) | | | |
| Detroit Lions | | | |
| ☐ 330 Eric Swann | .08 | .04 | .01 |
| Phoenix Cardinals | | | |
| ☐ 331 Bill Fralic | .05 | .02 | .01 |
| Atlanta Falcons | | | |
| ☐ 332 Rodney Peete | .08 | .04 | .01 |
| Detroit Lions | | | |
| ☐ 333 Jerry Gray | .05 | .02 | .01 |
| Los Angeles Rams | | | |
| ☐ 334 Ray Berry | .05 | .02 | .01 |
| Minnesota Vikings | | | |
| ☐ 335 Dennis Smith | .08 | .04 | .01 |
| Denver Broncos | | | |
| ☐ 336 Jeff Herrod | .05 | .02 | .01 |
| Indianapolis Colts | | | |
| ☐ 337 Tony Mandarich | .05 | .02 | .01 |
| Green Bay Packers | | | |
| ☐ 338 Matt Bahr | .05 | .02 | .01 |
| New York Giants | | | |
| ☐ 339 Mike Saxon | .05 | .02 | .01 |
| Dallas Cowboys | | | |
| ☐ 340 Bruce Matthews | .08 | .04 | .01 |
| Houston Oilers | | | |
| ☐ 341 Rickey Jackson | .08 | .04 | .01 |
| New Orleans Saints | | | |
| ☐ 342 Eric Allen | .08 | .04 | .01 |
| Philadelphia Eagles | | | |
| ☐ 343 Lonnie Young | .05 | .02 | .01 |
| New York Jets | | | |
| ☐ 344 Steve McMichael | .08 | .04 | .01 |
| Chicago Bears | | | |
| ☐ 345 Willie Gault | .08 | .04 | .01 |
| Los Angeles Raiders | | | |
| ☐ 346 Barry Word | .10 | .05 | .01 |
| Kansas City Chiefs | | | |
| ☐ 347 Rich Camarillo | .05 | .02 | .01 |
| Phoenix Cardinals | | | |
| ☐ 348 Bill Romanowski | .05 | .02 | .01 |
| San Francisco 49ers | | | |
| ☐ 349 Jim Lachey | .05 | .02 | .01 |
| Washington Redskins | | | |
| ☐ 350 Jim Ritcher | .05 | .02 | .01 |
| Buffalo Bills | | | |
| ☐ 351 Irving Fryar | .08 | .04 | .01 |
| New England Patriots | | | |
| ☐ 352 Gary Anderson | .05 | .02 | .01 |
| Pittsburgh Steelers | | | |
| ☐ 353 Henry Rolling | .05 | .02 | .01 |
| San Diego Chargers | | | |
| ☐ 354 Mark Bortz | .05 | .02 | .01 |
| Chicago Bears | | | |
| ☐ 355 Mark Clayton | .08 | .04 | .01 |
| Miami Dolphins | | | |
| ☐ 356 Keith Woodside | .05 | .02 | .01 |
| Green Bay Packers | | | |
| ☐ 357 Jonathan Hayes | .05 | .02 | .01 |
| Kansas City Chiefs | | | |
| ☐ 358 Derrick Fenner | .08 | .04 | .01 |
| Seattle Seahawks | | | |
| ☐ 359 Keith Byars | .08 | .04 | .01 |
| Philadelphia Eagles | | | |
| ☐ 360 Drew Hill | .08 | .04 | .01 |
| Houston Oilers | | | |
| ☐ 361 Harris Barton | .05 | .02 | .01 |
| San Francisco 49ers | | | |
| ☐ 362 John Kidd | .05 | .02 | .01 |
| San Diego Chargers | | | |
| ☐ 363 Aeneas Williams | .05 | .02 | .01 |
| Phoenix Cardinals | | | |
| ☐ 364 Brian Washington | .05 | .02 | .01 |
| New York Jets | | | |
| ☐ 365 John Stephens | .08 | .04 | .01 |
| New England Patriots | | | |
| ☐ 366 Norm Johnson | .05 | .02 | .01 |
| Atlanta Falcons | | | |
| ☐ 367 Darryl Henley | .05 | .02 | .01 |
| Los Angeles Rams | | | |
| ☐ 368 William White | .05 | .02 | .01 |
| Detroit Lions | | | |
| ☐ 369 Mark Murphy | .05 | .02 | .01 |

| | | | |
|---|---|---|---|
| Green Bay Packers | | | |
| ☐ 370 Myron Guyton | .05 | .02 | .01 |
| New York Giants | | | |
| ☐ 371 Leon Seals | .05 | .02 | .01 |
| Buffalo Bills | | | |
| ☐ 372 Rich Gannon | .08 | .04 | .01 |
| Minnesota Vikings | | | |
| ☐ 373 Toi Cook | .05 | .02 | .01 |
| New Orleans Saints | | | |
| ☐ 374 Anthony Johnson | .05 | .02 | .01 |
| Indianapolis Colts | | | |
| ☐ 375 Rod Woodson | .10 | .05 | .01 |
| Pittsburgh Steelers | | | |
| ☐ 376 Alexander Wright | .08 | .04 | .01 |
| Dallas Cowboys | | | |
| ☐ 377 Kevin Butler | .05 | .02 | .01 |
| Chicago Bears | | | |
| ☐ 378 Neil Smith | .10 | .05 | .01 |
| Kansas City Chiefs | | | |
| ☐ 379 Gary Anderson | .08 | .04 | .01 |
| Tampa Bay Buccaneers | | | |
| ☐ 380 Reggie Roby | .05 | .02 | .01 |
| Miami Dolphins | | | |
| ☐ 381 Jeff Bryant | .05 | .02 | .01 |
| Seattle Seahawks | | | |
| ☐ 382 Ray Crockett | .05 | .02 | .01 |
| Detroit Lions | | | |
| ☐ 383 Richard Johnson | .05 | .02 | .01 |
| Houston Oilers | | | |
| ☐ 384 Hassan Jones | .05 | .02 | .01 |
| Minnesota Vikings | | | |
| ☐ 385 Karl Mecklenburg | .08 | .04 | .01 |
| Denver Broncos | | | |
| ☐ 386 Jeff Jaeger | .05 | .02 | .01 |
| Los Angeles Raiders | | | |
| ☐ 387 Keith Willis | .05 | .02 | .01 |
| Pittsburgh Steelers | | | |
| ☐ 388 Phil Simms | .10 | .05 | .01 |
| New York Giants | | | |
| ☐ 389 Kevin Ross | .08 | .04 | .01 |
| Kansas City Chiefs | | | |
| ☐ 390 Chris Miller | .10 | .05 | .01 |
| Atlanta Falcons | | | |
| ☐ 391 Brian Noble | .05 | .02 | .01 |
| Green Bay Packers | | | |
| ☐ 392 Jamie Dukes | .05 | .02 | .01 |
| Atlanta Falcons | | | |
| ☐ 393 George Jamison | .05 | .02 | .01 |
| Detroit Lions | | | |
| ☐ 394 Rickey Dixon | .05 | .02 | .01 |
| Cincinnati Bengals | | | |
| ☐ 395 Carl Lee | .05 | .02 | .01 |
| Minnesota Vikings | | | |
| ☐ 396 Jon Hand | .05 | .02 | .01 |
| Indianapolis Colts | | | |
| ☐ 397 Kirby Jackson | .05 | .02 | .01 |
| Buffalo Bills | | | |
| ☐ 398 Pat Terrell | .05 | .02 | .01 |
| Los Angeles Rams | | | |
| ☐ 399 Howie Long | .08 | .04 | .01 |
| Los Angeles Raiders | | | |
| ☐ 400 Mike Young | .05 | .02 | .01 |
| Denver Broncos | | | |
| ☐ 401 Keith Sims | .05 | .02 | .01 |
| Miami Dolphins | | | |
| ☐ 402 Tommy Barnhardt | .05 | .02 | .01 |
| New Orleans Saints | | | |
| ☐ 403 Greg McMurtry | .05 | .02 | .01 |
| New England Patriots | | | |
| ☐ 404 Keith Van Horne | .05 | .02 | .01 |
| Chicago Bears | | | |
| ☐ 405 Seth Joyner | .08 | .04 | .01 |
| Philadelphia Eagles | | | |
| ☐ 406 Jim Jeffcoat | .05 | .02 | .01 |
| Dallas Cowboys | | | |
| ☐ 407 Courtney Hall | .05 | .02 | .01 |
| San Diego Chargers | | | |
| ☐ 408 Tony Covington | .05 | .02 | .01 |
| Tampa Bay Buccaneers | | | |
| ☐ 409 Jacob Green | .05 | .02 | .01 |
| Seattle Seahawks | | | |
| ☐ 410 Charles Haley | .08 | .04 | .01 |
| San Francisco 49ers | | | |
| ☐ 411 Darryl Talley | .08 | .04 | .01 |
| Buffalo Bills | | | |
| ☐ 412 Jeff Cross | .05 | .02 | .01 |
| Miami Dolphins | | | |
| ☐ 413 John Elway | .40 | .18 | .05 |
| Denver Broncos | | | |
| ☐ 414 Donald Evans | .05 | .02 | .01 |
| Pittsburgh Steelers | | | |
| ☐ 415 Jackie Slater | .08 | .04 | .01 |
| Los Angeles Rams | | | |
| ☐ 416 John Friesz | .08 | .04 | .01 |
| San Diego Chargers | | | |
| ☐ 417 Anthony Smith | .08 | .04 | .01 |
| Los Angeles Raiders | | | |
| ☐ 418 Gill Byrd | .08 | .04 | .01 |

| | | | |
|---|---|---|---|
| San Diego Chargers | | | |
| ☐ 419 Willie Drewrey | .05 | .02 | .01 |
| Tampa Bay Buccaneers | | | |
| ☐ 420 Jay Hilgenberg | .08 | .04 | .01 |
| Chicago Bears | | | |
| ☐ 421 David Treadwell | .05 | .02 | .01 |
| Denver Broncos | | | |
| ☐ 422 Curtis Duncan | .08 | .04 | .01 |
| Houston Oilers | | | |
| ☐ 423 Sammie Smith | .05 | .02 | .01 |
| Miami Dolphins | | | |
| ☐ 424 Henry Thomas | .05 | .02 | .01 |
| Minnesota Vikings | | | |
| ☐ 425 James Lofton | .10 | .05 | .01 |
| Buffalo Bills | | | |
| ☐ 426 Fred Marion | .05 | .02 | .01 |
| New England Patriots | | | |
| ☐ 427 Bryce Paup | .05 | .02 | .01 |
| Green Bay Packers | | | |
| ☐ 428 Michael Timpson | .25 | .11 | .03 |
| New England Patriots | | | |
| ☐ 429 Reyna Thompson | .05 | .02 | .01 |
| New York Giants | | | |
| ☐ 430 Mike Kenn | .08 | .04 | .01 |
| Atlanta Falcons | | | |
| ☐ 431 Bill Maas | .05 | .02 | .01 |
| Kansas City Chiefs | | | |
| ☐ 432 Quinn Early | .08 | .04 | .01 |
| New Orleans Saints | | | |
| ☐ 433 Everson Walls | .05 | .02 | .01 |
| New York Giants | | | |
| ☐ 434 Jimmie Jones | .05 | .02 | .01 |
| Dallas Cowboys | | | |
| ☐ 435 Dwight Stone | .05 | .02 | .01 |
| Pittsburgh Steelers | | | |
| ☐ 436 Harry Colon | .05 | .02 | .01 |
| New England Patriots | | | |
| ☐ 437 Don Mosebar | .05 | .02 | .01 |
| Los Angeles Raiders | | | |
| ☐ 438 Calvin Williams | .10 | .05 | .01 |
| Philadelphia Eagles | | | |
| ☐ 439 Tom Tupa | .08 | .04 | .01 |
| Phoenix Cardinals | | | |
| ☐ 440 Darrell Green | .08 | .04 | .01 |
| Washington Redskins | | | |
| ☐ 441 Eric Thomas | .05 | .02 | .01 |
| Cincinnati Bengals | | | |
| ☐ 442 Terry Wooden | .05 | .02 | .01 |
| Seattle Seahawks | | | |
| ☐ 443 Brett Perriman | .08 | .04 | .01 |
| Detroit Lions | | | |
| ☐ 444 Todd Marinovich | .05 | .02 | .01 |
| Los Angeles Raiders | | | |
| ☐ 445 Jim Breech | .05 | .02 | .01 |
| Cincinnati Bengals | | | |
| ☐ 446 Eddie Anderson | .05 | .02 | .01 |
| Los Angeles Raiders | | | |
| ☐ 447 Jay Schroeder | .08 | .04 | .01 |
| Los Angeles Raiders | | | |
| ☐ 448 William Roberts | .05 | .02 | .01 |
| New York Giants | | | |
| ☐ 449 Brad Edwards | .05 | .02 | .01 |
| Washington Redskins | | | |
| ☐ 450 Tunch Ilkin | .05 | .02 | .01 |
| Pittsburgh Steelers | | | |
| ☐ 451 Ivy Joe Hunter | .05 | .02 | .01 |
| New England Patriots | | | |
| ☐ 452 Robert Clark | .05 | .02 | .01 |
| Detroit Lions | | | |
| ☐ 453 Tim Barnett | .08 | .04 | .01 |
| Kansas City Chiefs | | | |
| ☐ 454 Jarrod Bunch | .05 | .02 | .01 |
| New York Giants | | | |
| ☐ 455 Tim Harris | .08 | .04 | .01 |
| San Francisco 49ers | | | |
| ☐ 456 James Brooks | .08 | .04 | .01 |
| Cincinnati Bengals | | | |
| ☐ 457 Trace Armstrong | .05 | .02 | .01 |
| Chicago Bears | | | |
| ☐ 458 Michael Brooks | .05 | .02 | .01 |
| Denver Broncos | | | |
| ☐ 459 Andy Heck | .05 | .02 | .01 |
| Seattle Seahawks | | | |
| ☐ 460 Greg Jackson | .05 | .02 | .01 |
| New York Giants | | | |
| ☐ 461 Vance Johnson | .08 | .04 | .01 |
| Denver Broncos | | | |
| ☐ 462 Kirk Lowdermilk | .05 | .02 | .01 |
| Minnesota Vikings | | | |
| ☐ 463 Erik McMillan | .05 | .02 | .01 |
| New York Jets | | | |
| ☐ 464 Scott Mersereau | .05 | .02 | .01 |
| New York Jets | | | |
| ☐ 465 Jeff Wright | .05 | .02 | .01 |
| Buffalo Bills | | | |
| ☐ 466 Mike Tomczak | .05 | .02 | .01 |
| Green Bay Packers | | | |
| ☐ 467 David Alexander | .05 | .02 | .01 |

| | | | |
|---|---|---|---|
| Philadelphia Eagles | | | |
| ☐ 468 Bryan Millard | .05 | .02 | .01 |
| Seattle Seahawks | | | |
| ☐ 469 John Randle | .05 | .02 | .01 |
| Minnesota Vikings | | | |
| ☐ 470 Joel Hilgenberg | .05 | .02 | .01 |
| New Orleans Saints | | | |
| ☐ 471 Bennie Thompson | .12 | .05 | .02 |
| New Orleans Saints | | | |
| ☐ 472 Freeman McNeil | .05 | .02 | .01 |
| New York Jets | | | |
| ☐ 473 Terry Orr | .15 | .07 | .02 |
| Washington Redskins | | | |
| ☐ 474 Mike Horan | .05 | .02 | .01 |
| Denver Broncos | | | |
| ☐ 475 Leroy Hoard | .08 | .04 | .01 |
| Cleveland Browns | | | |
| ☐ 476 Patrick Rowe DP | .10 | .05 | .01 |
| Cleveland Browns | | | |
| ☐ 477 Siran Stacy DP | .10 | .05 | .01 |
| Philadelphia Eagles | | | |
| ☐ 478 Amp Lee DP | .25 | .11 | .03 |
| San Francisco 49ers | | | |
| ☐ 479 Eddie Blake DP | .05 | .02 | .01 |
| Miami Dolphins | | | |
| ☐ 480 Joe Bowden DP | .05 | .02 | .01 |
| Houston Oilers | | | |
| ☐ 481 Roderick Milstead DP | .10 | .05 | .01 |
| Dallas Cowboys | | | |
| ☐ 482 Keith Hamilton DP | .15 | .07 | .02 |
| New York Giants | | | |
| ☐ 483 Darryl Williams DP | .20 | .09 | .03 |
| Cincinnati Bengals | | | |
| ☐ 484 Robert Porcher DP | .20 | .09 | .03 |
| Detroit Lions | | | |
| ☐ 485 Ed Cunningham DP | .05 | .02 | .01 |
| Phoenix Cardinals | | | |
| ☐ 486 Chris Mims DP | .25 | .11 | .03 |
| San Diego Chargers | | | |
| ☐ 487 Chris Hakel DP | .10 | .05 | .01 |
| Washington Redskins | | | |
| ☐ 488 Jimmy Smith DP | .10 | .05 | .01 |
| Dallas Cowboys | | | |
| ☐ 489 Todd Harrison DP | .10 | .05 | .01 |
| Chicago Bears | | | |
| ☐ 490 Edgar Bennett DP | .30 | .14 | .04 |
| Green Bay Packers | | | |
| ☐ 491 Dexter McNabb DP | .05 | .02 | .01 |
| Green Bay Packers | | | |
| ☐ 492 Leon Searcy DP | .05 | .02 | .01 |
| Pittsburgh Steelers | | | |
| ☐ 493 Tommy Vardell DP | .25 | .11 | .03 |
| Cleveland Browns | | | |
| ☐ 494 Terrell Buckley DP | .25 | .11 | .03 |
| Green Bay Packers | | | |
| ☐ 495 Kevin Turner DP | .20 | .09 | .03 |
| New England Patriots | | | |
| ☐ 496 Russ Campbell DP | .05 | .02 | .01 |
| Pittsburgh Steelers | | | |
| ☐ 497 Torrance Small DP | .10 | .05 | .01 |
| New Orleans Saints | | | |
| ☐ 498 Nate Turner DP | .10 | .05 | .01 |
| Buffalo Bills | | | |
| ☐ 499 Cornelius Benton DP | .05 | .02 | .01 |
| Pittsburgh Steelers | | | |
| ☐ 500 Matt Elliott DP | .05 | .02 | .01 |
| Washington Redskins | | | |
| ☐ 501 Robert Stewart DP | .10 | .05 | .01 |
| New Orleans Saints | | | |
| ☐ 502 Muhammad Shamsid-Deen... DP | .05 | .02 | .01 |
| Seattle Seahawks | | | |
| ☐ 503 George Williams DP | .05 | .02 | .01 |
| Cleveland Browns | | | |
| ☐ 504 Pumpy Tudors DP | .05 | .02 | .01 |
| Philadelphia Eagles | | | |
| ☐ 505 Matt LaBounty DP | .05 | .02 | .01 |
| San Francisco 49ers | | | |
| ☐ 506 Darryl Hardy DP | .05 | .02 | .01 |
| Atlanta Falcons | | | |
| ☐ 507 Derrick Moore DP | .40 | .18 | .05 |
| Atlanta Falcons | | | |
| ☐ 508 Willie Clay DP | .05 | .02 | .01 |
| Detroit Lions | | | |
| ☐ 509 Bob Whitfield DP | .10 | .05 | .01 |
| Atlanta Falcons | | | |
| ☐ 510 Ricardo McDonald DP | .10 | .05 | .01 |
| Cincinnati Bengals | | | |
| ☐ 511 Carlos Huerta DP | .05 | .02 | .01 |
| San Diego Chargers | | | |
| ☐ 512 Selwyn Jones DP | .15 | .07 | .02 |
| Cleveland Browns | | | |
| ☐ 513 Steve Gordon DP | .05 | .02 | .01 |
| New England Patriots | | | |
| ☐ 514 Bob Meeks DP | .05 | .02 | .01 |
| Denver Broncos | | | |
| ☐ 515 Bennie Blades CC | .05 | .02 | .01 |
| Detroit Lions | | | |

| | | | |
|---|---|---|---|
| ☐ 516 Andre Waters CC | .05 | .02 | .01 |
|     Philadelphia Eagles | | | |
| ☐ 517 Bubba McDowell CC | .05 | .02 | .01 |
|     Houston Oilers | | | |
| ☐ 518 Kevin Porter CC | .05 | .02 | .01 |
|     Kansas City Chiefs | | | |
| ☐ 519 Carnell Lake CC | .05 | .02 | .01 |
|     Pittsburgh Steelers | | | |
| ☐ 520 Leonard Russell ROY | .10 | .05 | .01 |
|     New England Patriots | | | |
| ☐ 521 Mike Croel ROY | .05 | .02 | .01 |
|     Denver Broncos | | | |
| ☐ 522 Lawrence Dawsey ROY | .08 | .04 | .01 |
|     Tampa Bay Buccaneers | | | |
| ☐ 523 Moe Gardner ROY | .05 | .02 | .01 |
|     Atlanta Falcons | | | |
| ☐ 524 Steve Broussard LBM | .05 | .02 | .01 |
|     Atlanta Falcons | | | |
| ☐ 525 Dave Meggett LBM | .05 | .02 | .01 |
|     New York Giants | | | |
| ☐ 526 Darrell Green LBM | .05 | .02 | .01 |
|     Washington Redskins | | | |
| ☐ 527 Tony Jones LBM | .05 | .02 | .01 |
|     Houston Oilers | | | |
| ☐ 528 Barry Sanders LBM | .30 | .14 | .04 |
|     Detroit Lions | | | |
| ☐ 529 Pat Swilling SA | .08 | .04 | .01 |
|     New Orleans Saints | | | |
| ☐ 530 Reggie White SA | .08 | .04 | .01 |
|     Philadelphia Eagles | | | |
| ☐ 531 William Fuller SA | .05 | .02 | .01 |
|     Houston Oilers | | | |
| ☐ 532 Simon Fletcher SA | .05 | .02 | .01 |
|     Denver Broncos | | | |
| ☐ 533 Derrick Thomas SA | .05 | .02 | .01 |
|     Kansas City Chiefs | | | |
| ☐ 534 Mark Rypien MOY | .08 | .04 | .01 |
|     Washington Redskins | | | |
| ☐ 535 John Mackey HOF | .05 | .02 | .01 |
| ☐ 536 John Riggins HOF | .05 | .02 | .01 |
| ☐ 537 Lem Barney HOF | .05 | .02 | .01 |
| ☐ 538 Shawn McCarthy 90 | .05 | .02 | .01 |
|     New England Patriots | | | |
| ☐ 539 Al Edwards 90 | .05 | .02 | .01 |
|     Buffalo Bills | | | |
| ☐ 540 Alexander Wright 90 | .05 | .02 | .01 |
|     Dallas Cowboys | | | |
| ☐ 541 Ray Crockett 90 | .05 | .02 | .01 |
|     Detroit Lions | | | |
| ☐ 542 Steve Young 90 and | .15 | .07 | .02 |
|     John Taylor 90 | | | |
|     San Francisco 49ers | | | |
| ☐ 543 Nate Lewis 90 | .05 | .02 | .01 |
|     San Diego Chargers | | | |
| ☐ 544 Dexter Carter 90 | .05 | .02 | .01 |
|     San Francisco 49ers | | | |
| ☐ 545 Reggie Rutland 90 | .05 | .02 | .01 |
|     Minnesota Vikings | | | |
| ☐ 546 Jon Vaughn 90 | .05 | .02 | .01 |
|     New England Patriots | | | |
| ☐ 547 Chris Martin 90 | .05 | .02 | .01 |
|     Kansas City Chiefs | | | |
| ☐ 548 Warren Moon HL | .10 | .05 | .01 |
|     Houston Oilers | | | |
| ☐ 549 Super Bowl Highlights | .05 | .02 | .01 |
| ☐ 550 Robb Thomas | .05 | .02 | .01 |
|     Kansas City Chiefs | | | |

which stands out against a background shot with a yellowish tint. The Score logo is gold-foil stamped at the lower left corner. On the back, a player profile is printed on a background that shades from tan to purple as one moves down the card face. The cards are numbered on the back.

| | MINT | EXC | G-VG |
|---|---|---|---|
| COMPLETE SET (25) | 80.00 | 36.00 | 10.00 |
| COMMON PLAYER (1-25) | 2.50 | 1.15 | .30 |
| ☐ 1 Michael Irvin | 15.00 | 6.75 | 1.90 |
|     Dallas Cowboys | | | |
| ☐ 2 Haywood Jeffires | 3.00 | 1.35 | .40 |
|     Houston Oilers | | | |
| ☐ 3 Emmitt Smith | 40.00 | 18.00 | 5.00 |
|     Dallas Cowboys | | | |
| ☐ 4 Barry Sanders | 22.00 | 10.00 | 2.80 |
|     Detroit Lions | | | |
| ☐ 5 Marv Cook | 2.50 | 1.15 | .30 |
|     New England Patriots | | | |
| ☐ 6 Bart Oates | 2.50 | 1.15 | .30 |
|     New York Giants | | | |
| ☐ 7 Steve Wisniewski | 2.50 | 1.15 | .30 |
|     Los Angeles Raiders | | | |
| ☐ 8 Randall McDaniel | 2.50 | 1.15 | .30 |
|     Minnesota Vikings | | | |
| ☐ 9 Jim Lachey | 2.50 | 1.15 | .30 |
|     Washington Redskins | | | |
| ☐ 10 Lomas Brown | 2.50 | 1.15 | .30 |
|     Detroit Lions | | | |
| ☐ 11 Reggie White | 4.00 | 1.80 | .50 |
|     Philadelphia Eagles | | | |
| ☐ 12 Clyde Simmons | 3.00 | 1.35 | .40 |
|     Philadelphia Eagles | | | |
| ☐ 13 Jerome Brown | 4.00 | 1.80 | .50 |
|     Philadelphia Eagles | | | |
| ☐ 14 Seth Joyner | 3.00 | 1.35 | .40 |
|     Philadelphia Eagles | | | |
| ☐ 15 Darryl Talley | 2.50 | 1.15 | .30 |
|     Buffalo Bills | | | |
| ☐ 16 Karl Mecklenburg | 2.50 | 1.15 | .30 |
|     Denver Broncos | | | |
| ☐ 17 Sam Mills | 2.50 | 1.15 | .30 |
|     New Orleans Saints | | | |
| ☐ 18 Darrell Green | 2.50 | 1.15 | .30 |
|     Washington Redskins | | | |
| ☐ 19 Steve Atwater | 2.50 | 1.15 | .30 |
|     Denver Broncos | | | |
| ☐ 20 Mark Carrier | 2.50 | 1.15 | .30 |
|     Chicago Bears | | | |
| ☐ 21 Jeff Gossett UER | 2.50 | 1.15 | .30 |
|     (Card says Rams, should | | | |
|     say Raiders) | | | |
|     Los Angeles Raiders | | | |
| ☐ 22 Chip Lohmiller | 2.50 | 1.15 | .30 |
|     Washington Redskins | | | |
| ☐ 23 Mel Gray | 2.50 | 1.15 | .30 |
|     Detroit Lions | | | |
| ☐ 24 Steve Tasker | 2.50 | 1.15 | .30 |
|     Buffalo Bills | | | |
| ☐ 25 Mark Rypien | 3.00 | 1.35 | .40 |
|     Washington Redskins | | | |

## 1992 Score Gridiron Stars

Three of these cards were inserted in each 1992 Score jumbo pack. The cards measure the standard size (2 1/2" by 3 1/2"). The fronts feature full-bleed color action player photos. Team color-coded stripes intersect a diamond carrying the team logo in the lower left corner. The vertical stripe has "Gridiron Stars" gold-foil stamped on it, while the player's name and position are printed in the horizontal stripe. On the backs, the team logo and color close-up photo appear on the top

## 1992 Score Dream Team

Randomly inserted in 1992 Score foil packs, this 25-card standard-size (2 1/2" by 3 1/2") set pays tribute to some of the NFL's finest players. The horizontal fronts are full-bleed and display on the left a close-up color head shot and on the right a color player action photo

half, while on the bottom half a white panel presents biography, statistics, and player profile. The cards are numbered on the back.

| | MINT | EXC | G-VG |
|---|---|---|---|
| COMPLETE SET (45) | 12.00 | 5.50 | 1.50 |
| COMMON PLAYER (1-45) | .25 | .11 | .03 |
| ☐ 1 Barry Sanders<br>Detroit Lions | 3.00 | 1.35 | .40 |
| ☐ 2 Mike Croel<br>Denver Broncos | .25 | .11 | .03 |
| ☐ 3 Thurman Thomas<br>Buffalo Bills | 1.25 | .55 | .16 |
| ☐ 4 Lawrence Dawsey<br>Tampa Bay Buccaneers | .30 | .14 | .04 |
| ☐ 5 Brad Baxter<br>New York Jets | .25 | .11 | .03 |
| ☐ 6 Moe Gardner<br>Atlanta Falcons | .25 | .11 | .03 |
| ☐ 7 Emmitt Smith<br>Dallas Cowboys | 5.00 | 2.30 | .60 |
| ☐ 8 Sammie Smith<br>Miami Dolphins | .25 | .11 | .03 |
| ☐ 9 Rodney Hampton<br>New York Giants | 1.25 | .55 | .16 |
| ☐ 10 Mark Carrier<br>Chicago Bears | .25 | .11 | .03 |
| ☐ 11 Mo Lewis<br>New York Jets | .25 | .11 | .03 |
| ☐ 12 Andre Rison<br>Atlanta Falcons | .35 | .16 | .04 |
| ☐ 13 Eric Green<br>Pittsburgh Steelers | .30 | .14 | .04 |
| ☐ 14 Richmond Webb<br>Miami Dolphins | .25 | .11 | .03 |
| ☐ 15 Johnny Bailey<br>Chicago Bears | .25 | .11 | .03 |
| ☐ 16 Mike Pritchard<br>Atlanta Falcons | .75 | .35 | .09 |
| ☐ 17 John Friesz<br>San Diego Chargers | .30 | .14 | .04 |
| ☐ 18 Leonard Russell<br>New England Patriots | 1.00 | .45 | .13 |
| ☐ 19 Derrick Thomas<br>Kansas City Chiefs | .35 | .16 | .04 |
| ☐ 20 Ken Harvey<br>Phoenix Cardinals | .25 | .11 | .03 |
| ☐ 21 Fred Barnett<br>Philadelphia Eagles | .30 | .14 | .04 |
| ☐ 22 Aeneas Williams<br>Phoenix Cardinals | .25 | .11 | .03 |
| ☐ 23 Marion Butts<br>San Diego Chargers | .30 | .14 | .04 |
| ☐ 24 Harold Green<br>Cincinnati Bengals | .30 | .14 | .04 |
| ☐ 25 Michael Irvin<br>Dallas Cowboys | 2.00 | .90 | .25 |
| ☐ 26 Dan Owens<br>Detroit Lions | .25 | .11 | .03 |
| ☐ 27 Curtis Duncan<br>Houston Oilers | .25 | .11 | .03 |
| ☐ 28 Rodney Peete<br>Detroit Lions | .30 | .14 | .04 |
| ☐ 29 Brian Blades<br>Seattle Seahawks | .25 | .11 | .03 |
| ☐ 30 Marv Cook<br>New England Patriots | .25 | .11 | .03 |
| ☐ 31 Burt Grossman<br>San Diego Chargers | .25 | .11 | .03 |
| ☐ 32 Michael Haynes<br>Atlanta Falcons | .75 | .35 | .09 |
| ☐ 33 Bennie Blades<br>Detroit Lions | .25 | .11 | .03 |
| ☐ 34 Cornelius Bennett<br>Buffalo Bills | .30 | .14 | .04 |
| ☐ 35 Louis Oliver<br>Miami Dolphins | .25 | .11 | .03 |
| ☐ 36 Rod Woodson<br>Pittsburgh Steelers | .30 | .14 | .04 |
| ☐ 37 Steve Wisniewski<br>Los Angeles Raiders | .25 | .11 | .03 |
| ☐ 38 Neil Smith<br>Kansas City Chiefs | .30 | .14 | .04 |
| ☐ 39 Gaston Green<br>Denver Broncos | .25 | .11 | .03 |
| ☐ 40 Jeff Lageman<br>New York Jets | .25 | .11 | .03 |
| ☐ 41 Chip Lohmiller<br>Washington Redskins | .25 | .11 | .03 |
| ☐ 42 Tim McDonald<br>Phoenix Cardinals | .25 | .11 | .03 |
| ☐ 43 John Elliott<br>New York Giants | .25 | .11 | .03 |
| ☐ 44 Steve Atwater<br>Denver Broncos | .25 | .11 | .03 |
| ☐ 45 Flipper Anderson<br>Los Angeles Rams | .25 | .11 | .03 |

# 1992 Score Young Superstars

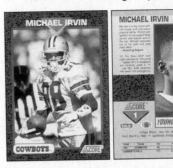

This 40-card boxed set features some of the young stars in the NFL. The cards measure the standard size (2 1/2 by 3 1/2"). The fronts feature glossy color action player photos inside a green inner border and a purple outer border speckled with black. The player's name appears in white lettering at the top, while the team name is printed at the lower left corner. On a gradated yellow background, the backs carry a color close-up photo, a scouting report feature, career highlights, biography, and statistics. The cards are numbered on the back.

| | MINT | EXC | G-VG |
|---|---|---|---|
| COMPLETE SET (40) | 6.00 | 2.40 | .60 |
| COMMON PLAYER (1-40) | .10 | .04 | .01 |
| ☐ 1 Michael Irvin<br>Dallas Cowboys | 1.00 | .40 | .10 |
| ☐ 2 Cortez Kennedy<br>Seattle Seahawks | .25 | .10 | .02 |
| ☐ 3 Ken Harvey<br>Phoenix Cardinals | .10 | .04 | .01 |
| ☐ 4 Bubba McDowell<br>Houston Oilers | .10 | .04 | .01 |
| ☐ 5 Mark Higgs<br>Miami Dolphins | .50 | .20 | .05 |
| ☐ 6 Andre Rison<br>Atlanta Falcons | .40 | .16 | .04 |
| ☐ 7 Lamar Lathon<br>Houston Oilers | .10 | .04 | .01 |
| ☐ 8 Bennie Blades<br>Detroit Lions | .10 | .04 | .01 |
| ☐ 9 Anthony Johnson<br>Indianapolis Colts | .15 | .06 | .01 |
| ☐ 10 Vince Buck<br>New Orleans Saints | .10 | .04 | .01 |
| ☐ 11 Pat Harlow<br>New England Patriots | .10 | .04 | .01 |
| ☐ 12 Mike Croel<br>Denver Broncos | .20 | .08 | .02 |
| ☐ 13 Myron Guyton<br>New York Giants | .10 | .04 | .01 |
| ☐ 14 Curtis Duncan<br>Houston Oilers | .15 | .06 | .01 |
| ☐ 15 Michael Haynes<br>Atlanta Falcons | .35 | .14 | .03 |
| ☐ 16 Alexander Wright<br>Dallas Cowboys | .15 | .06 | .01 |
| ☐ 17 Greg Lewis<br>Denver Broncos | .15 | .06 | .01 |
| ☐ 18 Chip Lohmiller<br>Washington Redskins | .10 | .04 | .01 |
| ☐ 19 Nate Lewis<br>San Diego Chargers | .10 | .04 | .01 |
| ☐ 20 Rodney Peete<br>Detroit Lions | .15 | .06 | .01 |
| ☐ 21 Marv Cook<br>New England Patriots | .10 | .04 | .01 |
| ☐ 22 Lawrence Dawsey<br>Tampa Bay Buccaneers | .20 | .08 | .02 |
| ☐ 23 Pat Terrell<br>Los Angeles Rams | .10 | .04 | .01 |
| ☐ 24 John Friesz<br>San Diego Chargers | .15 | .06 | .01 |
| ☐ 25 Tony Bennett<br>Green Bay Packers | .15 | .06 | .01 |
| ☐ 26 Gaston Green<br>Denver Broncos | .15 | .06 | .01 |
| ☐ 27 Kevin Porter<br>Kansas City Chiefs | .10 | .04 | .01 |
| ☐ 28 Mike Pritchard<br>Atlanta Falcons | .35 | .14 | .03 |
| ☐ 29 Keith Henderson<br>San Francisco 49ers | .10 | .04 | .01 |
| ☐ 30 Mo Lewis | .10 | .04 | .01 |

New York Jets
| | | | |
|---|---|---|---|
| ☐ 31 John Randle | .10 | .04 | .01 |
| Minnesota Vikings | | | |
| ☐ 32 Aeneas Williams | .10 | .04 | .01 |
| Phoenix Cardinals | | | |
| ☐ 33 Floyd Turner | .10 | .04 | .01 |
| New Orleans Saints | | | |
| ☐ 34 Neil Smith | .20 | .08 | .02 |
| Kansas City Chiefs | | | |
| ☐ 35 Tom Waddle | .25 | .10 | .02 |
| Chicago Bears | | | |
| ☐ 36 Jeff Lageman | .15 | .06 | .01 |
| New York Jets | | | |
| ☐ 37 Cris Carter | .20 | .08 | .02 |
| Minnesota Vikings | | | |
| ☐ 38 Leonard Russell | .40 | .16 | .04 |
| New England Patriots | | | |
| ☐ 39 Terry McDaniel | .10 | .04 | .01 |
| Los Angeles Raiders | | | |
| ☐ 40 Moe Gardner | .10 | .04 | .01 |
| Atlanta Falcons | | | |

## 1993 Score Samples

This six-card standard-size (2 1/2" by 3 1/2") set was issued to preview the 1993 Score regular series. The fronts feature color action player photos bordered in white. The player's name appears in the bottom white border, while the team name is printed vertically in a team color-coded bar that edges the left side of the picture. On team color-coded and pastel panels, the backs present a color head shot, biography, statistics, and player profile. These cards are also issued as an uncut sheet. The cards are numbered on the back. In a short yellow bar at the lower right corner, the cards are marked "sample card."

| | MINT | EXC | G-VG |
|---|---|---|---|
| COMPLETE SET (6) | 7.00 | 2.80 | .70 |
| COMMON PLAYER (1-6) | .75 | .30 | .07 |
| | | | |
| ☐ 1 Barry Sanders | 3.50 | 1.40 | .35 |
| Detroit Lions | | | |
| ☐ 2 Moe Gardner | .75 | .30 | .07 |
| Atlanta Falcons | | | |
| ☐ 3 Ricky Watters | 2.50 | 1.00 | .25 |
| San Francisco 49ers | | | |
| ☐ 4 Todd Lyght | 1.00 | .40 | .10 |
| Los Angeles Rams | | | |
| ☐ 5 Rodney Hampton | 1.50 | .60 | .15 |
| New York Giants | | | |
| ☐ 6 Curtis Duncan | 1.00 | .40 | .10 |
| Houston Oilers | | | |

## 1993 Score

The 1993 Score football set consists of 440 standard-size (2 1/2" by 3 1/2") cards. Each 16-card pack included one Pinnacle card from a 55-card "Men of Autumn" set not found in regular Pinnacle packs. A 28-card 1993 Score The Franchise subset was randomly inserted in 16-card foil packs, while a 26-card Dream Team subset was featured in 35-card super packs. Also dealers could receive one of 3,000 limited-edition autographed Dick Butkus cards for each order of 20 foil boxes. Topical subsets featured are Rookies (306-315), Super Bowl Highlights (411-412), Double Trouble (413-416), Rookie of the Year (417-420), 90 Plus Club (421-430), Highlights (431-434), and Hall of Fame (436-439). The set concludes with a Man of the Year card (440), honoring Steve Young. The cards are numbered on the back. Rookie Cards include Jerome Bettis, Drew Bledsoe, Curtis Conway and Garrison Hearst.

| | MINT | EXC | G-VG |
|---|---|---|---|
| COMPLETE SET (440) | 16.00 | 7.25 | 2.00 |
| COMMON PLAYER (1-440) | .05 | .02 | .01 |

| | | | |
|---|---|---|---|
| ☐ 1 Barry Sanders | .75 | .35 | .09 |
| Detroit Lions | | | |
| ☐ 2 Moe Gardner | .05 | .02 | .01 |
| Atlanta Falcons | | | |
| ☐ 3 Ricky Watters | .30 | .14 | .04 |
| San Francisco 49ers | | | |
| ☐ 4 Todd Lyght | .05 | .02 | .01 |
| Los Angeles Rams | | | |
| ☐ 5 Rodney Hampton | .30 | .14 | .04 |
| New York Giants | | | |
| ☐ 6 Curtis Duncan | .05 | .02 | .01 |
| Houston Oilers | | | |
| ☐ 7 Barry Word | .10 | .05 | .01 |
| Kansas City Chiefs | | | |
| ☐ 8 Reggie Cobb | .10 | .05 | .01 |
| Tampa Bay Buccaneers | | | |
| ☐ 9 Mike Kenn | .05 | .02 | .01 |
| Atlanta Falcons | | | |
| ☐ 10 Michael Irvin | .40 | .18 | .05 |
| Dallas Cowboys | | | |
| ☐ 11 Bryan Cox | .08 | .04 | .01 |
| Miami Dolphins | | | |
| ☐ 12 Chris Doleman | .08 | .04 | .01 |
| Minnesota Vikings | | | |
| ☐ 13 Rod Woodson | .10 | .05 | .01 |
| Pittsburgh Steelers | | | |
| ☐ 14 Emmitt Smith | 2.00 | .90 | .25 |
| Dallas Cowboys | | | |
| ☐ 15 Pete Stoyanovich | .05 | .02 | .01 |
| Miami Dolphins | | | |
| ☐ 16 Steve Young | .25 | .11 | .03 |
| San Francisco 49ers | | | |
| ☐ 17 Randall McDaniel | .05 | .02 | .01 |
| Minnesota Vikings | | | |
| ☐ 18 Cortez Kennedy | .10 | .05 | .01 |
| Seattle Seahawks | | | |
| ☐ 19 Mel Gray | .08 | .04 | .01 |
| Detroit Lions | | | |
| ☐ 20 Barry Foster | .25 | .11 | .03 |
| Pittsburgh Steelers | | | |
| ☐ 21 Tim Brown | .25 | .11 | .03 |
| Los Angeles Raiders | | | |
| ☐ 22 Todd McNair | .05 | .02 | .01 |
| Kansas City Chiefs | | | |
| ☐ 23 Anthony Johnson | .05 | .02 | .01 |
| Indianapolis Colts | | | |
| ☐ 24 Nate Odomes | .08 | .04 | .01 |
| Buffalo Bills | | | |
| ☐ 25 Brett Favre | .75 | .35 | .09 |
| Green Bay Packers | | | |
| ☐ 26 Jack Del Rio | .05 | .02 | .01 |
| Minnesota Vikings | | | |
| ☐ 27 Terry McDaniel | .05 | .02 | .01 |
| Los Angeles Raiders | | | |
| ☐ 28 Haywood Jeffires | .10 | .05 | .01 |
| Houston Oilers | | | |
| ☐ 29 Jay Novacek | .10 | .05 | .01 |
| Dallas Cowboys | | | |
| ☐ 30 Wilber Marshall | .08 | .04 | .01 |
| Washington Redskins | | | |
| ☐ 31 Richmond Webb | .05 | .02 | .01 |
| Miami Dolphins | | | |
| ☐ 32 Steve Atwater | .08 | .04 | .01 |
| Denver Broncos | | | |
| ☐ 33 James Lofton | .10 | .05 | .01 |
| Buffalo Bills | | | |
| ☐ 34 Harold Green | .08 | .04 | .01 |
| Cincinnati Bengals | | | |
| ☐ 35 Eric Metcalf | .10 | .05 | .01 |
| Cleveland Browns | | | |
| ☐ 36 Bruce Matthews | .08 | .04 | .01 |
| Houston Oilers | | | |
| ☐ 37 Albert Lewis | .05 | .02 | .01 |
| Kansas City Chiefs | | | |
| ☐ 38 Jeff Herrod | .05 | .02 | .01 |
| Indianapolis Colts | | | |
| ☐ 39 Vince Workman | .05 | .02 | .01 |

| | | | |
|---|---|---|---|
| Green Bay Packers | | | |
| ☐ 40 John Elway | .35 | .16 | .04 |
| Denver Broncos | | | |
| ☐ 41 Brett Perriman | .08 | .04 | .01 |
| Detroit Lions | | | |
| ☐ 42 Jon Vaughn | .05 | .02 | .01 |
| New England Patriots | | | |
| ☐ 43 Terry Allen | .10 | .05 | .01 |
| Minnesota Vikings | | | |
| ☐ 44 Clyde Simmons | .08 | .04 | .01 |
| Philadelphia Eagles | | | |
| ☐ 45 Bennie Thompson | .05 | .02 | .01 |
| Kansas City Chiefs | | | |
| ☐ 46 Wendell Davis | .08 | .04 | .01 |
| Chicago Bears | | | |
| ☐ 47 Bobby Hebert | .10 | .05 | .01 |
| New Orleans Saints | | | |
| ☐ 48 John Offerdahl | .05 | .02 | .01 |
| Miami Dolphins | | | |
| ☐ 49 Jeff Graham | .08 | .04 | .01 |
| Pittsburgh Steelers | | | |
| ☐ 50 Steve Wisniewski | .05 | .02 | .01 |
| Los Angeles Raiders | | | |
| ☐ 51 Louis Oliver | .05 | .02 | .01 |
| Miami Dolphins | | | |
| ☐ 52 Rohn Stark | .05 | .02 | .01 |
| Indianapolis Colts | | | |
| ☐ 53 Cleveland Gary | .08 | .04 | .01 |
| Los Angeles Rams | | | |
| ☐ 54 John Randle | .05 | .02 | .01 |
| Minnesota Vikings | | | |
| ☐ 55 Jim Everett | .05 | .02 | .01 |
| Los Angeles Rams | | | |
| ☐ 56 Donnell Woolford | .05 | .02 | .01 |
| Cincinnati Bengals | | | |
| ☐ 57 Pepper Johnson | .08 | .04 | .01 |
| New York Giants | | | |
| ☐ 58 Irving Fryar | .08 | .04 | .01 |
| New England Patriots | | | |
| ☐ 59 Greg Townsend | .05 | .02 | .01 |
| Los Angeles Raiders | | | |
| ☐ 60 Chris Burkett | .05 | .02 | .01 |
| New York Jets | | | |
| ☐ 61 Johnny Johnson | .10 | .05 | .01 |
| Phoenix Cardinals | | | |
| ☐ 62 Ronnie Harmon | .08 | .04 | .01 |
| San Diego Chargers | | | |
| ☐ 63 Don Griffin | .05 | .02 | .01 |
| San Francisco 49ers | | | |
| ☐ 64 Wayne Martin | .05 | .02 | .01 |
| New Orleans Saints | | | |
| ☐ 65 John L. Williams | .08 | .04 | .01 |
| Seattle Seahawks | | | |
| ☐ 66 Brad Edwards | .05 | .02 | .01 |
| Washington Redskins | | | |
| ☐ 67 Toi Cook | .05 | .02 | .01 |
| New Orleans Saints | | | |
| ☐ 68 Lawrence Dawsey | .10 | .05 | .01 |
| Tampa Bay Buccaneers | | | |
| ☐ 69 Johnny Bailey | .05 | .02 | .01 |
| Phoenix Cardinals | | | |
| ☐ 70 Mike Brim | .05 | .02 | .01 |
| New York Jets | | | |
| ☐ 71 Andre Rison | .25 | .11 | .03 |
| Atlanta Falcons | | | |
| ☐ 72 Cornelius Bennett | .10 | .05 | .01 |
| Buffalo Bills | | | |
| ☐ 73 Brad Muster | .08 | .04 | .01 |
| Chicago Bears | | | |
| ☐ 74 Broderick Thomas | .05 | .02 | .01 |
| Tampa Bay Buccaneers | | | |
| ☐ 75 Tom Waddle | .10 | .05 | .01 |
| Chicago Bears | | | |
| ☐ 76 Paul Gruber | .05 | .02 | .01 |
| Tampa Bay Buccaneers | | | |
| ☐ 77 Jackie Harris | .30 | .14 | .04 |
| Green Bay Packers | | | |
| ☐ 78 Kenneth Davis | .08 | .04 | .01 |
| Buffalo Bills | | | |
| ☐ 79 Norm Johnson | .05 | .02 | .01 |
| Atlanta Falcons | | | |
| ☐ 80 Jim Jeffcoat | .05 | .02 | .01 |
| Dallas Cowboys | | | |
| ☐ 81 Chris Warren | .15 | .07 | .02 |
| Seattle Seahawks | | | |
| ☐ 82 Greg Kragen | .05 | .02 | .01 |
| Denver Broncos | | | |
| ☐ 83 Ricky Reynolds | .05 | .02 | .01 |
| Tampa Bay Buccaneers | | | |
| ☐ 84 Hardy Nickerson | .05 | .02 | .01 |
| Pittsburgh Steelers | | | |
| ☐ 85 Brian Mitchell | .08 | .04 | .01 |
| Washington Redskins | | | |
| ☐ 86 Rufus Porter | .05 | .02 | .01 |
| Seattle Seahawks | | | |
| ☐ 87 Greg Jackson | .05 | .02 | .01 |
| New York Giants | | | |
| ☐ 88 Seth Joyner | .08 | .04 | .01 |

| | | | |
|---|---|---|---|
| Philadelphia Eagles | | | |
| ☐ 89 Tim Grunhard | .05 | .02 | .01 |
| Kansas City Chiefs | | | |
| ☐ 90 Tim Harris | .05 | .02 | .01 |
| San Francisco 49ers | | | |
| ☐ 91 Sterling Sharpe | .40 | .18 | .05 |
| Green Bay Packers | | | |
| ☐ 92 Daniel Stubbs | .05 | .02 | .01 |
| Cincinnati Bengals | | | |
| ☐ 93 Rob Burnett | .05 | .02 | .01 |
| Cincinnati Bengals | | | |
| ☐ 94 Rich Camarillo | .05 | .02 | .01 |
| Phoenix Cardinals | | | |
| ☐ 95 Al Smith | .05 | .02 | .01 |
| Houston Oilers | | | |
| ☐ 96 Thurman Thomas | .35 | .16 | .04 |
| Buffalo Bills | | | |
| ☐ 97 Morten Andersen | .08 | .04 | .01 |
| New Orleans Saints | | | |
| ☐ 98 Reggie White | .15 | .07 | .02 |
| Philadelphia Eagles | | | |
| ☐ 99 Gill Byrd | .08 | .04 | .01 |
| San Diego Chargers | | | |
| ☐ 100 Pierce Holt | .05 | .02 | .01 |
| San Francisco 49ers | | | |
| ☐ 101 Tim McGee | .05 | .02 | .01 |
| Cincinnati Bengals | | | |
| ☐ 102 Rickey Jackson | .08 | .04 | .01 |
| New Orleans Saints | | | |
| ☐ 103 Vince Newsome | .05 | .02 | .01 |
| Cleveland Browns | | | |
| ☐ 104 Chris Spielman | .05 | .02 | .01 |
| Detroit Lions | | | |
| ☐ 105 Tim McDonald | .05 | .02 | .01 |
| Phoenix Cardinals | | | |
| ☐ 106 James Francis | .05 | .02 | .01 |
| Cincinnati Bengals | | | |
| ☐ 107 Andre Tippett | .05 | .02 | .01 |
| New England Patriots | | | |
| ☐ 108 Sam Mills | .08 | .04 | .01 |
| New Orleans Saints | | | |
| ☐ 109 Hugh Millen | .05 | .02 | .01 |
| New England Patriots | | | |
| ☐ 110 Brad Baxter | .08 | .04 | .01 |
| New York Jets | | | |
| ☐ 111 Ricky Sanders | .08 | .04 | .01 |
| Washington Redskins | | | |
| ☐ 112 Marion Butts | .10 | .05 | .01 |
| San Diego Chargers | | | |
| ☐ 113 Fred Barnett | .10 | .05 | .01 |
| Philadelphia Eagles | | | |
| ☐ 114 Wade Wilson | .08 | .04 | .01 |
| Atlanta Falcons | | | |
| ☐ 115 Dave Meggett | .08 | .04 | .01 |
| New York Giants | | | |
| ☐ 116 Kevin Greene | .05 | .02 | .01 |
| Los Angeles Rams | | | |
| ☐ 117 Reggie Langhorne | .08 | .04 | .01 |
| Indianapolis Colts | | | |
| ☐ 118 Simon Fletcher | .08 | .04 | .01 |
| Denver Broncos | | | |
| ☐ 119 Tommy Vardell | .08 | .04 | .01 |
| Cleveland Browns | | | |
| ☐ 120 Darion Conner | .05 | .02 | .01 |
| Atlanta Falcons | | | |
| ☐ 121 Darren Lewis | .08 | .04 | .01 |
| Chicago Bears | | | |
| ☐ 122 Charles Mann | .08 | .04 | .01 |
| Washington Redskins | | | |
| ☐ 123 David Fulcher | .05 | .02 | .01 |
| Cincinnati Bengals | | | |
| ☐ 124 Tommy Kane | .05 | .02 | .01 |
| Seattle Seahawks | | | |
| ☐ 125 Richard Brown | .05 | .02 | .01 |
| Green Bay Packers | | | |
| ☐ 126 Nate Lewis | .08 | .04 | .01 |
| San Diego Chargers | | | |
| ☐ 127 Tony Tolbert | .05 | .02 | .01 |
| Dallas Cowboys | | | |
| ☐ 128 Greg Lloyd | .05 | .02 | .01 |
| Pittsburgh Steelers | | | |
| ☐ 129 Herman Moore | .35 | .16 | .04 |
| Detroit Lions | | | |
| ☐ 130 Robert Massey | .05 | .02 | .01 |
| New Orleans Saints | | | |
| ☐ 131 Chris Jacke | .05 | .02 | .01 |
| Green Bay Packers | | | |
| ☐ 132 Keith Byars | .08 | .04 | .01 |
| Philadelphia Eagles | | | |
| ☐ 133 William Fuller | .05 | .02 | .01 |
| Houston Oilers | | | |
| ☐ 134 Rob Moore | .10 | .05 | .01 |
| New York Jets | | | |
| ☐ 135 Duane Bickett | .05 | .02 | .01 |
| Indianapolis Colts | | | |
| ☐ 136 Jarrod Bunch | .08 | .04 | .01 |
| New York Giants | | | |
| ☐ 137 Ethan Horton | .05 | .02 | .01 |

| | | | |
|---|---|---|---|
| Los Angeles Raiders | | | |
| ☐ 138 Leonard Russell | .08 | .04 | .01 |
| New England Patriots | | | |
| ☐ 139 Darryl Henley | .05 | .02 | .01 |
| Los Angeles Rams | | | |
| ☐ 140 Tony Bennett | .05 | .02 | .01 |
| Green Bay Packers | | | |
| ☐ 141 Harry Newsome | .05 | .02 | .01 |
| Minnesota Vikings | | | |
| ☐ 142 Kelvin Martin | .08 | .04 | .01 |
| Dallas Cowboys | | | |
| ☐ 143 Audray McMillian | .05 | .02 | .01 |
| Minnesota Vikings | | | |
| ☐ 144 Chip Lohmiller | .05 | .02 | .01 |
| Washington Redskins | | | |
| ☐ 145 Henry Jones | .05 | .02 | .01 |
| Buffalo Bills | | | |
| ☐ 146 Rod Bernstine | .08 | .04 | .01 |
| San Diego Chargers | | | |
| ☐ 147 Darryl Talley | .05 | .02 | .01 |
| Buffalo Bills | | | |
| ☐ 148 Clarence Verdin | .05 | .02 | .01 |
| Indianapolis Colts | | | |
| ☐ 149 Derrick Thomas | .15 | .07 | .02 |
| Kansas City Chiefs | | | |
| ☐ 150 Raleigh McKenzie | .05 | .02 | .01 |
| Washington Redskins | | | |
| ☐ 151 Phil Hansen | .05 | .02 | .01 |
| Buffalo Bills | | | |
| ☐ 152 Lin Elliott | .05 | .02 | .01 |
| Dallas Cowboys | | | |
| ☐ 153 Chip Banks | .05 | .02 | .01 |
| Indianapolis Colts | | | |
| ☐ 154 Shannon Sharpe | .20 | .09 | .03 |
| Denver Broncos | | | |
| ☐ 155 David Williams | .05 | .02 | .01 |
| Houston Oilers | | | |
| ☐ 156 Gaston Green | .08 | .04 | .01 |
| Denver Broncos | | | |
| ☐ 157 Trace Armstrong | .05 | .02 | .01 |
| Chicago Bears | | | |
| ☐ 158 Todd Scott | .05 | .02 | .01 |
| Minnesota Vikings | | | |
| ☐ 159 Stan Humphries | .10 | .05 | .01 |
| San Diego Chargers | | | |
| ☐ 160 Christian Okoye | .08 | .04 | .01 |
| Kansas City Chiefs | | | |
| ☐ 161 Dennis Smith | .05 | .02 | .01 |
| Denver Broncos | | | |
| ☐ 162 Derek Kennard | .05 | .02 | .01 |
| New Orleans Saints | | | |
| ☐ 163 Melvin Jenkins | .05 | .02 | .01 |
| Detroit Lions | | | |
| ☐ 164 Tommy Barnhardt | .05 | .02 | .01 |
| New Orleans Saints | | | |
| ☐ 165 Eugene Robinson | .05 | .02 | .01 |
| Seattle Seahawks | | | |
| ☐ 166 Tom Rathman | .08 | .04 | .01 |
| San Francisco 49ers | | | |
| ☐ 167 Chris Chandler | .08 | .04 | .01 |
| Phoenix Cardinals | | | |
| ☐ 168 Steve Broussard | .05 | .02 | .01 |
| Atlanta Falcons | | | |
| ☐ 169 Wymon Henderson | .05 | .02 | .01 |
| Denver Broncos | | | |
| ☐ 170 Bryce Paup | .05 | .02 | .01 |
| Green Bay Packers | | | |
| ☐ 171 Kent Hull | .05 | .02 | .01 |
| Buffalo Bills | | | |
| ☐ 172 Willie Davis | .10 | .05 | .01 |
| Kansas City Chiefs | | | |
| ☐ 173 Richard Dent | .08 | .04 | .01 |
| Chicago Bears | | | |
| ☐ 174 Rodney Peete | .08 | .04 | .01 |
| Detroit Lions | | | |
| ☐ 175 Clay Matthews | .08 | .04 | .01 |
| Cleveland Browns | | | |
| ☐ 176 Erik Williams | .05 | .02 | .01 |
| Dallas Cowboys | | | |
| ☐ 177 Mike Cofer | .05 | .02 | .01 |
| San Francisco 49ers | | | |
| ☐ 178 Mark Kelso | .05 | .02 | .01 |
| Buffalo Bills | | | |
| ☐ 179 Kurt Gouveia | .05 | .02 | .01 |
| Washington Redskins | | | |
| ☐ 180 Keith McCants | .05 | .02 | .01 |
| Buffalo Bills | | | |
| ☐ 181 Jim Arnold | .05 | .02 | .01 |
| Detroit Lions | | | |
| ☐ 182 Sean Jones | .05 | .02 | .01 |
| Houston Oilers | | | |
| ☐ 183 Chuck Cecil | .05 | .02 | .01 |
| Green Bay Packers | | | |
| ☐ 184 Mark Rypien | .08 | .04 | .01 |
| Washington Redskins | | | |
| ☐ 185 William Perry | .08 | .04 | .01 |
| Chicago Bears | | | |
| ☐ 186 Mark Jackson | .08 | .04 | .01 |

| | | | |
|---|---|---|---|
| Denver Broncos | | | |
| ☐ 187 Jim Dombrowski | .05 | .02 | .01 |
| New Orleans Saints | | | |
| ☐ 188 Heath Sherman | .05 | .02 | .01 |
| Philadelphia Eagles | | | |
| ☐ 189 Bubba McDowell | .05 | .02 | .01 |
| Houston Oilers | | | |
| ☐ 190 Fuad Reveiz | .05 | .02 | .01 |
| Minnesota Vikings | | | |
| ☐ 191 Darren Perry | .05 | .02 | .01 |
| Pittsburgh Steelers | | | |
| ☐ 192 Karl Mecklenburg | .08 | .04 | .01 |
| Denver Broncos | | | |
| ☐ 193 Frank Reich | .08 | .04 | .01 |
| Buffalo Bills | | | |
| ☐ 194 Tony Casillas | .05 | .02 | .01 |
| Dallas Cowboys | | | |
| ☐ 195 Jerry Ball | .05 | .02 | .01 |
| Detroit Lions | | | |
| ☐ 196 Jessie Hester | .05 | .02 | .01 |
| Indianapolis Colts | | | |
| ☐ 197 David Lang | .05 | .02 | .01 |
| Los Angeles Rams | | | |
| ☐ 198 Sean Landeta | .05 | .02 | .01 |
| New York Giants | | | |
| ☐ 199 Jerry Gray | .05 | .02 | .01 |
| Houston Oilers | | | |
| ☐ 200 Mark Higgs | .10 | .05 | .01 |
| Miami Dolphins | | | |
| ☐ 201 Bruce Armstrong | .05 | .02 | .01 |
| New England Patriots | | | |
| ☐ 202 Vaughan Johnson | .05 | .02 | .01 |
| New Orleans Saints | | | |
| ☐ 203 Calvin Williams | .10 | .05 | .01 |
| Philadelphia Eagles | | | |
| ☐ 204 Leonard Marshall | .08 | .04 | .01 |
| New York Giants | | | |
| ☐ 205 Mike Munchak | .08 | .04 | .01 |
| Houston Oilers | | | |
| ☐ 206 Kevin Ross | .05 | .02 | .01 |
| Kansas City Chiefs | | | |
| ☐ 207 Daryl Johnston | .10 | .05 | .01 |
| Dallas Cowboys | | | |
| ☐ 208 Jay Schroeder | .05 | .02 | .01 |
| Los Angeles Raiders | | | |
| ☐ 209 Mo Lewis | .05 | .02 | .01 |
| New York Jets | | | |
| ☐ 210 Carlton Haselrig | .05 | .02 | .01 |
| Pittsburgh Steelers | | | |
| ☐ 211 Cris Carter | .10 | .05 | .01 |
| Minnesota Vikings | | | |
| ☐ 212 Marv Cook | .05 | .02 | .01 |
| New England Patriots | | | |
| ☐ 213 Mark Duper | .08 | .04 | .01 |
| Miami Dolphins | | | |
| ☐ 214 Jackie Slater | .05 | .02 | .01 |
| Los Angeles Rams | | | |
| ☐ 215 Mike Prior | .05 | .02 | .01 |
| Indianapolis Colts | | | |
| ☐ 216 Warren Moon | .15 | .07 | .02 |
| Houston Oilers | | | |
| ☐ 217 Mike Saxon | .05 | .02 | .01 |
| Dallas Cowboys | | | |
| ☐ 218 Derrick Fenner | .05 | .02 | .01 |
| Cincinnati Bengals | | | |
| ☐ 219 Brian Washington | .05 | .02 | .01 |
| New York Jets | | | |
| ☐ 220 Jessie Tuggle | .05 | .02 | .01 |
| Atlanta Falcons | | | |
| ☐ 221 Jeff Hostetler | .10 | .05 | .01 |
| New York Giants | | | |
| ☐ 222 Deion Sanders | .15 | .07 | .02 |
| Atlanta Falcons | | | |
| ☐ 223 Neal Anderson | .08 | .04 | .01 |
| Chicago Bears | | | |
| ☐ 224 Kevin Mack | .08 | .04 | .01 |
| Cleveland Browns | | | |
| ☐ 225 Tommy Maddox | .10 | .05 | .01 |
| Denver Broncos | | | |
| ☐ 226 Neil Smith | .10 | .05 | .01 |
| Kansas City Chiefs | | | |
| ☐ 227 Ronnie Lott | .10 | .05 | .01 |
| Los Angeles Raiders | | | |
| ☐ 228 Flipper Anderson | .08 | .04 | .01 |
| Los Angeles Rams | | | |
| ☐ 229 Keith Jackson | .10 | .05 | .01 |
| Miami Dolphins | | | |
| ☐ 230 Pat Swilling | .08 | .04 | .01 |
| New Orleans Saints | | | |
| ☐ 231 Carl Banks | .08 | .04 | .01 |
| New York Giants | | | |
| ☐ 232 Eric Allen | .08 | .04 | .01 |
| Philadelphia Eagles | | | |
| ☐ 233 Randal Hill | .10 | .05 | .01 |
| Phoenix Cardinals | | | |
| ☐ 234 Burt Grossman | .05 | .02 | .01 |
| San Diego Chargers | | | |
| ☐ 235 Jerry Rice | .50 | .23 | .06 |

San Francisco 49ers
☐ 236 Santana Dotson...................... .10 .05 .01
Tampa Bay Buccaneers
☐ 237 Andre Reed.......................... .10 .05 .01
Buffalo Bills
☐ 238 Troy Aikman.......................... 1.25 .55 .16
Dallas Cowboys
☐ 239 Ray Childress...................... .05 .02 .01
Houston Oilers
☐ 240 Phil Simms.......................... .10 .05 .01
New York Giants
☐ 241 Steve McMichael................. .05 .02 .01
Cincinnati Bengals
☐ 242 Browning Nagle.................. .08 .04 .01
New York Jets
☐ 243 Anthony Miller.................. .15 .07 .02
San Diego Chargers
☐ 244 Earnest Byner.................... .08 .04 .01
Washington Redskins
☐ 245 Jay Hilgenberg.................. .05 .02 .01
Cleveland Browns
☐ 246 Jeff George...................... .15 .07 .02
Indianapolis Colts
☐ 247 Marco Coleman.................. .08 .04 .01
Miami Dolphins
☐ 248 Mark Carrier...................... .08 .04 .01
Chicago Bears
☐ 249 Howie Long........................ .08 .04 .01
Los Angeles Raiders
☐ 250 Ed McCaffrey.................... .05 .02 .01
New York Giants
☐ 251 Jim Kelly.......................... .25 .11 .03
Buffalo Bills
☐ 252 Henry Ellard...................... .08 .04 .01
Los Angeles Rams
☐ 253 Joe Montana...................... 1.25 .55 .16
Kansas City Chiefs
☐ 254 Dale Carter........................ .10 .05 .01
Kansas City Chiefs
☐ 255 Boomer Esiason.................. .12 .05 .02
Cincinnati Bengals
☐ 256 Gary Clark........................ .08 .04 .01
Washington Redskins
☐ 257 Carl Pickens...................... .10 .05 .01
Cincinnati Bengals
☐ 258 Dave Krieg........................ .08 .04 .01
Kansas City Chiefs
☐ 259 Russell Maryland................ .10 .05 .01
Dallas Cowboys
☐ 260 Randall Cunningham.......... .10 .05 .01
Philadelphia Eagles
☐ 261 Leslie O'Neal.................... .08 .04 .01
San Diego Chargers
☐ 262 Vinny Testaverde................ .10 .05 .01
Tampa Bay Buccaneers
☐ 263 Ricky Ervins...................... .08 .04 .01
Washington Redskins
☐ 264 Chris Mims........................ .08 .04 .01
San Diego Chargers
☐ 265 Dan Marino........................ .75 .35 .09
Miami Dolphins
☐ 266 Eric Martin........................ .08 .04 .01
New Orleans Saints
☐ 267 Bruce Smith...................... .10 .05 .01
Buffalo Bills
☐ 268 Jim Harbaugh.................... .08 .04 .01
Chicago Bears
☐ 269 Steve Emtman.................... .08 .04 .01
Indianapolis Colts
☐ 270 Ricky Proehl...................... .08 .04 .01
Phoenix Cardinals
☐ 271 Vaughn Dunbar.................. .08 .04 .01
New Orleans Saints
☐ 272 Junior Seau........................ .10 .05 .01
San Diego Chargers
☐ 273 Sean Gilbert...................... .08 .04 .01
Los Angeles Rams
☐ 274 Jim Lachey........................ .05 .02 .01
Washington Redskins
☐ 275 Dalton Hilliard.................. .05 .02 .01
New Orleans Saints
☐ 276 David Klingler.................... .15 .07 .02
Cincinnati Bengals
☐ 277 Robert Jones...................... .05 .02 .01
Dallas Cowboys
☐ 278 David Treadwell.................. .05 .02 .01
Denver Broncos
☐ 279 Tracy Scroggins................ .08 .04 .01
Detroit Lions
☐ 280 Terrell Buckley.................. .10 .05 .01
Green Bay Packers
☐ 281 Quentin Coryatt................ .10 .05 .01
Indianapolis Colts
☐ 282 Jason Hanson.................... .05 .02 .01
Detroit Lions
☐ 283 Shane Conlan.................... .05 .02 .01
Buffalo Bills
☐ 284 Guy McIntyre.................... .05 .02 .01

San Francisco 49ers
☐ 285 Gary Zimmerman................ .05 .02 .01
Minnesota Vikings
☐ 286 Marty Carter...................... .05 .02 .01
Tampa Bay Buccaneers
☐ 287 Jim Sweeney...................... .05 .02 .01
New York Jets
☐ 288 Arthur Marshall.................. .25 .11 .03
Denver Broncos
☐ 289 Eugene Chung.................... .05 .02 .01
New England Patriots
☐ 290 Mike Pritchard.................. .10 .05 .01
Atlanta Falcons
☐ 291 Jim Ritcher........................ .05 .02 .01
Buffalo Bills
☐ 292 Todd Marinovich................ .05 .02 .01
Los Angeles Raiders
☐ 293 Courtney Hall.................... .05 .02 .01
San Diego Chargers
☐ 294 Mark Collins...................... .05 .02 .01
New York Giants
☐ 295 Troy Auzenne...................... .05 .02 .01
Cincinnati Bengals
☐ 296 Aeneas Williams................ .05 .02 .01
Phoenix Cardinals
☐ 297 Andy Heck.......................... .05 .02 .01
Seattle Seahawks
☐ 298 Shaun Gayle...................... .05 .02 .01
Chicago Bears
☐ 299 Kevin Fagan...................... .05 .02 .01
San Francisco 49ers
☐ 300 Carnell Lake...................... .05 .02 .01
Pittsburgh Steelers
☐ 301 Bernie Kosar...................... .10 .05 .01
Cleveland Browns
☐ 302 Maurice Hurst.................... .05 .02 .01
New England Patriots
☐ 303 Mike Merriweather.............. .05 .02 .01
Minnesota Vikings
☐ 304 Reggie Roby...................... .05 .02 .01
Miami Dolphins
☐ 305 Darryl Williams.................. .08 .04 .01
Cincinnati Bengals
☐ 306 Jerome Bettis.................... 3.00 1.35 .40
Los Angeles Rams
☐ 307 Curtis Conway.................... .50 .23 .06
Chicago Bears
☐ 308 Drew Bledsoe.................... 2.50 1.15 .30
Seattle Seahawks
☐ 309 John Copeland.................. .25 .11 .03
Cincinnati Bengals
☐ 310 Eric Curry.......................... .25 .11 .03
Tampa Bay Buccaneers
☐ 311 Lincoln Kennedy................ .15 .07 .02
Seattle Seahawks
☐ 312 Dan Williams...................... .10 .05 .01
Denver Broncos
☐ 313 Patrick Bates.................... .10 .05 .01
Los Angeles Raiders
☐ 314 Tom Carter........................ .25 .11 .03
Washington Redskins
☐ 315 Garrison Hearst.................. .60 .25 .08
Phoenix Cardinals
☐ 316 Joel Hilgenberg................ .05 .02 .01
New Orleans Saints
☐ 317 Harris Barton.................... .05 .02 .01
San Francisco 49ers
☐ 318 Jeff Lageman...................... .05 .02 .01
New York Jets
☐ 319 Charles Mincy.................... .20 .09 .03
Kansas City Chiefs
☐ 320 Ricardo McDonald.............. .05 .02 .01
Cincinnati Bengals
☐ 321 Lorenzo White.................... .08 .04 .01
Houston Oilers
☐ 322 Troy Vincent...................... .08 .04 .01
Miami Dolphins
☐ 323 Bennie Blades.................... .05 .02 .01
Detroit Lions
☐ 324 Dana Hall.......................... .08 .04 .01
San Francisco 49ers
☐ 325 Ken Norton Jr.................... .08 .04 .01
Dallas Cowboys
☐ 326 Will Wolford...................... .05 .02 .01
Buffalo Bills
☐ 327 Neil O'Donnell.................. .25 .11 .03
Pittsburgh Steelers
☐ 328 Tracy Simien...................... .05 .02 .01
Kansas City Chiefs
☐ 329 Darrell Green.................... .08 .04 .01
Washington Redskins
☐ 330 Kyle Clifton...................... .05 .02 .01
New York Jets
☐ 331 Elbert Shelley.................... .10 .05 .01
Atlanta Falcons
☐ 332 Jeff Wright........................ .05 .02 .01
Buffalo Bills
☐ 333 Mike Johnson.................... .05 .02 .01

Cleveland Browns

| | | | |
|---|---|---|---|
| ☐ 334 John Gesek | .05 | .02 | .01 |

Dallas Cowboys

| | | | |
|---|---|---|---|
| ☐ 335 Michael Brooks | .08 | .04 | .01 |

Denver Broncos

| | | | |
|---|---|---|---|
| ☐ 336 George Jamison | .05 | .02 | .01 |

Detroit Lions

| | | | |
|---|---|---|---|
| ☐ 337 Johnny Holland | .05 | .02 | .01 |

Green Bay Packers

| | | | |
|---|---|---|---|
| ☐ 338 Lamar Lathon | .05 | .02 | .01 |

Houston Oilers

| | | | |
|---|---|---|---|
| ☐ 339 Bern Brostek | .05 | .02 | .01 |

Los Angeles Rams

| | | | |
|---|---|---|---|
| ☐ 340 Steve Jordan | .08 | .04 | .01 |

Minnesota Vikings

| | | | |
|---|---|---|---|
| ☐ 341 Gene Atkins | .05 | .02 | .01 |

New Orleans Saints

| | | | |
|---|---|---|---|
| ☐ 342 Aaron Wallace | .05 | .02 | .01 |

Los Angeles Raiders

| | | | |
|---|---|---|---|
| ☐ 343 Adrian Cooper | .05 | .02 | .01 |

Pittsburgh Steelers

| | | | |
|---|---|---|---|
| ☐ 344 Amp Lee | .08 | .04 | .01 |

San Francisco 49ers

| | | | |
|---|---|---|---|
| ☐ 345 Vincent Brown | .05 | .02 | .01 |

New England Patriots

| | | | |
|---|---|---|---|
| ☐ 346 James Hasty | .05 | .02 | .01 |

New York Jets

| | | | |
|---|---|---|---|
| ☐ 347 Ron Hall | .05 | .02 | .01 |

Tampa Bay Buccaneers

| | | | |
|---|---|---|---|
| ☐ 348 Matt Elliott | .05 | .02 | .01 |

Washington Redskins

| | | | |
|---|---|---|---|
| ☐ 349 Tim Krumrie | .05 | .02 | .01 |

Cincinnati Bengals

| | | | |
|---|---|---|---|
| ☐ 350 Mark Stepnoski | .05 | .02 | .01 |

Dallas Cowboys

| | | | |
|---|---|---|---|
| ☐ 351 Matt Stover | .05 | .02 | .01 |

Cleveland Browns

| | | | |
|---|---|---|---|
| ☐ 352 James Washington | .05 | .02 | .01 |

Dallas Cowboys

| | | | |
|---|---|---|---|
| ☐ 353 Marc Spindler | .05 | .02 | .01 |

Dallas Cowboys

| | | | |
|---|---|---|---|
| ☐ 354 Frank Warren | .05 | .02 | .01 |

New Orleans Saints

| | | | |
|---|---|---|---|
| ☐ 355 Vai Sikahema | .05 | .02 | .01 |

Philadelphia Eagles

| | | | |
|---|---|---|---|
| ☐ 356 Dan Saleaumua | .05 | .02 | .01 |

Kansas City Chiefs

| | | | |
|---|---|---|---|
| ☐ 357 Mark Clayton | .08 | .04 | .01 |

Miami Dolphins

| | | | |
|---|---|---|---|
| ☐ 358 Brent Jones | .10 | .05 | .01 |

San Francisco 49ers

| | | | |
|---|---|---|---|
| ☐ 359 Andy Harmon | .05 | .02 | .01 |

Philadelphia Eagles

| | | | |
|---|---|---|---|
| ☐ 360 Anthony Parker | .05 | .02 | .01 |

Minnesota Vikings

| | | | |
|---|---|---|---|
| ☐ 361 Chris Hinton | .05 | .02 | .01 |

Indianapolis Colts

| | | | |
|---|---|---|---|
| ☐ 362 Greg Montgomery | .05 | .02 | .01 |

Houston Oilers

| | | | |
|---|---|---|---|
| ☐ 363 Greg McMurtry | .05 | .02 | .01 |

New England Patriots

| | | | |
|---|---|---|---|
| ☐ 364 Craig Heyward | .05 | .02 | .01 |

New Orleans Saints

| | | | |
|---|---|---|---|
| ☐ 365 David Johnson | .05 | .02 | .01 |

Pittsburgh Steelers

| | | | |
|---|---|---|---|
| ☐ 366 Bill Romanowski | .05 | .02 | .01 |

San Francisco 49ers

| | | | |
|---|---|---|---|
| ☐ 367 Steve Christie | .05 | .02 | .01 |

Buffalo Bills

| | | | |
|---|---|---|---|
| ☐ 368 Art Monk | .10 | .05 | .01 |

Washington Redskins

| | | | |
|---|---|---|---|
| ☐ 369 Howard Ballard | .05 | .02 | .01 |

Buffalo Bills

| | | | |
|---|---|---|---|
| ☐ 370 Andre Collins | .05 | .02 | .01 |

Washington Redskins

| | | | |
|---|---|---|---|
| ☐ 371 Alvin Harper | .25 | .11 | .03 |

Dallas Cowboys

| | | | |
|---|---|---|---|
| ☐ 372 Blaise Winter | .10 | .05 | .01 |

San Diego Chargers

| | | | |
|---|---|---|---|
| ☐ 373 Al Del Greco | .05 | .02 | .01 |

Houston Oilers

| | | | |
|---|---|---|---|
| ☐ 374 Eric Green | .10 | .05 | .01 |

Pittsburgh Steelers

| | | | |
|---|---|---|---|
| ☐ 375 Chris Mohr | .05 | .02 | .01 |

Buffalo Bills

| | | | |
|---|---|---|---|
| ☐ 376 Tom Newberry | .05 | .02 | .01 |

Los Angeles Rams

| | | | |
|---|---|---|---|
| ☐ 377 Cris Dishman | .05 | .02 | .01 |

Houston Oilers

| | | | |
|---|---|---|---|
| ☐ 378 James Geathers | .05 | .02 | .01 |

Washington Redskins

| | | | |
|---|---|---|---|
| ☐ 379 Don Mosebar | .05 | .02 | .01 |

Los Angeles Raiders

| | | | |
|---|---|---|---|
| ☐ 380 Andre Ware | .08 | .04 | .01 |

Detroit Lions

| | | | |
|---|---|---|---|
| ☐ 381 Marvin Washington | .05 | .02 | .01 |

Green Bay Packers

| | | | |
|---|---|---|---|
| ☐ 382 Bobby Humphrey | .08 | .04 | .01 |

Miami Dolphins

| | | | |
|---|---|---|---|
| ☐ 383 Marc Logan | .05 | .02 | .01 |

San Francisco 49ers

| | | | |
|---|---|---|---|
| ☐ 384 Lomas Brown | .05 | .02 | .01 |

Detroit Lions

| | | | |
|---|---|---|---|
| ☐ 385 Steve Tasker | .05 | .02 | .01 |

Buffalo Bills

| | | | |
|---|---|---|---|
| ☐ 386 Chris Miller | .10 | .05 | .01 |

Atlanta Falcons

| | | | |
|---|---|---|---|
| ☐ 387 Tony Paige | .05 | .02 | .01 |

Miami Dolphins

| | | | |
|---|---|---|---|
| ☐ 388 Charles Haley | .08 | .04 | .01 |

Dallas Cowboys

| | | | |
|---|---|---|---|
| ☐ 389 Rich Moran | .05 | .02 | .01 |

Green Bay Packers

| | | | |
|---|---|---|---|
| ☐ 390 Mike Sherrard | .05 | .02 | .01 |

San Francisco 49ers

| | | | |
|---|---|---|---|
| ☐ 391 Nick Lowery | .05 | .02 | .01 |

Kansas City Chiefs

| | | | |
|---|---|---|---|
| ☐ 392 Henry Thomas | .05 | .02 | .01 |

Minnesota Vikings

| | | | |
|---|---|---|---|
| ☐ 393 Keith Sims | .05 | .02 | .01 |

Miami Dolphins

| | | | |
|---|---|---|---|
| ☐ 394 Thomas Everett | .05 | .02 | .01 |

Dallas Cowboys

| | | | |
|---|---|---|---|
| ☐ 395 Steve Wallace | .05 | .02 | .01 |

San Francisco 49ers

| | | | |
|---|---|---|---|
| ☐ 396 John Carney | .05 | .02 | .01 |

San Diego Chargers

| | | | |
|---|---|---|---|
| ☐ 397 Tim Johnson | .05 | .02 | .01 |

Washington Redskins

| | | | |
|---|---|---|---|
| ☐ 398 Jeff Gossett | .05 | .02 | .01 |

Los Angeles Raiders

| | | | |
|---|---|---|---|
| ☐ 399 Anthony Smith | .05 | .02 | .01 |

Los Angeles Raiders

| | | | |
|---|---|---|---|
| ☐ 400 Kelvin Pritchett | .05 | .02 | .01 |

Detroit Lions

| | | | |
|---|---|---|---|
| ☐ 401 Dermontti Dawson | .05 | .02 | .01 |

Pittsburgh Steelers

| | | | |
|---|---|---|---|
| ☐ 402 Alfred Williams | .05 | .02 | .01 |

Cincinnati Bengals

| | | | |
|---|---|---|---|
| ☐ 403 Michael Haynes | .20 | .09 | .03 |

Atlanta Falcons

| | | | |
|---|---|---|---|
| ☐ 404 Bart Oates | .05 | .02 | .01 |

New York Giants

| | | | |
|---|---|---|---|
| ☐ 405 Ken Lanier | .05 | .02 | .01 |

Denver Broncos

| | | | |
|---|---|---|---|
| ☐ 406 Vencie Glenn | .05 | .02 | .01 |

San Diego Chargers

| | | | |
|---|---|---|---|
| ☐ 407 John Taylor | .10 | .05 | .01 |

San Francisco 49ers

| | | | |
|---|---|---|---|
| ☐ 408 Nate Newton | .05 | .02 | .01 |

Dallas Cowboys

| | | | |
|---|---|---|---|
| ☐ 409 Mark Carrier | .08 | .04 | .01 |

Tampa Bay Buccaneers

| | | | |
|---|---|---|---|
| ☐ 410 Ken Harvey | .05 | .02 | .01 |

Phoenix Cardinals

| | | | |
|---|---|---|---|
| ☐ 411 Troy Aikman SB | .50 | .23 | .06 |

Dallas Cowboys

| | | | |
|---|---|---|---|
| ☐ 412 Charles Haley SB | .05 | .02 | .01 |

Dallas Cowboys

| | | | |
|---|---|---|---|
| ☐ 413 Warren Moon DT | .12 | .05 | .02 |

Haywood Jeffires
Houston Oilers

| | | | |
|---|---|---|---|
| ☐ 414 Henry Jones DT | .05 | .02 | .01 |

Mark Kelso
Buffalo Bills

| | | | |
|---|---|---|---|
| ☐ 415 Rickey Jackson DT | .05 | .02 | .01 |

Sam Mills
New Orleans Saints

| | | | |
|---|---|---|---|
| ☐ 416 Clyde Simmons DT | .05 | .02 | .01 |

Reggie White
Philadelphia Eagles

| | | | |
|---|---|---|---|
| ☐ 417 Dale Carter ROY | .08 | .04 | .01 |

Kansas City Chiefs

| | | | |
|---|---|---|---|
| ☐ 418 Carl Pickens ROY | .08 | .04 | .01 |

Cincinnati Bengals

| | | | |
|---|---|---|---|
| ☐ 419 Vaughn Dunbar ROY | .05 | .02 | .01 |

New Orleans Saints

| | | | |
|---|---|---|---|
| ☐ 420 Santana Dotson ROY | .08 | .04 | .01 |

Tampa Bay Buccaneers

| | | | |
|---|---|---|---|
| ☐ 421 Steve Emtman 90 | .05 | .02 | .01 |

Indianapolis Colts

| | | | |
|---|---|---|---|
| ☐ 422 Louis Oliver 90 | .05 | .02 | .01 |

Miami Dolphins

| | | | |
|---|---|---|---|
| ☐ 423 Carl Pickens 90 | .10 | .05 | .01 |

Cincinnati Bengals

| | | | |
|---|---|---|---|
| ☐ 424 Eddie Anderson 90 | .05 | .02 | .01 |

Los Angeles Raiders

| | | | |
|---|---|---|---|
| ☐ 425 Deion Sanders 90 | .08 | .04 | .01 |

Atlanta Falcons

| | | | |
|---|---|---|---|
| ☐ 426 Jon Vaughn 90 | .05 | .02 | .01 |

New England Patriots

| | | | |
|---|---|---|---|
| ☐ 427 Darren Lewis 90 | .05 | .02 | .01 |

Chicago Bears

| | | | |
|---|---|---|---|
| ☐ 428 Kevin Ross 90 | .05 | .02 | .01 |

Kansas City Chiefs

| | | | |
|---|---|---|---|
| ☐ 429 David Brandon 90 | .05 | .02 | .01 |

Cleveland Browns
| | | | | |
|---|---|---|---|---|
| ☐ 430 Dave Meggett 90 | .08 | .04 | .01 |
| New York Giants | | | |
| ☐ 431 Jerry Rice HL | .25 | .11 | .03 |
| San Francisco 49ers | | | |
| ☐ 432 Sterling Sharpe HL | .20 | .09 | .03 |
| Green Bay Packers | | | |
| ☐ 433 Art Monk HL | .08 | .04 | .01 |
| Washington Redskins | | | |
| ☐ 434 James Lofton HL | .08 | .04 | .01 |
| Buffalo Bills | | | |
| ☐ 435 Lawrence Taylor | .10 | .05 | .01 |
| New York Giants | | | |
| ☐ 436 Bill Walsh HOF | .12 | .05 | .02 |
| San Francisco 49ers | | | |
| ☐ 437 Chuck Noll HOF | .05 | .02 | .01 |
| Pittsburgh Steelers | | | |
| ☐ 438 Dan Fouts HOF | .05 | .02 | .01 |
| San Diego Chargers | | | |
| ☐ 439 Larry Little HOF | .05 | .02 | .01 |
| Miami Dolphins | | | |
| ☐ 440 Steve Young MOY | .12 | .05 | .02 |
| San Francisco 49ers | | | |
| ☐ NNO Dick Butkus AU | 35.00 | 16.00 | 4.40 |
| (Certified Autograph) | | | |

| | | | | |
|---|---|---|---|---|
| ☐ 16 Clyde Simmons | .75 | .35 | .09 |
| Philadelphia Eagles | | | |
| ☐ 17 Reggie White | 1.00 | .45 | .13 |
| Philadelphia Eagles | | | |
| ☐ 18 Cortez Kennedy | .75 | .35 | .09 |
| Seattle Seahawks | | | |
| ☐ 19 Rod Woodson | .75 | .35 | .09 |
| Pittsburgh Steelers | | | |
| ☐ 20 Terry McDaniel | .60 | .25 | .08 |
| Los Angeles Raiders | | | |
| ☐ 21 Chuck Cecil | .60 | .25 | .08 |
| Green Bay Packers | | | |
| ☐ 22 Steve Atwater | .60 | .25 | .08 |
| Denver Broncos | | | |
| ☐ 23 Bryan Cox | .60 | .25 | .08 |
| Miami Dolphins | | | |
| ☐ 24 Derrick Thomas | .75 | .35 | .09 |
| Kansas City Chiefs | | | |
| ☐ 25 Wilber Marshall | .60 | .25 | .08 |
| Washington Redskins | | | |
| ☐ 26 Sam Mills | .60 | .25 | .08 |
| New Orleans Saints | | | |

## 1993 Score Dream Team

Randomly inserted in 1993 Score 35-card super packs, this 26-card set features the best offensive (1-13) and defensive (14-26) players by position as selected by Score. On a background consisting of a cloudy sky with a dark brown tint, the horizontal fronts have a color player cut-out emerging out of a black stripe on the left portion while the right portion displays a close-up color player cut-out. On the backs, the upper portion displays a larger, fuzzy version of the same player cut-out on the front left portion. The lower portion is a thick black stripe featuring a brief player profile. The team logo in a circle straddles the two portions. The cards are numbered on the back.

| | MINT | EXC | G-VG |
|---|---|---|---|
| COMPLETE SET (26) | 25.00 | 11.50 | 3.10 |
| COMMON PLAYER (1-26) | .60 | .25 | .08 |
| ☐ 1 Steve Young | 2.00 | .90 | .25 |
| San Francisco 49ers | | | |
| ☐ 2 Emmitt Smith | 14.00 | 6.25 | 1.75 |
| Dallas Cowboys | | | |
| ☐ 3 Barry Foster | 2.00 | .90 | .25 |
| Pittsburgh Steelers | | | |
| ☐ 4 Sterling Sharpe | 4.00 | 1.80 | .50 |
| Green Bay Packers | | | |
| ☐ 5 Jerry Rice | 5.00 | 2.30 | .60 |
| San Francisco 49ers | | | |
| ☐ 6 Keith Jackson | .75 | .35 | .09 |
| Philadelphia Eagles | | | |
| ☐ 7 Steve Wallace | .60 | .25 | .08 |
| San Francisco 49ers | | | |
| ☐ 8 Richmond Webb | .60 | .25 | .08 |
| Miami Dolphins | | | |
| ☐ 9 Guy McIntyre | .60 | .25 | .08 |
| San Francisco 49ers | | | |
| ☐ 10 Carlton Haselrig | .60 | .25 | .08 |
| Pittsburgh Steelers | | | |
| ☐ 11 Bruce Matthews | .60 | .25 | .08 |
| Houston Oilers | | | |
| ☐ 12 Morten Andersen | .60 | .25 | .08 |
| New Orleans Saints | | | |
| ☐ 13 Rich Camarillo | .60 | .25 | .08 |
| Phoenix Cardinals | | | |
| ☐ 14 Deion Sanders | 1.00 | .45 | .13 |
| Atlanta Falcons | | | |
| ☐ 15 Steve Tasker | .60 | .25 | .08 |
| Buffalo Bills | | | |

## 1993 Score Franchise

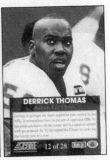

Randomly inserted in 1993 Score foil packs, this 28-card set features the top player on each of the NFL's 28 teams, as selected by Score. Score estimates that the chances of finding one of these cards are not less than one in 24 packs. The cards are standard size, 2 1/2" by 3 1/2".

| | MINT | EXC | G-VG |
|---|---|---|---|
| COMPLETE SET (28) | 150.00 | 70.00 | 19.00 |
| COMMON PLAYER (1-28) | 3.00 | 1.35 | .40 |
| ☐ 1 Andre Rison | 7.00 | 3.10 | .85 |
| Atlanta Falcons | | | |
| ☐ 2 Thurman Thomas | 12.00 | 5.50 | 1.50 |
| Buffalo Bills | | | |
| ☐ 3 Richard Dent | 3.00 | 1.35 | .40 |
| Chicago Bears | | | |
| ☐ 4 Harold Green | 3.50 | 1.55 | .45 |
| Cincinnati Bengals | | | |
| ☐ 5 Eric Metcalf | 3.50 | 1.55 | .45 |
| Cleveland Browns | | | |
| ☐ 6 Emmitt Smith | 60.00 | 27.00 | 7.50 |
| Dallas Cowboys | | | |
| ☐ 7 John Elway | 18.00 | 8.00 | 2.30 |
| Denver Broncos | | | |
| ☐ 8 Barry Sanders | 20.00 | 9.00 | 2.50 |
| Detroit Lions | | | |
| ☐ 9 Sterling Sharpe | 18.00 | 8.00 | 2.30 |
| Green Bay Packers | | | |
| ☐ 10 Warren Moon | 7.50 | 3.40 | .95 |
| Houston Oilers | | | |
| ☐ 11 Jeff Herrod | 3.00 | 1.35 | .40 |
| Indianapolis Colts | | | |
| ☐ 12 Derrick Thomas | 6.00 | 2.70 | .75 |
| Kansas City Chiefs | | | |
| ☐ 13 Steve Wisniewski | 3.00 | 1.35 | .40 |
| Los Angeles Raiders | | | |
| ☐ 14 Cleveland Gary | 3.00 | 1.35 | .40 |
| Los Angeles Rams | | | |
| ☐ 15 Dan Marino | 40.00 | 18.00 | 5.00 |
| Miami Dolphins | | | |
| ☐ 16 Chris Doleman | 3.00 | 1.35 | .40 |
| Minnesota Vikings | | | |
| ☐ 17 Marv Cook | 3.00 | 1.35 | .40 |
| New England Patriots | | | |
| ☐ 18 Rickey Jackson | 3.00 | 1.35 | .40 |
| New Orleans Saints | | | |
| ☐ 19 Rodney Hampton | 12.00 | 5.50 | 1.50 |
| New York Giants | | | |
| ☐ 20 Jeff Lageman | 3.00 | 1.35 | .40 |

New York Jets
| | | | |
|---|---|---|---|
| ☐ 21 Clyde Simmons | 3.50 | 1.55 | .45 |
| Philadelphia Eagles | | | |
| ☐ 22 Rich Camarillo | 3.00 | 1.35 | .40 |
| Phoenix Cardinals | | | |
| ☐ 23 Rod Woodson | 3.50 | 1.55 | .45 |
| Pittsburgh Steelers | | | |
| ☐ 24 Ronnie Harmon | 3.00 | 1.35 | .40 |
| San Diego Chargers | | | |
| ☐ 25 Steve Young | 12.00 | 5.50 | 1.50 |
| San Francisco 49ers | | | |
| ☐ 26 Cortez Kennedy | 3.50 | 1.55 | .45 |
| Seattle Seahawks | | | |
| ☐ 27 Reggie Cobb | 3.50 | 1.55 | .45 |
| Tampa Bay Buccaneers | | | |
| ☐ 28 Mark Rypien | 3.50 | 1.55 | .45 |
| Washington Redskins | | | |

## 1993 Score Ore-Ida QB Club

This set of 18 standard-size (2 1/2" by 3 1/2") cards could be obtained by the purchase of specially marked Ore-Ida products (Bagel Bites, Twice Baked, or Topped Baked Potatoes), filling out the order form on one of the packages, and mailing it plus six proofs-of-purchase and 1.50. Collectors would then receive two nine-card packs. For three proofs-of-purchase and 1.00, collectors could receive one nine-card set. The packs are sequentially numbered, with the first pack containing cards 1-9 and the second containing cards 10-18. Aside from sporting different color player action photos on their fronts (Hostetler and Esiason are pictured in their new Raiders and Jets uniforms, respectively), and the different numbering on the backs, the cards are identical in design to the regular 1993 Score issue.

| | MINT | EXC | G-VG |
|---|---|---|---|
| COMPLETE SET (18) | 15.00 | 6.00 | 1.50 |
| COMMON PLAYER (1-18) | .35 | .14 | .03 |
| ☐ 1 John Elway | 1.50 | .60 | .15 |
| Denver Broncos | | | |
| ☐ 2 Steve Young | 1.25 | .50 | .12 |
| San Francisco 49ers | | | |
| ☐ 3 Warren Moon | 1.00 | .40 | .10 |
| Houston Oilers | | | |
| ☐ 4 Randall Cunningham | .75 | .30 | .07 |
| Philadelphia Eagles | | | |
| ☐ 5 Jeff Hostetler | .50 | .20 | .05 |
| Los Angeles Raiders | | | |
| ☐ 6 Phil Simms | .75 | .30 | .07 |
| New York Giants | | | |
| ☐ 7 Jim Everett | .35 | .14 | .03 |
| Los Angeles Rams | | | |
| ☐ 8 David Klingler | .75 | .30 | .07 |
| Cincinnati Bengals | | | |
| ☐ 9 Brett Favre | 1.50 | .60 | .15 |
| Green Bay Packers | | | |
| ☐ 10 Troy Aikman | 3.50 | 1.40 | .35 |
| Dallas Cowboys | | | |
| ☐ 11 Dan Marino | 2.50 | 1.00 | .25 |
| Miami Dolphins | | | |
| ☐ 12 Mark Rypien | .35 | .14 | .03 |
| Washington Redskins | | | |
| ☐ 13 Jim Kelly | 1.00 | .40 | .10 |
| Buffalo Bills | | | |
| ☐ 14 Jim Harbaugh | .35 | .14 | .03 |
| Chicago Bears | | | |
| ☐ 15 Bernie Kosar | .50 | .20 | .05 |
| Cleveland Browns | | | |
| ☐ 16 Boomer Esiason | .50 | .20 | .05 |
| New York Jets | | | |
| ☐ 17 Chris Miller | .50 | .20 | .05 |
| Atlanta Falcons | | | |
| ☐ 18 Neil O'Donnell | .75 | .30 | .07 |
| Pittsburgh Steelers | | | |

## 1994 Score Samples

These nine sample cards were issued to herald the August release of the 1994 Score football set. The standard-size (2 1/2" by 3 1/2") cards feature on their fronts color player action shots with irregular purple and teal borders, except for the Glyn Milburn card (112), which is a sample foil card from the parallel Gold Zone set. The player's name appears in white lettering below the photo; his position appears in white lettering within a black box at the upper left. The multicolored back carries the player's name and team logo at the top, followed below by his position, biography, profile, and statistics. The player cards are numbered on the back.

| | MINT | EXC | G-VG |
|---|---|---|---|
| COMPLETE SET (9) | 9.00 | 3.75 | .90 |
| COMMON PLAYER | 1.00 | .40 | .10 |
| ☐ 0 Generic Rookie Card | 1.00 | .40 | .10 |
| ☐ 21 Jerome Bettis | 4.00 | 1.60 | .40 |
| Los Angeles Rams | | | |
| ☐ 25 Steve Jordan | 1.00 | .40 | .10 |
| Minnesota Vikings | | | |
| ☐ 50 Shannon Sharpe | 1.25 | .50 | .12 |
| Denver Broncos | | | |
| ☐ 112 Glyn Milburn FOIL | 2.00 | .80 | .20 |
| Denver Broncos | | | |
| ☐ 161 Ronnie Lott | 1.50 | .60 | .15 |
| New York Jets | | | |
| ☐ 257 Derrick Thomas | 1.50 | .60 | .15 |
| Kansas City Chiefs | | | |
| ☐ NNO Sample Redemption Card | 1.00 | .40 | .10 |
| ☐ NNO Score Ad Card | 1.00 | .40 | .10 |

## 1994 Score

The 1994 Score football set consists of 330 standard-size (2 1/2" by 3 1/2") cards. The fronts feature color action player photos with bright borders. The photos appear to be torn at the top and bottom. The player's name, position and team helmet also appear on the front. On a very colorful background, the backs contain a headshot, along with his name, biography and stats. Topical subsets featured are Rookies (276-305) and Team Checklists (306-319). A 330-card parallel set "Gold Zone" was inserted one card per pack. Ten randomly inserted redemption cards gave collectors an opportunity to receive ten top rookie players in their NFL uniforms.

| | MINT | EXC | G-VG |
|---|---|---|---|
| COMPLETE SET (330) | 22.00 | 10.00 | 2.80 |
| COMMON PLAYER (1-330) | .05 | .02 | .01 |
| ☐ 1 Barry Sanders | .60 | .25 | .08 |
| Detroit Lions | | | |

|  |  |  | | | |
|---|--------|------|---|---|---|
| ☐ 2 | Troy Aikman | Dallas Cowboys | 1.25 | .55 | .16 |
| ☐ 3 | Sterling Sharpe AP | Green Bay Packers | .30 | .14 | .04 |
| ☐ 4 | Deion Sanders AP | Atlanta Falcons | .15 | .07 | .02 |
| ☐ 5 | Bruce Smith AP | Buffalo Bills | .10 | .05 | .01 |
| ☐ 6 | Eric Metcalf AP | Cleveland Browns | .08 | .04 | .01 |
| ☐ 7 | John Elway | Denver Broncos | .40 | .18 | .05 |
| ☐ 8 | Bruce Matthews AP | Houston Oilers | .05 | .02 | .01 |
| ☐ 9 | Rickey Jackson | New Orleans Saints | .05 | .02 | .01 |
| ☐ 10 | Cortez Kennedy AP | Seattle Seahawks | .08 | .04 | .01 |
| ☐ 11 | Jerry Rice AP | San Francisco 49ers | .50 | .23 | .06 |
| ☐ 12 | Stanley Richard | San Diego Chargers | .05 | .02 | .01 |
| ☐ 13 | Rod Woodson AP | Pittsburgh Steelers | .10 | .05 | .01 |
| ☐ 14 | Eric Swann | Arizona Cardinals | .05 | .02 | .01 |
| ☐ 15 | Eric Allen | Philadelphia Eagles | .08 | .04 | .01 |
| ☐ 16 | Richard Dent | Chicago Bears | .10 | .05 | .01 |
| ☐ 17 | Carl Pickens | Cincinnati Bengals | .05 | .02 | .01 |
| ☐ 18 | Rohn Stark | Indianapolis Colts | .05 | .02 | .01 |
| ☐ 19 | Marcus Allen | Kansas City Chiefs | .10 | .05 | .01 |
| ☐ 20 | Steve Wisniewski AP | Los Angeles Raiders | .05 | .02 | .01 |
| ☐ 21 | Jerome Bettis AP | Los Angeles Rams | 2.00 | .90 | .25 |
| ☐ 22 | Darrell Green | Washington Redskins | .05 | .02 | .01 |
| ☐ 23 | Lawrence Dawsey | Tampa Bay Buccaneers | .05 | .02 | .01 |
| ☐ 24 | Larry Centers | Arizona Cardinals | .05 | .02 | .01 |
| ☐ 25 | Steve Jordan | Minnesota Vikings | .05 | .02 | .01 |
| ☐ 26 | Johnny Johnson | New York Jets | .08 | .04 | .01 |
| ☐ 27 | Phil Simms | New York Giants | .10 | .05 | .01 |
| ☐ 28 | Bruce Armstrong | New England Patriots | .05 | .02 | .01 |
| ☐ 29 | Willie Roaf | New Orleans Saints | .05 | .02 | .01 |
| ☐ 30 | Andre Rison | Atlanta Falcons | .15 | .07 | .02 |
| ☐ 31 | Henry Jones | Buffalo Bills | .05 | .02 | .01 |
| ☐ 32 | Warren Moon | Minnesota Vikings | .10 | .05 | .01 |
| ☐ 33 | Sean Gilbert | Los Angeles Rams | .05 | .02 | .01 |
| ☐ 34 | Ben Coates | New England Patriots | .05 | .02 | .01 |
| ☐ 35 | Seth Joyner AP | Arizona Cardinals | .05 | .02 | .01 |
| ☐ 36 | Ronnie Harmon | San Diego Chargers | .05 | .02 | .01 |
| ☐ 37 | Quentin Coryatt | Indianapolis Colts | .05 | .02 | .01 |
| ☐ 38 | Ricky Sanders | Atlanta Falcons | .05 | .02 | .01 |
| ☐ 39 | Gerald Williams | Pittsburgh Steelers | .05 | .02 | .01 |
| ☐ 40 | Emmitt Smith AP | Dallas Cowboys | 1.75 | .80 | .22 |
| ☐ 41 | Jason Hanson | Detroit Lions | .05 | .02 | .01 |
| ☐ 42 | Kevin Smith | Dallas Cowboys | .05 | .02 | .01 |
| ☐ 43 | Irving Fryar | Miami Dolphins | .08 | .04 | .01 |
| ☐ 44 | Boomer Esiason | New York Jets | .10 | .05 | .01 |
| ☐ 45 | Darryl Talley | Buffalo Bills | .05 | .02 | .01 |
| ☐ 46 | Paul Gruber | Tampa Bay Buccaneers | .05 | .02 | .01 |
| ☐ 47 | Anthony Smith | Los Angeles Raiders | .05 | .02 | .01 |
| ☐ 48 | John Copeland | Cincinnati Bengals | .05 | .02 | .01 |
| ☐ 49 | Michael Jackson | Cleveland Browns | .08 | .04 | .01 |
| ☐ 50 | Shannon Sharpe AP | Denver Broncos | .15 | .07 | .02 |
| ☐ 51 | Reggie White | Green Bay Packers | .15 | .07 | .02 |
| ☐ 52 | Andre Collins | Washington Redskins | .05 | .02 | .01 |
| ☐ 53 | Jack Del Rio | Minnesota Vikings | .05 | .02 | .01 |
| ☐ 54 | John Elliott | New York Giants | .05 | .02 | .01 |
| ☐ 55 | Kevin Greene | Pittsburgh Steelers | .05 | .02 | .01 |
| ☐ 56 | Steve Young AP | San Francisco 49ers | .15 | .07 | .02 |
| ☐ 57 | Erric Pegram | Atlanta Falcons | .25 | .11 | .03 |
| ☐ 58 | Donnell Woolford | Chicago Bears | .05 | .02 | .01 |
| ☐ 59 | Darryl Williams | Cincinnati Bengals | .05 | .02 | .01 |
| ☐ 60 | Michael Irvin | Dallas Cowboys | .30 | .14 | .04 |
| ☐ 61 | Mel Gray | Detroit Lions | .05 | .02 | .01 |
| ☐ 62 | Greg Montgomery AP | Houston Oilers | .05 | .02 | .01 |
| ☐ 63 | Neil Smith AP | Kansas City Chiefs | .05 | .02 | .01 |
| ☐ 64 | Andy Harmon | Philadelphia Eagles | .05 | .02 | .01 |
| ☐ 65 | Dan Marino | Miami Dolphins | .75 | .35 | .09 |
| ☐ 66 | Leonard Russell | New England Patriots | .05 | .02 | .01 |
| ☐ 67 | Joe Montana | Kansas City Chiefs | 1.25 | .55 | .16 |
| ☐ 68 | John Taylor | San Francisco 49ers | .08 | .04 | .01 |
| ☐ 69 | Cris Dishman | Houston Oilers | .05 | .02 | .01 |
| ☐ 70 | Cornelius Bennett | Buffalo Bills | .08 | .04 | .01 |
| ☐ 71 | Harold Green | Cincinnati Bengals | .05 | .02 | .01 |
| ☐ 72 | Anthony Pleasant | Cleveland Browns | .05 | .02 | .01 |
| ☐ 73 | Dennis Smith | Denver Broncos | .05 | .02 | .01 |
| ☐ 74 | Bryce Paup | Green Bay Packers | .08 | .04 | .01 |
| ☐ 75 | Jeff George | Atlanta Falcons | .08 | .04 | .01 |
| ☐ 76 | Henry Ellard | Washington Redskins | .05 | .02 | .01 |
| ☐ 77 | Randall McDaniel AP | Minnesota Vikings | .30 | .14 | .04 |
| ☐ 78 | Derek Brown | New Orleans Saints | .10 | .05 | .01 |
| ☐ 79 | Johnny Mitchell | New York Jets | .05 | .02 | .01 |
| ☐ 80 | Leroy Thompson | Pittsburgh Steelers | .10 | .05 | .01 |
| ☐ 81 | Junior Seau AP | San Diego Chargers | .05 | .02 | .01 |
| ☐ 82 | Kelvin Martin | Seattle Seahawks | .05 | .02 | .01 |
| ☐ 83 | Guy McIntyre | San Francisco 49ers | .05 | .02 | .01 |
| ☐ 84 | Elbert Shelley | Atlanta Falcons | .05 | .02 | .01 |
| ☐ 85 | Louis Oliver | Cincinnati Bengals | .08 | .04 | .01 |
| ☐ 86 | Tommy Vardell | Cleveland Browns | .05 | .02 | .01 |
| ☐ 87 | Jeff Herrod | Indianapolis Colts | .05 | .02 | .01 |
| ☐ 88 | Edgar Bennett | Green Bay Packers | .05 | .02 | .01 |
| ☐ 89 | Reggie Langhorne | Indianapolis Colts | .50 | .23 | .06 |
| ☐ 90 | Terry Kirby | Miami Dolphins | .05 | .02 | .01 |
| ☐ 91 | Marcus Robertson AP | Houston Oilers | .05 | .02 | .01 |
| ☐ 92 | Mark Collins | Kansas City Chiefs | .05 | .02 | .01 |
| ☐ 93 | Calvin Williams | Philadelphia Eagles | .15 | .07 | .02 |
| ☐ 94 | Barry Foster | Pittsburgh Steelers | .08 | .04 | .01 |
| ☐ 95 | Brent Jones | San Francisco 49ers | .08 | .04 | .01 |
| ☐ 96 | Reggie Cobb | Green Bay Packers | .05 | .02 | .01 |
| ☐ 97 | Ray Childress | Houston Oilers | .08 | .04 | .01 |
| ☐ 98 | Chris Miller | Los Angeles Rams | .05 | .02 | .01 |
| ☐ 99 | John Carney | | | | |

| | | | |
|---|---|---|---|
| San Diego Chargers | | | |
| ☐ 100 Ricky Proehl | .05 | .02 | .01 |
| Arizona Cardinals | | | |
| ☐ 101 Renaldo Turnbull AP | .05 | .02 | .01 |
| New Orleans Saints | | | |
| ☐ 102 John Randle AP | .05 | .02 | .01 |
| Minnesota Vikings | | | |
| ☐ 103 Flipper Anderson | .05 | .02 | .01 |
| Los Angeles Rams | | | |
| ☐ 104 Scottie Graham | .40 | .18 | .05 |
| Minnesota Vikings | | | |
| ☐ 105 Webster Slaughter | .05 | .02 | .01 |
| Houston Oilers | | | |
| ☐ 106 Tyrone Hughes AP | .05 | .02 | .01 |
| New Orleans Saints | | | |
| ☐ 107 Ken Norton Jr. | .08 | .04 | .01 |
| San Francisco 49ers | | | |
| ☐ 108 Jim Kelly | .20 | .09 | .03 |
| Buffalo Bills | | | |
| ☐ 109 Michael Haynes | .15 | .07 | .02 |
| New Orleans Saints | | | |
| ☐ 110 Mark Carrier | .05 | .02 | .01 |
| Chicago Bears | | | |
| ☐ 111 Eddie Murray | .05 | .02 | .01 |
| Philadelphia Eagles | | | |
| ☐ 112 Glyn Milburn | .20 | .09 | .03 |
| Denver Broncos | | | |
| ☐ 113 Jackie Harris | .15 | .07 | .02 |
| Green Bay Packers | | | |
| ☐ 114 Dean Biasucci | .05 | .02 | .01 |
| Indianapolis Colts | | | |
| ☐ 115 Tim Brown | .15 | .07 | .02 |
| Los Angeles Raiders | | | |
| ☐ 116 Mark Higgs | .05 | .02 | .01 |
| Miami Dolphins | | | |
| ☐ 117 Steve Emtman | .05 | .02 | .01 |
| Indianapolis Colts | | | |
| ☐ 118 Clay Matthews | .08 | .04 | .01 |
| Cleveland Browns | | | |
| ☐ 119 Clyde Simmons | .08 | .04 | .01 |
| Arizona Cardinals | | | |
| ☐ 120 Howard Ballard | .05 | .02 | .01 |
| Seattle Seahawks | | | |
| ☐ 121 Ricky Watters | .20 | .09 | .03 |
| San Francisco 49ers | | | |
| ☐ 122 William Fuller | .05 | .02 | .01 |
| Philadelphia Eagles | | | |
| ☐ 123 Robert Brooks | .05 | .02 | .01 |
| Green Bay Packers | | | |
| ☐ 124 Brian Blades | .05 | .02 | .01 |
| Seattle Seahawks | | | |
| ☐ 125 Leslie O'Neal | .05 | .02 | .01 |
| San Diego Chargers | | | |
| ☐ 126 Gary Clark | .10 | .05 | .01 |
| Arizona Cardinals | | | |
| ☐ 127 Jim Sweeney | .05 | .02 | .01 |
| New York Jets | | | |
| ☐ 128 Vaughan Johnson | .05 | .02 | .01 |
| New Orleans Saints | | | |
| ☐ 129 Gary Brown | .30 | .14 | .04 |
| Houston Oilers | | | |
| ☐ 130 Todd Lyght | .05 | .02 | .01 |
| Los Angeles Rams | | | |
| ☐ 131 Nick Lowery | .05 | .02 | .01 |
| Kansas City Chiefs | | | |
| ☐ 132 Ernest Givins | .08 | .04 | .01 |
| Houston Oilers | | | |
| ☐ 133 Lomas Brown | .05 | .02 | .01 |
| Detroit Lions | | | |
| ☐ 134 Craig Erickson | .08 | .04 | .01 |
| Tampa Bay Buccaneers | | | |
| ☐ 135 James Francis | .05 | .02 | .01 |
| Cincinnati Bengals | | | |
| ☐ 136 Andre Reed | .10 | .05 | .01 |
| Buffalo Bills | | | |
| ☐ 137 Jim Everett | .10 | .05 | .01 |
| New Orleans Saints | | | |
| ☐ 138 Nate Odomes | .05 | .02 | .01 |
| Seattle Seahawks | | | |
| ☐ 139 Tom Waddle | .08 | .04 | .01 |
| Chicago Bears | | | |
| ☐ 140 Stevon Moore | .05 | .02 | .01 |
| Cleveland Browns | | | |
| ☐ 141 Rod Bernstine | .05 | .02 | .01 |
| Denver Broncos | | | |
| ☐ 142 Brett Favre | .50 | .23 | .06 |
| Green Bay Packers | | | |
| ☐ 143 Roosevelt Potts | .08 | .04 | .01 |
| Indianapolis Colts | | | |
| ☐ 144 Chester McGlockton | .05 | .02 | .01 |
| Los Angeles Raiders | | | |
| ☐ 145 LeRoy Butler AP | .05 | .02 | .01 |
| Green Bay Packers | | | |
| ☐ 146 Charles Haley | .05 | .02 | .01 |
| Dallas Cowboys | | | |
| ☐ 147 Rodney Hampton | .25 | .11 | .03 |
| New York Giants | | | |

| | | | |
|---|---|---|---|
| ☐ 148 George Teague | .05 | .02 | .01 |
| Green Bay Packers | | | |
| ☐ 149 Gary Anderson | .05 | .02 | .01 |
| Pittsburgh Steelers | | | |
| ☐ 150 Mark Stepnoski | .05 | .02 | .01 |
| Dallas Cowboys | | | |
| ☐ 151 Courtney Hawkins | .05 | .02 | .01 |
| Tampa Bay Buccaneers | | | |
| ☐ 152 Tim Grunhard | .05 | .02 | .01 |
| Kansas City Chiefs | | | |
| ☐ 153 David Klingler | .15 | .07 | .02 |
| Cincinnati Bengals | | | |
| ☐ 154 Erik Williams AP | .05 | .02 | .01 |
| Dallas Cowboys | | | |
| ☐ 155 Herman Moore | .15 | .07 | .02 |
| Detroit Lions | | | |
| ☐ 156 Daryl Johnston | .08 | .04 | .01 |
| Dallas Cowboys | | | |
| ☐ 157 Chris Zorich | .05 | .02 | .01 |
| Chicago Bears | | | |
| ☐ 158 Shane Conlan | .05 | .02 | .01 |
| Los Angeles Rams | | | |
| ☐ 159 Santana Dotson | .05 | .02 | .01 |
| Tampa Bay Buccaneers | | | |
| ☐ 160 Sam Mills | .05 | .02 | .01 |
| New Orleans Saints | | | |
| ☐ 161 Ronnie Lott | .10 | .05 | .01 |
| New York Jets | | | |
| ☐ 162 Jesse Sapolu | .05 | .02 | .01 |
| San Francisco 49ers | | | |
| ☐ 163 Marion Butts | .08 | .04 | .01 |
| New England Patriots | | | |
| ☐ 164 Eugene Robinson AP | .05 | .02 | .01 |
| Seattle Seahawks | | | |
| ☐ 165 Mark Schlereth | .05 | .02 | .01 |
| Washington Redskins | | | |
| ☐ 166 John L. Williams | .05 | .02 | .01 |
| Pittsburgh Steelers | | | |
| ☐ 167 Anthony Miller | .15 | .07 | .02 |
| Denver Broncos | | | |
| ☐ 168 Rich Camarillo | .05 | .02 | .01 |
| Houston Oilers | | | |
| ☐ 169 Jeff Lageman | .05 | .02 | .01 |
| New York Jets | | | |
| ☐ 170 Michael Brooks | .05 | .02 | .01 |
| New York Giants | | | |
| ☐ 171 Scott Mitchell | .30 | .14 | .04 |
| Detroit Lions | | | |
| ☐ 172 Duane Bickett | .05 | .02 | .01 |
| Indianapolis Colts | | | |
| ☐ 173 Willie Davis | .08 | .04 | .01 |
| Kansas City Chiefs | | | |
| ☐ 174 Maurice Hurst | .05 | .02 | .01 |
| New England Patriots | | | |
| ☐ 175 Brett Perriman | .05 | .02 | .01 |
| Detroit Lions | | | |
| ☐ 176 Jay Novacek | .08 | .04 | .01 |
| Dallas Cowboys | | | |
| ☐ 177 Terry Allen | .05 | .02 | .01 |
| Minnesota Vikings | | | |
| ☐ 178 Pete Metzelaars | .05 | .02 | .01 |
| Buffalo Bills | | | |
| ☐ 179 Erik Kramer | .15 | .07 | .02 |
| Chicago Bears | | | |
| ☐ 180 Neal Anderson | .05 | .02 | .01 |
| Chicago Bears | | | |
| ☐ 181 Ethan Horton | .05 | .02 | .01 |
| Washington Redskins | | | |
| ☐ 182 Tony Bennett | .05 | .02 | .01 |
| Indianapolis Colts | | | |
| ☐ 183 Gary Zimmerman | .05 | .02 | .01 |
| Denver Broncos | | | |
| ☐ 184 Jeff Hostetler | .08 | .04 | .01 |
| Los Angeles Raiders | | | |
| ☐ 185 Jeff Cross | .05 | .02 | .01 |
| Miami Dolphins | | | |
| ☐ 186 Vincent Brown | .05 | .02 | .01 |
| New England Patriots | | | |
| ☐ 187 Herschel Walker | .10 | .05 | .01 |
| Philadelphia Eagles | | | |
| ☐ 188 Courtney Hall | .05 | .02 | .01 |
| San Diego Chargers | | | |
| ☐ 189 Norm Johnson AP | .05 | .02 | .01 |
| Atlanta Falcons | | | |
| ☐ 190 Hardy Nickerson AP | .05 | .02 | .01 |
| Tampa Bay Buccaneers | | | |
| ☐ 191 Greg Townsend | .05 | .02 | .01 |
| Los Angeles Raiders | | | |
| ☐ 192 Mike Munchak | .05 | .02 | .01 |
| Houston Oilers | | | |
| ☐ 193 Dante Jones | .05 | .02 | .01 |
| Chicago Bears | | | |
| ☐ 194 Vinny Testaverde | .08 | .04 | .01 |
| Cleveland Browns | | | |
| ☐ 195 Vance Johnson | .05 | .02 | .01 |
| San Diego Chargers | | | |
| ☐ 196 Chris Jacke AP | .05 | .02 | .01 |

| | | | |
|---|---|---|---|
| Green Bay Packers | | | |
| ☐ 197 Will Wolford | .05 | .02 | .01 |
| Indianapolis Colts | | | |
| ☐ 198 Terry McDaniel | .05 | .02 | .01 |
| Los Angeles Raiders | | | |
| ☐ 199 Bryan Cox | .05 | .02 | .01 |
| Miami Dolphins | | | |
| ☐ 200 Nate Newton | .05 | .02 | .01 |
| Dallas Cowboys | | | |
| ☐ 201 Keith Byars | .08 | .04 | .01 |
| Miami Dolphins | | | |
| ☐ 202 Neil O'Donnell | .12 | .05 | .02 |
| Pittsburgh Steelers | | | |
| ☐ 203 Harris Barton AP | .05 | .02 | .01 |
| San Francisco 49ers | | | |
| ☐ 204 Thurman Thomas | .25 | .11 | .03 |
| Buffalo Bills | | | |
| ☐ 205 Jeff Query | .05 | .02 | .01 |
| Cincinnati Bengals | | | |
| ☐ 206 Russell Maryland | .05 | .02 | .01 |
| Dallas Cowboys | | | |
| ☐ 207 Pat Swilling | .08 | .04 | .01 |
| Detroit Lions | | | |
| ☐ 208 Haywood Jeffires | .10 | .05 | .01 |
| Houston Oilers | | | |
| ☐ 209 John Alt | .05 | .02 | .01 |
| Kansas City Chiefs | | | |
| ☐ 210 O.J. McDuffie | .25 | .11 | .03 |
| Miami Dolphins | | | |
| ☐ 211 Keith Sims | .05 | .02 | .01 |
| Miami Dolphins | | | |
| ☐ 212 Eric Martin | .05 | .02 | .01 |
| New Orleans Saints | | | |
| ☐ 213 Kyle Clifton | .05 | .02 | .01 |
| New York Jets | | | |
| ☐ 214 Luis Sharpe | .05 | .02 | .01 |
| Arizona Cardinals | | | |
| ☐ 215 Thomas Everett | .05 | .02 | .01 |
| Tampa Bay Buccaneers | | | |
| ☐ 216 Chris Warren | .05 | .02 | .01 |
| Seattle Seahawks | | | |
| ☐ 217 Chris Doleman | .05 | .02 | .01 |
| Atlanta Falcons | | | |
| ☐ 218 Tony Jones | .05 | .02 | .01 |
| Cleveland Browns | | | |
| ☐ 219 Karl Mecklenburg | .05 | .02 | .01 |
| Denver Broncos | | | |
| ☐ 220 Rob Moore | .08 | .04 | .01 |
| New York Jets | | | |
| ☐ 221 Jessie Hester | .05 | .02 | .01 |
| Indianapolis Colts | | | |
| ☐ 222 Jeff Jaeger | .05 | .02 | .01 |
| Los Angeles Raiders | | | |
| ☐ 223 Keith Jackson | .10 | .05 | .01 |
| Miami Dolphins | | | |
| ☐ 224 Mo Lewis | .05 | .02 | .01 |
| New York Jets | | | |
| ☐ 225 Mike Horan | .05 | .02 | .01 |
| New York Giants | | | |
| ☐ 226 Eric Green | .08 | .04 | .01 |
| Pittsburgh Steelers | | | |
| ☐ 227 Jim Ritcher | .05 | .02 | .01 |
| Buffalo Bills | | | |
| ☐ 228 Eric Curry | .05 | .02 | .01 |
| Tampa Bay Buccaneers | | | |
| ☐ 229 Stan Humphries | .05 | .02 | .01 |
| San Diego Chargers | | | |
| ☐ 230 Mike Johnson | .05 | .02 | .01 |
| Detroit Lions | | | |
| ☐ 231 Alvin Harper | .08 | .04 | .01 |
| Dallas Cowboys | | | |
| ☐ 232 Bennie Blades | .05 | .02 | .01 |
| Detroit Lions | | | |
| ☐ 233 Cris Carter | .05 | .02 | .01 |
| Minnesota Vikings | | | |
| ☐ 234 Morten Andersen | .05 | .02 | .01 |
| New Orleans Saints | | | |
| ☐ 235 Brian Washington | .05 | .02 | .01 |
| New York Jets | | | |
| ☐ 236 Eric Hill | .05 | .02 | .01 |
| Arizona Cardinals | | | |
| ☐ 237 Natrone Means | .25 | .11 | .03 |
| San Diego Chargers | | | |
| ☐ 238 Carlton Bailey | .05 | .02 | .01 |
| New York Giants | | | |
| ☐ 239 Anthony Carter | .08 | .04 | .01 |
| Minnesota Vikings | | | |
| ☐ 240 Jessie Tuggle | .05 | .02 | .01 |
| Atlanta Falcons | | | |
| ☐ 241 Tim Irwin | .05 | .02 | .01 |
| Tampa Bay Buccaneers | | | |
| ☐ 242 Mark Carrier | .05 | .02 | .01 |
| Cleveland Browns | | | |
| ☐ 243 Steve Atwater | .05 | .02 | .01 |
| Denver Broncos | | | |
| ☐ 244 Sean Jones | .05 | .02 | .01 |
| Green Bay Packers | | | |

| | | | |
|---|---|---|---|
| ☐ 245 Bernie Kosar | .08 | .04 | .01 |
| Miami Dolphins | | | |
| ☐ 246 Richmond Webb | .05 | .02 | .01 |
| Miami Dolphins | | | |
| ☐ 247 Dave Meggett | .05 | .02 | .01 |
| New York Giants | | | |
| ☐ 248 Vincent Brisby | .30 | .14 | .04 |
| New England Patriots | | | |
| ☐ 249 Fred Barnett | .08 | .04 | .01 |
| Philadelphia Eagles | | | |
| ☐ 250 Greg Lloyd AP | .05 | .02 | .01 |
| Pittsburgh Steelers | | | |
| ☐ 251 Tim McDonald | .05 | .02 | .01 |
| San Francisco 49ers | | | |
| ☐ 252 Mike Pritchard | .05 | .02 | .01 |
| Denver Broncos | | | |
| ☐ 253 Greg Robinson | .10 | .05 | .01 |
| Los Angeles Raiders | | | |
| ☐ 254 Tony McGee | .05 | .02 | .01 |
| Cincinnati Bengals | | | |
| ☐ 255 Chris Spielman | .05 | .02 | .01 |
| Detroit Lions | | | |
| ☐ 256 Keith Loneker | .10 | .05 | .01 |
| Los Angeles Rams | | | |
| ☐ 257 Derrick Thomas | .15 | .07 | .02 |
| Kansas City Chiefs | | | |
| ☐ 258 Wayne Martin | .05 | .02 | .01 |
| New Orleans Saints | | | |
| ☐ 259 Art Monk | .10 | .05 | .01 |
| New York Jets | | | |
| ☐ 260 Andy Heck | .05 | .02 | .01 |
| Chicago Bears | | | |
| ☐ 261 Chip Lohmiller | .05 | .02 | .01 |
| Washington Redskins | | | |
| ☐ 262 Simon Fletcher | .05 | .02 | .01 |
| Denver Broncos | | | |
| ☐ 263 Ricky Reynolds | .05 | .02 | .01 |
| New England Patriots | | | |
| ☐ 264 Chris Hinton | .05 | .02 | .01 |
| Minnesota Vikings | | | |
| ☐ 265 Ron Moore | .40 | .18 | .05 |
| Arizona Cardinals | | | |
| ☐ 266 Rocket Ismail | .15 | .07 | .02 |
| Los Angeles Raiders | | | |
| ☐ 267 Pete Stoyanovich | .05 | .02 | .01 |
| Miami Dolphins | | | |
| ☐ 268 Mark Jackson | .05 | .02 | .01 |
| New York Giants | | | |
| ☐ 269 Randall Cunningham | .10 | .05 | .01 |
| Philadelphia Eagles | | | |
| ☐ 270 Dermontti Dawson AP | .05 | .02 | .01 |
| Pittsburgh Steelers | | | |
| ☐ 271 Bill Romanowski | .05 | .02 | .01 |
| Philadelphia Eagles | | | |
| ☐ 272 Tim Johnson | .05 | .02 | .01 |
| Washington Redskins | | | |
| ☐ 273 Steve Tasker AP | .05 | .02 | .01 |
| Buffalo Bills | | | |
| ☐ 274 Keith Hamilton | .05 | .02 | .01 |
| New York Giants | | | |
| ☐ 275 Pierce Holt | .05 | .02 | .01 |
| Atlanta Falcons | | | |
| ☐ 276 Heath Shuler R | 5.00 | 2.30 | .60 |
| Washington Redskins | | | |
| ☐ 277 Marshall Faulk R | 3.00 | 1.35 | .40 |
| Indianapolis Colts | | | |
| ☐ 278 Charles Johnson R | 1.00 | .45 | .13 |
| Pittsburgh Steelers | | | |
| ☐ 279 Sam Adams R | .25 | .11 | .03 |
| Seattle Seahawks | | | |
| ☐ 280 Trev Alberts R | .50 | .23 | .06 |
| Indianapolis Colts | | | |
| ☐ 281 Derrick Alexander R | .50 | .23 | .06 |
| Cleveland Browns | | | |
| ☐ 282 Bryant Young R | .25 | .11 | .03 |
| San Francisco 49ers | | | |
| ☐ 283 Greg Hill R | .75 | .35 | .09 |
| Kansas City Chiefs | | | |
| ☐ 284 Darnay Scott R | .40 | .18 | .05 |
| Cincinnati Bengals | | | |
| ☐ 285 Willie McGinest R | .50 | .23 | .06 |
| New England Patriots | | | |
| ☐ 286 Thomas Randolph R | .15 | .07 | .02 |
| New York Giants | | | |
| ☐ 287 Errict Rhett R | 1.00 | .45 | .13 |
| Tampa Bay Buccaneers | | | |
| ☐ 288 Lamar Smith R | .25 | .11 | .03 |
| Seattle Seahawks | | | |
| ☐ 289 William Floyd R | .50 | .23 | .06 |
| San Francisco 49ers | | | |
| ☐ 290 Johnnie Morton R | .75 | .35 | .09 |
| Detroit Lions | | | |
| ☐ 291 Jamir Miller R | .30 | .14 | .04 |
| Arizona Cardinals | | | |
| ☐ 292 David Palmer R | 1.00 | .45 | .13 |
| Minnesota Vikings | | | |
| ☐ 293 Dan Wilkinson R | .50 | .23 | .06 |

Cincinnati Bengals
| | | | |
|---|---|---|---|
| ☐ 294 Trent Dilfer R | 2.25 | 1.00 | .30 |
| Tampa Bay Buccaneers | | | |
| ☐ 295 Antonio Langham R | .30 | .14 | .04 |
| Cleveland Browns | | | |
| ☐ 296 Chuck Levy R | .60 | .25 | .08 |
| Arizona Cardinals | | | |
| ☐ 297 John Thierry R | .30 | .14 | .04 |
| Chicago Bears | | | |
| ☐ 298 Kevin Lee R | .30 | .14 | .04 |
| New England Patriots | | | |
| ☐ 299 Aaron Glenn R | .15 | .07 | .02 |
| New York Jets | | | |
| ☐ 300 Charlie Garner R | .60 | .25 | .08 |
| Philadelphia Eagles | | | |
| ☐ 301 Lonnie Johnson R | .15 | .07 | .02 |
| Buffalo Bills | | | |
| ☐ 302 LeShon Johnson R | .40 | .18 | .05 |
| Green Bay Packers | | | |
| ☐ 303 Thomas Lewis R | .40 | .18 | .05 |
| New York Giants | | | |
| ☐ 304 Ryan Yarborough R | .25 | .11 | .03 |
| New York Jets | | | |
| ☐ 305 Mario Bates R | .40 | .18 | .05 |
| New Orleans Saints | | | |
| ☐ 306 Buffalo Bills TC | .05 | .02 | .01 |
| Arizona Cardinals | | | |
| ☐ 307 Cincinnati Bengals TC | .05 | .02 | .01 |
| Atlanta Falcons | | | |
| ☐ 308 Cleveland Browns TC | .05 | .02 | .01 |
| Chicago Bears | | | |
| ☐ 309 Denver Broncos TC | .05 | .02 | .01 |
| Dallas Cowboys | | | |
| ☐ 310 Houston Oilers TC | .05 | .02 | .01 |
| Detroit Lions | | | |
| ☐ 311 Indianapolis Colts TC | .05 | .02 | .01 |
| Green Bay Packers | | | |
| ☐ 312 Kansas City Chiefs TC | .05 | .02 | .01 |
| Los Angeles Rams | | | |
| ☐ 313 Los Angeles Raiders TC | .05 | .02 | .01 |
| Minnesota Vikings | | | |
| ☐ 314 Miami Dolphins TC | .05 | .02 | .01 |
| New Orleans Saints | | | |
| ☐ 315 New England Patriots TC | .05 | .02 | .01 |
| New York Giants | | | |
| ☐ 316 New York Jets TC | .05 | .02 | .01 |
| Philadelphia Eagles | | | |
| ☐ 317 Pittsburgh Steelers TC | .05 | .02 | .01 |
| San Francisco 49ers | | | |
| ☐ 318 San Diego Charges TC | .05 | .02 | .01 |
| Tampa Bay Buccaneers | | | |
| ☐ 319 Seattle Seahawks TC | .05 | .02 | .01 |
| Washington Redskins | | | |
| ☐ 320 Garrison Hearst | .15 | .07 | .02 |
| Arizona Cardinals | | | |
| ☐ 321 Drew Bledsoe | 1.25 | .55 | .16 |
| New England Patriots | | | |
| ☐ 322 Tyrone Hughes | .05 | .02 | .01 |
| New Orleans Saints | | | |
| ☐ 323 James Jett | .20 | .09 | .03 |
| Los Angeles Raiders | | | |
| ☐ 324 Tom Carter | .05 | .02 | .01 |
| Washington Redskins | | | |
| ☐ 325 Reggie Brooks | .60 | .25 | .08 |
| Washington Redskins | | | |
| ☐ 326 Dana Stubblefield | .15 | .07 | .02 |
| San Francisco 49ers | | | |
| ☐ 327 Jerome Bettis | 1.00 | .45 | .13 |
| Los Angeles Rams | | | |
| ☐ 328 Chris Slade | .05 | .02 | .01 |
| New England Patriots | | | |
| ☐ 329 Rick Mirer | 1.25 | .55 | .16 |
| Seattle Seahawks | | | |
| ☐ 330 Emmitt Smith NFL MVP | .75 | .35 | .09 |
| Dallas Cowboys | | | |

## 1994 Score Gold

Inserted one card per pack, this 330-card standard size (2 1/2" by 3 1/2") set features the same design as the regular 1994 Score football cards, except that the fronts have a metallic sheen.

| | MINT | EXC | G-VG |
|---|---|---|---|
| COMPLETE SET (330) | 90.00 | 40.00 | 11.50 |
| COMMON PLAYER (1-330) | .20 | .09 | .03 |
| *GOLD STARS: 2.5X TO 5X VALUE | | | |
| *GOLD ROOKIES: 2X TO 4X VALUE | | | |
| | | | |
| ☐ 1 Barry Sanders | 3.00 | 1.35 | .40 |
| Detroit Lions | | | |
| ☐ 2 Troy Aikman | 7.00 | 3.10 | .85 |
| Dallas Cowboys | | | |
| ☐ 3 Sterling Sharpe AP | 1.50 | .65 | .19 |
| Green Bay Packers | | | |
| ☐ 7 John Elway | 2.00 | .90 | .25 |
| Denver Broncos | | | |

| | | | |
|---|---|---|---|
| ☐ 11 Jerry Rice AP | 2.50 | 1.15 | .30 |
| San Francisco 49ers | | | |
| ☐ 21 Jerome Bettis AP | 8.00 | 3.60 | 1.00 |
| Los Angeles Rams | | | |
| ☐ 40 Emmitt Smith AP | 10.00 | 4.50 | 1.25 |
| Dallas Cowboys | | | |
| ☐ 60 Michael Irvin | 1.50 | .65 | .19 |
| Dallas Cowboys | | | |
| ☐ 65 Dan Marino | 3.50 | 1.55 | .45 |
| Miami Dolphins | | | |
| ☐ 67 Joe Montana | 8.00 | 3.60 | 1.00 |
| Kansas City Chiefs | | | |
| ☐ 108 Jim Kelly | 1.00 | .45 | .13 |
| Buffalo Bills | | | |
| ☐ 121 Ricky Watters | 1.00 | .45 | .13 |
| San Francisco 49ers | | | |
| ☐ 129 Gary Brown | 1.25 | .55 | .16 |
| Houston Oilers | | | |
| ☐ 142 Brett Favre | 2.50 | 1.15 | .30 |
| Green Bay Packers | | | |
| ☐ 147 Rodney Hampton | 1.00 | .45 | .13 |
| New York Giants | | | |
| ☐ 171 Scott Mitchell | 1.25 | .55 | .16 |
| Detroit Lions | | | |
| ☐ 204 Thurman Thomas | 1.00 | .45 | .13 |
| Buffalo Bills | | | |
| ☐ 276 Heath Shuler RC | 14.00 | 6.25 | 1.75 |
| Washington Redskins | | | |
| ☐ 277 Marshall Faulk RC | 8.00 | 3.60 | 1.00 |
| Indianapolis Colts | | | |
| ☐ 278 Charles Johnson RC | 3.00 | 1.35 | .40 |
| Pittsburgh Steelers | | | |
| ☐ 283 Greg Hill RC | 2.25 | 1.00 | .30 |
| Kansas City Chiefs | | | |
| ☐ 287 Errict Rhett RC | 3.00 | 1.35 | .40 |
| Tampa Bay Buccaneers | | | |
| ☐ 290 Johnnie Morton RC | 2.25 | 1.00 | .30 |
| Detroit Lions | | | |
| ☐ 292 David Palmer RC | 3.00 | 1.35 | .40 |
| Minnesota Vikings | | | |
| ☐ 294 Trent Dilfer RC | 6.00 | 2.70 | .75 |
| Tampa Bay Buccaneers | | | |
| ☐ 296 Chuck Levy RC | 1.75 | .80 | .22 |
| Arizona Cardinals | | | |
| ☐ 300 Charlie Garner RC | 1.75 | .80 | .22 |
| Philadelphia Eagles | | | |
| ☐ 321 Drew Bledsoe | 6.00 | 2.70 | .75 |
| New England Patriots | | | |
| ☐ 325 Reggie Brooks | 3.00 | 1.35 | .40 |
| Washington Redskins | | | |
| ☐ 327 Jerome Bettis | 5.00 | 2.30 | .60 |
| Los Angeles Rams | | | |
| ☐ 329 Rick Mirer | 6.00 | 2.70 | .75 |
| Seattle Seahawks | | | |
| ☐ 330 Emmitt Smith NFL MVP | 6.00 | 2.70 | .75 |

## 1977 Seahawks Fred Meyer

Sponsored by Fred Meyer Department Stores and subtitled "Savings Selections Quality Service," this set consists of 11 photos (approximately 6" by 7 1/4") printed on thin glossy paper stock. The cards were reportedly given out one per week. The fronts feature either posed or action color player photos with black borders. The player's name, uniform number, and brief player information appear in one of the bottom corners. With the exception of the August photo, the other photos also feature a small color close-up photo immediately above the player information. The backs are blank. The cards are unnumbered and checklisted below in alphabetical order. The set features a card of Steve Largent in his Rookie Card year.

| | NRMT | VG-E | GOOD |
|---|---|---|---|
| COMPLETE SET (11) | 60.00 | 24.00 | 6.00 |
| COMMON PLAYER (1-11) | 5.00 | 2.00 | .50 |

| | | NRMT | VG-E | GOOD |
|---|---|---|---|---|
| ☐ 1 Steve August | | 5.00 | 2.00 | .50 |
| ☐ 2 Autry Beamon | | 5.00 | 2.00 | .50 |
| ☐ 3 Dennis Boyd | | 5.00 | 2.00 | .50 |
| ☐ 4 Sammy Green | | 5.00 | 2.00 | .50 |
| ☐ 5 Ron Howard | | 5.00 | 2.00 | .50 |
| ☐ 6 Steve Largent | | 25.00 | 10.00 | 2.50 |
| ☐ 7 Steve Myer | | 5.00 | 2.00 | .50 |
| ☐ 8 Steve Niehaus | | 6.00 | 2.40 | .60 |
| ☐ 9 Sherman Smith | | 6.00 | 2.40 | .60 |
| ☐ 10 Don Testerman | | 5.00 | 2.00 | .50 |
| ☐ 11 Jim Zorn | | 12.00 | 5.00 | 1.20 |

## 1977 Seahawks Team Issue

These ten blank-backed photos measure approximately 5" by 7" and feature black-and-white head shots of Seattle Seahawks players. The player's name, team, simulated autograph, and Seahawks logo appear near the bottom. The photos are unnumbered and checklisted below in alphabetical order.

| | NRMT | VG-E | GOOD |
|---|---|---|---|
| COMPLETE SET (10) | 60.00 | 24.00 | 6.00 |
| COMMON PLAYER (1-10) | 3.00 | 1.20 | .30 |
| ☐ 1 Ron Howard | 5.00 | 2.00 | .50 |
| ☐ 2 Steve Largent | 25.00 | 10.00 | 2.50 |
| ☐ 3 John Leypoldt | 5.00 | 2.00 | .50 |
| ☐ 4 Bob Lurstema | 5.00 | 2.00 | .50 |
| ☐ 5 Steve Myer | 5.00 | 2.00 | .50 |
| ☐ 6 Steve Niehaus | 6.00 | 2.40 | .60 |
| ☐ 7 Jack Patera CO | 6.00 | 2.40 | .60 |
| ☐ 8 Sherman Smith | 6.00 | 2.40 | .60 |
| ☐ 9 Don Testerman | 5.00 | 2.00 | .50 |
| ☐ 10 Jim Zorn | 12.00 | 5.00 | 1.20 |

## 1978-80 Seahawks Nalley's

The 1978-80 Nalley's Seattle Seahawks cards are actually the back panels of large (nine ounce) Nalley's boxes of Dippers, Barbecue Chips, and Potato Chips. The cards themselves measure approximately 9" by 10 3/4" and include a facsimile autograph. The back of the potato chip box features a color posed photo of the player with his facsimile autograph. One side of the box has the Seahawks game schedule, while the other side provides biographical and statistical information on the player. Cards 1-8 were issued in 1978, 9-16 in 1979, and 17-24 in 1980. All players in the set are members of the Seattle Seahawks. The prices listed below refer to complete boxes.

| | | NRMT | VG-E | GOOD |
|---|---|---|---|---|
| COMPLETE SET (24) | | 700.00 | 280.00 | 70.00 |
| COMMON CARD (1-8) | | 25.00 | 10.00 | 2.50 |
| COMMON CARD (9-16) | | 20.00 | 8.00 | 2.00 |
| COMMON CARD (17-24) | | 15.00 | 6.00 | 1.50 |
| ☐ 1 Steve Largent | | 300.00 | 120.00 | 30.00 |
| ☐ 2 Autry Beamon | | 25.00 | 10.00 | 2.50 |
| ☐ 3 Jim Zorn | | 50.00 | 20.00 | 5.00 |
| ☐ 4 Sherman Smith | | 35.00 | 14.00 | 3.50 |
| ☐ 5 Ron Coder | | 25.00 | 10.00 | 2.50 |
| ☐ 6 Terry Beeson | | 25.00 | 10.00 | 2.50 |
| ☐ 7 Steve Niehaus | | 30.00 | 12.00 | 3.00 |
| ☐ 8 Ron Howard | | 25.00 | 10.00 | 2.50 |
| ☐ 9 Steve Myer | | 20.00 | 8.00 | 2.00 |
| ☐ 10 Tom Lynch | | 20.00 | 8.00 | 2.00 |
| ☐ 11 David Sims | | 20.00 | 8.00 | 2.00 |
| ☐ 12 John Yarno | | 20.00 | 8.00 | 2.00 |
| ☐ 13 Bill Gregory | | 30.00 | 12.00 | 3.00 |
| ☐ 14 Steve Raible | | 30.00 | 12.00 | 3.00 |
| ☐ 15 Dennis Boyd | | 20.00 | 8.00 | 2.00 |
| ☐ 16 Steve August | | 20.00 | 8.00 | 2.00 |
| ☐ 17 Keith Simpson | | 15.00 | 6.00 | 1.50 |
| ☐ 18 Michael Jackson | | 15.00 | 6.00 | 1.50 |
| ☐ 19 Manu Tuiasosopo | | 20.00 | 8.00 | 2.00 |
| ☐ 20 Sam McCullum | | 20.00 | 8.00 | 2.00 |
| ☐ 21 Keith Butler | | 15.00 | 6.00 | 1.50 |
| ☐ 22 Sam Akins | | 15.00 | 6.00 | 1.50 |
| ☐ 23 Dan Doornink | | 20.00 | 8.00 | 2.00 |
| ☐ 24 Dave Brown | | 20.00 | 8.00 | 2.00 |

## 1980 Seahawks 7-Up

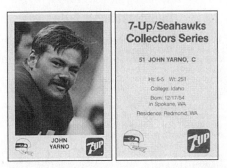

This 7-Up/Seahawks Collectors Series set measures approximately 2 3/8" by 3 1/4" and is printed on thin card stock. Card front carries a posed four-color player photo enclosed in a white border. The Seahawks helmet, player's name, and 7-Up logo appear in the bottom border. The card backs feature player statistics and sponsor logos. The cards are unnumbered and checklisted below alphabetically. Steve Largent and Jim Zorn were not included in the set due to their sponsorship of Darigold Dairy Products.

| | MINT | EXC | G-VG |
|---|---|---|---|
| COMPLETE SET (10) | 90.00 | 36.00 | 9.00 |
| COMMON PLAYER (1-10) | 10.00 | 4.00 | 1.00 |
| ☐ 1 Steve August | 10.00 | 4.00 | 1.00 |
| ☐ 2 Terry Beeson | 10.00 | 4.00 | 1.00 |
| ☐ 3 Dan Doornink | 12.00 | 5.00 | 1.20 |
| ☐ 4 Michael Jackson | 10.00 | 4.00 | 1.00 |
| ☐ 5 Tom Lynch | 10.00 | 4.00 | 1.00 |
| ☐ 6 Steve Myer | 10.00 | 4.00 | 1.00 |
| ☐ 7 Steve Raible | 15.00 | 6.00 | 1.50 |
| ☐ 8 Sherman Smith | 15.00 | 6.00 | 1.50 |
| ☐ 9 Manu Tuiasosopo | 12.00 | 5.00 | 1.20 |
| ☐ 10 John Yarno | 10.00 | 4.00 | 1.00 |

## 1981 Seahawks 7-Up

Sponsored by 7-Up and issued by the Seahawks, usually through mail requests, these 30 cards measure approximately 3 1/2" by 5 1/2" and are made of thin stock. The fronts feature color player action shots with the 7-Up logo and facsimile autograph. However, the Steve Largent and Jim Zorn photos do not have the 7-Up logo due to their association with Darigold Milk products at the time. The back carries a brief player biography. The cards are unnumbered and checklisted below in alphabetical order.

|  | MINT | EXC | G-VG |
|---|---|---|---|
| COMPLETE SET (30) | 90.00 | 36.00 | 9.00 |
| COMMON PLAYER (1-30) | 3.00 | 1.20 | .30 |
| | | | |
| ☐ 1 Sam Adkins | 3.00 | 1.20 | .30 |
| ☐ 2 Steve August | 3.00 | 1.20 | .30 |
| ☐ 3 Terry Beeson | 3.00 | 1.20 | .30 |
| ☐ 4 Dennis Boyd | 3.00 | 1.20 | .30 |
| ☐ 5 Dave Brown | 4.00 | 1.60 | .40 |
| ☐ 6 Louis Bullard | 3.00 | 1.20 | .30 |
| ☐ 7 Keith Butler | 3.00 | 1.20 | .30 |
| ☐ 8 Peter Cronan | 3.00 | 1.20 | .30 |
| ☐ 9 Dan Doornink | 4.00 | 1.60 | .40 |
| ☐ 10 Jacob Green | 5.00 | 2.00 | .50 |
| ☐ 11 Bill Gregory | 4.00 | 1.60 | .40 |
| ☐ 12 Robert Hardy | 3.00 | 1.20 | .30 |
| ☐ 13 Efren Herrera | 3.00 | 1.20 | .30 |
| ☐ 14 Michael Jackson | 3.00 | 1.20 | .30 |
| ☐ 15 Art Kuehn | 3.00 | 1.20 | .30 |
| ☐ 16 Steve Largent | 15.00 | 6.00 | 1.50 |
| ☐ 17 Tom Lynch | 3.00 | 1.20 | .30 |
| ☐ 18 Sam McCullum | 4.00 | 1.60 | .40 |
| ☐ 19 Steve Myer | 3.00 | 1.20 | .30 |
| ☐ 20 Jack Patera CO | 4.00 | 1.60 | .40 |
| ☐ 21 Steve Raible | 4.00 | 1.60 | .40 |
| ☐ 22 The Sea Gals | 4.00 | 1.60 | .40 |
| ☐ 23 The Seahawk Mascot | 4.00 | 1.60 | .40 |
| ☐ 24 Keith Simpson | 3.00 | 1.20 | .30 |
| ☐ 25 Sherman Smith | 4.00 | 1.60 | .40 |
| ☐ 26 Manu Tuiasosopo | 4.00 | 1.60 | .40 |
| ☐ 27 Herman Weaver | 3.00 | 1.20 | .30 |
| ☐ 28 Cornell Webster | 3.00 | 1.20 | .30 |
| ☐ 29 John Yarno | 3.00 | 1.20 | .30 |
| ☐ 30 Jim Zorn | 6.00 | 2.40 | .60 |

## 1982 Seahawks 7-Up

Sponsored by 7-Up and issued by the Seahawks, usually through mail requests, these 15 cards measure approximately 3 1/2" by 5 1/2" and are printed on thin stock. The fronts feature color player action shots with "Seahawks Fan Mail Courtesy," the 7-Up logo, and a facsimile autograph (which sometimes appears on the card back). The Steve Largent and Jim Zorn cards carry the Darigold logo, Gold-n-Soft Margarine," due to their association with Darigold Milk products at the time. The back carries a brief player biography, career highlights, or personal message. Some of the cards are horizontally oriented and some are vertically oriented. The cards are unnumbered and checklisted below in alphabetical order.

|  | MINT | EXC | G-VG |
|---|---|---|---|
| COMPLETE SET (15) | 60.00 | 24.00 | 6.00 |
| COMMON PLAYER (1-15) | 3.00 | 1.20 | .30 |
| | | | |
| ☐ 1 Edwin Bailey | 3.00 | 1.20 | .30 |
| ☐ 2 Dave Brown | 4.00 | 1.60 | .40 |
| ☐ 3 Ken Easley | 5.00 | 2.00 | .50 |
| ☐ 4 Ron Essink | 3.00 | 1.20 | .30 |
| ☐ 5 Jacob Green | 5.00 | 2.00 | .50 |
| (No facsimile autograph) | | | |
| ☐ 6 Robert Hardy | 3.00 | 1.20 | .30 |
| ☐ 7 John Harris | 3.00 | 1.20 | .30 |
| ☐ 8 David Hughes | 3.00 | 1.20 | .30 |
| ☐ 9 Paul Johns HOR | 3.00 | 1.20 | .30 |
| ☐ 10 Kerry Justin | 3.00 | 1.20 | .30 |
| ☐ 11 Dave Krieg | 7.50 | 3.00 | .75 |
| ☐ 12 Steve Largent | 15.00 | 6.00 | 1.50 |
| (Darigold logo or Gold-n-Soft) | | | |
| ☐ 13 Keith Simpson | 3.00 | 1.20 | .30 |
| ☐ 14 Manu Tuiasosopo | 4.00 | 1.60 | .40 |
| ☐ 15 Jim Zorn HOR | 6.00 | 2.40 | .60 |
| (Darigold logo or Gold-n-Soft) | | | |

## 1984 Seahawks GTE

Sponsored by GTE Communications and issued by the Seahawks, usually through mail requests, these 12 cards measure approximately 3 1/2" by 5 1/2" and are printed on thin stock. The fronts feature color player action shots with the GTE logo and facsimile autograph. A color player head shot is inset near one corner. The back carries a brief player biography. The cards are unnumbered and checklisted below in alphabetical order.

|  | MINT | EXC | G-VG |
|---|---|---|---|
| COMPLETE SET (12) | 40.00 | 16.00 | 4.00 |
| COMMON PLAYER (1-12) | 2.00 | .80 | .20 |
| | | | |
| ☐ 1 Kenny Easley | 3.00 | 1.20 | .30 |
| ☐ 2 Jacob Green | 3.00 | 1.20 | .30 |

|  | MINT | EXC | G-VG |
|---|---|---|---|
| ☐ 3 John Harris | 2.00 | .80 | .20 |
| ☐ 4 Norm Johnson | 3.00 | 1.20 | .30 |
| ☐ 5 Chuck Knox CO | 3.00 | 1.20 | .30 |
| ☐ 6 Dave Krieg | 6.00 | 2.40 | .60 |
| ☐ 7 Steve Largent | 15.00 | 6.00 | 1.50 |
| ☐ 8 Joe Nash | 2.00 | .80 | .20 |
| ☐ 9 Keith Simpson | 2.00 | .80 | .20 |
| ☐ 10 Mike Tice | 2.00 | .80 | .20 |
| ☐ 11 Curt Warner | 5.00 | 2.00 | .50 |
| ☐ 12 Charley Young | 3.00 | 1.20 | .30 |

## 1984 Seahawks Nalley's

The 1984 Nalley's Seahawks set was issued on large Nalley's Potato Chip boxes. The back of the box features a color photo of the player, with his facsimile autograph. One side of the box has the Seahawks 1984 schedule, while the other side provides biographical and statistical information on the player. The prices listed below refer to complete boxes. These cards are unnumbered and are listed below alphabetically.

|  | MINT | EXC | G-VG |
|---|---|---|---|
| COMPLETE SET (4) | 45.00 | 18.00 | 4.50 |
| COMMON PLAYER (1-4) | 7.50 | 3.00 | .75 |
| | | | |
| ☐ 1 Kenny Easley | 7.50 | 3.00 | .75 |
| ☐ 2 Dave Krieg | 12.00 | 5.00 | 1.20 |
| ☐ 3 Steve Largent | 25.00 | 10.00 | 2.50 |
| ☐ 4 Curt Warner | 10.00 | 4.00 | 1.00 |

## 1987 Seahawks Snyder's/Franz

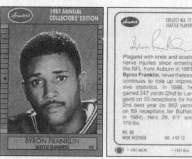

This 12-card set features players of the Seattle Seahawks. Cards were available only in Snyder's or Franz Bread loaves. The set was co-produced by Mike Schechter Associates on behalf of the NFL Players Association. Cards are standard size, 2 1/2" by 3 1/2", in full color, and are numbered on the back. The card fronts have a color photo within a blue border and the backs are printed in black ink on white card stock.

|  | MINT | EXC | G-VG |
|---|---|---|---|
| COMPLETE SET (12) | 50.00 | 20.00 | 5.00 |
| COMMON PLAYER (1-12) | 5.00 | 2.00 | .50 |
| | | | |
| ☐ 1 Jeff Bryant | 5.00 | 2.00 | .50 |
| ☐ 2 Keith Butler | 5.00 | 2.00 | .50 |
| ☐ 3 Randy Edwards | 5.00 | 2.00 | .50 |
| ☐ 4 Byron Franklin | 5.00 | 2.00 | .50 |
| ☐ 5 Jacob Green | 6.00 | 2.40 | .60 |
| ☐ 6 Dave Krieg | 10.00 | 4.00 | 1.00 |
| ☐ 7 Bryan Millard | 5.00 | 2.00 | .50 |
| ☐ 8 Paul Moyer | 5.00 | 2.00 | .50 |

| | MINT | EXC | G-VG |
|---|---|---|---|
| ☐ 9 Eugene Robinson | 6.00 | 2.40 | .60 |
| ☐ 10 Mike Tice | 6.00 | 2.40 | .60 |
| ☐ 11 Daryl Turner | 6.00 | 2.40 | .60 |
| ☐ 12 Curt Warner | 7.50 | 3.00 | .75 |

## 1988 Seahawks Domino's

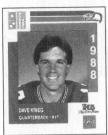 

This 50-card set was sponsored by Domino's Pizza and features Seattle Seahawks players and personnel. The cards were first distributed as a starter set of nine cards (1-9) perforated along with a team photo. Later cards were issued in strips of four or five players (10-13, 14-17, 18-21, 22-25, 26-29, 30-33, 34-38, 39-42, 43-46, and 47-50) along with a promotional coupon for a discount on pizza at Domino's. One strip was available each week with every Domino's pizza ordered. The discount coupons on strips 5, 6, and 8 were supposedly removed prior to distribution to the general public. The cards measure approximately 2 1/2" by 3" whereas the team photo is approximately 12 1/2" by 8 1/2". The set was also partially sponsored by Coca-Cola Classic and KING-5 TV.

| | MINT | EXC | G-VG |
|---|---|---|---|
| COMPLETE SET (50) | 40.00 | 16.00 | 4.00 |
| COMMON CARD (1-50) | .60 | .24 | .06 |
| | | | |
| ☐ 1 Steve Largent | 9.00 | 3.75 | .90 |
| ☐ 2 Kelly Stouffer | 1.00 | .40 | .10 |
| ☐ 3 Bobby Joe Edmonds | .75 | .30 | .07 |
| ☐ 4 Patrick Hunter | .75 | .30 | .07 |
| ☐ 5 Ventrella/Valle/Gellos | .75 | .30 | .07 |
| ☐ 6 Edwin Bailey | .60 | .24 | .06 |
| ☐ 7 Alonzo Mitz | .60 | .24 | .06 |
| ☐ 8 Tommy Kane | 1.00 | .40 | .10 |
| ☐ 9 Chuck Knox CO | 1.00 | .40 | .10 |
| ☐ 10 Curt Warner | 1.25 | .50 | .12 |
| ☐ 11 Alvin Powell | .60 | .24 | .06 |
| ☐ 12 Joe Nash | .60 | .24 | .06 |
| ☐ 13 Brian Blades | 2.50 | 1.00 | .25 |
| ☐ 14 Blair Bush | .75 | .30 | .07 |
| ☐ 15 Melvin Jenkins | .60 | .24 | .06 |
| ☐ 16 Ruben Rodriguez | .60 | .24 | .06 |
| ☐ 17 Tommie Agee | .75 | .30 | .07 |
| ☐ 18 Eugene Robinson | .75 | .30 | .07 |
| ☐ 19 Dwayne Harper | .60 | .24 | .06 |
| ☐ 20 Ray Butler | .75 | .30 | .07 |
| ☐ 21 Jeff Kemp | 1.00 | .40 | .10 |
| ☐ 22 Norm Johnson | .75 | .30 | .07 |
| ☐ 23 Bryan Millard | .60 | .24 | .06 |
| ☐ 24 Tony Woods | 1.00 | .40 | .10 |
| ☐ 25 Paul Skansi | .75 | .30 | .07 |
| ☐ 26 Jacob Green | 1.00 | .40 | .10 |
| ☐ 27 Randall Morris | .60 | .24 | .06 |
| ☐ 28 Mike Tice | .75 | .30 | .07 |
| ☐ 29 Kevin Harmon | .60 | .24 | .06 |
| ☐ 30 Dave Krieg | 2.00 | .80 | .20 |
| ☐ 31 Nesby Glasgow | .75 | .30 | .07 |
| ☐ 32 Bruce Scholtz | .60 | .24 | .06 |
| ☐ 33 John Spagnola | .60 | .24 | .06 |
| ☐ 34 Jeff Bryant | .75 | .30 | .07 |
| ☐ 35 Stan Eisenhooth | .60 | .24 | .06 |
| ☐ 36 Dave Wyman | .60 | .24 | .06 |
| ☐ 37 Greg Gaines | .60 | .24 | .06 |
| ☐ 38 Charlie Jones NBC ANN | .60 | .24 | .06 |
| ☐ 39 Terry Taylor | .75 | .30 | .07 |
| ☐ 40 Vernon Dean | .60 | .24 | .06 |
| ☐ 41 Mike Wilson | .60 | .24 | .06 |
| ☐ 42 Darrin Miller | .60 | .24 | .06 |
| ☐ 43 John L. Williams | 2.50 | 1.00 | .25 |
| ☐ 44 Grant Feasel | .60 | .24 | .06 |
| ☐ 45 M.L. Johnson | .60 | .24 | .06 |
| ☐ 46 Ken Clarke | .75 | .30 | .07 |
| ☐ 47 Brian Bosworth | .75 | .30 | .07 |
| ☐ 48 Ron Mattes | .60 | .24 | .06 |
| ☐ 49 Paul Moyer | .60 | .24 | .06 |
| ☐ 50 Rufus Porter | 1.00 | .40 | .10 |
| ☐ xx Team Photo | 6.00 | 2.40 | .60 |
| (Large size) | | | |

## 1988 Seahawks GTE

This 24-card set was sponsored by GTE and features members of the Seattle Seahawks. The cards measure approximately 3 5/8" by 5 1/2". The fronts show full-bleed color player photos with the player's signature and uniform number inscribed across the picture. The horizontal backs have career summary on the left portion; the right portion has a greeting and the player's signature and uniform number. The cards are unnumbered and checklisted below in alphabetical order.

| | MINT | EXC | G-VG |
|---|---|---|---|
| COMPLETE SET (24) | 50.00 | 20.00 | 5.00 |
| COMMON CARD (1-24) | 1.50 | .60 | .15 |
| | | | |
| ☐ 1 Edwin Bailey | 1.50 | .60 | .15 |
| ☐ 2 Brian Bosworth | 2.50 | 1.00 | .25 |
| ☐ 3 Dave Brown | 2.00 | .80 | .20 |
| ☐ 4 Jeff Bryant | 2.00 | .80 | .20 |
| ☐ 5 Bobby Joe Edmonds | 2.50 | 1.00 | .25 |
| ☐ 6 Jacob Green | 2.50 | 1.00 | .25 |
| ☐ 7 Michael Jackson | 1.50 | .60 | .15 |
| ☐ 8 Norm Johnson | 2.00 | .80 | .20 |
| ☐ 9 Jeff Kemp | 2.50 | 1.00 | .25 |
| ☐ 10 Chuck Knox CO | 2.50 | 1.00 | .25 |
| ☐ 11 Dave Krieg | 5.00 | 2.00 | .50 |
| ☐ 12 Steve Largent | 10.00 | 4.00 | 1.00 |
| ☐ 13 Ron Mattes | 1.50 | .60 | .15 |
| ☐ 14 Bryan Millard | 1.50 | .60 | .15 |
| ☐ 15 Paul Moyer | 1.50 | .60 | .15 |
| ☐ 16 Eugene Robinson | 2.00 | .80 | .20 |
| ☐ 17 Paul Skansi | 2.00 | .80 | .20 |
| ☐ 18 Kelly Stouffer | 2.00 | .80 | .20 |
| ☐ 19 Terry Taylor | 2.00 | .80 | .20 |
| ☐ 20 Mike Tice | 2.00 | .80 | .20 |
| ☐ 21 Daryl Turner | 2.00 | .80 | .20 |
| ☐ 22 Curt Warner | 3.00 | 1.20 | .30 |
| ☐ 23 John L. Williams | 4.00 | 1.60 | .40 |
| ☐ 24 Fredd Young | 2.00 | .80 | .20 |

## 1988 Seahawks Snyder's/Franz

This 12-card set features players of the Seattle Seahawks. Cards were available only in Snyder's or Franz Bread loaves. The set was co-produced by Mike Schechter Associates on behalf of the NFL Players Association. The cards are standard size, 2 1/2" by 3 1/2", in full color, and are numbered on the back. The card fronts have a color photo within a blue border and the backs are printed in black ink on white card stock.

|  | MINT | EXC | G-VG |
|---|---|---|---|
| COMPLETE SET (12)...................... | 30.00 | 12.00 | 3.00 |
| COMMON PLAYER (1-12)................ | 3.00 | 1.20 | .30 |
| ☐ 1 Dave Krieg........................... | 6.00 | 2.40 | .60 |
| ☐ 2 Curt Warner.......................... | 5.00 | 2.00 | .50 |
| ☐ 3 Byron Franklin....................... | 3.00 | 1.20 | .30 |
| ☐ 4 Eugene Robinson.................. | 4.00 | 1.60 | .40 |
| ☐ 5 Mike Tice............................. | 3.00 | 1.20 | .30 |
| ☐ 6 Daryl Turner......................... | 4.00 | 1.60 | .40 |
| ☐ 7 Paul Moyer........................... | 3.00 | 1.20 | .30 |
| ☐ 8 Bryan Millard........................ | 3.00 | 1.20 | .30 |
| ☐ 9 Jeff Bryant........................... | 3.00 | 1.20 | .30 |
| ☐ 10 Keith Butler......................... | 3.00 | 1.20 | .30 |
| ☐ 11 Randy Edwards.................... | 3.00 | 1.20 | .30 |
| ☐ 12 Jacob Green........................ | 4.00 | 1.60 | .40 |

## 1989 Seahawks Oroweat

The 1989 Oroweat Seahawks set contains 20 standard-size (2 1/2" by 3 1/2") cards. The cards have attractive silver borders and color action shots and were produced by Pacific Trading Cards for Oroweat. The horizontally-oriented backs have light blue borders with bios, stats, and career highlights. One card was distributed in each specially marked loaf of Oroweat's Oatnut Bread, sold only in the Pacific Northwest. It has been reported that 1.5 million cards were distributed.

|  | MINT | EXC | G-VG |
|---|---|---|---|
| COMPLETE SET (20)...................... | 25.00 | 10.00 | 2.50 |
| COMMON PLAYER (1-20)................ | .60 | .24 | .06 |
| ☐ 1 Paul Moyer........................... | .75 | .30 | .07 |
| ☐ 2 Dave Wyman......................... | .60 | .24 | .06 |
| ☐ 3 Tony Woods.......................... | 1.00 | .40 | .10 |
| ☐ 4 Kelly Stouffer........................ | 1.00 | .40 | .10 |
| ☐ 5 Brian Blades......................... | 2.50 | 1.00 | .25 |
| ☐ 6 Norm Johnson....................... | 1.00 | .40 | .10 |
| ☐ 7 Curt Warner.......................... | 1.50 | .60 | .15 |
| ☐ 8 John L. Williams.................... | 2.00 | .80 | .20 |
| ☐ 9 Edwin Bailey......................... | .60 | .24 | .06 |
| ☐ 10 Jacob Green........................ | 1.00 | .40 | .10 |
| ☐ 11 Paul Skansi......................... | .75 | .30 | .07 |
| ☐ 12 Jeff Bryant.......................... | .75 | .30 | .07 |
| ☐ 13 Bruce Scholtz...................... | .60 | .24 | .06 |
| ☐ 14 Dave Krieg.......................... | 2.00 | .80 | .20 |
| ☐ 15 Steve Largent...................... | 9.00 | 3.75 | .90 |
| ☐ 16 Joe Nash............................ | .75 | .30 | .07 |
| ☐ 17 Mike Wilson......................... | .60 | .24 | .06 |
| ☐ 18 Ron Mattes......................... | .60 | .24 | .06 |
| ☐ 19 Grant Feasel....................... | .60 | .24 | .06 |
| ☐ 20 Bryan Millard....................... | .60 | .24 | .06 |

## 1990 Seahawks Oroweat

This 50-card set of Seattle Seahawks was released in the Seattle area in various loaves of Oroweat products, Oat Nut, Health Nut, and Twelve Grain bread. The set was released in two series, 20 cards issued before the 1990 NFL season began and 30 cards released during the season. The fronts of the set feature full-color action shots within a silver border while the back of the card features a mix of statistical and biographical information. The cards each measure approximately 2 1/2" by 3 1/2" and were produced by Pacific Trading Cards for Oroweat.

|  | MINT | EXC | G-VG |
|---|---|---|---|
| COMPLETE SET (51)...................... | 30.00 | 12.00 | 3.00 |
| COMMON PLAYER (1-20)................ | .35 | .14 | .03 |
| COMMON PLAYER (21-50).............. | .50 | .20 | .05 |

|  | | | |
|---|---|---|---|
| ☐ 1 Dave Krieg........................... | 1.50 | .60 | .15 |
| ☐ 2 Rick Donnelly........................ | .35 | .14 | .03 |
| ☐ 3 Brian Blades......................... | 1.50 | .60 | .15 |
| ☐ 4 Cortez Kennedy..................... | 2.00 | .80 | .20 |
| ☐ 5 John L. Williams.................... | 2.00 | .80 | .20 |
| ☐ 6 Jeff Chadwick....................... | .50 | .20 | .05 |
| ☐ 7 Thom Kaumeyer..................... | .35 | .14 | .03 |
| ☐ 8 Bryan Millard........................ | .35 | .14 | .03 |
| ☐ 9 Eugene Robinson.................. | .50 | .20 | .05 |
| ☐ 10 Jacob Green........................ | .50 | .20 | .05 |
| ☐ 11 Willie Bouyer....................... | .35 | .14 | .03 |
| ☐ 12 Jeff Bryant.......................... | .50 | .20 | .05 |
| ☐ 13 Chris Warren....................... | 1.50 | .60 | .15 |
| ☐ 14 Derrick Fenner..................... | 1.00 | .40 | .10 |
| ☐ 15 Paul Skansi......................... | .50 | .20 | .05 |
| ☐ 16 Joe Cain............................. | .35 | .14 | .03 |
| ☐ 17 Tommy Kane........................ | .75 | .30 | .07 |
| ☐ 18 Tom Flores GM..................... | .50 | .20 | .05 |
| ☐ 19 Terry Wooden....................... | .50 | .20 | .05 |
| ☐ 20 Tony Woods......................... | .50 | .20 | .05 |
| ☐ 21 Ricky Andrews...................... | .50 | .20 | .05 |
| ☐ 22 Joe Tofflemire...................... | .50 | .20 | .05 |
| ☐ 23 Ned Bolcar......................... | .75 | .30 | .07 |
| ☐ 24A Kelly Stouffer..................... | 1.00 | .40 | .10 |
| ☐ 24B Melvin Jenkins.................... | .75 | .30 | .07 |
| ☐ 25 Does Not Exist..................... | .00 | .00 | .00 |
| ☐ 26 Norm Johnson...................... | .75 | .30 | .07 |
| ☐ 27 Eric Hayes.......................... | .50 | .20 | .05 |
| ☐ 28 Michael Morris...................... | .50 | .20 | .05 |
| ☐ 29 Edwin Bailey........................ | .50 | .20 | .05 |
| ☐ 30 Ron Heller........................... | .50 | .20 | .05 |
| ☐ 31 Darren Comeaux................... | .75 | .30 | .07 |
| ☐ 32 Andy Heck.......................... | .75 | .30 | .07 |
| ☐ 33 Ronnie Lee.......................... | .75 | .30 | .07 |
| ☐ 34 Robert Blackmon................... | .75 | .30 | .07 |
| ☐ 35 Joe Nash............................ | .75 | .30 | .07 |
| ☐ 36 Patrick Hunter...................... | .75 | .30 | .07 |
| ☐ 37 Darrick Brilz........................ | .50 | .20 | .05 |
| ☐ 38 Ron Mattes......................... | .50 | .20 | .05 |
| ☐ 39 Nesby Glasgow.................... | .75 | .30 | .07 |
| ☐ 40 Dwayne Harper..................... | .50 | .20 | .05 |
| ☐ 41 Chuck Knox CO.................... | .75 | .30 | .07 |
| ☐ 42 Travis McNeal...................... | .75 | .30 | .07 |
| ☐ 43 Derek Loville....................... | .50 | .20 | .05 |
| ☐ 44 Dave Wyman........................ | .50 | .20 | .05 |
| ☐ 45 Louis Clark.......................... | .50 | .20 | .05 |
| ☐ 46 Grant Feasel........................ | .50 | .20 | .05 |
| ☐ 47 James Jones....................... | .75 | .30 | .07 |
| ☐ 48 Rufus Porter........................ | 1.00 | .40 | .10 |
| ☐ 49 Jeff Kemp........................... | 1.00 | .40 | .10 |
| ☐ 50 James Jefferson................... | .75 | .30 | .07 |
| ☐ NNO Title Card......................... | 3.00 | 1.20 | .30 |

## 1991 Seahawks Oroweat

This 50-card set was sponsored by Oroweat and produced by Pacific. One card was included in every Oroweat loaf of bread throughout Washington, Oregon, and western portions of Idaho. Although cards were not sold in complete sets, five-card packs were given out at one of the Seahawks' games. The title cards were only available in the five-card packs. The fronts of these standard-size (2 1/2" by 3 1/2") cards feature glossy color action player photos, with the player's name written vertically in a purple stripe at the left side of the picture. The team name and position appear in a silver stripe below the picture. In a diagonal design, the horizontally oriented backs have biography, a color headshot of the player, statistics, and career summary. The cards are numbered on the back.

|  | MINT | EXC | G-VG |
|---|---|---|---|
| COMPLETE SET (51)...................... | 30.00 | 12.00 | 3.00 |
| COMMON PLAYER (1-50)................ | .50 | .20 | .05 |
| ☐ 1 Tommy Kane.......................... | 1.00 | .40 | .10 |
| ☐ 2 Norm Johnson....................... | .75 | .30 | .07 |

appear vertically in green lettering within a gray stripe on the left. The white-bordered horizontal back carries a color player close-up on the left and, alongside on the right, the player's name and position within a white strip near the top, followed below by biography, statistics, and career highlights within a green panel. The Oroweat and KIRO Newsradio logos on the back round out the card. The cards are numbered on the back.

|  | MINT | EXC | G-VG |
|---|---|---|---|
| COMPLETE SET (51) | 30.00 | 12.00 | 3.00 |
| COMMON PLAYER (1-50) | .50 | .20 | .05 |
| ☐ 1 Brian Blades | 1.00 | .40 | .10 |
| ☐ 2 Patrick Hunter | .75 | .30 | .07 |
| ☐ 3 Jeff Bryant | .50 | .20 | .05 |
| ☐ 4 Robert Blackmon | .50 | .20 | .05 |
| ☐ 5 Joe Cain | .50 | .20 | .05 |
| ☐ 6 Grant Feasel | .50 | .20 | .05 |
| ☐ 7 Dan McGwire | 1.00 | .40 | .10 |
| ☐ 8 David Wyman | .50 | .20 | .05 |
| ☐ 9 Jacob Green | .75 | .30 | .07 |
| ☐ 10 Theo Adams | .50 | .20 | .05 |
| ☐ 11 Brian Davis | .50 | .20 | .05 |
| ☐ 12 Andy Heck | .50 | .20 | .05 |
| ☐ 13 Bill Hitchcock | .50 | .20 | .05 |
| ☐ 14 Joe Nash | .50 | .20 | .05 |
| ☐ 15 Rod Stephens | .50 | .20 | .05 |
| ☐ 16 John Hunter | .50 | .20 | .05 |
| ☐ 17 Paul Green | .50 | .20 | .05 |
| ☐ 18 James Jones | .75 | .30 | .07 |
| ☐ 19 Robb Thomas | .75 | .30 | .07 |
| ☐ 20 Tony Woods | .75 | .30 | .07 |
| ☐ 21 Dedrick Dodge | .50 | .20 | .05 |
| ☐ 22 Tracy Johnson | .50 | .20 | .05 |
| ☐ 23 Darrick Brilz | .50 | .20 | .05 |
| ☐ 24 Joe Tofflemire | .50 | .20 | .05 |
| ☐ 25 Louis Clark | .50 | .20 | .05 |
| ☐ 26 Rueben Mayes | .75 | .30 | .07 |
| ☐ 27 Natu Tuatagaloa | .50 | .20 | .05 |
| ☐ 28 Terry Wooden | .75 | .30 | .07 |
| ☐ 29 Tommy Kane | .75 | .30 | .07 |
| ☐ 30 Stan Gelbaugh | .75 | .30 | .07 |
| ☐ 31 Nesby Glasgow | .50 | .20 | .05 |
| ☐ 32 Kelly Stouffer | .75 | .30 | .07 |
| ☐ 33 Ray Roberts | .75 | .30 | .07 |
| ☐ 34 Doug Thomas | .75 | .30 | .07 |
| ☐ 35 David Daniels | .75 | .30 | .07 |
| ☐ 36 John Kasay | .75 | .30 | .07 |
| ☐ 37 Cortez Kennedy | 1.50 | .60 | .15 |
| ☐ 38 Tyrone Rodgers | .50 | .20 | .05 |
| ☐ 39 Bryan Millard | .50 | .20 | .05 |
| ☐ 40 Eugene Robinson | .75 | .30 | .07 |
| ☐ 41 Malcolm Frank | .50 | .20 | .05 |
| ☐ 42 Dwayne Harper | .50 | .20 | .05 |
| ☐ 43 Ron Heller | .50 | .20 | .05 |
| ☐ 44 Rick Tuten | .50 | .20 | .05 |
| ☐ 45 Trey Junkin | .50 | .20 | .05 |
| ☐ 46 Bob Spitulski | .50 | .20 | .05 |
| ☐ 47 Chris Warren | 1.50 | .60 | .15 |
| ☐ 48 John L. Williams | 1.00 | .40 | .10 |
| ☐ 49 Ronnie Lee | .50 | .20 | .05 |
| ☐ 50 Rufus Porter | .75 | .30 | .07 |
| ☐ NNO Title/ad card | 1.00 | .40 | .10 |

| ☐ 3 Robert Blackmon | .75 | .30 | .07 |
|---|---|---|---|
| ☐ 4 Mike Tice | .75 | .30 | .07 |
| ☐ 5 Cortez Kennedy | 1.50 | .60 | .15 |
| ☐ 6 Bryan Millard | .50 | .20 | .05 |
| ☐ 7 Tony Woods | .75 | .30 | .07 |
| ☐ 8 Paul Skansi | .75 | .30 | .07 |
| ☐ 9 John L. Williams | 1.50 | .60 | .15 |
| ☐ 10 Terry Wooden | .75 | .30 | .07 |
| ☐ 11 Brian Blades | 1.50 | .60 | .15 |
| ☐ 12 Jacob Green | .75 | .30 | .07 |
| ☐ 13 Joe Nash | .75 | .30 | .07 |
| ☐ 14 Eugene Robinson | .75 | .30 | .07 |
| ☐ 15 Rufus Porter | .75 | .30 | .07 |
| ☐ 16 Andy Heck | .75 | .30 | .07 |
| ☐ 17 Derrick Fenner | 1.00 | .40 | .10 |
| ☐ 18 Nesby Glasgow | .75 | .30 | .07 |
| ☐ 19 Chris Warren | 1.25 | .50 | .12 |
| ☐ 20 Dave Krieg | 1.25 | .50 | .12 |
| ☐ 21 Vann McElroy | .75 | .30 | .07 |
| ☐ 22 Jeff Bryant | .75 | .30 | .07 |
| ☐ 23 Warren Wheat | .50 | .20 | .05 |
| ☐ 24 Marcus Cotton | .50 | .20 | .05 |
| ☐ 25 David Wyman | .50 | .20 | .05 |
| ☐ 26 Joe Cain | .50 | .20 | .05 |
| ☐ 27 Darrick Brilz | .50 | .20 | .05 |
| ☐ 28 Eric Hayes | .50 | .20 | .05 |
| ☐ 29 Ronnie Lee | .75 | .30 | .07 |
| ☐ 30 Louis Clark | .50 | .20 | .05 |
| ☐ 31 James Jones | .75 | .30 | .07 |
| ☐ 32 Dwayne Harper | .50 | .20 | .05 |
| ☐ 33 Grant Feasel | .50 | .20 | .05 |
| ☐ 34 Trey Junkin | .50 | .20 | .05 |
| ☐ 35 James Jefferson | .75 | .30 | .07 |
| ☐ 36 Edwin Bailey | .50 | .20 | .05 |
| ☐ 37 Derek Loville | .50 | .20 | .05 |
| ☐ 38 Travis McNeal | .75 | .30 | .07 |
| ☐ 39 Rick Donnelly | .50 | .20 | .05 |
| ☐ 40 Rod Stephens | .50 | .20 | .05 |
| ☐ 41 Darren Comeaux | .75 | .30 | .07 |
| ☐ 42 Brian Davis | .50 | .20 | .05 |
| ☐ 43 Bill Hitchcock | .50 | .20 | .05 |
| ☐ 44 Jeff Chadwick | .75 | .30 | .07 |
| ☐ 45 Patrick Hunter | .75 | .30 | .07 |
| ☐ 46 David Daniels | .75 | .30 | .07 |
| ☐ 47 Doug Thomas | .50 | .20 | .05 |
| ☐ 48 Dan McGwire | 1.00 | .40 | .10 |
| ☐ 49 John Kasay | .75 | .30 | .07 |
| ☐ 50 Jeff Kemp | .75 | .30 | .07 |
| ☐ NNO Title Card | 3.00 | 1.20 | .30 |

## 1992 Seahawks Oroweat

Inserted one card per Oroweat bread loaf, these 50 cards measure the standard size (2 1/2" by 3 1/2") and feature on their fronts white-bordered color player action shots. The player's name and position

## 1993 Seahawks Oroweat

Produced by Pacific, this 50-card standard-size (2 1/2" by 3 1/2") set was co-sponsored by Oroweat and KIRO News 710 AM. One card was included in each Oroweat loaf of bread throughout Washington, Oregon, and western portions of Idaho. Moreover, cello packs containing three player cards and one ad card were given away at home games. The fronts feature color action player photos that are tilted slightly to the left and set on a team color-coded gray and blue marbleized card face. The team helmet appears at the lower left corner, and the player's name and position are printed across the bottom of the picture. On a marbleized gray and blue background, the backs carry a second color player photo, biography, statistics, and player profile. The cards are numbered on the back.

| | MINT | EXC | G-VG |
|---|---|---|---|
| COMPLETE SET (50) | 25.00 | 10.00 | 2.50 |
| COMMON PLAYER (1-50) | .50 | .20 | .05 |
| ☐ 1 Cortez Kennedy | 1.50 | .60 | .15 |
| ☐ 2 Robb Thomas | .50 | .20 | .05 |
| ☐ 3 Rueben Mayes | .75 | .30 | .07 |
| ☐ 4 Rick Tuten | .50 | .20 | .05 |
| ☐ 5 Tracy Johnson | .50 | .20 | .05 |
| ☐ 6 Michael Bates | .75 | .30 | .07 |
| ☐ 7 Andy Heck | .50 | .20 | .05 |
| ☐ 8 Stan Gelbaugh | .75 | .30 | .07 |
| ☐ 9 Dan McGwire | 1.00 | .40 | .10 |
| ☐ 10 Mike Keim | .50 | .20 | .05 |
| ☐ 11 Grant Feasel | .50 | .20 | .05 |
| ☐ 12 Brian Blades | 1.00 | .40 | .10 |
| ☐ 13 Tyrone Rodgers | .50 | .20 | .05 |
| ☐ 14 Paul Green | .50 | .20 | .05 |
| ☐ 15 Rafael Robinson | .50 | .20 | .05 |
| ☐ 16 John Kasay | .75 | .30 | .07 |
| ☐ 17 Chris Warren | 1.50 | .60 | .15 |
| ☐ 18 Michael Sinclair | .50 | .20 | .05 |
| ☐ 19 John L. Williams | 1.00 | .40 | .10 |
| ☐ 20 Bob Spitulski | .50 | .20 | .05 |
| ☐ 21 Eugene Robinson | .75 | .30 | .07 |
| ☐ 22 Patrick Hunter | .75 | .30 | .07 |
| ☐ 23 Kevin Murphy | .75 | .30 | .07 |
| ☐ 24 Dave McCloughan | .50 | .20 | .05 |
| ☐ 25 Rick Mirer | 5.00 | 2.00 | .50 |
| ☐ 26 Ray Donaldson | .50 | .20 | .05 |
| ☐ 27 E.J. Junior | .75 | .30 | .07 |
| ☐ 28 Jeff Bryant | .75 | .30 | .07 |
| ☐ 29 Ferrell Edmunds | .75 | .30 | .07 |
| ☐ 30 Tommy Kane | .75 | .30 | .07 |
| ☐ 31 Terry Wooden | .75 | .30 | .07 |
| ☐ 32 Doug Thomas | .50 | .20 | .05 |
| ☐ 33 Carlton Gray | .50 | .20 | .05 |
| ☐ 34 Kelvin Martin | .75 | .30 | .07 |
| ☐ 35 Rod Stephens | .50 | .20 | .05 |
| ☐ 36 Darrick Brilz | .50 | .20 | .05 |
| ☐ 37 Joe Tofflemire | .50 | .20 | .05 |
| ☐ 38 James Jefferson | .50 | .20 | .05 |
| ☐ 39 Rufus Porter | .75 | .30 | .07 |
| ☐ 40 Jeff Blackshear | .50 | .20 | .05 |
| ☐ 41 Dwayne Harper | .50 | .20 | .05 |
| ☐ 42 Ray Roberts | .75 | .30 | .07 |
| ☐ 43 Robert Blackmon | .75 | .30 | .07 |
| ☐ 44 Joe Nash | .50 | .20 | .05 |
| ☐ 45 Michael McCrary | .50 | .20 | .05 |
| ☐ 46 Trey Junkin | .50 | .20 | .05 |
| ☐ 47 Natu Tuataagaloa | .50 | .20 | .05 |
| ☐ 48 Bill Hitchcock | .50 | .20 | .05 |
| ☐ 49 Jon Vaughn | 1.00 | .40 | .10 |
| ☐ 50 Dean Wells | .50 | .20 | .05 |

## 1982 Sears-Roebuck

These oversized 5" by 7" cards feature player photos on fronts. Reportedly these cards were issued in Sears 37 District Stores from January to December 1982. Reportedly because of the football players' strike, the promotion flopped, and consequently many cards were destroyed or thrown out. These cards look almost exactly like the Marketcom cards but say Sears Roebuck at the bottom of the reverse. These unnumbered cards are checklisted below in alphabetical order.

| | MINT | EXC | G-VG |
|---|---|---|---|
| COMPLETE SET (11) | 200.00 | 80.00 | 20.00 |
| COMMON CARD (1-11) | 8.00 | 3.25 | .80 |
| ☐ 1 Ken Anderson | 12.50 | 5.00 | 1.25 |
| Cincinnati Bengals | | | |
| ☐ 2 Terry Bradshaw | 25.00 | 10.00 | 2.50 |
| Pittsburgh Steelers | | | |
| ☐ 3 Earl Campbell | 30.00 | 12.00 | 3.00 |
| Houston Oilers | | | |
| ☐ 4 Dwight Clark | 8.00 | 3.25 | .80 |
| San Francisco 49ers | | | |
| ☐ 5 Cris Collinsworth | 8.00 | 3.25 | .80 |
| Cincinnati Bengals | | | |
| ☐ 6 Tony Dorsett | 20.00 | 8.00 | 2.00 |
| Dallas Cowboys | | | |
| ☐ 7 Dan Fouts | 15.00 | 6.00 | 1.50 |
| San Diego Chargers | | | |
| ☐ 8 Franco Harris | 20.00 | 8.00 | 2.00 |
| Pittsburgh Steelers | | | |
| ☐ 9 Joe Montana | 60.00 | 24.00 | 6.00 |
| San Francisco 49ers | | | |
| ☐ 10 Walter Payton | 30.00 | 12.00 | 3.00 |
| Chicago Bears | | | |
| ☐ 11 Kellen Winslow | 8.00 | 3.25 | .80 |
| San Diego Chargers | | | |

## 1993 Select

Available only through hobby dealers, the 1993 Select football set consists of 200 standard-size (2 1/2" by 3 1/2") cards. Production was reportedly limited to 2,950 cases. Randomly inserted throughout the foil packs was a ten-card "Gridiron Skills" subset featuring five quarterbacks and five wide receivers. The insert rate of these chase cards is reportedly one in every two boxes. Outstanding Rookies are showcased in a Rookie (166-185) subset. The cards feature color player action shots on their fronts. These photos are borderless on the top and one side. On the other side and bottom are oblique red and black borders set off by gold foil lines. The player's name appears in gold foil at a lower corner. The red and black back carries another irregularly shaped color player action shot in its upper right, with career highlights appearing alongside. Career and 1992 statistics follow below. The cards are numbered on the back. Rookie Cards include Jerome Bettis, Drew Bledsoe, Garrison Hearst, Natrone Means, Glyn Milburn and Rick Mirer.

| | MINT | EXC | G-VG |
|---|---|---|---|
| COMPLETE SET (200) | 60.00 | 27.00 | 7.50 |
| COMMON PLAYER (1-200) | .20 | .09 | .03 |
| ☐ 1 Steve Young | 1.00 | .45 | .13 |
| San Francisco 49ers | | | |
| ☐ 2 Andre Reed | .30 | .14 | .04 |
| Buffalo Bills | | | |
| ☐ 3 Deion Sanders | .50 | .23 | .06 |
| Atlanta Falcons | | | |
| ☐ 4 Harold Green | .25 | .11 | .03 |
| Cincinnati Bengals | | | |
| ☐ 5 Wendell Davis | .20 | .09 | .03 |
| Chicago Bears | | | |
| ☐ 6 Mike Johnson | .20 | .09 | .03 |
| Cleveland Browns | | | |
| ☐ 7 Troy Aikman | 7.00 | 3.10 | .85 |
| Dallas Cowboys | | | |
| ☐ 8 Johnny Mitchell | .75 | .35 | .09 |
| New York Jets | | | |
| ☐ 9 Dale Carter | .30 | .14 | .04 |
| Kansas City Chiefs | | | |
| ☐ 10 Bruce Matthews | .25 | .11 | .03 |
| Houston Oilers | | | |
| ☐ 11 Terrell Buckley | .30 | .14 | .04 |
| Green Bay Packers | | | |

| | | | |
|---|---|---|---|
| ☐ 12 Steve Emtman | .25 | .11 | .03 |
| Indianapolis Colts | | | |
| ☐ 13 Neil Smith | .30 | .14 | .04 |
| Kansas City Chiefs | | | |
| ☐ 14 Tim Brown | .60 | .25 | .08 |
| Los Angeles Raiders | | | |
| ☐ 15 Chris Doleman | .25 | .11 | .03 |
| Minnesota Vikings | | | |
| ☐ 16 Dan Marino | 4.00 | 1.80 | .50 |
| Miami Dolphins | | | |
| ☐ 17 Terry McDaniel | .20 | .09 | .03 |
| Los Angeles Raiders | | | |
| ☐ 18 Neal Anderson | .25 | .11 | .03 |
| Chicago Bears | | | |
| ☐ 19 Phil Simms | .30 | .14 | .04 |
| New York Giants | | | |
| ☐ 20 Jeff Lageman | .20 | .09 | .03 |
| New York Jets | | | |
| ☐ 21 Jerry Rice | 3.00 | 1.35 | .40 |
| San Francisco 49ers | | | |
| ☐ 22 Dermontti Dawson | .20 | .09 | .03 |
| Pittsburgh Steelers | | | |
| ☐ 23 Reggie Cobb | .30 | .14 | .04 |
| Tampa Bay Buccaneers | | | |
| ☐ 24 Junior Seau | .30 | .14 | .04 |
| San Diego Chargers | | | |
| ☐ 25 Darrell Green | .25 | .11 | .03 |
| Washington Redskins | | | |
| ☐ 26 Chris Warren | .50 | .23 | .06 |
| Seattle Seahawks | | | |
| ☐ 27 Randall Cunningham | .35 | .16 | .04 |
| Philadelphia Eagles | | | |
| ☐ 28 Bruce Smith | .30 | .14 | .04 |
| Buffalo Bills | | | |
| ☐ 29 Bryan Cox | .25 | .11 | .03 |
| Miami Dolphins | | | |
| ☐ 30 David Klingler | .60 | .25 | .08 |
| Cincinnati Bengals | | | |
| ☐ 31 Chip Lohmiller | .20 | .09 | .03 |
| Washington Redskins | | | |
| ☐ 32 Eric Metcalf | .30 | .14 | .04 |
| Cleveland Browns | | | |
| ☐ 33 Ken Norton Jr. | .25 | .11 | .03 |
| Dallas Cowboys | | | |
| ☐ 34 John Elway | 2.00 | .90 | .25 |
| Denver Broncos | | | |
| ☐ 35 Harris Barton | .20 | .09 | .03 |
| San Francisco 49ers | | | |
| ☐ 36 Tim Barnett | .25 | .11 | .03 |
| Kansas City Chiefs | | | |
| ☐ 37 Rodney Hampton | 1.00 | .45 | .13 |
| New York Giants | | | |
| ☐ 38 Desmond Howard | .60 | .25 | .08 |
| Washington Redskins | | | |
| ☐ 39 Tom Rathman | .25 | .11 | .03 |
| San Francisco 49ers | | | |
| ☐ 40 Derrick Thomas | .50 | .23 | .06 |
| Kansas City Chiefs | | | |
| ☐ 41 Randal Hill | .30 | .14 | .04 |
| Phoenix Cardinals | | | |
| ☐ 42 Steve Wisniewski | .20 | .09 | .03 |
| Los Angeles Raiders | | | |
| ☐ 43 Brett Favre | 3.00 | 1.35 | .40 |
| Green Bay Packers | | | |
| ☐ 44 Darryl Talley | .20 | .09 | .03 |
| Buffalo Bills | | | |
| ☐ 45 Shane Conlan | .20 | .09 | .03 |
| Los Angeles Rams | | | |
| ☐ 46 Anthony Miller | .60 | .25 | .08 |
| San Diego Chargers | | | |
| ☐ 47 Randall McDaniel | .20 | .09 | .03 |
| Minnesota Vikings | | | |
| ☐ 48 Rod Woodson | .30 | .14 | .04 |
| Pittsburgh Steelers | | | |
| ☐ 49 Eric Martin | .25 | .11 | .03 |
| New Orleans Saints | | | |
| ☐ 50 Ronnie Lott | .30 | .14 | .04 |
| New York Jets | | | |
| ☐ 51 Chris Spielman | .20 | .09 | .03 |
| Detroit Lions | | | |
| ☐ 52 Vincent Brown | .20 | .09 | .03 |
| New England Patriots | | | |
| ☐ 53 Donnell Woolford | .20 | .09 | .03 |
| Chicago Bears | | | |
| ☐ 54 Richmond Webb | .20 | .09 | .03 |
| Miami Dolphins | | | |
| ☐ 55 Emmittt Smith | 9.00 | 4.00 | 1.15 |
| Dallas Cowboys | | | |
| ☐ 56 Haywood Jeffires | .30 | .14 | .04 |
| Houston Oilers | | | |
| ☐ 57 Jim Kelly | 1.00 | .45 | .13 |
| Buffalo Bills | | | |
| ☐ 58 James Francis | .20 | .09 | .03 |
| Cincinnati Bengals | | | |
| ☐ 59 Steve Wallace | .20 | .09 | .03 |
| San Francisco 49ers | | | |
| ☐ 60 Jarrod Bunch | .20 | | |

| | | | |
|---|---|---|---|
| New York Giants | | | |
| ☐ 61 Lawrence Dawsey | .30 | .14 | .04 |
| Tampa Bay Buccaneers | | | |
| ☐ 62 Steve Atwater | .25 | .11 | .03 |
| Denver Broncos | | | |
| ☐ 63 Art Monk | .30 | .14 | .04 |
| Washington Redskins | | | |
| ☐ 64 Eric Green | .30 | .14 | .04 |
| Pittsburgh Steelers | | | |
| ☐ 65 Lawrence Taylor | .40 | .18 | .05 |
| New York Giants | | | |
| ☐ 66 Ronnie Harmon | .20 | .09 | .03 |
| San Diego Chargers | | | |
| ☐ 67 Fred Barnett | .30 | .14 | .04 |
| Philadelphia Eagles | | | |
| ☐ 68 Cortez Kennedy | .30 | .14 | .04 |
| Seattle Seahawks | | | |
| ☐ 69 Mark Collins | .20 | .09 | .03 |
| New York Giants | | | |
| ☐ 70 Howie Long | .25 | .11 | .03 |
| Los Angeles Raiders | | | |
| ☐ 71 Jackie Harris | .75 | .35 | .09 |
| Green Bay Packers | | | |
| ☐ 72 Irving Fryar | .20 | .09 | .03 |
| Miami Dolphins | | | |
| ☐ 73 Jim Everett | .20 | .09 | .03 |
| Los Angeles Rams | | | |
| ☐ 74 Troy Vincent | .25 | .11 | .03 |
| Miami Dolphins | | | |
| ☐ 75 Cris Carter | .30 | .14 | .04 |
| Minnesota Vikings | | | |
| ☐ 76 Boomer Esiason | .35 | .16 | .04 |
| New York Jets | | | |
| ☐ 77 Sam Mills | .25 | .11 | .03 |
| New Orleans Saints | | | |
| ☐ 78 Lorenzo White | .25 | .11 | .03 |
| Houston Oilers | | | |
| ☐ 79 Andre Rison | .60 | .25 | .08 |
| Atlanta Falcons | | | |
| ☐ 80 Quentin Coryatt | .30 | .14 | .04 |
| Indianapolis Colts | | | |
| ☐ 81 Steve McMichael | .20 | .09 | .03 |
| Chicago Bears | | | |
| ☐ 82 Nick Lowery | .20 | .09 | .03 |
| Kansas City Chiefs | | | |
| ☐ 83 Michael Irvin | 2.25 | 1.00 | .30 |
| Dallas Cowboys | | | |
| ☐ 84 Thurman Thomas | 1.50 | .65 | .19 |
| Buffalo Bills | | | |
| ☐ 85 Bill Romanowski | .20 | .09 | .03 |
| San Francisco 49ers | | | |
| ☐ 86 Carl Pickens | .25 | .11 | .03 |
| Cincinnati Bengals | | | |
| ☐ 87 Tim McDonald | .20 | .09 | .03 |
| San Francisco 49ers | | | |
| ☐ 88 Bernie Kosar | .30 | .14 | .04 |
| Cleveland Browns | | | |
| ☐ 89 Greg Lloyd | .20 | .09 | .03 |
| Pittsburgh Steelers | | | |
| ☐ 90 Barry Sanders | 3.50 | 1.55 | .45 |
| Detroit Lions | | | |
| ☐ 91 Shannon Sharpe | .75 | .35 | .09 |
| Denver Broncos | | | |
| ☐ 92 Henry Thomas | .20 | .09 | .03 |
| Minnesota Vikings | | | |
| ☐ 93 Barry Foster | 1.00 | .45 | .13 |
| Pittsburgh Steelers | | | |
| ☐ 94 Antone Davis | .20 | .09 | .03 |
| Philadelphia Eagles | | | |
| ☐ 95 Stan Humphries | .30 | .14 | .04 |
| San Diego Chargers | | | |
| ☐ 96 Eric Swann | .25 | .11 | .03 |
| Phoenix Cardinals | | | |
| ☐ 97 Mike Pritchard | .30 | .14 | .04 |
| Atlanta Falcons | | | |
| ☐ 98 Reggie White | .50 | .23 | .06 |
| Green Bay Packers | | | |
| ☐ 99 Jeff Hostetler | .30 | .14 | .04 |
| Los Angeles Raiders | | | |
| ☐ 100 Flipper Anderson | .25 | .11 | .03 |
| Los Angeles Rams | | | |
| ☐ 101 Gary Clark | .25 | .11 | .03 |
| Phoenix Cardinals | | | |
| ☐ 102 Morten Andersen | .25 | .11 | .03 |
| New Orleans Saints | | | |
| ☐ 103 Leonard Russell | .25 | .11 | .03 |
| New England Patriots | | | |
| ☐ 104 Chris Hinton | .20 | .09 | .03 |
| Atlanta Falcons | | | |
| ☐ 105 John Stephens | .20 | .09 | .03 |
| Green Bay Packers | | | |
| ☐ 106 Byron Evans | .20 | .09 | .03 |
| Philadelphia Eagles | | | |
| ☐ 107 Warren Moon | .50 | .23 | .06 |
| Houston Oilers | | | |
| ☐ 108 Marv Cook | .20 | .09 | .03 |
| New England Patriots | | | |
| ☐ 109 Carlton Gray | .50 | .23 | .06 |

Seattle Seahawks

| | | | | |
|---|---|---|---|---|
| ☐ 110 | Jay Novacek | .30 | .14 | .04 |

Dallas Cowboys

| | | | | |
|---|---|---|---|---|
| ☐ 111 | Gary Anderson | .20 | .09 | .03 |

Pittsburgh Steelers

| | | | | |
|---|---|---|---|---|
| ☐ 112 | Andre Tippett | .20 | .09 | .03 |

New England Patriots

| | | | | |
|---|---|---|---|---|
| ☐ 113 | Cornelius Bennett | .30 | .14 | .04 |

Buffalo Bills

| | | | | |
|---|---|---|---|---|
| ☐ 114 | Clyde Simmons | .25 | .11 | .03 |

Philadelphia Eagles

| | | | | |
|---|---|---|---|---|
| ☐ 115 | Jeff George | .60 | .25 | .08 |

Indianapolis Colts

| | | | | |
|---|---|---|---|---|
| ☐ 116 | Audray McMillian | .20 | .09 | .03 |

Minnesota Vikings

| | | | | |
|---|---|---|---|---|
| ☐ 117 | Mark Carrier | .25 | .11 | .03 |

Cleveland Browns

| | | | | |
|---|---|---|---|---|
| ☐ 118 | Vaughan Johnson | .20 | .09 | .03 |

New Orleans Saints

| | | | | |
|---|---|---|---|---|
| ☐ 119 | Kevin Greene | .20 | .09 | .03 |

Pittsburgh Steelers

| | | | | |
|---|---|---|---|---|
| ☐ 120 | John Taylor | .30 | .14 | .04 |

San Francisco 49ers

| | | | | |
|---|---|---|---|---|
| ☐ 121 | Jerry Ball | .20 | .09 | .03 |

Cleveland Browns

| | | | | |
|---|---|---|---|---|
| ☐ 122 | Pat Swilling | .25 | .11 | .03 |

Detroit Lions

| | | | | |
|---|---|---|---|---|
| ☐ 123 | George Teague | .50 | .23 | .06 |

Green Bay Packers

| | | | | |
|---|---|---|---|---|
| ☐ 124 | Ricky Reynolds | .20 | .09 | .03 |

Tampa Bay Buccaneers

| | | | | |
|---|---|---|---|---|
| ☐ 125 | Marcus Allen | .25 | .11 | .03 |

Kansas City Chiefs

| | | | | |
|---|---|---|---|---|
| ☐ 126 | Henry Jones | .20 | .09 | .03 |

Buffalo Bills

| | | | | |
|---|---|---|---|---|
| ☐ 127 | Ricky Watters | 1.25 | .55 | .16 |

San Francisco 49ers

| | | | | |
|---|---|---|---|---|
| ☐ 128 | Leon Searcy | .20 | .09 | .03 |

Pittsburgh Steelers

| | | | | |
|---|---|---|---|---|
| ☐ 129 | Chris Miller | .30 | .14 | .04 |

Atlanta Falcons

| | | | | |
|---|---|---|---|---|
| ☐ 130 | Jim Harbaugh | .25 | .11 | .03 |

Chicago Bears

| | | | | |
|---|---|---|---|---|
| ☐ 131 | Luis Sharpe | .20 | .09 | .03 |

Phoenix Cardinals

| | | | | |
|---|---|---|---|---|
| ☐ 132 | Simon Fletcher | .25 | .11 | .03 |

Denver Broncos

| | | | | |
|---|---|---|---|---|
| ☐ 133 | Eric Allen | .25 | .11 | .03 |

Philadelphia Eagles

| | | | | |
|---|---|---|---|---|
| ☐ 134 | Carlton Haselrig | .20 | .09 | .03 |

Pittsburgh Steelers

| | | | | |
|---|---|---|---|---|
| ☐ 135 | Harvey Williams | .40 | .18 | .05 |

Kansas City Chiefs

| | | | | |
|---|---|---|---|---|
| ☐ 136 | Leslie O'Neal | .25 | .11 | .03 |

San Diego Chargers

| | | | | |
|---|---|---|---|---|
| ☐ 137 | Sterling Sharpe | 2.25 | 1.00 | .30 |

Green Bay Packers

| | | | | |
|---|---|---|---|---|
| ☐ 138 | Tim Harris | .20 | .09 | .03 |

Philadelphia Eagles

| | | | | |
|---|---|---|---|---|
| ☐ 139 | Mark Rypien | .25 | .11 | .03 |

Washington Redskins

| | | | | |
|---|---|---|---|---|
| ☐ 140 | Harry Galbreath | .20 | .09 | .03 |

Green Bay Packers

| | | | | |
|---|---|---|---|---|
| ☐ 141 | Sean Gilbert | .25 | .11 | .03 |

Los Angeles Rams

| | | | | |
|---|---|---|---|---|
| ☐ 142 | Keith Jackson | .30 | .14 | .04 |

Miami Dolphins

| | | | | |
|---|---|---|---|---|
| ☐ 143 | Mark Clayton | .20 | .09 | .03 |

Green Bay Packers

| | | | | |
|---|---|---|---|---|
| ☐ 144 | Guy McIntyre | .20 | .09 | .03 |

San Francisco 49ers

| | | | | |
|---|---|---|---|---|
| ☐ 145 | Jessie Tuggle | .20 | .09 | .03 |

Atlanta Falcons

| | | | | |
|---|---|---|---|---|
| ☐ 146 | Leonard Marshall | .20 | .09 | .03 |

New York Jets

| | | | | |
|---|---|---|---|---|
| ☐ 147 | Willie Davis | .40 | .18 | .05 |

Kansas City Chiefs

| | | | | |
|---|---|---|---|---|
| ☐ 148 | Herman Moore | 1.00 | .45 | .13 |

Detroit Lions

| | | | | |
|---|---|---|---|---|
| ☐ 149 | Charles Haley | .25 | .11 | .03 |

Dallas Cowboys

| | | | | |
|---|---|---|---|---|
| ☐ 150 | Amp Lee | .25 | .11 | .03 |

San Francisco 49ers

| | | | | |
|---|---|---|---|---|
| ☐ 151 | Gary Zimmerman | .20 | .09 | .03 |

Denver Broncos

| | | | | |
|---|---|---|---|---|
| ☐ 152 | Bennie Blades | .20 | .09 | .03 |

Detroit Lions

| | | | | |
|---|---|---|---|---|
| ☐ 153 | Pierce Holt | .20 | .09 | .03 |

Atlanta Falcons

| | | | | |
|---|---|---|---|---|
| ☐ 154 | Edgar Bennett | .25 | .11 | .03 |

Green Bay Packers

| | | | | |
|---|---|---|---|---|
| ☐ 155 | Joe Montana | 6.00 | 2.70 | .75 |

Kansas City Chiefs

| | | | | |
|---|---|---|---|---|
| ☐ 156 | Ted Washington | .20 | .09 | .03 |

San Francisco 49ers

| | | | | |
|---|---|---|---|---|
| ☐ 157 | Hardy Nickerson | .20 | .09 | .03 |

Tampa Bay Buccaneers

| | | | | |
|---|---|---|---|---|
| ☐ 158 | Rohn Stark | .20 | .09 | .03 |

Indianapolis Colts

| | | | | |
|---|---|---|---|---|
| ☐ 159 | Brent Jones | .30 | .14 | .04 |

San Francisco 49ers

| | | | | |
|---|---|---|---|---|
| ☐ 160 | Eugene Robinson | .20 | .09 | .03 |

Seattle Seahawks

| | | | | |
|---|---|---|---|---|
| ☐ 161 | Pepper Johnson | .20 | .09 | .03 |

Cleveland Browns

| | | | | |
|---|---|---|---|---|
| ☐ 162 | Dan Saleaumua | .20 | .09 | .03 |

Kansas City Chiefs

| | | | | |
|---|---|---|---|---|
| ☐ 163 | Seth Joyner | .25 | .11 | .03 |

Philadelphia Eagles

| | | | | |
|---|---|---|---|---|
| ☐ 164 | Bruce Armstrong | .20 | .09 | .03 |

New England Patriots

| | | | | |
|---|---|---|---|---|
| ☐ 165 | Mike Munchak | .25 | .11 | .03 |

Houston Oilers

| | | | | |
|---|---|---|---|---|
| ☐ 166 | Drew Bledsoe | 12.00 | 5.50 | 1.50 |

New England Patriots

| | | | | |
|---|---|---|---|---|
| ☐ 167 | Curtis Conway | 1.50 | .65 | .19 |

Chicago Bears

| | | | | |
|---|---|---|---|---|
| ☐ 168 | Lincoln Kennedy | .50 | .23 | .06 |

Atlanta Falcons

| | | | | |
|---|---|---|---|---|
| ☐ 169 | Dana Stubblefield | 1.50 | .65 | .19 |

San Francisco 49ers

| | | | | |
|---|---|---|---|---|
| ☐ 170 | Wayne Simmons | .35 | .16 | .04 |

Green Bay Packers

| | | | | |
|---|---|---|---|---|
| ☐ 171 | Garrison Hearst | 2.25 | 1.00 | .30 |

Phoenix Cardinals

| | | | | |
|---|---|---|---|---|
| ☐ 172 | Troy Brown | 12.00 | 5.50 | 1.50 |

Los Angeles Rams

| | | | | |
|---|---|---|---|---|
| ☐ 173 | Eric Curry | .75 | .35 | .09 |

Tampa Bay Buccaneers

| | | | | |
|---|---|---|---|---|
| ☐ 174 | Natrone Means | 3.00 | 1.35 | .40 |

San Diego Chargers

| | | | | |
|---|---|---|---|---|
| ☐ 175 | Glyn Milburn | 2.50 | 1.15 | .30 |

Denver Broncos

| | | | | |
|---|---|---|---|---|
| ☐ 176 | Marvin Jones | .60 | .25 | .08 |

New York Jets

| | | | | |
|---|---|---|---|---|
| ☐ 177 | O.J. McDuffie | 4.00 | 1.80 | .50 |

Miami Dolphins

| | | | | |
|---|---|---|---|---|
| ☐ 178 | Dan Williams | .40 | .18 | .05 |

Denver Broncos

| | | | | |
|---|---|---|---|---|
| ☐ 179 | Rick Mirer | 12.00 | 5.50 | 1.50 |

Seattle Seahawks

| | | | | |
|---|---|---|---|---|
| ☐ 180 | John Copeland | .75 | .35 | .09 |

Cleveland Browns

| | | | | |
|---|---|---|---|---|
| ☐ 181 | Willie Roaf | .35 | .16 | .04 |

New Orleans Saints

| | | | | |
|---|---|---|---|---|
| ☐ 182 | Patrick Bates | .35 | .16 | .04 |

Los Angeles Raiders

| | | | | |
|---|---|---|---|---|
| ☐ 183 | Troy Drayton | .75 | .35 | .09 |

Los Angeles Rams

| | | | | |
|---|---|---|---|---|
| ☐ 184 | Vincent Brisby | 2.00 | .90 | .25 |

New England Patriots

| | | | | |
|---|---|---|---|---|
| ☐ 185 | Irv Smith | .75 | .35 | .09 |

New Orleans Saints

| | | | | |
|---|---|---|---|---|
| ☐ 186 | Marion Butts | .30 | .14 | .04 |

San Diego Chargers

| | | | | |
|---|---|---|---|---|
| ☐ 187 | Wayne Martin | .20 | .09 | .03 |

New Orleans Saints

| | | | | |
|---|---|---|---|---|
| ☐ 188 | Brian Blades | .25 | .11 | .03 |

Seattle Seahawks

| | | | | |
|---|---|---|---|---|
| ☐ 189 | Mel Gray | .20 | .09 | .03 |

Detroit Lions

| | | | | |
|---|---|---|---|---|
| ☐ 190 | Mark Stepnoski | .20 | .09 | .03 |

Dallas Cowboys

| | | | | |
|---|---|---|---|---|
| ☐ 191 | Ernest Givins | .25 | .11 | .03 |

Houston Oilers

| | | | | |
|---|---|---|---|---|
| ☐ 192 | Steve Tasker | .20 | .09 | .03 |

Buffalo Bills

| | | | | |
|---|---|---|---|---|
| ☐ 193 | Tim Grunhard | .20 | .09 | .03 |

Kansas City Chiefs

| | | | | |
|---|---|---|---|---|
| ☐ 194 | Stanley Richard | .20 | .09 | .03 |

San Diego Chargers

| | | | | |
|---|---|---|---|---|
| ☐ 195 | Jeff Wright | .20 | .09 | .03 |

Buffalo Bills

| | | | | |
|---|---|---|---|---|
| ☐ 196 | Rodney Peete | .25 | .11 | .03 |

Detroit Lions

| | | | | |
|---|---|---|---|---|
| ☐ 197 | Tunch Ilkin | .20 | .09 | .03 |

Green Bay Packers

| | | | | |
|---|---|---|---|---|
| ☐ 198 | Rich Camarillo | .20 | .09 | .03 |

Phoenix Cardinals

| | | | | |
|---|---|---|---|---|
| ☐ 199 | Erik Williams | .20 | .09 | .03 |

Dallas Cowboys

| | | | | |
|---|---|---|---|---|
| ☐ 200 | Pete Stoyanovich | .20 | .09 | .03 |

Miami Dolphins

# 1993 Select Gridiron Skills

Featuring five quarterbacks and five wide receivers, this ten-card "Gridiron Skills" subset was randomly inserted throughout the foil packs. The insert rate of these chase cards was reportedly one in every two boxes or not less than one in 72 packs. Each standard-size (2 1/2" by 3 1/2") card features on its front a color player action shot with a grainy metallic background. The photo is borderless, except at the bottom, where an oblique metallic red stripe carries the player's

name and skill. The back carries another color player action shot in its upper portion, with a description of his gridiron skill following below. The cards are numbered on the back as "X of 10."

| | MINT | EXC | G-VG |
|---|---|---|---|
| COMPLETE SET (10) | 450.00 | 200.00 | 57.50 |
| COMMON PLAYER (1-10) | 25.00 | 11.50 | 3.10 |
| ☐ 1 Warren Moon<br>Houston Oilers | 35.00 | 16.00 | 4.40 |
| ☐ 2 Steve Young<br>San Francisco 49ers | 50.00 | 23.00 | 6.25 |
| ☐ 3 Dan Marino<br>Miami Dolphins | 90.00 | 40.00 | 11.50 |
| ☐ 4 John Elway<br>Denver Broncos | 70.00 | 32.00 | 8.75 |
| ☐ 5 Troy Aikman<br>Dallas Cowboys | 125.00 | 57.50 | 15.50 |
| ☐ 6 Sterling Sharpe<br>Green Bay Packers | 60.00 | 27.00 | 7.50 |
| ☐ 7 Jerry Rice<br>San Francisco 49ers | 75.00 | 34.00 | 9.50 |
| ☐ 8 Andre Rison<br>Atlanta Falcons | 25.00 | 11.50 | 3.10 |
| ☐ 9 Haywood Jeffires<br>Houston Oilers | 25.00 | 11.50 | 3.10 |
| ☐ 10 Michael Irvin<br>Dallas Cowboys | 60.00 | 27.00 | 7.50 |

## 1993 Select Young Stars

This 38-card standard-size (2 1/2" by 3 1/2") set was sold in a hinged black leatherette box. Each set included a certificate of authenticity, providing the set serial number out of a total of 5,900 sets produced. Using Score's FX printing technology, the fronts display color action cutouts that extend beyond the arched-shape background. In block lettering, the set title "Young Stars" follows the curve of the arch, with the player's name in the upper left corner. The borders and the block lettering are team color-coded, and the entire fronts have a metallic sheen to them. On a team color-coded panel, the backs carry the team helmet and brief player profile. The cards are numbered on the back as "X of 38."

| | MINT | EXC | G-VG |
|---|---|---|---|
| COMPLETE SET (38) | 60.00 | 24.00 | 6.00 |
| COMMON PLAYER (1-38) | 1.00 | .40 | .10 |
| ☐ 1 Brett Favre<br>Green Bay Packers | 5.00 | 2.00 | .50 |
| ☐ 2 Anthony Miller<br>San Diego Chargers | 2.00 | .80 | .20 |
| ☐ 3 Rodney Hampton | 3.00 | 1.20 | .30 |

| | | | |
|---|---|---|---|
| | | | |
| New York Giants | | | |
| ☐ 4 Cortez Kennedy | 1.50 | .60 | .15 |
| Seattle Seahawks | | | |
| ☐ 5 Junior Seau | 1.50 | .60 | .15 |
| San Diego Chargers | | | |
| ☐ 6 Ricky Watters | 3.00 | 1.20 | .30 |
| San Francisco 49ers | | | |
| ☐ 7 Terry Allen | 2.00 | .80 | .20 |
| Minnesota Vikings | | | |
| ☐ 8 Drew Bledsoe | 10.00 | 4.00 | 1.00 |
| New England Patriots | | | |
| ☐ 9 Rick Mirer | 10.00 | 4.00 | 1.00 |
| Seattle Seahawks | | | |
| ☐ 10 Jeff Graham | 1.50 | .60 | .15 |
| Pittsburgh Steelers | | | |
| ☐ 11 Barry Foster | 2.50 | 1.00 | .25 |
| Pittsburgh Steelers | | | |
| ☐ 12 Eric Green | 1.50 | .60 | .15 |
| Pittsburgh Steelers | | | |
| ☐ 13 Troy Aikman | 10.00 | 4.00 | 1.00 |
| Dallas Cowboys | | | |
| ☐ 14 Michael Haynes | 3.00 | 1.20 | .30 |
| Atlanta Falcons | | | |
| ☐ 15 Johnny Mitchell | 1.50 | .60 | .15 |
| New York Jets | | | |
| ☐ 16 Lawrence Dawsey | 1.00 | .40 | .10 |
| Tampa Bay Buccaneers | | | |
| ☐ 17 Mo Lewis | 1.00 | .40 | .10 |
| New York Jets | | | |
| ☐ 18 Andre Ware | 1.50 | .60 | .15 |
| Detroit Lions | | | |
| ☐ 19 Neil O'Donnell | 2.50 | 1.00 | .25 |
| Pittsburgh Steelers | | | |
| ☐ 20 Broderick Thomas | 1.00 | .40 | .10 |
| Tampa Bay Buccaneers | | | |
| ☐ 21 Tim Barnett | 1.50 | .60 | .15 |
| Kansas City Chiefs | | | |
| ☐ 22 Fred Barnett | 1.50 | .60 | .15 |
| Philadelphia Eagles | | | |
| ☐ 23 Carl Pickens | 2.00 | .80 | .20 |
| Cincinnati Bengals | | | |
| ☐ 24 Santana Dotson | 1.50 | .60 | .15 |
| Tampa Bay Buccaneers | | | |
| ☐ 25 Sean Gilbert | 1.50 | .60 | .15 |
| Los Angeles Rams | | | |
| ☐ 26 Quentin Coryatt | 1.50 | .60 | .15 |
| Indianapolis Colts | | | |
| ☐ 27 Arthur Marshall | 1.50 | .60 | .15 |
| Denver Broncos | | | |
| ☐ 28 Dale Carter | 1.00 | .40 | .10 |
| Kansas City Chiefs | | | |
| ☐ 29 Henry Jones | 1.00 | .40 | .10 |
| Buffalo Bills | | | |
| ☐ 30 Terrell Buckley | 1.50 | .60 | .15 |
| Green Bay Packers | | | |
| ☐ 31 Tommy Vardell | 1.50 | .60 | .15 |
| Cleveland Browns | | | |
| ☐ 32 Russell Maryland | 1.50 | .60 | .15 |
| Dallas Cowboys | | | |
| ☐ 33 Steve Emtman | 1.00 | .40 | .10 |
| Indianapolis Colts | | | |
| ☐ 34 Jarrod Bunch | 1.00 | .40 | .10 |
| New York Giants | | | |
| ☐ 35 Alfred Williams | 1.00 | .40 | .10 |
| Cincinnati Bengals | | | |
| ☐ 36 Brian Mitchell | 1.00 | .40 | .10 |
| Washington Redskins | | | |
| ☐ 37 Chris Warren | 1.50 | .60 | .15 |
| Seattle Seahawks | | | |
| ☐ 38 Deion Sanders | 3.00 | 1.20 | .30 |
| Atlanta Falcons | | | |

## 1960 7-Eleven Dallas Texans

The cards measure the standard size 2 1/2" by 3 1/2" and are unnumbered. The front has a posed black and white photo of the player with no frame, with the player's name, position, and school listed below the picture. On many of the cards the team name is written from bottom to top on the right hand side. The back has biographical information running the length of the card in typewriter script. Since the cards are unnumbered, they are listed below alphabetically. Any additional cards that can be verifiably added to this list would be appreciated.

| | NRMT | VG-E | GOOD |
|---|---|---|---|
| COMPLETE SET (11) | 400.00 | 160.00 | 40.00 |
| COMMON PLAYER (1-11) | 30.00 | 12.00 | 3.00 |
| ☐ 1 Max Boydston | 30.00 | 12.00 | 3.00 |
| ☐ 2 Mel Branch | 35.00 | 14.00 | 3.50 |
| ☐ 3 Chris Burford | 40.00 | 16.00 | 4.00 |
| ☐ 4 Ray Collins UER<br>(No team name<br>on front) | 30.00 | 12.00 | 3.00 |

Abner Haynes
Halfback, North Texas

ABNER HAYNES--Halfback, North Texas. One of the greatest backs ever produced at North Texas State, a school which has gained renown for producing topflight professionals. Haynes was Missouri Valley "back of the year" in both 1958 and 1959. He is a quick, elusive runner and an excellent pass receiver. The 5-11, 180 pounder scored 158 points in his three seasons at North Tex.

| | | | |
|---|---|---|---|
| ☐ 5 Cotton Davidson | 40.00 | 16.00 | 4.00 |
| ☐ 6 Abner Haynes | 60.00 | 24.00 | 6.00 |
| ☐ 7 Sherrill Headrick | 40.00 | 16.00 | 4.00 |
| ☐ 8 Bill Krisher | 35.00 | 14.00 | 3.50 |
| ☐ 9 Paul Miller | 30.00 | 12.00 | 3.00 |
| ☐ 10 Johnny Robinson | 50.00 | 20.00 | 5.00 |
| ☐ 11 Jack Spikes | 35.00 | 14.00 | 3.50 |

## 1983 7-Eleven Coins

This set of 15 discs (coins), each measuring approximately 1 3/4" in diameter, features an alternating portrait and action picture of each of the players listed below. The set was sponsored by 7-Eleven Stores (Southland Corporation).

| | MINT | EXC | G-VG |
|---|---|---|---|
| COMPLETE SET (15) | 25.00 | 10.00 | 2.50 |
| COMMON PLAYER (1-15) | 1.00 | .40 | .10 |
| ☐ 1 Franco Harris | 4.00 | 1.60 | .40 |
| Pittsburgh Steelers | | | |
| ☐ 2 Dan Fouts | 3.00 | 1.20 | .30 |
| San Diego Chargers | | | |
| ☐ 3 Lee Roy Selmon | 1.25 | .50 | .12 |
| Tampa Bay Buccaneers | | | |
| ☐ 4 Nolan Cromwell | 1.25 | .50 | .12 |
| Los Angeles Rams | | | |
| ☐ 5 Marcus Allen | 4.00 | 1.60 | .40 |
| Los Angeles Raiders | | | |
| ☐ 6 Joe Montana | 9.00 | 3.75 | .90 |
| San Francisco 49ers | | | |
| ☐ 7 Kellen Winslow | 1.50 | .60 | .15 |
| San Diego Chargers | | | |
| ☐ 8 Hugh Green | 1.00 | .40 | .10 |
| Tampa Bay Buccaneers | | | |
| ☐ 9 Ted Hendricks | 2.00 | .80 | .20 |
| Los Angeles Raiders | | | |
| ☐ 10 Danny White | 1.50 | .60 | .15 |
| Dallas Cowboys | | | |
| ☐ 11 Wes Chandler | 1.00 | .40 | .10 |
| San Diego Chargers | | | |
| ☐ 12 Jimmie Giles | 1.00 | .40 | .10 |
| Tampa Bay Buccaneers | | | |
| ☐ 13 Jack Youngblood | 2.00 | .80 | .20 |
| Los Angeles Rams | | | |
| ☐ 14 Lester Hayes | 1.00 | .40 | .10 |
| Los Angeles Raiders | | | |
| ☐ 15 Vince Ferragamo | 1.50 | .60 | .15 |
| Los Angeles Rams | | | |

## 1984 7-Eleven Coins

This set of 40 discs (coins), each measuring approximately 1 3/4" in diameter, features an alternating portrait and action picture of each of the players listed below. The discs in the set are grouped into two

subsets, East (E prefix) and West (W prefix). Some players were included in both subsets.

| | MINT | EXC | G-VG |
|---|---|---|---|
| COMPLETE SET (40) | 50.00 | 20.00 | 5.00 |
| COMMON PLAYER (E1-E20) | .60 | .24 | .06 |
| COMMON PLAYER (W1-W20) | .60 | .24 | .06 |
| ☐ E1 Franco Harris | 2.00 | .80 | .20 |
| Pittsburgh Steelers | | | |
| ☐ E2 Lawrence Taylor | 1.50 | .60 | .15 |
| New York Giants | | | |
| ☐ E3 Mark Gastineau | .60 | .24 | .06 |
| New York Jets | | | |
| ☐ E4 Lee Roy Selmon | .75 | .30 | .07 |
| Tampa Bay Buccaneers | | | |
| ☐ E5 Ken Anderson | 1.25 | .50 | .12 |
| Cincinnati Bengals | | | |
| ☐ E6 Walter Payton | 3.50 | 1.40 | .35 |
| Chicago Bears | | | |
| ☐ E7 Ken Stabler | 1.25 | .50 | .12 |
| Los Angeles Raiders | | | |
| ☐ E8 Marcus Allen | 2.00 | .80 | .20 |
| Los Angeles Rams | | | |
| ☐ E9 Fred Smerlas | .60 | .24 | .06 |
| Buffalo Bills | | | |
| ☐ E10 Ozzie Newsome | 1.25 | .50 | .12 |
| Cleveland Browns | | | |
| ☐ E11 Steve Bartkowski | .75 | .30 | .07 |
| Atlanta Falcons | | | |
| ☐ E12 Tony Dorsett | 2.00 | .80 | .20 |
| Dallas Cowboys | | | |
| ☐ E13 John Riggins | 1.50 | .60 | .15 |
| Washington Redskins | | | |
| ☐ E14 Billy Sims | .75 | .30 | .07 |
| Detroit Lions | | | |
| ☐ E15 Dan Marino | 7.50 | 3.00 | .75 |
| Miami Dolphins | | | |
| ☐ E16 Tony Collins | .60 | .24 | .06 |
| New England Patriots | | | |
| ☐ E17 Curtis Dickey | .60 | .24 | .06 |
| Indianapolis Colts | | | |
| ☐ E18 Ron Jaworski | .75 | .30 | .07 |
| Philadelphia Eagles | | | |
| ☐ E19 William Andrews | .60 | .24 | .06 |
| Atlanta Falcons | | | |
| ☐ E20 Joe Theismann | 1.50 | .60 | .15 |
| Washington Redskins | | | |
| ☐ W1 Franco Harris | 2.00 | .80 | .20 |
| Pittsburgh Steelers | | | |
| ☐ W2 Joe Montana | 7.50 | 3.00 | .75 |
| San Francisco 49ers | | | |
| ☐ W3 Matt Blair | .60 | .24 | .06 |
| Minnesota Vikings | | | |
| ☐ W4 Warren Moon | 6.00 | 2.40 | .60 |
| Houston Oilers | | | |
| ☐ W5 Marcus Allen | 2.00 | .80 | .20 |
| Los Angeles Raiders | | | |
| ☐ W6 John Riggins | 1.50 | .60 | .15 |
| Washington Redskins | | | |
| ☐ W7 Walter Payton | 3.50 | 1.40 | .35 |
| Chicago Bears | | | |
| ☐ W8 Vince Ferragamo | .75 | .30 | .07 |
| Los Angeles Rams | | | |
| ☐ W9 Billy Sims | .75 | .30 | .07 |
| Detroit Lions | | | |
| ☐ W10 Ken Anderson | 1.25 | .50 | .12 |
| Cincinnati Bengals | | | |
| ☐ W11 Lynn Dickey | .60 | .24 | .06 |
| Green Bay Packers | | | |
| ☐ W12 Tony Dorsett | 2.00 | .80 | .20 |
| Dallas Cowboys | | | |
| ☐ W13 Bill Kenney | .60 | .24 | .06 |
| Kansas City Chiefs | | | |
| ☐ W14 Ottis Anderson | 1.00 | .40 | .10 |
| St. Louis Cardinals | | | |
| ☐ W15 Dan Fouts | 1.50 | .60 | .15 |
| San Diego Chargers | | | |
| ☐ W16 Eric Dickerson | 3.00 | 1.20 | .30 |
| Los Angeles Raiders | | | |
| ☐ W17 John Elway | 5.00 | 2.00 | .50 |
| Denver Broncos | | | |
| ☐ W18 Ozzie Newsome | 1.25 | .50 | .12 |

Cleveland Browns
☐ W19 Curt Warner ........................ .75 .30 .07
Seattle Seahawks
☐ W20 Joe Theismann ................... 1.50 .60 .15
Washington Redskins

# 1981 Shell Posters

This set of 96 posters was distributed by Shell Oil Co. across the country, with each major city distributing players from the local team. Those cities without a close NFL issuing team distributed the National set of six popular players (indicated as "National" in the checklist below: numbers 18, 21, 28, 35, 45, and 79). The pictures used are actually black and white drawings by artists, suitable for framing. These posters measure approximately 10 7/8" by 13 7/8"; most were (facsimile) signed by the artist. They are frequently available and offered by the team set of six. Several different artists are responsible for the artwork; they are K. Akins (KA), Nick Galloway (NG) and Tanenbawm (T). Those drawings which are not signed are asterisked in the checklist below. New Orleans and Houston are supposedly tougher to find than the other teams. The posters are numbered below alphabetically by team and alphabetically within team, Atlanta Falcons (1-6), Baltimore Colts (7-12), Chicago Bears (13-18), Cincinnati Bengals (19-24), Cleveland Browns (25-30), Dallas Cowboys (31-36), Detroit Lions (37-42), Houston Oilers (43-48), Miami Dolphins (49-54), New England Patriots (55-60), New Orleans Saints (61-66), New York Giants (67-72), New York Jets (73-78), St. Louis Cardinals (79-84), Tampa Bay Buccaneers (85-90), and Washington Redskins (91-96).

|  | MINT | EXC | G-VG |
|---|---|---|---|
| COMPLETE SET (96) | 350.00 | 140.00 | 35.00 |
| COMMON CARD (1-96) | 3.50 | 1.40 | .35 |

| | | | |
|---|---|---|---|
| ☐ 1 William Andrews NG | 5.00 | 2.00 | .50 |
| ☐ 2 Steve Bartkowski NG | 6.00 | 2.40 | .60 |
| ☐ 3 Buddy Curry NG | 3.50 | 1.40 | .35 |
| ☐ 4 Wallace Francis NG | 5.00 | 2.00 | .50 |
| ☐ 5 Mike Kenn NG | 5.00 | 2.00 | .50 |
| ☐ 6 Jeff Van Note NG | 5.00 | 2.00 | .50 |
| ☐ 7 Mike Barnes * | 3.50 | 1.40 | .35 |
| ☐ 8 Roger Carr KA | 3.50 | 1.40 | .35 |
| ☐ 9 Curtis Dickey KA | 5.00 | 2.00 | .50 |
| ☐ 10 Bert Jones KA | 6.00 | 2.40 | .60 |
| ☐ 11 Bruce Laird * | 3.50 | 1.40 | .35 |
| ☐ 12 Randy McMillan * | 5.00 | 2.00 | .50 |
| ☐ 13 Brian Baschnagel T | 3.50 | 1.40 | .35 |
| ☐ 14 Vince Evans T | 5.00 | 2.00 | .50 |
| ☐ 15 Gary Fencik T | 5.00 | 2.00 | .50 |
| ☐ 16 Roland Harper T | 3.50 | 1.40 | .35 |
| ☐ 17 Alan Page T | 7.50 | 3.00 | .75 |
| ☐ 18 Walter Payton T | 9.00 | 3.75 | .90 |
| (National) | | | |
| ☐ 19 Ken Anderson T | 7.50 | 3.00 | .75 |
| ☐ 20 Ross Browner T | 5.00 | 2.00 | .50 |
| ☐ 21 Archie Griffin T | 3.50 | 1.40 | .35 |
| (National) | | | |
| ☐ 22 Pat McInally T | 5.00 | 2.00 | .50 |
| ☐ 23 Anthony Munoz T | 7.50 | 3.00 | .75 |
| ☐ 24 Reggie Williams T | 5.00 | 2.00 | .50 |
| ☐ 25 Lyle Alzado KA | 6.00 | 2.40 | .60 |
| ☐ 26 Joe DeLamielleure KA | 3.50 | 1.40 | .35 |
| ☐ 27 Doug Dieken KA | 3.50 | 1.40 | .35 |
| ☐ 28 Dave Logan KA | 3.50 | 1.40 | .35 |
| (National) | | | |
| ☐ 29 Reggie Rucker KA | 5.00 | 2.00 | .50 |
| ☐ 30 Brian Sipe KA | 5.00 | 2.00 | .50 |
| ☐ 31 Benny Barnes T | 3.50 | 1.40 | .35 |
| ☐ 32 Bob Breunig T | 3.50 | 1.40 | .35 |
| ☐ 33 D.D. Lewis T | 3.50 | 1.40 | .35 |
| ☐ 34 Harvey Martin T | 5.00 | 2.00 | .50 |

| | | | |
|---|---|---|---|
| ☐ 35 Drew Pearson T | 3.50 | 1.40 | .35 |
| (National) | | | |
| ☐ 36 Rafael Septien T | 3.50 | 1.40 | .35 |
| ☐ 37 Al(Bubba) Baker KA | 5.00 | 2.00 | .50 |
| ☐ 38 Dexter Bussey KA | 3.50 | 1.40 | .35 |
| ☐ 39 Gary Danielson KA | 5.00 | 2.00 | .50 |
| ☐ 40 Freddie Scott KA | 3.50 | 1.40 | .35 |
| ☐ 41 Billy Sims KA | 6.00 | 2.40 | .60 |
| ☐ 42 Tom Skladany KA | 3.50 | 1.40 | .35 |
| ☐ 43 Robert Brazile T | 6.00 | 2.40 | .60 |
| ☐ 44 Ken Burrough T | 6.00 | 2.40 | .60 |
| ☐ 45 Earl Campbell T | 7.50 | 3.00 | .75 |
| (National) | | | |
| ☐ 46 Leon Gray T | 5.00 | 2.00 | .50 |
| ☐ 47 Carl Mauck T | 5.00 | 2.00 | .50 |
| ☐ 48 Ken Stabler T | 7.50 | 3.00 | .75 |
| ☐ 49 Bob Baumhower NG | 5.00 | 2.00 | .50 |
| ☐ 50 Jimmy Cefalo NG | 5.00 | 2.00 | .50 |
| ☐ 51 A.J. Duhe NG | 5.00 | 2.00 | .50 |
| ☐ 52 Nat Moore NG | 6.00 | 2.40 | .60 |
| ☐ 53 Ed Newman NG | 3.50 | 1.40 | .35 |
| ☐ 54 Uwe Von Schamann NG | 3.50 | 1.40 | .35 |
| ☐ 55 Steve Grogan NG | 6.00 | 2.40 | .60 |
| ☐ 56 John Hannah NG | 7.50 | 3.00 | .75 |
| ☐ 57 Don Hasselbeck NG | 3.50 | 1.40 | .35 |
| ☐ 58 Mike Haynes NG | 6.00 | 2.40 | .60 |
| ☐ 59 Harold Jackson NG | 5.00 | 2.00 | .50 |
| ☐ 60 Steve Nelson NG | 3.50 | 1.40 | .35 |
| ☐ 61 Elois Grooms | 5.00 | 2.00 | .50 |
| ☐ 62 Rickey Jackson NG | 7.50 | 3.00 | .75 |
| ☐ 63 Archie Manning T | 7.50 | 3.00 | .75 |
| ☐ 64 Tommy Myers | 5.00 | 2.00 | .50 |
| ☐ 65 Benny Ricardo T | 5.00 | 2.00 | .50 |
| ☐ 66 George Rogers NG | 6.00 | 2.40 | .60 |
| ☐ 67 Harry Carson NG | 6.00 | 2.40 | .60 |
| ☐ 68 Dave Jennings NG | 3.50 | 1.40 | .35 |
| ☐ 69 Gary Jeter NG | 3.50 | 1.40 | .35 |
| ☐ 70 Phil Simms NG | 7.50 | 3.00 | .75 |
| ☐ 71 Lawrence Taylor NG | 10.00 | 4.00 | 1.00 |
| ☐ 72 Brad Van Pelt NG | 5.00 | 2.00 | .50 |
| ☐ 73 Greg Buttle NG | 5.00 | 2.00 | .50 |
| ☐ 74 Bruce Harper NG | 3.50 | 1.40 | .35 |
| ☐ 75 Joe Klecko NG | 5.00 | 2.00 | .50 |
| ☐ 76 Randy Rasmussen NG | 3.50 | 1.40 | .35 |
| ☐ 77 Richard Todd NG | 5.00 | 2.00 | .50 |
| ☐ 78 Wesley Walker NG | 6.00 | 2.40 | .60 |
| ☐ 79 Ottis Anderson NG | 3.50 | 1.40 | .35 |
| (National) | | | |
| ☐ 80 Dan Dierdorf NG | 7.50 | 3.00 | .75 |
| ☐ 81 Mel Gray NG | 5.00 | 2.00 | .50 |
| ☐ 82 Jim Hart NG | 6.00 | 2.40 | .60 |
| ☐ 83 E.J. Junior NG | 5.00 | 2.00 | .50 |
| ☐ 84 Pat Tilley NG | 5.00 | 2.00 | .50 |
| ☐ 85 Jimmie Giles NG | 5.00 | 2.00 | .50 |
| ☐ 86 Charley Hannah NG | 3.50 | 1.40 | .35 |
| ☐ 87 Bill Kollar NG | 3.50 | 1.40 | .35 |
| ☐ 88 David Lewis NG | 3.50 | 1.40 | .35 |
| ☐ 89 Lee Roy Selmon NG | 6.00 | 2.40 | .60 |
| ☐ 90 Doug Williams NG | 5.00 | 2.00 | .50 |
| ☐ 91 Joe Lavender T | 3.50 | 1.40 | .35 |
| ☐ 92 Mark Moseley T | 5.00 | 2.00 | .50 |
| ☐ 93 Mark Murphy * | 3.50 | 1.40 | .35 |
| ☐ 94 Lemar Parrish T | 5.00 | 2.00 | .50 |
| ☐ 95 John Riggins T | 7.50 | 3.00 | .75 |
| ☐ 96 Joe Washington T | 5.00 | 2.00 | .50 |

# 1994 Signature Rookies

These 60 standard-size (2 1/2" by 3 1/2") cards feature borderless color action shots of top NFL prospects in their college uniforms. A wide gold-foil stripe adorns the left side and carries the words "1 of 45,000" or, for the autographed card included in every six-card pack, "Authentic Signature." The player's name and position appear at the bottom. Production was limited to 12,500 numbered boxes. Special subsets include the five-card Charlie Ward set, 2,500 cards of which were hand signed by the Heisman Trophy winner; the five-card "Hottest Prospect" set, 2,000 of which were hand signed by each of the five players; and also sets of Gale Sayers and Tony Dorsett, of which 2,000 and 1,000 cards, respectively, were autographed.

| | MINT | EXC | G-VG |
|---|---|---|---|
| COMPLETE SET (60) | 7.00 | 2.80 | .70 |
| COMMON PLAYER (1-60) | .05 | .02 | .00 |
| ☐ 1 Sam Adams | .15 | .06 | .01 |
| ☐ 2 Trev Alberts | .25 | .10 | .02 |
| ☐ 3 Derrick Alexander | .25 | .10 | .02 |
| ☐ 4 Larry Allen | .10 | .04 | .01 |
| ☐ 5 Aubrey Beavers | .12 | .05 | .01 |
| ☐ 6 Lou Benfatti | .10 | .04 | .01 |
| ☐ 7 James Bostic | .15 | .06 | .01 |
| ☐ 8 Tim Bowens | .12 | .05 | .01 |
| ☐ 9 Rich Braham | .10 | .04 | .01 |
| ☐ 10 Isaac Bruce | .15 | .06 | .01 |
| ☐ 11 Vaughn Bryant | .10 | .04 | .01 |
| ☐ 12 Brentson Buckner | .10 | .04 | .01 |
| ☐ 13 Jeff Burris | .25 | .10 | .02 |
| ☐ 14 Carlester Crumpler | .10 | .04 | .01 |
| ☐ 15 Lake Dawson | .25 | .10 | .02 |
| ☐ 16 Tyronne Drakeford | .10 | .04 | .01 |
| ☐ 17 Dan Eichloff | .05 | .02 | .00 |
| ☐ 18 Rob Fredrickson | .12 | .05 | .01 |
| ☐ 19 Gus Frerotte | .15 | .06 | .01 |
| ☐ 20 William Gaines | .10 | .04 | .01 |
| ☐ 21 Wayne Gandy | .12 | .05 | .01 |
| ☐ 22 Jason Gildon | .10 | .04 | .01 |
| ☐ 23 Lemanski Hall | .05 | .02 | .00 |
| ☐ 24 Shelby Hill | .10 | .04 | .01 |
| ☐ 25 Willie Jackson | .20 | .08 | .02 |
| ☐ 26 LeShon Johnson | .20 | .08 | .02 |
| ☐ 27 Tre Johnson | .10 | .04 | .01 |
| ☐ 28 Alan Kline | .05 | .02 | .00 |
| ☐ 29 Darren Krein | .10 | .04 | .01 |
| ☐ 30 Antonio Langham | .20 | .08 | .02 |
| ☐ 31 Corey Louchiey | .10 | .04 | .01 |
| ☐ 32 Keith Lyle | .10 | .04 | .01 |
| ☐ 33 Eric Mahlum | .10 | .04 | .01 |
| ☐ 34 Van Malone | .10 | .04 | .01 |
| ☐ 35 Chris Maumalanga | .10 | .04 | .01 |
| ☐ 36 Jamir Miller | .20 | .08 | .02 |
| ☐ 37 Jim Miller | .15 | .06 | .01 |
| ☐ 38 Byron(Bam) Morris | .20 | .08 | .02 |
| ☐ 39 Aaron Mundy | .05 | .02 | .00 |
| ☐ 40 Jeremy Nunley | .10 | .04 | .01 |
| ☐ 41 Turhonn O'Bannon | .05 | .02 | .00 |
| ☐ 42 Brad Ottis | .10 | .04 | .01 |
| ☐ 43 David Palmer | .50 | .20 | .05 |
| ☐ 44 Joe Panos | .10 | .04 | .01 |
| ☐ 45 Jim Pyne | .05 | .02 | .00 |
| ☐ 46 John Reece | .10 | .04 | .01 |
| ☐ 47 Errict Rhett | .50 | .20 | .05 |
| ☐ 48 Tony Richardson | .10 | .04 | .01 |
| ☐ 49 Sam Rogers | .10 | .04 | .01 |
| ☐ 50 Tim Ruddy | .10 | .04 | .01 |
| ☐ 51 Corey Sawyer | .12 | .05 | .01 |
| ☐ 52 Malcom Seabron | .12 | .05 | .01 |
| ☐ 53 Jason Sehorn | .10 | .04 | .01 |
| ☐ 54 John Thierry | .15 | .06 | .01 |
| ☐ 55 Jason Winrow | .05 | .02 | .00 |
| ☐ 56 Ronnie Woolfork | .10 | .04 | .01 |
| ☐ 57 Toby Wright | .10 | .04 | .01 |
| ☐ 58 Ryan Yarborough | .15 | .06 | .01 |
| ☐ 59 Eric Zomalt | .10 | .04 | .01 |
| ☐ 60 Checklist | .05 | .02 | .00 |

card pack of Signature Rookies. Production was limited to 12,500 numbered boxes. Each card was numbered out of 7750.

| | MINT | EXC | G-VG |
|---|---|---|---|
| COMPLETE SET (59) | 250.00 | 100.00 | 25.00 |
| COMMON SIGNATURE (1-59) | 3.50 | 1.40 | .35 |
| ☐ 1 Sam Adams | 5.00 | 2.00 | .50 |
| ☐ 2 Trev Alberts | 7.00 | 2.80 | .70 |
| ☐ 3 Derrick Alexander | 7.00 | 2.80 | .70 |
| ☐ 4 Larry Allen | 3.50 | 1.40 | .35 |
| ☐ 5 Aubrey Beavers | 4.00 | 1.60 | .40 |
| ☐ 6 Lou Benfatti | 3.50 | 1.40 | .35 |
| ☐ 7 James Bostic | 5.00 | 2.00 | .50 |
| ☐ 8 Tim Bowens | 4.00 | 1.60 | .40 |
| ☐ 9 Rich Braham | 3.50 | 1.40 | .35 |
| ☐ 10 Isaac Bruce | 5.00 | 2.00 | .50 |
| ☐ 11 Vaughn Bryant | 3.50 | 1.40 | .35 |
| ☐ 12 Brentson Buckner | 3.50 | 1.40 | .35 |
| ☐ 13 Jeff Burris | 7.00 | 2.80 | .70 |
| ☐ 14 Carlester Crumpler | 3.50 | 1.40 | .35 |
| ☐ 15 Lake Dawson | 7.00 | 2.80 | .70 |
| ☐ 16 Tyronne Drakeford | 3.50 | 1.40 | .35 |
| ☐ 17 Dan Eichloff | 3.50 | 1.40 | .35 |
| ☐ 18 Rob Fredrickson | 4.00 | 1.60 | .40 |
| ☐ 19 Gus Frerotte | 5.00 | 2.00 | .50 |
| ☐ 20 William Gaines | 3.50 | 1.40 | .35 |
| ☐ 21 Wayne Gandy | 4.00 | 1.60 | .40 |
| ☐ 22 Jason Gildon | 3.50 | 1.40 | .35 |
| ☐ 23 Lemanski Hall | 3.50 | 1.40 | .35 |
| ☐ 24 Shelby Hill | 3.50 | 1.40 | .35 |
| ☐ 25 Willie Jackson | 6.00 | 2.40 | .60 |
| ☐ 26 LeShon Johnson | 6.00 | 2.40 | .60 |
| ☐ 27 Tre Johnson | 3.50 | 1.40 | .35 |
| ☐ 28 Alan Kline | 3.50 | 1.40 | .35 |
| ☐ 29 Darren Krein | 3.50 | 1.40 | .35 |
| ☐ 30 Antonio Langham | 6.00 | 2.40 | .60 |
| ☐ 31 Corey Louchiey | 3.50 | 1.40 | .35 |
| ☐ 32 Keith Lyle | 3.50 | 1.40 | .35 |
| ☐ 33 Eric Mahlum | 3.50 | 1.40 | .35 |
| ☐ 34 Van Malone | 3.50 | 1.40 | .35 |
| ☐ 35 Chris Maumalanga | 3.50 | 1.40 | .35 |
| ☐ 36 Jamir Miller | 6.00 | 2.40 | .60 |
| ☐ 37 Jim Miller | 5.00 | 2.00 | .50 |
| ☐ 38 Byron(Bam) Morris | 6.00 | 2.40 | .60 |
| ☐ 39 Aaron Mundy | 3.50 | 1.40 | .35 |
| ☐ 40 Jeremy Nunley | 3.50 | 1.40 | .35 |
| ☐ 41 Turhonn O'Bannon | 3.50 | 1.40 | .35 |
| ☐ 42 Brad Ottis | 3.50 | 1.40 | .35 |
| ☐ 43 David Palmer | 16.00 | 6.50 | 1.60 |
| ☐ 44 Joe Panos | 3.50 | 1.40 | .35 |
| ☐ 45 Jim Pyne | 3.50 | 1.40 | .35 |
| ☐ 46 John Reece | 3.50 | 1.40 | .35 |
| ☐ 47 Errict Rhett | 16.00 | 6.50 | 1.60 |
| ☐ 48 Tony Richardson | 3.50 | 1.40 | .35 |
| ☐ 49 Sam Rogers | 3.50 | 1.40 | .35 |
| ☐ 50 Tim Ruddy | 3.50 | 1.40 | .35 |
| ☐ 51 Corey Sawyer | 4.00 | 1.60 | .40 |
| ☐ 52 Malcom Seabron | 4.00 | 1.60 | .40 |
| ☐ 53 Jason Sehorn | 3.50 | 1.40 | .35 |
| ☐ 54 John Thierry | 5.00 | 2.00 | .50 |
| ☐ 55 Jason Winrow | 3.50 | 1.40 | .35 |
| ☐ 56 Ronnie Woolfork | 3.50 | 1.40 | .35 |
| ☐ 57 Toby Wright | 3.50 | 1.40 | .35 |
| ☐ 58 Ryan Yarborough | 5.00 | 2.00 | .50 |
| ☐ 59 Eric Zomalt | 3.50 | 1.40 | .35 |

## 1992 SkyBox/Impel Impact/Primetime Promos

# 1994 Signature Rookies Signatures

These 59 standard-size (2 1/2" by 3 1/2") cards were also available in autographed form; an autographed card was promised in every six-

This two-card promotional set was distributed at the Super Bowl XXVI Show in Minneapolis in January, 1992. These cards were issued before Impel changed their corporate name to SkyBox and hence made some subtle changes in the promo cards to reflect their new identity. The cards are standard size, 2 1/2" by 3 1/2". The Byner card displays a full-bleed photo of him running with the ball, superimposed on a gray background. His name and jersey number are printed in maroon, with the team name in white on a maroon bar. Against the background of a crowd, the Kelly card shows him with the ball cocked, ready to pass. The backs of both cards have an advertisement for Impel's new Impact and Primetime series. The Byner card is trimmed in red, while the Kelly card is trimmed in blue. The cards are unnumbered.

|  | MINT | EXC | G-VG |
|---|---|---|---|
| COMPLETE SET (2).......................... | 6.00 | 2.40 | .60 |
| COMMON PLAYER.......................... | 1.25 | .50 | .12 |
| ☐ NNO Jim Kelly .............................<br>Impact<br>Buffalo Bills | 5.00 | 2.00 | .50 |
| ☐ NNO Earnest Byner ..................<br>PrimeTime<br>Washington Redskins | 1.25 | .50 | .12 |

## 1992 SkyBox Impact Promos

These three standard-size (2 1/2" by 3 1/2") cards were issued as a promo pack to show what the then-upcoming SkyBox Impact cards would be like. The fronts feature full-bleed color action photos, with the player's name in block lettering across the top of the picture. The team logo is superimposed at the lower left corner, and the SkyBox logo appears in the lower right corner. The backs show another color photo, career highlights, statistics, and the player's position by a diagram of "X's" and "O's." The photo displayed on the front of the Kelly card is almost identical to that used on the Impel promo given away at the Super Bowl XXVI card show. The cards are numbered on the back.

|  | MINT | EXC | G-VG |
|---|---|---|---|
| COMPLETE SET (3).......................... | 5.00 | 2.00 | .50 |
| COMMON PLAYER (1-3)................. | .75 | .30 | .07 |
| ☐ 1 Jim Kelly ............................. | 4.00 | 1.60 | .40 |
| ☐ 2 Michael Dean Perry.................. | 1.25 | .50 | .12 |
| ☐ 3 Reggie Roby ............................. | .75 | .30 | .07 |

## 1992 SkyBox Impact

The 1992 SkyBox Impact football set consists of 350 standard-size (2 1/2" by 3 1/2") cards. The cards were sold in 12-card foil packs and 24-card jumbo packs. Twenty Major Impact player cards were randomly inserted in jumbo packs, while two hologram cards

(featuring Jim Kelly and Lawrence Taylor) were inserted in foil packs. Four additional hologram cards were available as part of a mail-away promotion (H3-H6). The fronts feature full-bleed holograms with the player's last name in block lettering toward the bottom of the card. Five hundred Impact Playmakers cards featuring Magic Johnson and Jim Kelly bear autographs by both stars, and these cards were randomly inserted in the foil packs. Lastly, 2,500 gold foil-stamped Total Impact cards were autographed by Jim Kelly and randomly inserted in the foil packs. The full-bleed color action photos on the fronts have the player's last name printed in block lettering across the top of the picture. The team logo is superimposed at the lower left corner. The flipside shows another action photo, career highlights, biography, statistics, and the player's position by a diagram of "X's" and "O's." In addition to 276 player cards, the set includes the following subsets: Team Checklists (277-304), High Impact League Leaders (305-314), Sudden Impact Hardest Hitters (315-320), and Instant Impact Rookies (321-350). The cards are numbered on the back. The key Rookie Cards in this set are Edgar Bennett, Steve Bono, Terrell Buckley, Marco Coleman, Vaughn Dunbar, Steve Emtman, David Klingler, Tommy Maddox, and Carl Pickens.

|  | MINT | EXC | G-VG |
|---|---|---|---|
| COMPLETE SET (350)...................... | 12.00 | 5.50 | 1.50 |
| COMMON PLAYER (1-350).............. | .05 | .02 | .01 |
| ☐ 1 Jim Kelly .................................<br>Buffalo Bills | .25 | .11 | .03 |
| ☐ 2 Andre Rison...........................<br>Atlanta Falcons | .25 | .11 | .03 |
| ☐ 3 Michael Dean Perry...................<br>Cleveland Browns | .10 | .05 | .01 |
| ☐ 4 Herman Moore.........................<br>Detroit Lions | .30 | .14 | .04 |
| ☐ 5 Fred McAfee.............................<br>New Orleans Saints | .15 | .07 | .02 |
| ☐ 6 Ricky Proehl.............................<br>Phoenix Cardinals | .10 | .05 | .01 |
| ☐ 7 Jim Everett...............................<br>Los Angeles Rams | .05 | .02 | .01 |
| ☐ 8 Mark Carrier.............................<br>Chicago Bears | .08 | .04 | .01 |
| ☐ 9 Eric Martin...............................<br>New Orleans Saints | .08 | .04 | .01 |
| ☐ 10 John Elway.............................<br>Denver Broncos | .40 | .18 | .05 |
| ☐ 11 Michael Irvin .........................<br>Dallas Cowboys | .50 | .23 | .06 |
| ☐ 12 Keith McCants.........................<br>Tampa Bay Buccaneers | .05 | .02 | .01 |
| ☐ 13 Greg Lloyd .............................<br>Pittsburgh Steelers | .05 | .02 | .01 |
| ☐ 14 Lawrence Taylor......................<br>New York Giants | .10 | .05 | .01 |
| ☐ 15 Mike Tomczak.........................<br>Green Bay Packers | .05 | .02 | .01 |
| ☐ 16 Cortez Kennedy.......................<br>Seattle Seahawks | .10 | .05 | .01 |
| ☐ 17 William Fuller.........................<br>Houston Oilers | .05 | .02 | .01 |
| ☐ 18 James Lofton .........................<br>Buffalo Bills | .10 | .05 | .01 |
| ☐ 19 Kevin Fagan...........................<br>San Francisco 49ers | .05 | .02 | .01 |
| ☐ 20 Bill Brooks.............................<br>Indianapolis Colts | .08 | .04 | .01 |
| ☐ 21 Roger Craig UER.....................<br>(Text is about Vikings,<br>but Raiders logo<br>still on card)<br>Los Angeles Raiders | .08 | .04 | .01 |
| ☐ 22 Jay Novacek...........................<br>Dallas Cowboys | .15 | .07 | .02 |
| ☐ 23 Steve Sewell...........................<br>Denver Broncos | .05 | .02 | .01 |
| ☐ 24 William Perry UER .................<br>(Card has him injured<br>for 1988, but he did play)<br>Chicago Bears | .08 | .04 | .01 |
| ☐ 25 Jerry Rice...............................<br>San Francisco 49ers | .50 | .23 | .06 |
| ☐ 26 James Joseph.........................<br>Philadelphia Eagles | .05 | .02 | .01 |
| ☐ 27 Timm Rosenbach.....................<br>Phoenix Cardinals | .05 | .02 | .01 |
| ☐ 28 Pat Terrell .............................<br>Los Angeles Rams | .05 | .02 | .01 |
| ☐ 29 Jon Vaughn.............................<br>New England Patriots | .05 | .02 | .01 |
| ☐ 30 Steve Walsh...........................<br>New Orleans Saints | .05 | .02 | .01 |
| ☐ 31 James Hasty...........................<br>New York Jets | .05 | .02 | .01 |
| ☐ 32 Dwight Stone .........................<br>Pittsburgh Steelers | .05 | .02 | .01 |

| | | | | | | | | |
|---|---|---|---|---|---|---|---|---|
| ☐ 33 Derrick Fenner UER | .08 | .04 | .01 | ☐ 77 David Treadwell | .05 | .02 | .01 |
| (Text mentions Bengals, but Seahawks logo still on front) Seattle Seahawks | | | | Denver Broncos | | | |
| | | | | ☐ 78 Flipper Anderson | .08 | .04 | .01 |
| | | | | Los Angeles Rams | | | |
| ☐ 34 Mark Bortz | .05 | .02 | .01 | ☐ 79 Eric Allen | .08 | .04 | .01 |
| Chicago Bears | | | | Philadelphia Eagles | | | |
| ☐ 35 Dan Saleaumua | .05 | .02 | .01 | ☐ 80 Joe Jacoby | .05 | .02 | .01 |
| Kansas City Chiefs | | | | Washington Redskins | | | |
| ☐ 36 Sammie Smith UER | .05 | .02 | .01 | ☐ 81 Keith Sims | .05 | .02 | .01 |
| (Text mentions Broncos, but Dolphins logo still on front) Miami Dolphins | | | | Miami Dolphins | | | |
| | | | | ☐ 82 Bubba McDowell | .05 | .02 | .01 |
| | | | | Houston Oilers | | | |
| | | | | ☐ 83 Ronnie Lippett | .05 | .02 | .01 |
| ☐ 37 Antone Davis | .05 | .02 | .01 | New England Patriots | | | |
| Philadelphia Eagles | | | | ☐ 84 Cris Carter | .10 | .05 | .01 |
| ☐ 38 Steve Young | .35 | .16 | .04 | Minnesota Vikings | | | |
| San Francisco 49ers | | | | ☐ 85 Chris Burkett | .05 | .02 | .01 |
| ☐ 39 Mike Baab | .05 | .02 | .01 | New York Jets | | | |
| Cleveland Browns | | | | ☐ 86 Issiac Holt | .05 | .02 | .01 |
| ☐ 40 Rick Fenney | .05 | .02 | .01 | Dallas Cowboys | | | |
| Minnesota Vikings | | | | ☐ 87 Duane Bickett | .05 | .02 | .01 |
| ☐ 41 Chris Hinton | .05 | .02 | .01 | Indianapolis Colts | | | |
| Atlanta Falcons | | | | ☐ 88 Leslie O'Neal | .08 | .04 | .01 |
| ☐ 42 Bart Oates | .05 | .02 | .01 | San Diego Chargers | | | |
| New York Giants | | | | ☐ 89 Gill Fenerty | .05 | .02 | .01 |
| ☐ 43 Bryan Hinkle | .05 | .02 | .01 | New Orleans Saints | | | |
| Pittsburgh Steelers | | | | ☐ 90 Pierce Holt | .05 | .02 | .01 |
| ☐ 44 James Francis | .08 | .04 | .01 | San Francisco 49ers | | | |
| Cincinnati Bengals | | | | ☐ 91 Willie Drewrey | .05 | .02 | .01 |
| ☐ 45 Ray Crockett | .05 | .02 | .01 | Tampa Bay Buccaneers | | | |
| Detroit Lions | | | | ☐ 92 Brian Blades | .08 | .04 | .01 |
| ☐ 46 Eric Dickerson UER | .10 | .05 | .01 | Seattle Seahawks | | | |
| (Text mentions Raiders, but Colts logo still on front) Indianapolis Colts | | | | ☐ 93 Tony Martin | .05 | .02 | .01 |
| | | | | Miami Dolphins | | | |
| | | | | ☐ 94 Jessie Hester | .05 | .02 | .01 |
| | | | | Indianapolis Colts | | | |
| ☐ 47 Hart Lee Dykes | .05 | .02 | .01 | ☐ 95 John Stephens | .08 | .04 | .01 |
| New England Patriots | | | | New England Patriots | | | |
| ☐ 48 Percy Snow | .05 | .02 | .01 | ☐ 96 Keith Willis UER | .05 | .02 | .01 |
| Kansas City Chiefs | | | | (Text mentions Redskins, but Steelers logo still on front) Pittsburgh Steelers | | | |
| ☐ 49 Ron Hall | .05 | .02 | .01 | | | | |
| Tampa Bay Buccaneers | | | | | | | |
| ☐ 50 Warren Moon | .20 | .09 | .03 | ☐ 97 Vai Sikahema UER | .08 | .04 | .01 |
| Houston Oilers | | | | (Text mentions Eagles, but Cardinals logo still on front) Phoenix Cardinals | | | |
| ☐ 51 Ed West | .05 | .02 | .01 | | | | |
| Green Bay Packers | | | | | | | |
| ☐ 52 Clarence Verdin | .05 | .02 | .01 | ☐ 98 Mark Higgs | .10 | .05 | .01 |
| Indianapolis Colts | | | | Miami Dolphins | | | |
| ☐ 53 Eugene Lockhart | .05 | .02 | .01 | ☐ 99 Steve McMichael | .08 | .04 | .01 |
| New England Patriots | | | | Chicago Bears | | | |
| ☐ 54 Andre Reed | .10 | .05 | .01 | ☐ 100 Deion Sanders | .20 | .09 | .03 |
| Buffalo Bills | | | | Atlanta Falcons | | | |
| ☐ 55 Kevin Ross | .08 | .04 | .01 | ☐ 101 Marvin Washington | .05 | .02 | .01 |
| Kansas City Chiefs | | | | New York Jets | | | |
| ☐ 56 Al Noga | .05 | .02 | .01 | ☐ 102 Ken Norton | .08 | .04 | .01 |
| Minnesota Vikings | | | | Dallas Cowboys | | | |
| ☐ 57 Wes Hopkins | .05 | .02 | .01 | ☐ 103 Barry Word | .10 | .05 | .01 |
| Philadelphia Eagles | | | | Kansas City Chiefs | | | |
| ☐ 58 Rufus Porter | .05 | .02 | .01 | ☐ 104 Sean Jones | .05 | .02 | .01 |
| Seattle Seahawks | | | | Houston Oilers | | | |
| ☐ 59 Brian Mitchell | .08 | .04 | .01 | ☐ 105 Ronnie Harmon | .05 | .02 | .01 |
| Washington Redskins | | | | San Diego Chargers | | | |
| ☐ 60 Reggie Roby | .05 | .02 | .01 | ☐ 106 Donnell Woolford | .05 | .02 | .01 |
| Miami Dolphins | | | | Chicago Bears | | | |
| ☐ 61 Rodney Peete | .08 | .04 | .01 | ☐ 107 Ray Agnew | .05 | .02 | .01 |
| Detroit Lions | | | | New England Patriots | | | |
| ☐ 62 Jeff Herrod | .05 | .02 | .01 | ☐ 108 Lemuel Stinson | .05 | .02 | .01 |
| Indianapolis Colts | | | | Chicago Bears | | | |
| ☐ 63 Anthony Smith | .08 | .04 | .01 | ☐ 109 Dennis Smith | .08 | .04 | .01 |
| Los Angeles Raiders | | | | Denver Broncos | | | |
| ☐ 64 Brad Muster | .05 | .02 | .01 | ☐ 110 Lorenzo White | .08 | .04 | .01 |
| Chicago Bears | | | | Houston Oilers | | | |
| ☐ 65 Jessie Tuggle | .05 | .02 | .01 | ☐ 111 Craig Heyward | .05 | .02 | .01 |
| Atlanta Falcons | | | | New Orleans Saints | | | |
| ☐ 66 Al Smith | .05 | .02 | .01 | ☐ 112 Jeff Query UER | .05 | .02 | .01 |
| Houston Oilers | | | | (Text mentions Oilers, but Packers logo still on front) Green Bay Packers | | | |
| ☐ 67 Jeff Hostetler | .15 | .07 | .02 | | | | |
| New York Giants | | | | | | | |
| ☐ 68 John L. Williams | .08 | .04 | .01 | ☐ 113 Gary Plummer | .05 | .02 | .01 |
| Seattle Seahawks | | | | San Diego Chargers | | | |
| ☐ 69 Paul Gruber | .05 | .02 | .01 | ☐ 114 John Taylor | .10 | .05 | .01 |
| Tampa Bay Buccaneers | | | | San Francisco 49ers | | | |
| ☐ 70 Cornelius Bennett | .10 | .05 | .01 | ☐ 115 Rohn Stark | .05 | .02 | .01 |
| Buffalo Bills | | | | Indianapolis Colts | | | |
| ☐ 71 William White | .05 | .02 | .01 | ☐ 116 Tom Waddle | .10 | .05 | .01 |
| Detroit Lions | | | | Chicago Bears | | | |
| ☐ 72 Tom Rathman | .08 | .04 | .01 | ☐ 117 Jeff Cross | .05 | .02 | .01 |
| San Francisco 49ers | | | | Miami Dolphins | | | |
| ☐ 73 Boomer Esiason | .15 | .07 | .02 | ☐ 118 Tim Green | .05 | .02 | .01 |
| Cincinnati Bengals | | | | Atlanta Falcons | | | |
| ☐ 74 Neil Smith | .10 | .05 | .01 | ☐ 119 Anthony Munoz | .05 | .02 | .01 |
| Kansas City Chiefs | | | | Cincinnati Bengals | | | |
| ☐ 75 Sterling Sharpe | .50 | .23 | .06 | ☐ 120 Mel Gray | .08 | .04 | .01 |
| Green Bay Packers | | | | Detroit Lions | | | |
| ☐ 76 James Jones | .05 | .02 | .01 | | | | |
| Cleveland Browns | | | | | | | |

| | | | |
|---|---|---|---|
| ☐ 121 Ray Donaldson...................... | .05 | .02 | .01 |
| Indianapolis Colts | | | |
| ☐ 122 Dennis Byrd........................... | .08 | .04 | .01 |
| New York Jets | | | |
| ☐ 123 Carnell Lake....................... | .05 | .02 | .01 |
| Pittsburgh Steelers | | | |
| ☐ 124 Broderick Thomas................. | .05 | .02 | .01 |
| Tampa Bay Buccaneers | | | |
| ☐ 125 Charles Mann........................ | .08 | .04 | .01 |
| Washington Redskins | | | |
| ☐ 126 Darion Conner...................... | .05 | .02 | .01 |
| Atlanta Falcons | | | |
| ☐ 127 John Roper........................... | .05 | .02 | .01 |
| Chicago Bears | | | |
| ☐ 128 Jack Del Rio UER .................. | .05 | .02 | .01 |
| (Text mentions Vikings, | | | |
| but Cowboys logo | | | |
| still on front) | | | |
| Dallas Cowboys | | | |
| ☐ 129 Rickey Dixon ........................ | .05 | .02 | .01 |
| Cincinnati Bengals | | | |
| ☐ 130 Eddie Anderson...................... | .05 | .02 | .01 |
| Los Angeles Raiders | | | |
| ☐ 131 Steve Broussard.................... | .08 | .04 | .01 |
| Atlanta Falcons | | | |
| ☐ 132 Michael Young ...................... | .05 | .02 | .01 |
| Denver Broncos | | | |
| ☐ 133 Lamar Lathon........................ | .05 | .02 | .01 |
| Houston Oilers | | | |
| ☐ 134 Rickey Jackson ..................... | .08 | .04 | .01 |
| New Orleans Saints | | | |
| ☐ 135 Billy Ray Smith...................... | .05 | .02 | .01 |
| San Diego Chargers | | | |
| ☐ 136 Tony Casillas........................ | .05 | .02 | .01 |
| Dallas Cowboys | | | |
| ☐ 137 Ickey Woods ........................ | .05 | .02 | .01 |
| Cincinnati Bengals | | | |
| ☐ 138 Ray Childress........................ | .08 | .04 | .01 |
| Houston Oilers | | | |
| ☐ 139 Vance Johnson ...................... | .08 | .04 | .01 |
| Denver Broncos | | | |
| ☐ 140 Brett Perriman....................... | .08 | .04 | .01 |
| Detroit Lions | | | |
| ☐ 141 Calvin Williams ..................... | .10 | .05 | .01 |
| Philadelphia Eagles | | | |
| ☐ 142 Dino Hackett ........................ | .05 | .02 | .01 |
| Kansas City Chiefs | | | |
| ☐ 143 Jacob Green ......................... | .05 | .02 | .01 |
| Seattle Seahawks | | | |
| ☐ 144 Robert Delpino ...................... | .08 | .04 | .01 |
| Los Angeles Rams | | | |
| ☐ 145 Marv Cook............................ | .08 | .04 | .01 |
| New England Patriots | | | |
| ☐ 146 Dwayne Harper ..................... | .05 | .02 | .01 |
| Seattle Seahawks | | | |
| ☐ 147 Ricky Ervins ......................... | .08 | .04 | .01 |
| Washington Redskins | | | |
| ☐ 148 Kelvin Martin......................... | .08 | .04 | .01 |
| Dallas Cowboys | | | |
| ☐ 149 Leroy Hoard ......................... | .08 | .04 | .01 |
| Cleveland Browns | | | |
| ☐ 150 Dan Marino........................... | .75 | .35 | .09 |
| Miami Dolphins | | | |
| ☐ 151 Richard Johnson UER............ | .05 | .02 | .01 |
| (He and Carrier had 2 | | | |
| interceptions, only given | | | |
| credit for 1 on card) | | | |
| Houston Oilers | | | |
| ☐ 152 Henry Ellard ......................... | .08 | .04 | .01 |
| Los Angeles Rams | | | |
| ☐ 153 Al Toon ............................... | .08 | .04 | .01 |
| New York Jets | | | |
| ☐ 154 Dermontti Dawson ............... | .05 | .02 | .01 |
| Pittsburgh Steelers | | | |
| ☐ 155 Robert Blackmon .................. | .05 | .02 | .01 |
| Seattle Seahawks | | | |
| ☐ 156 Howie Long .......................... | .08 | .04 | .01 |
| Los Angeles Raiders | | | |
| ☐ 157 David Fulcher ....................... | .05 | .02 | .01 |
| Cincinnati Bengals | | | |
| ☐ 158 Mike Merriweather ................ | .05 | .02 | .01 |
| Minnesota Vikings | | | |
| ☐ 159 Gary Anderson ...................... | .05 | .02 | .01 |
| Pittsburgh Steelers | | | |
| ☐ 160 John Friesz .......................... | .08 | .04 | .01 |
| San Diego Chargers | | | |
| ☐ 161 Eugene Robinson ................... | .05 | .02 | .01 |
| Seattle Seahawks | | | |
| ☐ 162 Brad Baxter ......................... | .08 | .04 | .01 |
| New York Jets | | | |
| ☐ 163 Bennie Blades ...................... | .05 | .02 | .01 |
| Detroit Lions | | | |
| ☐ 164 Harold Green ........................ | .05 | .02 | .01 |
| Cincinnati Bengals | | | |
| ☐ 165 Ernest Givens........................ | .08 | .04 | .01 |
| Houston Oilers | | | |
| ☐ 166 Deron Cherry ........................ | .05 | .02 | .01 |
| Kansas City Chiefs | | | |

| | | | |
|---|---|---|---|
| ☐ 167 Carl Banks............................ | .08 | .04 | .01 |
| New York Giants | | | |
| ☐ 168 Keith Jackson....................... | .10 | .05 | .01 |
| Philadelphia Eagles | | | |
| ☐ 169 Pat Leahy ............................ | .08 | .04 | .01 |
| New York Jets | | | |
| ☐ 170 Alvin Harper ......................... | .40 | .18 | .05 |
| Dallas Cowboys | | | |
| ☐ 171 David Little .......................... | .05 | .02 | .01 |
| Pittsburgh Steelers | | | |
| ☐ 172 Anthony Carter ..................... | .08 | .04 | .01 |
| Minnesota Vikings | | | |
| ☐ 173 Willie Gault .......................... | .08 | .04 | .01 |
| Los Angeles Raiders | | | |
| ☐ 174 Bruce Armstrong................... | .05 | .02 | .01 |
| New England Patriots | | | |
| ☐ 175 Junior Seau .......................... | .15 | .07 | .02 |
| San Diego Chargers | | | |
| ☐ 176 Eric Metcalf .......................... | .10 | .05 | .01 |
| Cleveland Browns | | | |
| ☐ 177 Tony Mandarich .................... | .05 | .02 | .01 |
| Green Bay Packers | | | |
| ☐ 178 Ernie Jones .......................... | .05 | .02 | .01 |
| Phoenix Cardinals | | | |
| ☐ 179 Albert Bentley ...................... | .05 | .02 | .01 |
| Indianapolis Colts | | | |
| ☐ 180 Mike Pritchard....................... | .25 | .11 | .03 |
| Atlanta Falcons | | | |
| ☐ 181 Bubby Brister ....................... | .08 | .04 | .01 |
| Pittsburgh Steelers | | | |
| ☐ 182 Vaughan Johnson ................. | .08 | .04 | .01 |
| New Orleans Saints | | | |
| ☐ 183 Robert Clark UER .................. | .05 | .02 | .01 |
| (Text mentions Dolphins, | | | |
| but Seahawks logo | | | |
| on front) | | | |
| Detroit Lions | | | |
| ☐ 184 Lawrence Dawsey .................. | .10 | .05 | .01 |
| Tampa Bay Buccaneers | | | |
| ☐ 185 Eric Green ............................ | .10 | .05 | .01 |
| Pittsburgh Steelers | | | |
| ☐ 186 Jay Schroeder........................ | .08 | .04 | .01 |
| Los Angeles Raiders | | | |
| ☐ 187 Andre Tippett ........................ | .08 | .04 | .01 |
| New England Patriots | | | |
| ☐ 188 Vinny Testaverde ................... | .10 | .05 | .01 |
| Tampa Bay Buccaneers | | | |
| ☐ 189 Wendell Davis ...................... | .05 | .02 | .01 |
| Chicago Bears | | | |
| ☐ 190 Russell Maryland .................. | .15 | .07 | .02 |
| Dallas Cowboys | | | |
| ☐ 191 Chris Singleton ..................... | .05 | .02 | .01 |
| New England Patriots | | | |
| ☐ 192 Ken O'Brien.......................... | .08 | .04 | .01 |
| New York Jets | | | |
| ☐ 193 Merril Hoge .......................... | .08 | .04 | .01 |
| Pittsburgh Steelers | | | |
| ☐ 194 Steve Bono .......................... | .50 | .23 | .06 |
| San Francisco 49ers | | | |
| ☐ 195 Earnest Byner ....................... | .08 | .04 | .01 |
| Washington Redskins | | | |
| ☐ 196 Mike Singletary ..................... | .10 | .05 | .01 |
| Chicago Bears | | | |
| ☐ 197 Gaston Green ....................... | .08 | .04 | .01 |
| Denver Broncos | | | |
| ☐ 198 Mark Carrier ......................... | .08 | .04 | .01 |
| Tampa Bay Buccaneers | | | |
| ☐ 199 Harvey Williams ................... | .10 | .05 | .01 |
| Kansas City Chiefs | | | |
| ☐ 200 Randall Cunningham............. | .10 | .05 | .01 |
| Philadelphia Eagles | | | |
| ☐ 201 Cris Dishman ........................ | .08 | .04 | .01 |
| Houston Oilers | | | |
| ☐ 202 Greg Townsend ...................... | .05 | .02 | .01 |
| Los Angeles Raiders | | | |
| ☐ 203 Christian Okoye ..................... | .08 | .04 | .01 |
| Kansas City Chiefs | | | |
| ☐ 204 Sam Mills ............................ | .08 | .04 | .01 |
| New Orleans Saints | | | |
| ☐ 205 Kyle Clifton .......................... | .05 | .02 | .01 |
| New York Jets | | | |
| ☐ 206 Jim Harbaugh ....................... | .08 | .04 | .01 |
| Chicago Bears | | | |
| ☐ 207 Anthony Thompson............... | .05 | .02 | .01 |
| Phoenix Cardinals | | | |
| ☐ 208 Rob Moore ........................... | .10 | .05 | .01 |
| New York Jets | | | |
| ☐ 209 Irving Fryar .......................... | .08 | .04 | .01 |
| New England Patriots | | | |
| ☐ 210 Derrick Thomas ..................... | .15 | .07 | .02 |
| Kansas City Chiefs | | | |
| ☐ 211 Chris Miller .......................... | .10 | .05 | .01 |
| Atlanta Falcons | | | |
| ☐ 212 Doug Smith .......................... | .05 | .02 | .01 |
| Houston Oilers | | | |
| ☐ 213 Michael Haynes..................... | .30 | .14 | .04 |
| Atlanta Falcons | | | |

| | | | |
|---|---|---|---|
| ☐ 214 Phil Simms | .10 | .05 | .01 |
| New York Giants | | | |
| ☐ 215 Charles Haley | .08 | .04 | .01 |
| San Francisco 49ers | | | |
| ☐ 216 Burt Grossman | .05 | .02 | .01 |
| San Diego Chargers | | | |
| ☐ 217 Rod Bernstine | .08 | .04 | .01 |
| San Diego Chargers | | | |
| ☐ 218 Louis Lipps | .08 | .04 | .01 |
| Pittsburgh Steelers | | | |
| ☐ 219 Dan McGwire UER | .08 | .04 | .01 |
| (Actually drafted in | | | |
| 1991, not 1990) | | | |
| Seattle Seahawks | | | |
| ☐ 220 Ethan Horton | .05 | .02 | .01 |
| Los Angeles Raiders | | | |
| ☐ 221 Michael Carter | .05 | .02 | .01 |
| San Francisco 49ers | | | |
| ☐ 222 Neil O'Donnell | .50 | .23 | .06 |
| Pittsburgh Steelers | | | |
| ☐ 223 Anthony Miller | .15 | .07 | .02 |
| San Diego Chargers | | | |
| ☐ 224 Eric Swann | .08 | .04 | .01 |
| Phoenix Cardinals | | | |
| ☐ 225 Thurman Thomas | .40 | .18 | .05 |
| Buffalo Bills | | | |
| ☐ 226 Jeff George | .20 | .09 | .03 |
| Indianapolis Colts | | | |
| ☐ 227 Joe Montana | 1.00 | .45 | .13 |
| San Francisco 49ers | | | |
| ☐ 228 Leonard Marshall | .08 | .04 | .01 |
| New York Giants | | | |
| ☐ 229 Haywood Jeffires | .10 | .05 | .01 |
| Houston Oilers | | | |
| ☐ 230 Mark Clayton | .08 | .04 | .01 |
| Miami Dolphins | | | |
| ☐ 231 Chris Doleman | .08 | .04 | .01 |
| Minnesota Vikings | | | |
| ☐ 232 Troy Aikman | 1.25 | .55 | .16 |
| Dallas Cowboys | | | |
| ☐ 233 Gary Anderson | .08 | .04 | .01 |
| Tampa Bay Buccaneers | | | |
| ☐ 234 Pat Swilling | .08 | .04 | .01 |
| New Orleans Saints | | | |
| ☐ 235 Ronnie Lott | .10 | .05 | .01 |
| Los Angeles Raiders | | | |
| ☐ 236 Brian Jordan | .08 | .04 | .01 |
| Atlanta Falcons | | | |
| ☐ 237 Bruce Smith | .10 | .05 | .01 |
| Buffalo Bills | | | |
| ☐ 238 Tony Jones UER | .05 | .02 | .01 |
| (Text mentions Falcons, | | | |
| but Oilers logo | | | |
| still on front) | | | |
| Houston Oilers | | | |
| ☐ 239 Tim McKyer | .08 | .04 | .01 |
| Atlanta Falcons | | | |
| ☐ 240 Gary Clark | .08 | .04 | .01 |
| Washington Redskins | | | |
| ☐ 241 Mitchell Price | .05 | .02 | .01 |
| Los Angeles Rams | | | |
| ☐ 242 John Kasay | .05 | .02 | .01 |
| Atlanta Falcons | | | |
| ☐ 243 Stephone Paige | .05 | .02 | .01 |
| Kansas City Chiefs | | | |
| ☐ 244 Jeff Wright | .05 | .02 | .01 |
| Buffalo Bills | | | |
| ☐ 245 Shannon Sharpe | .25 | .11 | .03 |
| Denver Broncos | | | |
| ☐ 246 Keith Byars | .08 | .04 | .01 |
| Philadelphia Eagles | | | |
| ☐ 247 Charles Dimry | .05 | .02 | .01 |
| Denver Broncos | | | |
| ☐ 248 Steve Smith | .08 | .04 | .01 |
| Los Angeles Raiders | | | |
| ☐ 249 Erric Pegram | .40 | .18 | .05 |
| Atlanta Falcons | | | |
| ☐ 250 Bernie Kosar | .10 | .05 | .01 |
| Cleveland Browns | | | |
| ☐ 251 Peter Tom Willis | .05 | .02 | .01 |
| Chicago Bears | | | |
| ☐ 252 Mark Ingram | .08 | .04 | .01 |
| New York Giants | | | |
| ☐ 253 Keith McKeller | .05 | .02 | .01 |
| Buffalo Bills | | | |
| ☐ 254 Lewis Billups UER | .05 | .02 | .01 |
| (Text mentions Packers, | | | |
| but Bengals logo | | | |
| still on front) | | | |
| Cincinnati Bengals | | | |
| ☐ 255 Alton Montgomery | .05 | .02 | .01 |
| Houston Oilers | | | |
| ☐ 256 Jimmie Jones | .05 | .02 | .01 |
| Dallas Cowboys | | | |
| ☐ 257 Brent Williams | .05 | .02 | .01 |
| New England Patriots | | | |
| ☐ 258 Gene Atkins | .05 | .02 | .01 |
| New Orleans Saints | | | |
| ☐ 259 Reggie Rutland | .05 | .02 | .01 |
| Minnesota Vikings | | | |
| ☐ 260 Sam Seale UER | .05 | .02 | .01 |
| (Text mentions Raiders, | | | |
| but Chargers logo | | | |
| still on back) | | | |
| San Diego Chargers | | | |
| ☐ 261 Andre Ware | .08 | .04 | .01 |
| Detroit Lions | | | |
| ☐ 262 Fred Barnett | .10 | .05 | .01 |
| Philadelphia Eagles | | | |
| ☐ 263 Randal Hill | .10 | .05 | .01 |
| Phoenix Cardinals | | | |
| ☐ 264 Patrick Hunter | .05 | .02 | .01 |
| Seattle Seahawks | | | |
| ☐ 265 Johnny Rembert UER | .05 | .02 | .01 |
| (Card says DNP in 1991, | | | |
| but he played 12 games) | | | |
| New England Patriots | | | |
| ☐ 266 Monte Coleman | .05 | .02 | .01 |
| Washington Redskins | | | |
| ☐ 267 Aaron Wallace | .05 | .02 | .01 |
| Los Angeles Raiders | | | |
| ☐ 268 Ferrell Edmunds | .05 | .02 | .01 |
| Miami Dolphins | | | |
| ☐ 269 Stan Thomas | .05 | .02 | .01 |
| Chicago Bears | | | |
| ☐ 270 Robb Thomas | .05 | .02 | .01 |
| Kansas City Chiefs | | | |
| ☐ 271 Martin Bayless UER | .05 | .02 | .01 |
| (Text mentions Chiefs, | | | |
| but Chargers logo | | | |
| still on front) | | | |
| San Diego Chargers | | | |
| ☐ 272 Dean Biasucci | .05 | .02 | .01 |
| Indianapolis Colts | | | |
| ☐ 273 Keith Henderson | .05 | .02 | .01 |
| San Francisco 49ers | | | |
| ☐ 274 Vinnie Clark | .05 | .02 | .01 |
| Green Bay Packers | | | |
| ☐ 275 Emmitt Smith | 2.00 | .90 | .25 |
| Dallas Cowboys | | | |
| ☐ 276 Mark Rypien | .10 | .05 | .01 |
| Washington Redskins | | | |
| ☐ 277 Atlanta Falcons | .15 | .07 | .02 |
| Wing and a Prayer | | | |
| (Michael Haynes) | | | |
| ☐ 278 Buffalo Bills | .15 | .07 | .02 |
| Machine Gun | | | |
| (Jim Kelly) | | | |
| ☐ 279 Chicago Bears | .05 | .02 | .01 |
| Grizzly | | | |
| (Tom Waddle) | | | |
| ☐ 280 Cincinnati Bengals | .05 | .02 | .01 |
| Price is Right | | | |
| (Mitchell Price) | | | |
| ☐ 281 Cleveland Browns | .08 | .04 | .01 |
| Coasting | | | |
| (Bernie Kosar) | | | |
| ☐ 282 Dallas Cowboys | .25 | .11 | .03 |
| Gunned Down | | | |
| (Michael Irvin) | | | |
| ☐ 283 Denver Broncos | .15 | .07 | .02 |
| The Drive II | | | |
| (John Elway) | | | |
| ☐ 284 Detroit Lions | .05 | .02 | .01 |
| Lions Roar | | | |
| (Mel Gray) | | | |
| ☐ 285 Green Bay Packers | .20 | .09 | .03 |
| Razor Sharpe | | | |
| (Sterling Sharpe) | | | |
| ☐ 286 Houston Oilers | .10 | .05 | .01 |
| Oil's Well | | | |
| (Warren Moon) | | | |
| ☐ 287 Indianapolis Colts | .08 | .04 | .01 |
| Whew (Jeff George) | | | |
| ☐ 288 Kansas City Chiefs | .05 | .02 | .01 |
| Ambush | | | |
| (Derrick Thomas) | | | |
| ☐ 289 Los Angeles Raiders | .08 | .04 | .01 |
| Lott of Defense | | | |
| (Ronnie Lott) | | | |
| ☐ 290 Los Angeles Rams | .05 | .02 | .01 |
| Ram It | | | |
| (Robert Delpino) | | | |
| ☐ 291 Miami Dolphins | .25 | .11 | .03 |
| Miami Ice | | | |
| (Dan Marino) | | | |
| ☐ 292 Minnesota Vikings | .05 | .02 | .01 |
| Purple Blaze | | | |
| (Cris Carter) | | | |
| ☐ 293 New England Patriots | .05 | .02 | .01 |
| Surprise Attack | | | |
| (Irving Fryar) | | | |
| ☐ 294 New Orleans Saints | .05 | .02 | .01 |
| Marching In | | | |
| (Gene Atkins) | | | |

| | | | |
|---|---|---|---|
| ☐ 295 New York Giants | .08 | .04 | .01 |
| Almost Perfect | | | |
| (Phil Simms) | | | |
| ☐ 296 New York Jets | .05 | .02 | .01 |
| Playoff Bound | | | |
| (Ken O'Brien) | | | |
| ☐ 297 Philadelphia Eagles | .08 | .04 | .01 |
| Flying High | | | |
| (Keith Jackson) | | | |
| ☐ 298 Phoenix Cardinals | .05 | .02 | .01 |
| Airborne | | | |
| (Ricky Proehl) | | | |
| ☐ 299 Pittsburgh Steelers | .05 | .02 | .01 |
| Steel Curtain | | | |
| (Brian Hinkle) | | | |
| ☐ 300 San Diego Chargers | .05 | .02 | .01 |
| Lightning | | | |
| (John Friesz) | | | |
| ☐ 301 San Francisco 49ers | .25 | .11 | .03 |
| Instant Rice | | | |
| (Jerry Rice) | | | |
| ☐ 302 Seattle Seahawks | .05 | .02 | .01 |
| Defense Never Rests | | | |
| (Eugene Robinson) | | | |
| ☐ 303 Tampa Bay Buccaneers | .05 | .02 | .01 |
| Stunned | | | |
| (Broderick Thomas) | | | |
| ☐ 304 Washington Redskins | .08 | .04 | .01 |
| Super | | | |
| (Mark Rypien) | | | |
| ☐ 305 Jim Kelly LL | .15 | .07 | .02 |
| Buffalo Bills | | | |
| ☐ 306 Steve Young LL | .12 | .05 | .02 |
| San Francisco 49ers | | | |
| ☐ 307 Thurman Thomas LL | .20 | .09 | .03 |
| Buffalo Bills | | | |
| ☐ 308 Emmitt Smith LL | .75 | .35 | .09 |
| Dallas Cowboys | | | |
| ☐ 309 Haywood Jeffires LL | .08 | .04 | .01 |
| Houston Oilers | | | |
| ☐ 310 Michael Irvin LL | .25 | .11 | .03 |
| Dallas Cowboys | | | |
| ☐ 311 William Fuller LL | .05 | .02 | .01 |
| Houston Oilers | | | |
| ☐ 312 Pat Swilling LL | .08 | .04 | .01 |
| New Orleans Saints | | | |
| ☐ 313 Ronnie Lott LL | .08 | .04 | .01 |
| Los Angeles Raiders | | | |
| ☐ 314 Deion Sanders LL | .05 | .02 | .01 |
| Atlanta Falcons | | | |
| ☐ 315 Cornelius Bennett HH | .08 | .04 | .01 |
| Buffalo Bills | | | |
| ☐ 316 David Fulcher HH | .05 | .02 | .01 |
| Cincinnati Bengals | | | |
| ☐ 317 Ronnie Lott HH | .08 | .04 | .01 |
| Los Angeles Raiders | | | |
| ☐ 318 Pat Swilling HH | .08 | .04 | .01 |
| New Orleans Saints | | | |
| ☐ 319 Lawrence Taylor HH | .05 | .02 | .01 |
| New York Giants | | | |
| ☐ 320 Derrick Thomas HH | .05 | .02 | .01 |
| Kansas City Chiefs | | | |
| ☐ 321 Steve Emtman | .15 | .07 | .02 |
| Indianapolis Colts | | | |
| ☐ 322 Carl Pickens | .35 | .16 | .04 |
| Cincinnati Bengals | | | |
| ☐ 323 David Klingler | .50 | .23 | .06 |
| Cincinnati Bengals | | | |
| ☐ 324 Dale Carter | .25 | .11 | .03 |
| Kansas City Chiefs | | | |
| ☐ 325 Mike Gaddis | .05 | .02 | .01 |
| Minnesota Vikings | | | |
| ☐ 326 Quentin Coryatt | .30 | .14 | .04 |
| Indianapolis Colts | | | |
| ☐ 327 Darryl Williams | .20 | .09 | .03 |
| Cincinnati Bengals | | | |
| ☐ 328 Jeremy Lincoln | .15 | .07 | .02 |
| Chicago Bears | | | |
| ☐ 329 Robert Jones | .12 | .05 | .02 |
| Dallas Cowboys | | | |
| ☐ 330 Bucky Richardson | .20 | .09 | .03 |
| Houston Oilers | | | |
| ☐ 331 Tony Brooks | .05 | .02 | .01 |
| Philadelphia Eagles | | | |
| ☐ 332 Alonzo Spellman | .20 | .09 | .03 |
| Chicago Bears | | | |
| ☐ 333 Robert Brooks | .15 | .07 | .02 |
| Green Bay Packers | | | |
| ☐ 334 Marco Coleman | .30 | .14 | .04 |
| Miami Dolphins | | | |
| ☐ 335 Siran Stacy UER | .10 | .05 | .01 |
| (Misspelled Stacey) | | | |
| Philadelphia Eagles | | | |
| ☐ 336 Tommy Maddox | .40 | .18 | .05 |
| Denver Broncos | | | |
| ☐ 337 Steve Israel | .05 | .02 | .01 |
| Los Angeles Rams | | | |

| | | | |
|---|---|---|---|
| ☐ 338 Vaughn Dunbar | .20 | .09 | .03 |
| New Orleans Saints | | | |
| ☐ 339 Shane Collins | .15 | .07 | .02 |
| Washington Redskins | | | |
| ☐ 340 Kevin Smith | .25 | .11 | .03 |
| Dallas Cowboys | | | |
| ☐ 341 Chris Mims | .25 | .11 | .03 |
| San Diego Chargers | | | |
| ☐ 342 Chester McGlockton UER | .20 | .09 | .03 |
| (Misspelled McGlokton | | | |
| on both sides) | | | |
| Los Angeles Raiders | | | |
| ☐ 343 Tracy Scroggins | .20 | .09 | .03 |
| Detroit Lions | | | |
| ☐ 344 Howard Dinkins | .05 | .02 | .01 |
| Atlanta Falcons | | | |
| ☐ 345 Levon Kirkland | .15 | .07 | .02 |
| Pittsburgh Steelers | | | |
| ☐ 346 Terrell Buckley | .25 | .11 | .03 |
| Green Bay Packers | | | |
| ☐ 347 Marquez Pope | .10 | .05 | .01 |
| San Diego Chargers | | | |
| ☐ 348 Phillippi Sparks | .05 | .02 | .01 |
| New York Giants | | | |
| ☐ 349 Joe Bowden | .05 | .02 | .01 |
| Houston Oilers | | | |
| ☐ 350 Edgar Bennett | .30 | .14 | .04 |
| Green Bay Packers | | | |
| ☐ SP1 Jim Kelly | 7.00 | 3.10 | .85 |
| ☐ SP1AU Jim Kelly AUTO | 100.00 | 45.00 | 12.50 |
| ☐ SP2AU J.Kelly/Magic AUTO | 500.00 | 230.00 | 65.00 |

## 1992 SkyBox Impact Holograms

The 1992 SkyBox Impact Hologram set consists of six standard-size (2 1/2" by 3 1/2") cards. The first two hologram cards (featuring Jim Kelly and Lawrence Taylor) were randomly inserted in 12-card foil packs. Four additional hologram cards were available as part of a mail-away promotion (H3-H6). The fronts feature full-bleed holograms with the player's last name in block lettering toward the bottom of the card. The cards are numbered with an "H" prefix.

| | MINT | EXC | G-VG |
|---|---|---|---|
| COMPLETE SET (6) | 16.00 | 7.25 | 2.00 |
| COMMON PLAYER (H1-H2) | 2.00 | .90 | .25 |
| COMMON PLAYER (H3-H6) | 3.50 | 1.55 | .45 |
| | | | |
| ☐ H1 Jim Kelly | 3.00 | 1.35 | .40 |
| Buffalo Bills | | | |
| ☐ H2 Lawrence Taylor | 2.00 | .90 | .25 |
| New York Giants | | | |
| ☐ H3 Christian Okoye | 3.50 | 1.55 | .45 |
| Kansas City Chiefs | | | |
| ☐ H4 Mark Rypien | 3.50 | 1.55 | .45 |
| Washington Redskins | | | |
| ☐ H5 Pat Swilling | 3.50 | 1.55 | .45 |
| New Orleans Saints | | | |
| ☐ H6 Ricky Ervins | 3.50 | 1.55 | .45 |
| Washington Redskins | | | |

## 1992 SkyBox Impact Major Impact

This 20-card standard-size (2 1/2" by 3 1/2") set was randomly inserted into 1992 SkyBox Impact jumbo packs. The fronts feature full-bleed color player photos with the player's last name in silver-foil block lettering across the top of the picture. The backs carry a color player photo on the upper portion and player profile on the lower portion. The photos are separated from the text by a red stripe on AFC

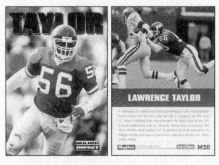

player cards (1-10) and by a blue stripe on NFC player cards (11-20). The cards are numbered on the back.

| | MINT | EXC | G-VG |
|---|---|---|---|
| COMPLETE SET (20) | 25.00 | 11.50 | 3.10 |
| COMMON PLAYER (1-20) | .50 | .23 | .06 |
| ☐ 1 Cornelius Bennett | .75 | .35 | .09 |
| Buffalo Bills | | | |
| ☐ 2 David Fulcher | .50 | .23 | .06 |
| Cincinnati Bengals | | | |
| ☐ 3 Haywood Jeffires | .75 | .35 | .09 |
| Houston Oilers | | | |
| ☐ 4 Ronnie Lott | .75 | .35 | .09 |
| Los Angeles Raiders | | | |
| ☐ 5 Dan Marino | 4.00 | 1.80 | .50 |
| Miami Dolphins | | | |
| ☐ 6 Warren Moon | 1.00 | .45 | .13 |
| Houston Oilers | | | |
| ☐ 7 Christian Okoye | .50 | .23 | .06 |
| Kansas City Chiefs | | | |
| ☐ 8 Andre Reed | .50 | .23 | .06 |
| Buffalo Bills | | | |
| ☐ 9 Derrick Thomas | .75 | .35 | .09 |
| Kansas City Chiefs | | | |
| ☐ 10 Thurman Thomas | 2.50 | 1.15 | .30 |
| Buffalo Bills | | | |
| ☐ 11 Troy Aikman | 6.00 | 2.70 | .75 |
| Dallas Cowboys | | | |
| ☐ 12 Randall Cunningham | 1.00 | .45 | .13 |
| Philadelphia Eagles | | | |
| ☐ 13 Michael Irvin | 3.00 | 1.35 | .40 |
| Dallas Cowboys | | | |
| ☐ 14 Jerry Rice | 3.00 | 1.35 | .40 |
| San Francisco 49ers | | | |
| ☐ 15 Joe Montana | 5.00 | 2.30 | .60 |
| San Francisco 49ers | | | |
| ☐ 16 Mark Rypien | .75 | .35 | .09 |
| Washington Redskins | | | |
| ☐ 17 Deion Sanders | 1.00 | .45 | .13 |
| Atlanta Falcons | | | |
| ☐ 18 Emmitt Smith | 8.00 | 3.60 | 1.00 |
| Dallas Cowboys | | | |
| ☐ 19 Pat Swilling | .50 | .23 | .06 |
| New Orleans Saints | | | |
| ☐ 20 Lawrence Taylor | .75 | .35 | .09 |
| New York Giants | | | |

## 1992 SkyBox Primetime Previews

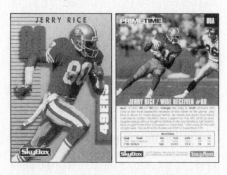

This five-card set was issued in cello packs to provide collectors with samples of SkyBox's Primetime series. The cards measure the standard size (2 1/2" by 3 1/2"). The fronts feature cut-out action color player photos superimposed on a computer generated gray background accented with a row of thin black lines. The player's name

is printed across the top. The player's jersey number is team color-coded while his team name is printed vertically in a team color-coded bar along the edge of the card. For example, the Elway card has a Broncos "purple" background featuring the picture of a horse. The backs display action color player photos on the upper half of the card. Biographical information, statistics, and career highlights appear below a team color-coded stripe on a white background. Except for the title card, the cards are numbered on the back at the upper right corner.

| | MINT | EXC | G-VG |
|---|---|---|---|
| COMPLETE SET (5) | 9.00 | 3.75 | .90 |
| COMMON PLAYER (A-D) | 1.00 | .40 | .10 |
| ☐ 0A Jerry Rice | 4.00 | 1.60 | .40 |
| San Francisco 49ers | | | |
| ☐ 0B Deion Sanders | 2.00 | .80 | .20 |
| Atlanta Falcons | | | |
| ☐ 0C John Elway | 3.00 | 1.20 | .30 |
| Denver Broncos | | | |
| ☐ 0D Vaughn Dunbar | 1.50 | .60 | .15 |
| New Orleans Saints | | | |
| ☐ NNO Title Card | 1.00 | .40 | .10 |
| (Advertisement) | | | |

## 1992 SkyBox Primetime

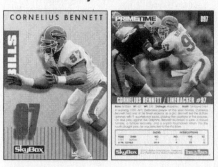

The 1992 SkyBox Primetime football set consists of 360 cards, measuring the standard size (2 1/2" by 3 1/2"). The production run was reportedly 5,000 20-box foil cases or 100,000 individually numbered display boxes. Eighteen special cards were randomly inserted throughout the foil packs: a Jim Kelly hologram, a Steve Emtman Horse-Power card, silver foil versions of the 15 Costacos Poster Art cards, and a Costacos Poster Art checklist card. By tilting the card, the hologram on the Kelly card alternates between a passing pose and Kelly celebrating a touchdown with his hands outstretched overhead. The back carries a color player photo on the upper half and Kelly's own description of the best game of his career. The front of the Emtman card sports a Costacos Brothers poster entitled "Horse Power." It introduces an etched, embossed foil Spectra-Etch. The back has a color player photo on the upper half and Kelly's evaluation of Emtman. Also there are five uncorrected errors involving misnumbered cards; see card numbers 38, 61, 138, 216, and 267. The fronts feature cut-out action color player photos superimposed on a computer generated gray background accented with a row of thin black lines. The player's name is printed across the top. The player's jersey number is team color-coded while his team name is printed vertically in a team color-coded bar along the edge of the card. The cards of rookies, including many in their NFL uniforms, have the round and the draft pick number on their fronts. The backs display action color player photos on the upper half of the card. Biographical information, statistics, and career highlights appear on a white background separated from the photo by a team-color colded stripe. The following cards make up the Team MVP subset (65, 68, 77, 90, 95, 101, 159, 168, 170, 172, 173, 176, 178, 181, 190, 209, 232, 243, 245, 257, 271, 273, 287, 288, 305, 307, 309, 332). Moreover, the set includes 15 Costacos Brothers Poster Art cards (23, 67, 86, 161, 165, 184, 197, 202, 211, 236, 272, 284, 313, 331, 344). The set closes with dual team checklists (347-360). The cards are numbered on the back. The key Rookie Cards in this set are Edgar Bennett, Terrell Buckley, Dale Carter, Marco Coleman, Quentin Coryatt, Vaughn Dunbar, Steve Emtman, David Klingler, Tommy Maddox, Carl Pickens, and Tony Smith.

| | MINT | EXC | G-VG |
|---|---|---|---|
| COMPLETE SET (360) | 30.00 | 13.50 | 3.80 |
| COMMON PLAYER (1-360) | .10 | .05 | .01 |

| | | | |
|---|---|---|---|
| ☐ 1 Deion Sanders............................ | .40 | .18 | .05 |
| Atlanta Falcons | | | |
| ☐ 2 Shane Collins UER .................... | .30 | .14 | .04 |
| (Photo actually | | | |
| Terry Smith; | | | |
| see also number 216) | | | |
| Washington Redskins | | | |
| ☐ 3 James Patton .......................... | .15 | .07 | .02 |
| Buffalo Bills | | | |
| ☐ 4 Reggie Roby ........................... | .10 | .05 | .01 |
| Miami Dolphins | | | |
| ☐ 5 Merril Hoge ............................ | .12 | .05 | .02 |
| Pittsburgh Steelers | | | |
| ☐ 6 Vinny Testaverde ..................... | .15 | .07 | .02 |
| Tampa Bay Buccaneers | | | |
| ☐ 7 Boomer Esiason ...................... | .25 | .11 | .03 |
| Cincinnati Bengals | | | |
| ☐ 8 Troy Aikman ........................... | 3.00 | 1.35 | .40 |
| Dallas Cowboys | | | |
| ☐ 9 Tommy Jeter ........................... | .15 | .07 | .02 |
| Philadelphia Eagles | | | |
| ☐ 10 Brent Williams ...................... | .10 | .05 | .01 |
| New England Patriots | | | |
| ☐ 11 Mark Rypien .......................... | .15 | .07 | .02 |
| Washington Redskins | | | |
| ☐ 12 Jim Kelly ............................... | .50 | .23 | .06 |
| Buffalo Bills | | | |
| ☐ 13 Dan Marino ........................... | 1.50 | .65 | .19 |
| Miami Dolphins | | | |
| ☐ 14 Bill Cowher CO ..................... | .10 | .05 | .01 |
| Pittsburgh Steelers | | | |
| ☐ 15 Leslie O'Neal ........................ | .12 | .05 | .02 |
| San Diego Chargers | | | |
| ☐ 16 Joe Montana .......................... | 2.00 | .90 | .25 |
| San Francisco 49ers | | | |
| ☐ 17 William Fuller ........................ | .10 | .05 | .01 |
| Houston Oilers | | | |
| ☐ 18 Paul Gruber ........................... | .10 | .05 | .01 |
| Tampa Bay Buccaneers | | | |
| ☐ 19 Bernie Kosar .......................... | .15 | .07 | .02 |
| Cleveland Browns | | | |
| ☐ 20 Rickey Jackson ...................... | .12 | .05 | .02 |
| New Orleans Saints | | | |
| ☐ 21 Earnest Byner ........................ | .12 | .05 | .02 |
| Washington Redskins | | | |
| ☐ 22 Emmitt Smith ......................... | 5.00 | 2.30 | .60 |
| Dallas Cowboys | | | |
| ☐ 23 Neal Anderson PC .................. | .10 | .05 | .01 |
| Chicago Bears | | | |
| ☐ 24 Greg Lloyd ............................ | .10 | .05 | .01 |
| Pittsburgh Steelers | | | |
| ☐ 25 Ronnie Harmon ...................... | .10 | .05 | .01 |
| San Diego Chargers | | | |
| ☐ 26 Ray Donaldson ....................... | .10 | .05 | .01 |
| Indianapolis Colts | | | |
| ☐ 27 Kevin Ross ............................ | .12 | .05 | .02 |
| Kansas City Chiefs | | | |
| ☐ 28 Irving Fryar ........................... | .12 | .05 | .02 |
| New England Patriots | | | |
| ☐ 29 John L. Williams ..................... | .12 | .05 | .02 |
| Seattle Seahawks | | | |
| ☐ 30 Chris Hinton .......................... | .10 | .05 | .01 |
| Atlanta Falcons | | | |
| ☐ 31 Tracy Scroggins ..................... | .40 | .18 | .05 |
| Detroit Lions | | | |
| ☐ 32 Rohn Stark ............................ | .10 | .05 | .01 |
| Indianapolis Colts | | | |
| ☐ 33 David Fulcher ........................ | .10 | .05 | .01 |
| Cincinnati Bengals | | | |
| ☐ 34 Thurman Thomas ................... | .75 | .35 | .09 |
| Buffalo Bills | | | |
| ☐ 35 Christian Okoye ..................... | .12 | .05 | .02 |
| Kansas City Chiefs | | | |
| ☐ 36 Vaughn Dunbar ...................... | .40 | .18 | .05 |
| New Orleans Saints | | | |
| ☐ 37 Joel Steed ............................. | .15 | .07 | .02 |
| Pittsburgh Steelers | | | |
| ☐ 38 James Francis UER ................ | .12 | .05 | .02 |
| Cincinnati Bengals | | | |
| (card number on back | | | |
| is actually 354) | | | |
| ☐ 39 Dermontti Dawson ................. | .10 | .05 | .01 |
| Pittsburgh Steelers | | | |
| ☐ 40 Mark Higgs ........................... | .15 | .07 | .02 |
| Miami Dolphins | | | |
| ☐ 41 Flipper Anderson UER ........... | .12 | .05 | .02 |
| Los Angeles Rams | | | |
| 5,301 receiving yards in 1991 | | | |
| ☐ 42 Ronnie Lott ........................... | .15 | .07 | .02 |
| Los Angeles Raiders | | | |
| ☐ 43 Jim Everett ............................ | .10 | .05 | .01 |
| Los Angeles Rams | | | |
| ☐ 44 Burt Grossman ....................... | .10 | .05 | .01 |
| San Diego Chargers | | | |
| ☐ 45 Charles Haley ......................... | .12 | .05 | .02 |
| Dallas Cowboys | | | |
| ☐ 46 Ricky Proehl .......................... | .15 | .07 | .02 |

| | | | |
|---|---|---|---|
| Phoenix Cardinals | | | |
| ☐ 47 Marquez Pope ....................... | .15 | .07 | .02 |
| San Diego Chargers | | | |
| ☐ 48 David Treadwell..................... | .10 | .05 | .01 |
| Denver Broncos | | | |
| ☐ 49 William White........................ | .10 | .05 | .01 |
| Detroit Lions | | | |
| ☐ 50 John Elway............................ | 1.00 | .45 | .13 |
| Denver Broncos | | | |
| ☐ 51 Mark Carrier.......................... | .12 | .05 | .02 |
| Tampa Bay Buccaneers | | | |
| ☐ 52 Brian Blades.......................... | .12 | .05 | .02 |
| Seattle Seahawks | | | |
| ☐ 53 Keith McKeller....................... | .10 | .05 | .01 |
| Buffalo Bills | | | |
| ☐ 54 Art Monk............................... | .15 | .07 | .02 |
| Washington Redskins | | | |
| ☐ 55 Lamar Lathon......................... | .10 | .05 | .01 |
| Houston Oilers | | | |
| ☐ 56 Pat Swilling............................ | .12 | .05 | .02 |
| New Orleans Saints | | | |
| ☐ 57 Steve Broussard...................... | .12 | .05 | .02 |
| Atlanta Falcons | | | |
| ☐ 58 Derrick Thomas....................... | .30 | .14 | .04 |
| Kansas City Chiefs | | | |
| ☐ 59 Keith Jackson......................... | .15 | .07 | .02 |
| Philadelphia Eagles | | | |
| ☐ 60 Leonard Marshall .................... | .12 | .05 | .02 |
| New York Giants | | | |
| ☐ 61 Eric Metcalf UER .................... | .15 | .07 | .02 |
| Cleveland Browns | | | |
| (card number on back | | | |
| is actually 350) | | | |
| ☐ 62 Andy Heck............................. | .10 | .05 | .01 |
| Seattle Seahawks | | | |
| ☐ 63 Mark Carrier.......................... | .12 | .05 | .02 |
| Chicago Bears | | | |
| ☐ 64 Neil O'Donnell....................... | 1.00 | .45 | .13 |
| Pittsburgh Steelers | | | |
| ☐ 65 Broderick Thomas MVP ......... | .10 | .05 | .01 |
| Tampa Bay Buccaneers | | | |
| ☐ 66 Eric Kramer........................... | .20 | .09 | .03 |
| Detroit Lions | | | |
| ☐ 67 Joe Montana PC...................... | .75 | .35 | .09 |
| San Francisco 49ers | | | |
| ☐ 68 Robert Delpino MVP .............. | .10 | .05 | .01 |
| Los Angeles Rams | | | |
| ☐ 69 Steve Israel .......................... | .10 | .05 | .01 |
| Los Angeles Rams | | | |
| ☐ 70 Herman Moore....................... | .60 | .25 | .08 |
| Detroit Lions | | | |
| ☐ 71 Jacob Green ........................... | .10 | .05 | .01 |
| Seattle Seahawks | | | |
| ☐ 72 Lorenzo White........................ | .12 | .05 | .02 |
| Houston Oilers | | | |
| ☐ 73 Nick Lowery.......................... | .12 | .05 | .02 |
| Kansas City Chiefs | | | |
| ☐ 74 Eugene Robinson..................... | .10 | .05 | .01 |
| Seattle Seahawks | | | |
| ☐ 75 Carl Banks............................. | .12 | .05 | .02 |
| New York Giants | | | |
| ☐ 76 Bruce Smith .......................... | .15 | .07 | .02 |
| Buffalo Bills | | | |
| ☐ 77 Mark Rypien MVP .................. | .12 | .05 | .02 |
| Washington Redskins | | | |
| ☐ 78 Anthony Munoz....................... | .10 | .05 | .01 |
| Cincinnati Bengals | | | |
| ☐ 79 Clayton Holmes....................... | .10 | .05 | .01 |
| Dallas Cowboys | | | |
| ☐ 80 Jerry Rice............................. | 1.25 | .55 | .16 |
| San Francisco 49ers | | | |
| ☐ 81 Henry Ellard .......................... | .12 | .05 | .02 |
| Los Angeles Rams | | | |
| ☐ 82 Tim McGee............................ | .10 | .05 | .01 |
| Cincinnati Bengals | | | |
| ☐ 83 Al Toon ................................ | .12 | .05 | .02 |
| New York Jets | | | |
| ☐ 84 Haywood Jeffires .................... | .15 | .07 | .02 |
| Houston Oilers | | | |
| ☐ 85 Mike Singletary ...................... | .15 | .07 | .02 |
| Chicago Bears | | | |
| ☐ 86 Thurman Thomas PC .............. | .40 | .18 | .05 |
| Buffalo Bills | | | |
| ☐ 87 Jessie Hester ......................... | .10 | .05 | .01 |
| Indianapolis Colts | | | |
| ☐ 88 Michael Irvin ......................... | 1.25 | .55 | .16 |
| Dallas Cowboys | | | |
| ☐ 89 Jack Del Rio .......................... | .10 | .05 | .01 |
| Minnesota Vikings | | | |
| ☐ 90 Seth Joyner MVP .................... | .12 | .05 | .02 |
| (No player photo) | | | |
| Philadelphia Eagles | | | |
| ☐ 91 Jeff Herrod ............................ | .10 | .05 | .01 |
| Indianapolis Colts | | | |
| ☐ 92 Michael Dean Perry .............. | .15 | .07 | .02 |
| Cleveland Browns | | | |
| ☐ 93 Louis Oliver........................... | .12 | .05 | .02 |
| Miami Dolphins | | | |

| | | | |
|---|---|---|---|
| ☐ 94 Dan McGwire | .12 | .05 | .02 |
| Seattle Seahawks | | | |
| ☐ 95 Cris Carter MVP | .12 | .05 | .02 |
| Minnesota Vikings | | | |
| ☐ 96 Dale Carter | .50 | .23 | .06 |
| Kansas City Chiefs | | | |
| ☐ 97 Cornelius Bennett | .15 | .07 | .02 |
| Buffalo Bills | | | |
| ☐ 98 Edgar Bennett | .60 | .25 | .08 |
| Green Bay Packers | | | |
| ☐ 99 Steve Young | .75 | .35 | .09 |
| San Francisco 49ers | | | |
| ☐ 100 Warren Moon | .35 | .16 | .04 |
| Houston Oilers | | | |
| ☐ 101 Deion Sanders MVP | .10 | .05 | .01 |
| Atlanta Falcons | | | |
| ☐ 102 Mel Gray | .12 | .05 | .02 |
| Detroit Lions | | | |
| ☐ 103 Mark Murphy | .10 | .05 | .01 |
| Green Bay Packers | | | |
| ☐ 104 Jeff George | .40 | .18 | .05 |
| Indianapolis Colts | | | |
| ☐ 105 Anthony Miller | .30 | .14 | .04 |
| San Diego Chargers | | | |
| ☐ 106 Tom Rathman | .12 | .05 | .02 |
| San Francisco 49ers | | | |
| ☐ 107 Fred McAfee | .30 | .14 | .04 |
| New Orleans Saints | | | |
| ☐ 108 Paul Siever | .15 | .07 | .02 |
| Washington Redskins | | | |
| ☐ 109 Lemuel Stinson | .10 | .05 | .01 |
| Chicago Bears | | | |
| ☐ 110 Vance Johnson | .12 | .05 | .02 |
| Denver Broncos | | | |
| ☐ 111 Jay Schroeder | .12 | .05 | .02 |
| Los Angeles Raiders | | | |
| ☐ 112 Calvin Williams | .15 | .07 | .02 |
| Philadelphia Eagles | | | |
| ☐ 113 Cortez Kennedy | .20 | .09 | .03 |
| Seattle Seahawks | | | |
| ☐ 114 Quentin Coryatt | .50 | .23 | .06 |
| Indianapolis Colts | | | |
| ☐ 115 Ronnie Lippett | .10 | .05 | .01 |
| New England Patriots | | | |
| ☐ 116 Brad Baxter | .12 | .05 | .02 |
| New York Jets | | | |
| ☐ 117 Bubba McDowell | .10 | .05 | .01 |
| Houston Oilers | | | |
| ☐ 118 Cris Carter | .15 | .07 | .02 |
| Minnesota Vikings | | | |
| ☐ 119 John Stephens | .12 | .05 | .02 |
| New England Patriots | | | |
| ☐ 120 James Hasty | .10 | .05 | .01 |
| New York Jets | | | |
| ☐ 121 Bubby Brister | .12 | .05 | .02 |
| Pittsburgh Steelers | | | |
| ☐ 122 Robert Jones | .20 | .09 | .03 |
| Dallas Cowboys | | | |
| ☐ 123 Sterling Sharpe | 1.25 | .55 | .16 |
| Green Bay Packers | | | |
| ☐ 124 Jason Hanson | .25 | .11 | .03 |
| Detroit Lions | | | |
| ☐ 125 Sam Mills | .12 | .05 | .02 |
| New Orleans Saints | | | |
| ☐ 126 Ernie Jones | .10 | .05 | .01 |
| Phoenix Cardinals | | | |
| ☐ 127 Chester McGlockton | .30 | .14 | .04 |
| Los Angeles Raiders | | | |
| ☐ 128 Troy Vincent | .20 | .09 | .03 |
| Miami Dolphins | | | |
| ☐ 129 Chuck Smith | .20 | .09 | .03 |
| Atlanta Falcons | | | |
| ☐ 130 Tim McKyer | .12 | .05 | .02 |
| Atlanta Falcons | | | |
| ☐ 131 Tom Newberry | .10 | .05 | .01 |
| Los Angeles Rams | | | |
| ☐ 132 Leonard Wheeler | .15 | .07 | .02 |
| Cincinnati Bengals | | | |
| ☐ 133 Patrick Rowe | .20 | .09 | .03 |
| Cleveland Browns | | | |
| ☐ 134 Eric Swann | .12 | .05 | .02 |
| Phoenix Cardinals | | | |
| ☐ 135 Jeremy Lincoln | .20 | .09 | .03 |
| Chicago Bears | | | |
| ☐ 136 Brian Noble | .10 | .05 | .01 |
| Green Bay Packers | | | |
| ☐ 137 Allen Pinkett | .10 | .05 | .01 |
| New Orleans Saints | | | |
| ☐ 138 Carl Pickens UER | .75 | .35 | .09 |
| Cincinnati Bengals | | | |
| (card number on back | | | |
| is actually 358) | | | |
| ☐ 139 Eric Green | .15 | .07 | .02 |
| Pittsburgh Steelers | | | |
| ☐ 140 Louis Lipps | .12 | .05 | .02 |
| Pittsburgh Steelers | | | |
| ☐ 141 Chris Singleton | .10 | .05 | .01 |

| | | | |
|---|---|---|---|
| New England Patriots | | | |
| ☐ 142 Gary Clark | .12 | .05 | .02 |
| Washington Redskins | | | |
| ☐ 143 Tim Green | .10 | .05 | .01 |
| Atlanta Falcons | | | |
| ☐ 144 Dennis Green CO | .10 | .05 | .01 |
| Minnesota Vikings | | | |
| ☐ 145 Gary Anderson | .10 | .05 | .01 |
| Pittsburgh Steelers | | | |
| ☐ 146 Mark Clayton | .12 | .05 | .02 |
| Miami Dolphins | | | |
| ☐ 147 Kelvin Martin | .12 | .05 | .02 |
| Dallas Cowboys | | | |
| ☐ 148 Mike Holmgren CO | .10 | .05 | .01 |
| Green Bay Packers | | | |
| ☐ 149 Gaston Green | .12 | .05 | .02 |
| Denver Broncos | | | |
| ☐ 150 Terrell Buckley | .50 | .23 | .06 |
| Green Bay Packers | | | |
| ☐ 151 Robert Brooks | .35 | .16 | .04 |
| Green Bay Packers | | | |
| ☐ 152 Anthony Smith | .12 | .05 | .02 |
| Los Angeles Raiders | | | |
| ☐ 153 Jay Novacek | .25 | .11 | .03 |
| Dallas Cowboys | | | |
| ☐ 154 Webster Slaughter | .12 | .05 | .02 |
| Cleveland Browns | | | |
| ☐ 155 John Roper | .10 | .05 | .01 |
| Chicago Bears | | | |
| ☐ 156 Steve Emtman | .20 | .09 | .03 |
| Indianapolis Colts | | | |
| ☐ 157 Tony Sacca | .25 | .11 | .03 |
| Phoenix Cardinals | | | |
| ☐ 158 Ray Crockett | .10 | .05 | .01 |
| Detroit Lions | | | |
| ☐ 159 Jerry Rice MVP | .60 | .25 | .08 |
| San Francisco 49ers | | | |
| ☐ 160 Alonzo Spellman | .40 | .18 | .05 |
| Chicago Bears | | | |
| ☐ 161 Deion Sanders PC | .10 | .05 | .01 |
| Atlanta Falcons | | | |
| ☐ 162 Robert Clark | .10 | .05 | .01 |
| Detroit Lions | | | |
| ☐ 163 Mark Ingram | .12 | .05 | .02 |
| New York Giants | | | |
| ☐ 164 Ricardo McDonald | .15 | .07 | .02 |
| Cincinnati Bengals | | | |
| ☐ 165 Emmitt Smith PC | 2.50 | 1.15 | .30 |
| Dallas Cowboys | | | |
| ☐ 166 Tommy Maddox | 1.00 | .45 | .13 |
| Denver Broncos | | | |
| ☐ 167 Tom Myslinski | .15 | .07 | .02 |
| Dallas Cowboys | | | |
| ☐ 168 Tony Bennett MVP | .12 | .05 | .02 |
| (No player photo on card) | | | |
| Green Bay Packers | | | |
| ☐ 169 Ernest Givins | .12 | .05 | .02 |
| Houston Oilers | | | |
| ☐ 170 Eugene Robinson MVP | .10 | .05 | .01 |
| Seattle Seahawks | | | |
| ☐ 171 Roger Craig | .12 | .05 | .02 |
| Los Angeles Raiders | | | |
| ☐ 172 Irving Fryar MVP | .10 | .05 | .01 |
| New England Patriots | | | |
| ☐ 173 Jeff Herrod MVP | .10 | .05 | .01 |
| Indianapolis Colts | | | |
| ☐ 174 Chris Mims | .40 | .18 | .05 |
| San Diego Chargers | | | |
| ☐ 175 Bart Oates | .10 | .05 | .01 |
| New York Giants | | | |
| ☐ 176 Michael Irvin MVP | .50 | .23 | .06 |
| Dallas Cowboys | | | |
| ☐ 177 Lawrence Dawsey | .15 | .07 | .02 |
| Tampa Bay Buccaneers | | | |
| ☐ 178 Warren Moon MVP | .20 | .09 | .03 |
| Houston Oilers | | | |
| ☐ 179 Timm Rosenbach | .10 | .05 | .01 |
| Phoenix Cardinals | | | |
| ☐ 180 Bobby Ross CO | .10 | .05 | .01 |
| San Diego Chargers | | | |
| ☐ 181 Chris Burkett MVP | .10 | .05 | .01 |
| New York Jets | | | |
| ☐ 182 Tony Brooks | .10 | .05 | .01 |
| Philadelphia Eagles | | | |
| ☐ 183 Clarence Verdin | .10 | .05 | .01 |
| Indianapolis Colts | | | |
| ☐ 184 Bernie Kosar PC | .12 | .05 | .02 |
| Cleveland Browns | | | |
| ☐ 185 Eric Martin | .12 | .05 | .02 |
| New Orleans Saints | | | |
| ☐ 186 Jeff Bryant | .10 | .05 | .01 |
| Seattle Seahawks | | | |
| ☐ 187 Carnell Lake | .10 | .05 | .01 |
| Pittsburgh Steelers | | | |
| ☐ 188 Darren Woodson | .30 | .14 | .04 |
| Dallas Cowboys | | | |
| ☐ 189 Dwayne Harper | .10 | .05 | .01 |
| Seattle Seahawks | | | |

| | | | |
|---|---|---|---|
| ☐ 190 Bernie Kosar MVP | .12 | .05 | .02 |
| Cleveland Browns | | | |
| ☐ 191 Keith Sims | .10 | .05 | .01 |
| Miami Dolphins | | | |
| ☐ 192 Rich Gannon | .12 | .05 | .02 |
| Minnesota Vikings | | | |
| ☐ 193 Broderick Thomas | .10 | .05 | .01 |
| Tampa Bay Buccaneers | | | |
| ☐ 194 Michael Young | .10 | .05 | .01 |
| Denver Broncos | | | |
| ☐ 195 Cris Dishman | .12 | .05 | .02 |
| Houston Oilers | | | |
| ☐ 196 Wes Hopkins | .10 | .05 | .01 |
| Philadelphia Eagles | | | |
| ☐ 197 Christian Okoye PC | .10 | .05 | .01 |
| Kansas City Chiefs | | | |
| ☐ 198 David Little | .10 | .05 | .01 |
| Pittsburgh Steelers | | | |
| ☐ 199 Chris Crooms | .15 | .07 | .02 |
| Los Angeles Rams | | | |
| ☐ 200 Lawrence Taylor | .20 | .09 | .03 |
| New York Giants | | | |
| ☐ 201 Marc Boutte | .10 | .05 | .01 |
| Los Angeles Rams | | | |
| ☐ 202 Mark Carrier PC | .10 | .05 | .01 |
| Chicago Bears | | | |
| ☐ 203 Keith McCants | .10 | .05 | .01 |
| Tampa Bay Buccaneers | | | |
| ☐ 204 Dwayne Sabb | .25 | .11 | .03 |
| New England Patriots | | | |
| ☐ 205 Brian Mitchell | .12 | .05 | .02 |
| Washington Redskins | | | |
| ☐ 206 Keith Byars | .12 | .05 | .02 |
| Philadelphia Eagles | | | |
| ☐ 207 Jeff Hostetler | .30 | .14 | .04 |
| New York Giants | | | |
| ☐ 208 Percy Snow | .10 | .05 | .01 |
| Kansas City Chiefs | | | |
| ☐ 209 Lawrence Taylor MVP | .10 | .05 | .01 |
| New York Giants | | | |
| ☐ 210 Troy Auzenne | .10 | .05 | .01 |
| Chicago Bears | | | |
| ☐ 211 Warren Moon PC | .15 | .07 | .02 |
| Houston Oilers | | | |
| ☐ 212 Mike Pritchard | .50 | .23 | .06 |
| Atlanta Falcons | | | |
| ☐ 213 Eric Dickerson | .15 | .07 | .02 |
| Los Angeles Raiders | | | |
| ☐ 214 Harvey Williams | .15 | .07 | .02 |
| Kansas City Chiefs | | | |
| ☐ 215 Phil Simms UER | .15 | .07 | .02 |
| (Misspelled Sims | | | |
| on card front) | | | |
| New York Giants | | | |
| ☐ 216 Sean Lumpkin UER | .25 | .11 | .03 |
| New Orleans Saints | | | |
| (Card number on back | | | |
| is actually 002) | | | |
| ☐ 217 Marco Coleman | .60 | .25 | .08 |
| Miami Dolphins | | | |
| ☐ 218 Phillippi Sparks | .10 | .05 | .01 |
| New York Giants | | | |
| ☐ 219 Gerald Dixon | .25 | .11 | .03 |
| Cleveland Browns | | | |
| ☐ 220 Steve Walsh | .10 | .05 | .01 |
| New Orleans Saints | | | |
| ☐ 221 Russell Maryland | .25 | .11 | .03 |
| Dallas Cowboys | | | |
| ☐ 222 Eddie Anderson | .10 | .05 | .01 |
| Los Angeles Raiders | | | |
| ☐ 223 Shane Dronett | .30 | .14 | .04 |
| Denver Broncos | | | |
| ☐ 224 Todd Collins | .25 | .11 | .03 |
| New England Patriots | | | |
| ☐ 225 Leon Searcy | .10 | .05 | .01 |
| Pittsburgh Steelers | | | |
| ☐ 226 Andre Rison | .40 | .18 | .05 |
| Atlanta Falcons | | | |
| ☐ 227 James Lofton | .15 | .07 | .02 |
| Buffalo Bills | | | |
| ☐ 228 Ken O'Brien | .12 | .05 | .02 |
| New York Jets | | | |
| ☐ 229 Mike Tomczak | .10 | .05 | .01 |
| Green Bay Packers | | | |
| ☐ 230 Nick Bell | .12 | .05 | .02 |
| Los Angeles Raiders | | | |
| ☐ 231 Ben Smith | .10 | .05 | .01 |
| Philadelphia Eagles | | | |
| ☐ 232 Wendell Davis MVP | .10 | .05 | .01 |
| Chicago Bears | | | |
| ☐ 233 Craig Thompson | .20 | .09 | .03 |
| Cincinnati Bengals | | | |
| ☐ 234 Dana Hall | .25 | .11 | .03 |
| San Francisco 49ers | | | |
| ☐ 235 Larry Webster | .10 | .05 | .01 |
| Miami Dolphins | | | |
| ☐ 236 Jerry Rice PC | .60 | .25 | .08 |
| San Francisco 49ers | | | |
| ☐ 237 Rod Bernstine | .12 | .05 | .02 |
| San Diego Chargers | | | |
| ☐ 238 David Klingler | 1.00 | .45 | .13 |
| Cincinnati Bengals | | | |
| ☐ 239 Greg Skrepenak | .15 | .07 | .02 |
| Los Angeles Raiders | | | |
| ☐ 240 Mark Wheeler | .15 | .07 | .02 |
| Tampa Bay Buccaneers | | | |
| ☐ 241 Kevin Smith | .50 | .23 | .06 |
| Dallas Cowboys | | | |
| ☐ 242 Charles Mann | .12 | .05 | .02 |
| Washington Redskins | | | |
| ☐ 243 Barry Sanders MVP | .10 | .05 | .01 |
| Detroit Lions | | | |
| ☐ 244 Curtis Whitley | .15 | .07 | .02 |
| San Diego Chargers | | | |
| ☐ 245 Ronnie Harmon MVP | .10 | .05 | .01 |
| San Diego Chargers | | | |
| ☐ 246 Brent Jones | .15 | .07 | .02 |
| San Francisco 49ers | | | |
| ☐ 247 Robert Harris | .10 | .05 | .01 |
| Minnesota Vikings | | | |
| ☐ 248 Ted Marchibroda CO | .10 | .05 | .01 |
| Indianapolis Colts | | | |
| ☐ 249 Willie Gault | .12 | .05 | .02 |
| Los Angeles Raiders | | | |
| ☐ 250 Siran Stacy | .20 | .09 | .03 |
| Philadelphia Eagles | | | |
| ☐ 251 Dennis Byrd | .12 | .05 | .02 |
| New York Jets | | | |
| ☐ 252 Corey Harris | .15 | .07 | .02 |
| Houston Oilers | | | |
| ☐ 253 Al Noga | .10 | .05 | .01 |
| Minnesota Vikings | | | |
| ☐ 254 David Shula CO | .10 | .05 | .01 |
| Cincinnati Bengals | | | |
| ☐ 255 Rob Moore | .15 | .07 | .02 |
| New York Jets | | | |
| ☐ 256 Marv Cook | .12 | .05 | .02 |
| New England Patriots | | | |
| ☐ 257 John Elway MVP | .30 | .14 | .04 |
| Denver Broncos | | | |
| ☐ 258 Harold Green | .12 | .05 | .02 |
| Cincinnati Bengals | | | |
| ☐ 259 Tom Flores CO | .10 | .05 | .01 |
| Seattle Seahawks | | | |
| ☐ 260 Andre Reed | .15 | .07 | .02 |
| Buffalo Bills | | | |
| ☐ 261 Anthony Thompson | .10 | .05 | .01 |
| Phoenix Cardinals | | | |
| ☐ 262 Issiac Holt | .10 | .05 | .01 |
| Dallas Cowboys | | | |
| ☐ 263 Mike Evans | .10 | .05 | .01 |
| Kansas City Chiefs | | | |
| ☐ 264 Jimmy Smith | .15 | .07 | .02 |
| Dallas Cowboys | | | |
| ☐ 265 Anthony Carter | .12 | .05 | .02 |
| Minnesota Vikings | | | |
| ☐ 266 Ashley Ambrose | .15 | .07 | .02 |
| Indianapolis Colts | | | |
| ☐ 267 John Fina | .10 | .05 | .01 |
| Buffalo Bills | | | |
| (card number on back | | | |
| is actually 357) | | | |
| ☐ 268 Sean Gilbert | .60 | .25 | .08 |
| Los Angeles Rams | | | |
| ☐ 269 Ken Norton Jr. | .12 | .05 | .02 |
| Dallas Cowboys | | | |
| ☐ 270 Barry Word | .15 | .07 | .02 |
| Kansas City Chiefs | | | |
| ☐ 271 Pat Swilling MVP | .12 | .05 | .02 |
| New Orleans Saints | | | |
| ☐ 272 Dan Marino PC | .60 | .25 | .08 |
| Miami Dolphins | | | |
| ☐ 273 David Fulcher MVP | .10 | .05 | .01 |
| Cincinnati Bengals | | | |
| ☐ 274 William Perry | .12 | .05 | .02 |
| Chicago Bears | | | |
| ☐ 275 Ed West | .10 | .05 | .01 |
| Green Bay Packers | | | |
| ☐ 276 Gene Atkins | .10 | .05 | .01 |
| New Orleans Saints | | | |
| ☐ 277 Neal Anderson | .12 | .05 | .02 |
| Chicago Bears | | | |
| ☐ 278 Dino Hackett | .10 | .05 | .01 |
| Kansas City Chiefs | | | |
| ☐ 279 Greg Townsend | .10 | .05 | .01 |
| Los Angeles Raiders | | | |
| ☐ 280 Andre Tippett | .12 | .05 | .02 |
| New England Patriots | | | |
| ☐ 281 Darryl Williams | .35 | .16 | .04 |
| Cincinnati Bengals | | | |
| ☐ 282 Kurt Barber | .15 | .07 | .02 |
| New York Jets | | | |
| ☐ 283 Pat Terrell | .10 | .05 | .01 |
| Los Angeles Rams | | | |
| ☐ 284 Derrick Thomas PC | .15 | .07 | .02 |

Kansas City Chiefs
| | | | | |
|---|---|---|---|---|
| ☐ 285 | Eddie Robinson | .20 | .09 | .03 |

Houston Oilers
| | | | | |
|---|---|---|---|---|
| ☐ 286 | Howie Long | .12 | .05 | .02 |

Los Angeles Raiders
| | | | | |
|---|---|---|---|---|
| ☐ 287 | Tim McDonald MVP | .12 | .05 | .02 |

(No player photo)
Phoenix Cardinals
| | | | | |
|---|---|---|---|---|
| ☐ 288 | Thurman Thomas MVP | .50 | .23 | .06 |

Buffalo Bills
| | | | | |
|---|---|---|---|---|
| ☐ 289 | Wendell Davis | .10 | .05 | .01 |

Chicago Bears
| | | | | |
|---|---|---|---|---|
| ☐ 290 | Jeff Cross | .10 | .05 | .01 |

Miami Dolphins
| | | | | |
|---|---|---|---|---|
| ☐ 291 | Duane Bickett | .10 | .05 | .01 |

Indianapolis Colts
| | | | | |
|---|---|---|---|---|
| ☐ 292 | Tony Smith | .40 | .18 | .05 |

Atlanta Falcons
| | | | | |
|---|---|---|---|---|
| ☐ 293 | Jerry Ball | .12 | .05 | .02 |

Detroit Lions
| | | | | |
|---|---|---|---|---|
| ☐ 294 | Jessie Tuggle | .10 | .05 | .01 |

Atlanta Falcons
| | | | | |
|---|---|---|---|---|
| ☐ 295 | Chris Burkett | .10 | .05 | .01 |

New York Jets
| | | | | |
|---|---|---|---|---|
| ☐ 296 | Eugene Chung | .10 | .05 | .01 |

New England Patriots
| | | | | |
|---|---|---|---|---|
| ☐ 297 | Chris Miller | .15 | .07 | .02 |

Atlanta Falcons
| | | | | |
|---|---|---|---|---|
| ☐ 298 | Albert Bentley | .10 | .05 | .01 |

Indianapolis Colts
| | | | | |
|---|---|---|---|---|
| ☐ 299 | Richard Johnson | .10 | .05 | .01 |

Houston Oilers
| | | | | |
|---|---|---|---|---|
| ☐ 300 | Randall Cunningham | .20 | .09 | .03 |

Philadelphia Eagles
| | | | | |
|---|---|---|---|---|
| ☐ 301 | Courtney Hawkins | .60 | .25 | .08 |

Tampa Bay Buccaneers
| | | | | |
|---|---|---|---|---|
| ☐ 302 | Ray Childress | .12 | .05 | .02 |

Houston Oilers
| | | | | |
|---|---|---|---|---|
| ☐ 303 | Rodney Peete | .12 | .05 | .02 |

Detroit Lions
| | | | | |
|---|---|---|---|---|
| ☐ 304 | Kevin Fagan | .10 | .05 | .01 |

San Francisco 49ers
| | | | | |
|---|---|---|---|---|
| ☐ 305 | Ronnie Lott MVP | .12 | .05 | .02 |

Los Angeles Raiders
| | | | | |
|---|---|---|---|---|
| ☐ 306 | Michael Carter | .10 | .05 | .01 |

San Francisco 49ers
| | | | | |
|---|---|---|---|---|
| ☐ 307 | Derrick Thomas MVP | .10 | .05 | .01 |

Kansas City Chiefs
| | | | | |
|---|---|---|---|---|
| ☐ 308 | Jarvis Williams | .10 | .05 | .01 |

Miami Dolphins
| | | | | |
|---|---|---|---|---|
| ☐ 309 | Greg Lloyd MVP | .10 | .05 | .01 |

Pittsburgh Steelers
| | | | | |
|---|---|---|---|---|
| ☐ 310 | Ethan Horton | .10 | .05 | .01 |

Los Angeles Raiders
| | | | | |
|---|---|---|---|---|
| ☐ 311 | Ricky Ervins | .12 | .05 | .02 |

Washington Redskins
| | | | | |
|---|---|---|---|---|
| ☐ 312 | Bennie Blades | .10 | .05 | .01 |

Detroit Lions
| | | | | |
|---|---|---|---|---|
| ☐ 313 | Troy Aikman PC | 1.50 | .65 | .19 |

Dallas Cowboys
| | | | | |
|---|---|---|---|---|
| ☐ 314 | Bruce Armstrong | .10 | .05 | .01 |

New England Patriots
| | | | | |
|---|---|---|---|---|
| ☐ 315 | Leroy Hoard | .12 | .05 | .02 |

Cleveland Browns
| | | | | |
|---|---|---|---|---|
| ☐ 316 | Gary Anderson | .12 | .05 | .02 |

Tampa Bay Buccaneers
| | | | | |
|---|---|---|---|---|
| ☐ 317 | Steve McMichael | .12 | .05 | .02 |

Chicago Bears
| | | | | |
|---|---|---|---|---|
| ☐ 318 | Junior Seau | .25 | .11 | .03 |

San Diego Chargers
| | | | | |
|---|---|---|---|---|
| ☐ 319 | Mark Thomas | .20 | .09 | .03 |

San Francisco 49ers
| | | | | |
|---|---|---|---|---|
| ☐ 320 | Fred Barnett | .15 | .07 | .02 |

Philadelphia Eagles
| | | | | |
|---|---|---|---|---|
| ☐ 321 | Mike Merriweather | .10 | .05 | .01 |

Minnesota Vikings
| | | | | |
|---|---|---|---|---|
| ☐ 322 | Keith Willis | .10 | .05 | .01 |

Pittsburgh Steelers
| | | | | |
|---|---|---|---|---|
| ☐ 323 | Brett Perriman | .12 | .05 | .02 |

Detroit Lions
| | | | | |
|---|---|---|---|---|
| ☐ 324 | Michael Haynes | .60 | .25 | .08 |

Atlanta Falcons
| | | | | |
|---|---|---|---|---|
| ☐ 325 | Jim Harbaugh | .12 | .05 | .02 |

Chicago Bears
| | | | | |
|---|---|---|---|---|
| ☐ 326 | Sammie Smith | .10 | .05 | .01 |

Denver Broncos
| | | | | |
|---|---|---|---|---|
| ☐ 327 | Robert Delpino | .12 | .05 | .02 |

Los Angeles Rams
| | | | | |
|---|---|---|---|---|
| ☐ 328 | Tony Mandarich | .10 | .05 | .01 |

Green Bay Packers
| | | | | |
|---|---|---|---|---|
| ☐ 329 | Mark Bortz | .10 | .05 | .01 |

Chicago Bears
| | | | | |
|---|---|---|---|---|
| ☐ 330 | Ray Etheridge | .10 | .05 | .01 |

San Diego Chargers
| | | | | |
|---|---|---|---|---|
| ☐ 331 | Jarvis Williams PC | .10 | .05 | .01 |

Miami Dolphins
Louis Oliver
Miami Dolphins

| | | | | |
|---|---|---|---|---|
| ☐ 332 | Dan Marino MVP | .75 | .35 | .09 |

Miami Dolphins
| | | | | |
|---|---|---|---|---|
| ☐ 333 | Dwight Stone | .10 | .05 | .01 |

Pittsburgh Steelers
| | | | | |
|---|---|---|---|---|
| ☐ 334 | Billy Ray Smith | .10 | .05 | .01 |

San Diego Chargers
| | | | | |
|---|---|---|---|---|
| ☐ 335 | Darion Conner | .10 | .05 | .01 |

Atlanta Falcons
| | | | | |
|---|---|---|---|---|
| ☐ 336 | Howard Dinkins | .10 | .05 | .01 |

Atlanta Falcons
| | | | | |
|---|---|---|---|---|
| ☐ 337 | Robert Porcher | .40 | .18 | .05 |

Detroit Lions
| | | | | |
|---|---|---|---|---|
| ☐ 338 | Chris Doleman | .12 | .05 | .02 |

Minnesota Vikings
| | | | | |
|---|---|---|---|---|
| ☐ 339 | Alvin Harper | .60 | .25 | .08 |

Dallas Cowboys
| | | | | |
|---|---|---|---|---|
| ☐ 340 | John Taylor | .15 | .07 | .02 |

San Francisco 49ers
| | | | | |
|---|---|---|---|---|
| ☐ 341 | Ray Agnew | .10 | .05 | .01 |

New England Patriots
| | | | | |
|---|---|---|---|---|
| ☐ 342 | Jon Vaughn | .10 | .05 | .01 |

New England Patriots
| | | | | |
|---|---|---|---|---|
| ☐ 343 | James Brown | .15 | .07 | .02 |

Dallas Cowboys
| | | | | |
|---|---|---|---|---|
| ☐ 344 | Michael Irvin PC | .50 | .23 | .06 |

Dallas Cowboys
| | | | | |
|---|---|---|---|---|
| ☐ 345 | Neil Smith | .15 | .07 | .02 |

Kansas City Chiefs
| | | | | |
|---|---|---|---|---|
| ☐ 346 | Vaughn Johnson | .10 | .05 | .01 |

New Orleans Saints
| | | | | |
|---|---|---|---|---|
| ☐ 347 | Checklist | .10 | .05 | .01 |

Atlanta Falcons
Buffalo Bills
| | | | | |
|---|---|---|---|---|
| ☐ 348 | Checklist | .10 | .05 | .01 |

Chicago Bears
Cincinnati Bengals
| | | | | |
|---|---|---|---|---|
| ☐ 349 | Checklist | .10 | .05 | .01 |

Cleveland Browns
Dallas Cowboys
| | | | | |
|---|---|---|---|---|
| ☐ 350 | Checklist | .10 | .05 | .01 |

(See also number 61)
Denver Broncos
Detroit Lions
| | | | | |
|---|---|---|---|---|
| ☐ 351 | Checklist | .10 | .05 | .01 |

Green Bay Packers
Houston Oilers
| | | | | |
|---|---|---|---|---|
| ☐ 352 | Checklist | .10 | .05 | .01 |

Indianapolis Colts
Kansas City Chiefs
| | | | | |
|---|---|---|---|---|
| ☐ 353 | Checklist | .10 | .05 | .01 |

Los Angeles Raiders
Los Angeles Rams
| | | | | |
|---|---|---|---|---|
| ☐ 354 | Checklist | .10 | .05 | .01 |

(See also number 38)
Miami Dolphins
Minnesota Vikings
| | | | | |
|---|---|---|---|---|
| ☐ 355 | Checklist | .10 | .05 | .01 |

New England Patriots
New Orleans Saints
| | | | | |
|---|---|---|---|---|
| ☐ 356 | Checklist | .10 | .05 | .01 |

New York Giants
New York Jets
| | | | | |
|---|---|---|---|---|
| ☐ 357 | Checklist | .10 | .05 | .01 |

(See also number 267)
Philadelphia Eagles
Phoenix Cardinals
| | | | | |
|---|---|---|---|---|
| ☐ 358 | Checklist | .10 | .05 | .01 |

(See also number 138)
Pittsburgh Steelers
San Diego Chargers
| | | | | |
|---|---|---|---|---|
| ☐ 359 | Checklist | .10 | .05 | .01 |

San Francisco 49ers
Seattle Seahawks
| | | | | |
|---|---|---|---|---|
| ☐ 360 | Checklist | .10 | .05 | .01 |

Tampa Bay Buccaneers
Washington Redskins
| | | | | |
|---|---|---|---|---|
| ☐ H1 | Jim Kelly | 4.00 | 1.80 | .50 |

(Flip Hologram)
Buffalo Bills
| | | | | |
|---|---|---|---|---|
| ☐ S1 | Steve Emtman | 2.50 | 1.15 | .30 |

(Spectra-Etch
"Horse Power")
Indianapolis Colts

# 1992 SkyBox Primetime Poster Cards

Randomly inserted throughout 1992 SkyBox Primetime foil packs, these cards present the same poster image as the regularly issued "Costacos" cards except that the borders of the cards are silver foil-stamped. A 16th Costacos Poster Art checklist card rounds out the insert set. The cards measure the standard size (2 1/2" by 3 1/2") and are numbered on the back with an "M" prefix. These metallic insert cards were available in 10,000 numbered cases distributed only to the

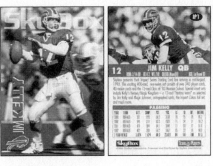

hobby. SkyBox estimated that two Costacos metallic poster cards would be found in each 36-pack box. The poster cards take the featured player out of the football arena and into an imaginary setting highlighting his nickname, image, or reputation.

| | MINT | EXC | G-VG |
|---|---|---|---|
| COMPLETE SET (16) | 60.00 | 27.00 | 7.50 |
| COMMON PLAYER (M1-M16) | 1.50 | .65 | .19 |
| ☐ M1 Bernie Kosar<br>Air Raid 19<br>Cleveland Browns | 1.50 | .65 | .19 |
| ☐ M2 Mark Carrier<br>Monster of the Midway<br>Chicago Bears | 1.50 | .65 | .19 |
| ☐ M3 Neal Anderson<br>The Bear Necessity<br>Chicago Bears | 1.50 | .65 | .19 |
| ☐ M4 Thurman Thomas<br>Thurmanator<br>Buffalo Bills | 5.00 | 2.30 | .60 |
| ☐ M5 Deion Sanders<br>PrimeTime<br>Atlanta Falcons | 2.25 | 1.00 | .30 |
| ☐ M6 Joe Montana<br>Sweet Sixteen<br>San Francisco 49ers | 10.00 | 4.50 | 1.25 |
| ☐ M7 Jerry Rice<br>Speed of Light<br>San Francisco 49ers | 7.00 | 3.10 | .85 |
| ☐ M8 Jarvis Williams<br>Louis Oliver<br>B2 Bombers<br>Miami Dolphins | 1.50 | .65 | .19 |
| ☐ M9 Dan Marino<br>Armed and Dangerous<br>Miami Dolphins | 8.00 | 3.60 | 1.00 |
| ☐ M10 Derrick Thomas<br>Sacred Ground<br>Kansas City Chiefs | 2.00 | .90 | .25 |
| ☐ M11 Christian Okoye<br>Nigerian Nightmare<br>Kansas City Chiefs | 1.50 | .65 | .19 |
| ☐ M12 Warren Moon<br>Moonlighting<br>Houston Oilers | 2.00 | .90 | .25 |
| ☐ M13 Michael Irvin<br>Playmaker<br>Dallas Cowboys | 7.00 | 3.10 | .85 |
| ☐ M14 Troy Aikman<br>Strong Arm of the Law<br>Dallas Cowboys | 14.00 | 6.25 | 1.75 |
| ☐ M15 Emmitt Smith<br>Catch 22<br>Dallas Cowboys | 20.00 | 9.00 | 2.50 |
| ☐ M16 Checklist | 1.50 | .65 | .19 |

## 1993 SkyBox Impact Promos

These two cards were issued to preview the design of the 1993 SkyBox Impact football set. Measuring the standard size (2 1/2" by 3 1/2"), the fronts feature full-bleed color action player photos with an unfocused background to make the featured player stand out. The player's name is printed vertically with the team logo beneath it. The top of the back has a second color photo, with biography, expanded four-year statistics, and career totals filling out the rest of the back. The cards are numbered on the back. A version of Jim Kelly was also issued at the 1993 Chicago National with a stamp to commemorating that event on the card front.

| | MINT | EXC | G-VG |
|---|---|---|---|
| COMPLETE SET (2) | 3.00 | 1.20 | .30 |
| COMMON PLAYER (IP1-IP2) | 1.50 | .60 | .15 |
| ☐ IP1 Jim Kelly<br>Buffalo Bills | 2.50 | 1.00 | .25 |
| ☐ IP2 Lawrence Taylor<br>New York Giants | 1.50 | .60 | .15 |

## 1993 SkyBox Promo Sheet

This promo sheet (approximately 8 1/2" by 15") was given away at the National Sports Collectors Convention, July 22, 1993, in Chicago, Illinois. The front of the sheet displays six SkyBox player cards on a variegated gray background. If the cards were cut, they would measure the standard size (2 1/2" by 3 1/2"). On the card fronts, the featured player stands out against a ghosted background that consists of two team color-coded panels. The team logo and the player's name are printed across the top of the card. The back carries an advertisement for SkyBox cards. The players are listed as they appear on the sheet from left to right, starting at the top.

| | MINT | EXC | G-VG |
|---|---|---|---|
| COMPLETE SET (1) | 3.00 | 1.20 | .30 |
| COMMON PANEL | 3.00 | 1.20 | .30 |
| ☐ 1 Promo Panel<br>Jim Kelly<br>Buffalo Bills<br>Derrick Thomas<br>Kansas City Chiefs<br>Lawrence Taylor<br>New York Giants<br>Neal Anderson<br>Chicago Bears<br>Marco Coleman<br>Miami Dolphins<br>Chris Doleman<br>Minnesota Vikings | 3.00 | 1.20 | .30 |

## 1993 SkyBox Celebrity Cycle Prototypes *

Measuring the standard size (2 1/2" by 3 1/2"), these four prototype cards feature celebrities and their bikes. On the fronts, the featured celebrity is pictured on his bike, and the varying backgrounds have a metallic sheen to them. The celebrity is identified by his name, position, and his team. (The mystery card pictures a Harley Davidson motocycle against an American flag background.) The backs are blank except for a red-inked stamp that reads "Unfinished SkyBox

Prototype." The cards are unnumbered and checklisted below in alphabetical order.

| | MINT | EXC | G-VG |
|---|---|---|---|
| COMPLETE SET (4) | 12.00 | 5.00 | 1.20 |
| COMMON PLAYER (1-4) | 2.50 | 1.00 | .25 |
| ☐ 1 Mitch Frerotte | 2.50 | 1.00 | .25 |
| Seattle Seahawks | | | |
| ☐ 2 Jerry Glanville CO | 3.50 | 1.40 | .35 |
| Atlanta Falcons | | | |
| ☐ 3 Kenny Lofton | 7.50 | 3.00 | .75 |
| Cleveland Indians | | | |
| ☐ 4 Mystery Celebrity | 2.50 | 1.00 | .25 |
| Cycle Card | | | |

# 1993 SkyBox

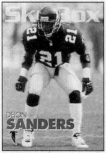

Marketed as an improved version of Skybox's NFL Primetime series, the 1993 SkyBox Premium football set consists of 270 standard-size (2 1/2" by 3 1/2") cards. Randomly inserted throughout the packs were a ten-card Costacos Brothers poster card subset, a ten-card Chris Mortensen's PrimeTime NFL Rookies subset, and a nine-card Thunder and Lightning subset. Production was limited to 5,000 numbered cases (equivalent to 100,000 numbered display boxes). Card 68, Jim Kelly, was repackaged in a three-card cello pack featuring SkyBox cards, such as Hoops and Star Trek. The cards measure the standard size (2 1/2" by 3 1/2"). The fronts display borderless color action player photos, the backgrounds of which are split horizontally or vertically into team color-coded screened halves. The player's name and team logo appear near the top. The backs carry a second color action photo, career synopsis, biography, four-year stats, and career totals. The cards are numbered on the back. Rookie Cards include Jerome Bettis, Drew Bledsoe, Garrison Hearst, O.J. McDuffie, Natrone Means and Rick Mirer.

| | MINT | EXC | G-VG |
|---|---|---|---|
| COMPLETE SET (270) | 32.00 | 14.50 | 4.00 |
| COMMON PLAYER (1-270) | .10 | .05 | .01 |
| ☐ 1 Eric Martin | .12 | .05 | .02 |
| New Orleans Saints | | | |
| ☐ 2 Earnest Byner | .12 | .05 | .02 |
| Washington Redskins | | | |
| ☐ 3 Ricky Proehl | .12 | .05 | .02 |
| Phoenix Cardinals | | | |
| ☐ 4 Mark Carrier | .12 | .05 | .02 |
| Cleveland Browns | | | |
| ☐ 5 Shannon Sharpe | .35 | .16 | .04 |
| Denver Broncos | | | |
| ☐ 6 Anthony Thompson | .10 | .05 | .01 |
| Los Angeles Rams | | | |
| ☐ 7 Drew Bledsoe | 6.00 | 2.70 | .75 |
| New England Patriots | | | |
| ☐ 8 Tom Carter | .40 | .18 | .05 |
| Washington Redskins | | | |
| ☐ 9 Ryan McNeil | .20 | .09 | .03 |
| Detroit Lions | | | |
| ☐ 10 Troy Aikman | 2.50 | 1.15 | .30 |
| Dallas Cowboys | | | |
| ☐ 11 Robert Jones | .10 | .05 | .01 |
| Dallas Cowboys | | | |
| ☐ 12 Rodney Peete | .12 | .05 | .02 |
| Detroit Lions | | | |
| ☐ 13 Wendell Davis | .10 | .05 | .01 |
| Chicago Bears | | | |
| ☐ 14 Thurman Thomas | .75 | .35 | .09 |
| Buffalo Bills | | | |
| ☐ 15 John Stephens | .10 | .05 | .01 |
| Green Bay Packers | | | |
| ☐ 16 Rodney Hampton | .75 | .35 | .09 |
| New York Giants | | | |

| | | | |
|---|---|---|---|
| ☐ 17 Eric Bieniemy | .12 | .05 | .02 |
| San Diego Chargers | | | |
| ☐ 18 Santana Dotson | .15 | .07 | .02 |
| Tampa Bay Buccaneers | | | |
| ☐ 19 Jeff George | .25 | .11 | .03 |
| Indianapolis Colts | | | |
| ☐ 20 John L. Williams | .12 | .05 | .02 |
| Seattle Seahawks | | | |
| ☐ 21 Barry Word | .15 | .07 | .02 |
| Kansas City Chiefs | | | |
| ☐ 22 Chris Miller | .15 | .07 | .02 |
| Atlanta Falcons | | | |
| ☐ 23 Jeff Hostetler | .15 | .07 | .02 |
| Los Angeles Raiders | | | |
| ☐ 24 Dwight Stone | .10 | .05 | .01 |
| Pittsburgh Steelers | | | |
| ☐ 25 Brad Baxter | .12 | .05 | .02 |
| New York Jets | | | |
| ☐ 26 Randall Cunningham | .20 | .09 | .03 |
| Philadelphia Eagles | | | |
| ☐ 27 Mark Higgs | .15 | .07 | .02 |
| Miami Dolphins | | | |
| ☐ 28 Vaughn Dunbar | .12 | .05 | .02 |
| New Orleans Saints | | | |
| ☐ 29 Ricky Ervins | .12 | .05 | .02 |
| Washington Redskins | | | |
| ☐ 30 Johnny Bailey | .10 | .05 | .01 |
| Phoenix Cardinals | | | |
| ☐ 31 Michael Jackson | .15 | .07 | .02 |
| Cleveland Browns | | | |
| ☐ 32 Mike Croel | .12 | .05 | .02 |
| Denver Broncos | | | |
| ☐ 33 Steve Young | .50 | .23 | .06 |
| San Francisco 49ers | | | |
| ☐ 34 Deon Figures | .30 | .14 | .04 |
| Pittsburgh Steelers | | | |
| ☐ 35 Robert Smith | .75 | .35 | .09 |
| Minnesota Vikings | | | |
| ☐ 36 Irv Smith | .40 | .18 | .05 |
| New Orleans Saints | | | |
| ☐ 37 Charles Haley | .12 | .05 | .02 |
| Dallas Cowboys | | | |
| ☐ 38 Cris Dishman | .10 | .05 | .01 |
| Houston Oilers | | | |
| ☐ 39 Barry Sanders | 1.50 | .65 | .19 |
| Detroit Lions | | | |
| ☐ 40 Jim Harbaugh | .10 | .05 | .01 |
| Chicago Bears | | | |
| ☐ 41 Darryl Talley | .10 | .05 | .01 |
| Buffalo Bills | | | |
| ☐ 42 Jackie Harris | .50 | .23 | .06 |
| Green Bay Packers | | | |
| ☐ 43 Phil Simms | .15 | .07 | .02 |
| New York Giants | | | |
| ☐ 44 Marion Butts | .15 | .07 | .02 |
| San Diego Chargers | | | |
| ☐ 45 Anthony Munoz | .12 | .05 | .02 |
| Tampa Bay Buccaneers | | | |
| ☐ 46 Steve Emtman | .12 | .05 | .02 |
| Indianapolis Colts | | | |
| ☐ 47 Kelvin Martin | .10 | .05 | .01 |
| Seattle Seahawks | | | |
| ☐ 48 Joe Montana | 2.00 | .90 | .25 |
| Kansas City Chiefs | | | |
| ☐ 49 Andre Rison | .40 | .18 | .05 |
| Atlanta Falcons | | | |
| ☐ 50 Ethan Horton | .10 | .05 | .01 |
| Los Angeles Raiders | | | |
| ☐ 51 Kevin Greene | .10 | .05 | .01 |
| Pittsburgh Steelers | | | |
| ☐ 52 Browning Nagle | .12 | .05 | .02 |
| New York Jets | | | |
| ☐ 53 Tim Harris | .10 | .05 | .01 |
| Philadelphia Eagles | | | |
| ☐ 54 Keith Byars | .12 | .05 | .02 |
| Miami Dolphins | | | |
| ☐ 55 Terry Allen | .15 | .07 | .02 |
| Minnesota Vikings | | | |
| ☐ 56 Chip Lohmiller | .10 | .05 | .01 |
| Washington Redskins | | | |
| ☐ 57 Robert Massey | .10 | .05 | .01 |
| Phoenix Cardinals | | | |
| ☐ 58 Michael Dean Perry | .15 | .07 | .02 |
| Cleveland Browns | | | |
| ☐ 59 Tommy Maddox | .25 | .11 | .03 |
| Denver Broncos | | | |
| ☐ 60 Jerry Rice | 1.25 | .55 | .16 |
| San Francisco 49ers | | | |
| ☐ 61 Lincoln Kennedy | .30 | .14 | .04 |
| Atlanta Falcons | | | |
| ☐ 62 Jerome Bettis | 6.00 | 2.70 | .75 |
| Los Angeles Rams | | | |
| ☐ 63 Coleman Rudolph | .20 | .09 | .03 |
| New York Jets | | | |
| ☐ 64 Emmitt Smith | 4.00 | 1.80 | .50 |
| Dallas Cowboys | | | |
| ☐ 65 Curtis Duncan | .10 | .05 | .01 |

| | | | | | | | | |
|---|---|---|---|---|---|---|---|---|
| Houston Oilers | | | | San Francisco 49ers | | | | |
| ☐ 66 Andre Ware | .12 | .05 | .02 | ☐ 115 Steve Everitt | .20 | .09 | .03 |
| Detroit Lions | | | | Cleveland Browns | | | | |
| ☐ 67 Neal Anderson | .12 | .05 | .02 | ☐ 116 Carlton Gray | .35 | .16 | .04 |
| Chicago Bears | | | | Seattle Seahawks | | | | |
| ☐ 68 Jim Kelly | .40 | .18 | .05 | ☐ 117 Eric Curry | .50 | .23 | .06 |
| Buffalo Bills | | | | Tampa Bay Buccaneers | | | | |
| ☐ 69 Reggie White | .25 | .11 | .03 | ☐ 118 Ken Norton Jr. | .12 | .05 | .02 |
| Green Bay Packers | | | | Dallas Cowboys | | | | |
| ☐ 70 Dave Meggett | .12 | .05 | .02 | ☐ 119 Lorenzo White | .12 | .05 | .02 |
| New York Giants | | | | Houston Oilers | | | | |
| ☐ 71 Junior Seau | .15 | .07 | .02 | ☐ 120 Pat Swilling | .12 | .05 | .02 |
| San Diego Chargers | | | | Detroit Lions | | | | |
| ☐ 72 Courtney Hawkins | .12 | .05 | .02 | ☐ 121 William Perry | .10 | .05 | .01 |
| Tampa Bay Buccaneers | | | | Chicago Bears | | | | |
| ☐ 73 Clarence Verdin | .10 | .05 | .01 | ☐ 122 Brett Favre | 1.50 | .65 | .19 |
| Indianapolis Colts | | | | Green Bay Packers | | | | |
| ☐ 74 Tommy Kane | .10 | .05 | .01 | ☐ 123 Jon Vaughn | .10 | .05 | .01 |
| Seattle Seahawks | | | | New England Patriots | | | | |
| ☐ 75 Dale Carter | .15 | .07 | .02 | ☐ 124 Mark Jackson | .12 | .05 | .02 |
| Kansas City Chiefs | | | | New York Giants | | | | |
| ☐ 76 Michael Haynes | .35 | .16 | .04 | ☐ 125 Stan Humphries | .15 | .07 | .02 |
| Atlanta Falcons | | | | San Diego Chargers | | | | |
| ☐ 77 Willie Gault | .12 | .05 | .02 | ☐ 126 Harold Green | .12 | .05 | .02 |
| Los Angeles Raiders | | | | Cincinnati Bengals | | | | |
| ☐ 78 Eric Green | .15 | .07 | .02 | ☐ 127 Anthony Johnson | .10 | .05 | .01 |
| Pittsburgh Steelers | | | | Indianapolis Colts | | | | |
| ☐ 79 Ronnie Lott | .15 | .07 | .02 | ☐ 128 Brian Blades | .12 | .05 | .02 |
| New York Jets | | | | Seattle Seahawks | | | | |
| ☐ 80 Vai Sikahema | .10 | .05 | .01 | ☐ 129 Willie Davis | .20 | .09 | .03 |
| Philadelphia Eagles | | | | Kansas City Chiefs | | | | |
| ☐ 81 Mark Ingram | .12 | .05 | .02 | ☐ 130 Bobby Hebert | .15 | .07 | .02 |
| Miami Dolphins | | | | Atlanta Falcons | | | | |
| ☐ 82 Anthony Carter | .12 | .05 | .02 | ☐ 131 Terry McDaniel | .10 | .05 | .01 |
| Minnesota Vikings | | | | Los Angeles Raiders | | | | |
| ☐ 83 Mark Rypien | .12 | .05 | .02 | ☐ 132 Jeff Graham | .12 | .05 | .02 |
| Washington Redskins | | | | Pittsburgh Steelers | | | | |
| ☐ 84 Gary Clark | .12 | .05 | .02 | ☐ 133 Jeff Lageman | .10 | .05 | .01 |
| Phoenix Cardinals | | | | New York Jets | | | | |
| ☐ 85 Bernie Kosar | .15 | .07 | .02 | ☐ 134 Andre Waters | .10 | .05 | .01 |
| Cleveland Browns | | | | Philadelphia Eagles | | | | |
| ☐ 86 Cleveland Gary | .12 | .05 | .02 | ☐ 135 Steve Walsh | .10 | .05 | .01 |
| Los Angeles Rams | | | | New Orleans Saints | | | | |
| ☐ 87 Tom Rathman | .12 | .05 | .02 | ☐ 136 Cris Carter | .15 | .07 | .02 |
| San Francisco 49ers | | | | Minnesota Vikings | | | | |
| ☐ 88 Tony McGee | .40 | .18 | .05 | ☐ 137 Tim McGee | .10 | .05 | .01 |
| Cincinnati Bengals | | | | Washington Redskins | | | | |
| ☐ 89 Rick Mirer | 6.00 | 2.70 | .75 | ☐ 138 Chuck Cecil | .10 | .05 | .01 |
| Seattle Seahawks | | | | Phoenix Cardinals | | | | |
| ☐ 90 John Copeland | .50 | .23 | .06 | ☐ 139 John Elway | 1.00 | .45 | .13 |
| Cincinnati Bengals | | | | Denver Broncos | | | | |
| ☐ 91 Michael Irvin | 1.00 | .45 | .13 | ☐ 140 Todd Lyght | .10 | .05 | .01 |
| Dallas Cowboys | | | | Los Angeles Rams | | | | |
| ☐ 92 Wilber Marshall | .12 | .05 | .02 | ☐ 141 Brent Jones | .15 | .07 | .02 |
| Houston Oilers | | | | San Francisco 49ers | | | | |
| ☐ 93 Mel Gray | .10 | .05 | .01 | ☐ 142 Patrick Bates | .25 | .11 | .03 |
| Detroit Lions | | | | Los Angeles Raiders | | | | |
| ☐ 94 Craig Heyward | .10 | .05 | .01 | ☐ 143 Darrien Gordon | .35 | .16 | .04 |
| Chicago Bears | | | | San Diego Chargers | | | | |
| ☐ 95 Don Beebe | .15 | .07 | .02 | ☐ 144 Michael Strahan | .20 | .09 | .03 |
| Buffalo Bills | | | | New York Giants | | | | |
| ☐ 96 Andre Tippett | .10 | .05 | .01 | ☐ 145 Jay Novacek | .15 | .07 | .02 |
| New England Patriots | | | | Dallas Cowboys | | | | |
| ☐ 97 Derek Brown | .12 | .05 | .02 | ☐ 146 Warren Moon | .30 | .14 | .04 |
| New York Giants | | | | Houston Oilers | | | | |
| ☐ 98 Ronnie Harmon | .10 | .05 | .01 | ☐ 147 Rodney Holman | .10 | .05 | .01 |
| San Diego Chargers | | | | New York Giants | | | | |
| ☐ 99 Derrick Fenner | .10 | .05 | .01 | ☐ 148 Anthony Morgan | .10 | .05 | .01 |
| Cincinnati Bengals | | | | Chicago Bears | | | | |
| ☐ 100 Rodney Culver | .10 | .05 | .01 | ☐ 149 Sterling Sharpe | 1.00 | .45 | .13 |
| Indianapolis Colts | | | | Green Bay Packers | | | | |
| ☐ 101 Cortez Kennedy | .15 | .07 | .02 | ☐ 150 Leonard Russell | .12 | .05 | .02 |
| Seattle Seahawks | | | | New England Patriots | | | | |
| ☐ 102 Marcus Allen | .12 | .05 | .02 | ☐ 151 Lawrence Taylor | .15 | .07 | .02 |
| Kansas City Chiefs | | | | New York Giants | | | | |
| ☐ 103 Steve Broussard | .10 | .05 | .01 | ☐ 152 Leslie O'Neal | .12 | .05 | .02 |
| Atlanta Falcons | | | | San Diego Chargers | | | | |
| ☐ 104 Tim Brown | .40 | .18 | .05 | ☐ 153 Carl Pickens | .15 | .07 | .02 |
| Los Angeles Raiders | | | | Cincinnati Bengals | | | | |
| ☐ 105 Merril Hoge | .10 | .05 | .01 | ☐ 154 Aaron Cox | .10 | .05 | .01 |
| Pittsburgh Steelers | | | | Indianapolis Colts | | | | |
| ☐ 106 Chris Burkett | .10 | .05 | .01 | ☐ 155 Ferrell Edmunds | .10 | .05 | .01 |
| New York Jets | | | | Seattle Seahawks | | | | |
| ☐ 107 Fred Barnett | .15 | .07 | .02 | ☐ 156 Neil O'Donnell | .50 | .23 | .06 |
| Philadelphia Eagles | | | | Pittsburgh Steelers | | | | |
| ☐ 108 Dan Marino | 1.50 | .65 | .19 | ☐ 157 Tony Smith | .10 | .05 | .01 |
| Miami Dolphins | | | | Atlanta Falcons | | | | |
| ☐ 109 Chris Doleman | .12 | .05 | .02 | ☐ 158 James Lofton | .15 | .07 | .02 |
| Minnesota Vikings | | | | Los Angeles Raiders | | | | |
| ☐ 110 Art Monk | .15 | .07 | .02 | ☐ 159 George Teague | .40 | .18 | .05 |
| Washington Redskins | | | | Green Bay Packers | | | | |
| ☐ 111 Ernie Jones | .10 | .05 | .01 | ☐ 160 Boomer Esiason | .25 | .11 | .03 |
| Phoenix Cardinals | | | | New York Jets | | | | |
| ☐ 112 Jay Hilgenberg | .10 | .05 | .01 | ☐ 161 Eric Allen | .12 | .05 | .02 |
| Cleveland Browns | | | | Philadelphia Eagles | | | | |
| ☐ 113 Jim Everett | .10 | .05 | .01 | ☐ 162 Floyd Turner | .10 | .05 | .01 |
| Los Angeles Rams | | | | New Orleans Saints | | | | |
| ☐ 114 John Taylor | .15 | .07 | .02 | ☐ 163 Esera Tuaolo | .10 | .05 | .01 |

|  |  |  |  |
|---|---|---|---|
| Minnesota Vikings | | | |
| ☐ 164 Darrell Green | .12 | .05 | .02 |
| Washington Redskins | | | |
| ☐ 165 Steve Beuerlein | .25 | .11 | .03 |
| Phoenix Cardinals | | | |
| ☐ 166 Vance Johnson | .12 | .05 | .02 |
| Denver Broncos | | | |
| ☐ 167 Flipper Anderson | .12 | .05 | .02 |
| Los Angeles Rams | | | |
| ☐ 168 Ricky Watters | .75 | .35 | .09 |
| San Francisco 49ers | | | |
| ☐ 169 Marvin Jones | .40 | .18 | .05 |
| New York Jets | | | |
| ☐ 170 Dana Stubblefield | 1.00 | .45 | .13 |
| San Francisco 49ers | | | |
| ☐ 171 Willie Roaf | .25 | .11 | .03 |
| New Orleans Saints | | | |
| ☐ 172 Russell Maryland | .15 | .07 | .02 |
| Dallas Cowboys | | | |
| ☐ 173 Ernest Givins | .12 | .05 | .02 |
| Houston Oilers | | | |
| ☐ 174 Willie Green | .12 | .05 | .02 |
| Detroit Lions | | | |
| ☐ 175 Bruce Smith | .15 | .07 | .02 |
| Buffalo Bills | | | |
| ☐ 176 Terrell Buckley | .15 | .07 | .02 |
| Green Bay Packers | | | |
| ☐ 177 Scott Zolak | .10 | .05 | .01 |
| New England Patriots | | | |
| ☐ 178 Mike Sherrard | .10 | .05 | .01 |
| New York Giants | | | |
| ☐ 179 Lawrence Dawsey | .15 | .07 | .02 |
| Tampa Bay Buccaneers | | | |
| ☐ 180 Jay Schroeder | .10 | .05 | .01 |
| Cincinnati Bengals | | | |
| ☐ 181 Quentin Coryatt | .15 | .07 | .02 |
| Indianapolis Colts | | | |
| ☐ 182 Harvey Williams | .15 | .07 | .02 |
| Kansas City Chiefs | | | |
| ☐ 183 Natrone Means | 2.00 | .90 | .25 |
| San Diego Chargers | | | |
| ☐ 184 Eric Dickerson | .15 | .07 | .02 |
| Atlanta Falcons | | | |
| ☐ 185 Gaston Green | .12 | .05 | .02 |
| Los Angeles Raiders | | | |
| ☐ 186 Thomas Smith | .25 | .11 | .03 |
| Buffalo Bills | | | |
| ☐ 187 Johnny Johnson | .15 | .07 | .02 |
| New York Jets | | | |
| ☐ 188 Marco Coleman | .12 | .05 | .02 |
| Miami Dolphins | | | |
| ☐ 189 Wade Wilson | .12 | .05 | .02 |
| New Orleans Saints | | | |
| ☐ 190 Rich Gannon | .12 | .05 | .02 |
| Washington Redskins | | | |
| ☐ 191 Brian Mitchell | .12 | .05 | .02 |
| Washington Redskins | | | |
| ☐ 192 Eric Metcalf | .15 | .07 | .02 |
| Cleveland Browns | | | |
| ☐ 193 Robert Delpino | .12 | .05 | .02 |
| Denver Broncos | | | |
| ☐ 194 Shane Conlan | .10 | .05 | .01 |
| Los Angeles Rams | | | |
| ☐ 195 Dexter Carter | .12 | .05 | .02 |
| San Francisco 49ers | | | |
| ☐ 196 Garrison Hearst | 1.00 | .45 | .13 |
| Los Angeles Rams | | | |
| ☐ 197 Chris Slade | .50 | .23 | .06 |
| New England Patriots | | | |
| ☐ 198 Troy Drayton | .50 | .23 | .06 |
| Los Angeles Rams | | | |
| ☐ 199 Lin Elliot | .10 | .05 | .01 |
| Dallas Cowboys | | | |
| ☐ 200 Haywood Jeffires | .15 | .07 | .02 |
| Houston Oilers | | | |
| ☐ 201 Herman Moore | .75 | .35 | .09 |
| Detroit Lions | | | |
| ☐ 202 Cornelius Bennett | .15 | .07 | .02 |
| Buffalo Bills | | | |
| ☐ 203 Mark Clayton | .10 | .05 | .01 |
| Green Bay Packers | | | |
| ☐ 204 Marv Cook | .10 | .05 | .01 |
| New England Patriots | | | |
| ☐ 205 Stephen Baker | .10 | .05 | .01 |
| New York Giants | | | |
| ☐ 206 Gary Anderson | .12 | .05 | .02 |
| Tampa Bay Buccaneers | | | |
| ☐ 207 Eddie Brown | .10 | .05 | .01 |
| Cincinnati Bengals | | | |
| ☐ 208 Will Wolford | .10 | .05 | .01 |
| Indianapolis Colts | | | |
| ☐ 209 Derrick Thomas | .30 | .14 | .04 |
| Kansas City Chiefs | | | |
| ☐ 210 Seth Joyner | .12 | .05 | .02 |
| Philadelphia Eagles | | | |
| ☐ 211 Mike Pritchard | .15 | .07 | .02 |
| Atlanta Falcons | | | |
| ☐ 212 Rod Woodson | .15 | .07 | .02 |
| Pittsburgh Steelers | | | |
| ☐ 213 Todd Kelly | .20 | .09 | .03 |
| San Francisco 49ers | | | |
| ☐ 214 Rob Moore | .15 | .07 | .02 |
| New York Jets | | | |
| ☐ 215 Keith Jackson | .15 | .07 | .02 |
| Miami Dolphins | | | |
| ☐ 216 Wesley Carroll | .10 | .05 | .01 |
| New Orleans Saints | | | |
| ☐ 217 Steve Jordan | .12 | .05 | .02 |
| Minnesota Vikings | | | |
| ☐ 218 Ricky Sanders | .12 | .05 | .02 |
| Washington Redskins | | | |
| ☐ 219 Tommy Vardell | .12 | .05 | .02 |
| Cleveland Browns | | | |
| ☐ 220 Rod Bernstine | .12 | .05 | .02 |
| Denver Broncos | | | |
| ☐ 221 Henry Ellard | .12 | .05 | .02 |
| Los Angeles Rams | | | |
| ☐ 222 Amp Lee | .12 | .05 | .02 |
| San Francisco 49ers | | | |
| ☐ 223 O.J. McDuffie | 2.50 | 1.15 | .30 |
| Miami Dolphins | | | |
| ☐ 224 Carl Simpson | .20 | .09 | .03 |
| Chicago Bears | | | |
| ☐ 225 Dan Williams | .20 | .09 | .03 |
| Denver Broncos | | | |
| ☐ 226 Thomas Everett | .10 | .05 | .01 |
| Dallas Cowboys | | | |
| ☐ 227 Webster Slaughter | .12 | .05 | .02 |
| Houston Oilers | | | |
| ☐ 228 Trace Armstrong | .10 | .05 | .01 |
| Chicago Bears | | | |
| ☐ 229 Kenneth Davis | .10 | .05 | .01 |
| Buffalo Bills | | | |
| ☐ 230 Tony Bennett | .10 | .05 | .01 |
| Green Bay Packers | | | |
| ☐ 231 Reyna Thompson | .10 | .05 | .01 |
| New York Giants | | | |
| ☐ 232 Anthony Miller | .30 | .14 | .04 |
| San Diego Chargers | | | |
| ☐ 233 Reggie Cobb | .15 | .07 | .02 |
| Tampa Bay Buccaneers | | | |
| ☐ 234 Mark Duper | .12 | .05 | .02 |
| Philadelphia Eagles | | | |
| ☐ 235 Chris Warren | .30 | .14 | .04 |
| Seattle Seahawks | | | |
| ☐ 236 Christian Okoye | .12 | .05 | .02 |
| Kansas City Chiefs | | | |
| ☐ 237 Irving Fryar | .10 | .05 | .01 |
| Miami Dolphins | | | |
| ☐ 238 Deion Sanders | .30 | .14 | .04 |
| Atlanta Falcons | | | |
| ☐ 239 Barry Foster | .60 | .25 | .08 |
| Pittsburgh Steelers | | | |
| ☐ 240 Ernest Dye | .20 | .09 | .03 |
| Phoenix Cardinals | | | |
| ☐ 241 Calvin Williams | .15 | .07 | .02 |
| Philadelphia Eagles | | | |
| ☐ 242 Louis Oliver | .10 | .05 | .01 |
| Miami Dolphins | | | |
| ☐ 243 Dalton Hilliard | .10 | .05 | .01 |
| New Orleans Saints | | | |
| ☐ 244 Roger Craig | .12 | .05 | .02 |
| Minnesota Vikings | | | |
| ☐ 245 Randal Hill | .15 | .07 | .02 |
| Phoenix Cardinals | | | |
| ☐ 246 Vinny Testaverde | .15 | .07 | .02 |
| Cleveland Browns | | | |
| ☐ 247 Steve Atwater | .12 | .05 | .02 |
| Denver Broncos | | | |
| ☐ 248 Jim Price | .10 | .05 | .01 |
| Los Angeles Rams | | | |
| ☐ 249 Martin Harrison | .35 | .16 | .04 |
| San Francisco 49ers | | | |
| ☐ 250 Curtis Conway | 1.00 | .45 | .13 |
| Chicago Bears | | | |
| ☐ 251 Demetrius DuBose | .30 | .14 | .04 |
| Tampa Bay Buccaneers | | | |
| ☐ 252 Leonard Renfro | .15 | .07 | .02 |
| Philadelphia Eagles | | | |
| ☐ 253 Alvin Harper | .50 | .23 | .06 |
| Dallas Cowboys | | | |
| ☐ 254 Leonard Harris | .10 | .05 | .01 |
| Houston Oilers | | | |
| ☐ 255 Tom Waddle | .15 | .07 | .02 |
| Chicago Bears | | | |
| ☐ 256 Andre Reed | .15 | .07 | .02 |
| Buffalo Bills | | | |
| ☐ 257 Sanjay Beach | .10 | .05 | .01 |
| Green Bay Packers | | | |
| ☐ 258 Michael Timpson | .10 | .05 | .01 |
| New England Patriots | | | |
| ☐ 259 Nate Lewis | .12 | .05 | .02 |
| San Diego Chargers | | | |
| ☐ 260 Steve DeBerg | .12 | .05 | .02 |
| Tampa Bay Buccaneers | | | |
| ☐ 261 David Klingler | .30 | .14 | .04 |

Cincinnati Bengals
| | | MINT | EXC | G-VG |
|---|---|---|---|---|
| ☐ 262 | Dan McGwire | .12 | .05 | .02 |
| | Seattle Seahawks | | | |
| ☐ 263 | Dave Krieg | .12 | .05 | .02 |
| | Kansas City Chiefs | | | |
| ☐ 264 | Brad Muster | .12 | .05 | .02 |
| | New Orleans Saints | | | |
| ☐ 265 | Nick Bell | .12 | .05 | .02 |
| | Los Angeles Raiders | | | |
| ☐ 266 | Checklist 1 | .10 | .05 | .01 |
| ☐ 267 | Checklist 2 | .10 | .05 | .01 |
| ☐ 268 | Checklist 3 | .10 | .05 | .01 |
| ☐ 269 | Checklsit 4 | .10 | .05 | .01 |
| ☐ 270 | Checklist 5 | .10 | .05 | .01 |

## 1993 SkyBox Poster Cards

This ten-card standard-size (2 1/2" by 3 1/2") subset of the 1993 SkyBox Premium set features on its fronts black-bordered reproductions of the Costacos Brothers Sports Posters. The back carries a color player action shot on its upper half, with the player's name appearing within a gold-colored stripe under the photo. The player's career highlights and team logo appear in the white bottom half. The cards are numbered on the back with a "CB" prefix.

| | | MINT | EXC | G-VG |
|---|---|---|---|---|
| COMPLETE SET (10) | | 5.00 | 2.30 | .60 |
| COMMON PLAYER (1-10) | | .30 | .14 | .04 |
| ☐ 1 | Dallas Cowboys Defense Doomsday Afternoon Leon Lett Tony Casillas Tony Tolbert Russell Maryland Jimmie Jones Charles Haley Jim Jeffcoat | .30 | .14 | .04 |
| ☐ 2 | Dallas Cowboys 1993 Word Champions Troy Aikman Michael Irvin Emmitt Smith Russell Maryland | 3.00 | 1.35 | .40 |
| ☐ 3 | Barry Foster Steel Wheels Pittsburgh Steelers | 1.00 | .45 | .13 |
| ☐ 4 | Art Monk The Art of Receiving Washington Redskins | .30 | .14 | .04 |
| ☐ 5 | Jerry Rice Wide Receiver San Francisco 49ers | 1.50 | .65 | .19 |
| ☐ 6 | Barry Sanders Roaring 20 Detroit Lions | 2.00 | .90 | .25 |
| ☐ 7 | Deion Sanders Big Time Atlanta Falcons | .75 | .35 | .09 |
| ☐ 8 | Junior Seau Shock Treatment San Diego Chargers | .30 | .14 | .04 |
| ☐ 9 | Derrick Thomas Neil Smith Rush Hour Kansas City Chiefs | .30 | .14 | .04 |
| ☐ 10 | Steve Young Run and Gun San Francisco 49ers | 1.00 | .45 | .13 |

## 1993 SkyBox Rookies

The chances of finding one of these ten standard-size (2 1/2" by 3 1/2") inserts in 1993 SkyBox Premium 12-card foil packs was one-in-18. Chris Mortensen of The Sporting News and ESPN selected these ten rookies who, in his estimation, will be "prime time" players during 1993 and beyond. Each front features a color action shot of the rookie in his college uniform against a two-tone (black and gold) metallic background. The player's name appears at the top of the broad black stripe at the left edge, and Mortensen's facsimile signature and set title appear at the bottom of that stripe. The back carries a color player photo in its upper half, with the player's name appearing within a gold-colored stripe beneath. The player's position and Mortensen's scouting report, along with a head shot of Mortensen, appear in the white bottom half. The cards are numbered on the back with a "PR" prefix.

| | | MINT | EXC | G-VG |
|---|---|---|---|---|
| COMPLETE SET (10) | | 100.00 | 45.00 | 12.50 |
| COMMON PLAYER (1-10) | | 2.25 | 1.00 | .30 |
| ☐ 1 | Patrick Bates Los Angeles Raiders | 2.25 | 1.00 | .30 |
| ☐ 2 | Drew Bledsoe New England Patriots | 35.00 | 16.00 | 4.40 |
| ☐ 3 | Darrien Gordon San Diego Chargers | 2.25 | 1.00 | .30 |
| ☐ 4 | Garrison Hearst Phoenix Cardinals | 10.00 | 4.50 | 1.25 |
| ☐ 5 | Marvin Jones New York Jets | 3.00 | 1.35 | .40 |
| ☐ 6 | Terry Kirby Miami Dolphins | 15.00 | 6.75 | 1.90 |
| ☐ 7 | Natrone Means San Diego Chargers | 15.00 | 6.75 | 1.90 |
| ☐ 8 | Rick Mirer Seattle Seahawks | 35.00 | 16.00 | 4.40 |
| ☐ 9 | Willie Roaf New Orleans Saints | 2.25 | 1.00 | .30 |
| ☐ 10 | Dan Williams Denver Broncos | 2.25 | 1.00 | .30 |

## 1993 SkyBox Thunder and Lightning

The chances of finding one of these nine standard-size (2 1/2" by 3 1/2") inserts in 1993 SkyBox Premium 12-card foil packs were one-in-nine. Each borderless and horizontal card features two players from the same team with a color action shot of each player appearing on either side. The player photo on the "Thunder" side has multiple ghosted images and appears upon a black- and gold-metallic background. The player photo on the "Lightning" side appears upon a black- and silver-metallic background, which is highlighted by filaments of lightning. Each side carries its player's name in white lettering near the bottom. The cards are numbered on the "Lightning" side with a "TL" prefix.

|                         | MINT  | EXC   | G-VG |
|-------------------------|-------|-------|------|
| COMPLETE SET (9)        | 40.00 | 18.00 | 5.00 |
| COMMON PLAYER (1-9)     | 3.00  | 1.35  | .40  |
| ☐ 1 Jim Kelly           | 6.00  | 2.70  | .75  |
|   Thurman Thomas |   |       |      |
|   Buffalo Bills |     |       |      |
| ☐ 2 Randall Cunningham  | 3.50  | 1.55  | .45  |
|   Fred Barnett |      |       |      |
|   Philadelphia Eagles |  |    |      |
| ☐ 3 Dan Marino          | 8.00  | 3.60  | 1.00 |
|   Keith Jackson |     |       |      |
|   Miami Dolphins |    |       |      |
| ☐ 4 Sam Mills           | 3.00  | 1.35  | .40  |
|   Vaughan Johnson |   |       |      |
|   New Orleans Saints | |       |      |
| ☐ 5 Warren Moon         | 5.00  | 2.30  | .60  |
|   Haywood Jeffires |  |       |      |
|   Houston Oilers |    |       |      |
| ☐ 6 Troy Aikman         | 18.00 | 8.00  | 2.30 |
|   Michael Irvin |     |       |      |
|   Dallas Cowboys |    |       |      |
| ☐ 7 Brett Favre         | 10.00 | 4.50  | 1.25 |
|   Sterling Sharpe |   |       |      |
|   Green Bay Packers | |       |      |
| ☐ 8 Steve Young         | 8.00  | 3.60  | 1.00 |
|   Jerry Rice |        |       |      |
|   San Francisco 49ers | |     |      |
| ☐ 9 Dennis Smith        | 3.00  | 1.35  | .40  |
|   Steve Atwater |     |       |      |
|   Denver Broncos |    |       |      |

## 1993 SkyBox Impact

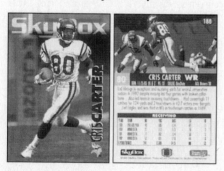

The 1993 SkyBox Impact football set consists of 400 cards, each measuring 2 1/2" by 3 1/2". The 12-card foil packs contained 11 regular issue or insert cards and one special SkyBox Colors foil card. (There are four different color foils, and each player card is reproduced in only one of the colors). These foil-stamped Colors cards combine to form a set of all 400 cards. A randomly inserted NFL Rookie Exchange (First Round Draft Pick Redemption) card could be redeemed by mail for a special set of up to 29 NFL Draft First Round selections. Also a 20-card update series was offered to collectors through a mail-in program. The fronts feature full-bleed color action player photos with unfocused backgrounds to make the featured player stand out. The player's name is printed vertically with the team logo beneath it. The top of the back has a second color photo, with biography, expanded four-year statistics, and career totals filling out the rest of the back. Randomly packed in the foil packs were 500 individually numbered redemption certificates that entitled the collector to a dual sport/autographed card of Jim Kelly and Magic Johnson. As a bonus, certificates number 12 and number 32, which correspond to Kelly and Johnson's uniform numbers, respectively, received the autographed cards personally presented by the superstar. The cards are numbered on the back and checklisted below alphabetically according to teams as follows: Atlanta Falcons (1-14), Buffalo Bills (15-30), Chicago Bears (31-43), Cincinnati Bengals (44-54), Cleveland Browns (55-65), Dallas Cowboys (66-80), Denver Broncos (81-94), Detroit Lions (95-107), Green Bay Packers (108-117), Houston Oilers (118-130), Indianapolis Colts (131-138), Kansas City Chiefs (139-150), Los Angeles Raiders (151-162), Los Angeles Rams (163-171), Miami Dolphins (172-185), Minnesota Vikings (186-196), New England Patriots (197-206), New Orleans Saints (207-219), New York Giants (220-230), New York Jets (231-242), Philadelphia Eagles (243-256), Phoenix Cardinals (257-268), Pittsburgh Steelers (269-280), San Diego Chargers (281-290), San Francisco 49ers (291-304), Seattle Seahawks (305-316), Tampa Bay Buccaneers (317-327), and Washington Redskins (328-340). The set closes with the following topical subsets: Class of '83 (341-352), Checklists (353-360), Rookies First Round (361-387), and Rookies Second Round (388-400). Rookie Cards include Jerome Bettis, Drew Bledsoe, Garrison Hearst, O.J. McDuffie, Natrone Means, Glyn Milburn and Rick Mirer.

|                         | MINT  | EXC   | G-VG |
|-------------------------|-------|-------|------|
| COMPLETE SET (400)      | 12.00 | 5.50  | 1.50 |
| COMMON PLAYER (1-400)   | .04   | .02   | .01  |
| ☐ 1 Steve Broussard     | .04   | .02   | .01  |
| ☐ 2 Michael Haynes      | .20   | .09   | .03  |
| ☐ 3 Tony Smith          | .04   | .02   | .01  |
| ☐ 4 Tory Epps           | .04   | .02   | .01  |
| ☐ 5 Chris Hinton        | .04   | .02   | .01  |
| ☐ 6 Bobby Hebert        | .10   | .05   | .01  |
| ☐ 7 Tim McKyer          | .08   | .04   | .01  |
| ☐ 8 Chris Miller        | .10   | .05   | .01  |
| ☐ 9 Bruce Pickens       | .04   | .02   | .01  |
| ☐ 10 Mike Pritchard     | .10   | .05   | .01  |
| ☐ 11 Andre Rison        | .25   | .11   | .03  |
| ☐ 12 Deion Sanders      | .15   | .07   | .02  |
| ☐ 13 Pierce Holt        | .04   | .02   | .01  |
| ☐ 14 Jessie Tuggle      | .04   | .02   | .01  |
| ☐ 15 Don Beebe          | .10   | .05   | .01  |
| ☐ 16 Cornelius Bennett  | .10   | .05   | .01  |
| ☐ 17 Kenneth Davis      | .08   | .04   | .01  |
| ☐ 18 Kent Hull          | .04   | .02   | .01  |
| ☐ 19 Jim Kelly          | .25   | .11   | .03  |
| ☐ 20 Mark Kelso         | .04   | .02   | .01  |
| ☐ 21 Keith McKeller UER | .04   | .02   | .01  |
|   (Name misspelled McKellar on front) | | | |
| ☐ 22 Andre Reed         | .10   | .05   | .01  |
| ☐ 23 Jim Richter        | .04   | .02   | .01  |
| ☐ 24 Bruce Smith        | .10   | .05   | .01  |
| ☐ 25 Thurman Thomas     | .35   | .16   | .04  |
| ☐ 26 Steve Christie     | .04   | .02   | .01  |
| ☐ 27 Darryl Talley UER  | .04   | .02   | .01  |
|   (Name misspelled Darrell on front) | | | |
| ☐ 28 Pete Metzelaars    | .04   | .02   | .01  |
| ☐ 29 Steve Tasker       | .04   | .02   | .01  |
| ☐ 30 Henry Jones        | .04   | .02   | .01  |
| ☐ 31 Neal Anderson      | .08   | .04   | .01  |
| ☐ 32 Trace Armstrong    | .04   | .02   | .01  |
| ☐ 33 Mark Bortz         | .04   | .02   | .01  |
| ☐ 34 Mark Carrier       | .08   | .04   | .01  |
| ☐ 35 Wendell Davis      | .08   | .04   | .01  |
| ☐ 36 Richard Dent       | .08   | .04   | .01  |
| ☐ 37 Jim Harbaugh       | .08   | .04   | .01  |
| ☐ 38 Steve McMichael    | .04   | .02   | .01  |
| ☐ 39 Craig Heyward      | .04   | .02   | .01  |
| ☐ 40 William Perry      | .08   | .04   | .01  |
| ☐ 41 Donnell Woolford   | .04   | .02   | .01  |
| ☐ 42 Tom Waddle         | .10   | .05   | .01  |
| ☐ 43 Anthony Morgan     | .08   | .04   | .01  |
| ☐ 44 Jim Breech         | .04   | .02   | .01  |
| ☐ 45 David Klingler     | .15   | .07   | .02  |
| ☐ 46 Derrick Fenner     | .04   | .02   | .01  |
| ☐ 47 David Fulcher      | .04   | .02   | .01  |
| ☐ 48 James Francis      | .04   | .02   | .01  |
| ☐ 49 Harold Green       | .08   | .04   | .01  |
| ☐ 50 Carl Pickens       | .10   | .05   | .01  |
| ☐ 51 Jay Schroeder      | .04   | .02   | .01  |
| ☐ 52 Alex Gordon        | .04   | .02   | .01  |
| ☐ 53 Eric Ball          | .04   | .02   | .01  |
| ☐ 54 Eddie Brown        | .04   | .02   | .01  |
| ☐ 55 Jay Hilgenberg UER | .04   | .02   | .01  |
|   (Name misspelled Hilgenburg on front) | | | |
| ☐ 56 Michael Jackson    | .10   | .05   | .01  |
| ☐ 57 Bernie Kosar       | .10   | .05   | .01  |
| ☐ 58 Kevin Mack         | .08   | .04   | .01  |
| ☐ 59 Eric Metcalf       | .10   | .05   | .01  |
| ☐ 60 Michael Dean Perry | .10   | .05   | .01  |
| ☐ 61 Tommy Vardell      | .08   | .04   | .01  |
| ☐ 62 Leroy Hoard        | .08   | .04   | .01  |
| ☐ 63 Clay Matthews      | .08   | .04   | .01  |
| ☐ 64 Vinny Testaverde   | .10   | .05   | .01  |
| ☐ 65 Mark Carrier       | .08   | .04   | .01  |
| ☐ 66 Troy Aikman        | 1.25  | .55   | .16  |
| ☐ 67 Lin Elliott UER    | .04   | .02   | .01  |
|   (Name misspelled Elliot on front) | | | |
| ☐ 68 Thomas Everett     | .04   | .02   | .01  |
| ☐ 69 Alvin Harper       | .25   | .11   | .03  |
| ☐ 70 Ray Horton         | .04   | .02   | .01  |
| ☐ 71 Michael Irvin      | .40   | .18   | .05  |
| ☐ 72 Russell Maryland   | .10   | .05   | .01  |
| ☐ 73 Jay Novacek        | .10   | .05   | .01  |

|  |  | | | |
|---|--------|------|------|------|
| ☐ 74 | Emmitt Smith | 2.00 | .90 | .25 |
| ☐ 75 | Tony Casillas | .04 | .02 | .01 |
| ☐ 76 | Robert Jones | .04 | .02 | .01 |
| ☐ 77 | Ken Norton Jr. | .08 | .04 | .01 |
| ☐ 78 | Daryl Johnston | .10 | .05 | .01 |
| ☐ 79 | Charles Haley | .08 | .04 | .01 |
| ☐ 80 | Leon Lett | .30 | .14 | .04 |
| ☐ 81 | Steve Atwater | .08 | .04 | .01 |
| ☐ 82 | Mike Croel | .08 | .04 | .01 |
| ☐ 83 | John Elway | .35 | .16 | .04 |
| ☐ 84 | Simon Fletcher | .08 | .04 | .01 |
| ☐ 85 | Vance Johnson | .08 | .04 | .01 |
| ☐ 86 | Shannon Sharpe | .20 | .09 | .03 |
| ☐ 87 | Rod Bernstine | .08 | .04 | .01 |
| ☐ 88 | Robert Delpino | .08 | .04 | .01 |
| ☐ 89 | Karl Mecklenburg | .08 | .04 | .01 |
| ☐ 90 | Steve Sewell | .04 | .02 | .01 |
| ☐ 91 | Tommy Maddox UER (Name misspelled Maddux on front and back) | .15 | .07 | .02 |
| ☐ 92 | Arthur Marshall | .25 | .11 | .03 |
| ☐ 93 | Dennis Smith | .04 | .02 | .01 |
| ☐ 94 | Derek Russell | .08 | .04 | .01 |
| ☐ 95 | Bennie Blades | .04 | .02 | .01 |
| ☐ 96 | Michael Cofer | .04 | .02 | .01 |
| ☐ 97 | Willie Green | .08 | .04 | .01 |
| ☐ 98 | Herman Moore | .35 | .16 | .04 |
| ☐ 99 | Rodney Peete | .08 | .04 | .01 |
| ☐ 100 | Andre Ware | .08 | .04 | .01 |
| ☐ 101 | Barry Sanders UER (Brett Perriman is pictured on front) | .75 | .35 | .09 |
| ☐ 102 | Chris Spielman | .04 | .02 | .01 |
| ☐ 103 | Jason Hanson | .04 | .02 | .01 |
| ☐ 104 | Mel Gray | .08 | .04 | .01 |
| ☐ 105 | Pat Swilling | .08 | .04 | .01 |
| ☐ 106 | Bill Fralic | .04 | .02 | .01 |
| ☐ 107 | Rodney Holman | .04 | .02 | .01 |
| ☐ 108 | Brett Favre | .75 | .35 | .09 |
| ☐ 109 | Sterling Sharpe | .40 | .18 | .05 |
| ☐ 110 | Reggie White | .15 | .07 | .02 |
| ☐ 111 | Terrell Buckley | .10 | .05 | .01 |
| ☐ 112 | Sanjay Beach | .04 | .02 | .01 |
| ☐ 113 | Tony Bennett | .04 | .02 | .01 |
| ☐ 114 | Jackie Harris | .30 | .14 | .04 |
| ☐ 115 | Bryce Paup | .04 | .02 | .01 |
| ☐ 116 | Shawn Patterson | .04 | .02 | .01 |
| ☐ 117 | John Stephens | .04 | .02 | .01 |
| ☐ 118 | Cris Dishman | .04 | .02 | .01 |
| ☐ 119 | Ernest Givins | .04 | .02 | .01 |
| ☐ 120 | Haywood Jeffires | .10 | .05 | .01 |
| ☐ 121 | Lamar Lathon | .04 | .02 | .01 |
| ☐ 122 | Warren Moon | .15 | .07 | .02 |
| ☐ 123 | Lorenzo White | .08 | .04 | .01 |
| ☐ 124 | Curtis Duncan | .08 | .04 | .01 |
| ☐ 125 | Webster Slaughter | .08 | .04 | .01 |
| ☐ 126 | Cody Carlson | .20 | .09 | .03 |
| ☐ 127 | Leonard Harris | .04 | .02 | .01 |
| ☐ 128 | Bruce Matthews | .08 | .04 | .01 |
| ☐ 129 | Ray Childress | .04 | .02 | .01 |
| ☐ 130 | Al Smith | .04 | .02 | .01 |
| ☐ 131 | Jeff George | .15 | .07 | .02 |
| ☐ 132 | Anthony Johnson | .04 | .02 | .01 |
| ☐ 133 | Steve Emtman | .08 | .04 | .01 |
| ☐ 134 | Quentin Coryatt | .10 | .05 | .01 |
| ☐ 135 | Rodney Culver | .08 | .04 | .01 |
| ☐ 136 | Jessie Hester | .04 | .02 | .01 |
| ☐ 137 | Aaron Cox | .04 | .02 | .01 |
| ☐ 138 | Clarence Verdin | .04 | .02 | .01 |
| ☐ 139 | Joe Montana | 1.00 | .45 | .13 |
| ☐ 140 | Dave Krieg | .08 | .04 | .01 |
| ☐ 141 | Harvey Williams | .10 | .05 | .01 |
| ☐ 142 | Derrick Thomas | .15 | .07 | .02 |
| ☐ 143 | Barry Word | .10 | .05 | .01 |
| ☐ 144 | Christian Okoye | .08 | .04 | .01 |
| ☐ 145 | Nick Lowery | .04 | .02 | .01 |
| ☐ 146 | Dale Carter | .10 | .05 | .01 |
| ☐ 147 | Willie Davis | .10 | .05 | .01 |
| ☐ 148 | Tim Barnett | .08 | .04 | .01 |
| ☐ 149 | Neil Smith UER (Name misspelled Neal on front) | .10 | .05 | .01 |
| ☐ 150 | Marcus Allen | .08 | .04 | .01 |
| ☐ 151 | Nick Bell | .08 | .04 | .01 |
| ☐ 152 | Tim Brown | .25 | .11 | .03 |
| ☐ 153 | Eric Dickerson | .10 | .05 | .01 |
| ☐ 154 | Willie Gault | .08 | .04 | .01 |
| ☐ 155 | Howie Long | .08 | .04 | .01 |
| ☐ 156 | Gaston Green | .08 | .04 | .01 |
| ☐ 157 | Chester McGlockton | .04 | .02 | .01 |
| ☐ 158 | Eddie Anderson | .04 | .02 | .01 |
| ☐ 159 | Ethan Horton | .04 | .02 | .01 |
| ☐ 160 | James Lofton | .10 | .05 | .01 |
| ☐ 161 | Jeff Hostetler | .10 | .05 | .01 |
| ☐ 162 | Terry McDaniel | .04 | .02 | .01 |
| ☐ 163 | Flipper Anderson | .08 | .04 | .01 |
| ☐ 164 | Shane Conlan | .04 | .02 | .01 |
| ☐ 165 | Jim Everett | .04 | .02 | .01 |
| ☐ 166 | Henry Ellard | .08 | .04 | .01 |
| ☐ 167 | Cleveland Gary | .08 | .04 | .01 |
| ☐ 168 | Todd Lyght | .04 | .02 | .01 |
| ☐ 169 | Sean Gilbert | .08 | .04 | .01 |
| ☐ 170 | Jim Price | .04 | .02 | .01 |
| ☐ 171 | Bill Hawkins | .04 | .02 | .01 |
| ☐ 172 | Mark Clayton (Green Bay Packers) | .08 | .04 | .01 |
| ☐ 173 | Mark Higgs | .10 | .05 | .01 |
| ☐ 174 | Dan Marino | .75 | .35 | .09 |
| ☐ 175 | Louis Oliver | .04 | .02 | .01 |
| ☐ 176 | Reggie Roby | .04 | .02 | .01 |
| ☐ 177 | Bobby Humphrey | .08 | .04 | .01 |
| ☐ 178 | Troy Vincent | .08 | .04 | .01 |
| ☐ 179 | Marco Coleman | .08 | .04 | .01 |
| ☐ 180 | Aaron Craver | .08 | .04 | .01 |
| ☐ 181 | Keith Jackson | .10 | .05 | .01 |
| ☐ 182 | Mark Duper | .08 | .04 | .01 |
| ☐ 183 | Pete Stoyanovich | .04 | .02 | .01 |
| ☐ 184 | Irving Fryar | .08 | .04 | .01 |
| ☐ 185 | Bryan Cox UER (Name misspelled Brian on front and back) | .08 | .04 | .01 |
| ☐ 186 | Terry Allen | .10 | .05 | .01 |
| ☐ 187 | Anthony Carter | .08 | .04 | .01 |
| ☐ 188 | Cris Carter | .10 | .05 | .01 |
| ☐ 189 | Chris Doleman | .08 | .04 | .01 |
| ☐ 190 | Rich Gannon | .08 | .04 | .01 |
| ☐ 191 | Sean Salisbury | .08 | .04 | .01 |
| ☐ 192 | Hassan Jones | .04 | .02 | .01 |
| ☐ 193 | Steve Jordan | .08 | .04 | .01 |
| ☐ 194 | Roger Craig | .08 | .04 | .01 |
| ☐ 195 | Todd Scott | .04 | .02 | .01 |
| ☐ 196 | Esera Tuaolo | .04 | .02 | .01 |
| ☐ 197 | Ray Agnew | .04 | .02 | .01 |
| ☐ 198 | Marv Cook | .04 | .02 | .01 |
| ☐ 199 | Tom Hodson | .04 | .02 | .01 |
| ☐ 200 | Chris Singleton | .04 | .02 | .01 |
| ☐ 201 | Michael Timpson | .04 | .02 | .01 |
| ☐ 202 | Jon Vaughn ERR (Photo on back is Keith Byars) | .04 | .02 | .01 |
| ☐ 203 | Leonard Russell | .08 | .04 | .01 |
| ☐ 204 | Scott Zolak | .04 | .02 | .01 |
| ☐ 205 | Reyna Thompson | .04 | .02 | .01 |
| ☐ 206 | Andre Tippett | .04 | .02 | .01 |
| ☐ 207 | Morten Andersen UER (Name misspelled Morton Anderson on front) | .08 | .04 | .01 |
| ☐ 208 | Wesley Carroll | .04 | .02 | .01 |
| ☐ 209 | Vince Buck | .04 | .02 | .01 |
| ☐ 210 | Rickey Jackson | .08 | .04 | .01 |
| ☐ 211 | Vaughan Johnson UER (Name misspelled Vaughn on front) | .08 | .04 | .01 |
| ☐ 212 | Eric Martin | .08 | .04 | .01 |
| ☐ 213 | Sam Mills | .08 | .04 | .01 |
| ☐ 214 | Steve Walsh | .04 | .02 | .01 |
| ☐ 215 | Wade Wilson | .08 | .04 | .01 |
| ☐ 216 | Vaughan Dunbar | .04 | .02 | .01 |
| ☐ 217 | Brad Muster | .08 | .04 | .01 |
| ☐ 218 | Dalton Hilliard | .04 | .02 | .01 |
| ☐ 219 | Floyd Turner | .04 | .02 | .01 |
| ☐ 220 | Stephen Baker | .04 | .02 | .01 |
| ☐ 221 | Mark Jackson | .08 | .04 | .01 |
| ☐ 222 | Jarrod Bunch | .08 | .04 | .01 |
| ☐ 223 | Mark Collins | .04 | .02 | .01 |
| ☐ 224 | Rodney Hampton | .30 | .14 | .04 |
| ☐ 225 | Phil Simms | .10 | .05 | .01 |
| ☐ 226 | Pepper Johnson | .04 | .02 | .01 |
| ☐ 227 | Dave Meggett | .08 | .04 | .01 |
| ☐ 228 | Derek Brown | .04 | .02 | .01 |
| ☐ 229 | Mike Sherrard | .04 | .02 | .01 |
| ☐ 230 | Lawrence Taylor | .10 | .05 | .01 |
| ☐ 231 | Leonard Marshall | .08 | .04 | .01 |
| ☐ 232 | Brad Baxter | .08 | .04 | .01 |
| ☐ 233 | Dennis Byrd | .08 | .04 | .01 |
| ☐ 234 | Ronnie Lott | .10 | .05 | .01 |
| ☐ 235 | Boomer Esiason | .10 | .05 | .01 |
| ☐ 236 | Browning Nagle | .08 | .04 | .01 |
| ☐ 237 | Rob Moore | .10 | .05 | .01 |
| ☐ 238 | Jeff Lageman | .04 | .02 | .01 |
| ☐ 239 | Johnny Mitchell | .25 | .11 | .03 |
| ☐ 240 | Chris Burkett | .04 | .02 | .01 |
| ☐ 241 | Eric Thomas | .04 | .02 | .01 |
| ☐ 242 | Johnny Johnson | .10 | .05 | .01 |
| ☐ 243 | Eric Allen | .08 | .04 | .01 |
| ☐ 244 | Fred Barnett | .10 | .05 | .01 |
| ☐ 245 | Keith Byars | .08 | .04 | .01 |
| ☐ 246 | Randall Cunningham | .10 | .05 | .01 |
| ☐ 247 | Heath Sherman | .04 | .02 | .01 |
| ☐ 248 | Calvin Williams | .10 | .05 | .01 |
| ☐ 249 | Erik McMillan | .04 | .02 | .01 |
| ☐ 250 | Byron Evans | .04 | .02 | .01 |

| | | | |
|---|---|---|---|
| ☐ 251 Seth Joyner | .08 | .04 | .01 |
| ☐ 252 Vai Sikahema | .04 | .02 | .01 |
| ☐ 253 Andre Waters | .04 | .02 | .01 |
| ☐ 254 Tim Harris | .04 | .02 | .01 |
| ☐ 255 Mark Bavaro | .08 | .04 | .01 |
| ☐ 256 Clyde Simmons | .08 | .04 | .01 |
| ☐ 257 Steve Beuerlein | .15 | .07 | .02 |
| ☐ 258 Randal Hill UER | .10 | .05 | .01 |
| (Name misspelled Randall on front) | | | |
| ☐ 259 Ernie Jones | .04 | .02 | .01 |
| ☐ 260 Robert Massey | .04 | .02 | .01 |
| ☐ 261 Ricky Proehl UER | .08 | .04 | .01 |
| (Name misspelled Rickey on front) | | | |
| ☐ 262 Aeneas Williams | .04 | .02 | .01 |
| ☐ 263 Johnny Bailey | .04 | .02 | .01 |
| ☐ 264 Chris Chandler UER | .08 | .04 | .01 |
| (Name misspelled Cris on front) | | | |
| ☐ 265 Anthony Thompson | .04 | .02 | .01 |
| (Los Angeles Rams) | | | |
| ☐ 266 Gary Clark | .08 | .04 | .01 |
| ☐ 267 Chuck Cecil | .04 | .02 | .01 |
| ☐ 268 Rich Camarillo | .04 | .02 | .01 |
| ☐ 269 Neil O'Donnell | .25 | .11 | .03 |
| ☐ 270 Gerald Williams | .04 | .02 | .01 |
| ☐ 271 Greg Lloyd | .04 | .02 | .01 |
| ☐ 272 Eric Green | .10 | .05 | .01 |
| ☐ 273 Merril Hoge | .04 | .02 | .01 |
| ☐ 274 Ernie Mills | .04 | .02 | .01 |
| ☐ 275 Rod Woodson | .10 | .05 | .01 |
| ☐ 276 Gary Anderson | .04 | .02 | .01 |
| ☐ 277 Barry Foster | .25 | .11 | .03 |
| ☐ 278 Jeff Graham | .08 | .04 | .01 |
| ☐ 279 Dwight Stone | .04 | .02 | .01 |
| ☐ 280 Kevin Greene | .04 | .02 | .01 |
| ☐ 281 Eric Bieniemy | .08 | .04 | .01 |
| ☐ 282 Marion Butts | .10 | .05 | .01 |
| ☐ 283 Gill Byrd | .04 | .02 | .01 |
| ☐ 284 Stan Humphries | .10 | .05 | .01 |
| ☐ 285 Anthony Miller | .15 | .07 | .02 |
| ☐ 286 Leslie O'Neal | .08 | .04 | .01 |
| ☐ 287 Junior Seau | .10 | .05 | .01 |
| ☐ 288 Ronnie Harmon | .08 | .04 | .01 |
| ☐ 289 Nate Lewis | .08 | .04 | .01 |
| ☐ 290 John Kidd | .04 | .02 | .01 |
| ☐ 291 Steve Young | .25 | .11 | .03 |
| ☐ 292 John Taylor | .10 | .05 | .01 |
| ☐ 293 Jerry Rice | .50 | .23 | .06 |
| ☐ 294 Tim McDonald | .04 | .02 | .01 |
| ☐ 295 Brent Jones | .10 | .05 | .01 |
| ☐ 296 Tom Rathman | .08 | .04 | .01 |
| ☐ 297 Dexter Carter | .08 | .04 | .01 |
| ☐ 298 Mike Cofer | .04 | .02 | .01 |
| ☐ 299 Ricky Watters | .30 | .14 | .04 |
| ☐ 300 Mervyn Fernandez | .04 | .02 | .01 |
| ☐ 301 Amp Lee | .08 | .04 | .01 |
| ☐ 302 Kevin Fagan | .04 | .02 | .01 |
| ☐ 303 Roy Foster | .04 | .02 | .01 |
| ☐ 304 Bill Romanowski | .04 | .02 | .01 |
| ☐ 305 Brian Blades | .08 | .04 | .01 |
| ☐ 306 John L. Williams | .08 | .04 | .01 |
| ☐ 307 Tommy Kane | .04 | .02 | .01 |
| ☐ 308 John Kasay | .04 | .02 | .01 |
| ☐ 309 Chris Warren | .15 | .07 | .02 |
| ☐ 310 Rufus Porter | .04 | .02 | .01 |
| ☐ 311 Cortez Kennedy | .10 | .05 | .01 |
| ☐ 312 Dan McGwire UER | .08 | .04 | .01 |
| (Name misspelled McGuire on front) | | | |
| ☐ 313 Stan Gelbaugh | .04 | .02 | .01 |
| ☐ 314 Kelvin Martin | .08 | .04 | .01 |
| ☐ 315 Ferrell Edmunds | .04 | .02 | .01 |
| ☐ 316 Eugene Robinson | .04 | .02 | .01 |
| ☐ 317 Gary Anderson | .04 | .02 | .01 |
| ☐ 318 Reggie Cobb | .10 | .05 | .01 |
| ☐ 319 Lawrence Dawsey | .10 | .05 | .01 |
| ☐ 320 Courtney Hawkins | .08 | .04 | .01 |
| ☐ 321 Santana Dotson | .10 | .05 | .01 |
| ☐ 322 Ron Hall | .04 | .02 | .01 |
| ☐ 323 Keith McCants | .04 | .02 | .01 |
| ☐ 324 Martin Mayhew | .04 | .02 | .01 |
| ☐ 325 Anthony Munoz | .08 | .04 | .01 |
| ☐ 326 Steve DeBerg | .08 | .04 | .01 |
| ☐ 327 Vince Workman | .04 | .02 | .01 |
| ☐ 328 Earnest Byner | .08 | .04 | .01 |
| ☐ 329 Ricky Ervins | .08 | .04 | .01 |
| ☐ 330 Jim Lachey | .04 | .02 | .01 |
| ☐ 331 Chip Lohmiller | .04 | .02 | .01 |
| ☐ 332 Ricky Sanders UER | .08 | .04 | .01 |
| (Name misspelled Rickey on front) | | | |
| ☐ 333 Brad Edwards | .04 | .02 | .01 |
| ☐ 334 Tim McGee | .04 | .02 | .01 |
| ☐ 335 Darrell Green | .08 | .04 | .01 |
| ☐ 336 Charles Mann | .08 | .04 | .01 |
| ☐ 337 Wilber Marshall | .08 | .04 | .01 |
| ☐ 338 Brian Mitchell | .08 | .04 | .01 |
| ☐ 339 Art Monk | .10 | .05 | .01 |
| ☐ 340 Mark Rypien | .08 | .04 | .01 |
| ☐ 341 John Elway | .15 | .07 | .02 |
| Denver Broncos | | | |
| ☐ 342 Jim Kelly | .10 | .05 | .01 |
| Buffalo Bills | | | |
| ☐ 343 Dan Marino | .25 | .11 | .03 |
| Miami Dolphins | | | |
| ☐ 344 Eric Dickerson | .10 | .05 | .01 |
| Los Angeles Rams | | | |
| ☐ 345 Willie Gault | .08 | .04 | .01 |
| Chicago Bears | | | |
| ☐ 346 Ken O'Brien | .08 | .04 | .01 |
| New York Jets | | | |
| ☐ 347 Darrell Green | .08 | .04 | .01 |
| Washington Redskins | | | |
| ☐ 348 Richard Dent | .08 | .04 | .01 |
| Chicago Bears | | | |
| ☐ 349 Karl Mecklenburg | .04 | .02 | .01 |
| Denver Broncos | | | |
| ☐ 350 Henry Ellard | .08 | .04 | .01 |
| Los Angeles Rams | | | |
| ☐ 351 Roger Craig | .08 | .04 | .01 |
| San Francisco 49ers | | | |
| ☐ 352 Charles Mann | .04 | .02 | .01 |
| Washington Redskins | | | |
| ☐ 353 Checklist A UER | .04 | .02 | .01 |
| (Misspellings) | | | |
| ☐ 354 Checklist B UER | .04 | .02 | .01 |
| (Misspellings) | | | |
| ☐ 355 Checklist C UER | .04 | .02 | .01 |
| (Numbering out of order) | | | |
| ☐ 356 Checklist D UER | .04 | .02 | .01 |
| (Misspellings and numbering out of order) | | | |
| ☐ 357 Checklist E UER | .04 | .02 | .01 |
| (Misspelling and numbering out of order) | | | |
| ☐ 358 Checklist F UER | .04 | .02 | .01 |
| (Misspelling and numbering out of order) | | | |
| ☐ 359 Checklist G UER | .04 | .02 | .01 |
| (Misspellings and numbering out of order) | | | |
| ☐ 360 Rookies Checklist UER | .04 | .02 | .01 |
| (Misspelling on 391) | | | |
| ☐ 361 Drew Bledsoe | 2.50 | 1.15 | .30 |
| New England Patriots | | | |
| ☐ 362 Rick Mirer | 2.50 | 1.15 | .30 |
| Seattle Seahawks | | | |
| ☐ 363 Garrison Hearst | .60 | .25 | .08 |
| Phoenix Cardinals | | | |
| ☐ 364 Marvin Jones | .15 | .07 | .02 |
| New York Jets | | | |
| ☐ 365 John Copeland | .25 | .11 | .03 |
| Cincinnati Bengals | | | |
| ☐ 366 Eric Curry | .25 | .11 | .03 |
| Tampa Bay Buccaneers | | | |
| ☐ 367 Curtis Conway | .50 | .23 | .06 |
| Chicago Bears | | | |
| ☐ 368 Willie Roaf | .10 | .05 | .01 |
| New Orleans Saints | | | |
| ☐ 369 Lincoln Kennedy | .15 | .07 | .02 |
| Atlanta Falcons | | | |
| ☐ 370 Jerome Bettis | 2.50 | 1.15 | .30 |
| Los Angeles Rams | | | |
| ☐ 371 Dan Williams | .10 | .05 | .01 |
| Denver Broncos | | | |
| ☐ 372 Patrick Bates | .10 | .05 | .01 |
| Los Angeles Raiders | | | |
| ☐ 373 Brad Hopkins | .10 | .05 | .01 |
| Houston Oilers | | | |
| ☐ 374 Steve Everitt | .10 | .05 | .01 |
| Cleveland Browns | | | |
| ☐ 375 Wayne Simmons | .10 | .05 | .01 |
| Green Bay Packers | | | |
| ☐ 376 Tom Carter | .25 | .11 | .03 |
| Washington Redskins | | | |
| ☐ 377 Ernest Dye | .10 | .05 | .01 |
| Phoenix Cardinals | | | |
| ☐ 378 Lester Holmes | .10 | .05 | .01 |
| Philadelphia Eagles | | | |
| ☐ 379 Irv Smith | .20 | .09 | .03 |
| New Orleans Saints | | | |
| ☐ 380 Robert Smith | .35 | .16 | .04 |
| Minnesota Vikings | | | |
| ☐ 381 Darrien Gordon | .20 | .09 | .03 |
| San Diego Chargers | | | |
| ☐ 382 Deon Figures | .15 | .07 | .02 |
| Pittsburgh Steelers | | | |
| ☐ 383 O.J. McDuffie | 1.25 | .55 | .16 |
| Miami Dolphins | | | |
| ☐ 384 Dana Stubblefield | .50 | .23 | .06 |
| San Francisco 49ers | | | |

| | | | |
|---|---|---|---|
| ☐ 385 Todd Kelly ............................ | .10 | .05 | .01 |
| San Francisco 49ers | | | |
| ☐ 386 Thomas Smith..................... | .10 | .05 | .01 |
| Buffalo Bills | | | |
| ☐ 387 George Teague.................... | .20 | .09 | .03 |
| Green Bay Packers | | | |
| ☐ 388 Carlton Gray...................... | .20 | .09 | .03 |
| Seattle Seahawks | | | |
| ☐ 389 Chris Slade........................ | .30 | .14 | .04 |
| New England Patriots | | | |
| ☐ 390 Ben Coleman...................... | .10 | .05 | .01 |
| Phoenix Cardinals | | | |
| ☐ 391 Ryan McNeil UER................ | .10 | .05 | .01 |
| Detroit Lions | | | |
| (Name misspelled | | | |
| McNeill on front) | | | |
| ☐ 392 Demetrius DuBose .............. | .15 | .07 | .02 |
| Tampa Bay Buccaneers | | | |
| ☐ 393 Carl Simpson ..................... | .10 | .05 | .01 |
| Chicago Bears | | | |
| ☐ 394 Coleman Rudolph ............... | .10 | .05 | .01 |
| New York Jets | | | |
| ☐ 395 Tony McGee ....................... | .20 | .09 | .03 |
| Cincinnati Bengals | | | |
| ☐ 396 Roger Harper ..................... | .15 | .07 | .02 |
| Atlanta Falcons | | | |
| ☐ 397 Troy Drayton ...................... | .25 | .11 | .03 |
| Los Angeles Rams | | | |
| ☐ 398 Michael Strahan ................. | .10 | .05 | .01 |
| New York Giants | | | |
| ☐ 399 Natrone Means.................... | 1.25 | .55 | .16 |
| San Diego Chargers | | | |
| ☐ 400 Glyn Milburn ...................... | .75 | .35 | .09 |
| Denver Broncos | | | |

## 1993 SkyBox Impact Kelly/Magic

Jim Kelly and Magic Johnson, spokesmen for SkyBox International, selected a fantasy team of their favorite NFL players, Kelly's Heroes and Magic's Kingdom. Measuring the standard size (2 1/2" by 3 1/2"), these 12 cards were foil stamped and randomly inserted into foil packs. Kelly's pick at the position is on one side, while Magic's pick is found on the other side. The cards are numbered on the back with a "T" prefix.

| | MINT | EXC | G-VG |
|---|---|---|---|
| COMPLETE SET (12)...................... | 20.00 | 9.00 | 2.50 |
| COMMON PAIR (1-12)..................... | 1.00 | .45 | .13 |
| | | | |
| ☐ 1 Title Card............................... | 1.50 | .65 | .19 |
| ☐ 2 Dan Marino ............................ | 4.00 | 1.80 | .50 |
| Jim Kelly | | | |
| ☐ 3 Jay Novacek........................... | 1.25 | .55 | .16 |
| Keith Jackson | | | |
| ☐ 4 Thurman Thomas..................... | 5.00 | 2.30 | .60 |
| Barry Sanders | | | |
| ☐ 5 Barry Sanders ........................ | 10.00 | 4.50 | 1.25 |
| Emmitt Smith | | | |
| ☐ 6 Jerry Rice .............................. | 5.00 | 2.30 | .60 |
| Sterling Sharpe | | | |
| ☐ 7 Andre Reed ............................ | 3.50 | 1.55 | .45 |
| Jerry Rice | | | |
| ☐ 8 Derrick Thomas....................... | 1.25 | .55 | .16 |
| Pat Swilling | | | |
| ☐ 9 Darryl Talley .......................... | 1.25 | .55 | .16 |
| Lawrence Taylor | | | |
| ☐ 10 Ron Woodson ....................... | 1.25 | .55 | .16 |
| Darrell Green | | | |
| ☐ 11 Steve Tasker ........................ | 1.00 | .45 | .13 |
| Elvis Patterson | | | |
| ☐ 12 Chip Lohmiller....................... | 1.00 | .45 | .13 |
| Morten Andersen | | | |
| ☐ AU1 Kelly/Magic Header AU ........ | 100.00 | 45.00 | 12.50 |

## 1993 SkyBox Impact Colors

The 1993 SkyBox Impact Colors football set consists of 400 cards, each measuring 2 1/2" by 3 1/2". The 12-card foil packs contained 11 regular issue or insert cards and one special SkyBox Colors foil card. These foil-stamped Colors cards combine to form a set of all 400 cards. The cards are similar to the regular issue Impact cards, except that they are UV coated and feature an Impact logo on the front highlighted in one of four different color foils (gold, silver, blue, and red). Each player card is reproduced in only one of the colors. The cards are numbered on the back; checklist cards were not issued for the Colors set.

| | MINT | EXC | G-VG |
|---|---|---|---|
| COMPLETE SET (392)...................... | 45.00 | 20.00 | 5.75 |
| COMMON COLOR CARD (1-400)...... | .15 | .07 | .02 |
| *COLOR STAR CARDS: 2X to 4X VALUE | | | |
| | | | |
| ☐ 19 Jim Kelly ............................. | 1.00 | .45 | .13 |
| ☐ 25 Thurman Thomas................... | 1.50 | .65 | .19 |
| ☐ 66 Troy Aikman......................... | 3.50 | 1.55 | .45 |
| ☐ 69 Alvin Harper ........................ | 1.50 | .65 | .19 |
| ☐ 71 Michael Irvin ....................... | 1.75 | .80 | .22 |
| ☐ 74 Emmitt Smith ....................... | 5.00 | 2.30 | .60 |
| ☐ 83 John Elway.......................... | 1.25 | .55 | .16 |
| ☐ 98 Herman Moore ..................... | 1.75 | .80 | .22 |
| ☐ 101 Barry Sanders ..................... | 2.25 | 1.00 | .30 |
| ☐ 108 Brett Favre.......................... | 2.25 | 1.00 | .30 |
| ☐ 109 Sterling Sharpe ................... | 1.75 | .80 | .22 |
| ☐ 139 Joe Montana ....................... | 3.00 | 1.35 | .40 |
| ☐ 174 Dan Marino ......................... | 2.50 | 1.15 | .30 |
| ☐ 277 Barry Foster ....................... | 1.00 | .45 | .13 |
| ☐ 291 Steve Young ....................... | 1.00 | .45 | .13 |
| ☐ 293 Jerry Rice ........................... | 2.00 | .90 | .25 |
| ☐ 299 Ricky Watters ...................... | 1.25 | .55 | .16 |
| ☐ 361 Drew Bledsoe ...................... | 5.00 | 2.30 | .60 |
| ☐ 362 Rick Mirer .......................... | 5.00 | 2.30 | .60 |
| ☐ 363 Garrison Hearst................... | 2.00 | .90 | .25 |
| ☐ 370 Jerome Bettis ...................... | 6.00 | 2.70 | .75 |
| ☐ 380 Robert Smith ...................... | 1.25 | .55 | .16 |
| ☐ 383 O.J. McDuffie ..................... | 2.00 | .90 | .25 |
| ☐ 399 Natrone Means..................... | 1.75 | .80 | .22 |
| ☐ 400 Glyn Milburn ...................... | 2.00 | .90 | .25 |

## 1993 SkyBox Impact Rookie Redemption

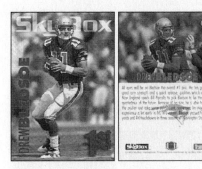

One NFL Rookie Exchange card was randomly inserted in approximately every 180 foil packs and could be redeemed by mail for this special set of 28 NFL Draft First Round selections in their pro uniforms. Collectors could also receive the insert set by sending in a postcard for an entry in the second chance drawing. The standard-size (2 1/2" by 3 1/2") cards feature borderless color player action shots on their fronts. The player's name appears vertically in team colors on one side, and his draft pick number appears within a lower corner. After the checklist card (1), the cards are arranged consecutively in order of the draft, from the first pick to the 29th pick. (The 16th 1993 NFL first-round draft pick, Sean Dawkins, is not represented in this set because of his exclusive contract with another card company.) The back carries another color player photo in its upper portion. The white lower part has player highlights that recount his on-field performance before being drafted, and his new NFL team's expectations of him. The cards are numbered on the back with an "R" prefix.

| | MINT | EXC | G-VG |
|---|---|---|---|
| COMPLETE SET (29)........................ | 25.00 | 11.50 | 3.10 |
| COMMON PLAYER (1-29)................. | .50 | .23 | .06 |

| | | | |
|---|---|---|---|
| ☐ 1 Drew Bledsoe | 2.00 | .90 | .25 |
| New England Patriots Title Card Checklist | | | |
| ☐ 2 Drew Bledsoe | 7.00 | 3.10 | .85 |
| New England Patriots | | | |
| ☐ 3 Rick Mirer | 7.00 | 3.10 | .85 |
| Seattle Seahawks | | | |
| ☐ 4 Garrison Hearst | 2.00 | .90 | .25 |
| Phoenix Cardinals | | | |
| ☐ 5 Marvin Jones | .75 | .35 | .09 |
| New York Jets | | | |
| ☐ 6 John Copeland | 1.00 | .45 | .13 |
| Cincinnati Bengals | | | |
| ☐ 7 Eric Curry UER | 1.00 | .45 | .13 |
| Tampa Bay Buccaneers (Card front states he was selected in sixth round instead of sixth pick) | | | |
| ☐ 8 Curtis Conway | 1.75 | .80 | .22 |
| Chicago Bears | | | |
| ☐ 9 Willie Roaf | .50 | .23 | .06 |
| New Orleans Saints | | | |
| ☐ 10 Lincoln Kennedy | .75 | .35 | .09 |
| Atlanta Falcons | | | |
| ☐ 11 Jerome Bettis | 7.00 | 3.10 | .85 |
| Los Angeles Rams | | | |
| ☐ 12 Dan Williams | .50 | .23 | .06 |
| Denver Broncos | | | |
| ☐ 13 Patrick Bates | .50 | .23 | .06 |
| Los Angeles Raiders | | | |
| ☐ 14 Brad Hopkins | .50 | .23 | .06 |
| Houston Oilers | | | |
| ☐ 15 Steve Everitt | .50 | .23 | .06 |
| Cleveland Browns | | | |
| ☐ 16 Wayne Simmons | .50 | .23 | .06 |
| Green Bay Packers | | | |
| ☐ 17 Tom Carter | .75 | .35 | .09 |
| Washington Redskins | | | |
| ☐ 18 Ernest Dye | .50 | .23 | .06 |
| Phoenix Cardinals | | | |
| ☐ 19 Lester Holmes | .50 | .23 | .06 |
| Philadelphia Eagles | | | |
| ☐ 20 Irv Smith | .75 | .35 | .09 |
| New Orleans Saints | | | |
| ☐ 21 Robert Smith | 1.00 | .45 | .13 |
| Minnesota Vikings | | | |
| ☐ 22 Darrien Gordon | .75 | .35 | .09 |
| San Diego Chargers | | | |
| ☐ 23 Deon Figures | .75 | .35 | .09 |
| Pittsburgh Steelers | | | |
| ☐ 24 Leonard Renfro | .50 | .23 | .06 |
| Philadelphia Eagles | | | |
| ☐ 25 O.J. McDuffie | 2.50 | 1.15 | .30 |
| Miami Dolphins | | | |
| ☐ 26 Dana Stubblefield | 1.00 | .45 | .13 |
| San Francisco 49ers | | | |
| ☐ 27 Todd Kelly | .50 | .23 | .06 |
| San Francisco 49ers | | | |
| ☐ 28 Thomas Smith | .75 | .35 | .09 |
| Buffalo Bills | | | |
| ☐ 29 George Teague | .75 | .35 | .09 |
| Green Bay Packers | | | |
| ☐ NNO Rookie Redemption | 3.00 | 1.35 | .40 |
| Card Expired | | | |

## 1993 SkyBox Impact Update

Focusing on NFL players who switched teams through free agency, SkyBox issued this 20-card standard-size (2 1/2" by 3 1/2") subset to depict these players in their new uniforms. The set could be obtained by sending in five Impact foil pack wrappers plus 3.99 for postage and handling. Each borderless front features a color player action shot showing him in his new team's uniform. This is cut out and superposed upon a black-and-white player photo showing him in his old team's uniform. The player's name appears in a lower corner in team-colored lettering. The back carries another color player photo in its upper portion. The white lower part has player highlights that recount his performance for his old team, and his new team's expectations of him. The cards are numbered on the back with a "U" prefix.

| | MINT | EXC | G-VG |
|---|---|---|---|
| COMPLETE SET (20) | 10.00 | 4.50 | 1.25 |
| COMMON PLAYER (1-20) | .25 | .11 | .03 |
| | | | |
| ☐ 1 Pierce Holt | .25 | .11 | .03 |
| Atlanta Falcons | | | |
| ☐ 2 Vinny Testaverde | .35 | .16 | .04 |
| Cleveland Browns | | | |
| ☐ 3 Rod Bernstine | .25 | .11 | .03 |
| Denver Broncos | | | |
| ☐ 4 Reggie White | .50 | .23 | .06 |
| Green Bay Packers | | | |
| ☐ 5 Mark Clayton | .25 | .11 | .03 |
| Green Bay Packers | | | |
| ☐ 6 Joe Montana | 4.00 | 1.80 | .50 |
| Kansas City Chiefs | | | |
| ☐ 7 Marcus Allen | .35 | .16 | .04 |
| Kansas City Chiefs | | | |
| ☐ 8 Jeff Hostetler | .35 | .16 | .04 |
| Los Angeles Raiders | | | |
| ☐ 9 Shane Conlan | .25 | .11 | .03 |
| Los Angeles Rams | | | |
| ☐ 10 Brad Muster | .25 | .11 | .03 |
| New Orleans Saints | | | |
| ☐ 11 Mike Sherrard | .25 | .11 | .03 |
| New York Giants | | | |
| ☐ 12 Ronnie Lott | .35 | .16 | .04 |
| New York Jets | | | |
| ☐ 13 Steve Beuerlein | .30 | .14 | .04 |
| Phoenix Cardinals | | | |
| ☐ 14 Gary Clark | .30 | .14 | .04 |
| Phoenix Cardinals | | | |
| ☐ 15 Kevin Greene | .25 | .11 | .03 |
| Pittsburgh Steelers | | | |
| ☐ 16 Tim McDonald | .25 | .11 | .03 |
| San Francisco 49ers | | | |
| ☐ 17 Wilber Marshall | .30 | .14 | .04 |
| Houston Oilers | | | |
| ☐ 18 Keith Byars | .30 | .14 | .04 |
| Miami Dolphins | | | |
| ☐ 19 Pat Swilling | .30 | .14 | .04 |
| Detroit Lions | | | |
| ☐ 20 Boomer Esiason | .30 | .14 | .04 |
| New York Jets | | | |

## 1994 SkyBox Impact Super Bowl Promo

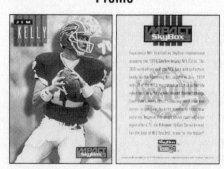

Distributed by SkyBox at the January 1994 NFL Experience show in Atlanta, this standard-size (2 1/2" by 3 1/2") card displays on its front a full-bleed color action player photo. The background of the picture is out of focus so as to contrast with the featured player. The player's name appears in the upper left corner on a short, black horizontal bar and on short, red vertical bars. On a white background featuring a ghosted Super Bowl XXVIII logo, the back presents an advertisement for the 1994 SkyBox Impact series. The card is unnumbered.

| | MINT | EXC | G-VG |
|---|---|---|---|
| COMPLETE SET (1) | 3.00 | 1.20 | .30 |
| COMMON PLAYER | 3.00 | 1.20 | .30 |
| | | | |
| ☐ NNO Jim Kelly | 3.00 | 1.20 | .30 |
| Buffalo Bills | | | |

# 1994 SkyBox Impact Promos

These six standard-size (2 1/2" by 3 1/2") promo cards feature on their fronts borderless color player action shots. The featured players stand out against faded backgrounds. The player's name appears within team-colored boxes in an upper corner. The horizontal back carries a color player action shot on the right, and upon which the player's NFL stats appear. His biography and career highlights appear to the left of the photo. The cards are numbered on the back with an "S" prefix.

|                               | MINT  | EXC  | G-VG |
|-------------------------------|-------|------|------|
| COMPLETE SET (6)              | 9.00  | 3.75 | .90  |
| COMMON PLAYER (S1-S6)         | 1.00  | .40  | .10  |
| ☐ S1 Marcus Allen            | 2.00  | .80  | .20  |
| Kansas City Chiefs            |       |      |      |
| ☐ S2 Chris Doleman           | 1.00  | .40  | .10  |
| Minnesota Vikings             |       |      |      |
| ☐ S3 Craig Erickson          | 2.00  | .80  | .20  |
| Tampa Bay Buccaneers          |       |      |      |
| ☐ S4 Jim Kelly               | 3.00  | 1.20 | .30  |
| Buffalo Bills                 |       |      |      |
| ☐ S5 Reggie Roby             | 1.00  | .40  | .10  |
| Washington Redskins           |       |      |      |
| ☐ S6 Rod Woodson             | 2.00  | .80  | .20  |
| Pittsburgh Steelers           |       |      |      |

# 1994 SkyBox Impact

These 300 standard-size (2 1/2" by 3 1/2") cards feature borderless color player action shots. The featured players stand out against a faded background. The player's name appears within team color-coded boxes in an upper corner, while the SkyBox Impact logo appears in a lower corner. The horizontal backs carry color player action shots on one side, with the player's NFL stats printed in the faded lower part of the photo. His biography and career highlights appear next to the picture. The cards are numbered on the back.

|                               | MINT  | EXC  | G-VG |
|-------------------------------|-------|------|------|
| COMPLETE SET (300)            | 20.00 | 9.00 | 2.50 |
| COMMON PLAYER (1-300)         | .05   | .02  | .01  |
| ☐ 1 Johnny Bailey            | .05   | .02  | .01  |
| Arizona Cardinals             |       |      |      |
| ☐ 2 Steve Beuerlein          | .10   | .05  | .01  |
| Arizona Cardinals             |       |      |      |
| ☐ 3 Gary Clark               | .08   | .04  | .01  |
| Arizona Cardinals             |       |      |      |
| ☐ 4 Garrison Hearst          | .15   | .07  | .02  |
| Arizona Cardinals             |       |      |      |

| ☐ 5 Ron Moore                | .50   | .23  | .06  |
| Arizona Cardinals             |       |      |      |
| ☐ 6 Ricky Proehl             | .08   | .04  | .01  |
| Arizona Cardinals             |       |      |      |
| ☐ 7 Eric Swann               | .05   | .02  | .01  |
| Arizona Cardinals             |       |      |      |
| ☐ 8 Aeneas Williams          | .05   | .02  | .01  |
| Arizona Cardinals             |       |      |      |
| ☐ 9 Robert Massey            | .05   | .02  | .01  |
| Detroit Lions                 |       |      |      |
| ☐ 10 Chuck Cecil             | .05   | .02  | .01  |
| Arizona Cardinals             |       |      |      |
| ☐ 11 Ken Harvey              | .08   | .04  | .01  |
| Washington Redskins           |       |      |      |
| ☐ 12 Michael Haynes          | .15   | .07  | .02  |
| New Orleans Saints            |       |      |      |
| ☐ 13 Tony Smith              | .05   | .02  | .01  |
| Atlanta Falcons               |       |      |      |
| ☐ 14 Bobby Hebert            | .10   | .05  | .01  |
| Atlanta Falcons               |       |      |      |
| ☐ 15 Mike Pritchard          | .10   | .05  | .01  |
| Denver Broncos                |       |      |      |
| ☐ 16 Andre Rison             | .15   | .07  | .02  |
| Atlanta Falcons               |       |      |      |
| ☐ 17 Deion Sanders           | .15   | .07  | .02  |
| Atlanta Falcons               |       |      |      |
| ☐ 18 Pierce Holt             | .05   | .02  | .01  |
| Atlanta Falcons               |       |      |      |
| ☐ 19 Erric Pegram            | .25   | .11  | .03  |
| Atlanta Falcons               |       |      |      |
| ☐ 20 Jessie Tuggle           | .05   | .02  | .01  |
| Atlanta Falcons               |       |      |      |
| ☐ 21 Steve Broussard         | .05   | .02  | .01  |
| Atlanta Falcons               |       |      |      |
| ☐ 22 Don Beebe               | .10   | .05  | .01  |
| Buffalo Bills                 |       |      |      |
| ☐ 23 Cornelius Bennett       | .10   | .05  | .01  |
| Buffalo Bills                 |       |      |      |
| ☐ 24 Kenneth Davis           | .05   | .02  | .01  |
| Buffalo Bills                 |       |      |      |
| ☐ 25 Bill Brooks             | .05   | .02  | .01  |
| Buffalo Bills                 |       |      |      |
| ☐ 26 Jim Kelly               | .20   | .09  | .03  |
| Buffalo Bills                 |       |      |      |
| ☐ 27 Andre Reed              | .10   | .05  | .01  |
| Buffalo Bills                 |       |      |      |
| ☐ 28 Bruce Smith             | .10   | .05  | .01  |
| Buffalo Bills                 |       |      |      |
| ☐ 29 Darryl Talley           | .05   | .02  | .01  |
| Buffalo Bills                 |       |      |      |
| ☐ 30 Thurman Thomas          | .25   | .11  | .03  |
| Buffalo Bills                 |       |      |      |
| ☐ 31 Steve Tasker            | .05   | .02  | .01  |
| Buffalo Bills                 |       |      |      |
| ☐ 32 Neal Anderson           | .08   | .04  | .01  |
| Chicago Bears                 |       |      |      |
| ☐ 33 Mark Carrier            | .08   | .04  | .01  |
| Chicago Bears                 |       |      |      |
| ☐ 34 Richard Dent            | .10   | .05  | .01  |
| Chicago Bears                 |       |      |      |
| ☐ 35 Jim Harbaugh            | .08   | .04  | .01  |
| Indianapolis Colts            |       |      |      |
| ☐ 36 Chris Gedney            | .05   | .02  | .01  |
| Chicago Bears                 |       |      |      |
| ☐ 37 Tom Waddle              | .10   | .05  | .01  |
| Chicago Bears                 |       |      |      |
| ☐ 38 Curtis Conway           | .15   | .07  | .02  |
| Chicago Bears                 |       |      |      |
| ☐ 39 Dante Jones             | .05   | .02  | .01  |
| Chicago Bears                 |       |      |      |
| ☐ 40 Donnell Woolford        | .05   | .02  | .01  |
| Chicago Bears                 |       |      |      |
| ☐ 41 Tim Worley              | .05   | .02  | .01  |
| Chicago Bears                 |       |      |      |
| ☐ 42 John Copeland           | .05   | .02  | .01  |
| Cincinnati Bengals            |       |      |      |
| ☐ 43 David Klingler          | .15   | .07  | .02  |
| Cincinnati Bengals            |       |      |      |
| ☐ 44 Derrick Fenner          | .05   | .02  | .01  |
| Cincinnati Bengals            |       |      |      |
| ☐ 45 Harold Green            | .08   | .04  | .01  |
| Cincinnati Bengals            |       |      |      |
| ☐ 46 Carl Pickens            | .10   | .05  | .01  |
| Cincinnati Bengals            |       |      |      |
| ☐ 47 Tony McGee              | .05   | .02  | .01  |
| Cincinnati Bengals            |       |      |      |
| ☐ 48 Darryl Williams         | .05   | .02  | .01  |
| Cincinnati Bengals            |       |      |      |
| ☐ 49 Steve Everitt           | .05   | .02  | .01  |
| Cleveland Browns              |       |      |      |
| ☐ 50 Michael Jackson         | .05   | .02  | .01  |
| Cleveland Browns              |       |      |      |
| ☐ 51 Eric Metcalf            | .10   | .05  | .01  |
| Cleveland Browns              |       |      |      |
| ☐ 52 Tommy Vardell           | .08   | .04  | .01  |
| Cleveland Browns              |       |      |      |
| ☐ 53 Vinny Testaverde        | .08   | .04  | .01  |

| | | | | | | | | |
|---|---|---|---|---|---|---|---|---|
| Cleveland Browns | | | | | Houston Oilers | | | |
| ☐ 54 Mark Carrier | .08 | .04 | .01 | | ☐ 103 Webster Slaughter | .08 | .04 | .01 |
| Cleveland Browns | | | | | Houston Oilers | | | |
| ☐ 55 Michael Dean Perry | .05 | .02 | .01 | | ☐ 104 Ray Childress | .05 | .02 | .01 |
| Cleveland Browns | | | | | Houston Oilers | | | |
| ☐ 56 Eric Turner | .05 | .02 | .01 | | ☐ 105 Wilber Marshall | .08 | .04 | .01 |
| Cleveland Browns | | | | | Houston Oilers | | | |
| ☐ 57 Troy Aikman | 1.25 | .55 | .16 | | ☐ 106 Gary Brown | .30 | .14 | .04 |
| Dallas Cowboys | | | | | Houston Oilers | | | |
| ☐ 58 Alvin Harper | .08 | .04 | .01 | | ☐ 107 Marcus Robertson | .05 | .02 | .01 |
| Dallas Cowboys | | | | | Houston Oilers | | | |
| ☐ 59 Michael Irvin | .30 | .14 | .04 | | ☐ 108 Sean Jones | .05 | .02 | .01 |
| Dallas Cowboys | | | | | Green Bay Packers | | | |
| ☐ 60 Leon Lett | .05 | .02 | .01 | | ☐ 109 Jeff George | .10 | .05 | .01 |
| Dallas Cowboys | | | | | Atlanta Falcons | | | |
| ☐ 61 Russell Maryland | .10 | .05 | .01 | | ☐ 110 Steve Emtman | .05 | .02 | .01 |
| Dallas Cowboys | | | | | Indianapolis Colts | | | |
| ☐ 62 Jay Novacek | .10 | .05 | .01 | | ☐ 111 Quentin Coryatt | .10 | .05 | .01 |
| Dallas Cowboys | | | | | Indianapolis Colts | | | |
| ☐ 63 Emmitt Smith | 1.75 | .80 | .22 | | ☐ 112 Sean Dawkins | .50 | .23 | .06 |
| Dallas Cowboys | | | | | Indianapolis Colts | | | |
| ☐ 64 Ken Norton | .08 | .04 | .01 | | ☐ 113 Jeff Herrod | .05 | .02 | .01 |
| San Francisco 49ers | | | | | Indianapolis Colts | | | |
| ☐ 65 Charles Haley | .08 | .04 | .01 | | ☐ 114 Roosevelt Potts | .08 | .04 | .01 |
| Dallas Cowboys | | | | | Indianapolis Colts | | | |
| ☐ 66 Daryl Johnston | .10 | .05 | .01 | | ☐ 115 Marcus Allen | .10 | .05 | .01 |
| Dallas Cowboys | | | | | Kansas City Chiefs | | | |
| ☐ 67 Kevin Smith | .05 | .02 | .01 | | ☐ 116 Kimble Anders | .15 | .07 | .02 |
| Dallas Cowboys | | | | | Kansas City Chiefs | | | |
| ☐ 68 James Washington | .05 | .02 | .01 | | ☐ 117 Tim Barnett | .08 | .04 | .01 |
| Dallas Cowboys | | | | | Kansas City Chiefs | | | |
| ☐ 69 Kevin Williams | .15 | .07 | .02 | | ☐ 118 J.J. Birden | .08 | .04 | .01 |
| Dallas Cowboys | | | | | Kansas City Chiefs | | | |
| ☐ 70 Bernie Kosar | .10 | .05 | .01 | | ☐ 119 Dale Carter | .05 | .02 | .01 |
| Miami Dolphins | | | | | Kansas City Chiefs | | | |
| ☐ 71 Mike Croel | .08 | .04 | .01 | | ☐ 120 Willie Davis | .08 | .04 | .01 |
| Denver Broncos | | | | | Kansas City Chiefs | | | |
| ☐ 72 John Elway | .40 | .18 | .05 | | ☐ 121 Nick Lowery | .05 | .02 | .01 |
| Denver Broncos | | | | | Kansas City Chiefs | | | |
| ☐ 73 Shannon Sharpe | .15 | .07 | .02 | | ☐ 122 Joe Montana | 1.25 | .55 | .16 |
| Denver Broncos | | | | | Kansas City Chiefs | | | |
| ☐ 74 Rod Bernstine | .08 | .04 | .01 | | ☐ 123 Kevin Ross | .05 | .02 | .01 |
| Denver Broncos | | | | | Atlanta Falcons | | | |
| ☐ 75 Simon Fletcher | .05 | .02 | .01 | | ☐ 124 Neil Smith | .10 | .05 | .01 |
| Denver Broncos | | | | | Kansas City Chiefs | | | |
| ☐ 76 Arthur Marshall | .05 | .02 | .01 | | ☐ 125 Derrick Thomas | .15 | .07 | .02 |
| New York Giants | | | | | Kansas City Chiefs | | | |
| ☐ 77 Glyn Milburn | .20 | .09 | .03 | | ☐ 126 Keith Cash | .05 | .02 | .01 |
| Denver Broncos | | | | | Kansas City Chiefs | | | |
| ☐ 78 Dennis Smith | .05 | .02 | .01 | | ☐ 127 Tim Brown | .15 | .07 | .02 |
| Denver Broncos | | | | | Los Angeles Raiders | | | |
| ☐ 79 Herman Moore | .15 | .07 | .02 | | ☐ 128 Raghib Ismail | .15 | .07 | .02 |
| Detroit Lions | | | | | Los Angeles Raiders | | | |
| ☐ 80 Rodney Peete | .08 | .04 | .01 | | ☐ 129 Ethan Horton | .05 | .02 | .01 |
| Dallas Cowboys | | | | | Washington Redskins | | | |
| ☐ 81 Barry Sanders | .60 | .25 | .08 | | ☐ 130 Jeff Hostetler | .10 | .05 | .01 |
| Detroit Lions | | | | | Los Angeles Raiders | | | |
| ☐ 82 Mel Gray | .05 | .02 | .01 | | ☐ 131 Patrick Bates | .05 | .02 | .01 |
| Detroit Lions | | | | | Los Angeles Raiders | | | |
| ☐ 83 Erik Kramer | .15 | .07 | .02 | | ☐ 132 Terry McDaniel | .05 | .02 | .01 |
| Chicago Bears | | | | | Los Angeles Raiders | | | |
| ☐ 84 Pat Swilling | .08 | .04 | .01 | | ☐ 133 Anthony Smith | .08 | .04 | .01 |
| Detroit Lions | | | | | Los Angeles Raiders | | | |
| ☐ 85 Willie Green | .05 | .02 | .01 | | ☐ 134 Greg Robinson | .10 | .05 | .01 |
| Detroit Lions | | | | | Los Angeles Raiders | | | |
| ☐ 86 Chris Spielman | .08 | .04 | .01 | | ☐ 135 James Jett | .30 | .14 | .04 |
| Detroit Lions | | | | | Los Angeles Raiders | | | |
| ☐ 87 Robert Porcher | .05 | .02 | .01 | | ☐ 136 Alexander Wright | .08 | .04 | .01 |
| Detroit Lions | | | | | Los Angeles Raiders | | | |
| ☐ 88 Derrick Moore | .08 | .04 | .01 | | ☐ 137 Flipper Anderson | .08 | .04 | .01 |
| Detroit Lions | | | | | Los Angeles Rams | | | |
| ☐ 89 Edgar Bennett | .10 | .05 | .01 | | ☐ 138 Shane Conlan | .08 | .04 | .01 |
| Green Bay Packers | | | | | Los Angeles Rams | | | |
| ☐ 90 Tony Bennett | .08 | .04 | .01 | | ☐ 139 Jim Everett | .10 | .05 | .01 |
| Indianapolis Colts | | | | | New Orleans Saints | | | |
| ☐ 91 LeRoy Butler | .05 | .02 | .01 | | ☐ 140 Henry Ellard | .08 | .04 | .01 |
| Green Bay Packers | | | | | Washington Redskins | | | |
| ☐ 92 Brett Favre | .50 | .23 | .06 | | ☐ 141 Jerome Bettis | 2.00 | .90 | .25 |
| Green Bay Packers | | | | | Los Angeles Rams | | | |
| ☐ 93 Jackie Harris | .15 | .07 | .02 | | ☐ 142 Troy Drayton | .08 | .04 | .01 |
| Green Bay Packers | | | | | Los Angeles Rams | | | |
| ☐ 94 Sterling Sharpe | .30 | .14 | .04 | | ☐ 143 Sean Gilbert | .05 | .02 | .01 |
| Green Bay Packers | | | | | Los Angeles Rams | | | |
| ☐ 95 Darrell Thompson | .05 | .02 | .01 | | ☐ 144 Chris Miller | .10 | .05 | .01 |
| Green Bay Packers | | | | | Los Angeles Rams | | | |
| ☐ 96 Reggie White | .15 | .07 | .02 | | ☐ 145 Keith Byars | .08 | .04 | .01 |
| Green Bay Packers | | | | | Miami Dolphins | | | |
| ☐ 97 Terrell Buckley | .10 | .05 | .01 | | ☐ 146 Marco Coleman | .05 | .02 | .01 |
| Green Bay Packers | | | | | Miami Dolphins | | | |
| ☐ 98 Cris Dishman | .05 | .02 | .01 | | ☐ 147 Bryan Cox | .05 | .02 | .01 |
| Houston Oilers | | | | | Miami Dolphins | | | |
| ☐ 99 Ernest Givins | .08 | .04 | .01 | | ☐ 148 Irving Fryar | .08 | .04 | .01 |
| Houston Oilers | | | | | Miami Dolphins | | | |
| ☐ 100 Haywood Jeffires | .10 | .05 | .01 | | ☐ 149 Mark Ingram | .05 | .02 | .01 |
| Houston Oilers | | | | | Miami Dolphins | | | |
| ☐ 101 Warren Moon | .10 | .05 | .01 | | ☐ 150 Keith Jackson | .10 | .05 | .01 |
| Minnesota Vikings | | | | | Miami Dolphins | | | |
| ☐ 102 Lorenzo White | .05 | .02 | .01 | | ☐ 151 Terry Kirby | .50 | .23 | .06 |

|  |  |  | | | |
|---|--------|------|------|------|------|
| ☐ 152 | Dan Marino | Miami Dolphins | .75 | .35 | .09 |
| ☐ 153 | O.J. McDuffie | Miami Dolphins | .25 | .11 | .03 |
| ☐ 154 | Scott Mitchell | Miami Dolphins | .30 | .14 | .04 |
| ☐ 155 | Anthony Carter | Detroit Lions | .08 | .04 | .01 |
| ☐ 156 | Cris Carter | Minnesota Vikings | .10 | .05 | .01 |
| ☐ 157 | Chris Doleman | Minnesota Vikings | .08 | .04 | .01 |
| ☐ 158 | Steve Jordan | Atlanta Falcons | .08 | .04 | .01 |
| ☐ 159 | Qadry Ismail | Minnesota Vikings | .15 | .07 | .02 |
| ☐ 160 | Randall McDaniel | Minnesota Vikings | .05 | .02 | .01 |
| ☐ 161 | John Randle | Minnesota Vikings | .05 | .02 | .01 |
| ☐ 162 | Robert Smith | Minnesota Vikings | .10 | .05 | .01 |
| ☐ 163 | Henry Thomas | Minnesota Vikings | .05 | .02 | .01 |
| ☐ 164 | Terry Allen | Minnesota Vikings | .10 | .05 | .01 |
| ☐ 165 | Scottie Graham | Minnesota Vikings | .40 | .18 | .05 |
| ☐ 166 | Drew Bledsoe | Minnesota Vikings | 2.00 | .90 | .25 |
| ☐ 167 | Vincent Brown | New England Patriots | .05 | .02 | .01 |
| ☐ 168 | Ben Coates | New England Patriots | .05 | .02 | .01 |
| ☐ 169 | Leonard Russell | New England Patriots | .10 | .05 | .01 |
| ☐ 170 | Andre Tippett | New England Patriots | .05 | .02 | .01 |
| ☐ 171 | Vincent Brisby | New England Patriots | .05 | .02 | .01 |
| ☐ 172 | Michael Timpson | New England Patriots | .05 | .02 | .01 |
| ☐ 173 | Bruce Armstrong | New England Patriots | .05 | .02 | .01 |
| ☐ 174 | Morten Andersen | New England Patriots | .08 | .04 | .01 |
| ☐ 175 | Derek Brown | New Orleans Saints | .20 | .09 | .03 |
| ☐ 176 | Quinn Early | New Orleans Saints | .08 | .04 | .01 |
| ☐ 177 | Rickey Jackson | New Orleans Saints | .08 | .04 | .01 |
| ☐ 178 | Vaughan Johnson | New Orleans Saints | .05 | .02 | .01 |
| ☐ 179 | Lorenzo Neal | New Orleans Saints | .15 | .07 | .02 |
| ☐ 180 | Sam Mills | New Orleans Saints | .08 | .04 | .01 |
| ☐ 181 | Irv Smith | New Orleans Saints | .05 | .02 | .01 |
| ☐ 182 | Renaldo Turnbull | New Orleans Saints | .08 | .04 | .01 |
| ☐ 183 | Wade Wilson | New Orleans Saints | .08 | .04 | .01 |
| ☐ 184 | Willie Roaf | New Orleans Saints | .08 | .04 | .01 |
| ☐ 185 | Michael Brooks | New Orleans Saints | .05 | .02 | .01 |
| ☐ 186 | Mark Jackson | New Orleans Saints | .08 | .04 | .01 |
| ☐ 187 | Rodney Hampton | New York Giants | .25 | .11 | .03 |
| ☐ 188 | Phil Simms | New York Giants | .10 | .05 | .01 |
| ☐ 189 | David Meggett | New York Giants | .10 | .05 | .01 |
| ☐ 190 | Mike Sherrard | New York Giants | .05 | .02 | .01 |
| ☐ 191 | Chris Calloway | New York Giants | .05 | .02 | .01 |
| ☐ 192 | Brad Baxter | New York Giants | .08 | .04 | .01 |
| ☐ 193 | Ronnie Lott | New York Jets | .10 | .05 | .01 |
| ☐ 194 | Boomer Esiason | New York Jets | .10 | .05 | .01 |
| ☐ 195 | Rob Moore | New York Jets | .10 | .05 | .01 |
| ☐ 196 | Johnny Johnson | New York Jets | .10 | .05 | .01 |
| ☐ 197 | Marvin Jones | New York Jets | .05 | .02 | .01 |
| ☐ 198 | Mo Lewis | New York Jets | .05 | .02 | .01 |
| ☐ 199 | Johnny Mitchell | New York Jets | .15 | .07 | .02 |
| ☐ 200 | Brian Washington | New York Jets | .05 | .02 | .01 |
| ☐ 201 | Eric Allen | New York Jets | .08 | .04 | .01 |
| ☐ 202 | Fred Barnett | Philadelphia Eagles | .10 | .05 | .01 |
| ☐ 203 | Mark Bavaro | Philadelphia Eagles | .08 | .04 | .01 |
| ☐ 204 | Randall Cunningham | Philadelphia Eagles | .10 | .05 | .01 |
| ☐ 205 | Vaughn Hebron | Philadelphia Eagles | .05 | .02 | .01 |
| ☐ 206 | Seth Joyner | Philadelphia Eagles | .10 | .05 | .01 |
| ☐ 207 | Clyde Simmons | Arizona Cardinals | .10 | .05 | .01 |
| ☐ 208 | Herschel Walker | Arizona Cardinals | .10 | .05 | .01 |
| ☐ 209 | Calvin Williams | Philadelphia Eagles | .10 | .05 | .01 |
| ☐ 210 | Neil O'Donnell | Philadelphia Eagles | .12 | .05 | .02 |
| ☐ 211 | Eric Green | Philadelphia Eagles | .10 | .05 | .01 |
| ☐ 212 | Leroy Thompson | Pittsburgh Steelers | .08 | .04 | .01 |
| ☐ 213 | Rod Woodson | Pittsburgh Steelers | .10 | .05 | .01 |
| ☐ 214 | Barry Foster | Pittsburgh Steelers | .15 | .07 | .02 |
| ☐ 215 | Jeff Graham | Philadelphia Eagles | .05 | .02 | .01 |
| ☐ 216 | Kevin Greene | Pittsburgh Steelers | .05 | .02 | .01 |
| ☐ 217 | Deon Figures | Pittsburgh Steelers | .05 | .02 | .01 |
| ☐ 218 | Greg Lloyd | Pittsburgh Steelers | .05 | .02 | .01 |
| ☐ 219 | Marion Butts | Pittsburgh Steelers | .10 | .05 | .01 |
| ☐ 220 | Chris Mims | New England Patriots | .05 | .02 | .01 |
| ☐ 221 | Eric Curry | San Diego Chargers | .05 | .02 | .01 |
| ☐ 222 | Ronnie Harmon | Tampa Bay Buccaneers | .05 | .02 | .01 |
| ☐ 223 | Stan Humphries | San Diego Chargers | .08 | .04 | .01 |
| ☐ 224 | Nate Lewis | San Diego Chargers | .05 | .02 | .01 |
| ☐ 225 | Natrone Means | San Diego Chargers | .25 | .11 | .03 |
| ☐ 226 | Anthony Miller | San Diego Chargers | .15 | .07 | .02 |
| ☐ 227 | Leslie O'Neal | Denver Broncos | .08 | .04 | .01 |
| ☐ 228 | Junior Seau | San Diego Chargers | .10 | .05 | .01 |
| ☐ 229 | Brent Jones | San Diego Chargers | .10 | .05 | .01 |
| ☐ 230 | Tim McDonald | San Francisco 49ers | .05 | .02 | .01 |
| ☐ 231 | Tom Rathman | San Francisco 49ers | .08 | .04 | .01 |
| ☐ 232 | Jerry Rice | San Francisco 49ers | .50 | .23 | .06 |
| ☐ 233 | Dana Stubblefield | San Francisco 49ers | .08 | .04 | .01 |
| ☐ 234 | John Taylor | San Francisco 49ers | .10 | .05 | .01 |
| ☐ 235 | Ricky Watters | San Francisco 49ers | .20 | .09 | .03 |
| ☐ 236 | Steve Young | San Francisco 49ers | .15 | .07 | .02 |
| ☐ 237 | Amp Lee | San Francisco 49ers | .05 | .02 | .01 |
| ☐ 238 | Robert Blackmon | San Francisco 49ers | .05 | .02 | .01 |
| ☐ 239 | Brian Blades | Seattle Seahawks | .08 | .04 | .01 |
| ☐ 240 | Cortez Kennedy | Seattle Seahawks | .10 | .05 | .01 |
| ☐ 241 | Kelvin Martin | Seattle Seahawks | .08 | .04 | .01 |
| ☐ 242 | Rick Mirer | Seattle Seahawks | 2.00 | .90 | .25 |
| ☐ 243 | Eugene Robinson | Seattle Seahawks | .05 | .02 | .01 |
| ☐ 244 | Chris Warren | Seattle Seahawks | .10 | .05 | .01 |
| ☐ 245 | John L. Williams | Seattle Seahawks | .08 | .04 | .01 |
| ☐ 246 | Jon Vaughn | Pittsburgh Steelers | .05 | .02 | .01 |
| ☐ 247 | Reggie Cobb | Seattle Seahawks | .10 | .05 | .01 |
| ☐ 248 | Horace Copeland | Green Bay Packers | .05 | .02 | .01 |
| ☐ 249 | Derrick Alexander | Tampa Bay Buccaneers | .50 | .23 | .06 |

| | | | |
|---|---|---|---|
| Cleveland Browns | | | |
| ☐ 250 Santana Dotson | .10 | .05 | .01 |
| Tampa Bay Buccaneers | | | |
| ☐ 251 Craig Erickson | .10 | .05 | .01 |
| Tampa Bay Buccaneers | | | |
| ☐ 252 Courtney Hawkins | .05 | .02 | .01 |
| Tampa Bay Buccaneers | | | |
| ☐ 253 Hardy Nickerson | .05 | .02 | .01 |
| Tampa Bay Buccaneers | | | |
| ☐ 254 Vince Workman | .05 | .02 | .01 |
| Tampa Bay Buccaneers | | | |
| ☐ 255 Paul Gruber | .05 | .02 | .01 |
| Tampa Bay Buccaneers | | | |
| ☐ 256 Reggie Brooks | .75 | .35 | .09 |
| Washington Redskins | | | |
| ☐ 257 Tom Carter | .05 | .02 | .01 |
| Washington Redskins | | | |
| ☐ 258 Andre Collins | .05 | .02 | .01 |
| Washington Redskins | | | |
| ☐ 259 Darrell Green | .08 | .04 | .01 |
| Washington Redskins | | | |
| ☐ 260 Desmond Howard | .15 | .07 | .02 |
| Washington Redskins | | | |
| ☐ 261 Tim McGee | .05 | .02 | .01 |
| Cincinnati Bengals | | | |
| ☐ 262 Brian Mitchell | .08 | .04 | .01 |
| Washington Redskins | | | |
| ☐ 263 Art Monk | .10 | .05 | .01 |
| Washington Redskins | | | |
| ☐ 264 John Friesz | .08 | .04 | .01 |
| Washington Redskins | | | |
| ☐ 265 Ricky Sanders | .08 | .04 | .01 |
| Atlanta Falcons | | | |
| ☐ 266 Checklist | .05 | .02 | .01 |
| ☐ 267 Checklist | .05 | .02 | .01 |
| ☐ 268 Checklist | .05 | .02 | .01 |
| ☐ 269 Checklist | .05 | .02 | .01 |
| ☐ 270 Checklist | .05 | .02 | .01 |
| ☐ 271 Carolina Panthers | .10 | .05 | .01 |
| Logo Card | | | |
| ☐ 272 Jacksonville Jaguars | .10 | .05 | .01 |
| Logo Card | | | |
| ☐ 273 Dan Wilkinson | .50 | .23 | .06 |
| Cincinnati Bengals | | | |
| ☐ 274 Marshall Faulk | 3.00 | 1.35 | .40 |
| Indianapolis Colts | | | |
| ☐ 275 Heath Shuler | 5.00 | 2.30 | .60 |
| Washington Redskins | | | |
| ☐ 276 Willie McGinest | .50 | .23 | .06 |
| New England Patriots | | | |
| ☐ 277 Trev Alberts | .50 | .23 | .06 |
| Indianapolis Colts | | | |
| ☐ 278 Trent Dilfer | 2.25 | 1.00 | .30 |
| Tampa Bay Buccaneers | | | |
| ☐ 279 Bryant Young | .25 | .11 | .03 |
| San Francisco 49ers | | | |
| ☐ 280 Sam Adams | .25 | .11 | .03 |
| Seattle Seahawks | | | |
| ☐ 281 Antonio Langham | .30 | .14 | .04 |
| Cleveland Browns | | | |
| ☐ 282 Jamir Miller | .30 | .14 | .04 |
| Arizona Cardinals | | | |
| ☐ 283 John Thierry | .30 | .14 | .04 |
| Chicago Bears | | | |
| ☐ 284 Aaron Glenn | .15 | .07 | .02 |
| New York Jets | | | |
| ☐ 285 Joe Johnson | .10 | .05 | .01 |
| New Orleans Saints | | | |
| ☐ 286 Bernard Williams | .10 | .05 | .01 |
| Philadelphia Eagles | | | |
| ☐ 287 Wayne Gandy | .10 | .05 | .01 |
| Los Angeles Rams | | | |
| ☐ 288 Aaron Taylor | .10 | .05 | .01 |
| Green Bay Packers | | | |
| ☐ 289 Charles Johnson | 1.00 | .45 | .13 |
| Pittsburgh Steelers | | | |
| ☐ 290 DeWayne Washington | .10 | .05 | .01 |
| Minnesota Vikings | | | |
| ☐ 291 Todd Steussie | .10 | .05 | .01 |
| Minnesota Vikings | | | |
| ☐ 292 Tim Bowens | .15 | .07 | .02 |
| Miami Dolphins | | | |
| ☐ 293 Johnnie Morton | .75 | .35 | .09 |
| Detroit Lions | | | |
| ☐ 294 Rob Frederickson | .10 | .05 | .01 |
| Los Angeles Raiders | | | |
| ☐ 295 Shante Carver | .20 | .09 | .03 |
| Dallas Cowboys | | | |
| ☐ 296 Thomas Lewis | .40 | .18 | .05 |
| New York Giants | | | |
| ☐ 297 Greg Hill | .75 | .35 | .09 |
| Kansas City Chiefs | | | |
| ☐ 298 Henry Ford | .10 | .05 | .01 |
| Houston Oilers | | | |
| ☐ 299 Jeff Burris | .15 | .07 | .02 |
| Buffalo Bills | | | |
| ☐ 300 William Floyd | .50 | .23 | .06 |
| San Francisco 49ers | | | |

| | | | |
|---|---|---|---|
| ☐ NNO Rookie Redemption | 24.00 | 11.00 | 3.00 |
| ☐ NNO Carolina Panthers HOLO | 40.00 | 18.00 | 5.00 |

## 1994 SkyBox Impact Instant Impact

These 12 standard-size (2 1/2" by 3 1/2") cards feature on their fronts borderless color player action shots. The featured players stand out against a faded background. The player's name appears within team color-coded boxes in an upper corner. The words "Instant Impact" appear in a gold-foil box in a lower corner. On a team-colored background, the horizontal backs carry color player action shots on one side, with player information next to the photo. The cards are numbered on the back with an "R" prefix.

| | MINT | EXC | G-VG |
|---|---|---|---|
| COMPLETE SET (12) | 40.00 | 18.00 | 5.00 |
| COMMON PLAYER (R1-R12) | 1.50 | .65 | .19 |
| ☐ R1 Rick Mirer | 12.00 | 5.50 | 1.50 |
| Seattle Seahawks | | | |
| ☐ R2 Jerome Bettis | 12.00 | 5.50 | 1.50 |
| Los Angeles Rams | | | |
| ☐ R3 Reggie Brooks | 6.00 | 2.70 | .75 |
| Washington Redskins | | | |
| ☐ R4 Terry Kirby | 4.00 | 1.80 | .50 |
| Miami Dolphins | | | |
| ☐ R5 Vincent Brisby | 1.50 | .65 | .19 |
| New England Patriots | | | |
| ☐ R6 James Jett | 2.00 | .90 | .25 |
| Los Angeles Raiders | | | |
| ☐ R7 Drew Bledsoe | 12.00 | 5.50 | 1.50 |
| New England Patriots | | | |
| ☐ R8 Dana Stubblefield | 1.50 | .65 | .19 |
| San Francisco 49ers | | | |
| ☐ R9 Natrone Means | 2.00 | .90 | .25 |
| San Diego Chargers | | | |
| ☐ R10 Curtis Conway | 1.50 | .65 | .19 |
| Chicago Bears | | | |
| ☐ R11 O.J. McDuffie | 2.00 | .90 | .25 |
| Miami Dolphins | | | |
| ☐ R12 Garrison Hearst | 2.00 | .90 | .25 |
| Arizona Cardinals | | | |

## 1994 SkyBox Impact Ultimate Impact

These 15 standard-size (2 1/2" by 3 1/2") cards feature borderless fronts with color action photos. The featured players stand out against a faded background. The player's name appears within team color-coded boxes in an upper corner. The words "Ultimate Impact" appear in a silver-foil box in a lower corner. On a team color-coded background, the horizontal backs carry color action shots on one side, with player information next to the photo. The cards are numbered on the back with a "U" prefix.

| | MINT | EXC | G-VG |
|---|---|---|---|
| COMPLETE SET (15)......................... | 50.00 | 23.00 | 6.25 |
| COMMON PLAYER (U1-U15)............. | 1.50 | .65 | .19 |
| ☐ U1 Troy Aikman ........................... Dallas Cowboys | 10.00 | 4.50 | 1.25 |
| ☐ U2 Emmitt Smith ......................... Dallas Cowboys | 12.00 | 5.50 | 1.50 |
| ☐ U3 Michael Irvin.......................... Dallas Cowboys | 3.50 | 1.55 | .45 |
| ☐ U4 Joe Montana.......................... Kansas City Chiefs | 10.00 | 4.50 | 1.25 |
| ☐ U5 Jerry Rice ............................. San Francisco 49ers | 4.00 | 1.80 | .50 |
| ☐ U6 Sterling Sharpe ...................... Green Bay Packers | 3.00 | 1.35 | .40 |
| ☐ U7 Steve Young .......................... San Francisco 49ers | 2.00 | .90 | .25 |
| ☐ U8 Ricky Watters ......................... San Francisco 49ers | 2.00 | .90 | .25 |
| ☐ U9 Barry Sanders ........................ Detroit Lions | 5.00 | 2.30 | .60 |
| ☐ U10 John Elway .......................... Denver Broncos | 3.00 | 1.35 | .40 |
| ☐ U11 Reggie White ........................ Green Bay Packers | 1.50 | .65 | .19 |
| ☐ U12 Jim Kelly ............................. Buffalo Bills | 2.00 | .90 | .25 |
| ☐ U13 Thurman Thomas ................... Buffalo Bills | 2.50 | 1.15 | .30 |
| ☐ U14 Dan Marino .......................... Miami Dolphins | 6.00 | 2.70 | .75 |
| ☐ U15 Brett Favre .......................... Green Bay Packers | 4.00 | 1.80 | .50 |

## 1992 Slam Thurman Thomas

This ten-card set showcases Thurman Thomas, the All-Pro Buffalo Bills' running back. The backs combine to present a biography of Thomas' life. The production run was reportedly 25,000 sets, and for every 25 sets ordered, the dealer received a limited edition (only 1,000 were reportedly produced) autograph card. Also a free promo card, numbered "Promo 1" in the upper right corner, was issued with every ten-card set. The fronts feature mostly color action or posed player photos inside a white frame. The card face shades from purple to white and back to purple. The player's name and the card subtitle are gold foil stamped in the bottom border. On a blue background inside a white frame, the backs carry career highlights, statistics, and a special "Slam-O-Meter" feature that summarizes his performance at that level. The cards are numbered on the back.

| | MINT | EXC | G-VG |
|---|---|---|---|
| COMPLETE SET (11)........................ | 12.00 | 5.00 | 1.20 |
| COMMON THOMAS (1-10) ............... | 1.50 | .60 | .15 |
| ☐ 1 Thurman Thomas...................... RB-Willowridge HS | 1.50 | .60 | .15 |
| ☐ 2 Thurman Thomas...................... HS-All American | 1.50 | .60 | .15 |
| ☐ 3 Thurman Thomas...................... Gator Bowl MVP | 1.50 | .60 | .15 |
| ☐ 4 Thurman Thomas...................... RB-Oklahoma State | 1.50 | .60 | .15 |
| ☐ 5 Thurman Thomas...................... All Big 8 | 1.50 | .60 | .15 |
| ☐ 6 Thurman Thomas...................... 1st Team All-American | 1.50 | .60 | .15 |
| ☐ 7 Thurman Thomas...................... | 1.50 | .60 | .15 |
| RB-Buffalo | | | |
| ☐ 8 Thurman Thomas...................... AFC All-Pro | 1.50 | .60 | .15 |
| ☐ 9 Thurman Thomas...................... AFC Rushing Champion | 1.50 | .60 | .15 |
| ☐ 10 Thurman Thomas...................... NFL Leader-Total Yards | 1.50 | .60 | .15 |
| ☐ AU Thurman Thomas AU ................ (Autographed) | 75.00 | 30.00 | 7.50 |
| ☐ P1 Thurman Thomas .................... (Promo 1) Buffalo Bills | 1.50 | .60 | .15 |

## 1993 Slam Jerome Bettis

This six-card set is comprised of five numbered cards and one unnumbered promo, and spotlights Jerome Bettis, the former Notre Dame star. One card in each set is hand autographed by Bettis, and a free promotional card is included with each set ordered. Each set also comes with a certificate of authenticity, which carries the production number out of 5,000 numbered sets produced. The cards measure 2 1/2" by 3 5/8" and feature on their fronts blue-bordered color action shots of Bettis in his Notre Dame uniform. His name and the card's title appear in gold foil within the bottom margin. The words "1st Round Pick" appear in gold foil within the top margin. The blue back is framed by a white line and carries a quote about Bettis from his coach at Notre Dame, Lou Holtz. Below this, each card carries stats and a graph representing Jerome's on-field yearly performance. Aside from the promo card, the cards are numbered on the back. The set is considered complete with one autographed card and the four others unsigned plus the promo card.

| | MINT | EXC | G-VG |
|---|---|---|---|
| COMPLETE SET (6)........................ | 20.00 | 8.00 | 2.00 |
| COMMON BETTIS (2-5) ................... | 2.00 | .80 | .20 |
| ☐ 1 Jerome Bettis AU...................... High School All-American | 2.00 | .80 | .20 |
| ☐ 1AU Jerome Bettis AU.................. High School All-American | 15.00 | 6.00 | 1.50 |
| ☐ 2 Jerome Bettis........................... Freshman Notre Dame | 2.00 | .80 | .20 |
| ☐ 2AU Jerome Bettis AU.................. Freshman Notre Dame | 15.00 | 6.00 | 1.50 |
| ☐ 3 Jerome Bettis........................... 1991 Notre Dame Co-MVP | 2.00 | .80 | .20 |
| ☐ 3AU Jerome Bettis AU.................. 1991 Notre Dame Co-MVP | 15.00 | 6.00 | 1.50 |
| ☐ 4 Jerome Bettis........................... All-American | 2.00 | .80 | .20 |
| ☐ 4AU Jerome Bettis AU.................. All-American | 15.00 | 6.00 | 1.50 |
| ☐ 5 Jerome Bettis........................... 10th Pick Overall | 2.00 | .80 | .20 |
| ☐ 5AU Jerome Bettis AU.................. 10th Pick Overall | 15.00 | 6.00 | 1.50 |
| ☐ P1 Jerome Bettis......................... (Promo 1) FB Notre Dame | 2.00 | .80 | .20 |

## 1978 Slim Jim

The 1978 Slim Jim football discs were obtained from the back of Slim Jim packages, each package back containing two discs. The complete set consists of 35 connected pairs or 70 individual discs. The individual discs measure approximately 2 3/8" in diameter whereas the complete panel is 3" by 5 3/4". The discs themselves are either yellow, red or brown with black lettering. The same two players are always

paired on a particular package. Cards are numbered for convenience in alphabetical order by the top player of the pair on the box; the top player is referenced first. The prices below are for each pair of discs. Prices for complete boxes would be one and a half times the values listed below.

| | NRMT | VG-E | GOOD |
|---|---|---|---|
| COMPLETE SET (35) | 300.00 | 120.00 | 30.00 |
| COMMON PAIR (1-35) | 7.50 | 3.00 | .75 |
| | | | |
| ☐ 1 Lyle Alzado | 15.00 | 6.00 | 1.50 |
| Archie Manning | | | |
| ☐ 2 Bill Bergey | 15.00 | 6.00 | 1.50 |
| John Riggins | | | |
| ☐ 3 Fred Biletnikoff | 15.00 | 6.00 | 1.50 |
| Dan Dierdorf | | | |
| ☐ 4 John Cappelletti | 7.50 | 3.00 | .75 |
| Bob Chandler | | | |
| ☐ 5 Tommy Casanova | 7.50 | 3.00 | .75 |
| Darryl Stingley | | | |
| ☐ 6 Billy Joe DuPree | 7.50 | 3.00 | .75 |
| Nat Moore | | | |
| ☐ 7 John Dutton | 7.50 | 3.00 | .75 |
| Paul Krause | | | |
| ☐ 8 Leon Gray | 7.50 | 3.00 | .75 |
| Richard Caster | | | |
| ☐ 9 Mel Gray | 7.50 | 3.00 | .75 |
| Claude Humphrey | | | |
| ☐ 10 Joe Greene | 12.00 | 5.00 | 1.20 |
| Dexter Bussey | | | |
| ☐ 11 Jack Gregory | 7.50 | 3.00 | .75 |
| Billy Johnson | | | |
| ☐ 12 Steve Grogan | 7.50 | 3.00 | .75 |
| Jerome Barkum | | | |
| ☐ 13 John Hannah | 10.00 | 4.00 | 1.00 |
| Isaac Curtis | | | |
| ☐ 14 Jim Hart | 7.50 | 3.00 | .75 |
| Otis Sistrunk | | | |
| ☐ 15 Tommy Hart | 7.50 | 3.00 | .75 |
| Ron Howard | | | |
| ☐ 16 Wilbur Jackson | 7.50 | 3.00 | .75 |
| Riley Odoms | | | |
| ☐ 17 Ron Jaworski | 10.00 | 4.00 | 1.00 |
| Mike Thomas | | | |
| ☐ 18 Larry Little | 10.00 | 4.00 | 1.00 |
| Isiah Robertson | | | |
| ☐ 19 Ron McDole | 7.50 | 3.00 | .75 |
| Willie Buchanon | | | |
| ☐ 20 Lydell Mitchell | 7.50 | 3.00 | .75 |
| Glen Edwards | | | |
| ☐ 21 Robert Newhouse | 7.50 | 3.00 | .75 |
| Glenn Doughty | | | |
| ☐ 22 Alan Page | 10.00 | 4.00 | 1.00 |
| Fred Carr | | | |
| ☐ 23 Walter Payton | 45.00 | 18.00 | 4.50 |
| Larry Csonka | | | |
| ☐ 24 Greg Pruitt | 7.50 | 3.00 | .75 |
| Doug Buffone | | | |

| | | | |
|---|---|---|---|
| ☐ 25 Ahmad Rashad | 12.00 | 5.00 | 1.20 |
| Jeff Van Note | | | |
| ☐ 26 Golden Richards | 10.00 | 4.00 | 1.00 |
| Rocky Bleier | | | |
| ☐ 27 Clarence Scott | 7.50 | 3.00 | .75 |
| Joe DeLamielleure | | | |
| ☐ 28 Lee Roy Selmon | 10.00 | 4.00 | 1.00 |
| Charlie Sanders | | | |
| ☐ 29 Bruce Taylor | 7.50 | 3.00 | .75 |
| Otis Armstrong | | | |
| ☐ 30 Emmitt Thomas | 7.50 | 3.00 | .75 |
| Elvin Bethea | | | |
| ☐ 31 Brad Van Pelt | 7.50 | 3.00 | .75 |
| Ted Washington | | | |
| ☐ 32 Gene Washington | 12.00 | 5.00 | 1.20 |
| Charlie Joiner | | | |
| ☐ 33 Clarence Williams | 7.50 | 3.00 | .75 |
| Lemar Parrish | | | |
| ☐ 34 Roger Wehrli | 10.00 | 4.00 | 1.00 |
| Gene Upshaw | | | |
| ☐ 35 Don Woods | 7.50 | 3.00 | .75 |
| Ron Jessie | | | |

# 1984 Smokey Invaders

This five-card set features the Oakland Invaders of the USFL. The theme of the set is Forestry, i.e., Smokey the Bear is pictured on each card. The set commemorates the 40th birthday of Smokey Bear and is sponsored by the California Forestry Department in conjunction with the U.S. Forest Service. The cards measure approximately 5" by 7". The front features a color posed photo of the football player with Smokey Bear. The player's signature, jersey number, and a public service announcement concerning wildfire prevention occur below the picture. Biographical information is provided on the back.

| | MINT | EXC | G-VG |
|---|---|---|---|
| COMPLETE SET (5) | 50.00 | 20.00 | 5.00 |
| COMMON CARD (1-5) | 10.00 | 4.00 | 1.00 |
| | | | |
| ☐ 1 Dupre Marshall | 10.00 | 4.00 | 1.00 |
| ☐ 2 Gary Plummer | 15.00 | 6.00 | 1.50 |
| ☐ 3 David Shaw | 10.00 | 4.00 | 1.00 |
| ☐ 4 Kevin Shea | 10.00 | 4.00 | 1.00 |
| ☐ 5 Smokey Bear | 10.00 | 4.00 | 1.00 |
| (With players above) | | | |

# 1985 Smokey 49ers

This set of seven large (approximately 2 15/16" by 4 3/8") cards was issued in the Summer of 1985 and features the San Francisco 49ers and Smokey Bear. The card backs are printed in black on a thin white card stock. Card backs have a cartoon fire safety message and a facsimile autograph of the player. Smokey Bear is pictured on each card along with the player (or players).

|  | MINT | EXC | G-VG |
|---|---|---|---|
| COMPLETE SET (7) | 20.00 | 8.00 | 2.00 |
| COMMON CARD (1-7) | 1.00 | .40 | .10 |
| ☐ 1 Group Picture with Smokey (Player list on back of card) | 4.00 | 1.60 | .40 |
| ☐ 2 Joe Montana | 12.50 | 5.00 | 1.25 |
| ☐ 3 Jack Reynolds | 1.50 | .60 | .15 |
| ☐ 4 Eric Wright | 1.00 | .40 | .10 |
| ☐ 5 Dwight Hicks | 1.00 | .40 | .10 |
| ☐ 6 Dwight Clark | 3.00 | 1.20 | .30 |
| ☐ 7 Keena Turner | 1.00 | .40 | .10 |

## 1985 Smokey Raiders

This four-card set of Los Angeles Raiders was also sponsored by Kodak. The cards measure approximately 2 5/8" by 4 1/8". It is technically a "fire safety" set as Smokey is not mentioned anywhere on the cards. The cards are numbered (and dated) on the back. The fire safety tip on the back is in the form of a cartoon. There are also two or three paragraphs of biographical information about the player on the card backs. The card fronts show a full-color photo inside a white border. The player's name, team, position, height, and weight are given at the bottom of the card front.

|  | MINT | EXC | G-VG |
|---|---|---|---|
| COMPLETE SET (4) | 2.50 | 1.00 | .25 |
| COMMON CARD (1-4) | .35 | .14 | .03 |
| ☐ 1 Marcus Allen | 1.25 | .50 | .12 |
| ☐ 2 Tom Flores CO | .50 | .20 | .05 |
| ☐ 3 Howie Long | .75 | .30 | .07 |
| ☐ 4 Rod Martin | .35 | .14 | .03 |

## 1985 Smokey Rams

This set of 24 cards was issued in the Summer of 1985 and features players of the Los Angeles Rams. The cards measure approximately 4" by 6". Each card photo also features Smokey Bear. The cards are numbered on the back essentially in alphabetical order; there are a few exceptions and two Smokey cards are unnumbered (listed at the end of the checklist below). Supposedly, LeRoy Irvin is more difficult to find than the other cards in the set.

|  | MINT | EXC | G-VG |
|---|---|---|---|
| COMPLETE SET (24) | 15.00 | 6.00 | 1.50 |
| COMMON CARD (1-24) | .50 | .20 | .05 |
| ☐ 1 George Andrews | .50 | .20 | .05 |
| ☐ 2 Bill Bain | .50 | .20 | .05 |
| ☐ 3 Russ Bolinger | .50 | .20 | .05 |
| ☐ 4 Jim Collins | .50 | .20 | .05 |
| ☐ 5 Nolan Cromwell | 1.00 | .40 | .10 |
| ☐ 6 Reggie Doss | .50 | .20 | .05 |
| ☐ 7 Carl Ekern | .50 | .20 | .05 |
| ☐ 8 Vince Ferragamo | 1.00 | .40 | .10 |
| ☐ 9 Gary Green | .60 | .24 | .06 |
| ☐ 10 Mike Guman | .50 | .20 | .05 |
| ☐ 11 David Hill | .50 | .20 | .05 |
| ☐ 12 LeRoy Irvin SP | 4.00 | 1.60 | .40 |
| ☐ 13 Mark Jerue | .50 | .20 | .05 |
| ☐ 14 Johnnie Johnson | .60 | .24 | .06 |
| ☐ 15 Jeff Kemp | 1.00 | .40 | .10 |
| ☐ 16 Mel Owens | .60 | .24 | .06 |
| ☐ 17 Irv Pankey | .50 | .20 | .05 |
| ☐ 18 Doug Smith | .60 | .24 | .06 |
| ☐ 19 Ivory Sully | .50 | .20 | .05 |
| ☐ 20 Jack Youngblood | 1.50 | .60 | .15 |
| ☐ 21 Mike McDonald | .50 | .20 | .05 |
| ☐ 22 Norwood Vann | .50 | .20 | .05 |
| ☐ 23 Smokey Bear (Unnumbered) | .50 | .20 | .05 |
| ☐ 24 Smokey Bear with Reggie Doss, Gary Green, Johnnie Johnson, and Carl Ekern (Unnumbered) | .75 | .30 | .07 |

## 1987 Smokey Chargers

This 48-card set features players of the San Diego Chargers in a set sponsored by the California Forestry Department. The cards measure approximately 5 1/2" by 8 1/2"; card fronts show a full-color action photo of the player. Card backs have a forestry safety tip cartoon with Smokey the Bear. Cards are unnumbered but are ordered below in alphabetical order according to the subject's last name. Cards of Donald Brown, Mike Douglass, and Fred Robinson were withdrawn after they were cut from the team and the card of Don Coryell was withdrawn after he was replaced as head coach.

|  | MINT | EXC | G-VG |
|---|---|---|---|
| COMPLETE SET (48) | 100.00 | 40.00 | 10.00 |
| COMMON PLAYER (1-48) | 1.50 | .60 | .15 |
| COMMON SP | 7.50 | 3.00 | .75 |
| ☐ 1 Curtis Adams | 1.50 | .60 | .15 |
| ☐ 2 Ty Allert | 1.50 | .60 | .15 |
| ☐ 3 Gary Anderson | 4.00 | 1.60 | .40 |
| ☐ 4 Rolf Benirschke | 2.50 | 1.00 | .25 |
| ☐ 5 Thomas Benson | 2.00 | .80 | .20 |
| ☐ 6 Donald Brown SP | 7.50 | 3.00 | .75 |
| ☐ 7 Gill Byrd | 3.00 | 1.20 | .30 |
| ☐ 8 Wes Chandler | 3.50 | 1.40 | .35 |
| ☐ 9 Sam Claphan | 1.50 | .60 | .15 |
| ☐ 10 Don Coryell CO SP | 7.50 | 3.00 | .75 |
| ☐ 11 Jeffery Dale | 1.50 | .60 | .15 |
| ☐ 12 Wayne Davis | 1.50 | .60 | .15 |
| ☐ 13 Mike Douglass SP | 7.50 | 3.00 | .75 |
| ☐ 14 Chuck Ehin | 1.50 | .60 | .15 |

| | | | |
|---|---|---|---|
| ☐ 15 James Fitzpatrick | 2.00 | .80 | .20 |
| ☐ 16 Tom Flick | 1.50 | .60 | .15 |
| ☐ 17 Dan Fouts | 9.00 | 3.75 | .90 |
| ☐ 18 Dee Hardison | 1.50 | .60 | .15 |
| ☐ 19 Andy Hawkins | 1.50 | .60 | .15 |
| ☐ 20 John Hendy | 1.50 | .60 | .15 |
| ☐ 21 Mark Herrmann | 2.00 | .80 | .20 |
| ☐ 22 Pete Holohan | 2.00 | .80 | .20 |
| ☐ 23 Lionel James | 2.00 | .80 | .20 |
| ☐ 24 Trumaine Johnson | 2.00 | .80 | .20 |
| ☐ 25 Charlie Joiner | 6.00 | 2.40 | .60 |
| ☐ 26 Gary Kowalski | 1.50 | .60 | .15 |
| ☐ 27 Jim Lachey | 2.50 | 1.00 | .25 |
| ☐ 28 Jim Leonard | 1.50 | .60 | .15 |
| ☐ 29 Woodrow Lowe | 2.00 | .80 | .20 |
| ☐ 30 Don Macek | 1.50 | .60 | .15 |
| ☐ 31 Buford McGee | 1.50 | .60 | .15 |
| ☐ 32 Dennis McKnight | 1.50 | .60 | .15 |
| ☐ 33 Ralf Mojsiejenko | 2.00 | .80 | .20 |
| ☐ 34 Derrie Nelson | 1.50 | .60 | .15 |
| ☐ 35 Leslie O'Neal | 3.50 | 1.40 | .35 |
| ☐ 36 Gary Plummer | 2.00 | .80 | .20 |
| ☐ 37 Fred Robinson SP | 7.50 | 3.00 | .75 |
| ☐ 38 Eric Sievers | 2.00 | .80 | .20 |
| ☐ 39 Billy Ray Smith | 2.50 | 1.00 | .25 |
| ☐ 40 Tim Spencer | 2.00 | .80 | .20 |
| ☐ 41 Kenny Taylor | 1.50 | .60 | .15 |
| ☐ 42 Terry Unrein | 1.50 | .60 | .15 |
| ☐ 43 Jeff Walker | 1.50 | .60 | .15 |
| ☐ 44 Danny Walters | 1.50 | .60 | .15 |
| ☐ 45 Lee Williams | 3.50 | 1.40 | .35 |
| ☐ 46 Earl Wilson | 1.50 | .60 | .15 |
| ☐ 47 Kellen Winslow | 6.00 | 2.40 | .60 |
| ☐ 48 Kevin Wyatt | 1.50 | .60 | .15 |

# 1987 Smokey Raiders Color-Grams

This set is actually a 14-page booklet featuring 13 player caricatures (all from the Los Angeles Raiders) and one of Smokey and Huddles. Each page includes a 5 5/8" by 3 11/16" postcard perforated with a card measuring 2 1/2" by 3 11/16". The booklet itself is approximately 8 1/8" by 3 11/16". The set is headlined as "Arsonbusters" in white over a black frame. The backs offer a fire prevention tip from Smokey. The cards are unnumbered, but are listed below according to booklet page number.

| | MINT | EXC | G-VG |
|---|---|---|---|
| COMPLETE SET (14) | 20.00 | 8.00 | 2.00 |
| COMMON PLAYER (1-14) | 1.00 | .40 | .10 |
| ☐ 1 Smokey and Huddles | 1.25 | .50 | .12 |
| ☐ 2 Matt Millen | 1.25 | .50 | .12 |
| ☐ 3 Rod Martin | 1.25 | .50 | .12 |
| ☐ 4 Sean Jones | 2.00 | .80 | .20 |
| ☐ 5 Dokie Williams | 1.25 | .50 | .12 |
| ☐ 6 Don Mosebar | 1.25 | .50 | .12 |
| ☐ 7 Todd Christensen | 2.00 | .80 | .20 |
| ☐ 8 Bill Pickel | 1.00 | .40 | .10 |
| ☐ 9 Marcus Allen | 6.00 | 2.40 | .60 |
| ☐ 10 Charley Hannah | 1.00 | .40 | .10 |
| ☐ 11 Howie Long | 2.00 | .80 | .20 |
| ☐ 12 Vann McElroy | 1.25 | .50 | .12 |

| | | | |
|---|---|---|---|
| ☐ 13 Reggie McKenzie | 1.00 | .40 | .10 |
| ☐ 14 Mike Haynes | 2.00 | .80 | .20 |

# 1988 Smokey Chargers

This 52-card set features players of the San Diego Chargers in a set sponsored by the California Forestry Department. The cards measure approximately 5" by 8"; card fronts show a full-color action photo of the player. Card backs have a forestry safety tip cartoon with Smokey Bear. Cards are unnumbered but are ordered below in numerical order according to the subject's uniform number as listed on the card's front and back. There is a variation on the Spanos card, which was originally issued indicating he bought the Chargers in 1987 and was quickly corrected to 1984. There are 35 cards which are easier to obtain as they were available all year and 18 cards (marked below as SP) who are more difficult to find as their cards were withdrawn after they were cut from the team, retired, traded, or put on injured reserve. The set is considered complete with only one Spanos card.

| | MINT | EXC | G-VG |
|---|---|---|---|
| COMPLETE SET (52) | 60.00 | 24.00 | 6.00 |
| COMMON PLAYER | .60 | .24 | .06 |
| ☐ 2 Ralf Mojsiejenko | .75 | .30 | .07 |
| ☐ 9 Mark Herrmann SP | 3.00 | 1.20 | .30 |
| ☐ 10 Vince Abbott | .75 | .30 | .07 |
| ☐ 13 Mark Vlasic | 1.25 | .50 | .12 |
| ☐ 14 Dan Fouts | 3.50 | 1.40 | .35 |
| ☐ 20 Barry Redden | .75 | .30 | .07 |
| ☐ 22 Gill Byrd | 1.00 | .40 | .10 |
| ☐ 23 Danny Walters SP | 2.50 | 1.00 | .25 |
| ☐ 25 Vencie Glenn | .75 | .30 | .07 |
| ☐ 26 Lionel James | 1.00 | .40 | .10 |
| ☐ 27 Daniel Hunter SP | 2.50 | 1.00 | .25 |
| ☐ 34 Elvis Patterson | .75 | .30 | .07 |
| ☐ 36 Mike Davis SP | 2.50 | 1.00 | .25 |
| ☐ 40 Gary Anderson | 1.50 | .60 | .15 |
| ☐ 42 Curtis Adams | .60 | .24 | .06 |
| ☐ 43 Tim Spencer | .75 | .30 | .07 |
| ☐ 44 Martin Bayless | .60 | .24 | .06 |
| ☐ 50 Gary Plummer | .75 | .30 | .07 |
| ☐ 52 Jeffrey Jackson | .60 | .24 | .06 |
| ☐ 54 Billy Ray Smith | 1.00 | .40 | .10 |
| ☐ 55 Steve Busick SP | 2.50 | 1.00 | .25 |
| ☐ 56 Chip Banks SP | 3.00 | 1.20 | .30 |
| ☐ 57 Thomas Benson SP | 2.50 | 1.00 | .25 |
| ☐ 58 David Brandon | .75 | .30 | .07 |
| ☐ 60 Dennis McKnight | .60 | .24 | .06 |
| ☐ 61 Ken Dallafior | .60 | .24 | .06 |
| ☐ 62 Don Macek | .60 | .24 | .06 |
| ☐ 68 Gary Kowalski | .60 | .24 | .06 |
| ☐ 69 Les Miller | .60 | .24 | .06 |
| ☐ 70 James Fitzpatrick | .60 | .24 | .06 |
| ☐ 71 Mike Charles | .60 | .24 | .06 |
| ☐ 72 Karl Wilson | .60 | .24 | .06 |
| ☐ 74 Jim Lachey SP | 3.00 | 1.20 | .30 |
| ☐ 75 Joe Phillips | .75 | .30 | .07 |
| ☐ 76 Broderick Thompson | .60 | .24 | .06 |
| ☐ 77 Sam Claphan SP | 2.50 | 1.00 | .25 |
| ☐ 78 Chuck Ehin SP | 2.50 | 1.00 | .25 |
| ☐ 79 Curtis Rouse SP | 2.50 | 1.00 | .25 |
| ☐ 80 Kellen Winslow | 2.00 | .80 | .20 |
| ☐ 81 Timmie Ware SP | 2.50 | 1.00 | .25 |
| ☐ 82 Rod Bernstine | 2.00 | .80 | .20 |
| ☐ 85 Eric Sievers | 1.00 | .40 | .10 |
| ☐ 86 Jamie Holland | .60 | .24 | .06 |
| ☐ 88 Pete Holohan SP | 2.50 | 1.00 | .25 |
| ☐ 89 Wes Chandler SP | 4.00 | 1.60 | .40 |
| ☐ 92 Dee Hardison SP | 2.50 | 1.00 | .25 |
| ☐ 94 Randy Kirk | .60 | .24 | .06 |

| | | | |
|---|---|---|---|
| ☐ 96 Keith Baldwin SP | 2.50 | 1.00 | .25 |
| ☐ 98 Terry Unrein SP | 2.50 | 1.00 | .25 |
| ☐ 99 Lee Williams | 1.25 | .50 | .12 |
| ☐ xx Al Saunders CO | .75 | .30 | .07 |
| ☐ xx Alex G. Spanos ERR SP | 6.00 | 2.40 | .60 |
| Chairman of the Board | | | |
| (purchased team 1987) | | | |
| ☐ xx Alex G. Spanos COR | 1.00 | .40 | .10 |
| Chairman of the Board | | | |
| (purchased team 1984) | | | |

## 1988 Smokey 49ers

This 35-card set features members of the San Francisco 49ers. The cards measure approximately 5" by 8". The printing on the card back is in black ink on white card stock. The cards are unnumbered except for uniform number; they are ordered below alphabetically for convenience. Each card back contains a fire safety cartoon (usually) featuring Smokey. Reportedly the Dwaine Board card is more difficult to find than the other cards in the set.

| | MINT | EXC | G-VG |
|---|---|---|---|
| COMPLETE SET (35) | 75.00 | 30.00 | 7.50 |
| COMMON PLAYER (1-35) | 1.00 | .40 | .10 |
| | | | |
| ☐ 1 Harris Barton | 1.00 | .40 | .10 |
| ☐ 2 Dwaine Board SP | 10.00 | 4.00 | 1.00 |
| ☐ 3 Michael Carter | 2.00 | .80 | .20 |
| ☐ 4 Bruce Collie | 1.00 | .40 | .10 |
| ☐ 5 Roger Craig | 3.00 | 1.20 | .30 |
| ☐ 6 Randy Cross | 2.00 | .80 | .20 |
| ☐ 7 Eddie DeBartolo Jr. | 2.00 | .80 | .20 |
| (Owner/President) | | | |
| ☐ 8 Riki Ellison | 1.00 | .40 | .10 |
| ☐ 9 Kevin Fagan | 1.00 | .40 | .10 |
| ☐ 10 Jim Fahnhorst | 1.00 | .40 | .10 |
| ☐ 11 John Frank | 1.50 | .60 | .15 |
| ☐ 12 Jeff Fuller | 1.00 | .40 | .10 |
| ☐ 13 Don Griffin | 1.25 | .50 | .12 |
| ☐ 14 Charles Haley | 2.50 | 1.00 | .25 |
| ☐ 15 Ron Heller | 1.25 | .50 | .12 |
| ☐ 16 Tom Holmoe | 1.00 | .40 | .10 |
| ☐ 17 Pete Kugler | 1.25 | .50 | .12 |
| ☐ 18 Ronnie Lott | 4.00 | 1.60 | .40 |
| ☐ 19 Tim McKyer | 1.50 | .60 | .15 |
| ☐ 20 Joe Montana | 20.00 | 8.00 | 2.00 |
| ☐ 21 Tory Nixon | 1.00 | .40 | .10 |
| ☐ 22 Bubba Paris | 1.00 | .40 | .10 |
| ☐ 23 John Paye | 1.50 | .60 | .15 |
| ☐ 24 Tom Rathman | 3.00 | 1.20 | .30 |
| ☐ 25 Jerry Rice | 12.00 | 5.00 | 1.20 |
| ☐ 26 Jeff Stover | 1.00 | .40 | .10 |
| ☐ 27 Harry Sydney | 1.00 | .40 | .10 |
| ☐ 28 John Taylor | 3.00 | 1.20 | .30 |
| ☐ 29 Keena Turner | 1.50 | .60 | .15 |
| ☐ 30 Steve Wallace | 1.25 | .50 | .12 |
| ☐ 31 Bill Walsh CO | 3.00 | 1.20 | .30 |
| ☐ 32 Michael Walter | 1.00 | .40 | .10 |
| ☐ 33 Mike Wilson | 1.25 | .50 | .12 |
| ☐ 34 Eric Wright | 1.00 | .40 | .10 |
| ☐ 35 Steve Young | 10.00 | 4.00 | 1.00 |

## 1988 Smokey Raiders

This 14-card set is distinguished by its thick black border on the front of every card as well as the presence of "Arsonbusters" in orange as a subtitle. The cards measure approximately 3" by 5". The set is not numbered although the players' uniform numbers are in small print on

the back; the list below has been ordered alphabetically. Each card back features a different fire safety cartoon starring Smokey.

| | MINT | EXC | G-VG |
|---|---|---|---|
| COMPLETE SET (14) | 15.00 | 6.00 | 1.50 |
| COMMON PLAYER (1-14) | .75 | .30 | .07 |
| | | | |
| ☐ 1 Marcus Allen | 3.00 | 1.20 | .30 |
| ☐ 2 Todd Christensen | 1.25 | .50 | .12 |
| ☐ 3 Bo Jackson | 5.00 | 2.00 | .50 |
| ☐ 4 James Lofton | 2.00 | .80 | .20 |
| ☐ 5 Howie Long | 1.25 | .50 | .12 |
| ☐ 6 Rod Martin | .75 | .30 | .07 |
| ☐ 7 Vann McElroy | .75 | .30 | .07 |
| ☐ 8 Don Mosebar | .75 | .30 | .07 |
| ☐ 9 Bill Pickel | .75 | .30 | .07 |
| ☐ 10 Jerry Robinson | .75 | .30 | .07 |
| ☐ 11 Mike Shanahan CO | .75 | .30 | .07 |
| ☐ 12 Smokey Bear | .75 | .30 | .07 |
| ☐ 13 Stacey Toran | .75 | .30 | .07 |
| ☐ 14 Greg Townsend | 1.00 | .40 | .10 |

## 1989 Smokey Chargers

This 48-card set is very similar in style to the Smokey Chargers set of the previous year. This set gives the 1989 date on the bottom of every reverse. Cards are unnumbered except for uniform number which appears on the card front and back. The cards are ordered below by uniform number. The cards measure approximately 5" by 8". Each card back shows a different fire safety cartoon.

| | MINT | EXC | G-VG |
|---|---|---|---|
| COMPLETE SET (48) | 40.00 | 16.00 | 4.00 |
| COMMON PLAYER | .75 | .30 | .07 |
| | | | |
| ☐ 2 Ralf Mojsiejenko | 1.00 | .40 | .10 |
| ☐ 6 Steve DeLine | .75 | .30 | .07 |
| ☐ 10 Vince Abbott | .75 | .30 | .07 |
| ☐ 13 Mark Vlasic | 1.25 | .50 | .12 |
| ☐ 16 Mark Malone | 1.25 | .50 | .12 |
| ☐ 20 Barry Redden | 1.25 | .50 | .12 |
| ☐ 22 Gill Byrd | 1.25 | .50 | .12 |
| ☐ 23 Roy Bennett | .75 | .30 | .07 |
| ☐ 25 Vencie Glenn | .75 | .30 | .07 |
| ☐ 26 Lionel James | 1.00 | .40 | .10 |
| ☐ 30 Sam Seale | 1.00 | .40 | .10 |
| ☐ 31 Leonard Coleman | .75 | .30 | .07 |

| | | | |
|---|---|---|---|
| ☐ 34 Elvis Patterson | 1.00 | .40 | .10 |
| ☐ 40 Gary Anderson | 2.00 | .80 | .20 |
| ☐ 42 Curtis Adams | .75 | .30 | .07 |
| ☐ 43 Tim Spencer | 1.00 | .40 | .10 |
| ☐ 44 Martin Bayless | 1.00 | .40 | .10 |
| ☐ 48 Pat Miller | .75 | .30 | .07 |
| ☐ 50 Gary Plummer | 1.00 | .40 | .10 |
| ☐ 51 Cedric Figaro | .75 | .30 | .07 |
| ☐ 52 Jeff Jackson | .75 | .30 | .07 |
| ☐ 53 Chuck Faucette | .75 | .30 | .07 |
| ☐ 54 Billy Ray Smith | 1.25 | .50 | .12 |
| ☐ 57 Keith Browner | .75 | .30 | .07 |
| ☐ 58 David Brandon | 1.00 | .40 | .10 |
| ☐ 59 Ken Woodard | .75 | .30 | .07 |
| ☐ 60 Dennis McKnight | .75 | .30 | .07 |
| ☐ 61 Ken Dallafior | .75 | .30 | .07 |
| ☐ 65 David Richards | 1.00 | .40 | .10 |
| ☐ 66 Dan Rosado | .75 | .30 | .07 |
| ☐ 69 Les Miller | .75 | .30 | .07 |
| ☐ 70 James Fitzpatrick | .75 | .30 | .07 |
| ☐ 71 Mike Charles | .75 | .30 | .07 |
| ☐ 72 Karl Wilson | .75 | .30 | .07 |
| ☐ 73 Darrick Brilz | 1.00 | .40 | .10 |
| ☐ 75 Joe Phillips | 1.00 | .40 | .10 |
| ☐ 76 Broderick Thompson | .75 | .30 | .07 |
| ☐ 82 Rod Bernstne | 2.00 | .80 | .20 |
| ☐ 83 Anthony Miller | 4.00 | 1.60 | .40 |
| ☐ 86 Jamie Holland | .75 | .30 | .07 |
| ☐ 87 Quinn Early | 1.25 | .50 | .12 |
| ☐ 88 Arthur Cox | 1.00 | .40 | .10 |
| ☐ 89 Darren Flutie | 1.00 | .40 | .10 |
| ☐ 91 Leslie O'Neal | 1.50 | .60 | .15 |
| ☐ 93 Tyrone Keys | .75 | .30 | .07 |
| ☐ 95 Joe Campbell | .75 | .30 | .07 |
| ☐ 97 George Hinkle | .75 | .30 | .07 |
| ☐ 99 Lee Williams | 1.50 | .60 | .15 |

| | | | |
|---|---|---|---|
| ☐ 41 Keith Byars | 3.00 | 1.20 | .30 |
| ☐ 42 Eric Everett | 1.50 | .60 | .15 |
| ☐ 43 Roynell Young | 2.00 | .80 | .20 |
| ☐ 46 Izel Jenkins | 1.50 | .60 | .15 |
| ☐ 48 Wes Hopkins | 2.00 | .80 | .20 |
| ☐ 50 Dave Rimington | 2.00 | .80 | .20 |
| ☐ 52 Todd Bell | 2.00 | .80 | .20 |
| ☐ 53 Dwayne Jiles | 1.50 | .60 | .15 |
| ☐ 55 Mike Reichenbach | 1.50 | .60 | .15 |
| ☐ 56 Byron Evans | 2.00 | .80 | .20 |
| ☐ 58 Ty Allert | 1.50 | .60 | .15 |
| ☐ 59 Seth Joyner | 4.00 | 1.60 | .40 |
| ☐ 61 Ben Tamburello | 1.50 | .60 | .15 |
| ☐ 63 Ron Baker | 1.50 | .60 | .15 |
| ☐ 66 Ken Reeves | 1.50 | .60 | .15 |
| ☐ 68 Reggie Singletary | 1.50 | .60 | .15 |
| ☐ 72 David Alexander | 1.50 | .60 | .15 |
| ☐ 73 Ron Heller | 1.50 | .60 | .15 |
| ☐ 74 Mike Pitts | 1.50 | .60 | .15 |
| ☐ 78 Matt Darwin | 1.50 | .60 | .15 |
| ☐ 80 Cris Carter | 4.00 | 1.60 | .40 |
| ☐ 81 Kenny Jackson | 3.00 | 1.20 | .30 |
| ☐ 82A Mike Quick | 3.50 | 1.40 | .35 |
|   (White jersey) | | | |
| ☐ 82B Mike Quick | 3.50 | 1.40 | .35 |
|   (Green jersey) | | | |
| ☐ 83 Jimmie Giles | 2.00 | .80 | .20 |
| ☐ 85 Ron Johnson | 2.00 | .80 | .20 |
| ☐ 86 Gregg Garrity | 1.50 | .60 | .15 |
| ☐ 88 Keith Jackson | 7.50 | 3.00 | .75 |
| ☐ 89 David Little | 2.00 | .80 | .20 |
| ☐ 90 Mike Golic | 2.00 | .80 | .20 |
| ☐ 91 Scott Curtis | 2.00 | .80 | .20 |
| ☐ 92 Reggie White | 10.00 | 4.00 | 1.00 |
| ☐ 96 Clyde Simmons | 4.00 | 1.60 | .40 |
| ☐ 97 John Klingel | 1.50 | .60 | .15 |
| ☐ 99 Jerome Brown | 4.00 | 1.60 | .40 |
| ☐ NNO Buddy Ryan CO | 7.50 | 3.00 | .75 |
|   (Wearing white cap) | | | |
| ☐ NNO Buddy Ryan CO | 7.50 | 3.00 | .75 |
|   (Wearing green cap) | | | |

## 1989 Smokey Eagles

This 49-card set features members of the Philadelphia Eagles. The cards measure approximately 3" by 5". The full-color photo on the front covers the complete card, although the player's name, number, and position are overprinted in the lower right corner. Each card back shows a different fire safety cartoon. Backs are printed in green ink in deference to the Eagles colors. Cards are unnumbered, except for uniform number which appears on the card front and back; cards are ordered below by uniform number. In a few cases, there were two cards produced of the same player; typically the two can be distinguished by home and away colors. The complete set price below includes all the variations listed.

| | MINT | EXC | G-VG |
|---|---|---|---|
| COMPLETE SET (49) | 125.00 | 50.00 | 12.50 |
| COMMON PLAYER | 1.50 | .60 | .15 |
| | | | |
| ☐ 6 Matt Cavanaugh | 2.50 | 1.00 | .25 |
| ☐ 8 Luis Zendejas | 2.00 | .80 | .20 |
| ☐ 9 Don McPherson | 2.50 | 1.00 | .25 |
| ☐ 10 John Teltschik | 1.50 | .60 | .15 |
| ☐ 12A Randall Cunningham | 12.00 | 5.00 | 1.20 |
|   (White jersey) | | | |
| ☐ 12B Randall Cunningham | 12.00 | 5.00 | 1.20 |
|   (Green jersey) | | | |
| ☐ 20 Andre Waters | 2.50 | 1.00 | .25 |
| ☐ 21 Eric Allen | 2.00 | .80 | .20 |
| ☐ 25 Anthony Toney | 2.00 | .80 | .20 |
| ☐ 33 William Frizzell | 1.50 | .60 | .15 |
| ☐ 34 Terry Hoage | 2.00 | .80 | .20 |
| ☐ 35 Mark Konecny | 2.00 | .80 | .20 |

## 1990 Smokey Chargers

This attractive 36-card set was distributed in the San Diego area and features members of the Chargers. The cards measure approximately 5" by 8" and are very similar in style to previous Chargers Smokey issues. Since the cards are unnumbered except for uniform number, they are ordered below in that manner. The cards backs contain a fire safety cartoon and very brief biographical information.

| | MINT | EXC | G-VG |
|---|---|---|---|
| COMPLETE SET (36) | 35.00 | 14.00 | 3.50 |
| COMMON PLAYER | .75 | .30 | .07 |
| | | | |
| ☐ 11 Billy Joe Tolliver | 2.50 | 1.00 | .25 |
| ☐ 13 Mark Vlasic | 1.25 | .50 | .12 |
| ☐ 15 David Archer | 2.00 | .80 | .20 |
| ☐ 20 Darrin Nelson | 1.25 | .50 | .12 |
| ☐ 22 Gill Byrd | 1.50 | .60 | .15 |
| ☐ 24 Lester Lyles | .75 | .30 | .07 |
| ☐ 25 Vencie Glenn | 1.00 | .40 | .10 |
| ☐ 30 Sam Seale | .75 | .30 | .07 |
| ☐ 31 Craig McEwen | .75 | .30 | .07 |
| ☐ 35 Marion Butts | 2.50 | 1.00 | .25 |
| ☐ 43 Tim Spencer | 1.00 | .40 | .10 |
| ☐ 44 Martin Bayless | 1.00 | .40 | .10 |
| ☐ 46 Joe Caravello | .75 | .30 | .07 |
| ☐ 50 Gary Plummer | 1.00 | .40 | .10 |
| ☐ 51 Cedric Figaro | .75 | .30 | .07 |
| ☐ 53 Courtney Hall | 1.00 | .40 | .10 |

| | | | |
|---|---|---|---|
| ☐ 54 Billy Ray Smith | 1.25 | .50 | .12 |
| ☐ 58 David Brandon | 1.00 | .40 | .10 |
| ☐ 59 Ken Woodard | .75 | .30 | .07 |
| ☐ 60 Dennis McKnight | .75 | .30 | .07 |
| ☐ 65 David Richards | .75 | .30 | .07 |
| ☐ 69 Les Miller | .75 | .30 | .07 |
| ☐ 75 Joe Phillips | .75 | .30 | .07 |
| ☐ 76 Broderick Thompson | .75 | .30 | .07 |
| ☐ 78 Joel Patten | .75 | .30 | .07 |
| ☐ 79 Joey Howard | .75 | .30 | .07 |
| ☐ 80 Wayne Walker | 1.00 | .40 | .10 |
| ☐ 82 Rod Bernstine | 2.00 | .80 | .20 |
| ☐ 83 Anthony Miller | 3.50 | 1.40 | .35 |
| ☐ 85 Andy Parker | .75 | .30 | .07 |
| ☐ 87 Quinn Early | 1.25 | .50 | .12 |
| ☐ 88 Arthur Cox | .75 | .30 | .07 |
| ☐ 91 Leslie O'Neal | 1.50 | .60 | .15 |
| ☐ 92 Burt Grossman | 1.25 | .50 | .12 |
| ☐ 97 George Hinkle | .75 | .30 | .07 |
| ☐ 99 Lee Williams | 1.50 | .60 | .15 |

# 1990 Smokey Raiders

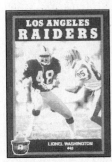

This 16-card standard size (2 1/2" by 3 1/2") set was issued by the USDA Forest Service in conjuction with the USDI Bureau of Land Management, USDI National Park Service, California Department of Forestry and Fire Prevention, and BDA. The set features solid black borders framing a full-color action shot with the Los Angeles Raiders team name in white. The player's name and uniform number is directly underneath the photo and there is a photo of the Smokey the Bear mascot in the lower left hand corner of the card. The back of the card has only the basic biographical information, as well as a fire safety tip. Surprisingly, there is no card of either Bo Jackson or Marcus Allen in this set. The set has been checklisted below in alphabetical order.

| | MINT | EXC | G-VG |
|---|---|---|---|
| COMPLETE SET (16) | 12.00 | 5.00 | 1.20 |
| COMMON PLAYER (1-16) | .75 | .30 | .07 |
| | | | |
| ☐ 1 Eddie Anderson | .90 | .36 | .09 |
| ☐ 2 Tom Benson | .90 | .36 | .09 |
| ☐ 3 Mervyn Fernandez | 1.25 | .50 | .12 |
| ☐ 4 Bob Golic | .90 | .36 | .09 |
| ☐ 5 Jeff Gossett | .75 | .30 | .07 |
| ☐ 6 Rory Graves | .75 | .30 | .07 |
| ☐ 7 Jeff Jaeger | .75 | .30 | .07 |
| ☐ 8 Howie Long | 1.50 | .60 | .15 |
| ☐ 9 Don Mosebar | .90 | .36 | .09 |
| ☐ 10 Jay Schroeder | 1.50 | .60 | .15 |
| ☐ 11 Art Shell CO | 1.75 | .70 | .17 |
| ☐ 12 Greg Townsend | 1.25 | .50 | .12 |
| ☐ 13 Lionel Washington | .75 | .30 | .07 |
| ☐ 14 Steve Wisniewski | .90 | .36 | .09 |
| ☐ 15 Commitment to Excellence (Helmet and Super Bowl trophies) | .75 | .30 | .07 |
| ☐ 16 Denise Franzen Cheerleader | .90 | .36 | .09 |

# 1992 Sport Decks Promo Aces

Produced by Junior Card and Toy Inc. and given away at the 1992 National Sports Collectors Convention in Atlanta, this four-card standard-size (2 1/2" by 3 1/2") set was produced to promote the premier edition of Sport Decks NFL playing cards. One card was given away on each of the four days of the convention. The color action player cut-outs on the fronts stand out against a full-bleed background that has a metallic sheen to it. A metallic bar overlays the photo at the top and bottom; the top bar carries the card's number, suit, and the

Team NFL logo, while the bottom bar has the team helmet, player's name and position, and the Sport Decks logo. All cards come in two varieties, with either gold or silver metallic bars on their fronts. The production figures for the silver were reportedly approximately 6,000, and for the gold, approximately 1,000. On a white background with hot pink and black lettering, the backs carry an advertisement, logos, and a list of players featured in the different card sets. All these cards are Aces, and this is indicated below by the number one followed by a letter indicating the suit. The silver versions are valued below; gold promos would be valued three times the prices below.

| | MINT | EXC | G-VG |
|---|---|---|---|
| COMPLETE SET (4) | 12.00 | 5.00 | 1.20 |
| COMMON PLAYER | 1.00 | .40 | .10 |
| | | | |
| ☐ 1C Emmitt Smith Dallas Cowboys | 6.00 | 2.40 | .60 |
| ☐ 1D Thurman Thomas Buffalo Bills | 2.00 | .80 | .20 |
| ☐ 1H Dan Marino Miami Dolphins | 5.00 | 2.00 | .50 |
| ☐ 1S Mark Rypien Washington Redskins | 1.00 | .40 | .10 |

# 1992 Sport Decks

This 55-card standard-size (2 1/2" by 3 1/2") set was issued in a box as if it were a playing card deck. According to Sport Decks, 294,632 decks were produced and 7,500 certified uncut sheets. The rounded-corner fronts feature full-bleed action color player photos. A ghosted stripe cuts across the top and bottom of the card. The card number and suit appear in the top stripe while the player's name, position and team helmet appear in the bottom stripe. The backs have the Official NFL 1992 Season Football Star Cards design on a blue-green football field with white borders. The design of these cards differ from the promo deck in that a Team NFL logo appears in the ghosted top stripe (promo issue has a NFL logo) and TM (trademark) is printed by the helmet. The back differs from the promo issue in that the Team NFL logo appears again, which slightly alters the back design. Since the set is similar to a playing card set, the set is arranged just like a card deck and checklisted below accordingly. In the checklist below S means Spades, D means Diamonds, C means Clubs, H means Hearts, and JK means Joker. The cards are checklisted below in playing card order by suits and numbers are assigned to Aces (1), Jacks (11), Queens (12), and Kings (13). The jokers are unnumbered and listed at the end.

| | MINT | EXC | G-VG |
|---|---|---|---|
| COMPLETE SET (55) | 4.00 | 1.60 | .40 |
| COMMON PLAYER | .05 | .02 | .00 |

☐ 1C Troy Aikman ............................ .75 .30 .07
　　Dallas Cowboys
☐ 1D Jim Kelly................................ .20 .08 .02
　　Buffalo Bills
☐ 1H Dan Marino ............................ .50 .20 .05
　　Miami Dolphins
☐ 1S Mark Rypien ........................... .10 .04 .01
　　Washington Redskins
☐ 2C Rodney Peete.......................... .08 .03 .01
　　Detroit Lions
☐ 2D John Friesz ............................ .08 .03 .01
　　San Diego Chargers
☐ 2H Anthony Munoz ....................... .05 .02 .00
　　Cincinnati Bengals
☐ 2S Phil Simms ............................. .10 .04 .01
　　New York Giants
☐ 3C Cris Carter.............................. .08 .03 .01
　　Minnesota Vikings
☐ 3D Gaston Green .......................... .05 .02 .00
　　Denver Broncos
☐ 3H Nick Bell ............................... .08 .03 .01
　　Los Angeles Raiders
☐ 3S Pat Swilling............................ .08 .03 .01
　　New Orleans Saints
☐ 4C Randal Hill ............................ .15 .06 .01
　　Phoenix Cardinals
☐ 4D Hugh Millen ........................... .05 .02 .00
　　New England Patriots
☐ 4H Michael Dean Perry ................. .05 .02 .00
　　Cleveland Browns
☐ 4S Jim Harbaugh ......................... .08 .03 .01
　　Chicago Bears
☐ 5C Jeff Hostetler ......................... .08 .03 .01
　　New York Giants
☐ 5D Dan McGwire .......................... .08 .03 .01
　　Seattle Seahawks
☐ 5H Haywood Jeffires..................... .10 .04 .01
　　Houston Oilers
☐ 5S Mike Singletary ....................... .10 .04 .01
　　Chicago Bears
☐ 6C Flipper Anderson..................... .05 .02 .00
　　Los Angeles Rams
☐ 6D Eric Green.............................. .05 .02 .00
　　Pittsburgh Steelers
☐ 6H Bubby Brister ......................... .05 .02 .00
　　Pittsburgh Steelers
☐ 6S Lawrence Taylor ...................... .12 .05 .01
　　New York Giants
☐ 7C Chris Miller ............................ .10 .04 .01
　　Atlanta Falcons
☐ 7D Christian Okoye ...................... .05 .02 .00
　　Kansas City Chiefs
☐ 7H Andre Reed ............................ .10 .04 .01
　　Buffalo Bills
☐ 7S John Taylor ............................ .08 .03 .01
　　San Francisco 49ers
☐ 8C Anthony Carter........................ .08 .03 .01
　　Minnesota Vikings
☐ 8D Ronnie Lott ............................ .10 .04 .01
　　Los Angeles Raiders
☐ 8H Anthony Miller ........................ .10 .04 .01
　　San Diego Chargers
☐ 8S Keith Jackson ......................... .10 .04 .01
　　Philadelphia Eagles
☐ 9C Timm Rosenbach...................... .08 .03 .01
　　Phoenix Cardinals
☐ 9D Rob Moore ............................. .10 .04 .01
　　New York Jets
☐ 9H Ken O'Brien ........................... .05 .02 .00
　　New York Jets
☐ 9S Vinny Testaverde ..................... .08 .03 .01
　　Tampa Bay Buccaneers
☐ 10C Sterling Sharpe ..................... .30 .12 .03
　　Green Bay Packers
☐ 10D Mark Clayton ........................ .08 .03 .01
　　Miami Dolphins
☐ 10H Bernie Kosar ......................... .10 .04 .01
　　Cleveland Browns
☐ 10S Andre Rison .......................... .15 .06 .01
　　Atlanta Falcons
☐ 11C Ricky Ervins .......................... .10 .04 .01
　　Washington Redskins
☐ 11D Thurman Thomas .................... .25 .10 .02
　　Buffalo Bills
☐ 11H Derrick Thomas ...................... .15 .06 .01
　　Kansas City Chiefs
☐ 11S Michael Irvin ......................... .30 .12 .03
　　Dallas Cowboys
☐ 12C Jerry Rice ............................ .35 .14 .03
　　San Francisco 49ers
☐ 12D John Elway ........................... .30 .12 .03
　　Denver Broncos
☐ 12H Jeff George .......................... .20 .08 .02
　　Indianapolis Colts
☐ 12S Earnest Byner ....................... .05 .02 .00
　　Washington Redskins
☐ 13C Emmitt Smith......................... .75 .30 .07

☐ 13D Warren Moon ........................ .20 .08 .02
　　Dallas Cowboys
☐ 13H Boomer Esiason ..................... .10 .04 .01
　　Houston Oilers
☐ 13S Randall Cunningham............... .15 .06 .01
　　Cincinnati Bengals
☐ JK Eric Dickerson ........................ .15 .06 .01
　　Philadelphia Eagles
☐ JK Jim Everett............................ .08 .03 .01
　　Indianapolis Colts
☐ NNO Title Card ............................ .05 .02 .00
　　Los Angeles Rams

# 1991 Stadium Club

The 1991 Topps Stadium Club set contains 500 cards measuring the standard size (2 1/2" by 3 1/2"). The fronts have full-bleed glossy color action photos. At the bottom, the player's name appears in an aqua stripe that is bordered in gold. On a colorful drawing of a football field and stadium background, the horizontally oriented backs have biography, The Sporting News Football Analysis Report (which consists of strengths and comments), and a miniature replica of the player's Topps Rookie Cards. The cards are numbered on the back. The key Rookie Cards in the set are Nick Bell, Mike Croel, Ricky Ervins, Brett Favre, Jeff Graham, Randal Hill, Todd Marinovich, Russell Maryland, Dan McGwire, Browning Nagle, Leonard Russell, Ricky Watters, and Harvey Williams. In conjunction with Super Bowl XXVI in Minneapolis, Topps issued cellophane packs containing Stadium Club cards. These cards differ from the basic issue in that an embossed Super Bowl XXVI logo appears at the top right or left corner of the card front. It is uncertain how many of the 500 cards were issued with this logo.

|  | MINT | EXC | G-VG |
|---|---|---|---|
| COMPLETE SET (500)..................... | 90.00 | 40.00 | 11.50 |
| COMMON PLAYER (1-500)............... | .15 | .07 | .02 |

☐ 1 Pepper Johnson.......................... .20 .09 .03
　　New York Giants
☐ 2 Emmitt Smith............................ 20.00 9.00 2.50
　　Dallas Cowboys
☐ 3 Deion Sanders........................... 1.50 .65 .19
　　Atlanta Falcons
☐ 4 Andre Collins ............................ .15 .07 .02
　　Washington Redskins
☐ 5 Eric Metcalf.............................. .25 .11 .03
　　Cleveland Browns
☐ 6 Richard Dent ............................ .20 .09 .03
　　Chicago Bears
☐ 7 Eric Martin .............................. .20 .09 .03
　　New Orleans Saints
☐ 8 Marcus Allen ............................ .75 .35 .09
　　Los Angeles Raiders
☐ 9 Gary Anderson .......................... .15 .07 .02
　　Pittsburgh Steelers
☐ 10 Joey Browner........................... .15 .07 .02
　　Minnesota Vikings
☐ 11 Lorenzo White.......................... .25 .11 .03
　　Houston Oilers
☐ 12 Bruce Smith............................ .25 .11 .03
　　Buffalo Bills
☐ 13 Mark Boyer ............................. .15 .07 .02
　　New York Jets
☐ 14 Mike Piel................................ .15 .07 .02
　　Los Angeles Rams
☐ 15 Albert Bentley .......................... .15 .07 .02
　　Indianapolis Colts
☐ 16 Bennie Blades .......................... .15 .07 .02
　　Detroit Lions
☐ 17 Jason Staurovsky....................... .15 .07 .02
　　New England Patriots
☐ 18 Anthony Toney .......................... .15 .07 .02

Philadelphia Eagles
| ☐ 19 Dave Krieg | .20 | .09 | .03 |
| Seattle Seahawks |
| ☐ 20 Harvey Williams | 1.00 | .45 | .13 |
| Kansas City Chiefs |
| ☐ 21 Bubba Paris | .15 | .07 | .02 |
| San Francisco 49ers |
| ☐ 22 Tim McGee | .20 | .09 | .03 |
| Cincinnati Bengals |
| ☐ 23 Brian Noble | .15 | .07 | .02 |
| Green Bay Packers |
| ☐ 24 Vinny Testaverde | .40 | .18 | .05 |
| Tampa Bay Buccaneers |
| ☐ 25 Doug Widell | .15 | .07 | .02 |
| Denver Broncos |
| ☐ 26 John Jackson | .30 | .14 | .04 |
| Phoenix Cardinals |
| ☐ 27 Marion Butts | .30 | .14 | .04 |
| San Diego Chargers |
| ☐ 28 Deron Cherry | .15 | .07 | .02 |
| Kansas City Chiefs |
| ☐ 29 Don Warren | .15 | .07 | .02 |
| Washington Redskins |
| ☐ 30 Rod Woodson | .75 | .35 | .09 |
| Pittsburgh Steelers |
| ☐ 31 Mike Baab | .15 | .07 | .02 |
| Cleveland Browns |
| ☐ 32 Greg Jackson | .30 | .14 | .04 |
| New York Giants |
| ☐ 33 Jerry Robinson | .15 | .07 | .02 |
| Los Angeles Raiders |
| ☐ 34 Dalton Hilliard | .15 | .07 | .02 |
| New Orleans Saints |
| ☐ 35 Brian Jordan | .35 | .16 | .04 |
| Atlanta Falcons |
| ☐ 36 James Thornton UER | .15 | .07 | .02 |
| Chicago Bears |
| (Misspelled Thorton |
| on card back) |
| ☐ 37 Michael Irvin | 5.00 | 2.30 | .60 |
| Dallas Cowboys |
| ☐ 38 Billy Joe Tolliver | .20 | .09 | .03 |
| San Diego Chargers |
| ☐ 39 Jeff Herrod | .15 | .07 | .02 |
| Indianapolis Colts |
| ☐ 40 Scott Norwood | .15 | .07 | .02 |
| Buffalo Bills |
| ☐ 41 Ferrell Edmunds | .15 | .07 | .02 |
| Miami Dolphins |
| ☐ 42 Andre Waters | .15 | .07 | .02 |
| Philadelphia Eagles |
| ☐ 43 Kevin Glover | .15 | .07 | .02 |
| Detroit Lions |
| ☐ 44 Ray Berry | .15 | .07 | .02 |
| Minnesota Vikings |
| ☐ 45 Timm Rosenbach | .20 | .09 | .03 |
| Phoenix Cardinals |
| ☐ 46 Reuben Davis | .15 | .07 | .02 |
| Tampa Bay Buccaneers |
| ☐ 47 Charles Wilson | .15 | .07 | .02 |
| Green Bay Packers |
| ☐ 48 Todd Marinovich | .20 | .09 | .03 |
| Los Angeles Raiders |
| ☐ 49 Harris Barton | .15 | .07 | .02 |
| San Francisco 49ers |
| ☐ 50 Jim Breech | .15 | .07 | .02 |
| Cincinnati Bengals |
| ☐ 51 Ron Holmes | .15 | .07 | .02 |
| Denver Broncos |
| ☐ 52 Chris Singleton | .15 | .07 | .02 |
| New England Patriots |
| ☐ 53 Pat Leahy | .20 | .09 | .03 |
| New York Jets |
| ☐ 54 Tom Newberry | .15 | .07 | .02 |
| Los Angeles Rams |
| ☐ 55 Greg Montgomery | .15 | .07 | .02 |
| Houston Oilers |
| ☐ 56 Robert Blackmon | .15 | .07 | .02 |
| Seattle Seahawks |
| ☐ 57 Jay Hilgenberg | .20 | .09 | .03 |
| Chicago Bears |
| ☐ 58 Rodney Hampton | 3.50 | 1.55 | .45 |
| New York Giants |
| ☐ 59 Brett Perriman | .40 | .18 | .05 |
| New Orleans Saints |
| ☐ 60 Ricky Watters | 9.00 | 4.00 | 1.15 |
| San Francisco 49ers |
| ☐ 61 Howie Long | .20 | .09 | .03 |
| Los Angeles Raiders |
| ☐ 62 Frank Cornish | .15 | .07 | .02 |
| San Diego Chargers |
| ☐ 63 Chris Miller | .25 | .11 | .03 |
| Atlanta Falcons |
| ☐ 64 Keith Taylor | .15 | .07 | .02 |
| Indianapolis Colts |
| ☐ 65 Tony Paige | .15 | .07 | .02 |
| Miami Dolphins |
| ☐ 66 Gary Zimmerman | .15 | .07 | .02 |

Minnesota Vikings
| ☐ 67 Mark Royals | .15 | .07 | .02 |
| Tampa Bay Buccaneers |
| ☐ 68 Ernie Jones | .15 | .07 | .02 |
| Phoenix Cardinals |
| ☐ 69 David Grant | .15 | .07 | .02 |
| Cincinnati Bengals |
| ☐ 70 Shane Conlan | .20 | .09 | .03 |
| Buffalo Bills |
| ☐ 71 Jerry Rice | 5.00 | 2.30 | .60 |
| San Francisco 49ers |
| ☐ 72 Christian Okoye | .20 | .09 | .03 |
| Kansas City Chiefs |
| ☐ 73 Eddie Murray | .20 | .09 | .03 |
| Detroit Lions |
| ☐ 74 Reggie White | 1.00 | .45 | .13 |
| Philadelphia Eagles |
| ☐ 75 Jeff Graham | 1.25 | .55 | .16 |
| Pittsburgh Steelers |
| ☐ 76 Mark Jackson | .20 | .09 | .03 |
| Denver Broncos |
| ☐ 77 David Grayson | .15 | .07 | .02 |
| Cleveland Browns |
| ☐ 78 Dan Stryzinski | .15 | .07 | .02 |
| Pittsburgh Steelers |
| ☐ 79 Sterling Sharpe | 5.00 | 2.30 | .60 |
| Green Bay Packers |
| ☐ 80 Cleveland Gary | .15 | .07 | .02 |
| Los Angeles Rams |
| ☐ 81 Johnny Meads | .15 | .07 | .02 |
| Houston Oilers |
| ☐ 82 Howard Cross | .15 | .07 | .02 |
| New York Giants |
| ☐ 83 Ken O'Brien | .20 | .09 | .03 |
| New York Jets |
| ☐ 84 Brian Blades | .25 | .11 | .03 |
| Seattle Seahawks |
| ☐ 85 Ethan Horton | .15 | .07 | .02 |
| Los Angeles Raiders |
| ☐ 86 Bruce Armstrong | .15 | .07 | .02 |
| New England Patriots |
| ☐ 87 James Washington | .50 | .23 | .06 |
| Dallas Cowboys |
| ☐ 88 Eugene Daniel | .15 | .07 | .02 |
| Indianapolis Colts |
| ☐ 89 James Lofton | .25 | .11 | .03 |
| Buffalo Bills |
| ☐ 90 Louis Oliver | .20 | .09 | .03 |
| Miami Dolphins |
| ☐ 91 Boomer Esiason | .60 | .25 | .08 |
| Cincinnati Bengals |
| ☐ 92 Seth Joyner | .20 | .09 | .03 |
| Philadelphia Eagles |
| ☐ 93 Mark Carrier | .20 | .09 | .03 |
| Tampa Bay Buccaneers |
| ☐ 94 Brett Favre UER | 15.00 | 6.75 | 1.90 |
| Atlanta Falcons |
| (Favre misspelled |
| as Farve) |
| ☐ 95 Lee Williams | .20 | .09 | .03 |
| San Diego Chargers |
| ☐ 96 Neal Anderson | .20 | .09 | .03 |
| Chicago Bears |
| ☐ 97 Brent Jones | .50 | .23 | .06 |
| San Francisco 49ers |
| ☐ 98 John Alt | .15 | .07 | .02 |
| Kansas City Chiefs |
| ☐ 99 Rodney Peete | .20 | .09 | .03 |
| Detroit Lions |
| ☐ 100 Steve Broussard | .20 | .09 | .03 |
| Atlanta Falcons |
| ☐ 101 Cedric Mack | .15 | .07 | .02 |
| Phoenix Cardinals |
| ☐ 102 Pat Swilling | .25 | .11 | .03 |
| New Orleans Saints |
| ☐ 103 Stan Humphries | 1.00 | .45 | .13 |
| Washington Redskins |
| ☐ 104 Darrell Thompson | .20 | .09 | .03 |
| Green Bay Packers |
| ☐ 105 Reggie Langhorne | .20 | .09 | .03 |
| Cleveland Browns |
| ☐ 106 Kenny Davidson | .15 | .07 | .02 |
| Pittsburgh Steelers |
| ☐ 107 Jim Everett | .20 | .09 | .03 |
| Los Angeles Rams |
| ☐ 108 Keith Millard | .20 | .09 | .03 |
| Minnesota Vikings |
| ☐ 109 Garry Lewis | .15 | .07 | .02 |
| Los Angeles Raiders |
| ☐ 110 Jeff Hostetler | 1.25 | .55 | .16 |
| New York Giants |
| ☐ 111 Lamar Lathon | .15 | .07 | .02 |
| Houston Oilers |
| ☐ 112 Johnny Bailey | .35 | .16 | .04 |
| Chicago Bears |
| ☐ 113 Cornelius Bennett | .25 | .11 | .03 |
| Buffalo Bills |
| ☐ 114 Travis McNeal | .15 | .07 | .02 |

Seattle Seahawks
| | | | |
|---|---|---|---|
| ☐ 115 Jeff Lageman | .15 | .07 | .02 |

New York Jets
| | | | |
|---|---|---|---|
| ☐ 116 Nick Bell | 1.00 | .45 | .13 |

Los Angeles Raiders
| | | | |
|---|---|---|---|
| ☐ 117 Calvin Williams | 1.25 | .55 | .16 |

Philadelphia Eagles
| | | | |
|---|---|---|---|
| ☐ 118 Shawn Lee | .40 | .18 | .05 |

Miami Dolphins
| | | | |
|---|---|---|---|
| ☐ 119 Anthony Munoz | .20 | .09 | .03 |

Cincinnati Bengals
| | | | |
|---|---|---|---|
| ☐ 120 Jay Novacek | .60 | .25 | .08 |

Dallas Cowboys
| | | | |
|---|---|---|---|
| ☐ 121 Kevin Fagan | .15 | .07 | .02 |

San Francisco 49ers
| | | | |
|---|---|---|---|
| ☐ 122 Leo Goeas | .15 | .07 | .02 |

San Diego Chargers
| | | | |
|---|---|---|---|
| ☐ 123 Vance Johnson | .20 | .09 | .03 |

Denver Broncos
| | | | |
|---|---|---|---|
| ☐ 124 Brent Williams | .15 | .07 | .02 |

New England Patriots
| | | | |
|---|---|---|---|
| ☐ 125 Clarence Verdin | .15 | .07 | .02 |

Indianapolis Colts
| | | | |
|---|---|---|---|
| ☐ 126 Luis Sharpe | .15 | .07 | .02 |

Phoenix Cardinals
| | | | |
|---|---|---|---|
| ☐ 127 Darrell Green | .15 | .07 | .02 |

Washington Redskins
| | | | |
|---|---|---|---|
| ☐ 128 Barry Word | .25 | .11 | .03 |

Kansas City Chiefs
| | | | |
|---|---|---|---|
| ☐ 129 Steve Walsh | .15 | .07 | .02 |

New Orleans Saints
| | | | |
|---|---|---|---|
| ☐ 130 Bryan Hinkle | .15 | .07 | .02 |

Pittsburgh Steelers
| | | | |
|---|---|---|---|
| ☐ 131 Ed West | .15 | .07 | .02 |

Green Bay Packers
| | | | |
|---|---|---|---|
| ☐ 132 Jeff Campbell | .15 | .07 | .02 |

Detroit Lions
| | | | |
|---|---|---|---|
| ☐ 133 Dennis Byrd | .50 | .23 | .06 |

New York Jets
| | | | |
|---|---|---|---|
| ☐ 134 Nate Odomes | .25 | .11 | .03 |

Buffalo Bills
| | | | |
|---|---|---|---|
| ☐ 135 Trace Armstrong | .15 | .07 | .02 |

Chicago Bears
| | | | |
|---|---|---|---|
| ☐ 136 Jarvis Williams | .15 | .07 | .02 |

Miami Dolphins
| | | | |
|---|---|---|---|
| ☐ 137 Warren Moon | 1.00 | .45 | .13 |

Houston Oilers
| | | | |
|---|---|---|---|
| ☐ 138 Eric Moten | .15 | .07 | .02 |

San Diego Chargers
| | | | |
|---|---|---|---|
| ☐ 139 Tony Woods | .15 | .07 | .02 |

Seattle Seahawks
| | | | |
|---|---|---|---|
| ☐ 140 Phil Simms | .25 | .11 | .03 |

New York Giants
| | | | |
|---|---|---|---|
| ☐ 141 Ricky Reynolds | .15 | .07 | .02 |

Tampa Bay Buccaneers
| | | | |
|---|---|---|---|
| ☐ 142 Frank Stams | .15 | .07 | .02 |

Los Angeles Rams
| | | | |
|---|---|---|---|
| ☐ 143 Kevin Mack | .20 | .09 | .03 |

Cleveland Browns
| | | | |
|---|---|---|---|
| ☐ 144 Wade Wilson | .20 | .09 | .03 |

Minnesota Vikings
| | | | |
|---|---|---|---|
| ☐ 145 Shawn Collins | .15 | .07 | .02 |

Atlanta Falcons
| | | | |
|---|---|---|---|
| ☐ 146 Roger Craig | .25 | .11 | .03 |

Los Angeles Raiders
| | | | |
|---|---|---|---|
| ☐ 147 Jeff Feagles | .15 | .07 | .02 |

Philadelphia Eagles
| | | | |
|---|---|---|---|
| ☐ 148 Norm Johnson | .15 | .07 | .02 |

Seattle Seahawks
| | | | |
|---|---|---|---|
| ☐ 149 Terance Mathis | .15 | .07 | .02 |

New York Jets
| | | | |
|---|---|---|---|
| ☐ 150 Reggie Cobb | 1.50 | .65 | .19 |

Tampa Bay Buccaneers
| | | | |
|---|---|---|---|
| ☐ 151 Chip Banks | .20 | .09 | .03 |

Indianapolis Colts
| | | | |
|---|---|---|---|
| ☐ 152 Darryl Pollard | .15 | .07 | .02 |

San Francisco 49ers
| | | | |
|---|---|---|---|
| ☐ 153 Karl Mecklenburg | .20 | .09 | .03 |

Denver Broncos
| | | | |
|---|---|---|---|
| ☐ 154 Ricky Proehl | .50 | .23 | .06 |

Phoenix Cardinals
| | | | |
|---|---|---|---|
| ☐ 155 Pete Stoyanovich | .20 | .09 | .03 |

Miami Dolphins
| | | | |
|---|---|---|---|
| ☐ 156 John Stephens | .20 | .09 | .03 |

New England Patriots
| | | | |
|---|---|---|---|
| ☐ 157 Ron Morris | .15 | .07 | .02 |

Chicago Bears
| | | | |
|---|---|---|---|
| ☐ 158 Steve DeBerg | .20 | .09 | .03 |

Kansas City Chiefs
| | | | |
|---|---|---|---|
| ☐ 159 Mike Munchak | .20 | .09 | .03 |

Houston Oilers
| | | | |
|---|---|---|---|
| ☐ 160 Brett Maxie | .15 | .07 | .02 |

New Orleans Saints
| | | | |
|---|---|---|---|
| ☐ 161 Don Beebe | .25 | .11 | .03 |

Buffalo Bills
| | | | |
|---|---|---|---|
| ☐ 162 Martin Mayhew | .15 | .07 | .02 |

Washington Redskins
| | | | |
|---|---|---|---|
| ☐ 163 Merril Hoge | .20 | .09 | .03 |

Pittsburgh Steelers
| | | | |
|---|---|---|---|
| ☐ 164 Kelvin Pritchett | .15 | .07 | .02 |

Detroit Lions
| | | | |
|---|---|---|---|
| ☐ 165 Jim Jeffcoat | .15 | .07 | .02 |

Dallas Cowboys
| | | | |
|---|---|---|---|
| ☐ 166 Myron Guyton | .15 | .07 | .02 |

New York Giants
| | | | |
|---|---|---|---|
| ☐ 167 Ickey Woods | .15 | .07 | .02 |

Cincinnati Bengals
| | | | |
|---|---|---|---|
| ☐ 168 Andre Ware | .40 | .18 | .05 |

Detroit Lions
| | | | |
|---|---|---|---|
| ☐ 169 Gary Plummer | .15 | .07 | .02 |

San Diego Chargers
| | | | |
|---|---|---|---|
| ☐ 170 Henry Ellard | .20 | .09 | .03 |

Los Angeles Rams
| | | | |
|---|---|---|---|
| ☐ 171 Scott Davis | .15 | .07 | .02 |

Los Angeles Raiders
| | | | |
|---|---|---|---|
| ☐ 172 Randall McDaniel | .15 | .07 | .02 |

Minnesota Vikings
| | | | |
|---|---|---|---|
| ☐ 173 Randal Hill | 1.75 | .80 | .22 |

Miami Dolphins
| | | | |
|---|---|---|---|
| ☐ 174 Anthony Bell | .15 | .07 | .02 |

Phoenix Cardinals
| | | | |
|---|---|---|---|
| ☐ 175 Gary Anderson | .20 | .09 | .03 |

Tampa Bay Buccaneers
| | | | |
|---|---|---|---|
| ☐ 176 Byron Evans | .20 | .09 | .03 |

Philadelphia Eagles
| | | | |
|---|---|---|---|
| ☐ 177 Tony Mandarich | .15 | .07 | .02 |

Green Bay Packers
| | | | |
|---|---|---|---|
| ☐ 178 Jeff George | 1.75 | .80 | .22 |

Indianapolis Colts
| | | | |
|---|---|---|---|
| ☐ 179 Art Monk | .25 | .11 | .03 |

Washington Redskins
| | | | |
|---|---|---|---|
| ☐ 180 Mike Kenn | .20 | .09 | .03 |

Atlanta Falcons
| | | | |
|---|---|---|---|
| ☐ 181 Sean Landeta | .15 | .07 | .02 |

New York Giants
| | | | |
|---|---|---|---|
| ☐ 182 Shaun Gayle | .15 | .07 | .02 |

Chicago Bears
| | | | |
|---|---|---|---|
| ☐ 183 Michael Carter | .15 | .07 | .02 |

San Francisco 49ers
| | | | |
|---|---|---|---|
| ☐ 184 Robb Thomas | .15 | .07 | .02 |

Kansas City Chiefs
| | | | |
|---|---|---|---|
| ☐ 185 Richmond Webb | .20 | .09 | .03 |

Miami Dolphins
| | | | |
|---|---|---|---|
| ☐ 186 Carnell Lake | .15 | .07 | .02 |

Pittsburgh Steelers
| | | | |
|---|---|---|---|
| ☐ 187 Rueben Mayes | .15 | .07 | .02 |

New Orleans Saints
| | | | |
|---|---|---|---|
| ☐ 188 Issiac Holt | .15 | .07 | .02 |

Dallas Cowboys
| | | | |
|---|---|---|---|
| ☐ 189 Leon Seals | .15 | .07 | .02 |

Buffalo Bills
| | | | |
|---|---|---|---|
| ☐ 190 Al Smith | .15 | .07 | .02 |

Houston Oilers
| | | | |
|---|---|---|---|
| ☐ 191 Steve Atwater | .25 | .11 | .03 |

Denver Broncos
| | | | |
|---|---|---|---|
| ☐ 192 Greg McMurtry | .15 | .07 | .02 |

New England Patriots
| | | | |
|---|---|---|---|
| ☐ 193 Al Toon | .20 | .09 | .03 |

New York Jets
| | | | |
|---|---|---|---|
| ☐ 194 Cortez Kennedy | 1.75 | .80 | .22 |

Seattle Seahawks
| | | | |
|---|---|---|---|
| ☐ 195 Gill Byrd | .15 | .07 | .02 |

San Diego Chargers
| | | | |
|---|---|---|---|
| ☐ 196 Carl Zander | .15 | .07 | .02 |

Cincinnati Bengals
| | | | |
|---|---|---|---|
| ☐ 197 Robert Brown | .15 | .07 | .02 |

Green Bay Packers
| | | | |
|---|---|---|---|
| ☐ 198 Buford McGee | .15 | .07 | .02 |

Los Angeles Rams
| | | | |
|---|---|---|---|
| ☐ 199 Mervyn Fernandez | .15 | .07 | .02 |

Los Angeles Raiders
| | | | |
|---|---|---|---|
| ☐ 200 Mike Dumas | .25 | .11 | .03 |

Houston Oilers
| | | | |
|---|---|---|---|
| ☐ 201 Rob Burnett | .50 | .23 | .06 |

Cleveland Browns
| | | | |
|---|---|---|---|
| ☐ 202 Brian Mitchell | .50 | .23 | .06 |

Washington Redskins
| | | | |
|---|---|---|---|
| ☐ 203 Randall Cunningham | .75 | .35 | .09 |

Philadelphia Eagles
| | | | |
|---|---|---|---|
| ☐ 204 Sammie Smith | .15 | .07 | .02 |

Miami Dolphins
| | | | |
|---|---|---|---|
| ☐ 205 Ken Clarke | .15 | .07 | .02 |

Minnesota Vikings
| | | | |
|---|---|---|---|
| ☐ 206 Floyd Dixon | .15 | .07 | .02 |

Atlanta Falcons
| | | | |
|---|---|---|---|
| ☐ 207 Ken Norton | .25 | .11 | .03 |

Dallas Cowboys
| | | | |
|---|---|---|---|
| ☐ 208 Tony Siragusa | .15 | .07 | .02 |

Indianapolis Colts
| | | | |
|---|---|---|---|
| ☐ 209 Louis Lipps | .20 | .09 | .03 |

Pittsburgh Steelers
| | | | |
|---|---|---|---|
| ☐ 210 Chris Martin | .15 | .07 | .02 |

Kansas City Chiefs
| | | | |
|---|---|---|---|
| ☐ 211 Jamie Mueller | .15 | .07 | .02 |

Buffalo Bills
| | | | |
|---|---|---|---|
| ☐ 212 Dave Waymer | .15 | .07 | .02 |

San Francisco 49ers
| ☐ 213 Donnell Woolford | .15 | .07 | .02 |
|---|---|---|---|

Chicago Bears
| ☐ 214 Paul Gruber | .20 | .09 | .03 |
|---|---|---|---|

Tampa Bay Buccaneers
| ☐ 215 Ken Harvey | .15 | .07 | .02 |
|---|---|---|---|

Phoenix Cardinals
| ☐ 216 Henry Jones | .50 | .23 | .06 |
|---|---|---|---|

Buffalo Bills
| ☐ 217 Tommy Barnhardt | .15 | .07 | .02 |
|---|---|---|---|

New Orleans Saints
| ☐ 218 Arthur Cox | .15 | .07 | .02 |
|---|---|---|---|

San Diego Chargers
| ☐ 219 Pat Terrell | .15 | .07 | .02 |
|---|---|---|---|

Los Angeles Rams
| ☐ 220 Curtis Duncan | .20 | .09 | .03 |
|---|---|---|---|

Houston Oilers
| ☐ 221 Jeff Jaeger | .15 | .07 | .02 |
|---|---|---|---|

Los Angeles Raiders
| ☐ 222 Scott Stephen | .15 | .07 | .02 |
|---|---|---|---|

Green Bay Packers
| ☐ 223 Rob Moore | .25 | .11 | .03 |
|---|---|---|---|

New York Jets
| ☐ 224 Chris Hinton | .15 | .07 | .02 |
|---|---|---|---|

Atlanta Falcons
| ☐ 225 Marv Cook | .15 | .07 | .02 |
|---|---|---|---|

New England Patriots
| ☐ 226 Patrick Hunter | .15 | .07 | .02 |
|---|---|---|---|

Seattle Seahawks
| ☐ 227 Earnest Byner | .25 | .11 | .03 |
|---|---|---|---|

Washington Redskins
| ☐ 228 Troy Aikman | 10.00 | 4.50 | 1.25 |
|---|---|---|---|

Dallas Cowboys
| ☐ 229 Kevin Walker | .15 | .07 | .02 |
|---|---|---|---|

Cincinnati Bengals
| ☐ 230 Keith Jackson | .60 | .25 | .08 |
|---|---|---|---|

Philadelphia Eagles
| ☐ 231 Russell Maryland UER | 1.50 | .65 | .19 |
|---|---|---|---|

(Card back says
Dallas Cowboy)
Dallas Cowboys
| ☐ 232 Charles Haley | .20 | .09 | .03 |
|---|---|---|---|

San Francisco 49ers
| ☐ 233 Nick Lowery | .20 | .09 | .03 |
|---|---|---|---|

Kansas City Chiefs
| ☐ 234 Erik Howard | .15 | .07 | .02 |
|---|---|---|---|

New York Giants
| ☐ 235 Leonard Smith | .15 | .07 | .02 |
|---|---|---|---|

Buffalo Bills
| ☐ 236 Tim Irwin | .15 | .07 | .02 |
|---|---|---|---|

Minnesota Vikings
| ☐ 237 Simon Fletcher | .20 | .09 | .03 |
|---|---|---|---|

Denver Broncos
| ☐ 238 Thomas Everett | .15 | .07 | .02 |
|---|---|---|---|

Pittsburgh Steelers
| ☐ 239 Reggie Roby | .20 | .09 | .03 |
|---|---|---|---|

Miami Dolphins
| ☐ 240 Leroy Hoard | .20 | .09 | .03 |
|---|---|---|---|

Cleveland Browns
| ☐ 241 Wayne Haddix | .15 | .07 | .02 |
|---|---|---|---|

Tampa Bay Buccaneers
| ☐ 242 Gary Clark | .15 | .07 | .02 |
|---|---|---|---|

Washington Redskins
| ☐ 243 Eric Andolsek | .15 | .07 | .02 |
|---|---|---|---|

Detroit Lions
| ☐ 244 Jim Wahler | .30 | .14 | .04 |
|---|---|---|---|

Phoenix Cardinals
| ☐ 245 Vaughan Johnson | .20 | .09 | .03 |
|---|---|---|---|

New Orleans Saints
| ☐ 246 Kevin Butler | .15 | .07 | .02 |
|---|---|---|---|

Chicago Bears
| ☐ 247 Steve Tasker | .20 | .09 | .03 |
|---|---|---|---|

Buffalo Bills
| ☐ 248 LeRoy Butler | .15 | .07 | .02 |
|---|---|---|---|

Green Bay Packers
| ☐ 249 Darion Conner | .15 | .07 | .02 |
|---|---|---|---|

Atlanta Falcons
| ☐ 250 Eric Turner | .50 | .23 | .06 |
|---|---|---|---|

Cleveland Browns
| ☐ 251 Kevin Ross | .20 | .09 | .03 |
|---|---|---|---|

Kansas City Chiefs
| ☐ 252 Stephen Baker | .15 | .07 | .02 |
|---|---|---|---|

New York Giants
| ☐ 253 Harold Green | .40 | .18 | .05 |
|---|---|---|---|

Cincinnati Bengals
| ☐ 254 Rohn Stark | .15 | .07 | .02 |
|---|---|---|---|

Indianapolis Colts
| ☐ 255 Joe Nash | .15 | .07 | .02 |
|---|---|---|---|

Seattle Seahawks
| ☐ 256 Jesse Sapolu | .15 | .07 | .02 |
|---|---|---|---|

San Francisco 49ers
| ☐ 257 Willie Gault | .20 | .09 | .03 |
|---|---|---|---|

Los Angeles Raiders
| ☐ 258 Jerome Brown | .20 | .09 | .03 |
|---|---|---|---|

Philadelphia Eagles
| ☐ 259 Ken Willis | .15 | .07 | .02 |
|---|---|---|---|

Dallas Cowboys
| ☐ 260 Courtney Hall | .15 | .07 | .02 |
|---|---|---|---|

San Diego Chargers
| ☐ 261 Hart Lee Dykes | .15 | .07 | .02 |
|---|---|---|---|

New England Patriots
| ☐ 262 William Fuller | .20 | .09 | .03 |
|---|---|---|---|

Houston Oilers
| ☐ 263 Stan Thomas | .15 | .07 | .02 |
|---|---|---|---|

Chicago Bears
| ☐ 264 Dan Marino | 6.00 | 2.70 | .75 |
|---|---|---|---|

Miami Dolphins
| ☐ 265 Ron Cox | .15 | .07 | .02 |
|---|---|---|---|

Chicago Bears
| ☐ 266 Eric Green | .75 | .35 | .09 |
|---|---|---|---|

Pittsburgh Steelers
| ☐ 267 Anthony Carter | .20 | .09 | .03 |
|---|---|---|---|

Minnesota Vikings
| ☐ 268 Jerry Ball | .20 | .09 | .03 |
|---|---|---|---|

Detroit Lions
| ☐ 269 Ron Hall | .15 | .07 | .02 |
|---|---|---|---|

Tampa Bay Buccaneers
| ☐ 270 Dennis Smith | .20 | .09 | .03 |
|---|---|---|---|

Denver Broncos
| ☐ 271 Eric Hill | .15 | .07 | .02 |
|---|---|---|---|

Phoenix Cardinals
| ☐ 272 Dan McGwire | .30 | .14 | .04 |
|---|---|---|---|

Seattle Seahawks
| ☐ 273 Lewis Billups UER | .15 | .07 | .02 |
|---|---|---|---|

Cincinnati Bengals
Louis on back
| ☐ 274 Rickey Jackson | .20 | .09 | .03 |
|---|---|---|---|

New Orleans Saints
| ☐ 275 Jim Sweeney | .15 | .07 | .02 |
|---|---|---|---|

New York Jets
| ☐ 276 Pat Beach | .15 | .07 | .02 |
|---|---|---|---|

Indianapolis Colts
| ☐ 277 Kevin Porter | .15 | .07 | .02 |
|---|---|---|---|

Kansas City Chiefs
| ☐ 278 Mike Sherrard | .20 | .09 | .03 |
|---|---|---|---|

San Francisco 49ers
| ☐ 279 Andy Heck | .15 | .07 | .02 |
|---|---|---|---|

Seattle Seahawks
| ☐ 280 Ron Brown | .15 | .07 | .02 |
|---|---|---|---|

Los Angeles Raiders
| ☐ 281 Lawrence Taylor | .75 | .35 | .09 |
|---|---|---|---|

New York Giants
| ☐ 282 Anthony Pleasant | .15 | .07 | .02 |
|---|---|---|---|

Cleveland Browns
| ☐ 283 Wes Hopkins | .15 | .07 | .02 |
|---|---|---|---|

Philadelphia Eagles
| ☐ 284 Jim Lachey | .15 | .07 | .02 |
|---|---|---|---|

Washington Redskins
| ☐ 285 Tim Harris | .20 | .09 | .03 |
|---|---|---|---|

Green Bay Packers
| ☐ 286 Tory Epps | .15 | .07 | .02 |
|---|---|---|---|

Atlanta Falcons
| ☐ 287 Wendell Davis | .15 | .07 | .02 |
|---|---|---|---|

Chicago Bears
| ☐ 288 Bubba McDowell | .15 | .07 | .02 |
|---|---|---|---|

Houston Oilers
| ☐ 289 Bubby Brister | .25 | .11 | .03 |
|---|---|---|---|

Pittsburgh Steelers
| ☐ 290 Chris Zorich | 1.00 | .45 | .13 |
|---|---|---|---|

Chicago Bears
| ☐ 291 Mike Merriweather | .15 | .07 | .02 |
|---|---|---|---|

Minnesota Vikings
| ☐ 292 Burt Grossman | .15 | .07 | .02 |
|---|---|---|---|

San Diego Chargers
| ☐ 293 Erik McMillan | .15 | .07 | .02 |
|---|---|---|---|

New York Jets
| ☐ 294 John Elway | 3.00 | 1.35 | .40 |
|---|---|---|---|

Denver Broncos
| ☐ 295 Toi Cook | .15 | .07 | .02 |
|---|---|---|---|

New Orleans Saints
| ☐ 296 Tom Rathman | .20 | .09 | .03 |
|---|---|---|---|

San Francisco 49ers
| ☐ 297 Matt Bahr | .15 | .07 | .02 |
|---|---|---|---|

New York Giants
| ☐ 298 Chris Spielman | .20 | .09 | .03 |
|---|---|---|---|

Detroit Lions
| ☐ 299 Freddie Joe Nunn | .50 | .23 | .06 |
|---|---|---|---|

Phoenix Cardinals
(Troy Aikman and
Emmitt Smith shown
in background)
| ☐ 300 Jim C. Jensen | .15 | .07 | .02 |
|---|---|---|---|

Miami Dolphins
| ☐ 301 David Fulcher UER | .15 | .07 | .02 |
|---|---|---|---|

Cincinnati Bengals
(Rookie card should
be '88, not '89)
| ☐ 302 Tommy Hodson | .15 | .07 | .02 |
|---|---|---|---|

New England Patriots
| ☐ 303 Stephone Paige | .20 | .09 | .03 |
|---|---|---|---|

Kansas City Chiefs
| ☐ 304 Greg Townsend | .15 | .07 | .02 |
|---|---|---|---|

Los Angeles Raiders
| ☐ 305 Dean Biasucci | .15 | .07 | .02 |
|---|---|---|---|

Indianapolis Colts
| ☐ 306 Jimmie Jones | .15 | .07 | .02 |
|---|---|---|---|

| | | | | |
|---|---|---|---|---|
| Dallas Cowboys | | | | |
| ☐ 307 Eugene Marve | .15 | .07 | .02 |
| Tampa Bay Buccaneers | | | |
| ☐ 308 Flipper Anderson | .20 | .09 | .03 |
| Los Angeles Rams | | | |
| ☐ 309 Darryl Talley | .20 | .09 | .03 |
| Buffalo Bills | | | |
| ☐ 310 Mike Croel | .75 | .35 | .09 |
| Denver Broncos | | | |
| ☐ 311 Thane Gash | .15 | .07 | .02 |
| Cleveland Browns | | | |
| ☐ 312 Perry Kemp | .15 | .07 | .02 |
| Green Bay Packers | | | |
| ☐ 313 Heath Sherman | .20 | .09 | .03 |
| Philadelphia Eagles | | | |
| ☐ 314 Mike Singletary | .25 | .11 | .03 |
| Chicago Bears | | | |
| ☐ 315 Chip Lohmiller | .20 | .09 | .03 |
| Washington Redskins | | | |
| ☐ 316 Tunch Ilkin | .15 | .07 | .02 |
| Pittsburgh Steelers | | | |
| ☐ 317 Junior Seau | 2.00 | .90 | .25 |
| San Diego Chargers | | | |
| ☐ 318 Mike Gann | .15 | .07 | .02 |
| Atlanta Falcons | | | |
| ☐ 319 Tim McDonald | .20 | .09 | .03 |
| Phoenix Cardinals | | | |
| ☐ 320 Kyle Clifton | .15 | .07 | .02 |
| New York Jets | | | |
| ☐ 321 Dan Owens | .15 | .07 | .02 |
| Detroit Lions | | | |
| ☐ 322 Tim Grunhard | .15 | .07 | .02 |
| Kansas City Chiefs | | | |
| ☐ 323 Stan Brock | .15 | .07 | .02 |
| New Orleans Saints | | | |
| ☐ 324 Rodney Holman | .15 | .07 | .02 |
| Cincinnati Bengals | | | |
| ☐ 325 Mark Ingram | .20 | .09 | .03 |
| New York Giants | | | |
| ☐ 326 Browning Nagle | .75 | .35 | .09 |
| New York Jets | | | |
| ☐ 327 Joe Montana | 6.00 | 2.70 | .75 |
| San Francisco 49ers | | | |
| ☐ 328 Carl Lee | .15 | .07 | .02 |
| Minnesota Vikings | | | |
| ☐ 329 John L. Williams | .20 | .09 | .03 |
| Seattle Seahawks | | | |
| ☐ 330 David Griggs | .15 | .07 | .02 |
| Miami Dolphins | | | |
| ☐ 331 Clarence Kay | .15 | .07 | .02 |
| Denver Broncos | | | |
| ☐ 332 Irving Fryar | .20 | .09 | .03 |
| New England Patriots | | | |
| ☐ 333 Doug Smith | .30 | .14 | .04 |
| Houston Oilers | | | |
| ☐ 334 Kent Hull | .15 | .07 | .02 |
| Buffalo Bills | | | |
| ☐ 335 Mike Wilcher | .15 | .07 | .02 |
| Los Angeles Rams | | | |
| ☐ 336 Ray Donaldson | .15 | .07 | .02 |
| Indianapolis Colts | | | |
| ☐ 337 Mark Carrier USC UER | .20 | .09 | .03 |
| Chicago Bears | | | |
| (Rookie card should | | | |
| be '90, not '89) | | | |
| ☐ 338 Kelvin Martin | .15 | .07 | .02 |
| Dallas Cowboys | | | |
| ☐ 339 Keith Byars | .25 | .11 | .03 |
| Philadelphia Eagles | | | |
| ☐ 340 Wilber Marshall | .20 | .09 | .03 |
| Washington Redskins | | | |
| ☐ 341 Ronnie Lott | .25 | .11 | .03 |
| Los Angeles Raiders | | | |
| ☐ 342 Blair Thomas | .20 | .09 | .03 |
| New York Jets | | | |
| ☐ 343 Ronnie Harmon | .15 | .07 | .02 |
| San Diego Chargers | | | |
| ☐ 344 Brian Brennan | .15 | .07 | .02 |
| Cleveland Browns | | | |
| ☐ 345 Charles McRae | .15 | .07 | .02 |
| Tampa Bay Buccaneers | | | |
| ☐ 346 Michael Cofer | .15 | .07 | .02 |
| Detroit Lions | | | |
| ☐ 347 Keith Willis | .15 | .07 | .02 |
| Pittsburgh Steelers | | | |
| ☐ 348 Bruce Kozerski | .15 | .07 | .02 |
| Cincinnati Bengals | | | |
| ☐ 349 Dave Meggett | .25 | .11 | .03 |
| New York Giants | | | |
| ☐ 350 John Taylor | .25 | .11 | .03 |
| San Francisco 49ers | | | |
| ☐ 351 Johnny Holland | .15 | .07 | .02 |
| Green Bay Packers | | | |
| ☐ 352 Steve Christie | .15 | .07 | .02 |
| Tampa Bay Buccaneers | | | |
| ☐ 353 Ricky Ervins | .90 | .40 | .11 |
| Washington Redskins | | | |
| ☐ 354 Robert Massey | .15 | .07 | .02 |

| | | | | |
|---|---|---|---|---|
| New Orleans Saints | | | | |
| ☐ 355 Derrick Thomas | 1.50 | .65 | .19 |
| Kansas City Chiefs | | | |
| ☐ 356 Tommy Kane | .15 | .07 | .02 |
| Seattle Seahawks | | | |
| ☐ 357 Melvin Bratton | .15 | .07 | .02 |
| Denver Broncos | | | |
| ☐ 358 Bruce Matthews | .20 | .09 | .03 |
| Houston Oilers | | | |
| ☐ 359 Mark Duper | .20 | .09 | .03 |
| Miami Dolphins | | | |
| ☐ 360 Jeff Wright | .30 | .14 | .04 |
| Buffalo Bills | | | |
| ☐ 361 Barry Sanders | 5.00 | 2.30 | .60 |
| Detroit Lions | | | |
| ☐ 362 Chuck Webb | .15 | .07 | .02 |
| Green Bay Packers | | | |
| ☐ 363 Darryl Grant | .15 | .07 | .02 |
| Washington Redskins | | | |
| ☐ 364 William Roberts | .15 | .07 | .02 |
| New York Giants | | | |
| ☐ 365 Reggie Rutland | .15 | .07 | .02 |
| Minnesota Vikings | | | |
| ☐ 366 Clay Matthews | .20 | .09 | .03 |
| Cleveland Browns | | | |
| ☐ 367 Anthony Miller | 1.00 | .45 | .13 |
| San Diego Chargers | | | |
| ☐ 368 Mike Prior | .15 | .07 | .02 |
| Indianapolis Colts | | | |
| ☐ 369 Jessie Tuggle | .15 | .07 | .02 |
| Atlanta Falcons | | | |
| ☐ 370 Brad Muster | .20 | .09 | .03 |
| Chicago Bears | | | |
| ☐ 371 Jay Schroeder | .20 | .09 | .03 |
| Los Angeles Raiders | | | |
| ☐ 372 Greg Lloyd | .15 | .07 | .02 |
| Pittsburgh Steelers | | | |
| ☐ 373 Mike Cofer | .15 | .07 | .02 |
| San Francisco 49ers | | | |
| ☐ 374 James Brooks | .20 | .09 | .03 |
| Cincinnati Bengals | | | |
| ☐ 375 Danny Noonan UER | .15 | .07 | .02 |
| Dallas Cowboys | | | |
| (Misspelled Noonen | | | |
| on card back) | | | |
| ☐ 376 Latin Berry | .15 | .07 | .02 |
| Los Angeles Rams | | | |
| ☐ 377 Brad Baxter | .20 | .09 | .03 |
| New York Jets | | | |
| ☐ 378 Godfrey Myles | .30 | .14 | .04 |
| Dallas Cowboys | | | |
| ☐ 379 Morten Andersen | .20 | .09 | .03 |
| New Orleans Saints | | | |
| ☐ 380 Keith Woodside | .15 | .07 | .02 |
| Green Bay Packers | | | |
| ☐ 381 Bobby Humphrey | .20 | .09 | .03 |
| Denver Broncos | | | |
| ☐ 382 Mike Golic | .15 | .07 | .02 |
| Philadelphia Eagles | | | |
| ☐ 383 Keith McCants | .15 | .07 | .02 |
| Tampa Bay Buccaneers | | | |
| ☐ 384 Anthony Thompson | .15 | .07 | .02 |
| Phoenix Cardinals | | | |
| ☐ 385 Mark Clayton | .20 | .09 | .03 |
| Miami Dolphins | | | |
| ☐ 386 Neil Smith | .25 | .11 | .03 |
| Kansas City Chiefs | | | |
| ☐ 387 Bryan Millard | .15 | .07 | .02 |
| Seattle Seahawks | | | |
| ☐ 388 Mel Gray UER | .20 | .09 | .03 |
| Detroit Lions | | | |
| (Wrong Mel Gray | | | |
| pictured on card back) | | | |
| ☐ 389 Ernest Givins | .20 | .09 | .03 |
| Houston Oilers | | | |
| ☐ 390 Reyna Thompson | .15 | .07 | .02 |
| New York Giants | | | |
| ☐ 391 Eric Bieniemy | .50 | .23 | .06 |
| San Diego Chargers | | | |
| ☐ 392 Jon Hand | .15 | .07 | .02 |
| Indianapolis Colts | | | |
| ☐ 393 Mark Rypien | .25 | .11 | .03 |
| Washington Redskins | | | |
| ☐ 394 Bill Romanowski | .15 | .07 | .02 |
| San Francisco 49ers | | | |
| ☐ 395 Thurman Thomas | 2.00 | .90 | .25 |
| Buffalo Bills | | | |
| ☐ 396 Jim Harbaugh | .20 | .09 | .03 |
| Chicago Bears | | | |
| ☐ 397 Don Mosebar | .15 | .07 | .02 |
| Los Angeles Raiders | | | |
| ☐ 398 Andre Rison | 1.50 | .65 | .19 |
| Atlanta Falcons | | | |
| ☐ 399 Mike Johnson | .15 | .07 | .02 |
| Cleveland Browns | | | |
| ☐ 400 Dermontti Dawson | .15 | .07 | .02 |
| Pittsburgh Steelers | | | |
| ☐ 401 Herschel Walker | .25 | .11 | .03 |

| | | | |
|---|---|---|---|
| Minnesota Vikings | | | |
| ☐ 402 Joe Prokop | .15 | .07 | .02 |
| New York Jets | | | |
| ☐ 403 Eddie Brown | .15 | .07 | .02 |
| Cincinnati Bengals | | | |
| ☐ 404 Nate Newton | .15 | .07 | .02 |
| Dallas Cowboys | | | |
| ☐ 405 Damone Johnson | .15 | .07 | .02 |
| Los Angeles Rams | | | |
| ☐ 406 Jessie Hester | .20 | .09 | .03 |
| Indianapolis Colts | | | |
| ☐ 407 Jim Arnold | .15 | .07 | .02 |
| Detroit Lions | | | |
| ☐ 408 Ray Agnew | .15 | .07 | .02 |
| New England Patriots | | | |
| ☐ 409 Michael Brooks | .15 | .07 | .02 |
| Denver Broncos | | | |
| ☐ 410 Keith Sims | .15 | .07 | .02 |
| Miami Dolphins | | | |
| ☐ 411 Carl Banks | .20 | .09 | .03 |
| New York Giants | | | |
| ☐ 412 Jonathan Hayes | .15 | .07 | .02 |
| Kansas City Chiefs | | | |
| ☐ 413 Richard Johnson | .15 | .07 | .02 |
| Houston Oilers | | | |
| ☐ 414 Darryll Lewis | .35 | .16 | .04 |
| Houston Oilers | | | |
| ☐ 415 Jeff Bryant | .15 | .07 | .02 |
| Seattle Seahawks | | | |
| ☐ 416 Leslie O'Neal | .20 | .09 | .03 |
| San Diego Chargers | | | |
| ☐ 417 Andre Reed | .50 | .23 | .06 |
| Buffalo Bills | | | |
| ☐ 418 Charles Mann | .20 | .09 | .03 |
| Washington Redskins | | | |
| ☐ 419 Keith DeLong | .15 | .07 | .02 |
| San Francisco 49ers | | | |
| ☐ 420 Bruce Hill | .15 | .07 | .02 |
| Tampa Bay Buccaneers | | | |
| ☐ 421 Matt Brock | .15 | .07 | .02 |
| Green Bay Packers | | | |
| ☐ 422 Johnny Johnson | 1.25 | .55 | .16 |
| Phoenix Cardinals | | | |
| ☐ 423 Mark Bortz | .15 | .07 | .02 |
| Chicago Bears | | | |
| ☐ 424 Ben Smith | .15 | .07 | .02 |
| Philadelphia Eagles | | | |
| ☐ 425 Jeff Cross | .15 | .07 | .02 |
| Miami Dolphins | | | |
| ☐ 426 Irv Pankey | .15 | .07 | .02 |
| Los Angeles Rams | | | |
| ☐ 427 Hassan Jones | .15 | .07 | .02 |
| Minnesota Vikings | | | |
| ☐ 428 Andre Tippett | .20 | .09 | .03 |
| New England Patriots | | | |
| ☐ 429 Tim Worley | .20 | .09 | .03 |
| Pittsburgh Steelers | | | |
| ☐ 430 Daniel Stubbs | .15 | .07 | .02 |
| Dallas Cowboys | | | |
| ☐ 431 Max Montoya | .15 | .07 | .02 |
| Los Angeles Rams | | | |
| ☐ 432 Jumbo Elliott | .15 | .07 | .02 |
| New York Giants | | | |
| ☐ 433 Duane Bickett | .15 | .07 | .02 |
| Indianapolis Colts | | | |
| ☐ 434 Nate Lewis | .75 | .35 | .09 |
| San Diego Chargers | | | |
| ☐ 435 Leonard Russell | 3.00 | 1.35 | .40 |
| New England Patriots | | | |
| ☐ 436 Hoby Brenner | .15 | .07 | .02 |
| New Orleans Saints | | | |
| ☐ 437 Ricky Sanders | .15 | .07 | .02 |
| Washington Redskins | | | |
| ☐ 438 Pierce Holt | .15 | .07 | .02 |
| San Francisco 49ers | | | |
| ☐ 439 Derrick Fenner | .20 | .09 | .03 |
| Seattle Seahawks | | | |
| ☐ 440 Drew Hill | .20 | .09 | .03 |
| Houston Oilers | | | |
| ☐ 441 Will Wolford | .15 | .07 | .02 |
| Buffalo Bills | | | |
| ☐ 442 Albert Lewis | .20 | .09 | .03 |
| Kansas City Chiefs | | | |
| ☐ 443 James Francis | .20 | .09 | .03 |
| Cincinnati Bengals | | | |
| ☐ 444 Chris Jacke | .15 | .07 | .02 |
| Green Bay Packers | | | |
| ☐ 445 Mike Farr | .15 | .07 | .02 |
| Detroit Lions | | | |
| ☐ 446 Stephen Braggs | .15 | .07 | .02 |
| Cleveland Browns | | | |
| ☐ 447 Michael Haynes | 3.00 | 1.35 | .40 |
| Atlanta Falcons | | | |
| ☐ 448 Freeman McNeil UER | .20 | .09 | .03 |
| New York Jets | | | |
| (2008 pounds, sic) | | | |
| ☐ 449 Kevin Donnalley | .15 | .07 | .02 |
| Houston Oilers | | | |

| | | | |
|---|---|---|---|
| ☐ 450 John Offerdahl | .20 | .09 | .03 |
| Miami Dolphins | | | |
| ☐ 451 Eric Allen | .20 | .09 | .03 |
| Philadelphia Eagles | | | |
| ☐ 452 Keith McKeller | .15 | .07 | .02 |
| Buffalo Bills | | | |
| ☐ 453 Kevin Greene | .20 | .09 | .03 |
| Los Angeles Rams | | | |
| ☐ 454 Ronnie Lippett | .15 | .07 | .02 |
| New England Patriots | | | |
| ☐ 455 Ray Childress | .20 | .09 | .03 |
| Houston Oilers | | | |
| ☐ 456 Mike Saxon | .15 | .07 | .02 |
| Dallas Cowboys | | | |
| ☐ 457 Mark Robinson | .15 | .07 | .02 |
| Tampa Bay Buccaneers | | | |
| ☐ 458 Greg Kragen | .15 | .07 | .02 |
| Denver Broncos | | | |
| ☐ 459 Steve Jordan | .20 | .09 | .03 |
| Minnesota Vikings | | | |
| ☐ 460 John Johnson | .15 | .07 | .02 |
| San Francisco 49ers | | | |
| ☐ 461 Sam Mills | .20 | .09 | .03 |
| New Orleans Saints | | | |
| ☐ 462 Bo Jackson | 1.50 | .65 | .19 |
| Los Angeles Raiders | | | |
| ☐ 463 Mark Collins | .15 | .07 | .02 |
| New York Giants | | | |
| ☐ 464 Percy Snow | .15 | .07 | .02 |
| Kansas City Chiefs | | | |
| ☐ 465 Jeff Bostic | .15 | .07 | .02 |
| Washington Redskins | | | |
| ☐ 466 Jacob Green | .15 | .07 | .02 |
| Seattle Seahawks | | | |
| ☐ 467 Dexter Carter | .20 | .09 | .03 |
| San Francisco 49ers | | | |
| ☐ 468 Rich Camarillo | .15 | .07 | .02 |
| Phoenix Cardinals | | | |
| ☐ 469 Bill Brooks | .20 | .09 | .03 |
| Indianapolis Colts | | | |
| ☐ 470 John Carney | .15 | .07 | .02 |
| San Diego Chargers | | | |
| ☐ 471 Don Majkowski | .20 | .09 | .03 |
| Green Bay Packers | | | |
| ☐ 472 Ralph Tamm | .35 | .16 | .04 |
| Cleveland Browns | | | |
| ☐ 473 Fred Barnett | 1.50 | .65 | .19 |
| Philadelphia Eagles | | | |
| ☐ 474 Jim Covert | .15 | .07 | .02 |
| Chicago Bears | | | |
| ☐ 475 Kenneth Davis | .15 | .07 | .02 |
| Buffalo Bills | | | |
| ☐ 476 Jerry Gray | .15 | .07 | .02 |
| Los Angeles Rams | | | |
| ☐ 477 Broderick Thomas | .15 | .07 | .02 |
| Tampa Bay Buccaneers | | | |
| ☐ 478 Chris Doleman | .20 | .09 | .03 |
| Minnesota Vikings | | | |
| ☐ 479 Haywood Jeffires | 1.25 | .55 | .16 |
| Houston Oilers | | | |
| ☐ 480 Craig Heyward | .15 | .07 | .02 |
| New Orleans Saints | | | |
| ☐ 481 Markus Koch | .15 | .07 | .02 |
| Washington Redskins | | | |
| ☐ 482 Tim Krumrie | .15 | .07 | .02 |
| Cincinnati Bengals | | | |
| ☐ 483 Robert Clark | .15 | .07 | .02 |
| Detroit Lions | | | |
| ☐ 484 Mike Rozier | .20 | .09 | .03 |
| Atlanta Falcons | | | |
| ☐ 485 Danny Villa | .15 | .07 | .02 |
| New England Patriots | | | |
| ☐ 486 Gerald Williams | .15 | .07 | .02 |
| Pittsburgh Steelers | | | |
| ☐ 487 Steve Wisniewski | .15 | .07 | .02 |
| Los Angeles Raiders | | | |
| ☐ 488 J.B. Brown | .15 | .07 | .02 |
| Miami Dolphins | | | |
| ☐ 489 Eugene Robinson | .15 | .07 | .02 |
| Seattle Seahawks | | | |
| ☐ 490 Ottis Anderson | .20 | .09 | .03 |
| New York Giants | | | |
| ☐ 491 Tony Stargell | .15 | .07 | .02 |
| New York Jets | | | |
| ☐ 492 Jack Del Rio | .15 | .07 | .02 |
| Dallas Cowboys | | | |
| ☐ 493 Lamar Rogers | .15 | .07 | .02 |
| Cincinnati Bengals | | | |
| ☐ 494 Ricky Nattiel | .15 | .07 | .02 |
| Denver Broncos | | | |
| ☐ 495 Dan Saleaumua | .15 | .07 | .02 |
| Kansas City Chiefs | | | |
| ☐ 496 Checklist 1-100 | .15 | .07 | .02 |
| ☐ 497 Checklist 101-200 | .15 | .07 | .02 |
| ☐ 498 Checklist 201-300 | .15 | .07 | .02 |
| ☐ 499 Checklist 301-400 | .15 | .07 | .02 |
| ☐ 500 Checklist 401-500 | .15 | .07 | .02 |

# 1992 Stadium Club Promo Sheet

This promo sheet was given away at the 13th National Sports Collectors Convention, July 10-12, 1992, in Atlanta, Georgia. The front of the sheet displays nine Stadium Club player cards. The purpose of the sheet is to demonstrate part of the production process. The cards pictured are larger than the finished product but have a gold foil line framing a portion of the photo (2 1/2" by 3 1/2") to show how the photos are cropped to achieve a full-bleed card front. The back has an advertisement for the convention and Topps. The players are listed as they appear on the sheet from left to right, starting at the top.

|                           | MINT  | EXC  | G-VG |
|---------------------------|-------|------|------|
| COMPLETE SET (1)          | 10.00 | 4.00 | 1.00 |
| COMMON SHEET              | 10.00 | 4.00 | 1.00 |
| ☐ NNO Promo Sheet         | 10.00 | 4.00 | 1.00 |
|   Barry Sanders |       |      |      |
|   Detroit Lions |       |      |      |
|   Gene Atkins   |       |      |      |
|   New Orleans Saints |  |      |      |
|   Louis Oliver  |       |      |      |
|   Miami Dolphins |      |      |      |
|   Paul Gruber   |       |      |      |
|   Tampa Bay Buccaneers | |     |      |
|   Emmitt Smith  |       |      |      |
|   Dallas Cowboys |      |      |      |
|   Steve Jordan  |       |      |      |
|   Minnesota Vikings |   |      |      |
|   Warren Moon   |       |      |      |
|   Houston Oilers |      |      |      |
|   Seth Joyner   |       |      |      |
|   Philadelpia Eagles |  |      |      |
|   Ronnie Lott   |       |      |      |
|   Los Angeles Raiders | |      |      |

# 1992 Stadium Club

The 1992 Topps Stadium Club football set was issued in three series and totaled 700 cards. The set includes 30 Members Choice (291-310, 601-610) cards. The cards measure the standard size (2 1/2" by 3 1/2"). The fronts feature full-bleed glossy color player photos. At the bottom, the player's name appears below the Stadium Club logo, and two gold foil stripes carry the team name. On a background consisting of an artistic rendition of a stadium and a football, the horizontal backs present biographical information, The Sporting News Skills Rating System, career summary, and a miniature reproduction of the player's Topps Rookie Card. The cards are numbered on the back. Rookie Cards include Edgar Bennett, Steve Bono, Terrell Buckley, Quentin Coryatt, Courtney Hawkins, Amp Lee, Dale Carter, Vaughn Dunbar, Steve Emtman, and Johnny Mitchell.

|                          | MINT   | EXC   | G-VG  |
|--------------------------|--------|-------|-------|
| COMPLETE SET (700)       | 120.00 | 55.00 | 15.00 |
| COMPLETE SERIES 1 (300)  | 15.00  | 6.75  | 1.90  |
| COMPLETE SERIES 2 (300)  | 15.00  | 6.75  | 1.90  |
| COMPLETE HI SERIES (100) | 90.00  | 40.00 | 11.50 |
| COMMON PLAYER (1-300)    | .08    | .04   | .01   |
| COMMON PLAYER (301-600)  | .08    | .04   | .01   |
| COMMON PLAYER (601-700)  | .50    | .23   | .06   |
| ☐ 1 Mark Rypien          | .12    | .05   | .02   |
|   Washington Redskins | |      |       |
| ☐ 2 Carlton Bailey       | .25    | .11   | .03   |
|   Buffalo Bills |       |       |       |
| ☐ 3 Kevin Glover         | .08    | .04   | .01   |
|   Detroit Lions |       |       |       |
| ☐ 4 Vance Johnson        | .10    | .05   | .01   |
|   Denver Broncos |      |       |       |
| ☐ 5 Jim Jeffcoat         | .08    | .04   | .01   |

|                          | | | |
|--------------------------|------|------|------|
|   Dallas Cowboys |    |      |      |
| ☐ 6 Dan Saleaumua        | .08  | .04  | .01  |
|   Kansas City Chiefs | |     |      |
| ☐ 7 Darion Conner        | .08  | .04  | .01  |
|   Atlanta Falcons |   |      |      |
| ☐ 8 Don Maggs            | .08  | .04  | .01  |
|   Houston Oilers |    |      |      |
| ☐ 9 Richard Dent         | .10  | .05  | .01  |
|   Chicago Bears |     |      |      |
| ☐ 10 Mark Murphy         | .08  | .04  | .01  |
|   Green Bay Packers | |      |      |
| ☐ 11 Wesley Carroll      | .10  | .05  | .01  |
|   New Orleans Saints | |     |      |
| ☐ 12 Chris Burkett       | .08  | .04  | .01  |
|   New York Jets |     |      |      |
| ☐ 13 Steve Wallace       | .08  | .04  | .01  |
|   San Francisco 49ers | |    |      |
| ☐ 14 Jacob Green         | .08  | .04  | .01  |
|   Seattle Seahawks |  |      |      |
| ☐ 15 Roger Ruzek         | .08  | .04  | .01  |
|   Philadelphia Eagles | |    |      |
| ☐ 16 J.B. Brown          | .08  | .04  | .01  |
|   Miami Dolphins |    |      |      |
| ☐ 17 Dave Meggett        | .10  | .05  | .01  |
|   New York Giants |   |      |      |
| ☐ 18 David Johnson       | .08  | .04  | .01  |
|   Pittsburgh Steelers | |    |      |
| ☐ 19 Rich Gannon         | .10  | .05  | .01  |
|   Minnesota Vikings | |      |      |
| ☐ 20 Kevin Mack          | .10  | .05  | .01  |
|   Cleveland Browns |  |      |      |
| ☐ 21A Reggie Cobb ERR    | .50  | .23  | .06  |
|   (Buccaneers upside down on card front) | | | |
|   Tampa Bay Buccaneers | |   |      |
| ☐ 21B Reggie Cobb COR    | .50  | .23  | .06  |
|   Tampa Bay Buccaneers | |   |      |
| ☐ 22 Nate Lewis          | .10  | .05  | .01  |
|   San Diego Chargers | |     |      |
| ☐ 23 Doug Smith          | .08  | .04  | .01  |
|   Los Angeles Rams |  |      |      |
| ☐ 24 Irving Fryar        | .10  | .05  | .01  |
|   New England Patriots | |   |      |
| ☐ 25 Anthony Thompson    | .08  | .04  | .01  |
|   Phoenix Cardinals | |      |      |
| ☐ 26 Duane Bickett       | .08  | .04  | .01  |
|   Indianapolis Colts | |     |      |
| ☐ 27 Don Majkowski       | .10  | .05  | .01  |
|   Green Bay Packers | |      |      |
| ☐ 28 Mark Schlereth      | .15  | .07  | .02  |
|   Washington Redskins | |    |      |
| ☐ 29 Melvin Jenkins      | .08  | .04  | .01  |
|   Detroit Lions |     |      |      |
| ☐ 30 Michael Haynes      | .60  | .25  | .08  |
|   Atlanta Falcons |   |      |      |
| ☐ 31 Greg Lewis          | .08  | .04  | .01  |
|   Denver Broncos |    |      |      |
| ☐ 32 Kenneth Davis       | .10  | .05  | .01  |
|   Buffalo Bills |     |      |      |
| ☐ 33 Derrick Thomas      | .30  | .14  | .04  |
|   Kansas City Chiefs | |     |      |
| ☐ 34 David Williams      | .08  | .04  | .01  |
|   Houston Oilers |    |      |      |
| ☐ 35 Neal Anderson       | .10  | .05  | .01  |
|   Chicago Bears |     |      |      |
| ☐ 36 Andre Collins       | .08  | .04  | .01  |
|   Washington Redskins | |    |      |
| ☐ 37 Jesse Solomon       | .08  | .04  | .01  |
|   Tampa Bay Buccaneers | |   |      |
| ☐ 38 Barry Sanders       | 2.00 | .90  | .25  |
|   Detroit Lions |     |      |      |
| ☐ 39 Jeff Gossett        | .08  | .04  | .01  |
|   Los Angeles Raiders | |    |      |
| ☐ 40 Rickey Jackson      | .10  | .05  | .01  |
|   New Orleans Saints | |     |      |
| ☐ 41 Ray Berry           | .08  | .04  | .01  |
|   Minnesota Vikings | |      |      |
| ☐ 42 Leroy Hoard         | .10  | .05  | .01  |
|   Cleveland Browns |  |      |      |
| ☐ 43 Eric Thomas         | .08  | .04  | .01  |
|   Cincinnati Bengals | |     |      |
| ☐ 44 Brian Washington    | .08  | .04  | .01  |
|   New York Jets |     |      |      |
| ☐ 45 Pat Terrell         | .08  | .04  | .01  |
|   Los Angeles Rams |  |      |      |
| ☐ 46 Eugene Robinson     | .08  | .04  | .01  |
|   Seattle Seahawks |  |      |      |
| ☐ 47 Luis Sharpe         | .08  | .04  | .01  |
|   Phoenix Cardinals | |      |      |
| ☐ 48 Jerome Brown        | .10  | .05  | .01  |
|   Philadelphia Eagles | |    |      |
| ☐ 49 Mark Collins        | .08  | .04  | .01  |
|   New York Giants |   |      |      |
| ☐ 50 Johnny Holland      | .08  | .04  | .01  |
|   Green Bay Packers | |      |      |
| ☐ 51 Tony Paige          | .08  | .04  | .01  |
|   Miami Dolphins |    |      |      |
| ☐ 52 Willie Green        | .08  | .04  | .01  |

|  |  |  | | | |
|---|--------|------|---|---|---|
| ☐ 53 | Steve Atwater | Detroit Lions | .10 | .05 | .01 |
| ☐ 54 | Brad Muster | Denver Broncos | .10 | .05 | .01 |
| ☐ 55 | Cris Dishman | Chicago Bears | .10 | .05 | .01 |
| ☐ 56 | Eddie Anderson | Houston Oilers | .08 | .04 | .01 |
| ☐ 57 | Sam Mills | Los Angeles Raiders | .10 | .05 | .01 |
| ☐ 58 | Donald Evans | New Orleans Saints | .08 | .04 | .01 |
| ☐ 59 | Jon Vaughn | Pittsburgh Steelers | .08 | .04 | .01 |
| ☐ 60 | Marion Butts | New England Patriots | .12 | .05 | .02 |
| ☐ 61 | Rodney Holman | San Diego Chargers | .08 | .04 | .01 |
| ☐ 62 | Dwayne White | Cincinnati Bengals | .08 | .04 | .01 |
| ☐ 63 | Martin Mayhew | New York Jets | .08 | .04 | .01 |
| ☐ 64 | Jonathan Hayes | Washington Redskins | .08 | .04 | .01 |
| ☐ 65 | Andre Rison | Kansas City Chiefs | .40 | .18 | .05 |
| ☐ 66 | Calvin Williams | Atlanta Falcons | .12 | .05 | .02 |
| ☐ 67 | James Washington | Philadelphia Eagles | .08 | .04 | .01 |
| ☐ 68 | Tim Harris | Dallas Cowboys | .10 | .05 | .01 |
| ☐ 69 | Jim Ritcher | San Francisco 49ers | .08 | .04 | .01 |
| ☐ 70 | Johnny Johnson | Buffalo Bills | .20 | .09 | .03 |
| ☐ 71 | John Offerdahl | Phoenix Cardinals | .10 | .05 | .01 |
| ☐ 72 | Herschel Walker | Miami Dolphins | .12 | .05 | .02 |
| ☐ 73 | Perry Kemp | Minnesota Vikings | .08 | .04 | .01 |
| ☐ 74 | Erik Howard | Green Bay Packers | .08 | .04 | .01 |
| ☐ 75 | Lamar Lathon | New York Giants | .08 | .04 | .01 |
| ☐ 76 | Greg Kragen | Houston Oilers | .08 | .04 | .01 |
| ☐ 77 | Jay Schroeder | Denver Broncos | .10 | .05 | .01 |
| ☐ 78 | Jim Arnold | Los Angeles Raiders | .08 | .04 | .01 |
| ☐ 79 | Chris Miller | Detroit Lions | .12 | .05 | .02 |
| ☐ 80 | Deron Cherry | Atlanta Falcons | .08 | .04 | .01 |
| ☐ 81 | Jim Harbaugh | Kansas City Chiefs | .10 | .05 | .01 |
| ☐ 82 | Gill Fenerty | Chicago Bears | .08 | .04 | .01 |
| ☐ 83 | Fred Stokes | New Orleans Saints | .08 | .04 | .01 |
| ☐ 84 | Roman Phifer | Washington Redskins | .08 | .04 | .01 |
| ☐ 85 | Clyde Simmons | Los Angeles Rams | .10 | .05 | .01 |
| ☐ 86 | Vince Newsome | Philadelphia Eagles | .08 | .04 | .01 |
| ☐ 87 | Lawrence Dawsey | Cleveland Browns | .12 | .05 | .02 |
| ☐ 88 | Eddie Brown | Tampa Bay Buccaneers | .08 | .04 | .01 |
| ☐ 89 | Greg Montgomery | Cincinnati Bengals | .08 | .04 | .01 |
| ☐ 90 | Jeff Lageman | Houston Oilers | .08 | .04 | .01 |
| ☐ 91 | Terry Wooden | New York Jets | .08 | .04 | .01 |
| ☐ 92 | Nate Newton | Seattle Seahawks | .08 | .04 | .01 |
| ☐ 93 | David Richards | Dallas Cowboys | .08 | .04 | .01 |
| ☐ 94 | Derek Russell | San Diego Chargers | .10 | .05 | .01 |
| ☐ 95 | Steve Jordan | Denver Broncos | .10 | .05 | .01 |
| ☐ 96 | Hugh Millen | Minnesota Vikings | .10 | .05 | .01 |
| ☐ 97 | Mark Duper | New England Patriots | .10 | .05 | .01 |
| ☐ 98 | Sean Landeta | Miami Dolphins | .08 | .04 | .01 |
| ☐ 99 | James Thornton | New York Giants | .08 | .04 | .01 |
| ☐ 100 | Darrell Green | Chicago Bears | .10 | .05 | .01 |
| ☐ 101 | Harris Barton | Washington Redskins | .08 | .04 | .01 |
| ☐ 102 | John Alt | San Francisco 49ers | .08 | .04 | .01 |
| ☐ 103 | Mike Farr | Kansas City Chiefs | .08 | .04 | .01 |
| ☐ 104 | Bob Golic | Detroit Lions | .08 | .04 | .01 |
| ☐ 105 | Gene Atkins | Los Angeles Raiders | .08 | .04 | .01 |
| ☐ 106 | Gary Anderson | New Orleans Saints | .08 | .04 | .01 |
| ☐ 107 | Norm Johnson | Pittsburgh Steelers | .08 | .04 | .01 |
| ☐ 108 | Eugene Daniel | Atlanta Falcons | .08 | .04 | .01 |
| ☐ 109 | Kent Hull | Indianapolis Colts | .08 | .04 | .01 |
| ☐ 110 | John Elway | Buffalo Bills | 1.00 | .45 | .13 |
| ☐ 111 | Rich Camarillo | Denver Broncos | .08 | .04 | .01 |
| ☐ 112 | Charles Wilson | Phoenix Cardinals | .08 | .04 | .01 |
| ☐ 113 | Matt Bahr | Green Bay Packers | .08 | .04 | .01 |
| ☐ 114 | Mark Carrier | New York Giants | .10 | .05 | .01 |
| ☐ 115 | Richmond Webb | Tampa Bay Buccaneers | .10 | .05 | .01 |
| ☐ 116 | Charles Mann | Miami Dolphins | .10 | .05 | .01 |
| ☐ 117 | Tim McGee | Washington Redskins | .08 | .04 | .01 |
| ☐ 118 | Wes Hopkins | Atlanta Falcons | .08 | .04 | .01 |
| ☐ 119 | Mo Lewis | Philadelphia Eagles | .08 | .04 | .01 |
| ☐ 120 | Warren Moon | New York Jets | .35 | .16 | .04 |
| ☐ 121 | Damone Johnson | Houston Oilers | .08 | .04 | .01 |
| ☐ 122 | Kevin Gogan | Los Angeles Rams | .08 | .04 | .01 |
| ☐ 123 | Joey Browner | Dallas Cowboys | .08 | .04 | .01 |
| ☐ 124 | Tommy Kane | Minnesota Vikings | .08 | .04 | .01 |
| ☐ 125 | Vincent Brown | Seattle Seahawks | .08 | .04 | .01 |
| ☐ 126 | Barry Word | New England Patriots | .12 | .05 | .02 |
| ☐ 127 | Michael Brooks | Kansas City Chiefs | .08 | .04 | .01 |
| ☐ 128 | Jumbo Elliott | Denver Broncos | .08 | .04 | .01 |
| ☐ 129 | Marcus Allen | New York Giants | .10 | .05 | .01 |
| ☐ 130 | Tom Waddle | Los Angeles Raiders | .12 | .05 | .02 |
| ☐ 131 | Jim Dombrowski | Chicago Bears | .08 | .04 | .01 |
| ☐ 132 | Aeneas Williams | New Orleans Saints | .08 | .04 | .01 |
| ☐ 133 | Clay Matthews | Phoenix Cardinals | .10 | .05 | .01 |
| ☐ 134 | Thurman Thomas | Cleveland Browns | .75 | .35 | .09 |
| ☐ 135 | Dean Biasucci | Buffalo Bills | .08 | .04 | .01 |
| ☐ 136 | Moe Gardner | Indianapolis Colts | .08 | .04 | .01 |
| ☐ 137 | James Campen | Atlanta Falcons | .08 | .04 | .01 |
| ☐ 138 | Tim Johnson | Green Bay Packers | .08 | .04 | .01 |
| ☐ 139 | Erik Kramer | Washington Redskins | .20 | .09 | .03 |
| ☐ 140 | Keith McCants | Detroit Lions | .08 | .04 | .01 |
| ☐ 141 | John Carney | Tampa Bay Buccaneers | .08 | .04 | .01 |
| ☐ 142 | Tunch Ilkin | San Diego Chargers | .08 | .04 | .01 |
| ☐ 143 | Louis Oliver | Pittsburgh Steelers | .10 | .05 | .01 |
| ☐ 144 | Bill Maas | Miami Dolphins | .08 | .04 | .01 |
| ☐ 145 | Wendell Davis | Kansas City Chiefs | .08 | .04 | .01 |
| ☐ 146 | Pepper Johnson | Chicago Bears | .10 | .05 | .01 |
| ☐ 147 | Howie Long | New York Giants | .10 | .05 | .01 |
| ☐ 148 | Brett Maxie | Los Angeles Raiders | .08 | .04 | .01 |
| ☐ 149 | Tony Casillas | New Orleans Saints | .08 | .04 | .01 |
| ☐ 150 | Michael Carter | Dallas Cowboys | .08 | .04 | .01 |

San Francisco 49ers
| | | | |
|---|---|---|---|
| ☐ 151 Byron Evans | .08 | .04 | .01 |

Philadelphia Eagles
| | | | |
|---|---|---|---|
| ☐ 152 Lorenzo White | .10 | .05 | .01 |

Houston Oilers
| | | | |
|---|---|---|---|
| ☐ 153 Larry Kelm | .08 | .04 | .01 |

Los Angeles Rams
| | | | |
|---|---|---|---|
| ☐ 154 Andy Heck | .08 | .04 | .01 |

Seattle Seahawks
| | | | |
|---|---|---|---|
| ☐ 155 Harry Newsome | .08 | .04 | .01 |

Minnesota Vikings
| | | | |
|---|---|---|---|
| ☐ 156 Chris Singleton | .08 | .04 | .01 |

Indianapolis Colts
| | | | |
|---|---|---|---|
| ☐ 157 Mike Kenn | .10 | .05 | .01 |

Atlanta Falcons
| | | | |
|---|---|---|---|
| ☐ 158 Jeff Faulkner | .08 | .04 | .01 |

Phoenix Cardinals
| | | | |
|---|---|---|---|
| ☐ 159 Ken Lanier | .08 | .04 | .01 |

Denver Broncos
| | | | |
|---|---|---|---|
| ☐ 160 Darryl Talley | .10 | .05 | .01 |

Buffalo Bills
| | | | |
|---|---|---|---|
| ☐ 161 Louie Aguiar | .08 | .04 | .01 |

New York Jets
| | | | |
|---|---|---|---|
| ☐ 162 Danny Copeland | .08 | .04 | .01 |

Washington Redskins
| | | | |
|---|---|---|---|
| ☐ 163 Kevin Porter | .08 | .04 | .01 |

Kansas City Chiefs
| | | | |
|---|---|---|---|
| ☐ 164 Trace Armstrong | .08 | .04 | .01 |

Chicago Bears
| | | | |
|---|---|---|---|
| ☐ 165 Dermontti Dawson | .08 | .04 | .01 |

Pittsburgh Steelers
| | | | |
|---|---|---|---|
| ☐ 166 Fred McAfee | .25 | .11 | .03 |

New Orleans Saints
| | | | |
|---|---|---|---|
| ☐ 167 Ronnie Lott | .12 | .05 | .02 |

Los Angeles Raiders
| | | | |
|---|---|---|---|
| ☐ 168 Tony Mandarich | .08 | .04 | .01 |

Green Bay Packers
| | | | |
|---|---|---|---|
| ☐ 169 Howard Cross | .08 | .04 | .01 |

New York Giants
| | | | |
|---|---|---|---|
| ☐ 170 Vestee Jackson | .08 | .04 | .01 |

Miami Dolphins
| | | | |
|---|---|---|---|
| ☐ 171 Jeff Herrod | .08 | .04 | .01 |

Indianapolis Colts
| | | | |
|---|---|---|---|
| ☐ 172 Randy Hilliard | .08 | .04 | .01 |

Cleveland Browns
| | | | |
|---|---|---|---|
| ☐ 173 Robert Wilson | .08 | .04 | .01 |

Tampa Bay Buccaneers
| | | | |
|---|---|---|---|
| ☐ 174 Joe Walter | .08 | .04 | .01 |

Cincinnati Bengals
| | | | |
|---|---|---|---|
| ☐ 175 Chris Spielman | .10 | .05 | .01 |

Detroit Lions
| | | | |
|---|---|---|---|
| ☐ 176 Darryl Henley | .08 | .04 | .01 |

Los Angeles Rams
| | | | |
|---|---|---|---|
| ☐ 177 Jay Hilgenberg | .10 | .05 | .01 |

Chicago Bears
| | | | |
|---|---|---|---|
| ☐ 178 John Kidd | .08 | .04 | .01 |

San Diego Chargers
| | | | |
|---|---|---|---|
| ☐ 179 Doug Widell | .08 | .04 | .01 |

Denver Broncos
| | | | |
|---|---|---|---|
| ☐ 180 Seth Joyner | .10 | .05 | .01 |

Philadelphia Eagles
| | | | |
|---|---|---|---|
| ☐ 181 Nick Bell | .10 | .05 | .01 |

Los Angeles Raiders
| | | | |
|---|---|---|---|
| ☐ 182 Don Griffin | .08 | .04 | .01 |

San Francisco 49ers
| | | | |
|---|---|---|---|
| ☐ 183 Johnny Meads | .08 | .04 | .01 |

Houston Oilers
| | | | |
|---|---|---|---|
| ☐ 184 Jeff Bostic | .08 | .04 | .01 |

Washington Redskins
| | | | |
|---|---|---|---|
| ☐ 185 Johnny Hector | .08 | .04 | .01 |

New York Jets
| | | | |
|---|---|---|---|
| ☐ 186 Jessie Tuggle | .08 | .04 | .01 |

Atlanta Falcons
| | | | |
|---|---|---|---|
| ☐ 187 Robb Thomas | .08 | .04 | .01 |

Kansas City Chiefs
| | | | |
|---|---|---|---|
| ☐ 188 Shane Conlan | .10 | .05 | .01 |

Buffalo Bills
| | | | |
|---|---|---|---|
| ☐ 189 Michael Zordich | .08 | .04 | .01 |

Phoenix Cardinals
| | | | |
|---|---|---|---|
| ☐ 190 Emmitt Smith | 5.00 | 2.30 | .60 |

Dallas Cowboys
| | | | |
|---|---|---|---|
| ☐ 191 Robert Blackmon | .08 | .04 | .01 |

Seattle Seahawks
| | | | |
|---|---|---|---|
| ☐ 192 Carl Lee | .08 | .04 | .01 |

Minnesota Vikings
| | | | |
|---|---|---|---|
| ☐ 193 Harry Galbreath | .08 | .04 | .01 |

Miami Dolphins
| | | | |
|---|---|---|---|
| ☐ 194 Ed King | .08 | .04 | .01 |

Cleveland Browns
| | | | |
|---|---|---|---|
| ☐ 195 Stan Thomas | .08 | .04 | .01 |

Chicago Bears
| | | | |
|---|---|---|---|
| ☐ 196 Andre Waters | .08 | .04 | .01 |

Philadelphia Eagles
| | | | |
|---|---|---|---|
| ☐ 197 Pat Harlow | .08 | .04 | .01 |

New England Patriots
| | | | |
|---|---|---|---|
| ☐ 198 Zefross Moss | .08 | .04 | .01 |

Indianapolis Colts
| | | | |
|---|---|---|---|
| ☐ 199 Bobby Hebert | .12 | .05 | .02 |

New Orleans Saints
| | | | |
|---|---|---|---|
| ☐ 200 Doug Riesenberg | .08 | .04 | .01 |

New York Giants
| | | | |
|---|---|---|---|
| ☐ 201 Mike Croel | .10 | .05 | .01 |

Denver Broncos
| | | | |
|---|---|---|---|
| ☐ 202 Jeff Jaeger | .08 | .04 | .01 |

Los Angeles Raiders
| | | | |
|---|---|---|---|
| ☐ 203 Gary Plummer | .08 | .04 | .01 |

San Diego Chargers
| | | | |
|---|---|---|---|
| ☐ 204 Chris Jacke | .08 | .04 | .01 |

Green Bay Packers
| | | | |
|---|---|---|---|
| ☐ 205 Neil O'Donnell | 1.00 | .45 | .13 |

Pittsburgh Steelers
| | | | |
|---|---|---|---|
| ☐ 206 Mark Bortz | .08 | .04 | .01 |

Chicago Bears
| | | | |
|---|---|---|---|
| ☐ 207 Tim Barnett | .10 | .05 | .01 |

Kansas City Chiefs
| | | | |
|---|---|---|---|
| ☐ 208 Jerry Ball | .10 | .05 | .01 |

Detroit Lions
| | | | |
|---|---|---|---|
| ☐ 209 Chip Lohmiller | .10 | .05 | .01 |

Washington Redskins
| | | | |
|---|---|---|---|
| ☐ 210 Jim Everett | .08 | .04 | .01 |

Los Angeles Rams
| | | | |
|---|---|---|---|
| ☐ 211 Tim McKyer | .10 | .05 | .01 |

Atlanta Falcons
| | | | |
|---|---|---|---|
| ☐ 212 Aaron Craver | .08 | .04 | .01 |

Miami Dolphins
| | | | |
|---|---|---|---|
| ☐ 213 John L. Williams | .10 | .05 | .01 |

Seattle Seahawks
| | | | |
|---|---|---|---|
| ☐ 214 Simon Fletcher | .10 | .05 | .01 |

Denver Broncos
| | | | |
|---|---|---|---|
| ☐ 215 Walter Reeves | .08 | .04 | .01 |

Phoenix Cardinals
| | | | |
|---|---|---|---|
| ☐ 216 Terance Mathis | .08 | .04 | .01 |

New York Jets
| | | | |
|---|---|---|---|
| ☐ 217 Mike Pitts | .08 | .04 | .01 |

Philadelphia Eagles
| | | | |
|---|---|---|---|
| ☐ 218 Bruce Matthews | .10 | .05 | .01 |

Houston Oilers
| | | | |
|---|---|---|---|
| ☐ 219 Howard Ballard | .08 | .04 | .01 |

Buffalo Bills
| | | | |
|---|---|---|---|
| ☐ 220 Leonard Russell | .60 | .25 | .08 |

New England Patriots
| | | | |
|---|---|---|---|
| ☐ 221 Michael Stewart | .08 | .04 | .01 |

Los Angeles Rams
| | | | |
|---|---|---|---|
| ☐ 222 Mike Merriweather | .08 | .04 | .01 |

Minnesota Vikings
| | | | |
|---|---|---|---|
| ☐ 223 Ricky Sanders | .10 | .05 | .01 |

Washington Redskins
| | | | |
|---|---|---|---|
| ☐ 224 Ray Horton | .08 | .04 | .01 |

Dallas Cowboys
| | | | |
|---|---|---|---|
| ☐ 225 Michael Jackson | .20 | .09 | .03 |

Cleveland Browns
| | | | |
|---|---|---|---|
| ☐ 226 Bill Romanowski | .08 | .04 | .01 |

San Francisco 49ers
| | | | |
|---|---|---|---|
| ☐ 227 Steve McMichael UER | .10 | .05 | .01 |

(His wife is former
Mrs. Illinois, not
Miss Illinois)
Chicago Bears
| | | | |
|---|---|---|---|
| ☐ 228 Chris Martin | .08 | .04 | .01 |

Kansas City Chiefs
| | | | |
|---|---|---|---|
| ☐ 229 Tim Green | .08 | .04 | .01 |

Atlanta Falcons
| | | | |
|---|---|---|---|
| ☐ 230 Karl Mecklenburg | .10 | .05 | .01 |

Denver Broncos
| | | | |
|---|---|---|---|
| ☐ 231 Felix Wright | .08 | .04 | .01 |

Minnesota Vikings
| | | | |
|---|---|---|---|
| ☐ 232 Charles McRae | .08 | .04 | .01 |

Tampa Bay Buccaneers
| | | | |
|---|---|---|---|
| ☐ 233 Pete Stoyanovich | .10 | .05 | .01 |

Miami Dolphins
| | | | |
|---|---|---|---|
| ☐ 234 Stephen Baker | .08 | .04 | .01 |

New York Giants
| | | | |
|---|---|---|---|
| ☐ 235 Herman Moore | .60 | .25 | .08 |

Detroit Lions
| | | | |
|---|---|---|---|
| ☐ 236 Terry McDaniel | .08 | .04 | .01 |

Los Angeles Raiders
| | | | |
|---|---|---|---|
| ☐ 237 Dalton Hilliard | .08 | .04 | .01 |

New Orleans Saints
| | | | |
|---|---|---|---|
| ☐ 238 Gill Byrd | .08 | .04 | .01 |

San Diego Chargers
| | | | |
|---|---|---|---|
| ☐ 239 Leon Seals | .08 | .04 | .01 |

Buffalo Bills
| | | | |
|---|---|---|---|
| ☐ 240 Rod Woodson | .12 | .05 | .02 |

Pittsburgh Steelers
| | | | |
|---|---|---|---|
| ☐ 241 Curtis Duncan | .10 | .05 | .01 |

Houston Oilers
| | | | |
|---|---|---|---|
| ☐ 242 Keith Jackson | .12 | .05 | .02 |

Philadelphia Eagles
| | | | |
|---|---|---|---|
| ☐ 243 Mark Stepnoski | .08 | .04 | .01 |

Dallas Cowboys
| | | | |
|---|---|---|---|
| ☐ 244 Art Monk | .12 | .05 | .02 |

Washington Redskins
| | | | |
|---|---|---|---|
| ☐ 245 Matt Stover | .08 | .04 | .01 |

Cleveland Browns
| | | | |
|---|---|---|---|
| ☐ 246 John Roper | .08 | .04 | .01 |

Chicago Bears

|  |  | | | |
|---|---|---|---|---|
| ☐ 247 | Rodney Hampton — New York Giants | .75 | .35 | .09 |
| ☐ 248 | Steve Wisniewski — Los Angeles Raiders | .08 | .04 | .01 |
| ☐ 249 | Bryan Millard — Seattle Seahawks | .08 | .04 | .01 |
| ☐ 250 | Todd Lyght — Los Angeles Rams | .08 | .04 | .01 |
| ☐ 251 | Marvin Washington — New York Jets | .08 | .04 | .01 |
| ☐ 252 | Eric Swann — Phoenix Cardinals | .10 | .05 | .01 |
| ☐ 253 | Bruce Kozerski — Cincinnati Bengals | .08 | .04 | .01 |
| ☐ 254 | Jon Hand — Indianapolis Colts | .08 | .04 | .01 |
| ☐ 255 | Scott Fulhage — Atlanta Falcons | .08 | .04 | .01 |
| ☐ 256 | Chuck Cecil — Green Bay Packers | .08 | .04 | .01 |
| ☐ 257 | Eric Martin — New Orleans Saints | .10 | .05 | .01 |
| ☐ 258 | Eric Metcalf — Cleveland Browns | .12 | .05 | .02 |
| ☐ 259 | T.J. Turner — Miami Dolphins | .08 | .04 | .01 |
| ☐ 260 | Kirk Lowdermilk — Minnesota Vikings | .08 | .04 | .01 |
| ☐ 261 | Keith McKeller — Buffalo Bills | .08 | .04 | .01 |
| ☐ 262 | Wymon Henderson — Denver Broncos | .08 | .04 | .01 |
| ☐ 263 | David Alexander — Philadelphia Eagles | .08 | .04 | .01 |
| ☐ 264 | George Jamison — Detroit Lions | .08 | .04 | .01 |
| ☐ 265 | Ken Norton Jr. — Dallas Cowboys | .10 | .05 | .01 |
| ☐ 266 | Jim Lachey — Washington Redskins | .08 | .04 | .01 |
| ☐ 267 | Bo Orlando — Houston Oilers | .30 | .14 | .04 |
| ☐ 268 | Nick Lowery — Kansas City Chiefs | .10 | .05 | .01 |
| ☐ 269 | Keith Van Horne — Chicago Bears | .08 | .04 | .01 |
| ☐ 270 | Dwight Stone — Pittsburgh Steelers | .08 | .04 | .01 |
| ☐ 271 | Keith DeLong — San Francisco 49ers | .08 | .04 | .01 |
| ☐ 272 | James Francis — Cincinnati Bengals | .10 | .05 | .01 |
| ☐ 273 | Greg McMurtry — New England Patriots | .08 | .04 | .01 |
| ☐ 274 | Ethan Horton — Los Angeles Raiders | .08 | .04 | .01 |
| ☐ 275 | Stan Brock — New Orleans Saints | .08 | .04 | .01 |
| ☐ 276 | Ken Harvey — Phoenix Cardinals | .08 | .04 | .01 |
| ☐ 277 | Ronnie Harmon — San Diego Chargers | .08 | .04 | .01 |
| ☐ 278 | Mike Pritchard — Atlanta Falcons | .50 | .23 | .06 |
| ☐ 279 | Kyle Clifton — New York Jets | .08 | .04 | .01 |
| ☐ 280 | Anthony Johnson — Indianapolis Colts | .08 | .04 | .01 |
| ☐ 281 | Esera Tuaolo — Green Bay Packers | .08 | .04 | .01 |
| ☐ 282 | Vernon Turner — Buffalo Bills | .08 | .04 | .01 |
| ☐ 283 | David Griggs — Miami Dolphins | .08 | .04 | .01 |
| ☐ 284 | Dino Hackett — Kansas City Chiefs | .08 | .04 | .01 |
| ☐ 285 | Carwell Gardner — Buffalo Bills | .08 | .04 | .01 |
| ☐ 286 | Ron Hall — Tampa Bay Buccaneers | .08 | .04 | .01 |
| ☐ 287 | Reggie White — Philadelphia Eagles | .30 | .14 | .04 |
| ☐ 288 | Checklist 1-100 | .08 | .04 | .01 |
| ☐ 289 | Checklist 101-200 | .08 | .04 | .01 |
| ☐ 290 | Checklist 201-300 | .08 | .04 | .01 |
| ☐ 291 | Mark Clayton MC — Miami Dolphins | .12 | .05 | .02 |
| ☐ 292 | Pat Swilling MC — New Orleans Saints | .12 | .05 | .02 |
| ☐ 293 | Ernest Givins MC — Houston Oilers | .12 | .05 | .02 |
| ☐ 294 | Broderick Thomas MC — Tampa Bay Buccaneers | .10 | .05 | .01 |
| ☐ 295 | John Friesz MC — San Diego Chargers | .12 | .05 | .02 |
| ☐ 296 | Cornelius Bennett MC — Buffalo Bills | .12 | .05 | .02 |
| ☐ 297 | Anthony Carter MC — Minnesota Vikings | .12 | .05 | .02 |
| ☐ 298 | Earnest Byner MC — Washington Redskins | .12 | .05 | .02 |
| ☐ 299 | Michael Irvin MC — Dallas Cowboys | 1.00 | .45 | .13 |
| ☐ 300 | Cortez Kennedy MC — Seattle Seahawks | .15 | .07 | .02 |
| ☐ 301 | Barry Sanders MC — Detroit Lions | 2.00 | .90 | .25 |
| ☐ 302 | Mike Croel MC — Denver Broncos | .12 | .05 | .02 |
| ☐ 303 | Emmitt Smith MC — Dallas Cowboys | 5.00 | 2.30 | .60 |
| ☐ 304 | Leonard Russell MC — New England Patriots | .20 | .09 | .03 |
| ☐ 305 | Neal Anderson MC — Chicago Bears | .12 | .05 | .02 |
| ☐ 306 | Derrick Thomas MC — Kansas City Chiefs | .20 | .09 | .03 |
| ☐ 307 | Mark Rypien MC — Washington Redskins | .12 | .05 | .02 |
| ☐ 308 | Reggie White MC — Philadelphia Eagles | .20 | .09 | .03 |
| ☐ 309 | Rod Woodson MC — Pittsburgh Steelers | .12 | .05 | .02 |
| ☐ 310 | Rodney Hampton MC — New York Giants | .35 | .16 | .04 |
| ☐ 311 | Carnell Lake — Pittsburgh Steelers | .08 | .04 | .01 |
| ☐ 312 | Robert Delpino — Los Angeles Rams | .10 | .05 | .01 |
| ☐ 313 | Brian Blades — Seattle Seahawks | .10 | .05 | .01 |
| ☐ 314 | Marc Spindler — Detroit Lions | .08 | .04 | .01 |
| ☐ 315 | Scott Norwood — Buffalo Bills | .08 | .04 | .01 |
| ☐ 316 | Frank Warren — New Orleans Saints | .08 | .04 | .01 |
| ☐ 317 | David Treadwell — Denver Broncos | .08 | .04 | .01 |
| ☐ 318 | Steve Broussard — Atlanta Falcons | .10 | .05 | .01 |
| ☐ 319 | Lorenzo Lynch — Phoenix Cardinals | .08 | .04 | .01 |
| ☐ 320 | Ray Agnew — New England Patriots | .08 | .04 | .01 |
| ☐ 321 | Derrick Walker — San Diego Chargers | .08 | .04 | .01 |
| ☐ 322 | Vinson Smith — Dallas Cowboys | .20 | .09 | .03 |
| ☐ 323 | Gary Clark — Washington Redskins | .10 | .05 | .01 |
| ☐ 324 | Charles Haley — San Francisco 49ers | .10 | .05 | .01 |
| ☐ 325 | Keith Byars — Philadelphia Eagles | .10 | .05 | .01 |
| ☐ 326 | Winston Moss — Los Angeles Raiders | .08 | .04 | .01 |
| ☐ 327 | Paul McJulien UER (Has Brett Perriman card back; see also 453) — Green Bay Packers | .08 | .04 | .01 |
| ☐ 328 | Tony Covington — Tampa Bay Buccaneers | .08 | .04 | .01 |
| ☐ 329 | Mark Carrier — Chicago Bears | .10 | .05 | .01 |
| ☐ 330 | Mark Tuinei — Dallas Cowboys | .08 | .04 | .01 |
| ☐ 331 | Tracy Simien — Kansas City Chiefs | .25 | .11 | .03 |
| ☐ 332 | Jeff Wright — Buffalo Bills | .08 | .04 | .01 |
| ☐ 333 | Bryan Cox — Miami Dolphins | .10 | .05 | .01 |
| ☐ 334 | Lonnie Young — New York Jets | .08 | .04 | .01 |
| ☐ 335 | Clarence Verdin — Indianapolis Colts | .08 | .04 | .01 |
| ☐ 336 | Dan Fike — Cleveland Browns | .08 | .04 | .01 |
| ☐ 337 | Steve Sewell — Denver Broncos | .08 | .04 | .01 |
| ☐ 338 | Gary Zimmerman — Minnesota Vikings | .08 | .04 | .01 |
| ☐ 339 | Barney Bussey — Cincinnati Bengals | .08 | .04 | .01 |
| ☐ 340 | William Perry — Chicago Bears | .10 | .05 | .01 |
| ☐ 341 | Jeff Hostetler — New York Giants | .30 | .14 | .04 |
| ☐ 342 | Doug Smith — Houston Oilers | .08 | .04 | .01 |
| ☐ 343 | Cleveland Gary — Los Angeles Rams | .10 | .05 | .01 |
| ☐ 344 | Todd Marinovich | .08 | .04 | .01 |

| | | | | |
|---|---|---|---|---|
| Los Angeles Raiders | | | | |
| ☐ 345 Rich Moran | .08 | .04 | .01 |
| Green Bay Packers | | | | |
| ☐ 346 Tony Woods | .08 | .04 | .01 |
| Seattle Seahawks | | | | |
| ☐ 347 Vaughan Johnson | .10 | .05 | .01 |
| New Orleans Saints | | | | |
| ☐ 348 Marv Cook | .10 | .05 | .01 |
| New England Patriots | | | | |
| ☐ 349 Pierce Holt | .08 | .04 | .01 |
| San Francisco 49ers | | | | |
| ☐ 350 Gerald Williams | .08 | .04 | .01 |
| Pittsburgh Steelers | | | | |
| ☐ 351 Kevin Butler | .08 | .04 | .01 |
| Chicago Bears | | | | |
| ☐ 352 William White | .08 | .04 | .01 |
| Detroit Lions | | | | |
| ☐ 353 Henry Rolling | .08 | .04 | .01 |
| San Diego Chargers | | | | |
| ☐ 354 James Joseph | .08 | .04 | .01 |
| Philadelphia Eagles | | | | |
| ☐ 355 Vinny Testaverde | .12 | .05 | .02 |
| Tampa Bay Buccaneers | | | | |
| ☐ 356 Scott Radecic | .08 | .04 | .01 |
| Indianapolis Colts | | | | |
| ☐ 357 Lee Johnson | .08 | .04 | .01 |
| Cincinnati Bengals | | | | |
| ☐ 358 Steve Tasker | .10 | .05 | .01 |
| Buffalo Bills | | | | |
| ☐ 359 David Lutz | .08 | .04 | .01 |
| Kansas City Chiefs | | | | |
| ☐ 360 Audray McMillian UER | .08 | .04 | .01 |
| (Name on back | | | | |
| misspelled Audrey) | | | | |
| Minnesota Vikings | | | | |
| ☐ 361 Brad Baxter | .10 | .05 | .01 |
| New York Jets | | | | |
| ☐ 362 Mark Dennis | .08 | .04 | .01 |
| Miami Dolphins | | | | |
| ☐ 363 Erric Pegram | .75 | .35 | .09 |
| Atlanta Falcons | | | | |
| ☐ 364 Sean Jones | .08 | .04 | .01 |
| Houston Oilers | | | | |
| ☐ 365 William Roberts | .08 | .04 | .01 |
| New York Giants | | | | |
| ☐ 366 Steve Young | .75 | .35 | .09 |
| San Francisco 49ers | | | | |
| ☐ 367 Joe Jacoby | .08 | .04 | .01 |
| Washington Redskins | | | | |
| ☐ 368 Richard Brown | .08 | .04 | .01 |
| Cleveland Browns | | | | |
| ☐ 369 Keith Kartz | .08 | .04 | .01 |
| Denver Broncos | | | | |
| ☐ 370 Freddie Joe Nunn | .08 | .04 | .01 |
| Phoenix Cardinals | | | | |
| ☐ 371 Darren Comeaux | .08 | .04 | .01 |
| Seattle Seahawks | | | | |
| ☐ 372 Larry Brown | .08 | .04 | .01 |
| Dallas Cowboys | | | | |
| ☐ 373 Haywood Jeffires | .12 | .05 | .02 |
| Houston Oilers | | | | |
| ☐ 374 Tom Newberry | .08 | .04 | .01 |
| Los Angeles Rams | | | | |
| ☐ 375 Steve Bono | 1.00 | .45 | .13 |
| San Francisco 49ers | | | | |
| ☐ 376 Kevin Ross | .10 | .05 | .01 |
| Kansas City Chiefs | | | | |
| ☐ 377 Kelvin Pritchett | .08 | .04 | .01 |
| Detroit Lions | | | | |
| ☐ 378 Jessie Hester | .08 | .04 | .01 |
| Indianapolis Colts | | | | |
| ☐ 379 Mitchell Price | .08 | .04 | .01 |
| Cincinnati Bengals | | | | |
| ☐ 380 Barry Foster | .75 | .35 | .09 |
| Pittsburgh Steelers | | | | |
| ☐ 381 Reyna Thompson | .08 | .04 | .01 |
| New York Giants | | | | |
| ☐ 382 Cris Carter | .12 | .05 | .02 |
| Minnesota Vikings | | | | |
| ☐ 383 Lemuel Stinson | .08 | .04 | .01 |
| Chicago Bears | | | | |
| ☐ 384 Rod Bernstine | .10 | .05 | .01 |
| San Diego Chargers | | | | |
| ☐ 385 James Lofton | .12 | .05 | .02 |
| Buffalo Bills | | | | |
| ☐ 386 Kevin Murphy | .08 | .04 | .01 |
| Tampa Bay Buccaneers | | | | |
| ☐ 387 Greg Townsend | .08 | .04 | .01 |
| Los Angeles Raiders | | | | |
| ☐ 388 Edgar Bennett | .60 | .25 | .08 |
| Green Bay Packers | | | | |
| ☐ 389 Rob Moore | .12 | .05 | .02 |
| New York Jets | | | | |
| ☐ 390 Eugene Lockhart | .08 | .04 | .01 |
| New England Patriots | | | | |
| ☐ 391 Bern Brostek | .08 | .04 | .01 |
| Los Angeles Rams | | | | |
| ☐ 392 Craig Heyward | .08 | .04 | .01 |

| | | | | |
|---|---|---|---|---|
| New Orleans Saints | | | | |
| ☐ 393 Ferrell Edmunds | .08 | .04 | .01 |
| Miami Dolphins | | | | |
| ☐ 394 John Kasay | .08 | .04 | .01 |
| Seattle Seahawks | | | | |
| ☐ 395 Jesse Sapolu | .08 | .04 | .01 |
| San Francisco 49ers | | | | |
| ☐ 396 Jim Breech | .08 | .04 | .01 |
| Cincinnati Bengals | | | | |
| ☐ 397 Neil Smith | .12 | .05 | .02 |
| Kansas City Chiefs | | | | |
| ☐ 398 Bryce Paup | .08 | .04 | .01 |
| Green Bay Packers | | | | |
| ☐ 399 Tony Tolbert | .08 | .04 | .01 |
| Dallas Cowboys | | | | |
| ☐ 400 Bubby Brister | .10 | .05 | .01 |
| Pittsburgh Steelers | | | | |
| ☐ 401 Dennis Smith | .10 | .05 | .01 |
| Denver Broncos | | | | |
| ☐ 402 Dan Owens | .08 | .04 | .01 |
| Detroit Lions | | | | |
| ☐ 403 Steve Beuerlein | .35 | .16 | .04 |
| Dallas Cowboys | | | | |
| ☐ 404 Rick Tuten | .08 | .04 | .01 |
| Seattle Seahawks | | | | |
| ☐ 405 Eric Allen | .10 | .05 | .01 |
| Philadelphia Eagles | | | | |
| ☐ 406 Eric Hill | .08 | .04 | .01 |
| Phoenix Cardinals | | | | |
| ☐ 407 Don Warren | .08 | .04 | .01 |
| Washington Redskins | | | | |
| ☐ 408 Greg Jackson | .08 | .04 | .01 |
| New York Giants | | | | |
| ☐ 409 Chris Doleman | .10 | .05 | .01 |
| Minnesota Vikings | | | | |
| ☐ 410 Anthony Munoz | .10 | .05 | .01 |
| Cincinnati Bengals | | | | |
| ☐ 411 Michael Young | .08 | .04 | .01 |
| Denver Broncos | | | | |
| ☐ 412 Cornelius Bennett | .12 | .05 | .02 |
| Buffalo Bills | | | | |
| ☐ 413 Ray Childress | .10 | .05 | .01 |
| Houston Oilers | | | | |
| ☐ 414 Kevin Call | .08 | .04 | .01 |
| Indianapolis Colts | | | | |
| ☐ 415 Burt Grossman | .08 | .04 | .01 |
| San Diego Chargers | | | | |
| ☐ 416 Scott Miller | .08 | .04 | .01 |
| Miami Dolphins | | | | |
| ☐ 417 Tim Newton | .08 | .04 | .01 |
| Tampa Bay Buccaneers | | | | |
| ☐ 418 Robert Young | .10 | .05 | .01 |
| Los Angeles Rams | | | | |
| ☐ 419 Tommy Vardell | .50 | .23 | .06 |
| Cleveland Browns | | | | |
| ☐ 420 Michael Walter | .08 | .04 | .01 |
| San Francisco 49ers | | | | |
| ☐ 421 Chris Port | .12 | .05 | .02 |
| New Orleans Saints | | | | |
| ☐ 422 Carlton Haselrig | .20 | .09 | .03 |
| Pittsburgh Steelers | | | | |
| ☐ 423 Rodney Peete | .10 | .05 | .01 |
| Detroit Lions | | | | |
| ☐ 424 Scott Stephen | .08 | .04 | .01 |
| Green Bay Packers | | | | |
| ☐ 425 Chris Warren | .40 | .18 | .05 |
| Seattle Seahawks | | | | |
| ☐ 426 Scott Galbraith | .08 | .04 | .01 |
| Cleveland Browns | | | | |
| ☐ 427 Fuad Reveiz UER | .08 | .04 | .01 |
| (Born in Colombia, | | | | |
| not Columbia) | | | | |
| Minnesota Vikings | | | | |
| ☐ 428 Irv Eatman | .08 | .04 | .01 |
| New York Jets | | | | |
| ☐ 429 David Szott | .08 | .04 | .01 |
| Kansas City Chiefs | | | | |
| ☐ 430 Brent Williams | .08 | .04 | .01 |
| New England Patriots | | | | |
| ☐ 431 Mike Horan | .08 | .04 | .01 |
| Denver Broncos | | | | |
| ☐ 432 Brent Jones | .12 | .05 | .02 |
| San Francisco 49ers | | | | |
| ☐ 433 Paul Gruber | .08 | .04 | .01 |
| Tampa Bay Buccaneers | | | | |
| ☐ 434 Carlos Huerta | .08 | .04 | .01 |
| San Diego Chargers | | | | |
| ☐ 435 Scott Case | .08 | .04 | .01 |
| Atlanta Falcons | | | | |
| ☐ 436 Greg Davis | .08 | .04 | .01 |
| Phoenix Cardinals | | | | |
| ☐ 437 Ken Clarke | .08 | .04 | .01 |
| Minnesota Vikings | | | | |
| ☐ 438 Alfred Williams | .08 | .04 | .01 |
| Cincinnati Bengals | | | | |
| ☐ 439 Jim C. Jensen | .08 | .04 | .01 |
| Miami Dolphins | | | | |
| ☐ 440 Louis Lipps | .10 | .05 | .01 |

| | | | |
|---|---|---|---|
| Pittsburgh Steelers | | | |
| ☐ 441 Larry Roberts | .08 | .04 | .01 |
| San Francisco 49ers | | | |
| ☐ 442 James Jones | .08 | .04 | .01 |
| Cleveland Browns | | | |
| ☐ 443 Don Mosebar | .08 | .04 | .01 |
| Los Angeles Raiders | | | |
| ☐ 444 Quinn Early | .10 | .05 | .01 |
| New Orleans Saints | | | |
| ☐ 445 Robert Brown | .08 | .04 | .01 |
| Green Bay Packers | | | |
| ☐ 446 Tom Thayer | .08 | .04 | .01 |
| Chicago Bears | | | |
| ☐ 447 Michael Irvin | 1.25 | .55 | .16 |
| Dallas Cowboys | | | |
| ☐ 448 Jarrod Bunch | .08 | .04 | .01 |
| New York Giants | | | |
| ☐ 449 Riki Ellison | .08 | .04 | .01 |
| Los Angeles Raiders | | | |
| ☐ 450 Joe Phillips | .08 | .04 | .01 |
| San Diego Chargers | | | |
| ☐ 451 Ernest Givins | .10 | .05 | .01 |
| Houston Oilers | | | |
| ☐ 452 Glenn Parker | .08 | .04 | .01 |
| Buffalo Bills | | | |
| ☐ 453 Brett Perriman UER | .20 | .09 | .03 |
| (Has Paul McJulien | | | |
| card back; see also 327) | | | |
| Detroit Lions | | | |
| ☐ 454 Jayice Pearson | .08 | .04 | .01 |
| Kansas City Chiefs | | | |
| ☐ 455 Mark Jackson | .10 | .05 | .01 |
| Denver Broncos | | | |
| ☐ 456 Siran Stacy | .20 | .09 | .03 |
| Philadelphia Eagles | | | |
| ☐ 457 Rufus Porter | .08 | .04 | .01 |
| Seattle Seahawks | | | |
| ☐ 458 Michael Ball | .08 | .04 | .01 |
| Indianapolis Colts | | | |
| ☐ 459 Craig Taylor | .08 | .04 | .01 |
| Cincinnati Bengals | | | |
| ☐ 460 George Thomas | .15 | .07 | .02 |
| Atlanta Falcons | | | |
| ☐ 461 Alvin Wright | .08 | .04 | .01 |
| Los Angeles Rams | | | |
| ☐ 462 Ron Hallstrom | .08 | .04 | .01 |
| Green Bay Packers | | | |
| ☐ 463 Mike Mooney | .20 | .09 | .03 |
| Houston Oilers | | | |
| ☐ 464 Dexter Carter | .10 | .05 | .01 |
| San Francisco 49ers | | | |
| ☐ 465 Marty Carter | .40 | .18 | .05 |
| Tampa Bay Buccaneers | | | |
| ☐ 466 Pat Swilling | .10 | .05 | .01 |
| New Orleans Saints | | | |
| ☐ 467 Mike Golic | .08 | .04 | .01 |
| Philadelphia Eagles | | | |
| ☐ 468 Reggie Roby | .08 | .04 | .01 |
| Miami Dolphins | | | |
| ☐ 469 Randall McDaniel | .08 | .04 | .01 |
| Minnesota Vikings | | | |
| ☐ 470 John Stephens | .10 | .05 | .01 |
| New England Patriots | | | |
| ☐ 471 Ricardo McDonald | .15 | .07 | .02 |
| Cincinnati Bengals | | | |
| ☐ 472 Wilber Marshall | .10 | .05 | .01 |
| Washington Redskins | | | |
| ☐ 473 Jim Sweeney | .08 | .04 | .01 |
| New York Jets | | | |
| ☐ 474 Ernie Jones | .08 | .04 | .01 |
| Phoenix Cardinals | | | |
| ☐ 475 Bennie Blades | .08 | .04 | .01 |
| Detroit Lions | | | |
| ☐ 476 Don Beebe | .12 | .05 | .02 |
| Buffalo Bills | | | |
| ☐ 477 Grant Feasel | .08 | .04 | .01 |
| Seattle Seahawks | | | |
| ☐ 478 Ernie Mills | .08 | .04 | .01 |
| Pittsburgh Steelers | | | |
| ☐ 479 Tony Jones | .08 | .04 | .01 |
| Cleveland Browns | | | |
| ☐ 480 Jeff Uhlenhake | .08 | .04 | .01 |
| Miami Dolphins | | | |
| ☐ 481 Gaston Green | .10 | .05 | .01 |
| Denver Broncos | | | |
| ☐ 482 John Taylor | .12 | .05 | .02 |
| San Francisco 49ers | | | |
| ☐ 483 Anthony Smith | .10 | .05 | .01 |
| Los Angeles Raiders | | | |
| ☐ 484 Tony Bennett | .10 | .05 | .01 |
| Green Bay Packers | | | |
| ☐ 485 David Brandon | .08 | .04 | .01 |
| Cleveland Browns | | | |
| ☐ 486 Shawn Jefferson | .08 | .04 | .01 |
| San Diego Chargers | | | |
| ☐ 487 Christian Okoye | .10 | .05 | .01 |
| Kansas City Chiefs | | | |
| ☐ 488 Leonard Marshall | .10 | .05 | .01 |

| | | | |
|---|---|---|---|
| New York Giants | | | |
| ☐ 489 Jay Novacek | .25 | .11 | .03 |
| Dallas Cowboys | | | |
| ☐ 490 Harold Green | .10 | .05 | .01 |
| Cincinnati Bengals | | | |
| ☐ 491 Bubba McDowell | .08 | .04 | .01 |
| Houston Oilers | | | |
| ☐ 492 Gary Anderson | .10 | .05 | .01 |
| Tampa Bay Buccaneers | | | |
| ☐ 493 Terrell Buckley | .50 | .23 | .06 |
| Green Bay Packers | | | |
| ☐ 494 Jamie Dukes | .08 | .04 | .01 |
| Atlanta Falcons | | | |
| ☐ 495 Morten Andersen | .10 | .05 | .01 |
| New Orleans Saints | | | |
| ☐ 496 Henry Thomas | .08 | .04 | .01 |
| Minnesota Vikings | | | |
| ☐ 497 Bill Lewis | .08 | .04 | .01 |
| Phoenix Cardinals | | | |
| ☐ 498 Jeff Cross | .08 | .04 | .01 |
| Miami Dolphins | | | |
| ☐ 499 Hardy Nickerson | .10 | .05 | .01 |
| Pittsburgh Steelers | | | |
| ☐ 500 Henry Ellard | .08 | .04 | .01 |
| Los Angeles Rams | | | |
| ☐ 501 Joe Bowden | .08 | .04 | .01 |
| Houston Oilers | | | |
| ☐ 502 Brian Noble | .08 | .04 | .01 |
| Green Bay Packers | | | |
| ☐ 503 Mike Cofer | .08 | .04 | .01 |
| San Francisco 49ers | | | |
| ☐ 504 Jeff Bryant | .08 | .04 | .01 |
| Seattle Seahawks | | | |
| ☐ 505 Lomas Brown | .08 | .04 | .01 |
| Detroit Lions | | | |
| ☐ 506 Chip Banks | .08 | .04 | .01 |
| Indianapolis Colts | | | |
| ☐ 507 Keith Traylor | .08 | .04 | .01 |
| Denver Broncos | | | |
| ☐ 508 Mark Kelso | .08 | .04 | .01 |
| Buffalo Bills | | | |
| ☐ 509 Dexter McNabb | .08 | .04 | .01 |
| Green Bay Packers | | | |
| ☐ 510 Gene Chilton | .08 | .04 | .01 |
| New England Patriots | | | |
| ☐ 511 George Thornton | .08 | .04 | .01 |
| San Diego Chargers | | | |
| ☐ 512 Jeff Criswell | .08 | .04 | .01 |
| New York Jets | | | |
| ☐ 513 Brad Edwards | .08 | .04 | .01 |
| Washington Redskins | | | |
| ☐ 514 Ron Heller | .08 | .04 | .01 |
| Philadelphia Eagles | | | |
| ☐ 515 Tim Brown | .40 | .18 | .05 |
| Los Angeles Raiders | | | |
| ☐ 516 Keith Hamilton | .25 | .11 | .03 |
| New York Giants | | | |
| ☐ 517 Mark Higgs | .15 | .07 | .02 |
| Miami Dolphins | | | |
| ☐ 518 Tommy Barnhardt | .08 | .04 | .01 |
| New Orleans Saints | | | |
| ☐ 519 Brian Jordan | .10 | .05 | .01 |
| Atlanta Falcons | | | |
| ☐ 520 Ray Crockett | .08 | .04 | .01 |
| Detroit Lions | | | |
| ☐ 521 Karl Wilson | .08 | .04 | .01 |
| Los Angeles Rams | | | |
| ☐ 522 Ricky Reynolds | .08 | .04 | .01 |
| Tampa Bay Buccaneers | | | |
| ☐ 523 Max Montoya | .08 | .04 | .01 |
| Los Angeles Raiders | | | |
| ☐ 524 David Little | .08 | .04 | .01 |
| Detroit Lions | | | |
| ☐ 525 Alonzo Mitz | .08 | .04 | .01 |
| Cincinnati Bengals | | | |
| ☐ 526 Darryll Lewis | .08 | .04 | .01 |
| Houston Oilers | | | |
| ☐ 527 Keith Henderson | .08 | .04 | .01 |
| San Francisco 49ers | | | |
| ☐ 528 LeRoy Butler | .08 | .04 | .01 |
| Green Bay Packers | | | |
| ☐ 529 Rob Burnett | .08 | .04 | .01 |
| Cleveland Browns | | | |
| ☐ 530 Chris Chandler | .10 | .05 | .01 |
| Phoenix Cardinals | | | |
| ☐ 531 Maury Buford | .08 | .04 | .01 |
| Chicago Bears | | | |
| ☐ 532 Mark Ingram | .10 | .05 | .01 |
| New York Giants | | | |
| ☐ 533 Mike Saxon | .08 | .04 | .01 |
| Dallas Cowboys | | | |
| ☐ 534 Bill Fralic | .08 | .04 | .01 |
| Atlanta Falcons | | | |
| ☐ 535 Craig Patterson | .08 | .04 | .01 |
| Phoenix Cardinals | | | |
| ☐ 536 John Randle | .08 | .04 | .01 |
| Minnesota Vikings | | | |
| ☐ 537 Dwayne Harper | .08 | .04 | .01 |

| | | | |
|---|---|---|---|
| Seattle Seahawks | | | |
| ☐ 538 Chris Hakel | .15 | .07 | .02 |
| Washington Redskins | | | |
| ☐ 539 Maurice Hurst | .08 | .04 | .01 |
| New England Patriots | | | |
| ☐ 540 Warren Powers UER | .08 | .04 | .01 |
| Denver Broncos | | | |
| (Front has photo of Ron Holmes) | | | |
| ☐ 541 Will Wolford | .08 | .04 | .01 |
| Buffalo Bills | | | |
| ☐ 542 Dennis Gibson | .08 | .04 | .01 |
| Detroit Lions | | | |
| ☐ 543 Jackie Slater | .10 | .05 | .01 |
| Los Angeles Rams | | | |
| ☐ 544 Floyd Turner | .08 | .04 | .01 |
| New Orleans Saints | | | |
| ☐ 545 Guy McIntyre | .10 | .05 | .01 |
| San Francisco 49ers | | | |
| ☐ 546 Eric Green | .12 | .05 | .02 |
| Pittsburgh Steelers | | | |
| ☐ 547 Rohn Stark | .08 | .04 | .01 |
| Indianapolis Colts | | | |
| ☐ 548 William Fuller | .08 | .04 | .01 |
| Houston Oilers | | | |
| ☐ 549 Alvin Harper | .60 | .25 | .08 |
| Dallas Cowboys | | | |
| ☐ 550 Mark Clayton | .10 | .05 | .01 |
| Miami Dolphins | | | |
| ☐ 551 Natu Tuatagaloa | .20 | .09 | .03 |
| Cincinnati Bengals | | | |
| ☐ 552 Fred Barnett | .12 | .05 | .02 |
| Philadelphia Eagles | | | |
| ☐ 553 Bob Whitfield | .20 | .09 | .03 |
| Atlanta Falcons | | | |
| ☐ 554 Courtney Hall | .08 | .04 | .01 |
| San Diego Chargers | | | |
| ☐ 555 Brian Mitchell | .10 | .05 | .01 |
| Washington Redskins | | | |
| ☐ 556 Patrick Hunter | .08 | .04 | .01 |
| Seattle Seahawks | | | |
| ☐ 557 Rick Bryan | .08 | .04 | .01 |
| Atlanta Falcons | | | |
| ☐ 558 Anthony Carter | .10 | .05 | .01 |
| Minnesota Vikings | | | |
| ☐ 559 Jim Wahler | .08 | .04 | .01 |
| Phoenix Cardinals | | | |
| ☐ 560 Joe Morris | .10 | .05 | .01 |
| Cleveland Browns | | | |
| ☐ 561 Tony Zendejas | .08 | .04 | .01 |
| Los Angeles Rams | | | |
| ☐ 562 Mervyn Fernandez | .08 | .04 | .01 |
| Los Angeles Raiders | | | |
| ☐ 563 Jamie Williams | .08 | .04 | .01 |
| San Francisco 49ers | | | |
| ☐ 564 Darrell Thompson | .10 | .05 | .01 |
| Green Bay Packers | | | |
| ☐ 565 Adrian Cooper | .08 | .04 | .01 |
| Pittsburgh Steelers | | | |
| ☐ 566 Chris Goode | .08 | .04 | .01 |
| Indianapolis Colts | | | |
| ☐ 567 Jeff Davidson | .08 | .04 | .01 |
| Denver Broncos | | | |
| ☐ 568 James Hasty | .08 | .04 | .01 |
| New York Jets | | | |
| ☐ 569 Chris Mims | .40 | .18 | .05 |
| San Diego Chargers | | | |
| ☐ 570 Ray Seals | .20 | .09 | .03 |
| Tampa Bay Buccaneers | | | |
| ☐ 571 Myron Guyton | .08 | .04 | .01 |
| New York Giants | | | |
| ☐ 572 Todd McNair | .08 | .04 | .01 |
| Kansas City Chiefs | | | |
| ☐ 573 Andre Tippett | .10 | .05 | .01 |
| New England Patriots | | | |
| ☐ 574 Kirby Jackson | .08 | .04 | .01 |
| Buffalo Bills | | | |
| ☐ 575 Mel Gray | .10 | .05 | .01 |
| Detroit Lions | | | |
| ☐ 576 Stephone Paige | .10 | .05 | .01 |
| Kansas City Chiefs | | | |
| ☐ 577 Scott Davis | .08 | .04 | .01 |
| Los Angeles Raiders | | | |
| ☐ 578 John Gesek | .08 | .04 | .01 |
| Dallas Cowboys | | | |
| ☐ 579 Earnest Byner | .10 | .05 | .01 |
| Washington Redskins | | | |
| ☐ 580 John Friesz | .10 | .05 | .01 |
| San Diego Chargers | | | |
| ☐ 581 Al Smith | .08 | .04 | .01 |
| Houston Oilers | | | |
| ☐ 582 Flipper Anderson | .10 | .05 | .01 |
| Los Angeles Rams | | | |
| ☐ 583 Amp Lee | .50 | .23 | .06 |
| San Francisco 49ers | | | |
| ☐ 584 Greg Lloyd | .08 | .04 | .01 |
| Pittsburgh Steelers | | | |
| ☐ 585 Cortez Kennedy | .20 | .09 | .03 |
| Seattle Seahawks | | | |

| | | | |
|---|---|---|---|
| ☐ 586 Keith Sims | .08 | .04 | .01 |
| Miami Dolphins | | | |
| ☐ 587 Terry Allen | .35 | .16 | .04 |
| Minnesota Vikings | | | |
| ☐ 588 David Fulcher | .08 | .04 | .01 |
| Cincinnati Bengals | | | |
| ☐ 589 Chris Hinton | .08 | .04 | .01 |
| Indianapolis Colts | | | |
| ☐ 590 Tim McDonald | .10 | .05 | .01 |
| Phoenix Cardinals | | | |
| ☐ 591 Bruce Armstrong | .08 | .04 | .01 |
| New England Patriots | | | |
| ☐ 592 Sterling Sharpe | 1.25 | .55 | .16 |
| Green Bay Packers | | | |
| ☐ 593 Tom Rathman | .10 | .05 | .01 |
| San Francisco 49ers | | | |
| ☐ 594 Bill Brooks | .10 | .05 | .01 |
| Indianapolis Colts | | | |
| ☐ 595 Broderick Thomas | .08 | .04 | .01 |
| Tampa Bay Buccaneers | | | |
| ☐ 596 Jim Wilks | .08 | .04 | .01 |
| New Orleans Saints | | | |
| ☐ 597 Tyrone Braxton UER | .08 | .04 | .01 |
| (Bio for Melvin Braxton) | | | |
| Denver Broncos | | | |
| ☐ 598 Checklist 301-400 UER | .08 | .04 | .01 |
| (Audray McMillian is | | | |
| misspelled Audrey) | | | |
| ☐ 599 Checklist 401-500 | .08 | .04 | .01 |
| ☐ 600 Checklist 501-600 | .08 | .04 | .01 |
| ☐ 601 Andre Reed MC | .75 | .35 | .09 |
| Buffalo Bills | | | |
| ☐ 602 Troy Aikman MC | 8.00 | 3.60 | 1.00 |
| Dallas Cowboys | | | |
| ☐ 603 Dan Marino MC | 5.00 | 2.30 | .60 |
| Miami Dolphins | | | |
| ☐ 604 Randall Cunningham MC | .75 | .35 | .09 |
| Philadelphia Eagles | | | |
| ☐ 605 Jim Kelly MC | 2.00 | .90 | .25 |
| Buffalo Bills | | | |
| ☐ 606 Deion Sanders MC | 1.25 | .55 | .16 |
| Atlanta Falcons | | | |
| ☐ 607 Junior Seau MC | 1.00 | .45 | .13 |
| San Diego Chargers | | | |
| ☐ 608 Jerry Rice MC | 4.00 | 1.80 | .50 |
| San Francisco 49ers | | | |
| ☐ 609 Bruce Smith MC | .75 | .35 | .09 |
| Buffalo Bills | | | |
| ☐ 610 Lawrence Taylor MC | 1.00 | .45 | .13 |
| New York Giants | | | |
| ☐ 611 Todd Collins | .75 | .35 | .09 |
| New England Patriots | | | |
| ☐ 612 Ty Detmer | .60 | .25 | .08 |
| Green Bay Packers | | | |
| ☐ 613 Browning Nagle | .60 | .25 | .08 |
| New York Jets | | | |
| ☐ 614 Tony Sacca UER | .75 | .35 | .09 |
| (Reverse negative | | | |
| photo on back) | | | |
| Phoenix Cardinals | | | |
| ☐ 615 Boomer Esiason | .75 | .35 | .09 |
| Cincinnati Bengals | | | |
| ☐ 616 Billy Joe Tolliver | .75 | .35 | .09 |
| Atlanta Falcons | | | |
| ☐ 617 Leslie O'Neal | .60 | .25 | .08 |
| San Diego Chargers | | | |
| ☐ 618 Mark Wheeler | .60 | .25 | .08 |
| Tampa Bay Buccaneers | | | |
| ☐ 619 Eric Dickerson | .75 | .35 | .09 |
| Los Angeles Raiders | | | |
| ☐ 620 Phil Simms | .75 | .35 | .09 |
| New York Giants | | | |
| ☐ 621 Troy Vincent | .50 | .23 | .06 |
| Miami Dolphins | | | |
| ☐ 622 Jason Hanson | .60 | .25 | .08 |
| Detroit Lions | | | |
| ☐ 623 Andre Reed | .75 | .35 | .09 |
| Buffalo Bills | | | |
| ☐ 624 Russell Maryland | 1.00 | .45 | .13 |
| Dallas Cowboys | | | |
| ☐ 625 Steve Emtman | .75 | .35 | .09 |
| Indianapolis Colts | | | |
| ☐ 626 Sean Gilbert | 2.00 | .90 | .25 |
| Los Angeles Rams | | | |
| ☐ 627 Dana Hall | 1.00 | .45 | .13 |
| San Francisco 49ers | | | |
| ☐ 628 Dan McGwire | .60 | .25 | .08 |
| Seattle Seahawks | | | |
| ☐ 629 Lewis Billups | .50 | .23 | .06 |
| Green Bay Packers | | | |
| ☐ 630 Darryl Williams | 1.25 | .55 | .16 |
| Cincinnati Bengals | | | |
| ☐ 631 Dwayne Sabb | .75 | .35 | .09 |
| New England Patriots | | | |
| ☐ 632 Mark Royals | .50 | .23 | .06 |
| Pittsburgh Steelers | | | |
| ☐ 633 Cary Conklin | .75 | .35 | .09 |

Washington Redskins
| | | | | |
|---|---|---|---|---|
| ☐ 634 | Al Toon | .75 | .35 | .09 |

New York Jets
| | | | | |
|---|---|---|---|---|
| ☐ 635 | Junior Seau | 1.50 | .65 | .19 |

San Diego Chargers
| | | | | |
|---|---|---|---|---|
| ☐ 636 | Greg Skrepenak UER | .75 | .35 | .09 |

(Card misnumbered 686)
Los Angeles Raiders
| | | | | |
|---|---|---|---|---|
| ☐ 637 | Deion Sanders | 1.50 | .65 | .19 |

Atlanta Falcons
| | | | | |
|---|---|---|---|---|
| ☐ 638 | Steve DeOssie | .50 | .23 | .06 |

New York Giants
| | | | | |
|---|---|---|---|---|
| ☐ 639 | Randall Cunningham | 1.00 | .45 | .13 |

Philadelphia Eagles
| | | | | |
|---|---|---|---|---|
| ☐ 640 | Jim Kelly | 2.00 | .90 | .25 |

Buffalo Bills
| | | | | |
|---|---|---|---|---|
| ☐ 641 | Michael Brandon | .75 | .35 | .09 |

Indianapolis Colts
| | | | | |
|---|---|---|---|---|
| ☐ 642 | Clayton Holmes | .50 | .23 | .06 |

Dallas Cowboys
| | | | | |
|---|---|---|---|---|
| ☐ 643 | Webster Slaughter | .75 | .35 | .09 |

Houston Oilers
| | | | | |
|---|---|---|---|---|
| ☐ 644 | Ricky Proehl | .75 | .35 | .09 |

Phoenix Cardinals
| | | | | |
|---|---|---|---|---|
| ☐ 645 | Jerry Rice | 6.00 | 2.70 | .75 |

San Francisco 49ers
| | | | | |
|---|---|---|---|---|
| ☐ 646 | Carl Banks | .75 | .35 | .09 |

New York Giants
| | | | | |
|---|---|---|---|---|
| ☐ 647 | J.J.Birden | .60 | .25 | .08 |

Kansas City Chiefs
| | | | | |
|---|---|---|---|---|
| ☐ 648 | Tracy Scroggins | 1.00 | .45 | .13 |

Detroit Lions
| | | | | |
|---|---|---|---|---|
| ☐ 649 | Alonzo Spellman | 1.00 | .45 | .13 |

Chicago Bears
| | | | | |
|---|---|---|---|---|
| ☐ 650 | Joe Montana | 15.00 | 6.75 | 1.90 |

San Francisco 49ers
| | | | | |
|---|---|---|---|---|
| ☐ 651 | Courtney Hawkins | 2.00 | .90 | .25 |

Tampa Bay Buccaneers
| | | | | |
|---|---|---|---|---|
| ☐ 652 | Corey Widmer | .75 | .35 | .09 |

New York Giants
| | | | | |
|---|---|---|---|---|
| ☐ 653 | Robert Brooks | .75 | .35 | .09 |

Green Bay Packers
| | | | | |
|---|---|---|---|---|
| ☐ 654 | Darren Woodson | 1.25 | .55 | .16 |

Dallas Cowboys
| | | | | |
|---|---|---|---|---|
| ☐ 655 | Derrick Fenner | .75 | .35 | .09 |

Cincinnati Bengals
| | | | | |
|---|---|---|---|---|
| ☐ 656 | Steve Christie | .50 | .23 | .06 |

Buffalo Bills
| | | | | |
|---|---|---|---|---|
| ☐ 657 | Chester McGlockton | 1.00 | .45 | .13 |

Los Angeles Raiders
| | | | | |
|---|---|---|---|---|
| ☐ 658 | Steve Israel | .50 | .23 | .06 |

Los Angeles Rams
| | | | | |
|---|---|---|---|---|
| ☐ 659 | Robert Harris | .50 | .23 | .06 |

Minnesota Vikings
| | | | | |
|---|---|---|---|---|
| ☐ 660 | Dan Marino | 8.00 | 3.60 | 1.00 |

Miami Dolphins
| | | | | |
|---|---|---|---|---|
| ☐ 661 | Ed McCaffrey | .60 | .25 | .08 |

New York Giants
| | | | | |
|---|---|---|---|---|
| ☐ 662 | Johnny Mitchell | 4.00 | 1.80 | .50 |

New York Jets
| | | | | |
|---|---|---|---|---|
| ☐ 663 | Timm Rosenbach | .50 | .23 | .06 |

Phoenix Cardinals
| | | | | |
|---|---|---|---|---|
| ☐ 664 | Anthony Miller | 1.25 | .55 | .16 |

San Diego Chargers
| | | | | |
|---|---|---|---|---|
| ☐ 665 | Merril Hoge | .75 | .35 | .09 |

Pittsburgh Steelers
| | | | | |
|---|---|---|---|---|
| ☐ 666 | Eugene Chung | .50 | .23 | .06 |

New England Patriots
| | | | | |
|---|---|---|---|---|
| ☐ 667 | Rueben Mayes | .50 | .23 | .06 |

Seattle Seahawks
| | | | | |
|---|---|---|---|---|
| ☐ 668 | Martin Bayless | .50 | .23 | .06 |

Kansas City Chiefs
| | | | | |
|---|---|---|---|---|
| ☐ 669 | Ashley Ambrose | .75 | .35 | .09 |

Indianapolis Colts
| | | | | |
|---|---|---|---|---|
| ☐ 670 | Michael Cofer UER | .50 | .23 | .06 |

(Back shows card for
Mike Cofer, the kicker)
Detroit Lions
| | | | | |
|---|---|---|---|---|
| ☐ 671 | Shane Dronett | 1.00 | .45 | .13 |

Denver Broncos
| | | | | |
|---|---|---|---|---|
| ☐ 672 | Bernie Kosar | .75 | .35 | .09 |

Cleveland Browns
| | | | | |
|---|---|---|---|---|
| ☐ 673 | Mike Singletary | .75 | .35 | .09 |

Chicago Bears
| | | | | |
|---|---|---|---|---|
| ☐ 674 | Mike Lodish | .50 | .23 | .06 |

Buffalo Bills
| | | | | |
|---|---|---|---|---|
| ☐ 675 | Phillippi Sparks | .50 | .23 | .06 |

New York Giants
| | | | | |
|---|---|---|---|---|
| ☐ 676 | Joel Steed | .75 | .35 | .09 |

Pittsburgh Steelers
| | | | | |
|---|---|---|---|---|
| ☐ 677 | Kevin Fagan | .50 | .23 | .06 |

San Francisco 49ers
| | | | | |
|---|---|---|---|---|
| ☐ 678 | Randal Hill | .75 | .35 | .09 |

Phoenix Cardinals
| | | | | |
|---|---|---|---|---|
| ☐ 679 | Ken O'Brien | .75 | .35 | .09 |

New York Jets
| | | | | |
|---|---|---|---|---|
| ☐ 680 | Lawrence Taylor | 1.00 | .45 | .13 |

New York Giants

| | | | | |
|---|---|---|---|---|
| ☐ 681 | Harvey Williams | .75 | .35 | .09 |

Kansas City Chiefs
| | | | | |
|---|---|---|---|---|
| ☐ 682 | Quentin Coryatt | 3.00 | 1.35 | .40 |

Indianapolis Colts
| | | | | |
|---|---|---|---|---|
| ☐ 683 | Brett Favre | 24.00 | 11.00 | 3.00 |

Green Bay Packers
| | | | | |
|---|---|---|---|---|
| ☐ 684 | Robert Jones | .75 | .35 | .09 |

Dallas Cowboys
| | | | | |
|---|---|---|---|---|
| ☐ 685 | Michael Dean Perry | .75 | .35 | .09 |

Cleveland Browns
| | | | | |
|---|---|---|---|---|
| ☐ 686 | Bruce Smith | .75 | .35 | .09 |

Buffalo Bills
| | | | | |
|---|---|---|---|---|
| ☐ 687 | Troy Auzenne | .50 | .23 | .06 |

Chicago Bears
| | | | | |
|---|---|---|---|---|
| ☐ 688 | Thomas McLemore | .60 | .25 | .08 |

Detroit Lions
| | | | | |
|---|---|---|---|---|
| ☐ 689 | Dale Carter | 2.00 | .90 | .25 |

Kansas City Chiefs
| | | | | |
|---|---|---|---|---|
| ☐ 690 | Marc Boutte | .50 | .23 | .06 |

Los Angeles Rams
| | | | | |
|---|---|---|---|---|
| ☐ 691 | Jeff George | 1.50 | .65 | .19 |

Indianapolis Colts
| | | | | |
|---|---|---|---|---|
| ☐ 692 | Dion Lambert UER | .50 | .23 | .06 |

New England Patriots
(Birthdate is 2/12/19; should
be 2/12/69)
| | | | | |
|---|---|---|---|---|
| ☐ 693 | Vaughn Dunbar | 1.00 | .45 | .13 |

New Orleans Saints
| | | | | |
|---|---|---|---|---|
| ☐ 694 | Derek Brown | .50 | .23 | .06 |

New York Giants
| | | | | |
|---|---|---|---|---|
| ☐ 695 | Troy Aikman | 20.00 | 9.00 | 2.50 |

Dallas Cowboys
| | | | | |
|---|---|---|---|---|
| ☐ 696 | John Fina | .50 | .23 | .06 |

Buffalo Bills
| | | | | |
|---|---|---|---|---|
| ☐ 697 | Kevin Smith | 2.00 | .90 | .25 |

Dallas Cowboys
| | | | | |
|---|---|---|---|---|
| ☐ 698 | Corey Miller | .75 | .35 | .09 |

New York Giants
| | | | | |
|---|---|---|---|---|
| ☐ 699 | Lance Olberding | .60 | .25 | .08 |

Cincinnati Bengals
| | | | | |
|---|---|---|---|---|
| ☐ 700 | Checklist 601-700 UER | .50 | .23 | .06 |

(Numbering sequence
off from 616 to 636)

## 1992 Stadium Club No.1 Draft Picks

Featuring three of the past Number One draft picks plus Rocket Ismail (who was apparently considered to be equivalent due to his early CFL signing), this four-card standard-size (2 1/2" by 3 1/2") set was inserted into Stadium Club high series packs. The cards are numbered on the back.

| | MINT | EXC | G-VG |
|---|---|---|---|
| COMPLETE SET (4) | 90.00 | 40.00 | 11.50 |
| COMMON PLAYER (1-4) | 20.00 | 9.00 | 2.50 |
| | | | |
| ☐ 1 Jeff George | 30.00 | 13.50 | 3.80 |
| Indianapolis Colts | | | |
| ☐ 2 Russell Maryland | 20.00 | 9.00 | 2.50 |
| Dallas Cowboys | | | |
| ☐ 3 Steve Emtman | 20.00 | 9.00 | 2.50 |
| Indianapolis Colts | | | |
| ☐ 4 Raghib Ismail | 30.00 | 13.50 | 3.80 |

## 1992 Stadium Club QB Legends

Featuring six of the greatest quarterbacks in NFL history, this six-card standard-size (2 1/2" by 3 1/2") set was inserted into Stadium Club Series II packs. Topps estimates that an average of one card would be found in every 72 packs. The fronts feature full-bleed action color

## 1993 Stadium Club

player photos, with the player's name beneath the Stadium Club logo in the lower right corner. A light blue bar intersects the logo and contains the words "Football Legend". A gold foil football helmet is printed in the lower left corner adjacent to the blue bar. In the top right corner, a lime green football icon edged in gold foil carries the year the player was elected to the Hall of Fame. Three varying length gold foil stripes run downward from the football. The horizontal backs are divided diagonally into kelly green and black areas and feature a close-up player picture, a gold foil facsimile signature, career passing statistics, and a mini-reproduction of the player's Topps Rookie Card. The cards are numbered on the back.

|  | MINT | EXC | G-VG |
|---|---|---|---|
| COMPLETE SET (6) | 20.00 | 9.00 | 2.50 |
| COMMON PLAYER (1-6) | 3.00 | 1.35 | .40 |
| ☐ 1 Y.A. Tittle | 3.00 | 1.35 | .40 |
| New York Giants |  |  |  |
| ☐ 2 Bart Starr | 3.50 | 1.55 | .45 |
| Green Bay Packers |  |  |  |
| ☐ 3 Johnny Unitas | 3.50 | 1.55 | .45 |
| Baltimore Colts |  |  |  |
| ☐ 4 George Blanda | 3.00 | 1.35 | .40 |
| Oakland Raiders |  |  |  |
| ☐ 5 Roger Staubach UER | 7.00 | 3.10 | .85 |
| (Card has his RC as 1974, was 1972) Dallas Cowboys |  |  |  |
| ☐ 6 Terry Bradshaw | 7.00 | 3.10 | .85 |
| Pittsburgh Steelers |  |  |  |

## 1993 Stadium Club Promo Sheet

This special nine-card promotional sheet was distributed by Topps at the July 1993 National Sports Collectors Convention in Chicago. It features original-size Stadium Club NFL player color photos prior to cropping. The pictures have gold frame lines that indicate the actual size of the standard-size (2 1/2" by 3 1/2") borderless cards. Each card has the player's name at the bottom in gold lettering and underscoring, printed over a broad green line. The Stadium Club logo appears above the player's name in gold, green, and red. The back of the sheet bears the logo of the National Sports Collectors Convention and Stadium Club's title for the promo sheet, "Beyond the Borders." The cards are unnumbered and are listed below as they appear on the sheet, from left to right, top to bottom.

|  | MINT | EXC | G-VG |
|---|---|---|---|
| COMPLETE SET (1) | 7.50 | 3.00 | .75 |
| COMMON SHEET | 7.50 | 3.00 | .75 |
| ☐ NNO Promo Sheet | 7.50 | 3.00 | .75 |
| Johnny Bailey |  |  |  |
| Phoenix Cardinals |  |  |  |
| Vai Sikahema |  |  |  |
| Philadelphia Eagles |  |  |  |
| Richard Dent |  |  |  |
| Chicago Bears |  |  |  |
| Sterling Sharpe |  |  |  |
| Green Bay Packers |  |  |  |
| Tommy Barnhardt |  |  |  |
| New Orleans Saints |  |  |  |
| Cris Carter |  |  |  |
| Minnesota Vikings |  |  |  |
| Cortez Kennedy |  |  |  |
| Seattle Seahawks |  |  |  |
| Christian Okoye |  |  |  |
| Kansas City Chiefs |  |  |  |
| Reggie Cobb |  |  |  |
| Tampa Bay Buccaneers |  |  |  |

The 1993 Stadium Club football set was issued in two series of 250 cards each and a 50-card Hi series for a total of 550 cards. The cards measure the standard size (2 1/2" by 3 1/2"). The card fronts feature full-bleed color action player photos. The player's name is gold foil-stamped on a green stripe edged on the bottom by gold foil. On a football field design, the backs carry a second color photo, a miniature representation of the player's Topps rookie card, biography, the Football News Skills Rating System, a "key stat" feature, and statistics (1992 season and career). The cards are numbered on the back. Every pack contains 14 regular cards plus one of the following special insert cards: Master Photo Winner, First Day Production, Special Chase or Stadium Club Membership Offer. With the exception of the Stadium Club Membership Offer cards, the inserts are randomly packed one in every 24 packs. The Master Photo redemption cards are redeemable for three Stadium Club Master Photos. The first series features 12 different Master Photos. Fewer than 1,000 1st Day Production cards were printed of each player card. The Special Chase cards are 28 Super Bowl XXVIII Super Team cards, one for each NFL team. Team cards featuring a division winner, conference championship team, or Super Bowl XXVIII winner were redeemable for the following special prizes: (1) 12 Stadium Club cards of players from the winning team, embossed with gold foil division winning logo (Division Winner card); (2) 12 Master Photos of the winning team, with special embossed gold foil Conference logo (AFC or NFC Conference Championship card); and (3) complete set of all 500 Stadium Club cards with official gold foil embossed Super Bowl logo (Super Bowl XXVIII Winner card; winners were also entered into a random drawing to win an official Super Bowl game ball). If the team pictured on the Super Team card wins more than one title, the collector may claim all of the corresponding prizes won by that card. The 1993 Draft Pick cards are scattered throughout the set (21, 40, 56, 73, 82, 108, 131, 134, 145, 154, 172, 180, 217, 226). The set concludes with a Member's Choice subset (241-250). The cards are numbered on the back. According to Topps, active members could purchase a 500-card Members Only factory set for 199.00. Reportedly only 10,000 sets were produced. The cards are identical to the regular set except for the gold-foil Members Only logo. Also, the member would receive an autographed Jerry Rice card that celebrates his 101st touchdown reception, 28 cards similar to the cards from the 1993 Stadium Club Super Team set, a special portfolio to store all of the cards, 24 1993 Stadium Club Master Photos, and a certificate of authenticity. The 1993 draft picks are featured on cards 280, 282, 301, 316, 317, 349, 359, 377, 384, 397, 409, 415, 469, 481, and 488. Rookie Cards include Reggie Brooks, Jerome Bettis, Drew Bledsoe, Garrison Hearst, Terry Kirby, O.J. McDuffie, Natrone Means, Glyn Milburn and Rick Mirer.

|  | MINT | EXC | G-VG |
|---|---|---|---|
| COMPLETE SET (550) | 50.00 | 23.00 | 6.25 |
| COMPLETE SERIES 1 (250) | 25.00 | 11.50 | 3.10 |
| COMPLETE SERIES 2 (250) | 18.00 | 8.00 | 2.30 |
| COMPLETE HI SERIES (50) | 9.00 | 4.00 | 1.15 |
| COMPLETE HI FACT.SET (51) | 14.00 | 6.25 | 1.75 |
| COMMON PLAYER (1-250) | .10 | .05 | .01 |
| COMMON PLAYER (251-500) | .10 | .05 | .01 |
| COMMON PLAYER (501-550) | .10 | .05 | .01 |
| ☐ 1 Sterling Sharpe | 1.00 | .45 | .13 |
| Green Bay Packers |  |  |  |
| ☐ 2 Chris Burkett | .10 | .05 | .01 |
| New York Jets |  |  |  |
| ☐ 3 Santana Dotson | .15 | .07 | .02 |
| Tampa Bay Buccaneers |  |  |  |
| ☐ 4 Michael Jackson | .15 | .07 | .02 |
| Cleveland Browns |  |  |  |
| ☐ 5 Neal Anderson | .12 | .05 | .02 |
| Chicago Bears |  |  |  |

| | | | |
|---|---|---|---|
| ☐ 6 Bryan Cox | .12 | .05 | .02 |
| Miami Dolphins | | | |
| ☐ 7 Dennis Gibson | .10 | .05 | .01 |
| Detroit Lions | | | |
| ☐ 8 Jeff Graham | .12 | .05 | .02 |
| Pittsburgh Steelers | | | |
| ☐ 9 Roger Ruzek | .10 | .05 | .01 |
| Philadelphia Eagles | | | |
| ☐ 10 Duane Bickett | .10 | .05 | .01 |
| Indianapolis Colts | | | |
| ☐ 11 Charles Mann | .12 | .05 | .02 |
| Washington Redskins | | | |
| ☐ 12 Tommy Maddox | .25 | .11 | .03 |
| Denver Broncos | | | |
| ☐ 13 Vaughn Dunbar | .12 | .05 | .02 |
| New Orleans Saints | | | |
| ☐ 14 Gary Plummer | .10 | .05 | .01 |
| San Diego Chargers | | | |
| ☐ 15 Chris Miller | .15 | .07 | .02 |
| Atlanta Falcons | | | |
| ☐ 16 Chris Warren | .30 | .14 | .04 |
| Seattle Seahawks | | | |
| ☐ 17 Alvin Harper | .50 | .23 | .06 |
| Dallas Cowboys | | | |
| ☐ 18 Eric Dickerson | .15 | .07 | .02 |
| Los Angeles Raiders | | | |
| ☐ 19 Mike Jones | .10 | .05 | .01 |
| Phoenix Cardinals | | | |
| ☐ 20 Ernest Givins | .12 | .05 | .02 |
| Houston Oilers | | | |
| ☐ 21 Natrone Means | 2.00 | .90 | .25 |
| San Diego Chargers | | | |
| ☐ 22 Doug Riesenberg | .10 | .05 | .01 |
| New York Giants | | | |
| ☐ 23 Barry Word | .15 | .07 | .02 |
| Kansas City Chiefs | | | |
| ☐ 24 Sean Salisbury | .12 | .05 | .02 |
| Minnesota Vikings | | | |
| ☐ 25 Derrick Fenner | .10 | .05 | .01 |
| Cincinnati Bengals | | | |
| ☐ 26 David Howard | .10 | .05 | .01 |
| New England Patriots | | | |
| ☐ 27 Mark Kelso | .10 | .05 | .01 |
| Buffalo Bills | | | |
| ☐ 28 Todd Lyght | .10 | .05 | .01 |
| Los Angeles Rams | | | |
| ☐ 29 Dana Hall | .12 | .05 | .02 |
| San Francisco 49ers | | | |
| ☐ 30 Eric Metcalf | .15 | .07 | .02 |
| Cleveland Browns | | | |
| ☐ 31 Jason Hanson | .10 | .05 | .01 |
| Detroit Lions | | | |
| ☐ 32 Dwight Stone | .10 | .05 | .01 |
| Pittsburgh Steelers | | | |
| ☐ 33 Johnny Mitchell | .50 | .23 | .06 |
| New York Jets | | | |
| ☐ 34 Reggie Roby | .10 | .05 | .01 |
| Miami Dolphins | | | |
| ☐ 35 Terrell Buckley | .15 | .07 | .02 |
| Green Bay Packers | | | |
| ☐ 36 Steve McMichael | .10 | .05 | .01 |
| Chicago Bears | | | |
| ☐ 37 Marty Carter | .10 | .05 | .01 |
| Tampa Bay Buccaneers | | | |
| ☐ 38 Seth Joyner | .12 | .05 | .02 |
| Philadelphia Eagles | | | |
| ☐ 39 Rohn Stark | .10 | .05 | .01 |
| Indianapolis Colts | | | |
| ☐ 40 Eric Curry | .50 | .23 | .06 |
| Tampa Bay Buccaneers | | | |
| ☐ 41 Tommy Barnhardt | .10 | .05 | .01 |
| New Orleans Saints | | | |
| ☐ 42 Karl Mecklenburg | .10 | .05 | .01 |
| Denver Broncos | | | |
| ☐ 43 Darion Conner | .10 | .05 | .01 |
| Atlanta Falcons | | | |
| ☐ 44 Ronnie Harmon | .12 | .05 | .02 |
| San Diego Chargers | | | |
| ☐ 45 Cortez Kennedy | .15 | .07 | .02 |
| Seattle Seahawks | | | |
| ☐ 46 Tim Brown | .40 | .18 | .05 |
| Los Angeles Raiders | | | |
| ☐ 47 Bill Lewis | .10 | .05 | .01 |
| New England Patriots | | | |
| ☐ 48 Randall McDaniel | .10 | .05 | .01 |
| Minnesota Vikings | | | |
| ☐ 49 Curtis Duncan | .12 | .05 | .02 |
| Houston Oilers | | | |
| ☐ 50 Troy Aikman | 2.50 | 1.15 | .30 |
| Dallas Cowboys | | | |
| ☐ 51 David Klingler | .30 | .14 | .04 |
| Cincinnati Bengals | | | |
| ☐ 52 Brent Jones | .15 | .07 | .02 |
| San Francisco 49ers | | | |
| ☐ 53 Dave Krieg | .12 | .05 | .02 |
| Kansas City Chiefs | | | |
| ☐ 54 Bruce Smith | .15 | .07 | .02 |

| | | | |
|---|---|---|---|
| Buffalo Bills | | | |
| ☐ 55 Vincent Brown | .10 | .05 | .01 |
| New England Patriots | | | |
| ☐ 56 O.J. McDuffie | 2.50 | 1.15 | .30 |
| Miami Dolphins | | | |
| ☐ 57 Cleveland Gary | .12 | .05 | .02 |
| Los Angeles Rams | | | |
| ☐ 58 Larry Centers | .40 | .18 | .05 |
| Phoenix Cardinals | | | |
| ☐ 59 Pepper Johnson | .10 | .05 | .01 |
| New York Giants | | | |
| ☐ 60 Dan Marino | 1.50 | .65 | .19 |
| Miami Dolphins | | | |
| ☐ 61 Robert Porcher | .12 | .05 | .02 |
| Detroit Lions | | | |
| ☐ 62 Jim Harbaugh | .12 | .05 | .02 |
| Chicago Bears | | | |
| ☐ 63 Sam Mills | .12 | .05 | .02 |
| New Orleans Saints | | | |
| ☐ 64 Gary Anderson | .12 | .05 | .02 |
| Tampa Bay Buccaneers | | | |
| ☐ 65 Neil O'Donnell | .50 | .23 | .06 |
| Pittsburgh Steelers | | | |
| ☐ 66 Keith Byars | .12 | .05 | .02 |
| Philadelphia Eagles | | | |
| ☐ 67 Jeff Herrod | .10 | .05 | .01 |
| Indianapolis Colts | | | |
| ☐ 68 Marion Butts | .15 | .07 | .02 |
| San Diego Chargers | | | |
| ☐ 69 Terry McDaniel | .10 | .05 | .01 |
| Los Angeles Raiders | | | |
| ☐ 70 John Elway | 1.00 | .45 | .13 |
| Denver Broncos | | | |
| ☐ 71 Steve Broussard | .10 | .05 | .01 |
| Atlanta Falcons | | | |
| ☐ 72 Kelvin Martin | .12 | .05 | .02 |
| Seattle Seahawks | | | |
| ☐ 73 Tom Carter | .40 | .18 | .05 |
| Washington Redskins | | | |
| ☐ 74 Bryce Paup | .10 | .05 | .01 |
| Green Bay Packers | | | |
| ☐ 75 Jim Kelly | .40 | .18 | .05 |
| Buffalo Bills | | | |
| ☐ 76 Bill Romanowski | .10 | .05 | .01 |
| San Francisco 49ers | | | |
| ☐ 77 Andre Collins | .10 | .05 | .01 |
| Washington Redskins | | | |
| ☐ 78 Mike Farr | .10 | .05 | .01 |
| New England Patriots | | | |
| ☐ 79 Henry Ellard | .12 | .05 | .02 |
| Los Angeles Rams | | | |
| ☐ 80 Dale Carter | .15 | .07 | .02 |
| Kansas City Chiefs | | | |
| ☐ 81 Johnny Bailey | .10 | .05 | .01 |
| Phoenix Cardinals | | | |
| ☐ 82 Garrison Hearst | 1.00 | .45 | .13 |
| Phoenix Cardinals | | | |
| ☐ 83 Brent Williams | .10 | .05 | .01 |
| New England Patriots | | | |
| ☐ 84 Ricardo McDonald | .10 | .05 | .01 |
| Cincinnati Bengals | | | |
| ☐ 85 Emmitt Smith | 4.00 | 1.80 | .50 |
| Dallas Cowboys | | | |
| ☐ 86 Vai Sikahema | .10 | .05 | .01 |
| Philadelphia Eagles | | | |
| ☐ 87 Jackie Harris | .50 | .23 | .06 |
| Green Bay Packers | | | |
| ☐ 88 Alonzo Spellman | .12 | .05 | .02 |
| Chicago Bears | | | |
| ☐ 89 Mark Wheeler | .10 | .05 | .01 |
| Tampa Bay Buccaneers | | | |
| ☐ 90 Dalton Hilliard | .10 | .05 | .01 |
| New Orleans Saints | | | |
| ☐ 91 Mark Higgs | .15 | .07 | .02 |
| Miami Dolphins | | | |
| ☐ 92 Aaron Wallace | .10 | .05 | .01 |
| Los Angeles Raiders | | | |
| ☐ 93 Earnest Byner | .12 | .05 | .02 |
| Washington Redskins | | | |
| ☐ 94 Stanley Richard | .10 | .05 | .01 |
| San Diego Chargers | | | |
| ☐ 95 Cris Carter | .15 | .07 | .02 |
| Minnesota Vikings | | | |
| ☐ 96 Bobby Houston | .20 | .09 | .03 |
| New York Jets | | | |
| ☐ 97 Craig Heyward | .10 | .05 | .01 |
| Chicago Bears | | | |
| ☐ 98 Bernie Kosar | .15 | .07 | .02 |
| Cleveland Browns | | | |
| ☐ 99 Mike Croel | .12 | .05 | .02 |
| Denver Broncos | | | |
| ☐ 100 Deion Sanders | .30 | .14 | .04 |
| Atlanta Falcons | | | |
| ☐ 101 Warren Moon | .30 | .14 | .04 |
| Houston Oilers | | | |
| ☐ 102 Christian Okoye | .12 | .05 | .02 |
| Kansas City Chiefs | | | |
| ☐ 103 Ricky Watters | .75 | .35 | .09 |

San Francisco 49ers
□ 104 Eric Swann .12 .05 .02
Phoenix Cardinals
□ 105 Rodney Hampton .75 .35 .09
New York Giants
□ 106 Daryl Johnston .15 .07 .02
Dallas Cowboys
□ 107 Andre Reed .15 .07 .02
Buffalo Bills
□ 108 Jerome Bettis 6.00 2.70 .75
Los Angeles Rams
□ 109 Eugene Daniel .10 .05 .01
Indianapolis Colts
□ 110 Leonard Russell .12 .05 .02
New England Patriots
□ 111 Darryl Williams .12 .05 .02
Cincinnati Bengals
□ 112 Rod Woodson .15 .07 .02
Pittsburgh Steelers
□ 113 Boomer Esiason .25 .11 .03
New York Jets
□ 114 James Hasty .10 .05 .01
New York Jets
□ 115 Marc Boutte .10 .05 .01
Los Angeles Rams
□ 116 Tom Waddle .15 .07 .02
Chicago Bears
□ 117 Lawrence Dawsey .15 .07 .02
Tampa Bay Buccaneers
□ 118 Mark Collins .10 .05 .01
New York Giants
□ 119 Willie Gault .12 .05 .02
Los Angeles Raiders
□ 120 Barry Sanders 1.50 .65 .19
Detroit Lions
□ 121 Leroy Hoard .12 .05 .02
Cleveland Browns
□ 122 Anthony Munoz .12 .05 .02
Tampa Bay Buccaneers
□ 123 Jesse Sapolu .10 .05 .01
San Francisco 49ers
□ 124 Art Monk .15 .07 .02
Washington Redskins
□ 125 Randal Hill .15 .07 .02
Phoenix Cardinals
□ 126 John Offerdahl .10 .05 .01
Miami Dolphins
□ 127 Carlos Jenkins .10 .05 .01
Minnesota Vikings
□ 128 Al Smith .10 .05 .01
Houston Oilers
□ 129 Michael Irvin 1.00 .45 .13
Dallas Cowboys
□ 130 Kenneth Davis .12 .05 .02
Buffalo Bills
□ 131 Curtis Conway 1.00 .45 .13
Chicago Bears
□ 132 Steve Atwater .12 .05 .02
Denver Broncos
□ 133 Neil Smith .15 .07 .02
Kansas City Chiefs
□ 134 Steve Everitt .20 .09 .03
Cleveland Browns
□ 135 Chris Mims .12 .05 .02
San Diego Chargers
□ 136 Rickey Jackson .12 .05 .02
New Orleans Saints
□ 137 Edgar Bennett .15 .07 .02
Green Bay Packers
□ 138 Mike Pritchard .15 .07 .02
Atlanta Falcons
□ 139 Richard Dent .12 .05 .02
Chicago Bears
□ 140 Barry Foster .50 .23 .06
Pittsburgh Steelers
□ 141 Eugene Robinson .10 .05 .01
Seattle Seahawks
□ 142 Jackie Slater .10 .05 .01
Los Angeles Rams
□ 143 Paul Gruber .10 .05 .01
Tampa Bay Buccaneers
□ 144 Rob Moore .15 .07 .02
New York Jets
□ 145 Robert Smith .75 .35 .09
Minnesota Vikings
□ 146 Lorenzo White .12 .05 .02
Houston Oilers
□ 147 Tommy Vardell .12 .05 .02
Cleveland Browns
□ 148 Dave Meggett .12 .05 .02
New York Giants
□ 149 Vince Workman .10 .05 .01
Tampa Bay Buccaneers
□ 150 Terry Allen .15 .07 .02
Minnesota Vikings
□ 151 Howie Long .12 .05 .02
Los Angeles Raiders
□ 152 Charles Haley .12 .05 .02

Dallas Cowboys
□ 153 Pete Metzelaars .10 .05 .01
Buffalo Bills
□ 154 John Copeland .75 .35 .09
Cincinnati Bengals
□ 155 Aeneas Williams .10 .05 .01
Phoenix Cardinals
□ 156 Ricky Sanders .12 .05 .02
Washington Redskins
□ 157 Andre Ware .12 .05 .02
Detroit Lions
□ 158 Tony Paige .10 .05 .01
Miami Dolphins
□ 159 Jerome Henderson .10 .05 .01
New England Patriots
□ 160 Harold Green .12 .05 .02
Cincinnati Bengals
□ 161 Wymon Henderson .10 .05 .01
New England Patriots
□ 162 Andre Rison .40 .18 .05
Atlanta Falcons
□ 163 Donald Evans .10 .05 .01
Pittsburgh Steelers
□ 164 Todd Scott .10 .05 .01
Minnesota Vikings
□ 165 Steve Emtman .12 .05 .02
Indianapolis Colts
□ 166 William Fuller .10 .05 .01
Houston Oilers
□ 167 Michael Dean Perry .15 .07 .02
Cleveland Browns
□ 168 Randall Cunningham .20 .09 .03
Philadelphia Eagles
□ 169 Toi Cook .10 .05 .01
New Orleans Saints
□ 170 Browning Nagle .12 .05 .02
New York Jets
□ 171 Darryl Henley .10 .05 .01
Los Angeles Rams
□ 172 George Teague .40 .18 .05
Green Bay Packers
□ 173 Derrick Thomas .30 .14 .04
Kansas City Chiefs
□ 174 Jay Novacek .15 .07 .02
Dallas Cowboys
□ 175 Mark Carrier .12 .05 .02
Chicago Bears
□ 176 Kevin Fagan .10 .05 .01
San Francisco 49ers
□ 177 Nate Lewis .12 .05 .02
San Diego Chargers
□ 178 Courtney Hawkins .12 .05 .02
Tampa Bay Buccaneers
□ 179 Robert Blackmon .10 .05 .01
Seattle Seahawks
□ 180 Rick Mirer 6.00 2.70 .75
Seattle Seahawks
□ 181 Mike Lodish .10 .05 .01
Buffalo Bills
□ 182 Jarrod Bunch .12 .05 .02
New York Giants
□ 183 Anthony Smith .10 .05 .01
Los Angeles Raiders
□ 184 Brian Noble .10 .05 .01
Green Bay Packers
□ 185 Eric Bieniemy .12 .05 .02
San Diego Chargers
□ 186 Keith Jackson .15 .07 .02
Miami Dolphins
□ 187 Eric Martin .12 .05 .02
New Orleans Saints
□ 188 Vance Johnson .12 .05 .02
Denver Broncos
□ 189 Kevin Mack .12 .05 .02
Cleveland Browns
□ 190 Rich Camarillo .10 .05 .01
Phoenix Cardinals
□ 191 Ashley Ambrose .10 .05 .01
Indianapolis Colts
□ 192 Ray Childress .10 .05 .01
Houston Oilers
□ 193 Jim Arnold .10 .05 .01
Detroit Lions
□ 194 Ricky Ervins .12 .05 .02
Washington Redskins
□ 195 Gary Anderson .10 .05 .01
Pittsburgh Steelers
□ 196 Eric Allen .12 .05 .02
Philadelphia Eagles
□ 197 Roger Craig .12 .05 .02
Minnesota Vikings
□ 198 Jon Vaughn .10 .05 .01
New England Patriots
□ 199 Tim McDonald .10 .05 .01
San Francisco 49ers
□ 200 Broderick Thomas .10 .05 .01
Tampa Bay Buccaneers
□ 201 Jessie Tuggle .10 .05 .01

| | | | |
|---|---|---|---|
| ☐ 202 Alonzo Mitz — Atlanta Falcons | .10 | .05 | .01 |
| ☐ 203 Harvey Williams — Cincinnati Bengals | .15 | .07 | .02 |
| ☐ 204 Russell Maryland — Kansas City Chiefs | .15 | .07 | .02 |
| ☐ 205 Marvin Washington — Dallas Cowboys | .10 | .05 | .01 |
| ☐ 206 Jim Everett — New York Jets | .10 | .05 | .01 |
| ☐ 207 Trace Armstrong — Los Angeles Rams | .10 | .05 | .01 |
| ☐ 208 Steve Young — Chicago Bears | .50 | .23 | .06 |
| ☐ 209 Tony Woods — San Francisco 49ers | .10 | .05 | .01 |
| ☐ 210 Brett Favre — Seattle Seahawks | 1.50 | .65 | .19 |
| ☐ 211 Nate Odomes — Green Bay Packers | .12 | .05 | .02 |
| ☐ 212 Ricky Proehl — Buffalo Bills | .12 | .05 | .02 |
| ☐ 213 Jim Dombrowski — Phoenix Cardinals | .10 | .05 | .01 |
| ☐ 214 Anthony Carter — New Orleans Saints | .12 | .05 | .02 |
| ☐ 215 Tracy Simien — Minnesota Vikings | .10 | .05 | .01 |
| ☐ 216 Clay Matthews — Kansas City Chiefs | .12 | .05 | .02 |
| ☐ 217 Patrick Bates — Cleveland Browns | .25 | .11 | .03 |
| ☐ 218 Jeff George — Los Angeles Raiders | .25 | .11 | .03 |
| ☐ 219 David Fulcher — Indianapolis Colts | .10 | .05 | .01 |
| ☐ 220 Phil Simms — Cincinnati Bengals | .15 | .07 | .02 |
| ☐ 221 Eugene Chung — New York Giants | .10 | .05 | .01 |
| ☐ 222 Reggie Cobb — New England Patriots | .15 | .07 | .02 |
| ☐ 223 Jim Sweeney — Tampa Bay Buccaneers | .10 | .05 | .01 |
| ☐ 224 Greg Lloyd — New York Jets | .10 | .05 | .01 |
| ☐ 225 Sean Jones — Pittsburgh Steelers | .10 | .05 | .01 |
| ☐ 226 Marvin Jones — Houston Oilers | .40 | .18 | .05 |
| ☐ 227 Bill Brooks — New York Jets | .12 | .05 | .02 |
| ☐ 228 Moe Gardner — Buffalo Bills | .10 | .05 | .01 |
| ☐ 229 Louis Oliver — Atlanta Falcons | .10 | .05 | .01 |
| ☐ 230 Flipper Anderson — Miami Dolphins | .12 | .05 | .02 |
| ☐ 231 Marc Spindler — Los Angeles Rams | .10 | .05 | .01 |
| ☐ 232 Jerry Rice — Detroit Lions | 1.25 | .55 | .16 |
| ☐ 233 Chip Lohmiller — San Francisco 49ers | .10 | .05 | .01 |
| ☐ 234 Nolan Harrison — Washington Redskins | .10 | .05 | .01 |
| ☐ 235 Heath Sherman — Los Angeles Raiders | .10 | .05 | .01 |
| ☐ 236 Reyna Thompson — Philadelphia Eagles | .10 | .05 | .01 |
| ☐ 237 Derrick Walker — New England Patriots | .10 | .05 | .01 |
| ☐ 238 Rufus Porter — San Diego Chargers | .10 | .05 | .01 |
| ☐ 239 Checklist 1-125 — Seattle Seahawks | .10 | .05 | .01 |
| ☐ 240 Checklist 126-250 | .10 | .05 | .01 |
| ☐ 241 John Elway MC | .30 | .14 | .04 |
| ☐ 242 Troy Aikman MC — Denver Broncos | 1.00 | .45 | .13 |
| ☐ 243 Steve Emtman MC — Dallas Cowboys | .12 | .05 | .02 |
| ☐ 244 Ricky Watters MC — Indianapolis Colts | .40 | .18 | .05 |
| ☐ 245 Barry Foster MC — San Francisco 49ers | .25 | .11 | .03 |
| ☐ 246 Dan Marino MC — Pittsburgh Steelers | .75 | .35 | .09 |
| ☐ 247 Reggie White MC — Miami Dolphins | .15 | .07 | .02 |
| ☐ 248 Thurman Thomas MC — Philadelphia Eagles | .50 | .23 | .06 |
| ☐ 249 Broderick Thomas MC — Buffalo Bills | .10 | .05 | .01 |
| ☐ 250 Joe Montana MC — Tampa Bay Buccaneers | 1.25 | .55 | .16 |
| ☐ 251 Tim Goad — Kansas City Chiefs | .10 | .05 | .01 |
| ☐ 252 Joe Nash — New England Patriots | .10 | .05 | .01 |
| ☐ 253 Anthony Johnson — Seattle Seahawks | .10 | .05 | .01 |
| ☐ 254 Carl Pickens — Indianapolis Colts | .15 | .07 | .02 |
| ☐ 255 Steve Beuerlein — Cincinnati Bengals | .25 | .11 | .03 |
| ☐ 256 Anthony Newman — Phoenix Cardinals | .10 | .05 | .01 |
| ☐ 257 Corey Miller — Los Angeles Rams | .10 | .05 | .01 |
| ☐ 258 Steve DeBerg — New York Giants | .12 | .05 | .02 |
| ☐ 259 Johnny Holland — Tampa Bay Buccaneers | .10 | .05 | .01 |
| ☐ 260 Jerry Ball — Green Bay Packers | .10 | .05 | .01 |
| ☐ 261 Siupeli Malamala — Detroit Lions | .15 | .07 | .02 |
| ☐ 262 Steve Wisniewski — New York Jets | .10 | .05 | .01 |
| ☐ 263 Kelvin Pritchett — Los Angeles Raiders | .10 | .05 | .01 |
| ☐ 264 Chris Gardocki — Detroit Lions | .10 | .05 | .01 |
| ☐ 265 Henry Thomas — New York Jets | .10 | .05 | .01 |
| ☐ 266 Arthur Marshall — Kansas City Chiefs | .35 | .16 | .04 |
| ☐ 267 Quinn Early — Denver Broncos | .12 | .05 | .02 |
| ☐ 268 Jonathan Hayes — New Orleans Saints | .10 | .05 | .01 |
| ☐ 269 Erric Pegram — Kansas City Chiefs | .50 | .23 | .06 |
| ☐ 270 Clyde Simmons — Atlanta Falcons | .12 | .05 | .02 |
| ☐ 271 Eric Moten — Philadelphia Eagles | .10 | .05 | .01 |
| ☐ 272 Brian Mitchell — San Diego Chargers | .12 | .05 | .02 |
| ☐ 273 Adrian Cooper — Washington Redskins | .10 | .05 | .01 |
| ☐ 274 Gaston Green — Pittsburgh Steelers | .12 | .05 | .02 |
| ☐ 275 John Taylor — Los Angeles Raiders | .15 | .07 | .02 |
| ☐ 276 Jeff Uhlenhake — San Francisco 49ers | .10 | .05 | .01 |
| ☐ 277 Phil Hansen — New York Jets | .10 | .05 | .01 |
| ☐ 278 Kevin Williams — Buffalo Bills | 1.00 | .45 | .13 |
| ☐ 279 Robert Massey — Dallas Cowboys | .10 | .05 | .01 |
| ☐ 280 Drew Bledsoe — Phoenix Cardinals (Card can be found with or without draft pick logo on front) | 6.00 | 2.70 | .75 |
| ☐ 281 Walter Reeves — New England Patriots | .10 | .05 | .01 |
| ☐ 282 Carlton Gray — Phoenix Cardinals (Card can be found with or without draft pick logo on front) | .35 | .16 | .04 |
| ☐ 283 Derek Brown — Seattle Seahawks | .12 | .05 | .02 |
| ☐ 284 Martin Mayhew — New York Giants | .10 | .05 | .01 |
| ☐ 285 Sean Gilbert — Tampa Bay Buccaneers | .12 | .05 | .02 |
| ☐ 286 Jessie Hester — Los Angeles Rams | .10 | .05 | .01 |
| ☐ 287 Mark Clayton — Indianapolis Colts | .10 | .05 | .01 |
| ☐ 288 Blair Thomas — Green Bay Packers | .12 | .05 | .02 |
| ☐ 289 J.J. Birden — New York Jets | .12 | .05 | .02 |
| ☐ 290 Shannon Sharpe — Kansas City Chiefs | .35 | .16 | .04 |
| ☐ 291 Richard Fain — Green Bay Packers | .15 | .07 | .02 |
| ☐ 292 Gene Atkins — Chicago Bears | .10 | .05 | .01 |
| ☐ 293 Burt Grossman — New York Giants | .10 | .05 | .01 |
| ☐ 294 Chris Doleman — San Diego Chargers | .12 | .05 | .02 |
| ☐ 295 Pat Swilling — Minnesota Vikings | .12 | .05 | .02 |
| ☐ 296 Mike Kenn — Detroit Lions | .10 | .05 | .01 |
| ☐ 297 Merril Hoge — Atlanta Falcons | .10 | .05 | .01 |
| ☐ 298 Don Mosebar — Pittsburgh Steelers | .10 | .05 | .01 |

Los Angeles Raiders
- [ ] 299 Kevin Smith ....................... .12 .05 .02
  Dallas Cowboys
- [ ] 300 Darrell Green ..................... .12 .05 .02
  Washington Redskins
- [ ] 301 Dan Footman ..................... .25 .11 .03
  Denver Broncos
  (Card can be found with or
  without draft pick logo on front)
- [ ] 302 Vestee Jackson .................... .10 .05 .01
  Miami Dolphins
- [ ] 303 Carwell Gardner ................... .10 .05 .01
  Buffalo Bills
- [ ] 304 Amp Lee .......................... .12 .05 .02
  San Francisco 49ers
- [ ] 305 Bruce Matthews ................... .12 .05 .02
  Houston Oilers
- [ ] 306 Antone Davis ...................... .10 .05 .01
  Philadelphia Eagles
- [ ] 307 Dean Biasucci ..................... .10 .05 .01
  Indianapolis Colts
- [ ] 308 Maurice Hurst ..................... .10 .05 .01
  New England Patriots
- [ ] 309 John Kasay ........................ .10 .05 .01
  Seattle Seahawks
- [ ] 310 Lawrence Taylor ................... .20 .09 .03
  New York Giants
- [ ] 311 Ken Harvey ........................ .10 .05 .01
  Phoenix Cardinals
- [ ] 312 Willie Davis ........................ .20 .09 .03
  Kansas City Chiefs
- [ ] 313 Tony Bennett ...................... .10 .05 .01
  Green Bay Packers
- [ ] 314 Jay Schroeder ...................... .10 .05 .01
  Cincinnati Bengals
- [ ] 315 Darren Perry ....................... .10 .05 .01
  Pittsburgh Steelers
- [ ] 316 Troy Drayton ....................... .50 .23 .06
  Los Angeles Rams
  (Card can be found with or
  without draft pick logo on front)
- [ ] 317 Dan Williams ...................... .20 .09 .03
  Denver Broncos
  (Card can be found with or
  without draft pick logo on front)
- [ ] 318 Michael Haynes .................... .10 .05 .01
  Atlanta Falcons
- [ ] 319 Renaldo Turnbull .................. .12 .05 .02
  New Orleans Saints
- [ ] 320 Junior Seau ........................ .15 .07 .02
  San Diego Chargers
- [ ] 321 Ray Crockett ....................... .10 .05 .01
  Detroit Lions
- [ ] 322 Will Furrer ......................... .10 .05 .01
  Chicago Bears
- [ ] 323 Byron Evans ....................... .10 .05 .01
  Philadelphia Eagles
- [ ] 324 Jim McMahon ...................... .15 .07 .02
  Cleveland Browns
- [ ] 325 Robert Jones ....................... .10 .05 .01
  Dallas Cowboys
- [ ] 326 Eric Davis .......................... .10 .05 .01
  San Francisco 49ers
- [ ] 327 Jeff Cross .......................... .10 .05 .01
  Philadelphia Eagles
- [ ] 328 Kyle Clifton ........................ .10 .05 .01
  New York Jets
- [ ] 329 Haywood Jeffires .................. .15 .07 .02
  Houston Oilers
- [ ] 330 Jeff Hostetler ...................... .15 .07 .02
  Los Angeles Raiders
- [ ] 331 Darryl Talley ....................... .10 .05 .01
  Buffalo Bills
- [ ] 332 Keith McCants ..................... .10 .05 .01
  New England Patriots
- [ ] 333 Mo Lewis ........................... .10 .05 .01
  New York Jets
- [ ] 334 Matt Stover ........................ .10 .05 .01
  Cleveland Browns
- [ ] 335 Ferrell Edmunds ................... .10 .05 .01
  Miami Dolphins
- [ ] 336 Matt Brock ......................... .10 .05 .01
  Green Bay Packers
- [ ] 337 Ernie Mills ......................... .10 .05 .01
  Pittsburgh Steelers
- [ ] 338 Shane Dronett ..................... .10 .05 .01
  Denver Broncos
- [ ] 339 Brad Muster ....................... .12 .05 .02
  New Orleans Saints
- [ ] 340 Jesse Solomon ..................... .10 .05 .01
  Atlanta Falcons
- [ ] 341 John Randle ........................ .10 .05 .01
  Minnesota Vikings
- [ ] 342 Chris Spielman ..................... .10 .05 .01
  Detroit Lions
- [ ] 343 David Whitmore .................... .10 .05 .01
  Kansas City Chiefs
- [ ] 344 Glenn Parker ....................... .10 .05 .01

Buffalo Bills
- [ ] 345 Marco Coleman ..................... .12 .05 .02
  Miami Dolphins
- [ ] 346 Kenneth Gant ...................... .10 .05 .01
  Dallas Cowboys
- [ ] 347 Cris Dishman ...................... .10 .05 .01
  Houston Oilers
- [ ] 348 Kenny Walker ...................... .10 .05 .01
  Denver Broncos
- [ ] 349 Roosevelt Potts .................... .50 .23 .06
  Indianapolis Colts
- [ ] 350 Reggie White ...................... .25 .11 .03
  Green Bay Packers
- [ ] 351 Gerald Robinson ................... .10 .05 .01
  Los Angeles Rams
- [ ] 352 Mark Rypien ....................... .12 .05 .02
  Washington Redskins
- [ ] 353 Stan Humphries .................... .15 .07 .02
  San Diego Chargers
- [ ] 354 Chris Singleton .................... .10 .05 .01
  New England Patriots
- [ ] 355 Herschel Walker ................... .15 .07 .02
  Philadelphia Eagles
- [ ] 356 Ron Hall ........................... .10 .05 .01
  Tampa Bay Buccaneers
- [ ] 357 Ethan Horton ...................... .10 .05 .01
  Los Angeles Raiders
- [ ] 358 Anthony Pleasant .................. .10 .05 .01
  Cleveland Browns
- [ ] 359 Thomas Smith ..................... .20 .09 .03
  Buffalo Bills
  (Card can be found with or
  without draft pick logo on front
- [ ] 360 Audray McMillian ................. .10 .05 .01
  Minnesota Vikings
- [ ] 361 D.J. Johnson ...................... .10 .05 .01
  Pittsburgh Steelers
- [ ] 362 Ron Heller ......................... .10 .05 .01
  Miami Dolphins
- [ ] 363 Bern Brostek ...................... .10 .05 .01
  Los Angeles Rams
- [ ] 364 Ronnie Lott ........................ .15 .07 .02
  New York Jets
- [ ] 365 Reggie Johnson .................... .10 .05 .01
  Denver Broncos
- [ ] 366 Lin Elliott .......................... .10 .05 .01
  Dallas Cowboys
- [ ] 367 Lemuel Stinson ................... .10 .05 .01
  Chicago Bears
- [ ] 368 William White ...................... .10 .05 .01
  Detroit Lions
- [ ] 369 Ernie Jones ........................ .10 .05 .01
  Los Angeles Rams
- [ ] 370 Tom Rathman ...................... .12 .05 .02
  San Francisco 49ers
- [ ] 371 Tommy Kane ....................... .10 .05 .01
  Seattle Seahawks
- [ ] 372 David Brandon ..................... .10 .05 .01
  Cleveland Browns
- [ ] 373 Lee Johnson ....................... .10 .05 .01
  Cincinnati Bengals
- [ ] 374 Wade Wilson ....................... .12 .05 .02
  New Orleans Saints
- [ ] 375 Nick Lowery ....................... .10 .05 .01
  Kansas City Chiefs
- [ ] 376 Bubba McDowell ................... .10 .05 .01
  Houston Oilers
- [ ] 377 Wayne Simmons .................. .25 .11 .03
  Green Bay Packers
  (Card can be found with or
  without draft pick logo on front)
- [ ] 378 Calvin Williams .................... .15 .07 .02
  Philadelphia Eagles
- [ ] 379 Courtney Hall ...................... .10 .05 .01
  San Diego Chargers
- [ ] 380 Troy Vincent ....................... .12 .05 .02
  Miami Dolphins
- [ ] 381 Tim McGee ......................... .10 .05 .01
  Washington Redskins
- [ ] 382 Russell Freeman ................... .15 .07 .02
  Denver Broncos
- [ ] 383 Steve Tasker ....................... .10 .05 .01
  Buffalo Bills
- [ ] 384 Michael Strahan ................... .20 .09 .03
  New York Giants
  (Card can be found with or
  without draft pick logo on front)
- [ ] 385 Greg Skrepenak .................... .10 .05 .01
  Los Angeles Raiders
- [ ] 386 Jake Reed .......................... .10 .05 .01
  Minnesota Vikings
- [ ] 387 Pete Stoyanovich .................. .10 .05 .01
  Miami Dolphins
- [ ] 388 Levon Kirkland ..................... .10 .05 .01
  Pittsburgh Steelers
- [ ] 389 Mel Gray ........................... .10 .05 .01
  Detroit Lions
- [ ] 390 Brian Washington .................. .10 .05 .01

| | | | |
|---|---|---|---|
| New York Jets | | | |
| ☐ 391 Don Griffin | .10 | .05 | .01 |
| San Francisco 49ers | | | |
| ☐ 392 Desmond Howard | .50 | .23 | .06 |
| Washington Redskins | | | |
| ☐ 393 Luis Sharpe | .10 | .05 | .01 |
| Phoenix Cardinals | | | |
| ☐ 394 Mike Johnson | .10 | .05 | .01 |
| Denver Broncos | | | |
| ☐ 395 Andre Tippett | .10 | .05 | .01 |
| New England Patriots | | | |
| ☐ 396 Donnell Woolford | .10 | .05 | .01 |
| Chicago Bears | | | |
| ☐ 397 Demetrius DuBose | .25 | .11 | .03 |
| Tampa Bay Buccaneers | | | |
| (Card can be found with or | | | |
| without draft pick logo on front) | | | |
| ☐ 398 Pat Terrell | .10 | .05 | .01 |
| Los Angeles Rams | | | |
| ☐ 399 Todd McNair | .10 | .05 | .01 |
| Kansas City Chiefs | | | |
| ☐ 400 Ken Norton | .12 | .05 | .02 |
| Dallas Cowboys | | | |
| ☐ 401 Keith Hamilton | .10 | .05 | .01 |
| New York Giants | | | |
| ☐ 402 Andy Heck | .10 | .05 | .01 |
| Seattle Seahawks | | | |
| ☐ 403 Jeff Gossett | .10 | .05 | .01 |
| Los Angeles Raiders | | | |
| ☐ 404 Dexter McNabb | .10 | .05 | .01 |
| Green Bay Packers | | | |
| ☐ 405 Richmond Webb | .10 | .05 | .01 |
| Miami Dolphins | | | |
| ☐ 406 Irving Fryar | .10 | .05 | .01 |
| Miami Dolphins | | | |
| ☐ 407 Brian Hansen | .10 | .05 | .01 |
| Cleveland Browns | | | |
| ☐ 408 David Little | .10 | .05 | .01 |
| Pittsburgh Steelers | | | |
| ☐ 409 Glyn Milburn | 1.50 | .65 | .19 |
| Denver Broncos | | | |
| ☐ 410 Doug Dawson | .10 | .05 | .01 |
| Houston Oilers | | | |
| ☐ 411 Scott Mersereau | .10 | .05 | .01 |
| New York Jets | | | |
| ☐ 412 Don Beebe | .15 | .07 | .02 |
| Buffalo Bills | | | |
| ☐ 413 Vaughan Johnson | .10 | .05 | .01 |
| New Orleans Saints | | | |
| ☐ 414 Jack Del Rio | .10 | .05 | .01 |
| Minnesota Vikings | | | |
| ☐ 415 Darrien Gordon | .35 | .16 | .04 |
| San Diego Chargers | | | |
| ☐ 416 Mark Schlereth | .10 | .05 | .01 |
| Washington Redskins | | | |
| ☐ 417 Lomas Brown | .10 | .05 | .01 |
| Detroit Lions | | | |
| ☐ 418 William Thomas | .10 | .05 | .01 |
| Philadelphia Eagles | | | |
| ☐ 419 James Francis | .10 | .05 | .01 |
| Cincinnati Bengals | | | |
| ☐ 420 Quentin Coryatt | .15 | .07 | .02 |
| Indianapolis Colts | | | |
| ☐ 421 Tyji Armstrong | .10 | .05 | .01 |
| Tampa Bay Buccaneers | | | |
| ☐ 422 Hugh Millen | .10 | .05 | .01 |
| Dallas Cowboys | | | |
| ☐ 423 Adrian White | .15 | .07 | .02 |
| New England Patriots | | | |
| ☐ 424 Eddie Anderson | .10 | .05 | .01 |
| Los Angeles Raiders | | | |
| ☐ 425 Mark Ingram | .12 | .05 | .02 |
| Miami Dolphins | | | |
| ☐ 426 Ken O'Brien | .12 | .05 | .02 |
| Green Bay Packers | | | |
| ☐ 427 Simon Fletcher | .12 | .05 | .02 |
| Denver Broncos | | | |
| ☐ 428 Tim McKyer | .12 | .05 | .02 |
| Detroit Lions | | | |
| ☐ 429 Leonard Marshall | .10 | .05 | .01 |
| New York Jets | | | |
| ☐ 430 Eric Green | .15 | .07 | .02 |
| Pittsburgh Steelers | | | |
| ☐ 431 Leonard Harris | .10 | .05 | .01 |
| Houston Oilers | | | |
| ☐ 432 Darin Jordan | .15 | .07 | .02 |
| San Francisco 49ers | | | |
| ☐ 433 Erik Howard | .10 | .05 | .01 |
| New York Giants | | | |
| ☐ 434 David Lang | .10 | .05 | .01 |
| Los Angeles Rams | | | |
| ☐ 435 Eric Turner | .12 | .05 | .02 |
| Cleveland Browns | | | |
| ☐ 436 Michael Cofer | .10 | .05 | .01 |
| Detroit Lions | | | |
| ☐ 437 Jeff Bryant | .10 | .05 | .01 |
| Seattle Seahawks | | | |
| ☐ 438 Charles McRae | .10 | .05 | .01 |

| | | | |
|---|---|---|---|
| Tampa Bay Buccaneers | | | |
| ☐ 439 Henry Jones | .10 | .05 | .01 |
| Buffalo Bills | | | |
| ☐ 440 Joe Montana | 3.00 | 1.35 | .40 |
| Kansas City Chiefs | | | |
| ☐ 441 Morten Andersen | .12 | .05 | .02 |
| New Orleans Saints | | | |
| ☐ 442 Jeff Jaeger | .10 | .05 | .01 |
| Los Angeles Raiders | | | |
| ☐ 443 Leslie O'Neal | .12 | .05 | .02 |
| San Diego Chargers | | | |
| ☐ 444 LeRoy Butler | .10 | .05 | .01 |
| Green Bay Packers | | | |
| ☐ 445 Steve Jordan | .12 | .05 | .02 |
| Minnesota Vikings | | | |
| ☐ 446 Brad Edwards | .10 | .05 | .01 |
| Washington Redskins | | | |
| ☐ 447 J.B. Brown | .10 | .05 | .01 |
| Miami Dolphins | | | |
| ☐ 448 Kerry Cash | .10 | .05 | .01 |
| Indianapolis Colts | | | |
| ☐ 449 Mark Tuinei | .10 | .05 | .01 |
| Dallas Cowboys | | | |
| ☐ 450 Rodney Peete | .12 | .05 | .02 |
| Detroit Lions | | | |
| ☐ 451 Sheldon White | .10 | .05 | .01 |
| Cincinnati Bengals | | | |
| ☐ 452 Wesley Carroll | .10 | .05 | .01 |
| New Orleans Saints | | | |
| ☐ 453 Brad Baxter | .12 | .05 | .02 |
| New York Jets | | | |
| ☐ 454 Mike Pitts | .10 | .05 | .01 |
| New England Patriots | | | |
| ☐ 455 Greg Montgomery | .10 | .05 | .01 |
| Houston Oilers | | | |
| ☐ 456 Kenny Davidson | .10 | .05 | .01 |
| Pittsburgh Steelers | | | |
| ☐ 457 Scott Fulhage | .10 | .05 | .01 |
| Atlanta Falcons | | | |
| ☐ 458 Greg Townsend | .10 | .05 | .01 |
| Los Angeles Raiders | | | |
| ☐ 459 Rod Bernstine | .12 | .05 | .02 |
| Denver Broncos | | | |
| ☐ 460 Gary Clark | .12 | .05 | .02 |
| Phoenix Cardinals | | | |
| ☐ 461 Hardy Nickerson | .10 | .05 | .01 |
| Pittsburgh Steelers | | | |
| ☐ 462 Sean Landeta | .10 | .05 | .01 |
| New York Giants | | | |
| ☐ 463 Rob Burnett | .10 | .05 | .01 |
| Cleveland Browns | | | |
| ☐ 464 Fred Barnett | .15 | .07 | .02 |
| Philadelphia Eagles | | | |
| ☐ 465 John L. Williams | .12 | .05 | .02 |
| Seattle Seahawks | | | |
| ☐ 466 Anthony Miller | .30 | .14 | .04 |
| San Diego Chargers | | | |
| ☐ 467 Roman Phifer | .10 | .05 | .01 |
| Los Angeles Rams | | | |
| ☐ 468 Rich Moran | .10 | .05 | .01 |
| Green Bay Packers | | | |
| ☐ 469 Willie Roaf | .20 | .09 | .03 |
| New Orleans Saints | | | |
| ☐ 470 William Perry | .10 | .05 | .01 |
| Chicago Bears | | | |
| ☐ 471 Marcus Allen | .25 | .11 | .03 |
| Kansas City Chiefs | | | |
| ☐ 472 Carl Lee | .10 | .05 | .01 |
| Minnesota Vikings | | | |
| ☐ 473 Kurt Gouveia | .10 | .05 | .01 |
| Washington Redskins | | | |
| ☐ 474 Jarvis Williams | .10 | .05 | .01 |
| Miami Dolphins | | | |
| ☐ 475 Alfred Williams | .10 | .05 | .01 |
| Cincinnati Bengals | | | |
| ☐ 476 Mark Stepnoski | .10 | .05 | .01 |
| Dallas Cowboys | | | |
| ☐ 477 Steve Wallace | .10 | .05 | .01 |
| San Francisco 49ers | | | |
| ☐ 478 Pat Harlow | .10 | .05 | .01 |
| New England Patriots | | | |
| ☐ 479 Chip Banks | .10 | .05 | .01 |
| Indianapolis Colts | | | |
| ☐ 480 Cornelius Bennett | .15 | .07 | .02 |
| Buffalo Bills | | | |
| ☐ 481 Ryan McNeil | .20 | .09 | .03 |
| Detroit Lions | | | |
| ☐ 482 Norm Johnson | .10 | .05 | .01 |
| Atlanta Falcons | | | |
| ☐ 483 Dermontti Dawson | .10 | .05 | .01 |
| Pittsburgh Steelers | | | |
| ☐ 484 Dwayne White | .10 | .05 | .01 |
| New York Jets | | | |
| ☐ 485 Derek Russell | .12 | .05 | .02 |
| Denver Broncos | | | |
| ☐ 486 Lionel Washington | .10 | .05 | .01 |
| Los Angeles Raiders | | | |
| ☐ 487 Eric Hill | .10 | .05 | .01 |

| | | | |
|---|---|---|---|
| Phoenix Cardinals | | | |
| ☐ 488 Micheal Barrow | .10 | .05 | .01 |
| Houston Oilers | | | |
| ☐ 489 Checklist 251-375 UER | .10 | .05 | .01 |
| (No. 277 Hansen misspelled Hanson) | | | |
| ☐ 490 Checklist 376-500 UER | .10 | .05 | .01 |
| (No. 488 Micheal Barrow misspelled Michael) | | | |
| ☐ 491 Emmitt Smith MC | 1.75 | .80 | .22 |
| Dallas Cowboys | | | |
| ☐ 492 Derrick Thomas MC | .15 | .07 | .02 |
| Kansas City Chiefs | | | |
| ☐ 493 Deion Sanders MC | .15 | .07 | .02 |
| Atlanta Falcons | | | |
| ☐ 494 Randall Cunningham MC | .15 | .07 | .02 |
| Philadelphia Eagles | | | |
| ☐ 495 Sterling Sharpe MC | .35 | .16 | .04 |
| Green Bay Packers | | | |
| ☐ 496 Barry Sanders MC | 1.00 | .45 | .13 |
| Detroit Lions | | | |
| ☐ 497 Thurman Thomas MC | .40 | .18 | .05 |
| Buffalo Bills | | | |
| ☐ 498 Brett Favre MC | .75 | .35 | .09 |
| Green Bay Packers | | | |
| ☐ 499 Vaughan Johnson MC | .10 | .05 | .01 |
| New Orleans Saints | | | |
| ☐ 500 Steve Young MC | .25 | .11 | .03 |
| San Francisco 49ers | | | |
| ☐ 501 Marvin Jones | .20 | .09 | .03 |
| New York Jets | | | |
| ☐ 502 Reggie Brooks | 2.50 | 1.15 | .30 |
| Washington Redskins | | | |
| ☐ 503 Eric Curry | .10 | .05 | .01 |
| Tampa Bay Buccaneers | | | |
| ☐ 504 Drew Bledsoe | 2.00 | .90 | .25 |
| New England Patriots | | | |
| ☐ 505 Glyn Milburn | .75 | .35 | .09 |
| Denver Broncos | | | |
| ☐ 506 Jerome Bettis | 2.00 | .90 | .25 |
| Los Angeles Rams | | | |
| ☐ 507 Robert Smith | .40 | .18 | .05 |
| Minnesota Vikings | | | |
| ☐ 508 Dana Stubblefield | .50 | .23 | .06 |
| San Francisco 49ers | | | |
| ☐ 509 Tom Carter | .10 | .05 | .01 |
| Washington Redskins | | | |
| ☐ 510 Rick Mirer | 2.00 | .90 | .25 |
| Seattle Seahawks | | | |
| ☐ 511 Russell Copeland | .25 | .11 | .03 |
| Buffalo Bills | | | |
| ☐ 512 Deon Figures | .30 | .14 | .04 |
| Pittsburgh Steelers | | | |
| ☐ 513 Tony McGee | .40 | .18 | .05 |
| Cincinnati Bengals | | | |
| ☐ 514 Derrick Lassic | .35 | .16 | .04 |
| Dallas Cowboys | | | |
| ☐ 515 Everett Lindsay | .15 | .07 | .02 |
| Minnesota Vikings | | | |
| ☐ 516 Derek Brown | 1.50 | .65 | .19 |
| New Orleans Saints | | | |
| ☐ 517 Harold Alexander | .15 | .07 | .02 |
| Atlanta Falcons | | | |
| ☐ 518 Tom Scott | .15 | .07 | .02 |
| Cincinnati Bengals | | | |
| ☐ 519 Elvis Grbac | .75 | .35 | .09 |
| San Francisco 49ers | | | |
| ☐ 520 Terry Kirby | 2.50 | 1.15 | .30 |
| Miami Dolphins | | | |
| ☐ 521 Doug Pelfrey | .15 | .07 | .02 |
| Cincinnati Bengals | | | |
| ☐ 522 Horace Copeland | .75 | .35 | .09 |
| Tampa Bay Buccaneers | | | |
| ☐ 523 Irv Smith | .40 | .18 | .05 |
| New Orleans Saints | | | |
| ☐ 524 Lincoln Kennedy | .30 | .14 | .04 |
| Atlanta Falcons | | | |
| ☐ 525 Jason Elam | .15 | .07 | .02 |
| Denver Broncos | | | |
| ☐ 526 Qadry Ismail | 1.00 | .45 | .13 |
| Minnesota Vikings | | | |
| ☐ 527 Artie Smith | .20 | .09 | .03 |
| San Francisco 49ers | | | |
| ☐ 528 Tyrone Hughes | .75 | .35 | .09 |
| New Orleans Saints | | | |
| ☐ 529 Lance Gunn | .30 | .14 | .04 |
| Cincinnati Bengals | | | |
| ☐ 530 Vincent Brisby | 1.00 | .45 | .13 |
| New England Patriots | | | |
| ☐ 531 Patrick Robinson | .20 | .09 | .03 |
| Cincinnati Bengals | | | |
| ☐ 532 Raghib Ismail | .75 | .35 | .09 |
| Los Angeles Raiders | | | |
| ☐ 533 Willie Beamon | .15 | .07 | .02 |
| New York Giants | | | |
| ☐ 534 Vaughn Hebron | .75 | .35 | .09 |
| Philadelphia Eagles | | | |
| ☐ 535 Darren Drozdov | .15 | .07 | .02 |
| Denver Broncos | | | |

| | | | |
|---|---|---|---|
| ☐ 536 James Jett | 1.50 | .65 | .19 |
| Los Angeles Raiders | | | |
| ☐ 537 Michael Bates | .50 | .23 | .06 |
| Seattle Seahawks | | | |
| ☐ 538 Tom Rouen | .20 | .09 | .03 |
| Denver Broncos | | | |
| ☐ 539 Michael Husted | .15 | .07 | .02 |
| Tampa Bay Buccaneers | | | |
| ☐ 540 Greg Robinson | 1.00 | .45 | .13 |
| Los Angeles Raiders | | | |
| ☐ 541 Carl Banks | .10 | .05 | .01 |
| Washington Redskins | | | |
| ☐ 542 Kevin Greene | .10 | .05 | .01 |
| Pittsburgh Steelers | | | |
| ☐ 543 Scott Mitchell | 1.00 | .45 | .13 |
| Miami Dolphins | | | |
| ☐ 544 Michael Brooks | .10 | .05 | .01 |
| New York Giants | | | |
| ☐ 545 Shane Conlan | .10 | .05 | .01 |
| Los Angeles Rams | | | |
| ☐ 546 Vinny Testaverde | .15 | .07 | .02 |
| Cleveland Browns | | | |
| ☐ 547 Robert Delpino | .12 | .05 | .02 |
| Denver Broncos | | | |
| ☐ 548 Bill Fralic | .10 | .05 | .01 |
| Detroit Lions | | | |
| ☐ 549 Carlton Bailey | .10 | .05 | .01 |
| New York Giants | | | |
| ☐ 550 Johnny Johnson | .15 | .07 | .02 |
| New York Jets | | | |
| ☐ NNO Jerry Rice RB UER | 16.00 | 7.25 | 2.00 |
| (San Francisco 49ers) | | | |
| (Wrong date for record touchdown) | | | |

# 1993 Stadium Club First Day Production

One of these standard-size (2 1/2" by 3 1/2") cards was randomly inserted in every 24 packs of 1993 Stadium Club. Fewer than 1,000 First Day Production cards were printed of each player card. In design, the cards are identical to the regular issue cards, except that each bears on its front a special holographic First Day Production logo. The cards are numbered on the back.

| | MINT | EXC | G-VG |
|---|---|---|---|
| COMPLETE SET (550) | 2100.00 | 950.00 | 275.00 |
| COMPLETE SERIES 1 (250) | 1100.00 | 500.00 | 140.00 |
| COMPLETE SERIES 2 (250) | 700.00 | 325.00 | 90.00 |
| COMPLETE HI SERIES (50) | 300.00 | 135.00 | 38.00 |
| COMMON FDP (1-250) | 2.25 | 1.00 | .30 |
| COMMON FDP (251-500) | 2.25 | 1.00 | .30 |
| COMMON FDP (501-550) | 2.25 | 1.00 | .30 |
| *FDP STARS: 15X to 35X VALUE | | | |

| | | | |
|---|---|---|---|
| ☐ 1 Sterling Sharpe | 60.00 | 27.00 | 7.50 |
| Green Bay Packers | | | |
| ☐ 21 Natrone Means | 40.00 | 18.00 | 5.00 |
| San Diego Chargers | | | |
| ☐ 50 Troy Aikman | 125.00 | 57.50 | 15.50 |
| Dallas Cowboys | | | |
| ☐ 56 O.J. McDuffie | 45.00 | 20.00 | 5.75 |
| Miami Dolphins | | | |
| ☐ 60 Dan Marino | 75.00 | 34.00 | 9.50 |
| Miami Dolphins | | | |
| ☐ 70 John Elway | 60.00 | 27.00 | 7.50 |
| Denver Broncos | | | |
| ☐ 75 Jim Kelly | 40.00 | 18.00 | 5.00 |
| Buffalo Bills | | | |
| ☐ 82 Garrison Hearst | 40.00 | 18.00 | 5.00 |
| Arizona Cardinals | | | |
| ☐ 85 Emmitt Smith | 175.00 | 80.00 | 22.00 |
| Dallas Cowboys | | | |

| | | | |
|---|---|---|---|
| ☐ 103 Ricky Watters............... | 40.00 | 18.00 | 5.00 |
| San Francisco 49ers | | | |
| ☐ 105 Rodney Hampton................ | 45.00 | 20.00 | 5.75 |
| New York Giants | | | |
| ☐ 108 Jerome Bettis...................... | 100.00 | 45.00 | 12.50 |
| Los Angeles Rams | | | |
| ☐ 120 Barry Sanders.................... | 75.00 | 34.00 | 9.50 |
| Detroit Lions | | | |
| ☐ 129 Michael Irvin...................... | 50.00 | 23.00 | 6.25 |
| Dallas Cowboys | | | |
| ☐ 180 Rick Mirer........................... | 100.00 | 45.00 | 12.50 |
| Seattle Seahawks | | | |
| ☐ 208 Steve Young........................ | 50.00 | 23.00 | 6.25 |
| San Francisco 49ers | | | |
| ☐ 210 Brett Favre.......................... | 70.00 | 32.00 | 8.75 |
| Green Bay Packers | | | |
| ☐ 232 Jerry Rice........................... | 75.00 | 34.00 | 9.50 |
| San Francisco 49ers | | | |
| ☐ 242 Troy Aikman MC.................. | 75.00 | 34.00 | 9.50 |
| Dallas Cowboys | | | |
| ☐ 246 Dan Marino MC.................... | 50.00 | 23.00 | 6.25 |
| Miami Dolphins | | | |
| ☐ 248 Thurman Thomas MC .......... | 35.00 | 16.00 | 4.40 |
| Buffalo Bills | | | |
| ☐ 250 Joe Montana MC.................. | 80.00 | 36.00 | 10.00 |
| Kansas City Chiefs | | | |
| ☐ 280 Drew Bledsoe...................... | 100.00 | 45.00 | 12.50 |
| New England Patriots | | | |
| ☐ 409 Glyn Milburn....................... | 40.00 | 18.00 | 5.00 |
| Denver Broncos | | | |
| ☐ 440 Joe Montana........................ | 125.00 | 57.50 | 15.50 |
| Kansas City Chiefs | | | |
| ☐ 491 Emmitt Smith MC................. | 90.00 | 40.00 | 11.50 |
| Dallas Cowboys | | | |
| ☐ 496 Barry Sanders MC ............... | 50.00 | 23.00 | 6.25 |
| Detroit Lions | | | |
| ☐ 497 Thurman Thomas MC .......... | 35.00 | 16.00 | 4.40 |
| Buffalo Bills | | | |
| ☐ 498 Brett Favre MC .................... | 40.00 | 18.00 | 5.00 |
| Green Bay Packers | | | |
| ☐ 502 Reggie Brooks..................... | 40.00 | 18.00 | 5.00 |
| Washington Redskins | | | |
| ☐ 504 Drew Bledsoe...................... | 40.00 | 18.00 | 5.00 |
| New England Patriots | | | |
| ☐ 506 Jerome Bettis...................... | 40.00 | 18.00 | 5.00 |
| Los Angeles Rams | | | |
| ☐ 510 Rick Mirer........................... | 40.00 | 18.00 | 5.00 |
| Seattle Seahawks | | | |
| ☐ 520 Terry Kirby.......................... | 40.00 | 18.00 | 5.00 |
| Miami Dolphins | | | |
| ☐ 530 Vincent Brisby..................... | 20.00 | 9.00 | 2.50 |
| New England Patriots | | | |
| ☐ 543 Scott Mitchell...................... | 20.00 | 9.00 | 2.50 |
| Miami Dolphins | | | |

# 1993 Stadium Club Master Photos I

Inserted one in every 24 packs, Master Photo redemption cards were redeemable for three Stadium Club Master Photos. The first series featured 12 different Master Photos. Carrying uncropped versions of regular Stadium Club cards, the front gives 17 percent more photo area than a regular card. The back has a narrative of the player along with a full-color graphic presentation of a key statistic. The photos are numbered on the back.

| | MINT | EXC | G-VG |
|---|---|---|---|
| COMPLETE SET (12)........................ | 15.00 | 6.75 | 1.90 |
| COMMON PLAYER (1-12)................ | .75 | .35 | .09 |
| ☐ 1 Barry Foster ........................ | 1.50 | .65 | .19 |
| Pittsburgh Steelers | | | |
| ☐ 2 Barry Sanders ...................... | 4.00 | 1.80 | .50 |
| Detroit Lions | | | |

| | | | |
|---|---|---|---|
| ☐ 3 Reggie Cobb ........................... | .75 | .35 | .09 |
| Tampa Bay Buccaneers | | | |
| ☐ 4 Cortez Kennedy ...................... | .75 | .35 | .09 |
| Seattle Seahawks | | | |
| ☐ 5 Steve Young ........................... | 2.00 | .90 | .25 |
| San Francisco 49ers | | | |
| ☐ 6 Ricky Watters ......................... | 2.00 | .90 | .25 |
| San Francisco 49ers | | | |
| ☐ 7 Rob Moore .............................. | .75 | .35 | .09 |
| New York Jets | | | |
| ☐ 8 Derrick Thomas....................... | .75 | .35 | .09 |
| Kansas City Chiefs | | | |
| ☐ 9 Jeff George ............................. | 1.25 | .55 | .16 |
| Indianapolis Colts | | | |
| ☐ 10 Sterling Sharpe ...................... | 2.50 | 1.15 | .30 |
| Green Bay Packers | | | |
| ☐ 11 Bruce Smith ........................... | .75 | .35 | .09 |
| Buffalo Bills | | | |
| ☐ 12 Deion Sanders........................ | 1.25 | .55 | .16 |
| Atlanta Falcons | | | |

# 1993 Stadium Club Master Photos II

Inserted one in every 24 packs, Master Photo redemption cards were redeemable, until 6/1/94, for three Stadium Club Master Photos II. The second series featured 12 different 5" by 7" Master Photos. Carrying uncropped versions of regular Stadium Club cards, the front gives 17 percent more photo area than a regular card. The back has a narrative player profile with the player's name printed vertically down the center of the card. The cards are numbered on the back "X of 12."

| | MINT | EXC | G-VG |
|---|---|---|---|
| COMPLETE SET (12)........................ | 9.00 | 4.00 | 1.15 |
| COMMON PLAYER (1-12)................ | .75 | .35 | .09 |
| ☐ 1 Morten Andersen ..................... | .75 | .35 | .09 |
| New Orleans Saints | | | |
| ☐ 2 Ken Norton.............................. | 1.00 | .45 | .13 |
| Dallas Cowboys | | | |
| ☐ 3 Clyde Simmons......................... | 1.00 | .45 | .13 |
| Philadelphia Eagles | | | |
| ☐ 4 Roman Phifer .......................... | .75 | .35 | .09 |
| Los Angeles Rams | | | |
| ☐ 5 Greg Townsend ....................... | .75 | .35 | .09 |
| Los Angeles Raiders | | | |
| ☐ 6 Darryl Talley ........................... | .75 | .35 | .09 |
| Buffalo Bills | | | |
| ☐ 7 Herschel Walker ...................... | 1.00 | .45 | .13 |
| Philadelphia Eagles | | | |
| ☐ 8 Reggie White ........................... | 1.00 | .45 | .13 |
| Green Bay Packers | | | |
| ☐ 9 Jesse Solomon ........................ | .75 | .35 | .09 |
| Atlanta Falcons | | | |
| ☐ 10 Joe Montana ........................... | 6.00 | 2.70 | .75 |
| Kansas City Chiefs | | | |
| ☐ 11 John Taylor.............................. | 1.00 | .45 | .13 |
| San Francisco 49ers | | | |
| ☐ 12 Cornelius Bennett..................... | 1.00 | .45 | .13 |
| Buffalo Bills | | | |

# 1993 Stadium Club Super Team

Measuring the standard-size (2 1/2" by 3 1/2"), one of these Super Team cards was randomly inserted in one pack of 1993 Stadium Club. Each of the 28 NFL teams is represented by a card. Team cards featuring a division winner, conference championship team, or Super Bowl XXVIII winner were redeemable for the following special prizes: (1) 12 Stadium Club cards of players from the winning team, embossed with gold foil division winning logo (Division Winner card);

(2) 12 Master Photos of the winning team, with special embossed gold foil Conference logo (AFC or NFC Conference Championship card); and (3) complete set of all 500 Stadium Club cards with official gold foil embossed Super Bowl logo (Super Bowl XXVIII Winner card; winners were also entered into a random drawing to win an official Super Bowl game ball). If the team pictured on the Super Team card wins more than one title, the collector may claim all of the corresponding prizes won by that card. The fronts feature full-bleed color action photos. The top and right side are edged by prismatic stripes. The team name in green is overprinted on the top prismatic border stripe. The player's name is featured from the team and the card subtitle "Super Team Card" are also printed in prismatic lettering. The backs are white and completely filled by instructions and conditions of the promotion. The cards are unnumbered and checklisted below alphabetically according to team name. Winning cards sent to Topps were returned with a "redeemed " stamp on the card back. In most cases, the stamped cards are valued at least 50 percent less than the non-stamped variety. Team cards that would have stamps are the Cowboys, Bills, Oilers, Lions, 49ers, Chiefs, Oilers.

| | MINT | EXC | G-VG |
|---|---|---|---|
| COMPLETE SET (28) | 75.00 | 34.00 | 9.50 |
| COMMON TEAM (1-28) | 1.50 | .65 | .19 |
| ☐ 1 Jim Harbaugh | 1.50 | .65 | .19 |
| Chicago Bears | | | |
| ☐ 2 David Klingler | 2.00 | .90 | .25 |
| Cincinnati Bengals | | | |
| ☐ 3 Jim Kelly | 5.00 | 2.30 | .60 |
| Buffalo Bills | | | |
| ☐ 4 John Elway | 4.00 | 1.80 | .50 |
| Denver Broncos | | | |
| ☐ 5 Bernie Kosar | 1.50 | .65 | .19 |
| Cleveland Browns | | | |
| ☐ 6 Reggie Cobb | 2.00 | .90 | .25 |
| Tampa Bay Buccaneers | | | |
| ☐ 7 Eric Swann | 1.50 | .65 | .19 |
| Phoenix Cardinals | | | |
| ☐ 8 Stan Humphries | 1.50 | .65 | .19 |
| San Diego Chargers | | | |
| ☐ 9 Derrick Thomas | 3.00 | 1.35 | .40 |
| Kansas City Chiefs | | | |
| ☐ 10 Steve Emtman | 1.50 | .65 | .19 |
| Indianapolis Colts | | | |
| ☐ 11 Emmitt Smith | 15.00 | 6.75 | 1.90 |
| Dallas Cowboys | | | |
| ☐ 12 Dan Marino | 5.00 | 2.30 | .60 |
| Miami Dolphins | | | |
| ☐ 13 Randall Cunningham | 2.25 | 1.00 | .30 |
| Philadelphia Eagles | | | |
| ☐ 14 Deion Sanders | 2.25 | 1.00 | .30 |
| Atlanta Falcons | | | |
| ☐ 15 Steve Young | 6.00 | 2.70 | .75 |
| San Francisco 49ers | | | |
| ☐ 16 Lawrence Taylor | 2.25 | 1.00 | .30 |
| New York Giants | | | |
| ☐ 17 Brad Baxter | 1.50 | .65 | .19 |
| New York Jets | | | |
| ☐ 18 Barry Sanders | 8.00 | 3.60 | 1.00 |
| Detroit Lions | | | |
| ☐ 19 Warren Moon | 4.00 | 1.80 | .50 |
| Houston Oilers | | | |
| ☐ 20 Brett Favre | 4.00 | 1.80 | .50 |
| Green Bay Packers | | | |
| ☐ 21 Brent Williams | 1.50 | .65 | .19 |
| New England Patriots | | | |
| ☐ 22 Howie Long | 1.50 | .65 | .19 |
| Los Angeles Raiders | | | |
| ☐ 23 Cleveland Gary | 1.50 | .65 | .19 |
| Los Angeles Rams | | | |
| ☐ 24 Mark Rypien | 2.00 | .90 | .25 |
| Washington Redskins | | | |
| ☐ 25 Sam Mills | 1.50 | .65 | .19 |
| New Orleans Saints | | | |

| | | | |
|---|---|---|---|
| ☐ 26 Cortez Kennedy | 2.00 | .90 | .25 |
| Seattle Seahawks | | | |
| ☐ 27 Barry Foster | 3.00 | 1.35 | .40 |
| Pittsburgh Steelers | | | |
| ☐ 28 Terry Allen | 2.00 | .90 | .25 |
| Minnesota Vikings | | | |

# 1993 Stadium Club Super Bowl Redemption

This 500-card standard-size (2 1/2" by 3 1/2") set was awarded to collectors who redeemed the 1993 Stadium Club Super Team Cowboys winner card. The set is identical to the first 500 regular Stadium Club cards, except for the addition of a gold-foil Super Bowl XXVIII logo stamped on the front. The set was packaged with a redeemed Super Team Cowboys card that also carried the Super Bowl logo. The cards are valued using a multiplier of the regular value.

| | MINT | EXC | G-VG |
|---|---|---|---|
| COMPLETE SET (500) | 150.00 | 67.50 | 15.00 |
| COMMON PLAYER (1-500) | .30 | .14 | .03 |
| STAMPED SERIES STARS 2X TO 4X VALUE | | | |

# 1993 Stadium Club Master Photos Bills

Featuring the AFC Champion Buffalo Bills, these 12 Master Photos measure approximately 5" by 7" each. Collectors who redeemed a Bills' Super Team card received this set as well as a Super Team card redemption set. Carrying uncropped versions of regular Stadium Club cards, the fronts give 17 percent more photo area than a regular card. A gold-prismatic "A" (for American Conference) edged by stars appears beneath each picture. The backs are blank except for Team NFL, NFLPA, and Topps logos. The cards are unnumbered and checklisted below in alphabetical order.

| | MINT | EXC | G-VG |
|---|---|---|---|
| COMPLETE SET (12) | 20.00 | 8.00 | 2.00 |
| COMMON PLAYER (1-12) | 1.00 | .40 | .10 |
| ☐ 1 Don Beebe | 2.50 | 1.00 | .25 |
| ☐ 2 Cornelius Bennett | 2.50 | 1.00 | .25 |
| ☐ 3 Bill Brooks | 2.50 | 1.00 | .25 |
| ☐ 4 Henry Jones | 2.00 | .80 | .20 |
| ☐ 5 Jim Kelly | 6.00 | 2.40 | .60 |
| ☐ 6 Mark Kelso | 1.00 | .40 | .10 |
| ☐ 7 Pete Metzelaars | 1.00 | .40 | .10 |
| ☐ 8 Nate Odomes | 1.00 | .40 | .10 |
| ☐ 9 Andre Reed | 3.00 | 1.20 | .30 |
| ☐ 10 Bruce Smith | 3.00 | 1.20 | .30 |
| ☐ 11 Darryl Talley | 2.00 | .80 | .20 |
| ☐ 12 Steve Tasker | 1.50 | .60 | .15 |

# 1993 Stadium Club AFC Winner Bills

Collectors who redeemed a Super Team card of a division winner received a Super Team card redemption set. If the team also won the conference championship, collectors were also entitled to receive a master photo set of the team. The cards measure the standard size (2 1/2" by 3 1/2"). The fronts feature vertical and horizontal full-bleed color action player photos. The player's name is gold foil-stamped on a green stripe edged on the bottom by gold foil. The words "Division

Winner" are also gold foil-stamped on the front. On a football field design, the backs carry a second color player photo, a miniature representation of the player's Topps rookie card, biography, the Football News Skills Rating System, a "key stat" feature, and statistics (1992 and career). The cards are numbered on the back.

|  | MINT | EXC | G-VG |
|---|---|---|---|
| COMPLETE SET (13) | 20.00 | 8.00 | 2.00 |
| COMMON PLAYER | 1.00 | .40 | .10 |
|  |  |  |  |
| ☐ 27 Mark Kelso | 1.00 | .40 | .10 |
| ☐ 54 Bruce Smith | 3.00 | 1.20 | .30 |
| ☐ 75 Jim Kelly | 6.00 | 2.40 | .60 |
| ☐ 107 Andre Reed | 3.00 | 1.20 | .30 |
| ☐ 153 Pete Metzelaars | 1.00 | .40 | .10 |
| ☐ 211 Nate Odomes | 1.00 | .40 | .10 |
| ☐ 227 Bill Brooks | 2.50 | 1.00 | .25 |
| ☐ 331 Darryl Talley | 2.00 | .80 | .20 |
| ☐ 383 Steve Tasker | 1.50 | .60 | .15 |
| ☐ 412 Don Beebe | 2.50 | 1.00 | .25 |
| ☐ 439 Henry Jones | 2.00 | .80 | .20 |
| ☐ 480 Cornelius Bennett | 2.50 | 1.00 | .25 |
| ☐ NNO Redemption Card | 2.50 | 1.00 | .25 |

## 1993 Stadium Club Master Photos Cowboys

Featuring the NFC Champion Dallas Cowboys, these 12 Master Photos measure approximately 5" by 7" each. Collectors who redeemed a Cowboys' Super Team card received this set as well as a Super Team card redemption set. Carrying uncropped versions of regular Stadium Club cards, the fronts give 17 percent more photo area than a regular card. A gold-prismatic "N" (for National Conference) edged by stars appears beneath each picture. The backs are blank except for Team NFL, NFLPA, and Topps logos. The cards are unnumbered and checklisted below in alphabetical order.

|  | MINT | EXC | G-VG |
|---|---|---|---|
| COMPLETE SET (12) | 30.00 | 12.00 | 3.00 |
| COMMON PLAYER (1-12) | 1.00 | .40 | .10 |
|  |  |  |  |
| ☐ 1 Troy Aikman | 6.00 | 2.40 | .60 |
| ☐ 2 Charles Haley | 1.50 | .60 | .15 |
| ☐ 3 Alvin Harper | 3.00 | 1.20 | .30 |
| ☐ 4 Michael Irvin | 3.00 | 1.20 | .30 |
| ☐ 5 Daryl Johnston | 2.00 | .80 | .20 |
| ☐ 6 Robert Jones | 1.00 | .40 | .10 |
| ☐ 7 Russell Maryland | 2.00 | .80 | .20 |
| ☐ 8 Ken Norton Jr | 1.50 | .60 | .15 |
| ☐ 9 Jay Novacek | 2.00 | .80 | .20 |
| ☐ 10 Emmitt Smith | 8.00 | 3.25 | .80 |
| ☐ 11 Kevin Smith | 1.50 | .60 | .15 |
| ☐ 12 Kevin Williams | 2.00 | .80 | .20 |

## 1993 Stadium Club NFC Winner Cowboys

Collectors who redeemed a Super Team card of a division winner received a Super Team card redemption set. If the team also won the conference championship, collectors were also entitled to receive a master photo set of the team. Finally, if the team was the Super Bowl XXVIII champion, they received additionally a factory set of 1993 Stadium Club cards with official gold foil embossed Super Bowl logo. The cards measure the standard size (2 1/2" by 3 1/2"). The fronts feature vertical and horizontal full-bleed color action player photos.

The player's name is gold foil-stamped on a green stripe edged on the bottom by gold foil. The words "Division Winner" are also gold foil-stamped on the front. On a football field design, the backs carry a second color player photo, a miniature representation of the player's Topps rookie card, biography, the Football News Skills Rating System, a "key stat" feature, and statistics (1992 and career). The cards are numbered on the back.

|  | MINT | EXC | G-VG |
|---|---|---|---|
| COMPLETE SET (13) | 30.00 | 12.00 | 3.00 |
| COMMON PLAYER | 1.00 | .40 | .10 |
|  |  |  |  |
| ☐ 17 Alvin Harper | 3.00 | 1.20 | .30 |
| ☐ 50 Troy Aikman | 6.00 | 2.40 | .60 |
| ☐ 85 Emmitt Smith | 8.00 | 3.25 | .80 |
| ☐ 106 Daryl Johnston | 2.00 | .80 | .20 |
| ☐ 129 Michael Irvin | 3.00 | 1.20 | .30 |
| ☐ 152 Charles Haley | 1.50 | .60 | .15 |
| ☐ 174 Jay Novacek | 2.00 | .80 | .20 |
| ☐ 204 Russell Maryland | 2.00 | .80 | .20 |
| ☐ 278 Kevin Williams | 2.00 | .80 | .20 |
| ☐ 299 Kevin Smith | 1.50 | .60 | .15 |
| ☐ 325 Robert Jones | 1.00 | .40 | .10 |
| ☐ 400 Ken Norton Jr | 1.50 | .60 | .15 |
| ☐ NNO Redemption Card | 6.00 | 2.40 | .60 |

## 1993 Stadium Club Division Winner Chiefs

Collectors who redeemed a Super Team card of a division winner received a Super Team card redemption set. If the team also won the conference championship, collectors were also entitled to receive a master photo set of the team. Finally, if the team was the Super Bowl XXVIII champion, they received additionally a factory set of 1993 Stadium Club cards with official gold foil embossed Super Bowl logo. The cards measure the standard size (2 1/2" by 3 1/2"). The fronts feature vertical and horizontal full-bleed color action player photos. The player's name is gold foil-stamped on a green stripe edged on the bottom by gold foil. The words "Division Winner" are also gold foil-stamped on the front. On a football field design, the backs carry a second color player photo, a miniature representation of the player's Topps rookie card, biography, the Football News Skills Rating System, a "key stat" feature, and statistics (1992 and career). The cards are numbered on the back.

|  | MINT | EXC | G-VG |
|---|---|---|---|
| COMPLETE SET (13) | 25.00 | 10.00 | 2.50 |
| COMMON PLAYER | 1.00 | .40 | .10 |

| | | | |
|---|---|---|---|
| ☐ 80 Dale Carter | 2.00 | .80 | .20 |
| ☐ 133 Neil Smith | 2.00 | .80 | .20 |
| ☐ 173 Derrick Thomas | 3.00 | 1.20 | .30 |
| ☐ 203 Harvey Williams | 2.00 | .80 | .20 |
| ☐ 215 Tracy Simien | 1.00 | .40 | .10 |
| ☐ 268 Jonathan Hayes | 1.00 | .40 | .10 |
| ☐ 289 J.J. Birden | 1.50 | .60 | .15 |
| ☐ 312 Willie Davis | 2.00 | .80 | .20 |
| ☐ 375 Nick Lowery | 1.50 | .60 | .15 |
| ☐ 399 Todd McNair | 1.00 | .40 | .10 |
| ☐ 440 Joe Montana | 10.00 | 4.00 | 1.00 |
| ☐ 471 Marcus Allen | 4.00 | 1.60 | .40 |
| ☐ NNO Redemption Card | 2.00 | .80 | .20 |

## 1993 Stadium Club Division Winner 49ers

Collectors who redeemed a Super Team card of a division winner received a Super Team card redemption set. If the team also won the conference championship, collectors were also entitled to receive a master photo set of the team. Finally, if the team was the Super Bowl XXVIII champion, they received additionally a factory set of 1993 Stadium Club cards with official gold foil embossed Super Bowl logo. The cards measure the standard size (2 1/2" by 3 1/2"). The fronts feature vertical and horizontal full-bleed color action player photos. The player's name is gold foil-stamped on a green stripe edged on the bottom by gold foil. The words "Division Winner" are also gold foil-stamped on the front. On a football field design, the backs carry a second color player photo, a miniature representation of the player's Topps rookie card, biography, the Football News Skills Rating System, a "key stat" feature, and statistics (1992 and career). The cards are numbered on the back.

| | MINT | EXC | G-VG |
|---|---|---|---|
| COMPLETE SET (13) | 25.00 | 10.00 | 2.50 |
| COMMON PLAYER | 1.00 | .40 | .10 |
| | | | |
| ☐ 29 Dana Hall | 1.50 | .60 | .15 |
| ☐ 52 Brent Jones | 2.00 | .80 | .20 |
| ☐ 76 Bill Romanowski | 1.00 | .40 | .10 |
| ☐ 103 Ricky Watters | 4.00 | 1.60 | .40 |
| ☐ 123 Jesse Sapolu | 1.00 | .40 | .10 |
| ☐ 176 Kevin Fagan | 1.00 | .40 | .10 |
| ☐ 199 Tim McDonald | 1.50 | .60 | .15 |
| ☐ 208 Steve Young | 5.00 | 2.00 | .50 |
| ☐ 232 Jerry Rice | 6.00 | 2.40 | .60 |
| ☐ 275 John Taylor | 2.00 | .80 | .20 |
| ☐ 326 Eric Davis | 1.00 | .40 | .10 |
| ☐ 370 Tom Rathman | 1.50 | .60 | .15 |
| ☐ NNO Redemption Card | 3.00 | 1.20 | .30 |

## 1993 Stadium Club Division Winner Lions

Collectors who redeemed a Super Team card of a division winner received a Super Team card redemption set. If the team also won the conference championship, collectors were also entitled to receive a master photo set of the team. Finally, if the team was the Super Bowl XXVIII champion, they received additionally a factory set of 1993 Stadium Club cards with official gold foil embossed Super Bowl logo. The cards measure the standard size (2 1/2" by 3 1/2"). The fronts feature vertical and horizontal full-bleed color action player photos. The player's name is gold foil-stamped on a green stripe edged on the bottom by gold foil. The words "Division Winner" are also gold foil-stamped on the front. On a football field design, the backs carry a

second color player photo, a miniature representation of the player's Topps rookie card, biography, the Football News Skills Rating System, a "key stat" feature, and statistics (1992 and career). The cards are numbered on the back.

| | MINT | EXC | G-VG |
|---|---|---|---|
| COMPLETE SET (13) | 20.00 | 8.00 | 2.00 |
| COMMON PLAYER | 1.00 | .40 | .10 |
| | | | |
| ☐ 7 Dennis Gibson | 1.00 | .40 | .10 |
| ☐ 31 Jason Hanson | 1.50 | .60 | .15 |
| ☐ 61 Robert Porcher | 1.50 | .60 | .15 |
| ☐ 120 Barry Sanders | 6.00 | 2.40 | .60 |
| ☐ 231 Marc Spindler | 1.00 | .40 | .10 |
| ☐ 263 Kelvin Pritchett | 1.50 | .60 | .15 |
| ☐ 295 Pat Swilling | 2.00 | .80 | .20 |
| ☐ 321 Ray Crockett | 1.00 | .40 | .10 |
| ☐ 342 Chris Spielman | 1.50 | .60 | .15 |
| ☐ 368 William White | 1.00 | .40 | .10 |
| ☐ 389 Mel Gray | 1.50 | .60 | .15 |
| ☐ 450 Rodney Peete | 2.00 | .80 | .20 |
| ☐ NNO Redemption Card | 3.00 | 1.20 | .30 |

## 1993 Stadium Club Division Winner Oilers

Collectors who redeemed a Super Team card of a division winner received a Super Team card redemption set. If the team also won the conference championship, collectors were also entitled to receive a master photo set of the team. Finally, if the team was the Super Bowl XXVIII champion, they received additionally a factory set of 1993 Stadium Club cards with official gold foil embossed Super Bowl logo. The cards measure the standard size (2 1/2" by 3 1/2"). The fronts feature vertical and horizontal full-bleed color action player photos. The player's name is gold foil-stamped on a green stripe edged on the bottom by gold foil. The words "Division Winner" are also gold foil-stamped on the front. On a football field design, the backs carry a second color player photo, a miniature representation of the player's Topps rookie card, biography, the Football News Skills Rating System, a "key stat" feature, and statistics (1992 and career). The cards are numbered on the back.

| | MINT | EXC | G-VG |
|---|---|---|---|
| COMPLETE SET (13) | 20.00 | 8.00 | 2.00 |
| COMMON PLAYER | 1.00 | .40 | .10 |
| | | | |
| ☐ 20 Ernest Givins | 2.50 | 1.00 | .25 |
| ☐ 101 Warren Moon | 5.00 | 2.00 | .50 |
| ☐ 128 Al Smith | 1.50 | .60 | .15 |
| ☐ 146 Lorenzo White | 2.00 | .80 | .20 |

| | | | |
|---|---|---|---|
| ☐ 166 William Fuller | 1.50 | .60 | .15 |
| ☐ 192 Ray Childress | 2.00 | .80 | .20 |
| ☐ 225 Sean Jones | 1.50 | .60 | .15 |
| ☐ 305 Bruce Matthews | 1.50 | .60 | .15 |
| ☐ 329 Haywood Jeffires | 2.50 | 1.00 | .25 |
| ☐ 347 Cris Dishman | 1.00 | .40 | .10 |
| ☐ 376 Bubba McDowell | 1.00 | .40 | .10 |
| ☐ 455 Greg Montgomery | 1.00 | .40 | .10 |
| ☐ NNO Redemption Card | 2.50 | 1.00 | .25 |

## 1963 Stancraft Playing Cards

This 54-card set, subtitled "Official NFL All-Time Greats," commemorates outstanding NFL players and was issued in conjunction with the opening of the Pro Football Hall of Fame in Canton, Ohio. It should be noted that several of the players in the set are (still) not in the Pro Football Hall of Fame. The back of the cards was produced two different ways. One style has a checkerboard pattern, with the NFL logo in the middle and logos for the 14 NFL teams surrounding it against a red background; the other style has the 14 NFL team helmets floating on a green background. The set was issued in a plastic box which fit into a cardboard outer slip-case box. Apart from the aces and two jokers (featuring the NFL logo), the fronts of the other cards have a skillfully drawn picture (in brown ink) of the player, with his name, position, year(s), and team below the drawing. The set was also reportedly made in a pinochle format. We have checklisted this set in playing card order by suits and assigned numbers to Aces (1), Jacks (11), Queens (12), and Kings (13). Each card measures approximately 2 1/4" by 3 1/2" with rounded corners.

| | NRMT | VG-E | GOOD |
|---|---|---|---|
| COMPLETE SET (54) | 100.00 | 40.00 | 10.00 |
| COMMON CARD (1-54) | 1.50 | .60 | .15 |
| | | | |
| ☐ 1C NFL Logo | 1.50 | .60 | .15 |
| ☐ 1D NFL Logo | 1.50 | .60 | .15 |
| ☐ 1H NFL Logo | 1.50 | .60 | .15 |
| ☐ 1S NFL Logo | 1.50 | .60 | .15 |
| ☐ 2C Johnny(Blood) McNally | 2.00 | .80 | .20 |
| ☐ 2D Frankie Albert | 1.50 | .60 | .15 |
| ☐ 2H Paul Hornung | 4.00 | 1.60 | .40 |
| ☐ 2S Eddie LeBaron | 1.50 | .60 | .15 |
| ☐ 3C Bobby Mitchell | 3.00 | 1.20 | .30 |
| ☐ 3D Del Shofner | 1.50 | .60 | .15 |
| ☐ 3H Johnny Unitas | 9.00 | 3.75 | .90 |
| ☐ 3S Don Hutson | 3.00 | 1.20 | .30 |
| ☐ 4C Bill Howton | 1.50 | .60 | .15 |
| ☐ 4D Ollie Matson | 4.00 | 1.60 | .40 |
| ☐ 4H Doak Walker | 4.00 | 1.60 | .40 |
| ☐ 4S Clarke Hinkle | 2.00 | .80 | .20 |
| ☐ 5C Wilbur(Fats) Henry | 2.00 | .80 | .20 |
| ☐ 5D Mike Ditka | 7.50 | 3.00 | .75 |
| ☐ 5H Tom Fears | 3.00 | 1.20 | .30 |
| ☐ 5S Charley Conerly | 2.50 | 1.00 | .25 |
| ☐ 6C Tony Canadeo | 2.00 | .80 | .20 |
| ☐ 6D Otto Graham | 5.00 | 2.00 | .50 |
| ☐ 6H Jim Thorpe | 9.00 | 3.75 | .90 |
| ☐ 6S Earl(Curly) Lambeau | 2.00 | .80 | .20 |
| ☐ 7C Clyde(Bulldog) Turner | 2.50 | 1.00 | .25 |
| ☐ 7D Chuck Bednarik | 4.00 | 1.60 | .40 |
| ☐ 7H Gino Marchetti | 3.00 | 1.20 | .30 |
| ☐ 7S Sid Luckman | 4.00 | 1.60 | .40 |
| ☐ 8C Charley Trippi | 2.00 | .80 | .20 |
| ☐ 8D Jim Taylor | 3.00 | 1.20 | .30 |
| ☐ 8H Claude(Buddy) Young | 1.50 | .60 | .15 |
| ☐ 8S Pete Pihos | 2.00 | .80 | .20 |
| ☐ 9C Tommy Mason | 1.50 | .60 | .15 |
| ☐ 9D Mel Hein | 2.00 | .80 | .20 |
| ☐ 9H Jim Benton | 1.50 | .60 | .15 |
| ☐ 9S Dante Lavelli | 2.00 | .80 | .20 |

| | | | |
|---|---|---|---|
| ☐ 10C Earl(Dutch) Clark | 2.00 | .80 | .20 |
| ☐ 10D Eddie Price | 1.50 | .60 | .15 |
| ☐ 10H Jim Brown | 12.00 | 5.00 | 1.20 |
| ☐ 10S Norm Van Brocklin | 4.00 | 1.60 | .40 |
| ☐ 11C Y.A. Tittle | 5.00 | 2.00 | .50 |
| ☐ 11D Sonny Randle | 1.50 | .60 | .15 |
| ☐ 11H George Halas | 4.00 | 1.60 | .40 |
| ☐ 11S Cloyce Box | 1.50 | .60 | .15 |
| ☐ 12C Lou Groza | 4.00 | 1.60 | .40 |
| ☐ 12D Joe Perry | 4.00 | 1.60 | .40 |
| ☐ 12H Sammy Baugh | 5.00 | 2.00 | .50 |
| ☐ 12S Joe Schmidt | 3.00 | 1.20 | .30 |
| ☐ 13C Bobby Layne | 5.00 | 2.00 | .50 |
| ☐ 13D Bob Waterfield | 4.00 | 1.60 | .40 |
| ☐ 13H Bill Dudley | 2.50 | 1.00 | .25 |
| ☐ 13S Elroy Hirsch | 3.00 | 1.20 | .30 |
| ☐ NNO Joker (NFL Logo) | 2.00 | .80 | .20 |
| ☐ NNO Joker (NFL Logo) | 2.00 | .80 | .20 |

## 1989 Star-Cal Decals

These decals were licensed by the NFL and NFL Players' Association. The first series features players from six NFL teams. The decals measure approximately 3" by 4 1/2" with rounded corners and a full-color action photo of the player. In the upper left corner, a silver logo with the words "First Edition 1989" distinguishes this series from future releases. As a bonus, each decal comes with a pennant-shaped miniature team banner decal in the player's team colors, with the team helmet and nickname on the banner. The decals are unnumbered and checklisted below alphabetically by player.

| | MINT | EXC | G-VG |
|---|---|---|---|
| COMPLETE SET (54) | 75.00 | 30.00 | 7.50 |
| COMMON PLAYER (1-54) | 1.00 | .40 | .10 |
| | | | |
| ☐ 1 Raul Allegre | 1.00 | .40 | .10 |
| New York Giants | | | |
| ☐ 2 Carl Banks | 1.50 | .60 | .15 |
| New York Giants | | | |
| ☐ 3 Cornelius Bennett | 2.00 | .80 | .20 |
| Buffalo Bills | | | |
| ☐ 4 Brian Blades | 2.50 | 1.00 | .25 |
| Seattle Seahawks | | | |
| ☐ 5 Kevin Butler | 1.00 | .40 | .10 |
| Chicago Bears | | | |
| ☐ 6 Harry Carson | 1.50 | .60 | .15 |
| New York Giants | | | |
| ☐ 7 Anthony Carter | 2.00 | .80 | .20 |
| Minnesota Vikings | | | |
| ☐ 8 Michael Carter | 1.50 | .60 | .15 |
| San Francisco 49ers | | | |
| ☐ 9 Shane Conlan | 2.00 | .80 | .20 |
| Buffalo Bills | | | |
| ☐ 10 Roger Craig | 2.50 | 1.00 | .25 |
| San Francisco 49ers | | | |
| ☐ 11 Richard Dent | 1.50 | .60 | .15 |
| Chicago Bears | | | |
| ☐ 12 Chris Doleman | 1.50 | .60 | .15 |
| Minnesota Vikings | | | |
| ☐ 13 Tony Dorsett | 4.00 | 1.60 | .40 |
| Denver Broncos | | | |
| ☐ 14 Dave Duerson | 1.00 | .40 | .10 |
| Chicago Bears | | | |
| ☐ 15 Charles Haley | 1.50 | .60 | .15 |
| San Francisco 49ers | | | |
| ☐ 16 Dan Hampton | 2.50 | 1.00 | .25 |
| Chicago Bears | | | |
| ☐ 17 Al Harris | 1.00 | .40 | .10 |
| Chicago Bears | | | |
| ☐ 18 Mark Jackson | 1.50 | .60 | .15 |
| Denver Broncos | | | |

| | | | |
|---|---|---|---|
| ☐ 19 Vance Johnson .................... | 1.50 | .60 | .15 |
| Denver Broncos | | | |
| ☐ 20 Steve Jordan ..................... | 1.50 | .60 | .15 |
| Minnesota Vikings | | | |
| ☐ 21 Clarence Kay ..................... | 1.00 | .40 | .10 |
| Denver Broncos | | | |
| ☐ 22 Jim Kelly ........................... | 5.00 | 2.00 | .50 |
| Buffalo Bills | | | |
| ☐ 23 Tommy Kramer .................... | 1.50 | .60 | .15 |
| Minnesota Vikings | | | |
| ☐ 24 Ronnie Lott ....................... | 2.50 | 1.00 | .25 |
| San Francisco 49ers | | | |
| ☐ 25 Lionel Manuel .................... | 1.00 | .40 | .10 |
| New York Giants | | | |
| ☐ 26 Guy McIntyre .................... | 1.00 | .40 | .10 |
| San Francisco 49ers | | | |
| ☐ 27 Steve McMichael ................ | 1.50 | .60 | .15 |
| Chicago Bears | | | |
| ☐ 28 Karl Mecklenburg ............... | 1.50 | .60 | .15 |
| Denver Broncos | | | |
| ☐ 29 Orson Mobley .................... | 1.00 | .40 | .10 |
| Denver Broncos | | | |
| ☐ 30 Joe Montana ..................... | 10.00 | 4.00 | 1.00 |
| San Francisco 49ers | | | |
| ☐ 31 Joe Morris ....................... | 1.50 | .60 | .15 |
| New York Giants | | | |
| ☐ 32 Joe Nash ......................... | 1.00 | .40 | .10 |
| Seattle Seahawks | | | |
| ☐ 33 Ricky Nattiel ..................... | 1.50 | .60 | .15 |
| Denver Broncos | | | |
| ☐ 34 Chuck Nelson .................... | 1.00 | .40 | .10 |
| Minnesota Vikings | | | |
| ☐ 35 Darrin Nelson .................... | 1.50 | .60 | .15 |
| Minnesota Vikings | | | |
| ☐ 36 Karl Nelson ...................... | 1.00 | .40 | .10 |
| New York Giants | | | |
| ☐ 37 Scott Norwood ................... | 1.00 | .40 | .10 |
| Buffalo Bills | | | |
| ☐ 38 Bart Oates ....................... | 1.00 | .40 | .10 |
| New York Giants | | | |
| ☐ 39 Rufus Porter ..................... | 1.50 | .60 | .15 |
| Seattle Seahawks | | | |
| ☐ 40 Andre Reed ...................... | 2.50 | 1.00 | .25 |
| Buffalo Bills | | | |
| ☐ 41 Phil Simms ....................... | 3.00 | 1.20 | .30 |
| New York Giants | | | |
| ☐ 42 Mike Singletary ................. | 2.00 | .80 | .20 |
| Chicago Bears | | | |
| ☐ 43 Fred Smerlas .................... | 1.50 | .60 | .15 |
| Buffalo Bills | | | |
| ☐ 44 Bruce Smith ..................... | 2.50 | 1.00 | .25 |
| Buffalo Bills | | | |
| ☐ 45 Kelly Stouffer .................... | 1.50 | .60 | .15 |
| Seattle Seahawks | | | |
| ☐ 46 Scott Studwell ................... | 1.00 | .40 | .10 |
| Minnesota Vikings | | | |
| ☐ 47 Matt Suhey ...................... | 1.00 | .40 | .10 |
| Chicago Bears | | | |
| ☐ 48 Steve Tasker .................... | 1.00 | .40 | .10 |
| Buffalo Bills | | | |
| ☐ 49 Keena Turner .................... | 1.00 | .40 | .10 |
| San Francisco 49ers | | | |
| ☐ 50 John L. Williams ................. | 1.50 | .60 | .15 |
| Seattle Seahawks | | | |
| ☐ 51 Wade Wilson ..................... | 2.00 | .80 | .20 |
| Minnesota Vikings | | | |
| ☐ 52 Sammy Winder ................... | 1.00 | .40 | .10 |
| Denver Broncos | | | |
| ☐ 53 Tony Woods ...................... | 1.50 | .60 | .15 |
| Seattle Seahawks | | | |
| ☐ 54 Eric Wright ....................... | 1.00 | .40 | .10 |
| San Francisco 49ers | | | |

## 1990 Star-Cal Decals

The 1990 Star-Cal decal set features six players from 12 of the most popular NFL teams and 36 NFL stars (most also represented in the team sets). The player decals measure approximately 3" by 4 1/2" and have on the fronts full-bleed color action player photos with rounded corners and a facsimile autograph. The player's name is printed on the lower left corner of the decal. The backs have instructions for applying the decals. Each player decal was issued with a pennant-shaped miniature team banner (3 1/2" by 2"), which displayed the team's helmet and name in the team's colors. The player decals are unnumbered and checklisted below according to player's name. The set is also known as the Grid-Star decal set.

| | MINT | EXC | G-VG |
|---|---|---|---|
| COMPLETE SET (108) ................ | 150.00 | 60.00 | 15.00 |
| COMMON PLAYER (1-108) ............. | 1.00 | .40 | .10 |
| ☐ 1 Eric Allen ........................... | 1.00 | .40 | .10 |
| Philadelphia Eagles | | | |
| ☐ 2 Marcus Allen ...................... | 2.50 | 1.00 | .25 |
| Los Angeles Raiders | | | |
| ☐ 3 Marcus Allen AS .................. | 2.50 | 1.00 | .25 |
| Los Angeles Raiders | | | |
| ☐ 4 Flipper Anderson ................. | 1.50 | .60 | .15 |
| Los Angeles Rams | | | |
| ☐ 5 Flipper Anderson AS ............ | 1.50 | .60 | .15 |
| Los Angeles Rams | | | |
| ☐ 6 Neal Anderson ..................... | 1.50 | .60 | .15 |
| Chicago Bears | | | |
| ☐ 7 Carl Banks ......................... | 1.50 | .60 | .15 |
| New York Giants | | | |
| ☐ 8 Mark Bavaro ....................... | 1.50 | .60 | .15 |
| New York Giants | | | |
| ☐ 9 Mark Bavaro AS .................. | 1.50 | .60 | .15 |
| New York Giants | | | |
| ☐ 10 Cornelius Bennett ............... | 1.50 | .60 | .15 |
| Buffalo Bills | | | |
| ☐ 11 Cornelius Bennett AS ........... | 1.50 | .60 | .15 |
| Buffalo Bills | | | |
| ☐ 12 Brian Blades ...................... | 1.50 | .60 | .15 |
| Seattle Seahawks | | | |
| ☐ 13 Joey Browner ..................... | 1.50 | .60 | .15 |
| Minnesota Vikings | | | |
| ☐ 14 Keith Byars ....................... | 1.50 | .60 | .15 |
| Philadelphia Eagles | | | |
| ☐ 15 Anthony Carter .................. | 1.50 | .60 | .15 |
| Minnesota Vikings | | | |
| ☐ 16 Anthony Carter AS .............. | 1.50 | .60 | .15 |
| Minnesota Vikings | | | |
| ☐ 17 Cris Carter ........................ | 1.50 | .60 | .15 |
| Philadelphia Eagles | | | |
| ☐ 18 Michael Carter ................... | 1.50 | .60 | .15 |
| San Francisco 49ers | | | |
| ☐ 19 Mark Collins ...................... | 1.00 | .40 | .10 |
| New York Giants | | | |
| ☐ 20 Shane Conlan ..................... | 1.50 | .60 | .15 |
| Buffalo Bills | | | |
| ☐ 21 Jimbo Covert ..................... | 1.00 | .40 | .10 |
| Chicago Bears | | | |
| ☐ 22 Roger Craig ....................... | 2.00 | .80 | .20 |
| San Francisco 49ers | | | |
| ☐ 23 Roger Craig AS ................... | 2.00 | .80 | .20 |
| San Francisco 49ers | | | |
| ☐ 24 Richard Dent ..................... | 1.50 | .60 | .15 |
| Chicago Bears | | | |
| ☐ 25 Richard Dent AS ................. | 1.50 | .60 | .15 |
| Chicago Bears | | | |
| ☐ 26 Chris Doleman ................... | 1.50 | .60 | .15 |
| Minnesota Vikings | | | |
| ☐ 27 Chris Doleman AS ............... | 1.50 | .60 | .15 |
| Minnesota Vikings | | | |
| ☐ 28 Dave Duerson ..................... | 1.00 | .40 | .10 |
| Chicago Bears | | | |
| ☐ 29 Dave Duerson AS ................ | 1.00 | .40 | .10 |
| Chicago Bears | | | |
| ☐ 30 Henry Ellard ...................... | 1.50 | .60 | .15 |
| Los Angeles Rams | | | |
| ☐ 31 Henry Ellard AS .................. | 1.50 | .60 | .15 |
| Los Angeles Rams | | | |
| ☐ 32 John Elway ....................... | 5.00 | 2.00 | .50 |
| Denver Broncos | | | |
| ☐ 33 John Elway AS .................... | 5.00 | 2.00 | .50 |
| Denver Broncos | | | |
| ☐ 34 Jim Everett ....................... | 2.00 | .80 | .20 |
| Los Angeles Rams | | | |
| ☐ 35 Jim Everett AS ................... | 2.00 | .80 | .20 |
| Los Angeles Rams | | | |
| ☐ 36 Mervyn Fernandez ............... | 1.50 | .60 | .15 |
| Los Angeles Raiders | | | |
| ☐ 37 Willie Gault ....................... | 1.50 | .60 | .15 |
| Los Angeles Raiders | | | |
| ☐ 38 Bob Golic ......................... | 1.00 | .40 | .10 |
| Los Angeles Raiders | | | |
| ☐ 39 Darrell Green ..................... | 1.50 | .60 | .15 |
| Washington Redskins | | | |
| ☐ 40 Kevin Greene ..................... | 1.50 | .60 | .15 |
| Los Angeles Rams | | | |

| | | | |
|---|---|---|---|
| ☐ 41 Charles Haley | 1.50 | .60 | .15 |
| San Francisco 49ers | | | |
| ☐ 42 Jay Hilgenberg | 1.00 | .40 | .10 |
| Chicago Bears | | | |
| ☐ 43 Pete Holohan | 1.00 | .40 | .10 |
| Los Angeles Rams | | | |
| ☐ 44 Kent Hull | 1.00 | .40 | .10 |
| Buffalo Bills | | | |
| ☐ 45 Bobby Humphery AS | 1.00 | .40 | .10 |
| New York Jets | | | |
| ☐ 46 Bobby Humphrey | 1.50 | .60 | .15 |
| Denver Broncos | | | |
| ☐ 47 Bo Jackson | 3.00 | 1.20 | .30 |
| Los Angeles Raiders | | | |
| ☐ 48 Bo Jackson AS | 3.00 | 1.20 | .30 |
| Los Angeles Raiders | | | |
| ☐ 49 Keith Jackson | 2.00 | .80 | .20 |
| Philadelphia Eagles | | | |
| ☐ 50 Keith Jackson AS | 2.00 | .80 | .20 |
| Philadelphia Eagles | | | |
| ☐ 51 Mark Jackson | 1.50 | .60 | .15 |
| Denver Broncos | | | |
| ☐ 52 Vance Johnson | 1.50 | .60 | .15 |
| Denver Broncos | | | |
| ☐ 53 Jim Kelly | 4.00 | 1.60 | .40 |
| Buffalo Bills | | | |
| ☐ 54 Jim Kelly AS | 4.00 | 1.60 | .40 |
| Buffalo Bills | | | |
| ☐ 55 Bernie Kosar | 2.50 | 1.00 | .25 |
| Cleveland Browns | | | |
| ☐ 56 Bernie Kosar AS | 2.50 | 1.00 | .25 |
| Cleveland Browns | | | |
| ☐ 57 Greg Kragen | 1.00 | .40 | .10 |
| Denver Broncos | | | |
| ☐ 58 Jeff Lageman | 1.00 | .40 | .10 |
| New York Jets | | | |
| ☐ 59 Pat Leahy | 1.00 | .40 | .10 |
| New York Jets | | | |
| ☐ 60 Howie Long | 1.50 | .60 | .15 |
| Los Angeles Raiders | | | |
| ☐ 61 Howie Long AS | 1.50 | .60 | .15 |
| Los Angeles Raiders | | | |
| ☐ 62 Ronnie Lott | 2.00 | .80 | .20 |
| San Francisco 49ers | | | |
| ☐ 63 Ronnie Lott AS | 2.00 | .80 | .20 |
| San Francisco 49ers | | | |
| ☐ 64 Kevin Mack | 1.50 | .60 | .15 |
| Cleveland Browns | | | |
| ☐ 65 Charles Mann AS | 1.00 | .40 | .10 |
| Washington Redskins | | | |
| ☐ 66 Leonard Marshall | 1.00 | .40 | .10 |
| New York Giants | | | |
| ☐ 67 Clay Matthews | 1.50 | .60 | .15 |
| Cleveland Browns | | | |
| ☐ 68 Clay Matthews AS | 1.50 | .60 | .15 |
| Cleveland Browns | | | |
| ☐ 69 Erik McMillan | 1.00 | .40 | .10 |
| New York Jets | | | |
| ☐ 70 Erik McMillan AS | 1.00 | .40 | .10 |
| New York Jets | | | |
| ☐ 71 Karl Mecklenburg | 1.00 | .40 | .10 |
| Denver Broncos | | | |
| ☐ 72 Karl Mecklenburg AS | 1.00 | .40 | .10 |
| Denver Broncos | | | |
| ☐ 73 Dave Meggett | 1.50 | .60 | .15 |
| New York Giants | | | |
| ☐ 74 Dave Meggett AS | 1.50 | .60 | .15 |
| New York Giants | | | |
| ☐ 75 Eric Metcalf | 1.50 | .60 | .15 |
| Cleveland Browns | | | |
| ☐ 76 Eric Metcalf AS | 1.50 | .60 | .15 |
| Cleveland Browns | | | |
| ☐ 77 Keith Millard | 1.00 | .40 | .10 |
| Minnesota Vikings | | | |
| ☐ 78 Frank Minnifield | 1.00 | .40 | .10 |
| Cleveland Browns | | | |
| ☐ 79 Joe Montana | 9.00 | 3.75 | .90 |
| San Francisco 49ers | | | |
| ☐ 80 Joe Montana AS | 9.00 | 3.75 | .90 |
| San Francisco 49ers | | | |
| ☐ 81 Joe Nash | 1.00 | .40 | .10 |
| Seattle Seahawks | | | |
| ☐ 82 Ken O'Brien | 1.50 | .60 | .15 |
| New York Jets | | | |
| ☐ 83 Ken O'Brien AS | 1.50 | .60 | .15 |
| New York Jets | | | |
| ☐ 84 Rufus Porter | 1.50 | .60 | .15 |
| Seattle Seahawks | | | |
| ☐ 85 Andre Reed | 2.00 | .80 | .20 |
| Buffalo Bills | | | |
| ☐ 86 Mickey Shuler | 1.00 | .40 | .10 |
| New York Jets | | | |
| ☐ 87 Clyde Simmons | 1.50 | .60 | .15 |
| Philadelphia Eagles | | | |
| ☐ 88 Phil Simms | 2.50 | 1.00 | .25 |
| New York Giants | | | |
| ☐ 89 Phil Simms AS | 2.50 | 1.00 | .25 |

| | | | |
|---|---|---|---|
| New York Giants | | | |
| ☐ 90 Mike Singletary | 1.50 | .60 | .15 |
| Chicago Bears | | | |
| ☐ 91 Mike Singletary AS | 1.50 | .60 | .15 |
| Chicago Bears | | | |
| ☐ 92 Jackie Slater | 1.50 | .60 | .15 |
| Los Angeles Rams | | | |
| ☐ 93 Bruce Smith | 2.00 | .80 | .20 |
| Buffalo Bills | | | |
| ☐ 94 Bruce Smith AS | 2.00 | .80 | .20 |
| Buffalo Bills | | | |
| ☐ 95 Kelly Stouffer | 1.50 | .60 | .15 |
| Seattle Seahawks | | | |
| ☐ 96 Kelly Stouffer AS | 1.50 | .60 | .15 |
| Seattle Seahawks | | | |
| ☐ 97 John Taylor | 1.50 | .60 | .15 |
| San Francisco 49ers | | | |
| ☐ 98 Al Toon | 1.50 | .60 | .15 |
| New York Jets | | | |
| ☐ 99 Al Toon AS | 1.50 | .60 | .15 |
| New York Jets | | | |
| ☐ 100 Lawyer Tillman | 1.50 | .60 | .15 |
| Cleveland Browns | | | |
| ☐ 101 Herschel Walker | 2.00 | .80 | .20 |
| Minnesota Vikings | | | |
| ☐ 102 Herschel Walker AS | 2.00 | .80 | .20 |
| Minnesota Vikings | | | |
| ☐ 103 Reggie White | 2.50 | 1.00 | .25 |
| Philadelphia Eagles | | | |
| ☐ 104 Reggie White AS | 2.50 | 1.00 | .25 |
| Philadelphia Eagles | | | |
| ☐ 105 John L. Williams | 1.50 | .60 | .15 |
| Seattle Seahawks | | | |
| ☐ 106 John L. Williams AS | 1.50 | .60 | .15 |
| Seattle Seahawks | | | |
| ☐ 107 Tony Woods | 1.50 | .60 | .15 |
| Seattle Seahawks | | | |
| ☐ 108 Gary Zimmerman | 1.00 | .40 | .10 |
| Minnesota Vikings | | | |

# 1991 Star Pics Promos

These promo cards measure the standard size, 2 1/2" by 3 1/2", and preview the style of the 1991 Star Pics football set. The cards were distributed in two-card panels with Mark Carrier paired with Aaron Craver and Dan McGwire paired with Eric Turner. These promos were quite plentiful because they were also bound into the Pro Football Weekly annual football preview publication. The fronts feature action color player photos. The photo is framed in white and bordered by footballs. The player's name appears in a maroon box at the bottom. The backs have a mint-green football field background with plays drawn in. Printed on the field is a close-up color photo, biography, career highlights, and player profile.

| | MINT | EXC | G-VG |
|---|---|---|---|
| COMPLETE SET (4) | 3.00 | 1.20 | .30 |
| COMMON PLAYER (1-4) | 1.00 | .40 | .10 |
| | | | |
| ☐ 1 Mark Carrier USC | 1.25 | .50 | .12 |
| ☐ 2 Aaron Craver | 1.00 | .40 | .10 |
| ☐ 3 Dan McGwire | 1.25 | .50 | .12 |
| ☐ 4 Eric Turner | 1.25 | .50 | .12 |

# 1991 Star Pics

This 112-card set is numbered on the back and measures the standard size, 2 1/2" by 3 1/2". The front features an action color photo enclosed by a thin white border against a background of footballs. The player's name appears in white print on a maroon-colored box below

the picture. The back has a full-color posed photo in the upper left hand corner and the card number (enclosed in a red star) in the upper right hand corner. The biographical information, including accomplishments, strengths, and weaknesses, is printed on a pale green diagram of a football field with a diagrammed play. The set also includes player agents and flashback cards of top young players. Autographed cards were inserted in some of the sets on a random basis. The key players in this set are Brett Favre, Alvin Harper, Randal Hill, Herman Moore, Mike Pritchard, and Ricky Watters.

|  | MINT | EXC | G-VG |
|---|---|---|---|
| COMPLETE SET (112) | 6.00 | 2.40 | .60 |
| COMMON CARD (1-112) | .04 | .02 | .00 |
| ☐ 1 1991 NFL Draft Overview | .04 | .02 | .00 |
| ☐ 2 Barry Sanders Flashback | .25 | .10 | .02 |
| ☐ 3 Nick Bell Iowa | .25 | .10 | .02 |
| ☐ 4 Kelvin Pritchett Mississippi | .15 | .06 | .01 |
| ☐ 5 Huey Richardson Florida | .07 | .03 | .01 |
| ☐ 6 Mike Croel Nebraska | .25 | .10 | .02 |
| ☐ 7 Paul Justin Arizona State | .04 | .02 | .00 |
| ☐ 8 Ivory Lee Brown Arkansas-Pine Bluff | .15 | .06 | .01 |
| ☐ 9 Herman Moore Virginia | 1.00 | .40 | .10 |
| ☐ 10 Derrick Thomas Flashback | .15 | .06 | .01 |
| ☐ 11 Keith Traylor Central State of Oklahoma | .04 | .02 | .00 |
| ☐ 12 Joe Johnson N.C. State | .04 | .02 | .00 |
| ☐ 13 Dan McGwire San Diego State | .15 | .06 | .01 |
| ☐ 14 Harvey Williams LSU | .25 | .10 | .02 |
| ☐ 15 Eric Moten Michigan State | .10 | .04 | .01 |
| ☐ 16 Steve Zucker Agent | .04 | .02 | .00 |
| ☐ 17 Randal Hill Miami (Florida) | .50 | .20 | .05 |
| ☐ 18 Browning Nagle Louisville | .12 | .05 | .01 |
| ☐ 19 Stan Thomas Texas | .10 | .04 | .01 |
| ☐ 20 Emmitt Smith Flashback | .50 | .20 | .05 |
| ☐ 21 Ted Washington Louisville | .10 | .04 | .01 |
| ☐ 22 Lamar Rogers Auburn | .04 | .02 | .00 |
| ☐ 23 Kenny Walker Nebraska | .07 | .03 | .01 |
| ☐ 24 Howard Griffith Illinois | .10 | .04 | .01 |
| ☐ 25 Reggie Johnson Florida State | .12 | .05 | .01 |
| ☐ 26 Lawrence Dawsey Florida State | .25 | .10 | .02 |
| ☐ 27 Joe Garten Colorado | .04 | .02 | .00 |
| ☐ 28 Moe Gardner Illinois | .15 | .06 | .01 |
| ☐ 29 Michael Stonebreaker Notre Dame | .07 | .03 | .01 |
| ☐ 30 Jeff George Flashback | .05 | .02 | .00 |
| ☐ 31 Leigh Steinberg Agent | .07 | .03 | .01 |
| ☐ 32 John Flannery Syracuse | .07 | .03 | .01 |
| ☐ 33 Pat Harlow USC | .10 | .04 | .01 |
| ☐ 34 Kanavis McGhee Colorado | .10 | .04 | .01 |
| ☐ 35 Mike Dumas Indiana | .10 | .04 | .01 |
| ☐ 36 Godfrey Myles Florida | .20 | .08 | .02 |
| ☐ 37 Shawn Moore Virginia | .25 | .10 | .02 |
| ☐ 38 Jeff Graham Ohio State | .30 | .12 | .03 |
| ☐ 39 Ricky Watters Notre Dame | 1.25 | .50 | .12 |
| ☐ 40 Andre Ware Flashback | .05 | .02 | .00 |
| ☐ 41 Henry Jones Illinois | .30 | .12 | .03 |
| ☐ 42 Eric Turner UCLA | .20 | .08 | .02 |
| ☐ 43 Bob Woolf Agent | .04 | .02 | .00 |
| ☐ 44 Randy Baldwin Mississippi | .15 | .06 | .01 |
| ☐ 45 Mo Lewis Georgia | .20 | .08 | .02 |
| ☐ 46 Jerry Evans Toledo University | .04 | .02 | .00 |
| ☐ 47 Derek Russell Arkansas | .25 | .10 | .02 |
| ☐ 48 Merton Hanks Iowa | .20 | .08 | .02 |
| ☐ 49 Kevin Donnalley North Carolina | .10 | .04 | .01 |
| ☐ 50 Troy Aikman Flashback | .35 | .14 | .03 |
| ☐ 51 William Thomas Texas A and M | .12 | .05 | .01 |
| ☐ 52 Chris Thome Minnesota | .04 | .02 | .00 |
| ☐ 53 Ricky Ervins USC | .20 | .08 | .02 |
| ☐ 54 Jake Reed Grambling | .12 | .05 | .01 |
| ☐ 55 Jerome Henderson Clemson | .10 | .04 | .01 |
| ☐ 56 Mark Vander Poel Colorado | .07 | .03 | .01 |
| ☐ 57 Bernard Ellison Nevada (Reno) | .04 | .02 | .00 |
| ☐ 58 Jack Mills Agent | .04 | .02 | .00 |
| ☐ 59 Jarrod Bunch Michigan | .25 | .10 | .02 |
| ☐ 60 Mark Carrier DB Flashback | .05 | .02 | .00 |
| ☐ 61 Rocen Keeton UCLA | .04 | .02 | .00 |
| ☐ 62 Louis Riddick Pittsburgh | .04 | .02 | .00 |
| ☐ 63 Bobby Wilson Michigan State | .10 | .04 | .01 |
| ☐ 64 Steve Jackson Purdue | .20 | .08 | .02 |
| ☐ 65 Brett Favre Southern Miss | 1.75 | .70 | .17 |
| ☐ 66 Ernie Mills Florida | .20 | .08 | .02 |
| ☐ 67 Joe Valerio Pennsylvania | .12 | .05 | .01 |
| ☐ 68 Chris Smith Brigham Young | .07 | .03 | .01 |
| ☐ 69 Ralph Cindrich Agent | .04 | .02 | .00 |
| ☐ 70 Christian Okoye Flashback | .05 | .02 | .00 |
| ☐ 71 Charles McRae Tennessee | .10 | .04 | .01 |
| ☐ 72 Jon Vaughn Michigan | .25 | .10 | .02 |
| ☐ 73 Eric Swann No college | .30 | .12 | .03 |
| ☐ 74 Bill Musgrave Oregon | .15 | .06 | .01 |
| ☐ 75 Eric Bieniemy Colorado | .20 | .08 | .02 |
| ☐ 76 Pat Tyrance Nebraska | .07 | .03 | .01 |
| ☐ 77 Vinnie Clark Ohio State | .12 | .05 | .01 |
| ☐ 78 Eugene Williams Iowa State | .10 | .04 | .01 |
| ☐ 79 Rob Carpenter | .15 | .06 | .01 |

| | | | | |
|---|---|---|---|---|
| ☐ 80 | Deion Sanders<br>Syracuse | .15 | .06 | .01 |
| ☐ 81 | Roman Phifer<br>Flashback | .15 | .06 | .01 |
| ☐ 82 | Greg Lewis<br>UCLA | .10 | .04 | .01 |
| ☐ 83 | John Johnson<br>Washington | .10 | .04 | .01 |
| ☐ 84 | Richard Howell<br>Clemson | .04 | .02 | .00 |
| ☐ 85 | Jesse Campbell<br>Agent | .10 | .04 | .01 |
| ☐ 86 | Stanley Richard<br>N.C. State | .25 | .10 | .02 |
| ☐ 87 | Alfred Williams<br>Texas | .15 | .06 | .01 |
| ☐ 88 | Mike Pritchard<br>Colorado | .75 | .30 | .07 |
| ☐ 89 | Mel Agee<br>Colorado | .10 | .04 | .01 |
| ☐ 90 | Aaron Craver<br>Illinois | .10 | .04 | .01 |
| ☐ 91 | Tim Barnett<br>Fresno State | .10 | .04 | .01 |
| ☐ 92 | Wesley Carroll<br>Jackson State | .10 | .04 | .01 |
| ☐ 93 | Kevin Scott<br>Miami (Florida) | .10 | .04 | .01 |
| ☐ 94 | Darren Lewis<br>Stanford | .10 | .04 | .01 |
| ☐ 95 | Tim Bruton<br>Texas A and M | .04 | .02 | .00 |
| ☐ 96 | Tim James<br>Missouri | .04 | .02 | .00 |
| ☐ 97 | Darryll Lewis<br>Colorado | .10 | .04 | .01 |
| ☐ 98 | Shawn Jefferson<br>Arizona | .10 | .04 | .01 |
| ☐ 99 | Mitch Donahue<br>Central Florida | .10 | .04 | .01 |
| ☐ 100 | Marvin Demoff<br>Wyoming | .04 | .02 | .00 |
| ☐ 101 | Adrian Cooper<br>Agent | .15 | .06 | .01 |
| ☐ 102 | Bruce Pickens<br>Oklahoma | .10 | .04 | .01 |
| ☐ 103 | Scott Zolak<br>Nebraska | .15 | .06 | .01 |
| ☐ 104 | Phil Hansen<br>Maryland | .20 | .08 | .02 |
| ☐ 105 | Ed King<br>No. Dakota State | .10 | .04 | .01 |
| ☐ 106 | Mike Jones<br>Auburn | .12 | .05 | .01 |
| ☐ 107 | Alvin Harper<br>N.C. State | .90 | .36 | .09 |
| ☐ 108 | Robert Young<br>Tennessee | .10 | .04 | .01 |
| ☐ 109 | Offensive Prospects<br>Mississippi State<br>Nick Bell<br>Brett Favre<br>Alvin Harper<br>Charles McRae | .10 | .04 | .01 |
| ☐ 110 | Defensive Prospects<br>Mike Croel<br>Eric Swann<br>Eric Turner | .05 | .02 | .00 |
| ☐ 111 | Checklist Card | .04 | .02 | .00 |
| ☐ 112 | Checklist Card | .04 | .02 | .00 |
| ☐ NNO | Salute/Advertisement<br>(American flag<br>background) | .05 | .02 | .00 |

# 1992 Star Pics

This 100-card standard-size (2 1/2" by 3 1/2") set highlights more than 80 of the top college prospects in the country. The set was available in ten-card foil StarPaks and factory sets, with randomly inserted autograph cards in both. It was reported that the production run did not exceed 195,000 factory sets and 12,000 ten-box foil cases. The fronts feature glossy color action photos bordered in white. A color stripe runs the length of the card on the right side, and the player's position and name are printed vertically. The Star Pics logo is superimposed at the lower right corner. The backs present an in-depth scouting report (accomplishments, strengths, and weaknesses), biographical information, and a color head shot in a circular format at the lower right corner. The five-card Flashback subset (10, 20, 30, 50, 70) displays illustrations by sports artist Scott Medlock. The StarStat subset, ten cards in all, compares the top pro prospects' stats to the collegiate stats of NFL greats; two of these were included in each set and eight others were randomly inserted in the foil packs. The cards

are numbered on the back. The key players in this set are Quentin Coryatt, Johnny Mitchell, Carl Pickens, and Tommy Vardell.

| | | MINT | EXC | G-VG |
|---|---|---|---|---|
| COMPLETE SET (100) | | 7.00 | 2.80 | .70 |
| COMMON PLAYER (1-100) | | .05 | .02 | .00 |
| ☐ 1 | Steve Emtman SS<br>Washington | .10 | .04 | .01 |
| ☐ 2 | Chris Hakel<br>William and Mary | .10 | .04 | .01 |
| ☐ 3 | Phillippi Sparks<br>Arizona State | .10 | .04 | .01 |
| ☐ 4 | Howard Dinkins<br>Florida State | .10 | .04 | .01 |
| ☐ 5 | Robert Brooks<br>South Carolina | .15 | .06 | .01 |
| ☐ 6 | Chris Pederson<br>Iowa State | .05 | .02 | .00 |
| ☐ 7 | Bucky Richardson<br>Texas A and M | .25 | .10 | .02 |
| ☐ 8 | Keith Goganious<br>Penn State | .10 | .04 | .01 |
| ☐ 9 | Robert Porcher<br>South Carolina State | .15 | .06 | .01 |
| ☐ 10 | Andre Rison<br>(Flashback) | .20 | .08 | .02 |
| ☐ 11 | Jason Hanson<br>Washington State | .35 | .14 | .03 |
| ☐ 12 | Tommy Vardell<br>Stanford | .60 | .24 | .06 |
| ☐ 13 | Kurt Barber<br>Southern California | .10 | .04 | .01 |
| ☐ 14 | Bernard Dafney<br>Tennessee | .10 | .04 | .01 |
| ☐ 15 | Levon Kirkland<br>Clemson | .15 | .06 | .01 |
| ☐ 16 | Corey Widmer<br>Montana State | .10 | .04 | .01 |
| ☐ 17 | Santana Dotson<br>Baylor | .30 | .12 | .03 |
| ☐ 18 | Chris Holder<br>Tuskegee | .05 | .02 | .00 |
| ☐ 19 | Elbert Turner<br>Illinois | .05 | .02 | .00 |
| ☐ 20 | Mike Croel<br>(Flashback) | .10 | .04 | .01 |
| ☐ 21 | Darren Perry<br>Penn State | .12 | .05 | .01 |
| ☐ 22 | Troy Vincent<br>Wisconsin | .10 | .04 | .01 |
| ☐ 23 | Quentin Coryatt<br>Texas A and M | .90 | .36 | .09 |
| ☐ 24 | John Brown III<br>Houston | .05 | .02 | .00 |
| ☐ 25 | John Ray<br>West Virginia | .05 | .02 | .00 |
| ☐ 26 | Vaughn Dunbar<br>Indiana | .25 | .10 | .02 |
| ☐ 27 | Stacey Dillard<br>Oklahoma | .10 | .04 | .01 |
| ☐ 28 | Alonzo Spellman<br>Ohio State | .20 | .08 | .02 |
| ☐ 29 | Darren Woodson<br>Arizona State | .25 | .10 | .02 |
| ☐ 30 | Pat Swilling<br>(Flashback) | .10 | .04 | .01 |
| ☐ 31 | Eddie Robinson<br>Alabama State | .20 | .08 | .02 |
| ☐ 32 | Tyji Armstrong<br>Mississippi | .15 | .06 | .01 |
| ☐ 33 | Bill Johnson<br>Michigan State | .10 | .04 | .01 |
| ☐ 34 | Eugene Chung<br>Virginia Tech | .12 | .05 | .01 |
| ☐ 35 | Ricardo McDonald<br>Pittsburgh | .10 | .04 | .01 |

| | | | |
|---|---|---|---|
| ☐ 36 Sean Lumpkin ....................... Minnesota | .10 | .04 | .01 |
| ☐ 37 Greg Skrepenak ..................... Michigan | .12 | .05 | .01 |
| ☐ 38 Ashley Ambrose ..................... Mississippi Valley St. | .15 | .06 | .01 |
| ☐ 39 Kevin Smith ........................... Texas A and M | .30 | .12 | .03 |
| ☐ 40 Todd Collins ........................... Carson-Newman | .15 | .06 | .01 |
| ☐ 41 Shane Dronett ....................... Texas | .20 | .08 | .02 |
| ☐ 42 Ronnie West ........................... Pittsburg State | .05 | .02 | .00 |
| ☐ 43 Darryl Williams ...................... Miami | .20 | .08 | .02 |
| ☐ 44 Rodney Blackshear ................ Texas Tech | .05 | .02 | .00 |
| ☐ 45 Dion Lambert ......................... UCLA | .10 | .04 | .01 |
| ☐ 46 Mike Saunders ....................... Iowa | .05 | .02 | .00 |
| ☐ 47 Keo Coleman ......................... Mississippi State | .10 | .04 | .01 |
| ☐ 48 Dana Hall .............................. Washington | .15 | .06 | .01 |
| ☐ 49 Arthur Marshall ...................... Georgia | .25 | .10 | .02 |
| ☐ 50 Leonard Russell ..................... (Flashback) | .15 | .06 | .01 |
| ☐ 51 Matt Rodgers ........................ Iowa | .05 | .02 | .00 |
| ☐ 52 Shane Collins ........................ Arizona State | .10 | .04 | .01 |
| ☐ 53 Courtney Hawkins ................. Michigan State | .40 | .16 | .04 |
| ☐ 54 Chuck Smith ......................... Tennessee | .12 | .05 | .01 |
| ☐ 55 Joe Bowden .......................... Oklahoma | .10 | .04 | .01 |
| ☐ 56 Gene McGuire ....................... Notre Dame | .10 | .04 | .01 |
| ☐ 57 Tracy Scroggins ..................... Tulsa | .15 | .06 | .01 |
| ☐ 58 Mark D'Onofrio ...................... Penn State | .10 | .04 | .01 |
| ☐ 59 Jimmy Smith.......................... Jackson State | .10 | .04 | .01 |
| ☐ 60 Carl Pickens .......................... Tennessee | 1.00 | .40 | .10 |
| ☐ 61 Robert Harris ........................ Southern | .10 | .04 | .01 |
| ☐ 62 Erick Anderson ...................... Michigan | .12 | .05 | .01 |
| ☐ 63 Doug Rigby ........................... Wyoming | .05 | .02 | .00 |
| ☐ 64 Keith Hamilton ...................... Pittsburgh | .30 | .12 | .03 |
| ☐ 65 Vaughn Dunbar SS................. Indiana | .10 | .04 | .01 |
| ☐ 66 Willie Clay ............................. Georgia Tech | .12 | .05 | .01 |
| ☐ 67 Robert Jones ......................... East Carolina | .20 | .08 | .02 |
| ☐ 68 Leon Searcy .......................... Miami | .12 | .05 | .01 |
| ☐ 69 Elliot Pilton ........................... Tennessee State | .05 | .02 | .00 |
| ☐ 70 Thurman Thomas.................... (Flashback) | .25 | .10 | .02 |
| ☐ 71 Mark Wheeler......................... Texas A and M | .10 | .04 | .01 |
| ☐ 72 Jeremy Lincoln ...................... Tennessee | .15 | .06 | .01 |
| ☐ 73 Tony McCoy ........................... Florida | .10 | .04 | .01 |
| ☐ 74 Charles Davenport.................. NC State | .15 | .06 | .01 |
| ☐ 75 Patrick Rowe .......................... San Diego State | .10 | .04 | .01 |
| ☐ 76 Tommy Jeter .......................... Texas | .10 | .04 | .01 |
| ☐ 77 Rod Smith ............................. Notre Dame | .10 | .04 | .01 |
| ☐ 78 Johnny Mitchell....................... Nebraska | 1.00 | .40 | .10 |
| ☐ 79 Corey Barlow......................... Auburn | .10 | .04 | .01 |
| ☐ 80 Scottie Graham ...................... Ohio State | .30 | .12 | .03 |
| ☐ 81 Mark Bounds.......................... Texas Tech | .05 | .02 | .00 |
| ☐ 82 Chester McGlockton................ Clemson | .15 | .06 | .01 |
| ☐ 83 Ray Roberts ........................... Virginia | .12 | .05 | .01 |
| ☐ 84 Dale Carter ............................ | .25 | .10 | .02 |

| | | | |
|---|---|---|---|
| Tennessee | | | |
| ☐ 85 James Patton ......................... Texas | .12 | .05 | .01 |
| ☐ 86 Tyrone Legette ....................... Nebraska | .10 | .04 | .01 |
| ☐ 87 Leodis Flowers ...................... Nebraska | .10 | .04 | .01 |
| ☐ 88 Rico Smith ............................. Colorado | .10 | .04 | .01 |
| ☐ 89 Kevin Turner .......................... Alabama | .20 | .08 | .02 |
| ☐ 90 Steve Emtman......................... Washington | .10 | .04 | .01 |
| ☐ 91 Rodney Culver ....................... Notre Dame | .25 | .10 | .02 |
| ☐ 92 Chris Mims ............................ Tennessee | .30 | .12 | .03 |
| ☐ 93 Carlos Snow........................... Ohio State | .05 | .02 | .00 |
| ☐ 94 Corey Harris .......................... Vanderbilt | .10 | .04 | .01 |
| ☐ 95 Nate Williams ........................ Mississippi State | .05 | .02 | .00 |
| ☐ 96 Timothy Roberts ..................... Southern Mississippi | .10 | .04 | .01 |
| ☐ 97 Steve Israel ........................... Pittsburgh | .10 | .04 | .01 |
| ☐ 98 Tony Smith (WR) ..................... Notre Dame | .10 | .04 | .01 |
| ☐ 99 Dwayne Sabb ........................ New Hampshire | .15 | .06 | .01 |
| ☐ 100 Checklist .............................. | .05 | .02 | .00 |

## 1992 Star Pics StarStat Bonus

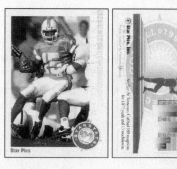

This eight-card standard-size (2 1/2" by 3 1/2") set highlights top college prospects. The cards were available as an insert in ten-card foil StarPaks. The StarStat concept compares top pro prospects' stats to the collegiate stats of NFL greats. The cards are numbered on the back.

| | MINT | EXC | G-VG |
|---|---|---|---|
| COMPLETE SET (8)........................... | 15.00 | 6.00 | 1.50 |
| COMMON PLAYER (SS1-SS8).......... | .60 | .24 | .06 |
| ☐ SS1 Dale Carter........................ Tennessee | 1.75 | .70 | .17 |
| ☐ SS2 Carl Pickens ...................... Tennessee | 5.00 | 2.00 | .50 |
| ☐ SS3 Alonzo Spellman ................ Ohio State | 1.50 | .60 | .15 |
| ☐ SS4 Jimmy Smith ...................... Jackson State | 1.00 | .40 | .10 |
| ☐ SS5 Quentin Coryatt................... Texas A and M | 4.00 | 1.60 | .40 |
| ☐ SS6 Troy Vincent ....................... Wisconsin | .60 | .24 | .06 |
| ☐ SS7 Darryl Williams.................... Miami | 1.75 | .70 | .17 |
| ☐ SS8 Courtney Hawkins................ Michigan State | 2.50 | 1.00 | .25 |

## 1961 Steelers Jay Publishing

This 12-card set features (approximately) 5" by 7" black-and-white player photos. The photos show players in traditional poses with the quarterback preparing to throw, the runner heading downfield, and the defenseman ready for the tackle. These cards were packaged 12 to a packet and originally sold for 25 cents. The backs are blank. The cards are unnumbered and checklisted below in alphabetical order.

| | NRMT | VG-E | GOOD |
|---|---|---|---|
| COMPLETE SET (12) | 60.00 | 24.00 | 6.00 |
| COMMON PLAYER (1-12) | 5.00 | 2.00 | .50 |
| ☐ 1 Preston Carpenter | 5.00 | 2.00 | .50 |
| ☐ 2 Dean Derby | 5.00 | 2.00 | .50 |
| ☐ 3 Buddy Dial | 6.00 | 2.40 | .60 |
| ☐ 4 John Henry Johnson | 9.00 | 3.75 | .90 |
| ☐ 5 Bobby Layne | 15.00 | 6.00 | 1.50 |
| ☐ 6 Gene Lipscomb | 7.50 | 3.00 | .75 |
| ☐ 7 Bill Mack | 5.00 | 2.00 | .50 |
| ☐ 8 Fred Mautino | 5.00 | 2.00 | .50 |
| ☐ 9 Lou Michaels | 5.00 | 2.00 | .50 |
| ☐ 10 Buddy Parker CO | 5.00 | 2.00 | .50 |
| ☐ 11 Myron Pottios | 6.00 | 2.40 | .60 |
| ☐ 12 Tom Tracy | 6.00 | 2.40 | .60 |

## 1963 Steelers IDL

ERNIE STAUTNER

This unnumbered black and white card set (featuring the Pittsburgh Steelers) is complete at 26 cards. The cards feature an identifying logo of IDL Drug Store on the front left corner of the card. The cards measure approximately 4" by 5". Cards are blank backed and unnumbered and hence are ordered alphabetically in the checklist below.

| | NRMT | VG-E | GOOD |
|---|---|---|---|
| COMPLETE SET (26) | 150.00 | 60.00 | 15.00 |
| COMMON PLAYER (1-26) | 6.00 | 2.40 | .60 |
| ☐ 1 Frank Atkinson | 6.00 | 2.40 | .60 |
| ☐ 2 Jim Bradshaw | 6.00 | 2.40 | .60 |
| ☐ 3 Ed Brown | 7.50 | 3.00 | .75 |
| ☐ 4 John Burrell | 6.00 | 2.40 | .60 |
| ☐ 5 Preston Carpenter | 7.50 | 3.00 | .75 |
| ☐ 6 Lou Cordileone | 6.00 | 2.40 | .60 |
| ☐ 7 Buddy Dial | 9.00 | 3.75 | .90 |
| ☐ 8 Bob Ferguson | 7.50 | 3.00 | .75 |
| ☐ 9 Glenn Glass | 6.00 | 2.40 | .60 |
| ☐ 10 Dick Haley | 6.00 | 2.40 | .60 |
| ☐ 11 Dick Hoak | 7.50 | 3.00 | .75 |
| ☐ 12 John Henry Johnson | 15.00 | 6.00 | 1.50 |
| ☐ 13 Brady Keys | 6.00 | 2.40 | .60 |
| ☐ 14 Joe Krupa | 6.00 | 2.40 | .60 |
| ☐ 15 Ray Lemek | 6.00 | 2.40 | .60 |
| ☐ 16 Bill(Red) Mack | 6.00 | 2.40 | .60 |
| ☐ 17 Lou Michaels | 7.50 | 3.00 | .75 |
| ☐ 18 Bill Nelsen | 9.00 | 3.75 | .90 |
| ☐ 19 Buzz Nutter | 6.00 | 2.40 | .60 |
| ☐ 20 Myron Pottios | 7.50 | 3.00 | .75 |
| ☐ 21 John Reger | 6.00 | 2.40 | .60 |
| ☐ 22 Mike Sandusky | 6.00 | 2.40 | .60 |
| ☐ 23 Ernie Stautner | 15.00 | 6.00 | 1.50 |
| ☐ 24 George Tarasovic | 6.00 | 2.40 | .60 |
| ☐ 25 Clendon Thomas | 6.00 | 2.40 | .60 |
| ☐ 26 Tom Tracy | 7.50 | 3.00 | .75 |

## 1968 Steelers KDKA

The 1968 KDKA Pittsburgh Steelers card set contains 15 cards with horizontal poses of several players per card. The cards measure approximately 2 3/8" by 4 1/8". Each card depicts players of a particular position (defensive backs, tight ends, linebackers). The backs are essentially advertisements for radio station KDKA, the

COLLECT THE ENTIRE SERIES OF STEELER CARDS

HEAR: HERE:
KDKA RADIO 1020 GROUP W

SEE: HERE:
KDKA-TV 2 GROUP W

PITTSBURGH STEELERS

sponsor of the card set. The cards are unnumbered and hence are listed below alphabetically by position name for convenience.

| | NRMT | VG-E | GOOD |
|---|---|---|---|
| COMPLETE SET (15) | 65.00 | 26.00 | 6.50 |
| COMMON CARD (1-15) | 5.00 | 2.00 | .50 |
| ☐ 1 Centers:<br>John Knight<br>Ray Mansfield | 5.00 | 2.00 | .50 |
| ☐ 2 Coaches:<br>Bill Austin (Head),<br>Fletcher, Torgeson,<br>McLaughlin, Taylor,<br>Heinrich, DePasqua,<br>Berlin (trainer) | 5.00 | 2.00 | .50 |
| ☐ 3 Defensive Backs:<br>Bob Hohn<br>Paul Martha<br>Marv Woodson | 6.00 | 2.40 | .60 |
| ☐ 4 Defensive Backs:<br>John Foruria<br>Clendon Thomas<br>Bob Morgan | 5.00 | 2.00 | .50 |
| ☐ 5 Defensive Linemen:<br>Ben McGhee<br>Chuck Hinton<br>Dick Arndt<br>Ken Kortas<br>Lloyd Voss | 5.00 | 2.00 | .50 |
| ☐ 6 Flankers:<br>Roy Jefferson<br>End-Kicker:<br>Ken Hebert | 6.00 | 2.40 | .60 |
| ☐ 7 Fullbacks:<br>Earl Gros<br>Bill Asbury | 5.00 | 2.00 | .50 |
| ☐ 8 Guards:<br>Larry Granger<br>Sam Davis<br>Bruce Van Dyke | 5.00 | 2.00 | .50 |
| ☐ 9 Linebackers:<br>Andy Russell<br>Bill Saul<br>John Campbell<br>Ray May | 6.00 | 2.40 | .60 |
| ☐ 10 Quarterbacks:<br>Dick Shiner<br>Kent Nix | 6.00 | 2.40 | .60 |
| ☐ 11 Rookies:<br>Ken Hebert<br>Ernie Ruple<br>Mike Taylor | 5.00 | 2.00 | .50 |
| ☐ 12 Running Backs:<br>Dick Hoak<br>Don Shy<br>Jim Butler | 6.00 | 2.40 | .60 |
| ☐ 13 Split Ends:<br>J.R. Wilburn<br>Dick Compton | 5.00 | 2.00 | .50 |
| ☐ 14 Tackles:<br>Fran O'Brien<br>Mike Haggerty<br>John Brown | 5.00 | 2.00 | .50 |
| ☐ 15 Tight Ends:<br>John Hilton<br>Chet Anderson | 5.00 | 2.00 | .50 |

# 1972 Steelers Photo Sheets

32 FRANCO HARRIS RB

This set consists of eight 10" by 8" sheets that display eight glossy black-and-white player photos each. Each photo measures approximately 2" by 3". The player's name, number, and position are printed below the photo. A Steelers helmet icon appears in the lower left corner of the sheet. The backs are blank. The sheets are unnumbered and checklisted below alphabetically according to the player featured in the upper left corner.

|  | NRMT | VG-E | GOOD |
|---|---|---|---|
| COMPLETE SET (8) | 50.00 | 20.00 | 5.00 |
| COMMON PLAYER (1-8) | 2.50 | 1.00 | .25 |
| ☐ 1 Ralph Anderson | 2.50 | 1.00 | .25 |
| Jim Clack |  |  |  |
| Bob Maples |  |  |  |
| Henry Davis |  |  |  |
| Jon Kolb |  |  |  |
| Ray Mansfield |  |  |  |
| Sam Davis |  |  |  |
| Chuck Allen |  |  |  |
| ☐ 2 Jim Brumfield | 7.50 | 3.00 | .75 |
| Chuck Beatty |  |  |  |
| Bobby Walden |  |  |  |
| Frank Lewis |  |  |  |
| Lee Calland |  |  |  |
| Warren Bankston |  |  |  |
| Mel Blount |  |  |  |
| John Rowser |  |  |  |
| ☐ 3 Bud Carson CO | 3.50 | 1.40 | .35 |
| Bob Fry CO |  |  |  |
| Dick Hoak CO |  |  |  |
| Babe Parilli CO |  |  |  |
| George Perles CO |  |  |  |
| Lou Riecke CO |  |  |  |
| Charley Sumner CO |  |  |  |
| Lionel Taylor CO |  |  |  |
| ☐ 4 Jack Ham | 7.50 | 3.00 | .75 |
| Ben McGee |  |  |  |
| Brian Stenger |  |  |  |
| Lloyd Voss |  |  |  |
| Bruce Van Dyke |  |  |  |
| L.C. Greenwood |  |  |  |
| Gerry Mullins |  |  |  |
| John Brown |  |  |  |
| ☐ 5 Joe Greene | 7.50 | 3.00 | .75 |
| Bert Askson UER |  |  |  |
| (Misspelled Burt) |  |  |  |
| Mel Holmes |  |  |  |
| Dwight White |  |  |  |
| Bob Adams |  |  |  |
| Larry Brown |  |  |  |
| Dave Smith |  |  |  |
| John McMakin |  |  |  |
| ☐ 6 Chuck Noll CO | 15.00 | 6.00 | 1.50 |
| Jon Staggers |  |  |  |
| Terry Hanratty |  |  |  |
| Roy Gerela |  |  |  |
| Terry Bradshaw |  |  |  |
| Bob Leahy |  |  |  |
| Joe Gilliam |  |  |  |
| Rocky Bleier |  |  |  |
| ☐ 7 Dick Post | 12.50 | 5.00 | 1.25 |
| Franco Harris |  |  |  |
| Dennis Meyer |  |  |  |
| Lorenzo Brinkley |  |  |  |
| Steve Furness |  |  |  |
| Gordon Gravelle |  |  |  |
| Rick Sharp |  |  |  |

| Dave Kalina |  |  |  |
|---|---|---|---|
| ☐ 8 Mike Wagner | 5.00 | 2.00 | .50 |
| Ron Shanklin |  |  |  |
| Preston Pearson |  |  |  |
| Glen Edwards |  |  |  |
| Al Young |  |  |  |
| John Fuqua |  |  |  |
| Andy Russell |  |  |  |
| Steve Davis |  |  |  |

# 1979 Stop'N'Go

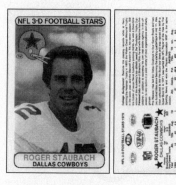

The 1979 Stop 'N' Go Markets set contains 18 3-D cards. The cards measure approximately 2 1/8" by 3 1/4". They are numbered and contain both a 1979 National Football League Players Association copyright date and a Xograph (predecessor of Sportflics and Score) trademark registration on the back. The set shows a heavy emphasis on players from the two Texas teams, the Dallas Cowboys and Houston Oilers, as they were issued primarily in the south.

|  | NRMT | VG-E | GOOD |
|---|---|---|---|
| COMPLETE SET (18) | 40.00 | 16.00 | 4.00 |
| COMMON PLAYER (1-18) | 1.00 | .40 | .10 |
| ☐ 1 Gregg Bingham | 1.00 | .40 | .10 |
| Houston Oilers |  |  |  |
| ☐ 2 Ken Burrough | 1.50 | .60 | .15 |
| Houston Oilers |  |  |  |
| ☐ 3 Preston Pearson | 1.50 | .60 | .15 |
| Dallas Cowboys |  |  |  |
| ☐ 4 Sam Cunningham | 1.50 | .60 | .15 |
| New England Patriots |  |  |  |
| ☐ 5 Robert Newhouse | 1.50 | .60 | .15 |
| Dallas Cowboys |  |  |  |
| ☐ 6 Walter Payton | 12.00 | 5.00 | 1.20 |
| Chicago Bears |  |  |  |
| ☐ 7 Robert Brazile | 1.50 | .60 | .15 |
| Houston Oilers |  |  |  |
| ☐ 8 Rocky Bleier | 2.50 | 1.00 | .25 |
| Pittsburgh Steelers |  |  |  |
| ☐ 9 Toni Fritsch | 1.00 | .40 | .10 |
| Houston Oilers |  |  |  |
| ☐ 10 Jack Ham | 3.00 | 1.20 | .30 |
| Pittsburgh Steelers |  |  |  |
| ☐ 11 Jay Saldi | 1.00 | .40 | .10 |
| Dallas Cowboys |  |  |  |
| ☐ 12 Roger Staubach | 15.00 | 6.00 | 1.50 |
| Dallas Cowboys |  |  |  |
| ☐ 13 Franco Harris | 6.00 | 2.40 | .60 |
| Pittsburgh Steelers |  |  |  |
| ☐ 14 Otis Armstrong | 2.00 | .80 | .20 |
| Denver Broncos |  |  |  |
| ☐ 15 Lyle Alzado | 2.00 | .80 | .20 |
| Denver Broncos |  |  |  |
| ☐ 16 Billy Johnson | 1.50 | .60 | .15 |
| Houston Oilers |  |  |  |
| ☐ 17 Elvin Bethea | 1.50 | .60 | .15 |
| Houston Oilers |  |  |  |
| ☐ 18 Joe Greene | 4.00 | 1.60 | .40 |
| Pittsburgh Steelers |  |  |  |

# 1980 Stop'N'Go

The 1980 Stop 'N' Go Markets football card set contains 48 3-D cards. The cards measure approximately 2 1/8" by 3 1/4". Although similar to the 1979 issue, the cards can easily be distinguished by the two stars surrounding the name plaque on the front of the 1980 set and the obvious copyright date on the respective backs. One card was given out with each soda fountain drink purchased through September.

While players from National Football League teams, other than those in Texas, are indeed contained in the set, the emphasis remains on the Cowboys and Oilers.

|  | MINT | EXC | G-VG |
|---|---|---|---|
| COMPLETE SET (48)...................... | 45.00 | 18.00 | 4.50 |
| COMMON PLAYER (1-48)................ | .60 | .24 | .06 |

| | | | |
|---|---|---|---|
| ☐ 1 John Jefferson ......................... San Diego Chargers | 1.00 | .40 | .10 |
| ☐ 2 Herbert Scott............................ Dallas Cowboys | .60 | .24 | .06 |
| ☐ 3 Pat Donovan ............................ Dallas Cowboys | .60 | .24 | .06 |
| ☐ 4 William Andrews....................... Atlanta Falcons | 1.25 | .50 | .12 |
| ☐ 5 Frank Corral ............................ Los Angeles Rams | .60 | .24 | .06 |
| ☐ 6 Fred Dryer .............................. Los Angeles Rams | 1.50 | .60 | .15 |
| ☐ 7 Franco Harris .......................... Pittsburgh Steelers | 4.00 | 1.60 | .40 |
| ☐ 8 Leon Gray .............................. Houston Oilers | .60 | .24 | .06 |
| ☐ 9 Gregg Bingham ........................ Houston Oilers | .60 | .24 | .06 |
| ☐ 10 Louie Kelcher ......................... San Diego Chargers | .60 | .24 | .06 |
| ☐ 11 Robert Newhouse .................... Dallas Cowboys | 1.00 | .40 | .10 |
| ☐ 12 Preston Pearson ..................... Dallas Cowboys | 1.00 | .40 | .10 |
| ☐ 13 Wallace Francis ...................... Atlanta Falcons | .75 | .30 | .07 |
| ☐ 14 Pat Haden ............................. Los Angeles Rams | 2.00 | .80 | .20 |
| ☐ 15 Jim Youngblood....................... Los Angeles Rams | .60 | .24 | .06 |
| ☐ 16 Rocky Bleier .......................... Pittsburgh Steelers | 1.50 | .60 | .15 |
| ☐ 17 Gifford Nielsen ....................... Houston Oilers | .60 | .24 | .06 |
| ☐ 18 Elvin Bethea .......................... Houston Oilers | 1.00 | .40 | .10 |
| ☐ 19 Charlie Joiner ........................ San Diego Chargers | 2.50 | 1.00 | .25 |
| ☐ 20 Tony Hill ............................... Dallas Cowboys | 1.00 | .40 | .10 |
| ☐ 21 Drew Pearson ........................ Dallas Cowboys | 1.25 | .50 | .12 |
| ☐ 22 Alfred Jenkins ........................ Atlanta Falcons | 1.00 | .40 | .10 |
| ☐ 23 Dave Elmendorf....................... Los Angeles Rams | .60 | .24 | .06 |
| ☐ 24 Jack Reynolds......................... Los Angeles Rams | 1.25 | .50 | .12 |
| ☐ 25 Joe Greene ............................ Pittsburgh Steelers | 3.00 | 1.20 | .30 |
| ☐ 26 Robert Brazile ........................ Houston Oilers | 1.00 | .40 | .10 |
| ☐ 27 Mike Reinfeldt......................... Houston Oilers | .60 | .24 | .06 |
| ☐ 28 Bob Griese ............................ Miami Dolphins | 4.00 | 1.60 | .40 |
| ☐ 29 Harold Carmichael.................... Philadelphia Eagles | 1.50 | .60 | .15 |
| ☐ 30 Ottis Anderson ....................... St. Louis Cardinals | 4.00 | 1.60 | .40 |
| ☐ 31 Ahmad Rashad........................ Minnesota Vikings | 3.00 | 1.20 | .30 |
| ☐ 32 Archie Manning........................ New Orleans Saints | 1.50 | .60 | .15 |
| ☐ 33 Ricky Bell ............................. Tampa Bay Buccaneers | 1.00 | .40 | .10 |
| ☐ 34 Jay Saldi .............................. Dallas Cowboys | .60 | .24 | .06 |
| ☐ 35 Ken Burrough......................... Houston Oilers | 1.00 | .40 | .10 |
| ☐ 36 Don Woods ........................... San Diego Chargers | .60 | .24 | .06 |
| ☐ 37 Henry Childs .......................... New Orleans Saints | .60 | .24 | .06 |
| ☐ 38 Wilbur Jackson ....................... San Francisco 49ers | .60 | .24 | .06 |
| ☐ 39 Steve DeBerg ......................... San Francisco 49ers | 1.50 | .60 | .15 |
| ☐ 40 Ron Jessie ............................ Los Angeles Rams | .75 | .30 | .07 |
| ☐ 41 Mel Blount ............................ Pittsburgh Steelers | 2.00 | .80 | .20 |
| ☐ 42 Cliff Branch ........................... Oakland Raiders | 1.50 | .60 | .15 |
| ☐ 43 Chuck Muncie ......................... San Diego Chargers | .75 | .30 | .07 |
| ☐ 44 Ken MacAfee .......................... San Francisco 49ers | .60 | .24 | .06 |
| ☐ 45 Charley Young......................... San Francisco 49ers | .75 | .30 | .07 |
| ☐ 46 Cody Jones ........................... Los Angeles Rams | .60 | .24 | .06 |
| ☐ 47 Jack Ham .............................. Pittsburgh Steelers | 2.00 | .80 | .20 |
| ☐ 48 Ray Guy ............................... Oakland Raiders | 1.50 | .60 | .15 |

# 1976 Sunbeam NFL Helmet Die-Cuts

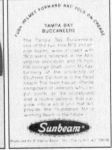

This 28-card set features cards of standard size, 2 1/2" by 3 1/2". The cards are die-cut so that they can stand up when the perforation is popped. The team's helmet, team nickname, and a generic player drawing are pictured on each card front. The card back features a narrative about the team and the Sunbeam logo. The cards are unnumbered. The set is dated by the fact that many of the card backs discuss the respective team's prospects for 1976.

|  | NRMT | VG-E | GOOD |
|---|---|---|---|
| COMPLETE SET (28)...................... | 100.00 | 40.00 | 10.00 |
| COMMON PLAYER (1-28)................ | 6.00 | 2.40 | .60 |

| | | | |
|---|---|---|---|
| ☐ 1 Atlanta Falcons........................ | 6.00 | 2.40 | .60 |
| ☐ 2 Baltimore Colts......................... | 6.00 | 2.40 | .60 |
| ☐ 3 Buffalo Bills ............................ | 6.00 | 2.40 | .60 |
| ☐ 4 Chicago Bears ......................... | 6.00 | 2.40 | .60 |
| ☐ 5 Cincinnati Bengals.................... | 6.00 | 2.40 | .60 |
| ☐ 6 Cleveland Browns ..................... | 6.00 | 2.40 | .60 |
| ☐ 7 Dallas Cowboys ....................... | 7.50 | 3.00 | .75 |
| ☐ 8 Denver Broncos ....................... | 6.00 | 2.40 | .60 |
| ☐ 9 Detroit Lions ........................... | 6.00 | 2.40 | .60 |
| ☐ 10 Green Bay Packers .................. | 6.00 | 2.40 | .60 |
| ☐ 11 Houston Oilers ....................... | 6.00 | 2.40 | .60 |
| ☐ 12 Kansas City Chiefs .................. | 6.00 | 2.40 | .60 |
| ☐ 13 Los Angeles Rams ................... | 6.00 | 2.40 | .60 |
| ☐ 14 Miami Dolphins ....................... | 7.50 | 3.00 | .75 |
| ☐ 15 Minnesota Vikings.................... | 6.00 | 2.40 | .60 |
| ☐ 16 New England Patriots................ | 6.00 | 2.40 | .60 |
| ☐ 17 New Orleans Saints.................. | 6.00 | 2.40 | .60 |
| ☐ 18 New York Giants...................... | 6.00 | 2.40 | .60 |
| ☐ 19 New York Jets ........................ | 6.00 | 2.40 | .60 |
| ☐ 20 Oakland Raiders...................... | 7.50 | 3.00 | .75 |
| ☐ 21 Philadelphia Eagles ................. | 6.00 | 2.40 | .60 |
| ☐ 22 Pittsburgh Steelers .................. | 6.00 | 2.40 | .60 |
| ☐ 23 St. Louis Cardinals .................. | 6.00 | 2.40 | .60 |
| ☐ 24 San Diego Chargers ................. | 6.00 | 2.40 | .60 |
| ☐ 25 San Francisco 49ers................. | 6.00 | 2.40 | .60 |
| ☐ 26 Seattle Seahawks .................... | 6.00 | 2.40 | .60 |
| ☐ 27 Tampa Bay Buccaneers............. | 6.00 | 2.40 | .60 |
| ☐ 28 Washington Redskins ............... | 6.00 | 2.40 | .60 |

## 1990-91 Sunkist Fun Fruits Wacky Players

This ten-card set features caricature cards of standard size, 2 1/2" by 3 1/2". One card was available in each specially marked box of Sunkist Fun Fruits Wacky Players Assorted Real Fruit Snacks. There were two years produced with the same players; the only difference was the stats on the card backs. The 1991 set features cards with stats for 1990 on the back. The side box panel contained a mail-in offer in which one could receive a free set of ten football Wacky Players cards for three UPC symbols. The cards are unnumbered, so they are listed below alphabetically by subject title.

|  | MINT | EXC | G-VG |
|---|---|---|---|
| COMPLETE SET (10) | 6.00 | 2.40 | .60 |
| COMMON PLAYER (1-10) | 1.00 | .40 | .10 |
| ☐ 1 Bullet Ben | 1.00 | .40 | .10 |
| ☐ 2 Coach | 1.00 | .40 | .10 |
| ☐ 3 Crusher | 1.00 | .40 | .10 |
| ☐ 4 Hollywood | 1.00 | .40 | .10 |
| ☐ 5 Krazy Karl | 1.00 | .40 | .10 |
| ☐ 6 Mixed-Up Mike | 1.00 | .40 | .10 |
| ☐ 7 Piled-On Pete | 1.00 | .40 | .10 |
| ☐ 8 Sacking Sam | 1.00 | .40 | .10 |
| ☐ 9 Sky-High Sly | 1.00 | .40 | .10 |
| ☐ 10 Spike | 1.00 | .40 | .10 |

## 1972 Sunoco Stamps

41 Phil Villapiano LLB
Oakland Raiders

In 1972, the Sun Oil Company issued a stamp set and two types of albums. Each stamp measures approximately 1 5/8" by 2 3/8" whereas the albums are approximately 10 3/8" by 10 15/16". The logo on the cover of the 56-page stamp album indicates "NFL Action '72". The other "deluxe" album contains 128 pages. Each team was represented with 12 offensive and 12 defensive player stamps. There are a total of 624 unnumbered stamps in the set, which made this stamp set the largest football set to date at that time. The albums indicate where each stamp is to be placed. The square for each player's stamp was marked by the player's number, name, position, height, weight, age, and college attended. When the album was issued, the back of the book included perforated sheets of stamps comprising more than one fourth of the set. The album also had sheets of tabs which were to be used for putting the stamps in the book, rather than licking the entire stamp. Each week of the promotion a purchase of gasoline yielded an additional nine-player perforated stamp sheet. The stamps and the album positions are unnumbered so they are ordered and numbered below according to the team order in which they appear in the book. The team order is alphabetical as well according to the city

name, i.e., Atlanta Falcons (1-24), Baltimore Colts (25-48), Buffalo Bills (49-72), Chicago Bears (73-96), Cincinnati Bengals (97-120), Cleveland Browns (121-144), Dallas Cowboys (145-168), Denver Broncos (169-192), Detroit Lions (193-216), Green Bay Packers (217-240), Houston Oilers (241-264), Kansas City Chiefs (265-288), Los Angeles Rams (289-312), Miami Dolphins (313-336), Minnesota Vikings (337-360), New England Patriots (361-384), New Orleans Saints (385-408), New York Giants (409-432), New York Jets (433-456), Oakland Raiders (457-480), Philadelphia Eagles (481-504), Pittsburgh Steelers (505-528), St. Louis Cardinals (529-552), San Diego Chargers (553-576), San Francisco 49ers (577-600), and Washington Redskins (601-624). Since the same 144 stamps were included as an insert with each album; these 144 stamps are easier to find and are marked as DP's in the checklist below. The stamp set is considered in very good condition at best when glued in the album. There are a number of players appearing in this set in (or before) their Rookie Card year: Lyle Alzado, Mel Blount, Harold Carmichael, Dan Dierdorf, L.C. Greenwood, Jack Ham, Cliff Harris, Ted Hendricks, Charlie Joiner, Bob Kuechenberg, Larry Little, Archie Manning, Ray Perkins, Jim Plunkett, John Riggins, Art Shell, Steve Spurrier, Roger Staubach, Gene Upshaw, Jeff Van Note, and Jack Youngblood.

|  | NRMT | VG-E | GOOD |
|---|---|---|---|
| COMPLETE SET (624) | 100.00 | 40.00 | 10.00 |
| COMMON PLAYER (1-624) | .10 | .04 | .01 |
| COMMON PLAYER DP (1-624) | .10 | .04 | .01 |
| ☐ 1 Ken Burrow | .10 | .04 | .01 |
| ☐ 2 Bill Sandeman | .10 | .04 | .01 |
| ☐ 3 Andy Maurer DP | .10 | .04 | .01 |
| ☐ 4 Jeff Van Note DP | .20 | .08 | .02 |
| ☐ 5 Malcolm Snider | .10 | .04 | .01 |
| ☐ 6 George Kunz | .20 | .08 | .02 |
| ☐ 7 Jim Mitchell | .10 | .04 | .01 |
| ☐ 8 Wes Chesson | .10 | .04 | .01 |
| ☐ 9 Bob Berry | .20 | .08 | .02 |
| ☐ 10 Dick Shiner | .10 | .04 | .01 |
| ☐ 11 Jim Butler | .10 | .04 | .01 |
| ☐ 12 Art Malone | .10 | .04 | .01 |
| ☐ 13 Claude Humphrey DP | .20 | .08 | .02 |
| ☐ 14 John Small DP | .10 | .04 | .01 |
| ☐ 15 Glen Condren | .10 | .04 | .01 |
| ☐ 16 John Zook | .20 | .08 | .02 |
| ☐ 17 Don Hansen | .10 | .04 | .01 |
| ☐ 18 Tommy Nobis | 1.00 | .40 | .10 |
| ☐ 19 Greg Brezina | .20 | .08 | .02 |
| ☐ 20 Ken Reaves | .10 | .04 | .01 |
| ☐ 21 Tom Hayes | .10 | .04 | .01 |
| ☐ 22 Tom McCauley DP | .10 | .04 | .01 |
| ☐ 23 Bill Bell DP | .10 | .04 | .01 |
| ☐ 24 Billy Lothridge | .20 | .08 | .02 |
| ☐ 25 Ed Hinton | .10 | .04 | .01 |
| ☐ 26 Bob Vogel DP | .10 | .04 | .01 |
| ☐ 27 Glenn Ressler | .10 | .04 | .01 |
| ☐ 28 Bill Curry DP | .30 | .12 | .03 |
| ☐ 29 John Williams | .10 | .04 | .01 |
| ☐ 30 Dan Sullivan | .10 | .04 | .01 |
| ☐ 31 Tom Mitchell | .10 | .04 | .01 |
| ☐ 32 John Mackey | 1.25 | .50 | .12 |
| ☐ 33 Ray Perkins | 1.50 | .60 | .15 |
| ☐ 34 John Unitas | 5.00 | 2.00 | .50 |
| ☐ 35 Tom Matte | .30 | .12 | .03 |
| ☐ 36 Norm Bulaich | .20 | .08 | .02 |
| ☐ 37 Bubba Smith DP | .75 | .30 | .07 |
| ☐ 38 Bill Newsome | .10 | .04 | .01 |
| ☐ 39 Fred Miller DP | .10 | .04 | .01 |
| ☐ 40 Roy Hilton | .10 | .04 | .01 |
| ☐ 41 Ray May DP | .10 | .04 | .01 |
| ☐ 42 Ted Hendricks | 1.25 | .50 | .12 |
| ☐ 43 Charlie Stukes | .10 | .04 | .01 |
| ☐ 44 Rex Kern | .30 | .12 | .03 |
| ☐ 45 Jerry Logan | .10 | .04 | .01 |
| ☐ 46 Rick Volk | .20 | .08 | .02 |
| ☐ 47 David Lee | .10 | .04 | .01 |
| ☐ 48 Jim O'Brien | .20 | .08 | .02 |
| ☐ 49 J.D. Hill | .20 | .08 | .02 |
| ☐ 50 Willie Young | .10 | .04 | .01 |
| ☐ 51 Jim Reilly | .10 | .04 | .01 |
| ☐ 52 Bruce Jarvis DP | .10 | .04 | .01 |
| ☐ 53 Levert Carr | .10 | .04 | .01 |
| ☐ 54 Donnie Green DP | .10 | .04 | .01 |
| ☐ 55 Jan White DP | .20 | .08 | .02 |
| ☐ 56 Marlin Briscoe | .30 | .12 | .03 |
| ☐ 57 Dennis Shaw | .20 | .08 | .02 |
| ☐ 58 O.J. Simpson | 10.00 | 4.00 | 1.00 |
| ☐ 59 Wayne Patrick | .10 | .04 | .01 |
| ☐ 60 John Leypoldt | .10 | .04 | .01 |
| ☐ 61 Al Cowlings | .50 | .20 | .05 |
| ☐ 62 Jim Dunaway DP | .20 | .08 | .02 |
| ☐ 63 Bob Tatarek | .10 | .04 | .01 |
| ☐ 64 Cal Snowden | .10 | .04 | .01 |
| ☐ 65 Paul Guidry | .10 | .04 | .01 |
| ☐ 66 Edgar Chandler | .20 | .08 | .02 |
| ☐ 67 Al Andrews DP | .10 | .04 | .01 |
| ☐ 68 Robert James | .10 | .04 | .01 |

|  |  | | | |
|---|---|---|---|---|
| ☐ 69 | Alvin Wyatt | .10 | .04 | .01 |
| ☐ 70 | John Pitts DP | .10 | .04 | .01 |
| ☐ 71 | Pete Richardson | .10 | .04 | .01 |
| ☐ 72 | Spike Jones | .10 | .04 | .01 |
| ☐ 73 | Dick Gordon | .20 | .08 | .02 |
| ☐ 74 | Randy Jackson DP | .10 | .04 | .01 |
| ☐ 75 | Glen Holloway | .10 | .04 | .01 |
| ☐ 76 | Rich Coady DP | .10 | .04 | .01 |
| ☐ 77 | Jim Cadile DP | .10 | .04 | .01 |
| ☐ 78 | Steve Wright | .10 | .04 | .01 |
| ☐ 79 | Bob Wallace | .10 | .04 | .01 |
| ☐ 80 | George Farmer | .10 | .04 | .01 |
| ☐ 81 | Bobby Douglass | .30 | .12 | .03 |
| ☐ 82 | Don Shy | .10 | .04 | .01 |
| ☐ 83 | Cyril Pinder | .10 | .04 | .01 |
| ☐ 84 | Mac Percival | .10 | .04 | .01 |
| ☐ 85 | Willie Holman | .10 | .04 | .01 |
| ☐ 86 | George Seals DP | .10 | .04 | .01 |
| ☐ 87 | Bill Staley | .10 | .04 | .01 |
| ☐ 88 | Ed O'Bradovich DP | .20 | .08 | .02 |
| ☐ 89 | Doug Buffone DP | .10 | .04 | .01 |
| ☐ 90 | Dick Butkus | 2.50 | 1.00 | .25 |
| ☐ 91 | Ross Brupbacher | .20 | .08 | .02 |
| ☐ 92 | Charlie Ford | .10 | .04 | .01 |
| ☐ 93 | Joe Taylor | .10 | .04 | .01 |
| ☐ 94 | Ron Smith | .20 | .08 | .02 |
| ☐ 95 | Jerry Moore | .10 | .04 | .01 |
| ☐ 96 | Bobby Joe Green | .10 | .04 | .01 |
| ☐ 97 | Chip Myers | .10 | .04 | .01 |
| ☐ 98 | Rufus Mayes DP | .10 | .04 | .01 |
| ☐ 99 | Howard Fest | .10 | .04 | .01 |
| ☐ 100 | Bob Johnson | .20 | .08 | .02 |
| ☐ 101 | Pat Matson DP | .10 | .04 | .01 |
| ☐ 102 | Vern Holland | .10 | .04 | .01 |
| ☐ 103 | Bruce Coslet | .50 | .20 | .05 |
| ☐ 104 | Bob Trumpy | .50 | .20 | .05 |
| ☐ 105 | Virgil Carter | .20 | .08 | .02 |
| ☐ 106 | Fred Willis | .10 | .04 | .01 |
| ☐ 107 | Jess Phillips | .10 | .04 | .01 |
| ☐ 108 | Horst Muhlmann | .10 | .04 | .01 |
| ☐ 109 | Royce Berry | .10 | .04 | .01 |
| ☐ 110 | Mike Reid DP | .50 | .20 | .05 |
| ☐ 111 | Steve Chomyszak DP | .10 | .04 | .01 |
| ☐ 112 | Ron Carpenter | .10 | .04 | .01 |
| ☐ 113 | Al Beauchamp DP | .10 | .04 | .01 |
| ☐ 114 | Bill Bergey | .40 | .16 | .04 |
| ☐ 115 | Ken Avery | .10 | .04 | .01 |
| ☐ 116 | Lemar Parrish | .30 | .12 | .03 |
| ☐ 117 | Ken Riley | .30 | .12 | .03 |
| ☐ 118 | Sandy Durko DP | .10 | .04 | .01 |
| ☐ 119 | Dave Lewis | .10 | .04 | .01 |
| ☐ 120 | Paul Robinson | .20 | .08 | .02 |
| ☐ 121 | Fair Hooker | .20 | .08 | .02 |
| ☐ 122 | Doug Dieken DP | .10 | .04 | .01 |
| ☐ 123 | John Demarie | .10 | .04 | .01 |
| ☐ 124 | Jim Copeland | .10 | .04 | .01 |
| ☐ 125 | Gene Hickerson DP | .10 | .04 | .01 |
| ☐ 126 | Bob McKay | .10 | .04 | .01 |
| ☐ 127 | Milt Morin | .20 | .08 | .02 |
| ☐ 128 | Frank Pitts | .10 | .04 | .01 |
| ☐ 129 | Mike Phipps | .30 | .12 | .03 |
| ☐ 130 | Leroy Kelly | 1.00 | .40 | .10 |
| ☐ 131 | Bo Scott | .20 | .08 | .02 |
| ☐ 132 | Don Cockroft | .10 | .04 | .01 |
| ☐ 133 | Ron Snidow | .10 | .04 | .01 |
| ☐ 134 | Walter Johnson DP | .10 | .04 | .01 |
| ☐ 135 | Jerry Sherk | .30 | .12 | .03 |
| ☐ 136 | Jack Gregory | .10 | .04 | .01 |
| ☐ 137 | Jim Houston DP | .10 | .04 | .01 |
| ☐ 138 | Dale Lindsey | .10 | .04 | .01 |
| ☐ 139 | Bill Andrews | .10 | .04 | .01 |
| ☐ 140 | Clarence Scott | .20 | .08 | .02 |
| ☐ 141 | Ernie Kellerman | .10 | .04 | .01 |
| ☐ 142 | Walt Sumner | .10 | .04 | .01 |
| ☐ 143 | Mike Howell DP | .10 | .04 | .01 |
| ☐ 144 | Reece Morrison | .10 | .04 | .01 |
| ☐ 145 | Bob Hayes | .75 | .30 | .07 |
| ☐ 146 | Ralph Neely | .20 | .08 | .02 |
| ☐ 147 | John Niland DP | .10 | .04 | .01 |
| ☐ 148 | Dave Manders | .20 | .08 | .02 |
| ☐ 149 | Blaine Nye | .10 | .04 | .01 |
| ☐ 150 | Rayfield Wright | .20 | .08 | .02 |
| ☐ 151 | Billy Truax | .10 | .04 | .01 |
| ☐ 152 | Lance Alworth | 2.00 | .80 | .20 |
| ☐ 153 | Roger Staubach | 9.00 | 3.75 | .90 |
| ☐ 154 | Duane Thomas | .50 | .20 | .05 |
| ☐ 155 | Walt Garrison | .30 | .12 | .03 |
| ☐ 156 | Mike Clark | .10 | .04 | .01 |
| ☐ 157 | Larry Cole DP | .10 | .04 | .01 |
| ☐ 158 | Jethro Pugh | .20 | .08 | .02 |
| ☐ 159 | Bob Lilly | 1.50 | .60 | .15 |
| ☐ 160 | George Andrie | .20 | .08 | .02 |
| ☐ 161 | Dave Edwards DP | .10 | .04 | .01 |
| ☐ 162 | Lee Roy Jordan | .75 | .30 | .07 |
| ☐ 163 | Chuck Howley | .30 | .12 | .03 |
| ☐ 164 | Herb Adderley DP | .75 | .30 | .07 |
| ☐ 165 | Mel Renfro | .60 | .24 | .06 |
| ☐ 166 | Cornell Green | .30 | .12 | .03 |
| ☐ 167 | Cliff Harris DP | .20 | .08 | .02 |
| ☐ 168 | Ron Widby | .10 | .04 | .01 |
| ☐ 169 | Jerry Simmons | .10 | .04 | .01 |
| ☐ 170 | Roger Shoals | .10 | .04 | .01 |
| ☐ 171 | Larron Jackson | .10 | .04 | .01 |
| ☐ 172 | George Goeddeke DP | .10 | .04 | .01 |
| ☐ 173 | Mike Schnitker | .10 | .04 | .01 |
| ☐ 174 | Mike Current | .10 | .04 | .01 |
| ☐ 175 | Billy Masters | .10 | .04 | .01 |
| ☐ 176 | Jack Gehrke | .10 | .04 | .01 |
| ☐ 177 | Don Horn | .20 | .08 | .02 |
| ☐ 178 | Floyd Little | .75 | .30 | .07 |
| ☐ 179 | Bobby Anderson | .30 | .12 | .03 |
| ☐ 180 | Jim Turner DP | .20 | .08 | .02 |
| ☐ 181 | Rich Jackson | .10 | .04 | .01 |
| ☐ 182 | Paul Smith DP | .10 | .04 | .01 |
| ☐ 183 | Dave Costa | .10 | .04 | .01 |
| ☐ 184 | Lyle Alzado DP | .75 | .30 | .07 |
| ☐ 185 | Olen Underwood | .10 | .04 | .01 |
| ☐ 186 | Fred Forsberg DP | .10 | .04 | .01 |
| ☐ 187 | Chip Myrtle | .10 | .04 | .01 |
| ☐ 188 | Leroy Mitchell | .10 | .04 | .01 |
| ☐ 189 | Billy Thompson DP | .20 | .08 | .02 |
| ☐ 190 | Charlie Greer | .10 | .04 | .01 |
| ☐ 191 | George Saimes | .20 | .08 | .02 |
| ☐ 192 | Billy Van Heusen | .10 | .04 | .01 |
| ☐ 193 | Earl McCullouch | .20 | .08 | .02 |
| ☐ 194 | Jim Yarbrough | .10 | .04 | .01 |
| ☐ 195 | Chuck Walton | .10 | .04 | .01 |
| ☐ 196 | Ed Flanagan | .10 | .04 | .01 |
| ☐ 197 | Frank Gallagher | .10 | .04 | .01 |
| ☐ 198 | Rockne Freitas | .10 | .04 | .01 |
| ☐ 199 | Charlie Sanders DP | .20 | .08 | .02 |
| ☐ 200 | Larry Walton | .10 | .04 | .01 |
| ☐ 201 | Greg Landry | .30 | .12 | .03 |
| ☐ 202 | Altie Taylor | .20 | .08 | .02 |
| ☐ 203 | Steve Owens | .40 | .16 | .04 |
| ☐ 204 | Errol Mann DP | .10 | .04 | .01 |
| ☐ 205 | Joe Robb | .10 | .04 | .01 |
| ☐ 206 | Dick Evey | .10 | .04 | .01 |
| ☐ 207 | Jerry Rush | .10 | .04 | .01 |
| ☐ 208 | Larry Hand DP | .10 | .04 | .01 |
| ☐ 209 | Paul Naumoff | .20 | .08 | .02 |
| ☐ 210 | Mike Lucci | .20 | .08 | .02 |
| ☐ 211 | Wayne Walker DP | .10 | .04 | .01 |
| ☐ 212 | Lem Barney DP | .75 | .30 | .07 |
| ☐ 213 | Dick LeBeau DP | .20 | .08 | .02 |
| ☐ 214 | Mike Weger | .10 | .04 | .01 |
| ☐ 215 | Wayne Rasmussen | .10 | .04 | .01 |
| ☐ 216 | Herman Weaver | .10 | .04 | .01 |
| ☐ 217 | John Spilis | .10 | .04 | .01 |
| ☐ 218 | Francis Peay DP | .10 | .04 | .01 |
| ☐ 219 | Bill Lueck | .10 | .04 | .01 |
| ☐ 220 | Ken Bowman DP | .10 | .04 | .01 |
| ☐ 221 | Gale Gillingham DP | .20 | .08 | .02 |
| ☐ 222 | Dick Himes DP | .10 | .04 | .01 |
| ☐ 223 | Rich McGeorge | .10 | .04 | .01 |
| ☐ 224 | Carroll Dale | .20 | .08 | .02 |
| ☐ 225 | Bart Starr | 2.50 | 1.00 | .25 |
| ☐ 226 | Scott Hunter | .30 | .12 | .03 |
| ☐ 227 | John Brockington | .30 | .12 | .03 |
| ☐ 228 | Dave Hampton | .20 | .08 | .02 |
| ☐ 229 | Clarence Williams | .10 | .04 | .01 |
| ☐ 230 | Mike McCoy | .20 | .08 | .02 |
| ☐ 231 | Bob Brown | .20 | .08 | .02 |
| ☐ 232 | Alden Roche | .10 | .04 | .01 |
| ☐ 233 | Dave Robinson DP | .20 | .08 | .02 |
| ☐ 234 | Jim Carter | .20 | .08 | .02 |
| ☐ 235 | Fred Carr | .20 | .08 | .02 |
| ☐ 236 | Ken Ellis | .10 | .04 | .01 |
| ☐ 237 | Doug Hart | .10 | .04 | .01 |
| ☐ 238 | Al Randolph | .10 | .04 | .01 |
| ☐ 239 | Al Matthews | .10 | .04 | .01 |
| ☐ 240 | Tim Webster | .10 | .04 | .01 |
| ☐ 241 | Jim Beirne DP | .10 | .04 | .01 |
| ☐ 242 | Bob Young | .10 | .04 | .01 |
| ☐ 243 | Elbert Drungo | .10 | .04 | .01 |
| ☐ 244 | Sam Walton | .20 | .08 | .02 |
| ☐ 245 | Alvin Reed | .10 | .04 | .01 |
| ☐ 246 | Charlie Joiner | 1.25 | .50 | .12 |
| ☐ 247 | Dan Pastorini | .30 | .12 | .03 |
| ☐ 248 | Charlie Johnson | .30 | .12 | .03 |
| ☐ 249 | Lynn Dickey | .30 | .12 | .03 |
| ☐ 250 | Woody Campbell | .10 | .04 | .01 |
| ☐ 251 | Robert Holmes | .20 | .08 | .02 |
| ☐ 252 | Mark Moseley | .30 | .12 | .03 |
| ☐ 253 | Pat Holmes | .10 | .04 | .01 |
| ☐ 254 | Mike Tilleman DP | .10 | .04 | .01 |
| ☐ 255 | Leo Brooks | .10 | .04 | .01 |
| ☐ 256 | Elvin Bethea | .30 | .12 | .03 |
| ☐ 257 | George Webster | .30 | .12 | .03 |
| ☐ 258 | Garland Boyette | .10 | .04 | .01 |
| ☐ 259 | Ron Pritchard | .10 | .04 | .01 |
| ☐ 260 | Zeke Moore DP | .10 | .04 | .01 |
| ☐ 261 | Willie Alexander | .10 | .04 | .01 |
| ☐ 262 | Ken Houston | 1.00 | .40 | .10 |

|  |  | | | |
|---|---|---|---|---|
| ☐ 263 | John Charles DP | .10 | .04 | .01 |
| ☐ 264 | Linzy Cole DP | .10 | .04 | .01 |
| ☐ 265 | Elmo Wright | .20 | .08 | .02 |
| ☐ 266 | Jim Tyrer DP | .20 | .08 | .02 |
| ☐ 267 | Ed Budde | .20 | .08 | .02 |
| ☐ 268 | Jack Rudnay DP | .10 | .04 | .01 |
| ☐ 269 | Mo Moorman | .10 | .04 | .01 |
| ☐ 270 | Dave Hill | .10 | .04 | .01 |
| ☐ 271 | Morris Stroud | .10 | .04 | .01 |
| ☐ 272 | Otis Taylor | .40 | .16 | .04 |
| ☐ 273 | Len Dawson | 2.00 | .80 | .20 |
| ☐ 274 | Ed Podolak | .30 | .12 | .03 |
| ☐ 275 | Wendell Hayes | .10 | .04 | .01 |
| ☐ 276 | Jan Stenerud | 1.00 | .40 | .10 |
| ☐ 277 | Marvin Upshaw DP | .10 | .04 | .01 |
| ☐ 278 | Curley Culp | .30 | .12 | .03 |
| ☐ 279 | Buck Buchanan | 1.00 | .40 | .10 |
| ☐ 280 | Aaron Brown | .10 | .04 | .01 |
| ☐ 281 | Bobby Bell | 1.00 | .40 | .10 |
| ☐ 282 | Willie Lanier | 1.25 | .50 | .12 |
| ☐ 283 | Jim Lynch | .20 | .08 | .02 |
| ☐ 284 | Jim Marsalis DP | .20 | .08 | .02 |
| ☐ 285 | Emmitt Thomas | .20 | .08 | .02 |
| ☐ 286 | Jim Kearney DP | .10 | .04 | .01 |
| ☐ 287 | Johnny Robinson | .40 | .16 | .04 |
| ☐ 288 | Jerrel Wilson DP | .10 | .04 | .01 |
| ☐ 289 | Jack Snow | .30 | .12 | .03 |
| ☐ 290 | Charlie Cowan | .10 | .04 | .01 |
| ☐ 291 | Tom Mack DP | .50 | .20 | .05 |
| ☐ 292 | Ken Iman | .10 | .04 | .01 |
| ☐ 293 | Joe Scibelli | .10 | .04 | .01 |
| ☐ 294 | Harry Schuh DP | .10 | .04 | .01 |
| ☐ 295 | Bob Klein | .20 | .08 | .02 |
| ☐ 296 | Lance Rentzel | .30 | .12 | .03 |
| ☐ 297 | Roman Gabriel | .60 | .24 | .06 |
| ☐ 298 | Les Josephson | .20 | .08 | .02 |
| ☐ 299 | Willie Ellison | .20 | .08 | .02 |
| ☐ 300 | David Ray | .10 | .04 | .01 |
| ☐ 301 | Jack Youngblood | 1.25 | .50 | .12 |
| ☐ 302 | Merlin Olsen | 1.50 | .60 | .15 |
| ☐ 303 | Phil Olsen | .10 | .04 | .01 |
| ☐ 304 | Coy Bacon | .10 | .04 | .01 |
| ☐ 305 | Jim Purnell DP | .10 | .04 | .01 |
| ☐ 306 | Marlin McKeever | .20 | .08 | .02 |
| ☐ 307 | Isiah Robertson | .30 | .12 | .03 |
| ☐ 308 | Jim Nettles DP | .10 | .04 | .01 |
| ☐ 309 | Gene Howard DP | .10 | .04 | .01 |
| ☐ 310 | Kermit Alexander | .20 | .08 | .02 |
| ☐ 311 | Dave Elmendorf DP | .10 | .04 | .01 |
| ☐ 312 | Pat Studstill | .20 | .08 | .02 |
| ☐ 313 | Paul Warfield | 1.50 | .60 | .15 |
| ☐ 314 | Doug Crusan | .10 | .04 | .01 |
| ☐ 315 | Bob Kuechenberg | .40 | .16 | .04 |
| ☐ 316 | Bob DeMarco DP | .20 | .08 | .02 |
| ☐ 317 | Larry Little | 1.00 | .40 | .10 |
| ☐ 318 | Norm Evans DP | .20 | .08 | .02 |
| ☐ 319 | Marv Fleming DP | .20 | .08 | .02 |
| ☐ 320 | Howard Twilley | .30 | .12 | .03 |
| ☐ 321 | Bob Griese | 2.00 | .80 | .20 |
| ☐ 322 | Jim Kiick | .40 | .16 | .04 |
| ☐ 323 | Larry Csonka | 1.50 | .60 | .15 |
| ☐ 324 | Garo Yepremian | .30 | .12 | .03 |
| ☐ 325 | Jim Riley DP | .10 | .04 | .01 |
| ☐ 326 | Manny Fernandez | .20 | .08 | .02 |
| ☐ 327 | Bob Heinz DP | .10 | .04 | .01 |
| ☐ 328 | Bill Stanfill | .30 | .12 | .03 |
| ☐ 329 | Doug Swift | .10 | .04 | .01 |
| ☐ 330 | Nick Buoniconti | .75 | .30 | .07 |
| ☐ 331 | Mike Kolen | .10 | .04 | .01 |
| ☐ 332 | Tim Foley | .30 | .12 | .03 |
| ☐ 333 | Curtis Johnson | .10 | .04 | .01 |
| ☐ 334 | Dick Anderson | .40 | .16 | .04 |
| ☐ 335 | Jake Scott | .40 | .16 | .04 |
| ☐ 336 | Larry Seiple | .10 | .04 | .01 |
| ☐ 337 | Gene Washington | .20 | .08 | .02 |
| ☐ 338 | Grady Alderman | .10 | .04 | .01 |
| ☐ 339 | Ed White DP | .20 | .08 | .02 |
| ☐ 340 | Mick Tingelhoff DP | .20 | .08 | .02 |
| ☐ 341 | Milt Sunde DP | .10 | .04 | .01 |
| ☐ 342 | Ron Yary | .40 | .16 | .04 |
| ☐ 343 | John Beasley | .10 | .04 | .01 |
| ☐ 344 | John Henderson | .10 | .04 | .01 |
| ☐ 345 | Fran Tarkenton | 3.50 | 1.40 | .35 |
| ☐ 346 | Clint Jones | .20 | .08 | .02 |
| ☐ 347 | Dave Osborn | .20 | .08 | .02 |
| ☐ 348 | Fred Cox | .20 | .08 | .02 |
| ☐ 349 | Carl Eller DP | .50 | .20 | .05 |
| ☐ 350 | Gary Larsen DP | .10 | .04 | .01 |
| ☐ 351 | Alan Page | 1.00 | .40 | .10 |
| ☐ 352 | Jim Marshall | 1.00 | .40 | .10 |
| ☐ 353 | Roy Winston | .20 | .08 | .02 |
| ☐ 354 | Lonnie Warwick | .10 | .04 | .01 |
| ☐ 355 | Wally Hilgenberg | .10 | .04 | .01 |
| ☐ 356 | Bobby Bryant | .10 | .04 | .01 |
| ☐ 357 | Ed Sharockman | .10 | .04 | .01 |
| ☐ 358 | Charlie West | .10 | .04 | .01 |
| ☐ 359 | Paul Krause | .50 | .20 | .05 |
| ☐ 360 | Bob Lee | .20 | .08 | .02 |
| ☐ 361 | Randy Vataha | .30 | .12 | .03 |
| ☐ 362 | Mike Montler DP | .10 | .04 | .01 |
| ☐ 363 | Halvor Hagen | .10 | .04 | .01 |
| ☐ 364 | Jon Morris DP | .10 | .04 | .01 |
| ☐ 365 | Len St. Jean | .10 | .04 | .01 |
| ☐ 366 | Tom Neville | .10 | .04 | .01 |
| ☐ 367 | Tom Beer | .10 | .04 | .01 |
| ☐ 368 | Ron Sellers | .20 | .08 | .02 |
| ☐ 369 | Jim Plunkett | 1.00 | .40 | .10 |
| ☐ 370 | Carl Garrett | .20 | .08 | .02 |
| ☐ 371 | Jim Nance | .30 | .12 | .03 |
| ☐ 372 | Charlie Gogolak | .20 | .08 | .02 |
| ☐ 373 | Ike Lassiter DP | .10 | .04 | .01 |
| ☐ 374 | Dave Rowe | .10 | .04 | .01 |
| ☐ 375 | Julius Adams | .20 | .08 | .02 |
| ☐ 376 | Dennis Wirgowski | .10 | .04 | .01 |
| ☐ 377 | Ed Weisacosky | .10 | .04 | .01 |
| ☐ 378 | Jim Cheyunski DP | .10 | .04 | .01 |
| ☐ 379 | Steve Kiner | .10 | .04 | .01 |
| ☐ 380 | Larry Carwell DP | .10 | .04 | .01 |
| ☐ 381 | John Outlaw | .10 | .04 | .01 |
| ☐ 382 | Rickie Harris | .10 | .04 | .01 |
| ☐ 383 | Don Webb DP | .10 | .04 | .01 |
| ☐ 384 | Tom Janik | .10 | .04 | .01 |
| ☐ 385 | Al Dodd DP | .10 | .04 | .01 |
| ☐ 386 | Don Morrison | .10 | .04 | .01 |
| ☐ 387 | Jake Kupp | .10 | .04 | .01 |
| ☐ 388 | John Didion | .10 | .04 | .01 |
| ☐ 389 | Del Williams | .10 | .04 | .01 |
| ☐ 390 | Glen Ray Hines | .10 | .04 | .01 |
| ☐ 391 | Dave Parks DP | .20 | .08 | .02 |
| ☐ 392 | Dan Abramowicz | .30 | .12 | .03 |
| ☐ 393 | Archie Manning | 2.00 | .80 | .20 |
| ☐ 394 | Bob Gresham | .10 | .04 | .01 |
| ☐ 395 | Virgil Robinson | .10 | .04 | .01 |
| ☐ 396 | Charlie Durkee | .10 | .04 | .01 |
| ☐ 397 | Richard Neal | .10 | .04 | .01 |
| ☐ 398 | Bob Pollard DP | .10 | .04 | .01 |
| ☐ 399 | Dave Long DP | .10 | .04 | .01 |
| ☐ 400 | Joe Owens | .10 | .04 | .01 |
| ☐ 401 | Carl Cunningham | .10 | .04 | .01 |
| ☐ 402 | Jim Flanigan | .10 | .04 | .01 |
| ☐ 403 | Wayne Colman | .10 | .04 | .01 |
| ☐ 404 | D'Artagnan Martin DP | .10 | .04 | .01 |
| ☐ 405 | Delles Howell | .10 | .04 | .01 |
| ☐ 406 | Hugo Hollas | .10 | .04 | .01 |
| ☐ 407 | Doug Wyatt DP | .10 | .04 | .01 |
| ☐ 408 | Julian Fagan | .10 | .04 | .01 |
| ☐ 409 | Don Herrmann | .10 | .04 | .01 |
| ☐ 410 | Willie Young | .10 | .04 | .01 |
| ☐ 411 | Bob Hyland | .10 | .04 | .01 |
| ☐ 412 | Greg Larson DP | .10 | .04 | .01 |
| ☐ 413 | Doug Van Horn | .10 | .04 | .01 |
| ☐ 414 | Charlie Harper DP | .10 | .04 | .01 |
| ☐ 415 | Bob Tucker | .20 | .08 | .02 |
| ☐ 416 | Joe Morrison | .20 | .08 | .02 |
| ☐ 417 | Randy Johnson | .20 | .08 | .02 |
| ☐ 418 | Tucker Frederickson | .30 | .12 | .03 |
| ☐ 419 | Ron Johnson | .30 | .12 | .03 |
| ☐ 420 | Pete Gogolak | .20 | .08 | .02 |
| ☐ 421 | Henry Reed | .10 | .04 | .01 |
| ☐ 422 | Jim Kanicki DP | .10 | .04 | .01 |
| ☐ 423 | Roland Lakes | .10 | .04 | .01 |
| ☐ 424 | John Douglas DP | .10 | .04 | .01 |
| ☐ 425 | Ron Hornsby DP | .10 | .04 | .01 |
| ☐ 426 | Jim Files | .10 | .04 | .01 |
| ☐ 427 | Willie Williams DP | .10 | .04 | .01 |
| ☐ 428 | Otto Brown | .10 | .04 | .01 |
| ☐ 429 | Scott Eaton | .10 | .04 | .01 |
| ☐ 430 | Carl Lockhart | .20 | .08 | .02 |
| ☐ 431 | Tom Blanchard | .20 | .08 | .02 |
| ☐ 432 | Rocky Thompson | .20 | .08 | .02 |
| ☐ 433 | Rich Caster | .30 | .12 | .03 |
| ☐ 434 | Randy Rasmussen | .10 | .04 | .01 |
| ☐ 435 | John Schmitt | .10 | .04 | .01 |
| ☐ 436 | Dave Herman DP | .20 | .08 | .02 |
| ☐ 437 | Winston Hill DP | .20 | .08 | .02 |
| ☐ 438 | Pete Lammons | .20 | .08 | .02 |
| ☐ 439 | Don Maynard | 1.50 | .60 | .15 |
| ☐ 440 | Joe Namath | 9.00 | 3.75 | .90 |
| ☐ 441 | Emerson Boozer | .30 | .12 | .03 |
| ☐ 442 | John Riggins | 3.00 | 1.20 | .30 |
| ☐ 443 | George Nock | .10 | .04 | .01 |
| ☐ 444 | Bobby Howfield | .10 | .04 | .01 |
| ☐ 445 | Gerry Philbin | .10 | .04 | .01 |
| ☐ 446 | John Little DP | .10 | .04 | .01 |
| ☐ 447 | Chuck Hinton | .10 | .04 | .01 |
| ☐ 448 | Mark Lomas | .10 | .04 | .01 |
| ☐ 449 | Ralph Baker | .10 | .04 | .01 |
| ☐ 450 | Al Atkinson DP | .10 | .04 | .01 |
| ☐ 451 | Larry Grantham DP | .20 | .08 | .02 |
| ☐ 452 | John Dockery | .10 | .04 | .01 |
| ☐ 453 | Earlie Thomas DP | .10 | .04 | .01 |
| ☐ 454 | Phil Wise | .10 | .04 | .01 |
| ☐ 455 | W.K. Hicks | .10 | .04 | .01 |
| ☐ 456 | Steve O'Neal | .10 | .04 | .01 |

| | | | |
|---|---|---|---|
| ☐ 457 Drew Buie | .10 | .04 | .01 |
| ☐ 458 Art Shell | 1.50 | .60 | .15 |
| ☐ 459 Gene Upshaw | 1.50 | .60 | .15 |
| ☐ 460 Jim Otto DP | .75 | .30 | .07 |
| ☐ 461 George Buehler | .10 | .04 | .01 |
| ☐ 462 Bob Brown | .40 | .16 | .04 |
| ☐ 463 Ray Chester | .40 | .16 | .04 |
| ☐ 464 Fred Biletnikoff | 2.00 | .80 | .20 |
| ☐ 465 Daryle Lamonica | .60 | .24 | .06 |
| ☐ 466 Marv Hubbard | .20 | .08 | .02 |
| ☐ 467 Clarence Davis | .20 | .08 | .02 |
| ☐ 468 George Blanda | 2.00 | .80 | .20 |
| ☐ 469 Tony Cline | .10 | .04 | .01 |
| ☐ 470 Art Thoms | .10 | .04 | .01 |
| ☐ 471 Tom Keating DP | .20 | .08 | .02 |
| ☐ 472 Ben Davidson | .75 | .30 | .07 |
| ☐ 473 Phil Villapiano | .40 | .16 | .04 |
| ☐ 474 Dan Conners DP | .10 | .04 | .01 |
| ☐ 475 Duane Benson DP | .10 | .04 | .01 |
| ☐ 476 Nemiah Wilson DP | .10 | .04 | .01 |
| ☐ 477 Willie Brown DP | .75 | .30 | .07 |
| ☐ 478 George Atkinson | .20 | .08 | .02 |
| ☐ 479 Jack Tatum | .40 | .16 | .04 |
| ☐ 480 Jerry DePoyster | .10 | .04 | .01 |
| ☐ 481 Harold Jackson | .50 | .20 | .05 |
| ☐ 482 Wade Key DP | .10 | .04 | .01 |
| ☐ 483 Henry Allison DP | .10 | .04 | .01 |
| ☐ 484 Mike Evans DP | .10 | .04 | .01 |
| ☐ 485 Steve Smith | .20 | .08 | .02 |
| ☐ 486 Harold Carmichael | 1.00 | .40 | .10 |
| ☐ 487 Ben Hawkins | .20 | .08 | .02 |
| ☐ 488 Pete Liske | .30 | .12 | .03 |
| ☐ 489 Rick Arrington | .10 | .04 | .01 |
| ☐ 490 Lee Bouggess | .10 | .04 | .01 |
| ☐ 491 Tom Woodeshick | .20 | .08 | .02 |
| ☐ 492 Tom Dempsey | .40 | .16 | .04 |
| ☐ 493 Richard Harris | .20 | .08 | .02 |
| ☐ 494 Don Hultz | .10 | .04 | .01 |
| ☐ 495 Ernie Calloway | .10 | .04 | .01 |
| ☐ 496 Mel Tom DP | .10 | .04 | .01 |
| ☐ 497 Steve Zabel | .20 | .08 | .02 |
| ☐ 498 Tim Rossovich DP | .20 | .08 | .02 |
| ☐ 499 Ron Porter | .10 | .04 | .01 |
| ☐ 500 Al Nelson | .10 | .04 | .01 |
| ☐ 501 Nate Ramsey | .10 | .04 | .01 |
| ☐ 502 Leroy Keyes | .40 | .16 | .04 |
| ☐ 503 Bill Bradley | .40 | .16 | .04 |
| ☐ 504 Tom McNeill | .10 | .04 | .01 |
| ☐ 505 Dave Smith | .10 | .04 | .01 |
| ☐ 506 Jon Kolb | .10 | .04 | .01 |
| ☐ 507 Gerry Mullins | .10 | .04 | .01 |
| ☐ 508 Ray Mansfield DP | .10 | .04 | .01 |
| ☐ 509 Bruce Van Dyke DP | .10 | .04 | .01 |
| ☐ 510 John Brown DP | .10 | .04 | .01 |
| ☐ 511 Ron Shanklin | .30 | .12 | .03 |
| ☐ 512 Terry Bradshaw | 6.00 | 2.40 | .60 |
| ☐ 513 Terry Hanratty | .40 | .16 | .04 |
| ☐ 514 Preston Pearson | .40 | .16 | .04 |
| ☐ 515 John Fuqua | .20 | .08 | .02 |
| ☐ 516 Roy Gerela | .10 | .04 | .01 |
| ☐ 517 L.C. Greenwood | .75 | .30 | .07 |
| ☐ 518 Joe Greene | 2.00 | .80 | .20 |
| ☐ 519 Lloyd Voss DP | .10 | .04 | .01 |
| ☐ 520 Dwight White DP | .20 | .08 | .02 |
| ☐ 521 Jack Ham | 2.00 | .80 | .20 |
| ☐ 522 Chuck Allen | .10 | .04 | .01 |
| ☐ 523 Brian Stenger | .10 | .04 | .01 |
| ☐ 524 Andy Russell | .40 | .16 | .04 |
| ☐ 525 John Rowser | .10 | .04 | .01 |
| ☐ 526 Mel Blount | 1.50 | .60 | .15 |
| ☐ 527 Mike Wagner | .20 | .08 | .02 |
| ☐ 528 Bobby Walden | .10 | .04 | .01 |
| ☐ 529 Mel Gray | .30 | .12 | .03 |
| ☐ 530 Bob Reynolds | .10 | .04 | .01 |
| ☐ 531 Dan Dierdorf DP | .50 | .20 | .05 |
| ☐ 532 Wayne Mulligan | .10 | .04 | .01 |
| ☐ 533 Clyde Williams | .10 | .04 | .01 |
| ☐ 534 Ernie McMillan | .10 | .04 | .01 |
| ☐ 535 Jackie Smith | .75 | .30 | .07 |
| ☐ 536 John Gilliam DP | .20 | .08 | .02 |
| ☐ 537 Jim Hart | .50 | .20 | .05 |
| ☐ 538 Pete Beathard | .40 | .16 | .04 |
| ☐ 539 Johnny Roland | .30 | .12 | .03 |
| ☐ 540 Jim Bakken | .30 | .12 | .03 |
| ☐ 541 Ron Yankowski DP | .10 | .04 | .01 |
| ☐ 542 Fred Heron | .10 | .04 | .01 |
| ☐ 543 Bob Rowe | .10 | .04 | .01 |
| ☐ 544 Chuck Walker | .10 | .04 | .01 |
| ☐ 545 Larry Stallings | .20 | .08 | .02 |
| ☐ 546 Jamie Rivers DP | .10 | .04 | .01 |
| ☐ 547 Mike McGill | .10 | .04 | .01 |
| ☐ 548 Miller Farr | .10 | .04 | .01 |
| ☐ 549 Roger Wehrli | .30 | .12 | .03 |
| ☐ 550 Larry Willingham DP | .10 | .04 | .01 |
| ☐ 551 Larry Wilson | 1.00 | .40 | .10 |
| ☐ 552 Chuck Latourette | .10 | .04 | .01 |
| ☐ 553 Billy Parks | .20 | .08 | .02 |

| | | | |
|---|---|---|---|
| ☐ 554 Terry Owens | .20 | .08 | .02 |
| ☐ 555 Doug Wilkerson | .10 | .04 | .01 |
| ☐ 556 Carl Mauck DP | .10 | .04 | .01 |
| ☐ 557 Walt Sweeney | .10 | .04 | .01 |
| ☐ 558 Russ Washington DP | .10 | .04 | .01 |
| ☐ 559 Pettis Norman | .20 | .08 | .02 |
| ☐ 560 Gary Garrison | .20 | .08 | .02 |
| ☐ 561 John Hadl | .50 | .20 | .05 |
| ☐ 562 Mike Montgomery | .10 | .04 | .01 |
| ☐ 563 Mike Garrett | .30 | .12 | .03 |
| ☐ 564 Dennis Partee DP | .10 | .04 | .01 |
| ☐ 565 Deacon Jones | 1.00 | .40 | .10 |
| ☐ 566 Ron East DP | .10 | .04 | .01 |
| ☐ 567 Kevin Hardy | .10 | .04 | .01 |
| ☐ 568 Steve DeLong | .20 | .08 | .02 |
| ☐ 569 Rick Redman DP | .10 | .04 | .01 |
| ☐ 570 Bob Babich | .10 | .04 | .01 |
| ☐ 571 Pete Barnes | .10 | .04 | .01 |
| ☐ 572 Bob Howard | .10 | .04 | .01 |
| ☐ 573 Joe Beauchamp | .10 | .04 | .01 |
| ☐ 574 Bryant Salter | .10 | .04 | .01 |
| ☐ 575 Chris Fletcher | .10 | .04 | .01 |
| ☐ 576 Jerry LeVias | .20 | .08 | .02 |
| ☐ 577 Dick Witcher | .10 | .04 | .01 |
| ☐ 578 Len Rohde | .10 | .04 | .01 |
| ☐ 579 Randy Beisler | .10 | .04 | .01 |
| ☐ 580 Forrest Blue | .20 | .08 | .02 |
| ☐ 581 Woody Peoples | .10 | .04 | .01 |
| ☐ 582 Cas Banaszek | .10 | .04 | .01 |
| ☐ 583 Ted Kwalick | .30 | .12 | .03 |
| ☐ 584 Gene Washington | .40 | .16 | .04 |
| ☐ 585 John Brodie | 1.25 | .50 | .12 |
| ☐ 586 Ken Willard | .40 | .16 | .04 |
| ☐ 587 Vic Washington | .20 | .08 | .02 |
| ☐ 588 Bruce Gossett DP | .10 | .04 | .01 |
| ☐ 589 Tommy Hart | .10 | .04 | .01 |
| ☐ 590 Charlie Krueger | .20 | .08 | .02 |
| ☐ 591 Earl Edwards | .10 | .04 | .01 |
| ☐ 592 Cedrick Hardman DP | .20 | .08 | .02 |
| ☐ 593 Dave Wilcox DP | .20 | .08 | .02 |
| ☐ 594 Frank Nunley | .10 | .04 | .01 |
| ☐ 595 Skip Vanderbundt DP | .10 | .04 | .01 |
| ☐ 596 Jimmy Johnson DP | .60 | .24 | .06 |
| ☐ 597 Bruce Taylor | .30 | .12 | .03 |
| ☐ 598 Mel Phillips | .10 | .04 | .01 |
| ☐ 599 Rosey Taylor | .20 | .08 | .02 |
| ☐ 600 Steve Spurrier | 2.00 | .80 | .20 |
| ☐ 601 Charley Taylor | 1.25 | .50 | .12 |
| ☐ 602 Jim Snowden DP | .10 | .04 | .01 |
| ☐ 603 Ray Schoenke | .10 | .04 | .01 |
| ☐ 604 Len Hauss DP | .20 | .08 | .02 |
| ☐ 605 John Wilbur | .10 | .04 | .01 |
| ☐ 606 Walt Rock DP | .10 | .04 | .01 |
| ☐ 607 Jerry Smith | .20 | .08 | .02 |
| ☐ 608 Roy Jefferson | .20 | .08 | .02 |
| ☐ 609 Bill Kilmer | .75 | .30 | .07 |
| ☐ 610 Larry Brown | .75 | .30 | .07 |
| ☐ 611 Charlie Harraway | .20 | .08 | .02 |
| ☐ 612 Curt Knight | .10 | .04 | .01 |
| ☐ 613 Ron McDole | .10 | .04 | .01 |
| ☐ 614 Manuel Sistrunk DP | .10 | .04 | .01 |
| ☐ 615 Diron Talbert | .20 | .08 | .02 |
| ☐ 616 Verlon Biggs DP | .10 | .04 | .01 |
| ☐ 617 Jack Pardee | .75 | .30 | .07 |
| ☐ 618 Myron Pottios | .20 | .08 | .02 |
| ☐ 619 Chris Hanburger | .40 | .16 | .04 |
| ☐ 620 Pat Fischer | .20 | .08 | .02 |
| ☐ 621 Mike Bass | .10 | .04 | .01 |
| ☐ 622 Richie Petitbon DP | .20 | .08 | .02 |
| ☐ 623 Brig Owens | .10 | .04 | .01 |
| ☐ 624 Mike Bragg | .10 | .04 | .01 |
| ☐ xx Album (64 pages) | 7.50 | 3.00 | .75 |
| ☐ xx Deluxe Album | 15.00 | 6.00 | 1.50 |
| (128 pages) | | | |

# 1972 Sunoco Stamps Update

The players listed below are those who are not explicitly listed in the 1972 Sunoco stamp album. They are otherwise indistinguishable from the 1972 Sunoco stamps listed immediately above. These unnumbered stamps are ordered below in team order and alphabetically within team. The stamps measure approximately 1 5/8" by 2 3/8" and were issued later in the year as part of complete team sheets. There are a number of players appearing in this set before their Rookie Card year: Cliff Branch, Tommy Casanova, Jim Langer, and Bobby Moore (later known as Ahmad Rashad).

| | NRMT | VG-E | GOOD |
|---|---|---|---|
| COMPLETE SET (82) | 65.00 | 26.00 | 6.50 |
| COMMON PLAYER (1-82) | .75 | .30 | .07 |
| | | | |
| ☐ 1 Clarence Ellis | 1.00 | .40 | .10 |
| Atlanta Falcons | | | |
| ☐ 2 Dave Hampton | 1.00 | .40 | .10 |
| Atlanta Falcons | | | |

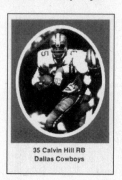

35 Calvin Hill RB
Dallas Cowboys

| | | | |
|---|---|---|---|
| ☐ 3 Dennis Havig | .75 | .30 | .07 |
| Atlanta Falcons | | | |
| ☐ 4 John James | .75 | .30 | .07 |
| Atlanta Falcons | | | |
| ☐ 5 Joe Profit | .75 | .30 | .07 |
| Atlanta Falcons | | | |
| ☐ 6 Lonnie Hepburn | .75 | .30 | .07 |
| Baltimore Colts | | | |
| ☐ 7 Dennis Nelson | .75 | .30 | .07 |
| Baltimore Colts | | | |
| ☐ 8 Mike McBath | 1.00 | .40 | .10 |
| Buffalo Bills | | | |
| ☐ 9 Walt Patulski | 1.00 | .40 | .10 |
| Buffalo Bills | | | |
| ☐ 10 Bob Asher | .75 | .30 | .07 |
| Chicago Bears | | | |
| ☐ 11 Steve DeLong | 1.00 | .40 | .10 |
| Chicago Bears | | | |
| ☐ 12 Tony McGee | .75 | .30 | .07 |
| Chicago Bears | | | |
| ☐ 13 James Osborne | .75 | .30 | .07 |
| Chicago Bears | | | |
| ☐ 14 Jim Seymour | .75 | .30 | .07 |
| Chicago Bears | | | |
| ☐ 15 Tommy Casanova | 1.50 | .60 | .15 |
| Cincinnati Bengals | | | |
| ☐ 16 Neil Craig | .75 | .30 | .07 |
| Cincinnati Bengals | | | |
| ☐ 17 Essex Johnson | 1.00 | .40 | .10 |
| Cincinnati Bengals | | | |
| ☐ 18 Sherman White | 1.00 | .40 | .10 |
| Cincinnati Bengals | | | |
| ☐ 19 Bob Briggs | .75 | .30 | .07 |
| Cleveland Browns | | | |
| ☐ 20 Thom Darden | 1.00 | .40 | .10 |
| Cleveland Browns | | | |
| ☐ 21 Marv Bateman | .75 | .30 | .07 |
| Dallas Cowboys | | | |
| ☐ 22 Toni Fritsch | .75 | .30 | .07 |
| Dallas Cowboys | | | |
| ☐ 23 Calvin Hill | 2.50 | 1.00 | .25 |
| Dallas Cowboys | | | |
| ☐ 24 Pat Toomay | .75 | .30 | .07 |
| Dallas Cowboys | | | |
| ☐ 25 Pete Duranko | .75 | .30 | .07 |
| Denver Broncos | | | |
| ☐ 26 Marv Montgomery | .75 | .30 | .07 |
| Denver Broncos | | | |
| ☐ 27 Rod Sherman | .75 | .30 | .07 |
| Denver Broncos | | | |
| ☐ 28 Bob Kowalkowski | .75 | .30 | .07 |
| Detroit Lions | | | |
| ☐ 29 Jim Mitchell | .75 | .30 | .07 |
| Detroit Lions | | | |
| ☐ 30 Larry Woods | .75 | .30 | .07 |
| Detroit Lions | | | |
| ☐ 31 Willie Buchanon | 1.25 | .50 | .12 |
| Green Bay Packers | | | |
| ☐ 32 Leland Glass | .75 | .30 | .07 |
| Green Bay Packers | | | |
| ☐ 33 MacArthur Lane | 1.25 | .50 | .12 |
| Green Bay Packers | | | |
| ☐ 34 Chester Marcol | 1.00 | .40 | .10 |
| Green Bay Packers | | | |
| ☐ 35 Ron Widby | .75 | .30 | .07 |
| Green Bay Packers | | | |
| ☐ 36 Ken Burrough | 1.50 | .60 | .15 |
| Houston Oilers | | | |
| ☐ 37 Calvin Hunt | .75 | .30 | .07 |
| Houston Oilers | | | |
| ☐ 38 Ron Saul | .75 | .30 | .07 |
| Houston Oilers | | | |
| ☐ 39 Greg Simpson | .75 | .30 | .07 |
| Houston Oilers | | | |
| ☐ 40 Mike Sensibaugh | 1.00 | .40 | .10 |
| Kansas City Chiefs | | | |

| | | | |
|---|---|---|---|
| ☐ 41 Dave Chapple | .75 | .30 | .07 |
| Los Angeles Rams | | | |
| ☐ 42 Jim Langer | 5.00 | 2.00 | .50 |
| Miami Dolphins | | | |
| ☐ 43 Mike Eischeid | .75 | .30 | .07 |
| Minnesota Vikings | | | |
| ☐ 44 John Gilliam | 1.25 | .50 | .12 |
| Minnesota Vikings | | | |
| ☐ 45 Ron Acks | .75 | .30 | .07 |
| New England Patriots | | | |
| ☐ 46 Bob Gladieux | .75 | .30 | .07 |
| New England Patriots | | | |
| ☐ 47 Honor Jackson | .75 | .30 | .07 |
| New England Patriots | | | |
| ☐ 48 Reggie Rucker | 1.00 | .40 | .10 |
| New England Patriots | | | |
| ☐ 49 Pat Studstill | 1.00 | .40 | .10 |
| New England Patriots | | | |
| ☐ 50 Bob Windsor | .75 | .30 | .07 |
| New England Patriots | | | |
| ☐ 51 Joe Federspiel | 1.00 | .40 | .10 |
| New Orleans Saints | | | |
| ☐ 52 Bob Newland | .75 | .30 | .07 |
| New Orleans Saints | | | |
| ☐ 53 Pete Athas | .75 | .30 | .07 |
| New York Giants | | | |
| ☐ 54 Charlie Evans | .75 | .30 | .07 |
| New York Giants | | | |
| ☐ 55 Jack Gregory | 1.00 | .40 | .10 |
| New York Giants | | | |
| ☐ 56 John Mendenhall | .75 | .30 | .07 |
| New York Giants | | | |
| ☐ 57 Ed Bell | .75 | .30 | .07 |
| New York Jets | | | |
| ☐ 58 John Elliott | .75 | .30 | .07 |
| New York Jets | | | |
| ☐ 59 Chris Farasopoulos | 1.00 | .40 | .10 |
| New York Jets | | | |
| ☐ 60 Bob Svihus | .75 | .30 | .07 |
| New York Jets | | | |
| ☐ 61 Steve Tannen | .75 | .30 | .07 |
| New York Jets | | | |
| ☐ 62 Cliff Branch | 2.50 | 1.00 | .25 |
| Oakland Raiders | | | |
| ☐ 63 Gus Otto | .75 | .30 | .07 |
| Oakland Raiders | | | |
| ☐ 64 Otis Sistrunk | 1.25 | .50 | .12 |
| Oakland Raiders | | | |
| ☐ 65 Charlie Smith | 1.00 | .40 | .10 |
| Oakland Raiders | | | |
| ☐ 66 John Reaves | 1.00 | .40 | .10 |
| Philadelphia Eagles | | | |
| ☐ 67 Larry Watkins | .75 | .30 | .07 |
| Philadelphia Eagles | | | |
| ☐ 68 Henry Davis | .75 | .30 | .07 |
| Pittsburgh Steelers | | | |
| ☐ 69 Ben McGee | .75 | .30 | .07 |
| Pittsburgh Steelers | | | |
| ☐ 70 Donny Anderson | 1.25 | .50 | .12 |
| St. Louis Cardinals | | | |
| ☐ 71 Walker Gillette | .75 | .30 | .07 |
| St. Louis Cardinals | | | |
| ☐ 72 Martin Imhoff | .75 | .30 | .07 |
| St. Louis Cardinals | | | |
| ☐ 73 Bobby Moore | 7.50 | 3.00 | .75 |
| (aka Ahmad Rashad) | | | |
| St. Louis Cardinals | | | |
| ☐ 74 Norm Thompson | 1.00 | .40 | .10 |
| St. Louis Cardinals | | | |
| ☐ 75 Lionel Aldridge | 1.00 | .40 | .10 |
| San Diego Chargers | | | |
| ☐ 76 Dave Costa | .75 | .30 | .07 |
| San Diego Chargers | | | |
| ☐ 77 Cid Edwards | 1.00 | .40 | .10 |
| San Diego Chargers | | | |
| ☐ 78 Tim Rossovich | 1.00 | .40 | .10 |
| San Diego Chargers | | | |
| ☐ 79 Dave Williams | 1.00 | .40 | .10 |
| San Diego Chargers | | | |
| ☐ 80 Johnny Fuller | .75 | .30 | .07 |
| San Francisco 49ers | | | |
| ☐ 81 Terry Hermeling | .75 | .30 | .07 |
| Washington Redskins | | | |
| ☐ 82 Paul Laaveg | .75 | .30 | .07 |
| Washington Redskins | | | |

# 1988 Swell Greats

The 1988 Swell Football Greats set contains 144 standard size (2 1/2" by 3 1/2") cards. Each card depicts a member of the Pro Football Hall of Fame. The fronts have blue borders and color photos. The backs are baby blue and contain each player's career highlights. This issue was distributed in wax packs of ten cards and also as a complete set. The factory-collated complete set cards are sometimes found with slight notches along the upper border; this does not seem to be the case

with the cards taken from wax packs. After each player's name below is listed his year of induction into the Hall of Fame. The set includes the 1988 Pro Football Hall of Fame inductees.

|  | MINT | EXC | G-VG |
|---|---|---|---|
| COMPLETE SET (144) | 10.00 | 4.00 | 1.00 |
| COMMON PLAYER (1-144) | .10 | .04 | .01 |
| ☐ 1 Pete Rozelle 85 | .30 | .12 | .03 |
| ☐ 2 Joe Namath 85 | 1.00 | .40 | .10 |
| ☐ 3 Frank Gatski 85 | .10 | .04 | .01 |
| ☐ 4 O.J. Simpson 85 | 1.00 | .40 | .10 |
| ☐ 5 Roger Staubach 85 | 1.00 | .40 | .10 |
| ☐ 6 Herb Adderley 80 | .10 | .04 | .01 |
| ☐ 7 Lance Alworth 78 | .20 | .08 | .02 |
| ☐ 8 Doug Atkins 82 | .10 | .04 | .01 |
| ☐ 9 Morris(Red) Badgro 81 | .10 | .04 | .01 |
| ☐ 10 Cliff Battles 68 | .10 | .04 | .01 |
| ☐ 11 Sammy Baugh 63 | .30 | .12 | .03 |
| ☐ 12 Raymond Berry 73 | .15 | .06 | .01 |
| ☐ 13 Charles W. Bidwill 67 | .10 | .04 | .01 |
| ☐ 14 Chuck Bednarik 67 | .15 | .06 | .01 |
| ☐ 15 Bert Bell 63 | .10 | .04 | .01 |
| ☐ 16 Bobby Bell 83 | .10 | .04 | .01 |
| ☐ 17 George Blanda 81 | .20 | .08 | .02 |
| ☐ 18 Jim Brown 71 | .75 | .30 | .07 |
| ☐ 19 Paul Brown 67 | .15 | .06 | .01 |
| ☐ 20 Roosevelt Brown 75 | .10 | .04 | .01 |
| ☐ 21 Ray Flaherty 76 | .10 | .04 | .01 |
| ☐ 22 Len Ford 76 | .10 | .04 | .01 |
| ☐ 23 Dan Fortmann 65 | .10 | .04 | .01 |
| ☐ 24 Bill George 74 | .10 | .04 | .01 |
| ☐ 25 Art Donovan 68 | .10 | .04 | .01 |
| ☐ 26 John(Paddy) Driscoll 65 | .10 | .04 | .01 |
| ☐ 27 Jimmy Conzelman 64 | .10 | .04 | .01 |
| ☐ 28 Willie Davis 81 | .10 | .04 | .01 |
| ☐ 29 Earl(Dutch) Clark 63 | .10 | .04 | .01 |
| ☐ 30 George Connor 75 | .10 | .04 | .01 |
| ☐ 31 Guy Chamberlain 65 | .10 | .04 | .01 |
| ☐ 32 Jack Christiansen 70 | .10 | .04 | .01 |
| ☐ 33 Tony Canadeo 74 | .10 | .04 | .01 |
| ☐ 34 Joe Carr 63 | .10 | .04 | .01 |
| ☐ 35 Willie Brown 84 | .10 | .04 | .01 |
| ☐ 36 Dick Butkus 79 | .30 | .12 | .03 |
| ☐ 37 Bill Dudley 66 | .10 | .04 | .01 |
| ☐ 38 Glen(Turk) Edwards 69 | .10 | .04 | .01 |
| ☐ 39 Weeb Ewbank 78 | .10 | .04 | .01 |
| ☐ 40 Tom Fears 70 | .10 | .04 | .01 |
| ☐ 41 Otto Graham 65 | .40 | .16 | .04 |
| ☐ 42 Harold(Red) Grange 63 | .40 | .16 | .04 |
| ☐ 43 Frank Gifford 77 | .40 | .16 | .04 |
| ☐ 44 Sid Gillman 83 | .10 | .04 | .01 |
| ☐ 45 Forrest Gregg 77 | .10 | .04 | .01 |
| ☐ 46 Lou Groza 74 | .20 | .08 | .02 |
| ☐ 47 Joe Guyon 66 | .10 | .04 | .01 |
| ☐ 48 George Halas 63 | .20 | .08 | .02 |
| ☐ 49 Ed Healey 64 | .10 | .04 | .01 |
| ☐ 50 Mel Hein 63 | .10 | .04 | .01 |
| ☐ 51 Wilbur(Fats) Henry 63 | .10 | .04 | .01 |
| ☐ 52 Arnie Herber 66 | .10 | .04 | .01 |
| ☐ 53 Bill Hewitt 71 | .10 | .04 | .01 |
| ☐ 54 Clarke Hinkle 64 | .10 | .04 | .01 |
| ☐ 55 Elroy Hirsch 68 (Crazylegs) | .15 | .06 | .01 |
| ☐ 56 Robert(Cal) Hubbard 63 | .10 | .04 | .01 |
| ☐ 57 Sam Huff 82 | .10 | .04 | .01 |
| ☐ 58 Lamar Hunt 72 | .10 | .04 | .01 |
| ☐ 59 Don Hutson 63 | .15 | .06 | .01 |
| ☐ 60 Deacon Jones 80 | .10 | .04 | .01 |
| ☐ 61 Sonny Jurgensen 83 | .15 | .06 | .01 |
| ☐ 62 Walt Kiesling 66 | .10 | .04 | .01 |
| ☐ 63 Frank(Bruiser) Kinard 71 | .10 | .04 | .01 |
| ☐ 64 Curly Lambeau 62 | .10 | .04 | .01 |
| ☐ 65 Dick Lane 65 (Night Train) 74 | .10 | .04 | .01 |
| ☐ 66 Yale Lary 79 | .10 | .04 | .01 |
| ☐ 67 Dante Lavelli 75 | .10 | .04 | .01 |
| ☐ 68 Bobby Layne 67 | .20 | .08 | .02 |
| ☐ 69 Tuffy Leemans 78 | .10 | .04 | .01 |
| ☐ 70 Bob Lilly 80 | .15 | .06 | .01 |
| ☐ 71 Vince Lombardi 71 | .25 | .10 | .02 |
| ☐ 72 Sid Luckman 65 | .20 | .08 | .02 |
| ☐ 73 William Roy Lyman (Link) 64 | .10 | .04 | .01 |
| ☐ 74 Tim Mara 63 | .10 | .04 | .01 |
| ☐ 75 Gino Marchetti 72 | .10 | .04 | .01 |
| ☐ 76 Geo.Preston Marshall 63 | .10 | .04 | .01 |
| ☐ 77 Ollie Matson 72 | .15 | .06 | .01 |
| ☐ 78 George McAfee 66 | .10 | .04 | .01 |
| ☐ 79 Mike McCormack 84 | .10 | .04 | .01 |
| ☐ 80 Hugh McElhenny 70 | .15 | .06 | .01 |
| ☐ 81 Johnny(Blood) McNally 63 | .10 | .04 | .01 |
| ☐ 82 Mike Michalske 64 | .10 | .04 | .01 |
| ☐ 83 Wayne Millner 68 | .10 | .04 | .01 |
| ☐ 84 Bobby Mitchell 83 | .10 | .04 | .01 |
| ☐ 85 Ron Mix 79 | .10 | .04 | .01 |
| ☐ 86 Lenny Moore 75 | .15 | .06 | .01 |
| ☐ 87 Marion Motley 68 | .15 | .06 | .01 |
| ☐ 88 George Musso 82 | .10 | .04 | .01 |
| ☐ 89 Bronko Nagurski 63 | .35 | .14 | .03 |
| ☐ 90 Earle(Greasy) Neale 69 | .10 | .04 | .01 |
| ☐ 91 Ernie Nevers 63 | .20 | .08 | .02 |
| ☐ 92 Ray Nitschke 78 | .15 | .06 | .01 |
| ☐ 93 Leo Nomellini 69 | .10 | .04 | .01 |
| ☐ 94 Merlin Olsen 82 | .15 | .06 | .01 |
| ☐ 95 Jim Otto 80 | .10 | .04 | .01 |
| ☐ 96 Steve Owen 66 | .10 | .04 | .01 |
| ☐ 97 Clarence(Ace) Parker 72 | .10 | .04 | .01 |
| ☐ 98 Jim Parker 73 | .10 | .04 | .01 |
| ☐ 99 Joe Perry 69 | .15 | .06 | .01 |
| ☐ 100 Pete Pihos 70 | .10 | .04 | .01 |
| ☐ 101 Hugh(Shorty) Ray 66 | .10 | .04 | .01 |
| ☐ 102 Dan Reeves 67 | .10 | .04 | .01 |
| ☐ 103 Jim Ringo 81 | .10 | .04 | .01 |
| ☐ 104 Andy Robustelli 71 | .10 | .04 | .01 |
| ☐ 105 Art Rooney 64 UER (Misspelled Janurary on card back) | .10 | .04 | .01 |
| ☐ 106 Gale Sayers 77 | .35 | .14 | .03 |
| ☐ 107 Joe Schmidt 73 | .10 | .04 | .01 |
| ☐ 108 Bart Starr 77 | .35 | .14 | .03 |
| ☐ 109 Ernie Stautner 69 | .15 | .06 | .01 |
| ☐ 110 Ken Strong 67 | .10 | .04 | .01 |
| ☐ 111 Joe Stydahar 67 | .10 | .04 | .01 |
| ☐ 112 Charley Taylor 84 | .15 | .06 | .01 |
| ☐ 113 Jim Taylor 76 | .15 | .06 | .01 |
| ☐ 114 Jim Thorpe 63 | .50 | .20 | .05 |
| ☐ 115 Y.A. Tittle 71 | .35 | .14 | .03 |
| ☐ 116 George Trafton 64 | .10 | .04 | .01 |
| ☐ 117 Charley Trippi 68 | .10 | .04 | .01 |
| ☐ 118 Emlen Tunnell 67 | .10 | .04 | .01 |
| ☐ 119 Clyde(Bulldog) Turner 66 | .10 | .04 | .01 |
| ☐ 120 Johnny Unitas 79 | .75 | .30 | .07 |
| ☐ 121 Norm Van Brocklin 71 | .20 | .08 | .02 |
| ☐ 122 Steve Van Buren 65 UER (Misspelled Lousianna and Decemer on back) | .15 | .06 | .01 |
| ☐ 123 Paul Warfield 83 | .15 | .06 | .01 |
| ☐ 124 Bob Waterfield 65 | .20 | .08 | .02 |
| ☐ 125 Arnie Weinmeister 84 | .10 | .04 | .01 |
| ☐ 126 Bill Willis 77 | .10 | .04 | .01 |
| ☐ 127 Larry Wilson 78 | .10 | .04 | .01 |
| ☐ 128 Alex Wojciechowicz 68 | .10 | .04 | .01 |
| ☐ 129 Doak Walker 86 | .15 | .06 | .01 |
| ☐ 130 Willie Lanier 86 | .10 | .04 | .01 |
| ☐ 131 Paul Hornung 86 | .25 | .10 | .02 |
| ☐ 132 Ken Houston 86 | .10 | .04 | .01 |
| ☐ 133 Fran Tarkenton 86 | .40 | .16 | .04 |
| ☐ 134 Don Maynard 87 | .15 | .06 | .01 |
| ☐ 135 Larry Csonka 87 | .25 | .10 | .02 |
| ☐ 136 Joe Greene 87 | .15 | .06 | .01 |
| ☐ 137 Len Dawson 87 | .15 | .06 | .01 |
| ☐ 138 Gene Upshaw 87 | .10 | .04 | .01 |
| ☐ 139 Jim Langer 87 | .10 | .04 | .01 |
| ☐ 140 John Henry Johnson 87 | .10 | .04 | .01 |
| ☐ 141 Fred Biletnikoff 88 | .15 | .06 | .01 |
| ☐ 142 Mike Ditka 88 | .40 | .16 | .04 |
| ☐ 143 Jack Ham 88 | .10 | .04 | .01 |
| ☐ 144 Alan Page 88 | .15 | .06 | .01 |

# 1989 Swell Greats

The 1989 Swell Football Greats set contains 150 standard-size (2 1/2" by 3 1/2") cards, depicting all Pro Football Hall of Famers. The fronts have white borders and vintage photos; the vertically oriented backs feature player profiles. The cards were available in ten-card wax packs.

Harold Grange
HALFBACK

|  | MINT | EXC | G-VG |
|---|---|---|---|
| COMPLETE SET (150) | 10.00 | 4.00 | 1.00 |
| COMMON PLAYER (1-150) | .10 | .04 | .01 |

| | | | |
|---|---|---|---|
| ☐ 1 Terry Bradshaw | .75 | .30 | .07 |
| ☐ 2 Bert Bell | .10 | .04 | .01 |
| ☐ 3 Joe Carr | .10 | .04 | .01 |
| ☐ 4 Earl(Dutch) Clark | .10 | .04 | .01 |
| ☐ 5 Harold(Red) Grange | .40 | .16 | .04 |
| ☐ 6 Wilbur(Fats) Henry | .10 | .04 | .01 |
| ☐ 7 Mel Hein | .10 | .04 | .01 |
| ☐ 8 Robert(Cal) Hubbard | .10 | .04 | .01 |
| ☐ 9 George Halas | .20 | .08 | .02 |
| ☐ 10 Don Hutson | .15 | .06 | .01 |
| ☐ 11 Curly Lambeau | .10 | .04 | .01 |
| ☐ 12 Tim Mara | .10 | .04 | .01 |
| ☐ 13 Geo.Preston Marshall | .10 | .04 | .01 |
| ☐ 14 Johnny(Blood) McNally | .10 | .04 | .01 |
| ☐ 15 Bronko Nagurski | .35 | .14 | .03 |
| ☐ 16 Ernie Nevers | .15 | .06 | .01 |
| ☐ 17 Jim Thorpe | .50 | .20 | .05 |
| ☐ 18 Ed Healey | .10 | .04 | .01 |
| ☐ 19 Clarke Hinkle | .10 | .04 | .01 |
| ☐ 20 Link Lyman | .10 | .04 | .01 |
| ☐ 21 Mike Michalske | .10 | .04 | .01 |
| ☐ 22 George Trafton | .10 | .04 | .01 |
| ☐ 23 Guy Chamberlin | .10 | .04 | .01 |
| ☐ 24 John(Paddy) Driscoll | .10 | .04 | .01 |
| ☐ 25 Dan Fortmann | .10 | .04 | .01 |
| ☐ 26 Otto Graham | .35 | .14 | .03 |
| ☐ 27A Sid Luckman ERR | .35 | .14 | .03 |
| (First name and first part of Chicago showing in upper left corner) | | | |
| ☐ 27B Sid Luckman COR | 1.00 | .40 | .10 |
| ☐ 28 Steve Van Buren | .15 | .06 | .01 |
| ☐ 29 Bob Waterfield | .20 | .08 | .02 |
| ☐ 30 Bill Dudley | .10 | .04 | .01 |
| ☐ 31 Joe Guyon | .10 | .04 | .01 |
| ☐ 32 Arnie Herber | .10 | .04 | .01 |
| ☐ 33 Walt Kiesling | .10 | .04 | .01 |
| ☐ 34 Jimmy Conzelman | .10 | .04 | .01 |
| ☐ 35 Art Rooney | .10 | .04 | .01 |
| ☐ 36 Willie Wood | .10 | .04 | .01 |
| ☐ 37 Art Shell | .15 | .06 | .01 |
| ☐ 38 Sammy Baugh | .35 | .14 | .03 |
| ☐ 39 Mel Blount | .10 | .04 | .01 |
| ☐ 40 Lamar Hunt | .15 | .06 | .01 |
| ☐ 41 Norm Van Brocklin | .20 | .08 | .02 |
| ☐ 42 Y.A. Tittle | .35 | .14 | .03 |
| ☐ 43 Andy Robustelli | .10 | .04 | .01 |
| ☐ 44 Vince Lombardi | .25 | .10 | .02 |
| ☐ 45 Frank(Bruiser) Kinard | .10 | .04 | .01 |
| ☐ 46 Bill Hewitt | .10 | .04 | .01 |
| ☐ 47 Jim Brown | .75 | .30 | .07 |
| ☐ 48 Pete Pihos | .10 | .04 | .01 |
| ☐ 49 Hugh McElhenny | .15 | .06 | .01 |
| ☐ 50 Tom Fears | .10 | .04 | .01 |
| ☐ 51 Jack Christiansen | .10 | .04 | .01 |
| ☐ 52 Ernie Stautner | .15 | .06 | .01 |
| ☐ 53 Joe Perry | .15 | .06 | .01 |
| ☐ 54 Leo Nomellini | .10 | .04 | .01 |
| ☐ 55 Earle(Greasy) Neale | .10 | .04 | .01 |
| ☐ 56 Glen(Turk) Edwards | .10 | .04 | .01 |
| ☐ 57 Alex Wojciechowicz | .10 | .04 | .01 |
| ☐ 58 Charley Trippi | .10 | .04 | .01 |
| ☐ 59 Marion Motley | .15 | .06 | .01 |
| ☐ 60 Wayne Millner | .10 | .04 | .01 |
| ☐ 61 Elroy Hirsch | .15 | .06 | .01 |
| ☐ 62 Art Donovan | .10 | .04 | .01 |
| ☐ 63 Cliff Battles | .10 | .04 | .01 |
| ☐ 64 Emlen Tunnell | .10 | .04 | .01 |
| ☐ 65 Joe Stydahar | .10 | .04 | .01 |
| ☐ 66 Ken Strong | .10 | .04 | .01 |
| ☐ 67 Dan Reeves | .10 | .04 | .01 |
| ☐ 68 Bobby Layne | .25 | .10 | .02 |
| ☐ 69 Paul Brown | .15 | .06 | .01 |
| ☐ 70 Charles W. Bidwill UER | .10 | .04 | .01 |

| | | | |
|---|---|---|---|
| (Name misspelled Biowill on front) | | | |
| ☐ 71 Chuck Bednarik | .15 | .06 | .01 |
| ☐ 72 Clyde(Bulldog) Turner | .10 | .04 | .01 |
| ☐ 73 Hugh(Shorty) Ray | .10 | .04 | .01 |
| ☐ 74 Steve Owen | .10 | .04 | .01 |
| ☐ 75 George McAfee | .10 | .04 | .01 |
| ☐ 76 Forrest Gregg | .10 | .04 | .01 |
| ☐ 77 Frank Gifford | .40 | .16 | .04 |
| ☐ 78 Jim Taylor | .15 | .06 | .01 |
| ☐ 79 Len Ford | .10 | .04 | .01 |
| ☐ 80 Ray Flaherty | .10 | .04 | .01 |
| ☐ 81 Lenny Moore | .15 | .06 | .01 |
| ☐ 82 Dante Lavelli | .10 | .04 | .01 |
| ☐ 83 George Connor | .10 | .04 | .01 |
| ☐ 84 Roosevelt Brown | .10 | .04 | .01 |
| ☐ 85 Dick Lane | .10 | .04 | .01 |
| ☐ 86 Lou Groza | .20 | .08 | .02 |
| ☐ 87 Bill George | .10 | .04 | .01 |
| ☐ 88 Tony Canadeo | .10 | .04 | .01 |
| ☐ 89 Joe Schmidt | .10 | .04 | .01 |
| ☐ 90 Jim Parker | .10 | .04 | .01 |
| ☐ 91 Raymond Berry | .15 | .06 | .01 |
| ☐ 92 Clarence(Ace) Parker | .10 | .04 | .01 |
| ☐ 93 Ollie Matson | .15 | .06 | .01 |
| ☐ 94 Gino Marchetti | .10 | .04 | .01 |
| ☐ 95 Larry Wilson | .10 | .04 | .01 |
| ☐ 96 Ray Nitschke | .15 | .06 | .01 |
| ☐ 97 Tuffy Leemans | .10 | .04 | .01 |
| ☐ 98 Weeb Ewbank UER | .10 | .04 | .01 |
| (Misspelled Uwbank on card front) | | | |
| ☐ 99 Lance Alworth | .20 | .08 | .02 |
| ☐ 100 Bill Willis | .10 | .04 | .01 |
| ☐ 101 Bart Starr | .35 | .14 | .03 |
| ☐ 102 Gale Sayers | .35 | .14 | .03 |
| ☐ 103 Herb Adderley | .10 | .04 | .01 |
| ☐ 104 Johnny Unitas | .75 | .30 | .07 |
| ☐ 105 Ron Mix | .10 | .04 | .01 |
| ☐ 106 Yale Lary | .10 | .04 | .01 |
| ☐ 107 Morris(Red) Badgro | .10 | .04 | .01 |
| ☐ 108 Jim Otto | .10 | .04 | .01 |
| ☐ 109 Bob Lilly | .15 | .06 | .01 |
| ☐ 110 Deacon Jones | .10 | .04 | .01 |
| ☐ 111 Doug Atkins | .10 | .04 | .01 |
| ☐ 112 Jim Ringo | .10 | .04 | .01 |
| ☐ 113 Willie Davis | .10 | .04 | .01 |
| ☐ 114 George Blanda | .25 | .10 | .02 |
| ☐ 115 Bobby Bell | .10 | .04 | .01 |
| ☐ 116 Merlin Olsen | .15 | .06 | .01 |
| ☐ 117 George Musso | .10 | .04 | .01 |
| ☐ 118 Sam Huff | .15 | .06 | .01 |
| ☐ 119 Paul Warfield | .15 | .06 | .01 |
| ☐ 120 Bobby Mitchell | .15 | .06 | .01 |
| ☐ 121 Sonny Jurgensen | .15 | .06 | .01 |
| ☐ 122 Sid Gillman UER | .10 | .04 | .01 |
| (Misspelled Gilman on card back) | | | |
| ☐ 123 Arnie Weinmeister | .10 | .04 | .01 |
| ☐ 124 Charley Taylor | .10 | .04 | .01 |
| ☐ 125 Mike McCormack | .10 | .04 | .01 |
| ☐ 126 Willie Brown | .10 | .04 | .01 |
| ☐ 127 O.J. Simpson | 1.00 | .40 | .10 |
| ☐ 128 Pete Rozelle | .25 | .10 | .02 |
| ☐ 129 Joe Namath | 1.00 | .40 | .10 |
| ☐ 130 Frank Gatski | .10 | .04 | .01 |
| ☐ 131 Willie Lanier | .10 | .04 | .01 |
| ☐ 132 Ken Houston | .10 | .04 | .01 |
| ☐ 133 Paul Hornung | .25 | .10 | .02 |
| ☐ 134 Roger Staubach | 1.00 | .40 | .10 |
| ☐ 135 Len Dawson | .15 | .06 | .01 |
| ☐ 136 Larry Csonka | .30 | .12 | .03 |
| ☐ 137 Doak Walker | .15 | .06 | .01 |
| ☐ 138 Fran Tarkenton | .40 | .16 | .04 |
| ☐ 139 Don Maynard | .15 | .06 | .01 |
| ☐ 140 Jim Langer | .10 | .04 | .01 |
| ☐ 141 John Henry Johnson | .10 | .04 | .01 |
| ☐ 142 Joe Greene | .20 | .08 | .02 |
| ☐ 143 Jack Ham | .10 | .04 | .01 |
| ☐ 144 Mike Ditka | .40 | .16 | .04 |
| ☐ 145 Alan Page | .10 | .04 | .01 |
| ☐ 146 Fred Biletnikoff | .10 | .04 | .01 |
| ☐ 147 Gene Upshaw | .10 | .04 | .01 |
| ☐ 148 Dick Butkus | .30 | .12 | .03 |
| ☐ 149 Checklist Card | .10 | .04 | .01 |
| ☐ 150 Checklist Card | .10 | .04 | .01 |

# 1990 Swell Greats

The 1990 Swell Greats set contains 160 standard size (2 1/2" by 3 1/2") cards, depicting all Pro Football Hall of Famers. The fronts have color photos, with a white border and blue and yellow lines. As in previous sets, some cards of the older players are sepia-toned. In fact, in several cases the same photos were reused from the previous two

years of Swell sets. The vertically-oriented backs feature player profiles. The cards were primarily available in the form of ten-card wax packs.

|  | MINT | EXC | G-VG |
|---|---|---|---|
| COMPLETE SET (160) | 10.00 | 4.00 | 1.00 |
| COMMON PLAYER (1-160) | .10 | .04 | .01 |

| | MINT | EXC | G-VG |
|---|---|---|---|
| ☐ 1 Terry Bradshaw | .75 | .30 | .07 |
| ☐ 2 Bert Bell | .10 | .04 | .01 |
| ☐ 3 Joe Carr | .10 | .04 | .01 |
| ☐ 4 Earl(Dutch) Clark | .10 | .04 | .01 |
| ☐ 5 Harold(Red) Grange | .40 | .16 | .04 |
| ☐ 6 Wilbur(Fats) Henry | .10 | .04 | .01 |
| ☐ 7 Mel Hein | .10 | .04 | .01 |
| ☐ 8 Robert(Cal) Hubbard | .10 | .04 | .01 |
| ☐ 9 George Halas | .20 | .08 | .02 |
| ☐ 10 Don Hutson | .15 | .06 | .01 |
| ☐ 11 Curly Lambeau | .10 | .04 | .01 |
| ☐ 12 Tim Mara | .10 | .04 | .01 |
| ☐ 13 Geo.Preston Marshall | .10 | .04 | .01 |
| ☐ 14 Johnny(Blood) McNally | .10 | .04 | .01 |
| ☐ 15 Bronko Nagurski | .35 | .14 | .03 |
| ☐ 16 Ernie Nevers | .15 | .06 | .01 |
| ☐ 17 Jim Thorpe | .50 | .20 | .05 |
| ☐ 18 Ed Healey | .10 | .04 | .01 |
| ☐ 19 Clarke Hinkle | .10 | .04 | .01 |
| ☐ 20 Link Lyman | .10 | .04 | .01 |
| ☐ 21 Mike Michalske | .10 | .04 | .01 |
| ☐ 22 George Trafton | .10 | .04 | .01 |
| ☐ 23 Guy Chamberlain | .10 | .04 | .01 |
| ☐ 24 Paddy Discoll | .10 | .04 | .01 |
| ☐ 25 Dan Fortmann | .10 | .04 | .01 |
| ☐ 26 Otto Graham | .35 | .14 | .03 |
| ☐ 27 Sid Luckman | .30 | .12 | .03 |
| ☐ 28 Steve Van Buren | .15 | .06 | .01 |
| ☐ 29 Bob Waterfield | .20 | .08 | .02 |
| ☐ 30 Bill Dudley | .10 | .04 | .01 |
| ☐ 31 Joe Guyon | .10 | .04 | .01 |
| ☐ 32 Arnie Herber | .10 | .04 | .01 |
| ☐ 33 Walt Kiesling | .10 | .04 | .01 |
| ☐ 34 Jimmy Conzelman | .10 | .04 | .01 |
| ☐ 35 Art Rooney | .10 | .04 | .01 |
| ☐ 36 Willie Wood | .15 | .06 | .01 |
| ☐ 37 Art Shell | .35 | .14 | .03 |
| ☐ 38 Sammy Baugh | .35 | .14 | .03 |
| ☐ 39 Mel Blount | .10 | .04 | .01 |
| ☐ 40 Lamar Hunt | .15 | .06 | .01 |
| ☐ 41 Norm Van Brocklin | .20 | .08 | .02 |
| ☐ 42 Y.A. Tittle | .30 | .12 | .03 |
| ☐ 43 Andy Robustelli | .10 | .04 | .01 |
| ☐ 44 Vince Lombardi | .25 | .10 | .02 |
| ☐ 45 Frank(Bruiser) Kinard | .10 | .04 | .01 |
| ☐ 46 Bill Hewitt | .10 | .04 | .01 |
| ☐ 47 Jim Brown | .75 | .30 | .07 |
| ☐ 48 Pete Pihos | .10 | .04 | .01 |
| ☐ 49 Hugh McElhenny | .15 | .06 | .01 |
| ☐ 50 Tom Fears | .10 | .04 | .01 |
| ☐ 51 Jack Christiansen | .15 | .06 | .01 |
| ☐ 52 Ernie Stautner | .15 | .06 | .01 |
| ☐ 53 Joe Perry | .15 | .06 | .01 |
| ☐ 54 Leo Nomellini | .10 | .04 | .01 |
| ☐ 55 Earle(Greasy) Neale | .10 | .04 | .01 |
| ☐ 56 Glen(Turk) Edwards | .10 | .04 | .01 |
| ☐ 57 Alex Wojciechowicz | .10 | .04 | .01 |
| ☐ 58 Charley Trippi | .10 | .04 | .01 |
| ☐ 59 Marion Motley | .15 | .06 | .01 |
| ☐ 60 Wayne Millner | .10 | .04 | .01 |
| ☐ 61 Elroy Hirsch | .15 | .06 | .01 |
| ☐ 62 Art Donovan | .10 | .04 | .01 |
| ☐ 63 Cliff Battles | .10 | .04 | .01 |
| ☐ 64 Emlen Tunnell | .10 | .04 | .01 |
| ☐ 65 Joe Stydahar | .10 | .04 | .01 |
| ☐ 66 Ken Strong | .10 | .04 | .01 |
| ☐ 67 Dan Reeves | .10 | .04 | .01 |
| ☐ 68 Bobby Layne | .25 | .10 | .02 |
| ☐ 69 Paul Brown | .15 | .06 | .01 |
| ☐ 70 Charles W. Bidwill | .10 | .04 | .01 |
| ☐ 71 Chuck Bednarik | .15 | .06 | .01 |
| ☐ 72 Clyde(Bulldog) Turner | .10 | .04 | .01 |
| ☐ 73 Hugh(Shorty) Ray | .10 | .04 | .01 |
| ☐ 74 Steve Owen | .10 | .04 | .01 |
| ☐ 75 George McAfee | .10 | .04 | .01 |
| ☐ 76 Forrest Gregg | .10 | .04 | .01 |
| ☐ 77 Frank Gifford | .35 | .14 | .03 |
| ☐ 78 Jim Taylor | .15 | .06 | .01 |
| ☐ 79 Len Ford | .10 | .04 | .01 |
| ☐ 80 Ray Flaherty | .10 | .04 | .01 |
| ☐ 81 Lenny Moore | .15 | .06 | .01 |
| ☐ 82 Dante Lavelli | .10 | .04 | .01 |
| ☐ 83 George Connor | .10 | .04 | .01 |
| ☐ 84 Roosevelt Brown | .10 | .04 | .01 |
| ☐ 85 Dick Lane | .20 | .08 | .02 |
| ☐ 86 Lou Groza | .20 | .08 | .02 |
| ☐ 87 Bill George | .10 | .04 | .01 |
| ☐ 88 Tony Canadeo | .10 | .04 | .01 |
| ☐ 89 Joe Schmidt | .10 | .04 | .01 |
| ☐ 90 Jim Parker | .10 | .04 | .01 |
| ☐ 91 Raymond Berry | .15 | .06 | .01 |
| ☐ 92 Clarence(Ace) Parker | .10 | .04 | .01 |
| ☐ 93 Ollie Matson | .15 | .06 | .01 |
| ☐ 94 Gino Marchetti | .10 | .04 | .01 |
| ☐ 95 Larry Wilson | .10 | .04 | .01 |
| ☐ 96 Ray Nitschke | .15 | .06 | .01 |
| ☐ 97 Tuffy Leemans | .10 | .04 | .01 |
| ☐ 98 Weeb Ewbank | .10 | .04 | .01 |
| ☐ 99 Lance Alworth | .20 | .08 | .02 |
| ☐ 100 Bill Willis | .10 | .04 | .01 |
| ☐ 101 Bart Starr | .30 | .12 | .03 |
| ☐ 102 Gale Sayers | .30 | .12 | .03 |
| ☐ 103 Herb Adderley | .10 | .04 | .01 |
| ☐ 104 Johnny Unitas | .75 | .30 | .07 |
| ☐ 105 Ron Mix | .10 | .04 | .01 |
| ☐ 106 Yale Lary | .10 | .04 | .01 |
| ☐ 107 Morris(Red) Badgro | .10 | .04 | .01 |
| ☐ 108 Jim Otto | .15 | .06 | .01 |
| ☐ 109 Bob Lilly | .10 | .04 | .01 |
| ☐ 110 Deacon Jones | .10 | .04 | .01 |
| ☐ 111 Doug Atkins | .10 | .04 | .01 |
| ☐ 112 Jim Ringo | .10 | .04 | .01 |
| ☐ 113 Willie Davis | .25 | .10 | .02 |
| ☐ 114 George Blanda | .10 | .04 | .01 |
| ☐ 115 Bobby Bell | .15 | .06 | .01 |
| ☐ 116 Merlin Olsen | .10 | .04 | .01 |
| ☐ 117 George Musso | .10 | .04 | .01 |
| ☐ 118 Sam Huff | .15 | .06 | .01 |
| ☐ 119 Paul Warfield | .10 | .04 | .01 |
| ☐ 120 Bobby Mitchell | .15 | .06 | .01 |
| ☐ 121 Sonny Jurgensen | .10 | .04 | .01 |
| ☐ 122 Sid Gillman | .10 | .04 | .01 |
| ☐ 123 Arnie Weinmeister | .10 | .04 | .01 |
| ☐ 124 Charley Taylor | .10 | .04 | .01 |
| ☐ 125 Mike McCormack | .10 | .04 | .01 |
| ☐ 126 Willie Brown | 1.00 | .40 | .10 |
| ☐ 127 O.J. Simpson | .25 | .10 | .02 |
| ☐ 128 Pete Rozelle | 1.00 | .40 | .10 |
| ☐ 129 Joe Namath | .10 | .04 | .01 |
| ☐ 130 Frank Gatski | .15 | .06 | .01 |
| ☐ 131 Willie Lanier | .10 | .04 | .01 |
| ☐ 132 Ken Houston | .25 | .10 | .02 |
| ☐ 133 Paul Hornung | 1.00 | .40 | .10 |
| ☐ 134 Roger Staubach | .15 | .06 | .01 |
| ☐ 135 Len Dawson | .25 | .10 | .02 |
| ☐ 136 Larry Csonka | .15 | .06 | .01 |
| ☐ 137 Doak Walker | .35 | .14 | .03 |
| ☐ 138 Fran Tarkenton | .15 | .06 | .01 |
| ☐ 139 Don Maynard | .10 | .04 | .01 |
| ☐ 140 Jim Langer | .10 | .04 | .01 |
| ☐ 141 John Henry Johnson | .20 | .08 | .02 |
| ☐ 142 Joe Greene | .10 | .04 | .01 |
| ☐ 143 Jack Ham | .40 | .16 | .04 |
| ☐ 144 Mike Ditka | .10 | .04 | .01 |
| ☐ 145 Alan Page | .15 | .06 | .01 |
| ☐ 146 Fred Biletnikoff | .10 | .04 | .01 |
| ☐ 147 Gene Upshaw | .30 | .12 | .03 |
| ☐ 148 Dick Butkus | .10 | .04 | .01 |
| ☐ 149 Buck Buchanan | .25 | .10 | .02 |
| ☐ 150 Franco Harris | .35 | .14 | .03 |
| ☐ 151 Tom Landry | .10 | .04 | .01 |
| ☐ 152 Ted Hendricks | .10 | .04 | .01 |
| ☐ 153 Bob St. Clair | .15 | .06 | .01 |
| ☐ 154 Jack Lambert | .20 | .08 | .02 |
| ☐ 155 Bob Griese | .10 | .04 | .01 |
| ☐ 156 Admission coupon | .10 | .04 | .01 |
| ☐ 157 Enshrinement Day | .10 | .04 | .01 |
| ☐ 158 Hall of Fame | .10 | .04 | .01 |
| ☐ 159 Checklist 1/2 | .10 | .04 | .01 |
| ☐ 160 Checklist 3/4 | .10 | .04 | .01 |

# 1981 TCMA Greats

**ROGER STAUBACH**
Navy, Quarterback
6' 2" 197 LBS. Navy

One of pro football's all-time great quarterbacks during his career with the Dallas Cowboys, Roger first attracted attention in his junior year at the United States Naval Academy in 1963 when he led the Middies to a 9-1 record and a berth in the Cotton Bowl. That year Staubach was the recipient of the Heisman Trophy as the outstanding collegiate player in the nation and was a first team All-America selection. At his graduation from Navy, Staubach received the Naval Academy's two most coveted awards—the one bestowed on the school's outstanding athlete and the other given to the cadet who had brought the greatest credit to the Academy through athletic achievement.

©TCMA Ltd. 1981

This 78-card set was put out by TCMA in 1981. The set features retired football players from the '50s and '60s. The cards are standard size, 2 1/2" by 3 1/2" and are in the popular "pure card" format where there is nothing on the card front except the color photo of the subject inside a simple white border. The card backs provide a short narrative printed in black ink on white card stock. The TCMA copyright is located in the lower right corner. The cards are numbered on the back at the top inside a football; however, some cards can be found without the card number inside the football. The unnumbered versions are valued at one and a half times the prices listed below.

|  | MINT | EXC | G-VG |
|---|---|---|---|
| COMPLETE SET (78) | 30.00 | 12.00 | 3.00 |
| COMMON PLAYER (1-78) | .25 | .10 | .02 |

| | MINT | EXC | G-VG |
|---|---|---|---|
| ☐ 1 Alex Karras | 1.25 | .50 | .12 |
| ☐ 2 Fran Tarkenton | 3.50 | 1.40 | .35 |
| ☐ 3 John Unitas | 5.00 | 2.00 | .50 |
| ☐ 4 Bobby Layne | 2.00 | .80 | .20 |
| ☐ 5 Roger Staubach | 6.00 | 2.40 | .60 |
| ☐ 6 Joe Namath | 6.00 | 2.40 | .60 |
| ☐ 7 1954 New York Giants Offense | .50 | .20 | .05 |
| ☐ 8 Jimmy Brown | 6.00 | 2.40 | .60 |
| ☐ 9 Ray Wietecha | .25 | .10 | .02 |
| ☐ 10 R.C. Owens | .25 | .10 | .02 |
| ☐ 11 Alex Webster | .35 | .14 | .03 |
| ☐ 12 Jim Otto UER (College was Miami, not Minnesota) | 1.25 | .50 | .12 |
| ☐ 13 Jim Taylor | 1.50 | .60 | .15 |
| ☐ 14 Kyle Rote | .75 | .30 | .07 |
| ☐ 15 Roger Ellis | .25 | .10 | .02 |
| ☐ 16 Nick Pietrosante | .35 | .14 | .03 |
| ☐ 17 Milt Plum | .35 | .14 | .03 |
| ☐ 18 Eddie LeBaron | .50 | .20 | .05 |
| ☐ 19 Jimmy Patton | .25 | .10 | .02 |
| ☐ 20 Yale Lary | 1.00 | .40 | .10 |
| ☐ 21 Leo Nomellini | 1.25 | .50 | .12 |
| ☐ 22 Johnny Olszewski | .25 | .10 | .02 |
| ☐ 23 Ernie Koy | .35 | .14 | .03 |
| ☐ 24 Bill Wade | .35 | .14 | .03 |
| ☐ 25 Billy Wells | .25 | .10 | .02 |
| ☐ 26 Ron Waller | .25 | .10 | .02 |
| ☐ 27 Pat Summerall | .75 | .30 | .07 |
| ☐ 28 Joe Schmidt | 1.25 | .50 | .12 |
| ☐ 29 Bob St.Clair | 1.00 | .40 | .10 |
| ☐ 30 Dick Lynch | .35 | .14 | .03 |
| ☐ 31 Tommy McDonald | .50 | .20 | .05 |
| ☐ 32 Earl Morrall | .50 | .20 | .05 |
| ☐ 33 Jim Martin | .25 | .10 | .02 |
| ☐ 34 Dick Modzelewski | .35 | .14 | .03 |
| ☐ 35 Dick LeBeau | .35 | .14 | .03 |
| ☐ 36 Dick Post | .25 | .10 | .02 |
| ☐ 37 Les Richter | .35 | .14 | .03 |
| ☐ 38 Andy Robustelli | 1.00 | .40 | .10 |
| ☐ 39 Pete Retzlaff | .35 | .14 | .03 |
| ☐ 40 Fred Biletnikoff | 2.00 | .80 | .20 |
| ☐ 41 Timmy Brown | .35 | .14 | .03 |
| ☐ 42 Babe Parilli | .35 | .14 | .03 |
| ☐ 43 Lance Alworth | 2.00 | .80 | .20 |
| ☐ 44 Sammy Baugh | 2.00 | .80 | .20 |
| ☐ 45 Paul(Tank) Younger | .35 | .14 | .03 |
| ☐ 46 Chuck Bednarik | 1.50 | .60 | .15 |
| ☐ 47 Art Donovan | 1.25 | .50 | .12 |
| ☐ 48 Len Dawson | 2.00 | .80 | .20 |
| ☐ 49 Don Maynard | 1.50 | .60 | .15 |
| ☐ 50 Joe Morrison | .35 | .14 | .03 |
| ☐ 51 John Elliott | .25 | .10 | .02 |
| ☐ 52 Jim Ringo | 1.00 | .40 | .10 |
| ☐ 53 Max McGee | .35 | .14 | .03 |
| ☐ 54 Art Powell | .35 | .14 | .03 |
| ☐ 55 Galen Fiss | .25 | .10 | .02 |

| | MINT | EXC | G-VG |
|---|---|---|---|
| ☐ 56 Jack Stroud | .25 | .10 | .02 |
| ☐ 57 Bake Turner | .35 | .14 | .03 |
| ☐ 58 Mike McCormack | 1.00 | .40 | .10 |
| ☐ 59 L.G. Dupre | .35 | .14 | .03 |
| ☐ 60 Bill McPeak | .25 | .10 | .02 |
| ☐ 61 Art Spinney | .25 | .10 | .02 |
| ☐ 62 Fran Rogel | .25 | .10 | .02 |
| ☐ 63 Ollie Matson | 1.50 | .60 | .15 |
| ☐ 64 Doak Walker | 1.25 | .50 | .12 |
| ☐ 65 Lenny Moore | 1.50 | .60 | .15 |
| ☐ 66 George Shaw and Bert Rechichar | .25 | .10 | .02 |
| ☐ 67 Kyle Rote, Jim Lee Howell, and Ray Krause | .35 | .14 | .03 |
| ☐ 68 Andy Robustelli, Roosevelt Grier, Dick Modzelewski, and Jim Katcavage | .75 | .30 | .07 |
| ☐ 69 Tucker Frederickson and Ernie Koy | .35 | .14 | .03 |
| ☐ 70 Gino Marchetti | 1.25 | .50 | .12 |
| ☐ 71 Earl Morrall and Allie Sherman | .50 | .20 | .05 |
| ☐ 72 Roosevelt Brown | 1.00 | .40 | .10 |
| ☐ 73 Howard Cassady (Hopalong) | .35 | .14 | .03 |
| ☐ 74 Don Chandler | .35 | .14 | .03 |
| ☐ 75 Joe Childress | .25 | .10 | .02 |
| ☐ 76 Rick Casares | .35 | .14 | .03 |
| ☐ 77 Charley Conerly | 1.25 | .50 | .12 |
| ☐ 78 1958 Giants QB's (Don Heinrich, Tom Dublinski, and Charley Conerly) | .50 | .20 | .05 |

## 1987 TCMA Update CMC

In 1987 CMC (the successor to TCMA) produced this 12-card set updating the 1981 TCMA issue. In fact the first 78 numbered cards were reissued at this time as part of a 90-card set; only the new-issue cards are listed below. Instead of copyright TCMA 1981, these 12 cards indicate copyright CMC 1987. The cards measure the standard size (2 1/2" by 3 1/2").

|  | MINT | EXC | G-VG |
|---|---|---|---|
| COMPLETE SET (12) | 20.00 | 8.00 | 2.00 |
| COMMON PLAYER (79-90) | .75 | .30 | .07 |

| | MINT | EXC | G-VG |
|---|---|---|---|
| ☐ 79 Fred Dryer | 1.50 | .60 | .15 |
| ☐ 80 Ed Marinaro | 1.50 | .60 | .15 |
| ☐ 81 O.J. Simpson | 9.00 | 3.75 | .90 |
| ☐ 82 Joe Theismann | 3.00 | 1.20 | .30 |
| ☐ 83 Roman Gabriel | 1.50 | .60 | .15 |
| ☐ 84 Terry Metcalf | 1.00 | .40 | .10 |
| ☐ 85 Lyle Alzado | 2.00 | .80 | .20 |
| ☐ 86 Jake Scott | .75 | .30 | .07 |
| ☐ 87 Cliff Branch | 2.00 | .80 | .20 |
| ☐ 88 Rocky Bleier | 1.50 | .60 | .15 |
| ☐ 89 Cliff Harris | 1.00 | .40 | .10 |
| ☐ 90 Archie Manning | 2.50 | 1.00 | .25 |

## 1961 Titans Jay Publishing

This 12-card set features (approximately) 5" by 7" black-and-white player photos of the New York Titans, one of the original AFL teams who later became the New York Jets. The photos show players in traditional poses with the quarterback preparing to throw, the runner heading downfield, and the defenseman ready for the tackle. The player's name and the team name appear in the wider bottom border. These cards were packaged 12 to a packet and originally sold for 25 cents. The backs are blank. The cards are unnumbered and checklisted below in alphabetical order.

|  | NRMT | VG-E | GOOD |
|---|---|---|---|
| COMPLETE SET (12) | 60.00 | 24.00 | 6.00 |
| COMMON PLAYER (1-12) | 5.00 | 2.00 | .50 |

| | NRMT | VG-E | GOOD |
|---|---|---|---|
| ☐ 1 Al Dorow | 6.00 | 2.40 | .60 |
| ☐ 2 Larry Grantham | 6.00 | 2.40 | .60 |
| ☐ 3 Mike Hagler | 5.00 | 2.00 | .50 |
| ☐ 4 Mike Hudock | 5.00 | 2.00 | .50 |
| ☐ 5 Bob Jewett | 5.00 | 2.00 | .50 |
| ☐ 6 Jack Klotz | 5.00 | 2.00 | .50 |
| ☐ 7 Don Maynard | 20.00 | 8.00 | 2.00 |
| ☐ 8 John McMullan | 5.00 | 2.00 | .50 |
| ☐ 9 Bob Mischak | 6.00 | 2.40 | .60 |
| ☐ 10 Art Powell | 8.00 | 3.25 | .80 |
| ☐ 11 Bob Reifsnyder | 6.00 | 2.40 | .60 |
| ☐ 12 Sid Youngelman | 6.00 | 2.40 | .60 |

# 1950 Topps Felt Backs

LEON VAN BILLINGHAM
Co-Captain and
Fullback
COLUMBIA UNIVERSITY

The 1950 Topps felt-back set contains 100 small cards, each measuring approximately 7/8" by 1 7/16". Cards are sometimes found connected as a sheet of 25 cards all with the same color background. The backs are made of felt and depict a college pennant. Cards with a yellow background are worth double the listed prices. The following players come with either brown or yellow (B variations) backgrounds: Boldin, Botula, Burnett, Cecconi, Gitschier, Hart, Hester, Jensen, Lee, Malekoff, Martin, Mathews, McKissack, J. Miller, Nagel, Perini, Royal, Shaw, Sitko, Stalloni, Teninga, Towler, Turek, Walker, and Zinaich. The key Rookie Cards in this set are Joe Paterno, Darrell Royal, and Ernie Stautner.

|  | NRMT | VG-E | GOOD |
|---|---|---|---|
| COMPLETE SET (100) | 3500.00 | 1600.00 | 450.00 |
| COMMON PLAYER (1-100) | 35.00 | 16.00 | 4.40 |
| ☐ 1 Lou Allen | 35.00 | 16.00 | 4.40 |
| Duke |  |  |  |
| ☐ 2 Morris Bailey | 35.00 | 16.00 | 4.40 |
| TCU |  |  |  |
| ☐ 3 George Bell | 35.00 | 16.00 | 4.40 |
| Oregon |  |  |  |
| ☐ 4 Lindy Berry HOR | 35.00 | 16.00 | 4.40 |
| TCU |  |  |  |
| ☐ 5A Mike Boldin | 35.00 | 16.00 | 4.40 |
| Pittsburgh |  |  |  |
| ☐ 5B Mike Boldin | 60.00 | 27.00 | 7.50 |
| Pittsburgh |  |  |  |
| ☐ 6A Bernie Botula | 35.00 | 16.00 | 4.40 |
| Washington and Jefferson |  |  |  |
| ☐ 6B Bernie Botula | 60.00 | 27.00 | 7.50 |
| Washington and Jefferson |  |  |  |
| ☐ 7 Bob Bowlby | 35.00 | 16.00 | 4.40 |
| NC State |  |  |  |
| ☐ 8 Bob Bucher | 35.00 | 16.00 | 4.40 |
| Bucknell |  |  |  |
| ☐ 9A Al Burnett | 35.00 | 16.00 | 4.40 |
| Rutgers |  |  |  |
| ☐ 9B Al Burnett | 60.00 | 27.00 | 7.50 |
| Rutgers |  |  |  |
| ☐ 10 Don Burson | 35.00 | 16.00 | 4.40 |
| Northwestern |  |  |  |
| ☐ 11 Paul Campbell | 35.00 | 16.00 | 4.40 |
| Texas |  |  |  |
| ☐ 12 Herb Carey | 35.00 | 16.00 | 4.40 |
| Dartmouth |  |  |  |
| ☐ 13A Bimbo Cecconi | 35.00 | 16.00 | 4.40 |
| Pittsburgh |  |  |  |
| ☐ 13B Bimbo Cecconi | 60.00 | 27.00 | 7.50 |
| Pittsburgh |  |  |  |
| ☐ 14 Bill Chauncey | 35.00 | 16.00 | 4.40 |
| Iowa State |  |  |  |
| ☐ 15 Dick Clark | 35.00 | 16.00 | 4.40 |
| Cornell |  |  |  |
| ☐ 16 Tom Coleman | 35.00 | 16.00 | 4.40 |
| Georgia |  |  |  |
| ☐ 17 Billy Conn | 35.00 | 16.00 | 4.40 |
| Georgetown |  |  |  |
| ☐ 18 John Cox | 35.00 | 16.00 | 4.40 |
| Florida |  |  |  |
| ☐ 19 Lou Creekmur | 45.00 | 20.00 | 5.75 |
| William and Mary |  |  |  |
| ☐ 20 Glen Davis | 50.00 | 23.00 | 6.25 |
| Ohio University |  |  |  |
| ☐ 21 Warren Davis | 35.00 | 16.00 | 4.40 |
| Colgate |  |  |  |
| ☐ 22 Bob Deuber | 35.00 | 16.00 | 4.40 |
| Pennsylvania |  |  |  |

| ☐ 23 Ray Dooney | 35.00 | 16.00 | 4.40 |
|---|---|---|---|
| Pennsylvania |  |  |  |
| ☐ 24 Tom Dublinski | 35.00 | 16.00 | 4.40 |
| Utah |  |  |  |
| ☐ 25 Jeff Fleischman | 35.00 | 16.00 | 4.40 |
| Cornell |  |  |  |
| ☐ 26 Jack Friedland | 35.00 | 16.00 | 4.40 |
| Duke |  |  |  |
| ☐ 27 Bob Fuchs | 35.00 | 16.00 | 4.40 |
| Missouri |  |  |  |
| ☐ 28 Arnold Galiffa | 35.00 | 16.00 | 4.40 |
| Army |  |  |  |
| ☐ 29 Dick Gilman | 35.00 | 16.00 | 4.40 |
| Kansas |  |  |  |
| ☐ 30A Frank Gitschier | 35.00 | 16.00 | 4.40 |
| Louisville |  |  |  |
| ☐ 30B Frank Gitschier | 60.00 | 27.00 | 7.50 |
| Louisville |  |  |  |
| ☐ 31 Gene Glick | 35.00 | 16.00 | 4.40 |
| Michigan State |  |  |  |
| ☐ 32 Bill Gregus | 35.00 | 16.00 | 4.40 |
| Wake Forest |  |  |  |
| ☐ 33 Harold Hagan | 35.00 | 16.00 | 4.40 |
| South Carolina |  |  |  |
| ☐ 34 Charles Hall | 35.00 | 16.00 | 4.40 |
| Arizona |  |  |  |
| ☐ 35A Leon Hart | 55.00 | 25.00 | 7.00 |
| Notre Dame |  |  |  |
| ☐ 35B Leon Hart | 110.00 | 50.00 | 14.00 |
| Notre Dame |  |  |  |
| ☐ 36A Bob Hester | 35.00 | 16.00 | 4.40 |
| Marquette |  |  |  |
| ☐ 36B Bob Hester | 60.00 | 27.00 | 7.50 |
| Marquette |  |  |  |
| ☐ 37 George Hughes | 35.00 | 16.00 | 4.40 |
| William and Mary |  |  |  |
| ☐ 38 Levi Jackson | 37.50 | 17.00 | 4.70 |
| Yale |  |  |  |
| ☐ 39A Jackie Jensen | 125.00 | 57.50 | 15.50 |
| California |  |  |  |
| ☐ 39B Jackie Jensen | 250.00 | 115.00 | 31.00 |
| California |  |  |  |
| ☐ 40 Charlie Justice | 100.00 | 45.00 | 12.50 |
| North Carolina |  |  |  |
| ☐ 41 Gary Kerkorian | 35.00 | 16.00 | 4.40 |
| Stanford |  |  |  |
| ☐ 42 Bernie Krueger | 35.00 | 16.00 | 4.40 |
| Illinois |  |  |  |
| ☐ 43 Bill Kuhn | 35.00 | 16.00 | 4.40 |
| North Carolina |  |  |  |
| ☐ 44 Dean Laun | 35.00 | 16.00 | 4.40 |
| Iowa State |  |  |  |
| ☐ 45 Chet Leach | 35.00 | 16.00 | 4.40 |
| Bucknell |  |  |  |
| ☐ 46A Bobby Lee | 35.00 | 16.00 | 4.40 |
| Pittsburgh |  |  |  |
| ☐ 46B Bobby Lee | 60.00 | 27.00 | 7.50 |
| Pittsburgh |  |  |  |
| ☐ 47 Roger Lehew | 35.00 | 16.00 | 4.40 |
| Tulsa |  |  |  |
| ☐ 48 Glenn Lippman | 35.00 | 16.00 | 4.40 |
| Texas A and M |  |  |  |
| ☐ 49 Melvin Lyle | 35.00 | 16.00 | 4.40 |
| Louisiana State |  |  |  |
| ☐ 50 Len Makowski | 35.00 | 16.00 | 4.40 |
| Tulsa |  |  |  |
| ☐ 51A Al Malekoff | 35.00 | 16.00 | 4.40 |
| Rutgers |  |  |  |
| ☐ 51B Al Malekoff | 60.00 | 27.00 | 7.50 |
| Rutgers |  |  |  |
| ☐ 52A Jim Martin | 45.00 | 20.00 | 5.75 |
| Notre Dame |  |  |  |
| ☐ 52B Jim Martin | 90.00 | 40.00 | 11.50 |
| Notre Dame |  |  |  |
| ☐ 53 Frank Mataya | 35.00 | 16.00 | 4.40 |
| Washington State |  |  |  |
| ☐ 54A Ray Mathews | 45.00 | 20.00 | 5.75 |
| Clemson |  |  |  |
| ☐ 54B Ray Mathews | 90.00 | 40.00 | 11.50 |
| Clemson |  |  |  |
| ☐ 55A Dick McKissack | 35.00 | 16.00 | 4.40 |
| SMU |  |  |  |
| ☐ 55B Dick McKissack | 60.00 | 27.00 | 7.50 |
| SMU |  |  |  |
| ☐ 56 Frank Miller | 35.00 | 16.00 | 4.40 |
| Cornell |  |  |  |
| ☐ 57A John Miller | 35.00 | 16.00 | 4.40 |
| Delaware |  |  |  |
| ☐ 57B John Miller | 60.00 | 27.00 | 7.50 |
| Delaware |  |  |  |
| ☐ 58 Ed Modzelewski | 45.00 | 20.00 | 5.75 |
| Maryland |  |  |  |
| ☐ 59 Don Mouser | 35.00 | 16.00 | 4.40 |
| Baylor |  |  |  |
| ☐ 60 James Murphy | 35.00 | 16.00 | 4.40 |
| Holy Cross |  |  |  |
| ☐ 61A Ray Nagle | 37.50 | 17.00 | 4.70 |

UCLA
☐ 61B Ray Nagle .......................... 65.00 29.00 8.25
UCLA
☐ 62 Leo Nomellini ...................... 135.00 60.00 17.00
Minnesota
☐ 63 James O'Day ....................... 35.00 16.00 4.40
Duquesne
☐ 64 Joe Paterno ......................... 375.00 170.00 47.50
Brown
☐ 65 Andy Pavich ........................ 35.00 16.00 4.40
Denver
☐ 66A Pete Perini ........................ 35.00 16.00 4.40
Ohio State
☐ 66B Pete Perini ........................ 60.00 27.00 7.50
Ohio State
☐ 67 Jim Powers ......................... 35.00 16.00 4.40
USC
☐ 68 Dave Rakestraw ................... 35.00 16.00 4.40
Tulsa
☐ 69 Herb Rich ........................... 35.00 16.00 4.40
Vanderbilt
☐ 70 Fran Rogel .......................... 35.00 16.00 4.40
Penn State
☐ 71A Darrell Royal ..................... 75.00 34.00 9.50
Oklahoma
☐ 71B Darrell Royal ..................... 150.00 70.00 19.00
Oklahoma
☐ 72 Steve Sawle ........................ 35.00 16.00 4.40
Northwestern
☐ 73 Nick Sebek .......................... 35.00 16.00 4.40
Indiana
☐ 74 Herb Seidell ........................ 35.00 16.00 4.40
Fordham
☐ 75A Charles Shaw ..................... 35.00 16.00 4.40
Oklahoma A and M
☐ 75B Charles Shaw ..................... 60.00 27.00 7.50
Oklahoma A and M
☐ 76A Emil Sitko ......................... 37.50 17.00 4.70
Notre Dame
☐ 76B Emil Sitko ......................... 65.00 29.00 8.25
Notre Dame
☐ 77 Ed(Butch) Songin .................. 45.00 20.00 5.75
Boston College
☐ 78A Mariano Stalloni ................. 35.00 16.00 4.40
Delaware
☐ 78B Mariano Stalloni ................. 60.00 27.00 7.50
Delaware
☐ 79 Ernie Stautner ..................... 135.00 60.00 17.00
Boston College
☐ 80 Don Stehley ........................ 35.00 16.00 4.40
Kansas State
☐ 81 Gil Stevenson ...................... 37.50 17.00 4.70
Army
☐ 82 Bishop Strickland .................. 35.00 16.00 4.40
South Carolina
☐ 83 Harry Szulborski ................... 35.00 16.00 4.40
Purdue
☐ 84A Wally Teninga .................... 35.00 16.00 4.40
Michigan
☐ 84B Wally Teninga .................... 60.00 27.00 7.50
Michigan
☐ 85 Clayton Tonnemaker .............. 35.00 16.00 4.40
Minnesota
☐ 86A Deacon Dan Towler .............. 55.00 25.00 7.00
Washington and
Jefferson
☐ 86B Deacon Dan Towler .............. 110.00 50.00 14.00
Washington and
Jefferson
☐ 87A Bert Turek ........................ 35.00 16.00 4.40
Marquette
☐ 87B Bert Turek ........................ 60.00 27.00 7.50
Marquette
☐ 88 Harry Ulinski ....................... 35.00 16.00 4.40
Kentucky
☐ 89 Leon Van Billingham .............. 35.00 16.00 4.40
Columbia
☐ 90 Langdon Viracola .................. 35.00 16.00 4.40
Fordham
☐ 91 Leo Wagner ........................ 35.00 16.00 4.40
CCNY
☐ 92A Doak Walker ...................... 150.00 70.00 19.00
SMU
☐ 92B Doak Walker ...................... 300.00 135.00 38.00
SMU
☐ 93 Jim Ward ........................... 35.00 16.00 4.40
Columbia
☐ 94 Art Weiner .......................... 35.00 16.00 4.40
North Carolina
☐ 95 Dick Weiss .......................... 35.00 16.00 4.40
North Carolina
☐ 96 Froggie Williams ................... 35.00 16.00 4.40
Rice
☐ 97 Robert(Red) Wilson ............... 37.50 17.00 4.70
Wisconsin
☐ 98 Roger(Red) Wilson ................ 35.00 16.00 4.40
South Carolina
☐ 99 Carl Wren ........................... 35.00 16.00 4.40

Rochester
☐ 100A Pete Zinaich ..................... 35.00 16.00 4.40
West Virginia
☐ 100B Pete Zinaich ..................... 60.00 20.00 5.75
West Virginia

# 1951 Topps Magic

The 1951 Topps Magic football set was Topps first major football "card" issue. The set features 75 cards of the country's best collegiate players. The cards measure approximately 2 1/16" by 2 15/16". The backs contain a scratch-off section which gives the answer to a football quiz. Cards with the scratch-off back intact are valued at 50 percent more than the prices listed below. The key Rookie Cards in this set are Marion Campbell, Vic Janowicz, Babe Parilli, and Bill Wade. The player's college nicknames are provided as they are listed physically on the card fronts.

|  | NRMT | VG-E | GOOD |
|---|---|---|---|
| COMPLETE SET (75) ...................... | 900.00 | 400.00 | 115.00 |
| COMMON PLAYER (1-75) ................ | 15.00 | 6.75 | 1.90 |
| *BACK UNSCRATCHED: 1.5X TO 2.5X | | | |

☐ 1 Jimmy Monahan .................. 22.00 6.50 2.20
Queensmen
☐ 2 Bill Wade .......................... 40.00 18.00 5.00
Commodores
☐ 3 Bill Reichardt ..................... 15.00 6.75 1.90
Hawkeyes
☐ 4 Babe Parilli ....................... 32.00 14.50 4.00
Wildcats
☐ 5 Billie Burkhalter ................. 15.00 6.75 1.90
Owls
☐ 6 Ed Weber .......................... 15.00 6.75 1.90
Indians
☐ 7 Tom Scott .......................... 15.00 6.75 1.90
Cavaliers
☐ 8 Frank Guthridge .................. 15.00 6.75 1.90
Blue Hens
☐ 9 John Karras ........................ 15.00 6.75 1.90
Fighting Illini
☐ 10 Vic Janowicz ..................... 55.00 25.00 7.00
Buckeyes
☐ 11 Lloyd Hill ........................ 15.00 6.75 1.90
Bruins
☐ 12 Jim Weatherall ................. 15.00 6.75 1.90
Sooners
☐ 13 Howard Hansen ................. 15.00 6.75 1.90
Lions
☐ 14 Lou D'Achille .................... 15.00 6.75 1.90
Hoosiers
☐ 15 Johnny Turco .................... 15.00 6.75 1.90
Crusaders
☐ 16 Jerrell Price ..................... 15.00 6.75 1.90
Red Raiders
☐ 17 John Coatta ...................... 15.00 6.75 1.90
Badgers
☐ 18 Bruce Patton ..................... 15.00 6.75 1.90
Hilltoppers
☐ 19 Marion Campbell ................ 30.00 13.50 3.80
Bulldogs
☐ 20 Blaine Earon ..................... 15.00 6.75 1.90
Blue Devils
☐ 21 Dewey McConnell ............... 15.00 6.75 1.90
Cowboys
☐ 22 Ray Beck .......................... 15.00 6.75 1.90
Yellow Jackets
☐ 23 Jim Prewett ...................... 15.00 6.75 1.90
Golden Hurricane
☐ 24 Bob Steele ........................ 15.00 6.75 1.90
Aggies
☐ 25 Art Betts .......................... 15.00 6.75 1.90

| | | | |
|---|---|---|---|
| Nittany Lions | | | |
| ☐ 26 Walt Trillhaase | 15.00 | 6.75 | 1.90 |
| Engineers | | | |
| ☐ 27 Gil Bartosh | 15.00 | 6.75 | 1.90 |
| Horned Frogs | | | |
| ☐ 28 Bob Bestwick | 15.00 | 6.75 | 1.90 |
| Panthers | | | |
| ☐ 29 Tom Rushing | 15.00 | 6.75 | 1.90 |
| Maroons | | | |
| ☐ 30 Bert Rechichar | 28.00 | 12.50 | 3.50 |
| Volunteers | | | |
| ☐ 31 Bill Owens | 15.00 | 6.75 | 1.90 |
| Raiders | | | |
| ☐ 32 Mike Goggins | 15.00 | 6.75 | 1.90 |
| Titans | | | |
| ☐ 33 John Petitbon | 17.00 | 7.75 | 2.10 |
| Fighting Irish | | | |
| ☐ 34 Byron Townsend | 15.00 | 6.75 | 1.90 |
| Longhorns | | | |
| ☐ 35 Ed Rotticci | 15.00 | 6.75 | 1.90 |
| Broncos | | | |
| ☐ 36 Steve Wadiak | 15.00 | 6.75 | 1.90 |
| Gamecocks | | | |
| ☐ 37 Bobby Marlow | 15.00 | 6.75 | 1.90 |
| Crimson Tide | | | |
| ☐ 38 Bill Fuchs | 15.00 | 6.75 | 1.90 |
| Tigers | | | |
| ☐ 39 Ralph Staub | 15.00 | 6.75 | 1.90 |
| Bearcats | | | |
| ☐ 40 Bill Vesprini | 15.00 | 6.75 | 1.90 |
| Indians | | | |
| ☐ 41 Zack Jordan | 15.00 | 6.75 | 1.90 |
| Tigers | | | |
| ☐ 42 Bob Smith | 17.00 | 7.75 | 2.10 |
| Aggies | | | |
| ☐ 43 Charles Hanson | 15.00 | 6.75 | 1.90 |
| Terriers | | | |
| ☐ 44 Glenn Smith | 15.00 | 6.75 | 1.90 |
| Tigers | | | |
| ☐ 45 Armand Kitto | 15.00 | 6.75 | 1.90 |
| Tigers | | | |
| ☐ 46 Vinnie Drake | 15.00 | 6.75 | 1.90 |
| Rams | | | |
| ☐ 47 Bill Putich | 15.00 | 6.75 | 1.90 |
| Wolverines | | | |
| ☐ 48 George Young | 30.00 | 13.50 | 3.80 |
| Bisons | | | |
| ☐ 49 Don McRae | 15.00 | 6.75 | 1.90 |
| Wildcats | | | |
| ☐ 50 Frank Smith | 15.00 | 6.75 | 1.90 |
| Hurricanes | | | |
| ☐ 51 Dick Hightower | 15.00 | 6.75 | 1.90 |
| Mustangs | | | |
| ☐ 52 Clyde Pickard | 15.00 | 6.75 | 1.90 |
| Deacons | | | |
| ☐ 53 Bob Reynolds | 15.00 | 6.75 | 1.90 |
| Cornhuskers | | | |
| ☐ 54 Dick Gregory | 15.00 | 6.75 | 1.90 |
| Gophers | | | |
| ☐ 55 Dale Samuels | 15.00 | 6.75 | 1.90 |
| Boilermakers | | | |
| ☐ 56 Gale Galloway | 15.00 | 6.75 | 1.90 |
| Bears | | | |
| ☐ 57 Vic Pujo | 15.00 | 6.75 | 1.90 |
| Big Red | | | |
| ☐ 58 Dave Waters | 15.00 | 6.75 | 1.90 |
| Generals | | | |
| ☐ 59 Joe Ernest | 15.00 | 6.75 | 1.90 |
| Green Wave | | | |
| ☐ 60 Elmer Costa | 15.00 | 6.75 | 1.90 |
| Wolfpack | | | |
| ☐ 61 Nick Liotta | 15.00 | 6.75 | 1.90 |
| Wildcats | | | |
| ☐ 62 John Dottley | 15.00 | 6.75 | 1.90 |
| Rebels | | | |
| ☐ 63 Hi Faubion | 15.00 | 6.75 | 1.90 |
| Wildcats | | | |
| ☐ 64 David Harr | 15.00 | 6.75 | 1.90 |
| Diplomats | | | |
| ☐ 65 Bill Matthews | 15.00 | 6.75 | 1.90 |
| Violets | | | |
| ☐ 66 Carroll McDonald | 15.00 | 6.75 | 1.90 |
| Gators | | | |
| ☐ 67 Dick Dewing | 15.00 | 6.75 | 1.90 |
| Wildcats | | | |
| ☐ 68 Joe Johnson | 15.00 | 6.75 | 1.90 |
| Eagles | | | |
| ☐ 69 Arnold Burwitz | 15.00 | 6.75 | 1.90 |
| Wildcats | | | |
| ☐ 70 Ed Dobrowolski | 15.00 | 6.75 | 1.90 |
| Orangemen | | | |
| ☐ 71 Joe Dudeck | 15.00 | 6.75 | 1.90 |
| Tar Heels | | | |
| ☐ 72 John Bright | 15.00 | 6.75 | 1.90 |
| Bulldogs | | | |
| ☐ 73 Harold Loehlein | 15.00 | 6.75 | 1.90 |
| Cadets | | | |
| ☐ 74 Lawrence Hairston | 15.00 | 6.75 | 1.90 |

| | | | |
|---|---|---|---|
| Wolfpack | | | |
| ☐ 75 Bob Carey | 18.00 | 6.75 | 1.90 |

# 1955 Topps All-American

JIM THORPE     Halfback

The 1955 Topps All-American set features 100 cards of college football greats. The cards measure approximately 2 5/8" by 3 5/8". There are some numbers which were printed in lesser supply; these short-printed cards are denoted in the checklist below by SP. The key rookies in this set are Doc Blanchard, The Four Horseman (Notre Dame backfield in 1924), Tommy Harmon, Don Hutson, Ernie Nevers, and Amos Alonzo Stagg.

| | NRMT | VG-E | GOOD |
|---|---|---|---|
| COMPLETE SET (100) | 3000.00 | 1350.00 | 375.00 |
| COMMON PLAYER (1-92) | 15.00 | 6.75 | 1.90 |
| COMMON PLAYER SP (93-100) | 30.00 | 13.50 | 3.80 |
| ☐ 1 Herman Hickman | 90.00 | 23.00 | 7.25 |
| Tennessee | | | |
| ☐ 2 John Kimbrough | 15.00 | 6.75 | 1.90 |
| Texas A and M | | | |
| ☐ 3 Ed Weir | 15.00 | 6.75 | 1.90 |
| Nebraska | | | |
| ☐ 4 Ernie Pinckert | 17.50 | 8.00 | 2.20 |
| USC | | | |
| ☐ 5 Bobby Grayson | 15.00 | 6.75 | 1.90 |
| Stanford | | | |
| ☐ 6 Nile Kinnick UER | 25.00 | 11.50 | 3.10 |
| Iowa | | | |
| (Misspelled Niles | | | |
| on card) | | | |
| ☐ 7 Andy Bershak | 15.00 | 6.75 | 1.90 |
| North Carolina | | | |
| ☐ 8 George Cafego | 17.50 | 8.00 | 2.20 |
| Tennessee | | | |
| ☐ 9 Tom Hamilton SP | 27.00 | 12.00 | 3.40 |
| Navy | | | |
| ☐ 10 Bill Dudley | 30.00 | 13.50 | 3.80 |
| Virginia | | | |
| ☐ 11 Bobby Dodd SP | 27.00 | 12.00 | 3.40 |
| Tennessee | | | |
| ☐ 12 Otto Graham | 175.00 | 80.00 | 22.00 |
| Northwestern | | | |
| ☐ 13 Aaron Rosenberg | 15.00 | 6.75 | 1.90 |
| USC | | | |
| ☐ 14A Gaynell Tinsley ERR | 25.00 | 11.50 | 3.10 |
| (Wrong back 21 with | | | |
| Whizzer White bio) | | | |
| LSU | | | |
| ☐ 14B Gaynell Tinsley COR | 20.00 | 9.00 | 2.50 |
| LSU | | | |
| ☐ 15 Ed Kaw SP | 27.00 | 12.00 | 3.40 |
| Cornell | | | |
| ☐ 16 Knute Rockne | 275.00 | 125.00 | 34.00 |
| Notre Dame | | | |
| ☐ 17 Bob Reynolds | 15.00 | 6.75 | 1.90 |
| Nebraska | | | |
| ☐ 18 Pudge Heffelfinger SP | 30.00 | 13.50 | 3.80 |
| Yale | | | |
| ☐ 19 Bruce Smith | 20.00 | 9.00 | 2.50 |
| Minnesota | | | |
| ☐ 20 Sammy Baugh | 180.00 | 80.00 | 23.00 |
| TCU | | | |
| ☐ 21A Whizzer White ERR SP | 40.00 | 18.00 | 5.00 |
| (Wrong back 14 with | | | |
| Gaynell Tinsley bio) | | | |
| Colorado | | | |
| ☐ 21B Whizzer White COR SP | 50.00 | 23.00 | 6.25 |
| Colorado | | | |
| ☐ 22 Brick Muller | 15.00 | 6.75 | 1.90 |
| California | | | |
| ☐ 23 Dick Kazmaier | 20.00 | 9.00 | 2.50 |

Princeton
| | | |
|---|---|---|
| ☐ 24 Ken Strong | 30.00 | 13.50 | 3.80 |

NYU
| | | |
|---|---|---|
| ☐ 25 Casimir Myslinski SP | 27.00 | 12.00 | 3.40 |

Army
| | | |
|---|---|---|
| ☐ 26 Larry Kelley SP | 30.00 | 13.50 | 3.80 |

Yale
| | | |
|---|---|---|
| ☐ 27 Red Grange UER | 300.00 | 135.00 | 38.00 |
(Card says he was QB, should say halfback)

Illinois
| | | |
|---|---|---|
| ☐ 28 Mel Hein SP | 30.00 | 13.50 | 3.80 |

Washington State
| | | |
|---|---|---|
| ☐ 29 Leo Nomellini SP | 35.00 | 16.00 | 4.40 |

Minnesota
| | | |
|---|---|---|
| ☐ 30 Wes E. Fesler | 15.00 | 6.75 | 1.90 |

Ohio State
| | | |
|---|---|---|
| ☐ 31 George Sauer Sr | 20.00 | 9.00 | 2.50 |

Nebraska
| | | |
|---|---|---|
| ☐ 32 Hank Foldberg | 15.00 | 6.75 | 1.90 |

Army
| | | |
|---|---|---|
| ☐ 33 Bob Higgins | 15.00 | 6.75 | 1.90 |

Penn State
| | | |
|---|---|---|
| ☐ 34 Davey O'Brien | 25.00 | 11.50 | 3.10 |

TCU
| | | |
|---|---|---|
| ☐ 35 Tom Harmon SP | 40.00 | 18.00 | 5.00 |

Michigan
| | | |
|---|---|---|
| ☐ 36 Turk Edwards SP | 30.00 | 13.50 | 3.80 |

Washington State
| | | |
|---|---|---|
| ☐ 37 Jim Thorpe | 300.00 | 135.00 | 38.00 |

Carlisle
| | | |
|---|---|---|
| ☐ 38A Amos Alonzo Stagg | 45.00 | 20.00 | 5.75 |
(Wrong back 19) ERR

Yale
| | | |
|---|---|---|
| ☐ 38B Amos Alonzo Stagg | 40.00 | 18.00 | 5.00 |
COR Yale
| | | |
|---|---|---|
| ☐ 39 Jerome Holland | 17.50 | 8.00 | 2.20 |

Cornell
| | | |
|---|---|---|
| ☐ 40 Donn Moomaw | 15.00 | 6.75 | 1.90 |

UCLA
| | | |
|---|---|---|
| ☐ 41 Joseph Alexander SP | 27.00 | 12.00 | 3.40 |

Syracuse
| | | |
|---|---|---|
| ☐ 42 J. Edward Tryon SP | 30.00 | 13.50 | 3.80 |

Colgate
| | | |
|---|---|---|
| ☐ 43 George Savitsky | 15.00 | 6.75 | 1.90 |

Pennsylvania
| | | |
|---|---|---|
| ☐ 44 Ed Garbisch | 15.00 | 6.75 | 1.90 |

Army
| | | |
|---|---|---|
| ☐ 45 Elmer Oliphant | 15.00 | 6.75 | 1.90 |

Army
| | | |
|---|---|---|
| ☐ 46 Arnold Lassman | 15.00 | 6.75 | 1.90 |

NYU
| | | |
|---|---|---|
| ☐ 47 Bo McMillan | 17.50 | 8.00 | 2.20 |

Centre
| | | |
|---|---|---|
| ☐ 48 Ed Widseth | 15.00 | 6.75 | 1.90 |

Minnesota
| | | |
|---|---|---|
| ☐ 49 Don Zimmerman | 15.00 | 6.75 | 1.90 |

Tulane
| | | |
|---|---|---|
| ☐ 50 Ken Kavanaugh | 20.00 | 9.00 | 2.50 |

LSU
| | | |
|---|---|---|
| ☐ 51 Duane Purvis SP | 27.00 | 12.00 | 3.40 |

Purdue
| | | |
|---|---|---|
| ☐ 52 John Lujack | 32.00 | 14.50 | 4.00 |

Notre Dame
| | | |
|---|---|---|
| ☐ 53 John F. Green | 15.00 | 6.75 | 1.90 |

Army
| | | |
|---|---|---|
| ☐ 54 Edwin Dooley SP | 27.00 | 12.00 | 3.40 |

Dartmouth
| | | |
|---|---|---|
| ☐ 55 Frank Merritt SP | 27.00 | 12.00 | 3.40 |

Army
| | | |
|---|---|---|
| ☐ 56 Ernie Nevers | 50.00 | 23.00 | 6.25 |

Stanford
| | | |
|---|---|---|
| ☐ 57 Vic Hanson SP | 27.00 | 12.00 | 3.40 |

Syracuse
| | | |
|---|---|---|
| ☐ 58 Ed Franco | 15.00 | 6.75 | 1.90 |

Fordham
| | | |
|---|---|---|
| ☐ 59 Doc Blanchard | 45.00 | 20.00 | 5.75 |

Army
| | | |
|---|---|---|
| ☐ 60 Dan Hill | 15.00 | 6.75 | 1.90 |

Duke
| | | |
|---|---|---|
| ☐ 61 Charles Brickley SP | 30.00 | 13.50 | 3.80 |

Harvard
| | | |
|---|---|---|
| ☐ 62 Harry Newman | 15.00 | 6.75 | 1.90 |

Michigan
| | | |
|---|---|---|
| ☐ 63 Charlie Justice | 22.00 | 10.00 | 2.80 |

North Carolina
| | | |
|---|---|---|
| ☐ 64 Benny Friedman | 17.50 | 8.00 | 2.20 |

Michigan
| | | |
|---|---|---|
| ☐ 65 Joe Donchess SP | 27.00 | 12.00 | 3.40 |

Pittsburgh
| | | |
|---|---|---|
| ☐ 66 Bruiser Kinard | 25.00 | 11.50 | 3.10 |

Ole Miss
| | | |
|---|---|---|
| ☐ 67 Frankie Albert | 18.00 | 8.00 | 2.30 |

Stanford
| | | |
|---|---|---|
| ☐ 68 Four Horsemen SP | 400.00 | 180.00 | 50.00 |
Jim Crowley
Elmer Layden
Creighton Miller

Harry Stuhldreher
Notre Dame
| | | |
|---|---|---|
| ☐ 69 Frank Sinkwich | 20.00 | 9.00 | 2.50 |

Georgia
| | | |
|---|---|---|
| ☐ 70 Bill Daddio | 15.00 | 6.75 | 1.90 |

Pittsburgh
| | | |
|---|---|---|
| ☐ 71 Bob Wilson | 15.00 | 6.75 | 1.90 |

SMU
| | | |
|---|---|---|
| ☐ 72 Chub Peabody | 15.00 | 6.75 | 1.90 |

Harvard
| | | |
|---|---|---|
| ☐ 73 Paul Governali | 17.50 | 8.00 | 2.20 |

Columbia
| | | |
|---|---|---|
| ☐ 74 Gene McEver | 15.00 | 6.75 | 1.90 |

Tennessee
| | | |
|---|---|---|
| ☐ 75 Hugh Gallarneau | 17.50 | 8.00 | 2.20 |

Stanford
| | | |
|---|---|---|
| ☐ 76 Angelo Bertelli | 18.00 | 8.00 | 2.30 |

Notre Dame
| | | |
|---|---|---|
| ☐ 77 Bowden Wyatt SP | 27.00 | 12.00 | 3.40 |

Tennessee
| | | |
|---|---|---|
| ☐ 78 Jay Berwanger | 20.00 | 9.00 | 2.50 |

Chicago
| | | |
|---|---|---|
| ☐ 79 Pug Lund | 15.00 | 6.75 | 1.90 |

Minnesota
| | | |
|---|---|---|
| ☐ 80 Bennie Oosterbaan | 17.50 | 8.00 | 2.20 |

Michigan
| | | |
|---|---|---|
| ☐ 81 Cotton Warburton | 15.00 | 6.75 | 1.90 |

USC
| | | |
|---|---|---|
| ☐ 82 Alex Wojciechowicz | 24.00 | 11.00 | 3.00 |

Fordham
| | | |
|---|---|---|
| ☐ 83 Ted Coy SP | 27.00 | 12.00 | 3.40 |

Yale
| | | |
|---|---|---|
| ☐ 84 Ace Parker SP | 45.00 | 20.00 | 5.75 |

Duke
| | | |
|---|---|---|
| ☐ 85 Sid Luckman | 75.00 | 34.00 | 9.50 |

Columbia
| | | |
|---|---|---|
| ☐ 86 Albie Booth SP | 27.00 | 12.00 | 3.40 |

Yale
| | | |
|---|---|---|
| ☐ 87 Adolph Schultz SP | 27.00 | 12.00 | 3.40 |

Michigan
| | | |
|---|---|---|
| ☐ 88 Ralph G. Kercheval | 15.00 | 6.75 | 1.90 |

Kentucky
| | | |
|---|---|---|
| ☐ 89 Marshall Goldberg | 17.50 | 8.00 | 2.20 |

Pittsburgh
| | | |
|---|---|---|
| ☐ 90 Charlie O'Rourke | 15.00 | 6.75 | 1.90 |

Boston College
| | | |
|---|---|---|
| ☐ 91 Bob Odell UER | 15.00 | 6.75 | 1.90 |
(Photo actually
Howard Odell)

Pennsylvania
| | | |
|---|---|---|
| ☐ 92 Biggie Munn | 15.00 | 6.75 | 1.90 |

Minnesota
| | | |
|---|---|---|
| ☐ 93 Willie Heston SP | 30.00 | 13.50 | 3.80 |

Michigan
| | | |
|---|---|---|
| ☐ 94 Joe Bernard SP | 30.00 | 13.50 | 3.80 |

Michigan
| | | |
|---|---|---|
| ☐ 95 Red Cagle SP | 30.00 | 13.50 | 3.80 |

Army
| | | |
|---|---|---|
| ☐ 96 Bill Hollenback SP | 30.00 | 13.50 | 3.80 |

Pennsylvania
| | | |
|---|---|---|
| ☐ 97 Don Hutson SP | 175.00 | 80.00 | 22.00 |

Alabama
| | | |
|---|---|---|
| ☐ 98 Beattie Feathers SP | 35.00 | 16.00 | 4.40 |

Tennessee
| | | |
|---|---|---|
| ☐ 99 Don Whitmire SP | 30.00 | 13.50 | 3.80 |

Alabama/Navy
| | | |
|---|---|---|
| ☐ 100 Fats Henry SP | 150.00 | 38.00 | 12.00 |
Washington and
Jefferson

# 1956 Topps

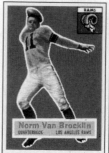

The 1956 Topps football set of 120 (numbered) cards contains NFL players. The cards measure 2 5/8" by 3 5/8". The first football team cards (produced by Topps) were included in this set. Players from the

Washington Redskins and the Chicago Cardinals were apparently produced in lesser quantities, as they are more difficult to find compared to the other teams. Some veteran collectors believe that cards of members of the Baltimore Colts, Chicago Bears, and Cleveland Browns are slightly more difficult to find as well. The card backs were printed in red and black on gray card stock. Statistical information from the immediate past season and career totals are given at the bottom of the reverse. A checklist card and six contest cards were also issued along with this set, although in much lesser quantities. The contest cards have advertisements on both sides for Bazooka Bubble Gum. Both sides have orange-red and blue type on an off-white background. The fronts of the contest cards feature an offer to win one of three prizes (basketball, football, or autographed baseball glove) in the Bazooka Bubble Gum football contest, and the rules governing the contest are listed on the back. Any eligible contestant (not over 15 years old) who mails in (before November 19th) the correct scores to the two NFL football games listed on the front of that particular card and includes five one-cent Bazooka Bubble Gum wrappers or one nickel Bazooka wrapper with the entry will receive a choice of one of the three above-mentioned prizes. The cards are either numbered (1-3) or lettered (A-C). The complete set price below refers to the 120 numbered cards plus the unnumbered checklist card. There also exists a three-card advertising panel consisting of the obverses of Lou Groza, Don Colo, and Darrell Brewster with ad copy on the reverse. The key Rookie Cards in this set are Roosevelt Brown, Bill George, Rosey Grier, Stan Jones, Lenny Moore, and Joe Schmidt.

|  | NRMT | VG-E | GOOD |
|---|---|---|---|
| COMPLETE SET (121) | 1600.00 | 700.00 | 200.00 |
| COMMON PLAYER (1-120) | 5.00 | 2.30 | .60 |
| ☐ 1 Jack Carson SP | 50.00 | 12.50 | 4.00 |
| Washington Redskins | | | |
| ☐ 2 Gordon Soltau | 5.00 | 2.30 | .60 |
| San Francisco 49ers | | | |
| ☐ 3 Frank Varrichione | 5.00 | 2.30 | .60 |
| Pittsburgh Steelers | | | |
| ☐ 4 Eddie Bell | 5.00 | 2.30 | .60 |
| Philadelphia Eagles | | | |
| ☐ 5 Alex Webster | 16.00 | 7.25 | 2.00 |
| New York Giants | | | |
| ☐ 6 Norm Van Brocklin | 27.00 | 12.00 | 3.40 |
| Los Angeles Rams | | | |
| ☐ 7 Green Bay Packers | 16.00 | 7.25 | 2.00 |
| Team Card | | | |
| ☐ 8 Lou Creekmur | 5.50 | 2.50 | .70 |
| Detroit Lions | | | |
| ☐ 9 Lou Groza | 25.00 | 11.50 | 3.10 |
| Cleveland Browns | | | |
| ☐ 10 Tom Bienemann SP | 22.00 | 10.00 | 2.80 |
| Chicago Cardinals | | | |
| ☐ 11 George Blanda | 45.00 | 20.00 | 5.75 |
| Chicago Bears | | | |
| ☐ 12 Alan Ameche | 12.00 | 5.50 | 1.50 |
| Baltimore Colts | | | |
| ☐ 13 Vic Janowicz SP | 22.00 | 10.00 | 2.80 |
| Washington Redskins | | | |
| ☐ 14 Dick Moegle | 6.00 | 2.70 | .75 |
| San Francisco 49ers | | | |
| ☐ 15 Fran Rogel | 5.00 | 2.30 | .60 |
| Pittsburgh Steelers | | | |
| ☐ 16 Harold Giancanelli | 5.00 | 2.30 | .60 |
| Philadelphia Eagles | | | |
| ☐ 17 Emlen Tunnell | 15.00 | 6.75 | 1.90 |
| New York Giants | | | |
| ☐ 18 Paul(Tank) Younger | 5.50 | 2.50 | .70 |
| Los Angeles Rams | | | |
| ☐ 19 Bill Howton | 8.00 | 3.60 | 1.00 |
| Green Bay Packers | | | |
| ☐ 20 Jack Christiansen | 14.00 | 6.25 | 1.75 |
| Detroit Lions | | | |
| ☐ 21 Darrell Brewster | 5.00 | 2.30 | .60 |
| Cleveland Browns | | | |
| ☐ 22 Chicago Cardinals SP | 75.00 | 34.00 | 9.50 |
| Team Card | | | |
| ☐ 23 Ed Brown | 6.00 | 2.70 | .75 |
| Chicago Bears | | | |
| ☐ 24 Joe Campanella | 5.00 | 2.30 | .60 |
| Baltimore Colts | | | |
| ☐ 25 Leon Heath SP | 18.00 | 8.00 | 2.30 |
| Washington Redskins | | | |
| ☐ 26 San Francisco 49ers | 16.00 | 7.25 | 2.00 |
| Team Card | | | |
| ☐ 27 Dick Flanagan | 5.00 | 2.30 | .60 |
| Pittsburgh Steelers | | | |
| ☐ 28 Chuck Bednarik | 25.00 | 11.50 | 3.10 |
| Philadelphia Eagles | | | |
| ☐ 29 Kyle Rote | 15.00 | 6.75 | 1.90 |
| New York Giants | | | |
| ☐ 30 Les Richter | 5.50 | 2.50 | .70 |
| Los Angeles Rams | | | |
| ☐ 31 Howard Ferguson | 5.50 | 2.50 | .70 |

| | | | |
|---|---|---|---|
| Green Bay Packers | | | |
| ☐ 32 Dorne Dibble | 5.00 | 2.30 | .60 |
| Detroit Lions | | | |
| ☐ 33 Kenny Konz | 5.00 | 2.30 | .60 |
| Cleveland Browns | | | |
| ☐ 34 Dave Mann SP | 22.00 | 10.00 | 2.80 |
| Chicago Cardinals | | | |
| ☐ 35 Rick Casares | 6.00 | 2.70 | .75 |
| Chicago Bears | | | |
| ☐ 36 Art Donovan | 15.00 | 6.75 | 1.90 |
| Baltimore Colts | | | |
| ☐ 37 Chuck Drazenovich SP | 18.00 | 8.00 | 2.30 |
| Washington Redskins | | | |
| ☐ 38 Joe Arenas | 5.00 | 2.30 | .60 |
| San Francisco 49ers | | | |
| ☐ 39 Lynn Chandnois | 5.00 | 2.30 | .60 |
| Pittsburgh Steelers | | | |
| ☐ 40 Philadelphia Eagles | 16.00 | 7.25 | 2.00 |
| Team Card | | | |
| ☐ 41 Roosevelt Brown | 40.00 | 18.00 | 5.00 |
| New York Giants | | | |
| ☐ 42 Tom Fears | 15.00 | 6.75 | 1.90 |
| Los Angeles Rams | | | |
| ☐ 43 Gary Knafelc | 5.00 | 2.30 | .60 |
| Green Bay Packers | | | |
| ☐ 44 Joe Schmidt | 45.00 | 20.00 | 5.75 |
| Detroit Lions | | | |
| ☐ 45 Cleveland Browns | 16.00 | 7.25 | 2.00 |
| Team Card UER | | | |
| (Card back does not | | | |
| credit the Browns with | | | |
| being Champs in 1955) | | | |
| ☐ 46 Len Teeuws SP | 5.00 | 2.30 | .60 |
| Chicago Cardinals | | | |
| ☐ 47 Bill George | 30.00 | 13.50 | 3.80 |
| Chicago Bears | | | |
| ☐ 48 Baltimore Colts | 16.00 | 7.25 | 2.00 |
| Team Card | | | |
| ☐ 49 Eddie LeBaron SP | 25.00 | 11.50 | 3.10 |
| Washington Redskins | | | |
| ☐ 50 Hugh McElhenny | 27.00 | 12.00 | 3.40 |
| San Francisco 49ers | | | |
| ☐ 51 Ted Marchibroda | 6.00 | 2.70 | .75 |
| Pittsburgh Steelers | | | |
| ☐ 52 Adrian Burk | 5.00 | 2.30 | .60 |
| Philadelphia Eagles | | | |
| ☐ 53 Frank Gifford | 110.00 | 50.00 | 14.00 |
| New York Giants | | | |
| ☐ 54 Charley Toogood | 5.00 | 2.30 | .60 |
| Los Angeles Rams | | | |
| ☐ 55 Tobin Rote | 8.00 | 3.60 | 1.00 |
| Green Bay Packers | | | |
| ☐ 56 Bill Stits | 5.00 | 2.30 | .60 |
| Detroit Lions | | | |
| ☐ 57 Don Colo | 5.00 | 2.30 | .60 |
| Cleveland Browns | | | |
| ☐ 58 Ollie Matson SP | 40.00 | 18.00 | 5.00 |
| Chicago Cardinals | | | |
| ☐ 59 Harlon Hill | 5.50 | 2.50 | .70 |
| Chicago Bears | | | |
| ☐ 60 Lenny Moore | 85.00 | 38.00 | 10.50 |
| Baltimore Colts | | | |
| ☐ 61 Washington Redskins | 75.00 | 34.00 | 9.50 |
| Team Card SP | | | |
| ☐ 62 Billy Wilson | 6.00 | 2.70 | .75 |
| San Francisco 49ers | | | |
| ☐ 63 Pittsburgh Steelers | 16.00 | 7.25 | 2.00 |
| Team Card | | | |
| ☐ 64 Bob Pellegrini | 5.00 | 2.30 | .60 |
| Philadelphia Eagles | | | |
| ☐ 65 Ken MacAfee | 5.50 | 2.50 | .70 |
| New York Giants | | | |
| ☐ 66 Willard Sherman | 5.00 | 2.30 | .60 |
| Los Angeles Rams | | | |
| ☐ 67 Roger Zatkoff | 5.00 | 2.30 | .60 |
| Green Bay Packers | | | |
| ☐ 68 Dave Middleton | 5.00 | 2.30 | .60 |
| Detroit Lions | | | |
| ☐ 69 Ray Renfro | 6.00 | 2.70 | .75 |
| Cleveland Browns | | | |
| ☐ 70 Don Stonesifer SP | 22.00 | 10.00 | 2.80 |
| Chicago Cardinals | | | |
| ☐ 71 Stan Jones | 30.00 | 13.50 | 3.80 |
| Chicago Bears | | | |
| ☐ 72 Jim Mutscheller | 5.00 | 2.30 | .60 |
| Baltimore Colts | | | |
| ☐ 73 Volney Peters SP | 18.00 | 8.00 | 2.30 |
| Washington Redskins | | | |
| ☐ 74 Leo Nomellini | 15.00 | 6.75 | 1.90 |
| San Francisco 49ers | | | |
| ☐ 75 Ray Mathews | 5.00 | 2.30 | .60 |
| Pittsburgh Steelers | | | |
| ☐ 76 Dick Bielski | 5.00 | 2.30 | .60 |
| Philadelphia Eagles | | | |
| ☐ 77 Charley Conerly | 25.00 | 11.50 | 3.10 |
| New York Giants | | | |
| ☐ 78 Elroy Hirsch | 25.00 | 11.50 | 3.10 |
| Los Angeles Rams | | | |

| | | | |
|---|---|---|---|
| ☐ 79 Bill Forester | 8.00 | 3.60 | 1.00 |
| Green Bay Packers | | | |
| ☐ 80 Jim Doran | 5.00 | 2.30 | .60 |
| Detroit Lions | | | |
| ☐ 81 Fred Morrison | 5.00 | 2.30 | .60 |
| Cleveland Browns | | | |
| ☐ 82 Jack Simmons SP | 22.00 | 10.00 | 2.80 |
| Chicago Cardinals | | | |
| ☐ 83 Bill McColl | 5.00 | 2.30 | .60 |
| Chicago Bears | | | |
| ☐ 84 Bert Rechichar | 5.00 | 2.30 | .60 |
| Baltimore Colts | | | |
| ☐ 85 Joe Scudero SP | 18.00 | 8.00 | 2.30 |
| Washington Redskins | | | |
| ☐ 86 Y.A. Tittle | 45.00 | 20.00 | 5.75 |
| San Francisco 49ers | | | |
| ☐ 87 Ernie Stautner | 15.00 | 6.75 | 1.90 |
| Pittsburgh Steelers | | | |
| ☐ 88 Norm Willey | 5.00 | 2.30 | .60 |
| Philadelphia Eagles | | | |
| ☐ 89 Bob Schnelker | 5.50 | 2.50 | .70 |
| New York Giants | | | |
| ☐ 90 Dan Towler | 8.00 | 3.60 | 1.00 |
| Los Angeles Rams | | | |
| ☐ 91 John Martinkovic | 5.00 | 2.30 | .60 |
| Green Bay Packers | | | |
| ☐ 92 Detroit Lions | 16.00 | 7.25 | 2.00 |
| Team Card | | | |
| ☐ 93 George Ratterman | 6.00 | 2.70 | .75 |
| Cleveland Browns | | | |
| ☐ 94 Chuck Ulrich SP | 22.00 | 10.00 | 2.80 |
| Chicago Cardinals | | | |
| ☐ 95 Bobby Watkins | 5.00 | 2.30 | .60 |
| Chicago Bears | | | |
| ☐ 96 Buddy Young | 6.00 | 2.70 | .75 |
| Baltimore Colts | | | |
| ☐ 97 Billy Wells SP | 18.00 | 8.00 | 2.30 |
| Washington Redskins | | | |
| ☐ 98 Bob Toneff | 5.00 | 2.30 | .60 |
| San Francisco 49ers | | | |
| ☐ 99 Bill McPeak | 5.00 | 2.30 | .60 |
| Pittsburgh Steelers | | | |
| ☐ 100 Bobby Thomason | 5.50 | 2.50 | .70 |
| Philadelphia Eagles | | | |
| ☐ 101 Roosevelt Grier | 30.00 | 13.50 | 3.80 |
| New York Giants | | | |
| ☐ 102 Ron Waller | 5.00 | 2.30 | .60 |
| Los Angeles Rams | | | |
| ☐ 103 Bobby Dillon | 5.50 | 2.50 | .70 |
| Green Bay Packers | | | |
| ☐ 104 Leon Hart | 7.00 | 3.10 | .85 |
| Detroit Lions | | | |
| ☐ 105 Mike McCormack | 14.00 | 6.25 | 1.75 |
| Cleveland Browns | | | |
| ☐ 106 John Olszewski SP | 22.00 | 10.00 | 2.80 |
| Chicago Cardinals | | | |
| ☐ 107 Bill Wightkin | 5.00 | 2.30 | .60 |
| Chicago Bears | | | |
| ☐ 108 George Shaw | 8.00 | 3.60 | 1.00 |
| Baltimore Colts | | | |
| ☐ 109 Dale Atkeson SP | 18.00 | 8.00 | 2.30 |
| Washington Redskins | | | |
| ☐ 110 Joe Perry | 25.00 | 11.50 | 3.10 |
| San Francisco 49ers | | | |
| ☐ 111 Dale Dodrill | 5.00 | 2.30 | .60 |
| Pittsburgh Steelers | | | |
| ☐ 112 Tom Scott | 5.00 | 2.30 | .60 |
| Philadelphia Eagles | | | |
| ☐ 113 New York Giants | 16.00 | 7.25 | 2.00 |
| Team Card | | | |
| ☐ 114 Los Angeles Rams | 16.00 | 7.25 | 2.00 |
| Team Card UER | | | |
| (back incorrect, Rams | | | |
| were not 1955 champs) | | | |
| ☐ 115 Al Carmichael | 5.00 | 2.30 | .60 |
| Green Bay Packers | | | |
| ☐ 116 Bobby Layne | 40.00 | 18.00 | 5.00 |
| Detroit Lions | | | |
| ☐ 117 Ed Modzelewski | 5.50 | 2.50 | .70 |
| Cleveland Browns | | | |
| ☐ 118 Lamar McHan SP | 5.00 | 2.30 | .60 |
| Chicago Cardinals | | | |
| ☐ 119 Chicago Bears | 16.00 | 7.25 | 2.00 |
| Team Card | | | |
| ☐ 120 Billy Vessels | 35.00 | 7.00 | 2.10 |
| Baltimore Colts | | | |
| ☐ C1 Sunday, October 14th | 50.00 | 23.00 | 6.25 |
| Colts vs. Packers | | | |
| Cards vs. Redskins | | | |
| (Numbered as 1) | | | |
| ☐ C2 Sunday, October 14th | 50.00 | 23.00 | 6.25 |
| Rams vs. Lions | | | |
| Giants vs. Browns | | | |
| (Numbered as 2) | | | |
| ☐ C3 Sunday, October 14th | 50.00 | 23.00 | 6.25 |
| Eagles vs. Steelers | | | |
| 49ers vs. Bears | | | |

| | | | |
|---|---|---|---|
| (Numbered as 3) | | | |
| ☐ CA Sunday, November 25th | 75.00 | 34.00 | 9.50 |
| Bears vs. Giants | | | |
| Rams vs. Colts | | | |
| (Numbered as A) | | | |
| ☐ CB Sunday, November 25th | 85.00 | 38.00 | 10.50 |
| Steelers vs. Cards | | | |
| 49ers vs. Eagles | | | |
| (Numbered as B) | | | |
| ☐ CC Sunday, November 25th | 300.00 | 135.00 | 38.00 |
| (Numbered as C) | | | |
| ☐ NNO Checklist Card | 325.00 | 80.00 | 27.00 |
| (unnumbered) | | | |

# 1957 Topps

The 1957 Topps football set contains 154 cards of NFL players, each card measuring 2 1/2" by 3 1/2". The fronts of the cards include both a bust and an action picture. The card backs were printed in red and black on gray card stock. Statistical information from the immediate past season and career totals are given at the bottom of the reverse. The Rookie Cards of Johnny Unitas, Bart Starr, and Paul Hornung are included in this set. Other notable Rookie Cards in this set are Raymond Berry, Dick "Night Train" Lane, Tommy McDonald, and Earl Morrall. The second series (89-154) is more difficult to obtain than the first series. Some collectors and dealers believe there are specific second series cards which were short printed. A checklist card was also issued along with this set. The checklist card was printed in red, yellow, and blue or in red, white, and blue; neither variety currently is recognized as having any additional premium value above the price listed below. There also exists a three-card advertising panel consisting of the obverses of Al Dorow, Harlon Hill, and Bert Rechichar with ad copy on the reverse of the first two and an Ollie Matson reverse on Rechichar. The complete set price below refers to the 154 numbered cards plus the unnumbered checklist card.

| | NRMT | VG-E | GOOD |
|---|---|---|---|
| COMPLETE SET (155) | 2500.00 | 1150.00 | 325.00 |
| COMMON PLAYER (1-88) | 4.00 | 1.80 | .50 |
| COMMON PLAYER (89-154) | 6.00 | 2.70 | .75 |
| ☐ 1 Eddie LeBaron | 30.00 | 6.00 | 1.80 |
| Washington Redskins | | | |
| ☐ 2 Pete Retzlaff | 8.00 | 3.60 | 1.00 |
| Philadelphia Eagles | | | |
| ☐ 3 Mike McCormack | 10.00 | 4.50 | 1.25 |
| Cleveland Browns | | | |
| ☐ 4 Lou Baldacci | 4.00 | 1.80 | .50 |
| Pittsburgh Steelers | | | |
| ☐ 5 Gino Marchetti | 12.00 | 5.50 | 1.50 |
| Baltimore Colts | | | |
| ☐ 6 Leo Nomellini | 14.00 | 6.25 | 1.75 |
| San Francisco 49ers | | | |
| ☐ 7 Bobby Watkins | 4.00 | 1.80 | .50 |
| Chicago Bears | | | |
| ☐ 8 Dave Middleton | 4.00 | 1.80 | .50 |
| Detroit Lions | | | |
| ☐ 9 Bobby Dillon | 4.50 | 2.00 | .55 |
| Green Bay Packers | | | |
| ☐ 10 Les Richter | 4.50 | 2.00 | .55 |
| Los Angeles Rams | | | |
| ☐ 11 Roosevelt Brown | 14.00 | 6.25 | 1.75 |
| New York Giants | | | |
| ☐ 12 Lavern Torgeson | 6.00 | 2.70 | .75 |
| Washington Redskins | | | |
| ☐ 13 Dick Bielski | 4.00 | 1.80 | .50 |
| Philadelphia Eagles | | | |
| ☐ 14 Pat Summerall | 15.00 | 6.75 | 1.90 |
| Chicago Cardinals | | | |
| ☐ 15 Jack Butler | 8.00 | 3.60 | 1.00 |
| Pittsburgh Steelers | | | |
| ☐ 16 John Henry Johnson | 14.00 | 6.25 | 1.75 |
| Cleveland Browns | | | |

| | Card | NM | EX | VG |
|---|---|---|---|---|
| ☐ | 17 Art Spinney — Baltimore Colts | 4.00 | 1.80 | .50 |
| ☐ | 18 Bob St. Clair — San Francisco 49ers | 10.00 | 4.50 | 1.25 |
| ☐ | 19 Perry Jeter — Chicago Bears | 4.00 | 1.80 | .50 |
| ☐ | 20 Lou Creekmur — Detroit Lions | 4.50 | 2.00 | .55 |
| ☐ | 21 Dave Hanner — Green Bay Packers | 4.50 | 2.00 | .55 |
| ☐ | 22 Norm Van Brocklin — Los Angeles Rams | 24.00 | 11.00 | 3.00 |
| ☐ | 23 Don Chandler — New York Giants | 8.00 | 3.60 | 1.00 |
| ☐ | 24 Al Dorow — Washington Redskins | 4.00 | 1.80 | .50 |
| ☐ | 25 Tom Scott — Philadelphia Eagles | 4.00 | 1.80 | .50 |
| ☐ | 26 Ollie Matson — Chicago Cardinals | 16.00 | 7.25 | 2.00 |
| ☐ | 27 Fran Rogel — Pittsburgh Steelers | 4.00 | 1.80 | .50 |
| ☐ | 28 Lou Groza — Cleveland Browns | 22.00 | 10.00 | 2.80 |
| ☐ | 29 Billy Vessels — Baltimore Colts | 4.50 | 2.00 | .55 |
| ☐ | 30 Y.A. Tittle — San Francisco 49ers | 32.00 | 14.50 | 4.00 |
| ☐ | 31 George Blanda — Chicago Bears | 40.00 | 18.00 | 5.00 |
| ☐ | 32 Bobby Layne — Detroit Lions | 30.00 | 13.50 | 3.80 |
| ☐ | 33 Bill Howton — Green Bay Packers | 4.50 | 2.00 | .55 |
| ☐ | 34 Bill Wade — Los Angeles Rams | 4.50 | 2.00 | .55 |
| ☐ | 35 Emlen Tunnell — New York Giants | 11.00 | 4.90 | 1.40 |
| ☐ | 36 Leo Elter — Washington Redskins | 4.00 | 1.80 | .50 |
| ☐ | 37 Clarence Peaks — Philadelphia Eagles | 7.00 | 3.10 | .85 |
| ☐ | 38 Don Stonesifer — Chicago Cardinals | 4.00 | 1.80 | .50 |
| ☐ | 39 George Tarasovic — Pittsburgh Steelers | 4.00 | 1.80 | .50 |
| ☐ | 40 Darrell Brewster — Cleveland Browns | 4.00 | 1.80 | .50 |
| ☐ | 41 Bert Rechichar — Baltimore Colts | 4.00 | 1.80 | .50 |
| ☐ | 42 Billy Wilson — San Francisco 49ers | 4.50 | 2.00 | .55 |
| ☐ | 43 Ed Brown — Chicago Bears | 4.50 | 2.00 | .55 |
| ☐ | 44 Gene Gedman — Detroit Lions | 4.00 | 1.80 | .50 |
| ☐ | 45 Gary Knafelc — Green Bay Packers | 4.00 | 1.80 | .50 |
| ☐ | 46 Elroy Hirsch — Los Angeles Rams | 20.00 | 9.00 | 2.50 |
| ☐ | 47 Don Heinrich — New York Giants | 4.50 | 2.00 | .55 |
| ☐ | 48 Gene Brito — Washington Redskins | 4.50 | 2.00 | .55 |
| ☐ | 49 Chuck Bednarik — Philadelphia Eagles | 16.00 | 7.25 | 2.00 |
| ☐ | 50 Dave Mann — Chicago Cardinals | 4.00 | 1.80 | .50 |
| ☐ | 51 Bill McPeak — Pittsburgh Steelers | 4.00 | 1.80 | .50 |
| ☐ | 52 Kenny Konz — Cleveland Browns | 4.00 | 1.80 | .50 |
| ☐ | 53 Alan Ameche — Baltimore Colts | 10.00 | 4.50 | 1.25 |
| ☐ | 54 Gordon Soltau — San Francisco 49ers | 4.00 | 1.80 | .50 |
| ☐ | 55 Rick Casares — Chicago Bears | 4.50 | 2.00 | .55 |
| ☐ | 56 Charlie Ane — Detroit Lions | 4.50 | 2.00 | .55 |
| ☐ | 57 Al Carmichael — Green Bay Packers | 4.00 | 1.80 | .50 |
| ☐ | 58A Willard Sherman ERR (no team on front) — Los Angeles Rams | 24.00 | 11.00 | 3.00 |
| ☐ | 58B Willard Sherman COR — Los Angeles Rams | 4.00 | 1.80 | .50 |
| ☐ | 59 Kyle Rote — New York Giants | 10.00 | 4.50 | 1.25 |
| ☐ | 60 Chuck Drazenovich — Washington Redskins | 4.00 | 1.80 | .50 |
| ☐ | 61 Bobby Walston — Philadelphia Eagles | 4.50 | 2.00 | .55 |
| ☐ | 62 John Olszewski — Chicago Cardinals | 4.00 | 1.80 | .50 |
| ☐ | 63 Ray Mathews — Pittsburgh Steelers | 4.00 | 1.80 | .50 |
| ☐ | 64 Maurice Bassett — Cleveland Browns | 4.00 | 1.80 | .50 |
| ☐ | 65 Art Donovan — Baltimore Colts | 14.00 | 6.25 | 1.75 |
| ☐ | 66 Joe Arenas — San Francisco 49ers | 4.00 | 1.80 | .50 |
| ☐ | 67 Harlon Hill — Chicago Bears | 4.50 | 2.00 | .55 |
| ☐ | 68 Yale Lary — Detroit Lions | 10.00 | 4.50 | 1.25 |
| ☐ | 69 Bill Forester — Green Bay Packers | 4.50 | 2.00 | .55 |
| ☐ | 70 Bob Boyd — Los Angeles Rams | 4.00 | 1.80 | .50 |
| ☐ | 71 Andy Robustelli — New York Giants | 14.00 | 6.25 | 1.75 |
| ☐ | 72 Sam Baker — Washington Redskins | 6.00 | 2.70 | .75 |
| ☐ | 73 Bob Pellegrini — Philadelphia Eagles | 4.00 | 1.80 | .50 |
| ☐ | 74 Leo Sanford — Chicago Cardinals | 4.00 | 1.80 | .50 |
| ☐ | 75 Sid Watson — Pittsburgh Steelers | 4.00 | 1.80 | .50 |
| ☐ | 76 Ray Renfro — Cleveland Browns | 4.50 | 2.00 | .55 |
| ☐ | 77 Carl Taseff — Baltimore Colts | 4.00 | 1.80 | .50 |
| ☐ | 78 Clyde Conner — San Francisco 49ers | 4.00 | 1.80 | .50 |
| ☐ | 79 J.C. Caroline — Chicago Bears | 4.50 | 2.00 | .55 |
| ☐ | 80 Howard Cassady ("Hopalong") — Detroit Lions | 11.00 | 4.90 | 1.40 |
| ☐ | 81 Tobin Rote — Green Bay Packers | 6.00 | 2.70 | .75 |
| ☐ | 82 Ron Waller — Los Angeles Rams | 4.00 | 1.80 | .50 |
| ☐ | 83 Jim Patton — New York Giants | 7.00 | 3.10 | .85 |
| ☐ | 84 Volney Peters — Washington Redskins | 4.00 | 1.80 | .50 |
| ☐ | 85 Dick Lane ("Night Train") — Chicago Cardinals | 40.00 | 18.00 | 5.00 |
| ☐ | 86 Royce Womble — Baltimore Colts | 4.00 | 1.80 | .50 |
| ☐ | 87 Duane Putnam — Los Angeles Rams | 6.00 | 2.70 | .75 |
| ☐ | 88 Frank Gifford — New York Giants | 90.00 | 40.00 | 11.50 |
| ☐ | 89 Steve Meilinger — Washington Redskins | 6.00 | 2.70 | .75 |
| ☐ | 90 Buck Lansford — Philadelphia Eagles | 6.00 | 2.70 | .75 |
| ☐ | 91 Lindon Crow — Chicago Cardinals | 6.00 | 2.70 | .75 |
| ☐ | 92 Ernie Stautner — Pittsburgh Steelers | 15.00 | 6.75 | 1.90 |
| ☐ | 93 Preston Carpenter — Cleveland Browns | 10.00 | 4.50 | 1.25 |
| ☐ | 94 Raymond Berry — Baltimore Colts | 90.00 | 40.00 | 11.50 |
| ☐ | 95 Hugh McElhenny — San Francisco 49ers | 25.00 | 11.50 | 3.10 |
| ☐ | 96 Stan Jones — Chicago Bears | 10.00 | 4.50 | 1.25 |
| ☐ | 97 Dorne Dibble — Detroit Lions | 6.00 | 2.70 | .75 |
| ☐ | 98 Joe Scudero — Washington Redskins | 6.00 | 2.70 | .75 |
| ☐ | 99 Eddie Bell — Philadelphia Eagles | 6.00 | 2.70 | .75 |
| ☐ | 100 Joe Childress — Chicago Cardinals | 6.00 | 2.70 | .75 |
| ☐ | 101 Elbert Nickel — Pittsburgh Steelers | 6.00 | 2.70 | .75 |
| ☐ | 102 Walt Michaels — Cleveland Browns | 6.50 | 2.90 | .80 |
| ☐ | 103 Jim Mutscheller — Baltimore Colts | 6.00 | 2.70 | .75 |
| ☐ | 104 Earl Morrall — San Francisco 49ers | 50.00 | 23.00 | 6.25 |
| ☐ | 105 Larry Strickland — Chicago Bears | 6.00 | 2.70 | .75 |
| ☐ | 106 Jack Christiansen — Detroit Lions | 14.00 | 6.25 | 1.75 |
| ☐ | 107 Fred Cone — Green Bay Packers | 6.50 | 2.90 | .80 |
| ☐ | 108 Bud McFadin — Los Angeles Rams | 10.00 | 4.50 | 1.25 |
| ☐ | 109 Charley Conerly — New York Giants | 25.00 | 11.50 | 3.10 |
| ☐ | 110 Tom Runnels — Washington Redskins | 6.00 | 2.70 | .75 |
| ☐ | 111 Ken Keller | 6.00 | 2.70 | .75 |

| | | | |
|---|---|---|---|
| Philadelphia Eagles | | | |
| ☐ 112 James Root | 6.00 | 2.70 | .75 |
| Chicago Cardinals | | | |
| ☐ 113 Ted Marchibroda | 6.50 | 2.90 | .80 |
| Pittsburgh Steelers | | | |
| ☐ 114 Don Paul | 6.00 | 2.70 | .75 |
| Cleveland Browns | | | |
| ☐ 115 George Shaw | 6.50 | 2.90 | .80 |
| Baltimore Colts | | | |
| ☐ 116 Dick Moegle | 6.50 | 2.90 | .80 |
| San Francisco 49ers | | | |
| ☐ 117 Don Bingham | 6.00 | 2.70 | .75 |
| Chicago Bears | | | |
| ☐ 118 Leon Hart | 8.00 | 3.60 | 1.00 |
| Detroit Lions | | | |
| ☐ 119 Bart Starr | 400.00 | 180.00 | 50.00 |
| Green Bay Packers | | | |
| ☐ 120 Paul Miller | 6.00 | 2.70 | .75 |
| Los Angeles Rams | | | |
| ☐ 121 Alex Webster | 8.00 | 3.60 | 1.00 |
| New York Giants | | | |
| ☐ 122 Ray Wietecha | 6.00 | 2.70 | .75 |
| New York Giants | | | |
| ☐ 123 Johnny Carson | 6.00 | 2.70 | .75 |
| Washington Redskins | | | |
| ☐ 124 Tommy McDonald | 15.00 | 6.75 | 1.90 |
| Philadelphia Eagles | | | |
| ☐ 125 Jerry Tubbs | 8.00 | 3.60 | 1.00 |
| Chicago Cardinals | | | |
| ☐ 126 Jack Scarbath | 6.00 | 2.70 | .75 |
| Pittsburgh Steelers | | | |
| ☐ 127 Ed Modzelewski | 6.50 | 2.90 | .80 |
| Cleveland Browns | | | |
| ☐ 128 Lenny Moore | 45.00 | 20.00 | 5.75 |
| Baltimore Colts | | | |
| ☐ 129 Joe Perry | 25.00 | 11.50 | 3.10 |
| San Francisco 49ers | | | |
| ☐ 130 Bill Wightkin | 6.00 | 2.70 | .75 |
| Chicago Bears | | | |
| ☐ 131 Jim Doran | 6.00 | 2.70 | .75 |
| Detroit Lions | | | |
| ☐ 132 Howard Ferguson | 6.00 | 2.70 | .75 |
| Green Bay Packers | | | |
| ☐ 133 Tom Wilson | 6.50 | 2.90 | .80 |
| Los Angeles Rams | | | |
| ☐ 134 Dick James | 6.00 | 2.70 | .75 |
| Washington Redskins | | | |
| ☐ 135 Jimmy Harris | 6.00 | 2.70 | .75 |
| Philadelphia Eagles | | | |
| ☐ 136 Chuck Ulrich | 6.00 | 2.70 | .75 |
| Chicago Cardinals | | | |
| ☐ 137 Lynn Chandnois | 6.00 | 2.70 | .75 |
| Pittsburgh Steelers | | | |
| ☐ 138 John Unitas | 450.00 | 200.00 | 57.50 |
| Baltimore Colts | | | |
| ☐ 139 Jim Ridlon | 6.00 | 2.70 | .75 |
| San Francisco 49ers | | | |
| ☐ 140 Zeke Bratkowski | 10.00 | 4.50 | 1.25 |
| Chicago Bears | | | |
| ☐ 141 Ray Krouse | 6.00 | 2.70 | .75 |
| Detroit Lions | | | |
| ☐ 142 John Martinkovic | 6.00 | 2.70 | .75 |
| Green Bay Packers | | | |
| ☐ 143 Jim Cason | 6.00 | 2.70 | .75 |
| Los Angeles Rams | | | |
| ☐ 144 Ken MacAfee | 6.50 | 2.90 | .80 |
| New York Giants | | | |
| ☐ 145 Sid Youngelman | 10.00 | 4.50 | 1.25 |
| Philadelphia Eagles | | | |
| ☐ 146 Paul Larson | 6.00 | 2.70 | .75 |
| Chicago Cardinals | | | |
| ☐ 147 Len Ford | 15.00 | 6.75 | 1.90 |
| Cleveland Browns | | | |
| ☐ 148 Bob Toneff | 6.00 | 2.70 | .75 |
| San Francisco 49ers | | | |
| ☐ 149 Ronnie Knox | 6.00 | 2.70 | .75 |
| Chicago Bears | | | |
| ☐ 150 Jim David | 10.00 | 4.50 | 1.25 |
| Detroit Lions | | | |
| ☐ 151 Paul Hornung | 400.00 | 180.00 | 50.00 |
| Green Bay Packers | | | |
| ☐ 152 Paul(Tank) Younger | 6.50 | 2.90 | .80 |
| Los Angeles Rams | | | |
| ☐ 153 Bill Svoboda | 6.00 | 2.70 | .75 |
| New York Giants | | | |
| ☐ 154 Fred Morrison | 40.00 | 8.00 | 2.40 |
| Cleveland Browns | | | |
| ☐ NNO Checklist Card SP | 475.00 | 120.00 | 47.50 |

# 1958 Topps

The 1958 Topps football set of 132 cards contains NFL players. After a one-year interruption, team cards are back in the Topps football cards. The cards measure 2 1/2" by 3 1/2". The backs are easily distinguished from other years, as they are printed in bright red ink on white stock.

CHUCK BEDNARIK
LINEBACKER • PHILADELPHIA EAGLES

The right-hand side of the reverse gives a trivia question; the answer could be obtained by rubbing with a coin over the blank space. The key Rookie Cards in this set are Jim Brown and Sonny Jurgensen. Topps also randomly inserted in packs a card with the words "Free Felt Initial" across the top. The horizontally oriented front pictures a boy in a red shirt and a girl in a blue shirt, with a large yellow "L" and "A" respectively on each of their shirts. The card back indicates an initial could be obtained by sending in three Bazooka or Blony wrappers and a self-addressed stamped envelope with the initial of choice printed on the front and back of the envelope.

| | NRMT | VG-E | GOOD |
|---|---|---|---|
| COMPLETE SET (132) | 1200.00 | 550.00 | 150.00 |
| COMMON PLAYER (1-132) | 3.00 | 1.35 | .40 |
| ☐ 1 Gene Filipski | 15.00 | 3.00 | .90 |
| New York Giants | | | |
| ☐ 2 Bobby Layne | 27.00 | 12.00 | 3.40 |
| Detroit Lions | | | |
| ☐ 3 Joe Schmidt | 9.00 | 4.00 | 1.15 |
| Detroit Lions | | | |
| ☐ 4 Bill Barnes | 3.00 | 1.35 | .40 |
| Philadelphia Eagles | | | |
| ☐ 5 Milt Plum | 8.00 | 3.60 | 1.00 |
| Cleveland Browns | | | |
| ☐ 6 Bill Howton UER | 3.50 | 1.55 | .45 |
| (Misspelled Billie on card front) Green Bay Packers | | | |
| ☐ 7 Howard Cassady | 5.00 | 2.30 | .60 |
| Detroit Lions | | | |
| ☐ 8 Jim Dooley | 3.50 | 1.55 | .45 |
| Chicago Bears | | | |
| ☐ 9 Cleveland Browns | 8.00 | 3.60 | 1.00 |
| Team Card | | | |
| ☐ 10 Lenny Moore | 16.00 | 7.25 | 2.00 |
| Baltimore Colts | | | |
| ☐ 11 Darrell Brewster UER | 3.00 | 1.35 | .40 |
| (Misspelled Darrel on card back) Cleveland Browns | | | |
| ☐ 12 Alan Ameche | 6.00 | 2.70 | .75 |
| Baltimore Colts | | | |
| ☐ 13 Jim David | 3.00 | 1.35 | .40 |
| Detroit Lions | | | |
| ☐ 14 Jim Mutscheller | 3.00 | 1.35 | .40 |
| Baltimore Colts | | | |
| ☐ 15 Andy Robustelli UER | 9.00 | 4.00 | 1.15 |
| (Never played for San Francisco) New York Giants | | | |
| ☐ 16 Gino Marchetti | 10.00 | 4.50 | 1.25 |
| Baltimore Colts | | | |
| ☐ 17 Ray Renfro | 3.50 | 1.55 | .45 |
| Cleveland Browns | | | |
| ☐ 18 Yale Lary | 8.00 | 3.60 | 1.00 |
| Detroit Lions | | | |
| ☐ 19 Gary Glick | 3.00 | 1.35 | .40 |
| Pittsburgh Steelers | | | |
| ☐ 20 Jon Arnett | 8.00 | 3.60 | 1.00 |
| Los Angeles Rams | | | |
| ☐ 21 Bob Boyd | 3.00 | 1.35 | .40 |
| Los Angeles Rams | | | |
| ☐ 22 John Unitas UER | 125.00 | 57.50 | 15.50 |
| (College: Pittsburgh should be Louisville) Baltimore Colts | | | |
| ☐ 23 Zeke Bratkowski | 4.00 | 1.80 | .50 |
| Chicago Bears | | | |
| ☐ 24 Sid Youngelman UER | 3.00 | 1.35 | .40 |
| (Misspelled Youngleman on card back) Philadelphia Eagles | | | |
| ☐ 25 Leo Elter | 3.00 | 1.35 | .40 |
| Washington Redskins | | | |
| ☐ 26 Kenny Konz | 3.00 | 1.35 | .40 |

| | | | |
|---|---|---|---|
| Cleveland Browns | | | |
| ☐ 27 Washington Redskins | 8.00 | 3.60 | 1.00 |
| Team Card | | | |
| ☐ 28 Carl Brettschneider | 3.00 | 1.35 | .40 |
| UER (Misspelled on back | | | |
| as Brettschneider) | | | |
| Chicago Cardinals | | | |
| ☐ 29 Chicago Bears | 8.00 | 3.60 | 1.00 |
| Team Card | | | |
| ☐ 30 Alex Webster | 4.00 | 1.80 | .50 |
| New York Giants | | | |
| ☐ 31 Al Carmichael | 3.00 | 1.35 | .40 |
| Green Bay Packers | | | |
| ☐ 32 Bobby Dillon | 3.50 | 1.55 | .45 |
| Green Bay Packers | | | |
| ☐ 33 Steve Meilinger | 3.00 | 1.35 | .40 |
| Washington Redskins | | | |
| ☐ 34 Sam Baker | 3.50 | 1.55 | .45 |
| Washington Redskins | | | |
| ☐ 35 Chuck Bednarik UER | 12.00 | 5.50 | 1.50 |
| (Misspelled Bednardk | | | |
| on card back) | | | |
| Philadelphia Eagles | | | |
| ☐ 36 Bert Vic Zucco | 3.00 | 1.35 | .40 |
| Chicago Bears | | | |
| ☐ 37 George Tarasovic | 3.00 | 1.35 | .40 |
| Pittsburgh Steelers | | | |
| ☐ 38 Bill Wade | 3.50 | 1.55 | .45 |
| Los Angeles Rams | | | |
| ☐ 39 Dick Stanfel | 3.50 | 1.55 | .45 |
| Washington Redskins | | | |
| ☐ 40 Jerry Norton | 3.00 | 1.35 | .40 |
| Philadelphia Eagles | | | |
| ☐ 41 San Francisco 49ers | 8.00 | 3.60 | 1.00 |
| Team Card | | | |
| ☐ 42 Emlen Tunnell | 10.00 | 4.50 | 1.25 |
| New York Giants | | | |
| ☐ 43 Jim Doran | 3.00 | 1.35 | .40 |
| Detroit Lions | | | |
| ☐ 44 Ted Marchibroda | 3.50 | 1.55 | .45 |
| Chicago Cardinals | | | |
| ☐ 45 Chet Hanulak | 3.00 | 1.35 | .40 |
| Cleveland Browns | | | |
| ☐ 46 Dale Dodrill | 3.00 | 1.35 | .40 |
| Pittsburgh Steelers | | | |
| ☐ 47 Johnny Carson | 3.00 | 1.35 | .40 |
| Washington Redskins | | | |
| ☐ 48 Dick Deschaine | 3.00 | 1.35 | .40 |
| Green Bay Packers | | | |
| ☐ 49 Billy Wells UER | 3.00 | 1.35 | .40 |
| (College should be | | | |
| Michigan State) | | | |
| Philadelphia Eagles | | | |
| ☐ 50 Larry Morris | 3.00 | 1.35 | .40 |
| Los Angeles Rams | | | |
| ☐ 51 Jack McClairen | 3.00 | 1.35 | .40 |
| Pittsburgh Steelers | | | |
| ☐ 52 Lou Groza | 18.00 | 8.00 | 2.30 |
| Cleveland Browns | | | |
| ☐ 53 Rick Casares | 3.50 | 1.55 | .45 |
| Chicago Bears | | | |
| ☐ 54 Don Chandler | 3.50 | 1.55 | .45 |
| New York Giants | | | |
| ☐ 55 Duane Putnam | 3.00 | 1.35 | .40 |
| Los Angeles Rams | | | |
| ☐ 56 Gary Knafelc | 3.00 | 1.35 | .40 |
| Green Bay Packers | | | |
| ☐ 57 Earl Morrall UER | 10.00 | 4.50 | 1.25 |
| (Misspelled Morall | | | |
| on card back) | | | |
| Pittsburgh Steelers | | | |
| ☐ 58 Ron Kramer | 5.00 | 2.30 | .60 |
| Green Bay Packers | | | |
| ☐ 59 Mike McCormack | 8.00 | 3.60 | 1.00 |
| Cleveland Browns | | | |
| ☐ 60 Gern Nagler | 3.00 | 1.35 | .40 |
| Chicago Cardinals | | | |
| ☐ 61 New York Giants | 8.00 | 3.60 | 1.00 |
| Team Card | | | |
| ☐ 62 Jim Brown | 350.00 | 160.00 | 45.00 |
| Cleveland Browns | | | |
| ☐ 63 Joe Marconi UER | 4.00 | 1.80 | .50 |
| (Avg. gain should be 4.4) | | | |
| Los Angeles Rams | | | |
| ☐ 64 R.C. Owens UER | 4.50 | 2.00 | .55 |
| San Francisco 49ers | | | |
| (Photo actually | | | |
| Don Owens) | | | |
| ☐ 65 Jimmy Carr | 4.00 | 1.80 | .50 |
| Chicago Cardinals | | | |
| ☐ 66 Bart Starr UER | 90.00 | 40.00 | 11.50 |
| Green Bay Packers | | | |
| (Life and year | | | |
| stats reversed) | | | |
| ☐ 67 Tom Wilson | 3.00 | 1.35 | .40 |
| Los Angeles Rams | | | |
| ☐ 68 Lamar McHan | 3.50 | 1.55 | .45 |
| Chicago Cardinals | | | |
| ☐ 69 Chicago Cardinals | 8.00 | 3.60 | 1.00 |
| Team Card | | | |
| ☐ 70 Jack Christiansen | 8.00 | 3.60 | 1.00 |
| Detroit Lions | | | |
| ☐ 71 Don McIlhenny | 4.00 | 1.80 | .50 |
| Green Bay Packers | | | |
| ☐ 72 Ron Waller | 3.00 | 1.35 | .40 |
| Los Angeles Rams | | | |
| ☐ 73 Frank Gifford | 65.00 | 29.00 | 8.25 |
| New York Giants | | | |
| ☐ 74 Bert Rechichar | 3.00 | 1.35 | .40 |
| Baltimore Colts | | | |
| ☐ 75 John Henry Johnson | 10.00 | 4.50 | 1.25 |
| Detroit Lions | | | |
| ☐ 76 Jack Butler | 3.00 | 1.35 | .40 |
| Pittsburgh Steelers | | | |
| ☐ 77 Frank Varrichione | 3.00 | 1.35 | .40 |
| Pittsburgh Steelers | | | |
| ☐ 78 Ray Mathews | 3.00 | 1.35 | .40 |
| Pittsburgh Steelers | | | |
| ☐ 79 Marv Matuszak UER | 3.00 | 1.35 | .40 |
| (Misspelled Matuzsak | | | |
| on card front) | | | |
| San Francisco 49ers | | | |
| ☐ 80 Harlon Hill UER | 3.50 | 1.55 | .45 |
| (Lifetime yards and | | | |
| Avg. gain incorrect) | | | |
| Chicago Bears | | | |
| ☐ 81 Lou Creekmur | 3.50 | 1.55 | .45 |
| Detroit Lions | | | |
| ☐ 82 Woodley Lewis UER | 3.00 | 1.35 | .40 |
| Chicago Cardinals | | | |
| (misspelled Woodly on | | | |
| front; end on front | | | |
| and halfback on back) | | | |
| ☐ 83 Don Heinrich | 3.50 | 1.55 | .45 |
| New York Giants | | | |
| ☐ 84 Charley Conerly UER | 14.00 | 6.25 | 1.75 |
| (Misspelled Charlie | | | |
| on card back) | | | |
| New York Giants | | | |
| ☐ 85 Los Angeles Rams | 8.00 | 3.60 | 1.00 |
| Team Card | | | |
| ☐ 86 Y.A. Tittle | 30.00 | 13.50 | 3.80 |
| San Francisco 49ers | | | |
| ☐ 87 Bobby Walston | 3.50 | 1.55 | .45 |
| Philadelphia Eagles | | | |
| ☐ 88 Earl Putman | 3.00 | 1.35 | .40 |
| Chicago Cardinals | | | |
| ☐ 89 Leo Nomellini | 9.00 | 4.00 | 1.15 |
| San Francisco 49ers | | | |
| ☐ 90 Sonny Jurgensen | 90.00 | 40.00 | 11.50 |
| Philadelphia Eagles | | | |
| ☐ 91 Don Paul | 3.00 | 1.35 | .40 |
| Cleveland Browns | | | |
| ☐ 92 Paige Cothren | 3.00 | 1.35 | .40 |
| Los Angeles Rams | | | |
| ☐ 93 Joe Perry | 15.00 | 6.75 | 1.90 |
| San Francisco 49ers | | | |
| ☐ 94 Tobin Rote | 4.00 | 1.80 | .50 |
| Detroit Lions | | | |
| ☐ 95 Billy Wilson | 3.50 | 1.55 | .45 |
| San Francisco 49ers | | | |
| ☐ 96 Green Bay Packers | 8.00 | 3.60 | 1.00 |
| Team Card | | | |
| ☐ 97 Lavern Torgeson | 3.00 | 1.35 | .40 |
| Washington Redskins | | | |
| ☐ 98 Milt Davis | 3.00 | 1.35 | .40 |
| Baltimore Colts | | | |
| ☐ 99 Larry Strickland | 3.00 | 1.35 | .40 |
| Chicago Bears | | | |
| ☐ 100 Matt Hazeltine | 4.00 | 1.80 | .50 |
| San Francisco 49ers | | | |
| ☐ 101 Walt Yowarski | 3.00 | 1.35 | .40 |
| New York Giants | | | |
| ☐ 102 Roosevelt Brown | 8.00 | 3.60 | 1.00 |
| New York Giants | | | |
| ☐ 103 Jim Ringo | 8.00 | 3.60 | 1.00 |
| Green Bay Packers | | | |
| ☐ 104 Joe Krupa | 3.00 | 1.35 | .40 |
| Pittsburgh Steelers | | | |
| ☐ 105 Les Richter | 3.50 | 1.55 | .45 |
| Los Angeles Rams | | | |
| ☐ 106 Art Donovan | 10.00 | 4.50 | 1.25 |
| Baltimore Colts | | | |
| ☐ 107 John Olszewski | 3.00 | 1.35 | .40 |
| Chicago Cardinals | | | |
| ☐ 108 Ken Keller | 3.00 | 1.35 | .40 |
| Philadelphia Eagles | | | |
| ☐ 109 Philadelphia Eagles | 8.00 | 3.60 | 1.00 |
| Team Card | | | |
| ☐ 110 Baltimore Colts | 8.00 | 3.60 | 1.00 |
| Team Card | | | |
| ☐ 111 Dick Bielski | 3.00 | 1.35 | .40 |
| Philadelphia Eagles | | | |
| ☐ 112 Eddie LeBaron | 5.00 | 2.30 | .60 |
| Washington Redskins | | | |

☐ 113 Gene Brito ............................ 3.50 1.55 .45
Washington Redskins
☐ 114 Willie Galimore ..................... 12.00 5.50 1.50
Chicago Bears
☐ 115 Detroit Lions ......................... 8.00 3.60 1.00
Team Card
☐ 116 Pittsburgh Steelers .............. 8.00 3.60 1.00
Team Card
☐ 117 L.G. Dupre ........................... 3.50 1.55 .45
Baltimore Colts
☐ 118 Babe Parilli .......................... 4.00 1.80 .50
Green Bay Packers
☐ 119 Bill George ........................... 7.50 3.40 .95
Chicago Bears
☐ 120 Raymond Berry ..................... 30.00 13.50 3.80
Baltimore Colts
☐ 121 Jim Podoley UER .................. 3.00 1.35 .40
Washington Redskins
(Photo actually
Volney Peters;
Podoly in cartoon)
☐ 122 Hugh McElhenny .................. 18.00 8.00 2.30
San Francisco 49ers
☐ 123 Ed Brown .............................. 3.50 1.55 .45
Chicago Bears
☐ 124 Dick Moegle .......................... 3.50 1.55 .45
San Francisco 49ers
☐ 125 Tom Scott .............................. 3.00 1.35 .40
Philadelphia Eagles
☐ 126 Tommy McDonald .................. 4.00 1.80 .50
Philadelphia Eagles
☐ 127 Ollie Matson .......................... 15.00 6.75 1.90
Chicago Cardinals
☐ 128 Preston Carpenter ................. 3.00 1.35 .40
Cleveland Browns
☐ 129 George Blanda ...................... 32.00 14.50 4.00
Chicago Bears
☐ 130 Gordon Soltau ....................... 3.00 1.35 .40
San Francisco 49ers
☐ 131 Dick Nolan ............................ 4.00 1.80 .50
Chicago Cardinals
☐ 132 Don Bosseler ......................... 16.00 3.20 .95
Washington Redskins
☐ NNO Free Felt Initial .................... 12.00 5.50 1.50

# 1959 Topps

ALEX KARRAS
DEF. TACKLE    DETROIT LIONS

103 ALEX KARRAS
DEFENSIVE TACKLE • DETROIT LIONS

RUB EDGE OF COIN OVER THIS
SPACE FOR MAGIC ANSWER

The 1959 Topps football set contains 176 cards which were issued in two series. The cards measure 2 1/2" by 3 1/2". Card backs include a scratch-off quiz. Team cards (with checklist backs) as well as team pennant cards are included in the set. The card backs were printed in gray on white card stock. Statistical information from the immediate past season and career totals are given on the reverse. The key Rookie Cards in this set are Sam Huff, Alex Karras, Jerry Kramer, Bobby Mitchell, Jim Parker, and Jim Taylor (although his card does not picture him).

|  | NRMT | VG-E | GOOD |
|---|---|---|---|
| COMPLETE SET (176) .............. | 900.00 | 400.00 | 115.00 |
| COMMON PLAYER (1-88) .......... | 2.50 | 1.15 | .30 |
| COMMON PLAYER (89-176) ....... | 2.00 | .90 | .25 |

☐ 1 Johnny Unitas ...................... 100.00 30.00 10.00
Baltimore Colts
☐ 2 Gene Brito .......................... 3.00 1.35 .40
Los Angeles Rams
☐ 3 Detroit Lions ...................... 5.00 1.25 .40
Team Card
(checklist back)
☐ 4 Max McGee .......................... 9.00 4.00 1.15
Green Bay Packers
☐ 5 Hugh McElhenny ................. 12.00 5.50 1.50
San Francisco 49ers
☐ 6 Joe Schmidt ........................ 7.50 3.40 .95

Detroit Lions
☐ 7 Kyle Rote ............................ 5.00 2.30 .60
New York Giants
☐ 8 Clarence Peaks ................... 2.50 1.15 .30
Philadelphia Eagles
☐ 9 Pittsburgh Steelers ............. 3.00 1.35 .40
Pennant Card
☐ 10 Jim Brown ........................... 125.00 57.50 15.50
Cleveland Browns
☐ 11 Ray Mathews ....................... 2.50 1.15 .30
Pittsburgh Steelers
☐ 12 Bobby Dillon ........................ 3.00 1.35 .40
Green Bay Packers
☐ 13 Joe Childress ...................... 2.50 1.15 .30
Chicago Cardinals
☐ 14 Terry Barr ........................... 2.50 1.15 .30
Detroit Lions
☐ 15 Del Shofner ......................... 5.00 2.30 .60
Los Angeles Rams
☐ 16 Bob Pellegrini UER .............. 2.50 1.15 .30
(Misspelled Pellagrini
on card back)
Philadelphia Eagles
☐ 17 Baltimore Colts ................... 5.00 1.25 .40
Team Card
(checklist back)
☐ 18 Preston Carpenter ............... 2.50 1.15 .30
Cleveland Browns
☐ 19 Leo Nomellini ...................... 7.50 3.40 .95
San Francisco 49ers
☐ 20 Frank Gifford ...................... 50.00 23.00 6.25
New York Giants
☐ 21 Charlie Ane ......................... 3.00 1.35 .40
Detroit Lions
☐ 22 Jack Butler .......................... 2.50 1.15 .30
Pittsburgh Steelers
☐ 23 Bart Starr ........................... 50.00 23.00 6.25
Green Bay Packers
☐ 24 Chicago Cardinals ............... 3.00 1.35 .40
Pennant Card
☐ 25 Bill Barnes .......................... 2.50 1.15 .30
Philadelphia Eagles
☐ 26 Walt Michaels ...................... 3.00 1.35 .40
Cleveland Browns
☐ 27 Clyde Conner UER ............... 2.50 1.15 .30
(Misspelled Connor
on card back)
San Francisco 49ers
☐ 28 Paige Cothren ..................... 2.50 1.15 .30
Los Angeles Rams
☐ 29 Roosevelt Grier ................... 6.00 2.70 .75
New York Giants
☐ 30 Alan Ameche ....................... 5.00 2.30 .60
Baltimore Colts
☐ 31 Philadelphia Eagles ............ 5.00 1.25 .40
Team Card
(checklist back)
☐ 32 Dick Nolan .......................... 3.00 1.35 .40
Chicago Cardinals
☐ 33 R.C. Owens .......................... 3.00 1.35 .40
San Francisco 49ers
☐ 34 Dale Dodrill ......................... 2.50 1.15 .30
Pittsburgh Steelers
☐ 35 Gene Gedman ...................... 2.50 1.15 .30
Detroit Lions
☐ 36 Gene Lipscomb .................... 8.00 3.60 1.00
Baltimore Colts
☐ 37 Ray Renfro .......................... 3.00 1.35 .40
Cleveland Browns
☐ 38 Cleveland Browns ................ 3.00 1.35 .40
Pennant Card
☐ 39 Bill Forester ........................ 3.00 1.35 .40
Green Bay Packers
☐ 40 Bobby Layne ........................ 25.00 11.50 3.10
Pittsburgh Steelers
☐ 41 Pat Summerall ..................... 9.00 4.00 1.15
New York Giants
☐ 42 Jerry Mertens ...................... 2.50 1.15 .30
San Francisco 49ers
☐ 43 Steve Myhra ......................... 2.50 1.15 .30
Baltimore Colts
☐ 44 John Henry Johnson .............. 8.00 3.60 1.00
Detroit Lions
☐ 45 Woodley Lewis UER .............. 2.50 1.15 .30
Chicago Cardinals
(misspelled Woody)
☐ 46 Green Bay Packers ............... 5.00 1.25 .40
Team Card
(checklist back)
☐ 47 Don Owens UER .................... 2.50 1.15 .30
(Def. Tackle on front,
Linebacker on back)
Philadelphia Eagles
☐ 48 Ed Beatty ............................ 2.50 1.15 .30
Pittsburgh Steelers
☐ 49 Don Chandler ....................... 3.00 1.35 .40
New York Giants
☐ 50 Ollie Matson ........................ 12.00 5.50 1.50

| | | | |
|---|---|---|---|
| Los Angeles Rams | | | |
| ☐ 51 Sam Huff | 40.00 | 18.00 | 5.00 |
| New York Giants | | | |
| ☐ 52 Tom Miner | 2.50 | 1.15 | .30 |
| Pittsburgh Steelers | | | |
| ☐ 53 New York Giants | 3.00 | 1.35 | .40 |
| Pennant Card | | | |
| ☐ 54 Kenny Konz | 2.50 | 1.15 | .30 |
| Cleveland Browns | | | |
| ☐ 55 Raymond Berry | 14.00 | 6.25 | 1.75 |
| Baltimore Colts | | | |
| ☐ 56 Howard Ferguson UER | 2.50 | 1.15 | .30 |
| (Misspelled Fergeson | | | |
| on card back) | | | |
| Green Bay Packers | | | |
| ☐ 57 Chuck Ulrich | 2.50 | 1.15 | .30 |
| Chicago Cardinals | | | |
| ☐ 58 Bob St. Clair | 5.00 | 2.30 | .60 |
| San Francisco 49ers | | | |
| ☐ 59 Don Burroughs | 3.00 | 1.35 | .40 |
| Los Angeles Rams | | | |
| ☐ 60 Lou Groza | 12.00 | 5.50 | 1.50 |
| Cleveland Browns | | | |
| ☐ 61 San Francisco 49ers | 5.00 | 1.25 | .40 |
| Team Card | | | |
| (checklist back) | | | |
| ☐ 62 Andy Nelson | 2.50 | 1.15 | .30 |
| Baltimore Colts | | | |
| ☐ 63 Hal Bradley | 2.50 | 1.15 | .30 |
| Philadelphia Eagles | | | |
| ☐ 64 Dave Hanner | 3.00 | 1.35 | .40 |
| Green Bay Packers | | | |
| ☐ 65 Charley Conerly | 12.00 | 5.50 | 1.50 |
| New York Giants | | | |
| ☐ 66 Gene Cronin | 2.50 | 1.15 | .30 |
| Detroit Lions | | | |
| ☐ 67 Duane Putnam | 2.50 | 1.15 | .30 |
| Los Angeles Rams | | | |
| ☐ 68 Baltimore Colts | 3.00 | 1.35 | .40 |
| Pennant Card | | | |
| ☐ 69 Ernie Stautner | 7.50 | 3.40 | .95 |
| Pittsburgh Steelers | | | |
| ☐ 70 Jon Arnett | 3.00 | 1.35 | .40 |
| Los Angeles Rams | | | |
| ☐ 71 Ken Panfil | 2.50 | 1.15 | .30 |
| Chicago Cardinals | | | |
| ☐ 72 Matt Hazeltine | 2.50 | 1.15 | .30 |
| San Francisco 49ers | | | |
| ☐ 73 Harley Sewell | 3.00 | 1.35 | .40 |
| Detroit Lions | | | |
| ☐ 74 Mike McCormack | 6.00 | 2.70 | .75 |
| Cleveland Browns | | | |
| ☐ 75 Jim Ringo | 6.00 | 2.70 | .75 |
| Green Bay Packers | | | |
| ☐ 76 Los Angeles Rams | 5.00 | 1.25 | .40 |
| Team Card | | | |
| (checklist back) | | | |
| ☐ 77 Bob Gain | 3.00 | 1.35 | .40 |
| Cleveland Browns | | | |
| ☐ 78 Buzz Nutter | 2.50 | 1.15 | .30 |
| Baltimore Colts | | | |
| ☐ 79 Jerry Norton | 2.50 | 1.15 | .30 |
| Philadelphia Eagles | | | |
| ☐ 80 Joe Perry | 12.00 | 5.50 | 1.50 |
| San Francisco 49ers | | | |
| ☐ 81 Carl Brettschneider | 2.50 | 1.15 | .30 |
| Chicago Cardinals | | | |
| ☐ 82 Paul Hornung | 60.00 | 27.00 | 7.50 |
| Green Bay Packers | | | |
| ☐ 83 Philadelphia Eagles | 3.00 | 1.35 | .40 |
| Pennant Card | | | |
| ☐ 84 Les Richter | 3.00 | 1.35 | .40 |
| Los Angeles Rams | | | |
| ☐ 85 Howard Cassady | 3.00 | 1.35 | .40 |
| ("Hopalong") | | | |
| Detroit Lions | | | |
| ☐ 86 Art Donovan | 8.00 | 3.60 | 1.00 |
| Baltimore Colts | | | |
| ☐ 87 Jim Patton | 3.00 | 1.35 | .40 |
| New York Giants | | | |
| ☐ 88 Pete Retzlaff | 3.00 | 1.35 | .40 |
| Philadelphia Eagles | | | |
| ☐ 89 Jim Mutscheller | 2.00 | .90 | .25 |
| Baltimore Colts | | | |
| ☐ 90 Zeke Bratkowski | 3.00 | 1.35 | .40 |
| Chicago Bears | | | |
| ☐ 91 Washington Redskins | 5.00 | 1.25 | .40 |
| Team Card | | | |
| (Checklist back) | | | |
| ☐ 92 Art Hunter | 2.00 | .90 | .25 |
| Cleveland Browns | | | |
| ☐ 93 Gern Nagler | 2.00 | .90 | .25 |
| Chicago Cardinals | | | |
| ☐ 94 Chuck Weber | 2.00 | .90 | .25 |
| Philadelphia Eagles | | | |
| ☐ 95 Lew Carpenter | 3.00 | 1.35 | .40 |
| Green Bay Packers | | | |
| ☐ 96 Stan Jones | 6.00 | 2.70 | .75 |
| Chicago Bears | | | |
| ☐ 97 Ralph Guglielmi UER | 2.50 | 1.15 | .30 |
| Washington Redskins | | | |
| (Misspelled Gugliemi | | | |
| on card front) | | | |
| ☐ 98 Green Bay Packers | 2.50 | 1.15 | .30 |
| Pennant Card | | | |
| ☐ 99 Ray Wietecha | 2.00 | .90 | .25 |
| New York Giants | | | |
| ☐ 100 Lenny Moore | 12.00 | 5.50 | 1.50 |
| Baltimore Colts | | | |
| ☐ 101 Jim Ray Smith UER | 3.00 | 1.35 | .40 |
| Cleveland Browns | | | |
| (Lions logo on front) | | | |
| ☐ 102 Abe Woodson | 4.00 | 1.80 | .50 |
| San Francisco 49ers | | | |
| ☐ 103 Alex Karras | 50.00 | 23.00 | 6.25 |
| Detroit Lions | | | |
| ☐ 104 Chicago Bears | 5.00 | 1.25 | .40 |
| Team Card | | | |
| (checklist back) | | | |
| ☐ 105 John David Crow | 10.00 | 4.50 | 1.25 |
| Chicago Cardinals | | | |
| ☐ 106 Joe Fortunato | 4.00 | 1.80 | .50 |
| Chicago Bears | | | |
| ☐ 107 Babe Parilli | 3.00 | 1.35 | .40 |
| Green Bay Packers | | | |
| ☐ 108 Proverb Jacobs | 2.00 | .90 | .25 |
| Philadelphia Eagles | | | |
| ☐ 109 Gino Marchetti | 7.00 | 3.10 | .85 |
| Baltimore Colts | | | |
| ☐ 110 Bill Wade | 2.50 | 1.15 | .30 |
| Los Angeles Rams | | | |
| ☐ 111 San Francisco 49ers | 2.50 | 1.15 | .30 |
| Pennant Card | | | |
| ☐ 112 Karl Rubke | 2.00 | .90 | .25 |
| San Francisco 49ers | | | |
| ☐ 113 Dave Middleton UER | 2.00 | .90 | .25 |
| Detroit Lions | | | |
| (Browns logo in | | | |
| upper left corner) | | | |
| ☐ 114 Roosevelt Brown | 6.00 | 2.70 | .75 |
| New York Giants | | | |
| ☐ 115 John Olszewski | 2.00 | .90 | .25 |
| Washington Redskins | | | |
| ☐ 116 Jerry Kramer | 25.00 | 11.50 | 3.10 |
| Green Bay Packers | | | |
| ☐ 117 King Hill | 3.50 | 1.55 | .45 |
| Chicago Cardinals | | | |
| ☐ 118 Chicago Cardinals | 5.00 | 1.25 | .40 |
| Team Card | | | |
| (Checklist back) | | | |
| ☐ 119 Frank Varrichione | 2.00 | .90 | .25 |
| Pittsburgh Steelers | | | |
| ☐ 120 Rick Casares | 2.50 | 1.15 | .30 |
| Chicago Bears | | | |
| ☐ 121 George Strugar | 2.00 | .90 | .25 |
| Los Angeles Rams | | | |
| ☐ 122 Bill Glass UER | 2.50 | 1.15 | .30 |
| (Center on front, | | | |
| tackle on back) | | | |
| Detroit Lions | | | |
| ☐ 123 Don Bosseler | 2.00 | .90 | .25 |
| Washington Redskins | | | |
| ☐ 124 John Reger | 2.00 | .90 | .25 |
| Pittsburgh Steelers | | | |
| ☐ 125 Jim Ninowski | 3.00 | 1.35 | .40 |
| Cleveland Browns | | | |
| ☐ 126 Los Angeles Rams | 2.50 | 1.15 | .30 |
| Pennant Card | | | |
| ☐ 127 Willard Sherman | 2.00 | .90 | .25 |
| Los Angeles Rams | | | |
| ☐ 128 Bob Schnelker | 2.00 | .90 | .25 |
| New York Giants | | | |
| ☐ 129 Ollie Spencer | 2.50 | 1.15 | .30 |
| Green Bay Packers | | | |
| ☐ 130 Y.A. Tittle | 25.00 | 11.50 | 3.10 |
| San Francisco 49ers | | | |
| ☐ 131 Yale Lary | 6.00 | 2.70 | .75 |
| Detroit Lions | | | |
| ☐ 132 Jim Parker | 25.00 | 11.50 | 3.10 |
| Baltimore Colts | | | |
| ☐ 133 New York Giants | 5.00 | 1.25 | .40 |
| Team Card | | | |
| (Checklist back) | | | |
| ☐ 134 Jim Schrader | 2.00 | .90 | .25 |
| Washington Redskins | | | |
| ☐ 135 M.C. Reynolds | 2.00 | .90 | .25 |
| Chicago Cardinals | | | |
| ☐ 136 Mike Sandusky | 2.00 | .90 | .25 |
| Pittsburgh Steelers | | | |
| ☐ 137 Ed Brown | 2.50 | 1.15 | .30 |
| Chicago Bears | | | |
| ☐ 138 Al Barry | 2.00 | .90 | .25 |
| New York Giants | | | |
| ☐ 139 Detroit Lions | 2.50 | 1.15 | .30 |
| Pennant Card | | | |
| ☐ 140 Bobby Mitchell | 40.00 | 18.00 | 5.00 |

| | | | | |
|---|---|---|---|---|
| Cleveland Browns | | | | |
| ☐ 141 Larry Morris | 2.00 | .90 | .25 | |
| Washington Redskins | | | | |
| ☐ 142 Jim Phillips | 3.00 | 1.35 | .40 | |
| Los Angeles Rams | | | | |
| ☐ 143 Jim David | 2.00 | .90 | .25 | |
| Detroit Lions | | | | |
| ☐ 144 Joe Krupa | 2.00 | .90 | .25 | |
| Pittsburgh Steelers | | | | |
| ☐ 145 Willie Galimore | 4.00 | 1.80 | .50 | |
| Chicago Bears | | | | |
| ☐ 146 Pittsburgh Steelers | 5.00 | 1.25 | .40 | |
| Team Card (Checklist back) | | | | |
| ☐ 147 Andy Robustelli | 7.00 | 3.10 | .85 | |
| New York Giants | | | | |
| ☐ 148 Billy Wilson | 2.50 | 1.15 | .30 | |
| San Francisco 49ers | | | | |
| ● ☐ 149 Leo Sanford | 2.00 | .90 | .25 | |
| Baltimore Colts | | | | |
| ☐ 150 Eddie LeBaron | 4.00 | 1.80 | .50 | |
| Washington Redskins | | | | |
| ☐ 151 Bill McColl | 2.00 | .90 | .25 | |
| Chicago Bears | | | | |
| ☐ 152 Buck Lansford UER | 2.00 | .90 | .25 | |
| (Tackle on front, guard on back) Los Angeles Rams | | | | |
| ☐ 153 Chicago Bears | 2.50 | 1.15 | .30 | |
| Pennant Card | | | | |
| ☐ 154 Leo Sugar | 2.00 | .90 | .25 | |
| Chicago Cardinals | | | | |
| ☐ 155 Jim Taylor UER | 18.00 | 8.00 | 2.30 | |
| (Photo actually other Jim Taylor, Cardinal LB) Green Bay Packers | | | | |
| ☐ 156 Lindon Crow | 2.00 | .90 | .25 | |
| New York Giants | | | | |
| ☐ 157 Jack McClairen | 2.00 | .90 | .25 | |
| Pittsburgh Steelers | | | | |
| ☐ 158 Vince Costello UER | 2.50 | 1.15 | .30 | |
| (Linebacker on front, Guard on back) Cleveland Browns | | | | |
| ● ☐ 159 Stan Wallace | 2.00 | .90 | .25 | |
| Chicago Bears | | | | |
| ☐ 160 Mel Triplett | 3.00 | 1.35 | .40 | |
| New York Giants | | | | |
| ☐ 161 Cleveland Browns | 5.00 | 1.25 | .40 | |
| Team Card (Checklist back) | | | | |
| ☐ 162 Dan Currie | 2.50 | 1.15 | .30 | |
| Green Bay Packers | | | | |
| ☐ 163 L.G. Dupre UER | 2.50 | 1.15 | .30 | |
| (Misspelled DuPre on back) Baltimore Colts | | | | |
| ☐ 164 John Morrow UER | 2.00 | .90 | .25 | |
| (Center on front, Linebacker on back) Los Angeles Rams | | | | |
| ☐ 165 Jim Podoley | 2.00 | .90 | .25 | |
| Washington Redskins | | | | |
| ☐ 166 Bruce Bosley | 2.50 | 1.15 | .30 | |
| San Francisco 49ers | | | | |
| ☐ 167 Harlon Hill | 2.50 | 1.15 | .30 | |
| Chicago Bears | | | | |
| ☐ 168 Washington Redskins | 2.50 | 1.15 | .30 | |
| Pennant Card | | | | |
| ☐ 169 Junior Wren | 2.00 | .90 | .25 | |
| Cleveland Browns | | | | |
| ☐ 170 Tobin Rote | 3.00 | 1.35 | .40 | |
| Detroit Lions | | | | |
| ☐ 171 Art Spinney | 2.00 | .90 | .25 | |
| Baltimore Colts | | | | |
| ☐ 172 Chuck Drazenovich UER | 2.00 | .90 | .25 | |
| (Linebacker on front, Defensive Back on back) Washington Redskins | | | | |
| ☐ 173 Bobby Joe Conrad | 4.00 | 1.80 | .50 | |
| Chicago Cardinals | | | | |
| ☐ 174 Jesse Richardson | 2.00 | .90 | .25 | |
| Philadelphia Eagles | | | | |
| ☐ 175 Sam Baker | 2.50 | 1.15 | .30 | |
| Washington Redskins | | | | |
| ☐ 176 Tom Tracy | 8.00 | 1.60 | .50 | |
| Pittsburgh Steelers | | | | |

# 1960 Topps

The 1960 Topps football set contains 132 cards, each measuring 2 1/2" by 3 1/2". The card backs are printed in green on white card stock. Statistical information from the immediate past season and career totals are given on the reverse. The set marks the debut of the Dallas

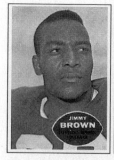

Cowboys into the National Football League. The backs feature a "Football Funnies" scratch-off quiz; answer was revealed by rubbing with an edge of a coin. The team cards feature numerical checklist backs. The (67-132) checklists all misspell 124 Don Bossler as Bosseler and 39 Doyle Nix is the only full name to appear on the checklists. The cards are numbered in team order, for example: Baltimore Colts (1-11), Chicago Bears (12-21), Cleveland Browns (22-31), Dallas Cowboys (32-40), Detroit Lions (41-50), Green Bay Packers (51-60), Los Angeles Rams (61-71), New York Giants (72-82), Philadelphia Eagles (83-92), Pittsburgh Steelers (93-102), St. Louis Cardinals (103-112), San Francisco 49ers (113-122), and Washington Redskins (123-132). The set marks the first apprearance of the St. Louis Cardinals after their move from Chicago. The key Rookie Card in this set is Forrest Gregg.

| | NRMT | VG-E | GOOD |
|---|---|---|---|
| COMPLETE SET (132) | 650.00 | 300.00 | 80.00 |
| COMMON PLAYER (1-132) | 2.00 | .90 | .25 |
| ☐ 1 John Unitas | 90.00 | 27.00 | 9.00 |
| ☐ 2 Alan Ameche | 5.00 | 2.30 | .60 |
| ☐ 3 Lenny Moore | 7.50 | 3.40 | .95 |
| ☐ 4 Raymond Berry | 8.00 | 3.60 | 1.00 |
| ☐ 5 Jim Parker | 7.50 | 3.40 | .95 |
| ☐ 6 George Preas | 2.00 | .90 | .25 |
| ☐ 7 Art Spinney | 2.00 | .90 | .25 |
| ☐ 8 Bill Pellington | 2.50 | 1.15 | .30 |
| ☐ 9 John Sample | 2.50 | 1.15 | .30 |
| ☐ 10 Gene Lipscomb UER (Def. Tackle on front, Tackle on back) | 3.00 | 1.35 | .40 |
| ☐ 11 Baltimore Colts Team Card (Checklist 67-132) | 5.00 | 1.25 | .40 |
| ☐ 12 Ed Brown | 2.50 | 1.15 | .30 |
| ☐ 13 Rick Casares | 2.50 | 1.15 | .30 |
| ☐ 14 Willie Galimore | 2.50 | 1.15 | .30 |
| ☐ 15 Jim Dooley | 2.50 | 1.15 | .30 |
| ☐ 16 Harlon Hill UER (Lifetime yards and Avg. gain incorrect) | 2.50 | 1.15 | .30 |
| ☐ 17 Stan Jones UER (Defensive ... All-Star Team, should be Offensive) | 4.00 | 1.80 | .50 |
| ☐ 18 Bill George | 4.00 | 1.80 | .50 |
| ☐ 19 Erich Barnes | 3.00 | 1.35 | .40 |
| ☐ 20 Doug Atkins UER (reversed negative) | 5.00 | 2.30 | .60 |
| ☐ 21 Chicago Bears Team Card (Checklist 1-66) | 5.00 | 1.25 | .40 |
| ☐ 22 Milt Plum | 2.50 | 1.15 | .30 |
| ☐ 23 Jim Brown | 80.00 | 36.00 | 10.00 |
| ☐ 24 Sam Baker | 2.50 | 1.15 | .30 |
| ☐ 25 Bobby Mitchell | 14.00 | 6.25 | 1.75 |
| ☐ 26 Ray Renfro | 2.50 | 1.15 | .30 |
| ☐ 27 Bill Howton | 2.50 | 1.15 | .30 |
| ☐ 28 Jim Ray Smith | 2.50 | 1.15 | .30 |
| ☐ 29 Jim Shofner | 3.50 | 1.55 | .45 |
| ☐ 30 Bob Gain | 2.00 | .90 | .25 |
| ☐ 31 Cleveland Browns Team Card (Checklist 1-66) | 5.00 | 1.25 | .40 |
| ☐ 32 Don Heinrich | 2.50 | 1.15 | .30 |
| ☐ 33 Ed Modzelewski UER (Lifetime yards and Avg. gain incorrect) | 2.50 | 1.15 | .30 |
| ☐ 34 Fred Cone | 2.50 | 1.15 | .30 |
| ☐ 35 L.G. Dupre | 2.50 | 1.15 | .30 |
| ☐ 36 Dick Bielski | 2.50 | 1.15 | .30 |
| ☐ 37 Charlie Ane UER (Misspelled Charley) | 2.50 | 1.15 | .30 |
| ☐ 38 Jerry Tubbs | 2.50 | 1.15 | .30 |
| ☐ 39 Doyle Nix | 2.50 | 1.15 | .30 |

| | | | |
|---|---|---|---|
| ☐ 40 Ray Krouse | 2.50 | 1.15 | .30 |
| ☐ 41 Earl Morrall | 5.00 | 2.30 | .60 |
| ☐ 42 Howard Cassady | 2.50 | 1.15 | .30 |
| ☐ 43 Dave Middleton | 2.00 | .90 | .25 |
| ☐ 44 Jim Gibbons | 2.50 | 1.15 | .30 |
| ☐ 45 Darris McCord | 2.00 | .90 | .25 |
| ☐ 46 Joe Schmidt | 6.00 | 2.70 | .75 |
| ☐ 47 Terry Barr | 2.00 | .90 | .25 |
| ☐ 48 Yale Lary UER | 5.00 | 2.30 | .60 |
| (Def.back on front, halfback on back) | | | |
| ☐ 49 Gil Mains | 2.00 | .90 | .25 |
| ☐ 50 Detroit Lions | 5.00 | 1.25 | .40 |
| Team Card (Checklist 1-66) | | | |
| ☐ 51 Bart Starr | 35.00 | 16.00 | 4.40 |
| ☐ 52 Jim Taylor UER | 8.00 | 3.60 | 1.00 |
| (photo actually Jim Taylor, Cardinal LB) | | | |
| ☐ 53 Lew Carpenter | 2.00 | .90 | .25 |
| ☐ 54 Paul Hornung UER | 30.00 | 13.50 | 3.80 |
| (Halfback on front, fullback on back) | | | |
| ☐ 55 Max McGee | 3.00 | 1.35 | .40 |
| ☐ 56 Forrest Gregg | 30.00 | 13.50 | 3.80 |
| ☐ 57 Jim Ringo | 4.00 | 1.80 | .50 |
| ☐ 58 Bill Forester | 2.00 | .90 | .25 |
| ☐ 59 Dave Hanner | 2.00 | .90 | .25 |
| ☐ 60 Green Bay Packers | 5.00 | 1.25 | .40 |
| Team Card (Checklist 67-132) | | | |
| ☐ 61 Bill Wade | 2.50 | 1.15 | .30 |
| ☐ 62 Frank Ryan | 7.00 | 3.10 | .85 |
| ☐ 63 Ollie Matson | 7.50 | 3.40 | .95 |
| ☐ 64 Jon Arnett | 2.50 | 1.15 | .30 |
| ☐ 65 Del Shofner | 2.50 | 1.15 | .30 |
| ☐ 66 Jim Phillips | 2.50 | 1.15 | .30 |
| ☐ 67 Art Hunter | 2.00 | .90 | .25 |
| ☐ 68 Les Richter | 2.50 | 1.15 | .30 |
| ☐ 69 Lou Michaels | 3.00 | 1.35 | .40 |
| ☐ 70 John Baker | 2.00 | .90 | .25 |
| ☐ 71 Los Angeles Rams | 5.00 | 1.25 | .40 |
| Team Card (Checklist 1-66) | | | |
| ☐ 72 Charley Conerly | 10.00 | 4.50 | 1.25 |
| ☐ 73 Mel Triplett | 2.00 | .90 | .25 |
| ☐ 74 Frank Gifford | 45.00 | 20.00 | 5.75 |
| ☐ 75 Alex Webster | 2.00 | .90 | .25 |
| ☐ 76 Bob Schnelker | 2.00 | .90 | .25 |
| ☐ 77 Pat Summerall | 7.00 | 3.10 | .85 |
| ☐ 78 Roosevelt Brown | 5.00 | 2.30 | .60 |
| ☐ 79 Jim Patton | 2.50 | 1.15 | .30 |
| ☐ 80 Sam Huff UER | 14.00 | 6.25 | 1.75 |
| (Def.tackle on front, linebacker on back) | | | |
| ☐ 81 Andy Robustelli | 6.00 | 2.70 | .75 |
| ☐ 82 New York Giants | 5.00 | 1.25 | .40 |
| Team Card (Checklist 1-66) | | | |
| ☐ 83 Clarence Peaks | 2.50 | 1.15 | .30 |
| ☐ 84 Bill Barnes | 2.00 | .90 | .25 |
| ☐ 85 Pete Retzlaff | 2.50 | 1.15 | .30 |
| ☐ 86 Bobby Walston | 2.50 | 1.15 | .30 |
| ☐ 87 Chuck Bednarik UER | 7.00 | 3.10 | .85 |
| (Misspelled Bednarick on both sides of card) | | | |
| ☐ 88 Bob Pellegrini | 2.00 | .90 | .25 |
| (Misspelled Pellagrini on both sides) | | | |
| ☐ 89 Tom Brookshier | 5.00 | 2.30 | .60 |
| ☐ 90 Marion Campbell | 2.50 | 1.15 | .30 |
| ☐ 91 Jesse Richardson | 2.00 | .90 | .25 |
| ☐ 92 Philadelphia Eagles | 5.00 | 1.25 | .40 |
| Team Card (Checklist 1-66) | | | |
| ☐ 93 Bobby Layne | 22.00 | 10.00 | 2.80 |
| ☐ 94 John Henry Johnson | 6.00 | 2.70 | .75 |
| ☐ 95 Tom Tracy UER | 2.50 | 1.15 | .30 |
| (Halfback on front, fullback on back) | | | |
| ☐ 96 Preston Carpenter | 2.00 | .90 | .25 |
| ☐ 97 Frank Varrichione UER | 2.00 | .90 | .25 |
| (Reversed negative) | | | |
| ☐ 98 John Nisby | 2.00 | .90 | .25 |
| ☐ 99 Dean Derby | 2.00 | .90 | .25 |
| ☐ 100 George Tarasovic | 2.00 | .90 | .25 |
| ☐ 101 Ernie Stautner | 5.00 | 2.30 | .60 |
| ☐ 102 Pittsburgh Steelers | 5.00 | 1.25 | .40 |
| Team Card (Checklist 67-132) | | | |
| ☐ 103 King Hill | 2.50 | 1.15 | .30 |
| ☐ 104 Mal Hammack | 2.00 | .90 | .25 |
| ☐ 105 John David Crow | 4.00 | 1.80 | .50 |
| ☐ 106 Bobby Joe Conrad | 2.50 | 1.15 | .30 |
| ☐ 107 Woodley Lewis | 2.00 | .90 | .25 |
| ☐ 108 Don Gillis | 2.00 | .90 | .25 |

| | | | |
|---|---|---|---|
| ☐ 109 Carl Brettschneider | 2.00 | .90 | .25 |
| ☐ 110 Leo Sugar | 2.00 | .90 | .25 |
| ☐ 111 Frank Fuller | 2.00 | .90 | .25 |
| ☐ 112 St. Louis Cardinals | 5.00 | 1.25 | .40 |
| Team Card (Checklist 67-132) | | | |
| ☐ 113 Y.A. Tittle | 22.00 | 10.00 | 2.80 |
| ☐ 114 Joe Perry | 7.50 | 3.40 | .95 |
| ☐ 115 J.D. Smith | 3.00 | 1.35 | .40 |
| ☐ 116 Hugh McElhenny | 7.50 | 3.40 | .95 |
| ☐ 117 Billy Wilson | 2.50 | 1.15 | .30 |
| ☐ 118 Bob St. Clair | 4.00 | 1.80 | .50 |
| ☐ 119 Matt Hazeltine | 2.00 | .90 | .25 |
| ☐ 120 Abe Woodson | 2.50 | 1.15 | .30 |
| ☐ 121 Leo Nomellini | 5.00 | 2.30 | .60 |
| ☐ 122 San Francisco 49ers | 5.00 | 1.25 | .40 |
| Team Card (Checklist 67-132) | | | |
| ☐ 123 Ralph Guglielmi UER | 2.50 | 1.15 | .30 |
| (Misspelled Gugliemi on card front) | | | |
| ☐ 124 Don Bosseler | 2.00 | .90 | .25 |
| ☐ 125 John Olszewski | 2.00 | .90 | .25 |
| ☐ 126 Bill Anderson UER | 2.00 | .90 | .25 |
| (Walt on back) | | | |
| ☐ 127 Joe Walton | 3.50 | 1.55 | .45 |
| ☐ 128 Jim Schrader | 2.00 | .90 | .25 |
| ☐ 129 Ralph Felton | 2.00 | .90 | .25 |
| ☐ 130 Gary Glick | 2.00 | .90 | .25 |
| ☐ 131 Bob Toneff | 2.00 | .90 | .25 |
| ☐ 132 Washington Redskins | 24.00 | 6.00 | 1.90 |
| Team Card (Checklist 67-132) | | | |

## 1960 Topps Metallic Inserts

This set of 33 metallic team emblem stickers was inserted with the 1960 Topps regular issue football set. The stickers are unnumbered and are ordered below alphabetically within type. NFL teams are listed first (1-13) followed by college teams (14-33). The stickers measure approximately 2 1/8" by 3 1/16". The sticker fronts are either silver, gold, or blue with a black border.

| | NRMT | VG-E | GOOD |
|---|---|---|---|
| COMPLETE SET (33) | 350.00 | 140.00 | 35.00 |
| COMMON CARD (1-13) | 15.00 | 6.00 | 1.50 |
| COMMON CARD (14-33) | 10.00 | 4.00 | 1.00 |
| ☐ 1 Baltimore Colts | 15.00 | 6.00 | 1.50 |
| ☐ 2 Chicago Bears | 18.00 | 7.25 | 1.80 |
| ☐ 3 Cleveland Browns | 15.00 | 6.00 | 1.50 |
| ☐ 4 Dallas Cowboys | 20.00 | 8.00 | 2.00 |
| ☐ 5 Detroit Lions | 15.00 | 6.00 | 1.50 |
| ☐ 6 Green Bay Packers | 15.00 | 6.00 | 1.50 |
| ☐ 7 Los Angeles Rams | 15.00 | 6.00 | 1.50 |
| ☐ 8 New York Giants | 18.00 | 7.25 | 1.80 |
| ☐ 9 Philadelphia Eagles | 15.00 | 6.00 | 1.50 |
| ☐ 10 Pittsburgh Steelers | 15.00 | 6.00 | 1.50 |
| ☐ 11 St. Louis Cardinals | 15.00 | 6.00 | 1.50 |
| ☐ 12 San Francisco 49ers | 15.00 | 6.00 | 1.50 |
| ☐ 13 Washington Redskins | 18.00 | 7.25 | 1.80 |
| ☐ 14 Air Force Academy | 10.00 | 4.00 | 1.00 |
| ☐ 15 Army | 15.00 | 6.00 | 1.50 |
| ☐ 16 California Golden Bears | 10.00 | 4.00 | 1.00 |
| ☐ 17 Dartmouth | 10.00 | 4.00 | 1.00 |
| ☐ 18 Duke Blue Devils | 12.00 | 5.00 | 1.20 |
| ☐ 19 LSU | 15.00 | 6.00 | 1.50 |
| ☐ 20 Michigan Wolverines | 20.00 | 8.00 | 2.00 |
| ☐ 21 Minnesota | 12.00 | 5.00 | 1.20 |
| ☐ 22 Mississippi Rebels | 10.00 | 4.00 | 1.00 |
| ☐ 23 Navy | 12.00 | 5.00 | 1.20 |
| ☐ 24 Notre Dame | 30.00 | 12.00 | 3.00 |
| ☐ 25 SMU Mustangs | 10.00 | 4.00 | 1.00 |

| | | | |
|---|---|---|---|
| ☐ 26 Southern California | 12.00 | 5.00 | 1.20 |
| ☐ 27 Syracuse Orange Men | 10.00 | 4.00 | 1.00 |
| ☐ 28 Tennessee Volunteers | 15.00 | 6.00 | 1.50 |
| ☐ 29 Texas Longhorns | 15.00 | 6.00 | 1.50 |
| ☐ 30 UCLA Bruins | 12.00 | 5.00 | 1.20 |
| ☐ 31 Washington Huskies | 12.00 | 5.00 | 1.20 |
| ☐ 32 Wisconsin Badgers | 10.00 | 4.00 | 1.00 |
| ☐ 33 Yale | 10.00 | 4.00 | 1.00 |

# 1961 Topps

ANDY ROBUSTELLI
DEFENSIVE END — NEW YORK GIANTS

The 1961 Topps football set of 198 cards contains NFL players (1-132) and AFL players (133-197). The cards measure 2 1/2" by 3 1/2". The fronts are very similar to the Topps 1961 baseball issue. The card backs are printed in light blue on white card stock. Statistical information from the immediate past season and career totals are given on the reverse. A "coin-rub" picture was featured on the right of the reverse. Cards are essentially numbered in team order, i.e., Baltimore Colts (1-9), Chicago Bears (10-18), Dallas Cowboys (19-28), Detroit Lions (29-37), Green Bay Packers (38-47), Los Angeles Rams (48-56), San Francisco 49ers (58-66), Cleveland Browns (68-77), Minnesota Vikings (78-84), New York Giants (85-94), Philadelphia Eagles (95-103), Pittsburgh Steelers (104-113), St. Louis Cardinals (114-121), and Washington Redskins (123-131) in the NFL; and Dallas Texans (133-140), Houston Oilers (141-148), New York Titans (149-156), Buffalo Bills (157-165), Los Angeles Chargers (166-173), Boston Patriots (174-181), Oakland Raiders (182-189), and Denver Broncos (190-197) in the AFL. There are three checklist cards in the set, numbers 67, 122, and 198. The key Rookie Cards in this set are John Brodie, Tom Flores, Don Maynard, and Jim Otto.

| | NRMT | VG-E | GOOD |
|---|---|---|---|
| COMPLETE SET (198) | 1100.00 | 500.00 | 140.00 |
| COMMON PLAYER (1-132) | 2.00 | .90 | .25 |
| COMMON PLAYER (133-198) | 2.50 | 1.15 | .30 |
| | | | |
| ☐ 1 Johnny Unitas | 100.00 | 30.00 | 10.00 |
| ☐ 2 Lenny Moore | 7.00 | 3.10 | .85 |
| ☐ 3 Alan Ameche | 4.00 | 1.80 | .50 |
| ☐ 4 Raymond Berry | 7.50 | 3.40 | .95 |
| ☐ 5 Jim Mutscheller | 2.00 | .90 | .25 |
| ☐ 6 Jim Parker | 5.00 | 2.30 | .60 |
| ☐ 7 Gino Marchetti | 6.00 | 2.70 | .75 |
| ☐ 8 Gene Lipscomb | 2.50 | 1.15 | .30 |
| ☐ 9 Baltimore Colts Team Card | 4.50 | 2.00 | .55 |
| ☐ 10 Bill Wade | 2.50 | 1.15 | .30 |
| ☐ 11 Johnny Morris UER (Years pro and return averages wrong) | 6.00 | 2.70 | .75 |
| ☐ 12 Rick Casares | 2.50 | 1.15 | .30 |
| ☐ 13 Harlon Hill | 2.50 | 1.15 | .30 |
| ☐ 14 Stan Jones | 4.00 | 1.80 | .50 |
| ☐ 15 Doug Atkins | 5.00 | 2.30 | .60 |
| ☐ 16 Bill George | 4.00 | 1.80 | .50 |
| ☐ 17 J.C. Caroline | 2.00 | .90 | .25 |
| ☐ 18 Chicago Bears Team Card | 4.50 | 2.00 | .55 |
| ☐ 19 Big Time Football Comes to Texas (Eddie LeBaron) | 3.00 | 1.35 | .40 |
| ☐ 20 Eddie LeBaron | 3.00 | 1.35 | .40 |
| ☐ 21 Don McIlhenny | 2.50 | 1.15 | .30 |
| ☐ 22 L.G. Dupre | 2.50 | 1.15 | .30 |
| ☐ 23 Jim Doran | 2.50 | 1.15 | .30 |
| ☐ 24 Bill Howton | 2.50 | 1.15 | .30 |
| ☐ 25 Buzz Guy | 2.00 | .90 | .25 |
| ☐ 26 Jack Patera | 2.50 | 1.15 | .30 |
| ☐ 27 Tom Frankhauser | 2.00 | .90 | .25 |
| ☐ 28 Dallas Cowboys Team Card | 7.50 | 3.40 | .95 |

| | | | |
|---|---|---|---|
| ☐ 29 Jim Ninowski | 2.50 | 1.15 | .30 |
| ☐ 30 Dan Lewis | 2.50 | 1.15 | .30 |
| ☐ 31 Nick Pietrosante | 3.50 | 1.55 | .45 |
| ☐ 32 Gail Cogdill | 3.00 | 1.35 | .40 |
| ☐ 33 Jim Gibbons | 2.00 | .90 | .25 |
| ☐ 34 Jim Martin | 2.50 | 1.15 | .30 |
| ☐ 35 Alex Karras | 18.00 | 8.00 | 2.30 |
| ☐ 36 Joe Schmidt | 5.00 | 2.30 | .60 |
| ☐ 37 Detroit Lions Team Card | 4.50 | 2.00 | .55 |
| ☐ 38 Packers' Hornung Sets NFL Scoring Record | 10.00 | 4.50 | 1.25 |
| ☐ 39 Bart Starr | 30.00 | 13.50 | 3.80 |
| ☐ 40 Paul Hornung | 30.00 | 13.50 | 3.80 |
| ☐ 41 Jim Taylor | 25.00 | 11.50 | 3.10 |
| ☐ 42 Max McGee | 2.50 | 1.15 | .30 |
| ☐ 43 Boyd Dowler | 5.00 | 2.30 | .60 |
| ☐ 44 Jim Ringo | 4.00 | 1.80 | .50 |
| ☐ 45 Henry Jordan | 5.00 | 2.30 | .60 |
| ☐ 46 Bill Forester | 2.00 | .90 | .25 |
| ☐ 47 Green Bay Packers Team Card | 4.50 | 2.00 | .55 |
| ☐ 48 Frank Ryan | 3.00 | 1.35 | .40 |
| ☐ 49 Jon Arnett | 2.50 | 1.15 | .30 |
| ☐ 50 Ollie Matson | 7.00 | 3.10 | .85 |
| ☐ 51 Jim Phillips | 2.50 | 1.15 | .30 |
| ☐ 52 Del Shofner | 2.50 | 1.15 | .30 |
| ☐ 53 Art Hunter | 2.00 | .90 | .25 |
| ☐ 54 Gene Brito | 2.50 | 1.15 | .30 |
| ☐ 55 Lindon Crow | 2.00 | .90 | .25 |
| ☐ 56 Los Angeles Rams Team Card | 4.50 | 2.00 | .55 |
| ☐ 57 Colts' Unitas 25 TD Passes | 15.00 | 6.75 | 1.90 |
| ☐ 58 Y.A. Tittle | 22.00 | 10.00 | 2.80 |
| ☐ 59 John Brodie | 50.00 | 23.00 | 6.25 |
| ☐ 60 J.D. Smith | 2.50 | 1.15 | .30 |
| ☐ 61 R.C. Owens | 2.50 | 1.15 | .30 |
| ☐ 62 Clyde Conner | 2.00 | .90 | .25 |
| ☐ 63 Bob St. Clair | 4.00 | 1.80 | .50 |
| ☐ 64 Leo Nomellini | 5.00 | 2.30 | .60 |
| ☐ 65 Abe Woodson | 2.50 | 1.15 | .30 |
| ☐ 66 San Francisco 49ers Team Card | 4.50 | 2.00 | .55 |
| ☐ 67 Checklist Card | 35.00 | 3.50 | .70 |
| ☐ 68 Milt Plum | 2.50 | 1.15 | .30 |
| ☐ 69 Ray Renfro | 2.50 | 1.15 | .30 |
| ☐ 70 Bobby Mitchell | 7.00 | 3.10 | .85 |
| ☐ 71 Jim Brown | 85.00 | 38.00 | 10.50 |
| ☐ 72 Mike McCormack | 4.00 | 1.80 | .50 |
| ☐ 73 Jim Ray Smith | 2.50 | 1.15 | .30 |
| ☐ 74 Sam Baker | 2.50 | 1.15 | .30 |
| ☐ 75 Walt Michaels | 2.50 | 1.15 | .30 |
| ☐ 76 Cleveland Browns Team Card | 4.50 | 2.00 | .55 |
| ☐ 77 Jimmy Brown Gains 1257 Yards | 25.00 | 11.50 | 3.10 |
| ☐ 78 George Shaw | 2.50 | 1.15 | .30 |
| ☐ 79 Hugh McElhenny | 7.50 | 3.40 | .95 |
| ☐ 80 Clancy Osborne | 2.00 | .90 | .25 |
| ☐ 81 Dave Middleton | 2.00 | .90 | .25 |
| ☐ 82 Frank Youso | 2.00 | .90 | .25 |
| ☐ 83 Don Joyce | 2.00 | .90 | .25 |
| ☐ 84 Ed Culpepper | 2.00 | .90 | .25 |
| ☐ 85 Charley Conerly | 8.00 | 3.60 | 1.00 |
| ☐ 86 Mel Triplett | 2.00 | .90 | .25 |
| ☐ 87 Kyle Rote | 4.00 | 1.80 | .50 |
| ☐ 88 Roosevelt Brown | 3.50 | 1.55 | .45 |
| ☐ 89 Ray Wietecha | 2.00 | .90 | .25 |
| ☐ 90 Andy Robustelli | 5.00 | 2.30 | .60 |
| ☐ 91 Sam Huff | 8.00 | 3.60 | 1.00 |
| ☐ 92 Jim Patton | 2.50 | 1.15 | .30 |
| ☐ 93 New York Giants Team Card | 4.50 | 2.00 | .55 |
| ☐ 94 Charley Conerly UER Leads Giants for 13th Year (Misspelled Charlie on card) | 5.00 | 2.30 | .60 |
| ☐ 95 Sonny Jurgensen | 20.00 | 9.00 | 2.50 |
| ☐ 96 Tommy McDonald | 2.50 | 1.15 | .30 |
| ☐ 97 Bill Barnes | 2.00 | .90 | .25 |
| ☐ 98 Bobby Walston | 2.50 | 1.15 | .30 |
| ☐ 99 Pete Retzlaff | 2.50 | 1.15 | .30 |
| ☐ 100 Jim McCusker | 2.00 | .90 | .25 |
| ☐ 101 Chuck Bednarik | 7.00 | 3.10 | .85 |
| ☐ 102 Tom Brookshier | 3.50 | 1.55 | .45 |
| ☐ 103 Philadelphia Eagles Team Card | 4.50 | 2.00 | .55 |
| ☐ 104 Bobby Layne | 22.00 | 10.00 | 2.80 |
| ☐ 105 John Henry Johnson | 6.00 | 2.70 | .75 |
| ☐ 106 Tom Tracy | 2.50 | 1.15 | .30 |
| ☐ 107 Buddy Dial | 3.00 | 1.35 | .40 |
| ☐ 108 Jimmy Orr | 4.50 | 2.00 | .55 |
| ☐ 109 Mike Sandusky | 2.00 | .90 | .25 |
| ☐ 110 John Reger | 2.00 | .90 | .25 |

☐ 111 Junior Wren .................. 2.00 .90 .25
☐ 112 Pittsburgh Steelers .............. 4.50 2.00 .55
    Team Card
☐ 113 Bobby Layne Sets .......... 7.00 3.10 .85
    New Passing Record
☐ 114 John Roach .................. 2.00 .90 .25
☐ 115 Sam Etcheverry .................. 3.00 1.35 .40
☐ 116 John David Crow .................. 3.00 1.35 .40
☐ 117 Mal Hammack .................. 2.00 .90 .25
☐ 118 Sonny Randle .................. 2.50 1.15 .30
☐ 119 Leo Sugar .................. 2.00 .90 .25
☐ 120 Jerry Norton .................. 2.00 .90 .25
☐ 121 St. Louis Cardinals .............. 4.50 2.00 .55
    Team Card
☐ 122 Checklist Card .................. 35.00 3.50 .70
☐ 123 Ralph Guglielmi .................. 2.50 1.15 .30
☐ 124 Dick James .................. 2.00 .90 .25
☐ 125 Don Bosseler .................. 2.00 .90 .25
☐ 126 Joe Walton .................. 2.00 .90 .25
☐ 127 Bill Anderson .................. 2.00 .90 .25
☐ 128 Vince Promuto .................. 2.50 1.15 .30
☐ 129 Bob Toneff .................. 2.00 .90 .25
☐ 130 John Paluck .................. 2.00 .90 .25
☐ 131 Washington Redskins .......... 4.50 2.00 .55
    Team Card
☐ 132 Browns' Plum Wins .............. 3.00 1.35 .40
    NFL Passing Title
☐ 133 Abner Haynes .................. 4.00 1.80 .50
☐ 134 Mel Branch UER .................. 3.00 1.35 .40
    (Def. Tackle on front,
    Def. End on back)
☐ 135 Jerry Cornelison UER .......... 2.50 1.15 .30
    (Misspelled Cornielson)
☐ 136 Bill Krisher .................. 2.50 1.15 .30
☐ 137 Paul Miller .................. 2.50 1.15 .30
☐ 138 Jack Spikes .................. 3.00 1.35 .40
☐ 139 Johnny Robinson .................. 6.00 2.70 .75
☐ 140 Cotton Davidson .................. 4.00 1.80 .50
☐ 141 Dave Smith .................. 2.50 1.15 .30
☐ 142 Bill Groman .................. 3.00 1.35 .40
☐ 143 Rich Michael .................. 2.50 1.15 .30
☐ 144 Mike Dukes .................. 2.50 1.15 .30
☐ 145 George Blanda .................. 25.00 11.50 3.10
☐ 146 Billy Cannon .................. 4.00 1.80 .50
☐ 147 Dennit Morris .................. 2.50 1.15 .30
☐ 148 Jacky Lee UER .................. 3.00 1.35 .40
    (Misspelled Jackie
    on card back)
☐ 149 Al Dorow .................. 2.50 1.15 .30
☐ 150 Don Maynard .................. 50.00 23.00 6.25
☐ 151 Art Powell .................. 6.00 2.70 .75
☐ 152 Sid Youngelman .................. 2.50 1.15 .30
☐ 153 Bob Mischak .................. 2.50 1.15 .30
☐ 154 Larry Grantham .................. 3.00 1.35 .40
☐ 155 Tom Saidock .................. 2.50 1.15 .30
☐ 156 Roger Donnahoo .................. 2.50 1.15 .30
☐ 157 Laverne Torczon .................. 2.50 1.15 .30
☐ 158 Archie Matsos .................. 3.50 1.55 .45
☐ 159 Elbert Dubenion .................. 3.00 1.35 .40
☐ 160 Wray Carlton .................. 3.50 1.55 .45
☐ 161 Rich McCabe .................. 2.50 1.15 .30
☐ 162 Ken Rice .................. 2.50 1.15 .30
☐ 163 Art Baker .................. 2.50 1.15 .30
☐ 164 Tom Rychlec .................. 2.50 1.15 .30
☐ 165 Mack Yoho .................. 2.50 1.15 .30
☐ 166 Jack Kemp .................. 175.00 80.00 22.00
☐ 167 Paul Lowe .................. 4.00 1.80 .50
☐ 168 Ron Mix .................. 9.00 4.00 1.15
☐ 169 Paul Maguire .................. 4.00 1.80 .50
☐ 170 Volney Peters .................. 2.50 1.15 .30
☐ 171 Ernie Wright .................. 2.50 1.15 .30
☐ 172 Ron Nery .................. 2.50 1.15 .30
☐ 173 Dave Kocourek .................. 3.00 1.35 .40
☐ 174 Jim Colclough .................. 2.50 1.15 .30
☐ 175 Babe Parilli .................. 3.00 1.35 .40
☐ 176 Billy Lott .................. 3.00 1.35 .40
☐ 177 Fred Bruney .................. 2.50 1.15 .30
☐ 178 Ross O'Hanley .................. 2.50 1.15 .30
☐ 179 Walt Cudzik .................. 2.50 1.15 .30
☐ 180 Charley Leo .................. 2.50 1.15 .30
☐ 181 Bob Dee .................. 2.50 1.15 .30
☐ 182 Jim Otto .................. 40.00 18.00 5.00
☐ 183 Eddie Macon .................. 2.50 1.15 .30
☐ 184 Dick Christy .................. 2.50 1.15 .30
☐ 185 Alan Miller .................. 2.50 1.15 .30
☐ 186 Tom Flores .................. 25.00 11.50 3.10
☐ 187 Joe Cannavino .................. 2.50 1.15 .30
☐ 188 Don Manoukian .................. 2.50 1.15 .30
☐ 189 Bob Coolbaugh .................. 8.00 3.60 1.00
☐ 190 Lionel Taylor .................. 2.50 1.15 .30
☐ 191 Bud McFadin .................. 4.00 1.80 .50
☐ 192 Goose Gonsoulin .................. 3.00 1.35 .40
☐ 193 Frank Tripucka .................. 4.00 1.80 .50
☐ 194 Gene Mingo .................. 3.00 1.35 .40
☐ 195 Eldon Danenhauer .................. 2.50 1.15 .30
☐ 196 Bob McNamara .................. 2.50 1.15 .30
☐ 197 Dave Rolle UER .................. 2.50 1.15 .30

    (End on front,
    Fullback on back)
☐ 198 Checklist Card UER .............. 90.00 9.50 1.90
    (135 Cornielson)

## 1961 Topps Flocked Stickers

This set of 48 flocked stickers was inserted with the 1961 Topps regular issue football set. The stickers are unnumbered and are ordered below alphabetically within type. NFL teams are listed first (1-15), followed by AFL teams (16-24), and college teams (25-48). The capital letters in the listing below signify the letter on the detachable tab. The stickers measure approximately 2" by 2 3/4" without the letter tab and 2" by 3 3/8" with the letter tab. The prices below are for the stickers with tabs intact; stickers without tabs would be considered VG-E at best. There are letter tab variations on 12 of the stickers as noted by the double letters below. The complete set price below considers the set complete with the 48 different distinct teams, i.e., not including all 60 different tab combinations.

| | NRMT | VG-E | GOOD |
|---|---|---|---|
| COMPLETE SET (48) .................. | 500.00 | 200.00 | 50.00 |
| COMMON NFL (1-15) .................. | 15.00 | 6.00 | 1.50 |
| COMMON AFL (16-24) .................. | 12.00 | 5.00 | 1.20 |
| COMMON COLLEGE (25-48) .......... | 10.00 | 4.00 | 1.00 |

☐ 1 NFL Emblem N .................. 15.00 6.00 1.50
☐ 2 Baltimore Colts U .................. 15.00 6.00 1.50
☐ 3 Chicago Bears H .................. 18.00 7.25 1.80
☐ 4 Cleveland Browns I .................. 15.00 6.00 1.50
☐ 5 Dallas Cowboys K .................. 20.00 8.00 2.00
☐ 6 Detroit Lions E .................. 15.00 6.00 1.50
☐ 7 Green Bay Packers A .................. 15.00 6.00 1.50
☐ 8 Los Angeles Rams M .................. 15.00 6.00 1.50
☐ 9 Minnesota Vikings R .................. 15.00 6.00 1.50
☐ 10 New York Giants D .................. 18.00 7.25 1.80
☐ 11 Philadelphia Eagles O .................. 15.00 6.00 1.50
☐ 12 Pittsburgh Steelers S .................. 15.00 6.00 1.50
☐ 13 San Francisco 49ers P .................. 15.00 6.00 1.50
☐ 14 St. Louis Cardinals L .................. 15.00 6.00 1.50
☐ 15 Washington Redskins J .......... 18.00 7.25 1.80
☐ 16 AFL Emblem A/G .................. 12.00 5.00 1.20
☐ 17 Boston Patriots F/T .................. 12.00 5.00 1.20
☐ 18 Buffalo Bills I/M .................. 15.00 6.00 1.50
☐ 19 Dallas Texans P/R .................. 20.00 8.00 2.00
☐ 20 Denver Broncos G/I .................. 18.00 7.25 1.80
☐ 21 Houston Oilers A/H .................. 15.00 6.00 1.50
☐ 22 Oakland Raiders B/O .................. 25.00 10.00 2.50
☐ 23 San Diego Chargers E/K .......... 12.00 5.00 1.20
☐ 24 New York Titans D/E .................. 15.00 6.00 1.50
☐ 25 Air Force V .................. 10.00 4.00 1.00
☐ 26 Alabama L .................. 15.00 6.00 1.50
☐ 27 Arkansas A .................. 15.00 6.00 1.50
☐ 28 Army G .................. 12.00 5.00 1.20
☐ 29 Baylor E .................. 10.00 4.00 1.00
☐ 30 California T .................. 10.00 4.00 1.00
☐ 31 Georgia Tech F .................. 12.00 5.00 1.20
☐ 32 Illinois C .................. 10.00 4.00 1.00
☐ 33 Kansas J .................. 12.00 5.00 1.20
☐ 34 Kentucky R .................. 10.00 4.00 1.00
☐ 35 Miami H .................. 12.00 5.00 1.20
☐ 36 Michigan W .................. 18.00 7.25 1.80
☐ 37 Missouri B .................. 10.00 4.00 1.00
☐ 38 Navy J/S .................. 10.00 4.00 1.00
☐ 39 Oregon C/N .................. 12.00 5.00 1.20
☐ 40 Penn State Z .................. 10.00 4.00 1.00
☐ 41 Pittsburgh G .................. 10.00 4.00 1.00
☐ 42 Purdue B .................. 10.00 4.00 1.00
☐ 43 Southern California Y .......... 12.00 5.00 1.20
☐ 44 Stanford L/O .................. 10.00 4.00 1.00
☐ 45 TCU C .................. 10.00 4.00 1.00
☐ 46 Virginia S .................. 10.00 4.00 1.00
☐ 47 Washington D .................. 12.00 5.00 1.20
☐ 48 Washington State M .................. 10.00 4.00 1.00

# 1962 Topps

The 1962 Topps football set contains 176 black-bordered cards. The cards measure 2 1/2" by 3 1/2". In designing the 1962 set, Topps chose a horizontally oriented card front for the first time since 1957. The black borders, which are prone to chipping, make it quite difficult to put together a set in Mint condition. The single-printed (SP) cards are in shorter supply than the others. The shortage is probably attributable to the fact that the set size is not the standard 132-card, single-sheet size; hence all cards were not printed in equal amounts. Cards are again organized numerically in team order, for example: Baltimore Colts (1-12), Chicago Bears (13-25), Cleveland Browns (26-37), Dallas Cowboys (38-49), Detroit Lions (50-62), Green Bay Packers (63-75), Los Angeles Rams (77-89), Minnesota Vikings (90-101), New York Giants (102-114), Philadelphia Eagles (115-126), Pittsburgh Steelers (127-138), St. Louis Cardinals (139-150), San Francisco 49ers (151-163), and Washington Redskins (164-175). The last card within each team grouping was a "rookie prospect" for that team. Many of the black and white inset photos on the card fronts (especially those of the rookie prospects) are not the player pictured and described on the card. The key Rookie Cards in this set are Ernie Davis, Mike Ditka, Roman Gabriel, Bill Kilmer, and Fran Tarkenton.

|  | NRMT | VG-E | GOOD |
|---|---|---|---|
| COMPLETE SET (176) | 1600.00 | 700.00 | 200.00 |
| COMMON PLAYER (1-176) | 3.00 | 1.35 | .40 |
| ☐ 1 John Unitas | 120.00 | 36.00 | 12.00 |
| ☐ 2 Lenny Moore | 8.00 | 3.60 | 1.00 |
| ☐ 3 Alex Hawkins SP | 8.00 | 3.60 | 1.00 |
| ☐ 4 Joe Perry | 8.00 | 3.60 | 1.00 |
| ☐ 5 Raymond Berry SP | 20.00 | 9.00 | 2.50 |
| ☐ 6 Steve Myhra | 3.00 | 1.35 | .40 |
| ☐ 7 Tom Gilburg SP | 7.00 | 3.10 | .85 |
| ☐ 8 Gino Marchetti | 6.50 | 2.90 | .80 |
| ☐ 9 Bill Pellington | 3.00 | 1.35 | .40 |
| ☐ 10 Andy Nelson | 3.00 | 1.35 | .40 |
| ☐ 11 Wendell Harris SP | 7.00 | 3.10 | .85 |
| ☐ 12 Baltimore Colts | 6.00 | 2.70 | .75 |
| Team Card |  |  |  |
| ☐ 13 Bill Wade SP | 7.50 | 3.40 | .95 |
| ☐ 14 Willie Galimore | 3.50 | 1.55 | .45 |
| ☐ 15 Johnny Morris SP | 7.50 | 3.40 | .95 |
| ☐ 16 Rick Casares | 3.50 | 1.55 | .45 |
| ☐ 17 Mike Ditka | 160.00 | 70.00 | 20.00 |
| ☐ 18 Stan Jones | 4.50 | 2.00 | .55 |
| ☐ 19 Roger LeClerc | 3.00 | 1.35 | .40 |
| ☐ 20 Angelo Coia | 3.00 | 1.35 | .40 |
| ☐ 21 Doug Atkins | 5.00 | 2.30 | .60 |
| ☐ 22 Bill George | 4.50 | 2.00 | .55 |
| ☐ 23 Richie Petitbon | 5.00 | 2.30 | .60 |
| ☐ 24 Ron Bull SP | 8.00 | 3.60 | 1.00 |
| ☐ 25 Chicago Bears | 6.00 | 2.70 | .75 |
| Team Card |  |  |  |
| ☐ 26 Howard Cassady | 3.50 | 1.55 | .45 |
| ☐ 27 Ray Renfro SP | 7.50 | 3.40 | .95 |
| ☐ 28 Jim Brown | 100.00 | 45.00 | 12.50 |
| ☐ 29 Rich Kreitling | 3.00 | 1.35 | .40 |
| ☐ 30 Jim Ray Smith | 3.50 | 1.55 | .45 |
| ☐ 31 John Morrow | 3.00 | 1.35 | .40 |
| ☐ 32 Lou Groza | 12.00 | 5.50 | 1.50 |
| ☐ 33 Bob Gain | 3.00 | 1.35 | .40 |
| ☐ 34 Bernie Parrish | 3.50 | 1.55 | .45 |
| ☐ 35 Jim Shofner | 3.50 | 1.55 | .45 |
| ☐ 36 Ernie Davis SP | 80.00 | 36.00 | 10.00 |
| ☐ 37 Cleveland Browns | 6.00 | 2.70 | .75 |
| Team Card |  |  |  |
| ☐ 38 Eddie LeBaron | 4.00 | 1.80 | .50 |
| ☐ 39 Don Meredith SP | 80.00 | 36.00 | 10.00 |
| ☐ 40 J.W. Lockett SP | 7.00 | 3.10 | .85 |
| ☐ 41 Don Perkins | 6.00 | 2.70 | .75 |
| ☐ 42 Bill Howton | 3.50 | 1.55 | .45 |
| ☐ 43 Dick Bielski | 3.00 | 1.35 | .40 |

| ☐ 44 Mike Connelly | 3.50 | 1.55 | .45 |
|---|---|---|---|
| ☐ 45 Jerry Tubbs SP | 7.50 | 3.40 | .95 |
| ☐ 46 Don Bishop SP | 7.50 | 3.40 | .95 |
| ☐ 47 Dick Moegle | 3.50 | 1.55 | .45 |
| ☐ 48 Bobby Plummer SP | 7.00 | 3.10 | .85 |
| ☐ 49 Dallas Cowboys | 10.00 | 4.50 | 1.25 |
| Team Card |  |  |  |
| ☐ 50 Milt Plum | 3.50 | 1.55 | .45 |
| ☐ 51 Dan Lewis | 3.00 | 1.35 | .40 |
| ☐ 52 Nick Pietrosante SP | 7.50 | 3.40 | .95 |
| ☐ 53 Gail Cogdill | 3.00 | 1.35 | .40 |
| ☐ 54 Jim Gibbons | 3.00 | 1.35 | .40 |
| ☐ 55 Jim Martin | 3.50 | 1.55 | .45 |
| ☐ 56 Yale Lary | 5.00 | 2.30 | .60 |
| ☐ 57 Darris McCord | 3.00 | 1.35 | .40 |
| ☐ 58 Alex Karras | 15.00 | 6.75 | 1.90 |
| ☐ 59 Joe Schmidt | 5.50 | 2.50 | .70 |
| ☐ 60 Dick Lane | 5.50 | 2.50 | .70 |
| ☐ 61 John Lomakoski SP | 7.00 | 3.10 | .85 |
| ☐ 62 Detroit Lions SP | 15.00 | 6.75 | 1.90 |
| Team Card |  |  |  |
| ☐ 63 Bart Starr SP | 50.00 | 23.00 | 6.25 |
| ☐ 64 Paul Hornung SP | 45.00 | 20.00 | 5.75 |
| ☐ 65 Tom Moore SP | 7.50 | 3.40 | .95 |
| ☐ 66 Jim Taylor SP | 32.00 | 14.50 | 4.00 |
| ☐ 67 Max McGee SP | 7.50 | 3.40 | .95 |
| ☐ 68 Jim Ringo SP | 14.00 | 6.25 | 1.75 |
| ☐ 69 Fuzzy Thurston SP | 14.00 | 6.25 | 1.75 |
| ☐ 70 Forrest Gregg | 5.00 | 2.30 | .60 |
| ☐ 71 Boyd Dowler | 3.50 | 1.55 | .45 |
| ☐ 72 Henry Jordan SP | 7.50 | 3.40 | .95 |
| ☐ 73 Bill Forester SP | 7.00 | 3.10 | .85 |
| ☐ 74 Earl Gros SP | 7.50 | 3.40 | .95 |
| ☐ 75 Green Bay Packers SP | 22.00 | 10.00 | 2.80 |
| Team Card |  |  |  |
| ☐ 76 Checklist SP | 80.00 | 8.00 | 1.60 |
| ☐ 77 Zeke Bratkowski SP | 7.50 | 3.40 | .95 |
| (Inset photo is Johnny Unitas) |  |  |  |
| ☐ 78 Jon Arnett SP | 7.50 | 3.40 | .95 |
| ☐ 79 Ollie Matson SP | 20.00 | 9.00 | 2.50 |
| ☐ 80 Dick Bass SP | 7.50 | 3.40 | .95 |
| ☐ 81 Jim Phillips | 3.50 | 1.55 | .45 |
| ☐ 82 Carroll Dale | 4.00 | 1.80 | .50 |
| ☐ 83 Frank Varrichione | 3.00 | 1.35 | .40 |
| ☐ 84 Art Hunter | 3.00 | 1.35 | .40 |
| ☐ 85 Danny Villanueva | 3.50 | 1.55 | .45 |
| ☐ 86 Les Richter SP | 7.50 | 3.40 | .95 |
| ☐ 87 Lindon Crow | 3.00 | 1.35 | .40 |
| ☐ 88 Roman Gabriel SP | 55.00 | 25.00 | 7.00 |
| (Inset photo is Y.A. Tittle) |  |  |  |
| ☐ 89 Los Angeles Rams SP | 15.00 | 6.75 | 1.90 |
| Team Card |  |  |  |
| ☐ 90 Fran Tarkenton SP UER | 275.00 | 125.00 | 34.00 |
| (Small photo actually Jurgensen with air-brushed jersey) |  |  |  |
| ☐ 91 Jerry Reichow SP | 7.00 | 3.10 | .85 |
| ☐ 92 Hugh McElhenny SP | 22.00 | 10.00 | 2.80 |
| ☐ 93 Mel Triplett SP | 7.00 | 3.10 | .85 |
| ☐ 94 Tommy Mason SP | 8.00 | 3.60 | 1.00 |
| ☐ 95 Dave Middleton SP | 7.00 | 3.10 | .85 |
| ☐ 96 Frank Youso SP | 7.00 | 3.10 | .85 |
| ☐ 97 Mike Mercer SP | 7.00 | 3.10 | .85 |
| ☐ 98 Rip Hawkins SP | 7.00 | 3.10 | .85 |
| ☐ 99 Cliff Livingston SP | 7.00 | 3.10 | .85 |
| ☐ 100 Roy Winston SP | 8.00 | 3.60 | 1.00 |
| ☐ 101 Minnesota Vikings SP | 20.00 | 9.00 | 2.50 |
| Team Card |  |  |  |
| ☐ 102 Y.A. Tittle | 25.00 | 11.50 | 3.10 |
| ☐ 103 Joe Walton | 3.00 | 1.35 | .40 |
| ☐ 104 Frank Gifford | 55.00 | 25.00 | 7.00 |
| ☐ 105 Alex Webster | 3.00 | 1.35 | .40 |
| ☐ 106 Del Shofner | 3.50 | 1.55 | .45 |
| ☐ 107 Don Chandler | 3.50 | 1.55 | .45 |
| ☐ 108 Andy Robustelli | 5.50 | 2.50 | .70 |
| ☐ 109 Jim Katcavage | 3.50 | 1.55 | .45 |
| ☐ 110 Sam Huff SP | 16.00 | 7.25 | 2.00 |
| ☐ 111 Erich Barnes | 3.50 | 1.55 | .45 |
| ☐ 112 Jim Patton | 3.50 | 1.55 | .45 |
| ☐ 113 Jerry Hillebrand SP | 7.00 | 3.10 | .85 |
| ☐ 114 New York Giants | 6.00 | 2.70 | .75 |
| Team Card |  |  |  |
| ☐ 115 Sonny Jurgensen | 24.00 | 11.00 | 3.00 |
| ☐ 116 Tommy McDonald | 3.50 | 1.55 | .45 |
| ☐ 117 Ted Dean SP | 7.00 | 3.10 | .85 |
| ☐ 118 Clarence Peaks | 3.00 | 1.35 | .40 |
| ☐ 119 Bobby Walston | 3.50 | 1.55 | .45 |
| ☐ 120 Pete Retzlaff SP | 7.50 | 3.40 | .95 |
| ☐ 121 Jim Schrader SP | 7.00 | 3.10 | .85 |
| ☐ 122 J.D. Smith | 3.00 | 1.35 | .40 |
| (tackle) |  |  |  |
| ☐ 123 King Hill | 3.50 | 1.55 | .45 |
| ☐ 124 Maxie Baughan | 3.50 | 1.55 | .45 |
| ☐ 125 Pete Case SP | 7.00 | 3.10 | .85 |
| ☐ 126 Philadelphia Eagles | 6.00 | 2.70 | .75 |

Team Card
| | | NRMT | VG-E | GOOD |
|---|---|---|---|---|
| ☐ 127 Bobby Layne UER | 25.00 | 11.50 | 3.10 |
| (Bears until 1958, should be Lions) | | | |
| ☐ 128 Tom Tracy | 3.50 | 1.55 | .45 |
| ☐ 129 John Henry Johnson | 7.00 | 3.10 | .85 |
| ☐ 130 Buddy Dial SP | 7.50 | 3.40 | .95 |
| ☐ 131 Preston Carpenter | 3.00 | 1.35 | .40 |
| ☐ 132 Lou Michaels SP | 7.50 | 3.40 | .95 |
| ☐ 133 Gene Lipscomb SP | 8.00 | 3.60 | 1.00 |
| ☐ 134 Ernie Stautner SP | 14.00 | 6.25 | 1.75 |
| ☐ 135 John Reger SP | 7.00 | 3.10 | .85 |
| ☐ 136 Myron Pottios | 3.50 | 1.55 | .45 |
| ☐ 137 Bob Ferguson SP | 7.50 | 3.40 | .95 |
| ☐ 138 Pittsburgh Steelers | 15.00 | 6.75 | 1.90 |
| Team Card SP | | | |
| ☐ 139 Sam Etcheverry | 3.50 | 1.55 | .45 |
| ☐ 140 John David Crow SP | 7.50 | 3.40 | .95 |
| ☐ 141 Bobby Joe Conrad SP | 7.50 | 3.40 | .95 |
| ☐ 142 Prentice Gautt SP | 8.00 | 3.60 | 1.00 |
| ☐ 143 Frank Mestnick | 3.00 | 1.35 | .40 |
| ☐ 144 Sonny Randle | 3.50 | 1.55 | .45 |
| ☐ 145 Gerry Perry UER | 3.00 | 1.35 | .40 |
| (T-K on both sides, but Def. End in bio) | | | |
| ☐ 146 Jerry Norton | 3.00 | 1.35 | .40 |
| ☐ 147 Jimmy Hill | 3.00 | 1.35 | .40 |
| ☐ 148 Bill Stacy | 3.00 | 1.35 | .40 |
| ☐ 149 Fate Echols SP | 7.00 | 3.10 | .85 |
| ☐ 150 St. Louis Cardinals | 6.00 | 2.70 | .75 |
| Team Card | | | |
| ☐ 151 Bill Kilmer | 25.00 | 11.50 | 3.10 |
| ☐ 152 John Brodie | 16.00 | 7.25 | 2.00 |
| ☐ 153 J.D. Smith | 3.50 | 1.55 | .45 |
| (Halfback) | | | |
| ☐ 154 C.R. Roberts SP | 7.00 | 3.10 | .85 |
| ☐ 155 Monty Stickles | 3.00 | 1.35 | .40 |
| ☐ 156 Clyde Conner UER | 3.00 | 1.35 | .40 |
| (Misspelled Connor on card back) | | | |
| ☐ 157 Bob St. Clair SP | 4.50 | 2.00 | .55 |
| ☐ 158 Tommy Davis | 3.50 | 1.55 | .45 |
| ☐ 159 Leo Nomellini | 5.50 | 2.50 | .70 |
| ☐ 160 Matt Hazeltine | 3.00 | 1.35 | .40 |
| ☐ 161 Abe Woodson | 3.50 | 1.55 | .45 |
| ☐ 162 Dave Baker | 3.00 | 1.35 | .40 |
| ☐ 163 San Francisco 49ers | 6.00 | 2.70 | .75 |
| Team Card | | | |
| ☐ 164 Norm Snead SP | 25.00 | 11.50 | 3.10 |
| ☐ 165 Dick James | 3.00 | 1.35 | .40 |
| (Inset photo is Don Bosseler) | | | |
| ☐ 166 Bobby Mitchell | 8.00 | 3.60 | 1.00 |
| ☐ 167 Sam Horner | 3.00 | 1.35 | .40 |
| ☐ 168 Bill Barnes | 3.00 | 1.35 | .40 |
| ☐ 169 Bill Anderson | 3.00 | 1.35 | .40 |
| ☐ 170 Fred Dugan | 3.00 | 1.35 | .40 |
| ☐ 171 John Aveni SP | 7.00 | 3.10 | .85 |
| ☐ 172 Bob Toneff | 3.00 | 1.35 | .40 |
| ☐ 173 Jim Kerr | 3.00 | 1.35 | .40 |
| ☐ 174 Leroy Jackson SP | 7.00 | 3.10 | .85 |
| ☐ 175 Washington Redskins | 6.00 | 2.70 | .75 |
| Team Card | | | |
| ☐ 176 Checklist | 100.00 | 10.00 | 2.00 |

## 1962 Topps Bucks

The 1962 Topps Football Bucks set contains 48 cards and was issued as an insert into wax packs of the 1962 Topps regular issue of football cards. Printing was done with black and green ink on off-white (very thin) paper stock. Bucks are typically found with a fold crease in the middle as they were inserted in packs in that manner. These "football bucks" measure approximately 1 1/4" by 4 1/4". Mike Ditka and Fran Tarkenton appear in their Rookie Card year.

| | NRMT | VG-E | GOOD |
|---|---|---|---|
| COMPLETE SET (48) | 400.00 | 160.00 | 40.00 |
| COMMON PLAYER (1-48) | 4.00 | 1.60 | .40 |
| ☐ 1 J.D. Smith | 4.00 | 1.60 | .40 |
| San Francisco 49ers | | | |
| ☐ 2 Bart Starr | 20.00 | 8.00 | 2.00 |
| Green Bay Packers | | | |
| ☐ 3 Dick James | 4.00 | 1.60 | .40 |
| Washington Redskins | | | |
| ☐ 4 Alex Webster | 5.00 | 2.00 | .50 |
| New York Giants | | | |
| ☐ 5 Paul Hornung | 15.00 | 6.00 | 1.50 |
| Green Bay Packers | | | |
| ☐ 6 John David Crow | 5.00 | 2.00 | .50 |
| St. Louis Cardinals | | | |
| ☐ 7 Jimmy Brown | 50.00 | 20.00 | 5.00 |
| Cleveland Browns | | | |
| ☐ 8 Don Perkins | 5.00 | 2.00 | .50 |
| Dallas Cowboys | | | |
| ☐ 9 Bobby Walston | 4.00 | 1.60 | .40 |
| Philadelphia Eagles | | | |
| ☐ 10 Jim Phillips | 4.00 | 1.60 | .40 |
| Los Angeles Rams | | | |
| ☐ 11 Y.A. Tittle | 15.00 | 6.00 | 1.50 |
| New York Giants | | | |
| ☐ 12 Sonny Randle | 4.00 | 1.60 | .40 |
| St. Louis Cardinals | | | |
| ☐ 13 Jerry Reichow | 4.00 | 1.60 | .40 |
| Minnesota Vikings | | | |
| ☐ 14 Yale Lary | 7.50 | 3.00 | .75 |
| Detroit Lions | | | |
| ☐ 15 Buddy Dial | 5.00 | 2.00 | .50 |
| Pittsburgh Steelers | | | |
| ☐ 16 Ray Renfro | 5.00 | 2.00 | .50 |
| Cleveland Browns | | | |
| ☐ 17 Norm Snead | 5.00 | 2.00 | .50 |
| Washington Redskins | | | |
| ☐ 18 Leo Nomellini | 7.50 | 3.00 | .75 |
| San Francisco 49ers | | | |
| ☐ 19 Hugh McElhenny | 10.00 | 4.00 | 1.00 |
| Minnesota Vikings | | | |
| ☐ 20 Eddie LeBaron | 5.00 | 2.00 | .50 |
| Dallas Cowboys | | | |
| ☐ 21 Bill Howton | 5.00 | 2.00 | .50 |
| Dallas Cowboys | | | |
| ☐ 22 Bobby Mitchell | 7.50 | 3.00 | .75 |
| Washington Redskins | | | |
| ☐ 23 Nick Pietrosante | 5.00 | 2.00 | .50 |
| Detroit Lions | | | |
| ☐ 24 John Unitas | 30.00 | 12.00 | 3.00 |
| Baltimore Colts | | | |
| ☐ 25 Raymond Berry | 10.00 | 4.00 | 1.00 |
| Baltimore Colts | | | |
| ☐ 26 Bill Kilmer | 7.50 | 3.00 | .75 |
| San Francisco 49ers | | | |
| ☐ 27 Lenny Moore | 10.00 | 4.00 | 1.00 |
| Baltimore Colts | | | |
| ☐ 28 Tommy McDonald | 5.00 | 2.00 | .50 |
| Philadelphia Eagles | | | |
| ☐ 29 Del Shofner | 5.00 | 2.00 | .50 |
| New York Giants | | | |
| ☐ 30 Jim Taylor | 12.00 | 5.00 | 1.20 |
| Green Bay Packers | | | |
| ☐ 31 Joe Schmidt | 7.50 | 3.00 | .75 |
| Detroit Lions | | | |
| ☐ 32 Bill George | 7.50 | 3.00 | .75 |
| Chicago Bears | | | |
| ☐ 33 Fran Tarkenton | 60.00 | 24.00 | 6.00 |
| Minnesota Vikings | | | |
| ☐ 34 Willie Galimore | 5.00 | 2.00 | .50 |
| Chicago Bears | | | |
| ☐ 35 Bobby Layne | 15.00 | 6.00 | 1.50 |
| Pittsburgh Steelers | | | |
| ☐ 36 Max McGee | 5.00 | 2.00 | .50 |
| Green Bay Packers | | | |
| ☐ 37 Jon Arnett | 5.00 | 2.00 | .50 |
| Los Angeles Rams | | | |
| ☐ 38 Lou Groza | 10.00 | 4.00 | 1.00 |
| Cleveland Browns | | | |
| ☐ 39 Frank Varrichione | 4.00 | 1.60 | .40 |
| Los Angeles Rams | | | |
| ☐ 40 Milt Plum | 5.00 | 2.00 | .50 |
| Detroit Lions | | | |
| ☐ 41 Prentice Gautt | 4.00 | 1.60 | .40 |
| St. Louis Cardinals | | | |
| ☐ 42 Bill Wade | 5.00 | 2.00 | .50 |
| Chicago Bears | | | |
| ☐ 43 Gino Marchetti | 7.50 | 3.00 | .75 |
| Baltimore Colts | | | |
| ☐ 44 John Brodie | 10.00 | 4.00 | 1.00 |
| San Francisco 49ers | | | |
| ☐ 45 Sonny Jurgensen UER | 10.00 | 4.00 | 1.00 |
| (Misspelled Jurgenson) | | | |
| Philadelphia Eagles | | | |
| ☐ 46 Clarence Peaks | 4.00 | 1.60 | .40 |
| Philadelphia Eagles | | | |
| ☐ 47 Mike Ditka | 35.00 | 14.00 | 3.50 |

Chicago Bears
☐ 48 John Henry Johnson ............. 7.50    3.00    .75
   Pittsburgh Steelers

# 1963 Topps

The 1963 Topps set contains 170 cards of NFL players grouped together by teams. The teams are ordered as follows: Baltimore Colts (1-12), Cleveland Browns (13-24), Detroit Lions (25-36), Los Angeles Rams (37-48), New York Giants (49-60), Chicago Bears (61-72), Dallas Cowboys (73-84), Green Bay Packers (86-97), Minnesota Vikings (98-109), Philadelphia Eagles (110-121), Pittsburgh Steelers (122-133), San Francisco 49ers (134-145), St. Louis Cardinals (146-157), and Washington Redskins (158-169). The cards measure 2 1/2" by 3 1/2". The card backs are printed in light orange ink on white card stock. Statistical information from the immediate past season and career totals are given on the reverse. The illustrated trivia question on the reverse (of each card) could be answered by placing red cellophane paper (which was inserted into wax packs) over the card. The 76 cards indicated by SP below are in shorter supply than the others because the set size is not the standard 132-card, single-sheet size; hence, all cards were not printed in equal amounts. There also exists a three-card advertising panel consisting of the obverses of Charlie Johnson, John David Crow, and Bobby Joe Conrad with ad copy on the reverse of the latter two and a Y.A. Tittle reverse on Johnson. The key Rookie Cards in this set are defensive stalwarts Deacon Jones, Bob Lilly, Jim Marshall, Ray Nitschke, Larry Wilson, and Willie Wood.

|  | NRMT | VG-E | GOOD |
|---|---|---|---|
| COMPLETE SET (170) .................... | 1350.00 | 600.00 | 170.00 |
| COMMON PLAYER (1-170) ............... | 2.00 | .90 | .25 |
| ☐ 1 John Unitas ............................. | 100.00 | 30.00 | 10.00 |
| ☐ 2 Lenny Moore ........................... | 7.00 | 3.10 | .85 |
| ☐ 3 Jimmy Orr .............................. | 2.25 | 1.00 | .30 |
| ☐ 4 Raymond Berry ........................ | 7.50 | 3.40 | .95 |
| ☐ 5 Jim Parker ............................. | 5.00 | 2.30 | .60 |
| ☐ 6 Alex Sandusky ........................ | 2.00 | .90 | .25 |
| ☐ 7 Dick Szymanski ....................... | 2.00 | .90 | .25 |
| ☐ 8 Gino Marchetti ........................ | 5.00 | 2.30 | .60 |
| ☐ 9 Billy Ray Smith ....................... | 3.00 | 1.35 | .40 |
| ☐ 10 Bill Pellington ....................... | 2.00 | .90 | .25 |
| ☐ 11 Bob Boyd ............................. | 2.50 | 1.15 | .30 |
| ☐ 12 Baltimore Colts SP ................. | 9.00 | 4.00 | 1.15 |
|    Team Card |  |  |  |
| ☐ 13 Frank Ryan SP ...................... | 6.50 | 2.90 | .80 |
| ☐ 14 Jim Brown SP ....................... | 150.00 | 70.00 | 19.00 |
| ☐ 15 Ray Renfro SP ...................... | 5.50 | 2.50 | .70 |
| ☐ 16 Rich Kreitling SP ................... | 5.00 | 2.30 | .60 |
| ☐ 17 Mike McCormack SP ............... | 8.00 | 3.60 | 1.00 |
| ☐ 18 Jim Ray Smith SP ................... | 5.00 | 2.30 | .60 |
| ☐ 19 Lou Groza SP ....................... | 16.00 | 7.25 | 2.00 |
| ☐ 20 Bill Glass SP ........................ | 5.50 | 2.50 | .70 |
| ☐ 21 Galen Fiss SP ....................... | 5.00 | 2.30 | .60 |
| ☐ 22 Don Fleming SP ..................... | 6.00 | 2.70 | .75 |
| ☐ 23 Bob Gain SP ......................... | 5.00 | 2.30 | .60 |
| ☐ 24 Cleveland Browns SP .............. | 9.00 | 4.00 | 1.15 |
|    Team Card |  |  |  |
| ☐ 25 Milt Plum ............................ | 2.25 | 1.00 | .30 |
| ☐ 26 Dan Lewis ........................... | 2.00 | .90 | .25 |
| ☐ 27 Nick Pietrosante .................... | 2.25 | 1.00 | .30 |
| ☐ 28 Gail Cogdill .......................... | 2.00 | .90 | .25 |
| ☐ 29 Harley Sewell ....................... | 2.25 | 1.00 | .30 |
| ☐ 30 Jim Gibbons ......................... | 2.00 | .90 | .25 |
| ☐ 31 Carl Brettschneider ................ | 2.00 | .90 | .25 |
| ☐ 32 Dick Lane ............................ | 4.00 | 1.80 | .50 |
| ☐ 33 Yale Lary ............................ | 4.00 | 1.80 | .50 |
| ☐ 34 Roger Brown ........................ | 3.00 | 1.35 | .40 |
| ☐ 35 Joe Schmidt ......................... | 5.00 | 2.30 | .60 |
| ☐ 36 Detroit Lions SP .................... | 9.00 | 4.00 | 1.15 |
|    Team Card |  |  |  |

| ☐ 37 Roman Gabriel ...................... | 7.50 | 3.40 | .95 |
|---|---|---|---|
| ☐ 38 Zeke Bratkowski .................... | 2.00 | .90 | .25 |
| ☐ 39 Dick Bass ............................ | 2.25 | 1.00 | .30 |
| ☐ 40 Jon Arnett ........................... | 2.25 | 1.00 | .30 |
| ☐ 41 Jim Phillips .......................... | 2.25 | 1.00 | .30 |
| ☐ 42 Frank Varrichione ................... | 2.00 | .90 | .25 |
| ☐ 43 Danny Villanueva ................... | 2.25 | 1.00 | .30 |
| ☐ 44 Deacon Jones ....................... | 55.00 | 25.00 | 7.00 |
| ☐ 45 Lindon Crow ......................... | 2.00 | .90 | .25 |
| ☐ 46 Marlin McKeever .................... | 2.25 | 1.00 | .30 |
| ☐ 47 Ed Meador ........................... | 3.00 | 1.35 | .40 |
| ☐ 48 Los Angeles Rams .................. | 4.00 | 1.80 | .50 |
|    Team Card |  |  |  |
| ☐ 49 Y.A. Tittle SP ....................... | 25.00 | 11.50 | 3.10 |
| ☐ 50 Del Shofner SP ...................... | 5.50 | 2.50 | .70 |
| ☐ 51 Alex Webster SP .................... | 6.00 | 2.70 | .75 |
| ☐ 52 Phil King SP ......................... | 5.00 | 2.30 | .60 |
| ☐ 53 Jack Stroud SP ...................... | 5.00 | 2.30 | .60 |
| ☐ 54 Darrell Dess SP ..................... | 5.00 | 2.30 | .60 |
| ☐ 55 Jim Katcavage SP .................. | 5.50 | 2.50 | .70 |
| ☐ 56 Roosevelt Grier SP ................. | 8.00 | 3.60 | 1.00 |
| ☐ 57 Erich Barnes SP ..................... | 5.50 | 2.50 | .70 |
| ☐ 58 Jim Patton SP ....................... | 5.50 | 2.50 | .70 |
| ☐ 59 Sam Huff SP ......................... | 15.00 | 6.75 | 1.90 |
| ☐ 60 New York Giants .................... | 4.00 | 1.80 | .50 |
|    Team Card |  |  |  |
| ☐ 61 Bill Wade ............................ | 2.25 | 1.00 | .30 |
| ☐ 62 Mike Ditka ........................... | 50.00 | 23.00 | 6.25 |
| ☐ 63 Johnny Morris ....................... | 2.25 | 1.00 | .30 |
| ☐ 64 Roger LeClerc ....................... | 2.00 | .90 | .25 |
| ☐ 65 Roger Davis .......................... | 2.00 | .90 | .25 |
| ☐ 66 Joe Marconi .......................... | 2.00 | .90 | .25 |
| ☐ 67 Herman Lee .......................... | 2.00 | .90 | .25 |
| ☐ 68 Doug Atkins .......................... | 5.00 | 2.30 | .60 |
| ☐ 69 Joe Fortunato ........................ | 2.25 | 1.00 | .30 |
| ☐ 70 Bill George ........................... | 4.00 | 1.80 | .50 |
| ☐ 71 Richie Petitbon ...................... | 2.25 | 1.00 | .30 |
| ☐ 72 Chicago Bears SP ................... | 9.00 | 4.00 | 1.15 |
|    Team Card |  |  |  |
| ☐ 73 Eddie LeBaron SP ................... | 6.00 | 2.70 | .75 |
| ☐ 74 Don Meredith SP .................... | 50.00 | 23.00 | 6.25 |
| ☐ 75 Don Perkins SP ...................... | 6.00 | 2.70 | .75 |
| ☐ 76 Amos Marsh SP ..................... | 5.25 | 2.40 | .65 |
| ☐ 77 Bill Howton SP ...................... | 5.50 | 2.50 | .70 |
| ☐ 78 Andy Cvercko SP ................... | 5.00 | 2.30 | .60 |
| ☐ 79 Sam Baker SP ....................... | 5.50 | 2.50 | .70 |
| ☐ 80 Jerry Tubbs SP ...................... | 5.50 | 2.50 | .70 |
| ☐ 81 Don Bishop SP ...................... | 5.25 | 2.40 | .65 |
| ☐ 82 Bob Lilly SP .......................... | 100.00 | 45.00 | 12.50 |
| ☐ 83 Jerry Norton SP ..................... | 5.00 | 2.30 | .60 |
| ☐ 84 Dallas Cowboys SP ................. | 16.00 | 7.25 | 2.00 |
|    Team Card |  |  |  |
| ☐ 85 Checklist Card ....................... | 25.00 | 2.50 | .50 |
| ☐ 86 Bart Starr ............................ | 30.00 | 13.50 | 3.80 |
| ☐ 87 Jim Taylor ........................... | 16.00 | 7.25 | 2.00 |
| ☐ 88 Boyd Dowler ......................... | 2.25 | 1.00 | .30 |
| ☐ 89 Forrest Gregg ....................... | 5.00 | 2.30 | .60 |
| ☐ 90 Fuzzy Thurston ..................... | 3.00 | 1.35 | .40 |
| ☐ 91 Jim Ringo ............................ | 4.00 | 1.80 | .50 |
| ☐ 92 Ron Kramer .......................... | 2.25 | 1.00 | .30 |
| ☐ 93 Henry Jordan ........................ | 2.25 | 1.00 | .30 |
| ☐ 94 Bill Forester ......................... | 2.00 | .90 | .25 |
| ☐ 95 Willie Wood .......................... | 27.00 | 12.00 | 3.40 |
| ☐ 96 Ray Nitschke ........................ | 70.00 | 32.00 | 8.75 |
| ☐ 97 Green Bay Packers ................. | 4.00 | 1.80 | .50 |
|    Team Card |  |  |  |
| ☐ 98 Fran Tarkenton ...................... | 70.00 | 32.00 | 8.75 |
| ☐ 99 Tommy Mason ...................... | 2.25 | 1.00 | .30 |
| ☐ 100 Mel Triplett ......................... | 2.00 | .90 | .25 |
| ☐ 101 Jerry Reichow ...................... | 2.00 | .90 | .25 |
| ☐ 102 Frank Youso ........................ | 2.00 | .90 | .25 |
| ☐ 103 Hugh McElhenny .................. | 7.00 | 3.10 | .85 |
| ☐ 104 Gerry Huth .......................... | 2.00 | .90 | .25 |
| ☐ 105 Ed Sharockman .................... | 2.00 | .90 | .25 |
| ☐ 106 Rip Hawkins ........................ | 2.00 | .90 | .25 |
| ☐ 107 Jim Marshall ........................ | 27.00 | 12.00 | 3.40 |
| ☐ 108 Jim Prestel ......................... | 2.00 | .90 | .25 |
| ☐ 109 Minnesota Vikings ................. | 4.00 | 1.80 | .50 |
|    Team Card |  |  |  |
| ☐ 110 Sonny Jurgensen SP .............. | 22.00 | 10.00 | 2.80 |
| ☐ 111 Tim Brown SP ...................... | 8.50 | 3.80 | 1.05 |
| ☐ 112 Tommy McDonald SP ............. | 5.50 | 2.50 | .70 |
| ☐ 113 Clarence Peaks SP ................ | 5.00 | 2.30 | .60 |
| ☐ 114 Pete Retzlaff SP ................... | 5.50 | 2.50 | .70 |
| ☐ 115 Jim Schrader SP ................... | 5.00 | 2.30 | .60 |
| ☐ 116 Jim McCusker SP .................. | 5.00 | 2.30 | .60 |
| ☐ 117 Don Burroughs SP ................. | 5.00 | 2.30 | .60 |
| ☐ 118 Maxie Baughan SP ................ | 5.50 | 2.50 | .70 |
| ☐ 119 Riley Gunnels SP .................. | 5.00 | 2.30 | .60 |
| ☐ 120 Jimmy Carr SP ..................... | 5.00 | 2.30 | .60 |
| ☐ 121 Philadelphia Eagles ............... | 9.00 | 4.00 | 1.15 |
|    Team Card SP |  |  |  |
| ☐ 122 Ed Brown SP ....................... | 5.50 | 2.50 | .70 |
| ☐ 123 John Henry Johnson SP .......... | 11.00 | 4.90 | 1.40 |
| ☐ 124 Buddy Dial SP ...................... | 5.50 | 2.50 | .70 |
| ☐ 125 Red Mack SP ....................... | 5.00 | 2.30 | .60 |
| ☐ 126 Preston Carpenter SP ............ | 5.00 | 2.30 | .60 |

| | | | |
|---|---|---|---|
| ☐ 127 Ray Lemek SP | 5.00 | 2.30 | .60 |
| ☐ 128 Buzz Nutter SP | 5.00 | 2.30 | .60 |
| ☐ 129 Ernie Stautner SP | 11.00 | 4.90 | 1.40 |
| ☐ 130 Lou Michaels SP | 5.00 | 2.30 | .60 |
| ☐ 131 Clendon Thomas SP | 7.00 | 3.10 | .85 |
| ☐ 132 Tom Bettis SP | 5.00 | 2.30 | .60 |
| ☐ 133 Pittsburgh Steelers Team Card SP | 9.00 | 4.00 | 1.15 |
| ☐ 134 John Brodie | 10.00 | 4.50 | 1.25 |
| ☐ 135 J.D. Smith | 2.25 | 1.00 | .30 |
| ☐ 136 Bill Kilmer UER (College listed as San Francisco 49ers) | 6.00 | 2.70 | .75 |
| ☐ 137 Bernie Casey | 4.00 | 1.80 | .50 |
| ☐ 138 Tommy Davis | 2.00 | .90 | .25 |
| ☐ 139 Ted Connolly | 2.00 | .90 | .25 |
| ☐ 140 Bob St. Clair | 4.00 | 1.80 | .50 |
| ☐ 141 Abe Woodson | 2.25 | 1.00 | .30 |
| ☐ 142 Matt Hazeltine | 2.00 | .90 | .25 |
| ☐ 143 Leo Nomellini | 5.00 | 2.30 | .60 |
| ☐ 144 Dan Colchico | 2.00 | .90 | .25 |
| ☐ 145 San Francisco 49ers Team Card SP | 9.00 | 4.00 | 1.15 |
| ☐ 146 Charlie Johnson | 9.00 | 4.00 | 1.15 |
| ☐ 147 John David Crow | 2.25 | 1.00 | .30 |
| ☐ 148 Bobby Joe Conrad | 2.25 | 1.00 | .30 |
| ☐ 149 Sonny Randle | 2.25 | 1.00 | .30 |
| ☐ 150 Prentice Gautt | 2.25 | 1.00 | .30 |
| ☐ 151 Taz Anderson | 2.00 | .90 | .25 |
| ☐ 152 Ernie McMillan | 3.00 | 1.35 | .40 |
| ☐ 153 Jimmy Hill | 2.00 | .90 | .25 |
| ☐ 154 Bill Koman | 2.00 | .90 | .25 |
| ☐ 155 Larry Wilson | 26.00 | 11.50 | 3.30 |
| ☐ 156 Don Owens | 2.00 | .90 | .25 |
| ☐ 157 St. Louis Cardinals Team Card SP | 9.00 | 4.00 | 1.15 |
| ☐ 158 Norm Snead SP | 8.00 | 3.60 | 1.00 |
| ☐ 159 Bobby Mitchell SP | 14.00 | 6.25 | 1.75 |
| ☐ 160 Bill Barnes SP | 5.00 | 2.30 | .60 |
| ☐ 161 Fred Dugan SP | 5.00 | 2.30 | .60 |
| ☐ 162 Don Bosseler SP | 5.00 | 2.30 | .60 |
| ☐ 163 John Nisby SP | 5.00 | 2.30 | .60 |
| ☐ 164 Riley Mattson SP | 5.00 | 2.30 | .60 |
| ☐ 165 Bob Toneff SP | 5.00 | 2.30 | .60 |
| ☐ 166 Rod Breedlove SP | 5.00 | 2.30 | .60 |
| ☐ 167 Dick James SP | 5.00 | 2.30 | .60 |
| ☐ 168 Claud Crabb SP | 5.00 | 2.30 | .60 |
| ☐ 169 Washington Redskins Team Card SP | 9.00 | 4.00 | 1.15 |
| ☐ 170 Checklist Card UER (108 Jim Prestal) | 60.00 | 6.00 | 1.20 |

## 1964 Topps

The 1964 Topps football set contains 176 American Football League (AFL) player cards. The cards measure the standard 2 1/2" by 3 1/2" and are grouped by teams. Because the cards were not printed on a standard 132-card sheet, some cards are printed in lesser quantities than others. These cards are marked in the checklist with SP for short print. The backs of the cards contain the card number, vital statistics, a short biography, the player's record for the past year and his career, and a cartoon-illustrated question and answer section. The cards are organized alphabetically within teams, for example: Boston Patriots (1-21), Buffalo Bills (22-43), Denver Broncos (44-65), Houston Oilers (66-88), Kansas City Chiefs (89-110), New York Jets (111-131), Oakland Raiders (132-153), and San Diego Chargers (154-175). The key Rookie Cards in this set are Bobby Bell, Buck Buchanan, John Hadl, and Daryle Lamonica.

| | NRMT | VG-E | GOOD |
|---|---|---|---|
| COMPLETE SET (176) | 1400.00 | 650.00 | 180.00 |
| COMMON PLAYER (1-176) | 3.50 | 1.55 | .45 |

| | | | |
|---|---|---|---|
| ☐ 1 Tommy Addison SP | 30.00 | 6.00 | 1.80 |
| ☐ 2 Houston Antwine | 4.00 | 1.80 | .50 |
| ☐ 3 Nick Buoniconti | 12.00 | 5.50 | 1.50 |
| ☐ 4 Ron Burton SP | 7.50 | 3.40 | .95 |
| ☐ 5 Gino Cappelletti UER (Misspelled Cappalletti on card front) | 5.50 | 2.50 | .70 |
| ☐ 6 Jim Colclough SP | 7.00 | 3.10 | .85 |
| ☐ 7 Bob Dee SP | 7.00 | 3.10 | .85 |
| ☐ 8 Larry Eisenhauer | 4.00 | 1.80 | .50 |
| ☐ 9 Dick Felt SP | 7.00 | 3.10 | .85 |
| ☐ 10 Larry Garron | 3.50 | 1.55 | .45 |
| ☐ 11 Art Graham | 3.50 | 1.55 | .45 |
| ☐ 12 Ron Hall | 3.50 | 1.55 | .45 |
| ☐ 13 Charles Long | 3.50 | 1.55 | .45 |
| ☐ 14 Don McKinnon | 3.50 | 1.55 | .45 |
| ☐ 15 Don Oakes SP | 7.00 | 3.10 | .85 |
| ☐ 16 Ross O'Hanley SP | 7.00 | 3.10 | .85 |
| ☐ 17 Babe Parilli SP | 7.50 | 3.40 | .95 |
| ☐ 18 Jesse Richardson SP | 7.00 | 3.10 | .85 |
| ☐ 19 Jack Rudolph SP | 7.00 | 3.10 | .85 |
| ☐ 20 Don Webb | 4.00 | 1.80 | .50 |
| ☐ 21 Boston Patriots Team Card | 8.00 | 3.60 | 1.00 |
| ☐ 22 Ray Abbruzzese | 3.50 | 1.55 | .45 |
| ☐ 23 Stew Barber | 4.00 | 1.80 | .50 |
| ☐ 24 Dave Behrman | 3.50 | 1.55 | .45 |
| ☐ 25 Al Bemiller | 3.50 | 1.55 | .45 |
| ☐ 26 Elbert Dubenion SP | 7.50 | 3.40 | .95 |
| ☐ 27 Jim Dunaway SP | 10.00 | 4.50 | 1.25 |
| ☐ 28 Booker Edgerson SP | 7.00 | 3.10 | .85 |
| ☐ 29 Cookie Gilchrist SP | 12.00 | 5.50 | 1.50 |
| ☐ 30 Jack Kemp SP | 200.00 | 90.00 | 25.00 |
| ☐ 31 Daryle Lamonica | 65.00 | 29.00 | 8.25 |
| ☐ 32 Bill Miller | 3.50 | 1.55 | .45 |
| ☐ 33 Herb Paterra | 4.00 | 1.80 | .50 |
| ☐ 34 Ken Rice SP | 7.00 | 3.10 | .85 |
| ☐ 35 Ed Rutkowski | 3.50 | 1.55 | .45 |
| ☐ 36 George Saimes | 5.00 | 2.30 | .60 |
| ☐ 37 Tom Sestak | 4.00 | 1.80 | .50 |
| ☐ 38 Billy Shaw SP | 7.00 | 3.10 | .85 |
| ☐ 39 Mike Stratton | 4.00 | 1.80 | .50 |
| ☐ 40 Gene Sykes | 3.50 | 1.55 | .45 |
| ☐ 41 John Tracey SP | 7.00 | 3.10 | .85 |
| ☐ 42 Sid Youngelman SP | 7.00 | 3.10 | .85 |
| ☐ 43 Buffalo Bills Team Card | 8.00 | 3.60 | 1.00 |
| ☐ 44 Eldon Danenhauer SP | 7.50 | 3.40 | .95 |
| ☐ 45 Jim Fraser SP | 7.00 | 3.10 | .85 |
| ☐ 46 Chuck Gavin SP | 7.00 | 3.10 | .85 |
| ☐ 47 Goose Gonsoulin SP | 7.50 | 3.40 | .95 |
| ☐ 48 Ernie Barnes | 4.00 | 1.80 | .50 |
| ☐ 49 Tom Janik | 3.50 | 1.55 | .45 |
| ☐ 50 Billy Joe | 5.00 | 2.30 | .60 |
| ☐ 51 Ike Lassiter | 4.00 | 1.80 | .50 |
| ☐ 52 John McCormick SP | 7.00 | 3.10 | .85 |
| ☐ 53 Bud McFadin SP | 7.00 | 3.10 | .85 |
| ☐ 54 Gene Mingo SP | 7.00 | 3.10 | .85 |
| ☐ 55 Charlie Mitchell | 3.50 | 1.55 | .45 |
| ☐ 56 John Nocera SP | 7.00 | 3.10 | .85 |
| ☐ 57 Tom Nomina | 3.50 | 1.55 | .45 |
| ☐ 58 Harold Olson SP | 7.00 | 3.10 | .85 |
| ☐ 59 Bob Scarpitto | 3.50 | 1.55 | .45 |
| ☐ 60 John Sklopan | 3.50 | 1.55 | .45 |
| ☐ 61 Mickey Slaughter | 3.50 | 1.55 | .45 |
| ☐ 62 Don Stone | 3.50 | 1.55 | .45 |
| ☐ 63 Jerry Sturm | 3.50 | 1.55 | .45 |
| ☐ 64 Lionel Taylor SP | 12.00 | 5.50 | 1.50 |
| ☐ 65 Denver Broncos SP Team Card | 16.00 | 7.25 | 2.00 |
| ☐ 66 Scott Appleton | 4.00 | 1.80 | .50 |
| ☐ 67 Tony Banfield SP | 7.00 | 3.10 | .85 |
| ☐ 68 George Blanda SP | 60.00 | 27.00 | 7.50 |
| ☐ 69 Billy Cannon | 5.50 | 2.50 | .70 |
| ☐ 70 Doug Cline SP | 7.00 | 3.10 | .85 |
| ☐ 71 Gary Cutsinger SP | 7.00 | 3.10 | .85 |
| ☐ 72 Willard Dewveall SP | 7.00 | 3.10 | .85 |
| ☐ 73 Don Floyd SP | 7.00 | 3.10 | .85 |
| ☐ 74 Freddy Glick SP | 7.00 | 3.10 | .85 |
| ☐ 75 Charlie Hennigan SP | 10.00 | 4.50 | 1.25 |
| ☐ 76 Ed Husmann SP | 7.00 | 3.10 | .85 |
| ☐ 77 Bobby Jancik SP | 7.50 | 3.40 | .95 |
| ☐ 78 Jacky Lee SP | 7.50 | 3.40 | .95 |
| ☐ 79 Bob McLeod SP | 7.00 | 3.10 | .85 |
| ☐ 80 Rich Michael SP | 7.00 | 3.10 | .85 |
| ☐ 81 Larry Onesti | 4.00 | 1.80 | .50 |
| ☐ 82 Checklist Card UER (16 Ross O'Hanldy) | 50.00 | 6.50 | 1.30 |
| ☐ 83 Bob Schmidt SP | 7.00 | 3.10 | .85 |
| ☐ 84 Walt Suggs SP | 7.00 | 3.10 | .85 |
| ☐ 85 Bob Talamini SP | 7.00 | 3.10 | .85 |
| ☐ 86 Charley Tolar SP | 7.50 | 3.40 | .95 |
| ☐ 87 Don Trull | 4.50 | 2.00 | .55 |
| ☐ 88 Houston Oilers Team Card | 8.00 | 3.60 | 1.00 |
| ☐ 89 Fred Arbanas | 4.00 | 1.80 | .50 |
| ☐ 90 Bobby Bell | 32.00 | 14.50 | 4.00 |

| | | | |
|---|---|---|---|
| ☐ 91 Mel Branch SP | 7.50 | 3.40 | .95 |
| ☐ 92 Buck Buchanan | 32.00 | 14.50 | 4.00 |
| ☐ 93 Ed Budde | 7.00 | 3.10 | .85 |
| ☐ 94 Chris Burford SP | 7.50 | 3.40 | .95 |
| ☐ 95 Walt Corey | 7.00 | 3.10 | .85 |
| ☐ 96 Len Dawson SP | 75.00 | 34.00 | 9.50 |
| ☐ 97 Dave Grayson | 4.00 | 1.80 | .50 |
| ☐ 98 Abner Haynes | 5.50 | 2.50 | .70 |
| ☐ 99 Sherrill Headrick SP | 7.50 | 3.40 | .95 |
| ☐ 100 E.J. Holub | 4.00 | 1.80 | .50 |
| ☐ 101 Bobby Hunt | 4.00 | 1.80 | .50 |
| ☐ 102 Frank Jackson SP | 7.50 | 3.40 | .95 |
| ☐ 103 Curtis McClinton | 4.00 | 1.80 | .50 |
| ☐ 104 Jerry Mays SP | 7.50 | 3.40 | .95 |
| ☐ 105 Johnny Robinson SP | 7.50 | 3.40 | .95 |
| ☐ 106 Jack Spikes SP | 7.50 | 3.40 | .95 |
| ☐ 107 Smokey Stover SP | 7.00 | 3.10 | .85 |
| ☐ 108 Jim Tyrer | 7.00 | 3.10 | .85 |
| ☐ 109 Duane Wood SP | 7.50 | 3.40 | .95 |
| ☐ 110 Kansas City Chiefs Team Card | 8.00 | 3.60 | 1.00 |
| ☐ 111 Dick Christy SP | 7.00 | 3.10 | .85 |
| ☐ 112 Dan Ficca SP | 7.00 | 3.10 | .85 |
| ☐ 113 Larry Grantham | 4.00 | 1.80 | .50 |
| ☐ 114 Curley Johnson SP | 7.00 | 3.10 | .85 |
| ☐ 115 Gene Heeter | 3.50 | 1.55 | .45 |
| ☐ 116 Jack Klotz | 3.50 | 1.55 | .45 |
| ☐ 117 Pete Liske | 4.00 | 1.80 | .50 |
| ☐ 118 Bob McAdam | 3.50 | 1.55 | .45 |
| ☐ 119 Dee Mackey SP | 7.00 | 3.10 | .85 |
| ☐ 120 Bill Mathis SP | 7.50 | 3.40 | .95 |
| ☐ 121 Don Maynard | 25.00 | 11.50 | 3.10 |
| ☐ 122 Dainard Paulson SP | 7.00 | 3.10 | .85 |
| ☐ 123 Gerry Philbin | 4.50 | 2.00 | .55 |
| ☐ 124 Mark Smolinski SP | 7.00 | 3.10 | .85 |
| ☐ 125 Matt Snell | 15.00 | 6.75 | 1.90 |
| ☐ 126 Mike Taliaferro | 3.50 | 1.55 | .45 |
| ☐ 127 Bake Turner SP | 12.00 | 5.50 | 1.50 |
| ☐ 128 Jeff Ware | 3.50 | 1.55 | .45 |
| ☐ 129 Clyde Washington | 3.50 | 1.55 | .45 |
| ☐ 130 Dick Wood | 4.00 | 1.80 | .50 |
| ☐ 131 New York Jets Team Card | 8.00 | 3.60 | 1.00 |
| ☐ 132 Dalva Allen SP | 7.00 | 3.10 | .85 |
| ☐ 133 Dan Birdwell | 3.50 | 1.55 | .45 |
| ☐ 134 Dave Costa | 4.00 | 1.80 | .50 |
| ☐ 135 Dobie Craig | 3.50 | 1.55 | .45 |
| ☐ 136 Clem Daniels | 4.00 | 1.80 | .50 |
| ☐ 137 Cotton Davidson SP | 7.50 | 3.40 | .95 |
| ☐ 138 Claude Gibson | 3.50 | 1.55 | .45 |
| ☐ 139 Tom Flores SP | 15.00 | 6.75 | 1.90 |
| ☐ 140 Wayne Hawkins SP | 7.00 | 3.10 | .85 |
| ☐ 141 Ken Herock | 3.50 | 1.55 | .45 |
| ☐ 142 Jon Jelacic SP | 7.00 | 3.10 | .85 |
| ☐ 143 Joe Krakoski | 3.50 | 1.55 | .45 |
| ☐ 144 Archie Matsos SP | 7.50 | 3.40 | .95 |
| ☐ 145 Mike Mercer | 3.50 | 1.55 | .45 |
| ☐ 146 Alan Miller SP | 7.00 | 3.10 | .85 |
| ☐ 147 Bob Mischak SP | 7.00 | 3.10 | .85 |
| ☐ 148 Jim Otto SP | 24.00 | 11.00 | 3.00 |
| ☐ 149 Clancy Osborne SP | 7.00 | 3.10 | .85 |
| ☐ 150 Art Powell SP | 10.00 | 4.50 | 1.25 |
| ☐ 151 Bo Roberson (Raider helmet placed over his foot) | 3.50 | 1.55 | .45 |
| ☐ 152 Fred Williamson SP | 12.00 | 5.50 | 1.50 |
| ☐ 153 Oakland Raiders Team Card | 8.00 | 3.60 | 1.00 |
| ☐ 154 Chuck Allen SP | 10.00 | 4.50 | 1.25 |
| ☐ 155 Lance Alworth | 40.00 | 18.00 | 5.00 |
| ☐ 156 George Blair | 3.50 | 1.55 | .45 |
| ☐ 157 Earl Faison | 4.00 | 1.80 | .50 |
| ☐ 158 Sam Gruniesen | 3.50 | 1.55 | .45 |
| ☐ 159 John Hadl | 35.00 | 16.00 | 4.40 |
| ☐ 160 Dick Harris SP | 7.00 | 3.10 | .85 |
| ☐ 161 Emil Karas SP | 7.00 | 3.10 | .85 |
| ☐ 162 Dave Kocourek SP | 7.50 | 3.40 | .95 |
| ☐ 163 Ernie Ladd | 5.50 | 2.50 | .70 |
| ☐ 164 Keith Lincoln | 5.50 | 2.50 | .70 |
| ☐ 165 Paul Lowe SP | 10.00 | 4.50 | 1.25 |
| ☐ 166 Charles McNeil | 3.50 | 1.55 | .45 |
| ☐ 167 Jacque MacKinnon SP | 7.00 | 3.10 | .85 |
| ☐ 168 Ron Mix SP | 15.00 | 6.75 | 1.90 |
| ☐ 169 Don Norton SP | 7.00 | 3.10 | .85 |
| ☐ 170 Don Rogers SP | 7.00 | 3.10 | .85 |
| ☐ 171 Tobin Rote SP | 10.00 | 4.50 | 1.25 |
| ☐ 172 Henry Schmidt SP | 7.00 | 3.10 | .85 |
| ☐ 173 Bud Whitehead | 3.50 | 1.55 | .45 |
| ☐ 174 Ernie Wright SP | 7.00 | 3.10 | .85 |
| ☐ 175 San Diego Chargers Team Card | 8.00 | 3.60 | 1.00 |
| ☐ 176 Checklist SP UER (155 Lance Allworth) | 150.00 | 21.00 | 4.30 |

## 1964 Topps Pennant Stickers

This set of 24 pennant stickers was inserted into the 1964 Topps regular issue AFL set. These inserts are actually 2 1/8" by 4 1/2" glassine type peel-offs on gray backing. The pennants are unnumbered and are ordered below alphabetically within type. The set consists of 8 AFL teams (1-8) and 16 college teams (9-24). The stickers were folded in order to fit into the 1964 Topps wax packs, so they are virtually always found with a crease or fold.

| | NRMT | VG-E | GOOD |
|---|---|---|---|
| COMPLETE SET (24) | 750.00 | 300.00 | 75.00 |
| COMMON AFL (1-8) | 40.00 | 16.00 | 4.00 |
| COMMON COLLEGE (9-24) | 25.00 | 10.00 | 2.50 |
| ☐ 1 Boston Patriots | 40.00 | 16.00 | 4.00 |
| ☐ 2 Buffalo Bills | 50.00 | 20.00 | 5.00 |
| ☐ 3 Denver Broncos | 60.00 | 24.00 | 6.00 |
| ☐ 4 Houston Oilers | 50.00 | 20.00 | 5.00 |
| ☐ 5 Kansas City Chiefs | 40.00 | 16.00 | 4.00 |
| ☐ 6 New York Jets | 50.00 | 20.00 | 5.00 |
| ☐ 7 Oakland Raiders | 75.00 | 30.00 | 7.50 |
| ☐ 8 San Diego Chargers | 40.00 | 16.00 | 4.00 |
| ☐ 9 Air Force Academy | 25.00 | 10.00 | 2.50 |
| ☐ 10 Army | 30.00 | 12.00 | 3.00 |
| ☐ 11 Dartmouth | 25.00 | 10.00 | 2.50 |
| ☐ 12 Duke | 30.00 | 12.00 | 3.00 |
| ☐ 13 Michigan | 40.00 | 16.00 | 4.00 |
| ☐ 14 Minnesota | 30.00 | 12.00 | 3.00 |
| ☐ 15 Mississippi | 25.00 | 10.00 | 2.50 |
| ☐ 16 Navy | 30.00 | 12.00 | 3.00 |
| ☐ 17 Notre Dame | 60.00 | 24.00 | 6.00 |
| ☐ 18 SMU | 25.00 | 10.00 | 2.50 |
| ☐ 19 Southern California | 30.00 | 12.00 | 3.00 |
| ☐ 20 Syracuse | 25.00 | 10.00 | 2.50 |
| ☐ 21 Texas | 30.00 | 12.00 | 3.00 |
| ☐ 22 Washington | 30.00 | 12.00 | 3.00 |
| ☐ 23 Wisconsin | 25.00 | 10.00 | 2.50 |
| ☐ 24 Yale | 25.00 | 10.00 | 2.50 |

## 1965 Topps

TOM FLORES quarterback

The 1965 Topps football card set contains 176 oversized (2 1/2" by 4 11/16") cards of American Football League players. The cards are grouped together and numbered in basic alphabetical order by teams: for example, Boston Patriots (1-22), Buffalo Bills (23-44), Denver Broncos (45-65), Houston Oilers (66-88), Kansas City Chiefs (89-

110), New York Jets (111-131), Oakland Raiders (132-153), and San Diego Chargers (154-175). Since this set was not printed in the standard fashion, many of the cards were printed in lesser quantities than others. These cards are marked in the checklist with SP for short print. This set is somewhat significant in that it contains the Rookie Card of Joe Namath. Other notable Rookie Cards in this set are Fred Biletnikoff, Willie Brown, and Ben Davidson.

| | NRMT | VG-E | GOOD |
|---|---|---|---|
| COMPLETE SET (176) | 4000.00 | 1800.00 | 500.00 |
| COMMON PLAYER (1-176) | 7.00 | 3.10 | .85 |
| ☐ 1 Tommy Addison SP | 35.00 | 7.00 | 2.10 |
| ☐ 2 Houston Antwine SP | 12.50 | 5.75 | 1.55 |
| ☐ 3 Nick Buoniconti SP | 25.00 | 11.50 | 3.10 |
| ☐ 4 Ron Burton SP | 15.00 | 6.75 | 1.90 |
| ☐ 5 Gino Cappelletti SP | 20.00 | 9.00 | 2.50 |
| ☐ 6 Jim Colclough | 7.00 | 3.10 | .85 |
| ☐ 7 Bob Dee SP | 12.50 | 5.75 | 1.55 |
| ☐ 8 Larry Eisenhauer | 8.00 | 3.60 | 1.00 |
| ☐ 9 J.D. Garrett | 7.00 | 3.10 | .85 |
| ☐ 10 Larry Garron | 7.00 | 3.10 | .85 |
| ☐ 11 Art Graham SP | 12.50 | 5.75 | 1.55 |
| ☐ 12 Ron Hall | 7.00 | 3.10 | .85 |
| ☐ 13 Charles Long | 7.00 | 3.10 | .85 |
| ☐ 14 Jon Morris | 10.00 | 4.50 | 1.25 |
| ☐ 15 Bill Neighbors SP | 12.50 | 5.75 | 1.55 |
| ☐ 16 Ross O'Hanley | 7.00 | 3.10 | .85 |
| ☐ 17 Babe Parilli SP | 15.00 | 6.75 | 1.90 |
| ☐ 18 Tony Romeo SP | 12.50 | 5.75 | 1.55 |
| ☐ 19 Jack Rudolph SP | 12.50 | 5.75 | 1.55 |
| ☐ 20 Bob Schmidt | 7.00 | 3.10 | .85 |
| ☐ 21 Don Webb SP | 12.50 | 5.75 | 1.55 |
| ☐ 22 Jim Whalen SP | 12.50 | 5.75 | 1.55 |
| ☐ 23 Stew Barber | 7.00 | 3.10 | .85 |
| ☐ 24 Glenn Bass SP | 12.50 | 5.75 | 1.55 |
| ☐ 25 Al Bemiller SP | 12.50 | 5.75 | 1.55 |
| ☐ 26 Wray Carlton SP | 15.00 | 6.75 | 1.90 |
| ☐ 27 Tom Day | 7.00 | 3.10 | .85 |
| ☐ 28 Elbert Dubenion SP | 15.00 | 6.75 | 1.90 |
| ☐ 29 Jim Dunaway | 7.00 | 3.10 | .85 |
| ☐ 30 Pete Gogolak SP | 18.00 | 8.00 | 2.30 |
| ☐ 31 Dick Hudson SP | 12.50 | 5.75 | 1.55 |
| ☐ 32 Harry Jacobs SP | 12.50 | 5.75 | 1.55 |
| ☐ 33 Billy Joe SP | 15.00 | 6.75 | 1.90 |
| ☐ 34 Tom Keating SP | 16.00 | 7.25 | 2.00 |
| ☐ 35 Jack Kemp SP | 250.00 | 115.00 | 31.00 |
| ☐ 36 Daryle Lamonica SP | 35.00 | 16.00 | 4.40 |
| ☐ 37 Paul Maguire SP | 20.00 | 9.00 | 2.50 |
| ☐ 38 Ron McDole SP | 16.00 | 7.25 | 2.00 |
| ☐ 39 George Saimes SP | 15.00 | 6.75 | 1.90 |
| ☐ 40 Tom Sestak SP | 15.00 | 6.75 | 1.90 |
| ☐ 41 Billy Shaw SP | 12.50 | 5.75 | 1.55 |
| ☐ 42 Mike Stratton SP | 12.50 | 5.75 | 1.55 |
| ☐ 43 John Tracey SP | 12.50 | 5.75 | 1.55 |
| ☐ 44 Ernie Warlick | 8.00 | 3.60 | 1.00 |
| ☐ 45 Odell Barry | 7.00 | 3.10 | .85 |
| ☐ 46 Willie Brown SP | 65.00 | 29.00 | 8.25 |
| ☐ 47 Gerry Bussell SP | 12.50 | 5.75 | 1.55 |
| ☐ 48 Eldon Danenhauer SP | 15.00 | 6.75 | 1.90 |
| ☐ 49 Al Denson SP | 12.50 | 5.75 | 1.55 |
| ☐ 50 Hewritt Dixon SP | 20.00 | 9.00 | 2.50 |
| ☐ 51 Cookie Gilchrist SP | 22.00 | 10.00 | 2.80 |
| ☐ 52 Goose Gonsoulin SP | 15.00 | 6.75 | 1.90 |
| ☐ 53 Abner Haynes SP | 20.00 | 9.00 | 2.50 |
| ☐ 54 Jerry Hopkins | 7.00 | 3.10 | .85 |
| ☐ 55 Ray Jacobs SP | 12.50 | 5.75 | 1.55 |
| ☐ 56 Jacky Lee SP | 15.00 | 6.75 | 1.90 |
| ☐ 57 John McCormick | 7.00 | 3.10 | .85 |
| ☐ 58 Bob McCullough SP | 12.50 | 5.75 | 1.55 |
| ☐ 59 John McGeever | 7.00 | 3.10 | .85 |
| ☐ 60 Charlie Mitchell SP | 12.50 | 5.75 | 1.55 |
| ☐ 61 Jim Perkins SP | 12.50 | 5.75 | 1.55 |
| ☐ 62 Bob Scarpitto SP | 12.50 | 5.75 | 1.55 |
| ☐ 63 Mickey Slaughter SP | 12.50 | 5.75 | 1.55 |
| ☐ 64 Jerry Sturm SP | 12.50 | 5.75 | 1.55 |
| ☐ 65 Lionel Taylor SP | 20.00 | 9.00 | 2.50 |
| ☐ 66 Scott Appleton SP | 15.00 | 6.75 | 1.90 |
| ☐ 67 Johnny Baker SP | 12.50 | 5.75 | 1.55 |
| ☐ 68 Sonny Bishop SP | 12.50 | 5.75 | 1.55 |
| ☐ 69 George Blanda SP | 90.00 | 40.00 | 11.50 |
| ☐ 70 Sid Blanks SP | 12.50 | 5.75 | 1.55 |
| ☐ 71 Ode Burrell SP | 12.50 | 5.75 | 1.55 |
| ☐ 72 Doug Cline SP | 12.50 | 5.75 | 1.55 |
| ☐ 73 Willard Dewveall | 7.00 | 3.10 | .85 |
| ☐ 74 Larry Elkins | 10.00 | 4.50 | 1.25 |
| ☐ 75 Don Floyd SP | 12.50 | 5.75 | 1.55 |
| ☐ 76 Freddy Glick | 7.00 | 3.10 | .85 |
| ☐ 77 Tom Goode SP | 12.50 | 5.75 | 1.55 |
| ☐ 78 Charlie Hennigan SP | 18.00 | 8.00 | 2.30 |
| ☐ 79 Ed Husmann | 7.00 | 3.10 | .85 |
| ☐ 80 Bobby Jancik SP | 12.50 | 5.75 | 1.55 |
| ☐ 81 Bud McFadin SP | 12.50 | 5.75 | 1.55 |
| ☐ 82 Bob McLeod SP | 12.50 | 5.75 | 1.55 |
| ☐ 83 Jim Norton SP | 12.50 | 5.75 | 1.55 |
| ☐ 84 Walt Suggs | 7.00 | 3.10 | .85 |
| ☐ 85 Bob Talamini | 7.00 | 3.10 | .85 |
| ☐ 86 Charley Tolar SP | 15.00 | 6.75 | 1.90 |
| ☐ 87 Checklist 1-88 SP | 150.00 | 30.00 | 10.00 |
| ☐ 88 Don Trull SP | 15.00 | 6.75 | 1.90 |
| ☐ 89 Fred Arbanas SP | 15.00 | 6.75 | 1.90 |
| ☐ 90 Pete Beathard SP | 20.00 | 9.00 | 2.50 |
| ☐ 91 Bobby Bell SP | 25.00 | 11.50 | 3.10 |
| ☐ 92 Mel Branch SP | 15.00 | 6.75 | 1.90 |
| ☐ 93 Tommy Brooker SP | 12.50 | 5.75 | 1.55 |
| ☐ 94 Buck Buchanan SP | 25.00 | 11.50 | 3.10 |
| ☐ 95 Ed Budde SP | 15.00 | 6.75 | 1.90 |
| ☐ 96 Chris Burford SP | 15.00 | 6.75 | 1.90 |
| ☐ 97 Walt Corey | 7.00 | 3.10 | .85 |
| ☐ 98 Jerry Cornelison | 7.00 | 3.10 | .85 |
| ☐ 99 Len Dawson SP | 80.00 | 36.00 | 10.00 |
| ☐ 100 Jon Gilliam SP | 12.50 | 5.75 | 1.55 |
| ☐ 101 Sherrill Headrick SP | 15.00 | 6.75 | 1.90 |
| ☐ 102 Dave Hill SP | 12.50 | 5.75 | 1.55 |
| ☐ 103 E.J. Holub SP | 15.00 | 6.75 | 1.90 |
| ☐ 104 Bobby Hunt SP | 15.00 | 6.75 | 1.90 |
| ☐ 105 Frank Jackson SP | 13.50 | 6.00 | 1.70 |
| ☐ 106 Jerry Mays | 8.00 | 3.60 | 1.00 |
| ☐ 107 Curtis McClinton SP | 15.00 | 6.75 | 1.90 |
| ☐ 108 Bobby Ply SP | 12.50 | 5.75 | 1.55 |
| ☐ 109 Johnny Robinson SP | 15.00 | 6.75 | 1.90 |
| ☐ 110 Jim Tyrer SP | 15.00 | 6.75 | 1.90 |
| ☐ 111 Bill Baird SP | 12.50 | 5.75 | 1.55 |
| ☐ 112 Ralph Baker SP | 16.00 | 7.25 | 2.00 |
| ☐ 113 Sam DeLuca SP | 12.50 | 5.75 | 1.55 |
| ☐ 114 Larry Grantham SP | 15.00 | 6.75 | 1.90 |
| ☐ 115 Gene Heeter SP | 12.50 | 5.75 | 1.55 |
| ☐ 116 Winston Hill SP | 20.00 | 9.00 | 2.50 |
| ☐ 117 John Huarte SP | 30.00 | 13.50 | 3.80 |
| ☐ 118 Cosmo Iacavazzi SP | 12.50 | 5.75 | 1.55 |
| ☐ 119 Curley Johnson SP | 12.50 | 5.75 | 1.55 |
| ☐ 120 Dee Mackey UER | 7.00 | 3.10 | .85 |
| (College WVU, should be East Texas State) | | | |
| ☐ 121 Don Maynard | 40.00 | 18.00 | 5.00 |
| ☐ 122 Joe Namath SP | 1600.00 | 700.00 | 200.00 |
| ☐ 123 Dainard Paulson | 7.00 | 3.10 | .85 |
| ☐ 124 Gerry Philbin SP | 13.50 | 6.00 | 1.70 |
| ☐ 125 Sherman Plunkett SP | 20.00 | 9.00 | 2.50 |
| ☐ 126 Mark Smolinski | 7.00 | 3.10 | .85 |
| ☐ 127 Matt Snell SP | 24.00 | 11.00 | 3.00 |
| ☐ 128 Mike Taliaferro SP | 12.50 | 5.75 | 1.55 |
| ☐ 129 Bake Turner SP | 7.00 | 3.10 | .85 |
| ☐ 130 Clyde Washington SP | 12.50 | 5.75 | 1.55 |
| ☐ 131 Verlon Biggs SP | 16.00 | 7.25 | 2.00 |
| ☐ 132 Dalva Allen | 7.00 | 3.10 | .85 |
| ☐ 133 Fred Biletnikoff SP | 185.00 | 85.00 | 23.00 |
| ☐ 134 Billy Cannon SP | 20.00 | 9.00 | 2.50 |
| ☐ 135 Dave Costa SP | 12.50 | 5.75 | 1.55 |
| ☐ 136 Clem Daniels SP | 15.00 | 6.75 | 1.90 |
| ☐ 137 Ben Davidson SP | 40.00 | 18.00 | 5.00 |
| ☐ 138 Cotton Davidson SP | 15.00 | 6.75 | 1.90 |
| ☐ 139 Tom Flores SP | 27.00 | 12.00 | 3.40 |
| ☐ 140 Claude Gibson | 7.00 | 3.10 | .85 |
| ☐ 141 Wayne Hawkins | 7.00 | 3.10 | .85 |
| ☐ 142 Archie Matsos SP | 15.00 | 6.75 | 1.90 |
| ☐ 143 Mike Mercer SP | 12.50 | 5.75 | 1.55 |
| ☐ 144 Bob Mischak SP | 12.50 | 5.75 | 1.55 |
| ☐ 145 Jim Otto SP | 25.00 | 11.50 | 3.10 |
| ☐ 146 Art Powell UER | 15.00 | 6.75 | 1.90 |
| (Photo actually Clem Daniels) | | | |
| ☐ 147 Warren Powers SP | 12.50 | 5.75 | 1.55 |
| ☐ 148 Ken Rice SP | 12.50 | 5.75 | 1.55 |
| ☐ 149 Bo Roberson SP | 12.50 | 5.75 | 1.55 |
| ☐ 150 Harry Schuh | 12.00 | 5.50 | 1.50 |
| ☐ 151 Larry Todd SP | 12.50 | 5.75 | 1.55 |
| ☐ 152 Fred Williamson SP | 20.00 | 9.00 | 2.50 |
| ☐ 153 J.R. Williamson | 7.00 | 3.10 | .85 |
| ☐ 154 Chuck Allen | 7.00 | 3.10 | .85 |
| ☐ 155 Lance Alworth | 65.00 | 29.00 | 8.25 |
| ☐ 156 Frank Buncom | 7.00 | 3.10 | .85 |
| ☐ 157 Steve DeLong SP | 18.00 | 8.00 | 2.30 |
| ☐ 158 Earl Faison SP | 15.00 | 6.75 | 1.90 |
| ☐ 159 Kenny Graham SP | 12.50 | 5.75 | 1.55 |
| ☐ 160 George Gross SP | 12.50 | 5.75 | 1.55 |
| ☐ 161 John Hadl SP | 27.00 | 12.00 | 3.40 |
| ☐ 162 Emil Karas SP | 12.50 | 5.75 | 1.55 |
| ☐ 163 Dave Kocourek SP | 15.00 | 6.75 | 1.90 |
| ☐ 164 Ernie Ladd SP | 20.00 | 9.00 | 2.50 |
| ☐ 165 Keith Lincoln SP | 18.00 | 8.00 | 2.30 |
| ☐ 166 Paul Lowe SP | 20.00 | 9.00 | 2.50 |
| ☐ 167 Jacque MacKinnon | 7.00 | 3.10 | .85 |
| ☐ 168 Ron Mix SP | 20.00 | 9.00 | 2.50 |
| ☐ 169 Don Norton SP | 12.50 | 5.75 | 1.55 |
| ☐ 170 Bob Petrich | 7.00 | 3.10 | .85 |
| ☐ 171 Rick Redman SP | 12.50 | 5.75 | 1.55 |
| ☐ 172 Pat Shea | 7.00 | 3.10 | .85 |
| ☐ 173 Walt Sweeney SP | 16.00 | 7.25 | 2.00 |
| ☐ 174 Dick Westmoreland | 12.50 | 5.50 | 1.50 |
| ☐ 175 Ernie Wright SP | 12.50 | 5.75 | 1.55 |
| ☐ 176 Checklist 89-176 SP | 200.00 | 30.00 | 10.00 |

## 1965 Topps Magic Rub-Off Inserts

This set of 36 rub-off team emblems was inserted into packs of the 1965 Topps AFL regular football issue. They are very similar to the 1961 Topps Baseball Magic Rub-Offs. Each rub-off measures 2" by 3"; eight AFL teams and 28 college teams are featured. The rub-offs are unnumbered and, hence, are numbered below alphabetically within type, i.e., AFL teams 1-8 and college teams 9-36.

|  | NRMT | VG-E | GOOD |
|---|---|---|---|
| COMPLETE SET (36) | 400.00 | 160.00 | 40.00 |
| COMMON CARD (1-8) | 15.00 | 6.00 | 1.50 |
| COMMON CARD (9-36) | 10.00 | 4.00 | 1.00 |
| ☐ 1 Boston Patriots | 15.00 | 6.00 | 1.50 |
| ☐ 2 Buffalo Bills | 20.00 | 8.00 | 2.00 |
| ☐ 3 Denver Broncos | 25.00 | 10.00 | 2.50 |
| ☐ 4 Houston Oilers | 20.00 | 8.00 | 2.00 |
| ☐ 5 Kansas City Chiefs | 15.00 | 6.00 | 1.50 |
| ☐ 6 New York Jets | 20.00 | 8.00 | 2.00 |
| ☐ 7 Oakland Raiders | 35.00 | 14.00 | 3.50 |
| ☐ 8 San Diego Chargers | 15.00 | 6.00 | 1.50 |
| ☐ 9 Alabama | 15.00 | 6.00 | 1.50 |
| ☐ 10 Air Force Academy | 10.00 | 4.00 | 1.00 |
| ☐ 11 Arkansas | 15.00 | 6.00 | 1.50 |
| ☐ 12 Army | 15.00 | 6.00 | 1.50 |
| ☐ 13 Boston College | 10.00 | 4.00 | 1.00 |
| ☐ 14 Duke | 15.00 | 6.00 | 1.50 |
| ☐ 15 Illinois | 10.00 | 4.00 | 1.00 |
| ☐ 16 Kansas | 12.00 | 5.00 | 1.20 |
| ☐ 17 Kentucky | 10.00 | 4.00 | 1.00 |
| ☐ 18 Maryland | 10.00 | 4.00 | 1.00 |
| ☐ 19 Miami | 12.00 | 5.00 | 1.20 |
| ☐ 20 Minnesota | 12.00 | 5.00 | 1.20 |
| ☐ 21 Mississippi | 12.00 | 5.00 | 1.20 |
| ☐ 22 Navy | 12.00 | 5.00 | 1.20 |
| ☐ 23 Nebraska | 15.00 | 6.00 | 1.50 |
| ☐ 24 Notre Dame | 35.00 | 14.00 | 3.50 |
| ☐ 25 Penn State | 12.00 | 5.00 | 1.20 |
| ☐ 26 Purdue | 10.00 | 4.00 | 1.00 |
| ☐ 27 SMU | 10.00 | 4.00 | 1.00 |
| ☐ 28 Southern California | 12.00 | 5.00 | 1.20 |
| ☐ 29 Stanford | 10.00 | 4.00 | 1.00 |
| ☐ 30 Syracuse | 10.00 | 4.00 | 1.00 |
| ☐ 31 TCU | 10.00 | 4.00 | 1.00 |
| ☐ 32 Texas | 15.00 | 6.00 | 1.50 |
| ☐ 33 Virginia | 10.00 | 4.00 | 1.00 |
| ☐ 34 Washington | 15.00 | 6.00 | 1.50 |
| ☐ 35 Wisconsin | 10.00 | 4.00 | 1.00 |
| ☐ 36 Yale | 10.00 | 4.00 | 1.00 |

## 1966 Topps

The 1966 Topps set of 132 cards contains AFL players grouped together and numbered alphabetically within teams, for example: Boston Patriots (1-14), Buffalo Bills (16-30), Denver Broncos (31-45), Houston Oilers (46-60), Kansas City Chiefs (62-75), Miami Dolphins (76-89), New York Jets (90-103), Oakland Raiders (104-117), and San Diego Chargers (118-131). The set marks the debut into the AFL of the Miami Dolphins. The cards measure standard size, 2 1/2" by 3 1/2". The card backs are printed in black and pink on white card stock. In actuality, card number 15 is not a football card at all but a "Funny Ring" checklist card; nevertheless, it is considered part of the set and is now regarded as the toughest card in the set to find in mint condition. Funny ring cards were inserted one per pack but measure only 2 1/2" by 3 3/8". The only notable Rookie Cards in this set are George Sauer Jr., Otis Taylor, and Jim Turner.

|  | NRMT | VG-E | GOOD |
|---|---|---|---|
| COMPLETE SET (132) | 1300.00 | 575.00 | 160.00 |
| COMMON PLAYER (1-132) | 4.50 | 2.00 | .55 |

| ☐ 1 Tommy Addison | 20.00 | 4.00 | 1.20 |
|---|---|---|---|
| ☐ 2 Houston Antwine | 4.50 | 2.00 | .55 |
| ☐ 3 Nick Buoniconti | 9.00 | 4.00 | 1.15 |
| ☐ 4 Gino Cappelletti | 6.00 | 2.70 | .75 |
| ☐ 5 Bob Dee | 4.50 | 2.00 | .55 |
| ☐ 6 Larry Garron | 4.50 | 2.00 | .55 |
| ☐ 7 Art Graham | 4.50 | 2.00 | .55 |
| ☐ 8 Ron Hall | 4.50 | 2.00 | .55 |
| ☐ 9 Charles Long | 4.50 | 2.00 | .55 |
| ☐ 10 Jon Morris | 4.50 | 2.00 | .55 |
| ☐ 11 Don Oakes | 4.50 | 2.00 | .55 |
| ☐ 12 Babe Parilli | 5.00 | 2.30 | .60 |
| ☐ 13 Don Webb | 4.50 | 2.00 | .55 |
| ☐ 14 Jim Whalen | 4.50 | 2.00 | .55 |
| ☐ 15 Funny Ring Checklist | 250.00 | 62.50 | 12.50 |
| ☐ 16 Stew Barber | 4.50 | 2.00 | .55 |
| ☐ 17 Glenn Bass | 4.50 | 2.00 | .55 |
| ☐ 18 Dave Behrman | 4.50 | 2.00 | .55 |
| ☐ 19 Al Bemiller | 4.50 | 2.00 | .55 |
| ☐ 20 George(Butch) Byrd | 6.00 | 2.70 | .75 |
| ☐ 21 Wray Carlton | 5.00 | 2.30 | .60 |
| ☐ 22 Tom Day | 4.50 | 2.00 | .55 |
| ☐ 23 Elbert Dubenion | 5.00 | 2.30 | .60 |
| ☐ 24 Jim Dunaway | 4.50 | 2.00 | .55 |
| ☐ 25 Dick Hudson | 4.50 | 2.00 | .55 |
| ☐ 26 Jack Kemp | 185.00 | 85.00 | 23.00 |
| ☐ 27 Daryle Lamonica | 10.00 | 4.50 | 1.25 |
| ☐ 28 Tom Sestak | 5.00 | 2.30 | .60 |
| ☐ 29 Billy Shaw | 4.50 | 2.00 | .55 |
| ☐ 30 Mike Stratton | 4.50 | 2.00 | .55 |
| ☐ 31 Eldon Danenhauer | 5.00 | 2.30 | .60 |
| ☐ 32 Cookie Gilchrist | 6.00 | 2.70 | .75 |
| ☐ 33 Goose Gonsoulin | 5.00 | 2.30 | .60 |
| ☐ 34 Wendell Hayes | 8.50 | 3.80 | 1.05 |
| ☐ 35 Abner Haynes | 5.00 | 2.30 | .60 |
| ☐ 36 Jerry Hopkins | 4.50 | 2.00 | .55 |
| ☐ 37 Ray Jacobs | 4.50 | 2.00 | .55 |
| ☐ 38 Charlie Janerette | 4.50 | 2.00 | .55 |
| ☐ 39 Ray Kubala | 4.50 | 2.00 | .55 |
| ☐ 40 John McCormick | 4.50 | 2.00 | .55 |
| ☐ 41 Leroy Moore | 4.50 | 2.00 | .55 |
| ☐ 42 Bob Scarpitto | 4.50 | 2.00 | .55 |
| ☐ 43 Mickey Slaughter | 4.50 | 2.00 | .55 |
| ☐ 44 Jerry Sturm | 4.50 | 2.00 | .55 |
| ☐ 45 Lionel Taylor | 6.00 | 2.70 | .75 |
| ☐ 46 Scott Appleton | 5.00 | 2.30 | .60 |
| ☐ 47 Johnny Baker | 4.50 | 2.00 | .55 |
| ☐ 48 George Blanda | 40.00 | 18.00 | 5.00 |
| ☐ 49 Sid Blanks | 4.50 | 2.00 | .55 |
| ☐ 50 Danny Brabham | 4.50 | 2.00 | .55 |
| ☐ 51 Ode Burrell | 4.50 | 2.00 | .55 |
| ☐ 52 Gary Cutsinger | 4.50 | 2.00 | .55 |
| ☐ 53 Larry Elkins | 4.50 | 2.00 | .55 |
| ☐ 54 Don Floyd | 4.50 | 2.00 | .55 |
| ☐ 55 Willie Frazier | 6.00 | 2.70 | .75 |
| ☐ 56 Freddy Glick | 4.50 | 2.00 | .55 |
| ☐ 57 Charlie Hennigan | 5.00 | 2.30 | .60 |
| ☐ 58 Bobby Jancik | 4.50 | 2.00 | .55 |
| ☐ 59 Rich Michael | 4.50 | 2.00 | .55 |
| ☐ 60 Don Trull | 5.00 | 2.30 | .60 |
| ☐ 61 Checklist Card | 45.00 | 5.75 | 1.15 |
| ☐ 62 Fred Arbanas | 4.50 | 2.00 | .55 |
| ☐ 63 Pete Beathard | 4.50 | 2.00 | .55 |
| ☐ 64 Bobby Bell | 9.00 | 4.00 | 1.15 |
| ☐ 65 Ed Budde | 5.00 | 2.30 | .60 |
| ☐ 66 Chris Burford | 4.50 | 2.00 | .55 |
| ☐ 67 Len Dawson | 32.00 | 14.50 | 4.00 |
| ☐ 68 Jon Gilliam | 4.50 | 2.00 | .55 |
| ☐ 69 Sherrill Headrick | 5.00 | 2.30 | .60 |
| ☐ 70 E.J. Holub UER | 5.00 | 2.30 | .60 |
| (College: TCU, should be Texas Tech) |  |  |  |
| ☐ 71 Bobby Hunt | 5.00 | 2.30 | .60 |
| ☐ 72 Curtis McClinton | 5.00 | 2.30 | .60 |
| ☐ 73 Jerry Mays | 5.00 | 2.30 | .60 |
| ☐ 74 Johnny Robinson | 5.00 | 2.30 | .60 |
| ☐ 75 Otis Taylor | 18.00 | 8.00 | 2.30 |

| | NRMT | VG-E | GOOD |
|---|---|---|---|
| ☐ 76 Tom Erlandson | 5.00 | 2.30 | .60 |
| ☐ 77 Norm Evans UER | 7.00 | 3.10 | .85 |
| (Flanker on front, tackle on back) | | | |
| ☐ 78 Tom Goode | 5.00 | 2.30 | .60 |
| ☐ 79 Mike Hudock | 5.00 | 2.30 | .60 |
| ☐ 80 Frank Jackson | 5.00 | 2.30 | .60 |
| ☐ 81 Billy Joe | 5.00 | 2.30 | .60 |
| ☐ 82 Dave Kocourek | 5.00 | 2.30 | .60 |
| ☐ 83 Bo Roberson | 5.00 | 2.30 | .60 |
| ☐ 84 Jack Spikes | 5.00 | 2.30 | .60 |
| ☐ 85 Jim Warren | 7.00 | 3.10 | .85 |
| ☐ 86 Willie West | 6.00 | 2.70 | .75 |
| ☐ 87 Dick Westmoreland | 5.00 | 2.30 | .60 |
| ☐ 88 Eddie Wilson | 5.00 | 2.30 | .60 |
| ☐ 89 Dick Wood | 5.00 | 2.30 | .60 |
| ☐ 90 Verlon Biggs | 5.00 | 2.30 | .60 |
| ☐ 91 Sam DeLuca | 4.50 | 2.00 | .55 |
| ☐ 92 Winston Hill | 4.50 | 2.00 | .55 |
| ☐ 93 Dee Mackey | 4.50 | 2.00 | .55 |
| ☐ 94 Bill Mathis | 5.00 | 2.30 | .60 |
| ☐ 95 Don Maynard | 25.00 | 11.50 | 3.10 |
| ☐ 96 Joe Namath | 325.00 | 145.00 | 40.00 |
| ☐ 97 Dainard Paulson | 4.50 | 2.00 | .55 |
| ☐ 98 Gerry Philbin | 5.00 | 2.30 | .60 |
| ☐ 99 Sherman Plunkett | 4.50 | 2.00 | .55 |
| ☐ 100 Paul Rochester | 4.50 | 2.00 | .55 |
| ☐ 101 George Sauer Jr. | 8.00 | 3.60 | 1.00 |
| ☐ 102 Matt Snell | 6.00 | 2.70 | .75 |
| ☐ 103 Jim Turner | 6.00 | 2.70 | .75 |
| ☐ 104 Fred Biletnikoff UER | 50.00 | 23.00 | 6.25 |
| (Misspelled on back as Bilentnikoff) | | | |
| ☐ 105 Bill Budness | 4.50 | 2.00 | .55 |
| ☐ 106 Billy Cannon | 6.00 | 2.70 | .75 |
| ☐ 107 Clem Daniels | 5.00 | 2.30 | .60 |
| ☐ 108 Ben Davidson | 7.00 | 3.10 | .85 |
| ☐ 109 Cotton Davidson | 5.00 | 2.30 | .60 |
| ☐ 110 Claude Gibson | 4.50 | 2.00 | .55 |
| ☐ 111 Wayne Hawkins | 4.50 | 2.00 | .55 |
| ☐ 112 Ken Herock | 4.50 | 2.00 | .55 |
| ☐ 113 Bob Mischak | 4.50 | 2.00 | .55 |
| ☐ 114 Gus Otto | 4.50 | 2.00 | .55 |
| ☐ 115 Jim Otto | 16.00 | 7.25 | 2.00 |
| ☐ 116 Art Powell | 6.00 | 2.70 | .75 |
| ☐ 117 Harry Schuh | 4.50 | 2.00 | .55 |
| ☐ 118 Chuck Allen | 4.50 | 2.00 | .55 |
| ☐ 119 Lance Alworth | 32.00 | 14.50 | 4.00 |
| ☐ 120 Frank Buncom | 4.50 | 2.00 | .55 |
| ☐ 121 Steve DeLong | 4.50 | 2.00 | .55 |
| ☐ 122 John Farris | 4.50 | 2.00 | .55 |
| ☐ 123 Kenny Graham | 4.50 | 2.00 | .55 |
| ☐ 124 Sam Gruniesen | 4.50 | 2.00 | .55 |
| ☐ 125 John Hadl | 9.00 | 4.00 | 1.15 |
| ☐ 126 Walt Sweeney | 5.00 | 2.30 | .60 |
| ☐ 127 Keith Lincoln | 5.50 | 2.50 | .70 |
| ☐ 128 Ron Mix | 8.50 | 3.80 | 1.05 |
| ☐ 129 Don Norton | 4.50 | 2.00 | .55 |
| ☐ 130 Pat Shea | 4.50 | 2.00 | .55 |
| ☐ 131 Ernie Wright | 4.50 | 2.00 | .55 |
| ☐ 132 Checklist Card | 90.00 | 13.50 | 4.50 |

## 1967 Topps

 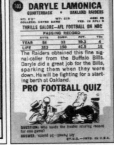

The 1967 Topps set of 132 cards contains AFL players only, with players grouped together and numbered by teams, for example: Boston Patriots (1-14), Buffalo Bills (15-29), Denver Broncos (30-43), Houston Oilers (44-58), Kansas City Chiefs (60-73), Miami Dolphins (74-88), New York Jets (89-102), Oakland Raiders (103-116), and San Diego Chargers (117-131). The cards measure 2 1/2" by 3 1/2". The card backs are printed in gold and black on white card stock. A question (with upside-down answer) is given on the bottom of the reverse. The only notable Rookie Card in this set is Wahoo McDaniel, who gained greater fame as a professional wrestler.

| | NRMT | VG-E | GOOD |
|---|---|---|---|
| COMPLETE SET (132) | 600.00 | 275.00 | 75.00 |
| COMMON PLAYER (1-132) | 3.00 | 1.35 | .40 |
| ☐ 1 John Huarte | 10.00 | 1.50 | .50 |
| ☐ 2 Babe Parilli | 3.25 | 1.45 | .40 |
| ☐ 3 Gino Cappelletti | 3.50 | 1.55 | .45 |
| ☐ 4 Larry Garron | 3.00 | 1.35 | .40 |
| ☐ 5 Tommy Addison | 3.00 | 1.35 | .40 |
| ☐ 6 Jon Morris | 3.00 | 1.35 | .40 |
| ☐ 7 Houston Antwine | 3.00 | 1.35 | .40 |
| ☐ 8 Don Oakes | 3.00 | 1.35 | .40 |
| ☐ 9 Larry Eisenhauer | 3.25 | 1.45 | .40 |
| ☐ 10 Jim Hunt | 3.00 | 1.35 | .40 |
| ☐ 11 Jim Whalen | 3.00 | 1.35 | .40 |
| ☐ 12 Art Graham | 3.00 | 1.35 | .40 |
| ☐ 13 Nick Buoniconti | 6.00 | 2.70 | .75 |
| ☐ 14 Bob Dee | 3.00 | 1.35 | .40 |
| ☐ 15 Keith Lincoln | 4.00 | 1.80 | .50 |
| ☐ 16 Tom Flores | 6.00 | 2.70 | .75 |
| ☐ 17 Art Powell | 3.50 | 1.55 | .45 |
| ☐ 18 Stew Barber | 3.00 | 1.35 | .40 |
| ☐ 19 Wray Carlton | 3.25 | 1.45 | .40 |
| ☐ 20 Elbert Dubenion | 3.25 | 1.45 | .40 |
| ☐ 21 Jim Dunaway | 3.00 | 1.35 | .40 |
| ☐ 22 Dick Hudson | 3.00 | 1.35 | .40 |
| ☐ 23 Harry Jacobs | 3.00 | 1.35 | .40 |
| ☐ 24 Jack Kemp | 100.00 | 45.00 | 12.50 |
| ☐ 25 Ron McDole | 3.00 | 1.35 | .40 |
| ☐ 26 George Saimes | 3.25 | 1.45 | .40 |
| ☐ 27 Tom Sestak | 3.25 | 1.45 | .40 |
| ☐ 28 Billy Shaw | 3.00 | 1.35 | .40 |
| ☐ 29 Mike Stratton | 3.00 | 1.35 | .40 |
| ☐ 30 Nemiah Wilson | 3.00 | 1.35 | .40 |
| ☐ 31 John McCormick | 3.00 | 1.35 | .40 |
| ☐ 32 Rex Mirich | 3.00 | 1.35 | .40 |
| ☐ 33 Dave Costa | 3.00 | 1.35 | .40 |
| ☐ 34 Goose Gonsoulin | 3.25 | 1.45 | .40 |
| ☐ 35 Abner Haynes | 3.50 | 1.55 | .45 |
| ☐ 36 Wendell Hayes | 3.25 | 1.45 | .40 |
| ☐ 37 Archie Matsos | 3.25 | 1.45 | .40 |
| ☐ 38 John Bramlett | 3.00 | 1.35 | .40 |
| ☐ 39 Jerry Sturm | 3.00 | 1.35 | .40 |
| ☐ 40 Max Leetzow | 3.00 | 1.35 | .40 |
| ☐ 41 Bob Scarpitto | 3.00 | 1.35 | .40 |
| ☐ 42 Lionel Taylor | 3.50 | 1.55 | .45 |
| ☐ 43 Al Denson | 3.00 | 1.35 | .40 |
| ☐ 44 Miller Farr | 3.50 | 1.55 | .45 |
| ☐ 45 Don Trull | 3.25 | 1.45 | .40 |
| ☐ 46 Jacky Lee | 3.25 | 1.45 | .40 |
| ☐ 47 Bobby Jancik | 3.00 | 1.35 | .40 |
| ☐ 48 Ode Burrell | 3.00 | 1.35 | .40 |
| ☐ 49 Larry Elkins | 3.00 | 1.35 | .40 |
| ☐ 50 W.K. Hicks | 3.00 | 1.35 | .40 |
| ☐ 51 Sid Blanks | 3.00 | 1.35 | .40 |
| ☐ 52 Jim Norton | 3.00 | 1.35 | .40 |
| ☐ 53 Bobby Maples | 3.50 | 1.55 | .45 |
| ☐ 54 Bob Talamini | 3.00 | 1.35 | .40 |
| ☐ 55 Walt Suggs | 3.00 | 1.35 | .40 |
| ☐ 56 Gary Cutsinger | 3.00 | 1.35 | .40 |
| ☐ 57 Danny Brabham | 3.00 | 1.35 | .40 |
| ☐ 58 Ernie Ladd | 4.00 | 1.80 | .50 |
| ☐ 59 Checklist Card | 40.00 | 4.37 | .88 |
| ☐ 60 Pete Beathard | 3.00 | 1.35 | .40 |
| ☐ 61 Len Dawson | 22.00 | 10.00 | 2.80 |
| ☐ 62 Bobby Hunt | 3.25 | 1.45 | .40 |
| ☐ 63 Bert Coan | 3.00 | 1.35 | .40 |
| ☐ 64 Curtis McClinton | 3.25 | 1.45 | .40 |
| ☐ 65 Johnny Robinson | 3.25 | 1.45 | .40 |
| ☐ 66 E.J. Holub | 3.25 | 1.45 | .40 |
| ☐ 67 Jerry Mays | 3.25 | 1.45 | .40 |
| ☐ 68 Jim Tyrer | 3.25 | 1.45 | .40 |
| ☐ 69 Bobby Bell | 5.50 | 2.50 | .70 |
| ☐ 70 Fred Arbanas | 3.00 | 1.35 | .40 |
| ☐ 71 Buck Buchanan | 5.50 | 2.50 | .70 |
| ☐ 72 Chris Burford | 3.00 | 1.35 | .40 |
| ☐ 73 Otis Taylor | 4.00 | 1.80 | .50 |
| ☐ 74 Cookie Gilchrist | 4.50 | 2.00 | .55 |
| ☐ 75 Earl Faison | 3.25 | 1.45 | .40 |
| ☐ 76 George Wilson Jr. | 3.00 | 1.35 | .40 |
| ☐ 77 Rick Norton | 3.00 | 1.35 | .40 |
| ☐ 78 Frank Jackson | 3.25 | 1.45 | .40 |
| ☐ 79 Joe Auer | 3.25 | 1.45 | .40 |
| ☐ 80 Willie West | 3.00 | 1.35 | .40 |
| ☐ 81 Jim Warren | 3.00 | 1.35 | .40 |
| ☐ 82 Wahoo McDaniel | 25.00 | 11.50 | 3.10 |
| ☐ 83 Ernie Park | 3.00 | 1.35 | .40 |
| ☐ 84 Bill Neighbors | 3.00 | 1.35 | .40 |
| ☐ 85 Norm Evans | 3.25 | 1.45 | .40 |
| ☐ 86 Tom Nomina | 3.00 | 1.35 | .40 |
| ☐ 87 Rich Zecher | 3.00 | 1.35 | .40 |
| ☐ 88 Dave Kocourek | 3.25 | 1.45 | .40 |
| ☐ 89 Bill Baird | 3.00 | 1.35 | .40 |
| ☐ 90 Ralph Baker | 3.00 | 1.35 | .40 |
| ☐ 91 Verlon Biggs | 3.25 | 1.45 | .40 |
| ☐ 92 Sam DeLuca | 3.00 | 1.35 | .40 |
| ☐ 93 Larry Grantham | 3.25 | 1.45 | .40 |
| ☐ 94 Jim Harris | 3.00 | 1.35 | .40 |

| | | NRMT | VG-E | GOOD |
|---|---|---|---|---|
| ☐ 95 | Winston Hill | 3.25 | 1.45 | .40 |
| ☐ 96 | Bill Mathis | 3.25 | 1.45 | .40 |
| ☐ 97 | Don Maynard | 20.00 | 9.00 | 2.50 |
| ☐ 98 | Joe Namath | 190.00 | 85.00 | 24.00 |
| ☐ 99 | Gerry Philbin | 3.25 | 1.45 | .40 |
| ☐ 100 | Paul Rochester | 3.00 | 1.35 | .40 |
| ☐ 101 | George Sauer Jr. | 3.50 | 1.55 | .45 |
| ☐ 102 | Matt Snell | 4.50 | 2.00 | .55 |
| ☐ 103 | Daryle Lamonica | 6.00 | 2.70 | .75 |
| ☐ 104 | Glenn Bass | 3.00 | 1.35 | .40 |
| ☐ 105 | Jim Otto | 6.00 | 2.70 | .75 |
| ☐ 106 | Fred Biletnikoff | 30.00 | 13.50 | 3.80 |
| ☐ 107 | Cotton Davidson | 3.25 | 1.45 | .40 |
| ☐ 108 | Larry Todd | 3.00 | 1.35 | .40 |
| ☐ 109 | Billy Cannon | 3.50 | 1.55 | .45 |
| ☐ 110 | Clem Daniels | 3.25 | 1.45 | .40 |
| ☐ 111 | Dave Grayson | 3.00 | 1.35 | .40 |
| ☐ 112 | Kent McCloughan | 3.00 | 1.35 | .40 |
| ☐ 113 | Bob Svihus | 3.00 | 1.35 | .40 |
| ☐ 114 | Ike Lassiter | 3.00 | 1.35 | .40 |
| ☐ 115 | Harry Schuh | 3.00 | 1.35 | .40 |
| ☐ 116 | Ben Davidson | 4.00 | 1.80 | .50 |
| ☐ 117 | Tom Day | 3.00 | 1.35 | .40 |
| ☐ 118 | Scott Appleton | 3.25 | 1.45 | .40 |
| ☐ 119 | Steve Tensi | 3.00 | 1.35 | .40 |
| ☐ 120 | John Hadl | 6.00 | 2.70 | .75 |
| ☐ 121 | Paul Lowe | 3.50 | 1.55 | .45 |
| ☐ 122 | Jim Allison | 3.00 | 1.35 | .40 |
| ☐ 123 | Lance Alworth | 22.00 | 10.00 | 2.80 |
| ☐ 124 | Jacque MacKinnon | 3.00 | 1.35 | .40 |
| ☐ 125 | Ron Mix | 5.50 | 2.50 | .70 |
| ☐ 126 | Bob Petrich | 3.00 | 1.35 | .40 |
| ☐ 127 | Howard Kindig | 3.00 | 1.35 | .40 |
| ☐ 128 | Steve DeLong | 3.00 | 1.35 | .40 |
| ☐ 129 | Chuck Allen | 3.00 | 1.35 | .40 |
| ☐ 130 | Frank Buncom | 3.00 | 1.35 | .40 |
| ☐ 131 | Speedy Duncan | 5.00 | 2.30 | .60 |
| ☐ 132 | Checklist Card | 60.00 | 11.00 | 3.20 |

## 1967 Topps Comic Pennants

This set was issued as an insert with the 1967 Topps regular issue football cards. The stickers are standard size, 2 1/2" by 3 1/2". Each sticker says "Peel off pennant carefully" on the front. The backs are blank. The set can also be found in non-adhesive form with the pennant merely printed on card stock. They are numbered in the upper right corner; although reportedly they can also occasionally be found without numbers. Many of the cards feature sayings or depictions that are in poor taste, i.e., sick humor. Perhaps they were discontinued or recalled before the end of the season, which would explain their relative scarcity.

| | | NRMT | VG-E | GOOD |
|---|---|---|---|---|
| COMPLETE SET (31) | | 600.00 | 240.00 | 60.00 |
| COMMON CARD (1-31) | | 20.00 | 8.00 | 2.00 |
| ☐ 1 | Navel Academy | 20.00 | 8.00 | 2.00 |
| ☐ 2 | City College of Useless Knowledge | 20.00 | 8.00 | 2.00 |
| ☐ 3 | Notre Dame (Hunchback of) | 40.00 | 16.00 | 4.00 |
| ☐ 4 | Psychedelic State | 20.00 | 8.00 | 2.00 |
| ☐ 5 | Minneapolis Mini-skirts | 20.00 | 8.00 | 2.00 |
| ☐ 6 | School of Art Go, Van Gogh | 20.00 | 8.00 | 2.00 |
| ☐ 7 | Washington Is Dead | 25.00 | 10.00 | 2.50 |
| ☐ 8 | School of Hard Knocks | 20.00 | 8.00 | 2.00 |
| ☐ 9 | Alaska (If I See Her ...) | 20.00 | 8.00 | 2.00 |
| ☐ 10 | Confused State | 20.00 | 8.00 | 2.00 |
| ☐ 11 | Yale Locks Are Tough to Pick | 20.00 | 8.00 | 2.00 |
| ☐ 12 | University of | 20.00 | 8.00 | 2.00 |

| | | NRMT | VG-E | GOOD |
|---|---|---|---|---|
| | Transylvania | | | |
| ☐ 13 | Down With Teachers | 20.00 | 8.00 | 2.00 |
| ☐ 14 | Cornell Caught Me Cheating | 20.00 | 8.00 | 2.00 |
| ☐ 15 | Houston Oilers (You're a Fink) | 25.00 | 10.00 | 2.50 |
| ☐ 16 | Harvard (Flunked Out) | 30.00 | 12.00 | 3.00 |
| ☐ 17 | Diskotech | 20.00 | 8.00 | 2.00 |
| ☐ 18 | Dropout U. | 20.00 | 8.00 | 2.00 |
| ☐ 19 | Air Force (Gas Masks) | 20.00 | 8.00 | 2.00 |
| ☐ 20 | Nutstu U. | 20.00 | 8.00 | 2.00 |
| ☐ 21 | Michigan State Pen | 20.00 | 8.00 | 2.00 |
| ☐ 22 | Denver Broncos (Girls Look Like) | 30.00 | 12.00 | 3.00 |
| ☐ 23 | Buffalo Bills (Without Paying My) | 25.00 | 10.00 | 2.50 |
| ☐ 24 | Army of Dropouts | 20.00 | 8.00 | 2.00 |
| ☐ 25 | Miami Dolphins (Bitten by Two) | 30.00 | 12.00 | 3.00 |
| ☐ 26 | Kansas City (Has Too Few Workers And Too Many) Chiefs | 20.00 | 8.00 | 2.00 |
| ☐ 27 | Boston Patriots (Banned In) | 20.00 | 8.00 | 2.00 |
| ☐ 28 | (Fat People In) Oakland (Are Usually Icebox) Raiders | 30.00 | 12.00 | 3.00 |
| ☐ 29 | (I'd Go) West (If You'd Just) Point (In The Right Direction) | 20.00 | 8.00 | 2.00 |
| ☐ 30 | New York Jets (Skies Are Crowded With) | 25.00 | 10.00 | 2.50 |
| ☐ 31 | San Diego Chargers (Police Will Press) | 20.00 | 8.00 | 2.00 |

## 1968 Topps

The 1968 Topps football set of 219 cards is Topps' first set in five years (since 1963) to contain NFL players. In fact, the set also includes AFL players even though the two rival leagues didn't formally merge until 1970. The set marks the AFL debut of the Cincinnati Bengals. The second series (132-219) is slightly more difficult to obtain than the first series. The cards in the second series have blue printing on the back whereas the cards in the first series had green printing on the back. Cards for players from the previous year's Super Bowl teams, the Green Bay Packers and the Oakland Raiders, are oriented horizontally; the rest of the cards are oriented vertically. The cards measure 2 1/2" by 3 1/2". Card backs of some of the cards in the second series can be used to form a ten-card puzzle of Bart Starr (141, 148, 153, 155, 168, 172, 186, 197, 201, and 213) or Len Dawson (145, 146, 151, 152, 163, 166, 170, 195, 199, and 200). The set features the Rookie Cards of quarterbacks Bob Griese, Jim Hart, and Craig Morton, and (ex-Syracuse) running backs Floyd Little and Jim Nance.

| | | NRMT | VG-E | GOOD |
|---|---|---|---|---|
| COMPLETE SET (219) | | 600.00 | 275.00 | 75.00 |
| COMMON PLAYER (1-131) | | 1.25 | .55 | .16 |
| COMMON PLAYER (132-219) | | 1.50 | .65 | .19 |
| ☐ 1 | Bart Starr Green Bay Packers | 32.00 | 9.50 | 3.20 |
| ☐ 2 | Dick Bass Los Angeles Rams | 1.50 | .65 | .19 |
| ☐ 3 | Grady Alderman Minnesota Vikings | 1.25 | .55 | .16 |
| ☐ 4 | Obert Logan New Orleans Saints | 1.25 | .55 | .16 |
| ☐ 5 | Ernie Koy New York Giants | 1.50 | .65 | .19 |

| | | | |
|---|---|---|---|
| ☐ 6 Don Hultz | 1.25 | .55 | .16 |
| Philadelphia Eagles | | | |
| ☐ 7 Earl Gros | 1.25 | .55 | .16 |
| Pittsburgh Steelers | | | |
| ☐ 8 Jim Bakken | 1.50 | .65 | .19 |
| St. Louis Cardinals | | | |
| ☐ 9 George Mira | 1.50 | .65 | .19 |
| San Francisco 49ers | | | |
| ☐ 10 Carl Kammerer | 1.25 | .55 | .16 |
| Washington Redskins | | | |
| ☐ 11 Willie Frazier | 1.50 | .65 | .19 |
| San Diego Chargers | | | |
| ☐ 12 Kent McCloughan UER | 1.50 | .65 | .19 |
| Oakland Raiders | | | |
| (McCloughlan on | | | |
| card back) | | | |
| ☐ 13 George Sauer Jr. | 1.50 | .65 | .19 |
| New York Jets | | | |
| ☐ 14 Jack Clancy | 1.50 | .65 | .19 |
| Miami Dolphins | | | |
| ☐ 15 Jim Tyrer | 1.50 | .65 | .19 |
| Kansas City Chiefs | | | |
| ☐ 16 Bobby Maples | 1.50 | .65 | .19 |
| Houston Oilers | | | |
| ☐ 17 Bo Hickey | 1.25 | .55 | .16 |
| Denver Broncos | | | |
| ☐ 18 Frank Buncom | 1.25 | .55 | .16 |
| Cincinnati Bengals | | | |
| ☐ 19 Keith Lincoln | 1.25 | .55 | .16 |
| Buffalo Bills | | | |
| ☐ 20 Jim Whalen | 1.25 | .55 | .16 |
| Boston Patriots | | | |
| ☐ 21 Junior Coffey | 1.25 | .55 | .16 |
| Atlanta Falcons | | | |
| ☐ 22 Billy Ray Smith | 1.25 | .55 | .16 |
| Baltimore Colts | | | |
| ☐ 23 Johnny Morris | 1.50 | .65 | .19 |
| Chicago Bears | | | |
| ☐ 24 Ernie Green | 1.50 | .65 | .19 |
| Cleveland Browns | | | |
| ☐ 25 Don Meredith | 20.00 | 9.00 | 2.50 |
| Dallas Cowboys | | | |
| ☐ 26 Wayne Walker | 1.50 | .65 | .19 |
| Detroit Lions | | | |
| ☐ 27 Carroll Dale | 1.50 | .65 | .19 |
| Green Bay Packers | | | |
| ☐ 28 Bernie Casey | 1.50 | .65 | .19 |
| Los Angeles Rams | | | |
| ☐ 29 Dave Osborn | 2.00 | .90 | .25 |
| Minnesota Vikings | | | |
| ☐ 30 Ray Poage | 1.25 | .55 | .16 |
| New Orleans Saints | | | |
| ☐ 31 Homer Jones | 1.50 | .65 | .19 |
| New York Giants | | | |
| ☐ 32 Sam Baker | 1.50 | .65 | .19 |
| Philadelphia Eagles | | | |
| ☐ 33 Bill Saul | 1.25 | .55 | .16 |
| Pittsburgh Steelers | | | |
| ☐ 34 Ken Willard | 1.50 | .65 | .19 |
| San Francisco 49ers | | | |
| ☐ 35 Bobby Mitchell | 4.00 | 1.80 | .50 |
| Washington Redskins | | | |
| ☐ 36 Gary Garrison | 1.50 | .65 | .19 |
| San Diego Chargers | | | |
| ☐ 37 Billy Cannon | 1.50 | .65 | .19 |
| Oakland Raiders | | | |
| ☐ 38 Ralph Baker | 1.25 | .55 | .16 |
| New York Jets | | | |
| ☐ 39 Howard Twilley | 3.50 | 1.55 | .45 |
| Miami Dolphins | | | |
| ☐ 40 Wendell Hayes | 1.50 | .65 | .19 |
| Kansas City Chiefs | | | |
| ☐ 41 Jim Norton | 1.25 | .55 | .16 |
| Houston Oilers | | | |
| ☐ 42 Tom Beer | 1.25 | .55 | .16 |
| Denver Broncos | | | |
| ☐ 43 Chris Burford | 1.25 | .55 | .16 |
| Cincinnati Bengals | | | |
| ☐ 44 Stew Barber | 1.25 | .55 | .16 |
| Buffalo Bills | | | |
| ☐ 45 Leroy Mitchell UER | 1.25 | .55 | .16 |
| (Lifetime Int. should | | | |
| be 3, not 2) | | | |
| Boston Patriots | | | |
| ☐ 46 Dan Grimm | 1.25 | .55 | .16 |
| Atlanta Falcons | | | |
| ☐ 47 Jerry Logan | 1.25 | .55 | .16 |
| Baltimore Colts | | | |
| ☐ 48 Andy Livingston | 1.25 | .55 | .16 |
| Chicago Bears | | | |
| ☐ 49 Paul Warfield | 10.00 | 4.50 | 1.25 |
| Cleveland Browns | | | |
| ☐ 50 Don Perkins | 1.50 | .65 | .19 |
| Dallas Cowboys | | | |
| ☐ 51 Ron Kramer | 1.50 | .65 | .19 |
| Detroit Lions | | | |
| ☐ 52 Bob Jeter | 1.25 | .55 | .16 |

| | | | |
|---|---|---|---|
| Green Bay Packers | | | |
| ☐ 53 Les Josephson | 1.75 | .80 | .22 |
| Los Angeles Rams | | | |
| ☐ 54 Bobby Walden | 1.25 | .55 | .16 |
| Minnesota Vikings | | | |
| ☐ 55 Checklist Card | 15.00 | 2.30 | .75 |
| ☐ 56 Walter Roberts | 1.25 | .55 | .16 |
| New Orleans Saints | | | |
| ☐ 57 Henry Carr | 1.50 | .65 | .19 |
| New York Giants | | | |
| ☐ 58 Gary Ballman | 1.25 | .55 | .16 |
| Philadelphia Eagles | | | |
| ☐ 59 J.R. Wilburn | 1.25 | .55 | .16 |
| Pittsburgh Steelers | | | |
| ☐ 60 Jim Hart | 8.00 | 3.60 | 1.00 |
| St. Louis Cardinals | | | |
| ☐ 61 Jim Johnson | 2.25 | 1.00 | .30 |
| San Francisco 49ers | | | |
| ☐ 62 Chris Hanburger | 2.00 | .90 | .25 |
| Washington Redskins | | | |
| ☐ 63 John Hadl | 3.50 | 1.55 | .45 |
| San Diego Chargers | | | |
| ☐ 64 Hewritt Dixon | 1.50 | .65 | .19 |
| Oakland Raiders | | | |
| ☐ 65 Joe Namath | 80.00 | 36.00 | 10.00 |
| New York Jets | | | |
| ☐ 66 Jim Warren | 1.25 | .55 | .16 |
| Miami Dolphins | | | |
| ☐ 67 Curtis McClinton | 1.50 | .65 | .19 |
| Kansas City Chiefs | | | |
| ☐ 68 Bob Talamini | 1.25 | .55 | .16 |
| Houston Oilers | | | |
| ☐ 69 Steve Tensi | 1.50 | .65 | .19 |
| Denver Broncos | | | |
| ☐ 70 Dick Van Raaphorst UER | 1.25 | .55 | .16 |
| Cincinnati Bengals | | | |
| (Van Raap Horst | | | |
| on card back) | | | |
| ☐ 71 Art Powell | 1.75 | .80 | .22 |
| Buffalo Bills | | | |
| ☐ 72 Jim Nance | 4.00 | 1.80 | .50 |
| Boston Patriots | | | |
| ☐ 73 Bob Riggle | 1.25 | .55 | .16 |
| Atlanta Falcons | | | |
| ☐ 74 John Mackey | 4.00 | 1.80 | .50 |
| Baltimore Colts | | | |
| ☐ 75 Gale Sayers | 60.00 | 27.00 | 7.50 |
| Chicago Bears | | | |
| ☐ 76 Gene Hickerson | 1.25 | .55 | .16 |
| Cleveland Browns | | | |
| ☐ 77 Dan Reeves | 8.00 | 3.60 | 1.00 |
| Dallas Cowboys | | | |
| ☐ 78 Tom Nowatzke | 1.25 | .55 | .16 |
| Detroit Lions | | | |
| ☐ 79 Elijah Pitts | 1.50 | .65 | .19 |
| Green Bay Packers | | | |
| ☐ 80 Lamar Lundy | 1.50 | .65 | .19 |
| Los Angeles Rams | | | |
| ☐ 81 Paul Flatley | 1.50 | .65 | .19 |
| Minnesota Vikings | | | |
| ☐ 82 Dave Whitsell | 1.25 | .55 | .16 |
| New Orleans Saints | | | |
| ☐ 83 Spider Lockhart | 1.50 | .65 | .19 |
| New York Giants | | | |
| ☐ 84 Dave Lloyd | 1.25 | .55 | .16 |
| Philadelphia Eagles | | | |
| ☐ 85 Roy Jefferson | 1.50 | .65 | .19 |
| Pittsburgh Steelers | | | |
| ☐ 86 Jackie Smith | 4.50 | 2.00 | .55 |
| St. Louis Cardinals | | | |
| ☐ 87 John David Crow | 1.50 | .65 | .19 |
| San Francisco 49ers | | | |
| ☐ 88 Sonny Jurgensen | 7.00 | 3.10 | .85 |
| Washington Redskins | | | |
| ☐ 89 Ron Mix | 3.50 | 1.55 | .45 |
| San Diego Chargers | | | |
| ☐ 90 Clem Daniels | 1.50 | .65 | .19 |
| Oakland Raiders | | | |
| ☐ 91 Cornell Gordon | 1.25 | .55 | .16 |
| New York Jets | | | |
| ☐ 92 Tom Goode | 1.25 | .55 | .16 |
| Miami Dolphins | | | |
| ☐ 93 Bobby Bell | 4.00 | 1.80 | .50 |
| Kansas City Chiefs | | | |
| ☐ 94 Walt Suggs | 1.25 | .55 | .16 |
| Houston Oilers | | | |
| ☐ 95 Eric Crabtree | 1.25 | .55 | .16 |
| Denver Broncos | | | |
| ☐ 96 Sherrill Headrick | 1.50 | .65 | .19 |
| Cincinnati Bengals | | | |
| ☐ 97 Wray Carlton | 1.50 | .65 | .19 |
| Buffalo Bills | | | |
| ☐ 98 Gino Cappelletti | 1.50 | .65 | .19 |
| Boston Patriots | | | |
| ☐ 99 Tommy McDonald | 1.50 | .65 | .19 |
| Atlanta Falcons | | | |
| ☐ 100 John Unitas | 25.00 | 11.50 | 3.10 |
| Baltimore Colts | | | |

| | | | | |
|---|---|---|---|---|
| ☐ 101 Richie Petitbon | 1.50 | .65 | .19 |
| Chicago Bears | | | |
| ☐ 102 Erich Barnes | 1.50 | .65 | .19 |
| Cleveland Browns | | | |
| ☐ 103 Bob Hayes | 2.50 | 1.15 | .30 |
| Dallas Cowboys | | | |
| ☐ 104 Milt Plum | 1.50 | .65 | .19 |
| Los Angeles Rams | | | |
| ☐ 105 Boyd Dowler | 1.50 | .65 | .19 |
| Green Bay Packers | | | |
| ☐ 106 Ed Meador | 1.50 | .65 | .19 |
| Los Angeles Rams | | | |
| ☐ 107 Fred Cox | 1.50 | .65 | .19 |
| Minnesota Vikings | | | |
| ☐ 108 Steve Stonebreaker | 1.25 | .55 | .16 |
| New Orleans Saints | | | |
| ☐ 109 Aaron Thomas | 1.50 | .65 | .19 |
| New York Giants | | | |
| ☐ 110 Norm Snead | 1.50 | .65 | .19 |
| Philadelphia Eagles | | | |
| ☐ 111 Paul Martha | 1.50 | .65 | .19 |
| Pittsburgh Steelers | | | |
| ☐ 112 Jerry Stovall | 1.50 | .65 | .19 |
| St. Louis Cardinals | | | |
| ☐ 113 Kay McFarland | 1.25 | .55 | .16 |
| San Francisco 49ers | | | |
| ☐ 114 Pat Richter | 1.25 | .55 | .16 |
| Washington Redskins | | | |
| ☐ 115 Rick Redman | 1.25 | .55 | .16 |
| San Diego Chargers | | | |
| ☐ 116 Tom Keating | 1.25 | .55 | .16 |
| Oakland Raiders | | | |
| ☐ 117 Matt Snell | 2.25 | 1.00 | .30 |
| New York Jets | | | |
| ☐ 118 Dick Westmoreland | 1.25 | .55 | .16 |
| Miami Dolphins | | | |
| ☐ 119 Jerry Mays | 1.50 | .65 | .19 |
| Kansas City Chiefs | | | |
| ☐ 120 Sid Blanks | 1.25 | .55 | .16 |
| Houston Oilers | | | |
| ☐ 121 Al Denson | 1.25 | .55 | .16 |
| Denver Broncos | | | |
| ☐ 122 Bobby Hunt | 1.25 | .55 | .16 |
| Cincinnati Bengals | | | |
| ☐ 123 Mike Mercer | 1.25 | .55 | .16 |
| Buffalo Bills | | | |
| ☐ 124 Nick Buoniconti | 3.00 | 1.35 | .40 |
| Boston Patriots | | | |
| ☐ 125 Ron Vanderkelen | 1.25 | .55 | .16 |
| Atlanta Falcons | | | |
| ☐ 126 Ordell Braase | 1.25 | .55 | .16 |
| Baltimore Colts | | | |
| ☐ 127 Dick Butkus | 35.00 | 16.00 | 4.40 |
| Chicago Bears | | | |
| ☐ 128 Gary Collins | 1.50 | .65 | .19 |
| Cleveland Browns | | | |
| ☐ 129 Mel Renfro | 1.75 | .80 | .22 |
| Dallas Cowboys | | | |
| ☐ 130 Alex Karras | 6.00 | 2.70 | .75 |
| Detroit Lions | | | |
| ☐ 131 Herb Adderley | 3.50 | 1.55 | .45 |
| Green Bay Packers | | | |
| ☐ 132 Roman Gabriel | 3.50 | 1.55 | .45 |
| Los Angeles Rams | | | |
| ☐ 133 Bill Brown | 1.75 | .80 | .22 |
| Minnesota Vikings | | | |
| ☐ 134 Kent Kramer | 1.50 | .65 | .19 |
| New Orleans Saints | | | |
| ☐ 135 Tucker Frederickson | 1.75 | .80 | .22 |
| New York Giants | | | |
| ☐ 136 Nate Ramsey | 1.50 | .65 | .19 |
| Philadelphia Eagles | | | |
| ☐ 137 Marv Woodson | 1.75 | .80 | .22 |
| Pittsburgh Steelers | | | |
| ☐ 138 Ken Gray | 1.75 | .80 | .22 |
| St. Louis Cardinals | | | |
| ☐ 139 John Brodie | 7.00 | 3.10 | .85 |
| San Francisco 49ers | | | |
| ☐ 140 Jerry Smith | 1.75 | .80 | .22 |
| Washington Redskins | | | |
| ☐ 141 Brad Hubbert | 1.50 | .65 | .19 |
| San Diego Chargers | | | |
| ☐ 142 George Blanda | 22.00 | 10.00 | 2.80 |
| Oakland Raiders | | | |
| ☐ 143 Pete Lammons | 1.75 | .80 | .22 |
| New York Jets | | | |
| ☐ 144 Doug Moreau | 1.75 | .80 | .22 |
| Miami Dolphins | | | |
| ☐ 145 E.J. Holub | 1.75 | .80 | .22 |
| Kansas City Chiefs | | | |
| ☐ 146 Ode Burrell | 1.50 | .65 | .19 |
| Houston Oilers | | | |
| ☐ 147 Bob Scarpitto | 1.50 | .65 | .19 |
| Denver Broncos | | | |
| ☐ 148 Andre White | 1.50 | .65 | .19 |
| Cincinnati Bengals | | | |
| ☐ 149 Jack Kemp | 55.00 | 25.00 | 7.00 |

| | | | | |
|---|---|---|---|---|
| Buffalo Bills | | | |
| ☐ 150 Art Graham | 1.50 | .65 | .19 |
| Boston Patriots | | | |
| ☐ 151 Tommy Nobis | 4.00 | 1.80 | .50 |
| Atlanta Falcons | | | |
| ☐ 152 Willie Richardson | 1.75 | .80 | .22 |
| Baltimore Colts | | | |
| ☐ 153 Jack Concannon | 1.75 | .80 | .22 |
| Chicago Bears | | | |
| ☐ 154 Bill Glass | 1.50 | .65 | .19 |
| Cleveland Browns | | | |
| ☐ 155 Craig Morton | 12.00 | 5.50 | 1.50 |
| Dallas Cowboys | | | |
| ☐ 156 Pat Studstill | 1.75 | .80 | .22 |
| Los Angeles Rams | | | |
| ☐ 157 Ray Nitschke | 4.50 | 2.00 | .55 |
| Green Bay Packers | | | |
| ☐ 158 Roger Brown | 1.75 | .80 | .22 |
| Los Angeles Rams | | | |
| ☐ 159 Joe Kapp | 5.00 | 2.30 | .60 |
| Minnesota Vikings | | | |
| ☐ 160 Jim Taylor | 10.00 | 4.50 | 1.25 |
| (Shown in uniform of | | | |
| Green Bay Packers) | | | |
| New Orleans Saints | | | |
| ☐ 161 Fran Tarkenton | 24.00 | 11.00 | 3.00 |
| New York Giants | | | |
| ☐ 162 Mike Ditka | 9.00 | 4.00 | 1.15 |
| Philadelphia Eagles | | | |
| ☐ 163 Andy Russell | 5.00 | 2.30 | .60 |
| Pittsburgh Steelers | | | |
| ☐ 164 Larry Wilson | 3.00 | 1.35 | .40 |
| St. Louis Cardinals | | | |
| ☐ 165 Tommy Davis | 1.50 | .65 | .19 |
| San Francisco 49ers | | | |
| ☐ 166 Paul Krause | 2.50 | 1.15 | .30 |
| Washington Redskins | | | |
| ☐ 167 Speedy Duncan | 1.75 | .80 | .22 |
| San Diego Chargers | | | |
| ☐ 168 Fred Biletnikoff | 10.00 | 4.50 | 1.25 |
| Oakland Raiders | | | |
| ☐ 169 Don Maynard | 10.00 | 4.50 | 1.25 |
| New York Jets | | | |
| ☐ 170 Frank Emanuel | 1.50 | .65 | .19 |
| Miami Dolphins | | | |
| ☐ 171 Len Dawson | 10.00 | 4.50 | 1.25 |
| Kansas City Chiefs | | | |
| ☐ 172 Miller Farr | 1.50 | .65 | .19 |
| Houston Oilers | | | |
| ☐ 173 Floyd Little | 18.00 | 8.00 | 2.30 |
| Denver Broncos | | | |
| ☐ 174 Lonnie Wright | 1.50 | .65 | .19 |
| Cincinnati Bengals | | | |
| ☐ 175 Paul Costa | 1.50 | .65 | .19 |
| Buffalo Bills | | | |
| ☐ 176 Don Trull | 1.75 | .80 | .22 |
| Boston Patriots | | | |
| ☐ 177 Jerry Simmons | 1.50 | .65 | .19 |
| Atlanta Falcons | | | |
| ☐ 178 Tom Matte | 1.75 | .80 | .22 |
| Baltimore Colts | | | |
| ☐ 179 Bennie McRae | 1.50 | .65 | .19 |
| Chicago Bears | | | |
| ☐ 180 Jim Kanicki | 1.50 | .65 | .19 |
| Cleveland Browns | | | |
| ☐ 181 Bob Lilly | 7.00 | 3.10 | .85 |
| Dallas Cowboys | | | |
| ☐ 182 Tom Watkins | 1.50 | .65 | .19 |
| Los Angeles Rams | | | |
| ☐ 183 Jim Grabowski | 2.50 | 1.15 | .30 |
| Green Bay Packers | | | |
| ☐ 184 Jack Snow | 4.00 | 1.80 | .50 |
| Los Angeles Rams | | | |
| ☐ 185 Gary Cuozzo | 1.75 | .80 | .22 |
| Minnesota Vikings | | | |
| ☐ 186 Bill Kilmer | 3.50 | 1.55 | .45 |
| New Orleans Saints | | | |
| ☐ 187 Jim Katcavage | 1.75 | .80 | .22 |
| New York Giants | | | |
| ☐ 188 Floyd Peters | 1.75 | .80 | .22 |
| Philadelphia Eagles | | | |
| ☐ 189 Bill Nelsen | 1.75 | .80 | .22 |
| Cleveland Browns | | | |
| ☐ 190 Bobby Joe Conrad | 1.75 | .80 | .22 |
| St. Louis Cardinals | | | |
| ☐ 191 Kermit Alexander | 1.50 | .65 | .19 |
| San Francisco 49ers | | | |
| ☐ 192 Charley Taylor UER | 7.00 | 3.10 | .85 |
| (Called Charley | | | |
| and Charlie on back) | | | |
| Washington Redskins | | | |
| ☐ 193 Lance Alworth | 12.00 | 5.50 | 1.50 |
| San Diego Chargers | | | |
| ☐ 194 Daryle Lamonica | 4.50 | 2.00 | .55 |
| Oakland Raiders | | | |
| ☐ 195 Al Atkinson | 1.50 | .65 | .19 |
| New York Jets | | | |
| ☐ 196 Bob Griese | 90.00 | 40.00 | 11.50 |

| | | | | |
|---|---|---|---|---|
| ☐ 197 Buck Buchanan | 4.00 | 1.80 | .50 |
| Miami Dolphins | | | |
| Kansas City Chiefs | | | |
| ☐ 198 Pete Beathard | 1.75 | .80 | .22 |
| Houston Oilers | | | |
| ☐ 199 Nemiah Wilson | 1.50 | .65 | .19 |
| Denver Broncos | | | |
| ☐ 200 Ernie Wright | 1.50 | .65 | .19 |
| Cincinnati Bengals | | | |
| ☐ 201 George Saimes | 1.75 | .80 | .22 |
| Buffalo Bills | | | |
| ☐ 202 John Charles | 1.50 | .65 | .19 |
| Boston Patriots | | | |
| ☐ 203 Randy Johnson | 1.75 | .80 | .22 |
| Atlanta Falcons | | | |
| ☐ 204 Tony Lorick | 1.50 | .65 | .19 |
| Baltimore Colts | | | |
| ☐ 205 Dick Evey | 1.50 | .65 | .19 |
| Chicago Bears | | | |
| ☐ 206 Leroy Kelly | 7.00 | 3.10 | .85 |
| Cleveland Browns | | | |
| ☐ 207 Lee Roy Jordan | 4.00 | 1.80 | .50 |
| Dallas Cowboys | | | |
| ☐ 208 Jim Gibbons | 1.50 | .65 | .19 |
| Detroit Lions | | | |
| ☐ 209 Donny Anderson | 4.00 | 1.80 | .50 |
| Green Bay Packers | | | |
| ☐ 210 Maxie Baughan | 1.75 | .80 | .22 |
| Los Angeles Rams | | | |
| ☐ 211 Joe Morrison | 1.75 | .80 | .22 |
| New York Giants | | | |
| ☐ 212 Jim Snowden | 1.50 | .65 | .19 |
| Washington Redskins | | | |
| ☐ 213 Lenny Lyles | 1.50 | .65 | .19 |
| Baltimore Colts | | | |
| ☐ 214 Bobby Joe Green | 1.50 | .65 | .19 |
| Chicago Bears | | | |
| ☐ 215 Frank Ryan | 1.75 | .80 | .22 |
| Cleveland Browns | | | |
| ☐ 216 Cornell Green | 1.75 | .80 | .22 |
| Dallas Cowboys | | | |
| ☐ 217 Karl Sweetan | 1.75 | .80 | .22 |
| Detroit Lions | | | |
| ☐ 218 Dave Williams | 1.75 | .80 | .22 |
| St. Louis Cardinals | | | |
| ☐ 219A Checklist 132-218 | 18.00 | 2.70 | .90 |
| (green print on back) | | | |
| ☐ 219B Checklist 132-218 | 20.00 | 3.00 | 1.00 |
| (blue print on back) | | | |

## 1968 Topps Posters

The 1968 Topps Football Posters set contains 16 NFL and AFL players on paper stock; the cards (posters) measure approximately 5" by 7". The posters, folded twice for insertion into first series wax packs, are numbered on the obverse at the lower left hand corner. The backs of these posters are blank. Fold marks are normal and do not detract from the poster's condition. These posters are the same style as the 1967 Topps baseball posters and are available on thin gray paper as well as on thicker white paper.

| | NRMT | VG-E | GOOD |
|---|---|---|---|
| COMPLETE SET (16) | 75.00 | 30.00 | 7.50 |
| COMMON PLAYER (1-16) | 2.00 | .80 | .20 |
| | | | |
| ☐ 1 Johnny Unitas | 15.00 | 6.00 | 1.50 |
| Baltimore Colts | | | |
| ☐ 2 Leroy Kelly | 4.50 | 1.80 | .45 |
| Cleveland Browns | | | |
| ☐ 3 Bob Hayes | 3.50 | 1.40 | .35 |
| Dallas Cowboys | | | |
| ☐ 4 Bart Starr | 10.00 | 4.00 | 1.00 |
| Green Bay Packers | | | |
| ☐ 5 Charley Taylor | 4.50 | 1.80 | .45 |
| Washington Redskins | | | |

| | | | | |
|---|---|---|---|---|
| ☐ 6 Fran Tarkenton | 12.00 | 5.00 | 1.20 |
| New York Giants | | | |
| ☐ 7 Jim Bakken | 2.00 | .80 | .20 |
| St. Louis Cardinals | | | |
| ☐ 8 Gale Sayers | 12.00 | 5.00 | 1.20 |
| Chicago Bears | | | |
| ☐ 9 Gary Cuozzo | 2.00 | .80 | .20 |
| New Orleans Saints | | | |
| ☐ 10 Les Josephson | 2.00 | .80 | .20 |
| Los Angeles Rams | | | |
| ☐ 11 Jim Nance | 2.50 | 1.00 | .25 |
| Boston Patriots | | | |
| ☐ 12 Brad Hubbert | 2.00 | .80 | .20 |
| San Diego Chargers | | | |
| ☐ 13 Keith Lincoln | 2.50 | 1.00 | .25 |
| Buffalo Bills | | | |
| ☐ 14 Don Maynard | 4.50 | 1.80 | .45 |
| New York Jets | | | |
| ☐ 15 Len Dawson | 6.50 | 2.60 | .65 |
| Kansas City Chiefs | | | |
| ☐ 16 Jack Clancy | 2.00 | .80 | .20 |
| Miami Dolphins | | | |

## 1968 Topps Stand-Ups

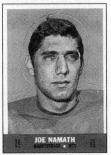

The 22-card 1968 Topps Football Stand-Ups set is unnumbered but has been numbered alphabetically in the checklist below for your convenience. The cards measure 2 1/2" by 3 1/2". The set features star players of the day with heavy emphasis on quarterbacks, running backs, and receivers. The card can be made to stand if the back is removed and appropriate folds are made. Values listed below are for complete cards; the value is greatly reduced if the backs are detached, and such a card can be considered fair to good at best. The cards were issued as an insert in second series packs of 1968 Topps football cards, one per pack. The cards are blank backed.

| | NRMT | VG-E | GOOD |
|---|---|---|---|
| COMPLETE SET (22) | 225.00 | 90.00 | 22.00 |
| COMMON PLAYER (1-22) | 5.00 | 2.00 | .50 |
| | | | |
| ☐ 1 Sid Blanks | 5.00 | 2.00 | .50 |
| Houston Oilers | | | |
| ☐ 2 John Brodie | 15.00 | 6.00 | 1.50 |
| San Francisco 49ers | | | |
| ☐ 3 Jack Concannon | 5.00 | 2.00 | .50 |
| Chicago Bears | | | |
| ☐ 4 Roman Gabriel | 7.50 | 3.00 | .75 |
| Los Angeles Rams | | | |
| ☐ 5 Art Graham | 5.00 | 2.00 | .50 |
| Boston Patriots | | | |
| ☐ 6 Jim Grabowski | 6.00 | 2.40 | .60 |
| Green Bay Packers | | | |
| ☐ 7 John Hadl | 6.00 | 2.40 | .60 |
| San Diego Chargers | | | |
| ☐ 8 Jim Hart | 7.50 | 3.00 | .75 |
| St. Louis Cardinals | | | |
| ☐ 9 Homer Jones | 5.00 | 2.00 | .50 |
| New York Giants | | | |
| ☐ 10 Sonny Jurgensen | 15.00 | 6.00 | 1.50 |
| Washington Redskins | | | |
| ☐ 11 Alex Karras | 9.00 | 3.75 | .90 |
| Detroit Lions | | | |
| ☐ 12 Billy Kilmer | 6.00 | 2.40 | .60 |
| New Orleans Saints | | | |
| ☐ 13 Daryle Lamonica | 7.50 | 3.00 | .75 |
| Oakland Raiders | | | |
| ☐ 14 Floyd Little | 7.50 | 3.00 | .75 |
| Denver Broncos | | | |
| ☐ 15 Curtis McClinton | 5.00 | 2.00 | .50 |
| Kansas City Chiefs | | | |
| ☐ 16 Don Meredith | 45.00 | 18.00 | 4.50 |
| Dallas Cowboys | | | |
| ☐ 17 Joe Namath | 90.00 | 36.00 | 9.00 |
| New York Jets | | | |

| | | | |
|---|---|---|---|
| ☐ 18 Bill Nelsen | 5.00 | 2.00 | .50 |
| Cleveland Browns | | | |
| ☐ 19 Dave Osborn | 5.00 | 2.00 | .50 |
| Minnesota Vikings | | | |
| ☐ 20 Willie Richardson | 5.00 | 2.00 | .50 |
| Baltimore Colts | | | |
| ☐ 21 Frank Ryan | 6.00 | 2.40 | .60 |
| Cleveland Browns | | | |
| ☐ 22 Norm Snead | 6.00 | 2.40 | .60 |
| Philadelphia Eagles | | | |

## 1968 Topps Test Teams

The 25-card set of team cards was a limited production by Topps. The obverse provides a black and white picture of the team, whereas the reverse gives the names of the players in the picture in red print on vanilla card stock. Due to their positioning within the pack, these test team cards are typically found with gum stains on the card backs. The cards measure approximately 2 1/2" by 4 11/16" and are numbered on the back.

| | NRMT | VG-E | GOOD |
|---|---|---|---|
| COMPLETE SET (25) | 2500.00 | 1000.00 | 300.00 |
| COMMON TEAM (1-25) | 100.00 | 40.00 | 10.00 |
| ☐ 1 Green Bay Packers | 125.00 | 50.00 | 12.50 |
| ☐ 2 New Orleans Saints | 100.00 | 40.00 | 10.00 |
| ☐ 3 New York Jets | 150.00 | 60.00 | 15.00 |
| ☐ 4 Miami Dolphins | 150.00 | 60.00 | 15.00 |
| ☐ 5 Pittsburgh Steelers | 125.00 | 50.00 | 12.50 |
| ☐ 6 Detroit Lions | 100.00 | 40.00 | 10.00 |
| ☐ 7 Los Angeles Rams | 100.00 | 40.00 | 10.00 |
| ☐ 8 Atlanta Falcons | 100.00 | 40.00 | 10.00 |
| ☐ 9 New York Giants | 125.00 | 50.00 | 12.50 |
| ☐ 10 Denver Broncos | 200.00 | 80.00 | 20.00 |
| ☐ 11 Dallas Cowboys | 200.00 | 80.00 | 20.00 |
| ☐ 12 Buffalo Bills | 125.00 | 50.00 | 12.50 |
| ☐ 13 Cleveland Browns | 100.00 | 40.00 | 10.00 |
| ☐ 14 San Francisco 49ers | 125.00 | 50.00 | 12.50 |
| ☐ 15 Baltimore Colts | 100.00 | 40.00 | 10.00 |
| ☐ 16 San Diego Chargers | 100.00 | 40.00 | 10.00 |
| ☐ 17 Oakland Raiders | 200.00 | 80.00 | 20.00 |
| ☐ 18 Houston Oilers | 125.00 | 50.00 | 12.50 |
| ☐ 19 Minnesota Vikings | 100.00 | 40.00 | 10.00 |
| ☐ 20 Washington Redskins | 150.00 | 60.00 | 15.00 |
| ☐ 21 St. Louis Cardinals | 100.00 | 40.00 | 10.00 |
| ☐ 22 Kansas City Chiefs | 100.00 | 40.00 | 10.00 |
| ☐ 23 Boston Patriots | 100.00 | 40.00 | 10.00 |
| ☐ 24 Chicago Bears | 150.00 | 60.00 | 15.00 |
| ☐ 25 Philadelphia Eagles | 100.00 | 40.00 | 10.00 |

## 1968 Topps Team Patch/Stickers

These team emblem cloth patches/stickers were distributed as an insert with the 1968 Topps Test Teams, one sticker per pack along with one test team. In fact according to the wrapper, these stickers were the featured item; however the hobby has deemed the team cards to be more collectible and hence more valuable than these rather bland, but scarce, logo stickers. The complete set of 44 patches consisted of team emblems, the letters A through Z, and the numbers 0 through 9. The letters and number patches contained two letters or numbers on each patch. The number patches are printed in black on a blue background, the letter patches are white on a red background,

and the team emblems were done in the team colors. The stickers measure 2 1/2" by 3 1/2". The backs are blank.

| | NRMT | VG-E | GOOD |
|---|---|---|---|
| COMPLETE SET (44) | 1500.00 | 650.00 | 165.00 |
| COMMON NUMBERS (1-5) | 10.00 | 4.00 | 1.00 |
| COMMON LETTERS (6-11) | 10.00 | 4.00 | 1.00 |
| COMMON NFL TEAM (12-22) | 60.00 | 24.00 | 6.00 |
| COMMON LETTERS (23-29) | 10.00 | 4.00 | 1.00 |
| COMMON NFL TEAM (30-34) | 60.00 | 24.00 | 6.00 |
| COMMON AFL TEAM (35-44) | 60.00 | 24.00 | 6.00 |
| ☐ 1 1 and 2 | 12.00 | 5.00 | 1.20 |
| ☐ 2 3 and 4 | 10.00 | 4.00 | 1.00 |
| ☐ 3 5 and 6 | 10.00 | 4.00 | 1.00 |
| ☐ 4 7 and 8 | 10.00 | 4.00 | 1.00 |
| ☐ 5 9 and 0 | 10.00 | 4.00 | 1.00 |
| ☐ 6 A and B | 10.00 | 4.00 | 1.00 |
| ☐ 7 C and D | 10.00 | 4.00 | 1.00 |
| ☐ 8 E and F | 10.00 | 4.00 | 1.00 |
| ☐ 9 G and H | 10.00 | 4.00 | 1.00 |
| ☐ 10 I and W | 10.00 | 4.00 | 1.00 |
| ☐ 11 J and X | 10.00 | 4.00 | 1.00 |
| ☐ 12 Atlanta Falcons | 60.00 | 24.00 | 6.00 |
| ☐ 13 Baltimore Colts | 60.00 | 24.00 | 6.00 |
| ☐ 14 Chicago Bears | 75.00 | 30.00 | 7.50 |
| ☐ 15 Cleveland Browns | 60.00 | 24.00 | 6.00 |
| ☐ 16 Dallas Cowboys | 125.00 | 50.00 | 12.50 |
| ☐ 17 Detroit Lions | 60.00 | 24.00 | 6.00 |
| ☐ 18 Green Bay Packers | 75.00 | 30.00 | 7.50 |
| ☐ 19 Los Angeles Rams | 60.00 | 24.00 | 6.00 |
| ☐ 20 Minnesota Vikings | 60.00 | 24.00 | 6.00 |
| ☐ 21 New Orleans Saints | 60.00 | 24.00 | 6.00 |
| ☐ 22 New York Giants | 75.00 | 30.00 | 7.50 |
| ☐ 23 K and L | 10.00 | 4.00 | 1.00 |
| ☐ 24 M and O | 10.00 | 4.00 | 1.00 |
| ☐ 25 N and P | 10.00 | 4.00 | 1.00 |
| ☐ 26 Q and R | 10.00 | 4.00 | 1.00 |
| ☐ 27 S and T | 10.00 | 4.00 | 1.00 |
| ☐ 28 U and V | 10.00 | 4.00 | 1.00 |
| ☐ 29 Y and Z | 10.00 | 4.00 | 1.00 |
| ☐ 30 Philadelphia Eagles | 60.00 | 24.00 | 6.00 |
| ☐ 31 Pittsburgh Steelers | 75.00 | 30.00 | 7.50 |
| ☐ 32 St. Louis Cardinals | 60.00 | 24.00 | 6.00 |
| ☐ 33 San Francisco 49ers | 75.00 | 30.00 | 7.50 |
| ☐ 34 Washington Redskins | 100.00 | 40.00 | 10.00 |
| ☐ 35 Boston Patriots | 60.00 | 24.00 | 6.00 |
| ☐ 36 Buffalo Bills | 75.00 | 30.00 | 7.50 |
| ☐ 37 Denver Broncos | 100.00 | 40.00 | 10.00 |
| ☐ 38 Houston Oilers | 75.00 | 30.00 | 7.50 |
| ☐ 39 Kansas City Chiefs | 60.00 | 24.00 | 6.00 |
| ☐ 40 Miami Dolphins | 100.00 | 40.00 | 10.00 |
| ☐ 41 New York Jets | 75.00 | 30.00 | 7.50 |
| ☐ 42 Oakland Raiders | 125.00 | 50.00 | 12.50 |
| ☐ 43 San Diego Chargers | 60.00 | 24.00 | 6.00 |
| ☐ 44 Cincinnati Bengals | 60.00 | 24.00 | 6.00 |

## 1969 Topps

The 1969 Topps football set of 263 cards contains 132 borderless cards (1-132), whereas the remaining 131 cards do have white borders. The lack of borders makes the first series especially difficult to find in mint condition. The checklist card 132 was obviously printed with each series as it is found in both styles (with and without borders). The cards in the set measure the standard 2 1/2" by 3 1/2". The backs of the cards are predominantly black, but with a green and white accent. Card backs of some of the cards in the second series can be used to form a ten-card puzzle of Fran Tarkenton (137, 145, 168, 174, 177, 194, 211, 219, 224, and 256). This set is distinctive in that it contains the late Brian Piccolo's only regular issue card. Another notable Rookie Card in this set is Larry Csonka.

| | NRMT | VG-E | GOOD |
|---|---|---|---|
| COMPLETE SET (263) | 575.00 | 250.00 | 70.00 |

| | | | |
|---|---|---|---|
| COMMON PLAYER (1-132) | 1.50 | .65 | .19 |
| COMMON PLAYER (133-263) | 1.50 | .65 | .19 |

| | | | |
|---|---|---|---|
| ☐ 1 Leroy Kelly | 12.00 | 2.40 | .70 |
| Cleveland Browns | | | |
| ☐ 2 Paul Flatley | 1.75 | .80 | .22 |
| Atlanta Falcons | | | |
| ☐ 3 Jim Cadile | 1.50 | .65 | .19 |
| Chicago Bears | | | |
| ☐ 4 Erich Barnes | 1.75 | .80 | .22 |
| Cleveland Browns | | | |
| ☐ 5 Willie Richardson | 1.75 | .80 | .22 |
| Baltimore Colts | | | |
| ☐ 6 Bob Hayes | 3.00 | 1.35 | .40 |
| Dallas Cowboys | | | |
| ☐ 7 Bob Jeter | 1.75 | .80 | .22 |
| Green Bay Packers | | | |
| ☐ 8 Jim Colclough | 1.50 | .65 | .19 |
| Boston Patriots | | | |
| ☐ 9 Sherrill Headrick | 1.75 | .80 | .22 |
| Cincinnati Bengals | | | |
| ☐ 10 Jim Dunaway | 1.50 | .65 | .19 |
| Buffalo Bills | | | |
| ☐ 11 Bill Munson | 1.75 | .80 | .22 |
| Detroit Lions | | | |
| ☐ 12 Jack Pardee | 2.00 | .90 | .25 |
| Los Angeles Rams | | | |
| ☐ 13 Jim Lindsey | 1.50 | .65 | .19 |
| Minnesota Vikings | | | |
| ☐ 14 Dave Whitsell | 1.50 | .65 | .19 |
| New Orleans Saints | | | |
| ☐ 15 Tucker Frederickson | 1.75 | .80 | .22 |
| New York Giants | | | |
| ☐ 16 Alvin Haymond | 1.50 | .65 | .19 |
| Philadelphia Eagles | | | |
| ☐ 17 Andy Russell | 1.75 | .80 | .22 |
| Pittsburgh Steelers | | | |
| ☐ 18 Tom Beer | 1.50 | .65 | .19 |
| Denver Broncos | | | |
| ☐ 19 Bobby Maples | 1.75 | .80 | .22 |
| Houston Oilers | | | |
| ☐ 20 Len Dawson | 8.00 | 3.60 | 1.00 |
| Kansas City Chiefs | | | |
| ☐ 21 Willis Crenshaw | 1.50 | .65 | .19 |
| St. Louis Cardinals | | | |
| ☐ 22 Tommy Davis | 1.50 | .65 | .19 |
| San Francisco 49ers | | | |
| ☐ 23 Rickie Harris | 1.50 | .65 | .19 |
| Washington Redskins | | | |
| ☐ 24 Jerry Simmons | 1.50 | .65 | .19 |
| Atlanta Falcons | | | |
| ☐ 25 John Unitas | 25.00 | 11.50 | 3.10 |
| Baltimore Colts | | | |
| ☐ 26 Brian Piccolo UER | 70.00 | 32.00 | 8.75 |
| Chicago Bears | | | |
| (Misspelled Bryon | | | |
| on back and Bryan | | | |
| on card front) | | | |
| ☐ 27 Bob Matheson | 1.75 | .80 | .22 |
| Cleveland Browns | | | |
| ☐ 28 Howard Twilley | 1.75 | .80 | .22 |
| Miami Dolphins | | | |
| ☐ 29 Jim Turner | 1.75 | .80 | .22 |
| New York Jets | | | |
| ☐ 30 Pete Banaszak | 1.75 | .80 | .22 |
| Oakland Raiders | | | |
| ☐ 31 Lance Rentzel | 1.75 | .80 | .22 |
| Dallas Cowboys | | | |
| ☐ 32 Bill Triplett | 1.50 | .65 | .19 |
| Detroit Lions | | | |
| ☐ 33 Boyd Dowler | 1.75 | .80 | .22 |
| Green Bay Packers | | | |
| ☐ 34 Merlin Olsen | 4.50 | 2.00 | .55 |
| Los Angeles Rams | | | |
| ☐ 35 Joe Kapp | 1.75 | .80 | .22 |
| Minnesota Vikings | | | |
| ☐ 36 Dan Abramowicz | 3.00 | 1.35 | .40 |

| | | | |
|---|---|---|---|
| New Orleans Saints | | | |
| ☐ 37 Spider Lockhart | 1.75 | .80 | .22 |
| New York Giants | | | |
| ☐ 38 Tom Day | 1.50 | .65 | .19 |
| San Diego Chargers | | | |
| ☐ 39 Art Graham | 1.50 | .65 | .19 |
| Boston Patriots | | | |
| ☐ 40 Bob Cappadona | 1.50 | .65 | .19 |
| Buffalo Bills | | | |
| ☐ 41 Gary Ballman | 1.50 | .65 | .19 |
| Philadelphia Eagles | | | |
| ☐ 42 Clendon Thomas | 1.50 | .65 | .19 |
| Pittsburgh Steelers | | | |
| ☐ 43 Jackie Smith | 3.00 | 1.35 | .40 |
| St. Louis Cardinals | | | |
| ☐ 44 Dave Wilcox | 1.50 | .65 | .19 |
| San Francisco 49ers | | | |
| ☐ 45 Jerry Smith | 1.75 | .80 | .22 |
| Washington Redskins | | | |
| ☐ 46 Dan Grimm | 1.50 | .65 | .19 |
| Atlanta Falcons | | | |
| ☐ 47 Tom Matte | 1.75 | .80 | .22 |
| Baltimore Colts | | | |
| ☐ 48 John Stofa | 1.50 | .65 | .19 |
| Cincinnati Bengals | | | |
| ☐ 49 Rex Mirich | 1.50 | .65 | .19 |
| Denver Broncos | | | |
| ☐ 50 Miller Farr | 1.50 | .65 | .19 |
| Houston Oilers | | | |
| ☐ 51 Gale Sayers | 55.00 | 25.00 | 7.00 |
| Chicago Bears | | | |
| ☐ 52 Bill Nelsen | 1.75 | .80 | .22 |
| Cleveland Browns | | | |
| ☐ 53 Bob Lilly | 6.00 | 2.70 | .75 |
| Dallas Cowboys | | | |
| ☐ 54 Wayne Walker | 1.75 | .80 | .22 |
| Detroit Lions | | | |
| ☐ 55 Ray Nitschke | 5.00 | 2.30 | .60 |
| Green Bay Packers | | | |
| ☐ 56 Ed Meador | 1.75 | .80 | .22 |
| Los Angeles Rams | | | |
| ☐ 57 Lonnie Warwick | 1.50 | .65 | .19 |
| Minnesota Vikings | | | |
| ☐ 58 Wendell Hayes | 1.75 | .80 | .22 |
| Kansas City Chiefs | | | |
| ☐ 59 Dick Anderson | 3.50 | 1.55 | .45 |
| Miami Dolphins | | | |
| ☐ 60 Don Maynard | 6.50 | 2.90 | .80 |
| New York Jets | | | |
| ☐ 61 Tony Lorick | 1.50 | .65 | .19 |
| New Orleans Saints | | | |
| ☐ 62 Pete Gogolak | 1.75 | .80 | .22 |
| New York Giants | | | |
| ☐ 63 Nate Ramsey | 1.50 | .65 | .19 |
| Philadelphia Eagles | | | |
| ☐ 64 Dick Shiner | 1.75 | .80 | .22 |
| Pittsburgh Steelers | | | |
| ☐ 65 Larry Wilson | 2.50 | 1.15 | .30 |
| St. Louis Cardinals | | | |
| ☐ 66 Ken Willard | 1.75 | .80 | .22 |
| San Francisco 49ers | | | |
| ☐ 67 Charley Taylor UER | 6.00 | 2.70 | .75 |
| Washington Redskins | | | |
| (Led Redskins in | | | |
| pass interceptions) | | | |
| ☐ 68 Billy Cannon | 1.75 | .80 | .22 |
| Oakland Raiders | | | |
| ☐ 69 Lance Alworth | 8.00 | 3.60 | 1.00 |
| San Diego Chargers | | | |
| ☐ 70 Jim Nance | 1.75 | .80 | .22 |
| Boston Patriots | | | |
| ☐ 71 Nick Rassas | 1.50 | .65 | .19 |
| Atlanta Falcons | | | |
| ☐ 72 Lenny Lyles | 1.50 | .65 | .19 |
| Baltimore Colts | | | |
| ☐ 73 Bennie McRae | 1.50 | .65 | .19 |
| Chicago Bears | | | |
| ☐ 74 Bill Glass | 1.50 | .65 | .19 |
| Cleveland Browns | | | |
| ☐ 75 Don Meredith | 20.00 | 9.00 | 2.50 |
| Dallas Cowboys | | | |
| ☐ 76 Dick LeBeau | 1.75 | .80 | .22 |
| Detroit Lions | | | |
| ☐ 77 Carroll Dale | 1.75 | .80 | .22 |
| Green Bay Packers | | | |
| ☐ 78 Ron McDole | 1.50 | .65 | .19 |
| Buffalo Bills | | | |
| ☐ 79 Charley King | 1.50 | .65 | .19 |
| Cincinnati Bengals | | | |
| ☐ 80 Checklist 1-132 UER | 16.00 | 2.40 | .80 |
| (26 Bryon Piccolo) | | | |
| ☐ 81 Dick Bass | 1.75 | .80 | .22 |
| Los Angeles Rams | | | |
| ☐ 82 Roy Winston | 1.50 | .65 | .19 |
| Minnesota Vikings | | | |
| ☐ 83 Don McCall | 1.50 | .65 | .19 |
| New Orleans Saints | | | |
| ☐ 84 Jim Katcavage | 1.75 | .80 | .22 |

| | | | |
|---|---|---|---|
| New York Giants | | | |
| ☐ 85 Norm Snead | 1.75 | .80 | .22 |
| Philadelphia Eagles | | | |
| ☐ 86 Earl Gros | 1.50 | .65 | .19 |
| Pittsburgh Steelers | | | |
| ☐ 87 Don Brumm | 1.50 | .65 | .19 |
| St. Louis Cardinals | | | |
| ☐ 88 Sonny Bishop | 1.50 | .65 | .19 |
| Houston Oilers | | | |
| ☐ 89 Fred Arbanas | 1.50 | .65 | .19 |
| Kansas City Chiefs | | | |
| ☐ 90 Karl Noonan | 1.50 | .65 | .19 |
| Miami Dolphins | | | |
| ☐ 91 Dick Witcher | 1.50 | .65 | .19 |
| San Francisco 49ers | | | |
| ☐ 92 Vince Promuto | 1.50 | .65 | .19 |
| Washington Redskins | | | |
| ☐ 93 Tommy Nobis | 3.00 | 1.35 | .40 |
| Atlanta Falcons | | | |
| ☐ 94 Jerry Hill | 1.50 | .65 | .19 |
| Baltimore Colts | | | |
| ☐ 95 Ed O'Bradovich | 1.75 | .80 | .22 |
| Chicago Bears | | | |
| ☐ 96 Ernie Kellerman | 1.50 | .65 | .19 |
| Cleveland Browns | | | |
| ☐ 97 Chuck Howley | 1.75 | .80 | .22 |
| Dallas Cowboys | | | |
| ☐ 98 Hewritt Dixon | 1.75 | .80 | .22 |
| Oakland Raiders | | | |
| ☐ 99 Ron Mix | 3.00 | 1.35 | .40 |
| San Diego Chargers | | | |
| ☐ 100 Joe Namath | 80.00 | 36.00 | 10.00 |
| New York Jets | | | |
| ☐ 101 Billy Gambrell | 1.50 | .65 | .19 |
| Detroit Lions | | | |
| ☐ 102 Elijah Pitts | 1.75 | .80 | .22 |
| Green Bay Packers | | | |
| ☐ 103 Billy Truax | 1.75 | .80 | .22 |
| Los Angeles Rams | | | |
| ☐ 104 Ed Sharockman | 1.50 | .65 | .19 |
| Minnesota Vikings | | | |
| ☐ 105 Doug Atkins | 3.00 | 1.35 | .40 |
| New Orleans Saints | | | |
| ☐ 106 Greg Larson | 1.50 | .65 | .19 |
| New York Giants | | | |
| ☐ 107 Israel Lang | 1.50 | .65 | .19 |
| Philadelphia Eagles | | | |
| ☐ 108 Houston Antwine | 1.50 | .65 | .19 |
| Boston Patriots | | | |
| ☐ 109 Paul Guidry | 1.50 | .65 | .19 |
| Buffalo Bills | | | |
| ☐ 110 Al Denson | 1.50 | .65 | .19 |
| Denver Broncos | | | |
| ☐ 111 Roy Jefferson | 1.75 | .80 | .22 |
| Pittsburgh Steelers | | | |
| ☐ 112 Chuck Latourette | 1.50 | .65 | .19 |
| St. Louis Cardinals | | | |
| ☐ 113 Jim Johnson | 2.25 | 1.00 | .30 |
| San Francisco 49ers | | | |
| ☐ 114 Bobby Mitchell | 4.00 | 1.80 | .50 |
| Washington Redskins | | | |
| ☐ 115 Randy Johnson | 1.75 | .80 | .22 |
| Atlanta Falcons | | | |
| ☐ 116 Lou Michaels | 1.50 | .65 | .19 |
| Baltimore Colts | | | |
| ☐ 117 Rudy Kuechenberg | 1.50 | .65 | .19 |
| Chicago Bears | | | |
| ☐ 118 Walt Suggs | 1.50 | .65 | .19 |
| Houston Oilers | | | |
| ☐ 119 Goldie Sellers | 1.50 | .65 | .19 |
| Kansas City Chiefs | | | |
| ☐ 120 Larry Csonka | 80.00 | 36.00 | 10.00 |
| Miami Dolphins | | | |
| ☐ 121 Jim Houston | 1.75 | .80 | .22 |
| Cleveland Browns | | | |
| ☐ 122 Craig Baynham | 1.50 | .65 | .19 |
| Dallas Cowboys | | | |
| ☐ 123 Alex Karras | 6.00 | 2.70 | .75 |
| Detroit Lions | | | |
| ☐ 124 Jim Grabowski | 1.75 | .80 | .22 |
| Green Bay Packers | | | |
| ☐ 125 Roman Gabriel | 3.50 | 1.55 | .45 |
| Los Angeles Rams | | | |
| ☐ 126 Larry Bowie | 1.50 | .65 | .19 |
| Minnesota Vikings | | | |
| ☐ 127 Dave Parks | 1.75 | .80 | .22 |
| New Orleans Saints | | | |
| ☐ 128 Ben Davidson | 2.00 | .90 | .25 |
| Oakland Raiders | | | |
| ☐ 129 Steve DeLong | 1.50 | .65 | .19 |
| San Diego Chargers | | | |
| ☐ 130 Fred Hill | 1.50 | .65 | .19 |
| Philadelphia Eagles | | | |
| ☐ 131 Ernie Koy | 1.75 | .80 | .22 |
| New York Giants | | | |
| ☐ 132A Checklist 133-263 | 16.00 | 2.40 | .80 |
| (no border) | | | |
| ☐ 132B Checklist 133-263 | 18.00 | 2.70 | .90 |

| | | | |
|---|---|---|---|
| (thin white border | | | |
| like second series) | | | |
| ☐ 133 Dick Hoak | 1.50 | .65 | .19 |
| Pittsburgh Steelers | | | |
| ☐ 134 Larry Stallings | 1.75 | .80 | .22 |
| St. Louis Cardinals | | | |
| ☐ 135 Clifton McNeil | 1.75 | .80 | .22 |
| San Francisco 49ers | | | |
| ☐ 136 Walter Rock | 1.50 | .65 | .19 |
| Washington Redskins | | | |
| ☐ 137 Billy Lothridge | 1.50 | .65 | .19 |
| Atlanta Falcons | | | |
| ☐ 138 Bob Vogel | 1.50 | .65 | .19 |
| Baltimore Colts | | | |
| ☐ 139 Dick Butkus | 25.00 | 11.50 | 3.10 |
| Chicago Bears | | | |
| ☐ 140 Frank Ryan | 1.75 | .80 | .22 |
| Cleveland Browns | | | |
| ☐ 141 Larry Garron | 1.50 | .65 | .19 |
| Boston Patriots | | | |
| ☐ 142 George Saimes | 1.75 | .80 | .22 |
| Buffalo Bills | | | |
| ☐ 143 Frank Buncom | 1.50 | .65 | .19 |
| Cincinnati Bengals | | | |
| ☐ 144 Don Perkins | 1.75 | .80 | .22 |
| Dallas Cowboys | | | |
| ☐ 145 Johnnie Robinson UER | 1.75 | .80 | .22 |
| (Misspelled Johnny) | | | |
| Detroit Lions | | | |
| ☐ 146 Lee Roy Caffey | 1.75 | .80 | .22 |
| Green Bay Packers | | | |
| ☐ 147 Bernie Casey | 1.75 | .80 | .22 |
| Los Angeles Rams | | | |
| ☐ 148 Billy Martin | 1.50 | .65 | .19 |
| Minnesota Vikings | | | |
| ☐ 149 Gene Howard | 1.50 | .65 | .19 |
| New Orleans Saints | | | |
| ☐ 150 Fran Tarkenton | 24.00 | 11.00 | 3.00 |
| New York Giants | | | |
| ☐ 151 Eric Crabtree | 1.50 | .65 | .19 |
| Denver Broncos | | | |
| ☐ 152 W.K. Hicks | 1.50 | .65 | .19 |
| Houston Oilers | | | |
| ☐ 153 Bobby Bell | 4.00 | 1.80 | .50 |
| Kansas City Chiefs | | | |
| ☐ 154 Sam Baker | 1.75 | .80 | .22 |
| Philadelphia Eagles | | | |
| ☐ 155 Marv Woodson | 1.50 | .65 | .19 |
| Pittsburgh Steelers | | | |
| ☐ 156 Dave Williams | 1.75 | .80 | .22 |
| St. Louis Cardinals | | | |
| ☐ 157 Bruce Bosley UER | 1.50 | .65 | .19 |
| (Considered one of the | | | |
| three centers in all | | | |
| of pro football) | | | |
| San Francisco 49ers | | | |
| ☐ 158 Carl Kammerer | 1.50 | .65 | .19 |
| Washington Redskins | | | |
| ☐ 159 Jim Burson | 1.50 | .65 | .19 |
| Atlanta Falcons | | | |
| ☐ 160 Roy Hilton | 1.50 | .65 | .19 |
| Baltimore Colts | | | |
| ☐ 161 Bob Griese | 30.00 | 13.50 | 3.80 |
| Miami Dolphins | | | |
| ☐ 162 Bob Talamini | 1.50 | .65 | .19 |
| New York Jets | | | |
| ☐ 163 Jim Otto | 4.00 | 1.80 | .50 |
| Oakland Raiders | | | |
| ☐ 164 Ron Bull | 1.50 | .65 | .19 |
| Chicago Bears | | | |
| ☐ 165 Walter Johnson | 1.75 | .80 | .22 |
| Cleveland Browns | | | |
| ☐ 166 Lee Roy Jordan | 3.50 | 1.55 | .45 |
| Dallas Cowboys | | | |
| ☐ 167 Mike Lucci | 1.75 | .80 | .22 |
| Detroit Lions | | | |
| ☐ 168 Willie Wood | 3.50 | 1.55 | .45 |
| Green Bay Packers | | | |
| ☐ 169 Maxie Baughan | 1.75 | .80 | .22 |
| Los Angeles Rams | | | |
| ☐ 170 Bill Brown | 1.75 | .80 | .22 |
| Minnesota Vikings | | | |
| ☐ 171 John Hadl | 3.00 | 1.35 | .40 |
| San Diego Chargers | | | |
| ☐ 172 Gino Cappelletti | 1.75 | .80 | .22 |
| Boston Patriots | | | |
| ☐ 173 George Byrd | 1.75 | .80 | .22 |
| Buffalo Bills | | | |
| ☐ 174 Steve Stonebreaker | 1.50 | .65 | .19 |
| New Orleans Saints | | | |
| ☐ 175 Joe Morrison | 1.75 | .80 | .22 |
| New York Giants | | | |
| ☐ 176 Joe Scarpati | 1.50 | .65 | .19 |
| Philadelphia Eagles | | | |
| ☐ 177 Bobby Walden | 1.50 | .65 | .19 |
| Pittsburgh Steelers | | | |
| ☐ 178 Roy Shivers | 1.75 | .80 | .22 |
| St. Louis Cardinals | | | |

| | | | |
|---|---|---|---|
| ☐ 179 Kermit Alexander<br>San Francisco 49ers | 1.50 | .65 | .19 |
| ☐ 180 Pat Richter<br>Washington Redskins | 1.50 | .65 | .19 |
| ☐ 181 Pete Perreault<br>Cincinnati Bengals | 1.50 | .65 | .19 |
| ☐ 182 Pete Duranko<br>Denver Broncos | 1.50 | .65 | .19 |
| ☐ 183 Leroy Mitchell<br>Houston Oilers | 1.50 | .65 | .19 |
| ☐ 184 Jim Simon<br>Atlanta Falcons | 1.50 | .65 | .19 |
| ☐ 185 Billy Ray Smith<br>Baltimore Colts | 1.50 | .65 | .19 |
| ☐ 186 Jack Concannon<br>Chicago Bears | 1.75 | .80 | .22 |
| ☐ 187 Ben Davis<br>Cleveland Browns | 1.50 | .65 | .19 |
| ☐ 188 Mike Clark<br>Dallas Cowboys | 1.50 | .65 | .19 |
| ☐ 189 Jim Gibbons<br>Detroit Lions | 1.50 | .65 | .19 |
| ☐ 190 Dave Robinson<br>Green Bay Packers | 1.75 | .80 | .22 |
| ☐ 191 Otis Taylor<br>Kansas City Chiefs | 1.75 | .80 | .22 |
| ☐ 192 Nick Buoniconti<br>Miami Dolphins | 3.00 | 1.35 | .40 |
| ☐ 193 Matt Snell<br>New York Jets | 2.50 | 1.15 | .30 |
| ☐ 194 Bruce Gossett<br>Los Angeles Rams | 1.50 | .65 | .19 |
| ☐ 195 Mick Tingelhoff<br>Minnesota Vikings | 1.75 | .80 | .22 |
| ☐ 196 Earl Leggett<br>New Orleans Saints | 1.50 | .65 | .19 |
| ☐ 197 Pete Case<br>New York Giants | 1.50 | .65 | .19 |
| ☐ 198 Tom Woodeshick<br>Philadelphia Eagles | 1.75 | .80 | .22 |
| ☐ 199 Ken Kortas<br>Pittsburgh Steelers | 1.50 | .65 | .19 |
| ☐ 200 Jim Hart<br>St. Louis Cardinals | 3.00 | 1.35 | .40 |
| ☐ 201 Fred Biletnikoff<br>Oakland Raiders | 10.00 | 4.50 | 1.25 |
| ☐ 202 Jacque MacKinnon<br>San Diego Chargers | 1.50 | .65 | .19 |
| ☐ 203 Jim Whalen<br>Boston Patriots | 1.50 | .65 | .19 |
| ☐ 204 Matt Hazeltine<br>San Francisco 49ers | 1.50 | .65 | .19 |
| ☐ 205 Charlie Gogolak<br>Washington Redskins | 1.75 | .80 | .22 |
| ☐ 206 Ray Ogden<br>Atlanta Falcons | 1.50 | .65 | .19 |
| ☐ 207 John Mackey<br>Baltimore Colts | 4.00 | 1.80 | .50 |
| ☐ 208 Roosevelt Taylor<br>Chicago Bears | 1.75 | .80 | .22 |
| ☐ 209 Gene Hickerson<br>Cleveland Browns | 1.50 | .65 | .19 |
| ☐ 210 Dave Edwards<br>Dallas Cowboys | 1.75 | .80 | .22 |
| ☐ 211 Tom Sestak<br>Buffalo Bills | 1.75 | .80 | .22 |
| ☐ 212 Ernie Wright<br>Cincinnati Bengals | 1.50 | .65 | .19 |
| ☐ 213 Dave Costa<br>Denver Broncos | 1.50 | .65 | .19 |
| ☐ 214 Tom Vaughn<br>Detroit Lions | 1.50 | .65 | .19 |
| ☐ 215 Bart Starr<br>Green Bay Packers | 25.00 | 11.50 | 3.10 |
| ☐ 216 Les Josephson<br>Los Angeles Rams | 1.75 | .80 | .22 |
| ☐ 217 Fred Cox<br>Minnesota Vikings | 1.75 | .80 | .22 |
| ☐ 218 Mike Tilleman<br>New Orleans Saints | 1.50 | .65 | .19 |
| ☐ 219 Darrell Dess<br>New York Giants | 1.50 | .65 | .19 |
| ☐ 220 Dave Lloyd<br>Philadelphia Eagles | 1.50 | .65 | .19 |
| ☐ 221 Pete Beathard<br>Houston Oilers | 1.75 | .80 | .22 |
| ☐ 222 Buck Buchanan<br>Kansas City Chiefs | 3.50 | 1.55 | .45 |
| ☐ 223 Frank Emanuel<br>Miami Dolphins | 1.50 | .65 | .19 |
| ☐ 224 Paul Martha<br>Pittsburgh Steelers | 1.50 | .65 | .19 |
| ☐ 225 Johnny Roland<br>St. Louis Cardinals | 1.50 | .65 | .19 |
| ☐ 226 Gary Lewis<br>San Francisco 49ers | 1.50 | .65 | .19 |
| ☐ 227 Sonny Jurgensen UER | 8.00 | 3.60 | 1.00 |

| | | | |
|---|---|---|---|
| Washington Redskins<br>(Chiefs logo) | | | |
| ☐ 228 Jim Butler<br>Atlanta Falcons | 1.50 | .65 | .19 |
| ☐ 229 Mike Curtis<br>Baltimore Colts | 4.50 | 2.00 | .55 |
| ☐ 230 Richie Petitbon<br>Chicago Bears | 1.75 | .80 | .22 |
| ☐ 231 George Sauer Jr.<br>New York Jets | 1.75 | .80 | .22 |
| ☐ 232 George Blanda<br>Oakland Raiders | 20.00 | 9.00 | 2.50 |
| ☐ 233 Gary Garrison<br>San Diego Chargers | 1.75 | .80 | .22 |
| ☐ 234 Gary Collins<br>Cleveland Browns | 1.75 | .80 | .22 |
| ☐ 235 Craig Morton<br>Dallas Cowboys | 4.00 | 1.80 | .50 |
| ☐ 236 Tom Nowatzke<br>Detroit Lions | 1.50 | .65 | .19 |
| ☐ 237 Donny Anderson<br>Green Bay Packers | 1.75 | .80 | .22 |
| ☐ 238 Deacon Jones<br>Los Angeles Rams | 4.00 | 1.80 | .50 |
| ☐ 239 Grady Alderman<br>Minnesota Vikings | 1.50 | .65 | .19 |
| ☐ 240 Bill Kilmer<br>New Orleans Saints | 3.00 | 1.35 | .40 |
| ☐ 241 Mike Taliaferro<br>Boston Patriots | 1.50 | .65 | .19 |
| ☐ 242 Stew Barber<br>Buffalo Bills | 1.50 | .65 | .19 |
| ☐ 243 Bobby Hunt<br>Cincinnati Bengals | 1.50 | .65 | .19 |
| ☐ 244 Homer Jones<br>New York Giants | 1.75 | .80 | .22 |
| ☐ 245 Bob Brown<br>Los Angeles Rams | 1.75 | .80 | .22 |
| ☐ 246 Bill Asbury<br>Pittsburgh Steelers | 1.50 | .65 | .19 |
| ☐ 247 Charlie Johnson UER<br>(Misspelled Charley<br>on both sides)<br>St. Louis Cardinals | 1.75 | .80 | .22 |
| ☐ 248 Chris Hanburger<br>Washington Redskins | 1.75 | .80 | .22 |
| ☐ 249 John Brodie<br>San Francisco 49ers | 7.50 | 3.40 | .95 |
| ☐ 250 Earl Morrall<br>Baltimore Colts | 2.00 | .90 | .25 |
| ☐ 251 Floyd Little<br>Denver Broncos | 5.00 | 2.30 | .60 |
| ☐ 252 Jerrel Wilson<br>Kansas City Chiefs | 1.75 | .80 | .22 |
| ☐ 253 Jim Keyes<br>Miami Dolphins | 1.50 | .65 | .19 |
| ☐ 254 Mel Renfro<br>Dallas Cowboys | 1.75 | .80 | .22 |
| ☐ 255 Herb Adderley<br>Green Bay Packers | 4.00 | 1.80 | .50 |
| ☐ 256 Jack Snow<br>Los Angeles Rams | 1.75 | .80 | .22 |
| ☐ 257 Charlie Durkee<br>New Orleans Saints | 1.50 | .65 | .19 |
| ☐ 258 Charlie Harper<br>New York Giants | 1.50 | .65 | .19 |
| ☐ 259 J.R. Wilburn<br>Pittsburgh Steelers | 1.50 | .65 | .19 |
| ☐ 260 Charlie Krueger<br>San Francisco 49ers | 1.75 | .80 | .22 |
| ☐ 261 Pete Jacques<br>Denver Broncos | 1.50 | .65 | .19 |
| ☐ 262 Gerry Philbin<br>New York Jets | 1.75 | .80 | .22 |
| ☐ 263 Daryle Lamonica<br>Oakland Raiders | 12.00 | 3.00 | .75 |

# 1969 Topps Four-in-One

The 1969 Topps Four-in-One set contains 66 cards (each measuring 2 1/2" by 3 1/2" standard size) with each card having four small (1" by 1 1/2") cardboard stamps on the front. Cards 27 and 28 are the same except for colors. The cards were issued as inserts to the 1969 Topps regular football card set. The cards are unnumbered, but have been numbered in the checklist below for convenience in alphabetical order by the player in the northwest quadrant of the card. Prices below are for complete cards; individual stamps are not priced. An album exists to house the stamps on these cards (see 1969 Topps Mini Albums). It is interesting to note that not all the players appearing in this set also appear in the 1969 Topps regular issue set especially since there are almost the same number of players in each set. Jack Kemp is included in this set but not in the regular 1969 Topps set. Bryan Piccolo also appears in his only Topps appearance other than the 1969 Topps regular issue set. There are 19 players in this set who do not appear in

the regular issue 1969 Topps set; they are marked by asterisks in the list below.

| | NRMT | VG-E | GOOD |
|---|---|---|---|
| COMPLETE SET (66) | 300.00 | 120.00 | 30.00 |
| COMMON CARD (1-66) | 3.00 | 1.20 | .30 |
| ☐ 1 Grady Alderman<br>Jerry Smith<br>Gale Sayers<br>Dick LeBeau | 12.00 | 5.00 | 1.20 |
| ☐ 2 Jim Allison *<br>Frank Buncom<br>Frank Emanuel<br>George Sauer Jr. | 3.00 | 1.20 | .30 |
| ☐ 3 Lance Alworth<br>Don Maynard<br>Ron McDole<br>Billy Cannon | 7.50 | 3.00 | .75 |
| ☐ 4 Dick Anderson<br>Mike Taliaferro<br>Fred Biletnikoff<br>Otis Taylor | 5.00 | 2.00 | .50 |
| ☐ 5 Ralph Baker<br>Speedy Duncan<br>Eric Crabtree<br>Bobby Bell | 4.00 | 1.60 | .40 |
| ☐ 6 Gary Ballman<br>Jerry Hill<br>Roy Jefferson<br>Boyd Dowler | 3.00 | 1.20 | .30 |
| ☐ 7 Tom Beer<br>Miller Farr<br>Jim Colclough<br>Steve DeLong | 3.00 | 1.20 | .30 |
| ☐ 8 Sonny Bishop<br>Pete Banaszak<br>Paul Guidry<br>Tom Day | 3.00 | 1.20 | .30 |
| ☐ 9 Bruce Bosley<br>J.R. Wilburn<br>Tom Nowatzke<br>Jim Simon | 3.00 | 1.20 | .30 |
| ☐ 10 Larry Bowie<br>Willis Crenshaw<br>Tommy Davis<br>Paul Flatley | 3.00 | 1.20 | .30 |
| ☐ 11 Nick Buoniconti<br>George Saimes<br>Jacque MacKinnon<br>Pete Duranko | 4.00 | 1.60 | .40 |
| ☐ 12 Jim Burson<br>Dan Abramowicz<br>Ed O'Bradovich<br>Dick Witcher | 3.00 | 1.20 | .30 |
| ☐ 13 Reg Carolan *<br>Larry Garron<br>W.K. Hicks<br>Pete Jacques | 3.00 | 1.20 | .30 |
| ☐ 14 Bert Coan *<br>John Hadl<br>Dan Birdwell *<br>Sam Brunelli * | 4.00 | 1.60 | .40 |
| ☐ 15 Hewritt Dixon<br>Goldie Sellers<br>Joe Namath<br>Howard Twilley | 30.00 | 12.00 | 3.00 |
| ☐ 16 Charlie Durkee<br>Clifton McNeil<br>Maxie Baughan<br>Fran Tarkenton | 10.00 | 4.00 | 1.00 |
| ☐ 17 Pete Gogolak<br>Ron Bull<br>Chuck Latourette<br>Willie Richardson | 3.00 | 1.20 | .30 |
| ☐ 18 Bob Griese<br>Jim LeMoine * | 7.50 | 3.00 | .75 |
| Dave Grayson<br>Walt Sweeney | | | |
| ☐ 19 Jim Hart<br>Darrell Dess<br>Kermit Alexander<br>Mick Tingelhoff | 4.00 | 1.60 | .40 |
| ☐ 20 Alvin Haymond<br>Elijah Pitts<br>Billy Ray Smith<br>Ken Willard | 3.00 | 1.20 | .30 |
| ☐ 21 Gene Hickerson<br>Donny Anderson<br>Dick Butkus<br>Mike Lucci | 10.00 | 4.00 | 1.00 |
| ☐ 22 Fred Hill<br>Ernie Koy<br>Tommy Nobis<br>Bennie McRae | 4.00 | 1.60 | .40 |
| ☐ 23 Dick Hoak<br>Roman Gabriel<br>Ed Sharockman<br>Dave Williams | 4.00 | 1.60 | .40 |
| ☐ 24 Jim Houston<br>Roy Shivers<br>Carroll Dale<br>Bill Asbury | 3.00 | 1.20 | .30 |
| ☐ 25 Gene Howard<br>Joe Morrison<br>Billy Martin<br>Ben Davis | 3.00 | 1.20 | .30 |
| ☐ 26 Chuck Howley<br>Brian Piccolo UER<br>Chris Hanburger<br>Erich Barnes | 25.00 | 10.00 | 2.50 |
| ☐ 27 Charlie Johnson (red)<br>Jim Katcavage<br>Gary Lewis<br>Bill Triplett<br>(white) | 4.00 | 1.60 | .40 |
| ☐ 28 Charlie Johnson<br>(white)<br>Jim Katcavage<br>Gary Lewis<br>Bill Triplett (red) | 4.00 | 1.60 | .40 |
| ☐ 29 Walter Johnson<br>Tucker Frederickson<br>Dave Lloyd<br>Bobby Walden | 3.00 | 1.20 | .30 |
| ☐ 30 Sonny Jurgensen<br>Dick Bass<br>Paul Martha<br>Dave Parks | 6.00 | 2.40 | .60 |
| ☐ 31 Leroy Kelly<br>Ed Meador<br>Bart Starr<br>Ray Ogden | 12.00 | 5.00 | 1.20 |
| ☐ 32 Charley King<br>Bob Cappadona<br>Fred Arbanas<br>Ben Davidson | 4.00 | 1.60 | .40 |
| ☐ 33 Daryle Lamonica<br>Carl Cunningham *<br>Bobby Hunt<br>Stew Barber | 4.00 | 1.60 | .40 |
| ☐ 34 Israel Lang<br>Bob Lilly<br>Jim Butler<br>John Brodie | 7.50 | 3.00 | .75 |
| ☐ 35 Jim Lindsey<br>Ray Nitschke<br>Rickie Harris<br>Bob Vogel | 4.00 | 1.60 | .40 |
| ☐ 36 Billy Lothridge<br>Herb Adderley<br>Charlie Gogolak<br>John Mackey | 5.00 | 2.00 | .50 |
| ☐ 37 Bobby Maples<br>Karl Noonan<br>Houston Antwine<br>Wendell Hayes | 3.00 | 1.20 | .30 |
| ☐ 38 Don Meredith<br>Gary Collins<br>Homer Jones<br>Marv Woodson | 10.00 | 4.00 | 1.00 |
| ☐ 39 Rex Mirich<br>Art Graham<br>Jim Turner<br>John Stofa | 3.00 | 1.20 | .30 |
| ☐ 40 Leroy Mitchell<br>Sid Blanks *<br>Paul Rochester *<br>Pete Perreault | 3.00 | 1.20 | .30 |
| ☐ 41 Jim Nance<br>Jim Dunaway<br>Larry Csonka<br>Ron Mix | 7.50 | 3.00 | .75 |
| ☐ 42 Bill Nelsen<br>Bill Munson | 3.00 | 1.20 | .30 |

|  | | | |
|---|---|---|---|
| Nate Ramsey | | | |
| Mike Curtis | | | |
| ☐ 43 Jim Otto | 4.00 | 1.60 | .40 |
| Dave Herman * | | | |
| Dave Costa | | | |
| Dennis Randall * | | | |
| ☐ 44 Jack Pardee | 4.00 | 1.60 | .40 |
| Norm Snead | | | |
| Craig Baynham | | | |
| Bob Jeter | | | |
| ☐ 45 Richie Petitbon | 4.00 | 1.60 | .40 |
| Johnny Robinson | | | |
| Mike Clark | | | |
| Jack Snow | | | |
| ☐ 46 Nick Rassas | 4.00 | 1.60 | .40 |
| Tom Matte | | | |
| Lance Rentzel | | | |
| Bobby Mitchell | | | |
| ☐ 47 Pat Richter | 4.00 | 1.60 | .40 |
| Dave Whitsell | | | |
| Joe Kapp | | | |
| Bill Glass | | | |
| ☐ 48 Johnny Roland | 4.00 | 1.60 | .40 |
| Craig Morton | | | |
| Bill Brown | | | |
| Sam Baker | | | |
| ☐ 49 Andy Russell | 5.00 | 2.00 | .50 |
| Randy Johnson | | | |
| Bob Matheson | | | |
| Alex Karras | | | |
| ☐ 50 Joe Scarpati | 3.00 | 1.20 | .30 |
| Walter Rock | | | |
| Jack Concannon | | | |
| Bernie Casey | | | |
| ☐ 51 Tom Sestak | 3.00 | 1.20 | .30 |
| Ernie Wright | | | |
| Doug Moreau * | | | |
| Matt Snell | | | |
| ☐ 52 Jerry Simmons | 5.00 | 2.00 | .50 |
| Bob Hayes | | | |
| Doug Atkins | | | |
| Spider Lockhart | | | |
| ☐ 53 Jackie Smith | 7.50 | 3.00 | .75 |
| Jim Grabowski | | | |
| Jim Johnson | | | |
| Charley Taylor | | | |
| ☐ 54 Larry Stallings | 3.00 | 1.20 | .30 |
| Rosey Taylor | | | |
| Jim Gibbons | | | |
| Bob Brown | | | |
| ☐ 55 Mike Stratton * | 3.00 | 1.20 | .30 |
| Marion Rushing * | | | |
| Solomon Brannan * | | | |
| Jim Keyes | | | |
| ☐ 56 Walt Suggs | 5.00 | 2.00 | .50 |
| Len Dawson | | | |
| Sherrill Headrick | | | |
| Al Denson | | | |
| ☐ 57 Bob Talamini | 40.00 | 16.00 | 4.00 |
| George Blanda | | | |
| Jim Whalen | | | |
| Jack Kemp * | | | |
| ☐ 58 Clendon Thomas | 4.00 | 1.60 | .40 |
| Don McCall | | | |
| Earl Morrall | | | |
| Lonnie Warwick | | | |
| ☐ 59 Don Trull * | 4.00 | 1.60 | .40 |
| Gerry Philbin | | | |
| Gary Garrison | | | |
| Buck Buchanan | | | |
| ☐ 60 John Unitas | 12.00 | 5.00 | 1.20 |
| Les Josephson | | | |
| Fred Cox | | | |
| Mel Renfro | | | |
| ☐ 61 Wayne Walker | 5.00 | 2.00 | .50 |
| Tony Lorick | | | |
| Dave Wilcox | | | |
| Merlin Olsen | | | |
| ☐ 62 Willie West * | 3.00 | 1.20 | .30 |
| Ken Herock * | | | |
| George Byrd | | | |
| Gino Cappelletti | | | |
| ☐ 63 Jerrel Wilson | 4.00 | 1.60 | .40 |
| John Bramlett | | | |
| Pete Beathard | | | |
| Floyd Little | | | |
| ☐ 64 Larry Wilson | 4.00 | 1.60 | .40 |
| Lou Michaels | | | |
| Billy Gambrell | | | |
| Earl Gros | | | |
| ☐ 65 Willie Wood | 4.00 | 1.60 | .40 |
| Steve Stonebreaker | | | |
| Vince Promuto | | | |
| Jim Cadile | | | |
| ☐ 66 Tom Woodeshick | 4.00 | 1.60 | .40 |
| Greg Larson | | | |
| Billy Kilmer | | | |
| Don Perkins | | | |

# 1969 Topps Mini-Albums

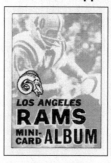

The 1969 Topps Mini-Card Team Albums is a set of 26 small (2 1/2" by 3 1/2") booklets which were issued in conjunction with the 1969 Four-in-One inserts. Each of these booklets has eight pages. A picture of each player is contained in the album, over which the stamps from the Four-in-One inserts were to be pasted. In order to be mint, the album must have no stamps pasted in it. The booklets are printed in blue and black ink on thick white paper and are numbered on the last page of the album. The card numbering cooresponds to an alphabetical listing by team name within each league.

|  | NRMT | VG-E | GOOD |
|---|---|---|---|
| COMPLETE SET (26) | 75.00 | 30.00 | 7.50 |
| COMMON ALBUM (1-26) | 3.50 | 1.40 | .35 |
| ☐ 1 Atlanta Falcons | 3.50 | 1.40 | .35 |
| ☐ 2 Baltimore Colts | 3.50 | 1.40 | .35 |
| ☐ 3 Chicago Bears | 5.00 | 2.00 | .50 |
| ☐ 4 Cleveland Browns | 3.50 | 1.40 | .35 |
| ☐ 5 Dallas Cowboys | 6.00 | 2.40 | .60 |
| ☐ 6 Detroit Lions | 3.50 | 1.40 | .35 |
| ☐ 7 Green Bay Packers | 6.00 | 2.40 | .60 |
| (Bart Starr | | | |
| pictured on front) | | | |
| ☐ 8 Los Angeles Rams | 3.50 | 1.40 | .35 |
| ☐ 9 Minnesota Vikings | 3.50 | 1.40 | .35 |
| ☐ 10 New Orleans Saints | 3.50 | 1.40 | .35 |
| ☐ 11 New York Giants | 5.00 | 2.00 | .50 |
| ☐ 12 Philadelphia Eagles | 3.50 | 1.40 | .35 |
| ☐ 13 Pittsburgh Steelers | 5.00 | 2.00 | .50 |
| ☐ 14 St. Louis Cardinals | 3.50 | 1.40 | .35 |
| ☐ 15 San Francisco 49ers | 5.00 | 2.00 | .50 |
| ☐ 16 Washington Redskins | 5.00 | 2.00 | .50 |
| ☐ 17 Boston Patriots | 3.50 | 1.40 | .35 |
| ☐ 18 Buffalo Bills | 5.00 | 2.00 | .50 |
| ☐ 19 Cincinnati Bengals | 3.50 | 1.40 | .35 |
| ☐ 20 Denver Broncos | 6.00 | 2.40 | .60 |
| ☐ 21 Houston Oilers | 5.00 | 2.00 | .50 |
| ☐ 22 Kansas City Chiefs | 3.50 | 1.40 | .35 |
| ☐ 23 Miami Dolphins | 5.00 | 2.00 | .50 |
| ☐ 24 New York Jets | 5.00 | 2.00 | .50 |
| ☐ 25 Oakland Raiders | 6.00 | 2.40 | .60 |
| ☐ 26 San Diego Chargers | 3.50 | 1.40 | .35 |

# 1970 Topps

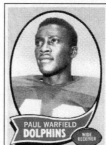

The 1970 Topps football set contains 263 cards. The cards measure 2 1/2" by 3 1/2". The second series was printed in slightly lesser quantities than the first series. There are no scarcities, although O.J. Simpson's Rookie Card appears in this set. Other notable Rookie Cards in this set are Lem Barney, Bill Bergey, Larry Brown, Fred Dryer, Calvin Hill, Harold Jackson, Tom Mack, Alan Page, Bubba Smith, Jan

Stenerud, Bob Trumpy, and both Gene Washingtons. The card backs are done in orange, purple, and white. In the second series, the offensive and defensive linemen are styled on the card back with no statistics and a coin rub-off cartoon rather than a printed cartoon as seen on all the other cards in the set.

| | NRMT | VG-E | GOOD |
|---|---|---|---|
| COMPLETE SET (263) | 475.00 | 210.00 | 60.00 |
| COMMON PLAYER (1-132) | .60 | .25 | .08 |
| COMMON PLAYER (133-263) | .75 | .35 | .09 |

| | NRMT | VG-E | GOOD |
|---|---|---|---|
| ☐ 1 Len Dawson UER Kansas City Chiefs (Cartoon caption says, "AFL AN NFL") | 15.00 | 3.00 | .90 |
| ☐ 2 Doug Hart Green Bay Packers | .60 | .25 | .08 |
| ☐ 3 Verlon Biggs New York Jets | .60 | .25 | .08 |
| ☐ 4 Ralph Neely Dallas Cowboys | 1.25 | .55 | .16 |
| ☐ 5 Harmon Wages Atlanta Falcons | .60 | .25 | .08 |
| ☐ 6 Dan Conners Oakland Raiders | .60 | .25 | .08 |
| ☐ 7 Gino Cappelletti Boston Patriots | 1.00 | .45 | .13 |
| ☐ 8 Erich Barnes Cleveland Browns | .75 | .35 | .09 |
| ☐ 9 Checklist 1-132 | 10.00 | 1.50 | .50 |
| ☐ 10 Bob Griese Miami Dolphins | 14.00 | 6.25 | 1.75 |
| ☐ 11 Ed Flanagan Detroit Lions | .60 | .25 | .08 |
| ☐ 12 George Seals Chicago Bears | .60 | .25 | .08 |
| ☐ 13 Harry Jacobs Buffalo Bills | .60 | .25 | .08 |
| ☐ 14 Mike Haffner Denver Broncos | .60 | .25 | .08 |
| ☐ 15 Bob Vogel Baltimore Colts | .60 | .25 | .08 |
| ☐ 16 Bill Peterson Cincinnati Bengals | .60 | .25 | .08 |
| ☐ 17 Spider Lockhart New York Giants | .75 | .35 | .09 |
| ☐ 18 Billy Truax Los Angeles Rams | .75 | .35 | .09 |
| ☐ 19 Jim Beirne Houston Oilers | .60 | .25 | .08 |
| ☐ 20 Leroy Kelly Cleveland Browns | 4.50 | 2.00 | .55 |
| ☐ 21 Dave Lloyd Philadelphia Eagles | .60 | .25 | .08 |
| ☐ 22 Mike Tilleman New Orleans Saints | .60 | .25 | .08 |
| ☐ 23 Gary Garrison San Diego Chargers | .75 | .35 | .09 |
| ☐ 24 Larry Brown Washington Redskins | 7.00 | 3.10 | .85 |
| ☐ 25 Jan Stenerud Kansas City Chiefs | 12.00 | 5.50 | 1.50 |
| ☐ 26 Rolf Krueger St. Louis Cardinals | .60 | .25 | .08 |
| ☐ 27 Roland Lakes San Francisco 49ers | .60 | .25 | .08 |
| ☐ 28 Dick Hoak Pittsburgh Steelers | .60 | .25 | .08 |
| ☐ 29 Gene Washington Minnesota Vikings | 1.25 | .55 | .16 |
| ☐ 30 Bart Starr Green Bay Packers | 22.00 | 10.00 | 2.80 |
| ☐ 31 Dave Grayson Oakland Raiders | .60 | .25 | .08 |
| ☐ 32 Jerry Rush Detroit Lions | .60 | .25 | .08 |
| ☐ 33 Len St. Jean Boston Patriots | .60 | .25 | .08 |
| ☐ 34 Randy Edmunds Miami Dolphins | .60 | .25 | .08 |
| ☐ 35 Matt Snell New York Jets | 1.25 | .55 | .16 |
| ☐ 36 Paul Costa Buffalo Bills | .60 | .25 | .08 |
| ☐ 37 Mike Pyle Chicago Bears | .60 | .25 | .08 |
| ☐ 38 Roy Hilton Baltimore Colts | .60 | .25 | .08 |
| ☐ 39 Steve Tensi Denver Broncos | .75 | .35 | .09 |
| ☐ 40 Tommy Nobis Atlanta Falcons | 2.00 | .90 | .25 |
| ☐ 41 Pete Case New York Giants | .60 | .25 | .08 |
| ☐ 42 Andy Rice Cincinnati Bengals | .60 | .25 | .08 |
| ☐ 43 Elvin Bethea | 3.50 | 1.55 | .45 |

| | NRMT | VG-E | GOOD |
|---|---|---|---|
| Houston Oilers | | | |
| ☐ 44 Jack Snow Los Angeles Rams | .75 | .35 | .09 |
| ☐ 45 Mel Renfro Dallas Cowboys | 1.25 | .55 | .16 |
| ☐ 46 Andy Livingston New Orleans Saints | .60 | .25 | .08 |
| ☐ 47 Gary Ballman Philadelphia Eagles | .60 | .25 | .08 |
| ☐ 48 Bob DeMarco St. Louis Cardinals | .60 | .25 | .08 |
| ☐ 49 Steve DeLong San Diego Chargers | .60 | .25 | .08 |
| ☐ 50 Daryle Lamonica Oakland Raiders | 3.00 | 1.35 | .40 |
| ☐ 51 Jim Lynch Kansas City Chiefs | 1.00 | .45 | .13 |
| ☐ 52 Mel Farr Detroit Lions | 1.00 | .45 | .13 |
| ☐ 53 Bob Long Washington Redskins | .60 | .25 | .08 |
| ☐ 54 John Elliott New York Jets | .60 | .25 | .08 |
| ☐ 55 Ray Nitschke Green Bay Packers | 4.00 | 1.80 | .50 |
| ☐ 56 Jim Shorter Pittsburgh Steelers | .60 | .25 | .08 |
| ☐ 57 Dave Wilcox San Francisco 49ers | .75 | .35 | .09 |
| ☐ 58 Eric Crabtree Cincinnati Bengals | .60 | .25 | .08 |
| ☐ 59 Alan Page Minnesota Vikings | 30.00 | 13.50 | 3.80 |
| ☐ 60 Jim Nance Boston Patriots | .75 | .35 | .09 |
| ☐ 61 Glen Ray Hines Houston Oilers | .60 | .25 | .08 |
| ☐ 62 John Mackey Baltimore Colts | 3.50 | 1.55 | .45 |
| ☐ 63 Ron McDole Buffalo Bills | .60 | .25 | .08 |
| ☐ 64 Tom Beier San Francisco 49ers | .60 | .25 | .08 |
| ☐ 65 Bill Nelsen Cleveland Browns | .75 | .35 | .09 |
| ☐ 66 Paul Flatley Atlanta Falcons | .75 | .35 | .09 |
| ☐ 67 Sam Brunelli Denver Broncos | .60 | .25 | .08 |
| ☐ 68 Jack Pardee Los Angeles Rams | 1.75 | .80 | .22 |
| ☐ 69 Brig Owens Washington Redskins | .60 | .25 | .08 |
| ☐ 70 Gale Sayers Chicago Bears | 35.00 | 16.00 | 4.40 |
| ☐ 71 Lee Roy Jordan Dallas Cowboys | 2.00 | .90 | .25 |
| ☐ 72 Harold Jackson Philadelphia Eagles | 8.00 | 3.60 | 1.00 |
| ☐ 73 John Hadl San Diego Chargers | 2.00 | .90 | .25 |
| ☐ 74 Dave Parks New Orleans Saints | .75 | .35 | .09 |
| ☐ 75 Lem Barney Detroit Lions | 15.00 | 6.75 | 1.90 |
| ☐ 76 Johnny Roland St. Louis Cardinals | .60 | .25 | .08 |
| ☐ 77 Ed Budde Kansas City Chiefs | .75 | .35 | .09 |
| ☐ 78 Ben McGee Pittsburgh Steelers | .60 | .25 | .08 |
| ☐ 79 Ken Bowman Green Bay Packers | .60 | .25 | .08 |
| ☐ 80 Fran Tarkenton New York Giants | 20.00 | 9.00 | 2.50 |
| ☐ 81 Gene Washington San Francisco 49ers | 4.00 | 1.80 | .50 |
| ☐ 82 Larry Grantham New York Jets | .75 | .35 | .09 |
| ☐ 83 Bill Brown Minnesota Vikings | .75 | .35 | .09 |
| ☐ 84 John Charles Boston Patriots | .60 | .25 | .08 |
| ☐ 85 Fred Biletnikoff Oakland Raiders | 7.00 | 3.10 | .85 |
| ☐ 86 Royce Berry Cincinnati Bengals | .60 | .25 | .08 |
| ☐ 87 Bob Lilly Dallas Cowboys | 5.00 | 2.30 | .60 |
| ☐ 88 Earl Morrall Baltimore Colts | 1.50 | .65 | .19 |
| ☐ 89 Jerry LeVias Houston Oilers | 1.00 | .45 | .13 |
| ☐ 90 O.J. Simpson Buffalo Bills | 175.00 | 80.00 | 22.00 |
| ☐ 91 Mike Howell Cleveland Browns | .60 | .25 | .08 |
| ☐ 92 Ken Gray | .75 | .35 | .09 |

| | | | |
|---|---|---|---|
| 93 Chris Hanburger | .75 | .35 | .09 |
| St. Louis Cardinals | | | |
| 94 Larry Seiple | 1.00 | .45 | .13 |
| Washington Redskins | | | |
| 95 Rich Jackson | 1.00 | .45 | .13 |
| Miami Dolphins | | | |
| 96 Rockne Freitas | .60 | .25 | .08 |
| Denver Broncos | | | |
| 97 Dick Post | 1.00 | .45 | .13 |
| Detroit Lions | | | |
| 98 Ben Hawkins | .60 | .25 | .08 |
| San Diego Chargers | | | |
| 99 Ken Reaves | .60 | .25 | .08 |
| Philadelphia Eagles | | | |
| 100 Roman Gabriel | 3.00 | 1.35 | .40 |
| Atlanta Falcons | | | |
| 101 Dave Rowe | .60 | .25 | .08 |
| Los Angeles Rams | | | |
| 102 Dave Robinson | .75 | .35 | .09 |
| New Orleans Saints | | | |
| 103 Otis Taylor | 1.25 | .55 | .16 |
| Green Bay Packers | | | |
| 104 Jim Turner | .75 | .35 | .09 |
| Kansas City Chiefs | | | |
| 105 Joe Morrison | .75 | .35 | .09 |
| New York Jets | | | |
| 106 Dick Evey | .60 | .25 | .08 |
| New York Giants | | | |
| 107 Ray Mansfield | .60 | .25 | .08 |
| Chicago Bears | | | |
| 108 Grady Alderman | .60 | .25 | .08 |
| Pittsburgh Steelers | | | |
| 109 Bruce Gossett | .60 | .25 | .08 |
| Minnesota Vikings | | | |
| 110 Bob Trumpy | 10.00 | 4.50 | 1.25 |
| San Francisco 49ers | | | |
| 111 Jim Hunt | .60 | .25 | .08 |
| Cincinnati Bengals | | | |
| 112 Larry Stallings | .60 | .25 | .08 |
| Boston Patriots | | | |
| 113A Lance Rentzel | 1.25 | .55 | .16 |
| St. Louis Cardinals | | | |
| Dallas Cowboys | | | |
| (name in red) | | | |
| 113B Lance Rentzel | 1.25 | .55 | .16 |
| Dallas Cowboys | | | |
| (name in black) | | | |
| 114 Bubba Smith | 30.00 | 13.50 | 3.80 |
| Baltimore Colts | | | |
| 115 Norm Snead | 1.00 | .45 | .13 |
| Philadelphia Eagles | | | |
| 116 Jim Otto | 3.00 | 1.35 | .40 |
| Oakland Raiders | | | |
| 117 Bo Scott | .60 | .25 | .08 |
| Cleveland Browns | | | |
| 118 Rick Redman | .60 | .25 | .08 |
| San Diego Chargers | | | |
| 119 George Byrd | .75 | .35 | .09 |
| Buffalo Bills | | | |
| 120 George Webster | 2.50 | 1.15 | .30 |
| Houston Oilers | | | |
| 121 Chuck Walton | .60 | .25 | .08 |
| Detroit Lions | | | |
| 122 Dave Costa | .60 | .25 | .08 |
| Denver Broncos | | | |
| 123 Al Dodd | .60 | .25 | .08 |
| New Orleans Saints | | | |
| 124 Len Hauss | .75 | .35 | .09 |
| Washington Redskins | | | |
| 125 Deacon Jones | 3.00 | 1.35 | .40 |
| Los Angeles Rams | | | |
| 126 Randy Johnson | .75 | .35 | .09 |
| Atlanta Falcons | | | |
| 127 Ralph Heck | .60 | .25 | .08 |
| New York Giants | | | |
| 128 Emerson Boozer | 2.50 | 1.15 | .30 |
| New York Jets | | | |
| 129 Johnny Robinson | .75 | .35 | .09 |
| Kansas City Chiefs | | | |
| 130 John Brodie | 6.00 | 2.70 | .75 |
| San Francisco 49ers | | | |
| 131 Gale Gillingham | .60 | .25 | .08 |
| Green Bay Packers | | | |
| 132 Checklist 133-263 DP | 6.00 | .90 | .30 |
| UER (145 Charley Taylor | | | |
| misspelled Charlie) | | | |
| 133 Chuck Walker | .75 | .35 | .09 |
| St. Louis Cardinals | | | |
| 134 Bennie McRae | .75 | .35 | .09 |
| Chicago Bears | | | |
| 135 Paul Warfield | 7.00 | 3.10 | .85 |
| Miami Dolphins | | | |
| 136 Dan Darragh | .75 | .35 | .09 |
| Buffalo Bills | | | |
| 137 Paul Robinson | .75 | .35 | .09 |
| Cincinnati Bengals | | | |
| 138 Ed Philpott | .75 | .35 | .09 |
| Boston Patriots | | | |
| 139 Craig Morton | 2.50 | 1.15 | .30 |
| Dallas Cowboys | | | |
| 140 Tom Dempsey | 4.00 | 1.80 | .50 |
| New Orleans Saints | | | |
| 141 Al Nelson | .75 | .35 | .09 |
| Philadelphia Eagles | | | |
| 142 Tom Matte | .90 | .40 | .11 |
| Baltimore Colts | | | |
| 143 Dick Schafrath | .75 | .35 | .09 |
| Cleveland Browns | | | |
| 144 Willie Brown | 4.00 | 1.80 | .50 |
| Oakland Raiders | | | |
| 145 Charley Taylor UER | 5.00 | 2.30 | .60 |
| (Misspelled Charlie | | | |
| on both sides) | | | |
| Washington Redskins | | | |
| 146 John Huard | .75 | .35 | .09 |
| Denver Broncos | | | |
| 147 Dave Osborn | .90 | .40 | .11 |
| Minnesota Vikings | | | |
| 148 Gene Mingo | .75 | .35 | .09 |
| Pittsburgh Steelers | | | |
| 149 Larry Hand | .75 | .35 | .09 |
| Detroit Lions | | | |
| 150 Joe Namath | 50.00 | 23.00 | 6.25 |
| New York Jets | | | |
| 151 Tom Mack | 7.00 | 3.10 | .85 |
| Los Angeles Rams | | | |
| 152 Kenny Graham | .75 | .35 | .09 |
| San Diego Chargers | | | |
| 153 Don Herrmann | .75 | .35 | .09 |
| New York Giants | | | |
| 154 Bobby Bell | 3.00 | 1.35 | .40 |
| Kansas City Chiefs | | | |
| 155 Hoyle Granger | .75 | .35 | .09 |
| Houston Oilers | | | |
| 156 Claude Humphrey | 2.50 | 1.15 | .30 |
| Atlanta Falcons | | | |
| 157 Clifton McNeil | .90 | .40 | .11 |
| New York Giants | | | |
| 158 Mick Tingelhoff | .90 | .40 | .11 |
| Minnesota Vikings | | | |
| 159 Don Horn | .75 | .35 | .09 |
| Green Bay Packers | | | |
| 160 Larry Wilson | 2.50 | 1.15 | .30 |
| St. Louis Cardinals | | | |
| 161 Tom Neville | .75 | .35 | .09 |
| Boston Patriots | | | |
| 162 Larry Csonka | 25.00 | 11.50 | 3.10 |
| Miami Dolphins | | | |
| 163 Doug Buffone | 1.25 | .55 | .16 |
| Chicago Bears | | | |
| 164 Cornell Green | .90 | .40 | .11 |
| Dallas Cowboys | | | |
| 165 Haven Moses | 1.75 | .80 | .22 |
| Buffalo Bills | | | |
| 166 Bill Kilmer | 2.25 | 1.00 | .30 |
| New Orleans Saints | | | |
| 167 Tim Rossovich | .75 | .35 | .09 |
| Philadelphia Eagles | | | |
| 168 Bill Bergey | 5.00 | 2.30 | .60 |
| Cincinnati Bengals | | | |
| 169 Gary Collins | .90 | .40 | .11 |
| Cleveland Browns | | | |
| 170 Floyd Little | 3.00 | 1.35 | .40 |
| Denver Broncos | | | |
| 171 Tom Keating | .75 | .35 | .09 |
| Oakland Raiders | | | |
| 172 Pat Fischer | .90 | .40 | .11 |
| Washington Redskins | | | |
| 173 Walt Sweeney | .90 | .40 | .11 |
| San Diego Chargers | | | |
| 174 Greg Larson | .75 | .35 | .09 |
| New York Giants | | | |
| 175 Carl Eller | 3.00 | 1.35 | .40 |
| Minnesota Vikings | | | |
| 176 George Sauer Jr. | .90 | .40 | .11 |
| New York Jets | | | |
| 177 Jim Hart | 2.25 | 1.00 | .30 |
| St. Louis Cardinals | | | |
| 178 Bob Brown | .90 | .40 | .11 |
| Los Angeles Rams | | | |
| 179 Mike Garrett | 4.00 | 1.80 | .50 |
| Kansas City Chiefs | | | |
| 180 John Unitas | 22.00 | 10.00 | 2.80 |
| Baltimore Colts | | | |
| 181 Tom Regner | .75 | .35 | .09 |
| Houston Oilers | | | |
| 182 Bob Jeter | .90 | .40 | .11 |
| Green Bay Packers | | | |
| 183 Gail Cogdill | .75 | .35 | .09 |
| Atlanta Falcons | | | |
| 184 Earl Gros | .75 | .35 | .09 |
| Pittsburgh Steelers | | | |
| 185 Dennis Partee | .75 | .35 | .09 |
| San Diego Chargers | | | |
| 186 Charlie Krueger | .90 | .40 | .11 |

| | | | |
|---|---|---|---|
| San Francisco 49ers | | | |
| ☐ 187 Martin Baccaglio | .75 | .35 | .09 |
| Cincinnati Bengals | | | |
| ☐ 188 Charles Long | .75 | .35 | .09 |
| Boston Patriots | | | |
| ☐ 189 Bob Hayes | 2.00 | .90 | .25 |
| Dallas Cowboys | | | |
| ☐ 190 Dick Butkus | 12.00 | 5.50 | 1.50 |
| Chicago Bears | | | |
| ☐ 191 Al Bemiller | .75 | .35 | .09 |
| Buffalo Bills | | | |
| ☐ 192 Dick Westmoreland | .75 | .35 | .09 |
| Minnesota Vikings | | | |
| ☐ 193 Joe Scarpati | .75 | .35 | .09 |
| New Orleans Saints | | | |
| ☐ 194 Ron Snidow | .75 | .35 | .09 |
| Cleveland Browns | | | |
| ☐ 195 Earl McCullouch | 1.25 | .55 | .16 |
| Detroit Lions | | | |
| ☐ 196 Jake Kupp | .75 | .35 | .09 |
| New Orleans Saints | | | |
| ☐ 197 Bob Lurtsema | .75 | .35 | .09 |
| New York Giants | | | |
| ☐ 198 Mike Current | .75 | .35 | .09 |
| Denver Broncos | | | |
| ☐ 199 Charlie Smith | .75 | .35 | .09 |
| Oakland Raiders | | | |
| ☐ 200 Sonny Jurgensen | 7.00 | 3.10 | .85 |
| Washington Redskins | | | |
| ☐ 201 Mike Curtis | 1.50 | .65 | .19 |
| Baltimore Colts | | | |
| ☐ 202 Aaron Brown | .75 | .35 | .09 |
| Kansas City Chiefs | | | |
| ☐ 203 Richie Petitbon | .90 | .40 | .11 |
| Los Angeles Rams | | | |
| ☐ 204 Walt Suggs | .75 | .35 | .09 |
| Houston Oilers | | | |
| ☐ 205 Roy Jefferson | .90 | .40 | .11 |
| Pittsburgh Steelers | | | |
| ☐ 206 Russ Washington | .75 | .35 | .09 |
| San Diego Chargers | | | |
| ☐ 207 Woody Peoples | .75 | .35 | .09 |
| San Francisco 49ers | | | |
| ☐ 208 Dave Williams | .90 | .40 | .11 |
| St. Louis Cardinals | | | |
| ☐ 209 John Zook | .75 | .35 | .09 |
| Atlanta Falcons | | | |
| ☐ 210 Tom Woodeshick | .75 | .35 | .09 |
| Philadelphia Eagles | | | |
| ☐ 211 Howard Fest | .75 | .35 | .09 |
| Cincinnati Bengals | | | |
| ☐ 212 Jack Concannon | .90 | .40 | .11 |
| Chicago Bears | | | |
| ☐ 213 Jim Marshall | 2.50 | 1.15 | .30 |
| Minnesota Vikings | | | |
| ☐ 214 Jon Morris | .75 | .35 | .09 |
| Boston Patriots | | | |
| ☐ 215 Dan Abramowicz | .90 | .40 | .11 |
| New Orleans Saints | | | |
| ☐ 216 Paul Martha | .75 | .35 | .09 |
| Denver Broncos | | | |
| ☐ 217 Ken Willard | .90 | .40 | .11 |
| San Francisco 49ers | | | |
| ☐ 218 Walter Rock | .75 | .35 | .09 |
| Washington Redskins | | | |
| ☐ 219 Garland Boyette | .75 | .35 | .09 |
| Houston Oilers | | | |
| ☐ 220 Buck Buchanan | 3.50 | 1.55 | .45 |
| Kansas City Chiefs | | | |
| ☐ 221 Bill Munson | .90 | .40 | .11 |
| Detroit Lions | | | |
| ☐ 222 David Lee | .75 | .35 | .09 |
| Baltimore Colts | | | |
| ☐ 223 Karl Noonan | .75 | .35 | .09 |
| Miami Dolphins | | | |
| ☐ 224 Harry Schuh | .75 | .35 | .09 |
| Oakland Raiders | | | |
| ☐ 225 Jackie Smith | 2.00 | .90 | .25 |
| St. Louis Cardinals | | | |
| ☐ 226 Gerry Philbin | .75 | .35 | .09 |
| New York Jets | | | |
| ☐ 227 Ernie Koy | .90 | .40 | .11 |
| New York Giants | | | |
| ☐ 228 Chuck Howley | .90 | .40 | .11 |
| Dallas Cowboys | | | |
| ☐ 229 Billy Shaw | .75 | .35 | .09 |
| Buffalo Bills | | | |
| ☐ 230 Jerry Hillebrand | .75 | .35 | .09 |
| Pittsburgh Steelers | | | |
| ☐ 231 Bill Thompson | 1.75 | .80 | .22 |
| Denver Broncos | | | |
| ☐ 232 Carroll Dale | .90 | .40 | .11 |
| Green Bay Packers | | | |
| ☐ 233 Gene Hickerson | .75 | .35 | .09 |
| Cleveland Browns | | | |
| ☐ 234 Jim Butler | .75 | .35 | .09 |
| Atlanta Falcons | | | |
| ☐ 235 Greg Cook | 1.75 | .80 | .22 |

| | | | |
|---|---|---|---|
| Cincinnati Bengals | | | |
| ☐ 236 Lee Roy Caffey | .90 | .40 | .11 |
| Chicago Bears | | | |
| ☐ 237 Merlin Olsen | 4.50 | 2.00 | .55 |
| Los Angeles Rams | | | |
| ☐ 238 Fred Cox | .90 | .40 | .11 |
| Minnesota Vikings | | | |
| ☐ 239 Nate Ramsey | .75 | .35 | .09 |
| Philadelphia Eagles | | | |
| ☐ 240 Lance Alworth | 6.50 | 2.90 | .80 |
| San Diego Chargers | | | |
| ☐ 241 Chuck Hinton | .75 | .35 | .09 |
| Pittsburgh Steelers | | | |
| ☐ 242 Jerry Smith | .90 | .40 | .11 |
| Washington Redskins | | | |
| ☐ 243 Tony Baker | .75 | .35 | .09 |
| New Orleans Saints | | | |
| ☐ 244 Nick Buoniconti | 2.50 | 1.15 | .30 |
| Miami Dolphins | | | |
| ☐ 245 Jim Johnson | 2.00 | .90 | .25 |
| San Francisco 49ers | | | |
| ☐ 246 Willie Richardson | .90 | .40 | .11 |
| Baltimore Colts | | | |
| ☐ 247 Fred Dryer | 15.00 | 6.75 | 1.90 |
| New York Giants | | | |
| ☐ 248 Bobby Maples | .90 | .40 | .11 |
| Houston Oilers | | | |
| ☐ 249 Alex Karras | 5.00 | 2.30 | .60 |
| Detroit Lions | | | |
| ☐ 250 Joe Kapp | 1.00 | .45 | .13 |
| Minnesota Vikings | | | |
| ☐ 251 Ben Davidson | 1.75 | .80 | .22 |
| Oakland Raiders | | | |
| ☐ 252 Mike Stratton | .75 | .35 | .09 |
| Buffalo Bills | | | |
| ☐ 253 Les Josephson | .90 | .40 | .11 |
| Los Angeles Rams | | | |
| ☐ 254 Don Maynard | 6.00 | 2.70 | .75 |
| New York Jets | | | |
| ☐ 255 Houston Antwine | .75 | .35 | .09 |
| Boston Patriots | | | |
| ☐ 256 Mac Percival | .75 | .35 | .09 |
| Chicago Bears | | | |
| ☐ 257 George Goeddeke | .75 | .35 | .09 |
| Denver Broncos | | | |
| ☐ 258 Homer Jones | .90 | .40 | .11 |
| Cleveland Browns | | | |
| ☐ 259 Bob Berry | .90 | .40 | .11 |
| Atlanta Falcons | | | |
| ☐ 260A Calvin Hill | 6.50 | 2.90 | .80 |
| Dallas Cowboys | | | |
| (Name in red) | | | |
| ☐ 260B Calvin Hill | 6.50 | 2.90 | .80 |
| Dallas Cowboys | | | |
| (Name in black) | | | |
| ☐ 261 Willie Wood | 2.50 | 1.15 | .30 |
| Green Bay Packers | | | |
| ☐ 262 Ed Weisacosky | .75 | .35 | .09 |
| Miami Dolphins | | | |
| ☐ 263 Jim Tyrer | 3.00 | .45 | .15 |
| Kansas City Chiefs | | | |

## 1970 Topps Super

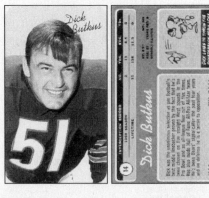

The 1970 Topps Super set contains 35 cards. The cards measure approximately 3 1/8" by 5 1/4". The backs of the cards are identical in format to the regular football issue of 1970. The cards were sold in packs of three with a stick of gum for a dime and are on very thick card stock. The last seven cards in the set were printed in smaller quantities, i.e., short printed; these seven are designated SP in the checklist below. The cards were printed in sheets of seven rows and nine columns or 63 cards; thus 28 cards were double printed and seven cards were single printed. The key cards in the set are Joe Namath and O.J. Simpson, appearing in his Rookie Card year.

| | NRMT | VG-E | GOOD |
|---|---|---|---|
| COMPLETE SET (35)........................ | 200.00 | 80.00 | 20.00 |
| COMMON PLAYER (1-28)................. | 2.00 | .80 | .20 |
| COMMON PLAYER (29-35) SP ........ | 4.00 | 1.60 | .40 |
| ☐ 1 Fran Tarkenton.......................... New York Giants | 12.00 | 5.00 | 1.20 |
| ☐ 2 Floyd Little .............................. Denver Broncos | 3.50 | 1.40 | .35 |
| ☐ 3 Bart Starr ................................ Green Bay Packers | 12.00 | 5.00 | 1.20 |
| ☐ 4 Len Dawson ............................ Kansas City Chiefs | 7.50 | 3.00 | .75 |
| ☐ 5 Dick Post................................ San Diego Chargers | 2.00 | .80 | .20 |
| ☐ 6 Sonny Jurgensen ...................... Washington Redskins | 7.50 | 3.00 | .75 |
| ☐ 7 Deacon Jones .......................... Los Angeles Rams | 4.50 | 1.80 | .45 |
| ☐ 8 Leroy Kelly ............................. Cleveland Browns | 4.50 | 1.80 | .45 |
| ☐ 9 Larry Wilson ........................... St. Louis Cardinals | 4.50 | 1.80 | .45 |
| ☐ 10 Greg Cook............................. Cincinnati Bengals | 2.50 | 1.00 | .25 |
| ☐ 11 Carl Eller.............................. Minnesota Vikings | 4.50 | 1.80 | .45 |
| ☐ 12 Lem Barney........................... Detroit Lions | 6.00 | 2.40 | .60 |
| ☐ 13 Lance Alworth........................ San Diego Chargers | 7.50 | 3.00 | .75 |
| ☐ 14 Dick Butkus........................... Chicago Bears | 10.00 | 4.00 | 1.00 |
| ☐ 15 John Unitas........................... Baltimore Colts | 15.00 | 6.00 | 1.50 |
| ☐ 16 Roy Jefferson........................ Pittsburgh Steelers | 2.00 | .80 | .20 |
| ☐ 17 Bobby Bell............................. Kansas City Chiefs | 4.50 | 1.80 | .45 |
| ☐ 18 John Brodie............................ San Francisco 49ers | 7.50 | 3.00 | .75 |
| ☐ 19 Dan Abramowicz...................... New Orleans Saints | 2.00 | .80 | .20 |
| ☐ 20 Matt Snell............................. New York Jets | 2.50 | 1.00 | .25 |
| ☐ 21 Tom Matte............................. Baltimore Colts | 2.50 | 1.00 | .25 |
| ☐ 22 Gale Sayers........................... Chicago Bears | 20.00 | 8.00 | 2.00 |
| ☐ 23 Tom Woodeshick...................... Philadelphia Eagles | 2.00 | .80 | .20 |
| ☐ 24 O.J. Simpson .......................... Buffalo Bills | 75.00 | 30.00 | 7.50 |
| ☐ 25 Roman Gabriel........................ Los Angeles Rams | 3.50 | 1.40 | .35 |
| ☐ 26 Jim Nance............................. Boston Patriots | 2.50 | 1.00 | .25 |
| ☐ 27 Joe Morrison.......................... New York Giants | 2.00 | .80 | .20 |
| ☐ 28 Calvin Hill............................. Dallas Cowboys | 3.50 | 1.40 | .35 |
| ☐ 29 Tommy Nobis SP...................... Atlanta Falcons | 6.00 | 2.40 | .60 |
| ☐ 30 Bob Hayes SP......................... Dallas Cowboys | 5.00 | 2.00 | .50 |
| ☐ 31 Joe Kapp SP.......................... Minnesota Vikings | 5.00 | 2.00 | .50 |
| ☐ 32 Daryle Lamonica SP.............. Oakland Raiders | 5.00 | 2.00 | .50 |
| ☐ 33 Joe Namath SP ...................... New York Jets | 50.00 | 20.00 | 5.00 |
| ☐ 34 George Webster SP.............. Houston Oilers | 4.00 | 1.60 | .40 |
| ☐ 35 Bob Griese SP........................ Miami Dolphins | 15.00 | 6.00 | 1.50 |

## 1970 Topps Glossy

The 1970 Topps Super Glossy football set features 33 full-color, thick-stock, glossy cards each measuring 2 1/4" by 3 1/4". The corners are rounded and the backs contain only the player's name, his position, his team and the card number. The set numbering follows the player's team location within league (NFC 1-20 and AFC 21-33). The cards are quite attractive and a favorite with collectors. The cards were inserted in 1970 Topps first series football wax packs. The key cards in the set are Joe Namath and O.J. Simpson, appearing in his Rookie Card year.

| | NRMT | VG-E | GOOD |
|---|---|---|---|
| COMPLETE SET (33)........................ | 250.00 | 100.00 | 25.00 |
| COMMON PLAYER (1-33)................. | 3.00 | 1.20 | .30 |

| | NRMT | VG-E | GOOD |
|---|---|---|---|
| ☐ 1 Tommy Nobis ........................... Atlanta Falcons | 6.00 | 2.40 | .60 |
| ☐ 2 John Unitas............................. Baltimore Colts | 20.00 | 8.00 | 2.00 |
| ☐ 3 Tom Matte.............................. Baltimore Colts | 4.00 | 1.60 | .40 |
| ☐ 4 Mac Percival........................... Chicago Bears | 3.00 | 1.20 | .30 |
| ☐ 5 Leroy Kelly ............................ Cleveland Browns | 6.00 | 2.40 | .60 |
| ☐ 6 Mel Renfro............................. Dallas Cowboys | 4.00 | 1.60 | .40 |
| ☐ 7 Bob Hayes.............................. Dallas Cowboys | 5.00 | 2.00 | .50 |
| ☐ 8 Earl McCullouch....................... Detroit Lions | 3.00 | 1.20 | .30 |
| ☐ 9 Bart Starr.............................. Green Bay Packers | 18.00 | 7.25 | 1.80 |
| ☐ 10 Willie Wood............................ Green Bay Packers | 6.00 | 2.40 | .60 |
| ☐ 11 Jack Snow............................. Los Angeles Rams | 4.00 | 1.60 | .40 |
| ☐ 12 Joe Kapp............................... Minnesota Vikings | 5.00 | 2.00 | .50 |
| ☐ 13 Dave Osborn .......................... Minnesota Vikings | 3.00 | 1.20 | .30 |
| ☐ 14 Dan Abramowicz....................... New Orleans Saints | 3.00 | 1.20 | .30 |
| ☐ 15 Fran Tarkenton........................ New York Giants | 20.00 | 8.00 | 2.00 |
| ☐ 16 Tom Woodeshick ...................... Philadelphia Eagles | 3.00 | 1.20 | .30 |
| ☐ 17 Roy Jefferson ........................ Pittsburgh Steelers | 3.00 | 1.20 | .30 |
| ☐ 18 Jackie Smith........................... St. Louis Cardinals | 6.00 | 2.40 | .60 |
| ☐ 19 Jim Johnson .......................... San Francisco 49ers | 6.00 | 2.40 | .60 |
| ☐ 20 Sonny Jurgensen ..................... Washington Redskins | 15.00 | 6.00 | 1.50 |
| ☐ 21 Houston Antwine....................... Boston Patriots | 3.00 | 1.20 | .30 |
| ☐ 22 O.J. Simpson .......................... Buffalo Bills | 75.00 | 30.00 | 7.50 |
| ☐ 23 Greg Cook.............................. Cincinnati Bengals | 4.00 | 1.60 | .40 |
| ☐ 24 Floyd Little............................ Denver Broncos | 5.00 | 2.00 | .50 |
| ☐ 25 Rich Jackson........................... Denver Broncos | 3.00 | 1.20 | .30 |
| ☐ 26 George Webster ...................... Houston Oilers | 4.00 | 1.60 | .40 |
| ☐ 27 Len Dawson ........................... Kansas City Chiefs | 9.00 | 3.75 | .90 |
| ☐ 28 Bob Griese............................. Miami Dolphins | 15.00 | 6.00 | 1.50 |
| ☐ 29 Joe Namath............................ New York Jets | 60.00 | 24.00 | 6.00 |
| ☐ 30 Matt Snell.............................. New York Jets | 4.00 | 1.60 | .40 |
| ☐ 31 Daryle Lamonica ...................... Oakland Raiders | 5.00 | 2.00 | .50 |
| ☐ 32 Fred Biletnikoff........................ Oakland Raiders | 7.50 | 3.00 | .75 |
| ☐ 33 Dick Post.............................. San Diego Chargers | 3.00 | 1.20 | .30 |

## 1970 Topps Poster Inserts

This insert set of 24 folded thin paper posters was issued with the 1970 Topps regular football card issue. The posters are approximately 8" by 10" and were inserted in wax packs along with the 1970 Topps regular issue (second series) football cards. The posters are blank backed.

the first series. There are no known scarcities, although the first cards of two Steeler greats, Terry Bradshaw and Mean Joe Greene, occur in this set. Other notable Rookie Cards in this set are Hall of Famers Ken Houston and Willie Lanier. The card backs are printed in black ink with a gold accent on gray card stock. The card fronts have red borders for AFC players, blue borders for NFC players, and blue over red borders for the respective conference All-Pros.

|  | NRMT | VG-E | GOOD |
|---|---|---|---|
| COMPLETE SET (263)...................... | 475.00 | 210.00 | 60.00 |
| COMMON PLAYER (1-132).............. | .60 | .25 | .08 |
| COMMON PLAYER (133-263)........... | .75 | .35 | .09 |
| ☐ 1 John Unitas............................. | 30.00 | 9.00 | 3.00 |
| Baltimore Colts | | | |
| ☐ 2 Jim Butler............................... | .60 | .25 | .08 |
| Atlanta Falcons | | | |
| ☐ 3 Marty Schottenheimer................ | 12.00 | 5.50 | 1.50 |
| New England Patriots | | | |
| ☐ 4 Joe O'Donnell.......................... | .60 | .25 | .08 |
| Buffalo Bills | | | |
| ☐ 5 Tom Dempsey........................... | 1.00 | .45 | .13 |
| New Orleans Saints | | | |
| ☐ 6 Chuck Allen............................. | .60 | .25 | .08 |
| Pittsburgh Steelers | | | |
| ☐ 7 Ernie Kellerman........................ | .60 | .25 | .08 |
| Cleveland Browns | | | |
| ☐ 8 Walt Garrison........................... | 2.50 | 1.15 | .30 |
| Dallas Cowboys | | | |
| ☐ 9 Bill Van Heusen........................ | .60 | .25 | .08 |
| Denver Broncos | | | |
| ☐ 10 Lance Alworth......................... | 5.00 | 2.30 | .60 |
| San Diego Chargers | | | |
| ☐ 11 Greg Landry........................... | 5.00 | 2.30 | .60 |
| Detroit Lions | | | |
| ☐ 12 Larry Krause........................... | .60 | .25 | .08 |
| Green Bay Packers | | | |
| ☐ 13 Buck Buchanan........................ | 2.50 | 1.15 | .30 |
| Kansas City Chiefs | | | |
| ☐ 14 Roy Gerela............................. | 1.00 | .45 | .13 |
| Houston Oilers | | | |
| ☐ 15 Clifton McNeil......................... | .75 | .35 | .09 |
| New York Giants | | | |
| ☐ 16 Bob Brown............................. | .75 | .35 | .09 |
| Los Angeles Rams | | | |
| ☐ 17 Lloyd Mumphord...................... | .75 | .35 | .09 |
| Miami Dolphins | | | |
| ☐ 18 Gary Cuozzo........................... | .75 | .35 | .09 |
| Minnesota Vikings | | | |
| ☐ 19 Don Maynard.......................... | 4.50 | 2.00 | .55 |
| New York Jets | | | |
| ☐ 20 Larry Wilson........................... | 2.25 | 1.00 | .30 |
| St. Louis Cardinals | | | |
| ☐ 21 Charlie Smith.......................... | .60 | .25 | .08 |
| Oakland Raiders | | | |
| ☐ 22 Ken Avery.............................. | .60 | .25 | .08 |
| Cincinnati Bengals | | | |
| ☐ 23 Billy Walik............................. | .60 | .25 | .08 |
| Philadelphia Eagles | | | |
| ☐ 24 Jim Johnson........................... | 1.75 | .80 | .22 |
| San Francisco 49ers | | | |
| ☐ 25 Dick Butkus............................ | 10.00 | 4.50 | 1.25 |
| Chicago Bears | | | |
| ☐ 26 Charley Taylor UER ................. | 4.00 | 1.80 | .50 |
| (Misspelled Charlie | | | |
| on both sides) | | | |
| Washington Redskins | | | |
| ☐ 27 Checklist 1-132 UER .............. | 8.00 | 1.20 | .40 |
| (26 Charlie Taylor | | | |
| should be Charley) | | | |
| ☐ 28 Lionel Aldridge........................ | 1.00 | .45 | .13 |
| Green Bay Packers | | | |
| ☐ 29 Billy Lothridge........................ | .60 | .25 | .08 |
| Atlanta Falcons | | | |
| ☐ 30 Terry Hanratty........................ | 1.25 | .55 | .16 |
| Pittsburgh Steelers | | | |
| ☐ 31 Lee Roy Jordan....................... | 1.75 | .80 | .22 |
| Dallas Cowboys | | | |
| ☐ 32 Rick Volk.............................. | 1.00 | .45 | .13 |
| Baltimore Colts | | | |
| ☐ 33 Howard Kindig......................... | .60 | .25 | .08 |
| Buffalo Bills | | | |
| ☐ 34 Carl Garrett............................ | 1.00 | .45 | .13 |
| New England Patriots | | | |
| ☐ 35 Bobby Bell............................. | 2.50 | 1.15 | .30 |
| Kansas City Chiefs | | | |
| ☐ 36 Gene Hickerson........................ | .60 | .25 | .08 |
| Cleveland Browns | | | |
| ☐ 37 Dave Parks............................. | .75 | .35 | .09 |
| New Orleans Saints | | | |
| ☐ 38 Paul Martha............................ | .60 | .25 | .08 |
| Denver Broncos | | | |
| ☐ 39 George Blanda......................... | 15.00 | 6.75 | 1.90 |
| Oakland Raiders | | | |
| ☐ 40 Tom Woodeshick ..................... | .60 | .25 | .08 |
| Philadelphia Eagles | | | |
| ☐ 41 Alex Karras............................ | 4.00 | 1.80 | .50 |

|  | NRMT | VG-E | GOOD |
|---|---|---|---|
| COMPLETE SET (24)...................... | 75.00 | 30.00 | 7.50 |
| COMMON PLAYER (1-24)............... | 2.00 | .80 | .20 |
| ☐ 1 Gale Sayers............................. | 12.00 | 5.00 | 1.20 |
| Chicago Bears | | | |
| ☐ 2 Bobby Bell............................... | 4.00 | 1.60 | .40 |
| Kansas City Chiefs | | | |
| ☐ 3 Roman Gabriel.......................... | 3.00 | 1.20 | .30 |
| Los Angeles Rams | | | |
| ☐ 4 Jim Tyrer................................ | 2.00 | .80 | .20 |
| Kansas City Chiefs | | | |
| ☐ 5 Willie Brown............................ | 4.00 | 1.60 | .40 |
| Oakland Raiders | | | |
| ☐ 6 Carl Eller............................... | 4.00 | 1.60 | .40 |
| Minnesota Vikings | | | |
| ☐ 7 Tom Mack............................... | 3.00 | 1.20 | .30 |
| Los Angeles Rams | | | |
| ☐ 8 Deacon Jones........................... | 4.00 | 1.60 | .40 |
| Los Angeles Rams | | | |
| ☐ 9 Johnny Robinson....................... | 2.50 | 1.00 | .25 |
| Kansas City Chiefs | | | |
| ☐ 10 Jan Stenerud.......................... | 5.00 | 2.00 | .50 |
| Kansas City Chiefs | | | |
| ☐ 11 Dick Butkus........................... | 9.00 | 3.75 | .90 |
| Chicago Bears | | | |
| ☐ 12 Lem Barney............................ | 5.00 | 2.00 | .50 |
| Detroit Lions | | | |
| ☐ 13 David Lee.............................. | 2.00 | .80 | .20 |
| Baltimore Colts | | | |
| ☐ 14 Larry Wilson........................... | 4.00 | 1.60 | .40 |
| St. Louis Cardinals | | | |
| ☐ 15 Gene Hickerson........................ | 2.00 | .80 | .20 |
| Cleveland Browns | | | |
| ☐ 16 Lance Alworth......................... | 5.00 | 2.00 | .50 |
| San Diego Chargers | | | |
| ☐ 17 Merlin Olsen........................... | 5.00 | 2.00 | .50 |
| Los Angeles Rams | | | |
| ☐ 18 Bob Trumpy............................ | 3.00 | 1.20 | .30 |
| Cincinnati Bengals | | | |
| ☐ 19 Bob Lilly.............................. | 5.00 | 2.00 | .50 |
| Dallas Cowboys | | | |
| ☐ 20 Mick Tingelhoff ...................... | 2.50 | 1.00 | .25 |
| Minnesota Vikings | | | |
| ☐ 21 Calvin Hill............................. | 2.50 | 1.00 | .25 |
| Dallas Cowboys | | | |
| ☐ 22 Paul Warfield.......................... | 5.00 | 2.00 | .50 |
| Miami Dolphins | | | |
| ☐ 23 Chuck Howley......................... | 2.50 | 1.00 | .25 |
| Dallas Cowboys | | | |
| ☐ 24 Bob Brown............................. | 2.00 | .80 | .20 |
| Los Angeles Rams | | | |

## 1971 Topps

The 1971 Topps set contains 263 cards. The cards measure 2 1/2" by 3 1/2". The second series was printed in slightly lesser quantities than

| | | | |
|---|---|---|---|
| Detroit Lions | | | |
| ☐ 42 Rick Redman | .60 | .25 | .08 |
| San Diego Chargers | | | |
| ☐ 43 Zeke Moore | .60 | .25 | .08 |
| Houston Oilers | | | |
| ☐ 44 Jack Snow | .75 | .35 | .09 |
| Los Angeles Rams | | | |
| ☐ 45 Larry Csonka | 12.00 | 5.50 | 1.50 |
| Miami Dolphins | | | |
| ☐ 46 Karl Kassulke | .60 | .25 | .08 |
| Minnesota Vikings | | | |
| ☐ 47 Jim Hart | 1.75 | .80 | .22 |
| St. Louis Cardinals | | | |
| ☐ 48 Al Atkinson | .60 | .25 | .08 |
| New York Jets | | | |
| ☐ 49 Horst Muhlmann | .60 | .25 | .08 |
| Cincinnati Bengals | | | |
| ☐ 50 Sonny Jurgensen | 5.50 | 2.50 | .70 |
| Washington Redskins | | | |
| ☐ 51 Ron Johnson | 2.00 | .90 | .25 |
| New York Giants | | | |
| ☐ 52 Cas Banaszek | .60 | .25 | .08 |
| San Francisco 49ers | | | |
| ☐ 53 Bubba Smith | 8.00 | 3.60 | 1.00 |
| Baltimore Colts | | | |
| ☐ 54 Bobby Douglass | 1.25 | .55 | .16 |
| Chicago Bears | | | |
| ☐ 55 Willie Wood | 3.00 | 1.35 | .40 |
| Green Bay Packers | | | |
| ☐ 56 Bake Turner | .75 | .35 | .09 |
| New England Patriots | | | |
| ☐ 57 Mike Morgan | .60 | .25 | .08 |
| New Orleans Saints | | | |
| ☐ 58 George Byrd | .75 | .35 | .09 |
| Buffalo Bills | | | |
| ☐ 59 Don Horn | .75 | .35 | .09 |
| Denver Broncos | | | |
| ☐ 60 Tommy Nobis | 1.75 | .80 | .22 |
| Atlanta Falcons | | | |
| ☐ 61 Jan Stenerud | 3.00 | 1.35 | .40 |
| Kansas City Chiefs | | | |
| ☐ 62 Altie Taylor | 1.00 | .45 | .13 |
| Detroit Lions | | | |
| ☐ 63 Gary Pettigrew | .60 | .25 | .08 |
| Philadelphia Eagles | | | |
| ☐ 64 Spike Jones | .60 | .25 | .08 |
| Houston Oilers | | | |
| ☐ 65 Duane Thomas | 2.50 | 1.15 | .30 |
| Dallas Cowboys | | | |
| ☐ 66 Marty Domres | 1.00 | .45 | .13 |
| San Diego Chargers | | | |
| ☐ 67 Dick Anderson | .90 | .40 | .11 |
| Miami Dolphins | | | |
| ☐ 68 Ken Iman | .60 | .25 | .08 |
| Los Angeles Rams | | | |
| ☐ 69 Miller Farr | .60 | .25 | .08 |
| St. Louis Cardinals | | | |
| ☐ 70 Daryle Lamonica | 2.50 | 1.15 | .30 |
| Oakland Raiders | | | |
| ☐ 71 Alan Page | 8.00 | 3.60 | 1.00 |
| Minnesota Vikings | | | |
| ☐ 72 Pat Matson | .60 | .25 | .08 |
| Cincinnati Bengals | | | |
| ☐ 73 Emerson Boozer | 1.00 | .45 | .13 |
| New York Jets | | | |
| ☐ 74 Pat Fischer | .75 | .35 | .09 |
| Washington Redskins | | | |
| ☐ 75 Gary Collins | .75 | .35 | .09 |
| Cleveland Browns | | | |
| ☐ 76 John Fuqua | 1.00 | .45 | .13 |
| Pittsburgh Steelers | | | |
| ☐ 77 Bruce Gossett | .60 | .25 | .08 |
| San Francisco 49ers | | | |
| ☐ 78 Ed O'Bradovich | .60 | .25 | .08 |
| Chicago Bears | | | |
| ☐ 79 Bob Tucker | 1.50 | .65 | .19 |
| New York Giants | | | |
| ☐ 80 Mike Curtis | .75 | .35 | .09 |
| Baltimore Colts | | | |
| ☐ 81 Rich Jackson | .60 | .25 | .08 |
| Denver Broncos | | | |
| ☐ 82 Tom Janik | .60 | .25 | .08 |
| New England Patriots | | | |
| ☐ 83 Gale Gillingham | .60 | .25 | .08 |
| Green Bay Packers | | | |
| ☐ 84 Jim Mitchell | .75 | .35 | .09 |
| Atlanta Falcons | | | |
| ☐ 85 Charlie Johnson | 1.00 | .45 | .13 |
| Houston Oilers | | | |
| ☐ 86 Edgar Chandler | .60 | .25 | .08 |
| Buffalo Bills | | | |
| ☐ 87 Cyril Pinder | .60 | .25 | .08 |
| Philadelphia Eagles | | | |
| ☐ 88 Johnny Robinson | .75 | .35 | .09 |
| Kansas City Chiefs | | | |
| ☐ 89 Ralph Neely | .75 | .35 | .09 |
| Dallas Cowboys | | | |
| ☐ 90 Dan Abramowicz | .75 | .35 | .09 |
| New Orleans Saints | | | |
| ☐ 91 Mercury Morris | 6.00 | 2.70 | .75 |
| Miami Dolphins | | | |
| ☐ 92 Steve DeLong | .60 | .25 | .08 |
| San Diego Chargers | | | |
| ☐ 93 Larry Stallings | .60 | .25 | .08 |
| St. Louis Cardinals | | | |
| ☐ 94 Tom Mack | 2.50 | 1.15 | .30 |
| Los Angeles Rams | | | |
| ☐ 95 Hewritt Dixon | .75 | .35 | .09 |
| Oakland Raiders | | | |
| ☐ 96 Fred Cox | .75 | .35 | .09 |
| Minnesota Vikings | | | |
| ☐ 97 Chris Hanburger | .75 | .35 | .09 |
| Washington Redskins | | | |
| ☐ 98 Gerry Philbin | .60 | .25 | .08 |
| New York Jets | | | |
| ☐ 99 Ernie Wright | .60 | .25 | .08 |
| Cincinnati Bengals | | | |
| ☐ 100 John Brodie | 5.00 | 2.30 | .60 |
| San Francisco 49ers | | | |
| ☐ 101 Tucker Frederickson | .75 | .35 | .09 |
| New York Giants | | | |
| ☐ 102 Bobby Walden | .60 | .25 | .08 |
| Pittsburgh Steelers | | | |
| ☐ 103 Dick Gordon | .75 | .35 | .09 |
| Chicago Bears | | | |
| ☐ 104 Walter Johnson | .60 | .25 | .08 |
| Cleveland Browns | | | |
| ☐ 105 Mike Lucci | .75 | .35 | .09 |
| Detroit Lions | | | |
| ☐ 106 Checklist 133-263 DP | 6.00 | .90 | .30 |
| ☐ 107 Ron Berger | .60 | .25 | .08 |
| New England Patriots | | | |
| ☐ 108 Dan Sullivan | .60 | .25 | .08 |
| Baltimore Colts | | | |
| ☐ 109 George Kunz | 1.75 | .80 | .22 |
| Atlanta Falcons | | | |
| ☐ 110 Floyd Little | 2.50 | 1.15 | .30 |
| Denver Broncos | | | |
| ☐ 111 Zeke Bratkowski | .60 | .25 | .08 |
| Green Bay Packers | | | |
| ☐ 112 Haven Moses | .75 | .35 | .09 |
| Buffalo Bills | | | |
| ☐ 113 Ken Houston | 20.00 | 9.00 | 2.50 |
| Houston Oilers | | | |
| ☐ 114 Willie Lanier | 20.00 | 9.00 | 2.50 |
| Kansas City Chiefs | | | |
| ☐ 115 Larry Brown | 2.00 | .90 | .25 |
| Washington Redskins | | | |
| ☐ 116 Tim Rossovich | .60 | .25 | .08 |
| Philadelphia Eagles | | | |
| ☐ 117 Errol Linden | .60 | .25 | .08 |
| New Orleans Saints | | | |
| ☐ 118 Mel Renfro | 1.25 | .55 | .16 |
| Dallas Cowboys | | | |
| ☐ 119 Mike Garrett | 1.00 | .45 | .13 |
| San Diego Chargers | | | |
| ☐ 120 Fran Tarkenton | 20.00 | 9.00 | 2.50 |
| New York Giants | | | |
| ☐ 121 Garo Yepremian | 3.00 | 1.35 | .40 |
| Miami Dolphins | | | |
| ☐ 122 Glen Condren | .60 | .25 | .08 |
| Atlanta Falcons | | | |
| ☐ 123 Johnny Roland | .60 | .25 | .08 |
| St. Louis Cardinals | | | |
| ☐ 124 Dave Herman | .60 | .25 | .08 |
| New York Jets | | | |
| ☐ 125 Merlin Olsen | 3.50 | 1.55 | .45 |
| Los Angeles Rams | | | |
| ☐ 126 Doug Buffone | .60 | .25 | .08 |
| Chicago Bears | | | |
| ☐ 127 Earl McCullouch | .75 | .35 | .09 |
| Detroit Lions | | | |
| ☐ 128 Spider Lockhart | .75 | .35 | .09 |
| New York Giants | | | |
| ☐ 129 Ken Willard | .75 | .35 | .09 |
| San Francisco 49ers | | | |
| ☐ 130 Gene Washington | .75 | .35 | .09 |
| Minnesota Vikings | | | |
| ☐ 131 Mike Phipps | 1.75 | .80 | .22 |
| Cleveland Browns | | | |
| ☐ 132 Andy Russell | .75 | .35 | .09 |
| Pittsburgh Steelers | | | |
| ☐ 133 Ray Nitschke | 4.00 | 1.80 | .50 |
| Green Bay Packers | | | |
| ☐ 134 Jerry Logan | .75 | .35 | .09 |
| Baltimore Colts | | | |
| ☐ 135 MacArthur Lane | 2.00 | .90 | .25 |
| St. Louis Cardinals | | | |
| ☐ 136 Jim Turner | .90 | .40 | .11 |
| Denver Broncos | | | |
| ☐ 137 Kent McCloughan | .90 | .40 | .11 |
| Oakland Raiders | | | |
| ☐ 138 Paul Guidry | .75 | .35 | .09 |
| Buffalo Bills | | | |
| ☐ 139 Otis Taylor | 1.25 | .55 | .16 |
| Kansas City Chiefs | | | |

| | | | |
|---|---|---|---|
| ☐ 140 Virgil Carter | 1.25 | .55 | .16 |
| Cincinnati Bengals | | | |
| ☐ 141 Joe Dawkins | .75 | .35 | .09 |
| Houston Oilers | | | |
| ☐ 142 Steve Preece | .75 | .35 | .09 |
| Philadelphia Eagles | | | |
| ☐ 143 Mike Bragg | 1.25 | .55 | .16 |
| Washington Redskins | | | |
| ☐ 144 Bob Lilly | 4.50 | 2.00 | .55 |
| Dallas Cowboys | | | |
| ☐ 145 Joe Kapp | 1.00 | .45 | .13 |
| New England Patriots | | | |
| ☐ 146 Al Dodd | .75 | .35 | .09 |
| New Orleans Saints | | | |
| ☐ 147 Nick Buoniconti | 2.25 | 1.00 | .30 |
| Miami Dolphins | | | |
| ☐ 148 Speedy Duncan | .90 | .40 | .11 |
| (Back mentions his | | | |
| trade to Redskins) | | | |
| San Diego Chargers | | | |
| ☐ 149 Cedrick Hardman | 1.25 | .55 | .16 |
| San Francisco 49ers | | | |
| ☐ 150 Gale Sayers | 30.00 | 13.50 | 3.80 |
| Chicago Bears | | | |
| ☐ 151 Jim Otto | 3.00 | 1.35 | .40 |
| Oakland Raiders | | | |
| ☐ 152 Billy Truax | .90 | .40 | .11 |
| Dallas Cowboys | | | |
| ☐ 153 John Elliott | .75 | .35 | .09 |
| New York Jets | | | |
| ☐ 154 Dick LeBeau | .90 | .40 | .11 |
| Detroit Lions | | | |
| ☐ 155 Bill Bergey | 1.75 | .80 | .22 |
| Cincinnati Bengals | | | |
| ☐ 156 Terry Bradshaw | 175.00 | 80.00 | 22.00 |
| Pittsburgh Steelers | | | |
| ☐ 157 Leroy Kelly | 4.00 | 1.80 | .50 |
| Cleveland Browns | | | |
| ☐ 158 Paul Krause | 1.75 | .80 | .22 |
| Minnesota Vikings | | | |
| ☐ 159 Ted Vactor | .75 | .35 | .09 |
| Washington Redskins | | | |
| ☐ 160 Bob Griese | 12.00 | 5.50 | 1.50 |
| Miami Dolphins | | | |
| ☐ 161 Ernie McMillan | .75 | .35 | .09 |
| St. Louis Cardinals | | | |
| ☐ 162 Donny Anderson | .90 | .40 | .11 |
| Green Bay Packers | | | |
| ☐ 163 John Pitts | .75 | .35 | .09 |
| Buffalo Bills | | | |
| ☐ 164 Dave Costa | .75 | .35 | .09 |
| Denver Broncos | | | |
| ☐ 165 Gene Washington | 1.25 | .55 | .16 |
| San Francisco 49ers | | | |
| ☐ 166 John Zook | .90 | .40 | .11 |
| Atlanta Falcons | | | |
| ☐ 167 Pete Gogolak | .90 | .40 | .11 |
| New York Giants | | | |
| ☐ 168 Erich Barnes | .90 | .40 | .11 |
| Cleveland Browns | | | |
| ☐ 169 Alvin Reed | .75 | .35 | .09 |
| Houston Oilers | | | |
| ☐ 170 Jim Nance | .90 | .40 | .11 |
| New England Patriots | | | |
| ☐ 171 Craig Morton | 2.00 | .90 | .25 |
| Dallas Cowboys | | | |
| ☐ 172 Gary Garrison | .90 | .40 | .11 |
| San Diego Chargers | | | |
| ☐ 173 Joe Scarpati | .75 | .35 | .09 |
| New Orleans Saints | | | |
| ☐ 174 Adrian Young UER | .75 | .35 | .09 |
| (Photo actually | | | |
| Rick Duncan) | | | |
| Philadelphia Eagles | | | |
| ☐ 175 John Mackey | 3.00 | 1.35 | .40 |
| Baltimore Colts | | | |
| ☐ 176 Mac Percival | .75 | .35 | .09 |
| Chicago Bears | | | |
| ☐ 177 Preston Pearson | 4.00 | 1.80 | .50 |
| Pittsburgh Steelers | | | |
| ☐ 178 Fred Biletnikoff | 6.00 | 2.70 | .75 |
| Oakland Raiders | | | |
| ☐ 179 Mike Battle | 1.25 | .55 | .16 |
| New York Jets | | | |
| ☐ 180 Len Dawson | 7.00 | 3.10 | .85 |
| Kansas City Chiefs | | | |
| ☐ 181 Les Josephson | .90 | .40 | .11 |
| Los Angeles Rams | | | |
| ☐ 182 Royce Berry | .75 | .35 | .09 |
| Cincinnati Bengals | | | |
| ☐ 183 Herman Weaver | .75 | .35 | .09 |
| Detroit Lions | | | |
| ☐ 184 Norm Snead | 1.25 | .55 | .16 |
| Minnesota Vikings | | | |
| ☐ 185 Sam Brunelli | .75 | .35 | .09 |
| Denver Broncos | | | |
| ☐ 186 Jim Kiick | 4.00 | 1.80 | .50 |

| | | | |
|---|---|---|---|
| Miami Dolphins | | | |
| ☐ 187 Austin Denney | .75 | .35 | .09 |
| Buffalo Bills | | | |
| ☐ 188 Roger Wehrli | 3.00 | 1.35 | .40 |
| St. Louis Cardinals | | | |
| ☐ 189 Dave Wilcox | .90 | .40 | .11 |
| San Francisco 49ers | | | |
| ☐ 190 Bob Hayes | 1.75 | .80 | .22 |
| Dallas Cowboys | | | |
| ☐ 191 Joe Morrison | .90 | .40 | .11 |
| New York Giants | | | |
| ☐ 192 Manny Sistrunk | .90 | .40 | .11 |
| Washington Redskins | | | |
| ☐ 193 Don Cockroft | 1.25 | .55 | .16 |
| Cleveland Browns | | | |
| ☐ 194 Lee Bouggess | .75 | .35 | .09 |
| Philadelphia Eagles | | | |
| ☐ 195 Bob Berry | .90 | .40 | .11 |
| Atlanta Falcons | | | |
| ☐ 196 Ron Sellers | .75 | .35 | .09 |
| New England Patriots | | | |
| ☐ 197 George Webster | .90 | .40 | .11 |
| Houston Oilers | | | |
| ☐ 198 Hoyle Granger | .75 | .35 | .09 |
| New Orleans Saints | | | |
| ☐ 199 Bob Vogel | .75 | .35 | .09 |
| Baltimore Colts | | | |
| ☐ 200 Bart Starr | 22.00 | 10.00 | 2.80 |
| Green Bay Packers | | | |
| ☐ 201 Mike Mercer | .75 | .35 | .09 |
| San Diego Chargers | | | |
| ☐ 202 Dave Smith | .75 | .35 | .09 |
| Pittsburgh Steelers | | | |
| ☐ 203 Lee Roy Caffey | .90 | .40 | .11 |
| Chicago Bears | | | |
| ☐ 204 Mick Tingelhoff | .90 | .40 | .11 |
| Minnesota Vikings | | | |
| ☐ 205 Matt Snell | 1.25 | .55 | .16 |
| New York Jets | | | |
| ☐ 206 Jim Tyrer | .90 | .40 | .11 |
| Kansas City Chiefs | | | |
| ☐ 207 Willie Brown | 3.00 | 1.35 | .40 |
| Oakland Raiders | | | |
| ☐ 208 Bob Johnson | 1.50 | .65 | .19 |
| Cincinnati Bengals | | | |
| ☐ 209 Deacon Jones | 3.00 | 1.35 | .40 |
| Los Angeles Rams | | | |
| ☐ 210 Charlie Sanders | 4.00 | 1.80 | .50 |
| Detroit Lions | | | |
| ☐ 211 Jake Scott | 4.50 | 2.00 | .55 |
| Miami Dolphins | | | |
| ☐ 212 Bob Anderson | 1.75 | .80 | .22 |
| Denver Broncos | | | |
| ☐ 213 Charlie Krueger | .90 | .40 | .11 |
| San Francisco 49ers | | | |
| ☐ 214 Jim Bakken | .90 | .40 | .11 |
| St. Louis Cardinals | | | |
| ☐ 215 Harold Jackson | 2.50 | 1.15 | .30 |
| Philadelphia Eagles | | | |
| ☐ 216 Bill Brundige | .75 | .35 | .09 |
| Washington Redskins | | | |
| ☐ 217 Calvin Hill | 2.00 | .90 | .25 |
| Dallas Cowboys | | | |
| ☐ 218 Claude Humphrey | .90 | .40 | .11 |
| Atlanta Falcons | | | |
| ☐ 219 Glen Ray Hines | .75 | .35 | .09 |
| Houston Oilers | | | |
| ☐ 220 Bill Nelsen | .90 | .40 | .11 |
| Cleveland Browns | | | |
| ☐ 221 Roy Hilton | .75 | .35 | .09 |
| Baltimore Colts | | | |
| ☐ 222 Don Herrmann | .75 | .35 | .09 |
| New York Giants | | | |
| ☐ 223 John Bramlett | .75 | .35 | .09 |
| New England Patriots | | | |
| ☐ 224 Ken Ellis | .75 | .35 | .09 |
| Green Bay Packers | | | |
| ☐ 225 Dave Osborn | .90 | .40 | .11 |
| Minnesota Vikings | | | |
| ☐ 226 Edd Hargett | 1.25 | .55 | .16 |
| New Orleans Saints | | | |
| ☐ 227 Gene Mingo | .75 | .35 | .09 |
| Pittsburgh Steelers | | | |
| ☐ 228 Larry Grantham | .90 | .40 | .11 |
| New York Jets | | | |
| ☐ 229 Dick Post | .75 | .35 | .09 |
| San Diego Chargers | | | |
| ☐ 230 Roman Gabriel | 3.00 | 1.35 | .40 |
| Los Angeles Rams | | | |
| ☐ 231 Mike Eischeid | .75 | .35 | .09 |
| Oakland Raiders | | | |
| ☐ 232 Jim Lynch | .90 | .40 | .11 |
| Kansas City Chiefs | | | |
| ☐ 233 Lemar Parrish | 3.00 | 1.35 | .40 |
| Cincinnati Bengals | | | |
| ☐ 234 Cecil Turner | .75 | .35 | .09 |
| Chicago Bears | | | |
| ☐ 235 Dennis Shaw | 1.25 | .55 | .16 |

| | | | | |
|---|---|---|---|---|
| | Buffalo Bills | | | |
| ☐ 236 | Mel Farr | .90 | .40 | .11 |
| | Detroit Lions | | | |
| ☐ 237 | Curt Knight | .75 | .35 | .09 |
| | Washington Redskins | | | |
| ☐ 238 | Chuck Howley | .90 | .40 | .11 |
| | Dallas Cowboys | | | |
| ☐ 239 | Bruce Taylor | 1.25 | .55 | .16 |
| | San Francisco 49ers | | | |
| ☐ 240 | Jerry LeVias | .90 | .40 | .11 |
| | Houston Oilers | | | |
| ☐ 241 | Bob Lurtsema | .75 | .35 | .09 |
| | New York Giants | | | |
| ☐ 242 | Earl Morrall | 2.00 | .90 | .25 |
| | Baltimore Colts | | | |
| ☐ 243 | Kermit Alexander | .75 | .35 | .09 |
| | Los Angeles Rams | | | |
| ☐ 244 | Jackie Smith | 2.00 | .90 | .25 |
| | St. Louis Cardinals | | | |
| ☐ 245 | Joe Greene | 50.00 | 23.00 | 6.25 |
| | Pittsburgh Steelers | | | |
| ☐ 246 | Harmon Wages | .75 | .35 | .09 |
| | Atlanta Falcons | | | |
| ☐ 247 | Errol Mann | .75 | .35 | .09 |
| | Detroit Lions | | | |
| ☐ 248 | Mike McCoy | .90 | .40 | .11 |
| | Green Bay Packers | | | |
| ☐ 249 | Milt Morin | 1.25 | .55 | .16 |
| | Cleveland Browns | | | |
| ☐ 250 | Joe Namath | 50.00 | 23.00 | 6.25 |
| | New York Jets | | | |
| ☐ 251 | Jackie Burkett | .75 | .35 | .09 |
| | New Orleans Saints | | | |
| ☐ 252 | Steve Chomyszak | .75 | .35 | .09 |
| | Cincinnati Bengals | | | |
| ☐ 253 | Ed Sharockman | .75 | .35 | .09 |
| | Minnesota Vikings | | | |
| ☐ 254 | Robert Holmes | 1.25 | .55 | .16 |
| | Kansas City Chiefs | | | |
| ☐ 255 | John Hadl | 1.75 | .80 | .22 |
| | San Diego Chargers | | | |
| ☐ 256 | Cornell Gordon | .75 | .35 | .09 |
| | Denver Broncos | | | |
| ☐ 257 | Mark Moseley | 5.00 | 2.30 | .60 |
| | Philadelphia Eagles | | | |
| ☐ 258 | Gus Otto | .75 | .35 | .09 |
| | Oakland Raiders | | | |
| ☐ 259 | Mike Taliaferro | .75 | .35 | .09 |
| | New England Patriots | | | |
| ☐ 260 | O.J. Simpson | 60.00 | 27.00 | 7.50 |
| | Buffalo Bills | | | |
| ☐ 261 | Paul Warfield | 7.00 | 3.10 | .85 |
| | Miami Dolphins | | | |
| ☐ 262 | Jack Concannon | .90 | .40 | .11 |
| | Chicago Bears | | | |
| ☐ 263 | Tom Matte | 3.00 | .45 | .15 |
| | Baltimore Colts | | | |

## 1971 Topps Game

 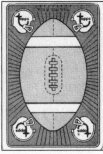

The 1971 Topps Game cards were issued as inserts with the 1971 regular issue football cards. The cards measure 2 1/4" by 3 1/4" with rounded corners. The cards can be used for a table game of football. The 52 player cards in the set are numbered and have light blue backs. The 53rd card (actually unnumbered) is a field position/first down marker which is used in the table game. Six of the cards in the set were double printed and are marked as DP in the checklist below. The key card in the set is Terry Bradshaw, appearing in his Rookie Card year.

| | NRMT | VG-E | GOOD |
|---|---|---|---|
| COMPLETE SET (53) | 125.00 | 50.00 | 12.50 |
| COMMON PLAYER (1-53) | .60 | .24 | .06 |

| | | | | |
|---|---|---|---|---|
| ☐ 1 | Dick Butkus DP | 6.00 | 2.40 | .60 |
| | Chicago Bears | | | |
| ☐ 2 | Bob Berry DP | .60 | .24 | .06 |
| | Atlanta Falcons | | | |
| ☐ 3 | Joe Namath DP | 15.00 | 6.00 | 1.50 |
| | New York Jets | | | |
| ☐ 4 | Mike Curtis | .75 | .30 | .07 |
| | Baltimore Colts | | | |
| ☐ 5 | Jim Nance | .75 | .30 | .07 |
| | New England Patriots | | | |
| ☐ 6 | Ron Berger | .60 | .24 | .06 |
| | New England Patriots | | | |
| ☐ 7 | O.J. Simpson | 25.00 | 10.00 | 2.50 |
| | Buffalo Bills | | | |
| ☐ 8 | Haven Moses | .60 | .24 | .06 |
| | Buffalo Bills | | | |
| ☐ 9 | Tommy Nobis | 1.50 | .60 | .15 |
| | Atlanta Falcons | | | |
| ☐ 10 | Gale Sayers | 12.00 | 5.00 | 1.20 |
| | Chicago Bears | | | |
| ☐ 11 | Virgil Carter | .60 | .24 | .06 |
| | Cincinnati Bengals | | | |
| ☐ 12 | Andy Russell DP | .60 | .24 | .06 |
| | Pittsburgh Steelers | | | |
| ☐ 13 | Bill Nelsen | .75 | .30 | .07 |
| | Cleveland Browns | | | |
| ☐ 14 | Gary Collins | .75 | .30 | .07 |
| | Cleveland Browns | | | |
| ☐ 15 | Duane Thomas | 1.00 | .40 | .10 |
| | Dallas Cowboys | | | |
| ☐ 16 | Bob Hayes | 1.25 | .50 | .12 |
| | Dallas Cowboys | | | |
| ☐ 17 | Floyd Little | 1.25 | .50 | .12 |
| | Denver Broncos | | | |
| ☐ 18 | Sam Brunelli | .60 | .24 | .06 |
| | Denver Broncos | | | |
| ☐ 19 | Charlie Sanders | .75 | .30 | .07 |
| | Detroit Lions | | | |
| ☐ 20 | Mike Lucci | .60 | .24 | .06 |
| | Detroit Lions | | | |
| ☐ 21 | Gene Washington | 1.00 | .40 | .10 |
| | San Francisco 49ers | | | |
| ☐ 22 | Willie Wood | 2.00 | .80 | .20 |
| | Green Bay Packers | | | |
| ☐ 23 | Jerry LeVias | .75 | .30 | .07 |
| | Houston Oilers | | | |
| ☐ 24 | Charlie Johnson | 1.00 | .40 | .10 |
| | Houston Oilers | | | |
| ☐ 25 | Len Dawson | 3.00 | 1.20 | .30 |
| | Kansas City Chiefs | | | |
| ☐ 26 | Bobby Bell | 2.00 | .80 | .20 |
| | Kansas City Chiefs | | | |
| ☐ 27 | Merlin Olsen | 3.00 | 1.20 | .30 |
| | Los Angeles Rams | | | |
| ☐ 28 | Roman Gabriel | 1.50 | .60 | .15 |
| | Los Angeles Rams | | | |
| ☐ 29 | Bob Griese | 4.00 | 1.60 | .40 |
| | Miami Dolphins | | | |
| ☐ 30 | Larry Csonka | 3.50 | 1.40 | .35 |
| | Miami Dolphins | | | |
| ☐ 31 | Dave Osborn | .60 | .24 | .06 |
| | Minnesota Vikings | | | |
| ☐ 32 | Gene Washington | .60 | .24 | .06 |
| | Minnesota Vikings | | | |
| ☐ 33 | Dan Abramowicz | .60 | .24 | .06 |
| | New Orleans Saints | | | |
| ☐ 34 | Tom Dempsey | .75 | .30 | .07 |
| | New Orleans Saints | | | |
| ☐ 35 | Fran Tarkenton | 10.00 | 4.00 | 1.00 |
| | New York Giants | | | |
| ☐ 36 | Clifton McNeil | .60 | .24 | .06 |
| | New York Giants | | | |
| ☐ 37 | John Unitas | 12.00 | 5.00 | 1.20 |
| | Baltimore Colts | | | |
| ☐ 38 | Matt Snell | .75 | .30 | .07 |
| | New York Jets | | | |
| ☐ 39 | Daryle Lamonica | 1.25 | .50 | .12 |
| | Oakland Raiders | | | |
| ☐ 40 | Hewritt Dixon | .75 | .30 | .07 |
| | Oakland Raiders | | | |
| ☐ 41 | Tom Woodeshick DP | .60 | .24 | .06 |
| | Philadelphia Eagles | | | |
| ☐ 42 | Harold Jackson | 1.00 | .40 | .10 |
| | Phildelphia Eagles | | | |
| ☐ 43 | Terry Bradshaw | 30.00 | 12.00 | 3.00 |
| | Pittsburgh Steelers | | | |
| ☐ 44 | Ken Avery | .60 | .24 | .06 |
| | Cincinnati Bengals | | | |
| ☐ 45 | MacArthur Lane | .75 | .30 | .07 |
| | St. Louis Cardinals | | | |
| ☐ 46 | Larry Wilson | 2.00 | .80 | .20 |
| | St. Louis Cardinals | | | |
| ☐ 47 | John Hadl | 1.00 | .40 | .10 |
| | San Diego Chargers | | | |
| ☐ 48 | Lance Alworth | 3.00 | 1.20 | .30 |
| | San Diego Chargers | | | |
| ☐ 49 | John Brodie | 3.50 | 1.40 | .35 |

| | NRMT | VG-E | GOOD |
|---|---|---|---|
| San Francisco 49ers | | | |
| ☐ 50 Bart Starr DP | 6.00 | 2.40 | .60 |
| Green Bay Packers | | | |
| ☐ 51 Sonny Jurgensen | 5.00 | 2.00 | .50 |
| Washington Redskins | | | |
| ☐ 52 Larry Brown | 1.25 | .50 | .12 |
| Washington Redskins | | | |
| ☐ NNO Field Marker | .60 | .24 | .06 |

## 1971 Topps Posters

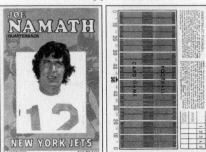

The 1971 Topps Football pin-up posters are a set of 32 paper inserts each folded twice for insertion into gum packs. The cards (small posters) measure 4 7/8" by 6 7/8". The lower left hand corner of the obverse contains the pin-up number while the back features a green simulated football field upon which a football card game could be played as well as the instructions to accompany the card insert game. Inexplicably the second half of the set seems to be somewhat more difficult to find.

| | NRMT | VG-E | GOOD |
|---|---|---|---|
| COMPLETE SET (32) | 60.00 | 24.00 | 6.00 |
| COMMON PLAYER (1-16) | .75 | .30 | .07 |
| COMMON PLAYER (17-32) | 1.00 | .40 | .10 |
| ☐ 1 Gene Washington | 1.00 | .40 | .10 |
| San Francisco 49ers | | | |
| ☐ 2 Andy Russell | 1.00 | .40 | .10 |
| Pittsburgh Steelers | | | |
| ☐ 3 Harold Jackson | 1.00 | .40 | .10 |
| Philadelphia Eagles | | | |
| ☐ 4 Joe Namath | 10.00 | 4.00 | 1.00 |
| New York Jets | | | |
| ☐ 5 Fran Tarkenton | 5.00 | 2.00 | .50 |
| New York Giants | | | |
| ☐ 6 Dave Osborn | .75 | .30 | .07 |
| Minnesota Vikings | | | |
| ☐ 7 Bob Griese | 3.00 | 1.20 | .30 |
| Miami Dolphins | | | |
| ☐ 8 Roman Gabriel | 1.25 | .50 | .12 |
| Los Angeles Rams | | | |
| ☐ 9 Jerry LeVias | 1.00 | .40 | .10 |
| Houston Oilers | | | |
| ☐ 10 Bart Starr | 4.00 | 1.60 | .40 |
| Green Bay Packers | | | |
| ☐ 11 Bob Hayes | 1.50 | .60 | .15 |
| Dallas Cowboys | | | |
| ☐ 12 Gale Sayers | 5.00 | 2.00 | .50 |
| Chicago Bears | | | |
| ☐ 13 O.J. Simpson | 12.00 | 5.00 | 1.20 |
| Buffalo Bills | | | |
| ☐ 14 Sam Brunelli | .75 | .30 | .07 |
| Denver Broncos | | | |
| ☐ 15 Jim Nance | 1.00 | .40 | .10 |
| New England Patriots | | | |
| ☐ 16 Bill Nelsen | .75 | .30 | .07 |
| Cleveland Browns | | | |
| ☐ 17 Sonny Jurgensen | 3.00 | 1.20 | .30 |
| Washington Redskins | | | |
| ☐ 18 John Brodie | 2.50 | 1.00 | .25 |
| San Francisco 49ers | | | |
| ☐ 19 Lance Alworth | 2.50 | 1.00 | .25 |
| Dallas Cowboys | | | |
| ☐ 20 Larry Wilson | 2.00 | .80 | .20 |
| St. Louis Cardinals | | | |
| ☐ 21 Daryle Lamonica | 1.50 | .60 | .15 |
| Oakland Raiders | | | |
| ☐ 22 Dan Abramowicz | 1.00 | .40 | .10 |
| New Orleans Saints | | | |
| ☐ 23 Gene Washington | 1.00 | .40 | .10 |
| Minnesota Vikings | | | |
| ☐ 24 Bobby Bell | 2.00 | .80 | .20 |
| Kansas City Chiefs | | | |
| ☐ 25 Merlin Olsen | 2.50 | 1.00 | .25 |

| | NRMT | VG-E | GOOD |
|---|---|---|---|
| Los Angeles Rams | | | |
| ☐ 26 Charlie Sanders | 1.25 | .50 | .12 |
| Detroit Lions | | | |
| ☐ 27 Virgil Carter | 1.00 | .40 | .10 |
| Cincinnati Bengals | | | |
| ☐ 28 Dick Butkus | 5.00 | 2.00 | .50 |
| Chicago Bears | | | |
| ☐ 29 John Unitas | 7.50 | 3.00 | .75 |
| Baltimore Colts | | | |
| ☐ 30 Tommy Nobis | 2.00 | .80 | .20 |
| Atlanta Falcons | | | |
| ☐ 31 Floyd Little | 1.50 | .60 | .15 |
| Denver Broncos | | | |
| ☐ 32 Larry Brown | 1.50 | .60 | .15 |
| Washington Redskins | | | |

## 1972 Topps

The 1972 Topps football set contains 351 cards. The cards measure 2 1/2" by 3 1/2". The second series was printed in slightly lesser quantities than the first series. The third series (264-351) is considerably more difficult to obtain than cards in the first two series. In-Action cards (IA in the checklist below) are included as numbers 119-132, 250-263, and 338-351, as are All-Pro selections (AP below) numbered 264-287. The first eight (1-8) cards in the set feature statistical league leaders for the AFC and NFC. Cards 133-139 show the results of the previous season's playoff action. The card backs are printed in blue and green on gray card stock. The key Rookie Cards in this set are Lyle Alzado, Ted Hendricks, Charlie Joiner, Larry Little, Archie Manning, Jim Plunkett, John Riggins, Steve Spurrier, Roger Staubach, and Gene Upshaw.

| | NRMT | VG-E | GOOD |
|---|---|---|---|
| COMPLETE SET (351) | 2400.00 | 1100.00 | 300.00 |
| COMMON PLAYER (1-132) | .50 | .23 | .06 |
| COMMON PLAYER (133-263) | .60 | .25 | .08 |
| COMMON PLAYER (264-351) | 20.00 | 9.00 | 2.50 |
| ☐ 1 AFC Rushing Leaders | 4.00 | 1.00 | .30 |
| Floyd Little | | | |
| Larry Csonka | | | |
| Marv Hubbard | | | |
| ☐ 2 NFC Rushing Leaders | 1.25 | .55 | .16 |
| John Brockington | | | |
| Steve Owens | | | |
| Willie Ellison | | | |
| ☐ 3 AFC Passing Leaders | 2.00 | .90 | .25 |
| Bob Griese | | | |
| Len Dawson | | | |
| Virgil Carter | | | |
| ☐ 4 NFC Passing Leaders | 5.00 | 2.30 | .60 |
| Roger Staubach | | | |
| Greg Landry | | | |
| Bill Kilmer | | | |
| ☐ 5 AFC Receiving Leaders | 1.00 | .45 | .13 |
| Fred Biletnikoff | | | |
| Otis Taylor | | | |
| Randy Vataha | | | |
| ☐ 6 NFC Receiving Leaders | 1.00 | .45 | .13 |
| Bob Tucker | | | |
| Ted Kwalick | | | |
| Harold Jackson | | | |
| Roy Jefferson | | | |
| ☐ 7 AFC Scoring Leaders | 1.25 | .55 | .16 |
| Garo Yepremian | | | |
| Jan Stenerud | | | |
| Jim O'Brien | | | |
| ☐ 8 NFC Scoring Leaders | 1.00 | .45 | .13 |
| Curt Knight | | | |
| Errol Mann | | | |
| Bruce Gossett | | | |
| ☐ 9 Jim Kiick | 1.25 | .55 | .16 |
| Miami Dolphins | | | |
| ☐ 10 Otis Taylor | 1.00 | .45 | .13 |

| | | | |
|---|---|---|---|
| Kansas City Chiefs | | | |
| ☐ 11 Bobby Joe Green | .50 | .23 | .06 |
| Chicago Bears | | | |
| ☐ 12 Ken Ellis | .50 | .23 | .06 |
| Green Bay Packers | | | |
| ☐ 13 John Riggins | 30.00 | 13.50 | 3.80 |
| New York Jets | | | |
| ☐ 14 Dave Parks | .60 | .25 | .08 |
| New Orleans Saints | | | |
| ☐ 15 John Hadl | 1.25 | .55 | .16 |
| San Diego Chargers | | | |
| ☐ 16 Ron Hornsby | .50 | .23 | .06 |
| New York Giants | | | |
| ☐ 17 Chip Myers | .50 | .23 | .06 |
| Cincinnati Bengals | | | |
| ☐ 18 Bill Kilmer | 1.25 | .55 | .16 |
| Washington Redskins | | | |
| ☐ 19 Fred Hoaglin | .50 | .23 | .06 |
| Cleveland Browns | | | |
| ☐ 20 Carl Eller | 1.25 | .55 | .16 |
| Minnesota Vikings | | | |
| ☐ 21 Steve Zabel | .50 | .23 | .06 |
| Philadelphia Eagles | | | |
| ☐ 22 Vic Washington | .75 | .35 | .09 |
| San Francisco 49ers | | | |
| ☐ 23 Len St. Jean | .50 | .23 | .06 |
| New England Patriots | | | |
| ☐ 24 Bill Thompson | .60 | .25 | .08 |
| Denver Broncos | | | |
| ☐ 25 Steve Owens | 2.50 | 1.15 | .30 |
| Detroit Lions | | | |
| ☐ 26 Ken Burrough | 1.25 | .55 | .16 |
| Houston Oilers | | | |
| ☐ 27 Mike Clark | .50 | .23 | .06 |
| Dallas Cowboys | | | |
| ☐ 28 Willie Brown | 2.50 | 1.15 | .30 |
| Oakland Raiders | | | |
| ☐ 29 Checklist 1-132 | 7.00 | 1.05 | .35 |
| ☐ 30 Marlin Briscoe | .50 | .23 | .06 |
| Buffalo Bills | | | |
| ☐ 31 Jerry Logan | .50 | .23 | .06 |
| Baltimore Colts | | | |
| ☐ 32 Donny Anderson | .60 | .25 | .08 |
| St. Louis Cardinals | | | |
| ☐ 33 Rich McGeorge | .50 | .23 | .06 |
| Green Bay Packers | | | |
| ☐ 34 Charlie Durkee | .50 | .23 | .06 |
| New Orleans Saints | | | |
| ☐ 35 Willie Lanier | 4.00 | 1.80 | .50 |
| Kansas City Chiefs | | | |
| ☐ 36 Chris Farasopoulos | .60 | .25 | .08 |
| New York Jets | | | |
| ☐ 37 Ron Shanklin | .50 | .23 | .06 |
| Pittsburgh Steelers | | | |
| ☐ 38 Forrest Blue | 1.25 | .55 | .16 |
| San Francisco 49ers | | | |
| ☐ 39 Ken Reaves | .50 | .23 | .06 |
| Atlanta Falcons | | | |
| ☐ 40 Roman Gabriel | 2.25 | 1.00 | .30 |
| Los Angeles Rams | | | |
| ☐ 41 Mac Percival | .50 | .23 | .06 |
| Chicago Bears | | | |
| ☐ 42 Lem Barney | 3.00 | 1.35 | .40 |
| Detroit Lions | | | |
| ☐ 43 Nick Buoniconti | 2.00 | .90 | .25 |
| Miami Dolphins | | | |
| ☐ 44 Charlie Gogolak | .60 | .25 | .08 |
| New England Patriots | | | |
| ☐ 45 Bill Bradley | 2.00 | .90 | .25 |
| Philadelphia Eagles | | | |
| ☐ 46 Joe Jones | .50 | .23 | .06 |
| Cleveland Browns | | | |
| ☐ 47 Dave Williams | .60 | .25 | .08 |
| San Diego Chargers | | | |
| ☐ 48 Pete Athas | .50 | .23 | .06 |
| New York Giants | | | |
| ☐ 49 Virgil Carter | .60 | .25 | .08 |
| Cincinnati Bengals | | | |
| ☐ 50 Floyd Little | 2.00 | .90 | .25 |
| Denver Broncos | | | |
| ☐ 51 Curt Knight | .50 | .23 | .06 |
| Washington Redskins | | | |
| ☐ 52 Bobby Maples | .60 | .25 | .08 |
| Houston Oilers | | | |
| ☐ 53 Charlie West | .60 | .25 | .08 |
| Minnesota Vikings | | | |
| ☐ 54 Marv Hubbard | 1.25 | .55 | .16 |
| Oakland Raiders | | | |
| ☐ 55 Archie Manning | 12.00 | 5.50 | 1.50 |
| New Orleans Saints | | | |
| ☐ 56 Jim O'Brien | 1.00 | .45 | .13 |
| Baltimore Colts | | | |
| ☐ 57 Wayne Patrick | .50 | .23 | .06 |
| Buffalo Bills | | | |
| ☐ 58 Ken Bowman | .50 | .23 | .06 |
| Green Bay Packers | | | |
| ☐ 59 Roger Wehrli | .60 | .25 | .08 |
| St. Louis Cardinals | | | |

| | | | |
|---|---|---|---|
| ☐ 60 Charlie Sanders UER | 1.00 | .45 | .13 |
| Detroit Lions | | | |
| (Front WR, back TE) | | | |
| ☐ 61 Jan Stenerud | 2.00 | .90 | .25 |
| Kansas City Chiefs | | | |
| ☐ 62 Willie Ellison | .60 | .25 | .08 |
| Los Angeles Rams | | | |
| ☐ 63 Walt Sweeney | .60 | .25 | .08 |
| San Diego Chargers | | | |
| ☐ 64 Ron Smith | .50 | .23 | .06 |
| Chicago Bears | | | |
| ☐ 65 Jim Plunkett | 20.00 | 9.00 | 2.50 |
| New England Patriots | | | |
| ☐ 66 Herb Adderley UER | 2.50 | 1.15 | .30 |
| Dallas Cowboys | | | |
| (misspelled Adderly) | | | |
| ☐ 67 Mike Reid | 4.00 | 1.80 | .50 |
| Cincinnati Bengals | | | |
| ☐ 68 Richard Caster | 1.25 | .55 | .16 |
| New York Jets | | | |
| ☐ 69 Dave Wilcox | .60 | .25 | .08 |
| San Francisco 49ers | | | |
| ☐ 70 Leroy Kelly | 2.00 | .90 | .25 |
| Cleveland Browns | | | |
| ☐ 71 Bob Lee | .75 | .35 | .09 |
| Minnesota Vikings | | | |
| ☐ 72 Verlon Biggs | .50 | .23 | .06 |
| Washington Redskins | | | |
| ☐ 73 Henry Allison | .50 | .23 | .06 |
| Philadelphia Eagles | | | |
| ☐ 74 Steve Ramsey | .60 | .25 | .08 |
| Denver Broncos | | | |
| ☐ 75 Claude Humphrey | .60 | .25 | .08 |
| Atlanta Falcons | | | |
| ☐ 76 Bob Grim | 1.00 | .45 | .13 |
| New York Giants | | | |
| ☐ 77 John Fuqua | .60 | .25 | .08 |
| Pittsburgh Steelers | | | |
| ☐ 78 Ken Houston | 4.00 | 1.80 | .50 |
| Houston Oilers | | | |
| ☐ 79 Checklist 133-263 DP | 5.00 | .75 | .25 |
| ☐ 80 Bob Griese | 8.00 | 3.60 | 1.00 |
| Miami Dolphins | | | |
| ☐ 81 Lance Rentzel | .60 | .25 | .08 |
| Los Angeles Rams | | | |
| ☐ 82 Ed Podolak | 1.75 | .80 | .22 |
| Kansas City Chiefs | | | |
| ☐ 83 Ike Hill | .50 | .23 | .06 |
| Buffalo Bills | | | |
| ☐ 84 George Farmer | .50 | .23 | .06 |
| Chicago Bears | | | |
| ☐ 85 John Brockington | 4.00 | 1.80 | .50 |
| Green Bay Packers | | | |
| ☐ 86 Jim Otto | 2.00 | .90 | .25 |
| Oakland Raiders | | | |
| ☐ 87 Richard Neal | .50 | .23 | .06 |
| New Orleans Saints | | | |
| ☐ 88 Jim Hart | 1.25 | .55 | .16 |
| St. Louis Cardinals | | | |
| ☐ 89 Bob Babich | .50 | .23 | .06 |
| San Diego Chargers | | | |
| ☐ 90 Gene Washington | .75 | .35 | .09 |
| San Francisco 49ers | | | |
| ☐ 91 John Zook | .50 | .23 | .06 |
| Atlanta Falcons | | | |
| ☐ 92 Bobby Duhon | .50 | .23 | .06 |
| New York Giants | | | |
| ☐ 93 Ted Hendricks | 20.00 | 9.00 | 2.50 |
| Baltimore Colts | | | |
| ☐ 94 Rockne Freitas | .50 | .23 | .06 |
| Detroit Lions | | | |
| ☐ 95 Larry Brown | 1.50 | .65 | .19 |
| Washington Redskins | | | |
| ☐ 96 Mike Phipps | .75 | .35 | .09 |
| Cleveland Browns | | | |
| ☐ 97 Julius Adams | .60 | .25 | .08 |
| New England Patriots | | | |
| ☐ 98 Dick Anderson | .75 | .35 | .09 |
| Miami Dolphins | | | |
| ☐ 99 Fred Willis | .50 | .23 | .06 |
| Cincinnati Bengals | | | |
| ☐ 100 Joe Namath | 35.00 | 16.00 | 4.40 |
| New York Jets | | | |
| ☐ 101 L.C. Greenwood | 18.00 | 8.00 | 2.30 |
| Pittsburgh Steelers | | | |
| ☐ 102 Mark Nordquist | .50 | .23 | .06 |
| Philadelphia Eagles | | | |
| ☐ 103 Robert Holmes | .50 | .23 | .06 |
| Houston Oilers | | | |
| ☐ 104 Ron Yary | 4.00 | 1.80 | .50 |
| Minnesota Vikings | | | |
| ☐ 105 Bob Hayes | 1.25 | .55 | .16 |
| Dallas Cowboys | | | |
| ☐ 106 Lyle Alzado | 14.00 | 6.25 | 1.75 |
| Denver Broncos | | | |
| ☐ 107 Bob Berry | .60 | .25 | .08 |
| Atlanta Falcons | | | |

| | | | |
|---|---|---|---|
| ☐ 108 Phil Villapiano .................... Oakland Raiders | 2.00 | .90 | .25 |
| ☐ 109 Dave Elmendorf .................... Los Angeles Rams | .60 | .25 | .08 |
| ☐ 110 Gale Sayers .................... Chicago Bears | 20.00 | 9.00 | 2.50 |
| ☐ 111 Jim Tyrer .................... Kansas City Chiefs | .60 | .25 | .08 |
| ☐ 112 Mel Gray .................... St. Louis Cardinals | 3.00 | 1.35 | .40 |
| ☐ 113 Gerry Philbin .................... New York Jets | .50 | .23 | .06 |
| ☐ 114 Bob James .................... Buffalo Bills | .50 | .23 | .06 |
| ☐ 115 Garo Yepremian .................... Miami Dolphins | 1.00 | .45 | .13 |
| ☐ 116 Dave Robinson .................... Green Bay Packers | .60 | .25 | .08 |
| ☐ 117 Jeff Queen .................... San Diego Chargers | .50 | .23 | .06 |
| ☐ 118 Norm Snead .................... New York Giants | .60 | .25 | .08 |
| ☐ 119 Jim Nance IA .................... New England Patriots | .50 | .23 | .06 |
| ☐ 120 Terry Bradshaw IA .................... Pittsburgh Steelers | 16.00 | 7.25 | 2.00 |
| ☐ 121 Jim Kiick IA .................... Miami Dolphins | .75 | .35 | .09 |
| ☐ 122 Roger Staubach IA .................... Dallas Cowboys | 20.00 | 9.00 | 2.50 |
| ☐ 123 Bo Scott IA .................... Cleveland Browns | .50 | .23 | .06 |
| ☐ 124 John Brodie IA .................... San Francisco 49ers | 2.00 | .90 | .25 |
| ☐ 125 Rick Volk IA .................... Baltimore Colts | .50 | .23 | .06 |
| ☐ 126 John Riggins IA .................... New York Jets | 8.00 | 3.60 | 1.00 |
| ☐ 127 Bubba Smith IA .................... Baltimore Colts | 1.75 | .80 | .22 |
| ☐ 128 Roman Gabriel IA .................... Los Angeles Rams | 1.00 | .45 | .13 |
| ☐ 129 Calvin Hill IA .................... Dallas Cowboys | .60 | .25 | .08 |
| ☐ 130 Bill Nelsen IA .................... Cleveland Browns | .50 | .23 | .06 |
| ☐ 131 Tom Matte IA .................... Baltimore Colts | .50 | .23 | .06 |
| ☐ 132 Bob Griese IA .................... Miami Dolphins | 4.00 | 1.80 | .50 |
| ☐ 133 AFC Semi-Final .................... Dolphins 27, Chiefs 24 | 1.50 | .65 | .19 |
| ☐ 134 NFC Semi-Final .................... Cowboys 20, Vikings 12 (Duane Thomas getting tackled) | 1.75 | .80 | .22 |
| ☐ 135 AFC Semi-Final .................... Colts 20, Browns 3 (Don Nottingham) | 1.50 | .65 | .19 |
| ☐ 136 NFC Semi-Final .................... 49ers 24, Redskins 20 | 1.50 | .65 | .19 |
| ☐ 137 AFC Title Game .................... Dolphins 21, Colts 0 (Johnny Unitas getting tackled) | 2.50 | 1.15 | .30 |
| ☐ 138 NFC Title Game .................... Cowboys 14, 49ers 3 (Bob Lilly making tackle) | 2.00 | .90 | .25 |
| ☐ 139 Super Bowl .................... Cowboys 24, Dolphins 3 (Roger Staubach rolling out) | 5.00 | 2.30 | .60 |
| ☐ 140 Larry Csonka .................... Miami Dolphins | 8.00 | 3.60 | 1.00 |
| ☐ 141 Rick Volk .................... Baltimore Colts | .60 | .25 | .08 |
| ☐ 142 Roy Jefferson .................... Washington Redskins | .75 | .35 | .09 |
| ☐ 143 Raymond Chester .................... Oakland Raiders | 1.75 | .80 | .22 |
| ☐ 144 Bobby Douglass .................... Chicago Bears | .75 | .35 | .09 |
| ☐ 145 Bob Lilly .................... Dallas Cowboys | 3.50 | 1.55 | .45 |
| ☐ 146 Harold Jackson .................... Philadelphia Eagles | 2.00 | .90 | .25 |
| ☐ 147 Pete Gogolak .................... New York Giants | .75 | .35 | .09 |
| ☐ 148 Art Malone .................... Atlanta Falcons | .60 | .25 | .08 |
| ☐ 149 Ed Flanagan .................... Detroit Lions | .60 | .25 | .08 |
| ☐ 150 Terry Bradshaw .................... Pittsburgh Steelers | 45.00 | 20.00 | 5.75 |
| ☐ 151 MacArthur Lane .................... Green Bay Packers | .75 | .35 | .09 |
| ☐ 152 Jack Snow .................... Los Angeles Rams | .75 | .35 | .09 |
| ☐ 153 Al Beauchamp .................... Cincinnati Bengals | .60 | .25 | .08 |
| ☐ 154 Bob Anderson .................... Denver Broncos | .60 | .25 | .08 |
| ☐ 155 Ted Kwalick .................... San Francisco 49ers | 1.50 | .65 | .19 |
| ☐ 156 Dan Pastorini .................... Houston Oilers | 2.50 | 1.15 | .30 |
| ☐ 157 Emmitt Thomas .................... Kansas City Chiefs | 1.25 | .55 | .16 |
| ☐ 158 Randy Vataha .................... New England Patriots | 1.00 | .45 | .13 |
| ☐ 159 Al Atkinson .................... New York Jets | .60 | .25 | .08 |
| ☐ 160 O.J. Simpson .................... Buffalo Bills | 35.00 | 16.00 | 4.40 |
| ☐ 161 Jackie Smith .................... St. Louis Cardinals | 1.25 | .55 | .16 |
| ☐ 162 Ernie Kellerman .................... Cleveland Browns | .60 | .25 | .08 |
| ☐ 163 Dennis Partee .................... San Diego Chargers | .60 | .25 | .08 |
| ☐ 164 Jake Kupp .................... New Orleans Saints | .60 | .25 | .08 |
| ☐ 165 John Unitas .................... Baltimore Colts | 20.00 | 9.00 | 2.50 |
| ☐ 166 Clint Jones .................... Minnesota Vikings | .75 | .35 | .09 |
| ☐ 167 Paul Warfield .................... Miami Dolphins | 6.00 | 2.70 | .75 |
| ☐ 168 Roland McDole .................... Washington Redskins | .60 | .25 | .08 |
| ☐ 169 Daryle Lamonica .................... Oakland Raiders | 2.00 | .90 | .25 |
| ☐ 170 Dick Butkus .................... Chicago Bears | 8.00 | 3.60 | 1.00 |
| ☐ 171 Jim Butler .................... Atlanta Falcons | .60 | .25 | .08 |
| ☐ 172 Mike McCoy .................... Green Bay Packers | .60 | .25 | .08 |
| ☐ 173 Dave Smith .................... Pittsburgh Steelers | .60 | .25 | .08 |
| ☐ 174 Greg Landry .................... Detroit Lions | 1.50 | .65 | .19 |
| ☐ 175 Tom Dempsey .................... Philadelphia Eagles | .75 | .35 | .09 |
| ☐ 176 John Charles .................... Houston Oilers | .60 | .25 | .08 |
| ☐ 177 Bobby Bell .................... Kansas City Chiefs | 2.25 | 1.00 | .30 |
| ☐ 178 Don Horn .................... Denver Broncos | .75 | .35 | .09 |
| ☐ 179 Bob Trumpy .................... Cincinnati Bengals | 2.00 | .90 | .25 |
| ☐ 180 Duane Thomas .................... Dallas Cowboys | 1.00 | .45 | .13 |
| ☐ 181 Merlin Olsen .................... Los Angeles Rams | 3.00 | 1.35 | .40 |
| ☐ 182 Dave Herman .................... New York Jets | .60 | .25 | .08 |
| ☐ 183 Jim Nance .................... New England Patriots | .75 | .35 | .09 |
| ☐ 184 Pete Beathard .................... St. Louis Cardinals | .75 | .35 | .09 |
| ☐ 185 Bob Tucker .................... New York Giants | .75 | .35 | .09 |
| ☐ 186 Gene Upshaw .................... Oakland Raiders | 14.00 | 6.25 | 1.75 |
| ☐ 187 Bo Scott .................... Cleveland Browns | .75 | .35 | .09 |
| ☐ 188 J.D. Hill .................... Buffalo Bills | 1.00 | .45 | .13 |
| ☐ 189 Bruce Gossett .................... San Francisco 49ers | .60 | .25 | .08 |
| ☐ 190 Bubba Smith .................... Baltimore Colts | 4.00 | 1.80 | .50 |
| ☐ 191 Edd Hargett .................... New Orleans Saints | .75 | .35 | .09 |
| ☐ 192 Gary Garrison .................... San Diego Chargers | .75 | .35 | .09 |
| ☐ 193 Jake Scott .................... Miami Dolphins | 1.50 | .65 | .19 |
| ☐ 194 Fred Cox .................... Minnesota Vikings | .75 | .35 | .09 |
| ☐ 195 Sonny Jurgensen .................... Washington Redskins | 4.50 | 2.00 | .55 |
| ☐ 196 Greg Brezina .................... Atlanta Falcons | 1.00 | .45 | .13 |
| ☐ 197 Ed O'Bradovich .................... | .60 | .25 | .08 |

| | | | |
|---|---|---|---|
| Chicago Bears | | | |
| ☐ 198 John Rowser | .60 | .25 | .08 |
| Pittsburgh Steelers | | | |
| ☐ 199 Altie Taylor UER | .75 | .35 | .09 |
| Detroit Lions | | | |
| (Taylor misspelled as | | | |
| Tayor on front) | | | |
| ☐ 200 Roger Staubach | 150.00 | 70.00 | 19.00 |
| Dallas Cowboys | | | |
| ☐ 201 Leroy Keyes | 1.00 | .45 | .13 |
| Philadelphia Eagles | | | |
| ☐ 202 Garland Boyette | .60 | .25 | .08 |
| Houston Oilers | | | |
| ☐ 203 Tom Beer | .60 | .25 | .08 |
| New England Patriots | | | |
| ☐ 204 Buck Buchanan | 2.00 | .90 | .25 |
| Kansas City Chiefs | | | |
| ☐ 205 Larry Wilson | 2.00 | .90 | .25 |
| St. Louis Cardinals | | | |
| ☐ 206 Scott Hunter | 1.00 | .45 | .13 |
| Green Bay Packers | | | |
| ☐ 207 Ron Johnson | .75 | .35 | .09 |
| New York Giants | | | |
| ☐ 208 Sam Brunelli | .60 | .25 | .08 |
| Denver Broncos | | | |
| ☐ 209 Deacon Jones | 2.25 | 1.00 | .30 |
| San Diego Chargers | | | |
| ☐ 210 Fred Biletnikoff | 5.00 | 2.30 | .60 |
| Oakland Raiders | | | |
| ☐ 211 Bill Nelsen | .75 | .35 | .09 |
| Cleveland Browns | | | |
| ☐ 212 George Nock | .60 | .25 | .08 |
| New York Jets | | | |
| ☐ 213 Dan Abramowicz | .75 | .35 | .09 |
| New Orleans Saints | | | |
| ☐ 214 Irv Goode | .60 | .25 | .08 |
| Buffalo Bills | | | |
| ☐ 215 Isiah Robertson | 2.00 | .90 | .25 |
| Los Angeles Rams | | | |
| ☐ 216 Tom Matte | .75 | .35 | .09 |
| Baltimore Colts | | | |
| ☐ 217 Pat Fischer | .75 | .35 | .09 |
| Washington Redskins | | | |
| ☐ 218 Gene Washington | .75 | .35 | .09 |
| Minnesota Vikings | | | |
| ☐ 219 Paul Robinson | .75 | .35 | .09 |
| Cincinnati Bengals | | | |
| ☐ 220 John Brodie | 4.50 | 2.00 | .55 |
| San Francisco 49ers | | | |
| ☐ 221 Manny Fernandez | 2.00 | .90 | .25 |
| Miami Dolphins | | | |
| ☐ 222 Errol Mann | .60 | .25 | .08 |
| Detroit Lions | | | |
| ☐ 223 Dick Gordon | .75 | .35 | .09 |
| Chicago Bears | | | |
| ☐ 224 Calvin Hill | 1.75 | .80 | .22 |
| Dallas Cowboys | | | |
| ☐ 225 Fran Tarkenton UER | 18.00 | 8.00 | 2.30 |
| (Plays in the Masters | | | |
| each spring) | | | |
| Minnesota Vikings | | | |
| ☐ 226 Jim Turner | .75 | .35 | .09 |
| Denver Broncos | | | |
| ☐ 227 Jim Mitchell | .75 | .35 | .09 |
| Atlanta Falcons | | | |
| ☐ 228 Pete Liske | .75 | .35 | .09 |
| Philadelphia Eagles | | | |
| ☐ 229 Carl Garrett | .60 | .25 | .08 |
| New England Patriots | | | |
| ☐ 230 Joe Greene | 16.00 | 7.25 | 2.00 |
| Pittsburgh Steelers | | | |
| ☐ 231 Gale Gillingham | .60 | .25 | .08 |
| Green Bay Packers | | | |
| ☐ 232 Norm Bulaich | 1.25 | .55 | .16 |
| Baltimore Colts | | | |
| ☐ 233 Spider Lockhart | .75 | .35 | .09 |
| New York Giants | | | |
| ☐ 234 Ken Willard | .75 | .35 | .09 |
| San Francisco 49ers | | | |
| ☐ 235 George Blanda | 12.00 | 5.50 | 1.50 |
| Oakland Raiders | | | |
| ☐ 236 Wayne Mulligan | .60 | .25 | .08 |
| St. Louis Cardinals | | | |
| ☐ 237 Dave Lewis | .60 | .25 | .08 |
| Cincinnati Bengals | | | |
| ☐ 238 Dennis Shaw | .75 | .35 | .09 |
| Buffalo Bills | | | |
| ☐ 239 Fair Hooker | .75 | .35 | .09 |
| Cleveland Browns | | | |
| ☐ 240 Larry Little | 15.00 | 6.75 | 1.90 |
| Miami Dolphins | | | |
| ☐ 241 Mike Garrett | 1.00 | .45 | .13 |
| San Diego Chargers | | | |
| ☐ 242 Glen Ray Hines | .60 | .25 | .08 |
| New Orleans Saints | | | |
| ☐ 243 Myron Pottios | .60 | .25 | .08 |
| Washington Redskins | | | |
| ☐ 244 Charlie Joiner | 25.00 | 11.50 | 3.10 |

| | | | |
|---|---|---|---|
| Houston Oilers | | | |
| ☐ 245 Len Dawson | 5.00 | 2.30 | .60 |
| Kansas City Chiefs | | | |
| ☐ 246 W.K. Hicks | .60 | .25 | .08 |
| New York Jets | | | |
| ☐ 247 Les Josephson | .75 | .35 | .09 |
| Los Angeles Rams | | | |
| ☐ 248 Lance Alworth UER | 5.00 | 2.30 | .60 |
| Dallas Cowboys | | | |
| (Front TE, back WR) | | | |
| ☐ 249 Frank Nunley | .60 | .25 | .08 |
| San Francisco 49ers | | | |
| ☐ 250 Mel Farr IA | .60 | .25 | .08 |
| Detroit Lions | | | |
| ☐ 251 Johnny Unitas IA | 8.00 | 3.60 | 1.00 |
| Baltimore Colts | | | |
| ☐ 252 George Farmer IA | .60 | .25 | .08 |
| Chicago Bears | | | |
| ☐ 253 Duane Thomas IA | .75 | .35 | .09 |
| Dallas Cowboys | | | |
| ☐ 254 John Hadl IA | 1.00 | .45 | .13 |
| San Diego Chargers | | | |
| ☐ 255 Vic Washington IA | .60 | .25 | .08 |
| San Francisco 49ers | | | |
| ☐ 256 Don Horn IA | .60 | .25 | .08 |
| Denver Broncos | | | |
| ☐ 257 L.C. Greenwood IA | 3.00 | 1.35 | .40 |
| Pittsburgh Steelers | | | |
| ☐ 258 Bob Lee IA | .60 | .25 | .08 |
| Minnesota Vikings | | | |
| ☐ 259 Larry Csonka IA | 4.00 | 1.80 | .50 |
| Miami Dolphins | | | |
| ☐ 260 Mike McCoy IA | .60 | .25 | .08 |
| Green Bay Packers | | | |
| ☐ 261 Greg Landry IA | .75 | .35 | .09 |
| Detroit Lions | | | |
| ☐ 262 Ray May IA | .60 | .25 | .08 |
| Baltimore Colts | | | |
| ☐ 263 Bobby Douglass IA | .60 | .25 | .08 |
| Chicago Bears | | | |
| ☐ 264 Charlie Sanders AP | 28.00 | 12.50 | 3.50 |
| Detroit Lions | | | |
| ☐ 265 Ron Yary AP | 28.00 | 12.50 | 3.50 |
| Minnesota Vikings | | | |
| ☐ 266 Rayfield Wright AP | 27.50 | 12.50 | 3.40 |
| Dallas Cowboys | | | |
| ☐ 267 Larry Little AP | 40.00 | 18.00 | 5.00 |
| Miami Dolphins | | | |
| ☐ 268 John Niland AP | 24.00 | 11.00 | 3.00 |
| Dallas Cowboys | | | |
| ☐ 269 Forrest Blue AP | 27.50 | 12.50 | 3.40 |
| San Francisco 49ers | | | |
| ☐ 270 Otis Taylor AP | 25.00 | 11.50 | 3.10 |
| Kansas City Chiefs | | | |
| ☐ 271 Paul Warfield AP | 50.00 | 23.00 | 6.25 |
| Miami Dolphins | | | |
| ☐ 272 Bob Griese AP | 75.00 | 34.00 | 9.50 |
| Miami Dolphins | | | |
| ☐ 273 John Brockington AP | 27.00 | 12.00 | 3.40 |
| Green Bay Packers | | | |
| ☐ 274 Floyd Little AP | 30.00 | 13.50 | 3.80 |
| Denver Broncos | | | |
| ☐ 275 Garo Yepremian AP | 30.00 | 13.50 | 3.80 |
| Miami Dolphins | | | |
| ☐ 276 Jerrel Wilson AP | 24.00 | 11.00 | 3.00 |
| Kansas City Chiefs | | | |
| ☐ 277 Carl Eller AP | 30.00 | 13.50 | 3.80 |
| Minnesota Vikings | | | |
| ☐ 278 Bubba Smith AP | 35.00 | 16.00 | 4.40 |
| Baltimore Colts | | | |
| ☐ 279 Alan Page AP | 40.00 | 18.00 | 5.00 |
| Minnesota Vikings | | | |
| ☐ 280 Bob Lilly AP | 48.00 | 22.00 | 6.00 |
| Dallas Cowboys | | | |
| ☐ 281 Ted Hendricks AP | 48.00 | 22.00 | 6.00 |
| Baltimore Colts | | | |
| ☐ 282 Dave Wilcox AP | 27.50 | 12.50 | 3.40 |
| San Francisco 49ers | | | |
| ☐ 283 Willie Lanier AP | 30.00 | 13.50 | 3.80 |
| Kansas City Chiefs | | | |
| ☐ 284 Jim Johnson AP | 30.00 | 13.50 | 3.80 |
| San Francisco 49ers | | | |
| ☐ 285 Willie Brown AP | 30.00 | 13.50 | 3.80 |
| Oakland Raiders | | | |
| ☐ 286 Bill Bradley AP | 25.00 | 11.50 | 3.10 |
| Philadelphia Eagles | | | |
| ☐ 287 Ken Houston AP | 30.00 | 13.50 | 3.80 |
| Houston Oilers | | | |
| ☐ 288 Mel Farr | 22.00 | 10.00 | 2.80 |
| Detroit Lions | | | |
| ☐ 289 Kermit Alexander | 20.00 | 9.00 | 2.50 |
| Los Angeles Rams | | | |
| ☐ 290 John Gilliam | 28.00 | 12.50 | 3.50 |
| Minnesota Vikings | | | |
| ☐ 291 Steve Spurrier | 85.00 | 38.00 | 10.50 |
| San Francisco 49ers | | | |
| ☐ 292 Walter Johnson | 20.00 | 9.00 | 2.50 |
| Cleveland Browns | | | |

| | | | |
|---|---|---|---|
| ☐ 293 Jack Pardee | 25.00 | 11.50 | 3.10 |
| Washington Redskins | | | |
| ☐ 294 Checklist 264-351 UER | 75.00 | 19.00 | 6.00 |
| (334 Charlie Taylor should be Charley) | | | |
| ☐ 295 Winston Hill | 22.00 | 10.00 | 2.80 |
| New York Jets | | | |
| ☐ 296 Hugo Hollas | 20.00 | 9.00 | 2.50 |
| New Orleans Saints | | | |
| ☐ 297 Ray May | 24.00 | 11.00 | 3.00 |
| Baltimore Colts | | | |
| ☐ 298 Jim Bakken | 22.00 | 10.00 | 2.80 |
| St. Louis Cardinals | | | |
| ☐ 299 Larry Carwell | 20.00 | 9.00 | 2.50 |
| New England Patriots | | | |
| ☐ 300 Alan Page | 35.00 | 16.00 | 4.40 |
| Minnesota Vikings | | | |
| ☐ 301 Walt Garrison | 25.00 | 11.50 | 3.10 |
| Dallas Cowboys | | | |
| ☐ 302 Mike Lucci | 22.00 | 10.00 | 2.80 |
| Detroit Lions | | | |
| ☐ 303 Nemiah Wilson | 20.00 | 9.00 | 2.50 |
| Oakland Raiders | | | |
| ☐ 304 Carroll Dale | 22.00 | 10.00 | 2.80 |
| Green Bay Packers | | | |
| ☐ 305 Jim Kanicki | 20.00 | 9.00 | 2.50 |
| New York Giants | | | |
| ☐ 306 Preston Pearson | 25.00 | 11.50 | 3.10 |
| Pittsburgh Steelers | | | |
| ☐ 307 Lemar Parrish | 22.00 | 10.00 | 2.80 |
| Cincinnati Bengals | | | |
| ☐ 308 Earl Morrall | 28.00 | 12.50 | 3.50 |
| Miami Dolphins | | | |
| ☐ 309 Tommy Nobis | 25.00 | 11.50 | 3.10 |
| Atlanta Falcons | | | |
| ☐ 310 Rich Jackson | 20.00 | 9.00 | 2.50 |
| Denver Broncos | | | |
| ☐ 311 Doug Cunningham | 20.00 | 9.00 | 2.50 |
| San Francisco 49ers | | | |
| ☐ 312 Jim Marsalis | 22.00 | 10.00 | 2.80 |
| Kansas City Chiefs | | | |
| ☐ 313 Jim Beirne | 20.00 | 9.00 | 2.50 |
| Houston Oilers | | | |
| ☐ 314 Tom McNeill | 20.00 | 9.00 | 2.50 |
| Philadelphia Eagles | | | |
| ☐ 315 Milt Morin | 20.00 | 9.00 | 2.50 |
| Cleveland Browns | | | |
| ☐ 316 Rayfield Wright | 25.00 | 11.50 | 3.10 |
| Dallas Cowboys | | | |
| ☐ 317 Jerry LeVias | 22.00 | 10.00 | 2.80 |
| San Diego Chargers | | | |
| ☐ 318 Travis Williams | 28.00 | 12.50 | 3.50 |
| Los Angeles Rams | | | |
| ☐ 319 Edgar Chandler | 20.00 | 9.00 | 2.50 |
| Buffalo Bills | | | |
| ☐ 320 Bob Wallace | 20.00 | 9.00 | 2.50 |
| Chicago Bears | | | |
| ☐ 321 Delles Howell | 20.00 | 9.00 | 2.50 |
| New Orleans Saints | | | |
| ☐ 322 Emerson Boozer | 22.00 | 10.00 | 2.80 |
| New York Jets | | | |
| ☐ 323 George Atkinson | 24.00 | 11.00 | 3.00 |
| Oakland Raiders | | | |
| ☐ 324 Mike Montler | 20.00 | 9.00 | 2.50 |
| New England Patriots | | | |
| ☐ 325 Randy Johnson | 22.00 | 10.00 | 2.80 |
| New York Giants | | | |
| ☐ 326 Mike Curtis UER | 22.00 | 10.00 | 2.80 |
| Baltimore Colts | | | |
| (Text on back states he was named Super Bowl MVP in 1972. Chuck Howley won the award) | | | |
| ☐ 327 Miller Farr | 20.00 | 9.00 | 2.50 |
| St. Louis Cardinals | | | |
| ☐ 328 Horst Muhlmann | 20.00 | 9.00 | 2.50 |
| Cincinnati Bengals | | | |
| ☐ 329 John Niland | 25.00 | 11.50 | 3.10 |
| Dallas Cowboys | | | |
| ☐ 330 Andy Russell | 22.00 | 10.00 | 2.80 |
| Pittsburgh Steelers | | | |
| ☐ 331 Mercury Morris | 35.00 | 16.00 | 4.40 |
| Miami Dolphins | | | |
| ☐ 332 Jim Johnson | 28.00 | 12.50 | 3.50 |
| San Francisco 49ers | | | |
| ☐ 333 Jerrel Wilson | 20.00 | 9.00 | 2.50 |
| Kansas City Chiefs | | | |
| ☐ 334 Charley Taylor UER | 40.00 | 18.00 | 5.00 |
| (Misspelled Charlie on both sides) | | | |
| Washington Redskins | | | |
| ☐ 335 Dick LeBeau | 22.00 | 10.00 | 2.80 |
| Detroit Lions | | | |
| ☐ 336 Jim Marshall | 28.00 | 12.50 | 3.50 |
| Minnesota Vikings | | | |
| ☐ 337 Tom Mack | 25.00 | 11.50 | 3.10 |
| Los Angeles Rams | | | |
| ☐ 338 Steve Spurrier IA | 48.00 | 22.00 | 6.00 |

| | | | |
|---|---|---|---|
| San Francisco 49ers | | | |
| ☐ 339 Floyd Little IA | 25.00 | 11.50 | 3.10 |
| Denver Broncos | | | |
| ☐ 340 Len Dawson IA | 40.00 | 18.00 | 5.00 |
| Kansas City Chiefs | | | |
| ☐ 341 Dick Butkus IA | 50.00 | 23.00 | 6.25 |
| Chicago Bears | | | |
| ☐ 342 Larry Brown IA | 25.00 | 11.50 | 3.10 |
| Washington Redskins | | | |
| ☐ 343 Joe Namath IA | 325.00 | 145.00 | 40.00 |
| New York Jets | | | |
| ☐ 344 Jim Turner IA | 22.00 | 10.00 | 2.80 |
| Denver Broncos | | | |
| ☐ 345 Doug Cunningham IA | 20.00 | 9.00 | 2.50 |
| San Francisco 49ers | | | |
| ☐ 346 Edd Hargett IA | 22.00 | 10.00 | 2.80 |
| New Orleans Saints | | | |
| ☐ 347 Steve Owens IA | 24.00 | 11.00 | 3.00 |
| Detroit Lions | | | |
| ☐ 348 George Blanda IA | 48.00 | 22.00 | 6.00 |
| Oakland Raiders | | | |
| ☐ 349 Ed Podolak IA | 22.00 | 10.00 | 2.80 |
| Kansas City Chiefs | | | |
| ☐ 350 Rich Jackson IA | 20.00 | 9.00 | 2.50 |
| Denver Broncos | | | |
| ☐ 351 Ken Willard IA | 35.00 | 9.00 | 2.50 |
| San Francisco 49ers | | | |

# 1973 Topps

The 1973 Topps football set marks the first of ten years in a row that Topps settled on a 528-card football set. This is Topps' first large football set which was not issued in series. The cards measure 2 1/2" by 3 1/2". The first six cards in the set are statistical league leader cards. Cards 133-139 show the results of the previous season's playoff games. Cards 265-267 are Kid Pictures (KP) showing the player in a boyhood photo. No known scarcities exist. The card backs are printed in blue ink with a red background on gray card stock. The bottom portion of each card back gives a cartoon and trivia question; the question's answer is given upside down. The key Rookie Cards in this set are Ken Anderson, Dan Dierdorf, Jack Ham, Franco Harris, Jim Langer, Art Shell, Ken Stabler, and Jack Youngblood.

| | NRMT | VG-E | GOOD |
|---|---|---|---|
| COMPLETE SET (528) | 425.00 | 190.00 | 52.50 |
| COMMON PLAYER (1-528) | .50 | .23 | .06 |
| ☐ 1 Rushing Leaders | 7.00 | 1.40 | .40 |
| Larry Brown | | | |
| O.J. Simpson | | | |
| ☐ 2 Passing Leaders | 1.00 | .45 | .13 |
| Norm Snead | | | |
| Earl Morrall | | | |
| ☐ 3 Receiving Leaders UER | 1.00 | .45 | .13 |
| Harold Jackson | | | |
| Fred Biletnikoff | | | |
| (Charley Taylor mis- spelled as Charlie) | | | |
| ☐ 4 Scoring Leaders | .75 | .35 | .09 |
| Chester Marcol | | | |
| Bobby Howfield | | | |
| ☐ 5 Interception Leaders | .75 | .35 | .09 |
| Bill Bradley | | | |
| Mike Sensibaugh | | | |
| ☐ 6 Punting Leaders | .75 | .35 | .09 |
| Dave Chapple | | | |
| Jerrel Wilson | | | |
| ☐ 7 Bob Trumpy | 1.25 | .55 | .16 |
| Cincinnati Bengals | | | |
| ☐ 8 Mel Tom | .50 | .23 | .06 |
| Philadelphia Eagles | | | |
| ☐ 9 Clarence Ellis | .50 | .23 | .06 |
| Atlanta Falcons | | | |
| ☐ 10 John Niland | .60 | .25 | .08 |

| | | |
|---|---|---|
| Dallas Cowboys | | |
| ☐ 11 Randy Jackson ....... .50 | .23 | .06 |
| San Francisco 49ers | | |
| ☐ 12 Greg Landry ....... 1.00 | .45 | .13 |
| Detroit Lions | | |
| ☐ 13 Cid Edwards ....... .50 | .23 | .06 |
| San Diego Chargers | | |
| ☐ 14 Phil Olsen ....... .50 | .23 | .06 |
| Los Angeles Rams | | |
| ☐ 15 Terry Bradshaw ....... 20.00 | 9.00 | 2.50 |
| Pittsburgh Steelers | | |
| ☐ 16 Al Cowlings ....... 2.50 | 1.15 | .30 |
| Buffalo Bills | | |
| ☐ 17 Walker Gillette ....... .60 | .25 | .08 |
| St. Louis Cardinals | | |
| ☐ 18 Bob Atkins ....... .50 | .23 | .06 |
| Houston Oilers | | |
| ☐ 19 Diron Talbert ....... 1.00 | .45 | .13 |
| Washington Redskins | | |
| ☐ 20 Jim Johnson ....... 1.25 | .55 | .16 |
| San Francisco 49ers | | |
| ☐ 21 Howard Twilley ....... .60 | .25 | .08 |
| Miami Dolphins | | |
| ☐ 22 Dick Enderle ....... .50 | .23 | .06 |
| New York Giants | | |
| ☐ 23 Wayne Colman ....... .50 | .23 | .06 |
| New Orleans Saints | | |
| ☐ 24 John Schmitt ....... .50 | .23 | .06 |
| New York Jets | | |
| ☐ 25 George Blanda ....... 8.00 | 3.60 | 1.00 |
| Oakland Raiders | | |
| ☐ 26 Milt Morin ....... .50 | .23 | .06 |
| Cleveland Browns | | |
| ☐ 27 Mike Current ....... .50 | .23 | .06 |
| Denver Broncos | | |
| ☐ 28 Rex Kern ....... .60 | .25 | .08 |
| Baltimore Colts | | |
| ☐ 29 MacArthur Lane ....... .60 | .25 | .08 |
| Green Bay Packers | | |
| ☐ 30 Alan Page ....... 3.00 | 1.35 | .40 |
| Minnesota Vikings | | |
| ☐ 31 Randy Vataha ....... .60 | .25 | .08 |
| New England Patriots | | |
| ☐ 32 Jim Kearney ....... .50 | .23 | .06 |
| Kansas City Chiefs | | |
| ☐ 33 Steve Smith ....... .50 | .23 | .06 |
| Philadelphia Eagles | | |
| ☐ 34 Ken Anderson ....... 25.00 | 11.50 | 3.10 |
| Cincinnati Bengals | | |
| ☐ 35 Calvin Hill ....... 1.00 | .45 | .13 |
| Dallas Cowboys | | |
| ☐ 36 Andy Maurer ....... .50 | .23 | .06 |
| Atlanta Falcons | | |
| ☐ 37 Joe Taylor ....... .50 | .23 | .06 |
| Chicago Bears | | |
| ☐ 38 Deacon Jones ....... 2.00 | .90 | .25 |
| San Diego Chargers | | |
| ☐ 39 Mike Weger ....... .50 | .23 | .06 |
| Detroit Lions | | |
| ☐ 40 Roy Gerela ....... .60 | .25 | .08 |
| Pittsburgh Steelers | | |
| ☐ 41 Les Josephson ....... .60 | .25 | .08 |
| Los Angeles Rams | | |
| ☐ 42 Dave Washington ....... .50 | .23 | .06 |
| Buffalo Bills | | |
| ☐ 43 Bill Curry ....... 1.00 | .45 | .13 |
| Houston Oilers | | |
| ☐ 44 Fred Heron ....... .50 | .23 | .06 |
| St. Louis Cardinals | | |
| ☐ 45 John Brodie ....... 4.00 | 1.80 | .50 |
| San Francisco 49ers | | |
| ☐ 46 Roy Winston ....... .50 | .23 | .06 |
| Minnesota Vikings | | |
| ☐ 47 Mike Bragg ....... .50 | .23 | .06 |
| Washington Redskins | | |
| ☐ 48 Mercury Morris ....... 1.50 | .65 | .19 |
| Miami Dolphins | | |
| ☐ 49 Jim Files ....... .50 | .23 | .06 |
| New York Giants | | |
| ☐ 50 Gene Upshaw ....... 3.50 | 1.55 | .45 |
| Oakland Raiders | | |
| ☐ 51 Hugo Hollas ....... .50 | .23 | .06 |
| New Orleans Saints | | |
| ☐ 52 Rod Sherman ....... .50 | .23 | .06 |
| Denver Broncos | | |
| ☐ 53 Ron Snidow ....... .50 | .23 | .06 |
| Cleveland Browns | | |
| ☐ 54 Steve Tannen ....... .50 | .23 | .06 |
| New York Jets | | |
| ☐ 55 Jim Carter ....... .50 | .23 | .06 |
| Green Bay Packers | | |
| ☐ 56 Lydell Mitchell ....... 3.00 | 1.35 | .40 |
| Baltimore Colts | | |
| ☐ 57 Jack Rudnay ....... .60 | .25 | .08 |
| Kansas City Chiefs | | |
| ☐ 58 Halvor Hagen ....... .50 | .23 | .06 |
| New England Patriots | | |
| ☐ 59 Tom Dempsey ....... .60 | .25 | .08 |

| | | |
|---|---|---|
| Philadelphia Eagles | | |
| ☐ 60 Fran Tarkenton ....... 15.00 | 6.75 | 1.90 |
| Minnesota Vikings | | |
| ☐ 61 Lance Alworth ....... 4.00 | 1.80 | .50 |
| Dallas Cowboys | | |
| ☐ 62 Vern Holland ....... .50 | .23 | .06 |
| Cincinnati Bengals | | |
| ☐ 63 Steve DeLong ....... .50 | .23 | .06 |
| Chicago Bears | | |
| ☐ 64 Art Malone ....... .50 | .23 | .06 |
| Atlanta Falcons | | |
| ☐ 65 Isiah Robertson ....... .60 | .25 | .08 |
| Los Angeles Rams | | |
| ☐ 66 Jerry Rush ....... .50 | .23 | .06 |
| Detroit Lions | | |
| ☐ 67 Bryant Salter ....... .50 | .23 | .06 |
| San Diego Chargers | | |
| ☐ 68 Checklist 1-132 ....... 4.50 | .45 | .14 |
| ☐ 69 J.D. Hill ....... .60 | .25 | .08 |
| Buffalo Bills | | |
| ☐ 70 Forrest Blue ....... .60 | .25 | .08 |
| San Francisco 49ers | | |
| ☐ 71 Myron Pottios ....... .60 | .25 | .08 |
| Washington Redskins | | |
| ☐ 72 Norm Thompson ....... .60 | .25 | .08 |
| St. Louis Cardinals | | |
| ☐ 73 Paul Robinson ....... .60 | .25 | .08 |
| Houston Oilers | | |
| ☐ 74 Larry Grantham ....... .60 | .25 | .08 |
| New York Jets | | |
| ☐ 75 Manny Fernandez ....... .60 | .25 | .08 |
| Miami Dolphins | | |
| ☐ 76 Kent Nix ....... .50 | .23 | .06 |
| New Orleans Saints | | |
| ☐ 77 Art Shell ....... 24.00 | 11.00 | 3.00 |
| Oakland Raiders | | |
| ☐ 78 George Saimes ....... .60 | .25 | .08 |
| Denver Broncos | | |
| ☐ 79 Don Cockroft ....... .60 | .25 | .08 |
| Cleveland Browns | | |
| ☐ 80 Bob Tucker ....... .60 | .25 | .08 |
| New York Giants | | |
| ☐ 81 Don McCauley ....... .75 | .35 | .09 |
| Baltimore Colts | | |
| ☐ 82 Bob Brown ....... .50 | .23 | .06 |
| Green Bay Packers | | |
| ☐ 83 Larry Carwell ....... .50 | .23 | .06 |
| New England Patriots | | |
| ☐ 84 Mo Moorman ....... .50 | .23 | .06 |
| Kansas City Chiefs | | |
| ☐ 85 John Gilliam ....... .60 | .25 | .08 |
| Minnesota Vikings | | |
| ☐ 86 Wade Key ....... .50 | .23 | .06 |
| Philadelphia Eagles | | |
| ☐ 87 Ross Brupbacher ....... .50 | .23 | .06 |
| Chicago Bears | | |
| ☐ 88 Dave Lewis ....... .50 | .23 | .06 |
| Cincinnati Bengals | | |
| ☐ 89 Franco Harris ....... 60.00 | 27.00 | 7.50 |
| Pittsburgh Steelers | | |
| ☐ 90 Tom Mack ....... .75 | .35 | .09 |
| Los Angeles Rams | | |
| ☐ 91 Mike Tilleman ....... .50 | .23 | .06 |
| Atlanta Falcons | | |
| ☐ 92 Carl Mauck ....... .50 | .23 | .06 |
| San Diego Chargers | | |
| ☐ 93 Larry Hand ....... .50 | .23 | .06 |
| Detroit Lions | | |
| ☐ 94 Dave Foley ....... .50 | .23 | .06 |
| Buffalo Bills | | |
| ☐ 95 Frank Nunley ....... .50 | .23 | .06 |
| San Francisco 49ers | | |
| ☐ 96 John Charles ....... .50 | .23 | .06 |
| Houston Oilers | | |
| ☐ 97 Jim Bakken ....... .60 | .25 | .08 |
| St. Louis Cardinals | | |
| ☐ 98 Pat Fischer ....... .60 | .25 | .08 |
| Washington Redskins | | |
| ☐ 99 Randy Rasmussen ....... .50 | .23 | .06 |
| New York Jets | | |
| ☐ 100 Larry Csonka ....... 5.00 | 2.30 | .60 |
| Miami Dolphins | | |
| ☐ 101 Mike Siani ....... .75 | .35 | .09 |
| Oakland Raiders | | |
| ☐ 102 Tom Roussel ....... .50 | .23 | .06 |
| New Orleans Saints | | |
| ☐ 103 Clarence Scott ....... .75 | .35 | .09 |
| Cleveland Browns | | |
| ☐ 104 Charlie Johnson ....... .60 | .25 | .08 |
| Denver Broncos | | |
| ☐ 105 Rick Volk ....... .50 | .23 | .06 |
| Baltimore Colts | | |
| ☐ 106 Willie Young ....... .50 | .23 | .06 |
| New York Giants | | |
| ☐ 107 Emmitt Thomas ....... .60 | .25 | .08 |
| Kansas City Chiefs | | |
| ☐ 108 Jon Morris ....... .50 | .23 | .06 |
| New England Patriots | | |

| | | | |
|---|---|---|---|
| ☐ 109 Clarence Williams | .50 | .23 | .06 |
| Green Bay Packers | | | |
| ☐ 110 Rayfield Wright | .50 | .23 | .06 |
| Dallas Cowboys | | | |
| ☐ 111 Norm Bulaich | .60 | .25 | .08 |
| Philadelphia Eagles | | | |
| ☐ 112 Mike Eischeid | .50 | .23 | .06 |
| Minnesota Vikings | | | |
| ☐ 113 Speedy Thomas | .50 | .23 | .06 |
| Cincinnati Bengals | | | |
| ☐ 114 Glen Holloway | .50 | .23 | .06 |
| Chicago Bears | | | |
| ☐ 115 Jack Ham | 25.00 | 11.50 | 3.10 |
| Pittsburgh Steelers | | | |
| ☐ 116 Jim Nettles | .50 | .23 | .06 |
| Los Angeles Rams | | | |
| ☐ 117 Errol Mann | .50 | .23 | .06 |
| Detroit Lions | | | |
| ☐ 118 John Mackey | 1.75 | .80 | .22 |
| San Diego Chargers | | | |
| ☐ 119 George Kunz | .60 | .25 | .08 |
| Atlanta Falcons | | | |
| ☐ 120 Bob James | .50 | .23 | .06 |
| Buffalo Bills | | | |
| ☐ 121 Garland Boyette | .50 | .23 | .06 |
| Houston Oilers | | | |
| ☐ 122 Mel Phillips | .50 | .23 | .06 |
| San Francisco 49ers | | | |
| ☐ 123 Johnny Roland | .50 | .23 | .06 |
| St. Louis Cardinals | | | |
| ☐ 124 Doug Swift | .60 | .25 | .08 |
| Miami Dolphins | | | |
| ☐ 125 Archie Manning | 3.00 | 1.35 | .40 |
| New Orleans Saints | | | |
| ☐ 126 Dave Herman | .50 | .23 | .06 |
| New York Jets | | | |
| ☐ 127 Carleton Oats | .50 | .23 | .06 |
| Oakland Raiders | | | |
| ☐ 128 Bill Van Heusen | .50 | .23 | .06 |
| Denver Broncos | | | |
| ☐ 129 Rich Jackson | .50 | .23 | .06 |
| Cleveland Browns | | | |
| ☐ 130 Len Hauss | .60 | .25 | .08 |
| Washington Redskins | | | |
| ☐ 131 Billy Parks | .75 | .35 | .09 |
| Dallas Cowboys | | | |
| ☐ 132 Ray May | .50 | .23 | .06 |
| Baltimore Colts | | | |
| ☐ 133 NFC Semi-Final | 3.50 | 1.55 | .45 |
| Cowboys 30, | | | |
| 49ers 28 | | | |
| (Roger Staubach | | | |
| dropping back) | | | |
| ☐ 134 AFC Semi-Final | .75 | .35 | .09 |
| Steelers 13, | | | |
| Raiders 7 | | | |
| (line play) | | | |
| ☐ 135 NFC Semi-Final | .75 | .35 | .09 |
| Redskins 16, | | | |
| Packers 3 | | | |
| (Redskins defense) | | | |
| ☐ 136 AFC Semi-Final | 2.00 | .90 | .25 |
| Dolphins 20, | | | |
| Browns 14 | | | |
| (Bob Griese | | | |
| handing off to | | | |
| Larry Csonka) | | | |
| ☐ 137 NFC Title Game | 1.50 | .65 | .19 |
| Redskins 26, | | | |
| Cowboys 3 | | | |
| (Bill Kilmer | | | |
| handing off to | | | |
| Larry Brown) | | | |
| ☐ 138 AFC Title Game | .75 | .35 | .09 |
| Dolphins 21, | | | |
| Steelers 17 | | | |
| (Miami defense | | | |
| stops Fuqua) | | | |
| ☐ 139 Super Bowl | 1.50 | .65 | .19 |
| Dolphins 14, | | | |
| Redskins 7 | | | |
| (Miami defense) | | | |
| ☐ 140 Dwight White UER | 2.25 | 1.00 | .30 |
| Pittsburgh Steelers | | | |
| (College North Texas | | | |
| State, should be | | | |
| East Texas State) | | | |
| ☐ 141 Jim Marsalis | .50 | .23 | .06 |
| Kansas City Chiefs | | | |
| ☐ 142 Doug Van Horn | .50 | .23 | .06 |
| New York Giants | | | |
| ☐ 143 Al Matthews | .50 | .23 | .06 |
| Green Bay Packers | | | |
| ☐ 144 Bob Windsor | .50 | .23 | .06 |
| New England Patriots | | | |
| ☐ 145 Dave Hampton | .75 | .35 | .09 |
| Atlanta Falcons | | | |
| ☐ 146 Horst Muhlmann | .50 | .23 | .06 |
| Cincinnati Bengals | | | |
| ☐ 147 Wally Hilgenberg | 1.00 | .45 | .13 |
| Minnesota Vikings | | | |
| ☐ 148 Ron Smith | .50 | .23 | .06 |
| Chicago Bears | | | |
| ☐ 149 Coy Bacon | 1.25 | .55 | .16 |
| San Diego Chargers | | | |
| ☐ 150 Winston Hill | .60 | .25 | .08 |
| New York Jets | | | |
| ☐ 151 Ron Jessie | 1.25 | .55 | .16 |
| Detroit Lions | | | |
| ☐ 152 Ken Iman | .50 | .23 | .06 |
| Los Angeles Rams | | | |
| ☐ 153 Ron Saul | .50 | .23 | .06 |
| Houston Oilers | | | |
| ☐ 154 Jim Braxton | 1.00 | .45 | .13 |
| Buffalo Bills | | | |
| ☐ 155 Bubba Smith | 3.00 | 1.35 | .40 |
| Baltimore Colts | | | |
| ☐ 156 Gary Cuozzo | .60 | .25 | .08 |
| St. Louis Cardinals | | | |
| ☐ 157 Charlie Krueger | .60 | .25 | .08 |
| San Francisco 49ers | | | |
| ☐ 158 Tim Foley | .75 | .35 | .09 |
| Miami Dolphins | | | |
| ☐ 159 Lee Roy Jordan | 2.00 | .90 | .25 |
| Dallas Cowboys | | | |
| ☐ 160 Bob Brown | .60 | .25 | .08 |
| Oakland Raiders | | | |
| ☐ 161 Margene Adkins | .50 | .23 | .06 |
| New Orleans Saints | | | |
| ☐ 162 Ron Widby | .60 | .25 | .08 |
| Green Bay Packers | | | |
| ☐ 163 Jim Houston | .60 | .25 | .08 |
| Cleveland Browns | | | |
| ☐ 164 Joe Dawkins | .50 | .23 | .06 |
| Denver Broncos | | | |
| ☐ 165 L.C. Greenwood | 4.00 | 1.80 | .50 |
| Pittsburgh Steelers | | | |
| ☐ 166 Richmond Flowers | .50 | .23 | .06 |
| New York Giants | | | |
| ☐ 167 Curley Culp | 2.00 | .90 | .25 |
| Kansas City Chiefs | | | |
| ☐ 168 Len St. Jean | .50 | .23 | .06 |
| New England Patriots | | | |
| ☐ 169 Walter Rock | .50 | .23 | .06 |
| Washington Redskins | | | |
| ☐ 170 Bill Bradley | .60 | .25 | .08 |
| Philadelphia Eagles | | | |
| ☐ 171 Ken Riley | 2.50 | 1.15 | .30 |
| Cincinnati Bengals | | | |
| ☐ 172 Rich Coady | .50 | .23 | .06 |
| Chicago Bears | | | |
| ☐ 173 Don Hansen | .50 | .23 | .06 |
| Atlanta Falcons | | | |
| ☐ 174 Lionel Aldridge | .50 | .23 | .06 |
| San Diego Chargers | | | |
| ☐ 175 Don Maynard | 3.00 | 1.35 | .40 |
| New York Jets | | | |
| ☐ 176 Dave Osborn | .60 | .25 | .08 |
| Minnesota Vikings | | | |
| ☐ 177 Jim Bailey | .50 | .23 | .06 |
| Baltimore Colts | | | |
| ☐ 178 John Pitts | .50 | .23 | .06 |
| Buffalo Bills | | | |
| ☐ 179 Dave Parks | .60 | .25 | .08 |
| Houston Oilers | | | |
| ☐ 180 Chester Marcol | .75 | .35 | .09 |
| Green Bay Packers | | | |
| ☐ 181 Len Rohde | .50 | .23 | .06 |
| San Francisco 49ers | | | |
| ☐ 182 Jeff Staggs | .50 | .23 | .06 |
| St. Louis Cardinals | | | |
| ☐ 183 Gene Hickerson | .50 | .23 | .06 |
| Cleveland Browns | | | |
| ☐ 184 Charlie Evans | .50 | .23 | .06 |
| New York Giants | | | |
| ☐ 185 Mel Renfro | 1.00 | .45 | .13 |
| Dallas Cowboys | | | |
| ☐ 186 Marvin Upshaw | .50 | .23 | .06 |
| Kansas City Chiefs | | | |
| ☐ 187 George Atkinson | .60 | .25 | .08 |
| Oakland Raiders | | | |
| ☐ 188 Norm Evans | .60 | .25 | .08 |
| Miami Dolphins | | | |
| ☐ 189 Steve Ramsey | .60 | .25 | .08 |
| Denver Broncos | | | |
| ☐ 190 Dave Chapple | .50 | .23 | .06 |
| Los Angeles Rams | | | |
| ☐ 191 Gerry Mullins | .50 | .23 | .06 |
| Pittsburgh Steelers | | | |
| ☐ 192 John Didion | .50 | .23 | .06 |
| New Orleans Saints | | | |
| ☐ 193 Bob Gladieux | .50 | .23 | .06 |
| New England Patriots | | | |
| ☐ 194 Don Hultz | .50 | .23 | .06 |

| | | | |
|---|---|---|---|
| Philadelphia Eagles | | | |
| ☐ 195 Mike Lucci | .60 | .25 | .08 |
| Detroit Lions | | | |
| ☐ 196 John Wilbur | .50 | .23 | .06 |
| Washington Redskins | | | |
| ☐ 197 George Farmer | .50 | .23 | .06 |
| Chicago Bears | | | |
| ☐ 198 Tommy Casanova | 1.25 | .55 | .16 |
| Cincinnati Bengals | | | |
| ☐ 199 Russ Washington | .50 | .23 | .06 |
| San Diego Chargers | | | |
| ☐ 200 Claude Humphrey | .60 | .25 | .08 |
| Atlanta Falcons | | | |
| ☐ 201 Pat Hughes | .50 | .23 | .06 |
| New York Giants | | | |
| ☐ 202 Zeke Moore | .50 | .23 | .06 |
| Houston Oilers | | | |
| ☐ 203 Chip Glass | .50 | .23 | .06 |
| Cleveland Browns | | | |
| ☐ 204 Glenn Ressler | .50 | .23 | .06 |
| Baltimore Colts | | | |
| ☐ 205 Willie Ellison | .60 | .25 | .08 |
| Kansas City Chiefs | | | |
| ☐ 206 John Leypoldt | .50 | .23 | .06 |
| Buffalo Bills | | | |
| ☐ 207 Johnny Fuller | .50 | .23 | .06 |
| San Francisco 49ers | | | |
| ☐ 208 Bill Hayhoe | .50 | .23 | .06 |
| Green Bay Packers | | | |
| ☐ 209 Ed Bell | .50 | .23 | .06 |
| New York Jets | | | |
| ☐ 210 Willie Brown | 1.75 | .80 | .22 |
| Oakland Raiders | | | |
| ☐ 211 Carl Eller | 1.00 | .45 | .13 |
| Minnesota Vikings | | | |
| ☐ 212 Mark Nordquist | .50 | .23 | .06 |
| Philadelphia Eagles | | | |
| ☐ 213 Larry Willingham | .50 | .23 | .06 |
| St. Louis Cardinals | | | |
| ☐ 214 Nick Buoniconti | 1.25 | .55 | .16 |
| Miami Dolphins | | | |
| ☐ 215 John Hadl | 1.00 | .45 | .13 |
| Los Angeles Rams | | | |
| ☐ 216 Jethro Pugh | 1.25 | .55 | .16 |
| Dallas Cowboys | | | |
| ☐ 217 Leroy Mitchell | .50 | .23 | .06 |
| Denver Broncos | | | |
| ☐ 218 Billy Newsome | .50 | .23 | .06 |
| New Orleans Saints | | | |
| ☐ 219 John McMakin | .50 | .23 | .06 |
| Pittsburgh Steelers | | | |
| ☐ 220 Larry Brown | 1.25 | .55 | .16 |
| Washington Redskins | | | |
| ☐ 221 Clarence Scott | .50 | .23 | .06 |
| New England Patriots | | | |
| ☐ 222 Paul Naumoff | .50 | .23 | .06 |
| Detroit Lions | | | |
| ☐ 223 Ted Fritsch Jr. | .60 | .25 | .08 |
| Atlanta Falcons | | | |
| ☐ 224 Checklist 133-264 | 4.50 | .45 | .14 |
| ☐ 225 Dan Pastorini | 1.00 | .45 | .13 |
| Houston Oilers | | | |
| ☐ 226 Joe Beauchamp UER | .50 | .23 | .06 |
| (Safety on front, Cornerback on back) | | | |
| San Diego Chargers | | | |
| ☐ 227 Pat Matson | .50 | .23 | .06 |
| Cincinnati Bengals | | | |
| ☐ 228 Tony McGee | .50 | .23 | .06 |
| Chicago Bears | | | |
| ☐ 229 Mike Phipps | .60 | .25 | .08 |
| Cleveland Browns | | | |
| ☐ 230 Harold Jackson | 1.25 | .55 | .16 |
| Philadelphia Eagles | | | |
| ☐ 231 Willie Williams | .50 | .23 | .06 |
| New York Giants | | | |
| ☐ 232 Spike Jones | .50 | .23 | .06 |
| Buffalo Bills | | | |
| ☐ 233 Jim Tyrer | .60 | .25 | .08 |
| Kansas City Chiefs | | | |
| ☐ 234 Roy Hilton | .50 | .23 | .06 |
| Baltimore Colts | | | |
| ☐ 235 Phil Villapiano | .60 | .25 | .08 |
| Oakland Raiders | | | |
| ☐ 236 Charley Taylor UER | 4.00 | 1.80 | .50 |
| (Misspelled Charlie on both sides) | | | |
| Washington Redskins | | | |
| ☐ 237 Malcolm Snider | .50 | .23 | .06 |
| Green Bay Packers | | | |
| ☐ 238 Vic Washington | .60 | .25 | .08 |
| San Francisco 49ers | | | |
| ☐ 239 Grady Alderman | .50 | .23 | .06 |
| Minnesota Vikings | | | |
| ☐ 240 Dick Anderson | .75 | .35 | .09 |
| Miami Dolphins | | | |
| ☐ 241 Ron Yankowski | .50 | .23 | .06 |
| St. Louis Cardinals | | | |

| | | | |
|---|---|---|---|
| ☐ 242 Billy Masters | .50 | .23 | .06 |
| Denver Broncos | | | |
| ☐ 243 Herb Adderley | 2.00 | .90 | .25 |
| Dallas Cowboys | | | |
| ☐ 244 David Ray | .50 | .23 | .06 |
| Los Angeles Rams | | | |
| ☐ 245 John Riggins | 8.00 | 3.60 | 1.00 |
| New York Jets | | | |
| ☐ 246 Mike Wagner | 1.75 | .80 | .22 |
| Pittsburgh Steelers | | | |
| ☐ 247 Don Morrison | .50 | .23 | .06 |
| New Orleans Saints | | | |
| ☐ 248 Earl McCullouch | .60 | .25 | .08 |
| Detroit Lions | | | |
| ☐ 249 Dennis Wirgowski | .50 | .23 | .06 |
| New England Patriots | | | |
| ☐ 250 Chris Hanburger | .60 | .25 | .08 |
| Washington Redskins | | | |
| ☐ 251 Pat Sullivan | 2.00 | .90 | .25 |
| Atlanta Falcons | | | |
| ☐ 252 Walt Sweeney | .60 | .25 | .08 |
| San Diego Chargers | | | |
| ☐ 253 Willie Alexander | .50 | .23 | .06 |
| Houston Oilers | | | |
| ☐ 254 Doug Dressler | .50 | .23 | .06 |
| Cincinnati Bengals | | | |
| ☐ 255 Walter Johnson | .50 | .23 | .06 |
| Cleveland Browns | | | |
| ☐ 256 Ron Hornsby | .50 | .23 | .06 |
| New York Giants | | | |
| ☐ 257 Ben Hawkins | .50 | .23 | .06 |
| Philadelphia Eagles | | | |
| ☐ 258 Donnie Green | .50 | .23 | .06 |
| Buffalo Bills | | | |
| ☐ 259 Fred Hoaglin | .50 | .23 | .06 |
| Baltimore Colts | | | |
| ☐ 260 Jerrel Wilson | .50 | .23 | .06 |
| Kansas City Chiefs | | | |
| ☐ 261 Horace Jones | .50 | .23 | .06 |
| Oakland Raiders | | | |
| ☐ 262 Woody Peoples | .50 | .23 | .06 |
| San Francisco 49ers | | | |
| ☐ 263 Jim Hill | .75 | .35 | .09 |
| Green Bay Packers | | | |
| ☐ 264 John Fuqua | .60 | .25 | .08 |
| Pittsburgh Steelers | | | |
| ☐ 265 Donny Anderson KP | .50 | .23 | .06 |
| St. Louis Cardinals | | | |
| ☐ 266 Roman Gabriel KP | .75 | .35 | .09 |
| Philadelphia Eagles | | | |
| ☐ 267 Mike Garrett KP | .50 | .23 | .06 |
| San Diego Chargers | | | |
| ☐ 268 Rufus Mayes | .60 | .25 | .08 |
| Cincinnati Bengals | | | |
| ☐ 269 Chip Myrtle | .50 | .23 | .06 |
| Denver Broncos | | | |
| ☐ 270 Bill Stanfill | 1.00 | .45 | .13 |
| Miami Dolphins | | | |
| ☐ 271 Clint Jones | .50 | .23 | .06 |
| Minnesota Vikings | | | |
| ☐ 272 Miller Farr | .50 | .23 | .06 |
| St. Louis Cardinals | | | |
| ☐ 273 Harry Schuh | .50 | .23 | .06 |
| Los Angeles Rams | | | |
| ☐ 274 Bob Hayes | 1.00 | .45 | .13 |
| Dallas Cowboys | | | |
| ☐ 275 Bobby Douglass | .60 | .25 | .08 |
| Chicago Bears | | | |
| ☐ 276 Gus Hollomon | .50 | .23 | .06 |
| New York Jets | | | |
| ☐ 277 Del Williams | .50 | .23 | .06 |
| New Orleans Saints | | | |
| ☐ 278 Julius Adams | .60 | .25 | .08 |
| New England Patriots | | | |
| ☐ 279 Herman Weaver | .50 | .23 | .06 |
| Detroit Lions | | | |
| ☐ 280 Joe Greene | 6.00 | 2.70 | .75 |
| Pittsburgh Steelers | | | |
| ☐ 281 Wes Chesson | .50 | .23 | .06 |
| Atlanta Falcons | | | |
| ☐ 282 Charlie Harraway | .50 | .23 | .06 |
| Washington Redskins | | | |
| ☐ 283 Paul Guidry | .50 | .23 | .06 |
| Houston Oilers | | | |
| ☐ 284 Terry Owens | .60 | .25 | .08 |
| San Diego Chargers | | | |
| ☐ 285 Jan Stenerud | 1.25 | .55 | .16 |
| Kansas City Chiefs | | | |
| ☐ 286 Pete Athas | .50 | .23 | .06 |
| New York Giants | | | |
| ☐ 287 Dale Lindsey | .50 | .23 | .06 |
| Cleveland Browns | | | |
| ☐ 288 Jack Tatum | 7.00 | 3.10 | .85 |
| Oakland Raiders | | | |
| ☐ 289 Floyd Little | 1.75 | .80 | .22 |
| Denver Broncos | | | |
| ☐ 290 Bob Johnson | .50 | .23 | .06 |

| | | | |
|---|---|---|---|
| Cincinnati Bengals | | | |
| ☐ 291 Tommy Hart | .50 | .23 | .06 |
| San Francisco 49ers | | | |
| ☐ 292 Tom Mitchell | .50 | .23 | .06 |
| Baltimore Colts | | | |
| ☐ 293 Walt Patulski | .75 | .35 | .09 |
| Buffalo Bills | | | |
| ☐ 294 Jim Skaggs | .50 | .23 | .06 |
| Philadelphia Eagles | | | |
| ☐ 295 Bob Griese | 7.00 | 3.10 | .85 |
| Miami Dolphins | | | |
| ☐ 296 Mike McCoy | .50 | .23 | .06 |
| Green Bay Packers | | | |
| ☐ 297 Mel Gray | 1.00 | .45 | .13 |
| St. Louis Cardinals | | | |
| ☐ 298 Bobby Bryant | .50 | .23 | .06 |
| Minnesota Vikings | | | |
| ☐ 299 Blaine Nye | .60 | .25 | .08 |
| Dallas Cowboys | | | |
| ☐ 300 Dick Butkus | 6.50 | 2.90 | .80 |
| Chicago Bears | | | |
| ☐ 301 Charlie Cowan | .50 | .23 | .06 |
| Los Angeles Rams | | | |
| ☐ 302 Mark Lomas | .50 | .23 | .06 |
| New York Jets | | | |
| ☐ 303 Josh Ashton | .50 | .23 | .06 |
| New England Patriots | | | |
| ☐ 304 Happy Feller | .50 | .23 | .06 |
| New Orleans Saints | | | |
| ☐ 305 Ron Shanklin | .50 | .23 | .06 |
| Pittsburgh Steelers | | | |
| ☐ 306 Wayne Rasmussen | .50 | .23 | .06 |
| Detroit Lions | | | |
| ☐ 307 Jerry Smith | .60 | .25 | .08 |
| Washington Redskins | | | |
| ☐ 308 Ken Reaves | .50 | .23 | .06 |
| Atlanta Falcons | | | |
| ☐ 309 Ron East | .50 | .23 | .06 |
| San Diego Chargers | | | |
| ☐ 310 Otis Taylor | .75 | .35 | .09 |
| Kansas City Chiefs | | | |
| ☐ 311 John Garlington | .50 | .23 | .06 |
| Cleveland Browns | | | |
| ☐ 312 Lyle Alzado | 3.50 | 1.55 | .45 |
| Denver Broncos | | | |
| ☐ 313 Remi Prudhomme | .50 | .23 | .06 |
| Buffalo Bills | | | |
| ☐ 314 Cornelius Johnson | .50 | .23 | .06 |
| Baltimore Colts | | | |
| ☐ 315 Lemar Parrish | .60 | .25 | .08 |
| Cincinnati Bengals | | | |
| ☐ 316 Jim Kiick | .75 | .35 | .09 |
| Miami Dolphins | | | |
| ☐ 317 Steve Zabel | .50 | .23 | .06 |
| Philadelphia Eagles | | | |
| ☐ 318 Alden Roche | .50 | .23 | .06 |
| Green Bay Packers | | | |
| ☐ 319 Tom Blanchard | .50 | .23 | .06 |
| New York Giants | | | |
| ☐ 320 Fred Biletnikoff | 4.00 | 1.80 | .50 |
| Oakland Raiders | | | |
| ☐ 321 Ralph Neely | .60 | .25 | .08 |
| Dallas Cowboys | | | |
| ☐ 322 Dan Dierdorf | 20.00 | 9.00 | 2.50 |
| St. Louis Cardinals | | | |
| ☐ 323 Richard Caster | .60 | .25 | .08 |
| New York Jets | | | |
| ☐ 324 Gene Howard | .50 | .23 | .06 |
| Los Angeles Rams | | | |
| ☐ 325 Elvin Bethea | .60 | .25 | .08 |
| Houston Oilers | | | |
| ☐ 326 Carl Garrett | .50 | .23 | .06 |
| Chicago Bears | | | |
| ☐ 327 Ron Billingsley | .50 | .23 | .06 |
| New Orleans Saints | | | |
| ☐ 328 Charlie West | .50 | .23 | .06 |
| Minnesota Vikings | | | |
| ☐ 329 Tom Neville | .50 | .23 | .06 |
| New England Patriots | | | |
| ☐ 330 Ted Kwalick | .60 | .25 | .08 |
| San Francisco 49ers | | | |
| ☐ 331 Rudy Redmond | .50 | .23 | .06 |
| Detroit Lions | | | |
| ☐ 332 Henry Davis | .50 | .23 | .06 |
| Pittsburgh Steelers | | | |
| ☐ 333 John Zook | .50 | .23 | .06 |
| Atlanta Falcons | | | |
| ☐ 334 Jim Turner | .60 | .25 | .08 |
| Denver Broncos | | | |
| ☐ 335 Len Dawson | 4.00 | 1.80 | .50 |
| Kansas City Chiefs | | | |
| ☐ 336 Bob Chandler | 1.25 | .55 | .16 |
| Buffalo Bills | | | |
| ☐ 337 Al Beauchamp | .50 | .23 | .06 |
| Cincinnati Bengals | | | |
| ☐ 338 Tom Matte | .60 | .25 | .08 |
| San Diego Chargers | | | |
| ☐ 339 Paul Laaveg | .50 | .23 | .06 |
| Washington Redskins | | | |
| ☐ 340 Ken Ellis | .50 | .23 | .06 |
| Green Bay Packers | | | |
| ☐ 341 Jim Langer | 14.00 | 6.25 | 1.75 |
| Miami Dolphins | | | |
| ☐ 342 Ron Porter | .50 | .23 | .06 |
| Philadelphia Eagles | | | |
| ☐ 343 Jack Youngblood | 15.00 | 6.75 | 1.90 |
| Los Angeles Rams | | | |
| ☐ 344 Cornell Green | .60 | .25 | .08 |
| Dallas Cowboys | | | |
| ☐ 345 Marv Hubbard | .60 | .25 | .08 |
| Oakland Raiders | | | |
| ☐ 346 Bruce Taylor | .60 | .25 | .08 |
| San Francisco 49ers | | | |
| ☐ 347 Sam Havrilak | .50 | .23 | .06 |
| Baltimore Colts | | | |
| ☐ 348 Walt Sumner | .50 | .23 | .06 |
| Cleveland Browns | | | |
| ☐ 349 Steve O'Neal | .50 | .23 | .06 |
| New York Jets | | | |
| ☐ 350 Ron Johnson | .60 | .25 | .08 |
| New York Giants | | | |
| ☐ 351 Rockne Freitas | .50 | .23 | .06 |
| Detroit Lions | | | |
| ☐ 352 Larry Stallings | .50 | .23 | .06 |
| St. Louis Cardinals | | | |
| ☐ 353 Jim Cadile | .50 | .23 | .06 |
| Chicago Bears | | | |
| ☐ 354 Ken Burrough | .60 | .25 | .08 |
| Houston Oilers | | | |
| ☐ 355 Jim Plunkett | 4.00 | 1.80 | .50 |
| New England Patriots | | | |
| ☐ 356 Dave Long | .50 | .23 | .06 |
| New Orleans Saints | | | |
| ☐ 357 Ralph Anderson | .50 | .23 | .06 |
| Pittsburgh Steelers | | | |
| ☐ 358 Checklist 265-396 | 4.50 | .45 | .14 |
| ☐ 359 Gene Washington | .60 | .25 | .08 |
| Minnesota Vikings | | | |
| ☐ 360 Dave Wilcox | .60 | .25 | .08 |
| San Francisco 49ers | | | |
| ☐ 361 Paul Smith | .60 | .25 | .08 |
| Denver Broncos | | | |
| ☐ 362 Alvin Wyatt | .50 | .23 | .06 |
| Buffalo Bills | | | |
| ☐ 363 Charlie Smith | .50 | .23 | .06 |
| Oakland Raiders | | | |
| ☐ 364 Royce Berry | .50 | .23 | .06 |
| Cincinnati Bengals | | | |
| ☐ 365 Dave Elmendorf | .60 | .25 | .08 |
| Los Angeles Rams | | | |
| ☐ 366 Scott Hunter | .60 | .25 | .08 |
| Green Bay Packers | | | |
| ☐ 367 Bob Kuechenberg | 3.50 | 1.55 | .45 |
| Miami Dolphins | | | |
| ☐ 368 Pete Gogolak | .60 | .25 | .08 |
| New York Giants | | | |
| ☐ 369 Dave Edwards | .50 | .23 | .06 |
| Dallas Cowboys | | | |
| ☐ 370 Lem Barney | 2.50 | 1.15 | .30 |
| Detroit Lions | | | |
| ☐ 371 Verlon Biggs | .50 | .23 | .06 |
| Washington Redskins | | | |
| ☐ 372 John Reaves | .60 | .25 | .08 |
| Philadelphia Eagles | | | |
| ☐ 373 Ed Podolak | .60 | .25 | .08 |
| Kansas City Chiefs | | | |
| ☐ 374 Chris Farasopoulos | .60 | .25 | .08 |
| New York Jets | | | |
| ☐ 375 Gary Garrison | .60 | .25 | .08 |
| San Diego Chargers | | | |
| ☐ 376 Tom Funchess | .50 | .23 | .06 |
| Houston Oilers | | | |
| ☐ 377 Bobby Joe Green | .50 | .23 | .06 |
| Chicago Bears | | | |
| ☐ 378 Don Brumm | .50 | .23 | .06 |
| St. Louis Cardinals | | | |
| ☐ 379 Jim O'Brien | .50 | .23 | .06 |
| Baltimore Colts | | | |
| ☐ 380 Paul Krause | 1.00 | .45 | .13 |
| Minnesota Vikings | | | |
| ☐ 381 Leroy Kelly | 1.75 | .80 | .22 |
| Cleveland Browns | | | |
| ☐ 382 Ray Mansfield | .50 | .23 | .06 |
| Pittsburgh Steelers | | | |
| ☐ 383 Dan Abramowicz | .60 | .25 | .08 |
| New Orleans Saints | | | |
| ☐ 384 John Outlaw | .60 | .25 | .08 |
| New England Patriots | | | |
| ☐ 385 Tommy Nobis | 1.25 | .55 | .16 |
| Atlanta Falcons | | | |
| ☐ 386 Tom Domres | .50 | .23 | .06 |
| Denver Broncos | | | |
| ☐ 387 Ken Willard | .60 | .25 | .08 |
| San Francisco 49ers | | | |
| ☐ 388 Mike Stratton | .50 | .23 | .06 |
| Buffalo Bills | | | |

| | | | | |
|---|---|---|---|---|
| ☐ 389 Fred Dryer | 3.00 | 1.35 | .40 |
| Los Angeles Rams | | | |
| ☐ 390 Jake Scott | .75 | .35 | .09 |
| Miami Dolphins | | | |
| ☐ 391 Rich Houston | .50 | .23 | .06 |
| New York Giants | | | |
| ☐ 392 Virgil Carter | .60 | .25 | .08 |
| Cincinnati Bengals | | | |
| ☐ 393 Tody Smith | .60 | .25 | .08 |
| Dallas Cowboys | | | |
| ☐ 394 Ernie Calloway | .50 | .23 | .06 |
| Philadelphia Eagles | | | |
| ☐ 395 Charlie Sanders | .60 | .25 | .08 |
| Detroit Lions | | | |
| ☐ 396 Fred Willis | .50 | .23 | .06 |
| Houston Oilers | | | |
| ☐ 397 Curt Knight | .50 | .23 | .06 |
| Washington Redskins | | | |
| ☐ 398 Nemiah Wilson | .50 | .23 | .06 |
| Oakland Raiders | | | |
| ☐ 399 Carroll Dale | .60 | .25 | .08 |
| Green Bay Packers | | | |
| ☐ 400 Joe Namath | 30.00 | 13.50 | 3.80 |
| New York Jets | | | |
| ☐ 401 Wayne Mulligan | .50 | .23 | .06 |
| St. Louis Cardinals | | | |
| ☐ 402 Jim Harrison | .50 | .23 | .06 |
| Chicago Bears | | | |
| ☐ 403 Tim Rossovich | .50 | .23 | .06 |
| San Diego Chargers | | | |
| ☐ 404 David Lee | .50 | .23 | .06 |
| Baltimore Colts | | | |
| ☐ 405 Frank Pitts | .50 | .23 | .06 |
| Cleveland Browns | | | |
| ☐ 406 Jim Marshall | 1.25 | .55 | .16 |
| Minnesota Vikings | | | |
| ☐ 407 Bob Brown | .50 | .23 | .06 |
| New Orleans Saints | | | |
| ☐ 408 John Rowser | .50 | .23 | .06 |
| Pittsburgh Steelers | | | |
| ☐ 409 Mike Montler | .50 | .23 | .06 |
| New England Patriots | | | |
| ☐ 410 Willie Lanier | 1.75 | .80 | .22 |
| Kansas City Chiefs | | | |
| ☐ 411 Bill Bell | .50 | .23 | .06 |
| Atlanta Falcons | | | |
| ☐ 412 Cedrick Hardman | .60 | .25 | .08 |
| San Francisco 49ers | | | |
| ☐ 413 Bob Anderson | .50 | .23 | .06 |
| Denver Broncos | | | |
| ☐ 414 Earl Morrall | 1.25 | .55 | .16 |
| Miami Dolphins | | | |
| ☐ 415 Ken Houston | 1.75 | .80 | .22 |
| Houston Oilers | | | |
| ☐ 416 Jack Snow | .60 | .25 | .08 |
| Los Angeles Rams | | | |
| ☐ 417 Dick Cunningham | .50 | .23 | .06 |
| Buffalo Bills | | | |
| ☐ 418 Greg Larson | .50 | .23 | .06 |
| New York Giants | | | |
| ☐ 419 Mike Bass | .60 | .25 | .08 |
| Washington Redskins | | | |
| ☐ 420 Mike Reid | 1.50 | .65 | .19 |
| Cincinnati Bengals | | | |
| ☐ 421 Walt Garrison | .60 | .25 | .08 |
| Dallas Cowboys | | | |
| ☐ 422 Pete Liske | .60 | .25 | .08 |
| Philadelphia Eagles | | | |
| ☐ 423 Jim Yarbrough | .50 | .23 | .06 |
| Detroit Lions | | | |
| ☐ 424 Rich McGeorge | .50 | .23 | .06 |
| Green Bay Packers | | | |
| ☐ 425 Bobby Howfield | .50 | .23 | .06 |
| New York Jets | | | |
| ☐ 426 Pete Banaszak | .60 | .25 | .08 |
| Oakland Raiders | | | |
| ☐ 427 Willie Holman | .50 | .23 | .06 |
| Chicago Bears | | | |
| ☐ 428 Dale Hackbart | .50 | .23 | .06 |
| St. Louis Cardinals | | | |
| ☐ 429 Fair Hooker | .50 | .23 | .06 |
| Cleveland Browns | | | |
| ☐ 430 Ted Hendricks | 4.00 | 1.80 | .50 |
| Baltimore Colts | | | |
| ☐ 431 Mike Garrett | .60 | .25 | .08 |
| San Diego Chargers | | | |
| ☐ 432 Glen Ray Hines | .50 | .23 | .06 |
| New Orleans Saints | | | |
| ☐ 433 Fred Cox | .60 | .25 | .08 |
| Minnesota Vikings | | | |
| ☐ 434 Bobby Walden | .50 | .23 | .06 |
| Pittsburgh Steelers | | | |
| ☐ 435 Bobby Bell | 1.75 | .80 | .22 |
| Kansas City Chiefs | | | |
| ☐ 436 Dave Rowe | .50 | .23 | .06 |
| New England Patriots | | | |
| ☐ 437 Bob Berry | .50 | .23 | .06 |

| | | | | |
|---|---|---|---|---|
| Atlanta Falcons | | | |
| ☐ 438 Bill Thompson | .60 | .25 | .08 |
| Denver Broncos | | | |
| ☐ 439 Jim Beirne | .50 | .23 | .06 |
| Houston Oilers | | | |
| ☐ 440 Larry Little | 3.00 | 1.35 | .40 |
| Miami Dolphins | | | |
| ☐ 441 Rocky Thompson | .50 | .23 | .06 |
| New York Giants | | | |
| ☐ 442 Brig Owens | .50 | .23 | .06 |
| Washington Redskins | | | |
| ☐ 443 Richard Neal | .50 | .23 | .06 |
| New York Jets | | | |
| ☐ 444 Al Nelson | .50 | .23 | .06 |
| Philadelphia Eagles | | | |
| ☐ 445 Chip Myers | .50 | .23 | .06 |
| Cincinnati Bengals | | | |
| ☐ 446 Ken Bowman | .50 | .23 | .06 |
| Green Bay Packers | | | |
| ☐ 447 Jim Purnell | .50 | .23 | .06 |
| Los Angeles Rams | | | |
| ☐ 448 Altie Taylor | .60 | .25 | .08 |
| Detroit Lions | | | |
| ☐ 449 Linzy Cole | .50 | .23 | .06 |
| Buffalo Bills | | | |
| ☐ 450 Bob Lilly | 3.50 | 1.55 | .45 |
| Dallas Cowboys | | | |
| ☐ 451 Charlie Ford | .50 | .23 | .06 |
| Chicago Bears | | | |
| ☐ 452 Milt Sunde | .50 | .23 | .06 |
| Minnesota Vikings | | | |
| ☐ 453 Doug Wyatt | .50 | .23 | .06 |
| New Orleans Saints | | | |
| ☐ 454 Don Nottingham | .75 | .35 | .09 |
| Baltimore Colts | | | |
| ☐ 455 John Unitas | 18.00 | 8.00 | 2.30 |
| San Diego Chargers | | | |
| ☐ 456 Frank Lewis | 1.25 | .55 | .16 |
| Pittsburgh Steelers | | | |
| ☐ 457 Roger Wehrli | .60 | .25 | .08 |
| St. Louis Cardinals | | | |
| ☐ 458 Jim Cheyunski | .50 | .23 | .06 |
| New England Patriots | | | |
| ☐ 459 Jerry Sherk | 1.00 | .45 | .13 |
| Cleveland Browns | | | |
| ☐ 460 Gene Washington | .50 | .23 | .06 |
| San Francisco 49ers | | | |
| ☐ 461 Jim Otto | 1.50 | .65 | .19 |
| Oakland Raiders | | | |
| ☐ 462 Ed Budde | .60 | .25 | .08 |
| Kansas City Chiefs | | | |
| ☐ 463 Jim Mitchell | .60 | .25 | .08 |
| Atlanta Falcons | | | |
| ☐ 464 Emerson Boozer | .60 | .25 | .08 |
| New York Jets | | | |
| ☐ 465 Garo Yepremian | .75 | .35 | .09 |
| Miami Dolphins | | | |
| ☐ 466 Pete Duranko | .50 | .23 | .06 |
| Denver Broncos | | | |
| ☐ 467 Charlie Joiner | 6.00 | 2.70 | .75 |
| Cincinnati Bengals | | | |
| ☐ 468 Spider Lockhart | .60 | .25 | .08 |
| New York Giants | | | |
| ☐ 469 Marty Domres | .60 | .25 | .08 |
| Baltimore Colts | | | |
| ☐ 470 John Brockington | 1.00 | .45 | .13 |
| Green Bay Packers | | | |
| ☐ 471 Ed Flanagan | .50 | .23 | .06 |
| Detroit Lions | | | |
| ☐ 472 Roy Jefferson | .60 | .25 | .08 |
| Washington Redskins | | | |
| ☐ 473 Julian Fagan | .50 | .23 | .06 |
| New Orleans Saints | | | |
| ☐ 474 Bill Brown | .60 | .25 | .08 |
| Minnesota Vikings | | | |
| ☐ 475 Roger Staubach | 40.00 | 18.00 | 5.00 |
| Dallas Cowboys | | | |
| ☐ 476 Jan White | .50 | .23 | .06 |
| Buffalo Bills | | | |
| ☐ 477 Pat Holmes | .50 | .23 | .06 |
| Houston Oilers | | | |
| ☐ 478 Bob DeMarco | .50 | .23 | .06 |
| Cleveland Browns | | | |
| ☐ 479 Merlin Olsen | 2.50 | 1.15 | .30 |
| Los Angeles Rams | | | |
| ☐ 480 Andy Russell | .60 | .25 | .08 |
| Pittsburgh Steelers | | | |
| ☐ 481 Steve Spurrier | 6.00 | 2.70 | .75 |
| San Francisco 49ers | | | |
| ☐ 482 Nate Ramsey | .50 | .23 | .06 |
| Philadelphia Eagles | | | |
| ☐ 483 Dennis Partee | .50 | .23 | .06 |
| San Diego Chargers | | | |
| ☐ 484 Jerry Simmons | .50 | .23 | .06 |
| Denver Broncos | | | |
| ☐ 485 Donny Anderson | .60 | .25 | .08 |
| St. Louis Cardinals | | | |
| ☐ 486 Ralph Baker | .50 | .23 | .06 |

New York Jets
| | | | |
|---|---|---|---|
| ☐ 487 Ken Stabler | 45.00 | 20.00 | 5.75 |

Oakland Raiders
| | | | |
|---|---|---|---|
| ☐ 488 Ernie McMillan | .50 | .23 | .06 |

St. Louis Cardinals
| | | | |
|---|---|---|---|
| ☐ 489 Ken Burrow | .50 | .23 | .06 |

Atlanta Falcons
| | | | |
|---|---|---|---|
| ☐ 490 Jack Gregory | .60 | .25 | .08 |

New York Giants
| | | | |
|---|---|---|---|
| ☐ 491 Larry Seiple | .60 | .25 | .08 |

Miami Dolphins
| | | | |
|---|---|---|---|
| ☐ 492 Mick Tingelhoff | .60 | .25 | .08 |

Minnesota Vikings
| | | | |
|---|---|---|---|
| ☐ 493 Craig Morton | 1.25 | .55 | .16 |

Dallas Cowboys
| | | | |
|---|---|---|---|
| ☐ 494 Cecil Turner | .50 | .23 | .06 |

Chicago Bears
| | | | |
|---|---|---|---|
| ☐ 495 Steve Owens | .60 | .25 | .08 |

Detroit Lions
| | | | |
|---|---|---|---|
| ☐ 496 Rickie Harris | .50 | .23 | .06 |

New England Patriots
| | | | |
|---|---|---|---|
| ☐ 497 Buck Buchanan | 1.50 | .65 | .19 |

Kansas City Chiefs
| | | | |
|---|---|---|---|
| ☐ 498 Checklist 397-528 | 4.50 | .45 | .14 |
| ☐ 499 Bill Kilmer | 1.00 | .45 | .13 |

Washington Redskins
| | | | |
|---|---|---|---|
| ☐ 500 O.J. Simpson | 30.00 | 13.50 | 3.80 |

Buffalo Bills
| | | | |
|---|---|---|---|
| ☐ 501 Bruce Gossett | .50 | .23 | .06 |

San Francisco 49ers
| | | | |
|---|---|---|---|
| ☐ 502 Art Thoms | .50 | .23 | .06 |

Oakland Raiders
| | | | |
|---|---|---|---|
| ☐ 503 Larry Kaminski | .50 | .23 | .06 |

Denver Broncos
| | | | |
|---|---|---|---|
| ☐ 504 Larry Smith | .50 | .23 | .06 |

Los Angeles Rams
| | | | |
|---|---|---|---|
| ☐ 505 Bruce Van Dyke | .50 | .23 | .06 |

Pittsburgh Steelers
| | | | |
|---|---|---|---|
| ☐ 506 Alvin Reed | .50 | .23 | .06 |

Houston Oilers
| | | | |
|---|---|---|---|
| ☐ 507 Delles Howell | .50 | .23 | .06 |

New York Jets
| | | | |
|---|---|---|---|
| ☐ 508 Leroy Keyes | .60 | .25 | .08 |

Philadelphia Eagles
| | | | |
|---|---|---|---|
| ☐ 509 Bo Scott | .60 | .25 | .08 |

Cleveland Browns
| | | | |
|---|---|---|---|
| ☐ 510 Ron Yary | 1.00 | .45 | .13 |

Minnesota Vikings
| | | | |
|---|---|---|---|
| ☐ 511 Paul Warfield | 4.50 | 2.00 | .55 |

Miami Dolphins
| | | | |
|---|---|---|---|
| ☐ 512 Mac Percival | .50 | .23 | .06 |

Chicago Bears
| | | | |
|---|---|---|---|
| ☐ 513 Essex Johnson | .50 | .23 | .06 |

Cincinnati Bengals
| | | | |
|---|---|---|---|
| ☐ 514 Jackie Smith | 1.00 | .45 | .13 |

St. Louis Cardinals
| | | | |
|---|---|---|---|
| ☐ 515 Norm Snead | .60 | .25 | .08 |

New York Giants
| | | | |
|---|---|---|---|
| ☐ 516 Charlie Stukes | .50 | .23 | .06 |

Baltimore Colts
| | | | |
|---|---|---|---|
| ☐ 517 Reggie Rucker | 1.50 | .65 | .19 |

New England Patriots
| | | | |
|---|---|---|---|
| ☐ 518 Bill Sandeman UER | .50 | .23 | .06 |

(Should be a period
between run and he
instead of a comma)
Atlanta Falcons
| | | | |
|---|---|---|---|
| ☐ 519 Mel Farr | .60 | .25 | .08 |

Detroit Lions
| | | | |
|---|---|---|---|
| ☐ 520 Raymond Chester | .60 | .25 | .08 |

Oakland Raiders
| | | | |
|---|---|---|---|
| ☐ 521 Fred Carr | 1.00 | .45 | .13 |

Green Bay Packers
| | | | |
|---|---|---|---|
| ☐ 522 Jerry LeVias | .60 | .25 | .08 |

San Diego Chargers
| | | | |
|---|---|---|---|
| ☐ 523 Jim Strong | .50 | .23 | .06 |

New Orleans Saints
| | | | |
|---|---|---|---|
| ☐ 524 Roland McDole | .50 | .23 | .06 |

Washington Redskins
| | | | |
|---|---|---|---|
| ☐ 525 Dennis Shaw | .60 | .25 | .08 |

Buffalo Bills
| | | | |
|---|---|---|---|
| ☐ 526 Dave Manders | .60 | .25 | .08 |

Dallas Cowboys
| | | | |
|---|---|---|---|
| ☐ 527 Skip Vanderbundt | .50 | .23 | .06 |

San Francisco 49ers
| | | | |
|---|---|---|---|
| ☐ 528 Mike Sensibaugh | 1.25 | .25 | .08 |

Kansas City Chiefs

## 1973 Topps Team Checklists

The 1973 Topps Team Checklist set contains 26 checklist cards, one for each of the 26 NFL teams. The cards measure 2 1/2" by 3 1/2" and were inserted into regular issue 1973 Topps football wax packs. The fronts show action scenes at the top of the card and a Topps helmet with the team name at its immediate right. The bottom portion of the

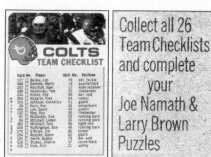

Collect all 26 Team Checklists and complete your Joe Namath & Larry Brown Puzzles

card contains the checklist, complete with boxes in which to place check marks. Uniform numbers and positions are also given with the player's name. The backs of the cards form puzzles of Joe Namath and Larry Brown. These unnumbered cards are numbered below for convenience in alphabetical order by team name. The cards can all be found with one or two asterisks on the front.

| | NRMT | VG-E | GOOD |
|---|---|---|---|
| COMPLETE SET (26) | 50.00 | 20.00 | 5.00 |
| COMMON TEAM (1-26) | 3.00 | 1.20 | .30 |
| | | | |
| ☐ 1 Atlanta Falcons | 3.00 | 1.20 | .30 |
| ☐ 2 Baltimore Colts | 3.00 | 1.20 | .30 |
| ☐ 3 Buffalo Bills | 3.00 | 1.20 | .30 |
| ☐ 4 Chicago Bears | 4.00 | 1.60 | .40 |
| ☐ 5 Cincinnati Bengals | 3.00 | 1.20 | .30 |
| ☐ 6 Cleveland Browns | 3.00 | 1.20 | .30 |
| ☐ 7 Dallas Cowboys | 5.00 | 2.00 | .50 |
| ☐ 8 Denver Broncos | 4.00 | 1.60 | .40 |
| ☐ 9 Detroit Lions | 3.00 | 1.20 | .30 |
| ☐ 10 Green Bay Packers | 3.00 | 1.20 | .30 |
| ☐ 11 Houston Oilers | 3.00 | 1.20 | .30 |
| ☐ 12 Kansas City Chiefs | 3.00 | 1.20 | .30 |
| ☐ 13 Los Angeles Rams | 3.00 | 1.20 | .30 |
| ☐ 14 Miami Dolphins | 4.00 | 1.60 | .40 |
| ☐ 15 Minnesota Vikings | 3.00 | 1.20 | .30 |
| ☐ 16 New England Patriots | 3.00 | 1.20 | .30 |
| ☐ 17 New Orleans Saints | 3.00 | 1.20 | .30 |
| ☐ 18 New York Giants | 4.00 | 1.60 | .40 |
| ☐ 19 New York Jets | 4.00 | 1.60 | .40 |
| ☐ 20 Oakland Raiders | 5.00 | 2.00 | .50 |
| ☐ 21 Philadelphia Eagles | 3.00 | 1.20 | .30 |
| ☐ 22 Pittsburgh Steelers | 4.00 | 1.60 | .40 |
| ☐ 23 St. Louis Cardinals | 3.00 | 1.20 | .30 |
| ☐ 24 San Diego Chargers | 3.00 | 1.20 | .30 |
| ☐ 25 San Francisco 49ers | 4.00 | 1.60 | .40 |
| ☐ 26 Washington Redskins | 4.00 | 1.60 | .40 |

## 1974 Topps

The 1974 Topps set contains 528 cards. The cards measure 2 1/2" by 3 1/2". Cards 328-333 present the statistical league leaders from each league. This set contains the Rookie Cards of Harold Carmichael, Chuck Foreman, Ray Guy, John Hannah, Bert Jones, Ed Marinaro, and Ahmad Rashad. No known scarcities exist. The card backs are printed in blue and yellow on gray card stock. The bottom of the reverse provided part of a simulated football game which could be played by drawing cards. All-Pro selections (AP) are provided as card numbers 121-144. Statistical league leaders are featured on cards 328-333. Post-season action is summarized on cards 460-463. The cards have either one or two asterisks on the back before the TCG notation. Cards with two asterisks include 26, 129, 130, 156, 162, 219, 265-364, 367-422, and 424-528; the rest have only one asterisk. Topps also printed a very similar (and very confusing) 50-card set for Parker Brothers in early 1974 as part of a football board game. The only players in this set (game) were offensive players (with an emphasis on the skill positions) and all come from the first 132 cards in the 1974 Topps football card set. There are several notable differences between these Parker Brothers Pro Draft cards and the 1974 Topps regular issue. Those cards with 1972 statistics on the back (unlike the 1974 Topps regular issue) are obviously Parker Brothers cards. Parker Brothers game cards can also be distinguished by the presence of two asterisks rather than one on the copyright line. However, as noted above, there are cards in the regular 1974 Topps set that do not have two asterisks but are not Parker Brothers Pro Draft cards. In fact, variations 23A, 49A, 116A, 124A, 126A, and 127A listed in this 1974 Topps checklist below are probably Parker Brothers cards, but they are impossible to identify as such, since they are exceptions to all the identification criteria with respect to Parker Brothers cards.

| | NRMT | VG-E | GOOD |
|---|---|---|---|
| COMPLETE SET (528) | 325.00 | 145.00 | 40.00 |
| COMMON PLAYER (1-528) | .40 | .18 | .05 |
| ☐ 1 O.J. Simpson RB UER | 27.00 | 6.75 | 2.20 |
| Buffalo Bills | | | |
| (Text on back says | | | |
| 100 years, should say | | | |
| 100 yards) | | | |
| ☐ 2 Blaine Nye | .40 | .18 | .05 |
| Dallas Cowboys | | | |
| ☐ 3 Don Hansen | .40 | .18 | .05 |
| Atlanta Falcons | | | |
| ☐ 4 Ken Bowman | .40 | .18 | .05 |
| Green Bay Packers | | | |
| ☐ 5 Carl Eller | 1.00 | .45 | .13 |
| Minnesota Vikings | | | |
| ☐ 6 Jerry Smith | .50 | .23 | .06 |
| Washington Redskins | | | |
| ☐ 7 Ed Podolak | .50 | .23 | .06 |
| Kansas City Chiefs | | | |
| ☐ 8 Mel Gray | .50 | .23 | .06 |
| St. Louis Cardinals | | | |
| ☐ 9 Pat Matson | .40 | .18 | .05 |
| Cincinnati Bengals | | | |
| ☐ 10 Floyd Little | 1.50 | .65 | .19 |
| Denver Broncos | | | |
| ☐ 11 Frank Pitts | .40 | .18 | .05 |
| Cleveland Browns | | | |
| ☐ 12 Vern Den Herder | .75 | .35 | .09 |
| Miami Dolphins | | | |
| ☐ 13 John Fuqua | .50 | .23 | .06 |
| Pittsburgh Steelers | | | |
| ☐ 14 Jack Tatum | 1.75 | .80 | .22 |
| Oakland Raiders | | | |
| ☐ 15 Winston Hill | .50 | .23 | .06 |
| New York Jets | | | |
| ☐ 16 John Beasley | .40 | .18 | .05 |
| New Orleans Saints | | | |
| ☐ 17 David Lee | .40 | .18 | .05 |
| Baltimore Colts | | | |
| ☐ 18 Rich Coady | .40 | .18 | .05 |
| Chicago Bears | | | |
| ☐ 19 Ken Willard | .50 | .23 | .06 |
| San Francisco 49ers | | | |
| ☐ 20 Coy Bacon | .50 | .23 | .06 |
| San Diego Chargers | | | |
| ☐ 21 Ben Hawkins | .40 | .18 | .05 |
| Philadelphia Eagles | | | |
| ☐ 22 Paul Guidry | .40 | .18 | .05 |
| Houston Oilers | | | |
| ☐ 23A Norm Snead | 5.00 | 2.30 | .60 |
| New York Giants | | | |
| (Vertical pose; 1973 | | | |
| stats; one asterisk | | | |
| before TCG on back) | | | |
| ☐ 23B Norm Snead HOR | 1.00 | .45 | .13 |
| New York Giants | | | |
| ☐ 24 Jim Yarbrough | .40 | .18 | .05 |
| Detroit Lions | | | |
| ☐ 25 Jack Reynolds | 2.50 | 1.15 | .30 |
| Los Angeles Rams | | | |
| ☐ 26 Josh Ashton | .40 | .18 | .05 |
| New England Patriots | | | |
| ☐ 27 Donnie Green | .40 | .18 | .05 |
| Buffalo Bills | | | |
| ☐ 28 Bob Hayes | 1.00 | .45 | .13 |
| Dallas Cowboys | | | |
| ☐ 29 John Zook | .40 | .18 | .05 |
| Atlanta Falcons | | | |
| ☐ 30 Bobby Bryant | .40 | .18 | .05 |
| Minnesota Vikings | | | |
| ☐ 31 Scott Hunter | .50 | .23 | .06 |
| Green Bay Packers | | | |
| ☐ 32 Dan Dierdorf | 4.00 | 1.80 | .50 |
| St. Louis Cardinals | | | |
| ☐ 33 Curt Knight | .40 | .18 | .05 |
| Washington Redskins | | | |
| ☐ 34 Elmo Wright | .60 | .25 | .08 |
| Kansas City Chiefs | | | |
| ☐ 35 Essex Johnson | .40 | .18 | .05 |
| Cincinnati Bengals | | | |
| ☐ 36 Walt Sumner | .40 | .18 | .05 |
| Cleveland Browns | | | |
| ☐ 37 Marv Montgomery | .40 | .18 | .05 |
| Denver Broncos | | | |
| ☐ 38 Tim Foley | .50 | .23 | .06 |
| Miami Dolphins | | | |
| ☐ 39 Mike Siani | .40 | .18 | .05 |
| Oakland Raiders | | | |
| ☐ 40 Joe Greene | 5.00 | 2.30 | .60 |
| Pittsburgh Steelers | | | |
| ☐ 41 Bobby Howfield | .40 | .18 | .05 |
| New York Jets | | | |
| ☐ 42 Del Williams | .40 | .18 | .05 |
| New Orleans Saints | | | |
| ☐ 43 Don McCauley | .40 | .18 | .05 |
| Baltimore Colts | | | |
| ☐ 44 Randy Jackson | .40 | .18 | .05 |
| Chicago Bears | | | |
| ☐ 45 Ron Smith | .40 | .18 | .05 |
| San Diego Chargers | | | |
| ☐ 46 Gene Washington | .40 | .18 | .05 |
| San Francisco 49ers | | | |
| ☐ 47 Po James | .50 | .23 | .06 |
| Philadelphia Eagles | | | |
| ☐ 48 Solomon Freelon | .40 | .18 | .05 |
| Houston Oilers | | | |
| ☐ 49A Bob Windsor | 3.00 | 1.35 | .40 |
| New England Patriots | | | |
| (Vertical pose; 1973 | | | |
| stats; one asterisk | | | |
| before TCG on back) | | | |
| ☐ 49B Bob Windsor HOR | .40 | .18 | .05 |
| New England Patriots | | | |
| ☐ 50 John Hadl | .75 | .35 | .09 |
| Los Angeles Rams | | | |
| ☐ 51 Greg Larson | .40 | .18 | .05 |
| New York Giants | | | |
| ☐ 52 Steve Owens | .50 | .23 | .06 |
| Detroit Lions | | | |
| ☐ 53 Jim Cheyunski | .40 | .18 | .05 |
| Buffalo Bills | | | |
| ☐ 54 Rayfield Wright | .40 | .18 | .05 |
| Dallas Cowboys | | | |
| ☐ 55 Dave Hampton | .40 | .18 | .05 |
| Atlanta Falcons | | | |
| ☐ 56 Ron Widby | .40 | .18 | .05 |
| Green Bay Packers | | | |
| ☐ 57 Milt Sunde | .40 | .18 | .05 |
| Minnesota Vikings | | | |
| ☐ 58 Bill Kilmer | .75 | .35 | .09 |
| Washington Redskins | | | |
| ☐ 59 Bobby Bell | 1.25 | .55 | .16 |
| Kansas City Chiefs | | | |
| ☐ 60 Jim Bakken | .50 | .23 | .06 |
| St. Louis Cardinals | | | |
| ☐ 61 Rufus Mayes | .40 | .18 | .05 |
| Cincinnati Bengals | | | |
| ☐ 62 Vic Washington | .50 | .23 | .06 |
| San Francisco 49ers | | | |
| ☐ 63 Gene Washington | .50 | .23 | .06 |
| Denver Broncos | | | |
| ☐ 64 Clarence Scott | .40 | .18 | .05 |
| Cleveland Browns | | | |
| ☐ 65 Gene Upshaw | 1.75 | .80 | .22 |
| Oakland Raiders | | | |
| ☐ 66 Larry Seiple | .50 | .23 | .06 |
| Miami Dolphins | | | |
| ☐ 67 John McMakin | .40 | .18 | .05 |
| Pittsburgh Steelers | | | |
| ☐ 68 Ralph Baker | .40 | .18 | .05 |
| New York Jets | | | |
| ☐ 69 Lydell Mitchell | 1.00 | .45 | .13 |
| Baltimore Colts | | | |
| ☐ 70 Archie Manning | 1.75 | .80 | .22 |
| New Orleans Saints | | | |
| ☐ 71 George Farmer | .40 | .18 | .05 |
| Chicago Bears | | | |
| ☐ 72 Ron East | .40 | .18 | .05 |
| San Diego Chargers | | | |
| ☐ 73 Al Nelson | .40 | .18 | .05 |
| Philadelphia Eagles | | | |
| ☐ 74 Pat Hughes | .40 | .18 | .05 |
| New York Giants | | | |
| ☐ 75 Fred Willis | .40 | .18 | .05 |
| Houston Oilers | | | |
| ☐ 76 Larry Walton | .40 | .18 | .05 |
| Detroit Lions | | | |
| ☐ 77 Tom Neville | .40 | .18 | .05 |
| New England Patriots | | | |
| ☐ 78 Ted Kwalick | .50 | .23 | .06 |
| San Francisco 49ers | | | |
| ☐ 79 Walt Patulski | .40 | .18 | .05 |
| Buffalo Bills | | | |

| | | | |
|---|---|---|---|
| ☐ 80 John Niland | .40 | .18 | .05 |
| Dallas Cowboys | | | |
| ☐ 81 Ted Fritsch Jr. | .50 | .23 | .06 |
| Atlanta Falcons | | | |
| ☐ 82 Paul Krause | .75 | .35 | .09 |
| Minnesota Vikings | | | |
| ☐ 83 Jack Snow | .50 | .23 | .06 |
| Los Angeles Rams | | | |
| ☐ 84 Mike Bass | .50 | .23 | .06 |
| Washington Redskins | | | |
| ☐ 85 Jim Tyrer | .50 | .23 | .06 |
| Kansas City Chiefs | | | |
| ☐ 86 Ron Yankowski | .40 | .18 | .05 |
| St. Louis Cardinals | | | |
| ☐ 87 Mike Phipps | .50 | .23 | .06 |
| Cleveland Browns | | | |
| ☐ 88 Al Beauchamp | .40 | .18 | .05 |
| Cincinnati Bengals | | | |
| ☐ 89 Riley Odoms | 2.00 | .90 | .25 |
| Denver Broncos | | | |
| ☐ 90 MacArthur Lane | .50 | .23 | .06 |
| Green Bay Packers | | | |
| ☐ 91 Art Thoms | .40 | .18 | .05 |
| Oakland Raiders | | | |
| ☐ 92 Marlin Briscoe | .50 | .23 | .06 |
| Miami Dolphins | | | |
| ☐ 93 Bruce Van Dyke | .40 | .18 | .05 |
| Pittsburgh Steelers | | | |
| ☐ 94 Tom Myers | .40 | .18 | .05 |
| New Orleans Saints | | | |
| ☐ 95 Calvin Hill | 1.00 | .45 | .13 |
| Dallas Cowboys | | | |
| ☐ 96 Bruce Laird | .40 | .18 | .05 |
| Baltimore Colts | | | |
| ☐ 97 Tony McGee | .40 | .18 | .05 |
| Chicago Bears | | | |
| ☐ 98 Len Rohde | .40 | .18 | .05 |
| San Francisco 49ers | | | |
| ☐ 99 Tom McNeill | .40 | .18 | .05 |
| Philadelphia Eagles | | | |
| ☐ 100 Delles Howell | .40 | .18 | .05 |
| New York Jets | | | |
| ☐ 101 Gary Garrison | .50 | .23 | .06 |
| San Diego Chargers | | | |
| ☐ 102 Dan Goich | .40 | .18 | .05 |
| New York Giants | | | |
| ☐ 103 Len St. Jean | .40 | .18 | .05 |
| New England Patriots | | | |
| ☐ 104 Zeke Moore | .40 | .18 | .05 |
| Houston Oilers | | | |
| ☐ 105 Ahmad Rashad | 18.00 | 8.00 | 2.30 |
| Buffalo Bills | | | |
| ☐ 106 Mel Renfro | 1.00 | .45 | .13 |
| Dallas Cowboys | | | |
| ☐ 107 Jim Mitchell | .40 | .18 | .05 |
| Detroit Lions | | | |
| ☐ 108 Ed Budde | .50 | .23 | .06 |
| Kansas City Chiefs | | | |
| ☐ 109 Harry Schuh | .40 | .18 | .05 |
| Los Angeles Rams | | | |
| ☐ 110 Greg Pruitt | 4.00 | 1.80 | .50 |
| Cleveland Browns | | | |
| ☐ 111 Ed Flanagan | .40 | .18 | .05 |
| Detroit Lions | | | |
| ☐ 112 Larry Stallings | .40 | .18 | .05 |
| St. Louis Cardinals | | | |
| ☐ 113 Chuck Foreman | 4.00 | 1.80 | .50 |
| Minnesota Vikings | | | |
| ☐ 114 Royce Berry | .40 | .18 | .05 |
| Cincinnati Bengals | | | |
| ☐ 115 Gale Gillingham | .40 | .18 | .05 |
| Green Bay Packers | | | |
| ☐ 116A Charlie Johnson | 5.00 | 2.30 | .60 |
| Denver Broncos | | | |
| (Vertical pose; 1973 | | | |
| stats; one asterisk | | | |
| before TCG on back) | | | |
| ☐ 116B Charlie Johnson HOR | 1.00 | .45 | .13 |
| Denver Broncos | | | |
| ☐ 117 Checklist 1-132 UER | 3.00 | .30 | .09 |
| (345 Hamburger) | | | |
| ☐ 118 Bill Butler | .40 | .18 | .05 |
| New Orleans Saints | | | |
| ☐ 119 Roy Jefferson | .50 | .23 | .06 |
| Washington Redskins | | | |
| ☐ 120 Bobby Douglass | .50 | .23 | .06 |
| Chicago Bears | | | |
| ☐ 121 Harold Carmichael AP | 16.00 | 7.25 | 2.00 |
| Philadelphia Eagles | | | |
| ☐ 122 George Kunz AP | .50 | .23 | .06 |
| Atlanta Falcons | | | |
| ☐ 123 Larry Little AP | 1.25 | .55 | .16 |
| Miami Dolphins | | | |
| ☐ 124A Forrest Blue AP | 3.00 | 1.35 | .40 |
| San Francisco 49ers | | | |
| (Not All-Pro style; 1973 | | | |
| stats; one asterisk | | | |

| | | | |
|---|---|---|---|
| before TCG on back) | | | |
| ☐ 124B Forrest Blue AP | .40 | .18 | .05 |
| San Francisco 49ers | | | |
| ☐ 125 Ron Yary AP | .75 | .35 | .09 |
| Minnesota Vikings | | | |
| ☐ 126A Tom Mack | 3.00 | 1.35 | .40 |
| Los Angeles Rams | | | |
| (Not All-Pro style; 1973 | | | |
| stats; one asterisk | | | |
| before TCG on back) | | | |
| ☐ 126B Tom Mack AP | .60 | .25 | .08 |
| Los Angeles Rams | | | |
| ☐ 127A Bob Tucker | 3.00 | 1.35 | .40 |
| New York Giants | | | |
| (Not All-Pro style; 1973 | | | |
| stats; one asterisk | | | |
| before TCG on back) | | | |
| ☐ 127B Bob Tucker AP | .50 | .23 | .06 |
| New York Giants | | | |
| ☐ 128 Paul Warfield AP | 4.00 | 1.80 | .50 |
| Miami Dolphins | | | |
| ☐ 129 Fran Tarkenton AP | 10.00 | 4.50 | 1.25 |
| Minnesota Vikings | | | |
| ☐ 130 O.J. Simpson AP | 20.00 | 9.00 | 2.50 |
| Buffalo Bills | | | |
| ☐ 131 Larry Csonka AP | 4.00 | 1.80 | .50 |
| Miami Dolphins | | | |
| ☐ 132 Bruce Gossett AP | .40 | .18 | .05 |
| San Francisco 49ers | | | |
| ☐ 133 Bill Stanfill AP | .50 | .23 | .06 |
| Miami Dolphins | | | |
| ☐ 134 Alan Page AP | 2.50 | 1.15 | .30 |
| Minnesota Vikings | | | |
| ☐ 135 Paul Smith AP | .40 | .18 | .05 |
| Denver Broncos | | | |
| ☐ 136 Claude Humphrey AP | .50 | .23 | .06 |
| Atlanta Falcons | | | |
| ☐ 137 Jack Ham AP | 7.00 | 3.10 | .85 |
| Pittsburgh Steelers | | | |
| ☐ 138 Lee Roy Jordan AP | 1.50 | .65 | .19 |
| Dallas Cowboys | | | |
| ☐ 139 Phil Villapiano AP | .50 | .23 | .06 |
| Oakland Raiders | | | |
| ☐ 140 Ken Ellis AP | .40 | .18 | .05 |
| Green Bay Packers | | | |
| ☐ 141 Willie Brown AP | 1.25 | .55 | .16 |
| Oakland Raiders | | | |
| ☐ 142 Dick Anderson AP | .60 | .25 | .08 |
| Miami Dolphins | | | |
| ☐ 143 Bill Bradley AP | .50 | .23 | .06 |
| Philadelphia Eagles | | | |
| ☐ 144 Jerrel Wilson AP | .40 | .18 | .05 |
| Kansas City Chiefs | | | |
| ☐ 145 Reggie Rucker | .60 | .25 | .08 |
| New England Patriots | | | |
| ☐ 146 Marty Domres | .50 | .23 | .06 |
| Baltimore Colts | | | |
| ☐ 147 Bob Kowalkowski | .40 | .18 | .05 |
| Detroit Lions | | | |
| ☐ 148 John Matuszak | 4.00 | 1.80 | .50 |
| Houston Oilers | | | |
| ☐ 149 Mike Adamle | .75 | .35 | .09 |
| New York Jets | | | |
| ☐ 150 John Unitas | 16.00 | 7.25 | 2.00 |
| San Diego Chargers | | | |
| ☐ 151 Charlie Ford | .40 | .18 | .05 |
| Chicago Bears | | | |
| ☐ 152 Bob Klein | .60 | .25 | .08 |
| Los Angeles Rams | | | |
| ☐ 153 Jim Merlo | .40 | .18 | .05 |
| New Orleans Saints | | | |
| ☐ 154 Willie Young | .40 | .18 | .05 |
| New York Giants | | | |
| ☐ 155 Donny Anderson | .50 | .23 | .06 |
| St. Louis Cardinals | | | |
| ☐ 156 Brig Owens | .40 | .18 | .05 |
| Washington Redskins | | | |
| ☐ 157 Bruce Jarvis | .40 | .18 | .05 |
| Buffalo Bills | | | |
| ☐ 158 Ron Carpenter | .40 | .18 | .05 |
| Cincinnati Bengals | | | |
| ☐ 159 Don Cockroft | .50 | .23 | .06 |
| Cleveland Browns | | | |
| ☐ 160 Tommy Nobis | 1.00 | .45 | .13 |
| Atlanta Falcons | | | |
| ☐ 161 Craig Morton | 1.00 | .45 | .13 |
| Dallas Cowboys | | | |
| ☐ 162 Jon Staggers | .40 | .18 | .05 |
| Green Bay Packers | | | |
| ☐ 163 Mike Eischeid | .40 | .18 | .05 |
| Minnesota Vikings | | | |
| ☐ 164 Jerry Sisemore | .50 | .23 | .06 |
| Philadelphia Eagles | | | |
| ☐ 165 Cedrick Hardman | .50 | .23 | .06 |
| San Francisco 49ers | | | |
| ☐ 166 Bill Thompson | .50 | .23 | .06 |
| Denver Broncos | | | |
| ☐ 167 Jim Lynch | .40 | .18 | .05 |

Kansas City Chiefs
| ☐ 168 Bob Moore | .50 | .23 | .06 |
|---|---|---|---|

Oakland Raiders
| ☐ 169 Glen Edwards | .50 | .23 | .06 |
|---|---|---|---|

Pittsburgh Steelers
| ☐ 170 Mercury Morris | 1.00 | .45 | .13 |
|---|---|---|---|

Miami Dolphins
| ☐ 171 Julius Adams | .40 | .18 | .05 |
|---|---|---|---|

New England Patriots
| ☐ 172 Cotton Speyrer | .50 | .23 | .06 |
|---|---|---|---|

Baltimore Colts
| ☐ 173 Bill Munson | .50 | .23 | .06 |
|---|---|---|---|

Detroit Lions
| ☐ 174 Benny Johnson | .40 | .18 | .05 |
|---|---|---|---|

Houston Oilers
| ☐ 175 Burgess Owens | .60 | .25 | .08 |
|---|---|---|---|

New York Jets
| ☐ 176 Cid Edwards | .40 | .18 | .05 |
|---|---|---|---|

San Diego Chargers
| ☐ 177 Doug Buffone | .40 | .18 | .05 |
|---|---|---|---|

Chicago Bears
| ☐ 178 Charlie Cowan | .40 | .18 | .05 |
|---|---|---|---|

Los Angeles Rams
| ☐ 179 Bob Newland | .40 | .18 | .05 |
|---|---|---|---|

New Orleans Saints
| ☐ 180 Ron Johnson | .50 | .23 | .06 |
|---|---|---|---|

New York Giants
| ☐ 181 Bob Rowe | .40 | .18 | .05 |
|---|---|---|---|

St. Louis Cardinals
| ☐ 182 Len Hauss | .50 | .23 | .06 |
|---|---|---|---|

Washington Redskins
| ☐ 183 Joe DeLamielleure | 2.00 | .90 | .25 |
|---|---|---|---|

Buffalo Bills
| ☐ 184 Sherman White | .75 | .35 | .09 |
|---|---|---|---|

Cincinnati Bengals
| ☐ 185 Fair Hooker | .40 | .18 | .05 |
|---|---|---|---|

Cleveland Browns
| ☐ 186 Nick Mike-Mayer | .40 | .18 | .05 |
|---|---|---|---|

Atlanta Falcons
| ☐ 187 Ralph Neely | .50 | .23 | .06 |
|---|---|---|---|

Dallas Cowboys
| ☐ 188 Rich McGeorge | .40 | .18 | .05 |
|---|---|---|---|

Green Bay Packers
| ☐ 189 Ed Marinaro | 4.50 | 2.00 | .55 |
|---|---|---|---|

Minnesota Vikings
| ☐ 190 Dave Wilcox | .50 | .23 | .06 |
|---|---|---|---|

San Francisco 49ers
| ☐ 191 Joe Owens | .40 | .18 | .05 |
|---|---|---|---|

New Orleans Saints
| ☐ 192 Bill Van Heusen | .40 | .18 | .05 |
|---|---|---|---|

Denver Broncos
| ☐ 193 Jim Kearney | .40 | .18 | .05 |
|---|---|---|---|

Kansas City Chiefs
| ☐ 194 Otis Sistrunk | 3.00 | 1.35 | .40 |
|---|---|---|---|

Oakland Raiders
| ☐ 195 Ron Shanklin | .40 | .18 | .05 |
|---|---|---|---|

Pittsburgh Steelers
| ☐ 196 Bill Lenkaitis | .40 | .18 | .05 |
|---|---|---|---|

New England Patriots
| ☐ 197 Tom Drougas | .40 | .18 | .05 |
|---|---|---|---|

Baltimore Colts
| ☐ 198 Larry Hand | .40 | .18 | .05 |
|---|---|---|---|

Detroit Lions
| ☐ 199 Mack Alston | .40 | .18 | .05 |
|---|---|---|---|

Houston Oilers
| ☐ 200 Bob Griese | 6.00 | 2.70 | .75 |
|---|---|---|---|

Miami Dolphins
| ☐ 201 Earlie Thomas | .40 | .18 | .05 |
|---|---|---|---|

New York Jets
| ☐ 202 Carl Gerbach | .40 | .18 | .05 |
|---|---|---|---|

San Diego Chargers
| ☐ 203 Jim Harrison | .40 | .18 | .05 |
|---|---|---|---|

Chicago Bears
| ☐ 204 Jake Kupp | .40 | .18 | .05 |
|---|---|---|---|

New Orleans Saints
| ☐ 205 Merlin Olsen | 2.25 | 1.00 | .30 |
|---|---|---|---|

Los Angeles Rams
| ☐ 206 Spider Lockhart | .50 | .23 | .06 |
|---|---|---|---|

New York Giants
| ☐ 207 Walker Gillette | .40 | .18 | .05 |
|---|---|---|---|

St. Louis Cardinals
| ☐ 208 Verlon Biggs | .40 | .18 | .05 |
|---|---|---|---|

Washington Redskins
| ☐ 209 Bob James | .40 | .18 | .05 |
|---|---|---|---|

Buffalo Bills
| ☐ 210 Bob Trumpy | 1.25 | .55 | .16 |
|---|---|---|---|

Cincinnati Bengals
| ☐ 211 Jerry Sherk HOR | .50 | .23 | .06 |
|---|---|---|---|

Cleveland Browns
| ☐ 212 Andy Maurer | .40 | .18 | .05 |
|---|---|---|---|

Atlanta Falcons
| ☐ 213 Fred Carr | .50 | .23 | .06 |
|---|---|---|---|

Green Bay Packers
| ☐ 214 Mick Tingelhoff | .50 | .23 | .06 |
|---|---|---|---|

Minnesota Vikings
| ☐ 215 Steve Spurrier | 3.00 | 1.35 | .40 |
|---|---|---|---|

San Francisco 49ers
| ☐ 216 Richard Harris | .40 | .18 | .05 |
|---|---|---|---|

Philadelphia Eagles
| ☐ 217 Charlie Greer | .40 | .18 | .05 |
|---|---|---|---|

Denver Broncos
| ☐ 218 Buck Buchanan | 1.25 | .55 | .16 |
|---|---|---|---|

Kansas City Chiefs
| ☐ 219 Ray Guy | 10.00 | 4.50 | 1.25 |
|---|---|---|---|

Oakland Raiders
| ☐ 220 Franco Harris | 20.00 | 9.00 | 2.50 |
|---|---|---|---|

Pittsburgh Steelers
| ☐ 221 Darryl Stingley | 2.50 | 1.15 | .30 |
|---|---|---|---|

New England Patriots
| ☐ 222 Rex Kern | .50 | .23 | .06 |
|---|---|---|---|

Baltimore Colts
| ☐ 223 Toni Fritsch | .50 | .23 | .06 |
|---|---|---|---|

Dallas Cowboys
| ☐ 224 Levi Johnson | .40 | .18 | .05 |
|---|---|---|---|

Detroit Lions
| ☐ 225 Bob Kuechenberg | .60 | .25 | .08 |
|---|---|---|---|

Miami Dolphins
| ☐ 226 Elvin Bethea | .50 | .23 | .06 |
|---|---|---|---|

Houston Oilers
| ☐ 227 Al Woodall | .50 | .23 | .06 |
|---|---|---|---|

New York Jets
| ☐ 228 Terry Owens | .40 | .18 | .05 |
|---|---|---|---|

San Diego Chargers
| ☐ 229 Bivian Lee | .40 | .18 | .05 |
|---|---|---|---|

New Orleans Saints
| ☐ 230 Dick Butkus | 6.00 | 2.70 | .75 |
|---|---|---|---|

Chicago Bears
| ☐ 231 Jim Bertelsen | .50 | .23 | .06 |
|---|---|---|---|

Los Angeles Rams
| ☐ 232 John Mendenhall | .50 | .23 | .06 |
|---|---|---|---|

New York Giants
| ☐ 233 Conrad Dobler | 2.50 | 1.15 | .30 |
|---|---|---|---|

St. Louis Cardinals
| ☐ 234 J.D. Hill | .50 | .23 | .06 |
|---|---|---|---|

Buffalo Bills
| ☐ 235 Ken Houston | 1.25 | .55 | .16 |
|---|---|---|---|

Washington Redskins
| ☐ 236 Dave Lewis | .40 | .18 | .05 |
|---|---|---|---|

Cincinnati Bengals
| ☐ 237 John Garlington | .40 | .18 | .05 |
|---|---|---|---|

Cleveland Browns
| ☐ 238 Bill Sandeman | .40 | .18 | .05 |
|---|---|---|---|

Atlanta Falcons
| ☐ 239 Alden Roche | .40 | .18 | .05 |
|---|---|---|---|

Green Bay Packers
| ☐ 240 John Gilliam | .50 | .23 | .06 |
|---|---|---|---|

Minnesota Vikings
| ☐ 241 Bruce Taylor | .40 | .18 | .05 |
|---|---|---|---|

San Francisco 49ers
| ☐ 242 Vern Winfield | .40 | .18 | .05 |
|---|---|---|---|

Philadelphia Eagles
| ☐ 243 Bobby Maples | .50 | .23 | .06 |
|---|---|---|---|

Denver Broncos
| ☐ 244 Wendell Hayes | .50 | .23 | .06 |
|---|---|---|---|

Kansas City Chiefs
| ☐ 245 George Blanda | 7.00 | 3.10 | .85 |
|---|---|---|---|

Oakland Raiders
| ☐ 246 Dwight White | .50 | .23 | .06 |
|---|---|---|---|

Pittsburgh Steelers
| ☐ 247 Sandy Durko | .40 | .18 | .05 |
|---|---|---|---|

New England Patriots
| ☐ 248 Tom Mitchell | .40 | .18 | .05 |
|---|---|---|---|

Baltimore Colts
| ☐ 249 Chuck Walton | .40 | .18 | .05 |
|---|---|---|---|

Detroit Lions
| ☐ 250 Bob Lilly | 3.50 | 1.55 | .45 |
|---|---|---|---|

Dallas Cowboys
| ☐ 251 Doug Swift | .40 | .18 | .05 |
|---|---|---|---|

Miami Dolphins
| ☐ 252 Lynn Dickey | 3.00 | 1.35 | .40 |
|---|---|---|---|

Houston Oilers
| ☐ 253 Jerome Barkum | 1.00 | .45 | .13 |
|---|---|---|---|

New York Jets
| ☐ 254 Clint Jones | .40 | .18 | .05 |
|---|---|---|---|

San Diego Chargers
| ☐ 255 Billy Newsome | .40 | .18 | .05 |
|---|---|---|---|

New Orleans Saints
| ☐ 256 Bob Asher | .40 | .18 | .05 |
|---|---|---|---|

Chicago Bears
| ☐ 257 Joe Scibelli | .50 | .23 | .06 |
|---|---|---|---|

Los Angeles Rams
| ☐ 258 Tom Blanchard | .40 | .18 | .05 |
|---|---|---|---|

New York Giants
| ☐ 259 Norm Thompson | .40 | .18 | .05 |
|---|---|---|---|

St. Louis Cardinals
| ☐ 260 Larry Brown | 1.00 | .45 | .13 |
|---|---|---|---|

Washington Redskins
| ☐ 261 Paul Seymour | .40 | .18 | .05 |
|---|---|---|---|

Buffalo Bills
| ☐ 262 Checklist 133-264 | 3.00 | .30 | .09 |
|---|---|---|---|
| ☐ 263 Doug Dieken | .60 | .25 | .08 |

Cleveland Browns
| ☐ 264 Lemar Parrish | .50 | .23 | .06 |
|---|---|---|---|

Cincinnati Bengals
| ☐ 265 Bob Lee UER | .50 | .23 | .06 |
|---|---|---|---|

Atlanta Falcons

(listed as Atlanta
Hawks on card back)

| | | | |
|---|---|---|---|
| ☐ 266 Bob Brown | .40 | .18 | .05 |
| Green Bay Packers | | | |
| ☐ 267 Roy Winston | .40 | .18 | .05 |
| Minnesota Vikings | | | |
| ☐ 268 Randy Beisler | .40 | .18 | .05 |
| San Francisco 49ers | | | |
| ☐ 269 Joe Dawkins | .40 | .18 | .05 |
| Denver Broncos | | | |
| ☐ 270 Tom Dempsey | .50 | .23 | .06 |
| Philadelphia Eagles | | | |
| ☐ 271 Jack Rudnay | .40 | .18 | .05 |
| Kansas City Chiefs | | | |
| ☐ 272 Art Shell | 6.00 | 2.70 | .75 |
| Oakland Raiders | | | |
| ☐ 273 Mike Wagner | .60 | .25 | .08 |
| Pittsburgh Steelers | | | |
| ☐ 274 Rick Cash | .40 | .18 | .05 |
| New England Patriots | | | |
| ☐ 275 Greg Landry | .75 | .35 | .09 |
| Detroit Lions | | | |
| ☐ 276 Glenn Ressler | .40 | .18 | .05 |
| Baltimore Colts | | | |
| ☐ 277 Billy Joe DuPree | 3.50 | 1.55 | .45 |
| Dallas Cowboys | | | |
| ☐ 278 Norm Evans | .50 | .23 | .06 |
| Miami Dolphins | | | |
| ☐ 279 Billy Parks | .40 | .18 | .05 |
| Houston Oilers | | | |
| ☐ 280 John Riggins | 6.00 | 2.70 | .75 |
| New York Jets | | | |
| ☐ 281 Lionel Aldridge | .40 | .18 | .05 |
| San Diego Chargers | | | |
| ☐ 282 Steve O'Neal | .40 | .18 | .05 |
| New Orleans Saints | | | |
| ☐ 283 Craig Clemons | .40 | .18 | .05 |
| Chicago Bears | | | |
| ☐ 284 Willie Williams | .40 | .18 | .05 |
| New York Giants | | | |
| ☐ 285 Isiah Robertson | .50 | .23 | .06 |
| Los Angeles Rams | | | |
| ☐ 286 Dennis Shaw | .50 | .23 | .06 |
| St. Louis Cardinals | | | |
| ☐ 287 Bill Brundige | .40 | .18 | .05 |
| Washington Redskins | | | |
| ☐ 288 John Leypoldt | .40 | .18 | .05 |
| Buffalo Bills | | | |
| ☐ 289 John DeMarie | .40 | .18 | .05 |
| Cleveland Browns | | | |
| ☐ 290 Mike Reid | 1.25 | .55 | .16 |
| Cincinnati Bengals | | | |
| ☐ 291 Greg Brezina | .40 | .18 | .05 |
| Atlanta Falcons | | | |
| ☐ 292 Willie Buchanon | 1.00 | .45 | .13 |
| Green Bay Packers | | | |
| ☐ 293 Dave Osborn | .50 | .23 | .06 |
| Minnesota Vikings | | | |
| ☐ 294 Mel Phillips | .40 | .18 | .05 |
| San Francisco 49ers | | | |
| ☐ 295 Haven Moses | .50 | .23 | .06 |
| Denver Broncos | | | |
| ☐ 296 Wade Key | .40 | .18 | .05 |
| Philadelphia Eagles | | | |
| ☐ 297 Marvin Upshaw | .40 | .18 | .05 |
| Kansas City Chiefs | | | |
| ☐ 298 Ray Mansfield | .40 | .18 | .05 |
| Pittsburgh Steelers | | | |
| ☐ 299 Edgar Chandler | .40 | .18 | .05 |
| New England Patriots | | | |
| ☐ 300 Marv Hubbard | .50 | .23 | .06 |
| Oakland Raiders | | | |
| ☐ 301 Herman Weaver | .40 | .18 | .05 |
| Detroit Lions | | | |
| ☐ 302 Jim Bailey | .40 | .18 | .05 |
| Baltimore Colts | | | |
| ☐ 303 D.D. Lewis | 1.50 | .65 | .19 |
| Dallas Cowboys | | | |
| ☐ 304 Ken Burrough | .50 | .23 | .06 |
| Houston Oilers | | | |
| ☐ 305 Jake Scott | .60 | .25 | .08 |
| Miami Dolphins | | | |
| ☐ 306 Randy Rasmussen | .40 | .18 | .05 |
| New York Jets | | | |
| ☐ 307 Pettis Norman | .50 | .23 | .06 |
| San Diego Chargers | | | |
| ☐ 308 Carl Johnson | .40 | .18 | .05 |
| New Orleans Saints | | | |
| ☐ 309 Joe Taylor | .40 | .18 | .05 |
| Chicago Bears | | | |
| ☐ 310 Pete Gogolak | .50 | .23 | .06 |
| New York Giants | | | |
| ☐ 311 Tony Baker | .40 | .18 | .05 |
| Los Angeles Rams | | | |
| ☐ 312 John Richardson | .40 | .18 | .05 |
| St. Louis Cardinals | | | |
| ☐ 313 Dave Robinson | .50 | .23 | .06 |
| Washington Redskins | | | |
| ☐ 314 Reggie McKenzie | 2.50 | 1.15 | .30 |
| Buffalo Bills | | | |
| ☐ 315 Isaac Curtis | 3.00 | 1.35 | .40 |
| Cincinnati Bengals | | | |
| ☐ 316 Thom Darden | .50 | .23 | .06 |
| Cleveland Browns | | | |
| ☐ 317 Ken Reaves | .40 | .18 | .05 |
| Atlanta Falcons | | | |
| ☐ 318 Malcolm Snider | .40 | .18 | .05 |
| Green Bay Packers | | | |
| ☐ 319 Jeff Siemon | 1.25 | .55 | .16 |
| Minnesota Vikings | | | |
| ☐ 320 Dan Abramowicz | .50 | .23 | .06 |
| San Francisco 49ers | | | |
| ☐ 321 Lyle Alzado | 2.00 | .90 | .25 |
| Denver Broncos | | | |
| ☐ 322 John Reaves | .50 | .23 | .06 |
| Philadelphia Eagles | | | |
| ☐ 323 Morris Stroud | .40 | .18 | .05 |
| Kansas City Chiefs | | | |
| ☐ 324 Bobby Walden | .40 | .18 | .05 |
| Pittsburgh Steelers | | | |
| ☐ 325 Randy Vataha | .50 | .23 | .06 |
| New England Patriots | | | |
| ☐ 326 Nemiah Wilson | .40 | .18 | .05 |
| Oakland Raiders | | | |
| ☐ 327 Paul Naumoff | .40 | .18 | .05 |
| Detroit Lions | | | |
| ☐ 328 Rushing Leaders | 5.00 | 2.30 | .60 |
| O.J. Simpson | | | |
| John Brockington | | | |
| ☐ 329 Passing Leaders | 4.00 | 1.80 | .50 |
| Ken Stabler | | | |
| Roger Staubach | | | |
| ☐ 330 Receiving Leaders | 1.25 | .55 | .16 |
| Fred Willis | | | |
| Harold Carmichael | | | |
| ☐ 331 Scoring Leaders | .60 | .25 | .08 |
| Roy Gerela | | | |
| David Ray | | | |
| ☐ 332 Interception Leaders | .60 | .25 | .08 |
| Dick Anderson | | | |
| Mike Wagner | | | |
| Bobby Bryant | | | |
| ☐ 333 Punting Leaders | .60 | .25 | .08 |
| Jerrel Wilson | | | |
| Tom Wittum | | | |
| ☐ 334 Dennis Nelson | .40 | .18 | .05 |
| Baltimore Colts | | | |
| ☐ 335 Walt Garrison | .50 | .23 | .06 |
| Dallas Cowboys | | | |
| ☐ 336 Tody Smith | .40 | .18 | .05 |
| Houston Oilers | | | |
| ☐ 337 Ed Bell | .40 | .18 | .05 |
| New York Jets | | | |
| ☐ 338 Bryant Salter | .40 | .18 | .05 |
| San Diego Chargers | | | |
| ☐ 339 Wayne Colman | .40 | .18 | .05 |
| New Orleans Saints | | | |
| ☐ 340 Garo Yepremian | .60 | .25 | .08 |
| Miami Dolphins | | | |
| ☐ 341 Bob Newton | .40 | .18 | .05 |
| Chicago Bears | | | |
| ☐ 342 Vince Clements | .50 | .23 | .06 |
| New York Giants | | | |
| ☐ 343 Ken Iman | .40 | .18 | .05 |
| Los Angeles Rams | | | |
| ☐ 344 Jim Tolbert | .40 | .18 | .05 |
| St. Louis Cardinals | | | |
| ☐ 345 Chris Hanburger | .50 | .23 | .06 |
| Washington Redskins | | | |
| ☐ 346 Dave Foley | .40 | .18 | .05 |
| Buffalo Bills | | | |
| ☐ 347 Tommy Casanova | .60 | .25 | .08 |
| Cincinnati Bengals | | | |
| ☐ 348 John James | .40 | .18 | .05 |
| Atlanta Falcons | | | |
| ☐ 349 Clarence Williams | .40 | .18 | .05 |
| Green Bay Packers | | | |
| ☐ 350 Leroy Kelly | 1.25 | .55 | .16 |
| Cleveland Browns | | | |
| ☐ 351 Stu Voigt | .75 | .35 | .09 |
| Minnesota Vikings | | | |
| ☐ 352 Skip Vanderbundt | .40 | .18 | .05 |
| San Francisco 49ers | | | |
| ☐ 353 Pete Duranko | .40 | .18 | .05 |
| Denver Broncos | | | |
| ☐ 354 John Outlaw | .40 | .18 | .05 |
| Philadelphia Eagles | | | |
| ☐ 355 Jan Stenerud | 1.00 | .45 | .13 |
| Kansas City Chiefs | | | |
| ☐ 356 Barry Pearson | .40 | .18 | .05 |
| Pittsburgh Steelers | | | |
| ☐ 357 Brian Dowling | .50 | .23 | .06 |
| New England Patriots | | | |
| ☐ 358 Dan Conners | .40 | .18 | .05 |
| Oakland Raiders | | | |

| | | | |
|---|---|---|---|
| ☐ 359 Bob Bell | .40 | .18 | .05 |
| Detroit Lions | | | |
| ☐ 360 Rick Volk | .40 | .18 | .05 |
| Baltimore Colts | | | |
| ☐ 361 Pat Toomay | .50 | .23 | .06 |
| Dallas Cowboys | | | |
| ☐ 362 Bob Gresham | .40 | .18 | .05 |
| Houston Oilers | | | |
| ☐ 363 John Schmitt | .40 | .18 | .05 |
| New York Jets | | | |
| ☐ 364 Mel Rogers | .40 | .18 | .05 |
| San Diego Chargers | | | |
| ☐ 365 Manny Fernandez | .50 | .23 | .06 |
| Miami Dolphins | | | |
| ☐ 366 Ernie Jackson | .40 | .18 | .05 |
| New Orleans Saints | | | |
| ☐ 367 Gary Huff | .75 | .35 | .09 |
| Chicago Bears | | | |
| ☐ 368 Bob Grim | .50 | .23 | .06 |
| New York Giants | | | |
| ☐ 369 Ernie McMillan | .40 | .18 | .05 |
| St. Louis Cardinals | | | |
| ☐ 370 Dave Elmendorf | .50 | .23 | .06 |
| Los Angeles Rams | | | |
| ☐ 371 Mike Bragg | .40 | .18 | .05 |
| Washington Redskins | | | |
| ☐ 372 John Skorupan | .40 | .18 | .05 |
| Buffalo Bills | | | |
| ☐ 373 Howard Fest | .40 | .18 | .05 |
| Cincinnati Bengals | | | |
| ☐ 374 Jerry Tagge | 1.00 | .45 | .13 |
| Green Bay Packers | | | |
| ☐ 375 Art Malone | .40 | .18 | .05 |
| Atlanta Falcons | | | |
| ☐ 376 Bob Babich | .40 | .18 | .05 |
| Cleveland Browns | | | |
| ☐ 377 Jim Marshall | 1.00 | .45 | .13 |
| Minnesota Vikings | | | |
| ☐ 378 Bob Hoskins | .40 | .18 | .05 |
| San Francisco 49ers | | | |
| ☐ 379 Don Zimmerman | .40 | .18 | .05 |
| Philadelphia Eagles | | | |
| ☐ 380 Ray May | .40 | .18 | .05 |
| Denver Broncos | | | |
| ☐ 381 Emmitt Thomas | .50 | .23 | .06 |
| Kansas City Chiefs | | | |
| ☐ 382 Terry Hanratty | .50 | .23 | .06 |
| Pittsburgh Steelers | | | |
| ☐ 383 John Hannah | 16.00 | 7.25 | 2.00 |
| New England Patriots | | | |
| ☐ 384 George Atkinson | .50 | .23 | .06 |
| Oakland Raiders | | | |
| ☐ 385 Ted Hendricks | 3.00 | 1.35 | .40 |
| Baltimore Colts | | | |
| ☐ 386 Jim O'Brien | .40 | .18 | .05 |
| Detroit Lions | | | |
| ☐ 387 Jethro Pugh | .50 | .23 | .06 |
| Dallas Cowboys | | | |
| ☐ 388 Elbert Drungo | .40 | .18 | .05 |
| Houston Oilers | | | |
| ☐ 389 Richard Caster | .50 | .23 | .06 |
| New York Jets | | | |
| ☐ 390 Deacon Jones | 1.75 | .80 | .22 |
| San Diego Chargers | | | |
| ☐ 391 Checklist 265-396 | 3.00 | .30 | .09 |
| ☐ 392 Jess Phillips | .40 | .18 | .05 |
| New Orleans Saints | | | |
| ☐ 393 Garry Lyle UER | .40 | .18 | .05 |
| (Misspelled Gary | | | |
| on card front) | | | |
| Chicago Bears | | | |
| ☐ 394 Jim Files | .40 | .18 | .05 |
| New York Giants | | | |
| ☐ 395 Jim Hart | 1.25 | .55 | .16 |
| St. Louis Cardinals | | | |
| ☐ 396 Dave Chapple | .40 | .18 | .05 |
| Los Angeles Rams | | | |
| ☐ 397 Jim Langer | 3.00 | 1.35 | .40 |
| Miami Dolphins | | | |
| ☐ 398 John Wilbur | .40 | .18 | .05 |
| Washington Redskins | | | |
| ☐ 399 Dwight Harrison | .40 | .18 | .05 |
| Buffalo Bills | | | |
| ☐ 400 John Brockington | .60 | .25 | .08 |
| Green Bay Packers | | | |
| ☐ 401 Ken Anderson | 7.00 | 3.10 | .85 |
| Cincinnati Bengals | | | |
| ☐ 402 Mike Tilleman | .40 | .18 | .05 |
| Atlanta Falcons | | | |
| ☐ 403 Charlie Hall | .40 | .18 | .05 |
| Cleveland Browns | | | |
| ☐ 404 Tommy Hart | .40 | .18 | .05 |
| San Francisco 49ers | | | |
| ☐ 405 Norm Bulaich | .50 | .23 | .06 |
| Philadelphia Eagles | | | |
| ☐ 406 Jim Turner | .50 | .23 | .06 |
| Denver Broncos | | | |

| | | | |
|---|---|---|---|
| ☐ 407 Mo Moorman | .40 | .18 | .05 |
| Kansas City Chiefs | | | |
| ☐ 408 Ralph Anderson | .40 | .18 | .05 |
| New England Patriots | | | |
| ☐ 409 Jim Otto | 1.50 | .65 | .19 |
| Oakland Raiders | | | |
| ☐ 410 Andy Russell | .50 | .23 | .06 |
| Pittsburgh Steelers | | | |
| ☐ 411 Glenn Doughty | .40 | .18 | .05 |
| Baltimore Colts | | | |
| ☐ 412 Altie Taylor | .50 | .23 | .06 |
| Detroit Lions | | | |
| ☐ 413 Marv Bateman | .40 | .18 | .05 |
| Dallas Cowboys | | | |
| ☐ 414 Willie Alexander | .40 | .18 | .05 |
| Houston Oilers | | | |
| ☐ 415 Bill Zapalac | .40 | .18 | .05 |
| New York Jets | | | |
| ☐ 416 Russ Washington | .40 | .18 | .05 |
| San Diego Chargers | | | |
| ☐ 417 Joe Federspiel | .40 | .18 | .05 |
| New Orleans Saints | | | |
| ☐ 418 Craig Cotton | .40 | .18 | .05 |
| Chicago Bears | | | |
| ☐ 419 Randy Johnson | .50 | .23 | .06 |
| New York Giants | | | |
| ☐ 420 Harold Jackson | 1.00 | .45 | .13 |
| Los Angeles Rams | | | |
| ☐ 421 Roger Wehrli | .50 | .23 | .06 |
| St. Louis Cardinals | | | |
| ☐ 422 Charlie Harraway | .40 | .18 | .05 |
| Washington Redskins | | | |
| ☐ 423 Spike Jones | .40 | .18 | .05 |
| Buffalo Bills | | | |
| ☐ 424 Bob Johnson | .40 | .18 | .05 |
| Cincinnati Bengals | | | |
| ☐ 425 Mike McCoy | .40 | .18 | .05 |
| Green Bay Packers | | | |
| ☐ 426 Dennis Havig HOR | .40 | .18 | .05 |
| Atlanta Falcons | | | |
| ☐ 427 Bob McKay | .40 | .18 | .05 |
| Cleveland Browns | | | |
| ☐ 428 Steve Zabel | .40 | .18 | .05 |
| Philadelphia Eagles | | | |
| ☐ 429 Horace Jones | .40 | .18 | .05 |
| Oakland Raiders | | | |
| ☐ 430 Jim Johnson | 1.25 | .55 | .16 |
| San Francisco 49ers | | | |
| ☐ 431 Roy Gerela | .50 | .23 | .06 |
| Pittsburgh Steelers | | | |
| ☐ 432 Tom Graham | .40 | .18 | .05 |
| Denver Broncos | | | |
| ☐ 433 Curley Culp | .50 | .23 | .06 |
| Kansas City Chiefs | | | |
| ☐ 434 Ken Mendenhall | .40 | .18 | .05 |
| Baltimore Colts | | | |
| ☐ 435 Jim Plunkett | 3.00 | 1.35 | .40 |
| New England Patriots | | | |
| ☐ 436 Julian Fagan | .40 | .18 | .05 |
| New York Jets | | | |
| ☐ 437 Mike Garrett | .50 | .23 | .06 |
| San Diego Chargers | | | |
| ☐ 438 Bobby Joe Green | .40 | .18 | .05 |
| Chicago Bears | | | |
| ☐ 439 Jack Gregory HOR | .40 | .18 | .05 |
| New York Giants | | | |
| ☐ 440 Charlie Sanders | .50 | .23 | .06 |
| Detroit Lions | | | |
| ☐ 441 Bill Curry | .50 | .23 | .06 |
| Houston Oilers | | | |
| ☐ 442 Bob Pollard | .40 | .18 | .05 |
| New Orleans Saints | | | |
| ☐ 443 David Ray | .40 | .18 | .05 |
| Los Angeles Rams | | | |
| ☐ 444 Terry Metcalf | 3.50 | 1.55 | .45 |
| St. Louis Cardinals | | | |
| ☐ 445 Pat Fischer | .50 | .23 | .06 |
| Washington Redskins | | | |
| ☐ 446 Bob Chandler | .50 | .23 | .06 |
| Buffalo Bills | | | |
| ☐ 447 Bill Bergey | 1.00 | .45 | .13 |
| Cincinnati Bengals | | | |
| ☐ 448 Walter Johnson | .40 | .18 | .05 |
| Cleveland Browns | | | |
| ☐ 449 Charley Young | 1.25 | .55 | .16 |
| Philadelphia Eagles | | | |
| ☐ 450 Chester Marcol | .50 | .23 | .06 |
| Green Bay Packers | | | |
| ☐ 451 Ken Stabler | 15.00 | 6.75 | 1.90 |
| Oakland Raiders | | | |
| ☐ 452 Preston Pearson | .75 | .35 | .09 |
| Pittsburgh Steelers | | | |
| ☐ 453 Mike Current | .40 | .18 | .05 |
| Denver Broncos | | | |
| ☐ 454 Ron Bolton | .40 | .18 | .05 |
| New England Patriots | | | |
| ☐ 455 Mark Lomas | .40 | .18 | .05 |

New York Jets
- ☐ 456 Raymond Chester ............... .50 .23 .06
  Baltimore Colts
- ☐ 457 Jerry LeVias ..................... .50 .23 .06
  San Diego Chargers
- ☐ 458 Skip Butler ...................... .40 .18 .05
  Houston Oilers
- ☐ 459 Mike Livingston ............... .75 .35 .09
  Kansas City Chiefs
- ☐ 460 AFC Semi-Finals ............... .75 .35 .09
  Raiders 33,
  Steelers 14 and
  Dolphins 34,
  Bengals 16
- ☐ 461 NFC Semi-Finals ............... 3.50 1.55 .45
  Vikings 27,
  Redskins 20 and
  Cowboys 27,
  Rams 16
  (Staubach)
- ☐ 462 Playoff Championship ......... 3.00 1.35 .40
  Dolphins 27,
  Raiders 10 and
  Vikings 27,
  Cowboys 10
  (Stabler/Tarkenton)
- ☐ 463 Super Bowl ..................... 2.50 1.15 .30
  Dolphins 24,
  Vikings 7
- ☐ 464 Wayne Mulligan ............... .40 .18 .05
  St. Louis Cardinals
- ☐ 465 Horst Muhlmann ............... .40 .18 .05
  Cincinnati Bengals
- ☐ 466 Milt Morin ...................... .40 .18 .05
  Cleveland Browns
- ☐ 467 Don Parish ..................... .40 .18 .05
  Denver Broncos
- ☐ 468 Richard Neal ................... .40 .18 .05
  New York Jets
- ☐ 469 Ron Jessie ..................... .50 .23 .06
  Detroit Lions
- ☐ 470 Terry Bradshaw ............... 20.00 9.00 2.50
  Pittsburgh Steelers
- ☐ 471 Fred Dryer ..................... 2.50 1.15 .30
  Los Angeles Rams
- ☐ 472 Jim Carter ..................... .40 .18 .05
  Green Bay Packers
- ☐ 473 Ken Burrow ..................... .40 .18 .05
  Atlanta Falcons
- ☐ 474 Wally Chambers ............... 1.00 .45 .13
  Chicago Bears
- ☐ 475 Dan Pastorini ................. .75 .35 .09
  Houston Oilers
- ☐ 476 Don Morrison .................. .40 .18 .05
  New Orleans Saints
- ☐ 477 Carl Mauck ..................... .40 .18 .05
  San Diego Chargers
- ☐ 478 Larry Cole ..................... .75 .35 .09
  Dallas Cowboys
- ☐ 479 Jim Kiick ....................... .60 .25 .08
  Miami Dolphins
- ☐ 480 Willie Lanier ................... 1.25 .55 .16
  Kansas City Chiefs
- ☐ 481 Don Herrmann ................. .40 .18 .05
  New York Giants
- ☐ 482 George Hunt .................... .40 .18 .05
  Baltimore Colts
- ☐ 483 Bob Howard .................... .40 .18 .05
  San Diego Chargers
- ☐ 484 Myron Pottios ................. .40 .18 .05
  Washington Redskins
- ☐ 485 Jackie Smith ................... 1.00 .45 .13
  St. Louis Cardinals
- ☐ 486 Vern Holland ................... .40 .18 .05
  Cincinnati Bengals
- ☐ 487 Jim Braxton .................... .40 .18 .05
  Buffalo Bills
- ☐ 488 Joe Reed ....................... .40 .18 .05
  San Francisco 49ers
- ☐ 489 Wally Hilgenberg ............. .40 .18 .05
  Minnesota Vikings
- ☐ 490 Fred Biletnikoff ............... 3.50 1.55 .45
  Oakland Raiders
- ☐ 491 Bob DeMarco HOR ............ .40 .18 .05
  Cleveland Browns
- ☐ 492 Mark Nordquist ............... .40 .18 .05
  Philadelphia Eagles
- ☐ 493 Larry Brooks ................... .40 .18 .05
  Los Angeles Rams
- ☐ 494 Pete Athas ..................... .40 .18 .05
  New York Giants
- ☐ 495 Emerson Boozer ............... .50 .23 .06
  New York Jets
- ☐ 496 L.C. Greenwood ............... 1.50 .65 .19
  Pittsburgh Steelers
- ☐ 497 Rockne Freitas ............... .40 .18 .05
  Detroit Lions
- ☐ 498 Checklist 397-528 UER ........ 3.00 .30 .09

(510 Charlie Taylor
should be Charley)
- ☐ 499 Joe Schmiesing................ .40 .18 .05
  Baltimore Colts
- ☐ 500 Roger Staubach ............... 27.00 12.00 3.40
  Dallas Cowboys
- ☐ 501 Al Cowlings UER ............... 1.50 .65 .19
  (Def. tackle on front,
  Def. End on back)
  Houston Oilers
- ☐ 502 Sam Cunningham ............. 2.00 .90 .25
  New England Patriots
- ☐ 503 Dennis Partee ................. .40 .18 .05
  San Diego Chargers
- ☐ 504 John Didion .................... .40 .18 .05
  New Orleans Saints
- ☐ 505 Nick Buoniconti ............... 1.00 .45 .13
  Miami Dolphins
- ☐ 506 Carl Garrett ................... .40 .18 .05
  Chicago Bears
- ☐ 507 Doug Van Horn ............... .40 .18 .05
  New York Giants
- ☐ 508 Jamie Rivers .................. .40 .18 .05
  St. Louis Cardinals
- ☐ 509 Jack Youngblood .............. 4.00 1.80 .50
  Los Angeles Rams
- ☐ 510 Charley Taylor UER ............ 2.50 1.15 .30
  (Misspelled Charlie
  on both sides)
  Washington Redskins
- ☐ 511 Ken Riley ....................... .60 .25 .08
  Cincinnati Bengals
- ☐ 512 Joe Ferguson .................. 2.50 1.15 .30
  Buffalo Bills
- ☐ 513 Bill Lueck ...................... .40 .18 .05
  Green Bay Packers
- ☐ 514 Ray Brown ..................... .40 .18 .05
  Atlanta Falcons
- ☐ 515 Fred Cox ....................... .50 .23 .06
  Minnesota Vikings
- ☐ 516 Joe Jones ...................... .40 .18 .05
  Cleveland Browns
- ☐ 517 Larry Schreiber ............... .40 .18 .05
  San Francisco 49ers
- ☐ 518 Dennis Wirgowski ............ .40 .18 .05
  Philadelphia Eagles
- ☐ 519 Leroy Mitchell ................. .40 .18 .05
  Denver Broncos
- ☐ 520 Otis Taylor ..................... .60 .25 .08
  Kansas City Chiefs
- ☐ 521 Henry Davis .................... .40 .18 .05
  Pittsburgh Steelers
- ☐ 522 Bruce Barnes .................. .40 .18 .05
  New England Patriots
- ☐ 523 Charlie Smith .................. .40 .18 .05
  Oakland Raiders
- ☐ 524 Bert Jones ..................... 4.50 2.00 .55
  Baltimore Colts
- ☐ 525 Lem Barney .................... 2.00 .90 .25
  Detroit Lions
- ☐ 526 John Fitzgerald ............... .50 .23 .06
  Dallas Cowboys
- ☐ 527 Tom Funchess .................. .40 .18 .05
  Houston Oilers
- ☐ 528 Steve Tannen .................. .75 .19 .06
  New York Jets

# 1974 Topps Team Checklists

The 1974 Topps Team Checklist set contains 26 cards. The cards measure 2 1/2" by 3 1/2" and were inserted into regular issue 1974 Topps football wax packs. The Topps logo and team name appear at the top of the card, while the mid-portion of the card contains the actual checklist giving each player's card number, check-off box, name, uniform number, and position. The lower portion of the card contains an ad to obtain all 26 team checklists. A picture of a boy collector is shown in the lower right corner. The back of the card contains rules for a football game to be played with the 1974 Topps football cards. These unnumbered cards are numbered below for convenience in alphabetical order by team name. Twenty of the 26 checklist cards show players out of alphabetical order on the card front. The cards can all be found with one or two asterisks on the front. The set was also available directly from Topps on a pair of unperforated uncut sheets, which had blank backs.

| | NRMT | VG-E | GOOD |
|---|---|---|---|
| COMPLETE SET (26) | 50.00 | 20.00 | 5.00 |
| COMMON TEAM (1-26) | 3.00 | 1.20 | .30 |
| ☐ 1 Atlanta Falcons | 3.00 | 1.20 | .30 |
| ☐ 2 Baltimore Colts | 3.00 | 1.20 | .30 |
| ☐ 3 Buffalo Bills | 3.00 | 1.20 | .30 |
| ☐ 4 Chicago Bears | 4.00 | 1.60 | .40 |
| ☐ 5 Cincinnati Bengals | 3.00 | 1.20 | .30 |
| ☐ 6 Cleveland Browns UER | 3.00 | 1.20 | .30 |
| (Reggie Rucher) | | | |
| ☐ 7 Dallas Cowboys | 5.00 | 2.00 | .50 |
| ☐ 8 Denver Broncos | 4.00 | 1.60 | .40 |
| ☐ 9 Detroit Lions | 3.00 | 1.20 | .30 |
| ☐ 10 Green Bay Packers | 3.00 | 1.20 | .30 |
| ☐ 11 Houston Oilers | 3.00 | 1.20 | .30 |
| ☐ 12 Kansas City Chiefs | 3.00 | 1.20 | .30 |
| ☐ 13 Los Angeles Rams | 3.00 | 1.20 | .30 |
| ☐ 14 Miami Dolphins | 4.00 | 1.60 | .40 |
| ☐ 15 Minnesota Vikings | 3.00 | 1.20 | .30 |
| ☐ 16 New England Patriots | 3.00 | 1.20 | .30 |
| ☐ 17 New Orleans Saints | 3.00 | 1.20 | .30 |
| ☐ 18 New York Giants | 4.00 | 1.60 | .40 |
| ☐ 19 New York Jets | 4.00 | 1.60 | .40 |
| ☐ 20 Oakland Raiders | 5.00 | 2.00 | .50 |
| ☐ 21 Philadelphia Eagles | 3.00 | 1.20 | .30 |
| ☐ 22 Pittsburgh Steelers | 4.00 | 1.60 | .40 |
| ☐ 23 St. Louis Cardinals | 3.00 | 1.20 | .30 |
| ☐ 24 San Diego Chargers | 3.00 | 1.20 | .30 |
| ☐ 25 San Francisco 49ers | 4.00 | 1.60 | .40 |
| ☐ 26 Washington Redskins UER | 4.00 | 1.60 | .40 |
| (Charley Taylor mis- | | | |
| spelled as Charlie) | | | |

## 1975 Topps

MERLIN OLSEN

The 1975 Topps football set contains 528 cards. The cards measure 2 1/2" by 3 1/2". The first six cards in the set depict the statistical league leaders from each league. Cards 7 and 8 both show George Blanda in a very similar pose but with a different color jersey. Cards 201-225 are the All-Pro (AP) selections at each position. Record Breakers (351-356) and Highlights (452-460) are also featured in this set. Post-season action is summarized on cards 526-528. No known scarcities exist. The card backs are printed in black ink with a green background on gray card stock. The key Rookie Cards in this set are Otis Armstrong, Rocky Bleier, Mel Blount, Cliff Branch, Dan Fouts, Cliff Harris, Drew Pearson, Lynn Swann, and Charlie Waters. The set also includes Joe Theismann's first American football card marking his return from the CFL.

| | NRMT | VG-E | GOOD |
|---|---|---|---|
| COMPLETE SET (528) | 325.00 | 145.00 | 40.00 |
| COMMON PLAYER (1-528) | .30 | .14 | .04 |
| ☐ 1 Rushing Leaders | 1.75 | .35 | .11 |
| Lawrence McCutcheon | | | |
| Otis Armstrong | | | |
| ☐ 2 Passing Leaders | 1.25 | .55 | .16 |
| Sonny Jurgensen | | | |
| Ken Anderson | | | |
| ☐ 3 Receiving Leaders | .60 | .25 | .08 |
| Charley Young | | | |

| | | | |
|---|---|---|---|
| Lydell Mitchell | | | |
| ☐ 4 Scoring Leaders | .60 | .25 | .08 |
| Chester Marcol | | | |
| Roy Gerela | | | |
| ☐ 5 Interception Leaders | .60 | .25 | .08 |
| Ray Brown | | | |
| Emmitt Thomas | | | |
| ☐ 6 Punting Leaders | .60 | .25 | .08 |
| Tom Blanchard | | | |
| Ray Guy | | | |
| ☐ 7 George Blanda | 5.00 | 2.30 | .60 |
| Oakland Raiders | | | |
| (Black jersey; | | | |
| highlights on back) | | | |
| ☐ 8 George Blanda | 5.00 | 2.30 | .60 |
| Oakland Raiders | | | |
| (White jersey; | | | |
| career record on back) | | | |
| ☐ 9 Ralph Baker | .30 | .14 | .04 |
| New York Jets | | | |
| ☐ 10 Don Woods | .30 | .14 | .04 |
| San Diego Chargers | | | |
| ☐ 11 Bob Asher | .30 | .14 | .04 |
| Chicago Bears | | | |
| ☐ 12 Mel Blount | 25.00 | 11.50 | 3.10 |
| Pittsburgh Steelers | | | |
| ☐ 13 Sam Cunningham | .60 | .25 | .08 |
| New England Patriots | | | |
| ☐ 14 Jackie Smith | .75 | .35 | .09 |
| St. Louis Cardinals | | | |
| ☐ 15 Greg Landry | .60 | .25 | .08 |
| Detroit Lions | | | |
| ☐ 16 Buck Buchanan | 1.00 | .45 | .13 |
| Kansas City Chiefs | | | |
| ☐ 17 Haven Moses | .35 | .16 | .04 |
| Denver Broncos | | | |
| ☐ 18 Clarence Ellis | .30 | .14 | .04 |
| Atlanta Falcons | | | |
| ☐ 19 Jim Carter | .30 | .14 | .04 |
| Green Bay Packers | | | |
| ☐ 20 Charley Taylor UER | 2.00 | .90 | .25 |
| Washington Redskins | | | |
| (Misspelled Charlie | | | |
| on card front) | | | |
| ☐ 21 Jess Phillips | .30 | .14 | .04 |
| New Orleans Saints | | | |
| ☐ 22 Larry Seiple | .35 | .16 | .04 |
| Miami Dolphins | | | |
| ☐ 23 Doug Dieken | .30 | .14 | .04 |
| Cleveland Browns | | | |
| ☐ 24 Ron Saul | .30 | .14 | .04 |
| Houston Oilers | | | |
| ☐ 25 Isaac Curtis UER | .75 | .35 | .09 |
| (Misspelled Issac | | | |
| on card front) | | | |
| Cincinnati Bengals | | | |
| ☐ 26 Gary Larsen | .75 | .35 | .09 |
| Minnesota Vikings | | | |
| ☐ 27 Bruce Jarvis | .30 | .14 | .04 |
| Buffalo Bills | | | |
| ☐ 28 Steve Zabel | .30 | .14 | .04 |
| Philadelphia Eagles | | | |
| ☐ 29 John Mendenhall | .30 | .14 | .04 |
| New York Giants | | | |
| ☐ 30 Rick Volk | .30 | .14 | .04 |
| Baltimore Colts | | | |
| ☐ 31 Checklist 1-132 | 2.50 | .25 | .08 |
| ☐ 32 Dan Abramowicz | .35 | .16 | .04 |
| San Francisco 49ers | | | |
| ☐ 33 Bubba Smith | 2.00 | .90 | .25 |
| Oakland Raiders | | | |
| ☐ 34 David Ray | .30 | .14 | .04 |
| Los Angeles Rams | | | |
| ☐ 35 Dan Dierdorf | 2.00 | .90 | .25 |
| St. Louis Cardinals | | | |
| ☐ 36 Randy Rasmussen | .30 | .14 | .04 |
| New York Jets | | | |
| ☐ 37 Bob Howard | .30 | .14 | .04 |
| San Diego Chargers | | | |
| ☐ 38 Gary Huff | .35 | .16 | .04 |
| Chicago Bears | | | |
| ☐ 39 Rocky Bleier | 12.00 | 5.50 | 1.50 |
| Pittsburgh Steelers | | | |
| ☐ 40 Mel Gray | .35 | .16 | .04 |
| St. Louis Cardinals | | | |
| ☐ 41 Tony McGee | .30 | .14 | .04 |
| New England Patriots | | | |
| ☐ 42 Larry Hand | .30 | .14 | .04 |
| Detroit Lions | | | |
| ☐ 43 Wendell Hayes | .35 | .16 | .04 |
| Kansas City Chiefs | | | |
| ☐ 44 Doug Wilkerson | .50 | .23 | .06 |
| San Diego Chargers | | | |
| ☐ 45 Paul Smith | .30 | .14 | .04 |
| Denver Broncos | | | |
| ☐ 46 Dave Robinson | .35 | .16 | .04 |
| Washington Redskins | | | |
| ☐ 47 Bivian Lee | .30 | .14 | .04 |

New Orleans Saints
| | | | | |
|---|---|---|---|---|
| ☐ 48 Jim Mandich | .50 | .23 | .06 |
| Miami Dolphins | | | |
| ☐ 49 Greg Pruitt | 1.00 | .45 | .13 |
| Cleveland Browns | | | |
| ☐ 50 Dan Pastorini UER | .60 | .25 | .08 |
| (5/26/39 birthdate incorrect) | | | |
| Houston Oilers | | | |
| ☐ 51 Ron Pritchard | .30 | .14 | .04 |
| Cincinnati Bengals | | | |
| ☐ 52 Dan Conners | .30 | .14 | .04 |
| Oakland Raiders | | | |
| ☐ 53 Fred Cox | .35 | .16 | .04 |
| Minnesota Vikings | | | |
| ☐ 54 Tony Greene | .30 | .14 | .04 |
| Buffalo Bills | | | |
| ☐ 55 Craig Morton | .75 | .35 | .09 |
| New York Giants | | | |
| ☐ 56 Jerry Sisemore | .35 | .16 | .04 |
| Philadelphia Eagles | | | |
| ☐ 57 Glenn Doughty | .30 | .14 | .04 |
| Baltimore Colts | | | |
| ☐ 58 Larry Schreiber | .30 | .14 | .04 |
| San Francisco 49ers | | | |
| ☐ 59 Charlie Waters | 4.00 | 1.80 | .50 |
| Dallas Cowboys | | | |
| ☐ 60 Jack Youngblood | 1.50 | .65 | .19 |
| Los Angeles Rams | | | |
| ☐ 61 Bill Lenkaitis | .30 | .14 | .04 |
| New England Patriots | | | |
| ☐ 62 Greg Brezina | .30 | .14 | .04 |
| Atlanta Falcons | | | |
| ☐ 63 Bob Pollard | .30 | .14 | .04 |
| New Orleans Saints | | | |
| ☐ 64 Mack Alston | .30 | .14 | .04 |
| Houston Oilers | | | |
| ☐ 65 Drew Pearson | 12.00 | 5.50 | 1.50 |
| Dallas Cowboys | | | |
| ☐ 66 Charlie Stukes | .30 | .14 | .04 |
| Los Angeles Rams | | | |
| ☐ 67 Emerson Boozer | .35 | .16 | .04 |
| New York Jets | | | |
| ☐ 68 Dennis Partee | .30 | .14 | .04 |
| San Diego Chargers | | | |
| ☐ 69 Bob Newton | .30 | .14 | .04 |
| Chicago Bears | | | |
| ☐ 70 Jack Tatum | .35 | .16 | .04 |
| Oakland Raiders | | | |
| ☐ 71 Frank Lewis | .35 | .16 | .04 |
| Pittsburgh Steelers | | | |
| ☐ 72 Bob Young | .30 | .14 | .04 |
| St. Louis Cardinals | | | |
| ☐ 73 Julius Adams | .30 | .14 | .04 |
| New England Patriots | | | |
| ☐ 74 Paul Naumoff | .30 | .14 | .04 |
| Detroit Lions | | | |
| ☐ 75 Otis Taylor | .60 | .25 | .08 |
| Kansas City Chiefs | | | |
| ☐ 76 Dave Hampton | .30 | .14 | .04 |
| Atlanta Falcons | | | |
| ☐ 77 Mike Current | .30 | .14 | .04 |
| Denver Broncos | | | |
| ☐ 78 Brig Owens | .30 | .14 | .04 |
| Washington Redskins | | | |
| ☐ 79 Bobby Scott | .35 | .16 | .04 |
| New Orleans Saints | | | |
| ☐ 80 Harold Carmichael | 3.00 | 1.35 | .40 |
| Philadelphia Eagles | | | |
| ☐ 81 Bill Stanfill | .35 | .16 | .04 |
| Miami Dolphins | | | |
| ☐ 82 Bob Babich | .30 | .14 | .04 |
| Cleveland Browns | | | |
| ☐ 83 Vic Washington | .35 | .16 | .04 |
| Houston Oilers | | | |
| ☐ 84 Mick Tingelhoff | .35 | .16 | .04 |
| Minnesota Vikings | | | |
| ☐ 85 Bob Trumpy | 1.00 | .45 | .13 |
| Cincinnati Bengals | | | |
| ☐ 86 Earl Edwards | .30 | .14 | .04 |
| Buffalo Bills | | | |
| ☐ 87 Ron Hornsby | .30 | .14 | .04 |
| New York Giants | | | |
| ☐ 88 Don McCauley | .30 | .14 | .04 |
| Baltimore Colts | | | |
| ☐ 89 Jim Johnson | 1.00 | .45 | .13 |
| San Francisco 49ers | | | |
| ☐ 90 Andy Russell | .35 | .16 | .04 |
| Pittsburgh Steelers | | | |
| ☐ 91 Cornell Green | .35 | .16 | .04 |
| Dallas Cowboys | | | |
| ☐ 92 Charlie Cowan | .30 | .14 | .04 |
| Los Angeles Rams | | | |
| ☐ 93 Jon Staggers | .30 | .14 | .04 |
| Green Bay Packers | | | |
| ☐ 94 Billy Newsome | .30 | .14 | .04 |
| New York Jets | | | |
| ☐ 95 Willie Brown | 1.00 | .45 | .13 |

Oakland Raiders
| | | | | |
|---|---|---|---|---|
| ☐ 96 Carl Mauck | .30 | .14 | .04 |
| San Diego Chargers | | | |
| ☐ 97 Doug Buffone | .30 | .14 | .04 |
| Chicago Bears | | | |
| ☐ 98 Preston Pearson | .60 | .25 | .08 |
| Pittsburgh Steelers | | | |
| ☐ 99 Jim Bakken | .35 | .16 | .04 |
| St. Louis Cardinals | | | |
| ☐ 100 Bob Griese | 5.00 | 2.30 | .60 |
| Miami Dolphins | | | |
| ☐ 101 Bob Windsor | .30 | .14 | .04 |
| New England Patriots | | | |
| ☐ 102 Rockne Freitas | .30 | .14 | .04 |
| Detroit Lions | | | |
| ☐ 103 Jim Marsalis | .30 | .14 | .04 |
| Kansas City Chiefs | | | |
| ☐ 104 Bill Thompson | .35 | .16 | .04 |
| Denver Broncos | | | |
| ☐ 105 Ken Burrow | .30 | .14 | .04 |
| Atlanta Falcons | | | |
| ☐ 106 Diron Talbert | .35 | .16 | .04 |
| Washington Redskins | | | |
| ☐ 107 Joe Federspiel | .30 | .14 | .04 |
| New Orleans Saints | | | |
| ☐ 108 Norm Bulaich | .35 | .16 | .04 |
| Philadelphia Eagles | | | |
| ☐ 109 Bob DeMarco | .30 | .14 | .04 |
| Cleveland Browns | | | |
| ☐ 110 Tom Wittum | .30 | .14 | .04 |
| San Francisco 49ers | | | |
| ☐ 111 Larry Hefner | .30 | .14 | .04 |
| Green Bay Packers | | | |
| ☐ 112 Tody Smith | .30 | .14 | .04 |
| Houston Oilers | | | |
| ☐ 113 Stu Voigt | .35 | .16 | .04 |
| Minnesota Vikings | | | |
| ☐ 114 Horst Muhlmann | .30 | .14 | .04 |
| Cincinnati Bengals | | | |
| ☐ 115 Ahmad Rashad | 5.00 | 2.30 | .60 |
| Buffalo Bills | | | |
| ☐ 116 Joe Dawkins | .30 | .14 | .04 |
| New York Giants | | | |
| ☐ 117 George Kunz | .35 | .16 | .04 |
| Atlanta Falcons | | | |
| ☐ 118 D.D. Lewis | .35 | .16 | .04 |
| Dallas Cowboys | | | |
| ☐ 119 Levi Johnson | .30 | .14 | .04 |
| Detroit Lions | | | |
| ☐ 120 Len Dawson | 3.50 | 1.55 | .45 |
| Kansas City Chiefs | | | |
| ☐ 121 Jim Bertelsen | .30 | .14 | .04 |
| Los Angeles Rams | | | |
| ☐ 122 Ed Bell | .30 | .14 | .04 |
| New York Jets | | | |
| ☐ 123 Art Thoms | .30 | .14 | .04 |
| Oakland Raiders | | | |
| ☐ 124 Joe Beauchamp | .30 | .14 | .04 |
| San Diego Chargers | | | |
| ☐ 125 Jack Ham | 5.00 | 2.30 | .60 |
| Pittsburgh Steelers | | | |
| ☐ 126 Carl Garrett | .30 | .14 | .04 |
| Chicago Bears | | | |
| ☐ 127 Roger Finnie | .30 | .14 | .04 |
| St. Louis Cardinals | | | |
| ☐ 128 Howard Twilley | .35 | .16 | .04 |
| Miami Dolphins | | | |
| ☐ 129 Bruce Barnes | .30 | .14 | .04 |
| New England Patriots | | | |
| ☐ 130 Nate Wright | .35 | .16 | .04 |
| Minnesota Vikings | | | |
| ☐ 131 Jerry Tagge | .35 | .16 | .04 |
| Green Bay Packers | | | |
| ☐ 132 Floyd Little | 1.25 | .55 | .16 |
| Denver Broncos | | | |
| ☐ 133 John Zook | .30 | .14 | .04 |
| Atlanta Falcons | | | |
| ☐ 134 Len Hauss | .35 | .16 | .04 |
| Washington Redskins | | | |
| ☐ 135 Archie Manning | 1.50 | .65 | .19 |
| New Orleans Saints | | | |
| ☐ 136 Po James | .30 | .14 | .04 |
| Philadelphia Eagles | | | |
| ☐ 137 Walt Sumner | .30 | .14 | .04 |
| Cleveland Browns | | | |
| ☐ 138 Randy Beisler | .30 | .14 | .04 |
| San Francisco 49ers | | | |
| ☐ 139 Willie Alexander | .30 | .14 | .04 |
| Houston Oilers | | | |
| ☐ 140 Garo Yepremian | .35 | .16 | .04 |
| Miami Dolphins | | | |
| ☐ 141 Chip Myers | .30 | .14 | .04 |
| Cincinnati Bengals | | | |
| ☐ 142 Jim Braxton | .30 | .14 | .04 |
| Buffalo Bills | | | |
| ☐ 143 Doug Van Horn | .30 | .14 | .04 |
| New York Giants | | | |
| ☐ 144 Stan White | .30 | .14 | .04 |

| | | | |
|---|---|---|---|
| Baltimore Colts | | | |
| ☐ 145 Roger Staubach | 24.00 | 11.00 | 3.00 |
| Dallas Cowboys | | | |
| ☐ 146 Herman Weaver | .30 | .14 | .04 |
| Detroit Lions | | | |
| ☐ 147 Marvin Upshaw | .30 | .14 | .04 |
| Kansas City Chiefs | | | |
| ☐ 148 Bob Klein | .30 | .14 | .04 |
| Los Angeles Rams | | | |
| ☐ 149 Earlie Thomas | .30 | .14 | .04 |
| New York Jets | | | |
| ☐ 150 John Brockington | .30 | .14 | .04 |
| Green Bay Packers | | | |
| ☐ 151 Mike Siani | .30 | .14 | .04 |
| Oakland Raiders | | | |
| ☐ 152 Sam Davis | .30 | .14 | .04 |
| Pittsburgh Steelers | | | |
| ☐ 153 Mike Wagner | .35 | .16 | .04 |
| Pittsburgh Steelers | | | |
| ☐ 154 Larry Stallings | .30 | .14 | .04 |
| St. Louis Cardinals | | | |
| ☐ 155 Wally Chambers | .35 | .16 | .04 |
| Chicago Bears | | | |
| ☐ 156 Randy Vataha | .35 | .16 | .04 |
| New England Patriots | | | |
| ☐ 157 Jim Marshall | 1.00 | .45 | .13 |
| Minnesota Vikings | | | |
| ☐ 158 Jim Turner | .35 | .16 | .04 |
| Denver Broncos | | | |
| ☐ 159 Walt Sweeney | .35 | .16 | .04 |
| Washington Redskins | | | |
| ☐ 160 Ken Anderson | 3.50 | 1.55 | .45 |
| Cincinnati Bengals | | | |
| ☐ 161 Ray Brown | .30 | .14 | .04 |
| Atlanta Falcons | | | |
| ☐ 162 John Didion | .30 | .14 | .04 |
| New Orleans Saints | | | |
| ☐ 163 Tom Dempsey | .35 | .16 | .04 |
| Los Angeles Rams | | | |
| ☐ 164 Clarence Scott | .30 | .14 | .04 |
| Cleveland Browns | | | |
| ☐ 165 Gene Washington | .30 | .14 | .04 |
| San Francisco 49ers | | | |
| ☐ 166 Willie Rogers | .30 | .14 | .04 |
| Houston Oilers | | | |
| ☐ 167 Doug Swift | .30 | .14 | .04 |
| Miami Dolphins | | | |
| ☐ 168 Rufus Mayes | .30 | .14 | .04 |
| Cincinnati Bengals | | | |
| ☐ 169 Marv Bateman | .30 | .14 | .04 |
| Buffalo Bills | | | |
| ☐ 170 Lydell Mitchell | .35 | .16 | .04 |
| Baltimore Colts | | | |
| ☐ 171 Ron Smith | .30 | .14 | .04 |
| Oakland Raiders | | | |
| ☐ 172 Bill Munson | .35 | .16 | .04 |
| Detroit Lions | | | |
| ☐ 173 Bob Grim | .35 | .16 | .04 |
| New York Giants | | | |
| ☐ 174 Ed Budde | .35 | .16 | .04 |
| Kansas City Chiefs | | | |
| ☐ 175 Bob Lilly UER | 3.00 | 1.35 | .40 |
| (Was first draft, | | | |
| not first player) | | | |
| Dallas Cowboys | | | |
| ☐ 176 Jim Youngblood | 1.75 | .80 | .22 |
| Los Angeles Rams | | | |
| ☐ 177 Steve Tannen | .30 | .14 | .04 |
| New York Jets | | | |
| ☐ 178 Rich McGeorge | .30 | .14 | .04 |
| Green Bay Packers | | | |
| ☐ 179 Jim Tyrer | .35 | .16 | .04 |
| Washington Redskins | | | |
| ☐ 180 Forrest Blue | .30 | .14 | .04 |
| San Francisco 49ers | | | |
| ☐ 181 Jerry LeVias | .35 | .16 | .04 |
| San Diego Chargers | | | |
| ☐ 182 Joe Gilliam | .60 | .25 | .08 |
| Pittsburgh Steelers | | | |
| ☐ 183 Jim Otis | 1.25 | .55 | .16 |
| St. Louis Cardinals | | | |
| ☐ 184 Mel Tom | .30 | .14 | .04 |
| Chicago Bears | | | |
| ☐ 185 Faul Seymour | .30 | .14 | .04 |
| Buffalo Bills | | | |
| ☐ 186 George Webster | .35 | .16 | .04 |
| New England Patriots | | | |
| ☐ 187 Pete Duranko | .30 | .14 | .04 |
| Denver Broncos | | | |
| ☐ 188 Essex Johnson | .30 | .14 | .04 |
| Cincinnati Bengals | | | |
| ☐ 189 Bob Lee | .35 | .16 | .04 |
| Atlanta Falcons | | | |
| ☐ 190 Gene Upshaw | 1.25 | .55 | .16 |
| Oakland Raiders | | | |
| ☐ 191 Tom Myers | .30 | .14 | .04 |
| New Orleans Saints | | | |
| ☐ 192 Don Zimmerman | .30 | .14 | .04 |

| | | | |
|---|---|---|---|
| Philadelphia Eagles | | | |
| ☐ 193 John Garlington | .30 | .14 | .04 |
| Cleveland Browns | | | |
| ☐ 194 Skip Butler | .30 | .14 | .04 |
| Houston Oilers | | | |
| ☐ 195 Tom Mitchell | .30 | .14 | .04 |
| San Francisco 49ers | | | |
| ☐ 196 Jim Langer | 1.25 | .55 | .16 |
| Miami Dolphins | | | |
| ☐ 197 Ron Carpenter | .30 | .14 | .04 |
| Cincinnati Bengals | | | |
| ☐ 198 Dave Foley | .30 | .14 | .04 |
| Buffalo Bills | | | |
| ☐ 199 Bert Jones | 1.25 | .55 | .16 |
| Baltimore Colts | | | |
| ☐ 200 Larry Brown | .75 | .35 | .09 |
| Washington Redskins | | | |
| ☐ 201 All Pro Receivers | 2.00 | .90 | .25 |
| Charley Taylor | | | |
| Fred Biletnikoff | | | |
| ☐ 202 All Pro Tackles | .60 | .25 | .08 |
| Rayfield Wright | | | |
| Russ Washington | | | |
| ☐ 203 All Pro Guards | 1.00 | .45 | .13 |
| Tom Mack | | | |
| Larry Little | | | |
| ☐ 204 All Pro Centers | .60 | .25 | .08 |
| Jeff Van Note | | | |
| Jack Rudnay | | | |
| ☐ 205 All Pro Guards | 1.00 | .45 | .13 |
| Gale Gillingham | | | |
| John Hannah | | | |
| ☐ 206 All Pro Tackles | .75 | .35 | .09 |
| Dan Dierdorf | | | |
| Winston Hill | | | |
| ☐ 207 All Pro Tight Ends | .60 | .25 | .08 |
| Charley Young | | | |
| Riley Odoms | | | |
| ☐ 208 All Pro Quarterbacks | 3.00 | 1.35 | .40 |
| Fran Tarkenton | | | |
| Ken Stabler | | | |
| ☐ 209 All Pro Backs | 4.00 | 1.80 | .50 |
| Lawrence McCutcheon | | | |
| O.J. Simpson | | | |
| ☐ 210 All Pro Backs | .75 | .35 | .09 |
| Terry Metcalf | | | |
| Otis Armstrong | | | |
| ☐ 211 All Pro Receivers | .60 | .25 | .08 |
| Mel Gray | | | |
| Isaac Curtis | | | |
| ☐ 212 All Pro Kickers | .60 | .25 | .08 |
| Chester Marcol | | | |
| Roy Gerela | | | |
| ☐ 213 All Pro Ends | .75 | .35 | .09 |
| Jack Youngblood | | | |
| Elvin Bethea | | | |
| ☐ 214 All Pro Tackles | .60 | .25 | .08 |
| Alan Page | | | |
| Otis Sistrunk | | | |
| ☐ 215 All Pro Tackles | 1.25 | .55 | .16 |
| Merlin Olsen | | | |
| Mike Reid | | | |
| ☐ 216 All Pro Ends | 1.00 | .45 | .13 |
| Carl Eller | | | |
| Lyle Alzado | | | |
| ☐ 217 All Pro Linebackers | 1.00 | .45 | .13 |
| Ted Hendricks | | | |
| Phil Villapiano | | | |
| ☐ 218 All Pro Linebackers | 1.00 | .45 | .13 |
| Lee Roy Jordan | | | |
| Willie Lanier | | | |
| ☐ 219 All Pro Linebackers | .60 | .25 | .08 |
| Isiah Robertson | | | |
| Andy Russell | | | |
| ☐ 220 All Pro Cornerbacks | .60 | .25 | .08 |
| Nate Wright | | | |
| Emmitt Thomas | | | |
| ☐ 221 All Pro Cornerbacks | .60 | .25 | .08 |
| Willie Buchanon | | | |
| Lemar Parrish | | | |
| ☐ 222 All Pro Safeties | 1.00 | .45 | .13 |
| Ken Houston | | | |
| Dick Anderson | | | |
| ☐ 223 All Pro Safeties | 1.00 | .45 | .13 |
| Cliff Harris | | | |
| Jack Tatum | | | |
| ☐ 224 All Pro Punters | .60 | .25 | .08 |
| Tom Wittum | | | |
| Ray Guy | | | |
| ☐ 225 All Pro Returners | .60 | .25 | .08 |
| Terry Metcalf | | | |
| Greg Pruitt | | | |
| ☐ 226 Ted Kwalick | .35 | .16 | .04 |
| San Francisco 49ers | | | |
| ☐ 227 Spider Lockhart | .35 | .16 | .04 |
| New York Giants | | | |
| ☐ 228 Mike Livingston | .35 | .16 | .04 |
| Kansas City Chiefs | | | |

| | | | | |
|---|---|---|---|---|
| ☐ 229 Larry Cole | .35 | .16 | .04 |
| Dallas Cowboys | | | |
| ☐ 230 Gary Garrison | .35 | .16 | .04 |
| San Diego Chargers | | | |
| ☐ 231 Larry Brooks | .30 | .14 | .04 |
| Los Angeles Rams | | | |
| ☐ 232 Bobby Howfield | .30 | .14 | .04 |
| New York Jets | | | |
| ☐ 233 Fred Carr | .35 | .16 | .04 |
| Green Bay Packers | | | |
| ☐ 234 Norm Evans | .35 | .16 | .04 |
| Miami Dolphins | | | |
| ☐ 235 Dwight White | .35 | .16 | .04 |
| Pittsburgh Steelers | | | |
| ☐ 236 Conrad Dobler | .35 | .16 | .04 |
| St. Louis Cardinals | | | |
| ☐ 237 Garry Lyle | .30 | .14 | .04 |
| Chicago Bears | | | |
| ☐ 238 Darryl Stingley | .75 | .35 | .09 |
| New England Patriots | | | |
| ☐ 239 Tom Graham | .30 | .14 | .04 |
| Denver Broncos | | | |
| ☐ 240 Chuck Foreman | 1.25 | .55 | .16 |
| Minnesota Vikings | | | |
| ☐ 241 Ken Riley | .35 | .16 | .04 |
| Cincinnati Bengals | | | |
| ☐ 242 Don Morrison | .30 | .14 | .04 |
| New Orleans Saints | | | |
| ☐ 243 Lynn Dickey | .75 | .35 | .09 |
| Houston Oilers | | | |
| ☐ 244 Don Cockroft | .35 | .16 | .04 |
| Cleveland Browns | | | |
| ☐ 245 Claude Humphrey | .35 | .16 | .04 |
| Atlanta Falcons | | | |
| ☐ 246 John Skorupan | .30 | .14 | .04 |
| Buffalo Bills | | | |
| ☐ 247 Raymond Chester | .35 | .16 | .04 |
| Baltimore Colts | | | |
| ☐ 248 Cas Banaszek | .30 | .14 | .04 |
| San Francisco 49ers | | | |
| ☐ 249 Art Malone | .30 | .14 | .04 |
| Philadelphia Eagles | | | |
| ☐ 250 Ed Flanagan | .30 | .14 | .04 |
| Detroit Lions | | | |
| ☐ 251 Checklist 133-264 | 2.50 | .25 | .08 |
| ☐ 252 Nemiah Wilson | .30 | .14 | .04 |
| Chicago Bears | | | |
| ☐ 253 Ron Jessie | .35 | .16 | .04 |
| Detroit Lions | | | |
| ☐ 254 Jim Lynch | .30 | .14 | .04 |
| Kansas City Chiefs | | | |
| ☐ 255 Bob Tucker | .35 | .16 | .04 |
| New York Giants | | | |
| ☐ 256 Terry Owens | .30 | .14 | .04 |
| San Diego Chargers | | | |
| ☐ 257 John Fitzgerald | .35 | .16 | .04 |
| Dallas Cowboys | | | |
| ☐ 258 Jack Snow | .35 | .16 | .04 |
| Los Angeles Rams | | | |
| ☐ 259 Garry Puetz | .30 | .14 | .04 |
| New York Jets | | | |
| ☐ 260 Mike Phipps | .35 | .16 | .04 |
| Cleveland Browns | | | |
| ☐ 261 Al Matthews | .30 | .14 | .04 |
| Green Bay Packers | | | |
| ☐ 262 Bob Kuechenberg | .40 | .18 | .05 |
| Miami Dolphins | | | |
| ☐ 263 Ron Yankowski | .30 | .14 | .04 |
| St. Louis Cardinals | | | |
| ☐ 264 Ron Shanklin | .30 | .14 | .04 |
| Pittsburgh Steelers | | | |
| ☐ 265 Bobby Douglass | .35 | .16 | .04 |
| Chicago Bears | | | |
| ☐ 266 Josh Ashton | .30 | .14 | .04 |
| New England Patriots | | | |
| ☐ 267 Bill Van Heusen | .30 | .14 | .04 |
| Denver Broncos | | | |
| ☐ 268 Jeff Siemon | .30 | .14 | .04 |
| Minnesota Vikings | | | |
| ☐ 269 Bob Newland | .30 | .14 | .04 |
| New Orleans Saints | | | |
| ☐ 270 Gale Gillingham | .30 | .14 | .04 |
| Green Bay Packers | | | |
| ☐ 271 Zeke Moore | .30 | .14 | .04 |
| Houston Oilers | | | |
| ☐ 272 Mike Tilleman | .30 | .14 | .04 |
| Atlanta Falcons | | | |
| ☐ 273 John Leypoldt | .30 | .14 | .04 |
| Buffalo Bills | | | |
| ☐ 274 Ken Mendenhall | .30 | .14 | .04 |
| Baltimore Colts | | | |
| ☐ 275 Norm Snead | .35 | .16 | .04 |
| San Francisco 49ers | | | |
| ☐ 276 Bill Bradley | .30 | .14 | .04 |
| Philadelphia Eagles | | | |
| ☐ 277 Jerry Smith | .35 | .16 | .04 |
| Washington Redskins | | | |

| | | | | |
|---|---|---|---|---|
| ☐ 278 Clarence Davis | .35 | .16 | .04 |
| Oakland Raiders | | | |
| ☐ 279 Jim Yarbrough | .30 | .14 | .04 |
| Detroit Lions | | | |
| ☐ 280 Lemar Parrish | .35 | .16 | .04 |
| Cincinnati Bengals | | | |
| ☐ 281 Bobby Bell | 1.00 | .45 | .13 |
| Kansas City Chiefs | | | |
| ☐ 282 Lynn Swann UER | 40.00 | 18.00 | 5.00 |
| Pittsburgh Steelers | | | |
| (Wide Reciever on front) | | | |
| ☐ 283 John Hicks | .30 | .14 | .04 |
| New York Giants | | | |
| ☐ 284 Coy Bacon | .35 | .16 | .04 |
| San Diego Chargers | | | |
| ☐ 285 Lee Roy Jordan | 1.25 | .55 | .16 |
| Dallas Cowboys | | | |
| ☐ 286 Willie Buchanon | .30 | .14 | .04 |
| Green Bay Packers | | | |
| ☐ 287 Al Woodall | .35 | .16 | .04 |
| New York Jets | | | |
| ☐ 288 Reggie Rucker | .35 | .16 | .04 |
| Cleveland Browns | | | |
| ☐ 289 John Schmitt | .30 | .14 | .04 |
| Green Bay Packers | | | |
| ☐ 290 Carl Eller | .75 | .35 | .09 |
| Minnesota Vikings | | | |
| ☐ 291 Jake Scott | .35 | .16 | .04 |
| Miami Dolphins | | | |
| ☐ 292 Donny Anderson | .35 | .16 | .04 |
| St. Louis Cardinals | | | |
| ☐ 293 Charley Wade | .30 | .14 | .04 |
| Chicago Bears | | | |
| ☐ 294 John Tanner | .30 | .14 | .04 |
| New England Patriots | | | |
| ☐ 295 Charlie Johnson | .35 | .16 | .04 |
| (Misspelled Charley | | | |
| on both sides) | | | |
| Denver Broncos | | | |
| ☐ 296 Tom Blanchard | .30 | .14 | .04 |
| New Orleans Saints | | | |
| ☐ 297 Curley Culp | .35 | .16 | .04 |
| Houston Oilers | | | |
| ☐ 298 Jeff Van Note | 1.25 | .55 | .16 |
| Atlanta Falcons | | | |
| ☐ 299 Bob James | .30 | .14 | .04 |
| Buffalo Bills | | | |
| ☐ 300 Franco Harris | 12.00 | 5.50 | 1.50 |
| Pittsburgh Steelers | | | |
| ☐ 301 Tim Berra | .35 | .16 | .04 |
| Baltimore Colts | | | |
| ☐ 302 Bruce Gossett | .30 | .14 | .04 |
| San Francisco 49ers | | | |
| ☐ 303 Verlon Biggs | .30 | .14 | .04 |
| Washington Redskins | | | |
| ☐ 304 Bob Kowalkowski | .30 | .14 | .04 |
| Detroit Lions | | | |
| ☐ 305 Marv Hubbard | .35 | .16 | .04 |
| Oakland Raiders | | | |
| ☐ 306 Ken Avery | .30 | .14 | .04 |
| Kansas City Chiefs | | | |
| ☐ 307 Mike Adamle | .30 | .14 | .04 |
| New York Jets | | | |
| ☐ 308 Don Herrmann | .30 | .14 | .04 |
| New York Giants | | | |
| ☐ 309 Chris Fletcher | .30 | .14 | .04 |
| San Diego Chargers | | | |
| ☐ 310 Roman Gabriel | 1.25 | .55 | .16 |
| Philadelphia Eagles | | | |
| ☐ 311 Billy Joe DuPree | 1.00 | .45 | .13 |
| Dallas Cowboys | | | |
| ☐ 312 Fred Dryer | 2.00 | .90 | .25 |
| Los Angeles Rams | | | |
| ☐ 313 John Riggins | 5.00 | 2.30 | .60 |
| New York Jets | | | |
| ☐ 314 Bob McKay | .30 | .14 | .04 |
| Cleveland Browns | | | |
| ☐ 315 Ted Hendricks | 1.25 | .55 | .16 |
| Green Bay Packers | | | |
| ☐ 316 Bobby Bryant | .30 | .14 | .04 |
| Minnesota Vikings | | | |
| ☐ 317 Don Nottingham | .30 | .14 | .04 |
| Miami Dolphins | | | |
| ☐ 318 John Hannah | 3.50 | 1.55 | .45 |
| New England Patriots | | | |
| ☐ 319 Rich Coady | .30 | .14 | .04 |
| Chicago Bears | | | |
| ☐ 320 Phil Villapiano | .35 | .16 | .04 |
| Oakland Raiders | | | |
| ☐ 321 Jim Plunkett | 2.00 | .90 | .25 |
| New England Patriots | | | |
| ☐ 322 Lyle Alzado | 1.25 | .55 | .16 |
| Denver Broncos | | | |
| ☐ 323 Ernie Jackson | .30 | .14 | .04 |
| New Orleans Saints | | | |
| ☐ 324 Billy Parks | .30 | .14 | .04 |
| Houston Oilers | | | |

| | | | |
|---|---|---|---|
| ☐ 325 Willie Lanier | 1.00 | .45 | .13 |
| Kansas City Chiefs | | | |
| ☐ 326 John James | .30 | .14 | .04 |
| Atlanta Falcons | | | |
| ☐ 327 Joe Ferguson | 1.00 | .45 | .13 |
| Buffalo Bills | | | |
| ☐ 328 Ernie Holmes | 1.00 | .45 | .13 |
| Pittsburgh Steelers | | | |
| ☐ 329 Bruce Laird | .30 | .14 | .04 |
| Baltimore Colts | | | |
| ☐ 330 Chester Marcol | .35 | .16 | .04 |
| Green Bay Packers | | | |
| ☐ 331 Dave Wilcox | .35 | .16 | .04 |
| San Francisco 49ers | | | |
| ☐ 332 Pat Fischer | .35 | .16 | .04 |
| Washington Redskins | | | |
| ☐ 333 Steve Owens | .35 | .16 | .04 |
| Detroit Lions | | | |
| ☐ 334 Royce Berry | .30 | .14 | .04 |
| Cincinnati Bengals | | | |
| ☐ 335 Russ Washington | .30 | .14 | .04 |
| San Diego Chargers | | | |
| ☐ 336 Walker Gillette | .30 | .14 | .04 |
| New York Giants | | | |
| ☐ 337 Mark Nordquist | .30 | .14 | .04 |
| Chicago Bears | | | |
| ☐ 338 James Harris | 1.00 | .45 | .13 |
| Los Angeles Rams | | | |
| ☐ 339 Warren Koegel | .30 | .14 | .04 |
| New York Jets | | | |
| ☐ 340 Emmitt Thomas | .35 | .16 | .04 |
| Kansas City Chiefs | | | |
| ☐ 341 Walt Garrison | .35 | .16 | .04 |
| Dallas Cowboys | | | |
| ☐ 342 Thom Darden | .30 | .14 | .04 |
| Cleveland Browns | | | |
| ☐ 343 Mike Eischeid | .30 | .14 | .04 |
| Minnesota Vikings | | | |
| ☐ 344 Ernie McMillan | .30 | .14 | .04 |
| St. Louis Cardinals | | | |
| ☐ 345 Nick Buoniconti | .75 | .35 | .09 |
| Miami Dolphins | | | |
| ☐ 346 George Farmer | .30 | .14 | .04 |
| Chicago Bears | | | |
| ☐ 347 Sam Adams | .30 | .14 | .04 |
| New England Patriots | | | |
| ☐ 348 Larry Cipa | .30 | .14 | .04 |
| New Orleans Saints | | | |
| ☐ 349 Bob Moore | .30 | .14 | .04 |
| Oakland Raiders | | | |
| ☐ 350 Otis Armstrong | 4.00 | 1.80 | .50 |
| Denver Broncos | | | |
| ☐ 351 George Blanda RB | 2.50 | 1.15 | .30 |
| All Time Scoring | | | |
| Leader | | | |
| ☐ 352 Fred Cox RB | .60 | .25 | .08 |
| 151 Straight PAT's | | | |
| ☐ 353 Tom Dempsey RB | .75 | .35 | .09 |
| 63 Yard FG | | | |
| ☐ 354 Ken Houston RB | .75 | .35 | .09 |
| 9th Int. for TD | | | |
| (Shown as Oiler, | | | |
| should be Redskin) | | | |
| ☐ 355 O.J. Simpson RB | 7.50 | 3.40 | .95 |
| 2003 Yard Season | | | |
| ☐ 356 Ron Smith RB | .60 | .25 | .08 |
| All Time Return | | | |
| Yardage Mark | | | |
| ☐ 357 Bob Atkins | .30 | .14 | .04 |
| Houston Oilers | | | |
| ☐ 358 Pat Sullivan | .35 | .16 | .04 |
| Atlanta Falcons | | | |
| ☐ 359 Joe DeLamielleure | .60 | .25 | .08 |
| Buffalo Bills | | | |
| ☐ 360 Lawrence McCutcheon | 2.50 | 1.15 | .30 |
| Los Angeles Rams | | | |
| ☐ 361 David Lee | .30 | .14 | .04 |
| Baltimore Colts | | | |
| ☐ 362 Mike McCoy | .30 | .14 | .04 |
| Green Bay Packers | | | |
| ☐ 363 Skip Vanderbundt | .30 | .14 | .04 |
| San Francisco 49ers | | | |
| ☐ 364 Mark Moseley | .60 | .25 | .08 |
| Washington Redskins | | | |
| ☐ 365 Lem Barney | 1.25 | .55 | .16 |
| Detroit Lions | | | |
| ☐ 366 Doug Dressler | .30 | .14 | .04 |
| Cincinnati Bengals | | | |
| ☐ 367 Dan Fouts | 55.00 | 25.00 | 7.00 |
| San Diego Chargers | | | |
| ☐ 368 Bob Hyland | .30 | .14 | .04 |
| New York Giants | | | |
| ☐ 369 John Outlaw | .30 | .14 | .04 |
| Philadelphia Eagles | | | |
| ☐ 370 Roy Gerela | .35 | .16 | .04 |
| Pittsburgh Steelers | | | |
| ☐ 371 Isiah Robertson | .35 | .16 | .04 |

| | | | |
|---|---|---|---|
| Los Angeles Rams | | | |
| ☐ 372 Jerome Barkum | .35 | .16 | .04 |
| New York Jets | | | |
| ☐ 373 Ed Podolak | .35 | .16 | .04 |
| Kansas City Chiefs | | | |
| ☐ 374 Milt Morin | .30 | .14 | .04 |
| Cleveland Browns | | | |
| ☐ 375 John Niland | .30 | .14 | .04 |
| Dallas Cowboys | | | |
| ☐ 376 Checklist 265-396 UER | 2.50 | .25 | .08 |
| (295 Charlie Johnson | | | |
| misspelled as Charley) | | | |
| ☐ 377 Ken Iman | .30 | .14 | .04 |
| St. Louis Cardinals | | | |
| ☐ 378 Manny Fernandez | .35 | .16 | .04 |
| Miami Dolphins | | | |
| ☐ 379 Dave Gallagher | .30 | .14 | .04 |
| Chicago Bears | | | |
| ☐ 380 Ken Stabler | 8.00 | 3.60 | 1.00 |
| Oakland Raiders | | | |
| ☐ 381 Mack Herron | .35 | .16 | .04 |
| New England Patriots | | | |
| ☐ 382 Bill McClard | .30 | .14 | .04 |
| New Orleans Saints | | | |
| ☐ 383 Ray May | .30 | .14 | .04 |
| Denver Broncos | | | |
| ☐ 384 Don Hansen | .30 | .14 | .04 |
| Atlanta Falcons | | | |
| ☐ 385 Elvin Bethea | .35 | .16 | .04 |
| Houston Oilers | | | |
| ☐ 386 Joe Scibelli | .35 | .16 | .04 |
| Los Angeles Rams | | | |
| ☐ 387 Neal Craig | .30 | .14 | .04 |
| Buffalo Bills | | | |
| ☐ 388 Marty Domres | .35 | .16 | .04 |
| Baltimore Colts | | | |
| ☐ 389 Ken Ellis | .30 | .14 | .04 |
| Green Bay Packers | | | |
| ☐ 390 Charley Young | .35 | .16 | .04 |
| Philadelphia Eagles | | | |
| ☐ 391 Tommy Hart | .30 | .14 | .04 |
| San Francisco 49ers | | | |
| ☐ 392 Moses Denson | .30 | .14 | .04 |
| Washington Redskins | | | |
| ☐ 393 Larry Walton | .30 | .14 | .04 |
| Detroit Lions | | | |
| ☐ 394 Dave Green | .30 | .14 | .04 |
| Cincinnati Bengals | | | |
| ☐ 395 Ron Johnson | .35 | .16 | .04 |
| New York Giants | | | |
| ☐ 396 Ed Bradley | .30 | .14 | .04 |
| Pittsburgh Steelers | | | |
| ☐ 397 J.T. Thomas | .35 | .16 | .04 |
| Pittsburgh Steelers | | | |
| ☐ 398 Jim Bailey | .30 | .14 | .04 |
| New York Jets | | | |
| ☐ 399 Barry Pearson | .30 | .14 | .04 |
| Kansas City Chiefs | | | |
| ☐ 400 Fran Tarkenton | 8.00 | 3.60 | 1.00 |
| Minnesota Vikings | | | |
| ☐ 401 Jack Rudnay | .30 | .14 | .04 |
| Kansas City Chiefs | | | |
| ☐ 402 Rayfield Wright | .30 | .14 | .04 |
| Dallas Cowboys | | | |
| ☐ 403 Roger Wehrli | .35 | .16 | .04 |
| St. Louis Cardinals | | | |
| ☐ 404 Vern Den Herder | .30 | .14 | .04 |
| Miami Dolphins | | | |
| ☐ 405 Fred Biletnikoff | 3.00 | 1.35 | .40 |
| Oakland Raiders | | | |
| ☐ 406 Ken Grandberry | .30 | .14 | .04 |
| Chicago Bears | | | |
| ☐ 407 Bob Adams | .30 | .14 | .04 |
| New England Patriots | | | |
| ☐ 408 Jim Merlo | .30 | .14 | .04 |
| New Orleans Saints | | | |
| ☐ 409 John Pitts | .30 | .14 | .04 |
| Denver Broncos | | | |
| ☐ 410 Dave Osborn | .35 | .16 | .04 |
| Minnesota Vikings | | | |
| ☐ 411 Dennis Havig | .30 | .14 | .04 |
| Atlanta Falcons | | | |
| ☐ 412 Bob Johnson | .30 | .14 | .04 |
| Cincinnati Bengals | | | |
| ☐ 413 Ken Burrough UER | .35 | .16 | .04 |
| (Misspelled Burrow | | | |
| on card front) | | | |
| Houston Oilers | | | |
| ☐ 414 Jim Cheyunski | .30 | .14 | .04 |
| Buffalo Bills | | | |
| ☐ 415 MacArthur Lane | .35 | .16 | .04 |
| Green Bay Packers | | | |
| ☐ 416 Joe Theismann | 25.00 | 11.50 | 3.10 |
| Washington Redskins | | | |
| ☐ 417 Mike Boryla | .50 | .23 | .06 |
| Philadelphia Eagles | | | |
| ☐ 418 Bruce Taylor | .30 | .14 | .04 |
| San Francisco 49ers | | | |

| | | | | |
|---|---|---|---|---|
| ☐ 419 Chris Hanburger | .35 | .16 | .04 |
| Washington Redskins | | | |
| ☐ 420 Tom Mack | .35 | .16 | .04 |
| Los Angeles Rams | | | |
| ☐ 421 Errol Mann | .30 | .14 | .04 |
| Detroit Lions | | | |
| ☐ 422 Jack Gregory | .30 | .14 | .04 |
| New York Giants | | | |
| ☐ 423 Harrison Davis | .30 | .14 | .04 |
| San Diego Chargers | | | |
| ☐ 424 Burgess Owens | .30 | .14 | .04 |
| New York Jets | | | |
| ☐ 425 Joe Greene | 4.00 | 1.80 | .50 |
| Pittsburgh Steelers | | | |
| ☐ 426 Morris Stroud | .30 | .14 | .04 |
| Houston Oilers | | | |
| ☐ 427 John DeMarie | .30 | .14 | .04 |
| Cleveland Browns | | | |
| ☐ 428 Mel Renfro | .75 | .35 | .09 |
| Dallas Cowboys | | | |
| ☐ 429 Cid Edwards | .30 | .14 | .04 |
| Chicago Bears | | | |
| ☐ 430 Mike Reid | 1.00 | .45 | .13 |
| Cincinnati Bengals | | | |
| ☐ 431 Jack Mildren | .35 | .16 | .04 |
| New England Patriots | | | |
| ☐ 432 Jerry Simmons | .30 | .14 | .04 |
| Denver Broncos | | | |
| ☐ 433 Ron Yary | .35 | .16 | .04 |
| Minnesota Vikings | | | |
| ☐ 434 Howard Stevens | .30 | .14 | .04 |
| New Orleans Saints | | | |
| ☐ 435 Ray Guy | 1.75 | .80 | .22 |
| Oakland Raiders | | | |
| ☐ 436 Tommy Nobis | .75 | .35 | .09 |
| Atlanta Falcons | | | |
| ☐ 437 Solomon Freelon | .30 | .14 | .04 |
| Houston Oilers | | | |
| ☐ 438 J.D. Hill | .35 | .16 | .04 |
| Buffalo Bills | | | |
| ☐ 439 Toni Linhart | .30 | .14 | .04 |
| Baltimore Colts | | | |
| ☐ 440 Dick Anderson | .40 | .18 | .05 |
| Miami Dolphins | | | |
| ☐ 441 Guy Morriss | .30 | .14 | .04 |
| Philadelphia Eagles | | | |
| ☐ 442 Bob Hoskins | .30 | .14 | .04 |
| San Francisco 49ers | | | |
| ☐ 443 John Hadl | .60 | .25 | .08 |
| Green Bay Packers | | | |
| ☐ 444 Roy Jefferson | .35 | .16 | .04 |
| Washington Redskins | | | |
| ☐ 445 Charlie Sanders | .35 | .16 | .04 |
| Detroit Lions | | | |
| ☐ 446 Pat Curran | .30 | .14 | .04 |
| Los Angeles Rams | | | |
| ☐ 447 David Knight | .30 | .14 | .04 |
| New York Jets | | | |
| ☐ 448 Bob Brown | .30 | .14 | .04 |
| San Diego Chargers | | | |
| ☐ 449 Pete Gogolak | .35 | .16 | .04 |
| New York Giants | | | |
| ☐ 450 Terry Metcalf | 1.00 | .45 | .13 |
| St. Louis Cardinals | | | |
| ☐ 451 Bill Bergey | .75 | .35 | .09 |
| Philadelphia Eagles | | | |
| ☐ 452 Dan Abramowicz HL | .60 | .25 | .08 |
| 105 Straight Games | | | |
| ☐ 453 Otis Armstrong HL | 1.00 | .45 | .13 |
| 183 Yard Game | | | |
| ☐ 454 Cliff Branch HL | 1.25 | .55 | .16 |
| 13 TD Passes | | | |
| ☐ 455 John James HL | .60 | .25 | .08 |
| Record 96 Punts | | | |
| ☐ 456 Lydell Mitchell HL | .60 | .25 | .08 |
| 13 Passes in Game | | | |
| ☐ 457 Lemar Parrish HL | .60 | .25 | .08 |
| 3 TD Punt Returns | | | |
| ☐ 458 Ken Stabler HL | 4.00 | 1.80 | .50 |
| 26 TD Passes | | | |
| in One Season | | | |
| ☐ 459 Lynn Swann HL | 7.00 | 3.10 | .85 |
| 577 Yards in | | | |
| Punt Returns | | | |
| ☐ 460 Emmitt Thomas HL | .60 | .25 | .08 |
| 73 Yd. Interception | | | |
| ☐ 461 Terry Bradshaw | 14.00 | 6.25 | 1.75 |
| Pittsburgh Steelers | | | |
| ☐ 462 Jerrel Wilson | .30 | .14 | .04 |
| Kansas City Chiefs | | | |
| ☐ 463 Walter Johnson | .30 | .14 | .04 |
| Cleveland Browns | | | |
| ☐ 464 Golden Richards | .35 | .16 | .04 |
| Dallas Cowboys | | | |
| ☐ 465 Tommy Casanova | .35 | .16 | .04 |
| Cincinnati Bengals | | | |
| ☐ 466 Randy Jackson | .30 | .14 | .04 |
| Chicago Bears | | | |
| ☐ 467 Ron Bolton | .30 | .14 | .04 |
| New England Patriots | | | |
| ☐ 468 Joe Owens | .30 | .14 | .04 |
| New Orleans Saints | | | |
| ☐ 469 Wally Hilgenberg | .30 | .14 | .04 |
| Minnesota Vikings | | | |
| ☐ 470 Riley Odoms | .50 | .23 | .06 |
| Denver Broncos | | | |
| ☐ 471 Otis Sistrunk | .35 | .16 | .04 |
| Oakland Raiders | | | |
| ☐ 472 Eddie Ray | .30 | .14 | .04 |
| Atlanta Falcons | | | |
| ☐ 473 Reggie McKenzie | .60 | .25 | .08 |
| Buffalo Bills | | | |
| ☐ 474 Elbert Drungo | .30 | .14 | .04 |
| Houston Oilers | | | |
| ☐ 475 Mercury Morris | .75 | .35 | .09 |
| Miami Dolphins | | | |
| ☐ 476 Dan Dickel | .30 | .14 | .04 |
| Baltimore Colts | | | |
| ☐ 477 Merritt Kersey | .30 | .14 | .04 |
| Philadelphia Eagles | | | |
| ☐ 478 Mike Holmes | .30 | .14 | .04 |
| San Francisco 49ers | | | |
| ☐ 479 Clarence Williams | .30 | .14 | .04 |
| Green Bay Packers | | | |
| ☐ 480 Bill Kilmer | .60 | .25 | .08 |
| Washington Redskins | | | |
| ☐ 481 Altie Taylor | .35 | .16 | .04 |
| Detroit Lions | | | |
| ☐ 482 Dave Elmendorf | .35 | .16 | .04 |
| Los Angeles Rams | | | |
| ☐ 483 Bob Rowe | .30 | .14 | .04 |
| St. Louis Cardinals | | | |
| ☐ 484 Pete Athas | .30 | .14 | .04 |
| New York Giants | | | |
| ☐ 485 Winston Hill | .35 | .16 | .04 |
| New York Jets | | | |
| ☐ 486 Bo Matthews | .30 | .14 | .04 |
| San Diego Chargers | | | |
| ☐ 487 Earl Thomas | .30 | .14 | .04 |
| St. Louis Cardinals | | | |
| ☐ 488 Jan Stenerud | .75 | .35 | .09 |
| Kansas City Chiefs | | | |
| ☐ 489 Steve Holden | .30 | .14 | .04 |
| Cleveland Browns | | | |
| ☐ 490 Cliff Harris | 4.00 | 1.80 | .50 |
| Dallas Cowboys | | | |
| ☐ 491 Boobie Clark | .50 | .23 | .06 |
| Cincinnati Bengals | | | |
| ☐ 492 Joe Taylor | .30 | .14 | .04 |
| Chicago Bears | | | |
| ☐ 493 Tom Neville | .30 | .14 | .04 |
| New England Patriots | | | |
| ☐ 494 Wayne Colman | .30 | .14 | .04 |
| New Orleans Saints | | | |
| ☐ 495 Jim Mitchell | .30 | .14 | .04 |
| Atlanta Falcons | | | |
| ☐ 496 Paul Krause | .75 | .35 | .09 |
| Minnesota Vikings | | | |
| ☐ 497 Jim Otto | 1.50 | .65 | .19 |
| Oakland Raiders | | | |
| ☐ 498 John Rowser | .30 | .14 | .04 |
| Denver Broncos | | | |
| ☐ 499 Larry Little | 1.00 | .45 | .13 |
| Miami Dolphins | | | |
| ☐ 500 O.J. Simpson | 15.00 | 6.75 | 1.90 |
| Buffalo Bills | | | |
| ☐ 501 John Dutton | 1.25 | .55 | .16 |
| Baltimore Colts | | | |
| ☐ 502 Pat Hughes | .30 | .14 | .04 |
| New York Giants | | | |
| ☐ 503 Malcolm Snider | .30 | .14 | .04 |
| Green Bay Packers | | | |
| ☐ 504 Fred Willis | .30 | .14 | .04 |
| Houston Oilers | | | |
| ☐ 505 Harold Jackson | .75 | .35 | .09 |
| Los Angeles Rams | | | |
| ☐ 506 Mike Bragg | .30 | .14 | .04 |
| Washington Redskins | | | |
| ☐ 507 Jerry Sherk | .35 | .16 | .04 |
| Cleveland Browns | | | |
| ☐ 508 Mirro Roder | .30 | .14 | .04 |
| Chicago Bears | | | |
| ☐ 509 Tom Sullivan | .30 | .14 | .04 |
| Philadelphia Eagles | | | |
| ☐ 510 Jim Hart | 1.00 | .45 | .13 |
| St. Louis Cardinals | | | |
| ☐ 511 Cedrick Hardman | .35 | .16 | .04 |
| San Francisco 49ers | | | |
| ☐ 512 Blaine Nye | .30 | .14 | .04 |
| Dallas Cowboys | | | |
| ☐ 513 Elmo Wright | .35 | .16 | .04 |
| Kansas City Chiefs | | | |
| ☐ 514 Herb Orvis | .30 | .14 | .04 |
| Detroit Lions | | | |
| ☐ 515 Richard Caster | .35 | .16 | .04 |

| | | | |
|---|---|---|---|
| **New York Jets** | | | |
| ☐ 516 Doug Kotar | .50 | .23 | .06 |
| **New York Giants** | | | |
| ☐ 517 Checklist 397-528 | 2.50 | .25 | .08 |
| ☐ 518 Jesse Freitas | .30 | .14 | .04 |
| **San Diego Chargers** | | | |
| ☐ 519 Ken Houston | 1.00 | .45 | .13 |
| **Washington Redskins** | | | |
| ☐ 520 Alan Page | 1.75 | .80 | .22 |
| **Minnesota Vikings** | | | |
| ☐ 521 Tim Foley | .35 | .16 | .04 |
| **Miami Dolphins** | | | |
| ☐ 522 Bill Olds | .30 | .14 | .04 |
| **Baltimore Colts** | | | |
| ☐ 523 Bobby Maples | .35 | .16 | .04 |
| **Denver Broncos** | | | |
| ☐ 524 Cliff Branch | 9.00 | 4.00 | 1.15 |
| **Oakland Raiders** | | | |
| ☐ 525 Merlin Olsen | 1.75 | .80 | .22 |
| **Los Angeles Rams** | | | |
| ☐ 526 AFC Champs | 3.00 | 1.35 | .40 |
| Pittsburgh 24, | | | |
| Oakland 13 | | | |
| (Bradshaw and | | | |
| Franco Harris) | | | |
| ☐ 527 NFC Champs | 1.00 | .45 | .13 |
| Minnesota 14, | | | |
| Los Angeles 10 | | | |
| (C.Foreman tackled) | | | |
| ☐ 528 Super Bowl IX | 4.00 | 1.00 | .30 |
| Steelers 16, | | | |
| Vikings 6 | | | |
| (Bradshaw watching | | | |
| pass) | | | |

## 1975 Topps Team Checklists

The 1975 Topps Team Checklist set contains 26 cards, one for each of the 26 NFL teams. The cards measure the standard 2 1/2" by 3 1/2". The front of the card has the 1975 schedule, while the back of the card contains the checklist, complete with boxes in which to place check marks. The player's position is also listed with his name. The set was only available directly from Topps as a send-off offer as an uncut sheet; the prices below apply equally to uncut sheets as they are frequently found in their original uncut condition. These unnumbered cards are numbered below for convenience in alphabetical order by team name.

| | NRMT | VG-E | GOOD |
|---|---|---|---|
| COMPLETE SET (26) | 150.00 | 60.00 | 15.00 |
| COMMON PLAYER (1-26) | 7.50 | 3.00 | .75 |
| | | | |
| ☐ 1 Atlanta Falcons | 7.50 | 3.00 | .75 |
| ☐ 2 Baltimore Colts | 7.50 | 3.00 | .75 |
| ☐ 3 Buffalo Bills | 7.50 | 3.00 | .75 |
| ☐ 4 Chicago Bears | 9.00 | 3.75 | .90 |
| ☐ 5 Cincinnati Bengals | 7.50 | 3.00 | .75 |
| ☐ 6 Cleveland Browns | 7.50 | 3.00 | .75 |
| ☐ 7 Dallas Cowboys | 10.00 | 4.00 | 1.00 |
| ☐ 8 Denver Broncos | 9.00 | 3.75 | .90 |
| ☐ 9 Detroit Lions | 7.50 | 3.00 | .75 |
| ☐ 10 Green Bay Packers | 7.50 | 3.00 | .75 |
| ☐ 11 Houston Oilers | 7.50 | 3.00 | .75 |
| ☐ 12 Kansas City Chiefs | 7.50 | 3.00 | .75 |
| ☐ 13 Los Angeles Rams | 7.50 | 3.00 | .75 |
| ☐ 14 Miami Dolphins | 9.00 | 3.75 | .90 |
| ☐ 15 Minnesota Vikings | 7.50 | 3.00 | .75 |
| ☐ 16 New England Patriots | 7.50 | 3.00 | .75 |
| ☐ 17 New York Giants | 9.00 | 3.75 | .90 |
| ☐ 18 New York Jets | 9.00 | 3.75 | .90 |
| ☐ 19 New Orleans Saints | 7.50 | 3.00 | .75 |
| ☐ 20 Oakland Raiders | 10.00 | 4.00 | 1.00 |
| ☐ 21 Philadelphia Eagles | 7.50 | 3.00 | .75 |
| ☐ 22 Pittsburgh Steelers | 9.00 | 3.75 | .90 |

| | | | |
|---|---|---|---|
| ☐ 23 St. Louis Cardinals | 7.50 | 3.00 | .75 |
| ☐ 24 San Diego Chargers | 7.50 | 3.00 | .75 |
| ☐ 25 San Francisco 49ers | 9.00 | 3.75 | .90 |
| ☐ 26 Washington Redskins | 9.00 | 3.75 | .90 |

## 1976 Topps

The 1976 Topps football set contains 528 cards. The cards measure 2 1/2" by 3 1/2". No known scarcities exist, although Walter Payton's first card is in great demand. Other notable Rookie Cards in this set are defensive stalwarts Randy Gradishar, Ed Too Tall Jones, Jack Lambert, Harvey Martin, and Randy White. The first eight cards are dedicated to Record-Breaking (RB) performances from the previous season. Statistical league leaders are depicted on cards 201-206. Post-season playoff action is summarized on cards 331-333. Cards 451-478 are team checklist cards. All-Pro (AP) selections are designated on the player's regular card, not a special card. The set marks the NFL debut of both the Seattle Seahawks and the Tampa Bay Buccaneers. The card backs are printed in orange and blue on gray card stock. An uncut sheet of team checklist cards was also available via a mail-in offer on wax packs.

| | NRMT | VG-E | GOOD |
|---|---|---|---|
| COMPLETE SET (528) | 375.00 | 170.00 | 47.50 |
| COMMON PLAYER (1-528) | .30 | .14 | .04 |
| | | | |
| ☐ 1 George Blanda RB | 5.00 | 1.00 | .30 |
| First to Score | | | |
| 2000 Points | | | |
| ☐ 2 Neal Colzie RB | .50 | .23 | .06 |
| Punt Returns | | | |
| ☐ 3 Chuck Foreman RB | .60 | .25 | .08 |
| Catches 73 Passes | | | |
| ☐ 4 Jim Marshall RB | .60 | .25 | .08 |
| 26th Fumble | | | |
| Recovery | | | |
| ☐ 5 Terry Metcalf RB | .60 | .25 | .08 |
| Most all-purpose yards; | | | |
| season | | | |
| ☐ 6 O.J. Simpson RB | 6.00 | 2.70 | .75 |
| 23 Touchdowns | | | |
| ☐ 7 Fran Tarkenton RB | 3.50 | 1.55 | .45 |
| Most Attempts;Season | | | |
| ☐ 8 Charley Taylor RB | 1.00 | .45 | .13 |
| Career Receptions | | | |
| ☐ 9 Ernie Holmes | .35 | .16 | .04 |
| Pittsburgh Steelers | | | |
| ☐ 10 Ken Anderson AP | 2.00 | .90 | .25 |
| Cincinnati Bengals | | | |
| ☐ 11 Bobby Bryant | .30 | .14 | .04 |
| Minnesota Vikings | | | |
| ☐ 12 Jerry Smith | .35 | .16 | .04 |
| Washington Redskins | | | |
| ☐ 13 David Lee | .30 | .14 | .04 |
| Baltimore Colts | | | |
| ☐ 14 Robert Newhouse | 1.50 | .65 | .19 |
| Dallas Cowboys | | | |
| ☐ 15 Vern Den Herder | .30 | .14 | .04 |
| Miami Dolphins | | | |
| ☐ 16 John Hannah | 1.75 | .80 | .22 |
| New England Patriots | | | |
| ☐ 17 J.D. Hill | .35 | .16 | .04 |
| Buffalo Bills | | | |
| ☐ 18 James Harris | .35 | .16 | .04 |
| Los Angeles Rams | | | |
| ☐ 19 Willie Buchanon | .35 | .16 | .04 |
| Green Bay Packers | | | |
| ☐ 20 Charley Young AP | .35 | .16 | .04 |
| Philadelphia Eagles | | | |
| ☐ 21 Jim Yarbrough | .30 | .14 | .04 |
| Detroit Lions | | | |
| ☐ 22 Ronnie Coleman | .30 | .14 | .04 |
| Houston Oilers | | | |

| | | | |
|---|---|---|---|
| ☐ 23 Don Cockroft | .35 | .16 | .04 |
| Cleveland Browns | | | |
| ☐ 24 Willie Lanier | 1.00 | .45 | .13 |
| Kansas City Chiefs | | | |
| ☐ 25 Fred Biletnikoff | 2.50 | 1.15 | .30 |
| Oakland Raiders | | | |
| ☐ 26 Ron Yankowski | .30 | .14 | .04 |
| St. Louis Cardinals | | | |
| ☐ 27 Spider Lockhart | .35 | .16 | .04 |
| New York Giants | | | |
| ☐ 28 Bob Johnson | .30 | .14 | .04 |
| Cincinnati Bengals | | | |
| ☐ 29 J.T. Thomas | .35 | .16 | .04 |
| Pittsburgh Steelers | | | |
| ☐ 30 Ron Yary AP | .35 | .16 | .04 |
| Minnesota Vikings | | | |
| ☐ 31 Brad Dusek | .50 | .23 | .06 |
| Washington Redskins | | | |
| ☐ 32 Raymond Chester | .35 | .16 | .04 |
| Baltimore Colts | | | |
| ☐ 33 Larry Little | 1.00 | .45 | .13 |
| Miami Dolphins | | | |
| ☐ 34 Pat Leahy | 2.50 | 1.15 | .30 |
| New York Jets | | | |
| ☐ 35 Steve Bartkowski | 4.00 | 1.80 | .50 |
| Atlanta Falcons | | | |
| ☐ 36 Tom Myers | .30 | .14 | .04 |
| New Orleans Saints | | | |
| ☐ 37 Bill Van Heusen | .30 | .14 | .04 |
| Denver Broncos | | | |
| ☐ 38 Russ Washington | .30 | .14 | .04 |
| San Diego Chargers | | | |
| ☐ 39 Tom Sullivan | .30 | .14 | .04 |
| Philadelphia Eagles | | | |
| ☐ 40 Curley Culp AP | .35 | .16 | .04 |
| Houston Oilers | | | |
| ☐ 41 Johnnie Gray | .30 | .14 | .04 |
| Green Bay Packers | | | |
| ☐ 42 Bob Klein | .30 | .14 | .04 |
| Los Angeles Rams | | | |
| ☐ 43 Lem Barney | 1.00 | .45 | .13 |
| Detroit Lions | | | |
| ☐ 44 Harvey Martin | 4.00 | 1.80 | .50 |
| Dallas Cowboys | | | |
| ☐ 45 Reggie Rucker | .35 | .16 | .04 |
| Cleveland Browns | | | |
| ☐ 46 Neil Clabo | .30 | .14 | .04 |
| Minnesota Vikings | | | |
| ☐ 47 Ray Hamilton | .35 | .16 | .04 |
| New England Patriots | | | |
| ☐ 48 Joe Ferguson | .75 | .35 | .09 |
| Buffalo Bills | | | |
| ☐ 49 Ed Podolak | .35 | .16 | .04 |
| Kansas City Chiefs | | | |
| ☐ 50 Ray Guy AP | 1.25 | .55 | .16 |
| Oakland Raiders | | | |
| ☐ 51 Glen Edwards | .35 | .16 | .04 |
| Pittsburgh Steelers | | | |
| ☐ 52 Jim LeClair | .35 | .16 | .04 |
| Cincinnati Bengals | | | |
| ☐ 53 Mike Barnes | .30 | .14 | .04 |
| Baltimore Colts | | | |
| ☐ 54 Nat Moore | 3.50 | 1.55 | .45 |
| Miami Dolphins | | | |
| ☐ 55 Bill Kilmer | .50 | .23 | .06 |
| Washington Redskins | | | |
| ☐ 56 Larry Stallings | .30 | .14 | .04 |
| St. Louis Cardinals | | | |
| ☐ 57 Jack Gregory | .30 | .14 | .04 |
| New York Giants | | | |
| ☐ 58 Steve Mike-Mayer | .30 | .14 | .04 |
| San Francisco 49ers | | | |
| ☐ 59 Virgil Livers | .30 | .14 | .04 |
| Chicago Bears | | | |
| ☐ 60 Jerry Sherk AP | .35 | .16 | .04 |
| Cleveland Browns | | | |
| ☐ 61 Guy Morriss | .30 | .14 | .04 |
| Philadelphia Eagles | | | |
| ☐ 62 Barty Smith | .30 | .14 | .04 |
| Green Bay Packers | | | |
| ☐ 63 Jerome Barkum | .35 | .16 | .04 |
| New York Jets | | | |
| ☐ 64 Ira Gordon | .30 | .14 | .04 |
| Tampa Bay Buccaneers | | | |
| ☐ 65 Paul Krause | .50 | .23 | .06 |
| Minnesota Vikings | | | |
| ☐ 66 John McMakin | .30 | .14 | .04 |
| Seattle Seahawks | | | |
| ☐ 67 Checklist 1-132 | 2.00 | .20 | .06 |
| ☐ 68 Charlie Johnson UER | .35 | .16 | .04 |
| (Misspelled Charley | | | |
| on both sides) | | | |
| Denver Broncos | | | |
| ☐ 69 Tommy Nobis | .60 | .25 | .08 |
| Atlanta Falcons | | | |
| ☐ 70 Lydell Mitchell | .35 | .16 | .04 |
| Baltimore Colts | | | |

| | | | |
|---|---|---|---|
| ☐ 71 Vern Holland | .30 | .14 | .04 |
| Cincinnati Bengals | | | |
| ☐ 72 Tim Foley | .35 | .16 | .04 |
| Miami Dolphins | | | |
| ☐ 73 Golden Richards | .35 | .16 | .04 |
| Dallas Cowboys | | | |
| ☐ 74 Bryant Salter | .30 | .14 | .04 |
| Washington Redskins | | | |
| ☐ 75 Terry Bradshaw | 14.00 | 6.25 | 1.75 |
| Pittsburgh Steelers | | | |
| ☐ 76 Ted Hendricks | 1.00 | .45 | .13 |
| Oakland Raiders | | | |
| ☐ 77 Rich Saul | .30 | .14 | .04 |
| Los Angeles Rams | | | |
| ☐ 78 John Smith | .30 | .14 | .04 |
| New England Patriots | | | |
| ☐ 79 Altie Taylor | .35 | .16 | .04 |
| Detroit Lions | | | |
| ☐ 80 Cedrick Hardman AP | .35 | .16 | .04 |
| San Francisco 49ers | | | |
| ☐ 81 Ken Payne | .30 | .14 | .04 |
| Green Bay Packers | | | |
| ☐ 82 Zeke Moore | .30 | .14 | .04 |
| Houston Oilers | | | |
| ☐ 83 Alvin Maxson | .30 | .14 | .04 |
| New Orleans Saints | | | |
| ☐ 84 Wally Hilgenberg | .30 | .14 | .04 |
| Minnesota Vikings | | | |
| ☐ 85 John Niland | .30 | .14 | .04 |
| Philadelphia Eagles | | | |
| ☐ 86 Mike Sensibaugh | .30 | .14 | .04 |
| Kansas City Chiefs | | | |
| ☐ 87 Ron Johnson | .35 | .16 | .04 |
| New York Giants | | | |
| ☐ 88 Winston Hill | .35 | .16 | .04 |
| New York Jets | | | |
| ☐ 89 Charlie Joiner | 2.00 | .90 | .25 |
| Cincinnati Bengals | | | |
| ☐ 90 Roger Wehrli AP | .35 | .16 | .04 |
| St. Louis Cardinals | | | |
| ☐ 91 Mike Bragg | .30 | .14 | .04 |
| Washington Redskins | | | |
| ☐ 92 Dan Dickel | .30 | .14 | .04 |
| Baltimore Colts | | | |
| ☐ 93 Earl Morrall | .60 | .25 | .08 |
| Miami Dolphins | | | |
| ☐ 94 Pat Toomay | .30 | .14 | .04 |
| Buffalo Bills | | | |
| ☐ 95 Gary Garrison | .35 | .16 | .04 |
| San Diego Chargers | | | |
| ☐ 96 Ken Geddes | .30 | .14 | .04 |
| Seattle Seahawks | | | |
| ☐ 97 Mike Current | .30 | .14 | .04 |
| Tampa Bay Buccaneers | | | |
| ☐ 98 Bob Avellini | .30 | .14 | .04 |
| Chicago Bears | | | |
| ☐ 99 Dave Pureifory | .35 | .16 | .04 |
| Green Bay Packers | | | |
| ☐ 100 Franco Harris AP | 8.00 | 3.60 | 1.00 |
| Pittsburgh Steelers | | | |
| ☐ 101 Randy Logan | .30 | .14 | .04 |
| Philadelphia Eagles | | | |
| ☐ 102 John Fitzgerald | .30 | .14 | .04 |
| Dallas Cowboys | | | |
| ☐ 103 Gregg Bingham | .40 | .18 | .05 |
| Houston Oilers | | | |
| ☐ 104 Jim Plunkett | 1.50 | .65 | .19 |
| New England Patriots | | | |
| ☐ 105 Carl Eller | .60 | .25 | .08 |
| Minnesota Vikings | | | |
| ☐ 106 Larry Walton | .30 | .14 | .04 |
| Detroit Lions | | | |
| ☐ 107 Clarence Scott | .30 | .14 | .04 |
| Cleveland Browns | | | |
| ☐ 108 Skip Vanderbundt | .30 | .14 | .04 |
| San Francisco 49ers | | | |
| ☐ 109 Boobie Clark | .35 | .16 | .04 |
| Cincinnati Bengals | | | |
| ☐ 110 Tom Mack AP | .35 | .16 | .04 |
| Los Angeles Rams | | | |
| ☐ 111 Bruce Laird | .30 | .14 | .04 |
| Baltimore Colts | | | |
| ☐ 112 Dave Dalby | .60 | .25 | .08 |
| Oakland Raiders | | | |
| ☐ 113 John Leypoldt | .30 | .14 | .04 |
| Buffalo Bills | | | |
| ☐ 114 Barry Pearson | .30 | .14 | .04 |
| Kansas City Chiefs | | | |
| ☐ 115 Larry Brown | .50 | .23 | .06 |
| Washington Redskins | | | |
| ☐ 116 Jackie Smith | .60 | .25 | .08 |
| St. Louis Cardinals | | | |
| ☐ 117 Pat Hughes | .30 | .14 | .04 |
| New York Giants | | | |
| ☐ 118 Al Woodall | .35 | .16 | .04 |
| New York Jets | | | |
| ☐ 119 John Zook | .30 | .14 | .04 |

| | | | | | | | | | |
|---|---|---|---|---|---|---|---|---|---|
| Atlanta Falcons | | | | | Cincinnati Bengals | | | | |
| ☐ 120 Jake Scott AP | .35 | .16 | .04 | | ☐ 169 Bob Berry | .30 | .14 | .04 |
| Miami Dolphins | | | | | Minnesota Vikings | | | | |
| ☐ 121 Rich Glover | .30 | .14 | .04 | | ☐ 170 Ken Houston AP | .75 | .35 | .09 |
| Philadelphia Eagles | | | | | Washington Redskins | | | | |
| ☐ 122 Ernie Jackson | .30 | .14 | .04 | | ☐ 171 Bill Olds | .30 | .14 | .04 |
| New Orleans Saints | | | | | Baltimore Colts | | | | |
| ☐ 123 Otis Armstrong | 1.00 | .45 | .13 | | ☐ 172 Larry Seiple | .35 | .16 | .04 |
| Denver Broncos | | | | | Miami Dolphins | | | | |
| ☐ 124 Bob Grim | .35 | .16 | .04 | | ☐ 173 Cliff Branch | 3.00 | 1.35 | .40 |
| Chicago Bears | | | | | Oakland Raiders | | | | |
| ☐ 125 Jeff Siemon | .35 | .16 | .04 | | ☐ 174 Reggie McKenzie | .35 | .16 | .04 |
| Minnesota Vikings | | | | | Buffalo Bills | | | | |
| ☐ 126 Harold Hart | .30 | .14 | .04 | | ☐ 175 Dan Pastorini | .50 | .23 | .06 |
| Tampa Bay Buccaneers | | | | | Houston Oilers | | | | |
| ☐ 127 John DeMarie | .30 | .14 | .04 | | ☐ 176 Paul Naumoff | .30 | .14 | .04 |
| Seattle Seahawks | | | | | Detroit Lions | | | | |
| ☐ 128 Dan Fouts | 20.00 | 9.00 | 2.50 | | ☐ 177 Checklist 133-264 | 2.00 | .20 | .06 |
| San Diego Chargers | | | | | ☐ 178 Durwood Keeton | .30 | .14 | .04 |
| ☐ 129 Jim Kearney | .30 | .14 | .04 | | Tampa Bay Buccaneers | | | | |
| Kansas City Chiefs | | | | | ☐ 179 Earl Thomas | .30 | .14 | .04 |
| ☐ 130 John Dutton AP | .30 | .14 | .04 | | St. Louis Cardinals | | | | |
| Baltimore Colts | | | | | ☐ 180 L.C. Greenwood AP | .75 | .35 | .09 |
| ☐ 131 Calvin Hill | .60 | .25 | .08 | | Pittsburgh Steelers | | | | |
| Washington Redskins | | | | | ☐ 181 John Outlaw | .30 | .14 | .04 |
| ☐ 132 Toni Fritsch | .30 | .14 | .04 | | Philadelphia Eagles | | | | |
| Dallas Cowboys | | | | | ☐ 182 Frank Nunley | .30 | .14 | .04 |
| ☐ 133 Ron Jessie | .35 | .16 | .04 | | San Francisco 49ers | | | | |
| Los Angeles Rams | | | | | ☐ 183 Dave Jennings | 1.00 | .45 | .13 |
| ☐ 134 Don Nottingham | .30 | .14 | .04 | | New York Giants | | | | |
| Miami Dolphins | | | | | ☐ 184 MacArthur Lane | .35 | .16 | .04 |
| ☐ 135 Lemar Parrish | .35 | .16 | .04 | | Kansas City Chiefs | | | | |
| Cincinnati Bengals | | | | | ☐ 185 Chester Marcol | .35 | .16 | .04 |
| ☐ 136 Russ Francis | 3.50 | 1.55 | .45 | | Green Bay Packers | | | | |
| New England Patriots | | | | | ☐ 186 J.J. Jones | .30 | .14 | .04 |
| ☐ 137 Joe Reed | .30 | .14 | .04 | | New York Jets | | | | |
| Detroit Lions | | | | | ☐ 187 Tom DeLeone | .30 | .14 | .04 |
| ☐ 138 C.L. Whittington | .30 | .14 | .04 | | Cleveland Browns | | | | |
| Houston Oilers | | | | | ☐ 188 Steve Zabel | .30 | .14 | .04 |
| ☐ 139 Otis Sistrunk | .35 | .16 | .04 | | New England Patriots | | | | |
| Oakland Raiders | | | | | ☐ 189 Ken Johnson | .30 | .14 | .04 |
| ☐ 140 Lynn Swann AP | 14.00 | 6.25 | 1.75 | | Cincinnati Bengals | | | | |
| Pittsburgh Steelers | | | | | ☐ 190 Rayfield Wright AP | .30 | .14 | .04 |
| ☐ 141 Jim Carter | .30 | .14 | .04 | | Dallas Cowboys | | | | |
| Green Bay Packers | | | | | ☐ 191 Brent McClanahan | .30 | .14 | .04 |
| ☐ 142 Mike Montler | .30 | .14 | .04 | | Minnesota Vikings | | | | |
| Buffalo Bills | | | | | ☐ 192 Pat Fischer | .35 | .16 | .04 |
| ☐ 143 Walter Johnson | .30 | .14 | .04 | | Washington Redskins | | | | |
| Cleveland Browns | | | | | ☐ 193 Roger Carr | .75 | .35 | .09 |
| ☐ 144 Doug Kotar | .30 | .14 | .04 | | Baltimore Colts | | | | |
| New York Giants | | | | | ☐ 194 Manny Fernandez | .35 | .16 | .04 |
| ☐ 145 Roman Gabriel | 1.00 | .45 | .13 | | Miami Dolphins | | | | |
| Philadelphia Eagles | | | | | ☐ 195 Roy Gerela | .35 | .16 | .04 |
| ☐ 146 Billy Newsome | .30 | .14 | .04 | | Pittsburgh Steelers | | | | |
| New York Jets | | | | | ☐ 196 Dave Elmendorf | .35 | .16 | .04 |
| ☐ 147 Ed Bradley | .30 | .14 | .04 | | Los Angeles Rams | | | | |
| Seattle Seahawks | | | | | ☐ 197 Bob Kowalkowski | .30 | .14 | .04 |
| ☐ 148 Walter Payton | 200.00 | 90.00 | 25.00 | | Detroit Lions | | | | |
| Chicago Bears | | | | | ☐ 198 Phil Villapiano | .35 | .16 | .04 |
| ☐ 149 Johnny Fuller | .30 | .14 | .04 | | Oakland Raiders | | | | |
| New Orleans Saints | | | | | ☐ 199 Will Wynn | .30 | .14 | .04 |
| ☐ 150 Alan Page AP | 1.25 | .55 | .16 | | Philadelphia Eagles | | | | |
| Minnesota Vikings | | | | | ☐ 200 Terry Metcalf | .50 | .23 | .06 |
| ☐ 151 Frank Grant | .30 | .14 | .04 | | St. Louis Cardinals | | | | |
| Washington Redskins | | | | | ☐ 201 Passing Leaders | 2.00 | .90 | .25 |
| ☐ 152 Dave Green | .30 | .14 | .04 | | Ken Anderson | | | | |
| Cincinnati Bengals | | | | | Fran Tarkenton | | | | |
| ☐ 153 Nelson Munsey | .30 | .14 | .04 | | ☐ 202 Receiving Leaders | .50 | .23 | .06 |
| Baltimore Colts | | | | | Reggie Rucker | | | | |
| ☐ 154 Jim Mandich | .30 | .14 | .04 | | Lydell Mitchell | | | | |
| Miami Dolphins | | | | | Chuck Foreman | | | | |
| ☐ 155 Lawrence McCutcheon | .75 | .35 | .09 | | ☐ 203 Rushing Leaders | 3.00 | 1.35 | .40 |
| Los Angeles Rams | | | | | O.J. Simpson | | | | |
| ☐ 156 Steve Ramsey | .35 | .16 | .04 | | Jim Otis | | | | |
| Denver Broncos | | | | | ☐ 204 Scoring Leaders | 3.00 | 1.35 | .40 |
| ☐ 157 Ed Flanagan | .30 | .14 | .04 | | O.J. Simpson | | | | |
| San Diego Chargers | | | | | Chuck Foreman | | | | |
| ☐ 158 Randy White | 27.00 | 12.00 | 3.40 | | ☐ 205 Interception Leaders | .75 | .35 | .09 |
| Dallas Cowboys | | | | | Mel Blount | | | | |
| ☐ 159 Gerry Mullins | .30 | .14 | .04 | | Paul Krause | | | | |
| Pittsburgh Steelers | | | | | ☐ 206 Punting Leaders | .50 | .23 | .06 |
| ☐ 160 Jan Stenerud | .60 | .25 | .08 | | Ray Guy | | | | |
| Kansas City Chiefs | | | | | Herman Weaver | | | | |
| ☐ 161 Steve Odom | .30 | .14 | .04 | | ☐ 207 Ken Ellis | .30 | .14 | .04 |
| Green Bay Packers | | | | | Green Bay Packers | | | | |
| ☐ 162 Roger Finnie | .30 | .14 | .04 | | ☐ 208 Ron Saul | .30 | .14 | .04 |
| St. Louis Cardinals | | | | | Houston Oilers | | | | |
| ☐ 163 Norm Snead | .35 | .16 | .04 | | ☐ 209 Toni Linhart | .30 | .14 | .04 |
| San Francisco 49ers | | | | | Baltimore Colts | | | | |
| ☐ 164 Jeff Van Note | .40 | .18 | .05 | | ☐ 210 Jim Langer AP | 1.00 | .45 | .13 |
| Atlanta Falcons | | | | | Miami Dolphins | | | | |
| ☐ 165 Bill Bergey | .50 | .23 | .06 | | ☐ 211 Jeff Wright | .30 | .14 | .04 |
| Philadelphia Eagles | | | | | Minnesota Vikings | | | | |
| ☐ 166 Allen Carter | .30 | .14 | .04 | | ☐ 212 Moses Denson | .30 | .14 | .04 |
| New England Patriots | | | | | Washington Redskins | | | | |
| ☐ 167 Steve Holden | .30 | .14 | .04 | | ☐ 213 Earl Edwards | .30 | .14 | .04 |
| Cleveland Browns | | | | | Buffalo Bills | | | | |
| ☐ 168 Sherman White | .30 | .14 | .04 | | ☐ 214 Walker Gillette | .30 | .14 | .04 |

| | | | |
|---|---|---|---|
| New York Giants | | | |
| ☐ 215 Bob Trumpy | .60 | .25 | .08 |
| Cincinnati Bengals | | | |
| ☐ 216 Emmitt Thomas | .35 | .16 | .04 |
| Kansas City Chiefs | | | |
| ☐ 217 Lyle Alzado | 1.00 | .45 | .13 |
| Denver Broncos | | | |
| ☐ 218 Carl Garrett | .30 | .14 | .04 |
| New York Jets | | | |
| ☐ 219 Van Green | .30 | .14 | .04 |
| Cleveland Browns | | | |
| ☐ 220 Jack Lambert AP | 27.00 | 12.00 | 3.40 |
| Pittsburgh Steelers | | | |
| ☐ 221 Spike Jones | .30 | .14 | .04 |
| Philadelphia Eagles | | | |
| ☐ 222 John Hadl | .50 | .23 | .06 |
| Green Bay Packers | | | |
| ☐ 223 Billy Johnson | 2.50 | 1.15 | .30 |
| Houston Oilers | | | |
| ☐ 224 Tony McGee | .30 | .14 | .04 |
| New England Patriots | | | |
| ☐ 225 Preston Pearson | .50 | .23 | .06 |
| Dallas Cowboys | | | |
| ☐ 226 Isiah Robertson | .35 | .16 | .04 |
| Los Angeles Rams | | | |
| ☐ 227 Errol Mann | .30 | .14 | .04 |
| Detroit Lions | | | |
| ☐ 228 Paul Seal | .30 | .14 | .04 |
| New Orleans Saints | | | |
| ☐ 229 Roland Harper | .60 | .25 | .08 |
| Chicago Bears | | | |
| ☐ 230 Ed White AP | .60 | .25 | .08 |
| Minnesota Vikings | | | |
| ☐ 231 Joe Theismann | 6.00 | 2.70 | .75 |
| Washington Redskins | | | |
| ☐ 232 Jim Cheyunski | .30 | .14 | .04 |
| Baltimore Colts | | | |
| ☐ 233 Bill Stanfill | .35 | .16 | .04 |
| Miami Dolphins | | | |
| ☐ 234 Marv Hubbard | .35 | .16 | .04 |
| Oakland Raiders | | | |
| ☐ 235 Tommy Casanova | .35 | .16 | .04 |
| Cincinnati Bengals | | | |
| ☐ 236 Bob Hyland | .30 | .14 | .04 |
| New York Giants | | | |
| ☐ 237 Jesse Freitas | .30 | .14 | .04 |
| San Diego Chargers | | | |
| ☐ 238 Norm Thompson | .30 | .14 | .04 |
| St. Louis Cardinals | | | |
| ☐ 239 Charlie Smith | .30 | .14 | .04 |
| Philadelphia Eagles | | | |
| ☐ 240 John James AP | .30 | .14 | .04 |
| Atlanta Falcons | | | |
| ☐ 241 Alden Roche | .30 | .14 | .04 |
| Green Bay Packers | | | |
| ☐ 242 Gordon Jolley | .30 | .14 | .04 |
| Seattle Seahawks | | | |
| ☐ 243 Larry Ely | .30 | .14 | .04 |
| Tampa Bay Buccaneers | | | |
| ☐ 244 Richard Caster | .35 | .16 | .04 |
| New York Jets | | | |
| ☐ 245 Joe Greene | 3.00 | 1.35 | .40 |
| Pittsburgh Steelers | | | |
| ☐ 246 Larry Schreiber | .30 | .14 | .04 |
| San Francisco 49ers | | | |
| ☐ 247 Terry Schmidt | .30 | .14 | .04 |
| New Orleans Saints | | | |
| ☐ 248 Jerrel Wilson | .30 | .14 | .04 |
| Kansas City Chiefs | | | |
| ☐ 249 Marty Domres | .35 | .16 | .04 |
| Baltimore Colts | | | |
| ☐ 250 Isaac Curtis AP | .35 | .16 | .04 |
| Cincinnati Bengals | | | |
| ☐ 251 Harold McLinton | .30 | .14 | .04 |
| Washington Redskins | | | |
| ☐ 252 Fred Dryer | 1.50 | .65 | .19 |
| Los Angeles Rams | | | |
| ☐ 253 Bill Lenkaitis | .30 | .14 | .04 |
| New England Patriots | | | |
| ☐ 254 Don Hardeman | .30 | .14 | .04 |
| Houston Oilers | | | |
| ☐ 255 Bob Griese | 4.50 | 2.00 | .55 |
| Miami Dolphins | | | |
| ☐ 256 Oscar Roan | .40 | .18 | .05 |
| Cleveland Browns | | | |
| ☐ 257 Randy Gradishar | 6.00 | 2.70 | .75 |
| Denver Broncos | | | |
| ☐ 258 Bob Thomas | .50 | .23 | .06 |
| Chicago Bears | | | |
| ☐ 259 Joe Owens | .30 | .14 | .04 |
| Seattle Seahawks | | | |
| ☐ 260 Cliff Harris AP | 1.25 | .55 | .16 |
| Dallas Cowboys | | | |
| ☐ 261 Frank Lewis | .35 | .16 | .04 |
| Pittsburgh Steelers | | | |
| ☐ 262 Mike McCoy | .30 | .14 | .04 |
| Green Bay Packers | | | |
| ☐ 263 Rickey Young | .50 | .23 | .06 |
| San Diego Chargers | | | |
| ☐ 264 Brian Kelley | .30 | .14 | .04 |
| New York Giants | | | |
| ☐ 265 Charlie Sanders | .35 | .16 | .04 |
| Detroit Lions | | | |
| ☐ 266 Jim Hart | .75 | .35 | .09 |
| St. Louis Cardinals | | | |
| ☐ 267 Greg Gantt | .30 | .14 | .04 |
| New York Jets | | | |
| ☐ 268 John Ward | .30 | .14 | .04 |
| Tampa Bay Buccaneers | | | |
| ☐ 269 Al Beauchamp | .30 | .14 | .04 |
| Cincinnati Bengals | | | |
| ☐ 270 Jack Tatum AP | .35 | .16 | .04 |
| Oakland Raiders | | | |
| ☐ 271 Jim Lash | .30 | .14 | .04 |
| Minnesota Vikings | | | |
| ☐ 272 Diron Talbert | .35 | .16 | .04 |
| Washington Redskins | | | |
| ☐ 273 Checklist 265-396 | 2.00 | .20 | .06 |
| ☐ 274 Steve Spurrier | 2.00 | .90 | .25 |
| San Francisco 49ers | | | |
| ☐ 275 Greg Pruitt | .60 | .25 | .08 |
| Cleveland Browns | | | |
| ☐ 276 Jim Mitchell | .30 | .14 | .04 |
| Atlanta Falcons | | | |
| ☐ 277 Jack Rudnay | .30 | .14 | .04 |
| Kansas City Chiefs | | | |
| ☐ 278 Freddie Solomon | 1.00 | .45 | .13 |
| Miami Dolphins | | | |
| ☐ 279 Frank LeMaster | .30 | .14 | .04 |
| Philadelphia Eagles | | | |
| ☐ 280 Wally Chambers AP | .35 | .16 | .04 |
| Chicago Bears | | | |
| ☐ 281 Mike Collier | .30 | .14 | .04 |
| Pittsburgh Steelers | | | |
| ☐ 282 Clarence Williams | .30 | .14 | .04 |
| Green Bay Packers | | | |
| ☐ 283 Mitch Hoopes | .30 | .14 | .04 |
| Dallas Cowboys | | | |
| ☐ 284 Ron Bolton | .30 | .14 | .04 |
| New England Patriots | | | |
| ☐ 285 Harold Jackson | .60 | .25 | .08 |
| Los Angeles Rams | | | |
| ☐ 286 Greg Landry | .50 | .23 | .06 |
| Detroit Lions | | | |
| ☐ 287 Tony Greene | .30 | .14 | .04 |
| Buffalo Bills | | | |
| ☐ 288 Howard Stevens | .30 | .14 | .04 |
| Baltimore Colts | | | |
| ☐ 289 Roy Jefferson | .35 | .16 | .04 |
| Washington Redskins | | | |
| ☐ 290 Jim Bakken AP | .35 | .16 | .04 |
| St. Louis Cardinals | | | |
| ☐ 291 Doug Sutherland | .35 | .16 | .04 |
| Minnesota Vikings | | | |
| ☐ 292 Marvin Cobb | .30 | .14 | .04 |
| Cincinnati Bengals | | | |
| ☐ 293 Mack Alston | .30 | .14 | .04 |
| Houston Oilers | | | |
| ☐ 294 Rod McNeil | .30 | .14 | .04 |
| New Orleans Saints | | | |
| ☐ 295 Gene Upshaw | 1.00 | .45 | .13 |
| Oakland Raiders | | | |
| ☐ 296 Dave Gallagher | .30 | .14 | .04 |
| New York Giants | | | |
| ☐ 297 Larry Ball | .30 | .14 | .04 |
| Tampa Bay Buccaneers | | | |
| ☐ 298 Ron Howard | .30 | .14 | .04 |
| Seattle Seahawks | | | |
| ☐ 299 Don Strock | 1.50 | .65 | .19 |
| Miami Dolphins | | | |
| ☐ 300 O.J. Simpson AP | 12.00 | 5.50 | 1.50 |
| Buffalo Bills | | | |
| ☐ 301 Ray Mansfield | .30 | .14 | .04 |
| Pittsburgh Steelers | | | |
| ☐ 302 Larry Marshall | .30 | .14 | .04 |
| Philadelphia Eagles | | | |
| ☐ 303 Dick Himes | .30 | .14 | .04 |
| Green Bay Packers | | | |
| ☐ 304 Ray Wersching | .50 | .23 | .06 |
| San Diego Chargers | | | |
| ☐ 305 John Riggins | 4.00 | 1.80 | .50 |
| New York Jets | | | |
| ☐ 306 Bob Parsons | .30 | .14 | .04 |
| Chicago Bears | | | |
| ☐ 307 Ray Brown | .30 | .14 | .04 |
| Atlanta Falcons | | | |
| ☐ 308 Len Dawson | 3.00 | 1.35 | .40 |
| Kansas City Chiefs | | | |
| ☐ 309 Andy Maurer | .30 | .14 | .04 |
| Minnesota Vikings | | | |
| ☐ 310 Jack Youngblood AP | 1.00 | .45 | .13 |
| Los Angeles Rams | | | |
| ☐ 311 Essex Johnson | .30 | .14 | .04 |
| Cincinnati Bengals | | | |
| ☐ 312 Stan White | .30 | .14 | .04 |
| Baltimore Colts | | | |

| | | | |
|---|---|---|---|
| ☐ 313 Drew Pearson | 4.00 | 1.80 | .50 |
| Dallas Cowboys | | | |
| ☐ 314 Rockne Freitas | .30 | .14 | .04 |
| Detroit Lions | | | |
| ☐ 315 Mercury Morris | .60 | .25 | .08 |
| Miami Dolphins | | | |
| ☐ 316 Willie Alexander | .30 | .14 | .04 |
| Houston Oilers | | | |
| ☐ 317 Paul Warfield | 3.00 | 1.35 | .40 |
| Cleveland Browns | | | |
| ☐ 318 Bob Chandler | .35 | .16 | .04 |
| Buffalo Bills | | | |
| ☐ 319 Bobby Walden | .30 | .14 | .04 |
| Pittsburgh Steelers | | | |
| ☐ 320 Riley Odoms AP | .35 | .16 | .04 |
| Denver Broncos | | | |
| ☐ 321 Mike Boryla | .30 | .14 | .04 |
| Philadelphia Eagles | | | |
| ☐ 322 Bruce Van Dyke | .30 | .14 | .04 |
| Green Bay Packers | | | |
| ☐ 323 Pete Banaszak | .35 | .16 | .04 |
| Oakland Raiders | | | |
| ☐ 324 Darryl Stingley | .50 | .23 | .06 |
| New England Patriots | | | |
| ☐ 325 John Mendenhall | .30 | .14 | .04 |
| New York Giants | | | |
| ☐ 326 Dan Dierdorf | 1.25 | .55 | .16 |
| St. Louis Cardinals | | | |
| ☐ 327 Bruce Taylor | .30 | .14 | .04 |
| San Francisco 49ers | | | |
| ☐ 328 Don McCauley | .30 | .14 | .04 |
| Baltimore Colts | | | |
| ☐ 329 John Reaves | .35 | .16 | .04 |
| Cincinnati Bengals | | | |
| ☐ 330 Chris Hanburger AP | .35 | .16 | .04 |
| Washington Redskins | | | |
| ☐ 331 NFC Champions | 3.00 | 1.35 | .40 |
| Cowboys 37, | | | |
| Rams 7 | | | |
| (Roger Staubach) | | | |
| ☐ 332 AFC Champions | 2.00 | .90 | .25 |
| Steelers 16, | | | |
| Raiders 10 | | | |
| (Franco Harris) | | | |
| ☐ 333 Super Bowl X | 2.50 | 1.15 | .30 |
| Steelers 21, | | | |
| Cowboys 17 | | | |
| (Terry Bradshaw) | | | |
| ☐ 334 Godwin Turk | .30 | .14 | .04 |
| New York Jets | | | |
| ☐ 335 Dick Anderson | .40 | .18 | .05 |
| Miami Dolphins | | | |
| ☐ 336 Woody Green | .30 | .14 | .04 |
| Kansas City Chiefs | | | |
| ☐ 337 Pat Curran | .30 | .14 | .04 |
| San Diego Chargers | | | |
| ☐ 338 Council Rudolph | .30 | .14 | .04 |
| Tampa Bay Buccaneers | | | |
| ☐ 339 Joe Lavender | .35 | .16 | .04 |
| Philadelphia Eagles | | | |
| ☐ 340 John Gilliam AP | .35 | .16 | .04 |
| Minnesota Vikings | | | |
| ☐ 341 Steve Furness | .75 | .35 | .09 |
| Pittsburgh Steelers | | | |
| ☐ 342 D.D. Lewis | .35 | .16 | .04 |
| Dallas Cowboys | | | |
| ☐ 343 Duane Carrell | .30 | .14 | .04 |
| Los Angeles Rams | | | |
| ☐ 344 Jon Morris | .30 | .14 | .04 |
| Detroit Lions | | | |
| ☐ 345 John Brockington | .35 | .16 | .04 |
| Green Bay Packers | | | |
| ☐ 346 Mike Phipps | .35 | .16 | .04 |
| Cleveland Browns | | | |
| ☐ 347 Lyle Blackwood | .50 | .23 | .06 |
| Seattle Seahawks | | | |
| ☐ 348 Julius Adams | .30 | .14 | .04 |
| New England Patriots | | | |
| ☐ 349 Terry Hermeling | .30 | .14 | .04 |
| Washington Redskins | | | |
| ☐ 350 Rolland Lawrence AP | .40 | .18 | .05 |
| Atlanta Falcons | | | |
| ☐ 351 Glenn Doughty | .30 | .14 | .04 |
| Baltimore Colts | | | |
| ☐ 352 Doug Swift | .30 | .14 | .04 |
| Miami Dolphins | | | |
| ☐ 353 Mike Strachan | .30 | .14 | .04 |
| New Orleans Saints | | | |
| ☐ 354 Craig Morton | .60 | .25 | .08 |
| New York Giants | | | |
| ☐ 355 George Blanda | 4.50 | 2.00 | .55 |
| Oakland Raiders | | | |
| ☐ 356 Garry Puetz | .30 | .14 | .04 |
| New York Jets | | | |
| ☐ 357 Carl Mauck | .30 | .14 | .04 |
| Houston Oilers | | | |
| ☐ 358 Walt Patulski | .30 | .14 | .04 |
| Buffalo Bills | | | |
| ☐ 359 Stu Voigt | .35 | .16 | .04 |
| Minnesota Vikings | | | |
| ☐ 360 Fred Carr AP | .35 | .16 | .04 |
| Green Bay Packers | | | |
| ☐ 361 Po James | .30 | .14 | .04 |
| Philadelphia Eagles | | | |
| ☐ 362 Otis Taylor | .50 | .23 | .06 |
| Kansas City Chiefs | | | |
| ☐ 363 Jeff West | .30 | .14 | .04 |
| St. Louis Cardinals | | | |
| ☐ 364 Gary Huff | .35 | .16 | .04 |
| Chicago Bears | | | |
| ☐ 365 Dwight White | .35 | .16 | .04 |
| Pittsburgh Steelers | | | |
| ☐ 366 Dan Ryczek | .30 | .14 | .04 |
| Tampa Bay Buccaneers | | | |
| ☐ 367 Jon Keyworth | .40 | .18 | .05 |
| Denver Broncos | | | |
| ☐ 368 Mel Renfro | .60 | .25 | .08 |
| Dallas Cowboys | | | |
| ☐ 369 Bruce Coslet | 1.00 | .45 | .13 |
| Cincinnati Bengals | | | |
| ☐ 370 Len Hauss AP | .35 | .16 | .04 |
| Washington Redskins | | | |
| ☐ 371 Rick Volk | .30 | .14 | .04 |
| Baltimore Colts | | | |
| ☐ 372 Howard Twilley | .35 | .16 | .04 |
| Miami Dolphins | | | |
| ☐ 373 Cullen Bryant | .50 | .23 | .06 |
| Los Angeles Rams | | | |
| ☐ 374 Bob Babich | .30 | .14 | .04 |
| Cleveland Browns | | | |
| ☐ 375 Herman Weaver | .30 | .14 | .04 |
| Detroit Lions | | | |
| ☐ 376 Steve Grogan | 8.00 | 3.60 | 1.00 |
| New England Patriots | | | |
| ☐ 377 Bubba Smith | 1.25 | .55 | .16 |
| Houston Oilers | | | |
| ☐ 378 Burgess Owens | .30 | .14 | .04 |
| New York Jets | | | |
| ☐ 379 Alvin Matthews | .30 | .14 | .04 |
| Green Bay Packers | | | |
| ☐ 380 Art Shell | 2.00 | .90 | .25 |
| Oakland Raiders | | | |
| ☐ 381 Larry Brown | .30 | .14 | .04 |
| Pittsburgh Steelers | | | |
| ☐ 382 Horst Muhlmann | .30 | .14 | .04 |
| Philadelphia Eagles | | | |
| ☐ 383 Ahmad Rashad | 2.50 | 1.15 | .30 |
| Buffalo Bills | | | |
| ☐ 384 Bobby Maples | .35 | .16 | .04 |
| Denver Broncos | | | |
| ☐ 385 Jim Marshall | .75 | .35 | .09 |
| Minnesota Vikings | | | |
| ☐ 386 Joe Dawkins | .30 | .14 | .04 |
| New York Giants | | | |
| ☐ 387 Dennis Partee | .30 | .14 | .04 |
| San Diego Chargers | | | |
| ☐ 388 Eddie McMillan | .30 | .14 | .04 |
| Seattle Seahawks | | | |
| ☐ 389 Randy Johnson | .35 | .16 | .04 |
| Washington Redskins | | | |
| ☐ 390 Bob Kuechenberg AP | .40 | .18 | .05 |
| Miami Dolphins | | | |
| ☐ 391 Rufus Mayes | .30 | .14 | .04 |
| Cincinnati Bengals | | | |
| ☐ 392 Lloyd Mumphord | .30 | .14 | .04 |
| Baltimore Colts | | | |
| ☐ 393 Ike Harris | .30 | .14 | .04 |
| St. Louis Cardinals | | | |
| ☐ 394 Dave Hampton | .30 | .14 | .04 |
| Atlanta Falcons | | | |
| ☐ 395 Roger Staubach | 16.00 | 7.25 | 2.00 |
| Dallas Cowboys | | | |
| ☐ 396 Doug Buffone | .30 | .14 | .04 |
| Chicago Bears | | | |
| ☐ 397 Howard Fest | .30 | .14 | .04 |
| Tampa Bay Buccaneers | | | |
| ☐ 398 Wayne Mulligan | .30 | .14 | .04 |
| New York Jets | | | |
| ☐ 399 Bill Bradley | .30 | .14 | .04 |
| Philadelphia Eagles | | | |
| ☐ 400 Chuck Foreman AP | .75 | .35 | .09 |
| Minnesota Vikings | | | |
| ☐ 401 Jack Snow | .35 | .16 | .04 |
| Los Angeles Rams | | | |
| ☐ 402 Bob Howard | .30 | .14 | .04 |
| New England Patriots | | | |
| ☐ 403 John Matuszak | 1.00 | .45 | .13 |
| Kansas City Chiefs | | | |
| ☐ 404 Bill Munson | .35 | .16 | .04 |
| Detroit Lions | | | |
| ☐ 405 Andy Russell | .35 | .16 | .04 |
| Pittsburgh Steelers | | | |
| ☐ 406 Skip Butler | .30 | .14 | .04 |
| Houston Oilers | | | |
| ☐ 407 Hugh McKinnis | .30 | .14 | .04 |

| | | | | |
|---|---|---|---|---|
| Cleveland Browns | | | | |
| ☐ 408 Bob Penchion | .30 | .14 | .04 |
| Seattle Seahawks | | | | |
| ☐ 409 Mike Bass | .35 | .16 | .04 |
| Washington Redskins | | | | |
| ☐ 410 George Kunz AP | .35 | .16 | .04 |
| Baltimore Colts | | | | |
| ☐ 411 Ron Pritchard | .30 | .14 | .04 |
| Cincinnati Bengals | | | | |
| ☐ 412 Barry Smith | .30 | .14 | .04 |
| Green Bay Packers | | | | |
| ☐ 413 Norm Bulaich | .35 | .16 | .04 |
| Miami Dolphins | | | | |
| ☐ 414 Marv Bateman | .30 | .14 | .04 |
| Buffalo Bills | | | | |
| ☐ 415 Ken Stabler | 6.00 | 2.70 | .75 |
| Oakland Raiders | | | | |
| ☐ 416 Conrad Dobler | .35 | .16 | .04 |
| St. Louis Cardinals | | | | |
| ☐ 417 Bob Tucker | .35 | .16 | .04 |
| New York Giants | | | | |
| ☐ 418 Gene Washington | .35 | .16 | .04 |
| San Francisco 49ers | | | | |
| ☐ 419 Ed Marinaro | .75 | .35 | .09 |
| Minnesota Vikings | | | | |
| ☐ 420 Jack Ham AP | 3.50 | 1.55 | .45 |
| Pittsburgh Steelers | | | | |
| ☐ 421 Jim Turner | .35 | .16 | .04 |
| Denver Broncos | | | | |
| ☐ 422 Chris Fletcher | .30 | .14 | .04 |
| San Diego Chargers | | | | |
| ☐ 423 Carl Barzilauskas | .30 | .14 | .04 |
| New York Jets | | | | |
| ☐ 424 Robert Brazile | 2.50 | 1.15 | .30 |
| Houston Oilers | | | | |
| ☐ 425 Harold Carmichael | 1.50 | .65 | .19 |
| Philadelphia Eagles | | | | |
| ☐ 426 Ron Jaworski | 4.00 | 1.80 | .50 |
| Los Angeles Rams | | | | |
| ☐ 427 Ed Too Tall Jones | 20.00 | 9.00 | 2.50 |
| Dallas Cowboys | | | | |
| ☐ 428 Larry McCarren | .30 | .14 | .04 |
| Green Bay Packers | | | | |
| ☐ 429 Mike Thomas | .50 | .23 | .06 |
| Washington Redskins | | | | |
| ☐ 430 Joe DeLamielleure AP | .35 | .16 | .04 |
| Buffalo Bills | | | | |
| ☐ 431 Tom Blanchard | .30 | .14 | .04 |
| New Orleans Saints | | | | |
| ☐ 432 Ron Carpenter | .30 | .14 | .04 |
| Cincinnati Bengals | | | | |
| ☐ 433 Levi Johnson | .30 | .14 | .04 |
| Detroit Lions | | | | |
| ☐ 434 Sam Cunningham | .35 | .16 | .04 |
| New England Patriots | | | | |
| ☐ 435 Garo Yepremian | .35 | .16 | .04 |
| Miami Dolphins | | | | |
| ☐ 436 Mike Livingston | .35 | .16 | .04 |
| Kansas City Chiefs | | | | |
| ☐ 437 Larry Csonka | 3.00 | 1.35 | .40 |
| New York Giants | | | | |
| ☐ 438 Doug Dieken | .30 | .14 | .04 |
| Cleveland Browns | | | | |
| ☐ 439 Bill Lueck | .30 | .14 | .04 |
| Philadelphia Eagles | | | | |
| ☐ 440 Tom MacLeod AP | .30 | .14 | .04 |
| Baltimore Colts | | | | |
| ☐ 441 Mick Tingelhoff | .35 | .16 | .04 |
| Minnesota Vikings | | | | |
| ☐ 442 Terry Hanratty | .35 | .16 | .04 |
| Pittsburgh Steelers | | | | |
| ☐ 443 Mike Siani | .30 | .14 | .04 |
| Oakland Raiders | | | | |
| ☐ 444 Dwight Harrison | .30 | .14 | .04 |
| Buffalo Bills | | | | |
| ☐ 445 Jim Otis | .35 | .16 | .04 |
| St. Louis Cardinals | | | | |
| ☐ 446 Jack Reynolds | .35 | .16 | .04 |
| Los Angeles Rams | | | | |
| ☐ 447 Jean Fugett | .40 | .18 | .05 |
| Dallas Cowboys | | | | |
| ☐ 448 Dave Beverly | .30 | .14 | .04 |
| Green Bay Packers | | | | |
| ☐ 449 Bernard Jackson | 1.00 | .45 | .13 |
| Cincinnati Bengals | | | | |
| ☐ 450 Charley Taylor | 1.75 | .80 | .22 |
| Washington Redskins | | | | |
| ☐ 451 Atlanta Falcons | 1.50 | .25 | .05 |
| Team Checklist | | | | |
| ☐ 452 Baltimore Colts | 1.50 | .25 | .05 |
| Team Checklist | | | | |
| ☐ 453 Buffalo Bills | 1.50 | .25 | .05 |
| Team Checklist | | | | |
| ☐ 454 Chicago Bears | 1.50 | .25 | .05 |
| Team Checklist | | | | |
| ☐ 455 Cincinnati Bengals | 1.50 | .25 | .05 |
| Team Checklist | | | | |
| ☐ 456 Cleveland Browns | 1.50 | .25 | .05 |

| | | | | |
|---|---|---|---|---|
| Team Checklist | | | | |
| ☐ 457 Dallas Cowboys | 1.50 | .25 | .05 |
| Team Checklist | | | | |
| ☐ 458 Denver Broncos UER | 1.50 | .25 | .05 |
| Team Checklist | | | | |
| (Charley Johnson | | | | |
| should be Charlie) | | | | |
| ☐ 459 Detroit Lions | 1.50 | .25 | .05 |
| Team Checklist | | | | |
| ☐ 460 Green Bay Packers | 1.50 | .25 | .05 |
| Team Checklist | | | | |
| ☐ 461 Houston Oilers | 1.50 | .25 | .05 |
| Team Checklist | | | | |
| ☐ 462 Kansas City Chiefs | 1.50 | .25 | .05 |
| Team Checklist | | | | |
| ☐ 463 Los Angeles Rams | 1.50 | .25 | .05 |
| Team Checklist | | | | |
| ☐ 464 Miami Dolphins | 1.50 | .25 | .05 |
| Team Checklist | | | | |
| ☐ 465 Minnesota Vikings | 1.50 | .25 | .05 |
| Team Checklist | | | | |
| ☐ 466 New England Patriots | 1.50 | .25 | .05 |
| Team Checklist | | | | |
| ☐ 467 New Orleans Saints | 1.50 | .25 | .05 |
| Team Checklist | | | | |
| ☐ 468 New York Giants | 1.50 | .25 | .05 |
| Team Checklist | | | | |
| ☐ 469 New York Jets | 1.50 | .25 | .05 |
| Team Checklist | | | | |
| ☐ 470 Oakland Raiders | 1.50 | .25 | .05 |
| Team Checklist | | | | |
| ☐ 471 Philadelphia Eagles | 1.50 | .25 | .05 |
| Team Checklist | | | | |
| ☐ 472 Pittsburgh Steelers | 1.50 | .25 | .05 |
| Team Checklist | | | | |
| ☐ 473 St. Louis Cardinals | 1.50 | .25 | .05 |
| Team Checklist | | | | |
| ☐ 474 San Diego Chargers | 1.50 | .25 | .05 |
| Team Checklist | | | | |
| ☐ 475 San Francisco 49ers | 1.50 | .25 | .05 |
| Team Checklist | | | | |
| ☐ 476 Seattle Seahawks | 1.50 | .25 | .05 |
| Team Checklist | | | | |
| ☐ 477 Tampa Bay Buccaneers | 1.50 | .25 | .05 |
| Team Checklist | | | | |
| ☐ 478 Washington Redskins | 1.50 | .25 | .05 |
| Team Checklist | | | | |
| ☐ 479 Fred Cox | .35 | .16 | .04 |
| Minnesota Vikings | | | | |
| ☐ 480 Mel Blount AP | 5.00 | 2.30 | .60 |
| Pittsburgh Steelers | | | | |
| ☐ 481 John Bunting | .30 | .14 | .04 |
| Philadelphia Eagles | | | | |
| ☐ 482 Ken Mendenhall | .30 | .14 | .04 |
| Baltimore Colts | | | | |
| ☐ 483 Will Harrell | .35 | .16 | .04 |
| Green Bay Packers | | | | |
| ☐ 484 Marlin Briscoe | .35 | .16 | .04 |
| Detroit Lions | | | | |
| ☐ 485 Archie Manning | 1.00 | .45 | .13 |
| New Orleans Saints | | | | |
| ☐ 486 Tody Smith | .30 | .14 | .04 |
| Houston Oilers | | | | |
| ☐ 487 George Hunt | .30 | .14 | .04 |
| New York Giants | | | | |
| ☐ 488 Roscoe Word | .30 | .14 | .04 |
| New York Jets | | | | |
| ☐ 489 Paul Seymour | .30 | .14 | .04 |
| Buffalo Bills | | | | |
| ☐ 490 Lee Roy Jordan AP | 1.00 | .45 | .13 |
| Dallas Cowboys | | | | |
| ☐ 491 Chip Myers | .30 | .14 | .04 |
| Cincinnati Bengals | | | | |
| ☐ 492 Norm Evans | .35 | .16 | .04 |
| Miami Dolphins | | | | |
| ☐ 493 Jim Bertelsen | .30 | .14 | .04 |
| Los Angeles Rams | | | | |
| ☐ 494 Mark Moseley | .50 | .23 | .06 |
| Washington Redskins | | | | |
| ☐ 495 George Buehler | .30 | .14 | .04 |
| Oakland Raiders | | | | |
| ☐ 496 Charlie Hall | .30 | .14 | .04 |
| Cleveland Browns | | | | |
| ☐ 497 Marvin Upshaw | .30 | .14 | .04 |
| Kansas City Chiefs | | | | |
| ☐ 498 Tom Banks | .50 | .23 | .06 |
| St. Louis Cardinals | | | | |
| ☐ 499 Randy Vataha | .35 | .16 | .04 |
| New England Patriots | | | | |
| ☐ 500 Fran Tarkenton AP | 7.00 | 3.10 | .85 |
| Minnesota Vikings | | | | |
| ☐ 501 Mike Wagner | .30 | .14 | .04 |
| Pittsburgh Steelers | | | | |
| ☐ 502 Art Malone | .30 | .14 | .04 |
| Philadelphia Eagles | | | | |
| ☐ 503 Fred Cook | .30 | .14 | .04 |
| Baltimore Colts | | | | |
| ☐ 504 Rich McGeorge | .30 | .14 | .04 |

| | | | | |
|---|---|---|---|---|
| | Green Bay Packers | | | |
| ☐ 505 | Ken Burrough | .35 | .16 | .04 |
| | Houston Oilers | | | |
| ☐ 506 | Nick Mike-Mayer | .30 | .14 | .04 |
| | Atlanta Falcons | | | |
| ☐ 507 | Checklist 397-528 | 2.00 | .20 | .06 |
| ☐ 508 | Steve Owens | .35 | .16 | .04. |
| | Detroit Lions | | | |
| ☐ 509 | Brad Van Pelt | .75 | .35 | .09 |
| | New York Giants | | | |
| ☐ 510 | Ken Riley AP | .35 | .16 | .04 |
| | Cincinnati Bengals | | | |
| ☐ 511 | Art Thoms | .30 | .14 | .04 |
| | Oakland Raiders | | | |
| ☐ 512 | Ed Bell | .30 | .14 | .04 |
| | New York Jets | | | |
| ☐ 513 | Tom Wittum | .30 | .14 | .04 |
| | San Francisco 49ers | | | |
| ☐ 514 | Jim Braxton | .30 | .14 | .04 |
| | Buffalo Bills | | | |
| ☐ 515 | Nick Buoniconti | .60 | .25 | .08 |
| | Miami Dolphins | | | |
| ☐ 516 | Brian Sipe | 3.50 | 1.55 | .45 |
| | Cleveland Browns | | | |
| ☐ 517 | Jim Lynch | .30 | .14 | .04 |
| | Kansas City Chiefs | | | |
| ☐ 518 | Prentice McCray | .30 | .14 | .04 |
| | New England Patriots | | | |
| ☐ 519 | Tom Dempsey | .35 | .16 | .04 |
| | Los Angeles Rams | | | |
| ☐ 520 | Mel Gray AP | .35 | .16 | .04 |
| | St. Louis Cardinals | | | |
| ☐ 521 | Nate Wright | .35 | .16 | .04 |
| | Minnesota Vikings | | | |
| ☐ 522 | Rocky Bleier | 2.50 | 1.15 | .30 |
| | Pittsburgh Steelers | | | |
| ☐ 523 | Dennis Johnson | .30 | .14 | .04 |
| | Washington Redskins | | | |
| ☐ 524 | Jerry Sisemore | .35 | .16 | .04 |
| | Philadelphia Eagles | | | |
| ☐ 525 | Bert Jones | 1.00 | .45 | .13 |
| | Baltimore Colts | | | |
| ☐ 526 | Perry Smith | .30 | .14 | .04 |
| | Green Bay Packers | | | |
| ☐ 527 | Blaine Nye | .30 | .14 | .04 |
| | Dallas Cowboys | | | |
| ☐ 528 | Bob Moore | .50 | .23 | .06 |
| | Oakland Raiders | | | |

## 1976 Topps Team Checklists

The 1976 Topps Team Checklist set contains 30 cards, one for each of the 28 NFL teams plus two checklist cards. The cards measure the standard 2 1/2" by 3 1/2". The front of the card has the 1976 Topps checklist for that particular team, complete with boxes in which to place check marks. The set was only available directly from Topps as a send-off offer as an uncut sheet; the prices below apply equally to uncut sheets as they are frequently found in their original uncut condition. These unnumbered cards are numbered below for convenience in alphabetical order by team name.

| | | NRMT | VG-E | GOOD |
|---|---|---|---|---|
| | COMPLETE SET (30) | 125.00 | 50.00 | 12.50 |
| | COMMON PLAYER (1-30) | 6.00 | 2.40 | .60 |
| ☐ 1 | Atlanta Falcons | 6.00 | 2.40 | .60 |
| ☐ 2 | Baltimore Colts | 6.00 | 2.40 | .60 |
| ☐ 3 | Buffalo Bills | 6.00 | 2.40 | .60 |
| ☐ 4 | Chicago Bears | 7.50 | 3.00 | .75 |
| ☐ 5 | Cincinnati Bengals | 6.00 | 2.40 | .60 |
| ☐ 6 | Cleveland Browns | 6.00 | 2.40 | .60 |
| ☐ 7 | Dallas Cowboys | 9.00 | 3.75 | .90 |
| ☐ 8 | Denver Broncos | 7.50 | 3.00 | .75 |
| ☐ 9 | Detroit Lions | 6.00 | 2.40 | .60 |

| | | | | |
|---|---|---|---|---|
| ☐ 10 | Green Bay Packers | 6.00 | 2.40 | .60 |
| ☐ 11 | Houston Oilers | 6.00 | 2.40 | .60 |
| ☐ 12 | Kansas City Chiefs | 6.00 | 2.40 | .60 |
| ☐ 13 | Los Angeles Rams | 6.00 | 2.40 | .60 |
| ☐ 14 | Miami Dolphins | 7.50 | 3.00 | .75 |
| ☐ 15 | Minnesota Vikings | 6.00 | 2.40 | .60 |
| ☐ 16 | New England Patriots | 6.00 | 2.40 | .60 |
| ☐ 17 | New York Giants | 7.50 | 3.00 | .75 |
| ☐ 18 | New York Jets | 7.50 | 3.00 | .75 |
| ☐ 19 | New Orleans Saints | 6.00 | 2.40 | .60 |
| ☐ 20 | Oakland Raiders | 9.00 | 3.75 | .90 |
| ☐ 21 | Philadelphia Eagles | 6.00 | 2.40 | .60 |
| ☐ 22 | Pittsburgh Steelers | 7.50 | 3.00 | .75 |
| ☐ 23 | St. Louis Cardinals | 6.00 | 2.40 | .60 |
| ☐ 24 | San Diego Chargers | 6.00 | 2.40 | .60 |
| ☐ 25 | San Francisco 49ers | 7.50 | 3.00 | .75 |
| ☐ 26 | Seattle Seahawks | 9.00 | 3.75 | .90 |
| ☐ 27 | Tampa Bay Buccaneers | 7.50 | 3.00 | .75 |
| ☐ 28 | Washington Redskins | 7.50 | 3.00 | .75 |
| ☐ 29 | Checklist 1-132 | 6.00 | 2.40 | .60 |
| ☐ 30 | Checklist 133-264 | 6.00 | 2.40 | .60 |

## 1977 Topps

The 1977 Topps football set contains 528 cards. The cards measure 2 1/2" by 3 1/2". The first six cards in the set are statistical league leaders from each conference. Cards 451 to 455 are Record Breaker (RB) cards featuring players breaking individual records during the previous season. Cards 201-228 are team checklist cards. The Falcons checklist erroneously does not list 79 Jim Mitchell. Cards 526-528 feature post-season action from the previous season. All-Pro (AP) selections are designated on the player's regular card, not a special card. No known scarcities exist. The card backs are printed in purple and black on gray card stock. The key Rookie Card in this set is Steve Largent. Other notable Rookie Cards include Harry Carson, Dave Casper, Archie Griffin, Lee Roy Selmon, Mike Webster, Danny White, and Jim Zorn. An uncut sheet of team checklist cards was also available via a mail-in offer on wax packs. There also exists a Mexican version of the Topps 1977 set. The Mexican set contains the same 528 players but is done in Spanish (front and back) and is obviously quite a bit rarer than the 1977 regular football issue. The Spanish cards are valued an average ten times the values listed below.

| | | NRMT | VG-E | GOOD |
|---|---|---|---|---|
| | COMPLETE SET (528) | 225.00 | 100.00 | 28.00 |
| | COMMON PLAYER (1-528) | .25 | .11 | .03 |
| ☐ 1 | Passing Leaders | 1.50 | .30 | .09 |
| | James Harris | | | |
| | Ken Stabler | | | |
| ☐ 2 | Receiving Leaders | .50 | .23 | .06 |
| | Drew Pearson | | | |
| | MacArthur Lane | | | |
| ☐ 3 | Rushing Leaders | 10.00 | 4.50 | 1.25 |
| | Walter Payton | | | |
| | O.J. Simpson | | | |
| ☐ 4 | Scoring Leaders | .40 | .18 | .05 |
| | Mark Moseley | | | |
| | Toni Linhart | | | |
| ☐ 5 | Interception Leaders | .40 | .18 | .05 |
| | Monte Jackson | | | |
| | Ken Riley | | | |
| ☐ 6 | Punting Leaders | .40 | .18 | .05 |
| | John James | | | |
| | Marv Bateman | | | |
| ☐ 7 | Mike Phipps | .30 | .14 | .04 |
| | Cleveland Browns | | | |
| ☐ 8 | Rick Volk | .25 | .11 | .03 |
| | New York Giants | | | |
| ☐ 9 | Steve Furness | .30 | .14 | .04 |
| | Pittsburgh Steelers | | | |
| ☐ 10 | Isaac Curtis | .30 | .14 | .04 |
| | Cincinnati Bengals | | | |

| | | | |
|---|---|---|---|
| ☐ 11 Nate Wright | .30 | .14 | .04 |
| Minnesota Vikings | | | |
| ☐ 12 Jean Fugett | .30 | .14 | .04 |
| Washington Redskins | | | |
| ☐ 13 Ken Mendenhall | .25 | .11 | .03 |
| Baltimore Colts | | | |
| ☐ 14 Sam Adams | .25 | .11 | .03 |
| New England Patriots | | | |
| ☐ 15 Charlie Waters | 1.00 | .45 | .13 |
| Dallas Cowboys | | | |
| ☐ 16 Bill Stanfill | .30 | .14 | .04 |
| Miami Dolphins | | | |
| ☐ 17 John Holland | .25 | .11 | .03 |
| Buffalo Bills | | | |
| ☐ 18 Pat Haden | 3.00 | 1.35 | .40 |
| Los Angeles Rams | | | |
| ☐ 19 Bob Young | .25 | .11 | .03 |
| St. Louis Cardinals | | | |
| ☐ 20 Wally Chambers AP | .30 | .14 | .04 |
| Chicago Bears | | | |
| ☐ 21 Lawrence Gaines | .25 | .11 | .03 |
| Detroit Lions | | | |
| ☐ 22 Larry McCarren | .25 | .11 | .03 |
| Green Bay Packers | | | |
| ☐ 23 Horst Muhlmann | .25 | .11 | .03 |
| Philadelphia Eagles | | | |
| ☐ 24 Phil Villapiano | .30 | .14 | .04 |
| Oakland Raiders | | | |
| ☐ 25 Greg Pruitt | .40 | .18 | .05 |
| Cleveland Browns | | | |
| ☐ 26 Ron Howard | .25 | .11 | .03 |
| Seattle Seahawks | | | |
| ☐ 27 Craig Morton | .50 | .23 | .06 |
| Denver Broncos | | | |
| ☐ 28 Rufus Mayes | .25 | .11 | .03 |
| Cincinnati Bengals | | | |
| ☐ 29 Lee Roy Selmon UER | 3.00 | 1.35 | .40 |
| Tampa Bay Buccaneers | | | |
| (Misspelled Leroy) | | | |
| ☐ 30 Ed White AP | .30 | .14 | .04 |
| Minnesota Vikings | | | |
| ☐ 31 Harold McLinton | .25 | .11 | .03 |
| Washington Redskins | | | |
| ☐ 32 Glenn Doughty | .25 | .11 | .03 |
| Baltimore Colts | | | |
| ☐ 33 Bob Kuechenberg | .35 | .16 | .04 |
| Miami Dolphins | | | |
| ☐ 34 Duane Carrell | .25 | .11 | .03 |
| New York Jets | | | |
| ☐ 35 Riley Odoms | .30 | .14 | .04 |
| Denver Broncos | | | |
| ☐ 36 Bobby Scott | .25 | .11 | .03 |
| New Orleans Saints | | | |
| ☐ 37 Nick Mike-Mayer | .25 | .11 | .03 |
| Atlanta Falcons | | | |
| ☐ 38 Bill Lenkaitis | .25 | .11 | .03 |
| New England Patriots | | | |
| ☐ 39 Roland Harper | .30 | .14 | .04 |
| Chicago Bears | | | |
| ☐ 40 Tommy Hart AP | .25 | .11 | .03 |
| San Francisco 49ers | | | |
| ☐ 41 Mike Sensibaugh | .25 | .11 | .03 |
| St. Louis Cardinals | | | |
| ☐ 42 Rusty Jackson | .25 | .11 | .03 |
| Los Angeles Rams | | | |
| ☐ 43 Levi Johnson | .25 | .11 | .03 |
| Detroit Lions | | | |
| ☐ 44 Mike McCoy | .25 | .11 | .03 |
| Green Bay Packers | | | |
| ☐ 45 Roger Staubach | 10.00 | 4.50 | 1.25 |
| Dallas Cowboys | | | |
| ☐ 46 Fred Cox | .30 | .14 | .04 |
| Minnesota Vikings | | | |
| ☐ 47 Bob Babich | .25 | .11 | .03 |
| Cleveland Browns | | | |
| ☐ 48 Reggie McKenzie | .30 | .14 | .04 |
| Buffalo Bills | | | |
| ☐ 49 Dave Jennings | .30 | .14 | .04 |
| New York Giants | | | |
| ☐ 50 Mike Haynes AP | 5.00 | 2.30 | .60 |
| New England Patriots | | | |
| ☐ 51 Larry Brown | .25 | .11 | .03 |
| Pittsburgh Steelers | | | |
| ☐ 52 Marvin Cobb | .25 | .11 | .03 |
| Cincinnati Bengals | | | |
| ☐ 53 Fred Cook | .25 | .11 | .03 |
| Baltimore Colts | | | |
| ☐ 54 Freddie Solomon | .30 | .14 | .04 |
| Miami Dolphins | | | |
| ☐ 55 John Riggins | 2.50 | 1.15 | .30 |
| Washington Redskins | | | |
| ☐ 56 John Bunting | .25 | .11 | .03 |
| Philadelphia Eagles | | | |
| ☐ 57 Ray Wersching | .30 | .14 | .04 |
| San Diego Chargers | | | |
| ☐ 58 Mike Livingston | .30 | .14 | .04 |
| Kansas City Chiefs | | | |
| ☐ 59 Billy Johnson | .50 | .23 | .06 |
| Houston Oilers | | | |
| ☐ 60 Mike Wagner AP | .25 | .11 | .03 |
| Pittsburgh Steelers | | | |
| ☐ 61 Waymond Bryant | .25 | .11 | .03 |
| Chicago Bears | | | |
| ☐ 62 Jim Otis | .30 | .14 | .04 |
| St. Louis Cardinals | | | |
| ☐ 63 Ed Galigher | .25 | .11 | .03 |
| New York Jets | | | |
| ☐ 64 Randy Vataha | .30 | .14 | .04 |
| New England Patriots | | | |
| ☐ 65 Jim Zorn | 4.00 | 1.80 | .50 |
| Seattle Seahawks | | | |
| ☐ 66 Jon Keyworth | .30 | .14 | .04 |
| Denver Broncos | | | |
| ☐ 67 Checklist 1-132 | 1.50 | .15 | .05 |
| ☐ 68 Henry Childs | .25 | .11 | .03 |
| New Orleans Saints | | | |
| ☐ 69 Thom Darden | .25 | .11 | .03 |
| Cleveland Browns | | | |
| ☐ 70 George Kunz AP | .30 | .14 | .04 |
| Baltimore Colts | | | |
| ☐ 71 Lenvil Elliott | .30 | .14 | .04 |
| Cincinnati Bengals | | | |
| ☐ 72 Curtis Johnson | .25 | .11 | .03 |
| Miami Dolphins | | | |
| ☐ 73 Doug Van Horn | .25 | .11 | .03 |
| New York Giants | | | |
| ☐ 74 Joe Theismann | 4.00 | 1.80 | .50 |
| Washington Redskins | | | |
| ☐ 75 Dwight White | .30 | .14 | .04 |
| Pittsburgh Steelers | | | |
| ☐ 76 Scott Laidlaw | .30 | .14 | .04 |
| Dallas Cowboys | | | |
| ☐ 77 Monte Johnson | .25 | .11 | .03 |
| Oakland Raiders | | | |
| ☐ 78 Dave Beverly | .25 | .11 | .03 |
| Green Bay Packers | | | |
| ☐ 79 Jim Mitchell | .25 | .11 | .03 |
| Atlanta Falcons | | | |
| ☐ 80 Jack Youngblood AP | .75 | .35 | .09 |
| Los Angeles Rams | | | |
| ☐ 81 Mel Gray | .30 | .14 | .04 |
| St. Louis Cardinals | | | |
| ☐ 82 Dwight Harrison | .25 | .11 | .03 |
| Buffalo Bills | | | |
| ☐ 83 John Hadl | .40 | .18 | .05 |
| Houston Oilers | | | |
| ☐ 84 Matt Blair | 1.75 | .80 | .22 |
| Minnesota Vikings | | | |
| ☐ 85 Charlie Sanders | .30 | .14 | .04 |
| Detroit Lions | | | |
| ☐ 86 Noah Jackson | .25 | .11 | .03 |
| Chicago Bears | | | |
| ☐ 87 Ed Marinaro | .50 | .23 | .06 |
| New York Jets | | | |
| ☐ 88 Bob Howard | .25 | .11 | .03 |
| New England Patriots | | | |
| ☐ 89 John McDaniel | .25 | .11 | .03 |
| Cincinnati Bengals | | | |
| ☐ 90 Dan Dierdorf AP | 1.00 | .45 | .13 |
| St. Louis Cardinals | | | |
| ☐ 91 Mark Moseley | .30 | .14 | .04 |
| Washington Redskins | | | |
| ☐ 92 Cleo Miller | .25 | .11 | .03 |
| Cleveland Browns | | | |
| ☐ 93 Andre Tillman | .30 | .14 | .04 |
| Miami Dolphins | | | |
| ☐ 94 Bruce Taylor | .25 | .11 | .03 |
| San Francisco 49ers | | | |
| ☐ 95 Bert Jones | .75 | .35 | .09 |
| Baltimore Colts | | | |
| ☐ 96 Anthony Davis | .75 | .35 | .09 |
| Tampa Bay Buccaneers | | | |
| ☐ 97 Don Goode | .25 | .11 | .03 |
| San Diego Chargers | | | |
| ☐ 98 Ray Rhodes | .25 | .11 | .03 |
| New York Giants | | | |
| ☐ 99 Mike Webster | 8.00 | 3.60 | 1.00 |
| Pittsburgh Steelers | | | |
| ☐ 100 O.J. Simpson AP | 10.00 | 4.50 | 1.25 |
| Buffalo Bills | | | |
| ☐ 101 Doug Plank | .75 | .35 | .09 |
| Chicago Bears | | | |
| ☐ 102 Efren Herrera | .30 | .14 | .04 |
| Dallas Cowboys | | | |
| ☐ 103 Charlie Smith | .25 | .11 | .03 |
| Philadelphia Eagles | | | |
| ☐ 104 Carlos Brown | .25 | .11 | .03 |
| Green Bay Packers | | | |
| ☐ 105 Jim Marshall | .60 | .25 | .08 |
| Minnesota Vikings | | | |
| ☐ 106 Paul Naumoff | .25 | .11 | .03 |
| Detroit Lions | | | |
| ☐ 107 Walter White | .25 | .11 | .03 |
| Kansas City Chiefs | | | |

| □ | Card | Player / Team | | | |
|---|---|---|---|---|---|
| □ | 108 | John Cappelletti — Los Angeles Rams | 2.50 | 1.15 | .30 |
| □ | 109 | Chip Myers — San Diego Chargers | .25 | .11 | .03 |
| □ | 110 | Ken Stabler AP — Oakland Raiders | 4.00 | 1.80 | .50 |
| □ | 111 | Joe Ehrmann — Baltimore Colts | .25 | .11 | .03 |
| □ | 112 | Rick Engles — Seattle Seahawks | .25 | .11 | .03 |
| □ | 113 | Jack Dolbin — Denver Broncos | .30 | .14 | .04 |
| □ | 114 | Ron Bolton — Cleveland Browns | .25 | .11 | .03 |
| □ | 115 | Mike Thomas — Washington Redskins | .30 | .14 | .04 |
| □ | 116 | Mike Fuller — San Diego Chargers | .25 | .11 | .03 |
| □ | 117 | John Hill — New Orleans Saints | .25 | .11 | .03 |
| □ | 118 | Richard Todd — New York Jets | 1.25 | .55 | .16 |
| □ | 119 | Duriel Harris — Miami Dolphins | .40 | .18 | .05 |
| □ | 120 | John James AP — Atlanta Falcons | .25 | .11 | .03 |
| □ | 121 | Lionel Antoine — Chicago Bears | .25 | .11 | .03 |
| □ | 122 | John Skorupan — Buffalo Bills | .25 | .11 | .03 |
| □ | 123 | Skip Butler — Houston Oilers | .25 | .11 | .03 |
| □ | 124 | Bob Tucker — New York Giants | .30 | .14 | .04 |
| □ | 125 | Paul Krause — Minnesota Vikings | .40 | .18 | .05 |
| □ | 126 | Dave Hampton — Philadelphia Eagles | .25 | .11 | .03 |
| □ | 127 | Tom Wittum — San Francisco 49ers | .25 | .11 | .03 |
| □ | 128 | Gary Huff — Tampa Bay Buccaneers | .30 | .14 | .04 |
| □ | 129 | Emmitt Thomas — Kansas City Chiefs | .30 | .14 | .04 |
| □ | 130 | Drew Pearson AP — Dallas Cowboys | 2.00 | .90 | .25 |
| □ | 131 | Ron Saul — Washington Redskins | .25 | .11 | .03 |
| □ | 132 | Steve Niehaus — Seattle Seahawks | .25 | .11 | .03 |
| □ | 133 | Fred Carr — Green Bay Packers | .30 | .14 | .04 |
| □ | 134 | Norm Bulaich — Miami Dolphins | .30 | .14 | .04 |
| □ | 135 | Bob Trumpy — Cincinnati Bengals | .40 | .18 | .05 |
| □ | 136 | Greg Landry — Detroit Lions | .50 | .23 | .06 |
| □ | 137 | George Buehler — Oakland Raiders | .25 | .11 | .03 |
| □ | 138 | Reggie Rucker — Cleveland Browns | .30 | .14 | .04 |
| □ | 139 | Julius Adams — New England Patriots | .25 | .11 | .03 |
| □ | 140 | Jack Ham AP — Pittsburgh Steelers | 2.50 | 1.15 | .30 |
| □ | 141 | Wayne Morris — St. Louis Cardinals | .25 | .11 | .03 |
| □ | 142 | Marv Bateman — Buffalo Bills | .25 | .11 | .03 |
| □ | 143 | Bobby Maples — Denver Broncos | .30 | .14 | .04 |
| □ | 144 | Harold Carmichael — Philadelphia Eagles | 1.00 | .45 | .13 |
| □ | 145 | Bob Avellini — Chicago Bears | .30 | .14 | .04 |
| □ | 146 | Harry Carson — New York Giants | 7.00 | 3.10 | .85 |
| □ | 147 | Lawrence Pillers — New York Jets | .25 | .11 | .03 |
| □ | 148 | Ed Williams — Tampa Bay Buccaneers | .25 | .11 | .03 |
| □ | 149 | Dan Pastorini — Houston Oilers | .40 | .18 | .05 |
| □ | 150 | Ron Yary AP — Minnesota Vikings | .30 | .14 | .04 |
| □ | 151 | Joe Lavender — Washington Redskins | .30 | .14 | .04 |
| □ | 152 | Pat McInally — Cincinnati Bengals | .75 | .35 | .09 |
| □ | 153 | Lloyd Mumphord — Baltimore Colts | .25 | .11 | .03 |
| □ | 154 | Cullen Bryant — Los Angeles Rams | .30 | .14 | .04 |
| □ | 155 | Willie Lanier — Kansas City Chiefs | .60 | .25 | .08 |
| □ | 156 | Gene Washington — San Francisco 49ers | .30 | .14 | .04 |
| □ | 157 | Scott Hunter — Atlanta Falcons | .30 | .14 | .04 |
| □ | 158 | Jim Merlo — New Orleans Saints | .25 | .11 | .03 |
| □ | 159 | Randy Grossman — Pittsburgh Steelers | .30 | .14 | .04 |
| □ | 160 | Blaine Nye AP — Dallas Cowboys | .25 | .11 | .03 |
| □ | 161 | Ike Harris — St. Louis Cardinals | .25 | .11 | .03 |
| □ | 162 | Doug Dieken — Cleveland Browns | .25 | .11 | .03 |
| □ | 163 | Guy Morriss — Philadelphia Eagles | .25 | .11 | .03 |
| □ | 164 | Bob Parsons — Chicago Bears | .25 | .11 | .03 |
| □ | 165 | Steve Grogan — New England Patriots | 2.00 | .90 | .25 |
| □ | 166 | John Brockington — Green Bay Packers | .30 | .14 | .04 |
| □ | 167 | Charlie Joiner — San Diego Chargers | 1.50 | .65 | .19 |
| □ | 168 | Ron Carpenter — Cincinnati Bengals | .25 | .11 | .03 |
| □ | 169 | Jeff Wright — Minnesota Vikings | .25 | .11 | .03 |
| □ | 170 | Chris Hanburger AP — Washington Redskins | .30 | .14 | .04 |
| □ | 171 | Roosevelt Leaks — Baltimore Colts | .40 | .18 | .05 |
| □ | 172 | Larry Little — Miami Dolphins | .60 | .25 | .08 |
| □ | 173 | John Matuszak — Oakland Raiders | .30 | .14 | .04 |
| □ | 174 | Joe Ferguson — Buffalo Bills | .50 | .23 | .06 |
| □ | 175 | Brad Van Pelt — New York Giants | .25 | .11 | .03 |
| □ | 176 | Dexter Bussey — Detroit Lions | .30 | .14 | .04 |
| □ | 177 | Steve Largent — Seattle Seahawks | 50.00 | 23.00 | 6.25 |
| □ | 178 | Dewey Selmon — Tampa Bay Buccaneers | .30 | .14 | .04 |
| □ | 179 | Randy Gradishar — Denver Broncos | 1.25 | .55 | .16 |
| □ | 180 | Mel Blount AP — Pittsburgh Steelers | 3.00 | 1.35 | .40 |
| □ | 181 | Dan Neal — Chicago Bears | .25 | .11 | .03 |
| □ | 182 | Rich Szaro — New Orleans Saints | .25 | .11 | .03 |
| □ | 183 | Mike Boryla — Philadelphia Eagles | .25 | .11 | .03 |
| □ | 184 | Steve Jones — St. Louis Cardinals | .25 | .11 | .03 |
| □ | 185 | Paul Warfield — Cleveland Browns | 2.25 | 1.00 | .30 |
| □ | 186 | Greg Buttle — New York Jets | .40 | .18 | .05 |
| □ | 187 | Rich McGeorge — Green Bay Packers | .25 | .11 | .03 |
| □ | 188 | Leon Gray — New England Patriots | .50 | .23 | .06 |
| □ | 189 | John Shinners — Cincinnati Bengals | .25 | .11 | .03 |
| □ | 190 | Toni Linhart AP — Baltimore Colts | .25 | .11 | .03 |
| □ | 191 | Robert Miller — Minnesota Vikings | .25 | .11 | .03 |
| □ | 192 | Jake Scott — Washington Redskins | .30 | .14 | .04 |
| □ | 193 | Jon Morris — Detroit Lions | .25 | .11 | .03 |
| □ | 194 | Randy Crowder — Miami Dolphins | .25 | .11 | .03 |
| □ | 195 | Lynn Swann UER — Pittsburgh Steelers (Interception Record on card back) | 8.00 | 3.60 | 1.00 |
| □ | 196 | Marsh White — New York Giants | .25 | .11 | .03 |
| □ | 197 | Rod Perry — Los Angeles Rams | .30 | .14 | .04 |
| □ | 198 | Willie Hall — Oakland Raiders | .25 | .11 | .03 |
| □ | 199 | Mike Hartenstine — Chicago Bears | .25 | .11 | .03 |
| □ | 200 | Jim Bakken AP — St. Louis Cardinals | .30 | .14 | .04 |
| □ | 201 | Atlanta Falcons UER (79 Jim Mitchell is not listed) Team Checklist | 1.00 | .15 | .03 |
| □ | 202 | Baltimore Colts Team Checklist | 1.00 | .15 | .03 |
| □ | 203 | Buffalo Bills | 1.00 | .15 | .03 |

| | | | |
|---|---|---|---|
| Team Checklist | | | |
| ☐ 204 Chicago Bears | 1.00 | .15 | .03 |
| Team Checklist | | | |
| ☐ 205 Cincinnati Bengals | 1.00 | .15 | .03 |
| Team Checklist | | | |
| ☐ 206 Cleveland Browns | 1.00 | .15 | .03 |
| Team Checklist | | | |
| ☐ 207 Dallas Cowboys | 1.00 | .15 | .03 |
| Team Checklist | | | |
| ☐ 208 Denver Broncos | 1.00 | .15 | .03 |
| Team Checklist | | | |
| ☐ 209 Detroit Lions | 1.00 | .15 | .03 |
| Team Checklist | | | |
| ☐ 210 Green Bay Packers | 1.00 | .15 | .03 |
| Team Checklist | | | |
| ☐ 211 Houston Oilers | 1.00 | .15 | .03 |
| Team Checklist | | | |
| ☐ 212 Kansas City Chiefs | 1.00 | .15 | .03 |
| Team Checklist | | | |
| ☐ 213 Los Angeles Rams | 1.00 | .15 | .03 |
| Team Checklist | | | |
| ☐ 214 Miami Dolphins | 1.00 | .15 | .03 |
| Team Checklist | | | |
| ☐ 215 Minnesota Vikings | 1.00 | .15 | .03 |
| Team Checklist | | | |
| ☐ 216 New England Patriots | 1.00 | .15 | .03 |
| Team Checklist | | | |
| ☐ 217 New Orleans Saints | 1.00 | .15 | .03 |
| Team Checklist | | | |
| ☐ 218 New York Giants | 1.00 | .15 | .03 |
| Team Checklist | | | |
| ☐ 219 New York Jets | 1.00 | .15 | .03 |
| Team Checklist | | | |
| ☐ 220 Oakland Raiders | 1.00 | .15 | .03 |
| Team Checklist | | | |
| ☐ 221 Philadelphia Eagles | 1.00 | .15 | .03 |
| Team Checklist | | | |
| ☐ 222 Pittsburgh Steelers | 1.00 | .15 | .03 |
| Team Checklist | | | |
| ☐ 223 St. Louis Cardinals | 1.00 | .15 | .03 |
| Team Checklist | | | |
| ☐ 224 San Diego Chargers | 1.00 | .15 | .03 |
| Team Checklist | | | |
| ☐ 225 San Francisco 49ers | 1.00 | .15 | .03 |
| Team Checklist | | | |
| ☐ 226 Seattle Seahawks | 1.00 | .15 | .03 |
| Team Checklist | | | |
| ☐ 227 Tampa Bay Buccaneers | 1.00 | .15 | .03 |
| Team Checklist UER | | | |
| (Lee Roy Selmon mis- | | | |
| spelled as Leroy) | | | |
| ☐ 228 Washington Redskins | 1.00 | .15 | .03 |
| Team Checklist | | | |
| ☐ 229 Sam Cunningham | .30 | .14 | .04 |
| New England Patriots | | | |
| ☐ 230 Alan Page AP | 1.00 | .45 | .13 |
| Minnesota Vikings | | | |
| ☐ 231 Eddie Brown | .25 | .11 | .03 |
| Washington Redskins | | | |
| ☐ 232 Stan White | .25 | .11 | .03 |
| Baltimore Colts | | | |
| ☐ 233 Vern Den Herder | .25 | .11 | .03 |
| Miami Dolphins | | | |
| ☐ 234 Clarence Davis | .25 | .11 | .03 |
| Oakland Raiders | | | |
| ☐ 235 Ken Anderson | 1.50 | .65 | .19 |
| Cincinnati Bengals | | | |
| ☐ 236 Karl Chandler | .25 | .11 | .03 |
| New York Giants | | | |
| ☐ 237 Will Harrell | .25 | .11 | .03 |
| Green Bay Packers | | | |
| ☐ 238 Clarence Scott | .25 | .11 | .03 |
| Cleveland Browns | | | |
| ☐ 239 Bo Rather | .30 | .14 | .04 |
| Chicago Bears | | | |
| ☐ 240 Robert Brazile AP | .40 | .18 | .05 |
| Houston Oilers | | | |
| ☐ 241 Bob Bell | .25 | .11 | .03 |
| St. Louis Cardinals | | | |
| ☐ 242 Rolland Lawrence | .30 | .14 | .04 |
| Atlanta Falcons | | | |
| ☐ 243 Tom Sullivan | .25 | .11 | .03 |
| Philadelphia Eagles | | | |
| ☐ 244 Larry Brunson | .25 | .11 | .03 |
| Kansas City Chiefs | | | |
| ☐ 245 Terry Bradshaw | 7.00 | 3.10 | .85 |
| Pittsburgh Steelers | | | |
| ☐ 246 Rich Saul | .25 | .11 | .03 |
| Los Angeles Rams | | | |
| ☐ 247 Cleveland Elam | .25 | .11 | .03 |
| San Francisco 49ers | | | |
| ☐ 248 Don Woods | .25 | .11 | .03 |
| San Diego Chargers | | | |
| ☐ 249 Bruce Laird | .25 | .11 | .03 |
| Baltimore Colts | | | |
| ☐ 250 Coy Bacon AP | .30 | .14 | .04 |
| Cincinnati Bengals | | | |
| ☐ 251 Russ Francis | .75 | .35 | .09 |

| | | | |
|---|---|---|---|
| New England Patriots | | | |
| ☐ 252 Jim Braxton | .25 | .11 | .03 |
| Buffalo Bills | | | |
| ☐ 253 Perry Smith | .25 | .11 | .03 |
| Green Bay Packers | | | |
| ☐ 254 Jerome Barkum | .25 | .11 | .03 |
| New York Jets | | | |
| ☐ 255 Garo Yepremian | .30 | .14 | .04 |
| Miami Dolphins | | | |
| ☐ 256 Checklist 133-264 | 1.50 | .15 | .05 |
| ☐ 257 Tony Galbreath | .50 | .23 | .06 |
| New Orleans Saints | | | |
| ☐ 258 Troy Archer | .25 | .11 | .03 |
| New York Giants | | | |
| ☐ 259 Brian Sipe | 1.00 | .45 | .13 |
| Cleveland Browns | | | |
| ☐ 260 Billy Joe DuPree AP | .50 | .23 | .06 |
| Dallas Cowboys | | | |
| ☐ 261 Bobby Walden | .25 | .11 | .03 |
| Pittsburgh Steelers | | | |
| ☐ 262 Larry Marshall | .25 | .11 | .03 |
| Philadelphia Eagles | | | |
| ☐ 263 Ted Fritsch Jr. | .30 | .14 | .04 |
| Washington Redskins | | | |
| ☐ 264 Larry Hand | .25 | .11 | .03 |
| Detroit Lions | | | |
| ☐ 265 Tom Mack | .30 | .14 | .04 |
| Los Angeles Rams | | | |
| ☐ 266 Ed Bradley | .25 | .11 | .03 |
| Seattle Seahawks | | | |
| ☐ 267 Pat Leahy | .60 | .25 | .08 |
| New York Jets | | | |
| ☐ 268 Louis Carter | .25 | .11 | .03 |
| Tampa Bay Buccaneers | | | |
| ☐ 269 Archie Griffin | 4.50 | 2.00 | .55 |
| Cincinnati Bengals | | | |
| ☐ 270 Art Shell AP | 1.25 | .55 | .16 |
| Oakland Raiders | | | |
| ☐ 271 Stu Voigt | .30 | .14 | .04 |
| Minnesota Vikings | | | |
| ☐ 272 Prentice McCray | .25 | .11 | .03 |
| New England Patriots | | | |
| ☐ 273 MacArthur Lane | .30 | .14 | .04 |
| Kansas City Chiefs | | | |
| ☐ 274 Dan Fouts | 8.00 | 3.60 | 1.00 |
| San Diego Chargers | | | |
| ☐ 275 Charley Young | .30 | .14 | .04 |
| Los Angeles Rams | | | |
| ☐ 276 Wilbur Jackson | .50 | .23 | .06 |
| San Francisco 49ers | | | |
| ☐ 277 John Hicks | .25 | .11 | .03 |
| New York Giants | | | |
| ☐ 278 Nat Moore | .60 | .25 | .08 |
| Miami Dolphins | | | |
| ☐ 279 Virgil Livers | .25 | .11 | .03 |
| Chicago Bears | | | |
| ☐ 280 Curley Culp AP | .30 | .14 | .04 |
| Houston Oilers | | | |
| ☐ 281 Rocky Bleier | 1.25 | .55 | .16 |
| Pittsburgh Steelers | | | |
| ☐ 282 John Zook | .25 | .11 | .03 |
| St. Louis Cardinals | | | |
| ☐ 283 Tom DeLeone | .25 | .11 | .03 |
| Cleveland Browns | | | |
| ☐ 284 Danny White | 5.00 | 2.30 | .60 |
| Dallas Cowboys | | | |
| ☐ 285 Otis Armstrong | .50 | .23 | .06 |
| Denver Broncos | | | |
| ☐ 286 Larry Walton | .25 | .11 | .03 |
| Detroit Lions | | | |
| ☐ 287 Jim Carter | .25 | .11 | .03 |
| Green Bay Packers | | | |
| ☐ 288 Don McCauley | .25 | .11 | .03 |
| Baltimore Colts | | | |
| ☐ 289 Frank Grant | .25 | .11 | .03 |
| Washington Redskins | | | |
| ☐ 290 Roger Wehrli AP | .30 | .14 | .04 |
| St. Louis Cardinals | | | |
| ☐ 291 Mick Tingelhoff | .30 | .14 | .04 |
| Minnesota Vikings | | | |
| ☐ 292 Bernard Jackson | .25 | .11 | .03 |
| Denver Broncos | | | |
| ☐ 293 Tom Owen | .30 | .14 | .04 |
| New England Patriots | | | |
| ☐ 294 Mike Esposito | .25 | .11 | .03 |
| Atlanta Falcons | | | |
| ☐ 295 Fred Biletnikoff | 2.00 | .90 | .25 |
| Oakland Raiders | | | |
| ☐ 296 Revie Sorey | .25 | .11 | .03 |
| Chicago Bears | | | |
| ☐ 297 John McMakin | .25 | .11 | .03 |
| Seattle Seahawks | | | |
| ☐ 298 Dan Ryczek | .25 | .11 | .03 |
| Tampa Bay Buccaneers | | | |
| ☐ 299 Wayne Moore | .25 | .11 | .03 |
| Miami Dolphins | | | |
| ☐ 300 Franco Harris AP | 4.00 | 1.80 | .50 |
| Pittsburgh Steelers | | | |

| | | | |
|---|---|---|---|
| ☐ 301 Rick Upchurch | 1.50 | .65 | .19 |
| Denver Broncos | | | |
| ☐ 302 Jim Stienke | .25 | .11 | .03 |
| New York Giants | | | |
| ☐ 303 Charlie Davis | .25 | .11 | .03 |
| St. Louis Cardinals | | | |
| ☐ 304 Don Cockroft | .30 | .14 | .04 |
| Cleveland Browns | | | |
| ☐ 305 Ken Burrough | .30 | .14 | .04 |
| Houston Oilers | | | |
| ☐ 306 Clark Gaines | .25 | .11 | .03 |
| New York Jets | | | |
| ☐ 307 Bobby Douglass | .30 | .14 | .04 |
| New Orleans Saints | | | |
| ☐ 308 Ralph Perretta | .25 | .11 | .03 |
| San Diego Chargers | | | |
| ☐ 309 Wally Hilgenberg | .25 | .11 | .03 |
| Minnesota Vikings | | | |
| ☐ 310 Monte Jackson AP | .40 | .18 | .05 |
| Los Angeles Rams | | | |
| ☐ 311 Chris Bahr | .40 | .18 | .05 |
| Cincinnati Bengals | | | |
| ☐ 312 Jim Cheyunski | .25 | .11 | .03 |
| Baltimore Colts | | | |
| ☐ 313 Mike Patrick | .25 | .11 | .03 |
| New England Patriots | | | |
| ☐ 314 Ed Too Tall Jones | 5.00 | 2.30 | .60 |
| Dallas Cowboys | | | |
| ☐ 315 Bill Bradley | .25 | .11 | .03 |
| Philadelphia Eagles | | | |
| ☐ 316 Benny Malone | .30 | .14 | .04 |
| Miami Dolphins | | | |
| ☐ 317 Paul Seymour | .25 | .11 | .03 |
| Buffalo Bills | | | |
| ☐ 318 Jim Laslavic | .25 | .11 | .03 |
| Detroit Lions | | | |
| ☐ 319 Frank Lewis | .30 | .14 | .04 |
| Pittsburgh Steelers | | | |
| ☐ 320 Ray Guy AP | .75 | .35 | .09 |
| Oakland Raiders | | | |
| ☐ 321 Allan Ellis | .25 | .11 | .03 |
| Chicago Bears | | | |
| ☐ 322 Conrad Dobler | .30 | .14 | .04 |
| St. Louis Cardinals | | | |
| ☐ 323 Chester Marcol | .30 | .14 | .04 |
| Green Bay Packers | | | |
| ☐ 324 Doug Kotar | .25 | .11 | .03 |
| New York Giants | | | |
| ☐ 325 Lemar Parrish | .30 | .14 | .04 |
| Cincinnati Bengals | | | |
| ☐ 326 Steve Holden | .25 | .11 | .03 |
| Cleveland Browns | | | |
| ☐ 327 Jeff Van Note | .30 | .14 | .04 |
| Atlanta Falcons | | | |
| ☐ 328 Howard Stevens | .25 | .11 | .03 |
| Baltimore Colts | | | |
| ☐ 329 Brad Dusek | .30 | .14 | .04 |
| Washington Redskins | | | |
| ☐ 330 Joe DeLamielleure AP | .30 | .14 | .04 |
| Buffalo Bills | | | |
| ☐ 331 Jim Plunkett | 1.00 | .45 | .13 |
| San Francisco 49ers | | | |
| ☐ 332 Checklist 265-396 | 1.50 | .15 | .05 |
| ☐ 333 Lou Piccone | .25 | .11 | .03 |
| New York Jets | | | |
| ☐ 334 Ray Hamilton | .25 | .11 | .03 |
| New England Patriots | | | |
| ☐ 335 Jan Stenerud | .50 | .23 | .06 |
| Kansas City Chiefs | | | |
| ☐ 336 Jeris White | .25 | .11 | .03 |
| Miami Dolphins | | | |
| ☐ 337 Sherman Smith | .30 | .14 | .04 |
| Seattle Seahawks | | | |
| ☐ 338 Dave Green | .25 | .11 | .03 |
| Tampa Bay Buccaneers | | | |
| ☐ 339 Terry Schmidt | .25 | .11 | .03 |
| Chicago Bears | | | |
| ☐ 340 Sammie White AP | 1.25 | .55 | .16 |
| Minnesota Vikings | | | |
| ☐ 341 Jon Kolb | .30 | .14 | .04 |
| Pittsburgh Steelers | | | |
| ☐ 342 Randy White | 7.00 | 3.10 | .85 |
| Dallas Cowboys | | | |
| ☐ 343 Bob Klein | .25 | .11 | .03 |
| Los Angeles Rams | | | |
| ☐ 344 Bob Kowalkowski | .25 | .11 | .03 |
| Detroit Lions | | | |
| ☐ 345 Terry Metcalf | .30 | .14 | .04 |
| St. Louis Cardinals | | | |
| ☐ 346 Joe Danelo | .25 | .11 | .03 |
| New York Giants | | | |
| ☐ 347 Ken Payne | .25 | .11 | .03 |
| Green Bay Packers | | | |
| ☐ 348 Neal Craig | .25 | .11 | .03 |
| Cleveland Browns | | | |
| ☐ 349 Dennis Johnson | .25 | .11 | .03 |
| Washington Redskins | | | |
| ☐ 350 Bill Bergey AP | .50 | .23 | .06 |
| Philadelphia Eagles | | | |
| ☐ 351 Raymond Chester | .30 | .14 | .04 |
| Baltimore Colts | | | |
| ☐ 352 Bob Matheson | .25 | .11 | .03 |
| Miami Dolphins | | | |
| ☐ 353 Mike Kadish | .25 | .11 | .03 |
| Buffalo Bills | | | |
| ☐ 354 Mark Van Eeghen | .75 | .35 | .09 |
| Oakland Raiders | | | |
| ☐ 355 L.C. Greenwood | .60 | .25 | .08 |
| Pittsburgh Steelers | | | |
| ☐ 356 Sam Hunt | .25 | .11 | .03 |
| New England Patriots | | | |
| ☐ 357 Darrell Austin | .25 | .11 | .03 |
| New York Jets | | | |
| ☐ 358 Jim Turner | .30 | .14 | .04 |
| Denver Broncos | | | |
| ☐ 359 Ahmad Rashad | 2.00 | .90 | .25 |
| Minnesota Vikings | | | |
| ☐ 360 Walter Payton AP | 32.00 | 14.50 | 4.00 |
| Chicago Bears | | | |
| ☐ 361 Mark Arneson | .25 | .11 | .03 |
| St. Louis Cardinals | | | |
| ☐ 362 Jerrel Wilson | .25 | .11 | .03 |
| Kansas City Chiefs | | | |
| ☐ 363 Steve Bartkowski | 1.00 | .45 | .13 |
| Atlanta Falcons | | | |
| ☐ 364 John Watson | .25 | .11 | .03 |
| San Francisco 49ers | | | |
| ☐ 365 Ken Riley | .30 | .14 | .04 |
| Cincinnati Bengals | | | |
| ☐ 366 Gregg Bingham | .25 | .11 | .03 |
| Houston Oilers | | | |
| ☐ 367 Golden Richards | .30 | .14 | .04 |
| Dallas Cowboys | | | |
| ☐ 368 Clyde Powers | .25 | .11 | .03 |
| New York Giants | | | |
| ☐ 369 Diron Talbert | .30 | .14 | .04 |
| Washington Redskins | | | |
| ☐ 370 Lydell Mitchell | .30 | .14 | .04 |
| Baltimore Colts | | | |
| ☐ 371 Bob Jackson | .25 | .11 | .03 |
| Cleveland Browns | | | |
| ☐ 372 Jim Mandich | .25 | .11 | .03 |
| Miami Dolphins | | | |
| ☐ 373 Frank LeMaster | .25 | .11 | .03 |
| Philadelphia Eagles | | | |
| ☐ 374 Benny Ricardo | .25 | .11 | .03 |
| Detroit Lions | | | |
| ☐ 375 Lawrence McCutcheon | .30 | .14 | .04 |
| Los Angeles Rams | | | |
| ☐ 376 Lynn Dickey | .50 | .23 | .06 |
| Green Bay Packers | | | |
| ☐ 377 Phil Wise | .25 | .11 | .03 |
| New York Jets | | | |
| ☐ 378 Tony McGee | .25 | .11 | .03 |
| New England Patriots | | | |
| ☐ 379 Norm Thompson | .25 | .11 | .03 |
| Baltimore Colts | | | |
| ☐ 380 Dave Casper AP | 5.00 | 2.30 | .60 |
| Oakland Raiders | | | |
| ☐ 381 Glen Edwards | .30 | .14 | .04 |
| Pittsburgh Steelers | | | |
| ☐ 382 Bob Thomas | .25 | .11 | .03 |
| Chicago Bears | | | |
| ☐ 383 Bob Chandler | .30 | .14 | .04 |
| Buffalo Bills | | | |
| ☐ 384 Rickey Young | .30 | .14 | .04 |
| San Diego Chargers | | | |
| ☐ 385 Carl Eller | .60 | .25 | .08 |
| Minnesota Vikings | | | |
| ☐ 386 Lyle Alzado | .75 | .35 | .09 |
| Denver Broncos | | | |
| ☐ 387 John Leypoldt | .25 | .11 | .03 |
| Seattle Seahawks | | | |
| ☐ 388 Gordon Bell | .25 | .11 | .03 |
| New York Giants | | | |
| ☐ 389 Mike Bragg | .25 | .11 | .03 |
| Washington Redskins | | | |
| ☐ 390 Jim Langer AP | .75 | .35 | .09 |
| Miami Dolphins | | | |
| ☐ 391 Vern Holland | .25 | .11 | .03 |
| Cincinnati Bengals | | | |
| ☐ 392 Nelson Munsey | .25 | .11 | .03 |
| Baltimore Colts | | | |
| ☐ 393 Mack Mitchell | .25 | .11 | .03 |
| Cleveland Browns | | | |
| ☐ 394 Tony Adams | .30 | .14 | .04 |
| Kansas City Chiefs | | | |
| ☐ 395 Preston Pearson | .30 | .14 | .04 |
| Dallas Cowboys | | | |
| ☐ 396 Emanuel Zanders | .25 | .11 | .03 |
| New Orleans Saints | | | |
| ☐ 397 Vince Papale | .25 | .11 | .03 |
| Philadelphia Eagles | | | |
| ☐ 398 Joe Fields | .30 | .14 | .04 |

| | | | | |
|---|---|---|---|---|
| New York Jets | | | | |
| ☐ 399 Craig Clemons | .25 | .11 | .03 |
| Chicago Bears | | | | |
| ☐ 400 Fran Tarkenton AP | 6.00 | 2.70 | .75 |
| Minnesota Vikings | | | | |
| ☐ 401 Andy Johnson | .30 | .14 | .04 |
| New England Patriots | | | | |
| ☐ 402 Willie Buchanon | .30 | .14 | .04 |
| Green Bay Packers | | | | |
| ☐ 403 Pat Curran | .25 | .11 | .03 |
| San Diego Chargers | | | | |
| ☐ 404 Ray Jarvis | .25 | .11 | .03 |
| Detroit Lions | | | | |
| ☐ 405 Joe Greene | 2.50 | 1.15 | .30 |
| Pittsburgh Steelers | | | | |
| ☐ 406 Bill Simpson | .25 | .11 | .03 |
| Los Angeles Rams | | | | |
| ☐ 407 Ronnie Coleman | .25 | .11 | .03 |
| Houston Oilers | | | | |
| ☐ 408 J.K. McKay | .30 | .14 | .04 |
| Tampa Bay Buccaneers | | | | |
| ☐ 409 Pat Fischer | .30 | .14 | .04 |
| Washington Redskins | | | | |
| ☐ 410 John Dutton AP | .30 | .14 | .04 |
| Baltimore Colts | | | | |
| ☐ 411 Boobie Clark | .30 | .14 | .04 |
| Cincinnati Bengals | | | | |
| ☐ 412 Pat Tilley | 1.00 | .45 | .13 |
| St. Louis Cardinals | | | | |
| ☐ 413 Don Strock | .30 | .14 | .04 |
| Miami Dolphins | | | | |
| ☐ 414 Brian Kelley | .25 | .11 | .03 |
| New York Giants | | | | |
| ☐ 415 Gene Upshaw | .75 | .35 | .09 |
| Oakland Raiders | | | | |
| ☐ 416 Mike Montler | .25 | .11 | .03 |
| Buffalo Bills | | | | |
| ☐ 417 Checklist 397-528 | 1.50 | .15 | .05 |
| ☐ 418 John Gilliam | .30 | .14 | .04 |
| Atlanta Falcons | | | | |
| ☐ 419 Brent McClanahan | .25 | .11 | .03 |
| Minnesota Vikings | | | | |
| ☐ 420 Jerry Sherk AP | .30 | .14 | .04 |
| Cleveland Browns | | | | |
| ☐ 421 Roy Gerela | .30 | .14 | .04 |
| Pittsburgh Steelers | | | | |
| ☐ 422 Tim Fox | .25 | .11 | .03 |
| New England Patriots | | | | |
| ☐ 423 John Ebersole | .25 | .11 | .03 |
| New York Jets | | | | |
| ☐ 424 James Scott | .25 | .11 | .03 |
| Chicago Bears | | | | |
| ☐ 425 Delvin Williams | .75 | .35 | .09 |
| San Francisco 49ers | | | | |
| ☐ 426 Spike Jones | .25 | .11 | .03 |
| Philadelphia Eagles | | | | |
| ☐ 427 Harvey Martin | 1.25 | .55 | .16 |
| Dallas Cowboys | | | | |
| ☐ 428 Don Herrmann | .25 | .11 | .03 |
| New Orleans Saints | | | | |
| ☐ 429 Calvin Hill | .40 | .18 | .05 |
| Washington Redskins | | | | |
| ☐ 430 Isiah Robertson AP | .30 | .14 | .04 |
| Los Angeles Rams | | | | |
| ☐ 431 Tony Greene | .25 | .11 | .03 |
| Buffalo Bills | | | | |
| ☐ 432 Bob Johnson | .25 | .11 | .03 |
| Cincinnati Bengals | | | | |
| ☐ 433 Lem Barney | .75 | .35 | .09 |
| Detroit Lions | | | | |
| ☐ 434 Eric Torkelson | .25 | .11 | .03 |
| Green Bay Packers | | | | |
| ☐ 435 John Mendenhall | .25 | .11 | .03 |
| New York Giants | | | | |
| ☐ 436 Larry Seiple | .30 | .14 | .04 |
| Miami Dolphins | | | | |
| ☐ 437 Art Kuehn | .25 | .11 | .03 |
| Seattle Seahawks | | | | |
| ☐ 438 John Vella | .25 | .11 | .03 |
| Oakland Raiders | | | | |
| ☐ 439 Greg Latta | .25 | .11 | .03 |
| Chicago Bears | | | | |
| ☐ 440 Roger Carr AP | .30 | .14 | .04 |
| Baltimore Colts | | | | |
| ☐ 441 Doug Sutherland | .25 | .11 | .03 |
| Minnesota Vikings | | | | |
| ☐ 442 Mike Kruczek | .25 | .11 | .03 |
| Pittsburgh Steelers | | | | |
| ☐ 443 Steve Zabel | .25 | .11 | .03 |
| New England Patriots | | | | |
| ☐ 444 Mike Pruitt | 1.00 | .45 | .13 |
| Cleveland Browns | | | | |
| ☐ 445 Harold Jackson | .50 | .23 | .06 |
| Los Angeles Rams | | | | |
| ☐ 446 George Jakowenko | .25 | .11 | .03 |
| Buffalo Bills | | | | |
| ☐ 447 John Fitzgerald | .25 | .11 | .03 |
| Dallas Cowboys | | | | |

| | | | | |
|---|---|---|---|---|
| ☐ 448 Carey Joyce | .25 | .11 | .03 |
| St. Louis Cardinals | | | | |
| ☐ 449 Jim LeClair | .25 | .11 | .03 |
| Cincinnati Bengals | | | | |
| ☐ 450 Ken Houston AP | .75 | .35 | .09 |
| Washington Redskins | | | | |
| ☐ 451 Steve Grogan RB | .60 | .25 | .08 |
| Most Touchdowns Rush-ing by QB, Season | | | | |
| ☐ 452 Jim Marshall RB | .50 | .23 | .06 |
| Most Games Played, Lifetime | | | | |
| ☐ 453 O.J. Simpson RB | 5.00 | 2.30 | .60 |
| Most Yardage, Rushing, Game | | | | |
| ☐ 454 Fran Tarkenton RB | 3.00 | 1.35 | .40 |
| Most Yardage, Passing, Lifetime | | | | |
| ☐ 455 Jim Zorn RB | .50 | .23 | .06 |
| Most Passing Yards Season, Rookie | | | | |
| ☐ 456 Robert Pratt | .25 | .11 | .03 |
| Baltimore Colts | | | | |
| ☐ 457 Walker Gillette | .25 | .11 | .03 |
| New York Giants | | | | |
| ☐ 458 Charlie Hall | .25 | .11 | .03 |
| Cleveland Browns | | | | |
| ☐ 459 Robert Newhouse | .30 | .14 | .04 |
| Dallas Cowboys | | | | |
| ☐ 460 John Hannah AP | 1.25 | .55 | .16 |
| New England Patriots | | | | |
| ☐ 461 Ken Reaves | .25 | .11 | .03 |
| St. Louis Cardinals | | | | |
| ☐ 462 Herman Weaver | .25 | .11 | .03 |
| Detroit Lions | | | | |
| ☐ 463 James Harris | .30 | .14 | .04 |
| Los Angeles Rams | | | | |
| ☐ 464 Howard Twilley | .30 | .14 | .04 |
| Miami Dolphins | | | | |
| ☐ 465 Jeff Siemon | .30 | .14 | .04 |
| Minnesota Vikings | | | | |
| ☐ 466 John Outlaw | .25 | .11 | .03 |
| Philadelphia Eagles | | | | |
| ☐ 467 Chuck Muncie | 1.25 | .55 | .16 |
| New Orleans Saints | | | | |
| ☐ 468 Bob Moore | .25 | .11 | .03 |
| Tampa Bay Buccaneers | | | | |
| ☐ 469 Robert Woods | .25 | .11 | .03 |
| New York Jets | | | | |
| ☐ 470 Cliff Branch AP | 1.50 | .65 | .19 |
| Oakland Raiders | | | | |
| ☐ 471 Johnnie Gray | .25 | .11 | .03 |
| Green Bay Packers | | | | |
| ☐ 472 Don Hardeman | .25 | .11 | .03 |
| Houston Oilers | | | | |
| ☐ 473 Steve Ramsey | .30 | .14 | .04 |
| New York Giants | | | | |
| ☐ 474 Steve Mike-Mayer | .25 | .11 | .03 |
| San Francisco 49ers | | | | |
| ☐ 475 Gary Garrison | .30 | .14 | .04 |
| San Diego Chargers | | | | |
| ☐ 476 Walter Johnson | .25 | .11 | .03 |
| Cleveland Browns | | | | |
| ☐ 477 Neil Clabo | .25 | .11 | .03 |
| Minnesota Vikings | | | | |
| ☐ 478 Len Hauss | .30 | .14 | .04 |
| Washington Redskins | | | | |
| ☐ 479 Darryl Stingley | .50 | .23 | .06 |
| New England Patriots | | | | |
| ☐ 480 Jack Lambert AP | 7.00 | 3.10 | .85 |
| Pittsburgh Steelers | | | | |
| ☐ 481 Mike Adamle | .25 | .11 | .03 |
| Chicago Bears | | | | |
| ☐ 482 David Lee | .25 | .11 | .03 |
| Baltimore Colts | | | | |
| ☐ 483 Tom Mullen | .25 | .11 | .03 |
| New York Giants | | | | |
| ☐ 484 Claude Humphrey | .30 | .14 | .04 |
| Atlanta Falcons | | | | |
| ☐ 485 Jim Hart | .60 | .25 | .08 |
| St. Louis Cardinals | | | | |
| ☐ 486 Bobby Thompson | .25 | .11 | .03 |
| Detroit Lions | | | | |
| ☐ 487 Jack Rudnay | .25 | .11 | .03 |
| Kansas City Chiefs | | | | |
| ☐ 488 Rich Sowells | .25 | .11 | .03 |
| New York Jets | | | | |
| ☐ 489 Reuben Gant | .25 | .11 | .03 |
| Buffalo Bills | | | | |
| ☐ 490 Cliff Harris AP | .75 | .35 | .09 |
| Dallas Cowboys | | | | |
| ☐ 491 Bob Brown | .25 | .11 | .03 |
| Cincinnati Bengals | | | | |
| ☐ 492 Don Nottingham | .25 | .11 | .03 |
| Miami Dolphins | | | | |
| ☐ 493 Ron Jessie | .30 | .14 | .04 |
| Los Angeles Rams | | | | |

| | NRMT | VG-E | GOOD |
|---|---|---|---|
| ☐ 494 Otis Sistrunk<br>Oakland Raiders | .30 | .14 | .04 |
| ☐ 495 Bill Kilmer<br>Washington Redskins | .50 | .23 | .06 |
| ☐ 496 Oscar Roan<br>Cleveland Browns | .30 | .14 | .04 |
| ☐ 497 Bill Van Heusen<br>Denver Broncos | .25 | .11 | .03 |
| ☐ 498 Randy Logan<br>Philadelphia Eagles | .25 | .11 | .03 |
| ☐ 499 John Smith<br>New England Patriots | .25 | .11 | .03 |
| ☐ 500 Chuck Foreman AP<br>Minnesota Vikings | .50 | .23 | .06 |
| ☐ 501 J.T. Thomas<br>Pittsburgh Steelers | .30 | .14 | .04 |
| ☐ 502 Steve Schubert<br>Chicago Bears | .25 | .11 | .03 |
| ☐ 503 Mike Barnes<br>Baltimore Colts | .25 | .11 | .03 |
| ☐ 504 J.V. Cain<br>St. Louis Cardinals | .25 | .11 | .03 |
| ☐ 505 Larry Csonka<br>New York Giants | 2.50 | 1.15 | .30 |
| ☐ 506 Elvin Bethea<br>Houston Oilers | .30 | .14 | .04 |
| ☐ 507 Ray Easterling<br>Atlanta Falcons | .25 | .11 | .03 |
| ☐ 508 Joe Reed<br>Detroit Lions | .25 | .11 | .03 |
| ☐ 509 Steve Odom<br>Green Bay Packers | .25 | .11 | .03 |
| ☐ 510 Tommy Casanova AP<br>Cincinnati Bengals | .30 | .14 | .04 |
| ☐ 511 Dave Dalby<br>Oakland Raiders | .30 | .14 | .04 |
| ☐ 512 Richard Caster<br>New York Jets | .30 | .14 | .04 |
| ☐ 513 Fred Dryer<br>Los Angeles Rams | 1.25 | .55 | .16 |
| ☐ 514 Jeff Kinney<br>Buffalo Bills | .25 | .11 | .03 |
| ☐ 515 Bob Griese<br>Miami Dolphins | 4.00 | 1.80 | .50 |
| ☐ 516 Butch Johnson<br>Dallas Cowboys | .75 | .35 | .09 |
| ☐ 517 Gerald Irons<br>Cleveland Browns | .25 | .11 | .03 |
| ☐ 518 Don Calhoun<br>New England Patriots | .25 | .11 | .03 |
| ☐ 519 Jack Gregory<br>New York Giants | .25 | .11 | .03 |
| ☐ 520 Tom Banks AP<br>St. Louis Cardinals | .30 | .14 | .04 |
| ☐ 521 Bobby Bryant<br>Minnesota Vikings | .25 | .11 | .03 |
| ☐ 522 Reggie Harrison<br>Pittsburgh Steelers | .25 | .11 | .03 |
| ☐ 523 Terry Hermeling<br>Washington Redskins | .25 | .11 | .03 |
| ☐ 524 David Taylor<br>Baltimore Colts | .25 | .11 | .03 |
| ☐ 525 Brian Baschnagel<br>Chicago Bears | .40 | .18 | .05 |
| ☐ 526 AFC Championship<br>Raiders 24,<br>Steelers 7<br>(Stabler) | .50 | .23 | .06 |
| ☐ 527 NFC Championship<br>Vikings 24,<br>Rams 13 | .50 | .23 | .06 |
| ☐ 528 Super Bowl XI<br>Raiders 32,<br>Vikings 14<br>(line play) | 1.25 | .25 | .08 |

## 1977 Topps Team Checklists

The 1977 Topps Team Checklist set contains 30 cards, one for each of the 28 NFL teams. The cards measure the standard 2 1/2" by 3 1/2". The front of the card has the 1977 Topps checklist for that particular team, complete with boxes in which to place check marks. The set was only available directly from Topps as a send-off offer as an uncut sheet; the prices below apply equally to uncut sheets as they are frequently found in their original uncut condition. These unnumbered cards are numbered below for convenience in alphabetical order by team name.

| | NRMT | VG-E | GOOD |
|---|---|---|---|
| COMPLETE SET (30) | 100.00 | 40.00 | 10.00 |
| COMMON PLAYER (1-30) | 4.50 | 1.80 | .45 |
| ☐ 1 Atlanta Falcons | 4.50 | 1.80 | .45 |
| ☐ 2 Baltimore Colts | 4.50 | 1.80 | .45 |

| | NRMT | VG-E | GOOD |
|---|---|---|---|
| ☐ 3 Buffalo Bills | 4.50 | 1.80 | .45 |
| ☐ 4 Chicago Bears | 6.00 | 2.40 | .60 |
| ☐ 5 Cincinnati Bengals | 4.50 | 1.80 | .45 |
| ☐ 6 Cleveland Browns | 4.50 | 1.80 | .45 |
| ☐ 7 Dallas Cowboys | 7.50 | 3.00 | .75 |
| ☐ 8 Denver Broncos | 6.00 | 2.40 | .60 |
| ☐ 9 Detroit Lions | 4.50 | 1.80 | .45 |
| ☐ 10 Green Bay Packers | 4.50 | 1.80 | .45 |
| ☐ 11 Houston Oilers | 4.50 | 1.80 | .45 |
| ☐ 12 Kansas City Chiefs | 4.50 | 1.80 | .45 |
| ☐ 13 Los Angeles Rams | 4.50 | 1.80 | .45 |
| ☐ 14 Miami Dolphins | 6.00 | 2.40 | .60 |
| ☐ 15 Minnesota Vikings | 4.50 | 1.80 | .45 |
| ☐ 16 New England Patriots | 4.50 | 1.80 | .45 |
| ☐ 17 New York Giants | 6.00 | 2.40 | .60 |
| ☐ 18 New York Jets | 6.00 | 2.40 | .60 |
| ☐ 19 New Orleans Saints | 4.50 | 1.80 | .45 |
| ☐ 20 Oakland Raiders | 7.50 | 3.00 | .75 |
| ☐ 21 Philadelphia Eagles | 4.50 | 1.80 | .45 |
| ☐ 22 Pittsburgh Steelers | 6.00 | 2.40 | .60 |
| ☐ 23 St. Louis Cardinals | 4.50 | 1.80 | .45 |
| ☐ 24 San Diego Chargers | 4.50 | 1.80 | .45 |
| ☐ 25 San Francisco 49ers | 6.00 | 2.40 | .60 |
| ☐ 26 Seattle Seahawks | 6.00 | 2.40 | .60 |
| ☐ 27 Tampa Bay Buccaneers | 4.50 | 1.80 | .45 |
| ☐ 28 Washington Redskins | 6.00 | 2.40 | .60 |
| ☐ 29 Checklist 1-132 | 4.50 | 1.80 | .45 |
| ☐ 30 Checklist 133-264 | 4.50 | 1.80 | .45 |

## 1977 Topps Holsum Packers/Vikings

In 1977 Topps produced a set of 11 Green Bay Packers (1-11) and 11 Minnesota Vikings (12-22) for Holsum Bread for distribution in the general area of those teams. One card was packed inside each loaf of bread. Unfortunately, nowhere on the card is Holsum mentioned leading to frequent misclassification of this set. The cards are in color and are standard size 2 1/2" by 3 1/2". An uncut production sheet was offered in the 1989 Topps Archives auction. The cards are numbered on the back. The personal data on the card back is printed in brown and orange.

| | NRMT | VG-E | GOOD |
|---|---|---|---|
| COMPLETE SET (22) | 45.00 | 18.00 | 4.50 |
| COMMON PLAYER (1-22) | 1.50 | .60 | .15 |
| ☐ 1 Lynn Dickey | 3.00 | 1.20 | .30 |
| ☐ 2 John Brockington | 3.00 | 1.20 | .30 |
| ☐ 3 Will Harrell | 2.00 | .80 | .20 |
| ☐ 4 Ken Payne | 1.50 | .60 | .15 |
| ☐ 5 Rich McGeorge | 1.50 | .60 | .15 |
| ☐ 6 Steve Odom | 2.00 | .80 | .20 |
| ☐ 7 Jim Carter | 2.00 | .80 | .20 |
| ☐ 8 Fred Carr | 2.50 | 1.00 | .25 |
| ☐ 9 Willie Buchanon | 2.50 | 1.00 | .25 |

| | NRMT | VG-E | GOOD |
|---|---|---|---|
| ☐ 10 Mike McCoy | 2.50 | 1.00 | .25 |
| ☐ 11 Chester Marcol | 2.00 | .80 | .20 |
| ☐ 12 Chuck Foreman | 4.00 | 1.60 | .40 |
| ☐ 13 Ahmad Rashad | 7.50 | 3.00 | .75 |
| ☐ 14 Sammie White | 3.00 | 1.20 | .30 |
| ☐ 15 Stu Voigt | 2.00 | .80 | .20 |
| ☐ 16 Fred Cox | 2.00 | .80 | .20 |
| ☐ 17 Carl Eller | 5.00 | 2.00 | .50 |
| ☐ 18 Alan Page | 5.00 | 2.00 | .50 |
| ☐ 19 Jeff Siemon | 2.00 | .80 | .20 |
| ☐ 20 Bobby Bryant | 1.50 | .60 | .15 |
| ☐ 21 Paul Krause | 2.50 | 1.00 | .25 |
| ☐ 22 Ron Yary | 2.00 | .80 | .20 |

# 1978 Topps

The 1978 Topps football set contains 528 cards. The cards measure 2 1/2" by 3 1/2". No known scarcities exist. The first six cards in the set feature Highlights (HL) of the previous season. Cards 501 through 528 are Team Leader (TL) cards depicting typically four individual team (statistical) leaders on the front and a team checklist on the back. Post-season playoff action is featured on cards 166-168. Statistical league leaders are depicted on cards 331-336. All-Pro (AP) selections are designated on the player's regular card, not a special card. The card backs are printed in black and green on gray card stock. The key Rookie Card in this set is Tony Dorsett. Other notable Rookie Cards in the set include Tom Jackson, Joe Klecko, Stanley Morgan, John Stallworth, Wesley Walker, and Reggie Williams.

| | NRMT | VG-E | GOOD |
|---|---|---|---|
| COMPLETE SET (528) | 125.00 | 57.50 | 15.50 |
| COMMON PLAYER (1-528) | .15 | .07 | .02 |
| ☐ 1 Gary Huff HL | .50 | .10 | .03 |
| Huff Leads Bucs to First Win | | | |
| ☐ 2 Craig Morton HL | .40 | .18 | .05 |
| Morton Passes Broncos to Super Bowl | | | |
| ☐ 3 Walter Payton HL | 4.00 | 1.80 | .50 |
| Rushes for 275 Yards | | | |
| ☐ 4 O.J. Simpson HL | 4.00 | 1.80 | .50 |
| Reaches 10,000 Yards | | | |
| ☐ 5 Fran Tarkenton HL | 2.00 | .90 | .25 |
| Completes 17 of 18 | | | |
| ☐ 6 Bob Thomas HL | .30 | .14 | .04 |
| Thomas' FG Sends Bears to Playoffs | | | |
| ☐ 7 Joe Pisarcik | .20 | .09 | .03 |
| New York Giants | | | |
| ☐ 8 Skip Thomas | .15 | .07 | .02 |
| Oakland Raiders | | | |
| ☐ 9 Roosevelt Leaks | .20 | .09 | .03 |
| Baltimore Colts | | | |
| ☐ 10 Ken Houston AP | .50 | .23 | .06 |
| Washington Redskins | | | |
| ☐ 11 Tom Blanchard | .15 | .07 | .02 |
| New Orleans Saints | | | |
| ☐ 12 Jim Turner | .20 | .09 | .03 |
| Denver Broncos | | | |
| ☐ 13 Tom DeLeone | .15 | .07 | .02 |
| Cleveland Browns | | | |
| ☐ 14 Jim LeClair | .15 | .07 | .02 |
| Cincinnati Bengals | | | |
| ☐ 15 Bob Avellini | .20 | .09 | .03 |
| Chicago Bears | | | |
| ☐ 16 Tony McGee | .15 | .07 | .02 |
| New England Patriots | | | |
| ☐ 17 James Harris | .20 | .09 | .03 |
| San Diego Chargers | | | |
| ☐ 18 Terry Nelson | .15 | .07 | .02 |
| Los Angeles Rams | | | |
| ☐ 19 Rocky Bleier | .75 | .35 | .09 |
| Pittsburgh Steelers | | | |
| ☐ 20 Joe DeLamielleure AP | .20 | .09 | .03 |
| Buffalo Bills | | | |
| ☐ 21 Richard Caster | .20 | .09 | .03 |
| New York Jets | | | |
| ☐ 22 A.J. Duhe | 1.00 | .45 | .13 |
| Miami Dolphins | | | |
| ☐ 23 John Outlaw | .15 | .07 | .02 |
| Philadelphia Eagles | | | |
| ☐ 24 Danny White | 1.50 | .65 | .19 |
| Dallas Cowboys | | | |
| ☐ 25 Larry Csonka | 1.75 | .80 | .22 |
| New York Giants | | | |
| ☐ 26 David Hill | .15 | .07 | .02 |
| Detroit Lions | | | |
| ☐ 27 Mark Arneson | .15 | .07 | .02 |
| St. Louis Cardinals | | | |
| ☐ 28 Jack Tatum | .20 | .09 | .03 |
| Oakland Raiders | | | |
| ☐ 29 Norm Thompson | .15 | .07 | .02 |
| Baltimore Colts | | | |
| ☐ 30 Sammie White | .25 | .11 | .03 |
| Minnesota Vikings | | | |
| ☐ 31 Dennis Johnson | .15 | .07 | .02 |
| Washington Redskins | | | |
| ☐ 32 Robin Earl | .15 | .07 | .02 |
| Chicago Bears | | | |
| ☐ 33 Don Cockroft | .20 | .09 | .03 |
| Cleveland Browns | | | |
| ☐ 34 Bob Johnson | .15 | .07 | .02 |
| Cincinnati Bengals | | | |
| ☐ 35 John Hannah | .75 | .35 | .09 |
| New England Patriots | | | |
| ☐ 36 Scott Hunter | .20 | .09 | .03 |
| Atlanta Falcons | | | |
| ☐ 37 Ken Burrough | .20 | .09 | .03 |
| Houston Oilers | | | |
| ☐ 38 Wilbur Jackson | .20 | .09 | .03 |
| San Francisco 49ers | | | |
| ☐ 39 Rich McGeorge | .15 | .07 | .02 |
| Green Bay Packers | | | |
| ☐ 40 Lyle Alzado AP | .60 | .25 | .08 |
| Denver Broncos | | | |
| ☐ 41 John Ebersole | .15 | .07 | .02 |
| New York Jets | | | |
| ☐ 42 Gary Green | .15 | .07 | .02 |
| Kansas City Chiefs | | | |
| ☐ 43 Art Kuehn | .15 | .07 | .02 |
| Seattle Seahawks | | | |
| ☐ 44 Glen Edwards | .20 | .09 | .03 |
| Pittsburgh Steelers | | | |
| ☐ 45 Lawrence McCutcheon | .20 | .09 | .03 |
| Los Angeles Rams | | | |
| ☐ 46 Duriel Harris | .20 | .09 | .03 |
| Miami Dolphins | | | |
| ☐ 47 Rich Szaro | .15 | .07 | .02 |
| New Orleans Saints | | | |
| ☐ 48 Mike Washington | .15 | .07 | .02 |
| Tampa Bay Buccaneers | | | |
| ☐ 49 Stan White | .15 | .07 | .02 |
| Baltimore Colts | | | |
| ☐ 50 Dave Casper AP | 1.25 | .55 | .16 |
| Oakland Raiders | | | |
| ☐ 51 Len Hauss | .20 | .09 | .03 |
| Washington Redskins | | | |
| ☐ 52 James Scott | .15 | .07 | .02 |
| Chicago Bears | | | |
| ☐ 53 Brian Sipe | .60 | .25 | .08 |
| Cleveland Browns | | | |
| ☐ 54 Gary Shirk | .15 | .07 | .02 |
| New York Giants | | | |
| ☐ 55 Archie Griffin | .60 | .25 | .08 |
| Cincinnati Bengals | | | |
| ☐ 56 Mike Patrick | .15 | .07 | .02 |
| New England Patriots | | | |
| ☐ 57 Mario Clark | .15 | .07 | .02 |
| Buffalo Bills | | | |
| ☐ 58 Jeff Siemon | .15 | .07 | .02 |
| Minnesota Vikings | | | |
| ☐ 59 Steve Mike-Mayer | .15 | .07 | .02 |
| Detroit Lions | | | |
| ☐ 60 Randy White AP | 2.50 | 1.15 | .30 |
| Dallas Cowboys | | | |
| ☐ 61 Darrell Austin | .15 | .07 | .02 |
| New York Jets | | | |
| ☐ 62 Tom Sullivan | .15 | .07 | .02 |
| Philadelphia Eagles | | | |
| ☐ 63 Johnny Rodgers | 1.25 | .55 | .16 |
| San Diego Chargers | | | |
| ☐ 64 Ken Reaves | .15 | .07 | .02 |
| St. Louis Cardinals | | | |
| ☐ 65 Terry Bradshaw | 6.00 | 2.70 | .75 |
| Pittsburgh Steelers | | | |
| ☐ 66 Fred Steinfort | .15 | .07 | .02 |
| Atlanta Falcons | | | |
| ☐ 67 Curley Culp | .20 | .09 | .03 |
| Houston Oilers | | | |
| ☐ 68 Ted Hendricks | .75 | .35 | .09 |

| | | | |
|---|---|---|---|
| Oakland Raiders | | | |
| ☐ 69 Raymond Chester | .20 | .09 | .03 |
| Baltimore Colts | | | |
| ☐ 70 Jim Langer AP | .50 | .23 | .06 |
| Miami Dolphins | | | |
| ☐ 71 Calvin Hill | .30 | .14 | .04 |
| Washington Redskins | | | |
| ☐ 72 Mike Hartenstine | .15 | .07 | .02 |
| Chicago Bears | | | |
| ☐ 73 Gerald Irons | .15 | .07 | .02 |
| Cleveland Browns | | | |
| ☐ 74 Billy Brooks | .20 | .09 | .03 |
| Cincinnati Bengals | | | |
| ☐ 75 John Mendenhall | .15 | .07 | .02 |
| New York Giants | | | |
| ☐ 76 Andy Johnson | .15 | .07 | .02 |
| New England Patriots | | | |
| ☐ 77 Tom Wittum | .15 | .07 | .02 |
| San Francisco 49ers | | | |
| ☐ 78 Lynn Dickey | .25 | .11 | .03 |
| Green Bay Packers | | | |
| ☐ 79 Carl Eller | .40 | .18 | .05 |
| Minnesota Vikings | | | |
| ☐ 80 Tom Mack | .20 | .09 | .03 |
| Los Angeles Rams | | | |
| ☐ 81 Clark Gaines | .15 | .07 | .02 |
| New York Jets | | | |
| ☐ 82 Lem Barney | .60 | .25 | .08 |
| Detroit Lions | | | |
| ☐ 83 Mike Montler | .15 | .07 | .02 |
| Denver Broncos | | | |
| ☐ 84 Jon Kolb | .20 | .09 | .03 |
| Pittsburgh Steelers | | | |
| ☐ 85 Bob Chandler | .20 | .09 | .03 |
| Buffalo Bills | | | |
| ☐ 86 Robert Newhouse | .20 | .09 | .03 |
| Dallas Cowboys | | | |
| ☐ 87 Frank LeMaster | .15 | .07 | .02 |
| Philadelphia Eagles | | | |
| ☐ 88 Jeff West | .15 | .07 | .02 |
| San Diego Chargers | | | |
| ☐ 89 Lyle Blackwood | .20 | .09 | .03 |
| Baltimore Colts | | | |
| ☐ 90 Gene Upshaw AP | .40 | .18 | .05 |
| Oakland Raiders | | | |
| ☐ 91 Frank Grant | .15 | .07 | .02 |
| Washington Redskins | | | |
| ☐ 92 Tom Hicks | .15 | .07 | .02 |
| Chicago Bears | | | |
| ☐ 93 Mike Pruitt | .30 | .14 | .04 |
| Cleveland Browns | | | |
| ☐ 94 Chris Bahr | .20 | .09 | .03 |
| Cincinnati Bengals | | | |
| ☐ 95 Russ Francis | .35 | .16 | .04 |
| New England Patriots | | | |
| ☐ 96 Norris Thomas | .15 | .07 | .02 |
| Miami Dolphins | | | |
| ☐ 97 Gary Barbaro | .35 | .16 | .04 |
| Kansas City Chiefs | | | |
| ☐ 98 Jim Merlo | .15 | .07 | .02 |
| New Orleans Saints | | | |
| ☐ 99 Karl Chandler | .15 | .07 | .02 |
| New York Giants | | | |
| ☐ 100 Fran Tarkenton | 4.00 | 1.80 | .50 |
| Minnesota Vikings | | | |
| ☐ 101 Abdul Salaam | .15 | .07 | .02 |
| New York Jets | | | |
| ☐ 102 Marv Kellum | .15 | .07 | .02 |
| St. Louis Cardinals | | | |
| ☐ 103 Herman Weaver | .15 | .07 | .02 |
| Seattle Seahawks | | | |
| ☐ 104 Roy Gerela | .20 | .09 | .03 |
| Pittsburgh Steelers | | | |
| ☐ 105 Harold Jackson | .40 | .18 | .05 |
| Los Angeles Rams | | | |
| ☐ 106 Dewey Selmon | .20 | .09 | .03 |
| Tampa Bay Buccaneers | | | |
| ☐ 107 Checklist 1-132 | 1.00 | .10 | .02 |
| ☐ 108 Clarence Davis | .15 | .07 | .02 |
| Oakland Raiders | | | |
| ☐ 109 Robert Pratt | .15 | .07 | .02 |
| Baltimore Colts | | | |
| ☐ 110 Harvey Martin AP | .60 | .25 | .08 |
| Dallas Cowboys | | | |
| ☐ 111 Brad Dusek | .20 | .09 | .03 |
| Washington Redskins | | | |
| ☐ 112 Greg Latta | .15 | .07 | .02 |
| Chicago Bears | | | |
| ☐ 113 Tony Peters | .20 | .09 | .03 |
| Cleveland Browns | | | |
| ☐ 114 Jim Braxton | .15 | .07 | .02 |
| Buffalo Bills | | | |
| ☐ 115 Ken Riley | .20 | .09 | .03 |
| Cincinnati Bengals | | | |
| ☐ 116 Steve Nelson | .15 | .07 | .02 |
| New England Patriots | | | |
| ☐ 117 Rick Upchurch | .30 | .14 | .04 |
| Denver Broncos | | | |

| | | | |
|---|---|---|---|
| ☐ 118 Spike Jones | .15 | .07 | .02 |
| Philadelphia Eagles | | | |
| ☐ 119 Doug Kotar | .15 | .07 | .02 |
| New York Giants | | | |
| ☐ 120 Bob Griese AP | 3.00 | 1.35 | .40 |
| Miami Dolphins | | | |
| ☐ 121 Burgess Owens | .15 | .07 | .02 |
| New York Jets | | | |
| ☐ 122 Rolf Benirschke | .50 | .23 | .06 |
| San Diego Chargers | | | |
| ☐ 123 Haskel Stanback | .15 | .07 | .02 |
| Atlanta Falcons | | | |
| ☐ 124 J.T. Thomas | .20 | .09 | .03 |
| Pittsburgh Steelers | | | |
| ☐ 125 Ahmad Rashad | 1.25 | .55 | .16 |
| Minnesota Vikings | | | |
| ☐ 126 Rick Kane | .15 | .07 | .02 |
| Detroit Lions | | | |
| ☐ 127 Elvin Bethea | .20 | .09 | .03 |
| Houston Oilers | | | |
| ☐ 128 Dave Dalby | .15 | .07 | .02 |
| Oakland Raiders | | | |
| ☐ 129 Mike Barnes | .15 | .07 | .02 |
| Baltimore Colts | | | |
| ☐ 130 Isiah Robertson | .20 | .09 | .03 |
| Los Angeles Rams | | | |
| ☐ 131 Jim Plunkett | .75 | .35 | .09 |
| San Francisco 49ers | | | |
| ☐ 132 Allan Ellis | .15 | .07 | .02 |
| Chicago Bears | | | |
| ☐ 133 Mike Bragg | .15 | .07 | .02 |
| Washington Redskins | | | |
| ☐ 134 Bob Jackson | .15 | .07 | .02 |
| Cleveland Browns | | | |
| ☐ 135 Coy Bacon | .20 | .09 | .03 |
| Cincinnati Bengals | | | |
| ☐ 136 John Smith | .15 | .07 | .02 |
| New England Patriots | | | |
| ☐ 137 Chuck Muncie | .30 | .14 | .04 |
| New Orleans Saints | | | |
| ☐ 138 Johnnie Gray | .15 | .07 | .02 |
| Green Bay Packers | | | |
| ☐ 139 Jimmy Robinson | .15 | .07 | .02 |
| New York Giants | | | |
| ☐ 140 Tom Banks | .20 | .09 | .03 |
| St. Louis Cardinals | | | |
| ☐ 141 Marvin Powell | .40 | .18 | .05 |
| New York Jets | | | |
| ☐ 142 Jerrel Wilson | .15 | .07 | .02 |
| Kansas City Chiefs | | | |
| ☐ 143 Ron Howard | .15 | .07 | .02 |
| Seattle Seahawks | | | |
| ☐ 144 Rob Lytle | .30 | .14 | .04 |
| Denver Broncos | | | |
| ☐ 145 L.C. Greenwood | .50 | .23 | .06 |
| Pittsburgh Steelers | | | |
| ☐ 146 Morris Owens | .15 | .07 | .02 |
| Tampa Bay Buccaneers | | | |
| ☐ 147 Joe Reed | .15 | .07 | .02 |
| Detroit Lions | | | |
| ☐ 148 Mike Kadish | .15 | .07 | .02 |
| Buffalo Bills | | | |
| ☐ 149 Phil Villapiano | .20 | .09 | .03 |
| Oakland Raiders | | | |
| ☐ 150 Lydell Mitchell | .20 | .09 | .03 |
| Baltimore Colts | | | |
| ☐ 151 Randy Logan | .15 | .07 | .02 |
| Philadelphia Eagles | | | |
| ☐ 152 Mike Williams | .15 | .07 | .02 |
| San Diego Chargers | | | |
| ☐ 153 Jeff Van Note | .20 | .09 | .03 |
| Atlanta Falcons | | | |
| ☐ 154 Steve Schubert | .15 | .07 | .02 |
| Chicago Bears | | | |
| ☐ 155 Bill Kilmer | .40 | .18 | .05 |
| Washington Redskins | | | |
| ☐ 156 Boobie Clark | .20 | .09 | .03 |
| Cincinnati Bengals | | | |
| ☐ 157 Charlie Hall | .15 | .07 | .02 |
| Cleveland Browns | | | |
| ☐ 158 Raymond Clayborn | .50 | .23 | .06 |
| New England Patriots | | | |
| ☐ 159 Jack Gregory | .15 | .07 | .02 |
| New York Giants | | | |
| ☐ 160 Cliff Harris AP | .50 | .23 | .06 |
| Dallas Cowboys | | | |
| ☐ 161 Joe Fields | .20 | .09 | .03 |
| New York Jets | | | |
| ☐ 162 Don Nottingham | .15 | .07 | .02 |
| Miami Dolphins | | | |
| ☐ 163 Ed White | .20 | .09 | .03 |
| Minnesota Vikings | | | |
| ☐ 164 Toni Fritsch | .15 | .07 | .02 |
| Houston Oilers | | | |
| ☐ 165 Jack Lambert | 2.50 | 1.15 | .30 |
| Pittsburgh Steelers | | | |
| ☐ 166 NFC Champions | 1.50 | .65 | .19 |

Cowboys 23,
Vikings 6
(Roger Staubach)
☐ 167 AFC Champions.................... .30 .14 .04
Broncos 20,
Raiders 17
(Lytle running)
☐ 168 Super Bowl XII .................... 2.50 1.15 .30
Cowboys 27,
Broncos 10
(Tony Dorsett)
☐ 169 Neal Colzie ......................... .15 .07 .02
Oakland Raiders
☐ 170 Cleveland Elam AP ............ .15 .07 .02
San Francisco 49ers
☐ 171 David Lee ........................... .15 .07 .02
Baltimore Colts
☐ 172 Jim Otis.............................. .20 .09 .03
St. Louis Cardinals
☐ 173 Archie Manning ................... .75 .35 .09
New Orleans Saints
☐ 174 Jim Carter ......................... .15 .07 .02
Green Bay Packers
☐ 175 Jean Fugett ........................ .20 .09 .03
Washington Redskins
☐ 176 Willie Parker ...................... .15 .07 .02
Buffalo Bills
☐ 177 Haven Moses ...................... .20 .09 .03
Denver Broncos
☐ 178 Horace King ....................... .15 .07 .02
Detroit Lions
☐ 179 Bob Thomas ....................... .15 .07 .02
Chicago Bears
☐ 180 Monte Jackson .................... .20 .09 .03
Los Angeles Rams
☐ 181 Steve Zabel ........................ .15 .07 .02
New England Patriots
☐ 182 John Fitzgerald.................... .15 .07 .02
Dallas Cowboys
☐ 183 Mike Livingston................... .20 .09 .03
Kansas City Chiefs
☐ 184 Larry Poole ........................ .15 .07 .02
Cleveland Browns
☐ 185 Isaac Curtis ....................... .20 .09 .03
Cincinnati Bengals
☐ 186 Chuck Ramsey ..................... .15 .07 .02
New York Jets
☐ 187 Bob Klein ........................... .15 .07 .02
San Diego Chargers
☐ 188 Ray Rhodes......................... .15 .07 .02
New York Giants
☐ 189 Otis Sistrunk ...................... .20 .09 .03
Oakland Raiders
☐ 190 Bill Bergey .......................... .30 .14 .04
Philadelphia Eagles
☐ 191 Sherman Smith .................... .15 .07 .02
Seattle Seahawks
☐ 192 Dave Green ........................ .15 .07 .02
Tampa Bay Buccaneers
☐ 193 Carl Mauck ........................ .15 .07 .02
Houston Oilers
☐ 194 Reggie Harrison ................... .15 .07 .02
Pittsburgh Steelers
☐ 195 Roger Carr ......................... .20 .09 .03
Baltimore Colts
☐ 196 Steve Bartkowski................. .75 .35 .09
Atlanta Falcons
☐ 197 Ray Wersching ..................... .20 .09 .03
San Francisco 49ers
☐ 198 Willie Buchanon .................. .20 .09 .03
Green Bay Packers
☐ 199 Neil Clabo .......................... .15 .07 .02
Minnesota Vikings
☐ 200 Walter Payton AP................. 18.00 8.00 2.30
Chicago Bears
UER (Born 7/5/54,
should be 7/25/54)
☐ 201 Sam Adams.......................... .15 .07 .02
New England Patriots
☐ 202 Larry Gordon....................... .20 .09 .03
Miami Dolphins
☐ 203 Pat Tilley ........................... .20 .09 .03
St. Louis Cardinals
☐ 204 Mack Mitchell...................... .15 .07 .02
Cleveland Browns
☐ 205 Ken Anderson ..................... 1.25 .55 .16
Cincinnati Bengals
☐ 206 Scott Dierking ..................... .15 .07 .02
New York Jets
☐ 207 Jack Rudnay ....................... .15 .07 .02
Kansas City Chiefs
☐ 208 Jim Stienke ........................ .15 .07 .02
New York Giants
☐ 209 Bill Simpson........................ .15 .07 .02
Los Angeles Rams
☐ 210 Errol Mann ......................... .15 .07 .02
Oakland Raiders
☐ 211 Bucky Dilts.......................... .15 .07 .02

Denver Broncos
☐ 212 Reuben Gant ....................... .15 .07 .02
Buffalo Bills
☐ 213 Thomas Henderson............... .50 .23 .06
Dallas Cowboys
☐ 214 Steve Furness ..................... .20 .09 .03
Pittsburgh Steelers
☐ 215 John Riggins......................... 2.00 .90 .25
Washington Redskins
☐ 216 Keith Krepfle ...................... .25 .11 .03
Philadelphia Eagles
☐ 217 Fred Dean........................... 1.00 .45 .13
San Diego Chargers
☐ 218 Emanuel Zanders ................. .15 .07 .02
New Orleans Saints
☐ 219 Don Testerman .................... .15 .07 .02
Seattle Seahawks
☐ 220 George Kunz ....................... .20 .09 .03
Baltimore Colts
☐ 221 Darryl Stingley .................... .25 .11 .03
New England Patriots
☐ 222 Ken Sanders........................ .15 .07 .02
Detroit Lions
☐ 223 Gary Huff............................ .20 .09 .03
Tampa Bay Buccaneers
☐ 224 Gregg Bingham .................... .15 .07 .02
Houston Oilers
☐ 225 Jerry Sherk ........................ .20 .09 .03
Cleveland Browns
☐ 226 Doug Plank ......................... .15 .07 .02
Chicago Bears
☐ 227 Ed Taylor............................ .15 .07 .02
New York Jets
☐ 228 Emery Moorehead................. .15 .07 .02
New York Giants
☐ 229 Reggie Williams ................... 2.25 1.00 .30
Cincinnati Bengals
☐ 230 Claude Humphrey ................. .20 .09 .03
Atlanta Falcons
☐ 231 Randy Cross ........................ 2.25 1.00 .30
San Francisco 49ers
☐ 232 Jim Hart............................. .50 .23 .06
St. Louis Cardinals
☐ 233 Bobby Bryant....................... .15 .07 .02
Minnesota Vikings
☐ 234 Larry Brown ........................ .15 .07 .02
Pittsburgh Steelers
☐ 235 Mark Van Eeghen ................. .20 .09 .03
Oakland Raiders
☐ 236 Terry Hermeling ................... .15 .07 .02
Washington Redskins
☐ 237 Steve Odom ........................ .15 .07 .02
Green Bay Packers
☐ 238 Jan Stenerud ...................... .40 .18 .05
Kansas City Chiefs
☐ 239 Andre Tillman ...................... .15 .07 .02
Miami Dolphins
☐ 240 Tom Jackson AP .................. 3.00 1.35 .40
Denver Broncos
☐ 241 Ken Mendenhall ................... .15 .07 .02
Baltimore Colts
☐ 242 Tim Fox .............................. .15 .07 .02
New England Patriots
☐ 243 Don Herrmann ..................... .15 .07 .02
New Orleans Saints
☐ 244 Eddie McMillan .................... .15 .07 .02
Seattle Seahawks
☐ 245 Greg Pruitt ......................... .30 .14 .04
Cleveland Browns
☐ 246 J.K. McKay ......................... .20 .09 .03
Tampa Bay Buccaneers
☐ 247 Larry Keller ........................ .15 .07 .02
New York Jets
☐ 248 Dave Jennings ..................... .20 .09 .03
New York Giants
☐ 249 Bo Harris............................ .15 .07 .02
Cincinnati Bengals
☐ 250 Revie Sorey ........................ .15 .07 .02
Chicago Bears
☐ 251 Tony Greene........................ .15 .07 .02
Buffalo Bills
☐ 252 Butch Johnson ..................... .20 .09 .03
Dallas Cowboys
☐ 253 Paul Naumoff ...................... .15 .07 .02
Detroit Lions
☐ 254 Rickey Young ...................... .20 .09 .03
San Diego Chargers
☐ 255 Dwight White ...................... .20 .09 .03
Pittsburgh Steelers
☐ 256 Joe Lavender ...................... .20 .09 .03
Washington Redskins
☐ 257 Checklist 133-264 ............... 1.00 .10 .02
☐ 258 Ronnie Coleman.................... .15 .07 .02
Houston Oilers
☐ 259 Charlie Smith ...................... .15 .07 .02
Philadelphia Eagles
☐ 260 Ray Guy AP......................... .50 .23 .06
Oakland Raiders

|  |  | | | |
|---|---|---|---|---|
| ☐ 261 | David Taylor — Baltimore Colts | .15 | .07 | .02 |
| ☐ 262 | Bill Lenkaitis — New England Patriots | .15 | .07 | .02 |
| ☐ 263 | Jim Mitchell — Atlanta Falcons | .15 | .07 | .02 |
| ☐ 264 | Delvin Williams — San Francisco 49ers | .20 | .09 | .03 |
| ☐ 265 | Jack Youngblood — Los Angeles Rams | .60 | .25 | .08 |
| ☐ 266 | Chuck Crist — New Orleans Saints | .15 | .07 | .02 |
| ☐ 267 | Richard Todd — New York Jets | .30 | .14 | .04 |
| ☐ 268 | Dave Logan — Cleveland Browns | .35 | .16 | .04 |
| ☐ 269 | Rufus Mayes — Cincinnati Bengals | .15 | .07 | .02 |
| ☐ 270 | Brad Van Pelt — New York Giants | .20 | .09 | .03 |
| ☐ 271 | Chester Marcol — Green Bay Packers | .20 | .09 | .03 |
| ☐ 272 | J.V. Cain — St. Louis Cardinals | .15 | .07 | .02 |
| ☐ 273 | Larry Seiple — Miami Dolphins | .20 | .09 | .03 |
| ☐ 274 | Brent McClanahan — Minnesota Vikings | .15 | .07 | .02 |
| ☐ 275 | Mike Wagner — Pittsburgh Steelers | .15 | .07 | .02 |
| ☐ 276 | Diron Talbert — Washington Redskins | .20 | .09 | .03 |
| ☐ 277 | Brian Baschnagel — Chicago Bears | .15 | .07 | .02 |
| ☐ 278 | Ed Podolak — Kansas City Chiefs | .20 | .09 | .03 |
| ☐ 279 | Don Goode — San Diego Chargers | .15 | .07 | .02 |
| ☐ 280 | John Dutton — Baltimore Colts | .20 | .09 | .03 |
| ☐ 281 | Don Calhoun — New England Patriots | .15 | .07 | .02 |
| ☐ 282 | Monte Johnson — Oakland Raiders | .15 | .07 | .02 |
| ☐ 283 | Ron Jessie — Los Angeles Rams | .20 | .09 | .03 |
| ☐ 284 | Jon Morris — Detroit Lions | .15 | .07 | .02 |
| ☐ 285 | Riley Odoms — Denver Broncos | .20 | .09 | .03 |
| ☐ 286 | Marv Bateman — Buffalo Bills | .15 | .07 | .02 |
| ☐ 287 | Joe Klecko — New York Jets | 2.00 | .90 | .25 |
| ☐ 288 | Oliver Davis — Cleveland Browns | .15 | .07 | .02 |
| ☐ 289 | John McDaniel — Cincinnati Bengals | .15 | .07 | .02 |
| ☐ 290 | Roger Staubach — Dallas Cowboys | 8.00 | 3.60 | 1.00 |
| ☐ 291 | Brian Kelley — New York Giants | .15 | .07 | .02 |
| ☐ 292 | Mike Hogan — Philadelphia Eagles | .15 | .07 | .02 |
| ☐ 293 | John Leypoldt — Seattle Seahawks | .15 | .07 | .02 |
| ☐ 294 | Jack Novak — Tampa Bay Buccaneers | .15 | .07 | .02 |
| ☐ 295 | Joe Greene — Pittsburgh Steelers | 1.50 | .65 | .19 |
| ☐ 296 | John Hill — New Orleans Saints | .15 | .07 | .02 |
| ☐ 297 | Danny Buggs — Washington Redskins | .20 | .09 | .03 |
| ☐ 298 | Ted Albrecht — Chicago Bears | .15 | .07 | .02 |
| ☐ 299 | Nelson Munsey — Baltimore Colts | .15 | .07 | .02 |
| ☐ 300 | Chuck Foreman — Minnesota Vikings | .40 | .18 | .05 |
| ☐ 301 | Dan Pastorini — Houston Oilers | .30 | .14 | .04 |
| ☐ 302 | Tommy Hart — Chicago Bears | .15 | .07 | .02 |
| ☐ 303 | Dave Beverly — Green Bay Packers | .15 | .07 | .02 |
| ☐ 304 | Tony Reed — Kansas City Chiefs | .15 | .07 | .02 |
| ☐ 305 | Cliff Branch — Oakland Raiders | 1.25 | .55 | .16 |
| ☐ 306 | Clarence Duren — San Diego Chargers | .15 | .07 | .02 |
| ☐ 307 | Randy Rasmussen — New York Jets | .15 | .07 | .02 |
| ☐ 308 | Oscar Roan — Cleveland Browns | .20 | .09 | .03 |
| ☐ 309 | Lenvil Elliott — Cincinnati Bengals | .15 | .07 | .02 |
| ☐ 310 | Dan Dierdorf AP — St. Louis Cardinals | 1.00 | .45 | .13 |
| ☐ 311 | Johnny Perkins — New York Giants | .15 | .07 | .02 |
| ☐ 312 | Rafael Septien — Los Angeles Rams | .25 | .11 | .03 |
| ☐ 313 | Terry Beeson — Seattle Seahawks | .15 | .07 | .02 |
| ☐ 314 | Lee Roy Selmon — Tampa Bay Buccaneers | .50 | .23 | .06 |
| ☐ 315 | Tony Dorsett — Dallas Cowboys | 32.00 | 14.50 | 4.00 |
| ☐ 316 | Greg Landry — Detroit Lions | .30 | .14 | .04 |
| ☐ 317 | Jake Scott — Washington Redskins | .20 | .09 | .03 |
| ☐ 318 | Dan Peiffer — Chicago Bears | .15 | .07 | .02 |
| ☐ 319 | John Bunting — Philadelphia Eagles | .15 | .07 | .02 |
| ☐ 320 | John Stallworth — Pittsburgh Steelers | 20.00 | 9.00 | 2.50 |
| ☐ 321 | Bob Howard — New England Patriots | .15 | .07 | .02 |
| ☐ 322 | Larry Little — Miami Dolphins | .50 | .23 | .06 |
| ☐ 323 | Reggie McKenzie — Buffalo Bills | .20 | .09 | .03 |
| ☐ 324 | Duane Carrell — St. Louis Cardinals | .15 | .07 | .02 |
| ☐ 325 | Ed Simonini — Baltimore Colts | .15 | .07 | .02 |
| ☐ 326 | John Vella — Oakland Raiders | .15 | .07 | .02 |
| ☐ 327 | Wesley Walker — New York Jets | 3.50 | 1.55 | .45 |
| ☐ 328 | Jon Keyworth — Denver Broncos | .20 | .09 | .03 |
| ☐ 329 | Ron Bolton — Cleveland Browns | .15 | .07 | .02 |
| ☐ 330 | Tommy Casanova — Cincinnati Bengals | .20 | .09 | .03 |
| ☐ 331 | Passing Leaders — Bob Griese / Roger Staubach | 4.00 | 1.80 | .50 |
| ☐ 332 | Receiving Leaders — Lydell Mitchell / Ahmad Rashad | .40 | .18 | .05 |
| ☐ 333 | Rushing Leaders — Mark Van Eeghen / Walter Payton | 2.50 | 1.15 | .30 |
| ☐ 334 | Scoring Leaders — Errol Mann / Walter Payton | 2.50 | 1.15 | .30 |
| ☐ 335 | Interception Leaders — Lyle Blackwood / Rolland Lawrence | .30 | .14 | .04 |
| ☐ 336 | Punting Leaders — Ray Guy / Tom Blanchard | .30 | .14 | .04 |
| ☐ 337 | Robert Brazile — Houston Oilers | .20 | .09 | .03 |
| ☐ 338 | Charlie Joiner — San Diego Chargers | 1.00 | .45 | .13 |
| ☐ 339 | Joe Ferguson — Buffalo Bills | .30 | .14 | .04 |
| ☐ 340 | Bill Thompson — Denver Broncos | .20 | .09 | .03 |
| ☐ 341 | Sam Cunningham — New England Patriots | .20 | .09 | .03 |
| ☐ 342 | Curtis Johnson — Miami Dolphins | .15 | .07 | .02 |
| ☐ 343 | Jim Marshall — Minnesota Vikings | .40 | .18 | .05 |
| ☐ 344 | Charlie Sanders — Detroit Lions | .20 | .09 | .03 |
| ☐ 345 | Willie Hall — Oakland Raiders | .15 | .07 | .02 |
| ☐ 346 | Pat Haden — Los Angeles Rams | .75 | .35 | .09 |
| ☐ 347 | Jim Bakken — St. Louis Cardinals | .20 | .09 | .03 |
| ☐ 348 | Bruce Taylor — San Francisco 49ers | .15 | .07 | .02 |
| ☐ 349 | Barty Smith — Green Bay Packers | .15 | .07 | .02 |
| ☐ 350 | Drew Pearson AP — Dallas Cowboys | 1.25 | .55 | .16 |
| ☐ 351 | Mike Webster — Pittsburgh Steelers | 2.00 | .90 | .25 |
| ☐ 352 | Bobby Hammond — New York Giants | .15 | .07 | .02 |
| ☐ 353 | Dave Mays — Cleveland Browns | .15 | .07 | .02 |
| ☐ 354 | Pat McInally — Cincinnati Bengals | .20 | .09 | .03 |
| ☐ 355 | Toni Linhart | .15 | .07 | .02 |

| | | | |
|---|---|---|---|
| Baltimore Colts | | | |
| ☐ 356 Larry Hand | .15 | .07 | .02 |
| Detroit Lions | | | |
| ☐ 357 Ted Fritsch Jr. | .20 | .09 | .03 |
| Washington Redskins | | | |
| ☐ 358 Larry Marshall | .15 | .07 | .02 |
| Philadelphia Eagles | | | |
| ☐ 359 Waymond Bryant | .15 | .07 | .02 |
| Chicago Bears | | | |
| ☐ 360 Louie Kelcher | .30 | .14 | .04 |
| San Diego Chargers | | | |
| ☐ 361 Stanley Morgan | 6.00 | 2.70 | .75 |
| New England Patriots | | | |
| ☐ 362 Bruce Harper | .25 | .11 | .03 |
| New York Jets | | | |
| ☐ 363 Bernard Jackson | .15 | .07 | .02 |
| Denver Broncos | | | |
| ☐ 364 Walter White | .15 | .07 | .02 |
| Kansas City Chiefs | | | |
| ☐ 365 Ken Stabler | 3.00 | 1.35 | .40 |
| Oakland Raiders | | | |
| ☐ 366 Fred Dryer | .75 | .35 | .09 |
| Los Angeles Rams | | | |
| ☐ 367 Ike Harris | .15 | .07 | .02 |
| New Orleans Saints | | | |
| ☐ 368 Norm Bulaich | .20 | .09 | .03 |
| Miami Dolphins | | | |
| ☐ 369 Merv Krakau | .15 | .07 | .02 |
| Buffalo Bills | | | |
| ☐ 370 John James | .15 | .07 | .02 |
| Atlanta Falcons | | | |
| ☐ 371 Bennie Cunningham | .30 | .14 | .04 |
| Pittsburgh Steelers | | | |
| ☐ 372 Doug Van Horn | .15 | .07 | .02 |
| New York Giants | | | |
| ☐ 373 Thom Darden | .15 | .07 | .02 |
| Cleveland Browns | | | |
| ☐ 374 Eddie Edwards | .15 | .07 | .02 |
| Cincinnati Bengals | | | |
| ☐ 375 Mike Thomas | .20 | .09 | .03 |
| Washington Redskins | | | |
| ☐ 376 Fred Cook | .15 | .07 | .02 |
| Baltimore Colts | | | |
| ☐ 377 Mike Phipps | .20 | .09 | .03 |
| Chicago Bears | | | |
| ☐ 378 Paul Krause | .20 | .09 | .03 |
| Minnesota Vikings | | | |
| ☐ 379 Harold Carmichael | .75 | .35 | .09 |
| Philadelphia Eagles | | | |
| ☐ 380 Mike Haynes AP | 1.00 | .45 | .13 |
| New England Patriots | | | |
| ☐ 381 Wayne Morris | .15 | .07 | .02 |
| St. Louis Cardinals | | | |
| ☐ 382 Greg Buttle | .20 | .09 | .03 |
| New York Jets | | | |
| ☐ 383 Jim Zorn | .60 | .25 | .08 |
| Seattle Seahawks | | | |
| ☐ 384 Jack Dolbin | .20 | .09 | .03 |
| Denver Broncos | | | |
| ☐ 385 Charlie Waters | .50 | .23 | .06 |
| Dallas Cowboys | | | |
| ☐ 386 Dan Ryczek | .15 | .07 | .02 |
| Los Angeles Rams | | | |
| ☐ 387 Joe Washington | 1.00 | .45 | .13 |
| San Diego Chargers | | | |
| ☐ 388 Checklist 265-396 | 1.00 | .10 | .02 |
| ☐ 389 James Hunter | .15 | .07 | .02 |
| Detroit Lions | | | |
| ☐ 390 Billy Johnson | .20 | .09 | .03 |
| Houston Oilers | | | |
| ☐ 391 Jim Allen | .15 | .07 | .02 |
| Pittsburgh Steelers | | | |
| ☐ 392 George Buehler | .15 | .07 | .02 |
| Oakland Raiders | | | |
| ☐ 393 Harry Carson | 1.50 | .65 | .19 |
| New York Giants | | | |
| ☐ 394 Cleo Miller | .15 | .07 | .02 |
| Cleveland Browns | | | |
| ☐ 395 Gary Burley | .15 | .07 | .02 |
| Cincinnati Bengals | | | |
| ☐ 396 Mark Moseley | .20 | .09 | .03 |
| Washington Redskins | | | |
| ☐ 397 Virgil Livers | .15 | .07 | .02 |
| Chicago Bears | | | |
| ☐ 398 Joe Ehrmann | .15 | .07 | .02 |
| Baltimore Colts | | | |
| ☐ 399 Freddie Solomon | .20 | .09 | .03 |
| Miami Dolphins | | | |
| ☐ 400 O.J. Simpson | 10.00 | 4.50 | 1.25 |
| San Francisco 49ers | | | |
| ☐ 401 Julius Adams | .15 | .07 | .02 |
| New England Patriots | | | |
| ☐ 402 Artimus Parker | .15 | .07 | .02 |
| New York Jets | | | |
| ☐ 403 Gene Washington | .20 | .09 | .03 |
| San Francisco 49ers | | | |
| ☐ 404 Herman Edwards | .15 | .07 | .02 |
| Philadelphia Eagles | | | |

| | | | |
|---|---|---|---|
| ☐ 405 Craig Morton | .50 | .23 | .06 |
| Denver Broncos | | | |
| ☐ 406 Alan Page | .75 | .35 | .09 |
| Minnesota Vikings | | | |
| ☐ 407 Larry McCarren | .15 | .07 | .02 |
| Green Bay Packers | | | |
| ☐ 408 Tony Galbreath | .20 | .09 | .03 |
| New Orleans Saints | | | |
| ☐ 409 Roman Gabriel | .60 | .25 | .08 |
| Los Angeles Rams | | | |
| ☐ 410 Efren Herrera AP | .15 | .07 | .02 |
| Dallas Cowboys | | | |
| ☐ 411 Jim Smith | .60 | .25 | .08 |
| Pittsburgh Steelers | | | |
| ☐ 412 Bill Bryant | .15 | .07 | .02 |
| New York Giants | | | |
| ☐ 413 Doug Dieken | .15 | .07 | .02 |
| Cleveland Browns | | | |
| ☐ 414 Marvin Cobb | .15 | .07 | .02 |
| Cincinnati Bengals | | | |
| ☐ 415 Fred Biletnikoff | 1.50 | .65 | .19 |
| Oakland Raiders | | | |
| ☐ 416 Joe Theismann | 2.50 | 1.15 | .30 |
| Washington Redskins | | | |
| ☐ 417 Roland Harper | .20 | .09 | .03 |
| Chicago Bears | | | |
| ☐ 418 Derrel Luce | .15 | .07 | .02 |
| Baltimore Colts | | | |
| ☐ 419 Ralph Perretta | .15 | .07 | .02 |
| San Diego Chargers | | | |
| ☐ 420 Louis Wright | 1.00 | .45 | .13 |
| Denver Broncos | | | |
| ☐ 421 Prentice McCray | .15 | .07 | .02 |
| New England Patriots | | | |
| ☐ 422 Garry Puetz | .15 | .07 | .02 |
| New York Jets | | | |
| ☐ 423 Alfred Jenkins | .50 | .23 | .06 |
| Atlanta Falcons | | | |
| ☐ 424 Paul Seymour | .15 | .07 | .02 |
| Buffalo Bills | | | |
| ☐ 425 Garo Yepremian | .20 | .09 | .03 |
| Miami Dolphins | | | |
| ☐ 426 Emmitt Thomas | .20 | .09 | .03 |
| Kansas City Chiefs | | | |
| ☐ 427 Dexter Bussey | .15 | .07 | .02 |
| Detroit Lions | | | |
| ☐ 428 John Sanders | .15 | .07 | .02 |
| Philadelphia Eagles | | | |
| ☐ 429 Ed Too Tall Jones | 2.00 | .90 | .25 |
| Dallas Cowboys | | | |
| ☐ 430 Ron Yary | .20 | .09 | .03 |
| Minnesota Vikings | | | |
| ☐ 431 Frank Lewis | .20 | .09 | .03 |
| Pittsburgh Steelers | | | |
| ☐ 432 Jerry Golsteyn | .15 | .07 | .02 |
| New York Giants | | | |
| ☐ 433 Clarence Scott | .15 | .07 | .02 |
| Cleveland Browns | | | |
| ☐ 434 Pete Johnson | .50 | .23 | .06 |
| Cincinnati Bengals | | | |
| ☐ 435 Charley Young | .20 | .09 | .03 |
| Los Angeles Rams | | | |
| ☐ 436 Harold McLinton | .15 | .07 | .02 |
| Washington Redskins | | | |
| ☐ 437 Noah Jackson | .15 | .07 | .02 |
| Chicago Bears | | | |
| ☐ 438 Bruce Laird | .15 | .07 | .02 |
| Baltimore Colts | | | |
| ☐ 439 John Matuszak | .20 | .09 | .03 |
| Oakland Raiders | | | |
| ☐ 440 Nat Moore AP | .30 | .14 | .04 |
| Miami Dolphins | | | |
| ☐ 441 Leon Gray | .20 | .09 | .03 |
| New England Patriots | | | |
| ☐ 442 Jerome Barkum | .15 | .07 | .02 |
| New York Jets | | | |
| ☐ 443 Steve Largent | 15.00 | 6.75 | 1.90 |
| Seattle Seahawks | | | |
| ☐ 444 John Zook | .15 | .07 | .02 |
| St. Louis Cardinals | | | |
| ☐ 445 Preston Pearson | .25 | .11 | .03 |
| Dallas Cowboys | | | |
| ☐ 446 Conrad Dobler | .20 | .09 | .03 |
| New Orleans Saints | | | |
| ☐ 447 Wilbur Summers | .15 | .07 | .02 |
| Detroit Lions | | | |
| ☐ 448 Lou Piccone | .15 | .07 | .02 |
| Buffalo Bills | | | |
| ☐ 449 Ron Jaworski | .60 | .25 | .08 |
| Philadelphia Eagles | | | |
| ☐ 450 Jack Ham AP | 1.50 | .65 | .19 |
| Pittsburgh Steelers | | | |
| ☐ 451 Mick Tingelhoff | .20 | .09 | .03 |
| Minnesota Vikings | | | |
| ☐ 452 Clyde Powers | .15 | .07 | .02 |
| New York Giants | | | |
| ☐ 453 John Cappelletti | .50 | .23 | .06 |

| | | | | |
|---|---|---|---|---|
| Los Angeles Rams | | | | |
| ☐ 454 Dick Ambrose | .15 | .07 | .02 | |
| Cleveland Browns | | | | |
| ☐ 455 Lemar Parrish | .20 | .09 | .03 | |
| Cincinnati Bengals | | | | |
| ☐ 456 Ron Saul | .15 | .07 | .02 | |
| Washington Redskins | | | | |
| ☐ 457 Bob Parsons | .15 | .07 | .02 | |
| Chicago Bears | | | | |
| ☐ 458 Glenn Doughty | .15 | .07 | .02 | |
| Baltimore Colts | | | | |
| ☐ 459 Don Woods | .15 | .07 | .02 | |
| San Diego Chargers | | | | |
| ☐ 460 Art Shell AP | 1.00 | .45 | .13 | |
| Oakland Raiders | | | | |
| ☐ 461 Sam Hunt | .15 | .07 | .02 | |
| New England Patriots | | | | |
| ☐ 462 Lawrence Pillers | .15 | .07 | .02 | |
| New York Jets | | | | |
| ☐ 463 Henry Childs | .15 | .07 | .02 | |
| New Orleans Saints | | | | |
| ☐ 464 Roger Wehrli | .20 | .09 | .03 | |
| St. Louis Cardinals | | | | |
| ☐ 465 Otis Armstrong | .30 | .14 | .04 | |
| Denver Broncos | | | | |
| ☐ 466 Bob Baumhower | .75 | .35 | .09 | |
| Miami Dolphins | | | | |
| ☐ 467 Ray Jarvis | .15 | .07 | .02 | |
| Detroit Lions | | | | |
| ☐ 468 Guy Morriss | .15 | .07 | .02 | |
| Philadelphia Eagles | | | | |
| ☐ 469 Matt Blair | .30 | .14 | .04 | |
| Minnesota Vikings | | | | |
| ☐ 470 Billy Joe DuPree | .30 | .14 | .04 | |
| Dallas Cowboys | | | | |
| ☐ 471 Roland Hooks | .15 | .07 | .02 | |
| Buffalo Bills | | | | |
| ☐ 472 Joe Danelo | .15 | .07 | .02 | |
| New York Giants | | | | |
| ☐ 473 Reggie Rucker | .20 | .09 | .03 | |
| Cleveland Browns | | | | |
| ☐ 474 Vern Holland | .15 | .07 | .02 | |
| Cincinnati Bengals | | | | |
| ☐ 475 Mel Blount | 1.25 | .55 | .16 | |
| Pittsburgh Steelers | | | | |
| ☐ 476 Eddie Brown | .15 | .07 | .02 | |
| Washington Redskins | | | | |
| ☐ 477 Bo Rather | .20 | .09 | .03 | |
| Chicago Bears | | | | |
| ☐ 478 Don McCauley | .15 | .07 | .02 | |
| Baltimore Colts | | | | |
| ☐ 479 Glen Walker | .15 | .07 | .02 | |
| Los Angeles Rams | | | | |
| ☐ 480 Randy Gradishar AP | .75 | .35 | .09 | |
| Denver Broncos | | | | |
| ☐ 481 Dave Rowe | .15 | .07 | .02 | |
| Oakland Raiders | | | | |
| ☐ 482 Pat Leahy | .40 | .18 | .05 | |
| New York Jets | | | | |
| ☐ 483 Mike Fuller | .15 | .07 | .02 | |
| San Diego Chargers | | | | |
| ☐ 484 David Lewis | .15 | .07 | .02 | |
| Tampa Bay Buccaneers | | | | |
| ☐ 485 Steve Grogan | .75 | .35 | .09 | |
| New England Patriots | | | | |
| ☐ 486 Mel Gray | .20 | .09 | .03 | |
| St. Louis Cardinals | | | | |
| ☐ 487 Eddie Payton | .30 | .14 | .04 | |
| Detroit Lions | | | | |
| ☐ 488 Checklist 397-528 | 1.00 | .10 | .02 | |
| ☐ 489 Stu Voigt | .20 | .09 | .03 | |
| Minnesota Vikings | | | | |
| ☐ 490 Rolland Lawrence AP | .20 | .09 | .03 | |
| Atlanta Falcons | | | | |
| ☐ 491 Nick Mike-Mayer | .15 | .07 | .02 | |
| Philadelphia Eagles | | | | |
| ☐ 492 Troy Archer | .15 | .07 | .02 | |
| New York Giants | | | | |
| ☐ 493 Benny Malone | .20 | .09 | .03 | |
| Miami Dolphins | | | | |
| ☐ 494 Golden Richards | .20 | .09 | .03 | |
| Dallas Cowboys | | | | |
| ☐ 495 Chris Hanburger | .20 | .09 | .03 | |
| Washington Redskins | | | | |
| ☐ 496 Dwight Harrison | .15 | .07 | .02 | |
| Buffalo Bills | | | | |
| ☐ 497 Gary Fencik | .60 | .25 | .08 | |
| Chicago Bears | | | | |
| ☐ 498 Rich Saul | .15 | .07 | .02 | |
| Los Angeles Rams | | | | |
| ☐ 499 Dan Fouts | 4.50 | 2.00 | .55 | |
| San Diego Chargers | | | | |
| ☐ 500 Franco Harris AP | 2.50 | 1.15 | .30 | |
| Pittsburgh Steelers | | | | |
| ☐ 501 Atlanta Falcons TL | .50 | .08 | .02 | |
| Haskel Stanback | | | | |
| Alfred Jenkins | | | | |
| Claude Humphrey | | | | |
| Jeff Merrow | | | | |
| Rolland Lawrence | | | | |
| ☐ 502 Baltimore Colts TL | .50 | .08 | .02 | |
| Lydell Mitchell | | | | |
| Lydell Mitchell | | | | |
| Lyle Blackwood | | | | |
| Fred Cook | | | | |
| ☐ 503 Buffalo Bills TL | 1.50 | .23 | .02 | |
| O.J. Simpson | | | | |
| Bob Chandler | | | | |
| Tony Greene | | | | |
| Sherman White | | | | |
| ☐ 504 Chicago Bears TL | 2.00 | .30 | .02 | |
| Walter Payton | | | | |
| James Scott | | | | |
| Allan Ellis | | | | |
| Ron Rydalch | | | | |
| ☐ 505 Cincinnati Bengals TL | .75 | .11 | .02 | |
| Pete Johnson | | | | |
| Billy Brooks | | | | |
| Lemar Parrish | | | | |
| Reggie Williams | | | | |
| Gary Burley | | | | |
| ☐ 506 Cleveland Browns TL | .50 | .08 | .02 | |
| Greg Pruitt | | | | |
| Reggie Rucker | | | | |
| Thom Darden | | | | |
| Mack Mitchell | | | | |
| ☐ 507 Dallas Cowboys TL | 2.00 | .30 | .02 | |
| Tony Dorsett | | | | |
| Drew Pearson | | | | |
| Cliff Harris | | | | |
| Harvey Martin | | | | |
| ☐ 508 Denver Broncos TL | .50 | .08 | .02 | |
| Otis Armstrong | | | | |
| Haven Moses | | | | |
| Bill Thompson | | | | |
| Rick Upchurch | | | | |
| ☐ 509 Detroit Lions TL | .50 | .08 | .02 | |
| Horace King | | | | |
| David Hill | | | | |
| James Hunter | | | | |
| Ken Sanders | | | | |
| ☐ 510 Green Bay Packers TL | .50 | .08 | .02 | |
| Barty Smith | | | | |
| Steve Odom | | | | |
| Steve Luke | | | | |
| Mike C. McCoy | | | | |
| Dave Pureifory | | | | |
| Dave Roller | | | | |
| ☐ 511 Houston Oilers TL | .50 | .08 | .02 | |
| Ronnie Coleman | | | | |
| Ken Burrough | | | | |
| Mike Reinfeldt | | | | |
| James Young | | | | |
| ☐ 512 Kansas City Chiefs TL | .50 | .08 | .02 | |
| Ed Podolak | | | | |
| Walter White | | | | |
| Gary Barbaro | | | | |
| Wilbur Young | | | | |
| ☐ 513 Los Angeles Rams TL | .50 | .08 | .02 | |
| Lawrence McCutcheon | | | | |
| Harold Jackson | | | | |
| Bill Simpson | | | | |
| Jack Youngblood | | | | |
| ☐ 514 Miami Dolphins TL | .50 | .08 | .02 | |
| Benny Malone | | | | |
| Nat Moore | | | | |
| Curtis Johnson | | | | |
| A.J. Duhe | | | | |
| ☐ 515 Minnesota Vikings TL | .50 | .08 | .02 | |
| Chuck Foreman | | | | |
| Sammie White | | | | |
| Bobby Bryant | | | | |
| Carl Eller | | | | |
| ☐ 516 New England Pats TL | .60 | .09 | .02 | |
| Sam Cunningham | | | | |
| Darryl Stingley | | | | |
| Mike Haynes | | | | |
| Tony McGee | | | | |
| ☐ 517 New Orleans Saints TL | .50 | .08 | .02 | |
| Chuck Muncie | | | | |
| Don Herrmann | | | | |
| Chuck Crist | | | | |
| Elois Grooms | | | | |
| ☐ 518 New York Giants TL | .50 | .08 | .02 | |
| Bobby Hammond | | | | |
| Jimmy Robinson | | | | |
| Bill Bryant | | | | |
| John Mendenhall | | | | |
| ☐ 519 New York Jets TL | .75 | .11 | .02 | |
| Clark Gaines | | | | |
| Wesley Walker | | | | |
| Burgess Owens | | | | |
| Joe Klecko | | | | |
| ☐ 520 Oakland Raiders TL | .60 | .09 | .02 | |
| Mark Van Eeghen | | | | |
| Dave Casper | | | | |

Jack Tatum
Neal Colzie

| | | NRMT | VG-E | GOOD |
|---|---|---|---|---|
| ☐ 521 | Philadelphia Eagles TL .......... | .50 | .08 | .02 |
| | Mike Hogan | | | |
| | Harold Carmichael | | | |
| | Herman Edwards | | | |
| | John Sanders | | | |
| | Lem Burnham | | | |
| ☐ 522 | Pittsburgh Steelers TL .......... | 1.00 | .15 | .02 |
| | Franco Harris | | | |
| | Jim Smith | | | |
| | Mel Blount | | | |
| | Steve Furness | | | |
| ☐ 523 | St.Louis Cardinals TL .......... | .50 | .08 | .02 |
| | Terry Metcalf | | | |
| | Mel Gray | | | |
| | Roger Wehrli | | | |
| | Mike Dawson | | | |
| ☐ 524 | San Diego Chargers TL .......... | .50 | .08 | .02 |
| | Rickey Young | | | |
| | Charlie Joiner | | | |
| | Mike Fuller | | | |
| | Gary Johnson | | | |
| ☐ 525 | San Francisco 49ers TL......... | .50 | .08 | .02 |
| | Delvin Williams | | | |
| | Gene Washington | | | |
| | Mel Phillips | | | |
| | Dave Washington | | | |
| | Cleveland Elam | | | |
| ☐ 526 | Seattle Seahawks TL .......... | 1.50 | .23 | .02 |
| | Sherman Smith | | | |
| | Steve Largent | | | |
| | Autry Beamon | | | |
| | Walter Packer | | | |
| ☐ 527 | Tampa Bay Bucs TL .............. | .50 | .08 | .02 |
| | Morris Owens | | | |
| | Isaac Hagins | | | |
| | Mike Washington | | | |
| | Lee Roy Selmon | | | |
| ☐ 528 | Wash. Redskins TL .............. | 1.00 | .15 | .02 |
| | Mike Thomas | | | |
| | Jean Fugett | | | |
| | Ken Houston | | | |
| | Dennis Johnson | | | |

## 1978 Topps Holsum

In 1978, Topps produced a set of 33 NFL players for Holsum Bread. One card was packed inside each loaf of bread. Unfortunately, nowhere on the card is Holsum mentioned, leading to frequent misclassification of this set. The cards are in color and are standard size, 2 1/2" by 3 1/2". An uncut production sheet was offered in the 1989 Topps Archives auction. The cards are numbered on the back. The personal data on the card back is printed in yellow and green. Each card can be found with either one or two asterisks on the copyright line.

| | NRMT | VG-E | GOOD |
|---|---|---|---|
| COMPLETE SET (33)........................ | 225.00 | 90.00 | 22.00 |
| COMMON PLAYER (1-33)................ | 3.00 | 1.20 | .30 |
| ☐ 1 Rolland Lawrence .................... | 3.00 | 1.20 | .30 |
| Atlanta Falcons | | | |
| ☐ 2 Walter Payton ........................ | 60.00 | 24.00 | 6.00 |
| Chicago Bears | | | |
| ☐ 3 Lydell Mitchell........................ | 4.00 | 1.60 | .40 |
| Baltimore Colts | | | |
| ☐ 4 Joe DeLamielleure................... | 3.00 | 1.20 | .30 |
| Buffalo Bills | | | |
| ☐ 5 Ken Anderson ........................ | 10.00 | 4.00 | 1.00 |
| Cincinnati Bengals | | | |
| ☐ 6 Greg Pruitt ............................ | 4.00 | 1.60 | .40 |
| Cleveland Browns | | | |
| ☐ 7 Harvey Martin ........................ | 5.00 | 2.00 | .50 |

Dallas Cowboys

| | | NRMT | VG-E | GOOD |
|---|---|---|---|---|
| ☐ 8 | Tom Jackson............................. | 5.00 | 2.00 | .50 |
| | Denver Broncos | | | |
| ☐ 9 | Chester Marcol......................... | 3.00 | 1.20 | .30 |
| | Green Bay Packers | | | |
| ☐ 10 | Jim Carter ............................... | 3.00 | 1.20 | .30 |
| | Green Bay Packers | | | |
| ☐ 11 | Will Harrell .............................. | 3.00 | 1.20 | .30 |
| | Green Bay Packers | | | |
| ☐ 12 | Greg Landry ............................. | 4.00 | 1.60 | .40 |
| | Detroit Lions | | | |
| ☐ 13 | Billy Johnson ........................... | 4.00 | 1.60 | .40 |
| | Houston Oilers | | | |
| ☐ 14 | Jan Stenerud........................... | 8.00 | 3.25 | .80 |
| | Kansas City Chiefs | | | |
| ☐ 15 | Lawrence McCutcheon............ | 4.00 | 1.60 | .40 |
| | Los Angeles Rams | | | |
| ☐ 16 | Bob Griese .............................. | 15.00 | 6.00 | 1.50 |
| | Miami Dolphins | | | |
| ☐ 17 | Chuck Foreman ......................... | 5.00 | 2.00 | .50 |
| | Minnesota Vikings | | | |
| ☐ 18 | Sammie White .......................... | 4.00 | 1.60 | .40 |
| | Minnesota Vikings | | | |
| ☐ 19 | Jeff Siemon ............................. | 4.00 | 1.60 | .40 |
| | Minnesota Vikings | | | |
| ☐ 20 | Mike Haynes ............................ | 6.00 | 2.40 | .60 |
| | New England Patriots | | | |
| ☐ 21 | Archie Manning........................ | 7.50 | 3.00 | .75 |
| | New Orleans Saints | | | |
| ☐ 22 | Brad Van Pelt ........................... | 4.00 | 1.60 | .40 |
| | New York Giants | | | |
| ☐ 23 | Richard Todd ........................... | 4.00 | 1.60 | .40 |
| | New York Jets | | | |
| ☐ 24 | Dave Casper............................. | 4.00 | 1.60 | .40 |
| | Oakland Raiders | | | |
| ☐ 25 | Bill Bergey ............................... | 4.00 | 1.60 | .40 |
| | Philadelphia Eagles | | | |
| ☐ 26 | Franco Harris ........................... | 20.00 | 8.00 | 2.00 |
| | Pittsburgh Steelers | | | |
| ☐ 27 | Mel Gray .................................. | 4.00 | 1.60 | .40 |
| | St. Louis Cardinals | | | |
| ☐ 28 | Louie Kelcher .......................... | 3.00 | 1.20 | .30 |
| | San Diego Chargers | | | |
| ☐ 29 | O.J. Simpson ........................... | 50.00 | 20.00 | 5.00 |
| | Buffalo Bills | | | |
| ☐ 30 | Jim Zorn .................................. | 5.00 | 2.00 | .50 |
| | Seattle Seahawks | | | |
| ☐ 31 | Lee Roy Selmon....................... | 5.00 | 2.00 | .50 |
| | Tampa Bay Buccaneers | | | |
| ☐ 32 | Ken Houston ............................ | 8.00 | 3.25 | .80 |
| | Washington Redskins | | | |
| ☐ 33 | Checklist Card .......................... | 6.00 | 2.40 | .60 |

## 1979 Topps

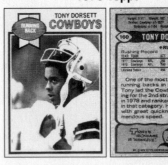

The 1979 Topps football set contains 528 cards. The cards measure 2 1/2" by 3 1/2". No known scarcities exist. The first six cards feature the AFC and NFC statistical leaders from the previous season. Post-season playoff action is summarized on cards 166-168. Record Breakers (RB) of the past season are featured on cards 331-336. Distributed throughout the set are Team Leader (TL) cards depicting, typically, four individual team (statistical) leaders on the front and a team checklist on the back. All-Pro (AP) selections are designated on the player's regular card, not a special card. The set features the first and only Topps cards of Earl Campbell. Other notable Rookie Cards in this set are Steve DeBerg, James Lofton, Ozzie Newsome, and Doug Williams. The card backs are printed in yellow and blue.

| | NRMT | VG-E | GOOD |
|---|---|---|---|
| COMPLETE SET (528)....................... | 125.00 | 57.50 | 15.50 |
| COMMON PLAYER (1-528)............... | .15 | .07 | .02 |
| ☐ 1 Passing Leaders........................ | 5.00 | 1.00 | .30 |
| Roger Staubach | | | |

| | | | |
|---|---|---|---|
| Terry Bradshaw | | | |
| ☐ 2 Receiving Leaders | .75 | .35 | .09 |
| Rickey Young | | | |
| Steve Largent | | | |
| ☐ 3 Rushing Leaders | 7.00 | 3.10 | .85 |
| Walter Payton | | | |
| Earl Campbell | | | |
| ☐ 4 Scoring Leaders | .30 | .14 | .04 |
| Frank Corral | | | |
| Pat Leahy | | | |
| ☐ 5 Interception Leaders | .30 | .14 | .04 |
| Willie Buchanon | | | |
| Ken Stone | | | |
| Thom Darden | | | |
| ☐ 6 Punting Leaders | .30 | .14 | .04 |
| Tom Skladany | | | |
| Pat McInally | | | |
| ☐ 7 Johnny Perkins | .15 | .07 | .02 |
| New York Giants | | | |
| ☐ 8 Charles Phillips | .15 | .07 | .02 |
| Oakland Raiders | | | |
| ☐ 9 Derrel Luce | .15 | .07 | .02 |
| Baltimore Colts | | | |
| ☐ 10 John Riggins | 1.25 | .55 | .16 |
| Washington Redskins | | | |
| ☐ 11 Chester Marcol | .20 | .09 | .03 |
| Green Bay Packers | | | |
| ☐ 12 Bernard Jackson | .15 | .07 | .02 |
| Denver Broncos | | | |
| ☐ 13 Dave Logan | .20 | .09 | .03 |
| Cleveland Browns | | | |
| ☐ 14 Bo Harris | .15 | .07 | .02 |
| Cincinnati Bengals | | | |
| ☐ 15 Alan Page | .60 | .25 | .08 |
| Chicago Bears | | | |
| ☐ 16 John Smith | .15 | .07 | .02 |
| New England Patriots | | | |
| ☐ 17 Dwight McDonald | .15 | .07 | .02 |
| San Diego Chargers | | | |
| ☐ 18 John Cappelletti | .30 | .14 | .04 |
| Los Angeles Rams | | | |
| ☐ 19 Pittsburgh Steelers TL | .75 | .11 | .03 |
| Franco Harris | | | |
| Larry Anderson | | | |
| Tony Dungy | | | |
| L.C. Greenwood | | | |
| ☐ 20 Bill Bergey AP | .20 | .09 | .03 |
| Philadelphia Eagles | | | |
| ☐ 21 Jerome Barkum | .15 | .07 | .02 |
| New York Jets | | | |
| ☐ 22 Larry Csonka | 1.50 | .65 | .19 |
| Miami Dolphins | | | |
| ☐ 23 Joe Ferguson | .25 | .11 | .03 |
| Buffalo Bills | | | |
| ☐ 24 Ed Too Tall Jones | 1.25 | .55 | .16 |
| Dallas Cowboys | | | |
| ☐ 25 Dave Jennings | .20 | .09 | .03 |
| New York Giants | | | |
| ☐ 26 Horace King | .15 | .07 | .02 |
| Detroit Lions | | | |
| ☐ 27 Steve Little | .15 | .07 | .02 |
| St. Louis Cardinals | | | |
| ☐ 28 Morris Bradshaw | .15 | .07 | .02 |
| Oakland Raiders | | | |
| ☐ 29 Joe Ehrmann | .15 | .07 | .02 |
| Baltimore Colts | | | |
| ☐ 30 Ahmad Rashad AP | .75 | .35 | .09 |
| Minnesota Vikings | | | |
| ☐ 31 Joe Lavender | .20 | .09 | .03 |
| Washington Redskins | | | |
| ☐ 32 Dan Neal | .15 | .07 | .02 |
| Chicago Bears | | | |
| ☐ 33 Johnny Evans | .15 | .07 | .02 |
| Cleveland Browns | | | |
| ☐ 34 Pete Johnson | .20 | .09 | .03 |
| Cincinnati Bengals | | | |
| ☐ 35 Mike Haynes AP | .40 | .18 | .05 |
| New England Patriots | | | |
| ☐ 36 Tim Mazzetti | .15 | .07 | .02 |
| Atlanta Falcons | | | |
| ☐ 37 Mike Barber | .20 | .09 | .03 |
| Houston Oilers | | | |
| ☐ 38 San Francisco 49ers TL | 1.50 | .23 | .02 |
| O.J. Simpson | | | |
| Freddie Solomon | | | |
| Chuck Crist | | | |
| Cedrick Hardman | | | |
| ☐ 39 Bill Gregory | .15 | .07 | .02 |
| Seattle Seahawks | | | |
| ☐ 40 Randy Gradishar AP | .50 | .23 | .06 |
| Denver Broncos | | | |
| ☐ 41 Richard Todd | .25 | .11 | .03 |
| New York Jets | | | |
| ☐ 42 Henry Marshall | .15 | .07 | .02 |
| Kansas City Chiefs | | | |
| ☐ 43 John Hill | .15 | .07 | .02 |
| New Orleans Saints | | | |
| ☐ 44 Sidney Thornton | .20 | .09 | .03 |

| | | | |
|---|---|---|---|
| Pittsburgh Steelers | | | |
| ☐ 45 Ron Jessie | .20 | .09 | .03 |
| Los Angeles Rams | | | |
| ☐ 46 Bob Baumhower | .20 | .09 | .03 |
| Miami Dolphins | | | |
| ☐ 47 Johnnie Gray | .15 | .07 | .02 |
| Green Bay Packers | | | |
| ☐ 48 Doug Williams | 2.00 | .90 | .25 |
| Tampa Bay Buccaneers | | | |
| ☐ 49 Don McCauley | .15 | .07 | .02 |
| Baltimore Colts | | | |
| ☐ 50 Ray Guy AP | .30 | .14 | .04 |
| Oakland Raiders | | | |
| ☐ 51 Bob Klein | .15 | .07 | .02 |
| San Diego Chargers | | | |
| ☐ 52 Golden Richards | .20 | .09 | .03 |
| Chicago Bears | | | |
| ☐ 53 Mark Miller | .15 | .07 | .02 |
| Cleveland Browns | | | |
| ☐ 54 John Sanders | .15 | .07 | .02 |
| Philadelphia Eagles | | | |
| ☐ 55 Gary Burley | .15 | .07 | .02 |
| Cincinnati Bengals | | | |
| ☐ 56 Steve Nelson | .15 | .07 | .02 |
| New England Patriots | | | |
| ☐ 57 Buffalo Bills TL | .50 | .08 | .02 |
| Terry Miller | | | |
| Frank Lewis | | | |
| Mario Clark | | | |
| Lucius Sanford | | | |
| ☐ 58 Bobby Bryant | .15 | .07 | .02 |
| Minnesota Vikings | | | |
| ☐ 59 Rick Kane | .15 | .07 | .02 |
| Detroit Lions | | | |
| ☐ 60 Larry Little | .30 | .14 | .04 |
| Miami Dolphins | | | |
| ☐ 61 Ted Fritsch Jr. | .20 | .09 | .03 |
| Washington Redskins | | | |
| ☐ 62 Larry Mallory | .15 | .07 | .02 |
| New York Giants | | | |
| ☐ 63 Marvin Powell | .20 | .09 | .03 |
| New York Jets | | | |
| ☐ 64 Jim Hart | .30 | .14 | .04 |
| St. Louis Cardinals | | | |
| ☐ 65 Joe Greene AP | 1.25 | .55 | .16 |
| Pittsburgh Steelers | | | |
| ☐ 66 Walter White | .15 | .07 | .02 |
| Kansas City Chiefs | | | |
| ☐ 67 Gregg Bingham | .15 | .07 | .02 |
| Houston Oilers | | | |
| ☐ 68 Errol Mann | .15 | .07 | .02 |
| Oakland Raiders | | | |
| ☐ 69 Bruce Laird | .15 | .07 | .02 |
| Baltimore Colts | | | |
| ☐ 70 Drew Pearson | .75 | .35 | .09 |
| Dallas Cowboys | | | |
| ☐ 71 Steve Bartkowski | .60 | .25 | .08 |
| Atlanta Falcons | | | |
| ☐ 72 Ted Albrecht | .15 | .07 | .02 |
| Chicago Bears | | | |
| ☐ 73 Charlie Hall | .15 | .07 | .02 |
| Cleveland Browns | | | |
| ☐ 74 Pat McInally | .20 | .09 | .03 |
| Cincinnati Bengals | | | |
| ☐ 75 Al(Bubba) Baker AP | 1.00 | .45 | .13 |
| Detroit Lions | | | |
| ☐ 76 New England Pats TL | .60 | .09 | .02 |
| Sam Cunningham | | | |
| Stanley Morgan | | | |
| Mike Haynes | | | |
| Tony McGee | | | |
| ☐ 77 Steve DeBerg | 6.00 | 2.70 | .75 |
| San Francisco 49ers | | | |
| ☐ 78 John Yarno | .15 | .07 | .02 |
| Seattle Seahawks | | | |
| ☐ 79 Stu Voigt | .20 | .09 | .03 |
| Minnesota Vikings | | | |
| ☐ 80 Frank Corral AP | .15 | .07 | .02 |
| Los Angeles Rams | | | |
| ☐ 81 Troy Archer | .15 | .07 | .02 |
| New York Giants | | | |
| ☐ 82 Bruce Harper | .15 | .07 | .02 |
| New York Jets | | | |
| ☐ 83 Tom Jackson | .75 | .35 | .09 |
| Denver Broncos | | | |
| ☐ 84 Larry Brown | .15 | .07 | .02 |
| Pittsburgh Steelers | | | |
| ☐ 85 Wilbert Montgomery AP | .75 | .35 | .09 |
| Philadelphia Eagles | | | |
| ☐ 86 Butch Johnson | .20 | .09 | .03 |
| Dallas Cowboys | | | |
| ☐ 87 Mike Kadish | .15 | .07 | .02 |
| Buffalo Bills | | | |
| ☐ 88 Ralph Perretta | .15 | .07 | .02 |
| San Diego Chargers | | | |
| ☐ 89 David Lee | .15 | .07 | .02 |
| Baltimore Colts | | | |
| ☐ 90 Mark Van Eeghen | .20 | .09 | .03 |

| | | | |
|---|---|---|---|
| Oakland Raiders | | | |
| ☐ 91 John McDaniel | .15 | .07 | .02 |
| Washington Redskins | | | |
| ☐ 92 Gary Fencik | .15 | .07 | .02 |
| Chicago Bears | | | |
| ☐ 93 Mack Mitchell | .15 | .07 | .02 |
| Cleveland Browns | | | |
| ☐ 94 Cincinnati Bengals TL | .50 | .08 | .02 |
| Pete Johnson | | | |
| Isaac Curtis | | | |
| Dick Jauron | | | |
| Ross Browner | | | |
| ☐ 95 Steve Grogan | .50 | .23 | .06 |
| New England Patriots | | | |
| ☐ 96 Garo Yepremian | .20 | .09 | .03 |
| Miami Dolphins | | | |
| ☐ 97 Barty Smith | .15 | .07 | .02 |
| Green Bay Packers | | | |
| ☐ 98 Frank Reed | .15 | .07 | .02 |
| Atlanta Falcons | | | |
| ☐ 99 Jim Clack | .15 | .07 | .02 |
| New York Giants | | | |
| ☐ 100 Chuck Foreman | .30 | .14 | .04 |
| Minnesota Vikings | | | |
| ☐ 101 Joe Klecko | .60 | .25 | .08 |
| New York Jets | | | |
| ☐ 102 Pat Tilley | .20 | .09 | .03 |
| St. Louis Cardinals | | | |
| ☐ 103 Conrad Dobler | .20 | .09 | .03 |
| New Orleans Saints | | | |
| ☐ 104 Craig Colquitt | .20 | .09 | .03 |
| Pittsburgh Steelers | | | |
| ☐ 105 Dan Pastorini | .20 | .09 | .03 |
| Houston Oilers | | | |
| ☐ 106 Rod Perry AP | .20 | .09 | .03 |
| Los Angeles Rams | | | |
| ☐ 107 Nick Mike-Mayer | .15 | .07 | .02 |
| Philadelphia Eagles | | | |
| ☐ 108 John Matuszak | .20 | .09 | .03 |
| Oakland Raiders | | | |
| ☐ 109 David Taylor | .15 | .07 | .02 |
| Baltimore Colts | | | |
| ☐ 110 Billy Joe DuPree AP | .20 | .09 | .03 |
| Dallas Cowboys | | | |
| ☐ 111 Harold McLinton | .15 | .07 | .02 |
| Washington Redskins | | | |
| ☐ 112 Virgil Livers | .15 | .07 | .02 |
| Chicago Bears | | | |
| ☐ 113 Cleveland Browns TL | .50 | .08 | .02 |
| Greg Pruitt | | | |
| Reggie Rucker | | | |
| Thom Darden | | | |
| Mack Mitchell | | | |
| ☐ 114 Checklist 1-132 | 1.00 | .10 | .03 |
| ☐ 115 Ken Anderson | 1.00 | .45 | .13 |
| Cincinnati Bengals | | | |
| ☐ 116 Bill Lenkaitis | .15 | .07 | .02 |
| New England Patriots | | | |
| ☐ 117 Bucky Dilts | .15 | .07 | .02 |
| Denver Broncos | | | |
| ☐ 118 Tony Greene | .15 | .07 | .02 |
| Buffalo Bills | | | |
| ☐ 119 Bobby Hammond | .15 | .07 | .02 |
| New York Giants | | | |
| ☐ 120 Nat Moore | .20 | .09 | .03 |
| Miami Dolphins | | | |
| ☐ 121 Pat Leahy AP | .30 | .14 | .04 |
| New York Jets | | | |
| ☐ 122 James Harris | .20 | .09 | .03 |
| San Diego Chargers | | | |
| ☐ 123 Lee Roy Selmon | .20 | .09 | .03 |
| Tampa Bay Buccaneers | | | |
| ☐ 124 Bennie Cunningham | .20 | .09 | .03 |
| Pittsburgh Steelers | | | |
| ☐ 125 Matt Blair AP | .20 | .09 | .03 |
| Minnesota Vikings | | | |
| ☐ 126 Jim Allen | .15 | .07 | .02 |
| Detroit Lions | | | |
| ☐ 127 Alfred Jenkins | .20 | .09 | .03 |
| Atlanta Falcons | | | |
| ☐ 128 Arthur Whittington | .20 | .09 | .03 |
| Oakland Raiders | | | |
| ☐ 129 Norm Thompson | .15 | .07 | .02 |
| Baltimore Colts | | | |
| ☐ 130 Pat Haden | .40 | .18 | .05 |
| Los Angeles Rams | | | |
| ☐ 131 Freddie Solomon | .20 | .09 | .03 |
| San Francisco 49ers | | | |
| ☐ 132 Chicago Bears TL | 2.00 | .30 | .02 |
| Walter Payton | | | |
| James Scott | | | |
| Gary Fencik | | | |
| Alan Page | | | |
| ☐ 133 Mark Moseley | .20 | .09 | .03 |
| Washington Redskins | | | |
| ☐ 134 Cleo Miller | .15 | .07 | .02 |
| Cleveland Browns | | | |
| ☐ 135 Ross Browner | .30 | .14 | .04 |
| Cincinnati Bengals | | | |
| ☐ 136 Don Calhoun | .15 | .07 | .02 |
| New England Patriots | | | |
| ☐ 137 David Whitehurst | .20 | .09 | .03 |
| Green Bay Packers | | | |
| ☐ 138 Terry Beeson | .15 | .07 | .02 |
| Seattle Seahawks | | | |
| ☐ 139 Ken Stone | .15 | .07 | .02 |
| St. Louis Cardinals | | | |
| ☐ 140 Brad Van Pelt AP | .20 | .09 | .03 |
| New York Giants | | | |
| ☐ 141 Wesley Walker AP | .75 | .35 | .09 |
| New York Jets | | | |
| ☐ 142 Jan Stenerud | .40 | .18 | .05 |
| Kansas City Chiefs | | | |
| ☐ 143 Henry Childs | .15 | .07 | .02 |
| New Orleans Saints | | | |
| ☐ 144 Otis Armstrong | .25 | .11 | .03 |
| Denver Broncos | | | |
| ☐ 145 Dwight White | .20 | .09 | .03 |
| Pittsburgh Steelers | | | |
| ☐ 146 Steve Wilson | .15 | .07 | .02 |
| Tampa Bay Buccaneers | | | |
| ☐ 147 Tom Skladany AP | .25 | .11 | .03 |
| Detroit Lions | | | |
| ☐ 148 Lou Piccone | .15 | .07 | .02 |
| Buffalo Bills | | | |
| ☐ 149 Monte Johnson | .15 | .07 | .02 |
| Oakland Raiders | | | |
| ☐ 150 Joe Washington | .15 | .07 | .02 |
| Baltimore Colts | | | |
| ☐ 151 Philadelphia Eagles TL | .60 | .09 | .02 |
| Wilbert Montgomery | | | |
| Harold Carmichael | | | |
| Herman Edwards | | | |
| Dennis Harrison | | | |
| ☐ 152 Fred Dean | .15 | .07 | .02 |
| San Diego Chargers | | | |
| ☐ 153 Rolland Lawrence | .20 | .09 | .03 |
| Atlanta Falcons | | | |
| ☐ 154 Brian Baschnagel | .15 | .07 | .02 |
| Chicago Bears | | | |
| ☐ 155 Joe Theismann | 1.75 | .80 | .22 |
| Washington Redskins | | | |
| ☐ 156 Marvin Cobb | .15 | .07 | .02 |
| Cincinnati Bengals | | | |
| ☐ 157 Dick Ambrose | .15 | .07 | .02 |
| Cleveland Browns | | | |
| ☐ 158 Mike Patrick | .15 | .07 | .02 |
| New England Patriots | | | |
| ☐ 159 Gary Shirk | .15 | .07 | .02 |
| New York Giants | | | |
| ☐ 160 Tony Dorsett | 8.00 | 3.60 | 1.00 |
| Dallas Cowboys | | | |
| ☐ 161 Greg Buttle | .20 | .09 | .03 |
| New York Jets | | | |
| ☐ 162 A.J. Duhe | .20 | .09 | .03 |
| Miami Dolphins | | | |
| ☐ 163 Mick Tingelhoff | .20 | .09 | .03 |
| Minnesota Vikings | | | |
| ☐ 164 Ken Burrough | .20 | .09 | .03 |
| Houston Oilers | | | |
| ☐ 165 Mike Wagner | .15 | .07 | .02 |
| Pittsburgh Steelers | | | |
| ☐ 166 AFC Championship | 1.00 | .45 | .13 |
| Steelers 34, | | | |
| Oilers 5 | | | |
| (Franco Harris) | | | |
| ☐ 167 NFC Championship | .35 | .16 | .04 |
| Cowboys 28, | | | |
| Rams 0 | | | |
| (line of scrimmage) | | | |
| ☐ 168 Super Bowl XIII | 1.25 | .55 | .16 |
| Steelers 35, | | | |
| Cowboys 31 | | | |
| (Franco Harris) | | | |
| ☐ 169 Oakland Raiders TL | .60 | .09 | .02 |
| Mark Van Eeghen | | | |
| Dave Casper | | | |
| Charles Phillips | | | |
| Ted Hendricks | | | |
| ☐ 170 O.J. Simpson | 8.00 | 3.60 | 1.00 |
| San Francisco 49ers | | | |
| ☐ 171 Doug Nettles | .15 | .07 | .02 |
| Baltimore Colts | | | |
| ☐ 172 Dan Dierdorf AP | .60 | .25 | .08 |
| St. Louis Cardinals | | | |
| ☐ 173 Dave Beverly | .15 | .07 | .02 |
| Green Bay Packers | | | |
| ☐ 174 Jim Zorn | .30 | .14 | .04 |
| Seattle Seahawks | | | |
| ☐ 175 Mike Thomas | .20 | .09 | .03 |
| Washington Redskins | | | |
| ☐ 176 John Outlaw | .15 | .07 | .02 |
| Philadelphia Eagles | | | |
| ☐ 177 Jim Turner | .20 | .09 | .03 |
| Denver Broncos | | | |
| ☐ 178 Freddie Scott | .15 | .07 | .02 |

Detroit Lions
| | | | |
|---|---|---|---|
| ☐ 179 Mike Phipps | .20 | .09 | .03 |

Chicago Bears
| | | | |
|---|---|---|---|
| ☐ 180 Jack Youngblood AP | .50 | .23 | .06 |

Los Angeles Rams
| | | | |
|---|---|---|---|
| ☐ 181 Sam Hunt | .15 | .07 | .02 |

New England Patriots
| | | | |
|---|---|---|---|
| ☐ 182 Tony Hill | 1.25 | .55 | .16 |

Dallas Cowboys
| | | | |
|---|---|---|---|
| ☐ 183 Gary Barbaro | .20 | .09 | .03 |

Kansas City Chiefs
| | | | |
|---|---|---|---|
| ☐ 184 Archie Griffin | .40 | .18 | .05 |

Cincinnati Bengals
| | | | |
|---|---|---|---|
| ☐ 185 Jerry Sherk | .20 | .09 | .03 |

Cleveland Browns
| | | | |
|---|---|---|---|
| ☐ 186 Bobby Jackson | .15 | .07 | .02 |

New York Jets
| | | | |
|---|---|---|---|
| ☐ 187 Don Woods | .15 | .07 | .02 |

San Diego Chargers
| | | | |
|---|---|---|---|
| ☐ 188 New York Giants TL | .50 | .08 | .02 |

Doug Kotar
Jimmy Robinson
Terry Jackson
George Martin
| | | | |
|---|---|---|---|
| ☐ 189 Raymond Chester | .20 | .09 | .03 |

Oakland Raiders
| | | | |
|---|---|---|---|
| ☐ 190 Joe DeLamielleure AP | .20 | .09 | .03 |

Buffalo Bills
| | | | |
|---|---|---|---|
| ☐ 191 Tony Galbreath | .20 | .09 | .03 |

New Orleans Saints
| | | | |
|---|---|---|---|
| ☐ 192 Robert Brazile AP | .20 | .09 | .03 |

Houston Oilers
| | | | |
|---|---|---|---|
| ☐ 193 Neil O'Donoghue | .15 | .07 | .02 |

Tampa Bay Buccaneers
| | | | |
|---|---|---|---|
| ☐ 194 Mike Webster AP | .75 | .35 | .09 |

Pittsburgh Steelers
| | | | |
|---|---|---|---|
| ☐ 195 Ed Simonini | .15 | .07 | .02 |

Baltimore Colts
| | | | |
|---|---|---|---|
| ☐ 196 Benny Malone | .20 | .09 | .03 |

Washington Redskins
| | | | |
|---|---|---|---|
| ☐ 197 Tom Wittum | .15 | .07 | .02 |

San Francisco 49ers
| | | | |
|---|---|---|---|
| ☐ 198 Steve Largent AP | 7.00 | 3.10 | .85 |

Seattle Seahawks
| | | | |
|---|---|---|---|
| ☐ 199 Tommy Hart | .15 | .07 | .02 |

Chicago Bears
| | | | |
|---|---|---|---|
| ☐ 200 Fran Tarkenton | 3.50 | 1.55 | .45 |

Minnesota Vikings
| | | | |
|---|---|---|---|
| ☐ 201 Leon Gray AP | .20 | .09 | .03 |

New England Patriots
| | | | |
|---|---|---|---|
| ☐ 202 Leroy Harris | .20 | .09 | .03 |

Miami Dolphins
| | | | |
|---|---|---|---|
| ☐ 203 Eric Williams | .15 | .07 | .02 |

St. Louis Cardinals
| | | | |
|---|---|---|---|
| ☐ 204 Thom Darden AP | .15 | .07 | .02 |

Cleveland Browns
| | | | |
|---|---|---|---|
| ☐ 205 Ken Riley | .20 | .09 | .03 |

Cincinnati Bengals
| | | | |
|---|---|---|---|
| ☐ 206 Clark Gaines | .15 | .07 | .02 |

New York Jets
| | | | |
|---|---|---|---|
| ☐ 207 Kansas City Chiefs TL | .50 | .08 | .02 |

Tony Reed
Tony Reed
Tim Gray
Art Still
| | | | |
|---|---|---|---|
| ☐ 208 Joe Danelo | .15 | .07 | .02 |

New York Giants
| | | | |
|---|---|---|---|
| ☐ 209 Glen Walker | .15 | .07 | .02 |

Los Angeles Rams
| | | | |
|---|---|---|---|
| ☐ 210 Art Shell | 1.00 | .45 | .13 |

Oakland Raiders
| | | | |
|---|---|---|---|
| ☐ 211 Jon Keyworth | .20 | .09 | .03 |

Denver Broncos
| | | | |
|---|---|---|---|
| ☐ 212 Herman Edwards | .15 | .07 | .02 |

Philadelphia Eagles
| | | | |
|---|---|---|---|
| ☐ 213 John Fitzgerald | .15 | .07 | .02 |

Dallas Cowboys
| | | | |
|---|---|---|---|
| ☐ 214 Jim Smith | .20 | .09 | .03 |

Pittsburgh Steelers
| | | | |
|---|---|---|---|
| ☐ 215 Coy Bacon | .20 | .09 | .03 |

Washington Redskins
| | | | |
|---|---|---|---|
| ☐ 216 Dennis Johnson | .15 | .07 | .02 |

Buffalo Bills
| | | | |
|---|---|---|---|
| ☐ 217 John Jefferson | 3.00 | 1.35 | .40 |

(Charlie Joiner
in background)
San Diego Chargers
| | | | |
|---|---|---|---|
| ☐ 218 Gary Weaver | .15 | .07 | .02 |

Green Bay Packers
| | | | |
|---|---|---|---|
| ☐ 219 Tom Blanchard | .15 | .07 | .02 |

New Orleans Saints
| | | | |
|---|---|---|---|
| ☐ 220 Bert Jones | .50 | .23 | .06 |

Baltimore Colts
| | | | |
|---|---|---|---|
| ☐ 221 Stanley Morgan | 1.75 | .80 | .22 |

New England Patriots
| | | | |
|---|---|---|---|
| ☐ 222 James Hunter | .15 | .07 | .02 |

Detroit Lions
| | | | |
|---|---|---|---|
| ☐ 223 Jim O'Bradovich | .15 | .07 | .02 |

Tampa Bay Buccaneers
| | | | |
|---|---|---|---|
| ☐ 224 Carl Mauck | .15 | .07 | .02 |

Houston Oilers
| | | | |
|---|---|---|---|
| ☐ 225 Chris Bahr | .15 | .07 | .02 |

Cincinnati Bengals
| | | | |
|---|---|---|---|
| ☐ 226 New York Jets TL | .60 | .25 | .08 |

Kevin Long
Wesley Walker
Bobby Jackson
Burgess Owens
Joe Klecko
| | | | |
|---|---|---|---|
| ☐ 227 Roland Harper | .20 | .09 | .03 |

Chicago Bears
| | | | |
|---|---|---|---|
| ☐ 228 Randy Dean | .15 | .07 | .02 |

New York Giants
| | | | |
|---|---|---|---|
| ☐ 229 Bob Jackson | .15 | .07 | .02 |

Cleveland Browns
| | | | |
|---|---|---|---|
| ☐ 230 Sammie White | .20 | .09 | .03 |

Minnesota Vikings
| | | | |
|---|---|---|---|
| ☐ 231 Mike Dawson | .15 | .07 | .02 |

St. Louis Cardinals
| | | | |
|---|---|---|---|
| ☐ 232 Checklist 133-264 | 1.00 | .10 | .03 |
| ☐ 233 Ken MacAfee | .20 | .09 | .03 |

San Francisco 49ers
| | | | |
|---|---|---|---|
| ☐ 234 Jon Kolb AP | .20 | .09 | .03 |

Pittsburgh Steelers
| | | | |
|---|---|---|---|
| ☐ 235 Willie Hall | .15 | .07 | .02 |

Oakland Raiders
| | | | |
|---|---|---|---|
| ☐ 236 Ron Saul AP | .15 | .07 | .02 |

Washington Redskins
| | | | |
|---|---|---|---|
| ☐ 237 Haskel Stanback | .15 | .07 | .02 |

Atlanta Falcons
| | | | |
|---|---|---|---|
| ☐ 238 Zenon Andrusyshyn | .15 | .07 | .02 |

Kansas City Chiefs
| | | | |
|---|---|---|---|
| ☐ 239 Norris Thomas | .15 | .07 | .02 |

Miami Dolphins
| | | | |
|---|---|---|---|
| ☐ 240 Rick Upchurch | .30 | .14 | .04 |

Denver Broncos
| | | | |
|---|---|---|---|
| ☐ 241 Robert Pratt | .15 | .07 | .02 |

Baltimore Colts
| | | | |
|---|---|---|---|
| ☐ 242 Julius Adams | .15 | .07 | .02 |

New England Patriots
| | | | |
|---|---|---|---|
| ☐ 243 Rich McGeorge | .15 | .07 | .02 |

Green Bay Packers
| | | | |
|---|---|---|---|
| ☐ 244 Seattle Seahawks TL | 1.00 | .15 | .02 |

Sherman Smith
Steve Largent
Cornell Webster
Bill Gregory
| | | | |
|---|---|---|---|
| ☐ 245 Blair Bush | .15 | .07 | .02 |

Cincinnati Bengals
| | | | |
|---|---|---|---|
| ☐ 246 Billy Johnson | .20 | .09 | .03 |

Houston Oilers
| | | | |
|---|---|---|---|
| ☐ 247 Randy Rasmussen | .15 | .07 | .02 |

New York Jets
| | | | |
|---|---|---|---|
| ☐ 248 Brian Kelley | .15 | .07 | .02 |

New York Giants
| | | | |
|---|---|---|---|
| ☐ 249 Mike Pruitt | .20 | .09 | .03 |

Cleveland Browns
| | | | |
|---|---|---|---|
| ☐ 250 Harold Carmichael AP | .60 | .25 | .08 |

Philadelphia Eagles
| | | | |
|---|---|---|---|
| ☐ 251 Mike Hartenstine | .15 | .07 | .02 |

Chicago Bears
| | | | |
|---|---|---|---|
| ☐ 252 Robert Newhouse | .20 | .09 | .03 |

Dallas Cowboys
| | | | |
|---|---|---|---|
| ☐ 253 Gary Danielson | .25 | .11 | .03 |

Detroit Lions
| | | | |
|---|---|---|---|
| ☐ 254 Mike Fuller | .15 | .07 | .02 |

San Diego Chargers
| | | | |
|---|---|---|---|
| ☐ 255 L.C. Greenwood AP | .40 | .18 | .05 |

Pittsburgh Steelers
| | | | |
|---|---|---|---|
| ☐ 256 Lemar Parrish | .20 | .09 | .03 |

Washington Redskins
| | | | |
|---|---|---|---|
| ☐ 257 Ike Harris | .15 | .07 | .02 |

New Orleans Saints
| | | | |
|---|---|---|---|
| ☐ 258 Ricky Bell | 1.25 | .55 | .16 |

Tampa Bay Buccaneers
| | | | |
|---|---|---|---|
| ☐ 259 Willie Parker | .15 | .07 | .02 |

Buffalo Bills
| | | | |
|---|---|---|---|
| ☐ 260 Gene Upshaw | .30 | .14 | .04 |

Oakland Raiders
| | | | |
|---|---|---|---|
| ☐ 261 Glenn Doughty | .15 | .07 | .02 |

Baltimore Colts
| | | | |
|---|---|---|---|
| ☐ 262 Steve Zabel | .15 | .07 | .02 |

New England Patriots
| | | | |
|---|---|---|---|
| ☐ 263 Atlanta Falcons TL | .50 | .08 | .02 |

Bubba Bean
Wallace Francis
Rolland Lawrence
Greg Brezina
| | | | |
|---|---|---|---|
| ☐ 264 Ray Wersching | .20 | .09 | .03 |

San Francisco 49ers
| | | | |
|---|---|---|---|
| ☐ 265 Lawrence McCutcheon | .20 | .09 | .03 |

Los Angeles Rams
| | | | |
|---|---|---|---|
| ☐ 266 Willie Buchanon AP | .20 | .09 | .03 |

Green Bay Packers
| | | | |
|---|---|---|---|
| ☐ 267 Matt Robinson | .20 | .09 | .03 |

New York Jets

| | | | |
|---|---|---|---|
| ☐ 268 Reggie Rucker | .20 | .09 | .03 |
| Cleveland Browns | | | |
| ☐ 269 Doug Van Horn | .15 | .07 | .02 |
| New York Giants | | | |
| ☐ 270 Lydell Mitchell | .20 | .09 | .03 |
| San Diego Chargers | | | |
| ☐ 271 Vern Holland | .15 | .07 | .02 |
| Cincinnati Bengals | | | |
| ☐ 272 Eason Ramson | .15 | .07 | .02 |
| St. Louis Cardinals | | | |
| ☐ 273 Steve Towle | .20 | .09 | .03 |
| Miami Dolphins | | | |
| ☐ 274 Jim Marshall | .30 | .14 | .04 |
| Minnesota Vikings | | | |
| ☐ 275 Mel Blount | 1.00 | .45 | .13 |
| Pittsburgh Steelers | | | |
| ☐ 276 Bob Kuziel | .15 | .07 | .02 |
| Washington Redskins | | | |
| ☐ 277 James Scott | .15 | .07 | .02 |
| Chicago Bears | | | |
| ☐ 278 Tony Reed | .20 | .09 | .03 |
| Kansas City Chiefs | | | |
| ☐ 279 Dave Green | .15 | .07 | .02 |
| Tampa Bay Buccaneers | | | |
| ☐ 280 Toni Linhart | .15 | .07 | .02 |
| Baltimore Colts | | | |
| ☐ 281 Andy Johnson | .15 | .07 | .02 |
| New England Patriots | | | |
| ☐ 282 Los Angeles Rams TL | .50 | .08 | .02 |
| Cullen Bryant | | | |
| Willie Miller | | | |
| Rod Perry | | | |
| Pat Thomas | | | |
| Larry Brooks | | | |
| ☐ 283 Phil Villapiano | .20 | .09 | .03 |
| Oakland Raiders | | | |
| ☐ 284 Dexter Bussey | .15 | .07 | .02 |
| Detroit Lions | | | |
| ☐ 285 Craig Morton | .35 | .16 | .04 |
| Denver Broncos | | | |
| ☐ 286 Guy Morriss | .15 | .07 | .02 |
| Philadelphia Eagles | | | |
| ☐ 287 Lawrence Pillers | .15 | .07 | .02 |
| New York Jets | | | |
| ☐ 288 Gerald Irons | .15 | .07 | .02 |
| Cleveland Browns | | | |
| ☐ 289 Scott Perry | .15 | .07 | .02 |
| Cincinnati Bengals | | | |
| ☐ 290 Randy White AP | 2.00 | .90 | .25 |
| Dallas Cowboys | | | |
| ☐ 291 Jack Gregory | .15 | .07 | .02 |
| New York Giants | | | |
| ☐ 292 Bob Chandler | .20 | .09 | .03 |
| Buffalo Bills | | | |
| ☐ 293 Rich Szaro | .15 | .07 | .02 |
| New Orleans Saints | | | |
| ☐ 294 Sherman Smith | .15 | .07 | .02 |
| Seattle Seahawks | | | |
| ☐ 295 Tom Banks AP | .20 | .09 | .03 |
| St. Louis Cardinals | | | |
| ☐ 296 Revie Sorey AP | .15 | .07 | .02 |
| Chicago Bears | | | |
| ☐ 297 Ricky Thompson | .15 | .07 | .02 |
| Washington Redskins | | | |
| ☐ 298 Ron Yary | .20 | .09 | .03 |
| Minnesota Vikings | | | |
| ☐ 299 Lyle Blackwood | .20 | .09 | .03 |
| Baltimore Colts | | | |
| ☐ 300 Franco Harris | 2.00 | .90 | .25 |
| Pittsburgh Steelers | | | |
| ☐ 301 Houston Oilers TL | 3.00 | .45 | .03 |
| Earl Campbell | | | |
| Ken Burrough | | | |
| Willie Alexander | | | |
| Elvin Bethea | | | |
| ☐ 302 Scott Bull | .15 | .07 | .02 |
| San Francisco 49ers | | | |
| ☐ 303 Dewey Selmon | .20 | .09 | .03 |
| Tampa Bay Buccaneers | | | |
| ☐ 304 Jack Rudnay | .15 | .07 | .02 |
| Kansas City Chiefs | | | |
| ☐ 305 Fred Biletnikoff | 1.25 | .55 | .16 |
| Oakland Raiders | | | |
| ☐ 306 Jeff West | .15 | .07 | .02 |
| San Diego Chargers | | | |
| ☐ 307 Shafer Suggs | .15 | .07 | .02 |
| New York Jets | | | |
| ☐ 308 Ozzie Newsome | 20.00 | 9.00 | 2.50 |
| Cleveland Browns | | | |
| ☐ 309 Boobie Clark | .20 | .09 | .03 |
| Cincinnati Bengals | | | |
| ☐ 310 James Lofton | 25.00 | 11.50 | 3.10 |
| Green Bay Packers | | | |
| ☐ 311 Joe Pisarcik | .20 | .09 | .03 |
| New York Giants | | | |
| ☐ 312 Bill Simpson AP | .15 | .07 | .02 |
| Los Angeles Rams | | | |

| | | | |
|---|---|---|---|
| ☐ 313 Haven Moses | .20 | .09 | .03 |
| Denver Broncos | | | |
| ☐ 314 Jim Merlo | .15 | .07 | .02 |
| New Orleans Saints | | | |
| ☐ 315 Preston Pearson | .20 | .09 | .03 |
| Dallas Cowboys | | | |
| ☐ 316 Larry Tearry | .15 | .07 | .02 |
| Detroit Lions | | | |
| ☐ 317 Tom Dempsey | .20 | .09 | .03 |
| Buffalo Bills | | | |
| ☐ 318 Greg Latta | .15 | .07 | .02 |
| Chicago Bears | | | |
| ☐ 319 Wash. Redskins TL | .75 | .11 | .03 |
| John Riggins | | | |
| John McDaniel | | | |
| Jake Scott | | | |
| Coy Bacon | | | |
| ☐ 320 Jack Ham AP | 1.25 | .55 | .16 |
| Pittsburgh Steelers | | | |
| ☐ 321 Harold Jackson | .30 | .14 | .04 |
| New England Patriots | | | |
| ☐ 322 George Roberts | .15 | .07 | .02 |
| Miami Dolphins | | | |
| ☐ 323 Ron Jaworski | .40 | .18 | .05 |
| Philadelphia Eagles | | | |
| ☐ 324 Jim Otis | .20 | .09 | .03 |
| St. Louis Cardinals | | | |
| ☐ 325 Roger Carr | .20 | .09 | .03 |
| Baltimore Colts | | | |
| ☐ 326 Jack Tatum | .20 | .09 | .03 |
| Oakland Raiders | | | |
| ☐ 327 Derrick Gaffney | .15 | .07 | .02 |
| New York Jets | | | |
| ☐ 328 Reggie Williams | .50 | .23 | .06 |
| Cincinnati Bengals | | | |
| ☐ 329 Doug Dieken | .15 | .07 | .02 |
| Cleveland Browns | | | |
| ☐ 330 Efren Herrera | .15 | .07 | .02 |
| Seattle Seahawks | | | |
| ☐ 331 Earl Campbell RB | 6.00 | 2.70 | .75 |
| Most Yards | | | |
| Rushing, Rookie | | | |
| ☐ 332 Tony Galbreath RB | .30 | .14 | .04 |
| Most Receptions, | | | |
| Running Back, Game | | | |
| ☐ 333 Bruce Harper RB | .30 | .14 | .04 |
| Most Combined Kick | | | |
| Return Yards, Season | | | |
| ☐ 334 John James RB | .30 | .14 | .04 |
| Most Punts, Season | | | |
| ☐ 335 Walter Payton RB | 4.00 | 1.80 | .50 |
| Most Combined | | | |
| Attempts, Season | | | |
| ☐ 336 Rickey Young RB | .30 | .14 | .04 |
| Most Receptions, | | | |
| Running Back, Season | | | |
| ☐ 337 Jeff Van Note | .20 | .09 | .03 |
| Atlanta Falcons | | | |
| ☐ 338 San Diego Chargers TL | .60 | .09 | .02 |
| Lydell Mitchell | | | |
| John Jefferson | | | |
| Mike Fuller | | | |
| Fred Dean | | | |
| ☐ 339 Stan Walters AP | .15 | .07 | .02 |
| Philadelphia Eagles | | | |
| ☐ 340 Louis Wright AP | .15 | .07 | .02 |
| Denver Broncos | | | |
| ☐ 341 Horace Ivory | .15 | .07 | .02 |
| New England Patriots | | | |
| ☐ 342 Andre Tillman | .15 | .07 | .02 |
| Miami Dolphins | | | |
| ☐ 343 Greg Coleman | .15 | .07 | .02 |
| Minnesota Vikings | | | |
| ☐ 344 Doug English AP | .50 | .23 | .06 |
| Detroit Lions | | | |
| ☐ 345 Ted Hendricks | .50 | .23 | .06 |
| Oakland Raiders | | | |
| ☐ 346 Rich Saul | .15 | .07 | .02 |
| Los Angeles Rams | | | |
| ☐ 347 Mel Gray | .20 | .09 | .03 |
| St. Louis Cardinals | | | |
| ☐ 348 Toni Fritsch | .15 | .07 | .02 |
| Houston Oilers | | | |
| ☐ 349 Cornell Webster | .15 | .07 | .02 |
| Seattle Seahawks | | | |
| ☐ 350 Ken Houston | .50 | .23 | .06 |
| Washington Redskins | | | |
| ☐ 351 Ron Johnson | .20 | .09 | .03 |
| Pittsburgh Steelers | | | |
| ☐ 352 Doug Kotar | .15 | .07 | .02 |
| New York Giants | | | |
| ☐ 353 Brian Sipe | .40 | .18 | .05 |
| Cleveland Browns | | | |
| ☐ 354 Billy Brooks | .20 | .09 | .03 |
| Cincinnati Bengals | | | |
| ☐ 355 John Dutton | .20 | .09 | .03 |
| Baltimore Colts | | | |

| Card | Price | | |
|---|---|---|---|
| ☐ 356 Don Goode | .15 | .07 | .02 |
| San Diego Chargers | | | |
| ☐ 357 Detroit Lions TL | .50 | .08 | .02 |
| Dexter Bussey | | | |
| David Hill | | | |
| Jim Allen | | | |
| Al(Bubba) Baker | | | |
| ☐ 358 Reuben Gant | .15 | .07 | .02 |
| Buffalo Bills | | | |
| ☐ 359 Bob Parsons | .15 | .07 | .02 |
| Chicago Bears | | | |
| ☐ 360 Cliff Harris AP | .40 | .18 | .05 |
| Dallas Cowboys | | | |
| ☐ 361 Raymond Clayborn | .15 | .07 | .02 |
| New England Patriots | | | |
| ☐ 362 Scott Dierking | .15 | .07 | .02 |
| New York Jets | | | |
| ☐ 363 Bill Bryan | .15 | .07 | .02 |
| Denver Broncos | | | |
| ☐ 364 Mike Livingston | .20 | .09 | .03 |
| Kansas City Chiefs | | | |
| ☐ 365 Otis Sistrunk | .20 | .09 | .03 |
| Oakland Raiders | | | |
| ☐ 366 Charley Young | .20 | .09 | .03 |
| Los Angeles Rams | | | |
| ☐ 367 Keith Wortman | .15 | .07 | .02 |
| St. Louis Cardinals | | | |
| ☐ 368 Checklist 265-396 | 1.00 | .10 | .03 |
| ☐ 369 Mike Michel | .15 | .07 | .02 |
| Philadelphia Eagles | | | |
| ☐ 370 Delvin Williams AP | .20 | .09 | .03 |
| Miami Dolphins | | | |
| ☐ 371 Steve Furness | .20 | .09 | .03 |
| Pittsburgh Steelers | | | |
| ☐ 372 Emery Moorehead | .15 | .07 | .02 |
| New York Giants | | | |
| ☐ 373 Clarence Scott | .15 | .07 | .02 |
| Cleveland Browns | | | |
| ☐ 374 Rufus Mayes | .15 | .07 | .02 |
| Cincinnati Bengals | | | |
| ☐ 375 Chris Hanburger | .20 | .09 | .03 |
| Washington Redskins | | | |
| ☐ 376 Baltimore Colts TL | .50 | .08 | .02 |
| Joe Washington | | | |
| Roger Carr | | | |
| Norm Thompson | | | |
| John Dutton | | | |
| ☐ 377 Bob Avellini | .20 | .09 | .03 |
| Chicago Bears | | | |
| ☐ 378 Jeff Siemon | .15 | .07 | .02 |
| Minnesota Vikings | | | |
| ☐ 379 Roland Hooks | .15 | .07 | .02 |
| Buffalo Bills | | | |
| ☐ 380 Russ Francis | .20 | .09 | .03 |
| New England Patriots | | | |
| ☐ 381 Roger Wehrli | .20 | .09 | .03 |
| St. Louis Cardinals | | | |
| ☐ 382 Joe Fields | .20 | .09 | .03 |
| New York Jets | | | |
| ☐ 383 Archie Manning | .50 | .23 | .06 |
| New Orleans Saints | | | |
| ☐ 384 Rob Lytle | .20 | .09 | .03 |
| Denver Broncos | | | |
| ☐ 385 Thomas Henderson | .20 | .09 | .03 |
| Dallas Cowboys | | | |
| ☐ 386 Morris Owens | .15 | .07 | .02 |
| Tampa Bay Buccaneers | | | |
| ☐ 387 Dan Fouts | 4.00 | 1.80 | .50 |
| San Diego Chargers | | | |
| ☐ 388 Chuck Crist | .15 | .07 | .02 |
| San Francisco 49ers | | | |
| ☐ 389 Ed O'Neil | .15 | .07 | .02 |
| Detroit Lions | | | |
| ☐ 390 Earl Campbell AP | 32.00 | 14.50 | 4.00 |
| Houston Oilers | | | |
| ☐ 391 Randy Grossman | .20 | .09 | .03 |
| Pittsburgh Steelers | | | |
| ☐ 392 Monte Jackson | .20 | .09 | .03 |
| Oakland Raiders | | | |
| ☐ 393 John Mendenhall | .15 | .07 | .02 |
| New York Giants | | | |
| ☐ 394 Miami Dolphins TL | .50 | .08 | .02 |
| Delvin Williams | | | |
| Duriel Harris | | | |
| Tim Foley | | | |
| Vern Den Herder | | | |
| ☐ 395 Isaac Curtis | .20 | .09 | .03 |
| Cincinnati Bengals | | | |
| ☐ 396 Mike Bragg | .15 | .07 | .02 |
| Washington Redskins | | | |
| ☐ 397 Doug Plank | .15 | .07 | .02 |
| Chicago Bears | | | |
| ☐ 398 Mike Barnes | .15 | .07 | .02 |
| Baltimore Colts | | | |
| ☐ 399 Calvin Hill | .20 | .09 | .03 |
| Cleveland Browns | | | |
| ☐ 400 Roger Staubach AP | 7.00 | 3.10 | .85 |
| Dallas Cowboys | | | |
| ☐ 401 Doug Beaudoin | .15 | .07 | .02 |
| New England Patriots | | | |
| ☐ 402 Chuck Ramsey | .15 | .07 | .02 |
| New York Jets | | | |
| ☐ 403 Mike Hogan | .15 | .07 | .02 |
| Philadelphia Eagles | | | |
| ☐ 404 Mario Clark | .15 | .07 | .02 |
| Buffalo Bills | | | |
| ☐ 405 Riley Odoms | .20 | .09 | .03 |
| Denver Broncos | | | |
| ☐ 406 Carl Eller | .30 | .14 | .04 |
| Minnesota Vikings | | | |
| ☐ 407 Green Bay Packers TL | 3.00 | .45 | .03 |
| Terdell Middleton | | | |
| James Lofton | | | |
| Willie Buchanon | | | |
| Ezra Johnson | | | |
| ☐ 408 Mark Arneson | .15 | .07 | .02 |
| St. Louis Cardinals | | | |
| ☐ 409 Vince Ferragamo | .60 | .25 | .08 |
| Los Angeles Rams | | | |
| ☐ 410 Cleveland Elam | .15 | .07 | .02 |
| San Francisco 49ers | | | |
| ☐ 411 Donnie Shell | 3.00 | 1.35 | .40 |
| Pittsburgh Steelers | | | |
| ☐ 412 Ray Rhodes | .15 | .07 | .02 |
| New York Giants | | | |
| ☐ 413 Don Cockroft | .20 | .09 | .03 |
| Cleveland Browns | | | |
| ☐ 414 Don Bass | .20 | .09 | .03 |
| Cincinnati Bengals | | | |
| ☐ 415 Cliff Branch | .75 | .35 | .09 |
| Oakland Raiders | | | |
| ☐ 416 Diron Talbert | .20 | .09 | .03 |
| Washington Redskins | | | |
| ☐ 417 Tom Hicks | .15 | .07 | .02 |
| Chicago Bears | | | |
| ☐ 418 Roosevelt Leaks | .20 | .09 | .03 |
| Baltimore Colts | | | |
| ☐ 419 Charlie Joiner | .75 | .35 | .09 |
| San Diego Chargers | | | |
| ☐ 420 Lyle Alzado AP | .50 | .23 | .06 |
| Denver Broncos | | | |
| ☐ 421 Sam Cunningham | .20 | .09 | .03 |
| New England Patriots | | | |
| ☐ 422 Larry Keller | .15 | .07 | .02 |
| New York Jets | | | |
| ☐ 423 Jim Mitchell | .15 | .07 | .02 |
| Atlanta Falcons | | | |
| ☐ 424 Randy Logan | .15 | .07 | .02 |
| Philadelphia Eagles | | | |
| ☐ 425 Jim Langer | .30 | .14 | .04 |
| Miami Dolphins | | | |
| ☐ 426 Gary Green | .15 | .07 | .02 |
| Kansas City Chiefs | | | |
| ☐ 427 Luther Blue | .15 | .07 | .02 |
| Detroit Lions | | | |
| ☐ 428 Dennis Johnson | .15 | .07 | .02 |
| Buffalo Bills | | | |
| ☐ 429 Danny White | .75 | .35 | .09 |
| Dallas Cowboys | | | |
| ☐ 430 Roy Gerela | .20 | .09 | .03 |
| Pittsburgh Steelers | | | |
| ☐ 431 Jimmy Robinson | .15 | .07 | .02 |
| New York Giants | | | |
| ☐ 432 Minnesota Vikings TL | .60 | .09 | .02 |
| Chuck Foreman | | | |
| Ahmad Rashad | | | |
| Bobby Bryant | | | |
| Mark Mullaney | | | |
| ☐ 433 Oliver Davis | .15 | .07 | .02 |
| Cleveland Browns | | | |
| ☐ 434 Lenvil Elliott | .15 | .07 | .02 |
| Cincinnati Bengals | | | |
| ☐ 435 Willie Miller | .20 | .09 | .03 |
| Los Angeles Rams | | | |
| ☐ 436 Brad Dusek | .20 | .09 | .03 |
| Washington Redskins | | | |
| ☐ 437 Bob Thomas | .15 | .07 | .02 |
| Chicago Bears | | | |
| ☐ 438 Ken Mendenhall | .15 | .07 | .02 |
| Baltimore Colts | | | |
| ☐ 439 Clarence Davis | .15 | .07 | .02 |
| Oakland Raiders | | | |
| ☐ 440 Bob Griese | 2.25 | 1.00 | .30 |
| Miami Dolphins | | | |
| ☐ 441 Tony McGee | .15 | .07 | .02 |
| New England Patriots | | | |
| ☐ 442 Ed Taylor | .15 | .07 | .02 |
| New York Jets | | | |
| ☐ 443 Ron Howard | .15 | .07 | .02 |
| Seattle Seahawks | | | |
| ☐ 444 Wayne Morris | .15 | .07 | .02 |
| St. Louis Cardinals | | | |
| ☐ 445 Charlie Waters | .40 | .18 | .05 |
| Dallas Cowboys | | | |
| ☐ 446 Rick Danmeier | .15 | .07 | .02 |

| | | | |
|---|---|---|---|
| Minnesota Vikings | | | |
| ☐ 447 Paul Naumoff | .15 | .07 | .02 |
| Detroit Lions | | | |
| ☐ 448 Keith Krepfle | .15 | .07 | .02 |
| Philadelphia Eagles | | | |
| ☐ 449 Rusty Jackson | .15 | .07 | .02 |
| Buffalo Bills | | | |
| ☐ 450 John Stallworth | 3.00 | 1.35 | .40 |
| Pittsburgh Steelers | | | |
| ☐ 451 New Orleans Saints TL | .50 | .08 | .02 |
| Tony Galbreath | | | |
| Henry Childs | | | |
| Tom Myers | | | |
| Elex Price | | | |
| ☐ 452 Ron Mikolajczyk | .15 | .07 | .02 |
| New York Giants | | | |
| ☐ 453 Fred Dryer | .50 | .23 | .06 |
| Los Angeles Rams | | | |
| ☐ 454 Jim LeClair | .15 | .07 | .02 |
| Cincinnati Bengals | | | |
| ☐ 455 Greg Pruitt | .25 | .11 | .03 |
| Cleveland Browns | | | |
| ☐ 456 Jake Scott | .20 | .09 | .03 |
| Washington Redskins | | | |
| ☐ 457 Steve Schubert | .15 | .07 | .02 |
| Chicago Bears | | | |
| ☐ 458 George Kunz | .20 | .09 | .03 |
| Baltimore Colts | | | |
| ☐ 459 Mike Williams | .15 | .07 | .02 |
| San Diego Chargers | | | |
| ☐ 460 Dave Casper AP | .20 | .09 | .03 |
| Oakland Raiders | | | |
| ☐ 461 Sam Adams | .15 | .07 | .02 |
| New England Patriots | | | |
| ☐ 462 Abdul Salaam | .15 | .07 | .02 |
| New York Jets | | | |
| ☐ 463 Terdell Middleton | .20 | .09 | .03 |
| Green Bay Packers | | | |
| ☐ 464 Mike Wood | .15 | .07 | .02 |
| St. Louis Cardinals | | | |
| ☐ 465 Bill Thompson AP | .20 | .09 | .03 |
| Denver Broncos | | | |
| ☐ 466 Larry Gordon | .15 | .07 | .02 |
| Miami Dolphins | | | |
| ☐ 467 Benny Ricardo | .15 | .07 | .02 |
| Detroit Lions | | | |
| ☐ 468 Reggie McKenzie | .20 | .09 | .03 |
| Buffalo Bills | | | |
| ☐ 469 Dallas Cowboys TL | 1.00 | .15 | .02 |
| Tony Dorsett | | | |
| Tony Hill | | | |
| Benny Barnes | | | |
| Harvey Martin | | | |
| Randy White | | | |
| ☐ 470 Rickey Young | .20 | .09 | .03 |
| Minnesota Vikings | | | |
| ☐ 471 Charlie Smith | .15 | .07 | .02 |
| Philadelphia Eagles | | | |
| ☐ 472 Al Dixon | .15 | .07 | .02 |
| New York Giants | | | |
| ☐ 473 Tom DeLeone | .15 | .07 | .02 |
| Cleveland Browns | | | |
| ☐ 474 Louis Breeden | .15 | .07 | .02 |
| Cincinnati Bengals | | | |
| ☐ 475 Jack Lambert | 2.00 | .90 | .25 |
| Pittsburgh Steelers | | | |
| ☐ 476 Terry Hermeling | .15 | .07 | .02 |
| Washington Redskins | | | |
| ☐ 477 J.K. McKay | .20 | .09 | .03 |
| Tampa Bay Buccaneers | | | |
| ☐ 478 Stan White | .15 | .07 | .02 |
| Baltimore Colts | | | |
| ☐ 479 Terry Nelson | .15 | .07 | .02 |
| Los Angeles Rams | | | |
| ☐ 480 Walter Payton AP | 12.00 | 5.50 | 1.50 |
| Chicago Bears | | | |
| ☐ 481 Dave Dalby | .15 | .07 | .02 |
| Oakland Raiders | | | |
| ☐ 482 Burgess Owens | .15 | .07 | .02 |
| New York Jets | | | |
| ☐ 483 Rolf Benirschke | .20 | .09 | .03 |
| San Diego Chargers | | | |
| ☐ 484 Jack Dolbin | .15 | .07 | .02 |
| Denver Broncos | | | |
| ☐ 485 John Hannah AP | .60 | .25 | .08 |
| New England Patriots | | | |
| ☐ 486 Checklist 397-528 | 1.00 | .10 | .03 |
| ☐ 487 Greg Landry | .25 | .11 | .03 |
| Detroit Lions | | | |
| ☐ 488 St. Louis Cardinals TL | .50 | .08 | .02 |
| Jim Otis | | | |
| Pat Tilley | | | |
| Ken Stone | | | |
| Mike Dawson | | | |
| ☐ 489 Paul Krause | .20 | .09 | .03 |
| Minnesota Vikings | | | |
| ☐ 490 John James | .15 | .07 | .02 |
| Atlanta Falcons | | | |

| | | | |
|---|---|---|---|
| ☐ 491 Merv Krakau | .15 | .07 | .02 |
| Buffalo Bills | | | |
| ☐ 492 Dan Doornink | .15 | .07 | .02 |
| New York Giants | | | |
| ☐ 493 Curtis Johnson | .15 | .07 | .02 |
| Miami Dolphins | | | |
| ☐ 494 Rafael Septien | .20 | .09 | .03 |
| Dallas Cowboys | | | |
| ☐ 495 Jean Fugett | .20 | .09 | .03 |
| Washington Redskins | | | |
| ☐ 496 Frank LeMaster | .15 | .07 | .02 |
| Philadelphia Eagles | | | |
| ☐ 497 Allan Ellis | .15 | .07 | .02 |
| Chicago Bears | | | |
| ☐ 498 Billy Waddy | .20 | .09 | .03 |
| Los Angeles Rams | | | |
| ☐ 499 Hank Bauer | .20 | .09 | .03 |
| San Diego Chargers | | | |
| ☐ 500 Terry Bradshaw AP UER | 5.00 | 2.30 | .60 |
| (Stat headers on back | | | |
| are for a runner) | | | |
| Pittsburgh Steelers | | | |
| ☐ 501 Larry McCarren | .15 | .07 | .02 |
| Green Bay Packers | | | |
| ☐ 502 Fred Cook | .15 | .07 | .02 |
| Baltimore Colts | | | |
| ☐ 503 Chuck Muncie | .20 | .09 | .03 |
| New Orleans Saints | | | |
| ☐ 504 Herman Weaver | .15 | .07 | .02 |
| Seattle Seahawks | | | |
| ☐ 505 Eddie Edwards | .15 | .07 | .02 |
| Cincinnati Bengals | | | |
| ☐ 506 Tony Peters | .20 | .09 | .03 |
| Cleveland Browns | | | |
| ☐ 507 Denver Broncos TL | .60 | .09 | .02 |
| Lonnie Perrin | | | |
| Riley Odoms | | | |
| Steve Foley | | | |
| Bernard Jackson | | | |
| Lyle Alzado | | | |
| ☐ 508 Jimbo Elrod | .15 | .07 | .02 |
| Kansas City Chiefs | | | |
| ☐ 509 David Hill | .15 | .07 | .02 |
| Detroit Lions | | | |
| ☐ 510 Harvey Martin | .30 | .14 | .04 |
| Dallas Cowboys | | | |
| ☐ 511 Terry Miller | .20 | .09 | .03 |
| Buffalo Bills | | | |
| ☐ 512 June Jones | 1.00 | .45 | .13 |
| Atlanta Falcons | | | |
| ☐ 513 Randy Cross | .30 | .14 | .04 |
| San Francisco 49ers | | | |
| ☐ 514 Duriel Harris | .20 | .09 | .03 |
| Miami Dolphins | | | |
| ☐ 515 Harry Carson | .75 | .35 | .09 |
| New York Giants | | | |
| ☐ 516 Tim Fox | .15 | .07 | .02 |
| New England Patriots | | | |
| ☐ 517 John Zook | .15 | .07 | .02 |
| St. Louis Cardinals | | | |
| ☐ 518 Bob Tucker | .20 | .09 | .03 |
| Minnesota Vikings | | | |
| ☐ 519 Kevin Long | .15 | .07 | .02 |
| New York Jets | | | |
| ☐ 520 Ken Stabler | 2.25 | 1.00 | .30 |
| Oakland Raiders | | | |
| ☐ 521 John Bunting | .15 | .07 | .02 |
| Philadelphia Eagles | | | |
| ☐ 522 Rocky Bleier | .60 | .25 | .08 |
| Pittsburgh Steelers | | | |
| ☐ 523 Noah Jackson | .15 | .07 | .02 |
| Chicago Bears | | | |
| ☐ 524 Cliff Parsley | .15 | .07 | .02 |
| Houston Oilers | | | |
| ☐ 525 Louie Kelcher AP | .20 | .09 | .03 |
| San Diego Chargers | | | |
| ☐ 526 Tampa Bay Bucs TL | .50 | .08 | .02 |
| Ricky Bell | | | |
| Morris Owens | | | |
| Cedric Brown | | | |
| Lee Roy Selmon | | | |
| ☐ 527 Bob Brudzinski | .15 | .07 | .02 |
| Los Angeles Rams | | | |
| ☐ 528 Danny Buggs | .20 | .09 | .03 |
| Washington Redskins | | | |

# 1980 Topps

The 1980 Topps football card set contains 528 cards of NFL players. The cards measure 2 1/2" by 3 1/2". The backs of the cards contain vital statistics, year-by-year career records, and a cartoon-illustrated fact section within a simulated football. No scarcities are known. The first six cards in the set recognize Record-Breaking (RB) performances from the previous season. Statistical league leaders are depicted on cards 331-336. Post-season playoff action is summarized

on cards 492-494. All-Pro selections are designated on the player's regular card and are indicated by AP in the checklist below. Distributed throughout the set are Team Leader (TL) cards depicting, typically, four individual team (statistical) leaders on the front and a team checklist on the back. The key Rookie Cards in this set are Ottis Anderson, Clay Mathews, and Phil Simms.

|  | MINT | EXC | G-VG |
|---|---|---|---|
| COMPLETE SET (528) | 70.00 | 32.00 | 8.75 |
| COMMON PLAYER (1-528) | .10 | .05 | .01 |

| | | | |
|---|---|---|---|
| ☐ 1 Ottis Anderson RB<br>Most Yardage,<br>Rushing, Rookie | 1.00 | .45 | .13 |
| ☐ 2 Harold Carmichael RB<br>Most Consec. Games,<br>One or More Receptions | .20 | .09 | .03 |
| ☐ 3 Dan Fouts RB<br>Most Yardage,<br>Passing, Season | 1.00 | .45 | .13 |
| ☐ 4 Paul Krause RB<br>Most Interceptions,<br>Lifetime | .15 | .07 | .02 |
| ☐ 5 Rick Upchurch RB<br>Most Punt Return<br>Yards, Lifetime | .15 | .07 | .02 |
| ☐ 6 Garo Yepremian RB<br>Most Consecutive<br>Field Goals | .15 | .07 | .02 |
| ☐ 7 Harold Jackson<br>New England Patriots | .25 | .11 | .03 |
| ☐ 8 Mike Williams<br>San Diego Chargers | .10 | .05 | .01 |
| ☐ 9 Calvin Hill<br>Cleveland Browns | .20 | .09 | .03 |
| ☐ 10 Jack Ham AP<br>Pittsburgh Steelers | 1.00 | .45 | .13 |
| ☐ 11 Dan Melville<br>San Francisco 49ers | .10 | .05 | .01 |
| ☐ 12 Matt Robinson<br>Denver Broncos | .12 | .05 | .02 |
| ☐ 13 Billy Campfield<br>Philadelphia Eagles | .10 | .05 | .01 |
| ☐ 14 Phil Tabor<br>New York Giants | .10 | .05 | .01 |
| ☐ 15 Randy Hughes UER<br>Dallas Cowboys<br>(Cowboys didn't play<br>in SB VII) | .12 | .05 | .02 |
| ☐ 16 Andre Tillman<br>Miami Dolphins | .10 | .05 | .01 |
| ☐ 17 Isaac Curtis<br>Cincinnati Bengals | .12 | .05 | .02 |
| ☐ 18 Charley Hannah<br>Tampa Bay Buccaneers | .10 | .05 | .01 |
| ☐ 19 Wash. Redskins TL<br>John Riggins<br>Danny Buggs<br>Joe Lavender<br>Coy Bacon | .50 | .08 | .02 |
| ☐ 20 Jim Zorn<br>Seattle Seahawks | .25 | .11 | .03 |
| ☐ 21 Brian Baschnagel<br>Chicago Bears | .10 | .05 | .01 |
| ☐ 22 Jon Keyworth<br>Denver Broncos | .12 | .05 | .02 |
| ☐ 23 Phil Villapiano<br>Oakland Raiders | .12 | .05 | .02 |
| ☐ 24 Richard Osborne<br>St. Louis Cardinals | .10 | .05 | .01 |
| ☐ 25 Rich Saul AP<br>Los Angeles Rams | .10 | .05 | .01 |
| ☐ 26 Doug Beaudoin<br>New England Patriots | .10 | .05 | .01 |
| ☐ 27 Cleveland Elam<br>Detroit Lions | .10 | .05 | .01 |
| ☐ 28 Charlie Joiner | .60 | .25 | .08 |

| | | | |
|---|---|---|---|
|  | San Diego Chargers | | |
| ☐ 29 Dick Ambrose | .10 | .05 | .01 |
|  | Cleveland Browns | | |
| ☐ 30 Mike Reinfeldt AP | .10 | .05 | .01 |
|  | Houston Oilers | | |
| ☐ 31 Matt Bahr | 1.75 | .80 | .22 |
|  | Pittsburgh Steelers | | |
| ☐ 32 Keith Krepfle | .10 | .05 | .01 |
|  | Philadelphia Eagles | | |
| ☐ 33 Herbert Scott | .12 | .05 | .02 |
|  | Dallas Cowboys | | |
| ☐ 34 Doug Kotar | .10 | .05 | .01 |
|  | New York Giants | | |
| ☐ 35 Bob Griese | 1.75 | .80 | .22 |
|  | Miami Dolphins | | |
| ☐ 36 Jerry Butler | .25 | .11 | .03 |
|  | Buffalo Bills | | |
| ☐ 37 Rolland Lawrence | .10 | .05 | .01 |
|  | Atlanta Falcons | | |
| ☐ 38 Gary Weaver | .10 | .05 | .01 |
|  | Green Bay Packers | | |
| ☐ 39 Kansas City Chiefs TL<br>Ted McKnight<br>J.T. Smith<br>Gary Barbaro<br>Art Still | .40 | .06 | .01 |
| ☐ 40 Chuck Muncie | .12 | .05 | .02 |
|  | New Orleans Saints | | |
| ☐ 41 Mike Hartenstine | .10 | .05 | .01 |
|  | Chicago Bears | | |
| ☐ 42 Sammie White | .15 | .07 | .02 |
|  | Minnesota Vikings | | |
| ☐ 43 Ken Clark | .10 | .05 | .01 |
|  | Los Angeles Rams | | |
| ☐ 44 Clarence Harmon | .10 | .05 | .01 |
|  | Washington Redskins | | |
| ☐ 45 Bert Jones | .30 | .14 | .04 |
|  | Baltimore Colts | | |
| ☐ 46 Mike Washington | .10 | .05 | .01 |
|  | Tampa Bay Buccaneers | | |
| ☐ 47 Joe Fields | .10 | .05 | .01 |
|  | New York Jets | | |
| ☐ 48 Mike Wood | .10 | .05 | .01 |
|  | San Diego Chargers | | |
| ☐ 49 Oliver Davis | .10 | .05 | .01 |
|  | Cleveland Browns | | |
| ☐ 50 Stan Walters AP | .12 | .05 | .02 |
|  | Philadelphia Eagles | | |
| ☐ 51 Riley Odoms | .12 | .05 | .02 |
|  | Denver Broncos | | |
| ☐ 52 Steve Pisarkiewicz | .12 | .05 | .02 |
|  | St. Louis Cardinals | | |
| ☐ 53 Tony Hill | .30 | .14 | .04 |
|  | Dallas Cowboys | | |
| ☐ 54 Scott Perry | .10 | .05 | .01 |
|  | San Francisco 49ers | | |
| ☐ 55 George Martin | .25 | .11 | .03 |
|  | New York Giants | | |
| ☐ 56 George Roberts | .10 | .05 | .01 |
|  | Miami Dolphins | | |
| ☐ 57 Seattle Seahawks TL<br>Sherman Smith<br>Steve Largent<br>Dave Brown<br>Manu Tuiasosopo | .75 | .11 | .02 |
| ☐ 58 Billy Johnson | .12 | .05 | .02 |
|  | Houston Oilers | | |
| ☐ 59 Reuben Gant | .10 | .05 | .01 |
|  | Buffalo Bills | | |
| ☐ 60 Dennis Harrah AP | .10 | .05 | .01 |
|  | Los Angeles Rams | | |
| ☐ 61 Rocky Bleier | .30 | .14 | .04 |
|  | Pittsburgh Steelers | | |
| ☐ 62 Sam Hunt | .10 | .05 | .01 |
|  | New England Patriots | | |
| ☐ 63 Allan Ellis | .10 | .05 | .01 |
|  | Chicago Bears | | |
| ☐ 64 Ricky Thompson | .10 | .05 | .01 |
|  | Washington Redskins | | |
| ☐ 65 Ken Stabler | 1.75 | .80 | .22 |
|  | Houston Oilers | | |
| ☐ 66 Dexter Bussey | .10 | .05 | .01 |
|  | Detroit Lions | | |
| ☐ 67 Ken Mendenhall | .10 | .05 | .01 |
|  | Baltimore Colts | | |
| ☐ 68 Woodrow Lowe | .10 | .05 | .01 |
|  | San Diego Chargers | | |
| ☐ 69 Thom Darden | .10 | .05 | .01 |
|  | Cleveland Browns | | |
| ☐ 70 Randy White AP | 1.50 | .65 | .19 |
|  | Dallas Cowboys | | |
| ☐ 71 Ken MacAfee | .10 | .05 | .01 |
|  | San Francisco 49ers | | |
| ☐ 72 Ron Jaworski | .30 | .14 | .04 |
|  | Philadelphia Eagles | | |
| ☐ 73 William Andrews | 1.00 | .45 | .13 |
|  | Atlanta Falcons | | |
| ☐ 74 Jimmy Robinson | .10 | .05 | .01 |

| | | | |
|---|---|---|---|
| New York Giants | | | |
| ☐ 75 Roger Wehrli AP | .12 | .05 | .02 |
| St. Louis Cardinals | | | |
| ☐ 76 Miami Dolphins TL | .50 | .08 | .02 |
| Larry Csonka | | | |
| Nat Moore | | | |
| Neal Colzie | | | |
| Gerald Small | | | |
| Vern Den Herder | | | |
| ☐ 77 Jack Rudnay | .10 | .05 | .01 |
| Kansas City Chiefs | | | |
| ☐ 78 James Lofton | 4.00 | 1.80 | .50 |
| Green Bay Packers | | | |
| ☐ 79 Robert Brazile | .12 | .05 | .02 |
| Houston Oilers | | | |
| ☐ 80 Russ Francis | .12 | .05 | .02 |
| New England Patriots | | | |
| ☐ 81 Ricky Bell | .30 | .14 | .04 |
| Tampa Bay Buccaneers | | | |
| ☐ 82 Bob Avellini | .12 | .05 | .02 |
| Chicago Bears | | | |
| ☐ 83 Bobby Jackson | .10 | .05 | .01 |
| New York Jets | | | |
| ☐ 84 Mike Bragg | .10 | .05 | .01 |
| Washington Redskins | | | |
| ☐ 85 Cliff Branch | .50 | .23 | .06 |
| Oakland Raiders | | | |
| ☐ 86 Blair Bush | .10 | .05 | .01 |
| Cincinnati Bengals | | | |
| ☐ 87 Sherman Smith | .10 | .05 | .01 |
| Seattle Seahawks | | | |
| ☐ 88 Glen Edwards | .10 | .05 | .01 |
| San Diego Chargers | | | |
| ☐ 89 Don Cockroft | .12 | .05 | .02 |
| Cleveland Browns | | | |
| ☐ 90 Louis Wright AP | .15 | .07 | .02 |
| Denver Broncos | | | |
| ☐ 91 Randy Grossman | .10 | .05 | .01 |
| Pittsburgh Steelers | | | |
| ☐ 92 Carl Hairston | .60 | .25 | .08 |
| Philadelphia Eagles | | | |
| ☐ 93 Archie Manning | .40 | .18 | .05 |
| New Orleans Saints | | | |
| ☐ 94 New York Giants TL | .30 | .05 | .01 |
| Billy Taylor | | | |
| Earnest Gray | | | |
| George Martin | | | |
| ☐ 95 Preston Pearson | .12 | .05 | .02 |
| Dallas Cowboys | | | |
| ☐ 96 Rusty Chambers | .12 | .05 | .02 |
| Miami Dolphins | | | |
| ☐ 97 Greg Coleman | .10 | .05 | .01 |
| Minnesota Vikings | | | |
| ☐ 98 Charley Young | .12 | .05 | .02 |
| Los Angeles Rams | | | |
| ☐ 99 Matt Cavanaugh | .25 | .11 | .03 |
| New England Patriots | | | |
| ☐ 100 Jesse Baker | .12 | .05 | .02 |
| Houston Oilers | | | |
| ☐ 101 Doug Plank | .10 | .05 | .01 |
| Chicago Bears | | | |
| ☐ 102 Checklist 1-132 | .60 | .06 | .02 |
| ☐ 103 Luther Bradley | .10 | .05 | .01 |
| Detroit Lions | | | |
| ☐ 104 Bob Kuziel | .10 | .05 | .01 |
| Washington Redskins | | | |
| ☐ 105 Craig Morton | .25 | .11 | .03 |
| Denver Broncos | | | |
| ☐ 106 Sherman White | .10 | .05 | .01 |
| Buffalo Bills | | | |
| ☐ 107 Jim Breech | .75 | .35 | .09 |
| Oakland Raiders | | | |
| ☐ 108 Hank Bauer | .10 | .05 | .01 |
| San Diego Chargers | | | |
| ☐ 109 Tom Blanchard | .10 | .05 | .01 |
| Tampa Bay Buccaneers | | | |
| ☐ 110 Ozzie Newsome AP | 4.00 | 1.80 | .50 |
| Cleveland Browns | | | |
| ☐ 111 Steve Furness | .12 | .05 | .02 |
| Pittsburgh Steelers | | | |
| ☐ 112 Frank LeMaster | .10 | .05 | .01 |
| Philadelphia Eagles | | | |
| ☐ 113 Dallas Cowboys TL | .75 | .11 | .02 |
| Tony Dorsett | | | |
| Tony Hill | | | |
| Harvey Martin | | | |
| ☐ 114 Doug Van Horn | .10 | .05 | .01 |
| New York Giants | | | |
| ☐ 115 Delvin Williams | .12 | .05 | .02 |
| Miami Dolphins | | | |
| ☐ 116 Lyle Blackwood | .12 | .05 | .02 |
| Baltimore Colts | | | |
| ☐ 117 Derrick Gaffney | .10 | .05 | .01 |
| New York Jets | | | |
| ☐ 118 Cornell Webster | .10 | .05 | .01 |
| Seattle Seahawks | | | |
| ☐ 119 Sam Cunningham | .12 | .05 | .02 |
| New England Patriots | | | |

| | | | |
|---|---|---|---|
| ☐ 120 Jim Youngblood AP | .12 | .05 | .02 |
| Los Angeles Rams | | | |
| ☐ 121 Bob Thomas | .10 | .05 | .01 |
| Chicago Bears | | | |
| ☐ 122 Jack Thompson | .15 | .07 | .02 |
| Cincinnati Bengals | | | |
| ☐ 123 Randy Cross | .12 | .05 | .02 |
| San Francisco 49ers | | | |
| ☐ 124 Karl Lorch | .10 | .05 | .01 |
| Washington Redskins | | | |
| ☐ 125 Mel Gray | .12 | .05 | .02 |
| St. Louis Cardinals | | | |
| ☐ 126 John James | .10 | .05 | .01 |
| Atlanta Falcons | | | |
| ☐ 127 Terdell Middleton | .10 | .05 | .01 |
| Green Bay Packers | | | |
| ☐ 128 Leroy Jones | .10 | .05 | .01 |
| San Diego Chargers | | | |
| ☐ 129 Tom DeLeone | .10 | .05 | .01 |
| Cleveland Browns | | | |
| ☐ 130 John Stallworth AP | 1.00 | .45 | .13 |
| Pittsburgh Steelers | | | |
| ☐ 131 Jimmie Giles | .25 | .11 | .03 |
| Tampa Bay Buccaneers | | | |
| ☐ 132 Philadelphia Eagles TL | .35 | .05 | .01 |
| Wilbert Montgomery | | | |
| Harold Carmichael | | | |
| Brenard Wilson | | | |
| Carl Hairston | | | |
| ☐ 133 Gary Green | .10 | .05 | .01 |
| Kansas City Chiefs | | | |
| ☐ 134 John Dutton | .12 | .05 | .02 |
| Dallas Cowboys | | | |
| ☐ 135 Harry Carson AP | .40 | .18 | .05 |
| New York Giants | | | |
| ☐ 136 Bob Kuechenberg | .15 | .07 | .02 |
| Miami Dolphins | | | |
| ☐ 137 Ike Harris | .10 | .05 | .01 |
| New Orleans Saints | | | |
| ☐ 138 Tommy Kramer | 1.00 | .45 | .13 |
| Minnesota Vikings | | | |
| ☐ 139 Sam Adams | .10 | .05 | .01 |
| New England Patriots | | | |
| ☐ 140 Doug English AP | .10 | .05 | .01 |
| Detroit Lions | | | |
| ☐ 141 Steve Schubert | .10 | .05 | .01 |
| Chicago Bears | | | |
| ☐ 142 Rusty Jackson | .10 | .05 | .01 |
| Buffalo Bills | | | |
| ☐ 143 Reese McCall | .10 | .05 | .01 |
| Baltimore Colts | | | |
| ☐ 144 Scott Dierking | .10 | .05 | .01 |
| New York Jets | | | |
| ☐ 145 Ken Houston AP | .40 | .18 | .05 |
| Washington Redskins | | | |
| ☐ 146 Bob Martin | .10 | .05 | .01 |
| San Francisco 49ers | | | |
| ☐ 147 Sam McCullum | .12 | .05 | .02 |
| Seattle Seahawks | | | |
| ☐ 148 Tom Banks | .12 | .05 | .02 |
| St. Louis Cardinals | | | |
| ☐ 149 Willie Buchanon | .12 | .05 | .02 |
| San Diego Chargers | | | |
| ☐ 150 Greg Pruitt | .20 | .09 | .03 |
| Cleveland Browns | | | |
| ☐ 151 Denver Broncos TL | .30 | .05 | .01 |
| Otis Armstrong | | | |
| Rick Upchurch | | | |
| Steve Foley | | | |
| Brison Manor | | | |
| ☐ 152 Don Smith | .10 | .05 | .01 |
| Atlanta Falcons | | | |
| ☐ 153 Pete Johnson | .12 | .05 | .02 |
| Cincinnati Bengals | | | |
| ☐ 154 Charlie Smith | .10 | .05 | .01 |
| Philadelphia Eagles | | | |
| ☐ 155 Mel Blount | .75 | .35 | .09 |
| Pittsburgh Steelers | | | |
| ☐ 156 John Mendenhall | .10 | .05 | .01 |
| New York Giants | | | |
| ☐ 157 Danny White | .50 | .23 | .06 |
| Dallas Cowboys | | | |
| ☐ 158 Jimmy Cefalo | .40 | .18 | .05 |
| Miami Dolphins | | | |
| ☐ 159 Richard Bishop AP | .10 | .05 | .01 |
| New England Patriots | | | |
| ☐ 160 Walter Payton AP | 8.00 | 3.60 | 1.00 |
| Chicago Bears | | | |
| ☐ 161 Dave Dalby | .10 | .05 | .01 |
| Oakland Raiders | | | |
| ☐ 162 Preston Dennard | .10 | .05 | .01 |
| Los Angeles Rams | | | |
| ☐ 163 Johnnie Gray | .10 | .05 | .01 |
| Green Bay Packers | | | |
| ☐ 164 Russell Erxleben | .10 | .05 | .01 |
| New Orleans Saints | | | |
| ☐ 165 Toni Fritsch AP | .10 | .05 | .01 |

| | | | |
|---|---|---|---|
| Houston Oilers | | | |
| ☐ 166 Terry Hermeling | .10 | .05 | .01 |
| Washington Redskins | | | |
| ☐ 167 Roland Hooks | .10 | .05 | .01 |
| Buffalo Bills | | | |
| ☐ 168 Roger Carr | .12 | .05 | .02 |
| Baltimore Colts | | | |
| ☐ 169 San Diego Chargers TL | .30 | .05 | .01 |
| Clarence Williams | | | |
| John Jefferson | | | |
| Woodrow Lowe | | | |
| Ray Preston | | | |
| Wilbur Young | | | |
| ☐ 170 Ottis Anderson AP | 5.00 | 2.30 | .60 |
| St. Louis Cardinals | | | |
| ☐ 171 Brian Sipe | .30 | .14 | .04 |
| Cleveland Browns | | | |
| ☐ 172 Leonard Thompson | .12 | .05 | .02 |
| Detroit Lions | | | |
| ☐ 173 Tony Reed | .12 | .05 | .02 |
| Kansas City Chiefs | | | |
| ☐ 174 Bob Tucker | .12 | .05 | .02 |
| Minnesota Vikings | | | |
| ☐ 175 Joe Greene | 1.00 | .45 | .13 |
| Pittsburgh Steelers | | | |
| ☐ 176 Jack Dolbin | .10 | .05 | .01 |
| Denver Broncos | | | |
| ☐ 177 Chuck Ramsey | .10 | .05 | .01 |
| New York Jets | | | |
| ☐ 178 Paul Hofer | .12 | .05 | .02 |
| San Francisco 49ers | | | |
| ☐ 179 Randy Logan | .10 | .05 | .01 |
| Philadelphia Eagles | | | |
| ☐ 180 David Lewis AP | .10 | .05 | .01 |
| Tampa Bay Buccaneers | | | |
| ☐ 181 Duriel Harris | .12 | .05 | .02 |
| Miami Dolphins | | | |
| ☐ 182 June Jones | .50 | .23 | .06 |
| Atlanta Falcons | | | |
| ☐ 183 Larry McCarren | .10 | .05 | .01 |
| Green Bay Packers | | | |
| ☐ 184 Ken Johnson | .10 | .05 | .01 |
| New York Giants | | | |
| ☐ 185 Charlie Waters | .30 | .14 | .04 |
| Dallas Cowboys | | | |
| ☐ 186 Noah Jackson | .10 | .05 | .01 |
| Chicago Bears | | | |
| ☐ 187 Reggie Williams | .25 | .11 | .03 |
| Cincinnati Bengals | | | |
| ☐ 188 New England Pats TL | .30 | .05 | .01 |
| Sam Cunningham | | | |
| Harold Jackson | | | |
| Raymond Clayborn | | | |
| Tony McGee | | | |
| ☐ 189 Carl Eller | .25 | .11 | .03 |
| Seattle Seahawks | | | |
| ☐ 190 Ed White AP | .12 | .05 | .02 |
| San Diego Chargers | | | |
| ☐ 191 Mario Clark | .10 | .05 | .01 |
| Buffalo Bills | | | |
| ☐ 192 Roosevelt Leaks | .12 | .05 | .02 |
| Baltimore Colts | | | |
| ☐ 193 Ted McKnight | .10 | .05 | .01 |
| Kansas City Chiefs | | | |
| ☐ 194 Danny Buggs | .12 | .05 | .02 |
| Washington Redskins | | | |
| ☐ 195 Lester Hayes | 2.50 | 1.15 | .30 |
| Oakland Raiders | | | |
| ☐ 196 Clarence Scott | .10 | .05 | .01 |
| Cleveland Browns | | | |
| ☐ 197 New Orleans Saints TL | .50 | .08 | .02 |
| Chuck Muncie | | | |
| Wes Chandler | | | |
| Tom Myers | | | |
| Elois Grooms | | | |
| Don Reese | | | |
| ☐ 198 Richard Caster | .12 | .05 | .02 |
| Houston Oilers | | | |
| ☐ 199 Louie Giammona | .10 | .05 | .01 |
| Philadelphia Eagles | | | |
| ☐ 200 Terry Bradshaw | 3.00 | 1.35 | .40 |
| Pittsburgh Steelers | | | |
| ☐ 201 Ed Newman | .12 | .05 | .02 |
| Miami Dolphins | | | |
| ☐ 202 Fred Dryer | .40 | .18 | .05 |
| Los Angeles Rams | | | |
| ☐ 203 Dennis Franks | .10 | .05 | .01 |
| Detroit Lions | | | |
| ☐ 204 Bob Breunig | .30 | .14 | .04 |
| Dallas Cowboys | | | |
| ☐ 205 Alan Page | .40 | .18 | .05 |
| Chicago Bears | | | |
| ☐ 206 Earnest Gray | .10 | .05 | .01 |
| New York Giants | | | |
| ☐ 207 Minnesota Vikings TL | .40 | .06 | .01 |
| Rickey Young | | | |
| Ahmad Rashad | | | |
| Tom Hannon | | | |

| | | | |
|---|---|---|---|
| Nate Wright | | | |
| Mark Mullaney | | | |
| ☐ 208 Horace Ivory | .10 | .05 | .01 |
| New England Patriots | | | |
| ☐ 209 Isaac Hagins | .10 | .05 | .01 |
| Tampa Bay Buccaneers | | | |
| ☐ 210 Gary Johnson AP | .12 | .05 | .02 |
| San Diego Chargers | | | |
| ☐ 211 Kevin Long | .10 | .05 | .01 |
| New York Jets | | | |
| ☐ 212 Bill Thompson | .12 | .05 | .02 |
| Denver Broncos | | | |
| ☐ 213 Don Bass | .10 | .05 | .01 |
| Cincinnati Bengals | | | |
| ☐ 214 George Starke | .10 | .05 | .01 |
| Washington Redskins | | | |
| ☐ 215 Efren Herrera | .10 | .05 | .01 |
| Seattle Seahawks | | | |
| ☐ 216 Theo Bell | .12 | .05 | .02 |
| Pittsburgh Steelers | | | |
| ☐ 217 Monte Jackson | .10 | .05 | .01 |
| Oakland Raiders | | | |
| ☐ 218 Reggie McKenzie | .12 | .05 | .02 |
| Buffalo Bills | | | |
| ☐ 219 Bucky Dilts | .10 | .05 | .01 |
| Baltimore Colts | | | |
| ☐ 220 Lyle Alzado | .40 | .18 | .05 |
| Cleveland Browns | | | |
| ☐ 221 Tim Foley | .12 | .05 | .02 |
| Miami Dolphins | | | |
| ☐ 222 Mark Arneson | .10 | .05 | .01 |
| St. Louis Cardinals | | | |
| ☐ 223 Fred Quillan | .10 | .05 | .01 |
| San Francisco 49ers | | | |
| ☐ 224 Benny Ricardo | .10 | .05 | .01 |
| Detroit Lions | | | |
| ☐ 225 Phil Simms | 18.00 | 8.00 | 2.30 |
| New York Giants | | | |
| ☐ 226 Chicago Bears TL | 1.00 | .15 | .03 |
| Walter Payton | | | |
| Brian Baschnagel | | | |
| Gary Fencik | | | |
| Terry Schmidt | | | |
| Jim Osborne | | | |
| ☐ 227 Max Runager | .10 | .05 | .01 |
| Philadelphia Eagles | | | |
| ☐ 228 Barty Smith | .10 | .05 | .01 |
| Green Bay Packers | | | |
| ☐ 229 Jay Saldi | .12 | .05 | .02 |
| Dallas Cowboys | | | |
| ☐ 230 John Hannah AP | .50 | .23 | .06 |
| New England Patriots | | | |
| ☐ 231 Tim Wilson | .10 | .05 | .01 |
| Houston Oilers | | | |
| ☐ 232 Jeff Van Note | .12 | .05 | .02 |
| Atlanta Falcons | | | |
| ☐ 233 Henry Marshall | .10 | .05 | .01 |
| Kansas City Chiefs | | | |
| ☐ 234 Diron Talbert | .12 | .05 | .02 |
| Washington Redskins | | | |
| ☐ 235 Garo Yepremian | .10 | .05 | .01 |
| New Orleans Saints | | | |
| ☐ 236 Larry Brown | .10 | .05 | .01 |
| Pittsburgh Steelers | | | |
| ☐ 237 Clarence Williams | .10 | .05 | .01 |
| San Diego Chargers | | | |
| ☐ 238 Burgess Owens | .10 | .05 | .01 |
| New York Jets | | | |
| ☐ 239 Vince Ferragamo | .20 | .09 | .03 |
| Los Angeles Rams | | | |
| ☐ 240 Rickey Young | .12 | .05 | .02 |
| Minnesota Vikings | | | |
| ☐ 241 Dave Logan | .12 | .05 | .02 |
| Cleveland Browns | | | |
| ☐ 242 Larry Gordon | .10 | .05 | .01 |
| Miami Dolphins | | | |
| ☐ 243 Terry Miller | .12 | .05 | .02 |
| Buffalo Bills | | | |
| ☐ 244 Baltimore Colts TL | .30 | .05 | .01 |
| Joe Washington | | | |
| Joe Washington | | | |
| Fred Cook | | | |
| ☐ 245 Steve DeBerg | 2.00 | .90 | .25 |
| San Francisco 49ers | | | |
| ☐ 246 Checklist 133-264 | .60 | .06 | .02 |
| ☐ 247 Greg Latta | .10 | .05 | .01 |
| Chicago Bears | | | |
| ☐ 248 Raymond Clayborn | .12 | .05 | .02 |
| New England Patriots | | | |
| ☐ 249 Jim Clack | .10 | .05 | .01 |
| New York Giants | | | |
| ☐ 250 Drew Pearson | .50 | .23 | .06 |
| Dallas Cowboys | | | |
| ☐ 251 John Bunting | .10 | .05 | .01 |
| Philadelphia Eagles | | | |
| ☐ 252 Rob Lytle | .12 | .05 | .02 |
| Denver Broncos | | | |
| ☐ 253 Jim Hart | .25 | .11 | .03 |

| | | | |
|---|---|---|---|
| St. Louis Cardinals | | | |
| ☐ 254 John McDaniel | .10 | .05 | .01 |
| Washington Redskins | | | |
| ☐ 255 Dave Pear AP | .10 | .05 | .01 |
| Oakland Raiders | | | |
| ☐ 256 Donnie Shell | .50 | .23 | .06 |
| Pittsburgh Steelers | | | |
| ☐ 257 Dan Doornink | .10 | .05 | .01 |
| Seattle Seahawks | | | |
| ☐ 258 Wallace Francis | .30 | .14 | .04 |
| Atlanta Falcons | | | |
| ☐ 259 Dave Beverly | .10 | .05 | .01 |
| Green Bay Packers | | | |
| ☐ 260 Lee Roy Selmon AP | .20 | .09 | .03 |
| Tampa Bay Buccaneers | | | |
| ☐ 261 Doug Dieken | .10 | .05 | .01 |
| Cleveland Browns | | | |
| ☐ 262 Gary Davis | .10 | .05 | .01 |
| Miami Dolphins | | | |
| ☐ 263 Bob Rush | .10 | .05 | .01 |
| San Diego Chargers | | | |
| ☐ 264 Buffalo Bills TL | .30 | .05 | .01 |
| Curtis Brown | | | |
| Frank Lewis | | | |
| Keith Moody | | | |
| Sherman White | | | |
| ☐ 265 Greg Landry | .20 | .09 | .03 |
| Baltimore Colts | | | |
| ☐ 266 Jan Stenerud | .25 | .11 | .03 |
| Kansas City Chiefs | | | |
| ☐ 267 Tom Hicks | .10 | .05 | .01 |
| Chicago Bears | | | |
| ☐ 268 Pat McInally | .12 | .05 | .02 |
| Cincinnati Bengals | | | |
| ☐ 269 Tim Fox | .10 | .05 | .01 |
| New England Patriots | | | |
| ☐ 270 Harvey Martin | .25 | .11 | .03 |
| Dallas Cowboys | | | |
| ☐ 271 Dan Lloyd | .10 | .05 | .01 |
| New York Giants | | | |
| ☐ 272 Mike Barber | .10 | .05 | .01 |
| Houston Oilers | | | |
| ☐ 273 Wendell Tyler | .60 | .25 | .08 |
| Los Angeles Rams | | | |
| ☐ 274 Jeff Komlo | .12 | .05 | .02 |
| Detroit Lions | | | |
| ☐ 275 Wes Chandler | 2.00 | .90 | .25 |
| New Orleans Saints | | | |
| ☐ 276 Brad Dusek | .12 | .05 | .02 |
| Washington Redskins | | | |
| ☐ 277 Charlie Johnson | .10 | .05 | .01 |
| Philadelphia Eagles | | | |
| ☐ 278 Dennis Swilley | .12 | .05 | .02 |
| Minnesota Vikings | | | |
| ☐ 279 Johnny Evans | .10 | .05 | .01 |
| Cleveland Browns | | | |
| ☐ 280 Jack Lambert AP | 1.50 | .65 | .19 |
| Pittsburgh Steelers | | | |
| ☐ 281 Vern Den Herder | .10 | .05 | .01 |
| Miami Dolphins | | | |
| ☐ 282 Tampa Bay Bucs TL | .30 | .05 | .01 |
| Ricky Bell | | | |
| Isaac Hagins | | | |
| Lee Roy Selmon | | | |
| ☐ 283 Bob Klein | .10 | .05 | .01 |
| San Diego Chargers | | | |
| ☐ 284 Jim Turner | .12 | .05 | .02 |
| Denver Broncos | | | |
| ☐ 285 Marvin Powell AP | .12 | .05 | .02 |
| New York Jets | | | |
| ☐ 286 Aaron Kyle | .12 | .05 | .02 |
| Dallas Cowboys | | | |
| ☐ 287 Dan Neal | .10 | .05 | .01 |
| Chicago Bears | | | |
| ☐ 288 Wayne Morris | .10 | .05 | .01 |
| St. Louis Cardinals | | | |
| ☐ 289 Steve Bartkowski | .30 | .14 | .04 |
| Atlanta Falcons | | | |
| ☐ 290 Dave Jennings AP | .12 | .05 | .02 |
| New York Giants | | | |
| ☐ 291 John Smith | .10 | .05 | .01 |
| New England Patriots | | | |
| ☐ 292 Bill Gregory | .10 | .05 | .01 |
| Seattle Seahawks | | | |
| ☐ 293 Frank Lewis | .12 | .05 | .02 |
| Buffalo Bills | | | |
| ☐ 294 Fred Cook | .10 | .05 | .01 |
| Baltimore Colts | | | |
| ☐ 295 David Hill AP | .10 | .05 | .01 |
| Detroit Lions | | | |
| ☐ 296 Wade Key | .10 | .05 | .01 |
| Philadelphia Eagles | | | |
| ☐ 297 Sidney Thornton | .12 | .05 | .02 |
| Pittsburgh Steelers | | | |
| ☐ 298 Charlie Hall | .10 | .05 | .01 |
| Cleveland Browns | | | |
| ☐ 299 Joe Lavender | .12 | .05 | .02 |
| Washington Redskins | | | |

| | | | |
|---|---|---|---|
| ☐ 300 Tom Rafferty | .10 | .05 | .01 |
| Dallas Cowboys | | | |
| ☐ 301 Mike Renfro | .10 | .05 | .01 |
| Houston Oilers | | | |
| ☐ 302 Wilbur Jackson | .12 | .05 | .02 |
| San Francisco 49ers | | | |
| ☐ 303 Green Bay Packers TL | 1.25 | .19 | .04 |
| Terdell Middleton | | | |
| James Lofton | | | |
| Johnnie Gray | | | |
| Robert Barber | | | |
| Ezra Johnson | | | |
| ☐ 304 Henry Childs | .10 | .05 | .01 |
| New Orleans Saints | | | |
| ☐ 305 Russ Washington AP | .10 | .05 | .01 |
| San Diego Chargers | | | |
| ☐ 306 Jim LeClair | .10 | .05 | .01 |
| Cincinnati Bengals | | | |
| ☐ 307 Tommy Hart | .10 | .05 | .01 |
| Chicago Bears | | | |
| ☐ 308 Gary Barbaro | .12 | .05 | .02 |
| Kansas City Chiefs | | | |
| ☐ 309 Billy Taylor | .12 | .05 | .02 |
| New York Giants | | | |
| ☐ 310 Ray Guy | .25 | .11 | .03 |
| Oakland Raiders | | | |
| ☐ 311 Don Hasselbeck | .12 | .05 | .02 |
| New England Patriots | | | |
| ☐ 312 Doug Williams | .60 | .25 | .08 |
| Tampa Bay Buccaneers | | | |
| ☐ 313 Nick Mike-Mayer | .10 | .05 | .01 |
| Buffalo Bills | | | |
| ☐ 314 Don McCauley | .10 | .05 | .01 |
| Baltimore Colts | | | |
| ☐ 315 Wesley Walker | .40 | .18 | .05 |
| New York Jets | | | |
| ☐ 316 Dan Dierdorf | .50 | .23 | .06 |
| St. Louis Cardinals | | | |
| ☐ 317 Dave Brown | .25 | .11 | .03 |
| Seattle Seahawks | | | |
| ☐ 318 Leroy Harris | .10 | .05 | .01 |
| Philadelphia Eagles | | | |
| ☐ 319 Pittsburgh Steelers TL | .75 | .11 | .02 |
| Franco Harris | | | |
| John Stallworth | | | |
| Jack Lambert | | | |
| Steve Furness | | | |
| L.C. Greenwood | | | |
| ☐ 320 Mark Moseley AP UER | .12 | .05 | .02 |
| (Bio on back refers | | | |
| to him as Mike) | | | |
| Washington Redskins | | | |
| ☐ 321 Mark Dennard | .12 | .05 | .02 |
| Miami Dolphins | | | |
| ☐ 322 Terry Nelson | .10 | .05 | .01 |
| Los Angeles Rams | | | |
| ☐ 323 Tom Jackson | .50 | .23 | .06 |
| Denver Broncos | | | |
| ☐ 324 Rick Kane | .10 | .05 | .01 |
| Detroit Lions | | | |
| ☐ 325 Jerry Sherk | .12 | .05 | .02 |
| Cleveland Browns | | | |
| ☐ 326 Ray Preston | .10 | .05 | .01 |
| San Diego Chargers | | | |
| ☐ 327 Golden Richards | .12 | .05 | .02 |
| Chicago Bears | | | |
| ☐ 328 Randy Dean | .10 | .05 | .01 |
| New York Giants | | | |
| ☐ 329 Rick Danmeier | .10 | .05 | .01 |
| Minnesota Vikings | | | |
| ☐ 330 Tony Dorsett | 4.00 | 1.80 | .50 |
| Dallas Cowboys | | | |
| ☐ 331 Passing Leaders | 2.50 | 1.15 | .30 |
| Dan Fouts | | | |
| Roger Staubach | | | |
| ☐ 332 Receiving Leaders | .20 | .09 | .03 |
| Joe Washington | | | |
| Ahmad Rashad | | | |
| ☐ 333 Sacks Leaders | .15 | .07 | .02 |
| Jesse Baker | | | |
| Al(Bubba) Baker | | | |
| Jack Youngblood | | | |
| ☐ 334 Scoring Leaders | .15 | .07 | .02 |
| John Smith | | | |
| Mark Moseley | | | |
| ☐ 335 Interception Leaders | .15 | .07 | .02 |
| Mike Reinfeldt | | | |
| Lemar Parrish | | | |
| ☐ 336 Punting Leaders | .15 | .07 | .02 |
| Bob Grupp | | | |
| Dave Jennings | | | |
| ☐ 337 Freddie Solomon | .12 | .05 | .02 |
| San Francisco 49ers | | | |
| ☐ 338 Cincinnati Bengals TL | .30 | .05 | .01 |
| Pete Johnson | | | |
| Don Bass | | | |
| Dick Jauron | | | |

| | | | |
|---|---|---|---|
| Gary Burley | | | |
| ☐ 339 Ken Stone | .10 | .05 | .01 |
| St. Louis Cardinals | | | |
| ☐ 340 Greg Buttle AP | .12 | .05 | .02 |
| New York Jets | | | |
| ☐ 341 Bob Baumhower | .12 | .05 | .02 |
| Miami Dolphins | | | |
| ☐ 342 Billy Waddy | .10 | .05 | .01 |
| Los Angeles Rams | | | |
| ☐ 343 Cliff Parsley | .10 | .05 | .01 |
| Houston Oilers | | | |
| ☐ 344 Walter White | .10 | .05 | .01 |
| Kansas City Chiefs | | | |
| ☐ 345 Mike Thomas | .12 | .05 | .02 |
| San Diego Chargers | | | |
| ☐ 346 Neil O'Donoghue | .10 | .05 | .01 |
| Tampa Bay Buccaneers | | | |
| ☐ 347 Freddie Scott | .10 | .05 | .01 |
| Detroit Lions | | | |
| ☐ 348 Joe Ferguson | .20 | .09 | .03 |
| Buffalo Bills | | | |
| ☐ 349 Doug Nettles | .10 | .05 | .01 |
| Baltimore Colts | | | |
| ☐ 350 Mike Webster AP | .50 | .23 | .06 |
| Pittsburgh Steelers | | | |
| ☐ 351 Ron Saul | .10 | .05 | .01 |
| Washington Redskins | | | |
| ☐ 352 Julius Adams | .10 | .05 | .01 |
| New England Patriots | | | |
| ☐ 353 Rafael Septien | .12 | .05 | .02 |
| Dallas Cowboys | | | |
| ☐ 354 Cleo Miller | .10 | .05 | .01 |
| Cleveland Browns | | | |
| ☐ 355 Keith Simpson AP | .10 | .05 | .01 |
| Seattle Seahawks | | | |
| ☐ 356 Johnny Perkins | .10 | .05 | .01 |
| New York Giants | | | |
| ☐ 357 Jerry Sisemore | .12 | .05 | .02 |
| Philadelphia Eagles | | | |
| ☐ 358 Arthur Whittington | .10 | .05 | .01 |
| Oakland Raiders | | | |
| ☐ 359 St. Louis Cardinals TL | .60 | .09 | .02 |
| Ottis Anderson | | | |
| Pat Tilley | | | |
| Ken Stone | | | |
| Bob Pollard | | | |
| ☐ 360 Rick Upchurch | .12 | .05 | .02 |
| Denver Broncos | | | |
| ☐ 361 Kim Bokamper | .20 | .09 | .03 |
| Miami Dolphins | | | |
| ☐ 362 Roland Harper | .10 | .05 | .01 |
| Chicago Bears | | | |
| ☐ 363 Pat Leahy | .10 | .05 | .01 |
| New York Jets | | | |
| ☐ 364 Louis Breeden | .10 | .05 | .01 |
| Cincinnati Bengals | | | |
| ☐ 365 John Jefferson | .75 | .35 | .09 |
| San Diego Chargers | | | |
| ☐ 366 Jerry Eckwood | .10 | .05 | .01 |
| Tampa Bay Buccaneers | | | |
| ☐ 367 David Whitehurst | .12 | .05 | .02 |
| Green Bay Packers | | | |
| ☐ 368 Willie Parker | .10 | .05 | .01 |
| Buffalo Bills | | | |
| ☐ 369 Ed Simonini | .10 | .05 | .01 |
| Baltimore Colts | | | |
| ☐ 370 Jack Youngblood AP | .40 | .18 | .05 |
| Los Angeles Rams | | | |
| ☐ 371 Don Warren | 1.00 | .45 | .13 |
| Washington Redskins | | | |
| ☐ 372 Andy Johnson | .10 | .05 | .01 |
| New England Patriots | | | |
| ☐ 373 D.D. Lewis | .12 | .05 | .02 |
| Dallas Cowboys | | | |
| ☐ 374A Beasley Reece ERR | .30 | .14 | .04 |
| (No S in position | | | |
| on front of card) | | | |
| New York Giants | | | |
| ☐ 374B Beasley Reece COR | .15 | .07 | .02 |
| New York Giants | | | |
| ☐ 375 L.C. Greenwood | .40 | .18 | .05 |
| Pittsburgh Steelers | | | |
| ☐ 376 Cleveland Browns TL | .30 | .05 | .01 |
| Mike Pruitt | | | |
| Dave Logan | | | |
| Thom Darden | | | |
| Jerry Sherk | | | |
| ☐ 377 Herman Edwards | .10 | .05 | .01 |
| Philadelphia Eagles | | | |
| ☐ 378 Rob Carpenter | .20 | .09 | .03 |
| Houston Oilers | | | |
| ☐ 379 Herman Weaver | .10 | .05 | .01 |
| Seattle Seahawks | | | |
| ☐ 380 Gary Fencik AP | .10 | .05 | .01 |
| Chicago Bears | | | |
| ☐ 381 Don Strock | .12 | .05 | .02 |
| Miami Dolphins | | | |
| ☐ 382 Art Shell | .50 | .23 | .06 |

| | | | |
|---|---|---|---|
| Oakland Raiders | | | |
| ☐ 383 Tim Mazzetti | .10 | .05 | .01 |
| Atlanta Falcons | | | |
| ☐ 384 Bruce Harper | .10 | .05 | .01 |
| New York Jets | | | |
| ☐ 385 Al(Bubba) Baker | .12 | .05 | .02 |
| Detroit Lions | | | |
| ☐ 386 Conrad Dobler | .12 | .05 | .02 |
| New Orleans Saints | | | |
| ☐ 387 Stu Voigt | .12 | .05 | .02 |
| Minnesota Vikings | | | |
| ☐ 388 Ken Anderson | .75 | .35 | .09 |
| Cincinnati Bengals | | | |
| ☐ 389 Pat Tilley | .12 | .05 | .02 |
| St. Louis Cardinals | | | |
| ☐ 390 John Riggins | 1.00 | .45 | .13 |
| Washington Redskins | | | |
| ☐ 391 Checklist 265-396 | .60 | .06 | .02 |
| ☐ 392 Fred Dean AP | .10 | .05 | .01 |
| San Diego Chargers | | | |
| ☐ 393 Benny Barnes | .12 | .05 | .02 |
| Dallas Cowboys | | | |
| ☐ 394 Los Angeles Rams TL | .30 | .05 | .01 |
| Wendell Tyler | | | |
| Preston Dennard | | | |
| Nolan Cromwell | | | |
| Jim Youngblood | | | |
| Jack Youngblood | | | |
| ☐ 395 Brad Van Pelt | .12 | .05 | .02 |
| New York Giants | | | |
| ☐ 396 Eddie Hare | .10 | .05 | .01 |
| New England Patriots | | | |
| ☐ 397 John Sciarra | .10 | .05 | .01 |
| Philadelphia Eagles | | | |
| ☐ 398 Bob Jackson | .10 | .05 | .01 |
| Cleveland Browns | | | |
| ☐ 399 John Yarno | .10 | .05 | .01 |
| Seattle Seahawks | | | |
| ☐ 400 Franco Harris AP | 1.50 | .65 | .19 |
| Pittsburgh Steelers | | | |
| ☐ 401 Ray Wersching | .12 | .05 | .02 |
| San Francisco 49ers | | | |
| ☐ 402 Virgil Livers | .10 | .05 | .01 |
| Chicago Bears | | | |
| ☐ 403 Raymond Chester | .12 | .05 | .02 |
| Oakland Raiders | | | |
| ☐ 404 Leon Gray | .12 | .05 | .02 |
| Houston Oilers | | | |
| ☐ 405 Richard Todd | .12 | .05 | .02 |
| New York Jets | | | |
| ☐ 406 Larry Little | .30 | .14 | .04 |
| Miami Dolphins | | | |
| ☐ 407 Ted Fritsch Jr. | .12 | .05 | .02 |
| Washington Redskins | | | |
| ☐ 408 Larry Mucker | .10 | .05 | .01 |
| Tampa Bay Buccaneers | | | |
| ☐ 409 Jim Allen | .10 | .05 | .01 |
| Detroit Lions | | | |
| ☐ 410 Randy Gradishar | .40 | .18 | .05 |
| Denver Broncos | | | |
| ☐ 411 Atlanta Falcons TL | .30 | .05 | .01 |
| William Andrews | | | |
| Wallace Francis | | | |
| Rolland Lawrence | | | |
| Don Smith | | | |
| ☐ 412 Louie Kelcher | .12 | .05 | .02 |
| San Diego Chargers | | | |
| ☐ 413 Robert Newhouse | .12 | .05 | .02 |
| Dallas Cowboys | | | |
| ☐ 414 Gary Shirk | .10 | .05 | .01 |
| New York Giants | | | |
| ☐ 415 Mike Haynes AP | .25 | .11 | .03 |
| New England Patriots | | | |
| ☐ 416 Craig Colquitt | .10 | .05 | .01 |
| Pittsburgh Steelers | | | |
| ☐ 417 Lou Piccone | .10 | .05 | .01 |
| Buffalo Bills | | | |
| ☐ 418 Clay Matthews | 8.00 | 3.60 | 1.00 |
| Cleveland Browns | | | |
| ☐ 419 Marvin Cobb | .10 | .05 | .01 |
| Cincinnati Bengals | | | |
| ☐ 420 Harold Carmichael AP | .50 | .23 | .06 |
| Philadelphia Eagles | | | |
| ☐ 421 Uwe Von Schamann | .12 | .05 | .02 |
| Miami Dolphins | | | |
| ☐ 422 Mike Phipps | .12 | .05 | .02 |
| Chicago Bears | | | |
| ☐ 423 Nolan Cromwell | 1.25 | .55 | .16 |
| Los Angeles Rams | | | |
| ☐ 424 Glenn Doughty | .10 | .05 | .01 |
| Baltimore Colts | | | |
| ☐ 425 Bob Young AP | .10 | .05 | .01 |
| St. Louis Cardinals | | | |
| ☐ 426 Tony Galbreath | .12 | .05 | .02 |
| New Orleans Saints | | | |
| ☐ 427 Luke Prestridge | .10 | .05 | .01 |
| Denver Broncos | | | |
| ☐ 428 Terry Beeson | .10 | .05 | .01 |

| | | | |
|---|---|---|---|
| Seattle Seahawks | | | |
| ☐ 429 Jack Tatum | .12 | .05 | .02 |
| Oakland Raiders | | | |
| ☐ 430 Lemar Parrish AP | .12 | .05 | .02 |
| Washington Redskins | | | |
| ☐ 431 Chester Marcol | .12 | .05 | .02 |
| Green Bay Packers | | | |
| ☐ 432 Houston Oilers TL | .30 | .05 | .01 |
| Dan Pastorini | | | |
| Ken Burrough | | | |
| Mike Reinfeldt | | | |
| Jesse Baker | | | |
| ☐ 433 John Fitzgerald | .10 | .05 | .01 |
| Dallas Cowboys | | | |
| ☐ 434 Gary Jeter | .30 | .14 | .04 |
| New York Giants | | | |
| ☐ 435 Steve Grogan | .40 | .18 | .05 |
| New England Patriots | | | |
| ☐ 436 Jon Kolb | .12 | .05 | .02 |
| Pittsburgh Steelers | | | |
| ☐ 437 Jim O'Bradovich UER | .10 | .05 | .01 |
| (Bio describes | | | |
| Neil O'Donoghue) | | | |
| Tampa Bay Buccaneers | | | |
| ☐ 438 Gerald Irons | .10 | .05 | .01 |
| Cleveland Browns | | | |
| ☐ 439 Jeff West | .10 | .05 | .01 |
| San Diego Chargers | | | |
| ☐ 440 Wilbert Montgomery | .25 | .11 | .03 |
| Philadelphia Eagles | | | |
| ☐ 441 Norris Thomas | .10 | .05 | .01 |
| Miami Dolphins | | | |
| ☐ 442 James Scott | .10 | .05 | .01 |
| Chicago Bears | | | |
| ☐ 443 Curtis Brown | .10 | .05 | .01 |
| Buffalo Bills | | | |
| ☐ 444 Ken Fantetti | .10 | .05 | .01 |
| Detroit Lions | | | |
| ☐ 445 Pat Haden | .30 | .14 | .04 |
| Los Angeles Rams | | | |
| ☐ 446 Carl Mauck | .10 | .05 | .01 |
| Houston Oilers | | | |
| ☐ 447 Bruce Laird | .10 | .05 | .01 |
| Baltimore Colts | | | |
| ☐ 448 Otis Armstrong | .20 | .09 | .03 |
| Denver Broncos | | | |
| ☐ 449 Gene Upshaw | .30 | .14 | .04 |
| Oakland Raiders | | | |
| ☐ 450 Steve Largent AP | 3.50 | 1.55 | .45 |
| Seattle Seahawks | | | |
| ☐ 451 Benny Malone | .12 | .05 | .02 |
| Washington Redskins | | | |
| ☐ 452 Steve Nelson | .10 | .05 | .01 |
| New England Patriots | | | |
| ☐ 453 Mark Cotney | .10 | .05 | .01 |
| Tampa Bay Buccaneers | | | |
| ☐ 454 Joe Danelo | .10 | .05 | .01 |
| New York Giants | | | |
| ☐ 455 Billy Joe DuPree | .12 | .05 | .02 |
| Dallas Cowboys | | | |
| ☐ 456 Ron Johnson | .12 | .05 | .02 |
| Pittsburgh Steelers | | | |
| ☐ 457 Archie Griffin | .25 | .11 | .03 |
| Cincinnati Bengals | | | |
| ☐ 458 Reggie Rucker | .12 | .05 | .02 |
| Cleveland Browns | | | |
| ☐ 459 Claude Humphrey | .12 | .05 | .02 |
| Philadelphia Eagles | | | |
| ☐ 460 Lydell Mitchell | .12 | .05 | .02 |
| San Diego Chargers | | | |
| ☐ 461 Steve Towle | .10 | .05 | .01 |
| Miami Dolphins | | | |
| ☐ 462 Revie Sorey | .10 | .05 | .01 |
| Chicago Bears | | | |
| ☐ 463 Tom Skladany | .10 | .05 | .01 |
| Detroit Lions | | | |
| ☐ 464 Clark Gaines | .10 | .05 | .01 |
| New York Jets | | | |
| ☐ 465 Frank Corral | .10 | .05 | .01 |
| Los Angeles Rams | | | |
| ☐ 466 Steve Fuller | .20 | .09 | .03 |
| Kansas City Chiefs | | | |
| ☐ 467 Ahmad Rashad AP | .75 | .35 | .09 |
| Minnesota Vikings | | | |
| ☐ 468 Oakland Raiders TL | .35 | .05 | .01 |
| Mark Van Eeghen | | | |
| Cliff Branch | | | |
| Lester Hayes | | | |
| Willie Jones | | | |
| ☐ 469 Brian Peets | .10 | .05 | .01 |
| Seattle Seahawks | | | |
| ☐ 470 Pat Donovan AP | .20 | .09 | .03 |
| Dallas Cowboys | | | |
| ☐ 471 Ken Burrough | .12 | .05 | .02 |
| Houston Oilers | | | |
| ☐ 472 Don Calhoun | .10 | .05 | .01 |
| New England Patriots | | | |
| ☐ 473 Bill Bryan | .10 | .05 | .01 |
| Denver Broncos | | | |
| ☐ 474 Terry Jackson | .10 | .05 | .01 |
| New York Giants | | | |
| ☐ 475 Joe Theismann | 1.25 | .55 | .16 |
| Washington Redskins | | | |
| ☐ 476 Jim Smith | .12 | .05 | .02 |
| Pittsburgh Steelers | | | |
| ☐ 477 Joe DeLamielleure | .12 | .05 | .02 |
| Buffalo Bills | | | |
| ☐ 478 Mike Pruitt AP | .12 | .05 | .02 |
| Cleveland Browns | | | |
| ☐ 479 Steve Mike-Mayer | .10 | .05 | .01 |
| Baltimore Colts | | | |
| ☐ 480 Bill Bergey | .15 | .07 | .02 |
| Philadelphia Eagles | | | |
| ☐ 481 Mike Fuller | .10 | .05 | .01 |
| San Diego Chargers | | | |
| ☐ 482 Bob Parsons | .10 | .05 | .01 |
| Chicago Bears | | | |
| ☐ 483 Billy Brooks | .12 | .05 | .02 |
| Cincinnati Bengals | | | |
| ☐ 484 Jerome Barkum | .10 | .05 | .01 |
| New York Jets | | | |
| ☐ 485 Larry Csonka | 1.25 | .55 | .16 |
| Miami Dolphins | | | |
| ☐ 486 John Hill | .10 | .05 | .01 |
| New Orleans Saints | | | |
| ☐ 487 Mike Dawson | .10 | .05 | .01 |
| St. Louis Cardinals | | | |
| ☐ 488 Detroit Lions TL | .30 | .05 | .01 |
| Dexter Bussey | | | |
| Freddie Scott | | | |
| Jim Allen | | | |
| Luther Bradley | | | |
| Al(Bubba) Baker | | | |
| ☐ 489 Ted Hendricks | .40 | .18 | .05 |
| Oakland Raiders | | | |
| ☐ 490 Dan Pastorini | .15 | .07 | .02 |
| Oakland Raiders | | | |
| ☐ 491 Stanley Morgan | .60 | .25 | .08 |
| New England Patriots | | | |
| ☐ 492 AFC Championship | .20 | .09 | .03 |
| Steelers 27, | | | |
| Oilers 13 | | | |
| (Rocky Bleier running) | | | |
| ☐ 493 NFC Championship | .20 | .09 | .03 |
| Rams 9, | | | |
| Buccaneers 0 | | | |
| (Vince Ferragamo) | | | |
| ☐ 494 Super Bowl XIV | .50 | .23 | .06 |
| Steelers 31, | | | |
| Rams 19 | | | |
| (line play) | | | |
| ☐ 495 Dwight White | .12 | .05 | .02 |
| Pittsburgh Steelers | | | |
| ☐ 496 Haven Moses | .12 | .05 | .02 |
| Denver Broncos | | | |
| ☐ 497 Guy Morriss | .10 | .05 | .01 |
| Philadelphia Eagles | | | |
| ☐ 498 Dewey Selmon | .12 | .05 | .02 |
| Tampa Bay Buccaneers | | | |
| ☐ 499 Dave Butz | 1.75 | .80 | .22 |
| Washington Redskins | | | |
| ☐ 500 Chuck Foreman | .20 | .09 | .03 |
| New England Patriots | | | |
| ☐ 501 Chris Bahr | .10 | .05 | .01 |
| Cincinnati Bengals | | | |
| ☐ 502 Mark Miller | .10 | .05 | .01 |
| Cleveland Browns | | | |
| ☐ 503 Tony Greene | .10 | .05 | .01 |
| Buffalo Bills | | | |
| ☐ 504 Brian Kelley | .10 | .05 | .01 |
| New York Giants | | | |
| ☐ 505 Joe Washington | .10 | .05 | .01 |
| Baltimore Colts | | | |
| ☐ 506 Butch Johnson | .12 | .05 | .02 |
| Dallas Cowboys | | | |
| ☐ 507 New York Jets TL | .35 | .05 | .01 |
| Clark Gaines | | | |
| Wesley Walker | | | |
| Burgess Owens | | | |
| Joe Klecko | | | |
| ☐ 508 Steve Little | .10 | .05 | .01 |
| St. Louis Cardinals | | | |
| ☐ 509 Checklist 397-528 | .60 | .06 | .02 |
| ☐ 510 Mark Van Eeghen | .12 | .05 | .02 |
| Oakland Raiders | | | |
| ☐ 511 Gary Danielson | .12 | .05 | .02 |
| Detroit Lions | | | |
| ☐ 512 Manu Tuiasosopo | .12 | .05 | .02 |
| Seattle Seahawks | | | |
| ☐ 513 Paul Coffman | .40 | .18 | .05 |
| Green Bay Packers | | | |
| ☐ 514 Cullen Bryant | .12 | .05 | .02 |
| Los Angeles Rams | | | |
| ☐ 515 Nat Moore | .12 | .05 | .02 |
| Miami Dolphins | | | |
| ☐ 516 Bill Lenkaitis | .10 | .05 | .01 |

| | | | |
|---|---|---|---|
| New England Patriots | | | |
| ☐ 517 Lynn Cain | .20 | .09 | .03 |
| Atlanta Falcons | | | |
| ☐ 518 Gregg Bingham | .10 | .05 | .01 |
| Houston Oilers | | | |
| ☐ 519 Ted Albrecht | .10 | .05 | .01 |
| Chicago Bears | | | |
| ☐ 520 Dan Fouts AP | 2.00 | .90 | .25 |
| San Diego Chargers | | | |
| ☐ 521 Bernard Jackson | .10 | .05 | .01 |
| Denver Broncos | | | |
| ☐ 522 Coy Bacon | .12 | .05 | .02 |
| Washington Redskins | | | |
| ☐ 523 Tony Franklin | .20 | .09 | .03 |
| Philadelphia Eagles | | | |
| ☐ 524 Bo Harris | .10 | .05 | .01 |
| Cincinnati Bengals | | | |
| ☐ 525 Bob Grupp AP | .10 | .05 | .01 |
| Kansas City Chiefs | | | |
| ☐ 526 San Francisco 49ers TL | .30 | .05 | .01 |
| Paul Hofer | | | |
| Freddie Solomon | | | |
| James Owens | | | |
| Dwaine Board | | | |
| ☐ 527 Steve Wilson | .10 | .05 | .01 |
| Tampa Bay Buccaneers | | | |
| ☐ 528 Bennie Cunningham | .12 | .05 | .02 |
| Pittsburgh Steelers | | | |

| | | | |
|---|---|---|---|
| St. Louis Cardinals | | | |
| ☐ 18 John Jefferson | .50 | .20 | .05 |
| San Diego Chargers | | | |
| ☐ 19 Jack Ham | 1.00 | .40 | .10 |
| Pittsburgh Steelers | | | |
| ☐ 20 Joe Greene | 1.50 | .60 | .15 |
| Pittsburgh Steelers | | | |
| ☐ 21 Chuck Muncie | .50 | .20 | .05 |
| San Diego Chargers | | | |
| ☐ 22 Ron Jaworski | .75 | .30 | .07 |
| Philadelphia Eagles | | | |
| ☐ 23 John Hannah | 1.00 | .40 | .10 |
| New England Patriots | | | |
| ☐ 24 Randy Gradishar | .50 | .20 | .05 |
| Denver Broncos | | | |
| ☐ 25 Jack Lambert | 1.50 | .60 | .15 |
| Pittsburgh Steelers | | | |
| ☐ 26 Ricky Bell | .50 | .20 | .05 |
| Tampa Bay Buccaneers | | | |
| ☐ 27 Drew Pearson | .75 | .30 | .07 |
| Dallas Cowboys | | | |
| ☐ 28 Rick Upchurch | .50 | .20 | .05 |
| Denver Broncos | | | |
| ☐ 29 Brad Van Pelt | .35 | .14 | .03 |
| New York Giants | | | |
| ☐ 30 Walter Payton | 6.00 | 2.40 | .60 |
| Chicago Bears | | | |

## 1980 Topps Super

The 1980 Topps Superstar Photo Football set features 30 large (approximately 4 7/8" by 6 7/8") and very colorful cards. This set, a football counterpart to Topps' Superstar Photo Baseball set of the same year, is numbered and is printed on white stock. The cards in this set, sold over the counter without gum at retail establishments, could be individually chosen by the buyer.

| | MINT | EXC | G-VG |
|---|---|---|---|
| COMPLETE SET (30) | 15.00 | 6.00 | 1.50 |
| COMMON PLAYER (1-30) | .35 | .14 | .03 |
| ☐ 1 Franco Harris | 2.00 | .80 | .20 |
| Pittsburgh Steelers | | | |
| ☐ 2 Bob Griese | 2.00 | .80 | .20 |
| Miami Dolphins | | | |
| ☐ 3 Archie Manning | 1.00 | .40 | .10 |
| New Orleans Saints | | | |
| ☐ 4 Harold Carmichael | .50 | .20 | .05 |
| Philadelphia Eagles | | | |
| ☐ 5 Wesley Walker | .50 | .20 | .05 |
| New York Jets | | | |
| ☐ 6 Richard Todd | .35 | .14 | .03 |
| New York Jets | | | |
| ☐ 7 Dan Fouts | 2.00 | .80 | .20 |
| San Diego Chargers | | | |
| ☐ 8 Ken Stabler | 2.00 | .80 | .20 |
| Houston Oilers | | | |
| ☐ 9 Jack Youngblood | 1.00 | .40 | .10 |
| Los Angeles Rams | | | |
| ☐ 10 Jim Zorn | .75 | .30 | .07 |
| Seattle Seahawks | | | |
| ☐ 11 Tony Dorsett | 2.00 | .80 | .20 |
| Dallas Cowboys | | | |
| ☐ 12 Lee Roy Selmon | .50 | .20 | .05 |
| Tampa Bay Buccaneers | | | |
| ☐ 13 Russ Francis | .35 | .14 | .03 |
| New England Patriots | | | |
| ☐ 14 John Stallworth | 1.00 | .40 | .10 |
| Pittsburgh Steelers | | | |
| ☐ 15 Terry Bradshaw | 4.00 | 1.60 | .40 |
| Pittsburgh Steelers | | | |
| ☐ 16 Joe Theismann | 2.00 | .80 | .20 |
| Washington Redskins | | | |
| ☐ 17 Ottis Anderson | 3.00 | 1.20 | .30 |

## 1981 Topps

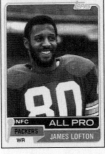 

The 1981 Topps football card set contains 528 cards of NFL players. The cards measure the standard 2 1/2" by 3 1/2". The backs of the cards contain player vital statistics, year-by-year records, and a short biography of the player. The fronts of the cards contain the name "Topps" in the frame line. The term SA refers to a Super Action card as stated on the obverse; the SA card is a special card issued in addition to the player's regular card. The first six cards in the set feature statistical league leaders from the previous season. Record-Breaking (RB) performances from the previous season are commemorated on cards 331-336. Post-season playoff action is summarized on cards 492-494. All-Pro (AP) selections are designated on the player's regular card, not a special card. Distributed throughout the set are Team Leader (TL) cards, typically, featuring four individual team statistical leaders on the front, as well as a team checklist on the back. The key Rookie Cards in this set are Art Monk, Joe Montana, and Kellen Winslow.

| | MINT | EXC | G-VG |
|---|---|---|---|
| COMPLETE SET (528) | 275.00 | 125.00 | 34.00 |
| COMMON PLAYER (1-528) | .07 | .03 | .01 |
| ☐ 1 Passing Leaders | .50 | .23 | .06 |
| Ron Jaworski | | | |
| Brian Sipe | | | |
| ☐ 2 Receiving Leaders | .50 | .23 | .06 |
| Earl Cooper | | | |
| Kellen Winslow | | | |
| ☐ 3 Sack Leaders | .15 | .07 | .02 |
| Al(Bubba) Baker | | | |
| Gary Johnson | | | |
| ☐ 4 Scoring Leaders | .15 | .07 | .02 |
| Ed Murray | | | |
| John Smith | | | |
| ☐ 5 Interception Leaders | .15 | .07 | .02 |
| Nolan Cromwell | | | |
| Lester Hayes | | | |
| ☐ 6 Punting Leaders | .15 | .07 | .02 |
| Dave Jennings | | | |
| Luke Prestridge | | | |
| ☐ 7 Don Calhoun | .07 | .03 | .01 |
| New England Patriots | | | |
| ☐ 8 Jack Tatum | .10 | .05 | .01 |
| Houston Oilers | | | |

|  | | | |
|---|---|---|---|
| 9 Reggie Rucker | .10 | .05 | .01 |
| Cleveland Browns | | | |
| 10 Mike Webster AP | .30 | .14 | .04 |
| Pittsburgh Steelers | | | |
| 11 Vince Evans | .75 | .35 | .09 |
| Chicago Bears | | | |
| 12 Ottis Anderson SA | .75 | .35 | .09 |
| St. Louis Cardinals | | | |
| 13 Leroy Harris | .07 | .03 | .01 |
| Philadelphia Eagles | | | |
| 14 Gordon King | .07 | .03 | .01 |
| New York Giants | | | |
| 15 Harvey Martin | .20 | .09 | .03 |
| Dallas Cowboys | | | |
| 16 Johnny "Lam" Jones | .07 | .03 | .01 |
| New York Jets | | | |
| 17 Ken Greene | .07 | .03 | .01 |
| St. Louis Cardinals | | | |
| 18 Frank Lewis | .10 | .05 | .01 |
| Buffalo Bills | | | |
| 19 Seattle Seahawks TL | .60 | .09 | .02 |
| Jim Jodat | | | |
| Dave Brown | | | |
| John Harris | | | |
| Steve Largent | | | |
| Jacob Green | | | |
| 20 Lester Hayes AP | .30 | .14 | .04 |
| Oakland Raiders | | | |
| 21 Uwe Von Schamann | .10 | .05 | .01 |
| Miami Dolphins | | | |
| 22 Joe Washington | .10 | .05 | .01 |
| Washington Redskins | | | |
| 23 Louie Kelcher | .10 | .05 | .01 |
| San Diego Chargers | | | |
| 24 Willie Miller | .10 | .05 | .01 |
| Los Angeles Rams | | | |
| 25 Steve Grogan | .30 | .14 | .04 |
| New England Patriots | | | |
| 26 John Hill | .07 | .03 | .01 |
| New Orleans Saints | | | |
| 27 Stan White | .07 | .03 | .01 |
| Detroit Lions | | | |
| 28 William Andrews SA | .10 | .05 | .01 |
| Atlanta Falcons | | | |
| 29 Clarence Scott | .07 | .03 | .01 |
| Cleveland Browns | | | |
| 30 Leon Gray AP | .10 | .05 | .01 |
| Houston Oilers | | | |
| 31 Craig Colquitt | .07 | .03 | .01 |
| Pittsburgh Steelers | | | |
| 32 Doug Williams | .30 | .14 | .04 |
| Tampa Bay Buccaneers | | | |
| 33 Bob Breunig | .10 | .05 | .01 |
| Dallas Cowboys | | | |
| 34 Billy Taylor | .07 | .03 | .01 |
| New York Giants | | | |
| 35 Harold Carmichael | .40 | .18 | .05 |
| Philadelphia Eagles | | | |
| 36 Ray Wersching | .10 | .05 | .01 |
| San Francisco 49ers | | | |
| 37 Dennis Johnson | .07 | .03 | .01 |
| Minnesota Vikings | | | |
| 38 Archie Griffin | .20 | .09 | .03 |
| Cincinnati Bengals | | | |
| 39 Los Angeles Rams TL | .25 | .04 | .01 |
| Cullen Bryant | | | |
| Billy Waddy | | | |
| Nolan Cromwell | | | |
| Jack Youngblood | | | |
| 40 Gary Fencik AP | .07 | .03 | .01 |
| Chicago Bears | | | |
| 41 Lynn Dickey | .10 | .05 | .01 |
| Green Bay Packers | | | |
| 42 Steve Bartkowski SA | .10 | .05 | .01 |
| Atlanta Falcons | | | |
| 43 Art Shell | .40 | .18 | .05 |
| Oakland Raiders | | | |
| 44 Wilbur Jackson | .10 | .05 | .01 |
| Washington Redskins | | | |
| 45 Frank Corral | .07 | .03 | .01 |
| Los Angeles Rams | | | |
| 46 Ted McKnight | .07 | .03 | .01 |
| Kansas City Chiefs | | | |
| 47 Joe Klecko | .30 | .14 | .04 |
| New York Jets | | | |
| 48 Dan Doornink | .07 | .03 | .01 |
| Seattle Seahawks | | | |
| 49 Doug Dieken | .07 | .03 | .01 |
| Cleveland Browns | | | |
| 50 Jerry Robinson AP | .60 | .25 | .08 |
| Philadelphia Eagles | | | |
| 51 Wallace Francis | .07 | .03 | .01 |
| Atlanta Falcons | | | |
| 52 Dave Preston | .07 | .03 | .01 |
| Denver Broncos | | | |
| 53 Jay Saldi | .07 | .03 | .01 |
| Dallas Cowboys | | | |
| 54 Rush Brown | .07 | .03 | .01 |
| St. Louis Cardinals | | | |
| 55 Phil Simms | 4.00 | 1.80 | .50 |
| New York Giants | | | |
| 56 Nick Mike-Mayer | .07 | .03 | .01 |
| Buffalo Bills | | | |
| 57 Wash. Redskins TL | 2.00 | .30 | .06 |
| Wilbur Jackson | | | |
| Art Monk | | | |
| Lemar Parrish | | | |
| Coy Bacon | | | |
| 58 Mike Renfro | .10 | .05 | .01 |
| Houston Oilers | | | |
| 59 Ted Brown SA | .07 | .03 | .01 |
| Minnesota Vikings | | | |
| 60 Steve Nelson AP | .07 | .03 | .01 |
| New England Patriots | | | |
| 61 Sidney Thornton | .10 | .05 | .01 |
| Pittsburgh Steelers | | | |
| 62 Kent Hill | .10 | .05 | .01 |
| Los Angeles Rams | | | |
| 63 Don Bessillieu | .07 | .03 | .01 |
| Miami Dolphins | | | |
| 64 Fred Cook | .07 | .03 | .01 |
| Baltimore Colts | | | |
| 65 Raymond Chester | .10 | .05 | .01 |
| Oakland Raiders | | | |
| 66 Rick Kane | .07 | .03 | .01 |
| Detroit Lions | | | |
| 67 Mike Fuller | .07 | .03 | .01 |
| San Diego Chargers | | | |
| 68 Dewey Selmon | .10 | .05 | .01 |
| Tampa Bay Buccaneers | | | |
| 69 Charles White | 1.00 | .45 | .13 |
| Cleveland Browns | | | |
| 70 Jeff Van Note AP | .10 | .05 | .01 |
| Atlanta Falcons | | | |
| 71 Robert Newhouse | .10 | .05 | .01 |
| Dallas Cowboys | | | |
| 72 Roynell Young | .07 | .03 | .01 |
| Philadelphia Eagles | | | |
| 73 Lynn Cain SA | .07 | .03 | .01 |
| Atlanta Falcons | | | |
| 74 Mike Friede | .07 | .03 | .01 |
| New York Giants | | | |
| 75 Earl Cooper | .10 | .05 | .01 |
| San Francisco 49ers | | | |
| 76 New Orleans Saints TL | .25 | .04 | .01 |
| Jimmy Rogers | | | |
| Wes Chandler | | | |
| Tom Myers | | | |
| Elois Grooms | | | |
| Derland Moore | | | |
| 77 Rick Danmeier | .07 | .03 | .01 |
| Minnesota Vikings | | | |
| 78 Darrol Ray | .07 | .03 | .01 |
| New York Jets | | | |
| 79 Gregg Bingham | .07 | .03 | .01 |
| Houston Oilers | | | |
| 80 John Hannah AP | .40 | .18 | .05 |
| New England Patriots | | | |
| 81 Jack Thompson | .10 | .05 | .01 |
| Cincinnati Bengals | | | |
| 82 Rick Upchurch | .10 | .05 | .01 |
| Denver Broncos | | | |
| 83 Mike Butler | .07 | .03 | .01 |
| Green Bay Packers | | | |
| 84 Don Warren | .30 | .14 | .04 |
| Washington Redskins | | | |
| 85 Mark Van Eeghen | .10 | .05 | .01 |
| Oakland Raiders | | | |
| 86 J.T. Smith | 1.00 | .45 | .13 |
| Kansas City Chiefs | | | |
| 87 Herman Weaver | .07 | .03 | .01 |
| Seattle Seahawks | | | |
| 88 Terry Bradshaw SA | 1.00 | .45 | .13 |
| Pittsburgh Steelers | | | |
| 89 Charlie Hall | .07 | .03 | .01 |
| Cleveland Browns | | | |
| 90 Donnie Shell | .25 | .11 | .03 |
| Pittsburgh Steelers | | | |
| 91 Ike Harris | .07 | .03 | .01 |
| New Orleans Saints | | | |
| 92 Charlie Johnson | .07 | .03 | .01 |
| Philadelphia Eagles | | | |
| 93 Rickey Watts | .07 | .03 | .01 |
| Chicago Bears | | | |
| 94 New England Pats TL | .30 | .05 | .01 |
| Vagas Ferguson | | | |
| Stanley Morgan | | | |
| Raymond Clayborn | | | |
| Julius Adams | | | |
| 95 Drew Pearson | .50 | .23 | .06 |
| Dallas Cowboys | | | |
| 96 Neil O'Donoghue | .07 | .03 | .01 |
| St. Louis Cardinals | | | |
| 97 Conrad Dobler | .10 | .05 | .01 |

Buffalo Bills
- ☐ 98 Jewel Thomas .07 .03 .01
  Los Angeles Rams
- ☐ 99 Mike Barber .07 .03 .01
  Houston Oilers
- ☐ 100 Billy Sims AP 1.50 .65 .19
  Detroit Lions
- ☐ 101 Vern Den Herder .07 .03 .01
  Miami Dolphins
- ☐ 102 Greg Landry .15 .07 .02
  Baltimore Colts
- ☐ 103 Joe Cribbs SA .07 .03 .01
  Buffalo Bills
- ☐ 104 Mark Murphy .07 .03 .01
  Washington Redskins
- ☐ 105 Chuck Muncie .10 .05 .01
  San Diego Chargers
- ☐ 106 Alfred Jackson .10 .05 .01
  Atlanta Falcons
- ☐ 107 Chris Bahr .07 .03 .01
  Oakland Raiders
- ☐ 108 Gordon Jones .10 .05 .01
  Tampa Bay Buccaneers
- ☐ 109 Willie Harper .10 .05 .01
  San Francisco 49ers
- ☐ 110 Dave Jennings AP .10 .05 .01
  New York Giants
- ☐ 111 Bennie Cunningham .10 .05 .01
  Pittsburgh Steelers
- ☐ 112 Jerry Sisemore .10 .05 .01
  Philadelphia Eagles
- ☐ 113 Cleveland Browns TL .30 .05 .01
  Mike Pruitt
  Dave Logan
  Ron Bolton
  Lyle Alzado
- ☐ 114 Rickey Young .10 .05 .01
  Minnesota Vikings
- ☐ 115 Ken Anderson .60 .25 .08
  Cincinnati Bengals
- ☐ 116 Randy Gradishar .30 .14 .04
  Denver Broncos
- ☐ 117 Eddie Lee Ivery .25 .11 .03
  Green Bay Packers
- ☐ 118 Wesley Walker .30 .14 .04
  New York Jets
- ☐ 119 Chuck Foreman .15 .07 .02
  New England Patriots
- ☐ 120 Nolan Cromwell AP .30 .14 .04
  Los Angeles Rams
  UER (Rushing TD's
  added wrong)
- ☐ 121 Curtis Dickey SA .10 .05 .01
  Baltimore Colts
- ☐ 122 Wayne Morris .07 .03 .01
  St. Louis Cardinals
- ☐ 123 Greg Stemrick .07 .03 .01
  Houston Oilers
- ☐ 124 Coy Bacon .10 .05 .01
  Washington Redskins
- ☐ 125 Jim Zorn .20 .09 .03
  (Steve Largent
  in background)
  Seattle Seahawks
- ☐ 126 Henry Childs .07 .03 .01
  New Orleans Saints
- ☐ 127 Checklist 1-132 .50 .05 .02
- ☐ 128 Len Walterscheid .07 .03 .01
  Chicago Bears
- ☐ 129 Johnny Evans .07 .03 .01
  Cleveland Browns
- ☐ 130 Gary Barbaro AP .10 .05 .01
  Kansas City Chiefs
- ☐ 131 Jim Smith .10 .05 .01
  Pittsburgh Steelers
- ☐ 132 New York Jets TL .25 .04 .01
  Scott Dierking
  Bruce Harper
  Ken Schroy
  Mark Gastineau
- ☐ 133 Curtis Brown .07 .03 .01
  Buffalo Bills
- ☐ 134 D.D. Lewis .10 .05 .01
  Dallas Cowboys
- ☐ 135 Jim Plunkett .50 .23 .06
  Oakland Raiders
- ☐ 136 Nat Moore .10 .05 .01
  Miami Dolphins
- ☐ 137 Don McCauley .07 .03 .01
  Baltimore Colts
- ☐ 138 Tony Dorsett SA .75 .35 .09
  Dallas Cowboys
- ☐ 139 Julius Adams .07 .03 .01
  New England Patriots
- ☐ 140 Ahmad Rashad AP .50 .23 .06
  Minnesota Vikings
- ☐ 141 Rich Saul .07 .03 .01
  Los Angeles Rams
- ☐ 142 Ken Fantetti .07 .03 .01
  Detroit Lions
- ☐ 143 Kenny Johnson .07 .03 .01
  Atlanta Falcons
- ☐ 144 Clark Gaines .07 .03 .01
  New York Jets
- ☐ 145 Mark Moseley .10 .05 .01
  Washington Redskins
- ☐ 146 Vernon Perry .20 .09 .03
  Houston Oilers
- ☐ 147 Jerry Eckwood .07 .03 .01
  Tampa Bay Buccaneers
- ☐ 148 Freddie Solomon .10 .05 .01
  San Francisco 49ers
- ☐ 149 Jerry Sherk .10 .05 .01
  Cleveland Browns
- ☐ 150 Kellen Winslow AP 12.00 5.50 1.50
  San Diego Chargers
- ☐ 151 Green Bay Packers TL .75 .11 .02
  Eddie Lee Ivery
  James Lofton
  Johnnie Gray
  Mike Butler
- ☐ 152 Ross Browner .10 .05 .01
  Cincinnati Bengals
- ☐ 153 Dan Fouts SA .75 .35 .09
  San Diego Chargers
- ☐ 154 Woody Peoples .07 .03 .01
  Philadelphia Eagles
- ☐ 155 Jack Lambert 1.00 .45 .13
  Pittsburgh Steelers
- ☐ 156 Mike Dennis .07 .03 .01
  New York Giants
- ☐ 157 Rafael Septien .07 .03 .01
  Dallas Cowboys
- ☐ 158 Archie Manning .30 .14 .04
  New Orleans Saints
- ☐ 159 Don Hasselbeck .07 .03 .01
  New England Patriots
- ☐ 160 Alan Page AP .40 .18 .05
  Chicago Bears
- ☐ 161 Arthur Whittington .07 .03 .01
  Oakland Raiders
- ☐ 162 Billy Waddy .07 .03 .01
  Los Angeles Rams
- ☐ 163 Horace Belton .07 .03 .01
  Kansas City Chiefs
- ☐ 164 Luke Prestridge .07 .03 .01
  Denver Broncos
- ☐ 165 Joe Theismann .75 .35 .09
  Washington Redskins
- ☐ 166 Morris Towns .07 .03 .01
  Houston Oilers
- ☐ 167 Dave Brown .07 .03 .01
  Seattle Seahawks
- ☐ 168 Ezra Johnson .07 .03 .01
  Green Bay Packers
- ☐ 169 Tampa Bay Bucs TL .25 .04 .01
  Ricky Bell
  Gordon Jones
  Mike Washington
  Lee Roy Selmon
- ☐ 170 Joe DeLamielleure AP .10 .05 .01
  Cleveland Browns
- ☐ 171 Earnest Gray SA .07 .03 .01
  New York Giants
- ☐ 172 Mike Thomas .10 .05 .01
  San Diego Chargers
- ☐ 173 Jim Haslett .07 .03 .01
  Buffalo Bills
- ☐ 174 David Woodley .30 .14 .04
  Miami Dolphins
- ☐ 175 Al(Bubba) Baker .10 .05 .01
  Detroit Lions
- ☐ 176 Nesby Glasgow .07 .03 .01
  Baltimore Colts
- ☐ 177 Pat Leahy .10 .05 .01
  New York Jets
- ☐ 178 Tom Brahaney .07 .03 .01
  St. Louis Cardinals
- ☐ 179 Herman Edwards .07 .03 .01
  Philadelphia Eagles
- ☐ 180 Junior Miller AP .25 .11 .03
  Atlanta Falcons
- ☐ 181 Richard Wood .07 .03 .01
  Tampa Bay Buccaneers
- ☐ 182 Lenvil Elliott .07 .03 .01
  San Francisco 49ers
- ☐ 183 Sammie White .15 .07 .02
  Minnesota Vikings
- ☐ 184 Russell Erxleben .07 .03 .01
  New Orleans Saints
- ☐ 185 Ed Too Tall Jones .75 .35 .09
  Dallas Cowboys
- ☐ 186 Ray Guy SA .10 .05 .01
  Oakland Raiders
- ☐ 187 Haven Moses .10 .05 .01

Denver Broncos
| ☐ 188 New York Giants TL | .25 | .04 | .01 |

Billy Taylor
Earnest Gray
Mike Dennis
Gary Jeter

| ☐ 189 David Whitehurst | .10 | .05 | .01 |

Green Bay Packers

| ☐ 190 John Jefferson AP | .25 | .11 | .03 |

San Diego Chargers

| ☐ 191 Terry Beeson | .07 | .03 | .01 |

Seattle Seahawks

| ☐ 192 Dan Ross | .50 | .23 | .06 |

Cincinnati Bengals

| ☐ 193 Dave Williams | .07 | .03 | .01 |

Chicago Bears

| ☐ 194 Art Monk | 30.00 | 13.50 | 3.80 |

Washington Redskins

| ☐ 195 Roger Wehrli | .10 | .05 | .01 |

St. Louis Cardinals

| ☐ 196 Ricky Feacher | .07 | .03 | .01 |

Cleveland Browns

| ☐ 197 Miami Dolphins TL | .30 | .05 | .01 |

Delvin Williams
Tony Nathan
Gerald Small
Kim Bokamper
A.J. Duhe

| ☐ 198 Carl Roaches | .07 | .03 | .01 |

Houston Oilers

| ☐ 199 Billy Campfield | .07 | .03 | .01 |

Philadelphia Eagles

| ☐ 200 Ted Hendricks AP | .30 | .14 | .04 |

Oakland Raiders

| ☐ 201 Fred Smerlas | .75 | .35 | .09 |

Buffalo Bills

| ☐ 202 Walter Payton SA | 2.50 | 1.15 | .30 |

Chicago Bears

| ☐ 203 Luther Bradley | .07 | .03 | .01 |

Detroit Lions

| ☐ 204 Herbert Scott | .10 | .05 | .01 |

Dallas Cowboys

| ☐ 205 Jack Youngblood | .30 | .14 | .04 |

Los Angeles Rams

| ☐ 206 Danny Pittman | .07 | .03 | .01 |

New York Giants

| ☐ 207 Houston Oilers TL | .30 | .14 | .04 |

Carl Roaches
Mike Barber
Jack Tatum
Jesse Baker
Robert Brazile

| ☐ 208 Vagas Ferguson | .07 | .03 | .01 |

New England Patriots

| ☐ 209 Mark Dennard | .07 | .03 | .01 |

Miami Dolphins

| ☐ 210 Lemar Parrish AP | .10 | .05 | .01 |

Washington Redskins

| ☐ 211 Bruce Harper | .07 | .03 | .01 |

New York Jets

| ☐ 212 Ed Simonini | .07 | .03 | .01 |

Baltimore Colts

| ☐ 213 Nick Lowery | 4.00 | 1.80 | .50 |

Kansas City Chiefs

| ☐ 214 Kevin House | .30 | .14 | .04 |

Tampa Bay Buccaneers

| ☐ 215 Mike Kenn | 1.50 | .65 | .19 |

Atlanta Falcons

| ☐ 216 Joe Montana | 200.00 | 90.00 | 25.00 |

San Francisco 49ers

| ☐ 217 Joe Senser | .10 | .05 | .01 |

Minnesota Vikings

| ☐ 218 Lester Hayes SA | .10 | .05 | .01 |

Oakland Raiders

| ☐ 219 Gene Upshaw | .25 | .11 | .03 |

Oakland Raiders

| ☐ 220 Franco Harris | 1.00 | .45 | .13 |

Pittsburgh Steelers

| ☐ 221 Ron Bolton | .07 | .03 | .01 |

Cleveland Browns

| ☐ 222 Charles Alexander | .07 | .03 | .01 |

Cincinnati Bengals

| ☐ 223 Matt Robinson | .10 | .05 | .01 |

Denver Broncos

| ☐ 224 Ray Oldham | .07 | .03 | .01 |

Detroit Lions

| ☐ 225 George Martin | .10 | .05 | .01 |

New York Giants

| ☐ 226 Buffalo Bills TL | .25 | .04 | .01 |

Joe Cribbs
Jerry Butler
Steve Freeman
Ben Williams

| ☐ 227 Tony Franklin | .10 | .05 | .01 |

Philadelphia Eagles

| ☐ 228 George Cumby | .07 | .03 | .01 |

Green Bay Packers

| ☐ 229 Butch Johnson | .10 | .05 | .01 |

Dallas Cowboys

| ☐ 230 Mike Haynes AP | .10 | .05 | .01 |

New England Patriots

| ☐ 231 Rob Carpenter | .10 | .05 | .01 |

Houston Oilers

| ☐ 232 Steve Fuller | .10 | .05 | .01 |

Kansas City Chiefs

| ☐ 233 John Sawyer | .07 | .03 | .01 |

Seattle Seahawks

| ☐ 234 Kenny King SA | .07 | .03 | .01 |

Oakland Raiders

| ☐ 235 Jack Ham | .75 | .35 | .09 |

Pittsburgh Steelers

| ☐ 236 Jimmy Rogers | .07 | .03 | .01 |

New Orleans Saints

| ☐ 237 Bob Parsons | .07 | .03 | .01 |

Chicago Bears

| ☐ 238 Marty Lyons | .60 | .25 | .08 |

New York Jets

| ☐ 239 Pat Tilley | .10 | .05 | .01 |

St. Louis Cardinals

| ☐ 240 Dennis Harrah AP | .10 | .05 | .01 |

Los Angeles Rams

| ☐ 241 Thom Darden | .07 | .03 | .01 |

Cleveland Browns

| ☐ 242 Rolf Benirschke | .10 | .05 | .01 |

San Diego Chargers

| ☐ 243 Gerald Small | .10 | .05 | .01 |

Miami Dolphins

| ☐ 244 Atlanta Falcons TL | .25 | .04 | .01 |

William Andrews
Alfred Jenkins
Al Richardson
Joel Williams

| ☐ 245 Roger Carr | .10 | .05 | .01 |

Baltimore Colts

| ☐ 246 Sherman White | .07 | .03 | .01 |

Buffalo Bills

| ☐ 247 Ted Brown | .10 | .05 | .01 |

Minnesota Vikings

| ☐ 248 Matt Cavanaugh | .10 | .05 | .01 |

New England Patriots

| ☐ 249 John Dutton | .10 | .05 | .01 |

Dallas Cowboys

| ☐ 250 Bill Bergey AP | .15 | .07 | .02 |

Philadelphia Eagles

| ☐ 251 Jim Allen | .07 | .03 | .01 |

Detroit Lions

| ☐ 252 Mike Nelms SA | .10 | .05 | .01 |

Washington Redskins

| ☐ 253 Tom Blanchard | .07 | .03 | .01 |

Tampa Bay Buccaneers

| ☐ 254 Ricky Thompson | .07 | .03 | .01 |

Washington Redskins

| ☐ 255 John Matuszak | .10 | .05 | .01 |

Oakland Raiders

| ☐ 256 Randy Grossman | .07 | .03 | .01 |

Pittsburgh Steelers

| ☐ 257 Ray Griffin | .07 | .03 | .01 |

Cincinnati Bengals

| ☐ 258 Lynn Cain | .10 | .05 | .01 |

Atlanta Falcons

| ☐ 259 Checklist 133-264 | .50 | .05 | .02 |
| ☐ 260 Mike Pruitt AP | .10 | .05 | .01 |

Cleveland Browns

| ☐ 261 Chris Ward | .07 | .03 | .01 |

New York Jets

| ☐ 262 Fred Steinfort | .07 | .03 | .01 |

Denver Broncos

| ☐ 263 James Owens | .10 | .05 | .01 |

San Francisco 49ers

| ☐ 264 Chicago Bears TL | 1.50 | .23 | .05 |

Walter Payton
James Scott
Len Walterscheid
Dan Hampton

| ☐ 265 Dan Fouts | 1.50 | .65 | .19 |

San Diego Chargers

| ☐ 266 Arnold Morgado | .07 | .03 | .01 |

Kansas City Chiefs

| ☐ 267 John Jefferson SA | .10 | .05 | .01 |

San Diego Chargers

| ☐ 268 Bill Lenkaitis | .07 | .03 | .01 |

New England Patriots

| ☐ 269 James Jones | .10 | .05 | .01 |

Dallas Cowboys

| ☐ 270 Brad Van Pelt | .10 | .05 | .01 |

New York Giants

| ☐ 271 Steve Largent | 1.50 | .65 | .19 |

Seattle Seahawks

| ☐ 272 Elvin Bethea | .10 | .05 | .01 |

Houston Oilers

| ☐ 273 Cullen Bryant | .10 | .05 | .01 |

Los Angeles Rams

| ☐ 274 Gary Danielson | .10 | .05 | .01 |

Detroit Lions

| ☐ 275 Tony Galbreath | .10 | .05 | .01 |

New Orleans Saints

| | | | |
|---|---|---|---|
| ☐ 276 Dave Butz | .25 | .11 | .03 |
| Washington Redskins | | | |
| ☐ 277 Steve Mike-Mayer | .07 | .03 | .01 |
| Baltimore Colts | | | |
| ☐ 278 Ron Johnson | .10 | .05 | .01 |
| Pittsburgh Steelers | | | |
| ☐ 279 Tom DeLeone | .07 | .03 | .01 |
| Cleveland Browns | | | |
| ☐ 280 Ron Jaworski | .20 | .09 | .03 |
| Philadelphia Eagles | | | |
| ☐ 281 Mel Gray | .10 | .05 | .01 |
| St. Louis Cardinals | | | |
| ☐ 282 San Diego Chargers TL | .30 | .05 | .01 |
| Chuck Muncie | | | |
| John Jefferson | | | |
| Glen Edwards | | | |
| Gary Johnson | | | |
| ☐ 283 Mark Brammer | .07 | .03 | .01 |
| Buffalo Bills | | | |
| ☐ 284 Alfred Jenkins SA | .10 | .05 | .01 |
| Atlanta Falcons | | | |
| ☐ 285 Greg Buttle | .10 | .05 | .01 |
| New York Jets | | | |
| ☐ 286 Randy Hughes | .07 | .03 | .01 |
| Dallas Cowboys | | | |
| ☐ 287 Delvin Williams | .10 | .05 | .01 |
| Miami Dolphins | | | |
| ☐ 288 Brian Baschnagel | .07 | .03 | .01 |
| Chicago Bears | | | |
| ☐ 289 Gary Jeter | .10 | .05 | .01 |
| New York Giants | | | |
| ☐ 290 Stanley Morgan AP | .50 | .23 | .06 |
| New England Patriots | | | |
| ☐ 291 Gerry Ellis | .07 | .03 | .01 |
| Green Bay Packers | | | |
| ☐ 292 Al Richardson | .07 | .03 | .01 |
| Atlanta Falcons | | | |
| ☐ 293 Jimmie Giles | .10 | .05 | .01 |
| Tampa Bay Buccaneers | | | |
| ☐ 294 Dave Jennings SA | .10 | .05 | .01 |
| New York Giants | | | |
| ☐ 295 Wilbert Montgomery | .15 | .07 | .02 |
| Philadelphia Eagles | | | |
| ☐ 296 Dave Pureifory | .07 | .03 | .01 |
| Detroit Lions | | | |
| ☐ 297 Greg Hawthorne | .07 | .03 | .01 |
| Pittsburgh Steelers | | | |
| ☐ 298 Dick Ambrose | .07 | .03 | .01 |
| Cleveland Browns | | | |
| ☐ 299 Terry Hermeling | .07 | .03 | .01 |
| Washington Redskins | | | |
| ☐ 300 Danny White | .40 | .18 | .05 |
| Dallas Cowboys | | | |
| ☐ 301 Ken Burrough | .10 | .05 | .01 |
| Houston Oilers | | | |
| ☐ 302 Paul Hofer | .07 | .03 | .01 |
| San Francisco 49ers | | | |
| ☐ 303 Denver Broncos TL | .25 | .04 | .01 |
| Jim Jensen | | | |
| Haven Moses | | | |
| Steve Foley | | | |
| Rulon Jones | | | |
| ☐ 304 Eddie Payton | .10 | .05 | .01 |
| Minnesota Vikings | | | |
| ☐ 305 Isaac Curtis | .10 | .05 | .01 |
| Cincinnati Bengals | | | |
| ☐ 306 Benny Ricardo | .07 | .03 | .01 |
| New Orleans Saints | | | |
| ☐ 307 Riley Odoms | .10 | .05 | .01 |
| Denver Broncos | | | |
| ☐ 308 Bob Chandler | .10 | .05 | .01 |
| Oakland Raiders | | | |
| ☐ 309 Larry Heater | .07 | .03 | .01 |
| New York Giants | | | |
| ☐ 310 Art Still AP | .50 | .23 | .06 |
| Kansas City Chiefs | | | |
| ☐ 311 Harold Jackson | .20 | .09 | .03 |
| New England Patriots | | | |
| ☐ 312 Charlie Joiner SA | .25 | .11 | .03 |
| San Diego Chargers | | | |
| ☐ 313 Jeff Nixon | .07 | .03 | .01 |
| Buffalo Bills | | | |
| ☐ 314 Aundra Thompson | .10 | .05 | .01 |
| Green Bay Packers | | | |
| ☐ 315 Richard Todd | .10 | .05 | .01 |
| New York Jets | | | |
| ☐ 316 Dan Hampton | 6.00 | 2.70 | .75 |
| Chicago Bears | | | |
| ☐ 317 Doug Marsh | .07 | .03 | .01 |
| St. Louis Cardinals | | | |
| ☐ 318 Louie Giammona | .07 | .03 | .01 |
| Philadelphia Eagles | | | |
| ☐ 319 San Francisco 49ers TL | .50 | .08 | .02 |
| Earl Cooper | | | |
| Dwight Clark | | | |
| Ricky Churchman | | | |
| Dwight Hicks | | | |
| Jim Stuckey | | | |
| ☐ 320 Manu Tuiasosopo | .07 | .03 | .01 |
| Seattle Seahawks | | | |
| ☐ 321 Rich Milot | .07 | .03 | .01 |
| Washington Redskins | | | |
| ☐ 322 Mike Guman | .07 | .03 | .01 |
| Los Angeles Rams | | | |
| ☐ 323 Bob Kuechenberg | .12 | .05 | .02 |
| Miami Dolphins | | | |
| ☐ 324 Tom Skladany | .07 | .03 | .01 |
| Detroit Lions | | | |
| ☐ 325 Dave Logan | .10 | .05 | .01 |
| Cleveland Browns | | | |
| ☐ 326 Bruce Laird | .07 | .03 | .01 |
| Baltimore Colts | | | |
| ☐ 327 James Jones SA | .07 | .03 | .01 |
| Dallas Cowboys | | | |
| ☐ 328 Joe Danelo | .07 | .03 | .01 |
| New York Giants | | | |
| ☐ 329 Kenny King | .07 | .03 | .01 |
| Oakland Raiders | | | |
| ☐ 330 Pat Donovan AP | .07 | .03 | .01 |
| Dallas Cowboys | | | |
| ☐ 331 Earl Cooper RB | .15 | .07 | .02 |
| Most Receptions, | | | |
| Running Back, | | | |
| Season, Rookie | | | |
| ☐ 332 John Jefferson RB | .15 | .07 | .02 |
| Most Cons. Seasons, | | | |
| 1000 Yards Receiving, | | | |
| Start of Career | | | |
| ☐ 333 Kenny King RB | .15 | .07 | .02 |
| Longest Pass Caught, | | | |
| Super Bowl History | | | |
| ☐ 334 Rod Martin RB | .15 | .07 | .02 |
| Most Interceptions | | | |
| Super Bowl Game | | | |
| ☐ 335 Jim Plunkett RB | .20 | .09 | .03 |
| Longest Pass, | | | |
| Super Bowl History | | | |
| ☐ 336 Bill Thompson RB | .15 | .07 | .02 |
| Most Touchdowns, | | | |
| Fumble Recoveries, | | | |
| Lifetime | | | |
| ☐ 337 John Cappelletti | .20 | .09 | .03 |
| San Diego Chargers | | | |
| ☐ 338 Detroit Lions TL | .40 | .06 | .01 |
| Billy Sims | | | |
| Freddie Scott | | | |
| Jim Allen | | | |
| James Hunter | | | |
| Al(Bubba) Baker | | | |
| ☐ 339 Don Smith | .07 | .03 | .01 |
| Atlanta Falcons | | | |
| ☐ 340 Rod Perry AP | .10 | .05 | .01 |
| Los Angeles Rams | | | |
| ☐ 341 David Lewis | .07 | .03 | .01 |
| Tampa Bay Buccaneers | | | |
| ☐ 342 Mark Gastineau | 1.00 | .45 | .13 |
| New York Jets | | | |
| ☐ 343 Steve Largent SA | .75 | .35 | .09 |
| Seattle Seahawks | | | |
| ☐ 344 Charley Young | .10 | .05 | .01 |
| San Francisco 49ers | | | |
| ☐ 345 Toni Fritsch | .07 | .03 | .01 |
| Houston Oilers | | | |
| ☐ 346 Matt Blair | .10 | .05 | .01 |
| Minnesota Vikings | | | |
| ☐ 347 Don Bass | .07 | .03 | .01 |
| Cincinnati Bengals | | | |
| ☐ 348 Jim Jensen | .25 | .11 | .03 |
| Denver Broncos | | | |
| ☐ 349 Karl Lorch | .07 | .03 | .01 |
| Washington Redskins | | | |
| ☐ 350 Brian Sipe AP | .25 | .11 | .03 |
| Cleveland Browns | | | |
| ☐ 351 Theo Bell | .07 | .03 | .01 |
| Pittsburgh Steelers | | | |
| ☐ 352 Sam Adams | .07 | .03 | .01 |
| New England Patriots | | | |
| ☐ 353 Paul Coffman | .10 | .05 | .01 |
| Green Bay Packers | | | |
| ☐ 354 Eric Harris | .07 | .03 | .01 |
| Kansas City Chiefs | | | |
| ☐ 355 Tony Hill | .20 | .09 | .03 |
| Dallas Cowboys | | | |
| ☐ 356 J.T. Turner | .07 | .03 | .01 |
| New York Giants | | | |
| ☐ 357 Frank LeMaster | .07 | .03 | .01 |
| Philadelphia Eagles | | | |
| ☐ 358 Jim Jodat | .07 | .03 | .01 |
| Seattle Seahawks | | | |
| ☐ 359 Oakland Raiders TL | .30 | .05 | .01 |
| Mark Van Eeghen | | | |
| Cliff Branch | | | |
| Lester Hayes | | | |
| Cedrick Hardman | | | |
| Ted Hendricks | | | |

| | | | |
|---|---|---|---|
| ☐ 360 Joe Cribbs AP | 1.00 | .45 | .13 |
| Buffalo Bills | | | |
| ☐ 361 James Lofton SA | 1.75 | .80 | .22 |
| Green Bay Packers | | | |
| ☐ 362 Dexter Bussey | .07 | .03 | .01 |
| Detroit Lions | | | |
| ☐ 363 Bobby Jackson | .07 | .03 | .01 |
| New York Jets | | | |
| ☐ 364 Steve DeBerg | .75 | .35 | .09 |
| San Francisco 49ers | | | |
| ☐ 365 Ottis Anderson | 1.00 | .45 | .13 |
| St. Louis Cardinals | | | |
| ☐ 366 Tom Myers | .07 | .03 | .01 |
| New Orleans Saints | | | |
| ☐ 367 John James | .07 | .03 | .01 |
| Atlanta Falcons | | | |
| ☐ 368 Reese McCall | .07 | .03 | .01 |
| Baltimore Colts | | | |
| ☐ 369 Jack Reynolds | .10 | .05 | .01 |
| Los Angeles Rams | | | |
| ☐ 370 Gary Johnson AP | .07 | .03 | .01 |
| San Diego Chargers | | | |
| ☐ 371 Jimmy Cefalo | .10 | .05 | .01 |
| Miami Dolphins | | | |
| ☐ 372 Horace Ivory | .07 | .03 | .01 |
| New England Patriots | | | |
| ☐ 373 Garo Yepremian | .07 | .03 | .01 |
| Tampa Bay Buccaneers | | | |
| ☐ 374 Brian Kelley | .07 | .03 | .01 |
| New York Giants | | | |
| ☐ 375 Terry Bradshaw | 2.50 | 1.15 | .30 |
| Pittsburgh Steelers | | | |
| ☐ 376 Dallas Cowboys TL | .60 | .09 | .02 |
| Tony Dorsett | | | |
| Tony Hill | | | |
| Dennis Thurman | | | |
| Charlie Waters | | | |
| Harvey Martin | | | |
| ☐ 377 Randy Logan | .07 | .03 | .01 |
| Philadelphia Eagles | | | |
| ☐ 378 Tim Wilson | .07 | .03 | .01 |
| Houston Oilers | | | |
| ☐ 379 Archie Manning SA | .15 | .07 | .02 |
| New Orleans Saints | | | |
| ☐ 380 Revie Sorey AP | .07 | .03 | .01 |
| Chicago Bears | | | |
| ☐ 381 Randy Holloway | .07 | .03 | .01 |
| Minnesota Vikings | | | |
| ☐ 382 Henry Lawrence | .07 | .03 | .01 |
| Oakland Raiders | | | |
| ☐ 383 Pat McInally | .10 | .05 | .01 |
| Cincinnati Bengals | | | |
| ☐ 384 Kevin Long | .07 | .03 | .01 |
| New York Jets | | | |
| ☐ 385 Louis Wright | .07 | .03 | .01 |
| Denver Broncos | | | |
| ☐ 386 Leonard Thompson | .07 | .03 | .01 |
| Detroit Lions | | | |
| ☐ 387 Jan Stenerud | .20 | .09 | .03 |
| Green Bay Packers | | | |
| ☐ 388 Raymond Butler | .25 | .11 | .03 |
| Baltimore Colts | | | |
| ☐ 389 Checklist 265-396 | .50 | .05 | .02 |
| ☐ 390 Steve Bartkowski AP | .25 | .11 | .03 |
| Atlanta Falcons | | | |
| ☐ 391 Clarence Harmon | .07 | .03 | .01 |
| Washington Redskins | | | |
| ☐ 392 Wilbert Montgomery SA | .10 | .05 | .01 |
| Philadelphia Eagles | | | |
| ☐ 393 Billy Joe DuPree | .10 | .05 | .01 |
| Dallas Cowboys | | | |
| ☐ 394 Kansas City Chiefs TL | .25 | .04 | .01 |
| Ted McKnight | | | |
| Henry Marshall | | | |
| Gary Barbaro | | | |
| Art Still | | | |
| ☐ 395 Earnest Gray | .07 | .03 | .01 |
| New York Giants | | | |
| ☐ 396 Ray Hamilton | .07 | .03 | .01 |
| New England Patriots | | | |
| ☐ 397 Brenard Wilson | .07 | .03 | .01 |
| Philadelphia Eagles | | | |
| ☐ 398 Calvin Hill | .10 | .05 | .01 |
| Cleveland Browns | | | |
| ☐ 399 Robin Cole | .10 | .05 | .01 |
| Pittsburgh Steelers | | | |
| ☐ 400 Walter Payton AP | 4.00 | 1.80 | .50 |
| Chicago Bears | | | |
| ☐ 401 Jim Hart | .20 | .09 | .03 |
| St. Louis Cardinals | | | |
| ☐ 402 Ron Yary | .10 | .05 | .01 |
| Minnesota Vikings | | | |
| ☐ 403 Cliff Branch | .40 | .18 | .05 |
| Oakland Raiders | | | |
| ☐ 404 Roland Hooks | .07 | .03 | .01 |
| Buffalo Bills | | | |
| ☐ 405 Ken Stabler | 1.25 | .55 | .16 |

| | | | |
|---|---|---|---|
| Houston Oilers | | | |
| ☐ 406 Chuck Ramsey | .07 | .03 | .01 |
| New York Jets | | | |
| ☐ 407 Mike Nelms | .07 | .03 | .01 |
| Washington Redskins | | | |
| ☐ 408 Ron Jaworski SA | .10 | .05 | .01 |
| Philadelphia Eagles | | | |
| ☐ 409 James Hunter | .07 | .03 | .01 |
| Detroit Lions | | | |
| ☐ 410 Lee Roy Selmon AP | .07 | .03 | .01 |
| Tampa Bay Buccaneers | | | |
| ☐ 411 Baltimore Colts TL | .25 | .04 | .01 |
| Curtis Dickey | | | |
| Roger Carr | | | |
| Bruce Laird | | | |
| Mike Barnes | | | |
| ☐ 412 Henry Marshall | .07 | .03 | .01 |
| Kansas City Chiefs | | | |
| ☐ 413 Preston Pearson | .10 | .05 | .01 |
| Dallas Cowboys | | | |
| ☐ 414 Richard Bishop | .07 | .03 | .01 |
| New England Patriots | | | |
| ☐ 415 Greg Pruitt | .07 | .03 | .01 |
| Cleveland Browns | | | |
| ☐ 416 Matt Bahr | .25 | .11 | .03 |
| Pittsburgh Steelers | | | |
| ☐ 417 Tom Mullady | .07 | .03 | .01 |
| New York Giants | | | |
| ☐ 418 Glen Edwards | .07 | .03 | .01 |
| San Diego Chargers | | | |
| ☐ 419 Sam McCullum | .10 | .05 | .01 |
| Seattle Seahawks | | | |
| ☐ 420 Stan Walters AP | .10 | .05 | .01 |
| Philadelphia Eagles | | | |
| ☐ 421 George Roberts | .07 | .03 | .01 |
| Miami Dolphins | | | |
| ☐ 422 Dwight Clark | 4.00 | 1.80 | .50 |
| San Francisco 49ers | | | |
| ☐ 423 Pat Thomas | .07 | .03 | .01 |
| Los Angeles Rams | | | |
| ☐ 424 Bruce Harper SA | .07 | .03 | .01 |
| New York Jets | | | |
| ☐ 425 Craig Morton | .20 | .09 | .03 |
| Denver Broncos | | | |
| ☐ 426 Derrick Gaffney | .07 | .03 | .01 |
| New York Jets | | | |
| ☐ 427 Pete Johnson | .10 | .05 | .01 |
| Cincinnati Bengals | | | |
| ☐ 428 Wes Chandler | .50 | .23 | .06 |
| New Orleans Saints | | | |
| ☐ 429 Burgess Owens | .07 | .03 | .01 |
| Oakland Raiders | | | |
| ☐ 430 James Lofton AP | 3.50 | 1.55 | .45 |
| Green Bay Packers | | | |
| ☐ 431 Tony Reed | .10 | .05 | .01 |
| Kansas City Chiefs | | | |
| ☐ 432 Minnesota Vikings TL | .40 | .06 | .01 |
| Ted Brown | | | |
| Ahmad Rashad | | | |
| John Turner | | | |
| Doug Sutherland | | | |
| ☐ 433 Ron Springs | .12 | .05 | .02 |
| Dallas Cowboys | | | |
| ☐ 434 Tim Fox | .07 | .03 | .01 |
| New England Patriots | | | |
| ☐ 435 Ozzie Newsome | 2.50 | 1.15 | .30 |
| Cleveland Browns | | | |
| ☐ 436 Steve Furness | .10 | .05 | .01 |
| Pittsburgh Steelers | | | |
| ☐ 437 Will Lewis | .07 | .03 | .01 |
| Seattle Seahawks | | | |
| ☐ 438 Mike Hartenstine | .07 | .03 | .01 |
| Chicago Bears | | | |
| ☐ 439 John Bunting | .07 | .03 | .01 |
| Philadelphia Eagles | | | |
| ☐ 440 Ed Murray | 1.50 | .65 | .19 |
| Detroit Lions | | | |
| ☐ 441 Mike Pruitt SA | .07 | .03 | .01 |
| Cleveland Browns | | | |
| ☐ 442 Larry Swider | .07 | .03 | .01 |
| St. Louis Cardinals | | | |
| ☐ 443 Steve Freeman | .07 | .03 | .01 |
| Buffalo Bills | | | |
| ☐ 444 Bruce Hardy | .10 | .05 | .01 |
| Miami Dolphins | | | |
| ☐ 445 Pat Haden | .25 | .11 | .03 |
| Los Angeles Rams | | | |
| ☐ 446 Curtis Dickey | .25 | .11 | .03 |
| Baltimore Colts | | | |
| ☐ 447 Doug Wilkerson | .07 | .03 | .01 |
| San Diego Chargers | | | |
| ☐ 448 Alfred Jenkins | .10 | .05 | .01 |
| Atlanta Falcons | | | |
| ☐ 449 Dave Dalby | .07 | .03 | .01 |
| Oakland Raiders | | | |
| ☐ 450 Robert Brazile AP | .07 | .03 | .01 |
| Houston Oilers | | | |
| ☐ 451 Bobby Hammond | .07 | .03 | .01 |

Washington Redskins
| | | | |
|---|---|---|---|
| ☐ 452 Raymond Clayborn .............. | .10 | .05 | .01 |

New England Patriots
| | | | |
|---|---|---|---|
| ☐ 453 Jim Miller ...................... | .07 | .03 | .01 |

San Francisco 49ers
| | | | |
|---|---|---|---|
| ☐ 454 Roy Simmons .................. | .07 | .03 | .01 |

New York Giants
| | | | |
|---|---|---|---|
| ☐ 455 Charlie Waters ................. | .25 | .11 | .03 |

Dallas Cowboys
| | | | |
|---|---|---|---|
| ☐ 456 Ricky Bell .................... | .10 | .05 | .01 |

Tampa Bay Buccaneers
| | | | |
|---|---|---|---|
| ☐ 457 Ahmad Rashad SA ................ | .25 | .11 | .03 |

Minnesota Vikings
| | | | |
|---|---|---|---|
| ☐ 458 Don Cockroft................... | .10 | .05 | .01 |

Cleveland Browns
| | | | |
|---|---|---|---|
| ☐ 459 Keith Krepfle ................. | .07 | .03 | .01 |

Philadelphia Eagles
| | | | |
|---|---|---|---|
| ☐ 460 Marvin Powell AP................ | .07 | .03 | .01 |

New York Jets
| | | | |
|---|---|---|---|
| ☐ 461 Tommy Kramer ................... | .30 | .14 | .04 |

Minnesota Vikings
| | | | |
|---|---|---|---|
| ☐ 462 Jim LeClair .................... | .07 | .03 | .01 |

Cincinnati Bengals
| | | | |
|---|---|---|---|
| ☐ 463 Freddie Scott .................. | .07 | .03 | .01 |

Detroit Lions
| | | | |
|---|---|---|---|
| ☐ 464 Rob Lytle....................... | .10 | .05 | .01 |

Denver Broncos
| | | | |
|---|---|---|---|
| ☐ 465 Johnnie Gray .................. | .07 | .03 | .01 |

Green Bay Packers
| | | | |
|---|---|---|---|
| ☐ 466 Doug France.................... | .07 | .03 | .01 |

Los Angeles Rams
| | | | |
|---|---|---|---|
| ☐ 467 Carlos Carson ................. | .25 | .11 | .03 |

Kansas City Chiefs
| | | | |
|---|---|---|---|
| ☐ 468 St. Louis Cardinals TL........... | .40 | .06 | .01 |

Ottis Anderson
Pat Tilley
Ken Stone
Curtis Greer
Steve Neils
| | | | |
|---|---|---|---|
| ☐ 469 Efren Herrera.................. | .07 | .03 | .01 |

Seattle Seahawks
| | | | |
|---|---|---|---|
| ☐ 470 Randy White AP ................. | 1.00 | .45 | .13 |

Dallas Cowboys
| | | | |
|---|---|---|---|
| ☐ 471 Richard Caster ................. | .10 | .05 | .01 |

Houston Oilers
| | | | |
|---|---|---|---|
| ☐ 472 Andy Johnson ................... | .07 | .03 | .01 |

New England Patriots
| | | | |
|---|---|---|---|
| ☐ 473 Billy Sims SA .................. | .30 | .14 | .04 |

Detroit Lions
| | | | |
|---|---|---|---|
| ☐ 474 Joe Lavender................... | .10 | .05 | .01 |

Washington Redskins
| | | | |
|---|---|---|---|
| ☐ 475 Harry Carson ................. | .30 | .14 | .04 |

New York Giants
| | | | |
|---|---|---|---|
| ☐ 476 John Stallworth.................. | .60 | .25 | .08 |

Pittsburgh Steelers
| | | | |
|---|---|---|---|
| ☐ 477 Bob Thomas..................... | .07 | .03 | .01 |

Chicago Bears
| | | | |
|---|---|---|---|
| ☐ 478 Keith Wright ................... | .07 | .03 | .01 |

Cleveland Browns
| | | | |
|---|---|---|---|
| ☐ 479 Ken Stone ..................... | .07 | .03 | .01 |

St. Louis Cardinals
| | | | |
|---|---|---|---|
| ☐ 480 Carl Hairston AP................ | .10 | .05 | .01 |

Philadelphia Eagles
| | | | |
|---|---|---|---|
| ☐ 481 Reggie McKenzie................ | .10 | .05 | .01 |

Buffalo Bills
| | | | |
|---|---|---|---|
| ☐ 482 Bob Griese .................... | 1.00 | .45 | .13 |

Miami Dolphins
| | | | |
|---|---|---|---|
| ☐ 483 Mike Bragg..................... | .07 | .03 | .01 |

Baltimore Colts
| | | | |
|---|---|---|---|
| ☐ 484 Scott Dierking ................. | .07 | .03 | .01 |

New York Jets
| | | | |
|---|---|---|---|
| ☐ 485 David Hill...................... | .07 | .03 | .01 |

Detroit Lions
| | | | |
|---|---|---|---|
| ☐ 486 Brian Sipe SA ................. | .10 | .05 | .01 |

Cleveland Browns
| | | | |
|---|---|---|---|
| ☐ 487 Rod Martin ..................... | .30 | .14 | .04 |

Oakland Raiders
| | | | |
|---|---|---|---|
| ☐ 488 Cincinnati Bengals TL........... | .25 | .04 | .01 |

Pete Johnson
Dan Ross
Louis Breeden
Eddie Edwards
| | | | |
|---|---|---|---|
| ☐ 489 Preston Dennard ................ | .07 | .03 | .01 |

Los Angeles Rams
| | | | |
|---|---|---|---|
| ☐ 490 John Smith AP .................. | .07 | .03 | .01 |

New England Patriots
| | | | |
|---|---|---|---|
| ☐ 491 Mike Reinfeldt.................. | .07 | .03 | .01 |

Houston Oilers
| | | | |
|---|---|---|---|
| ☐ 492 1980 NFC Champions ........... | .15 | .07 | .02 |

Eagles 20,
Cowboys 7
(Ron Jaworski)
| | | | |
|---|---|---|---|
| ☐ 493 1980 AFC Champions............ | .20 | .09 | .03 |

Raiders 34,
Chargers 27
(Jim Plunkett)
| | | | |
|---|---|---|---|
| ☐ 494 Super Bowl XV .................. | .50 | .23 | .06 |

Raiders 27,
Eagles 10
(Plunkett hand-
ing off to King)
| | | | |
|---|---|---|---|
| ☐ 495 Joe Greene ..................... | .75 | .35 | .09 |

Pittsburgh Steelers
| | | | |
|---|---|---|---|
| ☐ 496 Charlie Joiner................... | .50 | .23 | .06 |

San Diego Chargers
| | | | |
|---|---|---|---|
| ☐ 497 Rolland Lawrence ............... | .07 | .03 | .01 |

Atlanta Falcons
| | | | |
|---|---|---|---|
| ☐ 498 Al(Bubba) Baker SA ............. | .07 | .03 | .01 |

Detroit Lions
| | | | |
|---|---|---|---|
| ☐ 499 Brad Dusek .................... | .10 | .05 | .01 |

Washington Redskins
| | | | |
|---|---|---|---|
| ☐ 500 Tony Dorsett .................... | 2.50 | 1.15 | .30 |

Dallas Cowboys
| | | | |
|---|---|---|---|
| ☐ 501 Robin Earl .................... | .07 | .03 | .01 |

Chicago Bears
| | | | |
|---|---|---|---|
| ☐ 502 Theotis Brown .................. | .07 | .03 | .01 |

St. Louis Cardinals
| | | | |
|---|---|---|---|
| ☐ 503 Joe Ferguson ................... | .10 | .05 | .01 |

Buffalo Bills
| | | | |
|---|---|---|---|
| ☐ 504 Beasley Reece ................. | .07 | .03 | .01 |

New York Giants
| | | | |
|---|---|---|---|
| ☐ 505 Lyle Alzado .................... | .30 | .14 | .04 |

Cleveland Browns
| | | | |
|---|---|---|---|
| ☐ 506 Tony Nathan .................... | .50 | .23 | .06 |

Miami Dolphins
| | | | |
|---|---|---|---|
| ☐ 507 Philadelphia Eagles TL ......... | .25 | .04 | .01 |

Wilbert Montgomery
Charlie Smith
Brenard Wilson
Claude Humphrey
| | | | |
|---|---|---|---|
| ☐ 508 Herb Orvis ..................... | .07 | .03 | .01 |

Baltimore Colts
| | | | |
|---|---|---|---|
| ☐ 509 Clarence Williams ................ | .07 | .03 | .01 |

San Diego Chargers
| | | | |
|---|---|---|---|
| ☐ 510 Ray Guy AP .................... | .20 | .09 | .03 |

Oakland Raiders
| | | | |
|---|---|---|---|
| ☐ 511 Jeff Komlo...................... | .07 | .03 | .01 |

Detroit Lions
| | | | |
|---|---|---|---|
| ☐ 512 Freddie Solomon SA ............ | .07 | .03 | .01 |

San Francisco 49ers
| | | | |
|---|---|---|---|
| ☐ 513 Tim Mazzetti .................... | .07 | .03 | .01 |

Atlanta Falcons
| | | | |
|---|---|---|---|
| ☐ 514 Elvis Peacock ................... | .07 | .03 | .01 |

Los Angeles Rams
| | | | |
|---|---|---|---|
| ☐ 515 Russ Francis .................... | .10 | .05 | .01 |

New England Patriots
| | | | |
|---|---|---|---|
| ☐ 516 Roland Harper .................. | .07 | .03 | .01 |

Chicago Bears
| | | | |
|---|---|---|---|
| ☐ 517 Checklist 397-528 ................ | .50 | .05 | .02 |
| ☐ 518 Billy Johnson .................... | .10 | .05 | .01 |

Houston Oilers
| | | | |
|---|---|---|---|
| ☐ 519 Dan Dierdorf ................... | .40 | .18 | .05 |

St. Louis Cardinals
| | | | |
|---|---|---|---|
| ☐ 520 Fred Dean AP .................. | .10 | .05 | .01 |

San Diego Chargers
| | | | |
|---|---|---|---|
| ☐ 521 Jerry Butler ................... | .07 | .03 | .01 |

Buffalo Bills
| | | | |
|---|---|---|---|
| ☐ 522 Ron Saul ...................... | .07 | .03 | .01 |

Washington Redskins
| | | | |
|---|---|---|---|
| ☐ 523 Charlie Smith .................. | .07 | .03 | .01 |

Philadelphia Eagles
| | | | |
|---|---|---|---|
| ☐ 524 Kellen Winslow SA .............. | 3.00 | 1.35 | .40 |

San Diego Chargers
| | | | |
|---|---|---|---|
| ☐ 525 Bert Jones ..................... | .25 | .11 | .03 |

Baltimore Colts
| | | | |
|---|---|---|---|
| ☐ 526 Pittsburgh Steelers TL .......... | .60 | .09 | .02 |

Franco Harris
Theo Bell
Donnie Shell
L.C. Greenwood
| | | | |
|---|---|---|---|
| ☐ 527 Duriel Harris.................... | .10 | .05 | .01 |

Miami Dolphins
| | | | |
|---|---|---|---|
| ☐ 528 William Andrews ................ | .25 | .11 | .03 |

Atlanta Falcons

# 1982 Topps

The 1982 Topps football set features 528 cards. The cards measure 2 1/2" by 3 1/2". The team helmets appear on the fronts for the first time, as Topps apparently received permission from the teams for the use of their insignias. Again, the fronts contain the stylized Topps logo within the frame line. The backs contain blue and yellow-green ink on a gray card stock. Many special cards, e.g., Playoffs and Super Bowl (7-9), Record Breakers (RB, cards 1-6), and statistical leaders (257-262) are included in the set. Cards 263-270 feature brothers playing in the NFL. All-Pro (AP) selections are denoted on each player's regular card. Some players also have an additional special card with an In-Action (IA) pose. Distributed throughout the set are Team Leader (TL) cards typically featuring four individual team statistical leaders on the front, as well as a team checklist on the back. The set is organized in team order alphabetically by team within conference (and with players within teams in alphabetical order), for example, Baltimore Colts (10-

20), Buffalo Bills (21-35), Cincinnati Bengals (36-54), Cleveland Browns (55-75), Denver Broncos (76-91), Houston Oilers (92-108), Kansas City Chiefs (109-124), Miami Dolphins (125-140), New England Patriots (141-159), New York Jets (160-184), Oakland Raiders (185-201), Pittsburgh Steelers (202-222), San Diego Chargers (223-242), Seattle Seahawks (243-256), Atlanta Falcons (271-291), Chicago Bears (292-306), Detroit Lions (333-353), Green Bay Packers (354-368), Los Angeles Rams (369-388), Minnesota Vikings (389-403), New Orleans Saints (404-414), New York Giants (415-436), Philadelphia Eagles (437-461), St. Louis Cardinals (462-476), San Francisco 49ers (477-494), Tampa Bay Buccaneers (495-508), and Washington Redskins (509-524). The last four cards in the set (525-528) are checklist cards. The key Rookie Cards in this set are James Brooks, Ronnie Lott, Anthony Munoz, and Lawrence Taylor.

|  | MINT | EXC | G-VG |
|---|---|---|---|
| COMPLETE SET (528) | 90.00 | 40.00 | 11.50 |
| COMMON PLAYER (1-528) | .06 | .03 | .01 |
| ☐ 1 Ken Anderson RB | .50 | .23 | .06 |
| Cincinnati Bengals Most Completions, Super Bowl Game | | | |
| ☐ 2 Dan Fouts RB | .50 | .23 | .06 |
| San Diego Chargers Most Passing Yards, Playoff Game | | | |
| ☐ 3 LeRoy Irvin RB | .12 | .05 | .02 |
| Los Angeles Rams Most Punt Return Yardage, Game | | | |
| ☐ 4 Stump Mitchell RB | .12 | .05 | .02 |
| St. Louis Cardinals Most Return Yardage, Season | | | |
| ☐ 5 George Rogers RB | .15 | .07 | .02 |
| New Orleans Saints Most Rushing Yards, Rookie Season | | | |
| ☐ 6 Dan Ross RB | .12 | .05 | .02 |
| Cincinnati Bengals Most Receptions, Super Bowl Game | | | |
| ☐ 7 AFC Championship | .12 | .05 | .02 |
| Bengals 27, Chargers 7 (Ken Anderson handing off to Pete Johnson) | | | |
| ☐ 8 NFC Championship | .12 | .05 | .02 |
| 49ers 28, Cowboys 27 (Earl Cooper) | | | |
| ☐ 9 Super Bowl XVI | .75 | .35 | .09 |
| 49ers 26, Bengals 7 (Anthony Munoz blocking) | | | |
| ☐ 10 Baltimore Colts TL | .15 | .07 | .02 |
| Curtis Dickey Raymond Butler Larry Braziel Bruce Laird | | | |
| ☐ 11 Raymond Butler | .06 | .03 | .01 |
| ☐ 12 Roger Carr | .08 | .04 | .01 |
| ☐ 13 Curtis Dickey | .08 | .04 | .01 |
| ☐ 14 Zachary Dixon | .06 | .03 | .01 |
| ☐ 15 Nesby Glasgow | .06 | .03 | .01 |
| ☐ 16 Bert Jones | .15 | .07 | .02 |
| ☐ 17 Bruce Laird | .06 | .03 | .01 |
| ☐ 18 Reese McCall | .06 | .03 | .01 |
| ☐ 19 Randy McMillan | .08 | .04 | .01 |
| ☐ 20 Ed Simonini | .06 | .03 | .01 |
| ☐ 21 Buffalo Bills TL | .20 | .09 | .03 |

| | | | |
|---|---|---|---|
| Joe Cribbs Frank Lewis Mario Clark Fred Smerlas | | | |
| ☐ 22 Mark Brammer | .06 | .03 | .01 |
| ☐ 23 Curtis Brown | .06 | .03 | .01 |
| ☐ 24 Jerry Butler | .08 | .04 | .01 |
| ☐ 25 Mario Clark | .06 | .03 | .01 |
| ☐ 26 Joe Cribbs | .15 | .07 | .02 |
| ☐ 27 Joe Cribbs IA | .08 | .04 | .01 |
| ☐ 28 Joe Ferguson | .08 | .04 | .01 |
| ☐ 29 Jim Haslett | .06 | .03 | .01 |
| ☐ 30 Frank Lewis AP | .08 | .04 | .01 |
| ☐ 31 Frank Lewis IA | .06 | .03 | .01 |
| ☐ 32 Shane Nelson | .06 | .03 | .01 |
| ☐ 33 Charles Romes | .06 | .03 | .01 |
| ☐ 34 Bill Simpson | .06 | .03 | .01 |
| ☐ 35 Fred Smerlas | .06 | .03 | .01 |
| ☐ 36 Cincinnati Bengals TL | .25 | .11 | .03 |
| Pete Johnson Cris Collinsworth Ken Riley Reggie Williams | | | |
| ☐ 37 Charles Alexander | .06 | .03 | .01 |
| ☐ 38 Ken Anderson AP | .50 | .23 | .06 |
| ☐ 39 Ken Anderson IA | .25 | .11 | .03 |
| ☐ 40 Jim Breech | .06 | .03 | .01 |
| ☐ 41 Jim Breech IA | .06 | .03 | .01 |
| ☐ 42 Louis Breeden | .06 | .03 | .01 |
| ☐ 43 Ross Browner | .08 | .04 | .01 |
| ☐ 44 Cris Collinsworth | 2.00 | .90 | .25 |
| ☐ 45 Cris Collinsworth IA | 1.00 | .45 | .13 |
| ☐ 46 Isaac Curtis | .08 | .04 | .01 |
| ☐ 47 Pete Johnson | .08 | .04 | .01 |
| ☐ 48 Pete Johnson IA | .06 | .03 | .01 |
| ☐ 49 Steve Kreider | .06 | .03 | .01 |
| ☐ 50 Pat McInally AP | .08 | .04 | .01 |
| ☐ 51 Anthony Munoz AP | 7.00 | 3.10 | .85 |
| ☐ 52 Dan Ross | .08 | .04 | .01 |
| ☐ 53 David Verser | .06 | .03 | .01 |
| ☐ 54 Reggie Williams | .08 | .04 | .01 |
| ☐ 55 Cleveland Browns TL | .25 | .11 | .03 |
| Mike Pruitt Ozzie Newsome Clarence Scott Lyle Alzado | | | |
| ☐ 56 Lyle Alzado | .25 | .11 | .03 |
| ☐ 57 Dick Ambrose | .06 | .03 | .01 |
| ☐ 58 Ron Bolton | .06 | .03 | .01 |
| ☐ 59 Steve Cox | .06 | .03 | .01 |
| ☐ 60 Joe DeLamielleure | .08 | .04 | .01 |
| ☐ 61 Tom DeLeone | .06 | .03 | .01 |
| ☐ 62 Doug Dieken | .06 | .03 | .01 |
| ☐ 63 Ricky Feacher | .06 | .03 | .01 |
| ☐ 64 Don Goode | .06 | .03 | .01 |
| ☐ 65 Robert L. Jackson | .06 | .03 | .01 |
| ☐ 66 Dave Logan | .08 | .04 | .01 |
| ☐ 67 Ozzie Newsome | 1.25 | .55 | .16 |
| ☐ 68 Ozzie Newsome IA | .60 | .25 | .08 |
| ☐ 69 Greg Pruitt | .06 | .03 | .01 |
| ☐ 70 Mike Pruitt | .08 | .04 | .01 |
| ☐ 71 Mike Pruitt IA | .06 | .03 | .01 |
| ☐ 72 Reggie Rucker | .08 | .04 | .01 |
| ☐ 73 Clarence Scott | .06 | .03 | .01 |
| ☐ 74 Brian Sipe | .08 | .04 | .01 |
| ☐ 75 Charles White | .06 | .03 | .01 |
| ☐ 76 Denver Broncos TL | .15 | .07 | .02 |
| Rick Parros Steve Watson Steve Foley Rulon Jones | | | |
| ☐ 77 Rubin Carter | .06 | .03 | .01 |
| ☐ 78 Steve Foley | .06 | .03 | .01 |
| ☐ 79 Randy Gradishar | .25 | .11 | .03 |
| ☐ 80 Tom Jackson | .20 | .09 | .03 |
| ☐ 81 Craig Morton | .15 | .07 | .02 |
| ☐ 82 Craig Morton IA | .08 | .04 | .01 |
| ☐ 83 Riley Odoms | .08 | .04 | .01 |
| ☐ 84 Rick Parros | .06 | .03 | .01 |
| ☐ 85 Dave Preston | .06 | .03 | .01 |
| ☐ 86 Tony Reed | .08 | .04 | .01 |
| ☐ 87 Bob Swenson | .06 | .03 | .01 |
| ☐ 88 Bill Thompson | .08 | .04 | .01 |
| ☐ 89 Rick Upchurch | .08 | .04 | .01 |
| ☐ 90 Steve Watson AP | .25 | .11 | .03 |
| ☐ 91 Steve Watson IA | .06 | .03 | .01 |
| ☐ 92 Houston Oilers TL | .15 | .07 | .02 |
| Carl Roaches Ken Burrough Carter Hartwig Greg Stemrick Jesse Baker | | | |
| ☐ 93 Mike Barber | .06 | .03 | .01 |
| ☐ 94 Elvin Bethea | .08 | .04 | .01 |
| ☐ 95 Gregg Bingham | .06 | .03 | .01 |
| ☐ 96 Robert Brazile AP | .06 | .03 | .01 |
| ☐ 97 Ken Burrough | .08 | .04 | .01 |
| ☐ 98 Toni Fritsch | .06 | .03 | .01 |

|  |  | | | |
|---|---|---|---|---|
| ☐ 99 | Leon Gray | .08 | .04 | .01 |
| ☐ 100 | Gifford Nielsen | .20 | .09 | .03 |
| ☐ 101 | Vernon Perry | .06 | .03 | .01 |
| ☐ 102 | Mike Reinfeldt | .06 | .03 | .01 |
| ☐ 103 | Mike Renfro | .08 | .04 | .01 |
| ☐ 104 | Carl Roaches AP | .08 | .04 | .01 |
| ☐ 105 | Ken Stabler | 1.00 | .45 | .13 |
| ☐ 106 | Greg Stemrick | .06 | .03 | .01 |
| ☐ 107 | J.C. Wilson | .06 | .03 | .01 |
| ☐ 108 | Tim Wilson | .06 | .03 | .01 |
| ☐ 109 | Kansas City Chiefs TL | .15 | .07 | .02 |
| | Joe Delaney | | | |
| | J.T. Smith | | | |
| | Eric Harris | | | |
| | Ken Kremer | | | |
| ☐ 110 | Gary Barbaro AP | .08 | .04 | .01 |
| ☐ 111 | Brad Budde | .06 | .03 | .01 |
| ☐ 112 | Joe Delaney AP | .40 | .18 | .05 |
| ☐ 113 | Joe Delaney IA | .15 | .07 | .02 |
| ☐ 114 | Steve Fuller | .08 | .04 | .01 |
| ☐ 115 | Gary Green | .06 | .03 | .01 |
| ☐ 116 | James Hadnot | .06 | .03 | .01 |
| ☐ 117 | Eric Harris | .06 | .03 | .01 |
| ☐ 118 | Billy Jackson | .06 | .03 | .01 |
| ☐ 119 | Bill Kenney | .06 | .03 | .01 |
| ☐ 120 | Nick Lowery AP | 1.25 | .55 | .16 |
| ☐ 121 | Nick Lowery IA | .60 | .25 | .08 |
| ☐ 122 | Henry Marshall | .06 | .03 | .01 |
| ☐ 123 | J.T. Smith | .20 | .09 | .03 |
| ☐ 124 | Art Still | .06 | .03 | .01 |
| ☐ 125 | Miami Dolphins TL | .20 | .09 | .03 |
| | Tony Nathan | | | |
| | Duriel Harris | | | |
| | Glenn Blackwood | | | |
| | Bob Baumhower | | | |
| ☐ 126 | Bob Baumhower AP | .08 | .04 | .01 |
| ☐ 127 | Glenn Blackwood | .08 | .04 | .01 |
| ☐ 128 | Jimmy Cefalo | .08 | .04 | .01 |
| ☐ 129 | A.J. Duhe | .08 | .04 | .01 |
| ☐ 130 | Andra Franklin | .15 | .07 | .02 |
| ☐ 131 | Duriel Harris | .08 | .04 | .01 |
| ☐ 132 | Nat Moore | .08 | .04 | .01 |
| ☐ 133 | Tony Nathan | .08 | .04 | .01 |
| ☐ 134 | Ed Newman | .06 | .03 | .01 |
| ☐ 135 | Earnie Rhone | .08 | .04 | .01 |
| ☐ 136 | Don Strock | .08 | .04 | .01 |
| ☐ 137 | Tommy Vigorito | .08 | .04 | .01 |
| ☐ 138 | Uwe Von Schamann | .08 | .04 | .01 |
| ☐ 139 | Uwe Von Schamann IA | .06 | .03 | .01 |
| ☐ 140 | David Woodley | .08 | .04 | .01 |
| ☐ 141 | New England Pats TL | .15 | .07 | .02 |
| | Tony Collins | | | |
| | Stanley Morgan | | | |
| | Tim Fox | | | |
| | Rick Sanford | | | |
| | Tony McGee | | | |
| ☐ 142 | Julius Adams | .06 | .03 | .01 |
| ☐ 143 | Richard Bishop | .06 | .03 | .01 |
| ☐ 144 | Matt Cavanaugh | .08 | .04 | .01 |
| ☐ 145 | Raymond Clayborn | .08 | .04 | .01 |
| ☐ 146 | Tony Collins | .25 | .11 | .03 |
| ☐ 147 | Vagas Ferguson | .06 | .03 | .01 |
| ☐ 148 | Tim Fox | .06 | .03 | .01 |
| ☐ 149 | Steve Grogan | .25 | .11 | .03 |
| ☐ 150 | John Hannah AP | .30 | .14 | .04 |
| ☐ 151 | John Hannah IA | .15 | .07 | .02 |
| ☐ 152 | Don Hasselbeck | .06 | .03 | .01 |
| ☐ 153 | Mike Haynes | .08 | .04 | .01 |
| ☐ 154 | Harold Jackson | .08 | .04 | .01 |
| ☐ 155 | Andy Johnson | .06 | .03 | .01 |
| ☐ 156 | Stanley Morgan | .30 | .14 | .04 |
| ☐ 157 | Stanley Morgan IA | .15 | .07 | .02 |
| ☐ 158 | Steve Nelson | .06 | .03 | .01 |
| ☐ 159 | Rod Shoate | .06 | .03 | .01 |
| ☐ 160 | New York Jets TL | .40 | .18 | .05 |
| | Freeman McNeil | | | |
| | Wesley Walker | | | |
| | Darrol Ray | | | |
| | Joe Klecko | | | |
| ☐ 161 | Dan Alexander | .06 | .03 | .01 |
| ☐ 162 | Mike Augustyniak | .06 | .03 | .01 |
| ☐ 163 | Jerome Barkum | .06 | .03 | .01 |
| ☐ 164 | Greg Buttle | .08 | .04 | .01 |
| ☐ 165 | Scott Dierking | .06 | .03 | .01 |
| ☐ 166 | Joe Fields | .06 | .03 | .01 |
| ☐ 167 | Mark Gastineau AP | .20 | .09 | .03 |
| ☐ 168 | Mark Gastineau IA | .08 | .04 | .01 |
| ☐ 169 | Bruce Harper | .06 | .03 | .01 |
| ☐ 170 | Johnny "Lam" Jones | .08 | .04 | .01 |
| ☐ 171 | Joe Klecko AP | .25 | .11 | .03 |
| ☐ 172 | Joe Klecko IA | .08 | .04 | .01 |
| ☐ 173 | Pat Leahy | .08 | .04 | .01 |
| ☐ 174 | Pat Leahy IA | .06 | .03 | .01 |
| ☐ 175 | Marty Lyons | .06 | .03 | .01 |
| ☐ 176 | Freeman McNeil | 1.50 | .65 | .19 |
| ☐ 177 | Marvin Powell AP | .06 | .03 | .01 |
| ☐ 178 | Chuck Ramsey | .06 | .03 | .01 |
| ☐ 179 | Darrol Ray | .06 | .03 | .01 |
| ☐ 180 | Abdul Salaam | .06 | .03 | .01 |
| ☐ 181 | Richard Todd | .08 | .04 | .01 |
| ☐ 182 | Richard Todd IA | .08 | .04 | .01 |
| ☐ 183 | Wesley Walker | .25 | .11 | .03 |
| ☐ 184 | Chris Ward | .06 | .03 | .01 |
| ☐ 185 | Oakland Raiders TL | .15 | .07 | .02 |
| | Kenny King | | | |
| | Derrick Ramsey | | | |
| | Lester Hayes | | | |
| | Odis McKinney | | | |
| | Rod Martin | | | |
| ☐ 186 | Cliff Branch | .30 | .14 | .04 |
| ☐ 187 | Bob Chandler | .08 | .04 | .01 |
| ☐ 188 | Ray Guy | .15 | .07 | .02 |
| ☐ 189 | Lester Hayes AP | .08 | .04 | .01 |
| ☐ 190 | Ted Hendricks AP | .25 | .11 | .03 |
| ☐ 191 | Monte Jackson | .06 | .03 | .01 |
| ☐ 192 | Derrick Jensen | .06 | .03 | .01 |
| ☐ 193 | Kenny King | .08 | .04 | .01 |
| ☐ 194 | Rod Martin | .08 | .04 | .01 |
| ☐ 195 | John Matuszak | .08 | .04 | .01 |
| ☐ 196 | Matt Millen | .75 | .35 | .09 |
| ☐ 197 | Derrick Ramsey | .06 | .03 | .01 |
| ☐ 198 | Art Shell | .30 | .14 | .04 |
| ☐ 199 | Mark Van Eeghen | .08 | .04 | .01 |
| ☐ 200 | Arthur Whittington | .06 | .03 | .01 |
| ☐ 201 | Marc Wilson | .20 | .09 | .03 |
| ☐ 202 | Pittsburgh Steelers TL | .50 | .23 | .06 |
| | Franco Harris | | | |
| | John Stallworth | | | |
| | Mel Blount | | | |
| | Jack Lambert | | | |
| | Gary Dunn | | | |
| ☐ 203 | Mel Blount AP | .60 | .25 | .08 |
| ☐ 204 | Terry Bradshaw | 1.50 | .65 | .19 |
| ☐ 205 | Terry Bradshaw IA | .75 | .35 | .09 |
| ☐ 206 | Craig Colquitt | .06 | .03 | .01 |
| ☐ 207 | Bennie Cunningham | .08 | .04 | .01 |
| ☐ 208 | Russell Davis | .06 | .03 | .01 |
| ☐ 209 | Gary Dunn | .06 | .03 | .01 |
| ☐ 210 | Jack Ham | .60 | .25 | .08 |
| ☐ 211 | Franco Harris | .75 | .35 | .09 |
| ☐ 212 | Franco Harris IA | .35 | .16 | .04 |
| ☐ 213 | Jack Lambert AP | .75 | .35 | .09 |
| ☐ 214 | Jack Lambert IA | .35 | .16 | .04 |
| ☐ 215 | Mark Malone | .25 | .11 | .03 |
| ☐ 216 | Frank Pollard | .20 | .09 | .03 |
| ☐ 217 | Donnie Shell AP | .25 | .11 | .03 |
| ☐ 218 | Jim Smith | .08 | .04 | .01 |
| ☐ 219 | John Stallworth | .50 | .23 | .06 |
| ☐ 220 | John Stallworth IA | .25 | .11 | .03 |
| ☐ 221 | David Trout | .06 | .03 | .01 |
| ☐ 222 | Mike Webster AP | .25 | .11 | .03 |
| ☐ 223 | San Diego Chargers TL | .20 | .09 | .03 |
| | Chuck Muncie | | | |
| | Charlie Joiner | | | |
| | Willie Buchanon | | | |
| | Gary Johnson | | | |
| ☐ 224 | Rolf Benirschke | .06 | .03 | .01 |
| ☐ 225 | Rolf Benirschke IA | .06 | .03 | .01 |
| ☐ 226 | James Brooks | 3.00 | 1.35 | .40 |
| ☐ 227 | Willie Buchanon | .08 | .04 | .01 |
| ☐ 228 | Wes Chandler | .20 | .09 | .03 |
| ☐ 229 | Wes Chandler IA | .08 | .04 | .01 |
| ☐ 230 | Dan Fouts | 1.00 | .45 | .13 |
| ☐ 231 | Dan Fouts IA | .60 | .25 | .08 |
| ☐ 232 | Gary Johnson AP | .06 | .03 | .01 |
| ☐ 233 | Charlie Joiner | .40 | .18 | .05 |
| ☐ 234 | Charlie Joiner IA | .20 | .09 | .03 |
| ☐ 235 | Louie Kelcher | .08 | .04 | .01 |
| ☐ 236 | Chuck Muncie AP | .08 | .04 | .01 |
| ☐ 237 | Chuck Muncie IA | .06 | .03 | .01 |
| ☐ 238 | George Roberts | .06 | .03 | .01 |
| ☐ 239 | Ed White | .08 | .04 | .01 |
| ☐ 240 | Doug Wilkerson AP | .06 | .03 | .01 |
| ☐ 241 | Kellen Winslow AP | 2.00 | .90 | .25 |
| ☐ 242 | Kellen Winslow IA | 1.00 | .45 | .13 |
| ☐ 243 | Seattle Seahawks TL | .40 | .18 | .05 |
| | Theotis Brown | | | |
| | Steve Largent | | | |
| | John Harris | | | |
| | Jacob Green | | | |
| ☐ 244 | Theotis Brown | .06 | .03 | .01 |
| ☐ 245 | Dan Doornink | .06 | .03 | .01 |
| ☐ 246 | John Harris | .06 | .03 | .01 |
| ☐ 247 | Efren Herrera | .06 | .03 | .01 |
| ☐ 248 | David Hughes | .06 | .03 | .01 |
| ☐ 249 | Steve Largent | 1.25 | .55 | .16 |
| ☐ 250 | Steve Largent IA | .60 | .25 | .08 |
| ☐ 251 | Sam McCullum | .08 | .04 | .01 |
| ☐ 252 | Sherman Smith | .06 | .03 | .01 |
| ☐ 253 | Manu Tuiasosopo | .06 | .03 | .01 |
| ☐ 254 | Jim Yarno | .06 | .03 | .01 |
| ☐ 255 | Jim Zorn | .15 | .07 | .02 |
| | (Sitting with Dave Krieg) | | | |
| ☐ 256 | Jim Zorn IA | .08 | .04 | .01 |

| | | | |
|---|---|---|---|
| ☐ 257 Passing Leaders | 2.00 | .90 | .25 |
| Ken Anderson | | | |
| Joe Montana | | | |
| ☐ 258 Receiving Leaders | .50 | .23 | .06 |
| Kellen Winslow | | | |
| Dwight Clark | | | |
| ☐ 259 QB Sack Leaders | .12 | .05 | .02 |
| Joe Klecko | | | |
| Curtis Greer | | | |
| ☐ 260 Scoring Leaders | .12 | .05 | .02 |
| Jim Breech | | | |
| Nick Lowery | | | |
| Ed Murray | | | |
| Rafael Septien | | | |
| ☐ 261 Interception Leaders | .30 | .14 | .04 |
| John Harris | | | |
| Everson Walls | | | |
| ☐ 262 Punting Leaders | .12 | .05 | .02 |
| Pat McInally | | | |
| Tom Skladany | | | |
| ☐ 263 Brothers: Bahr | .12 | .05 | .02 |
| Chris and Matt | | | |
| ☐ 264 Brothers: Blackwood | .12 | .05 | .02 |
| Lyle and Glenn | | | |
| ☐ 265 Brothers: Brock | .12 | .05 | .02 |
| Pete and Stan | | | |
| ☐ 266 Brothers: Griffin | .12 | .05 | .02 |
| Archie and Ray | | | |
| ☐ 267 Brothers: Hannah | .15 | .07 | .02 |
| John and Charlie | | | |
| ☐ 268 Brothers: Jackson | .12 | .05 | .02 |
| Monte and Terry | | | |
| ☐ 269 Brothers: Payton | 1.25 | .55 | .16 |
| Eddie and Walter | | | |
| ☐ 270 Brothers: Selmon | .15 | .07 | .02 |
| Dewey and Lee Roy | | | |
| ☐ 271 Atlanta Falcons TL | .15 | .07 | .02 |
| William Andrews | | | |
| Alfred Jenkins | | | |
| Tom Pridemore | | | |
| Al Richardson | | | |
| ☐ 272 William Andrews | .08 | .04 | .01 |
| ☐ 273 William Andrews IA | .06 | .03 | .01 |
| ☐ 274 Steve Bartkowski | .25 | .11 | .03 |
| ☐ 275 Steve Bartkowski IA | .08 | .04 | .01 |
| ☐ 276 Bobby Butler | .06 | .03 | .01 |
| ☐ 277 Lynn Cain | .08 | .04 | .01 |
| ☐ 278 Wallace Francis | .06 | .03 | .01 |
| ☐ 279 Alfred Jackson | .06 | .03 | .01 |
| ☐ 280 John James | .06 | .03 | .01 |
| ☐ 281 Alfred Jenkins AP | .08 | .04 | .01 |
| ☐ 282 Alfred Jenkins IA | .06 | .03 | .01 |
| ☐ 283 Kenny Johnson | .06 | .03 | .01 |
| ☐ 284 Mike Kenn AP | .30 | .14 | .04 |
| ☐ 285 Fulton Kuykendall | .06 | .03 | .01 |
| ☐ 286 Mick Luckhurst | .06 | .03 | .01 |
| ☐ 287 Mick Luckhurst IA | .08 | .04 | .01 |
| ☐ 288 Junior Miller | .08 | .04 | .01 |
| ☐ 289 Al Richardson | .06 | .03 | .01 |
| ☐ 290 R.C. Thielemann | .06 | .03 | .01 |
| ☐ 291 Jeff Van Note | .08 | .04 | .01 |
| ☐ 292 Chicago Bears TL | .75 | .35 | .09 |
| Walter Payton | | | |
| Ken Margerum | | | |
| Gary Fencik | | | |
| Dan Hampton | | | |
| Alan Page | | | |
| ☐ 293 Brian Baschnagel | .06 | .03 | .01 |
| ☐ 294 Robin Earl | .06 | .03 | .01 |
| ☐ 295 Vince Evans | .35 | .16 | .04 |
| ☐ 296 Gary Fencik AP | .06 | .03 | .01 |
| ☐ 297 Dan Hampton | 2.00 | .90 | .25 |
| ☐ 298 Noah Jackson | .06 | .03 | .01 |
| ☐ 299 Ken Margerum | .08 | .04 | .01 |
| ☐ 300 Jim Osborne | .06 | .03 | .01 |
| ☐ 301 Bob Parsons | .06 | .03 | .01 |
| ☐ 302 Walter Payton | 3.50 | 1.55 | .45 |
| ☐ 303 Walter Payton IA | 1.75 | .80 | .22 |
| ☐ 304 Revie Sorey | .06 | .03 | .01 |
| ☐ 305 Matt Suhey | .30 | .14 | .04 |
| (Walter Payton | | | |
| in background) | | | |
| ☐ 306 Rickey Watts | .06 | .03 | .01 |
| ☐ 307 Dallas Cowboys TL | .50 | .23 | .06 |
| Tony Dorsett | | | |
| Tony Hill | | | |
| Everson Walls | | | |
| Harvey Martin | | | |
| ☐ 308 Bob Breunig | .08 | .04 | .01 |
| ☐ 309 Doug Cosbie | .25 | .11 | .03 |
| ☐ 310 Pat Donovan AP | .06 | .03 | .01 |
| ☐ 311 Tony Dorsett AP | 1.25 | .55 | .16 |
| ☐ 312 Tony Dorsett IA | .60 | .25 | .08 |
| ☐ 313 Michael Downs | .08 | .04 | .01 |
| ☐ 314 Billy Joe DuPree | .08 | .04 | .01 |
| ☐ 315 John Dutton | .08 | .04 | .01 |
| ☐ 316 Tony Hill | .08 | .04 | .01 |

| | | | |
|---|---|---|---|
| ☐ 317 Butch Johnson | .08 | .04 | .01 |
| ☐ 318 Ed Too Tall Jones AP | .50 | .23 | .06 |
| ☐ 319 James Jones | .06 | .03 | .01 |
| ☐ 320 Harvey Martin | .20 | .09 | .03 |
| ☐ 321 Drew Pearson | .30 | .14 | .04 |
| ☐ 322 Herbert Scott AP | .08 | .04 | .01 |
| ☐ 323 Rafael Septien AP | .06 | .03 | .01 |
| ☐ 324 Rafael Septien IA | .06 | .03 | .01 |
| ☐ 325 Ron Springs | .08 | .04 | .01 |
| ☐ 326 Dennis Thurman | .06 | .03 | .01 |
| ☐ 327 Everson Walls | .75 | .35 | .09 |
| ☐ 328 Everson Walls IA | .35 | .16 | .04 |
| ☐ 329 Danny White | .30 | .14 | .04 |
| ☐ 330 Danny White IA | .15 | .07 | .02 |
| ☐ 331 Randy White AP | .75 | .35 | .09 |
| ☐ 332 Randy White IA | .35 | .16 | .04 |
| ☐ 333 Detroit Lions TL | .15 | .07 | .02 |
| Billy Sims | | | |
| Freddie Scott | | | |
| Jim Allen | | | |
| Dave Pureifory | | | |
| ☐ 334 Jim Allen | .06 | .03 | .01 |
| ☐ 335 Al(Bubba) Baker | .08 | .04 | .01 |
| ☐ 336 Dexter Bussey | .06 | .03 | .01 |
| ☐ 337 Doug English AP | .08 | .04 | .01 |
| ☐ 338 Ken Fantetti | .06 | .03 | .01 |
| ☐ 339 William Gay | .06 | .03 | .01 |
| ☐ 340 David Hill | .06 | .03 | .01 |
| ☐ 341 Eric Hipple | .06 | .03 | .01 |
| ☐ 342 Rick Kane | .06 | .03 | .01 |
| ☐ 343 Ed Murray | .35 | .16 | .04 |
| ☐ 344 Ed Murray IA | .15 | .07 | .02 |
| ☐ 345 Ray Oldham | .06 | .03 | .01 |
| ☐ 346 Dave Pureifory | .06 | .03 | .01 |
| ☐ 347 Freddie Scott | .06 | .03 | .01 |
| ☐ 348 Freddie Scott IA | .06 | .03 | .01 |
| ☐ 349 Billy Sims AP | .40 | .18 | .05 |
| ☐ 350 Billy Sims IA | .15 | .07 | .02 |
| ☐ 351 Tom Skladany AP | .06 | .03 | .01 |
| ☐ 352 Leonard Thompson | .06 | .03 | .01 |
| ☐ 353 Stan White | .06 | .03 | .01 |
| ☐ 354 Green Bay Packers TL | .40 | .18 | .05 |
| Gerry Ellis | | | |
| James Lofton | | | |
| Maurice Harvey | | | |
| Mark Lee | | | |
| Mike Butler | | | |
| ☐ 355 Paul Coffman | .06 | .03 | .01 |
| ☐ 356 George Cumby | .06 | .03 | .01 |
| ☐ 357 Lynn Dickey | .08 | .04 | .01 |
| ☐ 358 Lynn Dickey IA | .08 | .04 | .01 |
| ☐ 359 Gerry Ellis | .06 | .03 | .01 |
| ☐ 360 Maurice Harvey | .06 | .03 | .01 |
| ☐ 361 Harlan Huckleby | .06 | .03 | .01 |
| ☐ 362 John Jefferson | .15 | .07 | .02 |
| ☐ 363 Mark Lee | .20 | .09 | .03 |
| ☐ 364 James Lofton AP | 1.50 | .65 | .19 |
| ☐ 365 James Lofton IA | .75 | .35 | .09 |
| ☐ 366 Jan Stenerud | .15 | .07 | .02 |
| ☐ 367 Jan Stenerud IA | .10 | .05 | .01 |
| ☐ 368 Rich Wingo | .06 | .03 | .01 |
| ☐ 369 Los Angeles Rams TL | .15 | .07 | .02 |
| Wendell Tyler | | | |
| Preston Dennard | | | |
| Nolan Cromwell | | | |
| Jack Youngblood | | | |
| ☐ 370 Frank Corral | .06 | .03 | .01 |
| ☐ 371 Nolan Cromwell AP | .25 | .11 | .03 |
| ☐ 372 Nolan Cromwell IA | .08 | .04 | .01 |
| ☐ 373 Preston Dennard | .06 | .03 | .01 |
| ☐ 374 Mike Fanning | .06 | .03 | .01 |
| ☐ 375 Doug France | .06 | .03 | .01 |
| ☐ 376 Mike Guman | .06 | .03 | .01 |
| ☐ 377 Pat Haden | .20 | .09 | .03 |
| ☐ 378 Dennis Harrah | .06 | .03 | .01 |
| ☐ 379 Drew Hill | 3.50 | 1.55 | .45 |
| ☐ 380 LeRoy Irvin | .40 | .18 | .05 |
| ☐ 381 Cody Jones | .06 | .03 | .01 |
| ☐ 382 Rod Perry | .08 | .04 | .01 |
| ☐ 383 Rich Saul AP | .06 | .03 | .01 |
| ☐ 384 Pat Thomas | .06 | .03 | .01 |
| ☐ 385 Wendell Tyler | .06 | .03 | .01 |
| ☐ 386 Wendell Tyler IA | .08 | .04 | .01 |
| ☐ 387 Billy Waddy | .06 | .03 | .01 |
| ☐ 388 Jack Youngblood | .25 | .11 | .03 |
| ☐ 389 Minnesota Vikings TL | .15 | .07 | .02 |
| Ted Brown | | | |
| Joe Senser | | | |
| Tom Hannon | | | |
| Willie Teal | | | |
| Matt Blair | | | |
| ☐ 390 Matt Blair AP | .08 | .04 | .01 |
| ☐ 391 Ted Brown | .08 | .04 | .01 |
| ☐ 392 Ted Brown IA | .06 | .03 | .01 |
| ☐ 393 Rick Danmeier | .06 | .03 | .01 |
| ☐ 394 Tommy Kramer | .20 | .09 | .03 |
| ☐ 395 Mark Mullaney | .08 | .04 | .01 |

| | | | |
|---|---|---|---|
| ☐ 396 Eddie Payton | .08 | .04 | .01 |
| ☐ 397 Ahmad Rashad | .30 | .14 | .04 |
| ☐ 398 Joe Senser | .08 | .04 | .01 |
| ☐ 399 Joe Senser IA | .06 | .03 | .01 |
| ☐ 400 Sammie White | .08 | .04 | .01 |
| ☐ 401 Sammie White IA | .08 | .04 | .01 |
| ☐ 402 Ron Yary | .08 | .04 | .01 |
| ☐ 403 Rickey Young | .08 | .04 | .01 |
| ☐ 404 New Orleans Saints TL | .50 | .23 | .06 |
| George Rogers | | | |
| Guido Merkens | | | |
| Dave Waymer | | | |
| Rickey Jackson | | | |
| ☐ 405 Russell Erxleben | .06 | .03 | .01 |
| ☐ 406 Elois Grooms | .06 | .03 | .01 |
| ☐ 407 Jack Holmes | .06 | .03 | .01 |
| ☐ 408 Archie Manning | .25 | .11 | .03 |
| ☐ 409 Derland Moore | .06 | .03 | .01 |
| ☐ 410 George Rogers | 1.00 | .45 | .13 |
| ☐ 411 George Rogers IA | .35 | .16 | .04 |
| ☐ 412 Toussaint Tyler | .06 | .03 | .01 |
| ☐ 413 Dave Waymer | .20 | .09 | .03 |
| ☐ 414 Wayne Wilson | .08 | .04 | .01 |
| ☐ 415 New York Giants TL | .15 | .07 | .02 |
| Rob Carpenter | | | |
| Johnny Perkins | | | |
| Beasley Reece | | | |
| George Martin | | | |
| ☐ 416 Scott Brunner | .06 | .03 | .01 |
| ☐ 417 Rob Carpenter | .08 | .04 | .01 |
| ☐ 418 Harry Carson AP | .25 | .11 | .03 |
| ☐ 419 Bill Currier | .06 | .03 | .01 |
| ☐ 420 Joe Danelo | .06 | .03 | .01 |
| ☐ 421 Joe Danelo IA | .06 | .03 | .01 |
| ☐ 422 Mark Haynes | .40 | .18 | .05 |
| ☐ 423 Terry Jackson | .06 | .03 | .01 |
| ☐ 424 Dave Jennings | .08 | .04 | .01 |
| ☐ 425 Gary Jeter | .06 | .03 | .01 |
| ☐ 426 Brian Kelley | .06 | .03 | .01 |
| ☐ 427 George Martin | .08 | .04 | .01 |
| ☐ 428 Curtis McGriff | .06 | .03 | .01 |
| ☐ 429 Bill Neill | .06 | .03 | .01 |
| ☐ 430 Johnny Perkins | .06 | .03 | .01 |
| ☐ 431 Beasley Reece | .06 | .03 | .01 |
| ☐ 432 Gary Shirk | .06 | .03 | .01 |
| ☐ 433 Phil Simms | 1.25 | .55 | .16 |
| ☐ 434 Lawrence Taylor AP | 35.00 | 16.00 | 4.40 |
| ☐ 435 Lawrence Taylor IA | 10.00 | 4.50 | 1.25 |
| ☐ 436 Brad Van Pelt | .08 | .04 | .01 |
| ☐ 437 Philadelphia Eagles TL | .20 | .09 | .03 |
| Wilbert Montgomery | | | |
| Harold Carmichael | | | |
| Brenard Wilson | | | |
| Carl Hairston | | | |
| ☐ 438 John Bunting | .06 | .03 | .01 |
| ☐ 439 Billy Campfield | .06 | .03 | .01 |
| ☐ 440 Harold Carmichael | .30 | .14 | .04 |
| ☐ 441 Harold Carmichael IA | .08 | .04 | .01 |
| ☐ 442 Herman Edwards | .06 | .03 | .01 |
| ☐ 443 Tony Franklin | .06 | .03 | .01 |
| ☐ 444 Tony Franklin IA | .06 | .03 | .01 |
| ☐ 445 Carl Hairston | .08 | .04 | .01 |
| ☐ 446 Dennis Harrison | .06 | .03 | .01 |
| ☐ 447 Ron Jaworski | .15 | .07 | .02 |
| ☐ 448 Charlie Johnson | .06 | .03 | .01 |
| ☐ 449 Keith Krepfle | .06 | .03 | .01 |
| ☐ 450 Frank LeMaster | .06 | .03 | .01 |
| ☐ 451 Randy Logan | .06 | .03 | .01 |
| ☐ 452 Wilbert Montgomery | .08 | .04 | .01 |
| ☐ 453 Wilbert Montgomery IA | .06 | .03 | .01 |
| ☐ 454 Hubert Oliver | .06 | .03 | .01 |
| ☐ 455 Jerry Robinson | .06 | .03 | .01 |
| ☐ 456 Jerry Robinson IA | .08 | .04 | .01 |
| ☐ 457 Jerry Sisemore | .06 | .03 | .01 |
| ☐ 458 Charlie Smith | .06 | .03 | .01 |
| ☐ 459 Stan Walters | .08 | .04 | .01 |
| ☐ 460 Brenard Wilson | .06 | .03 | .01 |
| ☐ 461 Roynell Young AP | .08 | .04 | .01 |
| ☐ 462 St. Louis Cardinals TL | .15 | .07 | .02 |
| Ottis Anderson | | | |
| Pat Tilley | | | |
| Ken Greene | | | |
| Curtis Greer | | | |
| ☐ 463 Ottis Anderson | .75 | .35 | .09 |
| ☐ 464 Ottis Anderson IA | .35 | .16 | .04 |
| ☐ 465 Carl Birdsong | .06 | .03 | .01 |
| ☐ 466 Rush Brown | .06 | .03 | .01 |
| ☐ 467 Mel Gray | .08 | .04 | .01 |
| ☐ 468 Ken Greene | .06 | .03 | .01 |
| ☐ 469 Jim Hart | .15 | .07 | .02 |
| ☐ 470 E.J. Junior | .50 | .23 | .06 |
| ☐ 471 Neil Lomax | .60 | .25 | .08 |
| ☐ 472 Stump Mitchell | .50 | .23 | .06 |
| ☐ 473 Wayne Morris | .06 | .03 | .01 |
| ☐ 474 Neil O'Donoghue | .06 | .03 | .01 |
| ☐ 475 Pat Tilley | .08 | .04 | .01 |
| ☐ 476 Pat Tilley IA | .06 | .03 | .01 |

| | | | |
|---|---|---|---|
| ☐ 477 San Francisco 49ers TL | .25 | .11 | .03 |
| Ricky Patton | | | |
| Dwight Clark | | | |
| Dwight Hicks | | | |
| Fred Dean | | | |
| ☐ 478 Dwight Clark | 1.00 | .45 | .13 |
| ☐ 479 Dwight Clark IA | .50 | .23 | .06 |
| ☐ 480 Earl Cooper | .08 | .04 | .01 |
| ☐ 481 Randy Cross AP | .08 | .04 | .01 |
| ☐ 482 Johnny Davis | .06 | .03 | .01 |
| ☐ 483 Fred Dean | .08 | .04 | .01 |
| ☐ 484 Fred Dean IA | .06 | .03 | .01 |
| ☐ 485 Dwight Hicks | .40 | .18 | .05 |
| ☐ 486 Ronnie Lott AP | 24.00 | 11.00 | 3.00 |
| ☐ 487 Ronnie Lott IA | 6.00 | 2.70 | .75 |
| ☐ 488 Joe Montana AP | 35.00 | 16.00 | 4.40 |
| ☐ 489 Joe Montana IA | 10.00 | 4.50 | 1.25 |
| ☐ 490 Ricky Patton | .08 | .04 | .01 |
| ☐ 491 Jack Reynolds | .08 | .04 | .01 |
| ☐ 492 Freddie Solomon | .08 | .04 | .01 |
| ☐ 493 Ray Wersching | .08 | .04 | .01 |
| ☐ 494 Charley Young | .08 | .04 | .01 |
| ☐ 495 Tampa Bay Bucs TL | .15 | .07 | .02 |
| Jerry Eckwood | | | |
| Kevin House | | | |
| Cedric Brown | | | |
| Lee Roy Selmon | | | |
| ☐ 496 Cedric Brown | .06 | .03 | .01 |
| ☐ 497 Neal Colzie | .06 | .03 | .01 |
| ☐ 498 Jerry Eckwood | .06 | .03 | .01 |
| ☐ 499 Jimmie Giles AP | .08 | .04 | .01 |
| ☐ 500 Hugh Green | .60 | .25 | .08 |
| ☐ 501 Kevin House | .08 | .04 | .01 |
| ☐ 502 Kevin House IA | .08 | .04 | .01 |
| ☐ 503 Cecil Johnson | .06 | .03 | .01 |
| ☐ 504 James Owens | .06 | .03 | .01 |
| ☐ 505 Lee Roy Selmon AP | .08 | .04 | .01 |
| ☐ 506 Mike Washington | .06 | .03 | .01 |
| ☐ 507 James Wilder | .60 | .25 | .08 |
| ☐ 508 Doug Williams | .20 | .09 | .03 |
| ☐ 509 Wash. Redskins TL | .75 | .35 | .09 |
| Joe Washington | | | |
| Art Monk | | | |
| Mark Murphy | | | |
| Perry Brooks | | | |
| ☐ 510 Perry Brooks | .06 | .03 | .01 |
| ☐ 511 Dave Butz | .08 | .04 | .01 |
| ☐ 512 Wilbur Jackson | .08 | .04 | .01 |
| ☐ 513 Joe Lavender | .08 | .04 | .01 |
| ☐ 514 Terry Metcalf | .08 | .04 | .01 |
| ☐ 515 Art Monk | 5.00 | 2.30 | .60 |
| ☐ 516 Mark Moseley | .08 | .04 | .01 |
| ☐ 517 Mark Murphy | .06 | .03 | .01 |
| ☐ 518 Mike Nelms AP | .08 | .04 | .01 |
| ☐ 519 Lemar Parrish | .08 | .04 | .01 |
| ☐ 520 John Riggins | .75 | .35 | .09 |
| ☐ 521 Joe Theismann | .75 | .35 | .09 |
| ☐ 522 Ricky Thompson | .06 | .03 | .01 |
| ☐ 523 Don Warren UER | .20 | .09 | .03 |
| (photo actually | | | |
| Ricky Thompson) | | | |
| ☐ 524 Joe Washington | .08 | .04 | .01 |
| ☐ 525 Checklist 1-132 | .35 | .03 | .01 |
| ☐ 526 Checklist 133-264 | .35 | .03 | .01 |
| ☐ 527 Checklist 265-396 | .35 | .03 | .01 |
| ☐ 528 Checklist 397-528 | .35 | .03 | .01 |

## 1983 Topps

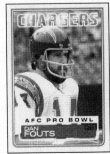

Although there are only 396 cards, a decrease from previous years, the set was printed on four sheets. As a result, there are 132 double-printed cards which are denoted in the checklist below by DP. The cards themselves contain the player's name at the bottom in a rectangular area, while the team names are in block letters at the top of the cards. The first nine cards in the set recognize Record-Breaking (RB) achievements occurring during the previous season. Cards 10-12 summarize the playoff action of the previous year. League leaders are recognized on cards 202-207. Players who appeared in the Pro Bowl game (designated PB in the checklist below) are identified as such on the card front. The backs of the cards are printed in black ink with red borders and a faintly identifiable helmet of the player's team covering the center of the back in a screened red color. The Team Leader (TL) cards are distributed throughout the set as the first card of the team sequence; this year only one leader (usually the team's rushing leader) is pictured and the backs contain team scoring information from the previous season. The team numbering is arranged alphabetically within each conference (with players ordered alphabetically within team) as follows: Atlanta Falcons (13-27), Chicago Bears (28-41), Dallas Cowboys (42-57), Detroit Lions (58-73), Green Bay Packers (74-85), Los Angeles Rams (86-96), Minnesota Vikings (97-108), New Orleans Saints (109-119), New York Giants (120-135), Philadelphia Eagles (136-151), St. Louis Cardinals (152-162), San Francisco 49ers (163-173), Tampa Bay Buccaneers (174-185), Washington Redskins (186-201), Baltimore Colts (208-218), Buffalo Bills (219-229), Cincinnati Bengals (230-243), Cleveland Browns (244-259), Denver Broncos (260-270), Houston Oilers (271-281), Kansas City Chiefs (282-292), Los Angeles Raiders (293-307), Miami Dolphins (308-323), New England Patriots (324-337), New York Jets (338-354), Pittsburgh Steelers (355-369), San Diego Chargers (370-382), and Seattle Seahawks (383-393). The last three cards in the set (394-396) are checklist cards. The key Rookie Cards in this set are Marcus Allen, Todd Christensen, Roy Green, Jim McMahon, and Mike Singletary.

|  | MINT | EXC | G-VG |
|---|---|---|---|
| COMPLETE SET (396) | 45.00 | 20.00 | 5.75 |
| COMMON PLAYER (1-396) | .05 | .02 | .01 |
| COMMON PLAYER DP | .04 | .02 | .01 |

| | | | |
|---|---|---|---|
| ☐ 1 Ken Anderson RB<br>20 Consecutive<br>Pass Completions | .30 | .14 | .04 |
| ☐ 2 Tony Dorsett RB<br>99 Yard Run | .30 | .14 | .04 |
| ☐ 3 Dan Fouts RB<br>30 Games Over<br>300 Yards Passing | .30 | .14 | .04 |
| ☐ 4 Joe Montana RB<br>Five Straight<br>300 Yard Games | 2.50 | 1.15 | .30 |
| ☐ 5 Mark Moseley RB<br>21 Straight<br>Field Goals | .10 | .05 | .01 |
| ☐ 6 Mike Nelms RB<br>Most Yards,<br>Punt Returns,<br>Super Bowl Game | .10 | .05 | .01 |
| ☐ 7 Darrol Ray RB<br>Longest Interception<br>Return, Playoff Game | .10 | .05 | .01 |
| ☐ 8 John Riggins RB<br>Most Yards Rushing,<br>Super Bowl Game | .25 | .11 | .03 |
| ☐ 9 Fulton Walker RB<br>Most Yards,<br>Kickoff Returns,<br>Super Bowl Game | .12 | .05 | .02 |
| ☐ 10 NFC Championship<br>Redskins 31,<br>Cowboys 17<br>(John Riggins tackled) | .10 | .05 | .01 |
| ☐ 11 AFC Championship<br>Dolphins 14,<br>Jets 0 | .10 | .05 | .01 |
| ☐ 12 Super Bowl XVII<br>Redskins 27,<br>Dolphins 17<br>(John Riggins running) | .40 | .18 | .05 |
| ☐ 13 Atlanta Falcons TL<br>William Andrews | .10 | .05 | .01 |
| ☐ 14 William Andrews DP PB | .06 | .03 | .01 |
| ☐ 15 Steve Bartkowski | .20 | .09 | .03 |
| ☐ 16 Bobby Butler | .05 | .02 | .01 |
| ☐ 17 Buddy Curry | .05 | .02 | .01 |
| ☐ 18 Alfred Jackson DP | .04 | .02 | .01 |
| ☐ 19 Alfred Jenkins | .07 | .03 | .01 |
| ☐ 20 Kenny Johnson | .05 | .02 | .01 |
| ☐ 21 Mike Kenn PB | .07 | .03 | .01 |
| ☐ 22 Mick Luckhurst | .05 | .02 | .01 |
| ☐ 23 Junior Miller | .07 | .03 | .01 |
| ☐ 24 Al Richardson | .05 | .02 | .01 |
| ☐ 25 Gerald Riggs DP | .75 | .35 | .09 |
| ☐ 26 R.C. Thielemann PB | .05 | .02 | .01 |
| ☐ 27 Jeff Van Note PB | .07 | .03 | .01 |
| ☐ 28 Chicago Bears TL<br>Walter Payton | .75 | .35 | .09 |
| ☐ 29 Brian Baschnagel | .05 | .02 | .01 |
| ☐ 30 Dan Hampton PB | 1.00 | .45 | .13 |
| ☐ 31 Mike Hartenstine | .05 | .02 | .01 |
| ☐ 32 Noah Jackson | .05 | .02 | .01 |
| ☐ 33 Jim McMahon | 6.00 | 2.70 | .75 |
| ☐ 34 Emery Moorehead DP | .04 | .02 | .01 |
| ☐ 35 Bob Parsons | .05 | .02 | .01 |
| ☐ 36 Walter Payton | 2.25 | 1.00 | .30 |
| ☐ 37 Terry Schmidt | .05 | .02 | .01 |
| ☐ 38 Mike Singletary | 7.50 | 3.40 | .95 |
| ☐ 39 Matt Suhey DP | .06 | .03 | .01 |
| ☐ 40 Rickey Watts DP | .04 | .02 | .01 |
| ☐ 41 Otis Wilson DP | .20 | .09 | .03 |
| ☐ 42 Dallas Cowboys TL<br>Tony Dorsett | .30 | .14 | .04 |
| ☐ 43 Bob Breunig PB | .07 | .03 | .01 |
| ☐ 44 Doug Cosbie | .07 | .03 | .01 |
| ☐ 45 Pat Donovan PB | .05 | .02 | .01 |
| ☐ 46 Tony Dorsett DP PB | .75 | .35 | .09 |
| ☐ 47 Tony Hill | .07 | .03 | .01 |
| ☐ 48 Butch Johnson DP | .06 | .03 | .01 |
| ☐ 49 Ed Jones DP PB | .25 | .11 | .03 |
| ☐ 50 Harvey Martin DP | .04 | .02 | .01 |
| ☐ 51 Drew Pearson | .25 | .11 | .03 |
| ☐ 52 Rafael Septien | .05 | .02 | .01 |
| ☐ 53 Ron Springs DP | .04 | .02 | .01 |
| ☐ 54 Dennis Thurman | .05 | .02 | .01 |
| ☐ 55 Everson Walls PB | .25 | .11 | .03 |
| ☐ 56 Danny White DP PB | .20 | .09 | .03 |
| ☐ 57 Randy White PB | .60 | .25 | .08 |
| ☐ 58 Detroit Lions TL<br>Billy Sims | .12 | .05 | .02 |
| ☐ 59 Al(Bubba) Baker DP | .06 | .03 | .01 |
| ☐ 60 Dexter Bussey DP | .04 | .02 | .01 |
| ☐ 61 Gary Danielson DP | .06 | .03 | .01 |
| ☐ 62 Keith Dorney DP PB | .05 | .02 | .01 |
| ☐ 63 Doug English PB | .07 | .03 | .01 |
| ☐ 64 Ken Fantetti DP | .04 | .02 | .01 |
| ☐ 65 Alvin Hall DP | .04 | .02 | .01 |
| ☐ 66 David Hill DP | .04 | .02 | .01 |
| ☐ 67 Eric Hipple | .07 | .03 | .01 |
| ☐ 68 Ed Murray DP | .15 | .07 | .02 |
| ☐ 69 Freddie Scott | .05 | .02 | .01 |
| ☐ 70 Billy Sims DP | .10 | .05 | .01 |
| ☐ 71 Tom Skladany DP | .04 | .02 | .01 |
| ☐ 72 Leonard Thompson DP | .04 | .02 | .01 |
| ☐ 73 Bobby Watkins | .05 | .02 | .01 |
| ☐ 74 Green Bay Packers TL<br>Eddie Lee Ivery | .10 | .05 | .01 |
| ☐ 75 John Anderson | .05 | .02 | .01 |
| ☐ 76 Paul Coffman PB | .05 | .02 | .01 |
| ☐ 77 Lynn Dickey | .07 | .03 | .01 |
| ☐ 78 Mike Douglass DP | .04 | .02 | .01 |
| ☐ 79 Eddie Lee Ivery | .07 | .03 | .01 |
| ☐ 80 John Jefferson DP PB | .15 | .07 | .02 |
| ☐ 81 Ezra Johnson | .05 | .02 | .01 |
| ☐ 82 Mark Lee | .07 | .03 | .01 |
| ☐ 83 James Lofton PB | 1.25 | .55 | .16 |
| ☐ 84 Larry McCarren PB | .05 | .02 | .01 |
| ☐ 85 Jan Stenerud DP | .15 | .07 | .02 |
| ☐ 86 Los Angeles Rams TL<br>Wendell Tyler | .10 | .05 | .01 |
| ☐ 87 Bill Bain DP | .04 | .02 | .01 |
| ☐ 88 Nolan Cromwell PB | .07 | .03 | .01 |
| ☐ 89 Preston Dennard | .05 | .02 | .01 |
| ☐ 90 Vince Ferragamo DP | .06 | .03 | .01 |
| ☐ 91 Mike Guman | .05 | .02 | .01 |
| ☐ 92 Kent Hill PB | .05 | .02 | .01 |
| ☐ 93 Mike Lansford DP | .05 | .02 | .01 |
| ☐ 94 Rod Perry | .07 | .03 | .01 |
| ☐ 95 Pat Thomas DP | .04 | .02 | .01 |
| ☐ 96 Jack Youngblood | .15 | .07 | .02 |
| ☐ 97 Minnesota Vikings TL<br>Ted Brown | .10 | .05 | .01 |
| ☐ 98 Matt Blair PB | .07 | .03 | .01 |
| ☐ 99 Ted Brown | .07 | .03 | .01 |
| ☐ 100 Greg Coleman | .05 | .02 | .01 |
| ☐ 101 Randy Holloway | .05 | .02 | .01 |
| ☐ 102 Tommy Kramer | .15 | .07 | .02 |
| ☐ 103 Doug Martin DP | .05 | .02 | .01 |
| ☐ 104 Mark Mullaney | .05 | .02 | .01 |
| ☐ 105 Joe Senser | .07 | .03 | .01 |
| ☐ 106 Willie Teal DP | .04 | .02 | .01 |
| ☐ 107 Sammie White | .07 | .03 | .01 |
| ☐ 108 Rickey Young | .05 | .02 | .01 |
| ☐ 109 New Orleans Saints TL<br>George Rogers | .10 | .05 | .01 |
| ☐ 110 Stan Brock | .30 | .14 | .04 |
| ☐ 111 Bruce Clark | .05 | .02 | .01 |
| ☐ 112 Russell Erxleben DP | .04 | .02 | .01 |
| ☐ 113 Russell Gary | .05 | .02 | .01 |
| ☐ 114 Jeff Groth DP | .05 | .02 | .01 |
| ☐ 115 John Hill DP | .05 | .02 | .01 |
| ☐ 116 Derland Moore | .05 | .02 | .01 |
| ☐ 117 George Rogers PB | .20 | .09 | .03 |
| ☐ 118 Ken Stabler | .75 | .35 | .09 |
| ☐ 119 Wayne Wilson | .05 | .02 | .01 |
| ☐ 120 New York Giants TL<br>Butch Woolfolk | .10 | .05 | .01 |

|  |  | | | |
|---|---|---|---|---|
| ☐ 121 | Scott Brunner | .05 | .02 | .01 |
| ☐ 122 | Rob Carpenter | .07 | .03 | .01 |
| ☐ 123 | Harry Carson PB | .20 | .09 | .03 |
| ☐ 124 | Joe Danelo DP | .04 | .02 | .01 |
| ☐ 125 | Earnest Gray | .05 | .02 | .01 |
| ☐ 126 | Mark Haynes DP PB | .04 | .02 | .01 |
| ☐ 127 | Terry Jackson | .05 | .02 | .01 |
| ☐ 128 | Dave Jennings PB | .07 | .03 | .01 |
| ☐ 129 | Brian Kelley | .05 | .02 | .01 |
| ☐ 130 | George Martin | .05 | .02 | .01 |
| ☐ 131 | Tom Mullady | .05 | .02 | .01 |
| ☐ 132 | Johnny Perkins | .05 | .02 | .01 |
| ☐ 133 | Lawrence Taylor PB | 8.00 | 3.60 | 1.00 |
| ☐ 134 | Brad Van Pelt | .07 | .03 | .01 |
| ☐ 135 | Butch Woolfolk DP | .06 | .03 | .01 |
| ☐ 136 | Philadelphia Eagles TL | .10 | .05 | .01 |
|  | Wilbert Montgomery | | | |
| ☐ 137 | Harold Carmichael | .25 | .11 | .03 |
| ☐ 138 | Herman Edwards | .05 | .02 | .01 |
| ☐ 139 | Tony Franklin DP | .04 | .02 | .01 |
| ☐ 140 | Carl Hairston DP | .06 | .03 | .01 |
| ☐ 141 | Dennis Harrison DP PB | .04 | .02 | .01 |
| ☐ 142 | Ron Jaworski DP | .07 | .03 | .01 |
| ☐ 143 | Frank LeMaster | .05 | .02 | .01 |
| ☐ 144 | Wilbert Montgomery DP | .06 | .03 | .01 |
| ☐ 145 | Guy Morriss | .05 | .02 | .01 |
| ☐ 146 | Jerry Robinson | .07 | .03 | .01 |
| ☐ 147 | Max Runager | .05 | .02 | .01 |
| ☐ 148 | Ron Smith DP | .04 | .02 | .01 |
| ☐ 149 | John Spagnola | .05 | .02 | .01 |
| ☐ 150 | Stan Walters DP | .06 | .03 | .01 |
| ☐ 151 | Roynell Young DP | .04 | .02 | .01 |
| ☐ 152 | St. Louis Cardinals TL | .10 | .05 | .01 |
|  | Ottis Anderson | | | |
| ☐ 153 | Ottis Anderson | .40 | .18 | .05 |
| ☐ 154 | Carl Birdsong | .05 | .02 | .01 |
| ☐ 155 | Dan Dierdorf DP | .15 | .07 | .02 |
| ☐ 156 | Roy Green | .75 | .35 | .09 |
| ☐ 157 | Elois Grooms | .05 | .02 | .01 |
| ☐ 158 | Neil Lomax DP | .05 | .02 | .01 |
| ☐ 159 | Wayne Morris | .05 | .02 | .01 |
| ☐ 160 | Tootie Robbins | .05 | .02 | .01 |
| ☐ 161 | Luis Sharpe | .30 | .14 | .04 |
| ☐ 162 | Pat Tilley | .07 | .03 | .01 |
| ☐ 163 | San Francisco 49ers TL | .10 | .05 | .01 |
|  | Jeff Moore | | | |
| ☐ 164 | Dwight Clark PB | .30 | .14 | .04 |
| ☐ 165 | Randy Cross PB | .07 | .03 | .01 |
| ☐ 166 | Russ Francis | .07 | .03 | .01 |
| ☐ 167 | Dwight Hicks PB | .07 | .03 | .01 |
| ☐ 168 | Ronnie Lott PB | 4.00 | 1.80 | .50 |
| ☐ 169 | Joe Montana DP | 12.00 | 5.50 | 1.50 |
| ☐ 170 | Jeff Moore | .05 | .02 | .01 |
| ☐ 171 | Renaldo Nehemiah DP | .15 | .07 | .02 |
| ☐ 172 | Freddie Solomon | .07 | .03 | .01 |
| ☐ 173 | Ray Wersching DP | .06 | .03 | .01 |
| ☐ 174 | Tampa Bay Bucs TL | .10 | .05 | .01 |
|  | James Wilder | | | |
| ☐ 175 | Cedric Brown | .05 | .02 | .01 |
| ☐ 176 | Bill Capece | .05 | .02 | .01 |
| ☐ 177 | Neal Colzie | .05 | .02 | .01 |
| ☐ 178 | Jimmie Giles PB | .07 | .03 | .01 |
| ☐ 179 | Hugh Green PB | .05 | .02 | .01 |
| ☐ 180 | Kevin House DP | .06 | .03 | .01 |
| ☐ 181 | James Owens | .05 | .02 | .01 |
| ☐ 182 | Lee Roy Selmon PB | .07 | .03 | .01 |
| ☐ 183 | Mike Washington | .05 | .02 | .01 |
| ☐ 184 | James Wilder | .15 | .07 | .02 |
| ☐ 185 | Doug Williams DP | .05 | .02 | .01 |
| ☐ 186 | Wash. Redskins TL | .25 | .11 | .03 |
|  | John Riggins | | | |
| ☐ 187 | Jeff Bostic DP | .25 | .11 | .03 |
| ☐ 188 | Charlie Brown PB | .05 | .02 | .01 |
| ☐ 189 | Vernon Dean DP | .06 | .03 | .01 |
| ☐ 190 | Joe Jacoby | .75 | .35 | .09 |
| ☐ 191 | Dexter Manley | .20 | .09 | .03 |
| ☐ 192 | Rich Milot | .05 | .02 | .01 |
| ☐ 193 | Art Monk DP | 2.00 | .90 | .25 |
| ☐ 194 | Mark Moseley DP PB | .06 | .03 | .01 |
| ☐ 195 | Mike Nelms PB | .05 | .02 | .01 |
| ☐ 196 | Neal Olkewicz DP | .06 | .03 | .01 |
| ☐ 197 | Tony Peters PB | .07 | .03 | .01 |
| ☐ 198 | John Riggins DP | .50 | .23 | .06 |
| ☐ 199 | Joe Theismann PB | .60 | .25 | .08 |
| ☐ 200 | Don Warren | .07 | .03 | .01 |
| ☐ 201 | Jeris White DP | .04 | .02 | .01 |
| ☐ 202 | Passing Leaders | .25 | .11 | .03 |
|  | Joe Theismann | | | |
|  | Ken Anderson | | | |
| ☐ 203 | Receiving Leaders | .15 | .07 | .02 |
|  | Dwight Clark | | | |
|  | Kellen Winslow | | | |
| ☐ 204 | Rushing Leaders | .50 | .23 | .06 |
|  | Tony Dorsett | | | |
|  | Freeman McNeil | | | |
| ☐ 205 | Scoring Leaders | .75 | .35 | .09 |
|  | Wendell Tyler | | | |
|  | Marcus Allen | | | |
| ☐ 206 | Interception Leaders | .10 | .05 | .01 |
|  | Everson Walls | | | |
|  | AFC Tie (Four) | | | |
| ☐ 207 | Punting Leaders | .10 | .05 | .01 |
|  | Carl Birdsong | | | |
|  | Luke Prestridge | | | |
| ☐ 208 | Baltimore Colts TL | .10 | .05 | .01 |
|  | Randy McMillan | | | |
| ☐ 209 | Matt Bouza | .05 | .02 | .01 |
| ☐ 210 | Johnie Cooks DP | .05 | .02 | .01 |
| ☐ 211 | Curtis Dickey | .07 | .03 | .01 |
| ☐ 212 | Nesby Glasgow DP | .04 | .02 | .01 |
| ☐ 213 | Derrick Hatchett | .05 | .02 | .01 |
| ☐ 214 | Randy McMillan | .05 | .02 | .01 |
| ☐ 215 | Mike Pagel | .15 | .07 | .02 |
| ☐ 216 | Rohn Stark DP | .30 | .14 | .04 |
| ☐ 217 | Donnell Thompson DP | .05 | .02 | .01 |
| ☐ 218 | Leo Wisniewski DP | .05 | .02 | .01 |
| ☐ 219 | Buffalo Bills TL | .10 | .05 | .01 |
|  | Joe Cribbs | | | |
| ☐ 220 | Curtis Brown | .05 | .02 | .01 |
| ☐ 221 | Jerry Butler | .07 | .03 | .01 |
| ☐ 222 | Greg Cater DP | .04 | .02 | .01 |
| ☐ 223 | Joe Cribbs | .07 | .03 | .01 |
| ☐ 224 | Joe Ferguson | .07 | .03 | .01 |
| ☐ 225 | Roosevelt Leaks | .07 | .03 | .01 |
| ☐ 226 | Frank Lewis | .07 | .03 | .01 |
| ☐ 227 | Eugene Marve | .05 | .02 | .01 |
| ☐ 228 | Fred Smerlas DP PB | .05 | .02 | .01 |
| ☐ 229 | Ben Williams DP PB | .04 | .02 | .01 |
| ☐ 230 | Cincinnati Bengals TL | .10 | .05 | .01 |
|  | Pete Johnson | | | |
| ☐ 231 | Charles Alexander | .05 | .02 | .01 |
| ☐ 232 | Ken Anderson DP PB | .30 | .14 | .04 |
| ☐ 233 | Jim Breech DP | .04 | .02 | .01 |
| ☐ 234 | Ross Browner | .07 | .03 | .01 |
| ☐ 235 | Cris Collinsworth | .30 | .14 | .04 |
|  | DP PB | | | |
| ☐ 236 | Isaac Curtis | .07 | .03 | .01 |
| ☐ 237 | Pete Johnson | .07 | .03 | .01 |
| ☐ 238 | Steve Kreider DP | .04 | .02 | .01 |
| ☐ 239 | Max Montoya | .05 | .02 | .01 |
| ☐ 240 | Anthony Munoz PB | 1.50 | .65 | .19 |
| ☐ 241 | Ken Riley | .07 | .03 | .01 |
| ☐ 242 | Dan Ross PB | .07 | .03 | .01 |
| ☐ 243 | Reggie Williams | .07 | .03 | .01 |
| ☐ 244 | Cleveland Browns TL | .10 | .05 | .01 |
|  | Mike Pruitt | | | |
| ☐ 245 | Chip Banks DP PB | .25 | .11 | .03 |
| ☐ 246 | Tom Cousineau DP | .05 | .02 | .01 |
| ☐ 247 | Joe DeLamielleure DP | .06 | .03 | .01 |
| ☐ 248 | Doug Dieken DP | .04 | .02 | .01 |
| ☐ 249 | Hanford Dixon | .05 | .02 | .01 |
| ☐ 250 | Ricky Feacher DP | .04 | .02 | .01 |
| ☐ 251 | Lawrence Johnson DP | .04 | .02 | .01 |
| ☐ 252 | Dave Logan | .06 | .03 | .01 |
| ☐ 253 | Paul McDonald DP | .06 | .03 | .01 |
| ☐ 254 | Ozzie Newsome DP | .40 | .18 | .05 |
| ☐ 255 | Mike Pruitt | .07 | .03 | .01 |
| ☐ 256 | Clarence Scott DP | .04 | .02 | .01 |
| ☐ 257 | Brian Sipe DP | .07 | .03 | .01 |
| ☐ 258 | Dwight Walker DP | .04 | .02 | .01 |
| ☐ 259 | Charles White | .07 | .03 | .01 |
| ☐ 260 | Denver Broncos TL | .10 | .05 | .01 |
|  | Gerald Willhite | | | |
| ☐ 261 | Steve DeBerg DP | .40 | .18 | .05 |
| ☐ 262 | Randy Gradishar DP PB | .15 | .07 | .02 |
| ☐ 263 | Rulon Jones DP | .05 | .02 | .01 |
| ☐ 264 | Rick Karlis DP | .04 | .02 | .01 |
| ☐ 265 | Don Latimer | .05 | .02 | .01 |
| ☐ 266 | Rick Parros DP | .04 | .02 | .01 |
| ☐ 267 | Luke Prestridge PB | .05 | .02 | .01 |
| ☐ 268 | Rick Upchurch PB | .07 | .03 | .01 |
| ☐ 269 | Steve Watson DP | .05 | .02 | .01 |
| ☐ 270 | Gerald Willhite DP | .06 | .03 | .01 |
| ☐ 271 | Houston Oilers TL | .10 | .05 | .01 |
|  | Gifford Nielsen | | | |
| ☐ 272 | Harold Bailey | .05 | .02 | .01 |
| ☐ 273 | Jesse Baker DP | .04 | .02 | .01 |
| ☐ 274 | Gregg Bingham DP | .04 | .02 | .01 |
| ☐ 275 | Robert Brazile DP PB | .04 | .02 | .01 |
| ☐ 276 | Donnie Craft | .05 | .02 | .01 |
| ☐ 277 | Daryl Hunt | .05 | .02 | .01 |
| ☐ 278 | Archie Manning DP | .15 | .07 | .02 |
| ☐ 279 | Gifford Nielsen | .07 | .03 | .01 |
| ☐ 280 | Mike Renfro | .07 | .03 | .01 |
| ☐ 281 | Carl Roaches DP | .06 | .03 | .01 |
| ☐ 282 | Kansas City Chiefs TL | .10 | .05 | .01 |
|  | Joe Delaney | | | |
| ☐ 283 | Gary Barbaro PB | .07 | .03 | .01 |
| ☐ 284 | Joe Delaney | .05 | .02 | .01 |
| ☐ 285 | Jeff Gossett | .50 | .23 | .06 |
| ☐ 286 | Gary Green PB | .04 | .02 | .01 |
| ☐ 287 | Eric Harris DP | .04 | .02 | .01 |
| ☐ 288 | Billy Jackson DP | .04 | .02 | .01 |
| ☐ 289 | Bill Kenney DP | .06 | .03 | .01 |
| ☐ 290 | Nick Lowery | .40 | .18 | .05 |

| | | | |
|---|---|---|---|
| ☐ 291 Henry Marshall | .05 | .02 | .01 |
| ☐ 292 Art Still DP PB | .06 | .03 | .01 |
| ☐ 293 Los Angeles Raiders TL | 1.00 | .45 | .13 |
|     Marcus Allen | | | |
| ☐ 294 Marcus Allen DP PB | 12.00 | 5.50 | 1.50 |
| ☐ 295 Lyle Alzado | .20 | .09 | .03 |
| ☐ 296 Chris Bahr DP | .04 | .02 | .01 |
| ☐ 297 Cliff Branch | .25 | .11 | .03 |
| ☐ 298 Todd Christensen | 2.00 | .90 | .25 |
| ☐ 299 Ray Guy | .15 | .07 | .02 |
| ☐ 300 Frank Hawkins DP | .04 | .02 | .01 |
| ☐ 301 Lester Hayes DP PB | .06 | .03 | .01 |
| ☐ 302 Ted Hendricks DP PB | .20 | .09 | .03 |
| ☐ 303 Kenny King DP | .06 | .03 | .01 |
| ☐ 304 Rod Martin | .07 | .03 | .01 |
| ☐ 305 Matt Millen DP | .15 | .07 | .01 |
| ☐ 306 Burgess Owens | .05 | .02 | .01 |
| ☐ 307 Jim Plunkett | .30 | .14 | .04 |
| ☐ 308 Miami Dolphins TL | .10 | .05 | .01 |
|     Andra Franklin | | | |
| ☐ 309 Bob Baumhower PB | .06 | .03 | .01 |
| ☐ 310 Glenn Blackwood | .07 | .03 | .01 |
| ☐ 311 Lyle Blackwood DP | .06 | .03 | .01 |
| ☐ 312 A.J. Duhe | .07 | .03 | .01 |
| ☐ 313 Andra Franklin PB | .07 | .03 | .01 |
| ☐ 314 Duriel Harris | .07 | .03 | .01 |
| ☐ 315 Bob Kuechenberg DP PB | .07 | .03 | .01 |
| ☐ 316 Don McNeal | .07 | .03 | .01 |
| ☐ 317 Tony Nathan | .07 | .03 | .01 |
| ☐ 318 Ed Newman PB | .05 | .02 | .01 |
| ☐ 319 Earnie Rhone DP | .04 | .02 | .01 |
| ☐ 320 Joe Rose DP | .06 | .03 | .01 |
| ☐ 321 Don Strock DP | .06 | .03 | .01 |
| ☐ 322 Uwe Von Schamann | .05 | .02 | .01 |
| ☐ 323 David Woodley DP | .06 | .03 | .01 |
| ☐ 324 New England Pats TL | .10 | .05 | .01 |
|     Tony Collins | | | |
| ☐ 325 Julius Adams | .05 | .02 | .01 |
| ☐ 326 Pete Brock | .05 | .02 | .01 |
| ☐ 327 Rich Camarillo DP | .25 | .11 | .03 |
| ☐ 328 Tony Collins DP | .06 | .03 | .01 |
| ☐ 329 Steve Grogan | .20 | .09 | .03 |
| ☐ 330 John Hannah PB | .25 | .11 | .03 |
| ☐ 331 Don Hasselbeck | .05 | .02 | .01 |
| ☐ 332 Mike Haynes PB | .07 | .03 | .01 |
| ☐ 333 Roland James | .05 | .02 | .01 |
| ☐ 334A Stanley Morgan ERR | .75 | .35 | .09 |
|     ("Inside Linebacker" | | | |
|     printed upside down | | | |
|     on card back) | | | |
| ☐ 334B Stanley Morgan COR | .25 | .11 | .03 |
| ☐ 335 Steve Nelson | .05 | .02 | .01 |
| ☐ 336 Kenneth Sims DP | .06 | .03 | .01 |
| ☐ 337 Mark Van Eeghen | .07 | .03 | .01 |
| ☐ 338 New York Jets TL | .10 | .05 | .01 |
|     Freeman McNeil | | | |
| ☐ 339 Greg Buttle | .07 | .03 | .01 |
| ☐ 340 Joe Fields PB | .05 | .02 | .01 |
| ☐ 341 Mark Gastineau DP PB | .06 | .03 | .01 |
| ☐ 342 Bruce Harper | .05 | .02 | .01 |
| ☐ 343 Bobby Jackson | .05 | .02 | .01 |
| ☐ 344 Bobby Jones | .05 | .02 | .01 |
| ☐ 345 Johnny "Lam" Jones DP | .07 | .03 | .01 |
| ☐ 346 Joe Klecko | .20 | .09 | .03 |
| ☐ 347 Marty Lyons | .07 | .03 | .01 |
| ☐ 348 Freeman McNeil PB | .50 | .23 | .06 |
| ☐ 349 Lance Mehl | .05 | .02 | .01 |
| ☐ 350 Marvin Powell DP PB | .04 | .02 | .01 |
| ☐ 351 Darrol Ray DP | .04 | .02 | .01 |
| ☐ 352 Abdul Salaam | .05 | .02 | .01 |
| ☐ 353 Richard Todd | .07 | .03 | .01 |
| ☐ 354 Wesley Walker PB | .20 | .09 | .03 |
| ☐ 355 Pittsburgh Steelers TL | .30 | .14 | .04 |
|     Franco Harris | | | |
| ☐ 356 Gary Anderson DP | .60 | .25 | .08 |
| ☐ 357 Mel Blount DP | .25 | .11 | .03 |
| ☐ 358 Terry Bradshaw DP | .75 | .35 | .09 |
| ☐ 359 Larry Brown PB | .05 | .02 | .01 |
| ☐ 360 Bennie Cunningham | .07 | .03 | .01 |
| ☐ 361 Gary Dunn | .05 | .02 | .01 |
| ☐ 362 Franco Harris | .75 | .35 | .09 |
| ☐ 363 Jack Lambert PB | .50 | .23 | .06 |
| ☐ 364 Frank Pollard | .07 | .03 | .01 |
| ☐ 365 Donnie Shell PB | .07 | .03 | .01 |
| ☐ 366 John Stallworth PB | .25 | .11 | .03 |
| ☐ 367 Loren Toews | .07 | .03 | .01 |
| ☐ 368 Mike Webster DP PB | .15 | .07 | .02 |
| ☐ 369 Dwayne Woodruff | .05 | .02 | .01 |
| ☐ 370 San Diego Chargers TL | .10 | .05 | .01 |
|     Chuck Muncie | | | |
| ☐ 371 Rolf Benirschke DP PB | .04 | .02 | .01 |
| ☐ 372 James Brooks | .60 | .25 | .08 |
| ☐ 373 Wes Chandler PB | .07 | .03 | .01 |
| ☐ 374 Dan Fouts DP PB | .75 | .35 | .09 |
| ☐ 375 Tim Fox | .05 | .02 | .01 |
| ☐ 376 Gary Johnson PB | .05 | .02 | .01 |
| ☐ 377 Charlie Joiner DP | .25 | .11 | .03 |

| | | | |
|---|---|---|---|
| ☐ 378 Louie Kelcher | .07 | .03 | .01 |
| ☐ 379 Chuck Muncie PB | .07 | .03 | .01 |
| ☐ 380 Cliff Thrift | .05 | .02 | .01 |
| ☐ 381 Doug Wilkerson PB | .05 | .02 | .01 |
| ☐ 382 Kellen Winslow PB | .75 | .35 | .09 |
| ☐ 383 Seattle Seahawks TL | .10 | .05 | .01 |
|     Sherman Smith | | | |
| ☐ 384 Kenny Easley PB | .40 | .18 | .05 |
| ☐ 385 Jacob Green | .60 | .25 | .08 |
| ☐ 386 John Harris | .05 | .02 | .01 |
| ☐ 387 Michael Jackson | .05 | .02 | .01 |
| ☐ 388 Norm Johnson | .50 | .23 | .06 |
| ☐ 389 Steve Largent | .75 | .35 | .09 |
| ☐ 390 Keith Simpson | .05 | .02 | .01 |
| ☐ 391 Sherman Smith | .05 | .02 | .01 |
| ☐ 392 Jeff West DP | .04 | .02 | .01 |
| ☐ 393 Jim Zorn DP | .04 | .02 | .01 |
| ☐ 394 Checklist 1-132 | .20 | .02 | .01 |
| ☐ 395 Checklist 133-264 | .20 | .02 | .01 |
| ☐ 396 Checklist 265-396 | .20 | .02 | .01 |

# 1983 Topps Sticker Inserts

The 1983 Topps Football Sticker Inserts come as a set of 33 full-sized (2 1/2" by 3 1/2") cards and were issued as inserts to the 1983 Topps wax packs. They were printed in the USA, whereas the smaller stickers of the previous two years were printed in Italy. The player's name, number, position, and team are included in a plaque at the bottom of the front of the card. The backs are parts of three puzzles, distinguished by either a red (A), blue (B), or green (C) border, each showing a different action scene from the previous year's Super Bowl between the Washington Redskins and Miami Dolphins. The actual set numbering is alphabetical by player's name.

| | MINT | EXC | G-VG |
|---|---|---|---|
| COMPLETE SET (33) | 15.00 | 6.00 | 1.50 |
| COMMON PLAYER (1-33) | .25 | .10 | .02 |
| | | | |
| ☐ 1 Marcus Allen | 5.00 | 2.00 | .50 |
|     (Completed red border | | | |
|     puzzle on back) | | | |
|     Los Angeles Raiders | | | |
| ☐ 2 Ken Anderson | .50 | .20 | .05 |
|     (Completed red border | | | |
|     puzzle on back) | | | |
|     Cincinnati Bengals | | | |
| ☐ 3 Ottis Anderson | .35 | .14 | .03 |
|     St. Louis Cardinals | | | |
| ☐ 4 William Andrews | .35 | .14 | .03 |
|     Atlanta Falcons | | | |
| ☐ 5 Terry Bradshaw | 1.25 | .50 | .12 |
|     Pittsburgh Steelers | | | |
| ☐ 6 Wes Chandler | .35 | .14 | .03 |
|     San Diego Chargers | | | |
| ☐ 7 Dwight Clark | .50 | .20 | .05 |
|     San Francisco 49ers | | | |
| ☐ 8 Cris Collinsworth | .35 | .14 | .03 |
|     Cincinnati Bengals | | | |
| ☐ 9 Joe Cribbs | .35 | .14 | .03 |
|     Buffalo Bills | | | |
| ☐ 10 Nolan Cromwell | .35 | .14 | .03 |
|     Los Angeles Rams | | | |
| ☐ 11 Tony Dorsett | 1.00 | .40 | .10 |
|     Dallas Cowboys | | | |
| ☐ 12 Dan Fouts | 1.00 | .40 | .10 |
|     San Diego Chargers | | | |
| ☐ 13 Mark Gastineau | .25 | .10 | .02 |
|     New York Jets | | | |
| ☐ 14 Jimmie Giles | .25 | .10 | .02 |
|     Tampa Bay Buccaneers | | | |
| ☐ 15 Franco Harris | 1.00 | .40 | .10 |
|     (Completed green border | | | |
|     puzzle on back) | | | |
|     Pittsburgh Steelers | | | |
| ☐ 16 Ted Hendricks | .60 | .24 | .06 |
|     Los Angeles Raiders | | | |
| ☐ 17 Tony Hill | .35 | .14 | .03 |

| Dallas Cowboys | | | |
|---|---|---|---|
| ☐ 18 John Jefferson | .25 | .10 | .02 |
| (Completed red border puzzle on back) Green Bay Packers | | | |
| ☐ 19 James Lofton | 1.25 | .50 | .12 |
| Green Bay Packers | | | |
| ☐ 20 Freeman McNeil | .50 | .20 | .05 |
| (Completed red border puzzle on back) New York Jets | | | |
| ☐ 21 Joe Montana | 5.00 | 2.00 | .50 |
| San Francisco 49ers | | | |
| ☐ 22 Mark Moseley | .25 | .10 | .02 |
| Washington Redskins | | | |
| ☐ 23 Ozzie Newsome | 1.00 | .40 | .10 |
| Cleveland Browns | | | |
| ☐ 24 Walter Payton | 3.00 | 1.20 | .30 |
| Chicago Bears | | | |
| ☐ 25 John Riggins | .75 | .30 | .07 |
| Washington Redskins | | | |
| ☐ 26 Billy Sims | .35 | .14 | .03 |
| Detroit Lions | | | |
| ☐ 27 John Stallworth | .50 | .20 | .05 |
| Pittsburgh Steelers | | | |
| ☐ 28 Lawrence Taylor | 2.50 | 1.00 | .25 |
| New York Giants | | | |
| ☐ 29 Joe Theismann | 1.00 | .40 | .10 |
| Washington Redskins | | | |
| ☐ 30 Richard Todd | .25 | .10 | .02 |
| (Completed green border puzzle on back) New York Jets | | | |
| ☐ 31 Wesley Walker | .35 | .14 | .03 |
| New York Jets | | | |
| ☐ 32 Danny White | .35 | .14 | .03 |
| Dallas Cowboys | | | |
| ☐ 33 Kellen Winslow | .50 | .20 | .05 |
| San Diego Chargers | | | |

## 1984 Topps

The 1984 Topps football card set contains 396 cards featuring players of the NFL. Cards are standard size, 2 1/2" by 3 1/2". The first six cards in the set recognize Record-Breaking (RB) achievements during the previous season. Post-season playoff games are featured on cards 7-9. Statistical league leaders are depicted on cards 202-207. The Team Leader (TL) cards are distributed throughout the set as the first card of the team sequence; this year only one leader (usually the team's rushing leader) is pictured and the backs contain team scoring information from the previous year. Instant Replay (IR) cards were issued as a special card for certain players in addition to (and immediately following) their regular card. Players who appeared in the Pro Bowl game (designated PB in the checklist below) are identified as such on the obverse of the player's regular card. Cards are numbered and alphabetically arranged within teams in the following order: Indianapolis Colts (10-20), Buffalo Bills (21-31), Cincinnati Bengals (32-46), Cleveland Browns (47-60), Denver Broncos (61-72), Houston Oilers (73-83), Kansas City Chiefs (84-96), Los Angeles Raiders (97-115), Miami Dolphins (116-130), New England Patriots (131-143), New York Jets (144-158), Pittsburgh Steelers (159-173), San Diego Chargers (174-187), Seattle Seahawks (188-201), Atlanta Falcons (208-220), Chicago Bears (221-234), Dallas Cowboys (235-249), Detroit Lions (250-262), Green Bay Packers (263-275), Los Angeles Rams (276-287), Minnesota Vikings (288-298), New Orleans Saints (299-309), New York Giants (310-324), Philadelphia Eagles (325-336), St. Louis Cardinals (337-348), San Francisco 49ers (349-363), Tampa Bay Buccaneers (364-374), and Washington Redskins (375-393). The teams themselves were ordered alphabetically by team name with the exception of Indianapolis, who had very recently moved from Baltimore. The last three cards in the set (394-396) are checklist cards. The set features the Rookie Cards of Morten Andersen, Roger Craig, Eric Dickerson, John Elway, Darrell Green, Rickey Jackson,

Dave Krieg, Howie Long, Dan Marino, and Curt Warner.

| | MINT | EXC | G-VG |
|---|---|---|---|
| COMPLETE SET (396) | 125.00 | 57.50 | 15.50 |
| COMMON PLAYER (1-396) | .05 | .02 | .01 |
| ☐ 1 Eric Dickerson RB | .60 | .25 | .08 |
| Sets Rookie Mark With 1808 Yards | | | |
| ☐ 2 Ali Haji-Sheikh RB | .10 | .05 | .01 |
| Sets Field Goal Mark as a Rookie | | | |
| ☐ 3 Franco Harris RB | .30 | .14 | .04 |
| Records Eighth 1000 Yard Year | | | |
| ☐ 4 Mark Moseley RB | .10 | .05 | .01 |
| 161 Points Sets Mark for Kickers | | | |
| ☐ 5 John Riggins RB | .25 | .11 | .03 |
| 24 Rushing TD's | | | |
| ☐ 6 Jan Stenerud RB | .12 | .05 | .02 |
| 338th Career FG | | | |
| ☐ 7 AFC Championship | .10 | .05 | .01 |
| Raiders 30, Seahawks 14 (Marcus Allen running) | | | |
| ☐ 8 NFC Championship | .10 | .05 | .01 |
| Redskins 24, 49ers 21 (John Riggins running) | | | |
| ☐ 9 Super Bowl XVIII UER | .35 | .16 | .04 |
| Raiders 38, Redskins 9 (hand-off to Marcus Allen; score wrong, 28-9 on card front) | | | |
| ☐ 10 Indianapolis Colts TL | .10 | .05 | .01 |
| Curtis Dickey | | | |
| ☐ 11 Raul Allegre | .05 | .02 | .01 |
| ☐ 12 Curtis Dickey | .08 | .04 | .01 |
| ☐ 13 Ray Donaldson | .05 | .02 | .01 |
| ☐ 14 Nesby Glasgow | .05 | .02 | .01 |
| ☐ 15 Chris Hinton PB | 1.50 | .65 | .19 |
| ☐ 16 Vernon Maxwell | .05 | .02 | .01 |
| ☐ 17 Randy McMillan | .05 | .02 | .01 |
| ☐ 18 Mike Pagel | .08 | .04 | .01 |
| ☐ 19 Rohn Stark | .08 | .04 | .01 |
| ☐ 20 Leo Wisniewski | .05 | .02 | .01 |
| ☐ 21 Buffalo Bills TL | .10 | .05 | .01 |
| Joe Cribbs | | | |
| ☐ 22 Jerry Butler | .08 | .04 | .01 |
| ☐ 23 Joe Danelo | .05 | .02 | .01 |
| ☐ 24 Joe Ferguson | .08 | .04 | .01 |
| ☐ 25 Steve Freeman | .05 | .02 | .01 |
| ☐ 26 Roosevelt Leaks | .08 | .04 | .01 |
| ☐ 27 Frank Lewis | .08 | .04 | .01 |
| ☐ 28 Eugene Marve | .05 | .02 | .01 |
| ☐ 29 Booker Moore | .05 | .02 | .01 |
| ☐ 30 Fred Smerlas PB | .08 | .04 | .01 |
| ☐ 31 Ben Williams | .05 | .02 | .01 |
| ☐ 32 Cincinnati Bengals TL | .10 | .05 | .01 |
| Cris Collinsworth | | | |
| ☐ 33 Charles Alexander | .05 | .02 | .01 |
| ☐ 34 Ken Anderson | .25 | .11 | .03 |
| ☐ 35 Ken Anderson IR | .12 | .05 | .02 |
| ☐ 36 Jim Breech | .05 | .02 | .01 |
| ☐ 37 Cris Collinsworth PB | .15 | .07 | .02 |
| ☐ 38 Cris Collinsworth IR | .08 | .04 | .01 |
| ☐ 39 Isaac Curtis | .08 | .04 | .01 |
| ☐ 40 Eddie Edwards | .05 | .02 | .01 |
| ☐ 41 Ray Horton | .15 | .07 | .02 |
| ☐ 42 Pete Johnson | .08 | .04 | .01 |
| ☐ 43 Steve Kreider | .05 | .02 | .01 |
| ☐ 44 Max Montoya | .05 | .02 | .01 |
| ☐ 45 Anthony Munoz PB | .60 | .25 | .08 |
| ☐ 46 Reggie Williams | .08 | .04 | .01 |
| ☐ 47 Cleveland Browns TL | .10 | .05 | .01 |
| Mike Pruitt | | | |
| ☐ 48 Matt Bahr | .08 | .04 | .01 |
| ☐ 49 Chip Banks PB | .05 | .02 | .01 |
| ☐ 50 Tom Cousineau | .08 | .04 | .01 |
| ☐ 51 Joe DeLamielleure | .08 | .04 | .01 |
| ☐ 52 Doug Dieken | .05 | .02 | .01 |
| ☐ 53 Bob Golic | 1.00 | .45 | .13 |
| ☐ 54 Bobby Jones | .05 | .02 | .01 |
| ☐ 55 Dave Logan | .08 | .04 | .01 |
| ☐ 56 Clay Matthews | 1.25 | .55 | .16 |
| ☐ 57 Paul McDonald | .08 | .04 | .01 |
| ☐ 58 Ozzie Newsome | .50 | .23 | .06 |
| ☐ 59 Ozzie Newsome IR | .25 | .11 | .03 |
| ☐ 60 Mike Pruitt | .08 | .04 | .01 |
| ☐ 61 Denver Broncos TL | .10 | .05 | .01 |
| Steve Watson | | | |
| ☐ 62 Barney Chavous | .20 | .09 | .03 |
| ☐ 63 John Elway | 32.00 | 14.50 | 4.00 |
| ☐ 64 Steve Foley | .05 | .02 | .01 |
| ☐ 65 Tom Jackson | .25 | .11 | .03 |
| ☐ 66 Rich Karlis | .05 | .02 | .01 |

| | | | |
|---|---|---|---|
| ☐ 67 Luke Prestridge | .05 | .02 | .01 |
| ☐ 68 Zack Thomas | .05 | .02 | .01 |
| ☐ 69 Rick Upchurch | .08 | .04 | .01 |
| ☐ 70 Steve Watson | .08 | .04 | .01 |
| ☐ 71 Sammy Winder | .20 | .09 | .03 |
| ☐ 72 Louis Wright PB | .08 | .04 | .01 |
| ☐ 73 Houston Oilers TL | .10 | .05 | .01 |
|     Tim Smith | | | |
| ☐ 74 Jesse Baker | .05 | .02 | .01 |
| ☐ 75 Gregg Bingham | .05 | .02 | .01 |
| ☐ 76 Robert Brazile | .05 | .02 | .01 |
| ☐ 77 Steve Brown | .05 | .02 | .01 |
| ☐ 78 Chris Dressel | .05 | .02 | .01 |
| ☐ 79 Doug France | .05 | .02 | .01 |
| ☐ 80 Florian Kempf | .05 | .02 | .01 |
| ☐ 81 Carl Roaches | .08 | .04 | .01 |
| ☐ 82 Tim Smith | .05 | .02 | .01 |
| ☐ 83 Willie Tullis | .05 | .02 | .01 |
| ☐ 84 Kansas City Chiefs TL | .10 | .05 | .01 |
|     Carlos Carson | | | |
| ☐ 85 Mike Bell | .08 | .04 | .01 |
| ☐ 86 Theotis Brown | .05 | .02 | .01 |
| ☐ 87 Carlos Carson PB | .15 | .07 | .02 |
| ☐ 88 Carlos Carson IR | .08 | .04 | .01 |
| ☐ 89 Deron Cherry PB | .60 | .25 | .08 |
| ☐ 90 Gary Green PB | .05 | .02 | .01 |
| ☐ 91 Billy Jackson | .05 | .02 | .01 |
| ☐ 92 Bill Kenney | .08 | .04 | .01 |
| ☐ 93 Bill Kenney IR | .05 | .02 | .01 |
| ☐ 94 Nick Lowery | .35 | .16 | .04 |
| ☐ 95 Henry Marshall | .05 | .02 | .01 |
| ☐ 96 Art Still | .08 | .04 | .01 |
| ☐ 97 Los Angeles Raiders TL | .13 | .06 | .02 |
|     Todd Christensen | | | |
| ☐ 98 Marcus Allen | 3.00 | 1.35 | .40 |
| ☐ 99 Marcus Allen IR | 1.50 | .65 | .19 |
| ☐ 100 Lyle Alzado | .25 | .11 | .03 |
| ☐ 101 Lyle Alzado IR | .08 | .04 | .01 |
| ☐ 102 Chris Bahr | .05 | .02 | .01 |
| ☐ 103 Malcolm Barnwell | .05 | .02 | .01 |
| ☐ 104 Cliff Branch | .25 | .11 | .03 |
| ☐ 105 Todd Christensen PB | .40 | .18 | .05 |
| ☐ 106 Todd Christensen IR | .20 | .09 | .03 |
| ☐ 107 Ray Guy | .25 | .11 | .03 |
| ☐ 108 Frank Hawkins | .05 | .02 | .01 |
| ☐ 109 Lester Hayes PB | .08 | .04 | .01 |
| ☐ 110 Ted Hendricks PB | .20 | .09 | .03 |
| ☐ 111 Howie Long PB | 4.00 | 1.80 | .50 |
| ☐ 112 Rod Martin PB | .08 | .04 | .01 |
| ☐ 113 Vann McElroy PB | .05 | .02 | .01 |
| ☐ 114 Jim Plunkett | .25 | .11 | .03 |
| ☐ 115 Greg Pruitt PB | .05 | .02 | .01 |
| ☐ 116 Miami Dolphins TL | .20 | .09 | .03 |
|     Mark Duper | | | |
| ☐ 117 Bob Baumhower PB | .08 | .04 | .01 |
| ☐ 118 Doug Betters PB | .08 | .04 | .01 |
| ☐ 119 A.J. Duhe | .08 | .04 | .01 |
| ☐ 120 Mark Duper PB | 1.50 | .65 | .19 |
| ☐ 121 Andra Franklin | .08 | .04 | .01 |
| ☐ 122 William Judson | .05 | .02 | .01 |
| ☐ 123 Dan Marino PB UER | 65.00 | 29.00 | 8.25 |
|     (Quaterback on back) | | | |
| ☐ 124 Dan Marino IR | 8.00 | 3.60 | 1.00 |
| ☐ 125 Nat Moore | .08 | .04 | .01 |
| ☐ 126 Ed Newman PB | .05 | .02 | .01 |
| ☐ 127 Reggie Roby | .50 | .23 | .06 |
| ☐ 128 Gerald Small | .05 | .02 | .01 |
| ☐ 129 Dwight Stephenson PB | .75 | .35 | .09 |
| ☐ 130 Uwe Von Schamann | .05 | .02 | .01 |
| ☐ 131 New England Pats TL | .10 | .05 | .01 |
|     Tony Collins | | | |
| ☐ 132 Rich Camarillo PB | .05 | .02 | .01 |
| ☐ 133 Tony Collins PB | .08 | .04 | .01 |
| ☐ 134 Tony Collins IR | .05 | .02 | .01 |
| ☐ 135 Bob Cryder | .05 | .02 | .01 |
| ☐ 136 Steve Grogan | .15 | .07 | .02 |
| ☐ 137 John Hannah PB | .25 | .11 | .03 |
| ☐ 138 Brian Holloway PB | .20 | .09 | .03 |
| ☐ 139 Roland James | .05 | .02 | .01 |
| ☐ 140 Stanley Morgan | .25 | .11 | .03 |
| ☐ 141 Rick Sanford | .05 | .02 | .01 |
| ☐ 142 Mosi Tatupu | .05 | .02 | .01 |
| ☐ 143 Andre Tippett | 1.00 | .45 | .13 |
| ☐ 144 New York Jets TL | .13 | .06 | .02 |
|     Wesley Walker | | | |
| ☐ 145 Jerome Barkum | .05 | .02 | .01 |
| ☐ 146 Mark Gastineau PB | .08 | .04 | .01 |
| ☐ 147 Mark Gastineau IR | .05 | .02 | .01 |
| ☐ 148 Bruce Harper | .05 | .02 | .01 |
| ☐ 149 Johnny "Lam" Jones | .08 | .04 | .01 |
| ☐ 150 Joe Klecko PB | .08 | .04 | .01 |
| ☐ 151 Pat Leahy | .08 | .04 | .01 |
| ☐ 152 Freeman McNeil | .20 | .09 | .03 |
| ☐ 153 Lance Mehl | .08 | .04 | .01 |
| ☐ 154 Marvin Powell PB | .05 | .02 | .01 |
| ☐ 155 Darrol Ray | .05 | .02 | .01 |
| ☐ 156 Pat Ryan | .05 | .02 | .01 |
| ☐ 157 Kirk Springs | .05 | .02 | .01 |
| ☐ 158 Wesley Walker | .20 | .09 | .03 |
| ☐ 159 Pittsburgh Steelers TL | .25 | .11 | .03 |
|     Franco Harris | | | |
| ☐ 160 Walter Abercrombie | .05 | .02 | .01 |
| ☐ 161 Gary Anderson PB | .08 | .04 | .01 |
| ☐ 162 Terry Bradshaw | 1.25 | .55 | .16 |
| ☐ 163 Craig Colquitt | .05 | .02 | .01 |
| ☐ 164 Bennie Cunningham | .08 | .04 | .01 |
| ☐ 165 Franco Harris | .50 | .23 | .06 |
| ☐ 166 Franco Harris IR | .25 | .11 | .03 |
| ☐ 167 Jack Lambert PB | .50 | .23 | .06 |
| ☐ 168 Jack Lambert IR | .25 | .11 | .03 |
| ☐ 169 Frank Pollard | .05 | .02 | .01 |
| ☐ 170 Donnie Shell | .08 | .04 | .01 |
| ☐ 171 Mike Webster PB | .20 | .09 | .03 |
| ☐ 172 Keith Willis | .05 | .02 | .01 |
| ☐ 173 Rick Woods | .05 | .02 | .01 |
| ☐ 174 San Diego Chargers TL | .25 | .11 | .03 |
|     Kellen Winslow | | | |
| ☐ 175 Rolf Benirschke | .05 | .02 | .01 |
| ☐ 176 James Brooks | .30 | .14 | .04 |
| ☐ 177 Maury Buford | .05 | .02 | .01 |
| ☐ 178 Wes Chandler PB | .08 | .04 | .01 |
| ☐ 179 Dan Fouts PB | .60 | .25 | .08 |
| ☐ 180 Dan Fouts IR | .30 | .14 | .04 |
| ☐ 181 Charlie Joiner | .30 | .14 | .04 |
| ☐ 182 Linden King | .05 | .02 | .01 |
| ☐ 183 Chuck Muncie | .08 | .04 | .01 |
| ☐ 184 Billy Ray Smith | .30 | .14 | .04 |
| ☐ 185 Danny Walters | .05 | .02 | .01 |
| ☐ 186 Kellen Winslow PB | .50 | .23 | .06 |
| ☐ 187 Kellen Winslow IR | .25 | .11 | .03 |
| ☐ 188 Seattle Seahawks TL | .15 | .07 | .02 |
|     Curt Warner | | | |
| ☐ 189 Steve August | .05 | .02 | .01 |
| ☐ 190 Dave Brown | .08 | .04 | .01 |
| ☐ 191 Zachary Dixon | .05 | .02 | .01 |
| ☐ 192 Kenny Easley | .08 | .04 | .01 |
| ☐ 193 Jacob Green | .20 | .09 | .03 |
| ☐ 194 Norm Johnson | .05 | .02 | .01 |
| ☐ 195 Dave Krieg | 2.50 | 1.15 | .30 |
| ☐ 196 Steve Largent | .75 | .35 | .09 |
| ☐ 197 Steve Largent IR | .35 | .16 | .04 |
| ☐ 198 Curt Warner PB | .50 | .23 | .06 |
| ☐ 199 Curt Warner IR | .25 | .11 | .03 |
| ☐ 200 Jeff West | .05 | .02 | .01 |
| ☐ 201 Charley Young | .08 | .04 | .01 |
| ☐ 202 Passing Leaders | 3.00 | 1.35 | .40 |
|     Dan Marino | | | |
|     Steve Bartkowski | | | |
| ☐ 203 Receiving Leaders | .13 | .06 | .02 |
|     Todd Christensen | | | |
|     Charlie Brown | | | |
|     Earnest Gray | | | |
|     Roy Green | | | |
| ☐ 204 Rushing Leaders | .50 | .23 | .06 |
|     Curt Warner | | | |
|     Eric Dickerson | | | |
| ☐ 205 Scoring Leaders | .10 | .05 | .01 |
|     Gary Anderson | | | |
|     Mark Moseley | | | |
| ☐ 206 Interception Leaders | .10 | .05 | .01 |
|     Vann McElroy | | | |
|     Ken Riley | | | |
|     Mark Murphy | | | |
| ☐ 207 Punting Leaders | .10 | .05 | .01 |
|     Rich Camarillo | | | |
|     Greg Coleman | | | |
| ☐ 208 Atlanta Falcons TL | .10 | .05 | .01 |
|     William Andrews | | | |
| ☐ 209 William Andrews PB | .08 | .04 | .01 |
| ☐ 210 William Andrews IR | .05 | .02 | .01 |
| ☐ 211 Stacey Bailey | .20 | .09 | .03 |
| ☐ 212 Steve Bartkowski | .20 | .09 | .03 |
| ☐ 213 Steve Bartkowski IR | .08 | .04 | .01 |
| ☐ 214 Ralph Giacomarro | .05 | .02 | .01 |
| ☐ 215 Billy Johnson PB | .08 | .04 | .01 |
| ☐ 216 Mike Kenn PB | .08 | .04 | .01 |
| ☐ 217 Mick Luckhurst | .05 | .02 | .01 |
| ☐ 218 Gerald Riggs | .15 | .07 | .02 |
| ☐ 219 R.C. Thielemann PB | .05 | .02 | .01 |
| ☐ 220 Jeff Van Note | .08 | .04 | .01 |
| ☐ 221 Chicago Bears TL | .75 | .35 | .09 |
|     Walter Payton | | | |
| ☐ 222 Jim Covert | .60 | .25 | .08 |
| ☐ 223 Leslie Frazier | .05 | .02 | .01 |
| ☐ 224 Willie Gault | 1.00 | .45 | .13 |
| ☐ 225 Mike Hartenstine | .05 | .02 | .01 |
| ☐ 226 Noah Jackson UER | .05 | .02 | .01 |
|     (photo actually | | | |
|     Jim Osborne) | | | |
| ☐ 227 Jim McMahon | 1.00 | .45 | .13 |
| ☐ 228 Walter Payton PB | 1.50 | .65 | .19 |
| ☐ 229 Walter Payton IR | .75 | .35 | .09 |
| ☐ 230 Mike Richardson | .15 | .07 | .02 |
| ☐ 231 Terry Schmidt | .05 | .02 | .01 |

| | | | |
|---|---|---|---|
| ☐ 232 Mike Singletary PB | 1.25 | .55 | .16 |
| ☐ 233 Matt Suhey | .08 | .04 | .01 |
| ☐ 234 Bob Thomas | .05 | .02 | .01 |
| ☐ 235 Dallas Cowboys TL | .35 | .16 | .04 |
| Tony Dorsett | | | |
| ☐ 236 Bob Breunig | .08 | .04 | .01 |
| ☐ 237 Doug Cosbie PB | .08 | .04 | .01 |
| ☐ 238 Tony Dorsett PB | .60 | .25 | .08 |
| ☐ 239 Tony Dorsett IR | .30 | .14 | .04 |
| ☐ 240 John Dutton | .08 | .04 | .01 |
| ☐ 241 Tony Hill | .08 | .04 | .01 |
| ☐ 242 Ed Jones PB | .25 | .11 | .03 |
| ☐ 243 Drew Pearson | .25 | .11 | .03 |
| ☐ 244 Rafael Septien | .05 | .02 | .01 |
| ☐ 245 Ron Springs | .05 | .02 | .01 |
| ☐ 246 Dennis Thurman | .05 | .02 | .01 |
| ☐ 247 Everson Walls PB | .05 | .02 | .01 |
| ☐ 248 Danny White | .25 | .11 | .03 |
| ☐ 249 Randy White PB | .50 | .23 | .06 |
| ☐ 250 Detroit Lions TL | .13 | .06 | .02 |
| Billy Sims | | | |
| ☐ 251 Jeff Chadwick | .25 | .11 | .03 |
| ☐ 252 Garry Cobb | .08 | .04 | .01 |
| ☐ 253 Doug English PB | .08 | .04 | .01 |
| ☐ 254 William Gay | .05 | .02 | .01 |
| ☐ 255 Eric Hipple | .08 | .04 | .01 |
| ☐ 256 James Jones | .20 | .09 | .03 |
| ☐ 257 Bruce McNorton | .08 | .04 | .01 |
| ☐ 258 Ed Murray | .08 | .04 | .01 |
| ☐ 259 Ulysses Norris | .05 | .02 | .01 |
| ☐ 260 Billy Sims | .05 | .02 | .01 |
| ☐ 261 Billy Sims IR | .08 | .04 | .01 |
| ☐ 262 Leonard Thompson | .05 | .02 | .01 |
| ☐ 263 Green Bay Packers TL | .30 | .14 | .04 |
| James Lofton | | | |
| ☐ 264 John Anderson | .05 | .02 | .01 |
| ☐ 265 Paul Coffman PB | .05 | .02 | .01 |
| ☐ 266 Lynn Dickey | .08 | .04 | .01 |
| ☐ 267 Gerry Ellis | .05 | .02 | .01 |
| ☐ 268 John Jefferson | .15 | .07 | .02 |
| ☐ 269 John Jefferson IR | .08 | .04 | .01 |
| ☐ 270 Ezra Johnson | .05 | .02 | .01 |
| ☐ 271 Tim Lewis | .08 | .04 | .01 |
| ☐ 272 James Lofton PB | 1.25 | .55 | .16 |
| ☐ 273 James Lofton IR | .60 | .25 | .08 |
| ☐ 274 Larry McCarren PB | .05 | .02 | .01 |
| ☐ 275 Jan Stenerud | .25 | .11 | .03 |
| ☐ 276 Los Angeles Rams TL | .75 | .35 | .09 |
| Eric Dickerson | | | |
| ☐ 277 Mike Barber | .05 | .02 | .01 |
| ☐ 278 Jim Collins | .05 | .02 | .01 |
| ☐ 279 Nolan Cromwell PB | .08 | .04 | .01 |
| ☐ 280 Eric Dickerson PB | 10.00 | 4.50 | 1.25 |
| ☐ 281 Eric Dickerson IR | 1.50 | .65 | .19 |
| ☐ 282 George Farmer | .05 | .02 | .01 |
| ☐ 283 Vince Ferragamo | .05 | .02 | .01 |
| ☐ 284 Kent Hill PB | .05 | .02 | .01 |
| ☐ 285 John Misko | .05 | .02 | .01 |
| ☐ 286 Jackie Slater PB | 2.00 | .90 | .25 |
| ☐ 287 Jack Youngblood | .20 | .09 | .03 |
| ☐ 288 Minnesota Vikings TL | .10 | .05 | .01 |
| Darrin Nelson | | | |
| ☐ 289 Ted Brown | .08 | .04 | .01 |
| ☐ 290 Greg Coleman | .05 | .02 | .01 |
| ☐ 291 Steve Dils | .05 | .02 | .01 |
| ☐ 292 Tony Galbreath | .08 | .04 | .01 |
| ☐ 293 Tommy Kramer | .08 | .04 | .01 |
| ☐ 294 Doug Martin | .05 | .02 | .01 |
| ☐ 295 Darrin Nelson | .20 | .09 | .03 |
| ☐ 296 Benny Ricardo | .05 | .02 | .01 |
| ☐ 297 John Swain | .05 | .02 | .01 |
| ☐ 298 John Turner | .05 | .02 | .01 |
| ☐ 299 New Orleans Saints TL | .10 | .05 | .01 |
| George Rogers | | | |
| ☐ 300 Morten Andersen | 2.25 | 1.00 | .30 |
| ☐ 301 Russell Erxleben | .05 | .02 | .01 |
| ☐ 302 Jeff Groth | .05 | .02 | .01 |
| ☐ 303 Rickey Jackson PB | 4.00 | 1.80 | .50 |
| ☐ 304 Johnnie Poe | .05 | .02 | .01 |
| ☐ 305 George Rogers | .15 | .07 | .02 |
| ☐ 306 Richard Todd | .05 | .02 | .01 |
| ☐ 307 Jim Wilks | .05 | .02 | .01 |
| ☐ 308 Dave Wilson | .05 | .02 | .01 |
| ☐ 309 Wayne Wilson | .05 | .02 | .01 |
| ☐ 310 New York Giants TL | .10 | .05 | .01 |
| Earnest Gray | | | |
| ☐ 311 Leon Bright | .05 | .02 | .01 |
| ☐ 312 Scott Brunner | .05 | .02 | .01 |
| ☐ 313 Rob Carpenter | .08 | .04 | .01 |
| ☐ 314 Harry Carson PB | .15 | .07 | .02 |
| ☐ 315 Earnest Gray | .05 | .02 | .01 |
| ☐ 316 Ali Haji-Sheikh PB | .05 | .02 | .01 |
| ☐ 317 Mark Haynes PB | .08 | .04 | .01 |
| ☐ 318 Dave Jennings | .08 | .04 | .01 |
| ☐ 319 Brian Kelley | .05 | .02 | .01 |
| ☐ 320 Phil Simms | 1.00 | .45 | .13 |
| ☐ 321 Lawrence Taylor PB | 2.50 | 1.15 | .30 |

| | | | |
|---|---|---|---|
| ☐ 322 Lawrence Taylor IR | 1.25 | .55 | .16 |
| ☐ 323 Brad Van Pelt | .08 | .04 | .01 |
| ☐ 324 Butch Woolfolk | .05 | .02 | .01 |
| ☐ 325 Philadelphia Eagles TL | .13 | .06 | .02 |
| Mike Quick | | | |
| ☐ 326 Harold Carmichael | .20 | .09 | .03 |
| ☐ 327 Herman Edwards | .05 | .02 | .01 |
| ☐ 328 Michael Haddix | .05 | .02 | .01 |
| ☐ 329 Dennis Harrison | .05 | .02 | .01 |
| ☐ 330 Ron Jaworski | .08 | .04 | .01 |
| ☐ 331 Wilbert Montgomery | .08 | .04 | .01 |
| ☐ 332 Hubert Oliver | .05 | .02 | .01 |
| ☐ 333 Mike Quick PB | .50 | .23 | .06 |
| ☐ 334 Jerry Robinson | .08 | .04 | .01 |
| ☐ 335 Max Runager | .05 | .02 | .01 |
| ☐ 336 Michael Williams | .05 | .02 | .01 |
| ☐ 337 St. Louis Cardinals TL | .15 | .07 | .02 |
| Ottis Anderson | | | |
| ☐ 338 Ottis Anderson | .40 | .18 | .05 |
| ☐ 339 Al(Bubba) Baker | .08 | .04 | .01 |
| ☐ 340 Carl Birdsong PB | .05 | .02 | .01 |
| ☐ 341 David Galloway | .05 | .02 | .01 |
| ☐ 342 Roy Green PB | .15 | .07 | .02 |
| ☐ 343 Roy Green IR | .08 | .04 | .01 |
| ☐ 344 Curtis Greer | .20 | .09 | .03 |
| ☐ 345 Neil Lomax | .08 | .04 | .01 |
| ☐ 346 Doug Marsh | .05 | .02 | .01 |
| ☐ 347 Stump Mitchell | .08 | .04 | .01 |
| ☐ 348 Lionel Washington | .35 | .16 | .04 |
| ☐ 349 San Francisco 49ers TL | .12 | .05 | .02 |
| Dwight Clark | | | |
| ☐ 350 Dwaine Board | .08 | .04 | .01 |
| ☐ 351 Dwight Clark | .25 | .11 | .03 |
| ☐ 352 Dwight Clark IR | .08 | .04 | .01 |
| ☐ 353 Roger Craig | 6.00 | 2.70 | .75 |
| ☐ 354 Fred Dean | .08 | .04 | .01 |
| ☐ 355 Fred Dean IR | .30 | .14 | .04 |
| ☐ 356 Dwight Hicks PB | .08 | .04 | .01 |
| ☐ 357 Ronnie Lott PB | 1.25 | .55 | .16 |
| ☐ 358 Joe Montana PB | 8.00 | 3.60 | 1.00 |
| ☐ 359 Joe Montana IR | 3.50 | 1.55 | .45 |
| ☐ 360 Freddie Solomon | .08 | .04 | .01 |
| ☐ 361 Wendell Tyler | .08 | .04 | .01 |
| ☐ 362 Ray Wersching | .08 | .04 | .01 |
| ☐ 363 Eric Wright | .15 | .07 | .02 |
| ☐ 364 Tampa Bay Bucs TL | .10 | .05 | .01 |
| Kevin House | | | |
| ☐ 365 Gerald Carter | .05 | .02 | .01 |
| ☐ 366 Hugh Green PB | .08 | .04 | .01 |
| ☐ 367 Kevin House | .08 | .04 | .01 |
| ☐ 368 Michael Morton | .05 | .02 | .01 |
| ☐ 369 James Owens | .05 | .02 | .01 |
| ☐ 370 Booker Reese | .05 | .02 | .01 |
| ☐ 371 Lee Roy Selmon PB | .08 | .04 | .01 |
| ☐ 372 Jack Thompson | .08 | .04 | .01 |
| ☐ 373 James Wilder | .05 | .02 | .01 |
| ☐ 374 Steve Wilson | .05 | .02 | .01 |
| ☐ 375 Wash. Redskins TL | .25 | .11 | .03 |
| John Riggins | | | |
| ☐ 376 Jeff Bostic PB | .05 | .02 | .01 |
| ☐ 377 Charlie Brown PB | .08 | .04 | .01 |
| ☐ 378 Charlie Brown IR | .05 | .02 | .01 |
| ☐ 379 Dave Butz PB | .08 | .04 | .01 |
| ☐ 380 Darrell Green | 1.50 | .65 | .19 |
| ☐ 381 Russ Grimm PB | .35 | .16 | .04 |
| ☐ 382 Joe Jacoby PB | .05 | .02 | .01 |
| ☐ 383 Dexter Manley | .08 | .04 | .01 |
| ☐ 384 Art Monk | 1.00 | .45 | .13 |
| ☐ 385 Mark Moseley | .08 | .04 | .01 |
| ☐ 386 Mark Murphy PB | .05 | .02 | .01 |
| ☐ 387 Mike Nelms | .05 | .02 | .01 |
| ☐ 388 John Riggins | .60 | .25 | .08 |
| ☐ 389 John Riggins IR | .30 | .14 | .04 |
| ☐ 390 Joe Theismann PB | .40 | .18 | .05 |
| ☐ 391 Joe Theismann IR | .20 | .09 | .03 |
| ☐ 392 Don Warren | .08 | .04 | .01 |
| ☐ 393 Joe Washington | .08 | .04 | .01 |
| ☐ 394 Checklist 1-132 | .20 | .02 | .01 |
| ☐ 395 Checklist 133-264 | .20 | .02 | .01 |
| ☐ 396 Checklist 265-396 | .20 | .02 | .01 |

## 1984 Topps Glossy Send-In

The 1984 Topps Glossy Send-In set contains 30 cards each measuring approximately 2 1/2" by 3 1/2" and was available via a send-in offer from Topps. The cards are numbered on the back.

| | MINT | EXC | G-VG |
|---|---|---|---|
| COMPLETE SET (30) | 15.00 | 6.00 | 1.50 |
| COMMON PLAYER (1-30) | .25 | .10 | .02 |
| | | | |
| ☐ 1 Marcus Allen | 1.25 | .50 | .12 |
| Los Angeles Raiders | | | |
| ☐ 2 John Riggins | 1.00 | .40 | .10 |
| Washington Redskins | | | |
| ☐ 3 Walter Payton | 2.50 | 1.00 | .25 |
| Chicago Bears | | | |

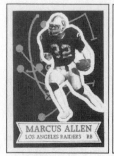
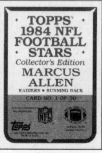

The 1984 Topps Glossy Inserts set contains 11 cards each with an attractive blue border. They are 2 1/2" by 3 1/2" as they were issued as an insert with the 1984 Topps football regular issue rack packs. The player selection appears to be based on conference-leading performers from the previous season in the categories of rushing, passing, receiving, and sacks. The key card in the set is Dan Marino appearing in his Rookie Card year.

| | MINT | EXC | G-VG |
|---|---|---|---|
| COMPLETE SET (11)............................. | 12.50 | 5.00 | 1.25 |
| COMMON PLAYER (1-11)................. | .25 | .10 | .02 |
| ☐ 1 Curt Warner ................................. | .50 | .20 | .05 |
|    Seattle Seahawks | | | |
| ☐ 2 Eric Dickerson........................... | 2.50 | 1.00 | .25 |
|    Los Angeles Rams | | | |
| ☐ 3 Dan Marino ................................ | 10.00 | 4.00 | 1.00 |
|    Miami Dolphins | | | |
| ☐ 4 Steve Bartkowski...................... | .35 | .14 | .03 |
|    Atlanta Falcons | | | |
| ☐ 5 Todd Christensen ..................... | .35 | .14 | .03 |
|    Los Angeles Raiders | | | |
| ☐ 6 Roy Green ................................. | .35 | .14 | .03 |
|    St. Louis Cardinals | | | |
| ☐ 7 Charlie Brown ........................... | .25 | .10 | .02 |
|    Washington Redskins | | | |
| ☐ 8 Earnest Gray ............................ | .25 | .10 | .02 |
|    New York Giants | | | |
| ☐ 9 Mark Gastineau ........................ | .25 | .10 | .02 |
|    New York Jets | | | |
| ☐ 10 Fred Dean............................... | .25 | .10 | .02 |
|    San Francisco 49ers | | | |
| ☐ 11 Lawrence Taylor...................... | 1.25 | .50 | .12 |
|    New York Giants | | | |

| | | | |
|---|---|---|---|
| ☐ 4 Tony Dorsett ............................. | 1.25 | .50 | .12 |
|    Dallas Cowboys | | | |
| ☐ 5 Franco Harris ............................ | 1.25 | .50 | .12 |
|    Pittsburgh Steelers | | | |
| ☐ 6 Curt Warner ............................... | .50 | .20 | .05 |
|    Seattle Seahawks | | | |
| ☐ 7 Eric Dickerson........................... | 2.50 | 1.00 | .25 |
|    Los Angeles Rams | | | |
| ☐ 8 Mike Pruitt ................................. | .25 | .10 | .02 |
|    Cleveland Browns | | | |
| ☐ 9 Ken Anderson ............................ | .75 | .30 | .07 |
|    Cincinnati Bengals | | | |
| ☐ 10 Dan Fouts ............................... | 1.00 | .40 | .10 |
|    San Diego Chargers | | | |
| ☐ 11 Terry Bradshaw....................... | 2.00 | .80 | .20 |
|    Pittsburgh Steelers | | | |
| ☐ 12 Joe Theismann........................ | 1.00 | .40 | .10 |
|    Washington Redskins | | | |
| ☐ 13 Joe Montana ........................... | 5.00 | 2.00 | .50 |
|    San Francisco 49ers | | | |
| ☐ 14 Danny White ........................... | .50 | .20 | .05 |
|    Dallas Cowboys | | | |
| ☐ 15 Kellen Winslow ........................ | .50 | .20 | .05 |
|    San Diego Chargers | | | |
| ☐ 16 Wesley Walker ......................... | .35 | .14 | .03 |
|    New York Jets | | | |
| ☐ 17 Drew Pearson .......................... | .50 | .20 | .05 |
|    Dallas Cowboys | | | |
| ☐ 18 James Lofton ........................... | 1.00 | .40 | .10 |
|    Green Bay Packers | | | |
| ☐ 19 Cris Collinsworth...................... | .35 | .14 | .03 |
|    Cincinnati Bengals | | | |
| ☐ 20 Dwight Clark ............................ | .50 | .20 | .05 |
|    San Francisco 49ers | | | |
| ☐ 21 Mark Gastineau ....................... | .25 | .10 | .02 |
|    New York Jets | | | |
| ☐ 22 Lawrence Taylor....................... | 1.25 | .50 | .12 |
|    New York Giants | | | |
| ☐ 23 Randy White ............................ | 1.00 | .40 | .10 |
|    Dallas Cowboys | | | |
| ☐ 24 Ed Too Tall Jones..................... | .75 | .30 | .07 |
|    Dallas Cowboys | | | |
| ☐ 25 Jack Lambert ........................... | 1.00 | .40 | .10 |
|    Pittsburgh Steelers | | | |
| ☐ 26 Fred Dean................................ | .25 | .10 | .02 |
|    San Francisco 49ers | | | |
| ☐ 27 Jan Stenerud ........................... | .50 | .20 | .05 |
|    Green Bay Packers | | | |
| ☐ 28 Bruce Harper............................ | .25 | .10 | .02 |
|    New York Jets | | | |
| ☐ 29 Todd Christensen ..................... | .50 | .20 | .05 |
|    Los Angeles Raiders | | | |
| ☐ 30 Greg Pruitt .............................. | .35 | .14 | .03 |
|    Los Angeles Raiders | | | |

## 1984 Topps Glossy Inserts

## 1984 Topps USFL

The 1984 Topps USFL set contains 132 cards, which were available as a pre-packaged set from Topps housed in its own specially made box. The cards are in full color and measure the standard 2 1/2" by 3 1/2". The cards in the set are numbered in alphabetical team order (with players arranged alphabetically within teams), for example, Arizona Wranglers (1-8), Birmingham Stallions (9-16), Chicago Blitz (17-24), Denver Gold (25-32), Houston Gamblers (33-38), Jacksonville Bulls (39-44), Los Angeles Express (45-52), Memphis Showboats (53-58), Michigan Panthers (59-66), New Jersey Generals (67-74), New Orleans Breakers (75-82), Oakland Invaders (83-90), Oklahoma Outlaws (91-96), Philadelphia Stars (97-104), Pittsburgh Maulers (105-110), San Antonio Gunslingers (111-116), Tampa Bay Bandits (117-124), and Washington Federals (125-131). The last card in the set is a checklist card. The key Extended Rookie Cards in this set are Gary Anderson, Anthony Carter, Bobby Hebert, Vaughan Johnson, Jim Kelly, Mike Rozier, Ricky Sanders, Herschel Walker, Reggie White, and Steve Young.

| | MINT | EXC | G-VG |
|---|---|---|---|
| COMPLETE FACT.SET (132) ............. | 375.00 | 170.00 | 47.50 |
| COMMON PLAYER (1-132)................. | 1.50 | .65 | .19 |
| ☐ 1 Luther Bradley........................... | 1.75 | .80 | .22 |
| ☐ 2 Frank Corral .............................. | 1.50 | .65 | .19 |
| ☐ 3 Trumaine Johnson .................... | 1.50 | .65 | .19 |
| ☐ 4 Greg Landry .............................. | 1.75 | .80 | .22 |
| ☐ 5 Kit Lathrop ................................ | 1.50 | .65 | .19 |
| ☐ 6 Kevin Long ................................ | 1.50 | .65 | .19 |
| ☐ 7 Tim Spencer ............................. | 1.75 | .80 | .22 |
| ☐ 8 Stan White ................................ | 1.50 | .65 | .19 |
| ☐ 9 Buddy Aydelette ........................ | 1.50 | .65 | .19 |
| ☐ 10 Tom Banks............................... | 1.75 | .80 | .22 |
| ☐ 11 Fred Bohannon......................... | 1.50 | .65 | .19 |
| ☐ 12 Joe Cribbs .............................. | 1.75 | .80 | .22 |
| ☐ 13 Joey Jones .............................. | 1.50 | .65 | .19 |
| ☐ 14 Scott Norwood......................... | 1.75 | .80 | .22 |

| | | | |
|---|---|---|---|
| ☐ 15 Jim Smith | 1.75 | .80 | .22 |
| ☐ 16 Cliff Stoudt | 1.75 | .80 | .22 |
| ☐ 17 Vince Evans | 2.00 | .90 | .25 |
| ☐ 18 Vagas Ferguson | 1.50 | .65 | .19 |
| ☐ 19 John Gillen | 1.50 | .65 | .19 |
| ☐ 20 Kris Haines | 1.50 | .65 | .19 |
| ☐ 21 Glenn Hyde | 1.50 | .65 | .19 |
| ☐ 22 Mark Keel | 1.50 | .65 | .19 |
| ☐ 23 Gary Lewis | 1.50 | .65 | .19 |
| ☐ 24 Doug Plank | 1.75 | .80 | .22 |
| ☐ 25 Neil Balholm | 1.50 | .65 | .19 |
| ☐ 26 David Dumars | 1.50 | .65 | .19 |
| ☐ 27 David Martin | 1.50 | .65 | .19 |
| ☐ 28 Craig Penrose | 1.50 | .65 | .19 |
| ☐ 29 Dave Stalls | 1.50 | .65 | .19 |
| ☐ 30 Harry Sydney | 1.75 | .80 | .22 |
| ☐ 31 Vincent White | 1.50 | .65 | .19 |
| ☐ 32 George Yarno | 1.50 | .65 | .19 |
| ☐ 33 Kiki DeAyala | 1.50 | .65 | .19 |
| ☐ 34 Sam Harrell | 1.50 | .65 | .19 |
| ☐ 35 Mike Hawkins | 1.50 | .65 | .19 |
| ☐ 36 Jim Kelly | 150.00 | 70.00 | 19.00 |
| ☐ 37 Mark Rush | 1.50 | .65 | .19 |
| ☐ 38 Ricky Sanders | 22.00 | 10.00 | 2.80 |
| ☐ 39 Paul Bergmann | 1.50 | .65 | .19 |
| ☐ 40 Tom Dinkel | 1.50 | .65 | .19 |
| ☐ 41 Wyatt Henderson | 1.50 | .65 | .19 |
| ☐ 42 Vaughan Johnson | 15.00 | 6.75 | 1.90 |
| ☐ 43 Willie McClendon | 1.50 | .65 | .19 |
| ☐ 44 Matt Robinson | 1.75 | .80 | .22 |
| ☐ 45 George Achica | 1.50 | .65 | .19 |
| ☐ 46 Mark Adickes | 1.50 | .65 | .19 |
| ☐ 47 Howard Carson | 1.50 | .65 | .19 |
| ☐ 48 Kevin Nelson | 1.50 | .65 | .19 |
| ☐ 49 Jeff Partridge | 1.50 | .65 | .19 |
| ☐ 50 Jo Jo Townsell | 1.75 | .80 | .22 |
| ☐ 51 Eddie Weaver | 1.50 | .65 | .19 |
| ☐ 52 Steve Young | 175.00 | 80.00 | 22.00 |
| ☐ 53 Derrick Crawford | 1.50 | .65 | .19 |
| ☐ 54 Walter Lewis | 1.50 | .65 | .19 |
| ☐ 55 Phil McKinnely | 1.50 | .65 | .19 |
| ☐ 56 Vic Minore | 1.50 | .65 | .19 |
| ☐ 57 Gary Shirk | 1.50 | .65 | .19 |
| ☐ 58 Reggie White | 75.00 | 34.00 | 9.50 |
| ☐ 59 Anthony Carter | 25.00 | 11.50 | 3.10 |
| ☐ 60 John Corker | 1.50 | .65 | .19 |
| ☐ 61 David Greenwood | 1.50 | .65 | .19 |
| ☐ 62 Bobby Hebert | 20.00 | 9.00 | 2.50 |
| ☐ 63 Derek Holloway | 1.50 | .65 | .19 |
| ☐ 64 Ken Lacy | 1.50 | .65 | .19 |
| ☐ 65 Tyrone McGriff | 1.50 | .65 | .19 |
| ☐ 66 Ray Pinney | 1.50 | .65 | .19 |
| ☐ 67 Gary Barbaro | 1.75 | .80 | .22 |
| ☐ 68 Sam Bowers | 1.50 | .65 | .19 |
| ☐ 69 Clarence Collins | 1.50 | .65 | .19 |
| ☐ 70 Willie Harper | 1.50 | .65 | .19 |
| ☐ 71 Jim LeClair | 1.50 | .65 | .19 |
| ☐ 72 Bob Leopold | 1.50 | .65 | .19 |
| ☐ 73 Brian Sipe | 2.00 | .90 | .25 |
| ☐ 74 Herschel Walker | 35.00 | 16.00 | 4.40 |
| ☐ 75 Junior Ah You | 1.50 | .65 | .19 |
| ☐ 76 Marcus Dupree | 1.75 | .80 | .22 |
| ☐ 77 Marcus Marek | 1.50 | .65 | .19 |
| ☐ 78 Tim Mazzetti | 1.50 | .65 | .19 |
| ☐ 79 Mike Robinson | 1.50 | .65 | .19 |
| ☐ 80 Dan Ross | 1.75 | .80 | .22 |
| ☐ 81 Mark Schellen | 1.50 | .65 | .19 |
| ☐ 82 Johnnie Walton | 1.50 | .65 | .19 |
| ☐ 83 Gordon Banks | 1.50 | .65 | .19 |
| ☐ 84 Fred Besana | 1.50 | .65 | .19 |
| ☐ 85 Dave Browning | 1.50 | .65 | .19 |
| ☐ 86 Eric Jordan | 1.50 | .65 | .19 |
| ☐ 87 Frank Manumaleuga | 1.50 | .65 | .19 |
| ☐ 88 Gary Plummer | 3.50 | 1.55 | .45 |
| ☐ 89 Stan Talley | 1.50 | .65 | .19 |
| ☐ 90 Arthur Whittington | 1.50 | .65 | .19 |
| ☐ 91 Terry Beeson | 1.50 | .65 | .19 |
| ☐ 92 Mel Gray | 1.75 | .80 | .22 |
| ☐ 93 Mike Katolin | 1.50 | .65 | .19 |
| ☐ 94 Dewey McClain | 1.50 | .65 | .19 |
| ☐ 95 Sidney Thornton | 1.50 | .65 | .19 |
| ☐ 96 Doug Williams | 2.00 | .90 | .25 |
| ☐ 97 Kelvin Bryant | 3.00 | 1.35 | .40 |
| ☐ 98 John Bunting | 1.50 | .65 | .19 |
| ☐ 99 Irv Eatman | 2.00 | .90 | .25 |
| ☐ 100 Scott Fitzkee | 1.50 | .65 | .19 |
| ☐ 101 Chuck Fusina | 1.75 | .80 | .22 |
| ☐ 102 Sean Landeta | 3.00 | 1.35 | .40 |
| ☐ 103 David Trout | 1.50 | .65 | .19 |
| ☐ 104 Scott Woerner | 1.50 | .65 | .19 |
| ☐ 105 Glenn Carano | 1.50 | .65 | .19 |
| ☐ 106 Ron Crosby | 1.50 | .65 | .19 |
| ☐ 107 Jerry Holmes | 1.50 | .65 | .19 |
| ☐ 108 Bruce Huther | 1.50 | .65 | .19 |
| ☐ 109 Mike Rozier | 5.00 | 2.30 | .60 |
| ☐ 110 Larry Swider | 1.50 | .65 | .19 |
| ☐ 111 Danny Buggs | 1.75 | .80 | .22 |

| | | | |
|---|---|---|---|
| ☐ 112 Putt Choate | 1.50 | .65 | .19 |
| ☐ 113 Rich Garza | 1.50 | .65 | .19 |
| ☐ 114 Joey Hackett | 1.50 | .65 | .19 |
| ☐ 115 Rick Neuheisel | 1.50 | .65 | .19 |
| ☐ 116 Mike St. Clair | 1.50 | .65 | .19 |
| ☐ 117 Gary Anderson | 7.00 | 3.10 | .85 |
| ☐ 118 Zenon Andrusyshyn | 1.50 | .65 | .19 |
| ☐ 119 Doug Beaudoin | 1.50 | .65 | .19 |
| ☐ 120 Mike Butler | 1.50 | .65 | .19 |
| ☐ 121 Willie Gillespie | 1.75 | .80 | .22 |
| ☐ 122 Fred Nordgren | 1.50 | .65 | .19 |
| ☐ 123 John Reaves | 1.75 | .80 | .22 |
| ☐ 124 Eric Truvillion | 1.50 | .65 | .19 |
| ☐ 125 Reggie Collier | 1.75 | .80 | .22 |
| ☐ 126 Mike Guess | 1.50 | .65 | .19 |
| ☐ 127 Mike Hohensee | 1.50 | .65 | .19 |
| ☐ 128 Craig James | 5.00 | 2.30 | .60 |
| ☐ 129 Eric Robinson | 1.50 | .65 | .19 |
| ☐ 130 Billy Taylor | 1.50 | .65 | .19 |
| ☐ 131 Joey Walters | 1.50 | .65 | .19 |
| ☐ 132 Checklist 1-132 | 2.00 | .65 | .19 |

## 1985 Topps

The 1985 Topps football card set contains 396 cards featuring players of the NFL. Cards are standard size 2 1/2" by 3 1/2". The set is distinguished by the black border on the fronts of the cards, as well as the horizontal orientation of the card fronts. The first six cards in the set recognize Record-Breaking (RB) achievements during the previous season. Cards 7-9 provide a summary of the post-season playoff action. Statistical league leaders are featured on cards 192-197. The Team Leader (TL) cards are distributed throughout the set as the first card of the team sequence; this year an action scene is pictured and captioned, and the backs contain team scoring information from the previous year. All-Pro (AP) selections are denoted on the player's regular card in small yellow print in the upper left black border of the obverse. The order of teams (alphabetically arranged by conference with players themselves alphabetically ordered within each team) is as follows: Atlanta Falcons (10-21), Chicago Bears (22-36), Dallas Cowboys (37-52), Detroit Lions (53-65), Green Bay Packers (66-76), Los Angeles Rams (77-88), Minnesota Vikings (89-99), New Orleans Saints (100-109), New York Giants (110-124), Philadelphia Eagles (125-136), St. Louis Cardinals (137-147), San Francisco 49ers (148-165), Tampa Bay Buccaneers (166-176), Washington Redskins (177-191), Buffalo Bills (198-208), Cincinnati Bengals (209-220), Cleveland Browns (221-234), Denver Broncos (235-247), Houston Oilers (248-257), Indianapolis Colts (258-268), Kansas City Chiefs (269-280), Los Angeles Raiders (281-299), Miami Dolphins (300-319), New England Patriots (320-334), New York Jets (335-350), Pittsburgh Steelers (351-366), San Diego Chargers (367-379), and Seattle Seahawks (380-393). The last three cards in the set (394-396) are checklist cards. Although they are not considered part of the complete set price, Topps also printed cards on the bottoms of the wax pack boxes. There were four different boxes, each with four different players. These box bottom cards are distinguished by their red border (instead of black) and the fact that they are "lettered" rather than numbered. The key Rookie Card in this set is Warren Moon (although he had already appeared in several JOGO CFL card issues). Other notable Rookie Cards in the set are Carl Banks, Gill Byrd, Mark Clayton, Richard Dent, Henry Ellard, Irving Fryar, Louis Lipps, Steve McMichael, and Darryl Talley.

| | MINT | EXC | G-VG |
|---|---|---|---|
| COMPLETE SET (396) | 75.00 | 34.00 | 9.50 |
| COMMON PLAYER (1-396) | .05 | .02 | .01 |
| | | | |
| ☐ 1 Mark Clayton RB | .60 | .25 | .08 |
| Most Touchdown Receptions, Season | | | |
| ☐ 2 Eric Dickerson RB | .40 | .18 | .05 |
| Most Yards | | | |

| | | | |
|---|---|---|---|
| Rushing, Season | | | |
| ☐ 3 Charlie Joiner RB | .15 | .07 | .02 |
| Most Receptions, | | | |
| Career | | | |
| ☐ 4 Dan Marino RB UER | 5.00 | 2.30 | .60 |
| Most Touchdown | | | |
| Passes, Season | | | |
| (Dolphins misspelled | | | |
| as Dophins) | | | |
| ☐ 5 Art Monk RB | .25 | .11 | .03 |
| Most Receptions, | | | |
| Season | | | |
| ☐ 6 Walter Payton RB | 1.00 | .45 | .13 |
| Most Yards | | | |
| Rushing, Career | | | |
| ☐ 7 NFC Championship | .10 | .05 | .01 |
| 49ers 23, Bears 0 | | | |
| (Matt Suhey tackled) | | | |
| ☐ 8 AFC Championship | .10 | .05 | .01 |
| Dolphins 45, | | | |
| Steelers 28 | | | |
| (Woody Bennett over) | | | |
| ☐ 9 Super Bowl XIX | .15 | .07 | .02 |
| 49ers 38, | | | |
| Dolphins 16 | | | |
| (Wendell Tyler) | | | |
| ☐ 10 Atlanta Falcons TL | .10 | .05 | .01 |
| Stretching For The | | | |
| First Down | | | |
| (Gerald Riggs) | | | |
| ☐ 11 William Andrews | .08 | .04 | .01 |
| ☐ 12 Stacey Bailey | .05 | .02 | .01 |
| ☐ 13 Steve Bartkowski | .15 | .07 | .02 |
| ☐ 14 Rick Bryan | .20 | .09 | .03 |
| ☐ 15 Alfred Jackson | .05 | .02 | .01 |
| ☐ 16 Kenny Johnson | .05 | .02 | .01 |
| ☐ 17 Mike Kenn AP | .08 | .04 | .01 |
| ☐ 18 Mike Pitts | .20 | .09 | .03 |
| ☐ 19 Gerald Riggs | .08 | .04 | .01 |
| ☐ 20 Sylvester Stamps | .05 | .02 | .01 |
| ☐ 21 R.C. Thielemann | .05 | .02 | .01 |
| ☐ 22 Chicago Bears TL | .75 | .35 | .09 |
| Sweetness Sets | | | |
| Record Straight | | | |
| (Walter Payton) | | | |
| ☐ 23 Todd Bell AP | .08 | .04 | .01 |
| ☐ 24 Richard Dent AP | 5.00 | 2.30 | .60 |
| ☐ 25 Gary Fencik | .05 | .02 | .01 |
| ☐ 26 Dave Finzer | .05 | .02 | .01 |
| ☐ 27 Leslie Frazier | .05 | .02 | .01 |
| ☐ 28 Steve Fuller | .08 | .04 | .01 |
| ☐ 29 Willie Gault | .40 | .18 | .05 |
| ☐ 30 Dan Hampton AP | .50 | .23 | .06 |
| ☐ 31 Jim McMahon | .60 | .25 | .08 |
| ☐ 32 Steve McMichael | 2.00 | .90 | .25 |
| ☐ 33 Walter Payton AP | 1.75 | .80 | .22 |
| ☐ 34 Mike Singletary | .75 | .35 | .09 |
| ☐ 35 Matt Suhey | .08 | .04 | .01 |
| ☐ 36 Bob Thomas | .05 | .02 | .01 |
| ☐ 37 Dallas Cowboys TL | .30 | .14 | .04 |
| Busting Through | | | |
| The Defense | | | |
| (Tony Dorsett) | | | |
| ☐ 38 Bill Bates | .60 | .25 | .08 |
| ☐ 39 Doug Cosbie | .08 | .04 | .01 |
| ☐ 40 Tony Dorsett | .60 | .25 | .08 |
| ☐ 41 Michael Downs | .05 | .02 | .01 |
| ☐ 42 Mike Hegman UER | .08 | .04 | .01 |
| (reference to SB VIII, | | | |
| should be SB XIII) | | | |
| ☐ 43 Tony Hill | .08 | .04 | .01 |
| ☐ 44 Gary Hogeboom | .05 | .02 | .01 |
| ☐ 45 Jim Jeffcoat | .75 | .35 | .09 |
| ☐ 46 Ed Too Tall Jones | .25 | .11 | .03 |
| ☐ 47 Mike Renfro | .08 | .04 | .01 |
| ☐ 48 Rafael Septien | .05 | .02 | .01 |
| ☐ 49 Dennis Thurman | .05 | .02 | .01 |
| ☐ 50 Everson Walls | .08 | .04 | .01 |
| ☐ 51 Danny White | .25 | .11 | .03 |
| ☐ 52 Randy White | .40 | .18 | .05 |
| ☐ 53 Detroit Lions TL | .10 | .05 | .01 |
| Popping One Loose | | | |
| (Lions' Defense) | | | |
| ☐ 54 Jeff Chadwick | .08 | .04 | .01 |
| ☐ 55 Mike Cofer | .20 | .09 | .03 |
| ☐ 56 Gary Danielson | .08 | .04 | .01 |
| ☐ 57 Keith Dorney | .05 | .02 | .01 |
| ☐ 58 Doug English | .08 | .04 | .01 |
| ☐ 59 William Gay | .05 | .02 | .01 |
| ☐ 60 Ken Jenkins | .05 | .02 | .01 |
| ☐ 61 James Jones | .08 | .04 | .01 |
| ☐ 62 Ed Murray | .08 | .04 | .01 |
| ☐ 63 Billy Sims | .08 | .04 | .01 |
| ☐ 64 Leonard Thompson | .05 | .02 | .01 |
| ☐ 65 Bobby Watkins | .05 | .02 | .01 |
| ☐ 66 Green Bay Packers TL | .10 | .05 | .01 |
| Spotting His | | | |
| Deep Receiver | | | |
| (Lynn Dickey) | | | |
| ☐ 67 Paul Coffman | .05 | .02 | .01 |
| ☐ 68 Lynn Dickey | .08 | .04 | .01 |
| ☐ 69 Mike Douglass | .05 | .02 | .01 |
| ☐ 70 Tom Flynn | .05 | .02 | .01 |
| ☐ 71 Eddie Lee Ivery | .05 | .02 | .01 |
| ☐ 72 Ezra Johnson | .05 | .02 | .01 |
| ☐ 73 Mark Lee | .05 | .02 | .01 |
| ☐ 74 Tim Lewis | .05 | .02 | .01 |
| ☐ 75 James Lofton | 1.00 | .45 | .13 |
| ☐ 76 Bucky Scribner | .05 | .02 | .01 |
| ☐ 77 Los Angeles Rams TL | .35 | .16 | .04 |
| Record-Setting | | | |
| Ground Attack | | | |
| (Eric Dickerson) | | | |
| ☐ 78 Nolan Cromwell | .08 | .04 | .01 |
| ☐ 79 Eric Dickerson AP | 2.00 | .90 | .25 |
| ☐ 80 Henry Ellard | 4.00 | 1.80 | .50 |
| ☐ 81 Kent Hill | .05 | .02 | .01 |
| ☐ 82 LeRoy Irvin | .08 | .04 | .01 |
| ☐ 83 Jeff Kemp | .25 | .11 | .03 |
| ☐ 84 Mike Lansford | .05 | .02 | .01 |
| ☐ 85 Barry Redden | .05 | .02 | .01 |
| ☐ 86 Jackie Slater | .40 | .18 | .05 |
| ☐ 87 Doug Smith | .50 | .23 | .06 |
| ☐ 88 Jack Youngblood | .15 | .07 | .02 |
| ☐ 89 Minnesota Vikings TL | .10 | .05 | .01 |
| Smothering The | | | |
| Opposition | | | |
| (Vikings' Defense) | | | |
| ☐ 90 Alfred Anderson | .15 | .07 | .02 |
| ☐ 91 Ted Brown | .08 | .04 | .01 |
| ☐ 92 Greg Coleman | .05 | .02 | .01 |
| ☐ 93 Tommy Hannon | .05 | .02 | .01 |
| ☐ 94 Tommy Kramer | .08 | .04 | .01 |
| ☐ 95 Leo Lewis | .15 | .07 | .02 |
| ☐ 96 Doug Martin | .05 | .02 | .01 |
| ☐ 97 Darrin Nelson | .08 | .04 | .01 |
| ☐ 98 Jan Stenerud AP | .15 | .07 | .02 |
| ☐ 99 Sammie White | .08 | .04 | .01 |
| ☐ 100 New Orleans Saints TL | .10 | .05 | .01 |
| Hurdling Over | | | |
| Front Line | | | |
| ☐ 101 Morten Andersen | .75 | .35 | .09 |
| ☐ 102 Hoby Brenner | .15 | .07 | .02 |
| ☐ 103 Bruce Clark | .05 | .02 | .01 |
| ☐ 104 Hokie Gajan | .08 | .04 | .01 |
| ☐ 105 Brian Hansen | .15 | .07 | .02 |
| ☐ 106 Rickey Jackson | 1.00 | .45 | .13 |
| ☐ 107 George Rogers | .08 | .04 | .01 |
| ☐ 108 Dave Wilson | .08 | .04 | .01 |
| ☐ 109 Tyrone Young | .05 | .02 | .01 |
| ☐ 110 New York Giants TL | .10 | .05 | .01 |
| Engulfing The | | | |
| Quarterback | | | |
| (Giants' Defense) | | | |
| ☐ 111 Carl Banks | 2.50 | 1.15 | .30 |
| ☐ 112 Jim Burt | .30 | .14 | .04 |
| ☐ 113 Rob Carpenter | .08 | .04 | .01 |
| ☐ 114 Harry Carson | .08 | .04 | .01 |
| ☐ 115 Earnest Gray | .05 | .02 | .01 |
| ☐ 116 Ali Haji-Sheikh | .05 | .02 | .01 |
| ☐ 117 Mark Haynes AP | .08 | .04 | .01 |
| ☐ 118 Bobby Johnson | .05 | .02 | .01 |
| ☐ 119 Lionel Manuel | .08 | .04 | .01 |
| ☐ 120 Joe Morris | .75 | .35 | .09 |
| ☐ 121 Zeke Mowatt | .08 | .04 | .01 |
| ☐ 122 Jeff Rutledge | .15 | .07 | .02 |
| ☐ 123 Phil Simms | .60 | .25 | .08 |
| ☐ 124 Lawrence Taylor AP | 1.25 | .55 | .16 |
| ☐ 125 Philadelphia Eagles TL | .10 | .05 | .01 |
| Finding The Wide | | | |
| Open Spaces | | | |
| (Wilbert Montgomery) | | | |
| ☐ 126 Greg Brown | .05 | .02 | .01 |
| ☐ 127 Ray Ellis | .05 | .02 | .01 |
| ☐ 128 Dennis Harrison | .05 | .02 | .01 |
| ☐ 129 Wes Hopkins | .50 | .23 | .06 |
| ☐ 130 Mike Horan | .08 | .04 | .01 |
| ☐ 131 Kenny Jackson | .15 | .07 | .02 |
| ☐ 132 Ron Jaworski | .08 | .04 | .01 |
| ☐ 133 Paul McFadden | .05 | .02 | .01 |
| ☐ 134 Wilbert Montgomery | .08 | .04 | .01 |
| ☐ 135 Mike Quick | .08 | .04 | .01 |
| ☐ 136 John Spagnola | .05 | .02 | .01 |
| ☐ 137 St.Louis Cardinals TL | .10 | .05 | .01 |
| Exploiting The | | | |
| Air Route | | | |
| (Neil Lomax) | | | |
| ☐ 138 Ottis Anderson | .30 | .14 | .04 |
| ☐ 139 Al(Bubba) Baker | .08 | .04 | .01 |
| ☐ 140 Roy Green | .08 | .04 | .01 |
| ☐ 141 Curtis Greer | .05 | .02 | .01 |
| ☐ 142 E.J. Junior AP | .08 | .04 | .01 |
| ☐ 143 Neil Lomax | .08 | .04 | .01 |
| ☐ 144 Stump Mitchell | .08 | .04 | .01 |
| ☐ 145 Neil O'Donoghue | .05 | .02 | .01 |
| ☐ 146 Pat Tilley | .08 | .04 | .01 |

| | | | |
|---|---|---|---|
| ☐ 147 Lionel Washington | .05 | .02 | .01 |
| ☐ 148 San Francisco 49ers TL | 1.00 | .45 | .13 |
| The Road To | | | |
| Super Bowl XIX | | | |
| (Joe Montana) | | | |
| ☐ 149 Dwaine Board | .08 | .04 | .01 |
| ☐ 150 Dwight Clark | .25 | .11 | .03 |
| ☐ 151 Roger Craig | 1.50 | .65 | .19 |
| ☐ 152 Randy Cross AP | .08 | .04 | .01 |
| ☐ 153 Fred Dean | .08 | .04 | .01 |
| ☐ 154 Keith Fahnhorst | .08 | .04 | .01 |
| ☐ 155 Dwight Hicks | .08 | .04 | .01 |
| ☐ 156 Ronnie Lott | 1.00 | .45 | .13 |
| ☐ 157 Joe Montana | 7.00 | 3.10 | .85 |
| ☐ 158 Renaldo Nehemiah | .08 | .04 | .01 |
| ☐ 159 Fred Quillan | .05 | .02 | .01 |
| ☐ 160 Jack Reynolds | .08 | .04 | .01 |
| ☐ 161 Freddie Solomon | .08 | .04 | .01 |
| ☐ 162 Keena Turner | .35 | .16 | .04 |
| ☐ 163 Wendell Tyler | .08 | .04 | .01 |
| ☐ 164 Ray Wersching | .08 | .04 | .01 |
| ☐ 165 Carlton Williamson | .08 | .04 | .01 |
| ☐ 166 Tampa Bay Bucs TL | .13 | .06 | .02 |
| Protecting The | | | |
| Quarterback | | | |
| (Steve DeBerg) | | | |
| ☐ 167 Gerald Carter | .05 | .02 | .01 |
| ☐ 168 Mark Cotney | .05 | .02 | .01 |
| ☐ 169 Steve DeBerg | .40 | .18 | .05 |
| ☐ 170 Sean Farrell | .08 | .04 | .01 |
| ☐ 171 Hugh Green | .08 | .04 | .01 |
| ☐ 172 Kevin House | .08 | .04 | .01 |
| ☐ 173 David Logan | .05 | .02 | .01 |
| ☐ 174 Michael Morton | .05 | .02 | .01 |
| ☐ 175 Lee Roy Selmon | .08 | .04 | .01 |
| ☐ 176 James Wilder | .08 | .04 | .01 |
| ☐ 177 Wash. Redskins TL | .20 | .09 | .03 |
| Diesel Named Desire | | | |
| (John Riggins) | | | |
| ☐ 178 Charlie Brown | .08 | .04 | .01 |
| ☐ 179 Monte Coleman | .75 | .35 | .09 |
| ☐ 180 Vernon Dean | .05 | .02 | .01 |
| ☐ 181 Darrell Green | .50 | .23 | .06 |
| ☐ 182 Russ Grimm | .08 | .04 | .01 |
| ☐ 183 Joe Jacoby | .08 | .04 | .01 |
| ☐ 184 Dexter Manley | .08 | .04 | .01 |
| ☐ 185 Art Monk AP | .75 | .35 | .09 |
| ☐ 186 Mark Moseley | .08 | .04 | .01 |
| ☐ 187 Calvin Muhammad | .08 | .04 | .01 |
| ☐ 188 Mike Nelms | .05 | .02 | .01 |
| ☐ 189 John Riggins | .50 | .23 | .06 |
| ☐ 190 Joe Theismann | .40 | .18 | .05 |
| ☐ 191 Joe Washington | .08 | .04 | .01 |
| ☐ 192 Passing Leaders | 7.00 | 3.10 | .85 |
| Dan Marino | | | |
| Joe Montana | | | |
| ☐ 193 Receiving Leaders | .35 | .16 | .04 |
| Ozzie Newsome | | | |
| Art Monk | | | |
| ☐ 194 Rushing Leaders | .30 | .14 | .04 |
| Earnest Jackson | | | |
| Eric Dickerson | | | |
| ☐ 195 Scoring Leaders | .10 | .05 | .01 |
| Gary Anderson | | | |
| Ray Wersching | | | |
| ☐ 196 Interception Leaders | .10 | .05 | .01 |
| Kenny Easley | | | |
| Tom Flynn | | | |
| ☐ 197 Punting Leaders | .10 | .05 | .01 |
| Jim Arnold | | | |
| Brian Hansen | | | |
| ☐ 198 Buffalo Bills TL | .10 | .05 | .01 |
| Rushing Toward | | | |
| Rookie Stardom | | | |
| (Greg Bell) | | | |
| ☐ 199 Greg Bell | .60 | .25 | .08 |
| ☐ 200 Preston Dennard | .05 | .02 | .01 |
| ☐ 201 Joe Ferguson | .08 | .04 | .01 |
| ☐ 202 Byron Franklin | .05 | .02 | .01 |
| ☐ 203 Steve Freeman | .05 | .02 | .01 |
| ☐ 204 Jim Haslett | .05 | .02 | .01 |
| ☐ 205 Charles Romes | .05 | .02 | .01 |
| ☐ 206 Fred Smerlas | .08 | .04 | .01 |
| ☐ 207 Darryl Talley | 2.00 | .90 | .25 |
| ☐ 208 Van Williams | .05 | .02 | .01 |
| ☐ 209 Cincinnati Bengals TL | .13 | .06 | .02 |
| Advancing The | | | |
| Ball Downfield | | | |
| (Ken Anderson and | | | |
| Larry Kinnebrew) | | | |
| ☐ 210 Ken Anderson | .20 | .09 | .03 |
| ☐ 211 Jim Breech | .05 | .02 | .01 |
| ☐ 212 Louis Breeden | .05 | .02 | .01 |
| ☐ 213 James Brooks | .20 | .09 | .03 |
| ☐ 214 Ross Browner | .08 | .04 | .01 |
| ☐ 215 Eddie Edwards | .05 | .02 | .01 |
| ☐ 216 M.L. Harris | .05 | .02 | .01 |
| ☐ 217 Bobby Kemp | .05 | .02 | .01 |
| ☐ 218 Larry Kinnebrew | .08 | .04 | .01 |
| ☐ 219 Anthony Munoz AP | .40 | .18 | .05 |
| ☐ 220 Reggie Williams | .08 | .04 | .01 |
| ☐ 221 Cleveland Browns TL | .10 | .05 | .01 |
| Evading The | | | |
| Defensive Pursuit | | | |
| (Boyce Green) | | | |
| ☐ 222 Matt Bahr | .08 | .04 | .01 |
| ☐ 223 Chip Banks | .08 | .04 | .01 |
| ☐ 224 Reggie Camp | .05 | .02 | .01 |
| ☐ 225 Tom Cousineau | .08 | .04 | .01 |
| ☐ 226 Joe DeLamielleure | .08 | .04 | .01 |
| ☐ 227 Ricky Feacher | .05 | .02 | .01 |
| ☐ 228 Boyce Green | .05 | .02 | .01 |
| ☐ 229 Al Gross | .05 | .02 | .01 |
| ☐ 230 Clay Matthews | .60 | .25 | .08 |
| ☐ 231 Paul McDonald | .08 | .04 | .01 |
| ☐ 232 Ozzie Newsome AP | .35 | .16 | .04 |
| ☐ 233 Mike Pruitt | .08 | .04 | .01 |
| ☐ 234 Don Rogers | .05 | .02 | .01 |
| ☐ 235 Denver Broncos TL | .60 | .25 | .08 |
| Thousand Yarder | | | |
| Gets The Ball | | | |
| (Sammy Winder and | | | |
| John Elway) | | | |
| ☐ 236 Rubin Carter | .05 | .02 | .01 |
| ☐ 237 Barney Chavous | .05 | .02 | .01 |
| ☐ 238 John Elway | 10.00 | 4.50 | 1.25 |
| ☐ 239 Steve Foley | .05 | .02 | .01 |
| ☐ 240 Mike Harden | .05 | .02 | .01 |
| ☐ 241 Tom Jackson | .20 | .09 | .03 |
| ☐ 242 Butch Johnson | .08 | .04 | .01 |
| ☐ 243 Rulon Jones | .05 | .02 | .01 |
| ☐ 244 Rich Karlis | .05 | .02 | .01 |
| ☐ 245 Steve Watson | .08 | .04 | .01 |
| ☐ 246 Gerald Willhite | .05 | .02 | .01 |
| ☐ 247 Sammy Winder | .08 | .04 | .01 |
| ☐ 248 Houston Oilers TL | .10 | .05 | .01 |
| Eluding A | | | |
| Traffic Jam | | | |
| (Larry Moriarty) | | | |
| ☐ 249 Jesse Baker | .05 | .02 | .01 |
| ☐ 250 Carter Hartwig | .05 | .02 | .01 |
| ☐ 251 Warren Moon | 20.00 | 9.00 | 2.50 |
| ☐ 252 Larry Moriarty | .05 | .02 | .01 |
| ☐ 253 Mike Munchak | 2.00 | .90 | .25 |
| ☐ 254 Carl Roaches | .08 | .04 | .01 |
| ☐ 255 Tim Smith | .05 | .02 | .01 |
| ☐ 256 Willie Tullis | .05 | .02 | .01 |
| ☐ 257 Jamie Williams | .05 | .02 | .01 |
| ☐ 258 Indianapolis Colts TL | .10 | .05 | .01 |
| Start Of A | | | |
| Long Gainer | | | |
| (Art Schlichter) | | | |
| ☐ 259 Raymond Butler | .05 | .02 | .01 |
| ☐ 260 Johnie Cooks | .05 | .02 | .01 |
| ☐ 261 Eugene Daniel | .05 | .02 | .01 |
| ☐ 262 Curtis Dickey | .08 | .04 | .01 |
| ☐ 263 Chris Hinton | .15 | .07 | .02 |
| ☐ 264 Vernon Maxwell | .08 | .04 | .01 |
| ☐ 265 Randy McMillan | .05 | .02 | .01 |
| ☐ 266 Art Schlichter | .15 | .07 | .02 |
| ☐ 267 Rohn Stark | .08 | .04 | .01 |
| ☐ 268 Leo Wisniewski | .05 | .02 | .01 |
| ☐ 269 Kansas City Chiefs TL | .10 | .05 | .01 |
| Pigskin About To | | | |
| Soar Upward | | | |
| (Bill Kenney) | | | |
| ☐ 270 Jim Arnold | .08 | .04 | .01 |
| ☐ 271 Mike Bell | .05 | .02 | .01 |
| ☐ 272 Todd Blackledge | .15 | .07 | .02 |
| ☐ 273 Carlos Carson | .08 | .04 | .01 |
| ☐ 274 Deron Cherry | .20 | .09 | .03 |
| ☐ 275 Herman Heard | .08 | .04 | .01 |
| ☐ 276 Bill Kenney | .08 | .04 | .01 |
| ☐ 277 Nick Lowery | .30 | .14 | .04 |
| ☐ 278 Bill Maas | .20 | .09 | .03 |
| ☐ 279 Henry Marshall | .05 | .02 | .01 |
| ☐ 280 Art Still | .08 | .04 | .01 |
| ☐ 281 Los Angeles Raiders TL | .40 | .18 | .05 |
| Diving For The | | | |
| Goal Line | | | |
| (Marcus Allen) | | | |
| ☐ 282 Marcus Allen | 2.00 | .90 | .25 |
| ☐ 283 Lyle Alzado | .20 | .09 | .03 |
| ☐ 284 Chris Bahr | .05 | .02 | .01 |
| ☐ 285 Malcolm Barnwell | .05 | .02 | .01 |
| ☐ 286 Cliff Branch | .15 | .07 | .02 |
| ☐ 287 Todd Christensen | .08 | .04 | .01 |
| ☐ 288 Ray Guy | .15 | .07 | .02 |
| ☐ 289 Lester Hayes | .08 | .04 | .01 |
| ☐ 290 Mike Haynes AP | .08 | .04 | .01 |
| ☐ 291 Henry Lawrence | .05 | .02 | .01 |
| ☐ 292 Howie Long | 1.25 | .55 | .16 |
| ☐ 293 Rod Martin AP | .08 | .04 | .01 |
| ☐ 294 Vann McElroy | .05 | .02 | .01 |

| | | | |
|---|---|---|---|
| ☐ 295 Matt Millen | .08 | .04 | .01 |
| ☐ 296 Bill Pickel | .15 | .07 | .02 |
| ☐ 297 Jim Plunkett | .20 | .09 | .03 |
| ☐ 298 Dokie Williams | .08 | .04 | .01 |
| ☐ 299 Marc Wilson | .08 | .04 | .01 |
| ☐ 300 Miami Dolphins TL | .10 | .05 | .01 |
| Super Duper | | | |
| Performance | | | |
| (Mark Duper) | | | |
| ☐ 301 Bob Baumhower | .05 | .02 | .01 |
| ☐ 302 Doug Betters | .05 | .02 | .01 |
| ☐ 303 Glenn Blackwood | .08 | .04 | .01 |
| ☐ 304 Lyle Blackwood | .08 | .04 | .01 |
| ☐ 305 Kim Bokamper | .08 | .04 | .01 |
| ☐ 306 Charles Bowser | .05 | .02 | .01 |
| ☐ 307 Jimmy Cefalo | .08 | .04 | .01 |
| ☐ 308 Mark Clayton AP | 4.00 | 1.80 | .50 |
| ☐ 309 A.J. Duhe | .08 | .04 | .01 |
| ☐ 310 Mark Duper | .25 | .11 | .03 |
| ☐ 311 Andra Franklin | .08 | .04 | .01 |
| ☐ 312 Bruce Hardy | .08 | .04 | .01 |
| ☐ 313 Pete Johnson | .08 | .04 | .01 |
| ☐ 314 Dan Marino AP UER | 20.00 | 9.00 | 2.50 |
| (Fouts 4802 yards in | | | |
| 1981, should be 4082) | | | |
| ☐ 315 Tony Nathan | .08 | .04 | .01 |
| ☐ 316 Ed Newman | .05 | .02 | .01 |
| ☐ 317 Reggie Roby AP | .15 | .07 | .02 |
| ☐ 318 Dwight Stephenson AP | .08 | .04 | .01 |
| ☐ 319 Uwe Von Schamann | .05 | .02 | .01 |
| ☐ 320 New England Pats TL | .10 | .05 | .01 |
| Refusing To | | | |
| Be Denied | | | |
| (Tony Collins) | | | |
| ☐ 321 Raymond Clayborn | .08 | .04 | .01 |
| ☐ 322 Tony Collins | .08 | .04 | .01 |
| ☐ 323 Tony Eason | .30 | .14 | .04 |
| ☐ 324 Tony Franklin | .05 | .02 | .01 |
| ☐ 325 Irving Fryar | 4.00 | 1.80 | .50 |
| ☐ 326 John Hannah AP | .20 | .09 | .03 |
| ☐ 327 Brian Holloway | .05 | .02 | .01 |
| ☐ 328 Craig James | .50 | .23 | .06 |
| ☐ 329 Stanley Morgan | .20 | .09 | .03 |
| ☐ 330 Steve Nelson AP | .05 | .02 | .01 |
| ☐ 331 Derrick Ramsey | .05 | .02 | .01 |
| ☐ 332 Stephen Starring | .05 | .02 | .01 |
| ☐ 333 Mosi Tatupu | .08 | .04 | .01 |
| ☐ 334 Andre Tippett | .05 | .02 | .01 |
| ☐ 335 New York Jets TL | .10 | .05 | .01 |
| Thwarting The | | | |
| Passing Game | | | |
| (Mark Gastineau | | | |
| and Joe Ferguson) | | | |
| ☐ 336 Russell Carter | .08 | .04 | .01 |
| ☐ 337 Mark Gastineau AP | .08 | .04 | .01 |
| ☐ 338 Bruce Harper | .05 | .02 | .01 |
| ☐ 339 Bobby Humphery | .08 | .04 | .01 |
| ☐ 340 Johnny "Lam" Jones | .08 | .04 | .01 |
| ☐ 341 Joe Klecko | .08 | .04 | .01 |
| ☐ 342 Pat Leahy | .08 | .04 | .01 |
| ☐ 343 Marty Lyons | .08 | .04 | .01 |
| ☐ 344 Freeman McNeil | .15 | .07 | .02 |
| ☐ 345 Lance Mehl | .05 | .02 | .01 |
| ☐ 346 Ken O'Brien | 1.00 | .45 | .13 |
| ☐ 347 Marvin Powell | .05 | .02 | .01 |
| ☐ 348 Pat Ryan | .05 | .02 | .01 |
| ☐ 349 Mickey Shuler | .25 | .11 | .03 |
| ☐ 350 Wesley Walker | .15 | .07 | .02 |
| ☐ 351 Pittsburgh Steelers TL | .10 | .05 | .01 |
| Testing Defensive | | | |
| Pass Coverage | | | |
| (Mark Malone) | | | |
| ☐ 352 Walter Abercrombie | .05 | .02 | .01 |
| ☐ 353 Gary Anderson | .08 | .04 | .01 |
| ☐ 354 Robin Cole | .05 | .02 | .01 |
| ☐ 355 Bennie Cunningham | .08 | .04 | .01 |
| ☐ 356 Rich Erenberg | .05 | .02 | .01 |
| ☐ 357 Jack Lambert | .40 | .18 | .05 |
| ☐ 358 Louis Lipps | 1.25 | .55 | .16 |
| ☐ 359 Mark Malone | .08 | .04 | .01 |
| ☐ 360 Mike Merriweather | .50 | .23 | .06 |
| ☐ 361 Frank Pollard | .05 | .02 | .01 |
| ☐ 362 Donnie Shell | .08 | .04 | .01 |
| ☐ 363 John Stallworth | .20 | .09 | .03 |
| ☐ 364 Sam Washington | .05 | .02 | .01 |
| ☐ 365 Mike Webster | .20 | .09 | .03 |
| ☐ 366 Dwayne Woodruff | .08 | .04 | .01 |
| ☐ 367 San Diego Chargers TL | .10 | .05 | .01 |
| Jarring The | | | |
| Ball Loose | | | |
| (Chargers' Defense) | | | |
| ☐ 368 Rolf Benirschke | .05 | .02 | .01 |
| ☐ 369 Gill Byrd | .75 | .35 | .09 |
| ☐ 370 Wes Chandler | .08 | .04 | .01 |
| ☐ 371 Bobby Duckworth | .05 | .02 | .01 |
| ☐ 372 Dan Fouts | .50 | .23 | .06 |
| ☐ 373 Mike Green | .05 | .02 | .01 |

| | | | |
|---|---|---|---|
| ☐ 374 Pete Holohan | .20 | .09 | .03 |
| ☐ 375 Earnest Jackson | .15 | .07 | .02 |
| ☐ 376 Lionel James | .20 | .09 | .03 |
| ☐ 377 Charlie Joiner | .30 | .14 | .04 |
| ☐ 378 Billy Ray Smith | .08 | .04 | .01 |
| ☐ 379 Kellen Winslow | .30 | .14 | .04 |
| ☐ 380 Seattle Seahawks TL | .10 | .05 | .01 |
| Setting Up For | | | |
| The Air Attack | | | |
| (Dave Krieg) | | | |
| ☐ 381 Dave Brown | .05 | .02 | .01 |
| ☐ 382 Jeff Bryant | .05 | .02 | .01 |
| ☐ 383 Dan Doornink | .05 | .02 | .01 |
| ☐ 384 Kenny Easley AP | .08 | .04 | .01 |
| ☐ 385 Jacob Green | .08 | .04 | .01 |
| ☐ 386 David Hughes | .05 | .02 | .01 |
| ☐ 387 Norm Johnson | .05 | .02 | .01 |
| ☐ 388 Dave Krieg | .50 | .23 | .06 |
| ☐ 389 Steve Largent | .60 | .25 | .08 |
| ☐ 390 Joe Nash | .15 | .07 | .02 |
| ☐ 391 Daryl Turner | .05 | .02 | .01 |
| ☐ 392 Curt Warner | .15 | .07 | .02 |
| ☐ 393 Fredd Young | .15 | .07 | .02 |
| ☐ 394 Checklist 1-132 | .15 | .02 | .01 |
| ☐ 395 Checklist 133-264 | .15 | .02 | .01 |
| ☐ 396 Checklist 265-396 | .15 | .02 | .01 |

## 1985 Topps Box Bottoms

This 16-card set, which measures 2 1/2" by 3 1/2", was issued on the bottom of 1985 Topps wax pack boxes. The cards are in the same design as the 1985 Topps regular issues except they are bordered in red and have the words "Topps Superstars" printed in very small letters above the players' photos. Similar to the regular issue, these cards have a horizontal orientation. The backs of the cards are just like the regular card in that they have biographical and complete statistical information. The cards are arranged in alphabetical order and include such stars as Joe Montana and Walter Payton.

| | MINT | EXC | G-VG |
|---|---|---|---|
| COMPLETE SET (16) | 12.50 | 5.00 | 1.25 |
| COMMON PLAYER (A-P) | .25 | .10 | .02 |
| ☐ A Marcus Allen | 1.25 | .50 | .12 |
| Los Angeles Raiders | | | |
| ☐ B Ottis Anderson | .35 | .14 | .03 |
| St. Louis Cardinals | | | |
| ☐ C Mark Clayton | 1.25 | .50 | .12 |
| Miami Dolphins | | | |
| ☐ D Eric Dickerson | 1.00 | .40 | .10 |
| Los Angeles Rams | | | |
| ☐ E Tony Dorsett | .75 | .30 | .07 |
| Dallas Cowboys | | | |
| ☐ F Dan Fouts | .75 | .30 | .07 |
| San Diego Chargers | | | |
| ☐ G Mark Gastineau | .25 | .10 | .02 |
| New York Jets | | | |
| ☐ H Charlie Joiner | .50 | .20 | .05 |
| San Diego Chargers | | | |
| ☐ I James Lofton | .75 | .30 | .07 |
| Green Bay Packers | | | |
| ☐ J Neil Lomax | .35 | .14 | .03 |
| St. Louis Cardinals | | | |
| ☐ K Dan Marino | 5.00 | 2.00 | .50 |
| Miami Dolphins | | | |
| ☐ L Art Monk | .75 | .30 | .07 |
| Washington Redskins | | | |
| ☐ M Joe Montana | 5.00 | 2.00 | .50 |
| San Francisco 49ers | | | |
| ☐ N Walter Payton | 2.00 | .80 | .20 |
| Chicago Bears | | | |
| ☐ O John Stallworth | .35 | .14 | .03 |
| Pittsburgh Steelers | | | |
| ☐ P Lawrence Taylor | .75 | .30 | .07 |
| New York Giants | | | |

## 1985 Topps Glossy Inserts

This red-bordered glossy insert set was distributed with rack packs of the 1985 Topps football regular issue. The backs of the cards are printed in red and blue on white card stock but provide very little about the player other than the most basic information. Cards are numbered on the back and measure the standard 2 1/2" by 3 1/2".

| | MINT | EXC | G-VG |
|---|---|---|---|
| COMPLETE SET (11) | 12.50 | 5.00 | 1.25 |
| COMMON PLAYER (1-11) | .35 | .14 | .03 |
| □ 1 Mark Clayton<br>Miami Dolphins | 1.50 | .60 | .15 |
| □ 2 Eric Dickerson<br>Los Angeles Rams | 1.00 | .40 | .10 |
| □ 3 John Elway<br>Denver Broncos | 3.00 | 1.20 | .30 |
| □ 4 Mark Gastineau<br>New York Jets | .35 | .14 | .03 |
| □ 5 Ronnie Lott UER<br>(Shown wearing 24)<br>San Francisco 49ers | .75 | .30 | .07 |
| □ 6 Dan Marino<br>Miami Dolphins | 5.00 | 2.00 | .50 |
| □ 7 Joe Montana<br>San Francisco 49ers | 5.00 | 2.00 | .50 |
| □ 8 Walter Payton<br>Chicago Bears | 2.00 | .80 | .20 |
| □ 9 John Riggins<br>Washington Redskins | 1.00 | .40 | .10 |
| □ 10 John Stallworth<br>Pittsburgh Steelers | .50 | .20 | .05 |
| □ 11 Lawrence Taylor<br>New York Giants | .75 | .30 | .07 |

## 1985 Topps USFL

The 1985 Topps USFL set contains 132 football cards, which were available as a pre-packaged set from Topps housed in its own specially made box. The cards are in full color and measure the standard, 2 1/2" by 3 1/2". The card backs are printed in red and blue on white card stock. The card fronts have a heavy red border with a blue and white stripe in the middle. Card backs describe each player's highlights of the previous USFL season. The cards in the set are ordered numerically by team location with players within teams also ordered alphabetically, i.e., Arizona Outlaws (1-9), Baltimore Stars (10-19), Birmingham Stallions (20-29), Denver Gold (30-38), Houston Gamblers (39-48), Jacksonville Bulls (49-57), Los Angeles Express (58-66), Memphis Showboats (67-76), New Jersey Generals (77-86), Oakland Invaders (87-96), Orlando Renegades (97-104), Portland Breakers (105-113), San Antonio Gunslingers (114-121), and Tampa Bay Bandits (122-131). The last card in the set is a checklist card. The key Extended Rookie Cards in this set are Gary Clark, Doug Flutie, and Sam Mills. Other key cards in the set include the second USFL cards of Jim Kelly, Herschel Walker, Reggie White, and Steve Young.

| | MINT | EXC | G-VG |
|---|---|---|---|
| COMPLETE FACT.SET (132) | 160.00 | 70.00 | 20.00 |
| COMMON PLAYER (1-132) | .40 | .18 | .05 |
| □ 1 Case DeBruijn | .40 | .18 | .05 |
| □ 2 Mike Katolin | .40 | .18 | .05 |
| □ 3 Bruce Laird | .40 | .18 | .05 |
| □ 4 Kit Lathrop | .40 | .18 | .05 |
| □ 5 Kevin Long | .40 | .18 | .05 |
| □ 6 Karl Lorch | .40 | .18 | .05 |
| □ 7 Dave Tipton | .40 | .18 | .05 |
| □ 8 Doug Williams | .50 | .23 | .06 |
| □ 9 Luis Zendejas | .50 | .23 | .06 |
| □ 10 Kelvin Bryant | .60 | .25 | .08 |
| □ 11 Willie Collier | .40 | .18 | .05 |
| □ 12 Irv Eatman | .50 | .23 | .06 |
| □ 13 Scott Fitzkee | .40 | .18 | .05 |
| □ 14 William Fuller | 7.00 | 3.10 | .85 |
| □ 15 Chuck Fusina | .50 | .23 | .06 |
| □ 16 Pete Kugler | .40 | .18 | .05 |
| □ 17 Garcia Lane | .40 | .18 | .05 |
| □ 18 Mike Lush | .40 | .18 | .05 |
| □ 19 Sam Mills | 7.00 | 3.10 | .85 |
| □ 20 Buddy Aydelette | .40 | .18 | .05 |
| □ 21 Joe Cribbs | .60 | .25 | .08 |
| □ 22 David Dumars | .40 | .18 | .05 |
| □ 23 Robin Earl | .40 | .18 | .05 |
| □ 24 Joey Jones | .40 | .18 | .05 |
| □ 25 Leon Perry | .40 | .18 | .05 |
| □ 26 Dave Pureifory | .40 | .18 | .05 |
| □ 27 Bill Roe | .40 | .18 | .05 |
| □ 28 Doug Smith | 2.00 | .90 | .25 |
| □ 29 Cliff Stoudt | .50 | .23 | .06 |
| □ 30 Jeff Delaney | .40 | .18 | .05 |
| □ 31 Vince Evans | .60 | .25 | .08 |
| □ 32 Leonard Harris | 1.75 | .80 | .22 |
| □ 33 Bill Johnson | .40 | .18 | .05 |
| □ 34 Marc Lewis | .40 | .18 | .05 |
| □ 35 David Martin | .40 | .18 | .05 |
| □ 36 Bruce Thornton | .40 | .18 | .05 |
| □ 37 Craig Walls | .40 | .18 | .05 |
| □ 38 Vincent White | .40 | .18 | .05 |
| □ 39 Luther Bradley | .50 | .23 | .06 |
| □ 40 Pete Catan | .40 | .18 | .05 |
| □ 41 Kiki DeAyala | .40 | .18 | .05 |
| □ 42 Toni Fritsch | .40 | .18 | .05 |
| □ 43 Sam Harrell | .40 | .18 | .05 |
| □ 44 Richard Johnson | 1.00 | .45 | .13 |
| □ 45 Jim Kelly | 50.00 | 23.00 | 6.25 |
| □ 46 Gerald McNeil | 1.00 | .45 | .13 |
| □ 47 Clarence Verdin | 4.00 | 1.80 | .50 |
| □ 48 Dale Walters | .40 | .18 | .05 |
| □ 49 Gary Clark | 35.00 | 16.00 | 4.40 |
| □ 50 Tom Dinkel | .40 | .18 | .05 |
| □ 51 Mike Edwards | .40 | .18 | .05 |
| □ 52 Brian Franco | .40 | .18 | .05 |
| □ 53 Bob Gruber | .40 | .18 | .05 |
| □ 54 Robbie Mahfouz | .40 | .18 | .05 |
| □ 55 Mike Rozier | 1.25 | .55 | .16 |
| □ 56 Brian Sipe | .50 | .23 | .06 |
| □ 57 J.T. Turner | .40 | .18 | .05 |
| □ 58 Howard Carson | .40 | .18 | .05 |
| □ 59 Wymon Henderson | .50 | .23 | .06 |
| □ 60 Kevin Nelson | .40 | .18 | .05 |
| □ 61 Jeff Partridge | .40 | .18 | .05 |
| □ 62 Ben Rudolph | .40 | .18 | .05 |
| □ 63 Jo Jo Townsell | .50 | .23 | .06 |
| □ 64 Eddie Weaver | .40 | .18 | .05 |
| □ 65 Steve Young | 70.00 | 32.00 | 8.75 |
| □ 66 Tony Zendejas | .75 | .35 | .09 |
| □ 67 Mossy Cade | .40 | .18 | .05 |
| □ 68 Leonard Coleman | .50 | .23 | .06 |
| □ 69 John Corker | .40 | .18 | .05 |
| □ 70 Derrick Crawford | .40 | .18 | .05 |
| □ 71 Art Kuehn | .40 | .18 | .05 |
| □ 72 Walter Lewis | .40 | .18 | .05 |
| □ 73 Tyrone McGriff | .40 | .18 | .05 |
| □ 74 Tim Spencer | .50 | .23 | .06 |
| □ 75 Reggie White | 26.00 | 11.50 | 3.30 |
| □ 76 Gizmo Williams | 1.75 | .80 | .22 |
| □ 77 Sam Bowers | .40 | .18 | .05 |
| □ 78 Maurice Carthon | 1.00 | .45 | .13 |
| □ 79 Clarence Collins | .40 | .18 | .05 |
| □ 80 Doug Flutie | 20.00 | 9.00 | 2.50 |
| □ 81 Freddie Gilbert | .40 | .18 | .05 |
| □ 82 Kerry Justin | .40 | .18 | .05 |
| □ 83 Dave Lapham | .40 | .18 | .05 |
| □ 84 Rick Partridge | .40 | .18 | .05 |
| □ 85 Roger Ruzek | 1.00 | .45 | .13 |
| □ 86 Herschel Walker | 14.00 | 6.25 | 1.75 |
| □ 87 Gordon Banks | .50 | .23 | .06 |
| □ 88 Monte Bennett | .40 | .18 | .05 |
| □ 89 Albert Bentley | 3.00 | 1.35 | .40 |
| □ 90 Novo Bojovic | .40 | .18 | .05 |
| □ 91 Dave Browning | .40 | .18 | .05 |

| | | | |
|---|---|---|---|
| ☐ 92 Anthony Carter | 6.50 | 2.90 | .80 |
| ☐ 93 Bobby Hebert | 6.50 | 2.90 | .80 |
| ☐ 94 Ray Pinney | .40 | .18 | .05 |
| ☐ 95 Stan Talley | .40 | .18 | .05 |
| ☐ 96 Ruben Vaughan | .40 | .18 | .05 |
| ☐ 97 Curtis Bledsoe | .40 | .18 | .05 |
| ☐ 98 Reggie Collier | .50 | .23 | .06 |
| ☐ 99 Jerry Doerger | .40 | .18 | .05 |
| ☐ 100 Jerry Golsteyn | .40 | .18 | .05 |
| ☐ 101 Bob Niziolek | .40 | .18 | .05 |
| ☐ 102 Joel Patten | .40 | .18 | .05 |
| ☐ 103 Ricky Simmons | .40 | .18 | .05 |
| ☐ 104 Joey Walters | .40 | .18 | .05 |
| ☐ 105 Marcus Dupree | .50 | .23 | .06 |
| ☐ 106 Jeff Gossett | .60 | .25 | .08 |
| ☐ 107 Frank Lockett | .40 | .18 | .05 |
| ☐ 108 Marcus Marek | .40 | .18 | .05 |
| ☐ 109 Kenny Neil | .40 | .18 | .05 |
| ☐ 110 Robert Pennywell | .40 | .18 | .05 |
| ☐ 111 Matt Robinson | .50 | .23 | .06 |
| ☐ 112 Dan Ross | .50 | .23 | .06 |
| ☐ 113 Doug Woodward | .40 | .18 | .05 |
| ☐ 114 Danny Buggs | .50 | .23 | .06 |
| ☐ 115 Putt Choate | .40 | .18 | .05 |
| ☐ 116 Greg Fields | .40 | .18 | .05 |
| ☐ 117 Ken Hartley | .40 | .18 | .05 |
| ☐ 118 Nick Mike-Mayer | .40 | .18 | .05 |
| ☐ 119 Rick Neuheisel | .40 | .18 | .05 |
| ☐ 120 Peter Raeford | .40 | .18 | .05 |
| ☐ 121 Gary Worthy | .40 | .18 | .05 |
| ☐ 122 Gary Anderson | 2.50 | 1.15 | .30 |
| ☐ 123 Zenon Andrusyshyn | .40 | .18 | .05 |
| ☐ 124 Greg Boone | .40 | .18 | .05 |
| ☐ 125 Mike Butler | .40 | .18 | .05 |
| ☐ 126 Mike Clark | .40 | .18 | .05 |
| ☐ 127 Willie Gillespie | .50 | .23 | .06 |
| ☐ 128 James Harrell | .40 | .18 | .05 |
| ☐ 129 Marvin Harvey | .40 | .18 | .05 |
| ☐ 130 John Reaves | .50 | .23 | .06 |
| ☐ 131 Eric Truvillion | .40 | .18 | .05 |
| ☐ 132 Checklist 1-132 | .50 | .18 | .05 |

## 1985 Topps USFL Generals

Topps produced this nine-card panel for the New Jersey Generals of the USFL. The entire panel measures approximately 7 1/2" by 10 1/2" and the individual cards, when cut, measure the standard 2 1/2" by 3 1/2". Card backs are printed in yellow and red on gray card stock. The panels were supposedly distributed to members of the Generals' Infantry Club, which was a fan club for youngsters. The values below are applicable also for uncut sheets as that is the most common way this set is seen.

| | MINT | EXC | G-VG |
|---|---|---|---|
| COMPLETE SET (9) | 30.00 | 12.00 | 3.00 |
| COMMON PLAYER (1-9) | 1.50 | .60 | .15 |
| | | | |
| ☐ 1 Walt Michaels CO | 2.00 | .80 | .20 |
| ☐ 2 Sam Bowers | 1.50 | .60 | .15 |
| ☐ 3 Clarence Collins | 1.50 | .60 | .15 |
| ☐ 4 Doug Flutie | 9.00 | 3.75 | .90 |
| ☐ 5 Gregory Johnson | 1.50 | .60 | .15 |
| ☐ 6 Jim LeClair | 2.00 | .80 | .20 |
| ☐ 7 Bobby Leopold | 1.50 | .60 | .15 |
| ☐ 8 Herschel Walker | 15.00 | 6.00 | 1.50 |
| ☐ 9 Membership card | 1.50 | .60 | .15 |
| (Schedule on back) | | | |

## 1986 Topps

The 1986 Topps football card set contains 396 cards featuring players of the NFL. Cards are standard size, 2 1/2" by 3 1/2". The set is distinguished by the green border on the fronts of the cards. The first seven cards in the set recognize Record-Breaking (RB) achievements during the previous season. Statistical league leaders are featured on cards 225-229. Team cards feature a distinctive yellow border on the

front with the team's results and leaders (from the previous season) listed on the back. All-Pro (AP) selections are designated on the player's regular card, not a special card. The set numbering is again ordered by teams, i.e., Chicago Bears (9-28), New England Patriots (29-43), Miami Dolphins (44-59), Los Angeles Raiders (60-75), Los Angeles Rams (76-93), New York Jets (94-110), Denver Broncos (111-123), Dallas Cowboys (124-136), New York Giants (137-154), San Francisco 49ers (155-169), Washington Redskins (170-184), Cleveland Browns (185-199), Seattle Seahawks (200-212), Green Bay Packers (213-224), San Diego Chargers (230-241), Detroit Lions (242-253), Cincinnati Bengals (254-267), Philadelphia Eagles (268-279), Pittsburgh Steelers (280-291), Minnesota Vikings (292-302), Kansas City Chiefs (303-313), Indianapolis Colts (314-325), St. Louis Cardinals (326-337), New Orleans Saints (338-348), Houston Oilers (349-359), Atlanta Falcons (360-371), Tampa Bay Buccaneers (372-382), and Buffalo Bills (383-393). The last three cards in the set (394-396) are checklist cards. Although they are not considered part of the complete set price, Topps also printed cards on the sides of the wax pack boxes. There were four different boxes each with a different playoff team pictured. These box cards are "lettered" rather than numbered and are listed at the end of the checklist below. The key Rookie Cards in this set are Mark Bavaro, Eddie Brown, Earnest Byner, Ray Childress, Boomer Esiason, Bernie Kosar, Charles Mann, Wilber Marshall, Karl Mecklenburg, William Perry, Andre Reed, Jerry Rice, Jay Schroeder, Bruce Smith, and Al Toon. In addition, Anthony Carter, Gary Clark, Bobby Hebert, Reggie White and Steve Young are Rookie Cards, although they had each appeared in a previous Topps USFL set.

| | MINT | EXC | G-VG |
|---|---|---|---|
| COMPLETE SET (396) | 100.00 | 45.00 | 12.50 |
| COMMON PLAYER (1-396) | .05 | .02 | .01 |
| | | | |
| ☐ 1 Marcus Allen RB | .60 | .25 | .08 |
| Los Angeles Raiders Most Yards From Scrimmage, Season | | | |
| ☐ 2 Eric Dickerson RB | .30 | .14 | .04 |
| Los Angeles Rams Most Yards Rushing, Playoff Game | | | |
| ☐ 3 Lionel James RB | .10 | .05 | .01 |
| San Diego Chargers Most All-Purpose Yards, Season | | | |
| ☐ 4 Steve Largent RB | .30 | .14 | .04 |
| Seattle Seahawks Most Seasons, 50 or More Receptions | | | |
| ☐ 5 George Martin RB | .10 | .05 | .01 |
| New York Giants Most Touchdowns, Def. Lineman, Career | | | |
| ☐ 6 Stephone Paige RB | .10 | .05 | .01 |
| Kansas City Chiefs Most Yards Receiving, Game | | | |
| ☐ 7 Walter Payton RB | .75 | .35 | .09 |
| Chicago Bears Most Consecutive Games, 100 or More Yards Rushing | | | |
| ☐ 8 Super Bowl XX | .15 | .07 | .02 |
| Bears 46, Patriots 10 (Jim McMahon handing off) | | | |
| ☐ 9 Chicago Bears | .60 | .25 | .08 |
| Team Card (Walter Payton in Motion) | | | |
| ☐ 10 Jim McMahon | .35 | .16 | .04 |
| ☐ 11 Walter Payton AP | 1.00 | .45 | .13 |
| ☐ 12 Matt Suhey | .08 | .04 | .01 |
| ☐ 13 Willie Gault | .25 | .11 | .03 |
| ☐ 14 Dennis McKinnon | .08 | .04 | .01 |

| | | | |
|---|---|---|---|
| ☐ 15 Emery Moorehead | .05 | .02 | .01 |
| ☐ 16 Jim Covert AP | .05 | .02 | .01 |
| ☐ 17 Jay Hilgenberg AP | 1.00 | .45 | .13 |
| ☐ 18 Kevin Butler | .75 | .35 | .09 |
| ☐ 19 Richard Dent AP | 1.00 | .45 | .13 |
| ☐ 20 William Perry | .75 | .35 | .09 |
| ☐ 21 Steve McMichael | .35 | .16 | .04 |
| ☐ 22 Dan Hampton | .30 | .14 | .04 |
| ☐ 23 Otis Wilson | .05 | .02 | .01 |
| ☐ 24 Mike Singletary | .60 | .25 | .08 |
| ☐ 25 Wilber Marshall | 3.00 | 1.35 | .40 |
| ☐ 26 Leslie Frazier | .05 | .02 | .01 |
| ☐ 27 Dave Duerson | .25 | .11 | .03 |
| ☐ 28 Gary Fencik | .05 | .02 | .01 |
| ☐ 29 New England Patriots | .13 | .06 | .02 |
| Team Card | | | |
| (Craig James on | | | |
| the Run) | | | |
| ☐ 30 Tony Eason | .05 | .02 | .01 |
| ☐ 31 Steve Grogan | .15 | .07 | .02 |
| ☐ 32 Craig James | .08 | .04 | .01 |
| ☐ 33 Tony Collins | .08 | .04 | .01 |
| ☐ 34 Irving Fryar | 1.00 | .45 | .13 |
| ☐ 35 Brian Holloway AP | .05 | .02 | .01 |
| ☐ 36 John Hannah AP | .15 | .07 | .02 |
| ☐ 37 Tony Franklin | .05 | .02 | .01 |
| ☐ 38 Garin Veris | .05 | .02 | .01 |
| ☐ 39 Andre Tippett AP | .05 | .02 | .01 |
| ☐ 40 Steve Nelson | .05 | .02 | .01 |
| ☐ 41 Raymond Clayborn | .08 | .04 | .01 |
| ☐ 42 Fred Marion | .08 | .04 | .01 |
| ☐ 43 Rich Camarillo | .05 | .02 | .01 |
| ☐ 44 Miami Dolphins | 1.25 | .55 | .16 |
| Team Card | | | |
| (Dan Marino Sets Up) | | | |
| ☐ 45 Dan Marino AP | 12.00 | 5.50 | 1.50 |
| ☐ 46 Tony Nathan | .08 | .04 | .01 |
| ☐ 47 Ron Davenport | .05 | .02 | .01 |
| ☐ 48 Mark Duper | .15 | .07 | .02 |
| ☐ 49 Mark Clayton | 1.25 | .55 | .16 |
| ☐ 50 Nat Moore | .08 | .04 | .01 |
| ☐ 51 Bruce Hardy | .05 | .02 | .01 |
| ☐ 52 Roy Foster | .05 | .02 | .01 |
| ☐ 53 Dwight Stephenson | .08 | .04 | .01 |
| ☐ 54 Fuad Reveiz | .20 | .09 | .03 |
| ☐ 55 Bob Baumhower | .05 | .02 | .01 |
| ☐ 56 Mike Charles | .05 | .02 | .01 |
| ☐ 57 Hugh Green | .08 | .04 | .01 |
| ☐ 58 Glenn Blackwood | .08 | .04 | .01 |
| ☐ 59 Reggie Roby | .08 | .04 | .01 |
| ☐ 60 Los Angeles Raiders | .30 | .14 | .04 |
| Team Card | | | |
| (Marcus Allen | | | |
| Cuts Upfield) | | | |
| ☐ 61 Marc Wilson | .08 | .04 | .01 |
| ☐ 62 Marcus Allen AP | 1.50 | .65 | .19 |
| ☐ 63 Dokie Williams | .08 | .04 | .01 |
| ☐ 64 Todd Christensen | .08 | .04 | .01 |
| ☐ 65 Chris Bahr | .05 | .02 | .01 |
| ☐ 66 Fulton Walker | .08 | .04 | .01 |
| ☐ 67 Howie Long | .50 | .23 | .06 |
| ☐ 68 Bill Pickel | .05 | .02 | .01 |
| ☐ 69 Ray Guy | .15 | .07 | .02 |
| ☐ 70 Greg Townsend | .75 | .35 | .09 |
| ☐ 71 Rod Martin | .08 | .04 | .01 |
| ☐ 72 Matt Millen | .08 | .04 | .01 |
| ☐ 73 Mike Haynes AP | .08 | .04 | .01 |
| ☐ 74 Lester Hayes | .08 | .04 | .01 |
| ☐ 75 Vann McElroy | .05 | .02 | .01 |
| ☐ 76 Los Angeles Rams | .25 | .11 | .03 |
| Team Card | | | |
| (Eric Dickerson | | | |
| Stiff-Arm) | | | |
| ☐ 77 Dieter Brock | .15 | .07 | .02 |
| ☐ 78 Eric Dickerson | .75 | .35 | .09 |
| ☐ 79 Henry Ellard | 1.00 | .45 | .13 |
| ☐ 80 Ron Brown | .25 | .11 | .03 |
| ☐ 81 Tony Hunter | .05 | .02 | .01 |
| ☐ 82 Kent Hill AP | .05 | .02 | .01 |
| ☐ 83 Doug Smith | .08 | .04 | .01 |
| ☐ 84 Dennis Harrah | .05 | .02 | .01 |
| ☐ 85 Jackie Slater | .25 | .11 | .03 |
| ☐ 86 Mike Lansford | .05 | .02 | .01 |
| ☐ 87 Gary Jeter | .05 | .02 | .01 |
| ☐ 88 Mike Wilcher | .05 | .02 | .01 |
| ☐ 89 Jim Collins | .05 | .02 | .01 |
| ☐ 90 LeRoy Irvin | .08 | .04 | .01 |
| ☐ 91 Gary Green | .05 | .02 | .01 |
| ☐ 92 Nolan Cromwell | .08 | .04 | .01 |
| ☐ 93 Dale Hatcher | .05 | .02 | .01 |
| ☐ 94 New York Jets | .13 | .06 | .02 |
| Team Card | | | |
| (Freeman McNeil | | | |
| Powers) | | | |
| ☐ 95 Ken O'Brien | .20 | .09 | .03 |
| ☐ 96 Freeman McNeil | .08 | .04 | .01 |
| ☐ 97 Tony Paige | .40 | .18 | .05 |

| | | | |
|---|---|---|---|
| ☐ 98 Johnny "Lam" Jones | .08 | .04 | .01 |
| ☐ 99 Wesley Walker | .08 | .04 | .01 |
| ☐ 100 Kurt Sohn | .05 | .02 | .01 |
| ☐ 101 Al Toon | 2.50 | 1.15 | .30 |
| ☐ 102 Mickey Shuler | .08 | .04 | .01 |
| ☐ 103 Marvin Powell | .05 | .02 | .01 |
| ☐ 104 Pat Leahy | .08 | .04 | .01 |
| ☐ 105 Mark Gastineau | .08 | .04 | .01 |
| ☐ 106 Joe Klecko AP | .08 | .04 | .01 |
| ☐ 107 Marty Lyons | .08 | .04 | .01 |
| ☐ 108 Lance Mehl | .05 | .02 | .01 |
| ☐ 109 Bobby Jackson | .05 | .02 | .01 |
| ☐ 110 Dave Jennings | .08 | .04 | .01 |
| ☐ 111 Denver Broncos | .10 | .05 | .01 |
| Team Card | | | |
| (Sammy Winder | | | |
| Up Middle) | | | |
| ☐ 112 John Elway | 6.00 | 2.70 | .75 |
| ☐ 113 Sammy Winder | .08 | .04 | .01 |
| ☐ 114 Gerald Willhite | .05 | .02 | .01 |
| ☐ 115 Steve Watson | .08 | .04 | .01 |
| ☐ 116 Vance Johnson | 1.25 | .55 | .16 |
| ☐ 117 Rich Karlis | .05 | .02 | .01 |
| ☐ 118 Rulon Jones | .05 | .02 | .01 |
| ☐ 119 Karl Mecklenburg AP | 2.50 | 1.15 | .30 |
| ☐ 120 Louis Wright | .08 | .04 | .01 |
| ☐ 121 Mike Harden | .05 | .02 | .01 |
| ☐ 122 Dennis Smith | 1.50 | .65 | .19 |
| ☐ 123 Steve Foley | .05 | .02 | .01 |
| ☐ 124 Dallas Cowboys | .10 | .05 | .01 |
| Team Card | | | |
| (Tony Hill Evades | | | |
| Defender) | | | |
| ☐ 125 Danny White | .15 | .07 | .02 |
| ☐ 126 Tony Dorsett | .50 | .23 | .06 |
| ☐ 127 Timmy Newsome | .05 | .02 | .01 |
| ☐ 128 Mike Renfro | .08 | .04 | .01 |
| ☐ 129 Tony Hill | .08 | .04 | .01 |
| ☐ 130 Doug Cosbie AP | .08 | .04 | .01 |
| ☐ 131 Rafael Septien | .05 | .02 | .01 |
| ☐ 132 Ed Too Tall Jones | .20 | .09 | .03 |
| ☐ 133 Randy White | .30 | .14 | .04 |
| ☐ 134 Jim Jeffcoat | .25 | .11 | .03 |
| ☐ 135 Everson Walls AP | .08 | .04 | .01 |
| ☐ 136 Dennis Thurman | .05 | .02 | .01 |
| ☐ 137 New York Giants | .10 | .05 | .01 |
| Team Card | | | |
| (Joe Morris Opening) | | | |
| ☐ 138 Phil Simms | .50 | .23 | .06 |
| ☐ 139 Joe Morris | .15 | .07 | .02 |
| ☐ 140 George Adams | .08 | .04 | .01 |
| ☐ 141 Lionel Manuel | .08 | .04 | .01 |
| ☐ 142 Bobby Johnson | .05 | .02 | .01 |
| ☐ 143 Phil McConkey | .20 | .09 | .03 |
| ☐ 144 Mark Bavaro | 3.00 | 1.35 | .40 |
| ☐ 145 Zeke Mowatt | .08 | .04 | .01 |
| ☐ 146 Brad Benson | .05 | .02 | .01 |
| ☐ 147 Bart Oates | .60 | .25 | .08 |
| ☐ 148 Leonard Marshall AP | 1.50 | .65 | .19 |
| ☐ 149 Jim Burt | .08 | .04 | .01 |
| ☐ 150 George Martin | .08 | .04 | .01 |
| ☐ 151 Lawrence Taylor AP | .60 | .25 | .08 |
| ☐ 152 Harry Carson AP | .08 | .04 | .01 |
| ☐ 153 Elvis Patterson | .25 | .11 | .03 |
| ☐ 154 Sean Landeta | .30 | .14 | .04 |
| ☐ 155 San Francisco 49ers | .20 | .09 | .03 |
| Team Card | | | |
| (Roger Craig | | | |
| Scampers) | | | |
| ☐ 156 Joe Montana | 5.00 | 2.30 | .60 |
| ☐ 157 Roger Craig | .60 | .25 | .08 |
| ☐ 158 Wendell Tyler | .08 | .04 | .01 |
| ☐ 159 Carl Monroe | .05 | .02 | .01 |
| ☐ 160 Dwight Clark | .20 | .09 | .03 |
| ☐ 161 Jerry Rice | 60.00 | 27.00 | 7.50 |
| ☐ 162 Randy Cross | .08 | .04 | .01 |
| ☐ 163 Keith Fahnhorst | .05 | .02 | .01 |
| ☐ 164 Jeff Stover | .05 | .02 | .01 |
| ☐ 165 Michael Carter | .60 | .25 | .08 |
| ☐ 166 Dwaine Board | .08 | .04 | .01 |
| ☐ 167 Eric Wright | .08 | .04 | .01 |
| ☐ 168 Ronnie Lott | .75 | .35 | .09 |
| ☐ 169 Carlton Williamson | .05 | .02 | .01 |
| ☐ 170 Washington Redskins | .10 | .05 | .01 |
| Team Card | | | |
| (Dave Butz Gets | | | |
| His Man) | | | |
| ☐ 171 Joe Theismann | .35 | .16 | .04 |
| ☐ 172 Jay Schroeder | .75 | .35 | .09 |
| ☐ 173 George Rogers | .08 | .04 | .01 |
| ☐ 174 Ken Jenkins | .05 | .02 | .01 |
| ☐ 175 Art Monk AP | .60 | .25 | .08 |
| ☐ 176 Gary Clark | 5.00 | 2.30 | .60 |
| ☐ 177 Joe Jacoby | .08 | .04 | .01 |
| ☐ 178 Russ Grimm | .08 | .04 | .01 |
| ☐ 179 Mark Moseley | .08 | .04 | .01 |
| ☐ 180 Dexter Manley | .08 | .04 | .01 |

| | | | |
|---|---|---|---|
| ☐ 181 Charles Mann | 1.00 | .45 | .13 |
| ☐ 182 Vernon Dean | .05 | .02 | .01 |
| ☐ 183 Raphel Cherry | .15 | .07 | .02 |
| ☐ 184 Curtis Jordan | .05 | .02 | .01 |
| ☐ 185 Cleveland Browns | .40 | .18 | .05 |
| Team Card | | | |
| (Bernie Kosar Fakes | | | |
| Handoff) | | | |
| ☐ 186 Gary Danielson | .08 | .04 | .01 |
| ☐ 187 Bernie Kosar | 6.00 | 2.70 | .75 |
| ☐ 188 Kevin Mack | .50 | .23 | .06 |
| ☐ 189 Earnest Byner | 2.50 | 1.15 | .30 |
| ☐ 190 Glen Young | .05 | .02 | .01 |
| ☐ 191 Ozzie Newsome | .30 | .14 | .04 |
| ☐ 192 Mike Baab | .05 | .02 | .01 |
| ☐ 193 Cody Risien | .08 | .04 | .01 |
| ☐ 194 Bob Golic | .08 | .04 | .01 |
| ☐ 195 Reggie Camp | .05 | .02 | .01 |
| ☐ 196 Chip Banks | .08 | .04 | .01 |
| ☐ 197 Tom Cousineau | .08 | .04 | .01 |
| ☐ 198 Frank Minnifield | .20 | .09 | .03 |
| ☐ 199 Al Gross | .05 | .02 | .01 |
| ☐ 200 Seattle Seahawks | .10 | .05 | .01 |
| Team Card | | | |
| (Curt Warner Breaks | | | |
| Free) | | | |
| ☐ 201 Dave Krieg | .20 | .09 | .03 |
| ☐ 202 Curt Warner | .08 | .04 | .01 |
| ☐ 203 Steve Largent AP | .50 | .23 | .06 |
| ☐ 204 Norm Johnson | .05 | .02 | .01 |
| ☐ 205 Daryl Turner | .05 | .02 | .01 |
| ☐ 206 Jacob Green | .08 | .04 | .01 |
| ☐ 207 Joe Nash | .08 | .04 | .01 |
| ☐ 208 Jeff Bryant | .05 | .02 | .01 |
| ☐ 209 Randy Edwards | .05 | .02 | .01 |
| ☐ 210 Fredd Young | .08 | .04 | .01 |
| ☐ 211 Kenny Easley | .08 | .04 | .01 |
| ☐ 212 John Harris | .05 | .02 | .01 |
| ☐ 213 Green Bay Packers | .10 | .05 | .01 |
| Team Card | | | |
| (Paul Coffman | | | |
| Conquers) | | | |
| ☐ 214 Lynn Dickey | .08 | .04 | .01 |
| ☐ 215 Gerry Ellis | .05 | .02 | .01 |
| ☐ 216 Eddie Lee Ivery | .05 | .02 | .01 |
| ☐ 217 Jessie Clark | .05 | .02 | .01 |
| ☐ 218 James Lofton | .50 | .23 | .06 |
| ☐ 219 Paul Coffman | .05 | .02 | .01 |
| ☐ 220 Alphonso Carreker | .05 | .02 | .01 |
| ☐ 221 Ezra Johnson | .05 | .02 | .01 |
| ☐ 222 Mike Douglass | .05 | .02 | .01 |
| ☐ 223 Tim Lewis | .05 | .02 | .01 |
| ☐ 224 Mark Murphy | .15 | .07 | .02 |
| ☐ 225 Passing Leaders: | 1.00 | .45 | .13 |
| Ken O'Brien AFC, | | | |
| New York Jets | | | |
| Joe Montana NFC, | | | |
| San Francisco 49ers | | | |
| ☐ 226 Receiving Leaders: | .13 | .06 | .02 |
| Lionel James AFC, | | | |
| San Diego Chargers | | | |
| Roger Craig NFC, | | | |
| San Francisco 49ers | | | |
| ☐ 227 Rushing Leaders: | .25 | .11 | .03 |
| Marcus Allen AFC, | | | |
| Los Angeles Raiders | | | |
| Gerald Riggs NFC, | | | |
| Atlanta Falcons | | | |
| ☐ 228 Scoring Leaders: | .10 | .05 | .01 |
| Gary Anderson AFC, | | | |
| Pittsburgh Steelers | | | |
| Kevin Butler NFC, | | | |
| Chicago Bears | | | |
| ☐ 229 Interception Leaders: | .10 | .05 | .01 |
| Eugene Daniel AFC, | | | |
| Indianapolis Colts | | | |
| Albert Lewis AFC, | | | |
| Kansas City Chiefs | | | |
| Everson Walls NFC, | | | |
| Dallas Cowboys | | | |
| ☐ 230 San Diego Chargers | .25 | .11 | .03 |
| Team Card | | | |
| (Dan Fouts Over Top) | | | |
| ☐ 231 Dan Fouts | .50 | .23 | .06 |
| ☐ 232 Lionel James | .08 | .04 | .01 |
| ☐ 233 Gary Anderson | 1.00 | .45 | .13 |
| ☐ 234 Tim Spencer | .08 | .04 | .01 |
| ☐ 235 Wes Chandler | .08 | .04 | .01 |
| ☐ 236 Charlie Joiner | .25 | .11 | .03 |
| ☐ 237 Kellen Winslow | .25 | .11 | .03 |
| ☐ 238 Jim Lachey | 1.50 | .65 | .19 |
| ☐ 239 Bob Thomas | .05 | .02 | .01 |
| ☐ 240 Jeffery Dale | .05 | .02 | .01 |
| ☐ 241 Ralf Mojsiejenko | .05 | .02 | .01 |
| ☐ 242 Detroit Lions | .10 | .05 | .01 |
| Team Card | | | |
| (Eric Hipple Spots | | | |

| | | | |
|---|---|---|---|
| Receiver) | | | |
| ☐ 243 Eric Hipple | .08 | .04 | .01 |
| ☐ 244 Billy Sims | .08 | .04 | .01 |
| ☐ 245 James Jones | .08 | .04 | .01 |
| ☐ 246 Pete Mandley | .05 | .02 | .01 |
| ☐ 247 Leonard Thompson | .05 | .02 | .01 |
| ☐ 248 Lomas Brown | .40 | .18 | .05 |
| ☐ 249 Ed Murray | .08 | .04 | .01 |
| ☐ 250 Curtis Green | .05 | .02 | .01 |
| ☐ 251 William Gay | .05 | .02 | .01 |
| ☐ 252 Jimmy Williams | .05 | .02 | .01 |
| ☐ 253 Bobby Watkins | .05 | .02 | .01 |
| ☐ 254 Cincinnati Bengals | .75 | .35 | .09 |
| Team Card | | | |
| (Boomer Esiason | | | |
| Zeroes In) | | | |
| ☐ 255 Boomer Esiason | 9.00 | 4.00 | 1.15 |
| ☐ 256 James Brooks | .08 | .04 | .01 |
| ☐ 257 Larry Kinnebrew | .05 | .02 | .01 |
| ☐ 258 Cris Collinsworth | .08 | .04 | .01 |
| ☐ 259 Mike Martin | .05 | .02 | .01 |
| ☐ 260 Eddie Brown | .75 | .35 | .09 |
| ☐ 261 Anthony Munoz | .25 | .11 | .03 |
| ☐ 262 Jim Breech | .05 | .02 | .01 |
| ☐ 263 Ross Browner | .08 | .04 | .01 |
| ☐ 264 Carl Zander | .05 | .02 | .01 |
| ☐ 265 James Griffin | .05 | .02 | .01 |
| ☐ 266 Robert Jackson | .05 | .02 | .01 |
| ☐ 267 Pat McInally | .08 | .04 | .01 |
| ☐ 268 Philadelphia Eagles | .10 | .05 | .01 |
| Team Card | | | |
| (Ron Jaworski Surveys) | | | |
| ☐ 269 Ron Jaworski | .08 | .04 | .01 |
| ☐ 270 Earnest Jackson | .08 | .04 | .01 |
| ☐ 271 Mike Quick | .08 | .04 | .01 |
| ☐ 272 John Spagnola | .05 | .02 | .01 |
| ☐ 273 Mark Dennard | .05 | .02 | .01 |
| ☐ 274 Paul McFadden | .05 | .02 | .01 |
| ☐ 275 Reggie White | 8.00 | 3.60 | 1.00 |
| ☐ 276 Greg Brown | .05 | .02 | .01 |
| ☐ 277 Herman Edwards | .05 | .02 | .01 |
| ☐ 278 Roynell Young | .05 | .02 | .01 |
| ☐ 279 Wes Hopkins AP | .05 | .02 | .01 |
| ☐ 280 Pittsburgh Steelers | .10 | .05 | .01 |
| Team Card | | | |
| (Walter Abercrombie | | | |
| Inches) | | | |
| ☐ 281 Mark Malone | .08 | .04 | .01 |
| ☐ 282 Frank Pollard | .05 | .02 | .01 |
| ☐ 283 Walter Abercrombie | .05 | .02 | .01 |
| ☐ 284 Louis Lipps | .30 | .14 | .04 |
| ☐ 285 John Stallworth | .20 | .09 | .03 |
| ☐ 286 Mike Webster | .08 | .04 | .01 |
| ☐ 287 Gary Anderson AP | .08 | .04 | .01 |
| ☐ 288 Keith Willis | .05 | .02 | .01 |
| ☐ 289 Mike Merriweather | .08 | .04 | .01 |
| ☐ 290 Dwayne Woodruff | .05 | .02 | .01 |
| ☐ 291 Donnie Shell | .08 | .04 | .01 |
| ☐ 292 Minnesota Vikings | .10 | .05 | .01 |
| Team Card | | | |
| (Tommy Kramer Audible) | | | |
| ☐ 293 Tommy Kramer | .08 | .04 | .01 |
| ☐ 294 Darrin Nelson | .08 | .04 | .01 |
| ☐ 295 Ted Brown | .08 | .04 | .01 |
| ☐ 296 Buster Rhymes | .08 | .04 | .01 |
| ☐ 297 Anthony Carter | 2.50 | 1.15 | .30 |
| ☐ 298 Steve Jordan | 1.00 | .45 | .13 |
| ☐ 299 Keith Millard | .50 | .23 | .06 |
| ☐ 300 Joey Browner | .75 | .35 | .09 |
| ☐ 301 John Turner | .05 | .02 | .01 |
| ☐ 302 Greg Coleman | .05 | .02 | .01 |
| ☐ 303 Kansas City Chiefs | .10 | .05 | .01 |
| Team Card | | | |
| (Todd Blackledge) | | | |
| ☐ 304 Bill Kenney | .08 | .04 | .01 |
| ☐ 305 Herman Heard | .05 | .02 | .01 |
| ☐ 306 Stephone Paige | .75 | .35 | .09 |
| ☐ 307 Carlos Carson | .08 | .04 | .01 |
| ☐ 308 Nick Lowery | .20 | .09 | .03 |
| ☐ 309 Mike Bell | .05 | .02 | .01 |
| ☐ 310 Bill Maas | .08 | .04 | .01 |
| ☐ 311 Art Still | .08 | .04 | .01 |
| ☐ 312 Albert Lewis | 1.25 | .55 | .16 |
| ☐ 313 Deron Cherry AP | .08 | .04 | .01 |
| ☐ 314 Indianapolis Colts | .10 | .05 | .01 |
| Team Card | | | |
| (Rohn Stark Booms It) | | | |
| ☐ 315 Mike Pagel | .08 | .04 | .01 |
| ☐ 316 Randy McMillan | .05 | .02 | .01 |
| ☐ 317 Albert Bentley | .30 | .14 | .04 |
| ☐ 318 George Wonsley | .05 | .02 | .01 |
| ☐ 319 Robbie Martin | .05 | .02 | .01 |
| ☐ 320 Pat Beach | .05 | .02 | .01 |
| ☐ 321 Chris Hinton | .08 | .04 | .01 |
| ☐ 322 Duane Bickett | .40 | .18 | .05 |
| ☐ 323 Eugene Daniel | .05 | .02 | .01 |
| ☐ 324 Cliff Odom | .08 | .04 | .01 |
| ☐ 325 Rohn Stark AP | .08 | .04 | .01 |

| | | | |
|---|---|---|---|
| ☐ 326 St. Louis Cardinals | .10 | .05 | .01 |
| Team Card | | | |
| (Stump Mitchell | | | |
| Outside) | | | |
| ☐ 327 Neil Lomax | .08 | .04 | .01 |
| ☐ 328 Stump Mitchell | .08 | .04 | .01 |
| ☐ 329 Ottis Anderson | .20 | .09 | .03 |
| ☐ 330 J.T. Smith | .08 | .04 | .01 |
| ☐ 331 Pat Tilley | .08 | .04 | .01 |
| ☐ 332 Roy Green | .08 | .04 | .01 |
| ☐ 333 Lance Smith | .05 | .02 | .01 |
| ☐ 334 Curtis Greer | .05 | .02 | .01 |
| ☐ 335 Freddie Joe Nunn | .40 | .18 | .05 |
| ☐ 336 E.J. Junior | .08 | .04 | .01 |
| ☐ 337 Lonnie Young | .15 | .07 | .02 |
| ☐ 338 New Orleans Saints | .10 | .05 | .01 |
| Team Card | | | |
| (Wayne Wilson running) | | | |
| ☐ 339 Bobby Hebert | 2.50 | 1.15 | .30 |
| ☐ 340 Dave Wilson | .08 | .04 | .01 |
| ☐ 341 Wayne Wilson | .05 | .02 | .01 |
| ☐ 342 Hoby Brenner | .05 | .02 | .01 |
| ☐ 343 Stan Brock | .05 | .02 | .01 |
| ☐ 344 Morten Andersen | .35 | .16 | .04 |
| ☐ 345 Bruce Clark | .05 | .02 | .01 |
| ☐ 346 Rickey Jackson | .50 | .23 | .06 |
| ☐ 347 Dave Waymer | .05 | .02 | .01 |
| ☐ 348 Brian Hansen | .05 | .02 | .01 |
| ☐ 349 Houston Oilers | .60 | .25 | .08 |
| Team Card | | | |
| (Warren Moon | | | |
| Throws Bomb) | | | |
| ☐ 350 Warren Moon | 3.50 | 1.55 | .45 |
| ☐ 351 Mike Rozier | .30 | .14 | .04 |
| ☐ 352 Butch Woolfolk | .05 | .02 | .01 |
| ☐ 353 Drew Hill | .30 | .14 | .04 |
| ☐ 354 Willie Drewrey | .08 | .04 | .01 |
| ☐ 355 Tim Smith | .05 | .02 | .01 |
| ☐ 356 Mike Munchak | .30 | .14 | .04 |
| ☐ 357 Ray Childress | 2.50 | 1.15 | .30 |
| ☐ 358 Frank Bush | .05 | .02 | .01 |
| ☐ 359 Steve Brown | .05 | .02 | .01 |
| ☐ 360 Atlanta Falcons | .10 | .05 | .01 |
| Team Card | | | |
| (Gerald Riggs | | | |
| Around End) | | | |
| ☐ 361 Dave Archer | .50 | .23 | .06 |
| ☐ 362 Gerald Riggs | .08 | .04 | .01 |
| ☐ 363 William Andrews | .08 | .04 | .01 |
| ☐ 364 Billy Johnson | .08 | .04 | .01 |
| ☐ 365 Arthur Cox | .05 | .02 | .01 |
| ☐ 366 Mike Kenn | .08 | .04 | .01 |
| ☐ 367 Bill Fralic | .75 | .35 | .09 |
| ☐ 368 Mick Luckhurst | .05 | .02 | .01 |
| ☐ 369 Rick Bryan | .05 | .02 | .01 |
| ☐ 370 Bobby Butler | .05 | .02 | .01 |
| ☐ 371 Rick Donnelly | .05 | .02 | .01 |
| ☐ 372 Tampa Bay Buccaneers | .10 | .05 | .01 |
| Team Card | | | |
| (James Wilder | | | |
| Sweeps Left) | | | |
| ☐ 373 Steve DeBerg | .25 | .11 | .03 |
| ☐ 374 Steve Young | 15.00 | 6.75 | 1.90 |
| ☐ 375 James Wilder | .08 | .04 | .01 |
| ☐ 376 Kevin House | .08 | .04 | .01 |
| ☐ 377 Gerald Carter | .05 | .02 | .01 |
| ☐ 378 Jimmie Giles | .08 | .04 | .01 |
| ☐ 379 Sean Farrell | .08 | .04 | .01 |
| ☐ 380 Donald Igwebuike | .05 | .02 | .01 |
| ☐ 381 David Logan | .05 | .02 | .01 |
| ☐ 382 Jeremiah Castille | .05 | .02 | .01 |
| ☐ 383 Buffalo Bills | .10 | .05 | .01 |
| Team Card | | | |
| (Greg Bell Sees | | | |
| Daylight) | | | |
| ☐ 384 Bruce Mathison | .05 | .02 | .01 |
| ☐ 385 Joe Cribbs | .08 | .04 | .01 |
| ☐ 386 Greg Bell | .08 | .04 | .01 |
| ☐ 387 Jerry Butler | .08 | .04 | .01 |
| ☐ 388 Andre Reed | 7.00 | 3.10 | .85 |
| ☐ 389 Bruce Smith | 7.00 | 3.10 | .85 |
| ☐ 390 Fred Smerlas | .08 | .04 | .01 |
| ☐ 391 Darryl Talley | .40 | .18 | .05 |
| ☐ 392 Jim Haslett | .05 | .02 | .01 |
| ☐ 393 Charles Romes | .05 | .02 | .01 |
| ☐ 394 Checklist 1-132 | .12 | .02 | .01 |
| ☐ 395 Checklist 133-264 | .12 | .02 | .01 |
| ☐ 396 Checklist 265-396 | .12 | .02 | .01 |

## 1986 Topps Box Bottoms

This four-card set, which measures 2 1/2" by 3 1/2", features the four teams which participated in the Super Bowl and in the Conference Championships. This set is arranged in order of how the teams finished, with the Super Bowl Champion Bears being the first team

listed. The fronts of the card feature a team photo and identification of all those players is pictured on the back of the card. The cards were issued one per wax box as the side panel of the box, not on the box bottom as was typical of similar sets.

| | MINT | EXC | G-VG |
|---|---|---|---|
| COMPLETE SET (4) | 6.00 | 2.40 | .60 |
| COMMON PLAYER (A-D) | 1.25 | .50 | .12 |
| ☐ A Chicago Bears | 3.00 | 1.20 | .30 |
| NFL Champions | | | |
| ☐ B New England Patriots | 1.50 | .60 | .15 |
| AFC Champions | | | |
| ☐ C Los Angeles Rams | 1.25 | .50 | .12 |
| NFC West Champions | | | |
| ☐ D Miami Dolphins | 2.00 | .80 | .20 |
| AFC East Champions | | | |

## 1986 Topps 1000 Yard Club

This 26-card set was distributed as an insert with the 1986 Topps regular issue football wax packs. Players featured are all members of the 1000-yard club, having gained over 1000 yards rushing or receiving during the previous season. The cards are numbered on back according to decreasing order of yardage gained. Roger Craig (22) actually gained over 1000 yards both rushing and receiving. Card backs have orange and red printing on white card stock. Cards measure the standard 2 1/2 by 3 1/2". The obverses have an ornate border design of green and yellow.

| | MINT | EXC | G-VG |
|---|---|---|---|
| COMPLETE SET (26) | 6.00 | 2.40 | .60 |
| COMMON PLAYER (1-26) | .25 | .10 | .02 |
| ☐ 1 Marcus Allen | .75 | .30 | .07 |
| Los Angeles Raiders | | | |
| ☐ 2 Gerald Riggs | .35 | .14 | .03 |
| Atlanta Falcons | | | |
| ☐ 3 Walter Payton | 1.50 | .60 | .15 |
| Chicago Bears | | | |
| ☐ 4 Joe Morris | .35 | .14 | .03 |
| New York Giants | | | |
| ☐ 5 Freeman McNeil | .35 | .14 | .03 |
| New York Jets | | | |
| ☐ 6 Tony Dorsett | .75 | .30 | .07 |
| Dallas Cowboys | | | |
| ☐ 7 James Wilder | .25 | .10 | .02 |
| Tampa Bay Buccaneers | | | |
| ☐ 8 Steve Largent | 1.00 | .40 | .10 |
| Seattle Seahawks | | | |
| ☐ 9 Mike Quick | .25 | .10 | .02 |
| Philadelphia Eagles | | | |
| ☐ 10 Eric Dickerson | 1.00 | .40 | .10 |
| Los Angeles Rams | | | |

| | | | |
|---|---|---|---|
| ☐ 11 Craig James | .50 | .20 | .05 |
| New England Patriots | | | |
| ☐ 12 Art Monk | .75 | .30 | .07 |
| Washington Redskins | | | |
| ☐ 13 Wes Chandler | .25 | .10 | .02 |
| San Diego Chargers | | | |
| ☐ 14 Drew Hill | .25 | .10 | .02 |
| Houston Oilers | | | |
| ☐ 15 James Lofton | .75 | .30 | .07 |
| Green Bay Packers | | | |
| ☐ 16 Louis Lipps | .35 | .14 | .03 |
| Pittsburgh Steelers | | | |
| ☐ 17 Cris Collinsworth | .35 | .14 | .03 |
| Cincinnati Bengals | | | |
| ☐ 18 Tony Hill | .25 | .10 | .02 |
| Dallas Cowboys | | | |
| ☐ 19 Kevin Mack | .25 | .10 | .02 |
| Cleveland Browns | | | |
| ☐ 20 Curt Warner | .35 | .14 | .03 |
| Seattle Seahawks | | | |
| ☐ 21 George Rogers | .25 | .10 | .02 |
| Washington Redskins | | | |
| ☐ 22 Roger Craig | .60 | .24 | .06 |
| San Francisco 49ers | | | |
| ☐ 23 Earnest Jackson | .25 | .10 | .02 |
| Philadelphia Eagles | | | |
| ☐ 24 Lionel James | .25 | .10 | .02 |
| San Diego Chargers | | | |
| ☐ 25 Stump Mitchell | .25 | .10 | .02 |
| St. Louis Cardinals | | | |
| ☐ 26 Earnest Byner | .35 | .14 | .03 |
| Cleveland Browns | | | |

## 1987 Topps

The 1987 Topps football set is standard size, 2 1/2" by 3 1/2", and consists of 396 cards featuring players of the NFL. The first eight cards in the set recognize the Super Bowl winning Giants and seven Record-Breaking (RB) achievements during the previous season. All-Pro (AP) selections are designated on the player's regular card, not a special card. Statistical league leaders are featured on cards 227-231. The set numbering is again ordered by teams, i.e., New York Giants (9-29), Denver Broncos (30-42), Chicago Bears (43-62), Washington Redskins (63-78), Cleveland Browns (79-95), New England Patriots (96-110), San Francisco 49ers (111-125), New York Jets (126-143), Los Angeles Rams (144-159), Kansas City Chiefs (160-171), Seattle Seahawks (172-183), Cincinnati Bengals (184-197), Minnesota Vikings (198-212), Los Angeles Raiders (213-226), Miami Dolphins (232-247), Atlanta Falcons (248-259), Dallas Cowboys (260-271), New Orleans Saints (272-282), Pittsburgh Steelers (283-293), Philadelphia Eagles (294-305), Houston Oilers (306-316), Detroit Lions (317-327), St. Louis Cardinals (328-338), San Diego Chargers (339-349), Green Bay Packers (350-360), Buffalo Bills (361-371), Indianapolis Colts (372-382), and Tampa Bay Buccaneers (383-393). The last three cards in the set (394-396) are checklist cards. Team cards feature an action photo on the front with the team's statistical leaders and week-by-week game results from the previous season. Although they are not considered part of the complete set price, Topps also printed cards on the bottoms of the wax pack boxes. There were four different boxes each with four different players. These box bottom cards are distinguished by their yellow border (instead of white) and the fact that they are "lettered" rather than numbered. The key Rookie Cards in this set are Randall Cunningham, Jim Everett, and Jim Kelly.

| | MINT | EXC | G-VG |
|---|---|---|---|
| COMPLETE SET (396) | 40.00 | 18.00 | 5.00 |
| COMPLETE FACT.SET (396) | 50.00 | 23.00 | 6.25 |
| COMMON PLAYER (1-396) | .05 | .02 | .01 |

| | | | |
|---|---|---|---|
| ☐ 1 Super Bowl XXI | .15 | .07 | .02 |
| Giants 39, | | | |

| | | | |
|---|---|---|---|
| Broncos 20 | | | |
| (Line play shown) | | | |
| ☐ 2 Todd Christensen RB | .07 | .03 | .01 |
| Most Seasons, | | | |
| 80 or More Receptions | | | |
| Los Angeles Raiders | | | |
| ☐ 3 Dave Jennings RB | .07 | .03 | .01 |
| Most Punts, Career | | | |
| New York Giants | | | |
| ☐ 4 Charlie Joiner RB | .10 | .05 | .01 |
| Most Receiving | | | |
| Yards, Career | | | |
| San Diego Chargers | | | |
| ☐ 5 Steve Largent RB | .25 | .11 | .03 |
| Most Cons. Games | | | |
| With a Reception | | | |
| Seattle Seahawks | | | |
| ☐ 6 Dan Marino RB | 2.00 | .90 | .25 |
| Most Cons. Seasons, | | | |
| 30 or More TD Passes | | | |
| Miami Dolphins | | | |
| ☐ 7 Donnie Shell RB | .07 | .03 | .01 |
| Most Interceptions, | | | |
| Strong Safety, Career | | | |
| Pittsburgh Steelers | | | |
| ☐ 8 Phil Simms RB | .15 | .07 | .02 |
| Highest Completion | | | |
| Percentage, Super Bowl | | | |
| New York Giants | | | |
| ☐ 9 New York Giants | .07 | .03 | .01 |
| Team Card | | | |
| (Mark Bavaro Pulls Free) | | | |
| ☐ 10 Phil Simms | .40 | .18 | .05 |
| ☐ 11 Joe Morris AP | .08 | .04 | .01 |
| ☐ 12 Maurice Carthon | .15 | .07 | .02 |
| ☐ 13 Lee Rouson | .05 | .02 | .01 |
| ☐ 14 Bobby Johnson | .05 | .02 | .01 |
| ☐ 15 Lionel Manuel | .05 | .02 | .01 |
| ☐ 16 Phil McConkey | .08 | .04 | .01 |
| ☐ 17 Mark Bavaro AP | .50 | .23 | .06 |
| ☐ 18 Zeke Mowatt | .05 | .02 | .01 |
| ☐ 19 Raul Allegre | .05 | .02 | .01 |
| ☐ 20 Sean Landeta | .08 | .04 | .01 |
| ☐ 21 Brad Benson | .05 | .02 | .01 |
| ☐ 22 Jim Burt | .08 | .04 | .01 |
| ☐ 23 Leonard Marshall | .40 | .18 | .05 |
| ☐ 24 Carl Banks | .40 | .18 | .05 |
| ☐ 25 Harry Carson | .08 | .04 | .01 |
| ☐ 26 Lawrence Taylor AP | .50 | .23 | .06 |
| ☐ 27 Terry Kinard | .15 | .07 | .02 |
| ☐ 28 Pepper Johnson | .75 | .35 | .09 |
| ☐ 29 Erik Howard | .15 | .07 | .02 |
| ☐ 30 Denver Broncos | .07 | .03 | .01 |
| Team Card | | | |
| (Gerald Willhite Dives) | | | |
| ☐ 31 John Elway | 3.50 | 1.55 | .45 |
| ☐ 32 Gerald Willhite | .05 | .02 | .01 |
| ☐ 33 Sammy Winder | .08 | .04 | .01 |
| ☐ 34 Ken Bell | .05 | .02 | .01 |
| ☐ 35 Steve Watson | .08 | .04 | .01 |
| ☐ 36 Rich Karlis | .05 | .02 | .01 |
| ☐ 37 Keith Bishop | .05 | .02 | .01 |
| ☐ 38 Rulon Jones | .05 | .02 | .01 |
| ☐ 39 Karl Mecklenburg AP | .50 | .23 | .06 |
| ☐ 40 Louis Wright | .08 | .04 | .01 |
| ☐ 41 Mike Harden | .05 | .02 | .01 |
| ☐ 42 Dennis Smith | .35 | .16 | .04 |
| ☐ 43 Chicago Bears | .50 | .23 | .06 |
| Team Card | | | |
| (Walter Payton Barrels) | | | |
| ☐ 44 Jim McMahon | .25 | .11 | .03 |
| ☐ 45 Doug Flutie | 2.50 | 1.15 | .30 |
| ☐ 46 Walter Payton | 1.00 | .45 | .13 |
| ☐ 47 Matt Suhey | .08 | .04 | .01 |
| ☐ 48 Willie Gault | .15 | .07 | .02 |
| ☐ 49 Dennis Gentry | .20 | .09 | .03 |
| ☐ 50 Kevin Butler | .25 | .11 | .03 |
| ☐ 51 Jim Covert AP | .08 | .04 | .01 |
| ☐ 52 Jay Hilgenberg | .25 | .11 | .03 |
| ☐ 53 Dan Hampton | .15 | .07 | .02 |
| ☐ 54 Steve McMichael | .08 | .04 | .01 |
| ☐ 55 William Perry | .15 | .07 | .02 |
| ☐ 56 Richard Dent | .40 | .18 | .05 |
| ☐ 57 Otis Wilson | .05 | .02 | .01 |
| ☐ 58 Mike Singletary AP | .35 | .16 | .04 |
| ☐ 59 Wilber Marshall | .40 | .18 | .05 |
| ☐ 60 Mike Richardson | .05 | .02 | .01 |
| ☐ 61 Dave Duerson | .08 | .04 | .01 |
| ☐ 62 Gary Fencik | .05 | .02 | .01 |
| ☐ 63 Washington Redskins | .07 | .03 | .01 |
| Team Card | | | |
| (George Rogers Plunges) | | | |
| ☐ 64 Jay Schroeder | .30 | .14 | .04 |
| ☐ 65 George Rogers | .08 | .04 | .01 |
| ☐ 66 Kelvin Bryant | .25 | .11 | .03 |
| ☐ 67 Ken Jenkins | .05 | .02 | .01 |
| ☐ 68 Gary Clark | 1.25 | .55 | .16 |
| ☐ 69 Art Monk | .40 | .18 | .05 |

| | | | |
|---|---|---|---|
| ☐ 70 Clint Didier | .15 | .07 | .02 |
| ☐ 71 Steve Cox | .05 | .02 | .01 |
| ☐ 72 Joe Jacoby | .08 | .04 | .01 |
| ☐ 73 Russ Grimm | .08 | .04 | .01 |
| ☐ 74 Charles Mann | .20 | .09 | .03 |
| ☐ 75 Dave Butz | .08 | .04 | .01 |
| ☐ 76 Dexter Manley AP | .08 | .04 | .01 |
| ☐ 77 Darrell Green AP | .25 | .11 | .03 |
| ☐ 78 Curtis Jordan | .05 | .02 | .01 |
| ☐ 79 Cleveland Browns Team Card (Harry Holt Sees Daylight) | .07 | .03 | .01 |
| ☐ 80 Bernie Kosar | 1.00 | .45 | .13 |
| ☐ 81 Curtis Dickey | .08 | .04 | .01 |
| ☐ 82 Kevin Mack | .05 | .02 | .01 |
| ☐ 83 Herman Fontenot | .05 | .02 | .01 |
| ☐ 84 Brian Brennan | .15 | .07 | .02 |
| ☐ 85 Ozzie Newsome | .20 | .09 | .03 |
| ☐ 86 Jeff Gossett | .05 | .02 | .01 |
| ☐ 87 Cody Risien AP | .08 | .04 | .01 |
| ☐ 88 Reggie Camp | .05 | .02 | .01 |
| ☐ 89 Bob Golic | .08 | .04 | .01 |
| ☐ 90 Carl Hairston | .05 | .02 | .01 |
| ☐ 91 Chip Banks | .08 | .04 | .01 |
| ☐ 92 Frank Minnifield | .05 | .02 | .01 |
| ☐ 93 Hanford Dixon AP | .05 | .02 | .01 |
| ☐ 94 Gerald McNeil | .20 | .09 | .03 |
| ☐ 95 Dave Puzzuoli | .05 | .02 | .01 |
| ☐ 96 New England Patriots Team Card (Andre Tippett Gets His Man (Marcus Allen) | .07 | .03 | .01 |
| ☐ 97 Tony Eason | .08 | .04 | .01 |
| ☐ 98 Craig James | .08 | .04 | .01 |
| ☐ 99 Tony Collins | .08 | .04 | .01 |
| ☐ 100 Mosi Tatupu | .08 | .04 | .01 |
| ☐ 101 Stanley Morgan | .08 | .04 | .01 |
| ☐ 102 Irving Fryar | .50 | .23 | .06 |
| ☐ 103 Stephen Starring | .05 | .02 | .01 |
| ☐ 104 Tony Franklin AP | .05 | .02 | .01 |
| ☐ 105 Rich Camarillo | .05 | .02 | .01 |
| ☐ 106 Garin Veris | .05 | .02 | .01 |
| ☐ 107 Andre Tippett AP | .08 | .04 | .01 |
| ☐ 108 Don Blackmon | .05 | .02 | .01 |
| ☐ 109 Ronnie Lippett | .20 | .09 | .03 |
| ☐ 110 Raymond Clayborn | .08 | .04 | .01 |
| ☐ 111 San Francisco 49ers Team Card (Roger Craig Up the Middle) | .12 | .05 | .02 |
| ☐ 112 Joe Montana | 3.50 | 1.55 | .45 |
| ☐ 113 Roger Craig | .20 | .09 | .03 |
| ☐ 114 Joe Cribbs | .08 | .04 | .01 |
| ☐ 115 Jerry Rice AP | 12.00 | 5.50 | 1.50 |
| ☐ 116 Dwight Clark | .20 | .09 | .03 |
| ☐ 117 Ray Wersching | .08 | .04 | .01 |
| ☐ 118 Max Runager | .05 | .02 | .01 |
| ☐ 119 Jeff Stover | .05 | .02 | .01 |
| ☐ 120 Dwaine Board | .05 | .02 | .01 |
| ☐ 121 Tim McKyer | .35 | .16 | .04 |
| ☐ 122 Don Griffin | .40 | .18 | .05 |
| ☐ 123 Ronnie Lott AP | .35 | .16 | .04 |
| ☐ 124 Tom Holmoe | .05 | .02 | .01 |
| ☐ 125 Charles Haley | 1.25 | .55 | .16 |
| ☐ 126 New York Jets Team Card (Mark Gastineau Seeks) | .07 | .03 | .01 |
| ☐ 127 Ken O'Brien | .08 | .04 | .01 |
| ☐ 128 Pat Ryan | .05 | .02 | .01 |
| ☐ 129 Freeman McNeil | .10 | .05 | .01 |
| ☐ 130 Johnny Hector | .30 | .14 | .04 |
| ☐ 131 Al Toon AP | .40 | .18 | .05 |
| ☐ 132 Wesley Walker | .08 | .04 | .01 |
| ☐ 133 Mickey Shuler | .08 | .04 | .01 |
| ☐ 134 Pat Leahy | .08 | .04 | .01 |
| ☐ 135 Mark Gastineau | .08 | .04 | .01 |
| ☐ 136 Joe Klecko | .08 | .04 | .01 |
| ☐ 137 Marty Lyons | .08 | .04 | .01 |
| ☐ 138 Bob Crable | .05 | .02 | .01 |
| ☐ 139 Lance Mehl | .05 | .02 | .01 |
| ☐ 140 Dave Jennings | .08 | .04 | .01 |
| ☐ 141 Harry Hamilton | .05 | .02 | .01 |
| ☐ 142 Lester Lyles | .05 | .02 | .01 |
| ☐ 143 Bobby Humphery UER (Misspelled Humphrey on card front) | .05 | .02 | .01 |
| ☐ 144 Los Angeles Rams Team Card (Eric Dickerson Through the Line) | .15 | .07 | .02 |
| ☐ 145 Jim Everett | 4.00 | 1.80 | .50 |
| ☐ 146 Eric Dickerson AP | .40 | .18 | .05 |
| ☐ 147 Barry Redden | .05 | .02 | .01 |
| ☐ 148 Ron Brown | .08 | .04 | .01 |
| ☐ 149 Kevin House | .08 | .04 | .01 |
| ☐ 150 Henry Ellard | .35 | .16 | .04 |

| | | | |
|---|---|---|---|
| ☐ 151 Doug Smith | .08 | .04 | .01 |
| ☐ 152 Dennis Harrah AP | .05 | .02 | .01 |
| ☐ 153 Jackie Slater | .15 | .07 | .02 |
| ☐ 154 Gary Jeter | .05 | .02 | .01 |
| ☐ 155 Carl Ekern | .05 | .02 | .01 |
| ☐ 156 Mike Wilcher | .05 | .02 | .01 |
| ☐ 157 Jerry Gray | .25 | .11 | .03 |
| ☐ 158 LeRoy Irvin | .05 | .02 | .01 |
| ☐ 159 Nolan Cromwell | .08 | .04 | .01 |
| ☐ 160 Kansas City Chiefs Team Card (Todd Blackledge Hands Off) | .07 | .03 | .01 |
| ☐ 161 Bill Kenney | .08 | .04 | .01 |
| ☐ 162 Stephone Paige | .05 | .02 | .01 |
| ☐ 163 Henry Marshall | .05 | .02 | .01 |
| ☐ 164 Carlos Carson | .08 | .04 | .01 |
| ☐ 165 Nick Lowery | .15 | .07 | .02 |
| ☐ 166 Irv Eatman | .08 | .04 | .01 |
| ☐ 167 Brad Budde | .05 | .02 | .01 |
| ☐ 168 Art Still | .08 | .04 | .01 |
| ☐ 169 Bill Maas AP | .08 | .04 | .01 |
| ☐ 170 Lloyd Burruss | .08 | .04 | .01 |
| ☐ 171 Deron Cherry AP | .08 | .04 | .01 |
| ☐ 172 Seattle Seahawks Team Card (Curt Warner Finds Opening) | .07 | .03 | .01 |
| ☐ 173 Dave Krieg | .15 | .07 | .02 |
| ☐ 174 Curt Warner | .08 | .04 | .01 |
| ☐ 175 John L. Williams | .75 | .35 | .09 |
| ☐ 176 Bobby Joe Edmonds | .15 | .07 | .02 |
| ☐ 177 Steve Largent | .50 | .23 | .06 |
| ☐ 178 Bruce Scholtz | .05 | .02 | .01 |
| ☐ 179 Norm Johnson | .05 | .02 | .01 |
| ☐ 180 Jacob Green | .08 | .04 | .01 |
| ☐ 181 Fredd Young | .05 | .02 | .01 |
| ☐ 182 Dave Brown | .05 | .02 | .01 |
| ☐ 183 Kenny Easley | .08 | .04 | .01 |
| ☐ 184 Cincinnati Bengals Team Card (James Brooks Stiff-Arm) | .07 | .03 | .01 |
| ☐ 185 Boomer Esiason | 1.75 | .80 | .22 |
| ☐ 186 James Brooks | .08 | .04 | .01 |
| ☐ 187 Larry Kinnebrew | .05 | .02 | .01 |
| ☐ 188 Cris Collinsworth | .08 | .04 | .01 |
| ☐ 189 Eddie Brown | .20 | .09 | .03 |
| ☐ 190 Tim McGee | .75 | .35 | .09 |
| ☐ 191 Jim Breech | .05 | .02 | .01 |
| ☐ 192 Anthony Munoz | .08 | .04 | .01 |
| ☐ 193 Max Montoya | .05 | .02 | .01 |
| ☐ 194 Eddie Edwards | .05 | .02 | .01 |
| ☐ 195 Ross Browner | .08 | .04 | .01 |
| ☐ 196 Emanuel King | .05 | .02 | .01 |
| ☐ 197 Louis Breeden | .05 | .02 | .01 |
| ☐ 198 Minnesota Vikings Team Card (Darrin Nelson In Motion) | .07 | .03 | .01 |
| ☐ 199 Tommy Kramer | .08 | .04 | .01 |
| ☐ 200 Darrin Nelson | .08 | .04 | .01 |
| ☐ 201 Allen Rice | .05 | .02 | .01 |
| ☐ 202 Anthony Carter | .35 | .16 | .04 |
| ☐ 203 Leo Lewis | .05 | .02 | .01 |
| ☐ 204 Steve Jordan | .25 | .11 | .03 |
| ☐ 205 Chuck Nelson | .05 | .02 | .01 |
| ☐ 206 Greg Coleman | .05 | .02 | .01 |
| ☐ 207 Gary Zimmerman | .30 | .14 | .04 |
| ☐ 208 Doug Martin | .05 | .02 | .01 |
| ☐ 209 Keith Millard | .08 | .04 | .01 |
| ☐ 210 Issiac Holt | .08 | .04 | .01 |
| ☐ 211 Joey Browner | .15 | .07 | .02 |
| ☐ 212 Rufus Bess | .05 | .02 | .01 |
| ☐ 213 Los Angeles Raiders Team Card (Marcus Allen Quick Feet) | .20 | .09 | .03 |
| ☐ 214 Jim Plunkett | .20 | .09 | .03 |
| ☐ 215 Marcus Allen | .60 | .25 | .08 |
| ☐ 216 Napoleon McCallum | .35 | .16 | .04 |
| ☐ 217 Dokie Williams | .08 | .04 | .01 |
| ☐ 218 Todd Christensen | .08 | .04 | .01 |
| ☐ 219 Chris Bahr | .05 | .02 | .01 |
| ☐ 220 Howie Long | .35 | .16 | .04 |
| ☐ 221 Bill Pickel | .05 | .02 | .01 |
| ☐ 222 Sean Jones | 1.50 | .65 | .19 |
| ☐ 223 Lester Hayes | .08 | .04 | .01 |
| ☐ 224 Mike Haynes | .08 | .04 | .01 |
| ☐ 225 Vann McElroy | .05 | .02 | .01 |
| ☐ 226 Fulton Walker | .05 | .02 | .01 |
| ☐ 227 Passing Leaders Tommy Kramer, Minnesota Vikings Dan Marino, Miami Dolphins | .60 | .25 | .08 |
| ☐ 228 Receiving Leaders | .50 | .23 | .06 |

Jerry Rice,
San Francisco 49ers
Todd Christensen,
Los Angeles Raiders

| | | | |
|---|---|---|---|
| ☐ 229 Rushing Leaders | .25 | .11 | .03 |

Eric Dickerson,
Los Angeles Rams
Curt Warner,
Seattle Seahawks

| | | | |
|---|---|---|---|
| ☐ 230 Scoring Leaders | .07 | .03 | .01 |

Kevin Butler,
Chicago Bears
Tony Franklin,
New England Patriots

| | | | |
|---|---|---|---|
| ☐ 231 Interception Leaders | .12 | .05 | .02 |

Ronnie Lott,
San Francisco 49ers
Deron Cherry,
Kansas City Chiefs

| | | | |
|---|---|---|---|
| ☐ 232 Miami Dolphins | .07 | .03 | .01 |

Team Card
(Reggie Roby Booms It)

| | | | |
|---|---|---|---|
| ☐ 233 Dan Marino AP | 7.50 | 3.40 | .95 |
| ☐ 234 Lorenzo Hampton | .08 | .04 | .01 |
| ☐ 235 Tony Nathan | .08 | .04 | .01 |
| ☐ 236 Mark Duper | .08 | .04 | .01 |
| ☐ 237 Mark Clayton | .40 | .18 | .05 |
| ☐ 238 Nat Moore | .08 | .04 | .01 |
| ☐ 239 Bruce Hardy | .05 | .02 | .01 |
| ☐ 240 Reggie Roby | .08 | .04 | .01 |
| ☐ 241 Roy Foster | .05 | .02 | .01 |
| ☐ 242 Dwight Stephenson AP | .08 | .04 | .01 |
| ☐ 243 Hugh Green | .08 | .04 | .01 |
| ☐ 244 John Offerdahl | .40 | .18 | .05 |
| ☐ 245 Mark Brown | .05 | .02 | .01 |
| ☐ 246 Doug Betters | .05 | .02 | .01 |
| ☐ 247 Bob Baumhower | .05 | .02 | .01 |
| ☐ 248 Atlanta Falcons | .07 | .03 | .01 |

Team Card
(Gerald Riggs Uses
Blockers)

| | | | |
|---|---|---|---|
| ☐ 249 Dave Archer | .05 | .02 | .01 |
| ☐ 250 Gerald Riggs | .08 | .04 | .01 |
| ☐ 251 William Andrews | .08 | .04 | .01 |
| ☐ 252 Charlie Brown | .08 | .04 | .01 |
| ☐ 253 Arthur Cox | .05 | .02 | .01 |
| ☐ 254 Rick Donnelly | .05 | .02 | .01 |
| ☐ 255 Bill Fralic AP | .08 | .04 | .01 |
| ☐ 256 Mike Gann | .05 | .02 | .01 |
| ☐ 257 Rick Bryan | .05 | .02 | .01 |
| ☐ 258 Bret Clark | .05 | .02 | .01 |
| ☐ 259 Mike Pitts | .05 | .02 | .01 |
| ☐ 260 Dallas Cowboys | .20 | .09 | .03 |

Team Card
(Tony Dorsett Cuts)

| | | | |
|---|---|---|---|
| ☐ 261 Danny White | .15 | .07 | .02 |
| ☐ 262 Steve Pelluer | .08 | .04 | .01 |
| ☐ 263 Tony Dorsett | .40 | .18 | .05 |
| ☐ 264 Herschel Walker UER | 2.25 | 1.00 | .30 |

(Stats show 12 TD's
in '86, text says 14)

| | | | |
|---|---|---|---|
| ☐ 265 Timmy Newsome | .05 | .02 | .01 |
| ☐ 266 Tony Hill | .08 | .04 | .01 |
| ☐ 267 Mike Sherrard | .75 | .35 | .09 |
| ☐ 268 Jim Jeffcoat | .08 | .04 | .01 |
| ☐ 269 Ron Fellows | .05 | .02 | .01 |
| ☐ 270 Bill Bates | .08 | .04 | .01 |
| ☐ 271 Michael Downs | .05 | .02 | .01 |
| ☐ 272 New Orleans Saints | .12 | .05 | .02 |

Team Card
(Bobby Hebert Fakes)

| | | | |
|---|---|---|---|
| ☐ 273 Dave Wilson | .08 | .04 | .01 |
| ☐ 274 Rueben Mayes UER | .20 | .09 | .03 |

(Stats show 1353 comple-
tions, should be yards)

| | | | |
|---|---|---|---|
| ☐ 275 Hoby Brenner | .05 | .02 | .01 |
| ☐ 276 Eric Martin | 1.50 | .65 | .19 |
| ☐ 277 Morten Andersen | .25 | .11 | .03 |
| ☐ 278 Brian Hansen | .05 | .02 | .01 |
| ☐ 279 Rickey Jackson | .40 | .18 | .05 |
| ☐ 280 Dave Waymer | .05 | .02 | .01 |
| ☐ 281 Bruce Clark | .05 | .02 | .01 |
| ☐ 282 James Geathers | .15 | .07 | .02 |
| ☐ 283 Pittsburgh Steelers | .07 | .03 | .01 |

Team Card
(Walter Abercrombie
Resists)

| | | | |
|---|---|---|---|
| ☐ 284 Mark Malone | .08 | .04 | .01 |
| ☐ 285 Earnest Jackson | .08 | .04 | .01 |
| ☐ 286 Walter Abercrombie | .05 | .02 | .01 |
| ☐ 287 Louis Lipps | .08 | .04 | .01 |
| ☐ 288 John Stallworth UER | .15 | .07 | .02 |

(Stats only go up
through 1981)

| | | | |
|---|---|---|---|
| ☐ 289 Gary Anderson | .08 | .04 | .01 |
| ☐ 290 Keith Willis | .05 | .02 | .01 |
| ☐ 291 Mike Merriweather | .08 | .04 | .01 |
| ☐ 292 Lupe Sanchez | .05 | .02 | .01 |

| | | | |
|---|---|---|---|
| ☐ 293 Donnie Shell | .08 | .04 | .01 |
| ☐ 294 Philadelphia Eagles | .35 | .16 | .04 |

Team Card
(Keith Byars
Inches Ahead)

| | | | |
|---|---|---|---|
| ☐ 295 Mike Reichenbach | .05 | .02 | .01 |
| ☐ 296 Randall Cunningham | 12.00 | 5.50 | 1.50 |
| ☐ 297 Keith Byars | 3.00 | 1.35 | .40 |
| ☐ 298 Mike Quick | .08 | .04 | .01 |
| ☐ 299 Kenny Jackson | .05 | .02 | .01 |
| ☐ 300 John Teltschik | .05 | .02 | .01 |
| ☐ 301 Reggie White AP | 2.00 | .90 | .25 |
| ☐ 302 Ken Clarke | .05 | .02 | .01 |
| ☐ 303 Greg Brown | .05 | .02 | .01 |
| ☐ 304 Roynell Young | .05 | .02 | .01 |
| ☐ 305 Andre Waters | .50 | .23 | .06 |
| ☐ 306 Houston Oilers | .40 | .18 | .05 |

Team Card
(Warren Moon
Plots Play)

| | | | |
|---|---|---|---|
| ☐ 307 Warren Moon | 2.00 | .90 | .25 |
| ☐ 308 Mike Rozier | .08 | .04 | .01 |
| ☐ 309 Drew Hill | .25 | .11 | .03 |
| ☐ 310 Ernest Givins | 2.00 | .90 | .25 |
| ☐ 311 Lee Johnson | .05 | .02 | .01 |
| ☐ 312 Kent Hill | .05 | .02 | .01 |
| ☐ 313 Dean Steinkuhler | .15 | .07 | .02 |
| ☐ 314 Ray Childress | .50 | .23 | .06 |
| ☐ 315 John Grimsley | .20 | .09 | .03 |
| ☐ 316 Jesse Baker | .05 | .02 | .01 |
| ☐ 317 Detroit Lions | .07 | .03 | .01 |

Team Card
(Eric Hipple Surveys)

| | | | |
|---|---|---|---|
| ☐ 318 Chuck Long | .12 | .05 | .02 |
| ☐ 319 James Jones | .05 | .02 | .01 |
| ☐ 320 Garry James | .08 | .04 | .01 |
| ☐ 321 Jeff Chadwick | .08 | .04 | .01 |
| ☐ 322 Leonard Thompson | .05 | .02 | .01 |
| ☐ 323 Pete Mandley | .05 | .02 | .01 |
| ☐ 324 Jimmie Giles | .08 | .04 | .01 |
| ☐ 325 Herman Hunter | .05 | .02 | .01 |
| ☐ 326 Keith Ferguson | .05 | .02 | .01 |
| ☐ 327 Devon Mitchell | .05 | .02 | .01 |
| ☐ 328 St. Louis Cardinals | .07 | .03 | .01 |

Team Card
(Neil Lomax Audible)

| | | | |
|---|---|---|---|
| ☐ 329 Neil Lomax | .08 | .04 | .01 |
| ☐ 330 Stump Mitchell | .08 | .04 | .01 |
| ☐ 331 Earl Ferrell | .08 | .04 | .01 |
| ☐ 332 Vai Sikahema | .60 | .25 | .08 |
| ☐ 333 Ron Wolfley | .15 | .07 | .02 |
| ☐ 334 J.T. Smith | .08 | .04 | .01 |
| ☐ 335 Roy Green | .08 | .04 | .01 |
| ☐ 336 Al(Bubba) Baker | .08 | .04 | .01 |
| ☐ 337 Freddie Joe Nunn | .08 | .04 | .01 |
| ☐ 338 Cedric Mack | .08 | .04 | .01 |
| ☐ 339 San Diego Chargers | .07 | .03 | .01 |

Team Card
(Gary Anderson Evades)

| | | | |
|---|---|---|---|
| ☐ 340 Dan Fouts | .35 | .16 | .04 |
| ☐ 341 Gary Anderson UER | .25 | .11 | .03 |

(Two Topps logos
on card front)

| | | | |
|---|---|---|---|
| ☐ 342 Wes Chandler | .08 | .04 | .01 |
| ☐ 343 Kellen Winslow | .15 | .07 | .02 |
| ☐ 344 Ralf Mojsiejenko | .05 | .02 | .01 |
| ☐ 345 Rolf Benirschke | .05 | .02 | .01 |
| ☐ 346 Lee Williams | .40 | .18 | .05 |
| ☐ 347 Leslie O'Neal | 3.00 | 1.35 | .40 |
| ☐ 348 Billy Ray Smith | .08 | .04 | .01 |
| ☐ 349 Gill Byrd | .05 | .02 | .01 |
| ☐ 350 Green Bay Packers | .07 | .03 | .01 |

Team Card
(Paul Ott Carruth
Around End)

| | | | |
|---|---|---|---|
| ☐ 351 Randy Wright | .08 | .04 | .01 |
| ☐ 352 Kenneth Davis | 1.75 | .80 | .22 |
| ☐ 353 Gerry Ellis | .05 | .02 | .01 |
| ☐ 354 James Lofton | .40 | .18 | .05 |
| ☐ 355 Phillip Epps | .05 | .02 | .01 |
| ☐ 356 Walter Stanley | .15 | .07 | .02 |
| ☐ 357 Eddie Lee Ivery | .05 | .02 | .01 |
| ☐ 358 Tim Harris | 1.25 | .55 | .16 |
| ☐ 359 Mark Lee UER | .05 | .02 | .01 |

(Red flag, rest of
Packers have yellow)

| | | | |
|---|---|---|---|
| ☐ 360 Mossy Cade | .05 | .02 | .01 |
| ☐ 361 Buffalo Bills | 1.00 | .45 | .13 |

Team Card
(Jim Kelly Works
Ground)

| | | | |
|---|---|---|---|
| ☐ 362 Jim Kelly | 10.00 | 4.50 | 1.25 |
| ☐ 363 Robb Riddick | .05 | .02 | .01 |
| ☐ 364 Greg Bell | .08 | .04 | .01 |
| ☐ 365 Andre Reed | 1.50 | .65 | .19 |
| ☐ 366 Pete Metzelaars | .50 | .23 | .06 |
| ☐ 367 Sean McNanie | .05 | .02 | .01 |

| | | | |
|---|---|---|---|
| ☐ 368 Fred Smerlas | .08 | .04 | .01 |
| ☐ 369 Bruce Smith | 1.50 | .65 | .19 |
| ☐ 370 Darryl Talley | .20 | .09 | .03 |
| ☐ 371 Charles Romes | .05 | .02 | .01 |
| ☐ 372 Indianapolis Colts | .07 | .03 | .01 |
|     Team Card | | | |
|     (Rohn Stark High | | | |
|     and Far) | | | |
| ☐ 373 Jack Trudeau | .25 | .11 | .03 |
| ☐ 374 Gary Hogeboom | .08 | .04 | .01 |
| ☐ 375 Randy McMillan | .05 | .02 | .01 |
| ☐ 376 Albert Bentley | .05 | .02 | .01 |
| ☐ 377 Matt Bouza | .05 | .02 | .01 |
| ☐ 378 Bill Brooks | 2.50 | 1.15 | .30 |
| ☐ 379 Rohn Stark AP | .08 | .04 | .01 |
| ☐ 380 Chris Hinton | .08 | .04 | .01 |
| ☐ 381 Ray Donaldson | .05 | .02 | .01 |
| ☐ 382 Jon Hand | .20 | .09 | .03 |
| ☐ 383 Tampa Bay Buccaneers | .07 | .03 | .01 |
|     Team Card | | | |
|     (James Wilder Braces) | | | |
| ☐ 384 Steve Young | 6.00 | 2.70 | .75 |
| ☐ 385 James Wilder | .08 | .04 | .01 |
| ☐ 386 Frank Garcia | .05 | .02 | .01 |
| ☐ 387 Gerald Carter | .05 | .02 | .01 |
| ☐ 388 Phil Freeman | .05 | .02 | .01 |
| ☐ 389 Calvin Magee | .05 | .02 | .01 |
| ☐ 390 Donald Igwebuike | .05 | .02 | .01 |
| ☐ 391 David Logan | .05 | .02 | .01 |
| ☐ 392 Jeff Davis | .05 | .02 | .01 |
| ☐ 393 Chris Washington | .05 | .02 | .01 |
| ☐ 394 Checklist 1-132 | .10 | .02 | .01 |
| ☐ 395 Checklist 133-264 | .10 | .02 | .01 |
| ☐ 396 Checklist 265-396 | .10 | .02 | .01 |

| | | | |
|---|---|---|---|
| ☐ M Lawrence Taylor | .60 | .24 | .06 |
|     New York Giants | | | |
| ☐ N Al Toon | .35 | .14 | .03 |
|     New York Jets | | | |
| ☐ O Curt Warner | .35 | .14 | .03 |
|     Seattle Seahawks | | | |
| ☐ P Reggie White | 1.00 | .40 | .10 |
|     Philadelphia Eagles | | | |

## 1987 Topps 1000 Yard Club

This glossy insert set was included one per wax pack with the regular issue 1987 Topps football cards. The set features, in order of yards gained, all players achieving 1000 yards gained either rushing or receiving. Cards have a light blue border on front; backs are blue and black print on white card stock. The cards are standard size, 2 1/2" by 3 1/2", and are numbered on the back. Card backs detail statistically the game by game performance of the player in terms of yards gained against each opponent. Ernest Givins appears in his Rookie Card year.

| | MINT | EXC | G-VG |
|---|---|---|---|
| COMPLETE SET (24) | 6.00 | 2.40 | .60 |
| COMMON PLAYER (1-24) | .25 | .10 | .02 |
| ☐ 1 Eric Dickerson | 1.00 | .40 | .10 |
|     Los Angeles Rams | | | |
| ☐ 2 Jerry Rice | 2.50 | 1.00 | .25 |
|     San Francisco 49ers | | | |
| ☐ 3 Joe Morris | .35 | .14 | .03 |
|     New York Giants | | | |
| ☐ 4 Stanley Morgan | .35 | .14 | .03 |
|     New England Patriots | | | |
| ☐ 5 Curt Warner | .35 | .14 | .03 |
|     Seattle Seahawks | | | |
| ☐ 6 Rueben Mayes | .25 | .10 | .02 |
|     New Orleans Saints | | | |
| ☐ 7 Walter Payton | 1.25 | .50 | .12 |
|     Chicago Bears | | | |
| ☐ 8 Gerald Riggs | .35 | .14 | .03 |
|     Atlanta Falcons | | | |
| ☐ 9 Mark Duper | .35 | .14 | .03 |
|     Miami Dolphins | | | |
| ☐ 10 Gary Clark | .75 | .30 | .07 |
|     Washington Redskins | | | |
| ☐ 11 George Rogers | .25 | .10 | .02 |
|     Washington Redskins | | | |
| ☐ 12 Al Toon | .35 | .14 | .03 |
|     New York Jets | | | |
| ☐ 13 Todd Christensen | .35 | .14 | .03 |
|     Los Angeles Raiders | | | |
| ☐ 14 Mark Clayton | .35 | .14 | .03 |
|     Miami Dolphins | | | |
| ☐ 15 Bill Brooks | .50 | .20 | .05 |
|     Indianapolis Colts | | | |
| ☐ 16 Drew Hill | .25 | .10 | .02 |
|     Houston Oilers | | | |
| ☐ 17 James Brooks | .35 | .14 | .03 |
|     Cincinnati Bengals | | | |
| ☐ 18 Steve Largent | 1.00 | .40 | .10 |
|     Seattle Seahawks | | | |
| ☐ 19 Art Monk | .75 | .30 | .07 |
|     Washington Redskins | | | |
| ☐ 20 Ernest Givins | 1.00 | .40 | .10 |
|     Houston Oilers | | | |
| ☐ 21 Cris Collinsworth | .35 | .14 | .03 |
|     Cincinnati Bengals | | | |
| ☐ 22 Wesley Walker | .25 | .10 | .02 |
|     New York Jets | | | |
| ☐ 23 J.T. Smith | .25 | .10 | .02 |
|     St. Louis Cardinals | | | |
| ☐ 24 Mark Bavaro | .35 | .14 | .03 |
|     New York Giants | | | |

## 1987 Topps Box Bottoms

This 16-card set, which measures the standard size 2 1/2" by 3 1/2", was issued on the bottom of 1987 Topps wax pack boxes. The cards are in the same design as the 1987 Topps regular issues except they are bordered in yellow. The backs of the cards are just like the regular card in that they have biographical and complete statistical information. The cards are arranged in alphabetical order and include such stars as Joe Montana, Walter Payton, and Jerry Rice.

| | MINT | EXC | G-VG |
|---|---|---|---|
| COMPLETE SET (16) | 8.00 | 3.25 | .80 |
| COMMON PLAYER (A-P) | .25 | .10 | .02 |
| ☐ A Mark Bavaro | .35 | .14 | .03 |
|     New York Giants | | | |
| ☐ B Todd Christensen | .50 | .20 | .05 |
|     Los Angeles Raiders | | | |
| ☐ C Eric Dickerson | .75 | .30 | .07 |
|     Los Angeles Rams | | | |
| ☐ D John Elway | 1.50 | .60 | .15 |
|     Denver Broncos | | | |
| ☐ E Rulon Jones | .25 | .10 | .02 |
|     Denver Broncos | | | |
| ☐ F Dan Marino | 3.00 | 1.20 | .30 |
|     Miami Dolphins | | | |
| ☐ G Karl Mecklenburg | .35 | .14 | .03 |
|     Denver Broncos | | | |
| ☐ H Joe Montana | 3.00 | 1.20 | .30 |
|     San Francisco 49ers | | | |
| ☐ I Joe Morris | .35 | .14 | .03 |
|     New York Giants | | | |
| ☐ J Walter Payton | 1.25 | .50 | .12 |
|     Chicago Bears | | | |
| ☐ K Jerry Rice | 3.00 | 1.20 | .30 |
|     San Francisco 49ers | | | |
| ☐ L Phil Simms | .50 | .20 | .05 |
|     New York Giants | | | |

# 1987 Topps American/UK

This mini-size version of 1987 football cards was distributed in the United Kingdom for British fans of American football. Cards measure only 2 1/8" by 3". The photos used are different from the regular issue Topps football cards, although the style is essentially the same. The card backs are colorful and feature a "Talking Football" section where a football term is explained. A collector box (with a complete set checklist on the side) is also available. The cards are arranged according to teams and checklisted below as follows: New York Giants (1-5), Denver Broncos (6-9), Chicago Bears (10-15), Washington Redskins (16-21), Cleveland Browns (22-24), New England Patriots (25-28), San Francisco 49ers (29-31), New York Jets (32-35), Los Angeles Rams (36-37), Kansas City Chiefs (38-39), Seattle Seahawks (40-42), Cincinnati Bengals (43-46), Minnesota Vikings (47), Los Angeles Raiders (48-50), Miami Dolphins (51-54), Atlanta Falcons (55-56), Dallas Cowboys (57-58), New Orleans Saints (59), Pittsburgh Steelers (60), Philadelphia Eagles (61), Houston Oilers (62-64), Detroit Lions (65-66), St. Louis Cardinals (67-68), San Diego Chargers (69-70), Green Bay Packers (71), Buffalo Bills (72-73), and Indianapolis Colts (74-75). Cards 76 through 87 are puzzle pieces, combining to show team action photos on their fronts and William "The Refrigerator" Perry on their backs.

|  | MINT | EXC | G-VG |
|---|---|---|---|
| COMPLETE SET (88) | 45.00 | 18.00 | 4.50 |
| COMMON PLAYER (1-88) | .15 | .06 | .01 |
| ☐ 1 Phil Simms | .75 | .30 | .07 |
| ☐ 2 Joe Morris | .35 | .14 | .03 |
| ☐ 3 Mark Bavaro | .25 | .10 | .02 |
| ☐ 4 Sean Landeta | .15 | .06 | .01 |
| ☐ 5 Lawrence Taylor | 1.00 | .40 | .10 |
| ☐ 6 John Elway | 4.00 | 1.60 | .40 |
| ☐ 7 Sammy Winder | .15 | .06 | .01 |
| ☐ 8 Rulon Jones | .15 | .06 | .01 |
| ☐ 9 Karl Mecklenburg | .25 | .10 | .02 |
| ☐ 10 Walter Payton | 4.00 | 1.60 | .40 |
| ☐ 11 Dennis Gentry | .15 | .06 | .01 |
| ☐ 12 Kevin Butler | .15 | .06 | .01 |
| ☐ 13 Jim Covert | .15 | .06 | .01 |
| ☐ 14 Richard Dent | .35 | .14 | .03 |
| ☐ 15 Mike Singletary | .50 | .20 | .05 |
| ☐ 16 Jay Schroeder | .50 | .20 | .05 |
| ☐ 17 George Rogers | .25 | .10 | .02 |
| ☐ 18 Gary Clark | .50 | .20 | .05 |
| ☐ 19 Art Monk | .50 | .20 | .05 |
| ☐ 20 Dexter Manley | .15 | .06 | .01 |
| ☐ 21 Darrell Green | .35 | .14 | .03 |
| ☐ 22 Bernie Kosar | 1.25 | .50 | .12 |
| ☐ 23 Cody Risien | .15 | .06 | .01 |
| ☐ 24 Hanford Dixon | .15 | .06 | .01 |
| ☐ 25 Tony Eason | .25 | .10 | .02 |
| ☐ 26 Stanley Morgan | .25 | .10 | .02 |
| ☐ 27 Tony Franklin | .15 | .06 | .01 |
| ☐ 28 Andre Tippett | .25 | .10 | .02 |
| ☐ 29 Joe Montana | 8.00 | 3.25 | .80 |
| ☐ 30 Jerry Rice | 8.00 | 3.25 | .80 |
| ☐ 31 Ronnie Lott | .75 | .30 | .07 |
| ☐ 32 Ken O'Brien | .25 | .10 | .02 |
| ☐ 33 Freeman McNeil | .25 | .10 | .02 |
| ☐ 34 Al Toon | .25 | .10 | .02 |
| ☐ 35 Wesley Walker | .25 | .10 | .02 |
| ☐ 36 Eric Dickerson | 2.00 | .80 | .20 |
| ☐ 37 Dennis Harrah | .15 | .06 | .01 |
| ☐ 38 Bill Maas | .15 | .06 | .01 |
| ☐ 39 Deron Cherry | .25 | .10 | .02 |
| ☐ 40 Curt Warner | .25 | .10 | .02 |
| ☐ 41 Bobby Joe Edmonds | .25 | .10 | .02 |
| ☐ 42 Steve Largent | 2.00 | .80 | .20 |
| ☐ 43 Boomer Esiason | 1.50 | .60 | .15 |
| ☐ 44 James Brooks | .25 | .10 | .02 |
| ☐ 45 Cris Collinsworth | .25 | .10 | .02 |
| ☐ 46 Tim McGee | .35 | .14 | .03 |
| ☐ 47 Tommy Kramer | .25 | .10 | .02 |
| ☐ 48 Marcus Allen | .75 | .30 | .07 |
| ☐ 49 Todd Christensen | .35 | .14 | .03 |
| ☐ 50 Sean Jones | .35 | .14 | .03 |
| ☐ 51 Dan Marino | 8.00 | 3.25 | .80 |
| ☐ 52 Mark Duper | .25 | .10 | .02 |
| ☐ 53 Mark Clayton | .35 | .14 | .03 |
| ☐ 54 Dwight Stephenson | .25 | .10 | .02 |
| ☐ 55 Gerald Riggs | .25 | .10 | .02 |
| ☐ 56 Bill Fralic | .25 | .10 | .02 |
| ☐ 57 Tony Dorsett | 1.25 | .50 | .12 |
| ☐ 58 Herschel Walker | 1.50 | .60 | .15 |
| ☐ 59 Rueben Mayes | .25 | .10 | .02 |
| ☐ 60 Lupe Sanchez | .15 | .06 | .01 |
| ☐ 61 Reggie White | 2.00 | .80 | .20 |
| ☐ 62 Warren Moon | 3.00 | 1.20 | .30 |
| ☐ 63 Ernest Givins | 1.50 | .60 | .15 |
| ☐ 64 Drew Hill | .25 | .10 | .02 |
| ☐ 65 Jeff Chadwick | .25 | .10 | .02 |
| ☐ 66 Herman Hunter | .15 | .06 | .01 |
| ☐ 67 Vai Sikahema | .25 | .10 | .02 |
| ☐ 68 J.T. Smith | .15 | .06 | .01 |
| ☐ 69 Dan Fouts | .75 | .30 | .07 |
| ☐ 70 Lee Williams | .50 | .20 | .05 |
| ☐ 71 Randy Wright | .25 | .10 | .02 |
| ☐ 72 Jim Kelly | 8.00 | 3.25 | .80 |
| ☐ 73 Bruce Smith | .75 | .30 | .07 |
| ☐ 74 Bill Brooks | .35 | .14 | .03 |
| ☐ 75 Rohn Stark | .15 | .06 | .01 |
| ☐ 76 Team Action | .15 | .06 | .01 |
| ☐ 77 Team Action | .15 | .06 | .01 |
| ☐ 78 Team Action | .15 | .06 | .01 |
| ☐ 79 Team Action | .15 | .06 | .01 |
| ☐ 80 Team Action | .15 | .06 | .01 |
| ☐ 81 Team Action | .15 | .06 | .01 |
| ☐ 82 Team Action | .15 | .06 | .01 |
| ☐ 83 Team Action | .15 | .06 | .01 |
| ☐ 84 Team Action | .15 | .06 | .01 |
| ☐ 85 Team Action | .15 | .06 | .01 |
| ☐ 86 Team Action | .15 | .06 | .01 |
| ☐ 87 Team Action | .15 | .06 | .01 |
| ☐ 88 Checklist Card | .15 | .06 | .01 |

# 1988 Topps

This 396-card set is essentially in team order as follows: Washington Redskins (7-21), Denver Broncos (22-36), San Francisco 49ers (37-53), New Orleans Saints (54-67), Chicago Bears (68-84), Cleveland Browns (85-101), Houston Oilers (102-115), Indianapolis Colts (116-129), Seattle Seahawks (130-145), Minnesota Vikings (146-161), Pittsburgh Steelers (162-174), New England Patriots (175-188), Miami Dolphins (189-202), San Diego Chargers (203-214), Buffalo Bills (220-232), Philadelphia Eagles (233-247), Phoenix Cardinals (248-258), Dallas Cowboys (259-270), New York Giants (271-286), Los Angeles Rams (287-300), New York Jets (301-313), Green Bay Packers (314-324), Los Angeles Raiders (325-338), Cincinnati Bengals (339-349), Tampa Bay Buccaneers (350-360), Kansas City Chiefs (361-371), Detroit Lions (372-382), and Atlanta Falcons (383-393). The cards are standard size 2 1/2" by 3 1/2". The Team Leader (TL) cards show an action scene for each team; the caption and featured players are identified in the checklist below. All-Pro selections are identified on the player's regular card. Some of the younger players are also designated by Topps as "Super Rookies" (SR). The wax box cards carry the theme of current pro players who were past college trophy winners, e.g., Heisman, Outland, or Lombardi. They are not included in the complete set price below. The key Rookie Cards in this set are Neal Anderson, Cornelius Bennett, Shane Conlan, Chris Doleman, Curtis Duncan, Dalton Hilliard, Bo Jackson, Seth Joyner, Christian Okoye, Tom Rathman, Clyde Simmons, Pat Swilling, and Vinny Testaverde.

|  | MINT | EXC | G-VG |
|---|---|---|---|
| COMPLETE SET (396) | 10.00 | 4.50 | 1.25 |
| COMPLETE FACT.SET (396) | 14.00 | 6.25 | 1.75 |
| COMMON PLAYER (1-396) | .04 | .02 | .01 |
| ☐ 1 Super Bowl XXII | .08 | .04 | .01 |
| Redskins 42, | | | |
| Broncos 10 | | | |
| (Redskins celebrating) | | | |
| ☐ 2 Vencie Glenn RB | .05 | .02 | .01 |
| Longest Interception | | | |
| Return | | | |
| San Diego Chargers | | | |
| ☐ 3 Steve Largent RB | .15 | .07 | .02 |
| Most Receptions, | | | |
| Career | | | |
| Seattle Seahawks | | | |
| ☐ 4 Joe Montana RB | .75 | .35 | .09 |
| Most Consecutive | | | |
| Pass Completions | | | |
| San Francisco 49ers | | | |
| ☐ 5 Walter Payton RB | .30 | .14 | .04 |
| Most Rushing | | | |
| Touchdowns, Career | | | |
| Chicago Bears | | | |
| ☐ 6 Jerry Rice RB | .75 | .35 | .09 |
| Most Touchdown | | | |
| Receptions, Season | | | |
| San Francisco 49ers | | | |
| ☐ 7 Redskins TL | .05 | .02 | .01 |
| Kelvin Bryant Sees | | | |
| Daylight | | | |
| ☐ 8 Doug Williams | .04 | .02 | .01 |
| ☐ 9 George Rogers | .06 | .03 | .01 |
| ☐ 10 Kelvin Bryant | .06 | .03 | .01 |
| ☐ 11 Timmy Smith SR | .06 | .03 | .01 |
| ☐ 12 Art Monk | .15 | .07 | .02 |
| ☐ 13 Gary Clark | .35 | .16 | .04 |
| ☐ 14 Ricky Sanders | .50 | .23 | .06 |
| ☐ 15 Steve Cox | .04 | .02 | .01 |
| ☐ 16 Joe Jacoby | .06 | .03 | .01 |
| ☐ 17 Charles Mann | .04 | .02 | .01 |
| ☐ 18 Dave Butz | .06 | .03 | .01 |
| ☐ 19 Darrell Green AP | .06 | .03 | .01 |
| ☐ 20 Dexter Manley | .06 | .03 | .01 |
| ☐ 21 Barry Wilburn | .04 | .02 | .01 |
| ☐ 22 Broncos TL | .05 | .02 | .01 |
| Sammy Winder Winds | | | |
| Through | | | |
| ☐ 23 John Elway AP | .75 | .35 | .09 |
| ☐ 24 Sammy Winder | .04 | .02 | .01 |
| ☐ 25 Vance Johnson | .15 | .07 | .02 |
| ☐ 26 Mark Jackson | .75 | .35 | .09 |
| ☐ 27 Ricky Nattiel SR | .04 | .02 | .01 |
| ☐ 28 Clarence Kay | .04 | .02 | .01 |
| ☐ 29 Rich Karlis | .04 | .02 | .01 |
| ☐ 30 Keith Bishop | .04 | .02 | .01 |
| ☐ 31 Mike Horan | .04 | .02 | .01 |
| ☐ 32 Rulon Jones | .04 | .02 | .01 |
| ☐ 33 Karl Mecklenburg | .04 | .02 | .01 |
| ☐ 34 Jim Ryan | .04 | .02 | .01 |
| ☐ 35 Mark Haynes | .06 | .03 | .01 |
| ☐ 36 Mike Harden | .04 | .02 | .01 |
| ☐ 37 49ers TL | .08 | .04 | .01 |
| Roger Craig Gallops | | | |
| For Yardage | | | |
| ☐ 38 Joe Montana | 1.25 | .55 | .16 |
| ☐ 39 Steve Young | 1.00 | .45 | .13 |
| ☐ 40 Roger Craig | .15 | .07 | .02 |
| ☐ 41 Tom Rathman | .40 | .18 | .05 |
| ☐ 42 Joe Cribbs | .06 | .03 | .01 |
| ☐ 43 Jerry Rice AP | 1.25 | .55 | .16 |
| ☐ 44 Mike Wilson | .04 | .02 | .01 |
| ☐ 45 Ron Heller | .10 | .05 | .01 |
| ☐ 46 Ray Wersching | .06 | .03 | .01 |
| ☐ 47 Michael Carter | .06 | .03 | .01 |
| ☐ 48 Dwaine Board | .04 | .02 | .01 |
| ☐ 49 Michael Walter | .06 | .03 | .01 |
| ☐ 50 Don Griffin | .06 | .03 | .01 |
| ☐ 51 Ronnie Lott | .25 | .11 | .03 |
| ☐ 52 Charles Haley | .20 | .09 | .03 |
| ☐ 53 Dana McLemore | .06 | .03 | .01 |
| ☐ 54 Saints TL | .08 | .04 | .01 |
| Bobby Hebert Hands Off | | | |
| ☐ 55 Bobby Hebert | .25 | .11 | .03 |
| ☐ 56 Rueben Mayes | .06 | .03 | .01 |
| ☐ 57 Dalton Hilliard | .30 | .14 | .04 |
| ☐ 58 Eric Martin | .25 | .11 | .03 |
| ☐ 59 John Tice | .10 | .05 | .01 |
| ☐ 60 Brad Edelman | .04 | .02 | .01 |
| ☐ 61 Morten Andersen AP | .10 | .05 | .01 |
| ☐ 62 Brian Hansen | .04 | .02 | .01 |
| ☐ 63 Mel Gray | .25 | .11 | .03 |
| ☐ 64 Rickey Jackson | .20 | .09 | .03 |
| ☐ 65 Sam Mills | .30 | .14 | .04 |
| ☐ 66 Pat Swilling | 1.00 | .45 | .13 |
| ☐ 67 Dave Waymer | .04 | .02 | .01 |
| ☐ 68 Bears TL | .08 | .04 | .01 |
| Willie Gault Powers | | | |
| Forward | | | |
| ☐ 69 Jim McMahon | .15 | .07 | .02 |
| ☐ 70 Mike Tomczak | .25 | .11 | .03 |
| ☐ 71 Neal Anderson | .75 | .35 | .09 |
| ☐ 72 Willie Gault | .06 | .03 | .01 |
| ☐ 73 Dennis Gentry | .06 | .03 | .01 |
| ☐ 74 Dennis McKinnon | .04 | .02 | .01 |
| ☐ 75 Kevin Butler | .04 | .02 | .01 |
| ☐ 76 Jim Covert | .06 | .03 | .01 |
| ☐ 77 Jay Hilgenberg | .04 | .02 | .01 |
| ☐ 78 Steve McMichael | .06 | .03 | .01 |
| ☐ 79 William Perry | .06 | .03 | .01 |
| ☐ 80 Richard Dent | .15 | .07 | .02 |
| ☐ 81 Ron Rivera | .04 | .02 | .01 |
| ☐ 82 Mike Singletary AP | .15 | .07 | .02 |
| ☐ 83 Dan Hampton | .06 | .03 | .01 |
| ☐ 84 Dave Duerson | .06 | .03 | .01 |
| ☐ 85 Browns TL | .08 | .04 | .01 |
| Bernie Kosar Lets | | | |
| It Go | | | |
| ☐ 86 Bernie Kosar | .25 | .11 | .03 |
| ☐ 87 Earnest Byner | .25 | .11 | .03 |
| ☐ 88 Kevin Mack | .06 | .03 | .01 |
| ☐ 89 Webster Slaughter | .75 | .35 | .09 |
| ☐ 90 Gerald McNeil | .04 | .02 | .01 |
| ☐ 91 Brian Brennan | .04 | .02 | .01 |
| ☐ 92 Ozzie Newsome | .15 | .07 | .02 |
| ☐ 93 Cody Risien | .06 | .03 | .01 |
| ☐ 94 Bob Golic | .04 | .02 | .01 |
| ☐ 95 Carl Hairston | .04 | .02 | .01 |
| ☐ 96 Mike Johnson | .15 | .07 | .02 |
| ☐ 97 Clay Matthews | .08 | .04 | .01 |
| ☐ 98 Frank Minnifield | .04 | .02 | .01 |
| ☐ 99 Hanford Dixon AP | .04 | .02 | .01 |
| ☐ 100 Dave Puzzuoli | .04 | .02 | .01 |
| ☐ 101 Felix Wright | .10 | .05 | .01 |
| ☐ 102 Oilers TL | .20 | .09 | .03 |
| Warren Moon Over | | | |
| The Top | | | |
| ☐ 103 Warren Moon | .60 | .25 | .08 |
| ☐ 104 Mike Rozier | .06 | .03 | .01 |
| ☐ 105 Alonzo Highsmith SR | .10 | .05 | .01 |
| ☐ 106 Drew Hill | .08 | .04 | .01 |
| ☐ 107 Ernest Givins | .40 | .18 | .05 |
| ☐ 108 Curtis Duncan | .50 | .23 | .06 |
| ☐ 109 Tony Zendejas | .04 | .02 | .01 |
| ☐ 110 Mike Munchak AP | .06 | .03 | .01 |
| ☐ 111 Kent Hill | .04 | .02 | .01 |
| ☐ 112 Ray Childress | .06 | .03 | .01 |
| ☐ 113 Al Smith | .25 | .11 | .03 |
| ☐ 114 Keith Bostic | .04 | .02 | .01 |
| ☐ 115 Jeff Donaldson | .04 | .02 | .01 |
| ☐ 116 Colts TL | .10 | .05 | .01 |
| Eric Dickerson Finds | | | |
| Opening | | | |
| ☐ 117 Jack Trudeau | .06 | .03 | .01 |
| ☐ 118 Eric Dickerson AP | .20 | .09 | .03 |
| ☐ 119 Albert Bentley | .06 | .03 | .01 |
| ☐ 120 Matt Bouza | .04 | .02 | .01 |
| ☐ 121 Bill Brooks | .30 | .14 | .04 |
| ☐ 122 Dean Biasucci | .10 | .05 | .01 |
| ☐ 123 Chris Hinton | .06 | .03 | .01 |
| ☐ 124 Ray Donaldson | .04 | .02 | .01 |
| ☐ 125 Ron Solt | .04 | .02 | .01 |
| ☐ 126 Donnell Thompson | .04 | .02 | .01 |
| ☐ 127 Barry Krauss | .04 | .02 | .01 |
| ☐ 128 Duane Bickett | .04 | .02 | .01 |
| ☐ 129 Mike Prior | .10 | .05 | .01 |
| ☐ 130 Seahawks TL | .05 | .02 | .01 |
| Curt Warner Follows | | | |
| Blocking | | | |
| ☐ 131 Dave Krieg | .06 | .03 | .01 |
| ☐ 132 Curt Warner | .06 | .03 | .01 |
| ☐ 133 John L. Williams | .15 | .07 | .02 |
| ☐ 134 Bobby Joe Edmonds | .06 | .03 | .01 |
| ☐ 135 Steve Largent | .30 | .14 | .04 |
| ☐ 136 Raymond Butler | .04 | .02 | .01 |
| ☐ 137 Norm Johnson | .04 | .02 | .01 |
| ☐ 138 Ruben Rodriguez | .04 | .02 | .01 |
| ☐ 139 Blair Bush | .04 | .02 | .01 |
| ☐ 140 Jacob Green | .06 | .03 | .01 |
| ☐ 141 Joe Nash | .04 | .02 | .01 |
| ☐ 142 Jeff Bryant | .04 | .02 | .01 |
| ☐ 143 Fredd Young AP | .04 | .02 | .01 |
| ☐ 144 Brian Bosworth SR | .10 | .05 | .01 |
| ☐ 145 Kenny Easley AP | .06 | .03 | .01 |
| ☐ 146 Vikings TL | .05 | .02 | .01 |
| Tommy Kramer Spots | | | |
| His Man | | | |
| ☐ 147 Wade Wilson | .40 | .18 | .05 |
| ☐ 148 Tommy Kramer | .06 | .03 | .01 |
| ☐ 149 Darrin Nelson | .06 | .03 | .01 |
| ☐ 150 D.J. Dozier SR | .04 | .02 | .01 |
| ☐ 151 Anthony Carter | .15 | .07 | .02 |
| ☐ 152 Leo Lewis | .04 | .02 | .01 |
| ☐ 153 Steve Jordan | .06 | .03 | .01 |
| ☐ 154 Gary Zimmerman | .06 | .03 | .01 |

| | | | |
|---|---|---|---|
| ☐ 155 Chuck Nelson | .04 | .02 | .01 |
| ☐ 156 Henry Thomas SR | .35 | .16 | .04 |
| ☐ 157 Chris Doleman | .50 | .23 | .06 |
| ☐ 158 Scott Studwell | .10 | .05 | .01 |
| ☐ 159 Jesse Solomon | .04 | .02 | .01 |
| ☐ 160 Joey Browner AP | .04 | .02 | .01 |
| ☐ 161 Neal Guggemos | .04 | .02 | .01 |
| ☐ 162 Steelers TL | .08 | .04 | .01 |
| Louis Lipps In a Crowd | | | |
| ☐ 163 Mark Malone | .06 | .03 | .01 |
| ☐ 164 Walter Abercrombie | .04 | .02 | .01 |
| ☐ 165 Earnest Jackson | .06 | .03 | .01 |
| ☐ 166 Frank Pollard | .04 | .02 | .01 |
| ☐ 167 Dwight Stone | .20 | .09 | .03 |
| ☐ 168 Gary Anderson | .06 | .03 | .01 |
| ☐ 169 Harry Newsome | .04 | .02 | .01 |
| ☐ 170 Keith Willis | .04 | .02 | .01 |
| ☐ 171 Keith Gary | .04 | .02 | .01 |
| ☐ 172 David Little | .10 | .05 | .01 |
| ☐ 173 Mike Merriweather | .06 | .03 | .01 |
| ☐ 174 Dwayne Woodruff | .04 | .02 | .01 |
| ☐ 175 Patriots TL | .07 | .03 | .01 |
| Irving Fryar One on One | | | |
| ☐ 176 Steve Grogan | .10 | .05 | .01 |
| ☐ 177 Tony Eason | .06 | .03 | .01 |
| ☐ 178 Tony Collins | .06 | .03 | .01 |
| ☐ 179 Mosi Tatupu | .06 | .03 | .01 |
| ☐ 180 Stanley Morgan | .06 | .03 | .01 |
| ☐ 181 Irving Fryar | .20 | .09 | .03 |
| ☐ 182 Stephen Starring | .04 | .02 | .01 |
| ☐ 183 Tony Franklin | .04 | .02 | .01 |
| ☐ 184 Rich Camarillo | .04 | .02 | .01 |
| ☐ 185 Garin Veris | .04 | .02 | .01 |
| ☐ 186 Andre Tippett AP | .06 | .03 | .01 |
| ☐ 187 Ronnie Lippett | .04 | .02 | .01 |
| ☐ 188 Fred Marion | .04 | .02 | .01 |
| ☐ 189 Dolphins TL | .40 | .18 | .05 |
| Dan Marino Play-Action Pass | | | |
| ☐ 190 Dan Marino | 1.25 | .55 | .16 |
| ☐ 191 Troy Stradford SR | .04 | .02 | .01 |
| ☐ 192 Lorenzo Hampton | .04 | .02 | .01 |
| ☐ 193 Mark Duper | .08 | .04 | .01 |
| ☐ 194 Mark Clayton | .20 | .09 | .03 |
| ☐ 195 Reggie Roby | .06 | .03 | .01 |
| ☐ 196 Dwight Stephenson AP | .06 | .03 | .01 |
| ☐ 197 T.J. Turner | .06 | .03 | .01 |
| ☐ 198 John Bosa SR | .04 | .02 | .01 |
| ☐ 199 Jackie Shipp | .04 | .02 | .01 |
| ☐ 200 John Offerdahl | .04 | .02 | .01 |
| ☐ 201 Mark Brown | .04 | .02 | .01 |
| ☐ 202 Paul Lankford | .04 | .02 | .01 |
| ☐ 203 Chargers TL | .05 | .02 | .01 |
| Kellen Winslow Sure Hands | | | |
| ☐ 204 Tim Spencer | .04 | .02 | .01 |
| ☐ 205 Gary Anderson | .04 | .02 | .01 |
| ☐ 206 Curtis Adams | .04 | .02 | .01 |
| ☐ 207 Lionel James | .06 | .03 | .01 |
| ☐ 208 Chip Banks | .06 | .03 | .01 |
| ☐ 209 Kellen Winslow | .10 | .05 | .01 |
| ☐ 210 Ralf Mojsiejenko | .04 | .02 | .01 |
| ☐ 211 Jim Lachey | .04 | .02 | .01 |
| ☐ 212 Lee Williams | .04 | .02 | .01 |
| ☐ 213 Billy Ray Smith | .06 | .03 | .01 |
| ☐ 214 Vencie Glenn | .04 | .02 | .01 |
| ☐ 215 Passing Leaders | .50 | .23 | .06 |
| Bernie Kosar Joe Montana | | | |
| ☐ 216 Receiving Leaders | .08 | .04 | .01 |
| Al Toon J.T. Smith | | | |
| ☐ 217 Rushing Leaders | .12 | .05 | .02 |
| Charles White Eric Dickerson | | | |
| ☐ 218 Scoring Leaders | .30 | .14 | .04 |
| Jim Breech Jerry Rice | | | |
| ☐ 219 Interception Leaders | .05 | .02 | .01 |
| Keith Bostic Mark Kelso Mike Prior Barry Wilburn | | | |
| ☐ 220 Bills TL | .25 | .11 | .03 |
| Jim Kelly Plots His Course | | | |
| ☐ 221 Jim Kelly | 1.00 | .45 | .13 |
| ☐ 222 Ronnie Harmon | .35 | .16 | .04 |
| ☐ 223 Robb Riddick | .04 | .02 | .01 |
| ☐ 224 Andre Reed | .40 | .18 | .05 |
| ☐ 225 Chris Burkett | .35 | .16 | .04 |
| ☐ 226 Pete Metzelaars | .04 | .02 | .01 |
| ☐ 227 Bruce Smith AP | .40 | .18 | .05 |
| ☐ 228 Darryl Talley | .04 | .02 | .01 |
| ☐ 229 Eugene Marve | .04 | .02 | .01 |
| ☐ 230 Cornelius Bennett SR | 1.00 | .45 | .13 |
| ☐ 231 Mark Kelso | .15 | .07 | .02 |

| | | | |
|---|---|---|---|
| ☐ 232 Shane Conlan SR | .50 | .23 | .06 |
| ☐ 233 Eagles TL | .15 | .07 | .02 |
| Randall Cunningham QB Keeper | | | |
| ☐ 234 Randall Cunningham | .60 | .25 | .08 |
| ☐ 235 Keith Byars | .40 | .18 | .05 |
| ☐ 236 Anthony Toney | .04 | .02 | .01 |
| ☐ 237 Mike Quick | .06 | .03 | .01 |
| ☐ 238 Kenny Jackson | .04 | .02 | .01 |
| ☐ 239 John Spagnola | .04 | .02 | .01 |
| ☐ 240 Paul McFadden | .04 | .02 | .01 |
| ☐ 241 Reggie White AP | .50 | .23 | .06 |
| ☐ 242 Ken Clarke | .04 | .02 | .01 |
| ☐ 243 Mike Pitts | .04 | .02 | .01 |
| ☐ 244 Clyde Simmons | .60 | .25 | .08 |
| ☐ 245 Seth Joyner | .75 | .35 | .09 |
| ☐ 246 Andre Waters | .04 | .02 | .01 |
| ☐ 247 Jerome Brown SR | .30 | .14 | .04 |
| ☐ 248 Cardinals TL | .05 | .02 | .01 |
| Stump Mitchell On the Run | | | |
| ☐ 249 Neil Lomax | .06 | .03 | .01 |
| ☐ 250 Stump Mitchell | .06 | .03 | .01 |
| ☐ 251 Earl Ferrell | .04 | .02 | .01 |
| ☐ 252 Vai Sikahema | .06 | .03 | .01 |
| ☐ 253 J.T. Smith AP | .04 | .02 | .01 |
| ☐ 254 Roy Green | .06 | .03 | .01 |
| ☐ 255 Robert Awalt SR | .04 | .02 | .01 |
| ☐ 256 Freddie Joe Nunn | .06 | .03 | .01 |
| ☐ 257 Leonard Smith | .04 | .02 | .01 |
| ☐ 258 Travis Curtis | .04 | .02 | .01 |
| ☐ 259 Cowboys TL | .15 | .07 | .02 |
| Herschel Walker Around End | | | |
| ☐ 260 Danny White | .10 | .05 | .01 |
| ☐ 261 Herschel Walker | .25 | .11 | .03 |
| ☐ 262 Tony Dorsett | .25 | .11 | .03 |
| ☐ 263 Doug Cosbie | .06 | .03 | .01 |
| ☐ 264 Roger Ruzek | .04 | .02 | .01 |
| ☐ 265 Darryl Clack | .06 | .03 | .01 |
| ☐ 266 Ed Too Tall Jones | .10 | .05 | .01 |
| ☐ 267 Jim Jeffcoat | .06 | .03 | .01 |
| ☐ 268 Everson Walls | .04 | .02 | .01 |
| ☐ 269 Bill Bates | .04 | .02 | .01 |
| ☐ 270 Michael Downs | .04 | .02 | .01 |
| ☐ 271 Giants TL | .05 | .02 | .01 |
| Mark Bavaro Drives Ahead | | | |
| ☐ 272 Phil Simms | .25 | .11 | .03 |
| ☐ 273 Joe Morris | .06 | .03 | .01 |
| ☐ 274 Lee Rouson | .04 | .02 | .01 |
| ☐ 275 George Adams | .04 | .02 | .01 |
| ☐ 276 Lionel Manuel | .04 | .02 | .01 |
| ☐ 277 Mark Bavaro AP | .06 | .03 | .01 |
| ☐ 278 Raul Allegre | .04 | .02 | .01 |
| ☐ 279 Sean Landeta | .06 | .03 | .01 |
| ☐ 280 Erik Howard | .04 | .02 | .01 |
| ☐ 281 Leonard Marshall | .04 | .02 | .01 |
| ☐ 282 Carl Banks AP | .04 | .02 | .01 |
| ☐ 283 Pepper Johnson | .04 | .02 | .01 |
| ☐ 284 Harry Carson | .06 | .03 | .01 |
| ☐ 285 Lawrence Taylor | .25 | .11 | .03 |
| ☐ 286 Terry Kinard | .06 | .03 | .01 |
| ☐ 287 Rams TL | .15 | .07 | .02 |
| Jim Everett Races Downfield | | | |
| ☐ 288 Jim Everett | .30 | .14 | .04 |
| ☐ 289 Charles White AP | .06 | .03 | .01 |
| ☐ 290 Ron Brown | .04 | .02 | .01 |
| ☐ 291 Henry Ellard | .20 | .09 | .03 |
| ☐ 292 Mike Lansford | .04 | .02 | .01 |
| ☐ 293 Dale Hatcher | .04 | .02 | .01 |
| ☐ 294 Doug Smith | .06 | .03 | .01 |
| ☐ 295 Jackie Slater AP | .06 | .03 | .01 |
| ☐ 296 Jim Collins | .04 | .02 | .01 |
| ☐ 297 Jerry Gray | .04 | .02 | .01 |
| ☐ 298 LeRoy Irvin | .04 | .02 | .01 |
| ☐ 299 Nolan Cromwell | .06 | .03 | .01 |
| ☐ 300 Kevin Greene | .50 | .23 | .06 |
| ☐ 301 Jets TL | .05 | .02 | .01 |
| Ken O'Brien Reads Defense | | | |
| ☐ 302 Ken O'Brien | .06 | .03 | .01 |
| ☐ 303 Freeman McNeil | .06 | .03 | .01 |
| ☐ 304 Johnny Hector | .06 | .03 | .01 |
| ☐ 305 Al Toon | .06 | .03 | .01 |
| ☐ 306 Jo Jo Townsell | .04 | .02 | .01 |
| ☐ 307 Mickey Shuler | .04 | .02 | .01 |
| ☐ 308 Pat Leahy | .06 | .03 | .01 |
| ☐ 309 Roger Vick | .06 | .03 | .01 |
| ☐ 310 Alex Gordon | .04 | .02 | .01 |
| ☐ 311 Troy Benson | .04 | .02 | .01 |
| ☐ 312 Bob Crable | .04 | .02 | .01 |
| ☐ 313 Harry Hamilton | .04 | .02 | .01 |
| ☐ 314 Packers TL | .05 | .02 | .01 |
| Phillip Epps Ready for Contact | | | |

| | | | |
|---|---|---|---|
| ☐ 315 Randy Wright | .06 | .03 | .01 |
| ☐ 316 Kenneth Davis | .20 | .09 | .03 |
| ☐ 317 Phillip Epps | .04 | .02 | .01 |
| ☐ 318 Walter Stanley | .06 | .03 | .01 |
| ☐ 319 Frankie Neal | .04 | .02 | .01 |
| ☐ 320 Don Bracken | .04 | .02 | .01 |
| ☐ 321 Brian Noble | .04 | .02 | .01 |
| ☐ 322 Johnny Holland SR | .04 | .02 | .01 |
| ☐ 323 Tim Harris | .15 | .07 | .02 |
| ☐ 324 Mark Murphy | .04 | .02 | .01 |
| ☐ 325 Raiders TL | .40 | .18 | .05 |
|     Bo Jackson All Alone | | | |
| ☐ 326 Marc Wilson | .06 | .03 | .01 |
| ☐ 327 Bo Jackson SR | 2.00 | .90 | .25 |
| ☐ 328 Marcus Allen | .30 | .14 | .04 |
| ☐ 329 James Lofton | .20 | .09 | .03 |
| ☐ 330 Todd Christensen | .06 | .03 | .01 |
| ☐ 331 Chris Bahr | .04 | .02 | .01 |
| ☐ 332 Stan Talley | .04 | .02 | .01 |
| ☐ 333 Howie Long | .08 | .04 | .01 |
| ☐ 334 Sean Jones | .06 | .03 | .01 |
| ☐ 335 Matt Millen | .06 | .03 | .01 |
| ☐ 336 Stacey Toran | .06 | .03 | .01 |
| ☐ 337 Vann McElroy | .04 | .02 | .01 |
| ☐ 338 Greg Townsend | .04 | .02 | .01 |
| ☐ 339 Bengals TL | .15 | .07 | .02 |
|     Boomer Esiason | | | |
|     Calls Signals | | | |
| ☐ 340 Boomer Esiason | .40 | .18 | .05 |
| ☐ 341 Larry Kinnebrew | .04 | .02 | .01 |
| ☐ 342 Stanford Jennings | .04 | .02 | .01 |
| ☐ 343 Eddie Brown | .04 | .02 | .01 |
| ☐ 344 Jim Breech | .04 | .02 | .01 |
| ☐ 345 Anthony Munoz AP | .06 | .03 | .01 |
| ☐ 346 Scott Fulhage | .04 | .02 | .01 |
| ☐ 347 Tim Krumrie | .15 | .07 | .02 |
| ☐ 348 Reggie Williams | .06 | .03 | .01 |
| ☐ 349 David Fulcher | .20 | .09 | .03 |
| ☐ 350 Buccaneers TL | .05 | .02 | .01 |
|     James Wilder Free | | | |
|     and Clear | | | |
| ☐ 351 Frank Garcia | .04 | .02 | .01 |
| ☐ 352 Vinny Testaverde SR | 1.00 | .45 | .13 |
| ☐ 353 James Wilder | .06 | .03 | .01 |
| ☐ 354 Jeff Smith | .04 | .02 | .01 |
| ☐ 355 Gerald Carter | .04 | .02 | .01 |
| ☐ 356 Calvin Magee | .04 | .02 | .01 |
| ☐ 357 Donald Igwebuike | .04 | .02 | .01 |
| ☐ 358 Ron Holmes | .04 | .02 | .01 |
| ☐ 359 Chris Washington | .04 | .02 | .01 |
| ☐ 360 Ervin Randle | .04 | .02 | .01 |
| ☐ 361 Chiefs TL | .05 | .02 | .01 |
|     Bill Kenney Ground | | | |
|     Attack | | | |
| ☐ 362 Bill Kenney | .06 | .03 | .01 |
| ☐ 363 Christian Okoye SR | .25 | .11 | .03 |
| ☐ 364 Paul Palmer | .06 | .03 | .01 |
| ☐ 365 Stephone Paige | .06 | .03 | .01 |
| ☐ 366 Carlos Carson | .06 | .03 | .01 |
| ☐ 367 Kelly Goodburn | .04 | .02 | .01 |
| ☐ 368 Bill Maas AP | .06 | .03 | .01 |
| ☐ 369 Mike Bell | .04 | .02 | .01 |
| ☐ 370 Dino Hackett | .04 | .02 | .01 |
| ☐ 371 Deron Cherry | .06 | .03 | .01 |
| ☐ 372 Lions TL | .05 | .02 | .01 |
|     James Jones Stretches | | | |
|     For More | | | |
| ☐ 373 Chuck Long | .06 | .03 | .01 |
| ☐ 374 Garry James | .04 | .02 | .01 |
| ☐ 375 James Jones | .04 | .02 | .01 |
| ☐ 376 Pete Mandley | .04 | .02 | .01 |
| ☐ 377 Gary Lee SR | .04 | .02 | .01 |
| ☐ 378 Ed Murray | .06 | .03 | .01 |
| ☐ 379 Jim Arnold | .04 | .02 | .01 |
| ☐ 380 Dennis Gibson SR | .04 | .02 | .01 |
| ☐ 381 Mike Cofer | .04 | .02 | .01 |
| ☐ 382 James Griffin | .04 | .02 | .01 |
| ☐ 383 Falcons TL | .05 | .02 | .01 |
|     Gerald Riggs Carries | | | |
|     Heavy Load | | | |
| ☐ 384 Scott Campbell | .04 | .02 | .01 |
| ☐ 385 Gerald Riggs | .06 | .03 | .01 |
| ☐ 386 Floyd Dixon | .04 | .02 | .01 |
| ☐ 387 Rick Donnelly AP | .04 | .02 | .01 |
| ☐ 388 Bill Fralic AP | .06 | .03 | .01 |
| ☐ 389 Major Everett | .04 | .02 | .01 |
| ☐ 390 Mike Gann | .04 | .02 | .01 |
| ☐ 391 Tony Casillas | .30 | .14 | .04 |
| ☐ 392 Rick Bryan | .04 | .02 | .01 |
| ☐ 393 John Rade | .04 | .02 | .01 |
| ☐ 394 Checklist 1-132 | .04 | .02 | .01 |
| ☐ 395 Checklist 133-264 | .04 | .02 | .01 |
| ☐ 396 Checklist 265-396 | .04 | .02 | .01 |

# 1988 Topps Box Bottoms

This 16-card set measures 3 1/2" by 2 1/2" and was issued on the bottom of 1988 Topps wax pack boxes. These cards feature NFL players who had won major awards while in college and they are displayed two players per card. The back of the card features brief biographical blurbs about how the players won the awards while they were in school. The set includes cards of Cornelius Bennett, Bo Jackson, and Vinny Testaverde during their rookie years for cards.

| | MINT | EXC | G-VG |
|---|---|---|---|
| COMPLETE SET (16) | 5.00 | 2.00 | .50 |
| COMMON PLAYER (A-P) | .25 | .10 | .02 |
| | | | |
| ☐ A Vinny Testaverde | .50 | .20 | .05 |
|     Tampa Bay Buccaneers | | | |
|     Jason Buck | | | |
|     Cincinnati Bengals | | | |
| ☐ B Dean Steinkuhler | .25 | .10 | .02 |
|     Houston Oilers | | | |
|     Dave Rimington | | | |
|     Cincinnati Bengals | | | |
| ☐ C George Rogers | .25 | .10 | .02 |
|     Washington Redskins | | | |
|     Mark May | | | |
|     Washington Redskins | | | |
| ☐ D Kenneth Sims | .25 | .10 | .02 |
|     New England Patriots | | | |
|     Hugh Green | | | |
|     Miami Dolphins | | | |
| ☐ E Cornelius Bennett | .50 | .20 | .05 |
|     Buffalo Bills | | | |
|     Tony Casillas | | | |
|     Atlanta Falcons | | | |
| ☐ F Bo Jackson | 1.25 | .50 | .12 |
|     Los Angeles Raiders | | | |
|     Mike Ruth | | | |
|     New England Patriots | | | |
| ☐ G Ross Browner | .35 | .14 | .03 |
|     Green Bay Packers | | | |
|     Randy White | | | |
|     Dallas Cowboys | | | |
| ☐ H Doug Flutie | 1.25 | .50 | .12 |
|     New England Patriots | | | |
|     Bruce Smith | | | |
|     Buffalo Bills | | | |
| ☐ I Herschel Walker | .50 | .20 | .05 |
|     Dallas Cowboys | | | |
|     Dave Rimington | | | |
|     Cincinnati Bengals | | | |
| ☐ J Jim Plunkett | .50 | .20 | .05 |
|     Los Angeles Raiders | | | |
|     Randy White | | | |
|     Dallas Cowboys | | | |
| ☐ K Charles White | .25 | .10 | .02 |
|     Los Angeles Rams | | | |
|     Jim Ritcher | | | |
|     Buffalo Bills | | | |
| ☐ L Brad Budde | .25 | .10 | .02 |
|     Kansas City Chiefs | | | |
|     Bruce Clark | | | |
|     New Orleans Saints | | | |
| ☐ M Marcus Allen | .50 | .20 | .05 |
|     Los Angeles Raiders | | | |
|     Dave Rimington | | | |
|     Cincinnati Bengals | | | |
| ☐ N Mike Rozier | .25 | .10 | .02 |
|     Houston Oilers | | | |
|     Dean Steinkuhler | | | |
|     Houston Oilers | | | |
| ☐ O Tony Dorsett | .50 | .20 | .05 |
|     Dallas Cowboys | | | |
|     Ross Browner | | | |
|     Green Bay Packers | | | |
| ☐ P Checklist | .25 | .10 | .02 |

## 1988 Topps 1000 Yard Club

This glossy insert set was included one per wax pack with the regular issue 1988 Topps football cards. The set typically features, in order of yards gained, all players achieving 1000 yards gained either rushing or receiving. However, this year, due to the players' strike which shortened the 1987 season, Topps projected 1,000 yard seasons for those players selected as noted in the checklist below. Cards have a green inner border on the front; backs are red and black print on white card stock. The cards are standard size, 2 1/2" by 3 1/2", and are numbered on the back. Card backs detail statistically the game by game performance of the player in terms of yards gained against each opponent.

|  | MINT | EXC | G-VG |
|---|---|---|---|
| COMPLETE SET (28) | 4.00 | 1.60 | .40 |
| COMMON PLAYER (1-28) | .25 | .10 | .02 |
| ☐ 1 Charles White | .25 | .10 | .02 |
| Los Angeles Rams | | | |
| ☐ 2 Eric Dickerson | .60 | .24 | .06 |
| Indianapolis Colts | | | |
| ☐ 3 J.T. Smith | .25 | .10 | .02 |
| St. Louis Cardinals | | | |
| ☐ 4 Jerry Rice | 1.25 | .50 | .12 |
| San Francisco 49ers | | | |
| ☐ 5 Gary Clark | .50 | .20 | .05 |
| Washington Redskins | | | |
| ☐ 6 Carlos Carson | .25 | .10 | .02 |
| Kansas City Chiefs | | | |
| ☐ 7 Drew Hill | .25 | .10 | .02 |
| Houston Oilers | | | |
| ☐ 8 Curt Warner UER | .35 | .14 | .03 |
| (Reversed negative) | | | |
| Seattle Seahawks | | | |
| ☐ 9 Al Toon | .35 | .14 | .03 |
| New York Jets | | | |
| ☐ 10 Mike Rozier | .35 | .14 | .03 |
| Houston Oilers | | | |
| ☐ 11 Ernest Givins | .50 | .20 | .05 |
| Houston Oilers | | | |
| ☐ 12 Anthony Carter | .35 | .14 | .03 |
| Minnesota Vikings | | | |
| ☐ 13 Rueben Mayes | .25 | .10 | .02 |
| New Orleans Saints | | | |
| ☐ 14 Steve Largent | 1.00 | .40 | .10 |
| Seattle Seahawks | | | |
| ☐ 15 Herschel Walker | .60 | .24 | .06 |
| Dallas Cowboys | | | |
| ☐ 16 James Lofton | .60 | .24 | .06 |
| Los Angeles Raiders | | | |
| ☐ 17 Gerald Riggs | .25 | .10 | .02 |
| Atlanta Falcons | | | |
| ☐ 18 Mark Bavaro | .25 | .10 | .02 |
| New York Giants | | | |
| ☐ 19 Roger Craig | .50 | .20 | .05 |
| San Francisco 49ers | | | |
| ☐ 20 Webster Slaughter | .35 | .14 | .03 |
| Cleveland Browns | | | |
| ☐ 21 Henry Ellard | .25 | .10 | .02 |
| Los Angeles Rams | | | |
| ☐ 22 Mike Quick | .25 | .10 | .02 |
| Philadelphia Eagles | | | |
| ☐ 23 Stump Mitchell | .25 | .10 | .02 |
| St. Louis Cardinals | | | |
| ☐ 24 Eric Martin | .35 | .14 | .03 |
| New Orleans Saints | | | |
| ☐ 25 Mark Clayton | .35 | .14 | .03 |
| Miami Dolphins | | | |
| ☐ 26 Chris Burkett | .25 | .10 | .02 |
| Buffalo Bills | | | |
| ☐ 27 Marcus Allen | .60 | .24 | .06 |
| Los Angeles Raiders | | | |
| ☐ 28 Andre Reed | .60 | .24 | .06 |
| Buffalo Bills | | | |

## 1989 Topps

This 396-card set is similar to the Topps football efforts of the past few years. The cards are standard size, 2 1/2" by 3 1/2". The cards are ordered in team order and the teams themselves are ordered according to their finish in the 1988 standings, e.g., San Francisco 49ers (6-22), Cincinnati Bengals (23-39), Buffalo Bills (40-56), Chicago Bears (57-73), Minnesota Vikings (74-89), Houston Oilers (90-105), Philadelphia Eagles (106-121), Los Angeles Rams (122-137), Cleveland Browns (138-151), New Orleans Saints (152-164), New York Giants (165-180), Seattle Seahawks (181-192), New England Patriots (193-204), Indianapolis Colts (205-216), New York Jets (222-237), Denver Broncos (238-249), Washington Redskins (250-263), Los Angeles Raiders (264-275), Phoenix Cardinals (276-289), Miami Dolphins (290-302), San Diego Chargers (303-313), Pittsburgh Steelers (314-324), Tampa Bay Buccaneers (325-335), Atlanta Falcons (336-347), Kansas City Chiefs (348-359), Detroit Lions (360-370), Green Bay Packers (371-381), and Dallas Cowboys (382-393). The card backs are printed in green and yellow on gray card stock. The team cards are actually Team Leader cards showing an action scene on the front and giving the recap of the team's success in the previous season on the back. Rookie Cards include Brian Blades, Tim Brown, Cris Carter, Michael Irvin, Keith Jackson, Don Majkowski, Anthony Miller, Chris Miller, Jay Novacek, Michael Dean Perry, Mark Rypien, Sterling Sharpe, John Taylor, Thurman Thomas and Rod Woodson.

|  | MINT | EXC | G-VG |
|---|---|---|---|
| COMPLETE SET (396) | 15.00 | 6.75 | 1.90 |
| COMPLETE FACT.SET (396) | 18.00 | 8.00 | 2.30 |
| COMMON PLAYER (1-396) | .04 | .02 | .01 |
| ☐ 1 Super Bowl XXIII | .40 | .18 | .05 |
| (Joe Montana back | | | |
| to pass) | | | |
| ☐ 2 Tim Brown RB | .60 | .25 | .08 |
| Most Combined Net | | | |
| Yards Gained, | | | |
| Rookie Season | | | |
| Los Angeles Raiders | | | |
| ☐ 3 Eric Dickerson RB | .05 | .02 | .01 |
| Most Consecutive | | | |
| Seasons, Start of | | | |
| Career, 1000 or More | | | |
| Yards Rushing | | | |
| Los Angeles Rams | | | |
| ☐ 4 Steve Largent RB | .12 | .05 | .02 |
| Most Yards Receiving, | | | |
| Career | | | |
| Seattle Seahawks | | | |
| ☐ 5 Dan Marino RB | .50 | .23 | .06 |
| Most Seasons 4000 or | | | |
| More Yards Passing | | | |
| Miami Dolphins | | | |
| ☐ 6 49ers Team | .30 | .14 | .04 |
| Joe Montana On The Run | | | |
| ☐ 7 Jerry Rice | 1.00 | .45 | .13 |
| ☐ 8 Roger Craig | .10 | .05 | .01 |
| ☐ 9 Ronnie Lott | .15 | .07 | .02 |
| ☐ 10 Michael Carter | .07 | .03 | .01 |
| ☐ 11 Charles Haley | .07 | .03 | .01 |
| ☐ 12 Joe Montana | 1.25 | .55 | .16 |
| ☐ 13 John Taylor | .75 | .35 | .09 |
| ☐ 14 Michael Walter | .04 | .02 | .01 |
| ☐ 15 Mike Cofer K | .10 | .05 | .01 |
| ☐ 16 Tom Rathman | .07 | .03 | .01 |
| ☐ 17 Danny Stubbs | .04 | .02 | .01 |
| ☐ 18 Keena Turner | .07 | .03 | .01 |
| ☐ 19 Tim McKyer | .07 | .03 | .01 |
| ☐ 20 Larry Roberts | .04 | .02 | .01 |
| ☐ 21 Jeff Fuller | .04 | .02 | .01 |
| ☐ 22 Bubba Paris | .07 | .03 | .01 |
| ☐ 23 Bengals Team UER | .10 | .05 | .01 |

Boomer Esiason Measures
Up (Should be versus
Steelers in week three)

| | | | |
|---|---|---|---|
| ☐ 24 Eddie Brown | .07 | .03 | .01 |
| ☐ 25 Boomer Esiason | .25 | .11 | .03 |
| ☐ 26 Tim Krumrie | .04 | .02 | .01 |
| ☐ 27 Ickey Woods | .07 | .03 | .01 |
| ☐ 28 Anthony Munoz | .07 | .03 | .01 |
| ☐ 29 Tim McGee | .07 | .03 | .01 |
| ☐ 30 Max Montoya | .04 | .02 | .01 |
| ☐ 31 David Grant | .04 | .02 | .01 |
| ☐ 32 Rodney Holman | .20 | .09 | .03 |

(Cincinnati Bengals on
card front is subject to
various printing errors)

| | | | |
|---|---|---|---|
| ☐ 33 David Fulcher | .07 | .03 | .01 |
| ☐ 34 Jim Skow | .04 | .02 | .01 |
| ☐ 35 James Brooks | .07 | .03 | .01 |
| ☐ 36 Reggie Williams | .07 | .03 | .01 |
| ☐ 37 Eric Thomas | .15 | .07 | .02 |
| ☐ 38 Stanford Jennings | .04 | .02 | .01 |
| ☐ 39 Jim Breech | .04 | .02 | .01 |
| ☐ 40 Bills Team | .15 | .07 | .02 |

Jim Kelly Reads Defense

| | | | |
|---|---|---|---|
| ☐ 41 Shane Conlan | .04 | .02 | .01 |
| ☐ 42 Scott Norwood | .04 | .02 | .01 |
| ☐ 43 Cornelius Bennett | .20 | .09 | .03 |
| ☐ 44 Bruce Smith | .20 | .09 | .03 |
| ☐ 45 Thurman Thomas | 2.50 | 1.15 | .30 |
| ☐ 46 Jim Kelly | .50 | .23 | .06 |
| ☐ 47 John Kidd | .07 | .03 | .01 |
| ☐ 48 Kent Hull | .12 | .05 | .02 |
| ☐ 49 Art Still | .07 | .03 | .01 |
| ☐ 50 Fred Smerlas | .07 | .03 | .01 |
| ☐ 51A Derrick Burroughs | .04 | .02 | .01 |

(White name plate)

| | | | |
|---|---|---|---|
| ☐ 51B Derrick Burroughs | .04 | .02 | .01 |

(Yellow name plate)

| | | | |
|---|---|---|---|
| ☐ 52 Andre Reed | .25 | .11 | .03 |
| ☐ 53 Robb Riddick | .04 | .02 | .01 |
| ☐ 54 Chris Burkett | .07 | .03 | .01 |
| ☐ 55 Ronnie Harmon | .20 | .09 | .03 |
| ☐ 56 Mark Kelso UER | .07 | .03 | .01 |

(team shown as
"Buffalo Bill")

| | | | |
|---|---|---|---|
| ☐ 57 Bears Team | .05 | .02 | .01 |

Thomas Sanders
Changes Pace

| | | | |
|---|---|---|---|
| ☐ 58 Mike Singletary | .10 | .05 | .01 |
| ☐ 59 Jay Hilgenberg UER | .07 | .03 | .01 |

(letter "g" is miss-
ing from Chicago)

| | | | |
|---|---|---|---|
| ☐ 60 Richard Dent | .07 | .03 | .01 |
| ☐ 61 Ron Rivera | .04 | .02 | .01 |
| ☐ 62 Jim McMahon | .10 | .05 | .01 |
| ☐ 63 Mike Tomczak | .07 | .03 | .01 |
| ☐ 64 Neal Anderson | .10 | .05 | .01 |
| ☐ 65 Dennis Gentry | .04 | .02 | .01 |
| ☐ 66 Dan Hampton | .07 | .03 | .01 |
| ☐ 67 David Tate | .07 | .03 | .01 |
| ☐ 68 Thomas Sanders | .04 | .02 | .01 |
| ☐ 69 Steve McMichael | .07 | .03 | .01 |
| ☐ 70 Dennis McKinnon | .04 | .02 | .01 |

(Neal Anderson in background)

| | | | |
|---|---|---|---|
| ☐ 71 Brad Muster | .20 | .09 | .03 |
| ☐ 72 Vestee Jackson | .10 | .05 | .01 |
| ☐ 73 Dave Duerson | .04 | .02 | .01 |
| ☐ 74 Vikings Team | .05 | .02 | .01 |

Millard Gets His Man

| | | | |
|---|---|---|---|
| ☐ 75 Joey Browner | .07 | .03 | .01 |
| ☐ 76 Carl Lee | .10 | .05 | .01 |
| ☐ 77 Gary Zimmerman | .07 | .03 | .01 |
| ☐ 78 Hassan Jones | .10 | .05 | .01 |
| ☐ 79 Anthony Carter | .10 | .05 | .01 |
| ☐ 80 Ray Berry | .04 | .02 | .01 |
| ☐ 81 Steve Jordan | .07 | .03 | .01 |
| ☐ 82 Issiac Holt | .04 | .02 | .01 |
| ☐ 83 Wade Wilson | .07 | .03 | .01 |
| ☐ 84 Chris Doleman | .15 | .07 | .02 |
| ☐ 85 Alfred Anderson | .04 | .02 | .01 |
| ☐ 86 Keith Millard | .07 | .03 | .01 |
| ☐ 87 Darrin Nelson | .07 | .03 | .01 |
| ☐ 88 D.J. Dozier | .07 | .03 | .01 |
| ☐ 89 Scott Studwell | .04 | .02 | .01 |
| ☐ 90 Oilers Team | .05 | .02 | .01 |

Tony Zendejas Big Boot

| | | | |
|---|---|---|---|
| ☐ 91 Bruce Matthews | .25 | .11 | .03 |
| ☐ 92 Curtis Duncan | .10 | .05 | .01 |
| ☐ 93 Warren Moon | .35 | .16 | .04 |
| ☐ 94 Johnny Meads | .04 | .02 | .01 |
| ☐ 95 Drew Hill | .07 | .03 | .01 |
| ☐ 96 Alonzo Highsmith | .04 | .02 | .01 |
| ☐ 97 Mike Munchak | .07 | .03 | .01 |
| ☐ 98 Mike Rozier | .07 | .03 | .01 |
| ☐ 99 Tony Zendejas | .04 | .02 | .01 |
| ☐ 100 Jeff Donaldson | .04 | .02 | .01 |
| ☐ 101 Ray Childress | .07 | .03 | .01 |
| ☐ 102 Sean Jones | .07 | .03 | .01 |

| | | | |
|---|---|---|---|
| ☐ 103 Ernest Givins | .10 | .05 | .01 |
| ☐ 104 William Fuller | .30 | .14 | .04 |
| ☐ 105 Allen Pinkett | .07 | .03 | .01 |
| ☐ 106 Eagles Team | .10 | .05 | .01 |

Randall Cunningham
Fakes Field

| | | | |
|---|---|---|---|
| ☐ 107 Keith Jackson | 1.25 | .55 | .16 |
| ☐ 108 Reggie White | .20 | .09 | .03 |
| ☐ 109 Clyde Simmons | .15 | .07 | .02 |
| ☐ 110 John Teltschik | .04 | .02 | .01 |
| ☐ 111 Wes Hopkins | .04 | .02 | .01 |
| ☐ 112 Keith Byars | .07 | .03 | .01 |
| ☐ 113 Jerome Brown | .07 | .03 | .01 |
| ☐ 114 Mike Quick | .07 | .03 | .01 |
| ☐ 115 Randall Cunningham | .30 | .14 | .04 |
| ☐ 116 Anthony Toney | .04 | .02 | .01 |
| ☐ 117 Ron Johnson | .07 | .03 | .01 |
| ☐ 118 Terry Hoage | .04 | .02 | .01 |
| ☐ 119 Seth Joyner | .20 | .09 | .03 |
| ☐ 120 Eric Allen | .30 | .14 | .04 |
| ☐ 121 Cris Carter | 1.00 | .45 | .13 |
| ☐ 122 Rams Team | .05 | .02 | .01 |

Greg Bell Runs To Glory

| | | | |
|---|---|---|---|
| ☐ 123 Tom Newberry | .15 | .07 | .02 |
| ☐ 124 Pete Holohan | .04 | .02 | .01 |
| ☐ 125 Robert Delpino UER | .25 | .11 | .03 |

(Listed as Raider
on card back)

| | | | |
|---|---|---|---|
| ☐ 126 Carl Ekern | .04 | .02 | .01 |
| ☐ 127 Greg Bell | .07 | .03 | .01 |
| ☐ 128 Mike Lansford | .04 | .02 | .01 |
| ☐ 129 Jim Everett | .15 | .07 | .02 |
| ☐ 130 Mike Wilcher | .04 | .02 | .01 |
| ☐ 131 Jerry Gray | .04 | .02 | .01 |
| ☐ 132 Dale Hatcher | .04 | .02 | .01 |
| ☐ 133 Doug Smith | .07 | .03 | .01 |
| ☐ 134 Kevin Greene | .07 | .03 | .01 |
| ☐ 135 Jackie Slater | .07 | .03 | .01 |
| ☐ 136 Aaron Cox | .10 | .05 | .01 |
| ☐ 137 Henry Ellard | .04 | .02 | .01 |
| ☐ 138 Browns Team | .10 | .05 | .01 |

Bernie Kosar Quick
Release

| | | | |
|---|---|---|---|
| ☐ 139 Frank Minnifield | .04 | .02 | .01 |
| ☐ 140 Webster Slaughter | .20 | .09 | .03 |
| ☐ 141 Bernie Kosar | .15 | .07 | .02 |
| ☐ 142 Charles Buchanan | .04 | .02 | .01 |
| ☐ 143 Clay Matthews | .07 | .03 | .01 |
| ☐ 144 Reggie Langhorne | .25 | .11 | .03 |
| ☐ 145 Hanford Dixon | .04 | .02 | .01 |
| ☐ 146 Brian Brennan | .04 | .02 | .01 |
| ☐ 147 Earnest Byner | .07 | .03 | .01 |
| ☐ 148 Michael Dean Perry | 1.00 | .45 | .13 |
| ☐ 149 Kevin Mack | .07 | .03 | .01 |
| ☐ 150 Matt Bahr | .04 | .02 | .01 |
| ☐ 151 Ozzie Newsome | .15 | .07 | .02 |
| ☐ 152 Saints Team | .05 | .02 | .01 |

Craig Heyward Motors
Forward

| | | | |
|---|---|---|---|
| ☐ 153 Morten Andersen | .07 | .03 | .01 |
| ☐ 154 Pat Swilling | .20 | .09 | .03 |
| ☐ 155 Sam Mills | .07 | .03 | .01 |
| ☐ 156 Lonzell Hill | .04 | .02 | .01 |
| ☐ 157 Dalton Hilliard | .07 | .03 | .01 |
| ☐ 158 Craig Heyward | .20 | .09 | .03 |
| ☐ 159 Vaughan Johnson | .25 | .11 | .03 |
| ☐ 160 Rueben Mayes | .07 | .03 | .01 |
| ☐ 161 Gene Atkins | .10 | .05 | .01 |
| ☐ 162 Bobby Hebert | .15 | .07 | .02 |
| ☐ 163 Rickey Jackson | .07 | .03 | .01 |
| ☐ 164 Eric Martin | .07 | .03 | .01 |
| ☐ 165 Giants Team | .05 | .02 | .01 |

Joe Morris Up
The Middle

| | | | |
|---|---|---|---|
| ☐ 166 Lawrence Taylor | .15 | .07 | .02 |
| ☐ 167 Bart Oates | .04 | .02 | .01 |
| ☐ 168 Carl Banks | .07 | .03 | .01 |
| ☐ 169 Eric Moore | .07 | .03 | .01 |
| ☐ 170 Sheldon White | .04 | .02 | .01 |
| ☐ 171 Mark Collins | .15 | .07 | .02 |
| ☐ 172 Phil Simms | .15 | .07 | .02 |
| ☐ 173 Jim Burt | .07 | .03 | .01 |
| ☐ 174 Stephen Baker | .10 | .05 | .01 |
| ☐ 175 Mark Bavaro | .07 | .03 | .01 |
| ☐ 176 Pepper Johnson | .07 | .03 | .01 |
| ☐ 177 Lionel Manuel | .04 | .02 | .01 |
| ☐ 178 Joe Morris | .07 | .03 | .01 |
| ☐ 179 John Elliott | .20 | .09 | .03 |
| ☐ 180 Gary Reasons | .04 | .02 | .01 |
| ☐ 181 Seahawks Team | .05 | .02 | .01 |

Dave Krieg Winds Up

| | | | |
|---|---|---|---|
| ☐ 182 Brian Blades | .75 | .35 | .09 |
| ☐ 183 Steve Largent | .25 | .11 | .03 |
| ☐ 184 Rufus Porter | .10 | .05 | .01 |
| ☐ 185 Ruben Rodriguez | .04 | .02 | .01 |
| ☐ 186 Curt Warner | .07 | .03 | .01 |
| ☐ 187 Paul Moyer | .04 | .02 | .01 |

|  |  | | | |
|---|---|---|---|---|
| ☐ 188 | Dave Krieg | .07 | .03 | .01 |
| ☐ 189 | Jacob Green | .07 | .03 | .01 |
| ☐ 190 | John L. Williams | .07 | .03 | .01 |
| ☐ 191 | Eugene Robinson | .25 | .11 | .03 |
| ☐ 192 | Brian Bosworth | .07 | .03 | .01 |
| ☐ 193 | Patriots Team<br>Tony Eason Behind<br>Blocking | .05 | .02 | .01 |
| ☐ 194 | John Stephens | .20 | .09 | .03 |
| ☐ 195 | Robert Perryman | .10 | .05 | .01 |
| ☐ 196 | Andre Tippett | .07 | .03 | .01 |
| ☐ 197 | Fred Marion | .04 | .02 | .01 |
| ☐ 198 | Doug Flutie | .30 | .14 | .04 |
| ☐ 199 | Stanley Morgan | .07 | .03 | .01 |
| ☐ 200 | Johnny Rembert | .04 | .02 | .01 |
| ☐ 201 | Tony Eason | .07 | .03 | .01 |
| ☐ 202 | Marvin Allen | .04 | .02 | .01 |
| ☐ 203 | Raymond Clayborn | .07 | .03 | .01 |
| ☐ 204 | Irving Fryar | .07 | .03 | .01 |
| ☐ 205 | Colts Team<br>Chris Chandler<br>All Alone | .05 | .02 | .01 |
| ☐ 206 | Eric Dickerson | .15 | .07 | .02 |
| ☐ 207 | Chris Hinton | .07 | .03 | .01 |
| ☐ 208 | Duane Bickett | .04 | .02 | .01 |
| ☐ 209 | Chris Chandler | .20 | .09 | .03 |
| ☐ 210 | Jon Hand | .04 | .02 | .01 |
| ☐ 211 | Ray Donaldson | .04 | .02 | .01 |
| ☐ 212 | Dean Biasucci | .04 | .02 | .01 |
| ☐ 213 | Bill Brooks | .07 | .03 | .01 |
| ☐ 214 | Chris Goode | .04 | .02 | .01 |
| ☐ 215 | Clarence Verdin | .15 | .07 | .02 |
| ☐ 216 | Albert Bentley | .04 | .02 | .01 |
| ☐ 217 | Passing Leaders<br>Wade Wilson<br>Boomer Esiason | .10 | .05 | .01 |
| ☐ 218 | Receiving Leaders<br>Henry Ellard<br>Al Toon | .10 | .05 | .01 |
| ☐ 219 | Rushing Leaders<br>Herschel Walker<br>Eric Dickerson | .10 | .05 | .01 |
| ☐ 220 | Scoring Leaders<br>Mike Cofer<br>Scott Norwood | .05 | .02 | .01 |
| ☐ 221 | Intercept Leaders<br>Scott Case<br>Erik McMillan | .05 | .02 | .01 |
| ☐ 222 | Jets Team<br>Ken O'Brien Surveys<br>Scene | .05 | .02 | .01 |
| ☐ 223 | Erik McMillan | .10 | .05 | .01 |
| ☐ 224 | James Hasty | .04 | .02 | .01 |
| ☐ 225 | Al Toon | .07 | .03 | .01 |
| ☐ 226 | John Booty | .10 | .05 | .01 |
| ☐ 227 | Johnny Hector | .04 | .02 | .01 |
| ☐ 228 | Ken O'Brien | .07 | .03 | .01 |
| ☐ 229 | Marty Lyons | .07 | .03 | .01 |
| ☐ 230 | Mickey Shuler | .04 | .02 | .01 |
| ☐ 231 | Robin Cole | .04 | .02 | .01 |
| ☐ 232 | Freeman McNeil | .07 | .03 | .01 |
| ☐ 233 | Marion Barber | .04 | .02 | .01 |
| ☐ 234 | Jo Jo Townsell | .04 | .02 | .01 |
| ☐ 235 | Wesley Walker | .07 | .03 | .01 |
| ☐ 236 | Roger Vick | .04 | .02 | .01 |
| ☐ 237 | Pat Leahy | .07 | .03 | .01 |
| ☐ 238 | Broncos Team UER<br>John Elway Ground Attack<br>(Score of week 15 says<br>42-21, should be 42-14) | .20 | .09 | .03 |
| ☐ 239 | Mike Horan | .04 | .02 | .01 |
| ☐ 240 | Tony Dorsett | .25 | .11 | .03 |
| ☐ 241 | John Elway | .75 | .35 | .09 |
| ☐ 242 | Mark Jackson | .07 | .03 | .01 |
| ☐ 243 | Sammy Winder | .04 | .02 | .01 |
| ☐ 244 | Rich Karlis | .04 | .02 | .01 |
| ☐ 245 | Vance Johnson | .07 | .03 | .01 |
| ☐ 246 | Steve Sewell | .04 | .02 | .01 |
| ☐ 247 | Karl Mecklenburg UER<br>(Drafted 2, should be 12) | .07 | .03 | .01 |
| ☐ 248 | Rulon Jones | .04 | .02 | .01 |
| ☐ 249 | Simon Fletcher | .25 | .11 | .03 |
| ☐ 250 | Redskins Team<br>Doug Williams Sets Up | .05 | .02 | .01 |
| ☐ 251 | Chip Lohmiller | .25 | .11 | .03 |
| ☐ 252 | Jamie Morris | .07 | .03 | .01 |
| ☐ 253 | Mark Rypien UER<br>(14 1988 completions,<br>should be 114) | .40 | .18 | .05 |
| ☐ 254 | Barry Wilburn | .04 | .02 | .01 |
| ☐ 255 | Mark May | .07 | .03 | .01 |
| ☐ 256 | Wilber Marshall | .07 | .03 | .01 |
| ☐ 257 | Charles Mann | .07 | .03 | .01 |
| ☐ 258 | Gary Clark | .10 | .05 | .01 |
| ☐ 259 | Doug Williams | .07 | .03 | .01 |
| ☐ 260 | Art Monk | .15 | .07 | .02 |
| ☐ 261 | Kelvin Bryant | .07 | .03 | .01 |
| ☐ 262 | Dexter Manley | .07 | .03 | .01 |
| ☐ 263 | Ricky Sanders | .07 | .03 | .01 |
| ☐ 264 | Raiders Team<br>Marcus Allen Through<br>the Line | .10 | .05 | .01 |
| ☐ 265 | Tim Brown | 1.50 | .65 | .19 |
| ☐ 266 | Jay Schroeder | .07 | .03 | .01 |
| ☐ 267 | Marcus Allen | .25 | .11 | .03 |
| ☐ 268 | Mike Haynes | .07 | .03 | .01 |
| ☐ 269 | Bo Jackson | .75 | .35 | .09 |
| ☐ 270 | Steve Beuerlein | .75 | .35 | .09 |
| ☐ 271 | Vann McElroy | .04 | .02 | .01 |
| ☐ 272 | Willie Gault | .07 | .03 | .01 |
| ☐ 273 | Howie Long | .10 | .05 | .01 |
| ☐ 274 | Greg Townsend | .07 | .03 | .01 |
| ☐ 275 | Mike Wise | .07 | .03 | .01 |
| ☐ 276 | Cardinals Team<br>Neil Lomax Looks Long | .05 | .02 | .01 |
| ☐ 277 | Luis Sharpe | .04 | .02 | .01 |
| ☐ 278 | Scott Dill | .04 | .02 | .01 |
| ☐ 279 | Vai Sikahema | .07 | .03 | .01 |
| ☐ 280 | Ron Wolfley | .04 | .02 | .01 |
| ☐ 281 | David Galloway | .04 | .02 | .01 |
| ☐ 282 | Jay Novacek | .75 | .35 | .09 |
| ☐ 283 | Neil Lomax | .07 | .03 | .01 |
| ☐ 284 | Robert Awalt | .04 | .02 | .01 |
| ☐ 285 | Cedric Mack | .04 | .02 | .01 |
| ☐ 286 | Freddie Joe Nunn | .07 | .03 | .01 |
| ☐ 287 | J.T. Smith | .04 | .02 | .01 |
| ☐ 288 | Stump Mitchell | .07 | .03 | .01 |
| ☐ 289 | Roy Green | .07 | .03 | .01 |
| ☐ 290 | Dolphins Team<br>Dan Marino High and Far | .25 | .11 | .03 |
| ☐ 291 | Jarvis Williams | .10 | .05 | .01 |
| ☐ 292 | Troy Stradford | .04 | .02 | .01 |
| ☐ 293 | Dan Marino | 1.25 | .55 | .16 |
| ☐ 294 | T.J. Turner | .04 | .02 | .01 |
| ☐ 295 | John Offerdahl | .07 | .03 | .01 |
| ☐ 296 | Ferrell Edmunds | .15 | .07 | .01 |
| ☐ 297 | Scott Schwedes | .07 | .03 | .01 |
| ☐ 298 | Lorenzo Hampton | .04 | .02 | .01 |
| ☐ 299 | Jim Jensen | .04 | .02 | .01 |
| ☐ 300 | Brian Sochia | .07 | .03 | .01 |
| ☐ 301 | Reggie Roby | .07 | .03 | .01 |
| ☐ 302 | Mark Clayton | .07 | .03 | .01 |
| ☐ 303 | Chargers Team<br>Tim Spencer Leads<br>the Way | .05 | .02 | .01 |
| ☐ 304 | Lee Williams | .07 | .03 | .01 |
| ☐ 305 | Gary Plummer | .10 | .05 | .01 |
| ☐ 306 | Gary Anderson | .07 | .03 | .01 |
| ☐ 307 | Gill Byrd | .07 | .03 | .01 |
| ☐ 308 | Jamie Holland | .04 | .02 | .01 |
| ☐ 309 | Billy Ray Smith | .07 | .03 | .01 |
| ☐ 310 | Lionel James | .07 | .03 | .01 |
| ☐ 311 | Mark Vlasic | .15 | .07 | .02 |
| ☐ 312 | Curtis Adams | .04 | .02 | .01 |
| ☐ 313 | Anthony Miller | 2.00 | .90 | .25 |
| ☐ 314 | Steelers Team<br>Frank Pollard Set<br>for Action | .05 | .02 | .01 |
| ☐ 315 | Bubby Brister | .25 | .11 | .03 |
| ☐ 316 | David Little | .04 | .02 | .01 |
| ☐ 317 | Tunch Ilkin | .04 | .02 | .01 |
| ☐ 318 | Louis Lipps | .07 | .03 | .01 |
| ☐ 319 | Warren Williams | .10 | .05 | .01 |
| ☐ 320 | Dwight Stone | .04 | .02 | .01 |
| ☐ 321 | Merril Hoge | .20 | .09 | .03 |
| ☐ 322 | Thomas Everett | .25 | .11 | .03 |
| ☐ 323 | Rod Woodson | 1.00 | .45 | .13 |
| ☐ 324 | Gary Anderson | .07 | .03 | .01 |
| ☐ 325 | Buccaneers Team<br>Ron Hall in Pursuit | .05 | .02 | .01 |
| ☐ 326 | Donnie Elder | .04 | .02 | .01 |
| ☐ 327 | Vinny Testaverde | .25 | .11 | .03 |
| ☐ 328 | Harry Hamilton | .04 | .02 | .01 |
| ☐ 329 | James Wilder | .07 | .03 | .01 |
| ☐ 330 | Lars Tate | .07 | .03 | .01 |
| ☐ 331 | Mark Carrier | .75 | .35 | .09 |
| ☐ 332 | Bruce Hill | .04 | .02 | .01 |
| ☐ 333 | Paul Gruber | .10 | .05 | .01 |
| ☐ 334 | Ricky Reynolds | .07 | .03 | .01 |
| ☐ 335 | Eugene Marve | .04 | .02 | .01 |
| ☐ 336 | Falcons Team<br>Joel Williams Holds On | .05 | .02 | .01 |
| ☐ 337 | Aundray Bruce | .10 | .05 | .01 |
| ☐ 338 | John Rade | .04 | .02 | .01 |
| ☐ 339 | Scott Case | .10 | .05 | .01 |
| ☐ 340 | Robert Moore | .04 | .02 | .01 |
| ☐ 341 | Chris Miller | .75 | .35 | .09 |
| ☐ 342 | Gerald Riggs | .07 | .03 | .01 |
| ☐ 343 | Gene Lang | .07 | .03 | .01 |
| ☐ 344 | Marcus Cotton | .04 | .02 | .01 |
| ☐ 345 | Rick Donnelly | .04 | .02 | .01 |
| ☐ 346 | John Settle | .04 | .02 | .01 |
| ☐ 347 | Bill Fralic | .07 | .03 | .01 |
| ☐ 348 | Chiefs Team | .05 | .02 | .01 |

Dino Hackett Zeros In

| | MINT | EXC | G-VG |
|---|---|---|---|
| ☐ 349 Steve DeBerg | .07 | .03 | .01 |
| ☐ 350 Mike Stensrud | .07 | .03 | .01 |
| ☐ 351 Dino Hackett | .04 | .02 | .01 |
| ☐ 352 Deron Cherry | .07 | .03 | .01 |
| ☐ 353 Christian Okoye | .07 | .03 | .01 |
| ☐ 354 Bill Maas | .07 | .03 | .01 |
| ☐ 355 Carlos Carson | .07 | .03 | .01 |
| ☐ 356 Albert Lewis | .07 | .03 | .01 |
| ☐ 357 Paul Palmer | .04 | .02 | .01 |
| ☐ 358 Nick Lowery | .07 | .03 | .01 |
| ☐ 359 Stephone Paige | .07 | .03 | .01 |
| ☐ 360 Lions Team | .05 | .02 | .01 |

Chuck Long Gets
the Snap

| | | | |
|---|---|---|---|
| ☐ 361 Chris Spielman | .25 | .11 | .03 |
| ☐ 362 Jim Arnold | .04 | .02 | .01 |
| ☐ 363 Devon Mitchell | .04 | .02 | .01 |
| ☐ 364 Mike Cofer | .04 | .02 | .01 |
| ☐ 365 Bennie Blades | .10 | .05 | .01 |
| ☐ 366 James Jones | .04 | .02 | .01 |
| ☐ 367 Garry James | .04 | .02 | .01 |
| ☐ 368 Pete Mandley | .04 | .02 | .01 |
| ☐ 369 Keith Ferguson | .04 | .02 | .01 |
| ☐ 370 Dennis Gibson | .04 | .02 | .01 |
| ☐ 371 Packers Team UER | .05 | .02 | .01 |

Johnny Holland Over
the Top (Week 16 has
vs. Vikings, but
they played Bears)

| | | | |
|---|---|---|---|
| ☐ 372 Brent Fullwood | .04 | .02 | .01 |
| ☐ 373 Don Majkowski UER | .15 | .07 | .02 |

(3 TD's in 1987,
should be 5)

| | | | |
|---|---|---|---|
| ☐ 374 Tim Harris | .04 | .02 | .01 |
| ☐ 375 Keith Woodside | .04 | .02 | .01 |
| ☐ 376 Mark Murphy | .04 | .02 | .01 |
| ☐ 377 Dave Brown | .04 | .02 | .01 |
| ☐ 378 Perry Kemp | .10 | .05 | .01 |
| ☐ 379 Sterling Sharpe | 3.50 | 1.55 | .45 |
| ☐ 380 Chuck Cecil | .25 | .11 | .03 |
| ☐ 381 Walter Stanley | .04 | .02 | .01 |
| ☐ 382 Cowboys Team | .05 | .02 | .01 |

Steve Pelluer Lets
It Go

| | | | |
|---|---|---|---|
| ☐ 383 Michael Irvin | 3.00 | 1.35 | .40 |
| ☐ 384 Bill Bates | .04 | .02 | .01 |
| ☐ 385 Herschel Walker | .15 | .07 | .02 |
| ☐ 386 Darryl Clack | .04 | .02 | .01 |
| ☐ 387 Danny Noonan | .07 | .03 | .01 |
| ☐ 388 Eugene Lockhart | .04 | .02 | .01 |
| ☐ 389 Ed Too Tall Jones | .10 | .05 | .01 |
| ☐ 390 Steve Pelluer | .07 | .03 | .01 |
| ☐ 391 Ray Alexander | .04 | .02 | .01 |
| ☐ 392 Nate Newton | .25 | .11 | .03 |
| ☐ 393 Garry Cobb | .04 | .02 | .01 |
| ☐ 394 Checklist 1-132 | .05 | .02 | .01 |
| ☐ 395 Checklist 133-264 | .05 | .02 | .01 |
| ☐ 396 Checklist 265-396 | .05 | .02 | .01 |

| | MINT | EXC | G-VG |
|---|---|---|---|
| ☐ C Wesley Walker | .35 | .14 | .03 |
| New York Jets | | | |
| Gary Jeter | | | |
| Los Angeles Rams | | | |
| ☐ D Jim Everett | .35 | .14 | .03 |
| Los Angeles Rams | | | |
| Danny Noonan | | | |
| Dallas Cowboys | | | |
| ☐ E Neil Lomax | .25 | .10 | .02 |
| Phoenix Cardinals | | | |
| Dexter Manley | | | |
| Washington Redskins | | | |
| ☐ F Kelvin Bryant | .25 | .10 | .02 |
| Washington Redskins | | | |
| Kevin Greene | | | |
| Los Angeles Rams | | | |
| ☐ G Roger Craig | .50 | .20 | .05 |
| San Francisco 49ers | | | |
| Tim Harris | | | |
| Green Bay Packers | | | |
| ☐ H Dan Marino | 1.50 | .60 | .15 |
| Miami Dolphins | | | |
| Carl Banks | | | |
| New York Giants | | | |
| ☐ I Drew Hill | .25 | .10 | .02 |
| Houston Oilers | | | |
| Robin Cole | | | |
| New York Jets | | | |
| ☐ J Neil Lomax | .50 | .20 | .05 |
| Phoenix Cardinals | | | |
| Lawrence Taylor | | | |
| New York Giants | | | |
| ☐ K Roy Green | .25 | .10 | .02 |
| Phoenix Cardinals | | | |
| Tim Krumrie | | | |
| Cincinnati Bengals | | | |
| ☐ L Bobby Hebert | .35 | .14 | .03 |
| New Orleans Saints | | | |
| Aundray Bruce | | | |
| Atlanta Falcons | | | |
| ☐ M Ickey Woods | .50 | .20 | .05 |
| Cincinnati Bengals | | | |
| Lawrence Taylor | | | |
| New York Giants | | | |
| ☐ N Louis Lipps | .35 | .14 | .03 |
| Pittsburgh Steelers | | | |
| Greg Townsend | | | |
| Los Angeles Raiders | | | |
| ☐ O Curt Warner | .35 | .14 | .03 |
| Seattle Seahawks | | | |
| Tim Harris | | | |
| Green Bay Packers | | | |
| ☐ P Dave Krieg | .25 | .10 | .02 |
| Seattle Seahawks | | | |
| Kevin Greene | | | |
| Los Angeles Rams | | | |

## 1989 Topps Box Bottoms

These cards were printed on the bottom of 1989 Topps wax pack boxes. This 16-card set measures the standard size (2 1/2" by 3 1/2") and features the NFL's offensive and defensive players of the week for each week in the 1989 season. Each card features two players on the front.

| | MINT | EXC | G-VG |
|---|---|---|---|
| COMPLETE SET (16) | 5.00 | 2.00 | .50 |
| COMMON PLAYER (A-P) | .25 | .10 | .02 |
| | | | |
| ☐ A Neal Anderson | .35 | .14 | .03 |
| Chicago Bears | | | |
| Terry Hoage | | | |
| Philadelphia Eagles | | | |
| ☐ B Boomer Esiason | .50 | .20 | .05 |
| Cincinnati Bengals | | | |
| Jacob Green | | | |
| Seattle Seahawks | | | |

## 1989 Topps 1000 Yard Club

This glossy insert set was included one per wax pack with the regular issue 1989 Topps football cards. The set features, in order of yards gained, all players achieving 1000 yards gained either rushing or receiving. The cards are standard size, 2 1/2" by 3 1/2" and are numbered on the back. The card numbers are actually a ranking of each player's standing with respect to total yards gained in 1988. Card backs detail statistically the game by game performance of the player in terms of yards gained against each opponent.

| | MINT | EXC | G-VG |
|---|---|---|---|
| COMPLETE SET (24) | 4.00 | 1.60 | .40 |
| COMMON PLAYER (1-24) | .25 | .10 | .02 |
| | | | |
| ☐ 1 Eric Dickerson | .60 | .24 | .06 |
| Indianapolis Colts | | | |

| | | | | |
|---|---|---|---|---|
| ☐ 2 Herschel Walker | .50 | .20 | .05 |
| Dallas Cowboys | | | |
| ☐ 3 Roger Craig | .50 | .20 | .05 |
| San Francisco 49ers | | | |
| ☐ 4 Henry Ellard | .25 | .10 | .02 |
| Los Angeles Rams | | | |
| ☐ 5 Jerry Rice | 1.00 | .40 | .10 |
| San Francisco 49ers | | | |
| ☐ 6 Eddie Brown | .25 | .10 | .02 |
| Cincinnati Bengals | | | |
| ☐ 7 Anthony Carter | .35 | .14 | .03 |
| Minnesota Vikings | | | |
| ☐ 8 Greg Bell | .25 | .10 | .02 |
| Los Angeles Rams | | | |
| ☐ 9 John Stephens | .50 | .20 | .05 |
| New England Patriots | | | |
| ☐ 10 Ricky Sanders | .35 | .14 | .03 |
| Washington Redskins | | | |
| ☐ 11 Drew Hill | .25 | .10 | .02 |
| Houston Oilers | | | |
| ☐ 12 Mark Clayton | .35 | .14 | .03 |
| Miami Dolphins | | | |
| ☐ 13 Gary Anderson | .35 | .14 | .03 |
| San Diego Chargers | | | |
| ☐ 14 Neal Anderson | .50 | .20 | .05 |
| Chicago Bears | | | |
| ☐ 15 Roy Green | .35 | .14 | .03 |
| Phoenix Cardinals | | | |
| ☐ 16 Eric Martin | .35 | .14 | .03 |
| New Orleans Saints | | | |
| ☐ 17 Joe Morris | .35 | .14 | .03 |
| New York Giants | | | |
| ☐ 18 Al Toon | .35 | .14 | .03 |
| New York Jets | | | |
| ☐ 19 Ickey Woods | .25 | .10 | .02 |
| Cincinnati Bengals | | | |
| ☐ 20 Bruce Hill | .25 | .10 | .02 |
| Tampa Bay Buccaneers | | | |
| ☐ 21 Lionel Manuel | .25 | .10 | .02 |
| New York Giants | | | |
| ☐ 22 Curt Warner | .35 | .14 | .03 |
| Seattle Seahawks | | | |
| ☐ 23 John Settle | .25 | .10 | .02 |
| Atlanta Falcons | | | |
| ☐ 24 Mike Rozier | .35 | .14 | .03 |
| Houston Oilers | | | |

## 1989 Topps Traded

The 1989 Topps Traded set contains 132 standard-size (2 1/2" by 3 1/2") cards, numbered with the suffix "T". The cards are nearly identical to the 1989 Topps regular issue football set, except this traded series was printed on white stock and was distributed only as a boxed set. The key Rookie Cards in this set are Troy Aikman, Marion Butts, Bobby Humphrey, Dave Meggett, Eric Metcalf, Rodney Peete, Frank Reich, Andre Rison, Barry Sanders, Deion Sanders, Sammie Smith, Derrick Thomas, Steve Walsh, and Lorenzo White.

| | MINT | EXC | G-VG |
|---|---|---|---|
| COMPLETE FACT.SET (132) | 7.00 | 3.10 | .85 |
| COMMON PLAYER (1T-132T) | .04 | .02 | .01 |
| | | | |
| ☐ 1T Eric Ball | .10 | .05 | .01 |
| Cincinnati Bengals | | | |
| ☐ 2T Tony Mandarich | .07 | .03 | .01 |
| Green Bay Packers | | | |
| ☐ 3T Shawn Collins | .10 | .05 | .01 |
| Atlanta Falcons | | | |
| ☐ 4T Ray Bentley | .15 | .07 | .02 |
| Buffalo Bills | | | |
| ☐ 5T Tony Casillas | .04 | .02 | .01 |
| Atlanta Falcons | | | |
| ☐ 6T Al Del Greco | .10 | .05 | .01 |
| Phoenix Cardinals | | | |

| | | | | |
|---|---|---|---|---|
| ☐ 7T Dan Saleaumua | .10 | .05 | .01 |
| Kansas City Chiefs | | | |
| ☐ 8T Keith Bishop | .04 | .02 | .01 |
| Denver Broncos | | | |
| ☐ 9T Rodney Peete | .35 | .16 | .04 |
| Detroit Lions | | | |
| ☐ 10T Lorenzo White | .20 | .09 | .03 |
| Houston Oilers | | | |
| ☐ 11T Steve Smith | .20 | .09 | .03 |
| Los Angeles Raiders | | | |
| ☐ 12T Pete Mandley | .04 | .02 | .01 |
| Kansas City Chiefs | | | |
| ☐ 13T Mervyn Fernandez | .04 | .02 | .01 |
| Los Angeles Raiders | | | |
| ☐ 14T Flipper Anderson | .25 | .11 | .03 |
| Los Angeles Rams | | | |
| ☐ 15T Louis Oliver | .15 | .07 | .02 |
| Miami Dolphins | | | |
| ☐ 16T Rick Fenney | .04 | .02 | .01 |
| Minnesota Vikings | | | |
| ☐ 17T Gary Jeter | .04 | .02 | .01 |
| New England Patriots | | | |
| ☐ 18T Greg Cox | .04 | .02 | .01 |
| New York Giants | | | |
| ☐ 19T Bubba McDowell | .15 | .07 | .02 |
| Houston Oilers | | | |
| ☐ 20T Ron Heller | .04 | .02 | .01 |
| Philadelphia Eagles | | | |
| ☐ 21T Tim McDonald | .20 | .09 | .03 |
| Phoenix Cardinals | | | |
| ☐ 22T Jerrol Williams | .10 | .05 | .01 |
| Pittsburgh Steelers | | | |
| ☐ 23T Marion Butts | .30 | .14 | .04 |
| San Diego Chargers | | | |
| ☐ 24T Steve Young | .50 | .23 | .06 |
| San Francisco 49ers | | | |
| ☐ 25T Mike Merriweather | .07 | .03 | .01 |
| Minnesota Vikings | | | |
| ☐ 26T Richard Johnson | .04 | .02 | .01 |
| Detroit Lions | | | |
| ☐ 27T Gerald Riggs | .07 | .03 | .01 |
| Washington Redskins | | | |
| ☐ 28T Dave Waymer | .04 | .02 | .01 |
| New Orleans Saints | | | |
| ☐ 29T Issiac Holt | .04 | .02 | .01 |
| Dallas Cowboys | | | |
| ☐ 30T Deion Sanders | .75 | .35 | .09 |
| Atlanta Falcons | | | |
| ☐ 31T Todd Blackledge | .07 | .03 | .01 |
| Pittsburgh Steelers | | | |
| ☐ 32T Jeff Cross | .25 | .11 | .03 |
| Miami Dolphins | | | |
| ☐ 33T Steve Wisniewski | .20 | .09 | .03 |
| Los Angeles Raiders | | | |
| ☐ 34T Ron Brown | .04 | .02 | .01 |
| Los Angeles Rams | | | |
| ☐ 35T Rod Bernstine | .35 | .16 | .04 |
| San Diego Chargers | | | |
| ☐ 36T Jeff Uhlenhake | .04 | .02 | .01 |
| Miami Dolphins | | | |
| ☐ 37T Donnell Woolford | .15 | .07 | .02 |
| Chicago Bears | | | |
| ☐ 38T Bob Gagliano | .10 | .05 | .01 |
| Detroit Lions | | | |
| ☐ 39T Ezra Johnson | .04 | .02 | .01 |
| Indianapolis Colts | | | |
| ☐ 40T Ron Jaworski | .07 | .03 | .01 |
| Kansas City Chiefs | | | |
| ☐ 41T Lawyer Tillman | .10 | .05 | .01 |
| Clevelands Browns | | | |
| ☐ 42T Lorenzo Lynch | .10 | .05 | .01 |
| Chicago Bears | | | |
| ☐ 43T Mike Alexander | .04 | .02 | .01 |
| Los Angeles Raiders | | | |
| ☐ 44T Tim Worley | .25 | .11 | .03 |
| Pittsburgh Steelers | | | |
| ☐ 45T Guy Bingham | .04 | .02 | .01 |
| Atlanta Falcons | | | |
| ☐ 46T Cleveland Gary | .15 | .07 | .02 |
| Los Angeles Rams | | | |
| ☐ 47T Danny Peebles | .07 | .03 | .01 |
| Tampa Bay Buccaneers | | | |
| ☐ 48T Clarence Weathers | .04 | .02 | .01 |
| Kansas City Chiefs | | | |
| ☐ 49T Jeff Lageman | .10 | .05 | .01 |
| New York Jets | | | |
| ☐ 50T Eric Metcalf | .40 | .18 | .05 |
| Cleveland Browns | | | |
| ☐ 51T Myron Guyton | .10 | .05 | .01 |
| New York Giants | | | |
| ☐ 52T Steve Atwater | .20 | .09 | .03 |
| Denver Broncos | | | |
| ☐ 53T John Fourcade | .04 | .02 | .01 |
| New Orleans Saints | | | |
| ☐ 54T Randall McDaniel | .15 | .07 | .02 |
| Minnesota Vikings | | | |
| ☐ 55T Al Noga | .20 | .09 | .03 |

Minnesota Vikings
- ☐ 56T Sammie Smith ............... .07 .03 .01
Miami Dolphins
- ☐ 57T Jesse Solomon ............... .04 .02 .01
Dallas Cowboys
- ☐ 58T Greg Kragen ............... .10 .05 .01
Denver Broncos
- ☐ 59T Don Beebe ............... .40 .18 .05
Buffalo Bills
- ☐ 60T Hart Lee Dykes ............... .04 .02 .01
New England Patriots
- ☐ 61T Trace Armstrong ............... .25 .11 .03
Chicago Bears
- ☐ 62T Steve Pelluer ............... .07 .03 .01
Kansas City Chiefs
- ☐ 63T Barry Krauss ............... .04 .02 .01
Miami Dolphins
- ☐ 64T Kevin Murphy ............... .07 .03 .01
Tampa Bay Buccaneers
- ☐ 65T Steve Tasker ............... .30 .14 .04
Buffalo Bills
- ☐ 66T Jessie Small ............... .04 .02 .01
Philadelphia Eagles
- ☐ 67T Dave Meggett ............... .20 .09 .03
New York Giants
- ☐ 68T Dean Hamel ............... .04 .02 .01
Dallas Cowboys
- ☐ 69T Jim Covert ............... .04 .02 .01
Chicago Bears
- ☐ 70T Troy Aikman ............... 3.50 1.55 .45
Dallas Cowboys
- ☐ 71T Raul Allegre ............... .04 .02 .01
New York Giants
- ☐ 72T Chris Jacke ............... .15 .07 .02
Green Bay Packers
- ☐ 73T Leslie O'Neal ............... .10 .05 .01
San Diego Chargers
- ☐ 74T Keith Taylor ............... .10 .05 .01
Indianapolis Colts
- ☐ 75T Steve Walsh ............... .10 .05 .01
Dallas Cowboys
- ☐ 76T Tracy Rocker ............... .04 .02 .01
Washington Redskins
- ☐ 77T Robert Massey ............... .10 .05 .01
New Orleans Saints
- ☐ 78T Bryan Wagner ............... .07 .03 .01
Cleveland Browns
- ☐ 79T Steve DeOssie ............... .04 .02 .01
New York Giants
- ☐ 80T Carnell Lake ............... .10 .05 .01
Pittsburgh Steelers
- ☐ 81T Frank Reich ............... .50 .23 .06
Buffalo Bills
- ☐ 82T Tyrone Braxton ............... .10 .05 .01
Denver Broncos
- ☐ 83T Barry Sanders ............... 3.00 1.35 .40
Detroit Lions
- ☐ 84T Pete Stoyanovich ............... .20 .09 .03
Miami Dolphins
- ☐ 85T Paul Palmer ............... .04 .02 .01
Dallas Cowboys
- ☐ 86T Billy Joe Tolliver ............... .10 .05 .01
San Diego Chargers
- ☐ 87T Eric Hill ............... .10 .05 .01
Phoenix Cardinals
- ☐ 88T Gerald McNeil ............... .04 .02 .01
Cleveland Browns
- ☐ 89T Bill Hawkins ............... .04 .02 .01
Los Angeles Rams
- ☐ 90T Derrick Thomas ............... .75 .35 .09
Kansas City Chiefs
- ☐ 91T Jim Harbaugh ............... .40 .18 .05
Chicago Bears
- ☐ 92T Brian Williams ............... .04 .02 .01
New York Giants
- ☐ 93T Jack Trudeau ............... .04 .02 .01
Indianapolis Colts
- ☐ 94T Leonard Smith ............... .04 .02 .01
Buffalo Bills
- ☐ 95T Gary Hogeboom ............... .07 .03 .01
Phoenix Cardinals
- ☐ 96T A.J. Johnson ............... .10 .05 .01
Washington Redskins
- ☐ 97T Jim McMahon ............... .10 .05 .01
San Diego Chargers
- ☐ 98T David Williams ............... .10 .05 .01
Houston Oilers
- ☐ 99T Rohn Stark ............... .07 .03 .01
Indianapolis Colts
- ☐ 100T Sean Landeta ............... .07 .03 .01
New York Giants
- ☐ 101T Tim Johnson ............... .10 .05 .01
Pittsburgh Steelers
- ☐ 102T Andre Rison ............... .75 .35 .09
Indianapolis Colts
- ☐ 103T Earnest Byner ............... .07 .03 .01
Washington Redskins
- ☐ 104T Don McPherson ............... .10 .05 .01

Philadelphia Eagles
- ☐ 105T Zefross Moss ............... .04 .02 .01
Indianapolis Colts
- ☐ 106T Frank Stams ............... .04 .02 .01
Los Angeles Rams
- ☐ 107T Courtney Hall ............... .15 .07 .02
San Diego Chargers
- ☐ 108T Marc Logan ............... .15 .07 .02
Miami Dolphins
- ☐ 109T James Lofton ............... .10 .05 .01
Buffalo Bills
- ☐ 110T Lewis Tillman ............... .20 .09 .03
New York Giants
- ☐ 111T Irv Pankey ............... .04 .02 .01
Los Angeles Rams
- ☐ 112T Ralf Mojsiejenko ............... .04 .02 .01
Washington Redskins
- ☐ 113T Bobby Humphrey ............... .08 .04 .01
Denver Broncos
- ☐ 114T Chris Burkett ............... .07 .03 .01
New York Jets
- ☐ 115T Greg Lloyd ............... .25 .11 .03
Pittsburgh Steelers
- ☐ 116T Matt Millen ............... .07 .03 .01
San Francisco 49ers
- ☐ 117T Carl Zander ............... .04 .02 .01
Cincinnati Bengals
- ☐ 118T Wayne Martin ............... .15 .07 .02
New Orleans Saints
- ☐ 119T Mike Saxon ............... .04 .02 .01
Dallas Cowboys
- ☐ 120T Herschel Walker ............... .10 .05 .01
Minnesota Vikings
- ☐ 121T Andy Heck ............... .10 .05 .01
Seattle Seahawks
- ☐ 122T Mark Robinson ............... .07 .03 .01
Tampa Bay Buccaneers
- ☐ 123T Keith Van Horne ............... .04 .02 .01
Chicago Bears
- ☐ 124T Ricky Hunley ............... .04 .02 .01
Los Angeles Raiders
- ☐ 125T Timm Rosenbach ............... .15 .07 .02
Phoenix Cardinals
- ☐ 126T Steve Grogan ............... .07 .03 .01
New England Patriots
- ☐ 127T Stephen Braggs ............... .04 .02 .01
Cleveland Browns
- ☐ 128T Terry Long ............... .04 .02 .01
Pittsburgh Steelers
- ☐ 129T Evan Cooper ............... .04 .02 .01
Atlanta Falcons
- ☐ 130T Robert Lyles ............... .04 .02 .01
Houston Oilers
- ☐ 131T Mike Webster ............... .07 .03 .01
Kansas City Chiefs
- ☐ 132T Checklist 1-132 ............... .05 .02 .01

# 1989 Topps American/UK

This 33-card set was sold in the United Kingdom as a boxed set. The style of the cards is very similar to the 1989 Topps regular issue set. The backs are different as this set was printed on white card stock. The cards are standard size, 2 1/2" by 3 1/2". The checklist for the set is on the back of the box. The set is populated with name players that, presumably, would be recognizable in England.

|  | MINT | EXC | G-VG |
| --- | --- | --- | --- |
| COMPLETE SET (33) ............... | 30.00 | 12.00 | 3.00 |
| COMMON PLAYER (1-33) ............... | .75 | .30 | .07 |

- ☐ 1 Anthony Carter ............... 1.00 .40 .10
Minnesota Vikings
- ☐ 2 Jim Kelly ............... 2.50 1.00 .25
Buffalo Bills
- ☐ 3 Bernie Kosar ............... 1.50 .60 .15

| | | | | |
|---|---|---|---|---|
| Cleveland Browns | | | | |
| ☐ 4 John Elway | 3.50 | 1.40 | .35 |
| Denver Broncos | | | | |
| ☐ 5 Andre Tippett | 1.00 | .40 | .10 |
| New England Patriots | | | | |
| ☐ 6 Henry Ellard | 1.00 | .40 | .10 |
| Los Angeles Rams | | | | |
| ☐ 7 Eddie Brown | 1.00 | .40 | .10 |
| Cincinnati Bengals | | | | |
| ☐ 8 Gary Anderson | 1.00 | .40 | .10 |
| San Diego Chargers | | | | |
| ☐ 9 Eric Martin | 1.00 | .40 | .10 |
| New Orleans Saints | | | | |
| ☐ 10 Ickey Woods | .75 | .30 | .07 |
| Cincinnati Bengals | | | | |
| ☐ 11 Mike Singletary | 1.00 | .40 | .10 |
| Chicago Bears | | | | |
| ☐ 12 Phil Simms | 1.50 | .60 | .15 |
| New York Giants | | | | |
| ☐ 13 Brian Bosworth | 1.00 | .40 | .10 |
| Seattle Seahawks | | | | |
| ☐ 14 Mark Clayton | 1.25 | .50 | .12 |
| Miami Dolphins | | | | |
| ☐ 15 Eric Dickerson | 1.50 | .60 | .15 |
| Indianapolis Colts | | | | |
| ☐ 16 John Stephens | 1.00 | .40 | .10 |
| New England Patriots | | | | |
| ☐ 17 Neal Anderson | 1.00 | .40 | .10 |
| Chicago Bears | | | | |
| ☐ 18 Al Toon | 1.00 | .40 | .10 |
| New York Jets | | | | |
| ☐ 19 Lionel Manuel | .75 | .30 | .07 |
| New York Giants | | | | |
| ☐ 20 Joe Montana | 6.00 | 2.40 | .60 |
| San Francisco 49ers | | | | |
| ☐ 21 Reggie White | 2.00 | .80 | .20 |
| Philadelphia Eagles | | | | |
| ☐ 22 Randall Cunningham | 2.00 | .80 | .20 |
| Philadelphia Eagles | | | | |
| ☐ 23 Lawrence Taylor | 1.50 | .60 | .15 |
| New York Giants | | | | |
| ☐ 24 Jim Everett | 1.25 | .50 | .12 |
| Los Angeles Rams | | | | |
| ☐ 25 Neil Lomax | .75 | .30 | .07 |
| Phoenix Cardinals | | | | |
| ☐ 26 Herschel Walker | 1.25 | .50 | .12 |
| Dallas Cowboys | | | | |
| ☐ 27 Roger Craig | 1.25 | .50 | .12 |
| San Francisco 49ers | | | | |
| ☐ 28 Greg Bell | .75 | .30 | .07 |
| Los Angeles Rams | | | | |
| ☐ 29 Ricky Sanders | 1.00 | .40 | .10 |
| Washington Redskins | | | | |
| ☐ 30 Joe Morris | 1.00 | .40 | .10 |
| New York Giants | | | | |
| ☐ 31 Curt Warner | 1.00 | .40 | .10 |
| Seattle Seahawks | | | | |
| ☐ 32 Boomer Esiason | 1.50 | .60 | .15 |
| Cincinnati Bengals | | | | |
| ☐ 33 Dan Marino | 6.00 | 2.40 | .60 |
| Miami Dolphins | | | | |

# 1990 Topps

This 528-card set is similar to the Topps football efforts of the past few years. The cards are standard size, 2 1/2" by 3 1/2". The cards are arranged in team order and the teams themselves are ordered according to their finish in the 1989 standings, e.g., San Francisco 49ers (6-27), Denver Broncos (29-47), New York Giants (48-66), Los Angeles Rams (67-83), Philadelphia Eagles (84-101), Minnesota Vikings (102-119), Washington Redskins (120-138), Green Bay Packers (139-155), Cleveland Browns (156-174), Pittsburgh Steelers (175-192), Buffalo Bills (194-211), Houston Oilers (212-228), New Orleans Saints (230-246), Kansas City Chiefs (247-264), Cincinnati

Bengals (265-279), Los Angeles Raiders (280-297), Indianapolis Colts (298-316), Miami Dolphins (317-334), Seattle Seahawks (335-348), Detroit Lions (349-364), Chicago Bears (365-381), San Diego Chargers (382-398), Tampa Bay Buccaneers (399-415), New England Patriots (416-430), Phoenix Cardinals (432-447), New York Jets (448-465), Atlanta Falcons (466-480), Dallas Cowboys (481-496), Checklists (497-500), and Team Action Cards (501-528). Certain Leader cards (28, 193, 229, and 431) as weel as all of the Team Action cards (501-528) can be found with or without the hashmarks on the bottom of the card. The regular issue cards were released in two distinct varieties; the NFL Properties disclaimer is either present or absent from the back each card. Topps also produced a Tiffany edition of the set; this upscale version features exactly the same cards, but with a glossy coating on white card stock. Individual card Tiffany values are approximately five times the values listed below. Rookie Cards include Barry Foster, Jeff George, Rodney Hampton, Michael Haynes, Haywood Jeffires, Daryl Johnston, Cortez Kennedy, Junior Seau, Blair Thomas, and Andre Ware.

| | MINT | EXC | G-VG |
|---|---|---|---|
| COMPLETE SET (528) | 8.00 | 3.60 | 1.00 |
| COMPLETE FACT.SET (528) | 10.00 | 4.50 | 1.25 |
| COMMON PLAYER (1-528) | .04 | .02 | .01 |
| ☐ 1 Joe Montana RB | .50 | .23 | .06 |
| Most TD Passes, | | | |
| Super Bowl | | | |
| ☐ 2 Flipper Anderson RB | .04 | .02 | .01 |
| Most Receiving | | | |
| Yards, Game | | | |
| ☐ 3 Troy Aikman RB | .60 | .25 | .08 |
| Most Passing Yards, | | | |
| Game, Rookie | | | |
| ☐ 4 Kevin Butler RB | .04 | .02 | .01 |
| Most Consecutive | | | |
| Field Goals | | | |
| ☐ 5 Super Bowl XXIV | .04 | .02 | .01 |
| 49ers 55 | | | |
| Broncos 10 | | | |
| (line of scrimmage) | | | |
| ☐ 6 Dexter Carter | .15 | .07 | .02 |
| ☐ 7 Matt Millen | .08 | .04 | .01 |
| ☐ 8 Jerry Rice | .75 | .35 | .09 |
| ☐ 9 Ronnie Lott | .10 | .05 | .01 |
| ☐ 10 John Taylor | .15 | .07 | .02 |
| ☐ 11 Guy McIntyre | .08 | .04 | .01 |
| ☐ 12 Roger Craig | .08 | .04 | .01 |
| ☐ 13 Joe Montana | 1.00 | .45 | .13 |
| ☐ 14 Brent Jones | .40 | .18 | .05 |
| ☐ 15 Tom Rathman | .08 | .04 | .01 |
| ☐ 16 Harris Barton | .04 | .02 | .01 |
| ☐ 17 Charles Haley | .08 | .04 | .01 |
| ☐ 18 Pierce Holt | .15 | .07 | .02 |
| ☐ 19 Michael Carter | .04 | .02 | .01 |
| ☐ 20 Chet Brooks | .04 | .02 | .01 |
| ☐ 21 Eric Wright | .04 | .02 | .01 |
| ☐ 22 Mike Cofer | .04 | .02 | .01 |
| ☐ 23 Jim Fahnhorst | .04 | .02 | .01 |
| ☐ 24 Keena Turner | .08 | .04 | .01 |
| ☐ 25 Don Griffin | .04 | .02 | .01 |
| ☐ 26 Kevin Fagan | .04 | .02 | .01 |
| ☐ 27 Bubba Paris | .08 | .04 | .01 |
| ☐ 28 Rushing Leaders | .15 | .07 | .02 |
| Barry Sanders | | | |
| Christian Okoye | | | |
| ☐ 29 Steve Atwater | .10 | .05 | .01 |
| ☐ 30 Tyrone Braxton | .04 | .02 | .01 |
| ☐ 31 Ron Holmes | .04 | .02 | .01 |
| ☐ 32 Bobby Humphrey | .08 | .04 | .01 |
| ☐ 33 Greg Kragen | .04 | .02 | .01 |
| ☐ 34 David Treadwell | .04 | .02 | .01 |
| ☐ 35 Karl Mecklenburg | .08 | .04 | .01 |
| ☐ 36 Dennis Smith | .08 | .04 | .01 |
| ☐ 37 John Elway | .40 | .18 | .05 |
| ☐ 38 Vance Johnson | .08 | .04 | .01 |
| ☐ 39 Simon Fletcher UER | .08 | .04 | .01 |
| (Front DL, back LB) | | | |
| ☐ 40 Jim Juriga | .04 | .02 | .01 |
| ☐ 41 Mark Jackson | .08 | .04 | .01 |
| ☐ 42 Melvin Bratton | .04 | .02 | .01 |
| ☐ 43 Wymon Henderson | .04 | .02 | .01 |
| ☐ 44 Ken Bell | .04 | .02 | .01 |
| ☐ 45 Sammy Winder | .04 | .02 | .01 |
| ☐ 46 Alphonso Carreker | .04 | .02 | .01 |
| ☐ 47 Orson Mobley | .04 | .02 | .01 |
| ☐ 48 Rodney Hampton | 1.50 | .65 | .19 |
| ☐ 49 Dave Meggett | .10 | .05 | .01 |
| ☐ 50 Myron Guyton | .04 | .02 | .01 |
| ☐ 51 Phil Simms | .10 | .05 | .01 |
| ☐ 52 Lawrence Taylor | .10 | .05 | .01 |
| ☐ 53 Carl Banks | .08 | .04 | .01 |
| ☐ 54 Pepper Johnson | .08 | .04 | .01 |
| ☐ 55 Leonard Marshall | .08 | .04 | .01 |
| ☐ 56 Mark Collins | .04 | .02 | .01 |
| ☐ 57 Erik Howard | .04 | .02 | .01 |

| | | | |
|---|---|---|---|
| ☐ 58 Eric Dorsey | .04 | .02 | .01 |
| ☐ 59 Ottis Anderson | .08 | .04 | .01 |
| ☐ 60 Mark Bavaro | .08 | .04 | .01 |
| ☐ 61 Odessa Turner | .15 | .07 | .02 |
| ☐ 62 Gary Reasons | .04 | .02 | .01 |
| ☐ 63 Maurice Carthon | .04 | .02 | .01 |
| ☐ 64 Lionel Manuel | .04 | .02 | .01 |
| ☐ 65 Sean Landeta | .08 | .04 | .01 |
| ☐ 66 Perry Williams | .04 | .02 | .01 |
| ☐ 67 Pat Terrell | .10 | .05 | .01 |
| ☐ 68 Flipper Anderson | .08 | .04 | .01 |
| ☐ 69 Jackie Slater | .08 | .04 | .01 |
| ☐ 70 Tom Newberry | .04 | .02 | .01 |
| ☐ 71 Jerry Gray | .04 | .02 | .01 |
| ☐ 72 Henry Ellard | .08 | .04 | .01 |
| ☐ 73 Doug Smith | .08 | .04 | .01 |
| ☐ 74 Kevin Greene | .08 | .04 | .01 |
| ☐ 75 Jim Everett | .08 | .04 | .01 |
| ☐ 76 Mike Lansford | .04 | .02 | .01 |
| ☐ 77 Greg Bell | .08 | .04 | .01 |
| ☐ 78 Pete Holohan | .04 | .02 | .01 |
| ☐ 79 Robert Delpino | .08 | .04 | .01 |
| ☐ 80 Mike Wilcher | .04 | .02 | .01 |
| ☐ 81 Mike Piel | .04 | .02 | .01 |
| ☐ 82 Mel Owens | .04 | .02 | .01 |
| ☐ 83 Michael Stewart | .04 | .02 | .01 |
| ☐ 84 Ben Smith | .10 | .05 | .01 |
| ☐ 85 Keith Jackson | .25 | .11 | .03 |
| ☐ 86 Reggie White | .15 | .07 | .02 |
| ☐ 87 Eric Allen | .08 | .04 | .01 |
| ☐ 88 Jerome Brown | .08 | .04 | .01 |
| ☐ 89 Robert Drummond | .04 | .02 | .01 |
| ☐ 90 Anthony Toney | .04 | .02 | .01 |
| ☐ 91 Keith Byars | .08 | .04 | .01 |
| ☐ 92 Cris Carter | .20 | .09 | .03 |
| ☐ 93 Randall Cunningham | .15 | .07 | .02 |
| ☐ 94 Ron Johnson | .08 | .04 | .01 |
| ☐ 95 Mike Quick | .08 | .04 | .01 |
| ☐ 96 Clyde Simmons | .08 | .04 | .01 |
| ☐ 97 Mike Pitts | .04 | .02 | .01 |
| ☐ 98 Izel Jenkins | .04 | .02 | .01 |
| ☐ 99 Seth Joyner | .08 | .04 | .01 |
| ☐ 100 Mike Schad | .04 | .02 | .01 |
| ☐ 101 Wes Hopkins | .04 | .02 | .01 |
| ☐ 102 Kirk Lowdermilk | .04 | .02 | .01 |
| ☐ 103 Rick Fenney | .04 | .02 | .01 |
| ☐ 104 Randall McDaniel | .04 | .02 | .01 |
| ☐ 105 Herschel Walker | .10 | .05 | .01 |
| ☐ 106 Al Noga | .04 | .02 | .01 |
| ☐ 107 Gary Zimmerman | .08 | .04 | .01 |
| ☐ 108 Chris Doleman | .08 | .04 | .01 |
| ☐ 109 Keith Millard | .08 | .04 | .01 |
| ☐ 110 Carl Lee | .04 | .02 | .01 |
| ☐ 111 Joey Browner | .08 | .04 | .01 |
| ☐ 112 Steve Jordan | .08 | .04 | .01 |
| ☐ 113 Reggie Rutland | .10 | .05 | .01 |
| ☐ 114 Wade Wilson | .08 | .04 | .01 |
| ☐ 115 Anthony Carter | .08 | .04 | .01 |
| ☐ 116 Rick Karlis | .04 | .02 | .01 |
| ☐ 117 Hassan Jones | .04 | .02 | .01 |
| ☐ 118 Henry Thomas | .04 | .02 | .01 |
| ☐ 119 Scott Studwell | .04 | .02 | .01 |
| ☐ 120 Ralf Mojsiejenko | .04 | .02 | .01 |
| ☐ 121 Earnest Byner | .08 | .04 | .01 |
| ☐ 122 Gerald Riggs | .08 | .04 | .01 |
| ☐ 123 Tracy Rocker | .04 | .02 | .01 |
| ☐ 124 A.J. Johnson | .04 | .02 | .01 |
| ☐ 125 Charles Mann | .08 | .04 | .01 |
| ☐ 126 Art Monk | .10 | .05 | .01 |
| ☐ 127 Ricky Sanders | .08 | .04 | .01 |
| ☐ 128 Gary Clark | .10 | .05 | .01 |
| ☐ 129 Jim Lachey | .08 | .04 | .01 |
| ☐ 130 Martin Mayhew | .15 | .07 | .02 |
| ☐ 131 Ravin Caldwell | .04 | .02 | .01 |
| ☐ 132 Don Warren | .04 | .02 | .01 |
| ☐ 133 Mark Rypien | .10 | .05 | .01 |
| ☐ 134 Ed Simmons | .10 | .05 | .01 |
| ☐ 135 Darryl Grant | .04 | .02 | .01 |
| ☐ 136 Darrell Green | .08 | .04 | .01 |
| ☐ 137 Chip Lohmiller | .08 | .04 | .01 |
| ☐ 138 Tony Bennett | .30 | .14 | .04 |
| ☐ 139 Tony Mandarich | .04 | .02 | .01 |
| ☐ 140 Sterling Sharpe | .75 | .35 | .09 |
| ☐ 141 Tim Harris | .08 | .04 | .01 |
| ☐ 142 Don Majkowski | .08 | .04 | .01 |
| ☐ 143 Rich Moran | .04 | .02 | .01 |
| ☐ 144 Jeff Query | .04 | .02 | .01 |
| ☐ 145 Brent Fullwood | .04 | .02 | .01 |
| ☐ 146 Chris Jacke | .04 | .02 | .01 |
| ☐ 147 Keith Woodside | .04 | .02 | .01 |
| ☐ 148 Perry Kemp | .04 | .02 | .01 |
| ☐ 149 Herman Fontenot | .04 | .02 | .01 |
| ☐ 150 Dave Brown | .04 | .02 | .01 |
| ☐ 151 Brian Noble | .04 | .02 | .01 |
| ☐ 152 Johnny Holland | .04 | .02 | .01 |
| ☐ 153 Mark Murphy | .04 | .02 | .01 |
| ☐ 154 Bob Nelson | .04 | .02 | .01 |
| ☐ 155 Darrell Thompson | .15 | .07 | .02 |
| ☐ 156 Lawyer Tillman | .04 | .02 | .01 |
| ☐ 157 Eric Metcalf | .15 | .07 | .02 |
| ☐ 158 Webster Slaughter | .08 | .04 | .01 |
| ☐ 159 Frank Minnifield | .04 | .02 | .01 |
| ☐ 160 Brian Brennan | .04 | .02 | .01 |
| ☐ 161 Thane Gash | .04 | .02 | .01 |
| ☐ 162 Robert Banks | .04 | .02 | .01 |
| ☐ 163 Bernie Kosar | .10 | .05 | .01 |
| ☐ 164 David Grayson | .04 | .02 | .01 |
| ☐ 165 Kevin Mack | .08 | .04 | .01 |
| ☐ 166 Mike Johnson | .04 | .02 | .01 |
| ☐ 167 Tim Manoa | .04 | .02 | .01 |
| ☐ 168 Ozzie Newsome | .10 | .05 | .01 |
| ☐ 169 Felix Wright | .04 | .02 | .01 |
| ☐ 170 Al(Bubba) Baker | .08 | .04 | .01 |
| ☐ 171 Reggie Langhorne | .08 | .04 | .01 |
| ☐ 172 Clay Matthews | .08 | .04 | .01 |
| ☐ 173 Andrew Stewart | .04 | .02 | .01 |
| ☐ 174 Barry Foster | 1.00 | .45 | .13 |
| ☐ 175 Tim Worley | .08 | .04 | .01 |
| ☐ 176 Tim Johnson | .04 | .02 | .01 |
| ☐ 177 Carnell Lake | .04 | .02 | .01 |
| ☐ 178 Greg Lloyd | .04 | .02 | .01 |
| ☐ 179 Rod Woodson | .20 | .09 | .03 |
| ☐ 180 Tunch Ilkin | .04 | .02 | .01 |
| ☐ 181 Dermontti Dawson | .04 | .02 | .01 |
| ☐ 182 Gary Anderson | .08 | .04 | .01 |
| ☐ 183 Bubby Brister | .10 | .05 | .01 |
| ☐ 184 Louis Lipps | .08 | .04 | .01 |
| ☐ 185 Merril Hoge | .08 | .04 | .01 |
| ☐ 186 Mike Mularkey | .04 | .02 | .01 |
| ☐ 187 Derek Hill | .04 | .02 | .01 |
| ☐ 188 Rodney Carter | .04 | .02 | .01 |
| ☐ 189 Dwayne Woodruff | .04 | .02 | .01 |
| ☐ 190 Keith Willis | .04 | .02 | .01 |
| ☐ 191 Jerry Olsavsky | .04 | .02 | .01 |
| ☐ 192 Mark Stock | .04 | .02 | .01 |
| ☐ 193 Sacks Leaders | .04 | .02 | .01 |
| Chris Doleman | | | |
| Lee Williams | | | |
| ☐ 194 Leonard Smith | .04 | .02 | .01 |
| ☐ 195 Darryl Talley | .08 | .04 | .01 |
| ☐ 196 Mark Kelso | .04 | .02 | .01 |
| ☐ 197 Kent Hull | .04 | .02 | .01 |
| ☐ 198 Nate Odomes | .25 | .11 | .03 |
| ☐ 199 Pete Metzelaars | .04 | .02 | .01 |
| ☐ 200 Don Beebe | .15 | .07 | .02 |
| ☐ 201 Ray Bentley | .04 | .02 | .01 |
| ☐ 202 Steve Tasker | .04 | .02 | .01 |
| ☐ 203 Scott Norwood | .04 | .02 | .01 |
| ☐ 204 Andre Reed | .15 | .07 | .02 |
| ☐ 205 Bruce Smith | .10 | .05 | .01 |
| ☐ 206 Thurman Thomas | .40 | .18 | .05 |
| ☐ 207 Jim Kelly | .30 | .14 | .04 |
| ☐ 208 Cornelius Bennett | .10 | .05 | .01 |
| ☐ 209 Shane Conlan | .08 | .04 | .01 |
| ☐ 210 Larry Kinnebrew | .04 | .02 | .01 |
| ☐ 211 Jeff Alm | .04 | .02 | .01 |
| ☐ 212 Robert Lyles | .04 | .02 | .01 |
| ☐ 213 Bubba McDowell | .04 | .02 | .01 |
| ☐ 214 Mike Munchak | .08 | .04 | .01 |
| ☐ 215 Bruce Matthews | .08 | .04 | .01 |
| ☐ 216 Warren Moon | .25 | .11 | .03 |
| ☐ 217 Drew Hill | .08 | .04 | .01 |
| ☐ 218 Ray Childress | .08 | .04 | .01 |
| ☐ 219 Steve Brown | .04 | .02 | .01 |
| ☐ 220 Alonzo Highsmith | .04 | .02 | .01 |
| ☐ 221 Allen Pinkett | .04 | .02 | .01 |
| ☐ 222 Sean Jones | .08 | .04 | .01 |
| ☐ 223 Johnny Meads | .04 | .02 | .01 |
| ☐ 224 John Grimsley | .04 | .02 | .01 |
| ☐ 225 Haywood Jeffires | 1.00 | .45 | .13 |
| ☐ 226 Curtis Duncan | .08 | .04 | .01 |
| ☐ 227 Greg Montgomery | .10 | .05 | .01 |
| ☐ 228 Ernest Givins | .08 | .04 | .01 |
| ☐ 229 Passing Leaders | .25 | .11 | .03 |
| Joe Montana | | | |
| Boomer Esiason | | | |
| ☐ 230 Robert Massey | .04 | .02 | .01 |
| ☐ 231 John Fourcade | .04 | .02 | .01 |
| ☐ 232 Dalton Hilliard | .08 | .04 | .01 |
| ☐ 233 Vaughan Johnson | .08 | .04 | .01 |
| ☐ 234 Hoby Brenner | .04 | .02 | .01 |
| ☐ 235 Pat Swilling | .10 | .05 | .01 |
| ☐ 236 Kevin Haverdink | .04 | .02 | .01 |
| ☐ 237 Bobby Hebert | .15 | .07 | .02 |
| ☐ 238 Sam Mills | .08 | .04 | .01 |
| ☐ 239 Eric Martin | .08 | .04 | .01 |
| ☐ 240 Lonzell Hill | .04 | .02 | .01 |
| ☐ 241 Steve Trapilo | .04 | .02 | .01 |
| ☐ 242 Rickey Jackson | .08 | .04 | .01 |
| ☐ 243 Craig Heyward | .08 | .04 | .01 |
| ☐ 244 Rueben Mayes | .08 | .04 | .01 |
| ☐ 245 Morten Andersen | .08 | .04 | .01 |
| ☐ 246 Percy Snow | .04 | .02 | .01 |
| ☐ 247 Pete Mandley | .04 | .02 | .01 |

|  |  | | | |
|---|---|---|---|---|
| 248 | Derrick Thomas | .25 | .11 | .03 |
| 249 | Dan Saleaumua | .04 | .02 | .01 |
| 250 | Todd McNair | .15 | .07 | .02 |
| 251 | Leonard Griffin | .04 | .02 | .01 |
| 252 | Jonathan Hayes | .04 | .02 | .01 |
| 253 | Christian Okoye | .08 | .04 | .01 |
| 254 | Albert Lewis | .08 | .04 | .01 |
| 255 | Nick Lowery | .08 | .04 | .01 |
| 256 | Kevin Ross | .08 | .04 | .01 |
| 257 | Steve DeBerg UER | .08 | .04 | .01 |
| | (Total 45,046, should be 25,046) | | | |
| 258 | Stephone Paige | .08 | .04 | .01 |
| 259 | James Saxon | .10 | .05 | .01 |
| 260 | Herman Heard | .04 | .02 | .01 |
| 261 | Deron Cherry | .08 | .04 | .01 |
| 262 | Dino Hackett | .04 | .02 | .01 |
| 263 | Neil Smith | .20 | .09 | .03 |
| 264 | Steve Pelluer | .04 | .02 | .01 |
| 265 | Eric Thomas | .04 | .02 | .01 |
| 266 | Eric Ball | .04 | .02 | .01 |
| 267 | Leon White | .04 | .02 | .01 |
| 268 | Tim Krumrie | .04 | .02 | .01 |
| 269 | Jason Buck | .04 | .02 | .01 |
| 270 | Boomer Esiason | .20 | .09 | .03 |
| 271 | Carl Zander | .04 | .02 | .01 |
| 272 | Eddie Brown | .04 | .02 | .01 |
| 273 | David Fulcher | .08 | .04 | .01 |
| 274 | Tim McGee | .08 | .04 | .01 |
| 275 | James Brooks | .08 | .04 | .01 |
| 276 | Rickey Dixon | .04 | .02 | .01 |
| 277 | Ickey Woods | .04 | .02 | .01 |
| 278 | Anthony Munoz | .08 | .04 | .01 |
| 279 | Rodney Holman | .04 | .02 | .01 |
| 280 | Mike Alexander | .04 | .02 | .01 |
| 281 | Mervyn Fernandez | .04 | .02 | .01 |
| 282 | Steve Wisniewski | .04 | .02 | .01 |
| 283 | Steve Smith | .08 | .04 | .01 |
| 284 | Howie Long | .08 | .04 | .01 |
| 285 | Bo Jackson | .40 | .18 | .05 |
| 286 | Mike Dyal | .04 | .02 | .01 |
| 287 | Thomas Benson | .04 | .02 | .01 |
| 288 | Willie Gault | .08 | .04 | .01 |
| 289 | Marcus Allen | .15 | .07 | .02 |
| 290 | Greg Townsend | .08 | .04 | .01 |
| 291 | Steve Beuerlein | .25 | .11 | .03 |
| 292 | Scott Davis | .04 | .02 | .01 |
| 293 | Eddie Anderson | .10 | .05 | .01 |
| 294 | Terry McDaniel | .04 | .02 | .01 |
| 295 | Tim Brown | .35 | .16 | .04 |
| 296 | Bob Golic | .04 | .02 | .01 |
| 297 | Jeff Jaeger | .04 | .02 | .01 |
| 298 | Jeff George | .75 | .35 | .09 |
| 299 | Chip Banks | .08 | .04 | .01 |
| 300 | Andre Rison UER | .25 | .11 | .03 |
| | (Photo actually Clarence Weathers) | | | |
| 301 | Rohn Stark | .08 | .04 | .01 |
| 302 | Keith Taylor | .04 | .02 | .01 |
| 303 | Jack Trudeau | .08 | .04 | .01 |
| 304 | Chris Hinton | .08 | .04 | .01 |
| 305 | Ray Donaldson | .04 | .02 | .01 |
| 306 | Jeff Herrod | .10 | .05 | .01 |
| 307 | Clarence Verdin | .04 | .02 | .01 |
| 308 | Jon Hand | .04 | .02 | .01 |
| 309 | Bill Brooks | .08 | .04 | .01 |
| 310 | Albert Bentley | .04 | .02 | .01 |
| 311 | Mike Prior | .04 | .02 | .01 |
| 312 | Pat Beach | .04 | .02 | .01 |
| 313 | Eugene Daniel | .04 | .02 | .01 |
| 314 | Duane Bickett | .04 | .02 | .01 |
| 315 | Dean Biasucci | .04 | .02 | .01 |
| 316 | Richmond Webb | .20 | .09 | .03 |
| 317 | Jeff Cross | .04 | .02 | .01 |
| 318 | Louis Oliver | .08 | .04 | .01 |
| 319 | Sammie Smith | .04 | .02 | .01 |
| 320 | Pete Stoyanovich | .08 | .04 | .01 |
| 321 | John Offerdahl | .08 | .04 | .01 |
| 322 | Ferrell Edmunds | .04 | .02 | .01 |
| 323 | Dan Marino | .75 | .35 | .09 |
| 324 | Andre Brown | .04 | .02 | .01 |
| 325 | Reggie Roby | .08 | .04 | .01 |
| 326 | Jarvis Williams | .04 | .02 | .01 |
| 327 | Roy Foster | .04 | .02 | .01 |
| 328 | Mark Clayton | .08 | .04 | .01 |
| 329 | Brian Sochia | .04 | .02 | .01 |
| 330 | Mark Duper | .08 | .04 | .01 |
| 331 | T.J. Turner | .04 | .02 | .01 |
| 332 | Jeff Uhlenhake | .04 | .02 | .01 |
| 333 | Jim Jensen | .04 | .02 | .01 |
| 334 | Cortez Kennedy | .75 | .35 | .09 |
| 335 | Andy Heck | .04 | .02 | .01 |
| 336 | Rufus Porter | .04 | .02 | .01 |
| 337 | Brian Blades | .15 | .07 | .02 |
| 338 | Dave Krieg | .08 | .04 | .01 |
| 339 | John L. Williams | .08 | .04 | .01 |
| 340 | David Wyman | .04 | .02 | .01 |
| 341 | Paul Skansi | .10 | .05 | .01 |
| 342 | Eugene Robinson | .04 | .02 | .01 |
| 343 | Joe Nash | .04 | .02 | .01 |
| 344 | Jacob Green | .04 | .02 | .01 |
| 345 | Jeff Bryant | .04 | .02 | .01 |
| 346 | Ruben Rodriguez | .04 | .02 | .01 |
| 347 | Norm Johnson | .04 | .02 | .01 |
| 348 | Darren Comeaux | .04 | .02 | .01 |
| 349 | Andre Ware | .15 | .07 | .02 |
| 350 | Richard Johnson | .04 | .02 | .01 |
| 351 | Rodney Peete | .08 | .04 | .01 |
| 352 | Barry Sanders | 1.00 | .45 | .13 |
| 353 | Chris Spielman | .08 | .04 | .01 |
| 354 | Eddie Murray | .08 | .04 | .01 |
| 355 | Jerry Ball | .08 | .04 | .01 |
| 356 | Mel Gray | .08 | .04 | .01 |
| 357 | Eric Williams | .10 | .05 | .01 |
| 358 | Robert Clark | .08 | .04 | .01 |
| 359 | Jason Phillips | .04 | .02 | .01 |
| 360 | Terry Taylor | .04 | .02 | .01 |
| 361 | Bennie Blades | .04 | .02 | .01 |
| 362 | Michael Cofer | .04 | .02 | .01 |
| 363 | Jim Arnold | .04 | .02 | .01 |
| 364 | Marc Spindler | .04 | .02 | .01 |
| 365 | Jim Covert | .04 | .02 | .01 |
| 366 | Jim Harbaugh | .12 | .05 | .02 |
| 367 | Neal Anderson | .08 | .04 | .01 |
| 368 | Mike Singletary | .10 | .05 | .01 |
| 369 | John Roper | .04 | .02 | .01 |
| 370 | Steve McMichael | .08 | .04 | .01 |
| 371 | Dennis Gentry | .04 | .02 | .01 |
| 372 | Brad Muster | .08 | .04 | .01 |
| 373 | Ron Morris | .04 | .02 | .01 |
| 374 | James Thornton | .04 | .02 | .01 |
| 375 | Kevin Butler | .04 | .02 | .01 |
| 376 | Richard Dent | .08 | .04 | .01 |
| 377 | Dan Hampton | .08 | .04 | .01 |
| 378 | Jay Hilgenberg | .08 | .04 | .01 |
| 379 | Donnell Woolford | .04 | .02 | .01 |
| 380 | Trace Armstrong | .04 | .02 | .01 |
| 381 | Junior Seau | .75 | .35 | .09 |
| 382 | Rod Bernstine | .15 | .07 | .02 |
| 383 | Marion Butts | .10 | .05 | .01 |
| 384 | Burt Grossman | .04 | .02 | .01 |
| 385 | Darrin Nelson | .08 | .04 | .01 |
| 386 | Leslie O'Neal | .08 | .04 | .01 |
| 387 | Billy Joe Tolliver | .04 | .02 | .01 |
| 388 | Courtney Hall | .04 | .02 | .01 |
| 389 | Lee Williams | .08 | .04 | .01 |
| 390 | Anthony Miller | .30 | .14 | .04 |
| 391 | Gill Byrd | .04 | .02 | .01 |
| 392 | Wayne Walker | .04 | .02 | .01 |
| 393 | Billy Ray Smith | .08 | .04 | .01 |
| 394 | Vencie Glenn | .04 | .02 | .01 |
| 395 | Tim Spencer | .04 | .02 | .01 |
| 396 | Gary Plummer | .04 | .02 | .01 |
| 397 | Arthur Cox | .04 | .02 | .01 |
| 398 | Jamie Holland | .04 | .02 | .01 |
| 399 | Keith McCants | .10 | .05 | .01 |
| 400 | Kevin Murphy | .04 | .02 | .01 |
| 401 | Danny Peebles | .04 | .02 | .01 |
| 402 | Mark Robinson | .04 | .02 | .01 |
| 403 | Broderick Thomas | .08 | .04 | .01 |
| 404 | Ron Hall | .04 | .02 | .01 |
| 405 | Mark Carrier | .10 | .05 | .01 |
| 406 | Paul Gruber | .08 | .04 | .01 |
| 407 | Vinny Testaverde | .15 | .07 | .02 |
| 408 | Bruce Hill | .04 | .02 | .01 |
| 409 | Lars Tate | .04 | .02 | .01 |
| 410 | Harry Hamilton | .04 | .02 | .01 |
| 411 | Ricky Reynolds | .04 | .02 | .01 |
| 412 | Donald Igwebuike | .04 | .02 | .01 |
| 413 | Reuben Davis | .04 | .02 | .01 |
| 414 | William Howard | .04 | .02 | .01 |
| 415 | Winston Moss | .04 | .02 | .01 |
| 416 | Chris Singleton | .10 | .05 | .01 |
| 417 | Hart Lee Dykes | .04 | .02 | .01 |
| 418 | Steve Grogan | .08 | .04 | .01 |
| 419 | Bruce Armstrong | .04 | .02 | .01 |
| 420 | Robert Perryman | .04 | .02 | .01 |
| 421 | Andre Tippett | .08 | .04 | .01 |
| 422 | Sammy Martin | .04 | .02 | .01 |
| 423 | Stanley Morgan | .08 | .04 | .01 |
| 424 | Cedric Jones | .04 | .02 | .01 |
| 425 | Sean Farrell | .04 | .02 | .01 |
| 426 | Marc Wilson | .08 | .04 | .01 |
| 427 | John Stephens | .08 | .04 | .01 |
| 428 | Eric Sievers | .04 | .02 | .01 |
| 429 | Maurice Hurst | .04 | .02 | .01 |
| 430 | Johnny Rembert | .04 | .02 | .01 |
| 431 | Receiving Leaders | .25 | .11 | .03 |
| | Jerry Rice Andre Reed | | | |
| 432 | Eric Hill | .04 | .02 | .01 |
| 433 | Gary Hogeboom | .08 | .04 | .01 |
| 434 | Timm Rosenbach UER | .04 | .02 | .01 |
| | (Born 1967 in Everett, | | | |

Wa., should be 1966
in Missoula, Mont.)

| | | | | |
|---|---|---|---|---|
| ☐ 435 Tim McDonald | .08 | .04 | .01 |
| ☐ 436 Rich Camarillo | .04 | .02 | .01 |
| ☐ 437 Luis Sharpe | .04 | .02 | .01 |
| ☐ 438 J.T. Smith | .04 | .02 | .01 |
| ☐ 439 Roy Green | .08 | .04 | .01 |
| ☐ 440 Ernie Jones | .15 | .07 | .02 |
| ☐ 441 Robert Awalt | .04 | .02 | .01 |
| ☐ 442 Vai Sikahema | .08 | .04 | .01 |
| ☐ 443 Joe Wolf | .04 | .02 | .01 |
| ☐ 444 Stump Mitchell | .08 | .04 | .01 |
| ☐ 445 David Galloway | .04 | .02 | .01 |
| ☐ 446 Ron Wolfley | .04 | .02 | .01 |
| ☐ 447 Freddie Joe Nunn | .08 | .04 | .01 |
| ☐ 448 Blair Thomas | .10 | .05 | .01 |
| ☐ 449 Jeff Lageman | .04 | .02 | .01 |
| ☐ 450 Tony Eason | .08 | .04 | .01 |
| ☐ 451 Erik McMillan | .04 | .02 | .01 |
| ☐ 452 Jim Sweeney | .04 | .02 | .01 |
| ☐ 453 Ken O'Brien | .08 | .04 | .01 |
| ☐ 454 Johnny Hector | .04 | .02 | .01 |
| ☐ 455 Jo Jo Townsell | .04 | .02 | .01 |
| ☐ 456 Roger Vick | .04 | .02 | .01 |
| ☐ 457 James Hasty | .04 | .02 | .01 |
| ☐ 458 Dennis Byrd | .25 | .11 | .03 |
| ☐ 459 Ron Stallworth | .04 | .02 | .01 |
| ☐ 460 Mickey Shuler | .04 | .02 | .01 |
| ☐ 461 Bobby Humphery | .04 | .02 | .01 |
| ☐ 462 Kyle Clifton | .04 | .02 | .01 |
| ☐ 463 Al Toon | .08 | .04 | .01 |
| ☐ 464 Freeman McNeil | .08 | .04 | .01 |
| ☐ 465 Pat Leahy | .08 | .04 | .01 |
| ☐ 466 Scott Case | .04 | .02 | .01 |
| ☐ 467 Shawn Collins | .04 | .02 | .01 |
| ☐ 468 Floyd Dixon | .04 | .02 | .01 |
| ☐ 469 Deion Sanders | .25 | .11 | .03 |
| ☐ 470 Tony Casillas | .04 | .02 | .01 |
| ☐ 471 Michael Haynes | 1.25 | .55 | .16 |
| ☐ 472 Chris Miller | .15 | .07 | .02 |
| ☐ 473 John Settle | .04 | .02 | .01 |
| ☐ 474 Aundray Bruce | .04 | .02 | .01 |
| ☐ 475 Gene Lang | .04 | .02 | .01 |
| ☐ 476 Tim Gordon | .04 | .02 | .01 |
| ☐ 477 Scott Fulhage | .04 | .02 | .01 |
| ☐ 478 Bill Fralic | .08 | .04 | .01 |
| ☐ 479 Jessie Tuggle | .25 | .11 | .03 |
| ☐ 480 Marcus Cotton | .04 | .02 | .01 |
| ☐ 481 Steve Walsh | .04 | .02 | .01 |
| ☐ 482 Troy Aikman | 1.25 | .55 | .16 |
| ☐ 483 Ray Horton | .04 | .02 | .01 |
| ☐ 484 Tony Tolbert | .20 | .09 | .03 |
| ☐ 485 Steve Folsom | .04 | .02 | .01 |
| ☐ 486 Ken Norton | .50 | .23 | .06 |
| ☐ 487 Kelvin Martin | .25 | .11 | .03 |
| ☐ 488 Jack Del Rio | .04 | .02 | .01 |
| ☐ 489 Daryl Johnston | .75 | .35 | .09 |
| ☐ 490 Bill Bates | .04 | .02 | .01 |
| ☐ 491 Jim Jeffcoat | .04 | .02 | .01 |
| ☐ 492 Vince Albritton | .04 | .02 | .01 |
| ☐ 493 Eugene Lockhart | .04 | .02 | .01 |
| ☐ 494 Mike Saxon | .04 | .02 | .01 |
| ☐ 495 James Dixon | .04 | .02 | .01 |
| ☐ 496 Willie Broughton | .04 | .02 | .01 |
| ☐ 497 Checklist 1-132 | .04 | .02 | .01 |
| ☐ 498 Checklist 133-264 | .04 | .02 | .01 |
| ☐ 499 Checklist 265-396 | .04 | .02 | .01 |
| ☐ 500 Checklist 397-528 | .04 | .02 | .01 |
| ☐ 501 Bears Team | .04 | .02 | .01 |
| Harbaugh Eludes | | | |
| The Pursuit | | | |
| ☐ 502 Bengals Team | .04 | .02 | .01 |
| Boomer Studies | | | |
| The Defense | | | |
| ☐ 503 Bills Team | .04 | .02 | .01 |
| Conlan Calls | | | |
| Defensive Scheme | | | |
| ☐ 504 Broncos Team | .04 | .02 | .01 |
| Bratton Breaks Away | | | |
| ☐ 505 Browns Team | .08 | .04 | .01 |
| Kosar Calls The Play | | | |
| ☐ 506 Buccaneers Team | .04 | .02 | .01 |
| Moss Assists In | | | |
| Squeeze Play | | | |
| ☐ 507 Cardinals Team | .04 | .02 | .01 |
| Zordich Saves The Day | | | |
| ☐ 508 Chargers Team | .04 | .02 | .01 |
| Williams Plugs | | | |
| The Hole | | | |
| ☐ 509 Chiefs Team | .04 | .02 | .01 |
| Cherry Applies The "D" | | | |
| ☐ 510 Colts Team | .04 | .02 | .01 |
| Trudeau Begins | | | |
| A Reverse | | | |
| ☐ 511 Cowboys Team | .60 | .25 | .08 |
| Aikman Directs | | | |
| Ground Attack | | | |
| ☐ 512 Dolphins Team | .04 | .02 | .01 |

| | | | | |
|---|---|---|---|---|
| Double-Decker By | | | |
| Oliver and Williams | | | |
| ☐ 513 Eagles Team | .04 | .02 | .01 |
| Toney Bangs Into | | | |
| The Line | | | |
| ☐ 514 Falcons Team | .04 | .02 | .01 |
| Tuggle Falls On Fumble | | | |
| ☐ 515 49ers Team | .25 | .11 | .03 |
| Montana To Craig, | | | |
| A Winning Duo | | | |
| ☐ 516 Giants Team | .08 | .04 | .01 |
| Simms Likes His O.J. | | | |
| ☐ 517 Jets Team | .04 | .02 | .01 |
| A Hasty Return | | | |
| ☐ 518 Lions Team | .04 | .02 | .01 |
| Gagliano Orchestrates | | | |
| The Offense | | | |
| ☐ 519 Oilers Team | .10 | .05 | .01 |
| Moon Scrambles | | | |
| To Daylight | | | |
| ☐ 520 Packers Team | .04 | .02 | .01 |
| A Bit Of Packer "Majik" | | | |
| ☐ 521 Patriots Team | .04 | .02 | .01 |
| Stephens Steams Ahead | | | |
| ☐ 522 Raiders Team | .10 | .05 | .01 |
| Bo Knows Yardage | | | |
| ☐ 523 Rams Team | .08 | .04 | .01 |
| Everett Rolls Right | | | |
| ☐ 524 Redskins Team | .08 | .04 | .01 |
| Riggs Rumbles | | | |
| Downfield | | | |
| ☐ 525 Saints Team | .04 | .02 | .01 |
| Mills Takes A Stand | | | |
| ☐ 526 Seahawks Team | .04 | .02 | .01 |
| Feasel Sets To Snap | | | |
| ☐ 527 Steelers Team | .04 | .02 | .01 |
| Brister Has A | | | |
| Clear Lane | | | |
| ☐ 528 Vikings Team | .04 | .02 | .01 |
| Fenney Spots Opening | | | |

## 1990 Topps Box Bottoms

These cards were printed on the bottom of the 1990 Topps Wax Boxes. This 16-card set measures the standard 2 1/2" by 3 1/2" and features the NFL's offensive and defensive player of the week for each week of the 1989 season. Each card features two players on the front and the back explains why they were the player of the week and what they did to earn the title. The cards are lettered rather than numbered. The set includes cards of Jim Kelly, Dan Marino, and Warren Moon. The set is checklisted in order of weeks of the season and is arranged alphabetically.

| | MINT | EXC | G-VG |
|---|---|---|---|
| COMPLETE SET (16) | 5.00 | 2.00 | .50 |
| COMMON PLAYER (A-P) | .25 | .10 | .02 |
| ☐ A Jim Kelly and | .50 | .20 | .05 |
| Buffalo Bills | | | |
| Dave Grayson | | | |
| Cleveland Browns | | | |
| ☐ B Henry Ellard and | .50 | .20 | .05 |
| Los Angeles Rams | | | |
| Derrick Thomas | | | |
| Kansas City Chiefs | | | |
| ☐ C Joe Montana and | 1.25 | .50 | .12 |
| San Francisco 49ers | | | |
| Vince Newsome | | | |
| Los Angeles Rams | | | |
| ☐ D Bubby Brister and | .25 | .10 | .02 |
| Pittsburgh Steelers | | | |
| Tim Harris | | | |
| Green Bay Packers | | | |
| ☐ E Christian Okoye and | .25 | .10 | .02 |

Kansas City Chiefs
Keith Millard
Minnesota Vikings

| | | | |
|---|---|---|---|
| ☐ F Warren Moon and .................... | .50 | .20 | .05 |
| Houston Oilers | | | |
| Jerome Brown | | | |
| Philadelphia Eagles | | | |
| ☐ G John Elway and .................... | .75 | .30 | .07 |
| Denver Broncos | | | |
| Mike Merriweather | | | |
| Minnesota Vikings | | | |
| ☐ H Webster Slaughter and ............ | .35 | .14 | .03 |
| Cleveland Browns | | | |
| Pat Swilling | | | |
| New Orleans Saints | | | |
| ☐ I Rick Karlis and .................... | .35 | .14 | .03 |
| Minnesota Vikings | | | |
| Lawrence Taylor | | | |
| New York Giants | | | |
| ☐ J Dan Marino and .................... | 1.00 | .40 | .10 |
| Miami Dolphins | | | |
| Greg Kragen | | | |
| Denver Broncos | | | |
| ☐ K Boomer Esiason and ............... | .35 | .14 | .03 |
| Cincinnati Bengals | | | |
| Brent Williams | | | |
| New England Patriots | | | |
| ☐ L Flipper Anderson and ............. | .25 | .10 | .02 |
| Los Angeles Rams | | | |
| Pierce Holt | | | |
| San Francisco 49ers | | | |
| ☐ M Richard Johnson and ............. | .25 | .10 | .02 |
| Detroit Lions | | | |
| David Fulcher | | | |
| Cincinnati Bengals | | | |
| ☐ N John Taylor and .................... | .35 | .14 | .03 |
| San Francisco 49ers | | | |
| Mike Prior | | | |
| Indianapolis Colts | | | |
| ☐ O Mark Rypien and .................... | .35 | .14 | .03 |
| Washington Redskins | | | |
| Brett Faryniarz | | | |
| Los Angeles Rams | | | |
| ☐ P Greg Bell and .................... | .25 | .10 | .02 |
| Los Angeles Rams | | | |
| Chris Doleman | | | |
| Minnesota Vikings | | | |

| | | | |
|---|---|---|---|
| ☐ 5 Mark Carrier .................... | .35 | .14 | .03 |
| Tampa Bay Buccaneers | | | |
| ☐ 6 Henry Ellard .................... | .25 | .10 | .02 |
| Los Angeles Rams | | | |
| ☐ 7 Andre Reed .................... | .50 | .20 | .05 |
| Buffalo Bills | | | |
| ☐ 8 Neal Anderson .................... | .35 | .14 | .03 |
| Chicago Bears | | | |
| ☐ 9 Dalton Hilliard .................... | .25 | .10 | .02 |
| New Orleans Saints | | | |
| ☐ 10 Anthony Miller .................... | .50 | .20 | .05 |
| San Diego Chargers | | | |
| ☐ 11 Thurman Thomas .................... | 1.00 | .40 | .10 |
| Buffalo Bills | | | |
| ☐ 12 James Brooks .................... | .35 | .14 | .03 |
| Cincinnati Bengals | | | |
| ☐ 13 Webster Slaughter .................... | .35 | .14 | .03 |
| Cleveland Browns | | | |
| ☐ 14 Gary Clark .................... | .35 | .14 | .03 |
| Washington Redskins | | | |
| ☐ 15 Tim McGee .................... | .25 | .10 | .02 |
| Cincinnati Bengals | | | |
| ☐ 16 Art Monk .................... | .50 | .20 | .05 |
| Washington Redskins | | | |
| ☐ 17 Bobby Humphrey .................... | .25 | .10 | .02 |
| Denver Broncos | | | |
| ☐ 18 Flipper Anderson .................... | .25 | .10 | .02 |
| Los Angeles Rams | | | |
| ☐ 19 Ricky Sanders .................... | .35 | .14 | .03 |
| Washington Redskins | | | |
| ☐ 20 Greg Bell .................... | .25 | .10 | .02 |
| Los Angeles Rams | | | |
| ☐ 21 Vance Johnson .................... | .25 | .10 | .02 |
| Denver Broncos | | | |
| ☐ 22 Richard Johnson UER .................... | .25 | .10 | .02 |
| Detroit Lions | | | |
| (Topps logo in upper | | | |
| right corner) | | | |
| ☐ 23 Eric Martin .................... | .35 | .14 | .03 |
| New Orleans Saints | | | |
| ☐ 24 John Taylor .................... | .35 | .14 | .03 |
| San Francisco 49ers | | | |
| ☐ 25 Mervyn Fernandez .................... | .35 | .14 | .03 |
| Los Angeles Raiders | | | |
| ☐ 26 Anthony Carter .................... | .35 | .14 | .03 |
| Minnesota Vikings | | | |
| ☐ 27 Brian Blades .................... | .35 | .14 | .03 |
| Seattle Seahawks | | | |
| ☐ 28 Roger Craig .................... | .35 | .14 | .03 |
| San Francisco 49ers | | | |
| ☐ 29 Ottis Anderson .................... | .35 | .14 | .03 |
| New York Giants | | | |
| ☐ 30 Mark Clayton .................... | .35 | .14 | .03 |
| Miami Dolphins | | | |

## 1990 Topps 1000 Yard Club

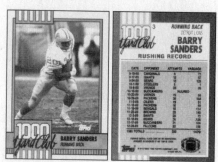

Topps once again in 1990 issued a card set which honored the players in the NFL who gained more than 1,000 yards in the 1989 season. These cards were included in every 1990 wax pack. The set consists of 30 standard size, 2 1/2" by 3 1/2", cards. The front features an attractive action photo of the player while the back has a game by game rundown of how the player achieved the 1,000 yard milestone. The set is arranged by Topps in order of number of yards gained in 1989. The cards in this set were released in two distinct varieties; the NFL Properties disclaimer is either present or absent from the back of each card.

| | MINT | EXC | G-VG |
|---|---|---|---|
| COMPLETE SET (30) .................... | 5.00 | 2.00 | .50 |
| COMMON PLAYER (1-30) ............... | .25 | .10 | .02 |
| ☐ 1 Jerry Rice .................... | 1.00 | .40 | .10 |
| San Francisco 49ers | | | |
| ☐ 2 Christian Okoye .................... | .35 | .14 | .03 |
| Kansas City Chiefs | | | |
| ☐ 3 Barry Sanders .................... | 1.50 | .60 | .15 |
| Detroit Lions | | | |
| ☐ 4 Sterling Sharpe .................... | 1.00 | .40 | .10 |
| Green Bay Packers | | | |

## 1990 Topps Traded

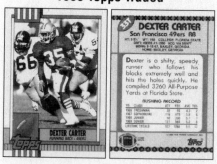

This 132-card set measures 2 1/2" by 3 1/2" and was released by Topps as an update to their regular issue set. The set features players who were traded after Topps printed their regular set and rookies who were not in the 1990 Topps football set. The set was issued in its own custom box and was distributed through the Topps hobby distribution system. The cards were printed on white card stock and are numbered on the back with a "T" suffix. The key Rookie Cards in the set are Fred Barnett, Reggie Cobb, Harold Green, Stan Humphries, Johnny Johnson, Rob Moore, and Emmitt Smith.

| | MINT | EXC | G-VG |
|---|---|---|---|
| COMPLETE FACT.SET (132) ............ | 9.00 | 4.00 | 1.15 |
| COMMON PLAYER (1T-132T) ........... | .04 | .02 | .01 |
| ☐ 1T Gerald McNeil .................... | .04 | .02 | .01 |
| Houston Oilers | | | |
| ☐ 2T Andre Rison .................... | .25 | .11 | .02 |

| | | | |
|---|---|---|---|
| Atlanta Falcons | | | |
| ☐ 3T Steve Walsh | .04 | .02 | .01 |
| New Orleans Saints | | | |
| ☐ 4T Lorenzo White | .10 | .05 | .01 |
| Houston Oilers | | | |
| ☐ 5T Max Montoya | .04 | .02 | .01 |
| Los Angeles Raiders | | | |
| ☐ 6T William Roberts | .10 | .05 | .01 |
| New York Giants | | | |
| ☐ 7T Alonzo Highsmith | .04 | .02 | .01 |
| Dallas Cowboys | | | |
| ☐ 8T Chris Hinton | .08 | .04 | .01 |
| Atlanta Falcons | | | |
| ☐ 9T Stanley Morgan | .08 | .04 | .01 |
| Indianapolis Colts | | | |
| ☐ 10T Mickey Shuler | .04 | .02 | .01 |
| Philadelphia Eagles | | | |
| ☐ 11T Bobby Humphery | .04 | .02 | .01 |
| Los Angeles Rams | | | |
| ☐ 12T Gary Anderson | .08 | .04 | .01 |
| Tampa Bay Buccaneers | | | |
| ☐ 13T Mike Tomczak | .08 | .04 | .01 |
| Chicago Bears | | | |
| ☐ 14T Anthony Pleasant | .10 | .05 | .01 |
| Cleveland Browns | | | |
| ☐ 15T Walter Stanley | .04 | .02 | .01 |
| Washington Redskins | | | |
| ☐ 16T Greg Bell | .08 | .04 | .01 |
| Los Angeles Raiders | | | |
| ☐ 17T Tony Martin | .15 | .07 | .02 |
| Miami Dolphins | | | |
| ☐ 18T Terry Kinard | .04 | .02 | .01 |
| Houston Oilers | | | |
| ☐ 19T Cris Carter | .20 | .09 | .03 |
| Minnesota Vikings | | | |
| ☐ 20T James Wilder | .08 | .04 | .01 |
| Detroit Lions | | | |
| ☐ 21T Jerry Kauric | .04 | .02 | .01 |
| Cleveland Browns | | | |
| ☐ 22T Irving Fryar | .08 | .04 | .01 |
| New England Patriots | | | |
| ☐ 23T Ken Harvey | .12 | .05 | .02 |
| Phoenix Cardinals | | | |
| ☐ 24T James Williams | .10 | .05 | .01 |
| Buffalo Bills | | | |
| ☐ 25T Ron Cox | .04 | .02 | .01 |
| Chicago Bears | | | |
| ☐ 26T Andre Ware | .10 | .05 | .01 |
| Detroit Lions | | | |
| ☐ 27T Emmitt Smith | 7.00 | 3.10 | .85 |
| Dallas Cowboys | | | |
| ☐ 28T Junior Seau | .75 | .35 | .09 |
| San Diego Chargers | | | |
| ☐ 29T Mark Carrier | .20 | .09 | .03 |
| Chicago Bears | | | |
| ☐ 30T Rodney Hampton | 1.00 | .45 | .13 |
| New York Giants | | | |
| ☐ 31T Rob Moore | .50 | .23 | .06 |
| New York Jets | | | |
| ☐ 32T Bern Brostek | .04 | .02 | .01 |
| Los Angeles Rams | | | |
| ☐ 33T Dexter Carter | .04 | .02 | .01 |
| San Francisco 49ers | | | |
| ☐ 34T Blair Thomas | .10 | .05 | .01 |
| New York Jets | | | |
| ☐ 35T Harold Green | .40 | .18 | .05 |
| Cincinnati Bengals | | | |
| ☐ 36T Darrell Thompson | .15 | .07 | .02 |
| Green Bay Packers | | | |
| ☐ 37T Eric Green | .40 | .18 | .05 |
| Pittsburgh Steelers | | | |
| ☐ 38T Renaldo Turnbull | .40 | .18 | .05 |
| New Orleans Saints | | | |
| ☐ 39T Leroy Hoard | .15 | .07 | .02 |
| Cleveland Browns | | | |
| ☐ 40T Anthony Thompson | .10 | .05 | .01 |
| Phoenix Cardinals | | | |
| ☐ 41T Jeff George | .60 | .25 | .08 |
| Indianapolis Colts | | | |
| ☐ 42T Alexander Wright | .10 | .05 | .01 |
| Dallas Cowboys | | | |
| ☐ 43T Richmond Webb | .20 | .09 | .03 |
| Miami Dolphins | | | |
| ☐ 44T Cortez Kennedy | .60 | .25 | .08 |
| Seattle Seahawks | | | |
| ☐ 45T Ray Agnew | .04 | .02 | .01 |
| New England Patriots | | | |
| ☐ 46T Percy Snow | .04 | .02 | .01 |
| Kansas City Chiefs | | | |
| ☐ 47T Chris Singleton | .04 | .02 | .01 |
| New England Patriots | | | |
| ☐ 48T James Francis | .20 | .09 | .03 |
| Cincinnati Bengals | | | |
| ☐ 49T Tony Bennett | .30 | .14 | .04 |
| Green Bay Packers | | | |
| ☐ 50T Reggie Cobb | .75 | .35 | .09 |
| Tampa Bay Buccaneers | | | |
| ☐ 51T Barry Foster | .75 | .35 | .09 |
| Pittsburgh Steelers | | | |
| ☐ 52T Ben Smith | .04 | .02 | .01 |
| Philadelphia Eagles | | | |
| ☐ 53T Anthony Smith | .40 | .18 | .05 |
| Los Angeles Raiders | | | |
| ☐ 54T Steve Christie | .15 | .07 | .02 |
| Tampa Bay Buccaneers | | | |
| ☐ 55T Johnny Bailey | .20 | .09 | .03 |
| Chicago Bears | | | |
| ☐ 56T Alan Grant | .04 | .02 | .01 |
| Indianapolis Colts | | | |
| ☐ 57T Eric Floyd | .04 | .02 | .01 |
| San Diego Chargers | | | |
| ☐ 58T Robert Blackmon | .10 | .05 | .01 |
| Seattle Seahawks | | | |
| ☐ 59T Brent Williams | .04 | .02 | .01 |
| New England Patriots | | | |
| ☐ 60T Raymond Clayborn | .08 | .04 | .01 |
| Cleveland Browns | | | |
| ☐ 61T Dave Duerson | .04 | .02 | .01 |
| New York Giants | | | |
| ☐ 62T Derrick Fenner | .15 | .07 | .02 |
| Seattle Seahawks | | | |
| ☐ 63T Ken Willis | .04 | .02 | .01 |
| Dallas Cowboys | | | |
| ☐ 64T Brad Baxter | .20 | .09 | .03 |
| New York Jets | | | |
| ☐ 65T Tony Paige | .04 | .02 | .01 |
| Miami Dolphins | | | |
| ☐ 66T Jay Schroeder | .08 | .04 | .01 |
| Los Angeles Raiders | | | |
| ☐ 67T Jim Breech | .04 | .02 | .01 |
| Cincinnati Bengals | | | |
| ☐ 68T Barry Word | .30 | .14 | .04 |
| Kansas City Chiefs | | | |
| ☐ 69T Anthony Dilweg | .04 | .02 | .01 |
| Green Bay Packers | | | |
| ☐ 70T Rich Gannon | .25 | .11 | .03 |
| Minnesota Vikings | | | |
| ☐ 71T Stan Humphries | .50 | .23 | .06 |
| Washington Redskins | | | |
| ☐ 72T Jay Novacek | .30 | .14 | .04 |
| Dallas Cowboys | | | |
| ☐ 73T Tommy Kane | .10 | .05 | .01 |
| Seattle Seahawks | | | |
| ☐ 74T Everson Walls | .04 | .02 | .01 |
| New York Giants | | | |
| ☐ 75T Mike Rozier | .08 | .04 | .01 |
| Atlanta Falcons | | | |
| ☐ 76T Robb Thomas | .04 | .02 | .01 |
| Kansas City Chiefs | | | |
| ☐ 77T Terance Mathis | .20 | .09 | .03 |
| New York Jets | | | |
| ☐ 78T LeRoy Irvin | .04 | .02 | .01 |
| Detroit Lions | | | |
| ☐ 79T Jeff Donaldson | .04 | .02 | .01 |
| Kansas City Chiefs | | | |
| ☐ 80T Ethan Horton | .15 | .07 | .02 |
| Los Angeles Raiders | | | |
| ☐ 81T J.B. Brown | .10 | .05 | .01 |
| Miami Dolphins | | | |
| ☐ 82T Joe Kelly | .04 | .02 | .01 |
| New York Jets | | | |
| ☐ 83T John Carney | .10 | .05 | .01 |
| San Diego Chargers | | | |
| ☐ 84T Dan Stryzinski | .04 | .02 | .01 |
| Pittsburgh Steelers | | | |
| ☐ 85T John Kidd | .04 | .02 | .01 |
| San Diego Chargers | | | |
| ☐ 86T Al Smith | .04 | .02 | .01 |
| Houston Oilers | | | |
| ☐ 87T Travis McNeal | .04 | .02 | .01 |
| Seattle Seahawks | | | |
| ☐ 88T Reyna Thompson | .10 | .05 | .01 |
| New York Giants | | | |
| ☐ 89T Rick Donnelly | .04 | .02 | .01 |
| Seattle Seahawks | | | |
| ☐ 90T Marv Cook | .20 | .09 | .03 |
| New England Patriots | | | |
| ☐ 91T Mike Farr | .10 | .05 | .01 |
| Detroit Lions | | | |
| ☐ 92T Daniel Stubbs | .04 | .02 | .01 |
| Dallas Cowboys | | | |
| ☐ 93T Jeff Campbell | .10 | .05 | .01 |
| Detroit Lions | | | |
| ☐ 94T Tim McKyer | .08 | .04 | .01 |
| Miami Dolphins | | | |
| ☐ 95T Ian Beckles | .04 | .02 | .01 |
| Tampa Bay Buccaneers | | | |
| ☐ 96T Lemuel Stinson | .04 | .02 | .01 |
| Chicago Bears | | | |
| ☐ 97T Frank Cornish | .04 | .02 | .01 |
| San Diego Chargers | | | |
| ☐ 98T Riki Ellison | .04 | .02 | .01 |
| Los Angeles Raiders | | | |
| ☐ 99T Jamie Mueller | .04 | .02 | .01 |
| Buffalo Bills | | | |
| ☐ 100T Brian Hansen | .04 | .02 | .01 |

New England Patriots
| | | | |
|---|---|---|---|
| ☐ 101T Warren Powers | .04 | .02 | .01 |

Denver Broncos
| | | | |
|---|---|---|---|
| ☐ 102T Howard Cross | .10 | .05 | .01 |

New York Giants
| | | | |
|---|---|---|---|
| ☐ 103T Tim Grunhard | .04 | .02 | .01 |

Kansas City Chiefs
| | | | |
|---|---|---|---|
| ☐ 104T Johnny Johnson | .75 | .35 | .09 |

Phoenix Cardinals
| | | | |
|---|---|---|---|
| ☐ 105T Calvin Williams | .60 | .25 | .08 |

Philadelphia Eagles
| | | | |
|---|---|---|---|
| ☐ 106T Keith McCants | .04 | .02 | .01 |

Tampa Bay Buccaneers
| | | | |
|---|---|---|---|
| ☐ 107T Lamar Lathon | .15 | .07 | .02 |

Houston Oilers
| | | | |
|---|---|---|---|
| ☐ 108T Steve Broussard | .10 | .05 | .01 |

Atlanta Falcons
| | | | |
|---|---|---|---|
| ☐ 109T Glenn Parker | .10 | .05 | .01 |

Buffalo Bills
| | | | |
|---|---|---|---|
| ☐ 110T Alton Montgomery | .10 | .05 | .01 |

Denver Broncos
| | | | |
|---|---|---|---|
| ☐ 111T Jim McMahon | .10 | .05 | .01 |

Philadelphia Eagles
| | | | |
|---|---|---|---|
| ☐ 112T Aaron Wallace | .15 | .07 | .02 |

Los Angeles Raiders
| | | | |
|---|---|---|---|
| ☐ 113T Keith Sims | .10 | .05 | .01 |

Miami Dolphins
| | | | |
|---|---|---|---|
| ☐ 114T Ervin Randle | .04 | .02 | .01 |

Tampa Bay Buccaneers
| | | | |
|---|---|---|---|
| ☐ 115T Walter Wilson | .04 | .02 | .01 |

San Diego Chargers
| | | | |
|---|---|---|---|
| ☐ 116T Terry Wooden | .10 | .05 | .01 |

Seattle Seahawks
| | | | |
|---|---|---|---|
| ☐ 117T Bernard Clark | .04 | .02 | .01 |

Cincinnati Bengals
| | | | |
|---|---|---|---|
| ☐ 118T Tony Stargell | .10 | .05 | .01 |

New York Jets
| | | | |
|---|---|---|---|
| ☐ 119T Jimmie Jones | .15 | .07 | .02 |

Dallas Cowboys
| | | | |
|---|---|---|---|
| ☐ 120T Andre Collins | .15 | .07 | .02 |

Washington Redskins
| | | | |
|---|---|---|---|
| ☐ 121T Ricky Proehl | .40 | .18 | .05 |

Phoenix Cardinals
| | | | |
|---|---|---|---|
| ☐ 122T Darion Conner | .10 | .05 | .01 |

Atlanta Falcons
| | | | |
|---|---|---|---|
| ☐ 123T Jeff Rutledge | .04 | .02 | .01 |

Washington Redskins
| | | | |
|---|---|---|---|
| ☐ 124T Heath Sherman | .15 | .07 | .02 |

Philadelphia Eagles
| | | | |
|---|---|---|---|
| ☐ 125T Tommie Agee | .04 | .02 | .01 |

Dallas Cowboys
| | | | |
|---|---|---|---|
| ☐ 126T Tory Epps | .04 | .02 | .01 |

Atlanta Falcons
| | | | |
|---|---|---|---|
| ☐ 127T Tommy Hodson | .15 | .07 | .02 |

New England Patriots
| | | | |
|---|---|---|---|
| ☐ 128T Jessie Hester | .25 | .11 | .03 |

Indianapolis Colts
| | | | |
|---|---|---|---|
| ☐ 129T Alfred Oglesby | .04 | .02 | .01 |

Miami Dolphins
| | | | |
|---|---|---|---|
| ☐ 130T Chris Chandler | .08 | .04 | .01 |

Tampa Bay Buccaneers
| | | | |
|---|---|---|---|
| ☐ 131T Fred Barnett | .50 | .23 | .06 |

Philadelphia Eagles
| | | | |
|---|---|---|---|
| ☐ 132T Checklist 1-132 | .05 | .02 | .01 |

## 1991 Topps

This 660-card standard size (2 1/2" by 3 1/2") set was issued by Topps. This set marked the largest football card set Topps had ever issued. The set numbering is according to teams as follows, Highlights (2-7), League Leaders (8-12), New York Giants (13-36), Buffalo Bills (37-59), San Francisco 49ers (60-82), Los Angeles Raiders (83-107), Miami Dolphins (108-129), Kansas City Chiefs (130-153), Chicago Bears (154-177), Washington Redskins (178-

200), Philadelphia Eagles (201-221), Houston Oilers (222-243), Cincinnati Bengals (244-265), Seattle Seahawks (266-287), Pittsburgh Steelers (288-309), New Orleans Saints (310-331), Indianapolis Colts (332-352), Dallas Cowboys (353-375), Minnesota Vikings (376-396), Detroit Lions (397-417), San Diego Chargers (418-438), Green Bay Packers (439-460), New York Jets (461-481), Tampa Bay Buccaneers (482-501), Phoenix Cardinals (502-522), Los Angeles Rams (523-544), Denver Broncos (545-566), Atlanta Falcons (567-588), Cleveland Browns (589-607), New England Patriots (608-627), Team Cards (628-655), and Checklist Cards (656-660). The key Rookie Cards in the set are Nick Bell, Ricky Ervins, Alvin Harper, Todd Marinovich, Dan McGwire, Herman Moore, Browning Nagle, and Harvey Williams.

| | MINT | EXC | G-VG |
|---|---|---|---|
| COMPLETE SET (660) | 12.00 | 5.50 | 1.50 |
| COMPLETE FACT.SET (660) | 18.00 | 8.00 | 2.30 |
| COMMON PLAYER (1-660) | .04 | .02 | .01 |
| ☐ 1 Super Bowl XXV | .08 | .04 | .01 |
| ☐ 2 Roger Craig HL | .08 | .04 | .01 |
| San Francisco 49ers | | | |
| ☐ 3 Derrick Thomas HL | .12 | .05 | .02 |
| Kansas City Chiefs | | | |
| ☐ 4 Pete Stoyanovich HL | .04 | .02 | .01 |
| Miami Dolphins | | | |
| ☐ 5 Ottis Anderson HL | .04 | .02 | .01 |
| New York Giants | | | |
| ☐ 6 Jerry Rice HL | .35 | .16 | .04 |
| San Francisco 49ers | | | |
| ☐ 7 Warren Moon HL | .10 | .05 | .01 |
| Houston Oilers | | | |
| ☐ 8 Leaders Passing Yards | .10 | .05 | .01 |
| Warren Moon | | | |
| Jim Everett | | | |
| ☐ 9 Leaders Rushing | .25 | .11 | .03 |
| Barry Sanders | | | |
| Thurman Thomas | | | |
| ☐ 10 Leaders Receiving | .20 | .09 | .03 |
| Jerry Rice | | | |
| Haywood Jeffires | | | |
| ☐ 11 Leaders Interceptions | .04 | .02 | .01 |
| Mark Carrier | | | |
| Richard Johnson | | | |
| ☐ 12 Leaders Sacks | .10 | .05 | .01 |
| Derrick Thomas | | | |
| Charles Haley | | | |
| ☐ 13 Jumbo Elliott | .04 | .02 | .01 |
| ☐ 14 Leonard Marshall | .08 | .04 | .01 |
| ☐ 15 William Roberts | .04 | .02 | .01 |
| ☐ 16 Lawrence Taylor | .10 | .05 | .01 |
| ☐ 17 Mark Ingram | .08 | .04 | .01 |
| ☐ 18 Rodney Hampton | .75 | .35 | .09 |
| ☐ 19 Carl Banks | .08 | .04 | .01 |
| ☐ 20 Ottis Anderson | .08 | .04 | .01 |
| ☐ 21 Mark Collins | .04 | .02 | .01 |
| ☐ 22 Pepper Johnson | .08 | .04 | .01 |
| ☐ 23 Dave Meggett | .10 | .05 | .01 |
| ☐ 24 Reyna Thompson | .04 | .02 | .01 |
| ☐ 25 Stephen Baker | .04 | .02 | .01 |
| ☐ 26 Mike Fox | .04 | .02 | .01 |
| ☐ 27 Maurice Carthon UER | .04 | .02 | .01 |
| (Herschel Walker mis- | | | |
| spelled as Herschell) | | | |
| ☐ 28 Jeff Hostetler | .25 | .11 | .03 |
| ☐ 29 Greg Jackson | .10 | .05 | .01 |
| ☐ 30 Sean Landeta | .04 | .02 | .01 |
| ☐ 31 Bart Oates | .04 | .02 | .01 |
| ☐ 32 Phil Simms | .10 | .05 | .01 |
| ☐ 33 Erik Howard | .04 | .02 | .01 |
| ☐ 34 Myron Guyton | .04 | .02 | .01 |
| ☐ 35 Mark Bavaro | .08 | .04 | .01 |
| ☐ 36 Jarrod Bunch | .15 | .07 | .02 |
| ☐ 37 Will Wolford | .04 | .02 | .01 |
| ☐ 38 Ray Bentley | .04 | .02 | .01 |
| ☐ 39 Nate Odomes | .10 | .05 | .01 |
| ☐ 40 Scott Norwood | .04 | .02 | .01 |
| ☐ 41 Darryl Talley | .08 | .04 | .01 |
| ☐ 42 Carwell Gardner | .04 | .02 | .01 |
| ☐ 43 James Lofton | .10 | .05 | .01 |
| ☐ 44 Shane Conlan | .08 | .04 | .01 |
| ☐ 45 Steve Tasker | .08 | .04 | .01 |
| ☐ 46 James Williams | .04 | .02 | .01 |
| ☐ 47 Kent Hull | .04 | .02 | .01 |
| ☐ 48 Al Edwards | .04 | .02 | .01 |
| ☐ 49 Frank Reich | .10 | .05 | .01 |
| ☐ 50 Leon Seals | .04 | .02 | .01 |
| ☐ 51 Keith McKeller | .04 | .02 | .01 |
| ☐ 52 Thurman Thomas | .40 | .18 | .05 |
| ☐ 53 Leonard Smith | .04 | .02 | .01 |
| ☐ 54 Andre Reed | .10 | .05 | .01 |
| ☐ 55 Kenneth Davis | .08 | .04 | .01 |
| ☐ 56 Jeff Wright | .10 | .05 | .01 |
| ☐ 57 Jamie Mueller | .04 | .02 | .01 |
| ☐ 58 Jim Ritcher | .04 | .02 | .01 |
| ☐ 59 Bruce Smith | .10 | .05 | .01 |

|  |  | | | |
|---|--------|---|---|---|
| ☐ 60 | Ted Washington | .04 | .02 | .01 |
| ☐ 61 | Guy McIntyre | .08 | .04 | .01 |
| ☐ 62 | Michael Carter | .04 | .02 | .01 |
| ☐ 63 | Pierce Holt | .04 | .02 | .01 |
| ☐ 64 | Darryl Pollard | .04 | .02 | .01 |
| ☐ 65 | Mike Sherrard | .08 | .04 | .01 |
| ☐ 66 | Dexter Carter | .08 | .04 | .01 |
| ☐ 67 | Bubba Paris | .04 | .02 | .01 |
| ☐ 68 | Harry Sydney | .04 | .02 | .01 |
| ☐ 69 | Tom Rathman | .08 | .04 | .01 |
| ☐ 70 | Jesse Sapolu | .04 | .02 | .01 |
| ☐ 71 | Mike Cofer | .04 | .02 | .01 |
| ☐ 72 | Keith DeLong | .04 | .02 | .01 |
| ☐ 73 | Joe Montana | 1.00 | .45 | .13 |
| ☐ 74 | Bill Romanowski | .04 | .02 | .01 |
| ☐ 75 | John Taylor | .10 | .05 | .01 |
| ☐ 76 | Brent Jones | .10 | .05 | .01 |
| ☐ 77 | Harris Barton | .04 | .02 | .01 |
| ☐ 78 | Charles Haley | .08 | .04 | .01 |
| ☐ 79 | Eric Davis | .04 | .02 | .01 |
| ☐ 80 | Kevin Fagan | .04 | .02 | .01 |
| ☐ 81 | Jerry Rice | .75 | .35 | .09 |
| ☐ 82 | Dave Waymer | .04 | .02 | .01 |
| ☐ 83 | Todd Marinovich | .08 | .04 | .01 |
| ☐ 84 | Steve Smith | .08 | .04 | .01 |
| ☐ 85 | Tim Brown | .20 | .09 | .03 |
| ☐ 86 | Ethan Horton | .04 | .02 | .01 |
| ☐ 87 | Marcus Allen | .15 | .07 | .02 |
| ☐ 88 | Terry McDaniel | .04 | .02 | .01 |
| ☐ 89 | Thomas Benson | .04 | .02 | .01 |
| ☐ 90 | Roger Craig | .08 | .04 | .01 |
| ☐ 91 | Don Mosebar | .04 | .02 | .01 |
| ☐ 92 | Aaron Wallace | .04 | .02 | .01 |
| ☐ 93 | Eddie Anderson | .04 | .02 | .01 |
| ☐ 94 | Willie Gault | .08 | .04 | .01 |
| ☐ 95 | Howie Long | .08 | .04 | .01 |
| ☐ 96 | Jay Schroeder | .08 | .04 | .01 |
| ☐ 97 | Ronnie Lott | .10 | .05 | .01 |
| ☐ 98 | Bob Golic | .04 | .02 | .01 |
| ☐ 99 | Bo Jackson | .35 | .16 | .04 |
| ☐ 100 | Max Montoya | .04 | .02 | .01 |
| ☐ 101 | Scott Davis | .04 | .02 | .01 |
| ☐ 102 | Greg Townsend | .04 | .02 | .01 |
| ☐ 103 | Garry Lewis | .04 | .02 | .01 |
| ☐ 104 | Mervyn Fernandez | .04 | .02 | .01 |
| ☐ 105 | Steve Wisniewski UER | .04 | .02 | .01 |
| | (Back has drafted, should be traded to) | | | |
| ☐ 106 | Jeff Jaeger | .04 | .02 | .01 |
| ☐ 107 | Nick Bell | .20 | .09 | .03 |
| ☐ 108 | Mark Dennis | .04 | .02 | .01 |
| ☐ 109 | Jarvis Williams | .04 | .02 | .01 |
| ☐ 110 | Mark Clayton | .08 | .04 | .01 |
| ☐ 111 | Harry Galbreath | .04 | .02 | .01 |
| ☐ 112 | Dan Marino | .75 | .35 | .09 |
| ☐ 113 | Louis Oliver | .08 | .04 | .01 |
| ☐ 114 | Pete Stoyanovich | .08 | .04 | .01 |
| ☐ 115 | Ferrell Edmunds | .04 | .02 | .01 |
| ☐ 116 | Jeff Cross | .04 | .02 | .01 |
| ☐ 117 | Richmond Webb | .08 | .04 | .01 |
| ☐ 118 | Jim C. Jensen | .04 | .02 | .01 |
| ☐ 119 | Keith Sims | .04 | .02 | .01 |
| ☐ 120 | Mark Duper | .08 | .04 | .01 |
| ☐ 121 | Shawn Lee | .10 | .05 | .01 |
| ☐ 122 | Reggie Roby | .04 | .02 | .01 |
| ☐ 123 | Jeff Uhlenhake | .04 | .02 | .01 |
| ☐ 124 | Sammie Smith | .04 | .02 | .01 |
| ☐ 125 | John Offerdahl | .08 | .04 | .01 |
| ☐ 126 | Hugh Green | .04 | .02 | .01 |
| ☐ 127 | Tony Paige | .04 | .02 | .01 |
| ☐ 128 | David Griggs | .04 | .02 | .01 |
| ☐ 129 | J.B. Brown | .04 | .02 | .01 |
| ☐ 130 | Harvey Williams | .20 | .09 | .03 |
| ☐ 131 | John Alt | .04 | .02 | .01 |
| ☐ 132 | Albert Lewis | .08 | .04 | .01 |
| ☐ 133 | Robb Thomas | .04 | .02 | .01 |
| ☐ 134 | Neil Smith | .10 | .05 | .01 |
| ☐ 135 | Stephone Paige | .08 | .04 | .01 |
| ☐ 136 | Nick Lowery | .08 | .04 | .01 |
| ☐ 137 | Steve DeBerg | .08 | .04 | .01 |
| ☐ 138 | Rich Baldinger | .04 | .02 | .01 |
| ☐ 139 | Percy Snow | .04 | .02 | .01 |
| ☐ 140 | Kevin Porter | .04 | .02 | .01 |
| ☐ 141 | Chris Martin | .04 | .02 | .01 |
| ☐ 142 | Deron Cherry | .04 | .02 | .01 |
| ☐ 143 | Derrick Thomas | .25 | .11 | .03 |
| ☐ 144 | Tim Grunhard | .04 | .02 | .01 |
| ☐ 145 | Todd McNair | .04 | .02 | .01 |
| ☐ 146 | David Szott | .04 | .02 | .01 |
| ☐ 147 | Dan Saleaumua | .04 | .02 | .01 |
| ☐ 148 | Jonathan Hayes | .04 | .02 | .01 |
| ☐ 149 | Christian Okoye | .08 | .04 | .01 |
| ☐ 150 | Dino Hackett | .04 | .02 | .01 |
| ☐ 151 | Bryan Barker | .04 | .02 | .01 |
| ☐ 152 | Kevin Ross | .08 | .04 | .01 |
| ☐ 153 | Barry Word | .10 | .05 | .01 |
| ☐ 154 | Stan Thomas | .04 | .02 | .01 |
| ☐ 155 | Brad Muster | .08 | .04 | .01 |
| ☐ 156 | Donnell Woolford | .04 | .02 | .01 |
| ☐ 157 | Neal Anderson | .08 | .04 | .01 |
| ☐ 158 | Jim Covert | .04 | .02 | .01 |
| ☐ 159 | Jim Harbaugh | .08 | .04 | .01 |
| ☐ 160 | Shaun Gayle | .04 | .02 | .01 |
| ☐ 161 | William Perry | .08 | .04 | .01 |
| ☐ 162 | Ron Morris | .04 | .02 | .01 |
| ☐ 163 | Mark Bortz | .04 | .02 | .01 |
| ☐ 164 | James Thornton | .04 | .02 | .01 |
| ☐ 165 | Ron Rivera | .04 | .02 | .01 |
| ☐ 166 | Kevin Butler | .04 | .02 | .01 |
| ☐ 167 | Jay Hilgenberg | .08 | .04 | .01 |
| ☐ 168 | Peter Tom Willis | .04 | .02 | .01 |
| ☐ 169 | Johnny Bailey | .08 | .04 | .01 |
| ☐ 170 | Ron Cox | .04 | .02 | .01 |
| ☐ 171 | Keith Van Horne | .04 | .02 | .01 |
| ☐ 172 | Mark Carrier | .08 | .04 | .01 |
| ☐ 173 | Richard Dent | .08 | .04 | .01 |
| ☐ 174 | Wendell Davis | .04 | .02 | .01 |
| ☐ 175 | Trace Armstrong | .04 | .02 | .01 |
| ☐ 176 | Mike Singletary | .10 | .05 | .01 |
| ☐ 177 | Chris Zorich | .25 | .11 | .03 |
| ☐ 178 | Gerald Riggs | .08 | .04 | .01 |
| ☐ 179 | Jeff Bostic | .04 | .02 | .01 |
| ☐ 180 | Kurt Gouveia | .20 | .09 | .03 |
| ☐ 181 | Stan Humphries | .15 | .07 | .02 |
| ☐ 182 | Chip Lohmiller | .08 | .04 | .01 |
| ☐ 183 | Raleigh McKenzie | .10 | .05 | .01 |
| ☐ 184 | Alvin Walton | .04 | .02 | .01 |
| ☐ 185 | Earnest Byner | .08 | .04 | .01 |
| ☐ 186 | Markus Koch | .04 | .02 | .01 |
| ☐ 187 | Art Monk | .10 | .05 | .01 |
| ☐ 188 | Ed Simmons | .04 | .02 | .01 |
| ☐ 189 | Bobby Wilson | .10 | .05 | .01 |
| ☐ 190 | Charles Mann | .08 | .04 | .01 |
| ☐ 191 | Darrell Green | .08 | .04 | .01 |
| ☐ 192 | Mark Rypien | .10 | .05 | .01 |
| ☐ 193 | Ricky Sanders | .08 | .04 | .01 |
| ☐ 194 | Jim Lachey | .04 | .02 | .01 |
| ☐ 195 | Martin Mayhew | .04 | .02 | .01 |
| ☐ 196 | Gary Clark | .10 | .05 | .01 |
| ☐ 197 | Wilber Marshall | .08 | .04 | .01 |
| ☐ 198 | Darryl Grant | .04 | .02 | .01 |
| ☐ 199 | Don Warren | .04 | .02 | .01 |
| ☐ 200 | Ricky Ervins UER | .20 | .09 | .03 |
| | (Front has Chiefs, back has Redskins) | | | |
| ☐ 201 | Eric Allen | .08 | .04 | .01 |
| ☐ 202 | Anthony Toney | .04 | .02 | .01 |
| ☐ 203 | Ben Smith UER | .04 | .02 | .01 |
| | (Front CB, back S) | | | |
| ☐ 204 | David Alexander | .04 | .02 | .01 |
| ☐ 205 | Jerome Brown | .08 | .04 | .01 |
| ☐ 206 | Mike Golic | .04 | .02 | .01 |
| ☐ 207 | Roger Ruzek | .04 | .02 | .01 |
| ☐ 208 | Andre Waters | .04 | .02 | .01 |
| ☐ 209 | Fred Barnett | .15 | .07 | .02 |
| ☐ 210 | Randall Cunningham | .10 | .05 | .01 |
| ☐ 211 | Mike Schad | .04 | .02 | .01 |
| ☐ 212 | Reggie White | .15 | .07 | .02 |
| ☐ 213 | Mike Bellamy | .04 | .02 | .01 |
| ☐ 214 | Jeff Feagles | .04 | .02 | .01 |
| ☐ 215 | Wes Hopkins | .08 | .04 | .01 |
| ☐ 216 | Clyde Simmons | .08 | .04 | .01 |
| ☐ 217 | Keith Byars | .08 | .04 | .01 |
| ☐ 218 | Seth Joyner | .08 | .04 | .01 |
| ☐ 219 | Byron Evans | .08 | .04 | .01 |
| ☐ 220 | Keith Jackson | .15 | .07 | .02 |
| ☐ 221 | Calvin Williams | .20 | .09 | .03 |
| ☐ 222 | Mike Dumas | .04 | .02 | .01 |
| ☐ 223 | Ray Childress | .08 | .04 | .01 |
| ☐ 224 | Ernest Givins | .04 | .02 | .01 |
| ☐ 225 | Lamar Lathon | .04 | .02 | .01 |
| ☐ 226 | Greg Montgomery | .08 | .04 | .01 |
| ☐ 227 | Mike Munchak | .04 | .02 | .01 |
| ☐ 228 | Al Smith | .04 | .02 | .01 |
| ☐ 229 | Bubba McDowell | .15 | .07 | .02 |
| ☐ 230 | Haywood Jeffires | .08 | .04 | .01 |
| ☐ 231 | Drew Hill | .08 | .04 | .01 |
| ☐ 232 | William Fuller | .20 | .09 | .03 |
| ☐ 233 | Warren Moon | .10 | .05 | .01 |
| ☐ 234 | Doug Smith | .15 | .07 | .02 |
| ☐ 235 | Cris Dishman | .04 | .02 | .01 |
| ☐ 236 | Teddy Garcia | .04 | .02 | .01 |
| ☐ 237 | Richard Johnson | .08 | .04 | .01 |
| ☐ 238 | Bruce Matthews | .04 | .02 | .01 |
| ☐ 239 | Gerald McNeil | .04 | .02 | .01 |
| ☐ 240 | Johnny Meads | .08 | .04 | .01 |
| ☐ 241 | Curtis Duncan | .08 | .04 | .01 |
| ☐ 242 | Sean Jones | .08 | .04 | .01 |
| ☐ 243 | Lorenzo White | .10 | .05 | .01 |
| ☐ 244 | Rob Carpenter | .04 | .02 | .01 |
| ☐ 245 | Bruce Reimers | .04 | .02 | .01 |
| ☐ 246 | Ickey Woods | .04 | .02 | .01 |
| ☐ 247 | Lewis Billups | .15 | .07 | .02 |
| ☐ 248 | Boomer Esiason | | | |

| | | | |
|---|---|---|---|
| ☐ 249 Tim Krumrie | .04 | .02 | .01 |
| ☐ 250 David Fulcher | .04 | .02 | .01 |
| ☐ 251 Jim Breech | .04 | .02 | .01 |
| ☐ 252 Mitchell Price | .04 | .02 | .01 |
| ☐ 253 Carl Zander | .04 | .02 | .01 |
| ☐ 254 Barney Bussey | .04 | .02 | .01 |
| ☐ 255 Leon White | .04 | .02 | .01 |
| ☐ 256 Eddie Brown | .04 | .02 | .01 |
| ☐ 257 James Francis | .08 | .04 | .01 |
| ☐ 258 Harold Green | .10 | .05 | .01 |
| ☐ 259 Anthony Munoz | .08 | .04 | .01 |
| ☐ 260 James Brooks | .08 | .04 | .01 |
| ☐ 261 Kevin Walker UER | .04 | .02 | .01 |
| (Hometown should be | | | |
| West Milford Township) | | | |
| ☐ 262 Bruce Kozerski | .04 | .02 | .01 |
| ☐ 263 David Grant | .04 | .02 | .01 |
| ☐ 264 Tim McGee | .04 | .02 | .01 |
| ☐ 265 Rodney Holman | .04 | .02 | .01 |
| ☐ 266 Dan McGwire | .10 | .05 | .01 |
| ☐ 267 Andy Heck | .04 | .02 | .01 |
| ☐ 268 Dave Krieg | .08 | .04 | .01 |
| ☐ 269 David Wyman | .04 | .02 | .01 |
| ☐ 270 Robert Blackmon | .04 | .02 | .01 |
| ☐ 271 Grant Feasel | .04 | .02 | .01 |
| ☐ 272 Patrick Hunter | .04 | .02 | .01 |
| ☐ 273 Travis McNeal | .04 | .02 | .01 |
| ☐ 274 John L. Williams | .08 | .04 | .01 |
| ☐ 275 Tony Woods | .04 | .02 | .01 |
| ☐ 276 Derrick Fenner | .08 | .04 | .01 |
| ☐ 277 Jacob Green | .04 | .02 | .01 |
| ☐ 278 Brian Blades | .10 | .05 | .01 |
| ☐ 279 Eugene Robinson | .04 | .02 | .01 |
| ☐ 280 Terry Wooden | .04 | .02 | .01 |
| ☐ 281 Jeff Bryant | .04 | .02 | .01 |
| ☐ 282 Norm Johnson | .04 | .02 | .01 |
| ☐ 283 Joe Nash UER | .04 | .02 | .01 |
| (Front DT, Back NT) | | | |
| ☐ 284 Rick Donnelly | .04 | .02 | .01 |
| ☐ 285 Chris Warren | .30 | .14 | .04 |
| ☐ 286 Tommy Kane | .04 | .02 | .01 |
| ☐ 287 Cortez Kennedy | .25 | .11 | .03 |
| ☐ 288 Ernie Mills | .10 | .05 | .01 |
| ☐ 289 Dermontti Dawson | .04 | .02 | .01 |
| ☐ 290 Tunch Ilkin | .04 | .02 | .01 |
| ☐ 291 Tim Worley | .08 | .04 | .01 |
| ☐ 292 David Little | .04 | .02 | .01 |
| ☐ 293 Gary Anderson | .04 | .02 | .01 |
| ☐ 294 Chris Calloway | .04 | .02 | .01 |
| ☐ 295 Carnell Lake | .04 | .02 | .01 |
| ☐ 296 Dan Stryzinski | .04 | .02 | .01 |
| ☐ 297 Rod Woodson | .10 | .05 | .01 |
| ☐ 298 Johnny Jackson | .10 | .05 | .01 |
| ☐ 299 Bubby Brister | .08 | .04 | .01 |
| ☐ 300 Thomas Everett | .04 | .02 | .01 |
| ☐ 301 Merril Hoge | .08 | .04 | .01 |
| ☐ 302 Eric Green | .15 | .07 | .02 |
| ☐ 303 Greg Lloyd | .04 | .02 | .01 |
| ☐ 304 Gerald Williams | .04 | .02 | .01 |
| ☐ 305 Bryan Hinkle | .04 | .02 | .01 |
| ☐ 306 Keith Willis | .04 | .02 | .01 |
| ☐ 307 Louis Lipps | .08 | .04 | .01 |
| ☐ 308 Donald Evans | .04 | .02 | .01 |
| ☐ 309 David Johnson | .04 | .02 | .01 |
| ☐ 310 Wesley Carroll | .10 | .05 | .01 |
| ☐ 311 Eric Martin | .08 | .04 | .01 |
| ☐ 312 Brett Maxie | .04 | .02 | .01 |
| ☐ 313 Rickey Jackson | .08 | .04 | .01 |
| ☐ 314 Robert Massey | .04 | .02 | .01 |
| ☐ 315 Pat Swilling | .08 | .04 | .01 |
| ☐ 316 Morten Andersen | .08 | .04 | .01 |
| ☐ 317 Toi Cook | .04 | .02 | .01 |
| ☐ 318 Sam Mills | .08 | .04 | .01 |
| ☐ 319 Steve Walsh | .04 | .02 | .01 |
| ☐ 320 Tommy Barnhardt | .04 | .02 | .01 |
| ☐ 321 Vince Buck | .04 | .02 | .01 |
| ☐ 322 Joel Hilgenberg | .04 | .02 | .01 |
| ☐ 323 Rueben Mayes | .04 | .02 | .01 |
| ☐ 324 Renaldo Turnbull | .08 | .04 | .01 |
| ☐ 325 Brett Perriman | .10 | .05 | .01 |
| ☐ 326 Vaughan Johnson | .08 | .04 | .01 |
| ☐ 327 Gill Fenerty | .08 | .04 | .01 |
| ☐ 328 Stan Brock | .04 | .02 | .01 |
| ☐ 329 Dalton Hilliard | .04 | .02 | .01 |
| ☐ 330 Hoby Brenner | .04 | .02 | .01 |
| ☐ 331 Craig Heyward | .04 | .02 | .01 |
| ☐ 332 Jon Hand | .04 | .02 | .01 |
| ☐ 333 Duane Bickett | .04 | .02 | .01 |
| ☐ 334 Jessie Hester | .08 | .04 | .01 |
| ☐ 335 Rohn Stark | .04 | .02 | .01 |
| ☐ 336 Zefross Moss | .04 | .02 | .01 |
| ☐ 337 Bill Brooks | .08 | .04 | .01 |
| ☐ 338 Clarence Verdin | .04 | .02 | .01 |
| ☐ 339 Mike Prior | .04 | .02 | .01 |
| ☐ 340 Chip Banks | .04 | .02 | .01 |
| ☐ 341 Dean Biasucci | .04 | .02 | .01 |
| ☐ 342 Ray Donaldson | .04 | .02 | .01 |

| | | | |
|---|---|---|---|
| ☐ 343 Jeff Herrod | .04 | .02 | .01 |
| ☐ 344 Donnell Thompson | .04 | .02 | .01 |
| ☐ 345 Chris Goode | .04 | .02 | .01 |
| ☐ 346 Eugene Daniel | .04 | .02 | .01 |
| ☐ 347 Pat Beach | .04 | .02 | .01 |
| ☐ 348 Keith Taylor | .04 | .02 | .01 |
| ☐ 349 Jeff George | .25 | .11 | .03 |
| ☐ 350 Tony Siragusa | .04 | .02 | .01 |
| ☐ 351 Randy Dixon | .04 | .02 | .01 |
| ☐ 352 Albert Bentley | .04 | .02 | .01 |
| ☐ 353 Russell Maryland | .40 | .18 | .05 |
| ☐ 354 Mike Saxon | .04 | .02 | .01 |
| ☐ 355 Godfrey Myles UER | .10 | .05 | .01 |
| (Misspelled Miles | | | |
| on card front) | | | |
| ☐ 356 Mark Stepnoski | .15 | .07 | .02 |
| ☐ 357 James Washington | .20 | .09 | .03 |
| ☐ 358 Jay Novacek | .15 | .07 | .02 |
| ☐ 359 Kelvin Martin | .08 | .04 | .01 |
| ☐ 360 Emmitt Smith UER | 2.00 | .90 | .25 |
| (Played for Florida, | | | |
| not Florida State) | | | |
| ☐ 361 Jim Jeffcoat | .04 | .02 | .01 |
| ☐ 362 Alexander Wright | .08 | .04 | .01 |
| ☐ 363 James Dixon UER | .04 | .02 | .01 |
| (Photo is not Dixon | | | |
| on card front) | | | |
| ☐ 364 Alonzo Highsmith | .04 | .02 | .01 |
| ☐ 365 Daniel Stubbs | .04 | .02 | .01 |
| ☐ 366 Jack Del Rio | .04 | .02 | .01 |
| ☐ 367 Mark Tuinei | .15 | .07 | .02 |
| ☐ 368 Michael Irvin | .50 | .23 | .06 |
| ☐ 369 John Gesek | .08 | .04 | .01 |
| ☐ 370 Ken Willis | .04 | .02 | .01 |
| ☐ 371 Troy Aikman | 1.25 | .55 | .16 |
| ☐ 372 Jimmie Jones | .04 | .02 | .01 |
| ☐ 373 Nate Newton | .04 | .02 | .01 |
| ☐ 374 Issiac Holt | .04 | .02 | .01 |
| ☐ 375 Alvin Harper | 1.00 | .45 | .13 |
| ☐ 376 Todd Kalis | .04 | .02 | .01 |
| ☐ 377 Wade Wilson | .04 | .02 | .01 |
| ☐ 378 Joey Browner | .04 | .02 | .01 |
| ☐ 379 Chris Doleman | .08 | .04 | .01 |
| ☐ 380 Hassan Jones | .04 | .02 | .01 |
| ☐ 381 Henry Thomas | .04 | .02 | .01 |
| ☐ 382 Darrell Fullington | .04 | .02 | .01 |
| ☐ 383 Steve Jordan | .08 | .04 | .01 |
| ☐ 384 Gary Zimmerman | .04 | .02 | .01 |
| ☐ 385 Ray Berry | .04 | .02 | .01 |
| ☐ 386 Cris Carter | .10 | .05 | .01 |
| ☐ 387 Mike Merriweather | .04 | .02 | .01 |
| ☐ 388 Carl Lee | .04 | .02 | .01 |
| ☐ 389 Keith Millard | .08 | .04 | .01 |
| ☐ 390 Reggie Rutland | .04 | .02 | .01 |
| ☐ 391 Anthony Carter | .08 | .04 | .01 |
| ☐ 392 Mark Dusbabek | .04 | .02 | .01 |
| ☐ 393 Kirk Lowdermilk | .04 | .02 | .01 |
| ☐ 394 Al Noga UER | .04 | .02 | .01 |
| (Card says DT, | | | |
| should be DE) | | | |
| ☐ 395 Herschel Walker | .10 | .05 | .01 |
| ☐ 396 Randall McDaniel | .04 | .02 | .01 |
| ☐ 397 Herman Moore | 1.00 | .45 | .13 |
| ☐ 398 Eddie Murray | .08 | .04 | .01 |
| ☐ 399 Lomas Brown | .04 | .02 | .01 |
| ☐ 400 Marc Spindler | .04 | .02 | .01 |
| ☐ 401 Bennie Blades | .04 | .02 | .01 |
| ☐ 402 Kevin Glover | .04 | .02 | .01 |
| ☐ 403 Aubrey Matthews | .04 | .02 | .01 |
| ☐ 404 Michael Cofer | .04 | .02 | .01 |
| ☐ 405 Robert Clark | .04 | .02 | .01 |
| ☐ 406 Eric Andolsek | .04 | .02 | .01 |
| ☐ 407 William White | .04 | .02 | .01 |
| ☐ 408 Rodney Peete | .08 | .04 | .01 |
| ☐ 409 Mel Gray | .04 | .02 | .01 |
| ☐ 410 Jim Arnold | .04 | .02 | .01 |
| ☐ 411 Jeff Campbell | .04 | .02 | .01 |
| ☐ 412 Chris Spielman | .08 | .04 | .01 |
| ☐ 413 Jerry Ball | .08 | .04 | .01 |
| ☐ 414 Dan Owens | .04 | .02 | .01 |
| ☐ 415 Barry Sanders | .75 | .35 | .09 |
| ☐ 416 Andre Ware | .10 | .05 | .01 |
| ☐ 417 Stanley Richard | .10 | .05 | .01 |
| ☐ 418 Gill Byrd | .08 | .04 | .01 |
| ☐ 419 John Kidd | .04 | .02 | .01 |
| ☐ 420 Sam Seale | .04 | .02 | .01 |
| ☐ 421 Gary Plummer | .04 | .02 | .01 |
| ☐ 422 Anthony Miller | .20 | .09 | .03 |
| ☐ 423 Ronnie Harmon | .04 | .02 | .01 |
| ☐ 424 Frank Cornish | .04 | .02 | .01 |
| ☐ 425 Marion Butts | .10 | .05 | .01 |
| ☐ 426 Leo Goeas | .04 | .02 | .01 |
| ☐ 427 Junior Seau | .25 | .11 | .03 |
| ☐ 428 Courtney Hall | .04 | .02 | .01 |
| ☐ 429 Leslie O'Neal | .08 | .04 | .01 |
| ☐ 430 Martin Bayless | .04 | .02 | .01 |
| ☐ 431 John Carney | .04 | .02 | .01 |

|  |  | | | |
|---|--------|----|----|----|
| ☐ 432 | Lee Williams | .08 | .04 | .01 |
| ☐ 433 | Arthur Cox | .04 | .02 | .01 |
| ☐ 434 | Burt Grossman | .04 | .02 | .01 |
| ☐ 435 | Nate Lewis | .25 | .11 | .03 |
| ☐ 436 | Rod Bernstine | .10 | .05 | .01 |
| ☐ 437 | Henry Rolling | .04 | .02 | .01 |
| ☐ 438 | Billy Joe Tolliver | .08 | .04 | .01 |
| ☐ 439 | Vinnie Clark | .04 | .02 | .01 |
| ☐ 440 | Brian Noble | .04 | .02 | .01 |
| ☐ 441 | Charles Wilson | .04 | .02 | .01 |
| ☐ 442 | Don Majkowski | .08 | .04 | .01 |
| ☐ 443 | Tim Harris | .08 | .04 | .01 |
| ☐ 444 | Scott Stephen | .04 | .02 | .01 |
| ☐ 445 | Perry Kemp | .04 | .02 | .01 |
| ☐ 446 | Darrell Thompson | .08 | .04 | .01 |
| ☐ 447 | Chris Jacke | .04 | .02 | .01 |
| ☐ 448 | Mark Murphy | .04 | .02 | .01 |
| ☐ 449 | Ed West | .04 | .02 | .01 |
| ☐ 450 | LeRoy Butler | .04 | .02 | .01 |
| ☐ 451 | Keith Woodside | .04 | .02 | .01 |
| ☐ 452 | Tony Bennett | .08 | .04 | .01 |
| ☐ 453 | Mark Lee | .04 | .02 | .01 |
| ☐ 454 | James Campen | .04 | .02 | .01 |
| ☐ 455 | Robert Brown | .04 | .02 | .01 |
| ☐ 456 | Sterling Sharpe | .50 | .23 | .06 |
| ☐ 457A | Tony Mandarich ERR<br>Denver Broncos | 2.50 | 1.15 | .30 |
| ☐ 457B | Tony Mandarich COR<br>Green Bay Packers | .08 | .04 | .01 |
| ☐ 458 | Johnny Holland | .04 | .02 | .01 |
| ☐ 459 | Matt Brock | .04 | .02 | .01 |
| ☐ 460A | Esera Tuaolo ERR<br>(See also 462; no 1991<br>NFL Draft Pick logo) | .20 | .09 | .03 |
| ☐ 460B | Esera Tuaolo COR<br>(See also 462; 1991 NFL<br>Draft Pick logo on front) | .08 | .04 | .01 |
| ☐ 461 | Freeman McNeil | .04 | .02 | .01 |
| ☐ 462 | Terance Mathis UER<br>(Card numbered in-<br>correctly as 460) | .04 | .02 | .01 |
| ☐ 463 | Rob Moore | .10 | .05 | .01 |
| ☐ 464 | Darrell Davis | .04 | .02 | .01 |
| ☐ 465 | Chris Burkett | .04 | .02 | .01 |
| ☐ 466 | Jeff Criswell | .04 | .02 | .01 |
| ☐ 467 | Tony Stargell | .04 | .02 | .01 |
| ☐ 468 | Ken O'Brien | .08 | .04 | .01 |
| ☐ 469 | Erik McMillan | .04 | .02 | .01 |
| ☐ 470 | Jeff Lageman UER<br>(Front DE, back LB) | .04 | .02 | .01 |
| ☐ 471 | Pat Leahy | .08 | .04 | .01 |
| ☐ 472 | Dennis Byrd | .08 | .04 | .01 |
| ☐ 473 | Jim Sweeney | .04 | .02 | .01 |
| ☐ 474 | Brad Baxter | .08 | .04 | .01 |
| ☐ 475 | Joe Kelly | .04 | .02 | .01 |
| ☐ 476 | Al Toon | .08 | .04 | .01 |
| ☐ 477 | Joe Prokop | .04 | .02 | .01 |
| ☐ 478 | Mark Boyer | .04 | .02 | .01 |
| ☐ 479 | Kyle Clifton | .04 | .02 | .01 |
| ☐ 480 | James Hasty | .04 | .02 | .01 |
| ☐ 481 | Browning Nagle | .20 | .09 | .03 |
| ☐ 482 | Gary Anderson | .08 | .04 | .01 |
| ☐ 483 | Mark Carrier | .08 | .04 | .01 |
| ☐ 484 | Ricky Reynolds | .04 | .02 | .01 |
| ☐ 485 | Bruce Hill | .04 | .02 | .01 |
| ☐ 486 | Steve Christie | .04 | .02 | .01 |
| ☐ 487 | Paul Gruber | .08 | .04 | .01 |
| ☐ 488 | Jesse Anderson | .04 | .02 | .01 |
| ☐ 489 | Reggie Cobb | .25 | .11 | .03 |
| ☐ 490 | Harry Hamilton | .04 | .02 | .01 |
| ☐ 491 | Vinny Testaverde | .10 | .05 | .01 |
| ☐ 492 | Mark Royals | .04 | .02 | .01 |
| ☐ 493 | Keith McCants | .04 | .02 | .01 |
| ☐ 494 | Ron Hall | .04 | .02 | .01 |
| ☐ 495 | Ian Beckles | .04 | .02 | .01 |
| ☐ 496 | Mark Robinson | .04 | .02 | .01 |
| ☐ 497 | Reuben Davis | .04 | .02 | .01 |
| ☐ 498 | Wayne Haddix | .04 | .02 | .01 |
| ☐ 499 | Kevin Murphy | .04 | .02 | .01 |
| ☐ 500 | Eugene Marve | .04 | .02 | .01 |
| ☐ 501 | Broderick Thomas | .08 | .04 | .01 |
| ☐ 502 | Eric Swann UER<br>(Draft pick logo miss-<br>ing from card front) | .20 | .09 | .03 |
| ☐ 503 | Ernie Jones | .04 | .02 | .01 |
| ☐ 504 | Rich Camarillo | .04 | .02 | .01 |
| ☐ 505 | Tim McDonald | .08 | .04 | .01 |
| ☐ 506 | Freddie Joe Nunn | .04 | .02 | .01 |
| ☐ 507 | Tim Jorden | .04 | .02 | .01 |
| ☐ 508 | Johnny Johnson | .25 | .11 | .03 |
| ☐ 509 | Eric Hill | .04 | .02 | .01 |
| ☐ 510 | Derek Kennard | .04 | .02 | .01 |
| ☐ 511 | Ricky Proehl | .10 | .05 | .01 |
| ☐ 512 | Bill Lewis | .04 | .02 | .01 |
| ☐ 513 | Roy Green | .08 | .04 | .01 |
| ☐ 514 | Anthony Bell | .04 | .02 | .01 |
| ☐ 515 | Timm Rosenbach | .08 | .04 | .01 |
| ☐ 516 | Jim Wahler | .10 | .05 | .01 |
| ☐ 517 | Anthony Thompson | .04 | .02 | .01 |
| ☐ 518 | Ken Harvey | .04 | .02 | .01 |
| ☐ 519 | Luis Sharpe | .04 | .02 | .01 |
| ☐ 520 | Walter Reeves | .04 | .02 | .01 |
| ☐ 521 | Lonnie Young | .04 | .02 | .01 |
| ☐ 522 | Rod Saddler | .04 | .02 | .01 |
| ☐ 523 | Todd Lyght | .10 | .05 | .01 |
| ☐ 524 | Alvin Wright | .04 | .02 | .01 |
| ☐ 525 | Flipper Anderson | .08 | .04 | .01 |
| ☐ 526 | Jackie Slater | .08 | .04 | .01 |
| ☐ 527 | Damone Johnson | .04 | .02 | .01 |
| ☐ 528 | Cleveland Gary | .08 | .04 | .01 |
| ☐ 529 | Mike Piel | .04 | .02 | .01 |
| ☐ 530 | Buford McGee | .04 | .02 | .01 |
| ☐ 531 | Michael Stewart | .04 | .02 | .01 |
| ☐ 532 | Jim Everett | .08 | .04 | .01 |
| ☐ 533 | Mike Wilcher | .04 | .02 | .01 |
| ☐ 534 | Irv Pankey | .04 | .02 | .01 |
| ☐ 535 | Bern Brostek | .04 | .02 | .01 |
| ☐ 536 | Henry Ellard | .08 | .04 | .01 |
| ☐ 537 | Doug Smith | .04 | .02 | .01 |
| ☐ 538 | Larry Kelm | .04 | .02 | .01 |
| ☐ 539 | Pat Terrell | .04 | .02 | .01 |
| ☐ 540 | Tom Newberry | .04 | .02 | .01 |
| ☐ 541 | Jerry Gray | .04 | .02 | .01 |
| ☐ 542 | Kevin Greene | .08 | .04 | .01 |
| ☐ 543 | Duval Love | .04 | .02 | .01 |
| ☐ 544 | Frank Stams | .04 | .02 | .01 |
| ☐ 545 | Mike Croel | .20 | .09 | .03 |
| ☐ 546 | Mark Jackson | .08 | .04 | .01 |
| ☐ 547 | Greg Kragen | .04 | .02 | .01 |
| ☐ 548 | Karl Mecklenburg | .08 | .04 | .01 |
| ☐ 549 | Simon Fletcher | .08 | .04 | .01 |
| ☐ 550 | Bobby Humphrey | .08 | .04 | .01 |
| ☐ 551 | Ken Lanier | .04 | .02 | .01 |
| ☐ 552 | Vance Johnson | .08 | .04 | .01 |
| ☐ 553 | Ron Holmes | .04 | .02 | .01 |
| ☐ 554 | John Elway | .35 | .16 | .04 |
| ☐ 555 | Melvin Bratton | .04 | .02 | .01 |
| ☐ 556 | Dennis Smith | .04 | .02 | .01 |
| ☐ 557 | Ricky Nattiel | .04 | .02 | .01 |
| ☐ 558 | Clarence Kay | .04 | .02 | .01 |
| ☐ 559 | Michael Brooks | .04 | .02 | .01 |
| ☐ 560 | Mike Horan | .04 | .02 | .01 |
| ☐ 561 | Warren Powers | .04 | .02 | .01 |
| ☐ 562 | Keith Kartz | .04 | .02 | .01 |
| ☐ 563 | Shannon Sharpe | .75 | .35 | .09 |
| ☐ 564 | Wymon Henderson | .04 | .02 | .01 |
| ☐ 565 | Steve Atwater | .10 | .05 | .01 |
| ☐ 566 | David Treadwell | .04 | .02 | .01 |
| ☐ 567 | Bruce Pickens | .10 | .05 | .01 |
| ☐ 568 | Jessie Tuggle | .04 | .02 | .01 |
| ☐ 569 | Chris Hinton | .04 | .02 | .01 |
| ☐ 570 | Keith Jones | .04 | .02 | .01 |
| ☐ 571 | Bill Fralic | .08 | .04 | .01 |
| ☐ 572 | Mike Rozier | .04 | .02 | .01 |
| ☐ 573 | Scott Fulhage | .04 | .02 | .01 |
| ☐ 574 | Floyd Dixon | .04 | .02 | .01 |
| ☐ 575 | Andre Rison | .25 | .11 | .03 |
| ☐ 576 | Darion Conner | .04 | .02 | .01 |
| ☐ 577 | Brian Jordan | .10 | .05 | .01 |
| ☐ 578 | Michael Haynes | .30 | .14 | .04 |
| ☐ 579 | Oliver Barnett | .04 | .02 | .01 |
| ☐ 580 | Shawn Collins | .04 | .02 | .01 |
| ☐ 581 | Tim Green | .04 | .02 | .01 |
| ☐ 582 | Deion Sanders | .25 | .11 | .03 |
| ☐ 583 | Mike Kenn | .08 | .04 | .01 |
| ☐ 584 | Mike Gann | .04 | .02 | .01 |
| ☐ 585 | Chris Miller | .10 | .05 | .01 |
| ☐ 586 | Tory Epps | .04 | .02 | .01 |
| ☐ 587 | Steve Broussard | .08 | .04 | .01 |
| ☐ 588 | Gary Wilkins | .04 | .02 | .01 |
| ☐ 589 | Eric Turner | .20 | .09 | .03 |
| ☐ 590 | Thane Gash | .04 | .02 | .01 |
| ☐ 591 | Clay Matthews | .08 | .04 | .01 |
| ☐ 592 | Mike Johnson | .04 | .02 | .01 |
| ☐ 593 | Raymond Clayborn | .08 | .04 | .01 |
| ☐ 594 | Leroy Hoard | .08 | .04 | .01 |
| ☐ 595 | Reggie Langhorne | .08 | .04 | .01 |
| ☐ 596 | Mike Baab | .04 | .02 | .01 |
| ☐ 597 | Anthony Pleasant | .04 | .02 | .01 |
| ☐ 598 | David Grayson | .04 | .02 | .01 |
| ☐ 599 | Rob Burnett | .15 | .07 | .02 |
| ☐ 600 | Frank Minnifield | .04 | .02 | .01 |
| ☐ 601 | Gregg Rakoczy | .04 | .02 | .01 |
| ☐ 602 | Eric Metcalf | .10 | .05 | .01 |
| ☐ 603 | Paul Farren | .04 | .02 | .01 |
| ☐ 604 | Brian Brennan | .04 | .02 | .01 |
| ☐ 605 | Tony Jones | .04 | .02 | .01 |
| ☐ 606 | Stephen Braggs | .08 | .04 | .01 |
| ☐ 607 | Kevin Mack | .08 | .04 | .01 |
| ☐ 608 | Pat Harlow | .10 | .05 | .01 |
| ☐ 609 | Marv Cook | .04 | .02 | .01 |
| ☐ 610 | John Stephens | .08 | .04 | .01 |
| ☐ 611 | Ed Reynolds | .04 | .02 | .01 |
| ☐ 612 | Tim Goad | .04 | .02 | .01 |

| | | | |
|---|---|---|---|
| ☐ 613 Chris Singleton | .04 | .02 | .01 |
| ☐ 614 Bruce Armstrong | .04 | .02 | .01 |
| ☐ 615 Tommy Hodson | .04 | .02 | .01 |
| ☐ 616 Sammy Martin | .04 | .02 | .01 |
| ☐ 617 Andre Tippett | .08 | .04 | .01 |
| ☐ 618 Johnny Rembert | .04 | .02 | .01 |
| ☐ 619 Maurice Hurst | .04 | .02 | .01 |
| ☐ 620 Vincent Brown | .04 | .02 | .01 |
| ☐ 621 Ray Agnew | .04 | .02 | .01 |
| ☐ 622 Ronnie Lippett | .04 | .02 | .01 |
| ☐ 623 Greg McMurtry | .04 | .02 | .01 |
| ☐ 624 Brent Williams | .04 | .02 | .01 |
| ☐ 625 Jason Staurovsky | .04 | .02 | .01 |
| ☐ 626 Marvin Allen | .04 | .02 | .01 |
| ☐ 627 Hart Lee Dykes | .04 | .02 | .01 |
| ☐ 628 Atlanta Falcons Team: (Keith) Jones Jumps for Yardage | .04 | .02 | .01 |
| ☐ 629 Buffalo Bills Team: (Jeff) Wright Goes for a Block | .04 | .02 | .01 |
| ☐ 630 Chicago Bears Team: (Jim) Harbaugh Makes Like a Halfback | .04 | .02 | .01 |
| ☐ 631 Cincinnati Bengals Team: (Stanford) Jennings Cuts Through Hole | .04 | .02 | .01 |
| ☐ 632 Cleveland Browns Team: (Eric) Metcalf Makes a Return | .08 | .04 | .01 |
| ☐ 633 Dallas Cowboys Team: (Kelvin) Martin Makes a Move | .04 | .02 | .01 |
| ☐ 634 Denver Broncos Team: (Shannon) Sharpe Into the Wedge | .08 | .04 | .01 |
| ☐ 635 Detroit Lions Team: (Rodney) Peete Hunted by a Bear (Mike Singletary) | .08 | .04 | .01 |
| ☐ 636 Green Bay Packers Team: (Don) Majkowski Orchestrates Some Magic | .04 | .02 | .01 |
| ☐ 637 Houston Oilers Team: (Warren) Moon Monitors the Action | .10 | .05 | .01 |
| ☐ 638 Indianapolis Colts Team: (Jeff) George Releases Just in Time | .15 | .07 | .02 |
| ☐ 639 Kansas City Chiefs Team: (Christian) Okoye Powers Ahead | .04 | .02 | .01 |
| ☐ 640 Los Angeles Raiders Team: (Marcus) Allen Crosses the Plane | .08 | .04 | .01 |
| ☐ 641 Los Angeles Rams Team: (Jim) Everett Connects With Soft Touch | .08 | .04 | .01 |
| ☐ 642 Miami Dolphins Team: (Pete) Stoyanovich Kicks It Through | .04 | .02 | .01 |
| ☐ 643 Minnesota Vikings Team: (Rich) Gannon Loads Cannon | .04 | .02 | .01 |
| ☐ 644 New Eng. Patriots Team: (John) Stephens Gets Stood Up | .04 | .02 | .01 |
| ☐ 645 New Orleans Saints Team: (Gill) Fenerty Finds Opening | .04 | .02 | .01 |
| ☐ 646 New York Giants Team: (Maurice) Carthon Inches Ahead | .04 | .02 | .01 |
| ☐ 647 New York Jets Team: (Pat) Leahy Perfect on Extra Point | .04 | .02 | .01 |
| ☐ 648 Philadelphia Eagles Team: (Randall) Cunningham Calls Own Play for TD | .08 | .04 | .01 |
| ☐ 649 Phoenix Cardinals Team: (Bill) Lewis Provides the Protection | .04 | .02 | .01 |
| ☐ 650 Pittsburgh Steelers Team: (Bubby) Brister Eyes Downfield Attack | .04 | .02 | .01 |
| ☐ 651 San Diego Chargers Team: (John) Friesz Finds the Passing Lane | .04 | .02 | .01 |
| ☐ 652 San Francisco 49ers Team: (Dexter) Carter Follows Rathman's Block | .04 | .02 | .01 |
| ☐ 653 Seattle Seahawks Team: (Derrick) Fenner With Fancy Footwork | .04 | .02 | .01 |
| ☐ 654 Tampa Bay Buccaneers Team: (Reggie) Cobb Hurdles His Way | .04 | .02 | .01 |
| to First Down | | | |
| ☐ 655 Washington Redskins Team: (Earnest) Byner Cuts Back to Follow Block | .04 | .02 | .01 |
| ☐ 656 Checklist 1-132 | .04 | .02 | .01 |
| ☐ 657 Checklist 132-264 | .04 | .02 | .01 |
| ☐ 658 Checklist 265-396 | .04 | .02 | .01 |
| ☐ 659 Checklist 397-528 | .04 | .02 | .01 |
| ☐ 660 Checklist 529-660 | .04 | .02 | .01 |

## 1991 Topps 1000 Yard Club

This 18-card set was issued by Topps to celebrate rushers and receivers who compiled 1000 yards or more in a season. The words "1000 Yard Club" appear at the top of the card. The color action player photo has a top red border, a red and purple left border, and no borders on the right and bottom. The player's name is given in an orange stripe toward the bottom of the picture. In blue and pink on white, the backs feature the rushing or receiving record of the player. The cards were inserted into regular issue 1991 Topps football wax packs. The cards are numbered on the back in the upper right corner.

| | MINT | EXC | G-VG |
|---|---|---|---|
| COMPLETE SET (18) | 5.00 | 2.00 | .50 |
| COMMON PLAYER (1-18) | .25 | .10 | .02 |
| ☐ 1 Jerry Rice San Francisco 49ers | .75 | .30 | .07 |
| ☐ 2 Barry Sanders Detroit Lions | 1.25 | .50 | .12 |
| ☐ 3 Thurman Thomas Buffalo Bills | .75 | .30 | .07 |
| ☐ 4 Henry Ellard Los Angeles Rams | .25 | .10 | .02 |
| ☐ 5 Marion Butts San Diego Chargers | .50 | .20 | .05 |
| ☐ 6 Earnest Byner Washington Redskins | .35 | .14 | .03 |
| ☐ 7 Andre Rison Atlanta Falcons | .50 | .20 | .05 |
| ☐ 8 Bobby Humphrey Denver Broncos | .25 | .10 | .02 |
| ☐ 9 Gary Clark Washington Redskins | .35 | .14 | .03 |
| ☐ 10 Sterling Sharpe Green Bay Packers | 1.00 | .40 | .10 |
| ☐ 11 Flipper Anderson Los Angeles Rams | .25 | .10 | .02 |
| ☐ 12 Neal Anderson Chicago Bears | .35 | .14 | .03 |
| ☐ 13 Haywood Jeffires Houston Oilers | .50 | .20 | .05 |
| ☐ 14 Stephone Paige Kansas City Chiefs | .35 | .14 | .03 |
| ☐ 15 Drew Hill Houston Oilers | .25 | .10 | .02 |
| ☐ 16 Barry Word Kansas City Chiefs | .35 | .14 | .03 |
| ☐ 17 Anthony Carter Minnesota Vikings | .35 | .14 | .03 |
| ☐ 18 James Brooks Cincinnati Bengals | .25 | .10 | .02 |

## 1992 Topps

The 1992 Topps football set was issued in three series and totaled 759 cards. Gold-foil ("ToppsGold") versions of each card were also produced, and these were inserted one per foil pack. The first two series were sold as a factory set with 20 gold cards, while the high number series was sold with ten gold cards and a four-card "No. 1 Draft Pick of the '90s" subset. Production figures for the high number

series were reportedly 5,000 20-box wax cases and 3,000 factory sets. The cards measure the standard size (2 1/2" by 3 1/2"). The fronts feature color action player photos inside a team color-coded picture frame and white outer borders. The player's name and team name appear in two short color bars toward the bottom of the picture. The backs carry biography, statistics, a photo of the team's stadium, and, where space permits, a player profile. The cards are numbered on the back. The key Rookie Cards in the set are Edgar Bennett, Steve Bono, Terrell Buckley, Quentin Coryatt, Vaughn Dunbar, Steve Emtman, David Klingler, Amp Lee, Tommy Maddox, Carl Pickens and Tommy Vardell.

|  | MINT | EXC | G-VG |
|---|---|---|---|
| COMPLETE SET (759) | 30.00 | 13.50 | 3.80 |
| COMPLETE FACT.SET (680) | 30.00 | 13.50 | 3.80 |
| COMPLETE SERIES 1 (330) | 14.00 | 6.25 | 1.75 |
| COMPLETE SERIES 2 (330) | 10.00 | 4.50 | 1.25 |
| COMPLETE HI SERIES (99) | 7.00 | 3.10 | .85 |
| COMPLETE FACT.HI SET (113) | 10.00 | 4.50 | 1.25 |
| COMMON PLAYER (1-330) | .05 | .02 | .01 |
| COMMON PLAYER (331-660) | .05 | .02 | .01 |
| COMMON PLAYER (661-759) | .05 | .02 | .01 |

| | | | |
|---|---|---|---|
| ☐ 1 Tim McGee<br>Atlanta Falcons | .05 | .02 | .01 |
| ☐ 2 Rich Camarillo<br>Phoenix Cardinals | .05 | .02 | .01 |
| ☐ 3 Anthony Johnson<br>Atlanta Falcons | .05 | .02 | .01 |
| ☐ 4 Larry Kelm<br>Los Angeles Rams | .05 | .02 | .01 |
| ☐ 5 Irving Fryar<br>New England Patriots | .08 | .04 | .01 |
| ☐ 6 Joey Browner<br>Minnesota Vikings | .05 | .02 | .01 |
| ☐ 7 Michael Walter<br>San Francisco 49ers | .05 | .02 | .01 |
| ☐ 8 Cortez Kennedy<br>Seattle Seahawks | .10 | .05 | .01 |
| ☐ 9 Reyna Thompson<br>New York Giants | .05 | .02 | .01 |
| ☐ 10 John Friesz<br>San Diego Chargers | .08 | .04 | .01 |
| ☐ 11 Leroy Hoard<br>Cleveland Browns | .08 | .04 | .01 |
| ☐ 12 Steve McMichael<br>Chicago Bears | .08 | .04 | .01 |
| ☐ 13 Marvin Washington<br>New York Jets | .05 | .02 | .01 |
| ☐ 14 Clyde Simmons<br>Philadelphia Eagles | .08 | .04 | .01 |
| ☐ 15 Stephone Paige<br>Kansas City Chiefs | .08 | .04 | .01 |
| ☐ 16 Mike Utley<br>Detroit Lions | .20 | .09 | .03 |
| ☐ 17 Tunch Ilkin<br>Pittsburgh Steelers | .05 | .02 | .01 |
| ☐ 18 Lawrence Dawsey<br>Tampa Bay Buccaneers | .10 | .05 | .01 |
| ☐ 19 Vance Johnson<br>Denver Broncos | .08 | .04 | .01 |
| ☐ 20 Bryce Paup<br>Green Bay Packers | .05 | .02 | .01 |
| ☐ 21 Jeff Wright<br>Buffalo Bills | .05 | .02 | .01 |
| ☐ 22 Gill Fenerty<br>New Orleans Saints | .05 | .02 | .01 |
| ☐ 23 Lamar Lathon<br>Houston Oilers | .05 | .02 | .01 |
| ☐ 24 Danny Copeland<br>Washington Redskins | .05 | .02 | .01 |
| ☐ 25 Marcus Allen<br>Los Angeles Raiders | .08 | .04 | .01 |
| ☐ 26 Tim Green<br>Atlanta Falcons | .05 | .02 | .01 |
| ☐ 27 Pete Stoyanovich | .08 | .04 | .01 |

| | | | |
|---|---|---|---|
| Miami Dolphins | | | |
| ☐ 28 Alvin Harper<br>Dallas Cowboys | .40 | .18 | .05 |
| ☐ 29 Roy Foster<br>San Francisco 49ers | .05 | .02 | .01 |
| ☐ 30 Eugene Daniel<br>Indianapolis Colts | .05 | .02 | .01 |
| ☐ 31 Luis Sharpe<br>Phoenix Cardinals | .05 | .02 | .01 |
| ☐ 32 Terry Wooden<br>Seattle Seahawks | .05 | .02 | .01 |
| ☐ 33 Jim Breech<br>Cincinnati Bengals | .05 | .02 | .01 |
| ☐ 34 Randy Hilliard<br>Cleveland Browns | .05 | .02 | .01 |
| ☐ 35 Roman Phifer<br>Los Angeles Rams | .05 | .02 | .01 |
| ☐ 36 Erik Howard<br>New York Giants | .05 | .02 | .01 |
| ☐ 37 Chris Singleton<br>Indianapolis Colts | .05 | .02 | .01 |
| ☐ 38 Matt Stover<br>Cleveland Browns | .05 | .02 | .01 |
| ☐ 39 Tim Irwin<br>Minnesota Vikings | .05 | .02 | .01 |
| ☐ 40 Karl Mecklenburg<br>Denver Broncos | .08 | .04 | .01 |
| ☐ 41 Joe Phillips<br>San Diego Chargers | .05 | .02 | .01 |
| ☐ 42 Bill Jones<br>Kansas City Chiefs | .05 | .02 | .01 |
| ☐ 43 Mark Carrier<br>Chicago Bears | .08 | .04 | .01 |
| ☐ 44 George Jamison<br>Detroit Lions | .05 | .02 | .01 |
| ☐ 45 Rob Taylor<br>Tampa Bay Buccaneers | .05 | .02 | .01 |
| ☐ 46 Jeff Jaeger<br>Los Angeles Raiders | .05 | .02 | .01 |
| ☐ 47 Don Majkowski<br>Green Bay Packers | .08 | .04 | .01 |
| ☐ 48 Al Edwards<br>Buffalo Bills | .05 | .02 | .01 |
| ☐ 49 Curtis Duncan<br>Houston Oilers | .08 | .04 | .01 |
| ☐ 50 Sam Mills<br>New Orleans Saints | .08 | .04 | .01 |
| ☐ 51 Terance Mathis<br>New York Jets | .05 | .02 | .01 |
| ☐ 52 Brian Mitchell<br>Washington Redskins | .08 | .04 | .01 |
| ☐ 53 Mike Pritchard<br>Atlanta Falcons | .25 | .11 | .03 |
| ☐ 54 Calvin Williams<br>Philadelphia Eagles | .10 | .05 | .01 |
| ☐ 55 Hardy Nickerson<br>Pittsburgh Steelers | .05 | .02 | .01 |
| ☐ 56 Nate Newton<br>Dallas Cowboys | .05 | .02 | .01 |
| ☐ 57 Steve Wallace<br>San Francisco 49ers | .05 | .02 | .01 |
| ☐ 58 John Offerdahl<br>Denver Broncos | .08 | .04 | .01 |
| ☐ 59 Aeneas Williams<br>Phoenix Cardinals | .05 | .02 | .01 |
| ☐ 60 Lee Johnson<br>San Diego Chargers | .05 | .02 | .01 |
| ☐ 61 Ricardo McDonald<br>Cincinnati Bengals | .10 | .05 | .01 |
| ☐ 62 David Richards<br>San Diego Chargers | .05 | .02 | .01 |
| ☐ 63 Paul Gruber<br>Tampa Bay Buccaneers | .05 | .02 | .01 |
| ☐ 64 Greg McMurtry<br>New England Patriots | .05 | .02 | .01 |
| ☐ 65 Jay Hilgenberg<br>Chicago Bears | .08 | .04 | .01 |
| ☐ 66 Tim Grunhard<br>Kansas City Chiefs | .05 | .02 | .01 |
| ☐ 67 Dwayne White<br>New York Jets | .05 | .02 | .01 |
| ☐ 68 Don Beebe<br>Buffalo Bills | .10 | .05 | .01 |
| ☐ 69 Simon Fletcher<br>Denver Broncos | .08 | .04 | .01 |
| ☐ 70 Warren Moon<br>Houston Oilers | .20 | .09 | .03 |
| ☐ 71 Chris Jacke<br>Green Bay Packers | .05 | .02 | .01 |
| ☐ 72 Steve Wisniewski UER<br>(Traded to Raiders,<br>not drafted by them)<br>Los Angeles Raiders | .05 | .02 | .01 |
| ☐ 73 Mike Cofer<br>San Francisco 49ers | .05 | .02 | .01 |
| ☐ 74 Tim Johnson UER<br>(No position listed<br>on back) | .05 | .02 | .01 |

| | | | |
|---|---|---|---|
| Washington Redskins | | | |
| ☐ 75 T.J. Turner | .05 | .02 | .01 |
| Miami Dolphins | | | |
| ☐ 76 Scott Case | .05 | .02 | .01 |
| Atlanta Falcons | | | |
| ☐ 77 Michael Jackson | .10 | .05 | .01 |
| Cleveland Browns | | | |
| ☐ 78 Jon Hand | .05 | .02 | .01 |
| Indianapolis Colts | | | |
| ☐ 79 Stan Brock | .05 | .02 | .01 |
| New Orleans Saints | | | |
| ☐ 80 Robert Blackmon | .05 | .02 | .01 |
| Seattle Seahawks | | | |
| ☐ 81 David Johnson | .05 | .02 | .01 |
| Pittsburgh Steelers | | | |
| ☐ 82 Damone Johnson | .05 | .02 | .01 |
| Los Angeles Rams | | | |
| ☐ 83 Marc Spindler | .05 | .02 | .01 |
| Detroit Lions | | | |
| ☐ 84 Larry Brown | .05 | .02 | .01 |
| Dallas Cowboys | | | |
| ☐ 85 Ray Berry | .05 | .02 | .01 |
| Minnesota Vikings | | | |
| ☐ 86 Andre Waters | .05 | .02 | .01 |
| Philadelphia Eagles | | | |
| ☐ 87 Carlos Huerta | .05 | .02 | .01 |
| San Diego Chargers | | | |
| ☐ 88 Brad Muster | .08 | .04 | .01 |
| Chicago Bears | | | |
| ☐ 89 Chuck Cecil | .05 | .02 | .01 |
| Green Bay Packers | | | |
| ☐ 90 Nick Lowery | .08 | .04 | .01 |
| Kansas City Chiefs | | | |
| ☐ 91 Cornelius Bennett | .10 | .05 | .01 |
| Buffalo Bills | | | |
| ☐ 92 Jessie Tuggle | .05 | .02 | .01 |
| Atlanta Falcons | | | |
| ☐ 93 Mark Schlereth | .10 | .05 | .01 |
| Washington Redskins | | | |
| ☐ 94 Vestee Jackson | .05 | .02 | .01 |
| Chicago Bears | | | |
| ☐ 95 Eric Bieniemy | .08 | .04 | .01 |
| San Diego Chargers | | | |
| ☐ 96 Jeff Hostetler | .15 | .07 | .02 |
| New York Giants | | | |
| ☐ 97 Ken Lanier | .05 | .02 | .01 |
| Denver Broncos | | | |
| ☐ 98 Wayne Haddix | .05 | .02 | .01 |
| Atlanta Falcons | | | |
| ☐ 99 Lorenzo White | .08 | .04 | .01 |
| Houston Oilers | | | |
| ☐ 100 Mervyn Fernandez | .05 | .02 | .01 |
| Los Angeles Raiders | | | |
| ☐ 101 Brent Williams | .05 | .02 | .01 |
| New England Patriots | | | |
| ☐ 102 Ian Beckles | .05 | .02 | .01 |
| Tampa Bay Buccaneers | | | |
| ☐ 103 Harris Barton | .05 | .02 | .01 |
| San Francisco 49ers | | | |
| ☐ 104 Edgar Bennett | .30 | .14 | .04 |
| Green Bay Packers | | | |
| ☐ 105 Mike Pitts | .05 | .02 | .01 |
| Philadelphia Eagles | | | |
| ☐ 106 Fuad Reveiz | .05 | .02 | .01 |
| Minnesota Vikings | | | |
| ☐ 107 Vernon Turner | .05 | .02 | .01 |
| Buffalo Bills | | | |
| ☐ 108 Tracy Hayworth | .05 | .02 | .01 |
| Detroit Lions | | | |
| ☐ 109 Checklist 1-110 | .05 | .02 | .01 |
| ☐ 110 Tom Waddle | .10 | .05 | .01 |
| Chicago Bears | | | |
| ☐ 111 Fred Stokes | .05 | .02 | .01 |
| Washington Redskins | | | |
| ☐ 112 Howard Ballard | .05 | .02 | .01 |
| Buffalo Bills | | | |
| ☐ 113 David Szott | .05 | .02 | .01 |
| Kansas City Chiefs | | | |
| ☐ 114 Tim McKyer | .08 | .04 | .01 |
| Atlanta Falcons | | | |
| ☐ 115 Kyle Clifton | .05 | .02 | .01 |
| New York Jets | | | |
| ☐ 116 Tony Bennett | .08 | .04 | .01 |
| Green Bay Packers | | | |
| ☐ 117 Joel Hilgenberg | .05 | .02 | .01 |
| New Orleans Saints | | | |
| ☐ 118 Dwayne Harper | .05 | .02 | .01 |
| Seattle Seahawks | | | |
| ☐ 119 Mike Baab | .05 | .02 | .01 |
| Cleveland Browns | | | |
| ☐ 120 Mark Clayton | .08 | .04 | .01 |
| Miami Dolphins | | | |
| ☐ 121 Eric Swann | .08 | .04 | .01 |
| Phoenix Cardinals | | | |
| ☐ 122 Neil O'Donnell | .50 | .23 | .06 |
| Pittsburgh Steelers | | | |
| ☐ 123 Mike Munchak | .08 | .04 | .01 |
| Houston Oilers | | | |

| | | | |
|---|---|---|---|
| ☐ 124 Howie Long | .08 | .04 | .01 |
| Los Angeles Raiders | | | |
| ☐ 125 John Elway UER | .40 | .18 | .05 |
| (Card says 6-year | | | |
| vet, should be 9) | | | |
| Denver Broncos | | | |
| ☐ 126 Joe Prokop | .05 | .02 | .01 |
| New York Jets | | | |
| ☐ 127 Pepper Johnson | .08 | .04 | .01 |
| New York Giants | | | |
| ☐ 128 Richard Dent | .08 | .04 | .01 |
| Chicago Bears | | | |
| ☐ 129 Robert Porcher | .20 | .09 | .03 |
| Detroit Lions | | | |
| ☐ 130 Earnest Byner | .08 | .04 | .01 |
| Washington Redskins | | | |
| ☐ 131 Kent Hull | .05 | .02 | .01 |
| Buffalo Bills | | | |
| ☐ 132 Mike Merriweather | .05 | .02 | .01 |
| Minnesota Vikings | | | |
| ☐ 133 Scott Fulhage | .05 | .02 | .01 |
| Atlanta Falcons | | | |
| ☐ 134 Kevin Porter | .05 | .02 | .01 |
| Kansas City Chiefs | | | |
| ☐ 135 Tony Casillas | .05 | .02 | .01 |
| Dallas Cowboys | | | |
| ☐ 136 Dean Biasucci | .05 | .02 | .01 |
| Indianapolis Colts | | | |
| ☐ 137 Ben Smith | .05 | .02 | .01 |
| Philadelphia Eagles | | | |
| ☐ 138 Bruce Kozerski | .05 | .02 | .01 |
| Cincinnati Bengals | | | |
| ☐ 139 Jeff Campbell | .05 | .02 | .01 |
| Detroit Lions | | | |
| ☐ 140 Kevin Greene | .08 | .04 | .01 |
| Los Angeles Rams | | | |
| ☐ 141 Gary Plummer | .05 | .02 | .01 |
| San Diego Chargers | | | |
| ☐ 142 Vincent Brown | .05 | .02 | .01 |
| New England Patriots | | | |
| ☐ 143 Ron Hall | .05 | .02 | .01 |
| Tampa Bay Buccaneers | | | |
| ☐ 144 Louie Aguiar | .05 | .02 | .01 |
| New York Jets | | | |
| ☐ 145 Mark Duper | .08 | .04 | .01 |
| Miami Dolphins | | | |
| ☐ 146 Jesse Sapolu | .05 | .02 | .01 |
| San Francisco 49ers | | | |
| ☐ 147 Jeff Gossett | .05 | .02 | .01 |
| Los Angeles Raiders | | | |
| ☐ 148 Brian Noble | .05 | .02 | .01 |
| Green Bay Packers | | | |
| ☐ 149 Derek Russell | .08 | .04 | .01 |
| Denver Broncos | | | |
| ☐ 150 Carlton Bailey | .20 | .09 | .03 |
| Buffalo Bills | | | |
| ☐ 151 Kelly Goodburn | .05 | .02 | .01 |
| Washington Redskins | | | |
| ☐ 152 Audray McMillian UER | .05 | .02 | .01 |
| (Misspelled Audrey) | | | |
| Minnesota Vikings | | | |
| ☐ 153 Neal Anderson | .08 | .04 | .01 |
| Chicago Bears | | | |
| ☐ 154 Bill Maas | .05 | .02 | .01 |
| Kansas City Chiefs | | | |
| ☐ 155 Rickey Jackson | .08 | .04 | .01 |
| Denver Broncos | | | |
| ☐ 156 Chris Miller | .10 | .05 | .01 |
| Atlanta Falcons | | | |
| ☐ 157 Darren Comeaux | .05 | .02 | .01 |
| Seattle Seahawks | | | |
| ☐ 158 David Williams | .05 | .02 | .01 |
| Houston Oilers | | | |
| ☐ 159 Rich Gannon | .08 | .04 | .01 |
| Minnesota Vikings | | | |
| ☐ 160 Kevin Mack | .08 | .04 | .01 |
| Cleveland Browns | | | |
| ☐ 161 Jim Arnold | .05 | .02 | .01 |
| Detroit Lions | | | |
| ☐ 162 Reggie White | .15 | .07 | .02 |
| Philadelphia Eagles | | | |
| ☐ 163 Leonard Russell | .30 | .14 | .04 |
| New England Patriots | | | |
| ☐ 164 Doug Smith | .05 | .02 | .01 |
| Los Angeles Rams | | | |
| ☐ 165 Tony Mandarich | .05 | .02 | .01 |
| Green Bay Packers | | | |
| ☐ 166 Greg Lloyd | .05 | .02 | .01 |
| Pittsburgh Steelers | | | |
| ☐ 167 Jumbo Elliott | .05 | .02 | .01 |
| New York Giants | | | |
| ☐ 168 Jonathan Hayes | .05 | .02 | .01 |
| Kansas City Chiefs | | | |
| ☐ 169 Jim Ritcher | .05 | .02 | .01 |
| Buffalo Bills | | | |
| ☐ 170 Mike Kenn | .08 | .04 | .01 |
| Atlanta Falcons | | | |

| | | | |
|---|---|---|---|
| ☐ 171 James Washington | .05 | .02 | .01 |
| Dallas Cowboys | | | |
| ☐ 172 Tim Harris | .08 | .04 | .01 |
| San Francisco 49ers | | | |
| ☐ 173 James Thornton | .05 | .02 | .01 |
| Chicago Bears | | | |
| ☐ 174 John Brandes | .05 | .02 | .01 |
| Washington Redskins | | | |
| ☐ 175 Fred McAfee | .15 | .07 | .02 |
| New Orleans Saints | | | |
| ☐ 176 Henry Rolling | .05 | .02 | .01 |
| San Diego Chargers | | | |
| ☐ 177 Tony Paige | .05 | .02 | .01 |
| Miami Dolphins | | | |
| ☐ 178 Jay Schroeder | .08 | .04 | .01 |
| Los Angeles Raiders | | | |
| ☐ 179 Jeff Herrod | .05 | .02 | .01 |
| Indianapolis Colts | | | |
| ☐ 180 Emmitt Smith | 2.00 | .90 | .25 |
| Dallas Cowboys | | | |
| ☐ 181 Wymon Henderson | .05 | .02 | .01 |
| San Francisco 49ers | | | |
| ☐ 182 Rob Moore | .10 | .05 | .01 |
| New York Jets | | | |
| ☐ 183 Robert Wilson | .05 | .02 | .01 |
| Tampa Bay Buccaneers | | | |
| ☐ 184 Michael Zordich | .05 | .02 | .01 |
| Phoenix Cardinals | | | |
| ☐ 185 Jim Harbaugh | .08 | .04 | .01 |
| Chicago Bears | | | |
| ☐ 186 Vince Workman | .08 | .04 | .01 |
| Green Bay Packers | | | |
| ☐ 187 Ernest Givins | .08 | .04 | .01 |
| Houston Oilers | | | |
| ☐ 188 Herschel Walker | .10 | .05 | .01 |
| Minnesota Vikings | | | |
| ☐ 189 Dan Fike | .05 | .02 | .01 |
| Cleveland Browns | | | |
| ☐ 190 Seth Joyner | .08 | .04 | .01 |
| Philadelphia Eagles | | | |
| ☐ 191 Steve Young | .35 | .16 | .04 |
| San Francisco 49ers | | | |
| ☐ 192 Dennis Gibson | .05 | .02 | .01 |
| Detroit Lions | | | |
| ☐ 193 Darryl Talley | .08 | .04 | .01 |
| Buffalo Bills | | | |
| ☐ 194 Emile Harry | .05 | .02 | .01 |
| Kansas City Chiefs | | | |
| ☐ 195 Bill Fralic | .05 | .02 | .01 |
| Atlanta Falcons | | | |
| ☐ 196 Michael Stewart | .05 | .02 | .01 |
| Los Angeles Rams | | | |
| ☐ 197 James Francis | .08 | .04 | .01 |
| Cincinnati Bengals | | | |
| ☐ 198 Jerome Henderson | .05 | .02 | .01 |
| New England Patriots | | | |
| ☐ 199 John L. Williams | .08 | .04 | .01 |
| Seattle Seahawks | | | |
| ☐ 200 Rod Woodson | .10 | .05 | .01 |
| Pittsburgh Steelers | | | |
| ☐ 201 Mike Farr | .05 | .02 | .01 |
| Detroit Lions | | | |
| ☐ 202 Greg Montgomery | .05 | .02 | .01 |
| Houston Oilers | | | |
| ☐ 203 Andre Collins | .05 | .02 | .01 |
| Washington Redskins | | | |
| ☐ 204 Scott Miller | .05 | .02 | .01 |
| Miami Dolphins | | | |
| ☐ 205 Clay Matthews | .08 | .04 | .01 |
| Cleveland Browns | | | |
| ☐ 206 Ethan Horton | .05 | .02 | .01 |
| Los Angeles Raiders | | | |
| ☐ 207 Rich Miano | .05 | .02 | .01 |
| Philadelphia Eagles | | | |
| ☐ 208 Chris Mims | .25 | .11 | .03 |
| San Diego Chargers | | | |
| ☐ 209 Anthony Morgan | .05 | .02 | .01 |
| Chicago Bears | | | |
| ☐ 210 Rodney Hampton | .40 | .18 | .05 |
| New York Giants | | | |
| ☐ 211 Chris Hinton | .05 | .02 | .01 |
| Indianapolis Colts | | | |
| ☐ 212 Esera Tuaolo | .05 | .02 | .01 |
| Green Bay Packers | | | |
| ☐ 213 Shane Conlan | .08 | .04 | .01 |
| Buffalo Bills | | | |
| ☐ 214 John Carney | .05 | .02 | .01 |
| San Diego Chargers | | | |
| ☐ 215 Kenny Walker | .05 | .02 | .01 |
| Denver Broncos | | | |
| ☐ 216 Scott Radecic | .05 | .02 | .01 |
| Indianapolis Colts | | | |
| ☐ 217 Chris Martin | .05 | .02 | .01 |
| Kansas City Chiefs | | | |
| ☐ 218 Checklist 111-220 UER | .05 | .02 | .01 |
| (152 Audray McMillian misspelled Audrey) | | | |

| | | | |
|---|---|---|---|
| ☐ 219 Wesley Carroll UER | .08 | .04 | .01 |
| (Stats say 1st round pick, bio correctly has 2nd) | | | |
| New Orleans Saints | | | |
| ☐ 220 Bill Romanowski | .05 | .02 | .01 |
| San Francisco 49ers | | | |
| ☐ 221 Reggie Cobb | .10 | .05 | .01 |
| Tampa Bay Buccaneers | | | |
| ☐ 222 Alfred Anderson | .05 | .02 | .01 |
| Minnesota Vikings | | | |
| ☐ 223 Cleveland Gary | .08 | .04 | .01 |
| Los Angeles Rams | | | |
| ☐ 224 Eddie Blake | .05 | .02 | .01 |
| Miami Dolphins | | | |
| ☐ 225 Chris Spielman | .08 | .04 | .01 |
| Detroit Lions | | | |
| ☐ 226 John Roper | .05 | .02 | .01 |
| Chicago Bears | | | |
| ☐ 227 George Thomas | .10 | .05 | .01 |
| Atlanta Falcons | | | |
| ☐ 228 Jeff Faulkner | .05 | .02 | .01 |
| Phoenix Cardinals | | | |
| ☐ 229 Chip Lohmiller UER | .08 | .04 | .01 |
| (RFK Stadium not identified on back) | | | |
| Washington Redskins | | | |
| ☐ 230 Hugh Millen | .08 | .04 | .01 |
| New England Patriots | | | |
| ☐ 231 Ray Horton | .05 | .02 | .01 |
| Dallas Cowboys | | | |
| ☐ 232 James Campen | .05 | .02 | .01 |
| Green Bay Packers | | | |
| ☐ 233 Howard Cross | .05 | .02 | .01 |
| New York Giants | | | |
| ☐ 234 Keith McKeller | .05 | .02 | .01 |
| Buffalo Bills | | | |
| ☐ 235 Dino Hackett | .05 | .02 | .01 |
| Kansas City Chiefs | | | |
| ☐ 236 Jerome Brown | .08 | .04 | .01 |
| Philadelphia Eagles | | | |
| ☐ 237 Andy Heck | .05 | .02 | .01 |
| Seattle Seahawks | | | |
| ☐ 238 Rodney Holman | .05 | .02 | .01 |
| Cincinnati Bengals | | | |
| ☐ 239 Bruce Matthews | .08 | .04 | .01 |
| Houston Oilers | | | |
| ☐ 240 Jeff Lageman | .05 | .02 | .01 |
| New York Jets | | | |
| ☐ 241 Bobby Hebert | .10 | .05 | .01 |
| New Orleans Saints | | | |
| ☐ 242 Gary Anderson | .05 | .02 | .01 |
| Pittsburgh Steelers | | | |
| ☐ 243 Mark Bortz | .05 | .02 | .01 |
| Chicago Bears | | | |
| ☐ 244 Rich Moran | .05 | .02 | .01 |
| Green Bay Packers | | | |
| ☐ 245 Jeff Uhlenhake | .05 | .02 | .01 |
| Miami Dolphins | | | |
| ☐ 246 Ricky Sanders | .08 | .04 | .01 |
| Washington Redskins | | | |
| ☐ 247 Clarence Kay | .05 | .02 | .01 |
| Denver Broncos | | | |
| ☐ 248 Ed King | .05 | .02 | .01 |
| Cleveland Browns | | | |
| ☐ 249 Eddie Anderson | .05 | .02 | .01 |
| Los Angeles Raiders | | | |
| ☐ 250 Amp Lee | .25 | .11 | .03 |
| San Francisco 49ers | | | |
| ☐ 251 Norm Johnson | .05 | .02 | .01 |
| Atlanta Falcons | | | |
| ☐ 252 Michael Carter | .05 | .02 | .01 |
| San Francisco 49ers | | | |
| ☐ 253 Felix Wright | .05 | .02 | .01 |
| Minnesota Vikings | | | |
| ☐ 254 Leon Seals | .05 | .02 | .01 |
| Buffalo Bills | | | |
| ☐ 255 Nate Lewis | .08 | .04 | .01 |
| San Diego Chargers | | | |
| ☐ 256 Kevin Call | .05 | .02 | .01 |
| Indianapolis Colts | | | |
| ☐ 257 Darryl Henley | .05 | .02 | .01 |
| Los Angeles Rams | | | |
| ☐ 258 Jon Vaughn | .05 | .02 | .01 |
| New England Patriots | | | |
| ☐ 259 Matt Bahr | .05 | .02 | .01 |
| New York Giants | | | |
| ☐ 260 Johnny Johnson | .10 | .05 | .01 |
| Phoenix Cardinals | | | |
| ☐ 261 Ken Norton | .08 | .04 | .01 |
| Dallas Cowboys | | | |
| ☐ 262 Wendell Davis | .05 | .02 | .01 |
| Chicago Bears | | | |
| ☐ 263 Eugene Robinson | .05 | .02 | .01 |
| Seattle Seahawks | | | |
| ☐ 264 David Treadwell | .05 | .02 | .01 |
| Denver Broncos | | | |

| | | | |
|---|---|---|---|
| ☐ 265 Michael Haynes | .30 | .14 | .04 |
| Atlanta Falcons | | | |
| ☐ 266 Robb Thomas | .05 | .02 | .01 |
| Kansas City Chiefs | | | |
| ☐ 267 Nate Odomes | .08 | .04 | .01 |
| Buffalo Bills | | | |
| ☐ 268 Martin Mayhew | .05 | .02 | .01 |
| Washington Redskins | | | |
| ☐ 269 Perry Kemp | .05 | .02 | .01 |
| Green Bay Packers | | | |
| ☐ 270 Jerry Ball | .08 | .04 | .01 |
| Detroit Lions | | | |
| ☐ 271 Tommy Vardell | .30 | .14 | .04 |
| Cleveland Browns | | | |
| ☐ 272 Ernie Mills | .05 | .02 | .01 |
| Pittsburgh Steelers | | | |
| ☐ 273 Mo Lewis | .05 | .02 | .01 |
| New York Jets | | | |
| ☐ 274 Roger Ruzek | .05 | .02 | .01 |
| Philadelphia Eagles | | | |
| ☐ 275 Steve Smith | .08 | .04 | .01 |
| Los Angeles Raiders | | | |
| ☐ 276 Bo Orlando | .15 | .07 | .02 |
| Houston Oilers | | | |
| ☐ 277 Louis Oliver | .08 | .04 | .01 |
| Miami Dolphins | | | |
| ☐ 278 Toi Cook | .05 | .02 | .01 |
| New Orleans Saints | | | |
| ☐ 279 Eddie Brown | .05 | .02 | .01 |
| Cincinnati Bengals | | | |
| ☐ 280 Keith McCants | .05 | .02 | .01 |
| Tampa Bay Buccaneers | | | |
| ☐ 281 Rob Burnett | .05 | .02 | .01 |
| Cleveland Browns | | | |
| ☐ 282 Keith DeLong | .05 | .02 | .01 |
| San Francisco 49ers | | | |
| ☐ 283 Stan Thomas UER | .05 | .02 | .01 |
| (9th line bio notes, | | | |
| the word of is in caps) | | | |
| Chicago Bears | | | |
| ☐ 284 Robert Brown | .05 | .02 | .01 |
| Green Bay Packers | | | |
| ☐ 285 John Alt | .05 | .02 | .01 |
| Kansas City Chiefs | | | |
| ☐ 286 Randy Dixon | .05 | .02 | .01 |
| Indianapolis Colts | | | |
| ☐ 287 Siran Stacy | .10 | .05 | .01 |
| Philadelphia Eagles | | | |
| ☐ 288 Ray Agnew | .05 | .02 | .01 |
| New England Patriots | | | |
| ☐ 289 Darion Conner | .05 | .02 | .01 |
| Atlanta Falcons | | | |
| ☐ 290 Kirk Lowdermilk | .05 | .02 | .01 |
| Minnesota Vikings | | | |
| ☐ 291 Greg Jackson | .05 | .02 | .01 |
| New York Giants | | | |
| ☐ 292 Ken Harvey | .05 | .02 | .01 |
| Phoenix Cardinals | | | |
| ☐ 293 Jacob Green | .05 | .02 | .01 |
| Seattle Seahawks | | | |
| ☐ 294 Mark Tuinei | .05 | .02 | .01 |
| Dallas Cowboys | | | |
| ☐ 295 Mark Rypien | .10 | .05 | .01 |
| Washington Redskins | | | |
| ☐ 296 Gerald Robinson | .05 | .02 | .01 |
| Los Angeles Rams | | | |
| ☐ 297 Broderick Thompson | .05 | .02 | .01 |
| San Diego Chargers | | | |
| ☐ 298 Doug Widell | .05 | .02 | .01 |
| Denver Broncos | | | |
| ☐ 299 Carwell Gardner | .05 | .02 | .01 |
| Buffalo Bills | | | |
| ☐ 300 Barry Sanders | .75 | .35 | .09 |
| Detroit Lions | | | |
| ☐ 301 Eric Metcalf | .10 | .05 | .01 |
| Cleveland Browns | | | |
| ☐ 302 Eric Thomas | .05 | .02 | .01 |
| Cleveland Browns | | | |
| ☐ 303 Terrell Buckley | .25 | .11 | .03 |
| Green Bay Packers | | | |
| ☐ 304 Byron Evans | .05 | .02 | .01 |
| Philadelphia Eagles | | | |
| ☐ 305 Johnny Hector | .05 | .02 | .01 |
| New York Jets | | | |
| ☐ 306 Steve Broussard | .08 | .04 | .01 |
| Atlanta Falcons | | | |
| ☐ 307 Gene Atkins | .05 | .02 | .01 |
| New Orleans Saints | | | |
| ☐ 308 Terry McDaniel | .05 | .02 | .01 |
| Los Angeles Raiders | | | |
| ☐ 309 Charles McRae | .05 | .02 | .01 |
| Tampa Bay Buccaneers | | | |
| ☐ 310 Jim Lachey | .05 | .02 | .01 |
| Washington Redskins | | | |
| ☐ 311 Pat Harlow | .05 | .02 | .01 |
| New England Patriots | | | |
| ☐ 312 Kevin Butler | .05 | .02 | .01 |
| Chicago Bears | | | |
| ☐ 313 Scott Stephen | .05 | .02 | .01 |
| Green Bay Packers | | | |
| ☐ 314 Dermontti Dawson | .05 | .02 | .01 |
| Pittsburgh Steelers | | | |
| ☐ 315 Johnny Meads | .05 | .02 | .01 |
| Houston Oilers | | | |
| ☐ 316 Checklist 221-330 | .05 | .02 | .01 |
| ☐ 317 Aaron Craver | .05 | .02 | .01 |
| Miami Dolphins | | | |
| ☐ 318 Michael Brooks | .05 | .02 | .01 |
| Denver Broncos | | | |
| ☐ 319 Guy McIntyre | .08 | .04 | .01 |
| San Francisco 49ers | | | |
| ☐ 320 Thurman Thomas | .40 | .18 | .05 |
| Buffalo Bills | | | |
| ☐ 321 Courtney Hall | .05 | .02 | .01 |
| San Diego Chargers | | | |
| ☐ 322 Dan Saleaumua | .05 | .02 | .01 |
| Kansas City Chiefs | | | |
| ☐ 323 Vinson Smith | .10 | .05 | .01 |
| Dallas Cowboys | | | |
| ☐ 324 Steve Jordan | .08 | .04 | .01 |
| Minnesota Vikings | | | |
| ☐ 325 Walter Reeves | .05 | .02 | .01 |
| Phoenix Cardinals | | | |
| ☐ 326 Erik Kramer | .15 | .07 | .02 |
| Detroit Lions | | | |
| ☐ 327 Duane Bickett | .05 | .02 | .01 |
| Indianapolis Colts | | | |
| ☐ 328 Tom Newberry | .05 | .02 | .01 |
| Los Angeles Rams | | | |
| ☐ 329 John Kasay | .05 | .02 | .01 |
| Seattle Seahawks | | | |
| ☐ 330 Dave Meggett | .08 | .04 | .01 |
| New York Giants | | | |
| ☐ 331 Kevin Ross | .08 | .04 | .01 |
| Kansas City Chiefs | | | |
| ☐ 332 Keith Hamilton | .15 | .07 | .02 |
| New York Giants | | | |
| ☐ 333 Dwight Stone | .05 | .02 | .01 |
| Pittsburgh Steelers | | | |
| ☐ 334 Mel Gray | .05 | .02 | .01 |
| Detroit Lions | | | |
| ☐ 335 Harry Galbreath | .05 | .02 | .01 |
| Miami Dolphins | | | |
| ☐ 336 William Perry | .08 | .04 | .01 |
| Chicago Bears | | | |
| ☐ 337 Brian Blades | .08 | .04 | .01 |
| Seattle Seahawks | | | |
| ☐ 338 Randall McDaniel | .05 | .02 | .01 |
| Minnesota Vikings | | | |
| ☐ 339 Pat Coleman | .10 | .05 | .01 |
| Houston Oilers | | | |
| ☐ 340 Michael Irvin | .50 | .23 | .06 |
| Dallas Cowboys | | | |
| ☐ 341 Checklist 331-440 | .05 | .02 | .01 |
| ☐ 342 Chris Mohr | .05 | .02 | .01 |
| Buffalo Bills | | | |
| ☐ 343 Greg Davis | .05 | .02 | .01 |
| Phoenix Cardinals | | | |
| ☐ 344 Dave Cadigan | .05 | .02 | .01 |
| New York Jets | | | |
| ☐ 345 Art Monk | .10 | .05 | .01 |
| Washington Redskins | | | |
| ☐ 346 Tim Goad | .05 | .02 | .01 |
| New England Patriots | | | |
| ☐ 347 Vinnie Clark | .05 | .02 | .01 |
| Green Bay Packers | | | |
| ☐ 348 David Fulcher | .05 | .02 | .01 |
| Cincinnati Bengals | | | |
| ☐ 349 Craig Heyward | .05 | .02 | .01 |
| New Orleans Saints | | | |
| ☐ 350 Ronnie Lott | .10 | .05 | .01 |
| Los Angeles Raiders | | | |
| ☐ 351 Dexter Carter | .08 | .04 | .01 |
| San Francisco 49ers | | | |
| ☐ 352 Mark Jackson | .08 | .04 | .01 |
| Denver Broncos | | | |
| ☐ 353 Brian Jordan | .08 | .04 | .01 |
| Atlanta Falcons | | | |
| ☐ 354 Ray Donaldson | .05 | .02 | .01 |
| Indianapolis Colts | | | |
| ☐ 355 Jim Price | .05 | .02 | .01 |
| Los Angeles Rams | | | |
| ☐ 356 Rod Bernstine | .08 | .04 | .01 |
| San Diego Chargers | | | |
| ☐ 357 Tony Mayberry | .05 | .02 | .01 |
| Tampa Bay Buccaneers | | | |
| ☐ 358 Richard Brown | .05 | .02 | .01 |
| Cleveland Browns | | | |
| ☐ 359 David Alexander | .05 | .02 | .01 |
| Philadelphia Eagles | | | |
| ☐ 360 Haywood Jeffires | .10 | .05 | .01 |
| Houston Oilers | | | |
| ☐ 361 Henry Thomas | .05 | .02 | .01 |
| Minnesota Vikings | | | |
| ☐ 362 Jeff Graham | .08 | .04 | .01 |

| | | | |
|---|---|---|---|
| Pittsburgh Steelers | | | |
| ☐ 363 Don Warren.................... | .05 | .02 | .01 |
| Washington Redskins | | | |
| ☐ 364 Scott Davis..................... | .05 | .02 | .01 |
| Los Angeles Raiders | | | |
| ☐ 365 Harlon Barnett................ | .05 | .02 | .01 |
| Cleveland Browns | | | |
| ☐ 366 Mark Collins.................. | .05 | .02 | .01 |
| New York Giants | | | |
| ☐ 367 Rick Tuten..................... | .05 | .02 | .01 |
| Green Bay Packers | | | |
| ☐ 368 Lonnie Marts UER.......... | .15 | .07 | .02 |
| (Injured Reserved | | | |
| should be Reserve) | | | |
| Kansas City Chiefs | | | |
| ☐ 369 Dennis Smith ................. | .08 | .04 | .01 |
| Denver Broncos | | | |
| ☐ 370 Steve Tasker ................. | .08 | .04 | .01 |
| Buffalo Bills | | | |
| ☐ 371 Robert Massey ............... | .05 | .02 | .01 |
| Phoenix Cardinals | | | |
| ☐ 372 Ricky Reynolds .............. | .05 | .02 | .01 |
| Tampa Bay Buccaneers | | | |
| ☐ 373 Alvin Wright .................. | .05 | .02 | .01 |
| Los Angeles Rams | | | |
| ☐ 374 Kelvin Martin ................. | .08 | .04 | .01 |
| Dallas Cowboys | | | |
| ☐ 375 Vince Buck ................... | .05 | .02 | .01 |
| New Orleans Saints | | | |
| ☐ 376 John Kidd .................... | .05 | .02 | .01 |
| San Diego Chargers | | | |
| ☐ 377 William White................. | .05 | .02 | .01 |
| Detroit Lions | | | |
| ☐ 378 Bryan Cox .................... | .08 | .04 | .01 |
| Miami Dolphins | | | |
| ☐ 379 Jamie Dukes ................. | .05 | .02 | .01 |
| Atlanta Falcons | | | |
| ☐ 380 Anthony Munoz............... | .08 | .04 | .01 |
| Cincinnati Bengals | | | |
| ☐ 381 Mark Gunn .................... | .10 | .05 | .01 |
| New York Jets | | | |
| ☐ 382 Keith Henderson ............ | .05 | .02 | .01 |
| San Francisco 49ers | | | |
| ☐ 383 Charles Wilson .............. | .05 | .02 | .01 |
| Green Bay Packers | | | |
| ☐ 384 Shawn McCarthy............. | .05 | .02 | .01 |
| New England Patriots | | | |
| ☐ 385 Ernie Jones .................. | .05 | .02 | .01 |
| Phoenix Cardinals | | | |
| ☐ 386 Nick Bell ..................... | .08 | .04 | .01 |
| Los Angeles Raiders | | | |
| ☐ 387 Derrick Walker .............. | .05 | .02 | .01 |
| Kansas City Chiefs | | | |
| ☐ 388 Mark Stepnoski .............. | .05 | .02 | .01 |
| Dallas Cowboys | | | |
| ☐ 389 Broderick Thomas ........... | .05 | .02 | .01 |
| Tampa Bay Buccaneers | | | |
| ☐ 390 Reggie Roby ................. | .05 | .02 | .01 |
| Miami Dolphins | | | |
| ☐ 391 Bubba McDowell............. | .05 | .02 | .01 |
| Houston Oilers | | | |
| ☐ 392 Eric Martin ................... | .08 | .04 | .01 |
| New Orleans Saints | | | |
| ☐ 393 Toby Caston ................. | .05 | .02 | .01 |
| Detroit Lions | | | |
| ☐ 394 Bern Brostek ................ | .05 | .02 | .01 |
| Los Angeles Rams | | | |
| ☐ 395 Christian Okoye ............. | .08 | .04 | .01 |
| Kansas City Chiefs | | | |
| ☐ 396 Frank Minnifield ............ | .05 | .02 | .01 |
| Cleveland Browns | | | |
| ☐ 397 Mike Golic ................... | .05 | .02 | .01 |
| Philadelphia Eagles | | | |
| ☐ 398 Grant Feasel ................. | .05 | .02 | .01 |
| Seattle Seahawks | | | |
| ☐ 399 Michael Ball.................. | .05 | .02 | .01 |
| Detroit Lions | | | |
| ☐ 400 Mike Croel.................... | .08 | .04 | .01 |
| Denver Broncos | | | |
| ☐ 401 Maury Buford ................ | .05 | .02 | .01 |
| Chicago Bears | | | |
| ☐ 402 Jeff Bostic UER ............. | .05 | .02 | .01 |
| (Signed as free agent | | | |
| in 1980, not 1984) | | | |
| Washington Redskins | | | |
| ☐ 403 Sean Landeta ................ | .05 | .02 | .01 |
| New York Giants | | | |
| ☐ 404 Terry Allen................... | .20 | .09 | .03 |
| Minnesota Vikings | | | |
| ☐ 405 Donald Evans ................ | .05 | .02 | .01 |
| Pittsburgh Steelers | | | |
| ☐ 406 Don Mosebar ................ | .05 | .02 | .01 |
| Los Angeles Raiders | | | |
| ☐ 407 D.J. Dozier .................. | .08 | .04 | .01 |
| Detroit Lions | | | |
| ☐ 408 Bruce Pickens ............... | .05 | .02 | .01 |
| Atlanta Falcons | | | |
| ☐ 409 Jim Dombrowski................. | .05 | .02 | .01 |

| | | | |
|---|---|---|---|
| New Orleans Saints | | | |
| ☐ 410 Deron Cherry................ | .05 | .02 | .01 |
| Kansas City Chiefs | | | |
| ☐ 411 Richard Johnson................ | .05 | .02 | .01 |
| Houston Oilers | | | |
| ☐ 412 Alexander Wright ............ | .08 | .04 | .01 |
| Dallas Cowboys | | | |
| ☐ 413 Tom Rathman ................. | .08 | .04 | .01 |
| San Francisco 49ers | | | |
| ☐ 414 Mark Dennis.................. | .05 | .02 | .01 |
| Miami Dolphins | | | |
| ☐ 415 Phil Hansen................... | .05 | .02 | .01 |
| Buffalo Bills | | | |
| ☐ 416 Lonnie Young................. | .05 | .02 | .01 |
| New York Jets | | | |
| ☐ 417 Burt Grossman .............. | .05 | .02 | .01 |
| San Diego Chargers | | | |
| ☐ 418 Tony Covington.............. | .05 | .02 | .01 |
| Tampa Bay Buccaneers | | | |
| ☐ 419 John Stephens .............. | .08 | .04 | .01 |
| New England Patriots | | | |
| ☐ 420 Jim Everett.................. | .05 | .02 | .01 |
| Los Angeles Rams | | | |
| ☐ 421 Johnny Holland .............. | .05 | .02 | .01 |
| Green Bay Packers | | | |
| ☐ 422 Mike Barber................. | .10 | .05 | .01 |
| Cincinnati Bengals | | | |
| ☐ 423 Carl Lee ...................... | .05 | .02 | .01 |
| Minnesota Vikings | | | |
| ☐ 424 Craig Patterson ............. | .05 | .02 | .01 |
| Phoenix Cardinals | | | |
| ☐ 425 Greg Townsend............... | .05 | .02 | .01 |
| Los Angeles Raiders | | | |
| ☐ 426 Brett Perriman .............. | .08 | .04 | .01 |
| Green Bay Packers | | | |
| ☐ 427 Morten Andersen ............ | .08 | .04 | .01 |
| New Orleans Saints | | | |
| ☐ 428 John Gesek ................... | .05 | .02 | .01 |
| Dallas Cowboys | | | |
| ☐ 429 Bryan Barker ................. | .05 | .02 | .01 |
| Kansas City Chiefs | | | |
| ☐ 430 John Taylor .................. | .10 | .05 | .01 |
| San Francisco 49ers | | | |
| ☐ 431 Donnell Woolford.............. | .05 | .02 | .01 |
| Chicago Bears | | | |
| ☐ 432 Ron Holmes .................. | .05 | .02 | .01 |
| Denver Broncos | | | |
| ☐ 433 Lee Williams ................. | .08 | .04 | .01 |
| Houston Oilers | | | |
| ☐ 434 Alfred Oglesby................ | .05 | .02 | .01 |
| Miami Dolphins | | | |
| ☐ 435 Jarrod Bunch ................ | .05 | .02 | .01 |
| New York Giants | | | |
| ☐ 436 Carlton Haselrig ............ | .10 | .05 | .01 |
| Pittsburgh Steelers | | | |
| ☐ 437 Rufus Porter ................ | .05 | .02 | .01 |
| Seattle Seahawks | | | |
| ☐ 438 Rohn Stark................... | .05 | .02 | .01 |
| Indianapolis Colts | | | |
| ☐ 439 Tony Jones .................. | .05 | .02 | .01 |
| Houston Oilers | | | |
| ☐ 440 Andre Rison .................. | .25 | .11 | .03 |
| Atlanta Falcons | | | |
| ☐ 441 Eric Hill ..................... | .05 | .02 | .01 |
| Phoenix Cardinals | | | |
| ☐ 442 Jesse Solomon ............... | .05 | .02 | .01 |
| Tampa Bay Buccaneers | | | |
| ☐ 443 Jackie Slater................. | .08 | .04 | .01 |
| Los Angeles Rams | | | |
| ☐ 444 Donnie Elder ................. | .05 | .02 | .01 |
| San Diego Chargers | | | |
| ☐ 445 Brett Maxie................... | .05 | .02 | .01 |
| New Orleans Saints | | | |
| ☐ 446 Max Montoya ................. | .05 | .02 | .01 |
| Los Angeles Raiders | | | |
| ☐ 447 Will Wolford.................. | .05 | .02 | .01 |
| Buffalo Bills | | | |
| ☐ 448 Craig Taylor.................. | .05 | .02 | .01 |
| Cincinnati Bengals | | | |
| ☐ 449 Jimmie Jones ................ | .05 | .02 | .01 |
| Dallas Cowboys | | | |
| ☐ 450 Anthony Carter............... | .08 | .04 | .01 |
| Minnesota Vikings | | | |
| ☐ 451 Brian Bollinger .............. | .05 | .02 | .01 |
| San Francisco 49ers | | | |
| ☐ 452 Checklist 441-550............. | .05 | .02 | .01 |
| ☐ 453 Brad Edwards................. | .05 | .02 | .01 |
| Washington Redskins | | | |
| ☐ 454 Gene Chilton ................. | .05 | .02 | .01 |
| New England Patriots | | | |
| ☐ 455 Eric Allen .................... | .08 | .04 | .01 |
| Philadelphia Eagles | | | |
| ☐ 456 William Roberts ............... | .05 | .02 | .01 |
| New York Giants | | | |
| ☐ 457 Eric Green ................... | .10 | .05 | .01 |
| Pittsburgh Steelers | | | |
| ☐ 458 Irv Eatman................... | .05 | .02 | .01 |
| New York Jets | | | |

| | | | |
|---|---|---|---|
| ☐ 459 Derrick Thomas | .15 | .07 | .02 |
| Kansas City Chiefs | | | |
| ☐ 460 Tommy Kane | .05 | .02 | .01 |
| Seattle Seahawks | | | |
| ☐ 461 LeRoy Butler | .05 | .02 | .01 |
| Green Bay Packers | | | |
| ☐ 462 Oliver Barnett | .05 | .02 | .01 |
| Atlanta Falcons | | | |
| ☐ 463 Anthony Smith | .08 | .04 | .01 |
| Los Angeles Raiders | | | |
| ☐ 464 Cris Dishman | .08 | .04 | .01 |
| Houston Oilers | | | |
| ☐ 465 Pat Terrell | .05 | .02 | .01 |
| Los Angeles Rams | | | |
| ☐ 466 Greg Kragen | .05 | .02 | .01 |
| Denver Broncos | | | |
| ☐ 467 Rodney Peete | .08 | .04 | .01 |
| Detroit Lions | | | |
| ☐ 468 Willie Drewrey | .05 | .02 | .01 |
| Tampa Bay Buccaneers | | | |
| ☐ 469 Jim Wilks | .05 | .02 | .01 |
| New Orleans Saints | | | |
| ☐ 470 Vince Newsome | .05 | .02 | .01 |
| Cleveland Browns | | | |
| ☐ 471 Chris Gardocki | .05 | .02 | .01 |
| Chicago Bears | | | |
| ☐ 472 Chris Chandler | .08 | .04 | .01 |
| Tampa Bay Buccaneers | | | |
| ☐ 473 George Thornton | .05 | .02 | .01 |
| San Diego Chargers | | | |
| ☐ 474 Albert Lewis | .08 | .04 | .01 |
| Kansas City Chiefs | | | |
| ☐ 475 Kevin Glover | .05 | .02 | .01 |
| Detroit Lions | | | |
| ☐ 476 Joe Bowden | .05 | .02 | .01 |
| Houston Oilers | | | |
| ☐ 477 Harry Sydney | .05 | .02 | .01 |
| San Francisco 49ers | | | |
| ☐ 478 Bob Golic | .05 | .02 | .01 |
| Los Angeles Raiders | | | |
| ☐ 479 Tony Zendejas | .05 | .02 | .01 |
| Los Angeles Rams | | | |
| ☐ 480 Brad Baxter | .08 | .04 | .01 |
| New York Jets | | | |
| ☐ 481 Steve Beuerlein | .20 | .09 | .03 |
| Dallas Cowboys | | | |
| ☐ 482 Mark Higgs | .10 | .05 | .01 |
| Miami Dolphins | | | |
| ☐ 483 Drew Hill | .08 | .04 | .01 |
| Houston Oilers | | | |
| ☐ 484 Bryan Millard | .05 | .02 | .01 |
| Seattle Seahawks | | | |
| ☐ 485 Mark Kelso | .05 | .02 | .01 |
| Buffalo Bills | | | |
| ☐ 486 David Grant | .05 | .02 | .01 |
| Cincinnati Bengals | | | |
| ☐ 487 Gary Zimmerman | .05 | .02 | .01 |
| Minnesota Vikings | | | |
| ☐ 488 Leonard Marshall | .08 | .04 | .01 |
| New York Giants | | | |
| ☐ 489 Keith Jackson | .10 | .05 | .01 |
| Philadelphia Eagles | | | |
| ☐ 490 Sterling Sharpe | .50 | .23 | .06 |
| Green Bay Packers | | | |
| ☐ 491 Ferrell Edmunds | .05 | .02 | .01 |
| Miami Dolphins | | | |
| ☐ 492 Wilber Marshall | .08 | .04 | .01 |
| Washington Redskins | | | |
| ☐ 493 Charles Haley | .08 | .04 | .01 |
| San Francisco 49ers | | | |
| ☐ 494 Riki Ellison | .05 | .02 | .01 |
| San Francisco 49ers | | | |
| ☐ 495 Bill Brooks | .08 | .04 | .01 |
| Indianapolis Colts | | | |
| ☐ 496 Bill Hawkins | .05 | .02 | .01 |
| Los Angeles Rams | | | |
| ☐ 497 Erik Williams | .05 | .02 | .01 |
| Dallas Cowboys | | | |
| ☐ 498 Leon Searcy | .05 | .02 | .01 |
| Pittsburgh Steelers | | | |
| ☐ 499 Mike Horan | .05 | .02 | .01 |
| Denver Broncos | | | |
| ☐ 500 Pat Swilling | .08 | .04 | .01 |
| New Orleans Saints | | | |
| ☐ 501 Maurice Hurst | .05 | .02 | .01 |
| New England Patriots | | | |
| ☐ 502 William Fuller | .05 | .02 | .01 |
| Houston Oilers | | | |
| ☐ 503 Tim Newton | .05 | .02 | .01 |
| Tampa Bay Buccaneers | | | |
| ☐ 504 Lorenzo Lynch | .05 | .02 | .01 |
| Phoenix Cardinals | | | |
| ☐ 505 Tim Barnett | .08 | .04 | .01 |
| Kansas City Chiefs | | | |
| ☐ 506 Tom Thayer | .05 | .02 | .01 |
| Chicago Bears | | | |
| ☐ 507 Chris Burkett | .05 | .02 | .01 |
| New York Jets | | | |
| ☐ 508 Ronnie Harmon | .05 | .02 | .01 |
| San Diego Chargers | | | |
| ☐ 509 James Brooks | .08 | .04 | .01 |
| Cincinnati Bengals | | | |
| ☐ 510 Bennie Blades | .05 | .02 | .01 |
| Detroit Lions | | | |
| ☐ 511 Roger Craig | .08 | .04 | .01 |
| Minnesota Vikings | | | |
| ☐ 512 Tony Woods | .05 | .02 | .01 |
| Seattle Seahawks | | | |
| ☐ 513 Greg Lewis | .05 | .02 | .01 |
| Denver Broncos | | | |
| ☐ 514 Erric Pegram | .40 | .18 | .05 |
| Atlanta Falcons | | | |
| ☐ 515 Elvis Patterson | .05 | .02 | .01 |
| Los Angeles Raiders | | | |
| ☐ 516 Jeff Cross | .05 | .02 | .01 |
| Miami Dolphins | | | |
| ☐ 517 Myron Guyton | .05 | .02 | .01 |
| New York Giants | | | |
| ☐ 518 Jay Novacek | .15 | .07 | .02 |
| Dallas Cowboys | | | |
| ☐ 519 Leo Barker | .05 | .02 | .01 |
| Cincinnati Bengals | | | |
| ☐ 520 Keith Byars | .08 | .04 | .01 |
| Philadelphia Eagles | | | |
| ☐ 521 Dalton Hilliard | .05 | .02 | .01 |
| New Orleans Saints | | | |
| ☐ 522 Ted Washington | .05 | .02 | .01 |
| San Francisco 49ers | | | |
| ☐ 523 Dexter McNabb | .05 | .02 | .01 |
| Green Bay Packers | | | |
| ☐ 524 Frank Reich | .08 | .04 | .01 |
| Buffalo Bills | | | |
| ☐ 525 Henry Ellard | .08 | .04 | .01 |
| Los Angeles Rams | | | |
| ☐ 526 Barry Foster | .35 | .16 | .04 |
| Pittsburgh Steelers | | | |
| ☐ 527 Barry Word | .10 | .05 | .01 |
| Kansas City Chiefs | | | |
| ☐ 528 Gary Anderson | .08 | .04 | .01 |
| Tampa Bay Buccaneers | | | |
| ☐ 529 Reggie Rutland | .05 | .02 | .01 |
| Minnesota Vikings | | | |
| ☐ 530 Stephen Baker | .05 | .02 | .01 |
| New York Giants | | | |
| ☐ 531 John Flannery | .05 | .02 | .01 |
| Houston Oilers | | | |
| ☐ 532 Steve Wright | .05 | .02 | .01 |
| Los Angeles Raiders | | | |
| ☐ 533 Eric Sanders | .05 | .02 | .01 |
| Detroit Lions | | | |
| ☐ 534 Bob Whitfield | .10 | .05 | .01 |
| Atlanta Falcons | | | |
| ☐ 535 Gaston Green | .08 | .04 | .01 |
| Denver Broncos | | | |
| ☐ 536 Anthony Pleasant | .05 | .02 | .01 |
| Cleveland Browns | | | |
| ☐ 537 Jeff Bryant | .05 | .02 | .01 |
| Seattle Seahawks | | | |
| ☐ 538 Jarvis Williams | .05 | .02 | .01 |
| Miami Dolphins | | | |
| ☐ 539 Jim Morrissey | .05 | .02 | .01 |
| Chicago Bears | | | |
| ☐ 540 Andre Tippett | .08 | .04 | .01 |
| New England Patriots | | | |
| ☐ 541 Gill Byrd | .08 | .04 | .01 |
| San Diego Chargers | | | |
| ☐ 542 Raleigh McKenzie | .05 | .02 | .01 |
| Washington Redskins | | | |
| ☐ 543 Jim Sweeney | .05 | .02 | .01 |
| New York Jets | | | |
| ☐ 544 David Lutz | .05 | .02 | .01 |
| Kansas City Chiefs | | | |
| ☐ 545 Wayne Martin | .05 | .02 | .01 |
| New Orleans Saints | | | |
| ☐ 546 Karl Wilson | .05 | .02 | .01 |
| Los Angeles Rams | | | |
| ☐ 547 Pierce Holt | .05 | .02 | .01 |
| San Francisco 49ers | | | |
| ☐ 548 Doug Smith | .05 | .02 | .01 |
| Houston Oilers | | | |
| ☐ 549 Nolan Harrison | .10 | .05 | .01 |
| Los Angeles Raiders | | | |
| ☐ 550 Freddie Joe Nunn | .05 | .02 | .01 |
| Phoenix Cardinals | | | |
| ☐ 551 Eric Moore | .05 | .02 | .01 |
| New York Giants | | | |
| ☐ 552 Cris Carter | .10 | .05 | .01 |
| Minnesota Vikings | | | |
| ☐ 553 Kevin Gogan | .05 | .02 | .01 |
| Dallas Cowboys | | | |
| ☐ 554 Harold Green | .08 | .04 | .01 |
| Cincinnati Bengals | | | |
| ☐ 555 Kenneth Davis | .08 | .04 | .01 |
| Buffalo Bills | | | |
| ☐ 556 Travis McNeal | .05 | .02 | .01 |

| | | | |
|---|---|---|---|
| Seattle Seahawks | | | |
| ☐ 557 Jim C. Jensen | .05 | .02 | .01 |
| Miami Dolphins | | | |
| ☐ 558 Willie Green | .05 | .02 | .01 |
| Detroit Lions | | | |
| ☐ 559 Scott Galbraith UER | .05 | .02 | .01 |
| (Drafted in 1990, not 1989) | | | |
| Cleveland Browns | | | |
| ☐ 560 Louis Lipps | .08 | .04 | .01 |
| Pittsburgh Steelers | | | |
| ☐ 561 Matt Brock | .05 | .02 | .01 |
| Green Bay Packers | | | |
| ☐ 562 Mike Prior | .05 | .02 | .01 |
| Indianapolis Colts | | | |
| ☐ 563 Checklist 551-660 | .05 | .02 | .01 |
| ☐ 564 Robert Delpino | .08 | .04 | .01 |
| Los Angeles Rams | | | |
| ☐ 565 Vinny Testaverde | .10 | .05 | .01 |
| Tampa Bay Buccaneers | | | |
| ☐ 566 Willie Gault | .08 | .04 | .01 |
| Los Angeles Raiders | | | |
| ☐ 567 Quinn Early | .08 | .04 | .01 |
| New Orleans Saints | | | |
| ☐ 568 Eric Moten | .05 | .02 | .01 |
| San Diego Chargers | | | |
| ☐ 569 Lance Smith | .05 | .02 | .01 |
| Phoenix Cardinals | | | |
| ☐ 570 Darrell Green | .08 | .04 | .01 |
| Washington Redskins | | | |
| ☐ 571 Moe Gardner | .05 | .02 | .01 |
| Atlanta Falcons | | | |
| ☐ 572 Steve Atwater | .08 | .04 | .01 |
| Denver Broncos | | | |
| ☐ 573 Ray Childress | .08 | .04 | .01 |
| Houston Oilers | | | |
| ☐ 574 Dave Krieg | .08 | .04 | .01 |
| Seattle Seahawks | | | |
| ☐ 575 Bruce Armstrong | .05 | .02 | .01 |
| New England Patriots | | | |
| ☐ 576 Fred Barnett | .10 | .05 | .01 |
| Philadelphia Eagles | | | |
| ☐ 577 Don Griffin | .05 | .02 | .01 |
| San Francisco 49ers | | | |
| ☐ 578 David Brandon | .05 | .02 | .01 |
| Cleveland Browns | | | |
| ☐ 579 Robert Young | .08 | .04 | .01 |
| Los Angeles Rams | | | |
| ☐ 580 Keith Van Horne | .05 | .02 | .01 |
| Chicago Bears | | | |
| ☐ 581 Jeff Criswell | .05 | .02 | .01 |
| New York Jets | | | |
| ☐ 582 Lewis Tillman | .08 | .04 | .01 |
| New York Giants | | | |
| ☐ 583 Bubby Brister | .08 | .04 | .01 |
| Pittsburgh Steelers | | | |
| ☐ 584 Aaron Wallace | .05 | .02 | .01 |
| Los Angeles Raiders | | | |
| ☐ 585 Chris Doleman | .08 | .04 | .01 |
| Minnesota Vikings | | | |
| ☐ 586 Marty Carter | .20 | .09 | .03 |
| Tampa Bay Buccaneers | | | |
| ☐ 587 Chris Warren | .25 | .11 | .03 |
| Seattle Seahawks | | | |
| ☐ 588 David Griggs | .05 | .02 | .01 |
| Miami Dolphins | | | |
| ☐ 589 Darrell Thompson | .08 | .04 | .01 |
| Green Bay Packers | | | |
| ☐ 590 Marion Butts | .10 | .05 | .01 |
| San Diego Chargers | | | |
| ☐ 591 Scott Norwood | .05 | .02 | .01 |
| Buffalo Bills | | | |
| ☐ 592 Lomas Brown | .05 | .02 | .01 |
| Detroit Lions | | | |
| ☐ 593 Daryl Johnston | .10 | .05 | .01 |
| Dallas Cowboys | | | |
| ☐ 594 Alonzo Mitz | .05 | .02 | .01 |
| Cincinnati Bengals | | | |
| ☐ 595 Tommy Barnhardt | .05 | .02 | .01 |
| New Orleans Saints | | | |
| ☐ 596 Tim Jorden | .05 | .02 | .01 |
| Phoenix Cardinals | | | |
| ☐ 597 Neil Smith | .10 | .05 | .01 |
| Kansas City Chiefs | | | |
| ☐ 598 Todd Marinovich | .05 | .02 | .01 |
| Los Angeles Raiders | | | |
| ☐ 599 Sean Jones | .05 | .02 | .01 |
| Houston Oilers | | | |
| ☐ 600 Clarence Verdin | .05 | .02 | .01 |
| Indianapolis Colts | | | |
| ☐ 601 Trace Armstrong | .05 | .02 | .01 |
| Chicago Bears | | | |
| ☐ 602 Steve Bono | .50 | .23 | .06 |
| San Francisco 49ers | | | |
| ☐ 603 Mark Ingram | .08 | .04 | .01 |
| New York Giants | | | |
| ☐ 604 Flipper Anderson | .08 | .04 | .01 |
| Los Angeles Rams | | | |

| | | | |
|---|---|---|---|
| ☐ 605 James Jones | .05 | .02 | .01 |
| Cleveland Browns | | | |
| ☐ 606 Al Noga | .05 | .02 | .01 |
| Minnesota Vikings | | | |
| ☐ 607 Rick Bryan | .05 | .02 | .01 |
| Atlanta Falcons | | | |
| ☐ 608 Eugene Lockhart | .05 | .02 | .01 |
| New England Patriots | | | |
| ☐ 609 Charles Mann | .08 | .04 | .01 |
| Washington Redskins | | | |
| ☐ 610 James Hasty | .05 | .02 | .01 |
| New York Jets | | | |
| ☐ 611 Jeff Feagles | .05 | .02 | .01 |
| New York Jets | | | |
| ☐ 612 Tim Brown | .25 | .11 | .03 |
| Los Angeles Raiders | | | |
| ☐ 613 David Little | .05 | .02 | .01 |
| Pittsburgh Steelers | | | |
| ☐ 614 Keith Sims | .05 | .02 | .01 |
| Miami Dolphins | | | |
| ☐ 615 Kevin Murphy | .05 | .02 | .01 |
| Tampa Bay Buccaneers | | | |
| ☐ 616 Ray Crockett | .05 | .02 | .01 |
| Detroit Lions | | | |
| ☐ 617 Jim Jeffcoat | .05 | .02 | .01 |
| Dallas Cowboys | | | |
| ☐ 618 Patrick Hunter | .05 | .02 | .01 |
| Seattle Seahawks | | | |
| ☐ 619 Keith Kartz | .05 | .02 | .01 |
| Denver Broncos | | | |
| ☐ 620 Peter Tom Willis | .08 | .04 | .01 |
| Chicago Bears | | | |
| ☐ 621 Vaughan Johnson | .08 | .04 | .01 |
| New Orleans Saints | | | |
| ☐ 622 Shawn Jefferson | .05 | .02 | .01 |
| San Diego Chargers | | | |
| ☐ 623 Anthony Thompson | .05 | .02 | .01 |
| Phoenix Cardinals | | | |
| ☐ 624 John Rienstra | .05 | .02 | .01 |
| Cleveland Browns | | | |
| ☐ 625 Don Maggs | .05 | .02 | .01 |
| Houston Oilers | | | |
| ☐ 626 Todd Lyght | .05 | .02 | .01 |
| Los Angeles Rams | | | |
| ☐ 627 Brent Jones | .10 | .05 | .01 |
| San Francisco 49ers | | | |
| ☐ 628 Todd McNair | .05 | .02 | .01 |
| Kansas City Chiefs | | | |
| ☐ 629 Winston Moss | .05 | .02 | .01 |
| Los Angeles Raiders | | | |
| ☐ 630 Mark Carrier | .08 | .04 | .01 |
| Tampa Bay Buccaneers | | | |
| ☐ 631 Dan Owens | .05 | .02 | .01 |
| Detroit Lions | | | |
| ☐ 632 Sammie Smith UER | .05 | .02 | .01 |
| (Old team front, correct new team back; acquired via trade, not draft) | | | |
| Miami Dolphins | | | |
| ☐ 633 James Lofton | .10 | .05 | .01 |
| Buffalo Bills | | | |
| ☐ 634 Paul McJulien | .05 | .02 | .01 |
| Green Bay Packers | | | |
| ☐ 635 Tony Tolbert | .05 | .02 | .01 |
| Dallas Cowboys | | | |
| ☐ 636 Carnell Lake | .05 | .02 | .01 |
| Pittsburgh Steelers | | | |
| ☐ 637 Gary Clark | .08 | .04 | .01 |
| Washington Redskins | | | |
| ☐ 638 Brian Washington | .05 | .02 | .01 |
| New York Jets | | | |
| ☐ 639 Jessie Hester | .05 | .02 | .01 |
| Indianapolis Colts | | | |
| ☐ 640 Doug Riesenberg | .05 | .02 | .01 |
| New York Giants | | | |
| ☐ 641 Joe Walter | .05 | .02 | .01 |
| Cincinnati Bengals | | | |
| ☐ 642 John Rade | .05 | .02 | .01 |
| Atlanta Falcons | | | |
| ☐ 643 Wes Hopkins | .05 | .02 | .01 |
| Philadelphia Eagles | | | |
| ☐ 644 Kelly Stouffer | .05 | .02 | .01 |
| Seattle Seahawks | | | |
| ☐ 645 Marv Cook | .08 | .04 | .01 |
| New England Patriots | | | |
| ☐ 646 Ken Clarke | .05 | .02 | .01 |
| Indianapolis Colts | | | |
| ☐ 647 Bobby Humphrey UER | .08 | .04 | .01 |
| (Old team front, correct new team back; acquired via trade, not draft) | | | |
| Denver Broncos | | | |
| ☐ 648 Tim McDonald | .08 | .04 | .01 |
| Phoenix Cardinals | | | |
| ☐ 649 Donald Frank | .05 | .02 | .01 |

| | | | |
|---|---|---|---|
| San Diego Chargers | | | |
| ☐ 650 Richmond Webb | .08 | .04 | .01 |
| Miami Dolphins | | | |
| ☐ 651 Lemuel Stinson | .05 | .02 | .01 |
| Chicago Bears | | | |
| ☐ 652 Merton Hanks | .05 | .02 | .01 |
| San Francisco 49ers | | | |
| ☐ 653 Frank Warren | .05 | .02 | .01 |
| New Orleans Saints | | | |
| ☐ 654 Thomas Benson | .05 | .02 | .01 |
| Los Angeles Raiders | | | |
| ☐ 655 Al Smith | .05 | .02 | .01 |
| Houston Oilers | | | |
| ☐ 656 Steve DeBerg | .08 | .04 | .01 |
| Tampa Bay Buccaneers | | | |
| ☐ 657 Jayice Pearson | .05 | .02 | .01 |
| Kansas City Chiefs | | | |
| ☐ 658 Joe Morris | .08 | .04 | .01 |
| Cleveland Browns | | | |
| ☐ 659 Fred Strickland | .05 | .02 | .01 |
| Los Angeles Rams | | | |
| ☐ 660 Kelvin Pritchett | .05 | .02 | .01 |
| Detroit Lions | | | |
| ☐ 661 Lewis Billups | .05 | .02 | .01 |
| Green Bay Packers | | | |
| ☐ 662 Todd Collins | .15 | .07 | .02 |
| New England Patriots | | | |
| ☐ 663 Corey Miller | .15 | .07 | .02 |
| New York Giants | | | |
| ☐ 664 Levon Kirkland | .15 | .07 | .02 |
| Pittsburgh Steelers | | | |
| ☐ 665 Jerry Rice | .50 | .23 | .06 |
| San Francisco 49ers | | | |
| ☐ 666 Mike Lodish | .05 | .02 | .01 |
| Buffalo Bills | | | |
| ☐ 667 Chuck Smith | .10 | .05 | .01 |
| Atlanta Falcons | | | |
| ☐ 668 Lance Olberding | .05 | .02 | .01 |
| Cincinnati Bengals | | | |
| ☐ 669 Kevin Smith | .25 | .11 | .03 |
| Dallas Cowboys | | | |
| ☐ 670 Dale Carter | .25 | .11 | .03 |
| Kansas City Chiefs | | | |
| ☐ 671 Sean Gilbert | .30 | .14 | .04 |
| Los Angeles Rams | | | |
| ☐ 672 Ken O'Brien | .08 | .04 | .01 |
| New York Jets | | | |
| ☐ 673 Ricky Proehl | .10 | .05 | .01 |
| Phoenix Cardinals | | | |
| ☐ 674 Junior Seau | .15 | .07 | .02 |
| San Diego Chargers | | | |
| ☐ 675 Courtney Hawkins | .25 | .11 | .03 |
| Tampa Bay Buccaneers | | | |
| ☐ 676 Eddie Robinson | .10 | .05 | .01 |
| Houston Oilers | | | |
| ☐ 677 Tom Jeter | .10 | .05 | .01 |
| Philadelphia Eagles | | | |
| ☐ 678 Jeff George | .20 | .09 | .03 |
| Indianapolis Colts | | | |
| ☐ 679 Cary Conklin | .10 | .05 | .01 |
| Washington Redskins | | | |
| ☐ 680 Rueben Mayes | .05 | .02 | .01 |
| New Orleans Saints | | | |
| ☐ 681 Sean Lumpkin | .10 | .05 | .01 |
| New Orleans Saints | | | |
| ☐ 682 Dan Marino | .75 | .35 | .09 |
| Miami Dolphins | | | |
| ☐ 683 Ed McDaniel | .10 | .05 | .01 |
| Minnesota Vikings | | | |
| ☐ 684 Greg Skrepenak | .10 | .05 | .01 |
| Los Angeles Raiders | | | |
| ☐ 685 Tracy Scroggins | .20 | .09 | .03 |
| Detroit Lions | | | |
| ☐ 686 Tommy Maddox | .50 | .23 | .06 |
| Denver Broncos | | | |
| ☐ 687 Mike Singletary | .10 | .05 | .01 |
| Chicago Bears | | | |
| ☐ 688 Patrick Rowe | .10 | .05 | .01 |
| Cleveland Browns | | | |
| ☐ 689 Phillippi Sparks | .05 | .02 | .01 |
| New York Giants | | | |
| ☐ 690 Joel Steed | .10 | .05 | .01 |
| Pittsburgh Steelers | | | |
| ☐ 691 Kevin Fagan | .05 | .02 | .01 |
| San Francisco 49ers | | | |
| ☐ 692 Deion Sanders | .20 | .09 | .03 |
| Atlanta Falcons | | | |
| ☐ 693 Bruce Smith | .10 | .05 | .01 |
| Buffalo Bills | | | |
| ☐ 694 David Klingler | .50 | .23 | .06 |
| Cincinnati Bengals | | | |
| ☐ 695 Clayton Holmes | .05 | .02 | .01 |
| Dallas Cowboys | | | |
| ☐ 696 Brett Favre | 1.00 | .45 | .13 |
| Green Bay Packers | | | |
| ☐ 697 Marc Boutte | .05 | .02 | .01 |
| Los Angeles Rams | | | |
| ☐ 698 Dwayne Sabb | .12 | .05 | .02 |
| New England Patriots | | | |
| ☐ 699 Ed McCaffrey | .08 | .04 | .01 |
| New York Giants | | | |
| ☐ 700 Randall Cunningham | .10 | .05 | .01 |
| Philadelphia Eagles | | | |
| ☐ 701 Quentin Coryatt | .30 | .14 | .04 |
| Indianapolis Colts | | | |
| ☐ 702 Bernie Kosar | .10 | .05 | .01 |
| Cleveland Browns | | | |
| ☐ 703 Vaughn Dunbar | .20 | .09 | .03 |
| New Orleans Saints | | | |
| ☐ 704 Browning Nagle | .08 | .04 | .01 |
| New York Jets | | | |
| ☐ 705 Mark Wheeler | .10 | .05 | .01 |
| Tampa Bay Buccaneers | | | |
| ☐ 706 Paul Siever | .10 | .05 | .01 |
| Washington Redskins | | | |
| ☐ 707 Anthony Miller | .15 | .07 | .02 |
| San Diego Chargers | | | |
| ☐ 708 Corey Widmer | .10 | .05 | .01 |
| New York Giants | | | |
| ☐ 709 Eric Dickerson | .10 | .05 | .01 |
| Los Angeles Raiders | | | |
| ☐ 710 Martin Bayless | .05 | .02 | .01 |
| Kansas City Chiefs | | | |
| ☐ 711 Jason Hanson | .15 | .07 | .02 |
| Detroit Lions | | | |
| ☐ 712 Michael Dean Perry | .10 | .05 | .01 |
| Cleveland Browns | | | |
| ☐ 713 Billy Joe Tolliver UER | .08 | .04 | .01 |
| (Stats say 1991 Chargers, | | | |
| should be Falcons) | | | |
| Atlanta Falcons | | | |
| ☐ 714 Chad Hennings | .15 | .07 | .02 |
| Dallas Cowboys | | | |
| ☐ 715 Bucky Richardson | .20 | .09 | .03 |
| Houston Oilers | | | |
| ☐ 716 Steve Israel | .05 | .02 | .01 |
| Los Angeles Rams | | | |
| ☐ 717 Robert Harris | .05 | .02 | .01 |
| Minnesota Vikings | | | |
| ☐ 718 Timm Rosenbach | .05 | .02 | .01 |
| Phoenix Cardinals | | | |
| ☐ 719 Joe Montana | 1.00 | .45 | .13 |
| San Francisco 49ers | | | |
| ☐ 720 Derek Brown | .10 | .05 | .01 |
| New York Giants | | | |
| ☐ 721 Robert Brooks | .15 | .07 | .02 |
| Green Bay Packers | | | |
| ☐ 722 Boomer Esiason | .15 | .07 | .02 |
| Cincinnati Bengals | | | |
| ☐ 723 Troy Auzenne | .05 | .02 | .01 |
| Chicago Bears | | | |
| ☐ 724 John Fina | .05 | .02 | .01 |
| Buffalo Bills | | | |
| ☐ 725 Chris Crooms | .10 | .05 | .01 |
| Los Angeles Rams | | | |
| ☐ 726 Eugene Chung | .05 | .02 | .01 |
| New England Patriots | | | |
| ☐ 727 Darren Woodson | .20 | .09 | .03 |
| Dallas Cowboys | | | |
| ☐ 728 Leslie O'Neal | .08 | .04 | .01 |
| San Diego Chargers | | | |
| ☐ 729 Dan McGwire | .08 | .04 | .01 |
| Seattle Seahawks | | | |
| ☐ 730 Al Toon | .08 | .04 | .01 |
| New York Jets | | | |
| ☐ 731 Michael Brandon | .10 | .05 | .01 |
| Indianapolis Colts | | | |
| ☐ 732 Steve DeOssie | .05 | .02 | .01 |
| New York Giants | | | |
| ☐ 733 Jim Kelly | .25 | .11 | .03 |
| Buffalo Bills | | | |
| ☐ 734 Webster Slaughter | .08 | .04 | .01 |
| Houston Oilers | | | |
| ☐ 735 Tony Smith | .15 | .07 | .02 |
| Atlanta Falcons | | | |
| ☐ 736 Shane Collins | .15 | .07 | .02 |
| Washington Redskins | | | |
| ☐ 737 Randal Hill | .10 | .05 | .01 |
| Phoenix Cardinals | | | |
| ☐ 738 Chris Holder | .05 | .02 | .01 |
| Green Bay Packers | | | |
| ☐ 739 Russell Maryland | .15 | .07 | .02 |
| Dallas Cowboys | | | |
| ☐ 740 Carl Pickens | .40 | .18 | .05 |
| Cincinnati Bengals | | | |
| ☐ 741 Andre Reed | .10 | .05 | .01 |
| Buffalo Bills | | | |
| ☐ 742 Steve Emtman | .15 | .07 | .02 |
| Indianapolis Colts | | | |
| ☐ 743 Carl Banks | .08 | .04 | .01 |
| New York Giants | | | |
| ☐ 744 Troy Aikman | 1.25 | .55 | .16 |
| Dallas Cowboys | | | |
| ☐ 745 Mark Royals | .05 | .02 | .01 |
| Pittsburgh Steelers | | | |
| ☐ 746 J.J. Birden | .12 | .05 | .02 |

| | | | | |
|---|---|---|---|---|
| Kansas City Chiefs | | | | |
| ☐ 747 Michael Cofer ...................... | .05 | .02 | .01 |
| Detroit Lions | | | |
| ☐ 748 Darryl Ashmore ..................... | .05 | .02 | .01 |
| Los Angeles Rams | | | |
| ☐ 749 Dion Lambert ........................ | .05 | .02 | .01 |
| New England Patriots | | | |
| ☐ 750 Phil Simms .......................... | .10 | .05 | .01 |
| New York Giants | | | |
| ☐ 751 Reggie E. White .................... | .10 | .05 | .01 |
| San Diego Chargers | | | |
| ☐ 752 Harvey Williams .................... | .10 | .05 | .01 |
| Kansas City Chiefs | | | |
| ☐ 753 Ty Detmer ........................... | .08 | .04 | .01 |
| Green Bay Packers | | | |
| ☐ 754 Tony Brooks ........................ | .05 | .02 | .01 |
| Philadelphia Eagles | | | |
| ☐ 755 Steve Christie ...................... | .05 | .02 | .01 |
| Tampa Bay Buccaneers | | | |
| ☐ 756 Lawrence Taylor .................... | .10 | .05 | .01 |
| New York Giants | | | |
| ☐ 757 Merril Hoge ......................... | .08 | .04 | .01 |
| Pittsburgh Steelers | | | |
| ☐ 758 Robert Jones ....................... | .12 | .05 | .02 |
| Dallas Cowboys | | | |
| ☐ 759 Checklist 661-759 ................. | .05 | .02 | .01 |

## 1992 Topps Gold

Topps issued all three series of football cards in a gold version. In addition, all checklist cards were replaced by new player cards. The cards are standard size (2 1/2" by 3 1/2") and are distinguished from the regular cards by the gold embossing of the player's name and team on the card front. The gold versions are valued approximately four to ten times the regular card values. The gold cards were issued in several ways: one per wax pack, three per rack pack, 20 per 660-card factory set, and ten per 99-card high-number factory set.

| | MINT | EXC | G-VG |
|---|---|---|---|
| COMPLETE SET (759) ..................... | 170.00 | 75.00 | 21.00 |
| COMPLETE SERIES 1 (330) .............. | 80.00 | 36.00 | 10.00 |
| COMPLETE SERIES 2 (330) .............. | 60.00 | 27.00 | 7.50 |
| COMPLETE HI SERIES (99) .............. | 30.00 | 13.50 | 3.80 |
| COMMON GOLD (1G-330G) ............. | .15 | .07 | .02 |
| COMMON GOLD (331G-660G) ......... | .15 | .07 | .02 |
| COMMON GOLD (661G-759G) ......... | .15 | .07 | .02 |
| *GOLD STAR CARDS: 3X TO 6X VALUE | | | |
| ☐ 109G Freeman McNeil UER .......... | .75 | .35 | .09 |
| (Text on back | | | |
| upside down) | | | |
| ☐ 218G David Daniels ..................... | .75 | .35 | .09 |
| ☐ 316G Chris Hakel ....................... | .75 | .35 | .09 |
| ☐ 327G Duane Bickett UER .............. | .40 | .18 | .05 |
| (Misspelled Beckett | | | |
| on the card front) | | | |
| ☐ 341G Ottis Anderson ................... | .75 | .35 | .09 |
| ☐ 452G Shawn Moore .................... | 1.00 | .45 | .13 |
| ☐ 563G Mike Mooney ..................... | .90 | .40 | .11 |
| ☐ 737G Randal Hill UER ................. | 2.00 | .90 | .25 |
| (Number on back is 37) | | | |
| ☐ 759G Curtis Whitley .................... | 1.50 | .65 | .19 |

## 1992 Topps No.1 Draft Picks

In addition to being individually inserted randomly in Topps high-series packs, this four-card subset was inserted into each 1992 Topps "High Series" factory set. It features the Number 1 draft pick for 1990, 1991, and 1992 as well as a card for Raghib "Rocket" Ismail, who many experts feel could have been the number 1 pick if he had entered the NFL draft. The cards measure the standard size (2 1/2" by 3 1/2").

Inside white borders, the fronts display color action player photos. The words "No. 1 Draft Pick of the 90's" are printed above the picture, while the player's name and team name appear respectively in two short color bars at the bottom. On a football design, the backs carry a color close-up photo and biographical information. The cards are numbered on the back.

| | MINT | EXC | G-VG |
|---|---|---|---|
| COMPLETE SET (4) .......................... | 5.00 | 2.30 | .60 |
| COMMON PLAYER (1-4) ................... | 1.00 | .45 | .13 |
| ☐ 1 Jeff George ............................. | 1.50 | .65 | .19 |
| Indianapolis Colts | | | |
| ☐ 2 Russell Maryland ...................... | 1.00 | .45 | .13 |
| Dallas Cowboys | | | |
| ☐ 3 Steve Emtman .......................... | 1.00 | .45 | .13 |
| Indianapolis Colts | | | |
| ☐ 4 Raghib(Rocket) Ismail ............... | 1.50 | .65 | .19 |

## 1992 Topps Finest

Manufactured with Topps Poly-tech process, this 44-card set features 33 established NFL stars and 11 top rookies. Just 3,000 cases were produced, with 20 sets per case. The cards measure the standard size (2 1/2" by 3 1/2"). The fronts feature action color player photos with a foil and lacquer finish. The background of each picture has a metallic look. The photos of veteran players are bordered in blue and gold against a black card face. The photos of rookies are bordered in red and gold. The player's name and team appear in a blue bar, and the words "Limited Edition" appear in a gold bar near the bottom. The set name at the top and a football icon round out the front design. The backs are white and show the words "Football's Finest" in white-edged royal blue lettering against a gradated red panel. The player's name appears in large black print and partially overlaps a royal blue helmet icon. Biographical information finishes the back. The cards are numbered on the back and checklisted below alphabetically according to veterans (1-33) and rookies (34-44).

| | MINT | EXC | G-VG |
|---|---|---|---|
| COMPLETE FACT. SET (45) .............. | 25.00 | 10.00 | 2.50 |
| COMMON PLAYER (1-44) ................. | .50 | .20 | .05 |
| ☐ 1 Neal Anderson .......................... | .75 | .30 | .07 |
| Chicago Bears | | | |
| ☐ 2 Cornelius Bennett ..................... | .75 | .30 | .07 |
| Buffalo Bills | | | |
| ☐ 3 Marion Butts ............................ | .75 | .30 | .07 |
| San Diego Chargers | | | |
| ☐ 4 Anthony Carter ......................... | .75 | .30 | .07 |
| Minnesota Vikings | | | |
| ☐ 5 Mike Croel .............................. | .75 | .30 | .07 |

| | | | |
|---|---|---|---|
| Denver Broncos | | | |
| ☐ 6 John Elway | 3.00 | 1.20 | .30 |
| Denver Broncos | | | |
| ☐ 7 Jim Everett | .75 | .30 | .07 |
| Los Angeles Rams | | | |
| ☐ 8 Ernest Givins | .75 | .30 | .07 |
| Houston Oilers | | | |
| ☐ 9 Rodney Hampton | 2.00 | .80 | .20 |
| New York Giants | | | |
| ☐ 10 Alvin Harper | 2.00 | .80 | .20 |
| Dallas Cowboys | | | |
| ☐ 11 Michael Irvin | 3.00 | 1.20 | .30 |
| Dallas Cowboys | | | |
| ☐ 12 Rickey Jackson | .50 | .20 | .05 |
| New Orleans Saints | | | |
| ☐ 13 Seth Joyner | .50 | .20 | .05 |
| Philadelphia Eagles | | | |
| ☐ 14 James Lofton | .75 | .30 | .07 |
| Buffalo Bills | | | |
| ☐ 15 Ronnie Lott | .75 | .30 | .07 |
| Los Angeles Raiders | | | |
| ☐ 16 Eric Metcalf | .75 | .30 | .07 |
| Cleveland Browns | | | |
| ☐ 17 Chris Miller | 1.00 | .40 | .10 |
| Atlanta Falcons | | | |
| ☐ 18 Art Monk | 1.00 | .40 | .10 |
| Washington Redskins | | | |
| ☐ 19 Warren Moon | 1.50 | .60 | .15 |
| Houston Oilers | | | |
| ☐ 20 Rob Moore | 1.25 | .50 | .12 |
| New York Jets | | | |
| ☐ 21 Anthony Munoz | .75 | .30 | .07 |
| Cincinnati Bengals | | | |
| ☐ 22 Christian Okoye | .75 | .30 | .07 |
| Kansas City Chiefs | | | |
| ☐ 23 Andre Rison | 1.00 | .40 | .10 |
| Atlanta Falcons | | | |
| ☐ 24 Leonard Russell | 1.25 | .50 | .12 |
| New England Patriots | | | |
| ☐ 25 Mark Rypien | .75 | .30 | .07 |
| Washington Redskins | | | |
| ☐ 26 Barry Sanders | 5.00 | 2.00 | .50 |
| Detroit Lions | | | |
| ☐ 27 Emmitt Smith | 9.00 | 3.75 | .90 |
| Dallas Cowboys | | | |
| ☐ 28 Pat Swilling | .75 | .30 | .07 |
| New Orleans Saints | | | |
| ☐ 29 John Taylor | .75 | .30 | .07 |
| San Francisco 49ers | | | |
| ☐ 30 Derrick Thomas | 1.50 | .60 | .15 |
| Kansas City Chiefs | | | |
| ☐ 31 Thurman Thomas | 2.50 | 1.00 | .25 |
| Buffalo Bills | | | |
| ☐ 32 Reggie White | 1.50 | .60 | .15 |
| Philadelphia Eagles | | | |
| ☐ 33 Rod Woodson | 1.00 | .40 | .10 |
| Pittsburgh Steelers | | | |
| ☐ 34 Edgar Bennett | 1.00 | .40 | .10 |
| Green Bay Packers | | | |
| ☐ 35 Terrell Buckley | 1.00 | .40 | .10 |
| Green Bay Packers | | | |
| ☐ 36 Keith Hamilton | .75 | .30 | .07 |
| New York Giants | | | |
| ☐ 37 Amp Lee | 1.00 | .40 | .10 |
| San Francisco 49ers | | | |
| ☐ 38 Ricardo McDonald | .75 | .30 | .07 |
| Cincinnati Bengals | | | |
| ☐ 39 Chris Mims | 1.00 | .40 | .10 |
| San Diego Chargers | | | |
| ☐ 40 Robert Porcher | .50 | .20 | .05 |
| Detroit Lions | | | |
| ☐ 41 Leon Searcy | .50 | .20 | .05 |
| Pittsburgh Steelers | | | |
| ☐ 42 Siran Stacy | .50 | .20 | .05 |
| Philadelphia Eagles | | | |
| ☐ 43 Tommy Vardell | 1.25 | .50 | .12 |
| Cleveland Browns | | | |
| ☐ 44 Bob Whitfield | .50 | .20 | .05 |
| Atlanta Falcons | | | |
| ☐ NNO Checklist | .50 | .20 | .05 |

## 1992 Topps 1000 Yard Club

This 20-card set was issued to celebrate rushers and receivers who compiled 1000 yards or more in the 1991 season. The fronts display color action player photos with white borders. A two-color picture frame overlays the picture; the words "1000 Yard Club" lay on the top crossbar of this frame. The player's name appears in a green-and-white striped bar that overlays the bottom crossbar. The design of the card fronts is enhanced by the use of red foil lettering for the number "1000" and the player's name. Receiving or rushing statistics for 1991 appear in a lime green panel against the background of a football field with white yard lines. The cards are numbered on the back.

| | MINT | EXC | G-VG |
|---|---|---|---|
| COMPLETE SET (20) | 16.00 | 7.25 | 2.00 |
| COMMON PLAYER (1-20) | .50 | .23 | .06 |
| ☐ 1 Emmitt Smith | 8.00 | 3.60 | 1.00 |
| Dallas Cowboys | | | |
| ☐ 2 Barry Sanders | 4.00 | 1.80 | .50 |
| Detroit Lions | | | |
| ☐ 3 Michael Irvin | 3.00 | 1.35 | .40 |
| Dallas Cowboys | | | |
| ☐ 4 Thurman Thomas | 2.50 | 1.15 | .30 |
| Buffalo Bills | | | |
| ☐ 5 Gary Clark | .60 | .25 | .08 |
| Washington Redskins | | | |
| ☐ 6 Haywood Jeffires | .60 | .25 | .08 |
| Houston Oilers | | | |
| ☐ 7 Michael Haynes | 1.25 | .55 | .16 |
| Atlanta Falcons | | | |
| ☐ 8 Drew Hill | .50 | .23 | .06 |
| Houston Oilers | | | |
| ☐ 9 Mark Duper | .50 | .23 | .06 |
| Miami Dolphins | | | |
| ☐ 10 James Lofton | .60 | .25 | .08 |
| Buffalo Bills | | | |
| ☐ 11 Rodney Hampton | 2.50 | 1.15 | .30 |
| New York Giants | | | |
| ☐ 12 Mark Clayton | .50 | .23 | .06 |
| Miami Dolphins | | | |
| ☐ 13 Henry Ellard | .75 | .35 | .09 |
| Los Angeles Rams | | | |
| ☐ 14 Art Monk | .60 | .25 | .08 |
| Washington Redskins | | | |
| ☐ 15 Earnest Byner | .50 | .23 | .06 |
| Washington Redskins | | | |
| ☐ 16 Gaston Green | .50 | .23 | .06 |
| Denver Broncos | | | |
| ☐ 17 Christian Okoye | .50 | .23 | .06 |
| Kansas City Chiefs | | | |
| ☐ 18 Irving Fryar | .50 | .23 | .06 |
| New England Patriots | | | |
| ☐ 19 John Taylor | .50 | .23 | .06 |
| San Francisco 49ers | | | |
| ☐ 20 Brian Blades | .50 | .23 | .06 |
| Seattle Seahawks | | | |

## 1993 Topps

The first series of the 1993 Topps football set consists of 660 standard-size (2 1/2" by 3 1/2") cards. The set also includes 30 rookies from the first three rounds of the 1993 draft. Each pack contained 14 cards plus one Topps Gold card. Factory set contain 13 gold cards. Reportedly in every 48th pack, one Topps Black Gold card was inserted in place of the Topps Gold card. The fronts feature color action player photos bordered in white. The player's name and team affiliation appear below the picture, and team color-coded diagonal bars accent the bottom corners of the photo. On team color-coded diagonal panels, the backs carry a color close-up photo, biography, and statistics, and career highlights. Special cards or topical subsets featured are Record Breakers (1-2), Franchise Players (82-90), Team Leaders (171-184, 261-274), League Leaders (216-220), and Field Generals (291-300). Draft Pick 1993 cards are scattered throughout the set (12, 22, 34, 64, 101, 130, 143, 152, 166, 187, 189, 204, 209, 215, 230, 232, 237, 243, 259, 275, 285, 307, 314, 317, 324, 326). The cards are numbered on the back. Rookie Cards include Jerome Bettis, Drew Bledsoe, Reggie Brooks, Garrison Hearst, O.J. McDuffie, Natrone Means, Rick Mirer and Ron Moore..

| | MINT | EXC | G-VG |
|---|---|---|---|
| COMPLETE SET (660) | 25.00 | 11.50 | 3.10 |
| COMPLETE FACT.SET (673) | 38.00 | 17.00 | 4.70 |
| COMPLETE SERIES 1 (330) | 15.00 | 6.75 | 1.90 |
| COMPLETE SERIES 2 (330) | 10.00 | 4.50 | 1.25 |
| COMMON PLAYER (1-330) | .05 | .02 | .01 |
| COMMON PLAYER (331-660) | .05 | .02 | .01 |

| | | | |
|---|---|---|---|
| ☐ 1 Art Monk RB | .08 | .04 | .01 |
| Washington Redskins | | | |
| ☐ 2 Jerry Rice RB | .25 | .11 | .03 |
| San Francisco 49ers | | | |
| ☐ 3 Stanley Richard | .05 | .02 | .01 |
| San Diego Chargers | | | |
| ☐ 4 Ron Hall | .05 | .02 | .01 |
| Tampa Bay Buccaneers | | | |
| ☐ 5 Daryl Johnston | .10 | .05 | .01 |
| Dallas Cowboys | | | |
| ☐ 6 Wendell Davis | .08 | .04 | .01 |
| Chicago Bears | | | |
| ☐ 7 Vaughn Dunbar | .08 | .04 | .01 |
| New Orleans Saints | | | |
| ☐ 8 Mike Jones | .05 | .02 | .01 |
| Phoenix Cardinals | | | |
| ☐ 9 Anthony Johnson | .05 | .02 | .01 |
| Indianapolis Colts | | | |
| ☐ 10 Chris Miller | .10 | .05 | .01 |
| Atlanta Falcons | | | |
| ☐ 11 Kyle Clifton | .05 | .02 | .01 |
| New York Jets | | | |
| ☐ 12 Curtis Conway | .50 | .23 | .06 |
| Chicago Bears | | | |
| ☐ 13 Lionel Washington | .05 | .02 | .01 |
| Los Angeles Raiders | | | |
| ☐ 14 Reggie Johnson | .05 | .02 | .01 |
| Denver Broncos | | | |
| ☐ 15 David Little | .05 | .02 | .01 |
| Pittsburgh Steelers | | | |
| ☐ 16 Nick Lowery | .05 | .02 | .01 |
| Kansas City Chiefs | | | |
| ☐ 17 Darryl Williams | .08 | .04 | .01 |
| Cincinnati Bengals | | | |
| ☐ 18 Brent Jones | .10 | .05 | .01 |
| San Francisco 49ers | | | |
| ☐ 19 Bruce Matthews | .08 | .04 | .01 |
| Houston Oilers | | | |
| ☐ 20 Heath Sherman | .05 | .02 | .01 |
| Philadelphia Eagles | | | |
| ☐ 21 John Kasay UER | .05 | .02 | .01 |
| Seattle Seahawks | | | |
| (Text on back states he did not | | | |
| attempt any FG's over 50 yds. | | | |
| but made 8) | | | |
| ☐ 22 Troy Drayton | .25 | .11 | .03 |
| Los Angeles Rams | | | |
| ☐ 23 Eric Metcalf | .10 | .05 | .01 |
| Cleveland Browns | | | |
| ☐ 24 Andre Tippett | .05 | .02 | .01 |
| New England Patriots | | | |
| ☐ 25 Rodney Hampton | .30 | .14 | .04 |
| New York Giants | | | |
| ☐ 26 Henry Jones | .05 | .02 | .01 |
| Buffalo Bills | | | |
| ☐ 27 Jim Everett | .05 | .02 | .01 |
| Los Angeles Rams | | | |
| ☐ 28 Steve Jordan | .08 | .04 | .01 |
| Minnesota Vikings | | | |
| ☐ 29 LeRoy Butler | .05 | .02 | .01 |
| Green Bay Packers | | | |
| ☐ 30 Troy Vincent | .08 | .04 | .01 |
| Miami Dolphins | | | |
| ☐ 31 Nate Lewis | .08 | .04 | .01 |
| San Diego Chargers | | | |
| ☐ 32 Rickey Jackson | .08 | .04 | .01 |
| New Orleans Saints | | | |
| ☐ 33 Darion Conner | .05 | .02 | .01 |
| Atlanta Falcons | | | |
| ☐ 34 Tom Carter | .25 | .11 | .03 |
| Washington Redskins | | | |
| ☐ 35 Jeff George | .15 | .07 | .02 |
| Indianapolis Colts | | | |
| ☐ 36 Larry Centers | .20 | .09 | .03 |
| Phoenix Cardinals | | | |

| | | | |
|---|---|---|---|
| ☐ 37 Reggie Cobb | .10 | .05 | .01 |
| Tampa Bay Buccaneers | | | |
| ☐ 38 Mike Saxon | .05 | .02 | .01 |
| Dallas Cowboys | | | |
| ☐ 39 Brad Baxter | .08 | .04 | .01 |
| New York Jets | | | |
| ☐ 40 Reggie White | .15 | .07 | .02 |
| Green Bay Packers | | | |
| ☐ 41 Haywood Jeffires | .10 | .05 | .01 |
| Houston Oilers | | | |
| ☐ 42 Alfred Williams | .05 | .02 | .01 |
| Cincinnati Bengals | | | |
| ☐ 43 Aaron Wallace | .05 | .02 | .01 |
| Los Angeles Raiders | | | |
| ☐ 44 Tracy Simien | .05 | .02 | .01 |
| Kansas City Chiefs | | | |
| ☐ 45 Pat Harlow | .05 | .02 | .01 |
| New England Patriots | | | |
| ☐ 46 David Johnson | .05 | .02 | .01 |
| Pittsburgh Steelers | | | |
| ☐ 47 Don Griffin | .05 | .02 | .01 |
| San Francisco 49ers | | | |
| ☐ 48 Flipper Anderson | .08 | .04 | .01 |
| Los Angeles Rams | | | |
| ☐ 49 Keith Kartz | .05 | .02 | .01 |
| Denver Broncos | | | |
| ☐ 50 Bernie Kosar | .10 | .05 | .01 |
| Cleveland Browns | | | |
| ☐ 51 Kent Hull | .05 | .02 | .01 |
| Buffalo Bills | | | |
| ☐ 52 Erik Howard | .05 | .02 | .01 |
| New York Giants | | | |
| ☐ 53 Pierce Holt | .05 | .02 | .01 |
| Atlanta Falcons | | | |
| ☐ 54 Dwayne Harper | .05 | .02 | .01 |
| Seattle Seahawks | | | |
| ☐ 55 Bennie Blades | .05 | .02 | .01 |
| Detroit Lions | | | |
| ☐ 56 Mark Duper | .08 | .04 | .01 |
| Miami Dolphins | | | |
| ☐ 57 Brian Noble | .05 | .02 | .01 |
| Green Bay Packers | | | |
| ☐ 58 Jeff Feagles | .05 | .02 | .01 |
| Philadelphia Eagles | | | |
| ☐ 59 Michael Haynes | .20 | .09 | .03 |
| Atlanta Falcons | | | |
| ☐ 60 Junior Seau | .10 | .05 | .01 |
| San Diego Chargers | | | |
| ☐ 61 Gary Anderson | .08 | .04 | .01 |
| Tampa Bay Buccaneers | | | |
| ☐ 62 Jon Hand | .05 | .02 | .01 |
| Indianapolis Colts | | | |
| ☐ 63 Lin Elliott | .05 | .02 | .01 |
| Dallas Cowboys | | | |
| ☐ 64 Dana Stubblefield | .50 | .23 | .06 |
| San Francisco 49ers | | | |
| ☐ 65 Vaughan Johnson | .05 | .02 | .01 |
| New Orleans Saints | | | |
| ☐ 66 Mo Lewis | .05 | .02 | .01 |
| New York Jets | | | |
| ☐ 67 Aeneas Williams | .05 | .02 | .01 |
| Phoenix Cardinals | | | |
| ☐ 68 David Fulcher | .05 | .02 | .01 |
| Cincinnati Bengals | | | |
| ☐ 69 Chip Lohmiller | .05 | .02 | .01 |
| Washington Redskins | | | |
| ☐ 70 Greg Townsend | .05 | .02 | .01 |
| Los Angeles Raiders | | | |
| ☐ 71 Simon Fletcher | .08 | .04 | .01 |
| Denver Broncos | | | |
| ☐ 72 Sean Salisbury | .08 | .04 | .01 |
| Minnesota Vikings | | | |
| ☐ 73 Christian Okoye | .08 | .04 | .01 |
| Kansas City Chiefs | | | |
| ☐ 74 Jim Arnold | .05 | .02 | .01 |
| Detroit Lions | | | |
| ☐ 75 Bruce Smith | .10 | .05 | .01 |
| Buffalo Bills | | | |
| ☐ 76 Fred Barnett | .10 | .05 | .01 |
| Philadelphia Eagles | | | |
| ☐ 77 Bill Romanowski | .05 | .02 | .01 |
| San Francisco 49ers | | | |
| ☐ 78 Dermontti Dawson | .05 | .02 | .01 |
| Pittsburgh Steelers | | | |
| ☐ 79 Bern Brostek | .05 | .02 | .01 |
| Los Angeles Rams | | | |
| ☐ 80 Warren Moon | .15 | .07 | .02 |
| Houston Oilers | | | |
| ☐ 81 Bill Fralic | .05 | .02 | .01 |
| Detroit Lions | | | |
| ☐ 82 Lomas Brown FP | .05 | .02 | .01 |
| Detroit Lions | | | |
| ☐ 83 Duane Bickett FP | .05 | .02 | .01 |
| Indianapolis Colts | | | |
| ☐ 84 Neil Smith FP | .10 | .05 | .01 |
| Kansas City Chiefs | | | |
| ☐ 85 Reggie White FP | .08 | .04 | .01 |

| | | | | |
|---|---|---|---|---|
| Philadelphia Eagles | | | | |
| ☐ 86 Tim McDonald FP | .05 | .02 | .01 |
| San Francisco 49ers | | | | |
| ☐ 87 Leslie O'Neal FP | .05 | .02 | .01 |
| San Diego Chargers | | | | |
| ☐ 88 Steve Young FP | .12 | .05 | .02 |
| San Francisco 49ers | | | | |
| ☐ 89 Paul Gruber FP | .05 | .02 | .01 |
| Tampa Bay Buccaneers | | | | |
| ☐ 90 Wilber Marshall FP | .08 | .04 | .01 |
| Washington Redskins | | | | |
| ☐ 91 Trace Armstrong | .05 | .02 | .01 |
| Chicago Bears | | | | |
| ☐ 92 Bobby Houston | .10 | .05 | .01 |
| New York Jets | | | | |
| ☐ 93 George Thornton | .05 | .02 | .01 |
| San Diego Chargers | | | | |
| ☐ 94 Keith McCants | .05 | .02 | .01 |
| Tampa Bay Buccaneers | | | | |
| ☐ 95 Ricky Sanders | .08 | .04 | .01 |
| Washington Redskins | | | | |
| ☐ 96 Jackie Harris | .30 | .14 | .04 |
| Green Bay Packers | | | | |
| ☐ 97 Todd Marinovich | .05 | .02 | .01 |
| Los Angeles Raiders | | | | |
| ☐ 98 Henry Thomas | .05 | .02 | .01 |
| Minnesota Vikings | | | | |
| ☐ 99 Jeff Wright | .05 | .02 | .01 |
| Buffalo Bills | | | | |
| ☐ 100 John Elway | .35 | .16 | .04 |
| Denver Broncos | | | | |
| ☐ 101 Garrison Hearst | .60 | .25 | .08 |
| Phoenix Cardinals | | | | |
| ☐ 102 Roy Foster | .05 | .02 | .01 |
| San Francisco 49ers | | | | |
| ☐ 103 David Lang | .05 | .02 | .01 |
| Los Angeles Rams | | | | |
| ☐ 104 Matt Stover | .05 | .02 | .01 |
| Cleveland Browns | | | | |
| ☐ 105 Lawrence Taylor | .10 | .05 | .01 |
| New York Giants | | | | |
| ☐ 106 Pete Stoyanovich | .05 | .02 | .01 |
| Miami Dolphins | | | | |
| ☐ 107 Jessie Tuggle | .05 | .02 | .01 |
| Atlanta Falcons | | | | |
| ☐ 108 William White | .05 | .02 | .01 |
| Detroit Lions | | | | |
| ☐ 109 Andy Harmon | .05 | .02 | .01 |
| Philadelphia Eagles | | | | |
| ☐ 110 John L. Williams | .08 | .04 | .01 |
| Seattle Seahawks | | | | |
| ☐ 111 Jon Vaughn | .05 | .02 | .01 |
| New England Patriots | | | | |
| ☐ 112 John Alt | .05 | .02 | .01 |
| Kansas City Chiefs | | | | |
| ☐ 113 Chris Jacke | .05 | .02 | .01 |
| Green Bay Packers | | | | |
| ☐ 114 Jim Breech | .05 | .02 | .01 |
| Cincinnati Bengals | | | | |
| ☐ 115 Eric Martin | .08 | .04 | .01 |
| New Orleans Saints | | | | |
| ☐ 116 Derrick Walker | .05 | .02 | .01 |
| San Diego Chargers | | | | |
| ☐ 117 Ricky Ervins | .08 | .04 | .01 |
| Washington Redskins | | | | |
| ☐ 118 Roger Craig | .08 | .04 | .01 |
| Minnesota Vikings | | | | |
| ☐ 119 Jeff Gossett | .05 | .02 | .01 |
| Los Angeles Raiders | | | | |
| ☐ 120 Emmitt Smith | 2.00 | .90 | .25 |
| Dallas Cowboys | | | | |
| ☐ 121 Bob Whitfield | .05 | .02 | .01 |
| Atlanta Falcons | | | | |
| ☐ 122 Alonzo Spellman | .08 | .04 | .01 |
| Chicago Bears | | | | |
| ☐ 123 David Klingler | .15 | .07 | .02 |
| Cincinnati Bengals | | | | |
| ☐ 124 Tommy Maddox | .10 | .05 | .01 |
| Denver Broncos | | | | |
| ☐ 125 Robert Porcher | .08 | .04 | .01 |
| Detroit Lions | | | | |
| ☐ 126 Edgar Bennett | .10 | .05 | .01 |
| Green Bay Packers | | | | |
| ☐ 127 Harvey Williams | .10 | .05 | .01 |
| Kansas City Chiefs | | | | |
| ☐ 128 Dave Brown | .75 | .35 | .09 |
| New York Giants | | | | |
| ☐ 129 Johnny Mitchell | .25 | .11 | .03 |
| New York Jets | | | | |
| ☐ 130 Drew Bledsoe | 3.00 | 1.35 | .40 |
| New England Patriots | | | | |
| ☐ 131 Zefross Moss | .05 | .02 | .01 |
| Indianapolis Colts | | | | |
| ☐ 132 Nate Odomes | .08 | .04 | .01 |
| Buffalo Bills | | | | |
| ☐ 133 Rufus Porter | .05 | .02 | .01 |
| Seattle Seahawks | | | | |
| ☐ 134 Jackie Slater | .05 | .02 | .01 |

| | | | | |
|---|---|---|---|---|
| Los Angeles Rams | | | | |
| ☐ 135 Steve Young | .25 | .11 | .03 |
| San Francisco 49ers | | | | |
| ☐ 136 Chris Calloway | .05 | .02 | .01 |
| New York Giants | | | | |
| ☐ 137 Steve Atwater | .08 | .04 | .01 |
| Denver Broncos | | | | |
| ☐ 138 Mark Carrier | .08 | .04 | .01 |
| Chicago Bears | | | | |
| ☐ 139 Marvin Washington | .05 | .02 | .01 |
| New York Jets | | | | |
| ☐ 140 Barry Foster | .25 | .11 | .03 |
| Pittsburgh Steelers | | | | |
| ☐ 141 Ricky Reynolds | .05 | .02 | .01 |
| Tampa Bay Buccaneers | | | | |
| ☐ 142 Bubba McDowell | .05 | .02 | .01 |
| Houston Oilers | | | | |
| ☐ 143 Dan Footman | .15 | .07 | .02 |
| Cleveland Browns | | | | |
| ☐ 144 Richmond Webb | .05 | .02 | .01 |
| Miami Dolphins | | | | |
| ☐ 145 Mike Pritchard | .10 | .05 | .01 |
| Atlanta Falcons | | | | |
| ☐ 146 Chris Spielman | .05 | .02 | .01 |
| Detroit Lions | | | | |
| ☐ 147 Dave Krieg | .08 | .04 | .01 |
| Kansas City Chiefs | | | | |
| ☐ 148 Nick Bell | .08 | .04 | .01 |
| Los Angeles Raiders | | | | |
| ☐ 149 Vincent Brown | .05 | .02 | .01 |
| New England Patriots | | | | |
| ☐ 150 Seth Joyner | .08 | .04 | .01 |
| Philadelphia Eagles | | | | |
| ☐ 151 Tommy Kane | .05 | .02 | .01 |
| Seattle Seahawks | | | | |
| ☐ 152 Carlton Gray | .20 | .09 | .03 |
| Seattle Seahawks | | | | |
| ☐ 153 Harry Newsome | .05 | .02 | .01 |
| Minnesota Vikings | | | | |
| ☐ 154 Rohn Stark | .05 | .02 | .01 |
| Indianapolis Colts | | | | |
| ☐ 155 Shannon Sharpe | .20 | .09 | .03 |
| Denver Broncos | | | | |
| ☐ 156 Charles Haley | .08 | .04 | .01 |
| Dallas Cowboys | | | | |
| ☐ 157 Cornelius Bennett | .10 | .05 | .01 |
| Buffalo Bills | | | | |
| ☐ 158 Doug Riesenberg | .05 | .02 | .01 |
| New York Giants | | | | |
| ☐ 159 Amp Lee | .08 | .04 | .01 |
| San Francisco 49ers | | | | |
| ☐ 160 Sterling Sharpe UER | .40 | .18 | .05 |
| Green Bay Packers | | | | |
| (Card front pictures Edgar Bennett) | | | | |
| ☐ 161 Alonzo Mitz | .05 | .02 | .01 |
| Cincinnati Bengals | | | | |
| ☐ 162 Pat Terrell | .05 | .02 | .01 |
| Los Angeles Rams | | | | |
| ☐ 163 Mark Schlereth | .05 | .02 | .01 |
| Washington Redskins | | | | |
| ☐ 164 Gary Anderson | .05 | .02 | .01 |
| Pittsburgh Steelers | | | | |
| ☐ 165 Quinn Early | .08 | .04 | .01 |
| New Orleans Saints | | | | |
| ☐ 166 Jerome Bettis | 3.00 | 1.35 | .40 |
| Los Angeles Rams | | | | |
| ☐ 167 Lawrence Dawsey | .10 | .05 | .01 |
| Tampa Bay Buccaneers | | | | |
| ☐ 168 Derrick Thomas | .15 | .07 | .02 |
| Kansas City Chiefs | | | | |
| ☐ 169 Rodney Peete | .08 | .04 | .01 |
| Detroit Lions | | | | |
| ☐ 170 Jim Kelly | .25 | .11 | .03 |
| Buffalo Bills | | | | |
| ☐ 171 Deion Sanders TL | .08 | .04 | .01 |
| Atlanta Falcons | | | | |
| ☐ 172 Richard Dent TL | .05 | .02 | .01 |
| Chicago Bears | | | | |
| ☐ 173 Emmitt Smith TL | .75 | .35 | .09 |
| Dallas Cowboys | | | | |
| ☐ 174 Barry Sanders TL | .35 | .16 | .04 |
| Detroit Lions | | | | |
| ☐ 175 Sterling Sharpe TL | .20 | .09 | .03 |
| Green Bay Packers | | | | |
| ☐ 176 Cleveland Gary TL | .05 | .02 | .01 |
| Los Angeles Rams | | | | |
| ☐ 177 Terry Allen TL | .08 | .04 | .01 |
| Minnesota Vikings | | | | |
| ☐ 178 Vaughan Johnson TL | .05 | .02 | .01 |
| New Orleans Saints | | | | |
| ☐ 179 Rodney Hampton TL | .15 | .07 | .02 |
| New York Giants | | | | |
| ☐ 180 Randall Cunningham TL | .08 | .04 | .01 |
| Philadelphia Eagles | | | | |
| ☐ 181 Ricky Proehl TL | .05 | .02 | .01 |
| Phoenix Cardinals | | | | |
| ☐ 182 Jerry Rice TL | .25 | .11 | .03 |
| San Francisco 49ers | | | | |

|  |  | | | |
|---|---|---|---|---|
| □ 183 | Reggie Cobb TL — Tampa Bay Buccaneers | .05 | .02 | .01 |
| □ 184 | Earnest Byner TL — Washington Redskins | .05 | .02 | .01 |
| □ 185 | Jeff Lageman — New York Jets | .05 | .02 | .01 |
| □ 186 | Carlos Jenkins — Minnesota Vikings | .05 | .02 | .01 |
| □ 187 | Cardinals Draft Picks — Ernest Dye / Ronald Moore / Garrison Hearst / Ben Coleman — Phoenix Cardinals | 1.25 | .55 | .16 |
| □ 188 | Todd Lyght — Los Angeles Rams | .05 | .02 | .01 |
| □ 189 | Carl Simpson — Chicago Bears | .10 | .05 | .01 |
| □ 190 | Barry Sanders — Detroit Lions | .75 | .35 | .09 |
| □ 191 | Jim Harbaugh — Chicago Bears | .08 | .04 | .01 |
| □ 192 | Roger Ruzek — Philadelphia Eagles | .05 | .02 | .01 |
| □ 193 | Brent Williams — New England Patriots | .05 | .02 | .01 |
| □ 194 | Chip Banks — Indianapolis Colts | .05 | .02 | .01 |
| □ 195 | Mike Croel — Denver Broncos | .08 | .04 | .01 |
| □ 196 | Marion Butts — San Diego Chargers | .10 | .05 | .01 |
| □ 197 | James Washington — Dallas Cowboys | .05 | .02 | .01 |
| □ 198 | John Offerdahl — Miami Dolphins | .05 | .02 | .01 |
| □ 199 | Tom Rathman — San Francisco 49ers | .08 | .04 | .01 |
| □ 200 | Joe Montana — Kansas City Chiefs | 1.25 | .55 | .16 |
| □ 201 | Pepper Johnson — New York Giants | .05 | .02 | .01 |
| □ 202 | Cris Dishman — Houston Oilers | .05 | .02 | .01 |
| □ 203 | Adrian White — New England Patriots | .10 | .05 | .01 |
| □ 204 | Reggie Brooks — Washington Redskins | 1.75 | .80 | .22 |
| □ 205 | Cortez Kennedy — Seattle Seahawks | .10 | .05 | .01 |
| □ 206 | Robert Massey — Phoenix Cardinals | .05 | .02 | .01 |
| □ 207 | Toi Cook — New Orleans Saints | .05 | .02 | .01 |
| □ 208 | Harry Sydney — Green Bay Packers | .05 | .02 | .01 |
| □ 209 | Lincoln Kennedy — Atlanta Falcons | .15 | .07 | .02 |
| □ 210 | Randall McDaniel — Minnesota Vikings | .05 | .02 | .01 |
| □ 211 | Eugene Daniel — Indianapolis Colts | .05 | .02 | .01 |
| □ 212 | Rob Burnett — Cleveland Browns | .05 | .02 | .01 |
| □ 213 | Steve Broussard — Atlanta Falcons | .05 | .02 | .01 |
| □ 214 | Brian Washington — New York Jets | .05 | .02 | .01 |
| □ 215 | Leonard Renfro — Philadelphia Eagles | .10 | .05 | .01 |
| □ 216 | Audray McMillian LL — Minnesota Vikings — Henry Jones — Buffalo Bills | .05 | .02 | .01 |
| □ 217 | Sterling Sharpe LL — Green Bay Packers — Anthony Miller — San Diego Chargers | .15 | .07 | .02 |
| □ 218 | Clyde Simmons LL — Philadelphia Eagles — Leslie O'Neal — San Diego Chargers | .05 | .02 | .01 |
| □ 219 | Emmitt Smith LL — Dallas Cowboys — Barry Foster — Pittsburgh Steelers | .50 | .23 | .06 |
| □ 220 | Steve Young LL — San Francisco 49ers — Warren Moon — Houston Oilers | .10 | .05 | .01 |
| □ 221 | Mel Gray — Detroit Lions | .05 | .02 | .01 |
| □ 222 | Luis Sharpe — Phoenix Cardinals | .05 | .02 | .01 |
| □ 223 | Eric Moten — San Diego Chargers | .05 | .02 | .01 |
| □ 224 | Albert Lewis — Kansas City Chiefs | .05 | .02 | .01 |
| □ 225 | Alvin Harper — Dallas Cowboys | .25 | .11 | .03 |
| □ 226 | Steve Wallace — San Francisco 49ers | .05 | .02 | .01 |
| □ 227 | Mark Higgs — Miami Dolphins | .10 | .05 | .01 |
| □ 228 | Eugene Lockhart — New England Patriots | .05 | .02 | .01 |
| □ 229 | Sean Jones — Houston Oilers | .05 | .02 | .01 |
| □ 230 | Buccaneers Draft Picks — Eric Curry / Lamar Thomas / Demetrious DuBose / John Lynch — Tampa Bay Buccaneers | .15 | .07 | .02 |
| □ 231 | Jimmy Williams — Tampa Bay Buccaneers (Text states drafted in 1992; he was drafted in 1982) | .05 | .02 | .01 |
| □ 232 | Demetrius DuBose — Los Angeles Rams | .15 | .07 | .02 |
| □ 233 | John Roper — Chicago Bears | .05 | .02 | .01 |
| □ 234 | Keith Hamilton — New York Giants | .05 | .02 | .01 |
| □ 235 | Donald Evans — Pittsburgh Steelers | .05 | .02 | .01 |
| □ 236 | Kenneth Davis — Buffalo Bills | .08 | .04 | .01 |
| □ 237 | John Copeland — Cincinnati Bengals | .25 | .11 | .03 |
| □ 238 | Leonard Russell — New England Patriots | .08 | .04 | .01 |
| □ 239 | Ken Harvey — Phoenix Cardinals | .05 | .02 | .01 |
| □ 240 | Dale Carter — Kansas City Chiefs | .10 | .05 | .01 |
| □ 241 | Anthony Pleasant — Cleveland Browns | .05 | .02 | .01 |
| □ 242 | Darrell Green — Washington Redskins | .08 | .04 | .01 |
| □ 243 | Natrone Means — San Diego Chargers | 1.25 | .55 | .16 |
| □ 244 | Rob Moore — New York Jets | .10 | .05 | .01 |
| □ 245 | Chris Doleman — Minnesota Vikings | .08 | .04 | .01 |
| □ 246 | J.B. Brown — Miami Dolphins | .05 | .02 | .01 |
| □ 247 | Ray Crockett — Detroit Lions | .05 | .02 | .01 |
| □ 248 | John Taylor — San Francisco 49ers | .10 | .05 | .01 |
| □ 249 | Russell Maryland — Dallas Cowboys | .10 | .05 | .01 |
| □ 250 | Brett Favre — Green Bay Packers | .75 | .35 | .09 |
| □ 251 | Carl Pickens — Cincinnati Bengals | .10 | .05 | .01 |
| □ 252 | Andy Heck — Seattle Seahawks | .05 | .02 | .01 |
| □ 253 | Jerome Henderson — New England Patriots | .05 | .02 | .01 |
| □ 254 | Deion Sanders — Atlanta Falcons | .15 | .07 | .02 |
| □ 255 | Steve Emtman — Indianapolis Colts | .08 | .04 | .01 |
| □ 256 | Calvin Williams — Philadelphia Eagles | .10 | .05 | .01 |
| □ 257 | Sean Gilbert — Los Angeles Rams | .08 | .04 | .01 |
| □ 258 | Don Beebe — Buffalo Bills | .10 | .05 | .01 |
| □ 259 | Robert Smith — Minnesota Vikings | .35 | .16 | .04 |
| □ 260 | Robert Blackmon — Seattle Seahawks | .05 | .02 | .01 |
| □ 261 | Jim Kelly TL — Buffalo Bills | .10 | .05 | .01 |
| □ 262 | Harold Green TL UER — Cincinnati Bengals (Harold Green is identified as Gaston Green) | .05 | .02 | .01 |
| □ 263 | Clay Matthews TL — Cleveland Browns | .08 | .04 | .01 |
| □ 264 | John Elway TL — Denver Broncos | .15 | .07 | .02 |
| □ 265 | Warren Moon TL — Houston Oilers | .10 | .05 | .01 |
| □ 266 | Jeff George TL — Indianapolis Colts | .05 | .02 | .01 |
| □ 267 | Derrick Thomas TL — Kansas City Chiefs | .08 | .04 | .01 |
| □ 268 | Howie Long TL — Los Angeles Raiders | .08 | .04 | .01 |
| □ 269 | Dan Marino TL | .30 | .14 | .04 |

| | | | |
|---|---|---|---|
| Miami Dolphins | | | |
| ☐ 270 Jon Vaughn TL | .05 | .02 | .01 |
| New England Patriots | | | |
| ☐ 271 Chris Burkett TL | .05 | .02 | .01 |
| New York Jets | | | |
| ☐ 272 Barry Foster TL | .10 | .05 | .01 |
| Pittsburgh Steelers | | | |
| ☐ 273 Marion Butts TL | .08 | .04 | .01 |
| San Diego Chargers | | | |
| ☐ 274 Chris Warren TL | .05 | .02 | .01 |
| Seattle Seahawks | | | |
| ☐ 275 Michael Strahan and | .15 | .07 | .02 |
| Marcus Buckley | | | |
| Giants Draft Picks | | | |
| New York Giants | | | |
| ☐ 276 Tony Casillas | .05 | .02 | .01 |
| Dallas Cowboys | | | |
| ☐ 277 Jarrod Bunch | .08 | .04 | .01 |
| New York Giants | | | |
| ☐ 278 Eric Green | .10 | .05 | .01 |
| Pittsburgh Steelers | | | |
| ☐ 279 Stan Brock | .05 | .02 | .01 |
| New Orleans Saints | | | |
| ☐ 280 Chester McGlockton | .05 | .02 | .01 |
| Los Angeles Raiders | | | |
| ☐ 281 Ricky Watters | .30 | .14 | .04 |
| San Francisco 49ers | | | |
| ☐ 282 Dan Saleaumua | .05 | .02 | .01 |
| Kansas City Chiefs | | | |
| ☐ 283 Rich Camarillo | .05 | .02 | .01 |
| Phoenix Cardinals | | | |
| ☐ 284 Cris Carter | .10 | .05 | .01 |
| Minnesota Vikings | | | |
| ☐ 285 Rick Mirer | 3.00 | 1.35 | .40 |
| Seattle Seahawks | | | |
| ☐ 286 Matt Brock | .05 | .02 | .01 |
| Green Bay Packers | | | |
| ☐ 287 Burt Grossman | .05 | .02 | .01 |
| San Diego Chargers | | | |
| ☐ 288 Andre Collins | .05 | .02 | .01 |
| Washington Redskins | | | |
| ☐ 289 Mark Jackson | .08 | .04 | .01 |
| New York Giants | | | |
| ☐ 290 Dan Marino | .75 | .35 | .09 |
| Miami Dolphins | | | |
| ☐ 291 Cornelius Bennett FG | .08 | .04 | .01 |
| Buffalo Bills | | | |
| ☐ 292 Steve Atwater FG | .05 | .02 | .01 |
| Denver Broncos | | | |
| ☐ 293 Bryan Cox FG | .05 | .02 | .01 |
| Miami Dolphins | | | |
| ☐ 294 Sam Mills FG | .05 | .02 | .01 |
| New Orleans Saints | | | |
| ☐ 295 Pepper Johnson FG | .05 | .02 | .01 |
| New York Giants | | | |
| ☐ 296 Seth Joyner FG | .08 | .04 | .01 |
| Philadelphia Eagles | | | |
| ☐ 297 Chris Spielman FG | .05 | .02 | .01 |
| Detroit Lions | | | |
| ☐ 298 Junior Seau FG | .05 | .02 | .01 |
| San Diego Chargers | | | |
| ☐ 299 Cortez Kennedy FG | .08 | .04 | .01 |
| Seattle Seahawks | | | |
| ☐ 300 Broderick Thomas FG | .05 | .02 | .01 |
| Tampa Bay Buccaneers | | | |
| ☐ 301 Todd McNair | .05 | .02 | .01 |
| Kansas City Chiefs | | | |
| ☐ 302 Nate Newton | .05 | .02 | .01 |
| Dallas Cowboys | | | |
| ☐ 303 Mike Walter | .05 | .02 | .01 |
| San Francisco 49ers | | | |
| ☐ 304 Clyde Simmons | .08 | .04 | .01 |
| Philadelphia Eagles | | | |
| ☐ 305 Ernie Mills | .05 | .02 | .01 |
| Pittsburgh Steelers | | | |
| ☐ 306 Steve Wisniewski | .05 | .02 | .01 |
| Los Angeles Raiders | | | |
| ☐ 307 Coleman Rudolph | .10 | .05 | .01 |
| New York Jets | | | |
| ☐ 308 Thurman Thomas | .35 | .16 | .04 |
| Buffalo Bills | | | |
| ☐ 309 Reggie Roby | .05 | .02 | .01 |
| Miami Dolphins | | | |
| ☐ 310 Eric Swann | .08 | .04 | .01 |
| Phoenix Cardinals | | | |
| ☐ 311 Mark Wheeler | .05 | .02 | .01 |
| Tampa Bay Buccaneers | | | |
| ☐ 312 Jeff Herrod | .05 | .02 | .01 |
| Indianapolis Colts | | | |
| ☐ 313 Leroy Hoard | .08 | .04 | .01 |
| Cleveland Browns | | | |
| ☐ 314 Patrick Bates | .10 | .05 | .01 |
| Los Angeles Raiders | | | |
| ☐ 315 Earnest Byner | .08 | .04 | .01 |
| Washington Redskins | | | |
| ☐ 316 Dave Meggett | .08 | .04 | .01 |
| New York Giants | | | |
| ☐ 317 George Teague | .20 | .09 | .03 |

| | | | |
|---|---|---|---|
| Green Bay Packers | | | |
| ☐ 318 Ray Childress | .05 | .02 | .01 |
| Houston Oilers | | | |
| ☐ 319 Mike Kenn | .05 | .02 | .01 |
| Atlanta Falcons | | | |
| ☐ 320 Jason Hanson | .05 | .02 | .01 |
| Detroit Lions | | | |
| ☐ 321 Gary Clark | .08 | .04 | .01 |
| Phoenix Cardinals | | | |
| ☐ 322 Chris Gardocki | .05 | .02 | .01 |
| Chicago Bears | | | |
| ☐ 323 Ken Norton | .08 | .04 | .01 |
| Dallas Cowboys | | | |
| ☐ 324 Eric Curry | .25 | .11 | .03 |
| Tampa Bay Buccaneers | | | |
| ☐ 325 Byron Evans | .05 | .02 | .01 |
| Philadelphia Eagles | | | |
| ☐ 326 O.J. McDuffie | 1.25 | .55 | .16 |
| Miami Dolphins | | | |
| ☐ 327 Dwight Stone | .05 | .02 | .01 |
| Pittsburgh Steelers | | | |
| ☐ 328 Tommy Barnhardt | .05 | .02 | .01 |
| New Orleans Saints | | | |
| ☐ 329 Checklist 1-165 | .05 | .02 | .01 |
| ☐ 330 Checklist 166-329 | .05 | .02 | .01 |
| ☐ 331 Erik Williams | .05 | .02 | .01 |
| Dallas Cowboys | | | |
| ☐ 332 Phil Hansen | .05 | .02 | .01 |
| Buffalo Bills | | | |
| ☐ 333 Martin Harrison | .20 | .09 | .03 |
| San Francisco 49ers | | | |
| ☐ 334 Mark Ingram | .08 | .04 | .01 |
| Miami Dolphins | | | |
| ☐ 335 Mark Rypien | .08 | .04 | .01 |
| Washington Redskins | | | |
| ☐ 336 Anthony Miller | .15 | .07 | .02 |
| San Diego Chargers | | | |
| ☐ 337 Antone Davis | .05 | .02 | .01 |
| Philadelphia Eagles | | | |
| ☐ 338 Mike Munchak | .08 | .04 | .01 |
| Houston Oilers | | | |
| ☐ 339 Wayne Martin | .05 | .02 | .01 |
| New Orleans Saints | | | |
| ☐ 340 Joe Montana | 1.25 | .55 | .16 |
| Kansas City Chiefs | | | |
| ☐ 341 Deon Figures | .15 | .07 | .02 |
| Pittsburgh Steelers | | | |
| ☐ 342 Ed McDaniel | .05 | .02 | .01 |
| Minnesota Vikings | | | |
| ☐ 343 Chris Burkett | .05 | .02 | .01 |
| New York Jets | | | |
| ☐ 344 Tony Smith | .05 | .02 | .01 |
| Atlanta Falcons | | | |
| ☐ 345 James Lofton | .10 | .05 | .01 |
| Los Angeles Raiders | | | |
| ☐ 346 Courtney Hawkins | .08 | .04 | .01 |
| Tampa Bay Buccaneers | | | |
| ☐ 347 Dennis Smith | .05 | .02 | .01 |
| Denver Broncos | | | |
| ☐ 348 Anthony Morgan | .05 | .02 | .01 |
| Chicago Bears | | | |
| ☐ 349 Chris Goode | .05 | .02 | .01 |
| Indianapolis Colts | | | |
| ☐ 350 Phil Simms | .10 | .05 | .01 |
| New York Giants | | | |
| ☐ 351 Patrick Hunter | .05 | .02 | .01 |
| Seattle Seahawks | | | |
| ☐ 352 Brett Perriman | .08 | .04 | .01 |
| Detroit Lions | | | |
| ☐ 353 Corey Miller | .05 | .02 | .01 |
| New York Giants | | | |
| ☐ 354 Harry Galbreath | .05 | .02 | .01 |
| Green Bay Packers | | | |
| ☐ 355 Mark Carrier WR | .08 | .04 | .01 |
| Cleveland Browns | | | |
| ☐ 356 Troy Drayton | .05 | .02 | .01 |
| Los Angeles Rams | | | |
| ☐ 357 Greg Davis | .05 | .02 | .01 |
| Phoenix Cardinals | | | |
| ☐ 358 Tim Krumrie | .05 | .02 | .01 |
| Cleveland Browns | | | |
| ☐ 359 Tim McDonald | .05 | .02 | .01 |
| San Francisco 49ers | | | |
| ☐ 360 Webster Slaughter | .08 | .04 | .01 |
| Houston Oilers | | | |
| ☐ 361 Steve Christie | .05 | .02 | .01 |
| Buffalo Bills | | | |
| ☐ 362 Courtney Hall | .05 | .02 | .01 |
| San Diego Chargers | | | |
| ☐ 363 Charles Mann | .05 | .02 | .01 |
| Washington Redskins | | | |
| ☐ 364 Vestee Jackson | .05 | .02 | .01 |
| Miami Dolphins | | | |
| ☐ 365 Robert Jones | .05 | .02 | .01 |
| Dallas Cowboys | | | |
| ☐ 366 Rich Miano | .05 | .02 | .01 |
| Philadelphia Eagles | | | |
| ☐ 367 Morten Andersen | .08 | .04 | .01 |

| | | | |
|---|---|---|---|
| New Orleans Saints | | | |
| ☐ 368 Jeff Graham | .08 | .04 | .01 |
| Pittsburgh Steelers | | | |
| ☐ 369 Martin Mayhew | .05 | .02 | .01 |
| Tampa Bay Buccaneers | | | |
| ☐ 370 Anthony Carter | .08 | .04 | .01 |
| Minnesota Vikings | | | |
| ☐ 371 Greg Kragen | .05 | .02 | .01 |
| Denver Broncos | | | |
| ☐ 372 Ron Cox | .05 | .02 | .01 |
| Chicago Bears | | | |
| ☐ 373 Perry Williams | .05 | .02 | .01 |
| New York Giants | | | |
| ☐ 374 Willie Gault | .08 | .04 | .01 |
| Los Angeles Raiders | | | |
| ☐ 375 Chris Warren | .15 | .07 | .02 |
| Seattle Seahawks | | | |
| ☐ 376 Reyna Thompson | .05 | .02 | .01 |
| New England Patriots | | | |
| ☐ 377 Bennie Thompson | .05 | .02 | .01 |
| Kansas City Chiefs | | | |
| ☐ 378 Kevin Mack | .05 | .02 | .01 |
| Cleveland Browns | | | |
| ☐ 379 Clarence Verdin | .05 | .02 | .01 |
| Indianapolis Colts | | | |
| ☐ 380 Marc Boutte | .05 | .02 | .01 |
| Los Angeles Rams | | | |
| ☐ 381 Marvin Jones | .15 | .07 | .02 |
| New York Jets | | | |
| ☐ 382 Greg Jackson | .05 | .02 | .01 |
| New York Giants | | | |
| ☐ 383 Steve Bono | .15 | .07 | .02 |
| San Francisco 49ers | | | |
| ☐ 384 Terrell Buckley | .10 | .05 | .01 |
| Green Bay Packers | | | |
| ☐ 385 Garrison Hearst | .35 | .16 | .04 |
| Phoenix Cardinals | | | |
| ☐ 386 Mike Brim | .05 | .02 | .01 |
| Cincinnati Bengals | | | |
| ☐ 387 Jesse Sapolu | .05 | .02 | .01 |
| San Francisco 49ers | | | |
| ☐ 388 Carl Lee | .05 | .02 | .01 |
| Minnesota Vikings | | | |
| ☐ 389 Jeff Cross | .05 | .02 | .01 |
| Miami Dolphins | | | |
| ☐ 390 Karl Mecklenburg | .05 | .02 | .01 |
| Denver Broncos | | | |
| ☐ 391 Chad Hennings | .05 | .02 | .01 |
| Dallas Cowboys | | | |
| ☐ 392 Oliver Barnett | .05 | .02 | .01 |
| Buffalo Bills | | | |
| ☐ 393 Dalton Hilliard | .05 | .02 | .01 |
| New Orleans Saints | | | |
| ☐ 394 Broderick Thompson | .05 | .02 | .01 |
| Tampa Bay Buccaneers | | | |
| ☐ 395 Raghib Ismail | .40 | .18 | .05 |
| Los Angeles Raiders | | | |
| ☐ 396 John Kidd | .05 | .02 | .01 |
| San Diego Chargers | | | |
| ☐ 397 Eddie Anderson | .05 | .02 | .01 |
| Los Angeles Raiders | | | |
| ☐ 398 Lamar Lathon | .05 | .02 | .01 |
| Houston Oilers | | | |
| ☐ 399 Darren Perry | .05 | .02 | .01 |
| Pittsburgh Steelers | | | |
| ☐ 400 Drew Bledsoe | 1.25 | .55 | .16 |
| New England Patriots | | | |
| ☐ 401 Ferrell Edmunds | .05 | .02 | .01 |
| Seattle Seahawks | | | |
| ☐ 402 Lomas Brown | .05 | .02 | .01 |
| Detroit Lions | | | |
| ☐ 403 Drew Hill | .08 | .04 | .01 |
| Atlanta Falcons | | | |
| ☐ 404 David Whitmore | .05 | .02 | .01 |
| Kansas City Chiefs | | | |
| ☐ 405 Mike Johnson | .05 | .02 | .01 |
| Cleveland Browns | | | |
| ☐ 406 Paul Gruber | .05 | .02 | .01 |
| Tampa Bay Buccaneers | | | |
| ☐ 407 Kirk Lowdermilk | .05 | .02 | .01 |
| Indianapolis Colts | | | |
| ☐ 408 Curtis Conway | .25 | .11 | .03 |
| Chicago Bears | | | |
| ☐ 409 Bryce Paup | .05 | .02 | .01 |
| Green Bay Packers | | | |
| ☐ 410 Boomer Esiason | .10 | .05 | .01 |
| New York Jets | | | |
| ☐ 411 Jay Schroeder | .05 | .02 | .01 |
| Cincinnati Bengals | | | |
| ☐ 412 Anthony Newman | .05 | .02 | .01 |
| Los Angeles Rams | | | |
| ☐ 413 Ernie Jones | .05 | .02 | .01 |
| Phoenix Cardinals | | | |
| ☐ 414 Carlton Bailey | .05 | .02 | .01 |
| New York Giants | | | |
| ☐ 415 Kenneth Gant | .05 | .02 | .01 |
| Dallas Cowboys | | | |
| ☐ 416 Todd Scott | .05 | .02 | .01 |
| Minnesota Vikings | | | |
| ☐ 417 Anthony Smith | .05 | .02 | .01 |
| Los Angeles Raiders | | | |
| ☐ 418 Erik McMillan | .05 | .02 | .01 |
| Philadelphia Eagles | | | |
| ☐ 419 Ronnie Harmon | .05 | .02 | .01 |
| San Diego Chargers | | | |
| ☐ 420 Andre Reed | .10 | .05 | .01 |
| Buffalo Bills | | | |
| ☐ 421 Wymon Henderson | .05 | .02 | .01 |
| Denver Broncos | | | |
| ☐ 422 Carnell Lake | .05 | .02 | .01 |
| Pittsburgh Steelers | | | |
| ☐ 423 Al Noga | .05 | .02 | .01 |
| Washington Redskins | | | |
| ☐ 424 Curtis Duncan | .05 | .02 | .01 |
| Houston Oilers | | | |
| ☐ 425 Mike Gann | .05 | .02 | .01 |
| Atlanta Falcons | | | |
| ☐ 426 Eugene Robinson | .05 | .02 | .01 |
| Seattle Seahawks | | | |
| ☐ 427 Scott Mersereau | .05 | .02 | .01 |
| New York Jets | | | |
| ☐ 428 Chris Singleton | .05 | .02 | .01 |
| New England Patriots | | | |
| ☐ 429 Gerald Robinson | .05 | .02 | .01 |
| Los Angeles Raiders | | | |
| ☐ 430 Pat Swilling | .08 | .04 | .01 |
| Detroit Lions | | | |
| ☐ 431 Ed McCaffrey | .05 | .02 | .01 |
| New York Giants | | | |
| ☐ 432 Neal Anderson | .08 | .04 | .01 |
| Cincinnati Bengals | | | |
| ☐ 433 Joe Phillips | .05 | .02 | .01 |
| Kansas City Chiefs | | | |
| ☐ 434 Jerry Ball | .05 | .02 | .01 |
| Cleveland Browns | | | |
| ☐ 435 Tyrone Stowe | .05 | .02 | .01 |
| Phoenix Cardinals | | | |
| ☐ 436 Dana Stubblefield | .25 | .11 | .03 |
| San Francisco 49ers | | | |
| ☐ 437 Eric Curry | .15 | .07 | .02 |
| Tampa Bay Buccaneers | | | |
| ☐ 438 Derrick Fenner | .05 | .02 | .01 |
| Cincinnati Bengals | | | |
| ☐ 439 Mark Clayton | .05 | .02 | .01 |
| Green Bay Packers | | | |
| ☐ 440 Quentin Coryatt | .10 | .05 | .01 |
| Indianapolis Colts | | | |
| ☐ 441 Willie Roaf | .10 | .05 | .01 |
| New Orleans Saints | | | |
| ☐ 442 Ernest Dye | .05 | .02 | .01 |
| Phoenix Cardinals | | | |
| ☐ 443 Jeff Jaeger | .05 | .02 | .01 |
| Los Angeles Rams | | | |
| ☐ 444 Stan Humphries | .10 | .05 | .01 |
| San Diego Chargers | | | |
| ☐ 445 Johnny Johnson | .10 | .05 | .01 |
| New York Jets | | | |
| ☐ 446 Larry Brown | .05 | .02 | .01 |
| Dallas Cowboys | | | |
| ☐ 447 Kurt Gouveia | .05 | .02 | .01 |
| Washington Redskins | | | |
| ☐ 448 Qadry Ismail | .50 | .23 | .06 |
| Minnesota Vikings | | | |
| ☐ 449 Dan Footman | .05 | .02 | .01 |
| Cleveland Browns | | | |
| ☐ 450 Tom Waddle | .10 | .05 | .01 |
| Cincinnati Bengals | | | |
| ☐ 451 Kelvin Martin | .05 | .02 | .01 |
| Seattle Seahawks | | | |
| ☐ 452 Kanavis McGhee | .05 | .02 | .01 |
| New York Giants | | | |
| ☐ 453 Herman Moore | .35 | .16 | .04 |
| Detroit Lions | | | |
| ☐ 454 Jesse Solomon | .05 | .02 | .01 |
| Atlanta Falcons | | | |
| ☐ 455 Shane Conlan | .05 | .02 | .01 |
| Buffalo Bills | | | |
| ☐ 456 Joel Steed | .05 | .02 | .01 |
| Pittsburgh Steelers | | | |
| ☐ 457 Charles Arbuckle | .05 | .02 | .01 |
| Indianapolis Colts | | | |
| ☐ 458 Shane Dronett | .05 | .02 | .01 |
| Denver Broncos | | | |
| ☐ 459 Steve Tasker | .05 | .02 | .01 |
| Buffalo Bills | | | |
| ☐ 460 Herschel Walker | .10 | .05 | .01 |
| Philadelphia Eagles | | | |
| ☐ 461 Willie Davis | .10 | .05 | .01 |
| Kansas City Chiefs | | | |
| ☐ 462 Al Smith | .05 | .02 | .01 |
| Houston Oilers | | | |
| ☐ 463 O.J. McDuffie | .50 | .23 | .06 |
| Miami Dolphins | | | |
| ☐ 464 Kevin Fagan | .05 | .02 | .01 |
| San Francisco 49ers | | | |
| ☐ 465 Hardy Nickerson | .05 | .02 | .01 |

Tampa Bay Buccaneers

| | | | |
|---|---|---|---|
| ☐ 466 Leonard Marshall | .05 | .02 | .01 |

New York Jets

| | | | |
|---|---|---|---|
| ☐ 467 John Baylor | .05 | .02 | .01 |

Indianapolis Colts

| | | | |
|---|---|---|---|
| ☐ 468 Jay Novacek | .10 | .05 | .01 |

Dallas Cowboys

| | | | |
|---|---|---|---|
| ☐ 469 Wayne Simmons | .10 | .05 | .01 |

Green Bay Packers

| | | | |
|---|---|---|---|
| ☐ 470 Tommy Vardell | .08 | .04 | .01 |

Cleveland Browns

| | | | |
|---|---|---|---|
| ☐ 471 Cleveland Gary | .08 | .04 | .01 |

Los Angeles Rams

| | | | |
|---|---|---|---|
| ☐ 472 Mark Collins | .05 | .02 | .01 |

New York Giants

| | | | |
|---|---|---|---|
| ☐ 473 Craig Heyward | .05 | .02 | .01 |

Chicago Bears

| | | | |
|---|---|---|---|
| ☐ 474 John Copeland UER | .10 | .05 | .01 |

Cincinnati Bengals
(Bio states he was born 0-29-70
instead of 9-29-70)

| | | | |
|---|---|---|---|
| ☐ 475 Jeff Hostetler | .10 | .05 | .01 |

Los Angeles Raiders

| | | | |
|---|---|---|---|
| ☐ 476 Brian Mitchell | .08 | .04 | .01 |

Washington Redskins

| | | | |
|---|---|---|---|
| ☐ 477 Natrone Means | .50 | .23 | .06 |

San Diego Chargers

| | | | |
|---|---|---|---|
| ☐ 478 Brad Muster | .08 | .04 | .01 |

New Orleans Saints

| | | | |
|---|---|---|---|
| ☐ 479 David Lutz | .05 | .02 | .01 |

Detroit Lions

| | | | |
|---|---|---|---|
| ☐ 480 Andre Rison | .25 | .11 | .03 |

Atlanta Falcons

| | | | |
|---|---|---|---|
| ☐ 481 Michael Zordich | .05 | .02 | .01 |

Phoenix Cardinals

| | | | |
|---|---|---|---|
| ☐ 482 Jim McMahon | .10 | .05 | .01 |

Minnesota Vikings

| | | | |
|---|---|---|---|
| ☐ 483 Carlton Gray | .05 | .02 | .01 |

Seattle Seahawks

| | | | |
|---|---|---|---|
| ☐ 484 Chris Mohr | .05 | .02 | .01 |

Buffalo Bills

| | | | |
|---|---|---|---|
| ☐ 485 Ernest Givins | .08 | .04 | .01 |

Houston Oilers

| | | | |
|---|---|---|---|
| ☐ 486 Tony Tolbert | .05 | .02 | .01 |

Dallas Cowboys

| | | | |
|---|---|---|---|
| ☐ 487 Vai Sikahema | .05 | .02 | .01 |

Phoenix Cardinals

| | | | |
|---|---|---|---|
| ☐ 488 Larry Webster | .05 | .02 | .01 |

Miami Dolphins

| | | | |
|---|---|---|---|
| ☐ 489 James Hasty | .05 | .02 | .01 |

New York Jets

| | | | |
|---|---|---|---|
| ☐ 490 Reggie White | .15 | .07 | .02 |

Green Bay Packers

| | | | |
|---|---|---|---|
| ☐ 491 Reggie Rivers | .20 | .09 | .03 |

Denver Broncos

| | | | |
|---|---|---|---|
| ☐ 492 Roman Phifer | .05 | .02 | .01 |

Los Angeles Raiders

| | | | |
|---|---|---|---|
| ☐ 493 Levon Kirkland | .05 | .02 | .01 |

Pittsburgh Steelers

| | | | |
|---|---|---|---|
| ☐ 494 Demetrius DuBose | .10 | .05 | .01 |

Tampa Bay Buccaneers

| | | | |
|---|---|---|---|
| ☐ 495 William Perry | .05 | .02 | .01 |

Chicago Bears

| | | | |
|---|---|---|---|
| ☐ 496 Clay Matthews | .08 | .04 | .01 |

Cleveland Browns

| | | | |
|---|---|---|---|
| ☐ 497 Aaron Jones | .05 | .02 | .01 |

New England Patriots

| | | | |
|---|---|---|---|
| ☐ 498 Jack Trudeau | .05 | .02 | .01 |

Indianapolis Colts

| | | | |
|---|---|---|---|
| ☐ 499 Michael Brooks | .05 | .02 | .01 |

New York Giants

| | | | |
|---|---|---|---|
| ☐ 500 Jerry Rice | .50 | .23 | .06 |

San Francisco 49ers

| | | | |
|---|---|---|---|
| ☐ 501 Lonnie Marts | .05 | .02 | .01 |

Kansas City Chiefs

| | | | |
|---|---|---|---|
| ☐ 502 Tim McGee | .05 | .02 | .01 |

Washington Redskins

| | | | |
|---|---|---|---|
| ☐ 503 Kelvin Pritchett | .05 | .02 | .01 |

Detroit Lions

| | | | |
|---|---|---|---|
| ☐ 504 Bobby Hebert | .10 | .05 | .01 |

Atlanta Falcons

| | | | |
|---|---|---|---|
| ☐ 505 Audray McMillian | .05 | .02 | .01 |

Minnesota Vikings

| | | | |
|---|---|---|---|
| ☐ 506 Chuck Cecil | .05 | .02 | .01 |

Phoenix Cardinals

| | | | |
|---|---|---|---|
| ☐ 507 Leonard Renfro | .05 | .02 | .01 |

Philadelphia Eagles

| | | | |
|---|---|---|---|
| ☐ 508 Ethan Horton | .05 | .02 | .01 |

Los Angeles Raiders

| | | | |
|---|---|---|---|
| ☐ 509 Kevin Smith | .08 | .04 | .01 |

Dallas Cowboys

| | | | |
|---|---|---|---|
| ☐ 510 Louis Oliver | .05 | .02 | .01 |

Miami Dolphins

| | | | |
|---|---|---|---|
| ☐ 511 John Stephens | .05 | .02 | .01 |

Green Bay Packers

| | | | |
|---|---|---|---|
| ☐ 512 Browning Nagle | .08 | .04 | .01 |

New York Jets

| | | | |
|---|---|---|---|
| ☐ 513 Ricardo McDonald | .05 | .02 | .01 |

Cincinnati Bengals

| | | | |
|---|---|---|---|
| ☐ 514 Leslie O'Neal | .08 | .04 | .01 |

San Diego Chargers

| | | | |
|---|---|---|---|
| ☐ 515 Lorenzo White | .08 | .04 | .01 |

Houston Oilers

| | | | |
|---|---|---|---|
| ☐ 516 Thomas Smith | .10 | .05 | .01 |

Buffalo Bills

| | | | |
|---|---|---|---|
| ☐ 517 Tony Woods | .05 | .02 | .01 |

Seattle Seahawks

| | | | |
|---|---|---|---|
| ☐ 518 Darryl Henley | .05 | .02 | .01 |

Los Angeles Rams

| | | | |
|---|---|---|---|
| ☐ 519 Robert Delpino | .08 | .04 | .01 |

Denver Broncos

| | | | |
|---|---|---|---|
| ☐ 520 Rod Woodson | .10 | .05 | .01 |

Pittsburgh Steelers

| | | | |
|---|---|---|---|
| ☐ 521 Phillippi Sparks | .05 | .02 | .01 |

New York Giants

| | | | |
|---|---|---|---|
| ☐ 522 Jessie Hester | .05 | .02 | .01 |

Indianapolis Colts

| | | | |
|---|---|---|---|
| ☐ 523 Shaun Gayle | .05 | .02 | .01 |

Chicago Bears

| | | | |
|---|---|---|---|
| ☐ 524 Brad Edwards | .05 | .02 | .01 |

Washington Redskins

| | | | |
|---|---|---|---|
| ☐ 525 Randall Cunningham | .10 | .05 | .01 |

Philadelphia Eagles

| | | | |
|---|---|---|---|
| ☐ 526 Marv Cook | .05 | .02 | .01 |

New England Patriots

| | | | |
|---|---|---|---|
| ☐ 527 Dennis Gibson | .05 | .02 | .01 |

Detroit Lions

| | | | |
|---|---|---|---|
| ☐ 528 Erric Pegram | .25 | .11 | .03 |

Atlanta Falcons

| | | | |
|---|---|---|---|
| ☐ 529 Terry McDaniel | .05 | .02 | .01 |

Los Angeles Raiders

| | | | |
|---|---|---|---|
| ☐ 530 Troy Aikman | 1.25 | .55 | .16 |

Dallas Cowboys

| | | | |
|---|---|---|---|
| ☐ 531 Irving Fryar | .05 | .02 | .01 |

Miami Dolphins

| | | | |
|---|---|---|---|
| ☐ 532 Blair Thomas | .08 | .04 | .01 |

New York Jets

| | | | |
|---|---|---|---|
| ☐ 533 Jim Wilks | .05 | .02 | .01 |

New Orleans Saints

| | | | |
|---|---|---|---|
| ☐ 534 Michael Jackson | .10 | .05 | .01 |

Cleveland Browns

| | | | |
|---|---|---|---|
| ☐ 535 Eric Davis | .05 | .02 | .01 |

San Francisco 49ers

| | | | |
|---|---|---|---|
| ☐ 536 James Campen | .05 | .02 | .01 |

Green Bay Packers

| | | | |
|---|---|---|---|
| ☐ 537 Steve Beuerlein | .15 | .07 | .02 |

Phoenix Cardinals

| | | | |
|---|---|---|---|
| ☐ 538 Robert Smith | .15 | .07 | .02 |

Minnesota Vikings

| | | | |
|---|---|---|---|
| ☐ 539 J.J. Birden | .08 | .04 | .01 |

Kansas City Chiefs

| | | | |
|---|---|---|---|
| ☐ 540 Broderick Thomas | .05 | .02 | .01 |

Tampa Bay Buccaneers

| | | | |
|---|---|---|---|
| ☐ 541 Darryl Talley | .05 | .02 | .01 |

Buffalo Bills

| | | | |
|---|---|---|---|
| ☐ 542 Russell Freeman | .10 | .05 | .01 |

Denver Broncos

| | | | |
|---|---|---|---|
| ☐ 543 David Alexander | .05 | .02 | .01 |

Philadelphia Eagles

| | | | |
|---|---|---|---|
| ☐ 544 Chris Mims | .08 | .04 | .01 |

San Diego Chargers

| | | | |
|---|---|---|---|
| ☐ 545 Coleman Rudolph | .05 | .02 | .01 |

New York Jets

| | | | |
|---|---|---|---|
| ☐ 546 Steve McMichael | .05 | .02 | .01 |

Chicago Bears

| | | | |
|---|---|---|---|
| ☐ 547 David Williams | .05 | .02 | .01 |

Houston Oilers

| | | | |
|---|---|---|---|
| ☐ 548 Chris Hinton | .05 | .02 | .01 |

Indianapolis Colts

| | | | |
|---|---|---|---|
| ☐ 549 Jim Jeffcoat | .05 | .02 | .01 |

Dallas Cowboys

| | | | |
|---|---|---|---|
| ☐ 550 Howie Long | .08 | .04 | .01 |

Los Angeles Raiders

| | | | |
|---|---|---|---|
| ☐ 551 Roosevelt Potts | .25 | .11 | .03 |

Indianapolis Colts

| | | | |
|---|---|---|---|
| ☐ 552 Bryan Cox | .08 | .04 | .01 |

Miami Dolphins

| | | | |
|---|---|---|---|
| ☐ 553 David Richards UER | .05 | .02 | .01 |

Houston Oilers
(Photo on front is Stanley Richards)

| | | | |
|---|---|---|---|
| ☐ 554 Reggie Brooks | .75 | .35 | .09 |

Washington Redskins

| | | | |
|---|---|---|---|
| ☐ 555 Neil O'Donnell | .25 | .11 | .03 |

Pittsburgh Steelers

| | | | |
|---|---|---|---|
| ☐ 556 Irv Smith | .20 | .09 | .03 |

New Orleans Saints

| | | | |
|---|---|---|---|
| ☐ 557 Henry Ellard | .08 | .04 | .01 |

Los Angeles Rams

| | | | |
|---|---|---|---|
| ☐ 558 Steve DeBerg | .08 | .04 | .01 |

Tampa Bay Buccaneers

| | | | |
|---|---|---|---|
| ☐ 559 Jim Sweeney | .05 | .02 | .01 |

New York Jets

| | | | |
|---|---|---|---|
| ☐ 560 Harold Green | .08 | .04 | .01 |

Cleveland Browns

| | | | |
|---|---|---|---|
| ☐ 561 Darrell Thompson | .08 | .04 | .01 |

Green Bay Packers

| | | | |
|---|---|---|---|
| ☐ 562 Vinny Testaverde | .10 | .05 | .01 |
| Cleveland Browns | | | |
| ☐ 563 Bubby Brister | .05 | .02 | .01 |
| Philadelphia Eagles | | | |
| ☐ 564 Sean Landeta | .05 | .02 | .01 |
| New York Giants | | | |
| ☐ 565 Neil Smith | .10 | .05 | .01 |
| Kansas City Chiefs | | | |
| ☐ 566 Craig Erickson | .10 | .05 | .01 |
| Tampa Bay Buccaneers | | | |
| ☐ 567 Jim Ritcher | .05 | .02 | .01 |
| Washington Redskins | | | |
| ☐ 568 Don Mosebar | .05 | .02 | .01 |
| Los Angeles Raiders | | | |
| ☐ 569 John Gesek | .05 | .02 | .01 |
| Dallas Cowboys | | | |
| ☐ 570 Gary Plummer | .05 | .02 | .01 |
| San Diego Chargers | | | |
| ☐ 571 Norm Johnson | .05 | .02 | .01 |
| Atlanta Falcons | | | |
| ☐ 572 Ron Heller | .05 | .02 | .01 |
| Miami Dolphins | | | |
| ☐ 573 Carl Simpson | .05 | .02 | .01 |
| Chicago Bears | | | |
| ☐ 574 Greg Montgomery | .05 | .02 | .01 |
| Houston Oilers | | | |
| ☐ 575 Dana Hall | .05 | .02 | .01 |
| San Francisco 49ers | | | |
| ☐ 576 Vencie Glenn | .05 | .02 | .01 |
| Miami Dolphins | | | |
| ☐ 577 Dean Biasucci | .05 | .02 | .01 |
| Indianapolis Colts | | | |
| ☐ 578 Rod Bernstine UER | .08 | .04 | .01 |
| Denver Broncos | | | |
| (Name spelled Bernstein on front) | | | |
| ☐ 579 Randal Hill | .10 | .05 | .01 |
| Phoenix Cardinals | | | |
| ☐ 580 Sam Mills | .08 | .04 | .01 |
| New Orleans Saints | | | |
| ☐ 581 Santana Dotson | .10 | .05 | .01 |
| Tampa Bay Buccaneers | | | |
| ☐ 582 Greg Lloyd | .05 | .02 | .01 |
| Pittsburgh Steelers | | | |
| ☐ 583 Eric Thomas | .05 | .02 | .01 |
| New York Jets | | | |
| ☐ 584 Henry Rolling | .05 | .02 | .01 |
| Los Angeles Rams | | | |
| ☐ 585 Tony Bennett | .05 | .02 | .01 |
| Green Bay Packers | | | |
| ☐ 586 Sheldon White | .05 | .02 | .01 |
| Cincinnati Bengals | | | |
| ☐ 587 Mark Kelso | .05 | .02 | .01 |
| Buffalo Bills | | | |
| ☐ 588 Marc Spindler | .05 | .02 | .01 |
| Detroit Lions | | | |
| ☐ 589 Greg McMurtry | .05 | .02 | .01 |
| New England Patriots | | | |
| ☐ 590 Art Monk | .10 | .05 | .01 |
| Washington Redskins | | | |
| ☐ 591 Marco Coleman | .08 | .04 | .01 |
| Miami Dolphins | | | |
| ☐ 592 Tony Jones | .05 | .02 | .01 |
| Atlanta Falcons | | | |
| ☐ 593 Melvin Jenkins | .05 | .02 | .01 |
| Atlanta Falcons | | | |
| ☐ 594 Kevin Ross | .05 | .02 | .01 |
| Kansas City Chiefs | | | |
| ☐ 595 William Fuller | .05 | .02 | .01 |
| Houston Oilers | | | |
| ☐ 596 James Joseph | .05 | .02 | .01 |
| Philadelphia Eagles | | | |
| ☐ 597 Lamar McGriggs | .15 | .07 | .02 |
| New York Giants | | | |
| ☐ 598 Gill Byrd | .05 | .02 | .01 |
| San Diego Chargers | | | |
| ☐ 599 Alexander Wright | .08 | .04 | .01 |
| Seattle Seahawks | | | |
| ☐ 600 Rick Mirer | 1.25 | .55 | .16 |
| Seattle Seahawks | | | |
| ☐ 601 Richard Dent | .08 | .04 | .01 |
| Chicago Bears | | | |
| ☐ 602 Thomas Everett | .05 | .02 | .01 |
| Dallas Cowboys | | | |
| ☐ 603 Jack Del Rio | .05 | .02 | .01 |
| Minnesota Vikings | | | |
| ☐ 604 Jerome Bettis | 1.25 | .55 | .16 |
| Los Angeles Rams | | | |
| ☐ 605 Ronnie Lott | .10 | .05 | .01 |
| New York Jets | | | |
| ☐ 606 Marty Carter | .05 | .02 | .01 |
| Tampa Bay Buccaneers | | | |
| ☐ 607 Arthur Marshall | .25 | .11 | .03 |
| Denver Broncos | | | |
| ☐ 608 Lee Johnson | .05 | .02 | .01 |
| Cleveland Browns | | | |
| ☐ 609 Bruce Armstrong | .05 | .02 | .01 |
| New England Patriots | | | |
| ☐ 610 Ricky Proehl | .08 | .04 | .01 |
| Phoenix Cardinals | | | |
| ☐ 611 Will Wolford | .05 | .02 | .01 |
| Buffalo Bills | | | |
| ☐ 612 Mike Prior | .05 | .02 | .01 |
| Indianapolis Colts | | | |
| ☐ 613 George Jamison | .05 | .02 | .01 |
| Detroit Lions | | | |
| ☐ 614 Gene Atkins | .05 | .02 | .01 |
| New Orleans Saints | | | |
| ☐ 615 Merril Hoge | .05 | .02 | .01 |
| Pittsburgh Steelers | | | |
| ☐ 616 Desmond Howard UER | .25 | .11 | .03 |
| Washington Redskins | | | |
| (Stats indicate 8 TD's receiving; | | | |
| he had 0) | | | |
| ☐ 617 Jarvis Williams | .05 | .02 | .01 |
| Miami Dolphins | | | |
| ☐ 618 Marcus Allen | .15 | .07 | .02 |
| Kansas City Chiefs | | | |
| ☐ 619 Gary Brown | .60 | .25 | .08 |
| Houston Oilers | | | |
| ☐ 620 Bill Brooks | .05 | .02 | .01 |
| Buffalo Bills | | | |
| ☐ 621 Eric Allen | .08 | .04 | .01 |
| Philadelphia Eagles | | | |
| ☐ 622 Todd Kelly | .05 | .02 | .01 |
| San Francisco 49ers | | | |
| ☐ 623 Michael Dean Perry | .10 | .05 | .01 |
| Cleveland Browns | | | |
| ☐ 624 David Braxton | .05 | .02 | .01 |
| Phoenix Cardinals | | | |
| ☐ 625 Mike Sherrard | .05 | .02 | .01 |
| New York Giants | | | |
| ☐ 626 Jeff Bryant | .05 | .02 | .01 |
| Seattle Seahawks | | | |
| ☐ 627 Eric Bieniemy | .08 | .04 | .01 |
| San Diego Chargers | | | |
| ☐ 628 Tim Brown | .25 | .11 | .03 |
| Los Angeles Rams | | | |
| ☐ 629 Troy Auzenne | .05 | .02 | .01 |
| Chicago Bears | | | |
| ☐ 630 Michael Irvin | .40 | .18 | .05 |
| Dallas Cowboys | | | |
| ☐ 631 Maurice Hurst | .05 | .02 | .01 |
| New England Patriots | | | |
| ☐ 632 Duane Bickett | .05 | .02 | .01 |
| Indianapolis Colts | | | |
| ☐ 633 George Teague | .05 | .02 | .01 |
| Minnesota Vikings | | | |
| ☐ 634 Vince Workman | .05 | .02 | .01 |
| Tampa Bay Buccaneers | | | |
| ☐ 635 Renaldo Turnbull | .08 | .04 | .01 |
| New Orleans Saints | | | |
| ☐ 636 Johnny Bailey | .05 | .02 | .01 |
| Phoenix Cardinals | | | |
| ☐ 637 Dan Williams | .10 | .05 | .01 |
| Denver Broncos | | | |
| ☐ 638 James Thornton | .05 | .02 | .01 |
| New York Jets | | | |
| ☐ 639 Terry Allen | .10 | .05 | .01 |
| Minnesota Vikings | | | |
| ☐ 640 Kevin Greene | .05 | .02 | .01 |
| Pittsburgh Steelers | | | |
| ☐ 641 Tony Zendejas | .05 | .02 | .01 |
| Los Angeles Rams | | | |
| ☐ 642 Scott Kowalkowski | .10 | .05 | .01 |
| Philadelphia Eagles | | | |
| ☐ 643 Jeff Query UER | .05 | .02 | .01 |
| Cleveland Browns | | | |
| (Text states he played for Packers | | | |
| in `92; he played for Bengals) | | | |
| ☐ 644 Brian Blades | .08 | .04 | .01 |
| Seattle Seahawks | | | |
| ☐ 645 Keith Jackson | .10 | .05 | .01 |
| Miami Dolphins | | | |
| ☐ 646 Monte Coleman | .05 | .02 | .01 |
| Miami Dolphins | | | |
| ☐ 647 Guy McIntyre | .05 | .02 | .01 |
| San Francisco 49ers | | | |
| ☐ 648 Barry Word | .10 | .05 | .01 |
| Minnesota Vikings | | | |
| ☐ 649 Steve Everitt | .10 | .05 | .01 |
| Cleveland Browns | | | |
| ☐ 650 Patrick Bates | .05 | .02 | .01 |
| Los Angeles Raiders | | | |
| ☐ 651 Marcus Robertson | .15 | .07 | .02 |
| Houston Oilers | | | |
| ☐ 652 John Carney | .05 | .02 | .01 |
| San Diego Chargers | | | |
| ☐ 653 Derek Brown | .08 | .04 | .01 |
| New York Giants | | | |
| ☐ 654 Carwell Gardner | .05 | .02 | .01 |
| Buffalo Bills | | | |
| ☐ 655 Moe Gardner | .05 | .02 | .01 |
| Atlanta Falcons | | | |
| ☐ 656 Andre Ware | .08 | .04 | .01 |

| | | MINT | EXC | G-VG |
|---|---|---|---|---|
| | Detroit Lions | | | |
| ☐ 657 Keith Van Horne | | .05 | .02 | .01 |
| | Chicago Bears | | | |
| ☐ 658 Hugh Millen | | .05 | .02 | .01 |
| | Dallas Cowboys | | | |
| ☐ 659 Checklist 330-495 | | .05 | .02 | .01 |
| ☐ 660 Checklist 496-660 | | .05 | .02 | .01 |

## 1993 Topps Black Gold

One Topps Black Gold card was inserted in approximately every 48 packs of 1993 Topps football. Card numbers 1-22 were randomly inserted in first series wax packs while card numbers 23-44 were featured in second series packs. Collectors could obtain the set by collecting individual random insert cards or receive 11, 22, or 44 Black Gold cards through the mail by sending in special "You've Just Won" cards, entitling the holder to receive Group A (1-11), Group B (12-22), or Groups A and B (1-22). Likewise, four "You've Just Won" cards were inserted in second series packs and entitled the holder to receive Group C (23-33), Group D (34-44), Groups C and D (23-44), or Groups A-D (1-44). As a bonus for mailing in the special cards, the collector received a special "You've Just Won" and a congratulatory letter notifying the collector that his/her name has been entered into a drawing for one of 500 uncut sheets of all 44 Topps Black Gold cards in a leatherette frame. Inside a white border, the fronts feature color action player photos that are edged above and below by a gold foil screened background. Each of these gold foil areas is curved, and in the bottom one appears a black stripe carrying the player's name. Showing a black-and-white pinstripe background inside a white border, the horizontal backs carry a color close-up cut-out and, on a greenish-blue panel, career summary. The first series cards are numbered on the back "X of 22."

| | MINT | EXC | G-VG |
|---|---|---|---|
| COMPLETE SET (44) | 30.00 | 13.50 | 3.80 |
| COMPLETE SERIES 1 (22) | 14.00 | 6.25 | 1.75 |
| COMPLETE SERIES 2 (22) | 16.00 | 7.25 | 2.00 |
| COMMON PLAYER (1-22) | .50 | .23 | .06 |
| COMMON PLAYER (23-44) | .50 | .23 | .06 |

| | | | |
|---|---|---|---|
| ☐ 1 Kelvin Martin | .50 | .23 | .06 |
| Seattle Seahawks | | | |
| ☐ 2 Audray McMillian | .50 | .23 | .06 |
| Minnesota Vikings | | | |
| ☐ 3 Terry Allen | .50 | .23 | .06 |
| Minnesota Vikings | | | |
| ☐ 4 Vai Sikahema | .50 | .23 | .06 |
| Philadelphia Eagles | | | |
| ☐ 5 Clyde Simmons | .60 | .25 | .08 |
| Philadelphia Eagles | | | |
| ☐ 6 Lorenzo White | .60 | .25 | .08 |
| Houston Oilers | | | |
| ☐ 7 Michael Irvin | 2.50 | 1.15 | .30 |
| Dallas Cowboys | | | |
| ☐ 8 Troy Aikman | 6.00 | 2.70 | .75 |
| Dallas Cowboys | | | |
| ☐ 9 Mark Kelso | .50 | .23 | .06 |
| Buffalo Bills | | | |
| ☐ 10 Cleveland Gary | .60 | .25 | .08 |
| Los Angeles Rams | | | |
| ☐ 11 Greg Montgomery | .50 | .23 | .06 |
| Houston Oilers | | | |
| ☐ 12 Jerry Rice | 3.00 | 1.35 | .40 |
| San Francisco 49ers | | | |
| ☐ 13 Rod Woodson | .75 | .35 | .09 |
| Pittsburgh Steelers | | | |
| ☐ 14 Leslie O'Neal | .50 | .23 | .06 |
| San Diego Chargers | | | |
| ☐ 15 Harold Green | .75 | .35 | .09 |
| Cincinnati Bengals | | | |
| ☐ 16 Randall Cunningham | .50 | .23 | .06 |

| | | | |
|---|---|---|---|
| | Philadelphia Eagles | | | |
| ☐ 17 Ricky Watters | 2.00 | .90 | .25 |
| San Francisco 49ers | | | |
| ☐ 18 Andre Rison | 1.00 | .45 | .13 |
| Atlanta Falcons | | | |
| ☐ 19 Eugene Robinson | .50 | .23 | .06 |
| Seattle Seahawks | | | |
| ☐ 20 Wayne Martin | .50 | .23 | .06 |
| New Orleans Saints | | | |
| ☐ 21 Chris Warren | .60 | .25 | .08 |
| Seattle Seahawks | | | |
| ☐ 22 Anthony Miller | 1.00 | .45 | .13 |
| San Diego Chargers | | | |
| ☐ 23 Steve Young | 1.25 | .55 | .16 |
| San Francisco 49ers | | | |
| ☐ 24 Tim Harris | .50 | .23 | .06 |
| San Francisco 49ers | | | |
| ☐ 25 Emmitt Smith | 8.00 | 3.60 | 1.00 |
| Dallas Cowboys | | | |
| ☐ 26 Sterling Sharpe | 2.50 | 1.15 | .30 |
| Green Bay Packers | | | |
| ☐ 27 Henry Jones | .50 | .23 | .06 |
| Buffalo Bills | | | |
| ☐ 28 Warren Moon | .75 | .35 | .09 |
| Houston Oilers | | | |
| ☐ 29 Barry Foster | 1.25 | .55 | .16 |
| Detroit Lions | | | |
| ☐ 30 Dale Carter | .50 | .23 | .06 |
| Kansas City Chiefs | | | |
| ☐ 31 Mel Gray | .50 | .23 | .06 |
| Detroit Lions | | | |
| ☐ 32 Barry Sanders | 3.00 | 1.35 | .40 |
| Detroit Lions | | | |
| ☐ 33 Dan Marino | 4.00 | 1.80 | .50 |
| Miami Dolphins | | | |
| ☐ 34 Fred Barnett | .50 | .23 | .06 |
| Philadelphia Eagles | | | |
| ☐ 35 Deion Sanders | 1.00 | .45 | .13 |
| Atlanta Falcons | | | |
| ☐ 36 Simon Fletcher | .50 | .23 | .06 |
| Denver Broncos | | | |
| ☐ 37 Donnell Woolford | .50 | .23 | .06 |
| Chicago Bears | | | |
| ☐ 38 Reggie Cobb | .50 | .23 | .06 |
| Tampa Bay Buccaneers | | | |
| ☐ 39 Brett Favre | 3.00 | 1.35 | .40 |
| Green Bay Packers | | | |
| ☐ 40 Thurman Thomas | 2.25 | 1.00 | .30 |
| Buffalo Bills | | | |
| ☐ 41 Rodney Hampton | 1.50 | .65 | .19 |
| New York Giants | | | |
| ☐ 42 Eric Martin | .50 | .23 | .06 |
| New Orleans Saints | | | |
| ☐ 43 Pete Stoyanovich | .50 | .23 | .06 |
| Miami Dolphins | | | |
| ☐ 44 Herschel Walker | .50 | .23 | .06 |
| Philadelphia Eagles | | | |
| ☐ A Winner A 1-11 | 2.00 | .90 | .25 |
| ☐ AB Winner AB 1-22 | 3.00 | 1.35 | .40 |
| ☐ B Winner B 12-22 UER | 2.00 | .90 | .25 |
| (Card No. 17 listed as | | | |
| Herschel Walker instead of Ricky Watters) | | | |
| ☐ C Winner C 23-33 | 2.00 | .90 | .25 |
| ☐ CD Winner C/D 23-44 | 3.00 | 1.35 | .40 |
| ☐ D Winner D 34-44 | 2.00 | .90 | .25 |

## 1993 Topps FantaSports

According to Topps, this was the first interactive Fantasy game that incorporated trading cards as a key playing element. The set of 200 cards was provided that featured key players. The card backs carried graphs of the players' three-year performances on all FantaSports criteria, comparisons with other players in that position, and scouting reports. The cards were used by contestants to make draft choices and trades throughout the season. The cost of playing the game was 159.00. Included were the cards, entry into the league, stat book, worksheets, and instructions. The person who earned the best 18-game NFL fantasy score won four tickets to Super Bowl XXVIII. The game was test-marketed in four cities (Houston, Kansas City, Buffalo, and Washington D.C.) and the cards were not offered at retail in those cities. The black-bordered 3" by 5" cards feature color player action shots on their fronts. The player's name and team appears in black lettering within gold-foil stripes at the bottom. The set's title appears in gold foil within the upper margin. The horizontal white back carries a color action player photo on the right, with the player's name, position, team, three-year performance graphs, and scouting report shown on the left. The cards are numbered on the back arranged by position, quarterbacks (1-30), running backs (31-89), wide receivers (90-137), tight ends (138-150), kickers (151-162), punters (163-172), and defensive players (173-200).

| | MINT | EXC | G-VG |
|---|---|---|---|
| COMPLETE SET (200) | 125.00 | 50.00 | 12.50 |
| COMMON PLAYER (1-200) | .50 | .20 | .05 |

| | | MINT | EXC | G-VG |
|---|---|---|---|---|
| ☐ 1 | Chris Miller<br>Atlanta Falcons | 1.00 | .40 | .10 |
| ☐ 2 | Jim Kelly<br>Buffalo Bills | 2.50 | 1.00 | .25 |
| ☐ 3 | Jim Harbaugh<br>Chicago Bears | .75 | .30 | .07 |
| ☐ 4 | David Klingler<br>Cincinnati Bengals | 1.00 | .40 | .10 |
| ☐ 5 | Bernie Kosar<br>Cleveland Browns | 1.25 | .50 | .12 |
| ☐ 6 | Troy Aikman<br>Dallas Cowboys | 7.50 | 3.00 | .75 |
| ☐ 7 | John Elway<br>Denver Broncos | 5.00 | 2.00 | .50 |
| ☐ 8 | Tommy Maddox<br>Denver Broncos | 1.00 | .40 | .10 |
| ☐ 9 | Rodney Peete<br>Detroit Lions | .75 | .30 | .07 |
| ☐ 10 | Andre Ware<br>Detroit Lions | .75 | .30 | .07 |
| ☐ 11 | Brett Favre<br>Green Bay Packers | 3.00 | 1.20 | .30 |
| ☐ 12 | Warren Moon<br>Houston Oilers | 3.00 | 1.20 | .30 |
| ☐ 13 | Jeff George<br>Indianapolis Colts | 2.50 | 1.00 | .25 |
| ☐ 14 | Dave Krieg<br>Kansas City Chiefs | .75 | .30 | .07 |
| ☐ 15 | Joe Montana<br>Kansas City Chiefs | 7.50 | 3.00 | .75 |
| ☐ 16 | Todd Marinovich<br>Los Angeles Raiders | .50 | .20 | .05 |
| ☐ 17 | Jim Everett<br>Los Angeles Rams | 1.00 | .40 | .10 |
| ☐ 18 | Dan Marino<br>Miami Dolphins | 7.50 | 3.00 | .75 |
| ☐ 19 | Sean Salisbury<br>Minnesota Vikings | .50 | .20 | .05 |
| ☐ 20 | Drew Bledsoe<br>New England Patriots | 7.50 | 3.00 | .75 |
| ☐ 21 | Dave Brown<br>New York Giants | 2.00 | .80 | .20 |
| ☐ 22 | Phil Simms<br>New York Giants | 2.00 | .80 | .20 |
| ☐ 23 | Boomer Esiason<br>New York Jets | 1.00 | .40 | .10 |
| ☐ 24 | Browning Nagle<br>New York Jets | .75 | .30 | .07 |
| ☐ 25 | Randall Cunningham<br>Philadelphia Eagles | 2.50 | 1.00 | .25 |
| ☐ 26 | Neil O'Donnell<br>Pittsburgh Steelers | 1.50 | .60 | .15 |
| ☐ 27 | Stan Humphries<br>San Diego Chargers | 1.00 | .40 | .10 |
| ☐ 28 | Steve Young<br>San Francisco 49ers | 4.00 | 1.60 | .40 |
| ☐ 29 | Rick Mirer<br>Seattle Seahawks | 7.50 | 3.00 | .75 |
| ☐ 30 | Mark Rypien<br>Washington Redskins | .75 | .30 | .07 |
| ☐ 31 | Kenneth Davis<br>Buffalo Bills | .75 | .30 | .07 |
| ☐ 32 | Thurman Thomas<br>Buffalo Bills | 2.50 | 1.00 | .25 |
| ☐ 33 | Steve Broussard<br>Atlanta Falcons | .50 | .20 | .05 |
| ☐ 34 | Neal Anderson<br>Chicago Bears | .75 | .30 | .07 |
| ☐ 35 | Craig Heyward<br>Chicago Bears | .50 | .20 | .05 |
| ☐ 36 | Derrick Fenner | .50 | .20 | .05 |

| | | MINT | EXC | G-VG |
|---|---|---|---|---|
| ☐ 37 | Harold Green<br>Cincinnati Bengals | .75 | .30 | .07 |
| ☐ 38 | Leroy Hoard<br>Cincinnati Bengals | .50 | .20 | .05 |
| ☐ 39 | Kevin Mack<br>Cleveland Browns | .50 | .20 | .05 |
| ☐ 40 | Eric Metcalf<br>Cleveland Browns | 1.00 | .40 | .10 |
| ☐ 41 | Tommy Vardell<br>Cleveland Browns | 1.00 | .40 | .10 |
| ☐ 42 | Daryl Johnston<br>Dallas Cowboys | 1.00 | .40 | .10 |
| ☐ 43 | Emmitt Smith<br>Dallas Cowboys | 7.50 | 3.00 | .75 |
| ☐ 44 | Barry Sanders<br>Detroit Lions | 5.00 | 2.00 | .50 |
| ☐ 45 | Edgar Bennett<br>Green Bay Packers | 1.00 | .40 | .10 |
| ☐ 46 | Lorenzo White<br>Houston Oilers | .75 | .30 | .07 |
| ☐ 47 | Anthony Johnson<br>Indianapolis Colts | .50 | .20 | .05 |
| ☐ 48 | Todd McNair<br>Kansas City Chiefs | .50 | .20 | .05 |
| ☐ 49 | Christian Okoye<br>Kansas City Chiefs | .75 | .30 | .07 |
| ☐ 50 | Harvey Williams<br>Kansas City Chiefs | .75 | .30 | .07 |
| ☐ 51 | Barry Word<br>Kansas City Chiefs | .50 | .20 | .05 |
| ☐ 52 | Nick Bell<br>Los Angeles Raiders | .75 | .30 | .07 |
| ☐ 53 | Eric Dickerson<br>Los Angeles Raiders | 1.00 | .40 | .10 |
| ☐ 54 | Jerome Bettis<br>Los Angeles Rams | 7.50 | 3.00 | .75 |
| ☐ 55 | Cleveland Gary<br>Los Angeles Rams | .50 | .20 | .05 |
| ☐ 56 | Mark Higgs<br>Miami Dolphins | .75 | .30 | .07 |
| ☐ 57 | Tony Paige<br>Miami Dolphins | .50 | .20 | .05 |
| ☐ 58 | Terry Allen<br>Minnesota Vikings | .75 | .30 | .07 |
| ☐ 59 | Roger Craig<br>Minnesota Vikings | .75 | .30 | .07 |
| ☐ 60 | Robert Smith<br>Minnesota Vikings | 1.00 | .40 | .10 |
| ☐ 61 | Leonard Russell<br>New England Patriots | 1.00 | .40 | .10 |
| ☐ 62 | Jon Vaughn<br>New England Patriots | .75 | .30 | .07 |
| ☐ 63 | Vaughn Dunbar<br>New Orleans Saints | .75 | .30 | .07 |
| ☐ 64 | Dalton Hilliard<br>New Orleans Saints | .50 | .20 | .05 |
| ☐ 65 | Jarrod Bunch<br>New York Giants | .50 | .20 | .05 |
| ☐ 66 | Rodney Hampton<br>New York Giants | 2.00 | .80 | .20 |
| ☐ 67 | Dave Meggett<br>New York Giants | .75 | .30 | .07 |
| ☐ 68 | Brad Baxter<br>New York Jets | .75 | .30 | .07 |
| ☐ 69 | Heath Sherman<br>Philadelphia Eagles | .50 | .20 | .05 |
| ☐ 70 | Vai Sikahema<br>Philadelphia Eagles | .50 | .20 | .05 |
| ☐ 71 | Johnny Bailey<br>Phoenix Cardinals | .50 | .20 | .05 |
| ☐ 72 | Larry Centers<br>Phoenix Cardinals | .50 | .20 | .05 |
| ☐ 73 | Garrison Hearst<br>Phoenix Cardinals | 1.50 | .60 | .15 |
| ☐ 74 | Barry Foster<br>Pittsburgh Steelers | 1.50 | .60 | .15 |
| ☐ 75 | Eric Bieniemy<br>San Diego Chargers | .50 | .20 | .05 |
| ☐ 76 | Marion Butts<br>San Diego Chargers | 1.00 | .40 | .10 |
| ☐ 77 | Ronnie Harmon<br>San Diego Chargers | .50 | .20 | .05 |
| ☐ 78 | Natrone Means<br>San Diego Chargers | 2.50 | 1.00 | .25 |
| ☐ 79 | Amp Lee<br>San Francisco 49ers | .75 | .30 | .07 |
| ☐ 80 | Tom Rathman<br>San Francisco 49ers | .75 | .30 | .07 |
| ☐ 81 | Ricky Watters<br>San Francisco 49ers | 2.00 | .80 | .20 |
| ☐ 82 | Chris Warren<br>Seattle Seahawks | 1.00 | .40 | .10 |
| ☐ 83 | John L. Williams<br>Seattle Seahawks | .75 | .30 | .07 |
| ☐ 84 | Gary Anderson<br>Tampa Bay Buccaneers | .50 | .20 | .05 |
| ☐ 85 | Reggie Cobb | 1.25 | .50 | .12 |

| | | | | |
|---|---|---|---|---|
| Tampa Bay Buccaneers | | | | |
| ☐ 86 Vince Workman | .50 | .20 | .05 | |
| Tampa Bay Buccaneers | | | | |
| ☐ 87 Reggie Brooks | 3.00 | 1.20 | .30 | |
| Washington Redskins | | | | |
| ☐ 88 Earnest Byner | .75 | .30 | .07 | |
| Washington Redskins | | | | |
| ☐ 89 Ricky Ervins | .75 | .30 | .07 | |
| Washington Redskins | | | | |
| ☐ 90 Michael Haynes | 1.00 | .40 | .10 | |
| Atlanta Falcons | | | | |
| ☐ 91 Mike Pritchard | 1.25 | .50 | .12 | |
| Atlanta Falcons | | | | |
| ☐ 92 Andre Rison | 2.00 | .80 | .20 | |
| Atlanta Falcons | | | | |
| ☐ 93 Don Beebe | 1.00 | .40 | .10 | |
| Buffalo Bills | | | | |
| ☐ 94 Andre Reed | 2.00 | .80 | .20 | |
| Buffalo Bills | | | | |
| ☐ 95 Curtis Conway | 2.00 | .80 | .20 | |
| Chicago Bears | | | | |
| ☐ 96 Wendell Davis | .75 | .30 | .07 | |
| Chicago Bears | | | | |
| ☐ 97 Tom Waddle | .75 | .30 | .07 | |
| Chicago Bears | | | | |
| ☐ 98 Carl Pickens | 1.00 | .40 | .10 | |
| Cincinnati Bengals | | | | |
| ☐ 99 Michael Jackson | 1.00 | .40 | .10 | |
| Cleveland Browns | | | | |
| ☐ 100 Alvin Harper | 2.00 | .80 | .20 | |
| Dallas Cowboys | | | | |
| ☐ 101 Michael Irvin | 3.00 | 1.20 | .30 | |
| Dallas Cowboys | | | | |
| ☐ 102 Vance Johnson | .75 | .30 | .07 | |
| Denver Broncos | | | | |
| ☐ 103 Mel Gray | .50 | .20 | .05 | |
| Detroit Lions | | | | |
| ☐ 104 Sterling Sharpe | 3.00 | 1.20 | .30 | |
| Green Bay Packers | | | | |
| ☐ 105 Curtis Duncan | .75 | .30 | .07 | |
| Houston Oilers | | | | |
| ☐ 106 Ernest Givins | 1.00 | .40 | .10 | |
| Houston Oilers | | | | |
| ☐ 107 Haywood Jeffires | 2.00 | .80 | .20 | |
| Houston Oilers | | | | |
| ☐ 108 Tim Brown | 2.50 | 1.00 | .25 | |
| Los Angeles Raiders | | | | |
| ☐ 109 Willie Gault | .75 | .30 | .07 | |
| Los Angeles Raiders | | | | |
| ☐ 110 Flipper Anderson | .50 | .20 | .05 | |
| Los Angeles Rams | | | | |
| ☐ 111 Henry Ellard | .75 | .30 | .07 | |
| Los Angeles Rams | | | | |
| ☐ 112 Mark Duper | .50 | .20 | .05 | |
| Miami Dolphins | | | | |
| ☐ 113 O.J. McDuffie | 2.00 | .80 | .20 | |
| Miami Dolphins | | | | |
| ☐ 114 Anthony Carter | 1.00 | .40 | .10 | |
| Minnesota Vikings | | | | |
| ☐ 115 Cris Carter | 1.00 | .40 | .10 | |
| Minnesota Vikings | | | | |
| ☐ 116 Mike Farr | .50 | .20 | .05 | |
| New England Patriots | | | | |
| ☐ 117 Quinn Early | .50 | .20 | .05 | |
| New Orleans Saints | | | | |
| ☐ 118 Eric Martin | .75 | .30 | .07 | |
| New Orleans Saints | | | | |
| ☐ 119 Chris Calloway | .50 | .20 | .05 | |
| New York Giants | | | | |
| ☐ 120 Mark Jackson | .75 | .30 | .07 | |
| New York Giants | | | | |
| ☐ 121 Rob Moore | 1.00 | .40 | .10 | |
| New York Jets | | | | |
| ☐ 122 Fred Barnett | 1.00 | .40 | .10 | |
| Philadelphia Eagles | | | | |
| ☐ 123 Calvin Williams | 1.00 | .40 | .10 | |
| Philadelphia Eagles | | | | |
| ☐ 124 Gary Clark | 1.00 | .40 | .10 | |
| Phoenix Cardinals | | | | |
| ☐ 125 Randal Hill | 1.00 | .40 | .10 | |
| Phoenix Cardinals | | | | |
| ☐ 126 Ricky Proehl | .75 | .30 | .07 | |
| Phoenix Cardinals | | | | |
| ☐ 127 Jeff Graham | 1.00 | .40 | .10 | |
| Pittsburgh Steelers | | | | |
| ☐ 128 Ernie Mills | .75 | .30 | .07 | |
| Pittsburgh Steelers | | | | |
| ☐ 129 Dwight Stone | .50 | .20 | .05 | |
| Pittsburgh Steelers | | | | |
| ☐ 130 Nate Lewis | .50 | .20 | .05 | |
| San Diego Chargers | | | | |
| ☐ 131 Jerry Rice | 5.00 | 2.00 | .50 | |
| San Francisco 49ers | | | | |
| ☐ 132 John Taylor | 1.00 | .40 | .10 | |
| San Francisco 49ers | | | | |
| ☐ 133 Tommy Kane | .50 | .20 | .05 | |
| Seattle Seahawks | | | | |

| | | | | |
|---|---|---|---|---|
| ☐ 134 Kelvin Martin | .50 | .20 | .05 | |
| Seattle Seahawks | | | | |
| ☐ 135 Lawrence Dawsey | .50 | .20 | .05 | |
| Tampa Bay Buccaneers | | | | |
| ☐ 136 Courtney Hawkins | 1.25 | .50 | .12 | |
| Tampa Bay Buccaneers | | | | |
| ☐ 137 Art Monk | 1.50 | .60 | .15 | |
| Washington Redskins | | | | |
| ☐ 138 Pete Metzelaars | .50 | .20 | .05 | |
| Buffalo Bills | | | | |
| ☐ 139 Jay Novacek | 1.25 | .50 | .12 | |
| Dallas Cowboys | | | | |
| ☐ 140 Reggie Johnson | .50 | .20 | .05 | |
| Cleveland Browns | | | | |
| ☐ 141 Shannon Sharpe | 1.50 | .60 | .15 | |
| Denver Broncos | | | | |
| ☐ 142 Jackie Harris | 1.50 | .60 | .15 | |
| Green Bay Packers | | | | |
| ☐ 143 Troy Drayton | 1.25 | .50 | .12 | |
| Los Angeles Rams | | | | |
| ☐ 144 Keith Jackson | 1.50 | .60 | .15 | |
| Miami Dolphins | | | | |
| ☐ 145 Steve Jordan | .75 | .30 | .07 | |
| Minnesota Vikings | | | | |
| ☐ 146 Johnny Mitchell | 1.00 | .40 | .10 | |
| New York Jets | | | | |
| ☐ 147 Eric Green | 1.00 | .40 | .10 | |
| Pittsburgh Steelers | | | | |
| ☐ 148 Derrick Walker | .50 | .20 | .05 | |
| San Diego Chargers | | | | |
| ☐ 149 Brent Jones | .75 | .30 | .07 | |
| San Francisco 49ers | | | | |
| ☐ 150 Ron Hall | .50 | .20 | .05 | |
| Tampa Bay Buccaneers | | | | |
| ☐ 151 Norm Johnson | .50 | .20 | .05 | |
| Atlanta Falcons | | | | |
| ☐ 152 Jim Breech | .50 | .20 | .05 | |
| Cincinnati Bengals | | | | |
| ☐ 153 Matt Stover | .50 | .20 | .05 | |
| Cleveland Browns | | | | |
| ☐ 154 Lin Elliott | .50 | .20 | .05 | |
| Dallas Cowboys | | | | |
| ☐ 155 Jason Hanson | .75 | .30 | .07 | |
| Detroit Lions | | | | |
| ☐ 156 Chris Jacke | .75 | .30 | .07 | |
| Green Bay Packers | | | | |
| ☐ 157 Nick Lowery | .75 | .30 | .07 | |
| Kansas City Chiefs | | | | |
| ☐ 158 Pete Stoyanovich | .75 | .30 | .07 | |
| Miami Dolphins | | | | |
| ☐ 159 Roger Ruzek | .50 | .20 | .05 | |
| Philadelphia Eagles | | | | |
| ☐ 160 Gary Anderson | .50 | .20 | .05 | |
| Pittsburgh Steelers | | | | |
| ☐ 161 John Kasay | .50 | .20 | .05 | |
| Seattle Seahawks | | | | |
| ☐ 162 Chip Lohmiller | .75 | .30 | .07 | |
| Washington Redskins | | | | |
| ☐ 163 Chris Gardocki | .50 | .20 | .05 | |
| Chicago Bears | | | | |
| ☐ 164 Mike Saxon | .50 | .20 | .05 | |
| Dallas Cowboys | | | | |
| ☐ 165 Jim Arnold | .50 | .20 | .05 | |
| Detroit Lions | | | | |
| ☐ 166 Rohn Stark | .50 | .20 | .05 | |
| Indianapolis Colts | | | | |
| ☐ 167 Jeff Gossett | .50 | .20 | .05 | |
| Los Angeles Raiders | | | | |
| ☐ 168 Reggie Roby | .50 | .20 | .05 | |
| Miami Dolphins | | | | |
| ☐ 169 Harry Newsome | .50 | .20 | .05 | |
| Minnesota Vikings | | | | |
| ☐ 170 Tommy Barnhardt | .50 | .20 | .05 | |
| New Orleans Saints | | | | |
| ☐ 171 Jeff Feagles | .50 | .20 | .05 | |
| Philadelphia Eagles | | | | |
| ☐ 172 Rick Camarillo | .50 | .20 | .05 | |
| Phoenix Cardinals | | | | |
| ☐ 173 Deion Sanders | 2.50 | 1.00 | .25 | |
| Falcons Defense | | | | |
| ☐ 174 Cornelius Bennett | 1.00 | .40 | .10 | |
| Bills Defense | | | | |
| ☐ 175 Mark Carrier | .50 | .20 | .05 | |
| Bears Defense | | | | |
| ☐ 176 Darryl Williams | .50 | .20 | .05 | |
| Bengals Defense | | | | |
| ☐ 177 Michael Dean Perry | .75 | .30 | .07 | |
| Browns Defense | | | | |
| ☐ 178 Russell Maryland | 1.00 | .40 | .10 | |
| Cowboys Defense | | | | |
| ☐ 179 Steve Atwater | .75 | .30 | .07 | |
| Broncos Defense | | | | |
| ☐ 180 Bennie Blades | .50 | .20 | .05 | |
| Lions Defense | | | | |
| ☐ 181 Reggie White | 1.50 | .60 | .15 | |
| Packers Defense | | | | |
| ☐ 182 Cris Dishman | .50 | .20 | .05 | |

| | | | |
|---|---|---|---|
| Oilers Defense | | | |
| ☐ 183 Steve Emtman | .75 | .30 | .07 |
| Colts Defense | | | |
| ☐ 184 Derrick Thomas | 1.50 | .60 | .15 |
| Chiefs Defense | | | |
| ☐ 185 Howie Long | 1.00 | .40 | .10 |
| Raiders Defense | | | |
| ☐ 186 Sean Gilbert | 1.00 | .40 | .10 |
| Rams Defense | | | |
| ☐ 187 John Offerdahl | .50 | .20 | .05 |
| Dolphins Defense | | | |
| ☐ 188 Chris Doleman | .50 | .20 | .05 |
| Vikings Defense | | | |
| ☐ 189 Andre Tippett | .50 | .20 | .05 |
| Patriots Defense | | | |
| ☐ 190 Sam Mills | .50 | .20 | .05 |
| Saints Defense | | | |
| ☐ 191 Lawrence Taylor | 2.00 | .80 | .20 |
| Giants Defense | | | |
| ☐ 192 James Hasty | .50 | .20 | .05 |
| Jets Defense | | | |
| ☐ 193 Clyde Simmons | .75 | .30 | .07 |
| Eagles Defense | | | |
| ☐ 194 Eric Swann | .75 | .30 | .07 |
| Cardinals Defense | | | |
| ☐ 195 Greg Lloyd | .50 | .20 | .05 |
| Steelers Defense | | | |
| ☐ 196 Junior Seau | 1.25 | .50 | .12 |
| Chargers Defense | | | |
| ☐ 197 Kevin Fagan | .50 | .20 | .05 |
| 49ers Defense | | | |
| ☐ 198 Cortez Kennedy | 1.00 | .40 | .10 |
| Seahawks Defense | | | |
| ☐ 199 Broderick Thomas | .75 | .30 | .07 |
| Buccaneers Defense | | | |
| ☐ 200 Darrell Green | 1.00 | .40 | .10 |
| Redskins Defense | | | |

## 1993 Topps Gold

The 1993 Topps Gold set consists of 660 standard-size (2 1/2" by 3 1/2") cards. The cards were inserted one per foil pack, three per rack pack, and five per jumbo pack. In design, the cards are identical to the regular issue cards, except that the color-coded stripes carrying player information are replaced by gold foil stripes. The cards are numbered on the back. The checklist cards in the regular set were replaced by the player cards 329, 330, 659, and 660, listed below.

| | MINT | EXC | G-VG |
|---|---|---|---|
| COMPLETE SET (660) | 90.00 | 40.00 | 11.50 |
| COMPLETE SERIES 1 (330) | 50.00 | 23.00 | 6.25 |
| COMPLETE SERIES 2 (330) | 40.00 | 18.00 | 5.00 |
| COMMON GOLD (1G-330G) | .20 | .09 | .03 |
| COMMON GOLD (331G-660G) | .20 | .09 | .03 |
| *GOLD STAR CARDS: 2X to 4X VALUE | | | |

| | | | |
|---|---|---|---|
| ☐ 2 Jerry Rice RB | 1.50 | .65 | .19 |
| San Francisco 49ers | | | |
| ☐ 40 Reggie White | 1.00 | .45 | .13 |
| Green Bay Packers | | | |
| ☐ 80 Warren Moon | 1.50 | .65 | .19 |
| Houston Oilers | | | |
| ☐ 100 John Elway | 2.00 | .90 | .25 |
| Denver Broncos | | | |
| ☐ 120 Emmitt Smith | 8.00 | 3.60 | 1.00 |
| Dallas Cowboys | | | |
| ☐ 130 Drew Bledsoe | 8.00 | 3.60 | 1.00 |
| New England Patriots | | | |
| ☐ 135 Steve Young | 2.00 | .90 | .25 |
| San Francisco 49ers | | | |
| ☐ 140 Barry Foster | 2.00 | .90 | .25 |
| Pittsburgh Steelers | | | |
| ☐ 160 Sterling Sharpe | 3.00 | 1.35 | .40 |
| Green Bay Packers | | | |
| ☐ 166 Jerome Bettis | 8.00 | 3.60 | 1.00 |
| Los Angeles Rams | | | |
| ☐ 168 Derrick Thomas | 1.00 | .45 | .13 |
| Kansas City Chiefs | | | |
| ☐ 170 Jim Kelly | 1.50 | .65 | .19 |
| Buffalo Bills | | | |
| ☐ 173 Emmitt Smith TL | 3.00 | 1.35 | .40 |
| Dallas Cowboys | | | |
| ☐ 174 Barry Sanders TL | 1.75 | .80 | .22 |
| Detroit Lions | | | |
| ☐ 175 Sterling Sharpe TL | 1.25 | .55 | .16 |
| Green Bay Packers | | | |
| ☐ 182 Jerry Rice TL | 1.50 | .65 | .19 |
| San Francisco 49ers | | | |
| ☐ 187 Cardinals Draft Picks | 3.00 | 1.35 | .40 |
| Ernest Dye | | | |
| Ronald Moore | | | |
| Garrison Hearst | | | |
| Ben Coleman | | | |

| | | | |
|---|---|---|---|
| Phoenix Cardinals | | | |
| ☐ 190 Barry Sanders | 3.50 | 1.55 | .45 |
| Detroit Lions | | | |
| ☐ 200 Joe Montana | 6.00 | 2.70 | .75 |
| Kansas City Chiefs | | | |
| ☐ 204 Reggie Brooks | 4.50 | 2.00 | .55 |
| Washington Redskins | | | |
| ☐ 219 Emmitt Smith LL | 2.25 | 1.00 | .30 |
| Dallas Cowboys | | | |
| Barry Foster | | | |
| Pittsburgh Steelers | | | |
| ☐ 225 Alvin Harper | 2.50 | 1.15 | .30 |
| Dallas Cowboys | | | |
| ☐ 243 Natrone Means | 3.50 | 1.55 | .45 |
| San Diego Chargers | | | |
| ☐ 250 Brett Favre | 4.00 | 1.80 | .50 |
| Green Bay Packers | | | |
| ☐ 269 Dan Marino TL | 1.75 | .80 | .22 |
| Miami Dolphins | | | |
| ☐ 281 Ricky Watters | 2.25 | 1.00 | .30 |
| San Francisco 49ers | | | |
| ☐ 285 Rick Mirer | 8.00 | 3.60 | 1.00 |
| Seattle Seahawks | | | |
| ☐ 290 Dan Marino | 3.50 | 1.55 | .45 |
| Miami Dolphins | | | |
| ☐ 308 Thurman Thomas | 2.50 | 1.15 | .30 |
| Buffalo Bills | | | |
| ☐ 326 O.J. McDuffie | 4.00 | 1.80 | .50 |
| Miami Dolphins | | | |
| ☐ 329 Terance Mathis | .50 | .23 | .06 |
| New York Jets | | | |
| ☐ 330 John Wojchiechowski UER | .50 | .23 | .06 |
| Chicago Bears | | | |
| (Name spelled Wojociekowski both sides) | | | |
| ☐ 340 Joe Montana | 6.00 | 2.70 | .75 |
| Kansas City Chiefs | | | |
| ☐ 385 Garrison Hearst | 1.50 | .65 | .19 |
| Phoenix Cardinals | | | |
| ☐ 400 Drew Bledsoe | 4.00 | 1.80 | .50 |
| New England Patriots | | | |
| ☐ 448 Qadry Ismail | 1.00 | .45 | .13 |
| Minnesota Vikings | | | |
| ☐ 453 Herman Moore | 2.50 | 1.15 | .30 |
| Detroit Lions | | | |
| ☐ 463 O.J. McDuffie | 1.25 | .55 | .16 |
| Miami Dolphins | | | |
| ☐ 477 Natrone Means | 1.50 | .65 | .19 |
| San Diego Chargers | | | |
| ☐ 500 Jerry Rice | 3.50 | 1.55 | .45 |
| San Francisco 49ers | | | |
| ☐ 530 Troy Aikman | 6.00 | 2.70 | .75 |
| Dallas Cowboys | | | |
| ☐ 554 Reggie Brooks | 2.00 | .90 | .25 |
| Washington Redskins | | | |
| ☐ 600 Rick Mirer | 4.00 | 1.80 | .50 |
| Seattle Seahawks | | | |
| ☐ 604 Jerome Bettis | 4.00 | 1.80 | .50 |
| Los Angeles Rams | | | |
| ☐ 619 Gary Brown | 2.25 | 1.00 | .30 |
| Houston Oilers | | | |
| ☐ 630 Michael Irvin | 3.00 | 1.35 | .40 |
| Dallas Cowboys | | | |
| ☐ 659 Pat Chaffey | .50 | .23 | .06 |
| New York Jets | | | |
| ☐ 660 Milton Mack | .50 | .23 | .06 |
| Tampa Bay Buccaneers | | | |

## 1994 Topps

The 1994 Topps football set consists of 330 standard-size (2 1/2" by 3 1/2") cards. The fronts feature white-bordered, football-shaped color action player photos highlighted by gold-foil borders and placed on a pebble grain football background. The player's name in gold foil appears at the bottom, along with the team name and the player's position. The horizontal white-bordered backs carry a color action player photo on the right, with the player's name, biography, stats, and career highlights next to the photo. Topical subsets include League Leaders (116-120), Tools of the Game (196-205), Career Active Leaders (272-275), and Measure of Greatness (316-319). A 330-card parallel set "Special Effects" was inserted one card per pack. The cards are numbered on the back.

|  | MINT | EXC | G-VG |
|---|---|---|---|
| COMPLETE SET (330) | 20.00 | 9.00 | 2.50 |
| COMMON PLAYER (1-330) | .05 | .02 | .01 |
| ☐ 1 Emmitt Smith | 1.75 | .80 | .22 |
| Dallas Cowboys |  |  |  |
| ☐ 2 Russell Copeland | .05 | .02 | .01 |
| Buffalo Bills |  |  |  |
| ☐ 3 Jesse Sapolu | .05 | .02 | .01 |
| San Francisco 49ers |  |  |  |
| ☐ 4 David Szott | .05 | .02 | .01 |
| Kansas City Chiefs |  |  |  |
| ☐ 5 Rodney Hampton | .25 | .11 | .03 |
| New York Giants |  |  |  |
| ☐ 6 Bubba McDowell | .05 | .02 | .01 |
| Houston Oilers |  |  |  |
| ☐ 7 Bryce Paup | .05 | .02 | .01 |
| Green Bay Packers |  |  |  |
| ☐ 8 Winston Moss | .05 | .02 | .01 |
| Los Angeles Raiders |  |  |  |
| ☐ 9 Brett Perriman | .05 | .02 | .01 |
| Detroit Lions |  |  |  |
| ☐ 10 Rod Woodson | .10 | .05 | .01 |
| Pittsburgh Steelers |  |  |  |
| ☐ 11 John Randle | .05 | .02 | .01 |
| Minnesota Vikings |  |  |  |
| ☐ 12 David Wyman | .05 | .02 | .01 |
| Denver Broncos |  |  |  |
| ☐ 13 Jeff Cross | .05 | .02 | .01 |
| Miami Dolphins |  |  |  |
| ☐ 14 Richard Cooper | .05 | .02 | .01 |
| New Orleans Saints |  |  |  |
| ☐ 15 Johnny Mitchell | .10 | .05 | .01 |
| New York Jets |  |  |  |
| ☐ 16 David Alexander | .05 | .02 | .01 |
| Philadelphia Eagles |  |  |  |
| ☐ 17 Ronnie Harmon | .05 | .02 | .01 |
| San Diego Chargers |  |  |  |
| ☐ 18 Tyronne Stowe | .05 | .02 | .01 |
| Arizona Cardinals |  |  |  |
| ☐ 19 Chris Zorich | .05 | .02 | .01 |
| Chicago Bears |  |  |  |
| ☐ 20 Rob Burnett | .05 | .02 | .01 |
| Cleveland Browns |  |  |  |
| ☐ 21 Harold Alexander | .05 | .02 | .01 |
| Atlanta Falcons |  |  |  |
| ☐ 22 Rod Stephens | .05 | .02 | .01 |
| Seattle Seahawks |  |  |  |
| ☐ 23 Mark Wheeler | .05 | .02 | .01 |
| Tampa Bay Buccaneers |  |  |  |
| ☐ 24 Dwayne Sabb | .05 | .02 | .01 |
| New England Patriots |  |  |  |
| ☐ 25 Troy Drayton | .08 | .04 | .01 |
| Los Angeles Rams |  |  |  |
| ☐ 26 Kurt Gouveia | .05 | .02 | .01 |
| Washington Redskins |  |  |  |
| ☐ 27 Warren Moon | .10 | .05 | .01 |
| Minnesota Vikings |  |  |  |
| ☐ 28 Jeff Query | .05 | .02 | .01 |
| Cincinnati Bengals |  |  |  |
| ☐ 29 Chuck Levy | .60 | .25 | .08 |
| Arizona Cardinals |  |  |  |
| ☐ 30 Bruce Smith | .05 | .02 | .01 |
| Buffalo Bills |  |  |  |
| ☐ 31 Doug Riesenberg | .05 | .02 | .01 |
| New York Giants |  |  |  |
| ☐ 32 Willie Drewrey | .05 | .02 | .01 |
| Houston Oilers |  |  |  |
| ☐ 33 Nate Newton | .05 | .02 | .01 |
| Dallas Cowboys |  |  |  |
| ☐ 34 James Jett | .30 | .14 | .04 |
| Los Angeles Raiders |  |  |  |
| ☐ 35 George Teague | .05 | .02 | .01 |
| Green Bay Packers |  |  |  |
| ☐ 36 Marc Spindler | .05 | .02 | .01 |
| Detroit Lions |  |  |  |
| ☐ 37 Jack Del Rio | .05 | .02 | .01 |
| Minnesota Vikings |  |  |  |
| ☐ 38 Dale Carter | .05 | .02 | .01 |
| Kansas City Chiefs |  |  |  |
| ☐ 39 Steve Atwater | .05 | .02 | .01 |
| Denver Broncos |  |  |  |
| ☐ 40 Herschel Walker | .10 | .05 | .01 |
| Philadelphia Eagles |  |  |  |
| ☐ 41 James Hasty | .05 | .02 | .01 |
| New York Jets |  |  |  |
| ☐ 42 Seth Joyner | .08 | .04 | .01 |
| Arizona Cardinals |  |  |  |
| ☐ 43 Keith Jackson | .10 | .05 | .01 |
| Miami Dolphins |  |  |  |
| ☐ 44 Tommy Vardell | .08 | .04 | .01 |
| Cleveland Browns |  |  |  |
| ☐ 45 Antonio Langham | .30 | .14 | .04 |
| Cleveland Browns |  |  |  |
| ☐ 46 Derek Brown | .30 | .14 | .04 |
| New Orleans Saints |  |  |  |
| ☐ 47 John Wojciechowski | .05 | .02 | .01 |
| Chicago Bears |  |  |  |
| ☐ 48 Horace Copeland | .05 | .02 | .01 |
| Tampa Bay Buccaneers |  |  |  |
| ☐ 49 Luis Sharpe | .05 | .02 | .01 |
| Arizona Cardinals |  |  |  |
| ☐ 50 Pat Harlow | .05 | .02 | .01 |
| New England Patriots |  |  |  |
| ☐ 51 David Palmer | 1.00 | .45 | .13 |
| Minnesota Vikings |  |  |  |
| ☐ 52 Tony Smith | .05 | .02 | .01 |
| Atlanta Falcons |  |  |  |
| ☐ 53 Tim Johnson | .05 | .02 | .01 |
| Washington Redskins |  |  |  |
| ☐ 54 Anthony Newman | .05 | .02 | .01 |
| Los Angeles Rams |  |  |  |
| ☐ 55 Terry Wooden | .05 | .02 | .01 |
| Seattle Seahawks |  |  |  |
| ☐ 56 Derrick Fenner | .05 | .02 | .01 |
| Cincinnati Bengals |  |  |  |
| ☐ 57 Mike Fox | .05 | .02 | .01 |
| New York Giants |  |  |  |
| ☐ 58 Brad Hopkins | .05 | .02 | .01 |
| Houston Oilers |  |  |  |
| ☐ 59 Daryl Johnston | .08 | .04 | .01 |
| Dallas Cowboys |  |  |  |
| ☐ 60 Steve Young | .15 | .07 | .02 |
| San Francisco 49ers |  |  |  |
| ☐ 61 Scottie Graham | .40 | .18 | .05 |
| Minnesota Vikings |  |  |  |
| ☐ 62 Nolan Harrison | .05 | .02 | .01 |
| Los Angeles Raiders |  |  |  |
| ☐ 63 David Richards | .05 | .02 | .01 |
| Detroit Lions |  |  |  |
| ☐ 64 Chris Mohr | .05 | .02 | .01 |
| Buffalo Bills |  |  |  |
| ☐ 65 Hardy Nickerson | .05 | .02 | .01 |
| Tampa Bay Buccaneers |  |  |  |
| ☐ 66 Heath Sherman | .05 | .02 | .01 |
| Philadelphia Eagles |  |  |  |
| ☐ 67 Irving Fryar | .08 | .04 | .01 |
| Miami Dolphins |  |  |  |
| ☐ 68 Ray Buchanan | .05 | .02 | .01 |
| Indianapolis Colts |  |  |  |
| ☐ 69 Jay Taylor | .05 | .02 | .01 |
| Kansas City Chiefs |  |  |  |
| ☐ 70 Shannon Sharpe | .15 | .07 | .02 |
| Denver Broncos |  |  |  |
| ☐ 71 Vinny Testaverde | .05 | .02 | .01 |
| Cleveland Browns |  |  |  |
| ☐ 72 Renaldo Turnbull | .05 | .02 | .01 |
| New Orleans Saints |  |  |  |
| ☐ 73 Dwight Stone | .05 | .02 | .01 |
| Pittsburgh Steelers |  |  |  |
| ☐ 74 Willie McGinest | .50 | .23 | .06 |
| New England Patriots |  |  |  |
| ☐ 75 Darrell Green | .08 | .04 | .01 |
| Washington Redskins |  |  |  |
| ☐ 76 Kyle Clifton | .05 | .02 | .01 |
| New York Jets |  |  |  |
| ☐ 77 Leo Coeas | .05 | .02 | .01 |
| Los Angeles Rams |  |  |  |
| ☐ 78 Ken Ruettgers | .05 | .02 | .01 |
| Green Bay Packers |  |  |  |
| ☐ 79 Craig Heyward | .05 | .02 | .01 |
| Chicago Bears |  |  |  |
| ☐ 80 Andre Rison | .15 | .07 | .02 |
| Atlanta Falcons |  |  |  |
| ☐ 81 Chris Mims | .05 | .02 | .01 |
| San Diego Chargers |  |  |  |
| ☐ 82 Gary Clark | .10 | .05 | .01 |
| Arizona Cardinals |  |  |  |
| ☐ 83 Ricardo McDonald | .05 | .02 | .01 |
| Cincinnati Bengals |  |  |  |
| ☐ 84 Patrick Hunter | .05 | .02 | .01 |
| Seattle Seahawks |  |  |  |
| ☐ 85 Bruce Matthews | .05 | .02 | .01 |
| Houston Oilers |  |  |  |
| ☐ 86 Russell Maryland | .08 | .04 | .01 |
| Dallas Cowboys |  |  |  |
| ☐ 87 Gary Anderson | .05 | .02 | .01 |
| Pittsburgh Steelers |  |  |  |
| ☐ 88 Brad Edwards | .05 | .02 | .01 |
| Washington Redskins |  |  |  |
| ☐ 89 Carlton Bailey | .05 | .02 | .01 |
| New York Giants |  |  |  |
| ☐ 90 Qadry Ismail | .15 | .07 | .02 |
| Minnesota Vikings |  |  |  |

| | | | |
|---|---|---|---|
| ☐ 91 Terry McDaniel | .05 | .02 | .01 |
| Los Angeles Raiders | | | |
| ☐ 92 Willie Green | .05 | .02 | .01 |
| Detroit Lions | | | |
| ☐ 93 Cornelius Bennett | .05 | .02 | .01 |
| Buffalo Bills | | | |
| ☐ 94 Paul Gruber | .05 | .02 | .01 |
| Tampa Bay Buccaneers | | | |
| ☐ 95 Pete Stoyanovich | .05 | .02 | .01 |
| Miami Dolphins | | | |
| ☐ 96 Merton Hanks | .05 | .02 | .01 |
| San Francisco 49ers | | | |
| ☐ 97 Tre' Johnson | .10 | .05 | .01 |
| Washington Redskins | | | |
| ☐ 98 Jonathan Hayes | .05 | .02 | .01 |
| Kansas City Chiefs | | | |
| ☐ 99 Jason Elam | .05 | .02 | .01 |
| Denver Broncos | | | |
| ☐ 100 Jerome Bettis | 2.00 | .90 | .25 |
| Los Angeles Rams | | | |
| ☐ 101 Ronnie Lott | .10 | .05 | .01 |
| New York Jets | | | |
| ☐ 102 Maurice Hurst | .05 | .02 | .01 |
| New England Patriots | | | |
| ☐ 103 Kirk Lowdermilk | .05 | .02 | .01 |
| Indianapolis Colts | | | |
| ☐ 104 Tony Jones | .05 | .02 | .01 |
| Cleveland Browns | | | |
| ☐ 105 Steve Beuerlein | .05 | .02 | .01 |
| Arizona Cardinals | | | |
| ☐ 106 Isaac Davis | .15 | .07 | .02 |
| San Diego Chargers | | | |
| ☐ 107 Vaughan Johnson | .05 | .02 | .01 |
| New Orleans Saints | | | |
| ☐ 108 Terrell Buckley | .05 | .02 | .01 |
| Green Bay Packers | | | |
| ☐ 109 Pierce Holt | .05 | .02 | .01 |
| Atlanta Falcons | | | |
| ☐ 110 Alonzo Spellman | .05 | .02 | .01 |
| Chicago Bears | | | |
| ☐ 111 Patrick Robinson | .05 | .02 | .01 |
| Cincinnati Bengals | | | |
| ☐ 112 Cortez Kennedy | .10 | .05 | .01 |
| Seattle Seahawks | | | |
| ☐ 113 Kevin Williams | .15 | .07 | .02 |
| Dallas Cowboys | | | |
| ☐ 114 Danny Copeland | .05 | .02 | .01 |
| Washington Redskins | | | |
| ☐ 115 Chris Doleman | .05 | .02 | .01 |
| Minnesota Vikings | | | |
| ☐ 116 Jerry Rice LL | .25 | .11 | .03 |
| San Francisco 49ers | | | |
| ☐ 117 Neil Smith LL | .05 | .02 | .01 |
| Kansas City Chiefs | | | |
| ☐ 118 Emmitt Smith LL | .60 | .25 | .08 |
| Dallas Cowboys | | | |
| ☐ 119 Eugene Robinson LL | .05 | .02 | .01 |
| Seattle Seahawks | | | |
| Nate Odomes | | | |
| Buffalo Bills | | | |
| ☐ 120 Steve Young LL | .08 | .04 | .01 |
| San Francisco 49ers | | | |
| ☐ 121 Carnell Lake | .05 | .02 | .01 |
| Pittsburgh Steelers | | | |
| ☐ 122 Ernest Givins | .08 | .04 | .01 |
| Houston Oilers | | | |
| ☐ 123 Henry Jones | .05 | .02 | .01 |
| Buffalo Bills | | | |
| ☐ 124 Michael Brooks | .05 | .02 | .01 |
| New York Giants | | | |
| ☐ 125 Jason Hanson | .05 | .02 | .01 |
| Detroit Lions | | | |
| ☐ 126 Andy Harmon | .05 | .02 | .01 |
| Philadelphia Eagles | | | |
| ☐ 127 Errict Rhett | 1.00 | .45 | .13 |
| Tampa Bay Buccaneers | | | |
| ☐ 128 Harris Barton | .05 | .02 | .01 |
| San Francisco 49ers | | | |
| ☐ 129 Greg Robinson | .10 | .05 | .01 |
| Los Angeles Raiders | | | |
| ☐ 130 Derrick Thomas | .15 | .07 | .02 |
| Kansas City Chiefs | | | |
| ☐ 131 Keith Kartz | .05 | .02 | .01 |
| Denver Broncos | | | |
| ☐ 132 Lincoln Kennedy | .05 | .02 | .01 |
| Atlanta Falcons | | | |
| ☐ 133 Leslie O'Neal | .05 | .02 | .01 |
| San Diego Chargers | | | |
| ☐ 134 Tim Goad | .05 | .02 | .01 |
| New England Patriots | | | |
| ☐ 135 Rohn Stark | .05 | .02 | .01 |
| Indianapolis Colts | | | |
| ☐ 136 O.J. McDuffie | .25 | .11 | .03 |
| Miami Dolphins | | | |
| ☐ 137 Donnell Woolford | .05 | .02 | .01 |
| Chicago Bears | | | |
| ☐ 138 Jamir Miller | .30 | .14 | .04 |
| Arizona Cardinals | | | |
| ☐ 139 Eric Thomas | .05 | .02 | .01 |
| New York Jets | | | |
| ☐ 140 William Roaf | .05 | .02 | .01 |
| New Orleans Saints | | | |
| ☐ 141 Wayne Gandy | .10 | .05 | .01 |
| Los Angeles Rams | | | |
| ☐ 142 Mike Brim | .05 | .02 | .01 |
| Cincinnati Bengals | | | |
| ☐ 143 Kelvin Martin | .05 | .02 | .01 |
| Seattle Seahawks | | | |
| ☐ 144 Edgar Bennett | .05 | .02 | .01 |
| Green Bay Packers | | | |
| ☐ 145 Michael Dean Perry | .05 | .02 | .01 |
| Cleveland Browns | | | |
| ☐ 146 Shante Carver | .15 | .07 | .02 |
| Dallas Cowboys | | | |
| ☐ 147 Jesse Armstead | .05 | .02 | .01 |
| New York Giants | | | |
| ☐ 148 Mo Elewonibi | .05 | .02 | .01 |
| Washington Redskins | | | |
| ☐ 149 Dana Stubblefield | .15 | .07 | .02 |
| San Francisco 49ers | | | |
| ☐ 150 Cody Carlson | .05 | .02 | .01 |
| Houston Oilers | | | |
| ☐ 151 Vencie Glenn | .05 | .02 | .01 |
| Minnesota Vikings | | | |
| ☐ 152 Levon Kirkland | .05 | .02 | .01 |
| Pittsburgh Steelers | | | |
| ☐ 153 Derrick Moore | .08 | .04 | .01 |
| Detroit Lions | | | |
| ☐ 154 John Fina | .05 | .02 | .01 |
| Buffalo Bills | | | |
| ☐ 155 Jeff Hostetler | .08 | .04 | .01 |
| Los Angeles Raiders | | | |
| ☐ 156 Courtney Hawkins | .05 | .02 | .01 |
| Tampa Bay Buccaneers | | | |
| ☐ 157 Todd Collins | .05 | .02 | .01 |
| New England Patriots | | | |
| ☐ 158 Neil Smith | .08 | .04 | .01 |
| Kansas City Chiefs | | | |
| ☐ 159 Simon Fletcher | .05 | .02 | .01 |
| Denver Broncos | | | |
| ☐ 160 Dan Marino | .75 | .35 | .09 |
| Miami Dolphins | | | |
| ☐ 161 Sam Adams | .25 | .11 | .03 |
| Seattle Seahawks | | | |
| ☐ 162 Marvin Washington | .05 | .02 | .01 |
| New York Jets | | | |
| ☐ 163 John Copeland | .05 | .02 | .01 |
| Cincinnati Bengals | | | |
| ☐ 164 Eugene Robinson | .05 | .02 | .01 |
| Seattle Seahawks | | | |
| ☐ 165 Mark Carrier | .05 | .02 | .01 |
| Chicago Bears | | | |
| ☐ 166 Mike Kenn | .05 | .02 | .01 |
| Atlanta Falcons | | | |
| ☐ 167 Tyrone Hughes | .05 | .02 | .01 |
| New Orleans Saints | | | |
| ☐ 168 Darren Carrington | .05 | .02 | .01 |
| San Diego Chargers | | | |
| ☐ 169 Shane Conlan | .05 | .02 | .01 |
| Los Angeles Rams | | | |
| ☐ 170 Ricky Proehl | .08 | .04 | .01 |
| Arizona Cardinals | | | |
| ☐ 171 Jeff Herrod | .05 | .02 | .01 |
| Indianapolis Colts | | | |
| ☐ 172 Mark Carrier | .05 | .02 | .01 |
| Cleveland Browns | | | |
| ☐ 173 George Koonce | .05 | .02 | .01 |
| Green Bay Packers | | | |
| ☐ 174 Desmond Howard | .15 | .07 | .02 |
| Washington Redskins | | | |
| ☐ 175 David Meggett | .08 | .04 | .01 |
| New York Giants | | | |
| ☐ 176 Charles Haley | .05 | .02 | .01 |
| Dallas Cowboys | | | |
| ☐ 177 Steve Wisniewski | .05 | .02 | .01 |
| Los Angeles Raiders | | | |
| ☐ 178 Dermontti Dawson | .05 | .02 | .01 |
| Pittsburgh Steelers | | | |
| ☐ 179 Tim McDonald | .05 | .02 | .01 |
| San Francisco 49ers | | | |
| ☐ 180 Broderick Thomas | .05 | .02 | .01 |
| Tampa Bay Buccaneers | | | |
| ☐ 181 Bernard Dafney | .05 | .02 | .01 |
| Minnesota Vikings | | | |
| ☐ 182 Bo Orlando | .05 | .02 | .01 |
| Houston Oilers | | | |
| ☐ 183 Andre Reed | .10 | .05 | .01 |
| Buffalo Bills | | | |
| ☐ 184 Randall Cunningham | .10 | .05 | .01 |
| Philadelphia Eagles | | | |
| ☐ 185 Chris Spielman | .05 | .02 | .01 |
| Detroit Lions | | | |
| ☐ 186 Keith Byars | .08 | .04 | .01 |
| Miami Dolphins | | | |

| | | | |
|---|---|---|---|
| ☐ 187 Ben Coates | .05 | .02 | .01 |
| New England Patriots | | | |
| ☐ 188 Tracy Simien | .05 | .02 | .01 |
| Kansas City Chiefs | | | |
| ☐ 189 Carl Pickens | .05 | .02 | .01 |
| Cincinnati Bengals | | | |
| ☐ 190 Reggie White | .15 | .07 | .02 |
| Green Bay Packers | | | |
| ☐ 191 Norm Johnson | .05 | .02 | .01 |
| Atlanta Falcons | | | |
| ☐ 192 Brian Washington | .05 | .02 | .01 |
| New York Jets | | | |
| ☐ 193 Stan Humphries | .05 | .02 | .01 |
| San Diego Chargers | | | |
| ☐ 194 Fred Stokes | .05 | .02 | .01 |
| Los Angeles Rams | | | |
| ☐ 195 Dan Williams | .05 | .02 | .01 |
| Denver Broncos | | | |
| ☐ 196 John Elway TOG | .20 | .09 | .03 |
| Denver Broncos | | | |
| ☐ 197 Eric Allen TOG | .05 | .02 | .01 |
| Philadelphia Eagles | | | |
| ☐ 198 Hardy Nickerson TOG | .05 | .02 | .01 |
| Tampa Bay Buccaneers | | | |
| ☐ 199 Jerome Bettis TOG | 1.00 | .45 | .13 |
| Los Angeles Rams | | | |
| ☐ 200 Troy Aikman TOG | .75 | .35 | .09 |
| Dallas Cowboys | | | |
| ☐ 201 Thurman Thomas TOG | .12 | .05 | .02 |
| Buffalo Bills | | | |
| ☐ 202 Cornelius Bennett TOG | .05 | .02 | .01 |
| Buffalo Bills | | | |
| ☐ 203 Michael Irvin TOG | .15 | .07 | .02 |
| Dallas Cowboys | | | |
| ☐ 204 Jim Kelly TOG | .15 | .07 | .02 |
| Buffalo Bills | | | |
| ☐ 205 Junior Seau TOG | .08 | .04 | .01 |
| San Diego Chargers | | | |
| ☐ 206 Heath Shuler | 5.00 | 2.30 | .60 |
| Washington Redskins | | | |
| ☐ 207 Howard Cross | .05 | .02 | .01 |
| New York Giants | | | |
| ☐ 208 Pat Swilling | .08 | .04 | .01 |
| Detroit Lions | | | |
| ☐ 209 Pete Metzelaars | .05 | .02 | .01 |
| Buffalo Bills | | | |
| ☐ 210 Tony McGee | .05 | .02 | .01 |
| Cincinnati Bengals | | | |
| ☐ 211 Neil O'Donnell | .12 | .05 | .02 |
| Pittsburgh Steelers | | | |
| ☐ 212 Eugene Chung | .05 | .02 | .01 |
| New England Patriots | | | |
| ☐ 213 J.B. Brown | .05 | .02 | .01 |
| Miami Dolphins | | | |
| ☐ 214 Marcus Allen | .10 | .05 | .01 |
| Kansas City Chiefs | | | |
| ☐ 215 Harry Newsome | .05 | .02 | .01 |
| Minnesota Vikings | | | |
| ☐ 216 Greg Hill | .75 | .35 | .09 |
| Kansas City Chiefs | | | |
| ☐ 217 Ryan Yarborough | .05 | .02 | .01 |
| New York Jets | | | |
| ☐ 218 Marty Carter | .05 | .02 | .01 |
| Tampa Bay Buccaneers | | | |
| ☐ 219 Bern Brostek | .05 | .02 | .01 |
| Los Angeles Rams | | | |
| ☐ 220 Boomer Esiason | .10 | .05 | .01 |
| New York Jets | | | |
| ☐ 221 Vince Buck | .05 | .02 | .01 |
| New Orleans Saints | | | |
| ☐ 222 Jim Jeffcoat | .05 | .02 | .01 |
| Dallas Cowboys | | | |
| ☐ 223 Bob Dahl | .05 | .02 | .01 |
| Cleveland Browns | | | |
| ☐ 224 Marion Butts | .08 | .04 | .01 |
| San Diego Chargers | | | |
| ☐ 225 Ronald Moore | .50 | .23 | .06 |
| Arizona Cardinals | | | |
| ☐ 226 Robert Blackmon | .05 | .02 | .01 |
| Seattle Seahawks | | | |
| ☐ 227 Curtis Conway | .15 | .07 | .02 |
| Chicago Bears | | | |
| ☐ 228 Jon Hand | .05 | .02 | .01 |
| Indianapolis Colts | | | |
| ☐ 229 Shane Dronett | .05 | .02 | .01 |
| Denver Broncos | | | |
| ☐ 230 Erik Williams | .05 | .02 | .01 |
| Dallas Cowboys | | | |
| ☐ 231 Dennis Brown | .05 | .02 | .01 |
| Denver Broncos | | | |
| ☐ 232 Ray Childress | .05 | .02 | .01 |
| Houston Oilers | | | |
| ☐ 233 Johnnie Morton | .75 | .35 | .09 |
| Detroit Lions | | | |
| ☐ 234 Kent Hull | .05 | .02 | .01 |
| Buffalo Bills | | | |
| ☐ 235 John Elliott | .05 | .02 | .01 |
| New York Giants | | | |
| ☐ 236 Ron Heller | .05 | .02 | .01 |
| Miami Dolphins | | | |
| ☐ 237 J.J. Birden | .05 | .02 | .01 |
| Kansas City Chiefs | | | |
| ☐ 238 Thomas Randolph | .15 | .07 | .02 |
| New York Giants | | | |
| ☐ 239 Chip Lohmiller | .05 | .02 | .01 |
| Washington Redskins | | | |
| ☐ 240 Tim Brown | .15 | .07 | .02 |
| Los Angeles Raiders | | | |
| ☐ 241 Steve Tovar | .05 | .02 | .01 |
| Cincinnati Bengals | | | |
| ☐ 242 Moe Gardner | .05 | .02 | .01 |
| Atlanta Falcons | | | |
| ☐ 243 Vincent Brown | .05 | .02 | .01 |
| New England Patriots | | | |
| ☐ 244 Tony Zendejas | .05 | .02 | .01 |
| Los Angeles Rams | | | |
| ☐ 245 Eric Allen | .08 | .04 | .01 |
| Philadelphia Eagles | | | |
| ☐ 246 Joe King | .10 | .05 | .01 |
| Tampa Bay Buccaneers | | | |
| ☐ 247 Mo Lewis | .05 | .02 | .01 |
| New York Jets | | | |
| ☐ 248 Rod Bernstine | .05 | .02 | .01 |
| Denver Broncos | | | |
| ☐ 249 Tom Waddle | .08 | .04 | .01 |
| Chicago Bears | | | |
| ☐ 250 Junior Seau | .10 | .05 | .01 |
| San Diego Chargers | | | |
| ☐ 251 Eric Metcalf | .08 | .04 | .01 |
| Cleveland Browns | | | |
| ☐ 252 Cris Carter | .08 | .04 | .01 |
| Minnesota Vikings | | | |
| ☐ 253 Bill Hitchcock | .05 | .02 | .01 |
| Seattle Seahawks | | | |
| ☐ 254 Zefross Moss | .05 | .02 | .01 |
| Indianapolis Colts | | | |
| ☐ 255 Morten Andersen | .05 | .02 | .01 |
| New Orleans Saints | | | |
| ☐ 256 Keith Rucker | .10 | .05 | .01 |
| Arizona Cardinals | | | |
| ☐ 257 Chris Jacke | .05 | .02 | .01 |
| Green Bay Packers | | | |
| ☐ 258 Richmond Webb | .05 | .02 | .01 |
| Miami Dolphins | | | |
| ☐ 259 Herman Moore | .15 | .07 | .02 |
| Detroit Lions | | | |
| ☐ 260 Phil Simms | .10 | .05 | .01 |
| New York Giants | | | |
| ☐ 261 Mark Tuinei | .05 | .02 | .01 |
| Dallas Cowboys | | | |
| ☐ 262 Don Beebe | .08 | .04 | .01 |
| Buffalo Bills | | | |
| ☐ 263 Marc Logan | .05 | .02 | .01 |
| San Francisco 49ers | | | |
| ☐ 264 Willie Davis | .08 | .04 | .01 |
| Kansas City Chiefs | | | |
| ☐ 265 David Klingler | .15 | .07 | .02 |
| Cincinnati Bengals | | | |
| ☐ 266 Martin Mayhew | .05 | .02 | .01 |
| Tampa Bay Buccaneers | | | |
| ☐ 267 Mark Bavaro | .08 | .04 | .01 |
| Philadelphia Eagles | | | |
| ☐ 268 Greg Lloyd | .05 | .02 | .01 |
| Pittsburgh Steelers | | | |
| ☐ 269 Al Del Greco | .05 | .02 | .01 |
| Houston Oilers | | | |
| ☐ 270 Reggie Brooks | .75 | .35 | .09 |
| Washington Redskins | | | |
| ☐ 271 Greg Townsend | .05 | .02 | .01 |
| Los Angeles Raiders | | | |
| ☐ 272 Rohn Stark CAL | .05 | .02 | .01 |
| Indianapolis Colts | | | |
| ☐ 273 Marcus Allen CAL | .08 | .04 | .01 |
| Kansas City Chiefs | | | |
| ☐ 274 Ronnie Lott CAL | .08 | .04 | .01 |
| New York Jets | | | |
| ☐ 275 Dan Marino CAL | .40 | .18 | .05 |
| Miami Dolphins | | | |
| ☐ 276 Sean Gilbert | .05 | .02 | .01 |
| Los Angeles Rams | | | |
| ☐ 277 LeRoy Butler | .05 | .02 | .01 |
| Green Bay Packers | | | |
| ☐ 278 Troy Auzenne | .05 | .02 | .01 |
| Chicago Bears | | | |
| ☐ 279 Eric Swann | .05 | .02 | .01 |
| Arizona Cardinals | | | |
| ☐ 280 Quentin Coryatt | .05 | .02 | .01 |
| Indianapolis Colts | | | |
| ☐ 281 Anthony Pleasant | .05 | .02 | .01 |
| Cleveland Browns | | | |
| ☐ 282 Brad Baxter | .05 | .02 | .01 |
| New York Jets | | | |
| ☐ 283 Carl Lee | .05 | .02 | .01 |
| Minnesota Vikings | | | |

| | | | | |
|---|---|---|---|---|
| ☐ 284 Courtney Hall | .05 | .02 | .01 |
| San Diego Chargers | | | |
| ☐ 285 Quinn Early | .05 | .02 | .01 |
| New Orleans Saints | | | |
| ☐ 286 Eddie Robinson | .05 | .02 | .01 |
| Houston Oilers | | | |
| ☐ 287 Marco Coleman | .05 | .02 | .01 |
| Miami Dolphins | | | |
| ☐ 288 Harold Green | .05 | .02 | .01 |
| Cincinnati Bengals | | | |
| ☐ 289 Santana Dotson | .08 | .04 | .01 |
| Tampa Bay Buccaneers | | | |
| ☐ 290 Robert Porcher | .05 | .02 | .01 |
| Detroit Lions | | | |
| ☐ 291 Joe Phillips | .05 | .02 | .01 |
| Kansas City Chiefs | | | |
| ☐ 292 Mark McMillian | .05 | .02 | .01 |
| Philadelphia Eagles | | | |
| ☐ 293 Eric Davis | .05 | .02 | .01 |
| San Francisco 49ers | | | |
| ☐ 294 Mark Jackson | .05 | .02 | .01 |
| New York Giants | | | |
| ☐ 295 Darryl Talley | .05 | .02 | .01 |
| Buffalo Bills | | | |
| ☐ 296 Curtis Duncan | .05 | .02 | .01 |
| Houston Oilers | | | |
| ☐ 297 Bruce Armstrong | .05 | .02 | .01 |
| New England Patriots | | | |
| ☐ 298 Eric Hill | .05 | .02 | .01 |
| Arizona Cardinals | | | |
| ☐ 299 Andre Collins | .05 | .02 | .01 |
| Washington Redskins | | | |
| ☐ 300 Jay Novacek | .08 | .04 | .01 |
| Dallas Cowboys | | | |
| ☐ 301 Roosevelt Potts | .08 | .04 | .01 |
| Indianapolis Colts | | | |
| ☐ 302 Eric Martin | .05 | .02 | .01 |
| New Orleans Saints | | | |
| ☐ 303 Chris Warren | .05 | .02 | .01 |
| Seattle Seahawks | | | |
| ☐ 304 Deral Boykin | .10 | .05 | .01 |
| Los Angeles Rams | | | |
| ☐ 305 Jessie Tuggle | .05 | .02 | .01 |
| Atlanta Falcons | | | |
| ☐ 306 Glyn Milburn | .20 | .09 | .03 |
| Denver Broncos | | | |
| ☐ 307 Terry Obee | .15 | .07 | .02 |
| Chicago Bears | | | |
| ☐ 308 Eric Turner | .05 | .02 | .01 |
| Cleveland Browns | | | |
| ☐ 309 Dewayne Washington | .10 | .05 | .01 |
| Minnesota Vikings | | | |
| ☐ 310 Sterling Sharpe | .30 | .14 | .04 |
| Green Bay Packers | | | |
| ☐ 311 Jeff Gossett | .05 | .02 | .01 |
| Los Angeles Raiders | | | |
| ☐ 312 John Carney | .05 | .02 | .01 |
| San Diego Chargers | | | |
| ☐ 313 Aaron Glenn | .15 | .07 | .02 |
| New York Jets | | | |
| ☐ 314 Nick Lowery | .05 | .02 | .01 |
| Kansas City Chiefs | | | |
| ☐ 315 Thurman Thomas | .25 | .11 | .03 |
| Buffalo Bills | | | |
| ☐ 316 Troy Aikman MOG | .75 | .35 | .09 |
| Dallas Cowboys | | | |
| ☐ 317 Thurman Thomas MOG | .12 | .05 | .02 |
| Buffalo Bills | | | |
| ☐ 318 Michael Irvin MOG | .15 | .07 | .02 |
| Dallas Cowboys | | | |
| ☐ 319 Steve Beuerlein MOG | .05 | .02 | .01 |
| Arizona Cardinals | | | |
| ☐ 320 Jerry Rice | .50 | .23 | .06 |
| San Francisco 49ers | | | |
| ☐ 321 Alexander Wright | .05 | .02 | .01 |
| Los Angeles Raiders | | | |
| ☐ 322 Michael Bates | .05 | .02 | .01 |
| Seattle Seahawks | | | |
| ☐ 323 Greg Davis | .05 | .02 | .01 |
| Arizona Cardinals | | | |
| ☐ 324 Mark Bortz | .05 | .02 | .01 |
| Chicago Bears | | | |
| ☐ 325 Kevin Greene | .05 | .02 | .01 |
| Pittsburgh Steelers | | | |
| ☐ 326 Wayne Simmons | .05 | .02 | .01 |
| Green Bay Packers | | | |
| ☐ 327 Wayne Martin | .05 | .02 | .01 |
| New Orleans Saints | | | |
| ☐ 328 Michael Irvin | .30 | .14 | .04 |
| Dallas Cowboys | | | |
| ☐ 329 Checklist 1 of 4 | .05 | .02 | .01 |
| ☐ 330 Checklist 2 of 4 | .05 | .02 | .01 |

# 1994 Topps Special Effects

Randomly inserted in packs, these 330 standard-size (2 1/2" by 3 1/2") cards are identical to the regular 1994 Topps set except that the photos feature a clear plastic prismatic overcoating with a holographic stripe. The cards are numbered on the back.

| | MINT | EXC | G-VG |
|---|---|---|---|
| COMPLETE SET (330) | 125.00 | 57.50 | 15.50 |
| COMMON PLAYER (1-330) | .30 | .14 | .04 |
| *UNLISTED STARS: 4X TO 7X VALUE | | | |
| *UNLISTED ROOKIES: 3X TO 5X VALUE | | | |

| | | | |
|---|---|---|---|
| ☐ 1 Emmitt Smith | 8.00 | 3.60 | 1.00 |
| Dallas Cowboys | | | |
| ☐ 5 Rodney Hampton | 1.25 | .55 | .16 |
| New York Giants | | | |
| ☐ 29 Chuck Levy | 2.25 | 1.00 | .30 |
| Arizona Cardinals | | | |
| ☐ 34 James Jett | 1.50 | .65 | .19 |
| Los Angeles Raiders | | | |
| ☐ 46 Derek Brown | 1.50 | .65 | .19 |
| New Orleans Saints | | | |
| ☐ 51 David Palmer | 4.00 | 1.80 | .50 |
| Minnesota Vikings | | | |
| ☐ 74 Willie McGinest | 1.50 | .65 | .19 |
| New England Patriots | | | |
| ☐ 100 Jerome Bettis | 8.00 | 3.60 | 1.00 |
| Los Angeles Rams | | | |
| ☐ 116 Jerry Rice LL | 1.25 | .55 | .16 |
| San Francisco 49ers | | | |
| ☐ 118 Emmitt Smith LL | 3.00 | 1.35 | .40 |
| Dallas Cowboys | | | |
| ☐ 127 Errict Rhett | 4.00 | 1.80 | .50 |
| Tampa Bay Buccaneers | | | |
| ☐ 136 O.J. McDuffie | 1.25 | .55 | .16 |
| Miami Dolphins | | | |
| ☐ 160 Dan Marino | 3.50 | 1.55 | .45 |
| Miami Dolphins | | | |
| ☐ 196 John Elway TOG | 1.00 | .45 | .13 |
| Denver Broncos | | | |
| ☐ 199 Jerome Bettis TOG | 4.00 | 1.80 | .50 |
| Los Angeles Rams | | | |
| ☐ 200 Troy Aikman TOG | 3.00 | 1.35 | .40 |
| Dallas Cowboys | | | |
| ☐ 206 Heath Shuler | 16.00 | 7.25 | 2.00 |
| Washington Redskins | | | |
| ☐ 216 Greg Hill | 2.50 | 1.15 | .30 |
| Kansas City Chiefs | | | |
| ☐ 225 Ronald Moore | 2.00 | .90 | .25 |
| Arizona Cardinals | | | |
| ☐ 233 Johnnie Morton | 2.50 | 1.15 | .30 |
| Detroit Lions | | | |
| ☐ 270 Reggie Brooks | 3.00 | 1.35 | .40 |
| Washington Redskins | | | |
| ☐ 275 Dan Marino CAL | 2.00 | .90 | .25 |
| Miami Dolphins | | | |
| ☐ 306 Glyn Milburn | 1.00 | .45 | .13 |
| Denver Broncos | | | |
| ☐ 310 Sterling Sharpe | 1.50 | .65 | .19 |
| Green Bay Packers | | | |
| ☐ 315 Thurman Thomas | 1.25 | .55 | .16 |
| Buffalo Bills | | | |
| ☐ 316 Troy Aikman MOG | 3.00 | 1.35 | .40 |
| Dallas Cowboys | | | |
| ☐ 320 Jerry Rice | 2.50 | 1.15 | .30 |
| San Francisco 49ers | | | |
| ☐ 328 Michael Irvin | 1.50 | .65 | .19 |
| Dallas Cowboys | | | |

# 1994 Topps Finest Inserts

Randomly inserted in first series Topps packs, these 32 standard-size (2 1/2" by 3 1/2") cards feature metallic fronts with color player action cutouts set on silver-bordered multicolored designs. The player's name appears near the bottom in a colored bar. The white-bordered backs carry a color action cutout set to one side. The player's name, position and team name appear at the top, followed below by statistics. The cards are numbered on the back as "X of 32." The first 20 cards are of running backs and wide receivers; the last 12 are quarterbacks.

|  | MINT | EXC | G-VG |
|---|---|---|---|
| COMPLETE SET (32) | 225.00 | 100.00 | 28.00 |
| COMMON PLAYER (1-32) | 3.00 | 1.35 | .40 |
| ☐ 1 Jerry Rice | 14.00 | 6.25 | 1.75 |
| San Francisco 49ers |  |  |  |
| ☐ 2 Chris Warren | 3.50 | 1.55 | .45 |
| Seattle Seahawks |  |  |  |
| ☐ 3 Leonard Russell | 4.00 | 1.80 | .50 |
| New England Patriots |  |  |  |
| ☐ 4 Gary Brown | 5.00 | 2.30 | .60 |
| Houston Oilers |  |  |  |
| ☐ 5 Tim Brown | 4.00 | 1.80 | .50 |
| Los Angeles Raiders |  |  |  |
| ☐ 6 Erric Pegram | 4.00 | 1.80 | .50 |
| Atlanta Falcons |  |  |  |
| ☐ 7 Irving Fryar | 3.00 | 1.35 | .40 |
| Miami Dolphins |  |  |  |
| ☐ 8 Anthony Miller | 4.00 | 1.80 | .50 |
| Denver Broncos |  |  |  |
| ☐ 9 Reggie Langhorne | 3.00 | 1.35 | .40 |
| Indianapolis Colts |  |  |  |
| ☐ 10 Thurman Thomas | 10.00 | 4.50 | 1.25 |
| Buffalo Bills |  |  |  |
| ☐ 11 Reggie Brooks | 14.00 | 6.25 | 1.75 |
| Washington Redskins |  |  |  |
| ☐ 12 Andre Rison | 4.00 | 1.80 | .50 |
| Atlanta Falcons |  |  |  |
| ☐ 13 Ron Moore | 4.00 | 1.80 | .50 |
| Arizona Cardinals |  |  |  |
| ☐ 14 Michael Irvin | 12.00 | 5.50 | 1.50 |
| Dallas Cowboys |  |  |  |
| ☐ 15 Barry Sanders | 18.00 | 8.00 | 2.30 |
| Detroit Lions |  |  |  |
| ☐ 16 Cris Carter | 3.50 | 1.55 | .45 |
| Minnesota Vikings |  |  |  |
| ☐ 17 Rodney Hampton | 10.00 | 4.50 | 1.25 |
| New York Giants |  |  |  |
| ☐ 18 Jerome Bettis | 30.00 | 13.50 | 3.80 |
| Los Angeles Rams |  |  |  |
| ☐ 19 Sterling Sharpe | 12.00 | 5.50 | 1.50 |
| Green Bay Packers |  |  |  |
| ☐ 20 Emmit Smith | 40.00 | 18.00 | 5.00 |
| Dallas Cowboys |  |  |  |
| ☐ 21 John Elway | 10.00 | 4.50 | 1.25 |
| Denver Broncos |  |  |  |
| ☐ 22 Brett Favre | 12.00 | 5.50 | 1.50 |
| Green Bay Packers |  |  |  |
| ☐ 23 Jim Kelly | 5.00 | 2.30 | .60 |
| Buffalo Bills |  |  |  |
| ☐ 24 Warren Moon | 5.00 | 2.30 | .60 |
| Minnesota Vikings |  |  |  |
| ☐ 25 Phil Simms | 3.50 | 1.55 | .45 |
| New York Giants |  |  |  |
| ☐ 26 Craig Erickson | 3.00 | 1.35 | .40 |
| Tampa Bay Buccaneers |  |  |  |
| ☐ 27 Neil O'Donnell | 4.00 | 1.80 | .50 |
| Pittsburgh Steelers |  |  |  |
| ☐ 28 Steve Young | 5.00 | 2.30 | .60 |
| San Francisco 49ers |  |  |  |
| ☐ 29 Steve Beuerlein | 3.50 | 1.55 | .45 |
| Arizona Cardinals |  |  |  |
| ☐ 30 Troy Aikman | 30.00 | 13.50 | 3.80 |
| Dallas Cowboys |  |  |  |
| ☐ 31 Jeff Hostetler | 3.50 | 1.55 | .45 |
| Los Angeles Raiders |  |  |  |
| ☐ 32 Boomer Esiason | 3.50 | 1.55 | .45 |
| New York Jets |  |  |  |

# 1994 Topps Finest

The 1994 Topps Finest football set consists of 220 standard-size (2 1/2" by 3 1/2") cards. Specially designed refracting foil cards were produced for each of the 220 cards. One of these foil cards was inserted in every nine packs. Thirty-eight rookie cards displayed a special rookie design, and one of these rookie cards was included in each five-card pack. Moreover, oversized 4" by 6" versions of these 38 rookie cards were produced and inserted at a rate of one in each 24-count box. The fronts feature colorful metallic fronts that carry color player action shots. The player's name appears within a colored bar near the bottom of the frame. The white-bordered horizontal back carries another color player action shot in a simulated picture frame on the left. The back is filled out by biography, statistics, and copy detailing each player's "Finest Moment."

|  | MINT | EXC | G-VG |
|---|---|---|---|
| COMPLETE SET (220) | 225.00 | 100.00 | 28.00 |
| COMMON PLAYER (1-220) | .75 | .35 | .09 |
| ☐ 1 Emmitt Smith | 25.00 | 11.50 | 3.10 |
| Dallas Cowboys |  |  |  |
| ☐ 2 Calvin Williams | 1.25 | .55 | .16 |
| Philadelphia Eagles |  |  |  |
| ☐ 3 Mark Collins | .75 | .35 | .09 |
| New York Giants |  |  |  |
| ☐ 4 Steve McMichael | .75 | .35 | .09 |
| Chicago Bears |  |  |  |
| ☐ 5 Jim Kelly | 5.00 | 2.30 | .60 |
| Buffalo Bills |  |  |  |
| ☐ 6 Michael Dean Perry | 1.25 | .55 | .16 |
| Cleveland Browns |  |  |  |
| ☐ 7 Wayne Simmons | .75 | .35 | .09 |
| Green Bay Packers |  |  |  |
| ☐ 8 Raghib Ismail | 2.50 | 1.15 | .30 |
| Los Angeles Raiders |  |  |  |
| ☐ 9 Mark Rypien | 1.00 | .45 | .13 |
| Washington Redskins |  |  |  |
| ☐ 10 Brian Blades | 1.00 | .45 | .13 |
| Seattle Seahawks |  |  |  |
| ☐ 11 Barry Word | 1.00 | .45 | .13 |
| Kansas City Chiefs |  |  |  |
| ☐ 12 Jerry Rice | 8.00 | 3.60 | 1.00 |
| San Francisco 49ers |  |  |  |
| ☐ 13 Derrick Fenner | .75 | .35 | .09 |
| Cincinnati Bengals |  |  |  |
| ☐ 14 Karl Mecklenburg | .75 | .35 | .09 |
| Denver Broncos |  |  |  |
| ☐ 15 Reggie Cobb | 1.25 | .55 | .16 |
| Tampa Bay Buccaneers |  |  |  |
| ☐ 16 Eric Swann | 1.00 | .45 | .13 |
| Phoenix Cardinals |  |  |  |
| ☐ 17 Neil Smith | 1.25 | .55 | .16 |
| Kansas City Chiefs |  |  |  |
| ☐ 18 Barry Foster | 5.00 | 2.30 | .60 |
| Pittsburgh Steelers |  |  |  |
| ☐ 19 Willie Roaf | .75 | .35 | .09 |
| New Orleans Saints |  |  |  |
| ☐ 20 Troy Drayton | .75 | .35 | .09 |
| Los Angeles Rams |  |  |  |
| ☐ 21 Warren Moon | 2.50 | 1.15 | .30 |
| Houston Oilers |  |  |  |
| ☐ 22 Richmond Webb | .75 | .35 | .09 |
| Miami Dolphins |  |  |  |
| ☐ 23 Anthony Miller | 2.00 | .90 | .25 |
| San Diego Chargers |  |  |  |

| | | | |
|---|---|---|---|
| ☐ 24 Chris Slade | 1.50 | .65 | .19 |
| New England Patriots | | | |
| ☐ 25 Mel Gray | .75 | .35 | .09 |
| Detroit Lions | | | |
| ☐ 26 Ronnie Lott | 1.25 | .55 | .16 |
| New York Jets | | | |
| ☐ 27 Andre Rison | 2.25 | 1.00 | .30 |
| Atlanta Falcons | | | |
| ☐ 28 Jeff George | 2.00 | .90 | .25 |
| Indianapolis Colts | | | |
| ☐ 29 John Copeland | .75 | .35 | .09 |
| Cincinnati Bengals | | | |
| ☐ 30 Derrick Thomas | 1.50 | .65 | .19 |
| Kansas City Chiefs | | | |
| ☐ 31 Sterling Sharpe | 8.00 | 3.60 | 1.00 |
| Green Bay Packers | | | |
| ☐ 32 Chris Doleman | 1.00 | .45 | .13 |
| Minnesota Vikings | | | |
| ☐ 33 Monte Coleman | .75 | .35 | .09 |
| Washington Redskins | | | |
| ☐ 34 Mark Bavaro | .75 | .35 | .09 |
| Philadelphia Eagles | | | |
| ☐ 35 Kevin Williams | 3.00 | 1.35 | .40 |
| Dallas Cowboys | | | |
| ☐ 36 Eric Metcalf | 1.25 | .55 | .16 |
| Cleveland Browns | | | |
| ☐ 37 Brent Jones | 1.25 | .55 | .16 |
| San Francisco 49ers | | | |
| ☐ 38 Steve Tasker | .75 | .35 | .09 |
| Buffalo Bills | | | |
| ☐ 39 Dave Meggett | 1.00 | .45 | .13 |
| New York Giants | | | |
| ☐ 40 Howie Long | 1.00 | .45 | .13 |
| Los Angeles Raiders | | | |
| ☐ 41 Rick Mirer | 20.00 | 9.00 | 2.50 |
| Seattle Seahawks | | | |
| ☐ 42 Jerome Bettis | 20.00 | 9.00 | 2.50 |
| Los Angeles Rams | | | |
| ☐ 43 Marion Butts | 1.25 | .55 | .16 |
| San Diego Chargers | | | |
| ☐ 44 Barry Sanders | 10.00 | 4.50 | 1.25 |
| Detroit Lions | | | |
| ☐ 45 Jason Elam | .75 | .35 | .09 |
| Denver Broncos | | | |
| ☐ 46 Broderick Thomas | .75 | .35 | .09 |
| Tampa Bay Buccaneers | | | |
| ☐ 47 Derek Brown RB | 4.00 | 1.80 | .50 |
| New Orleans Saints | | | |
| ☐ 48 Lorenzo White | 1.00 | .45 | .13 |
| Houston Oilers | | | |
| ☐ 49 Neil O'Donnell | 1.50 | .65 | .19 |
| Pittsburgh Steelers | | | |
| ☐ 50 Chris Burkett | .75 | .35 | .09 |
| New York Jets | | | |
| ☐ 51 John Offerdahl | .75 | .35 | .09 |
| Miami Dolphins | | | |
| ☐ 52 Rohn Stark | .75 | .35 | .09 |
| Indianapolis Colts | | | |
| ☐ 53 Neal Anderson | 1.00 | .45 | .13 |
| Chicago Bears | | | |
| ☐ 54 Steve Beuerlein | 1.25 | .55 | .16 |
| Phoenix Cardinals | | | |
| ☐ 55 Bruce Armstrong | .75 | .35 | .09 |
| New England Patriots | | | |
| ☐ 56 Lincoln Kennedy | .75 | .35 | .09 |
| Atlanta Falcons | | | |
| ☐ 57 Darrell Green | 1.00 | .45 | .13 |
| Washington Redskins | | | |
| ☐ 58 Ricardo McDonald | .75 | .35 | .09 |
| Cincinnati Bengals | | | |
| ☐ 59 Chris Warren | .75 | .35 | .09 |
| Seattle Seahawks | | | |
| ☐ 60 Mark Jackson | 1.00 | .45 | .13 |
| New York Giants | | | |
| ☐ 61 Pepper Johnson | .75 | .35 | .09 |
| Cleveland Browns | | | |
| ☐ 62 Chris Spielman | .75 | .35 | .09 |
| Detroit Lions | | | |
| ☐ 63 Marcus Allen | 4.00 | 1.80 | .50 |
| Kansas City Chiefs | | | |
| ☐ 64 Jim Everett | 1.25 | .55 | .16 |
| Los Angeles Rams | | | |
| ☐ 65 Greg Townsend | .75 | .35 | .09 |
| Los Angeles Raiders | | | |
| ☐ 66 Cris Carter | 1.25 | .55 | .16 |
| Minnesota Vikings | | | |
| ☐ 67 Don Beebe | 1.25 | .55 | .16 |
| Buffalo Bills | | | |
| ☐ 68 Reggie Langhorne | 1.00 | .45 | .13 |
| Indianapolis Colts | | | |
| ☐ 69 Randall Cunningham | 1.50 | .65 | .19 |
| Philadelphia Eagles | | | |
| ☐ 70 Johnny Holland | .75 | .35 | .09 |
| Green Bay Packers | | | |
| ☐ 71 Morten Andersen | 1.00 | .45 | .13 |
| New Orleans Saints | | | |
| ☐ 72 Leonard Marshall | .75 | .35 | .09 |

| | | | |
|---|---|---|---|
| New York Jets | | | |
| ☐ 73 Keith Jackson | 1.25 | .55 | .16 |
| Miami Dolphins | | | |
| ☐ 74 Leslie O'Neal | 1.00 | .45 | .13 |
| San Diego Chargers | | | |
| ☐ 75 Hardy Nickerson | .75 | .35 | .09 |
| Pittsburgh Steelers | | | |
| ☐ 76 Dan Williams | .75 | .35 | .09 |
| Denver Broncos | | | |
| ☐ 77 Steve Young | 5.00 | 2.30 | .60 |
| San Francisco 49ers | | | |
| ☐ 78 Deon Figures | .75 | .35 | .09 |
| Pittsburgh Steelers | | | |
| ☐ 79 Michael Irvin | 8.00 | 3.60 | 1.00 |
| Dallas Cowboys | | | |
| ☐ 80 Luis Sharpe | .75 | .35 | .09 |
| Phoenix Cardinals | | | |
| ☐ 81 Andre Tippett | .75 | .35 | .09 |
| New England Patriots | | | |
| ☐ 82 Ricky Sanders | 1.00 | .45 | .13 |
| Washington Redskins | | | |
| ☐ 83 Erric Pegram | 3.00 | 1.35 | .40 |
| Atlanta Falcons | | | |
| ☐ 84 Albert Lewis | .75 | .35 | .09 |
| Kansas City Chiefs | | | |
| ☐ 85 Anthony Blaylock | .75 | .35 | .09 |
| Chicago Bears | | | |
| ☐ 86 Pat Swilling | 1.00 | .45 | .13 |
| Detroit Lions | | | |
| ☐ 87 Duane Bickett | .75 | .35 | .09 |
| Indianapolis Colts | | | |
| ☐ 88 Myron Guyton | .75 | .35 | .09 |
| New York Giants | | | |
| ☐ 89 Clay Matthews | 1.00 | .45 | .13 |
| Cleveland Browns | | | |
| ☐ 90 Jim McMahon | 1.25 | .55 | .16 |
| Minnesota Vikings | | | |
| ☐ 91 Bruce Smith | 1.25 | .55 | .16 |
| Buffalo Bills | | | |
| ☐ 92 Reggie White | 1.50 | .65 | .19 |
| Green Bay Packers | | | |
| ☐ 93 Shannon Sharpe | 2.50 | 1.15 | .30 |
| Denver Broncos | | | |
| ☐ 94 Rickey Jackson | 1.00 | .45 | .13 |
| New Orleans Saints | | | |
| ☐ 95 Ronnie Harmon | .75 | .35 | .09 |
| San Diego Chargers | | | |
| ☐ 96 Terry McDaniel | .75 | .35 | .09 |
| Los Angeles Raiders | | | |
| ☐ 97 Bryan Cox | 1.00 | .45 | .13 |
| Miami Dolphins | | | |
| ☐ 98 Webster Slaughter | 1.00 | .45 | .13 |
| Houston Oilers | | | |
| ☐ 99 Boomer Esiason | 1.25 | .55 | .16 |
| New York Jets | | | |
| ☐ 100 Tim Krumrie | .75 | .35 | .09 |
| Cincinnati Bengals | | | |
| ☐ 101 Cortez Kennedy | 1.25 | .55 | .16 |
| Seattle Seahawks | | | |
| ☐ 102 Henry Ellard | 1.00 | .45 | .13 |
| Los Angeles Rams | | | |
| ☐ 103 Clyde Simmons | 1.00 | .45 | .13 |
| Philadelphia Eagles | | | |
| ☐ 104 Craig Erickson | 1.25 | .55 | .16 |
| Tampa Bay Buccaneers | | | |
| ☐ 105 Eric Green | 1.25 | .55 | .16 |
| Pittsburgh Steelers | | | |
| ☐ 106 Gary Clark | 1.00 | .45 | .13 |
| Phoenix Cardinals | | | |
| ☐ 107 Jay Novacek | 1.25 | .55 | .16 |
| Dallas Cowboys | | | |
| ☐ 108 Dana Stubblefield | 2.50 | 1.15 | .30 |
| San Francisco 49ers | | | |
| ☐ 109 Mike Johnson | .75 | .35 | .09 |
| Cleveland Browns | | | |
| ☐ 110 Ray Crockett | .75 | .35 | .09 |
| Detroit Lions | | | |
| ☐ 111 Leonard Russell | 1.00 | .45 | .13 |
| New England Patriots | | | |
| ☐ 112 Robert Smith | 2.50 | 1.15 | .30 |
| Minnesota Vikings | | | |
| ☐ 113 Art Monk | 1.25 | .55 | .16 |
| Washington Redskins | | | |
| ☐ 114 Ray Childress | .75 | .35 | .09 |
| Houston Oilers | | | |
| ☐ 115 O.J. McDuffie | 6.00 | 2.70 | .75 |
| Miami Dolphins | | | |
| ☐ 116 Tim Brown | 1.00 | .45 | .13 |
| Los Angeles Raiders | | | |
| ☐ 117 Kevin Ross | .75 | .35 | .09 |
| Kansas City Chiefs | | | |
| ☐ 118 Richard Dent | 1.00 | .45 | .13 |
| Chicago Bears | | | |
| ☐ 119 John Elway | 10.00 | 4.50 | 1.25 |
| Denver Broncos | | | |
| ☐ 120 James Hasty | .75 | .35 | .09 |
| New York Jets | | | |
| ☐ 121 Gary Plummer | .75 | .35 | .09 |

| | | | |
|---|---|---|---|
| San Diego Chargers | | | |
| ☐ 122 Pierce Holt | .75 | .35 | .09 |
| Atlanta Falcons | | | |
| ☐ 123 Eric Martin | 1.00 | .45 | .13 |
| New Orleans Saints | | | |
| ☐ 124 Bret Favre | 10.00 | 4.50 | 1.25 |
| Green Bay Packers | | | |
| ☐ 125 Cornelius Bennett | 1.25 | .55 | .16 |
| Buffalo Bills | | | |
| ☐ 126 Jessie Hester | .75 | .35 | .09 |
| Indianapolis Colts | | | |
| ☐ 127 Lewis Tillman | 1.00 | .45 | .13 |
| New York Giants | | | |
| ☐ 128 Qadry Ismail | 3.00 | 1.35 | .40 |
| Minnesota Vikings | | | |
| ☐ 129 Jay Schroeder | 1.00 | .45 | .13 |
| Cincinnati Bengals | | | |
| ☐ 130 Curtis Conway | 3.00 | 1.35 | .40 |
| Chicago Bears | | | |
| ☐ 131 Santana Dotson | 1.25 | .55 | .16 |
| Tampa Bay Buccaneers | | | |
| ☐ 132 Nick Lowery | .75 | .35 | .09 |
| Kansas City Chiefs | | | |
| ☐ 133 Lomas Brown | .75 | .35 | .09 |
| Detroit Lions | | | |
| ☐ 134 Reggie Roby | .75 | .35 | .09 |
| Washington Redskins | | | |
| ☐ 135 John L. Williams | 1.00 | .45 | .13 |
| Seattle Seahawks | | | |
| ☐ 136 Vinny Testaverde | 1.25 | .55 | .16 |
| Cleveland Browns | | | |
| ☐ 137 Seth Joyner | 1.00 | .45 | .13 |
| Philadelphia Eagles | | | |
| ☐ 138 Ethan Horton | .75 | .35 | .09 |
| Los Angeles Raiders | | | |
| ☐ 139 Jackie Slater | .75 | .35 | .09 |
| Los Angeles Rams | | | |
| ☐ 140 Rod Bernstine | 1.00 | .45 | .13 |
| Denver Broncos | | | |
| ☐ 141 Rob Moore | 1.25 | .55 | .16 |
| New York Jets | | | |
| ☐ 142 Dan Marino | 15.00 | 6.75 | 1.90 |
| Miami Dolphins | | | |
| ☐ 143 Ken Harvey | .75 | .35 | .09 |
| Phoenix Cardinals | | | |
| ☐ 144 Ernest Givins | 1.00 | .45 | .13 |
| Houston Oilers | | | |
| ☐ 145 Russell Maryland | 1.25 | .55 | .16 |
| Dallas Cowboys | | | |
| ☐ 146 Drew Bledsoe | 20.00 | 9.00 | 2.50 |
| New Orleans Saints | | | |
| ☐ 147 Kevin Greene | .75 | .35 | .09 |
| Pittsburgh Steelers | | | |
| ☐ 148 Bobby Hebert | 1.25 | .55 | .16 |
| Atlanta Falcons | | | |
| ☐ 149 Junior Seau | 1.25 | .55 | .16 |
| San Diego Chargers | | | |
| ☐ 150 Tim McDonald | .75 | .35 | .09 |
| San Francisco 49ers | | | |
| ☐ 151 Thurman Thomas | 6.00 | 2.70 | .75 |
| Buffalo Bills | | | |
| ☐ 152 Phil Simms | 1.25 | .55 | .16 |
| New York Giants | | | |
| ☐ 153 Terrell Buckley | 1.25 | .55 | .16 |
| Green Bay Packers | | | |
| ☐ 154 Sam Mills | 1.00 | .45 | .13 |
| New Orleans Saints | | | |
| ☐ 155 Anthony Carter | 1.00 | .45 | .13 |
| Minnesota Vikings | | | |
| ☐ 156 Kelvin Martin | .75 | .35 | .09 |
| Seattle Seahawks | | | |
| ☐ 157 Shane Conlan | .75 | .35 | .09 |
| Los Angeles Rams | | | |
| ☐ 158 Irving Fryar | 1.00 | .45 | .13 |
| Miami Dolphins | | | |
| ☐ 159 Demetrius DuBose | .75 | .35 | .09 |
| Tampa Bay Buccaneers | | | |
| ☐ 160 David Klingler | 1.50 | .65 | .19 |
| Cincinnati Bengals | | | |
| ☐ 161 Herman Moore | 4.00 | 1.80 | .50 |
| Detroit Lions | | | |
| ☐ 162 Jeff Hostetler | 1.25 | .55 | .16 |
| Los Angeles Raiders | | | |
| ☐ 163 Tommy Vardell | 1.00 | .45 | .13 |
| Cleveland Browns | | | |
| ☐ 164 Craig Heyward | .75 | .35 | .09 |
| Chicago Bears | | | |
| ☐ 165 Wilber Marshall | 1.00 | .45 | .13 |
| Houston Oilers | | | |
| ☐ 166 Quentin Coryatt | 1.25 | .55 | .16 |
| Indianapolis Colts | | | |
| ☐ 167 Glyn Milburn | 5.00 | 2.30 | .60 |
| Denver Broncos | | | |
| ☐ 168 Fred Barnett | 1.25 | .55 | .16 |
| Philadelphia Eagles | | | |
| ☐ 169 Charles Haley | 1.00 | .45 | .13 |
| Dallas Cowboys | | | |

| | | | |
|---|---|---|---|
| ☐ 170 Carl Banks | .75 | .35 | .09 |
| Washington Redskins | | | |
| ☐ 171 Ricky Proehl | 1.00 | .45 | .13 |
| Phoenix Cardinals | | | |
| ☐ 172 Joe Montana | 25.00 | 11.50 | 3.10 |
| Kansas City Chiefs | | | |
| ☐ 173 Johnny Mitchell | 1.00 | .45 | .13 |
| New York Jets | | | |
| ☐ 174 Andre Reed | 1.25 | .55 | .16 |
| Buffalo Bills | | | |
| ☐ 175 Marco Coleman | 1.00 | .45 | .13 |
| Miami Dolphins | | | |
| ☐ 176 Vaughan Johnson | .75 | .35 | .09 |
| New Orleans Saints | | | |
| ☐ 177 Carl Pickens | 1.25 | .55 | .16 |
| Cincinnati Bengals | | | |
| ☐ 178 Dwight Stone | .75 | .35 | .09 |
| Pittsburgh Steelers | | | |
| ☐ 179 Ricky Watters | 6.00 | 2.70 | .75 |
| San Francisco 49ers | | | |
| ☐ 180 Michael Haynes | 2.25 | 1.00 | .30 |
| Atlanta Falcons | | | |
| ☐ 181 Roger Craig | 1.00 | .45 | .13 |
| Minnesota Vikings | | | |
| ☐ 182 Cleveland Gary | 1.00 | .45 | .13 |
| Los Angeles Rams | | | |
| ☐ 183 Steve Emtman | 1.00 | .45 | .13 |
| Indianapolis Colts | | | |
| ☐ 184 Patrick Bates | .75 | .35 | .09 |
| Los Angeles Raiders | | | |
| ☐ 185 Mark Carrier WR | 1.00 | .45 | .13 |
| Cleveland Browns | | | |
| ☐ 186 Brad Hopkins | .75 | .35 | .09 |
| Houston Oilers | | | |
| ☐ 187 Dennis Smith | .75 | .35 | .09 |
| Denver Broncos | | | |
| ☐ 188 Natrone Means | 7.00 | 3.10 | .85 |
| San Diego Chargers | | | |
| ☐ 189 Michael Jackson | 1.25 | .55 | .16 |
| Cleveland Browns | | | |
| ☐ 190 Ken Norton Jr. | 1.00 | .45 | .13 |
| Dallas Cowboys | | | |
| ☐ 191 Carlton Gray | .75 | .35 | .09 |
| Seattle Seahawks | | | |
| ☐ 192 Edgar Bennett | .75 | .35 | .09 |
| Green Bay Packers | | | |
| ☐ 193 Lawrence Taylor | 1.50 | .65 | .19 |
| New York Giants | | | |
| ☐ 194 Marv Cook | .75 | .35 | .09 |
| New England Patriots | | | |
| ☐ 195 Eric Curry | .75 | .35 | .09 |
| Tampa Bay Buccaneers | | | |
| ☐ 196 Victor Bailey | .75 | .35 | .09 |
| Philadelphia Eagles | | | |
| ☐ 197 Ryan McNeil | .75 | .35 | .09 |
| Detroit Lions | | | |
| ☐ 198 Rod Woodson | 1.25 | .55 | .16 |
| Pittsburgh Steelers | | | |
| ☐ 199 Ernest Byner | 1.00 | .45 | .13 |
| Washington Redskins | | | |
| ☐ 200 Marvin Jones | .75 | .35 | .09 |
| New York Jets | | | |
| ☐ 201 Thomas Smith | .75 | .35 | .09 |
| Buffalo Bills | | | |
| ☐ 202 Troy Aikman | 20.00 | 9.00 | 2.50 |
| Dallas Cowboys | | | |
| ☐ 203 Audray McMillian | .75 | .35 | .09 |
| Minnesota Vikings | | | |
| ☐ 204 Wade Wilson | 1.00 | .45 | .13 |
| New Orleans Saints | | | |
| ☐ 205 George Teague | .75 | .35 | .09 |
| Green Bay Packers | | | |
| ☐ 206 Deion Sanders | 2.00 | .90 | .25 |
| Atlanta Falcons | | | |
| ☐ 207 Will Shields | .75 | .35 | .09 |
| Kansas City Chiefs | | | |
| ☐ 208 John Taylor | 1.25 | .55 | .16 |
| San Francisco 49ers | | | |
| ☐ 209 Jim Harbaugh | 1.00 | .45 | .13 |
| Chicago Bears | | | |
| ☐ 210 Micheal Barrow | .75 | .35 | .09 |
| Houston Oilers | | | |
| ☐ 211 Harold Green | 1.00 | .45 | .13 |
| Cincinnati Bengals | | | |
| ☐ 212 Steve Everitt | .75 | .35 | .09 |
| Cleveland Browns | | | |
| ☐ 213 Flipper Anderson | 1.00 | .45 | .13 |
| Los Angeles Rams | | | |
| ☐ 214 Rodney Hampton | 4.00 | 1.80 | .50 |
| New York Giants | | | |
| ☐ 215 Steve Atwater | 1.00 | .45 | .13 |
| Denver Broncos | | | |
| ☐ 216 James Trapp | .75 | .35 | .09 |
| Los Angeles Raiders | | | |
| ☐ 217 Terry Kirby | 6.00 | 2.70 | .75 |
| Miami Dolphins | | | |
| ☐ 218 Garrison Hearst | 5.00 | 2.30 | .60 |

Phoenix Cardinals
☐ 219 Jeff Bryant............................ .75 .35 .09
Seattle Seahawks
☐ 220 Roosevelt Potts.................... 1.50 .65 .19
Indianapolis Colts

# 1994 Topps Finest Refractors

These specially designed refracting foil cards were produced for each of the 220 regular-issue 1994 Topps Finest cards. One of these standard-size (2 1/2" by 3 1/2") foil cards was inserted in every nine packs. Aside from the rainbow-effect of the special Refractors' foil, the cards are identical to the regular Topps Finest cards. The cards are numbered on the back.

| | MINT | EXC | G-VG |
|---|---|---|---|
| COMPLETE SET (220).................... | 3000.00 | 1350.00 | 375.00 |
| COMMON PLAYER (1-220)............. | 5.00 | 2.30 | .60 |
| *UNLISTED STARS: 5X to 10X VALUE | | | |

| | | MINT | EXC | G-VG |
|---|---|---|---|---|
| ☐ 1 | Emmitt Smith............................ | 250.00 | 115.00 | 31.00 |
| | Dallas Cowboys | | | |
| ☐ 12 | Jerry Rice................................. | 75.00 | 34.00 | 9.50 |
| | San Francisco 49ers | | | |
| ☐ 31 | Sterling Sharpe........................ | 60.00 | 27.00 | 7.50 |
| | Green Bay Packers | | | |
| ☐ 41 | Rick Mirer................................. | 150.00 | 70.00 | 19.00 |
| | Seattle Seahawks | | | |
| ☐ 42 | Jerome Bettis........................... | 150.00 | 70.00 | 19.00 |
| | Los Angeles Rams | | | |
| ☐ 44 | Barry Sanders.......................... | 100.00 | 45.00 | 12.50 |
| | Detroit Lions | | | |
| ☐ 77 | Steve Young............................. | 60.00 | 27.00 | 7.50 |
| | San Francisco 49ers | | | |
| ☐ 79 | Michael Irvin............................ | 60.00 | 27.00 | 7.50 |
| | Dallas Cowboys | | | |
| ☐ 119 | John Elway............................... | 80.00 | 36.00 | 10.00 |
| | Denver Broncos | | | |
| ☐ 124 | Bret Favre................................ | 60.00 | 27.00 | 7.50 |
| | Green Bay Packers | | | |
| ☐ 142 | Dan Marino............................... | 150.00 | 70.00 | 19.00 |
| | Miami Dolphins | | | |
| ☐ 146 | Drew Bledsoe........................... | 150.00 | 70.00 | 19.00 |
| | New Orleans Saints | | | |
| ☐ 151 | Thurman Thomas................... | 50.00 | 23.00 | 6.25 |
| | Buffalo Bills | | | |
| ☐ 172 | Joe Montana............................ | 250.00 | 115.00 | 31.00 |
| | Kansas City Chiefs | | | |
| ☐ 202 | Troy Aikman............................. | 150.00 | 70.00 | 19.00 |
| | Dallas Cowboys | | | |

# 1994 Topps Finest Rookie Jumbos

These oversized (4 1/4" by 6") versions of the 38 Rookie Cards from the 1994 Topps Finest set were inserted at a rate of one in each 24-count box. One of every six Rookie Jumbo inserts was enhanced with refracting foil. Aside from their larger size, the cards are identical to their regular Topps Finest counterparts. The cards are numbered on the back.

| | MINT | EXC | G-VG |
|---|---|---|---|
| COMPLETE SET (38)........................ | 350.00 | 160.00 | 45.00 |
| COMMON PLAYER............................ | 8.00 | 3.60 | 1.00 |

| | | MINT | EXC | G-VG |
|---|---|---|---|---|
| ☐ 7 | Wayne Simmons...................... | 8.00 | 3.60 | 1.00 |
| | Green Bay Packers | | | |
| ☐ 19 | Willie Roaf............................... | 8.00 | 3.60 | 1.00 |
| | New Orleans Saints | | | |

| | | MINT | EXC | G-VG |
|---|---|---|---|---|
| ☐ 20 | Troy Drayton........................... | 10.00 | 4.50 | 1.25 |
| | Los Angeles Rams | | | |
| ☐ 24 | Chris Slade.............................. | 10.00 | 4.50 | 1.25 |
| | New England Patriots | | | |
| ☐ 29 | John Copeland......................... | 10.00 | 4.50 | 1.25 |
| | Cincinnati Bengals | | | |
| ☐ 35 | Kevin Williams........................ | 8.00 | 3.60 | 1.00 |
| | Dallas Cowboys | | | |
| ☐ 41 | Rick Mirer................................ | 45.00 | 20.00 | 5.75 |
| | Seattle Seahawks | | | |
| ☐ 42 | Jerome Bettis.......................... | 45.00 | 20.00 | 5.75 |
| | Los Angeles Rams | | | |
| ☐ 45 | Jason Elam.............................. | 8.00 | 3.60 | 1.00 |
| | Denver Broncos | | | |
| ☐ 47 | Derek Brown RB...................... | 12.00 | 5.50 | 1.50 |
| | New Orleans Saints | | | |
| ☐ 56 | Lincoln Kennedy ..................... | 8.00 | 3.60 | 1.00 |
| | Atlanta Falcons | | | |
| ☐ 76 | Dan Williams.......................... | 8.00 | 3.60 | 1.00 |
| | Denver Broncos | | | |
| ☐ 78 | Deon Figures........................... | 10.00 | 4.50 | 1.25 |
| | Pittsburgh Steelers | | | |
| ☐ 108 | Dana Stubblefield.................. | 10.00 | 4.50 | 1.25 |
| | San Francisco 49ers | | | |
| ☐ 112 | Robert Smith........................... | 10.00 | 4.50 | 1.25 |
| | Minnesota Vikings | | | |
| ☐ 115 | O.J. McDuffie ......................... | 12.00 | 5.50 | 1.50 |
| | Miami Dolphins | | | |
| ☐ 128 | Qadry Ismail............................ | 10.00 | 4.50 | 1.25 |
| | Minnesota Vikings | | | |
| ☐ 130 | Curtis Conway......................... | 12.00 | 5.50 | 1.50 |
| | Chicago Bears | | | |
| ☐ 146 | Drew Bledsoe........................... | 45.00 | 20.00 | 5.75 |
| | New Orleans Saints | | | |
| ☐ 159 | Demetrius DuBose................... | 10.00 | 4.50 | 1.25 |
| | Tampa Bay Buccaneers | | | |
| ☐ 167 | Glyn Milburn .......................... | 15.00 | 6.75 | 1.90 |
| | Denver Broncos | | | |
| ☐ 184 | Patrick Bates.......................... | 8.00 | 3.60 | 1.00 |
| | Los Angeles Raiders | | | |
| ☐ 186 | Brad Hopkins.......................... | 8.00 | 3.60 | 1.00 |
| | Houston Oilers | | | |
| ☐ 188 | Natrone Means...................... | 20.00 | 9.00 | 2.50 |
| | San Diego Chargers | | | |
| ☐ 191 | Carlton Gray............................ | 8.00 | 3.60 | 1.00 |
| | Seattle Seahawks | | | |
| ☐ 195 | Eric Curry................................ | 10.00 | 4.50 | 1.25 |
| | Tampa Bay Buccaneers | | | |
| ☐ 196 | Victor Bailey........................... | 8.00 | 3.60 | 1.00 |
| | Philadelphia Eagles | | | |
| ☐ 197 | Ryan McNeil............................ | 8.00 | 3.60 | 1.00 |
| | Detroit Lions | | | |
| ☐ 200 | Marvin Jones .......................... | 8.00 | 3.60 | 1.00 |
| | New York Jets | | | |
| ☐ 201 | Thomas Smith......................... | 8.00 | 3.60 | 1.00 |
| | Buffalo Bills | | | |
| ☐ 205 | George Teague........................ | 8.00 | 3.60 | 1.00 |
| | Green Bay Packers | | | |
| ☐ 207 | Will Shields............................. | 8.00 | 3.60 | 1.00 |
| | Kansas City Chiefs | | | |
| ☐ 210 | Micheal Barrow...................... | 8.00 | 3.60 | 1.00 |
| | Houston Oilers | | | |
| ☐ 212 | Steve Everitt............................ | 8.00 | 3.60 | 1.00 |
| | Cleveland Browns | | | |
| ☐ 216 | James Trapp ........................... | 8.00 | 3.60 | 1.00 |
| | Los Angeles Raiders | | | |
| ☐ 217 | Terry Kirby.............................. | 20.00 | 9.00 | 2.50 |
| | Miami Dolphins | | | |
| ☐ 218 | Garrison Hearst...................... | 15.00 | 6.75 | 1.90 |
| | Phoenix Cardinals | | | |
| ☐ 220 | Roosevelt Potts....................... | 10.00 | 4.50 | 1.25 |
| | Indianapolis Colts | | | |

# 1994 Topps Archives 1956

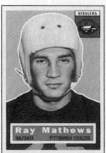

Topps reprinted all 274 cards in the original 1956 and 1957 sets. The 1956 reprint set contained 120 cards, not including the unnumbered checklist card which was not reprinted. The suggested retail for a 12-card pack was 2.00. The cards measure the standard-size (2 1/2" by 3 1/2"). Factual and grammatical errors in the original cards were not changed in reprints. The fronts feature action player cutouts on bright color backgrounds. The backs were printed in red and black on gray card stock. The cards are numbered on the back. Gold versions of each card were produced and are valued at three times the values listed below.

|  | MINT | EXC | G-VG |
|---|---|---|---|
| COMPLETE SET (120)................ | 25.00 | 10.00 | 2.50 |
| COMMON PLAYER (1-120).............. | .10 | .04 | .01 |
| ☐ 1 Jack Carson ....................... | .30 | .12 | .03 |
| ☐ 2 Gordon Soltau..................... | .10 | .04 | .01 |
| ☐ 3 Frank Varrichione................. | .10 | .04 | .01 |
| ☐ 4 Eddie Bell ......................... | .10 | .04 | .01 |
| ☐ 5 Alex Webster ...................... | .20 | .08 | .02 |
| ☐ 6 Norm Van Brocklin ................ | 2.00 | .80 | .20 |
| ☐ 7 Green Bay Packers ................ | .50 | .20 | .05 |
| Team Card |  |  |  |
| ☐ 8 Lou Creekmur ..................... | .10 | .04 | .01 |
| ☐ 9 Lou Groza ......................... | 1.50 | .60 | .15 |
| ☐ 10 Tom Bienemann ................... | .10 | .04 | .01 |
| ☐ 11 George Blanda ................... | 1.00 | .40 | .10 |
| ☐ 12 Alan Ameche ..................... | .50 | .20 | .05 |
| ☐ 13 Vic Janowicz..................... | .30 | .12 | .03 |
| ☐ 14 Dick Moegle...................... | .10 | .04 | .01 |
| ☐ 15 Fran Rogel ....................... | .10 | .04 | .01 |
| ☐ 16 Harold Giancanelli............... | .10 | .04 | .01 |
| ☐ 17 Emlen Tunnell.................... | .75 | .30 | .07 |
| ☐ 18 Paul(Tank) Younger............... | .20 | .08 | .02 |
| ☐ 19 Bill Howton ...................... | .20 | .08 | .02 |
| ☐ 20 Jack Christiansen................ | .75 | .30 | .07 |
| ☐ 21 Darrell Brewster................. | .10 | .04 | .01 |
| ☐ 22 Chicago Cardinals ............... | .50 | .20 | .05 |
| Team Card |  |  |  |
| ☐ 23 Ed Brown......................... | .20 | .08 | .02 |
| ☐ 24 Joe Campanella................... | .10 | .04 | .01 |
| ☐ 25 Leon Heath ...................... | .10 | .04 | .01 |
| ☐ 26 San Francisco 49ers.............. | .50 | .20 | .05 |
| Team Card |  |  |  |
| ☐ 27 Dick Flanagan.................... | .10 | .04 | .01 |
| ☐ 28 Chuck Bednarik................... | 1.00 | .40 | .10 |
| ☐ 29 Kyle Rote ........................ | .75 | .30 | .07 |
| ☐ 30 Les Richter ...................... | .20 | .08 | .02 |
| ☐ 31 Howard Ferguson.................. | .10 | .04 | .01 |
| ☐ 32 Dorne Dibble..................... | .10 | .04 | .01 |
| ☐ 33 Kenny Konz....................... | .10 | .04 | .01 |
| ☐ 34 Dave Mann ....................... | .10 | .04 | .01 |
| ☐ 35 Rick Casares ..................... | .20 | .08 | .02 |
| ☐ 36 Art Donovan...................... | .75 | .30 | .07 |
| ☐ 37 Chuck Drazenovich................ | .10 | .04 | .01 |
| ☐ 38 Joe Arenas....................... | .10 | .04 | .01 |
| ☐ 39 Lynn Chandnois................... | .10 | .04 | .01 |
| ☐ 40 Philadelphia Eagles.............. | .50 | .20 | .05 |
| Team Card |  |  |  |
| ☐ 41 Roosevelt Brown.................. | 1.00 | .40 | .10 |
| ☐ 42 Tom Fears........................ | .75 | .30 | .07 |
| ☐ 43 Gary Knafelc..................... | .10 | .04 | .01 |
| ☐ 44 Joe Schmidt...................... | 1.25 | .50 | .12 |
| ☐ 45 Cleveland Browns ................ | .50 | .20 | .05 |
| Team Card UER |  |  |  |
| (Card back does not |  |  |  |
| credit the Browns with |  |  |  |
| being Champs in 1955) |  |  |  |
| ☐ 46 Len Teeuws....................... | .10 | .04 | .01 |
| ☐ 47 Bill George ...................... | 1.00 | .40 | .10 |
| ☐ 48 Baltimore Colts ................. | .50 | .20 | .05 |
| Team Card |  |  |  |
| ☐ 49 Eddie LeBaron.................... | .50 | .20 | .05 |
| ☐ 50 Hugh McElhenny................... | 1.25 | .50 | .12 |
| ☐ 51 Ted Marchibroda.................. | .20 | .08 | .02 |
| ☐ 52 Adrian Burk...................... | .10 | .04 | .01 |
| ☐ 53 Frank Gifford.................... | 3.00 | 1.20 | .30 |
| ☐ 54 Charley Toogood.................. | .10 | .04 | .01 |
| ☐ 55 Tobin Rote ...................... | .20 | .08 | .02 |
| ☐ 56 Bill Stits....................... | .10 | .04 | .01 |
| ☐ 57 Don Colo ........................ | .10 | .04 | .01 |
| ☐ 58 Ollie Matson..................... | 1.50 | .60 | .15 |
| ☐ 59 Harlon Hill...................... | .20 | .08 | .02 |
| ☐ 60 Lenny Moore ..................... | 5.00 | 2.00 | .50 |
| ☐ 61 Washington Redskins ............. | .50 | .20 | .05 |
| Team Card |  |  |  |
| ☐ 62 Billy Wilson..................... | .20 | .08 | .02 |
| ☐ 63 Pittsburgh Steelers ............. | .50 | .20 | .05 |
| Team Card |  |  |  |
| ☐ 64 Bob Pellegrini................... | .10 | .04 | .01 |
| ☐ 65 Ken MacAfee...................... | .20 | .08 | .02 |
| ☐ 66 Willard Sherman.................. | .10 | .04 | .01 |
| ☐ 67 Roger Zatkoff.................... | .10 | .04 | .01 |
| ☐ 68 Dave Middleton................... | .10 | .04 | .01 |
| ☐ 69 Ray Renfro ...................... | .20 | .08 | .02 |
| ☐ 70 Don Stonesifer................... | .10 | .04 | .01 |
| ☐ 71 Stan Jones ...................... | 1.00 | .40 | .10 |
| ☐ 72 Jim Mutscheller.................. | .10 | .04 | .01 |
| ☐ 73 Volney Peters.................... | .10 | .04 | .01 |
| ☐ 74 Leo Nomellini.................... | 1.00 | .40 | .10 |
| ☐ 75 Ray Mathews...................... | .10 | .04 | .01 |
| ☐ 76 Dick Bielski..................... | .10 | .04 | .01 |
| ☐ 77 Charley Conerly.................. | 1.00 | .40 | .10 |
| ☐ 78 Elroy Hirsch..................... | 1.00 | .40 | .10 |
| ☐ 79 Bill Forester.................... | .20 | .08 | .02 |
| ☐ 80 Jim Doran ....................... | .10 | .04 | .01 |
| ☐ 81 Fred Morrison.................... | .10 | .04 | .01 |
| ☐ 82 Jack Simmons..................... | .10 | .04 | .01 |
| ☐ 83 Bill McColl...................... | .10 | .04 | .01 |
| ☐ 84 Bert Rechichar................... | .10 | .04 | .01 |
| ☐ 85 Joe Scudero...................... | .10 | .04 | .01 |
| ☐ 86 Y.A. Tittle...................... | 2.50 | 1.00 | .25 |
| ☐ 87 Ernie Stautner................... | 1.25 | .50 | .12 |
| ☐ 88 Norm Willey...................... | .10 | .04 | .01 |
| ☐ 89 Bob Schnelker.................... | .20 | .08 | .02 |
| ☐ 90 Dan Towler....................... | .20 | .08 | .02 |
| ☐ 91 John Martinkovic................. | .10 | .04 | .01 |
| ☐ 92 Detroit Lions.................... | .50 | .20 | .05 |
| Team Card |  |  |  |
| ☐ 93 George Ratterman................. | .20 | .08 | .02 |
| ☐ 94 Chuck Ulrich..................... | .10 | .04 | .01 |
| ☐ 95 Bobby Watkins.................... | .10 | .04 | .01 |
| ☐ 96 Buddy Young...................... | .30 | .12 | .03 |
| ☐ 97 Billy Wells...................... | .10 | .04 | .01 |
| ☐ 98 Bob Toneff....................... | .10 | .04 | .01 |
| ☐ 99 Bill McPeak...................... | .10 | .04 | .01 |
| ☐ 100 Bobby Thomason.................. | .20 | .08 | .02 |
| ☐ 101 Roosevelt Grier................. | 1.50 | .60 | .15 |
| ☐ 102 Ron Waller...................... | .10 | .04 | .01 |
| ☐ 103 Bobby Dillon.................... | .10 | .04 | .01 |
| ☐ 104 Leon Hart....................... | .30 | .12 | .03 |
| ☐ 105 Mike McCormack.................. | .75 | .30 | .07 |
| ☐ 106 John Olszewski.................. | .20 | .08 | .02 |
| ☐ 107 Bill Wightkin................... | .10 | .04 | .01 |
| ☐ 108 George Shaw..................... | .20 | .08 | .02 |
| ☐ 109 Dale Atkeson.................... | .10 | .04 | .01 |
| ☐ 110 Joe Perry....................... | 1.50 | .60 | .15 |
| ☐ 111 Dale Dodrill.................... | .10 | .04 | .01 |
| ☐ 112 Tom Scott ...................... | .10 | .04 | .01 |
| ☐ 113 New York Giants ................ | .50 | .20 | .05 |
| Team Card |  |  |  |
| ☐ 114 Los Angeles Rams ............... | .50 | .20 | .05 |
| Team Card UER |  |  |  |
| (Back incorrect, Rams |  |  |  |
| were not 1955 champs) |  |  |  |
| ☐ 115 Al Carmichael................... | .10 | .04 | .01 |
| ☐ 116 Bobby Layne..................... | 2.50 | 1.00 | .25 |
| ☐ 117 Ed Modzelewski.................. | .20 | .08 | .02 |
| ☐ 118 Lamar McHan .................... | .20 | .08 | .02 |
| ☐ 119 Chicago Bears .................. | .50 | .20 | .05 |
| Team Card |  |  |  |
| ☐ 120 Billy Vessels.................. | 1.00 | .40 | .10 |

# 1994 Topps Archives 1957

Topps reprinted all 274 cards in the original 1956 and 1957 sets. The 1957 reprint set contained 154 cards, not including the unnumbered checklist card which was not reprinted. The suggested retail for a 12-card pack was 2.00. The cards measure the standard-size (2 1/2" by 3 1/2"). Factual and grammatical errors in the original cards were not changed in reprints. The fronts feature action player cutouts on bright color backgrounds. The backs were printed in red and black on gray card stock. The cards are numbered on the back. Gold versions of each card were produced and are valued at three times the values listed below.

| | MINT | EXC | G-VG |
|---|---|---|---|
| COMPLETE SET (154) | 30.00 | 12.00 | 3.00 |
| COMMON PLAYER (1-154) | .10 | .04 | .01 |

| | | | |
|---|---|---|---|
| ☐ 1 Eddie LeBaron | .30 | .12 | .03 |
| ☐ 2 Pete Retzlaff | .20 | .08 | .02 |
| ☐ 3 Mike McCormack | .75 | .30 | .07 |
| ☐ 4 Lou Baldacci | .10 | .04 | .01 |
| ☐ 5 Gino Marchetti | 1.00 | .40 | .10 |
| ☐ 6 Leo Nomellini | 1.00 | .40 | .10 |
| ☐ 7 Bobby Watkins | .10 | .04 | .01 |
| ☐ 8 Dave Middleton | .10 | .04 | .01 |
| ☐ 9 Bobby Dillon | .10 | .04 | .01 |
| ☐ 10 Les Richter | .20 | .08 | .02 |
| ☐ 11 Roosevelt Brown | .75 | .30 | .07 |
| ☐ 12 Lavern Torgeson | .20 | .08 | .02 |
| ☐ 13 Dick Bielski | .10 | .04 | .01 |
| ☐ 14 Pat Summerall | 1.00 | .40 | .10 |
| ☐ 15 Jack Butler | .10 | .04 | .01 |
| ☐ 16 John Henry Johnson | 1.00 | .40 | .10 |
| ☐ 17 Art Spinney | .10 | .04 | .01 |
| ☐ 18 Bob St. Clair | 1.00 | .40 | .10 |
| ☐ 19 Perry Jeter | .10 | .04 | .01 |
| ☐ 20 Lou Creekmur | .20 | .08 | .02 |
| ☐ 21 Dave Hanner | .20 | .08 | .02 |
| ☐ 22 Norm Van Brocklin | 2.00 | .80 | .20 |
| ☐ 23 Don Chandler | .30 | .12 | .03 |
| ☐ 24 Al Dorow | .10 | .04 | .01 |
| ☐ 25 Tom Scott | .10 | .04 | .01 |
| ☐ 26 Ollie Matson | 1.50 | .60 | .15 |
| ☐ 27 Fran Rogel | .10 | .04 | .01 |
| ☐ 28 Lou Groza | 1.50 | .60 | .15 |
| ☐ 29 Billy Vessels | .20 | .08 | .02 |
| ☐ 30 Y.A. Tittle | 2.50 | 1.00 | .25 |
| ☐ 31 George Blanda | 2.00 | .80 | .20 |
| ☐ 32 Bobby Layne | 2.50 | 1.00 | .25 |
| ☐ 33 Bill Howton | .20 | .08 | .02 |
| ☐ 34 Bill Wade | .20 | .08 | .02 |
| ☐ 35 Emlen Tunnell | 1.50 | .60 | .15 |
| ☐ 36 Leo Elter | .10 | .04 | .01 |
| ☐ 37 Clarence Peaks | .20 | .08 | .02 |
| ☐ 38 Don Stonesifer | .10 | .04 | .01 |
| ☐ 39 George Tarasovic | .10 | .04 | .01 |
| ☐ 40 Darrell Brewster | .10 | .04 | .01 |
| ☐ 41 Bert Rechichar | .10 | .04 | .01 |
| ☐ 42 Billy Wilson | .20 | .08 | .02 |
| ☐ 43 Ed Brown | .20 | .08 | .02 |
| ☐ 44 Gene Gedman | .10 | .04 | .01 |
| ☐ 45 Gary Knafelc | .10 | .04 | .01 |
| ☐ 46 Elroy Hirsch | 1.50 | .60 | .15 |
| ☐ 47 Don Heinrich | .20 | .08 | .02 |
| ☐ 48 Gene Brito | .20 | .08 | .02 |
| ☐ 49 Chuck Bednarik | 1.00 | .40 | .10 |
| ☐ 50 Dave Mann | .20 | .08 | .02 |
| ☐ 51 Bill McPeak | .10 | .04 | .01 |
| ☐ 52 Kenny Konz | .10 | .04 | .01 |
| ☐ 53 Alan Ameche | .50 | .20 | .05 |
| ☐ 54 Gordon Soltau | .10 | .04 | .01 |
| ☐ 55 Rick Casares | .30 | .12 | .03 |
| ☐ 56 Charlie Ane | .10 | .04 | .01 |
| ☐ 57 Al Carmichael | .10 | .04 | .01 |
| ☐ 58 Willard Sherman | .10 | .04 | .01 |
| ☐ 59 Kyle Rote | .75 | .30 | .07 |
| ☐ 60 Chuck Drazenovich | .10 | .04 | .01 |
| ☐ 61 Bobby Walston | .10 | .04 | .01 |
| ☐ 62 John Olszewski | .10 | .04 | .01 |
| ☐ 63 Ray Mathews | .10 | .04 | .01 |
| ☐ 64 Maurice Bassett | .10 | .04 | .01 |
| ☐ 65 Art Donovan | 1.00 | .40 | .10 |
| ☐ 66 Joe Arenas | .10 | .04 | .01 |
| ☐ 67 Harlon Hill | .20 | .08 | .02 |
| ☐ 68 Yale Lary | 1.00 | .40 | .10 |
| ☐ 69 Bill Forester | .30 | .12 | .03 |
| ☐ 70 Bob Boyd | .10 | .04 | .01 |
| ☐ 71 Andy Robustelli | .75 | .30 | .07 |
| ☐ 72 Sam Baker | .30 | .12 | .03 |
| ☐ 73 Bob Pellegrini | .10 | .04 | .01 |
| ☐ 74 Leo Sanford | .10 | .04 | .01 |
| ☐ 75 Sid Watson | .10 | .04 | .01 |
| ☐ 76 Ray Renfro | .30 | .12 | .03 |
| ☐ 77 Carl Taseff | .10 | .04 | .01 |
| ☐ 78 Clyde Conner | .10 | .04 | .01 |
| ☐ 79 J.C. Caroline | .20 | .08 | .02 |
| ☐ 80 Howard Cassady | .75 | .30 | .07 |
| **Detroit Lions** | | | |
| ☐ 81 Tobin Rote | .30 | .12 | .03 |
| ☐ 82 Ron Waller | .10 | .04 | .01 |
| ☐ 83 Jim Patton | .30 | .12 | .03 |
| ☐ 84 Volney Peters | .10 | .04 | .01 |
| ☐ 85 Dick Lane | 1.00 | .40 | .10 |
| ☐ 86 Royce Womble | .10 | .04 | .01 |
| ☐ 87 Duane Putnam | .20 | .08 | .02 |
| ☐ 88 Frank Gifford | 3.00 | 1.20 | .30 |
| ☐ 89 Steve Meilinger | .10 | .04 | .01 |
| ☐ 90 Buck Lansford | .10 | .04 | .01 |
| ☐ 91 Lindon Crow | .10 | .04 | .01 |
| ☐ 92 Ernie Stautner | 1.00 | .40 | .10 |
| ☐ 93 Preston Carpenter | .20 | .08 | .02 |
| ☐ 94 Raymond Berry | 1.50 | .60 | .15 |
| ☐ 95 Hugh McElhenny | 1.25 | .50 | .12 |
| ☐ 96 Stan Jones | 1.00 | .40 | .10 |
| ☐ 97 Dorne Dibble | .10 | .04 | .01 |
| ☐ 98 Joe Scudero | .10 | .04 | .01 |
| ☐ 99 Eddie Bell | .10 | .04 | .01 |
| ☐ 100 Joe Childress | .10 | .04 | .01 |
| ☐ 101 Elbert Nickel | .10 | .04 | .01 |
| ☐ 102 Walt Michaels | .20 | .08 | .02 |
| ☐ 103 Jim Mutscheller | .10 | .04 | .01 |
| ☐ 104 Earl Morrall | .50 | .20 | .05 |
| ☐ 105 Larry Strickland | .10 | .04 | .01 |
| ☐ 106 Jack Christiansen | 1.25 | .50 | .12 |
| ☐ 107 Fred Cone | .10 | .04 | .01 |
| ☐ 108 Bud McFadin | .20 | .08 | .02 |
| ☐ 109 Charley Conerly | 1.00 | .40 | .10 |
| ☐ 110 Tom Runnels | .10 | .04 | .01 |
| ☐ 111 Ken Keller | .10 | .04 | .01 |
| ☐ 112 James Root | .10 | .04 | .01 |
| ☐ 113 Ted Marchibroda | .30 | .12 | .03 |
| ☐ 114 Don Paul | .10 | .04 | .01 |
| ☐ 115 George Shaw | .30 | .12 | .03 |
| ☐ 116 Dick Moegle | .20 | .08 | .02 |
| ☐ 117 Don Bingham | .10 | .04 | .01 |
| ☐ 118 Leon Hart | .30 | .12 | .03 |
| ☐ 119 Bart Starr | 4.00 | 1.60 | .40 |
| ☐ 120 Paul Miller | .10 | .04 | .01 |
| ☐ 121 Alex Webster | .20 | .08 | .02 |
| ☐ 122 Ray Wietecha | .10 | .04 | .01 |
| ☐ 123 Johnny Carson | .10 | .04 | .01 |
| ☐ 124 Tommy McDonald | .50 | .20 | .05 |
| ☐ 125 Jerry Tubbs | .30 | .12 | .03 |
| ☐ 126 Jack Scarbath | .10 | .04 | .01 |
| ☐ 127 Ed Modzelewski | .20 | .08 | .02 |
| ☐ 128 Lenny Moore | 2.50 | 1.00 | .25 |
| ☐ 129 Joe Perry | 2.00 | .80 | .20 |
| ☐ 130 Bill Wightkin | .10 | .04 | .01 |
| ☐ 131 Jim Doran | .10 | .04 | .01 |
| ☐ 132 Howard Ferguson | .10 | .04 | .01 |
| ☐ 133 Tom Wilson | .20 | .08 | .02 |
| ☐ 134 Dick James | .10 | .04 | .01 |
| ☐ 135 Jimmy Harris | .10 | .04 | .01 |
| ☐ 136 Chuck Ulrich | .10 | .04 | .01 |
| ☐ 137 Lynn Chandnois | .10 | .04 | .01 |
| ☐ 138 John Unitas | 5.00 | 2.00 | .50 |
| ☐ 139 Jim Ridlon | .10 | .04 | .01 |
| ☐ 140 Zeke Bratkowski | .30 | .12 | .03 |
| ☐ 141 Ray Krouse | .10 | .04 | .01 |
| ☐ 142 John Martinkovic | .10 | .04 | .01 |
| ☐ 143 Jim Cason | .10 | .04 | .01 |
| ☐ 144 Ken MacAfee | .20 | .08 | .02 |
| ☐ 145 Sid Youngelman | .10 | .04 | .01 |
| ☐ 146 Paul Larson | .10 | .04 | .01 |
| ☐ 147 Len Ford | 1.50 | .60 | .15 |
| ☐ 148 Bob Toneff | .10 | .04 | .01 |
| ☐ 149 Ronnie Knox | .30 | .12 | .03 |
| ☐ 150 Jim David | .30 | .12 | .03 |
| ☐ 151 Paul Hornung | 4.00 | 1.60 | .40 |
| ☐ 152 Paul(Tank) Younger | .30 | .12 | .03 |
| ☐ 153 Bill Svoboda | .30 | .12 | .03 |
| ☐ 154 Fred Morrison | 1.00 | .40 | .10 |

# 1981 Topps Stickers

Like the 1981 baseball stickers, the 1981 Topps football stickers were also printed in Italy, each sticker measuring 1 15/16" by 2 9/16". The 262-card (sticker) set contains 22 All-Pro foil cards (numbers 121-142). The foil cards are somewhat more difficult to obtain, and a premium price is placed upon them. The card numbers begin with players from the AFC East teams and continue through the AFC Central and West divisions with teams within each division listed alphabetically. Card number 151 begins the NFC East teams, and a similar progression through the NFC divisions completes the remaining cards of the set. Team groupings include: Baltimore Colts

226

*DAVID LEWIS*
LINEBACKER
**BUCCANEERS**

TO COLLECT YOUR STICKERS...
Ask your dealer for the
**TOPPS Football Sticker ALBUM**

© 1981 Topps Chewing Gum, Inc.

(9-16), Buffalo Bills (17-24), Miami Dolphins (25-32), New England Patriots (33-40), New York Jets (41-48), Cincinnati Bengals (49-56), Cleveland Browns (57-64), Houston Oilers (65-72), Pittsburgh Steelers (73-80), Denver Broncos (81-88), Kansas City Chiefs (89-96), Oakland Raiders (97-104), San Diego Chargers (105-112), Seattle Seahawks (113-120), Dallas Cowboys (151-158), New York Giants (159-166), Philadelphia Eagles (167-174), St. Louis Cardinals (175-182), Washington Redskins (183-190), Chicago Bears (191-198), Detroit Lions (199-206), Green Bay Packers (207-214), Minnesota Vikings (215-222), Tampa Bay Buccaneers (223-230), Atlanta Falcons (231-238), Los Angeles Rams (239-246), New Orleans Saints (247-254), and San Francisco 49ers (25-262). The backs contain a 1981 copyright date. On the inside back cover of the sticker album the company offered (via direct mail-order) any ten different stickers (but no more than two foil) of your choice for 1.00; this is one reason why the values of the most popular players in these sticker sets are somewhat depressed compared to traditional card set prices. The front cover of the sticker album features a Buffalo Bills player. The following players are shown in their Rookie Card year or earlier: Dwight Clark, Jacob Green (two years early), Dan Hampton, Art Monk, Anthony Munoz (one year early), and Kellen Winslow.

|  | MINT | EXC | G-VG |
|---|---|---|---|
| COMPLETE SET (262) | 20.00 | 8.00 | 2.00 |
| COMMON PLAYER (1-120) | .05 | .02 | .00 |
| COMMON FOIL (121-142) | .15 | .06 | .01 |
| COMMON PLAYER (143-262) | .05 | .02 | .00 |

| | | | |
|---|---|---|---|
| ☐ 1 Brian Sipe<br>AFC Passing Leader | .10 | .04 | .01 |
| ☐ 2 Dan Fouts<br>AFC Passing<br>Yardage Leader | .30 | .12 | .03 |
| ☐ 3 John Jefferson<br>AFC Receiving<br>Yardage Leader | .08 | .03 | .01 |
| ☐ 4 Bruce Harper<br>AFC Kickoff Return<br>Yardage Leader | .05 | .02 | .00 |
| ☐ 5 J.T. Smith<br>AFC Punt Return<br>Yardage Leader | .05 | .02 | .00 |
| ☐ 6 Luke Prestridge<br>AFC Punting Leader | .05 | .02 | .00 |
| ☐ 7 Lester Hayes<br>AFC Interceptions Leader | .05 | .02 | .00 |
| ☐ 8 Gary Johnson<br>AFC Sacks Leader | .05 | .02 | .00 |
| ☐ 9 Bert Jones | .15 | .06 | .01 |
| ☐ 10 Fred Cook | .05 | .02 | .00 |
| ☐ 11 Roger Carr | .05 | .02 | .00 |
| ☐ 12 Greg Landry | .08 | .03 | .01 |
| ☐ 13 Raymond Butler | .08 | .03 | .01 |
| ☐ 14 Bruce Laird | .05 | .02 | .00 |
| ☐ 15 Ed Simonini | .05 | .02 | .00 |
| ☐ 16 Curtis Dickey | .08 | .03 | .01 |
| ☐ 17 Joe Cribbs | .10 | .04 | .01 |
| ☐ 18 Joe Ferguson | .10 | .04 | .01 |
| ☐ 19 Ben Williams | .05 | .02 | .00 |
| ☐ 20 Jerry Butler | .08 | .03 | .01 |
| ☐ 21 Roland Hooks | .05 | .02 | .00 |
| ☐ 22 Fred Smerlas | .08 | .03 | .01 |
| ☐ 23 Frank Lewis | .05 | .02 | .00 |
| ☐ 24 Mark Brammer | .05 | .02 | .00 |
| ☐ 25 Dave Woodley | .08 | .03 | .01 |
| ☐ 26 Nat Moore | .08 | .03 | .01 |
| ☐ 27 Uwe Von Schamann | .05 | .02 | .00 |
| ☐ 28 Vern Den Herder | .05 | .02 | .00 |
| ☐ 29 Tony Nathan | .08 | .03 | .01 |
| ☐ 30 Duriel Harris | .08 | .03 | .01 |
| ☐ 31 Don McNeal | .05 | .02 | .00 |
| ☐ 32 Delvin Williams | .05 | .02 | .00 |
| ☐ 33 Stanley Morgan | .12 | .05 | .01 |

| | | | |
|---|---|---|---|
| ☐ 34 John Hannah | .15 | .06 | .01 |
| ☐ 35 Horace Ivory | .05 | .02 | .00 |
| ☐ 36 Steve Nelson | .05 | .02 | .00 |
| ☐ 37 Steve Grogan | .15 | .06 | .01 |
| ☐ 38 Vagas Ferguson | .08 | .03 | .01 |
| ☐ 39 John Smith | .05 | .02 | .00 |
| ☐ 40 Mike Haynes | .12 | .05 | .01 |
| ☐ 41 Mark Gastineau | .10 | .04 | .01 |
| ☐ 42 Wesley Walker | .15 | .06 | .01 |
| ☐ 43 Joe Klecko | .10 | .04 | .01 |
| ☐ 44 Chris Ward | .05 | .02 | .00 |
| ☐ 45 Johnny Lam Jones | .08 | .03 | .01 |
| ☐ 46 Marvin Powell | .08 | .03 | .01 |
| ☐ 47 Richard Todd | .12 | .05 | .01 |
| ☐ 48 Greg Buttle | .08 | .03 | .01 |
| ☐ 49 Eddie Edwards | .05 | .02 | .00 |
| ☐ 50 Dan Ross | .08 | .03 | .01 |
| ☐ 51 Ken Anderson | .30 | .12 | .03 |
| ☐ 52 Ross Browner | .08 | .03 | .01 |
| ☐ 53 Don Bass | .08 | .03 | .01 |
| ☐ 54 Jim LeClair | .05 | .02 | .00 |
| ☐ 55 Pete Johnson | .08 | .03 | .01 |
| ☐ 56 Anthony Munoz | 1.00 | .40 | .10 |
| ☐ 57 Brian Sipe | .12 | .05 | .01 |
| ☐ 58 Mike Pruitt | .10 | .04 | .01 |
| ☐ 59 Greg Pruitt | .10 | .04 | .01 |
| ☐ 60 Thom Darden | .05 | .02 | .00 |
| ☐ 61 Ozzie Newsome | .30 | .12 | .03 |
| ☐ 62 Dave Logan | .05 | .02 | .00 |
| ☐ 63 Lyle Alzado | .15 | .06 | .01 |
| ☐ 64 Reggie Rucker | .08 | .03 | .01 |
| ☐ 65 Robert Brazile | .08 | .03 | .01 |
| ☐ 66 Mike Barber | .08 | .03 | .01 |
| ☐ 67 Carl Roaches | .08 | .03 | .01 |
| ☐ 68 Ken Stabler | .30 | .12 | .03 |
| ☐ 69 Gregg Bingham | .08 | .03 | .01 |
| ☐ 70 Mike Renfro | .08 | .03 | .01 |
| ☐ 71 Leon Gray | .05 | .02 | .00 |
| ☐ 72 Rob Carpenter | .08 | .03 | .01 |
| ☐ 73 Franco Harris | .40 | .16 | .04 |
| ☐ 74 Jack Lambert | .30 | .12 | .03 |
| ☐ 75 Jim Smith | .08 | .03 | .01 |
| ☐ 76 Mike Webster | .15 | .06 | .01 |
| ☐ 77 Sidney Thornton | .05 | .02 | .00 |
| ☐ 78 Joe Greene | .30 | .12 | .03 |
| ☐ 79 John Stallworth | .20 | .08 | .02 |
| ☐ 80 Tyrone McGriff | .05 | .02 | .00 |
| ☐ 81 Randy Gradishar | .15 | .06 | .01 |
| ☐ 82 Haven Moses | .08 | .03 | .01 |
| ☐ 83 Riley Odoms | .08 | .03 | .01 |
| ☐ 84 Matt Robinson | .05 | .02 | .00 |
| ☐ 85 Craig Morton | .12 | .05 | .01 |
| ☐ 86 Rulon Jones | .05 | .02 | .00 |
| ☐ 87 Rick Upchurch | .08 | .03 | .01 |
| ☐ 88 Jim Jensen | .05 | .02 | .00 |
| ☐ 89 Art Still | .08 | .03 | .01 |
| ☐ 90 J.T. Smith | .12 | .05 | .01 |
| ☐ 91 Steve Fuller | .05 | .02 | .00 |
| ☐ 92 Gary Barbaro | .08 | .03 | .01 |
| ☐ 93 Ted McKnight | .05 | .02 | .00 |
| ☐ 94 Bob Grupp | .05 | .02 | .00 |
| ☐ 95 Henry Marshall | .05 | .02 | .00 |
| ☐ 96 Mike Williams | .05 | .02 | .00 |
| ☐ 97 Jim Plunkett | .15 | .06 | .01 |
| ☐ 98 Lester Hayes | .12 | .05 | .01 |
| ☐ 99 Cliff Branch | .15 | .06 | .01 |
| ☐ 100 John Matuszak | .10 | .04 | .01 |
| ☐ 101 Matt Millen | .10 | .04 | .01 |
| ☐ 102 Kenny King | .08 | .03 | .01 |
| ☐ 103 Ray Guy | .15 | .06 | .01 |
| ☐ 104 Ted Hendricks | .20 | .08 | .02 |
| ☐ 105 John Jefferson | .12 | .05 | .01 |
| ☐ 106 Fred Dean | .08 | .03 | .01 |
| ☐ 107 Dan Fouts | .35 | .14 | .03 |
| ☐ 108 Charlie Joiner | .25 | .10 | .02 |
| ☐ 109 Kellen Winslow | 1.00 | .40 | .10 |
| ☐ 110 Gary Johnson | .08 | .03 | .01 |
| ☐ 111 Mike Thomas | .05 | .02 | .00 |
| ☐ 112 Louie Kelcher | .08 | .03 | .01 |
| ☐ 113 Jim Zorn | .12 | .05 | .01 |
| ☐ 114 Terry Beeson | .05 | .02 | .00 |
| ☐ 115 Jacob Green | .35 | .14 | .03 |
| ☐ 116 Steve Largent | 1.00 | .40 | .10 |
| ☐ 117 Dan Doornink | .05 | .02 | .00 |
| ☐ 118 Manu Tuiasosopo | .05 | .02 | .00 |
| ☐ 119 John Sawyer | .05 | .02 | .00 |
| ☐ 120 Jim Jodat | .05 | .02 | .00 |
| ☐ 121 Walter Payton<br>All-Pro FOIL | 1.25 | .50 | .12 |
| ☐ 122 Brian Sipe<br>All-Pro FOIL | .20 | .08 | .02 |
| ☐ 123 Joe Cribbs<br>All-Pro FOIL | .20 | .08 | .02 |
| ☐ 124 James Lofton<br>All-Pro FOIL | .50 | .20 | .05 |
| ☐ 125 John Jefferson<br>All-Pro FOIL | .20 | .08 | .02 |

| | | | |
|---|---|---|---|
| ☐ 126 Leon Gray | .15 | .06 | .01 |
| All-Pro FOIL | | | |
| ☐ 127 Joe DeLamielleure | .15 | .06 | .01 |
| All-Pro FOIL | | | |
| ☐ 128 Mike Webster | .25 | .10 | .02 |
| All-Pro FOIL | | | |
| ☐ 129 John Hannah | .25 | .10 | .02 |
| All-Pro FOIL | | | |
| ☐ 130 Mike Kenn | .20 | .08 | .02 |
| All-Pro FOIL | | | |
| ☐ 131 Kellen Winslow | 1.25 | .50 | .12 |
| All-Pro FOIL | | | |
| ☐ 132 Lee Roy Selmon | .25 | .10 | .02 |
| All-Pro FOIL | | | |
| ☐ 133 Randy White | .30 | .12 | .03 |
| All-Pro FOIL | | | |
| ☐ 134 Gary Johnson | .15 | .06 | .01 |
| All-Pro FOIL | | | |
| ☐ 135 Art Still | .15 | .06 | .01 |
| All-Pro FOIL | | | |
| ☐ 136 Robert Brazile | .20 | .08 | .02 |
| All-Pro FOIL | | | |
| ☐ 137 Nolan Cromwell | .20 | .08 | .02 |
| All-Pro FOIL | | | |
| ☐ 138 Ted Hendricks | .30 | .12 | .03 |
| All-Pro FOIL | | | |
| ☐ 139 Lester Hayes | .20 | .08 | .02 |
| All-Pro FOIL | | | |
| ☐ 140 Randy Gradishar | .30 | .12 | .03 |
| All-Pro FOIL | | | |
| ☐ 141 Lemar Parrish | .20 | .08 | .02 |
| All-Pro FOIL | | | |
| ☐ 142 Donnie Shell | .20 | .08 | .02 |
| All-Pro FOIL | | | |
| ☐ 143 Ron Jaworski | .12 | .05 | .01 |
| NFC Passing Leader | | | |
| ☐ 144 Archie Manning | .15 | .06 | .01 |
| NFC Passing Yardage Leader | | | |
| ☐ 145 Walter Payton | .60 | .24 | .06 |
| NFC Rushing Yardage Leader | | | |
| ☐ 146 Billy Sims | .20 | .08 | .02 |
| NFC Rushing Touchdowns Leader | | | |
| ☐ 147 James Lofton | .25 | .10 | .02 |
| NFC Receiving Yardage Leader | | | |
| ☐ 148 Dave Jennings | .05 | .02 | .00 |
| NFC Punting Leader | | | |
| ☐ 149 Nolan Cromwell | .08 | .03 | .01 |
| NFC Interceptions Leader | | | |
| ☐ 150 Al(Bubba) Baker | .08 | .03 | .01 |
| NFC Sacks Leader | | | |
| ☐ 151 Tony Dorsett | .40 | .16 | .04 |
| ☐ 152 Harvey Martin | .15 | .06 | .01 |
| ☐ 153 Danny White | .20 | .08 | .02 |
| ☐ 154 Pat Donovan | .05 | .02 | .00 |
| ☐ 155 Drew Pearson | .15 | .06 | .01 |
| ☐ 156 Robert Newhouse | .08 | .03 | .01 |
| ☐ 157 Randy White | .30 | .12 | .03 |
| ☐ 158 Butch Johnson | .10 | .04 | .01 |
| ☐ 159 Dave Jennings | .05 | .02 | .00 |
| ☐ 160 Brad Van Pelt | .08 | .03 | .01 |
| ☐ 161 Phil Simms | .40 | .16 | .04 |
| ☐ 162 Mike Friede | .05 | .02 | .00 |
| ☐ 163 Billy Taylor | .08 | .03 | .01 |
| ☐ 164 Gary Jeter | .08 | .03 | .01 |
| ☐ 165 George Martin | .05 | .02 | .00 |
| ☐ 166 Earnest Gray | .05 | .02 | .00 |
| ☐ 167 Ron Jaworski | .15 | .06 | .01 |
| ☐ 168 Bill Bergey | .10 | .04 | .01 |
| ☐ 169 Wilbert Montgomery | .10 | .04 | .01 |
| ☐ 170 Charlie Smith | .05 | .02 | .00 |
| ☐ 171 Jerry Robinson | .08 | .03 | .01 |
| ☐ 172 Herman Edwards | .05 | .02 | .00 |
| ☐ 173 Harold Carmichael | .15 | .06 | .01 |
| ☐ 174 Claude Humphrey | .08 | .03 | .01 |
| ☐ 175 Ottis Anderson | .30 | .12 | .03 |
| ☐ 176 Jim Hart | .15 | .06 | .01 |
| ☐ 177 Pat Tilley | .08 | .03 | .01 |
| ☐ 178 Rush Brown | .05 | .02 | .00 |
| ☐ 179 Tom Brahaney | .05 | .02 | .00 |
| ☐ 180 Dan Dierdorf | .20 | .08 | .02 |
| ☐ 181 Wayne Morris | .05 | .02 | .00 |
| ☐ 182 Doug Marsh | .05 | .02 | .00 |
| ☐ 183 Art Monk | 2.50 | 1.00 | .25 |
| ☐ 184 Clarence Harmon | .05 | .02 | .00 |
| ☐ 185 Lemar Parrish | .08 | .03 | .01 |
| ☐ 186 Joe Theismann | .35 | .14 | .03 |
| ☐ 187 Joe Lavender | .05 | .02 | .00 |
| ☐ 188 Wilbur Jackson | .05 | .02 | .00 |
| ☐ 189 Dave Butz | .08 | .03 | .01 |
| ☐ 190 Coy Bacon | .05 | .02 | .00 |
| ☐ 191 Walter Payton | 1.25 | .50 | .12 |
| ☐ 192 Alan Page | .15 | .06 | .01 |
| ☐ 193 Vince Evans | .15 | .06 | .01 |

| | | | |
|---|---|---|---|
| ☐ 194 Roland Harper | .08 | .03 | .01 |
| ☐ 195 Dan Hampton | .75 | .30 | .07 |
| ☐ 196 Gary Fencik | .08 | .03 | .01 |
| ☐ 197 Mike Hartenstine | .05 | .02 | .00 |
| ☐ 198 Robin Earl | .05 | .02 | .00 |
| ☐ 199 Billy Sims | .25 | .10 | .02 |
| ☐ 200 Leonard Thompson | .05 | .02 | .00 |
| ☐ 201 Jeff Komlo | .05 | .02 | .00 |
| ☐ 202 Al(Bubba) Baker | .10 | .04 | .01 |
| ☐ 203 Eddie Murray | .15 | .06 | .01 |
| ☐ 204 Dexter Bussey | .05 | .02 | .00 |
| ☐ 205 Tom Ginn | .05 | .02 | .00 |
| ☐ 206 Freddie Scott | .08 | .03 | .01 |
| ☐ 207 James Lofton | .40 | .16 | .04 |
| ☐ 208 Mike Butler | .05 | .02 | .00 |
| ☐ 209 Lynn Dickey | .12 | .05 | .01 |
| ☐ 210 Gerry Ellis | .05 | .02 | .00 |
| ☐ 211 Eddie Lee Ivery | .10 | .04 | .01 |
| ☐ 212 Ezra Johnson | .05 | .02 | .00 |
| ☐ 213 Paul Coffman | .08 | .03 | .01 |
| ☐ 214 Aundra Thompson | .05 | .02 | .00 |
| ☐ 215 Ahmad Rashad | .25 | .10 | .02 |
| ☐ 216 Tommy Kramer | .12 | .05 | .01 |
| ☐ 217 Matt Blair | .08 | .03 | .01 |
| ☐ 218 Sammie White | .08 | .03 | .01 |
| ☐ 219 Ted Brown | .08 | .03 | .01 |
| ☐ 220 Joe Senser | .08 | .03 | .01 |
| ☐ 221 Rickey Young | .08 | .03 | .01 |
| ☐ 222 Randy Holloway | .05 | .02 | .00 |
| ☐ 223 Lee Roy Selmon | .15 | .06 | .01 |
| ☐ 224 Doug Williams | .15 | .06 | .01 |
| ☐ 225 Ricky Bell | .10 | .04 | .01 |
| ☐ 226 David Lewis | .05 | .02 | .00 |
| ☐ 227 Gordon Jones | .08 | .03 | .01 |
| ☐ 228 Dewey Selmon | .08 | .03 | .01 |
| ☐ 229 Jimmie Giles | .08 | .03 | .01 |
| ☐ 230 Mike Washington | .05 | .02 | .00 |
| ☐ 231 William Andrews | .15 | .06 | .01 |
| ☐ 232 Jeff Van Note | .08 | .03 | .01 |
| ☐ 233 Steve Bartkowski | .15 | .06 | .01 |
| ☐ 234 Junior Miller | .08 | .03 | .01 |
| ☐ 235 Lynn Cain | .08 | .03 | .01 |
| ☐ 236 Joel Williams | .05 | .02 | .00 |
| ☐ 237 Alfred Jenkins | .08 | .03 | .01 |
| ☐ 238 Kenny Johnson | .05 | .02 | .00 |
| ☐ 239 Jack Youngblood | .20 | .08 | .02 |
| ☐ 240 Elvis Peacock | .08 | .03 | .01 |
| ☐ 241 Cullen Bryant | .05 | .02 | .00 |
| ☐ 242 Dennis Harrah | .05 | .02 | .00 |
| ☐ 243 Billy Waddy | .05 | .02 | .00 |
| ☐ 244 Nolan Cromwell | .10 | .04 | .01 |
| ☐ 245 Doug France | .05 | .02 | .00 |
| ☐ 246 Johnnie Johnson | .08 | .03 | .01 |
| ☐ 247 Archie Manning | .20 | .08 | .02 |
| ☐ 248 Tony Galbreath | .08 | .03 | .01 |
| ☐ 249 Wes Chandler | .15 | .06 | .01 |
| ☐ 250 Stan Brock | .05 | .02 | .00 |
| ☐ 251 Ike Harris | .05 | .02 | .00 |
| ☐ 252 Russell Erxleben | .05 | .02 | .00 |
| ☐ 253 Jimmy Rogers | .05 | .02 | .00 |
| ☐ 254 Tom Myers | .05 | .02 | .00 |
| ☐ 255 Dwight Clark | .60 | .24 | .06 |
| ☐ 256 Earl Cooper | .05 | .02 | .00 |
| ☐ 257 Steve DeBerg | .25 | .10 | .02 |
| ☐ 258 Randy Cross | .10 | .04 | .01 |
| ☐ 259 Freddie Solomon | .08 | .03 | .01 |
| ☐ 260 Jim Miller | .05 | .02 | .00 |
| ☐ 261 Charley Young | .08 | .03 | .01 |
| ☐ 262 Bobby Leopold | .05 | .02 | .00 |
| ☐ xx Sticker Album | 1.25 | .50 | .12 |

# 1981 Topps Red Border Stickers

This set of 28 red-bordered stickers was distributed as a separate issue (inside a football capsule) unlike the "Coming Soon" subsets, which were inserted in with the regular football card wax packs. They are the same size as the regular Topps stickers (as 1 15/16" by 2 9/16") and tougher to find than the other "Coming Soon" sticker subsets distributed in later years. The numbering in this set is completely different from the sticker numbering in the 1981 Topps 262-sticker set. There was one sticker issued for each team.

| | MINT | EXC | G-VG |
|---|---|---|---|
| COMPLETE SET (28) | 20.00 | 8.00 | 2.00 |
| COMMON PLAYER (1-28) | .35 | .14 | .03 |
| | | | |
| ☐ 1 Steve Bartkowski | .75 | .30 | .07 |
| Atlanta Falcons | | | |
| ☐ 2 Bert Jones | .75 | .30 | .07 |
| Baltimore Colts | | | |
| ☐ 3 Joe Cribbs | .60 | .24 | .06 |
| Buffalo Bills | | | |
| ☐ 4 Walter Payton | 5.00 | 2.00 | .50 |

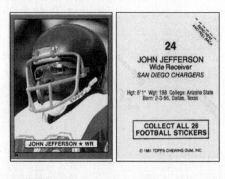

"Coming Soon" stickers were inserted in the regular issue 1982 Topps football card wax packs. They are the same size as the regular Topps stickers with the same sticker numbers as well; hence the set is skip-numbered.

|  | MINT | EXC | G-VG |
|---|---|---|---|
| COMPLETE SET (16) | 6.00 | 2.40 | .60 |
| COMMON PLAYER | .20 | .08 | .02 |
| ☐ 5 MVP Super Bowl XVI | 2.50 | 1.00 | .25 |
| (Joe Montana) | | | |
| ☐ 6 NFC Championship | .20 | .08 | .02 |
| ☐ 9 Super Bowl XVI | 2.00 | .80 | .20 |
| (Joe Montana | | | |
| handing off) | | | |
| ☐ 71 Tommy Kramer | .30 | .12 | .03 |
| Minnesota Vikings | | | |
| ☐ 73 George Rogers | .30 | .12 | .03 |
| Washington Redskins | | | |
| ☐ 75 Tom Skladany | .20 | .08 | .02 |
| Detroit Lions | | | |
| ☐ 139 Nolan Cromwell AP | .30 | .12 | .03 |
| Los Angeles Rams | | | |
| ☐ 143 Jack Lambert AP | .50 | .20 | .05 |
| Pittsburgh Steelers | | | |
| ☐ 144 Lawrence Taylor AP | 2.00 | .80 | .20 |
| New York Giants | | | |
| ☐ 150 Billy Sims AP | .40 | .16 | .04 |
| Detroit Lions | | | |
| ☐ 154 Ken Anderson AP | .40 | .16 | .04 |
| Cincinnati Bengals | | | |
| ☐ 159 John Hannah AP | .40 | .16 | .04 |
| New England Patriots | | | |
| ☐ 160 Anthony Munoz AP | 1.00 | .40 | .10 |
| Cincinnati Bengals | | | |
| ☐ 220 Ken Anderson | .50 | .20 | .05 |
| Cincinnati Bengals | | | |
| ☐ 221 Dan Fouts | .50 | .20 | .05 |
| San Diego Chargers | | | |
| ☐ 222 Frank Lewis | .20 | .08 | .02 |
| Buffalo Bills | | | |

| | | | |
|---|---|---|---|
| Chicago Bears | | | |
| ☐ 5 Ross Browner | .35 | .14 | .03 |
| Cincinnati Bengals | | | |
| ☐ 6 Brian Sipe | .50 | .20 | .05 |
| Cleveland Browns | | | |
| ☐ 7 Tony Dorsett | 2.00 | .80 | .20 |
| Dallas Cowboys | | | |
| ☐ 8 Randy Gradishar | .60 | .24 | .06 |
| Denver Broncos | | | |
| ☐ 9 Billy Sims | 1.00 | .40 | .10 |
| Detroit Lions | | | |
| ☐ 10 James Lofton | 2.00 | .80 | .20 |
| Green Bay Packers | | | |
| ☐ 11 Mike Barber | .35 | .14 | .03 |
| Houston Oilers | | | |
| ☐ 12 Art Still | .50 | .20 | .05 |
| Kansas City Chiefs | | | |
| ☐ 13 Jack Youngblood | .75 | .30 | .07 |
| Los Angeles Rams | | | |
| ☐ 14 David Woodley | .50 | .20 | .05 |
| Miami Dolphins | | | |
| ☐ 15 Ahmad Rashad | 1.25 | .50 | .12 |
| Minnesota Vikings | | | |
| ☐ 16 Russ Francis | .50 | .20 | .05 |
| New England Patriots | | | |
| ☐ 17 Archie Manning | .75 | .30 | .07 |
| New Orleans Saints | | | |
| ☐ 18 Dave Jennings | .35 | .14 | .03 |
| New York Giants | | | |
| ☐ 19 Richard Todd | .50 | .20 | .05 |
| New York Jets | | | |
| ☐ 20 Lester Hayes | .50 | .20 | .05 |
| Oakland Raiders | | | |
| ☐ 21 Ron Jaworski | .50 | .20 | .05 |
| Philadelphia Eagles | | | |
| ☐ 22 Franco Harris | 2.00 | .80 | .20 |
| Pittsburgh Steelers | | | |
| ☐ 23 Ottis Anderson | 1.00 | .40 | .10 |
| St. Louis Cardinals | | | |
| ☐ 24 John Jefferson | .50 | .20 | .05 |
| San Diego Chargers | | | |
| ☐ 25 Freddie Solomon | .35 | .14 | .03 |
| San Francisco 49ers | | | |
| ☐ 26 Steve Largent | 3.50 | 1.40 | .35 |
| Seattle Seahawks | | | |
| ☐ 27 Lee Roy Selmon | .60 | .24 | .06 |
| Tampa Bay Buccaneers | | | |
| ☐ 28 Art Monk | 7.50 | 3.00 | .75 |
| Washington Redskins | | | |

## 1982 Topps "Coming Soon" Stickers

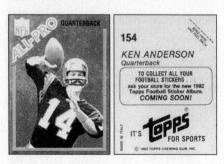

This 16-sticker set advertises "Coming Soon" on the sticker backs. All stickers in this small set were gold bordered foil stickers; these

## 1982 Topps Stickers

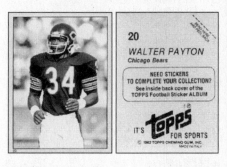

The 1982 Topps football sticker set contains 288 stickers and is similar in format to the 1981 sticker set. The stickers measure 1 15/16" by 2 9/16". This year's stickers have yellow borders compared to the white borders of the previous year. Stickers numbered 1-10, 70-77, 139-160, and 220-227 are foils. Stickers numbered 1 and 2 combine to portray the San Francisco 49ers, Super Bowl XVI Champions. Sticker numbers 3 and 4 combine to form the Super Bowl XVI theme art trophy. Stickers are numbered essentially in team order, with the teams themselves ordered alphabetically by team name within conference, e.g., Atlanta Falcons (11-18), Chicago Bears (19-27), Dallas Cowboys (28-36), Detroit Lions (37-45), Green Bay Packers (46-53), Los Angeles Rams (54-61), Minnesota Vikings (62-69), New Orleans Saints (78-85), New York Giants (86-94), Philadelphia Eagles (95-103), St. Louis Cardinals (104-112), San Francisco 49ers (113-121), Tampa Bay Buccaneers (122-129), Washington Redskins (130-138), Baltimore Colts (161-168), Buffalo Bills (169-177), Cincinnati Bengals (178-186), Cleveland Browns (187-195), Denver Broncos (196-203), Houston Oilers (204-211), Kansas City Chiefs (212-219), Miami Dolphins (228-236), New England Patriots (237-245), New York Jets (246-254), Oakland Raiders (255-262), Pittsburgh Steelers (263-271), San Diego Chargers (272-280), and Seattle Seahawks (281-288). Those stickers that are asterisked in the checklist below are those that were also included in the "Coming Soon" sticker set inserted in early 1982 football wax packs. The backs contain a 1982 copyright date. On the inside back cover of the sticker album the company offered (via direct mail-order) any ten different stickers (but no more than two foil) of your choice for 1.00; this is one reason why the values of the most popular players in these sticker sets are somewhat depressed compared to traditional card set prices. The front cover of the sticker album features Joe Montana. The following players are shown in their Rookie Card year: James Brooks, Cris Collinsworth, Ronnie Lott, Anthony Munoz, Lawrence Taylor, and Everson Walls.

| | MINT | EXC | G-VG |
|---|---|---|---|
| COMPLETE SET (288) | 25.00 | 10.00 | 2.50 |
| COMMON PLAYER (1-288) | .05 | .02 | .00 |
| COMMON FOIL | .15 | .06 | .01 |
| ☐ 1 Super Bowl XVI Champs, San Francisco 49ers Team (L) FOIL | .25 | .10 | .02 |
| ☐ 2 Super Bowl XVI Champs, San Francisco 49ers Team (R) FOIL | .15 | .06 | .01 |
| ☐ 3 Super Bowl XVI Theme Art trophy (top) FOIL | .15 | .06 | .01 |
| ☐ 4 Super Bowl XVI Theme Art trophy (bottom) FOIL | .15 | .06 | .01 |
| ☐ 5 MVP Joe Montana Super Bowl XVI * FOIL | 3.00 | 1.20 | .30 |
| ☐ 6 1981 NFC Champions 49'ers * FOIL | .15 | .06 | .01 |
| ☐ 7 1981 AFC Champions (Ken Anderson handing off) FOIL | .25 | .10 | .02 |
| ☐ 8 Super Bowl XVI (Ken Anderson dropping back) FOIL | .25 | .10 | .02 |
| ☐ 9 Super Bowl XVI (Joe Montana handing off) * FOIL | 2.50 | 1.00 | .25 |
| ☐ 10 Super Bowl XVI (line blocking) FOIL | .15 | .06 | .01 |
| ☐ 11 Steve Bartkowski | .15 | .06 | .01 |
| ☐ 12 William Andrews | .10 | .04 | .01 |
| ☐ 13 Lynn Cain | .08 | .03 | .01 |
| ☐ 14 Wallace Francis | .08 | .03 | .01 |
| ☐ 15 Alfred Jackson | .08 | .03 | .01 |
| ☐ 16 Alfred Jenkins | .10 | .04 | .01 |
| ☐ 17 Mike Kenn | .08 | .03 | .01 |
| ☐ 18 Junior Miller | .08 | .03 | .01 |
| ☐ 19 Vince Evans | .10 | .04 | .01 |
| ☐ 20 Walter Payton | 1.00 | .40 | .10 |
| ☐ 21 Dave Williams | .05 | .02 | .00 |
| ☐ 22 Brian Baschnagel | .05 | .02 | .00 |
| ☐ 23 Rickey Watts | .05 | .02 | .00 |
| ☐ 24 Ken Margerum | .08 | .03 | .01 |
| ☐ 25 Revie Sorey | .05 | .02 | .00 |
| ☐ 26 Gary Fencik | .08 | .03 | .01 |
| ☐ 27 Matt Suhey | .05 | .02 | .00 |
| ☐ 28 Danny White | .15 | .06 | .01 |
| ☐ 29 Tony Dorsett | .35 | .14 | .03 |
| ☐ 30 Drew Pearson | .15 | .06 | .01 |
| ☐ 31 Rafael Septien | .08 | .03 | .01 |
| ☐ 32 Pat Donovan | .05 | .02 | .00 |
| ☐ 33 Herbert Scott | .05 | .02 | .00 |
| ☐ 34 Ed Too Tall Jones | .15 | .06 | .01 |
| ☐ 35 Randy White | .25 | .10 | .02 |
| ☐ 36 Tony Hill | .08 | .03 | .01 |
| ☐ 37 Eric Hipple | .08 | .03 | .01 |
| ☐ 38 Billy Sims | .20 | .08 | .02 |
| ☐ 39 Dexter Bussey | .05 | .02 | .00 |
| ☐ 40 Freddie Scott | .08 | .03 | .01 |
| ☐ 41 David Hill | .05 | .02 | .00 |
| ☐ 42 Eddie Murray | .08 | .03 | .01 |
| ☐ 43 Tom Skladany | .05 | .02 | .00 |
| ☐ 44 Doug English | .08 | .03 | .01 |
| ☐ 45 Al(Bubba) Baker | .08 | .03 | .01 |
| ☐ 46 Lynn Dickey | .12 | .05 | .01 |
| ☐ 47 Gerry Ellis | .05 | .02 | .00 |
| ☐ 48 Harlan Huckleby | .08 | .03 | .01 |
| ☐ 49 James Lofton | .35 | .14 | .03 |
| ☐ 50 John Jefferson | .08 | .03 | .01 |
| ☐ 51 Paul Coffman | .05 | .02 | .00 |
| ☐ 52 Jan Stenerud | .15 | .06 | .01 |
| ☐ 53 Rich Wingo | .05 | .02 | .00 |
| ☐ 54 Wendell Tyler | .08 | .03 | .01 |
| ☐ 55 Preston Dennard | .05 | .02 | .00 |
| ☐ 56 Billy Waddy | .05 | .02 | .00 |
| ☐ 57 Frank Corral | .05 | .02 | .00 |
| ☐ 58 Jack Youngblood | .15 | .06 | .01 |
| ☐ 59 Pat Thomas | .05 | .02 | .00 |
| ☐ 60 Rod Perry | .08 | .03 | .01 |
| ☐ 61 Nolan Cromwell | .10 | .04 | .01 |
| ☐ 62 Tommy Kramer | .10 | .04 | .01 |
| ☐ 63 Rickey Young | .08 | .03 | .01 |
| ☐ 64 Ted Brown | .08 | .03 | .01 |
| ☐ 65 Ahmad Rashad | .25 | .10 | .02 |
| ☐ 66 Sammie White | .08 | .03 | .01 |
| ☐ 67 Joe Senser | .08 | .03 | .01 |
| ☐ 68 Ron Yary | .08 | .03 | .01 |
| ☐ 69 Matt Blair | .08 | .03 | .01 |
| ☐ 70 Joe Montana FOIL NFC Passing Leader | 2.50 | 1.00 | .25 |
| ☐ 71 Tommy Kramer * FOIL NFC Passing Yardage Leader | .20 | .08 | .02 |
| ☐ 72 Alfred Jenkins FOIL NFC Receiving Yardage Leader | .15 | .06 | .01 |
| ☐ 73 George Rogers * FOIL NFC Rushing Yardage Leader | .20 | .08 | .02 |
| ☐ 74 Wendell Tyler FOIL NFC Rushing Touchdowns Leader | .20 | .08 | .02 |
| ☐ 75 Tom Skladany * FOIL NFC Punting Leader | .15 | .06 | .01 |
| ☐ 76 Everson Walls FOIL NFC Interceptions Leader | .35 | .14 | .03 |
| ☐ 77 Curtis Greer FOIL NFC Sacks Leader | .15 | .06 | .01 |
| ☐ 78 Archie Manning | .20 | .08 | .02 |
| ☐ 79 Dave Waymer | .08 | .03 | .01 |
| ☐ 80 George Rogers | .20 | .08 | .02 |
| ☐ 81 Jack Holmes | .05 | .02 | .00 |
| ☐ 82 Toussaint Tyler | .05 | .02 | .00 |
| ☐ 83 Wayne Wilson | .05 | .02 | .00 |
| ☐ 84 Russell Erxleben | .05 | .02 | .00 |
| ☐ 85 Elois Grooms | .05 | .02 | .00 |
| ☐ 86 Phil Simms | .20 | .08 | .02 |
| ☐ 87 Scott Brunner | .08 | .03 | .01 |
| ☐ 88 Rob Carpenter | .08 | .03 | .01 |
| ☐ 89 Johnny Perkins | .05 | .02 | .00 |
| ☐ 90 Dave Jennings | .05 | .02 | .00 |
| ☐ 91 Harry Carson | .12 | .05 | .01 |
| ☐ 92 Lawrence Taylor | 2.00 | .80 | .20 |
| ☐ 93 Beasley Reece | .05 | .02 | .00 |
| ☐ 94 Mark Haynes | .08 | .03 | .01 |
| ☐ 95 Ron Jaworski | .12 | .05 | .01 |
| ☐ 96 Wilbert Montgomery | .08 | .03 | .01 |
| ☐ 97 Hubert Oliver | .05 | .02 | .00 |
| ☐ 98 Harold Carmichael | .12 | .05 | .01 |
| ☐ 99 Jerry Robinson | .08 | .03 | .01 |
| ☐ 100 Stan Walters | .05 | .02 | .00 |
| ☐ 101 Charlie Johnson | .05 | .02 | .00 |
| ☐ 102 Roynell Young | .08 | .03 | .01 |
| ☐ 103 Tony Franklin | .05 | .02 | .00 |
| ☐ 104 Neil Lomax | .15 | .06 | .01 |
| ☐ 105 Jim Hart | .15 | .06 | .01 |
| ☐ 106 Ottis Anderson | .20 | .08 | .02 |
| ☐ 107 Stump Mitchell | .10 | .04 | .01 |
| ☐ 108 Pat Tilley | .08 | .03 | .01 |
| ☐ 109 Rush Brown | .05 | .02 | .00 |
| ☐ 110 E.J. Junior | .08 | .03 | .01 |
| ☐ 111 Ken Greene | .05 | .02 | .00 |
| ☐ 112 Mel Gray | .08 | .03 | .01 |
| ☐ 113 Joe Montana | 2.00 | .80 | .20 |
| ☐ 114 Ricky Patton | .05 | .02 | .00 |
| ☐ 115 Earl Cooper | .05 | .02 | .00 |
| ☐ 116 Dwight Clark | .25 | .10 | .02 |
| ☐ 117 Freddie Solomon | .08 | .03 | .01 |
| ☐ 118 Randy Cross | .10 | .04 | .01 |
| ☐ 119 Fred Dean | .08 | .03 | .01 |
| ☐ 120 Ronnie Lott | 2.00 | .80 | .20 |
| ☐ 121 Dwight Hicks | .08 | .03 | .01 |
| ☐ 122 Doug Williams | .15 | .06 | .01 |
| ☐ 123 Jerry Eckwood | .08 | .03 | .01 |
| ☐ 124 James Owens | .08 | .03 | .01 |
| ☐ 125 Kevin House | .08 | .03 | .01 |
| ☐ 126 Jimmie Giles | .08 | .03 | .01 |
| ☐ 127 Charley Hannah | .05 | .02 | .00 |
| ☐ 128 Lee Roy Selmon | .15 | .06 | .01 |
| ☐ 129 Hugh Green | .12 | .05 | .01 |
| ☐ 130 Joe Theismann | .30 | .12 | .03 |
| ☐ 131 Joe Washington | .08 | .03 | .01 |
| ☐ 132 John Riggins | .25 | .10 | .02 |
| ☐ 133 Art Monk | .50 | .20 | .05 |
| ☐ 134 Ricky Thompson | .05 | .02 | .00 |
| ☐ 135 Don Warren | .08 | .03 | .01 |
| ☐ 136 Perry Brooks | .05 | .02 | .00 |
| ☐ 137 Mike Nelms | .08 | .03 | .01 |
| ☐ 138 Mark Moseley | .08 | .03 | .01 |
| ☐ 139 Nolan Cromwell * AP FOIL | .20 | .08 | .02 |
| ☐ 140 Dwight Hicks AP FOIL | .15 | .06 | .01 |
| ☐ 141 Ronnie Lott AP FOIL | 2.50 | 1.00 | .25 |
| ☐ 142 Harry Carson AP FOIL | .20 | .08 | .02 |
| ☐ 143 Jack Lambert * AP FOIL | .30 | .12 | .03 |
| ☐ 144 Lawrence Taylor * AP FOIL | 2.50 | 1.00 | .25 |
| ☐ 145 Mel Blount | .25 | .10 | .02 |

| | | | |
|---|---|---|---|
| AP FOIL | | | |
| ☐ 146 Joe Klecko | .15 | .06 | .01 |
| AP FOIL | | | |
| ☐ 147 Randy White | .30 | .12 | .03 |
| AP FOIL | | | |
| ☐ 148 Doug English | .15 | .06 | .01 |
| AP FOIL | | | |
| ☐ 149 Fred Dean | .15 | .06 | .01 |
| AP FOIL | | | |
| ☐ 150 Billy Sims * | .25 | .10 | .02 |
| AP FOIL | | | |
| ☐ 151 Tony Dorsett | .60 | .24 | .06 |
| AP FOIL | | | |
| ☐ 152 James Lofton | .60 | .24 | .06 |
| AP FOIL | | | |
| ☐ 153 Alfred Jenkins | .20 | .08 | .02 |
| AP FOIL | | | |
| ☐ 154 Ken Anderson * | .35 | .14 | .03 |
| AP FOIL | | | |
| ☐ 155 Kellen Winslow | .40 | .16 | .04 |
| AP FOIL | | | |
| ☐ 156 Marvin Powell | .15 | .06 | .01 |
| AP FOIL | | | |
| ☐ 157 Randy Cross | .20 | .08 | .02 |
| AP FOIL | | | |
| ☐ 158 Mike Webster | .25 | .10 | .02 |
| AP FOIL | | | |
| ☐ 159 John Hannah * | .30 | .12 | .03 |
| AP FOIL | | | |
| ☐ 160 Anthony Munoz * | 1.00 | .40 | .10 |
| AP FOIL | | | |
| ☐ 161 Curtis Dickey | .08 | .03 | .01 |
| ☐ 162 Randy McMillan | .08 | .03 | .01 |
| ☐ 163 Roger Carr | .08 | .03 | .01 |
| ☐ 164 Raymond Butler | .08 | .03 | .01 |
| ☐ 165 Reese McCall | .05 | .02 | .00 |
| ☐ 166 Ed Simonini | .05 | .02 | .00 |
| ☐ 167 Herb Orvis | .05 | .02 | .00 |
| ☐ 168 Nesby Glasgow | .05 | .02 | .00 |
| ☐ 169 Joe Ferguson | .10 | .04 | .01 |
| ☐ 170 Joe Cribbs | .10 | .04 | .01 |
| ☐ 171 Jerry Butler | .08 | .03 | .01 |
| ☐ 172 Frank Lewis | .08 | .03 | .01 |
| ☐ 173 Mark Brammer | .05 | .02 | .00 |
| ☐ 174 Fred Smerlas | .08 | .03 | .01 |
| ☐ 175 Jim Haslett | .05 | .02 | .00 |
| ☐ 176 Charles Romes | .05 | .02 | .00 |
| ☐ 177 Bill Simpson | .05 | .02 | .00 |
| ☐ 178 Ken Anderson | .20 | .08 | .02 |
| ☐ 179 Charles Alexander | .05 | .02 | .00 |
| ☐ 180 Pete Johnson | .08 | .03 | .01 |
| ☐ 181 Isaac Curtis | .08 | .03 | .01 |
| ☐ 182 Cris Collinsworth | .50 | .20 | .05 |
| ☐ 183 Pat McInally | .08 | .03 | .01 |
| ☐ 184 Anthony Munoz | .50 | .20 | .05 |
| ☐ 185 Louis Breeden | .05 | .02 | .00 |
| ☐ 186 Jim Breech | .05 | .02 | .00 |
| ☐ 187 Brian Sipe | .10 | .04 | .01 |
| ☐ 188 Charles White | .10 | .04 | .01 |
| ☐ 189 Mike Pruitt | .08 | .03 | .01 |
| ☐ 190 Reggie Rucker | .08 | .03 | .01 |
| ☐ 191 Dave Logan | .05 | .02 | .00 |
| ☐ 192 Ozzie Newsome | .30 | .12 | .03 |
| ☐ 193 Dick Ambrose | .05 | .02 | .00 |
| ☐ 194 Joe DeLamielleure | .05 | .02 | .00 |
| ☐ 195 Ricky Feacher | .05 | .02 | .00 |
| ☐ 196 Craig Morton | .12 | .05 | .01 |
| ☐ 197 Dave Preston | .05 | .02 | .00 |
| ☐ 198 Rick Parros | .05 | .02 | .00 |
| ☐ 199 Rick Upchurch | .08 | .03 | .01 |
| ☐ 200 Steve Watson | .08 | .03 | .01 |
| ☐ 201 Riley Odoms | .08 | .03 | .01 |
| ☐ 202 Randy Gradishar | .10 | .04 | .01 |
| ☐ 203 Steve Foley | .05 | .02 | .00 |
| ☐ 204 Ken Stabler | .30 | .12 | .03 |
| ☐ 205 Gifford Nielsen | .08 | .03 | .01 |
| ☐ 206 Tim Wilson | .05 | .02 | .00 |
| ☐ 207 Ken Burrough | .08 | .03 | .01 |
| ☐ 208 Mike Renfro | .08 | .03 | .01 |
| ☐ 209 Greg Stemrick | .05 | .02 | .00 |
| ☐ 210 Robert Brazile | .08 | .03 | .01 |
| ☐ 211 Gregg Bingham | .08 | .03 | .01 |
| ☐ 212 Steve Fuller | .08 | .03 | .01 |
| ☐ 213 Bill Kenney | .08 | .03 | .01 |
| ☐ 214 Joe Delaney | .15 | .06 | .01 |
| ☐ 215 Henry Marshall | .05 | .02 | .00 |
| ☐ 216 Nick Lowery | .10 | .04 | .01 |
| ☐ 217 Art Still | .08 | .03 | .01 |
| ☐ 218 Gary Green | .05 | .02 | .00 |
| ☐ 219 Gary Barbaro | .08 | .03 | .01 |
| ☐ 220 Ken Anderson * FOIL | .35 | .14 | .03 |
| AFC Passing Leader | | | |
| ☐ 221 Dan Fouts * FOIL | .40 | .16 | .04 |
| AFC Passing Yardage Leader | | | |
| ☐ 222 Frank Lewis * FOIL | .15 | .06 | .01 |
| AFC Receiving Yardage Leader | | | |

| | | | |
|---|---|---|---|
| ☐ 222 Steve Watson FOIL | .15 | .06 | .01 |
| AFC Receiving Yardage Leader | | | |
| ☐ 223 James Brooks FOIL | .60 | .24 | .06 |
| AFC Kickoff Return Yardage Leader | | | |
| ☐ 224 Chuck Muncie FOIL | .20 | .08 | .02 |
| AFC Rushing Touchdowns Leader | | | |
| ☐ 225 Pat McInally FOIL | .15 | .06 | .01 |
| AFC Punting Leader | | | |
| ☐ 226 John Harris FOIL | .15 | .06 | .01 |
| AFC Interceptions Leader | | | |
| ☐ 227 Joe Klecko FOIL | .15 | .06 | .01 |
| AFC Sacks Leader | | | |
| ☐ 228 Dave Woodley | .08 | .03 | .01 |
| ☐ 229 Tony Nathan | .08 | .03 | .01 |
| ☐ 230 Andra Franklin | .08 | .03 | .01 |
| ☐ 231 Nat Moore | .08 | .03 | .01 |
| ☐ 232 Duriel Harris | .08 | .03 | .01 |
| ☐ 233 Uwe Von Schamann | .05 | .02 | .00 |
| ☐ 234 Bob Baumhower | .08 | .03 | .01 |
| ☐ 235 Glenn Blackwood | .08 | .03 | .01 |
| ☐ 236 Tommy Vigorito | .05 | .02 | .00 |
| ☐ 237 Steve Grogan | .12 | .05 | .01 |
| ☐ 238 Matt Cavanaugh | .08 | .03 | .01 |
| ☐ 239 Tony Collins | .08 | .03 | .01 |
| ☐ 240 Vagas Ferguson | .08 | .03 | .01 |
| ☐ 241 John Smith | .05 | .02 | .00 |
| ☐ 242 Stanley Morgan | .10 | .04 | .01 |
| ☐ 243 John Hannah | .15 | .06 | .01 |
| ☐ 244 Steve Nelson | .05 | .02 | .00 |
| ☐ 245 Don Hasselbeck | .05 | .02 | .00 |
| ☐ 246 Richard Todd | .10 | .04 | .01 |
| ☐ 247 Bruce Harper | .05 | .02 | .00 |
| ☐ 248 Wesley Walker | .12 | .05 | .01 |
| ☐ 249 Jerome Barkum | .08 | .03 | .01 |
| ☐ 250 Marvin Powell | .08 | .03 | .01 |
| ☐ 251 Mark Gastineau | .08 | .03 | .01 |
| ☐ 252 Joe Klecko | .08 | .03 | .01 |
| ☐ 253 Darrol Ray | .05 | .02 | .00 |
| ☐ 254 Marty Lyons | .08 | .03 | .01 |
| ☐ 255 Marc Wilson | .10 | .04 | .01 |
| ☐ 256 Kenny King | .08 | .03 | .01 |
| ☐ 257 Mark Van Eeghen | .08 | .03 | .01 |
| ☐ 258 Cliff Branch | .12 | .05 | .01 |
| ☐ 259 Bob Chandler | .08 | .03 | .01 |
| ☐ 260 Ray Guy | .15 | .06 | .01 |
| ☐ 261 Ted Hendricks | .20 | .08 | .02 |
| ☐ 262 Lester Hayes | .10 | .04 | .01 |
| ☐ 263 Terry Bradshaw | .60 | .24 | .06 |
| ☐ 264 Franco Harris | .35 | .14 | .03 |
| ☐ 265 John Stallworth | .15 | .06 | .01 |
| ☐ 266 Jim Smith | .05 | .02 | .00 |
| ☐ 267 Mike Webster | .12 | .05 | .01 |
| ☐ 268 Jack Lambert | .20 | .08 | .02 |
| ☐ 269 Mel Blount | .15 | .06 | .01 |
| ☐ 270 Donnie Shell | .08 | .03 | .01 |
| ☐ 271 Bennie Cunningham | .05 | .02 | .00 |
| ☐ 272 Dan Fouts | .35 | .14 | .03 |
| ☐ 273 Chuck Muncie | .10 | .04 | .01 |
| ☐ 274 James Brooks | .50 | .20 | .05 |
| ☐ 275 Charlie Joiner | .20 | .08 | .02 |
| ☐ 276 Wes Chandler | .12 | .05 | .01 |
| ☐ 277 Kellen Winslow | .25 | .10 | .02 |
| ☐ 278 Doug Wilkerson | .05 | .02 | .00 |
| ☐ 279 Gary Johnson | .08 | .03 | .01 |
| ☐ 280 Rolf Benirschke | .08 | .03 | .01 |
| ☐ 281 Jim Zorn | .12 | .05 | .01 |
| ☐ 282 Theotis Brown | .08 | .03 | .01 |
| ☐ 283 Dan Doornink | .05 | .02 | .00 |
| ☐ 284 Steve Largent | 1.00 | .40 | .10 |
| ☐ 285 Sam McCullum | .08 | .03 | .01 |
| ☐ 286 Efren Herrera | .05 | .02 | .00 |
| ☐ 287 Manu Tuiasosopo | .05 | .02 | .00 |
| ☐ 288 John Harris | .05 | .02 | .00 |
| ☐ 288 Sticker Album | 2.00 | .80 | .20 |
| (Joe Montana) | | | |

# 1983 Topps Sticker Boxes

The 1983 Topps Sticker Box set contains 12 boxes each containing two large cards (24 cards total) on the side of the box itself and 35 stickers inside. Cards, when cut, measure approximately 2 1/2" by 3 1/2". These blank-backed cards are unnumbered but each box is numbered on a white box tab. The player on top is offense and the lower player is defense. Number 10 was not issued. Prices below reflect the value of the uncut boxes not including the stickers inside the box.

| | MINT | EXC | G-VG |
|---|---|---|---|
| COMPLETE SET (12) | 10.00 | 4.00 | 1.00 |
| COMMON PAIR (1-13) | 1.00 | .40 | .10 |

and 264-271. The numbering sequence is ordered in the following way: Double Foils (1-4), Running Backs (5-14), Baltimore Colts (15-22), Buffalo Bills (23-30), Cincinnati Bengals (31-39), Cleveland Browns (40-48), Denver Broncos (49-56), Houston Oilers (57-64), Kansas City Chiefs (65-72), AFC Foils (73-80), Los Angeles Raiders (81-89), Miami Dolphins (90-98), New England Patriots (99-107), New York Jets (108-116), Pittsburgh Steelers (117-125), San Diego Chargers (126-134), Seattle Seahawks (135-142), Double Foils (143-152), Atlanta Falcons (203-211), Chicago Bears (212-219), Dallas Cowboys (220-228), Detroit Lions (229-237), Green Bay Packers (238-246), Los Angeles Rams (247-254), Minnesota Vikings (255-262), NFC Foils (264-271), New Orleans Saints (272-279), New York Giants (280-287), Philadelphia Eagles (288-295), St. Louis Cardinals (296-304), San Francisco 49ers (305-312), Tampa Bay Buccaneers (313-321), and Washington Redskins (322-330). On the inside back cover of the sticker album the company offered (via direct mail-order) any ten different stickers (but no more than two foil) of your choice for 1.00; this is one reason why the values of the most popular players in these sticker sets are somewhat depressed compared to traditional card set prices. The following players are shown in their Rookie Card year: Marcus Allen, Jim McMahon, and Mike Singletary.

| | MINT | EXC | G-VG |
|---|---|---|---|
| COMPLETE SET (330) | 25.00 | 10.00 | 2.50 |
| COMMON STICKER (1-330) | .05 | .02 | .00 |
| COMMON FOIL | .15 | .06 | .01 |
| ☐ 1 Franco Harris | .50 | .20 | .05 |
| (Left half) FOIL | | | |
| ☐ 2 Franco Harris | .30 | .12 | .03 |
| (Right half) FOIL | | | |
| ☐ 3 Walter Payton | 1.00 | .40 | .10 |
| (Left half) FOIL | | | |
| ☐ 4 Walter Payton | 1.00 | .40 | .10 |
| (Right half) FOIL | | | |
| ☐ 5 John Riggins | .30 | .12 | .03 |
| ☐ 6 Tony Dorsett | .30 | .12 | .03 |
| ☐ 7 Mark Van Eeghen | .08 | .03 | .01 |
| ☐ 8 Chuck Muncie | .08 | .03 | .01 |
| ☐ 9 Wilbert Montgomery | .08 | .03 | .01 |
| ☐ 10 Greg Pruitt | .08 | .03 | .01 |
| ☐ 11 Sam Cunningham | .08 | .03 | .01 |
| ☐ 12 Ottis Anderson | .15 | .06 | .01 |
| ☐ 13 Mike Pruitt | .08 | .03 | .01 |
| ☐ 14 Dexter Bussey | .05 | .02 | .00 |
| ☐ 15 Mike Pagel | .08 | .03 | .01 |
| ☐ 16 Curtis Dickey | .08 | .03 | .01 |
| ☐ 17 Randy McMillan | .08 | .03 | .01 |
| ☐ 18 Raymond Butler | .08 | .03 | .01 |
| ☐ 19 Nesby Glasgow | .05 | .02 | .00 |
| ☐ 20 Zachary Dixon | .05 | .02 | .00 |
| ☐ 21 Matt Bouza | .08 | .03 | .01 |
| ☐ 22 Johnie Cooks | .08 | .03 | .01 |
| ☐ 23 Curtis Brown | .05 | .02 | .00 |
| ☐ 24 Joe Cribbs | .08 | .03 | .01 |
| ☐ 25 Roosevelt Leaks | .08 | .03 | .01 |
| ☐ 26 Jerry Butler | .08 | .03 | .01 |
| ☐ 27 Frank Lewis | .08 | .03 | .01 |
| ☐ 28 Fred Smerlas | .08 | .03 | .01 |
| ☐ 29 Ben Williams | .05 | .02 | .00 |
| ☐ 30 Joe Ferguson | .10 | .04 | .01 |
| ☐ 31 Isaac Curtis | .08 | .03 | .01 |
| ☐ 32 Cris Collinsworth | .15 | .06 | .01 |
| ☐ 33 Anthony Munoz | .20 | .08 | .02 |
| ☐ 34 Max Montoya | .08 | .03 | .01 |
| ☐ 35 Ross Browner | .08 | .03 | .01 |
| ☐ 36 Reggie Williams | .10 | .04 | .01 |
| ☐ 37 Ken Riley | .08 | .03 | .01 |
| ☐ 38 Pete Johnson | .08 | .03 | .01 |
| ☐ 39 Ken Anderson | .20 | .08 | .02 |
| ☐ 40 Charles White | .10 | .04 | .01 |
| ☐ 41 Dave Logan | .05 | .02 | .00 |
| ☐ 42 Doug Dieken | .05 | .02 | .00 |
| ☐ 43 Ozzie Newsome | .20 | .08 | .02 |
| ☐ 44 Tom Cousineau | .10 | .04 | .01 |
| ☐ 45 Bob Golic | .10 | .04 | .01 |
| ☐ 46 Brian Sipe | .10 | .04 | .01 |
| ☐ 47 Paul McDonald | .05 | .02 | .00 |
| ☐ 48 Mike Pruitt | .08 | .03 | .01 |
| ☐ 49 Luke Prestridge | .05 | .02 | .00 |
| ☐ 50 Randy Gradishar | .10 | .04 | .01 |
| ☐ 51 Rulon Jones | .08 | .03 | .01 |
| ☐ 52 Rick Parros | .05 | .02 | .00 |
| ☐ 53 Steve DeBerg | .15 | .06 | .01 |
| ☐ 54 Tom Jackson | .10 | .04 | .01 |
| ☐ 55 Rick Upchurch | .08 | .03 | .01 |
| ☐ 56 Steve Watson | .08 | .03 | .01 |
| ☐ 57 Robert Brazile | .08 | .03 | .01 |
| ☐ 58 Willie Tullis | .05 | .02 | .00 |
| ☐ 59 Archie Manning | .15 | .06 | .01 |
| ☐ 60 Gifford Nielsen | .08 | .03 | .01 |
| ☐ 61 Harold Bailey | .05 | .02 | .00 |
| ☐ 62 Carl Roaches | .08 | .03 | .01 |
| ☐ 63 Gregg Bingham | .05 | .02 | .00 |
| ☐ 64 Daryl Hunt | .05 | .02 | .00 |

| | | | |
|---|---|---|---|
| ☐ 1 Pat Donovan and | 1.00 | .40 | .10 |
| Dallas Cowboys | | | |
| Mark Gastineau | | | |
| New York Jets | | | |
| ☐ 2 Wes Chandler and | 1.25 | .50 | .12 |
| San Diego Chargers | | | |
| Nolan Cromwell | | | |
| Los Angeles Rams | | | |
| ☐ 3 Marvin Powell and | 1.25 | .50 | .12 |
| New York Jets | | | |
| Ed Too Tall Jones | | | |
| Dallas Cowboys | | | |
| ☐ 4 Ken Anderson and | 1.25 | .50 | .12 |
| Cincinnati Bengals | | | |
| Tony Peters | | | |
| Washington Redskins | | | |
| ☐ 5 Freeman McNeil and | 2.00 | .80 | .20 |
| New York Jets | | | |
| Lawrence Taylor | | | |
| New York Giants | | | |
| ☐ 6 Mark Moseley and | 1.00 | .40 | .10 |
| Washington Redskins | | | |
| Dave Jennings | | | |
| New York Giants | | | |
| ☐ 7 Dwight Clark and | 1.25 | .50 | .12 |
| San Francisco 49ers | | | |
| Mark Haynes | | | |
| New England Patriots | | | |
| ☐ 8 Jeff Van Note and | 1.00 | .40 | .10 |
| Atlanta Falcons | | | |
| Harry Carson | | | |
| New York Giants | | | |
| ☐ 9 Tony Dorsett and | 2.00 | .80 | .20 |
| Dallas Cowboys | | | |
| Hugh Green | | | |
| Tampa Bay Buccaneers | | | |
| ☐ 11 Randy Cross and | 1.00 | .40 | .10 |
| San Francisco 49ers | | | |
| Gary Johnson | | | |
| San Diego Chargers | | | |
| ☐ 12 Kellen Winslow and | 1.25 | .50 | .12 |
| San Diego Chargers | | | |
| Lester Hayes | | | |
| Los Angeles Raiders | | | |
| ☐ 13 John Hannah and | 2.00 | .80 | .20 |
| New England Patriots | | | |
| Randy White | | | |
| Dallas Cowboys | | | |

# 1983 Topps Stickers

The 1983 Topps football sticker set (330) is similar to the previous years in that it contains stickers, foil stickers, and an accompanying album to house one's sticker collection. The foil stickers are noted in the checklist below by "FOIL"; foils are numbers 1-4, 73-80, 143-152,

|  | | | |
|---|---|---|---|
| ☐ 65 Gary Green | .08 | .03 | .01 |
| ☐ 66 Gary Barbaro | .08 | .03 | .01 |
| ☐ 67 Bill Kenney | .08 | .03 | .01 |
| ☐ 68 Joe Delaney | .10 | .04 | .01 |
| ☐ 69 Henry Marshall | .05 | .02 | .00 |
| ☐ 70 Nick Lowery | .10 | .04 | .01 |
| ☐ 71 Jeff Gossett | .05 | .02 | .00 |
| ☐ 72 Art Still | .08 | .03 | .01 |
| ☐ 73 Ken Anderson FOIL AFC Passing Leader | .35 | .14 | .03 |
| ☐ 74 Dan Fouts FOIL AFC Passing Yardage Leader | .40 | .16 | .04 |
| ☐ 75 Wes Chandler FOIL AFC Receiving Yardage Leader | .20 | .08 | .02 |
| ☐ 76 James Brooks FOIL AFC Kickoff Return Yardage Leader | .30 | .12 | .03 |
| ☐ 77 Rick Upchurch FOIL AFC Punt Return Yardage Leader | .20 | .08 | .02 |
| ☐ 78 Luke Prestridge FOIL AFC Punting Leader | .15 | .06 | .01 |
| ☐ 79 Jesse Baker FOIL AFC Sacks Leader | .15 | .06 | .01 |
| ☐ 80 Freeman McNeil FOIL AFC Rushing Yardage Leader | .35 | .14 | .03 |
| ☐ 81 Ray Guy | .15 | .06 | .01 |
| ☐ 82 Jim Plunkett | .15 | .06 | .01 |
| ☐ 83 Lester Hayes | .08 | .03 | .01 |
| ☐ 84 Kenny King | .08 | .03 | .01 |
| ☐ 85 Cliff Branch | .12 | .05 | .01 |
| ☐ 86 Todd Christensen | .12 | .05 | .01 |
| ☐ 87 Lyle Alzado | .15 | .06 | .01 |
| ☐ 88 Ted Hendricks | .20 | .08 | .02 |
| ☐ 89 Rod Martin | .08 | .03 | .01 |
| ☐ 90 Dave Woodley | .08 | .03 | .01 |
| ☐ 91 Ed Newman | .05 | .02 | .00 |
| ☐ 92 Earnie Rhone | .05 | .02 | .00 |
| ☐ 93 Don McNeal | .05 | .02 | .00 |
| ☐ 94 Glenn Blackwood | .08 | .03 | .01 |
| ☐ 95 Andra Franklin | .08 | .03 | .01 |
| ☐ 96 Nat Moore | .08 | .03 | .01 |
| ☐ 97 Lyle Blackwood | .08 | .03 | .01 |
| ☐ 98 A.J. Duhe | .08 | .03 | .01 |
| ☐ 99 Tony Collins | .08 | .03 | .01 |
| ☐ 100 Stanley Morgan | .10 | .04 | .01 |
| ☐ 101 Pete Brock | .05 | .02 | .00 |
| ☐ 102 Steve Nelson | .05 | .02 | .00 |
| ☐ 103 Steve Grogan | .12 | .05 | .01 |
| ☐ 104 Mark Van Eeghen | .08 | .03 | .01 |
| ☐ 105 Don Hasselbeck | .05 | .02 | .00 |
| ☐ 106 John Hannah | .15 | .06 | .01 |
| ☐ 107 Mike Haynes | .12 | .05 | .01 |
| ☐ 108 Wesley Walker | .10 | .04 | .01 |
| ☐ 109 Marvin Powell | .08 | .03 | .01 |
| ☐ 110 Joe Klecko | .08 | .03 | .01 |
| ☐ 111 Bobby Jackson | .05 | .02 | .00 |
| ☐ 112 Richard Todd | .10 | .04 | .01 |
| ☐ 113 Lance Mehl | .08 | .03 | .01 |
| ☐ 114 Johnny Lam Jones | .08 | .03 | .01 |
| ☐ 115 Mark Gastineau | .08 | .03 | .01 |
| ☐ 116 Freeman McNeil | .15 | .06 | .01 |
| ☐ 117 Franco Harris | .30 | .12 | .03 |
| ☐ 118 Mike Webster | .15 | .06 | .01 |
| ☐ 119 Mel Blount | .15 | .06 | .01 |
| ☐ 120 Donnie Shell | .08 | .03 | .01 |
| ☐ 121 Terry Bradshaw | .50 | .20 | .05 |
| ☐ 122 John Stallworth | .12 | .05 | .01 |
| ☐ 123 Jack Lambert | .20 | .08 | .02 |
| ☐ 124 Dwayne Woodruff | .05 | .02 | .00 |
| ☐ 125 Bennie Cunningham | .05 | .02 | .00 |
| ☐ 126 Charlie Joiner | .20 | .08 | .02 |
| ☐ 127 Kellen Winslow | .20 | .08 | .02 |
| ☐ 128 Rolf Benirschke | .08 | .03 | .01 |
| ☐ 129 Louie Kelcher | .08 | .03 | .01 |
| ☐ 130 Chuck Muncie | .08 | .03 | .01 |
| ☐ 131 Wes Chandler | .10 | .04 | .01 |
| ☐ 132 Gary Johnson | .08 | .03 | .01 |
| ☐ 133 James Brooks | .15 | .06 | .01 |
| ☐ 134 Dan Fouts | .35 | .14 | .03 |
| ☐ 135 Jacob Green | .10 | .04 | .01 |
| ☐ 136 Michael Jackson | .05 | .02 | .00 |
| ☐ 137 Jim Zorn | .12 | .05 | .01 |
| ☐ 138 Sherman Smith | .08 | .03 | .01 |
| ☐ 139 Keith Simpson | .05 | .02 | .00 |
| ☐ 140 Steve Largent | 1.00 | .40 | .10 |
| ☐ 141 John Harris | .05 | .02 | .00 |
| ☐ 142 Jeff West | .05 | .02 | .00 |
| ☐ 143 Ken Anderson (top) FOIL | .35 | .14 | .03 |
| ☐ 144 Ken Anderson (bottom) FOIL | .35 | .14 | .03 |
| ☐ 145 Tony Dorsett (top) FOIL | .40 | .16 | .04 |
| ☐ 146 Tony Dorsett (bottom) FOIL | .40 | .16 | .04 |
| ☐ 147 Dan Fouts (top) FOIL | .40 | .16 | .04 |
| ☐ 148 Dan Fouts (bottom) FOIL | .40 | .16 | .04 |
| ☐ 149 Joe Montana (top) FOIL | 1.50 | .60 | .15 |
| ☐ 150 Joe Montana (bottom) FOIL | 1.50 | .60 | .15 |
| ☐ 151 Mark Moseley (top) FOIL | .15 | .06 | .01 |
| ☐ 152 Mark Moseley (bottom) FOIL | .15 | .06 | .01 |
| ☐ 153 Richard Todd | .08 | .03 | .01 |
| ☐ 154 Butch Johnson | .08 | .03 | .01 |
| ☐ 155 Gary Hogeboom UER (Bill on back) | .08 | .03 | .01 |
| ☐ 156 A.J. Duhe | .08 | .03 | .01 |
| ☐ 157 Kurt Sohn | .05 | .02 | .00 |
| ☐ 158 Drew Pearson | .10 | .04 | .01 |
| ☐ 159 John Riggins | .25 | .10 | .02 |
| ☐ 160 Pat Donovan | .05 | .02 | .00 |
| ☐ 161 John Hannah | .15 | .06 | .01 |
| ☐ 162 Jeff Van Note | .08 | .03 | .01 |
| ☐ 163 Randy Cross | .10 | .04 | .01 |
| ☐ 164 Marvin Powell | .08 | .03 | .01 |
| ☐ 165 Kellen Winslow | .20 | .08 | .02 |
| ☐ 166 Dwight Clark | .20 | .08 | .02 |
| ☐ 167 Wes Chandler | .08 | .03 | .01 |
| ☐ 168 Tony Dorsett | .30 | .12 | .03 |
| ☐ 169 Freeman McNeil | .12 | .05 | .01 |
| ☐ 170 Ken Anderson | .25 | .10 | .02 |
| ☐ 171 Mark Moseley | .08 | .03 | .01 |
| ☐ 172 Mark Gastineau | .08 | .03 | .01 |
| ☐ 173 Gary Johnson | .05 | .02 | .00 |
| ☐ 174 Randy White | .20 | .08 | .02 |
| ☐ 175 Ed Too Tall Jones | .12 | .05 | .01 |
| ☐ 176 Hugh Green | .08 | .03 | .01 |
| ☐ 177 Harry Carson | .08 | .03 | .01 |
| ☐ 178 Lawrence Taylor | .30 | .12 | .03 |
| ☐ 179 Lester Hayes | .08 | .03 | .01 |
| ☐ 180 Mark Haynes | .08 | .03 | .01 |
| ☐ 181 Dave Jennings | .05 | .02 | .00 |
| ☐ 182 Nolan Cromwell | .08 | .03 | .01 |
| ☐ 183 Tony Peters | .05 | .02 | .00 |
| ☐ 184 Jimmy Cefalo | .08 | .03 | .01 |
| ☐ 185 A.J. Duhe | .08 | .03 | .01 |
| ☐ 186 John Riggins | .25 | .10 | .02 |
| ☐ 187 Charlie Brown | .08 | .03 | .01 |
| ☐ 188 Mike Nelms | .05 | .02 | .00 |
| ☐ 189 Mark Murphy | .05 | .02 | .00 |
| ☐ 190 Fulton Walker | .05 | .02 | .00 |
| ☐ 191 Marcus Allen | 2.00 | .80 | .20 |
| ☐ 192 Chip Banks | .08 | .03 | .01 |
| ☐ 193 Charlie Brown | .08 | .03 | .01 |
| ☐ 194 Bob Crable | .08 | .03 | .01 |
| ☐ 195 Vernon Dean | .05 | .02 | .00 |
| ☐ 196 Jim McMahon | .75 | .30 | .07 |
| ☐ 197 Tootie Robbins | .08 | .03 | .01 |
| ☐ 198 Luis Sharpe | .08 | .03 | .01 |
| ☐ 199 Rohn Stark | .08 | .03 | .01 |
| ☐ 200 Lester Williams | .05 | .02 | .00 |
| ☐ 201 Leo Wisniewski | .05 | .02 | .00 |
| ☐ 202 Butch Woolfolk | .08 | .03 | .01 |
| ☐ 203 Mike Kenn | .08 | .03 | .01 |
| ☐ 204 R.C. Thielemann | .05 | .02 | .00 |
| ☐ 205 Buddy Curry | .05 | .02 | .00 |
| ☐ 206 Steve Bartkowski | .12 | .05 | .01 |
| ☐ 207 Alfred Jackson | .08 | .03 | .01 |
| ☐ 208 Don Smith | .05 | .02 | .00 |
| ☐ 209 Alfred Jenkins | .08 | .03 | .01 |
| ☐ 210 Fulton Kuykendall | .05 | .02 | .00 |
| ☐ 211 William Andrews | .10 | .04 | .01 |
| ☐ 212 Gary Fencik | .08 | .03 | .01 |
| ☐ 213 Walter Payton | 1.00 | .40 | .10 |
| ☐ 214 Mike Singletary | 1.00 | .40 | .10 |
| ☐ 215 Otis Wilson | .08 | .03 | .01 |
| ☐ 216 Matt Suhey | .05 | .02 | .00 |
| ☐ 217 Dan Hampton | .20 | .08 | .02 |
| ☐ 218 Emery Moorehead | .05 | .02 | .00 |
| ☐ 219 Mike Hartenstine | .05 | .02 | .00 |
| ☐ 220 Danny White | .15 | .06 | .01 |
| ☐ 221 Drew Pearson | .10 | .04 | .01 |
| ☐ 222 Rafael Septien | .05 | .02 | .00 |
| ☐ 223 Ed Too Tall Jones | .12 | .05 | .01 |
| ☐ 224 Everson Walls | .10 | .04 | .01 |
| ☐ 225 Randy White | .20 | .08 | .02 |
| ☐ 226 Harvey Martin | .10 | .04 | .01 |
| ☐ 227 Tony Hill | .08 | .03 | .01 |
| ☐ 228 Tony Dorsett | .30 | .12 | .03 |
| ☐ 229 Billy Sims | .20 | .08 | .02 |
| ☐ 230 Leonard Thompson | .05 | .02 | .00 |
| ☐ 231 Eddie Murray | .08 | .03 | .01 |
| ☐ 232 Doug English | .08 | .03 | .01 |
| ☐ 233 Ken Fantetti | .05 | .02 | .00 |
| ☐ 234 Tom Skladany | .05 | .02 | .00 |

| | | | |
|---|---|---|---|
| ☐ 235 Freddie Scott | .05 | .02 | .00 |
| ☐ 236 Eric Hipple | .08 | .03 | .01 |
| ☐ 237 David Hill | .05 | .02 | .00 |
| ☐ 238 John Jefferson | .08 | .03 | .01 |
| ☐ 239 Paul Coffman | .08 | .03 | .01 |
| ☐ 240 Ezra Johnson | .05 | .02 | .00 |
| ☐ 241 Mike Douglass | .05 | .02 | .00 |
| ☐ 242 Mark Lee | .08 | .03 | .01 |
| ☐ 243 John Anderson | .08 | .03 | .01 |
| ☐ 244 Jan Stenerud | .15 | .06 | .01 |
| ☐ 245 Lynn Dickey | .10 | .04 | .01 |
| ☐ 246 James Lofton | .30 | .12 | .03 |
| ☐ 247 Vince Ferragamo | .12 | .05 | .01 |
| ☐ 248 Preston Dennard | .05 | .02 | .00 |
| ☐ 249 Jack Youngblood | .15 | .06 | .01 |
| ☐ 250 Mike Guman | .05 | .02 | .00 |
| ☐ 251 LeRoy Irvin | .08 | .03 | .01 |
| ☐ 252 Mike Lansford | .05 | .02 | .00 |
| ☐ 253 Kent Hill | .05 | .02 | .00 |
| ☐ 254 Nolan Cromwell | .08 | .03 | .01 |
| ☐ 255 Doug Martin | .05 | .02 | .00 |
| ☐ 256 Greg Coleman | .05 | .02 | .00 |
| ☐ 257 Ted Brown | .08 | .03 | .01 |
| ☐ 258 Mark Mullaney | .05 | .02 | .00 |
| ☐ 259 Joe Senser | .08 | .03 | .01 |
| ☐ 260 Randy Holloway | .05 | .02 | .00 |
| ☐ 261 Matt Blair | .08 | .03 | .01 |
| ☐ 262 Sammie White | .08 | .03 | .01 |
| ☐ 263 Tommy Kramer | .10 | .04 | .01 |
| ☐ 264 Joe Theismann FOIL NFC Passing Leader | .40 | .16 | .04 |
| ☐ 265 Joe Montana FOIL NFC Passing Yardage Leader | 1.25 | .50 | .12 |
| ☐ 266 Dwight Clark FOIL NFC Receiving Yardage Leader | .25 | .10 | .02 |
| ☐ 267 Mike Nelms FOIL NFC Kickoff Return Yardage Leader | .15 | .06 | .01 |
| ☐ 268 Carl Birdsong FOIL NFC Punting Leader | .15 | .06 | .01 |
| ☐ 269 Everson Walls FOIL NFC Interceptions Leader | .20 | .08 | .02 |
| ☐ 270 Doug Martin FOIL NFC Sacks Leader | .15 | .06 | .01 |
| ☐ 271 Tony Dorsett FOIL NFC Rushing Yardage Leader | .40 | .16 | .04 |
| ☐ 272 Russell Erxleben | .05 | .02 | .00 |
| ☐ 273 Stan Brock | .05 | .02 | .00 |
| ☐ 274 Jeff Groth | .05 | .02 | .00 |
| ☐ 275 Bruce Clark | .08 | .03 | .01 |
| ☐ 276 Ken Stabler | .30 | .12 | .03 |
| ☐ 277 George Rogers | .10 | .04 | .01 |
| ☐ 278 Derland Moore | .08 | .03 | .01 |
| ☐ 279 Wayne Wilson | .05 | .02 | .00 |
| ☐ 280 Lawrence Taylor | .35 | .14 | .03 |
| ☐ 281 Harry Carson | .10 | .04 | .01 |
| ☐ 282 Brian Kelley | .05 | .02 | .00 |
| ☐ 283 Brad Van Pelt | .08 | .03 | .01 |
| ☐ 284 Earnest Gray | .05 | .02 | .00 |
| ☐ 285 Dave Jennings | .05 | .02 | .00 |
| ☐ 286 Rob Carpenter | .05 | .02 | .00 |
| ☐ 287 Scott Brunner | .08 | .03 | .01 |
| ☐ 288 Ron Jaworski | .12 | .05 | .01 |
| ☐ 289 Jerry Robinson | .08 | .03 | .01 |
| ☐ 290 Frank LeMaster | .05 | .02 | .00 |
| ☐ 291 Wilbert Montgomery | .08 | .03 | .01 |
| ☐ 292 Tony Franklin | .05 | .02 | .00 |
| ☐ 293 Harold Carmichael | .10 | .04 | .01 |
| ☐ 294 John Spagnola | .05 | .02 | .00 |
| ☐ 295 Herman Edwards | .05 | .02 | .00 |
| ☐ 296 Ottis Anderson | .15 | .06 | .01 |
| ☐ 297 Carl Birdsong | .05 | .02 | .00 |
| ☐ 298 Doug Marsh | .08 | .03 | .01 |
| ☐ 299 Neil Lomax | .12 | .05 | .01 |
| ☐ 300 Rush Brown | .05 | .02 | .00 |
| ☐ 301 Pat Tilley | .08 | .03 | .01 |
| ☐ 302 Wayne Morris | .08 | .03 | .01 |
| ☐ 303 Dan Dierdorf | .15 | .06 | .01 |
| ☐ 304 Roy Green | .20 | .08 | .02 |
| ☐ 305 Joe Montana | 1.25 | .50 | .12 |
| ☐ 306 Randy Cross | .10 | .04 | .01 |
| ☐ 307 Freddie Solomon | .08 | .03 | .01 |
| ☐ 308 Jack Reynolds | .10 | .04 | .01 |
| ☐ 309 Ronnie Lott | .40 | .16 | .04 |
| ☐ 310 Renaldo Nehemiah | .15 | .06 | .01 |
| ☐ 311 Russ Francis | .08 | .03 | .01 |
| ☐ 312 Dwight Clark | .20 | .08 | .02 |
| ☐ 313 Doug Williams | .10 | .04 | .01 |
| ☐ 314 Bill Capece | .05 | .02 | .00 |
| ☐ 315 Mike Washington | .05 | .02 | .00 |
| ☐ 316 Hugh Green | .10 | .04 | .01 |
| ☐ 317 Kevin House | .08 | .03 | .01 |
| ☐ 318 Lee Roy Selmon | .12 | .05 | .01 |
| ☐ 319 Neal Colzie | .05 | .02 | .00 |

| | | | |
|---|---|---|---|
| ☐ 320 Jimmie Giles | .08 | .03 | .01 |
| ☐ 321 Cedric Brown | .05 | .02 | .00 |
| ☐ 322 Tony Peters | .05 | .02 | .00 |
| ☐ 323 Neal Olkewicz | .05 | .02 | .00 |
| ☐ 324 Dexter Manley | .08 | .03 | .01 |
| ☐ 325 Joe Theismann | .30 | .12 | .03 |
| ☐ 326 Rich Milot | .05 | .02 | .00 |
| ☐ 327 Mark Moseley | .08 | .03 | .01 |
| ☐ 328 Art Monk | .35 | .14 | .03 |
| ☐ 329 Mike Nelms | .08 | .03 | .01 |
| ☐ 330 John Riggins | .25 | .10 | .02 |
| ☐ xx Sticker Album | 1.25 | .50 | .12 |

## 1984 Topps Stickers

The 1984 Topps Football sticker set (283) is similar to the previous years in that it contains stickers, foil stickers, and an accompanying album to house one's sticker collection. Many of these stickers came two to a card. In the checklist below the other player on these two player stickers is listed parenthetically by number; players listed without any parenthetical number have the whole sticker card to themselves. The foil stickers are noted by "FOIL" in the checklist below. Numbers within the set are organized by subgroups: Super Bowl Foils (1-5), Chicago Bears (6-14), Tampa Bay Buccaneers (15-23), St. Louis Cardinals (24-32), Dallas Cowboys (33-41), Philadelphia Eagles (42-50), Atlanta Falcons (51-59), San Francisco 49ers (60-68), New York Giants (69-77), Detroit Lions (78-86), Green Bay Packers (87-95), Los Angeles Rams (96-104), Washington Redskins (105-113), New Orleans Saints (114-122), Minnesota Vikings (123-131), All Pro Half Foils (132-155), Cincinnati Bengals (156-164), Buffalo Bills (165-173), Denver Broncos (174-182), Cleveland Browns (183-191), San Diego Chargers (192-200), Kansas City Chiefs (201-209), Indianapolis Colts (210-218), Miami Dolphins (219-227), New York Jets (228-236), Houston Oilers (237-245), New England Patriots (246-254), Los Angeles Raiders (255-263), Seattle Seahawks (264-272), Pittsburgh Steelers (273-281), and Foil Pairs (282-283). On the inside back cover of the sticker album the company offered (via direct mail-order) any 10 different stickers of your choice for 1.00; this is one reason why the values of the most popular players in these sticker sets are somewhat depressed compared to traditional card set prices. The sticker album features Charlie Joiner on the front cover and Dan Fouts on the back cover. The following players are shown in their Rookie Card year: Deron Cherry, Roger Craig, Eric Dickerson, Mark Duper, John Elway, Chris Hinton, Howie Long, Dan Marino, and Jackie Slater.

| | MINT | EXC | G-VG |
|---|---|---|---|
| COMPLETE SET (283) | 18.00 | 7.25 | 1.80 |
| COMMON STICKER (1-283) | .05 | .02 | .00 |
| COMMON HALF STICKER | .03 | .01 | .00 |
| COMMON FOILS | .15 | .06 | .01 |
| COMMON HALF FOILS | .10 | .04 | .01 |
| | | | |
| ☐ 1 Super Bowl XVIII FOIL Plunkett/Allen UL | .25 | .10 | .02 |
| ☐ 2 Super Bowl XVIII FOIL Plunkett/Allen UR | .15 | .06 | .01 |
| ☐ 3 Super Bowl XVIII FOIL Plunkett/Allen LL | .15 | .06 | .01 |
| ☐ 4 Super Bowl XVIII FOIL Plunkett/Allen LR | .15 | .06 | .01 |
| ☐ 5 Marcus Allen FOIL (Super Bowl MVP) | .50 | .20 | .05 |
| ☐ 6 Walter Payton | .75 | .30 | .07 |
| ☐ 7 Mike Richardson (157) | .03 | .01 | .00 |
| ☐ 8 Jim McMahon (158) | .10 | .04 | .01 |
| ☐ 9 Mike Hartenstine (159) | .03 | .01 | .00 |

|  |  | | | |
|---|---|---|---|---|
| ☐ 10 | Mike Singletary | .20 | .08 | .02 |
| ☐ 11 | Willie Gault | .10 | .04 | .01 |
| ☐ 12 | Terry Schmidt (162) | .03 | .01 | .00 |
| ☐ 13 | Emery Moorehead (163) | .03 | .01 | .00 |
| ☐ 14 | Leslie Frazier (164) | .03 | .01 | .00 |
| ☐ 15 | Jack Thompson (165) | .03 | .01 | .00 |
| ☐ 16 | Booker Reese (166) | .03 | .01 | .00 |
| ☐ 17 | James Wilder (167) | .05 | .02 | .00 |
| ☐ 18 | Lee Roy Selmon | .08 | .03 | .01 |
| ☐ 19 | Hugh Green | .06 | .02 | .00 |
| ☐ 20 | Gerald Carter (170) | .03 | .01 | .00 |
| ☐ 21 | Steve Wilson (171) | .03 | .01 | .00 |
| ☐ 22 | Michael Morton (172) | .03 | .01 | .00 |
| ☐ 23 | Kevin House | .05 | .02 | .00 |
| ☐ 24 | Ottis Anderson | .12 | .05 | .01 |
| ☐ 25 | Lionel Washington (175) | .08 | .03 | .01 |
| ☐ 26 | Pat Tilley (176) | .03 | .01 | .00 |
| ☐ 27 | Curtis Greer (177) | .03 | .01 | .00 |
| ☐ 28 | Roy Green | .08 | .03 | .01 |
| ☐ 29 | Carl Birdsong | .05 | .02 | .00 |
| ☐ 30 | Neil Lomax (180) | .06 | .02 | .00 |
| ☐ 31 | Lee Nelson (181) | .03 | .01 | .00 |
| ☐ 32 | Stump Mitchell (182) | .04 | .02 | .00 |
| ☐ 33 | Tony Hill (183) | .05 | .02 | .00 |
| ☐ 34 | Everson Walls (184) | .05 | .02 | .00 |
| ☐ 35 | Danny White (185) | .08 | .03 | .01 |
| ☐ 36 | Tony Dorsett | .30 | .12 | .03 |
| ☐ 37 | Ed Too Tall Jones | .12 | .05 | .01 |
| ☐ 38 | Rafael Septien (188) | .03 | .01 | .00 |
| ☐ 39 | Doug Cosbie (189) | .03 | .01 | .00 |
| ☐ 40 | Drew Pearson (190) | .06 | .02 | .00 |
| ☐ 41 | Randy White | .20 | .08 | .02 |
| ☐ 42 | Ron Jaworski | .10 | .04 | .01 |
| ☐ 43 | Anthony Griggs (193) | .03 | .01 | .00 |
| ☐ 44 | Hubert Oliver (194) | .03 | .01 | .00 |
| ☐ 45 | Wilbert Montgomery (195) | .05 | .02 | .00 |
| ☐ 46 | Dennis Harrison | .05 | .02 | .00 |
| ☐ 47 | Mike Quick | .08 | .03 | .01 |
| ☐ 48 | Jerry Robinson (198) | .04 | .02 | .00 |
| ☐ 49 | Michael Williams (199) | .03 | .01 | .00 |
| ☐ 50 | Herman Edwards (200) | .03 | .01 | .00 |
| ☐ 51 | Steve Bartkowski (201) | .06 | .02 | .00 |
| ☐ 52 | Mick Luckhurst (202) | .03 | .01 | .00 |
| ☐ 53 | Mike Pitts (203) | .03 | .01 | .00 |
| ☐ 54 | William Andrews | .10 | .04 | .01 |
| ☐ 55 | R.C. Thielemann | .05 | .02 | .00 |
| ☐ 56 | Buddy Curry (206) | .03 | .01 | .00 |
| ☐ 57 | Billy Johnson (207) | .04 | .02 | .00 |
| ☐ 58 | Ralph Giacomarro (208) | .03 | .01 | .00 |
| ☐ 59 | Mike Kenn | .08 | .03 | .01 |
| ☐ 60 | Joe Montana | 1.25 | .50 | .12 |
| ☐ 61 | Fred Dean (211) | .03 | .01 | .00 |
| ☐ 62 | Dwight Clark (212) | .10 | .04 | .01 |
| ☐ 63 | Wendell Tyler (213) | .05 | .02 | .00 |
| ☐ 64 | Dwight Hicks | .05 | .02 | .00 |
| ☐ 65 | Ronnie Lott | .25 | .10 | .02 |
| ☐ 66 | Roger Craig (216) | .50 | .20 | .05 |
| ☐ 67 | Fred Solomon (217) | .03 | .01 | .00 |
| ☐ 68 | Ray Wersching (218) | .03 | .01 | .00 |
| ☐ 69 | Brad Van Pelt (219) | .03 | .01 | .00 |
| ☐ 70 | Butch Woolfolk (220) | .03 | .01 | .00 |
| ☐ 71 | Terry Kinard (221) | .03 | .01 | .00 |
| ☐ 72 | Lawrence Taylor | .30 | .12 | .03 |
| ☐ 73 | Ali Haji-Sheikh | .05 | .02 | .00 |
| ☐ 74 | Mark Haynes (224) | .03 | .01 | .00 |
| ☐ 75 | Rob Carpenter (225) | .03 | .01 | .00 |
| ☐ 76 | Earnest Gray (226) | .03 | .01 | .00 |
| ☐ 77 | Harry Carson | .10 | .04 | .01 |
| ☐ 78 | Billy Sims | .15 | .06 | .01 |
| ☐ 79 | Eddie Murray (229) | .05 | .02 | .00 |
| ☐ 80 | William Gay (230) | .03 | .01 | .00 |
| ☐ 81 | Leonard Thompson (231) | .03 | .01 | .00 |
| ☐ 82 | Doug English | .08 | .03 | .01 |
| ☐ 83 | Eric Hipple | .08 | .03 | .01 |
| ☐ 84 | Ken Fantetti (234) | .03 | .01 | .00 |
| ☐ 85 | Bruce McNorton (235) | .03 | .01 | .00 |
| ☐ 86 | James Jones (236) | .05 | .02 | .00 |
| ☐ 87 | Lynn Dickey (237) | .06 | .02 | .00 |
| ☐ 88 | Ezra Johnson (238) | .03 | .01 | .00 |
| ☐ 89 | Jan Stenerud (239) | .08 | .03 | .01 |
| ☐ 90 | James Lofton | .20 | .08 | .02 |
| ☐ 91 | Larry McCarren | .05 | .02 | .00 |
| ☐ 92 | John Jefferson (242) | .05 | .02 | .00 |
| ☐ 93 | Mike Douglass (243) | .03 | .01 | .00 |
| ☐ 94 | Gerry Ellis (244) | .03 | .01 | .00 |
| ☐ 95 | Paul Coffman | .05 | .02 | .00 |
| ☐ 96 | Eric Dickerson | 1.00 | .40 | .10 |
| ☐ 97 | Jackie Slater (247) | .20 | .08 | .02 |
| ☐ 98 | Carl Ekern (248) | .03 | .01 | .00 |
| ☐ 99 | Vince Ferragamo (249) | .06 | .02 | .00 |
| ☐ 100 | Kent Hill | .05 | .02 | .00 |
| ☐ 101 | Nolan Cromwell | .08 | .03 | .01 |
| ☐ 102 | Jack Youngblood (252) | .10 | .04 | .01 |
| ☐ 103 | John Misko (253) | .03 | .01 | .00 |
| ☐ 104 | Mike Barber (254) | .03 | .01 | .00 |
| ☐ 105 | Jeff Bostic (255) | .05 | .02 | .00 |
| ☐ 106 | Mark Murphy (256) | .03 | .01 | .00 |
| ☐ 107 | Joe Jacoby (257) | .05 | .02 | .00 |
| ☐ 108 | John Riggins | .25 | .10 | .02 |
| ☐ 109 | Joe Theismann | .30 | .12 | .03 |
| ☐ 110 | Russ Grimm (260) | .03 | .01 | .00 |
| ☐ 111 | Neal Olkewicz (261) | .03 | .01 | .00 |
| ☐ 112 | Charlie Brown (262) | .05 | .02 | .00 |
| ☐ 113 | Dave Butz | .08 | .03 | .01 |
| ☐ 114 | George Rogers | .10 | .04 | .01 |
| ☐ 115 | Jim Kovach (265) | .03 | .01 | .00 |
| ☐ 116 | Dave Wilson (266) | .03 | .01 | .00 |
| ☐ 117 | Johnnie Poe (267) | .03 | .01 | .00 |
| ☐ 118 | Russell Erxleben | .05 | .02 | .00 |
| ☐ 119 | Rickey Jackson | .50 | .20 | .05 |
| ☐ 120 | Jeff Groth (270) | .03 | .01 | .00 |
| ☐ 121 | Richard Todd (271) | .06 | .02 | .00 |
| ☐ 122 | Wayne Wilson (272) | .03 | .01 | .00 |
| ☐ 123 | Steve Dils (273) | .03 | .01 | .00 |
| ☐ 124 | Benny Ricardo (274) | .03 | .01 | .00 |
| ☐ 125 | John Turner (275) | .03 | .01 | .00 |
| ☐ 126 | Ted Brown | .05 | .02 | .00 |
| ☐ 127 | Greg Coleman | .05 | .02 | .00 |
| ☐ 128 | Darrin Nelson (278) | .06 | .02 | .00 |
| ☐ 129 | Scott Studwell (279) | .06 | .02 | .00 |
| ☐ 130 | Tommy Kramer (280) | .06 | .02 | .00 |
| ☐ 131 | Doug Martin | .05 | .02 | .00 |
| ☐ 132 | Nolan Cromwell (144) All-Pro FOIL | .10 | .04 | .01 |
| ☐ 133 | Carl Birdsong (145) All-Pro FOIL | .10 | .04 | .01 |
| ☐ 134 | Deron Cherry (146) All-Pro FOIL | .20 | .08 | .02 |
| ☐ 135 | Ronnie Lott (147) All-Pro FOIL | .25 | .10 | .02 |
| ☐ 136 | Lester Hayes (148) All-Pro FOIL | .10 | .04 | .01 |
| ☐ 137 | Lawrence Taylor (149) All-Pro FOIL | .30 | .12 | .03 |
| ☐ 138 | Jack Lambert (150) All-Pro FOIL | .20 | .08 | .02 |
| ☐ 139 | Chip Banks (151) All-Pro FOIL | .10 | .04 | .01 |
| ☐ 140 | Lee Roy Selmon (152) All-Pro FOIL | .12 | .05 | .01 |
| ☐ 141 | Fred Smerlas (153) All-Pro FOIL | .10 | .04 | .01 |
| ☐ 142 | Doug English (154) All-Pro FOIL | .10 | .04 | .01 |
| ☐ 143 | Doug Betters (155) All-Pro FOIL | .10 | .04 | .01 |
| ☐ 144 | Dan Marino (132) All-Pro FOIL | 2.00 | .80 | .20 |
| ☐ 145 | Ali Haji-Sheikh (133) All-Pro FOIL | .10 | .04 | .01 |
| ☐ 146 | Eric Dickerson (134) All-Pro FOIL | .75 | .30 | .07 |
| ☐ 147 | Curt Warner (135) All-Pro FOIL | .15 | .06 | .01 |
| ☐ 148 | James Lofton (136) All-Pro FOIL | .25 | .10 | .02 |
| ☐ 149 | Todd Christensen (137) All-Pro FOIL | .15 | .06 | .01 |
| ☐ 150 | Cris Collinsworth (138) All-Pro FOIL | .15 | .06 | .01 |
| ☐ 151 | Mike Kenn (139) All-Pro FOIL | .10 | .04 | .01 |
| ☐ 152 | Russ Grimm (140) All-Pro FOIL | .10 | .04 | .01 |
| ☐ 153 | Jeff Bostic (141) All-Pro FOIL | .10 | .04 | .01 |
| ☐ 154 | John Hannah (142) All-Pro FOIL | .15 | .06 | .01 |
| ☐ 155 | Anthony Munoz (143) All-Pro FOIL | .20 | .08 | .02 |
| ☐ 156 | Ken Anderson | .30 | .12 | .03 |
| ☐ 157 | Pete Johnson (7) | .05 | .02 | .00 |
| ☐ 158 | Reggie Williams (8) | .06 | .02 | .00 |
| ☐ 159 | Isaac Curtis (9) | .05 | .02 | .00 |
| ☐ 160 | Anthony Munoz | .20 | .08 | .02 |
| ☐ 161 | Cris Collinsworth | .15 | .06 | .01 |
| ☐ 162 | Charles Alexander(12) | .03 | .01 | .00 |
| ☐ 163 | Ray Horton (13) | .05 | .02 | .00 |
| ☐ 164 | Steve Kreider (14) | .03 | .01 | .00 |
| ☐ 165 | Ben Williams (15) | .03 | .01 | .00 |
| ☐ 166 | Frank Lewis (16) | .03 | .01 | .00 |
| ☐ 167 | Roosevelt Leaks (17) | .03 | .01 | .00 |
| ☐ 168 | Joe Ferguson | .08 | .03 | .01 |
| ☐ 169 | Fred Smerlas | .08 | .03 | .01 |
| ☐ 170 | Joe Danelo (20) | .03 | .01 | .00 |
| ☐ 171 | Chris Keating (21) | .03 | .01 | .00 |
| ☐ 172 | Jerry Butler (22) | .03 | .01 | .00 |

| | | | |
|---|---|---|---|
| ☐ 173 Eugene Marve | .05 | .02 | .00 |
| ☐ 174 Louis Wright | .08 | .03 | .01 |
| ☐ 175 Barney Chavous (25) | .03 | .01 | .00 |
| ☐ 176 Zack Thomas (26) | .03 | .01 | .00 |
| ☐ 177 Luke Prestridge (27) | .03 | .01 | .00 |
| ☐ 178 Steve Watson | .08 | .03 | .01 |
| ☐ 179 John Elway | 2.00 | .80 | .20 |
| ☐ 180 Steve Foley (30) | .03 | .01 | .00 |
| ☐ 181 Sammy Winder (31) | .03 | .01 | .00 |
| ☐ 182 Rick Upchurch (32) | .05 | .02 | .00 |
| ☐ 183 Bobby Jones (33) | .03 | .01 | .00 |
| ☐ 184 Matt Bahr (34) | .03 | .01 | .00 |
| ☐ 185 Doug Dieken (35) | .03 | .01 | .00 |
| ☐ 186 Mike Pruitt | .08 | .03 | .01 |
| ☐ 187 Chip Banks | .08 | .03 | .01 |
| ☐ 188 Tom Cousineau (38) | .05 | .02 | .00 |
| ☐ 189 Paul McDonald (39) | .05 | .02 | .00 |
| ☐ 190 Clay Matthews (40) | .08 | .03 | .01 |
| ☐ 191 Ozzie Newsome | .20 | .08 | .02 |
| ☐ 192 Dan Fouts | .30 | .12 | .03 |
| ☐ 193 Chuck Muncie (43) | .05 | .02 | .00 |
| ☐ 194 Linden King (44) | .03 | .01 | .00 |
| ☐ 195 Charlie Joiner (45) | .08 | .03 | .01 |
| ☐ 196 Wes Chandler | .08 | .03 | .01 |
| ☐ 197 Kellen Winslow | .20 | .08 | .02 |
| ☐ 198 James Brooks (48) | .10 | .04 | .01 |
| ☐ 199 Mike Green (49) | .03 | .01 | .00 |
| ☐ 200 Rolf Benirschke (58) | .05 | .02 | .00 |
| ☐ 201 Henry Marshall (51) | .03 | .01 | .00 |
| ☐ 202 Nick Lowery (52) | .06 | .02 | .00 |
| ☐ 203 Jerry Blanton (53) | .03 | .01 | .00 |
| ☐ 204 Bill Kenney | .08 | .03 | .01 |
| ☐ 205 Carlos Carson | .08 | .03 | .01 |
| ☐ 206 Billy Jackson (56) | .03 | .01 | .00 |
| ☐ 207 Art Still (57) | .05 | .02 | .00 |
| ☐ 208 Theotis Brown (58) | .03 | .01 | .00 |
| ☐ 209 Deron Cherry | .25 | .10 | .02 |
| ☐ 210 Curtis Dickey | .08 | .03 | .01 |
| ☐ 211 Nesby Glasgow (61) | .03 | .01 | .00 |
| ☐ 212 Mike Pagel (62) | .05 | .02 | .00 |
| ☐ 213 Ray Donaldson (63) | .03 | .01 | .00 |
| ☐ 214 Raul Allegre | .05 | .02 | .00 |
| ☐ 215 Chris Hinton | .35 | .14 | .03 |
| ☐ 216 Rohn Stark (66) | .05 | .02 | .00 |
| ☐ 217 Randy McMillan (67) | .04 | .02 | .00 |
| ☐ 218 Vernon Maxwell (68) | .03 | .01 | .00 |
| ☐ 219 A.J. Duhe (69) | .03 | .01 | .00 |
| ☐ 220 Andra Franklin (70) | .03 | .01 | .00 |
| ☐ 221 Ed Newman (71) | .03 | .01 | .00 |
| ☐ 222 Dan Marino | 4.00 | 1.60 | .40 |
| ☐ 223 Doug Betters | .08 | .03 | .01 |
| ☐ 224 Bob Baumhower (74) | .03 | .01 | .00 |
| ☐ 225 Reggie Roby (75) | .08 | .03 | .01 |
| ☐ 226 Dwight Stephenson (76) | .04 | .02 | .00 |
| ☐ 227 Mark Duper | .35 | .14 | .03 |
| ☐ 228 Mark Gastineau | .10 | .04 | .01 |
| ☐ 229 Freeman McNeil (79) | .08 | .03 | .01 |
| ☐ 230 Bruce Harper (80) | .03 | .01 | .00 |
| ☐ 231 Wesley Walker (81) | .06 | .02 | .00 |
| ☐ 232 Marvin Powell | .08 | .03 | .01 |
| ☐ 233 Joe Klecko | .08 | .03 | .01 |
| ☐ 234 Johnny Lam Jones (84) | .05 | .02 | .00 |
| ☐ 235 Lance Mehl (85) | .03 | .01 | .00 |
| ☐ 236 Pat Ryan (86) | .05 | .02 | .00 |
| ☐ 237 Florian Kempf (87) | .03 | .01 | .00 |
| ☐ 238 Carl Roaches (88) | .03 | .01 | .00 |
| ☐ 239 Gregg Bingham (89) | .03 | .01 | .00 |
| ☐ 240 Tim Smith | .05 | .02 | .00 |
| ☐ 241 Jesse Baker | .05 | .02 | .00 |
| ☐ 242 Doug France (92) | .03 | .01 | .00 |
| ☐ 243 Chris Dressel (93) | .03 | .01 | .00 |
| ☐ 244 Willie Tullis (94) | .03 | .01 | .00 |
| ☐ 245 Robert Brazile | .08 | .03 | .01 |
| ☐ 246 Tony Collins | .08 | .03 | .01 |
| ☐ 247 Brian Holloway (97) | .03 | .01 | .00 |
| ☐ 248 Stanley Morgan (98) | .06 | .02 | .00 |
| ☐ 249 Rick Sanford (99) | .03 | .01 | .00 |
| ☐ 250 John Hannah | .15 | .06 | .01 |
| ☐ 251 Rich Camarillo | .05 | .02 | .00 |
| ☐ 252 Andre Tippett (102) | .08 | .03 | .01 |
| ☐ 253 Steve Grogan (103) | .08 | .03 | .01 |
| ☐ 254 Clayton Weishuhn (104) | .03 | .01 | .00 |
| ☐ 255 Jim Plunkett (105) | .08 | .03 | .01 |
| ☐ 256 Rod Martin (106) | .03 | .01 | .00 |
| ☐ 257 Lester Hayes (107) | .05 | .02 | .00 |
| ☐ 258 Marcus Allen | .50 | .20 | .05 |
| ☐ 259 Todd Christensen | .10 | .04 | .01 |
| ☐ 260 Ted Hendricks (110) | .08 | .03 | .01 |
| ☐ 261 Greg Pruitt (111) | .05 | .02 | .00 |
| ☐ 262 Howie Long (112) | .50 | .20 | .05 |
| ☐ 263 Vann McElroy (113) | .05 | .02 | .00 |
| ☐ 264 Curt Warner | .25 | .10 | .02 |
| ☐ 265 Jacob Green (115) | .06 | .02 | .00 |
| ☐ 266 Bruce Scholtz (116) | .03 | .01 | .00 |
| ☐ 267 Steve Largent (117) | .50 | .20 | .05 |

| | | | |
|---|---|---|---|
| ☐ 268 Kenny Easley | .08 | .03 | .01 |
| ☐ 269 Dave Krieg | .35 | .14 | .03 |
| ☐ 270 Dave Brown (120) | .03 | .01 | .00 |
| ☐ 271 Zachary Dixon (121) | .03 | .01 | .00 |
| ☐ 272 Norm Johnson (122) | .05 | .02 | .00 |
| ☐ 273 Terry Bradshaw (123) | .30 | .12 | .03 |
| ☐ 274 Keith Willis (124) | .03 | .01 | .00 |
| ☐ 275 Gary Anderson (125) | .03 | .01 | .00 |
| ☐ 276 Franco Harris | .35 | .14 | .03 |
| ☐ 277 Mike Webster | .15 | .06 | .01 |
| ☐ 278 Calvin Sweeney (128) | .03 | .01 | .00 |
| ☐ 279 Rick Woods (129) | .03 | .01 | .00 |
| ☐ 280 Bennie Cunningham (130) | .03 | .01 | .00 |
| ☐ 281 Jack Lambert | .15 | .06 | .01 |
| ☐ 282 Curt Warner (283) FOIL | .30 | .12 | .03 |
| ☐ 283 Todd Christensen (282) FOIL | .12 | .05 | .01 |
| ☐ xx Sticker Album (Charlie Joiner and Dan Fouts) | 1.25 | .50 | .12 |

## 1985 Topps "Coming Soon" Stickers

This set of 30 white-bordered stickers are usually referred to as the "Coming Soon" stickers as they were inserted in the regular issue 1985 Topps football card wax packs and prominently mention "Coming Soon" on the sticker backs. They are the same size as the regular Topps stickers (approximately 2 1/8" by 3") and were not very difficult to find. Unlike many of the sticker cards in the regular set, this subset only contains one player per sticker. This is a skip-numbered set due to the fact that these stickers have the same numbers as the regular sticker issue.

| | MINT | EXC | G-VG |
|---|---|---|---|
| COMPLETE SET (30) | 5.00 | 2.00 | .50 |
| COMMON PLAYER | .10 | .04 | .01 |
| ☐ 6 Ken Anderson Cincinnati Bengals | .30 | .12 | .03 |
| ☐ 15 Greg Bell Buffalo Bills | .15 | .06 | .01 |
| ☐ 24 John Elway Denver Broncos | .75 | .30 | .07 |
| ☐ 33 Ozzie Newsome Cleveland Browns | .25 | .10 | .02 |
| ☐ 42 Charlie Joiner San Diego Chargers | .25 | .10 | .02 |
| ☐ 51 Bill Kenney Kansas City Chiefs | .15 | .06 | .01 |
| ☐ 60 Randy McMillan Indianapolis Colts | .10 | .04 | .01 |
| ☐ 69 Dan Marino Miami Dolphins | 2.00 | .80 | .20 |
| ☐ 77 Mark Clayton Miami Dolphins | .50 | .20 | .05 |
| ☐ 78 Mark Gastineau New York Jets | .10 | .04 | .01 |
| ☐ 87 Warren Moon Houston Oilers | 2.00 | .80 | .20 |
| ☐ 96 Tony Eason New England Patriots | .15 | .06 | .01 |
| ☐ 105 Marcus Allen Los Angeles Raiders | .50 | .20 | .05 |
| ☐ 114 Steve Largent Seattle Seahawks | .60 | .24 | .06 |
| ☐ 123 John Stallworth Pittsburgh Steelers | .20 | .08 | .02 |
| ☐ 156 Walter Payton Chicago Bears | 1.00 | .40 | .10 |
| ☐ 165 James Wilder | .10 | .04 | .01 |

| | | | |
|---|---|---|---|
| Tampa Bay Buccaneers | | | |
| ☐ 174 Neil Lomax | .15 | .06 | .01 |
| St. Louis Cardinals | | | |
| ☐ 183 Tony Dorsett | .30 | .12 | .03 |
| Dallas Cowboys | | | |
| ☐ 192 Mike Quick | .15 | .06 | .01 |
| Philadelphia Eagles | | | |
| ☐ 201 William Andrews | .15 | .06 | .01 |
| Atlanta Falcons | | | |
| ☐ 210 Joe Montana | 2.00 | .80 | .20 |
| San Francisco 49ers | | | |
| ☐ 214 Dwight Clark | .30 | .12 | .03 |
| San Francisco 49ers | | | |
| ☐ 219 Lawrence Taylor | .40 | .16 | .04 |
| New York Giants | | | |
| ☐ 228 Billy Sims | .15 | .06 | .01 |
| Detroit Lions | | | |
| ☐ 237 James Lofton | .35 | .14 | .03 |
| Green Bay Packers | | | |
| ☐ 246 Eric Dickerson | .60 | .24 | .06 |
| Los Angeles Rams | | | |
| ☐ 255 John Riggins | .25 | .10 | .02 |
| Washington Redskins | | | |
| ☐ 268 George Rogers | .15 | .06 | .01 |
| New Orleans Saints | | | |
| ☐ 281 Tommy Kramer | .10 | .04 | .01 |
| Minnesota Vikings | | | |

# 1985 Topps Stickers

The 1985 Topps Football sticker set is similar to the previous years in that it contains stickers and an accompanying album to house one's sticker collection. However, there are no foil stickers in this set. Some of the stickers are half the size of others; those paired stickers sharing a card with another player are indicated parenthetically by the other player's sticker number in the checklist below. On the inside back cover of the sticker album the company offered (via direct mail-order) any ten different stickers of your choice for 1.00; this is one reason why the values of the most popular players in these sticker sets are somewhat depressed compared to traditional card set prices. The front cover of the sticker album features Dan Marino, Joe Montana, Walter Payton, Eric Dickerson, Art Monk, and Charlie Joiner; the back cover shows a team photo of the San Francisco 49ers. The stickers are checklisted below according to special subsets and teams as follows: Super Bowl puzzle (1-5), Cincinnati Bengals (6-14), Buffalo Bills (15-23), Denver Broncos (24-32), Cleveland Browns (33-41), San Diego Chargers (42-50), Kansas City Chiefs (51-59), Indianapolis Colts (60-68), Miami Dolphins (69-77), New York Jets (78-86), Houston Oilers (87-95), New England Patriots (96-104), Los Angeles Raiders (105-113), Seattle Seahawks (114-122), Pittsburgh Steelers (123-131), Chicago Bears (156-164), Tampa Bay Buccaneers (165-173), St. Louis Cardinals (174-182), Dallas Cowboys (183-191), Philadelphia Eagles (192-200), Atlanta Falcons (201-209), San Francisco 49ers (210-218), New York Giants (219-227), Detroit Lions (228-236), Green Bay Packers (237-245), Los Angeles Rams (246-254), Washington Redskins (255-263), New Orleans Saints (264-272), Minnesota Vikings (273-281), and Leaders (282-285). The following players are shown in their Rookie Card year or earlier: Gill Byrd, Mark Clayton, Richard Dent, Henry Ellard, Boomer Esiason (one year early), Craig James, Louis Lipps, Mike Merriweather, Warren Moon, Ken O'Brien, and Darryl Talley.

| | MINT | EXC | G-VG |
|---|---|---|---|
| COMPLETE SET (285) | 15.00 | 6.00 | 1.50 |
| COMMON PLAYER (1-285) | .05 | .02 | .00 |
| COMMON HALF STICKER | .03 | .01 | .00 |

| | | | |
|---|---|---|---|
| ☐ 1 Super Bowl XIX | 1.00 | .40 | .10 |
| Joe Montana LH | | | |
| ☐ 2 Super Bowl XIX | .75 | .30 | .07 |
| Joe Montana RH | | | |
| ☐ 3 Super Bowl XIX | .10 | .04 | .01 |
| Roger Craig LH | | | |
| ☐ 4 Super Bowl XIX | .10 | .04 | .01 |
| Roger Craig RH | | | |
| ☐ 5 Super Bowl XIX | .08 | .03 | .01 |
| Wendell Tyler | | | |
| ☐ 6 Ken Anderson | .25 | .10 | .02 |
| ☐ 7 M.L. Harris (157) | .03 | .01 | .00 |
| ☐ 8 Eddie Edwards (157) | .03 | .01 | .00 |
| ☐ 9 Louis Breeden (159) | .03 | .01 | .00 |
| ☐ 10 Larry Kinnebrew | .05 | .02 | .00 |
| ☐ 11 Isaac Curtis (161) | .06 | .02 | .00 |
| ☐ 12 James Brooks (162) | .08 | .03 | .01 |
| ☐ 13 Jim Breech (163) | .03 | .01 | .00 |
| ☐ 14 Boomer Esiason (164) | .75 | .30 | .07 |
| ☐ 15 Greg Bell | .10 | .04 | .01 |
| ☐ 16 Fred Smerlas (166) | .03 | .01 | .00 |
| ☐ 17 Joe Ferguson (167) | .06 | .02 | .00 |
| ☐ 18 Ken Johnson (168) | .03 | .01 | .00 |
| ☐ 19 Darryl Talley (169) | .25 | .10 | .02 |
| ☐ 20 Preston Dennard (170) | .03 | .01 | .00 |
| ☐ 21 Charles Romes (171) | .03 | .01 | .00 |
| ☐ 22 Jim Haslett (172) | .03 | .01 | .00 |
| ☐ 23 Byron Franklin | .05 | .02 | .00 |
| ☐ 24 John Elway | 1.00 | .40 | .10 |
| ☐ 25 Rulon Jones (175) | .03 | .01 | .00 |
| ☐ 26 Butch Johnson (176) | .03 | .01 | .00 |
| ☐ 27 Rick Karlis (177) | .03 | .01 | .00 |
| ☐ 28 Sammy Winder | .05 | .02 | .00 |
| ☐ 29 Tom Jackson (179) | .06 | .02 | .00 |
| ☐ 30 Mike Harden (180) | .03 | .01 | .00 |
| ☐ 31 Steve Watson (181) | .03 | .01 | .00 |
| ☐ 32 Steve Foley (182) | .03 | .01 | .00 |
| ☐ 33 Ozzie Newsome | .20 | .08 | .02 |
| ☐ 34 Al Gross (184) | .03 | .01 | .00 |
| ☐ 35 Paul McDonald (185) | .03 | .01 | .00 |
| ☐ 36 Matt Bahr (186) | .03 | .01 | .00 |
| ☐ 37 Charles White (187) | .06 | .02 | .00 |
| ☐ 38 Don Rogers (188) | .03 | .01 | .00 |
| ☐ 39 Mike Pruitt (189) | .05 | .02 | .00 |
| ☐ 40 Reggie Camp (190) | .03 | .01 | .00 |
| ☐ 41 Boyce Green | .05 | .02 | .00 |
| ☐ 42 Charlie Joiner | .15 | .06 | .01 |
| ☐ 43 Dan Fouts (193) | .15 | .06 | .01 |
| ☐ 44 Keith Ferguson (194) | .03 | .01 | .00 |
| ☐ 45 Pete Holohan (195) | .03 | .01 | .00 |
| ☐ 46 Earnest Jackson | .08 | .03 | .01 |
| ☐ 47 Wes Chandler (197) | .06 | .02 | .00 |
| ☐ 48 Gill Byrd (198) | .15 | .06 | .01 |
| ☐ 49 Kellen Winslow (199) | .10 | .04 | .01 |
| ☐ 50 Billy Ray Smith (200) | .06 | .02 | .00 |
| ☐ 51 Bill Kenney | .08 | .03 | .01 |
| ☐ 52 Herman Heard (202) | .03 | .01 | .00 |
| ☐ 53 Art Still (203) | .05 | .02 | .00 |
| ☐ 54 Nick Lowery (204) | .05 | .02 | .00 |
| ☐ 55 Deron Cherry (205) | .08 | .03 | .01 |
| ☐ 56 Henry Marshall (206) | .03 | .01 | .00 |
| ☐ 57 Mike Bell (207) | .03 | .01 | .00 |
| ☐ 58 Todd Blackledge (208) | .05 | .02 | .00 |
| ☐ 59 Carlos Carson | .08 | .03 | .01 |
| ☐ 60 Randy McMillan | .05 | .02 | .00 |
| ☐ 61 Donnell Thompson (211) | .03 | .01 | .00 |
| ☐ 62 Raymond Butler (212) | .04 | .02 | .00 |
| ☐ 63 Ray Donaldson (213) | .03 | .01 | .00 |
| ☐ 64 Art Schlichter | .15 | .06 | .01 |
| ☐ 65 Rohn Stark (215) | .05 | .02 | .00 |
| ☐ 66 Johnie Cooks (216) | .04 | .02 | .00 |
| ☐ 67 Mike Pagel (217) | .04 | .02 | .00 |
| ☐ 68 Eugene Daniel (218) | .03 | .01 | .00 |
| ☐ 69 Dan Marino | 2.00 | .80 | .20 |
| ☐ 70 Pete Johnson (220) | .05 | .02 | .00 |
| ☐ 71 Tony Nathan (221) | .05 | .02 | .00 |
| ☐ 72 Glenn Blackwood (222) | .05 | .02 | .00 |
| ☐ 73 Woody Bennett (223) | .03 | .01 | .00 |
| ☐ 74 Dwight Stephenson (224) | .05 | .02 | .00 |
| ☐ 75 Mark Duper (225) | .10 | .04 | .01 |
| ☐ 76 Doug Betters (226) | .03 | .01 | .00 |
| ☐ 77 Mark Clayton | .50 | .20 | .05 |
| ☐ 78 Mark Gastineau | .08 | .03 | .01 |
| ☐ 79 Johnny Lam Jones (229) | .03 | .01 | .00 |
| ☐ 80 Mickey Shuler (230) | .03 | .01 | .00 |
| ☐ 81 Tony Paige (231) | .15 | .06 | .01 |
| ☐ 82 Freeman McNeil | .12 | .05 | .01 |
| ☐ 83 Russell Carter (233) | .06 | .02 | .00 |
| ☐ 84 Wesley Walker (234) | .06 | .02 | .00 |
| ☐ 85 Bruce Harper (235) | .03 | .01 | .00 |
| ☐ 86 Ken O'Brien (236) | .15 | .06 | .01 |
| ☐ 87 Warren Moon | 2.00 | .80 | .20 |
| ☐ 88 Jesse Baker (238) | .03 | .01 | .00 |
| ☐ 89 Carl Roaches (239) | .03 | .01 | .00 |
| ☐ 90 Carter Hartwig (240) | .03 | .01 | .00 |
| ☐ 91 Larry Moriarty (241) | .03 | .01 | .00 |
| ☐ 92 Robert Brazile (242) | .05 | .02 | .00 |
| ☐ 93 Oliver Luck (243) | .05 | .02 | .00 |

| | | | |
|---|---|---|---|
| ☐ 94 Willie Tullis (244) | .03 | .01 | .00 |
| ☐ 95 Tim Smith | .05 | .02 | .00 |
| ☐ 96 Tony Eason | .10 | .04 | .01 |
| ☐ 97 Stanley Morgan (247) | .08 | .03 | .01 |
| ☐ 98 Mosi Tatupu (248) | .03 | .01 | .00 |
| ☐ 99 Raymond Clayborn (249) | .03 | .01 | .00 |
| ☐ 100 Andre Tippett | .10 | .04 | .01 |
| ☐ 101 Craig James (251) | .12 | .05 | .01 |
| ☐ 102 Derrick Ramsey (252) | .03 | .01 | .00 |
| ☐ 103 Tony Collins (253) | .03 | .01 | .00 |
| ☐ 104 Tony Franklin (254) | .03 | .01 | .00 |
| ☐ 105 Marcus Allen | .30 | .12 | .03 |
| ☐ 106 Chris Bahr (256) | .03 | .01 | .00 |
| ☐ 107 Marc Wilson (257) | .05 | .02 | .00 |
| ☐ 108 Howie Long (258) | .10 | .04 | .01 |
| ☐ 109 Bill Pickel (259) | .03 | .01 | .00 |
| ☐ 110 Mike Haynes (260) | .08 | .03 | .01 |
| ☐ 111 Malcolm Barnwell (261) | .03 | .01 | .00 |
| ☐ 112 Rod Martin (262) | .03 | .01 | .00 |
| ☐ 113 Todd Christensen | .10 | .04 | .01 |
| ☐ 114 Steve Largent | .75 | .30 | .07 |
| ☐ 115 Curt Warner (265) | .08 | .03 | .01 |
| ☐ 116 Kenny Easley (266) | .05 | .02 | .00 |
| ☐ 117 Jacob Green (267) | .05 | .02 | .00 |
| ☐ 118 Daryl Turner | .08 | .03 | .01 |
| ☐ 119 Norm Johnson (269) | .05 | .02 | .00 |
| ☐ 120 Dave Krieg (270) | .10 | .04 | .01 |
| ☐ 121 Eric Lane (271) | .03 | .01 | .00 |
| ☐ 122 Jeff Bryant (272) | .03 | .01 | .00 |
| ☐ 123 John Stallworth | .12 | .05 | .01 |
| ☐ 124 Donnie Shell (274) | .05 | .02 | .00 |
| ☐ 125 Gary Anderson (275) | .03 | .01 | .00 |
| ☐ 126 Mark Malone (276) | .04 | .02 | .00 |
| ☐ 127 Sam Washington (277) | .03 | .01 | .00 |
| ☐ 128 Frank Pollard (278) | .03 | .01 | .00 |
| ☐ 129 Mike Merriweather (279) | .10 | .04 | .01 |
| ☐ 130 Walter Abercrombie (280) | .03 | .01 | .00 |
| ☐ 131 Louis Lipps | .40 | .16 | .04 |
| ☐ 132 Mark Clayton (144) | .35 | .14 | .03 |
| ☐ 133 Randy Cross (145) | .06 | .02 | .00 |
| ☐ 134 Eric Dickerson (146) | .30 | .12 | .03 |
| ☐ 135 John Hannah (147) | .10 | .04 | .01 |
| ☐ 136 Mike Kenn (148) | .05 | .02 | .00 |
| ☐ 137 Dan Marino (149) | 1.00 | .40 | .10 |
| ☐ 138 Art Monk (150) | .15 | .06 | .01 |
| ☐ 139 Anthony Munoz (151) | .10 | .04 | .01 |
| ☐ 140 Ozzie Newsome (152) | .10 | .04 | .01 |
| ☐ 141 Walter Payton (153) | .40 | .16 | .04 |
| ☐ 142 Jan Stenerud (154) | .08 | .03 | .01 |
| ☐ 143 Dwight Stephenson (155) | .05 | .02 | .00 |
| ☐ 144 Todd Bell (132) | .03 | .01 | .00 |
| ☐ 145 Richard Dent (133) | .50 | .20 | .05 |
| ☐ 146 Kenny Easley (134) | .05 | .02 | .00 |
| ☐ 147 Mark Gastineau (135) | .06 | .02 | .00 |
| ☐ 148 Dan Hampton (136) | .10 | .04 | .01 |
| ☐ 149 Mark Haynes (137) | .05 | .02 | .00 |
| ☐ 150 Mike Haynes (138) | .06 | .02 | .00 |
| ☐ 151 E.J. Junior (139) | .05 | .02 | .00 |
| ☐ 152 Rod Martin (140) | .03 | .01 | .00 |
| ☐ 153 Steve Nelson (141) | .03 | .01 | .00 |
| ☐ 154 Reggie Roby (142) | .05 | .02 | .00 |
| ☐ 155 Lawrence Taylor (143) | .15 | .06 | .01 |
| ☐ 156 Walter Payton | .60 | .24 | .06 |
| ☐ 157 Dan Hampton (7) | .06 | .02 | .00 |
| ☐ 158 Willie Gault (8) | .03 | .01 | .00 |
| ☐ 159 Matt Suhey (9) | .03 | .01 | .00 |
| ☐ 160 Richard Dent | 1.00 | .40 | .10 |
| ☐ 161 Mike Singletary (11) | .10 | .04 | .01 |
| ☐ 162 Gary Fencik (12) | .05 | .02 | .00 |
| ☐ 163 Jim McMahon (13) | .10 | .04 | .01 |
| ☐ 164 Bob Thomas (14) | .03 | .01 | .00 |
| ☐ 165 James Wilder | .08 | .03 | .01 |
| ☐ 166 Steve DeBerg (16) | .08 | .03 | .01 |
| ☐ 167 Mark Cotney (17) | .03 | .01 | .00 |
| ☐ 168 Adger Armstrong (18) | .03 | .01 | .00 |
| ☐ 169 Gerald Carter (19) | .03 | .01 | .00 |
| ☐ 170 David Logan (20) | .03 | .01 | .00 |
| ☐ 171 Hugh Green (21) | .05 | .02 | .00 |
| ☐ 172 Lee Roy Selmon (22) | .06 | .02 | .00 |
| ☐ 173 Kevin House | .08 | .03 | .01 |
| ☐ 174 Neil Lomax | .12 | .05 | .01 |
| ☐ 175 Ottis Anderson | .10 | .04 | .01 |
| ☐ 176 Al(Bubba) Baker (26) | .05 | .02 | .00 |
| ☐ 177 E.J. Junior (27) | .04 | .02 | .00 |
| ☐ 178 Roy Green | .10 | .04 | .01 |
| ☐ 179 Pat Tilley (29) | .03 | .01 | .00 |
| ☐ 180 Stump Mitchell (30) | .05 | .02 | .00 |
| ☐ 181 Lionel Washington (31) | .03 | .01 | .00 |
| ☐ 182 Curtis Greer (32) | .03 | .01 | .00 |
| ☐ 183 Tony Dorsett | .25 | .10 | .02 |
| ☐ 184 Gary Hogeboom (34) | .06 | .02 | .00 |
| ☐ 185 Jim Jeffcoat (35) | .06 | .02 | .00 |
| ☐ 186 Danny White (36) | .08 | .03 | .01 |
| ☐ 187 Michael Downs (37) | .03 | .01 | .00 |
| ☐ 188 Doug Cosbie (38) | .04 | .02 | .00 |
| ☐ 189 Tony Hill (39) | .05 | .02 | .00 |
| ☐ 190 Rafael Septien (40) | .03 | .01 | .00 |
| ☐ 191 Randy White | .15 | .06 | .01 |
| ☐ 192 Mike Quick | .08 | .03 | .01 |
| ☐ 193 Ray Ellis (43) | .03 | .01 | .00 |
| ☐ 194 John Spagnola (44) | .03 | .01 | .00 |
| ☐ 195 Dennis Harrison (45) | .03 | .01 | .00 |
| ☐ 196 Wilbert Montgomery | .08 | .03 | .01 |
| ☐ 197 Greg Brown (47) | .03 | .01 | .00 |
| ☐ 198 Ron Jaworski (48) | .08 | .03 | .01 |
| ☐ 199 Paul McFadden (49) | .03 | .01 | .00 |
| ☐ 200 Wes Hopkins (50) | .03 | .01 | .00 |
| ☐ 201 William Andrews | .10 | .04 | .01 |
| ☐ 202 Mike Pitts (52) | .03 | .01 | .00 |
| ☐ 203 Steve Bartkowski (53) | .08 | .03 | .01 |
| ☐ 204 Gerald Riggs (54) | .08 | .03 | .01 |
| ☐ 205 Alfred Jackson (55) | .05 | .02 | .00 |
| ☐ 206 Don Smith (56) | .03 | .01 | .00 |
| ☐ 207 Mike Kenn (57) | .05 | .02 | .00 |
| ☐ 208 Kenny Johnson (58) | .03 | .01 | .00 |
| ☐ 209 Stacey Bailey | .05 | .02 | .00 |
| ☐ 210 Joe Montana | 1.25 | .50 | .12 |
| ☐ 211 Wendell Tyler (61) | .05 | .02 | .00 |
| ☐ 212 Keena Turner (62) | .03 | .01 | .00 |
| ☐ 213 Ray Wersching (63) | .03 | .01 | .00 |
| ☐ 214 Dwight Clark | .15 | .06 | .01 |
| ☐ 215 Dwaine Board (65) | .03 | .01 | .00 |
| ☐ 216 Roger Craig (66) | .15 | .06 | .01 |
| ☐ 217 Ronnie Lott (67) | .15 | .06 | .01 |
| ☐ 218 Freddie Solomon (68) | .03 | .01 | .00 |
| ☐ 219 Lawrence Taylor | .25 | .10 | .02 |
| ☐ 220 Zeke Mowatt (70) | .04 | .02 | .00 |
| ☐ 221 Harry Carson (71) | .06 | .02 | .00 |
| ☐ 222 Rob Carpenter (72) | .03 | .01 | .00 |
| ☐ 223 Bobby Johnson (73) | .03 | .01 | .00 |
| ☐ 224 Joe Morris (74) | .07 | .03 | .01 |
| ☐ 225 Mark Haynes (75) | .04 | .02 | .00 |
| ☐ 226 Lionel Manuel (76) | .04 | .02 | .00 |
| ☐ 227 Phil Simms | .15 | .06 | .01 |
| ☐ 228 Billy Sims | .12 | .05 | .01 |
| ☐ 229 Leonard Thompson (79) | .03 | .01 | .00 |
| ☐ 230 James Jones (80) | .05 | .02 | .00 |
| ☐ 231 Eddie Murray (81) | .05 | .02 | .00 |
| ☐ 232 William Gay | .05 | .02 | .00 |
| ☐ 233 Gary Danielson (83) | .05 | .02 | .00 |
| ☐ 234 Curtis Green (84) | .03 | .01 | .00 |
| ☐ 235 Bobby Watkins (85) | .03 | .01 | .00 |
| ☐ 236 Doug English (86) | .05 | .02 | .00 |
| ☐ 237 James Lofton | .20 | .08 | .02 |
| ☐ 238 Eddie Lee Ivery (88) | .06 | .02 | .00 |
| ☐ 239 Mike Douglass (89) | .03 | .01 | .00 |
| ☐ 240 Gerry Ellis (90) | .03 | .01 | .00 |
| ☐ 241 Tim Lewis (91) | .03 | .01 | .00 |
| ☐ 242 Paul Coffman (92) | .05 | .02 | .00 |
| ☐ 243 Tom Flynn (93) | .03 | .01 | .00 |
| ☐ 244 Ezra Johnson (94) | .03 | .01 | .00 |
| ☐ 245 Lynn Dickey | .08 | .03 | .01 |
| ☐ 246 Eric Dickerson | .60 | .24 | .06 |
| ☐ 247 Jack Youngblood (97) | .08 | .03 | .01 |
| ☐ 248 Doug Smith (98) | .05 | .02 | .00 |
| ☐ 249 Jeff Kemp (99) | .05 | .02 | .00 |
| ☐ 250 Kent Hill | .03 | .01 | .00 |
| ☐ 251 Mike Lansford (101) | .03 | .01 | .00 |
| ☐ 252 Henry Ellard (102) | .35 | .14 | .03 |
| ☐ 253 LeRoy Irvin (103) | .03 | .01 | .00 |
| ☐ 254 Ron Brown (104) | .06 | .02 | .00 |
| ☐ 255 John Riggins | .20 | .08 | .02 |
| ☐ 256 Dexter Manley (106) | .06 | .02 | .00 |
| ☐ 257 Darrell Green (107) | .10 | .04 | .01 |
| ☐ 258 Joe Theismann (108) | .15 | .06 | .01 |
| ☐ 259 Mark Moseley (109) | .05 | .02 | .00 |
| ☐ 260 Clint Didier (110) | .03 | .01 | .00 |
| ☐ 261 Vernon Dean (111) | .03 | .01 | .00 |
| ☐ 262 Calvin Muhammad (112) | .03 | .01 | .00 |
| ☐ 263 Art Monk | .20 | .08 | .02 |
| ☐ 264 Bruce Clark | .08 | .03 | .01 |
| ☐ 265 Hoby Brenner (115) | .03 | .01 | .00 |
| ☐ 266 Dave Wilson (116) | .03 | .01 | .00 |
| ☐ 267 Hokie Gajan (117) | .03 | .01 | .00 |
| ☐ 268 George Rogers | .10 | .04 | .01 |
| ☐ 269 Rickey Jackson (119) | .08 | .03 | .01 |
| ☐ 270 Brian Hansen (120) | .04 | .02 | .00 |
| ☐ 271 Dave Waymer (121) | .03 | .01 | .00 |
| ☐ 272 Richard Todd (122) | .05 | .02 | .00 |
| ☐ 273 Jan Stenerud | .15 | .06 | .01 |
| ☐ 274 Ted Brown (124) | .04 | .02 | .00 |
| ☐ 275 Leo Lewis (125) | .03 | .01 | .00 |
| ☐ 276 Scott Studwell (126) | .04 | .02 | .00 |
| ☐ 277 Alfred Anderson (127) | .04 | .02 | .00 |
| ☐ 278 Rufus Bess (128) | .03 | .01 | .00 |
| ☐ 279 Darrin Nelson (129) | .05 | .02 | .00 |

| | MINT | EXC | G-VG |
|---|---|---|---|
| ☐ 280 Greg Coleman (130) | .03 | .01 | .00 |
| ☐ 281 Tommy Kramer | .08 | .03 | .01 |
| ☐ 282 Joe Montana (283) | .75 | .30 | .07 |
| ☐ 283 Dan Marino (282) | .75 | .30 | .07 |
| ☐ 284 Brian Hansen (285) | .03 | .01 | .00 |
| ☐ 285 Jim Arnold (284) | .03 | .01 | .00 |
| ☐ xx Sticker Album | 1.25 | .50 | .12 |

# 1986 Topps Stickers

The 1986 Topps Football sticker set is similar to the previous years in that it contains stickers, foil stickers, and an accompanying album to house one's sticker collection. The stickers measure approximately 2 1/8" by 3". The sticker design shows an inverted L-shaped border in an accent color. The stickers are numbered on the front and on the back. The sticker backs are printed in brown ink on white stock. Sticker pairs are identified below by parenthetically listing the other member of the pair. On the inside back cover of the sticker album the company offered (via direct mail-order) any ten different stickers of your choice for 1.00; this is one reason why the values of the most popular players in these sticker sets are somewhat depressed compared to traditional card set prices. The front cover of the sticker album features Walter Payton and several other Chicago Bears players; the back cover shows a team photo of the Chicago Bears. The stickers are checklisted below according to special subsets and teams as follows: Super Bowl puzzle (1-5), Chicago Bears (6-14), Tampa Bay Buccaneers (15-23), St. Louis Cardinals (24-32), Dallas Cowboys (33-41), Philadelphia Eagles (42-50), Atlanta Falcons (51-59), San Francisco 49ers (60-68), New York Giants (69-77), Detroit Lions (78-86), Green Bay Packers (87-95), Los Angeles Rams (96-104), Washington Redskins (105-113), New Orleans Saints (114-122), Minnesota Vikings (123-131), All-Pros (132-155), Cincinnati Bengals (156-164), Buffalo Bills (165-173), Denver Broncos (174-182), Cleveland Browns (183-191), San Diego Chargers (192-200), Kansas City Chiefs (201-209), Indianapolis Colts (210-218), Miami Dolphins (219-227), New York Jets (228-236), Houston Oilers (237-245), New England Patriots (246-254), Los Angeles Raiders (255-263), Seattle Seahawks (264-272), Pittsburgh Steelers (273-281), and Leaders (282-285). The following players are shown in their Rookie Card year: Duane Bickett, Joey Browner, Earnest Byner, Anthony Carter, Gary Clark, Bobby Hebert, Steve Jordan, Bernie Kosar, Albert Lewis, Keith Millard, Stephone Paige, Andre Reed, Bruce Smith, Al Toon, Reggie White, and Steve Young.

| | MINT | EXC | G-VG |
|---|---|---|---|
| COMPLETE SET (285) | 15.00 | 6.00 | 1.50 |
| COMMON PLAYER (1-285) | .05 | .02 | .00 |
| COMMON HALF STICKER | .03 | .01 | .00 |
| COMMON FOILS | .15 | .06 | .01 |
| COMMON HALF FOILS | .10 | .04 | .01 |
| | | | |
| ☐ 1 Walter Payton LH | .50 | .20 | .05 |
| ☐ 2 Walter Payton RH | .40 | .16 | .04 |
| ☐ 3 Richard Dent LH | .10 | .04 | .01 |
| ☐ 4 Richard Dent RH | .10 | .04 | .01 |
| ☐ 5 Richard Dent FOIL | .40 | .16 | .04 |
| Super Bowl MVP | | | |
| ☐ 6 Walter Payton | .75 | .30 | .07 |
| ☐ 7 William Perry | .12 | .05 | .01 |
| ☐ 8 Jim McMahon (158) | .10 | .04 | .01 |
| ☐ 9 Richard Dent (159) | .10 | .04 | .01 |
| ☐ 10 Jim Covert (160) | .05 | .02 | .00 |
| ☐ 11 Dan Hampton (161) | .08 | .03 | .01 |
| ☐ 12 Mike Singletary (162) | .08 | .03 | .01 |
| ☐ 13 Jay Hilgenberg (163) | .06 | .02 | .00 |
| ☐ 14 Otis Wilson (164) | .04 | .02 | .00 |
| ☐ 15 Jimmie Giles | .05 | .02 | .00 |
| ☐ 16 Kevin House (166) | .03 | .01 | .00 |
| ☐ 17 Jeremiah Castille (167) | .03 | .01 | .00 |
| ☐ 18 James Wilder | .05 | .02 | .00 |
| ☐ 19 Donald Igwebuike (169) | .03 | .01 | .00 |
| ☐ 20 David Logan (170) | .03 | .01 | .00 |
| ☐ 21 Jeff Davis (171) | .03 | .01 | .00 |
| ☐ 22 Frank Garcia (172) | .03 | .01 | .00 |
| ☐ 23 Steve Young (173) | .75 | .30 | .07 |
| ☐ 24 Stump Mitchell | .08 | .03 | .01 |
| ☐ 25 E.J. Junior | .08 | .03 | .01 |
| ☐ 26 J.T. Smith (176) | .05 | .02 | .00 |
| ☐ 27 Pat Tilley (177) | .04 | .02 | .00 |
| ☐ 28 Neil Lomax (178) | .06 | .02 | .00 |
| ☐ 29 Leonard Smith (179) | .03 | .01 | .00 |
| ☐ 30 Ottis Anderson (180) | .08 | .03 | .01 |
| ☐ 31 Curtis Greer (181) | .04 | .02 | .00 |
| ☐ 32 Roy Green (182) | .06 | .02 | .00 |
| ☐ 33 Tony Dorsett | .25 | .10 | .02 |
| ☐ 34 Tony Hill (184) | .05 | .02 | .00 |
| ☐ 35 Doug Cosbie (185) | .04 | .02 | .00 |
| ☐ 36 Everson Walls | .08 | .03 | .01 |
| ☐ 37 Randy White (187) | .10 | .04 | .01 |
| ☐ 38 Rafael Septien (188) | .03 | .01 | .00 |
| ☐ 39 Mike Renfro (189) | .03 | .01 | .00 |
| ☐ 40 Danny White (190) | .06 | .02 | .00 |
| ☐ 41 Ed Too Tall Jones (191) | .07 | .03 | .01 |
| ☐ 42 Earnest Jackson | .08 | .03 | .01 |
| ☐ 43 Mike Quick | .08 | .03 | .01 |
| ☐ 44 Wes Hopkins (194) | .03 | .01 | .00 |
| ☐ 45 Reggie White (195) | .60 | .24 | .06 |
| ☐ 46 Greg Brown (196) | .03 | .01 | .00 |
| ☐ 47 Paul McFadden (197) | .02 | .01 | .00 |
| ☐ 48 John Spagnola (198) | .02 | .01 | .00 |
| ☐ 49 Ron Jaworski (199) | .05 | .02 | .00 |
| ☐ 50 Herman Hunter (200) | .03 | .01 | .00 |
| ☐ 51 Gerald Riggs | .10 | .04 | .01 |
| ☐ 52 Mike Pitts (202) | .03 | .01 | .00 |
| ☐ 53 Buddy Curry (203) | .03 | .01 | .00 |
| ☐ 54 Billy Johnson | .08 | .03 | .01 |
| ☐ 55 Rick Donnelly (205) | .03 | .01 | .00 |
| ☐ 56 Rick Bryan (206) | .08 | .03 | .01 |
| ☐ 57 Bobby Butler (207) | .03 | .01 | .00 |
| ☐ 58 Mick Luckhurst (208) | .03 | .01 | .00 |
| ☐ 59 Mike Kenn (209) | .05 | .02 | .00 |
| ☐ 60 Roger Craig | .25 | .10 | .02 |
| ☐ 61 Joe Montana | 1.25 | .50 | .12 |
| ☐ 62 Michael Carter (212) | .10 | .04 | .01 |
| ☐ 63 Eric Wright (213) | .03 | .01 | .00 |
| ☐ 64 Dwight Clark (214) | .10 | .04 | .01 |
| ☐ 65 Ronnie Lott (215) | .12 | .05 | .01 |
| ☐ 66 Carlton Williamson (216) | .03 | .01 | .00 |
| ☐ 67 Wendell Tyler (217) | .03 | .01 | .00 |
| ☐ 68 Dwaine Board (218) | .03 | .01 | .00 |
| ☐ 69 Joe Morris | .12 | .05 | .01 |
| ☐ 70 Leonard Marshall (220) | .04 | .02 | .00 |
| ☐ 71 Lionel Manuel (221) | .04 | .02 | .00 |
| ☐ 72 Harry Carson | .10 | .04 | .01 |
| ☐ 73 Phil Simms (223) | .10 | .04 | .01 |
| ☐ 74 Sean Landeta (224) | .03 | .01 | .00 |
| ☐ 75 Lawrence Taylor (225) | .15 | .06 | .01 |
| ☐ 76 Elvis Patterson (226) | .03 | .01 | .00 |
| ☐ 77 George Adams (227) | .08 | .03 | .01 |
| ☐ 78 James Jones | .08 | .03 | .01 |
| ☐ 79 Leonard Thompson | .05 | .02 | .00 |
| ☐ 80 William Graham (230) | .03 | .01 | .00 |
| ☐ 81 Mark Nichols (231) | .03 | .01 | .00 |
| ☐ 82 William Gay (232) | .03 | .01 | .00 |
| ☐ 83 Jimmy Williams (233) | .03 | .01 | .00 |
| ☐ 84 Billy Sims (234) | .10 | .04 | .01 |
| ☐ 85 Bobby Watkins (235) | .03 | .01 | .00 |
| ☐ 86 Eddie Murray (236) | .05 | .02 | .00 |
| ☐ 87 James Lofton (237) | .25 | .10 | .02 |
| ☐ 88 Jessie Clark (238) | .03 | .01 | .00 |
| ☐ 89 Tim Lewis (239) | .03 | .01 | .00 |
| ☐ 90 Eddie Lee Ivery | .08 | .03 | .01 |
| ☐ 91 Phillip Epps (241) | .05 | .02 | .00 |
| ☐ 92 Ezra Johnson (242) | .03 | .01 | .00 |
| ☐ 93 Mike Douglass (243) | .03 | .01 | .00 |
| ☐ 94 Paul Coffman (244) | .05 | .02 | .00 |
| ☐ 95 Randy Scott (245) | .03 | .01 | .00 |
| ☐ 96 Eric Dickerson | .50 | .20 | .05 |
| ☐ 97 Dale Hatcher | .05 | .02 | .00 |
| ☐ 98 Ron Brown (248) | .05 | .02 | .00 |
| ☐ 99 LeRoy Irvin (249) | .05 | .02 | .00 |
| ☐ 100 Kent Hill (250) | .03 | .01 | .00 |
| ☐ 101 Dennis Harrah (251) | .03 | .01 | .00 |
| ☐ 102 Jackie Slater (252) | .08 | .03 | .01 |
| ☐ 103 Mike Wilcher (253) | .03 | .01 | .00 |
| ☐ 104 Doug Smith (254) | .03 | .01 | .00 |
| ☐ 105 Art Monk | .25 | .10 | .02 |
| ☐ 106 Joe Jacoby (256) | .05 | .02 | .00 |
| ☐ 107 Russ Grimm (257) | .05 | .02 | .00 |
| ☐ 108 George Rogers | .08 | .03 | .01 |
| ☐ 109 Dexter Manley (259) | .03 | .01 | .00 |
| ☐ 110 Jay Schroeder (260) | .15 | .06 | .01 |

|  |  | | | |
|---|---|---|---|---|
| ☐ 111 | Gary Clark (261) | .40 | .16 | .04 |
| ☐ 112 | Curtis Jordan (262) | .03 | .01 | .00 |
| ☐ 113 | Charles Mann (263) | .08 | .03 | .01 |
| ☐ 114 | Morten Andersen | .08 | .03 | .01 |
| ☐ 115 | Rickey Jackson | .10 | .04 | .01 |
| ☐ 116 | Glen Redd (266) | .03 | .01 | .00 |
| ☐ 117 | Bobby Hebert (267) | .20 | .08 | .02 |
| ☐ 118 | Hoby Brenner (268) | .03 | .01 | .00 |
| ☐ 119 | Brian Hansen (269) | .03 | .01 | .00 |
| ☐ 120 | Dave Waymer (270) | .03 | .01 | .00 |
| ☐ 121 | Bruce Clark (271) | .03 | .01 | .00 |
| ☐ 122 | Wayne Wilson (272) | .03 | .01 | .00 |
| ☐ 123 | Joey Browner | .25 | .10 | .02 |
| ☐ 124 | Darrin Nelson (274) | .03 | .01 | .00 |
| ☐ 125 | Keith Millard (275) | .15 | .06 | .01 |
| ☐ 126 | Anthony Carter | .40 | .16 | .04 |
| ☐ 127 | Buster Rhymes (277) | .04 | .02 | .00 |
| ☐ 128 | Steve Jordan (278) | .20 | .08 | .02 |
| ☐ 129 | Greg Coleman (279) | .03 | .01 | .00 |
| ☐ 130 | Ted Brown (280) | .03 | .01 | .00 |
| ☐ 131 | John Turner (281) | .03 | .01 | .00 |
| ☐ 132 | Harry Carson (144) AP FOIL | .15 | .06 | .01 |
| ☐ 133 | Deron Cherry (145) AP FOIL | .10 | .04 | .01 |
| ☐ 134 | Richard Dent (146) AP FOIL | .20 | .08 | .02 |
| ☐ 135 | Mike Haynes (147) AP FOIL | .12 | .05 | .01 |
| ☐ 136 | Wes Hopkins (148) AP FOIL | .10 | .04 | .01 |
| ☐ 137 | Joe Klecko (149) AP FOIL | .10 | .04 | .01 |
| ☐ 138 | Leonard Marshall (150) AP FOIL | .10 | .04 | .01 |
| ☐ 139 | Karl Mecklenburg (151) AP FOIL | .12 | .05 | .01 |
| ☐ 140 | Rohn Stark (152) AP FOIL | .10 | .04 | .01 |
| ☐ 141 | Lawrence Taylor (153) AP FOIL | .25 | .10 | .02 |
| ☐ 142 | Andre Tippett (154) AP FOIL | .12 | .05 | .01 |
| ☐ 143 | Everson Walls (155) AP FOIL | .12 | .05 | .01 |
| ☐ 144 | Marcus Allen (132) AP FOIL | .25 | .10 | .02 |
| ☐ 145 | Gary Anderson (133) AP FOIL | .10 | .04 | .01 |
| ☐ 146 | Doug Cosbie (134) AP FOIL | .10 | .04 | .01 |
| ☐ 147 | Jim Covert (135) AP FOIL | .10 | .04 | .01 |
| ☐ 148 | John Hannah (136) AP FOIL | .15 | .06 | .01 |
| ☐ 149 | Jay Hilgenberg (137) AP FOIL | .12 | .05 | .01 |
| ☐ 150 | Kent Hill (138) AP FOIL | .10 | .04 | .01 |
| ☐ 151 | Brian Holloway (139) AP FOIL | .10 | .04 | .01 |
| ☐ 152 | Steve Largent (140) AP FOIL | .60 | .24 | .06 |
| ☐ 153 | Dan Marino (141) AP FOIL | 1.00 | .40 | .10 |
| ☐ 154 | Art Monk (142) AP FOIL | .25 | .10 | .02 |
| ☐ 155 | Walter Payton (143) AP FOIL | .60 | .24 | .06 |
| ☐ 156 | Anthony Munoz | .15 | .06 | .01 |
| ☐ 157 | Boomer Esiason | .40 | .16 | .04 |
| ☐ 158 | Cris Collinsworth (8) | .06 | .02 | .00 |
| ☐ 159 | Eddie Edwards (9) | .03 | .01 | .00 |
| ☐ 160 | James Griffin (10) | .03 | .01 | .00 |
| ☐ 161 | Jim Breech (11) | .03 | .01 | .00 |
| ☐ 162 | Eddie Brown (12) | .05 | .02 | .00 |
| ☐ 163 | Ross Browner (13) | .03 | .01 | .00 |
| ☐ 164 | James Brooks (14) | .07 | .03 | .01 |
| ☐ 165 | Greg Bell | .08 | .03 | .01 |
| ☐ 166 | Jerry Butler (16) | .03 | .01 | .00 |
| ☐ 167 | Don Wilson (17) | .03 | .01 | .00 |
| ☐ 168 | Andre Reed | .75 | .30 | .07 |
| ☐ 169 | Jim Haslett (19) | .03 | .01 | .00 |
| ☐ 170 | Bruce Mathison (20) | .03 | .01 | .00 |
| ☐ 171 | Bruce Smith (21) | .40 | .16 | .04 |
| ☐ 172 | Joe Cribbs (22) | .05 | .02 | .00 |
| ☐ 173 | Charles Romes (23) | .03 | .01 | .00 |
| ☐ 174 | Karl Mecklenburg | .08 | .03 | .01 |
| ☐ 175 | Rulon Jones | .05 | .02 | .00 |
| ☐ 176 | John Elway (26) | .40 | .16 | .04 |
| ☐ 177 | Sammy Winder (27) | .03 | .01 | .00 |
| ☐ 178 | Louis Wright (28) | .04 | .02 | .00 |
| ☐ 179 | Steve Watson (29) | .03 | .01 | .00 |
| ☐ 180 | Dennis Smith (30) | .03 | .01 | .00 |
| ☐ 181 | Mike Harden (31) | .03 | .01 | .00 |
| ☐ 182 | Vance Johnson (32) | .07 | .03 | .01 |
| ☐ 183 | Kevin Mack | .10 | .04 | .01 |
| ☐ 184 | Chip Banks (34) | .05 | .02 | .00 |
| ☐ 185 | Bob Golic (35) | .05 | .02 | .00 |
| ☐ 186 | Earnest Byner | .35 | .14 | .03 |
| ☐ 187 | Ozzie Newsome (37) | .12 | .05 | .01 |
| ☐ 188 | Bernie Kosar (38) | .60 | .24 | .06 |
| ☐ 189 | Don Rogers (39) | .03 | .01 | .00 |
| ☐ 190 | Al Gross (40) | .03 | .01 | .00 |
| ☐ 191 | Clarence Weathers (41) | .03 | .01 | .00 |
| ☐ 192 | Lionel James | .08 | .03 | .01 |
| ☐ 193 | Dan Fouts | .30 | .12 | .03 |
| ☐ 194 | Wes Chandler (44) | .06 | .02 | .00 |
| ☐ 195 | Kellen Winslow (45) | .10 | .04 | .01 |
| ☐ 196 | Gary Anderson (46) | .07 | .03 | .01 |
| ☐ 197 | Charlie Joiner (47) | .08 | .03 | .01 |
| ☐ 198 | Ralf Mojsiejenko (48) | .03 | .01 | .00 |
| ☐ 199 | Bob Thomas (49) | .03 | .01 | .00 |
| ☐ 200 | Tim Spencer (50) | .03 | .01 | .00 |
| ☐ 201 | Deron Cherry | .10 | .04 | .01 |
| ☐ 202 | Bill Maas (52) | .05 | .02 | .00 |
| ☐ 203 | Herman Heard (53) | .03 | .01 | .00 |
| ☐ 204 | Carlos Carson | .08 | .03 | .01 |
| ☐ 205 | Nick Lowery (55) | .05 | .02 | .00 |
| ☐ 206 | Bill Kenney (56) | .05 | .02 | .00 |
| ☐ 207 | Albert Lewis (57) | .25 | .10 | .02 |
| ☐ 208 | Art Still (58) | .05 | .02 | .00 |
| ☐ 209 | Stephone Paige (59) | .25 | .10 | .02 |
| ☐ 210 | Rohn Stark | .05 | .02 | .00 |
| ☐ 211 | Chris Hinton | .10 | .04 | .01 |
| ☐ 212 | Albert Bentley (62) | .10 | .04 | .01 |
| ☐ 213 | Eugene Daniel (63) | .03 | .01 | .00 |
| ☐ 214 | Pat Beach (64) | .03 | .01 | .00 |
| ☐ 215 | Cliff Odom (65) | .03 | .01 | .00 |
| ☐ 216 | Duane Bickett (66) | .20 | .08 | .02 |
| ☐ 217 | George Wonsley (67) | .03 | .01 | .00 |
| ☐ 218 | Randy McMillan (68) | .03 | .01 | .00 |
| ☐ 219 | Dan Marino | 1.25 | .50 | .12 |
| ☐ 220 | Dwight Stephenson (70) | .05 | .02 | .00 |
| ☐ 221 | Roy Foster (71) | .03 | .01 | .00 |
| ☐ 222 | Mark Clayton | .20 | .08 | .02 |
| ☐ 223 | Mark Duper (73) | .05 | .02 | .00 |
| ☐ 224 | Fuad Reveiz (74) | .05 | .02 | .00 |
| ☐ 225 | Reggie Roby (75) | .05 | .02 | .00 |
| ☐ 226 | Tony Nathan (76) | .05 | .02 | .00 |
| ☐ 227 | Ron Davenport (77) | .03 | .01 | .00 |
| ☐ 228 | Freeman McNeil | .10 | .04 | .01 |
| ☐ 229 | Joe Klecko | .08 | .03 | .01 |
| ☐ 230 | Mark Gastineau (80) | .05 | .02 | .00 |
| ☐ 231 | Ken O'Brien (81) | .06 | .02 | .00 |
| ☐ 232 | Lance Mehl (82) | .03 | .01 | .00 |
| ☐ 233 | Al Toon (83) | .25 | .10 | .02 |
| ☐ 234 | Mickey Shuler (84) | .03 | .01 | .00 |
| ☐ 235 | Pat Leahy (85) | .05 | .02 | .00 |
| ☐ 236 | Wesley Walker (86) | .06 | .02 | .00 |
| ☐ 237 | Drew Hill | .10 | .04 | .01 |
| ☐ 238 | Warren Moon (88) | .40 | .16 | .04 |
| ☐ 239 | Mike Rozier (89) | .10 | .04 | .01 |
| ☐ 240 | Mike Munchak | .10 | .04 | .01 |
| ☐ 241 | Tim Smith (91) | .03 | .01 | .00 |
| ☐ 242 | Butch Woolfolk (92) | .04 | .02 | .00 |
| ☐ 243 | Willie Drewrey (93) | .03 | .01 | .00 |
| ☐ 244 | Keith Bostic (94) | .03 | .01 | .00 |
| ☐ 245 | Jesse Baker (95) | .03 | .01 | .00 |
| ☐ 246 | Craig James | .12 | .05 | .01 |
| ☐ 247 | John Hannah | .12 | .05 | .01 |
| ☐ 248 | Tony Eason (98) | .06 | .02 | .00 |
| ☐ 249 | Andre Tippett (99) | .06 | .02 | .00 |
| ☐ 250 | Tony Collins (100) | .03 | .01 | .00 |
| ☐ 251 | Brian Holloway (101) | .03 | .01 | .00 |
| ☐ 252 | Irving Fryar (102) | .10 | .04 | .01 |
| ☐ 253 | Raymond Clayborn (103) | .03 | .01 | .00 |
| ☐ 254 | Steve Nelson (104) | .03 | .01 | .00 |
| ☐ 255 | Marcus Allen | .25 | .10 | .02 |
| ☐ 256 | Mike Haynes (106) | .06 | .02 | .00 |
| ☐ 257 | Todd Christensen (107) | .06 | .02 | .00 |
| ☐ 258 | Howie Long | .12 | .05 | .01 |
| ☐ 259 | Lester Hayes (109) | .05 | .02 | .00 |
| ☐ 260 | Rod Martin (110) | .03 | .01 | .00 |
| ☐ 261 | Dokie Williams (111) | .03 | .01 | .00 |
| ☐ 262 | Chris Bahr (112) | .03 | .01 | .00 |
| ☐ 263 | Bill Pickel (113) | .10 | .04 | .01 |
| ☐ 264 | Curt Warner (114) | .50 | .20 | .05 |
| ☐ 265 | Steve Largent | .50 | .20 | .05 |
| ☐ 266 | Fredd Young (116) | .06 | .02 | .00 |
| ☐ 267 | Dave Krieg (117) | .08 | .03 | .01 |
| ☐ 268 | Daryl Turner (118) | .03 | .01 | .00 |
| ☐ 269 | John Harris (119) | .03 | .01 | .00 |
| ☐ 270 | Randy Edwards (120) | .03 | .01 | .00 |
| ☐ 271 | Kenny Easley (121) | .05 | .02 | .00 |
| ☐ 272 | Jacob Green (122) | .05 | .02 | .00 |
| ☐ 273 | Gary Anderson | .05 | .02 | .00 |
| ☐ 274 | Mike Webster (124) | .07 | .03 | .01 |
| ☐ 275 | Walter Abercrombie (125) | .03 | .01 | .00 |

| | | | |
|---|---|---|---|
| ☐ 276 Louis Lipps ........................ | .10 | .04 | .01 |
| ☐ 277 Frank Pollard (127) ............... | .03 | .01 | .00 |
| ☐ 278 Mike Merriweather ............... (128) | .05 | .02 | .00 |
| ☐ 279 Mark Malone (129) .............. | .04 | .02 | .00 |
| ☐ 280 Donnie Shell (130) ............... | .04 | .02 | .00 |
| ☐ 281 John Stallworth (131) ........... | .06 | .02 | .00 |
| ☐ 282 Marcus Allen (284) .............. FOIL | .40 | .16 | .04 |
| ☐ 283 Ken O'Brien (285) ............... FOIL | .15 | .06 | .01 |
| ☐ 284 Kevin Butler (282) .............. FOIL | .10 | .04 | .01 |
| ☐ 285 Roger Craig (283) ............... FOIL | .30 | .12 | .03 |
| ☐ xx Sticker Album ...................... | 1.25 | .50 | .12 |

## 1987 Topps Stickers

The 1987 Topps Football sticker set is similar to the previous years in that it contains stickers, foil stickers, and an accompanying album to house one's sticker collection. The stickers are approximately 2 1/8" by 3" and are in full-color with a white border with little footballs in each corner. The stickers are numbered on the front in the lower left hand border. Several of the stickers are two players per sticker card; they are designated in the checklist below with the number of the paired player in parentheses. The sticker backs are printed in red on white stock. There are 14 foil stickers, individual (half-size) player stickers numbered 132-155 and 282-285. On the inside back cover of the sticker album the company offered (via direct mail-order) any ten different stickers of your choice for 1.00; this is one reason why the values of the most popular players in these sticker sets are somewhat depressed compared to traditional card set prices. The front cover of the sticker album shows New York Giants art. The stickers are checklisted below according to special subsets and teams as follows: Super Bowl puzzle (1-5), Chicago Bears (6-14), Tampa Bay Buccaneers (15-23), St. Louis Cardinals (24-32), Dallas Cowboys (33-41), Philadelphia Eagles (42-50), Atlanta Falcons (51-59), San Francisco 49ers (60-68), New York Giants (69-77), Detroit Lions (78-86), Green Bay Packers (87-95), Los Angeles Rams (96-104), Washington Redskins (105-113), New Orleans Saints (114-122), Minnesota Vikings (123-131), All-Pros (132-155), Cincinnati Bengals (156-164), Buffalo Bills (165-173), Denver Broncos (174-182), Cleveland Browns (183-191), San Diego Chargers (192-200), Kansas City Chiefs (201-209), Indianapolis Colts (210-218), Miami Dolphins (219-227), New York Jets (228-236), Houston Oilers (237-245), New England Patriots (246-254), Los Angeles Raiders (255-263), Seattle Seahawks (264-272), Pittsburgh Steelers (273-281), and Leaders (282-285). The following players are shown in their Rookie Card year: Keith Byars, Randall Cunningham, Kenneth Davis, Jim Everett, Doug Flutie, Ernest Givins, Tim Harris, Jim Kelly, Tim McGee, John Offerdahl, Leslie O'Neal, Mike Sherrard, Herschel Walker, and Lee Williams.

| | MINT | EXC | G-VG |
|---|---|---|---|
| COMPLETE SET (285)...................... | 12.00 | 5.00 | 1.20 |
| COMMON PLAYER (1-285)............... | .05 | .02 | .00 |
| COMMON HALF STICKER................ | .03 | .01 | .00 |
| COMMON HALF FOILS..................... | .10 | .04 | .01 |
| | | | |
| ☐ 1 Phil Simms ........................ Super Bowl MVP | .25 | .10 | .02 |
| ☐ 2 Super Bowl XXI .................... Phil Simms UL | .10 | .04 | .01 |
| ☐ 3 Super Bowl XXI .................... Phil Simms UR | .10 | .04 | .01 |
| ☐ 4 Super Bowl XXI .................... Phil Simms LL | .10 | .04 | .01 |

| | | | |
|---|---|---|---|
| ☐ 5 Super Bowl XXI .................... Phil Simms LR | .10 | .04 | .01 |
| ☐ 6 Mike Singletary ..................... | .12 | .05 | .01 |
| ☐ 7 Jim Covert (156)................... | .04 | .02 | .00 |
| ☐ 8 Willie Gault (157)................. | .06 | .02 | .00 |
| ☐ 9 Jim McMahon (158)............... | .08 | .03 | .01 |
| ☐ 10 Doug Flutie (159)............... | .35 | .14 | .03 |
| ☐ 11 Richard Dent (160).............. | .08 | .03 | .01 |
| ☐ 12 Kevin Butler (161).............. | .03 | .01 | .00 |
| ☐ 13 Wilber Marshall (162).......... | .08 | .03 | .01 |
| ☐ 14 Walter Payton .................... | .60 | .24 | .06 |
| ☐ 15 Calvin Magee .................... | .05 | .02 | .00 |
| ☐ 16 David Logan (165)............... | .03 | .01 | .00 |
| ☐ 17 Jeff Davis (166).................. | .03 | .01 | .00 |
| ☐ 18 Gerald Carter (167)............. | .03 | .01 | .00 |
| ☐ 19 James Wilder .................... | .05 | .02 | .00 |
| ☐ 20 Chris Washington ............... (168) | .03 | .01 | .00 |
| ☐ 21 Phil Freeman (169).............. | .03 | .01 | .00 |
| ☐ 22 Frank Garcia (170).............. | .03 | .01 | .00 |
| ☐ 23 Donald Igwebuike ............... (171) | .03 | .01 | .00 |
| ☐ 24 Al(Bubba) Baker (175).......... | .05 | .02 | .00 |
| ☐ 25 Vai Sikahema (176).............. | .05 | .02 | .00 |
| ☐ 26 Leonard Smith (177)............. | .03 | .01 | .00 |
| ☐ 27 Ron Wolfley (178)............... | .03 | .01 | .00 |
| ☐ 28 J.T. Smith ........................ | .08 | .03 | .01 |
| ☐ 29 Roy Green (179)................. | .06 | .02 | .00 |
| ☐ 30 Cedric Mack (180).............. | .03 | .01 | .00 |
| ☐ 31 Neil Lomax (181)............... | .06 | .02 | .00 |
| ☐ 32 Stump Mitchell................... | .08 | .03 | .01 |
| ☐ 33 Herschel Walker ................. | .40 | .16 | .04 |
| ☐ 34 Danny White (184).............. | .06 | .02 | .00 |
| ☐ 35 Michael Downs (185)........... | .03 | .01 | .00 |
| ☐ 36 Randy White (186).............. | .08 | .03 | .01 |
| ☐ 37 Eugene Lockhart (188).......... | .05 | .02 | .00 |
| ☐ 38 Mike Sherrard (189)............ | .20 | .08 | .02 |
| ☐ 39 Jim Jeffcoat (190).............. | .03 | .01 | .00 |
| ☐ 40 Tony Hill (191).................. | .04 | .02 | .00 |
| ☐ 41 Tony Dorsett ..................... | .25 | .10 | .02 |
| ☐ 42 Keith Byars (192)............... | .25 | .10 | .02 |
| ☐ 43 Andre Waters (193)............. | .06 | .02 | .00 |
| ☐ 44 Kenny Jackson (194) ........... | .03 | .01 | .00 |
| ☐ 45 John Teltschik (195)............ | .03 | .01 | .00 |
| ☐ 46 Roynell Young (196)............ | .03 | .01 | .00 |
| ☐ 47 Randall Cunningham ........... (197) | .75 | .30 | .07 |
| ☐ 48 Mike Reichenbach ............... (198) | .03 | .01 | .00 |
| ☐ 49 Reggie White .................... | .35 | .14 | .03 |
| ☐ 50 Mike Quick ...................... | .08 | .03 | .01 |
| ☐ 51 Bill Fralic (201)................. | .03 | .01 | .00 |
| ☐ 52 Sylvester Stamps ............... (202) | .03 | .01 | .00 |
| ☐ 53 Bret Clark (203)................. | .03 | .01 | .00 |
| ☐ 54 William Andrews (204).......... | .05 | .02 | .00 |
| ☐ 55 Buddy Curry (205).............. | .03 | .01 | .00 |
| ☐ 56 Dave Archer (206).............. | .10 | .04 | .01 |
| ☐ 57 Rick Bryan (207)................ | .05 | .02 | .00 |
| ☐ 58 Gerald Riggs .................... | .10 | .04 | .01 |
| ☐ 59 Charlie Brown ................... | .05 | .02 | .00 |
| ☐ 60 Joe Montana .................... | 1.50 | .60 | .15 |
| ☐ 61 Jerry Rice........................ | 1.50 | .60 | .15 |
| ☐ 62 Carlton Williamson ............. (212) | .03 | .01 | .00 |
| ☐ 63 Roger Craig (213)............... | .12 | .05 | .01 |
| ☐ 64 Ronnie Lott (214)............... | .15 | .06 | .01 |
| ☐ 65 Dwight Clark (215).............. | .10 | .04 | .01 |
| ☐ 66 Jeff Stover (216)................ | .03 | .01 | .00 |
| ☐ 67 Charles Haley (217)............. | .15 | .06 | .01 |
| ☐ 68 Ray Wersching (218)............ | .03 | .01 | .00 |
| ☐ 69 Lawrence Taylor ................ | .25 | .10 | .02 |
| ☐ 70 Joe Morris........................ | .12 | .05 | .01 |
| ☐ 71 Carl Banks (221)................ | .08 | .03 | .01 |
| ☐ 72 Mark Bavaro (222)............. | .06 | .02 | .00 |
| ☐ 73 Harry Carson (223)............. | .05 | .02 | .00 |
| ☐ 74 Phil Simms (224)............... | .10 | .04 | .01 |
| ☐ 75 Jim Burt (225) .................. | .03 | .01 | .00 |
| ☐ 76 Brad Benson (226).............. | .03 | .01 | .00 |
| ☐ 77 Leonard Marshall ............... (227) | .03 | .01 | .00 |
| ☐ 78 Jeff Chadwick.................... | .05 | .02 | .00 |
| ☐ 79 Devon Mitchell (228)........... | .03 | .01 | .00 |
| ☐ 80 Chuck Long (229)............... | .06 | .02 | .00 |
| ☐ 81 Demetrious Johnson ............ (230) | .03 | .01 | .00 |
| ☐ 82 Herman Hunter (231)........... | .03 | .01 | .00 |
| ☐ 83 Keith Ferguson (232)........... | .03 | .01 | .00 |
| ☐ 84 Garry James (233).............. | .04 | .02 | .00 |
| ☐ 85 Leonard Thompson............... (234) | .03 | .01 | .00 |
| ☐ 86 James Jones ..................... | .08 | .03 | .01 |
| ☐ 87 Kenneth Davis ................... | .30 | .12 | .03 |
| ☐ 88 Brian Noble (237).............. | .03 | .01 | .00 |
| ☐ 89 Al Del Greco (238).............. | .03 | .01 | .00 |
| ☐ 90 Mark Lee (239).................. | .05 | .02 | .00 |
| ☐ 91 Randy Wright..................... | .08 | .03 | .01 |

|  |  | | | |
|---|---|---|---|---|
| ☐ 92 | Tim Harris (240) | .25 | .10 | .02 |
| ☐ 93 | Phillip Epps (241) | .03 | .01 | .00 |
| ☐ 94 | Walter Stanley (242) | .10 | .04 | .01 |
| ☐ 95 | Eddie Lee Ivery (243) | .05 | .02 | .00 |
| ☐ 96 | Doug Smith (247) | .03 | .01 | .00 |
| ☐ 97 | Jerry Gray (248) | .05 | .02 | .00 |
| ☐ 98 | Dennis Harrah (249) | .03 | .01 | .00 |
| ☐ 99 | Jim Everett (250) | .50 | .20 | .05 |
| ☐ 100 | Jackie Slater (251) | .06 | .02 | .00 |
| ☐ 101 | Vince Newsome (252) | .03 | .01 | .00 |
| ☐ 102 | LeRoy Irvin (253) | .03 | .01 | .00 |
| ☐ 103 | Henry Ellard | .10 | .04 | .01 |
| ☐ 104 | Eric Dickerson | .50 | .20 | .05 |
| ☐ 105 | George Rogers (256) | .06 | .02 | .00 |
| ☐ 106 | Darrell Green (257) | .07 | .03 | .01 |
| ☐ 107 | Art Monk (258) | .10 | .04 | .01 |
| ☐ 108 | Neal Olkewicz (260) | .03 | .01 | .00 |
| ☐ 109 | Russ Grimm (261) | .03 | .01 | .00 |
| ☐ 110 | Dexter Manley (262) | .03 | .01 | .00 |
| ☐ 111 | Kelvin Bryant (263) | .05 | .02 | .00 |
| ☐ 112 | Jay Schroeder | .15 | .06 | .01 |
| ☐ 113 | Gary Clark | .15 | .06 | .01 |
| ☐ 114 | Rickey Jackson | .08 | .03 | .01 |
| ☐ 115 | Eric Martin (264) | .07 | .03 | .01 |
| ☐ 116 | Dave Waymer (265) | .03 | .01 | .00 |
| ☐ 117 | Morten Andersen (266) | .06 | .02 | .00 |
| ☐ 118 | Bruce Clark (267) | .03 | .01 | .00 |
| ☐ 119 | Hoby Brenner (269) | .03 | .01 | .00 |
| ☐ 120 | Brian Hansen (270) | .03 | .01 | .00 |
| ☐ 121 | Dave Wilson (271) | .04 | .02 | .00 |
| ☐ 122 | Rueben Mayes | .10 | .04 | .01 |
| ☐ 123 | Tommy Kramer | .08 | .03 | .01 |
| ☐ 124 | Mark Malone (274) | .04 | .02 | .00 |
| ☐ 125 | Anthony Carter (275) | .10 | .04 | .01 |
| ☐ 126 | Keith Millard (276) | .08 | .03 | .01 |
| ☐ 127 | Steve Jordan | .12 | .05 | .01 |
| ☐ 128 | Chuck Nelson (277) | .03 | .01 | .00 |
| ☐ 129 | Issiac Holt (278) | .04 | .02 | .00 |
| ☐ 130 | Darrin Nelson (279) | .05 | .02 | .00 |
| ☐ 131 | Gary Zimmerman (280) | .05 | .02 | .00 |
| ☐ 132 | Mark Bavaro (146) All-Pro FOIL | .10 | .04 | .01 |
| ☐ 133 | Jim Covert (147) All-Pro FOIL | .10 | .04 | .01 |
| ☐ 134 | Eric Dickerson (148) All-Pro FOIL | .30 | .12 | .03 |
| ☐ 135 | Bill Fralic (149) All-Pro FOIL | .10 | .04 | .01 |
| ☐ 136 | Tony Franklin (150) All-Pro FOIL | .10 | .04 | .01 |
| ☐ 137 | Dennis Harrah (151) All-Pro FOIL | .10 | .04 | .01 |
| ☐ 138 | Dan Marino (152) All-Pro FOIL | .75 | .30 | .07 |
| ☐ 139 | Joe Morris (153) All-Pro FOIL | .15 | .06 | .01 |
| ☐ 140 | Jerry Rice (154) All-Pro FOIL | .75 | .30 | .07 |
| ☐ 141 | Cody Risien (155) All-Pro FOIL | .10 | .04 | .01 |
| ☐ 142 | Dwight Stephenson (282) All-Pro FOIL | .10 | .04 | .01 |
| ☐ 143 | Al Toon (283) All-Pro FOIL | .15 | .06 | .01 |
| ☐ 144 | Deron Cherry (284) All-Pro FOIL | .12 | .05 | .01 |
| ☐ 145 | Hanford Dixon (285) All-Pro FOIL | .10 | .04 | .01 |
| ☐ 146 | Darrell Green (132) All-Pro FOIL | .15 | .06 | .01 |
| ☐ 147 | Ronnie Lott (133) All-Pro FOIL | .20 | .08 | .02 |
| ☐ 148 | Bill Maas (134) All-Pro FOIL | .10 | .04 | .01 |
| ☐ 149 | Dexter Manley (135) All-Pro FOIL | .10 | .04 | .01 |
| ☐ 150 | Karl Mecklenburg (136) All-Pro FOIL | .12 | .05 | .01 |
| ☐ 151 | Mike Singletary (137) All-Pro FOIL | .20 | .08 | .02 |
| ☐ 152 | Rohn Stark (138) All-Pro FOIL | .10 | .04 | .01 |
| ☐ 153 | Lawrence Taylor (139) All-Pro FOIL | .25 | .10 | .02 |
| ☐ 154 | Andre Tippett (140) All-Pro FOIL | .10 | .04 | .01 |
| ☐ 155 | Reggie White (141) All-Pro FOIL | .35 | .14 | .03 |
| ☐ 156 | Boomer Esiason (7) | .15 | .06 | .01 |
| ☐ 157 | Anthony Munoz (8) | .10 | .04 | .01 |
| ☐ 158 | Tim McGee (9) | .20 | .08 | .02 |
| ☐ 159 | Max Montoya (10) | .05 | .02 | .00 |
| ☐ 160 | Jim Breech (11) | .03 | .01 | .00 |
| ☐ 161 | Tim Krumrie (12) | .03 | .01 | .00 |
| ☐ 162 | Eddie Brown (13) | .06 | .02 | .00 |
| ☐ 163 | James Brooks | .10 | .04 | .01 |
| ☐ 164 | Cris Collinsworth | .10 | .04 | .01 |
| ☐ 165 | Charles Romes (16) | .03 | .01 | .00 |
| ☐ 166 | Robb Riddick (17) | .03 | .01 | .00 |
| ☐ 167 | Eugene Marve (18) | .03 | .01 | .00 |
| ☐ 168 | Chris Burkett (20) | .10 | .04 | .01 |
| ☐ 169 | Bruce Smith (21) | .12 | .05 | .01 |
| ☐ 170 | Greg Bell (22) | .05 | .02 | .00 |
| ☐ 171 | Pete Metzelaars (23) | .03 | .01 | .00 |
| ☐ 172 | Jim Kelly | 1.50 | .60 | .15 |
| ☐ 173 | Andre Reed | .30 | .12 | .03 |
| ☐ 174 | John Elway | .60 | .24 | .06 |
| ☐ 175 | Mike Harden (24) | .03 | .01 | .00 |
| ☐ 176 | Gerald Willhite (25) | .03 | .01 | .00 |
| ☐ 177 | Rulon Jones (26) | .03 | .01 | .00 |
| ☐ 178 | Ricky Hunley (27) | .03 | .01 | .00 |
| ☐ 179 | Mark Jackson (29) | .04 | .02 | .00 |
| ☐ 180 | Rich Karlis (30) | .03 | .01 | .00 |
| ☐ 181 | Sammy Winder (31) | .03 | .01 | .00 |
| ☐ 182 | Karl Mecklenburg | .08 | .03 | .01 |
| ☐ 183 | Bernie Kosar | .35 | .14 | .03 |
| ☐ 184 | Kevin Mack (34) | .05 | .02 | .00 |
| ☐ 185 | Bob Golic (35) | .03 | .01 | .00 |
| ☐ 186 | Ozzie Newsome (36) | .08 | .03 | .01 |
| ☐ 187 | Brian Brennan | .05 | .02 | .00 |
| ☐ 188 | Gerald McNeil (37) | .05 | .02 | .00 |
| ☐ 189 | Hanford Dixon (38) | .03 | .01 | .00 |
| ☐ 190 | Cody Risien (39) | .03 | .01 | .00 |
| ☐ 191 | Chris Rockins (40) | .03 | .01 | .00 |
| ☐ 192 | Gill Byrd (42) | .05 | .02 | .00 |
| ☐ 193 | Kellen Winslow (43) | .08 | .03 | .01 |
| ☐ 194 | Billy Ray Smith (44) | .05 | .02 | .00 |
| ☐ 195 | Wes Chandler (45) | .05 | .02 | .00 |
| ☐ 196 | Leslie O'Neal (46) | .25 | .10 | .02 |
| ☐ 197 | Ralf Mojsiejenko (47) | .03 | .01 | .00 |
| ☐ 198 | Lee Williams (48) | .20 | .08 | .02 |
| ☐ 199 | Gary Anderson | .08 | .03 | .01 |
| ☐ 200 | Dan Fouts | .30 | .12 | .03 |
| ☐ 201 | Stephone Paige (51) | .08 | .03 | .01 |
| ☐ 202 | Irv Eatman (52) | .03 | .01 | .00 |
| ☐ 203 | Bill Kenney (53) | .04 | .02 | .00 |
| ☐ 204 | Dino Hackett (54) | .03 | .01 | .00 |
| ☐ 205 | Carlos Carson (55) | .03 | .01 | .00 |
| ☐ 206 | Art Still (56) | .04 | .02 | .00 |
| ☐ 207 | Lloyd Burruss (57) | .03 | .01 | .00 |
| ☐ 208 | Deron Cherry | .08 | .03 | .01 |
| ☐ 209 | Bill Maas | .05 | .02 | .00 |
| ☐ 210 | Gary Hogeboom | .08 | .03 | .01 |
| ☐ 211 | Rohn Stark | .05 | .02 | .00 |
| ☐ 212 | Cliff Odom (62) | .03 | .01 | .00 |
| ☐ 213 | Randy McMillan (63) | .05 | .02 | .00 |
| ☐ 214 | Chris Hinton (64) | .03 | .01 | .00 |
| ☐ 215 | Matt Bouza (65) | .03 | .01 | .00 |
| ☐ 216 | Ray Donaldson (66) | .03 | .01 | .00 |
| ☐ 217 | Bill Brooks (67) | .06 | .02 | .00 |
| ☐ 218 | Jack Trudeau (68) | .06 | .02 | .00 |
| ☐ 219 | Mark Duper | .10 | .04 | .01 |
| ☐ 220 | Dan Marino | 1.25 | .50 | .12 |
| ☐ 221 | Dwight Stephenson (71) | .05 | .02 | .00 |
| ☐ 222 | Mark Clayton (72) | .10 | .04 | .01 |
| ☐ 223 | Roy Foster (73) | .03 | .01 | .00 |
| ☐ 224 | John Offerdahl (74) | .20 | .08 | .02 |
| ☐ 225 | Lorenzo Hampton (75) | .04 | .02 | .00 |
| ☐ 226 | Reggie Roby (76) | .04 | .02 | .00 |
| ☐ 227 | Tony Nathan (77) | .05 | .02 | .00 |
| ☐ 228 | Johnny Hector (79) | .05 | .02 | .00 |
| ☐ 229 | Wesley Walker (80) | .06 | .02 | .00 |
| ☐ 230 | Mark Gastineau (81) | .04 | .02 | .00 |
| ☐ 231 | Ken O'Brien (82) | .05 | .02 | .00 |
| ☐ 232 | Dave Jennings (83) | .03 | .01 | .00 |
| ☐ 233 | Mickey Shuler (84) | .05 | .02 | .00 |
| ☐ 234 | Joe Klecko (85) | .05 | .02 | .00 |
| ☐ 235 | Freeman McNeil | .10 | .04 | .01 |
| ☐ 236 | Al Toon | .08 | .03 | .01 |
| ☐ 237 | Warren Moon (88) | .35 | .14 | .03 |
| ☐ 238 | Dean Steinkuhler (89) | .05 | .02 | .00 |
| ☐ 239 | Mike Rozier (90) | .06 | .02 | .00 |
| ☐ 240 | Ray Childress (92) | .08 | .03 | .01 |
| ☐ 241 | Tony Zendejas (93) | .03 | .01 | .00 |
| ☐ 242 | John Grimsley (94) | .03 | .01 | .00 |
| ☐ 243 | Jesse Baker (95) | .03 | .01 | .00 |
| ☐ 244 | Ernest Givins | .50 | .20 | .05 |
| ☐ 245 | Drew Hill | .10 | .04 | .01 |
| ☐ 246 | Tony Franklin | .05 | .02 | .00 |
| ☐ 247 | Steve Grogan (96) | .06 | .02 | .00 |
| ☐ 248 | Garin Veris (97) | .03 | .01 | .00 |
| ☐ 249 | Stanley Morgan (98) | .06 | .02 | .00 |
| ☐ 250 | Fred Marion (99) | .03 | .01 | .00 |
| ☐ 251 | Raymond Clayborn (100) | .03 | .01 | .00 |
| ☐ 252 | Mosi Tatupu (101) | .03 | .01 | .00 |
| ☐ 253 | Tony Eason (102) | .05 | .02 | .00 |
| ☐ 254 | Andre Tippett (102) | .08 | .03 | .01 |
| ☐ 255 | Todd Christensen | .08 | .03 | .01 |
| ☐ 256 | Howie Long (105) | .06 | .02 | .00 |
| ☐ 257 | Marcus Allen (106) | .12 | .05 | .01 |
| ☐ 258 | Vann McElroy (107) | .03 | .01 | .00 |
| ☐ 259 | Dokie Williams | .05 | .02 | .00 |

| | | | |
|---|---|---|---|
| ☐ 260 Mike Haynes (108) | .06 | .02 | .00 |
| ☐ 261 Sean Jones (109) | .08 | .03 | .01 |
| ☐ 262 Jim Plunkett (110) | .07 | .03 | .01 |
| ☐ 263 Chris Bahr (111) | .03 | .01 | .00 |
| ☐ 264 Dave Krieg (115) | .08 | .03 | .01 |
| ☐ 265 Jacob Green (116) | .05 | .02 | .00 |
| ☐ 266 Norm Johnson (117) | .05 | .02 | .00 |
| ☐ 267 Fredd Young (118) | .05 | .02 | .00 |
| ☐ 268 Steve Largent | .50 | .20 | .05 |
| ☐ 269 Dave Brown (119) | .04 | .02 | .00 |
| ☐ 270 Kenny Easley (120) | .05 | .02 | .00 |
| ☐ 271 Bobby Joe Edmonds (121) | .05 | .02 | .00 |
| ☐ 272 Curt Warner | .10 | .04 | .01 |
| ☐ 273 Mike Merriweather | .08 | .03 | .01 |
| ☐ 274 Mark Malone (124) | .04 | .02 | .00 |
| ☐ 275 Bryan Hinkle (125) | .03 | .01 | .00 |
| ☐ 276 Earnest Jackson (126) | .04 | .02 | .00 |
| ☐ 277 Keith Willis (128) | .03 | .01 | .00 |
| ☐ 278 Walter Abercrombie (129) | .03 | .01 | .00 |
| ☐ 279 Donnie Shell (130) | .04 | .02 | .00 |
| ☐ 280 John Stallworth (131) | .06 | .02 | .00 |
| ☐ 281 Louis Lipps | .10 | .04 | .01 |
| ☐ 282 Eric Dickerson (142) FOIL | .25 | .10 | .02 |
| ☐ 283 Dan Marino (143) FOIL | .75 | .30 | .07 |
| ☐ 284 Tony Franklin (144) FOIL | .10 | .04 | .01 |
| ☐ 285 Todd Christensen (145) FOIL | .12 | .05 | .01 |
| ☐ xx Sticker Album | 1.25 | .50 | .12 |

# 1988 Topps Stickers

The 1988 Topps Football sticker set is very similar to the previous years in that it contains stickers, foil stickers, and an accompanying album to house one's sticker collection. The stickers measure approximately 2 1/8" by 3" and have a distinctive red border with an inner frame of small yellow footballs. The stickers are numbered on the front. The sticker backs are actually part of a different set. Sticker pairs are identified below by parenthetically listing the other member of the pair. The foil stickers are pairs of All-Pros (AP) and are so indicated in the checklist below on stickers. Stickers 2-5 are actually a large four-part action photo of Super Bowl XXII action with Doug Williams handing off to Timmy Smith. On the inside back cover of the sticker album the company offered (via direct mail-order) any ten different stickers of your choice for 1.00; this is one reason why the values of the most popular players in these sticker sets are somewhat depressed compared to traditional card set prices. The front cover of the sticker album features an actrion photo of the Washington Redskins; the back cover depicts Doug Williams artwork. The stickers are checklisted below according to special subsets and teams as follows: Super Bowl puzzle (1-5), Chicago Bears (6-14), Tampa Bay Buccaneers (15-23), Phoenix Cardinals (24-32), Dallas Cowboys (33-41), Philadelphia Eagles (42-50), Atlanta Falcons (51-59), San Francisco 49ers (60-68), New York Giants (69-77), Detroit Lions (78-86), Green Bay Packers (87-95), Los Angeles Rams (96-104), Washington Redskins (105-113), New Orleans Saints (114-122), Minnesota Vikings (123-131), All-Pros (132-155), Cincinnati Bengals (156-164), Buffalo Bills (165-173), Denver Broncos (174-182), Cleveland Browns (183-191), San Diego Chargers (192-200), Kansas City Chiefs (201-209), Indianapolis Colts (210-218), Miami Dolphins (219-227), New York Jets (228-236), Houston Oilers (237-245), New England Patriots (246-254), Los Angeles Raiders (255-263), Seattle Seahawks (264-272), Pittsburgh Steelers (273-281), and Leaders (282-285). The following players are shown in their Rookie Card year: Neal Anderson, Cornelius Bennett, Brian Bosworth, Jerome Brown, Tony Casillas, Shane Conlan, Chris Doleman, Ronnie Harmon, Alonzo

Highsmith, Dalton Hilliard, Johnny Holland, Bo Jackson, Christian Okoye, Clyde Simmons, Webster Slaughter, Al Smith, Pat Swilling, Vinny Testaverde, and Wade Wilson.

| | MINT | EXC | G-VG |
|---|---|---|---|
| COMPLETE SET (285) | 10.00 | 4.00 | 1.00 |
| COMMON PLAYER (1-131) | .05 | .02 | .00 |
| COMMON PLAYER (156-285) | .05 | .02 | .00 |
| COMMON HALF STICKER | .03 | .01 | .00 |
| COMMON HALF FOIL | .10 | .04 | .01 |
| | | | |
| ☐ 1 Super Bowl XXII MVP Doug Williams | .10 | .04 | .01 |
| ☐ 2 Super Bowl XXII Redskins vs. Broncos Doug Williams UL | .03 | .01 | .00 |
| ☐ 3 Super Bowl XXII Redskins vs. Broncos Doug Williams UR | .03 | .01 | .00 |
| ☐ 4 Super Bowl XXII Redskins vs. Broncos Doug Williams LL | .03 | .01 | .00 |
| ☐ 5 Super Bowl XXII Redskins vs. Broncos Doug Williams LR | .03 | .01 | .00 |
| ☐ 6 Neal Anderson (234) | .20 | .08 | .02 |
| ☐ 7 Willie Gault (224) | .05 | .02 | .00 |
| ☐ 8 Dennis Gentry (219) | .03 | .01 | .00 |
| ☐ 9 Dave Duerson (197) | .03 | .01 | .00 |
| ☐ 10 Steve McMichael (266) | .05 | .02 | .00 |
| ☐ 11 Dennis McKinnon (230) | .03 | .01 | .00 |
| ☐ 12 Mike Singletary (209) | .08 | .03 | .01 |
| ☐ 13 Jim McMahon | .12 | .05 | .01 |
| ☐ 14 Richard Dent | .10 | .04 | .01 |
| ☐ 15 Vinny Testaverde (167) | .15 | .06 | .01 |
| ☐ 16 Gerald Carter (187) | .03 | .01 | .00 |
| ☐ 17 Jeff Smith (185) | .03 | .01 | .00 |
| ☐ 18 Chris Washington (212) | .03 | .01 | .00 |
| ☐ 19 Bobby Futrell (231) | .03 | .01 | .00 |
| ☐ 20 Calvin Magee (182) | .03 | .01 | .00 |
| ☐ 21 Ron Holmes (169) | .03 | .01 | .00 |
| ☐ 22 Ervin Randle | .05 | .02 | .00 |
| ☐ 23 James Wilder | .05 | .02 | .00 |
| ☐ 24 Neil Lomax | .08 | .03 | .01 |
| ☐ 25 Robert Awalt (161) | .03 | .01 | .00 |
| ☐ 26 Leonard Smith (177) | .03 | .01 | .00 |
| ☐ 27 Stump Mitchell (178) | .05 | .02 | .00 |
| ☐ 28 Vai Sikahema (280) | .03 | .01 | .00 |
| ☐ 29 Freddie Joe Nunn (222) | .05 | .02 | .00 |
| ☐ 30 Earl Ferrell (223) | .03 | .01 | .00 |
| ☐ 31 Roy Green (157) | .06 | .02 | .00 |
| ☐ 32 J.T. Smith | .08 | .03 | .01 |
| ☐ 33 Michael Downs | .05 | .02 | .00 |
| ☐ 34 Herschel Walker | .30 | .12 | .03 |
| ☐ 35 Roger Ruzek (269) | .03 | .01 | .00 |
| ☐ 36 Ed Too Tall Jones (245) | .07 | .03 | .01 |
| ☐ 37 Everson Walls (252) | .04 | .02 | .00 |
| ☐ 38 Bill Bates (213) | .04 | .02 | .00 |
| ☐ 39 Doug Cosbie (179) | .04 | .02 | .00 |
| ☐ 40 Eugene Lockhart (186) | .03 | .01 | .00 |
| ☐ 41 Danny White (205) | .07 | .03 | .01 |
| ☐ 42 Randall Cunningham | .40 | .16 | .04 |
| ☐ 43 Reggie White | .30 | .12 | .03 |
| ☐ 44 Anthony Toney (256) | .03 | .01 | .00 |
| ☐ 45 Mike Quick (248) | .05 | .02 | .00 |
| ☐ 46 John Spagnola (235) | .03 | .01 | .00 |
| ☐ 47 Clyde Simmons (275) | .20 | .08 | .02 |
| ☐ 48 Andre Waters (261) | .05 | .02 | .00 |
| ☐ 49 Keith Byars (265) | .07 | .03 | .01 |
| ☐ 50 Jerome Brown (240) | .15 | .06 | .01 |
| ☐ 51 John Rade | .05 | .02 | .00 |
| ☐ 52 Rick Donnelly | .05 | .02 | .00 |
| ☐ 53 Scott Campbell (160) | .04 | .02 | .00 |
| ☐ 54 Floyd Dixon (246) | .03 | .01 | .00 |
| ☐ 55 Gerald Riggs (236) | .06 | .02 | .00 |
| ☐ 56 Bill Fralic (267) | .05 | .02 | .00 |
| ☐ 57 Mike Gann (165) | .03 | .01 | .00 |
| ☐ 58 Tony Casillas (168) | .15 | .06 | .01 |
| ☐ 59 Rick Bryan (257) | .04 | .02 | .00 |
| ☐ 60 Jerry Rice | .60 | .24 | .06 |
| ☐ 61 Ronnie Lott | .15 | .06 | .01 |
| ☐ 62 Ray Wersching (220) | .03 | .01 | .00 |
| ☐ 63 Charles Haley (281) | .06 | .02 | .00 |
| ☐ 64 Joe Montana (190) | .75 | .30 | .07 |
| ☐ 65 Joe Cribbs (221) | .04 | .02 | .00 |
| ☐ 66 Mike Wilson (203) | .03 | .01 | .00 |
| ☐ 67 Roger Craig (251) | .12 | .05 | .01 |
| ☐ 68 Michael Walter (162) | .03 | .01 | .00 |
| ☐ 69 Mark Bavaro | .08 | .03 | .01 |
| ☐ 70 Carl Banks | .08 | .03 | .01 |
| ☐ 71 George Adams (274) | .03 | .01 | .00 |
| ☐ 72 Phil Simms (216) | .08 | .03 | .01 |
| ☐ 73 Lawrence Taylor (181) | .12 | .05 | .01 |

|  |  | | | |
|---|---|---|---|---|
| ☐ 74 | Joe Morris (198) | .06 | .02 | .00 |
| ☐ 75 | Lionel Manuel (204) | .03 | .01 | .00 |
| ☐ 76 | Sean Landeta (210) | .03 | .01 | .00 |
| ☐ 77 | Harry Carson (159) | .05 | .02 | .00 |
| ☐ 78 | Chuck Long (166) | .05 | .02 | .00 |
| ☐ 79 | James Jones (259) | .03 | .01 | .00 |
| ☐ 80 | Garry James (158) | .03 | .01 | .00 |
| ☐ 81 | Gary Lee (176) | .03 | .01 | .00 |
| ☐ 82 | Jim Arnold (260) | .03 | .01 | .00 |
| ☐ 83 | Dennis Gibson (232) | .03 | .01 | .00 |
| ☐ 84 | Mike Cofer (242) | .03 | .01 | .00 |
| ☐ 85 | Pete Mandley | .05 | .02 | .00 |
| ☐ 86 | James Griffin | .05 | .02 | .00 |
| ☐ 87 | Randy Wright (206) | .03 | .01 | .00 |
| ☐ 88 | Phillip Epps (191) | .03 | .01 | .00 |
| ☐ 89 | Brian Noble (249) | .03 | .01 | .00 |
| ☐ 90 | Johnny Holland (258) | .10 | .04 | .01 |
| ☐ 91 | Dave Brown (156) | .03 | .01 | .00 |
| ☐ 92 | Brent Fullwood (207) | .03 | .01 | .00 |
| ☐ 93 | Kenneth Davis (194) | .08 | .03 | .01 |
| ☐ 94 | Tim Harris | .15 | .06 | .01 |
| ☐ 95 | Walter Stanley | .08 | .03 | .01 |
| ☐ 96 | Charles White | .08 | .03 | .01 |
| ☐ 97 | Jackie Slater | .08 | .03 | .01 |
| ☐ 98 | Jim Everett (271) | .12 | .05 | .01 |
| ☐ 99 | Mike Lansford (200) | .03 | .01 | .00 |
| ☐ 100 | Henry Ellard (199) | .06 | .02 | .00 |
| ☐ 101 | Dale Hatcher (170) | .03 | .01 | .00 |
| ☐ 102 | Jim Collins (268) | .03 | .01 | .00 |
| ☐ 103 | Jerry Gray (214) | .03 | .01 | .00 |
| ☐ 104 | LeRoy Irvin (276) | .03 | .01 | .00 |
| ☐ 105 | Darrell Green (214) | .12 | .05 | .01 |
| ☐ 106 | Doug Williams | .10 | .04 | .01 |
| ☐ 107 | Gary Clark (247) | .10 | .04 | .01 |
| ☐ 108 | Charles Mann (171) | .05 | .02 | .00 |
| ☐ 109 | Art Monk (270) | .12 | .05 | .01 |
| ☐ 110 | Barry Wilburn (196) | .03 | .01 | .00 |
| ☐ 111 | Alvin Walton (188) | .03 | .01 | .00 |
| ☐ 112 | Dexter Manley (233) | .05 | .02 | .00 |
| ☐ 113 | Kelvin Bryant (180) | .04 | .02 | .00 |
| ☐ 114 | Morten Andersen | .08 | .03 | .01 |
| ☐ 115 | Rueben Mayes (244) | .06 | .02 | .00 |
| ☐ 116 | Brian Hansen (279) | .03 | .01 | .00 |
| ☐ 117 | Dalton Hilliard (241) | .10 | .04 | .01 |
| ☐ 118 | Rickey Jackson (195) | .06 | .02 | .00 |
| ☐ 119 | Eric Martin (189) | .06 | .02 | .00 |
| ☐ 120 | Mel Gray (278) | .05 | .02 | .00 |
| ☐ 121 | Bobby Hebert (215) | .08 | .03 | .01 |
| ☐ 122 | Pat Swilling | .40 | .16 | .04 |
| ☐ 123 | Anthony Carter | .12 | .05 | .01 |
| ☐ 124 | Wade Wilson (225) | .20 | .08 | .02 |
| ☐ 125 | Darrin Nelson (250) | .04 | .02 | .00 |
| ☐ 126 | D.J. Dozier (239) | .06 | .02 | .00 |
| ☐ 127 | Chris Doleman | .30 | .12 | .03 |
| ☐ 128 | Henry Thomas (255) | .03 | .01 | .00 |
| ☐ 129 | Jesse Solomon (211) | .04 | .02 | .00 |
| ☐ 130 | Neal Guggemos (243) | .03 | .01 | .00 |
| ☐ 131 | Joey Browner (208) | .06 | .02 | .00 |
| ☐ 132 | Carl Banks AP (152) FOIL | .10 | .04 | .01 |
| ☐ 133 | Joey Browner AP (145) FOIL | .10 | .04 | .01 |
| ☐ 134 | Hanford Dixon AP (147) FOIL | .10 | .04 | .01 |
| ☐ 135 | Rick Donnelly AP (149) FOIL | .10 | .04 | .01 |
| ☐ 136 | Kenny Easley AP (155) FOIL | .10 | .04 | .01 |
| ☐ 137 | Darrell Green AP (151) FOIL | .15 | .06 | .01 |
| ☐ 138 | Bill Maas AP (148) FOIL | .10 | .04 | .01 |
| ☐ 139 | Mike Singletary AP (153) FOIL | .15 | .06 | .01 |
| ☐ 140 | Bruce Smith AP (154) FOIL | .15 | .06 | .01 |
| ☐ 141 | Andre Tippett AP (146) FOIL | .10 | .04 | .01 |
| ☐ 142 | Reggie White AP (150) FOIL | .20 | .08 | .02 |
| ☐ 143 | Fredd Young AP (144) FOIL | .10 | .04 | .01 |
| ☐ 144 | Morten Andersen AP (143) FOIL | .10 | .04 | .01 |
| ☐ 145 | Mark Bavaro AP (133) FOIL | .10 | .04 | .01 |
| ☐ 146 | Eric Dickerson AP (141) FOIL | .30 | .12 | .03 |
| ☐ 147 | John Elway AP (134) FOIL | .60 | .24 | .06 |
| ☐ 148 | Bill Fralic AP (138) FOIL | .10 | .04 | .01 |
| ☐ 149 | Mike Munchak AP (135) FOIL | .10 | .04 | .01 |
| ☐ 150 | Anthony Munoz AP (142) FOIL | .15 | .06 | .01 |
| ☐ 151 | Jerry Rice AP (137) | .75 | .30 | .07 |
| | FOIL | | | |
| ☐ 152 | Jackie Slater AP (132) FOIL | .12 | .05 | .01 |
| ☐ 153 | J.T. Smith AP (139) FOIL | .10 | .04 | .01 |
| ☐ 154 | Dwight Stephenson AP (140) FOIL | .10 | .04 | .01 |
| ☐ 155 | Charles White AP (136) FOIL | .10 | .04 | .01 |
| ☐ 156 | Larry Kinnebrew (91) | .03 | .01 | .00 |
| ☐ 157 | Stanford Jennings (31) | .03 | .01 | .00 |
| ☐ 158 | Eddie Brown (80) | .05 | .02 | .00 |
| ☐ 159 | Scott Fulhage (77) | .03 | .01 | .00 |
| ☐ 160 | Boomer Esiason (53) | .12 | .05 | .01 |
| ☐ 161 | Tim Krumrie (25) | .03 | .01 | .00 |
| ☐ 162 | Anthony Munoz (68) | .08 | .03 | .01 |
| ☐ 163 | Jim Breech | .05 | .02 | .00 |
| ☐ 164 | Reggie Williams | .08 | .03 | .01 |
| ☐ 165 | Andre Reed (57) | .12 | .05 | .01 |
| ☐ 166 | Cornelius Bennett (78) | .30 | .12 | .03 |
| ☐ 167 | Ronnie Harmon (15) | .15 | .06 | .01 |
| ☐ 168 | Shane Conlan (58) | .15 | .06 | .01 |
| ☐ 169 | Chris Burkett (21) | .03 | .01 | .00 |
| ☐ 170 | Mark Kelso (101) | .04 | .02 | .00 |
| ☐ 171 | Robb Riddick (108) | .03 | .01 | .00 |
| ☐ 172 | Bruce Smith | .15 | .06 | .01 |
| ☐ 173 | Jim Kelly | .60 | .24 | .06 |
| ☐ 174 | Jim Ryan | .03 | .01 | .00 |
| ☐ 175 | John Elway | .60 | .24 | .06 |
| ☐ 176 | Sammy Winder (81) | .04 | .02 | .00 |
| ☐ 177 | Karl Mecklenburg (26) | .05 | .02 | .00 |
| ☐ 178 | Mark Haynes (27) | .03 | .01 | .00 |
| ☐ 179 | Rulon Jones (39) | .03 | .01 | .00 |
| ☐ 180 | Ricky Nattiel (113) | .04 | .02 | .00 |
| ☐ 181 | Vance Johnson (73) | .05 | .02 | .00 |
| ☐ 182 | Mike Harden (20) | .03 | .01 | .00 |
| ☐ 183 | Frank Minnifield | .05 | .02 | .00 |
| ☐ 184 | Bernie Kosar | .25 | .10 | .02 |
| ☐ 185 | Earnest Byner (17) | .08 | .03 | .01 |
| ☐ 186 | Webster Slaughter (40) | .15 | .06 | .01 |
| ☐ 187 | Brian Brennan (16) | .03 | .01 | .00 |
| ☐ 188 | Carl Hairston (111) | .03 | .01 | .00 |
| ☐ 189 | Mike Johnson (119) | .03 | .01 | .00 |
| ☐ 190 | Clay Matthews (64) | .06 | .02 | .00 |
| ☐ 191 | Kevin Mack (88) | .06 | .02 | .00 |
| ☐ 192 | Kellen Winslow | .12 | .05 | .01 |
| ☐ 193 | Billy Ray Smith | .08 | .03 | .01 |
| ☐ 194 | Gary Anderson (93) | .06 | .02 | .00 |
| ☐ 195 | Chip Banks (118) | .05 | .02 | .00 |
| ☐ 196 | Elvis Patterson (110) | .03 | .01 | .00 |
| ☐ 197 | Lee Williams (9) | .07 | .03 | .01 |
| ☐ 198 | Curtis Adams (74) | .03 | .01 | .00 |
| ☐ 199 | Vencie Glenn (100) | .03 | .01 | .00 |
| ☐ 200 | Ralf Mojsiejenko (99) | .03 | .01 | .00 |
| ☐ 201 | Carlos Carson | .05 | .02 | .00 |
| ☐ 202 | Bill Maas | .05 | .02 | .00 |
| ☐ 203 | Christian Okoye (66) | .15 | .06 | .01 |
| ☐ 204 | Deron Cherry (75) | .05 | .02 | .00 |
| ☐ 205 | Dino Hackett (41) | .03 | .01 | .00 |
| ☐ 206 | Mike Bell (87) | .03 | .01 | .00 |
| ☐ 207 | Stephone Paige (92) | .06 | .02 | .00 |
| ☐ 208 | Bill Kenney (131) | .04 | .02 | .00 |
| ☐ 209 | Paul Palmer (12) | .05 | .02 | .00 |
| ☐ 210 | Jack Trudeau (76) | .06 | .02 | .00 |
| ☐ 211 | Albert Bentley (129) | .06 | .02 | .00 |
| ☐ 212 | Bill Brooks (18) | .06 | .02 | .00 |
| ☐ 213 | Dean Biasucci (38) | .03 | .01 | .00 |
| ☐ 214 | Cliff Odom (103) | .03 | .01 | .00 |
| ☐ 215 | Barry Krauss (121) | .03 | .01 | .00 |
| ☐ 216 | Mike Prior (72) | .03 | .01 | .00 |
| ☐ 217 | Eric Dickerson | .30 | .12 | .03 |
| ☐ 218 | Duane Bickett (29) | .08 | .03 | .01 |
| ☐ 219 | Dwight Stephenson (8) | .05 | .02 | .00 |
| ☐ 220 | John Offerdahl (62) | .06 | .02 | .00 |
| ☐ 221 | Troy Stradford (65) | .06 | .02 | .00 |
| ☐ 222 | John Bosa (29) | .04 | .02 | .00 |
| ☐ 223 | Jackie Shipp (30) | .03 | .01 | .00 |
| ☐ 224 | Paul Lankford (7) | .03 | .01 | .00 |
| ☐ 225 | Mark Duper (124) | .07 | .03 | .01 |
| ☐ 226 | Dan Marino | 1.00 | .40 | .10 |
| ☐ 227 | Mark Clayton | .15 | .06 | .01 |
| ☐ 228 | Bob Crable | .05 | .02 | .00 |
| ☐ 229 | Al Toon | .08 | .03 | .01 |
| ☐ 230 | Freeman McNeil (11) | .06 | .02 | .00 |
| ☐ 231 | Johnny Hector (19) | .05 | .02 | .00 |
| ☐ 232 | Pat Leahy (83) | .04 | .02 | .00 |
| ☐ 233 | Ken O'Brien (112) | .05 | .02 | .00 |
| ☐ 234 | Alex Gordon (6) | .03 | .01 | .00 |
| ☐ 235 | Harry Hamilton (46) | .03 | .01 | .00 |
| ☐ 236 | Mickey Shuler (55) | .03 | .01 | .00 |
| ☐ 237 | Mike Rozier | .08 | .03 | .01 |
| ☐ 238 | Al Smith | .15 | .06 | .01 |
| ☐ 239 | Ernest Givins (126) | .10 | .04 | .01 |
| ☐ 240 | Warren Moon (50) | .25 | .10 | .02 |

| | | | |
|---|---|---|---|
| ☐ 241 Drew Hill (117) | .07 | .03 | .01 |
| ☐ 242 Alonzo Highsmith (84) | .10 | .04 | .01 |
| ☐ 243 Mike Munchak (130) | .06 | .02 | .00 |
| ☐ 244 Keith Bostic (115) | .03 | .01 | .00 |
| ☐ 245 Sean Jones (36) | .06 | .02 | .00 |
| ☐ 246 Stanley Morgan (54) | .06 | .02 | .00 |
| ☐ 247 Garin Veris (107) | .03 | .01 | .00 |
| ☐ 248 Stephen Starring (45) | .03 | .01 | .00 |
| ☐ 249 Steve Grogan (89) | .06 | .02 | .00 |
| ☐ 250 Irving Fryar (125) | .06 | .02 | .00 |
| ☐ 251 Rich Camarillo (67) | .03 | .01 | .00 |
| ☐ 252 Ronnie Lippett (37) | .04 | .02 | .00 |
| ☐ 253 Andre Tippett | .08 | .03 | .01 |
| ☐ 254 Fred Marion | .05 | .02 | .00 |
| ☐ 255 Howie Long (128) | .07 | .03 | .01 |
| ☐ 256 James Lofton (44) | .12 | .05 | .01 |
| ☐ 257 Vance Mueller (59) | .03 | .01 | .00 |
| ☐ 258 Jerry Robinson (90) | .04 | .02 | .00 |
| ☐ 259 Todd Christensen (79) | .06 | .02 | .00 |
| ☐ 260 Vann McElroy (82) | .03 | .01 | .00 |
| ☐ 261 Greg Townsend (48) | .07 | .03 | .01 |
| ☐ 262 Bo Jackson | 1.00 | .40 | .10 |
| ☐ 263 Marcus Allen | .20 | .08 | .02 |
| ☐ 264 Curt Warner | .08 | .03 | .01 |
| ☐ 265 Jacob Green (49) | .06 | .02 | .00 |
| ☐ 266 Norm Johnson (10) | .05 | .02 | .00 |
| ☐ 267 Brian Bosworth (56) | .10 | .04 | .01 |
| ☐ 268 Bobby Joe Edmonds (102) | .05 | .02 | .00 |
| ☐ 269 Dave Krieg (35) | .07 | .03 | .01 |
| ☐ 270 Kenny Easley (109) | .04 | .02 | .00 |
| ☐ 271 Steve Largent (98) | .30 | .12 | .03 |
| ☐ 272 Fredd Young | .05 | .02 | .00 |
| ☐ 273 David Little | .03 | .01 | .00 |
| ☐ 274 Frank Pollard (71) | .03 | .01 | .00 |
| ☐ 275 Dwight Stone (47) | .08 | .03 | .01 |
| ☐ 276 Mike Merriweather (104) | .03 | .01 | .00 |
| ☐ 277 Earnest Jackson | .05 | .02 | .00 |
| ☐ 278 Delton Hall (120) | .03 | .01 | .00 |
| ☐ 279 Gary Anderson (116) | .03 | .01 | .00 |
| ☐ 280 Harry Newsome (28) | .03 | .01 | .00 |
| ☐ 281 Dwayne Woodruff (63) | .03 | .01 | .00 |
| ☐ 282 J.T. Smith (283) | .04 | .02 | .00 |
| ☐ 283 Charles White (282) | .05 | .02 | .00 |
| ☐ 284 Reggie White (285) | .15 | .06 | .01 |
| ☐ 285 Morten Andersen (284) | .05 | .02 | .00 |
| ☐ xx Sticker Album | 1.25 | .50 | .12 |

## 1988 Topps Sticker Backs

These cards are actually the backs of the Topps stickers. These cards are numbered in fine print in the statistical section of the card. The 67 cards in the set are generally a selection of popular players with all of them being quarterbacks, running backs, or receivers. The cards measure approximately 2 1/8" by 3". The cards are checklisted below alphabetically according to teams as follows: Washington Redskins (1-2), Denver Broncos (3-5), San Francisco 49ers (6-8), New Orleans Saints (9-10), Chicago Bears (11-12), Cleveland Browns (13-15), Houston Oilers (16-18), Indianapolis Colts (19-20), Seattle Seahawks (21-22), Minnesota Vikings (23-24), Pittsburgh Steelers (25-26), New England Patriots (27-28), Miami Dolphins (29-31), San Diego Chargers (32-33), Buffalo Bills (34-36), Philadelphia Eagles (37-39), Phoenix Cardinals (40-42), Dallas Cowboys (43-44), New York Giants (45-46), Los Angeles Rams (47-48), New York Jets (49-51), Green Bay Packers (52-53), Los Angeles Raiders (54-55), Cincinnati Bengals (56-58), Tampa Bay Buccaneers (59-60), Kansas City Chiefs (61-62), Detroit Lions (63-64), and Atlanta Falcons (65-66).

| | MINT | EXC | G-VG |
|---|---|---|---|
| COMPLETE SET (67) | 5.00 | 2.00 | .50 |
| COMMON PLAYER (1-67) | .07 | .03 | .01 |
| ☐ 1 Doug Williams | .10 | .04 | .01 |
| ☐ 2 Gary Clark | .15 | .06 | .01 |
| ☐ 3 John Elway | .50 | .20 | .05 |
| ☐ 4 Sammy Winder | .07 | .03 | .01 |
| ☐ 5 Vance Johnson | .07 | .03 | .01 |
| ☐ 6 Joe Montana | 1.00 | .40 | .10 |
| ☐ 7 Roger Craig | .15 | .06 | .01 |
| ☐ 8 Jerry Rice | .75 | .30 | .07 |
| ☐ 9 Rueben Mayes | .10 | .04 | .01 |
| ☐ 10 Eric Martin | .10 | .04 | .01 |
| ☐ 11 Neal Anderson | .30 | .12 | .03 |
| ☐ 12 Willie Gault | .10 | .04 | .01 |
| ☐ 13 Bernie Kosar | .25 | .10 | .02 |
| ☐ 14 Kevin Mack | .07 | .03 | .01 |
| ☐ 15 Webster Slaughter | .15 | .06 | .01 |
| ☐ 16 Warren Moon | .40 | .16 | .04 |
| ☐ 17 Mike Rozier | .10 | .04 | .01 |
| ☐ 18 Drew Hill | .10 | .04 | .01 |
| ☐ 19 Eric Dickerson | .30 | .12 | .03 |
| ☐ 20 Bill Brooks | .07 | .03 | .01 |
| ☐ 21 Curt Warner | .10 | .04 | .01 |
| ☐ 22 Steve Largent | .40 | .16 | .04 |
| ☐ 23 Darrin Nelson | .07 | .03 | .01 |
| ☐ 24 Anthony Carter | .15 | .06 | .01 |
| ☐ 25 Earnest Jackson | .07 | .03 | .01 |
| ☐ 26 Weegie Thompson | .07 | .03 | .01 |
| ☐ 27 Stephen Starring | .07 | .03 | .01 |
| ☐ 28 Stanley Morgan | .10 | .04 | .01 |
| ☐ 29 Dan Marino | 1.00 | .40 | .10 |
| ☐ 30 Troy Stradford | .10 | .04 | .01 |
| ☐ 31 Mark Clayton | .15 | .06 | .01 |
| ☐ 32 Curtis Adams | .07 | .03 | .01 |
| ☐ 33 Kellen Winslow | .15 | .06 | .01 |
| ☐ 34 Jim Kelly | .50 | .20 | .05 |
| ☐ 35 Ronnie Harmon | .25 | .10 | .02 |
| ☐ 36 Chris Burkett | .07 | .03 | .01 |
| ☐ 37 Randall Cunningham | .35 | .14 | .03 |
| ☐ 38 Anthony Toney | .07 | .03 | .01 |
| ☐ 39 Mike Quick | .10 | .04 | .01 |
| ☐ 40 Neil Lomax | .10 | .04 | .01 |
| ☐ 41 Stump Mitchell | .10 | .04 | .01 |
| ☐ 42 J.T. Smith | .07 | .03 | .01 |
| ☐ 43 Herschel Walker | .25 | .10 | .02 |
| ☐ 44 Herschel Walker | .25 | .10 | .02 |
| ☐ 45 Joe Morris | .10 | .04 | .01 |
| ☐ 46 Mark Bavaro | .10 | .04 | .01 |
| ☐ 47 Charles White | .10 | .04 | .01 |
| ☐ 48 Henry Ellard | .10 | .04 | .01 |
| ☐ 49 Ken O'Brien | .10 | .04 | .01 |
| ☐ 50 Freeman McNeil | .10 | .04 | .01 |
| ☐ 51 Al Toon | .10 | .04 | .01 |
| ☐ 52 Kenneth Davis | .10 | .04 | .01 |
| ☐ 53 Walter Stanley | .07 | .03 | .01 |
| ☐ 54 Marcus Allen | .30 | .12 | .03 |
| ☐ 55 James Lofton | .25 | .10 | .02 |
| ☐ 56 Boomer Esiason | .20 | .08 | .02 |
| ☐ 57 Larry Kinnebrew | .07 | .03 | .01 |
| ☐ 58 Eddie Brown | .10 | .04 | .01 |
| ☐ 59 James Wilder | .07 | .03 | .01 |
| ☐ 60 Gerald Carter | .07 | .03 | .01 |
| ☐ 61 Christian Okoye | .20 | .08 | .02 |
| ☐ 62 Carlos Carson | .07 | .03 | .01 |
| ☐ 63 James Jones | .07 | .03 | .01 |
| ☐ 64 Pete Mandley | .07 | .03 | .01 |
| ☐ 65 Gerald Riggs | .10 | .04 | .01 |
| ☐ 66 Floyd Dixon | .07 | .03 | .01 |
| ☐ 67 Checklist Card | .10 | .04 | .01 |

## 1977 Touchdown Club

This 50-card set was initially targeted toward football autograph collectors as the set featured only living (at the time) ex-football players many of whom were or are now in the Pro Football Hall of Fame in Canton, Ohio. The set was originally sold as a complete set along with a printed address list for the players in the set. The cards are black and white (typically showing the player in his prime) and are numbered on the back. The cards measure approximately 2 1/4" by 3 1/4". Card backs list career honors the player received.

| | NRMT | VG-E | GOOD |
|---|---|---|---|
| COMPLETE SET (50) | 50.00 | 20.00 | 5.00 |
| COMMON CARD (1-50) | .80 | .32 | .08 |
| ☐ 1 Harold(Red) Grange | 5.00 | 2.00 | .50 |
| ☐ 2 George Halas | 2.00 | .80 | .20 |
| ☐ 3 Benny Friedman | .80 | .32 | .08 |
| ☐ 4 Cliff Battles | 1.00 | .40 | .10 |
| ☐ 5 Mike Michalske | .80 | .32 | .08 |
| ☐ 6 George McAfee | 1.00 | .40 | .10 |

Sid Luckman

cards, although some collectors and dealers consider Howard Fest, Harry Gunner, and Warren McVea to be somewhat more difficult to find as well. The backs contain biographical and statistical data of the player and the Tresler Comet logo. An offer to obtain a free set of these cards at a Tresler Comet (gasoline) dealer is stated at the bottom on the back.

|  | NRMT | VG-E | GOOD |
|---|---|---|---|
| COMPLETE SET (20) | 200.00 | 80.00 | 20.00 |
| COMMON PLAYER (1-20) | 5.00 | 2.00 | .50 |
| ☐ 1 Al Beauchamp | 5.00 | 2.00 | .50 |
| ☐ 2 Bill Bergey | 10.00 | 4.00 | 1.00 |
| ☐ 3 Royce Berry | 5.00 | 2.00 | .50 |
| ☐ 4 Paul Brown CO | 12.00 | 5.00 | 1.20 |
| ☐ 5 Frank Buncom | 5.00 | 2.00 | .50 |
| ☐ 6 Greg Cook | 10.00 | 4.00 | 1.00 |
| ☐ 7 Howard Fest SP | 12.00 | 5.00 | 1.20 |
| ☐ 8 Harry Gunner SP | 12.00 | 5.00 | 1.20 |
| ☐ 9 Bobby Hunt | 5.00 | 2.00 | .50 |
| ☐ 10 Bob Johnson SP | 100.00 | 40.00 | 10.00 |
| ☐ 11 Charley King | 5.00 | 2.00 | .50 |
| ☐ 12 Dale Livingston | 5.00 | 2.00 | .50 |
| ☐ 13 Warren McVea SP | 15.00 | 6.00 | 1.50 |
| ☐ 14 Bill Peterson | 6.00 | 2.40 | .60 |
| ☐ 15 Jess Phillips | 5.00 | 2.00 | .50 |
| ☐ 16 Andy Rice | 5.00 | 2.00 | .50 |
| ☐ 17 Bill Staley | 5.00 | 2.00 | .50 |
| ☐ 18 Bob Trumpy | 12.00 | 5.00 | 1.20 |
| ☐ 19 Ernie Wright | 5.00 | 2.00 | .50 |
| ☐ 20 Sam Wyche | 18.00 | 7.25 | 1.80 |

| | | | |
|---|---|---|---|
| ☐ 7 Beattie Feathers | 1.00 | .40 | .10 |
| ☐ 8 Ernie Caddel | .80 | .32 | .08 |
| ☐ 9 George Musso | 1.00 | .40 | .10 |
| ☐ 10 Sid Luckman | 2.00 | .80 | .20 |
| ☐ 11 Cecil Isbell | .80 | .32 | .08 |
| ☐ 12 Bronko Nagurski | 2.50 | 1.00 | .25 |
| ☐ 13 Hunk Anderson | .80 | .32 | .08 |
| ☐ 14 Dick Farman | .80 | .32 | .08 |
| ☐ 15 Aldo Forte | .80 | .32 | .08 |
| ☐ 16 Ki Aldrich | .80 | .32 | .08 |
| ☐ 17 Jim Lee Howell | .80 | .32 | .08 |
| ☐ 18 Ray Flaherty | .80 | .32 | .08 |
| ☐ 19 Hampton Pool | .80 | .32 | .08 |
| ☐ 20 Alex Wojciechowicz | 1.00 | .40 | .10 |
| ☐ 21 Bill Osmanski | .80 | .32 | .08 |
| ☐ 22 Hank Soar | .80 | .32 | .08 |
| ☐ 23 Earl(Dutch) Clark | 1.00 | .40 | .10 |
| ☐ 24 Joe Muha | .80 | .32 | .08 |
| ☐ 25 Don Hutson | 1.50 | .60 | .15 |
| ☐ 26 Jim Poole | .80 | .32 | .08 |
| ☐ 27 Charley Malone | .80 | .32 | .08 |
| ☐ 28 Charley Trippi | 1.25 | .50 | .12 |
| ☐ 29 Andy Farkas | .80 | .32 | .08 |
| ☐ 30 Clarke Hinkle | 1.00 | .40 | .10 |
| ☐ 31 Gary Famiglietti | .80 | .32 | .08 |
| ☐ 32 Clyde(Bulldog) Turner | 1.25 | .50 | .12 |
| ☐ 33 Sammy Baugh | 2.50 | 1.00 | .25 |
| ☐ 34 Pat Harder | .80 | .32 | .08 |
| ☐ 35 Tuffy Leemans | 1.00 | .40 | .10 |
| ☐ 36 Ken Strong | 1.00 | .40 | .10 |
| ☐ 37 Barney Poole | .80 | .32 | .08 |
| ☐ 38 Frank(Bruiser) Kinard | 1.00 | .40 | .10 |
| ☐ 39 Buford Ray | .80 | .32 | .08 |
| ☐ 40 Clarence(Ace) Parker | 1.25 | .50 | .12 |
| ☐ 41 Buddy Parker | .80 | .32 | .08 |
| ☐ 42 Mel Hein | 1.00 | .40 | .10 |
| ☐ 43 Ed Danowski | .80 | .32 | .08 |
| ☐ 44 Bill Dudley | 1.25 | .50 | .12 |
| ☐ 45 Paul Stenn | .80 | .32 | .08 |
| ☐ 46 George Connor | 1.00 | .40 | .10 |
| ☐ 47 George Sauer | .80 | .32 | .08 |
| ☐ 48 Armand Niccolai | .80 | .32 | .08 |
| ☐ 49 Tony Canadeo | 1.00 | .40 | .10 |
| ☐ 50 Bill Willis | 1.50 | .60 | .15 |

## 1969 Tresler Comet Bengals

The 1969 Tresler Comet set contains 20 cards featuring Cincinnati Bengals only. The cards measure 2 1/2" by 3 1/2". The set is quite attractive in its sepia and orange color front with a facsimile autograph of the player portrayed. The cards are unnumbered but have been listed below in alphabetical order for convenience. The card of Bob Johnson (not alphabetized below) is much scarcer than the other

## 1989 TV-4 NFL Quarterbacks

The 1989 TV-4 NFL Quarterbacks set features 20 cards measuring approximately 2 7/16" by 3 1/8". The fronts are borderless and show attractive color action and portrait drawings of each quarterback. The drawings were performed by artist J.C. Ford. The vertically oriented backs list career highlights. The TV-4 refers to a London (England) television station, which distributed the cards. The cards were distributed in England and were intended to promote the National Football League, which had begun playing pre-season games there.

|  | MINT | EXC | G-VG |
|---|---|---|---|
| COMPLETE SET (20) | 15.00 | 6.00 | 1.50 |
| COMMON PLAYER (1-20) | .50 | .20 | .05 |
| ☐ 1 Earl(Dutch) Clark | .50 | .20 | .05 |
| ☐ 2 Sammy Baugh | 1.00 | .40 | .10 |
| ☐ 3 Bob Waterfield | .75 | .30 | .07 |
| ☐ 4 Sid Luckman | .75 | .30 | .07 |
| ☐ 5 Otto Graham | 1.00 | .40 | .10 |
| ☐ 6 Bobby Layne | .75 | .30 | .07 |
| ☐ 7 Norm Van Brocklin | .75 | .30 | .07 |
| ☐ 8 George Blanda | 1.00 | .40 | .10 |
| ☐ 9 Y.A. Tittle | 2.00 | .80 | .20 |
| ☐ 10 Johnny Unitas | 1.25 | .50 | .12 |
| ☐ 11 Bart Starr | 1.00 | .40 | .10 |
| ☐ 12 Sonny Jurgensen | 2.50 | 1.00 | .25 |
| ☐ 13 Joe Namath | 1.50 | .60 | .15 |
| ☐ 14 Fran Tarkenton | 2.50 | 1.00 | .25 |
| ☐ 15 Roger Staubach | 2.00 | .80 | .20 |
| ☐ 16 Terry Bradshaw | 1.25 | .50 | .12 |
| ☐ 17 Dan Fouts | 4.00 | 1.60 | .40 |
| ☐ 18 Joe Montana | 2.00 | .80 | .20 |
| ☐ 19 John Elway | 4.00 | 1.60 | .40 |
| ☐ 20 Dan Marino | | | |

# 1992 Ultimate WLAF

The 1992 Ultimate WLAF football set consists of 200 standard-size (2 1/2" by 3 1/2") cards. Twelve nine-card foil packs were packaged in each coliseum display box, and each box came with a mini-poster and one hologram card. There were ten different hologram cards produced, one for each WLAF team logo. In addition, each foil pack contained a giveaway game card, and the individual who collected all five letters to spell W-O-R-L-D would win one million dollars. On a white card face, the fronts display color action player photos accented on the right and bottom by borders in the team's color. The team name, player's name, and position appear in these borders. The top left and bottom right corners of the picture are peeled back to create space for the Ultimate and World League logos. The backs feature another color photo, with biography, player profile, and a trivia note on a silver background. Some cards have a "Power Meter" for measuring each player's skills. The cards are numbered on the back and checklisted below alphabetically according to teams as follows: Barcelona Dragons (1-18), Birmingham Fire (19-35), Frankfurt Galaxy (36-55), London Monarchs (56-75), Montreal Machine (76-93), New York/New Jersey Knights (94-113), Orlando Thunder (114-130), Sacramento Surge (131-147), and San Antonio Riders (148-165). The Ohio Glory are represented by card numbers 166-179. The set closes with two topical subsets: How to Play the Game (180-192) and How To Collect Cards (193-200).

|  | MINT | EXC | G-VG |
|---|---|---|---|
| COMPLETE SET (200) | 8.00 | 3.25 | .80 |
| COMMON PLAYER (1-200) | .05 | .02 | .00 |
| ☐ 1 Barcelona Dragons '91 Team Statistics Thomas Woods | .10 | .04 | .01 |
| ☐ 2 Demetrius Davis | .15 | .06 | .01 |
| ☐ 3 Tim Egerton | .05 | .02 | .00 |
| ☐ 4 Scott Erney | .10 | .04 | .01 |
| ☐ 5 Tony Baker '91 Rushing Attempt Leader | .15 | .06 | .01 |
| ☐ 6 Anthony Greene | .10 | .04 | .01 |
| ☐ 7 Mike Hinnant UER (No position on front) | .05 | .02 | .00 |
| ☐ 8 Erik Naposki | .10 | .04 | .01 |
| ☐ 9 Paul Palmer | .15 | .06 | .01 |
| ☐ 10 Gene Taylor | .05 | .02 | .00 |
| ☐ 11 Thomas Woods | .05 | .02 | .00 |
| ☐ 12 Tony Rice | .35 | .14 | .03 |
| ☐ 13 Terry O'Shea | .05 | .02 | .00 |
| ☐ 14 Brett Wiese | .05 | .02 | .00 |
| ☐ 15 Phil Alexander Kicking Leader | .10 | .04 | .01 |
| ☐ 16 Eric Wilkerson Rushing/Scoring Leader | .15 | .06 | .01 |
| ☐ 17 Barcelona Dragons Team Picture | .10 | .04 | .01 |
| ☐ 18 Barcelona Dragons Checklist | .05 | .02 | .00 |
| ☐ 19 Birmingham Fire '91 Team Statistics | .05 | .02 | .00 |
| ☐ 20 Eric Jones | .05 | .02 | .00 |
| ☐ 21 Steven Avery | .05 | .02 | .00 |
| ☐ 22 Willie Bouyer | .05 | .02 | .00 |
| ☐ 23 Anthony Parker '91 Interception Leader | .15 | .06 | .01 |
| ☐ 24 Elroy Harris | .05 | .02 | .00 |
| ☐ 25 James Henry | .05 | .02 | .00 |
| ☐ 26 John Holland | .10 | .04 | .01 |
| ☐ 27 Mark Hopkins | .05 | .02 | .00 |
| ☐ 28 Arthur Hunter | .05 | .02 | .00 |
| ☐ 29 Danny Lockett '91 Sacking Leader | .15 | .06 | .01 |
| ☐ 30 Kirk Maggio | .05 | .02 | .00 |
| ☐ 31 John Miller | .05 | .02 | .00 |
| ☐ 32 Ricky Shaw | .05 | .02 | .00 |
| ☐ 33 Phil Ross | .05 | .02 | .00 |
| ☐ 34 Mike Norseth | .15 | .06 | .01 |
| ☐ 35 Birmingham Fire Checklist | .05 | .02 | .00 |
| ☐ 36 Frankfurt Galaxy '91 Team Statistics | .05 | .02 | .00 |
| ☐ 37 Anthony Wallace | .05 | .02 | .00 |
| ☐ 38 Lew Barnes | .05 | .02 | .00 |
| ☐ 39 Richard Buchanan | .05 | .02 | .00 |
| ☐ 40 Yepi Pau'u | .05 | .02 | .00 |
| ☐ 41 Pat McGuirk UER (Played for Raleigh-Durham in 1991) | .05 | .02 | .00 |
| ☐ 42 Tony Baker | .15 | .06 | .01 |
| ☐ 43 1992 TV Schedule 1 | .05 | .02 | .00 |
| ☐ 44 Tim Broady | .10 | .04 | .01 |
| ☐ 45 Lonnie Finch | .05 | .02 | .00 |
| ☐ 46 Chad Fortune | .05 | .02 | .00 |
| ☐ 47 Harry Jackson | .05 | .02 | .00 |
| ☐ 48 Jason Johnson | .05 | .02 | .00 |
| ☐ 49 Pat Moorer | .05 | .02 | .00 |
| ☐ 50 Mike Perez | .25 | .10 | .02 |
| ☐ 51 Mark Seals | .05 | .02 | .00 |
| ☐ 52 Cedric Stallworth | .05 | .02 | .00 |
| ☐ 53 Tom Whelihan | .05 | .02 | .00 |
| ☐ 54 Joe Johnson | .15 | .06 | .01 |
| ☐ 55 Frankfurt Galaxy Checklist | .05 | .02 | .00 |
| ☐ 56 London Monarchs '91 Team Statistics Stan Gelbaugh | .15 | .06 | .01 |
| ☐ 57 Stan Gelbaugh | .35 | .14 | .03 |
| ☐ 58 Jeffery Alexander | .05 | .02 | .00 |
| ☐ 59 Dana Brinson | .05 | .02 | .00 |
| ☐ 60 Marlon Brown | .05 | .02 | .00 |
| ☐ 61 Dedrick Dodge | .05 | .02 | .00 |
| ☐ 62 Judd Garrett | .25 | .10 | .02 |
| ☐ 63 Greg Horne | .05 | .02 | .00 |
| ☐ 64 Jon Horton | .05 | .02 | .00 |
| ☐ 65 Danny Lockett | .20 | .08 | .02 |
| ☐ 66 Andre Riley | .05 | .02 | .00 |
| ☐ 67 Charlie Young | .10 | .04 | .01 |
| ☐ 68 David Smith | .05 | .02 | .00 |
| ☐ 69 Irvin Smith | .05 | .02 | .00 |
| ☐ 70 Rickey Williams | .10 | .04 | .01 |
| ☐ 71 Roland Smith | .05 | .02 | .00 |
| ☐ 72 William Kirksey | .05 | .02 | .00 |
| ☐ 73 Phil Alexander | .05 | .02 | .00 |
| ☐ 74 London Monarchs Team Picture | .10 | .04 | .01 |
| ☐ 75 London Monarchs Checklist | .05 | .02 | .00 |
| ☐ 76 Montreal Machine '91 Team Statistics | .05 | .02 | .00 |
| ☐ 77 Rollin Putzier | .10 | .04 | .01 |
| ☐ 78 Adam Bob | .10 | .04 | .01 |
| ☐ 79 K.D. Dunn | .05 | .02 | .00 |
| ☐ 80 Darryl Holmes | .05 | .02 | .00 |
| ☐ 81 Ricky Johnson | .05 | .02 | .00 |
| ☐ 82 Michael Finn | .05 | .02 | .00 |
| ☐ 83 Chris Mohr | .15 | .06 | .01 |
| ☐ 84 Don Murray | .05 | .02 | .00 |
| ☐ 85 Bjorn Nittmo | .15 | .06 | .01 |
| ☐ 86 Michael Proctor | .05 | .02 | .00 |
| ☐ 87 Broderick Sargent | .05 | .02 | .00 |
| ☐ 88 Richard Shelton | .15 | .06 | .01 |
| ☐ 89 Emanuel King | .05 | .02 | .00 |
| ☐ 90 Pete Mandley | .15 | .06 | .01 |
| ☐ 91 Kris McCall | .05 | .02 | .00 |
| ☐ 92 1992 TV Schedule 2 | .05 | .02 | .00 |
| ☐ 93 Montreal Machine Checklist | .05 | .02 | .00 |
| ☐ 94 NY/NJ Knights '91 Team Statistics | .05 | .02 | .00 |
| ☐ 95 Andre Alexander | .05 | .02 | .00 |
| ☐ 96 Pat Marlatt | .05 | .02 | .00 |
| ☐ 97 Cecil Fletcher | .05 | .02 | .00 |
| ☐ 98 Lonnie Turner | .05 | .02 | .00 |
| ☐ 99 Monty Gilbreath | .05 | .02 | .00 |
| ☐ 100 Tony Jones UER (Should be DB, not WR) | .10 | .04 | .01 |
| ☐ 101 Kip Lewis | .05 | .02 | .00 |
| ☐ 102 Bobby Lilljedahl | .05 | .02 | .00 |
| ☐ 103 Mark Moore | .05 | .02 | .00 |
| ☐ 104 Falanda Newton | .10 | .04 | .01 |
| ☐ 105 Anthony Parker UER (Played for Chiefs in 1991, not Bears; was released by the Bears) | .15 | .06 | .01 |
| ☐ 106 Kendall Trainor | .15 | .06 | .01 |
| ☐ 107 Eric Wilkerson | .15 | .06 | .01 |
| ☐ 108 Tony Woods | .10 | .04 | .01 |
| ☐ 109 Reggie Slack | .25 | .10 | .02 |
| ☐ 110 Joey Banes | .05 | .02 | .00 |
| ☐ 111 Ron Sancho | .10 | .04 | .01 |
| ☐ 112 Mike Husar | .05 | .02 | .00 |

| | | | |
|---|---|---|---|
| ☐ 113 NY/NJ Knights........................ Checklist | .05 | .02 | .00 |
| ☐ 114 Orlando Thunder ................... '91 Team Statistics | .05 | .02 | .00 |
| ☐ 115 Byron Williams UER ............. (Waived by Orlando and picked up by NY-NJ) | .05 | .02 | .00 |
| ☐ 116 Charlie Baumann................... | .15 | .06 | .01 |
| ☐ 117 Kevin Bell ............................. | .10 | .04 | .01 |
| ☐ 118 Rodney Lossow .................... | .05 | .02 | .00 |
| ☐ 119 Myron Jones ......................... | .05 | .02 | .00 |
| ☐ 120 Bruce Lasane ....................... | .05 | .02 | .00 |
| ☐ 121 Eric Mitchel .......................... | .20 | .08 | .02 |
| ☐ 122 Billy Owens .......................... | .10 | .04 | .01 |
| ☐ 123 1992 TV Schedule 3 ............. | .05 | .02 | .00 |
| ☐ 124 Chris Roscoe ........................ | .05 | .02 | .00 |
| ☐ 125 Tommie Stowers .................... | .05 | .02 | .00 |
| ☐ 126 Wayne Dickson UER ............. (Not a rookie, he played for Orlando in 1991) | .05 | .02 | .00 |
| ☐ 127 Scott Mitchell........................ | 1.00 | .40 | .10 |
| ☐ 128 Karl Dunbar .......................... | .05 | .02 | .00 |
| ☐ 129 Dana Brinson ........................ '91 Punt Return Leader | .10 | .04 | .01 |
| ☐ 130 Orlando Thunder .................... Checklist | .05 | .02 | .00 |
| ☐ 131 Sacramento Surge ................ Team Statistics | .05 | .02 | .00 |
| ☐ 132 1992 TV Schedule 4 ............. | .05 | .02 | .00 |
| ☐ 133 Mike Adams .......................... | .05 | .02 | .00 |
| ☐ 134 Greg Coauette....................... | .05 | .02 | .00 |
| ☐ 135 Mel Farr Jr. .......................... (Should be TE, not FB) | .15 | .06 | .01 |
| ☐ 136 Victor Floyd .......................... | .05 | .02 | .00 |
| ☐ 137 Paul Frazier .......................... | .05 | .02 | .00 |
| ☐ 138 Tom Gerhart .......................... | .05 | .02 | .00 |
| ☐ 139 Pete Najarian ....................... | .05 | .02 | .00 |
| ☐ 140 John Nies ............................. | .05 | .02 | .00 |
| ☐ 141 Carl Parker ........................... | .05 | .02 | .00 |
| ☐ 142 Saute Sapolu ........................ | .05 | .02 | .00 |
| ☐ 143 George Bethune .................... | .10 | .04 | .01 |
| ☐ 144 David Archer ......................... | .25 | .10 | .02 |
| ☐ 145 John Buddenberg................... | .05 | .02 | .00 |
| ☐ 146 Jon Horton UER .................... (Incorrect stats on back) '91 Receiving Yardage Leader | .10 | .04 | .01 |
| ☐ 147 Sacramento Surge ................ Checklist | .05 | .02 | .00 |
| ☐ 148 San Antonio Riders ............... '91 Team Statistics | .05 | .02 | .00 |
| ☐ 149 Ricky Blake .......................... | .25 | .10 | .02 |
| ☐ 150 Jim Gallery ........................... | .05 | .02 | .00 |
| ☐ 151 Jason Garrett ........................ | .35 | .14 | .03 |
| ☐ 152 John Garrett .......................... | .20 | .08 | .02 |
| ☐ 153 Broderick Graves................... | .05 | .02 | .00 |
| ☐ 154 Bill Hess .............................. | .05 | .02 | .00 |
| ☐ 155 Mike Johnson ....................... | .05 | .02 | .00 |
| ☐ 156 Lee Morris............................ | .05 | .02 | .00 |
| ☐ 157 Dwight Pickens ..................... | .05 | .02 | .00 |
| ☐ 158 Kent Sullivan ........................ | .05 | .02 | .00 |
| ☐ 159 Ken Watson .......................... | .05 | .02 | .00 |
| ☐ 160 Ronnie Williams..................... | .05 | .02 | .00 |
| ☐ 161 Titus Dixon ........................... | .05 | .02 | .00 |
| ☐ 162 Mike Kiselak ........................ | .05 | .02 | .00 |
| ☐ 163 Greg Lee .............................. | .05 | .02 | .00 |
| ☐ 164 Judd Garrett UER .................. '91 Receiving Leader (Had 71 receptions in 1991, not 18; game high was 12, not 13) | .20 | .08 | .02 |
| ☐ 165 San Antonio Riders ............... Checklist | .05 | .02 | .00 |
| ☐ 166 Tenth Week Summaries ........ | .05 | .02 | .00 |
| ☐ 167 Randy Bethel ........................ | .05 | .02 | .00 |
| ☐ 168 Melvin Patterson ................... | .05 | .02 | .00 |
| ☐ 169 Eric Harmon .......................... | .05 | .02 | .00 |
| ☐ 170 Patrick Jackson ..................... | .05 | .02 | .00 |
| ☐ 171 Tim James ........................... | .05 | .02 | .00 |
| ☐ 172 George Koonce ..................... | .05 | .02 | .00 |
| ☐ 173 Babe Laufenberg ................... | .20 | .08 | .02 |
| ☐ 174 Amir Rasul ........................... | .05 | .02 | .00 |
| ☐ 175 Stan Gelbaugh....................... '91 Passing Leader | .20 | .08 | .02 |
| ☐ 176 Jason Wallace ...................... | .05 | .02 | .00 |
| ☐ 177 Walter Wilson ....................... | .05 | .02 | .00 |
| ☐ 178 Power Meter Info ................... | .10 | .04 | .01 |
| ☐ 179 Ohio Glory Checklist ............. | .05 | .02 | .00 |
| ☐ 180 The Football Field ................. Jim Kelly | .15 | .06 | .01 |
| ☐ 181 Moving the Ball ..................... Jim Kelly | .10 | .04 | .01 |
| ☐ 182 Defense/Back Field ............... Cornerbacks and Safeties Lawrence Taylor | .10 | .04 | .01 |
| ☐ 183 Defense/Linebackers ............. Lawrence Taylor | .10 | .04 | .01 |

| | | | |
|---|---|---|---|
| ☐ 184 Defense/Defensive Line ......... Defensive Tackles and Ends Lawrence Taylor | .10 | .04 | .01 |
| ☐ 185 Offense/Offensive Line .......... Centers, Guards, Tackles and Tight Ends Jim Kelly | .15 | .06 | .01 |
| ☐ 186 Offense/Receivers ................. Lawrence Taylor | .10 | .04 | .01 |
| ☐ 187 Offense/Running Backs.......... Jim Kelly | .15 | .06 | .01 |
| ☐ 188 Offensive/Quarterback........... Jim Kelly | .15 | .06 | .01 |
| ☐ 189 Special Teams....................... | .10 | .04 | .01 |
| ☐ 190 Rules and Regulations .......... WL Rules that differ from NFL 1990 Rules | .05 | .02 | .00 |
| ☐ 191 Defensive Overview ............... Scoring Touchdowns and Extra Points | .05 | .02 | .00 |
| ☐ 192 Offensive Overview ............... Scoring, Field Goals and Safeties | .05 | .02 | .00 |
| ☐ 193 How to Collect....................... What is a Set Lawrence Taylor | .10 | .04 | .01 |
| ☐ 194 How to Collect....................... What is a Wax Pack Lawrence Taylor | .10 | .04 | .01 |
| ☐ 195 How to Collect....................... Premier Editions Lawrence Taylor | .10 | .04 | .01 |
| ☐ 196 How to Collect....................... What Creates Value Lawrence Taylor | .10 | .04 | .01 |
| ☐ 197 How to Collect....................... Rookie Cards Jim Kelly | .15 | .06 | .01 |
| ☐ 198 How to Collect....................... Grading Your Cards Jim Kelly | .15 | .06 | .01 |
| ☐ 199 How to Collect....................... Storing Your Cards Jim Kelly | .15 | .06 | .01 |
| ☐ 200 How to Collect....................... Trading Your Cards Jim Kelly | .15 | .06 | .01 |

# 1992 Ultimate WLAF Logo Holograms

The 1992 Ultimate WLAF Team Logo Hologram set consists of ten standard-size (2 1/2" by 3 1/2") cards. Twelve nine-card foil packs were packaged in each coliseum display box, and each box came with a mini-poster and one hologram card. There were ten different hologram cards produced, one for each WLAF team logo.

| | MINT | EXC | G-VG |
|---|---|---|---|
| COMPLETE SET (10)........................ | 7.00 | 2.80 | .70 |
| COMMON PLAYER (1-10)................. | 1.00 | .40 | .10 |
| | | | |
| ☐ 1 Barcelona Dragons.................... | 1.00 | .40 | .10 |
| ☐ 2 Birmingham Fire ....................... | 1.00 | .40 | .10 |
| ☐ 3 Frankfurt Galaxy ...................... | 1.00 | .40 | .10 |
| ☐ 4 London Monarchs...................... | 1.00 | .40 | .10 |
| ☐ 5 Montreal Machine ..................... | 1.00 | .40 | .10 |
| ☐ 6 NY/NJ Knights.......................... | 1.00 | .40 | .10 |
| ☐ 7 Ohio Glory ............................... | 1.00 | .40 | .10 |
| ☐ 8 Orlando Thunder ....................... | 1.00 | .40 | .10 |
| ☐ 9 Sacramento Surge ................... | 1.00 | .40 | .10 |
| ☐ 10 San Antonio Riders ................. | 1.00 | .40 | .10 |

# 1991 Ultra

The 1991 Fleer Ultra football set contains 300 cards measuring the standard size (2 1/2" by 3 1/2"). The front design has a color action player photo, bleeding to the card sides but with silver borders above and beneath the picture. Player information is given in white lettering in the bottom silver border. The backs have a yellow fading to orange and green background, with the same silver borders as on the fronts. A color head shot of the player in a shield format is sandwiched between two smaller action shots of the player. Brief biographical information and statistics appear at the bottom of the back. The cards are numbered on the back and checklisted below alphabetically within and according to teams in the AFC and NFC as follows: Buffalo Bills (1-10), Cincinnati Bengals (11-24), Cleveland Browns (25-32), Denver Broncos (33-43), Houston Oilers (44-55), Indianapolis Colts (56-63), Kansas City Chiefs (64-74), Los Angeles Raiders (75-85), Miami Dolphins (86-93), New England Patriots (94-99), New York Jets (100-108), Pittsburgh Steelers (109-118), San Diego Chargers (119-131), Seattle Seahawks (132-142), Atlanta Falcons (143-150), Chicago Bears (151-161), Dallas Cowboys (162-165), Detroit Lions (166-169), Green Bay Packers (170-180), Los Angeles Rams (181-190), Minnesota Vikings (191-203), New Orleans Saints (204-213), New York Giants (214-226), Philadelphia Eagles (227-236), Phoenix Cardinals (237-244), San Francisco 49ers (245-256), Tampa Bay Buccaneers (257-267), and Washington Redskins (268-278). The last subset included in this set was Rookie Prospects (279-298). The key Rookie Cards in this set are Nick Bell, Mike Croel, Brett Favre, Randal Hill, Todd Marinovich, Russell Maryland, Dan McGwire, Herman Moore, Browning Nagle, Mike Pritchard, and Ricky Watters.

|  | MINT | EXC | G-VG |
|---|---|---|---|
| COMPLETE SET (300) | 12.00 | 5.50 | 1.50 |
| COMMON PLAYER (1-300) | .05 | .02 | .01 |

| | | | |
|---|---|---|---|
| ☐ 1 Don Beebe | .10 | .05 | .01 |
| ☐ 2 Shane Conlan | .08 | .04 | .01 |
| ☐ 3 Pete Metzelaars | .05 | .02 | .01 |
| ☐ 4 Jamie Mueller | .05 | .02 | .01 |
| ☐ 5 Scott Norwood | .05 | .02 | .01 |
| ☐ 6 Andre Reed | .10 | .05 | .01 |
| ☐ 7 Leon Seals | .05 | .02 | .01 |
| ☐ 8 Bruce Smith | .10 | .05 | .01 |
| ☐ 9 Leonard Smith | .05 | .02 | .01 |
| ☐ 10 Thurman Thomas | .40 | .18 | .05 |
| ☐ 11 Lewis Billups | .05 | .02 | .01 |
| ☐ 12 Jim Breech | .05 | .02 | .01 |
| ☐ 13 James Brooks | .08 | .04 | .01 |
| ☐ 14 Eddie Brown | .05 | .02 | .01 |
| ☐ 15 Boomer Esiason | .15 | .07 | .02 |
| ☐ 16 David Fulcher | .05 | .02 | .01 |
| ☐ 17 Rodney Holman | .05 | .02 | .01 |
| ☐ 18 Bruce Kozerski | .05 | .02 | .01 |
| ☐ 19 Tim Krumrie | .05 | .02 | .01 |
| ☐ 20 Tim McGee | .05 | .02 | .01 |
| ☐ 21 Anthony Munoz | .08 | .04 | .01 |
| ☐ 22 Leon White | .05 | .02 | .01 |
| ☐ 23 Ickey Woods | .05 | .02 | .01 |
| ☐ 24 Carl Zander | .05 | .02 | .01 |
| ☐ 25 Brian Brennan | .05 | .02 | .01 |
| ☐ 26 Thane Gash | .05 | .02 | .01 |
| ☐ 27 Leroy Hoard | .08 | .04 | .01 |
| ☐ 28 Mike Johnson | .05 | .02 | .01 |
| ☐ 29 Reggie Langhorne | .08 | .04 | .01 |
| ☐ 30 Kevin Mack | .08 | .04 | .01 |
| ☐ 31 Clay Matthews | .08 | .04 | .01 |
| ☐ 32 Eric Metcalf | .10 | .05 | .01 |
| ☐ 33 Steve Atwater | .10 | .05 | .01 |
| ☐ 34 Melvin Bratton | .05 | .02 | .01 |
| ☐ 35 John Elway | .35 | .16 | .04 |
| ☐ 36 Bobby Humphrey | .08 | .04 | .01 |
| ☐ 37 Mark Jackson | .08 | .04 | .01 |
| ☐ 38 Vance Johnson | .08 | .04 | .01 |
| ☐ 39 Ricky Nattiel | .05 | .02 | .01 |
| ☐ 40 Steve Sewell | .05 | .02 | .01 |
| ☐ 41 Dennis Smith | .08 | .04 | .01 |
| ☐ 42 David Treadwell | .05 | .02 | .01 |
| ☐ 43 Mike Young | .05 | .02 | .01 |
| ☐ 44 Ray Childress | .08 | .04 | .01 |
| ☐ 45 Cris Dishman | .15 | .07 | .02 |
| ☐ 46 William Fuller | .08 | .04 | .01 |
| ☐ 47 Ernest Givins | .08 | .04 | .01 |
| ☐ 48 John Grimsley UER | .05 | .02 | .01 |
| (Acquired line should be Trade '91, not Draft 6-'84) | | | |
| ☐ 49 Drew Hill | .08 | .04 | .01 |
| ☐ 50 Haywood Jeffires | .15 | .07 | .02 |
| ☐ 51 Sean Jones | .08 | .04 | .01 |
| ☐ 52 Johnny Meads | .05 | .02 | .01 |
| ☐ 53 Warren Moon | .20 | .09 | .03 |
| ☐ 54 Al Smith | .05 | .02 | .01 |
| ☐ 55 Lorenzo White | .08 | .04 | .01 |
| ☐ 56 Albert Bentley | .05 | .02 | .01 |
| ☐ 57 Duane Bickett | .05 | .02 | .01 |
| ☐ 58 Bill Brooks | .08 | .04 | .01 |
| ☐ 59 Jeff George | .25 | .11 | .03 |
| ☐ 60 Mike Prior | .05 | .02 | .01 |
| ☐ 61 Rohn Stark | .05 | .02 | .01 |
| ☐ 62 Jack Trudeau | .05 | .02 | .01 |
| ☐ 63 Clarence Verdin | .05 | .02 | .01 |
| ☐ 64 Steve DeBerg | .08 | .04 | .01 |
| ☐ 65 Emile Harry | .05 | .02 | .01 |
| ☐ 66 Albert Lewis | .08 | .04 | .01 |
| ☐ 67 Nick Lowery UER | .08 | .04 | .01 |
| (NFL Exp. has 12 years, should be 13) | | | |
| ☐ 68 Todd McNair | .05 | .02 | .01 |
| ☐ 69 Christian Okoye | .08 | .04 | .01 |
| ☐ 70 Stephone Paige | .08 | .04 | .01 |
| ☐ 71 Kevin Porter UER | .05 | .02 | .01 |
| (Front has traded logo, but he has been a Chief all career) | | | |
| ☐ 72 Derrick Thomas | .25 | .11 | .03 |
| ☐ 73 Robb Thomas | .05 | .02 | .01 |
| ☐ 74 Barry Word | .10 | .05 | .01 |
| ☐ 75 Marcus Allen | .15 | .07 | .02 |
| ☐ 76 Eddie Anderson | .05 | .02 | .01 |
| ☐ 77 Tim Brown | .20 | .09 | .03 |
| ☐ 78 Mervyn Fernandez | .05 | .02 | .01 |
| ☐ 79 Willie Gault | .08 | .04 | .01 |
| ☐ 80 Ethan Horton | .05 | .02 | .01 |
| ☐ 81 Howie Long | .08 | .04 | .01 |
| ☐ 82 Vance Mueller | .05 | .02 | .01 |
| ☐ 83 Jay Schroeder | .08 | .04 | .01 |
| ☐ 84 Steve Smith | .08 | .04 | .01 |
| ☐ 85 Greg Townsend | .05 | .02 | .01 |
| ☐ 86 Mark Clayton | .08 | .04 | .01 |
| ☐ 87 Jim C. Jensen | .05 | .02 | .01 |
| ☐ 88 Dan Marino | .75 | .35 | .09 |
| ☐ 89 Tim McKyer UER | .08 | .04 | .01 |
| (Acquired line should be Trade '91, not Trade '90) | | | |
| ☐ 90 John Offerdahl | .08 | .04 | .01 |
| ☐ 91 Louis Oliver | .08 | .04 | .01 |
| ☐ 92 Reggie Roby | .05 | .02 | .01 |
| ☐ 93 Sammie Smith | .05 | .02 | .01 |
| ☐ 94 Hart Lee Dykes | .05 | .02 | .01 |
| ☐ 95 Irving Fryar | .08 | .04 | .01 |
| ☐ 96 Tommy Hodson | .05 | .02 | .01 |
| ☐ 97 Maurice Hurst | .05 | .02 | .01 |
| ☐ 98 John Stephens | .08 | .04 | .01 |
| ☐ 99 Andre Tippett | .08 | .04 | .01 |
| ☐ 100 Mark Boyer | .05 | .02 | .01 |
| ☐ 101 Kyle Clifton | .05 | .02 | .01 |
| ☐ 102 James Hasty | .05 | .02 | .01 |
| ☐ 103 Erik McMillan | .05 | .02 | .01 |
| ☐ 104 Rob Moore | .10 | .05 | .01 |
| ☐ 105 Joe Mott | .05 | .02 | .01 |
| ☐ 106 Ken O'Brien | .08 | .04 | .01 |
| ☐ 107 Ron Stallworth UER | .05 | .02 | .01 |
| (Acquired line should be Trade '91, not Draft 4-'89) | | | |
| ☐ 108 Al Toon | .08 | .04 | .01 |
| ☐ 109 Gary Anderson | .05 | .02 | .01 |
| ☐ 110 Bubby Brister | .08 | .04 | .01 |
| ☐ 111 Thomas Everett | .05 | .02 | .01 |
| ☐ 112 Merril Hoge | .08 | .04 | .01 |
| ☐ 113 Louis Lipps | .08 | .04 | .01 |
| ☐ 114 Greg Lloyd | .05 | .02 | .01 |
| ☐ 115 Hardy Nickerson | .05 | .02 | .01 |
| ☐ 116 Dwight Stone | .05 | .02 | .01 |
| ☐ 117 Rod Woodson | .10 | .05 | .01 |
| ☐ 118 Tim Worley | .08 | .04 | .01 |
| ☐ 119 Rod Bernstine | .10 | .05 | .01 |
| ☐ 120 Marion Butts | .10 | .05 | .01 |
| ☐ 121 Gill Byrd | .08 | .04 | .01 |

| | | | |
|---|---|---|---|
| ☐ 122 Arthur Cox | .05 | .02 | .01 |
| ☐ 123 Burt Grossman | .05 | .02 | .01 |
| ☐ 124 Ronnie Harmon | .05 | .02 | .01 |
| ☐ 125 Anthony Miller | .10 | .05 | .01 |
| ☐ 126 Leslie O'Neal | .08 | .04 | .01 |
| ☐ 127 Gary Plummer | .05 | .02 | .01 |
| ☐ 128 Sam Seale | .05 | .02 | .01 |
| ☐ 129 Junior Seau | .25 | .11 | .03 |
| ☐ 130 Broderick Thompson | .05 | .02 | .01 |
| ☐ 131 Billy Joe Tolliver | .08 | .04 | .01 |
| ☐ 132 Brian Blades | .10 | .05 | .01 |
| ☐ 133 Jeff Bryant | .05 | .02 | .01 |
| ☐ 134 Derrick Fenner | .08 | .04 | .01 |
| ☐ 135 Jacob Green | .05 | .02 | .01 |
| ☐ 136 Andy Heck | .05 | .02 | .01 |
| ☐ 137 Patrick Hunter UER (Photos on back show 23 and 27) | .05 | .02 | .01 |
| ☐ 138 Norm Johnson | .05 | .02 | .01 |
| ☐ 139 Tommy Kane | .05 | .02 | .01 |
| ☐ 140 Dave Krieg | .08 | .04 | .01 |
| ☐ 141 John L. Williams | .08 | .04 | .01 |
| ☐ 142 Terry Wooden | .05 | .02 | .01 |
| ☐ 143 Steve Broussard | .08 | .04 | .01 |
| ☐ 144 Keith Jones | .05 | .02 | .01 |
| ☐ 145 Brian Jordan | .10 | .05 | .01 |
| ☐ 146 Chris Miller | .10 | .05 | .01 |
| ☐ 147 John Rade | .05 | .02 | .01 |
| ☐ 148 Andre Rison | .25 | .11 | .03 |
| ☐ 149 Mike Rozier | .08 | .04 | .01 |
| ☐ 150 Deion Sanders | .25 | .11 | .03 |
| ☐ 151 Neal Anderson | .08 | .04 | .01 |
| ☐ 152 Trace Armstrong | .05 | .02 | .01 |
| ☐ 153 Kevin Butler | .05 | .02 | .01 |
| ☐ 154 Mark Carrier | .08 | .04 | .01 |
| ☐ 155 Richard Dent | .08 | .04 | .01 |
| ☐ 156 Dennis Gentry | .05 | .02 | .01 |
| ☐ 157 Jim Harbaugh | .08 | .04 | .01 |
| ☐ 158 Brad Muster | .08 | .04 | .01 |
| ☐ 159 William Perry | .08 | .04 | .01 |
| ☐ 160 Mike Singletary | .10 | .05 | .01 |
| ☐ 161 Lemuel Stinson | .05 | .02 | .01 |
| ☐ 162 Troy Aikman | 1.25 | .55 | .16 |
| ☐ 163 Michael Irvin | .50 | .23 | .06 |
| ☐ 164 Mike Saxon | .05 | .02 | .01 |
| ☐ 165 Emmitt Smith | 2.00 | .90 | .25 |
| ☐ 166 Jerry Ball | .08 | .04 | .01 |
| ☐ 167 Michael Cofer | .05 | .02 | .01 |
| ☐ 168 Rodney Peete | .08 | .04 | .01 |
| ☐ 169 Barry Sanders | .75 | .35 | .09 |
| ☐ 170 Robert Brown | .05 | .02 | .01 |
| ☐ 171 Anthony Dilweg | .08 | .04 | .01 |
| ☐ 172 Tim Harris | .08 | .04 | .01 |
| ☐ 173 Johnny Holland | .05 | .02 | .01 |
| ☐ 174 Perry Kemp | .05 | .02 | .01 |
| ☐ 175 Don Majkowski | .08 | .04 | .01 |
| ☐ 176 Brian Noble | .05 | .02 | .01 |
| ☐ 177 Jeff Query | .05 | .02 | .01 |
| ☐ 178 Sterling Sharpe | .50 | .23 | .06 |
| ☐ 179 Charles Wilson | .05 | .02 | .01 |
| ☐ 180 Keith Woodside | .05 | .02 | .01 |
| ☐ 181 Flipper Anderson UER (Back photo not him) | .08 | .04 | .01 |
| ☐ 182 Bern Brostek | .05 | .02 | .01 |
| ☐ 183 Pat Carter | .15 | .07 | .02 |
| ☐ 184 Aaron Cox | .05 | .02 | .01 |
| ☐ 185 Henry Ellard | .08 | .04 | .01 |
| ☐ 186 Jim Everett | .08 | .04 | .01 |
| ☐ 187 Cleveland Gary | .08 | .04 | .01 |
| ☐ 188 Jerry Gray | .05 | .02 | .01 |
| ☐ 189 Kevin Greene | .08 | .04 | .01 |
| ☐ 190 Mike Wilcher | .05 | .02 | .01 |
| ☐ 191 Alfred Anderson | .05 | .02 | .01 |
| ☐ 192 Joey Browner | .05 | .02 | .01 |
| ☐ 193 Anthony Carter | .08 | .04 | .01 |
| ☐ 194 Chris Doleman | .08 | .04 | .01 |
| ☐ 195 Rick Fenney | .05 | .02 | .01 |
| ☐ 196 Darrell Fullington | .05 | .02 | .01 |
| ☐ 197 Rich Gannon | .08 | .04 | .01 |
| ☐ 198 Hassan Jones | .05 | .02 | .01 |
| ☐ 199 Steve Jordan | .08 | .04 | .01 |
| ☐ 200 Mike Merriweather | .05 | .02 | .01 |
| ☐ 201 Al Noga | .05 | .02 | .01 |
| ☐ 202 Herschel Walker | .10 | .05 | .01 |
| ☐ 203 Wade Wilson | .08 | .04 | .01 |
| ☐ 204 Morten Andersen | .08 | .04 | .01 |
| ☐ 205 Gene Atkins | .05 | .02 | .01 |
| ☐ 206 Toi Cook | .05 | .02 | .01 |
| ☐ 207 Craig Heyward | .08 | .04 | .01 |
| ☐ 208 Dalton Hilliard | .05 | .02 | .01 |
| ☐ 209 Vaughan Johnson | .08 | .04 | .01 |
| ☐ 210 Eric Martin | .08 | .04 | .01 |
| ☐ 211 Brett Perriman | .10 | .05 | .01 |
| ☐ 212 Pat Swilling | .08 | .04 | .01 |
| ☐ 213 Steve Walsh | .05 | .02 | .01 |
| ☐ 214 Ottis Anderson | .08 | .04 | .01 |
| ☐ 215 Carl Banks | .08 | .04 | .01 |
| ☐ 216 Maurice Carthon | .05 | .02 | .01 |
| ☐ 217 Mark Collins | .05 | .02 | .01 |
| ☐ 218 Rodney Hampton | .75 | .35 | .09 |
| ☐ 219 Erik Howard | .05 | .02 | .01 |
| ☐ 220 Mark Ingram | .08 | .04 | .01 |
| ☐ 221 Pepper Johnson | .08 | .04 | .01 |
| ☐ 222 Dave Meggett | .10 | .05 | .01 |
| ☐ 223 Phil Simms | .10 | .05 | .01 |
| ☐ 224 Lawrence Taylor | .08 | .04 | .01 |
| ☐ 225 Lewis Tillman | .05 | .02 | .01 |
| ☐ 226 Everson Walls | .05 | .02 | .01 |
| ☐ 227 Fred Barnett | .15 | .07 | .02 |
| ☐ 228 Jerome Brown | .08 | .04 | .01 |
| ☐ 229 Keith Byars | .08 | .04 | .01 |
| ☐ 230 Randall Cunningham | .10 | .05 | .01 |
| ☐ 231 Byron Evans | .08 | .04 | .01 |
| ☐ 232 Wes Hopkins | .05 | .02 | .01 |
| ☐ 233 Keith Jackson | .15 | .07 | .02 |
| ☐ 234 Heath Sherman | .08 | .04 | .01 |
| ☐ 235 Anthony Toney | .05 | .02 | .01 |
| ☐ 236 Reggie White | .15 | .07 | .02 |
| ☐ 237 Rich Camarillo | .05 | .02 | .01 |
| ☐ 238 Ken Harvey | .05 | .02 | .01 |
| ☐ 239 Eric Hill | .05 | .02 | .01 |
| ☐ 240 Johnny Johnson | .25 | .11 | .03 |
| ☐ 241 Ernie Jones | .05 | .02 | .01 |
| ☐ 242 Tim McDonald | .08 | .04 | .01 |
| ☐ 243 Timm Rosenbach | .08 | .04 | .01 |
| ☐ 244 Jay Taylor | .05 | .02 | .01 |
| ☐ 245 Dexter Carter | .08 | .04 | .01 |
| ☐ 246 Mike Cofer | .05 | .02 | .01 |
| ☐ 247 Kevin Fagan | .05 | .02 | .01 |
| ☐ 248 Don Griffin | .05 | .02 | .01 |
| ☐ 249 Charles Haley | .08 | .04 | .01 |
| ☐ 250 Brent Jones | .10 | .05 | .01 |
| ☐ 251 Joe Montana UER (Born: Monongahela, not New Eagle) | 1.00 | .45 | .13 |
| ☐ 252 Darryl Pollard | .05 | .02 | .01 |
| ☐ 253 Tom Rathman | .08 | .04 | .01 |
| ☐ 254 Jerry Rice | .75 | .35 | .09 |
| ☐ 255 John Taylor | .10 | .05 | .01 |
| ☐ 256 Steve Young | .50 | .23 | .06 |
| ☐ 257 Gary Anderson | .08 | .04 | .01 |
| ☐ 258 Mark Carrier | .08 | .04 | .01 |
| ☐ 259 Chris Chandler | .08 | .04 | .01 |
| ☐ 260 Reggie Cobb | .25 | .11 | .03 |
| ☐ 261 Reuben Davis | .05 | .02 | .01 |
| ☐ 262 Willie Drewrey | .05 | .02 | .01 |
| ☐ 263 Ron Hall | .05 | .02 | .01 |
| ☐ 264 Eugene Marve | .05 | .02 | .01 |
| ☐ 265 Winston Moss UER (Acquired line should be Trade '91, not Draft 2-'87) | .05 | .02 | .01 |
| ☐ 266 Vinny Testaverde | .10 | .05 | .01 |
| ☐ 267 Broderick Thomas | .08 | .04 | .01 |
| ☐ 268 Jeff Bostic | .05 | .02 | .01 |
| ☐ 269 Earnest Byner | .08 | .04 | .01 |
| ☐ 270 Gary Clark | .08 | .04 | .01 |
| ☐ 271 Darrell Green | .08 | .04 | .01 |
| ☐ 272 Jim Lachey | .05 | .02 | .01 |
| ☐ 273 Wilber Marshall | .08 | .04 | .01 |
| ☐ 274 Art Monk | .10 | .05 | .01 |
| ☐ 275 Gerald Riggs | .08 | .04 | .01 |
| ☐ 276 Mark Rypien | .10 | .05 | .01 |
| ☐ 277 Ricky Sanders | .08 | .04 | .01 |
| ☐ 278 Alvin Walton | .05 | .02 | .01 |
| ☐ 279 Nick Bell Los Angeles Raiders | .20 | .09 | .03 |
| ☐ 280 Eric Bieniemy San Diego Chargers | .15 | .07 | .02 |
| ☐ 281 Jarrod Bunch New York Giants | .15 | .07 | .02 |
| ☐ 282 Mike Croel Denver Broncos | .20 | .09 | .03 |
| ☐ 283 Brett Favre Atlanta Falcons | 2.00 | .90 | .25 |
| ☐ 284 Moe Gardner Atlanta Falcons | .10 | .05 | .01 |
| ☐ 285 Pat Harlow New England Patriots | .10 | .05 | .01 |
| ☐ 286 Randal Hill Miami Dolphins | .30 | .14 | .04 |
| ☐ 287 Todd Marinovich Los Angeles Raiders | .08 | .04 | .01 |
| ☐ 288 Russell Maryland Dallas Cowboys | .40 | .18 | .05 |
| ☐ 289 Dan McGwire Seattle Seahawks | .10 | .05 | .01 |
| ☐ 290 Ernie Mills UER Pittsburgh Steelers (Patterns misspelled as pattersn in first sentence) | .10 | .05 | .01 |
| ☐ 291 Herman Moore Detroit Lions | 1.00 | .45 | .13 |

| | | | |
|---|---|---|---|
| ☐ 292 Godfrey Myles................ | .10 | .05 | .01 |
| Dallas Cowboys | | | |
| ☐ 293 Browning Nagle................ | .20 | .09 | .03 |
| New York Jets | | | |
| ☐ 294 Mike Pritchard................ | .75 | .35 | .09 |
| Atlanta Falcons | | | |
| ☐ 295 Esera Tuaolo................ | .05 | .02 | .01 |
| Green Bay Packers | | | |
| ☐ 296 Mark Vander Poel............ | .05 | .02 | .01 |
| Indianapolis Colts | | | |
| ☐ 297 Ricky Watters UER........... | 1.25 | .55 | .16 |
| San Francisco 49ers | | | |
| (Photo on back act- | | | |
| ually Ray Griggs) | | | |
| ☐ 298 Chris Zorich................ | .25 | .11 | .03 |
| Chicago Bears | | | |
| ☐ 299 Checklist Card................ | .10 | .05 | .01 |
| (Randall Cunningham | | | |
| and Emmitt Smith) | | | |
| ☐ 300 Checklist Card................ | .10 | .05 | .01 |
| (Randall Cunningham | | | |
| and Emmitt Smith) | | | |

## 1991 Ultra All-Stars

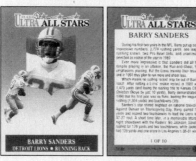

The 1991 Fleer Ultra All-Stars set consists of 10 standard-size (2 1/2" by 3 1/2") cards. On the fronts, a color head shot of the player in a shield format is sandwiched between two smaller action shots of the player. The card face is gold, with player information provided in a green stripe at the bottom. Within a gold border on a white background, the backs present player profile. The cards are numbered on the back and were issued as inserts into the regular 1991 Fleer Ultra packs that were sold in black boxes.

| | MINT | EXC | G-VG |
|---|---|---|---|
| COMPLETE SET (10)................ | 7.00 | 3.10 | .85 |
| COMMON PLAYER (1-10)................ | .50 | .23 | .06 |
| ☐ 1 Barry Sanders................ | 3.50 | 1.55 | .45 |
| Detroit Lions | | | |
| ☐ 2 Keith Jackson................ | .75 | .35 | .09 |
| Philadelphia Eagles | | | |
| ☐ 3 Bruce Smith................ | .50 | .23 | .06 |
| Buffalo Bills | | | |
| ☐ 4 Randall Cunningham................ | .75 | .35 | .09 |
| Philadelphia Eagles | | | |
| ☐ 5 Dan Marino................ | 3.50 | 1.55 | .45 |
| Miami Dolphins | | | |
| ☐ 6 Charles Haley................ | .50 | .23 | .06 |
| San Francisco 49ers | | | |
| ☐ 7 John L. Williams................ | .50 | .23 | .06 |
| Seattle Seahawks | | | |
| ☐ 8 Darrell Green................ | .50 | .23 | .06 |
| Washington Redskins | | | |
| ☐ 9 Stephone Paige................ | .50 | .23 | .06 |
| Kansas City Chiefs | | | |
| ☐ 10 Kevin Greene................ | .50 | .23 | .06 |
| Los Angeles Rams | | | |

## 1991 Ultra Performances

This ten-card standard-size (2 1/2" by 3 1/2") set was produced by Fleer to showcase outstanding NFL football players. The front features a color action player photo, banded above and below by silver stripes but bleeding to the edge of the card on the sides. To highlight the featured player, the background and other players in the picture are washed out. Inside black and silver borders, the back presents player profile. The cards are numbered on the back and were issued as inserts into the regular 1991 Fleer Ultra packs that were sold in green boxes.

| | MINT | EXC | G-VG |
|---|---|---|---|
| COMPLETE SET (10)................ | 12.00 | 5.50 | 1.50 |
| COMMON PLAYER (1-10)................ | .50 | .23 | .06 |
| ☐ 1 Emmitt Smith................ | 6.00 | 2.70 | .75 |
| Dallas Cowboys | | | |
| ☐ 2 Andre Rison................ | 1.00 | .45 | .13 |
| Atlanta Falcons | | | |
| ☐ 3 Derrick Thomas................ | 1.00 | .45 | .13 |
| Kansas City Chiefs | | | |
| ☐ 4 Joe Montana................ | 3.00 | 1.35 | .40 |
| San Francisco 49ers | | | |
| ☐ 5 Warren Moon................ | .75 | .35 | .09 |
| Houston Oilers | | | |
| ☐ 6 Mike Singletary................ | .50 | .23 | .06 |
| Chicago Bears | | | |
| ☐ 7 Thurman Thomas................ | 1.50 | .65 | .19 |
| Buffalo Bills | | | |
| ☐ 8 Rod Woodson................ | .50 | .23 | .06 |
| Pittsburgh Steelers | | | |
| ☐ 9 Jerry Rice................ | 2.00 | .90 | .25 |
| San Francisco 49ers | | | |
| ☐ 10 Reggie White................ | .75 | .35 | .09 |
| Philadelphia Eagles | | | |

## 1991 Ultra Update

This 100-card set was produced by Fleer and featured some of the leading rookies and players who switched franchises during the 1991 season. The cards are standard size, 2 1/2" by 3 1/2". The front design has a color action player photo, bleeding to the card sides but with silver borders above and beneath the picture. On most of the card backs, a color head shot of the player in a shield format is sandwiched between two smaller action shots of the player. The backs are accented in blue and green, with biography and statistics (1990 and career) at the bottom. The cards are numbered on the back and checklisted below alphabetically according to and within teams as follows: Atlanta Falcons (1-5), Buffalo Bills (6-10), Chicago Bears (11-13), Cincinnati Bengals (14-15), Cleveland Browns (16-19), Dallas Cowboys (20-22), Denver Broncos (23-25), Detroit Lions (26-29), Green Bay Packers (30-33), Houston Oilers (34-36), Kansas City Chiefs (37-39), Los Angeles Raiders (40-43), Los Angeles Rams (44-46), Miami Dolphins (47-49), Minnesota Vikings (50-51), New England Patriots (52-57), New Orleans Saints (58-61), New York Giants (62-66), New York Jets (67-69), Philadelphia Eagles (70-73), Phoenix Cardinals (74-76), Pittsburgh Steelers (77-80), San Diego Chargers (81-84), San Francisco 49ers (85-89), Seattle Seahawks (90-91), Tampa Bay Buccaneers (92-95), and Washington Redskins (96-98). The key Rookie Cards in this set are Lawrence Dawsey, Ricky Ervins, Jeff Graham, Mark Higgs, Michael Jackson, Ed McCaffrey,

Hugh Millen, Neil O'Donnell, Leonard Russell, Jon Vaughn, and Harvey Williams. The card numbers carry a "U" prefix.

| | MINT | EXC | G-VG |
|---|---|---|---|
| COMPLETE FACT.SET (100) | 16.00 | 7.25 | 2.00 |
| COMMON PLAYER (U1-U100) | .08 | .04 | .01 |
| ☐ U1 Brett Favre | 7.00 | 3.10 | .85 |
| ☐ U2 Moe Gardner | .10 | .05 | .01 |
| ☐ U3 Tim McKyer | .10 | .05 | .01 |
| ☐ U4 Bruce Pickens | .20 | .09 | .03 |
| ☐ U5 Mike Pritchard | 1.00 | .45 | .13 |
| ☐ U6 Cornelius Bennett | .12 | .05 | .02 |
| ☐ U7 Phil Hansen | .30 | .14 | .04 |
| ☐ U8 Henry Jones | .50 | .23 | .06 |
| ☐ U9 Mark Kelso | .08 | .04 | .01 |
| ☐ U10 James Lofton | .12 | .05 | .02 |
| ☐ U11 Anthony Morgan | .20 | .09 | .03 |
| ☐ U12 Stan Thomas | .08 | .04 | .01 |
| ☐ U13 Chris Zorich | .35 | .16 | .04 |
| ☐ U14 Reggie Rembert | .08 | .04 | .01 |
| ☐ U15 Alfred Williams | .25 | .11 | .03 |
| ☐ U16 Michael Jackson | 1.50 | .65 | .19 |
| ☐ U17 Ed King | .08 | .04 | .01 |
| ☐ U18 Joe Morris | .10 | .04 | .01 |
| ☐ U19 Vince Newsome | .08 | .04 | .01 |
| ☐ U20 Tony Casillas | .08 | .04 | .01 |
| ☐ U21 Russell Maryland | .50 | .23 | .06 |
| ☐ U22 Jay Novacek | .30 | .14 | .04 |
| ☐ U23 Mike Croel | .25 | .11 | .03 |
| ☐ U24 Gaston Green | .10 | .05 | .01 |
| ☐ U25 Kenny Walker | .08 | .04 | .01 |
| ☐ U26 Melvin Jenkins | .20 | .09 | .03 |
| ☐ U27 Herman Moore | 3.00 | 1.35 | .40 |
| ☐ U28 Kelvin Pritchett | .08 | .04 | .01 |
| ☐ U29 Chris Spielman | .10 | .05 | .01 |
| ☐ U30 Vinnie Clark | .08 | .04 | .01 |
| ☐ U31 Allen Rice | .08 | .04 | .01 |
| ☐ U32 Vai Sikahema | .10 | .05 | .01 |
| ☐ U33 Esera Tuaolo | .08 | .04 | .01 |
| ☐ U34 Mike Dumas | .10 | .05 | .01 |
| ☐ U35 John Flannery | .08 | .04 | .01 |
| ☐ U36 Allen Pinkett | .08 | .04 | .01 |
| ☐ U37 Tim Barnett | .35 | .16 | .04 |
| ☐ U38 Dan Saleaumua | .08 | .04 | .01 |
| ☐ U39 Harvey Williams | .35 | .16 | .04 |
| ☐ U40 Nick Bell | .35 | .16 | .04 |
| ☐ U41 Roger Craig | .10 | .05 | .01 |
| ☐ U42 Ronnie Lott | .12 | .05 | .02 |
| ☐ U43 Todd Marinovich | .10 | .05 | .01 |
| ☐ U44 Robert Delpino | .10 | .05 | .01 |
| ☐ U45 Todd Lyght | .10 | .05 | .01 |
| ☐ U46 Robert Young | .35 | .16 | .04 |
| ☐ U47 Aaron Craver | .08 | .04 | .01 |
| ☐ U48 Mark Higgs | 1.25 | .55 | .16 |
| ☐ U49 Vestee Jackson | .08 | .04 | .01 |
| ☐ U50 Carl Lee | .08 | .04 | .01 |
| ☐ U51 Felix Wright | .08 | .04 | .01 |
| ☐ U52 Darrell Fullington | .08 | .04 | .01 |
| ☐ U53 Pat Harlow | .10 | .05 | .01 |
| ☐ U54 Eugene Lockhart | .08 | .04 | .01 |
| ☐ U55 Hugh Millen | .25 | .11 | .03 |
| ☐ U56 Leonard Russell | 2.50 | 1.15 | .30 |
| ☐ U57 Jon Vaughn | .25 | .11 | .03 |
| ☐ U58 Quinn Early | .10 | .05 | .01 |
| ☐ U59 Bobby Hebert | .12 | .05 | .02 |
| ☐ U60 Rickey Jackson | .10 | .05 | .01 |
| ☐ U61 Sam Mills | .10 | .05 | .01 |
| ☐ U62 Jarrod Bunch | .15 | .07 | .02 |
| ☐ U63 John Elliott | .08 | .04 | .01 |
| ☐ U64 Jeff Hostetler | .25 | .11 | .03 |
| ☐ U65 Ed McCaffrey | .30 | .14 | .04 |
| ☐ U66 Kanavis McGhee | .10 | .05 | .01 |
| ☐ U67 Mo Lewis | .15 | .07 | .02 |
| ☐ U68 Browning Nagle | .25 | .11 | .03 |
| ☐ U69 Blair Thomas | .10 | .05 | .01 |
| ☐ U70 Antone Davis | .08 | .04 | .01 |
| ☐ U71 Brad Goebel | .20 | .09 | .03 |
| (See card U74) | | | |
| ☐ U72 Jim McMahon | .12 | .05 | .02 |
| ☐ U73 Clyde Simmons | .10 | .05 | .01 |
| ☐ U74 Randal Hill UER | .75 | .35 | .09 |
| (Card number on back U71 instead of U74) | | | |
| ☐ U75 Eric Swann | .50 | .23 | .06 |
| ☐ U76 Tom Tupa | .10 | .05 | .01 |
| ☐ U77 Jeff Graham | 1.00 | .45 | .13 |
| ☐ U78 Eric Green | .20 | .09 | .03 |
| ☐ U79 Neil O'Donnell | 3.50 | 1.55 | .45 |
| ☐ U80 Huey Richardson | .08 | .04 | .01 |
| ☐ U81 Eric Bieniemy | .15 | .07 | .02 |
| ☐ U82 John Friesz | .15 | .07 | .02 |
| ☐ U83 Eric Moten | .08 | .04 | .01 |
| ☐ U84 Stanley Richard | .10 | .05 | .01 |
| ☐ U85 Todd Bowles | .08 | .04 | .01 |
| ☐ U86 Merton Hanks | .20 | .09 | .03 |
| ☐ U87 Tim Harris | .10 | .05 | .01 |
| ☐ U88 Pierce Holt | .08 | .04 | .01 |
| ☐ U89 Ted Washington | .08 | .04 | .01 |
| ☐ U90 John Kasay | .20 | .09 | .03 |
| ☐ U91 Dan McGwire | .15 | .07 | .02 |
| ☐ U92 Lawrence Dawsey | .50 | .23 | .06 |
| ☐ U93 Charles McRae | .08 | .04 | .01 |
| ☐ U94 Jesse Solomon | .08 | .04 | .01 |
| ☐ U95 Robert Wilson | .08 | .04 | .01 |
| ☐ U96 Ricky Ervins | .40 | .18 | .05 |
| ☐ U97 Charles Mann | .10 | .05 | .01 |
| ☐ U98 Bobby Wilson | .10 | .05 | .01 |
| ☐ U99 Jerry Rice | 1.25 | .55 | .16 |
| Pro-Visions | | | |
| ☐ U100 Checklist 1-100 | .10 | .05 | .01 |
| (Nick Bell and Jim McMahon) | | | |

# 1992 Ultra

This 450-card set measures the standard size (2 1/2" by 3 1/2") and features full-bleed color action player photos. The pictures are full-bleed except at the bottom where a diagonal gold foil stripe separates the photo from a green marbleized area. Within this area are bars in the team's colors that contain the player's name, team name, and position. The horizontal backs display both close-up and action cut-out player photos against a team-color coded football field design. Superimposed over the pictures are the player's name and statistics in bars matching the team colors. Rounding out the back is a green marbleized area on the right edge containing the team logo and a player biography. The cards are numbered on the back and checklisted below alphabetically according to teams as follows: Atlanta Falcons (1-16), Buffalo Bills (17-33), Chicago Bears (34-50), Cincinnati Bengals (51-63), Cleveland Browns (64-76), Dallas Cowboys (77-92), Denver Broncos (93-110), Detroit Lions (111-125), Green Bay Packers (126-139), Houston Oilers (140-156), Indianapolis Colts (157-166), Kansas City Chiefs (167-184), Los Angeles Raiders (185-202), Los Angeles Rams (203-215), Miami Dolphins (216-229), Minnesota Vikings (230-242), New England Patriots (243-255), New Orleans Saints (256-271), New York Giants (272-288), New York Jets (289-303), Philadelphia Eagles (304-316), Phoenix Cardinals (317-328), Pittsburgh Steelers (329-340), San Diego Chargers (341-355), San Francisco 49ers (356-371), Seattle Seahawks (372-384), Tampa Bay Buccaneers (385-398), and Washington Redskins (399-416). The set closes with Draft Picks (417-446) and Checklists (447-450). Rookie Cards include Edgar Bennett, Steve Bono, Terrell Buckley, Amp Lee, and Tommy Vardell.

| | MINT | EXC | G-VG |
|---|---|---|---|
| COMPLETE SET (450) | 20.00 | 9.00 | 2.50 |
| COMMON PLAYER (1-450) | .05 | .02 | .01 |
| ☐ 1 Steve Broussard | .10 | .05 | .01 |
| ☐ 2 Rick Bryan | .05 | .02 | .01 |
| ☐ 3 Scott Case | .05 | .02 | .01 |
| ☐ 4 Darion Conner | .05 | .02 | .01 |
| ☐ 5 Bill Fralic | .05 | .02 | .01 |
| ☐ 6 Moe Gardner | .05 | .02 | .01 |
| ☐ 7 Tim Green | .05 | .02 | .01 |
| ☐ 8 Michael Haynes | .50 | .23 | .06 |
| ☐ 9 Chris Hinton | .05 | .02 | .01 |
| ☐ 10 Mike Kenn | .08 | .04 | .01 |
| ☐ 11 Tim McKyer | .08 | .04 | .01 |
| ☐ 12 Chris Miller | .10 | .05 | .01 |
| ☐ 13 Erric Pegram | .50 | .23 | .06 |
| ☐ 14 Mike Pritchard | .50 | .23 | .06 |
| ☐ 15 Andre Rison | .40 | .18 | .05 |
| ☐ 16 Jessie Tuggle | .05 | .02 | .01 |
| ☐ 17 Carlton Bailey | .30 | .14 | .04 |
| ☐ 18 Howard Ballard | .05 | .02 | .01 |
| ☐ 19 Cornelius Bennett | .10 | .05 | .01 |
| ☐ 20 Shane Conlan | .08 | .04 | .01 |
| ☐ 21 Kenneth Davis | .08 | .04 | .01 |

| Card | Price 1 | Price 2 | Price 3 |
|---|---|---|---|
| ☐ 22 Kent Hull | .05 | .02 | .01 |
| ☐ 23 Mark Kelso | .05 | .02 | .01 |
| ☐ 24 James Lofton | .10 | .05 | .01 |
| ☐ 25 Keith McKeller | .05 | .02 | .01 |
| ☐ 26 Nate Odomes | .08 | .04 | .01 |
| ☐ 27 Jim Ritcher | .05 | .02 | .01 |
| ☐ 28 Leon Seals | .05 | .02 | .01 |
| ☐ 29 Darryl Talley | .08 | .04 | .01 |
| ☐ 30 Steve Tasker | .08 | .04 | .01 |
| ☐ 31 Thurman Thomas | .60 | .25 | .08 |
| ☐ 32 Will Wolford | .05 | .02 | .01 |
| ☐ 33 Jeff Wright | .05 | .02 | .01 |
| ☐ 34 Neal Anderson | .08 | .04 | .01 |
| ☐ 35 Trace Armstrong | .05 | .02 | .01 |
| ☐ 36 Mark Carrier | .08 | .04 | .01 |
| ☐ 37 Wendell Davis | .05 | .02 | .01 |
| ☐ 38 Richard Dent | .08 | .04 | .01 |
| ☐ 39 Shaun Gayle | .05 | .02 | .01 |
| ☐ 40 Jim Harbaugh | .08 | .04 | .01 |
| ☐ 41 Jay Hilgenberg | .08 | .04 | .01 |
| ☐ 42 Darren Lewis | .05 | .02 | .01 |
| ☐ 43 Steve McMichael | .08 | .04 | .01 |
| ☐ 44 Anthony Morgan | .05 | .02 | .01 |
| ☐ 45 Brad Muster | .08 | .04 | .01 |
| ☐ 46 William Perry | .08 | .04 | .01 |
| ☐ 47 John Roper | .05 | .02 | .01 |
| ☐ 48 Lemuel Stinson | .05 | .02 | .01 |
| ☐ 49 Tom Waddle | .10 | .05 | .01 |
| ☐ 50 Donnell Woolford | .05 | .02 | .01 |
| ☐ 51 Leo Barker | .05 | .02 | .01 |
| ☐ 52 Eddie Brown | .05 | .02 | .01 |
| ☐ 53 James Francis | .08 | .04 | .01 |
| ☐ 54 David Fulcher UER | .05 | .02 | .01 |
| (Photo on back actually Eddie Brown) | | | |
| ☐ 55 David Grant | .05 | .02 | .01 |
| ☐ 56 Harold Green | .08 | .04 | .01 |
| ☐ 57 Rodney Holman | .05 | .02 | .01 |
| ☐ 58 Lee Johnson | .05 | .02 | .01 |
| ☐ 59 Tim Krumrie | .05 | .02 | .01 |
| ☐ 60 Tim McGee | .05 | .02 | .01 |
| ☐ 61 Alonzo Mitz | .05 | .02 | .01 |
| ☐ 62 Anthony Munoz | .08 | .04 | .01 |
| ☐ 63 Alfred Williams | .05 | .02 | .01 |
| ☐ 64 Stephen Braggs | .05 | .02 | .01 |
| ☐ 65 Richard Brown | .05 | .02 | .01 |
| ☐ 66 Randy Hilliard | .05 | .02 | .01 |
| ☐ 67 Leroy Hoard | .08 | .04 | .01 |
| ☐ 68 Michael Jackson | .15 | .07 | .02 |
| ☐ 69 Mike Johnson | .05 | .02 | .01 |
| ☐ 70 James Jones | .05 | .02 | .01 |
| ☐ 71 Tony Jones | .05 | .02 | .01 |
| ☐ 72 Ed King | .05 | .02 | .01 |
| ☐ 73 Kevin Mack | .08 | .04 | .01 |
| ☐ 74 Clay Matthews | .08 | .04 | .01 |
| ☐ 75 Eric Metcalf | .10 | .05 | .01 |
| ☐ 76 Vince Newsome | .05 | .02 | .01 |
| ☐ 77 Steve Beuerlein | .30 | .14 | .04 |
| ☐ 78 Larry Brown | .05 | .02 | .01 |
| ☐ 79 Tony Casillas | .05 | .02 | .01 |
| ☐ 80 Alvin Harper | .40 | .18 | .05 |
| ☐ 81 Issiac Holt | .05 | .02 | .01 |
| ☐ 82 Ray Horton | .05 | .02 | .01 |
| ☐ 83 Michael Irvin | .75 | .35 | .09 |
| ☐ 84 Daryl Johnston | .10 | .05 | .01 |
| ☐ 85 Kelvin Martin | .08 | .04 | .01 |
| ☐ 86 Ken Norton | .08 | .04 | .01 |
| ☐ 87 Jay Novacek | .25 | .11 | .03 |
| ☐ 88 Emmitt Smith | 4.00 | 1.80 | .50 |
| ☐ 89 Vinson Smith | .20 | .09 | .03 |
| ☐ 90 Mark Stepnoski | .05 | .02 | .01 |
| ☐ 91 Tony Tolbert | .05 | .02 | .01 |
| ☐ 92 Alexander Wright | .08 | .04 | .01 |
| ☐ 93 Steve Atwater | .08 | .04 | .01 |
| ☐ 94 Tyrone Braxton | .05 | .02 | .01 |
| ☐ 95 Michael Brooks | .05 | .02 | .01 |
| ☐ 96 Mike Croel | .08 | .04 | .01 |
| ☐ 97 John Elway | .75 | .35 | .09 |
| ☐ 98 Simon Fletcher | .08 | .04 | .01 |
| ☐ 99 Gaston Green | .08 | .04 | .01 |
| ☐ 100 Mark Jackson | .08 | .04 | .01 |
| ☐ 101 Keith Kartz | .05 | .02 | .01 |
| ☐ 102 Greg Kragen | .05 | .02 | .01 |
| ☐ 103 Greg Lewis | .05 | .02 | .01 |
| ☐ 104 Karl Mecklenburg | .08 | .04 | .01 |
| ☐ 105 Derek Russell | .08 | .04 | .01 |
| ☐ 106 Steve Sewell | .05 | .02 | .01 |
| ☐ 107 Dennis Smith | .08 | .04 | .01 |
| ☐ 108 David Treadwell | .05 | .02 | .01 |
| ☐ 109 Kenny Walker | .05 | .02 | .01 |
| ☐ 110 Michael Young | .05 | .02 | .01 |
| ☐ 111 Jerry Ball | .08 | .04 | .01 |
| ☐ 112 Bennie Blades | .05 | .02 | .01 |
| ☐ 113 Lomas Brown | .05 | .02 | .01 |
| ☐ 114 Scott Conover | .15 | .07 | .02 |
| ☐ 115 Ray Crockett | .05 | .02 | .01 |
| ☐ 116 Mel Gray | .05 | .02 | .01 |
| ☐ 117 Willie Green | .05 | .02 | .01 |
| ☐ 118 Erik Kramer | .15 | .07 | .02 |
| ☐ 119 Dan Owens | .05 | .02 | .01 |
| ☐ 120 Rodney Peete | .08 | .04 | .01 |
| ☐ 121 Brett Perriman | .08 | .04 | .01 |
| ☐ 122 Barry Sanders | 2.00 | .90 | .25 |
| ☐ 123 Chris Spielman | .08 | .04 | .01 |
| ☐ 124 Marc Spindler | .05 | .02 | .01 |
| ☐ 125 Willie White | .05 | .02 | .01 |
| ☐ 126 Tony Bennett | .08 | .04 | .01 |
| ☐ 127 Matt Brock | .05 | .02 | .01 |
| ☐ 128 LeRoy Butler | .05 | .02 | .01 |
| ☐ 129 Chuck Cecil | .05 | .02 | .01 |
| ☐ 130 Johnny Holland | .05 | .02 | .01 |
| ☐ 131 Perry Kemp | .05 | .02 | .01 |
| ☐ 132 Don Majkowski | .08 | .04 | .01 |
| ☐ 133 Tony Mandarich | .05 | .02 | .01 |
| ☐ 134 Brian Noble | .05 | .02 | .01 |
| ☐ 135 Bryce Paup | .05 | .02 | .01 |
| ☐ 136 Sterling Sharpe | .75 | .35 | .09 |
| ☐ 137 Darrell Thompson | .08 | .04 | .01 |
| ☐ 138 Mike Tomczak | .05 | .02 | .01 |
| ☐ 139 Vince Workman | .08 | .04 | .01 |
| ☐ 140 Ray Childress | .08 | .04 | .01 |
| ☐ 141 Cris Dishman | .08 | .04 | .01 |
| ☐ 142 Curtis Duncan | .08 | .04 | .01 |
| ☐ 143 William Fuller | .05 | .02 | .01 |
| ☐ 144 Ernest Givins | .08 | .04 | .01 |
| ☐ 145 Haywood Jeffires | .10 | .05 | .01 |
| ☐ 146 Sean Jones | .05 | .02 | .01 |
| ☐ 147 Lamar Lathon | .05 | .02 | .01 |
| ☐ 148 Bruce Matthews | .08 | .04 | .01 |
| ☐ 149 Bubba McDowell | .05 | .02 | .01 |
| ☐ 150 Johnny Meads | .05 | .02 | .01 |
| ☐ 151 Warren Moon | .35 | .16 | .04 |
| ☐ 152 Mike Munchak | .08 | .04 | .01 |
| ☐ 153 Bo Orlando | .30 | .14 | .04 |
| ☐ 154 Al Smith | .05 | .02 | .01 |
| ☐ 155 Doug Smith | .05 | .02 | .01 |
| ☐ 156 Lorenzo White | .08 | .04 | .01 |
| ☐ 157 Chip Banks | .05 | .02 | .01 |
| ☐ 158 Duane Bickett | .05 | .02 | .01 |
| ☐ 159 Bill Brooks | .08 | .04 | .01 |
| ☐ 160 Jon Hand | .05 | .02 | .01 |
| ☐ 161 Jeff Herrod | .05 | .02 | .01 |
| ☐ 162 Jessie Hester | .05 | .02 | .01 |
| ☐ 163 Scott Radecic | .05 | .02 | .01 |
| ☐ 164 Rohn Stark | .05 | .02 | .01 |
| ☐ 165 Clarence Verdin | .05 | .02 | .01 |
| ☐ 166 Eugene Daniel | .05 | .02 | .01 |
| ☐ 167 John Alt | .05 | .02 | .01 |
| ☐ 168 Tim Barnett | .08 | .04 | .01 |
| ☐ 169 Tim Grunhard | .05 | .02 | .01 |
| ☐ 170 Dino Hackett | .05 | .02 | .01 |
| ☐ 171 Jonathan Hayes | .05 | .02 | .01 |
| ☐ 172 Bill Maas | .05 | .02 | .01 |
| ☐ 173 Chris Martin | .05 | .02 | .01 |
| ☐ 174 Christian Okoye | .08 | .04 | .01 |
| ☐ 175 Stephone Paige | .08 | .04 | .01 |
| ☐ 176 Jayice Pearson | .05 | .02 | .01 |
| ☐ 177 Kevin Porter | .05 | .02 | .01 |
| ☐ 178 Kevin Ross | .08 | .04 | .01 |
| ☐ 179 Dan Saleaumua | .05 | .02 | .01 |
| ☐ 180 Tracy Simien | .25 | .11 | .03 |
| ☐ 181 Neil Smith | .10 | .05 | .01 |
| ☐ 182 Derrick Thomas | .20 | .09 | .03 |
| ☐ 183 Robb Thomas | .05 | .02 | .01 |
| ☐ 184 Barry Word | .10 | .05 | .01 |
| ☐ 185 Marcus Allen | .08 | .04 | .01 |
| ☐ 186 Eddie Anderson | .05 | .02 | .01 |
| ☐ 187 Nick Bell | .08 | .04 | .01 |
| ☐ 188 Tim Brown | .30 | .14 | .04 |
| ☐ 189 Mervyn Fernandez | .05 | .02 | .01 |
| ☐ 190 Willie Gault | .08 | .04 | .01 |
| ☐ 191 Jeff Gossett | .05 | .02 | .01 |
| ☐ 192 Ethan Horton | .05 | .02 | .01 |
| ☐ 193 Jeff Jaeger | .05 | .02 | .01 |
| ☐ 194 Howie Long | .08 | .04 | .01 |
| ☐ 195 Ronnie Lott | .10 | .05 | .01 |
| ☐ 196 Todd Marinovich | .05 | .02 | .01 |
| ☐ 197 Don Mosebar | .05 | .02 | .01 |
| ☐ 198 Jay Schroeder | .08 | .04 | .01 |
| ☐ 199 Anthony Smith | .08 | .04 | .01 |
| ☐ 200 Greg Townsend | .05 | .02 | .01 |
| ☐ 201 Lionel Washington | .05 | .02 | .01 |
| ☐ 202 Steve Wisniewski | .05 | .02 | .01 |
| ☐ 203 Flipper Anderson | .08 | .04 | .01 |
| ☐ 204 Robert Delpino | .08 | .04 | .01 |
| ☐ 205 Henry Ellard | .08 | .04 | .01 |
| ☐ 206 Jim Everett | .10 | .05 | .01 |
| ☐ 207 Kevin Greene | .08 | .04 | .01 |
| ☐ 208 Darryl Henley | .05 | .02 | .01 |
| ☐ 209 Damone Johnson | .05 | .02 | .01 |
| ☐ 210 Larry Kelm | .05 | .02 | .01 |
| ☐ 211 Todd Lyght | .05 | .02 | .01 |
| ☐ 212 Jackie Slater | .08 | .04 | .01 |
| ☐ 213 Michael Stewart | .05 | .02 | .01 |

|  |  | | | |
|---|------|-----|-----|-----|
| ☐ 214 | Pat Terrell | .05 | .02 | .01 |
| ☐ 215 | Robert Young | .08 | .04 | .01 |
| ☐ 216 | Mark Clayton | .08 | .04 | .01 |
| ☐ 217 | Bryan Cox | .08 | .04 | .01 |
| ☐ 218 | Jeff Cross | .05 | .02 | .01 |
| ☐ 219 | Mark Duper | .08 | .04 | .01 |
| ☐ 220 | Harry Galbreath | .05 | .02 | .01 |
| ☐ 221 | David Griggs | .05 | .02 | .01 |
| ☐ 222 | Mark Higgs | .12 | .05 | .02 |
| ☐ 223 | Vestee Jackson | .05 | .02 | .01 |
| ☐ 224 | John Offerdahl | .08 | .04 | .01 |
| ☐ 225 | Louis Oliver | .08 | .04 | .01 |
| ☐ 226 | Tony Paige | .05 | .02 | .01 |
| ☐ 227 | Reggie Roby | .05 | .02 | .01 |
| ☐ 228 | Pete Stoyanovich | .08 | .04 | .01 |
| ☐ 229 | Richmond Webb | .08 | .04 | .01 |
| ☐ 230 | Terry Allen | .30 | .14 | .04 |
| ☐ 231 | Ray Berry | .05 | .02 | .01 |
| ☐ 232 | Anthony Carter | .08 | .04 | .01 |
| ☐ 233 | Cris Carter | .10 | .05 | .01 |
| ☐ 234 | Chris Doleman | .08 | .04 | .01 |
| ☐ 235 | Rich Gannon | .08 | .04 | .01 |
| ☐ 236 | Steve Jordan | .08 | .04 | .01 |
| ☐ 237 | Carl Lee | .05 | .02 | .01 |
| ☐ 238 | Randall McDaniel | .05 | .02 | .01 |
| ☐ 239 | Mike Merriweather | .05 | .02 | .01 |
| ☐ 240 | Harry Newsome | .05 | .02 | .01 |
| ☐ 241 | John Randle | .05 | .02 | .01 |
| ☐ 242 | Henry Thomas | .05 | .02 | .01 |
| ☐ 243 | Bruce Armstrong | .05 | .02 | .01 |
| ☐ 244 | Vincent Brown | .05 | .02 | .01 |
| ☐ 245 | Marv Cook | .08 | .04 | .01 |
| ☐ 246 | Irving Fryar | .08 | .04 | .01 |
| ☐ 247 | Pat Harlow | .05 | .02 | .01 |
| ☐ 248 | Maurice Hurst | .05 | .02 | .01 |
| ☐ 249 | Eugene Lockhart | .05 | .02 | .01 |
| ☐ 250 | Greg McMurtry | .05 | .02 | .01 |
| ☐ 251 | Hugh Millen | .08 | .04 | .01 |
| ☐ 252 | Leonard Russell | .35 | .16 | .04 |
| ☐ 253 | Chris Singleton | .05 | .02 | .01 |
| ☐ 254 | Andre Tippett | .08 | .04 | .01 |
| ☐ 255 | Jon Vaughn | .05 | .02 | .01 |
| ☐ 256 | Morten Andersen | .08 | .04 | .01 |
| ☐ 257 | Gene Atkins | .05 | .02 | .01 |
| ☐ 258 | Wesley Caroll | .05 | .02 | .01 |
| ☐ 259 | Jim Dombrowski | .05 | .02 | .01 |
| ☐ 260 | Quinn Early | .08 | .04 | .01 |
| ☐ 261 | Bobby Hebert | .10 | .05 | .01 |
| ☐ 262 | Joel Hilgenberg | .05 | .02 | .01 |
| ☐ 263 | Rickey Jackson | .08 | .04 | .01 |
| ☐ 264 | Vaughan Johnson | .08 | .04 | .01 |
| ☐ 265 | Eric Martin | .08 | .04 | .01 |
| ☐ 266 | Brett Maxie | .05 | .02 | .01 |
| ☐ 267 | Fred McAfee | .25 | .11 | .03 |
| ☐ 268 | Sam Mills | .08 | .04 | .01 |
| ☐ 269 | Pat Swilling | .08 | .04 | .01 |
| ☐ 270 | Floyd Turner | .05 | .02 | .01 |
| ☐ 271 | Steve Walsh | .05 | .02 | .01 |
| ☐ 272 | Stephen Baker | .05 | .02 | .01 |
| ☐ 273 | Jarrod Bunch | .05 | .02 | .01 |
| ☐ 274 | Mark Collins | .05 | .02 | .01 |
| ☐ 275 | John Elliott | .05 | .02 | .01 |
| ☐ 276 | Myron Guyton | .05 | .02 | .01 |
| ☐ 277 | Rodney Hampton | .60 | .25 | .08 |
| ☐ 278 | Jeff Hostetler | .20 | .09 | .03 |
| ☐ 279 | Mark Ingram | .05 | .02 | .01 |
| ☐ 280 | Pepper Johnson | .08 | .04 | .01 |
| ☐ 281 | Sean Landeta | .05 | .02 | .01 |
| ☐ 282 | Leonard Marshall | .08 | .04 | .01 |
| ☐ 283 | Kanavis McGhee | .05 | .02 | .01 |
| ☐ 284 | Dave Meggett | .08 | .04 | .01 |
| ☐ 285 | Bart Oates | .05 | .02 | .01 |
| ☐ 286 | Phil Simms | .10 | .05 | .01 |
| ☐ 287 | Reyna Thompson | .05 | .02 | .01 |
| ☐ 288 | Lewis Tillman | .08 | .04 | .01 |
| ☐ 289 | Brad Baxter | .08 | .04 | .01 |
| ☐ 290 | Mike Brim | .05 | .02 | .01 |
| ☐ 291 | Chris Burkett | .05 | .02 | .01 |
| ☐ 292 | Kyle Clifton | .05 | .02 | .01 |
| ☐ 293 | James Hasty | .05 | .02 | .01 |
| ☐ 294 | Joe Kelly | .05 | .02 | .01 |
| ☐ 295 | Jeff Lageman | .05 | .02 | .01 |
| ☐ 296 | Mo Lewis | .05 | .02 | .01 |
| ☐ 297 | Erik McMillan | .05 | .02 | .01 |
| ☐ 298 | Scott Mersereau | .05 | .02 | .01 |
| ☐ 299 | Rob Moore | .10 | .05 | .01 |
| ☐ 300 | Tony Stargell | .05 | .02 | .01 |
| ☐ 301 | Jim Sweeney | .05 | .02 | .01 |
| ☐ 302 | Marvin Washington | .05 | .02 | .01 |
| ☐ 303 | Lonnie Young | .05 | .02 | .01 |
| ☐ 304 | Eric Allen | .08 | .04 | .01 |
| ☐ 305 | Fred Barnett | .10 | .05 | .01 |
| ☐ 306 | Keith Byars | .08 | .04 | .01 |
| ☐ 307 | Byron Evans | .05 | .02 | .01 |
| ☐ 308 | Wes Hopkins | .05 | .02 | .01 |
| ☐ 309 | Keith Jackson | .10 | .05 | .01 |
| ☐ 310 | James Joseph | .05 | .02 | .01 |
| ☐ 311 | Seth Joyner | .08 | .04 | .01 |
| ☐ 312 | Roger Ruzek | .05 | .02 | .01 |
| ☐ 313 | Clyde Simmons | .08 | .04 | .01 |
| ☐ 314 | William Thomas | .05 | .02 | .01 |
| ☐ 315 | Reggie White | .30 | .14 | .04 |
| ☐ 316 | Calvin Williams | .10 | .05 | .01 |
| ☐ 317 | Rich Camarillo | .05 | .02 | .01 |
| ☐ 318 | Jeff Faulkner | .05 | .02 | .01 |
| ☐ 319 | Ken Harvey | .05 | .02 | .01 |
| ☐ 320 | Eric Hill | .05 | .02 | .01 |
| ☐ 321 | Johnny Johnson | .15 | .07 | .02 |
| ☐ 322 | Ernie Jones | .05 | .02 | .01 |
| ☐ 323 | Tim McDonald | .08 | .04 | .01 |
| ☐ 324 | Freddie Joe Nunn | .05 | .02 | .01 |
| ☐ 325 | Luis Sharpe | .05 | .02 | .01 |
| ☐ 326 | Eric Swann | .08 | .04 | .01 |
| ☐ 327 | Aeneas Williams | .05 | .02 | .01 |
| ☐ 328 | Mike Zordich | .05 | .02 | .01 |
| ☐ 329 | Gary Anderson | .05 | .02 | .01 |
| ☐ 330 | Bubby Brister | .08 | .04 | .01 |
| ☐ 331 | Barry Foster | .50 | .23 | .06 |
| ☐ 332 | Eric Green | .10 | .05 | .01 |
| ☐ 333 | Bryan Hinkle | .05 | .02 | .01 |
| ☐ 334 | Tunch Ilkin | .05 | .02 | .01 |
| ☐ 335 | Carnell Lake | .05 | .02 | .01 |
| ☐ 336 | Louis Lipps | .08 | .04 | .01 |
| ☐ 337 | David Little | .05 | .02 | .01 |
| ☐ 338 | Greg Lloyd | .05 | .02 | .01 |
| ☐ 339 | Neil O'Donnell | .75 | .35 | .09 |
| ☐ 340 | Rod Woodson | .10 | .05 | .01 |
| ☐ 341 | Rod Bernstine | .08 | .04 | .01 |
| ☐ 342 | Marion Butts | .10 | .05 | .01 |
| ☐ 343 | Gill Byrd | .08 | .04 | .01 |
| ☐ 344 | John Friesz | .08 | .04 | .01 |
| ☐ 345 | Burt Grossman | .05 | .02 | .01 |
| ☐ 346 | Courtney Hall | .05 | .02 | .01 |
| ☐ 347 | Ronnie Harmon | .05 | .02 | .01 |
| ☐ 348 | Shawn Jefferson | .05 | .02 | .01 |
| ☐ 349 | Nate Lewis | .08 | .04 | .01 |
| ☐ 350 | Craig McEwen | .05 | .02 | .01 |
| ☐ 351 | Eric Moten | .05 | .02 | .01 |
| ☐ 352 | Gary Plummer | .05 | .02 | .01 |
| ☐ 353 | Henry Rolling | .05 | .02 | .01 |
| ☐ 354 | Broderick Thompson | .05 | .02 | .01 |
| ☐ 355 | Derrick Walker | .05 | .02 | .01 |
| ☐ 356 | Harris Barton | .05 | .02 | .01 |
| ☐ 357 | Steve Bono | 1.00 | .45 | .13 |
| ☐ 358 | Todd Bowles | .05 | .02 | .01 |
| ☐ 359 | Dexter Carter | .08 | .04 | .01 |
| ☐ 360 | Michael Carter | .05 | .02 | .01 |
| ☐ 361 | Keith DeLong | .05 | .02 | .01 |
| ☐ 362 | Charles Haley | .08 | .04 | .01 |
| ☐ 363 | Merton Hanks | .08 | .04 | .01 |
| ☐ 364 | Tim Harris | .05 | .02 | .01 |
| ☐ 365 | Brent Jones | .10 | .05 | .01 |
| ☐ 366 | Guy McIntyre | .08 | .04 | .01 |
| ☐ 367 | Tom Rathman | .08 | .04 | .01 |
| ☐ 368 | Bill Romanowski | .05 | .02 | .01 |
| ☐ 369 | Jesse Sapolu | .05 | .02 | .01 |
| ☐ 370 | John Taylor | .10 | .05 | .01 |
| ☐ 371 | Steve Young | .75 | .35 | .09 |
| ☐ 372 | Robert Blackmon | .05 | .02 | .01 |
| ☐ 373 | Brian Blades | .08 | .04 | .01 |
| ☐ 374 | Jacob Green | .05 | .02 | .01 |
| ☐ 375 | Dwayne Harper | .05 | .02 | .01 |
| ☐ 376 | Andy Heck | .05 | .02 | .01 |
| ☐ 377 | Tommy Kane | .05 | .02 | .01 |
| ☐ 378 | John Kasay | .05 | .02 | .01 |
| ☐ 379 | Cortez Kennedy | .20 | .09 | .03 |
| ☐ 380 | Bryan Millard | .05 | .02 | .01 |
| ☐ 381 | Rufus Porter | .05 | .02 | .01 |
| ☐ 382 | Eugene Robinson | .05 | .02 | .01 |
| ☐ 383 | John L. Williams | .08 | .04 | .01 |
| ☐ 384 | Terry Wooden | .05 | .02 | .01 |
| ☐ 385 | Gary Anderson | .08 | .04 | .01 |
| ☐ 386 | Ian Beckles | .05 | .02 | .01 |
| ☐ 387 | Mark Carrier | .08 | .04 | .01 |
| ☐ 388 | Reggie Cobb | .10 | .05 | .01 |
| ☐ 389 | Tony Covington | .05 | .02 | .01 |
| ☐ 390 | Lawrence Dawsey | .10 | .05 | .01 |
| ☐ 391 | Ron Hall | .05 | .02 | .01 |
| ☐ 392 | Keith McCants | .05 | .02 | .01 |
| ☐ 393 | Charles McRae | .05 | .02 | .01 |
| ☐ 394 | Tim Newton | .05 | .02 | .01 |
| ☐ 395 | Jesse Solomon | .05 | .02 | .01 |
| ☐ 396 | Vinny Testaverde | .10 | .05 | .01 |
| ☐ 397 | Broderick Thomas | .05 | .02 | .01 |
| ☐ 398 | Robert Wilson | .05 | .02 | .01 |
| ☐ 399 | Earnest Byner | .08 | .04 | .01 |
| ☐ 400 | Gary Clark | .08 | .04 | .01 |
| ☐ 401 | Andre Collins | .05 | .02 | .01 |
| ☐ 402 | Brad Edwards | .05 | .02 | .01 |
| ☐ 403 | Kurt Gouveia | .05 | .02 | .01 |
| ☐ 404 | Darrell Green | .08 | .04 | .01 |
| ☐ 405 | Joe Jacoby | .05 | .02 | .01 |
| ☐ 406 | Jim Lachey | .05 | .02 | .01 |
| ☐ 407 | Chip Lohmiller | .08 | .04 | .01 |

| | | | |
|---|---|---|---|
| ☐ 408 Charles Mann | .08 | .04 | .01 |
| ☐ 409 Wilber Marshall | .08 | .04 | .01 |
| ☐ 410 Brian Mitchell | .08 | .04 | .01 |
| ☐ 411 Art Monk | .10 | .05 | .01 |
| ☐ 412 Mark Rypien | .10 | .05 | .01 |
| ☐ 413 Ricky Sanders | .08 | .04 | .01 |
| ☐ 414 Mark Schlereth | .15 | .07 | .02 |
| ☐ 415 Fred Stokes | .05 | .02 | .01 |
| ☐ 416 Bobby Wilson | .05 | .02 | .01 |
| ☐ 417 Corey Barlow | .15 | .07 | .02 |
| ☐ 418 Edgar Bennett | .50 | .23 | .06 |
| ☐ 419 Eddie Blake | .05 | .02 | .01 |
| ☐ 420 Terrell Buckley | .50 | .23 | .06 |
| ☐ 421 Willie Clay | .05 | .02 | .01 |
| ☐ 422 Rodney Culver | .20 | .09 | .03 |
| ☐ 423 Ed Cunningham | .05 | .02 | .01 |
| ☐ 424 Mark D'Onofrio | .05 | .02 | .01 |
| ☐ 425 Matt Darby | .05 | .02 | .01 |
| ☐ 426 Charles Davenport | .05 | .02 | .01 |
| ☐ 427 Will Furrer | .25 | .11 | .03 |
| ☐ 428 Keith Goganious | .05 | .02 | .01 |
| ☐ 429 Mario Bailey | .15 | .07 | .02 |
| ☐ 430 Chris Hakel | .15 | .07 | .02 |
| ☐ 431 Keith Hamilton | .25 | .11 | .03 |
| ☐ 432 Aaron Pierce | .15 | .07 | .02 |
| ☐ 433 Amp Lee | .50 | .23 | .06 |
| ☐ 434 Scott Lockwood | .15 | .07 | .02 |
| ☐ 435 Ricardo McDonald | .15 | .07 | .02 |
| ☐ 436 Dexter McNabb | .05 | .02 | .01 |
| ☐ 437 Chris Mims | .35 | .16 | .04 |
| ☐ 438 Mike Mooney | .20 | .09 | .03 |
| ☐ 439 Ray Roberts | .05 | .02 | .01 |
| ☐ 440 Patrick Rowe | .20 | .09 | .03 |
| ☐ 441 Leon Searcy | .05 | .02 | .01 |
| ☐ 442 Siran Stacy | .15 | .07 | .02 |
| ☐ 443 Kevin Turner | .30 | .14 | .04 |
| ☐ 444 Tommy Vardell | .40 | .18 | .05 |
| ☐ 445 Bob Whitfield | .20 | .09 | .03 |
| ☐ 446 Darryl Williams | .30 | .14 | .04 |
| ☐ 447 Checklist 1-110 | .05 | .02 | .01 |
| ☐ 448 Checklist 111-224 | .05 | .02 | .01 |
| ☐ 449 Checklist 230-340 UER (Missing 225-229) | .05 | .02 | .01 |
| ☐ 450 Checklist 341-450 | .05 | .02 | .01 |

| | | | |
|---|---|---|---|
| Pro Football Weekly NFL Offensive POY Buffalo Bills | | | |
| ☐ 6 Michael Irvin | 4.00 | 1.80 | .50 |
| Pro Bowl MVP Dallas Cowboys | | | |
| ☐ 7 Mike Croel | 1.25 | .55 | .16 |
| UPI AFC ROY Denver Broncos | | | |
| ☐ 8 Barry Sanders | 6.00 | 2.70 | .75 |
| Maxwell Club POY Detroit Lions | | | |
| ☐ 9 Pat Swilling | 1.25 | .55 | .16 |
| AP Defensive POY New Orleans Saints | | | |
| ☐ 10 Leonard Russell | 2.25 | 1.00 | .30 |
| Pro Football Weekly NFL Offensive ROY New England Patriots | | | |

## 1992 Ultra Chris Miller

Randomly inserted in the foil packs, this ten-card set is part of Fleer's signature series. Miller signed over 2,000 of his subset cards. Card numbers 11-12 were available only by mail for ten '92 Ultra wrappers plus 2.00. The cards measure the standard size (2 1/2" by 3 1/2"). The fronts display color action player photos with a grayish-black inner border and a maroon marbleized outer border. The player's name and the set title "Performance Highlights" appear in gold foil lettering in the bottom border. On a dusty rose marbleized background, the backs carry a color head shot and summary of Miller's football career. The cards are numbered on the back.

| | MINT | EXC | G-VG |
|---|---|---|---|
| COMPLETE SET (12) | 15.00 | 6.75 | 1.90 |
| COMMON C.MILLER (1-10) | 1.50 | .65 | .19 |
| COMMON SEND-OFF (11-12) | 2.00 | .90 | .25 |
| ☐ 1 Chris Miller (Rolling out to pass white jersey) | 1.50 | .65 | .19 |
| ☐ 2 Chris Miller (Ready to hand off ball, black jersey) | 1.50 | .65 | .19 |
| ☐ 3 Chris Miller (Standing in pocket; prepared to pass) | 1.50 | .65 | .19 |
| ☐ 4 Chris Miller (Ready to hand off) | 1.50 | .65 | .19 |
| ☐ 5 Chris Miller (Poised to pass; ball held in one hand; black uniform) | 1.50 | .65 | .19 |
| ☐ 6 Chris Miller (Poised to pass; both hands on ball) | 1.50 | .65 | .19 |
| ☐ 7 Chris Miller (Running up field; black uniform) | 1.50 | .65 | .19 |
| ☐ 8 Chris Miller (Rolling out and looking for receiver) | 1.50 | .65 | .19 |
| ☐ 9 Chris Miller (Passing; arm cocked back) | 1.50 | .65 | .19 |
| ☐ 10 Chris Miller (Running to right with ball at waist) | 1.50 | .65 | .19 |
| ☐ 11 Chris Miller (Left side shot; ball cocked behind head) | 2.00 | .90 | .25 |
| ☐ 12 Chris Miller (Front shot; just | 2.00 | .90 | .25 |

## 1992 Ultra Award Winners

This ten-card set was randomly inserted in 1992 Fleer Ultra foil packs. Each player featured was a recipient of an award for his performance during the 1991 season. The cards are standard size, 2 1/2" by 3 1/2". The player photos are full-bleed except at the bottom where a diagonal gold foil stripe separates the picture from a black marbleized area. The player's name and the award won are printed in gold foil in this marbleized area, and a black emblem with "Award Winner" and a banner in gold foil is superimposed toward the lower right corner.

| | MINT | EXC | G-VG |
|---|---|---|---|
| COMPLETE SET (10) | 16.00 | 7.25 | 2.00 |
| COMMON PLAYER (1-10) | 1.25 | .55 | .16 |
| ☐ 1 Mark Rypien Super Bowl XXVI MVP Washington Redskins | 1.75 | .80 | .22 |
| ☐ 2 Cornelius Bennett UPI AFC Defensive POY Buffalo Bills | 1.75 | .80 | .22 |
| ☐ 3 Anthony Munoz NFL Man of the Year Cincinnati Bengals | 1.25 | .55 | .16 |
| ☐ 4 Lawrence Dawsey UPI NFC ROY Tampa Bay Buccaneers | 1.25 | .55 | .16 |
| ☐ 5 Thurman Thomas | 3.00 | 1.35 | .40 |

after ball released)
☐ AU Chris Miller AU ........................ 65.00  29.00  8.25
(Certified autograph)

## 1992 Ultra Reggie White

Randomly inserted in the foil packs, this ten-card set is part of Fleer's signature series. White signed over 2,000 of his subset cards. Card numbers 11-12 were available only by mail for ten '92 Ultra wrappers plus 2.00. The cards measure the standard size (2 1/2" by 3 1/2"). The fronts display color action player photos with a green inner border and a gray marbleized outer border. The player's name and the set title "Career Highlights" appear in gold foil lettering in the bottom border. On a gray marbleized background, the backs carry a color head shot and summary of White's football career. Card numbers 11-12 have rose-colored backs. The cards are numbered on the back.

|  | MINT | EXC | G-VG |
| --- | --- | --- | --- |
| COMPLETE SET (12) | 20.00 | 9.00 | 2.50 |
| COMMON R.WHITE (1-10) | 1.75 | .80 | .22 |
| COMMON SEND-OFF (11-12) | 2.50 | 1.15 | .30 |
| ☐ 1 Reggie White (Rushing passer and being held by Cardinal) | 1.75 | .80 | .22 |
| ☐ 2 Reggie White (Tackling George Rogers) | 1.75 | .80 | .22 |
| ☐ 3 Reggie White (Rushing passer and beating Raider lineman) | 1.75 | .80 | .22 |
| ☐ 4 Reggie White (Rushing passer with Redskin Don Warren in background) | 1.75 | .80 | .22 |
| ☐ 5 Reggie White (Defensive posture in open field) | 1.75 | .80 | .22 |
| ☐ 6 Reggie White (Rushing passer in dark green jersey) | 1.75 | .80 | .22 |
| ☐ 7 Reggie White (Rushing passer with arms extended) | 1.75 | .80 | .22 |
| ☐ 8 Reggie White (Fighting off block of Redskin Ed Simmons) | 1.75 | .80 | .22 |
| ☐ 9 Reggie White (Watching from the sideline) | 1.75 | .80 | .22 |
| ☐ 10 Reggie White (Fighting off block of Cardinal Walter Reeves) | 1.75 | .80 | .22 |
| ☐ 11 Reggie White (Front shot; adjusting chin strap on helmet) | 2.50 | 1.15 | .30 |
| ☐ 12 Reggie White (Pass rushing to his left) | 2.50 | 1.15 | .30 |
| ☐ AU Reggie White AU (Certified autograph) | 100.00 | 45.00 | 12.50 |

## 1993 Ultra

The 1993 Fleer Ultra set comprises 500 standard-size (2 1/2" by 3 1/2") cards. The front carries a color action player shot that is borderless, except at the bottom, where a black marbleized area set off by a gold-foil line carries the player's team name and position in gold foil. A team-colored marbleized bar immediately above carries the player's name. The horizontal back sports a close-up and action cut-out player photo against a football stadium graphic. The player's name, biography, and 1992 statistics all appear toward the lower left. The cards are numbered on the back and checklisted below alphabetically according to teams as follows: Atlanta Falcons (1-18), Buffalo Bills (19-37), Chicago Bears (38-54), Cincinnati Bengals (55-69), Cleveland Browns (70-84), Dallas Cowboys (85-105), Denver Broncos (106-122), Detroit Lions (123-139), Green Bay Packers (140-157), Houston Oilers (158-176), Indianapolis Colts (177-192), Kansas City Chiefs (193-211), Los Angeles Raiders (212-230), Los Angeles Rams (231-247), Miami Dolphins (248-265), Minnesota Vikings (266-280), New England Patriots (281-296), New Orleans Saints (297-315), New York Giants (316-332), New York Jets (333-351), Philadelphia Eagles (352-370), Phoenix Cardinals (371-388), Pittsburgh Steelers (389-405), San Diego Chargers (406-424), San Francisco 49ers (425-444), Seattle Seahawks (445-461), Tampa Bay Buccaneers (462-477), and Washington Redskins (478-495). Rookie Cards include Jerome Bettis, Drew Bledsoe, Reggie Brooks, Terry Kirby, O.J. McDuffie, Natrone Means, Glyn Milburn and Rick Mirer.

|  | MINT | EXC | G-VG |
| --- | --- | --- | --- |
| COMPLETE SET (500) | 32.00 | 14.50 | 4.00 |
| COMMON PLAYER (1-500) | .10 | .05 | .01 |
| ☐ 1 Vinnie Clark | .10 | .05 | .01 |
| ☐ 2 Darion Conner | .10 | .05 | .01 |
| ☐ 3 Eric Dickerson | .15 | .07 | .02 |
| ☐ 4 Moe Gardner | .10 | .05 | .01 |
| ☐ 5 Tim Green | .10 | .05 | .01 |
| ☐ 6 Roger Harper | .25 | .11 | .03 |
| ☐ 7 Michael Haynes | .35 | .16 | .04 |
| ☐ 8 Bobby Hebert | .15 | .07 | .02 |
| ☐ 9 Chris Hinton | .10 | .05 | .01 |
| ☐ 10 Pierce Holt | .10 | .05 | .01 |
| ☐ 12 Lincoln Kennedy | .25 | .11 | .03 |
| ☐ 13 Chris Miller | .15 | .07 | .02 |
| ☐ 14 Mike Pritchard | .15 | .07 | .02 |
| ☐ 15 Andre Rison | .40 | .18 | .05 |
| ☐ 16 Deion Sanders | .30 | .14 | .04 |
| ☐ 17 Tony Smith | .10 | .05 | .01 |
| ☐ 18 Jessie Tuggle | .10 | .05 | .01 |
| ☐ 19 Howard Ballard | .10 | .05 | .01 |
| ☐ 20 Don Beebe | .15 | .07 | .02 |
| ☐ 21 Cornelius Bennett | .15 | .07 | .02 |
| ☐ 22 Bill Brooks | .10 | .05 | .01 |
| ☐ 23 Kenneth Davis | .10 | .05 | .01 |
| ☐ 24 Phil Hansen | .10 | .05 | .01 |
| ☐ 25 Henry Jones | .10 | .05 | .01 |
| ☐ 26 Jim Kelly | .40 | .18 | .05 |
| ☐ 27 Nate Odomes | .12 | .05 | .02 |
| ☐ 28 John Parrella | .15 | .07 | .02 |
| ☐ 29 Andre Reed | .15 | .07 | .02 |
| ☐ 30 Frank Reich | .12 | .05 | .02 |
| ☐ 31 Jim Ritcher | .10 | .05 | .01 |
| ☐ 32 Bruce Smith | .15 | .07 | .02 |
| ☐ 33 Thomas Smith | .20 | .09 | .03 |
| ☐ 34 Darryl Talley | .10 | .05 | .01 |
| ☐ 35 Steve Tasker | .10 | .05 | .01 |
| ☐ 36 Thurman Thomas | .75 | .35 | .09 |
| ☐ 37 Jeff Wright | .10 | .05 | .01 |
| ☐ 38 Neal Anderson | .12 | .05 | .02 |
| ☐ 39 Trace Armstrong | .10 | .05 | .01 |
| ☐ 40 Mark Carrier USC | .12 | .05 | .02 |
| ☐ 41 Curtis Conway | 1.00 | .45 | .13 |
| ☐ 42 Wendell Davis | .10 | .05 | .01 |
| ☐ 43 Richard Dent | .12 | .05 | .02 |
| ☐ 44 Shaun Gayle | .10 | .05 | .01 |
| ☐ 45 Jim Harbaugh | .12 | .05 | .02 |
| ☐ 46 Craig Heyward | .10 | .05 | .01 |
| ☐ 47 Darren Lewis | .10 | .05 | .01 |
| ☐ 48 Steve McMichael | .10 | .05 | .01 |
| ☐ 49 William Perry | .10 | .05 | .01 |
| ☐ 50 Carl Simpson | .20 | .09 | .03 |
| ☐ 51 Alonzo Spellman | .12 | .05 | .02 |
| ☐ 52 Keith Van Horne | .10 | .05 | .01 |
| ☐ 53 Tom Waddle | .15 | .07 | .02 |

| | | | |
|---|---|---|---|
| 54 Donnell Woolford | .10 | .05 | .01 |
| 55 John Copeland | .50 | .23 | .06 |
| 56 Derrick Fenner | .10 | .05 | .01 |
| 57 James Francis | .10 | .05 | .01 |
| 58 Harold Green | .12 | .05 | .02 |
| 59 David Klingler | .30 | .14 | .04 |
| 60 Tim Krumrie | .10 | .05 | .01 |
| 61 Ricardo McDonald | .10 | .05 | .01 |
| 62 Tony McGee | .40 | .18 | .05 |
| 63 Carl Pickens | .15 | .07 | .02 |
| 64 Lamar Rogers | .10 | .05 | .01 |
| 65 Jay Schroeder | .10 | .05 | .01 |
| 66 Daniel Stubbs | .10 | .05 | .01 |
| 67 Steve Tovar | .20 | .09 | .03 |
| 68 Alfred Williams | .10 | .05 | .01 |
| 69 Darryl Williams | .12 | .05 | .02 |
| 70 Jerry Ball | .10 | .05 | .01 |
| 71 David Brandon | .10 | .05 | .01 |
| 72 Rob Burnett | .10 | .05 | .01 |
| 73 Mark Carrier WR | .12 | .05 | .02 |
| 74 Steve Everitt | .20 | .09 | .03 |
| 75 Dan Footman | .25 | .11 | .03 |
| 76 Leroy Hoard | .12 | .05 | .02 |
| 77 Michael Jackson | .15 | .07 | .02 |
| 78 Mike Johnson | .10 | .05 | .01 |
| 79 Bernie Kosar | .15 | .07 | .02 |
| 80 Clay Matthews | .12 | .05 | .02 |
| 81 Eric Metcalf | .15 | .07 | .02 |
| 82 Michael Dean Perry | .15 | .07 | .02 |
| 83 Vinny Testaverde | .15 | .07 | .02 |
| 84 Tommy Vardell | .12 | .05 | .02 |
| 85 Troy Aikman | 2.50 | 1.15 | .30 |
| 86 Larry Brown | .10 | .05 | .01 |
| 87 Tony Casillas | .10 | .05 | .01 |
| 88 Thomas Everett | .10 | .05 | .01 |
| 89 Charles Haley | .12 | .05 | .02 |
| 90 Alvin Harper | .50 | .23 | .06 |
| 91 Michael Irvin | 1.00 | .45 | .13 |
| 92 Jim Jeffcoat | .10 | .05 | .01 |
| 93 Daryl Johnston | .15 | .07 | .02 |
| 94 Robert Jones | .10 | .05 | .01 |
| 95 Leon Lett | .60 | .25 | .08 |
| 96 Russell Maryland | .15 | .07 | .02 |
| 97 Nate Newton | .10 | .05 | .01 |
| 98 Ken Norton | .12 | .05 | .02 |
| 99 Jay Novacek | .15 | .07 | .02 |
| 100 Darrin Smith | .60 | .25 | .08 |
| 101 Emmitt Smith | 4.00 | 1.80 | .50 |
| 102 Kevin Smith | .12 | .05 | .02 |
| 103 Mark Stepnoski | .10 | .05 | .01 |
| 104 Tony Tolbert | .10 | .05 | .01 |
| 105 Kevin Williams | 1.00 | .45 | .13 |
| 106 Steve Atwater | .12 | .05 | .02 |
| 107 Rod Bernstine | .12 | .05 | .02 |
| 108 Mike Croel | .12 | .05 | .02 |
| 109 Robert Delpino | .12 | .05 | .02 |
| 110 Shane Dronett | .10 | .05 | .01 |
| 111 John Elway | 1.00 | .45 | .13 |
| 112 Simon Fletcher | .12 | .05 | .02 |
| 113 Greg Kragen | .10 | .05 | .01 |
| 114 Tommy Maddox | .25 | .11 | .03 |
| 115 Arthur Marshall | .40 | .18 | .05 |
| 116 Karl Mecklenburg | .10 | .05 | .01 |
| 117 Glyn Milburn | 1.75 | .80 | .22 |
| 118 Reggie Rivers | .35 | .16 | .04 |
| 119 Shannon Sharpe | .35 | .16 | .04 |
| 120 Dennis Smith | .10 | .05 | .01 |
| 121 Kenny Walker | .10 | .05 | .01 |
| 122 Dan Williams | .25 | .11 | .03 |
| 123 Bennie Blades | .10 | .05 | .01 |
| 124 Lomas Brown | .10 | .05 | .01 |
| 125 Bill Fralic | .10 | .05 | .01 |
| 126 Mel Gray | .10 | .05 | .01 |
| 127 Willie Green | .12 | .05 | .02 |
| 128 Jason Hanson | .10 | .05 | .01 |
| 129 Antonio London | .20 | .09 | .03 |
| 130 Ryan McNeil | .20 | .09 | .03 |
| 131 Herman Moore | .75 | .35 | .09 |
| 132 Rodney Peete | .12 | .05 | .02 |
| 133 Brett Perriman | .12 | .05 | .02 |
| 134 Kelvin Pritchett | .10 | .05 | .01 |
| 135 Barry Sanders | 1.50 | .65 | .19 |
| 136 Tracy Scroggins | .12 | .05 | .02 |
| 137 Chris Spielman | .10 | .05 | .01 |
| 138 Pat Swilling | .12 | .05 | .02 |
| 139 Andre Ware | .12 | .05 | .02 |
| 140 Edgar Bennett | .15 | .07 | .02 |
| 141 Tony Bennett | .10 | .05 | .01 |
| 142 Matt Brock | .10 | .05 | .01 |
| 143 Terrell Buckley | .15 | .07 | .02 |
| 144 LeRoy Butler | .10 | .05 | .01 |
| 145 Mark Clayton | .10 | .05 | .01 |
| 146 Brett Favre | 1.50 | .65 | .19 |
| 147 Jackie Harris | .50 | .23 | .06 |
| 148 Johnny Holland | .10 | .05 | .01 |
| 149 Bill Maas | .10 | .05 | .01 |
| 150 Brian Noble | .10 | .05 | .01 |

| | | | |
|---|---|---|---|
| 151 Bryce Paup | .10 | .05 | .01 |
| 152 Ken Ruettgers | .10 | .05 | .01 |
| 153 Sterling Sharpe | 1.00 | .45 | .13 |
| 154 Wayne Simmons | .25 | .11 | .03 |
| 155 John Stephens | .10 | .05 | .01 |
| 156 George Teague | .35 | .16 | .04 |
| 157 Reggie White | .25 | .11 | .03 |
| 158 Micheal Barrow | .10 | .05 | .01 |
| 159 Cody Carlson | .30 | .14 | .04 |
| 160 Ray Childress | .10 | .05 | .01 |
| 161 Cris Dishman | .10 | .05 | .01 |
| 162 Curtis Duncan | .10 | .05 | .01 |
| 163 William Fuller | .10 | .05 | .01 |
| 164 Ernest Givins | .12 | .05 | .02 |
| 165 Brad Hopkins | .20 | .09 | .03 |
| 166 Haywood Jeffires | .15 | .07 | .02 |
| 167 Lamar Lathon | .10 | .05 | .01 |
| 168 Wilber Marshall | .12 | .05 | .02 |
| 169 Bruce Matthews | .12 | .05 | .02 |
| 170 Bubba McDowell | .10 | .05 | .01 |
| 171 Warren Moon | .30 | .14 | .04 |
| 172 Mike Munchak | .12 | .05 | .02 |
| 173 Eddie Robinson | .10 | .05 | .01 |
| 174 Al Smith | .10 | .05 | .01 |
| 175 Lorenzo White | .12 | .05 | .02 |
| 176 Lee Williams | .10 | .05 | .01 |
| 177 Chip Banks | .10 | .05 | .01 |
| 178 John Baylor | .10 | .05 | .01 |
| 179 Duane Bickett | .10 | .05 | .01 |
| 180 Kerry Cash | .10 | .05 | .01 |
| 181 Quentin Coryatt | .15 | .07 | .02 |
| 182 Rodney Culver | .25 | .05 | .01 |
| 183 Steve Emtman | .12 | .05 | .02 |
| 184 Jeff George | .30 | .14 | .04 |
| 185 Jeff Herrod | .10 | .05 | .01 |
| 186 Jessie Hester | .10 | .05 | .01 |
| 187 Anthony Johnson | .10 | .05 | .01 |
| 188 Reggie Langhorne | .10 | .05 | .02 |
| 189 Roosevelt Potts | .50 | .23 | .06 |
| 190 Rohn Stark | .10 | .05 | .01 |
| 191 Clarence Verdin | .10 | .05 | .01 |
| 192 Will Wolford | .10 | .05 | .01 |
| 193 Marcus Allen | .25 | .11 | .03 |
| 194 John Alt | .10 | .05 | .01 |
| 195 Tim Barnett | .12 | .05 | .02 |
| 196 J.J.Birden | .10 | .05 | .01 |
| 197 Dale Carter | .15 | .07 | .02 |
| 198 Willie Davis | .20 | .09 | .03 |
| 199 Jaime Fields | .15 | .07 | .02 |
| 200 Dave Krieg | .15 | .05 | .02 |
| 201 Nick Lowery | .10 | .05 | .01 |
| 202 Charles Mincy | .30 | .14 | .04 |
| 203 Joe Montana | 3.00 | 1.35 | .40 |
| 204 Christian Okoye | .12 | .05 | .01 |
| 205 Dan Saleaumua | .10 | .05 | .01 |
| 206 Will Shields | .15 | .07 | .02 |
| 207 Tracy Simien | .10 | .05 | .01 |
| 208 Neil Smith | .15 | .07 | .02 |
| 209 Derrick Thomas | .30 | .14 | .04 |
| 210 Harvey Williams | .15 | .07 | .02 |
| 211 Barry Word | .15 | .07 | .02 |
| 212 Eddie Anderson | .10 | .05 | .01 |
| 213 Patrick Bates | .20 | .09 | .03 |
| 214 Nick Bell | .12 | .05 | .02 |
| 215 Tim Brown | .40 | .18 | .05 |
| 216 Willie Gault | .12 | .05 | .02 |
| 217 Gaston Green | .12 | .05 | .02 |
| 218 Billy Joe Hobert | .75 | .35 | .09 |
| 219 Ethan Horton | .10 | .05 | .01 |
| 220 Jeff Hostetler | .15 | .07 | .02 |
| 221 James Lofton | .15 | .07 | .02 |
| 222 Howie Long | .12 | .05 | .02 |
| 223 Todd Marinovich | .10 | .05 | .01 |
| 224 Terry McDaniel | .10 | .05 | .01 |
| 225 Winston Moss | .10 | .05 | .01 |
| 226 Anthony Smith | .10 | .05 | .01 |
| 227 Greg Townsend | .10 | .05 | .01 |
| 228 Aaron Wallace | .10 | .05 | .01 |
| 229 Lionel Washington | .10 | .05 | .01 |
| 230 Steve Wisniewski | .10 | .05 | .01 |
| 231 Willie Anderson | .10 | .05 | .01 |
| 232 Jerome Bettis | 6.00 | 2.70 | .75 |
| 233 Marc Boutte | .10 | .05 | .01 |
| 234 Shane Conlan | .10 | .05 | .01 |
| 235 Troy Drayton | .50 | .23 | .06 |
| 236 Henry Ellard | .12 | .05 | .02 |
| 237 Jim Everett | .12 | .05 | .01 |
| 238 Cleveland Gary | .12 | .05 | .02 |
| 239 Sean Gilbert | .12 | .05 | .02 |
| 240 Darryl Henley | .10 | .05 | .01 |
| 241 David Lang | .10 | .05 | .01 |
| 242 Todd Lyght | .10 | .05 | .01 |
| 243 Anthony Newman | .10 | .05 | .01 |
| 244 Roman Phifer | .10 | .05 | .01 |
| 245 Gerald Robinson | .10 | .05 | .01 |
| 246 Henry Rolling | .10 | .05 | .01 |
| 247 Jackie Slater | .10 | .05 | .01 |

| □ | | | | |
|---|---|---|---|---|
| 248 Keith Byars | .12 | .05 | .02 |
| 249 Marco Coleman | .12 | .05 | .02 |
| 250 Bryan Cox | .12 | .05 | .02 |
| 251 Jeff Cross | .10 | .05 | .01 |
| 252 Irving Fryar | .10 | .05 | .01 |
| 253 Mark Higgs | .15 | .07 | .02 |
| 254 Dwight Hollier | .15 | .07 | .02 |
| 255 Mark Ingram | .12 | .05 | .02 |
| 256 Keith Jackson | .10 | .05 | .01 |
| 257 Terry Kirby | 2.50 | 1.15 | .30 |
| 258 Dan Marino | 1.50 | .65 | .19 |
| 259 O.J.McDuffie | 2.50 | 1.15 | .30 |
| 260 John Offerdahl | .10 | .05 | .01 |
| 261 Louis Oliver | .10 | .05 | .01 |
| 262 Pete Stoyanovich | .10 | .05 | .01 |
| 263 Troy Vincent | .12 | .05 | .02 |
| 264 Richmond Webb | .10 | .05 | .01 |
| 265 Jarvis Williams | .10 | .05 | .01 |
| 266 Terry Allen | .15 | .07 | .02 |
| 267 Anthony Carter | .12 | .05 | .02 |
| 268 Cris Carter | .15 | .07 | .02 |
| 269 Roger Craig | .12 | .05 | .02 |
| 270 Jack Del Rio | .10 | .05 | .01 |
| 271 Chris Doleman | .12 | | |
| 272 Qadry Ismail | 1.00 | .45 | .13 |
| 273 Steve Jordan | .12 | .05 | .02 |
| 274 Randall McDaniel | .10 | .05 | .01 |
| 275 Audray McMillian | .10 | .05 | .01 |
| 276 John Randle | .10 | .05 | .01 |
| 277 Sean Salisbury | .12 | .05 | .02 |
| 278 Todd Scott | .10 | .05 | .01 |
| 279 Robert Smith | .75 | .35 | .09 |
| 280 Henry Thomas | .10 | .05 | .01 |
| 281 Ray Agnew | .10 | .05 | .01 |
| 282 Bruce Armstrong | .10 | .05 | .01 |
| 283 Drew Bledsoe | 6.00 | 2.70 | .75 |
| 284 Vincent Brisby | 1.00 | .45 | .13 |
| 285 Vincent Brown | .10 | .05 | .01 |
| 286 Eugene Chung | .10 | .05 | .01 |
| 287 Marv Cook | .10 | .05 | .01 |
| 288 Pat Harlow | .10 | .05 | .01 |
| 289 Jerome Henderson | .10 | .05 | .01 |
| 290 Greg McMurtry | .10 | .05 | .01 |
| 291 Leonard Russell | .12 | .05 | .02 |
| 292 Chris Singleton | .10 | .05 | .01 |
| 293 Chris Slade | .50 | .23 | .06 |
| 294 Andre Tippett | .10 | .05 | .01 |
| 295 Brent Williams | .10 | .05 | .01 |
| 296 Scott Zolak | .10 | .05 | .01 |
| 297 Morten Andersen | .12 | .05 | .02 |
| 298 Gene Atkins | .10 | .05 | .01 |
| 299 Mike Buck | .10 | .05 | .01 |
| 300 Toi Cook | .10 | .05 | .01 |
| 301 Jim Dombrowski | .10 | .05 | .01 |
| 302 Vaughn Dunbar | .12 | .05 | .02 |
| 303 Quinn Early | .12 | .05 | .02 |
| 304 Joel Hilgenberg | .10 | .05 | .01 |
| 305 Dalton Hilliard | .10 | .05 | .01 |
| 306 Rickey Jackson | .12 | .05 | .02 |
| 307 Vaughan Johnson | .10 | .05 | .01 |
| 308 Reginald Jones | .10 | .05 | .01 |
| 309 Eric Martin | .12 | .05 | .02 |
| 310 Wayne Martin | .10 | .05 | .01 |
| 311 Sam Mills | .12 | .05 | .02 |
| 312 Brad Muster | .12 | .05 | .02 |
| 313 Willie Roaf | .20 | .09 | .03 |
| 314 Irv Smith | .40 | .18 | .05 |
| 315 Wade Wilson | .12 | .05 | .02 |
| 316 Carlton Bailey | .10 | .05 | .01 |
| 317 Michael Brooks | .10 | .05 | .01 |
| 318 Derek Brown | .12 | .05 | .02 |
| 319 Marcus Buckley | .15 | .07 | .02 |
| 320 Jarrod Bunch | .10 | .05 | .01 |
| 321 Mark Collins | .10 | .05 | .01 |
| 322 Eric Dorsey | .10 | .05 | .01 |
| 323 Rodney Hampton | .75 | .35 | .09 |
| 324 Mark Jackson | .12 | .05 | .02 |
| 325 Pepper Johnson | .10 | .05 | .01 |
| 326 Ed McCaffrey | .10 | .05 | .01 |
| 327 David Meggett | .12 | .05 | .02 |
| 328 Bart Oates | .10 | .05 | .01 |
| 329 Mike Sherrard | .10 | .05 | .01 |
| 330 Phil Simms | .15 | .07 | .02 |
| 331 Michael Strahan | .20 | .09 | .03 |
| 332 Lawrence Taylor | .15 | .07 | .02 |
| 333 Brad Baxter | .12 | .05 | .02 |
| 334 Chris Burkett | .10 | .05 | .01 |
| 335 Kyle Clifton | .10 | .05 | .01 |
| 336 Boomer Esiason | .25 | .11 | .03 |
| 337 James Hasty | .10 | .05 | .01 |
| 338 Johnny Johnson | .15 | .07 | .02 |
| 339 Marvin Jones | .40 | .18 | .05 |
| 340 Jeff Lageman | .10 | .05 | .01 |
| 341 Mo Lewis | .10 | .05 | .01 |
| 342 Ronnie Lott | .15 | .07 | .02 |
| 343 Leonard Marshall | .10 | .05 | .01 |
| 344 Johnny Mitchell | .50 | .23 | .06 |
| 345 Rob Moore | .15 | .07 | .02 |
| 346 Browning Nagle | .12 | .05 | .02 |
| 347 Coleman Rudolph | .20 | .09 | .03 |
| 348 Blair Thomas | .12 | .05 | .02 |
| 349 Eric Thomas | .10 | .05 | .01 |
| 350 Brian Washington | .10 | .05 | .01 |
| 351 Marvin Washington | .10 | .05 | .01 |
| 352 Eric Allen | .12 | .05 | .02 |
| 353 Victor Bailey | .60 | .25 | .08 |
| 354 Fred Barnett | .15 | .07 | .02 |
| 355 Mark Bavaro | .10 | .05 | .01 |
| 356 Randall Cunningham | .20 | .09 | .03 |
| 357 Byron Evans | .10 | .05 | .01 |
| 358 Andy Harmon | .10 | .05 | .01 |
| 359 Tim Harris | .10 | .05 | .01 |
| 360 Lester Holmes | .10 | .05 | .01 |
| 361 Seth Joyner | .12 | .05 | .02 |
| 362 Keith Millard | .10 | .05 | .01 |
| 363 Leonard Renfro | .15 | .07 | .02 |
| 364 Heath Sherman | .10 | .05 | .01 |
| 365 Vai Sikahema | .10 | .05 | .01 |
| 366 Clyde Simmons | .12 | .05 | .02 |
| 367 William Thomas | .10 | .05 | .01 |
| 368 Herschel Walker | .15 | .07 | .02 |
| 369 Andre Waters | .10 | .05 | .01 |
| 370 Calvin Williams | .15 | .07 | .02 |
| 371 Johnny Bailey | .10 | .05 | .01 |
| 372 Steve Beuerlein | .25 | .11 | .03 |
| 373 Rich Camarillo | .10 | .05 | .01 |
| 374 Chuck Cecil | .10 | .05 | .01 |
| 375 Chris Chandler | .12 | .05 | .02 |
| 376 Gary Clark | .12 | .05 | .02 |
| 377 Ben Coleman | .15 | .07 | .02 |
| 378 Ernest Dye | .20 | .09 | .03 |
| 379 Ken Harvey | .10 | .05 | .01 |
| 380 Garrison Hearst | 1.25 | .55 | .16 |
| 381 Randal Hill | .15 | .07 | .02 |
| 382 Robert Massey | .10 | .05 | .01 |
| 383 Freddie Joe Nunn | .10 | .05 | .01 |
| 384 Ricky Proehl | .12 | .05 | .02 |
| 385 Luis Sharpe | .10 | .05 | .01 |
| 386 Tyronne Stowe | .10 | .05 | .01 |
| 387 Eric Swann | .12 | .05 | .02 |
| 388 Aeneas Williams | .10 | .05 | .01 |
| 389 Chad Brown | .15 | .07 | .02 |
| 390 Dermontti Dawson | .10 | .05 | .01 |
| 391 Donald Evans | .10 | .05 | .01 |
| 392 Deon Figures | .30 | .14 | .04 |
| 393 Barry Foster | .50 | .23 | .06 |
| 394 Jeff Graham | .12 | .05 | .02 |
| 395 Eric Green | .15 | .07 | .02 |
| 396 Kevin Greene | .10 | .05 | .01 |
| 397 Carlton Haselrig | .10 | .05 | .01 |
| 398 Andre Hastings | .40 | .18 | .05 |
| 399 D.J. Johnson | .10 | .05 | .01 |
| 400 Carnell Lake | .10 | .05 | .01 |
| 401 Greg Lloyd | .10 | .05 | .01 |
| 402 Neil O'Donnell | .50 | .23 | .06 |
| 403 Darren Perry | .10 | .05 | .01 |
| 404 Mike Tomczak | .10 | .05 | .01 |
| 405 Rod Woodson | .15 | .07 | .02 |
| 406 Eric Bieniemy | .12 | .05 | .02 |
| 407 Marion Butts | .15 | .07 | .02 |
| 408 Gill Byrd | .10 | .05 | .01 |
| 409 Darren Carrington | .20 | .09 | .03 |
| 410 Darrien Gordon | .35 | .16 | .04 |
| 411 Burt Grossman | .10 | .05 | .01 |
| 412 Courtney Hall | .10 | .05 | .01 |
| 413 Ronnie Harmon | .15 | .07 | .02 |
| 414 Stan Humphries | .10 | .05 | .01 |
| 415 Nate Lewis | .12 | .05 | .02 |
| 416 Natrone Means | 2.00 | .90 | .25 |
| 417 Anthony Miller | .30 | .14 | .04 |
| 418 Chris Mims | .12 | .05 | .02 |
| 419 Leslie O'Neal | .12 | .05 | .02 |
| 420 Gary Plummer | .10 | .05 | .01 |
| 421 Stanley Richard | .10 | .05 | .01 |
| 422 Junior Seau | .15 | .07 | .02 |
| 423 Harry Swayne | .10 | .05 | .01 |
| 424 Jerrol Williams | .10 | .05 | .01 |
| 425 Harris Barton | .10 | .05 | .01 |
| 426 Steve Bono | .25 | .11 | .03 |
| 427 Kevin Fagan | .10 | .05 | .01 |
| 428 Don Griffin | .10 | .05 | .01 |
| 429 Dana Hall | .10 | .05 | .01 |
| 430 Adrian Hardy | .10 | .05 | .01 |
| 431 Brent Jones | .15 | .07 | .02 |
| 432 Todd Kelly | .15 | .07 | .02 |
| 433 Amp Lee | .12 | .05 | .02 |
| 434 Tim McDonald | .10 | .05 | .01 |
| 435 Guy McIntyre | .10 | .05 | .01 |
| 436 Tom Rathman | .12 | .05 | .02 |
| 437 Jerry Rice | 1.25 | .55 | .16 |
| 438 Bill Romanowski | .10 | .05 | .01 |
| 439 Dana Stubblefield | 1.00 | .45 | .13 |
| 440 John Taylor | .15 | .07 | .02 |
| 441 Steve Wallace | .10 | .05 | .01 |

| | | | |
|---|---|---|---|
| ☐ 442 Mike Walter | .10 | .05 | .01 |
| ☐ 443 Ricky Watters | .75 | .35 | .09 |
| ☐ 444 Steve Young | .50 | .23 | .06 |
| ☐ 445 Robert Blackmon | .10 | .05 | .01 |
| ☐ 446 Brian Blades | .12 | .05 | .02 |
| ☐ 447 Jeff Bryant | .10 | .05 | .01 |
| ☐ 448 Ferrell Edmunds | .10 | .05 | .01 |
| ☐ 449 Carlton Gray | .35 | .16 | .04 |
| ☐ 450 Dwayne Harper | .10 | .05 | .01 |
| ☐ 451 Andy Heck | .10 | .05 | .01 |
| ☐ 452 Tommy Kane | .10 | .05 | .01 |
| ☐ 453 Cortez Kennedy | .15 | .07 | .02 |
| ☐ 454 Kelvin Martin | .10 | .05 | .01 |
| ☐ 455 Dan McGwire | .12 | .05 | .02 |
| ☐ 456 Rick Mirer | 6.00 | 2.70 | .75 |
| ☐ 457 Rufus Porter | .10 | .05 | .01 |
| ☐ 458 Ray Roberts | .10 | .05 | .01 |
| ☐ 459 Eugene Robinson | .10 | .05 | .01 |
| ☐ 460 Chris Warren | .30 | .14 | .04 |
| ☐ 461 John L. Williams | .12 | .05 | .02 |
| ☐ 462 Gary Anderson | .10 | .05 | .01 |
| ☐ 463 Tyji Armstrong | .10 | .05 | .01 |
| ☐ 464 Reggie Cobb | .15 | .07 | .02 |
| ☐ 465 Eric Curry | .50 | .23 | .06 |
| ☐ 466 Lawrence Dawsey | .15 | .07 | .02 |
| ☐ 467 Steve DeBerg | .12 | .05 | .02 |
| ☐ 468 Santana Dotson | .15 | .07 | .02 |
| ☐ 469 Demetrius DuBose | .30 | .14 | .04 |
| ☐ 470 Paul Gruber | .10 | .05 | .01 |
| ☐ 471 Ron Hall | .10 | .05 | .01 |
| ☐ 472 Courtney Hawkins | .12 | .05 | .02 |
| ☐ 473 Hardy Nickerson | .10 | .05 | .01 |
| ☐ 474 Ricky Reynolds | .10 | .05 | .01 |
| ☐ 475 Broderick Thomas | .10 | .05 | .01 |
| ☐ 476 Mark Wheeler | .10 | .05 | .01 |
| ☐ 477 Jimmy Williams | .10 | .05 | .01 |
| ☐ 478 Carl Banks | .10 | .05 | .01 |
| ☐ 479 Reggie Brooks | 4.00 | 1.80 | .50 |
| ☐ 480 Earnest Byner | .12 | .05 | .02 |
| ☐ 481 Tom Carter | .40 | .18 | .05 |
| ☐ 482 Andre Collins | .10 | .05 | .01 |
| ☐ 483 Brad Edwards | .10 | .05 | .01 |
| ☐ 484 Ricky Ervins | .12 | .05 | .02 |
| ☐ 485 Kurt Gouveia | .10 | .05 | .01 |
| ☐ 486 Darrell Green | .12 | .05 | .02 |
| ☐ 487 Desmond Howard | .50 | .23 | .06 |
| ☐ 488 Jim Lachey | .10 | .05 | .01 |
| ☐ 489 Chip Lohmiller | .10 | .05 | .01 |
| ☐ 490 Charles Mann | .10 | .05 | .01 |
| ☐ 491 Tim McGee | .10 | .05 | .01 |
| ☐ 492 Brian Mitchell | .12 | .05 | .02 |
| ☐ 493 Art Monk | .15 | .07 | .02 |
| ☐ 494 Mark Rypien | .12 | .05 | .02 |
| ☐ 495 Ricky Sanders | .12 | .05 | .02 |
| ☐ 496 Checklist 1-126 Chip Lohmiller | .10 | .05 | .01 |
| ☐ 497 Checklist 127-254 Ricky Proehl | .10 | .05 | .01 |
| ☐ 498 Checklist 255-382 Randall Cunningham | .10 | .05 | .01 |
| ☐ 499 Checklist 383-500 Dave Meggett | .10 | .05 | .01 |
| ☐ 500 Inserts Checklist William Perry | .10 | .05 | .01 |

## 1993 Ultra All-Rookies

The 1993 Fleer All-Rookies set compises 10 standard-size (2 1/2" by 3 1/2") cards, randomly inserted in Fleer Ultra 14- and 19-card foil packs. The set spotlights 10 first-year players in the NFL. The full-bleed fronts feature action player cut-outs on bright orange scorched-earth backgrounds. Stamped in gold-foil at the bottom of the picture is the set title and the player's name. The horizontal back displays a background of orange fading to yellow with a close-up player cut-out

on the left side, and a white panel containing the player's name and highlights on the right. The cards are numbered on the back "X of 10."

| | MINT | EXC | G-VG |
|---|---|---|---|
| COMPLETE SET (10) | 50.00 | 23.00 | 6.25 |
| COMMON PLAYER (1-10) | 1.25 | .55 | .16 |
| ☐ 1 Patrick Bates Los Angeles Raiders | 1.25 | .55 | .16 |
| ☐ 2 Jerome Bettis Los Angeles Rams | 16.00 | 7.25 | 2.00 |
| ☐ 3 Drew Bledsoe New England Patriots | 16.00 | 7.25 | 2.00 |
| ☐ 4 Curtis Conway Cincinnati Bengals | 3.00 | 1.35 | .40 |
| ☐ 5 Garrison Hearst Phoenix Cardinals | 4.00 | 1.80 | .50 |
| ☐ 6 Qadry Ismail Minnesota Vikings | 3.00 | 1.35 | .40 |
| ☐ 7 Marvin Jones New York Jets | 1.25 | .55 | .16 |
| ☐ 8 Glyn Milburn Denver Broncos | 4.00 | 1.80 | .50 |
| ☐ 9 Rick Mirer Seattle Seahawks | 16.00 | 7.25 | 2.00 |
| ☐ 10 Kevin Williams Dallas Cowboys | 3.00 | 1.35 | .40 |

## 1993 Ultra Award Winners

The 1993 Fleer Ultra Award Winners set comprises ten standard-size (2 1/2" by 3 1/2") cards, randomly inserted in Fleer Ultra 14- and 19-card foil packs. The set spotlights MVP's of the AFC and NFC, Rookies of the Year and other awards. The borderless fronts feature close-up posed or action player cut-outs on gold metallic backgrounds. The set title appears at the top, with the player's name printed across the bottom. The back sports a player cut-out on a gold metallic background with light gold rays radiating from the center. The set title and player's name are stamped in silver foil at the top followed by the player's 1992 award and career highlights. The cards are numbered on the back "X of 10."

| | MINT | EXC | G-VG |
|---|---|---|---|
| COMPLETE SET (10) | 50.00 | 23.00 | 6.25 |
| COMMON PLAYER (1-10) | 2.50 | 1.15 | .30 |
| ☐ 1 Troy Aikman Dallas Cowboys | 20.00 | 9.00 | 2.50 |
| ☐ 2 Dale Carter Kansas City Chiefs | 2.50 | 1.15 | .30 |
| ☐ 3 Chris Doleman Minnesota Vikings | 2.50 | 1.15 | .30 |
| ☐ 4 Santana Dotson Tampa Bay Buccaneers | 2.50 | 1.15 | .30 |
| ☐ 5 Barry Foster Pittsburgh Steelers | 6.00 | 2.70 | .75 |
| ☐ 6 Jason Hanson Detroit Lions | 2.50 | 1.15 | .30 |
| ☐ 7 Cortez Kennedy Seattle Seahawks | 3.00 | 1.35 | .40 |
| ☐ 8 Carl Pickens Cincinnati Bengals | 3.00 | 1.35 | .40 |
| ☐ 9 Steve Tasker Buffalo Bills | 2.50 | 1.15 | .30 |
| ☐ 10 Steve Young San Francisco 49ers | 6.00 | 2.70 | .75 |

## 1993 Ultra Michael Irvin

Subtitled Performance Highlights and randomly inserted in 1993 Fleer Ultra packs, these ten standard-size (2 1/2" by 3 1/2") cards feature on their fronts color action shots of Irvin that are borderless, except at

| | MINT | EXC | G-VG |
|---|---|---|---|
| Houston Oilers | | | |
| ☐ 2 Henry Jones | 3.00 | 1.35 | .40 |
| Buffalo Bills | | | |
| ☐ 3 Audray McMillian | 3.00 | 1.35 | .40 |
| Minnesota Vikings | | | |
| ☐ 4 Warren Moon | 4.00 | 1.80 | .50 |
| Houston Oilers | | | |
| ☐ 5 Leslie O'Neal | 3.00 | 1.35 | .40 |
| San Diego Chargers | | | |
| ☐ 6 Deion Sanders | 4.00 | 1.80 | .50 |
| Atlanta Falcons | | | |
| ☐ 7 Sterling Sharpe | 8.00 | 3.60 | 1.00 |
| Green Bay Packers | | | |
| ☐ 8 Clyde Simmons | 3.50 | 1.55 | .45 |
| Philadelphia Eagles | | | |
| ☐ 9 Emmitt Smith | 30.00 | 13.50 | 3.80 |
| Dallas Cowboys | | | |
| ☐ 10 Thurman Thomas | 6.00 | 2.70 | .75 |
| Buffalo Bills | | | |

the bottom, where the card is edged with a black marbleized stripe that carries the set's subtitle in silver-foil lettering. The set's logo appears in one corner. The back carries a color photo of Irvin, which is again bordered only on the bottom by a black marbleized stripe. Career highlights appear in silver-foil lettering within a blue-screened panel framed by a silver-foil line. The cards are numbered on the back.

| | MINT | EXC | G-VG |
|---|---|---|---|
| COMPLETE SET (10) | 15.00 | 6.75 | 1.90 |
| COMMON M.IRVIN (1-10) | 1.75 | .80 | .22 |
| | | | |
| ☐ 1 Michael Irvin | 1.75 | .80 | .22 |
| The New Wave | | | |
| ☐ 2 Michael Irvin | 1.75 | .80 | .22 |
| Eye of the Hurricane | | | |
| ☐ 3 Michael Irvin | 1.75 | .80 | .22 |
| Dallas Delight | | | |
| ☐ 4 Michael Irvin | 1.75 | .80 | .22 |
| Passing the Torch | | | |
| ☐ 5 Michael Irvin | 1.75 | .80 | .22 |
| First Impressions | | | |
| ☐ 6 Michael Irvin | 1.75 | .80 | .22 |
| Setback | | | |
| ☐ 7 Michael Irvin | 1.75 | .80 | .22 |
| The Comeback Trail | | | |
| ☐ 8 Michael Irvin | 1.75 | .80 | .22 |
| The Playmaker | | | |
| ☐ 9 Michael Irvin | 1.75 | .80 | .22 |
| The Big Time | | | |
| ☐ 10 Michael Irvin | 1.75 | .80 | .22 |
| All the Way | | | |
| ☐ AU Michael Irvin | 125.00 | 57.50 | 15.50 |

## 1993 Ultra League Leaders

The 1993 Fleer Ultra League Leaders set comprises ten standard-size (2 1/2" by 3 1/2") cards, randomly inserted in Fleer Ultra 14- and 19-card foil packs. The set spotlights players who led their respective conferences in specific defensive or offensive categories. The borderless fronts feature close-up posed or action player cut-outs on silver metallic backgrounds. The set title appears at the top, with the player's name printed across the bottom. The back sports a player cut-out on a silver metallic background with light silver rays radiating from the center. The set title and player's name are stamped in silver foil at the top, followed by the category the player led in the 1992 season, and career highlights. The cards are numbered on the back "X of 10."

| | MINT | EXC | G-VG |
|---|---|---|---|
| COMPLETE SET (10) | 50.00 | 23.00 | 6.25 |
| COMMON PLAYER (1-10) | 3.00 | 1.35 | .40 |
| | | | |
| ☐ 1 Haywood Jeffires | 3.50 | 1.55 | .45 |

## 1993 Ultra Stars

The 1993 Fleer Ultra Stars set comprises ten standard-size (2 1/2" by 3 1/2") cards, randomly inserted in Fleer Ultra 19-card foil packs. The set spotlights ten outstanding NFL players. The fronts feature close-up action player cut-outs superposed upon a ghosted U.S. flag and black-and-white background. Except for the gray marbleized stripe edging the bottom, the front is borderless. Stamped in gold-foil across the bottom of the picture are the set title, the player's name, and a motion-streaked football icon. The back sports a close-up player cutout on one side, and career highlights on the other. The cards are numbered on the back "X of 10."

| | MINT | EXC | G-VG |
|---|---|---|---|
| COMPLETE SET (10) | 40.00 | 18.00 | 5.00 |
| COMMON PLAYER (1-10) | 2.50 | 1.15 | .30 |
| | | | |
| ☐ 1 Brett Favre | 8.00 | 3.60 | 1.00 |
| Green Bay Packers | | | |
| ☐ 2 Barry Foster | 4.00 | 1.80 | .50 |
| Pittsburgh Steelers | | | |
| ☐ 3 Michael Irvin | 8.00 | 3.60 | 1.00 |
| Dallas Cowboys | | | |
| ☐ 4 Cortez Kennedy | 2.50 | 1.15 | .30 |
| Seattle Seahawks | | | |
| ☐ 5 Deion Sanders | 3.50 | 1.55 | .45 |
| Atlanta Falcons | | | |
| ☐ 6 Junior Seau | 2.50 | 1.15 | .30 |
| San Diego Chargers | | | |
| ☐ 7 Derrick Thomas | 2.50 | 1.15 | .30 |
| Kansas City Chiefs | | | |
| ☐ 8 Ricky Watters | 4.00 | 1.80 | .50 |
| San Francisco 49ers | | | |
| ☐ 9 Reggie White | 3.50 | 1.55 | .45 |
| Green Bay Packers | | | |
| ☐ 10 Steve Young | 4.00 | 1.80 | .50 |
| San Francisco 49ers | | | |

## 1993 Ultra Touchdown Kings

The 1993 Fleer Ultra Touchdown Kings set comprises ten standard-size (2 1/2" by 3 1/2") cards, randomly inserted exclusively in Fleer Ultra 14-card foil packs. The set spotlights the NFL's best offensive players. The front features a close-up action player cutout superposed upon a ghosted design of a football field and play diagrams. Stamped in gold foil across the bottom of the picture are the set title and the player's name. Except for a green marbleized lower edge, the front is borderless. The white back sports a close-up player cutout on a background of play diagrams, and includes the player's career highlights. The cards are numbered on the back "X of 10."

|  | MINT | EXC | G-VG |
|---|---|---|---|
| COMPLETE SET (10) | 45.00 | 20.00 | 5.75 |
| COMMON PLAYER (1-10) | 1.00 | .45 | .13 |
| ☐ 1 Rodney Hampton<br>New York Giants | 2.00 | .90 | .25 |
| ☐ 2 Dan Marino<br>Miami Dolphins | 9.00 | 4.00 | 1.15 |
| ☐ 3 Art Monk<br>Washington Redskins | 1.00 | .45 | .13 |
| ☐ 4 Joe Montana<br>Kansas City Chiefs | 14.00 | 6.25 | 1.75 |
| ☐ 5 Jerry Rice<br>San Francisco 49ers | 6.00 | 2.70 | .75 |
| ☐ 6 Andre Rison<br>Atlanta Falcons | 1.50 | .65 | .19 |
| ☐ 7 Barry Sanders<br>Detroit Lions | 6.00 | 2.70 | .75 |
| ☐ 8 Sterling Sharpe<br>Green Bay Packers | 4.00 | 1.80 | .50 |
| ☐ 9 Emmitt Smith<br>Dallas Cowboys | 20.00 | 9.00 | 2.50 |
| ☐ 10 Thurman Thomas<br>Buffalo Bills | 3.00 | 1.35 | .40 |

## 1991 Upper Deck Promos

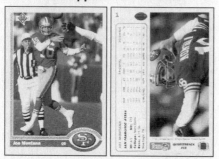

These two standard size (2 1/2" by 3 1/2") promo cards differ from these players' cards in the regular set in both numbering and in the color photos displayed on both sides of the card. The basic design remains the same: the front photo has white borders and is accented by stripes in the team's colors, while biographical and statistical information appears in a box on the flipside. It was reported that 10,000 sets were produced originally, but it is considered possible even more were produced for the nationwide give-away through a 900-number promotion sponsored by Upper Deck. The cards are numbered on the back.

|  | MINT | EXC | G-VG |
|---|---|---|---|
| COMPLETE SET (2) | 6.00 | 2.40 | .60 |
| COMMON PLAYER | 2.50 | 1.00 | .25 |
| ☐ 1 Joe Montana<br>San Francisco 49ers | 4.00 | 1.60 | .40 |
| ☐ 500 Barry Sanders<br>Detroit Lions | 2.50 | 1.00 | .25 |

## 1991 Upper Deck

This 700-card, standard size (2 1/2" by 3 1/2") set was the first football card set produced by Upper Deck. The set was released in two series. The first series contains 500 cards and the high-number series contains 200 additional cards numbered in continuation of the low series. The cards have the typical Upper Deck look to them with attractive color photos on both sides of the card and statistics and a brief biography on the back. The front photos are accented by two color border stripes reflecting the team's colors, and the team's emblem appears in the lower right corner. Cards 72-99 feature team checklists with Vernon Wells drawings. Other special subsets included are Star Rookies (1-29), Aerial Threats (30-35), Season Leaders (401-406), and Team MVP's (450-487). The second series includes a Rookie Force subset depicting 50 top rookies in their NFL uniforms (AFC 601-626 and NFC 627-652) and an Arch Rivals subset with split-photo cards presenting one-on-one rivalries (653-658). Rookie Cards include Cody Carlson, Bryan Cox, Lawrence Dawsey, Ricky Ervins, Brett Favre, Jeff Graham, Alvin Harper, Mark Higgs, Randal Hill, Michael Jackson, Todd Marinovich, Dan McGwire, Herman Moore, Erric Pegram, Mike Pritchard, Leonard Russell, Ricky Watters, Harvey Williams, and Vince Workman. There were nine different "Football Heroes" insert cards spotlighting Hall of Famer Joe Namath along with 2,500 Namath autographed cards which were randomly inserted in high series 12-card foil packs. The final three Game Breaker hologram insert cards were included with the second series only and round out the nine-card hologram set. A special insert card (SP2) commemorating Don Shula's historic 300th NFL victory was also randomly inserted in these Upper Deck high series foil packs.

|  | MINT | EXC | G-VG |
|---|---|---|---|
| COMPLETE SET (700) | 20.00 | 9.00 | 2.50 |
| COMPLETE FACT.SET (700) | 20.00 | 9.00 | 2.50 |
| COMPLETE LO SERIES (500) | 15.00 | 6.75 | 1.90 |
| COMPLETE HI SERIES (200) | 5.00 | 2.30 | .60 |
| COMPLETE FACT.HI SET (200) | 5.00 | 2.30 | .60 |
| COMMON PLAYER (1-500) | .04 | .02 | .01 |
| COMMON PLAYER (501-700) | .04 | .02 | .01 |
| ☐ 1 Star Rookie Checklist<br>Dan McGwire | .04 | .02 | .01 |
| ☐ 2 Eric Bieniemy<br>San Diego Chargers | .15 | .07 | .02 |
| ☐ 3 Mike Dumas<br>Houston Oilers | .06 | .03 | .01 |
| ☐ 4 Mike Croel<br>Denver Broncos | .20 | .09 | .03 |
| ☐ 5 Russell Maryland<br>Dallas Cowboys | .40 | .18 | .05 |
| ☐ 6 Charles McRae<br>Tampa Bay Buccaneers | .06 | .03 | .01 |
| ☐ 7 Dan McGwire<br>Seattle Seahawks | .10 | .05 | .01 |
| ☐ 8 Mike Pritchard<br>Atlanta Falcons | .75 | .35 | .09 |
| ☐ 9 Ricky Watters<br>San Francisco 49ers | 1.25 | .55 | .16 |
| ☐ 10 Chris Zorich<br>Chicago Bears | .25 | .11 | .03 |
| ☐ 11 Browning Nagle<br>New York Jets | .20 | .09 | .03 |
| ☐ 12 Wesley Carroll<br>New Orleans Saints | .10 | .05 | .01 |
| ☐ 13 Brett Favre<br>Atlanta Falcons | 2.00 | .90 | .25 |
| ☐ 14 Rob Carpenter<br>Cincinnati Bengals | .10 | .05 | .01 |
| ☐ 15 Eric Swann<br>Phoenix Cardinals | .20 | .09 | .03 |
| ☐ 16 Stanley Richard<br>San Diego Chargers | .10 | .05 | .01 |
| ☐ 17 Herman Moore<br>Detroit Lions | 1.00 | .45 | .13 |
| ☐ 18 Todd Marinovich<br>Los Angeles Raiders | .10 | .05 | .01 |
| ☐ 19 Aaron Craver<br>Miami Dolphins | .06 | .03 | .01 |
| ☐ 20 Chuck Webb<br>Green Bay Packers | .06 | .03 | .01 |

| | | | |
|---|---|---|---|
| ☐ 21 Todd Lyght............................. | .10 | .05 | .01 |
| Los Angeles Rams | | | |
| ☐ 22 Greg Lewis.............................. | .06 | .03 | .01 |
| Denver Broncos | | | |
| ☐ 23 Eric Turner............................. | .20 | .09 | .03 |
| Cleveland Browns | | | |
| ☐ 24 Alvin Harper........................... | 1.00 | .45 | .13 |
| Dallas Cowboys | | | |
| ☐ 25 Jarrod Bunch.......................... | .15 | .07 | .02 |
| New York Giants | | | |
| ☐ 26 Bruce Pickens........................ | .10 | .05 | .01 |
| Atlanta Falcons | | | |
| ☐ 27 Harvey Williams...................... | .20 | .09 | .03 |
| Kansas City Chiefs | | | |
| ☐ 28 Randal Hill............................. | .30 | .14 | .04 |
| Miami Dolphins | | | |
| ☐ 29 Nick Bell................................ | .20 | .09 | .03 |
| Los Angeles Raiders | | | |
| ☐ 30 Jim Everett AT......................... | .04 | .02 | .01 |
| Henry Ellard | | | |
| Los Angeles Rams | | | |
| ☐ 31 Randall Cunningham AT.......... | .10 | .05 | .01 |
| Keith Jackson | | | |
| Philadelphia Eagles | | | |
| ☐ 32 Steve DeBerg AT..................... | .04 | .02 | .01 |
| Stephone Paige | | | |
| Kansas City Chiefs | | | |
| ☐ 33 Warren Moon AT..................... | .10 | .05 | .01 |
| Drew Hill | | | |
| Houston Oilers | | | |
| ☐ 34 Dan Marino AT........................ | .20 | .09 | .03 |
| Mark Clayton | | | |
| Miami Dolphins | | | |
| ☐ 35 Joe Montana AT...................... | .35 | .16 | .04 |
| Jerry Rice | | | |
| San Francisco 49ers | | | |
| ☐ 36 Percy Snow............................ | .04 | .02 | .01 |
| Kansas City Chiefs | | | |
| ☐ 37 Kelvin Martin.......................... | .08 | .04 | .01 |
| Dallas Cowboys | | | |
| ☐ 38 Scott Case............................. | .04 | .02 | .01 |
| Atlanta Falcons | | | |
| ☐ 39 John Gesek............................ | .08 | .04 | .01 |
| Dallas Cowboys | | | |
| ☐ 40 Barry Word............................. | .10 | .05 | .01 |
| Kansas City Chiefs | | | |
| ☐ 41 Cornelius Bennett................... | .10 | .05 | .01 |
| Buffalo Bills | | | |
| ☐ 42 Mike Kenn.............................. | .08 | .04 | .01 |
| Atlanta Falcons | | | |
| ☐ 43 Andre Reed............................ | .10 | .05 | .01 |
| Buffalo Bills | | | |
| ☐ 44 Bobby Hebert......................... | .10 | .05 | .01 |
| New Orleans Saints | | | |
| ☐ 45 William Perry.......................... | .08 | .04 | .01 |
| Chicago Bears | | | |
| ☐ 46 Dennis Byrd........................... | .08 | .04 | .01 |
| New York Jets | | | |
| ☐ 47 Martin Mayhew....................... | .04 | .02 | .01 |
| Washington Redskins | | | |
| ☐ 48 Issaic Holt............................. | .04 | .02 | .01 |
| Dallas Cowboys | | | |
| ☐ 49 William White......................... | .04 | .02 | .01 |
| Detroit Lions | | | |
| ☐ 50 JoJo Townsell......................... | .04 | .02 | .01 |
| New York Jets | | | |
| ☐ 51 Jarvis Williams....................... | .04 | .02 | .01 |
| Miami Dolphins | | | |
| ☐ 52 Joey Browner......................... | .04 | .02 | .01 |
| Minnesota Vikings | | | |
| ☐ 53 Pat Terrell............................. | .04 | .02 | .01 |
| Los Angeles Rams | | | |
| ☐ 54 Joe Montana UER ................... | 1.00 | .45 | .13 |
| San Francisco 49ers | | | |
| (Born Monongahela, | | | |
| not New Eagle) | | | |
| ☐ 55 Jeff Herrod............................ | .04 | .02 | .01 |
| Indianapolis Colts | | | |
| ☐ 56 Cris Carter............................. | .10 | .05 | .01 |
| Minnesota Vikings | | | |
| ☐ 57 Jerry Rice.............................. | .75 | .35 | .09 |
| San Francisco 49ers | | | |
| ☐ 58 Brett Perriman........................ | .10 | .05 | .01 |
| New Orleans Saints | | | |
| ☐ 59 Kevin Fagan........................... | .04 | .02 | .01 |
| San Francisco 49ers | | | |
| ☐ 60 Wayne Haddix......................... | .04 | .02 | .01 |
| Tampa Bay Buccaneers | | | |
| ☐ 61 Tommy Kane........................... | .04 | .02 | .01 |
| Seattle Seahawks | | | |
| ☐ 62 Pat Beach.............................. | .04 | .02 | .01 |
| Indianapolis Colts | | | |
| ☐ 63 Jeff Lageman.......................... | .04 | .02 | .01 |
| New York Jets | | | |
| ☐ 64 Hassan Jones......................... | .04 | .02 | .01 |
| Minnesota Vikings | | | |
| ☐ 65 Bennie Blades ....................... | .04 | .02 | .01 |

| | | | |
|---|---|---|---|
| Detroit Lions | | | |
| ☐ 66 Tim McGee............................ | .04 | .02 | .01 |
| Cincinnati Bengals | | | |
| ☐ 67 Robert Blackmon ................... | .04 | .02 | .01 |
| Seattle Seahawks | | | |
| ☐ 68 Fred Stokes........................... | .20 | .09 | .03 |
| Washington Redskins | | | |
| ☐ 69 Barney Bussey....................... | .04 | .02 | .01 |
| Cincinnati Bengals | | | |
| ☐ 70 Eric Metcalf........................... | .10 | .05 | .01 |
| Cleveland Browns | | | |
| ☐ 71 Mark Kelso............................ | .04 | .02 | .01 |
| Buffalo Bills | | | |
| ☐ 72 Neal Anderson TC................... | .04 | .02 | .01 |
| Chicago Bears | | | |
| ☐ 73 Boomer Esiason TC................. | .08 | .04 | .01 |
| Cincinnati Bengals | | | |
| ☐ 74 Thurman Thomas TC ............... | .20 | .09 | .03 |
| Buffalo Bills | | | |
| ☐ 75 John Elway TC ........................ | .15 | .07 | .02 |
| Denver Broncos | | | |
| ☐ 76 Eric Metcalf TC....................... | .08 | .04 | .01 |
| Cleveland Browns | | | |
| ☐ 77 Vinny Testaverde TC ............... | .08 | .04 | .01 |
| Tampa Bay Buccaneers | | | |
| ☐ 78 Johnny Johnson TC ................. | .12 | .05 | .02 |
| Phoenix Cardinals | | | |
| ☐ 79 Anthony Miller TC ................... | .10 | .05 | .01 |
| San Diego Chargers | | | |
| ☐ 80 Derrick Thomas TC ................. | .12 | .05 | .02 |
| Kansas City Chiefs | | | |
| ☐ 81 Jeff George TC ...................... | .10 | .05 | .01 |
| Indianapolis Colts | | | |
| ☐ 82 Troy Aikman TC ...................... | .60 | .25 | .08 |
| Dallas Cowboys | | | |
| ☐ 83 Dan Marino TC........................ | .35 | .16 | .04 |
| Miami Dolphins | | | |
| ☐ 84 Randall Cunningham TC........... | .08 | .04 | .01 |
| Philadelphia Eagles | | | |
| ☐ 85 Deion Sanders TC ................... | .12 | .05 | .02 |
| Atlanta Falcons | | | |
| ☐ 86 Jerry Rice TC ......................... | .35 | .16 | .04 |
| San Francisco 49ers | | | |
| ☐ 87 Lawrence Taylor TC ................ | .04 | .02 | .01 |
| New York Giants | | | |
| ☐ 88 Al Toon TC ............................ | .04 | .02 | .01 |
| New York Jets | | | |
| ☐ 89 Barry Sanders TC ................... | .35 | .16 | .04 |
| Detroit Lions | | | |
| ☐ 90 Warren Moon TC...................... | .10 | .05 | .01 |
| Houston Oilers | | | |
| ☐ 91 Sterling Sharpe TC ................. | .25 | .11 | .03 |
| Green Bay Packers | | | |
| ☐ 92 Andre Tippett TC .................... | .04 | .02 | .01 |
| New England Patriots | | | |
| ☐ 93 Bo Jackson TC ....................... | .15 | .07 | .02 |
| Los Angeles Raiders | | | |
| ☐ 94 Jim Everett TC ....................... | .04 | .02 | .01 |
| Los Angeles Rams | | | |
| ☐ 95 Art Monk TC .......................... | .08 | .04 | .01 |
| Washington Redskins | | | |
| ☐ 96 Morten Andersen TC ............... | .04 | .02 | .01 |
| New Orleans Saints | | | |
| ☐ 97 John L. Williams TC ................ | .04 | .02 | .01 |
| Seattle Seahawks | | | |
| ☐ 98 Rod Woodson TC..................... | .08 | .04 | .01 |
| Pittsburgh Steelers | | | |
| ☐ 99 Herschel Walker TC................. | .08 | .04 | .01 |
| Minnesota Vikings | | | |
| ☐ 100 Checklist 1-100 ..................... | .04 | .02 | .01 |
| ☐ 101 Steve Young.......................... | .50 | .23 | .06 |
| San Francisco 49ers | | | |
| ☐ 102 Jim Lachey............................ | .04 | .02 | .01 |
| Washington Redskins | | | |
| ☐ 103 Tom Rathman......................... | .08 | .04 | .01 |
| San Francisco 49ers | | | |
| ☐ 104 Earnest Byner........................ | .08 | .04 | .01 |
| Washington Redskins | | | |
| ☐ 105 Karl Mecklenburg................... | .08 | .04 | .01 |
| Denver Broncos | | | |
| ☐ 106 Wes Hopkins.......................... | .04 | .02 | .01 |
| Philadelphia Eagles | | | |
| ☐ 107 Michael Irvin ......................... | .50 | .23 | .06 |
| Dallas Cowboys | | | |
| ☐ 108 Burt Grossman....................... | .04 | .02 | .01 |
| San Diego Chargers | | | |
| ☐ 109 Jay Novacek UER ................... | .15 | .07 | .02 |
| Dallas Cowboys | | | |
| (Wearing 82, but card | | | |
| says he wears 84) | | | |
| ☐ 110 Ben Smith............................. | .04 | .02 | .01 |
| Philadelphia Eagles | | | |
| ☐ 111 Rod Woodson........................ | .10 | .05 | .01 |
| Pittsburgh Steelers | | | |
| ☐ 112 Ernie Jones.......................... | .04 | .02 | .01 |
| Phoenix Cardinals | | | |
| ☐ 113 Bryan Hinkle.......................... | .04 | .02 | .01 |
| Pittsburgh Steelers | | | |

| | | | |
|---|---|---|---|
| ☐ 114 Vai Sikahema | .08 | .04 | .01 |
| Phoenix Cardinals | | | |
| ☐ 115 Bubby Brister | .08 | .04 | .01 |
| Pittsburgh Steelers | | | |
| ☐ 116 Brian Blades | .10 | .05 | .01 |
| Seattle Seahawks | | | |
| ☐ 117 Don Majkowski | .08 | .04 | .01 |
| Green Bay Packers | | | |
| ☐ 118 Rod Bernstine | .10 | .05 | .01 |
| San Diego Chargers | | | |
| ☐ 119 Brian Noble | .04 | .02 | .01 |
| Green Bay Packers | | | |
| ☐ 120 Eugene Robinson | .04 | .02 | .01 |
| Seattle Seahawks | | | |
| ☐ 121 John Taylor | .10 | .05 | .01 |
| San Francisco 49ers | | | |
| ☐ 122 Vance Johnson | .08 | .04 | .01 |
| Denver Broncos | | | |
| ☐ 123 Art Monk | .10 | .05 | .01 |
| Washington Redskins | | | |
| ☐ 124 John Elway | .35 | .16 | .04 |
| Denver Broncos | | | |
| ☐ 125 Dexter Carter | .08 | .04 | .01 |
| San Francisco 49ers | | | |
| ☐ 126 Anthony Miller | .20 | .09 | .03 |
| San Diego Chargers | | | |
| ☐ 127 Keith Jackson | .15 | .07 | .02 |
| Philadelphia Eagles | | | |
| ☐ 128 Albert Lewis | .08 | .04 | .01 |
| Kansas City Chiefs | | | |
| ☐ 129 Billy Ray Smith | .04 | .02 | .01 |
| San Diego Chargers | | | |
| ☐ 130 Clyde Simmons | .08 | .04 | .01 |
| Philadelphia Eagles | | | |
| ☐ 131 Merril Hoge | .08 | .04 | .01 |
| Pittsburgh Steelers | | | |
| ☐ 132 Ricky Proehl | .10 | .05 | .01 |
| Phoenix Cardinals | | | |
| ☐ 133 Tim McDonald | .08 | .04 | .01 |
| Phoenix Cardinals | | | |
| ☐ 134 Louis Lipps | .08 | .04 | .01 |
| Pittsburgh Steelers | | | |
| ☐ 135 Ken Harvey | .04 | .02 | .01 |
| Phoenix Cardinals | | | |
| ☐ 136 Sterling Sharpe | .50 | .23 | .06 |
| Green Bay Packers | | | |
| ☐ 137 Gill Byrd | .08 | .04 | .01 |
| San Diego Chargers | | | |
| ☐ 138 Tim Harris | .08 | .04 | .01 |
| Green Bay Packers | | | |
| ☐ 139 Derrick Fenner | .08 | .04 | .01 |
| Seattle Seahawks | | | |
| ☐ 140 Johnny Holland | .04 | .02 | .01 |
| Green Bay Packers | | | |
| ☐ 141 Ricky Sanders | .08 | .04 | .01 |
| Washington Redskins | | | |
| ☐ 142 Bobby Humphrey | .08 | .04 | .01 |
| Denver Broncos | | | |
| ☐ 143 Roger Craig | .08 | .04 | .01 |
| San Francisco 49ers | | | |
| ☐ 144 Steve Atwater | .10 | .05 | .01 |
| Denver Broncos | | | |
| ☐ 145 Ickey Woods | .04 | .02 | .01 |
| Cincinnati Bengals | | | |
| ☐ 146 Randall Cunningham | .10 | .05 | .01 |
| Philadelphia Eagles | | | |
| ☐ 147 Marion Butts | .10 | .05 | .01 |
| San Diego Chargers | | | |
| ☐ 148 Reggie White | .15 | .07 | .02 |
| Philadelphia Eagles | | | |
| ☐ 149 Ronnie Harmon | .04 | .02 | .01 |
| San Diego Chargers | | | |
| ☐ 150 Mike Saxon | .04 | .02 | .01 |
| Dallas Cowboys | | | |
| ☐ 151 Greg Townsend | .04 | .02 | .01 |
| Los Angeles Raiders | | | |
| ☐ 152 Troy Aikman | 1.25 | .55 | .16 |
| Dallas Cowboys | | | |
| ☐ 153 Shane Conlan | .08 | .04 | .01 |
| Buffalo Bills | | | |
| ☐ 154 Deion Sanders | .25 | .11 | .03 |
| Atlanta Falcons | | | |
| ☐ 155 Bo Jackson | .35 | .16 | .04 |
| Los Angeles Raiders | | | |
| ☐ 156 Jeff Hostetler | .25 | .11 | .03 |
| New York Giants | | | |
| ☐ 157 Albert Bentley | .04 | .02 | .01 |
| Indianapolis Colts | | | |
| ☐ 158 James Williams | .04 | .02 | .01 |
| Buffalo Bills | | | |
| ☐ 159 Bill Brooks | .08 | .04 | .01 |
| Indianapolis Colts | | | |
| ☐ 160 Nick Lowery | .08 | .04 | .01 |
| Kansas City Chiefs | | | |
| ☐ 161 Ottis Anderson | .08 | .04 | .01 |
| New York Giants | | | |
| ☐ 162 Kevin Greene | .08 | .04 | .01 |

| | | | |
|---|---|---|---|
| Los Angeles Rams | | | |
| ☐ 163 Neil Smith | .10 | .05 | .01 |
| Kansas City Chiefs | | | |
| ☐ 164 Jim Everett | .08 | .04 | .01 |
| Los Angeles Rams | | | |
| ☐ 165 Derrick Thomas | .25 | .11 | .03 |
| Kansas City Chiefs | | | |
| ☐ 166 John L. Williams | .08 | .04 | .01 |
| Seattle Seahawks | | | |
| ☐ 167 Timm Rosenbach | .08 | .04 | .01 |
| Phoenix Cardinals | | | |
| ☐ 168 Leslie O'Neal | .08 | .04 | .01 |
| San Diego Chargers | | | |
| ☐ 169 Clarence Verdin | .04 | .02 | .01 |
| Indianapolis Colts | | | |
| ☐ 170 Dave Krieg | .08 | .04 | .01 |
| Seattle Seahawks | | | |
| ☐ 171 Steve Broussard | .08 | .04 | .01 |
| Atlanta Falcons | | | |
| ☐ 172 Emmitt Smith | 2.00 | .90 | .25 |
| Dallas Cowboys | | | |
| ☐ 173 Andre Rison | .25 | .11 | .03 |
| Atlanta Falcons | | | |
| ☐ 174 Bruce Smith | .10 | .05 | .01 |
| Buffalo Bills | | | |
| ☐ 175 Mark Clayton | .08 | .04 | .01 |
| Miami Dolphins | | | |
| ☐ 176 Christian Okoye | .08 | .04 | .01 |
| Kansas City Chiefs | | | |
| ☐ 177 Duane Bickett | .04 | .02 | .01 |
| Indianapolis Colts | | | |
| ☐ 178 Stephone Paige | .08 | .04 | .01 |
| Kansas City Chiefs | | | |
| ☐ 179 Fredd Young | .04 | .02 | .01 |
| Indianapolis Colts | | | |
| ☐ 180 Mervyn Fernandez | .04 | .02 | .01 |
| Los Angeles Raiders | | | |
| ☐ 181 Phil Simms | .10 | .05 | .01 |
| New York Giants | | | |
| ☐ 182 Pete Holohan | .04 | .02 | .01 |
| Los Angeles Rams | | | |
| ☐ 183 Pepper Johnson | .08 | .04 | .01 |
| New York Giants | | | |
| ☐ 184 Jackie Slater | .08 | .04 | .01 |
| Los Angeles Rams | | | |
| ☐ 185 Stephen Baker | .04 | .02 | .01 |
| New York Giants | | | |
| ☐ 186 Frank Cornish | .04 | .02 | .01 |
| San Diego Chargers | | | |
| ☐ 187 Dave Waymer | .04 | .02 | .01 |
| San Francisco 49ers | | | |
| ☐ 188 Terance Mathis | .04 | .02 | .01 |
| New York Jets | | | |
| ☐ 189 Darryl Talley | .08 | .04 | .01 |
| Buffalo Bills | | | |
| ☐ 190 James Hasty | .04 | .02 | .01 |
| New York Jets | | | |
| ☐ 191 Jay Schroeder | .08 | .04 | .01 |
| Los Angeles Raiders | | | |
| ☐ 192 Kenneth Davis | .08 | .04 | .01 |
| Buffalo Bills | | | |
| ☐ 193 Chris Miller | .10 | .05 | .01 |
| Atlanta Falcons | | | |
| ☐ 194 Scott Davis | .04 | .02 | .01 |
| Los Angeles Raiders | | | |
| ☐ 195 Tim Green | .04 | .02 | .01 |
| Atlanta Falcons | | | |
| ☐ 196 Dan Saleaumua | .04 | .02 | .01 |
| Kansas City Chiefs | | | |
| ☐ 197 Rohn Stark | .04 | .02 | .01 |
| Indianapolis Colts | | | |
| ☐ 198 John Alt | .04 | .02 | .01 |
| Kansas City Chiefs | | | |
| ☐ 199 Steve Tasker | .08 | .04 | .01 |
| Buffalo Bills | | | |
| ☐ 200 Checklist 101-200 | .04 | .02 | .01 |
| ☐ 201 Freddie Joe Nunn | .04 | .02 | .01 |
| Phoenix Cardinals | | | |
| ☐ 202 Jim Breech | .04 | .02 | .01 |
| Cincinnati Bengals | | | |
| ☐ 203 Roy Green | .08 | .04 | .01 |
| Phoenix Cardinals | | | |
| ☐ 204 Gary Anderson | .08 | .04 | .01 |
| Tampa Bay Buccaneers | | | |
| ☐ 205 Rich Camarillo | .04 | .02 | .01 |
| Phoenix Cardinals | | | |
| ☐ 206 Mark Bortz | .04 | .02 | .01 |
| Chicago Bears | | | |
| ☐ 207 Eddie Brown | .04 | .02 | .01 |
| Cincinnati Bengals | | | |
| ☐ 208 Brad Muster | .08 | .04 | .01 |
| Chicago Bears | | | |
| ☐ 209 Anthony Munoz | .08 | .04 | .01 |
| Cincinnati Bengals | | | |
| ☐ 210 Dalton Hilliard | .04 | .02 | .01 |
| New Orleans Saints | | | |
| ☐ 211 Erik McMillan | .04 | .02 | .01 |
| New York Jets | | | |

|  |  |  | | | |
|---|--------|------|------|------|------|
| ☐ 212 | Perry Kemp | Green Bay Packers | .04 | .02 | .01 |
| ☐ 213 | Jim Thornton | Chicago Bears | .04 | .02 | .01 |
| ☐ 214 | Anthony Dilweg | Green Bay Packers | .08 | .04 | .01 |
| ☐ 215 | Cleveland Gary | Los Angeles Rams | .08 | .04 | .01 |
| ☐ 216 | Leo Goeas | San Diego Chargers | .04 | .02 | .01 |
| ☐ 217 | Mike Merriweather | Minnesota Vikings | .04 | .02 | .01 |
| ☐ 218 | Courtney Hall | San Diego Chargers | .04 | .02 | .01 |
| ☐ 219 | Wade Wilson | Minnesota Vikings | .08 | .04 | .01 |
| ☐ 220 | Billy Joe Tolliver | San Diego Chargers | .08 | .04 | .01 |
| ☐ 221 | Harold Green | Cincinnati Bengals | .10 | .05 | .01 |
| ☐ 222 | Al (Bubba) Baker | Cleveland Browns | .04 | .02 | .01 |
| ☐ 223 | Carl Zander | Cincinnati Bengals | .04 | .02 | .01 |
| ☐ 224 | Thane Gash | Cleveland Browns | .04 | .02 | .01 |
| ☐ 225 | Kevin Mack | Cleveland Browns | .08 | .04 | .01 |
| ☐ 226 | Morten Andersen | New Orleans Saints | .08 | .04 | .01 |
| ☐ 227 | Dennis Gentry | Chicago Bears | .04 | .02 | .01 |
| ☐ 228 | Vince Buck | New Orleans Saints | .04 | .02 | .01 |
| ☐ 229 | Mike Singletary | Chicago Bears | .10 | .05 | .01 |
| ☐ 230 | Rueben Mayes | New Orleans Saints | .04 | .02 | .01 |
| ☐ 231 | Mark Carrier | Tampa Bay Buccaneers | .08 | .04 | .01 |
| ☐ 232 | Tony Mandarich | Green Bay Packers | .04 | .02 | .01 |
| ☐ 233 | Al Toon | New York Jets | .08 | .04 | .01 |
| ☐ 234 | Renaldo Turnbull | New Orleans Saints | .08 | .04 | .01 |
| ☐ 235 | Broderick Thomas | Tampa Bay Buccaneers | .08 | .04 | .01 |
| ☐ 236 | Anthony Carter | Minnesota Vikings | .08 | .04 | .01 |
| ☐ 237 | Flipper Anderson | Los Angeles Rams | .08 | .04 | .01 |
| ☐ 238 | Jerry Robinson | Los Angeles Raiders | .04 | .02 | .01 |
| ☐ 239 | Vince Newsome | Los Angeles Rams | .04 | .02 | .01 |
| ☐ 240 | Keith Millard | Minnesota Vikings | .08 | .04 | .01 |
| ☐ 241 | Reggie Langhorne | Cleveland Browns | .08 | .04 | .01 |
| ☐ 242 | James Francis | Cincinnati Bengals | .08 | .04 | .01 |
| ☐ 243 | Felix Wright | Cleveland Browns | .04 | .02 | .01 |
| ☐ 244 | Neal Anderson | Chicago Bears | .08 | .04 | .01 |
| ☐ 245 | Boomer Esiason | Cincinnati Bengals | .15 | .07 | .02 |
| ☐ 246 | Pat Swilling | New Orleans Saints | .08 | .04 | .01 |
| ☐ 247 | Richard Dent | Chicago Bears | .08 | .04 | .01 |
| ☐ 248 | Craig Heyward | New Orleans Saints | .04 | .02 | .01 |
| ☐ 249 | Ron Morris | Chicago Bears | .04 | .02 | .01 |
| ☐ 250 | Eric Martin | New Orleans Saints | .08 | .04 | .01 |
| ☐ 251 | Jim C. Jensen | Miami Dolphins | .04 | .02 | .01 |
| ☐ 252 | Anthony Toney | Philadelphia Eagles | .04 | .02 | .01 |
| ☐ 253 | Sammie Smith | Miami Dolphins | .04 | .02 | .01 |
| ☐ 254 | Calvin Williams | Philadelphia Eagles | .20 | .09 | .03 |
| ☐ 255 | Dan Marino | Miami Dolphins | .75 | .35 | .09 |
| ☐ 256 | Warren Moon | Houston Oilers | .20 | .09 | .03 |
| ☐ 257 | Tommie Agee | Dallas Cowboys | .04 | .02 | .01 |
| ☐ 258 | Haywood Jeffires | Houston Oilers | .15 | .07 | .02 |
| ☐ 259 | Eugene Lockhart | Dallas Cowboys | .04 | .02 | .01 |
| ☐ 260 | Drew Hill | Houston Oilers | .08 | .04 | .01 |
| ☐ 261 | Vinny Testaverde | Tampa Bay Buccaneers | .10 | .05 | .01 |
| ☐ 262 | Jim Arnold | Detroit Lions | .04 | .02 | .01 |
| ☐ 263 | Steve Christie | Tampa Bay Buccaneers | .04 | .02 | .01 |
| ☐ 264 | Chris Spielman | Detroit Lions | .08 | .04 | .01 |
| ☐ 265 | Reggie Cobb | Tampa Bay Buccaneers | .25 | .11 | .03 |
| ☐ 266 | John Stephens | New England Patriots | .08 | .04 | .01 |
| ☐ 267 | Jay Hilgenberg | Chicago Bears | .08 | .04 | .01 |
| ☐ 268 | Brent Williams | New England Patriots | .04 | .02 | .01 |
| ☐ 269 | Rodney Hampton | New York Giants | .75 | .35 | .09 |
| ☐ 270 | Irving Fryar | New England Patriots | .08 | .04 | .01 |
| ☐ 271 | Terry McDaniel | Los Angeles Raiders | .04 | .02 | .01 |
| ☐ 272 | Reggie Roby | Miami Dolphins | .04 | .02 | .01 |
| ☐ 273 | Allen Pinkett | Houston Oilers | .04 | .02 | .01 |
| ☐ 274 | Tim McKyer | Miami Dolphins | .08 | .04 | .01 |
| ☐ 275 | Bob Golic | Los Angeles Raiders | .04 | .02 | .01 |
| ☐ 276 | Wilber Marshall | Washington Redskins | .08 | .04 | .01 |
| ☐ 277 | Ray Childress | Houston Oilers | .08 | .04 | .01 |
| ☐ 278 | Charles Mann | Washington Redskins | .08 | .04 | .01 |
| ☐ 279 | Cris Dishman | Houston Oilers | .15 | .07 | .02 |
| ☐ 280 | Mark Rypien | Washington Redskins | .10 | .05 | .01 |
| ☐ 281 | Michael Cofer | Detroit Lions | .04 | .02 | .01 |
| ☐ 282 | Keith Byars | Philadelphia Eagles | .08 | .04 | .01 |
| ☐ 283 | Mike Rozier | Atlanta Falcons | .08 | .04 | .01 |
| ☐ 284 | Seth Joyner | Philadelphia Eagles | .08 | .04 | .01 |
| ☐ 285 | Jessie Tuggle | Atlanta Falcons | .04 | .02 | .01 |
| ☐ 286 | Mark Bavaro | New York Giants | .08 | .04 | .01 |
| ☐ 287 | Eddie Anderson | Los Angeles Raiders | .04 | .02 | .01 |
| ☐ 288 | Sean Landeta | New York Giants | .04 | .02 | .01 |
| ☐ 289 | Howie Long (With George Brett) | Los Angeles Raiders | .15 | .07 | .02 |
| ☐ 290 | Reyna Thompson | New York Giants | .04 | .02 | .01 |
| ☐ 291 | Ferrell Edmunds | Miami Dolphins | .04 | .02 | .01 |
| ☐ 292 | Willie Gault | Los Angeles Raiders | .08 | .04 | .01 |
| ☐ 293 | John Offerdahl | Miami Dolphins | .08 | .04 | .01 |
| ☐ 294 | Tim Brown | Los Angeles Raiders | .20 | .09 | .03 |
| ☐ 295 | Bruce Matthews | Houston Oilers | .08 | .04 | .01 |
| ☐ 296 | Kevin Ross | Kansas City Chiefs | .08 | .04 | .01 |
| ☐ 297 | Lorenzo White | Houston Oilers | .08 | .04 | .01 |
| ☐ 298 | Dino Hackett | Kansas City Chiefs | .04 | .02 | .01 |
| ☐ 299 | Curtis Duncan | Houston Oilers | .08 | .04 | .01 |
| ☐ 300 | Checklist 201-300 | | .04 | .02 | .01 |
| ☐ 301 | Andre Ware | Detroit Lions | .10 | .05 | .01 |
| ☐ 302 | David Little | Pittsburgh Steelers | .04 | .02 | .01 |
| ☐ 303 | Jerry Ball | Detroit Lions | .08 | .04 | .01 |
| ☐ 304 | Dwight Stone UER (He's a WR, not RB) | Pittsburgh Steelers | .04 | .02 | .01 |
| ☐ 305 | Rodney Peete | Detroit Lions | .08 | .04 | .01 |
| ☐ 306 | Mike Baab | Cleveland Browns | .04 | .02 | .01 |
| ☐ 307 | Tim Worley | Pittsburgh Steelers | .08 | .04 | .01 |
| ☐ 308 | Paul Farren | Cleveland Browns | .04 | .02 | .01 |

| | | | | | | | | | |
|---|---|---|---|---|---|---|---|---|---|
| ☐ 309 Carnell Lake | .04 | .02 | .01 | | Philadelphia Eagles | | | | |
| Pittsburgh Steelers | | | | | ☐ 358 James Lofton | .10 | .05 | .01 |
| ☐ 310 Clay Matthews | .08 | .04 | .01 | | Buffalo Bills | | | | |
| Cleveland Browns | | | | | ☐ 359 William Frizzell | .04 | .02 | .01 |
| ☐ 311 Alton Montgomery | .04 | .02 | .01 | | Philadelphia Eagles | | | | |
| Denver Broncos | | | | | ☐ 360 Keith McKeller | .04 | .02 | .01 |
| ☐ 312 Ernest Givins | .08 | .04 | .01 | | Buffalo Bills | | | | |
| Houston Oilers | | | | | ☐ 361 Rodney Holman | .04 | .02 | .01 |
| ☐ 313 Mike Horan | .04 | .02 | .01 | | Cincinnati Bengals | | | | |
| Denver Broncos | | | | | ☐ 362 Henry Ellard | .08 | .04 | .01 |
| ☐ 314 Sean Jones | .08 | .04 | .01 | | Los Angeles Rams | | | | |
| Houston Oilers | | | | | ☐ 363 David Fulcher | .04 | .02 | .01 |
| ☐ 315 Leonard Smith | .04 | .02 | .01 | | Cincinnati Bengals | | | | |
| Buffalo Bills | | | | | ☐ 364 Jerry Gray | .04 | .02 | .01 |
| ☐ 316 Carl Banks | .08 | .04 | .01 | | Los Angeles Rams | | | | |
| New York Giants | | | | | ☐ 365 James Brooks | .08 | .04 | .01 |
| ☐ 317 Jerome Brown | .08 | .04 | .01 | | Cincinnati Bengals | | | | |
| Philadelphia Eagles | | | | | ☐ 366 Tony Stargell | .04 | .02 | .01 |
| ☐ 318 Everson Walls | .04 | .02 | .01 | | New York Jets | | | | |
| New York Giants | | | | | ☐ 367 Keith McCants | .04 | .02 | .01 |
| ☐ 319 Ron Heller | .04 | .02 | .01 | | Tampa Bay Buccaneers | | | | |
| Philadelphia Eagles | | | | | ☐ 368 Lewis Billups | .04 | .02 | .01 |
| ☐ 320 Mark Collins | .04 | .02 | .01 | | Cincinnati Bengals | | | | |
| New York Giants | | | | | ☐ 369 Ervin Randle | .04 | .02 | .01 |
| ☐ 321 Eddie Murray | .08 | .04 | .01 | | Tampa Bay Buccaneers | | | | |
| Detroit Lions | | | | | ☐ 370 Pat Leahy | .08 | .04 | .01 |
| ☐ 322 Jim Harbaugh | .08 | .04 | .01 | | New York Jets | | | | |
| Chicago Bears | | | | | ☐ 371 Bruce Armstrong | .04 | .02 | .01 |
| ☐ 323 Mel Gray | .04 | .02 | .01 | | New England Patriots | | | | |
| Detroit Lions | | | | | ☐ 372 Steve DeBerg | .08 | .04 | .01 |
| ☐ 324 Keith Van Horne | .04 | .02 | .01 | | Kansas City Chiefs | | | | |
| Chicago Bears | | | | | ☐ 373 Guy McIntyre | .08 | .04 | .01 |
| ☐ 325 Lomas Brown | .04 | .02 | .01 | | San Francisco 49ers | | | | |
| Detroit Lions | | | | | ☐ 374 Deron Cherry | .04 | .02 | .01 |
| ☐ 326 Carl Lee | .04 | .02 | .01 | | Kansas City Chiefs | | | | |
| Minnesota Vikings | | | | | ☐ 375 Fred Marion | .04 | .02 | .01 |
| ☐ 327 Ken O'Brien | .08 | .04 | .01 | | New England Patriots | | | | |
| New York Jets | | | | | ☐ 376 Michael Haddix | .04 | .02 | .01 |
| ☐ 328 Dermontti Dawson | .04 | .02 | .01 | | Green Bay Packers | | | | |
| Pittsburgh Steelers | | | | | ☐ 377 Kent Hull | .04 | .02 | .01 |
| ☐ 329 Brad Baxter | .08 | .04 | .01 | | Buffalo Bills | | | | |
| New York Jets | | | | | ☐ 378 Jerry Holmes | .04 | .02 | .01 |
| ☐ 330 Chris Doleman | .08 | .04 | .01 | | Green Bay Packers | | | | |
| Minnesota Vikings | | | | | ☐ 379 Jim Richter | .04 | .02 | .01 |
| ☐ 331 Louis Oliver | .08 | .04 | .01 | | Buffalo Bills | | | | |
| Miami Dolphins | | | | | ☐ 380 Ed West | .04 | .02 | .01 |
| ☐ 332 Frank Stams | .04 | .02 | .01 | | Green Bay Packers | | | | |
| Los Angeles Rams | | | | | ☐ 381 Richmond Webb | .08 | .04 | .01 |
| ☐ 333 Mike Munchak | .08 | .04 | .01 | | Miami Dolphins | | | | |
| Houston Oilers | | | | | ☐ 382 Mark Jackson | .08 | .04 | .01 |
| ☐ 334 Fred Strickland | .04 | .02 | .01 | | Denver Broncos | | | | |
| Los Angeles Rams | | | | | ☐ 383 Tom Newberry | .04 | .02 | .01 |
| ☐ 335 Mark Duper | .08 | .04 | .01 | | Los Angeles Rams | | | | |
| Miami Dolphins | | | | | ☐ 384 Ricky Nattiel | .04 | .02 | .01 |
| ☐ 336 Jacob Green | .04 | .02 | .01 | | Denver Broncos | | | | |
| Seattle Seahawks | | | | | ☐ 385 Keith Sims | .04 | .02 | .01 |
| ☐ 337 Tony Paige | .04 | .02 | .01 | | Miami Dolphins | | | | |
| Miami Dolphins | | | | | ☐ 386 Ron Hall | .04 | .02 | .01 |
| ☐ 338 Jeff Bryant | .04 | .02 | .01 | | Tampa Bay Buccaneers | | | | |
| Seattle Seahawks | | | | | ☐ 387 Ken Norton | .10 | .05 | .01 |
| ☐ 339 Lemuel Stinson | .04 | .02 | .01 | | Dallas Cowboys | | | | |
| Chicago Bears | | | | | ☐ 388 Paul Gruber | .08 | .04 | .01 |
| ☐ 340 David Wyman | .04 | .02 | .01 | | Tampa Bay Buccaneers | | | | |
| Seattle Seahawks | | | | | ☐ 389 Danny Stubbs | .04 | .02 | .01 |
| ☐ 341 Lee Williams | .08 | .04 | .01 | | Dallas Cowboys | | | | |
| San Diego Chargers | | | | | ☐ 390 Ian Beckles | .04 | .02 | .01 |
| ☐ 342 Trace Armstrong | .04 | .02 | .01 | | Tampa Bay Buccaneers | | | | |
| Chicago Bears | | | | | ☐ 391 Hoby Brenner | .04 | .02 | .01 |
| ☐ 343 Junior Seau | .25 | .11 | .03 | | New Orleans Saints | | | | |
| San Diego Chargers | | | | | ☐ 392 Tory Epps | .04 | .02 | .01 |
| ☐ 344 John Roper | .04 | .02 | .01 | | Atlanta Falcons | | | | |
| Chicago Bears | | | | | ☐ 393 Sam Mills | .08 | .04 | .01 |
| ☐ 345 Jeff George | .25 | .11 | .03 | | New Orleans Saints | | | | |
| Indianapolis Colts | | | | | ☐ 394 Chris Hinton | .04 | .02 | .01 |
| ☐ 346 Herschel Walker | .10 | .05 | .01 | | Atlanta Falcons | | | | |
| Minnesota Vikings | | | | | ☐ 395 Steve Walsh | .04 | .02 | .01 |
| ☐ 347 Sam Clancy | .04 | .02 | .01 | | New Orleans Saints | | | | |
| Indianapolis Colts | | | | | ☐ 396 Simon Fletcher | .08 | .04 | .01 |
| ☐ 348 Steve Jordan | .08 | .04 | .01 | | Denver Broncos | | | | |
| Minnesota Vikings | | | | | ☐ 397 Tony Bennett | .08 | .04 | .01 |
| ☐ 349 Nate Odomes | .10 | .05 | .01 | | Green Bay Packers | | | | |
| Buffalo Bills | | | | | ☐ 398 Aundray Bruce | .04 | .02 | .01 |
| ☐ 350 Martin Bayless | .04 | .02 | .01 | | Atlanta Falcons | | | | |
| San Diego Chargers | | | | | ☐ 399 Mark Murphy | .04 | .02 | .01 |
| ☐ 351 Brent Jones | .10 | .05 | .01 | | Green Bay Packers | | | | |
| San Francisco 49ers | | | | | ☐ 400 Checklist 301-400 | .04 | .02 | .01 |
| ☐ 352 Ray Agnew | .04 | .02 | .01 | | ☐ 401 Barry Sanders LL | .35 | .16 | .04 |
| New England Patriots | | | | | Detroit Lions | | | | |
| ☐ 353 Charles Haley | .08 | .04 | .01 | | ☐ 402 Jerry Rice LL | .35 | .16 | .04 |
| San Francisco 49ers | | | | | San Francisco 49ers | | | | |
| ☐ 354 Andre Tippett | .08 | .04 | .01 | | ☐ 403 Warren Moon LL | .10 | .05 | .01 |
| New England Patriots | | | | | Houston Oilers | | | | |
| ☐ 355 Ronnie Lott | .10 | .05 | .01 | | ☐ 404 Derrick Thomas LL | .12 | .05 | .02 |
| San Francisco 49ers | | | | | Kansas City Chiefs | | | | |
| ☐ 356 Thurman Thomas | .40 | .18 | .05 | | ☐ 405 Nick Lowery LL | .04 | .02 | .01 |
| Buffalo Bills | | | | | Kansas City Chiefs | | | | |
| ☐ 357 Fred Barnett | .15 | .07 | .02 | | ☐ 406 Mark Carrier LL | .04 | .02 | .01 |
| | | | | | Chicago Bears | | | | |

| | | | |
|---|---|---|---|
| ☐ 407 Michael Carter | .04 | .02 | .01 |
| San Francisco 49ers | | | |
| ☐ 408 Chris Singleton | .04 | .02 | .01 |
| New England Patriots | | | |
| ☐ 409 Matt Millen | .08 | .04 | .01 |
| San Francisco 49ers | | | |
| ☐ 410 Ronnie Lippett | .04 | .02 | .01 |
| New England Patriots | | | |
| ☐ 411 E.J. Junior | .04 | .02 | .01 |
| Miami Dolphins | | | |
| ☐ 412 Ray Donaldson | .04 | .02 | .01 |
| Indianapolis Colts | | | |
| ☐ 413 Keith Willis | .04 | .02 | .01 |
| Pittsburgh Steelers | | | |
| ☐ 414 Jessie Hester | .08 | .04 | .01 |
| Indianapolis Colts | | | |
| ☐ 415 Jeff Cross | .04 | .02 | .01 |
| Miami Dolphins | | | |
| ☐ 416 Greg Jackson | .10 | .05 | .01 |
| New York Giants | | | |
| ☐ 417 Alvin Walton | .04 | .02 | .01 |
| Washington Redskins | | | |
| ☐ 418 Bart Oates | .04 | .02 | .01 |
| New York Giants | | | |
| ☐ 419 Chip Lohmiller | .08 | .04 | .01 |
| Washington Redskins | | | |
| ☐ 420 John Elliott | .04 | .02 | .01 |
| New York Giants | | | |
| ☐ 421 Randall McDaniel | .04 | .02 | .01 |
| Minnesota Vikings | | | |
| ☐ 422 Richard Johnson | .04 | .02 | .01 |
| Houston Oilers | | | |
| ☐ 423 Al Noga | .04 | .02 | .01 |
| Minnesota Vikings | | | |
| ☐ 424 Lamar Lathon | .04 | .02 | .01 |
| Houston Oilers | | | |
| ☐ 425 Rick Fenney | .04 | .02 | .01 |
| Minnesota Vikings | | | |
| ☐ 426 Jack Del Rio | .04 | .02 | .01 |
| Dallas Cowboys | | | |
| ☐ 427 Don Mosebar | .04 | .02 | .01 |
| Los Angeles Raiders | | | |
| ☐ 428 Luis Sharpe | .04 | .02 | .01 |
| Phoenix Cardinals | | | |
| ☐ 429 Steve Wisniewski | .04 | .02 | .01 |
| Los Angeles Raiders | | | |
| ☐ 430 Jimmie Jones | .04 | .02 | .01 |
| Dallas Cowboys | | | |
| ☐ 431 Freeman McNeil | .04 | .02 | .01 |
| New York Jets | | | |
| ☐ 432 Ron Rivera | .04 | .02 | .01 |
| Chicago Bears | | | |
| ☐ 433 Hart Lee Dykes | .08 | .04 | .01 |
| New England Patriots | | | |
| ☐ 434 Mark Carrier | .10 | .05 | .01 |
| Chicago Bears | | | |
| ☐ 435 Rob Moore | .08 | .04 | .01 |
| New York Jets | | | |
| ☐ 436 Gary Clark | .08 | .04 | .01 |
| Washington Redskins | | | |
| ☐ 437 Heath Sherman | .08 | .04 | .01 |
| Philadelphia Eagles | | | |
| ☐ 438 Darrell Green | .04 | .02 | .01 |
| Washington Redskins | | | |
| ☐ 439 Jessie Small | .04 | .02 | .01 |
| Philadelphia Eagles | | | |
| ☐ 440 Monte Coleman | .08 | .04 | .01 |
| Washington Redskins | | | |
| ☐ 441 Leonard Marshall | .04 | .02 | .01 |
| New York Giants | | | |
| ☐ 442 Richard Johnson | .10 | .05 | .01 |
| Detroit Lions | | | |
| ☐ 443 Dave Meggett | .10 | .05 | .01 |
| New York Giants | | | |
| ☐ 444 Barry Sanders | .75 | .35 | .09 |
| Detroit Lions | | | |
| ☐ 445 Lawrence Taylor | .10 | .05 | .01 |
| New York Giants | | | |
| ☐ 446 Marcus Allen | .08 | .04 | .01 |
| Los Angeles Raiders | | | |
| ☐ 447 Johnny Johnson | .25 | .11 | .03 |
| Phoenix Cardinals | | | |
| ☐ 448 Aaron Wallace | .04 | .02 | .01 |
| Los Angeles Raiders | | | |
| ☐ 449 Anthony Thompson | .04 | .02 | .01 |
| Phoenix Cardinals | | | |
| ☐ 450 Steve DeBerg | .10 | .05 | .01 |
| Kansas City Chiefs | | | |
| and Dan Marino | | | |
| Miami Dolphins | | | |
| Team MVP CL 453-473 | | | |
| ☐ 451 Andre Rison MVP | .12 | .05 | .02 |
| Atlanta Falcons | | | |
| ☐ 452 Thurman Thomas MVP | .20 | .09 | .03 |
| Buffalo Bills | | | |
| ☐ 453 Neal Anderson MVP | .04 | .02 | .01 |
| Chicago Bears | | | |
| ☐ 454 Boomer Esiason MVP | .08 | .04 | .01 |
| Cincinnati Bengals | | | |
| ☐ 455 Eric Metcalf MVP | .08 | .04 | .01 |
| Cleveland Browns | | | |
| ☐ 456 Emmitt Smith MVP | 1.00 | .45 | .13 |
| Dallas Cowboys | | | |
| ☐ 457 Bobby Humphrey MVP | .04 | .02 | .01 |
| Denver Broncos | | | |
| ☐ 458 Barry Sanders MVP | .35 | .16 | .04 |
| Detroit Lions | | | |
| ☐ 459 Sterling Sharpe MVP | .25 | .11 | .03 |
| Green Bay Packers | | | |
| ☐ 460 Warren Moon MVP | .10 | .05 | .01 |
| Houston Oilers | | | |
| ☐ 461 Albert Bentley MVP | .04 | .02 | .01 |
| Indianapolis Colts | | | |
| ☐ 462 Steve DeBerg MVP | .08 | .04 | .01 |
| Kansas City Chiefs | | | |
| ☐ 463 Greg Townsend MVP | .04 | .02 | .01 |
| Los Angeles Raiders | | | |
| ☐ 464 Henry Ellard MVP | .08 | .04 | .01 |
| Los Angeles Rams | | | |
| ☐ 465 Dan Marino MVP | .35 | .16 | .04 |
| Miami Dolphins | | | |
| ☐ 466 Anthony Carter MVP | .08 | .04 | .01 |
| Minnesota Vikings | | | |
| ☐ 467 John Stephens MVP | .08 | .04 | .01 |
| New England Patriots | | | |
| ☐ 468 Pat Swilling MVP | .08 | .04 | .01 |
| New Orleans Saints | | | |
| ☐ 469 Ottis Anderson MVP | .08 | .04 | .01 |
| New York Giants | | | |
| ☐ 470 Dennis Byrd MVP | .04 | .02 | .01 |
| New York Jets | | | |
| ☐ 471 Randall Cunningham MVP | .04 | .02 | .01 |
| Philadelphia Eagles | | | |
| ☐ 472 Johnny Johnson MVP | .12 | .05 | .02 |
| Phoenix Cardinals | | | |
| ☐ 473 Rod Woodson MVP | .08 | .04 | .01 |
| Pittsburgh Steelers | | | |
| ☐ 474 Anthony Miller MVP | .10 | .05 | .01 |
| San Diego Chargers | | | |
| ☐ 475 Jerry Rice MVP | .35 | .16 | .04 |
| San Francisco 49ers | | | |
| ☐ 476 John L.Williams MVP | .08 | .04 | .01 |
| Seattle Seahawks | | | |
| ☐ 477 Wayne Haddix MVP | .04 | .02 | .01 |
| Tampa Bay Buccaneers | | | |
| ☐ 478 Earnest Byner MVP | .04 | .02 | .01 |
| Washington Redskins | | | |
| ☐ 479 Doug Widell | .04 | .02 | .01 |
| Denver Broncos | | | |
| ☐ 480 Tommy Hodson | .04 | .02 | .01 |
| New England Patriots | | | |
| ☐ 481 Shawn Collins | .04 | .02 | .01 |
| Atlanta Falcons | | | |
| ☐ 482 Rickey Jackson | .08 | .04 | .01 |
| New Orleans Saints | | | |
| ☐ 483 Tony Casillas | .04 | .02 | .01 |
| Atlanta Falcons | | | |
| ☐ 484 Vaughan Johnson | .08 | .04 | .01 |
| New Orleans Saints | | | |
| ☐ 485 Floyd Dixon | .04 | .02 | .01 |
| Atlanta Falcons | | | |
| ☐ 486 Eric Green | .15 | .07 | .02 |
| Pittsburgh Steelers | | | |
| ☐ 487 Harry Hamilton | .04 | .02 | .01 |
| Tampa Bay Buccaneers | | | |
| ☐ 488 Gary Anderson | .04 | .02 | .01 |
| Pittsburgh Steelers | | | |
| ☐ 489 Bruce Hill | .04 | .02 | .01 |
| Tampa Bay Buccaneers | | | |
| ☐ 490 Gerald Williams | .04 | .02 | .01 |
| Pittsburgh Steelers | | | |
| ☐ 491 Cortez Kennedy | .25 | .11 | .03 |
| Seattle Seahawks | | | |
| ☐ 492 Chet Brooks | .04 | .02 | .01 |
| San Francisco 49ers | | | |
| ☐ 493 Dwayne Harper | .15 | .07 | .02 |
| Seattle Seahawks | | | |
| ☐ 494 Don Griffin | .04 | .02 | .01 |
| San Francisco 49ers | | | |
| ☐ 495 Andy Heck | .04 | .02 | .01 |
| Seattle Seahawks | | | |
| ☐ 496 David Treadwell | .04 | .02 | .01 |
| Denver Broncos | | | |
| ☐ 497 Irv Pankey | .04 | .02 | .01 |
| Los Angeles Rams | | | |
| ☐ 498 Dennis Smith | .08 | .04 | .01 |
| Denver Broncos | | | |
| ☐ 499 Marcus Dupree | .08 | .04 | .01 |
| Los Angeles Rams | | | |
| ☐ 500 Checklist 401-500 | .04 | .02 | .01 |
| ☐ 501 Wendell Davis | .04 | .02 | .01 |
| Chicago Bears | | | |
| ☐ 502 Matt Bahr | .04 | .02 | .01 |
| New York Giants | | | |

| | | | |
|---|---|---|---|
| 503 Rob Burnett | .15 | .07 | .02 |
| Cleveland Browns | | | |
| 504 Maurice Carthon | .04 | .02 | .01 |
| New York Giants | | | |
| 505 Donnell Woolford | .04 | .02 | .01 |
| Chicago Bears | | | |
| 506 Howard Ballard | .04 | .02 | .01 |
| Buffalo Bills | | | |
| 507 Mark Boyer | .04 | .02 | .01 |
| New York Jets | | | |
| 508 Eugene Marve | .04 | .02 | .01 |
| Tampa Bay Buccaneers | | | |
| 509 Joe Kelly | .04 | .02 | .01 |
| New York Jets | | | |
| 510 Will Wolford | .04 | .02 | .01 |
| Buffalo Bills | | | |
| 511 Robert Clark | .04 | .02 | .01 |
| Detroit Lions | | | |
| 512 Matt Brock | .04 | .02 | .01 |
| Green Bay Packers | | | |
| 513 Chris Warren | .30 | .14 | .04 |
| Seattle Seahawks | | | |
| 514 Ken Willis | .04 | .02 | .01 |
| Dallas Cowboys | | | |
| 515 George Jamison | .04 | .02 | .01 |
| Detroit Lions | | | |
| 516 Rufus Porter | .04 | .02 | .01 |
| Seattle Seahawks | | | |
| 517 Mark Higgs | .60 | .25 | .08 |
| Miami Dolphins | | | |
| 518 Thomas Everett | .04 | .02 | .01 |
| Pittsburgh Steelers | | | |
| 519 Robert Brown | .04 | .02 | .01 |
| Green Bay Packers | | | |
| 520 Gene Atkins | .04 | .02 | .01 |
| New Orleans Saints | | | |
| 521 Hardy Nickerson | .04 | .02 | .01 |
| Pittsburgh Steelers | | | |
| 522 Johnny Bailey | .08 | .04 | .01 |
| Chicago Bears | | | |
| 523 William Frizzell | .04 | .02 | .01 |
| Tampa Bay Buccaneers | | | |
| 524 Steve McMichael | .08 | .04 | .01 |
| Chicago Bears | | | |
| 525 Kevin Porter | .04 | .02 | .01 |
| Kansas City Chiefs | | | |
| 526 Carwell Gardner | .04 | .02 | .01 |
| Buffalo Bills | | | |
| 527 Eugene Daniel | .04 | .02 | .01 |
| Indianapolis Colts | | | |
| 528 Vestee Jackson | .04 | .02 | .01 |
| Miami Dolphins | | | |
| 529 Chris Goode | .04 | .02 | .01 |
| Indianapolis Colts | | | |
| 530 Leon Seals | .04 | .02 | .01 |
| Buffalo Bills | | | |
| 531 Darion Conner | .04 | .02 | .01 |
| Atlanta Falcons | | | |
| 532 Stan Brock | .04 | .02 | .01 |
| New Orleans Saints | | | |
| 533 Kirby Jackson | .04 | .02 | .01 |
| Buffalo Bills | | | |
| 534 Marv Cook | .04 | .02 | .01 |
| New England Patriots | | | |
| 535 Bill Fralic | .04 | .02 | .01 |
| Atlanta Falcons | | | |
| 536 Keith Woodside | .04 | .02 | .01 |
| Green Bay Packers | | | |
| 537 Hugh Green | .04 | .02 | .01 |
| Miami Dolphins | | | |
| 538 Grant Feasel | .04 | .02 | .01 |
| Seattle Seahawks | | | |
| 539 Bubba McDowell | .04 | .02 | .01 |
| Houston Oilers | | | |
| 540 Vai Sikahema | .08 | .04 | .01 |
| Green Bay Packers | | | |
| 541 Aaron Cox | .04 | .02 | .01 |
| Los Angeles Rams | | | |
| 542 Roger Craig | .08 | .04 | .01 |
| Los Angeles Raiders | | | |
| 543 Robb Thomas | .04 | .02 | .01 |
| Kansas City Chiefs | | | |
| 544 Ronnie Lott | .10 | .05 | .01 |
| Los Angeles Raiders | | | |
| 545 Robert Delpino | .08 | .04 | .01 |
| Los Angeles Rams | | | |
| 546 Greg McMurtry | .04 | .02 | .01 |
| New England Patriots | | | |
| 547 Jim Morrissey | .15 | .07 | .02 |
| Chicago Bears | | | |
| 548 Johnny Rembert | .04 | .02 | .01 |
| New England Patriots | | | |
| 549 Markus Paul | .10 | .05 | .01 |
| Chicago Bears | | | |
| 550 Karl Wilson | .10 | .05 | .01 |
| Los Angeles Rams | | | |
| 551 Gaston Green | .08 | .04 | .01 |
| Denver Broncos | | | |
| 552 Willie Drewrey | .04 | .02 | .01 |
| Tampa Bay Buccaneers | | | |
| 553 Michael Young | .04 | .02 | .01 |
| Denver Broncos | | | |
| 554 Tom Tupa | .08 | .04 | .01 |
| Phoenix Cardinals | | | |
| 555 John Friesz | .10 | .05 | .01 |
| San Diego Chargers | | | |
| 556 Cody Carlson | .75 | .35 | .09 |
| Houston Oilers | | | |
| 557 Eric Allen | .08 | .04 | .01 |
| Philadelphia Eagles | | | |
| 558 Tom Benson | .04 | .02 | .01 |
| Los Angeles Raiders | | | |
| 559 Scott Mersereau | .04 | .02 | .01 |
| New York Jets | | | |
| 560 Lionel Washington | .04 | .02 | .01 |
| Los Angeles Raiders | | | |
| 561 Brian Brennan | .04 | .02 | .01 |
| Cleveland Browns | | | |
| 562 Jim Jeffcoat | .04 | .02 | .01 |
| Dallas Cowboys | | | |
| 563 Jeff Jaeger | .04 | .02 | .01 |
| Los Angeles Raiders | | | |
| 564 David Johnson | .04 | .02 | .01 |
| Pittsburgh Steelers | | | |
| 565 Danny Villa | .04 | .02 | .01 |
| New England Patriots | | | |
| 566 Don Beebe | .10 | .05 | .01 |
| Buffalo Bills | | | |
| 567 Michael Haynes | .30 | .14 | .04 |
| Atlanta Falcons | | | |
| 568 Brett Faryniarz | .04 | .02 | .01 |
| Los Angeles Rams | | | |
| 569 Mike Prior | .04 | .02 | .01 |
| Indianapolis Colts | | | |
| 570 John Davis | .04 | .02 | .01 |
| Buffalo Bills | | | |
| 571 Vernon Turner | .10 | .05 | .01 |
| Los Angeles Rams | | | |
| 572 Michael Brooks | .04 | .02 | .01 |
| Denver Broncos | | | |
| 573 Mike Gann | .04 | .02 | .01 |
| Atlanta Falcons | | | |
| 574 Ron Holmes | .04 | .02 | .01 |
| Denver Broncos | | | |
| 575 Gary Plummer | .04 | .02 | .01 |
| San Diego Chargers | | | |
| 576 Bill Romanowski | .04 | .02 | .01 |
| San Francisco 49ers | | | |
| 577 Chris Jacke | .04 | .02 | .01 |
| Green Bay Packers | | | |
| 578 Gary Reasons | .04 | .02 | .01 |
| New York Giants | | | |
| 579 Tim Jorden | .04 | .02 | .01 |
| Phoenix Cardinals | | | |
| 580 Tim McKyer | .08 | .04 | .01 |
| Atlanta Falcons | | | |
| 581 Johnny Jackson | .04 | .02 | .01 |
| San Francisco 49ers | | | |
| 582 Ethan Horton | .04 | .02 | .01 |
| Los Angeles Raiders | | | |
| 583 Pete Stoyanovich | .08 | .04 | .01 |
| Miami Dolphins | | | |
| 584 Jeff Query | .04 | .02 | .01 |
| Green Bay Packers | | | |
| 585 Frank Reich | .10 | .05 | .01 |
| Buffalo Bills | | | |
| 586 Riki Ellison | .04 | .02 | .01 |
| Los Angeles Raiders | | | |
| 587 Eric Hill | .04 | .02 | .01 |
| Phoenix Cardinals | | | |
| 588 Anthony Shelton | .04 | .02 | .01 |
| San Diego Chargers | | | |
| 589 Steve Smith | .08 | .04 | .01 |
| Los Angeles Raiders | | | |
| 590 Garth Jax | .04 | .02 | .01 |
| Phoenix Cardinals | | | |
| 591 Greg Davis | .10 | .05 | .01 |
| Phoenix Cardinals | | | |
| 592 Bill Maas | .04 | .02 | .01 |
| Kansas City Chiefs | | | |
| 593 Henry Rolling | .04 | .02 | .01 |
| San Diego Chargers | | | |
| 594 Keith Jones | .04 | .02 | .01 |
| Atlanta Falcons | | | |
| 595 Tootie Robbins | .04 | .02 | .01 |
| Phoenix Cardinals | | | |
| 596 Brian Jordan | .10 | .05 | .01 |
| Atlanta Falcons | | | |
| 597 Derrick Walker | .04 | .02 | .01 |
| San Diego Chargers | | | |
| 598 Jonathan Hayes | .04 | .02 | .01 |
| Kansas City Chiefs | | | |
| 599 Nate Lewis | .25 | .11 | .03 |
| San Diego Chargers | | | |
| 600 Checklist 501-600 | .04 | .02 | .01 |

|  |  |  | | | |
|---|--------|------|---|---|---|
| □ 601 | AFC Checklist RF | | .15 | .07 | .02 |
| | Mike Croel | | | | |
| | Greg Lewis | | | | |
| | Keith Traylor | | | | |
| | Kenny Walker | | | | |
| | | Denver Broncos | | | |
| □ 602 | James Jones RF | | .15 | .07 | .02 |
| | | Cleveland Browns | | | |
| □ 603 | Tim Barnett RF | | .15 | .07 | .02 |
| | | Kansas City Chiefs | | | |
| □ 604 | Ed King RF | | .06 | .03 | .01 |
| | | Cleveland Browns | | | |
| □ 605 | Shane Curry RF | | .06 | .03 | .01 |
| | | Indianapolis Colts | | | |
| □ 606 | Mike Croel RF | | .10 | .05 | .01 |
| | | Denver Broncos | | | |
| □ 607 | Bryan Cox RF | | .40 | .18 | .05 |
| | | Miami Dolphins | | | |
| □ 608 | Shawn Jefferson RF | | .10 | .05 | .01 |
| | | San Diego Chargers | | | |
| □ 609 | Kenny Walker RF | | .06 | .03 | .01 |
| | | Denver Broncos | | | |
| □ 610 | Michael Jackson RF | | .75 | .35 | .09 |
| | | Cleveland Browns | | | |
| □ 611 | Jon Vaughn RF | | .20 | .09 | .03 |
| | | New England Patriots | | | |
| □ 612 | Greg Lewis RF | | .06 | .03 | .01 |
| | | Denver Broncos | | | |
| □ 613 | Joe Valerio RF | | .06 | .03 | .01 |
| | | Kansas City Chiefs | | | |
| □ 614 | Pat Harlow RF | | .10 | .05 | .01 |
| | | New England Patriots | | | |
| □ 615 | Henry Jones RF | | .25 | .11 | .03 |
| | | Buffalo Bills | | | |
| □ 616 | Jeff Graham RF | | .35 | .16 | .04 |
| | | Pittsburgh Steelers | | | |
| □ 617 | Darryll Lewis RF | | .10 | .05 | .01 |
| | | Houston Oilers | | | |
| □ 618 | Keith Traylor RF UER | | .06 | .03 | .01 |
| | | Denver Broncos | | | |
| | (Bronchos on back) | | | | |
| □ 619 | Scott Miller RF | | .06 | .03 | .01 |
| | | Miami Dolphins | | | |
| □ 620 | Nick Bell RF | | .10 | .05 | .01 |
| | | Los Angeles Raiders | | | |
| □ 621 | John Flannery RF | | .06 | .03 | .01 |
| | | Houston Oilers | | | |
| □ 622 | Leonard Russell RF | | 1.00 | .45 | .13 |
| | | New England Patriots | | | |
| □ 623 | Alfred Williams RF | | .15 | .07 | .02 |
| | | Cincinnati Bengals | | | |
| □ 624 | Browning Nagle RF | | .10 | .05 | .01 |
| | | New York Jets | | | |
| □ 625 | Harvey Williams RF | | .10 | .05 | .01 |
| | | Kansas City Chiefs | | | |
| □ 626 | Dan McGwire RF | | .06 | .03 | .01 |
| | | Seattle Seahawks | | | |
| □ 627 | NFC Checklist RF | | .25 | .11 | .03 |
| | Brett Favre | | | | |
| | Moe Gardner | | | | |
| | Erric Pegram | | | | |
| | Bruce Pickens | | | | |
| | Mike Pritchard | | | | |
| | | Atlanta Falcons | | | |
| □ 628 | William Thomas RF | | .06 | .03 | .01 |
| | | Philadelphia Eagles | | | |
| □ 629 | Lawrence Dawsey RF | | .20 | .09 | .03 |
| | | Tampa Bay Buccaneers | | | |
| □ 630 | Aeneas Williams RF | | .15 | .07 | .02 |
| | | Phoenix Cardinals | | | |
| □ 631 | Stan Thomas RF | | .06 | .03 | .01 |
| | | Chicago Bears | | | |
| □ 632 | Randal Hill RF | | .15 | .07 | .02 |
| | | Phoenix Cardinals | | | |
| □ 633 | Moe Gardner RF | | .10 | .05 | .01 |
| | | Atlanta Falcons | | | |
| □ 634 | Alvin Harper RF | | .50 | .23 | .06 |
| | | Dallas Cowboys | | | |
| □ 635 | Esera Tuaolo RF | | .06 | .03 | .01 |
| | | Green Bay Packers | | | |
| □ 636 | Russell Maryland RF | | .15 | .07 | .02 |
| | | Dallas Cowboys | | | |
| □ 637 | Anthony Morgan RF | | .10 | .05 | .01 |
| | | Chicago Bears | | | |
| □ 638 | Erric Pegram RF | | 1.25 | .55 | .16 |
| | | Atlanta Falcons | | | |
| □ 639 | Herman Moore RF | | .50 | .23 | .06 |
| | | Detroit Lions | | | |
| □ 640 | Ricky Ervins RF | | .20 | .09 | .03 |
| | | Washington Redskins | | | |
| □ 641 | Kelvin Pritchett RF | | .06 | .03 | .01 |
| | | Detroit Lions | | | |
| □ 642 | Roman Phifer RF | | .10 | .05 | .01 |
| | | Los Angeles Rams | | | |
| □ 643 | Antone Davis RF | | .06 | .03 | .01 |
| | | Philadelphia Eagles | | | |
| □ 644 | Mike Pritchard RF | | .40 | .18 | .05 |
| | | Atlanta Falcons | | | |
| □ 645 | Vinnie Clark RF | | .06 | .03 | .01 |
| | | Green Bay Packers | | | |
| □ 646 | Jake Reed RF | | .15 | .07 | .02 |
| | | Minnesota Vikings | | | |
| □ 647 | Brett Favre RF | | 1.00 | .45 | .13 |
| | | Atlanta Falcons | | | |
| □ 648 | Todd Lyght RF | | .06 | .03 | .01 |
| | | Los Angeles Rams | | | |
| □ 649 | Bruce Pickens RF | | .06 | .03 | .01 |
| | | Atlanta Falcons | | | |
| □ 650 | Darren Lewis RF | | .20 | .09 | .03 |
| | | Chicago Bears | | | |
| □ 651 | Wesley Carroll RF | | .06 | .03 | .01 |
| | | New Orleans Saints | | | |
| □ 652 | James Joseph RF | | .20 | .09 | .03 |
| | | Philadelphia Eagles | | | |
| □ 653 | Robert Delpino AR | | .04 | .02 | .01 |
| | | Los Angeles Rams | | | |
| | Tim McDonald | | | | |
| | | Phoenix Cardinals | | | |
| □ 654 | Vencie Glenn AR | | .10 | .05 | .01 |
| | | New Orleans Saints | | | |
| | Deion Sanders | | | | |
| | | Atlanta Falcons | | | |
| □ 655 | Jerry Rice AR | | .20 | .09 | .03 |
| | | San Francisco 49ers | | | |
| | Terry McDaniel | | | | |
| | | Los Angeles Rams | | | |
| □ 656 | Barry Sanders AR | | .30 | .14 | .04 |
| | | Detroit Lions | | | |
| | Derrick Thomas | | | | |
| | | Kansas City Chiefs | | | |
| □ 657 | Ken Tippins AR | | .04 | .02 | .01 |
| | | Atlanta Falcons | | | |
| | Lorenzo White | | | | |
| | | Houston Oilers | | | |
| □ 658 | Christian Okoye AR | | .08 | .04 | .01 |
| | | Kansas City Chiefs | | | |
| | Jacob Green | | | | |
| | | Seattle Seahawks | | | |
| □ 659 | Rich Gannon | | .08 | .04 | .01 |
| | | Minnesota Vikings | | | |
| □ 660 | Johnny Meads | | .04 | .02 | .01 |
| | | Houston Oilers | | | |
| □ 661 | J.J. Birden | | .40 | .18 | .05 |
| | | Kansas City Chiefs | | | |
| □ 662 | Bruce Kozerski | | .04 | .02 | .01 |
| | | Cincinnati Bengals | | | |
| □ 663 | Felix Wright | | .04 | .02 | .01 |
| | | Minnesota Vikings | | | |
| □ 664 | Al Smith | | .04 | .02 | .01 |
| | | Houston Oilers | | | |
| □ 665 | Stan Humphries | | .20 | .09 | .03 |
| | | Washington Redskins | | | |
| □ 666 | Alfred Anderson | | .04 | .02 | .01 |
| | | Minnesota Vikings | | | |
| □ 667 | Nate Newton | | .04 | .02 | .01 |
| | | Dallas Cowboys | | | |
| □ 668 | Vince Workman | | .40 | .18 | .05 |
| | | Green Bay Packers | | | |
| □ 669 | Ricky Reynolds | | .04 | .02 | .01 |
| | | Tampa Bay Buccaneers | | | |
| □ 670 | Bryce Paup | | .25 | .11 | .03 |
| | | Green Bay Packers | | | |
| □ 671 | Gill Fenerty | | .08 | .04 | .01 |
| | | New Orleans Saints | | | |
| □ 672 | Darrell Thompson | | .08 | .04 | .01 |
| | | Green Bay Packers | | | |
| □ 673 | Anthony Smith | | .08 | .04 | .01 |
| | | Los Angeles Raiders | | | |
| □ 674 | Darryl Henley | | .04 | .02 | .01 |
| | | Los Angeles Rams | | | |
| □ 675 | Brett Maxie | | .04 | .02 | .01 |
| | | New Orleans Saints | | | |
| □ 676 | Craig Taylor | | .04 | .02 | .01 |
| | | Cincinnati Bengals | | | |
| □ 677 | Steve Wallace | | .04 | .02 | .01 |
| | | San Francisco 49ers | | | |
| □ 678 | Jeff Feagles | | .04 | .02 | .01 |
| | | Philadelphia Eagles | | | |
| □ 679 | James Washington | | .20 | .09 | .03 |
| | | Dallas Cowboys | | | |
| □ 680 | Tim Harris | | .08 | .04 | .01 |
| | | San Francisco 49ers | | | |
| □ 681 | Dennis Gibson | | .04 | .02 | .01 |
| | | Detroit Lions | | | |
| □ 682 | Toi Cook | | .04 | .02 | .01 |
| | | New Orleans Saints | | | |
| □ 683 | Lorenzo Lynch | | .04 | .02 | .01 |
| | | Phoenix Cardinals | | | |
| □ 684 | Brad Edwards | | .04 | .02 | .01 |
| | | Washington Redskins | | | |
| □ 685 | Ray Crockett | | .10 | .05 | .01 |
| | | Detroit Lions | | | |
| □ 686 | Harris Barton | | .04 | .02 | .01 |
| | | San Francisco 49ers | | | |
| □ 687 | Byron Evans | | .08 | .04 | .01 |

Philadelphia Eagles

| | | MINT | EXC | G-VG |
|---|---|---|---|---|
| ☐ 688 | Eric Thomas | .04 | .02 | .01 |
| | Cincinnati Bengals | | | |
| ☐ 689 | Jeff Criswell | .04 | .02 | .01 |
| | New York Jets | | | |
| ☐ 690 | Eric Ball | .04 | .02 | .01 |
| | Cincinnati Bengals | | | |
| ☐ 691 | Brian Mitchell | .15 | .07 | .02 |
| | Washington Redskins | | | |
| ☐ 692 | Quinn Early | .08 | .04 | .01 |
| | New Orleans Saints | | | |
| ☐ 693 | Aaron Jones | .04 | .02 | .01 |
| | Philadelphia Eagles | | | |
| ☐ 694 | Jim Dombrowski | .04 | .02 | .01 |
| | New Orleans Saints | | | |
| ☐ 695 | Jeff Bostic | .04 | .02 | .01 |
| | Washington Redskins | | | |
| ☐ 696 | Tony Casillas | .04 | .02 | .01 |
| | Dallas Cowboys | | | |
| ☐ 697 | Ken Lanier | .04 | .02 | .01 |
| | Denver Broncos | | | |
| ☐ 698 | Henry Thomas | .04 | .02 | .01 |
| | Minnesota Vikings | | | |
| ☐ 699 | Steve Beuerlein | .20 | .09 | .03 |
| | Dallas Cowboys | | | |
| ☐ 700 | Checklist 601-700 | .04 | .02 | .01 |
| ☐ SP1 | Darrell Green | 2.00 | .90 | .25 |
| | NFL's Fastest Man | | | |
| ☐ SP2 | Don Shula CO | 2.00 | .90 | .25 |
| | 300th Victory | | | |

## 1991 Upper Deck Heroes Joe Montana

This ten-card Joe Montana set introduces Upper Deck's "Football Heroes" series, which were randomly inserted into 1991 Upper Deck first series foil packs. Montana personally autographed 2,500 of these cards, which feature a diamond hologram as a sign of authenticity. The cards measure the standard size (2 1/2" by 3 1/2"). The front design has color player photos in an oval frame with white and blue borders, on a card face that shades from mustard to brown as one moves from top to bottom. The Upper Deck Football Heroes logo is superimposed at the lower left corner. The backs have a green football field design and summarize various high points in his career. Card number 9 features a portrait of Montana by noted sports artist Vernon Wells. The cards are numbered on the back.

| | MINT | EXC | G-VG |
|---|---|---|---|
| COMPLETE SET (10) | 15.00 | 6.75 | 1.90 |
| COMMON MONTANA (1-9) | 1.00 | .45 | .13 |
| ☐ 1 1974-78 College Years | 1.00 | .45 | .13 |
| ☐ 2 1981 A Star is Born | 1.00 | .45 | .13 |
| ☐ 3 1984 Super Bowl MVP | 1.00 | .45 | .13 |
| ☐ 4 1987 1st Passing Title | 1.00 | .45 | .13 |
| ☐ 5 1988 Rematch | 1.00 | .45 | .13 |
| ☐ 6 1989 NFL's MVP | 1.00 | .45 | .13 |
| ☐ 7 1989 Back-to-Back | 1.00 | .45 | .13 |
| ☐ 8 1990 Career Highs | 1.00 | .45 | .13 |
| ☐ 9 Checklist Heroes 1-9 | 1.00 | .45 | .13 |
| (Vernon Wells portrait of Joe Montana) | | | |
| ☐ AU Joe Montana AU | 300.00 | 135.00 | 38.00 |
| (Certified Autograph) | | | |
| ☐ NNO Title/Header Card SP | 10.00 | 4.50 | 1.25 |

## 1991 Upper Deck Heroes Montana Box Bottoms

These eight oversized "cards" (approximately 5 1/4" by 7 1/4") were featured on the bottom of 1991 Upper Deck low series wax boxes. They are identical in design to the Montana Football Heroes insert cards, with the same color player photos in an oval frame. The backs are blank and the cards are unnumbered. We have checklisted them below according to their Heroes card numbering.

| | MINT | EXC | G-VG |
|---|---|---|---|
| COMPLETE SET (8) | 6.00 | 2.40 | .60 |
| COMMON CARD (1-8) | 1.00 | .40 | .10 |
| ☐ 1 1974-78 College Years | 1.00 | .40 | .10 |
| ☐ 2 1981 A Star is Born | 1.00 | .40 | .10 |
| ☐ 3 1984 Super Bowl MVP | 1.00 | .40 | .10 |
| ☐ 4 1987 1st Passing Title | 1.00 | .40 | .10 |
| ☐ 5 1988 Rematch | 1.00 | .40 | .10 |
| ☐ 6 1989 NFL's MVP | 1.00 | .40 | .10 |
| ☐ 7 1989 Back-to-Back | 1.00 | .40 | .10 |
| ☐ 8 1990 Career Highs | 1.00 | .40 | .10 |

## 1991 Upper Deck Game Breaker Holograms

This nine-card hologram set spotlights outstanding NFL running backs. Holograms 1-6 were randomly inserted in Upper Deck low series wax packs, and holograms 7-9 were inserted in the high series. The standard-size (2 1/2" by 3 1/2") holograms feature a player action shot against the background of a football play diagram with X's and O's. The player's name appears in a stripe toward the bottom, with the words "Game Breaker" in the lower right corner. The backs have the team logo and career summary. The cards are numbered on the back.

| | MINT | EXC | G-VG |
|---|---|---|---|
| COMPLETE SET (9) | 7.00 | 3.10 | .85 |
| COMMON PLAYER (GB1-GB9) | .60 | .25 | .08 |
| ☐ GB1 Barry Sanders | 2.50 | 1.15 | .30 |
| Detroit Lions | | | |
| ☐ GB2 Thurman Thomas | 1.50 | .65 | .19 |
| Buffalo Bills | | | |
| ☐ GB3 Bobby Humphrey | .60 | .25 | .08 |
| Denver Broncos | | | |
| ☐ GB4 Earnest Byner | .60 | .25 | .08 |
| Washington Redskins | | | |
| ☐ GB5 Emmitt Smith | 4.00 | 1.80 | .50 |
| Dallas Cowboys | | | |
| ☐ GB6 Neal Anderson | .60 | .25 | .08 |

Chicago Bears
| | MINT | EXC | G-VG |
|---|---|---|---|
| ☐ GB7 Marion Butts........................ | .60 | .25 | .08 |
| San Diego Chargers | | | |
| ☐ GB8 James Brooks...................... | .60 | .25 | .08 |
| Cincinnati Bengals | | | |
| ☐ GB9 Marcus Allen ...................... | .60 | .25 | .08 |
| Los Angeles Raiders | | | |

## 1991 Upper Deck Heroes Joe Namath

This ten-card Joe Namath set is part of Upper Deck's "Football Heroes" series, which were inserted in its High Number Series packs. Namath personally autographed 2,500 of these cards, and every 100th card was signed "Broadway Joe." The cards measure the standard size (2 1/2" by 3 1/2"). The front design has color player photos in an oval frame with white and blue borders, on a card face that shades from mustard to brown as one moves from top to bottom. The Upper Deck Football Heroes logo is superimposed at the lower left corner. The backs have a green football field design and summarize various high points in his career. Card number 18 features a portrait of Namath by noted sports artist Vernon Wells. The cards are numbered on the back.

| | MINT | EXC | G-VG |
|---|---|---|---|
| COMPLETE SET (10)................... | 14.00 | 6.25 | 1.75 |
| COMMON NAMATH (10-18) ............ | 1.00 | .45 | .13 |
| ☐ 10 1962-65 Crimson Tide ............ | 1.00 | .45 | .13 |
| ☐ 11 1965 Broadway Joe ................ | 1.00 | .45 | .13 |
| ☐ 12 1967 4,000 Yards .................... | 1.00 | .45 | .13 |
| Passing | | | |
| ☐ 13 1968 AFL MVP ...................... | 1.00 | .45 | .13 |
| ☐ 14 1969 Super Bowl III ................ | 1.00 | .45 | .13 |
| ☐ 15 1969 All-Pro......................... | 1.00 | .45 | .13 |
| ☐ 16 1972 400 Yards ...................... | 1.00 | .45 | .13 |
| ☐ 17 1985 Hall of Fame .................. | 1.00 | .45 | .13 |
| ☐ 18 Checklist Heroes 10-18.......... | 1.00 | .45 | .13 |
| (Vernon Wells portrait | | | |
| of Joe Namath) | | | |
| ☐ AU Joe Montana AU ..................... | 300.00 | 135.00 | 38.00 |
| (Certified Autograph) | | | |
| ☐ NNO Title/Header Card SP .......... | 8.00 | 3.60 | 1.00 |

## 1991 Upper Deck Heroes Namath Box Bottoms

These eight oversized "cards" (approximately 5 1/4" by 7 1/4") were featured on the bottom of 1991 Upper Deck high series wax boxes.

They are identical in design to the Namath Football Heroes insert cards, with the same color player photos in an oval frame. The backs are blank and the cards are unnumbered. We have checklisted them below according to the numbering of the Heroes cards.

| | MINT | EXC | G-VG |
|---|---|---|---|
| COMPLETE SET (8)........................ | 6.00 | 2.40 | .60 |
| COMMON CARD (10-17) ................. | 1.00 | .40 | .10 |
| ☐ 10 1962-65 Crimson Tide ............ | 1.00 | .40 | .10 |
| ☐ 11 1965 Broadway Joe ............... | 1.00 | .40 | .10 |
| ☐ 12 1967 4,000 Yards .................. | 1.00 | .40 | .10 |
| Passing | | | |
| ☐ 13 1968 AFL MVP ...................... | 1.00 | .40 | .10 |
| ☐ 14 1969 Super Bowl III ................ | 1.00 | .40 | .10 |
| ☐ 15 1969 All-Pro ........................ | 1.00 | .40 | .10 |
| ☐ 16 1972 400 Yards ..................... | 1.00 | .40 | .10 |
| ☐ 17 1985 Hall of Fame .................. | 1.00 | .40 | .10 |

## 1991 Upper Deck Sheets

Upper Deck issued two football sheets in 1991. The 8 1/2" by 11" sheet to honor the Super Bowl XXV Champions features six Upper Deck Giants cards, which are listed as they appear counterclockwise beginning from the upper left corner. The background is a green football field design. At the top are the words, "Washington Redskins vs. New York Giants" and "The Upper Deck Company Salutes The Super Bowl XXV Champions" in yellow lettering. In the center are game highlights in red lettering. The sheet is bordered by two blue and one red stripe. The issue date appears in the lower right corner as do the production run and issue number, which appear in the Upper Deck gold foil stamp. The Rams sheet commemorated the 40th anniversary of the 1951 Rams championship team. Reportedly 60,000 sheets were distributed but were not individually numbered; this sheet was slightly larger than the other typical Upper Deck sheets. The backs of both sheets are blank.

| | MINT | EXC | G-VG |
|---|---|---|---|
| COMPLETE SET (2)......................... | 15.00 | 6.00 | 1.50 |
| COMMON SHEET (1-2) ................... | 8.00 | 3.25 | .80 |
| ☐ 1 Los Angeles Rams ................... | 8.00 | 3.25 | .80 |
| Commemorative Sheet | | | |
| October 1991 (60,000) | | | |
| ☐ 2 New York Giants ...................... | 8.00 | 3.25 | .80 |
| vs. Washington Redskins | | | |
| October 27, 1991 | | | |
| (SB XXV Champions (72,000) | | | |
| Rodney Hampton | | | |
| Lawrence Taylor | | | |
| Dave Meggett | | | |
| Jeff Hostetler | | | |
| Mark Collins | | | |
| Ottis Anderson | | | |

## 1992 Upper Deck SCD Sheets

Upper Deck produced eight different sheets for insertion into the Sept. 18, 1992, issue of Sports Collector's Digest. Reportedly 8,000 of each sheet were produced, and one was inserted into each SCD issue. The 11" by 8 1/2" sheet features two rows of three cards each, on a speckled granite background. The backs are covered by the phrase "Upper Deck Limited Edition Commemorative Sheet." The sheets are numbered at the lower left corner "Version X of 8."

| | MINT | EXC | G-VG |
|---|---|---|---|
| COMPLETE SET (8)......................... | 50.00 | 20.00 | 5.00 |
| COMMON SHEET (1-8) .................... | 6.00 | 2.40 | .60 |
| ☐ 1 Randall Cunningham................. | 12.00 | 5.00 | 1.20 |
| Philadelphia Eagles | | | |
| David Klingler | | | |
| Cincinnati Bengals | | | |
| Dan Marino | | | |

Miami Dolphins
Troy Aikman
Dallas Cowboys
Jim Kelly
Buffalo Bills
Bernie Kosar
Cleveland Browns
☐ 2 Phillippi Sparks ....................... 6.00 2.40 .60
New York Giants
Dale Carter
Kansas City Chiefs
Steve Emtman
Indianapolis Colts
Kevin Smith
Dallas Cowboys
Marco Coleman
Miami Dolphins
Carl Pickens
Cincinnati Bengals
☐ 3 Quentin Coryatt ....................... 6.00 2.40 .60
Indianapolis Colts
Greg Skrepenak
Los Angeles Raiders
Chester McGlockton
Los Angeles Raiders
Kurt Barber
New York Jets
Vaughn Dunbar
New Orleans Saints
Ashley Ambrose
Indianapolis Colts
☐ 4 Ty Detmer ............................... 6.00 2.40 .60
Green Bay Packers
Steve Israel
Los Angeles Rams
Tracy Scroggins
Detroit Lions
Todd Collins
New England Patriots
Alonzo Spellman
Chicago Bears
Marquez Pope
San Diego Chargers
☐ 5 Eric Dickerson ......................... 10.00 4.00 1.00
Los Angeles Raiders
Randal Hill
Phoenix Cardinals
Jim Kelly
Buffalo Bills
Bernie Kosar
Cleveland Browns
Deion Sanders
Atlanta Falcons
Andre Reed
Buffalo Bills
☐ 6 Joe Montana ........................... 10.00 4.00 1.00
San Francisco 49ers
Mike Singletary
Chicago Bears
Randall Cunningham
Philadelphia Eagles
Anthony Miller
San Diego Chargers
Dan McGwire
Seattle Seahawks
Harvey Williams
Kansas City Chiefs
☐ 7 Al Toon .................................... 10.00 4.00 1.00

New York Jets
Michael Dean Perry
Cleveland Browns
Troy Aikman
Dallas Cowboys
Jeff George
Indianapolis Colts
Carl Banks
New York Giants
Junior Seau
San Diego Chargers
☐ 8 Dan Marino .............................. 10.00 4.00 1.00
Miami Dolphins
Tommy Maddox
Denver Broncos
Bruce Smith
Buffalo Bills
Leslie O'Neal
San Diego Chargers
Lawrence Taylor
New York Giants
Jerry Rice
San Francisco 49ers

# 1992 Upper Deck NFL Sheets

As an advertising promotion, Upper Deck released 8 1/2" by 11" commemorative sheets printed on card stock and picturing a series of Upper Deck cards. The fronts feature either captions indicating the event the sheet commemorates, or text advertising Upper Deck cards. The sheets have an Upper Deck stamp indicating the production run and serial number. The backs of the game sheets are blank. The backs of the advertising sheets are printed in black with the words "Upper Deck Limited Edition Commemorative Sheet." The AFC and NFC championship game commemorative sheets were distributed at Upper Deck's Super Bowl Card Show III and at the NFL Experience in Minneapolis. The Super Bowl XXVI sheet was given away at the downtown Hyatt and other area hotels hosting Super Bowl guests in Minneapolis. In the listing of sheets below, the players cards are listed beginning in the upper left corner of the sheet and moving toward the lower right corner. A sheet was also issued to promote Upper Deck's 1992 Comic Ball Comic Bowl IV cards. The front features a color photo of Lawrence Taylor, Jerry Rice, Thurman Thomas, Dan Marino, and various Looney Tunes characters set against a blue sky background. A green bottom border carries the issue number and production run in the Upper Deck gold foil stamp, the Looney Tunes logo, and product information. The Comic Ball logo overlaps the green border and the photo. The entire sheet is bordered by a thin black and wider white border.

| | MINT | EXC | G-VG |
|---|---|---|---|
| COMPLETE SET (4) ........................ | 30.00 | 12.00 | 3.00 |
| COMMON SHEET (1-4) .................... | 7.50 | 3.00 | .75 |
| ☐ 1 AFC Championship ................... | 7.50 | 3.00 | .75 |
| Denver Broncos | | | |
| vs. Buffalo Bills | | | |
| Jan. 12, 1992 (30,000) | | | |
| Thurman Thomas | | | |
| Cornelius Bennett | | | |
| Andre Reed | | | |
| John Elway | | | |
| Steve Atwater | | | |
| Gaston Green | | | |
| ☐ 2 NFC Championship .................. | 7.50 | 3.00 | .75 |
| Detroit Lions | | | |
| vs. Washington Redskins | | | |
| Jan. 12, 1992 (30,000) | | | |
| Mark Rypien | | | |
| Ricky Ervins | | | |
| Charles Mann | | | |
| Barry Sanders | | | |
| Chris Spielman | | | |
| Mel Gray | | | |
| ☐ 3 Super Bowl XXVI ...................... | 10.00 | 4.00 | 1.00 |

Washington Redskins
Jan. 26, 1992 (15,000)
Mark Rypien
Ricky Ervins
Charles Mann
Gary Clark
Darrell Green
Earnest Byner

| | MINT | EXC | G-VG |
|---|---|---|---|
| ☐ 4 Comic Ball IV | 15.00 | 6.00 | 1.50 |

(15,000)
Lawrence Taylor
Jerry Rice
Thurman Thomas
Dan Marino
Looney Tunes Characters

# 1992 Upper Deck

The 1992 Upper Deck football set was issued in two series and totaled 620 cards. The cards measure the standard size (2 1/2" by 3 1/2"). No low series cards were included in this year's second series packs. First series packs featured the following random insert sets: a ten-card Walter Payton "Football Heroes"; a 15-card Pro Bowl; and five Game Breaker holograms (GB1, GB3, GB4, GB6, and GB8). Randomly inserted throughout series II foil packs were a ten-card Dan Marino "Football Heroes" subset, special sets of James Lofton (SP3) and Art Monk (SP4), and three Game Breaker holograms (GB2, GB5, and GB7). A 20-card "Coach's Report" subset was featured only in hobby packs while ten "Fanimation" cards were included only in retail packs. Inside white borders, the fronts display color action player photos with shadow borders. The team logo appears on a granite slab at the lower left corner, and the player's name and position are printed on a granite bar extending to the right. A team color-coded bar accents the granite bar. The backs carry a second color player photo as well as biographical and statistical information on a granite slab. Topical subsets featured are Star Rookie (1-29), All-Rookie (30-55), Team Checklists (73-100), Season Leader (301-311), Team MVP (350-378), Rookie Force (401-426), and NFL Scrapbook (511-520). The cards are numbered on the back. Rookie Cards include Edgar Bennett, Steve Bono, Terrell Buckley, Amp Lee, Tommy Vardell, Courtney Hawkins, Robert Jones, Johnny Mitchell, Derek Moore, Todd Philcox and Troy Vincent.

| | MINT | EXC | G-VG |
|---|---|---|---|
| COMPLETE SET (620) | 20.00 | 9.00 | 2.50 |
| COMPLETE SERIES 1 (400) | 14.00 | 6.25 | 1.75 |
| COMPLETE SERIES 2 (220) | 6.00 | 2.70 | .75 |
| COMMON PLAYER (1-400) | .05 | .02 | .01 |
| COMMON PLAYER (401-620) | .05 | .02 | .01 |
| ☐ 1 Star Rookie Checklist | .25 | .11 | .03 |
|    Edgar Bennett | | | |
|    Terrell Buckley | | | |
|    Dexter McNabb | | | |
| ☐ 2 Edgar Bennett | .30 | .14 | .04 |
|    Green Bay Packers | | | |
| ☐ 3 Eddie Blake | .05 | .02 | .01 |
|    Miami Dolphins | | | |
| ☐ 4 Brian Bollinger | .05 | .02 | .01 |
|    San Francisco 49ers | | | |
| ☐ 5 Joe Bowden | .05 | .02 | .01 |
|    Houston Oilers | | | |
| ☐ 6 Terrell Buckley | .25 | .11 | .03 |
|    Green Bay Packers | | | |
| ☐ 7 Willie Clay | .05 | .02 | .01 |
|    Detroit Lions | | | |
| ☐ 8 Ed Cunningham | .05 | .02 | .01 |
|    Phoenix Cardinals | | | |
| ☐ 9 Matt Darby | .05 | .02 | .01 |
|    Buffalo Bills | | | |
| ☐ 10 Will Furrer | .15 | .07 | .02 |
|    Chicago Bears | | | |
| ☐ 11 Chris Hakel | .10 | .05 | .01 |
|    Washington Redskins | | | |
| ☐ 12 Carlos Huerta | .05 | .02 | .01 |
|    San Diego Chargers | | | |
| ☐ 13 Amp Lee | .25 | .11 | .03 |
|    San Francisco 49ers | | | |
| ☐ 14 Ricardo McDonald | .10 | .05 | .01 |
|    Cincinnati Bengals | | | |
| ☐ 15 Dexter McNabb | .05 | .02 | .01 |
|    Green Bay Packers | | | |
| ☐ 16 Chris Mims | .25 | .11 | .03 |
|    San Diego Chargers | | | |
| ☐ 17 Derrick Moore | .40 | .18 | .05 |
|    Atlanta Falcons | | | |
| ☐ 18 Mark D'Onofrio | .05 | .02 | .01 |
|    Green Bay Packers | | | |
| ☐ 19 Patrick Rowe | .10 | .05 | .01 |
|    Cleveland Browns | | | |
| ☐ 20 Leon Searcy | .05 | .02 | .01 |
|    Pittsburgh Steelers | | | |
| ☐ 21 Torrance Small | .10 | .05 | .01 |
|    New Orleans Saints | | | |
| ☐ 22 Jimmy Smith | .10 | .05 | .01 |
|    Dallas Cowboys | | | |
| ☐ 23 Tony Smith | .10 | .05 | .01 |
|    Kansas City Chiefs | | | |
| ☐ 24 Siran Stacy | .10 | .05 | .01 |
|    Philadelphia Eagles | | | |
| ☐ 25 Kevin Turner | .20 | .09 | .03 |
|    New England Patriots | | | |
| ☐ 26 Tommy Vardell | .30 | .14 | .04 |
|    Cleveland Browns | | | |
| ☐ 27 Bob Whitfield | .12 | .05 | .02 |
|    Atlanta Falcons | | | |
| ☐ 28 Darryl Williams | .20 | .09 | .03 |
|    Cincinnati Bengals | | | |
| ☐ 29 Jeff Sydner | .12 | .05 | .02 |
|    Philadelphia Eagles | | | |
| ☐ 30 All-Rookie Checklist | .12 | .05 | .02 |
|    Mike Croel | | | |
|    Leonard Russell | | | |
| ☐ 31 Todd Marinovich AR | .05 | .02 | .01 |
|    Los Angeles Raiders | | | |
| ☐ 32 Leonard Russell AR | .12 | .05 | .02 |
|    New England Patriots | | | |
| ☐ 33 Nick Bell AR | .05 | .02 | .01 |
|    Los Angeles Raiders | | | |
| ☐ 34 Alvin Harper AR | .20 | .09 | .03 |
|    Dallas Cowboys | | | |
| ☐ 35 Mike Pritchard AR | .25 | .11 | .03 |
|    Atlanta Falcons | | | |
| ☐ 36 Lawrence Dawsey AR | .08 | .04 | .01 |
|    Tampa Bay Buccaneers | | | |
| ☐ 37 Tim Barnett AR | .05 | .02 | .01 |
|    Kansas City Chiefs | | | |
| ☐ 38 John Flannery AR | .05 | .02 | .01 |
|    Houston Oilers | | | |
| ☐ 39 Stan Thomas AR | .05 | .02 | .01 |
|    Chicago Bears | | | |
| ☐ 40 Ed King AR | .05 | .02 | .01 |
|    Cleveland Browns | | | |
| ☐ 41 Charles McRae AR | .05 | .02 | .01 |
|    Tampa Bay Buccaneers | | | |
| ☐ 42 Eric Moten AR | .05 | .02 | .01 |
|    San Diego Chargers | | | |
| ☐ 43 Moe Gardner AR | .05 | .02 | .01 |
|    Atlanta Falcons | | | |
| ☐ 44 Kenny Walker AR | .05 | .02 | .01 |
|    Denver Broncos | | | |
| ☐ 45 Esera Tuaolo AR | .05 | .02 | .01 |
|    Green Bay Packers | | | |
| ☐ 46 Alfred Williams AR | .05 | .02 | .01 |
|    Cincinnati Bengals | | | |
| ☐ 47 Bryan Cox AR | .05 | .02 | .01 |
|    Miami Dolphins | | | |
| ☐ 48 Mo Lewis AR | .05 | .02 | .01 |
|    New York Jets | | | |
| ☐ 49 Mike Croel AR | .05 | .02 | .01 |
|    Denver Broncos | | | |
| ☐ 50 Stanley Richard AR | .05 | .02 | .01 |
|    San Diego Chargers | | | |
| ☐ 51 Tony Covington AR | .05 | .02 | .01 |
|    Tampa Bay Buccaneers | | | |
| ☐ 52 Larry Brown AR | .05 | .02 | .01 |
|    Dallas Cowboys | | | |
| ☐ 53 Aeneas Williams AR | .05 | .02 | .01 |
|    Phoenix Cardinals | | | |
| ☐ 54 John Kasay AR | .05 | .02 | .01 |
|    Seattle Seahawks | | | |
| ☐ 55 Jon Vaughn AR | .05 | .02 | .01 |
|    New England Patriots | | | |
| ☐ 56 David Fulcher | .05 | .02 | .01 |
|    Cincinnati Bengals | | | |
| ☐ 57 Barry Foster | .35 | .16 | .04 |
|    Pittsburgh Steelers | | | |
| ☐ 58 Terry Wooden | .05 | .02 | .01 |
|    Seattle Seahawks | | | |

| | | | |
|---|---|---|---|
| 59 Gary Anderson | .05 | .02 | .01 |
| Pittsburgh Steelers | | | |
| 60 Alfred Williams | .05 | .02 | .01 |
| Cincinnati Bengals | | | |
| 61 Robert Blackmon | .05 | .02 | .01 |
| Seattle Seahawks | | | |
| 62 Brian Noble | .05 | .02 | .01 |
| Green Bay Packers | | | |
| 63 Terry Allen | .20 | .09 | .03 |
| Minnesota Vikings | | | |
| 64 Darrell Green | .08 | .04 | .01 |
| Washington Redskins | | | |
| 65 Darren Comeaux | .05 | .02 | .01 |
| Seattle Seahawks | | | |
| 66 Rob Burnett | .05 | .02 | .01 |
| Cleveland Browns | | | |
| 67 Jarrod Bunch | .05 | .02 | .01 |
| New York Giants | | | |
| 68 Michael Jackson | .10 | .05 | .01 |
| Cleveland Browns | | | |
| 69 Greg Lloyd | .05 | .02 | .01 |
| Pittsburgh Steelers | | | |
| 70 Richard Brown | .05 | .02 | .01 |
| Cleveland Browns | | | |
| 71 Harold Green | .08 | .04 | .01 |
| Cincinnati Bengals | | | |
| 72 William Fuller | .05 | .02 | .01 |
| Houston Oilers | | | |
| 73 Mark Carrier TC | .05 | .02 | .01 |
| Chicago Bears | | | |
| 74 David Fulcher TC | .05 | .02 | .01 |
| Cincinnati Bengals | | | |
| 75 Cornelius Bennett TC | .08 | .04 | .01 |
| Buffalo Bills | | | |
| 76 Steve Atwater TC | .05 | .02 | .01 |
| Denver Broncos | | | |
| 77 Kevin Mack TC | .05 | .02 | .01 |
| Cleveland Browns | | | |
| 78 Mark Carrier TC | .05 | .02 | .01 |
| Tampa Bay Buccaneers | | | |
| 79 Tim McDonald TC | .05 | .02 | .01 |
| Phoenix Cardinals | | | |
| 80 Marion Butts TC | .08 | .04 | .01 |
| San Diego Chargers | | | |
| 81 Christian Okoye TC | .05 | .02 | .01 |
| Kansas City Chiefs | | | |
| 82 Jeff Herrod TC | .05 | .02 | .01 |
| Indianapolis Colts | | | |
| 83 Emmitt Smith TC | 1.00 | .45 | .13 |
| Dallas Cowboys | | | |
| 84 Mark Duper TC | .05 | .02 | .01 |
| Miami Dolphins | | | |
| 85 Keith Jackson TC | .08 | .04 | .01 |
| Philadelphia Eagles | | | |
| 86 Andre Rison TC | .10 | .05 | .01 |
| Atlanta Falcons | | | |
| 87 John Taylor TC | .08 | .04 | .01 |
| San Francisco 49ers | | | |
| 88 Rodney Hampton TC | .15 | .07 | .02 |
| New York Giants | | | |
| 89 Rob Moore TC | .08 | .04 | .01 |
| New York Jets | | | |
| 90 Chris Spielman TC | .05 | .02 | .01 |
| Detroit Lions | | | |
| 91 Haywood Jeffires TC | .08 | .04 | .01 |
| Houston Oilers | | | |
| 92 Sterling Sharpe TC | .20 | .09 | .03 |
| Green Bay Packers | | | |
| 93 Irvin Fryar TC | .05 | .02 | .01 |
| New England Patriots | | | |
| 94 Marcus Allen TC | .08 | .04 | .01 |
| Los Angeles Raiders | | | |
| 95 Henry Ellard TC | .05 | .02 | .01 |
| Los Angeles Rams | | | |
| 96 Mark Rypien TC | .08 | .04 | .01 |
| Washington Redskins | | | |
| 97 Pat Swilling TC | .08 | .04 | .01 |
| New Orleans Saints | | | |
| 98 Brian Blades TC | .05 | .02 | .01 |
| Seattle Seahawks | | | |
| 99 Eric Green TC | .05 | .02 | .01 |
| Pittsburgh Steelers | | | |
| 100 Anthony Carter TC | .05 | .02 | .01 |
| Minnesota Vikings | | | |
| 101 Burt Grossman | .05 | .02 | .01 |
| San Diego Chargers | | | |
| 102 Gary Anderson | .08 | .04 | .01 |
| Tampa Bay Buccaneers | | | |
| 103 Neil Smith | .10 | .05 | .01 |
| Kansas City Chiefs | | | |
| 104 Jeff Feagles | .05 | .02 | .01 |
| Philadelphia Eagles | | | |
| 105 Shane Conlan | .05 | .02 | .01 |
| Buffalo Bills | | | |
| 106 Jay Novacek | .15 | .07 | .02 |
| Dallas Cowboys | | | |
| 107 Billy Brooks | .08 | .04 | .01 |
| Indianapolis Colts | | | |
| 108 Mark Ingram | .08 | .04 | .01 |
| New York Giants | | | |
| 109 Anthony Munoz | .08 | .04 | .01 |
| Cincinnati Bengals | | | |
| 110 Wendell Davis | .05 | .02 | .01 |
| Chicago Bears | | | |
| 111 Jim Everett | .05 | .02 | .01 |
| Los Angeles Rams | | | |
| 112 Bruce Matthews | .08 | .04 | .01 |
| Houston Oilers | | | |
| 113 Mark Higgs | .10 | .05 | .01 |
| Miami Dolphins | | | |
| 114 Chris Warren | .25 | .11 | .03 |
| Seattle Seahawks | | | |
| 115 Brad Baxter | .08 | .04 | .01 |
| New York Jets | | | |
| 116 Greg Townsend | .05 | .02 | .01 |
| Los Angeles Raiders | | | |
| 117 Al Smith | .05 | .02 | .01 |
| Houston Oilers | | | |
| 118 Jeff Cross | .05 | .02 | .01 |
| Miami Dolphins | | | |
| 119 Terry McDaniel | .05 | .02 | .01 |
| Los Angeles Raiders | | | |
| 120 Ernest Givins | .08 | .04 | .01 |
| Houston Oilers | | | |
| 121 Fred Barnett | .10 | .05 | .01 |
| Philadelphia Eagles | | | |
| 122 Flipper Anderson | .08 | .04 | .01 |
| Los Angeles Rams | | | |
| 123 Floyd Turner | .05 | .02 | .01 |
| New Orleans Saints | | | |
| 124 Stephen Baker | .05 | .02 | .01 |
| New York Giants | | | |
| 125 Tim Johnson | .05 | .02 | .01 |
| Washington Redskins | | | |
| 126 Brent Jones | .10 | .05 | .01 |
| San Francisco 49ers | | | |
| 127 Leonard Marshall | .08 | .04 | .01 |
| New York Giants | | | |
| 128 Jim Price | .05 | .02 | .01 |
| Los Angeles Rams | | | |
| 129 Jessie Hester | .05 | .02 | .01 |
| Indianapolis Colts | | | |
| 130 Mark Carrier | .08 | .04 | .01 |
| Tampa Bay Buccaneers | | | |
| 131 Bubba McDowell | .05 | .02 | .01 |
| Houston Oilers | | | |
| 132 Andre Tippett | .08 | .04 | .01 |
| New England Patriots | | | |
| 133 James Hasty | .05 | .02 | .01 |
| New York Jets | | | |
| 134 Mel Gray | .05 | .02 | .01 |
| Detroit Lions | | | |
| 135 Christian Okoye | .08 | .04 | .01 |
| Kansas City Chiefs | | | |
| 136 Earnest Byner | .08 | .04 | .01 |
| Washington Redskins | | | |
| 137 Ferrell Edmunds | .05 | .02 | .01 |
| Miami Dolphins | | | |
| 138 Henry Ellard | .08 | .04 | .01 |
| Los Angeles Rams | | | |
| 139 Rob Moore | .10 | .05 | .01 |
| New York Jets | | | |
| 140 Brian Jordan | .08 | .04 | .01 |
| Atlanta Falcons | | | |
| 141 Clarence Verdin | .05 | .02 | .01 |
| Indianapolis Colts | | | |
| 142 Cornelius Bennett | .10 | .05 | .01 |
| Buffalo Bills | | | |
| 143 John Taylor | .10 | .05 | .01 |
| San Francisco 49ers | | | |
| 144 Derrick Thomas | .15 | .07 | .02 |
| Kansas City Chiefs | | | |
| 145 Thurman Thomas | .40 | .18 | .05 |
| Buffalo Bills | | | |
| 146 Warren Moon | .20 | .09 | .03 |
| Houston Oilers | | | |
| 147 Vinny Testaverde | .10 | .05 | .01 |
| Tampa Bay Buccaneers | | | |
| 148 Steve Bono | .50 | .23 | .06 |
| San Francisco 49ers | | | |
| 149 Robb Thomas | .05 | .02 | .01 |
| Kansas City Chiefs | | | |
| 150 John Friesz | .08 | .04 | .01 |
| San Diego Chargers | | | |
| 151 Richard Dent | .08 | .04 | .01 |
| Chicago Bears | | | |
| 152 Eddie Anderson | .05 | .02 | .01 |
| Los Angeles Raiders | | | |
| 153 Kevin Greene | .08 | .04 | .01 |
| Los Angeles Rams | | | |
| 154 Marion Butts | .10 | .05 | .01 |
| San Diego Chargers | | | |
| 155 Barry Sanders | .75 | .35 | .09 |
| Detroit Lions | | | |
| 156 Andre Rison | .25 | .11 | .03 |

| | | | | | | | |
|---|---|---|---|---|---|---|---|
| Atlanta Falcons | | | | Los Angeles Rams | | | |
| ☐ 157 Ronnie Lott | .10 | .05 | .01 | ☐ 206 Andre Ware | .08 | .04 | .01 |
| Los Angeles Raiders | | | | Detroit Lions | | | |
| ☐ 158 Eric Allen | .08 | .04 | .01 | ☐ 207 Dave Waymer | .05 | .02 | .01 |
| Philadelphia Eagles | | | | San Francisco 49ers | | | |
| ☐ 159 Mark Clayton | .08 | .04 | .01 | ☐ 208 Darren Lewis | .05 | .02 | .01 |
| Miami Dolphins | | | | Chicago Bears | | | |
| ☐ 160 Terance Mathis | .05 | .02 | .01 | ☐ 209 Joey Browner | .05 | .02 | .01 |
| New York Jets | | | | Minnesota Vikings | | | |
| ☐ 161 Darryl Talley | .08 | .04 | .01 | ☐ 210 Rich Miano | .05 | .02 | .01 |
| Buffalo Bills | | | | Philadelphia Eagles | | | |
| ☐ 162 Eric Metcalf | .10 | .05 | .01 | ☐ 211 Marcus Allen | .08 | .04 | .01 |
| Cleveland Browns | | | | Los Angeles Raiders | | | |
| ☐ 163 Reggie Cobb | .10 | .05 | .01 | ☐ 212 Steve Broussard | .08 | .04 | .01 |
| Tampa Bay Buccaneers | | | | Atlanta Falcons | | | |
| ☐ 164 Ernie Jones | .05 | .02 | .01 | ☐ 213 Joel Hilgenberg | .05 | .02 | .01 |
| Phoenix Cardinals | | | | New Orleans Saints | | | |
| ☐ 165 David Griggs | .05 | .02 | .01 | ☐ 214 Bo Orlando | .15 | .07 | .02 |
| Miami Dolphins | | | | Houston Oilers | | | |
| ☐ 166 Tom Rathman | .08 | .04 | .01 | ☐ 215 Clay Matthews | .08 | .04 | .01 |
| San Francisco 49ers | | | | Cleveland Browns | | | |
| ☐ 167 Bubby Brister | .08 | .04 | .01 | ☐ 216 Chris Hinton | .05 | .02 | .01 |
| Pittsburgh Steelers | | | | Atlanta Falcons | | | |
| ☐ 168 Broderick Thomas | .05 | .02 | .01 | ☐ 217 Al Edwards | .05 | .02 | .01 |
| Tampa Bay Buccaneers | | | | Buffalo Bills | | | |
| ☐ 169 Chris Doleman | .08 | .04 | .01 | ☐ 218 Tim Brown | .25 | .11 | .03 |
| Minnesota Vikings | | | | Los Angeles Raiders | | | |
| ☐ 170 Charles Haley | .08 | .04 | .01 | ☐ 219 Sam Mills | .08 | .04 | .01 |
| San Francisco 49ers | | | | New Orleans Saints | | | |
| ☐ 171 Michael Haynes | .30 | .14 | .04 | ☐ 220 Don Majkowski | .08 | .04 | .01 |
| Atlanta Falcons | | | | Green Bay Packers | | | |
| ☐ 172 Rodney Hampton | .40 | .18 | .05 | ☐ 221 James Francis | .08 | .04 | .01 |
| New York Giants | | | | Cincinnati Bengals | | | |
| ☐ 173 Nick Bell | .08 | .04 | .01 | ☐ 222 Steve Hendrickson | .05 | .02 | .01 |
| Los Angeles Raiders | | | | San Diego Chargers | | | |
| ☐ 174 Gene Atkins | .05 | .02 | .01 | ☐ 223 James Thornton | .05 | .02 | .01 |
| New Orleans Saints | | | | Chicago Bears | | | |
| ☐ 175 Mike Merriweather | .05 | .02 | .01 | ☐ 224 Byron Evans | .05 | .02 | .01 |
| Minnesota Vikings | | | | Philadelphia Eagles | | | |
| ☐ 176 Reggie Roby | .05 | .02 | .01 | ☐ 225 Pepper Johnson | .08 | .04 | .01 |
| Miami Dolphins | | | | New York Giants | | | |
| ☐ 177 Bennie Blades | .05 | .02 | .01 | ☐ 226 Darryl Henley | .05 | .02 | .01 |
| Detroit Lions | | | | Los Angeles Rams | | | |
| ☐ 178 John L. Williams | .08 | .04 | .01 | ☐ 227 Simon Fletcher | .08 | .04 | .01 |
| Seattle Seahawks | | | | Denver Broncos | | | |
| ☐ 179 Rodney Peete | .08 | .04 | .01 | ☐ 228 Hugh Millen | .08 | .04 | .01 |
| Detroit Lions | | | | New England Patriots | | | |
| ☐ 180 Greg Montgomery | .05 | .02 | .01 | ☐ 229 Tim McGee | .05 | .02 | .01 |
| Houston Oilers | | | | Cincinnati Bengals | | | |
| ☐ 181 Vince Newsome | .05 | .02 | .01 | ☐ 230 Richmond Webb | .08 | .04 | .01 |
| Cleveland Browns | | | | Miami Dolphins | | | |
| ☐ 182 Andre Collins | .05 | .02 | .01 | ☐ 231 Tony Bennett | .08 | .04 | .01 |
| Washington Redskins | | | | Green Bay Packers | | | |
| ☐ 183 Erik Kramer | .15 | .07 | .02 | ☐ 232 Nate Odomes | .08 | .04 | .01 |
| Detroit Lions | | | | Buffalo Bills | | | |
| ☐ 184 Bryan Hinkle | .05 | .02 | .01 | ☐ 233 Scott Case | .05 | .02 | .01 |
| Pittsburgh Steelers | | | | Atlanta Falcons | | | |
| ☐ 185 Reggie White | .15 | .07 | .02 | ☐ 234 Dalton Hilliard | .05 | .02 | .01 |
| Philadelphia Eagles | | | | New Orleans Saints | | | |
| ☐ 186 Bruce Armstrong | .05 | .02 | .01 | ☐ 235 Paul Gruber | .05 | .02 | .01 |
| New England Patriots | | | | Tampa Bay Buccaneers | | | |
| ☐ 187 Anthony Carter | .08 | .04 | .01 | ☐ 236 Jeff Lageman | .05 | .02 | .01 |
| Minnesota Vikings | | | | New York Jets | | | |
| ☐ 188 Pat Swilling | .08 | .04 | .01 | ☐ 237 Tony Mandarich | .05 | .02 | .01 |
| New Orleans Saints | | | | Green Bay Packers | | | |
| ☐ 189 Robert Delpino | .08 | .04 | .01 | ☐ 238 Cris Dishman | .08 | .04 | .01 |
| Los Angeles Rams | | | | Houston Oilers | | | |
| ☐ 190 Brent Williams | .05 | .02 | .01 | ☐ 239 Steve Walsh | .05 | .02 | .01 |
| New England Patriots | | | | New Orleans Saints | | | |
| ☐ 191 Johnny Johnson | .10 | .05 | .01 | ☐ 240 Moe Gardner | .05 | .02 | .01 |
| Phoenix Cardinals | | | | Atlanta Falcons | | | |
| ☐ 192 Aaron Craver | .05 | .02 | .01 | ☐ 241 Bill Romanowski | .05 | .02 | .01 |
| Miami Dolphins | | | | San Francisco 49ers | | | |
| ☐ 193 Vincent Brown | .05 | .02 | .01 | ☐ 242 Chris Zorich | .08 | .04 | .01 |
| New England Patriots | | | | Chicago Bears | | | |
| ☐ 194 Herschel Walker | .10 | .05 | .01 | ☐ 243 Stephone Paige | .08 | .04 | .01 |
| Minnesota Vikings | | | | Kansas City Chiefs | | | |
| ☐ 195 Tim McDonald | .08 | .04 | .01 | ☐ 244 Mike Croel | .08 | .04 | .01 |
| Phoenix Cardinals | | | | Denver Broncos | | | |
| ☐ 196 Gaston Green | .08 | .04 | .01 | ☐ 245 Leonard Russell | .30 | .14 | .04 |
| Denver Broncos | | | | New England Patriots | | | |
| ☐ 197 Brian Blades | .08 | .04 | .01 | ☐ 246 Mark Rypien | .10 | .05 | .01 |
| Seattle Seahawks | | | | Washington Redskins | | | |
| ☐ 198 Rod Bernstine | .08 | .04 | .01 | ☐ 247 Aeneas Williams | .05 | .02 | .01 |
| San Diego Chargers | | | | Phoenix Cardinals | | | |
| ☐ 199 Brett Perriman | .08 | .04 | .01 | ☐ 248 Steve Atwater | .08 | .04 | .01 |
| Detroit Lions | | | | Denver Broncos | | | |
| ☐ 200 John Elway | .40 | .18 | .05 | ☐ 249 Michael Stewart | .05 | .02 | .01 |
| Denver Broncos | | | | Los Angeles Rams | | | |
| ☐ 201 Michael Carter | .05 | .02 | .01 | ☐ 250 Pierce Holt | .05 | .02 | .01 |
| San Francisco 49ers | | | | San Francisco 49ers | | | |
| ☐ 202 Mark Carrier | .08 | .04 | .01 | ☐ 251 Kevin Mack | .08 | .04 | .01 |
| Chicago Bears | | | | Cleveland Browns | | | |
| ☐ 203 Cris Carter | .10 | .05 | .01 | ☐ 252 Sterling Sharpe | .50 | .23 | .06 |
| Minnesota Vikings | | | | Green Bay Packers | | | |
| ☐ 204 Kyle Clifton | .05 | .02 | .01 | ☐ 253 Lawrence Dawsey | .10 | .05 | .01 |
| New York Jets | | | | Tampa Bay Buccaneers | | | |
| ☐ 205 Alvin Wright | .05 | .02 | .01 | ☐ 254 Emmitt Smith | 2.00 | .90 | .25 |

| | | | | | | | | |
|---|---|---|---|---|---|---|---|---|
| Dallas Cowboys | | | | | Dallas Cowboys | | | |
| ☐ 255 Todd Marinovich | .05 | .02 | .01 | | ☐ 304 Warren Moon SL | .10 | .05 | .01 |
| Los Angeles Raiders | | | | | Houston Oilers | | | |
| ☐ 256 Neal Anderson | .08 | .04 | .01 | | ☐ 305 Chip Lohmiller SL | .08 | .04 | .01 |
| Chicago Bears | | | | | Washington Redskins | | | |
| ☐ 257 Mo Lewis | .05 | .02 | .01 | | ☐ 306 Barry Sanders SL | .35 | .16 | .04 |
| New York Jets | | | | | Detroit Lions | | | |
| ☐ 258 Vance Johnson | .08 | .04 | .01 | | ☐ 307 Ronnie Lott SL | .08 | .04 | .01 |
| Denver Broncos | | | | | Los Angeles Raiders | | | |
| ☐ 259 Rickey Jackson | .08 | .04 | .01 | | ☐ 308 Pat Swilling SL | .08 | .04 | .01 |
| New Orleans Saints | | | | | New Orleans Saints | | | |
| ☐ 260 Esera Tuaolo | .05 | .02 | .01 | | ☐ 309 Thurman Thomas SL | .20 | .09 | .03 |
| Green Bay Packers | | | | | Buffalo Bills | | | |
| ☐ 261 Wilber Marshall | .08 | .04 | .01 | | ☐ 310 Reggie Roby SL | .05 | .02 | .01 |
| Washington Redskins | | | | | Miami Dolphins | | | |
| ☐ 262 Keith Henderson | .05 | .02 | .01 | | ☐ 311 Season Leader CL | .15 | .07 | .02 |
| San Francisco 49ers | | | | | Warren Moon | | | |
| ☐ 263 William Thomas | .05 | .02 | .01 | | Michael Irvin | | | |
| Philadelphia Eagles | | | | | Thurman Thomas | | | |
| ☐ 264 Rickey Dixon | .05 | .02 | .01 | | ☐ 312 Jacob Green | .05 | .02 | .01 |
| Cincinnati Bengals | | | | | Seattle Seahawks | | | |
| ☐ 265 Dave Meggett | .08 | .04 | .01 | | ☐ 313 Stephen Braggs | .05 | .02 | .01 |
| New York Giants | | | | | Cleveland Browns | | | |
| ☐ 266 Gerald Riggs | .08 | .04 | .01 | | ☐ 314 Haywood Jeffires | .10 | .05 | .01 |
| Washington Redskins | | | | | Houston Oilers | | | |
| ☐ 267 Tim Harris | .08 | .04 | .01 | | ☐ 315 Freddie Joe Nunn | .05 | .02 | .01 |
| San Francisco 49ers | | | | | Phoenix Cardinals | | | |
| ☐ 268 Ken Harvey | .05 | .02 | .01 | | ☐ 316 Gary Clark | .08 | .04 | .01 |
| Phoenix Cardinals | | | | | Washington Redskins | | | |
| ☐ 269 Clyde Simmons | .08 | .04 | .01 | | ☐ 317 Tim Barnett | .08 | .04 | .01 |
| Philadelphia Eagles | | | | | Kansas City Chiefs | | | |
| ☐ 270 Irving Fryar | .08 | .04 | .01 | | ☐ 318 Mark Duper | .08 | .04 | .01 |
| New England Patriots | | | | | Miami Dolphins | | | |
| ☐ 271 Darion Conner | .05 | .02 | .01 | | ☐ 319 Eric Green | .10 | .05 | .01 |
| Atlanta Falcons | | | | | Pittsburgh Steelers | | | |
| ☐ 272 Vince Workman | .08 | .04 | .01 | | ☐ 320 Robert Wilson | .05 | .02 | .01 |
| Green Bay Packers | | | | | Tampa Bay Buccaneers | | | |
| ☐ 273 Jim Harbaugh | .08 | .04 | .01 | | ☐ 321 Michael Ball | .05 | .02 | .01 |
| Chicago Bears | | | | | Indianapolis Colts | | | |
| ☐ 274 Lorenzo White | .08 | .04 | .01 | | ☐ 322 Eric Martin | .08 | .04 | .01 |
| Houston Oilers | | | | | New Orleans Saints | | | |
| ☐ 275 Bobby Hebert | .10 | .05 | .01 | | ☐ 323 Alexander Wright | .08 | .04 | .01 |
| New Orleans Saints | | | | | Dallas Cowboys | | | |
| ☐ 276 Duane Bickett | .05 | .02 | .01 | | ☐ 324 Jessie Tuggle | .05 | .02 | .01 |
| Indianapolis Colts | | | | | Atlanta Falcons | | | |
| ☐ 277 Jeff Bryant | .05 | .02 | .01 | | ☐ 325 Ronnie Harmon | .05 | .02 | .01 |
| Seattle Seahawks | | | | | San Diego Chargers | | | |
| ☐ 278 Scott Stephen | .05 | .02 | .01 | | ☐ 326 Jeff Hostetler | .15 | .07 | .02 |
| Green Bay Packers | | | | | New York Giants | | | |
| ☐ 279 Bob Golic | .05 | .02 | .01 | | ☐ 327 Eugene Daniel | .05 | .02 | .01 |
| Los Angeles Raiders | | | | | Indianapolis Colts | | | |
| ☐ 280 Steve McMichael | .08 | .04 | .01 | | ☐ 328 Ken Norton Jr. | .08 | .04 | .01 |
| Chicago Bears | | | | | Dallas Cowboys | | | |
| ☐ 281 Jeff Graham | .08 | .04 | .01 | | ☐ 329 Reyna Thompson | .05 | .02 | .01 |
| Pittsburgh Steelers | | | | | New York Giants | | | |
| ☐ 282 Keith Jackson | .10 | .05 | .01 | | ☐ 330 Jerry Ball | .08 | .04 | .01 |
| Philadelphia Eagles | | | | | Detroit Lions | | | |
| ☐ 283 Howard Ballard | .05 | .02 | .01 | | ☐ 331 Leroy Hoard | .08 | .04 | .01 |
| Buffalo Bills | | | | | Cleveland Browns | | | |
| ☐ 284 Michael Brooks | .05 | .02 | .01 | | ☐ 332 Chris Martin | .05 | .02 | .01 |
| Denver Broncos | | | | | Kansas City Chiefs | | | |
| ☐ 285 Freeman McNeil | .05 | .02 | .01 | | ☐ 333 Keith McKeller | .05 | .02 | .01 |
| New York Jets | | | | | Buffalo Bills | | | |
| ☐ 286 Rodney Holman | .05 | .02 | .01 | | ☐ 334 Brian Washington | .05 | .02 | .01 |
| Cincinnati Bengals | | | | | New York Jets | | | |
| ☐ 287 Eric Bieniemy | .08 | .04 | .01 | | ☐ 335 Eugene Robinson | .05 | .02 | .01 |
| San Diego Chargers | | | | | Seattle Seahawks | | | |
| ☐ 288 Seth Joyner | .08 | .04 | .01 | | ☐ 336 Maurice Hurst | .05 | .02 | .01 |
| Philadelphia Eagles | | | | | New England Patriots | | | |
| ☐ 289 Carwell Gardner | .05 | .02 | .01 | | ☐ 337 Dan Saleaumua | .05 | .02 | .01 |
| Buffalo Bills | | | | | Kansas City Chiefs | | | |
| ☐ 290 Brian Mitchell | .08 | .04 | .01 | | ☐ 338 Neil O'Donnell | .50 | .23 | .06 |
| Washington Redskins | | | | | Pittsburgh Steelers | | | |
| ☐ 291 Chris Miller | .10 | .05 | .01 | | ☐ 339 Dexter Davis | .05 | .02 | .01 |
| Atlanta Falcons | | | | | Phoenix Cardinals | | | |
| ☐ 292 Ray Berry | .05 | .02 | .01 | | ☐ 340 Keith McCants | .05 | .02 | .01 |
| Minnesota Vikings | | | | | Tampa Bay Buccaneers | | | |
| ☐ 293 Matt Brock | .05 | .02 | .01 | | ☐ 341 Steve Beuerlein | .20 | .09 | .03 |
| Green Bay Packers | | | | | Dallas Cowboys | | | |
| ☐ 294 Eric Thomas | .05 | .02 | .01 | | ☐ 342 Roman Phifer | .05 | .02 | .01 |
| Cincinnati Bengals | | | | | Los Angeles Rams | | | |
| ☐ 295 John Kasay | .05 | .02 | .01 | | ☐ 343 Bryan Cox | .08 | .04 | .01 |
| Seattle Seahawks | | | | | Miami Dolphins | | | |
| ☐ 296 Jay Hilgenberg | .08 | .04 | .01 | | ☐ 344 Art Monk | .10 | .05 | .01 |
| Chicago Bears | | | | | Washington Redskins | | | |
| ☐ 297 Darrell Thompson | .08 | .04 | .01 | | ☐ 345 Michael Irvin | .50 | .23 | .06 |
| Green Bay Packers | | | | | Dallas Cowboys | | | |
| ☐ 298 Rich Gannon | .08 | .04 | .01 | | ☐ 346 Vaughan Johnson | .08 | .04 | .01 |
| Minnesota Vikings | | | | | New Orleans Saints | | | |
| ☐ 299 Steve Young | .35 | .16 | .04 | | ☐ 347 Jeff Herrod | .05 | .02 | .01 |
| San Francisco 49ers | | | | | Indianapolis Colts | | | |
| ☐ 300 Mike Kenn | .08 | .04 | .01 | | ☐ 348 Stanley Richard | .05 | .02 | .01 |
| Atlanta Falcons | | | | | San Diego Chargers | | | |
| ☐ 301 Emmitt Smith SL | 1.00 | .45 | .13 | | ☐ 349 Michael Young | .05 | .02 | .01 |
| Dallas Cowboys | | | | | Denver Broncos | | | |
| ☐ 302 Haywood Jeffires SL | .08 | .04 | .01 | | ☐ 350 Team MVP Checklist | .05 | .02 | .01 |
| Houston Oilers | | | | | Rodney Hampton | | | |
| ☐ 303 Michael Irvin SL | .25 | .11 | .03 | | Reggie Cobb | | | |

| | | | | |
|---|---|---|---|---|
| ☐ 351 | Jim Harbaugh MVP | .05 | .02 | .01 |
| | Chicago Bears | | | |
| ☐ 352 | David Fulcher MVP | .05 | .02 | .01 |
| | Cincinnati Bengals | | | |
| ☐ 353 | Thurman Thomas MVP | .20 | .09 | .03 |
| | Buffalo Bills | | | |
| ☐ 354 | Gaston Green MVP | .05 | .02 | .01 |
| | Denver Broncos | | | |
| ☐ 355 | Leroy Hoard MVP | .08 | .04 | .01 |
| | Cleveland Browns | | | |
| ☐ 356 | Reggie Cobb MVP | .08 | .04 | .01 |
| | Tampa Bay Buccaneers | | | |
| ☐ 357 | Tim McDonald MVP | .05 | .02 | .01 |
| | Phoenix Cardinals | | | |
| ☐ 358 | Ronnie Harmon MVP UER | .05 | .02 | .01 |
| | (Bernstine misspelled | | | |
| | as Bernstein) | | | |
| | San Diego Chargers | | | |
| ☐ 359 | Derrick Thomas MVP | .08 | .04 | .01 |
| | Kansas City Chiefs | | | |
| ☐ 360 | Jeff Herrod MVP | .05 | .02 | .01 |
| | Indianapolis Colts | | | |
| ☐ 361 | Michael Irvin MVP | .25 | .11 | .03 |
| | Dallas Cowboys | | | |
| ☐ 362 | Mark Higgs MVP | .05 | .02 | .01 |
| | Miami Dolphins | | | |
| ☐ 363 | Reggie White MVP | .08 | .04 | .01 |
| | Philadelphia Eagles | | | |
| ☐ 364 | Chris Miller MVP | .08 | .04 | .01 |
| | Atlanta Falcons | | | |
| ☐ 365 | Steve Young MVP | .12 | .05 | .02 |
| | San Francisco 49ers | | | |
| ☐ 366 | Rodney Hampton MVP | .15 | .07 | .02 |
| | New York Giants | | | |
| ☐ 367 | Jeff Lageman MVP | .05 | .02 | .01 |
| | New York Jets | | | |
| ☐ 368 | Barry Sanders MVP | .35 | .16 | .04 |
| | Detroit Lions | | | |
| ☐ 369 | Haywood Jeffires MVP | .08 | .04 | .01 |
| | Houston Oilers | | | |
| ☐ 370 | Tony Bennett MVP | .05 | .02 | .01 |
| | Green Bay Packers | | | |
| ☐ 371 | Leonard Russell MVP | .12 | .05 | .02 |
| | New England Patriots | | | |
| ☐ 372 | Jeff Jaeger MVP | .05 | .02 | .01 |
| | Los Angeles Raiders | | | |
| ☐ 373 | Robert Delpino MVP | .05 | .02 | .01 |
| | Los Angeles Rams | | | |
| ☐ 374 | Mark Rypien MVP | .08 | .04 | .01 |
| | Washington Redskins | | | |
| ☐ 375 | Pat Swilling MVP | .08 | .04 | .01 |
| | New Orleans Saints | | | |
| ☐ 376 | Cortez Kennedy MVP | .08 | .04 | .01 |
| | Seattle Seahawks | | | |
| ☐ 377 | Eric Green MVP | .05 | .02 | .01 |
| | Pittsburgh Steelers | | | |
| ☐ 378 | Cris Carter MVP | .08 | .04 | .01 |
| | Minnesota Vikings | | | |
| ☐ 379 | John Roper | .05 | .02 | .01 |
| | Chicago Bears | | | |
| ☐ 380 | Barry Word | .10 | .05 | .01 |
| | Kansas City Chiefs | | | |
| ☐ 381 | Shawn Jefferson | .05 | .02 | .01 |
| | San Diego Chargers | | | |
| ☐ 382 | Tony Casillas | .05 | .02 | .01 |
| | Dallas Cowboys | | | |
| ☐ 383 | John Baylor | .05 | .02 | .01 |
| | Indianapolis Colts | | | |
| ☐ 384 | Al Noga | .05 | .02 | .01 |
| | Minnesota Vikings | | | |
| ☐ 385 | Charles Mann | .08 | .04 | .01 |
| | Washington Redskins | | | |
| ☐ 386 | Gill Byrd | .08 | .04 | .01 |
| | San Diego Chargers | | | |
| ☐ 387 | Chris Singleton | .05 | .02 | .01 |
| | New England Patriots | | | |
| ☐ 388 | James Joseph | .05 | .02 | .01 |
| | Philadelphia Eagles | | | |
| ☐ 389 | Larry Brown | .05 | .02 | .01 |
| | Dallas Cowboys | | | |
| ☐ 390 | Chris Spielman | .08 | .04 | .01 |
| | Detroit Lions | | | |
| ☐ 391 | Anthony Thompson | .05 | .02 | .01 |
| | Phoenix Cardinals | | | |
| ☐ 392 | Karl Mecklenburg | .08 | .04 | .01 |
| | Denver Broncos | | | |
| ☐ 393 | Joe Kelly | .05 | .02 | .01 |
| | New York Jets | | | |
| ☐ 394 | Kanavis McGhee | .05 | .02 | .01 |
| | New York Giants | | | |
| ☐ 395 | Bill Maas | .05 | .02 | .01 |
| | Kansas City Chiefs | | | |
| ☐ 396 | Marv Cook | .08 | .04 | .01 |
| | New England Patriots | | | |
| ☐ 397 | Louis Lipps | .08 | .04 | .01 |
| | Pittsburgh Steelers | | | |
| ☐ 398 | Marty Carter | .20 | .09 | .03 |

| | | | | |
|---|---|---|---|---|
| | Tampa Bay Buccaneers | | | |
| ☐ 399 | Louis Oliver | .08 | .04 | .01 |
| | Miami Dolphins | | | |
| ☐ 400 | Eric Swann | .08 | .04 | .01 |
| | Phoenix Cardinals | | | |
| ☐ 401 | Troy Auzenne | .05 | .02 | .01 |
| | Chicago Bears | | | |
| ☐ 402 | Kurt Barber | .05 | .02 | .01 |
| | New York Jets | | | |
| ☐ 403 | Marc Boutte | .05 | .02 | .01 |
| | Los Angeles Rams | | | |
| ☐ 404 | Dale Carter | .10 | .05 | .01 |
| | Kansas City Chiefs | | | |
| ☐ 405 | Marco Coleman | .15 | .07 | .02 |
| | Miami Dolphins | | | |
| ☐ 406 | Quentin Coryatt | .40 | .18 | .05 |
| | Indianapolis Colts | | | |
| ☐ 407 | Shane Dronett | .20 | .09 | .03 |
| | Denver Broncos | | | |
| ☐ 408 | Vaughn Dunbar | .25 | .11 | .03 |
| | New Orleans Saints | | | |
| ☐ 409 | Steve Emtman | .15 | .07 | .02 |
| | Indianapolis Colts | | | |
| ☐ 410 | Dana Hall | .15 | .07 | .02 |
| | San Francisco 49ers | | | |
| ☐ 411 | Jason Hanson | .15 | .07 | .02 |
| | Detroit Lions | | | |
| ☐ 412 | Courtney Hawkins | .25 | .11 | .03 |
| | Tampa Bay Buccaneers | | | |
| ☐ 413 | Terrell Buckley | .12 | .05 | .02 |
| | Green Bay Packers | | | |
| ☐ 414 | Robert Jones | .12 | .05 | .02 |
| | Dallas Cowboys | | | |
| ☐ 415 | David Klingler | .30 | .14 | .04 |
| | Cincinnati Bengals | | | |
| ☐ 416 | Tommy Maddox | .40 | .18 | .05 |
| | Denver Broncos | | | |
| ☐ 417 | Johnny Mitchell | .50 | .23 | .06 |
| | New York Jets | | | |
| ☐ 418 | Carl Pickens | .30 | .14 | .04 |
| | Cincinnati Bengals | | | |
| ☐ 419 | Tracy Scroggins | .10 | .05 | .01 |
| | Detroit Lions | | | |
| ☐ 420 | Tony Sacca | .12 | .05 | .02 |
| | Phoenix Cardinals | | | |
| ☐ 421 | Kevin Smith | .20 | .09 | .03 |
| | Dallas Cowboys | | | |
| ☐ 422 | Alonzo Spellman | .10 | .05 | .01 |
| | Chicago Bears | | | |
| ☐ 423 | Troy Vincent | .10 | .05 | .01 |
| | Miami Dolphins | | | |
| ☐ 424 | Sean Gilbert | .30 | .14 | .04 |
| | Los Angeles Rams | | | |
| ☐ 425 | Larry Webster | .05 | .02 | .01 |
| | Miami Dolphins | | | |
| ☐ 426 | Rookie Force Checklist | .15 | .07 | .02 |
| | Carl Pickens | | | |
| | David Klingler | | | |
| | Cincinnati Bengals | | | |
| ☐ 427 | Bill Fralic | .05 | .02 | .01 |
| | Atlanta Falcons | | | |
| ☐ 428 | Kevin Murphy | .05 | .02 | .01 |
| | Tampa Bay Buccaneers | | | |
| ☐ 429 | Lemuel Stinson | .05 | .02 | .01 |
| | Chicago Bears | | | |
| ☐ 430 | Harris Barton | .05 | .02 | .01 |
| | San Francisco 49ers | | | |
| ☐ 431 | Dino Hackett | .05 | .02 | .01 |
| | Kansas City Chiefs | | | |
| ☐ 432 | John Stephens | .08 | .04 | .01 |
| | New England Patriots | | | |
| ☐ 433 | Keith Jennings | .05 | .02 | .01 |
| | Chicago Bears | | | |
| ☐ 434 | Derrick Fenner | .08 | .04 | .01 |
| | Cincinnati Bengals | | | |
| ☐ 435 | Kenneth Gant | .25 | .11 | .03 |
| | Dallas Cowboys | | | |
| ☐ 436 | Willie Gault | .08 | .04 | .01 |
| | Los Angeles Raiders | | | |
| ☐ 437 | Steve Jordan | .08 | .04 | .01 |
| | Minnesota Vikings | | | |
| ☐ 438 | Charles Haley | .08 | .04 | .01 |
| | Dallas Cowboys | | | |
| ☐ 439 | Keith Kartz | .05 | .02 | .01 |
| | Denver Broncos | | | |
| ☐ 440 | Nate Lewis | .08 | .04 | .01 |
| | San Diego Chargers | | | |
| ☐ 441 | Doug Widell | .05 | .02 | .01 |
| | Denver Broncos | | | |
| ☐ 442 | William White | .05 | .02 | .01 |
| | Detroit Lions | | | |
| ☐ 443 | Eric Hill | .05 | .02 | .01 |
| | Phoenix Cardinals | | | |
| ☐ 444 | Melvin Jenkins | .05 | .02 | .01 |
| | Detroit Lions | | | |
| ☐ 445 | David Wyman | .05 | .02 | .01 |
| | Seattle Seahawks | | | |
| ☐ 446 | Ed West | .05 | .02 | .01 |

Green Bay Packers
| | | | |
|---|---|---|---|
| ☐ 447 Brad Muster | .08 | .04 | .01 |

Chicago Bears
| | | | |
|---|---|---|---|
| ☐ 448 Ray Childress | .08 | .04 | .01 |

Houston Oilers
| | | | |
|---|---|---|---|
| ☐ 449 Kevin Ross | .08 | .04 | .01 |

Kansas City Chiefs
| | | | |
|---|---|---|---|
| ☐ 450 Johnnie Jackson | .05 | .02 | .01 |

San Francisco 49ers
| | | | |
|---|---|---|---|
| ☐ 451 Tracy Simien | .15 | .07 | .02 |

Kansas City Chiefs
| | | | |
|---|---|---|---|
| ☐ 452 Don Mosebar | .05 | .02 | .01 |

Los Angeles Raiders
| | | | |
|---|---|---|---|
| ☐ 453 Jay Hilgenberg | .08 | .04 | .01 |

Cleveland Browns
| | | | |
|---|---|---|---|
| ☐ 454 Wes Hopkins | .05 | .02 | .01 |

Philadelphia Eagles
| | | | |
|---|---|---|---|
| ☐ 455 Jay Schroeder | .08 | .04 | .01 |

Los Angeles Raiders
| | | | |
|---|---|---|---|
| ☐ 456 Jeff Bostic | .05 | .02 | .01 |

Washington Redskins
| | | | |
|---|---|---|---|
| ☐ 457 Bryce Paup | .05 | .02 | .01 |

Green Bay Packers
| | | | |
|---|---|---|---|
| ☐ 458 Dave Waymer | .05 | .02 | .01 |

Los Angeles Raiders
| | | | |
|---|---|---|---|
| ☐ 459 Toi Cook | .05 | .02 | .01 |

New Orleans Saints
| | | | |
|---|---|---|---|
| ☐ 460 Anthony Smith | .08 | .04 | .01 |

Los Angeles Raiders
| | | | |
|---|---|---|---|
| ☐ 461 Don Griffin | .05 | .02 | .01 |

San Francisco 49ers
| | | | |
|---|---|---|---|
| ☐ 462 Bill Hawkins | .05 | .02 | .01 |

Los Angeles Rams
| | | | |
|---|---|---|---|
| ☐ 463 Courtney Hall | .05 | .02 | .01 |

San Diego Chargers
| | | | |
|---|---|---|---|
| ☐ 464 Jeff Ulenhake | .05 | .02 | .01 |

Miami Dolphins
| | | | |
|---|---|---|---|
| ☐ 465 Mike Sherrard | .08 | .04 | .01 |

San Francisco 49ers
| | | | |
|---|---|---|---|
| ☐ 466 James Jones | .05 | .02 | .01 |

Cleveland Browns
| | | | |
|---|---|---|---|
| ☐ 467 Jerrol Williams | .05 | .02 | .01 |

Pittsburgh Steelers
| | | | |
|---|---|---|---|
| ☐ 468 Eric Ball | .05 | .02 | .01 |

Cincinnati Bengals
| | | | |
|---|---|---|---|
| ☐ 469 Randall McDaniel | .05 | .02 | .01 |

Minnesota Vikings
| | | | |
|---|---|---|---|
| ☐ 470 Alvin Harper | .40 | .18 | .05 |

Dallas Cowboys
| | | | |
|---|---|---|---|
| ☐ 471 Tom Waddle | .10 | .05 | .01 |

Chicago Bears
| | | | |
|---|---|---|---|
| ☐ 472 Tony Woods | .05 | .02 | .01 |

Seattle Seahawks
| | | | |
|---|---|---|---|
| ☐ 473 Kelvin Martin | .08 | .04 | .01 |

Dallas Cowboys
| | | | |
|---|---|---|---|
| ☐ 474 Jon Vaughn | .05 | .02 | .01 |

New England Patriots
| | | | |
|---|---|---|---|
| ☐ 475 Gill Fenerty | .05 | .02 | .01 |

New Orleans Saints
| | | | |
|---|---|---|---|
| ☐ 476 Aundray Bruce | .05 | .02 | .01 |

Los Angeles Raiders
| | | | |
|---|---|---|---|
| ☐ 477 Morten Andersen | .08 | .04 | .01 |

New Orleans Saints
| | | | |
|---|---|---|---|
| ☐ 478 Lamar Lathon | .05 | .02 | .01 |

Houston Oilers
| | | | |
|---|---|---|---|
| ☐ 479 Steve DeOssie | .05 | .02 | .01 |

New York Giants
| | | | |
|---|---|---|---|
| ☐ 480 Marvin Washington | .05 | .02 | .01 |

New York Jets
| | | | |
|---|---|---|---|
| ☐ 481 Herschel Walker | .10 | .05 | .01 |

Philadelphia Eagles
| | | | |
|---|---|---|---|
| ☐ 482 Howie Long | .08 | .04 | .01 |

Los Angeles Raiders
| | | | |
|---|---|---|---|
| ☐ 483 Calvin Williams | .10 | .05 | .01 |

Philadelphia Eagles
| | | | |
|---|---|---|---|
| ☐ 484 Brett Favre | 1.00 | .45 | .13 |

Green Bay Packers
| | | | |
|---|---|---|---|
| ☐ 485 Johnny Bailey | .05 | .02 | .01 |

Phoenix Cardinals
| | | | |
|---|---|---|---|
| ☐ 486 Jeff Gossett | .05 | .02 | .01 |

Los Angeles Raiders
| | | | |
|---|---|---|---|
| ☐ 487 Carnell Lake | .05 | .02 | .01 |

Pittsburgh Steelers
| | | | |
|---|---|---|---|
| ☐ 488 Michael Zordich | .05 | .02 | .01 |

Phoenix Cardinals
| | | | |
|---|---|---|---|
| ☐ 489 Henry Rolling | .05 | .02 | .01 |

San Diego Chargers
| | | | |
|---|---|---|---|
| ☐ 490 Steve Smith | .08 | .04 | .01 |

Los Angeles Raiders
| | | | |
|---|---|---|---|
| ☐ 491 Vestee Jackson | .05 | .02 | .01 |

Miami Dolphins
| | | | |
|---|---|---|---|
| ☐ 492 Ray Crockett | .05 | .02 | .01 |

Detroit Lions
| | | | |
|---|---|---|---|
| ☐ 493 Dexter Carter | .08 | .04 | .01 |

San Francisco 49ers
| | | | |
|---|---|---|---|
| ☐ 494 Nick Lowery | .08 | .04 | .01 |

Kansas City Chiefs
| | | | |
|---|---|---|---|
| ☐ 495 Cortez Kennedy | .10 | .05 | .01 |

Seattle Seahawks
| | | | |
|---|---|---|---|
| ☐ 496 Cleveland Gary | .08 | .04 | .01 |

Los Angeles Rams
| | | | |
|---|---|---|---|
| ☐ 497 Kelly Stouffer | .05 | .02 | .01 |

Seattle Seahawks
| | | | |
|---|---|---|---|
| ☐ 498 Carl Carter | .05 | .02 | .01 |

Tampa Bay Buccaneers
| | | | |
|---|---|---|---|
| ☐ 499 Shannon Sharpe | .25 | .11 | .03 |

Denver Broncos
| | | | |
|---|---|---|---|
| ☐ 500 Roger Craig | .08 | .04 | .01 |

Minnesota Vikings
| | | | |
|---|---|---|---|
| ☐ 501 Willie Drewery | .05 | .02 | .01 |

Tampa Bay Buccaneers
| | | | |
|---|---|---|---|
| ☐ 502 Mark Schlereth | .10 | .05 | .01 |

Washington Redskins
| | | | |
|---|---|---|---|
| ☐ 503 Tony Martin | .05 | .02 | .01 |

Miami Dolphins
| | | | |
|---|---|---|---|
| ☐ 504 Tom Newberry | .05 | .02 | .01 |

Los Angeles Rams
| | | | |
|---|---|---|---|
| ☐ 505 Ron Hall | .05 | .02 | .01 |

Tampa Bay Buccaneers
| | | | |
|---|---|---|---|
| ☐ 506 Scott Miller | .05 | .02 | .01 |

Miami Dolphins
| | | | |
|---|---|---|---|
| ☐ 507 Donnell Woolford | .05 | .02 | .01 |

Chicago Bears
| | | | |
|---|---|---|---|
| ☐ 508 Dave Krieg | .08 | .04 | .01 |

Kansas City Chiefs
| | | | |
|---|---|---|---|
| ☐ 509 Erric Pegram | .40 | .18 | .05 |

Atlanta Falcons
| | | | |
|---|---|---|---|
| ☐ 510 Checklist 401-510 | .05 | .02 | .01 |
| ☐ 511 Barry Sanders SBK | .35 | .16 | .04 |

Detroit Lions
| | | | |
|---|---|---|---|
| ☐ 512 Thurman Thomas SBK | .20 | .09 | .03 |

Buffalo Bills
| | | | |
|---|---|---|---|
| ☐ 513 Warren Moon SBK | .10 | .05 | .01 |

Houston Oilers
| | | | |
|---|---|---|---|
| ☐ 514 John Elway SBK | .20 | .09 | .03 |

Denver Broncos
| | | | |
|---|---|---|---|
| ☐ 515 Ronnie Lott SBK | .08 | .04 | .01 |

Los Angeles Raiders
| | | | |
|---|---|---|---|
| ☐ 516 Emmitt Smith SBK | 1.00 | .45 | .13 |

Dallas Cowboys
| | | | |
|---|---|---|---|
| ☐ 517 Andre Rison SBK | .08 | .04 | .01 |

Atlanta Falcons
| | | | |
|---|---|---|---|
| ☐ 518 Steve Atwater SBK | .05 | .02 | .01 |

Denver Broncos
| | | | |
|---|---|---|---|
| ☐ 519 Steve Young SBK | .08 | .04 | .01 |

San Francisco 49ers
| | | | |
|---|---|---|---|
| ☐ 520 Mark Rypien SBK | .08 | .04 | .01 |

Washington Redskins
| | | | |
|---|---|---|---|
| ☐ 521 Rich Camarillo | .05 | .02 | .01 |

Phoenix Cardinals
| | | | |
|---|---|---|---|
| ☐ 522 Mark Bavaro | .05 | .02 | .01 |

Cleveland Browns
| | | | |
|---|---|---|---|
| ☐ 523 Brad Edwards | .05 | .02 | .01 |

Washington Redskins
| | | | |
|---|---|---|---|
| ☐ 524 Chad Hennings | .15 | .07 | .02 |

Dallas Cowboys
| | | | |
|---|---|---|---|
| ☐ 525 Tony Paige | .05 | .02 | .01 |

Miami Dolphins
| | | | |
|---|---|---|---|
| ☐ 526 Shawn Moore | .05 | .02 | .01 |

Denver Broncos
| | | | |
|---|---|---|---|
| ☐ 527 Sidney Johnson | .05 | .02 | .01 |

Washington Redskins
| | | | |
|---|---|---|---|
| ☐ 528 Sanjay Beach | .10 | .05 | .01 |

Green Bay Packers
| | | | |
|---|---|---|---|
| ☐ 529 Kelvin Pritchett | .05 | .02 | .01 |

Detroit Lions
| | | | |
|---|---|---|---|
| ☐ 530 Jerry Holmes | .05 | .02 | .01 |

Green Bay Packers
| | | | |
|---|---|---|---|
| ☐ 531 Al Del Greco | .05 | .02 | .01 |

Houston Oilers
| | | | |
|---|---|---|---|
| ☐ 532 Bob Gagliano | .05 | .02 | .01 |

San Diego Chargers
| | | | |
|---|---|---|---|
| ☐ 533 Drew Hill | .08 | .04 | .01 |

Atlanta Falcons
| | | | |
|---|---|---|---|
| ☐ 534 Donald Frank | .05 | .02 | .01 |

San Diego Chargers
| | | | |
|---|---|---|---|
| ☐ 535 Pio Sagapolutele | .10 | .05 | .01 |

Cleveland Browns
| | | | |
|---|---|---|---|
| ☐ 536 Jackie Slater | .08 | .04 | .01 |

Los Angeles Rams
| | | | |
|---|---|---|---|
| ☐ 537 Vernon Turner | .05 | .02 | .01 |

Los Angeles Rams
| | | | |
|---|---|---|---|
| ☐ 538 Bobby Humphrey | .08 | .04 | .01 |

Miami Dolphins
| | | | |
|---|---|---|---|
| ☐ 539 Audray McMillian | .05 | .02 | .01 |

Minnesota Vikings
| | | | |
|---|---|---|---|
| ☐ 540 Gary Brown | 2.00 | .90 | .25 |

Houston Oilers
| | | | |
|---|---|---|---|
| ☐ 541 Wesley Carroll | .08 | .04 | .01 |

New Orleans Saints
| | | | |
|---|---|---|---|
| ☐ 542 Nate Newton | .05 | .02 | .01 |

Dallas Cowboys
| | | | |
|---|---|---|---|
| ☐ 543 Vai Sikahema | .08 | .04 | .01 |

Philadelphia Eagles
| | | | |
|---|---|---|---|
| ☐ 544 Chris Chandler | .08 | .04 | .01 |

Phoenix Cardinals

| | | | |
|---|---|---|---|
| ☐ 545 Nolan Harrison .......................... | .10 | .05 | .01 |
| Los Angeles Raiders | | | |
| ☐ 546 Mark Green ............................ | .05 | .02 | .01 |
| Chicago Bears | | | |
| ☐ 547 Ricky Watters ......................... | .50 | .23 | .06 |
| San Francisco 49ers | | | |
| ☐ 548 J.J. Birden .............................. | .08 | .04 | .01 |
| Kansas City Chiefs | | | |
| ☐ 549 Cody Carlson ........................... | .20 | .09 | .03 |
| Houston Oilers | | | |
| ☐ 550 Tim Green ............................... | .05 | .02 | .01 |
| Atlanta Falcons | | | |
| ☐ 551 Mark Jackson .......................... | .08 | .04 | .01 |
| Denver Broncos | | | |
| ☐ 552 Vince Buck ............................. | .05 | .02 | .01 |
| New Orleans Saints | | | |
| ☐ 553 George Jamison ........................ | .05 | .02 | .01 |
| Detroit Lions | | | |
| ☐ 554 Anthony Pleasant ...................... | .05 | .02 | .01 |
| Cleveland Browns | | | |
| ☐ 555 Reggie Johnson ........................ | .05 | .02 | .01 |
| Denver Broncos | | | |
| ☐ 556 John Jackson ........................... | .05 | .02 | .01 |
| Phoenix Cardinals | | | |
| ☐ 557 Ian Beckles ............................ | .05 | .02 | .01 |
| Tampa Bay Buccaneers | | | |
| ☐ 558 Buford McGee .......................... | .05 | .02 | .01 |
| Green Bay Packers | | | |
| ☐ 559 Fuad Reveiz UER ...................... | .05 | .02 | .01 |
| (Born in Colombia, | | | |
| not Columbia) | | | |
| Minnesota Vikings | | | |
| ☐ 560 Joe Montana ............................ | 1.00 | .45 | .13 |
| San Francisco 49ers | | | |
| ☐ 561 Phil Simms ............................. | .10 | .05 | .01 |
| New York Giants | | | |
| ☐ 562 Greg McMurtry ......................... | .05 | .02 | .01 |
| New England Patriots | | | |
| ☐ 563 Gerald Williams ........................ | .05 | .02 | .01 |
| Pittsburgh Steelers | | | |
| ☐ 564 Dave Cadigan ........................... | .05 | .02 | .01 |
| New York Jets | | | |
| ☐ 565 Rufus Porter ........................... | .05 | .02 | .01 |
| Seattle Seahawks | | | |
| ☐ 566 Jim Kelly ............................... | .25 | .11 | .03 |
| Buffalo Bills | | | |
| ☐ 567 Deion Sanders .......................... | .20 | .09 | .03 |
| Atlanta Falcons | | | |
| ☐ 568 Mike Singletary ........................ | .10 | .05 | .01 |
| Chicago Bears | | | |
| ☐ 569 Boomer Esiason ........................ | .15 | .07 | .02 |
| Cincinnati Bengals | | | |
| ☐ 570 Andre Reed ............................. | .10 | .05 | .01 |
| Buffalo Bills | | | |
| ☐ 571 James Washington ..................... | .05 | .02 | .01 |
| Dallas Cowboys | | | |
| ☐ 572 Jack Del Rio ........................... | .05 | .02 | .01 |
| Minnesota Vikings | | | |
| ☐ 573 Gerald Perry ........................... | .05 | .02 | .01 |
| Los Angeles Rams | | | |
| ☐ 574 Vinnie Clark ............................ | .05 | .02 | .01 |
| Green Bay Packers | | | |
| ☐ 575 Mike Piel .............................. | .05 | .02 | .01 |
| Los Angeles Rams | | | |
| ☐ 576 Michael Dean Perry .................... | .10 | .05 | .01 |
| Cleveland Browns | | | |
| ☐ 577 Ricky Proehl ........................... | .10 | .05 | .01 |
| Phoenix Cardinals | | | |
| ☐ 578 Leslie O'Neal ........................... | .08 | .04 | .01 |
| San Diego Chargers | | | |
| ☐ 579 Russell Maryland ...................... | .15 | .07 | .02 |
| Dallas Cowboys | | | |
| ☐ 580 Eric Dickerson ......................... | .10 | .05 | .01 |
| Los Angeles Raiders | | | |
| ☐ 581 Fred Strickland ........................ | .05 | .02 | .01 |
| Los Angeles Rams | | | |
| ☐ 582 Nick Lowery ........................... | .08 | .04 | .01 |
| Kansas City Chiefs | | | |
| ☐ 583 Joe Milinichik ......................... | .05 | .02 | .01 |
| Los Angeles Rams | | | |
| ☐ 584 Mark Vlasic ............................ | .08 | .04 | .01 |
| Kansas City Chiefs | | | |
| ☐ 585 James Lofton ........................... | .10 | .05 | .01 |
| Buffalo Bills | | | |
| ☐ 586 Bruce Smith ............................ | .10 | .05 | .01 |
| Buffalo Bills | | | |
| ☐ 587 Harvey Williams ....................... | .10 | .05 | .01 |
| Kansas City Chiefs | | | |
| ☐ 588 Bernie Kosar ........................... | .10 | .05 | .01 |
| Cleveland Browns | | | |
| ☐ 589 Carl Banks ............................. | .08 | .04 | .01 |
| New York Giants | | | |
| ☐ 590 Jeff George ............................. | .20 | .09 | .03 |
| Indianapolis Colts | | | |
| ☐ 591 Fred Jones ............................. | .15 | .07 | .02 |
| Kansas City Chiefs | | | |
| ☐ 592 Todd Scott .............................. | .05 | .02 | .01 |

| | | | |
|---|---|---|---|
| Minnesota Vikings | | | |
| ☐ 593 Keith Jones ............................ | .05 | .02 | .01 |
| Atlanta Falcons | | | |
| ☐ 594A Tootie Robbins ERR ............... | .05 | .02 | .01 |
| (Card has him as | | | |
| a Denver Bronco) | | | |
| Green Bay Packers | | | |
| ☐ 594B Tootie Robbins COR ............. | .05 | .02 | .01 |
| Green Bay Packers | | | |
| ☐ 595 Todd Philcox ........................... | .25 | .11 | .03 |
| Cleveland Browns | | | |
| ☐ 596 Browning Nagle......................... | .08 | .04 | .01 |
| New York Jets | | | |
| ☐ 597 Troy Aikman ........................... | 1.25 | .55 | .16 |
| Dallas Cowboys | | | |
| ☐ 598 Dan Marino ............................ | .75 | .35 | .09 |
| Miami Dolphins | | | |
| ☐ 599 Lawrence Taylor........................ | .10 | .05 | .01 |
| New York Giants | | | |
| ☐ 600 Webster Slaughter ..................... | .08 | .04 | .01 |
| Cleveland Browns | | | |
| ☐ 601 Aaron Cox .............................. | .05 | .02 | .01 |
| Los Angeles Rams | | | |
| ☐ 602 Matt Stover ............................ | .05 | .02 | .01 |
| Cleveland Browns | | | |
| ☐ 603 Keith Sims .............................. | .05 | .02 | .01 |
| Miami Dolphins | | | |
| ☐ 604 Dennis Smith ........................... | .08 | .04 | .01 |
| Denver Broncos | | | |
| ☐ 605 Kevin Porter ........................... | .05 | .02 | .01 |
| Kansas City Chiefs | | | |
| ☐ 606 Anthony Miller.......................... | .15 | .07 | .02 |
| San Diego Chargers | | | |
| ☐ 607 Ken O'Brien ............................ | .08 | .04 | .01 |
| New York Jets | | | |
| ☐ 608 Randall Cunningham .................. | .10 | .05 | .01 |
| Philadelphia Eagles | | | |
| ☐ 609 Timm Rosenbach ...................... | .05 | .02 | .01 |
| Phoenix Cardinals | | | |
| ☐ 610 Junior Seau ............................. | .15 | .07 | .02 |
| San Diego Chargers | | | |
| ☐ 611 Johnny Rembert ....................... | .05 | .02 | .01 |
| New England Patriots | | | |
| ☐ 612 Rick Tuten .............................. | .05 | .02 | .01 |
| Seattle Seahawks | | | |
| ☐ 613 Willie Green............................. | .05 | .02 | .01 |
| Detroit Lions | | | |
| ☐ 614 Sean Salisbury UER ................. | .50 | .23 | .06 |
| Minnesota Vikings | | | |
| (He is listed with Lions in 1990 | | | |
| and Chargers in 1991 when | | | |
| he was Vikings both years) | | | |
| ☐ 615 Martin Bayless ........................ | .05 | .02 | .01 |
| Kansas City Chiefs | | | |
| ☐ 616 Jerry Rice.............................. | .60 | .25 | .08 |
| San Francisco 49ers | | | |
| ☐ 617 Randal Hill ............................. | .10 | .05 | .01 |
| Phoenix Cardinals | | | |
| ☐ 618 Dan McGwire .......................... | .08 | .04 | .01 |
| Seattle Seahawks | | | |
| ☐ 619 Merril Hoge ............................ | .08 | .04 | .01 |
| Pittsburgh Steelers | | | |
| ☐ 620 Checklist 571-620 ..................... | .05 | .02 | .01 |
| ☐ SP3 James Lofton Yardage.......... | 2.50 | 1.15 | .30 |
| Buffalo Bills | | | |
| ☐ SP4 Art Monk Catches ................. | 2.50 | 1.15 | .30 |
| Washington Redskins | | | |

# 1992 Upper Deck Coach's Report

These 20 cards were randomly inserted throughout 1992 Upper Deck II hobby foil packs only. The set features Chuck Noll, former Steelers' head coach, analyzing this year's crop of rookies along with outstanding second-year players on their potential to achieve stardom in the NFL. The cards measure the standard size (2 1/2" by 3 1/2"). The fronts feature full-bleed color action photos with the "Coach's Report" logo at one of the upper corners. The player's name and his position are printed on a short pencil toward the bottom of the card. The back has a yellow spiral-bound notepad resting on top of a chalkboard and wooden desk, with grass visible in the background. The top page has the words "From the desk of Chuck Noll" with his evaluation of the player's strengths as well as a color photograph taped to the page. The cards are numbered (with a "CR" prefix) on a white stripe that cuts across the top of the card.

|  | MINT | EXC | G-VG |
|---|---|---|---|
| COMPLETE SET (20) | 20.00 | 9.00 | 2.50 |
| COMMON PLAYER (CR1-CR20) | .75 | .35 | .09 |
| □ CR1 Mike Pritchard | 2.00 | .90 | .25 |
| Atlanta Falcons |  |  |  |
| □ CR2 Will Furrer | .75 | .35 | .09 |
| Chicago Bears |  |  |  |
| □ CR3 Alfred Williams | .75 | .35 | .09 |
| Cincinnati Bengals |  |  |  |
| □ CR4 Tommy Vardell | 1.50 | .65 | .19 |
| Cleveland Browns |  |  |  |
| □ CR5 Brett Favre | 5.00 | 2.30 | .60 |
| Green Bay Packers |  |  |  |
| □ CR6 Alvin Harper | 4.00 | 1.80 | .50 |
| Dallas Cowboys |  |  |  |
| □ CR7 Mike Croel | .75 | .35 | .09 |
| Denver Broncos |  |  |  |
| □ CR8 Herman Moore | 4.00 | 1.80 | .50 |
| Detroit Lions |  |  |  |
| □ CR9 Edgar Bennett | 1.50 | .65 | .19 |
| Green Bay Packers |  |  |  |
| □ CR10 Todd Marinovich | .75 | .35 | .09 |
| Los Angeles Raiders |  |  |  |
| □ CR11 Aeneas Williams | .75 | .35 | .09 |
| Phoenix Cardinals |  |  |  |
| □ CR12 Ricky Watters | 4.00 | 1.80 | .50 |
| San Francisco 49ers |  |  |  |
| □ CR13 Amp Lee | 1.50 | .65 | .19 |
| San Francisco 49ers |  |  |  |
| □ CR14 Terrell Buckley | .75 | .35 | .09 |
| Green Bay Packers |  |  |  |
| □ CR15 Tim Barnett | .75 | .35 | .09 |
| Kansas City Chiefs |  |  |  |
| □ CR16 Nick Bell | .75 | .35 | .09 |
| Los Angeles Raiders |  |  |  |
| □ CR17 Leonard Russell | 2.50 | 1.15 | .30 |
| New England Patriots |  |  |  |
| □ CR18 Lawrence Dawsey | .75 | .35 | .09 |
| Tampa Bay Buccaneers |  |  |  |
| □ CR19 Robert Porcher | .75 | .35 | .09 |
| Detroit Lions |  |  |  |
| □ CR20 Checklist | 1.50 | .65 | .19 |
| (Ricky Watters) |  |  |  |

## 1992 Upper Deck Fanimation

These ten cards were randomly inserted throughout 1992 Upper Deck II retail foil packs only and were the work of artists Jim Lee and Rob Liefeld. The standard-size (2 1/2" by 3 1/2") cards feature on the fronts full-bleed color cartoon illustrations that are based on NFL stars. The "Fanimation" logo appears in one of the lower corners. On a background that shades from red to orange to yellow, the backs have a head shot, biography (including topics such as "Armament" and "Special Features"), and a discussion of the character's strengths. The cards are numbered on the back in the upper left corner with an "F" prefix. The player's nickname is mentioned in the listing below.

|  | MINT | EXC | G-VG |
|---|---|---|---|
| COMPLETE SET (10) | 30.00 | 13.50 | 3.80 |
| COMMON PLAYER (F1-F10) | 2.25 | 1.00 | .30 |
| □ F1 Jim Kelly | 4.00 | 1.80 | .50 |
| (Shotgun Kelly) |  |  |  |
| Buffalo Bills |  |  |  |
| □ F2 Dan Marino | 6.00 | 2.70 | .75 |
| (Machine Gun) |  |  |  |
| Miami Dolphins |  |  |  |
| □ F3 Lawrence Taylor | 2.25 | 1.00 | .30 |
| (The Giant) |  |  |  |
| New York Giants |  |  |  |
| □ F4 Deion Sanders | 4.00 | 1.80 | .50 |
| (Neon Deion) |  |  |  |
| Atlanta Falcons |  |  |  |
| □ F5 Troy Aikman | 10.00 | 4.50 | 1.25 |
| (The Marshall) |  |  |  |
| Dallas Cowboys |  |  |  |
| □ F6 Junior Seau | 2.25 | 1.00 | .30 |
| (The Warrior) |  |  |  |
| San Diego Chargers |  |  |  |
| □ F7 Mike Singletary | 2.25 | 1.00 | .30 |
| (Samurai) |  |  |  |
| Chicago Bears |  |  |  |
| □ F8 Eric Dickerson | 2.25 | 1.00 | .30 |
| (The Raider) |  |  |  |
| Los Angeles Raiders |  |  |  |
| □ F9 Jerry Rice | 6.00 | 2.70 | .75 |
| (Goldfinger) |  |  |  |
| San Francisco 49ers |  |  |  |
| □ F10 Checklist Card | 3.00 | 1.35 | .40 |

## 1992 Upper Deck Game Breaker Holograms

This nine-card hologram set showcases some of the NFL's standout wide receivers. Card numbers 1, 3, 4, 6, 8, and 9 were randomly inserted in 1992 Upper Deck first series packs while card numbers 2, 5, and 7 were found in the second series. The cards measure the standard size (2 1/2" by 3 1/2"). The fronts feature holographic action images of the players with a football field in the background and Roman architecture bordering the edges. The player's name appears at the bottom. The Upper Deck logo is at the lower left corner. On a white card face, the backs have a beige marble-textured tablet with verdigris borders. The tablet contains career highlights and is accented by football icons and a red diagonal stripe at three corners. The fourth corner shows the team logo. The words "Game Breakers" are at the top in verdigris marble-texture block letters. The player's name is printed in a beige bar to the left. The cards are numbered on the back with a "GB" prefix.

|  | MINT | EXC | G-VG |
|---|---|---|---|
| COMPLETE SET (9) | 12.00 | 5.50 | 1.50 |
| COMMON PLAYER (GB1-GB9) | 1.50 | .65 | .19 |
| □ GB1 Art Monk | 1.75 | .80 | .22 |
| Washington Redskins |  |  |  |
| □ GB2 Drew Hill | 1.50 | .65 | .19 |
| Atlanta Falcons |  |  |  |
| □ GB3 Haywood Jeffires | 1.75 | .80 | .22 |
| Houston Oilers |  |  |  |
| □ GB4 Andre Rison | 2.00 | .90 | .25 |
| Atlanta Falcons |  |  |  |
| □ GB5 Mark Clayton | 1.50 | .65 | .19 |
| Miami Dolphins |  |  |  |
| □ GB6 Jerry Rice | 3.00 | 1.35 | .40 |
| San Francisco 49ers |  |  |  |
| □ GB7 Michael Haynes | 2.00 | .90 | .25 |
| Atlanta Falcons |  |  |  |
| □ GB8 Andre Reed | 1.75 | .80 | .22 |
| Buffalo Bills |  |  |  |
| □ GB9 Michael Irvin | 3.00 | 1.35 | .40 |
| Dallas Cowboys |  |  |  |

# 1992 Upper Deck Gold

These 50 standard-size (2 1/2" by 3 1/2") cards feature players licensed by NFL Properties. Each low series foil box contained one 15-card foil pack of these cards. Two Game Breaker holograms of Jerry Rice and Andre Reed were randomly inserted throughout these packs. The fronts of all cards display color action player photos bordered in white. On the Quarterback Club cards, the player's name is printed in a black stripe along the left edge, while the other cards have the player's name and position printed in different designs at the bottom. Though the backs of the Prospects cards feature a career summary, the backs of the remaining cards carry a color close-up photo as well as biography, statistics, or player profile. Two distinguishing features of the backs are a gold (instead of silver) Upper Deck hologram image and the NFL Properties logo. The cards are numbered on the back with a "G" prefix and subdivided into NFL Top Prospects (1-20), Quarterback Club (21-25), and veteran players (26-50). The key Rookie Cards in this set are Quentin Coryatt, Vaughn Dunbar, Steve Emtman, David Klingler, Tommy Maddox, and Carl Pickens.

|  | MINT | EXC | G-VG |
|---|---|---|---|
| COMPLETE SET (50) | 15.00 | 6.75 | 1.90 |
| COMMON PLAYER (G1-G50) | .15 | .07 | .02 |
| ☐ G1 Steve Emtman | .30 | .14 | .04 |
| Indianapolis Colts |  |  |  |
| ☐ G2 Carl Pickens | .60 | .25 | .08 |
| Cincinnati Bengals |  |  |  |
| ☐ G3 Dale Carter | .50 | .23 | .06 |
| Kansas City Chiefs |  |  |  |
| ☐ G4 Greg Skrepenak | .20 | .09 | .03 |
| Los Angeles Raiders |  |  |  |
| ☐ G5 Kevin Smith | .50 | .23 | .06 |
| Dallas Cowboys |  |  |  |
| ☐ G6 Marco Coleman | .50 | .23 | .06 |
| Miami Dolphins |  |  |  |
| ☐ G7 David Klingler | 1.25 | .55 | .16 |
| Cincinnati Bengals |  |  |  |
| ☐ G8 Phillippi Sparks | .15 | .07 | .02 |
| New York Giants |  |  |  |
| ☐ G9 Tommy Maddox | 1.00 | .45 | .13 |
| Denver Broncos |  |  |  |
| ☐ G10 Quentin Coryatt | .75 | .35 | .09 |
| Indianapolis Colts |  |  |  |
| ☐ G11 Ty Detmer | .20 | .09 | .03 |
| Green Bay Packers |  |  |  |
| ☐ G12 Vaughn Dunbar | .40 | .18 | .05 |
| New Orleans Saints |  |  |  |
| ☐ G13 Ashley Ambrose | .30 | .14 | .04 |
| Indianapolis Colts |  |  |  |
| ☐ G14 Kurt Barber | .20 | .09 | .03 |
| New York Jets |  |  |  |
| ☐ G15 Chester McGlockton | .20 | .09 | .03 |
| Los Angeles Raiders |  |  |  |
| ☐ G16 Todd Collins | .30 | .14 | .04 |
| New England Patriots |  |  |  |
| ☐ G17 Steve Israel | .15 | .07 | .02 |
| Los Angeles Rams |  |  |  |
| ☐ G18 Marquez Pope | .25 | .11 | .03 |
| San Diego Chargers |  |  |  |
| ☐ G19 Alonzo Spellman | .50 | .23 | .06 |
| Chicago Bears |  |  |  |
| ☐ G20 Tracy Scroggins | .50 | .23 | .06 |
| Detroit Lions |  |  |  |
| ☐ G21 Jim Kelly QC | .50 | .23 | .06 |
| Buffalo Bills |  |  |  |
| ☐ G22 Troy Aikman QC | 1.25 | .55 | .16 |
| Dallas Cowboys |  |  |  |
| ☐ G23 Randall Cunningham QC | .40 | .18 | .05 |
| Philadelphia Eagles |  |  |  |
| ☐ G24 Bernie Kosar QC | .30 | .14 | .04 |
| Cleveland Browns |  |  |  |
| ☐ G25 Dan Marino QC | 1.00 | .45 | .13 |
| Miami Dolphins |  |  |  |
| ☐ G26 Andre Reed | .25 | .11 | .03 |
| Buffalo Bills |  |  |  |
| ☐ G27 Deion Sanders | .40 | .18 | .05 |
| Atlanta Falcons |  |  |  |
| ☐ G28 Randal Hill | .25 | .11 | .03 |
| Phoenix Cardinals |  |  |  |
| ☐ G29 Eric Dickerson | .25 | .11 | .03 |
| Los Angeles Raiders |  |  |  |
| ☐ G30 Jim Kelly | .60 | .25 | .08 |
| Buffalo Bills |  |  |  |
| ☐ G31 Bernie Kosar | .25 | .11 | .03 |
| Cleveland Browns |  |  |  |
| ☐ G32 Mike Singletary | .25 | .11 | .03 |
| Chicago Bears |  |  |  |
| ☐ G33 Anthony Miller | .35 | .16 | .04 |
| San Diego Chargers |  |  |  |
| ☐ G34 Harvey Williams | .25 | .11 | .03 |
| Kansas City Chiefs |  |  |  |
| ☐ G35 Randall Cunningham | .35 | .16 | .04 |
| Philadelphia Eagles |  |  |  |
| ☐ G36 Joe Montana | 2.00 | .90 | .25 |
| San Francisco 49ers |  |  |  |
| ☐ G37 Dan McGwire | .20 | .09 | .03 |
| Seattle Seahawks |  |  |  |
| ☐ G38 Al Toon | .15 | .07 | .02 |
| New York Jets |  |  |  |
| ☐ G39 Carl Banks | .15 | .07 | .02 |
| New York Giants |  |  |  |
| ☐ G40 Troy Aikman | 2.50 | 1.15 | .30 |
| Dallas Cowboys |  |  |  |
| ☐ G41 Junior Seau | .35 | .16 | .04 |
| San Diego Chargers |  |  |  |
| ☐ G42 Jeff George | .50 | .23 | .06 |
| Indianapolis Colts |  |  |  |
| ☐ G43 Michael Dean Perry | .25 | .11 | .03 |
| Cleveland Browns |  |  |  |
| ☐ G44 Lawrence Taylor | .30 | .14 | .04 |
| New York Giants |  |  |  |
| ☐ G45 Dan Marino | 1.50 | .65 | .19 |
| Miami Dolphins |  |  |  |
| ☐ G46 Jerry Rice | 1.50 | .65 | .19 |
| San Francisco 49ers |  |  |  |
| ☐ G47 Boomer Esiason | .25 | .11 | .03 |
| Cincinnati Bengals |  |  |  |
| ☐ G48 Bruce Smith | .25 | .11 | .03 |
| Buffalo Bills |  |  |  |
| ☐ G49 Leslie O'Neal | .15 | .07 | .02 |
| San Diego Chargers |  |  |  |
| ☐ G50 Checklist Card | .20 | .09 | .03 |

# 1992 Upper Deck Heroes Dan Marino

This ten-card set chronicles the collegiate and professional career of Dan Marino. The cards were randomly inserted in 1992 Upper Deck second series foil packs. The cards measure the standard size (2 1/2" by 3 1/2"). The fronts feature color photos of Marino at various stages of his career within an oval picture frame on a marbleized slab. A shadow border makes the slab appear to hover over the white card face. The card subtitle appears in the lower right corner of the slab. The back design displays career highlights on a marbleized plaque framed by verdigris marbleized borders. The cards are numbered on the back in continuation of the Walter Payton Football Heroes subset.

|  | MINT | EXC | G-VG |
|---|---|---|---|
| COMPLETE SET (10) | 28.00 | 12.50 | 3.50 |
| COMMON MARINO (28-36) | 3.00 | 1.35 | .40 |
| ☐ 28 1979-82 College Years | 3.00 | 1.35 | .40 |
| ☐ 29 1983 Rookie-of-the-Year | 3.00 | 1.35 | .40 |
| ☐ 30 1984 5,000 Yards Passing | 3.00 | 1.35 | .40 |
| ☐ 31 1985 Super Bowl XIX | 3.00 | 1.35 | .40 |
| ☐ 32 1986 4,000 Yards | 3.00 | 1.35 | .40 |

Passing

| | | MINT | EXC | G-VG |
|---|---|---|---|---|
| ☐ 33 | 1989 200th Touchdown Pass UER (Jurgensen misspelled as Jurgenson) | 3.00 | 1.35 | .40 |
| ☐ 34 | 1990 30,000 Yards | 3.00 | 1.35 | .40 |
| ☐ 35 | 1992 Still Counting | 3.00 | 1.35 | .40 |
| ☐ 36 | Checklist Heroes 28-36 | 3.00 | 1.35 | .40 |
| ☐ NNO | Title/Header card | 8.00 | 3.60 | 1.00 |

## 1992 Upper Deck Heroes Marino Box Bottom

This oversized "card" (approximately 5 1/4" by 7 1/4") was featured on the bottoms of 1992 Upper Deck second series waxboxes. It is identical in design to the Marino Football Heroes insert card number 36. The back is blank and the card is unnumbered.

| | MINT | EXC | G-VG |
|---|---|---|---|
| COMPLETE SET (1) | 1.00 | .40 | .10 |
| COMMON CARD | 1.00 | .40 | .10 |
| ☐ 36 Dan Marino Box Bottom (Art Card) | 1.00 | .40 | .10 |

## 1992 Upper Deck Heroes Walter Payton

Randomly inserted in series II foil packs, this ten-card set depicts the former Chicago Bears running back Walter Payton during various stages of his career. The cards measure the standard size (2 1/2" by 3 1/2"). The fronts feature color photos within an oval picture frame on a marbleized slab. A shadow border makes the slab appear to hover over the white card face. The back design displays capsule summaries on a marbleized plaque framed by dark gray marbleized borders. The cards are numbered on the back.

| | MINT | EXC | G-VG |
|---|---|---|---|
| COMPLETE SET (10) | 28.00 | 12.50 | 3.50 |
| COMMON PAYTON (19-27) | 3.00 | 1.35 | .40 |
| ☐ 19 College Years 1971-74 | 3.00 | 1.35 | .40 |
| ☐ 20 Sweetness 1975 | 3.00 | 1.35 | .40 |
| ☐ 21 Career Year 1977 | 3.00 | 1.35 | .40 |
| ☐ 22 NFL Rushing Rec. 1984 | 3.00 | 1.35 | .40 |
| ☐ 23 2,000 Yard Seasons 1983-1985 | 3.00 | 1.35 | .40 |
| ☐ 24 Super Bowl XX 1986 | 3.00 | 1.35 | .40 |

| | | MINT | EXC | G-VG |
|---|---|---|---|---|
| ☐ 25 | Walter Payton Day 1987 | 3.00 | 1.35 | .40 |
| ☐ 26 | Hall of Fame Bound 1992 | 3.00 | 1.35 | .40 |
| ☐ 27 | Checklist Heroes 19-27 | 3.00 | 1.35 | .40 |
| ☐ NNO | Title/Header Card | 8.00 | 3.60 | 1.00 |

## 1992 Upper Deck Heroes Payton Box Bottoms

These eight oversized "cards" (approximately 5 1/4" by 7 1/4") were featured on the bottoms of 1992 Upper Deck first series waxboxes. They are identical in design to the Payton Football Heroes insert cards, with the same color player photos in an oval picture frame. The backs are blank and the cards are unnumbered. We have checklisted them below according to the numbering of the Heroes cards.

| | MINT | EXC | G-VG |
|---|---|---|---|
| COMPLETE SET (8) | 6.00 | 2.40 | .60 |
| COMMON CARD (19-26) | 1.00 | .40 | .10 |
| ☐ 19 College Years 1971-74 | 1.00 | .40 | .10 |
| ☐ 20 Sweetness 1975 | 1.00 | .40 | .10 |
| ☐ 21 Career Year 1977 | 1.00 | .40 | .10 |
| ☐ 22 NFL Rushing Record 1984 | 1.00 | .40 | .10 |
| ☐ 23 2,000 Yard Seasons 1983-1985 | 1.00 | .40 | .10 |
| ☐ 24 Super Bowl XX 1986 | 1.00 | .40 | .10 |
| ☐ 25 Walter Payton Day 1987 | 1.00 | .40 | .10 |
| ☐ 26 Hall of Fame Bound 1992 | 1.00 | .40 | .10 |

## 1992 Upper Deck Pro Bowl

Randomly inserted in series I foil packs, this 16-card standard-size (2 1/2" by 3 1/2") set featured players from the 1992 Pro Bowl in Hawaii. The horizontal fronts carry two full-bleed player photos; the left one features an AFC Pro Bowl player, while the right one has a NFC Pro Bowl player. The photos are separated by a rainbow consisting of six different color bands and overprinted with "Pro Bowl" in silver foil lettering. When rotated under a light, the bands reflect light in different directions. This unique look was produced by a process called prismatic lithography. The player's name in silver foil lettering at the bottom rounds out the front. On two rainbow-colored panels, the horizontal backs present a career summary for each player. The cards are numbered on the back with a "PB" prefix.

| | MINT | EXC | G-VG |
|---|---|---|---|
| COMPLETE SET (16) | 30.00 | 13.50 | 3.80 |
| COMMON PAIR (PB1-PB16) | 1.50 | .65 | .19 |
| ☐ PB1 Haywood Jeffires | 4.00 | 1.80 | .50 |

Houston Oilers
Michael Irvin
Dallas Cowboys

| | | | |
|---|---|---|---|
| ☐ PB2 Mark Clayton | 2.00 | .90 | .25 |
| Miami Dolphins | | | |
| Gary Clark | | | |
| Washington Redskins | | | |
| ☐ PB3 Anthony Munoz | 1.50 | .65 | .19 |
| Cincinnati Bengals | | | |
| Jim Lachey | | | |
| Washington Redskins | | | |
| ☐ PB4 Warren Moon | 2.00 | .90 | .25 |
| Houston Oilers | | | |
| Mark Rypien | | | |
| Washington Redskins | | | |
| ☐ PB5 Thurman Thomas | 8.00 | 3.60 | 1.00 |
| Buffalo Bills | | | |
| Barry Sanders | | | |
| Detroit Lions | | | |
| ☐ PB6 Marion Butts | 12.00 | 5.50 | 1.50 |
| San Diego Chargers | | | |
| Emmitt Smith | | | |
| Dallas Cowboys | | | |
| ☐ PB7 Greg Townsend | 2.00 | .90 | .25 |
| Los Angeles Raiders | | | |
| Reggie White | | | |
| Philadelphia Eagles | | | |
| ☐ PB8 Cornelius Bennett | 2.00 | .90 | .25 |
| Buffalo Bills | | | |
| Seth Joyner | | | |
| Philadelphia Eagles | | | |
| ☐ PB9 Derrick Thomas | 2.00 | .90 | .25 |
| Kansas City Chiefs | | | |
| Pat Swilling | | | |
| New Orleans Saints | | | |
| ☐ PB10 Darryl Talley | 1.50 | .65 | .19 |
| Buffalo Bills | | | |
| Chris Spielman | | | |
| Detroit Lions | | | |
| ☐ PB11 Ronnie Lott | 2.00 | .90 | .25 |
| Los Angeles Raiders | | | |
| Mark Carrier | | | |
| Chicago Bears | | | |
| ☐ PB12 Steve Atwater | 1.50 | .65 | .19 |
| Denver Broncos | | | |
| Shaun Gayle | | | |
| Chicago Bears | | | |
| ☐ PB13 Rod Woodson | 2.00 | .90 | .25 |
| Pittsburgh Steelers | | | |
| Darrell Green | | | |
| Washington Redskins | | | |
| ☐ PB14 Jeff Gossett | 1.50 | .65 | .19 |
| Los Angeles Raiders | | | |
| Chip Lohmiller | | | |
| Washington Redskins | | | |
| ☐ PB15 Tim Brown | 2.00 | .90 | .25 |
| Los Angeles Raiders | | | |
| Mel Gray | | | |
| Detroit Lions | | | |
| ☐ PB16 Checklist Card | 2.50 | 1.15 | .30 |

# 1992-93 Upper Deck NFL Experience

This 50-card set commemorates the stars of previous Super Bowls and potential stars of tomorrow. The set was produced in conjunction with the NFL Experience, a theme park held January 28-31, 1993, at the Rose Bowl (Pasadena, California), the site of Super Bowl XXVII. The set was available only through hobby dealers and was introduced at the Super Bowl Card Show at the NFL Experience. The fronts of card numbers 1-20 have full-bleed color player photos that are edged on two sides by various border stripes, while the fronts of cards numbers 21-50 feature color player photos tilted slightly to the left and bordered in the remaining area by a ghosted background. Some cards are accented with silver foil highlights, with at least one set in every case having gold-foil highlights. The gold set is valued at approximately five times the prices listed below. The backs present a color close-up photo, player profile, game performance summary, or player quote. The set is subdivided as follows: Super Bowl MVPs (1-5), Super Bowl Moments (6-10), Future Champions (11-20), and Super Bowl Dreams (21-50). The cards are numbered on the back.

| | MINT | EXC | G-VG |
|---|---|---|---|
| COMPLETE SET (50) | 10.00 | 4.00 | 1.00 |
| COMMON PLAYER (1-50) | .10 | .04 | .01 |
| ☐ 1 Joe Montana MVP | 1.50 | .60 | .15 |
| San Francisco 49ers | | | |
| ☐ 2 Roger Staubach MVP | .60 | .24 | .06 |
| Dallas Cowboys | | | |
| ☐ 3 Bart Starr MVP | .25 | .10 | .02 |
| Green Bay Packers | | | |
| ☐ 4 Len Dawson MVP | .20 | .08 | .02 |
| Kansas City Chiefs | | | |
| ☐ 5 Fred Biletnikoff MVP | .20 | .08 | .02 |
| Oakland Raiders | | | |
| ☐ 6 Jim Plunkett | .15 | .06 | .01 |
| Oakland Raiders | | | |
| ☐ 7 Terry Bradshaw | .50 | .20 | .05 |
| Pittsburgh Steelers | | | |
| ☐ 8 Jerry Rice | 1.00 | .40 | .10 |
| San Francisco 49ers | | | |
| ☐ 9 Doug Williams | .10 | .04 | .01 |
| Washington Redskins | | | |
| ☐ 10 Dan Marino | 1.25 | .50 | .12 |
| Miami Dolphins | | | |
| ☐ 11 David Klingler | .75 | .30 | .07 |
| Cincinnati Bengals | | | |
| ☐ 12 Steve Emtman | .15 | .06 | .01 |
| Indianapolis Colts | | | |
| ☐ 13 Dale Carter | .20 | .08 | .02 |
| Kansas City Chiefs | | | |
| ☐ 14 Quentin Coryatt | .35 | .14 | .03 |
| Indianapolis Colts | | | |
| ☐ 15 Tommy Maddox | .75 | .30 | .07 |
| Denver Broncos | | | |
| ☐ 16 Vaughn Dunbar | .20 | .08 | .02 |
| New Orleans Saints | | | |
| ☐ 17 Marco Coleman | .20 | .08 | .02 |
| Miami Dolphins | | | |
| ☐ 18 Carl Pickens | .40 | .16 | .04 |
| Cincinnati Bengals | | | |
| ☐ 19 Sean Gilbert | .30 | .12 | .03 |
| Los Angeles Rams | | | |
| ☐ 20 Tony Smith | .20 | .08 | .02 |
| Atlanta Falcons | | | |
| ☐ 21 Jim Kelly | .40 | .16 | .04 |
| Buffalo Bills | | | |
| ☐ 22 Dan Marino | 1.25 | .50 | .12 |
| Miami Dolphins | | | |
| ☐ 23 Boomer Esiason | .20 | .08 | .02 |
| Cincinnati Bengals | | | |
| ☐ 24 Bernie Kosar | .20 | .08 | .02 |
| Cleveland Browns | | | |
| ☐ 25 Ken O'Brien | .10 | .04 | .01 |
| New York Jets | | | |
| ☐ 26 Deion Sanders | .30 | .12 | .03 |
| Atlanta Falcons | | | |
| ☐ 27 Mike Singletary | .15 | .06 | .01 |
| Chicago Bears | | | |
| ☐ 28 Andre Reed | .20 | .08 | .02 |
| Buffalo Bills | | | |
| ☐ 29 Michael Dean Perry | .15 | .06 | .01 |
| Cleveland Browns | | | |
| ☐ 30 Ricky Proehl | .10 | .04 | .01 |
| Phoenix Cardinals | | | |
| ☐ 31 Leslie O'Neal | .10 | .04 | .01 |
| San Diego Chargers | | | |
| ☐ 32 Jerry Rice | 1.00 | .40 | .10 |
| San Francisco 49ers | | | |
| ☐ 33 Eric Dickerson | .25 | .10 | .02 |
| Los Angeles Raiders | | | |
| ☐ 34 Troy Aikman | 1.50 | .60 | .15 |
| Dallas Cowboys | | | |
| ☐ 35 Bruce Smith | .20 | .08 | .02 |
| Buffalo Bills | | | |
| ☐ 36 Browning Nagle | .15 | .06 | .01 |
| New York Jets | | | |
| ☐ 37 Carl Banks | .10 | .04 | .01 |
| New York Giants | | | |
| ☐ 38 Harvey Williams | .25 | .10 | .02 |
| Kansas City Chiefs | | | |
| ☐ 39 Jeff George | .25 | .10 | .02 |
| Indianapolis Colts | | | |
| ☐ 40 Lawrence Taylor | .25 | .10 | .02 |
| New York Giants | | | |
| ☐ 41 Webster Slaughter | .10 | .04 | .01 |
| Houston Oilers | | | |
| ☐ 42 Anthony Miller | .25 | .10 | .02 |
| San Diego Chargers | | | |
| ☐ 43 Randall Cunningham | .35 | .14 | .03 |
| Philadelphia Eagles | | | |

| | MINT | EXC | G-VG |
|---|---|---|---|
| ☐ 44 Timm Rosenbach | .15 | .06 | .01 |
| Phoenix Cardinals | | | |
| ☐ 45 Russell Maryland | .20 | .08 | .02 |
| Dallas Cowboys | | | |
| ☐ 46 Randal Hill | .25 | .10 | .02 |
| Phoenix Cardinals | | | |
| ☐ 47 Dan McGwire | .15 | .06 | .01 |
| Seattle Seahawks | | | |
| ☐ 48 Merril Hoge | .10 | .04 | .01 |
| Pittsburgh Steelers | | | |
| ☐ 49 Kevin Fagan | .10 | .04 | .01 |
| San Francisco 49ers | | | |
| ☐ 50 Junior Seau | .20 | .08 | .02 |
| San Diego Chargers | | | |

## 1993 Upper Deck

The 1993 Upper Deck football set was issued in a single series consisting of 530 standard-size (2 1/2" by 3 1/2") cards. Randomly inserted throughout various Upper Deck products were the following: a "Trade Upper Deck" card (all packs), a ten-card Future Heroes subset (all packs), a 20-card Pro Bowl subset (retail foil packs), a 15-card America's team subset (hobby foil packs), and a 29-card Team MVP subset (jumbo foil packs). The fronts feature color action player photos, with two stripes in the player's team colors at the bottom. The player's name and position are printed in the top stripe. On the left side of the card, the team name is printed in the teams' dominant color against a ghosted background. The backs carry a color close-up photo alongside biographical and statistical information that run the length of the card. The cards are numbered on the back. Topical subsets featured are Star Rookies (1-29), All-Rookie Team (30-55), Hitmen (56-62), Team Checklists (63-90), Season Leaders (421-431), and Berman's Best (432-442). Rookie Cards include Jerome Bettis, Drew Bledsoe, Reggie Brooks, Terry Kirby, O.J. McDuffie, Natrone Means and Rick Mirer.

| | MINT | EXC | G-VG |
|---|---|---|---|
| COMPLETE SET (530) | 32.00 | 14.50 | 4.00 |
| COMMON PLAYER (1-530) | .05 | .02 | .01 |
| ☐ 1 Star Rookie Checklist | .30 | .14 | .04 |
| Rick Mirer | | | |
| Garrison Hearst | | | |
| Curtis Conway | | | |
| Lincoln Kennedy | | | |
| ☐ 2 Eric Curry SR | .25 | .11 | .03 |
| Tampa Bay Buccaneers | | | |
| ☐ 3 Rick Mirer SR | 3.50 | 1.55 | .45 |
| Seattle Seahawks | | | |
| ☐ 4 Dan Williams SR | .15 | .07 | .02 |
| Denver Broncos | | | |
| ☐ 5 Marvin Jones SR | .20 | .09 | .03 |
| New York Jets | | | |
| ☐ 6 Willie Roaf SR | .12 | .05 | .02 |
| New Orleans Saints | | | |
| ☐ 7 Reggie Brooks SR | 2.00 | .90 | .25 |
| Washington Redskins | | | |
| ☐ 8 Horace Copeland SR | .60 | .25 | .08 |
| Tampa Bay Buccaneers | | | |
| ☐ 9 Lincoln Kennedy SR | .15 | .07 | .02 |
| Atlanta Falcons | | | |
| ☐ 10 Curtis Conway SR | .50 | .23 | .06 |
| Chicago Bears | | | |
| ☐ 11 Drew Bledsoe SR | 3.50 | 1.55 | .45 |
| New England Patriots | | | |
| ☐ 12 Patrick Bates SR | .12 | .05 | .02 |
| Los Angeles Raiders | | | |
| ☐ 13 Wayne Simmons SR | .12 | .05 | .02 |
| Green Bay Packers | | | |
| ☐ 14 Irv Smith SR | .20 | .09 | .03 |
| Tampa Bay Buccaneers | | | |
| ☐ 15 Robert Smith SR | .35 | .16 | .04 |
| Minnesota Vikings | | | |

| | MINT | EXC | G-VG |
|---|---|---|---|
| ☐ 16 O.J. McDuffie SR | 1.25 | .55 | .16 |
| Miami Dolphins | | | |
| ☐ 17 Darrien Gordon SR | .15 | .07 | .02 |
| San Diego Chargers | | | |
| ☐ 18 John Copeland SR | .25 | .11 | .03 |
| Cincinnati Bengals | | | |
| ☐ 19 Derek Brown SR | .75 | .35 | .09 |
| New Orleans Saints | | | |
| ☐ 20 Jerome Bettis SR | 3.50 | 1.55 | .45 |
| Los Angeles Rams | | | |
| ☐ 21 Deon Figures SR | .15 | .07 | .02 |
| Pittsburgh Steelers | | | |
| ☐ 22 Glyn Milburn SR | .75 | .35 | .09 |
| Denver Broncos | | | |
| ☐ 23 Garrison Hearst SR | .60 | .25 | .08 |
| Phoenix Cardinals | | | |
| ☐ 24 Qadry Ismail SR | .50 | .23 | .06 |
| Minnesota Vikings | | | |
| ☐ 25 Terry Kirby SR | 1.50 | .65 | .19 |
| Miami Dolphins | | | |
| ☐ 26 Lamar Thomas SR | .25 | .11 | .03 |
| Tampa Bay Buccaneers | | | |
| ☐ 27 Tom Carter SR | .25 | .11 | .03 |
| Washington Redskins | | | |
| ☐ 28 Andre Hastings SR | .20 | .09 | .03 |
| Pittsburgh Steelers | | | |
| ☐ 29 George Teague SR | .20 | .09 | .03 |
| Green Bay Packers | | | |
| ☐ 30 All-Rookie Team CL | .05 | .02 | .01 |
| Tommy Maddox | | | |
| ☐ 31 David Klingler ART | .10 | .05 | .01 |
| Cincinnati Bengals | | | |
| ☐ 32 Tommy Maddox ART | .05 | .02 | .01 |
| Denver Broncos | | | |
| ☐ 33 Vaughn Dunbar ART | .05 | .02 | .01 |
| New Orleans Saints | | | |
| ☐ 34 Rodney Culver ART | .05 | .02 | .01 |
| Indianapolis Colts | | | |
| ☐ 35 Carl Pickens ART | .08 | .04 | .01 |
| Cincinnati Bengals | | | |
| ☐ 36 Courtney Hawkins ART | .05 | .02 | .01 |
| Tampa Bay Buccaneers | | | |
| ☐ 37 Tyji Armstrong ART | .05 | .02 | .01 |
| Tampa Bay Buccaneers | | | |
| ☐ 38 Ray Roberts ART | .05 | .02 | .01 |
| Seattle Seahawks | | | |
| ☐ 39 Troy Auzenne ART | .05 | .02 | .01 |
| Chicago Bears | | | |
| ☐ 40 Shane Dronett ART | .05 | .02 | .01 |
| Denver Broncos | | | |
| ☐ 41 Chris Mims ART | .05 | .02 | .01 |
| San Diego Chargers | | | |
| ☐ 42 Sean Gilbert ART | .05 | .02 | .01 |
| Los Angeles Rams | | | |
| ☐ 43 Steve Emtman ART | .05 | .02 | .01 |
| Indianapolis Colts | | | |
| ☐ 44 Robert Jones ART | .05 | .02 | .01 |
| Dallas Cowboys | | | |
| ☐ 45 Marco Coleman ART | .05 | .02 | .01 |
| Miami Dolphins | | | |
| ☐ 46 Ricardo McDonald ART | .05 | .02 | .01 |
| Cincinnati Bengals | | | |
| ☐ 47 Quentin Coryatt ART | .08 | .04 | .01 |
| Indianapolis Colts | | | |
| ☐ 48 Dana Hall ART | .05 | .02 | .01 |
| San Francisco 49ers | | | |
| ☐ 49 Darren Perry ART | .05 | .02 | .01 |
| Pittsburgh Steelers | | | |
| ☐ 50 Darryl Williams ART | .05 | .02 | .01 |
| Cincinnati Bengals | | | |
| ☐ 51 Kevin Smith ART | .08 | .04 | .01 |
| Dallas Cowboys | | | |
| ☐ 52 Terrell Buckley ART | .10 | .05 | .01 |
| Green Bay Packers | | | |
| ☐ 53 Troy Vincent ART | .08 | .04 | .01 |
| Miami Dolphins | | | |
| ☐ 54 Lin Elliot ART | .05 | .02 | .01 |
| Dallas Cowboys | | | |
| ☐ 55 Dale Carter ART | .08 | .04 | .01 |
| Kansas City Chiefs | | | |
| ☐ 56 Steve Atwater HIT | .05 | .02 | .01 |
| Denver Broncos | | | |
| ☐ 57 Junior Seau HIT | .05 | .02 | .01 |
| San Diego Chargers | | | |
| ☐ 58 Ronnie Lott HIT | .08 | .04 | .01 |
| New York Jets | | | |
| ☐ 59 Louis Oliver HIT | .05 | .02 | .01 |
| Miami Dolphins | | | |
| ☐ 60 Cortez Kennedy HIT | .08 | .04 | .01 |
| Seattle Seahawks | | | |
| ☐ 61 Pat Swilling HIT | .05 | .02 | .01 |
| New Orleans Saints | | | |
| ☐ 62 Hitmen Checklist | .05 | .02 | .01 |
| ☐ 63 Curtis Conway TC | .25 | .11 | .03 |
| Chicago Bears | | | |
| ☐ 64 Alfred Williams TC | .05 | .02 | .01 |
| Cincinnati Bengals | | | |

| | | | |
|---|---|---|---|
| ☐ 65 Jim Kelly TC | .12 | .05 | .02 |
| Buffalo Bills | | | |
| ☐ 66 Simon Fletcher TC | .05 | .02 | .01 |
| Denver Broncos | | | |
| ☐ 67 Eric Metcalf TC | .08 | .04 | .01 |
| Cleveland Browns | | | |
| ☐ 68 Lawrence Dawsey TC | .08 | .04 | .01 |
| Tampa Bay Buccaneers | | | |
| ☐ 69 Garrison Hearst TC | .30 | .14 | .04 |
| Phoenix Cardinals | | | |
| ☐ 70 Anthony Miller TC | .15 | .07 | .02 |
| San Diego Chargers | | | |
| ☐ 71 Neil Smith TC | .08 | .04 | .01 |
| Kansas City Chiefs | | | |
| ☐ 72 Jeff George TC | .05 | .02 | .01 |
| Indianapolis Colts | | | |
| ☐ 73 Emmitt Smith TC | .75 | .35 | .09 |
| Dallas Cowboys | | | |
| ☐ 74 Dan Marino TC | .35 | .16 | .04 |
| Miami Dolphins | | | |
| ☐ 75 Clyde Simmons TC | .05 | .02 | .01 |
| Philadelphia Eagles | | | |
| ☐ 76 Deion Sanders TC | .08 | .04 | .01 |
| Atlanta Falcons | | | |
| ☐ 77 Ricky Watters TC | .20 | .09 | .03 |
| San Francisco 49ers | | | |
| ☐ 78 Rodney Hampton TC | .15 | .07 | .02 |
| New York Giants | | | |
| ☐ 79 Brad Baxter TC | .05 | .02 | .01 |
| New York Jets | | | |
| ☐ 80 Barry Sanders TC | .35 | .16 | .04 |
| Detroit Lions | | | |
| ☐ 81 Warren Moon TC | .10 | .05 | .01 |
| Houston Oilers | | | |
| ☐ 82 Brett Favre TC | .40 | .18 | .05 |
| Green Bay Packers | | | |
| ☐ 83 Drew Bledsoe TC | 1.25 | .55 | .16 |
| New England Patriots | | | |
| ☐ 84 Eric Dickerson TC | .08 | .04 | .01 |
| Los Angeles Raiders | | | |
| ☐ 85 Cleveland Gary TC | .05 | .02 | .01 |
| Los Angeles Rams | | | |
| ☐ 86 Earnest Byner TC | .05 | .02 | .01 |
| Washington Redskins | | | |
| ☐ 87 Wayne Martin TC | .05 | .02 | .01 |
| New Orleans Saints | | | |
| ☐ 88 Rick Mirer TC | 1.25 | .55 | .16 |
| Seattle Seahawks | | | |
| ☐ 89 Barry Foster TC | .10 | .05 | .01 |
| Pittsburgh Steelers | | | |
| ☐ 90 Terry Allen TC | .08 | .04 | .01 |
| Minnesota Vikings | | | |
| ☐ 91 Vinnie Clark | .05 | .02 | .01 |
| Green Bay Packers | | | |
| ☐ 92 Howard Ballard | .05 | .02 | .01 |
| Buffalo Bills | | | |
| ☐ 93 Eric Ball | .05 | .02 | .01 |
| Cincinnati Bengals | | | |
| ☐ 94 Marc Boutte | .05 | .02 | .01 |
| Los Angeles Rams | | | |
| ☐ 95 Larry Centers | .25 | .11 | .03 |
| Phoenix Cardinals | | | |
| ☐ 96 Gary Brown | .60 | .25 | .08 |
| Houston Oilers | | | |
| ☐ 97 Hugh Millen | .05 | .02 | .01 |
| New England Patriots | | | |
| ☐ 98 Anthony Newman | .05 | .02 | .01 |
| Los Angeles Rams | | | |
| ☐ 99 Darrell Thompson | .08 | .04 | .01 |
| Green Bay Packers | | | |
| ☐ 100 George Jamison | .05 | .02 | .01 |
| Detroit Lions | | | |
| ☐ 101 James Francis | .05 | .02 | .01 |
| Cincinnati Bengals | | | |
| ☐ 102 Leonard Harris | .05 | .02 | .01 |
| Houston Oilers | | | |
| ☐ 103 Lomas Brown | .05 | .02 | .01 |
| Detroit Lions | | | |
| ☐ 104 James Lofton | .10 | .05 | .01 |
| Buffalo Bills | | | |
| ☐ 105 Jamie Dukes | .05 | .02 | .01 |
| Atlanta Falcons | | | |
| ☐ 106 Quinn Early | .08 | .04 | .01 |
| New Orleans Saints | | | |
| ☐ 107 Ernie Jones | .05 | .02 | .01 |
| Phoenix Cardinals | | | |
| ☐ 108 Torrance Small | .05 | .02 | .01 |
| New Orleans Saints | | | |
| ☐ 109 Michael Carter | .05 | .02 | .01 |
| San Francisco 49ers | | | |
| ☐ 110 Aeneas Williams | .05 | .02 | .01 |
| Phoenix Cardinals | | | |
| ☐ 111 Renaldo Turnbull | .08 | .04 | .01 |
| New Orleans Saints | | | |
| ☐ 112 Al Smith | .05 | .02 | .01 |
| Houston Oilers | | | |
| ☐ 113 Troy Auzenne | .05 | .02 | .01 |
| Chicago Bears | | | |
| ☐ 114 Stephen Baker | .05 | .02 | .01 |
| New York Giants | | | |
| ☐ 115 Daniel Stubbs | .05 | .02 | .01 |
| Cincinnati Bengals | | | |
| ☐ 116 Dana Hall | .08 | .04 | .01 |
| San Francisco 49ers | | | |
| ☐ 117 Lawrence Taylor | .10 | .05 | .01 |
| New York Giants | | | |
| ☐ 118 Ron Hall | .05 | .02 | .01 |
| Tampa Bay Buccaneers | | | |
| ☐ 119 Derrick Fenner | .05 | .02 | .01 |
| Cincinnati Bengals | | | |
| ☐ 120 Martin Mayhew | .05 | .02 | .01 |
| Washington Redskins | | | |
| ☐ 121 Jay Schroeder | .05 | .02 | .01 |
| Los Angeles Raiders | | | |
| ☐ 122 Michael Zordich | .05 | .02 | .01 |
| Phoenix Cardinals | | | |
| ☐ 123 Ed McCaffrey | .05 | .02 | .01 |
| New York Giants | | | |
| ☐ 124 John Stephens | .05 | .02 | .01 |
| New England Patriots | | | |
| ☐ 125 Brad Edwards | .05 | .02 | .01 |
| Washington Redskins | | | |
| ☐ 126 Don Griffin | .05 | .02 | .01 |
| San Francisco 49ers | | | |
| ☐ 127 Broderick Thomas | .05 | .02 | .01 |
| Tampa Bay Buccaneers | | | |
| ☐ 128 Ted Washington | .05 | .02 | .01 |
| San Francisco 49ers | | | |
| ☐ 129 Haywood Jeffires | .10 | .05 | .01 |
| Houston Oilers | | | |
| ☐ 130 Gary Plummer | .05 | .02 | .01 |
| San Diego Chargers | | | |
| ☐ 131 Mark Wheeler | .05 | .02 | .01 |
| Tampa Bay Buccaneers | | | |
| ☐ 132 Ty Detmer | .08 | .04 | .01 |
| Green Bay Packers | | | |
| ☐ 133 Derrick Walker | .05 | .02 | .01 |
| San Diego Chargers | | | |
| ☐ 134 Henry Ellard | .08 | .04 | .01 |
| Los Angeles Rams | | | |
| ☐ 135 Neal Anderson | .08 | .04 | .01 |
| Chicago Bears | | | |
| ☐ 136 Bruce Smith | .10 | .05 | .01 |
| Buffalo Bills | | | |
| ☐ 137 Cris Carter | .10 | .05 | .01 |
| Minnesota Vikings | | | |
| ☐ 138 Vaughn Dunbar | .08 | .04 | .01 |
| New Orleans Saints | | | |
| ☐ 139 Dan Marino | .75 | .35 | .09 |
| Miami Dolphins | | | |
| ☐ 140 Troy Aikman | 1.25 | .55 | .16 |
| Dallas Cowboys | | | |
| ☐ 141 Randall Cunningham | .10 | .05 | .01 |
| Philadelphia Eagles | | | |
| ☐ 142 Darryl Johnston | .10 | .05 | .01 |
| Dallas Cowboys | | | |
| ☐ 143 Mark Clayton | .08 | .04 | .01 |
| Miami Dolphins | | | |
| ☐ 144 Rich Gannon | .08 | .04 | .01 |
| Minnesota Vikings | | | |
| ☐ 145 Nate Newton | .05 | .02 | .01 |
| Dallas Cowboys | | | |
| ☐ 146 Willie Gault | .08 | .04 | .01 |
| Los Angeles Raiders | | | |
| ☐ 147 Brian Washington | .05 | .02 | .01 |
| New York Jets | | | |
| ☐ 148 Fred Barnett | .10 | .05 | .01 |
| Philadelphia Eagles | | | |
| ☐ 149 Gill Byrd | .05 | .02 | .01 |
| San Diego Chargers | | | |
| ☐ 150 Art Monk | .10 | .05 | .01 |
| Washington Redskins | | | |
| ☐ 151 Stan Humphries | .10 | .05 | .01 |
| San Diego Chargers | | | |
| ☐ 152 Charles Mann | .08 | .04 | .01 |
| Washington Redskins | | | |
| ☐ 153 Greg Lloyd | .05 | .02 | .01 |
| Pittsburgh Steelers | | | |
| ☐ 154 Marvin Washington | .05 | .02 | .01 |
| New York Jets | | | |
| ☐ 155 Bernie Kosar | .10 | .05 | .01 |
| Cleveland Browns | | | |
| ☐ 156 Pete Metzelaars | .05 | .02 | .01 |
| Buffalo Bills | | | |
| ☐ 157 Chris Hinton | .05 | .02 | .01 |
| Atlanta Falcons | | | |
| ☐ 158 Jim Harbaugh | .08 | .04 | .01 |
| Chicago Bears | | | |
| ☐ 159 Willie Davis | .10 | .05 | .01 |
| Kansas City Chiefs | | | |
| ☐ 160 Leroy Thompson | .08 | .04 | .01 |
| Pittsburgh Steelers | | | |
| ☐ 161 Scott Miller | .05 | .02 | .01 |
| Miami Dolphins | | | |
| ☐ 162 Eugene Robinson | .05 | .02 | .01 |

| | | | | |
|---|---|---|---|---|
| Seattle Seahawks | | | | |
| ☐ 163 David Little | .05 | .02 | .01 |
| Pittsburgh Steelers | | | | |
| ☐ 164 Pierce Holt | .05 | .02 | .01 |
| Atlanta Falcons | | | | |
| ☐ 165 James Hasty | .05 | .02 | .01 |
| New York Jets | | | | |
| ☐ 166 Dave Krieg | .08 | .04 | .01 |
| Kansas City Chiefs | | | | |
| ☐ 167 Gerald Williams | .05 | .02 | .01 |
| Pittsburgh Steelers | | | | |
| ☐ 168 Kyle Clifton | .05 | .02 | .01 |
| New York Jets | | | | |
| ☐ 169 Bill Brooks | .08 | .04 | .01 |
| Indianapolis Colts | | | | |
| ☐ 170 Vance Johnson | .08 | .04 | .01 |
| Denver Broncos | | | | |
| ☐ 171 Greg Townsend | .05 | .02 | .01 |
| Los Angeles Raiders | | | | |
| ☐ 172 Jason Belser | .05 | .02 | .01 |
| Indianapolis Colts | | | | |
| ☐ 173 Brett Perriman | .08 | .04 | .01 |
| Detroit Lions | | | | |
| ☐ 174 Steve Jordan | .08 | .04 | .01 |
| Minnesota Vikings | | | | |
| ☐ 175 Kelvin Martin | .08 | .04 | .01 |
| Dallas Cowboys | | | | |
| ☐ 176 Greg Kragen | .05 | .02 | .01 |
| Denver Broncos | | | | |
| ☐ 177 Kerry Cash | .05 | .02 | .01 |
| Indianapolis Colts | | | | |
| ☐ 178 Chester McGlockton | .05 | .02 | .01 |
| Los Angeles Raiders | | | | |
| ☐ 179 Jim Kelly | .25 | .11 | .03 |
| Buffalo Bills | | | | |
| ☐ 180 Todd McNair | .05 | .02 | .01 |
| Kansas City Chiefs | | | | |
| ☐ 181 Leroy Hoard | .08 | .04 | .01 |
| Cleveland Browns | | | | |
| ☐ 182 Seth Joyner | .08 | .04 | .01 |
| Philadelphia Eagles | | | | |
| ☐ 183 Sam Gash | .10 | .05 | .01 |
| New England Patriots | | | | |
| ☐ 184 Joe Nash | .05 | .02 | .01 |
| Seattle Seahawks | | | | |
| ☐ 185 Lin Elliott | .05 | .02 | .01 |
| Dallas Cowboys | | | | |
| ☐ 186 Robert Porcher | .08 | .04 | .01 |
| Detroit Lions | | | | |
| ☐ 187 Tom Hodson | .05 | .02 | .01 |
| New England Patriots | | | | |
| ☐ 188 Greg Lewis | .05 | .02 | .01 |
| Denver Broncos | | | | |
| ☐ 189 Dan Saleaumua | .05 | .02 | .01 |
| Kansas City Chiefs | | | | |
| ☐ 190 Chris Goode | .05 | .02 | .01 |
| Indianapolis Colts | | | | |
| ☐ 191 Henry Thomas | .05 | .02 | .01 |
| Minnesota Vikings | | | | |
| ☐ 192 Bobby Hebert | .10 | .05 | .01 |
| New Orleans Saints | | | | |
| ☐ 193 Clay Matthews | .08 | .04 | .01 |
| Cleveland Browns | | | | |
| ☐ 194 Mark(WR) Carrier | .08 | .04 | .01 |
| Tampa Bay Buccaneers | | | | |
| ☐ 195 Anthony Pleasant | .05 | .02 | .01 |
| Cleveland Browns | | | | |
| ☐ 196 Eric Dorsey | .05 | .02 | .01 |
| New York Giants | | | | |
| ☐ 197 Clarence Verdin | .05 | .02 | .01 |
| Indianapolis Colts | | | | |
| ☐ 198 Marc Spindler | .05 | .02 | .01 |
| Detroit Lions | | | | |
| ☐ 199 Tommy Maddox | .10 | .05 | .01 |
| Denver Broncos | | | | |
| ☐ 200 Wendell Davis | .08 | .04 | .01 |
| Chicago Bears | | | | |
| ☐ 201 John Fina | .05 | .02 | .01 |
| Buffalo Bills | | | | |
| ☐ 202 Alonzo Spellman | .08 | .04 | .01 |
| Chicago Bears | | | | |
| ☐ 203 Darryl Williams | .08 | .04 | .01 |
| Cincinnati Bengals | | | | |
| ☐ 204 Mike Croel | .08 | .04 | .01 |
| Denver Broncos | | | | |
| ☐ 205 Ken Norton Jr. | .08 | .04 | .01 |
| Dallas Cowboys | | | | |
| ☐ 206 Mel Gray | .08 | .04 | .01 |
| Detroit Lions | | | | |
| ☐ 207 Chuck Cecil | .05 | .02 | .01 |
| Green Bay Packers | | | | |
| ☐ 208 John Flannery | .05 | .02 | .01 |
| Houston Oilers | | | | |
| ☐ 209 Chip Banks | .05 | .02 | .01 |
| Indianapolis Colts | | | | |
| ☐ 210 Chris Martin | .05 | .02 | .01 |
| Kansas City Chiefs | | | | |
| ☐ 211 Dennis Brown | .05 | .02 | .01 |

| | | | | |
|---|---|---|---|---|
| San Francisco 49ers | | | | |
| ☐ 212 Vinny Testaverde | .10 | .05 | .01 |
| Tampa Bay Buccaneers | | | | |
| ☐ 213 Nick Bell | .08 | .04 | .01 |
| Los Angeles Raiders | | | | |
| ☐ 214 Robert Delpino | .08 | .04 | .01 |
| Los Angeles Rams | | | | |
| ☐ 215 Mark Higgs | .10 | .05 | .01 |
| Miami Dolphins | | | | |
| ☐ 216 Al Noga | .05 | .02 | .01 |
| Minnesota Vikings | | | | |
| ☐ 217 Andre Tippett | .05 | .02 | .01 |
| New England Patriots | | | | |
| ☐ 218 Pat Swilling | .08 | .04 | .01 |
| New Orleans Saints | | | | |
| ☐ 219 Phil Simms | .10 | .05 | .01 |
| New York Giants | | | | |
| ☐ 220 Ricky Proehl | .08 | .04 | .01 |
| Phoenix Cardinals | | | | |
| ☐ 221 William Thomas | .05 | .02 | .01 |
| Philadelphia Eagles | | | | |
| ☐ 222 Jeff Graham | .08 | .04 | .01 |
| Pittsburgh Steelers | | | | |
| ☐ 223 Darion Conner | .05 | .02 | .01 |
| Atlanta Falcons | | | | |
| ☐ 224 Mark (USC) Carrier | .08 | .04 | .01 |
| Chicago Bears | | | | |
| ☐ 225 Willie Green | .08 | .04 | .01 |
| Detroit Lions | | | | |
| ☐ 226 Reggie Rivers | .25 | .11 | .03 |
| Denver Broncos | | | | |
| ☐ 227 Andre Reed | .10 | .05 | .01 |
| Buffalo Bills | | | | |
| ☐ 228 Deion Sanders | .15 | .07 | .02 |
| Atlanta Falcons | | | | |
| ☐ 229 Chris Doleman | .08 | .04 | .01 |
| Minnesota Vikings | | | | |
| ☐ 230 Jerry Ball | .05 | .02 | .01 |
| Detroit Lions | | | | |
| ☐ 231 Eric Dickerson | .10 | .05 | .01 |
| Los Angeles Raiders | | | | |
| ☐ 232 Carlos Jenkins | .05 | .02 | .01 |
| Minnesota Vikings | | | | |
| ☐ 233 Mike Johnson | .05 | .02 | .01 |
| Cleveland Browns | | | | |
| ☐ 234 Marco Coleman | .08 | .04 | .01 |
| Miami Dolphins | | | | |
| ☐ 235 Leslie O'Neal | .08 | .04 | .01 |
| San Diego Chargers | | | | |
| ☐ 236 Browning Nagle | .08 | .04 | .01 |
| New York Jets | | | | |
| ☐ 237 Carl Pickens | .10 | .05 | .01 |
| Cincinnati Bengals | | | | |
| ☐ 238 Steve Emtman | .08 | .04 | .01 |
| Indianapolis Colts | | | | |
| ☐ 239 Alvin Harper | .25 | .11 | .03 |
| Dallas Cowboys | | | | |
| ☐ 240 Keith Jackson | .10 | .05 | .01 |
| Miami Dolphins | | | | |
| ☐ 241 Jerry Rice | .60 | .25 | .08 |
| San Francisco 49ers | | | | |
| ☐ 242 Cortez Kennedy | .10 | .05 | .01 |
| Seattle Seahawks | | | | |
| ☐ 243 Tyji Armstrong | .05 | .02 | .01 |
| Tampa Bay Buccaneers | | | | |
| ☐ 244 Troy Vincent | .08 | .04 | .01 |
| Miami Dolphins | | | | |
| ☐ 245 Randal Hill | .10 | .05 | .01 |
| Phoenix Cardinals | | | | |
| ☐ 246 Robert Blackmon | .05 | .02 | .01 |
| Seattle Seahawks | | | | |
| ☐ 247 Junior Seau | .10 | .05 | .01 |
| San Diego Chargers | | | | |
| ☐ 248 Sterling Sharpe | .40 | .18 | .05 |
| Green Bay Packers | | | | |
| ☐ 249 Thurman Thomas | .35 | .16 | .04 |
| Buffalo Bills | | | | |
| ☐ 250 David Klingler | .15 | .07 | .02 |
| Cincinnati Bengals | | | | |
| ☐ 251 Jeff George | .15 | .07 | .02 |
| Indianapolis Colts | | | | |
| ☐ 252 Anthony Miller | .10 | .05 | .01 |
| San Diego Chargers | | | | |
| ☐ 253 Earnest Byner | .08 | .04 | .01 |
| Washington Redskins | | | | |
| ☐ 254 Eric Swann | .08 | .04 | .01 |
| Phoenix Cardinals | | | | |
| ☐ 255 Jeff Herrod | .05 | .02 | .01 |
| Indianapolis Colts | | | | |
| ☐ 256 Eddie Robinson | .05 | .02 | .01 |
| Houston Oilers | | | | |
| ☐ 257 Eric Allen | .08 | .04 | .01 |
| Philadelphia Eagles | | | | |
| ☐ 258 John Taylor | .10 | .05 | .01 |
| San Francisco 49ers | | | | |
| ☐ 259 Sean Gilbert | .08 | .04 | .01 |
| Los Angeles Raiders | | | | |
| ☐ 260 Ray Childress | .05 | .02 | .01 |

| | | | |
|---|---|---|---|
| Houston Oilers | | | |
| ☐ 261 Michael Haynes | .20 | .09 | .03 |
| Atlanta Falcons | | | |
| ☐ 262 Greg McMurtry | .05 | .02 | .01 |
| New England Patriots | | | |
| ☐ 263 Bill Romanowski | .05 | .02 | .01 |
| San Francisco 49ers | | | |
| ☐ 264 Todd Lyght | .05 | .02 | .01 |
| Los Angeles Raiders | | | |
| ☐ 265 Clyde Simmons | .08 | .04 | .01 |
| Philadelphia Eagles | | | |
| ☐ 266 Webster Slaughter | .08 | .04 | .01 |
| Houston Oilers | | | |
| ☐ 267 J.J. Birden | .08 | .04 | .01 |
| Kansas City Chiefs | | | |
| ☐ 268 Aaron Wallace | .05 | .02 | .01 |
| Los Angeles Raiders | | | |
| ☐ 269 Carl Banks | .05 | .02 | .01 |
| New York Giants | | | |
| ☐ 270 Ricardo McDonald | .05 | .02 | .01 |
| Cincinnati Bengals | | | |
| ☐ 271 Michael Brooks | .05 | .02 | .01 |
| Denver Broncos | | | |
| ☐ 272 Dale Carter | .10 | .05 | .01 |
| Kansas City Chiefs | | | |
| ☐ 273 Mike Pritchard | .10 | .05 | .01 |
| Atlanta Falcons | | | |
| ☐ 274 Derek Brown | .08 | .04 | .01 |
| New York Giants | | | |
| ☐ 275 Burt Grossman | .05 | .02 | .01 |
| San Diego Chargers | | | |
| ☐ 276 Mark Schlereth | .05 | .02 | .01 |
| Washington Redskins | | | |
| ☐ 277 Karl Mecklenburg | .08 | .04 | .01 |
| Denver Broncos | | | |
| ☐ 278 Rickey Jackson | .08 | .04 | .01 |
| New Orleans Saints | | | |
| ☐ 279 Ricky Ervins | .08 | .04 | .01 |
| Washington Redskins | | | |
| ☐ 280 Jeff Bryant | .05 | .02 | .01 |
| Seattle Seahawks | | | |
| ☐ 281 Eric Martin | .08 | .04 | .01 |
| New Orleans Saints | | | |
| ☐ 282 Carlton Haselrig | .05 | .02 | .01 |
| Pittsburgh Steelers | | | |
| ☐ 283 Kevin Mack | .08 | .04 | .01 |
| Cleveland Browns | | | |
| ☐ 284 Brad Muster | .08 | .04 | .01 |
| Chicago Bears | | | |
| ☐ 285 Kelvin Pritchett | .05 | .02 | .01 |
| Detroit Lions | | | |
| ☐ 286 Courtney Hawkins | .08 | .04 | .01 |
| Tampa Bay Buccaneers | | | |
| ☐ 287 Levon Kirkland | .05 | .02 | .01 |
| Pittsburgh Steelers | | | |
| ☐ 288 Steve DeBerg | .08 | .04 | .01 |
| Tampa Bay Buccaneers | | | |
| ☐ 289 Edgar Bennett | .10 | .05 | .01 |
| Green Bay Packers | | | |
| ☐ 290 Michael Dean Perry | .10 | .05 | .01 |
| Cleveland Browns | | | |
| ☐ 291 Richard Dent | .08 | .04 | .01 |
| Chicago Bears | | | |
| ☐ 292 Howie Long | .08 | .04 | .01 |
| Los Angeles Raiders | | | |
| ☐ 293 Chris Mims | .08 | .04 | .01 |
| San Diego Chargers | | | |
| ☐ 294 Kurt Barber | .05 | .02 | .01 |
| New York Jets | | | |
| ☐ 295 Wilber Marshall | .08 | .04 | .01 |
| Washington Redskins | | | |
| ☐ 296 Ethan Horton | .05 | .02 | .01 |
| Los Angeles Raiders | | | |
| ☐ 297 Tony Bennett | .05 | .02 | .01 |
| Green Bay Packers | | | |
| ☐ 298 Johnny Johnson | .10 | .05 | .01 |
| New York Jets | | | |
| ☐ 299 Craig Heyward | .05 | .02 | .01 |
| New Orleans Saints | | | |
| ☐ 300 Steve Israel | .05 | .02 | .01 |
| Los Angeles Raiders | | | |
| ☐ 301 Kenneth Gant | .05 | .02 | .01 |
| Dallas Cowboys | | | |
| ☐ 302 Eugene Chung | .05 | .02 | .01 |
| New England Patriots | | | |
| ☐ 303 Harvey Williams | .10 | .05 | .01 |
| Kansas City Chiefs | | | |
| ☐ 304 Jarrod Bunch | .08 | .04 | .01 |
| New York Giants | | | |
| ☐ 305 Darren Perry | .05 | .02 | .01 |
| Pittsburgh Steelers | | | |
| ☐ 306 Steve Christie | .05 | .02 | .01 |
| Buffalo Bills | | | |
| ☐ 307 John Randle | .05 | .02 | .01 |
| Minnesota Vikings | | | |
| ☐ 308 Warren Moon | .15 | .07 | .02 |
| Houston Oilers | | | |
| ☐ 309 Charles Haley | .08 | .04 | .01 |

| | | | |
|---|---|---|---|
| Dallas Cowboys | | | |
| ☐ 310 Tony Smith | .05 | .02 | .01 |
| Atlanta Falcons | | | |
| ☐ 311 Steve Broussard | .05 | .02 | .01 |
| Atlanta Falcons | | | |
| ☐ 312 Alfred Williams | .05 | .02 | .01 |
| Cincinnati Bengals | | | |
| ☐ 313 Terrell Buckley | .10 | .05 | .01 |
| Green Bay Packers | | | |
| ☐ 314 Trace Armstrong | .05 | .02 | .01 |
| Chicago Bears | | | |
| ☐ 315 Brian Mitchell | .08 | .04 | .01 |
| Washington Redskins | | | |
| ☐ 316 Steve Atwater | .08 | .04 | .01 |
| Denver Broncos | | | |
| ☐ 317 Nate Lewis | .08 | .04 | .01 |
| San Diego Chargers | | | |
| ☐ 318 Richard Brown | .05 | .02 | .01 |
| Cleveland Browns | | | |
| ☐ 319 Rufus Porter | .05 | .02 | .01 |
| Seattle Seahawks | | | |
| ☐ 320 Pat Harlow | .05 | .02 | .01 |
| New England Patriots | | | |
| ☐ 321 Anthony Smith | .05 | .02 | .01 |
| Los Angeles Raiders | | | |
| ☐ 322 Jack Del Rio | .05 | .02 | .01 |
| Minnesota Vikings | | | |
| ☐ 323 Darryl Talley | .05 | .02 | .01 |
| Buffalo Bills | | | |
| ☐ 324 Sam Mills | .08 | .04 | .01 |
| New Orleans Saints | | | |
| ☐ 325 Chris Miller | .10 | .05 | .01 |
| Atlanta Falcons | | | |
| ☐ 326 Ken Harvey | .05 | .02 | .01 |
| Phoenix Cardinals | | | |
| ☐ 327 Rod Woodson | .10 | .05 | .01 |
| Pittsburgh Steelers | | | |
| ☐ 328 Tony Tolbert | .05 | .02 | .01 |
| Dallas Cowboys | | | |
| ☐ 329 Todd Kinchen | .08 | .04 | .01 |
| Los Angeles Rams | | | |
| ☐ 330 Brian Noble | .05 | .02 | .01 |
| Green Bay Packers | | | |
| ☐ 331 David Meggett | .08 | .04 | .01 |
| New York Giants | | | |
| ☐ 332 Chris Spielman | .05 | .02 | .01 |
| Detroit Lions | | | |
| ☐ 333 Barry Word | .10 | .05 | .01 |
| Kansas City Chiefs | | | |
| ☐ 334 Jessie Hester | .05 | .02 | .01 |
| Indianapolis Colts | | | |
| ☐ 335 Michael Jackson | .10 | .05 | .01 |
| Cleveland Browns | | | |
| ☐ 336 Mitchell Price | .05 | .02 | .01 |
| Cincinnati Bengals | | | |
| ☐ 337 Michael Irvin | .50 | .23 | .06 |
| Dallas Cowboys | | | |
| ☐ 338 Simon Fletcher | .08 | .04 | .01 |
| Denver Broncos | | | |
| ☐ 339 Keith Jennings | .05 | .02 | .01 |
| Chicago Bears | | | |
| ☐ 340 Vai Sikahema | .05 | .02 | .01 |
| Philadelphia Eagles | | | |
| ☐ 341 Roger Craig | .08 | .04 | .01 |
| Minnesota Vikings | | | |
| ☐ 342 Ricky Watters | .30 | .14 | .04 |
| San Francisco 49ers | | | |
| ☐ 343 Reggie Cobb | .10 | .05 | .01 |
| Tampa Bay Buccaneers | | | |
| ☐ 344 Kanavis McGhee | .05 | .02 | .01 |
| New York Giants | | | |
| ☐ 345 Barry Foster | .25 | .11 | .03 |
| Pittsburgh Steelers | | | |
| ☐ 346 Marion Butts | .10 | .05 | .01 |
| San Diego Chargers | | | |
| ☐ 347 Bryan Cox | .08 | .04 | .01 |
| Miami Dolphins | | | |
| ☐ 348 Wayne Martin | .05 | .02 | .01 |
| New Orleans Saints | | | |
| ☐ 349 Jim Everett | .05 | .02 | .01 |
| Los Angeles Rams | | | |
| ☐ 350 Nate Odomes | .08 | .04 | .01 |
| Buffalo Bills | | | |
| ☐ 351 Anthony Johnson | .05 | .02 | .01 |
| Indianapolis Colts | | | |
| ☐ 352 Rodney Hampton | .30 | .14 | .04 |
| New York Giants | | | |
| ☐ 353 Terry Allen | .10 | .05 | .01 |
| Minnesota Vikings | | | |
| ☐ 354 Derrick Thomas | .15 | .07 | .02 |
| Kansas City Chiefs | | | |
| ☐ 355 Calvin Williams | .10 | .05 | .01 |
| Philadelphia Eagles | | | |
| ☐ 356 Pepper Johnson | .05 | .02 | .01 |
| New York Giants | | | |
| ☐ 357 John Elway | .35 | .16 | .04 |
| Denver Broncos | | | |
| ☐ 358 Steve Young | .25 | .11 | .03 |

| | | | | | | | | |
|---|---|---|---|---|---|---|---|---|
| | San Francisco 49ers | | | | | New York Jets | | |
| ☐ 359 | Emmitt Smith | 2.00 | .90 | .25 | ☐ 408 | Tommy Vardell | .08 | .04 | .01 |
| | Dallas Cowboys | | | | | Cleveland Browns | | |
| ☐ 360 | Brett Favre | .75 | .35 | .09 | ☐ 409 | Gene Atkins | .05 | .02 | .01 |
| | Green Bay Packers | | | | | New Orleans Saints | | |
| ☐ 361 | Cody Carlson | .20 | .09 | .03 | ☐ 410 | Sean Salisbury | .08 | .04 | .01 |
| | Houston Oilers | | | | | Minnesota Vikings | | |
| ☐ 362 | Vincent Brown | .05 | .02 | .01 | ☐ 411 | Kenneth Davis | .08 | .04 | .01 |
| | New England Patriots | | | | | Buffalo Bills | | |
| ☐ 363 | Gary Anderson | .08 | .04 | .01 | ☐ 412 | John L. Williams | .08 | .04 | .01 |
| | Tampa Bay Buccaneers | | | | | Seattle Seahawks | | |
| ☐ 364 | Jon Vaughn | .05 | .02 | .01 | ☐ 413 | Roman Phifer | .05 | .02 | .01 |
| | New England Patriots | | | | | Los Angeles Rams | | |
| ☐ 365 | Todd Marinovich | .05 | .02 | .01 | ☐ 414 | Bennie Blades | .05 | .02 | .01 |
| | Los Angeles Raiders | | | | | Detroit Lions | | |
| ☐ 366 | Carnell Lake | .05 | .02 | .01 | ☐ 415 | Tim Brown | .25 | .11 | .03 |
| | Pittsburgh Steelers | | | | | Los Angeles Raiders | | |
| ☐ 367 | Kurt Gouveia | .05 | .02 | .01 | ☐ 416 | Lorenzo White | .08 | .04 | .01 |
| | Washington Redskins | | | | | Houston Oilers | | |
| ☐ 368 | Lawrence Dawsey | .10 | .05 | .01 | ☐ 417 | Tony Casillas | .05 | .02 | .01 |
| | Tampa Bay Buccaneers | | | | | Dallas Cowboys | | |
| ☐ 369 | Neil O'Donnell | .25 | .11 | .03 | ☐ 418 | Tom Waddle | .10 | .05 | .01 |
| | Pittsburgh Steelers | | | | | Chicago Bears | | |
| ☐ 370 | Duane Bickett | .05 | .02 | .01 | ☐ 419 | David Fulcher | .05 | .02 | .01 |
| | Indianapolis Colts | | | | | Cincinnati Bengals | | |
| ☐ 371 | Ronnie Harmon | .08 | .04 | .01 | ☐ 420 | Jessie Tuggle | .05 | .02 | .01 |
| | San Diego Chargers | | | | | Atlanta Falcons | | |
| ☐ 372 | Rodney Peete | .08 | .04 | .01 | ☐ 421 | Emmitt Smith SL | .75 | .35 | .09 |
| | Detroit Lions | | | | | Dallas Cowboys | | |
| ☐ 373 | Cornelius Bennett | .10 | .05 | .01 | ☐ 422 | Clyde Simmons SL | .05 | .02 | .01 |
| | Buffalo Bills | | | | | Philadelphia Eagles | | |
| ☐ 374 | Brad Baxter | .08 | .04 | .01 | ☐ 423 | Sterling Sharpe SL | .20 | .09 | .03 |
| | New York Jets | | | | | Green Bay Packers | | |
| ☐ 375 | Ernest Givins | .05 | .02 | .01 | ☐ 424 | Sterling Sharpe SL | .20 | .09 | .03 |
| | Houston Oilers | | | | | Green Bay Packers | | |
| ☐ 376 | Keith Byars | .08 | .04 | .01 | ☐ 425 | Emmitt Smith SL | .75 | .35 | .09 |
| | Philadelphia Eagles | | | | | Dallas Cowboys | | |
| ☐ 377 | Eric Bieniemy | .08 | .04 | .01 | ☐ 426 | Dan Marino SL | .35 | .16 | .04 |
| | San Diego Chargers | | | | | Miami Dolphins | | |
| ☐ 378 | Mike Brim | .05 | .02 | .01 | ☐ 427 | Henry Jones SL | .05 | .02 | .01 |
| | New York Jets | | | | | Buffalo Bills | | |
| ☐ 379 | Darren Lewis | .08 | .04 | .01 | | Audray McMillan | | |
| | Chicago Bears | | | | | Minnesota Vikings | | |
| ☐ 380 | Heath Sherman | .05 | .02 | .01 | ☐ 428 | Thurman Thomas SL | .15 | .07 | .02 |
| | Philadelphia Eagles | | | | | Buffalo Bills | | |
| ☐ 381 | Leonard Russell | .08 | .04 | .01 | ☐ 429 | Greg Montgomery SL | .05 | .02 | .01 |
| | New England Patriots | | | | | Houston Oilers | | |
| ☐ 382 | Brent Jones | .10 | .05 | .01 | ☐ 430 | Pete Stoyanovich SL | .05 | .02 | .01 |
| | San Francisco 49ers | | | | | Miami Dolphins | | |
| ☐ 383 | David Whitmore | .05 | .02 | .01 | ☐ 431 | Season Leaders CL | .25 | .11 | .03 |
| | San Francisco 49ers | | | | | Emmitt Smith | | |
| ☐ 384 | Ray Roberts | .05 | .02 | .01 | ☐ 432 | Steve Young BB | .12 | .05 | .02 |
| | Seattle Seahawks | | | | | San Francisco 49ers | | |
| ☐ 385 | John Offerdahl | .05 | .02 | .01 | ☐ 433 | Jerry Rice BB | .25 | .11 | .03 |
| | Miami Dolphins | | | | | San Francisco 49ers | | |
| ☐ 386 | Keith McCants | .05 | .02 | .01 | ☐ 434 | Ricky Watters BB | .15 | .07 | .02 |
| | Tampa Bay Buccaneers | | | | | San Francisco 49ers | | |
| ☐ 387 | John Baylor | .05 | .02 | .01 | ☐ 435 | Barry Foster BB | .10 | .05 | .01 |
| | Indianapolis Colts | | | | | Pittsburgh Steelers | | |
| ☐ 388 | Amp Lee | .08 | .04 | .01 | ☐ 436 | Cortez Kennedy BB | .08 | .04 | .01 |
| | San Francisco 49ers | | | | | Seattle Seahawks | | |
| ☐ 389 | Chris Warren | .15 | .07 | .02 | ☐ 437 | Warren Moon BB | .10 | .05 | .01 |
| | Seattle Seahawks | | | | | Houston Oilers | | |
| ☐ 390 | Herman Moore | .35 | .16 | .04 | ☐ 438 | Thurman Thomas BB | .15 | .07 | .02 |
| | Detroit Lions | | | | | Buffalo Bills | | |
| ☐ 391 | Johnny Bailey | .05 | .02 | .01 | ☐ 439 | Brett Favre BB | .35 | .16 | .04 |
| | Phoenix Cardinals | | | | | Green Bay Packers | | |
| ☐ 392 | Tim Johnson | .05 | .02 | .01 | ☐ 440 | Andre Rison BB | .08 | .04 | .01 |
| | Washington Redskins | | | | | Atlanta Falcons | | |
| ☐ 393 | Eric Metcalf | .10 | .05 | .01 | ☐ 441 | Barry Sanders BB | .40 | .18 | .05 |
| | Cleveland Browns | | | | | Detroit Lions | | |
| ☐ 394 | Chris Chandler | .08 | .04 | .01 | ☐ 442 | Berman's Best CL | .15 | .07 | .02 |
| | Phoenix Cardinals | | | | | Chris Berman | | |
| ☐ 395 | Mark Rypien | .08 | .04 | .01 | ☐ 443 | Moe Gardner | .05 | .02 | .01 |
| | Washington Redskins | | | | | Atlanta Falcons | | |
| ☐ 396 | Christian Okoye | .08 | .04 | .01 | ☐ 444 | Robert Jones | .05 | .02 | .01 |
| | Kansas City Chiefs | | | | | Dallas Cowboys | | |
| ☐ 397 | Shannon Sharpe | .20 | .09 | .03 | ☐ 445 | Reggie Langhorne | .08 | .04 | .01 |
| | Denver Broncos | | | | | Indianapolis Colts | | |
| ☐ 398 | Eric Hill | .05 | .02 | .01 | ☐ 446 | Flipper Anderson | .08 | .04 | .01 |
| | Phoenix Cardinals | | | | | Los Angeles Rams | | |
| ☐ 399 | David Lang | .05 | .02 | .01 | ☐ 447 | James Washington | .05 | .02 | .01 |
| | Los Angeles Rams | | | | | Dallas Cowboys | | |
| ☐ 400 | Bruce Matthews | .08 | .04 | .01 | ☐ 448 | Aaron Craver | .08 | .04 | .01 |
| | Houston Oilers | | | | | Miami Dolphins | | |
| ☐ 401 | Harold Green | .08 | .04 | .01 | ☐ 449 | Jack Trudeau | .05 | .02 | .01 |
| | Cincinnati Bengals | | | | | Indianapolis Colts | | |
| ☐ 402 | Mo Lewis | .05 | .02 | .01 | ☐ 450 | Neil Smith | .10 | .05 | .01 |
| | New York Jets | | | | | Kansas City Chiefs | | |
| ☐ 403 | Terry McDaniel | .05 | .02 | .01 | ☐ 451 | Chris Burkett | .05 | .02 | .01 |
| | Los Angeles Raiders | | | | | New York Jets | | |
| ☐ 404 | Wesley Carroll | .05 | .02 | .01 | ☐ 452 | Russell Maryland | .05 | .02 | .01 |
| | New Orleans Saints | | | | | Dallas Cowboys | | |
| ☐ 405 | Richmond Webb | .05 | .02 | .01 | ☐ 453 | Drew Hill | .08 | .04 | .01 |
| | Miami Dolphins | | | | | Atlanta Falcons | | |
| ☐ 406 | Andre Rison | .25 | .11 | .03 | ☐ 454 | Barry Sanders | .75 | .35 | .09 |
| | Atlanta Falcons | | | | | Detroit Lions | | |
| ☐ 407 | Lonnie Young | .05 | .02 | .01 | ☐ 455 | Jeff Cross | .05 | .02 | .01 |

| | | | | |
|---|---|---|---|---|
| Miami Dolphins | | | | |
| ☐ 456 Bennie Thompson | .05 | .02 | .01 | |
| Kansas City Chiefs | | | | |
| ☐ 457 Marcus Allen | .08 | .04 | .01 | |
| Los Angeles Raiders | | | | |
| ☐ 458 Tracy Scroggins | .08 | .04 | .01 | |
| Detroit Lions | | | | |
| ☐ 459 LeRoy Butler | .05 | .02 | .01 | |
| Green Bay Packers | | | | |
| ☐ 460 Joe Montana | 1.25 | .55 | .16 | |
| Kansas City Chiefs | | | | |
| ☐ 461 Eddie Anderson | .05 | .02 | .01 | |
| Los Angeles Raiders | | | | |
| ☐ 462 Tim McDonald | .05 | .02 | .01 | |
| Phoenix Cardinals | | | | |
| ☐ 463 Ronnie Lott | .10 | .05 | .01 | |
| Los Angeles Raiders | | | | |
| ☐ 464 Gaston Green | .08 | .04 | .01 | |
| Denver Broncos | | | | |
| ☐ 465 Shane Conlan | .05 | .02 | .01 | |
| Buffalo Bills | | | | |
| ☐ 466 Leonard Marshall | .08 | .04 | .01 | |
| New York Giants | | | | |
| ☐ 467 Melvin Jenkins | .05 | .02 | .01 | |
| Detroit Lions | | | | |
| ☐ 468 Don Beebe | .10 | .05 | .01 | |
| Buffalo Bills | | | | |
| ☐ 469 Johnny Mitchell | .25 | .11 | .03 | |
| New York Jets | | | | |
| ☐ 470 Darryl Henley | .05 | .02 | .01 | |
| Los Angeles Rams | | | | |
| ☐ 471 Boomer Esiason | .12 | .05 | .02 | |
| Cincinnati Bengals | | | | |
| ☐ 472 Mark Kelso | .05 | .02 | .01 | |
| Buffalo Bills | | | | |
| ☐ 473 John Booty | .05 | .02 | .01 | |
| Philadelphia Eagles | | | | |
| ☐ 474 Pete Stoyanovich | .05 | .02 | .01 | |
| Miami Dolphins | | | | |
| ☐ 475 Thomas Smith | .12 | .05 | .02 | |
| Buffalo Bills | | | | |
| ☐ 476 Carlton Gray | .20 | .09 | .03 | |
| Seattle Seahawks | | | | |
| ☐ 477 Dana Stubblefield | .50 | .23 | .06 | |
| San Francisco 49ers | | | | |
| ☐ 478 Ryan McNeil | .10 | .05 | .01 | |
| Miami Dolphins | | | | |
| ☐ 479 Natrone Means | 1.25 | .55 | .16 | |
| San Diego Chargers | | | | |
| ☐ 480 Carl Simpson | .10 | .05 | .01 | |
| Chicago Bears | | | | |
| ☐ 481 Robert O'Neal | .10 | .05 | .01 | |
| Miami Dolphins | | | | |
| ☐ 482 Demetrius DuBose | .15 | .07 | .02 | |
| Tampa Bay Buccaneers | | | | |
| ☐ 483 Darrin Smith | .30 | .14 | .04 | |
| Dallas Cowboys | | | | |
| ☐ 484 Micheal Barrow | .05 | .02 | .01 | |
| Houston Oilers | | | | |
| ☐ 485 Chris Slade | .30 | .14 | .04 | |
| New England Patriots | | | | |
| ☐ 486 Steve Tovar | .10 | .05 | .01 | |
| Cincinnati Bengals | | | | |
| ☐ 487 Ron George | .05 | .02 | .01 | |
| Atlanta Falcons | | | | |
| ☐ 488 Steve Tasker | .05 | .02 | .01 | |
| Buffalo Bills | | | | |
| ☐ 489 Will Furrer | .05 | .02 | .01 | |
| Chicago Bears | | | | |
| ☐ 490 Reggie White | .15 | .07 | .02 | |
| Green Bay Packers | | | | |
| ☐ 491 Sean Jones | .05 | .02 | .01 | |
| Houston Oilers | | | | |
| ☐ 492 Gary Clark | .08 | .04 | .01 | |
| Washington Redskins | | | | |
| ☐ 493 Donnell Woolford | .05 | .02 | .01 | |
| Chicago Bears | | | | |
| ☐ 494 Steve Beuerlein | .15 | .07 | .02 | |
| Dallas Cowboys | | | | |
| ☐ 495 Anthony Carter | .08 | .04 | .01 | |
| Minnesota Vikings | | | | |
| ☐ 496 Louis Oliver | .05 | .02 | .01 | |
| Miami Dolphins | | | | |
| ☐ 497 Chris Zorich | .08 | .04 | .01 | |
| Chicago Bears | | | | |
| ☐ 498 David Brandon | .05 | .02 | .01 | |
| Cleveland Browns | | | | |
| ☐ 499 Bubba McDowell | .05 | .02 | .01 | |
| Houston Oilers | | | | |
| ☐ 500 Adrian Cooper | .05 | .02 | .01 | |
| Pittsburgh Steelers | | | | |
| ☐ 501 Bill Johnson | .05 | .02 | .01 | |
| Cleveland Browns | | | | |
| ☐ 502 Shawn Jefferson | .05 | .02 | .01 | |
| San Diego Chargers | | | | |
| ☐ 503 Siran Stacy | .05 | .02 | .01 | |
| Philadelphia Eagles | | | | |
| ☐ 504 James Jones | .05 | .02 | .01 | |

| | | | |
|---|---|---|---|
| Cleveland Browns | | | |
| ☐ 505 Tom Rathman | .08 | .04 | .01 |
| San Francisco 49ers | | | |
| ☐ 506 Vince Buck | .05 | .02 | .01 |
| New Orleans Saints | | | |
| ☐ 507 Kent Graham | .60 | .25 | .08 |
| New York Giants | | | |
| ☐ 508 Darren Carrington | .12 | .05 | .02 |
| San Diego Chargers | | | |
| ☐ 509 Rickey Dixon | .05 | .02 | .01 |
| Cincinnati Bengals | | | |
| ☐ 510 Toi Cook | .05 | .02 | .01 |
| New Orleans Saints | | | |
| ☐ 511 Steve Smith | .08 | .04 | .01 |
| Los Angeles Raiders | | | |
| ☐ 512 Ostell Miles | .05 | .02 | .01 |
| Cincinnati Bengals | | | |
| ☐ 513 Phillippi Sparks | .05 | .02 | .01 |
| New York Giants | | | |
| ☐ 514 Lee Williams | .05 | .02 | .01 |
| Houston Oilers | | | |
| ☐ 515 Gary Reasons | .05 | .02 | .01 |
| Cincinnati Bengals | | | |
| ☐ 516 Shane Dronett | .05 | .02 | .01 |
| Denver Broncos | | | |
| ☐ 517 Jay Novacek | .10 | .05 | .01 |
| Dallas Cowboys | | | |
| ☐ 518 Kevin Greene | .05 | .02 | .01 |
| Los Angeles Rams | | | |
| ☐ 519 Derek Russell | .08 | .04 | .01 |
| Denver Broncos | | | |
| ☐ 520 Quentin Coryatt | .10 | .05 | .01 |
| Indianapolis Colts | | | |
| ☐ 521 Santana Dotson | .10 | .05 | .01 |
| Tampa Bay Buccaneers | | | |
| ☐ 522 Donald Frank | .05 | .02 | .01 |
| San Diego Chargers | | | |
| ☐ 523 Mike Prior | .05 | .02 | .01 |
| Indianapolis Colts | | | |
| ☐ 524 Dwight Hollier | .15 | .07 | .02 |
| Miami Dolphins | | | |
| ☐ 525 Eric Davis | .05 | .02 | .01 |
| San Francisco 49ers | | | |
| ☐ 526 Dalton Hilliard | .05 | .02 | .01 |
| New Orleans Saints | | | |
| ☐ 527 Rodney Culver | .08 | .04 | .01 |
| Indianapolis Colts | | | |
| ☐ 528 Jeff Hostetler | .10 | .05 | .01 |
| New York Giants | | | |
| ☐ 529 Ernie Mills | .05 | .02 | .01 |
| Pittsburgh Steelers | | | |
| ☐ 530 Craig Erickson | .10 | .05 | .01 |
| Tampa Bay Buccaneers | | | |

## 1993 Upper Deck America's Team

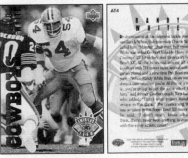

Randomly inserted in hobby foil packs, this 15-card standard-size (2 1/2" by 3 1/2") set showcases past and present Super Bowl champions from the Dallas Cowboys. Card numbers 1-6 feature Cowboys who participated in Super Bowl XII while card numbers 7-13 highlight Cowboys from Super Bowl XXVII. The fronts display full-bleed color action player photos; the team name and the player's name are silver foil-stamped and run up the edge of the card. A special "America's Team" emblem adorns the bottom corner. With a faded and enlarged version of this special emblem as a background, the backs presents a career summary, highlighting the player's performance in the Super Bowl. The cards are numbered on the back with an "AT" prefix.

| | MINT | EXC | G-VG |
|---|---|---|---|
| COMPLETE SET (15) | 140.00 | 65.00 | 17.50 |
| COMMON PLAYER (AT1-AT14) | 6.00 | 2.70 | .75 |
| | | | |
| ☐ AT1 Roger Staubach | 12.00 | 5.50 | 1.50 |
| ☐ AT2 Chuck Howley | 6.00 | 2.70 | .75 |

| | | MINT | EXC | G-VG |
|---|---|---|---|---|
| ☐ | AT3 Harvey Martin | 6.00 | 2.70 | .75 |
| ☐ | AT4 Randy White | 7.00 | 3.10 | .85 |
| ☐ | AT5 Bob Lilly | 7.00 | 3.10 | .85 |
| ☐ | AT6 Drew Pearson | 6.00 | 2.70 | .75 |
| ☐ | AT7 Emmitt Smith | 40.00 | 18.00 | 5.00 |
| ☐ | AT8 Troy Aikman | 30.00 | 13.50 | 3.80 |
| ☐ | AT9 Ken Norton Jr. | 6.00 | 2.70 | .75 |
| ☐ | AT10 Robert Jones | 6.00 | 2.70 | .75 |
| ☐ | AT11 Russell Maryland | 6.00 | 2.70 | .75 |
| ☐ | AT12 Jay Novacek | 6.00 | 2.70 | .75 |
| ☐ | AT13 Michael Irvin | 16.00 | 7.25 | 2.00 |
| ☐ | AT14 Checklist Card<br>Troy Aikman | 15.00 | 6.75 | 1.90 |
| ☐ | NNO Header Card<br>Emmitt Smith | 18.00 | 8.00 | 2.30 |

# 1993 Upper Deck Future Heroes

Randomly inserted in all types of single series packs, this ten-card set focuses on eight stars whose current performance may one day land them in the Pro Football Hall of Fame. The cards measure the standard size (2 1/2" by 3 1/2"). The color action player photos are full-bleed on three sides but edged on the left by a team color-coded stripe carrying the player's name. Short diagonal stripes and a "1993 Future Heroes" logo are done in gold foil and accent the card front. The backs have a team color-coded panel tilted to the left and carrying player profile and a small color player photo that bleeds off the left edge. Player identification as well as card number appear in a stripe at the top.

| | MINT | EXC | G-VG |
|---|---|---|---|
| COMPLETE SET (10) | 20.00 | 9.00 | 2.50 |
| COMMON PLAYER (37-45) | .60 | .25 | .08 |
| ☐ 37 Barry Foster<br>Pittsburgh Steelers | 1.50 | .65 | .19 |
| ☐ 38 Junior Seau<br>San Diego Chargers | .60 | .25 | .08 |
| ☐ 39 Emmitt Smith<br>Dallas Cowboys | 6.00 | 2.70 | .75 |
| ☐ 40 Troy Aikman<br>Dallas Cowboys | 4.00 | 1.80 | .50 |
| ☐ 41 David Klingler<br>Cincinnati Bengals | .75 | .35 | .09 |
| ☐ 42 Ricky Watters<br>San Francisco 49ers | 1.50 | .65 | .19 |
| ☐ 43 Barry Sanders<br>Detroit Lions | 3.00 | 1.35 | .40 |
| ☐ 44 Brett Favre<br>Green Bay Packers | 2.50 | 1.15 | .30 |
| ☐ 45 Emmitt Smith Checklist | 2.50 | 1.15 | .30 |
| ☐ NNO Header Card<br>Ricky Watters CL | 1.50 | .65 | .19 |

# 1993 Upper Deck
# Montana Box Bottom

This oversized "card" (approximately 5 1/4" by 7 1/4") was featured on the bottoms of 1993 Upper Deck waxboxes. It is identical in design to the 1993 Upper Deck football card number 460. The back is blank and the card is unnumbered.

| | MINT | EXC | G-VG |
|---|---|---|---|
| COMPLETE SET (1) | 1.00 | .40 | .10 |
| COMMON CARD | 1.00 | .40 | .10 |
| ☐ NNO Joe Montana<br>Box Bottom<br>(Same pose as card 460<br>in regular set) | 1.00 | .40 | .10 |

# 1993 Upper Deck Pro Bowl

Randomly inserted in retail foil packs, this 15-card set highlights the top NFC and AFC participants in last year's Pro Bowl. Measuring the standard size (2 1/2" by 3 1/2") and produced with Upper Deck's new "Electric" printing technology, the horizontal fronts display glossy color player photos that are full-bleed on the top and right and bordered on the left and bottom by holographic stripes. A second color player photo is inset on the right portion of the card, while the 1993 Pro Bowl logo appears at the lower left corner. On a panel that shades from blue to white, the horizontal backs present career summary. The cards are numbered on the back with a "PB" prefix.

| | MINT | EXC | G-VG |
|---|---|---|---|
| COMPLETE SET (20) | 130.00 | 57.50 | 16.50 |
| COMMON PLAYER (PB1-PB20) | 5.00 | 2.30 | .60 |
| ☐ PB1 Andre Reed<br>Buffalo Bills | 6.00 | 2.70 | .75 |
| ☐ PB2 Dan Marino<br>Miami Dolphins | 20.00 | 9.00 | 2.50 |
| ☐ PB3 Warren Moon<br>Houston Oilers | 7.00 | 3.10 | .85 |
| ☐ PB4 Anthony Miller<br>San Diego Chargers | 6.00 | 2.70 | .75 |
| ☐ PB5 Barry Foster<br>Pittsburgh Steelers | 7.00 | 3.10 | .85 |
| ☐ PB6 Steve Atwater<br>Denver Broncos | 5.00 | 2.30 | .60 |
| ☐ PB7 Cortez Kennedy<br>Seattle Seahawks | 6.00 | 2.70 | .75 |
| ☐ PB8 Junior Seau<br>San Diego Chargers | 6.00 | 2.70 | .75 |
| ☐ PB9 Jerry Rice<br>San Francisco 49ers | 15.00 | 6.75 | 1.90 |
| ☐ PB10 Michael Irvin<br>Dallas Cowboys | 14.00 | 6.25 | 1.75 |
| ☐ PB11 Sterling Sharpe<br>Green Bay Packers | 14.00 | 6.25 | 1.75 |
| ☐ PB12 Steve Young<br>San Francisco 49ers | 7.00 | 3.10 | .85 |
| ☐ PB13 Troy Aikman<br>Dallas Cowboys | 25.00 | 11.50 | 3.10 |
| ☐ PB14 Brett Favre<br>Green Bay Packers | 12.00 | 5.50 | 1.50 |
| ☐ PB15 Emmitt Smith<br>Dallas Cowboys | 30.00 | 13.50 | 3.80 |
| ☐ PB16 Rodney Hampton<br>New York Giants | 8.00 | 3.60 | 1.00 |
| ☐ PB17 Barry Sanders<br>Detroit Lions | 15.00 | 6.75 | 1.90 |
| ☐ PB18 Ricky Watters<br>San Francisco 49ers | 7.00 | 3.10 | .85 |

| | | MINT | EXC | G-VG |
|---|---|---|---|---|
| ☐ PB19 Pat Swilling | | 5.00 | 2.30 | .60 |
| New Orleans Saints | | | | |
| ☐ PB20 Checklist Card | | 10.00 | 4.50 | 1.25 |

# 1993 Upper Deck Rookie Exchange

Produced by Upper Deck's "Electric" printing technology, this seven-card standard-size (2 1/2" by 3 1/2") set was obtainable by redeeming the "Trade Upper Deck" card. One of these special cards was reportedly inserted in every 72 packs. The fronts feature borderless color player action shots that have the metallic quality of the "Electric" printing process. The player's name and position appear within a team color-coded bar near the bottom, and his team's name appears in silver lettering below. The back carries another color player photo on the left side, with his 1993 season highlights shown on the right, all overlaid upon a team color-coded background that lightens toward the bottom left. The player's name and position are again shown within a team color-coded bar, this time near the top. The cards are numbered on the back with an "RE" prefix.

| | MINT | EXC | G-VG |
|---|---|---|---|
| COMPLETE SET (6) | 20.00 | 9.00 | 2.50 |
| COMMON PLAYER (RE2-RE7) | 1.25 | .55 | .16 |
| | | | |
| ☐ RE1 Trade Upper Deck | 2.00 | .90 | .25 |
| Card Expired | | | |
| ☐ RE1X Trade Upper Deck | 2.00 | .90 | .25 |
| Card Punched | | | |
| ☐ RE2 Drew Bledsoe | 6.00 | 2.70 | .75 |
| New England Patriots | | | |
| ☐ RE3 Rick Mirer | 6.00 | 2.70 | .75 |
| Seattle Seahawks | | | |
| ☐ RE4 Garrison Hearst | 2.00 | .90 | .25 |
| Phoenix Cardinals | | | |
| ☐ RE5 Marvin Jones | 1.25 | .55 | .16 |
| New York Jets | | | |
| ☐ RE6 Curtis Conway | 1.50 | .65 | .19 |
| Chicago Bears | | | |
| ☐ RE7 Jerome Bettis | 6.00 | 2.70 | .75 |
| Los Angeles Rams | | | |

# 1993 Upper Deck Team MVPs

Randomly inserted in jumbo foil packs, this 29-card standard-size (2 1/2" by 3 1/2") set spotlights the Most Valuable Player on each of the NFL's 28 teams. The fronts carry full-bleed color action player photos. The player's name and team name appear respectively on two team color-coded stripes that intersect a Team MVP logo at the bottom center. Inside team color-coded stripes that edge the left and top, the gray-fading-to white backs have different color player photos

alongside career highlights. The cards are numbered on the back with a "TM" prefix.

| | MINT | EXC | G-VG |
|---|---|---|---|
| COMPLETE SET (29) | 25.00 | 11.50 | 3.10 |
| COMMON PLAYER (TM1-TM29) | .50 | .23 | .06 |
| | | | |
| ☐ TM1 Neal Anderson | .50 | .23 | .06 |
| Chicago Bears | | | |
| ☐ TM2 Harold Green | .60 | .25 | .08 |
| Cincinnati Bengals | | | |
| ☐ TM3 Thurman Thomas | 2.00 | .90 | .25 |
| Buffalo Bills | | | |
| ☐ TM4 John Elway | 2.00 | .90 | .25 |
| Denver Broncos | | | |
| ☐ TM5 Eric Metcalf | .60 | .25 | .08 |
| Cleveland Browns | | | |
| ☐ TM6 Reggie Cobb | .60 | .25 | .08 |
| Tampa Bay Buccaneers | | | |
| ☐ TM7 Johnny Bailey | .50 | .23 | .06 |
| Phoenix Cardinals | | | |
| ☐ TM8 Junior Seau | .60 | .25 | .08 |
| San Diego Chargers | | | |
| ☐ TM9 Derrick Thomas | .50 | .23 | .06 |
| Kansas City Chiefs | | | |
| ☐ TM10 Steve Emtman | .50 | .23 | .06 |
| Indianapolis Colts | | | |
| ☐ TM11 Troy Aikman | 6.00 | 2.70 | .75 |
| Dallas Cowboys | | | |
| ☐ TM12 Dan Marino | 5.00 | 2.30 | .60 |
| Miami Dolphins | | | |
| ☐ TM13 Clyde Simmons | .60 | .25 | .08 |
| Philadelphia Eagles | | | |
| ☐ TM14 Andre Rison | 1.00 | .45 | .13 |
| Atlanta Falcons | | | |
| ☐ TM15 Steve Young | 1.50 | .65 | .19 |
| San Francisco 49ers | | | |
| ☐ TM16 Rodney Hampton | 2.00 | .90 | .25 |
| New York Giants | | | |
| ☐ TM17 Rob Moore | .50 | .23 | .06 |
| New York Jets | | | |
| ☐ TM18 Barry Sanders | 4.00 | 1.80 | .50 |
| Detroit Lions | | | |
| ☐ TM19 Warren Moon | 1.00 | .45 | .13 |
| Houston Oilers | | | |
| ☐ TM20 Sterling Sharpe | 2.50 | 1.15 | .30 |
| Green Bay Packers | | | |
| ☐ TM21 Jon Vaughn | .50 | .23 | .06 |
| New England Patriots | | | |
| ☐ TM22 Tim Brown | .60 | .25 | .08 |
| Los Angeles Raiders | | | |
| ☐ TM23 Jim Everett | .60 | .25 | .08 |
| Los Angeles Rams | | | |
| ☐ TM24 Gary Clark | .60 | .25 | .08 |
| Washington Redskins | | | |
| ☐ TM25 Wayne Martin | .50 | .23 | .06 |
| New Orleans Saints | | | |
| ☐ TM26 Cortez Kennedy | .60 | .25 | .08 |
| Seattle Seahawks | | | |
| ☐ TM27 Barry Foster | 2.00 | .90 | .25 |
| Pittsburgh Steelers | | | |
| ☐ TM28 Terry Allen | .60 | .25 | .08 |
| Minnesota Vikings | | | |
| ☐ TM29 Checklist Card | .50 | .23 | .06 |

# 1993 Upper Deck SP Promo

Issued to promote the debut of Upper Deck's 270-card SP football set, this standard-size (2 1/2" by 3 1/2") promo card features on its front a color action shot of Montana in his Chiefs' home jersey. The photo is borderless, except at the bottom, where the card is edged by a team-red stripe, which fades to white from left to right and carries his name and position. His gold-foil team name appears in an arc near the top, underscored by a gold-foil line that extends down the right side and terminates short of the gold-foil SP logo at the bottom right. The back carries another action shot of Montana in its upper portion. Alternate team-colored checks form a stripe on the photo's right edge, and his name and position appear beneath the photo. His biography, stats, and career highlights follow below. The card is numbered on the back. This card is not marked as a promo, but its card number (19) contrasts with Montana's card number (122) in the regular series.

|  | MINT | EXC | G-VG |
|---|---|---|---|
| COMPLETE SET (1) | 4.00 | 1.60 | .40 |
| COMMON PLAYER | 4.00 | 1.60 | .40 |
| ☐ 19 Joe Montana | 4.00 | 1.60 | .40 |
| Kansas City Chiefs | | | |

# 1993 Upper Deck SP

The 270 standard-size (2 1/2" by 3 1/2") cards comprising Upper Deck's SP football set feature on their fronts color player action shots that are borderless, except at the bottom, where the card is edged by a team color-coded stripe, which fades to white from left to right and carries the player's name and position. His gold-foil team name appears in an arc near the top, underscored by a gold-foil line that extends down the right side and terminates short of the gold-foil SP logo at the bottom right. The back carries another color player action shot in its upper portion. Alternate team color-coded checks form a stripe on the photo's right edge, and the player's name and position appear beneath the photo. His biography, stats, and career highlights follow below. The gold-foil Upper Deck football hologram in the lower right rounds out the card. The cards are numbered on the back. After a Premier Prospects (1-18) subset, the cards are arranged alphabetically according to and within teams as follows: Atlanta Falcons (19-27), Buffalo Bills (28-36), Chicago Bears (37-45), Cincinnati Bengals (46-54), Cleveland Browns (55-63), Dallas Cowboys (64-72), Denver Broncos (73-81), Detroit Lions (82-90), Green Bay Packers (91-99), Houston Oilers (100-108), Indianapolis Colts (109-117), Kansas City Chiefs (118-126), Los Angeles Raiders (127-135), Los Angeles Rams (136-144), Miami Dolphins (145-153), Minnesota Vikings (154-162), New England Patriots (163-171), New Orleans Saints (172-180), New York Giants (181-189), New York Jets (190-198), Philadelphia Eagles (199-207), Phoenix Cardinals (208-216), Pittsburgh Steelers (217-225), San Diego Chargers (226-234), San Francisco 49ers (235-243), Seattle Seahawks (244-252), Tampa Bay Buccaneers (253-261), and Washington Redskins (262-270). The cards are numbered on the back. Rookie Cards include Jerome Bettis, Drew Bledsoe, Reggie Brooks and Rick Mirer.

|  | MINT | EXC | G-VG |
|---|---|---|---|
| COMPLETE SET (270) | 75.00 | 34.00 | 9.50 |
| COMMON PLAYER (1-270) | .20 | .09 | .03 |
| ☐ 1 Curtis Conway | 1.75 | .80 | .22 |
| Chicago Bears | | | |
| ☐ 2 John Copeland | 1.00 | .45 | .13 |
| Cincinnati Bengals | | | |
| ☐ 3 Kevin Williams | 1.75 | .80 | .22 |
| Dallas Cowboys | | | |
| ☐ 4 Dan Williams | .40 | .18 | .05 |
| Denver Broncos | | | |
| ☐ 5 Patrick Bates | .40 | .18 | .05 |
| Los Angeles Raiders | | | |
| ☐ 6 Jerome Bettis | 15.00 | 6.75 | 1.90 |
| Los Angeles Rams | | | |
| ☐ 7 O.J. McDuffie | 4.00 | 1.80 | .50 |
| Miami Dolphins | | | |
| ☐ 8 Robert Smith | 1.25 | .55 | .16 |
| Minnesota Vikings | | | |
| ☐ 9 Drew Bledsoe | 15.00 | 6.75 | 1.90 |
| New England Patriots | | | |
| ☐ 10 Irv Smith | .60 | .25 | .08 |

| | | | |
|---|---|---|---|
| New Orleans Saints | | | |
| ☐ 11 Marvin Jones | .50 | .23 | .06 |
| New York Jets | | | |
| ☐ 12 Victor Bailey | 1.00 | .45 | .13 |
| Philadelphia Eagles | | | |
| ☐ 13 Garrison Hearst | 2.25 | 1.00 | .30 |
| Phoenix Cardinals | | | |
| ☐ 14 Natrone Means | 4.00 | 1.80 | .50 |
| San Diego Chargers | | | |
| ☐ 15 Todd Kelly | .35 | .16 | .04 |
| San Francisco 49ers | | | |
| ☐ 16 Rick Mirer | 15.00 | 6.75 | 1.90 |
| Seattle Seahawks | | | |
| ☐ 17 Eric Curry | .75 | .35 | .09 |
| Tampa Bay Buccaneers | | | |
| ☐ 18 Reggie Brooks | 8.00 | 3.60 | 1.00 |
| Washington Redskins | | | |
| ☐ 19 Eric Dickerson | .35 | .16 | .04 |
| ☐ 20 Roger Harper | .35 | .16 | .04 |
| ☐ 21 Michael Haynes | .20 | .09 | .03 |
| ☐ 22 Bobby Hebert | .35 | .16 | .04 |
| ☐ 23 Lincoln Kennedy | .50 | .23 | .06 |
| ☐ 24 Chris Miller | .35 | .16 | .04 |
| ☐ 25 Mike Pritchard | .35 | .16 | .04 |
| ☐ 26 Andre Rison | .60 | .25 | .08 |
| ☐ 27 Deion Sanders | .50 | .23 | .06 |
| ☐ 28 Cornelius Bennett | .25 | .11 | .03 |
| ☐ 29 Kenneth Davis | .20 | .09 | .03 |
| ☐ 30 Henry Jones | .20 | .09 | .03 |
| ☐ 31 Jim Kelly | 1.00 | .45 | .13 |
| ☐ 32 John Parrella | .30 | .14 | .04 |
| ☐ 33 Andre Reed | .35 | .16 | .04 |
| ☐ 34 Bruce Smith | .35 | .16 | .04 |
| ☐ 35 Thomas Smith | .35 | .16 | .04 |
| ☐ 36 Thurman Thomas | 1.50 | .65 | .19 |
| ☐ 37 Neal Anderson | .25 | .11 | .03 |
| ☐ 38 Myron Baker | .40 | .18 | .05 |
| ☐ 39 Mark Carrier | .25 | .11 | .03 |
| ☐ 40 Richard Dent | .25 | .11 | .03 |
| ☐ 41 Chris Gedney | .30 | .14 | .04 |
| ☐ 42 Jim Harbaugh | .25 | .11 | .03 |
| ☐ 43 Craig Heyward | .20 | .09 | .03 |
| ☐ 44 Carl Simpson | .30 | .14 | .04 |
| ☐ 45 Alonzo Spellman | .25 | .11 | .03 |
| ☐ 46 Derrick Fenner | .20 | .09 | .03 |
| ☐ 47 Harold Green | .25 | .11 | .03 |
| ☐ 48 David Klingler | .60 | .25 | .08 |
| ☐ 49 Ricardo McDonald | .20 | .09 | .03 |
| ☐ 50 Tony McGee | .50 | .23 | .06 |
| ☐ 51 Carl Pickens | .25 | .11 | .03 |
| ☐ 52 Steve Tovar | .30 | .14 | .04 |
| ☐ 53 Alfred Williams | .20 | .09 | .03 |
| ☐ 54 Darryl Williams | .25 | .11 | .03 |
| ☐ 55 Jerry Ball | .20 | .09 | .03 |
| ☐ 56 Michael Caldwell | .30 | .14 | .04 |
| ☐ 57 Mark Carrier | .25 | .11 | .03 |
| ☐ 58 Steve Everitt | .30 | .14 | .04 |
| ☐ 59 Dan Footman | .40 | .18 | .05 |
| ☐ 60 Pepper Johnson | .20 | .09 | .03 |
| ☐ 61 Bernie Kosar | .35 | .16 | .04 |
| ☐ 62 Eric Metcalf | .35 | .16 | .04 |
| ☐ 63 Michael Dean Perry | .35 | .16 | .04 |
| ☐ 64 Troy Aikman | 8.00 | 3.60 | 1.00 |
| ☐ 65 Charles Haley | .25 | .11 | .03 |
| ☐ 66 Michael Irvin | 2.25 | 1.00 | .30 |
| ☐ 67 Robert Jones | .20 | .09 | .03 |
| ☐ 68 Derrick Lassic | .50 | .23 | .06 |
| ☐ 69 Russell Maryland | .35 | .16 | .04 |
| ☐ 70 Ken Norton Jr. | .25 | .11 | .03 |
| ☐ 71 Darrin Smith | 1.00 | .45 | .13 |
| ☐ 72 Emmitt Smith | 10.00 | 4.50 | 1.25 |
| ☐ 73 Steve Atwater | .25 | .11 | .03 |
| ☐ 74 Rod Bernstine | .25 | .11 | .03 |
| ☐ 75 Jason Elam | .35 | .16 | .04 |
| ☐ 76 John Elway | 2.00 | .90 | .25 |
| ☐ 77 Simon Fletcher | .25 | .11 | .03 |
| ☐ 78 Tommy Maddox | .50 | .23 | .06 |
| ☐ 79 Glyn Milburn | 2.50 | 1.15 | .30 |
| ☐ 80 Derek Russell | .25 | .11 | .03 |
| ☐ 81 Shannon Sharpe | .75 | .35 | .09 |
| ☐ 82 Bennie Blades | .20 | .09 | .03 |
| ☐ 83 Willie Green | .25 | .11 | .03 |
| ☐ 84 Antonio London | .25 | .11 | .03 |
| ☐ 85 Ryan McNeil | .35 | .16 | .04 |
| ☐ 86 Herman Moore | 1.00 | .45 | .13 |
| ☐ 87 Rodney Peete | .25 | .11 | .03 |
| ☐ 88 Barry Sanders | 3.50 | 1.55 | .45 |
| ☐ 89 Chris Spielman | .20 | .09 | .03 |
| ☐ 90 Pat Swilling | .25 | .11 | .03 |
| ☐ 91 Mark Brunell | .75 | .35 | .09 |
| ☐ 92 Terrell Buckley | .35 | .16 | .04 |
| ☐ 93 Brett Favre | 3.50 | 1.55 | .45 |
| ☐ 94 Jackie Harris | .75 | .35 | .09 |
| ☐ 95 Sterling Sharpe | 2.25 | 1.00 | .30 |
| ☐ 96 John Stephens | .20 | .09 | .03 |
| ☐ 97 Wayne Simmons | .35 | .16 | .04 |
| ☐ 98 George Teague | .60 | .25 | .08 |
| ☐ 99 Reggie White | .50 | .23 | .06 |

| | | | |
|---|---|---|---|
| ☐ 100 Micheal Barrow | .20 | .09 | .03 |
| ☐ 101 Cody Carlson | .60 | .25 | .08 |
| ☐ 102 Ray Childress | .20 | .09 | .03 |
| ☐ 103 Brad Hopkins | .30 | .14 | .04 |
| ☐ 104 Haywood Jeffires | .35 | .16 | .04 |
| ☐ 105 Wilber Marshall | .25 | .11 | .03 |
| ☐ 106 Warren Moon | .50 | .23 | .06 |
| ☐ 107 Webster Slaughter | .25 | .11 | .03 |
| ☐ 108 Lorenzo White | .25 | .11 | .03 |
| ☐ 109 John Baylor | .20 | .09 | .03 |
| ☐ 110 Duane Bickett | .20 | .09 | .03 |
| ☐ 111 Quentin Coryatt | .35 | .16 | .04 |
| ☐ 112 Steve Emtman | .25 | .11 | .03 |
| ☐ 113 Jeff George | .50 | .23 | .06 |
| ☐ 114 Jessie Hester | .20 | .09 | .03 |
| ☐ 115 Anthony Johnson | .20 | .09 | .03 |
| ☐ 116 Reggie Langhome | .20 | .09 | .03 |
| ☐ 117 Roosevelt Potts | .75 | .35 | .09 |
| ☐ 118 Marcus Allen | .40 | .18 | .05 |
| ☐ 119 J.J. Birden | .25 | .11 | .03 |
| ☐ 120 Willie Davis | .30 | .14 | .04 |
| ☐ 121 Jaime Fields | .25 | .11 | .03 |
| ☐ 122 Joe Montana | 8.00 | 3.60 | 1.00 |
| ☐ 123 Will Shields | .25 | .11 | .03 |
| ☐ 124 Neil Smith | .35 | .16 | .04 |
| ☐ 125 Derrick Thomas | .40 | .18 | .05 |
| ☐ 126 Harvey Williams | .35 | .16 | .04 |
| ☐ 127 Tim Brown | .60 | .25 | .08 |
| ☐ 128 Billy Joe Hobert | .75 | .35 | .09 |
| ☐ 129 Jeff Hostetler | .35 | .16 | .04 |
| ☐ 130 Ethan Horton | .20 | .09 | .03 |
| ☐ 131 Raghib Ismail | 1.00 | .45 | .13 |
| ☐ 132 Howie Long | .25 | .11 | .03 |
| ☐ 133 Terry McDaniel | .20 | .09 | .03 |
| ☐ 134 Greg Robinson | 2.00 | .90 | .25 |
| ☐ 135 Anthony Smith | .20 | .09 | .03 |
| ☐ 136 Flipper Anderson | .25 | .11 | .03 |
| ☐ 137 Marc Boutte | .20 | .09 | .03 |
| ☐ 138 Shane Conlan | .20 | .09 | .03 |
| ☐ 139 Troy Drayton | .75 | .35 | .09 |
| ☐ 140 Henry Ellard | .25 | .11 | .03 |
| ☐ 141 Jim Everett | .20 | .09 | .03 |
| ☐ 142 Cleveland Gary | .25 | .11 | .03 |
| ☐ 143 Sean Gilbert | .25 | .11 | .03 |
| ☐ 144 Robert Young | .25 | .11 | .03 |
| ☐ 145 Marco Coleman | .25 | .11 | .03 |
| ☐ 146 Bryan Cox | .25 | .11 | .03 |
| ☐ 147 Irving Fryar | .20 | .09 | .03 |
| ☐ 148 Keith Jackson | .35 | .16 | .04 |
| ☐ 149 Terry Kirby | 4.00 | 1.80 | .50 |
| ☐ 150 Dan Marino | 4.00 | 1.80 | .50 |
| ☐ 151 Scott Mitchell | 2.50 | 1.15 | .30 |
| ☐ 152 Louis Oliver | .20 | .09 | .03 |
| ☐ 153 Troy Vincent | .25 | .11 | .03 |
| ☐ 154 Anthony Carter | .25 | .11 | .03 |
| ☐ 155 Cris Carter | .35 | .16 | .04 |
| ☐ 156 Roger Craig | .25 | .11 | .03 |
| ☐ 157 Chris Doleman | .25 | .11 | .03 |
| ☐ 158 Qadry Ismail | 1.50 | .65 | .19 |
| ☐ 159 Steve Jordan | .25 | .11 | .03 |
| ☐ 160 Randall McDaniel | .20 | .09 | .03 |
| ☐ 161 Audray McMillian | .20 | .09 | .03 |
| ☐ 162 Barry Word | .35 | .16 | .04 |
| ☐ 163 Vincent Brown | .20 | .09 | .03 |
| ☐ 164 Marv Cook | .20 | .09 | .03 |
| ☐ 165 Sam Gash | .25 | .11 | .03 |
| ☐ 166 Pat Harlow | .20 | .09 | .03 |
| ☐ 167 Greg McMurtry | .20 | .09 | .03 |
| ☐ 168 Todd Rucci | .25 | .11 | .03 |
| ☐ 169 Leonard Russell | .20 | .09 | .03 |
| ☐ 170 Scott Sisson | .25 | .11 | .03 |
| ☐ 171 Chris Slade | .90 | .40 | .11 |
| ☐ 172 Morten Andersen | .25 | .11 | .03 |
| ☐ 173 Derek Brown | 2.25 | 1.00 | .30 |
| ☐ 174 Reggie Freeman | .25 | .11 | .03 |
| ☐ 175 Rickey Jackson | .25 | .11 | .03 |
| ☐ 176 Eric Martin | .25 | .11 | .03 |
| ☐ 177 Wayne Martin | .20 | .09 | .03 |
| ☐ 178 Brad Muster | .25 | .11 | .03 |
| ☐ 179 Willie Roaf | .35 | .16 | .04 |
| ☐ 180 Renaldo Turnbull | .25 | .11 | .03 |
| ☐ 181 Derek Brown | .25 | .11 | .03 |
| ☐ 182 Marcus Buckley | .25 | .11 | .03 |
| ☐ 183 Jarrod Bunch | .20 | .09 | .03 |
| ☐ 184 Rodney Hampton | 1.00 | .45 | .13 |
| ☐ 185 Ed McCaffrey | .20 | .09 | .03 |
| ☐ 186 Kanavis McGhee | .20 | .09 | .03 |
| ☐ 187 Mike Sherrard | .20 | .09 | .03 |
| ☐ 188 Phil Simms | .35 | .16 | .04 |
| ☐ 189 Lawrence Taylor | .40 | .18 | .05 |
| ☐ 190 Kurt Barber | .20 | .09 | .03 |
| ☐ 191 Boomer Esiason | .35 | .16 | .04 |
| ☐ 192 Johnny Johnson | .35 | .16 | .04 |
| ☐ 193 Ronnie Lott | .35 | .16 | .04 |
| ☐ 194 Johnny Mitchell | .75 | .35 | .09 |
| ☐ 195 Rob Moore | .35 | .16 | .04 |
| ☐ 196 Adrian Murrell | .30 | .14 | .04 |

| | | | |
|---|---|---|---|
| ☐ 197 Browning Nagle | .25 | .11 | .03 |
| ☐ 198 Marvin Washington | .20 | .09 | .03 |
| ☐ 199 Eric Allen | .25 | .11 | .03 |
| ☐ 200 Fred Barnett | .35 | .16 | .04 |
| ☐ 201 Randall Cunningham | .35 | .16 | .04 |
| ☐ 202 Byron Evans | .20 | .09 | .03 |
| ☐ 203 Tim Harris | .20 | .09 | .03 |
| ☐ 204 Seth Joyner | .25 | .11 | .03 |
| ☐ 205 Leonard Renfro | .25 | .11 | .03 |
| ☐ 206 Heath Sherman | .20 | .09 | .03 |
| ☐ 207 Clyde Simmons | .25 | .11 | .03 |
| ☐ 208 Johnny Bailey | .20 | .09 | .03 |
| ☐ 209 Steve Beuerlein | .40 | .18 | .05 |
| ☐ 210 Chuck Cecil | .20 | .09 | .03 |
| ☐ 211 Larry Centers | .60 | .25 | .08 |
| ☐ 212 Gary Clark | .25 | .11 | .03 |
| ☐ 213 Ernest Dye | .25 | .11 | .03 |
| ☐ 214 Ken Harvey | .20 | .09 | .03 |
| ☐ 215 Randal Hill | .35 | .16 | .04 |
| ☐ 216 Ricky Proehl | .25 | .11 | .03 |
| ☐ 217 Deon Figures | .50 | .23 | .06 |
| ☐ 218 Barry Foster | 1.00 | .45 | .13 |
| ☐ 219 Eric Green | .35 | .16 | .04 |
| ☐ 220 Kevin Greene | .20 | .09 | .03 |
| ☐ 221 Carlton Haselring | .20 | .09 | .03 |
| ☐ 222 Andre Hastings | .60 | .25 | .08 |
| ☐ 223 Greg Lloyd | .20 | .09 | .03 |
| ☐ 224 Neil O'Donnell | .75 | .35 | .09 |
| ☐ 225 Rod Woodson | .35 | .16 | .04 |
| ☐ 226 Marion Butts | .35 | .16 | .04 |
| ☐ 227 Darren Carrington | .35 | .16 | .04 |
| ☐ 228 Darrien Gordon | .50 | .23 | .06 |
| ☐ 229 Ronnie Harmon | .20 | .09 | .03 |
| ☐ 230 Stan Humphries | .35 | .16 | .04 |
| ☐ 231 Anthony Miller | .50 | .23 | .06 |
| ☐ 232 Chris Mims | .25 | .11 | .03 |
| ☐ 233 Leslie O'Neal | .25 | .11 | .03 |
| ☐ 234 Junior Seau | .35 | .16 | .04 |
| ☐ 235 Dana Hall | .20 | .09 | .03 |
| ☐ 236 Adrian Hardy | .20 | .09 | .03 |
| ☐ 237 Brent Jones | .35 | .16 | .04 |
| ☐ 238 Tim McDonald | .20 | .09 | .03 |
| ☐ 239 Tom Rathman | .25 | .11 | .03 |
| ☐ 240 Jerry Rice | 3.00 | 1.35 | .40 |
| ☐ 241 Dana Stubblefield | 1.50 | .65 | .19 |
| ☐ 242 Ricky Watters | 1.25 | .55 | .16 |
| ☐ 243 Steve Young | 1.00 | .45 | .13 |
| ☐ 244 Brian Blades | .25 | .11 | .03 |
| ☐ 245 Ferrell Edmunds | .20 | .09 | .03 |
| ☐ 246 Carlton Gray | .50 | .23 | .06 |
| ☐ 247 Cortez Kennedy | .35 | .16 | .04 |
| ☐ 248 Kelvin Martin | .20 | .09 | .03 |
| ☐ 249 Dan McGwire | .25 | .11 | .03 |
| ☐ 250 Jon Vaughn | .20 | .09 | .03 |
| ☐ 251 Chris Warren | .50 | .23 | .06 |
| ☐ 252 John L. Williams | .25 | .11 | .03 |
| ☐ 253 Reggie Cobb | .35 | .16 | .04 |
| ☐ 254 Horace Copeland | 1.25 | .55 | .16 |
| ☐ 255 Lawrence Dawsey | .35 | .16 | .04 |
| ☐ 256 Demetrius DuBose | .40 | .18 | .05 |
| ☐ 257 Craig Erickson | .35 | .16 | .04 |
| ☐ 258 Courtney Hawkins | .25 | .11 | .03 |
| ☐ 259 John Lynch | .25 | .11 | .03 |
| ☐ 260 Hardy Nickerson | .20 | .09 | .03 |
| ☐ 261 Lamar Thomas | 1.00 | .45 | .13 |
| ☐ 262 Carl Banks | .20 | .09 | .03 |
| ☐ 263 Tom Carter | .60 | .25 | .08 |
| ☐ 264 Brad Edwards | .20 | .09 | .03 |
| ☐ 265 Kurt Gouveia | .20 | .09 | .03 |
| ☐ 266 Desmond Howard | .75 | .35 | .09 |
| ☐ 267 Charles Mann | .20 | .09 | .03 |
| ☐ 268 Art Monk | .35 | .16 | .04 |
| ☐ 269 Mark Rypien | .25 | .11 | .03 |
| ☐ 270 Ricky Sanders | .25 | .11 | .03 |

## 1993 Upper Deck SP All-Pros

Randomly inserted in 1993 Upper Deck SP football packs, these 15 standard-size (2 1/2" by 3 1/2") cards are distinguished by the gold-foil-accented arcs cut into their top edges, and feature on their fronts color player action cut-outs superposed upon black backgrounds that carry multicolored lettering. The player's name appears within the gold-foil arc at the top, and the gold-foil embossed All-Pro logo rests in the lower right. The back carries another color player action shot over the black and multicolor-lettered background in its upper portion. The player's name and team appear vertically near the left edge. Season highlights printed in the white area below the photo round out the card. The cards are numbered on the back with an "AP" prefix.

| | MINT | EXC | G-VG |
|---|---|---|---|
| COMPLETE SET (15) | 200.00 | 90.00 | 25.00 |
| COMMON PLAYER (1-15) | 6.00 | 2.70 | .75 |
| ☐ 1 Steve Young | 12.00 | 5.50 | 1.50 |
| San Francisco 49ers | | | |
| ☐ 2 Warren Moon | 8.00 | 3.60 | 1.00 |
| Houston Oilers | | | |
| ☐ 3 Troy Aikman | 50.00 | 23.00 | 6.25 |
| Dallas Cowboys | | | |
| ☐ 4 Dan Marino | 40.00 | 18.00 | 5.00 |
| Miami Dolphins | | | |
| ☐ 5 Barry Sanders | 24.00 | 11.00 | 3.00 |
| Detroit Lions | | | |
| ☐ 6 Barry Foster | 10.00 | 4.50 | 1.25 |
| Pittsburgh Steelers | | | |
| ☐ 7 Emmitt Smith | 75.00 | 34.00 | 9.50 |
| Dallas Cowboys | | | |
| ☐ 8 Thurman Thomas | 10.00 | 4.50 | 1.25 |
| Buffalo Bills | | | |
| ☐ 9 Jerry Rice | 25.00 | 11.50 | 3.10 |
| San Francisco 49ers | | | |
| ☐ 10 Sterling Sharpe | 18.00 | 8.00 | 2.30 |
| Green Bay Packers | | | |
| ☐ 11 Anthony Miller | 8.00 | 3.60 | 1.00 |
| San Diego Chargers | | | |
| ☐ 12 Haywood Jeffires | 6.00 | 2.70 | .75 |
| Houston Oilers | | | |
| ☐ 13 Junior Seau | 6.00 | 2.70 | .75 |
| San Diego Chargers | | | |
| ☐ 14 Reggie White | 8.00 | 3.60 | 1.00 |
| Green Bay Packers | | | |
| ☐ 15 Derrick Thomas | 6.00 | 2.70 | .75 |
| Kansas City Chiefs | | | |

## 1993 Upper Deck Team Chiefs

The 1993 Upper Deck Chiefs Team Set consists of 25 cards which measure standard size (2 1/2" by 3 1/2"). The fronts display a color action player photo with white borders and two team color-coded stripes at the bottom. The player's name and position are printed in the top stripe. On the left side of the card, the team name is printed in a team color against a ghosted background. The backs carry a second photo alongside biographical and statistical information. The cards are numbered on the back with a "KC" prefix.

| | MINT | EXC | G-VG |
|---|---|---|---|
| COMPLETE SET (25) | 6.00 | 2.40 | .60 |
| COMMON PLAYER (KC1-KC25) | .15 | .06 | .01 |
| ☐ KC1 Nick Lowery | .15 | .06 | .01 |
| ☐ KC2 Lonnie Marts | .15 | .06 | .01 |
| ☐ KC3 Marcus Allen | .75 | .30 | .07 |
| ☐ KC4 Bennie Thompson | .15 | .06 | .01 |
| ☐ KC5 Bryan Barker | .15 | .06 | .01 |
| ☐ KC6 Christian Okoye | .25 | .10 | .02 |
| ☐ KC7 Dale Carter | .25 | .10 | .02 |
| ☐ KC8 Dan Saleaumua | .15 | .06 | .01 |
| ☐ KC9 Dave Krieg | .25 | .10 | .02 |
| ☐ KC10 Derrick Thomas | .75 | .30 | .07 |

| | MINT | EXC | G-VG |
|---|---|---|---|
| ☐ KC11 Doug Terry | .15 | .06 | .01 |
| ☐ KC12 Fred Jones | .15 | .06 | .01 |
| ☐ KC13 Harvey Williams | .50 | .20 | .05 |
| ☐ KC14 J.J. Birden | .25 | .10 | .02 |
| ☐ KC15 Joe Montana | 2.50 | 1.00 | .25 |
| ☐ KC16 John Alt | .25 | .10 | .02 |
| ☐ KC17 Leonard Griffin | .15 | .06 | .01 |
| ☐ KC18 Matt Blundin | .50 | .20 | .05 |
| ☐ KC19 Neil Smith | .35 | .14 | .03 |
| ☐ KC20 Tim Barnett | .25 | .10 | .02 |
| ☐ KC21 Tim Grunhard | .15 | .06 | .01 |
| ☐ KC22 Todd McNair | .25 | .10 | .02 |
| ☐ KC23 Tracy Simien | .15 | .06 | .01 |
| ☐ KC24 Willie Davis | .35 | .14 | .03 |
| ☐ KC25 Joe Montana | 1.25 | .50 | .12 |
| (Checklist back) | | | |

## 1993 Upper Deck Team Cowboys

The 1993 Upper Deck Cowboys Team Set consists of 25 cards which measure standard size (2 1/2" by 3 1/2"). The fronts display a color action player photo with white borders and two team color-coded stripes at the bottom. The player's name and position are printed in the top stripe. On the left side of the card, the team name is printed in a team color against a ghosted background. The backs carry a second photo alongside biographical and statistical information. The cards are numbered on the back with a "D" prefix.

| | MINT | EXC | G-VG |
|---|---|---|---|
| COMPLETE SET (25) | 6.00 | 2.40 | .60 |
| COMMON PLAYER (D1-D25) | .15 | .06 | .01 |
| ☐ D1 Alvin Harper | .50 | .20 | .05 |
| ☐ D2 Charles Haley | .25 | .10 | .02 |
| ☐ D3 Jimmy Smith | .25 | .10 | .02 |
| ☐ D4 Darrin Smith | .25 | .10 | .02 |
| ☐ D5 Jim Jeffcoat | .25 | .10 | .02 |
| ☐ D6 Daryl Johnston | .75 | .30 | .07 |
| ☐ D7 Dixon Edwards | .25 | .10 | .02 |
| ☐ D8 Emmitt Smith | 2.00 | .80 | .20 |
| ☐ D9 James Washington | .25 | .10 | .02 |
| ☐ D10 Jay Novacek | .35 | .14 | .03 |
| ☐ D11 Ken Norton Jr. | .35 | .14 | .03 |
| ☐ D12 Kenneth Gant | .25 | .10 | .02 |
| ☐ D13 Larry Brown | .25 | .10 | .02 |
| ☐ D14 Leon Lett | .25 | .10 | .02 |
| ☐ D15 Lin Elliott | .25 | .10 | .02 |
| ☐ D16 Mark Tuinei | .25 | .10 | .02 |
| ☐ D17 Michael Irvin | 1.00 | .40 | .10 |
| ☐ D18 Nate Newton | .25 | .10 | .02 |
| ☐ D19 Robert Jones | .25 | .10 | .02 |
| ☐ D20 Thomas Everett UER | .25 | .10 | .02 |
| (Brock Marion pictured | | | |
| on card) | | | |
| ☐ D21 Tony Casillas | .25 | .10 | .02 |
| ☐ D22 Tony Tolbert | .25 | .10 | .02 |
| ☐ D23 Troy Aikman | 2.00 | .80 | .20 |
| ☐ D24 Russell Maryland | .50 | .20 | .05 |
| ☐ D25 Troy Aikman | 1.00 | .40 | .10 |
| (Checklist back) | | | |

## 1993 Upper Deck Team 49ers

The 1993 Upper Deck 49ers Team Set consists of 25 cards which measure standard size (2 1/2" by 3 1/2"). The fronts display a color action player photo with white borders and two team color-coded stripes at the bottom. The player's name and position are printed in the top stripe. On the left side of the card, the team name is printed in a team color against a ghosted background. The backs carry a second photo alongside biographical and statistical information. The cards are numbered on the back with an "SF" prefix.

| | MINT | EXC | G-VG |
|---|---|---|---|
| COMPLETE SET (25)......................... | 6.00 | 2.40 | .60 |
| COMMON PLAYER (SF1-SF25)......... | .15 | .06 | .01 |
| | | | |
| ☐ SF1 Amp Lee.............................. | .35 | .14 | .03 |
| ☐ SF2 Bill Romanowski ................... | .25 | .10 | .02 |
| ☐ SF3 Brent Jones.......................... | .50 | .20 | .05 |
| ☐ SF4 Dana Hall............................ | .25 | .10 | .02 |
| ☐ SF5 Dana Stubblefield ................ | .75 | .30 | .07 |
| ☐ SF6 Dennis Brown ...................... | .15 | .06 | .01 |
| ☐ SF7 Dexter Carter....................... | .25 | .10 | .02 |
| ☐ SF8 Don Griffin .......................... | .15 | .06 | .01 |
| ☐ SF9 Eric Davis ........................... | .25 | .10 | .02 |
| ☐ SF10 Guy McIntyre ..................... | .15 | .06 | .01 |
| ☐ SF11 Jamie Williams ................... | .15 | .06 | .01 |
| ☐ SF12 Jerry Rice .......................... | 1.50 | .60 | .15 |
| ☐ SF13 John Taylor......................... | .35 | .14 | .03 |
| ☐ SF14 Keith DeLong ..................... | .25 | .10 | .02 |
| ☐ SF15 Marc Logan ....................... | .15 | .06 | .01 |
| ☐ SF16 Mike Walter........................ | .15 | .06 | .01 |
| ☐ SF17 Mike Cofer......................... | .15 | .06 | .01 |
| ☐ SF18 Odessa Turner.................... | .15 | .06 | .01 |
| ☐ SF19 Ricky Watters ..................... | .75 | .30 | .07 |
| ☐ SF20 Steve Bono......................... | .50 | .20 | .05 |
| ☐ SF21 Steve Young........................ | 1.25 | .50 | .12 |
| ☐ SF22 Ted Washington .................. | .15 | .06 | .01 |
| ☐ SF23 Tom Rathman...................... | .35 | .14 | .03 |
| ☐ SF24 Jesse Sapolu ..................... | .15 | .06 | .01 |
| ☐ SF25 Steve Young........................ | .60 | .24 | .06 |
| (Checklist back) | | | |

## 1993-94 Upper Deck Miller Lite SB

Sponsored by Miller Lite Beer and Tombstone Pizza, the 1993 Upper Deck Super Bowl Showdown Series consists of five cards measuring approximately 5" by 3 1/2". One card was included in specially-marked half-cases of Miller Lite beer. Furthermore, the set could be obtained by mailing in the official certificate (included in each specially-marked case), along with three UPC symbols from three 24-packs (or case equivalents) of 12-ounce Miller Lite cans and the dated cash register receipt. All certificates must be received by March 18, 1994. All entries were entered in a random drawing for 1,000 sweepstakes prizes of a Joe Montana personally autographed collector sheet. The horizontal card fronts feature the starting quarterbacks from competing Super Bowl teams. On each side of the front is a color action player cut-out photo superimposed over a ghosted game photo. The quarterbacks' last names appear in the center of the card in white print above the Super Bowl depicted on the card, the final score, and the date all printed in gold foil lettering. A blue stripe intersects the lower portion of the left photo containing the words "Super Bowl," and "Showdowns" appears on a red stripe intersecting the right photo. A ghosted Super Bowl logo for the play-off depicted on the front, serves

as a background for highlights of the quarterbacks' accomplishments during the game. The backs are bordered in team color-coded borders that fade to a metallic silver. Sponsor logos are printed on the lower edge. The cards are numbered on the front.

| | MINT | EXC | G-VG |
|---|---|---|---|
| COMPLETE SET (5)........................... | 25.00 | 10.00 | 2.50 |
| COMMON PLAYER (1-5).................. | 3.00 | 1.20 | .30 |
| | | | |
| ☐ 1 Troy Aikman.............................. | 6.00 | 2.40 | .60 |
| Dallas Cowboys | | | |
| Jim Kelly | | | |
| Buffalo Bills | | | |
| Super Bowl XXVII | | | |
| ☐ 2 Jim Kelly ................................. | 3.00 | 1.20 | .30 |
| Buffalo Bills | | | |
| Mark Rypien | | | |
| Washington Redskins | | | |
| Super Bowl XXVI | | | |
| ☐ 3 John Elway............................... | 7.50 | 3.00 | .75 |
| Denver Broncos | | | |
| Joe Montana | | | |
| San Francisco 49ers | | | |
| Super Bowl XXIV | | | |
| ☐ 4 John Elway............................... | 4.00 | 1.60 | .40 |
| Denver Broncos | | | |
| Phil Simms | | | |
| New York Giants | | | |
| Super Bowl XXI | | | |
| ☐ 5 Joe Montana ............................ | 9.00 | 3.75 | .90 |
| San Francisco 49ers | | | |
| Dan Marino | | | |
| Miami Dolphins | | | |
| Super Bowl XIX | | | |

## 1994 Upper Deck Collector's Choice Prototype

This standard-size (2 1/2" by 3 1/2") prototype features a white-bordered color action shot of Joe Montana in his Chiefs uniform. The set's title appears at the upper left, Montana's name and team appear at the lower left, and his position appears at the lower right. The white-bordered back carries Montana's NFL career statistics on a ghosted action photo background. The card is numbered on the back.

| | MINT | EXC | G-VG |
|---|---|---|---|
| COMPLETE SET ............................... | 3.00 | 1.20 | .30 |
| COMMON PLAYER.......................... | 3.00 | 1.20 | .30 |
| | | | |
| ☐ 19 Joe Montana .......................... | 3.00 | 1.20 | .30 |
| Kansas City Chiefs | | | |

## 1994 Upper Deck National Samples

Measuring the standard-size (2 1/2" by 3 1/2"), this six-card sample set spotlights players who participated in the Pro Bowl. The cards were originally passed out at the National Convention in Houston. On the left edge, the horizontal fronts have a purple stripe carrying the player's name, team name, and a holographic headshot framed by a black border. The rest of the front displays a full-bleed color action player photo with a metallic sheen. On a white screened background of a gray Upper Deck logos, the backs have the disclaimer "SAMPLE CARD" printed diagonally. The cards are unnumbered and checklisted below in alphabetical order.

| | MINT | EXC | G-VG |
|---|---|---|---|
| COMPLETE SET (6).......................... | 25.00 | 10.00 | 2.50 |
| COMMON PLAYER (1-6).................. | 2.00 | .80 | .20 |
| | | | |
| ☐ 1 Jerome Bettis............................ | 10.00 | 4.00 | 1.00 |

| | MINT | EXC | G-VG |
|---|---|---|---|
| Los Angeles Rams | | | |
| ☐ 2 Brett Favre | 5.00 | 2.00 | .50 |
| Green Bay Packers | | | |
| ☐ 3 John Elway | 5.00 | 2.00 | .50 |
| Denver Broncos | | | |
| ☐ 4 Thurman Thomas | 4.00 | 1.60 | .40 |
| Buffalo Bills | | | |
| ☐ 5 Jerry Rice | 6.00 | 2.40 | .60 |
| San Francisco 49ers | | | |
| ☐ 6 Steve Young | 4.00 | 1.60 | .40 |
| San Francisco 49ers | | | |

# 1994 Upper Deck Collector's Choice

This standard-size (2 1/2" by 3 1/2") 384-card set features color action player photos. The set's title appears at the upper left while the player's name and team appear at the lower left. The player's position is at lower right. The white-bordered backs carry color action player photos with the player's name, position, biography, and NFL career statistics under the photo. The cards are numbered on the back. A 384-card silver-foil parallel set was inserted one card per pack.

| | MINT | EXC | G-VG |
|---|---|---|---|
| COMPLETE SET (384) | 22.00 | 10.00 | 2.80 |
| COMMON PLAYER (1-384) | .05 | .02 | .01 |
| ☐ 1 Antonio Langham | .30 | .14 | .04 |
| Cleveland Browns | | | |
| ☐ 2 Aaron Glenn | .15 | .07 | .02 |
| New York Jets | | | |
| ☐ 3 Sam Adams | .25 | .11 | .03 |
| Seattle Seahawks | | | |
| ☐ 4 DeWayne Washington | .10 | .05 | .01 |
| Minnesota Vikings | | | |
| ☐ 5 Dan Wilkinson | .50 | .23 | .06 |
| Cincinnati Bengals | | | |
| ☐ 6 Bryant Young | .25 | .11 | .03 |
| San Francisco 49ers | | | |
| ☐ 7 Aaron Taylor | .10 | .05 | .01 |
| Green Bay Packers | | | |
| ☐ 8 Willie McGinest | .50 | .23 | .06 |
| New England Patriots | | | |
| ☐ 9 Trev Alberts | .50 | .23 | .06 |
| Indianapolis Colts | | | |
| ☐ 10 Jamir Miller | .30 | .14 | .04 |
| Arizona Cardinals | | | |
| ☐ 11 John Thierry | .30 | .14 | .04 |
| Chicago Bears | | | |
| ☐ 12 Heath Shuler | 5.00 | 2.30 | .60 |
| Washington Redskins | | | |
| ☐ 13 Trent Dilfer | 2.25 | 1.00 | .30 |
| Tampa Bay Buccaneers | | | |
| ☐ 14 Marshall Faulk | 3.00 | 1.35 | .40 |
| Indianapolis Colts | | | |
| ☐ 15 Greg Hill | .75 | .35 | .09 |
| Kansas City Chiefs | | | |
| ☐ 16 William Floyd | .50 | .23 | .06 |
| San Francisco 49ers | | | |
| ☐ 17 Chuck Levy | .60 | .25 | .08 |
| Arizona Cardinals | | | |
| ☐ 18 Charlie Garner | .60 | .25 | .08 |
| Philadelphia Eagles | | | |
| ☐ 19 Mario Bates | .40 | .18 | .05 |
| New Orleans Saints | | | |
| ☐ 20 Donnell Bennett | .20 | .09 | .03 |
| Kansas City Chiefs | | | |
| ☐ 21 LeShon Johnson | .50 | .23 | .06 |
| Green Bay Packers | | | |
| ☐ 22 Calvin Jones | .60 | .25 | .08 |
| Los Angeles Raiders | | | |
| ☐ 23 Darnay Scott | .40 | .18 | .05 |
| Cincinnati Bengals | | | |
| ☐ 24 Charles Johnson | 1.00 | .45 | .13 |
| Pittsburgh Steelers | | | |
| ☐ 25 Johnnie Morton | .75 | .35 | .09 |
| Detroit Lions | | | |
| ☐ 26 Shante Carver | .15 | .07 | .02 |
| Dallas Cowboys | | | |
| ☐ 27 Derrick Alexander | .50 | .23 | .06 |
| Cleveland Browns | | | |
| ☐ 28 David Palmer | 1.00 | .45 | .13 |
| Minnesota Vikings | | | |
| ☐ 29 Ryan Yarborough | .25 | .11 | .03 |
| New York Jets | | | |
| ☐ 30 Errict Rhett | 1.00 | .45 | .13 |
| Tampa Bay Buccaneers | | | |
| ☐ 31 James Washington | .05 | .02 | .01 |
| Dallas Cowboys | | | |
| ☐ 32 Sterling Sharpe | .15 | .07 | .02 |
| Green Bay Packers | | | |
| ☐ 33 Drew Bledsoe | .75 | .35 | .09 |
| New England Patriots | | | |
| ☐ 34 Eric Allen | .05 | .02 | .01 |
| Philadelphia Eagles | | | |
| ☐ 35 Jerome Bettis | .75 | .35 | .09 |
| Los Angeles Rams | | | |
| ☐ 36 Joe Montana | .60 | .25 | .08 |
| Kansas City Chiefs | | | |
| ☐ 37 John Carney | .05 | .02 | .01 |
| San Diego Chargers | | | |
| ☐ 38 Emmitt Smith | 1.00 | .45 | .13 |
| Dallas Cowboys | | | |
| ☐ 39 Chris Warren | .08 | .04 | .01 |
| Seattle Seahawks | | | |
| ☐ 40 Reggie Brooks | .35 | .16 | .04 |
| Washington Redskins | | | |
| ☐ 41 Gary Brown | .15 | .07 | .02 |
| Houston Oilers | | | |
| ☐ 42 Tim Brown | .10 | .05 | .01 |
| Los Angeles Raiders | | | |
| ☐ 43 Erric Pegram | .12 | .05 | .02 |
| Atlanta Falcons | | | |
| ☐ 44 Ron Moore | .20 | .09 | .03 |
| Arizona Cardinals | | | |
| ☐ 45 Jerry Rice | .25 | .11 | .03 |
| San Francisco 49ers | | | |
| ☐ 46 Ricky Watters | .10 | .05 | .01 |
| San Francisco 49ers | | | |
| ☐ 47 Joe Montana | .60 | .25 | .08 |
| Kansas City Chiefs | | | |
| ☐ 48 Reggie Brooks | .35 | .16 | .04 |
| Washington Redskins | | | |
| ☐ 49 Rick Mirer | .75 | .35 | .09 |
| Seattle Seahawks | | | |
| ☐ 50 Raghib Ismail | .10 | .05 | .01 |
| Los Angeles Raiders | | | |
| ☐ 51 Curtis Conway | .08 | .04 | .01 |
| Chicago Bears | | | |
| ☐ 52 Junior Seau | .10 | .05 | .01 |
| San Diego Chargers | | | |
| ☐ 53 Mark Carrier | .05 | .02 | .01 |
| Chicago Bears | | | |
| ☐ 54 Ronnie Lott | .10 | .05 | .01 |
| New York Jets | | | |
| ☐ 55 Marcus Allen | .10 | .05 | .01 |
| Kansas City Chiefs | | | |
| ☐ 56 Michael Irvin | .15 | .07 | .02 |
| Dallas Cowboys | | | |
| ☐ 57 Bennie Blades | .05 | .02 | .01 |
| Detroit Lions | | | |
| ☐ 58 Randal Hill | .08 | .04 | .01 |
| Arizona Cardinals | | | |
| ☐ 59 Brian Blades | .05 | .02 | .01 |
| Seattle Seahawks | | | |
| ☐ 60 Russell Maryland | .08 | .04 | .01 |
| Dallas Cowboys | | | |
| ☐ 61 Jim Kelly | .20 | .09 | .03 |
| Buffalo Bills | | | |
| ☐ 62 Arthur Marshall | .05 | .02 | .01 |
| Denver Broncos | | | |
| ☐ 63 Webster Slaughter | .05 | .02 | .01 |

| | | | |
|---|---|---|---|
| Houston Oilers | | | |
| ☐ 64 Dave Krieg | .05 | .02 | .01 |
| Kansas City Chiefs | | | |
| ☐ 65 Steve Jordan | .05 | .02 | .01 |
| Minnesota Vikings | | | |
| ☐ 66 Neil O'Donnell | .12 | .05 | .02 |
| Pittsburgh Steelers | | | |
| ☐ 67 Andre Reed | .10 | .05 | .01 |
| Buffalo Bills | | | |
| ☐ 68 Mike Croel | .05 | .02 | .01 |
| Denver Broncos | | | |
| ☐ 69 Al Smith | .05 | .02 | .01 |
| Houston Oilers | | | |
| ☐ 70 Joe Montana | 1.25 | .55 | .16 |
| Kansas City Chiefs | | | |
| ☐ 71 Randall McDaniel | .05 | .02 | .01 |
| Minnesota Vikings | | | |
| ☐ 72 Greg Lloyd | .05 | .02 | .01 |
| Pittsburgh Steelers | | | |
| ☐ 73 Thomas Smith | .05 | .02 | .01 |
| Buffalo Bills | | | |
| ☐ 74 Glyn Milburn | .20 | .09 | .03 |
| Denver Broncos | | | |
| ☐ 75 Lorenzo White | .05 | .02 | .01 |
| Houston Oilers | | | |
| ☐ 76 Neil Smith | .08 | .04 | .01 |
| Kansas City Chiefs | | | |
| ☐ 77 John Randle | .05 | .02 | .01 |
| Minnesota Vikings | | | |
| ☐ 78 Rod Woodson | .10 | .05 | .01 |
| Pittsburgh Steelers | | | |
| ☐ 79 Russell Maryland | .10 | .05 | .01 |
| Dallas Cowboys | | | |
| ☐ 80 Rodney Peete | .08 | .04 | .01 |
| Detroit Lions | | | |
| ☐ 81 Jackie Harris | .15 | .07 | .02 |
| Green Bay Packers | | | |
| ☐ 82 James Jett | .30 | .14 | .04 |
| Los Angeles Raiders | | | |
| ☐ 83 Rodney Hampton | .25 | .11 | .03 |
| New York Giants | | | |
| ☐ 84 Bill Romanowski | .05 | .02 | .01 |
| San Francisco 49ers | | | |
| ☐ 85 Ken Norton Jr. | .08 | .04 | .01 |
| Dallas Cowboys | | | |
| ☐ 86 Barry Sanders | .60 | .25 | .08 |
| Detroit Lions | | | |
| ☐ 87 Johnny Holland | .05 | .02 | .01 |
| Green Bay Packers | | | |
| ☐ 88 Terry McDaniel | .05 | .02 | .01 |
| Los Angeles Raiders | | | |
| ☐ 89 Greg Jackson | .05 | .02 | .01 |
| New York Giants | | | |
| ☐ 90 Dana Stubblefield | .15 | .07 | .02 |
| San Francisco 49ers | | | |
| ☐ 91 Jay Novacek | .08 | .04 | .01 |
| Dallas Cowboys | | | |
| ☐ 92 Chris Spielman | .05 | .02 | .01 |
| Detroit Lions | | | |
| ☐ 93 Ken Ruettgers | .05 | .02 | .01 |
| Green Bay Packers | | | |
| ☐ 94 Greg Robinson | .10 | .05 | .01 |
| Los Angeles Raiders | | | |
| ☐ 95 Mark Jackson | .05 | .02 | .01 |
| New York Giants | | | |
| ☐ 96 John Taylor | .08 | .04 | .01 |
| San Francisco 49ers | | | |
| ☐ 97 Roger Harper | .05 | .02 | .01 |
| Atlanta Falcons | | | |
| ☐ 98 Jerry Ball | .05 | .02 | .01 |
| Cleveland Browns | | | |
| ☐ 99 Keith Byars | .08 | .04 | .01 |
| Miami Dolphins | | | |
| ☐ 100 Morten Andersen | .05 | .02 | .01 |
| New Orleans Saints | | | |
| ☐ 101 Eric Allen | .08 | .04 | .01 |
| Philadelphia Eagles | | | |
| ☐ 102 Marion Butts | .08 | .04 | .01 |
| San Diego Chargers | | | |
| ☐ 103 Michael Haynes | .15 | .07 | .02 |
| Atlanta Falcons | | | |
| ☐ 104 Rob Burnett | .05 | .02 | .01 |
| Cleveland Browns | | | |
| ☐ 105 Marco Coleman | .05 | .02 | .01 |
| Miami Dolphins | | | |
| ☐ 106 Derek Brown | .30 | .14 | .04 |
| New Orleans Saints | | | |
| ☐ 107 Andy Harmon | .05 | .02 | .01 |
| Philadelphia Eagles | | | |
| ☐ 108 Darren Carrington | .05 | .02 | .01 |
| San Diego Chargers | | | |
| ☐ 109 Bobby Hebert | .08 | .04 | .01 |
| Atlanta Falcons | | | |
| ☐ 110 Mark Carrier | .05 | .02 | .01 |
| Cleveland Browns | | | |
| ☐ 111 Bryan Cox | .05 | .02 | .01 |
| Miami Dolphins | | | |
| ☐ 112 Toi Cook | .05 | .02 | .01 |

| | | | |
|---|---|---|---|
| New Orleans Saints | | | |
| ☐ 113 Tim Harris | .05 | .02 | .01 |
| Philadelphia Eagles | | | |
| ☐ 114 John Friesz | .08 | .04 | .01 |
| San Diego Chargers | | | |
| ☐ 115 Neal Anderson | .05 | .02 | .01 |
| Chicago Bears | | | |
| ☐ 116 Jerome Bettis | 2.00 | .90 | .25 |
| Los Angeles Rams | | | |
| ☐ 117 Bruce Armstrong | .05 | .02 | .01 |
| New England Patriots | | | |
| ☐ 118 Brad Baxter | .05 | .02 | .01 |
| New York Jets | | | |
| ☐ 119 Johnny Bailey | .05 | .02 | .01 |
| Arizona Cardinals | | | |
| ☐ 120 Brian Blades | .05 | .02 | .01 |
| Seattle Seahawks | | | |
| ☐ 121 Mark Carrier | .05 | .02 | .01 |
| Chicago Bears | | | |
| ☐ 122 Shane Conlan | .05 | .02 | .01 |
| Los Angeles Rams | | | |
| ☐ 123 Drew Bledsoe | 2.00 | .90 | .25 |
| New England Patriots | | | |
| ☐ 124 Chris Burkett | .05 | .02 | .01 |
| New York Jets | | | |
| ☐ 125 Steve Beuerlein | .08 | .04 | .01 |
| Arizona Cardinals | | | |
| ☐ 126 Ferrell Edmunds | .05 | .02 | .01 |
| Seattle Seahawks | | | |
| ☐ 127 Curtis Conway | .15 | .07 | .02 |
| Chicago Bears | | | |
| ☐ 128 Troy Drayton | .08 | .04 | .01 |
| Los Angeles Rams | | | |
| ☐ 129 Vincent Brown | .05 | .02 | .01 |
| New England Patriots | | | |
| ☐ 130 Boomer Esiason | .10 | .05 | .01 |
| New York Jets | | | |
| ☐ 131 Larry Centers | .05 | .02 | .01 |
| Arizona Cardinals | | | |
| ☐ 132 Carlton Gray | .05 | .02 | .01 |
| Seattle Seahawks | | | |
| ☐ 133 Chris Miller | .08 | .04 | .01 |
| Atlanta Falcons | | | |
| ☐ 134 Eric Metcalf | .08 | .04 | .01 |
| Cleveland Browns | | | |
| ☐ 135 Mark Higgs | .08 | .04 | .01 |
| Miami Dolphins | | | |
| ☐ 136 Tyrone Hughes | .05 | .02 | .01 |
| New Orleans Saints | | | |
| ☐ 137 Randall Cunningham | .10 | .05 | .01 |
| Philadelphia Eagles | | | |
| ☐ 138 Ronnie Harmon | .05 | .02 | .01 |
| San Diego Chargers | | | |
| ☐ 139 Andre Rison | .15 | .07 | .02 |
| Atlanta Falcons | | | |
| ☐ 140 Eric Turner | .05 | .02 | .01 |
| Cleveland Browns | | | |
| ☐ 141 Terry Kirby | .50 | .23 | .06 |
| Miami Dolphins | | | |
| ☐ 142 Eric Martin | .05 | .02 | .01 |
| New Orleans Saints | | | |
| ☐ 143 Seth Joyner | .08 | .04 | .01 |
| Philadelphia Eagles | | | |
| ☐ 144 Stan Humphries | .08 | .04 | .01 |
| San Diego Chargers | | | |
| ☐ 145 Deion Sanders | .15 | .07 | .02 |
| Atlanta Falcons | | | |
| ☐ 146 Vinny Testaverde | .08 | .04 | .01 |
| Cleveland Browns | | | |
| ☐ 147 Dan Marino | .75 | .35 | .09 |
| Miami Dolphins | | | |
| ☐ 148 Renaldo Turnbull | .05 | .02 | .01 |
| New Orleans Saints | | | |
| ☐ 149 Herschel Walker | .05 | .02 | .01 |
| Philadelphia Eagles | | | |
| ☐ 150 Anthony Miller | .15 | .07 | .02 |
| San Diego Chargers | | | |
| ☐ 151 Richard Dent | .10 | .05 | .01 |
| Chicago Bears | | | |
| ☐ 152 Jim Everett | .10 | .05 | .01 |
| Los Angeles Rams | | | |
| ☐ 153 Ben Coates | .05 | .02 | .01 |
| New England Patriots | | | |
| ☐ 154 Jeff Lageman | .05 | .02 | .01 |
| New York Jets | | | |
| ☐ 155 Garrison Hearst | .20 | .09 | .03 |
| Arizona Cardinals | | | |
| ☐ 156 Kelvin Martin | .05 | .02 | .01 |
| Seattle Seahawks | | | |
| ☐ 157 Dante Jones | .05 | .02 | .01 |
| Chicago Bears | | | |
| ☐ 158 Sean Gilbert | .05 | .02 | .01 |
| Los Angeles Rams | | | |
| ☐ 159 Leonard Russell | .08 | .04 | .01 |
| New England Patriots | | | |
| ☐ 160 Ronnie Lott | .10 | .05 | .01 |
| New York Jets | | | |
| ☐ 161 Randal Hill | .08 | .04 | .01 |

| | | | |
|---|---|---|---|
| Arizona Cardinals | | | |
| ☐ 162 Rick Mirer | 2.00 | .90 | .25 |
| Seattle Seahawks | | | |
| ☐ 163 Alonzo Spellman | .05 | .02 | .01 |
| Chicago Bears | | | |
| ☐ 164 Todd Lyght | .05 | .02 | .01 |
| Los Angeles Rams | | | |
| ☐ 165 Chris Slade | .05 | .02 | .01 |
| New England Patriots | | | |
| ☐ 166 Johnny Mitchell | .10 | .05 | .01 |
| New York Jets | | | |
| ☐ 167 Ron Moore | .40 | .18 | .05 |
| Arizona Cardinals | | | |
| ☐ 168 Eugene Robinson | .05 | .02 | .01 |
| Seattle Seahawks | | | |
| ☐ 169 Chris Hinton | .05 | .02 | .01 |
| Atlanta Falcons | | | |
| ☐ 170 Dan Footman | .05 | .02 | .01 |
| Cleveland Browns | | | |
| ☐ 171 Keith Jackson | .10 | .05 | .01 |
| Miami Dolphins | | | |
| ☐ 172 Rickey Jackson | .05 | .02 | .01 |
| New Orleans Saints | | | |
| ☐ 173 Heath Sherman | .05 | .02 | .01 |
| Philadelphia Eagles | | | |
| ☐ 174 Chris Mims | .05 | .02 | .01 |
| San Diego Chargers | | | |
| ☐ 175 Erric Pegram | .25 | .11 | .03 |
| Atlanta Falcons | | | |
| ☐ 176 Leroy Hoard | .05 | .02 | .01 |
| Cleveland Browns | | | |
| ☐ 177 O.J. McDuffie | .25 | .11 | .03 |
| Miami Dolphins | | | |
| ☐ 178 Wayne Martin | .05 | .02 | .01 |
| New Orleans Saints | | | |
| ☐ 179 Clyde Simmons | .08 | .04 | .01 |
| Philadelphia Eagles | | | |
| ☐ 180 Leslie O'Neal | .05 | .02 | .01 |
| San Diego Chargers | | | |
| ☐ 181 Mike Pritchard | .08 | .04 | .01 |
| Atlanta Falcons | | | |
| ☐ 182 Michael Jackson | .05 | .02 | .01 |
| Cleveland Browns | | | |
| ☐ 183 Scott Mitchell | .30 | .14 | .04 |
| Miami Dolphins | | | |
| ☐ 184 Lorenzo Neal | .15 | .07 | .02 |
| New Orleans Saints | | | |
| ☐ 185 William Thomas | .05 | .02 | .01 |
| Philadelphia Eagles | | | |
| ☐ 186 Junior Seau | .10 | .05 | .01 |
| San Diego Chargers | | | |
| ☐ 187 Chris Gedney | .05 | .02 | .01 |
| Chicago Bears | | | |
| ☐ 188 Tim Lester | .05 | .02 | .01 |
| Los Angeles Rams | | | |
| ☐ 189 Sam Gash | .05 | .02 | .01 |
| New England Patriots | | | |
| ☐ 190 Johnny Johnson | .05 | .02 | .01 |
| New York Jets | | | |
| ☐ 191 Chuck Cecil | .05 | .02 | .01 |
| Arizona Cardinals | | | |
| ☐ 192 Cortez Kennedy | .10 | .05 | .01 |
| Seattle Seahawks | | | |
| ☐ 193 Jim Harbaugh | .08 | .04 | .01 |
| Chicago Bears | | | |
| ☐ 194 Roman Phifer | .05 | .02 | .01 |
| Los Angeles Rams | | | |
| ☐ 195 Pat Harlow | .05 | .02 | .01 |
| New England Patriots | | | |
| ☐ 196 Rob Moore | .05 | .02 | .01 |
| New York Jets | | | |
| ☐ 197 Gary Clark | .10 | .05 | .01 |
| Arizona Cardinals | | | |
| ☐ 198 Jon Vaughn | .05 | .02 | .01 |
| Seattle Seahawks | | | |
| ☐ 199 Craig Heyward | .05 | .02 | .01 |
| Chicago Bears | | | |
| ☐ 200 Michael Stewart | .05 | .02 | .01 |
| Los Angeles Rams | | | |
| ☐ 201 Greg McMurtry | .05 | .02 | .01 |
| New England Patriots | | | |
| ☐ 202 Brian Washington | .05 | .02 | .01 |
| New York Jets | | | |
| ☐ 203 Ken Harvey | .05 | .02 | .01 |
| Arizona Cardinals | | | |
| ☐ 204 Chris Warren | .08 | .04 | .01 |
| Seattle Seahawks | | | |
| ☐ 205 Bruce Smith | .10 | .05 | .01 |
| Buffalo Bills | | | |
| ☐ 206 Tom Rouen | .05 | .02 | .01 |
| Denver Broncos | | | |
| ☐ 207 Cris Dishman | .05 | .02 | .01 |
| Houston Oilers | | | |
| ☐ 208 Keith Cash | .05 | .02 | .01 |
| Kansas City Chiefs | | | |
| ☐ 209 Carlos Jenkins | .05 | .02 | .01 |
| Minnesota Vikings | | | |
| ☐ 210 Levon Kirkland | .05 | .02 | .01 |

| | | | |
|---|---|---|---|
| Pittsburgh Steelers | | | |
| ☐ 211 Pete Metzelaars | .05 | .02 | .01 |
| Buffalo Bills | | | |
| ☐ 212 Shannon Sharpe | .15 | .07 | .02 |
| Denver Broncos | | | |
| ☐ 213 Cody Carlson | .08 | .04 | .01 |
| Houston Oilers | | | |
| ☐ 214 Derrick Thomas | .15 | .07 | .02 |
| Kansas City Chiefs | | | |
| ☐ 215 Emmitt Smith | 1.75 | .80 | .22 |
| Dallas Cowboys | | | |
| ☐ 216 Robert Porcher | .05 | .02 | .01 |
| Detroit Lions | | | |
| ☐ 217 Sterling Sharpe | .30 | .14 | .04 |
| Green Bay Packers | | | |
| ☐ 218 Anthony Smith | .05 | .02 | .01 |
| Los Angeles Raiders | | | |
| ☐ 219 Mike Sherrard | .05 | .02 | .01 |
| New York Giants | | | |
| ☐ 220 Tom Rathman | .05 | .02 | .01 |
| San Francisco 49ers | | | |
| ☐ 221 Nate Newton | .05 | .02 | .01 |
| Dallas Cowboys | | | |
| ☐ 222 Pat Swilling | .05 | .02 | .01 |
| Detroit Lions | | | |
| ☐ 223 George Teague | .05 | .02 | .01 |
| Green Bay Packers | | | |
| ☐ 224 Greg Townsend | .05 | .02 | .01 |
| Los Angeles Raiders | | | |
| ☐ 225 Eric Guliford | .30 | .14 | .04 |
| Minnesota Vikings | | | |
| ☐ 226 Leroy Thompson | .05 | .02 | .01 |
| Pittsburgh Steelers | | | |
| ☐ 227 Thurman Thomas | .25 | .11 | .03 |
| Buffalo Bills | | | |
| ☐ 228 Dan Williams | .05 | .02 | .01 |
| Denver Broncos | | | |
| ☐ 229 Bubba McDowell | .05 | .02 | .01 |
| Houston Oilers | | | |
| ☐ 230 Tracy Simien | .05 | .02 | .01 |
| Kansas City Chiefs | | | |
| ☐ 231 Scottie Graham | .40 | .18 | .05 |
| Minnesota Vikings | | | |
| ☐ 232 Eric Green | .08 | .04 | .01 |
| Pittsburgh Steelers | | | |
| ☐ 233 Phil Simms | .10 | .05 | .01 |
| New York Giants | | | |
| ☐ 234 Ricky Watters | .20 | .09 | .03 |
| San Francisco 49ers | | | |
| ☐ 235 Kevin Williams | .15 | .07 | .02 |
| Dallas Cowboys | | | |
| ☐ 236 Brett Perriman | .05 | .02 | .01 |
| Detroit Lions | | | |
| ☐ 237 Reggie White | .15 | .07 | .02 |
| Green Bay Packers | | | |
| ☐ 238 Steve Wisniewski | .05 | .02 | .01 |
| Los Angeles Rams | | | |
| ☐ 239 Mark Collins | .05 | .02 | .01 |
| New York Giants | | | |
| ☐ 240 Steve Young | .15 | .07 | .02 |
| San Francisco 49ers | | | |
| ☐ 241 Steve Tovar | .05 | .02 | .01 |
| Cincinnati Bengals | | | |
| ☐ 242 Jason Belser | .05 | .02 | .01 |
| Indianapolis Colts | | | |
| ☐ 243 Ray Seals | .05 | .02 | .01 |
| Tampa Bay Buccaneers | | | |
| ☐ 244 Ernest Byner | .05 | .02 | .01 |
| Washington Redskins | | | |
| ☐ 245 Ricky Proehl | .08 | .04 | .01 |
| Arizona Cardinals | | | |
| ☐ 246 Rich Miano | .05 | .02 | .01 |
| Philadelphia Eagles | | | |
| ☐ 247 Alfred Williams | .05 | .02 | .01 |
| Cincinnati Bengals | | | |
| ☐ 248 Ray Buchanan | .05 | .02 | .01 |
| Indianapolis Colts | | | |
| ☐ 249 Hardy Nickerson | .05 | .02 | .01 |
| Tampa Bay Buccaneers | | | |
| ☐ 250 Brad Edwards | .05 | .02 | .01 |
| Washington Redskins | | | |
| ☐ 251 Jerrol Williams | .05 | .02 | .01 |
| San Diego Chargers | | | |
| ☐ 252 Marvin Washington | .05 | .02 | .01 |
| New York Jets | | | |
| ☐ 253 Tony McGee | .05 | .02 | .01 |
| Cincinnati Bengals | | | |
| ☐ 254 Jeff George | .10 | .05 | .01 |
| Indianapolis Colts | | | |
| ☐ 255 Ron Hall | .05 | .02 | .01 |
| Tampa Bay Buccaneers | | | |
| ☐ 256 Tim Johnson | .05 | .02 | .01 |
| Washington Redskins | | | |
| ☐ 257 Willie Roaf | .05 | .02 | .01 |
| New Orleans Saints | | | |
| ☐ 258 Corwin Brown | .10 | .05 | .01 |
| New England Patriots | | | |
| ☐ 259 Ricardo McDonald | .05 | .02 | .01 |

| | | | | | | | | |
|---|---|---|---|---|---|---|---|---|
| Cincinnati Bengals | | | | Detroit Lions | | | | |
| ☐ 260 Jeff Herrod | .05 | .02 | .01 | ☐ 309 Brett Favre | .50 | .23 | .06 | |
| Indianapolis Colts | | | | Green Bay Packers | | | | |
| ☐ 261 Demetrius DuBose | .05 | .02 | .01 | ☐ 310 Raghib Ismail | .15 | .07 | .02 | |
| Tampa Bay Buccaneers | | | | Los Angeles Raiders | | | | |
| ☐ 262 Ricky Sanders | .05 | .02 | .01 | ☐ 311 Jarrod Bunch | .05 | .02 | .01 | |
| Washington Redskins | | | | New York Giants | | | | |
| ☐ 263 John L. Williams | .05 | .02 | .01 | ☐ 312 Don Beebe | .05 | .02 | .01 | |
| Seattle Seahawks | | | | Buffalo Bills | | | | |
| ☐ 264 John Lynch | .05 | .02 | .01 | ☐ 313 Steve Atwater | .05 | .02 | .01 | |
| Tampa Bay Buccaneers | | | | Denver Broncos | | | | |
| ☐ 265 Lance Gunn | .05 | .02 | .01 | ☐ 314 Gary Brown | .30 | .14 | .04 | |
| Cincinnati Bengals | | | | Houston Oilers | | | | |
| ☐ 266 Jessie Hester | .05 | .02 | .01 | ☐ 315 Marcus Allen | .10 | .05 | .01 | |
| Indianapolis Colts | | | | Kansas City Chiefs | | | | |
| ☐ 267 Mark Wheeler | .05 | .02 | .01 | ☐ 316 Terry Allen | .08 | .04 | .01 | |
| Tampa Bay Buccaneers | | | | Minnesota Vikings | | | | |
| ☐ 268 Chip Lohmiller | .05 | .02 | .01 | ☐ 317 Chad Brown | .05 | .02 | .01 | |
| Washington Redskins | | | | Pittsburgh Steelers | | | | |
| ☐ 269 Eric Swann | .05 | .02 | .01 | ☐ 318 Cornelius Bennett | .08 | .04 | .01 | |
| Arizona Cardinals | | | | Buffalo Bills | | | | |
| ☐ 270 Byron Evans | .05 | .02 | .01 | ☐ 319 Rod Bernstine | .05 | .02 | .01 | |
| Philadelphia Eagles | | | | Denver Broncos | | | | |
| ☐ 271 Gary Plummer | .05 | .02 | .01 | ☐ 320 Greg Montgomery | .05 | .02 | .01 | |
| San Diego Chargers | | | | Houston Oilers | | | | |
| ☐ 272 Roger Duffy | .10 | .05 | .01 | ☐ 321 Kimble Anders | .15 | .07 | .02 | |
| New York Jets | | | | Kansas City Chiefs | | | | |
| ☐ 273 Irv Smith | .05 | .02 | .01 | ☐ 322 Charles Haley | .05 | .02 | .01 | |
| New Orleans Saints | | | | Dallas Cowboys | | | | |
| ☐ 274 Todd Collins | .05 | .02 | .01 | ☐ 323 Mel Gray | .05 | .02 | .01 | |
| New England Patriots | | | | Detroit Lions | | | | |
| ☐ 275 Robert Blackmon | .05 | .02 | .01 | ☐ 324 Edgar Bennett | .05 | .02 | .01 | |
| Seattle Seahawks | | | | Green Bay Packers | | | | |
| ☐ 276 Reggie Roby | .05 | .02 | .01 | ☐ 325 Eddie Anderson | .05 | .02 | .01 | |
| Washington Redskins | | | | Los Angeles Raiders | | | | |
| ☐ 277 Russell Copeland | .05 | .02 | .01 | ☐ 326 Derek Brown | .05 | .02 | .01 | |
| Buffalo Bills | | | | New York Giants | | | | |
| ☐ 278 Simon Fletcher | .05 | .02 | .01 | ☐ 327 Steve Bono | .08 | .04 | .01 | |
| Denver Broncos | | | | San Francisco 49ers | | | | |
| ☐ 279 Ernest Givins | .10 | .05 | .01 | ☐ 328 Alvin Harper | .08 | .04 | .01 | |
| Houston Oilers | | | | Dallas Cowboys | | | | |
| ☐ 280 Tim Barnett | .05 | .02 | .01 | ☐ 329 Willie Green | .05 | .02 | .01 | |
| Kansas City Chiefs | | | | Detroit Lions | | | | |
| ☐ 281 Chris Doleman | .05 | .02 | .01 | ☐ 330 Robert Brooks | .05 | .02 | .01 | |
| Minnesota Vikings | | | | Green Bay Packers | | | | |
| ☐ 282 Jeff Graham | .05 | .02 | .01 | ☐ 331 Patrick Bates | .05 | .02 | .01 | |
| Pittsburgh Steelers | | | | Los Angeles Raiders | | | | |
| ☐ 283 Kenneth Davis | .05 | .02 | .01 | ☐ 332 Anthony Carter | .05 | .02 | .01 | |
| Buffalo Bills | | | | Minnesota Vikings | | | | |
| ☐ 284 Vance Johnson | .05 | .02 | .01 | ☐ 333 Barry Foster | .15 | .07 | .02 | |
| Denver Broncos | | | | Pittsburgh Steelers | | | | |
| ☐ 285 Haywood Jeffires | .10 | .05 | .01 | ☐ 334 Billy Brooks | .08 | .04 | .01 | |
| Houston Oilers | | | | Buffalo Bills | | | | |
| ☐ 286 Todd McNair | .05 | .02 | .01 | ☐ 335 Jason Elam | .05 | .02 | .01 | |
| Kansas City Chiefs | | | | Denver Broncos | | | | |
| ☐ 287 Daryl Johnston | .08 | .04 | .01 | ☐ 336 Ray Childress | .05 | .02 | .01 | |
| Dallas Cowboys | | | | Houston Oilers | | | | |
| ☐ 288 Ryan McNeil | .05 | .02 | .01 | ☐ 337 J.J. Birden | .05 | .02 | .01 | |
| Detroit Lions | | | | Kansas City Chiefs | | | | |
| ☐ 289 Terrell Buckley | .05 | .02 | .01 | ☐ 338 Cris Carter | .08 | .04 | .01 | |
| Green Bay Packers | | | | Minnesota Vikings | | | | |
| ☐ 290 Ethan Horton | .05 | .02 | .01 | ☐ 339 Deon Figures | .05 | .02 | .01 | |
| Los Angeles Raiders | | | | Pittsburgh Steelers | | | | |
| ☐ 291 Corey Miller | .05 | .02 | .01 | ☐ 340 Carlton Bailey | .05 | .02 | .01 | |
| New York Giants | | | | New York Giants | | | | |
| ☐ 292 Marc Logan | .05 | .02 | .01 | ☐ 341 Brent Jones | .08 | .04 | .01 | |
| San Francisco 49ers | | | | San Francisco 49ers | | | | |
| ☐ 293 Lincoln Coleman | .25 | .11 | .03 | ☐ 342 Troy Aikman | 1.25 | .55 | .16 | |
| Dallas Cowboys | | | | Dallas Cowboys | | | | |
| ☐ 294 Derrick Moore | .05 | .02 | .01 | ☐ 343 Rodney Holman | .05 | .02 | .01 | |
| Detroit Lions | | | | Detroit Lions | | | | |
| ☐ 295 LeRoy Butler | .05 | .02 | .01 | ☐ 344 Tony Bennett | .05 | .02 | .01 | |
| Green Bay Packers | | | | Green Bay Packers | | | | |
| ☐ 296 Jeff Hostetler | .08 | .04 | .01 | ☐ 345 Tim Brown | .15 | .07 | .02 | |
| Los Angeles Raiders | | | | Los Angeles Raiders | | | | |
| ☐ 297 Qadry Ismail | .15 | .07 | .02 | ☐ 346 Michael Brooks | .05 | .02 | .01 | |
| Minnesota Vikings | | | | New York Giants | | | | |
| ☐ 298 Andre Hastings | .05 | .02 | .01 | ☐ 347 Martin Harrison | .05 | .02 | .01 | |
| Pittsburgh Steelers | | | | San Francisco 49ers | | | | |
| ☐ 299 Henry Jones | .05 | .02 | .01 | ☐ 348 Jerry Rice | .50 | .23 | .06 | |
| Buffalo Bills | | | | San Francisco 49ers | | | | |
| ☐ 300 John Elway | .40 | .18 | .05 | ☐ 349 John Copeland | .05 | .02 | .01 | |
| Denver Broncos | | | | Cincinnati Bengals | | | | |
| ☐ 301 Warren Moon | .10 | .05 | .01 | ☐ 350 Kerry Cash | .05 | .02 | .01 | |
| Houston Oilers | | | | Indianapolis Colts | | | | |
| ☐ 302 Willie Davis | .08 | .04 | .01 | ☐ 351 Reggie Cobb | .08 | .04 | .01 | |
| Kansas City Chiefs | | | | Tampa Bay Buccaneers | | | | |
| ☐ 303 Vencie Glenn | .05 | .02 | .01 | ☐ 352 Brian Mitchell | .05 | .02 | .01 | |
| Minnesota Vikings | | | | Washington Redskins | | | | |
| ☐ 304 Kevin Greene | .05 | .02 | .01 | ☐ 353 Derrick Fenner | .05 | .02 | .01 | |
| Pittsburgh Steelers | | | | Cincinnati Bengals | | | | |
| ☐ 305 Marcus Buckley | .05 | .02 | .01 | ☐ 354 Roosevelt Potts | .08 | .04 | .01 | |
| New York Giants | | | | Indianapolis Colts | | | | |
| ☐ 306 Tim McDonald | .05 | .02 | .01 | ☐ 355 Courtney Hawkins | .05 | .02 | .01 | |
| San Francisco 49ers | | | | Tampa Bay Buccaneers | | | | |
| ☐ 307 Michael Irvin | .30 | .14 | .04 | ☐ 356 Carl Banks | .05 | .02 | .01 | |
| Dallas Cowboys | | | | Washington Redskins | | | | |
| ☐ 308 Herman Moore | .15 | .07 | .02 | ☐ 357 Harold Green | .05 | .02 | .01 | |

| | | | |
|---|---|---|---|
| Cincinnati Bengals | | | |
| ☐ 358 Steve Emtman | .05 | .02 | .01 |
| Indianapolis Colts | | | |
| ☐ 359 Santana Dotson | .08 | .04 | .01 |
| Tampa Bay Buccaneers | | | |
| ☐ 360 Reggie Brooks | .75 | .35 | .09 |
| Washington Redskins | | | |
| ☐ 361 Terry Obee | .15 | .07 | .02 |
| Chicago Bears | | | |
| ☐ 362 David Klingler | .15 | .07 | .02 |
| Cincinnati Bengals | | | |
| ☐ 363 Quentin Coryatt | .05 | .02 | .01 |
| Indianapolis Colts | | | |
| ☐ 364 Craig Erickson | .08 | .04 | .01 |
| Tampa Bay Buccaneers | | | |
| ☐ 365 Desmond Howard | .15 | .07 | .02 |
| Washington Redskins | | | |
| ☐ 366 Carl Pickens | .08 | .04 | .01 |
| Cincinnati Bengals | | | |
| ☐ 367 Lawrence Dawsey | .05 | .02 | .01 |
| Tampa Bay Buccaneers | | | |
| ☐ 368 Henry Ellard | .08 | .04 | .01 |
| Los Angeles Rams | | | |
| ☐ 369 Shaun Gayle | .05 | .02 | .01 |
| Chicago Bears | | | |
| ☐ 370 David Lang | .05 | .02 | .01 |
| Los Angeles Rams | | | |
| ☐ 371 Anthony Johnson | .05 | .02 | .01 |
| Indianapolis Colts | | | |
| ☐ 372 Darnell Walker | .10 | .05 | .01 |
| Atlanta Falcons | | | |
| ☐ 373 Pepper Johnson | .05 | .02 | .01 |
| Cleveland Browns | | | |
| ☐ 374 Kurt Gouveia | .05 | .02 | .01 |
| Washington Redskins | | | |
| ☐ 375 Louis Oliver | .05 | .02 | .01 |
| Miami Dolphins | | | |
| ☐ 376 Lincoln Kennedy | .05 | .02 | .01 |
| Atlanta Falcons | | | |
| ☐ 377 Anthony Pleasant | .05 | .02 | .01 |
| Cleveland Browns | | | |
| ☐ 378 Irving Fryar | .08 | .04 | .01 |
| Miami Dolphins | | | |
| ☐ 379 Carolina Pathers | .15 | .07 | .02 |
| Expansion Team Cards | | | |
| ☐ 380 Jacksonville Jaguars | .15 | .07 | .02 |
| Expansion Team Cards | | | |
| ☐ 381 Checklist UER | .05 | .02 | .01 |
| (Front has 193-288) | | | |
| Sterling Sharpe | | | |
| ☐ 382 Checklist | .05 | .02 | .01 |
| Dan Marino | | | |
| ☐ 383 Checklist UER | .05 | .02 | .01 |
| (Front has 289-384) | | | |
| Jerry Rice | | | |
| ☐ 384 Checklist UER | .05 | .02 | .01 |
| (Front has 1-96) | | | |
| Joe Montana | | | |
| ☐ NNO "You Crash The Game" | 4.00 | 1.80 | .50 |
| Instant Win Card | | | |

| | | | |
|---|---|---|---|
| ☐ 12 Heath Shuler | 14.00 | 6.25 | 1.75 |
| ☐ 13 Trent Dilfer | 6.00 | 2.70 | .75 |
| ☐ 14 Marshall Faulk | 8.00 | 3.60 | 1.00 |
| ☐ 15 Greg Hill | 2.25 | 1.00 | .30 |
| ☐ 17 Chuck Levy | 1.75 | .80 | .22 |
| ☐ 18 Charlie Garner | 1.75 | .80 | .22 |
| ☐ 22 Calvin Jones | 1.75 | .80 | .22 |
| ☐ 24 Charles Johnson | 3.00 | 1.35 | .40 |
| ☐ 25 Johnnie Morton | 2.25 | 1.00 | .30 |
| ☐ 28 David Palmer | 3.00 | 1.35 | .40 |
| ☐ 30 Errict Rhett | 3.00 | 1.35 | .40 |
| ☐ 33 Drew Bledsoe I93 | 3.50 | 1.55 | .45 |
| ☐ 35 Jerome Bettis I93 | 3.50 | 1.55 | .45 |
| ☐ 36 Joe Montana I93 | 3.00 | 1.35 | .40 |
| ☐ 38 Emmitt Smith I93 | 5.00 | 2.30 | .60 |
| ☐ 40 Reggie Brooks I93 | 1.75 | .80 | .22 |
| ☐ 45 Jerry Rice I93 | 1.00 | .45 | .13 |
| ☐ 47 Joe Montana TE | 3.00 | 1.35 | .40 |
| ☐ 48 Reggie Brooks TE | 1.75 | .80 | .22 |
| ☐ 49 Rick Mirer TE | 3.50 | 1.55 | .45 |
| ☐ 61 Jim Kelly | 1.00 | .45 | .13 |
| ☐ 70 Joe Montana | 8.00 | 3.60 | 1.00 |
| ☐ 83 Rodney Hampton | 1.00 | .45 | .13 |
| ☐ 86 Barry Sanders | 3.00 | 1.35 | .40 |
| ☐ 116 Jerome Bettis | 8.00 | 3.60 | 1.00 |
| ☐ 123 Drew Bledsoe | 8.00 | 3.60 | 1.00 |
| ☐ 141 Terry Kirby | 2.50 | 1.15 | .30 |
| ☐ 147 Dan Marino | 3.50 | 1.55 | .45 |
| ☐ 162 Rick Mirer | 8.00 | 3.60 | 1.00 |
| ☐ 183 Scott Mitchell | 1.25 | .55 | .16 |
| ☐ 215 Emmitt Smith | 10.00 | 4.50 | 1.25 |
| ☐ 217 Sterling Sharpe | 1.50 | .65 | .19 |
| ☐ 227 Thurman Thomas | 1.00 | .45 | .13 |
| ☐ 234 Ricky Watters | 1.00 | .45 | .13 |
| ☐ 300 John Elway | 2.00 | .90 | .25 |
| ☐ 307 Michael Irvin | 1.50 | .65 | .19 |
| ☐ 309 Brett Favre | 2.50 | 1.15 | .30 |
| ☐ 314 Gary Brown | 1.25 | .55 | .16 |
| ☐ 342 Troy Aikman | 7.00 | 3.10 | .85 |
| ☐ 348 Jerry Rice | 2.50 | 1.15 | .30 |
| ☐ 360 Reggie Brooks | 3.50 | 1.55 | .45 |

# 1994 U.S. Playing Cards
## Ditka's Picks

Part of the Bicycle Sports Collection, these 56 playing cards, featuring Mike Ditka's NFL player picks, measure the standard-size (2 1/2" by 3 1/2") and have rounded corners. The fronts feature borderless color player action shots with slightly ghosted backgrounds. The player's name appears in white lettering within a green rectangle at the bottom. His team name and helmet appear at the upper right. The backs are black, gold, and green, and besides carrying the set's title, also display the logos for the Bicycle Sports Collection, NFL, and NFLPA. The set is checklisted below in playing card order by suits and assigned numbers to Aces (1), Jacks (11), Queens (12), and Kings (13).

| | MINT | EXC | G-VG |
|---|---|---|---|
| COMPLETE SET (56) | 5.00 | 2.00 | .50 |
| COMMON PLAYER | .05 | .02 | .00 |
| | | | |
| ☐ 1C Steve Young | .25 | .10 | .02 |
| ☐ 1D Joe Montana | .75 | .30 | .07 |
| ☐ 1H Dan Marino | .50 | .20 | .05 |
| ☐ 1S Troy Aikman | .75 | .30 | .07 |
| ☐ 2C Jim Lachey | .05 | .02 | .00 |
| ☐ 2D Richmond Webb | .05 | .02 | .00 |
| ☐ 2H Wilber Marshall | .10 | .04 | .01 |
| ☐ 2S Ronnie Lott | .15 | .06 | .01 |
| ☐ 3C Sean Gilbert | .15 | .06 | .01 |
| ☐ 3D Clay Matthews | .15 | .06 | .01 |
| ☐ 3H Jeff Lageman | .05 | .02 | .00 |
| ☐ 3S Audray McMillian | .05 | .02 | .00 |
| ☐ 4C Morten Andersen | .05 | .02 | .00 |

# 1994 Upper Deck
## Collector's Choice Silver

Inserted one in every pack, this standard-size (2 1/2" by 3 1/2") 384-card set features a similar design to the regular 1994 Upper Deck Collector's Choice issue. The difference being that the team's name appears in big silver foil letters above the player's name on the front.

| | MINT | EXC | G-VG |
|---|---|---|---|
| COMPLETE SET (384) | 100.00 | 45.00 | 12.50 |
| COMMON PLAYER (1-384) | .20 | .09 | .03 |
| *SILVER STARS: 2.5X TO 5X VALUE | | | |
| *SILVER ROOKIES: 2X TO 4X VALUE | | | |

| | | | |
|---|---|---|---|
| ☐ 4D Pete Stoyanovich | .05 | .02 | .00 |
| ☐ 4H Rohn Stark | .05 | .02 | .00 |
| ☐ 4S Sean Landeta | .05 | .02 | .00 |
| ☐ 5C Broderick Thomas | .05 | .02 | .00 |
| ☐ 5D James Francis | .05 | .02 | .00 |
| ☐ 5H Derrick Thomas | .20 | .08 | .02 |
| ☐ 5S Tony Bennett | .10 | .04 | .01 |
| ☐ 6C Seth Joyner | .05 | .02 | .00 |
| ☐ 6D Percy Snow | .05 | .02 | .00 |
| ☐ 6H Junior Seau | .20 | .08 | .02 |
| ☐ 6S Chris Spielman | .10 | .04 | .01 |
| ☐ 7C Pierce Holt | .10 | .04 | .01 |
| ☐ 7D Rod Woodson | .15 | .06 | .01 |
| ☐ 7H Ray Childress | .10 | .04 | .01 |
| ☐ 7S Deion Sanders | .25 | .10 | .02 |
| ☐ 8C Jay Novacek | .15 | .06 | .01 |
| ☐ 8D Eric Green | .10 | .04 | .01 |
| ☐ 8H Marv Cook | .05 | .02 | .00 |
| ☐ 8S Brent Jones | .10 | .04 | .01 |
| ☐ 9C Randall McDaniel | .05 | .02 | .00 |
| ☐ 9D Mike Munchak | .05 | .02 | .00 |
| ☐ 9H Bruce Matthews | .05 | .02 | .00 |
| ☐ 9S Mark Stepnoski | .05 | .02 | .00 |
| ☐ 10C Harris Barton | .05 | .02 | .00 |
| ☐ 10D Steve Atwater | .10 | .04 | .01 |
| ☐ 10H Henry Jones | .10 | .04 | .01 |
| ☐ 10S Chuck Cecil | .05 | .02 | .00 |
| ☐ 11C Sterling Sharpe | .30 | .12 | .03 |
| ☐ 11D Anthony Miller | .15 | .06 | .01 |
| ☐ 11H Haywood Jeffires | .15 | .06 | .01 |
| ☐ 11S Jerry Rice | .35 | .14 | .03 |
| ☐ 12C Reggie White | .20 | .08 | .02 |
| ☐ 12D Howie Long | .10 | .04 | .01 |
| ☐ 12H Cortez Kennedy | .15 | .06 | .01 |
| ☐ 12S Chris Doleman | .10 | .04 | .01 |
| ☐ 13C Emmitt Smith | .75 | .30 | .07 |
| ☐ 13D Thurman Thomas | .30 | .12 | .03 |
| ☐ 13H Barry Foster | .30 | .12 | .03 |
| ☐ 13S Barry Sanders | .45 | .18 | .04 |
| ☐ NNO Ditka's AFC Picks | .10 | .04 | .01 |
| ☐ NNO Ditka's NFC Picks | .10 | .04 | .01 |
| ☐ WILD Tom Waddle | .10 | .04 | .01 |
| ☐ WILD Steve Wisniewski | .05 | .02 | .00 |

## 1967-68 Vikings

These large photo cards are approximately 8" by 10", black-and-white. These white border cards have blank backs and are printed on glossy thick paper, not photographs. The cards are unnumbered and checklisted below in alphabetical order. The set is dated by the fact that 1967 was the only or last year with the Vikings for Paul Flatley, Don Hansen, Jeff Jordan, Marlin McKeever, Dave Tobey, Ron Vanderkelen, and Bobby Walden and that 1968 was the first year with the Vikings for Gary Cuozzo.

| | NRMT | VG-E | GOOD |
|---|---|---|---|
| COMPLETE SET (29) | 75.00 | 30.00 | 7.50 |
| COMMON PLAYER (1-29) | 3.00 | 1.20 | .30 |
| ☐ 1 Grady Alderman (Tackle) | 3.00 | 1.20 | .30 |
| ☐ 2 Grady Alderman (Offensive lineman) | 3.00 | 1.20 | .30 |
| ☐ 3 John Beasley | 3.00 | 1.20 | .30 |
| ☐ 4 Bob Berry | 4.00 | 1.60 | .40 |
| ☐ 5 Larry Bowie | 3.00 | 1.20 | .30 |
| ☐ 6 Gary Cuozzo | 4.00 | 1.60 | .40 |
| ☐ 7 Doug Davis | 3.00 | 1.20 | .30 |
| ☐ 8 Paul Dickinson | 3.00 | 1.20 | .30 |
| ☐ 9 Paul Flatley | 4.00 | 1.60 | .40 |
| ☐ 10 Bob Grim | 4.00 | 1.60 | .40 |
| ☐ 11 Dale Hackbart | 3.00 | 1.20 | .30 |
| ☐ 12 Don Hansen | 3.00 | 1.20 | .30 |
| ☐ 13 Jim Hargrove | 3.00 | 1.20 | .30 |
| ☐ 14 Clint Jones | 4.00 | 1.60 | .40 |
| ☐ 15 Jeff Jordan | 3.00 | 1.20 | .30 |
| ☐ 16 Joe Kapp | 6.00 | 2.40 | .60 |
| ☐ 17 John Kirby | 3.00 | 1.20 | .30 |
| ☐ 18 Gary Larsen | 4.00 | 1.60 | .40 |
| ☐ 19 Earsell Mackbee | 3.00 | 1.20 | .30 |
| ☐ 20 Marlin McKeever | 4.00 | 1.60 | .40 |
| ☐ 21 Milt Sunde | 3.00 | 1.20 | .30 |
| ☐ 22 Dave Tobey | 3.00 | 1.20 | .30 |
| ☐ 23 Ron Vanderkelen | 5.00 | 2.00 | .50 |
| ☐ 24 Jim Vellone | 3.00 | 1.20 | .30 |
| ☐ 25 Bobby Walden | 3.00 | 1.20 | .30 |
| ☐ 26 Lonnie Warwick | 3.00 | 1.20 | .30 |
| ☐ 27 Gene Washington (Wide receiver) | 4.00 | 1.60 | .40 |
| ☐ 28 Gene Washington (End) | 4.00 | 1.60 | .40 |
| ☐ 29 Roy Winston | 4.00 | 1.60 | .40 |

## 1971 Vikings Photos

Issued in the late summer of 1971 (preseason), this team-issued set consists of 34 four-color close-up photos printed on thin paper stock. Each photo measures approximately 5" by 7 7/16". The player's name, position, and team name appear in a white bottom border. The backs are blank. The cards are unnumbered and checklisted below in alphabetical order.

| | MINT | EXC | G-VG |
|---|---|---|---|
| COMPLETE SET (49) | 90.00 | 36.00 | 9.00 |
| COMMON CARD (1-49) | 1.50 | .60 | .15 |
| ☐ 1 Grady Alderman | 2.00 | .80 | .20 |
| ☐ 2 Neill Armstrong CO | 2.00 | .80 | .20 |
| ☐ 3 Bill Brown | 3.00 | 1.20 | .30 |
| ☐ 4 Bob Brown | 2.00 | .80 | .20 |
| ☐ 5 Bob Bryant | 2.00 | .80 | .20 |
| ☐ 6 Jerry Burns CO | 2.50 | 1.00 | .25 |
| ☐ 7 Fred Cox | 2.00 | .80 | .20 |
| ☐ 8 Gary Cuozzo | 2.50 | 1.00 | .25 |
| ☐ 9 Doug Davis | 1.50 | .60 | .15 |
| ☐ 10 Al Denson | 1.50 | .60 | .15 |
| ☐ 11 Paul Dickson | 1.50 | .60 | .15 |
| ☐ 12 Carl Eller | 6.00 | 2.40 | .60 |
| ☐ 13 Bud Grant CO | 6.00 | 2.40 | .60 |
| ☐ 14 Bob Grim | 2.50 | 1.00 | .25 |
| ☐ 15 Leo Hayden | 1.50 | .60 | .15 |
| ☐ 16 John Henderson | 1.50 | .60 | .15 |
| ☐ 17 Wally Hilgenberg | 2.50 | 1.00 | .25 |
| ☐ 18 Noel Jenke | 1.50 | .60 | .15 |
| ☐ 19 Clint Jones | 2.00 | .80 | .20 |
| ☐ 20 Karl Kassulke | 1.50 | .60 | .15 |
| ☐ 21 Paul Krause | 4.00 | 1.60 | .40 |
| ☐ 22 Gary Larsen | 2.00 | .80 | .20 |
| ☐ 23 Bob Lee | 2.00 | .80 | .20 |
| ☐ 24 Jim Lindsey | 1.50 | .60 | .15 |
| ☐ 25 Jim Marshall | 6.00 | 2.40 | .60 |
| ☐ 26 Bus Mertes CO | 1.50 | .60 | .15 |
| ☐ 27 John Michels CO | 1.50 | .60 | .15 |
| ☐ 28 Jocko Nelson CO | 1.50 | .60 | .15 |
| ☐ 29 Dave Osborn | 2.50 | 1.00 | .25 |
| ☐ 30 Alan Page | 6.00 | 2.40 | .60 |
| ☐ 31 Jack Patera CO | 2.50 | 1.00 | .25 |
| ☐ 32 Jerry Patton | 1.50 | .60 | .15 |
| ☐ 33 Pete Perreault | 1.50 | .60 | .15 |
| ☐ 34 Oscar Reed | 1.50 | .60 | .15 |
| ☐ 35 Ed Sharockman | 2.00 | .80 | .20 |
| ☐ 36 Norm Snead | 4.00 | 1.60 | .40 |
| ☐ 37 Milt Sunde | 2.00 | .80 | .20 |
| ☐ 38 Mick Tingelhoff | 3.00 | 1.20 | .30 |
| ☐ 39 Stu Voigt | 3.00 | 1.20 | .30 |
| ☐ 40 John Ward | 1.50 | .60 | .15 |
| ☐ 41 Lonnie Warwick | 2.00 | .80 | .20 |
| ☐ 42 Gene Washington | 3.00 | 1.20 | .30 |
| ☐ 43 Charlie West | 2.00 | .80 | .20 |
| ☐ 44 Ed White | 2.50 | 1.00 | .25 |
| ☐ 45 Carl Winfrey | 1.50 | .60 | .15 |
| ☐ 46 Roy Winston | 3.00 | 1.20 | .30 |
| ☐ 47 Jeff Wright | 2.00 | .80 | .20 |
| ☐ 48 Nate Wright | 2.00 | .80 | .20 |
| ☐ 49 Ron Yary | 3.00 | 1.20 | .30 |

## 1971 Vikings Postcards

This 18-card set measures approximately 5" by 7 7/16" and features posed color close-up photos on the fronts. These cards were issued after the season had begun and may have been sold at the stadium. The player's name, position, and team name appear in a white bottom border. As with a postcard, the horizontal backs are divided into two sections by a thin black stripe. Brief biographical information is given

mug shots; the backs are white and have sparse bio and stats. One disc was included in each specially-marked Taystee product, distributed only in the Minnesota area. The discs are numbered on the backs.

at the upper left corner, while a box for the stamp is printed at the upper right corner. The cards are unnumbered and checklisted below in alphabetical order.

|  | NRMT | VG-E | GOOD |
|---|---|---|---|
| COMPLETE SET (18) | 35.00 | 14.00 | 3.50 |
| COMMON CARD (1-18) | 1.50 | .60 | .15 |
| ☐ 1 Grady Alderman | 2.00 | .80 | .20 |
| ☐ 2 Neill Armstrong CO | 2.00 | .80 | .20 |
| ☐ 3 John Beasley | 1.50 | .60 | .15 |
| ☐ 4 Bud Grant CO | 6.00 | 2.40 | .60 |
| ☐ 5 Wally Hilgenberg | 2.50 | 1.00 | .25 |
| ☐ 6 Noel Jenke | 1.50 | .60 | .15 |
| ☐ 7 Paul Krause | 4.00 | 1.60 | .40 |
| ☐ 8 Gary Larsen | 2.00 | .80 | .20 |
| ☐ 9 Dave Osborn | 2.50 | 1.00 | .25 |
| ☐ 10 Alan Page | 6.00 | 2.40 | .60 |
| ☐ 11 Jerry Patton | 1.50 | .60 | .15 |
| ☐ 12 Doug Sutherland | 2.00 | .80 | .20 |
| ☐ 13 Mick Tingelhoff | 3.00 | 1.20 | .30 |
| ☐ 14 Lonnie Warwick | 2.00 | .80 | .20 |
| ☐ 15 Charlie West | 2.00 | .80 | .20 |
| ☐ 16 Jeff Wright | 2.00 | .80 | .20 |
| ☐ 17 Nate Wright | 2.00 | .80 | .20 |
| ☐ 18 Godfrey Zaunbrecher | 1.50 | .60 | .15 |

|  | MINT | EXC | G-VG |
|---|---|---|---|
| COMPLETE SET (12) | 6.00 | 2.40 | .60 |
| COMMON PLAYER (1-12) | .50 | .20 | .05 |
| ☐ 1 Anthony Carter | 1.25 | .50 | .12 |
| ☐ 2 Chris Doleman | .90 | .36 | .09 |
| ☐ 3 Joey Browner | .90 | .36 | .09 |
| ☐ 4 Steve Jordan | .90 | .36 | .09 |
| ☐ 5 Scott Studwell | .60 | .24 | .06 |
| ☐ 6 Wade Wilson | .90 | .36 | .09 |
| ☐ 7 Kirk Lowdermilk | .50 | .20 | .05 |
| ☐ 8 Tommy Kramer | .90 | .36 | .09 |
| ☐ 9 Keith Millard | .90 | .36 | .09 |
| ☐ 10 Rick Fenney | .60 | .24 | .06 |
| ☐ 11 Gary Zimmerman | .50 | .20 | .05 |
| ☐ 12 Darrin Nelson | .60 | .24 | .06 |

## 1978 Vikings Country Kitchen

This seven-card set was sponsored by Country Kitchen Restaurants and measures approximately 5" by 7". The front features a black and white head shot of the player. The card backs have biographical and statistical information. The cards are unnumbered and hence are listed alphabetically below.

|  | NRMT | VG-E | GOOD |
|---|---|---|---|
| COMPLETE SET (7) | 30.00 | 12.00 | 3.00 |
| COMMON PLAYER (1-7) | 3.50 | 1.40 | .35 |
| ☐ 1 Bobby Bryant | 3.50 | 1.40 | .35 |
| ☐ 2 Tommy Kramer | 6.00 | 2.40 | .60 |
| ☐ 3 Paul Krause | 6.00 | 2.40 | .60 |
| ☐ 4 Ahmad Rashad | 8.00 | 3.25 | .80 |
| ☐ 5 Jeff Siemon | 5.00 | 2.00 | .50 |
| ☐ 6 Mick Tingelhoff | 5.00 | 2.00 | .50 |
| ☐ 7 Sammie White | 5.00 | 2.00 | .50 |

## 1989 Vikings Taystee Discs

The 1989 Taystee Minnesota Vikings set contains 12 white-bordered, approximately 2 3/4" diameter discs. The fronts have helmetless color

## 1988 Wagon Wheel

This attractive set of eight large cards was issued in the United Kingdom by Burtons as an insert in a box of Chocolate Biscuits (cookies). Players in the set are recognizable but not explicitly identified on the card. The theme of the set is the explanation of American football to the British. The cards measure approximately 6 5/16" by 4 5/16" and are unnumbered. The card backs provide information on related mail order products available until May 31, 1988.

|  | NRMT | VG-E | GOOD |
|---|---|---|---|
| COMPLETE SET (8) | 60.00 | 24.00 | 6.00 |
| COMMON PLAYER (1-8) | 6.00 | 2.40 | .60 |
| ☐ 1 Defensive Back<br>(Todd Bowles covering Mark Bavaro) | 6.00 | 2.40 | .60 |
| ☐ 2 Defensive Lineman<br>(Ed Too Tall Jones and Neil Lomax) | 9.00 | 3.75 | .90 |
| ☐ 3 Kicker<br>(Kevin Butler) | 6.00 | 2.40 | .60 |
| ☐ 4 Linebacker<br>(Bob Brudzinski) | 6.00 | 2.40 | .60 |
| ☐ 5 Offensive Lineman<br>(Keith Van Horne leading Walter Payton) | 12.00 | 5.00 | 1.20 |
| ☐ 6 Quarterback<br>(John Elway) | 20.00 | 8.00 | 2.00 |
| ☐ 7 Receiver<br>(Steve Largent between Vann McElroy and Mike Haynes) | 9.00 | 3.75 | .90 |
| ☐ 8 Running Back<br>(Rodney Carter of the Steelers) | 6.00 | 2.40 | .60 |

# 1964 Wheaties Stamps

This set of 74 stamps was issued perforated within a 48-page album. There were 70 players and four team logo stamps bound into the album as six pages of 12 stamps each plus two stamps attached to the inside front cover. In fact, they are typically found this way, still bound into the album. The stamps measure approximately 2 1/2" by 2 3/4" and are unnumbered. The album itself measures approximately 8 1/8" by 11" and is entitled "Pro Bowl Football Player Stamp Album". The stamp list below has been alphabetized for convenience. Each player stamp has a facsimile autograph on the front. Note that there are no spaces in the album for Joe Schmidt, Y.A.Tittle, or the four team emblem stamps.

| | NRMT | VG-E | GOOD |
|---|---|---|---|
| COMPLETE SET (74) | 200.00 | 80.00 | 20.00 |
| COMMON PLAYER (1-74) | 2.00 | .80 | .20 |
| ☐ 1 Herb Adderley — Green Bay Packers | 5.00 | 2.00 | .50 |
| ☐ 2 Grady Alderman — Minnesota Vikings | 2.00 | .80 | .20 |
| ☐ 3 Doug Atkins — Chicago Bears | 4.00 | 1.60 | .40 |
| ☐ 4 Sam Baker — Philadelphia Eagles (In Cowboys' uniform) | 2.00 | .80 | .20 |
| ☐ 5 Erich Barnes — New York Giants (In Bears' jersey) | 2.00 | .80 | .20 |
| ☐ 6 Terry Barr — Detroit Lions | 2.00 | .80 | .20 |
| ☐ 7 Dick Bass — Los Angeles Rams | 2.00 | .80 | .20 |
| ☐ 8 Maxie Baughan — Philadelphia Eagles | 3.00 | 1.20 | .30 |
| ☐ 9 Raymond Berry — Baltimore Colts | 6.00 | 2.40 | .60 |
| ☐ 10 Charley Bradshaw — Pittsburgh Steelers (In Rams' jersey) | 2.00 | .80 | .20 |
| ☐ 11 Jim Brown — Cleveland Browns | 30.00 | 12.00 | 3.00 |
| ☐ 12 Roger Brown — Detroit Lions | 2.00 | .80 | .20 |
| ☐ 13 Timmy Brown — Philadelphia Eagles | 3.00 | 1.20 | .30 |
| ☐ 14 Gail Cogdill — Detroit Lions | 2.00 | .80 | .20 |
| ☐ 15 Tommy Davis — San Francisco 49ers | 2.00 | .80 | .20 |
| ☐ 16 Willie Davis — Green Bay Packers | 5.00 | 2.00 | .50 |
| ☐ 17 Bob DeMarco — St. Louis Cardinals | 2.00 | .80 | .20 |
| ☐ 18 Darrell Dess — New York Giants | 2.00 | .80 | .20 |
| ☐ 19 Buddy Dial — Dallas Cowboys (In Steelers' jersey) | 3.00 | 1.20 | .30 |
| ☐ 20 Mike Ditka — Chicago Bears | 15.00 | 6.00 | 1.50 |
| ☐ 21 Galen Fiss — Cleveland Browns | 2.00 | .80 | .20 |
| ☐ 22 Lee Folkins — Dallas Cowboys | 2.00 | .80 | .20 |
| ☐ 23 Joe Fortunato — Chicago Bears | 2.00 | .80 | .20 |
| ☐ 24 Bill Glass — Cleveland Browns | 3.00 | 1.20 | .30 |
| ☐ 25 John Gordy — Detroit Lions | 2.00 | .80 | .20 |
| ☐ 26 Ken Gray — St. Louis Cardinals | 2.00 | .80 | .20 |
| ☐ 27 Forrest Gregg — Green Bay Packers | 4.00 | 1.60 | .40 |
| ☐ 28 Rip Hawkins — Minnesota Vikings | 2.00 | .80 | .20 |
| ☐ 29 Charlie Johnson — St. Louis Cardinals | 3.00 | 1.20 | .30 |
| ☐ 30 John Henry Johnson — Pittsburgh Steelers | 4.00 | 1.60 | .40 |
| ☐ 31 Henry Jordan — Green Bay Packers | 3.00 | 1.20 | .30 |
| ☐ 32 Jim Katcavage — New York Giants | 2.00 | .80 | .20 |
| ☐ 33 Jerry Kramer — Green Bay Packers | 4.00 | 1.60 | .40 |
| ☐ 34 Joe Krupa — Pittsburgh Steelers | 2.00 | .80 | .20 |
| ☐ 35 John LoVetere — New York Giants (In Rams' jersey) | 2.00 | .80 | .20 |
| ☐ 36 Dick Lynch — New York Giants | 2.00 | .80 | .20 |
| ☐ 37 Gino Marchetti — Baltimore Colts | 5.00 | 2.00 | .50 |
| ☐ 38 Joe Marconi — Chicago Bears | 2.00 | .80 | .20 |
| ☐ 39 Tommy Mason — Minnesota Vikings | 3.00 | 1.20 | .30 |
| ☐ 40 Dale Meinert — St. Louis Cardinals | 2.00 | .80 | .20 |
| ☐ 41 Lou Michaels — Pittsburgh Steelers | 2.00 | .80 | .20 |
| ☐ 42 Minnesota Vikings Emblem | 3.00 | 1.20 | .30 |
| ☐ 43 Bobby Mitchell — Washington Redskins | 5.00 | 2.00 | .50 |
| ☐ 44 John Morrow — Cleveland Browns | 2.00 | .80 | .20 |
| ☐ 45 New York Giants Emblem | 3.00 | 1.20 | .30 |
| ☐ 46 Merlin Olsen — Los Angeles Rams | 8.00 | 3.25 | .80 |
| ☐ 47 Jack Pardee — Los Angeles Rams | 4.00 | 1.60 | .40 |
| ☐ 48 Jim Parker — Baltimore Colts | 4.00 | 1.60 | .40 |
| ☐ 49 Bernie Parrish — Cleveland Browns | 2.00 | .80 | .20 |
| ☐ 50 Don Perkins — Dallas Cowboys | 3.00 | 1.20 | .30 |
| ☐ 51 Richie Petitbon — Chicago Bears | 3.00 | 1.20 | .30 |
| ☐ 52 Vince Promuto — Washington Redskins | 2.00 | .80 | .20 |
| ☐ 53 Myron Pottios — Pittsburgh Steelers | 2.00 | .80 | .20 |
| ☐ 54 Mike Pyle — Chicago Bears | 2.00 | .80 | .20 |
| ☐ 55 Pete Retzlaff — Philadelphia Eagles | 3.00 | 1.20 | .30 |
| ☐ 56 Jim Ringo — Philadelphia Eagles (In Packers' jersey) | 4.00 | 1.60 | .40 |
| ☐ 57 Joe Rutgens — Washington Redskins | 2.00 | .80 | .20 |
| ☐ 58 St. Louis Cardinals Emblem | 3.00 | 1.20 | .30 |
| ☐ 59 San Francisco 49ers Emblem | 3.00 | 1.20 | .30 |
| ☐ 60 Dick Schafrath — Cleveland Browns | 2.00 | .80 | .20 |
| ☐ 61 Joe Schmidt — Detroit Lions | 5.00 | 2.00 | .50 |
| ☐ 62 Del Shofner — New York Giants | 3.00 | 1.20 | .30 |
| ☐ 63 Norm Snead — Philadelphia Eagles | 3.00 | 1.20 | .30 |
| ☐ 64 Bart Starr — Green Bay Packers | 12.00 | 5.00 | 1.20 |
| ☐ 65 Jim Taylor — Green Bay Packers | 6.00 | 2.40 | .60 |
| ☐ 66 Roosevelt Taylor — Chicago Bears | 2.00 | .80 | .20 |
| ☐ 67 Clendon Thomas — Pittsburgh Steelers (In Rams' jersey) | 2.00 | .80 | .20 |
| ☐ 68 Y.A. Tittle — New York Giants (In 49ers' jersey) | 10.00 | 4.00 | 1.00 |
| ☐ 69 John Unitas — Baltimore Colts | 15.00 | 6.00 | 1.50 |
| ☐ 70 Bill Wade — Chicago Bears | 3.00 | 1.20 | .30 |
| ☐ 71 Wayne Walker — Detroit Lions | 2.00 | .80 | .20 |
| ☐ 72 Jesse Whittenton — Green Bay Packers | 2.00 | .80 | .20 |
| ☐ 73 Larry Wilson — St. Louis Cardinals | 5.00 | 2.00 | .50 |
| ☐ 74 Abe Woodson — San Francisco 49ers | 2.00 | .80 | .20 |
| ☐ xx Stamp Album | 20.00 | 8.00 | 2.00 |

## 1987 Wheaties

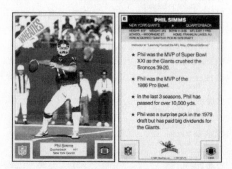

This 26-card set was distributed one per box in the specially marked packages of Wheaties cereal. Each "card" (actually they are more like mini-posters) came folded and inside a thin cellophane wrap. These 5" by 7" color photos are attractive. Individual player information and statistics are printed in black and white on the card backs. The cards are numbered on the back in the upper left corner. This project was organized by Mike Schechter Associates and produced by Starline Inc. in conjunction with the NFL Players Association. Bernie Kosar is very difficult to find and is not even listed as being in the set on the checklists Wheaties provides on the cereal box. Kosar may have been pulled from the set since, apparently, Ohio Edison held Bernie's advertising rights with some exclusivity.

|  | MINT | EXC | G-VG |
|---|---|---|---|
| COMPLETE SET (26) | 100.00 | 40.00 | 10.00 |
| COMMON PLAYER (1-26) | 2.00 | .80 | .20 |
| ☐ 1 Tony Dorsett | 4.00 | 1.60 | .40 |
| Dallas Cowboys |  |  |  |
| ☐ 2 Herschel Walker | 5.00 | 2.00 | .50 |
| Dallas Cowboys |  |  |  |
| ☐ 3 Marcus Allen | 5.00 | 2.00 | .50 |
| Los Angeles Raiders |  |  |  |
| ☐ 4 Eric Dickerson | 6.00 | 2.40 | .60 |
| Los Angeles Rams |  |  |  |
| ☐ 5 Walter Payton | 10.00 | 4.00 | 1.00 |
| Chicago Bears |  |  |  |
| ☐ 6 Phil Simms | 4.00 | 1.60 | .40 |
| New York Giants |  |  |  |
| ☐ 7 Tommy Kramer | 2.00 | .80 | .20 |
| Minnesota Vikings |  |  |  |
| ☐ 8 Joe Morris | 2.50 | 1.00 | .25 |
| New York Giants |  |  |  |
| ☐ 9 Roger Craig | 4.00 | 1.60 | .40 |
| San Francisco 49ers |  |  |  |
| ☐ 10 Curt Warner | 2.50 | 1.00 | .25 |
| Seattle Seahawks |  |  |  |
| ☐ 11 Andre Tippett | 2.50 | 1.00 | .25 |
| New England Patriots |  |  |  |
| ☐ 12 Joe Montana | 15.00 | 6.00 | 1.50 |
| San Francisco 49ers |  |  |  |
| ☐ 13 Jim McMahon | 3.00 | 1.20 | .30 |
| Chicago Bears |  |  |  |
| ☐ 14 Bernie Kosar SP | 25.00 | 10.00 | 2.50 |
| Cleveland Browns |  |  |  |
| ☐ 15 Jay Schroeder | 2.50 | 1.00 | .25 |
| Washington Redskins |  |  |  |
| ☐ 16 Al Toon | 2.00 | .80 | .20 |
| New York Jets |  |  |  |
| ☐ 17 Mark Gastineau | 2.00 | .80 | .20 |
| New York Jets |  |  |  |
| ☐ 18 Kenny Easley | 2.00 | .80 | .20 |
| Seattle Seahawks |  |  |  |
| ☐ 19 Howie Long | 2.50 | 1.00 | .25 |
| Los Angeles Raiders |  |  |  |
| ☐ 20 Dan Marino | 15.00 | 6.00 | 1.50 |
| Miami Dolphins |  |  |  |
| ☐ 21 Karl Mecklenburg | 2.50 | 1.00 | .25 |
| Denver Broncos |  |  |  |
| ☐ 22 John Elway | 10.00 | 4.00 | 1.00 |
| Denver Broncos |  |  |  |
| ☐ 23 Boomer Esiason | 5.00 | 2.00 | .50 |
| Cincinnati Bengals |  |  |  |
| ☐ 24 Dan Fouts | 4.00 | 1.60 | .40 |
| San Diego Chargers |  |  |  |
| ☐ 25 Jim Kelly | 9.00 | 3.75 | .90 |
| Buffalo Bills |  |  |  |
| ☐ 26 Louis Lipps | 2.50 | 1.00 | .25 |
| Pittsburgh Steelers |  |  |  |

## 1991 Wild Card National Promos

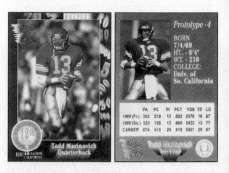

These cards were given away at the 1991 12th Annual Sports Collectors Convention in Anaheim, California. The fronts of these standard-size (2 1/2" by 3 1/2") cards have high gloss color player photos on a black card face with different colored numbers above and to the right of the picture. On a background that changes from fuchsia to purple as one moves down the card, the backs have a color player photo, biography, and statistics. Striped versions of these cards with a football-shaped hologram in the upper left corner were also issued. The cards are numbered in the upper right corner as "Prototype-2" and following.

|  | MINT | EXC | G-VG |
|---|---|---|---|
| COMPLETE SET (3) | 5.00 | 2.00 | .50 |
| COMMON PLAYER (P2-P4) | 2.00 | .80 | .20 |
| ☐ P2 Dan McGwire | 2.00 | .80 | .20 |
| San Diego State |  |  |  |
| ☐ P3 Randal Hill | 2.00 | .80 | .20 |
| Miami |  |  |  |
| ☐ P4 Todd Marinovich | 2.00 | .80 | .20 |
| USC |  |  |  |

## 1991 Wild Card Draft

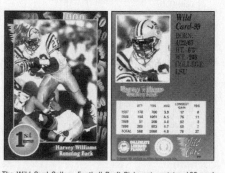

The Wild Card College Football Draft Picks set contains 160 cards measuring the standard size (2 1/2" by 3 1/2"). Reportedly, production quantities were limited to 20,000 numbered cases (or 630,000 sets). The front design features glossy color action player photos, on a black card face with an orange frame around the picture and different color numbers appearing in the top and right borders. The words "1st edition" in a circular emblem overlay the lower left corner of the picture. The backs have different shades of purple and a color headshot, biography, and complete college statistics (1987-90). One out of every 100 cards is "wild," with a numbered stripe to indicate how many cards it can be redeemed for. There are 5, 10, 20, 50, 100, and 1,000 denominations, with the highest numbers the scarcest. Whatever the number, the card can be redeemed for that number of regular cards of the same player, after paying a redemption fee of 4.95 per order. The secondary market value of the striped cards has not proven to be as strong as Wild Card may have anticipated. There have been numerous examples available at card shows and stores of higher stripe cards being offered at 50 percent of their theoretical value based on multiplying the stripe number times the single card value. The set included three surprise wild cards (1, 15, and 22). If these cards were redeemed before April 30, 1992, the collector received three cards to complete the set and a bonus set of six 1992 collegiate football prototype cards. Collectors who redeemed their cards after April 30 did not receive the prototype cards. Also, Kenny Anderson and Larry Johnson promo cards, numbers P2 and P1 respectively, were randomly inserted, and they may be redeemed after January 2, 1992 for then-unknown player cards. The cards are numbered on the back. The key cards in this set are Bryan Cox, Craig Erickson, Brett Favre, Alvin Harper, Randal Hill, Rocket Ismail (issued as a surprise card), Herman Moore, Mike Pritchard, Leonard Russell, and Ricky Watters.

| | MINT | EXC | G-VG |
|---|---|---|---|
| COMPLETE SET (166) | 8.00 | 3.25 | .80 |
| COMPLETE SET (160) | 6.00 | 2.40 | .60 |
| COMMON PLAYER (1-160) | .04 | .02 | .00 |

| | MINT | EXC | G-VG |
|---|---|---|---|
| ☐ 1A Wild Card 1 | .20 | .08 | .02 |
| ☐ 1B Todd Lyght | .25 | .10 | .02 |
| Notre Dame | | | |
| ☐ 2 Kelvin Pritchett | .15 | .06 | .01 |
| Mississippi | | | |
| ☐ 3 Robert Young | .10 | .04 | .01 |
| Mississippi State | | | |
| ☐ 4 Reggie Johnson | .07 | .03 | .01 |
| Arizona | | | |
| ☐ 5 Eric Turner | .20 | .08 | .02 |
| UCLA | | | |
| ☐ 6 Pat Tyrance | .07 | .03 | .01 |
| Nebraska | | | |
| ☐ 7 Curvin Richards | .07 | .03 | .01 |
| Pittsburgh | | | |
| ☐ 8 Calvin Stephens | .07 | .03 | .01 |
| South Carolina | | | |
| ☐ 9 Corey Miller | .15 | .06 | .01 |
| South Carolina | | | |
| ☐ 10 Michael Jackson | .75 | .30 | .07 |
| Southern Mississippi | | | |
| ☐ 11 Simmie Carter | .04 | .02 | .00 |
| Southern Mississippi | | | |
| ☐ 12 Roland Smith | .07 | .03 | .01 |
| Miami (Florida) | | | |
| ☐ 13 Pat O'Hara | .07 | .03 | .01 |
| Southern California | | | |
| ☐ 14 Scott Conover | .10 | .04 | .01 |
| Purdue | | | |
| ☐ 15A Wild Card 2 | .25 | .10 | .02 |
| ☐ 15B Russell Maryland | .40 | .16 | .04 |
| Miami | | | |
| ☐ 16 Greg Amsler | .04 | .02 | .00 |
| Tennessee | | | |
| ☐ 17 Moe Gardner | .15 | .06 | .01 |
| Illinois | | | |
| ☐ 18 Howard Griffith | .10 | .04 | .01 |
| Illinois | | | |
| ☐ 19 David Daniels | .07 | .03 | .01 |
| Penn State | | | |
| ☐ 20 Henry Jones | .30 | .12 | .03 |
| Illinois | | | |
| ☐ 21 Don Davey | .10 | .04 | .01 |
| Wisconsin | | | |
| ☐ 22A Wild Card 3 | 1.25 | .50 | .12 |
| ☐ 22B Raghib(Rocket) Ismail | 1.75 | .70 | .17 |
| Notre Dame | | | |
| ☐ 23 Richie Andrews | .04 | .02 | .00 |
| Florida State | | | |
| ☐ 24 Shawn Moore | .25 | .10 | .02 |
| Virginia | | | |
| ☐ 25 Anthony Moss | .04 | .02 | .00 |
| Florida State | | | |
| ☐ 26 Vince Moore | .04 | .02 | .00 |
| Tennessee | | | |
| ☐ 27 Leroy Thompson | .30 | .12 | .03 |
| Penn State | | | |
| ☐ 28 Darrick Brownlow | .07 | .03 | .01 |
| Illinois | | | |
| ☐ 29 Mel Agee | .10 | .04 | .01 |
| Illinois | | | |
| ☐ 30 Darryll Lewis UER | .10 | .04 | .01 |
| Arizona | | | |
| (Misspelled Darryl | | | |
| on both sides) | | | |
| ☐ 31 Hyland Hickson | .04 | .02 | .00 |
| Michigan State | | | |
| ☐ 32 Leonard Russell | .75 | .30 | .07 |
| Arizona State | | | |
| ☐ 33 Floyd Fields | .10 | .04 | .01 |
| Arizona State | | | |
| ☐ 34 Esera Tuaolo | .10 | .04 | .01 |
| Oregon State | | | |
| ☐ 35 Todd Marinovich | .10 | .04 | .01 |
| USC | | | |
| ☐ 36 Gary Wellman | .25 | .10 | .02 |
| USC | | | |
| ☐ 37 Ricky Ervins | .20 | .08 | .02 |
| USC | | | |
| ☐ 38 Pat Harlow | .10 | .04 | .01 |
| USC | | | |
| ☐ 39 Mo Lewis | .20 | .08 | .02 |
| Georgia | | | |
| ☐ 40 John Kasay | .25 | .10 | .02 |

| | MINT | EXC | G-VG |
|---|---|---|---|
| Georgia | | | |
| ☐ 41 Phil Hansen | .20 | .08 | .02 |
| North Dakota | | | |
| ☐ 42 Kevin Donnalley | .10 | .04 | .01 |
| North Carolina | | | |
| ☐ 43 Dexter Davis | .10 | .04 | .01 |
| Clemson | | | |
| ☐ 44 Vance Hammond | .04 | .02 | .00 |
| Clemson | | | |
| ☐ 45 Chris Gardocki | .12 | .05 | .01 |
| Clemson | | | |
| ☐ 46 Bruce Pickens | .10 | .04 | .01 |
| Nebraska | | | |
| ☐ 47 Godfrey Myles | .20 | .08 | .02 |
| Florida | | | |
| ☐ 48 Ernie Mills | .20 | .08 | .02 |
| Florida | | | |
| ☐ 49 Derek Russell | .25 | .10 | .02 |
| Arkansas | | | |
| ☐ 50 Chris Zorich | .35 | .14 | .03 |
| Notre Dame | | | |
| ☐ 51 Alfred Williams | .15 | .06 | .01 |
| Colorado | | | |
| ☐ 52 Jon Vaughn | .25 | .10 | .02 |
| Michigan | | | |
| ☐ 53 Adrian Cooper | .15 | .06 | .01 |
| Oklahoma | | | |
| ☐ 54 Eric Bieniemy | .20 | .08 | .02 |
| Colorado | | | |
| ☐ 55 Robert Bailey | .04 | .02 | .00 |
| Miami | | | |
| ☐ 56 Ricky Watters | 1.25 | .50 | .12 |
| Notre Dame | | | |
| ☐ 57 Mark Vander Poel | .07 | .03 | .01 |
| Colorado | | | |
| ☐ 58 James Joseph | .25 | .10 | .02 |
| Auburn | | | |
| ☐ 59 Darren Lewis | .10 | .04 | .01 |
| Texas A and M | | | |
| ☐ 60 Wesley Carroll | .10 | .04 | .01 |
| Miami | | | |
| ☐ 61 Dave Key | .04 | .02 | .00 |
| Michigan | | | |
| ☐ 62 Mike Pritchard | .75 | .30 | .07 |
| Colorado | | | |
| ☐ 63 Craig Erickson | .50 | .20 | .05 |
| Miami | | | |
| ☐ 64 Browning Nagle | .12 | .05 | .01 |
| Louisville | | | |
| ☐ 65 Mike Dumas | .10 | .04 | .01 |
| Indiana | | | |
| ☐ 66 Andre Jones | .04 | .02 | .00 |
| Notre Dame | | | |
| ☐ 67 Herman Moore | 1.00 | .40 | .10 |
| Virginia | | | |
| ☐ 68 Greg Lewis | .10 | .04 | .01 |
| Washington | | | |
| ☐ 69 James Goode | .04 | .02 | .00 |
| Oklahoma | | | |
| ☐ 70 Stan Thomas | .10 | .04 | .01 |
| Texas | | | |
| ☐ 71 Jerome Henderson | .10 | .04 | .01 |
| Clemson | | | |
| ☐ 72 Doug Thomas | .15 | .06 | .01 |
| Clemson | | | |
| ☐ 73 Tony Covington | .07 | .03 | .01 |
| Virginia | | | |
| ☐ 74 Charles Mincy | .15 | .06 | .01 |
| Washington | | | |
| ☐ 75 Kanavis McGhee | .10 | .04 | .01 |
| Colorado | | | |
| ☐ 76 Tom Backes | .04 | .02 | .00 |
| Oklahoma | | | |
| ☐ 77 Fernandus Vinson | .10 | .04 | .01 |
| North Carolina State | | | |
| ☐ 78 Marcus Robertson | .20 | .08 | .02 |
| Iowa State | | | |
| ☐ 79 Eric Harmon | .04 | .02 | .00 |
| Clemson | | | |
| ☐ 80 Rob Selby | .10 | .04 | .01 |
| Auburn | | | |
| ☐ 81 Ed Kelly | .10 | .04 | .01 |
| Auburn | | | |
| ☐ 82 William Thomas | .12 | .05 | .01 |
| Texas A and M | | | |
| ☐ 83 Mike Jones | .12 | .05 | .01 |
| North Carolina State | | | |
| ☐ 84 Paul Justin | .07 | .03 | .01 |
| Arizona State | | | |
| ☐ 85 Robert Wilson | .07 | .03 | .01 |
| Texas A and M | | | |
| ☐ 86 Jesse Campbell | .10 | .04 | .01 |
| North Carolina State | | | |
| ☐ 87 Hayward Haynes | .04 | .02 | .00 |
| Florida State | | | |
| ☐ 88 Mike Croel | .25 | .10 | .02 |
| Nebraska | | | |
| ☐ 89 Jeff Graham | .30 | .12 | .03 |

| | | | | |
|---|---|---|---|---|
| | Ohio State | | | |
| ☐ 90 | Vinnie Clark | .12 | .05 | .01 |
| | Ohio State | | | |
| ☐ 91 | Keith Cash | .25 | .10 | .02 |
| | Texas | | | |
| ☐ 92 | Tim Ryan | .12 | .05 | .01 |
| | Notre Dame | | | |
| ☐ 93 | Jarrod Bunch | .25 | .10 | .02 |
| | Michigan | | | |
| ☐ 94 | Stanley Richard | .25 | .10 | .02 |
| | Texas | | | |
| ☐ 95 | Alvin Harper | .90 | .36 | .09 |
| | Tennessee | | | |
| ☐ 96 | Bob Dahl | .10 | .04 | .01 |
| | Notre Dame | | | |
| ☐ 97 | Mark Gunn | .10 | .04 | .01 |
| | Pittsburgh | | | |
| ☐ 98 | Frank Blevins | .04 | .02 | .00 |
| | Oklahoma | | | |
| ☐ 99 | Harvey Williams | .25 | .10 | .02 |
| | LSU | | | |
| ☐ 100 | Dixon Edwards | .15 | .06 | .01 |
| | Michigan State | | | |
| ☐ 101 | Blake Miller | .04 | .02 | .00 |
| | LSU | | | |
| ☐ 102 | Bobby Wilson | .10 | .04 | .01 |
| | Michigan State | | | |
| ☐ 103 | Chuck Webb | .07 | .03 | .01 |
| | Tennessee | | | |
| ☐ 104 | Randal Hill | .50 | .20 | .05 |
| | Miami | | | |
| ☐ 105 | Shane Curry | .04 | .02 | .00 |
| | Miami | | | |
| ☐ 106 | Barry Sanders FLB | .25 | .10 | .02 |
| | Oklahoma State | | | |
| ☐ 107 | Richard Fain | .07 | .03 | .01 |
| | Florida | | | |
| ☐ 108 | Joe Garten | .07 | .03 | .01 |
| | Colorado | | | |
| ☐ 109 | Dean Dingman | .04 | .02 | .00 |
| | Michigan | | | |
| ☐ 110 | Mark Tucker | .04 | .02 | .00 |
| | USC | | | |
| ☐ 111 | Dan McGwire UER | .15 | .06 | .01 |
| | San Diego State | | | |
| | (TD stats say 29, | | | |
| | should be 27) | | | |
| ☐ 112 | Paul Glonek | .04 | .02 | .00 |
| | Arizona | | | |
| ☐ 113 | Tom Dohring | .04 | .02 | .00 |
| | Michigan | | | |
| ☐ 114 | Joe Sims | .10 | .04 | .01 |
| | Nebraska | | | |
| ☐ 115 | Bryan Cox | .40 | .16 | .04 |
| | Western Illinois | | | |
| ☐ 116 | Bobby Olive | .04 | .02 | .00 |
| | Ohio State | | | |
| ☐ 117 | Blaise Bryant | .07 | .03 | .01 |
| | Iowa State | | | |
| ☐ 118 | Charles Johnson | .10 | .04 | .01 |
| | Colorado | | | |
| ☐ 119 | Brett Favre | 1.75 | .70 | .17 |
| | Southern Mississippi | | | |
| ☐ 120 | Luis Cristobal | .04 | .02 | .00 |
| | Miami | | | |
| ☐ 121 | Don Gibson | .04 | .02 | .00 |
| | USC | | | |
| ☐ 122 | Scott Ross | .04 | .02 | .00 |
| | USC | | | |
| ☐ 123 | Huey Richardson | .07 | .03 | .01 |
| | Florida | | | |
| ☐ 124 | Chris Smith | .07 | .03 | .01 |
| | Brigham Young | | | |
| ☐ 125 | Duane Young | .10 | .04 | .01 |
| | Michigan State | | | |
| ☐ 126 | Eric Swann | .30 | .12 | .03 |
| | (No College) | | | |
| ☐ 127 | Jeff Fite | .04 | .02 | .00 |
| | Memphis State | | | |
| ☐ 128 | Eugene Williams | .10 | .04 | .01 |
| | Iowa State | | | |
| ☐ 129 | Harlan Davis | .04 | .02 | .00 |
| | Tennessee | | | |
| ☐ 130 | James Bradley | .04 | .02 | .00 |
| | Michigan State | | | |
| ☐ 131 | Rob Carpenter | .15 | .06 | .01 |
| | Syracuse | | | |
| ☐ 132 | Dennis Ransom | .04 | .02 | .00 |
| | Texas A and M | | | |
| ☐ 133 | Mike Arthur | .10 | .04 | .01 |
| | Texas A and M | | | |
| ☐ 134 | Chuck Weatherspoon | .07 | .03 | .01 |
| | Houston | | | |
| ☐ 135 | Darrell Malone | .12 | .05 | .01 |
| | Jacksonville State | | | |
| ☐ 136 | George Thornton | .07 | .03 | .01 |
| | Alabama | | | |
| ☐ 137 | Lamar McGriggs | .20 | .08 | .02 |

| | | | | |
|---|---|---|---|---|
| | Western Illinois | | | |
| ☐ 138 | Alex Johnson | .04 | .02 | .00 |
| | Miami | | | |
| ☐ 139 | Eric Moten | .10 | .04 | .01 |
| | Michigan State | | | |
| ☐ 140 | Joe Valerio | .12 | .05 | .01 |
| | Pennsylvania | | | |
| ☐ 141 | Jake Reed | .12 | .05 | .01 |
| | Grambling | | | |
| ☐ 142 | Ernie Thompson | .10 | .04 | .01 |
| | Indiana | | | |
| ☐ 143 | Roland Poles | .04 | .02 | .00 |
| | Tennessee | | | |
| ☐ 144 | Randy Bethel | .04 | .02 | .00 |
| | Miami (Florida) | | | |
| ☐ 145 | Terry Bagsby | .04 | .02 | .00 |
| | East Texas State | | | |
| ☐ 146 | Tim James | .04 | .02 | .00 |
| | Colorado | | | |
| ☐ 147 | Kenny Walker | .07 | .03 | .01 |
| | Nebraska | | | |
| ☐ 148 | Nolan Harrison | .12 | .05 | .01 |
| | Indiana | | | |
| ☐ 149 | Keith Traylor | .07 | .03 | .01 |
| | Central Oklahoma | | | |
| ☐ 150 | Nick Subis | .04 | .02 | .00 |
| | San Diego State | | | |
| ☐ 151 | Scott Zolak | .15 | .06 | .01 |
| | Maryland | | | |
| ☐ 152 | Pio Sagapolutele | .10 | .04 | .01 |
| | San Diego State | | | |
| ☐ 153 | James Jones | .10 | .04 | .01 |
| | Northern Iowa | | | |
| ☐ 154 | Mike Sullivan | .10 | .04 | .01 |
| | Miami (Florida) | | | |
| ☐ 155 | Joe Johnson | .04 | .02 | .00 |
| | North Carolina State | | | |
| ☐ 156 | Todd Scott | .30 | .12 | .03 |
| | Southwest Louisiana | | | |
| ☐ 157 | Checklist 1 | .04 | .02 | .00 |
| ☐ 158 | Checklist 2 | .04 | .02 | .00 |
| ☐ 159 | Checklist 3 | .04 | .02 | .00 |
| ☐ 160 | Checklist 4 | .04 | .02 | .00 |

# 1991 Wild Card NFL Prototypes

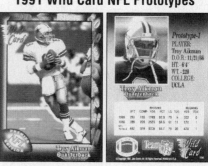

This six-card Wild Card Prototype set features cards measuring the standard-size (2 1/2" by 3 1/2"). The front design features glossy color action player photos, on a black card face with yellow highlighting around the picture and different color numbers appearing in the top and right borders. A football icon with the words "NFL Premier Edition" overlays the lower left corner of the picture. The backs shade from black to yellow and have a color headshot, biography, and statistics for the last three years. The cards are numbered in the upper right corner.

| | | MINT | EXC | G-VG |
|---|---|---|---|---|
| | COMPLETE SET (6) | 20.00 | 8.00 | 2.00 |
| | COMMON PLAYER (1-6) | 2.00 | .80 | .20 |
| ☐ 1 | Troy Aikman | 6.00 | 2.40 | .60 |
| | Dallas Cowboys | | | |
| ☐ 2 | Barry Sanders | 4.00 | 1.60 | .40 |
| | Detroit Lions | | | |
| ☐ 3 | Thurman Thomas | 3.00 | 1.20 | .30 |
| | Buffalo Bills | | | |
| ☐ 4 | Emmitt Smith | 8.00 | 3.25 | .80 |
| | Dallas Cowboys | | | |
| ☐ 5 | Jerry Rice | 4.00 | 1.60 | .40 |
| | San Francisco 49ers | | | |
| ☐ 6 | Lawrence Taylor | 2.00 | .80 | .20 |
| | New York Giants | | | |

# 1991 Wild Card

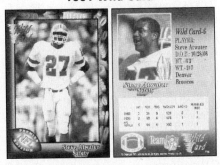

The Wild Card NFL Football set contains 160 cards measuring the standard size (2 1/2" by 3 1/2"). Reportedly production quantities were limited to 30,000 numbered ten-box cases. The series included three bonus cards (Wild Card Case Card, Wild Card Box Card, and Wild Card Hat Card) that were redeemable for the item pictured. Surprise wild card number 126 could be exchanged for a ten-card NFL Experience set, featuring five players each from the Washington Redskins and the Buffalo Bills. This set resembles that given away at the Super Bowl Show, except that the cards bear no date. The front design features glossy color action player photos, highlighted in mustard on a black card face. Different color numbers appear in the top and right borders. The words "NFL Premier Edition" in a football icon overlay the lower left corner of the picture. The backs shade from black to mustard and carry a color headshot, biography, statistics, and card number. The secondary market value of the striped cards has not proven to be as strong as Wild Card may have anticipated. There have been numerous examples available at card shows and stores of higher stripe cards being offered at 50 percent of their theoretical value based on multiplying the stripe number times the single card value. The key Rookie Cards in this set are Ricky Ervins, Alvin Harper, Randal Hill, Michael Jackson, Todd Marinovich, Dan McGwire, Hugh Millen, Herman Moore, Browning Nagle, Neil O'Donnell, Mike Pritchard, and Leonard Russell.

|  | MINT | EXC | G-VG |
|---|---|---|---|
| COMPLETE SET (160) | 10.00 | 4.50 | 1.25 |
| COMMON PLAYER (1-160) | .05 | .02 | .01 |

*5/10/20 STRIPES: .30X to .75X VALUE
*50/100 STRIPES: .25X to .60X VALUE
*1000 STRIPES: .20X to .50X VALUE

| | | | |
|---|---|---|---|
| ☐ 1 Jeff George<br>Indianapolis Colts | .25 | .11 | .03 |
| ☐ 2 Sean Jones<br>Houston Oilers | .08 | .04 | .01 |
| ☐ 3 Duane Bickett<br>Indianapolis Colts | .05 | .02 | .01 |
| ☐ 4 John Elway<br>Denver Broncos | .35 | .16 | .04 |
| ☐ 5 Christian Okoye<br>Kansas City Chiefs | .08 | .04 | .01 |
| ☐ 6 Steve Atwater<br>Denver Broncos | .10 | .05 | .01 |
| ☐ 7 Anthony Munoz<br>Cincinnati Bengals | .08 | .04 | .01 |
| ☐ 8 Dave Krieg<br>Seattle Seahawks | .08 | .04 | .01 |
| ☐ 9 Nick Lowery<br>Kansas City Chiefs | .08 | .04 | .01 |
| ☐ 10 Albert Bentley<br>Indianapolis Colts | .05 | .02 | .01 |
| ☐ 11 Mark Jackson<br>Denver Broncos | .08 | .04 | .01 |
| ☐ 12 Jeff Bryant<br>Seattle Seahawks | .05 | .02 | .01 |
| ☐ 13 Johnny Hector<br>New York Jets | .05 | .02 | .01 |
| ☐ 14 John L. Williams<br>Seattle Seahawks | .08 | .04 | .01 |
| ☐ 15 Jim Everett<br>Los Angeles Rams | .08 | .04 | .01 |
| ☐ 16 Mark Duper<br>Miami Dolphins | .08 | .04 | .01 |
| ☐ 17 Drew Hill UER<br>(Reversed negative<br>on card front)<br>Houston Oilers | .08 | .04 | .01 |
| ☐ 18 Randal Hill<br>Phoenix Cardinals | .30 | .14 | .04 |
| ☐ 19 Ernest Givins<br>Houston Oilers | .08 | .04 | .01 |
| ☐ 20 Ken O'Brien<br>New York Jets | .08 | .04 | .01 |
| ☐ 21 Blair Thomas UER<br>(Says he caught 204<br>passes in 1990)<br>New York Jets | .08 | .04 | .01 |
| ☐ 22 Derrick Thomas<br>Kansas City Chiefs | .25 | .11 | .03 |
| ☐ 23 Harvey Williams<br>Kansas City Chiefs | .20 | .09 | .03 |
| ☐ 24 Simon Fletcher<br>Denver Broncos | .08 | .04 | .01 |
| ☐ 25 Stephone Paige<br>Kansas City Chiefs | .08 | .04 | .01 |
| ☐ 26 Barry Word<br>Kansas City Chiefs | .10 | .05 | .01 |
| ☐ 27 Warren Moon<br>Houston Oilers | .20 | .09 | .03 |
| ☐ 28 Derrick Fenner<br>Seattle Seahawks | .08 | .04 | .01 |
| ☐ 29 Shane Conlan<br>Buffalo Bills | .08 | .04 | .01 |
| ☐ 30 Karl Mecklenburg<br>Denver Broncos | .08 | .04 | .01 |
| ☐ 31 Gary Anderson<br>Tampa Bay Buccaneers | .08 | .04 | .01 |
| ☐ 32 Sammie Smith<br>Miami Dolphins | .05 | .02 | .01 |
| ☐ 33 Steve DeBerg<br>Kansas City Chiefs | .08 | .04 | .01 |
| ☐ 34 Dan McGwire UER<br>(TD stats say 29,<br>should be 27)<br>Seattle Seahawks | .10 | .05 | .01 |
| ☐ 35 Roger Craig<br>Los Angeles Raiders | .08 | .04 | .01 |
| ☐ 36 Tom Tupa<br>Phoenix Cardinals | .08 | .04 | .01 |
| ☐ 37 Rod Woodson<br>Pittsburgh Steelers | .10 | .05 | .01 |
| ☐ 38 Junior Seau<br>San Diego Chargers | .25 | .11 | .03 |
| ☐ 39 Bruce Pickens<br>Atlanta Falcons | .10 | .05 | .01 |
| ☐ 40 Greg Townsend<br>Los Angeles Raiders | .05 | .02 | .01 |
| ☐ 41 Gary Clark<br>Washington Redskins | .08 | .04 | .01 |
| ☐ 42 Broderick Thomas<br>Tampa Bay Buccaneers | .08 | .04 | .01 |
| ☐ 43 Charles Mann<br>Washington Redskins | .08 | .04 | .01 |
| ☐ 44 Browning Nagle<br>New York Jets | .15 | .07 | .02 |
| ☐ 45 James Joseph<br>Philadelphia Eagles | .20 | .09 | .03 |
| ☐ 46 Emmitt Smith UER<br>Dallas Cowboys<br>(Scoring 1 TD,<br>should be 11) | 2.00 | .90 | .25 |
| ☐ 47 Cornelius Bennett<br>Buffalo Bills | .10 | .05 | .01 |
| ☐ 48 Maurice Hurst<br>New England Patriots | .05 | .02 | .01 |
| ☐ 49 Art Monk<br>Washington Redskins | .10 | .05 | .01 |
| ☐ 50 Louis Lipps<br>Pittsburgh Steelers | .08 | .04 | .01 |
| ☐ 51 Mark Rypien<br>Washington Redskins | .10 | .05 | .01 |
| ☐ 52 Bubby Brister<br>Pittsburgh Steelers | .08 | .04 | .01 |
| ☐ 53 John Stephens<br>New England Patriots | .08 | .04 | .01 |
| ☐ 54 Merril Hoge<br>Pittsburgh Steelers | .08 | .04 | .01 |
| ☐ 55 Kevin Mack<br>Cleveland Browns | .08 | .04 | .01 |
| ☐ 56 Al Toon<br>New York Jets | .08 | .04 | .01 |
| ☐ 57 Ronnie Lott<br>Los Angeles Raiders | .10 | .05 | .01 |
| ☐ 58 Eric Metcalf<br>Cleveland Browns | .10 | .05 | .01 |
| ☐ 59 Vinny Testaverde<br>Tampa Bay Buccaneers | .10 | .05 | .01 |
| ☐ 60 Darrell Green<br>Washington Redskins | .08 | .04 | .01 |
| ☐ 61 Randall Cunningham<br>Philadelphia Eagles | .10 | .05 | .01 |
| ☐ 62 Charles Haley<br>San Francisco 49ers | .08 | .04 | .01 |
| ☐ 63 Mark Carrier<br>Chicago Bears | .08 | .04 | .01 |
| ☐ 64 Jim Harbaugh<br>Chicago Bears | .08 | .04 | .01 |
| ☐ 65 Richard Dent | .08 | .04 | .01 |

| | | | |
|---|---|---|---|
| Chicago Bears | | | |
| ☐ 66 Stan Thomas | .05 | .02 | .01 |
| Chicago Bears | | | |
| ☐ 67 Neal Anderson | .05 | .02 | .01 |
| Chicago Bears | | | |
| ☐ 68 Troy Aikman | 1.25 | .55 | .16 |
| Dallas Cowboys | | | |
| ☐ 69 Mike Pritchard | .75 | .35 | .09 |
| Atlanta Falcons | | | |
| ☐ 70 Deion Sanders | .25 | .11 | .03 |
| Atlanta Falcons | | | |
| ☐ 71 Andre Rison | .25 | .11 | .03 |
| Atlanta Falcons | | | |
| ☐ 72 Keith Millard | .08 | .04 | .01 |
| Minnesota Vikings | | | |
| ☐ 73 Jerry Rice | .75 | .35 | .09 |
| San Francisco 49ers | | | |
| ☐ 74 Johnny Johnson | .25 | .11 | .03 |
| Phoenix Cardinals | | | |
| ☐ 75 Tim McDonald | .08 | .04 | .01 |
| Phoenix Cardinals | | | |
| ☐ 76 Leonard Russell | 1.00 | .45 | .13 |
| New England Patriots | | | |
| ☐ 77 Keith Jackson | .15 | .07 | .02 |
| Philadelphia Eagles | | | |
| ☐ 78 Keith Byars | .08 | .04 | .01 |
| Philadelphia Eagles | | | |
| ☐ 79 Ricky Proehl | .10 | .05 | .01 |
| Phoenix Cardinals | | | |
| ☐ 80 Dexter Carter | .08 | .04 | .01 |
| San Francisco 49ers | | | |
| ☐ 81 Alvin Harper | 1.00 | .45 | .13 |
| Dallas Cowboys | | | |
| ☐ 82 Irving Fryar | .08 | .04 | .01 |
| New England Patriots | | | |
| ☐ 83 Marion Butts | .10 | .05 | .01 |
| San Diego Chargers | | | |
| ☐ 84 Alfred Williams | .15 | .07 | .02 |
| Cincinnati Bengals | | | |
| ☐ 85 Timm Rosenbach | .08 | .04 | .01 |
| Phoenix Cardinals | | | |
| ☐ 86 Steve Young | .50 | .23 | .06 |
| San Francisco 49ers | | | |
| ☐ 87 Albert Lewis | .08 | .04 | .01 |
| Kansas City Chiefs | | | |
| ☐ 88 Rodney Peete | .08 | .04 | .01 |
| Detroit Lions | | | |
| ☐ 89 Barry Sanders | .75 | .35 | .09 |
| Detroit Lions | | | |
| ☐ 90 Bennie Blades | .05 | .02 | .01 |
| Detroit Lions | | | |
| ☐ 91 Chris Spielman | .08 | .04 | .01 |
| Detroit Lions | | | |
| ☐ 92 John Friesz | .10 | .05 | .01 |
| San Diego Chargers | | | |
| ☐ 93 Jerome Brown | .08 | .04 | .01 |
| Philadelphia Eagles | | | |
| ☐ 94 Reggie White | .15 | .07 | .02 |
| Philadelphia Eagles | | | |
| ☐ 95 Michael Irvin | .50 | .23 | .06 |
| Dallas Cowboys | | | |
| ☐ 96 Keith McCants | .05 | .02 | .01 |
| Tampa Bay Buccaneers | | | |
| ☐ 97 Vinnie Clark | .05 | .02 | .01 |
| Green Bay Packers | | | |
| ☐ 98 Louis Oliver | .08 | .04 | .01 |
| Miami Dolphins | | | |
| ☐ 99 Mark Clayton | .08 | .04 | .01 |
| Miami Dolphins | | | |
| ☐ 100 John Offerdahl | .08 | .04 | .01 |
| Miami Dolphins | | | |
| ☐ 101 Michael Carter | .05 | .02 | .01 |
| San Francisco 49ers | | | |
| ☐ 102 John Taylor | .10 | .05 | .01 |
| San Francisco 49ers | | | |
| ☐ 103 William Perry | .08 | .04 | .01 |
| Chicago Bears | | | |
| ☐ 104 Gill Byrd | .08 | .04 | .01 |
| San Diego Chargers | | | |
| ☐ 105 Burt Grossman | .05 | .02 | .01 |
| San Diego Chargers | | | |
| ☐ 106 Herman Moore | 1.00 | .45 | .13 |
| Detroit Lions | | | |
| ☐ 107 Howie Long | .08 | .04 | .01 |
| Los Angeles Raiders | | | |
| ☐ 108 Bo Jackson | .35 | .16 | .04 |
| Los Angeles Raiders | | | |
| ☐ 109 Kelvin Pritchett | .05 | .02 | .01 |
| Detroit Lions | | | |
| ☐ 110 Jacob Green | .05 | .02 | .01 |
| Seattle Seahawks | | | |
| ☐ 111 Chris Doleman | .08 | .04 | .01 |
| Minnesota Vikings | | | |
| ☐ 112 Herschel Walker | .10 | .05 | .01 |
| Minnesota Vikings | | | |
| ☐ 113 Russell Maryland | .40 | .18 | .05 |
| Dallas Cowboys | | | |
| ☐ 114 Anthony Carter | .08 | .04 | .01 |

| | | | |
|---|---|---|---|
| Minnesota Vikings | | | |
| ☐ 115 Joey Browner | .05 | .02 | .01 |
| Minnesota Vikings | | | |
| ☐ 116 Tony Mandarich | .05 | .02 | .01 |
| Green Bay Packers | | | |
| ☐ 117 Don Majkowski | .08 | .04 | .01 |
| Green Bay Packers | | | |
| ☐ 118 Ricky Ervins | .20 | .09 | .03 |
| Washington Redskins | | | |
| ☐ 119 Sterling Sharpe | .50 | .23 | .06 |
| Green Bay Packers | | | |
| ☐ 120 Tim Harris | .08 | .04 | .01 |
| San Francisco 49ers | | | |
| ☐ 121 Hugh Millen | .10 | .05 | .01 |
| New England Patriots | | | |
| ☐ 122 Mike Rozier | .08 | .04 | .01 |
| Atlanta Falcons | | | |
| ☐ 123 Chris Miller | .10 | .05 | .01 |
| Atlanta Falcons | | | |
| ☐ 124 Morten Andersen | .08 | .04 | .01 |
| New Orleans Saints | | | |
| ☐ 125 Neil O'Donnell | 1.50 | .65 | .19 |
| Pittsburgh Steelers | | | |
| ☐ 126 Surprise Wild Card | 1.50 | .65 | .19 |
| (Exchangeable for | | | |
| ten-card NFL | | | |
| Experience set) | | | |
| ☐ 127 Eddie Brown | .05 | .02 | .01 |
| Cincinnati Bengals | | | |
| ☐ 128 James Francis | .08 | .04 | .01 |
| Cincinnati Bengals | | | |
| ☐ 129 James Brooks | .08 | .04 | .01 |
| Cincinnati Bengals | | | |
| ☐ 130 David Fulcher | .05 | .02 | .01 |
| Cincinnati Bengals | | | |
| ☐ 131 Michael Jackson | .75 | .35 | .09 |
| Cleveland Browns | | | |
| ☐ 132 Clay Matthews | .08 | .04 | .01 |
| Cleveland Browns | | | |
| ☐ 133 Scott Norwood | .05 | .02 | .01 |
| Buffalo Bills | | | |
| ☐ 134 Wesley Carroll | .10 | .05 | .01 |
| New Orleans Saints | | | |
| ☐ 135 Thurman Thomas | .40 | .18 | .05 |
| Buffalo Bills | | | |
| ☐ 136 Mark Ingram | .08 | .04 | .01 |
| New York Giants | | | |
| ☐ 137 Bobby Hebert | .10 | .05 | .01 |
| New Orleans Saints | | | |
| ☐ 138 Bobby Wilson | .10 | .05 | .01 |
| Washington Redskins | | | |
| ☐ 139 Craig Heyward | .05 | .02 | .01 |
| New Orleans Saints | | | |
| ☐ 140 Dalton Hilliard | .05 | .02 | .01 |
| New Orleans Saints | | | |
| ☐ 141 Jeff Hostetler | .25 | .11 | .03 |
| New York Giants | | | |
| ☐ 142 Dave Meggett | .10 | .05 | .01 |
| New York Giants | | | |
| ☐ 143 Cris Dishman | .15 | .07 | .02 |
| Houston Oilers | | | |
| ☐ 144 Lawrence Taylor | .10 | .05 | .01 |
| New York Giants | | | |
| ☐ 145 Leonard Marshall | .08 | .04 | .01 |
| New York Giants | | | |
| ☐ 146 Pepper Johnson | .08 | .04 | .01 |
| New York Giants | | | |
| ☐ 147 Todd Marinovich | .08 | .04 | .01 |
| Los Angeles Raiders | | | |
| ☐ 148 Mike Croel | .20 | .09 | .03 |
| Denver Broncos | | | |
| ☐ 149 Erik McMillan | .05 | .02 | .01 |
| New York Jets | | | |
| ☐ 150 Flipper Anderson | .08 | .04 | .01 |
| Los Angeles Rams | | | |
| ☐ 151 Cleveland Gary | .08 | .04 | .01 |
| Los Angeles Rams | | | |
| ☐ 152 Henry Ellard | .08 | .04 | .01 |
| Los Angeles Rams | | | |
| ☐ 153 Kevin Greene | .08 | .04 | .01 |
| Los Angeles Rams | | | |
| ☐ 154 Michael Cofer | .05 | .02 | .01 |
| Detroit Lions | | | |
| ☐ 155 Todd Lyght | .10 | .05 | .01 |
| Los Angeles Rams | | | |
| ☐ 156 Bruce Smith | .10 | .05 | .01 |
| Buffalo Bills | | | |
| ☐ 157 Checklist 1 | .05 | .02 | .01 |
| ☐ 158 Checklist 2 | .05 | .02 | .01 |
| ☐ 159 Checklist 3 | .05 | .02 | .01 |
| ☐ 160 Checklist 4 | .05 | .02 | .01 |

# 1991 Wild Card
# NFL Redemption Cards

This ten-card standard-size (2 1/2" by 3 1/2") set commemorates Super Bowl XXVI and features five players from each team. These cards were exchanged for Wild Card surprise card number 126, and thus they are numbered 126A-J. Cards 126A-126E feature Washington Redskins, whereas cards 126F-126J feature Buffalo Bills. In design, these redemption cards are identical to the 1991 Wild Card NFL Super Bowl Promos/NFL Experience set. The only detectible difference is that the Super Bowl promos have the date and location of the Super Bowl Card Show III on the back, while these redemption cards do not carry that information and are numbered differently.

|  | MINT | EXC | G-VG |
|---|---|---|---|
| COMPLETE SET (10) | 3.00 | 1.20 | .30 |
| COMMON PLAYER (126A-126J) | .15 | .06 | .01 |
| ☐ 126A Mark Rypien | .35 | .14 | .03 |
| ☐ 126B Ricky Ervins | .35 | .14 | .03 |
| ☐ 126C Darrell Green | .35 | .14 | .03 |
| ☐ 126D Charles Mann | .15 | .06 | .01 |
| ☐ 126E Art Monk | .50 | .20 | .05 |
| ☐ 126F Thurman Thomas | 1.00 | .40 | .10 |
| ☐ 126G Bruce Smith | .35 | .14 | .03 |
| ☐ 126H Cornelius Bennett | .25 | .10 | .02 |
| ☐ 126I Scott Norwood | .15 | .06 | .01 |
| ☐ 126J Shane Conlan | .25 | .10 | .02 |

# 1991 Wild Card
# NFL Super Bowl Promos

This ten-card standard-size (2 1/2" by 3 1/2") set commemorates Super Bowl XXVI and features five players from each team. The cards were given away during the SuperBowl Card Show III by Wild Card, a corporate sponsor of the show. Prominently displayed on the card front is the "NFL Experience" logo. The fronts have high gloss color player photos, on a black and yellow card face that has different colored numbers above and to the right of the picture. On a background that shades from black to yellow and to black again, the backs have a color head shot, biography, and a sponsor's advertisement. The cards are numbered in the upper right corner. Cards 1-5 feature Washington Redskins, whereas cards 6-10 feature Buffalo Bills.

|  | MINT | EXC | G-VG |
|---|---|---|---|
| COMPLETE SET (10) | 15.00 | 6.00 | 1.50 |
| COMMON PLAYER (1-10) | .50 | .20 | .05 |

|  | | | |
|---|---|---|---|
| ☐ 1 Mark Rypien | 1.75 | .70 | .17 |
| ☐ 2 Ricky Ervins | 1.75 | .70 | .17 |
| ☐ 3 Darrell Green | 1.75 | .70 | .17 |
| ☐ 4 Charles Mann | .75 | .30 | .07 |
| ☐ 5 Art Monk | 2.50 | 1.00 | .25 |
| ☐ 6 Thurman Thomas | 5.00 | 2.00 | .50 |
| ☐ 7 Bruce Smith | 1.75 | .70 | .17 |
| ☐ 8 Cornelius Bennett | 1.25 | .50 | .12 |
| ☐ 9 Scott Norwood | .75 | .30 | .07 |
| ☐ 10 Shane Conlan | 1.25 | .50 | .12 |

# 1991-92 Wild Card
# Redemption Prototypes

Collectors who redeemed their three Collegiate Football Surprise wild cards before April 30, 1992 received as a bonus this six-card set of 1992 Collegiate Football Redemption Prototype cards. The standard-size (2 1/2" by 3 1/2") cards feature glossy color player photos bordered in white. Different color numbers (100, 100, 50, 20, 10 and 5) edge the top and right side of the photo in the white border, and the team name and team colors frame the picture on the left side and bottom. The player's name and position appear in the bottom white border. The backs shade from purple to white and back to purple and carry a color head shot, biography, and statistics. The cards are numbered on the back with a "P" prefix.

|  | MINT | EXC | G-VG |
|---|---|---|---|
| COMPLETE SET (6) | 3.00 | 1.20 | .30 |
| COMMON PLAYER (P1-P6) | .10 | .04 | .01 |
| ☐ P1 Edgar Bennett<br>Florida State | 1.25 | .50 | .12 |
| ☐ P2 Jimmy Smith<br>Jackson State | .10 | .04 | .01 |
| ☐ P3 Will Furrer<br>Virginia Tech | .30 | .12 | .03 |
| ☐ P4 Terrell Buckley<br>Florida State | .60 | .24 | .06 |
| ☐ P5 Tommy Vardell<br>Stanford | .60 | .24 | .06 |
| ☐ P6 Amp Lee<br>Florida State | .50 | .20 | .05 |

# 1992 Wild Card NFL Prototypes

This 12-card Wild Card Prototype set features cards measuring the standard-size (2 1/2" by 3 1/2"). The front design is the samer as the regular issue 1992 Wild Card NFL cards. The cards are numbered in the upper right corner of the reverse with a "P" prefix. The set numbering starts where the 1991 Wild Card Prototypes set left off.

|  | MINT | EXC | G-VG |
|---|---|---|---|
| COMPLETE SET (12) | 25.00 | 10.00 | 2.50 |
| COMMON PLAYER (P7-P18) | 1.50 | .60 | .15 |
| ☐ P7 Barry Sanders<br>Detroit Lions | 4.00 | 1.60 | .40 |
| ☐ P8 John Taylor<br>San Francisco 49ers | 2.00 | .80 | .20 |
| ☐ P9 John Elway<br>Denver Broncos | 4.00 | 1.60 | .40 |
| ☐ P10 Eric Kramer<br>Detroit Lions | 2.00 | .80 | .20 |
| ☐ P11 Christian Okoye<br>Kansas City Chiefs | 1.50 | .60 | .15 |
| ☐ P12 Leonard Russell<br>New England Patriots | 2.50 | 1.00 | .25 |
| ☐ P13 Barry Sanders<br>Detroit Lions | 4.00 | 1.60 | .40 |
| ☐ P14 Earnest Byner<br>Washington Redskins | 1.50 | .60 | .15 |
| ☐ P15 Warren Moon<br>Houston Oilers | 3.00 | 1.20 | .30 |
| ☐ P16 Ronnie Lott<br>Los Angeles Raiders | 2.00 | .80 | .20 |
| ☐ P17 Michael Irvin<br>Dallas Cowboys | 3.00 | 1.20 | .30 |
| ☐ P18 Haywood Jeffires<br>Houston Oilers | 2.50 | 1.00 | .25 |

# 1992 Wild Card

The 1992 Wild Card NFL football set contains 460 standard-size (2 1/2" by 3 1/2") cards issued in two series of 250 and 210 cards, respectively. It is reported that the first series production run was limited to 30,000 ten-box numbered foil cases. One hundred case cards and one thousand box cards were randomly inserted into the foil packs. Also cards from the Red Hot Rookie subset were inserted in the packs. The left half of the card face is white while the right half shades from gray to black. The fronts display glossy color action photos, with the player's name and position beneath the picture. In the lower left corner, the pictures are accented by a two-color stripe (reflecting the team's colors); a numbered stripe with the denominations 5, 10, 20, 50, 100, and 1,000 accents the upper right corner. The backs exhibit different shades of jade and present biographical and statistical information. At the bottom, a color head shot appears inside a football. The cards are numbered on the back and checklisted below according to teams as follows: Los Angeles Rams (2-9), Philadelphia Eagles (10-17), Miami Dolphins (18-25), San Diego Chargers (26-33), Phoenix Cardinals (34-40), Tampa Bay Buccaneers (41-48), Green Bay Packers (49-57), Minnesota Vikings (58-65), Los Angeles Raiders (70-75, 101, 160), Kansas City Chiefs (76-84), Houston Oilers (85-93), San Francisco 49ers (94-100, 102), Detroit Lions (104-111), Denver Broncos (112-119), New England Patriots (69, 120-128), Washington Redskins (129-137), Chicago Bears (138-145), Atlanta Falcons (103, 146-154), Indianapolis Colts (155-159), Dallas Cowboys (161-166), Cleveland Browns (167-174), New York Jets (175-180), New York Giants (181-188), Cincinnati Bengals (189-196), Pittsburgh Steelers (197-200), Buffalo Bills (201-206), New Orleans Saints (207-217), and Seattle Seahawks (218-222). The set closes with Draft Picks (223-239), League Leaders (240-245), and Checklists (246-250). Through a mail-in offer, the surprise card could be exchanged for a four-card cello pack featuring a P1 Barry Sanders (with first series Surprise Card 1) or P2 Emmitt Smith (with second series Surprise Card 251) Stat Smasher field card, a Red Hot Rookie card, a Field Force card, and either a silver or gold Field Force card. Every jumbo pack included ten Series I cards, ten Series II cards, one Stat Smasher, one gold or silver foil Red Hot Rookie, and one gold or silver foil Running Wild.

Rookie Cards include Edgar Bennett, Steve Bono, Terrell Buckley, Marco Coleman, David Klingler, Amp Lee, Johnny Mitchell, Tommy Vardell, Tommy Maddox, and Tony Smith.

|  | MINT | EXC | G-VG |
|---|---|---|---|
| COMPLETE SET (460) | 15.00 | 6.75 | 1.90 |
| COMPLETE SERIES 1 (250) | 8.00 | 3.60 | 1.00 |
| COMPLETE SERIES 2 (210) | 8.00 | 3.60 | 1.00 |
| COMMON PLAYER (1-250) | .04 | .02 | .01 |
| COMMON PLAYER (251-460) | .04 | .02 | .01 |
| *5/10/20 STRIPES: .30X to .75X VALUE | | | |
| *50/100 STRIPES: .25X to .60 VALUE | | | |
| *1000 STRIPES: .20X to .50X VALUE | | | |
| ☐ 1 Surprise Card | 1.50 | .65 | .19 |
| ☐ 2 Marcus Dupree | .08 | .04 | .01 |
| ☐ 3 Jackie Slater | .08 | .04 | .01 |
| ☐ 4 Robert Delpino | .08 | .04 | .01 |
| ☐ 5 Jerry Gray | .04 | .02 | .01 |
| ☐ 6 Jim Everett | .04 | .02 | .01 |
| ☐ 7 Roman Phifer | .04 | .02 | .01 |
| ☐ 8 Alvin Wright | .04 | .02 | .01 |
| ☐ 9 Todd Lyght | .04 | .02 | .01 |
| ☐ 10 Reggie White | .15 | .07 | .02 |
| ☐ 11 Randal Hill | .10 | .05 | .01 |
| ☐ 12 Keith Byars | .08 | .04 | .01 |
| ☐ 13 Clyde Simmons | .08 | .04 | .01 |
| ☐ 14 Keith Jackson | .10 | .05 | .01 |
| ☐ 15 Seth Joyner | .08 | .04 | .01 |
| ☐ 16 James Joseph | .04 | .02 | .01 |
| ☐ 17 Eric Allen | .08 | .04 | .01 |
| ☐ 18 Sammie Smith | .04 | .02 | .01 |
| ☐ 19 Mark Clayton | .08 | .04 | .01 |
| ☐ 20 Aaron Craver | .04 | .02 | .01 |
| ☐ 21 Hugh Green | .04 | .02 | .01 |
| ☐ 22 John Offerdahl | .08 | .04 | .01 |
| ☐ 23 Jeff Cross | .04 | .02 | .01 |
| ☐ 24 Ferrell Edmunds | .04 | .02 | .01 |
| ☐ 25 Mark Duper | .08 | .04 | .01 |
| ☐ 26 Ronnie Harmon | .04 | .02 | .01 |
| ☐ 27 Derrick Walker | .04 | .02 | .01 |
| ☐ 28 Gary Plummer | .04 | .02 | .01 |
| ☐ 29 Rod Bernstine | .08 | .04 | .01 |
| ☐ 30 Burt Grossman | .04 | .02 | .01 |
| ☐ 31 Donnie Elder | .04 | .02 | .01 |
| ☐ 32 John Friesz | .08 | .04 | .01 |
| ☐ 33 Billy Ray Smith | .04 | .02 | .01 |
| ☐ 34 Luis Sharpe | .04 | .02 | .01 |
| ☐ 35 Aeneas Williams | .04 | .02 | .01 |
| ☐ 36 Ken Harvey | .04 | .02 | .01 |
| ☐ 37 Johnny Johnson UER<br>(1990 rushing stats<br>are wrong) | .10 | .05 | .01 |
| ☐ 38 Eric Swann | .08 | .04 | .01 |
| ☐ 39 Tom Tupa | .08 | .04 | .01 |
| ☐ 40 Anthony Thompson | .04 | .02 | .01 |
| ☐ 41 Broderick Thomas | .04 | .02 | .01 |
| ☐ 42 Vinny Testaverde | .10 | .05 | .01 |
| ☐ 43 Mark Carrier | .08 | .04 | .01 |
| ☐ 44 Gary Anderson | .08 | .04 | .01 |
| ☐ 45 Keith McCants | .04 | .02 | .01 |
| ☐ 46 Reggie Cobb | .10 | .05 | .01 |
| ☐ 47 Lawrence Dawsey | .10 | .05 | .01 |
| ☐ 48 Kevin Murphy | .04 | .02 | .01 |
| ☐ 49 Keith Woodside | .04 | .02 | .01 |
| ☐ 50 Darrell Thompson | .08 | .04 | .01 |
| ☐ 51 Vinnie Clark | .04 | .02 | .01 |
| ☐ 52 Sterling Sharpe | .50 | .23 | .06 |
| ☐ 53 Mike Tomczak | .04 | .02 | .01 |
| ☐ 54A Don Majikowski ERR<br>(Listed as Dan) | .10 | .05 | .01 |
| ☐ 54B Don Majikowski COR | .10 | .05 | .01 |
| ☐ 55 Tony Mandarich | .04 | .02 | .01 |
| ☐ 56 Mark Murphy | .04 | .02 | .01 |
| ☐ 57 Dexter McNabb | .04 | .02 | .01 |
| ☐ 58 Rick Fenney | .04 | .02 | .01 |
| ☐ 59 Cris Carter | .10 | .05 | .01 |
| ☐ 60 Wade Wilson | .08 | .04 | .01 |
| ☐ 61 Mike Merriweather | .04 | .02 | .01 |
| ☐ 62 Rich Gannon | .08 | .04 | .01 |
| ☐ 63 Herschel Walker | .10 | .05 | .01 |
| ☐ 64 Chris Doleman | .08 | .04 | .01 |
| ☐ 65 Al Noga UER<br>(On front, he's a DE;<br>on back, he's a DT) | .04 | .02 | .01 |
| ☐ 66 Chris Mims | .25 | .11 | .03 |
| ☐ 67 Ed Cunningham | .04 | .02 | .01 |
| ☐ 68 Marcus Allen | .08 | .04 | .01 |
| ☐ 69 Kevin Turner | .20 | .09 | .03 |
| ☐ 70 Howie Long | .08 | .04 | .01 |
| ☐ 71 Tim Brown | .25 | .11 | .03 |
| ☐ 72 Nick Bell | .08 | .04 | .01 |
| ☐ 73 Todd Marinovich | .04 | .02 | .01 |
| ☐ 74 Jay Schroeder | .08 | .04 | .01 |
| ☐ 75 Mervyn Fernandez | .04 | .02 | .01 |
| ☐ 76 Tony Smith | .10 | .05 | .01 |
| ☐ 77 John Alt | .04 | .02 | .01 |

| | | | |
|---|---|---|---|
| ☐ 78 Christian Okoye | .08 | .04 | .01 |
| ☐ 79 Nick Lowery | .08 | .04 | .01 |
| ☐ 80 Derrick Thomas | .15 | .07 | .02 |
| ☐ 81 Bill Maas | .04 | .02 | .01 |
| ☐ 82 Dino Hackett | .04 | .02 | .01 |
| ☐ 83 Deron Cherry | .04 | .02 | .01 |
| ☐ 84 Barry Word | .10 | .05 | .01 |
| ☐ 85 Mike Mooney | .10 | .05 | .01 |
| ☐ 86 Cris Dishman | .08 | .04 | .01 |
| ☐ 87 Bruce Matthews | .08 | .04 | .01 |
| ☐ 88 Tony Jones | .04 | .02 | .01 |
| ☐ 89 William Fuller | .04 | .02 | .01 |
| ☐ 90 Ray Childress | .08 | .04 | .01 |
| ☐ 91 Warren Moon | .20 | .09 | .03 |
| ☐ 92 Lorenzo White | .08 | .04 | .01 |
| ☐ 93 Joe Bowden | .04 | .02 | .01 |
| ☐ 94 Tom Rathman | .08 | .04 | .01 |
| ☐ 95 Keith Henderson | .04 | .02 | .01 |
| ☐ 96 Jesse Sapolu | .04 | .02 | .01 |
| ☐ 97 Charles Haley | .08 | .04 | .01 |
| ☐ 98 Steve Young | .35 | .16 | .04 |
| ☐ 99 John Taylor | .10 | .05 | .01 |
| ☐ 100 Tim Harris | .08 | .04 | .01 |
| ☐ 101 Scott Davis | .04 | .02 | .01 |
| ☐ 102 Steve Bono | .50 | .23 | .06 |
| ☐ 103 Mike Kenn | .08 | .04 | .01 |
| ☐ 104 Mike Farr | .04 | .02 | .01 |
| ☐ 105 Rodney Peete | .08 | .04 | .01 |
| ☐ 106 Jerry Ball | .08 | .04 | .01 |
| ☐ 107 Chris Spielman | .08 | .04 | .01 |
| ☐ 108 Barry Sanders | .75 | .35 | .09 |
| ☐ 109 Bennie Blades | .04 | .02 | .01 |
| ☐ 110 Herman Moore | .30 | .14 | .04 |
| ☐ 111 Erik Kramer | .10 | .05 | .01 |
| ☐ 112 Vance Johnson | .08 | .04 | .01 |
| ☐ 113 Mike Croel | .08 | .04 | .01 |
| ☐ 114 Mark Jackson | .08 | .04 | .01 |
| ☐ 115 Steve Atwater | .08 | .04 | .01 |
| ☐ 116 Gaston Green | .08 | .04 | .01 |
| ☐ 117 John Elway | .40 | .18 | .05 |
| ☐ 118 Simon Fletcher | .08 | .04 | .01 |
| ☐ 119 Karl Mecklenburg | .08 | .04 | .01 |
| ☐ 120 Hart Lee Dykes | .04 | .02 | .01 |
| ☐ 121 Jerome Henderson | .04 | .02 | .01 |
| ☐ 122 Chris Singleton | .04 | .02 | .01 |
| ☐ 123 Marv Cook | .08 | .04 | .01 |
| ☐ 124 Leonard Russell | .30 | .14 | .04 |
| ☐ 125 Hugh Millen | .08 | .04 | .01 |
| ☐ 126 Pat Harlow | .04 | .02 | .01 |
| ☐ 127 Andre Tippett | .08 | .04 | .01 |
| ☐ 128 Bruce Armstrong | .04 | .02 | .01 |
| ☐ 129 Gary Clark | .08 | .04 | .01 |
| ☐ 130 Art Monk | .10 | .05 | .01 |
| ☐ 131 Darrell Green | .08 | .04 | .01 |
| ☐ 132 Wilber Marshall | .08 | .04 | .01 |
| ☐ 133 Jim Lachey | .04 | .02 | .01 |
| ☐ 134 Earnest Byner | .08 | .04 | .01 |
| ☐ 135 Chip Lohmiller | .08 | .04 | .01 |
| ☐ 136 Mark Rypien | .10 | .05 | .01 |
| ☐ 137 Ricky Sanders | .08 | .04 | .01 |
| ☐ 138 Stan Thomas | .04 | .02 | .01 |
| ☐ 139 Neal Anderson | .08 | .04 | .01 |
| ☐ 140 Trace Armstrong | .04 | .02 | .01 |
| ☐ 141 Kevin Butler | .04 | .02 | .01 |
| ☐ 142 Mark Carrier | .08 | .04 | .01 |
| ☐ 143 Dennis Gentry | .04 | .02 | .01 |
| ☐ 144 Jim Harbaugh | .08 | .04 | .01 |
| ☐ 145 Richard Dent | .08 | .04 | .01 |
| ☐ 146 Andre Rison | .25 | .11 | .03 |
| ☐ 147 Bruce Pickens | .04 | .02 | .01 |
| ☐ 148 Chris Hinton UER | .04 | .02 | .01 |
| (Dealt to Falcons in 1990, not 1989) | | | |
| ☐ 149 Brian Jordan | .08 | .04 | .01 |
| ☐ 150 Chris Miller | .10 | .05 | .01 |
| ☐ 151 Moe Gardner | .04 | .02 | .01 |
| ☐ 152 Bill Fralic | .04 | .02 | .01 |
| ☐ 153 Michael Haynes | .30 | .14 | .04 |
| ☐ 154 Mike Pritchard | .25 | .11 | .03 |
| ☐ 155 Dean Biasucci | .04 | .02 | .01 |
| ☐ 156 Clarence Verdin | .04 | .02 | .01 |
| ☐ 157 Donnell Thompson | .04 | .02 | .01 |
| ☐ 158 Duane Bickett | .04 | .02 | .01 |
| ☐ 159 Jon Hand | .04 | .02 | .01 |
| ☐ 160 Sam Graddy | .20 | .09 | .03 |
| ☐ 161 Emmitt Smith | 2.00 | .90 | .25 |
| ☐ 162 Michael Irvin | .50 | .23 | .06 |
| ☐ 163 Danny Noonan | .04 | .02 | .01 |
| ☐ 164 Jack Del Rio | .04 | .02 | .01 |
| ☐ 165 Jim Jeffcoat | .04 | .02 | .01 |
| ☐ 166 Alexander Wright | .08 | .04 | .01 |
| ☐ 167 Frank Minnifield | .04 | .02 | .01 |
| ☐ 168 Ed King | .04 | .02 | .01 |
| ☐ 169 Reggie Langhorne | .08 | .04 | .01 |
| ☐ 170 Mike Baab | .04 | .02 | .01 |
| ☐ 171 Eric Metcalf | .10 | .05 | .01 |
| ☐ 172 Clay Matthews | .08 | .04 | .01 |

| | | | |
|---|---|---|---|
| ☐ 173 Kevin Mack | .08 | .04 | .01 |
| ☐ 174 Mike Johnson | .04 | .02 | .01 |
| ☐ 175 Jeff Lageman | .04 | .02 | .01 |
| ☐ 176 Freeman McNeil | .04 | .02 | .01 |
| ☐ 177 Erik McMillan | .04 | .02 | .01 |
| ☐ 178 James Hasty | .04 | .02 | .01 |
| ☐ 179 Kyle Clifton | .04 | .02 | .01 |
| ☐ 180 Joe Kelly | .04 | .02 | .01 |
| ☐ 181 Phil Simms | .10 | .05 | .01 |
| ☐ 182 Everson Walls | .04 | .02 | .01 |
| ☐ 183 Jeff Hostetler | .15 | .07 | .02 |
| ☐ 184 Dave Meggett | .08 | .04 | .01 |
| ☐ 185 Matt Bahr | .04 | .02 | .01 |
| ☐ 186 Mark Ingram | .08 | .04 | .01 |
| ☐ 187 Rodney Hampton | .40 | .18 | .05 |
| ☐ 188 Kanavis McGhee | .04 | .02 | .01 |
| ☐ 189 Tim McGee | .04 | .02 | .01 |
| ☐ 190 Eddie Brown | .04 | .02 | .01 |
| ☐ 191 Rodney Holman | .04 | .02 | .01 |
| ☐ 192 Harold Green | .08 | .04 | .01 |
| ☐ 193 James Francis | .08 | .04 | .01 |
| ☐ 194 Anthony Munoz | .08 | .04 | .01 |
| ☐ 195 David Fulcher | .04 | .02 | .01 |
| ☐ 196 Tim Krumrie | .04 | .02 | .01 |
| ☐ 197 Bubby Brister | .08 | .04 | .01 |
| ☐ 198 Rod Woodson | .10 | .05 | .01 |
| ☐ 199 Louis Lipps | .08 | .04 | .01 |
| ☐ 200 Carnell Lake | .04 | .02 | .01 |
| ☐ 201 Don Beebe | .10 | .05 | .01 |
| ☐ 202 Thurman Thomas | .40 | .18 | .05 |
| ☐ 203 Cornelius Bennett | .10 | .05 | .01 |
| ☐ 204 Mark Kelso | .04 | .02 | .01 |
| ☐ 205 James Lofton | .10 | .05 | .01 |
| ☐ 206 Darryl Talley | .08 | .04 | .01 |
| ☐ 207 Morten Andersen | .08 | .04 | .01 |
| ☐ 208 Vince Buck | .04 | .02 | .01 |
| ☐ 209 Wesley Carroll | .08 | .04 | .01 |
| ☐ 210 Bobby Hebert | .10 | .05 | .01 |
| ☐ 211 Craig Heyward | .04 | .02 | .01 |
| ☐ 212 Dalton Hilliard | .04 | .02 | .01 |
| ☐ 213 Rickey Jackson | .08 | .04 | .01 |
| ☐ 214 Eric Martin | .08 | .04 | .01 |
| ☐ 215 Pat Swilling | .08 | .04 | .01 |
| ☐ 216 Steve Walsh | .04 | .02 | .01 |
| ☐ 217 Torrance Small | .10 | .05 | .01 |
| ☐ 218 Jacob Green | .04 | .02 | .01 |
| ☐ 219 Cortez Kennedy | .10 | .05 | .01 |
| ☐ 220 John L. Williams | .08 | .04 | .01 |
| ☐ 221 Terry Wooden | .04 | .02 | .01 |
| ☐ 222 Grant Feasel | .04 | .02 | .01 |
| ☐ 223 Siran Stacy | .10 | .05 | .01 |
| Philadelphia Eagles | | | |
| ☐ 224 Chris Hakel | .10 | .05 | .01 |
| Washington Redskins | | | |
| ☐ 225 Todd Harrison | .10 | .05 | .01 |
| Chicago Bears | | | |
| ☐ 226 Bob Whitfield | .15 | .07 | .02 |
| Atlanta Falcons | | | |
| ☐ 227 Eddie Blake | .10 | .05 | .01 |
| Miami Dolphins | | | |
| ☐ 228 Keith Hamilton | .15 | .07 | .02 |
| New York Giants | | | |
| ☐ 229 Darryl Williams | .20 | .09 | .03 |
| Cincinnati Bengals | | | |
| ☐ 230 Ricardo McDonald | .10 | .05 | .01 |
| Cincinnati Bengals | | | |
| ☐ 231 Alan Haller | .10 | .05 | .01 |
| Pittsburgh Steelers | | | |
| ☐ 232 Leon Searcy | .10 | .05 | .01 |
| Pittsburgh Steelers | | | |
| ☐ 233 Patrick Rowe | .10 | .05 | .01 |
| Cleveland Browns | | | |
| ☐ 234 Edgar Bennett | .30 | .14 | .04 |
| Green Bay Packers | | | |
| ☐ 235 Terrell Buckley | .25 | .11 | .03 |
| Green Bay Packers | | | |
| ☐ 236 Will Furrer | .15 | .07 | .02 |
| Chicago Bears | | | |
| ☐ 237 Amp Lee UER | .25 | .11 | .03 |
| (Front photo actually Edgar Bennett) San Francisco 49ers | | | |
| ☐ 238 Jimmy Smith | .12 | .05 | .02 |
| Dallas Cowboys | | | |
| ☐ 239 Tommy Vardell | .30 | .14 | .04 |
| Cleveland Browns | | | |
| ☐ 240 Leonard Russell | .12 | .05 | .02 |
| New England Patriots '91 Offensive ROY | | | |
| ☐ 241 Mike Croel | .08 | .04 | .01 |
| Denver Broncos '91 Defensive ROY | | | |
| ☐ 242 Warren Moon | .10 | .05 | .01 |
| Houston Oilers '91 AFC Passing Leader | | | |
| ☐ 243 Mark Rypien | .10 | .05 | .01 |
| Washington Redskins | | | |

| | | | |
|---|---|---|---|
| '91 NFC Passing Leader | | | |
| ☐ 244 Thurman Thomas | .20 | .09 | .03 |
| Buffalo Bills | | | |
| '91 AFC Rushing Leader | | | |
| ☐ 245 Emmitt Smith | .75 | .35 | .09 |
| Dallas Cowboys | | | |
| '91 NFC Rushing Leader | | | |
| ☐ 246 Checklist 1-50 | .04 | .02 | .01 |
| ☐ 247 Checklist 51-100 | .04 | .02 | .01 |
| ☐ 248 Checklist 101-150 | .04 | .02 | .01 |
| ☐ 249 Checklist 151-200 | .04 | .02 | .01 |
| ☐ 250 Checklist 201-250 | .04 | .02 | .01 |
| ☐ 251 Surprise Card | 1.50 | .65 | .19 |
| ☐ 252 Erric Pegram | .40 | .18 | .05 |
| Atlanta Falcons | | | |
| ☐ 253 Anthony Carter | .08 | .04 | .01 |
| Minnesota Vikings | | | |
| ☐ 254 Roger Craig | .08 | .04 | .01 |
| Minnesota Vikings | | | |
| ☐ 255 Hassan Jones | .04 | .02 | .01 |
| Minnesota Vikings | | | |
| ☐ 256 Steve Jordan | .08 | .04 | .01 |
| Minnesota Vikings | | | |
| ☐ 257 Randall McDaniel | .04 | .02 | .01 |
| Minnesota Vikings | | | |
| ☐ 258 Henry Thomas | .04 | .02 | .01 |
| Minnesota Vikings | | | |
| ☐ 259 Carl Lee | .04 | .02 | .01 |
| Minnesota Vikings | | | |
| ☐ 260 Ray Agnew | .04 | .02 | .01 |
| New England Patriots | | | |
| ☐ 261 Irving Fryar | .08 | .04 | .01 |
| New England Patriots | | | |
| ☐ 262 Tom Waddle | .10 | .05 | .01 |
| Chicago Bears | | | |
| ☐ 263 Greg McMurtry | .04 | .02 | .01 |
| New England Patriots | | | |
| ☐ 264 Stephen Baker | .04 | .02 | .01 |
| New York Giants | | | |
| ☐ 265 Mark Collins | .04 | .02 | .01 |
| New York Giants | | | |
| ☐ 266 Howard Cross | .04 | .02 | .01 |
| New York Giants | | | |
| ☐ 267 Pepper Johnson | .08 | .04 | .01 |
| New York Giants | | | |
| ☐ 268 Fred Barnett | .10 | .05 | .01 |
| Philadelphia Eagles | | | |
| ☐ 269 Heath Sherman | .08 | .04 | .01 |
| Philadelphia Eagles | | | |
| ☐ 270 William Thomas | .04 | .02 | .01 |
| Philadelphia Eagles | | | |
| ☐ 271 Bill Bates | .04 | .02 | .01 |
| Dallas Cowboys | | | |
| ☐ 272 Issiac Holt | .04 | .02 | .01 |
| Dallas Cowboys | | | |
| ☐ 273 Emmitt Smith | 2.00 | .90 | .25 |
| Dallas Cowboys | | | |
| ☐ 274 Eric Bieniemy | .08 | .04 | .01 |
| San Diego Chargers | | | |
| ☐ 275 Marion Butts | .10 | .05 | .01 |
| San Diego Chargers | | | |
| ☐ 276 Gill Byrd | .08 | .04 | .01 |
| San Diego Chargers | | | |
| ☐ 277 Robert Blackmon | .04 | .02 | .01 |
| Seattle Seahawks | | | |
| ☐ 278 Brian Blades | .08 | .04 | .01 |
| Seattle Seahawks | | | |
| ☐ 279 Joe Nash | .04 | .02 | .01 |
| Seattle Seahawks | | | |
| ☐ 280 Bill Brooks | .08 | .04 | .01 |
| Indianapolis Colts | | | |
| ☐ 281 Mel Gray | .04 | .02 | .01 |
| Detroit Lions | | | |
| ☐ 282 Andre Ware | .08 | .04 | .01 |
| Detroit Lions | | | |
| ☐ 283 Steve McMichael | .08 | .04 | .01 |
| Chicago Bears | | | |
| ☐ 284 Brad Muster | .08 | .04 | .01 |
| Chicago Bears | | | |
| ☐ 285 Ron Rivera | .04 | .02 | .01 |
| Chicago Bears | | | |
| ☐ 286 Chris Zorich | .08 | .04 | .01 |
| Chicago Bears | | | |
| ☐ 287 Chris Burkett | .04 | .02 | .01 |
| New York Jets | | | |
| ☐ 288 Irv Eatman | .04 | .02 | .01 |
| New York Jets | | | |
| ☐ 289 Rob Moore | .10 | .05 | .01 |
| New York Jets | | | |
| ☐ 290 Joe Mott | .04 | .02 | .01 |
| New York Jets | | | |
| ☐ 291 Brian Washington | .04 | .02 | .01 |
| New York Jets | | | |
| ☐ 292 Michael Carter | .04 | .02 | .01 |
| San Francisco 49ers | | | |
| ☐ 293 Dexter Carter | .08 | .04 | .01 |
| San Francisco 49ers | | | |
| ☐ 294 Don Griffin | .04 | .02 | .01 |
| San Francisco 49ers | | | |
| ☐ 295 John Taylor | .10 | .05 | .01 |
| San Francisco 49ers | | | |
| ☐ 296 Ted Washington | .04 | .02 | .01 |
| San Francisco 49ers | | | |
| ☐ 297 Monte Coleman | .04 | .02 | .01 |
| Washington Redskins | | | |
| ☐ 298 Andre Collins | .04 | .02 | .01 |
| Washington Redskins | | | |
| ☐ 299 Charles Mann | .08 | .04 | .01 |
| Washington Redskins | | | |
| ☐ 300 Shane Conlon | .04 | .02 | .01 |
| Buffalo Bills | | | |
| ☐ 301 Keith McKeller | .04 | .02 | .01 |
| Buffalo Bills | | | |
| ☐ 302 Nate Odomes | .08 | .04 | .01 |
| Buffalo Bills | | | |
| ☐ 303 Riki Ellison | .04 | .02 | .01 |
| Los Angeles Raiders | | | |
| ☐ 304 Willie Gault | .08 | .04 | .01 |
| Los Angeles Raiders | | | |
| ☐ 305 Bob Golic | .04 | .02 | .01 |
| Los Angeles Raiders | | | |
| ☐ 306 Ethan Horton | .04 | .02 | .01 |
| Los Angeles Raiders | | | |
| ☐ 307 Ronnie Lott | .10 | .05 | .01 |
| Los Angeles Raiders | | | |
| ☐ 308 Don Mosebar | .04 | .02 | .01 |
| Los Angeles Raiders | | | |
| ☐ 309 Aaron Wallace | .04 | .02 | .01 |
| Los Angeles Raiders | | | |
| ☐ 310 Wymon Henderson | .04 | .02 | .01 |
| Denver Broncos | | | |
| ☐ 311 Vance Johnson | .08 | .04 | .01 |
| Denver Broncos | | | |
| ☐ 312 Ken Lanier | .04 | .02 | .01 |
| Denver Broncos | | | |
| ☐ 313 Steve Sewell | .04 | .02 | .01 |
| Denver Broncos | | | |
| ☐ 314 Dennis Smith | .08 | .04 | .01 |
| Denver Broncos | | | |
| ☐ 315 Kenny Walker | .04 | .02 | .01 |
| Denver Broncos | | | |
| ☐ 316 Chris Martin | .04 | .02 | .01 |
| Kansas City Chiefs | | | |
| ☐ 317 Albert Lewis | .08 | .04 | .01 |
| Kansas City Chiefs | | | |
| ☐ 318 Todd McNair | .04 | .02 | .01 |
| Kansas City Chiefs | | | |
| ☐ 319 Tracy Simien | .12 | .05 | .02 |
| Kansas City Chiefs | | | |
| ☐ 320 Percy Snow | .04 | .02 | .01 |
| Kansas City Chiefs | | | |
| ☐ 321 Mark Rypien | .10 | .05 | .01 |
| Washington Redskins | | | |
| ☐ 322 Bryan Hinkle | .04 | .02 | .01 |
| Pittsburgh Steelers | | | |
| ☐ 323 David Little | .04 | .02 | .01 |
| Pittsburgh Steelers | | | |
| ☐ 324 Dwight Stone | .04 | .02 | .01 |
| Pittsburgh Steelers | | | |
| ☐ 325 Van Waiters | .04 | .02 | .01 |
| Cleveland Browns | | | |
| ☐ 326 Pio Sagapolutele | .10 | .05 | .01 |
| Cleveland Browns | | | |
| ☐ 327 Michael Jackson | .10 | .05 | .01 |
| Cleveland Browns | | | |
| ☐ 328 Vestee Jackson | .04 | .02 | .01 |
| Miami Dolphins | | | |
| ☐ 329 Tony Paige | .04 | .02 | .01 |
| Miami Dolphins | | | |
| ☐ 330 Reggie Roby | .04 | .02 | .01 |
| Miami Dolphins | | | |
| ☐ 331 Haywood Jeffires | .10 | .05 | .01 |
| Houston Oilers | | | |
| ☐ 332 Lamar Lathon | .04 | .02 | .01 |
| Houston Oilers | | | |
| ☐ 333 Bubba McDowell | .04 | .02 | .01 |
| Houston Oilers | | | |
| ☐ 334 Doug Smith | .04 | .02 | .01 |
| Houston Oilers | | | |
| ☐ 335 Dean Steinkuhler | .04 | .02 | .01 |
| Houston Oilers | | | |
| ☐ 336 Jessie Tuggle | .04 | .02 | .01 |
| Atlanta Falcons | | | |
| ☐ 337 Freddie Joe Nunn | .04 | .02 | .01 |
| Phoenix Cardinals | | | |
| ☐ 338 Pat Terrell | .04 | .02 | .01 |
| Los Angeles Rams | | | |
| ☐ 339 Tom McHale | .04 | .02 | .01 |
| Tampa Bay Buccaneers | | | |
| ☐ 340 Sam Mills | .08 | .04 | .01 |
| New Orleans Saints | | | |
| ☐ 341 John Tice | .04 | .02 | .01 |
| New Orleans Saints | | | |
| ☐ 342 Brent Jones | .10 | .05 | .01 |
| San Francisco 49ers | | | |
| ☐ 343 Robert Porcher | .20 | .09 | .03 |

| | | | |
|---|---|---|---|
| Detroit Lions | | | |
| ☐ 344 Mark D'Onofrio | .04 | .02 | .01 |
| Green Bay Packers | | | |
| ☐ 345 David Tate | .04 | .02 | .01 |
| Chicago Bears | | | |
| ☐ 346 Courtney Hawkins | .25 | .11 | .03 |
| Tampa Bay Buccaneers | | | |
| ☐ 347 Ricky Watters | .50 | .23 | .06 |
| San Francisco 49ers | | | |
| ☐ 348 Amp Lee | .10 | .05 | .01 |
| San Francisco 49ers | | | |
| ☐ 349 Steve Young | .35 | .16 | .04 |
| San Francisco 49ers | | | |
| ☐ 350 Natu Tuatagaloa | .10 | .05 | .01 |
| Cincinnati Bengals | | | |
| ☐ 351 Alfred Williams | .04 | .02 | .01 |
| Cincinnati Bengals | | | |
| ☐ 352 Derek Brown | .10 | .05 | .01 |
| New York Giants | | | |
| ☐ 353 Marco Coleman UER | .30 | .14 | .04 |
| (Back photo actually a Denver Bronco) | | | |
| Miami Dolphins | | | |
| ☐ 354 Tommy Maddox | .35 | .16 | .04 |
| Denver Broncos | | | |
| ☐ 355 Siran Stacy | .04 | .02 | .01 |
| Philadelphia Eagles | | | |
| ☐ 356 Greg Lewis | .04 | .02 | .01 |
| Denver Broncos | | | |
| ☐ 357 Paul Gruber | .04 | .02 | .01 |
| Tampa Bay Buccaneers | | | |
| ☐ 358 Troy Vincent | .10 | .05 | .01 |
| Miami Dolphins | | | |
| ☐ 359 Robert Wilson | .04 | .02 | .01 |
| Tampa Bay Buccaneers | | | |
| ☐ 360 Jessie Hester | .04 | .02 | .01 |
| Indianapolis Colts | | | |
| ☐ 361 Shaun Gayle | .04 | .02 | .01 |
| Chicago Bears | | | |
| ☐ 362 Deron Cherry | .04 | .02 | .01 |
| Kansas City Chiefs | | | |
| ☐ 363 Wendell Davis | .04 | .02 | .01 |
| Chicago Bears | | | |
| ☐ 364 David Klingler UER | .50 | .23 | .06 |
| (Bio misspells his name as Klinger) | | | |
| Cincinnati Bengals | | | |
| ☐ 365 Jason Hanson | .15 | .07 | .02 |
| Detroit Lions | | | |
| ☐ 366 Marquez Pope | .10 | .05 | .01 |
| San Diego Chargers | | | |
| ☐ 367 Robert Williams | .10 | .05 | .01 |
| Dallas Cowboys | | | |
| ☐ 368 Kelvin Pritchett | .04 | .02 | .01 |
| Detroit Lions | | | |
| ☐ 369 Dana Hall | .15 | .07 | .02 |
| San Francisco 49ers | | | |
| ☐ 370 David Brandon | .04 | .02 | .01 |
| Cleveland Browns | | | |
| ☐ 371 Tim McKyer | .08 | .04 | .01 |
| Atlanta Falcons | | | |
| ☐ 372 Darion Conner | .04 | .02 | .01 |
| Atlanta Falcons | | | |
| ☐ 373 Derrick Fenner | .08 | .04 | .01 |
| Cincinnati Bengals | | | |
| ☐ 374 Hugh Millen | .08 | .04 | .01 |
| New England Patriots | | | |
| ☐ 375 Bill Jones | .04 | .02 | .01 |
| Kansas City Chiefs | | | |
| ☐ 376 J.J. Birden | .08 | .04 | .01 |
| Kansas City Chiefs | | | |
| ☐ 377 Ty Detmer | .08 | .04 | .01 |
| Green Bay Packers | | | |
| ☐ 378 Alonzo Spellman | .20 | .09 | .03 |
| Chicago Bears | | | |
| ☐ 379 Sammie Smith | .04 | .02 | .01 |
| Miami Dolphins | | | |
| ☐ 380 Al Smith | .04 | .02 | .01 |
| Houston Oilers | | | |
| ☐ 381 Louis Clark | .04 | .02 | .01 |
| Seattle Seahawks | | | |
| ☐ 382 Vernice Smith | .04 | .02 | .01 |
| Phoenix Cardinals | | | |
| ☐ 383 Tony Martin | .04 | .02 | .01 |
| Miami Dolphins | | | |
| ☐ 384 Willie Green | .04 | .02 | .01 |
| Detroit Lions | | | |
| ☐ 385 Sean Gilbert | .30 | .14 | .04 |
| Los Angeles Rams | | | |
| ☐ 386 Eugene Chung | .04 | .02 | .01 |
| New England Patriots | | | |
| ☐ 387 Toi Cook | .04 | .02 | .01 |
| New Orleans Saints | | | |
| ☐ 388 Brett Maxie | .04 | .02 | .01 |
| New Orleans Saints | | | |
| ☐ 389 Steve Israel | .04 | .02 | .01 |
| Los Angeles Rams | | | |
| ☐ 390 Mike Mularkey | .04 | .02 | .01 |
| Pittsburgh Steeelers | | | |
| ☐ 391 Barry Foster | .35 | .16 | .04 |
| Pittsburgh Steelers | | | |
| ☐ 392 Hardy Nickerson | .04 | .02 | .01 |
| Pittsburgh Steelers | | | |
| ☐ 393 Johnny Mitchell | .50 | .23 | .06 |
| New York Jets | | | |
| ☐ 394 Thurman Thomas | .40 | .18 | .05 |
| Buffalo Bills | | | |
| ☐ 395 Tony Smith | .15 | .07 | .02 |
| Atlanta Falcons | | | |
| ☐ 396 Keith Goganious | .04 | .02 | .01 |
| Buffalo Bills | | | |
| ☐ 397 Matt Darby | .04 | .02 | .01 |
| Buffalo Bills | | | |
| ☐ 398 Nate Turner | .10 | .05 | .01 |
| Buffalo Bills | | | |
| ☐ 399 Keith Jennings | .04 | .02 | .01 |
| Chicago Bears | | | |
| ☐ 400 Mitchell Benson | .04 | .02 | .01 |
| San Diego Chargers | | | |
| ☐ 401 Kurt Barber | .10 | .05 | .01 |
| New York Jets | | | |
| ☐ 402 Tony Sacca | .12 | .05 | .02 |
| Phoenix Cardinals | | | |
| ☐ 403 Steve Hendrickson | .04 | .02 | .01 |
| San Diego Chargers | | | |
| ☐ 404 Johnny Johnson | .10 | .05 | .01 |
| Phoenix Cardinals | | | |
| ☐ 405 Lorenzo Lynch | .04 | .02 | .01 |
| Phoenix Cardinals | | | |
| ☐ 406 Luis Sharpe | .04 | .02 | .01 |
| Phoenix Cardinals | | | |
| ☐ 407 Jim Everett | .08 | .04 | .01 |
| Los Angeles Rams | | | |
| ☐ 408 Neal Anderson | .10 | .05 | .01 |
| Chicago Bears | | | |
| ☐ 409 Ashley Ambrose | .04 | .02 | .01 |
| Indianapolis Colts | | | |
| ☐ 410 George Williams | .04 | .02 | .01 |
| Cleveland Browns | | | |
| ☐ 411 Clarence Kay | .08 | .04 | .01 |
| Denver Broncos | | | |
| ☐ 412 Dave Krieg | .10 | .05 | .01 |
| Kansas City Chiefs | | | |
| ☐ 413 Terrell Buckley | .04 | .02 | .01 |
| Green Bay Packers | | | |
| ☐ 414 Ricardo McDonald | .04 | .02 | .01 |
| Cincinnati Bengals | | | |
| ☐ 415 Kelly Stouffer | .04 | .02 | .01 |
| Seattle Seahawks | | | |
| ☐ 416 Barney Bussey | .04 | .02 | .01 |
| Cincinnati Bengals | | | |
| ☐ 417 Ray Roberts | .15 | .07 | .02 |
| Seattle Seahawks | | | |
| ☐ 418 Fred McAfee | .04 | .02 | .01 |
| San Diego Chargers | | | |
| ☐ 419 Fred Banks | .08 | .04 | .01 |
| Miami Dolphins | | | |
| ☐ 420 Tim McDonald | .04 | .02 | .01 |
| Phoenix Cardinals | | | |
| ☐ 421 Darryl Williams | .04 | .02 | .01 |
| Cincinnati Bengals | | | |
| ☐ 422 Bobby Abrams | .15 | .07 | .02 |
| New York Giants | | | |
| ☐ 423 Tommy Vardell | .04 | .02 | .01 |
| Cleveland Browns | | | |
| ☐ 424 William White | .04 | .02 | .01 |
| Detroit Lions | | | |
| ☐ 425 Billy Ray Smith | .04 | .02 | .01 |
| San Diego Chargers | | | |
| ☐ 426 Lemuel Stinson | .20 | .09 | .03 |
| Chicago Bears | | | |
| ☐ 427 Brad Johnson | .10 | .05 | .01 |
| Minnesota Vikings | | | |
| ☐ 428 Herschel Walker | .04 | .02 | .01 |
| Philadelphia Eagles | | | |
| ☐ 429 Eric Thomas | .04 | .02 | .01 |
| Cincinnati Bengals | | | |
| ☐ 430 Anthony Thompson | .04 | .02 | .01 |
| Phoenix Cardinals | | | |
| ☐ 431 Ed West | .12 | .05 | .02 |
| Green Bay Packers | | | |
| ☐ 432 Edgar Bennett | .04 | .02 | .01 |
| Green Bay Packers | | | |
| ☐ 433 Warren Powers | .04 | .02 | .01 |
| Denver Broncos | | | |
| ☐ 434 Byron Evans | .10 | .05 | .01 |
| Philadelphia Eagles | | | |
| ☐ 435 Rodney Culver | .04 | .02 | .01 |
| Indianapolis Colts | | | |
| ☐ 436 Ray Horton | .08 | .04 | .01 |
| Dallas Cowboys | | | |
| ☐ 437 Richmond Webb | .10 | .05 | .01 |
| Miami Dolphins | | | |
| ☐ 438 Mark McMillian | .04 | .02 | .01 |
| Philadelphia Eagles | | | |
| ☐ 439 Subset Checklist | .04 | .02 | .01 |

| | | | |
|---|---|---|---|
| ☐ 440 Lawrence Pete..................... Detroit Lions | .10 | .05 | .01 |
| ☐ 441 Rodney Smith ..................... New England Patriots | .10 | .05 | .01 |
| ☐ 442 Mark Rodenhauser................ Chicago Bears | .04 | .02 | .01 |
| ☐ 443 Scott Lockwood ................... New England Patriots | .04 | .02 | .01 |
| ☐ 444 Charles Davenport............... Pittsburgh Steelers | .04 | .02 | .01 |
| ☐ 445 Terry McDaniel.................... Los Angeles Raiders | .04 | .02 | .01 |
| ☐ 446 Darren Perry ...................... Pittsburgh Steelers | .15 | .07 | .02 |
| ☐ 447 Darrick Owens..................... Detroit Lions | .04 | .02 | .01 |
| ☐ 448 Alvin Wright ....................... Los Angeles Rams | .04 | .02 | .01 |
| ☐ 449 Frank Stams ....................... Los Angeles Rams | .04 | .02 | .01 |
| ☐ 450 Santana Dotson.................... Tampa Bay Buccaneers | .25 | .11 | .03 |
| ☐ 451 Mark Carrier....................... Chicago Bears | .08 | .04 | .01 |
| ☐ 452 Kevin Murphy ..................... Tampa Bay Buccaneers | .04 | .02 | .01 |
| ☐ 453 Jeff Bryant ......................... Seattle Seahawks | .04 | .02 | .01 |
| ☐ 454 Eric Allen .......................... Philadelphia Eagles | .08 | .04 | .01 |
| ☐ 455 Brian Bollinger .................... San Francisco 49ers | .04 | .02 | .01 |
| ☐ 456 Elston Ridgle ...................... Cincinnati Bengals | .04 | .02 | .01 |
| ☐ 457 Jim Riggs .......................... Cincinnati Bengals | .04 | .02 | .01 |
| ☐ 458 Checklist 251-320 ................ | .04 | .02 | .01 |
| ☐ 459 Checklist 321-391 ................ | .04 | .02 | .01 |
| ☐ 460 Checklist 392-460 ................ | .04 | .02 | .01 |

## 1992 Wild Card Field Force

This 30-card set was randomly inserted in 1992 Wild Card NFL II foil packs. The cards measure the standard size (2 1/2" by 3 1/2"), and gold and silver foil versions of each card were also produced and randomly inserted in the packs. The front design features glossy color player photos. Against a dark plum background, a silver or gold foil pattern similar to the teeth on a comb runs the length of the card on the left. The remaining border is purple and turns into wavy purple lines on white as one moves toward the right card edge. The backs carry a second color player photo and player profile or statistics are presented on a pastel green panel. The cards are numbered on the back. The gold and silver versions are valued at 2X and 4X, respectively, of the values listed below.

| | MINT | EXC | G-VG |
|---|---|---|---|
| COMPLETE SET (30)...................... | 20.00 | 9.00 | 2.50 |
| COMMON PLAYER (1-30)................. | .30 | .14 | .04 |
| *5/10/20 STRIPES: .3X TO .75X VALUE | | | |
| *50/100 STRIPES: .25X TO .60X VALUE | | | |
| *1000 STRIPES: .2X TO .5X VALUE | | | |
| *SILVER CARDS: 2X VALUE | | | |
| *GOLD CARDS: 4X VALUE | | | |
| | | | |
| ☐ 1 Joe Montana ......................... San Francisco 49ers | 3.00 | 1.35 | .40 |
| ☐ 2 Quentin Coryatt ..................... Indianapolis Colts | .60 | .25 | .08 |
| ☐ 3 Tommy Vardell ...................... Cleveland Browns | .50 | .23 | .06 |
| ☐ 4 Jim Kelly ............................. Buffalo Bills | 1.00 | .45 | .13 |
| ☐ 5 John Elway........................... Denver Broncos | 1.50 | .65 | .19 |

| | | | |
|---|---|---|---|
| ☐ 6 Ricky Watters ....................... San Francisco 49ers | 1.50 | .65 | .19 |
| ☐ 7 Vinny Testaverde.................... Tampa Bay Buccaneers | .40 | .18 | .05 |
| ☐ 8 Randal Hill........................... Phoenix Cardinals | .40 | .18 | .05 |
| ☐ 9 Amp Lee .............................. San Francisco 49ers | .40 | .18 | .05 |
| ☐ 10 Vaughn Dunbar..................... New Orleans Saints | .40 | .18 | .05 |
| ☐ 11 Troy Aikman ....................... Dallas Cowboys | 3.50 | 1.55 | .45 |
| ☐ 12 Deion Sanders...................... Atlanta Falcons | .50 | .23 | .06 |
| ☐ 13 Rodney Hampton ................... New York Giants | 1.50 | .65 | .19 |
| ☐ 14 Brett Favre.......................... Atlanta Falcons | 2.00 | .90 | .25 |
| ☐ 15 Warren Moon ....................... Houston Oilers | .50 | .23 | .06 |
| ☐ 16 Browning Nagle..................... New York Jets | .30 | .14 | .04 |
| ☐ 17 Terrell Buckley ..................... Green Bay Packers | .40 | .18 | .05 |
| ☐ 18 Barry Sanders ...................... Detroit Lions | 2.50 | 1.15 | .30 |
| ☐ 19 Dan Marino ......................... Miami Dolphins | 2.00 | .90 | .25 |
| ☐ 20 Carl Pickens ........................ Cincinnati Bengals | .50 | .23 | .06 |
| ☐ 21 Herschel Walker .................... Philadelphia Eagles | .40 | .18 | .05 |
| ☐ 22 Ronnie Lott ......................... Los Angeles Raiders | .40 | .18 | .05 |
| ☐ 23 Steve Emtman....................... Indianapolis Colts | .40 | .18 | .05 |
| ☐ 24 Mark Rypien......................... Washington Redskins | .40 | .18 | .05 |
| ☐ 25 Bobby Hebert ....................... New Orleans Saints | .30 | .14 | .04 |
| ☐ 26 Dan McGwire ....................... Seattle Seahawks | .30 | .14 | .04 |
| ☐ 27 Neil O'Donnell ...................... Pittsburgh Steelers | 1.00 | .45 | .13 |
| ☐ 28 Cris Carter........................... Minnesota Vikings | .30 | .14 | .04 |
| ☐ 29 Randall Cunningham ............... Philadelphia Eagles | .50 | .23 | .06 |
| ☐ 30 Jerry Rice........................... San Francisco 49ers | 1.50 | .65 | .19 |

## 1992 Wild Card Pro Picks

This eight-card set was randomly inserted one per card in retail jumbo packs. The cards measure the standard size (2 1/2" by 3 1/2") and feature color action player photos with thin black borders. The picture is set against a black and white card face with multi-colored numbers on the top and right edge. A football icon at the lower left is printed with the words "Pro Picks". The player's name and position appear in the lower right corner. The backs are magenta shading to burgundy and sport a close-up, football-shaped shot, biographical information, and statistics. The cards are numbered on the back.

| | MINT | EXC | G-VG |
|---|---|---|---|
| COMPLETE SET (8)......................... | 12.00 | 5.50 | 1.50 |
| COMMON PLAYER (1-8)................... | .50 | .23 | .06 |
| | | | |
| ☐ 1 Emmitt Smith ........................ Dallas Cowboys | 5.00 | 2.30 | .60 |
| ☐ 2 Mark Rypien .......................... Washington Redskins | .50 | .23 | .06 |
| ☐ 3 Warren Moon ......................... Houston Oilers | 1.00 | .45 | .13 |

| | MINT | EXC | G-VG |
|---|---|---|---|
| ☐ 4 Leonard Russell ....................... <br> New England Patriots | 1.50 | .65 | .19 |
| ☐ 5 Thurman Thomas..................... <br> Buffalo Bills | 1.75 | .80 | .22 |
| ☐ 6 John Elway............................... <br> Denver Broncos | 2.00 | .90 | .25 |
| ☐ 7 Barry Sanders .......................... <br> Detroit Lions | 3.00 | 1.35 | .40 |
| ☐ 8 Steve Young............................. <br> San Francisco 49ers | 1.50 | .65 | .19 |

## 1992 Wild Card Red Hot Rookies

This 30-card set was randomly inserted in 1992 Wild Card NFL II foil packs. The cards measure the standard size (2 1/2" by 3 1/2"). The fronts feature glossy color player photos inside black inner borders. The outer borders shade from red to white and then to black as one moves from left to right across the card face, and the customary series of colored numbers (1000, 100, 50, 20, 10, and 5) form a right angle at the upper right corner of the photo. A flaming football with the words "Red Hot Rookies" appears at the lower left corner. The backs are streaked with different shades of red and bordered in white. A player profile appears on a pastel green panel. A color head shot inside a football-shaped icon rounds out the back. The cards are numbered on the back. Gold and silver versions were also available one per jumbo pack.

| | MINT | EXC | G-VG |
|---|---|---|---|
| COMPLETE SET (30)........................ | 18.00 | 8.00 | 2.30 |
| COMPLETE SERIES 1 (10)................ | 6.00 | 2.70 | .75 |
| COMPLETE SERIES 2 (20)................ | 12.00 | 5.50 | 1.50 |
| COMMON PLAYER (1-10)................ | .50 | .23 | .06 |
| COMMON PLAYER (11-30)............... | .50 | .23 | .06 |
| *5/10/20 STRIPES: .30X TO .75X VALUE | | | |
| *50/100 STRIPES: .25X TO .60X VALUE | | | |
| *1000 STRIPES: .20X TO .50X VALUE | | | |
| *GOLD CARDS: .75X to 1X VALUE | | | |
| *SILVER CARDS: .50X TO .75X VALUE | | | |
| ☐ 1 Darryl Williams ........................ <br> Cincinnati Bengals | .75 | .35 | .09 |
| ☐ 2 Amp Lee.................................. <br> San Francisco 49ers | .75 | .35 | .09 |
| ☐ 3 Will Furrer ............................... <br> Chicago Bears | .75 | .35 | .09 |
| ☐ 4 Edgar Bennett ......................... <br> Green Bay Packers | .75 | .35 | .09 |
| ☐ 5 Terrell Buckley ........................ <br> Green Bay Packers | .75 | .35 | .09 |
| ☐ 6 Bob Whitfield .......................... <br> Atlanta Falcons | .50 | .23 | .06 |
| ☐ 7 Siran Stacy ............................. <br> Philadelphia Eagles | .75 | .35 | .09 |
| ☐ 8 Jimmy Smith ........................... <br> Dallas Cowboys | .75 | .35 | .09 |
| ☐ 9 Kevin Turner ........................... <br> New England Patriots | .50 | .23 | .06 |
| ☐ 10 Tommy Vardell........................ <br> Cleveland Browns | 1.00 | .45 | .13 |
| ☐ 11 Surprise Card.......................... | 1.25 | .55 | .16 |
| ☐ 12 Derek Brown ........................... <br> New York Giants | .75 | .35 | .09 |
| ☐ 13 Marco Coleman........................ <br> Miami Dolphins | .75 | .35 | .09 |
| ☐ 14 Quentin Coryatt ...................... <br> Indianapolis Colts | 1.00 | .45 | .13 |
| ☐ 15 Rodney Culver......................... <br> Indianapolis Colts | .75 | .35 | .09 |
| ☐ 16 Ty Detmer............................... <br> Green Bay Packers | .75 | .35 | .09 |
| ☐ 17 Vaughn Dunbar........................ <br> New Orleans Saints | .75 | .35 | .09 |

| | MINT | EXC | G-VG |
|---|---|---|---|
| ☐ 18 Steve Emtman.......................... <br> Indianapolis Colts | .75 | .35 | .09 |
| ☐ 19 Sean Gilbert .......................... <br> Los Angeles Rams | 1.00 | .45 | .13 |
| ☐ 20 Courtney Hawkins..................... <br> Tampa Bay Buccaneers | 1.00 | .45 | .13 |
| ☐ 21 David Klingler.......................... <br> Cincinnati Bengals | 1.75 | .80 | .22 |
| ☐ 22 Amp Lee ................................. <br> San Francisco 49ers | .75 | .35 | .09 |
| ☐ 23 Tommy Maddox...................... <br> Denver Broncos | 1.50 | .65 | .19 |
| ☐ 24 Johnny Mitchell........................ <br> New York Jets | 1.50 | .65 | .19 |
| ☐ 25 Darren Perry ........................... <br> Pittsburgh Steelers | .50 | .23 | .06 |
| ☐ 26 Carl Pickens ........................... <br> Cincinnati Bengals | 1.00 | .45 | .13 |
| ☐ 27 Robert Porcher ....................... <br> Detroit Lions | .75 | .35 | .09 |
| ☐ 28 Tony Smith ............................. <br> Atlanta Falcons | .75 | .35 | .09 |
| ☐ 29 Alonzo Spellman ..................... <br> Chicago Bears | .75 | .35 | .09 |
| ☐ 30 Troy Vincent............................ <br> Miami Dolphins | .75 | .35 | .09 |

## 1992 Wild Card Running Wild Silver

This 40-card set was inserted one card per pack in 1992 Wild Card NFL II jumbo packs. The cards measure the standard size (2 1/2" by 3 1/2") and feature action color player photos set in a parallelogram shape against a background that shades from white to black. Near the bottom of the picture, a gradated green arrow icon runs from left to right stamped in gold foil with the words "Running Wild". Thin black lines emanating from the letters give the impression of motion. Smaller versions of the arrow icon appear at the right edge of the photo as though they are running behind it. The player's name and team appear at the bottom right in red. The backs have white borders and display action color player photos in a parallelogram shape similar to but smaller than the one on the front. A narrow light blue-green parallelogram runs next to the picture and contains statistics that are printed horizontally. The cards are numbered on the back at the upper right with the numbers printed on a pale green and white striped graphic design.

| | MINT | EXC | G-VG |
|---|---|---|---|
| COMPLETE SET (40)........................ | 20.00 | 9.00 | 2.50 |
| COMMON PLAYER (1-40)................. | .50 | .23 | .06 |
| *5/10/20 STRIPES: .30X TO .75X VALUE | | | |
| *50/100 STRIPES: .25X TO .60X VALUE | | | |
| *1000 STRIPES: .20X TO .50X VALUE | | | |
| *GOLD CARDS: 1.1X TO 1.5X VALUE | | | |
| ☐ 1 Terry Allen .............................. <br> Minnesota Vikings | 1.00 | .45 | .13 |
| ☐ 2 Neal Anderson.......................... <br> Chicago Bears | .75 | .35 | .09 |
| ☐ 3 Eric Ball.................................. <br> Cincinnati Bengals | .50 | .23 | .06 |
| ☐ 4 Nick Bell ................................. <br> Los Angeles Raiders | .50 | .23 | .06 |
| ☐ 5 Edgar Bennett .......................... <br> Green Bay Packers | .75 | .35 | .09 |
| ☐ 6 Rod Bernstine .......................... <br> San Diego Chargers | .50 | .23 | .06 |
| ☐ 7 Marion Butts............................ <br> San Diego Chargers | .75 | .35 | .09 |
| ☐ 8 Keith Byars .............................. <br> Philadelphia Eagles | .50 | .23 | .06 |
| ☐ 9 Earnest Byner .......................... <br> Washington Redskins | .75 | .35 | .09 |

| | | | |
|---|---|---|---|
| ☐ 10 Reggie Cobb | .75 | .35 | .09 |
| Tampa Bay Buccaneers | | | |
| ☐ 11 Roger Craig | .75 | .35 | .09 |
| Minnesota Vikings | | | |
| ☐ 12 Rodney Culver | .75 | .35 | .09 |
| Indianapolis Colts | | | |
| ☐ 13 Barry Foster | 1.50 | .65 | .19 |
| Pittsburgh Steelers | | | |
| ☐ 14 Cleveland Gary | .50 | .23 | .06 |
| Los Angeles Rams | | | |
| ☐ 15 Harold Green | .75 | .35 | .09 |
| Cincinnati Bengals | | | |
| ☐ 16 Gaston Green | .50 | .23 | .06 |
| Denver Broncos | | | |
| ☐ 17 Rodney Hampton | 1.50 | .65 | .19 |
| New York Giants | | | |
| ☐ 18 Mark Higgs | .50 | .23 | .06 |
| Miami Dolphins | | | |
| ☐ 19 Dalton Hilliard | .50 | .23 | .06 |
| New Orleans Saints | | | |
| ☐ 20 Bobby Humphrey UER | .50 | .23 | .06 |
| Miami Dolphins | | | |
| (Misspelled Humphries) | | | |
| ☐ 21 Amp Lee | .75 | .35 | .09 |
| San Francisco 49ers | | | |
| ☐ 22 Kevin Mack | .50 | .23 | .06 |
| Cleveland Browns | | | |
| ☐ 23 Eric Metcalf | .75 | .35 | .09 |
| Cleveland Browns | | | |
| ☐ 24 Brad Muster | .50 | .23 | .06 |
| Chicago Bears | | | |
| ☐ 25 Christian Okoye | .50 | .23 | .06 |
| Kansas City Chiefs | | | |
| ☐ 26 Tom Rathman | .50 | .23 | .06 |
| San Francisco 49ers | | | |
| ☐ 27 Leonard Russell | 1.25 | .55 | .16 |
| New England Patriots | | | |
| ☐ 28 Barry Sanders | 3.00 | 1.35 | .40 |
| Detroit Lions | | | |
| ☐ 29 Heath Sherman | .50 | .23 | .06 |
| Philadelphia Eagles | | | |
| ☐ 30 Emmitt Smith | 6.00 | 2.70 | .75 |
| Dallas Cowboys | | | |
| ☐ 31 Blair Thomas | .75 | .35 | .09 |
| New York Jets | | | |
| ☐ 32 Thurman Thomas | 1.50 | .65 | .19 |
| Buffalo Bills | | | |
| ☐ 33 Tommy Vardell | .75 | .35 | .09 |
| Cleveland Browns | | | |
| ☐ 34 Herschel Walker | .75 | .35 | .09 |
| Philadelphia Eagles | | | |
| ☐ 35 Chris Warren | .75 | .35 | .09 |
| Seattle Seahawks | | | |
| ☐ 36 Ricky Watters | 2.25 | 1.00 | .30 |
| San Francisco 49ers | | | |
| ☐ 37 Lorenzo White | .50 | .23 | .06 |
| Houston Oilers | | | |
| ☐ 38 John L. Williams | .50 | .23 | .06 |
| Seattle Seahawks | | | |
| ☐ 39 Barry Word | .75 | .35 | .09 |
| Kansas City Chiefs | | | |
| ☐ 40 Vince Workman | .75 | .35 | .09 |
| Green Bay Packers | | | |

# 1992 Wild Card Stat Smashers

This 52-card subset was randomly inserted in 1992 Wild Card NFL packs. Card numbers 1-16 were randomly inserted in 1992 Wild Card NFL II foil packs, while card numbers 17-52 were inserted one per pack in Series II jumbo packs. The collector could also obtain a Barry Sanders Stat Smasher card through a mail-in offer in exchange for the surprise card in series I. The cards measure the standard size (2 1/2 by 3 1/2"). The fronts feature color player cut-outs superimposed on a full-bleed metallic foil background texturized in various patterns. The

player's name, team name, and his position appear in lilac and purple stripes that cut across the bottom of the card face. Each stripe becomes jagged at the right edge of the card. The Stat Smashers icon in the upper right completes the front. The backs have black borders and display a panel that shades from violet to a deep, brownish-purple from top to bottom. Featured on the panel are a color head shot, biography, and a 1991 season summary of the player's achievements. The cards are numbered on the back with an "SS" prefix.

| | MINT | EXC | G-VG |
|---|---|---|---|
| COMPLETE SET (52) | 60.00 | 27.00 | 7.50 |
| COMPLETE SERIES 1 (16) | 35.00 | 16.00 | 4.40 |
| COMPLETE SERIES 2 (36) | 25.00 | 11.50 | 3.10 |
| COMMON PLAYER (SS1-SS16) | 1.50 | .65 | .19 |
| COMMON PLAYER (SS17-SS52) | .50 | .23 | .06 |
| *5/10/20 STRIPES: .3X TO .8X VALUE | | | |
| *50/100 STRIPES: .25X TO .65X VALUE | | | |
| *1000 STRIPES: .2X TO .5X VALUE | | | |

| | | | |
|---|---|---|---|
| ☐ SS1 Barry Sanders | 6.00 | 2.70 | .75 |
| Detroit Lions | | | |
| ☐ SS2 Leonard Russell | 2.25 | 1.00 | .30 |
| New England Patriots | | | |
| ☐ SS3 Thurman Thomas | 3.00 | 1.35 | .40 |
| Buffalo Bills | | | |
| ☐ SS4 John Elway | 5.00 | 2.30 | .60 |
| Denver Broncos | | | |
| ☐ SS5 Steve Young | 3.00 | 1.35 | .40 |
| San Francisco 49ers | | | |
| ☐ SS6 Warren Moon | 2.25 | 1.00 | .30 |
| Houston Oilers | | | |
| ☐ SS7 Terrell Buckley | 1.50 | .65 | .19 |
| Green Bay Packers | | | |
| ☐ SS8 Randall Cunningham | 2.00 | .90 | .25 |
| Philadelphia Eagles | | | |
| ☐ SS9 Steve Emtman | 1.50 | .65 | .19 |
| Indianapolis Colts | | | |
| ☐ SS10 Dan Marino | 6.00 | 2.70 | .75 |
| Miami Dolphins | | | |
| ☐ SS11 Joe Montana | 8.00 | 3.60 | 1.00 |
| San Francisco 49ers | | | |
| ☐ SS12 Carl Pickens | 1.50 | .65 | .19 |
| Cincinnati Bengals | | | |
| ☐ SS13 Jerry Rice | 5.00 | 2.30 | .60 |
| San Francisco 49ers | | | |
| ☐ SS14 Deion Sanders | 2.25 | 1.00 | .30 |
| Atlanta Falcons | | | |
| ☐ SS15 Tommy Vardell | 2.00 | .90 | .25 |
| Cleveland Browns | | | |
| ☐ SS16 Ricky Watters | 4.00 | 1.80 | .50 |
| San Francisco 49ers | | | |
| ☐ SS17 Troy Aikman | 6.00 | 2.70 | .75 |
| Dallas Cowboys | | | |
| ☐ SS18 Dale Carter | .75 | .35 | .09 |
| Kansas City Chiefs | | | |
| ☐ SS19 Quentin Coryatt | .75 | .35 | .09 |
| Indianapolis Colts | | | |
| ☐ SS20 Vaughn Dunbar | .60 | .25 | .08 |
| New Orleans Saints | | | |
| ☐ SS21 Mark Duper | .50 | .23 | .06 |
| Miami Dolphins | | | |
| ☐ SS22 Eric Metcalf | .50 | .23 | .06 |
| Cleveland Browns | | | |
| ☐ SS23 Brett Favre | 4.00 | 1.80 | .50 |
| Green Bay Packers | | | |
| ☐ SS24 Barry Foster | 2.25 | 1.00 | .30 |
| Pittsburgh Steelers | | | |
| ☐ SS25 Jeff George | .75 | .35 | .09 |
| Indianapolis Colts | | | |
| ☐ SS26 Sean Gilbert UER | .75 | .35 | .09 |
| Los Angeles Rams | | | |
| ("Stan" on front) | | | |
| ☐ SS27 Jim Harbaugh | .50 | .23 | .06 |
| Chicago Bears | | | |
| ☐ SS28 Courtney Hawkins | 1.00 | .45 | .13 |
| Tampa Bay Buccaneers | | | |
| ☐ SS29 Charles Haley | .50 | .23 | .06 |
| Dallas Cowboys | | | |
| ☐ SS30 Bobby Hebert | .50 | .23 | .06 |
| New Orleans Saints | | | |
| ☐ SS31 Stan Humphries | .60 | .25 | .08 |
| San Diego Chargers | | | |
| ☐ SS32 Michael Irvin | 2.50 | 1.15 | .30 |
| Dallas Cowboys | | | |
| ☐ SS33 Jim Kelly | 1.50 | .65 | .19 |
| Buffalo Bills | | | |
| ☐ SS34 David Klingler | 1.25 | .55 | .16 |
| Cincinnati Bengals | | | |
| ☐ SS35 Ronnie Lott | .60 | .25 | .08 |
| Los Angeles Raiders | | | |
| ☐ SS36 Tommy Maddox | 1.00 | .45 | .13 |
| Denver Broncos | | | |
| ☐ SS37 Todd Marinovich | .50 | .23 | .06 |
| Los Angeles Raiders | | | |
| ☐ SS38 Hugh Millen | .50 | .23 | .06 |
| New England Patriots | | | |

| | MINT | EXC | G-VG |
|---|---|---|---|
| ☐ SS39 Art Monk............ | .60 | .25 | .08 |
| Washington Redskins | | | |
| ☐ SS40 Browning Nagle ................. | .50 | .23 | .06 |
| New York Jets | | | |
| ☐ SS41 Neil O'Donnell.................... | 1.25 | .55 | .16 |
| Pittsburgh Steelers | | | |
| ☐ SS42 Tom Rathman................... | .50 | .23 | .06 |
| San Francisco 49ers | | | |
| ☐ SS43 Andre Rison ................... | 1.00 | .45 | .13 |
| Atlanta Falcons | | | |
| ☐ SS44 Mike Singletary.................. | .60 | .25 | .08 |
| Chicago Bears | | | |
| ☐ SS45 Tony Smith..................... | .60 | .25 | .08 |
| Atlanta Falcons | | | |
| ☐ SS46 Emmitt Smith................... | 10.00 | 4.50 | 1.25 |
| Dallas Cowboys | | | |
| ☐ SS47 Pete Stoyanovich............... | .50 | .23 | .06 |
| Miami Dolphins | | | |
| ☐ SS48 John Taylor ..................... | .60 | .25 | .08 |
| San Francisco 49ers | | | |
| ☐ SS49 Troy Vincent ..................... | .50 | .23 | .06 |
| Miami Dolphins | | | |
| ☐ SS50 Herschel Walker ................. | .50 | .23 | .06 |
| Philadelphia Eagles | | | |
| ☐ SS51 Lorenzo White ................. | .50 | .23 | .06 |
| Houston Oilers | | | |
| ☐ SS52 Rodney Culver................... | .60 | .25 | .08 |
| Indianapolis Colts | | | |
| ☐ P1 Barry Sanders...................... | 3.50 | 1.55 | .45 |
| Detroit Lions | | | |
| ☐ P2 Emmitt Smith........................ | 5.00 | 2.30 | .60 |
| Dallas Cowboys | | | |

## 1992 Wild Card WLAF

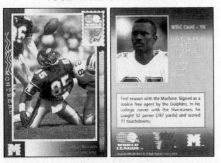

The Wild Card WLAF Football set contains 150 cards measuring the standard size (2 1/2" by 3 1/2"). It is reported that the production run was limited to 6,000 numbered ten-box cases, and that no factory sets were produced. The fronts display glossy color action player photos, on a black and gray card face with a white frame around the picture and different color numbers in the right border. The Wild Card World League logo resembles a postage stamp in the upper right corner. On a background with different shades of blue, the backs have a head shot, biography, and career highlights. The cards are numbered on the back and checklisted below according to teams as follows: Montreal Machine (2-15, 57), San Antonio Riders (16-30), Ohio Glory (31-43), Sacramento Surge (44-56), Orlando Thunder (58-69, 138, 140, 142), New York-New Jersey Knights (70-85), Frankfurt Galaxy (86-88, 90-91, 93-95, 124-128), Birmingham Fire (96-110, 143-144), London Monarchs (111-123, 139, 141, 145-147), and Barcelona Dragons (89, 92, 129-137).

| | MINT | EXC | G-VG |
|---|---|---|---|
| COMPLETE SET (150).................. | 7.50 | 3.00 | .75 |
| COMMON PLAYER (1-150)............... | .05 | .02 | .00 |
| | | | |
| ☐ 1 World Bowl Champs ............... | .15 | .06 | .01 |
| ☐ 2 Pete Mandley ......................... | .15 | .06 | .01 |
| ☐ 3 Steve Williams ....................... | .05 | .02 | .00 |
| ☐ 4 Dee Thomas .......................... | .05 | .02 | .00 |
| ☐ 5 Emanuel King ......................... | .15 | .06 | .01 |
| ☐ 6 Anthony Dilweg ..................... | .25 | .10 | .02 |
| ☐ 7 Ben Brown ............................ | .05 | .02 | .00 |
| ☐ 8 Darryl Harris .......................... | .05 | .02 | .00 |
| ☐ 9 Aaron Emanuel....................... | .25 | .10 | .02 |
| ☐ 10 Andre Brown........................ | .10 | .04 | .01 |
| ☐ 11 Reggie McKenzie .................. | .15 | .06 | .01 |
| ☐ 12 Darryl Holmes ...................... | .05 | .02 | .00 |
| ☐ 13 Michael Proctor..................... | .05 | .02 | .00 |
| ☐ 14 Ricky Johnson ...................... | .05 | .02 | .00 |
| ☐ 15 Ray Savage .......................... | .05 | .02 | .00 |
| ☐ 16 George Searcy....................... | .05 | .02 | .00 |
| ☐ 17 Titus Dixon........................... | .05 | .02 | .00 |
| ☐ 18 Willie Fears ........................... | .15 | .06 | .01 |
| ☐ 19 Terrence Cooks ...................... | .05 | .02 | .00 |
| ☐ 20 Ivory Lee Brown..................... | .25 | .10 | .02 |
| ☐ 21 Mike Johnson ........................ | .05 | .02 | .00 |
| ☐ 22 Doug Williams ....................... | .15 | .06 | .01 |
| ☐ 23 Brad Goebel .......................... | .25 | .10 | .02 |
| ☐ 24 Tony Boles ........................... | .15 | .06 | .01 |
| ☐ 25 Cisco Richard........................ | .05 | .02 | .00 |
| ☐ 26 Robb White ........................... | .05 | .02 | .00 |
| ☐ 27 Darrell Colbert........................ | .05 | .02 | .00 |
| ☐ 28 Wayne Walker ....................... | .15 | .06 | .01 |
| ☐ 29 Ronnie Williams ..................... | .05 | .02 | .00 |
| ☐ 30 Erik Norgard.......................... | .05 | .02 | .00 |
| ☐ 31 Darren Willis ......................... | .05 | .02 | .00 |
| ☐ 32 Kent Wells ............................ | .05 | .02 | .00 |
| ☐ 33 Phil Logan ............................ | .05 | .02 | .00 |
| ☐ 34 Pat O'Hara............................ | .05 | .02 | .00 |
| ☐ 35 Melvin Patterson ..................... | .05 | .02 | .00 |
| ☐ 36 Amir Rasul ........................... | .05 | .02 | .00 |
| ☐ 37 Tom Rouen ........................... | .15 | .06 | .01 |
| ☐ 38 Chris Cochrane ...................... | .05 | .02 | .00 |
| ☐ 39 Randy Bethel ........................ | .05 | .02 | .00 |
| ☐ 40 Eric Harmon .......................... | .05 | .02 | .00 |
| ☐ 41 Archie Herring ....................... | .05 | .02 | .00 |
| ☐ 42 Tim James ............................ | .05 | .02 | .00 |
| ☐ 43 Babe Laufenberg .................... | .15 | .06 | .01 |
| ☐ 44 Herb Welch ........................... | .05 | .02 | .00 |
| ☐ 45 Stefon Adams ....................... | .05 | .02 | .00 |
| ☐ 46 Tony Burse ........................... | .10 | .04 | .01 |
| ☐ 47 Carl Parker ........................... | .05 | .02 | .00 |
| ☐ 48 Mike Prugle .......................... | .05 | .02 | .00 |
| ☐ 49 Michael Jones ....................... | .05 | .02 | .00 |
| ☐ 50 David Archer .......................... | .25 | .10 | .02 |
| ☐ 51 Corian Freeman ..................... | .05 | .02 | .00 |
| ☐ 52 Eddie Brown.......................... | .15 | .06 | .01 |
| ☐ 53 Paul Green ........................... | .05 | .02 | .00 |
| ☐ 54 Basil Proctor ......................... | .05 | .02 | .00 |
| ☐ 55 Mike Sinclair ......................... | .05 | .02 | .00 |
| ☐ 56 Louis Riddick ........................ | .05 | .02 | .00 |
| ☐ 57 Roman Matuez ....................... | .05 | .02 | .00 |
| ☐ 58 Darryl Clack .......................... | .10 | .04 | .01 |
| ☐ 59 Willie Davis ........................... | .75 | .30 | .07 |
| ☐ 60 Glen Rodgers ........................ | .05 | .02 | .00 |
| ☐ 61 Grantis Bell .......................... | .05 | .02 | .00 |
| ☐ 62 Joe Howard-Johnson.............. | .15 | .06 | .01 |
| ☐ 63 Rocen Keeton ........................ | .10 | .04 | .01 |
| ☐ 64 Dean Witkowski ..................... | .05 | .02 | .00 |
| ☐ 65 Stacey Simmons ..................... | .15 | .06 | .01 |
| ☐ 66 Roger Vick ........................... | .15 | .06 | .01 |
| ☐ 67 Scott Mitchell ........................ | .75 | .30 | .07 |
| ☐ 68 Todd Krumm.......................... | .05 | .02 | .00 |
| ☐ 69 Kerwin Bell ........................... | .15 | .06 | .01 |
| ☐ 70 Richard Carey ....................... | .05 | .02 | .00 |
| ☐ 71 Kip Lewis ............................. | .05 | .02 | .00 |
| ☐ 72 Andre Alexander..................... | .05 | .02 | .00 |
| ☐ 73 Reggie Slack ......................... | .20 | .08 | .02 |
| ☐ 74 Falanda Newton ..................... | .10 | .04 | .01 |
| ☐ 75 Tony Woods.......................... | .10 | .04 | .01 |
| ☐ 76 Chris McLemore ..................... | .05 | .02 | .00 |
| ☐ 77 Eric Wilkerson ....................... | .10 | .04 | .01 |
| ☐ 78 Cornell Burbage ..................... | .10 | .04 | .01 |
| ☐ 79 Doug Pederson ...................... | .05 | .02 | .00 |
| ☐ 80 Brent Pease .......................... | .15 | .06 | .01 |
| ☐ 81 Monty Gilbreath ..................... | .05 | .02 | .00 |
| ☐ 82 Wes Pritchett ........................ | .05 | .02 | .00 |
| ☐ 83 Byron Williams ...................... | .05 | .02 | .00 |
| ☐ 84 Ron Sancho .......................... | .10 | .04 | .01 |
| ☐ 85 Tony Jones ........................... | .10 | .04 | .01 |
| ☐ 86 Anthony Wallace .................... | .05 | .02 | .00 |
| ☐ 87 Mike Perez ........................... | .20 | .08 | .02 |
| ☐ 88 Steve Bartalo ........................ | .05 | .02 | .00 |
| ☐ 89 Teddy Garcia ........................ | .05 | .02 | .00 |
| ☐ 90 Joe Greenwood ...................... | .05 | .02 | .00 |
| ☐ 91 Tony Baker ........................... | .05 | .02 | .00 |
| ☐ 92 Glenn Cobb .......................... | .05 | .02 | .00 |
| ☐ 93 Mark Tucker .......................... | .05 | .02 | .00 |
| ☐ 94 Lyneil Mayo........................... | .05 | .02 | .00 |
| ☐ 95 Alex Espinoza ....................... | .05 | .02 | .00 |
| ☐ 96 Mike Norseth......................... | .15 | .06 | .01 |
| ☐ 97 Steve Avery .......................... | .05 | .02 | .00 |
| ☐ 98 John Brantley......................... | .10 | .04 | .01 |
| ☐ 99 Eddie Britton ......................... | .05 | .02 | .00 |
| ☐ 100 Philip Doyle ......................... | .05 | .02 | .00 |
| ☐ 101 Elroy Harris ......................... | .05 | .02 | .00 |
| ☐ 102 John R. Holland .................... | .10 | .04 | .01 |
| ☐ 103 Mark Hopkins ...................... | .05 | .02 | .00 |
| ☐ 104 Arthur Hunter ...................... | .05 | .02 | .00 |
| ☐ 105 Paul McGowan ..................... | .05 | .02 | .00 |
| ☐ 106 John Miller .......................... | .05 | .02 | .00 |
| ☐ 107 Shawn Moore....................... | .15 | .06 | .01 |
| ☐ 108 Phil Ross ............................ | .05 | .02 | .00 |
| ☐ 109 Eugene Rowell ..................... | .05 | .02 | .00 |
| ☐ 110 Joe Valerio .......................... | .15 | .06 | .01 |
| ☐ 111 Harvey Wilson ...................... | .05 | .02 | .00 |
| ☐ 112 Irvin Smith .......................... | .05 | .02 | .00 |
| ☐ 113 Tony Sargent........................ | .05 | .02 | .00 |
| ☐ 114 Ricky Shaw .......................... | .05 | .02 | .00 |

| | | | |
|---|---|---|---|
| ☐ 115 Curtis Moore | .05 | .02 | .00 |
| ☐ 116 Fred McNair | .05 | .02 | .00 |
| ☐ 117 Danny Lockett | .15 | .06 | .01 |
| ☐ 118 William Kirksey | .05 | .02 | .00 |
| ☐ 119 Stan Gelbaugh | .25 | .10 | .02 |
| ☐ 120 Judd Garrett | .20 | .08 | .02 |
| ☐ 121 Dedrick Dodge | .05 | .02 | .00 |
| ☐ 122 Dan Crossman | .05 | .02 | .00 |
| ☐ 123 Jeff Alexander | .05 | .02 | .00 |
| ☐ 124 Lew Barnes | .05 | .02 | .00 |
| ☐ 125 Willie Don Wright | .05 | .02 | .00 |
| ☐ 126 Johnny Thomas | .05 | .02 | .00 |
| ☐ 127 Richard Buchanan | .05 | .02 | .00 |
| ☐ 128 Chad Fortune | .05 | .02 | .00 |
| ☐ 129 Eric Lindstrom | .05 | .02 | .00 |
| ☐ 130 Ron Goetz | .05 | .02 | .00 |
| ☐ 131 Bruce Clark | .10 | .04 | .01 |
| ☐ 132 Anthony Greene | .15 | .06 | .01 |
| ☐ 133 Demetrius Davis | .10 | .04 | .01 |
| ☐ 134 Mike Roth | .05 | .02 | .00 |
| ☐ 135 Tony Moss | .05 | .02 | .00 |
| ☐ 136 Scott Erney | .10 | .04 | .01 |
| ☐ 137 Brad Henke | .05 | .02 | .00 |
| ☐ 138 Malcolm Frank | .05 | .02 | .00 |
| ☐ 139 Sean Foster | .05 | .02 | .00 |
| ☐ 140 Michael Titley | .05 | .02 | .00 |
| ☐ 141 Rickey Williams | .05 | .02 | .00 |
| ☐ 142 Karl Dunbar | .05 | .02 | .00 |
| ☐ 143 Carl Bax | .05 | .02 | .00 |
| ☐ 144 Willie Bouyer | .05 | .02 | .00 |
| ☐ 145 Howard Feggins | .05 | .02 | .00 |
| ☐ 146 David Smith | .05 | .02 | .00 |
| ☐ 147 Bernard Ford | .10 | .04 | .01 |
| ☐ 148 Checklist 1 | .05 | .02 | .00 |
| ☐ 149 Checklist 2 | .05 | .02 | .00 |
| ☐ 150 Checklist 3 | .05 | .02 | .00 |
| ☐ NNO Box Card | 1.00 | .40 | .10 |

(Redeemable for box of WLAF; inserted in various Wild Card products)

## 1992 Wild Card Class Back Attack

This five-card set was randomly inserted in 1992 Wild Card WLAF foil packs. The cards measure the standard size (2 1/2" by 3 1/2") and feature color action player photos with white borders. The picture is set against a black and green card face with multi-colored numbers on the right edge and a mustard graphic design on the left. A football icon at the lower left is printed with the words "Class Back Attack" (1-4) or "Red Hot Rookie" (5). The player's name and position appear in the lower right corner. The backs are green and sport a close-up shot and biographical information. A pale green box with a red border contains an explanation of the odds of getting a wild card in packs or boxes. David Klingler was redeemable for a Surprise Card. The cards are numbered on the back.

| | MINT | EXC | G-VG |
|---|---|---|---|
| COMPLETE SET (5) | 20.00 | 8.00 | 2.00 |
| COMMON PLAYER (SP1-SP5) | 2.00 | .80 | .20 |
| ☐ SP1 Vaughn Dunbar | 2.00 | .80 | .20 |
|     New Orleans Saints | | | |
| ☐ SP2 Barry Sanders | 5.00 | 2.00 | .50 |
|     Detroit Lions | | | |
| ☐ SP3 Emmitt Smith | 10.00 | 4.00 | 1.00 |
|     Dallas Cowboys | | | |
| ☐ SP4 Thurman Thomas | 4.00 | 1.60 | .40 |
|     Buffalo Bills | | | |
| ☐ SP5 David Klingler | 4.00 | 1.60 | .40 |
|     (Red Hot Rookie; Surprise Card Redemption) Cincinnati Bengals | | | |

## 1992 Wild Card NASDAM

These five promo cards were given away at the NASDAM trade show in Orlando in the spring of 1992. The standard-size (2 1/2" by 3 1/2") cards features color action player photos with white borders. Team color-coded stripes form a right angle at the lower left corner, while the customary series of colored numbers (1000, 100, 50, 20, 10, and 5) form a right angle at the upper right corner of the photo. On a blue and white background, the backs carry a color headshot, biography, and statistics. The cards are numbered on the back.

| | MINT | EXC | G-VG |
|---|---|---|---|
| COMPLETE SET (5) | 7.00 | 2.80 | .70 |
| COMMON PLAYER (1-5) | 1.25 | .50 | .12 |
| ☐ 1 Edgar Bennett | 2.00 | .80 | .20 |
|     Florida State | | | |
| ☐ 2 Amp Lee | 2.00 | .80 | .20 |
|     Florida State | | | |
| ☐ 3 Terrell Buckley | 2.00 | .80 | .20 |
|     Florida State | | | |
| ☐ 4 Tony Smith | 1.25 | .50 | .12 |
|     Southern Mississippi | | | |
| ☐ 5 Will Furrer UER | 1.25 | .50 | .12 |
|     (Misspelled Furer) Virginia Tech | | | |

## 1992 Wild Card NASDAM/SCAI Miami

Exclusively featuring Miami Dolphins, this six-card standard-size (2 1/2" by 3 1/2") set was given out at the NASDAM/SCAI annual conference in Miami during November, 1992. The glossy color player photos have borders shading from white to black as one moves across the card face. The team color-coded stripes form a right angle at the lower left corner, while the customary series of colored numbers (1000, 100, 50, 20, 10, and 5) form a right angle at the upper right corner of the photo. On the back statistics appear on a pastel green panel. A color head shot inside a football-shaped icon and biographical information rounds out the back. The cards are numbered on the back.

| | MINT | EXC | G-VG |
|---|---|---|---|
| COMPLETE SET (6) | 7.00 | 2.80 | .70 |
| COMMON PLAYER (1-6) | 1.25 | .50 | .12 |
| ☐ 1 Mark Clayton | 2.00 | .80 | .20 |
| ☐ 2 Aaron Craver | 1.25 | .50 | .12 |
| ☐ 3 Tony Paige | 1.25 | .50 | .12 |
| ☐ 4 Mark Duper | 1.50 | .60 | .15 |

| | MINT | EXC | G-VG |
|---|---|---|---|
| ☐ 5 Tony Martin | 1.25 | .50 | .12 |
| ☐ 6 Reggie Roby | 1.25 | .50 | .12 |

## 1992 Wild Card Sacramento CardFest

This six-card set (of San Francisco 49ers) measures the standard size (2 1/2" by 3 1/2") and features color action player photos with thin black borders. The picture is set against a black and white card face with multi-colored numbers on the top and right edge. A Sacramento CardFest icon is superimposed on the photo at the lower left. The player's name and position appear in the lower right corner. The backs are blue-green shading to black and sport a close-up, football-shaped picture, biographical information, and statistics. The cards are numbered on the back.

| | MINT | EXC | G-VG |
|---|---|---|---|
| COMPLETE SET (6) | 10.00 | 4.00 | 1.00 |
| COMMON PLAYER (1-6) | 1.25 | .50 | .12 |
| ☐ 1 Tom Rathman | 1.50 | .60 | .15 |
| ☐ 2 Steve Young | 3.00 | 1.20 | .30 |
| ☐ 3 Steve Bono | 2.00 | .80 | .20 |
| ☐ 4 Brent Jones | 1.25 | .50 | .12 |
| ☐ 5 Ricky Watters | 4.00 | 1.60 | .40 |
| ☐ 6 Amp Lee | 2.00 | .80 | .20 |

## 1992-93 Wild Card San Francisco

Exclusively featuring San Francisco 49ers, this six-card, standard-size (2 1/2" by 3 1/2") set was originally given out at the Sports Collectors Card Expo held in San Francisco in September, 1992 and then reissued (with a slightly different show logo, different individual card numbers, and two replacement players) at the Spring National Sports Collectors Convention in San Francisco in March 1993. The two sets are indistinguishable except for the different show logo in the lower left corner of each obverse and the card numbering. The two sets currently are valued equally. The glossy color player photos have borders shading from white to black as one moves across the card face. The team color-coded stripes form a right angle at the lower left corner, while the customary series of colored numbers (1000, 100, 50, 20, 10, and 5) form a right angle at the upper right corner of the photo. On the back statistics appear on a pastel green panel. A color head shot inside a football-shaped icon and biographical information rounds out the back. The cards are numbered on the back; cards designated below as A are from the original 1992 set, whereas the B versions are from the 1993 reissue set. The complete set below applies to either set.

| | MINT | EXC | G-VG |
|---|---|---|---|
| COMPLETE SET (6) | 8.00 | 3.25 | .80 |
| COMMON PLAYER (1-6) | 1.25 | .50 | .12 |
| ☐ 1A John Taylor | 1.50 | .60 | .15 |
| ☐ 1B Tom Rathman | 1.50 | .60 | .15 |
| ☐ 2A Amp Lee | 2.00 | .80 | .20 |
| ☐ 2B Steve Young | 3.00 | 1.20 | .30 |
| ☐ 3A Steve Bono | 2.00 | .80 | .20 |
| ☐ 3B Steve Bono | 2.00 | .80 | .20 |
| ☐ 4A Steve Young | 3.00 | 1.20 | .30 |
| ☐ 4B Brent Jones | 1.50 | .60 | .15 |
| ☐ 5A Tom Rathman | 1.50 | .60 | .15 |
| ☐ 5B Ricky Watters | 3.00 | 1.20 | .30 |
| ☐ 6A Don Griffin | 1.25 | .50 | .12 |
| ☐ 6B Amp Lee | 2.00 | .80 | .20 |

## 1993 Wild Card NFL Prototypes

These six promo cards were given away at the 1993 National Sports Collectors Convention in Chicago, Ill. The standard-size (2 1/2" by 3 1/2") cards feature full-bleed color action player photos. The player's name and team name appear in a gold lightning stripe that cuts across the bottom of the card. Against a background of the home team's city skyline, the horizontal backs carry a second, smaller color action photo, biography, and career summary. The cards are numbered on the back with a "P" prefix. The set numbering starts where the 1992 Wild Card Prototypes left off.

| | MINT | EXC | G-VG |
|---|---|---|---|
| COMPLETE SET (6) | 9.00 | 3.75 | .90 |
| COMMON PLAYER (P19-P24) | 1.00 | .40 | .10 |
| ☐ P19 Emmitt Smith<br>Dallas Cowboys | 3.00 | 1.20 | .30 |
| ☐ P20 Ricky Watters<br>San Francisco 49ers | 1.50 | .60 | .15 |
| ☐ P21 Drew Bledsoe<br>New England Patriots | 3.00 | 1.20 | .30 |
| ☐ P22 Garrison Hearst<br>Phoenix Cardinals | 1.50 | .60 | .15 |
| ☐ P23 Barry Foster<br>Pittsburgh Steelers | 1.00 | .40 | .10 |
| ☐ P24 Rick Mirer<br>Seattle Seahawks | 3.00 | 1.20 | .30 |

## 1993 Wild Card

The 1993 Wild Card set consists of 260 cards. Randomly inserted in early 1993 Wild Card packs were cards from the 1993 Stat Smashers, Field Force, and Red Hot Rookies sets. A different packaging scheme begun early in 1994 featured six Superchrome counterparts to the regular cards inserted in special Superchrome 15-card low-series and 13-card high-series hobby packs, and are valued up to five times the value of the regular issue. One of ten Superchrome Back-to-Back inserts, featuring a Field Force player on the front and a Red Hot Rookie on the back, was inserted in each 18-pack box. Also, special striped cards were randomly inserted into regular Wild Card packs. These cards came in varying "denominations" of stripes, ranging from five to 1,000, and the corresponding values for them are noted in the header below.

| | MINT | EXC | G-VG |
|---|---|---|---|
| COMPLETE SET (260) | 14.00 | 6.25 | 1.75 |
| COMPLETE SERIES 1 (200) | 6.00 | 2.70 | .75 |
| COMPLETE SERIES 2 (60) | 8.00 | 3.60 | 1.00 |
| COMMON PLAYER (1-200) | .04 | .02 | .01 |
| COMMON PLAYER (201-260) | .05 | .02 | .01 |
| *5/10/20 STRIPES: .30X to .75X VALUE | | | |
| *50/100 STRIPES: .25X to .60X VALUE | | | |
| *1000 STRIPES: .20X to .50X VALUE | | | |
| COMP.SUPERCHROME 1 (200) | 60.00 | 27.00 | 7.50 |
| COMP.SUPERCHROME 2 (60) | 25.00 | 11.50 | 3.10 |
| *SUPERCHROMES: .2X to .5X VALUE | | | |

| | | | |
|---|---|---|---|
| ☐ 1 Surprise Card | 1.00 | .45 | .13 |
| ☐ 2 Steve Young | .25 | .11 | .03 |
| ☐ 3 John Taylor | .09 | .04 | .01 |
| ☐ 4 Jerry Rice | .50 | .23 | .06 |
| ☐ 5 Brent Jones | .09 | .04 | .01 |
| ☐ 6 Ricky Watters | .25 | .11 | .03 |
| ☐ 7 Elvis Grbac | .50 | .23 | .06 |
| ☐ 8 Amp Lee | .07 | .03 | .01 |
| ☐ 9 Steve Bono | .15 | .07 | .02 |
| ☐ 10 Wendell Davis | .07 | .03 | .01 |
| ☐ 11 Mark Carrier | .07 | .03 | .01 |
| ☐ 12 Jim Harbaugh | .07 | .03 | .01 |
| ☐ 13 Curtis Conway | .50 | .23 | .06 |
| ☐ 14 Neal Anderson | .07 | .03 | .01 |
| ☐ 15 Tom Waddle | .09 | .04 | .01 |
| ☐ 16 Jeff Query | .04 | .02 | .01 |
| ☐ 17 David Klingler | .15 | .07 | .02 |
| ☐ 18 Eric Ball | .04 | .02 | .01 |
| ☐ 19 Derrick Fenner | .04 | .02 | .01 |
| ☐ 20 Steve Tovar | .10 | .05 | .01 |
| ☐ 21 Carl Pickens | .10 | .05 | .01 |
| ☐ 22 Ricardo McDonald | .04 | .02 | .01 |
| ☐ 23 Harold Green | .07 | .03 | .01 |
| ☐ 24 Keith McKeller | .04 | .02 | .01 |
| ☐ 25 Steve Christie | .04 | .02 | .01 |
| ☐ 26 Andre Reed | .09 | .04 | .01 |
| ☐ 27 Kenneth Davis | .07 | .03 | .01 |
| ☐ 28 Frank Reich | .07 | .03 | .01 |
| ☐ 29 Jim Kelly | .25 | .11 | .03 |
| ☐ 30 Bruce Smith | .09 | .04 | .01 |
| ☐ 31 Thurman Thomas | .35 | .16 | .04 |
| ☐ 32 Glyn Milburn | .75 | .35 | .09 |
| ☐ 33 John Elway | .35 | .16 | .04 |
| ☐ 34 Vance Johnson | .07 | .03 | .01 |
| ☐ 35 Greg Lewis | .04 | .02 | .01 |
| ☐ 36 Steve Atwater | .07 | .03 | .01 |
| ☐ 37 Shannon Sharpe | .20 | .09 | .03 |
| ☐ 38 Mike Croel | .07 | .03 | .01 |
| ☐ 39 Kevin Mack | .07 | .03 | .01 |
| ☐ 40 Lawyer Tillman | .04 | .02 | .01 |
| ☐ 41 Tommy Vardell | .07 | .03 | .01 |
| ☐ 42 Bernie Kosar | .09 | .04 | .01 |
| ☐ 43 Eric Metcalf | .09 | .04 | .01 |
| ☐ 44 Clay Matthews | .07 | .03 | .01 |
| ☐ 45 Keith McCants | .04 | .02 | .01 |
| ☐ 46 Broderick Thomas | .04 | .02 | .01 |
| ☐ 47 Lawrence Dawsey | .09 | .04 | .01 |
| ☐ 48 Reggie Cobb | .09 | .04 | .01 |
| ☐ 49 Lamar Thomas | .25 | .11 | .03 |
| ☐ 50 Courtney Hawkins | .07 | .03 | .01 |
| ☐ 51 Ivory Lee Brown | .15 | .07 | .02 |
| ☐ 52 Ernie Jones | .04 | .02 | .01 |
| ☐ 53 Freddie Joe Nunn | .04 | .02 | .01 |
| ☐ 54 Chris Chandler | .07 | .03 | .01 |
| ☐ 55 Randal Hill | .09 | .04 | .01 |
| ☐ 56 Lorenzo Lynch | .04 | .02 | .01 |
| ☐ 57 Garrison Hearst | .60 | .25 | .08 |
| ☐ 58 Marion Butts | .09 | .04 | .01 |
| ☐ 59 Anthony Miller | .15 | .07 | .02 |
| ☐ 60 Eric Bieniemy | 25.03 | 11.50 | 3.10 |
| ☐ 61 Ronnie Harmon | .07 | .03 | .01 |
| ☐ 62 Junior Seau | .09 | .04 | .01 |
| ☐ 63 Gill Byrd | .07 | .03 | .01 |
| ☐ 64 Stan Humphries | .09 | .04 | .01 |
| ☐ 65 John Friesz | .07 | .03 | .01 |
| ☐ 66 J.J. Birden | .07 | .03 | .01 |
| ☐ 67 Joe Montana | 1.25 | .55 | .16 |
| ☐ 68 Christian Okoye | .07 | .03 | .01 |
| ☐ 69 Dale Carter | .09 | .04 | .01 |
| ☐ 70 Barry Word | .09 | .04 | .01 |
| ☐ 71 Derrick Thomas | .15 | .07 | .02 |
| ☐ 72 Todd McNair | .04 | .02 | .01 |

| | | | |
|---|---|---|---|
| ☐ 73 Harvey Williams | .09 | .04 | .01 |
| ☐ 74 Jack Trudeau | .04 | .02 | .01 |
| ☐ 75 Rodney Culver | .07 | .03 | .01 |
| ☐ 76 Anthony Johnson | .04 | .02 | .01 |
| ☐ 77 Steve Emtman | .07 | .03 | .01 |
| ☐ 78 Quentin Coryatt | .09 | .04 | .01 |
| ☐ 79 Kerry Cash | .04 | .02 | .01 |
| ☐ 80 Jeff George | .15 | .07 | .02 |
| ☐ 81 Darrin Smith | .30 | .14 | .04 |
| ☐ 82 Jay Novacek | .09 | .04 | .01 |
| ☐ 83 Michael Irvin | .40 | .18 | .05 |
| ☐ 84 Alvin Harper | .25 | .11 | .03 |
| ☐ 85 Kevin Williams | .50 | .23 | .06 |
| ☐ 86 Troy Aikman | 1.25 | .55 | .16 |
| ☐ 87 Emmitt Smith | 2.00 | .90 | .25 |
| ☐ 88 O.J. McDuffie | 1.25 | .55 | .16 |
| ☐ 89 Mike Williams | .10 | .05 | .01 |
| ☐ 90 Dan Marino | .75 | .35 | .09 |
| ☐ 91 Aaron Craver | .07 | .03 | .01 |
| ☐ 92 Troy Vincent | .07 | .03 | .01 |
| ☐ 93 Keith Jackson | .09 | .04 | .01 |
| ☐ 94 Marco Coleman | .07 | .03 | .01 |
| ☐ 95 Mark Higgs | .09 | .04 | .01 |
| ☐ 96 Fred Barnett | .09 | .04 | .01 |
| ☐ 97 Wes Hopkins | .04 | .02 | .01 |
| ☐ 98 Randall Cunningham | .10 | .05 | .01 |
| ☐ 99 Heath Sherman | .04 | .02 | .01 |
| ☐ 100 Vai Sikahema | .04 | .02 | .01 |
| ☐ 101 Tony Smith | .04 | .02 | .01 |
| ☐ 102 Andre Rison | .25 | .11 | .03 |
| ☐ 103 Chris Miller | .09 | .04 | .01 |
| ☐ 104 Deion Sanders | .15 | .07 | .02 |
| ☐ 105 Mike Pritchard | .09 | .04 | .01 |
| ☐ 106 Steve Broussard | .04 | .02 | .01 |
| ☐ 107 Stephen Baker | .04 | .02 | .01 |
| ☐ 108 Carl Banks | .07 | .03 | .01 |
| ☐ 109 Jarrod Bunch | .07 | .03 | .01 |
| ☐ 110 Phil Simms | .09 | .04 | .01 |
| ☐ 111 Rodney Hampton | .30 | .14 | .04 |
| ☐ 112 Dave Meggett | .07 | .03 | .01 |
| ☐ 113 Pepper Johnson | .04 | .02 | .01 |
| ☐ 114 Coleman Rudolph | .10 | .05 | .01 |
| ☐ 115 Boomer Esiason | .10 | .05 | .01 |
| ☐ 116 Browning Nagle | .07 | .03 | .01 |
| ☐ 117 Rob Moore | .09 | .04 | .01 |
| ☐ 118 Marvin Jones | .15 | .07 | .02 |
| ☐ 119 Herman Moore | .35 | .16 | .04 |
| ☐ 120 Bennie Blades | .04 | .02 | .01 |
| ☐ 121 Erik Kramer | .15 | .07 | .02 |
| ☐ 122 Mel Gray | .07 | .03 | .01 |
| ☐ 123 Rodney Peete | .07 | .03 | .01 |
| ☐ 124 Barry Sanders | .75 | .35 | .09 |
| ☐ 125 Chris Spielman | .04 | .02 | .01 |
| ☐ 126 Lamar Lathon | .04 | .02 | .01 |
| ☐ 127 Ernest Givins | .04 | .02 | .01 |
| ☐ 128 Lorenzo White | .07 | .03 | .01 |
| ☐ 129 Micheal Barrow | .04 | .02 | .01 |
| ☐ 130 Warren Moon | .15 | .07 | .02 |
| ☐ 131 Cody Carlson | .20 | .09 | .03 |
| ☐ 132 Reggie White | .15 | .07 | .02 |
| ☐ 133 Terrell Buckley | .09 | .04 | .01 |
| ☐ 134 Ed West | .04 | .02 | .01 |
| ☐ 135 Mark Brunell | .25 | .11 | .03 |
| ☐ 136 Brett Favre | .75 | .35 | .09 |
| ☐ 137 Edgar Bennett | .10 | .05 | .01 |
| ☐ 138 Sterling Sharpe | .40 | .18 | .05 |
| ☐ 139 George Teague | .15 | .07 | .02 |
| ☐ 140 Leonard Russell | .07 | .03 | .01 |
| ☐ 141 Drew Bledsoe | 2.00 | .90 | .25 |
| ☐ 142 Eugene Chung | .04 | .02 | .01 |
| ☐ 143 Walter Stanley | .04 | .02 | .01 |
| ☐ 144 Scott Zolak | .04 | .02 | .01 |
| ☐ 145 Jon Vaughn | .04 | .02 | .01 |
| ☐ 146 Andre Tippett | .04 | .02 | .01 |
| ☐ 147 Alexander Wright | .07 | .03 | .01 |
| ☐ 148 Billy Joe Hobert | .25 | .11 | .03 |
| ☐ 149 Terry McDaniel | .04 | .02 | .01 |
| ☐ 150 Tim Brown | .25 | .11 | .03 |
| ☐ 151 Willie Gault | .07 | .03 | .01 |
| ☐ 152 Howie Long | .07 | .03 | .01 |
| ☐ 153 Todd Marinovich | .04 | .02 | .01 |
| ☐ 154 Jim Everett | .04 | .02 | .01 |
| ☐ 155 David Lang | .04 | .02 | .01 |
| ☐ 156 Henry Ellard | .07 | .03 | .01 |
| ☐ 157 Cleveland Gary | .07 | .03 | .01 |
| ☐ 158 Steve Israel | .04 | .02 | .01 |
| ☐ 159 Jerome Bettis | 2.00 | .90 | .25 |
| ☐ 160 Jackie Slater | .04 | .02 | .01 |
| ☐ 161 Art Monk | .09 | .04 | .01 |
| ☐ 162 Ricky Sanders | .07 | .03 | .01 |
| ☐ 163 Brian Mitchell | .07 | .03 | .01 |
| ☐ 164 Reggie Brooks | 1.50 | .65 | .19 |
| ☐ 165 Mark Rypien | .07 | .03 | .01 |
| ☐ 166 Earnest Byner | .07 | .03 | .01 |
| ☐ 167 Andre Collins | .04 | .02 | .01 |
| ☐ 168 Quinn Early | .07 | .03 | .01 |
| ☐ 169 Fred McAfee | .04 | .02 | .01 |

| | | | |
|---|---|---|---|
| ☐ 170 Wesley Carroll | .04 | .02 | .01 |
| ☐ 171 Gene Atkins | .04 | .02 | .01 |
| ☐ 172 Derek Brown UER | .75 | .35 | .09 |
| (Name spelled Derrek on front) | | | |
| ☐ 173 Vaughn Dunbar | .07 | .03 | .01 |
| ☐ 174 Rickey Jackson UER | .07 | .03 | .01 |
| (Name spelled Ricky on front) | | | |
| ☐ 175 John L. Williams | .07 | .03 | .01 |
| ☐ 176 Carlton Gray | .20 | .09 | .03 |
| ☐ 177 Cortez Kennedy | .09 | .04 | .01 |
| ☐ 178 Kelly Stouffer | .04 | .02 | .01 |
| ☐ 179 Rick Mirer | 2.00 | .90 | .25 |
| ☐ 180 Dan McGwire | .07 | .03 | .01 |
| ☐ 181 Chris Warren | .15 | .07 | .02 |
| ☐ 182 Barry Foster | .25 | .11 | .03 |
| ☐ 183 Merril Hoge | .04 | .02 | .01 |
| ☐ 184 Darren Perry | .04 | .02 | .01 |
| ☐ 185 Deon Figures | .15 | .07 | .02 |
| ☐ 186A Jeff Graham UER | .15 | .07 | .02 |
| (Name misspelled Grahm on front) | | | |
| ☐ 186B Jeff Graham UER | .15 | .07 | .02 |
| (Name misspelled Grahm on front) | | | |
| ☐ 187 Dwight Stone | .04 | .02 | .01 |
| ☐ 188 Neil O'Donnell | .25 | .11 | .03 |
| ☐ 189 Rod Woodson | .09 | .04 | .01 |
| ☐ 190 Alex Van Pelt | .15 | .07 | .02 |
| ☐ 191 Steve Jordan | .07 | .03 | .01 |
| ☐ 192 Roger Craig | .07 | .03 | .01 |
| ☐ 193 Qadry Ismail UER | .50 | .23 | .06 |
| (Misspelled Quadry on card front) | | | |
| ☐ 194 Robert Smith | .35 | .16 | .04 |
| ☐ 195 Gino Torretta | .30 | .14 | .04 |
| ☐ 196 Anthony Carter | .07 | .03 | .01 |
| ☐ 197 Terry Allen | .09 | .04 | .01 |
| ☐ 198 Rich Gannon | .07 | .03 | .01 |
| ☐ 199 Checklist Card | .05 | .02 | .01 |
| ☐ 200 Checklist Card | 60.00 | 27.00 | 7.50 |
| ☐ 201 Victor Bailey | .30 | .14 | .04 |
| Philadelphia Eagles | | | |
| ☐ 202 Micheal Barrow | .05 | .02 | .01 |
| Houston Oilers | | | |
| ☐ 203 Patrick Bates | .10 | .05 | .01 |
| Los Angeles Raiders | | | |
| ☐ 204 Jerome Bettis | 1.00 | .45 | .13 |
| Los Angeles Rams | | | |
| ☐ 205 Drew Bledsoe | 1.00 | .45 | .13 |
| New England Patriots | | | |
| ☐ 206 Vincent Brisby | .50 | .23 | .06 |
| New England Patriots | | | |
| ☐ 207 Reggie Brooks | .60 | .25 | .08 |
| Washington Redskins | | | |
| ☐ 208 Derek Brown | .30 | .14 | .04 |
| New Orleans Saints | | | |
| ☐ 209 Keith Byars | .08 | .04 | .01 |
| Miami Dolphins | | | |
| ☐ 210 Tom Carter | .25 | .11 | .03 |
| Washington Redskins | | | |
| ☐ 211 Curtis Conway | .20 | .09 | .03 |
| Chicago Bears | | | |
| ☐ 212 Russell Copeland | .15 | .07 | .02 |
| Buffalo Bills | | | |
| ☐ 213 John Copeland | .20 | .09 | .03 |
| Cincinnati Bengals | | | |
| ☐ 214 Eric Curry | .25 | .11 | .03 |
| Tampa Bay Buccaneers | | | |
| ☐ 215 Troy Drayton | .50 | .23 | .06 |
| Los Angeles Rams | | | |
| ☐ 216 Jason Elam | .10 | .05 | .01 |
| Denver Broncos | | | |
| ☐ 217 Steve Everitt | .10 | .05 | .01 |
| Cleveland Browns | | | |
| ☐ 218 Deon Figures | .05 | .02 | .01 |
| Pittsburgh Steelers | | | |
| ☐ 219 Irving Fryar | .08 | .04 | .01 |
| Miami Dolphins | | | |
| ☐ 220 Darrien Gordon | .20 | .09 | .03 |
| San Diego Chargers | | | |
| ☐ 221 Carlton Gray | .05 | .02 | .01 |
| Seattle Seahawks | | | |
| ☐ 222 Kevin Greene | .05 | .02 | .01 |
| Pittsburgh Steelers | | | |
| ☐ 223 Andre Hastings | .20 | .09 | .03 |
| Pittsburgh Steelers | | | |
| ☐ 224 Michael Haynes | .20 | .09 | .03 |
| Atlanta Falcons | | | |
| ☐ 225 Garrison Hearst | .30 | .14 | .04 |
| Phoenix Cardinals | | | |
| ☐ 226 Bobby Hebert | .08 | .04 | .01 |
| New Orleans Saints | | | |
| ☐ 227 Lester Holmes | .08 | .04 | .01 |
| Philadelphia Eagles | | | |
| ☐ 228 Jeff Hostetler | .08 | .04 | .01 |
| Los Angeles Raiders | | | |
| ☐ 229 Desmond Howard | .20 | .09 | .03 |
| Washington Redskins | | | |
| ☐ 230 Tyrone Hughes | .30 | .14 | .04 |

| | | | |
|---|---|---|---|
| New Orleans Saints | | | |
| ☐ 231 Quadry Ismail | .25 | .11 | .03 |
| Minnesota Vikings | | | |
| ☐ 232 Rocket Ismail | .25 | .11 | .03 |
| Los Angeles Raiders | | | |
| ☐ 233 James Jett | .60 | .25 | .08 |
| Los Angeles Raiders | | | |
| ☐ 234 Marvin Jones | .05 | .02 | .01 |
| New York Jets | | | |
| ☐ 235 Todd Kelly | .10 | .05 | .01 |
| San Francisco 49ers | | | |
| ☐ 236 Lincoln Kennedy | .15 | .07 | .02 |
| Atlanta Falcons | | | |
| ☐ 237 Terry Kirby | 1.25 | .55 | .16 |
| Miami Dolphins | | | |
| ☐ 238 Bernie Kosar | .10 | .05 | .01 |
| Dallas Cowboys | | | |
| ☐ 239 Derrick Lassic | .20 | .09 | .03 |
| Dallas Cowboys | | | |
| ☐ 240 Wilber Marshall | .08 | .04 | .01 |
| Houston Oilers | | | |
| ☐ 241 O.J. McDuffie | .50 | .23 | .06 |
| Miami Dolphins | | | |
| ☐ 242 Ryan McNeil | .10 | .05 | .01 |
| Detroit Lions | | | |
| ☐ 243 Natrone Means | 1.00 | .45 | .13 |
| San Diego Chargers | | | |
| ☐ 244 Glyn Milburn | .30 | .14 | .04 |
| Denver Broncos | | | |
| ☐ 245 Rick Mirer | 1.00 | .45 | .13 |
| Seattle Seahawks | | | |
| ☐ 246 Scott Mitchell | .40 | .18 | .05 |
| Miami Dolphins | | | |
| ☐ 247 Ronald Moore | 1.50 | .65 | .19 |
| Phoenix Cardinals | | | |
| ☐ 248 Lorenzo Neal | .40 | .18 | .05 |
| New Orleans Saints | | | |
| ☐ 249 Erric Pegram | .25 | .11 | .03 |
| Atlanta Falcons | | | |
| ☐ 250 Roosevelt Potts | .25 | .11 | .03 |
| Indianapolis Colts | | | |
| ☐ 251 Leonard Renfro | .10 | .05 | .01 |
| Philadelphia Eagles | | | |
| ☐ 252 Greg Robinson | .60 | .25 | .08 |
| Los Angeles Raiders | | | |
| ☐ 253 Wayne Simmons | .10 | .05 | .01 |
| Green Bay Packers | | | |
| ☐ 254 Chris Slade | .30 | .14 | .04 |
| New England Patriots | | | |
| ☐ 255 Irv Smith | .20 | .09 | .03 |
| New Orleans Saints | | | |
| ☐ 256 Robert Smith | .15 | .07 | .02 |
| Minnesota Vikings | | | |
| ☐ 257 Dana Stubblefield | .40 | .18 | .05 |
| San Francisco 49ers | | | |
| ☐ 258 George Teague | .05 | .02 | .01 |
| Green Bay Packers | | | |
| ☐ 259 Kevin Williams WR | .25 | .11 | .03 |
| Dallas Cowboys | | | |
| ☐ 260 Checklist | .05 | .02 | .01 |

## 1993 Wild Card Bomb Squad

One of these 30 standard-size (2 1/2" by 3 1/2") cards was inserted in each 1993 Wild Card high-number (201-260) pack. Reportedly, 10,000 Bomb Squad sets were produced. The cards feature on their metallic fronts embossed color action photos of the NFL's top receivers within lined silver and bronze borders. The player's name, team, and position appear at the bottom. The orangeish back carries the player's name, team, and position at the top, followed below by biography, a horizontal stat table, and player action shot. The cards are numbered on the back.

|  | MINT | EXC | G-VG |
|---|---|---|---|
| COMPLETE SET (30)........................ | 25.00 | 11.50 | 3.10 |
| COMMON PLAYER (1-30)................ | .50 | .23 | .06 |
| ☐ 1 Jerry Rice................................ | 2.00 | .90 | .25 |
| San Francisco 49ers | | | |
| ☐ 2 John Taylor.............................. | .75 | .35 | .09 |
| San Francisco 49ers | | | |
| ☐ 3 J.J. Birden.............................. | .50 | .23 | .06 |
| Kansas City Chiefs | | | |
| ☐ 4 Stephen Baker......................... | .50 | .23 | .06 |
| New York Giants | | | |
| ☐ 5 Victor Bailey........................... | .75 | .35 | .09 |
| Philadelphia Eagles | | | |
| ☐ 6 O.J. McDuffie.......................... | 2.00 | .90 | .25 |
| Miami Dolphins | | | |
| ☐ 7 Haywood Jeffires..................... | .75 | .35 | .09 |
| Houston Oilers | | | |
| ☐ 8 Eric Green.............................. | .75 | .35 | .09 |
| Pittsburgh Steelers | | | |
| ☐ 9 Johnny Mitchell....................... | .75 | .35 | .09 |
| New York Jets | | | |
| ☐ 10 Art Monk............................... | .75 | .35 | .09 |
| Washington Redskins | | | |
| ☐ 11 Quinn Early........................... | .50 | .23 | .06 |
| New Orleans Saints | | | |
| ☐ 12 Troy Drayton......................... | 1.00 | .45 | .13 |
| Los Angeles Rams | | | |
| ☐ 13 Vincent Brisby....................... | 1.25 | .55 | .16 |
| New England Patriots | | | |
| ☐ 14 Courtney Hawkins................... | .50 | .23 | .06 |
| Tampa Bay Buccaneers | | | |
| ☐ 15 Tom Waddle........................... | .50 | .23 | .06 |
| Chicago Bears | | | |
| ☐ 16 Curtis Conway........................ | 1.00 | .45 | .13 |
| Chicago Bears | | | |
| ☐ 17 Andre Reed............................ | .75 | .35 | .09 |
| Buffalo Bills | | | |
| ☐ 18 Carl Pickens.......................... | .75 | .35 | .09 |
| Cincinnati Bengals | | | |
| ☐ 19 Sterling Sharpe...................... | 2.00 | .90 | .25 |
| Green Bay Packers | | | |
| ☐ 20 Shannon Sharpe..................... | 1.00 | .45 | .13 |
| Denver Broncos | | | |
| ☐ 21 Quadry Ismail........................ | 1.25 | .55 | .16 |
| Minnesota Vikings | | | |
| ☐ 22 Rocket Ismail........................ | 1.00 | .45 | .13 |
| Los Angeles Raiders | | | |
| ☐ 23 Andre Rison........................... | 1.00 | .45 | .13 |
| Atlanta Falcons | | | |
| ☐ 24 Michael Haynes...................... | 1.00 | .45 | .13 |
| Atlanta Falcons | | | |
| ☐ 25 Alvin Harper........................... | 1.00 | .45 | .13 |
| Dallas Cowboys | | | |
| ☐ 26 Michael Irvin.......................... | 1.50 | .65 | .19 |
| Dallas Cowboys | | | |
| ☐ 27 Michael Jackson..................... | .75 | .35 | .09 |
| Cleveland Browns | | | |
| ☐ 28 Herman Moore....................... | 1.25 | .55 | .16 |
| Detroit Lions | | | |
| ☐ 29 Anthony Miller........................ | .75 | .35 | .09 |
| San Diego Chargers | | | |
| ☐ 30 Gary Clark............................. | .75 | .35 | .09 |
| Phoenix Cardinals | | | |

|  | MINT | EXC | G-VG |
|---|---|---|---|
| COMPLETE SET (15)........................ | 75.00 | 34.00 | 9.50 |
| COMMON PAIR (1-15)................... | 4.00 | 1.80 | .50 |
| ☐ 1 Jerry Rice................................ | 10.00 | 4.50 | 1.25 |
| John Taylor | | | |
| San Francisco 49ers | | | |
| ☐ 2 Tom Waddle............................ | 4.00 | 1.80 | .50 |
| Curtis Conway | | | |
| Chicago Bears | | | |
| ☐ 3 Andre Reed.............................. | 5.00 | 2.30 | .60 |
| Buffalo Bills | | | |
| Carl Pickens | | | |
| Cincinnati Bengals | | | |
| ☐ 4 Sterling Sharpe........................ | 10.00 | 4.50 | 1.25 |
| Green Bay Packers | | | |
| Shannon Sharpe | | | |
| Denver Broncos | | | |
| ☐ 5 Quadry Ismail.......................... | 6.00 | 2.70 | .75 |
| Minnesota Vikings | | | |
| Rocket Ismail | | | |
| Los Angeles Raiders | | | |
| ☐ 6 Andre Rison............................. | 6.00 | 2.70 | .75 |
| Michael Haynes | | | |
| Atlanta Falcons | | | |
| ☐ 7 Alvin Harper............................ | 10.00 | 4.50 | 1.25 |
| Michael Irwin | | | |
| Dallas Cowboys | | | |
| ☐ 8 Michael Jackson....................... | 6.00 | 2.70 | .75 |
| Cleveland Browns | | | |
| Herman Moore | | | |
| Detroit Lions | | | |
| ☐ 9 Anthony Miller.......................... | 5.00 | 2.30 | .60 |
| San Diego Chargers | | | |
| Gary Clark | | | |
| Phoenix Cardinals | | | |
| ☐ 10 J.J. Birden............................. | 4.00 | 1.80 | .50 |
| Kansas City Chiefs | | | |
| Stephen Baker | | | |
| New York Giants | | | |
| ☐ 11 Victor Bailey.......................... | 8.00 | 3.60 | 1.00 |
| Philadelphia Eagles | | | |
| O.J. McDuffie | | | |
| Miami Dolphins | | | |
| ☐ 12 Haywood Jeffires.................... | 5.00 | 2.30 | .60 |
| Houston Oilers | | | |
| Eric Green | | | |
| Pittsburgh Steelers | | | |
| ☐ 13 Johnny Mitchell...................... | 4.00 | 1.80 | .50 |
| New York Jets | | | |
| Art Monk | | | |
| Washington Redskins | | | |
| ☐ 14 Quinn Early............................ | 4.00 | 1.80 | .50 |
| New Orleans Saints | | | |
| Troy Drayton | | | |
| Los Angeles Rams | | | |
| ☐ 15 Vincent Brisby........................ | 6.00 | 2.70 | .75 |
| New England Patriots | | | |
| Courtney Hawkins | | | |
| Tampa Bay Buccaneers | | | |

## 1993 Wild Card Field Force

Randomly inserted in foil packs, this 90-card standard-size (2 1/2" by 3 1/2") set features players from the AFC and NFC Western Divisions. The series will continue with players from the Central and Eastern Divisions of both conferences. The obverse features bordered glossy color player action photos. The composite border is black and blue straight lines on the left side, blending into blue and white wavy lines on the right. The player's name and position appear in red on the right side of the bottom border, and the team name, also in red, appears vertically on the left. The Field Force logo appears at the lower left

## 1993 Wild Card Bomb Squad B/B

These 15 standard-size (2 1/2" by 3 1/2") cards are double-front (two-player) versions of the 30-card Bomb Squad set. One was randomly inserted in each 20-pack box of 1993 Wild Card high-number jumbo packs. Reportedly, 1,000 of these double-sided sets were made. The cards' designs are identical to the fronts of the regular Bomb Squad cards. The cards are numbered on one side.

corner. The white-bordered reverse sports another color player action photo on the left side, with stats appearing horizontally in a green box on the right. The cards are numbered on the back with a "WFF" prefix. Cards 61-90 are numbered with a "EFF" prefix, cards 91-120 with a "CFF" prefix. Early in 1994, Superchrome counterparts to 10 Field Force cards were randomly inserted in Wild Card Superchrome foil packs. These Superchrome Field Force cards are valued at four to ten times the value of the regular issue cards.

| | MINT | EXC | G-VG |
|---|---|---|---|
| COMPLETE SET (90) | 50.00 | 23.00 | 6.25 |
| COMPLETE WEST SERIES (30) | 18.00 | 8.00 | 2.30 |
| COMPLETE EAST SERIES (30) | 18.00 | 8.00 | 2.30 |
| COMPLETE CENT.SERIES (30) | 18.00 | 8.00 | 2.30 |
| COMMON PLAYER (31-60) | .40 | .18 | .05 |
| COMMON PLAYER (61-90) | .40 | .18 | .05 |
| COMMON PLAYER (91-120) | .40 | .18 | .05 |

*5/10/20 STRIPES: .30X to .75 VALUE
*50/100 STRIPES: .25X to .60X VALUE
*1000 STRIPES: .20X to .50X VALUE
*SILVER CARDS: 1X to 1.5X VALUE
*GOLD CARDS: 1.25X to 2.5X VALUE

| | | | |
|---|---|---|---|
| ☐ 31 Jerry Rice | 2.00 | .90 | .25 |
| San Francisco 49ers | | | |
| ☐ 32 Ricky Watters | 1.00 | .45 | .13 |
| San Francisco 49ers | | | |
| ☐ 33 Steve Bono | .75 | .35 | .09 |
| San Francisco 49ers | | | |
| ☐ 34 Amp Lee | .40 | .18 | .05 |
| San Francisco 49ers | | | |
| ☐ 35 Steve Young | 1.00 | .45 | .13 |
| San Francisco 49ers | | | |
| ☐ 36 Tommy Maddox | .65 | .30 | .08 |
| Denver Broncos | | | |
| ☐ 37 Cleveland Gary | .40 | .18 | .05 |
| Los Angeles Rams | | | |
| ☐ 38 John Elway | 1.25 | .55 | .16 |
| Denver Broncos | | | |
| ☐ 39 Glyn Milburn | 1.00 | .45 | .13 |
| Denver Broncos | | | |
| ☐ 40 Stan Humphries | .40 | .18 | .05 |
| San Diego Chargers | | | |
| ☐ 41 Junior Seau | .65 | .30 | .08 |
| San Diego Chargers | | | |
| ☐ 42 Natrone Means | 2.00 | .90 | .25 |
| San Diego Chargers | | | |
| ☐ 43 Dale Carter | .65 | .30 | .08 |
| Kansas City Chiefs | | | |
| ☐ 44 Joe Montana | 3.00 | 1.35 | .40 |
| Kansas City Chiefs | | | |
| ☐ 45 Christian Okoye | .40 | .18 | .05 |
| Kansas City Chiefs | | | |
| ☐ 46 Deion Sanders | .75 | .35 | .09 |
| Atlanta Falcons | | | |
| ☐ 47 Roger Harper | .65 | .30 | .08 |
| Atlanta Falcons | | | |
| ☐ 48 Steve Broussard | .40 | .18 | .05 |
| Atlanta Falcons | | | |
| ☐ 49 Todd Marinovich | .40 | .18 | .05 |
| Los Angeles Raiders | | | |
| ☐ 50 Billy Joe Hobert | .75 | .35 | .09 |
| Los Angeles Raiders | | | |
| ☐ 51 Patrick Bates | .65 | .30 | .08 |
| Los Angeles Raiders | | | |
| ☐ 52 Jerome Bettis | 5.00 | 2.30 | .60 |
| Los Angeles Rams | | | |
| ☐ 53 Flipper Anderson | .40 | .18 | .05 |
| Los Angeles Rams | | | |
| ☐ 54 Irv Smith | .65 | .30 | .08 |
| New Orleans Saints | | | |
| ☐ 55 Quinn Early | .40 | .18 | .05 |
| New Orleans Saints | | | |
| ☐ 56 Vaughn Dunbar | .65 | .30 | .08 |
| New Orleans Saints | | | |
| ☐ 57 Rick Mirer | 5.00 | 2.30 | .60 |
| Seattle Seahawks | | | |
| ☐ 58 Carlton Gray | .65 | .30 | .08 |
| Seattle Seahawks | | | |
| ☐ 59 Chris Warren | .65 | .30 | .08 |
| Seattle Seahawks | | | |
| ☐ 60 Dan McGwire | .40 | .18 | .05 |
| Seattle Seahawks | | | |
| ☐ 61 Pete Metzelaars | .40 | .18 | .05 |
| Buffalo Bills | | | |
| ☐ 62 Kenneth Davis | .40 | .18 | .05 |
| Buffalo Bills | | | |
| ☐ 63 Thurman Thomas | 1.00 | .45 | .13 |
| Buffalo Bills | | | |
| ☐ 64 Chris Chandler | .40 | .18 | .05 |
| Phoenix Cardinals | | | |
| ☐ 65 Garrison Hearst | .75 | .35 | .09 |
| Phoenix Cardinals | | | |
| ☐ 66 Rick Proehl | .40 | .18 | .05 |
| Phoenix Cardinals | | | |
| ☐ 67 Steve Emtman | .40 | .18 | .05 |
| Indianapolis Colts | | | |
| ☐ 68 Jeff George | .65 | .30 | .08 |
| Indianapolis Colts | | | |
| ☐ 69 Clarence Verdin | .40 | .18 | .05 |
| Indianapolis Colts | | | |
| ☐ 70 Troy Aikman | 4.00 | 1.80 | .50 |
| Dallas Cowboys | | | |
| ☐ 71 Emmitt Smith | 4.50 | 2.00 | .55 |
| Dallas Cowboys | | | |
| ☐ 72 Alvin Harper | 1.00 | .45 | .13 |
| Dallas Cowboys | | | |
| ☐ 73 Michael Irvin | 1.50 | .65 | .19 |
| Dallas Cowboys | | | |
| ☐ 74 O.J. McDuffie | 1.00 | .45 | .13 |
| Miami Dolphins | | | |
| ☐ 75 .Troy Vincent | .40 | .18 | .05 |
| Miami Dolphins | | | |
| ☐ 76 Keith Jackson | .65 | .30 | .08 |
| Miami Dolphins | | | |
| ☐ 77 Dan Marino | 2.00 | .90 | .25 |
| Miami Dolphins | | | |
| ☐ 78 Leonard Renfro | .40 | .18 | .05 |
| Philadelphia Eagles | | | |
| ☐ 79 Heath Sherman | .40 | .18 | .05 |
| Philadelphia Eagles | | | |
| ☐ 80 Derek Brown | .40 | .18 | .05 |
| New York Giants | | | |
| ☐ 81 Rodney Hampton | 1.00 | .45 | .13 |
| New York Giants | | | |
| ☐ 82 James Hasty | .40 | .18 | .05 |
| New York Jets | | | |
| ☐ 83 Johnny Mitchell | .65 | .30 | .08 |
| New York Jets | | | |
| ☐ 84 Brad Baxter | .40 | .18 | .05 |
| New York Jets | | | |
| ☐ 85 Leonard Russell | .40 | .18 | .05 |
| New England Patriots | | | |
| ☐ 86 Marv Cook | .40 | .18 | .05 |
| New England Patriots | | | |
| ☐ 87 Drew Bledsoe | 5.00 | 2.30 | .60 |
| New England Patriots | | | |
| ☐ 88 Ricky Ervins | .40 | .18 | .05 |
| Washington Redskins | | | |
| ☐ 89 Art Monk | .65 | .30 | .08 |
| Washington Redskins | | | |
| ☐ 90 Earnest Byner | .40 | .18 | .05 |
| Washington Redskins | | | |
| ☐ 91 Tom Waddle | .40 | .18 | .05 |
| Chicago Bears | | | |
| ☐ 92 Neal Anderson | .40 | .18 | .05 |
| Chicago Bears | | | |
| ☐ 93 Curtis Conway | .75 | .35 | .09 |
| Chicago Bears | | | |
| ☐ 94 Harold Green | .65 | .30 | .08 |
| Cincinnati Bengals | | | |
| ☐ 95 Jeff Query | .40 | .18 | .05 |
| Cincinnati Bengals | | | |
| ☐ 96 Carl Pickens | .65 | .30 | .08 |
| Cincinnati Bengals | | | |
| ☐ 97 David Klingler | .75 | .35 | .09 |
| Cincinnati Bengals | | | |
| ☐ 98 Michael Jackson | .65 | .30 | .08 |
| Cleveland Browns | | | |
| ☐ 99 Eric Metcalf | .40 | .18 | .05 |
| Cleveland Browns | | | |
| ☐ 100 Courtney Hawkins | .40 | .18 | .05 |
| Tampa Bay Buccaneers | | | |
| ☐ 101 Eric Curry | .65 | .30 | .08 |
| Tampa Bay Buccaneers | | | |
| ☐ 102 Reggie Cobb | .65 | .30 | .08 |
| Tampa Bay Buccaneers | | | |
| ☐ 103 Mel Gray | .40 | .18 | .05 |
| Detroit Lions | | | |
| ☐ 104 Barry Sanders | 2.00 | .90 | .25 |
| Detroit Lions | | | |
| ☐ 105 Rodney Peete | .40 | .18 | .05 |
| Detroit Lions | | | |
| ☐ 106 Haywood Jeffires | .65 | .30 | .08 |
| Houston Oilers | | | |
| ☐ 107 Cody Carlson | .65 | .30 | .08 |
| Houston Oilers | | | |
| ☐ 108 Curtis Duncan | .40 | .18 | .05 |
| Houston Oilers | | | |
| ☐ 109 Edgar Bennett | .65 | .30 | .08 |
| Green Bay Packers | | | |
| ☐ 110 George Teague | .65 | .30 | .08 |
| Green Bay Packers | | | |
| ☐ 111 Terrell Buckley | .65 | .30 | .08 |
| Green Bay Packers | | | |
| ☐ 112 Brett Favre | 2.00 | .90 | .25 |
| Green Bay Packers | | | |
| ☐ 113 Deon Figures | .65 | .30 | .08 |
| Pittsburgh Steelers | | | |
| ☐ 114 Rod Woodson | .65 | .30 | .08 |
| Pittsburgh Steelers | | | |
| ☐ 115 Neil O'Donnell | .75 | .35 | .09 |
| Pittsburgh Steelers | | | |
| ☐ 116 Barry Foster | .75 | .35 | .09 |

Pittsburgh Steelers

| | | | | |
|---|---|---|---|---|
| ☐ 117 | Cris Carter | .40 | .18 | .05 |
| | Minnesota Vikings | | | |
| ☐ 118 | Gino Torretta | .65 | .30 | .08 |
| | Minnesota Vikings | | | |
| ☐ 119 | Terry Allen | .65 | .30 | .08 |
| | Minnesota Vikings | | | |
| ☐ 120 | Qadry Ismail | .40 | .18 | .05 |
| | Minnesota Vikings | | | |

# 1993 Wild Card
# Field Force Superchrome

These standard-size (2 1/2" by 3 1/2") cards were randomly inserted in superchrome packs. These cards are identical in design and color to the regular Field Force cards, except that their fronts have a metallic sheen to them. Also, their numbering on the back with an "SCF" prefix is another distinguishing feature.

| | | MINT | EXC | G-VG |
|---|---|---|---|---|
| | COMPLETE SET (10) | 50.00 | 20.00 | 5.00 |
| | COMMON PLAYER (1-10) | 3.00 | 1.20 | .30 |
| ☐ 1 | Jerry Rice | 5.00 | 2.00 | .50 |
| | San Francisco 49ers | | | |
| ☐ 2 | Glyn Milburn | 3.00 | 1.20 | .30 |
| | Denver Broncos | | | |
| ☐ 3 | Joe Montana | 10.00 | 4.00 | 1.00 |
| | Kansas City Chiefs | | | |
| ☐ 4 | Rick Mirer | 12.00 | 5.00 | 1.20 |
| | Seattle Seahawks | | | |
| ☐ 5 | Troy Aikman | 10.00 | 4.00 | 1.00 |
| | Dallas Cowboys | | | |
| ☐ 6 | Emmitt Smith | 12.00 | 5.00 | 1.20 |
| | Dallas Cowboys | | | |
| ☐ 7 | Dan Marino | 7.50 | 3.00 | .75 |
| | Miami Dolphins | | | |
| ☐ 8 | Drew Bledsoe | 12.00 | 5.00 | 1.20 |
| | New England Patriots | | | |
| ☐ 9 | Barry Sanders | 5.00 | 2.00 | .50 |
| | Detroit Lions | | | |
| ☐ 10 | Brett Favre | 5.00 | 2.00 | .50 |
| | Green Bay Packers | | | |

# 1993 Wild Card Red Hot Rookies

Randomly inserted in foil packs, this 30-card standard-size (2 1/2" by 3 1/2") set features players from the AFC and NFC Western Divisions. The series will continue with players from the Central and Eastern Divisions of both conferences. The fronts feature bordered glossy color player action photos. Different color numbers and stripes appear in the top and right borders. A football icon with the words "Red Hot Rookies" straddles the lower left corner of the photo and border. The player's name and position appear in the lower right of the border, and the team name appears vertically on the left, both in mustard yellow. The white-bordered back has a posed color player close-up within a football icon in the lower right and stats displayed horizontally in a green rectangle down the left side, all on a reddish brown background. Cards 31-40 are numbered on the back with a "WRHR" prefix. Cards 41-50 are numbered with a "ERHR" prefix and cards 51-60 with a "CRHR" prefix. Early in 1994, Superchrome counterparts to 10 Red Hot Rookies cards were randomly inserted in Wild Card Superchrome foil packs. The Supercrome Red Hot Rookies cards are valued at three to six times the value of the regular issue cards.

| | | MINT | EXC | G-VG |
|---|---|---|---|---|
| | COMPLETE SET (30) | 35.00 | 16.00 | 4.40 |
| | COMPLETE WEST SERIES (10) | 14.00 | 6.25 | 1.75 |
| | COMPLETE EAST SERIES (10) | 12.00 | 5.50 | 1.50 |
| | COMPLETE CENT.SERIES (10) | 10.00 | 4.50 | 1.25 |
| | COMMON PLAYER (31-40) | .50 | .23 | .06 |
| | COMMON PLAYER (41-50) | .50 | .23 | .06 |
| | COMMON PLAYER (51-60) | .50 | .23 | .06 |
| | *5/10/20 STRIPES: .30X to .75X VALUE | | | |
| | *50/100 STRIPES: .25X to .60X VALUE | | | |
| | *1000 STRIPES: .20X to .50X VALUE | | | |
| ☐ 31 | Dana Stubblefield | 1.00 | .45 | .13 |
| | San Francisco 49ers | | | |
| ☐ 32 | Todd Kelly | .75 | .35 | .09 |
| | San Francisco 49ers | | | |
| ☐ 33 | Dan Williams | .50 | .23 | .06 |
| | Denver Broncos | | | |
| ☐ 34 | Glyn Milburn | 1.50 | .65 | .19 |
| | Denver Broncos | | | |
| ☐ 35 | Natrone Means | 2.00 | .90 | .25 |
| | San Diego Chargers | | | |
| ☐ 36 | Lincoln Kennedy | .75 | .35 | .09 |
| | Atlanta Falcons | | | |
| ☐ 37 | Patrick Bates | .50 | .23 | .06 |
| | Los Angeles Raiders | | | |
| ☐ 38 | Jerome Bettis | 5.00 | 2.30 | .60 |
| | Los Angeles Rams | | | |
| ☐ 39 | Irv Smith | .75 | .35 | .09 |
| | New Orleans Saints | | | |
| ☐ 40 | Rick Mirer | 5.00 | 2.30 | .60 |
| | Seattle Seahawks | | | |
| ☐ 41 | Garrison Hearst | 1.50 | .65 | .19 |
| | Phoenix Cardinals | | | |
| ☐ 42 | Kevin Williams | 1.00 | .45 | .13 |
| | Dallas Cowboys | | | |
| ☐ 43 | Terry Kirby | 2.00 | .90 | .25 |
| | Miami Dolphins | | | |
| ☐ 44 | O.J. McDuffie | 2.00 | .90 | .25 |
| | Miami Dolphins | | | |
| ☐ 45 | Leonard Renfro | .50 | .23 | .06 |
| | Philadelphia Eagles | | | |
| ☐ 46 | Victor Bailey | 1.00 | .45 | .13 |
| | Philadelphia Eagles | | | |
| ☐ 47 | Marvin Jones | .50 | .23 | .06 |
| | New York Jets | | | |
| ☐ 48 | Drew Bledsoe | 5.00 | 2.30 | .60 |
| | New England Patriots | | | |
| ☐ 49 | Reggie Brooks | 2.50 | 1.15 | .30 |
| | Washington Redskins | | | |
| ☐ 50 | Tom Carter | .75 | .35 | .09 |
| | Washington Redskins | | | |
| ☐ 51 | Curtis Conway | 1.25 | .55 | .16 |
| | Chicago Bears | | | |
| ☐ 52 | Dan Footman | .50 | .23 | .06 |
| | Cleveland Browns | | | |
| ☐ 53 | Lamar Thomas | .75 | .35 | .09 |
| | Tampa Bay Buccaneers | | | |
| ☐ 54 | Eric Curry | .75 | .35 | .09 |
| | Tampa Bay Buccaneers | | | |
| ☐ 55 | Ryan McNeil | .50 | .23 | .06 |
| | Detroit Lions | | | |
| ☐ 56 | Micheal Barrow | .50 | .23 | .06 |
| | Houston Oilers | | | |
| ☐ 57 | Wayne Simmons | .50 | .23 | .06 |
| | Green Bay Packers | | | |
| ☐ 58 | George Teague | .75 | .35 | .09 |
| | Green Bay Packers | | | |
| ☐ 59 | Robert Smith | 1.00 | .45 | .13 |
| | Minnesota Vikings | | | |
| ☐ 60 | Qadry Ismail | 1.25 | .55 | .16 |
| | Minnesota Vikings | | | |

# 1993 Wild Card
# Red Hot Rookies Superchrome

This ten-card standard-size (2 1/2" by 3 1/2") set was randomly inserted in superchrome packs. These cards are identical in design and color to the regular Red Hot Rookies cards, except that their fronts have a metallic sheen to them. Also, their numbering on the back with an "SCR" prefix is another distinguishing feature.

| | MINT | EXC | G-VG |
|---|---|---|---|
| COMPLETE SET (10) | 50.00 | 20.00 | 5.00 |
| COMMON PLAYER (1-10) | 3.00 | 1.20 | .30 |
| ☐ 1 Dana Stubblefield | 3.00 | 1.20 | .30 |
| San Francisco 49ers | | | |
| ☐ 2 Glyn Milburn | 3.00 | 1.20 | .30 |
| Denver Broncos | | | |
| ☐ 3 Jerome Bettis | 12.00 | 5.00 | 1.20 |
| Los Angeles Rams | | | |
| ☐ 4 Rick Mirer | 12.00 | 5.00 | 1.20 |
| Seattle Seahawks | | | |
| ☐ 5 Garrison Hearst | 5.00 | 2.00 | .50 |
| Phoenix Cardinals | | | |
| ☐ 6 Terry Kirby | 5.00 | 2.00 | .50 |
| Miami Dolphins | | | |
| ☐ 7 Victor Bailey | 3.00 | 1.20 | .30 |
| Philadelphia Eagles | | | |
| ☐ 8 Drew Bledsoe | 12.00 | 5.00 | 1.20 |
| New England Patriots | | | |
| ☐ 9 Reggie Brooks | 6.00 | 2.40 | .60 |
| Washington Redskins | | | |
| ☐ 10 Qadry Ismail | 4.00 | 1.60 | .40 |
| Minnesota Vikings | | | |

# 1993 Wild Card
# Superchrome FF/RHR B/B

This set is frequently called "Red Hot Rookies and Field Force -- Back to Back." Measuring the standard-size (2 1/2" by 3 1/2"), these cards were randomly inserted in Superchrome series II packs. The cards are double-sided, with a Red Hot Rookies on one side and a Field Force on the other. The cards are unnumbered and checklisted below alphabetically by the Field Force player.

| | MINT | EXC | G-VG |
|---|---|---|---|
| COMPLETE SET (10) | 50.00 | 20.00 | 5.00 |
| COMMON PAIR (1-10) | 3.00 | 1.20 | .30 |
| ☐ 1 Troy Aikman | 3.00 | 1.35 | .40 |
| Dana Stubblefield | | | |

| ☐ 2 Drew Bledsoe | 3.00 | 1.35 | .40 |
|---|---|---|---|
| Drew Bledsoe | | | |
| ☐ 3 Brett Favre | 3.00 | 1.35 | .40 |
| Terry Kirby | | | |
| ☐ 4 Dan Marino | 3.00 | 1.35 | .40 |
| Reggie Brooks | | | |
| ☐ 5 Glyn Milburn | 3.00 | 1.35 | .40 |
| Rick Mirer | | | |
| ☐ 6 Rick Mirer | 3.00 | 1.35 | .40 |
| Glyn Milburn | | | |
| ☐ 7 Joe Montana | 3.00 | 1.35 | .40 |
| Jerome Bettis | | | |
| ☐ 8 Jerry Rice | 3.00 | 1.35 | .40 |
| Garrison Hearst | | | |
| ☐ 9 Barry Sanders | 3.00 | 1.35 | .40 |
| Victor Bailey | | | |
| ☐ 10 Emmitt Smith | 3.00 | 1.35 | .40 |
| Quadry Ismail UER | | | |
| (Misspelled Quadry) | | | |

# 1993 Wild Card Stat Smashers

Randomly inserted in foil packs, this 60-card standard-size (2 1/2" by 3 1/2") set features players from the AFC and NFC Western Divisions. The series will continue with players from the Central and Eastern Divisions of both conferences. The action player photos on the fronts stand out against action scenes that have a silver metallic sheen to them. The player's name as well as team name and position appear on colored stripes that jut across the bottom of the picture. The black-bordered backs carry biographical information and a close-up player photo (in the lower left corner), with career summary appearing horizontally in a box on the right portion.

| | MINT | EXC | G-VG |
|---|---|---|---|
| COMPLETE SET (60) | 100.00 | 45.00 | 12.50 |
| COMPLETE WEST SERIES (20) | 35.00 | 16.00 | 4.40 |
| COMPLETE EAST SERIES (20) | 35.00 | 16.00 | 4.40 |
| COMPLETE CENT.SERIES (20) | 35.00 | 16.00 | 4.40 |
| COMMON PLAYER (53-72) | 1.00 | .45 | .13 |
| COMMON PLAYER (73-92) | 1.00 | .45 | .13 |
| COMMON PLAYER (93-112) | 1.00 | .45 | .13 |
| *5/10/20 STRIPES: .30X to .75X VALUE | | | |
| *50/100 STRIPES: .25X to .60X VALUE | | | |
| *1000 STRIPES: .20X to .50X VALUE | | | |
| *GOLD CARDS: 1X to 2X VALUE | | | |
| ☐ 53 Ricky Watters | 2.00 | .90 | .25 |
| San Francisco 49ers | | | |
| ☐ 54 Jerry Rice | 4.00 | 1.80 | .50 |
| San Francisco 49ers | | | |
| ☐ 55 Steve Young | 2.50 | 1.15 | .30 |
| San Francisco 49ers | | | |
| ☐ 56 Shannon Sharpe | 1.50 | .65 | .19 |
| Denver Broncos | | | |
| ☐ 57 John Elway | 3.00 | 1.35 | .40 |
| Denver Broncos | | | |
| ☐ 58 Glyn Milburn | 3.00 | 1.35 | .40 |
| Denver Broncos | | | |
| ☐ 59 Marion Butts | 1.00 | .45 | .13 |
| San Diego Chargers | | | |
| ☐ 60 Junior Seau | 1.00 | .45 | .13 |
| San Diego Chargers | | | |
| ☐ 61 Natrone Means | 3.50 | 1.55 | .45 |
| San Diego Chargers | | | |
| ☐ 62 Joe Montana | 7.00 | 3.10 | .85 |
| Kansas City Chiefs | | | |
| ☐ 63 J.J. Birden | 1.00 | .45 | .13 |
| Kansas City Chiefs | | | |
| ☐ 64 Michael Haynes | 2.00 | .90 | .25 |
| Atlanta Falcons | | | |
| ☐ 65 Deion Sanders | 2.00 | .90 | .25 |
| Atlanta Falcons | | | |

| | | | |
|---|---|---|---|
| ☐ 66 Billy Joe Hobert<br>Los Angeles Raiders | 2.00 | .90 | .25 |
| ☐ 67 Nick Bell<br>Los Angeles Raiders | 1.00 | .45 | .13 |
| ☐ 68 Jerome Bettis<br>Los Angeles Rams | 6.00 | 2.70 | .75 |
| ☐ 69 Vaughn Dunbar<br>New Orleans Saints | 1.00 | .45 | .13 |
| ☐ 70 Quinn Early<br>New Orleans Saints | 1.00 | .45 | .13 |
| ☐ 71 Dan McGwire<br>Seattle Seahawks | 1.00 | .45 | .13 |
| ☐ 72 Rick Mirer<br>Seattle Seahawks | 7.00 | 3.10 | .85 |
| ☐ 73 Kenneth Davis<br>Buffalo Bills | 1.00 | .45 | .13 |
| ☐ 74 Thurman Thomas<br>Buffalo Bills | 3.00 | 1.35 | .40 |
| ☐ 75 Garrison Hearst<br>Phoenix Cardinals | 2.50 | 1.15 | .30 |
| ☐ 76 Ricky Proehl<br>Phoenix Cardinals | 1.00 | .45 | .13 |
| ☐ 77 Jeff George<br>Indianapolis Colts | 2.00 | .90 | .25 |
| ☐ 78 Rodney Culver<br>Indianapolis Colts | 1.00 | .45 | .13 |
| ☐ 79 Troy Aikman<br>Dallas Cowboys | 7.00 | 3.10 | .85 |
| ☐ 80 Emmitt Smith<br>Dallas Cowboys | 9.00 | 4.00 | 1.15 |
| ☐ 81 Michael Irvin<br>Dallas Cowboys | 3.50 | 1.55 | .45 |
| ☐ 82 O.J. McDuffie<br>Miami Dolphins | 4.00 | 1.80 | .50 |
| ☐ 83 Keith Jackson<br>Miami Dolphins | 1.50 | .65 | .19 |
| ☐ 84 Dan Marino<br>Miami Dolphins | 5.00 | 2.30 | .60 |
| ☐ 85 Heath Sherman<br>Philadelphia Eagles | 1.00 | .45 | .13 |
| ☐ 86 Fred Barnett<br>Philadelphia Eagles | 1.50 | .65 | .19 |
| ☐ 87 Rodney Hampton<br>New York Giants | 3.00 | 1.35 | .40 |
| ☐ 88 Marvin Jones<br>New York Jets | 1.50 | .65 | .19 |
| ☐ 89 Brad Baxter<br>New York Jets | 1.00 | .45 | .13 |
| ☐ 90 Drew Bledsoe<br>New England Patriots | 7.00 | 3.10 | .85 |
| ☐ 91 Ricky Ervins<br>Washington Redskins | 1.00 | .45 | .13 |
| ☐ 92 Art Monk<br>Washington Redskins | 1.50 | .65 | .19 |
| ☐ 93 Neal Anderson<br>Chicago Bears | 1.00 | .45 | .13 |
| ☐ 94 Curtis Conway<br>Chicago Bears | 2.50 | 1.15 | .30 |
| ☐ 95 John Copeland<br>Cincinnati Bengals | 1.50 | .65 | .19 |
| ☐ 96 Carl Pickens<br>Cincinnati Bengals | 1.50 | .65 | .19 |
| ☐ 97 David Klingler<br>Cincinnati Bengals | 1.75 | .80 | .22 |
| ☐ 98 Michael Jackson<br>Cleveland Browns | 1.50 | .65 | .19 |
| ☐ 99 Kevin Mack<br>Cleveland Browns | 1.00 | .45 | .13 |
| ☐ 100 Eric Curry<br>Tampa Bay Buccaneers | 1.50 | .65 | .19 |
| ☐ 101 Reggie Cobb<br>Tampa Bay Buccaneers | 1.50 | .65 | .19 |
| ☐ 102 Willie Green<br>Detroit Lions | 1.00 | .45 | .13 |
| ☐ 103 Barry Sanders<br>Detroit Lions | 4.00 | 1.80 | .50 |
| ☐ 104 Haywood Jeffires<br>Houston Oilers | 1.50 | .65 | .19 |
| ☐ 105 Lorenzo White<br>Houston Oilers | 1.00 | .45 | .13 |
| ☐ 106 Sterling Sharpe<br>Green Bay Packers | 4.00 | 1.80 | .50 |
| ☐ 107 Brett Favre<br>Green Bay Packers | 5.00 | 2.30 | .60 |
| ☐ 108 Neil O'Donnell<br>Pittsburgh Steelers | 2.00 | .90 | .25 |
| ☐ 109 Barry Foster<br>Pittsburgh Steelers | 2.50 | 1.15 | .30 |
| ☐ 110 Rich Gannon<br>Minnesota Vikings | 1.00 | .45 | .13 |
| ☐ 111 Robert Smith<br>Minnesota Vikings | 2.00 | .90 | .25 |
| ☐ 112 Qadry Ismail<br>Minnesota Vikings | 2.25 | 1.00 | .30 |

# 1993 Wild Card
# Stat Smashers Rookies

Inserted in each 20-card 1993 Wild Card high-number (201-260) jumbo pack was one of 52 standard-size (2 1/2" by 3 1/2") metallic silver cards that have designs similar to the first-series Stat Smasher inserts. Four packs in each 20-pack high-number box carried a gold Stat Smasher insert instead of the regular silver. These gold versions are valued up to 2.5 times the regular silver cards. Reportedly, 4,500 regular silver and 1,200 gold sets were produced. The cards are numbered on the back with an "SS" prefix.

| | MINT | EXC | G-VG |
|---|---|---|---|
| COMPLETE SET (52) | 30.00 | 13.50 | 3.80 |
| COMMON PLAYER (1-52) | .50 | .23 | .06 |
| *GOLD CARDS: 1.5X to 2.5X VALUE | | | |

| | | | |
|---|---|---|---|
| ☐ 1 Todd Kelly<br>San Francisco 49ers | .75 | .35 | .09 |
| ☐ 2 Dana Stubblefield<br>San Francisco 49ers | 1.00 | .45 | .13 |
| ☐ 3 Curtis Conway<br>Chicago Bears | 1.00 | .45 | .13 |
| ☐ 4 John Copeland<br>Cincinnati Bengals | .75 | .35 | .09 |
| ☐ 5 Russell Copeland<br>Buffalo Bills | .75 | .35 | .09 |
| ☐ 6 Thomas Smith<br>Buffalo Bills | .75 | .35 | .09 |
| ☐ 7 Glyn Milburn<br>Denver Broncos | 1.50 | .65 | .19 |
| ☐ 8 Jason Elam<br>Denver Broncos | .50 | .23 | .06 |
| ☐ 9 Steve Everitt<br>Cleveland Browns | .50 | .23 | .06 |
| ☐ 10 Eric Curry<br>Tampa Bay Buccaneers | .75 | .35 | .09 |
| ☐ 11 Horace Copeland<br>Tampa Bay Buccaneers | .75 | .35 | .09 |
| ☐ 12 Ronald Moore<br>Phoenix Cardinals | 2.00 | .90 | .25 |
| ☐ 13 Garrison Hearst<br>Phoenix Cardinals | 1.00 | .45 | .13 |
| ☐ 14 Natrone Means<br>San Diego Chargers | 2.00 | .90 | .25 |
| ☐ 15 Darrien Gordon<br>San Diego Chargers | .75 | .35 | .09 |
| ☐ 16 Roosevelt Potts<br>Indianapolis Colts | .75 | .35 | .09 |
| ☐ 17 Kevin Williams<br>Dallas Cowboys | 1.25 | .55 | .16 |
| ☐ 18 Derrick Lassic<br>Dallas Cowboys | .75 | .35 | .09 |
| ☐ 19 O.J. McDuffie<br>Miami Dolphins | 2.00 | .90 | .25 |
| ☐ 20 Terry Kirby<br>Miami Dolphins | 1.50 | .65 | .19 |
| ☐ 21 Scott Mitchell<br>Miami Dolphins | 1.00 | .45 | .13 |
| ☐ 22 Victor Bailey<br>Philadelphia Eagles | 1.00 | .45 | .13 |
| ☐ 23 Vaughn Hebron<br>Philadelphia Eagles | .50 | .23 | .06 |
| ☐ 24 Lincoln Kennedy<br>Atlanta Falcons | .75 | .35 | .09 |
| ☐ 25 Michael Strahan<br>New York Giants | .50 | .23 | .06 |
| ☐ 26 Marvin Jones<br>New York Jets | .75 | .35 | .09 |
| ☐ 27 Tony McGee<br>Cincinnati Bengals | .50 | .23 | .06 |
| ☐ 28 Ryan McNeil<br>Detroit Lions | .50 | .23 | .06 |

| | | | |
|---|---|---|---|
| ☐ 29 Micheal Barrow<br>Houston Oilers | .50 | .23 | .06 |
| ☐ 30 Wayne Simmons<br>Green Bay Packers | .75 | .35 | .09 |
| ☐ 31 George Teague<br>Green Bay Packers | .75 | .35 | .09 |
| ☐ 32 Vincent Brisby<br>Green Bay Packers | 1.00 | .45 | .13 |
| ☐ 33 Drew Bledsoe<br>New England Patriots | 4.00 | 1.80 | .50 |
| ☐ 34 Rocket Ismail<br>Los Angeles Raiders | 1.00 | .45 | .13 |
| ☐ 35 Patrick Bates<br>Los Angeles Raiders | .50 | .23 | .06 |
| ☐ 36 James Jett<br>Los Angeles Raiders | 1.25 | .55 | .16 |
| ☐ 37 Jerome Bettis<br>Los Angeles Rams | 4.00 | 1.80 | .50 |
| ☐ 38 Troy Drayton<br>Los Angeles Rams | 1.50 | .65 | .19 |
| ☐ 39 Tom Carter<br>Washington Redskins | .75 | .35 | .09 |
| ☐ 40 Reggie Brooks<br>Washington Redskins | 2.00 | .90 | .25 |
| ☐ 41 Lorenzo Neal<br>New Orleans Saints | 1.00 | .45 | .13 |
| ☐ 42 Derek Brown<br>New Orleans Saints | 1.25 | .55 | .16 |
| ☐ 43 Tyrone Hughes<br>New Orleans Saints | 1.00 | .45 | .13 |
| ☐ 44 Rick Mirer<br>Seattle Seahawks | 4.00 | 1.80 | .50 |
| ☐ 45 Carlton Gray<br>Seattle Seahawks | .50 | .23 | .06 |
| ☐ 46 Andre Hastings<br>Pittsburgh Steelers | .75 | .35 | .09 |
| ☐ 47 Deon Figures<br>Pittsburgh Steelers | .50 | .23 | .06 |
| ☐ 48 Quadry Ismail<br>Minnesota Vikings | 1.00 | .45 | .13 |
| ☐ 49 Robert Smith<br>Minnesota Vikings | .75 | .35 | .09 |
| ☐ 50 Irv Smith<br>New Orleans Saints | .75 | .35 | .09 |
| ☐ 51 Chris Slade<br>New England Patriots | .75 | .35 | .09 |
| ☐ 52 Willie Roaf<br>New Orleans Saints | .50 | .23 | .06 |

## 1993 Wild Card
## Superchrome Promos

These six standard-size (2 1/2" by 3 1/2") promo cards feature on their fronts borderless metallic color player action shots, with the player's name, team, and position appearing within the jagged gold stripe at the bottom. The borderless horizontal back carries the player's name, team, and position at the top, followed by biography, statistics, and, on the right, another color player action shot. The cards are numbered on the back with an "SCP" prefix.

| | MINT | EXC | G-VG |
|---|---|---|---|
| COMPLETE SET (6) | 15.00 | 6.00 | 1.50 |
| COMMON PLAYER (1-6) | 1.50 | .60 | .15 |
| ☐ 1 Emmitt Smith<br>Dallas Cowboys | 5.00 | 2.00 | .50 |
| ☐ 2 Ricky Watters<br>San Francisco 49ers | 2.00 | .80 | .20 |
| ☐ 3 Drew Bledsoe | 5.00 | 2.00 | .50 |

| | | | |
|---|---|---|---|
| New England Patriots | | | |
| ☐ 4 Garrison Hearst<br>Phoenix Cardinals | 2.50 | 1.00 | .25 |
| ☐ 5 Barry Foster<br>Pittsburgh Steelers | 1.50 | .60 | .15 |
| ☐ 6 Rick Mirer<br>Seattle Seahawks | 5.00 | 2.00 | .50 |

## 1993 Wild Card
## Superchrome Rookies Promos

These five standard-size (2 1/2" by 3 1/2") promo cards feature on their fronts metallic purple-bordered color player action shots set within gold elliptical inner borders. The player's name, team, and position appear within the gold inner border. The "Sample" disclaimer appears near the bottom of the photo. The black- and purple-bordered horizontal back carries the player's name, team, and position at the top, followed below by biography, statistics, and, on the right, another color player action shot. The cards are numbered on the back with a "P" prefix.

| | MINT | EXC | G-VG |
|---|---|---|---|
| COMPLETE SET (5) | 15.00 | 6.00 | 1.50 |
| COMMON PLAYER (P1-P5) | 1.50 | .60 | .15 |
| ☐ P1 Rick Mirer<br>Seattle Seahawks | 5.00 | 2.00 | .50 |
| ☐ P2 Reggie Brooks<br>Washington Redskins | 3.00 | 1.20 | .30 |
| ☐ P3 Glyn Milburn<br>Denver Broncos | 1.50 | .60 | .15 |
| ☐ P4 Drew Bledsoe<br>New England Patriots | 5.00 | 2.00 | .50 |
| ☐ P5 Jerome Bettis<br>Los Angeles Rams | 5.00 | 2.00 | .50 |

## 1993 Wild Card
## Superchrome Rookies

These 50 standard-size (2 1/2" by 3 1/2") cards issued early in 1994 were inserted, six per pack, in each special Superchrome Rookies 15-

card foil pack. (The remaining cards in the pack were regular 1993 Wild Cards.) They feature on their foil fronts color player action shots with multicolored borders. The player's name, team, and position appear within the oval gold-colored inner border. The black- and purple-bordered horizontal back carries the player's name, team and position at the top, followed below by biography and statistics. A small color player action shot appears on the right. The cards are numbered on the back. After beginning with the San Francisco 49ers (1-2), and except for card number 28 (Chiefs), the cards are arranged alphabetically according to team names as follows: Chicago Bears (3), Cincinnati Bengals (4-5), Buffalo Bills (6-7), Denver Broncos (8-9), Cleveland Browns (10), Tampa Bay Buccaneers (11-12), Phoenix Cardinals (13-14), San Diego Chargers (15-16), Indianapolis Colts (17), Dallas Cowboys (18-19), Miami Dolphins (20-22), Philadelphia Eagles (23-24), Atlanta Falcons (25), New York Giants (26), New York Jets (27), Kansas City Chiefs (28), Detroit Lions (29), Houston Oilers (30), Green Bay Packers (31-32), New England Patriots (33-34), Los Angeles Raiders (35-37), Los Angeles Rams (38-39), Washington Redskins (40-41), New Orleans Saints (42-44), Seattle Seahawks (45-46), Pittsburgh Steelers (47-48), and Minnesota Vikings (49-50).

|  | MINT | EXC | G-VG |
|---|---|---|---|
| COMPLETE SET (50) | 25.00 | 11.50 | 3.10 |
| COMMON PLAYER (1-50) | .30 | .14 | .04 |
| | | | |
| ☐ 1 Dana Stubblefield | .30 | .14 | .04 |
| ☐ 2 Todd Kelly | .50 | .23 | .06 |
| ☐ 3 Curtis Conway | 1.00 | .45 | .13 |
| ☐ 4 John Copeland | .50 | .23 | .06 |
| ☐ 5 Tony McGee | .30 | .14 | .04 |
| ☐ 6 Russell Copeland | .50 | .23 | .06 |
| ☐ 7 Thomas Smith | .30 | .14 | .04 |
| ☐ 8 Jason Elam | .30 | .14 | .04 |
| ☐ 9 Glyn Milburn | 2.25 | 1.00 | .30 |
| ☐ 10 Steve Everitt | .30 | .14 | .04 |
| ☐ 11 Demetrius DuBose | .50 | .23 | .06 |
| ☐ 12 Eric Curry | .50 | .23 | .06 |
| ☐ 13 Garrison Hearst | 1.75 | .80 | .22 |
| ☐ 14 Ronald Moore | 2.50 | 1.15 | .30 |
| ☐ 15 Darrien Gordon | .50 | .23 | .06 |
| ☐ 16 Natrone Means | 2.50 | 1.15 | .30 |
| ☐ 17 Roosevelt Potts | .75 | .35 | .09 |
| ☐ 18 Derrick Lassic | .75 | .35 | .09 |
| ☐ 19 Kevin Williams | 1.50 | .65 | .19 |
| ☐ 20 Scott Mitchell | 1.50 | .65 | .19 |
| ☐ 21 O.J. McDuffie | 2.25 | 1.00 | .30 |
| ☐ 22 Terry Kirby | 2.00 | .90 | .25 |
| ☐ 23 Vaughn Hebron | .30 | .14 | .04 |
| ☐ 24 Victor Bailey | .30 | .14 | .04 |
| ☐ 25 Lincoln Kennedy | .50 | .23 | .06 |
| ☐ 26 Michael Strahan | .30 | .14 | .04 |
| ☐ 27 Marvin Jones | .50 | .23 | .06 |
| ☐ 28 Will Shields | .30 | .14 | .04 |
| ☐ 29 Ryan McNeil | .30 | .14 | .04 |
| ☐ 30 Micheal Barrow | .30 | .14 | .04 |
| ☐ 31 George Teague | .50 | .23 | .06 |
| ☐ 32 Wayne Simmons | .30 | .14 | .04 |
| ☐ 33 Vincent Brisby | 1.25 | .55 | .16 |
| ☐ 34 Drew Bledsoe | 7.00 | 3.10 | .85 |
| ☐ 35 Patrick Bates | .30 | .14 | .04 |
| ☐ 36 James Jett | 2.00 | .90 | .25 |
| ☐ 37 Rocket Ismail | 1.50 | .65 | .19 |
| ☐ 38 Troy Drayton | .50 | .23 | .06 |
| ☐ 39 Jerome Bettis | 7.00 | 3.10 | .85 |
| ☐ 40 Tom Carter | .50 | .23 | .06 |
| ☐ 41 Reggie Brooks | 4.00 | 1.80 | .50 |
| ☐ 42 Tyrone Hughes | 1.00 | .45 | .13 |
| ☐ 43 Derek Brown | 1.50 | .65 | .19 |
| ☐ 44 Willie Roaf | .30 | .14 | .04 |
| ☐ 45 Carlton Gray | .30 | .14 | .04 |
| ☐ 46 Rick Mirer | 8.00 | 3.60 | 1.00 |
| ☐ 47 Andre Hastings | .50 | .23 | .06 |
| ☐ 48 Deon Figures | .50 | .23 | .06 |
| ☐ 49 Quadry Ismail | 1.25 | .55 | .16 |
| ☐ 50 Robert Smith | 1.00 | .45 | .13 |

# 1993 Wild Card Superchrome Rookies B/B

Randomly inserted in 1993 Wild Card Superchrome Rookies foil packs, these 25 standard-size (2 1/2" by 3 1/2") cards feature on both metallic sides embossed color action shots of NFL rookies in their NFL uniforms within purple, black, blue, and gold borders. The player's name, team, and position appear above the photo within the oval gold inner border. The cards are unnumbered and checklisted below in alphabetical order.

|  | MINT | EXC | G-VG |
|---|---|---|---|
| COMPLETE SET (25) | 75.00 | 34.00 | 9.50 |
| COMMON PAIR (1-25) | 2.00 | .90 | .25 |
| | | | |
| ☐ 1 Victor Bailey | 2.00 | .90 | .25 |
| Philadelphia Eagles | | | |
| Vaughn Hebron | | | |
| Philadelphia Eagles | | | |
| ☐ 2 Micheal Barrow | 2.00 | .90 | .25 |
| Houston Oilers | | | |
| Ryan McNeil | | | |
| Detroit Lions | | | |
| ☐ 3 Patrick Bates | 2.00 | .90 | .25 |
| Los Angeles Raiders | | | |
| Vincent Brisby | | | |
| New England Patriots | | | |
| ☐ 4 Jerome Bettis | 30.00 | 13.50 | 3.80 |
| Los Angeles Rams | | | |
| Natrone Means | | | |
| San Diego Chargers | | | |
| ☐ 5 Drew Bledsoe | 40.00 | 18.00 | 5.00 |
| New England Patriots | | | |
| Rick Mirer | | | |
| Seattle Seahawks | | | |
| ☐ 6 Reggie Brooks | 15.00 | 6.75 | 1.90 |
| Washington Redskins | | | |
| Glyn Milburn | | | |
| Denver Broncos | | | |
| ☐ 7 Derek Brown | 7.00 | 3.10 | .85 |
| New Orleans Saints | | | |
| Tyrone Hughes | | | |
| New Orleans Saints | | | |
| ☐ 8 Tom Carter | 2.00 | .90 | .25 |
| Washington Redskins | | | |
| Jason Elam | | | |
| Denver Broncos | | | |
| ☐ 9 Curtis Conway | 4.00 | 1.80 | .50 |
| Chicago Bears | | | |
| Steve Everitt | | | |
| Cleveland Browns | | | |
| ☐ 10 John Copeland | 2.00 | .90 | .25 |
| Cincinnati Bengals | | | |
| Tony McGee | | | |
| Cincinnati Bengals | | | |
| ☐ 11 Russell Copeland | 2.00 | .90 | .25 |
| Buffalo Bills | | | |
| Thomas Smith | | | |
| Buffalo Bills | | | |
| ☐ 12 Eric Curry | 2.00 | .90 | .25 |
| Tampa Bay Buccaneers | | | |
| Demetrius DuBose | | | |
| Tampa Bay Buccaneers | | | |
| ☐ 13 Troy Drayton | 4.00 | 1.80 | .50 |
| Los Angeles Rams | | | |
| Darrien Gordon | | | |
| San Diego Chargers | | | |
| ☐ 14 Deon Figures | 2.00 | .90 | .25 |
| Pittsburgh Steelers | | | |
| Andre Hastings | | | |
| Pittsburgh Steelers | | | |
| ☐ 15 Carlton Gray | 2.00 | .90 | .25 |
| Seattle Seahawks | | | |
| Willie Roaf | | | |
| New Orleans Saints | | | |
| ☐ 16 Garrison Hearst | 12.00 | 5.50 | 1.50 |
| Phoenix Cardinals | | | |
| Ronald Moore | | | |
| Phoenix Cardinals | | | |
| ☐ 17 Qadry Ismail | 6.00 | 2.70 | .75 |
| Minnesota Vikings | | | |
| Rocket Ismail | | | |
| Los Angeles Raiders | | | |
| ☐ 18 James Jett | 7.00 | 3.10 | .85 |
| Los Angeles Raiders | | | |
| Robert Smith | | | |
| Minnesota Vikings | | | |
| ☐ 19 Marvin Jones | 2.00 | .90 | .25 |
| New York Jets | | | |
| Will Shields | | | |
| Kansas City Chiefs | | | |
| ☐ 20 Todd Kelly | 2.00 | .90 | .25 |
| San Francisco 49ers | | | |
| Dana Stubblefield | | | |
| San Francisco 49ers | | | |
| ☐ 21 Lincoln Kennedy | 2.00 | .90 | .25 |
| Atlanta Falcons | | | |
| Michael Strahan | | | |
| New York Giants | | | |
| ☐ 22 Terry Kirby | 12.00 | 5.50 | 1.50 |
| Miami Dolphins | | | |
| O.J. McDuffie | | | |
| Miami Dolphins | | | |
| ☐ 23 Derrick Lassic | 6.00 | 2.70 | .75 |
| Dallas Cowboys | | | |
| Kevin Williams | | | |
| Dallas Cowboys | | | |
| ☐ 24 Scott Mitchell | 7.00 | 3.10 | .85 |
| Miami Dolphins | | | |

Roosevelt Potts
Indianapolis Colts
☐ 25 Wayne Simmons.................... 2.00 .90 .25
Green Bay Packers
George Teague
Green Bay Packers

## 1994 Ted Williams Promos

These two standard-size (2 1/2" by 3 1/2") promo cards were issued to herald the release of the 1994 Ted Williams Roger Staubach's NFL Preview set. The fronts feature borderless color player action shots. The player's name appears in vertical silver lettering near the left edge. The set's embossed logo appears in one corner. The back of Staubach's promo carries his position, biography, stats, and career highlights within a silver-colored plaque highlighted by flags. His name appears in white lettering within a red banner near the bottom. The back of Bradshaw's promo carries his name at the top followed below by career highlights, all in white lettering upon a background consisting of the letters "G-O-L-D" resting on artificial turf. The cards are numbered on the back with a "P" prefix. Moreover, these two promos are easily distinguished from the correspondingly-numbered regular series cards by different front photos.

|  | MINT | EXC | G-VG |
|---|---|---|---|
| COMPLETE SET (2)........................ | 5.00 | 2.00 | .50 |
| COMMON PLAYER........................... | 3.00 | 1.20 | .30 |
| ☐ 1 Roger Staubach ....................... Dallas Cowboys | 3.00 | 1.20 | .30 |
| ☐ 73 Terry Bradshaw....................... Pittsburgh Steelers | 3.00 | 1.20 | .30 |

## 1994 Ted Williams

The 1994 Ted Williams Roger Staubach's NFL Football Preview Edition consists of 90 standard-size (2 1/2" by 3 1/2") cards. Only 5,000 twelve box cases were produced. The fronts feature borderless color player action shots superimposed on a ghosted action player photo. The player's name appears in vertical silver lettering near the left edge. The set's embossed logo appears in the lower left corner. The navy blue backs carry the player's position, biography, stats, and career highlights within a silver-colored, oval plaque highlighted by flags. The

cards are numbered on the back and checklisted below according to teams as follows: Dallas Cowboys (1-3), Baltimore Colts (4-6), Buffalo Bills (7-8), Chicago Bears (9-12), Cincinnati Bengals (13), Cleveland Browns (14-16), Denver Broncos (17-18), Detroit Lions (19-21), Green Bay Packers (22-23), Houston Oilers (24), Kansas City Chiefs (25-27), Los Angeles Rams (28-31), Miami Dolphins (32), Minnesota Vikings (33-34), New England Patriots (35-36), New Orleans Saints (37-38), New York Giants (39-41), New York Jets (42-44), Oakland Raiders (45-47), Philadelphia Eagles (48-49), Pittsburgh Steelers (50-52), San Diego Chargers (53-54), San Francisco 49ers (55), Seattle Seahawks (56-57), St. Louis Cardinals (58-59), Tampa Bay Buccaneers (60), and Washington Redskins (61-62). The series closes with three topical subsets: Chalkboard Legends (64-72), Golden Arms (73-81), and Dawning of a Legacy (82-90). The cards are numbered on the back. Randomly inserted in foil packs were three special chase cards, Charles Barkley, Fred Dryer, and Ted Williams.

|  | MINT | EXC | G-VG |
|---|---|---|---|
| COMPLETE SET (90)........................ | 12.00 | 5.00 | 1.20 |
| COMMON PLAYER (1-90)................. | .10 | .04 | .01 |
| ☐ 1 Roger Staubach ......................... | 1.25 | .50 | .12 |
| ☐ 2 Tony Dorsett ............................. | .50 | .20 | .05 |
| ☐ 3 Bob Lilly................................... | .35 | .14 | .03 |
| ☐ 4 Art Donovan .............................. | .25 | .10 | .02 |
| ☐ 5 Bert Jones ................................ | .25 | .10 | .02 |
| ☐ 6 Johnny Unitas ........................... | 1.00 | .40 | .10 |
| ☐ 7 Jack Kemp ................................ | 1.00 | .40 | .10 |
| ☐ 8 O.J. Simpson ............................ | 1.50 | .60 | .15 |
| ☐ 9 Dick Butkus .............................. | .60 | .24 | .06 |
| ☐ 10 Gale Sayers ............................ | .75 | .30 | .07 |
| ☐ 11 Mike Singletary ....................... | .25 | .10 | .02 |
| ☐ 12 Bronko Nagurski ...................... | .25 | .10 | .02 |
| ☐ 13 Ken Anderson .......................... | .25 | .10 | .02 |
| ☐ 14 Otto Graham ........................... | .35 | .14 | .03 |
| ☐ 15 Lou Groza .............................. | .25 | .10 | .02 |
| ☐ 16 Marion Motley.......................... | .25 | .10 | .02 |
| ☐ 17 Floyd Little ............................. | .15 | .06 | .01 |
| ☐ 18 Haven Moses .......................... | .10 | .04 | .01 |
| ☐ 19 Lem Barney ............................ | .25 | .10 | .02 |
| ☐ 20 Dick(Night Train) Lane .......... | .25 | .10 | .02 |
| ☐ 21 Bobby Layne ........................... | .35 | .14 | .03 |
| ☐ 22 Ray Nitschke ........................... | .25 | .10 | .02 |
| ☐ 23 Willie Wood............................. | .25 | .10 | .02 |
| ☐ 24 Billy(White Shoes) Johnson | .10 | .04 | .01 |
| ☐ 25 Mike Bell ............................... | .10 | .04 | .01 |
| ☐ 26 Buck Buchanan ....................... | .25 | .10 | .02 |
| ☐ 27 Len Dawson ............................ | .35 | .14 | .03 |
| ☐ 28 Roman Gabriel ........................ | .20 | .08 | .02 |
| ☐ 29 LeRoy Irvin ............................ | .10 | .04 | .01 |
| ☐ 30 Deacon Jones .......................... | .25 | .10 | .02 |
| ☐ 31 Bob Waterfield ........................ | .35 | .14 | .03 |
| ☐ 32 Bob Griese .............................. | .75 | .30 | .07 |
| ☐ 33 Carl Eller ............................... | .25 | .10 | .02 |
| ☐ 34 Fran Tarkenton ........................ | .75 | .30 | .07 |
| ☐ 35 John Hannah ........................... | .25 | .10 | .02 |
| ☐ 36 Jim Plunkett ........................... | .20 | .08 | .02 |
| ☐ 37 Tom Dempsey .......................... | .10 | .04 | .01 |
| ☐ 38 Archie Manning ....................... | .25 | .10 | .02 |
| ☐ 39 Sam Huff ............................... | .25 | .10 | .02 |
| ☐ 40 Andy Robustelli ....................... | .25 | .10 | .02 |
| ☐ 41 Charley Conerly ....................... | .25 | .10 | .02 |
| ☐ 42 Don Maynard ........................... | .25 | .10 | .02 |
| ☐ 43 Matt Snell .............................. | .15 | .06 | .01 |
| ☐ 44 Wesley Walker ........................ | .15 | .06 | .01 |
| ☐ 45 George Blanda ......................... | .35 | .14 | .03 |
| ☐ 46 Ben Davidson .......................... | .15 | .06 | .01 |
| ☐ 47 Jim Otto ................................. | .25 | .10 | .02 |
| ☐ 48 Norm Van Brocklin ................... | .35 | .14 | .03 |
| ☐ 49 Harold Carmichael................... | .15 | .06 | .01 |
| ☐ 50 Joe Greene ............................. | .30 | .12 | .03 |
| ☐ 51 L.C. Greenwood ....................... | .15 | .06 | .01 |
| ☐ 52 Jack Lambert .......................... | .30 | .12 | .03 |
| ☐ 53 Lance Alworth .......................... | .35 | .14 | .03 |
| ☐ 54 Dan Fouts .............................. | .35 | .14 | .03 |
| ☐ 55 John Brodie............................. | .30 | .12 | .03 |
| ☐ 56 Steve Largent .......................... | .35 | .14 | .03 |
| ☐ 57 Jim Zorn ................................ | .15 | .06 | .01 |
| ☐ 58 Jim Hart ................................ | .15 | .06 | .01 |
| ☐ 59 Mel Gray ................................ | .15 | .06 | .01 |
| ☐ 60 Lee Roy Selmon ....................... | .10 | .04 | .01 |
| ☐ 61 Sonny Jurgensen ...................... | .30 | .12 | .03 |
| ☐ 62 Sammy Baugh........................... | .50 | .20 | .05 |
| ☐ 63 Checklist UER ......................... (Players on card nos. 61 and 62 reversed) | .10 | .04 | .01 |
| ☐ 64 George Allen CO ...................... Washington Redskins | .15 | .06 | .01 |
| ☐ 65 George Halas CO...................... Chicago Bears | .35 | .14 | .03 |
| ☐ 66 Tom Landry CO........................ Dallas Cowboys | .50 | .20 | .05 |
| ☐ 67 Vince Lombardi CO.................. Green Bay Packers | .50 | .20 | .05 |

| | | | |
|---|---|---|---|
| ☐ 68 John Madden CO | .35 | .14 | .03 |
| Oakland Raiders | | | |
| ☐ 69 Chuck Noll CO | .20 | .08 | .02 |
| Pittsburgh Steelers | | | |
| ☐ 70 Don Shula CO | .25 | .10 | .02 |
| Miami Dolphins | | | |
| ☐ 71 Hank Stram CO | .15 | .06 | .01 |
| Kansas City Chiefs | | | |
| ☐ 72 Checklist | .10 | .04 | .01 |
| ☐ 73 Terry Bradshaw | .75 | .30 | .07 |
| ☐ 74 Len Dawson | .35 | .14 | .03 |
| ☐ 75 Dan Fouts | .35 | .14 | .03 |
| ☐ 76 Bart Starr | .50 | .20 | .05 |
| ☐ 77 Roger Staubach | 1.25 | .50 | .12 |
| ☐ 78 Fran Tarkenton | .60 | .24 | .06 |
| ☐ 79 Y.A. Tittle | .35 | .14 | .03 |
| ☐ 80 Johnny Unitas | 1.00 | .40 | .10 |
| ☐ 81 Checklist | .10 | .04 | .01 |
| ☐ 82 Brett Favre | .50 | .20 | .05 |
| Pack-ing Up | | | |
| ☐ 83 Brett Favre | .50 | .20 | .05 |
| A Memorable Week | | | |
| ☐ 84 Brett Favre | .50 | .20 | .05 |
| What A Year | | | |
| ☐ 85 Brett Favre | .50 | .20 | .05 |
| Ready for 1993 | | | |
| ☐ 86 Neil O'Donnell | .20 | .08 | .02 |
| 1991 | | | |
| ☐ 87 Neil O'Donnell | .20 | .08 | .02 |
| College | | | |
| ☐ 88 Neil O'Donnell | .20 | .08 | .02 |
| High Notes | | | |
| ☐ 89 Neil O'Donnell | .20 | .08 | .02 |
| 1992 | | | |
| ☐ 90 Checklist Card | .10 | .04 | .01 |
| ☐ CB1 Charles Barkley | 5.00 | 2.00 | .50 |
| ☐ CB1AU Charles Barkley AU | 900.00 | 360.00 | 90.00 |
| (Certified autograph) | | | |
| AU/34 | | | |
| ☐ HM1 Fred Dryer | 5.00 | 2.00 | .50 |
| Hollywood Makeovers | | | |
| ☐ TW1 Ted Williams | 20.00 | 8.00 | 2.00 |
| Teddy Football | | | |
| ☐ TW1AU Ted Williams AU/54 | 500.00 | 200.00 | 50.00 |
| (Certified autograph) | | | |

## 1994 Ted Williams Auckland Collection

Randomly inserted in hobby packs only, the nine-card set consists of an illustrated series by one of the country's foremost sports artists, Jim Auckland. The cards measure standard-size (2 1/2" by 3 1/2") and are printed on a special matte finish paper stock. The white bordered fronts have illustrations from noted sports artist, Jim Auckland. The red and white bordered backs have a ghosted multi-player illustration with a player summary. The cards are numbered on the back with an "AC" prefix.

| | MINT | EXC | G-VG |
|---|---|---|---|
| COMPLETE SET (9) | 35.00 | 14.00 | 3.50 |
| COMMON PLAYER (AC1-AC9) | 3.00 | 1.20 | .30 |
| | | | |
| ☐ AC1 Brett Favre | 6.00 | 2.40 | .60 |
| ☐ AC2 Vince Lombardi | 7.00 | 2.80 | .70 |
| ☐ AC3 Walter Payton | 9.00 | 3.75 | .90 |
| ☐ AC4 Phil Simms | 5.00 | 2.00 | .50 |
| ☐ AC5 Bart Starr | 7.00 | 2.80 | .70 |
| ☐ AC6 Roger Staubach | 10.00 | 4.00 | 1.00 |
| ☐ AC7 Jim Thorpe | 6.00 | 2.40 | .60 |

| | | | |
|---|---|---|---|
| ☐ AC8 Johnny Unitas | 8.00 | 3.25 | .80 |
| ☐ AC9 Checklist | 3.00 | 1.20 | .30 |

## 1994 Ted Williams Etched In Stone Unitas

Randomly inserted in packs, this nine-card 1994 Ted Williams Etched in Stone set highlights the career of football legend Johnny Unitas. The full-bleed color and sepia photos have a gold edged upper left and lower right corner. Unitas' name is printed within the lower right gold corner and the set title appears in the lower left corner. The backs are brick red with a puzzle design. When all nine cards are placed in a protective card sheet, the words "Etched in Stone," a gold star, and a stone mallet become visible. The narrative format on the back chronicals Unitas' career beginning with college football. The cards are numbered on the back with an "ES" prefix.

| | MINT | EXC | G-VG |
|---|---|---|---|
| COMPLETE SET (9) | 20.00 | 8.00 | 2.00 |
| COMMON PLAYER (ES1-ES9) | 2.50 | 1.00 | .25 |
| | | | |
| ☐ ES1 Johnny Unitas | 2.50 | 1.00 | .25 |
| 1970 Championship Game | | | |
| ☐ ES2 Johnny Unitas | 2.50 | 1.00 | .25 |
| Super Bowl V | | | |
| ☐ ES3 Johnny Unitas | 2.50 | 1.00 | .25 |
| Memories | | | |
| ☐ ES4 Johnny Unitas | 2.50 | 1.00 | .25 |
| Injuries | | | |
| ☐ ES5 Johnny Unitas | 2.50 | 1.00 | .25 |
| 1959 Rematch | | | |
| ☐ ES6 Johnny Unitas | 2.50 | 1.00 | .25 |
| College Days | | | |
| ☐ ES7 Johnny Unitas | 2.50 | 1.00 | .25 |
| 1972 | | | |
| ☐ ES8 Johnny Unitas | 2.50 | 1.00 | .25 |
| Greatest Game Ever | | | |
| ☐ ES9 Checklist Card | 2.50 | 1.00 | .25 |

## 1994 Ted Williams Instant Replays

Randomly inserted in hobby packs only, this 17-card set highlights four of the greatest dynasties in NFL history. The four teams were distributed by region. The cards measure standard-size (2 1/2" by 3 1/2"). The card front features a color or sepia-toned action player photo with gold film strip designed borders to the left and right side of the photo. The photo has a striped finish effect somewhat similar to a Sportflic card, but with only a single player photo. The set name is printed in the lower left corner and the player's name appears on a film strip styled stripe across the bottom. The orange backs have a ghosted star wrapped with gray film strip and carry player summary and highlights. The player's name is printed on a gold bar across the top. The set is organized according to teams as follows: New York Giants (1-4), Green Bay Packers (5-8), Pittsburgh Steelers (9-12), and Oakland/L.A. Raiders (13-16). The cards are numbered on the back with an "IR" prefix.

|  | MINT | EXC | G-VG |
|---|---|---|---|
| COMPLETE SET (17) | 30.00 | 12.00 | 3.00 |
| COMMON PLAYER (IR1-IR17) | 1.00 | .40 | .10 |
| ☐ IR1 Phil Simms | 2.50 | 1.00 | .25 |
| ☐ IR2 Y.A. Tittle | 3.00 | 1.20 | .30 |
| ☐ IR3 Sam Huff | 2.00 | .80 | .20 |
| ☐ IR4 Brad Van Pelt | 1.00 | .40 | .10 |
| ☐ IR5 Brett Favre | 4.00 | 1.60 | .40 |
| ☐ IR6 Bart Starr | 5.00 | 2.00 | .50 |
| ☐ IR7 Paul Hornung | 4.00 | 1.60 | .40 |
| ☐ IR8 Ray Nitschke | 2.50 | 1.00 | .25 |
| ☐ IR9 Neil O'Donnell | 2.00 | .80 | .20 |
| ☐ IR10 Terry Bradshaw | 5.00 | 2.00 | .50 |
| ☐ IR11 Joe Greene | 2.50 | 1.00 | .25 |
| ☐ IR12 Jack Lambert | 2.50 | 1.00 | .25 |
| ☐ IR13 Jeff Hostetler | 2.00 | .80 | .20 |
| ☐ IR14 Lyle Alzado | 1.50 | .60 | .15 |
| ☐ IR15 Dave Casper | 1.00 | .40 | .10 |
| ☐ IR16 Ken Stabler | 3.00 | 1.20 | .30 |
| ☐ IR17 Checklist Card | 1.00 | .40 | .10 |

# 1994 Ted Williams Path to Greatness

Randomly inserted into packs, this nine-card set features collegiate players who went on to successful NFL careers. The standard-size (3 1/2" by 2 1/2") cards feature great collegiate players and coaches who went on to successful NFL careers. The fronts carry sepia-toned or color action player photos. A narrow gold border is located along the upper and left side. The photo has a striped finish effect somewhat similar to a Sportflic card, but with only a single player photo. In gold foil, the player's name is stamped on a white banner across the bottom of the picture. The set title appears in the lower left corner. The colorful backs are borderless with gray stairs leading from a torch in the lower left corner. The player's name is printed on a white banner across the top. The player's collegiate football highlights are listed in narrative format. The cards are numbered on the back with a "PG" prefix.

|  | MINT | EXC | G-VG |
|---|---|---|---|
| COMPLETE SET (9) | 25.00 | 10.00 | 2.50 |
| COMMON PLAYER (PG1-PG9) | 1.00 | .40 | .10 |
| ☐ PG1 Tony Dorsett | 4.00 | 1.60 | .40 |
| ☐ PG2 Red Grange | 3.00 | 1.20 | .30 |
| ☐ PG3 Bob Griese | 4.00 | 1.60 | .40 |
| ☐ PG4 Jeff Hostetler | 1.50 | .60 | .15 |
| ☐ PG5 Neil O'Donnell | 1.50 | .60 | .15 |
| ☐ PG6 Jim Plunkett | 2.50 | 1.00 | .25 |
| ☐ PG7 O.J. Simpson | 10.00 | 4.00 | 1.00 |
| ☐ PG8 Roger Staubach | 6.00 | 2.40 | .60 |
| ☐ PG9 Checklist Card | 1.00 | .40 | .10 |

# 1994 Ted Williams Walter Payton

Available only in jumbo packs sold in mass market retail outlets, this nine-card set spotlights the career of one of football's greatest running backs, Walter Payton. The standard size (2 1/2" by 3 1/2") cards feature full-bleed color action shots. The photo has a striped finish effect somewhat similar to a Sportflic card, but with only a single photo exposure. The set title appears in the lower right corner. The borderless blue backs have a sun design at the top, with the title of the card appearing below Payton's name. Each card chronicles a specific time of Payton's career beginning with college, and including a card listing career statistics. The cards are numbered on the back with a "WP" prefix.

|  | MINT | EXC | G-VG |
|---|---|---|---|
| COMPLETE SET (9) | 15.00 | 6.00 | 1.50 |
| COMMON PLAYER (WP1-WP9) | 2.00 | .80 | .20 |
| ☐ WP1 Walter Payton<br>Ditka On Payton | 2.00 | .80 | .20 |
| ☐ WP2 Walter Payton<br>Winning It All | 2.00 | .80 | .20 |
| ☐ WP3 Walter Payton<br>Rookie | 2.00 | .80 | .20 |
| ☐ WP4 Walter Payton<br>1977 | 2.00 | .80 | .20 |
| ☐ WP5 Walter Payton<br>College | 2.00 | .80 | .20 |
| ☐ WP6 Walter Payton<br>Payton vs. O.J. | 3.00 | 1.20 | .30 |
| ☐ WP7 Walter Payton<br>Sweetness | 2.00 | .80 | .20 |
| ☐ WP8 Walter Payton<br>The Records | 2.00 | .80 | .20 |
| ☐ WP9 Checklist Card | 2.00 | .80 | .20 |

# 1994 Ted Williams POG Cards

The 1994 Ted Williams POG's were inserted in every foil pack of the 1994 Ted Williams Roger Staubach football cards. A total of 18 POG cards with 34 different players and a checklist were produced. On a dark blue background, each POG or Milk Cap card contains two POG's, each measuring approximately 1 5/8" in diameter. The cards measure standard size (2 1/2" by 3 1/2"). The fronts feature a head shot of the player in color or black and white with the player's name printed above or below the photo. The white backs are blank. The cards are numbered on the front.

| | MINT | EXC | G-VG |
|---|---|---|---|
| COMPLETE SET (18) | 5.00 | 2.00 | .50 |
| COMMON PLAYER (1-18) | .25 | .10 | .02 |
| ☐ 1 Roger Staubach<br>Brett Favre | .75 | .30 | .07 |
| ☐ 2 Roman Gabriel<br>Lee Roy Jordan | .30 | .12 | .03 |
| ☐ 3 Dan Fouts<br>John Brodie | .40 | .16 | .04 |
| ☐ 4 Terry Bradshaw<br>Bart Starr | .75 | .30 | .07 |
| ☐ 5 O.J. Simpson<br>Floyd Little | 1.00 | .40 | .10 |
| ☐ 6 Pete Pihos<br>Larry Csonka | .30 | .12 | .03 |
| ☐ 7 Dick(Night Train) Lane<br>Carl Eller | .40 | .16 | .04 |
| ☐ 8 Sam Huff<br>Ben Davidson | .40 | .16 | .04 |
| ☐ 9 Jack Lambert<br>Jethro Pugh | .35 | .14 | .03 |
| ☐ 10 Mike Singletary<br>Harold Carmichael | .30 | .12 | .03 |
| ☐ 11 Chuck Noll CO<br>Bud Grant CO | .25 | .10 | .02 |
| ☐ 12 John Madden CO<br>Lyle Alzado | .25 | .10 | .02 |
| ☐ 13 Walter Payton<br>Gale Sayers | 1.00 | .40 | .10 |
| ☐ 14 Fred Dryer<br>Ron Mix | .30 | .12 | .03 |
| ☐ 15 Bob Griese<br>Doug Williams | .35 | .14 | .03 |
| ☐ 16 Tony Dorsett<br>Red Grange | .50 | .20 | .05 |
| ☐ 17 Sonny Jurgensen<br>Jeff Hostetler | .35 | .14 | .03 |
| ☐ 18 Checklist Card | .25 | .10 | .02 |

## 1974 Wonder Bread

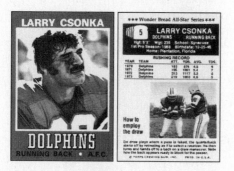

The 1974 Wonder Bread Football set features 30 cards with colored borders and color photographs of the players on the obverse. The cards measure 2 1/2" by 3 1/2". Season by season records are given on the back of the cards as well as a particular football technique. A "Topps Chewing Gum, Inc." copyright appears on the reverse. The cards were also produced by Town Talk Bread; these Town Talk cards are slightly more difficult to find (valued roughly 1.5X) and are distinguished by the absence of a credit line at the top of the reverse of each card.

| | NRMT | VG-E | GOOD |
|---|---|---|---|
| COMPLETE SET (30) | 20.00 | 8.00 | 2.00 |
| COMMON PLAYER (1-30) | .50 | .20 | .05 |
| ☐ 1 Jim Bakken<br>St. Louis Cardinals | .50 | .20 | .05 |
| ☐ 2 Forrest Blue<br>San Francisco 49ers | .50 | .20 | .05 |
| ☐ 3 Bill Bradley<br>Philadelphia Eagles | .50 | .20 | .05 |
| ☐ 4 Willie Brown<br>Oakland Raiders | 1.50 | .60 | .15 |
| ☐ 5 Larry Csonka<br>Miami Dolphins | 3.00 | 1.20 | .30 |
| ☐ 6 Ken Ellis<br>Green Bay Packers | .50 | .20 | .05 |
| ☐ 7 Bruce Gossett<br>San Francisco 49ers | .50 | .20 | .05 |

| | | | |
|---|---|---|---|
| ☐ 8 Bob Griese<br>Miami Dolphins | 3.00 | 1.20 | .30 |
| ☐ 9 Chris Hanburger<br>Washington Redskins | .75 | .30 | .07 |
| ☐ 10 Winston Hill<br>New York Jets | .50 | .20 | .05 |
| ☐ 11 Jim Johnson<br>San Francisco 49ers | 1.25 | .50 | .12 |
| ☐ 12 Paul Krause<br>Minnesota Vikings | .75 | .30 | .07 |
| ☐ 13 Ted Kwalick<br>San Francisco 49ers | .75 | .30 | .07 |
| ☐ 14 Willie Lanier<br>Kansas City Chiefs | 1.50 | .60 | .15 |
| ☐ 15 Tom Mack<br>Los Angeles Rams | 1.00 | .40 | .10 |
| ☐ 16 Jim Otto<br>Oakland Raiders | 1.50 | .60 | .15 |
| ☐ 17 Alan Page<br>Minnesota Vikings | 1.50 | .60 | .15 |
| ☐ 18 Frank Pitts<br>Cleveland Browns | .50 | .20 | .05 |
| ☐ 19 Jim Plunkett<br>New England Patriots | 1.50 | .60 | .15 |
| ☐ 20 Mike Reid<br>Cincinnati Bengals | 1.00 | .40 | .10 |
| ☐ 21 Paul Smith<br>Denver Broncos | .50 | .20 | .05 |
| ☐ 22 Bob Tucker<br>New York Giants | .75 | .30 | .07 |
| ☐ 23 Jim Tyrer<br>Kansas City Chiefs | .75 | .30 | .07 |
| ☐ 24 Eugene Upshaw<br>Oakland Raiders | 1.50 | .60 | .15 |
| ☐ 25 Phil Villapiano<br>Oakland Raiders | .75 | .30 | .07 |
| ☐ 26 Paul Warfield<br>Miami Dolphins | 2.00 | .80 | .20 |
| ☐ 27 Dwight White<br>Pittsburgh Steelers | .50 | .20 | .05 |
| ☐ 28 Steve Owens<br>Detroit Lions | .75 | .30 | .07 |
| ☐ 29 Jerrel Wilson<br>Kansas City Chiefs | .50 | .20 | .05 |
| ☐ 30 Ron Yary<br>Minnesota Vikings | .75 | .30 | .07 |

## 1975 Wonder Bread

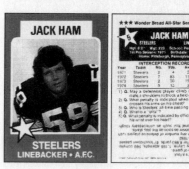

The 1975 Wonder Bread Football card set contains 24 cards with either blue (7-18) or red (1-6 and 19-24) borders. The cards measure 2 1/2" by 3 1/2". The backs feature several questions (about the player and the game of football) whose answers could be determined by turning the card upside down and reading the answers to the corresponding questions. The words "Topps Chewing Gum, Inc." appears at the bottom of the reverse of the card. The cards were also produced by Town Talk Bread; these Town Talk cards are more slightly difficult to find (valued roughly 1.5X) and are distinguished by the different credit line at the top of the reverse of each card. Wonder Bread also produced a saver sheet and album for this set.

| | NRMT | VG-E | GOOD |
|---|---|---|---|
| COMPLETE SET (24) | 15.00 | 6.00 | 1.50 |
| COMMON PLAYER (1-24) | .40 | .16 | .04 |
| ☐ 1 Alan Page<br>Minnesota Vikings | 1.50 | .60 | .15 |
| ☐ 2 Emmitt Thomas<br>Kansas City Chiefs | .40 | .16 | .04 |
| ☐ 3 John Mendenhall | .40 | .16 | .04 |

|  |  |  |  |
|---|---|---|---|
| New York Giants |  |  |  |
| ☐ 4 Ken Houston | 1.25 | .50 | .12 |
| Washington Redskins |  |  |  |
| ☐ 5 Jack Ham | 1.25 | .50 | .12 |
| Pittsburgh Steelers |  |  |  |
| ☐ 6 L.C. Greenwood | .60 | .24 | .06 |
| Pittsburgh Steelers |  |  |  |
| ☐ 7 Tom Mack | .75 | .30 | .07 |
| Los Angeles Rams |  |  |  |
| ☐ 8 Winston Hill | .40 | .16 | .04 |
| New York Jets |  |  |  |
| ☐ 9 Isaac Curtis | .50 | .20 | .05 |
| Cincinnati Bengals |  |  |  |
| ☐ 10 Terry Owens | .50 | .20 | .05 |
| San Diego Chargers |  |  |  |
| ☐ 11 Drew Pearson | .60 | .24 | .06 |
| Dallas Cowboys |  |  |  |
| ☐ 12 Don Cockroft | .40 | .16 | .04 |
| Cleveland Browns |  |  |  |
| ☐ 13 Bob Griese | 2.00 | .80 | .20 |
| Miami Dolphins |  |  |  |
| ☐ 14 Riley Odoms | .50 | .20 | .05 |
| Denver Broncos |  |  |  |
| ☐ 15 Chuck Foreman | .60 | .24 | .06 |
| Minnesota Vikings |  |  |  |
| ☐ 16 Forrest Blue | .40 | .16 | .04 |
| San Francisco 49ers |  |  |  |
| ☐ 17 Franco Harris | 3.00 | 1.20 | .30 |
| Pittsburgh Steelers |  |  |  |
| ☐ 18 Larry Little | 1.00 | .40 | .10 |
| Miami Dolphins |  |  |  |
| ☐ 19 Bill Bergey | .60 | .24 | .06 |
| Philadelphia Eagles |  |  |  |
| ☐ 20 Ray Guy | 1.00 | .40 | .10 |
| Oakland Raiders |  |  |  |
| ☐ 21 Ted Hendricks | 1.25 | .50 | .12 |
| Oakland Raiders |  |  |  |
| ☐ 22 Levi Johnson | .40 | .16 | .04 |
| Detroit Lions |  |  |  |
| ☐ 23 Jack Mildren | .50 | .20 | .05 |
| New England Patriots |  |  |  |
| ☐ 24 Mel Tom | .40 | .16 | .04 |
| Chicago Bears |  |  |  |

|  |  |  |  |
|---|---|---|---|
| St. Louis Cardinals |  |  |  |
| ☐ 5 Charley Taylor | .60 | .24 | .06 |
| Washington Redskins |  |  |  |
| ☐ 6 Rich Caster | .25 | .10 | .02 |
| New York Jets |  |  |  |
| ☐ 7 George Kunz | .25 | .10 | .02 |
| Baltimore Colts |  |  |  |
| ☐ 8 Rayfield Wright | .25 | .10 | .02 |
| Dallas Cowboys |  |  |  |
| ☐ 9 Gene Upshaw | .75 | .30 | .07 |
| Oakland Raiders |  |  |  |
| ☐ 10 Tom Mack | .50 | .20 | .05 |
| Los Angeles Rams |  |  |  |
| ☐ 11 Len Hauss | .35 | .14 | .03 |
| Washington Redskins |  |  |  |
| ☐ 12 Garo Yepremian | .25 | .10 | .02 |
| Miami Dolphins |  |  |  |
| ☐ 13 Cedrick Hardman | .25 | .10 | .02 |
| San Francisco 49ers |  |  |  |
| ☐ 14 Jack Youngblood | .75 | .30 | .07 |
| Los Angeles Rams |  |  |  |
| ☐ 15 Wally Chambers | .25 | .10 | .02 |
| Chicago Bears |  |  |  |
| ☐ 16 Jerry Sherk | .25 | .10 | .02 |
| Cleveland Browns |  |  |  |
| ☐ 17 Bill Bergey | .35 | .14 | .03 |
| Philadelphia Eagles |  |  |  |
| ☐ 18 Jack Ham | .75 | .30 | .07 |
| Pittsburgh Steelers |  |  |  |
| ☐ 19 Fred Carr | .25 | .10 | .02 |
| Green Bay Packers |  |  |  |
| ☐ 20 Jack Tatum | .35 | .14 | .03 |
| Oakland Raiders |  |  |  |
| ☐ 21 Cliff Harris | .35 | .14 | .03 |
| Dallas Cowboys |  |  |  |
| ☐ 22 Emmitt Thomas | .25 | .10 | .02 |
| Kansas City Chiefs |  |  |  |
| ☐ 23 Ken Riley | .25 | .10 | .02 |
| Cincinnati Bengals |  |  |  |
| ☐ 24 Ray Guy | .75 | .30 | .07 |
| Oakland Raiders |  |  |  |

## 1976 Wonder Bread

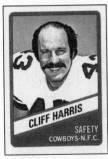 

The 1976 Wonder Bread Football Card set features 24 colored cards with red or blue frame lines and white borders. The first 12 cards (1-12) in the set feature offensive players with a blue frame and the last 12 cards (13-24) feature defensive players with a red frame. The cards measure 2 1/2 by 3 1/2". The backs feature one of coach Hank Stram's favorite plays, with a football diagram and a text listing each offensive player's assignments of the particular play. The "Topps Chewing Gum, Inc." copyright appears at the bottom on the reverse of the card. The cards were also produced by Town Talk Bread; these Town Talk cards are more difficult to find (valued roughly double) and are distinguished by the different credit line at the top of the reverse of each card.

|  | NRMT | VG-E | GOOD |
|---|---|---|---|
| COMPLETE SET (24) | 5.00 | 2.00 | .50 |
| COMMON PLAYER (1-24) | .25 | .10 | .02 |
| ☐ 1 Craig Morton | .35 | .14 | .03 |
| New York Giants |  |  |  |
| ☐ 2 Chuck Foreman | .35 | .14 | .03 |
| Minnesota Vikings |  |  |  |
| ☐ 3 Franco Harris | 1.00 | .40 | .10 |
| Pittsburgh Steelers |  |  |  |
| ☐ 4 Mel Gray | .35 | .14 | .03 |

## 1984 Wranglers Carl's Jr.

This ten-card USFL set was sponsored by Carl's Jr. Restaurants and distributed by the local police department in Tempe, Arizona. The cards measure approximately 2 1/2" by 3 5/8". On the front, the company logo and name appears in the lower right hand corner, and the USFL logo in the lower left hand corner. These emblems and the team name "Arizona Wranglers" on the top are in red print. The black and white posed photo in the middle has the player's name and position below in black ink. The back includes biographical information and an advertisement for Carl's Jr. Restaurants. The cards are listed below alphabetically, with the jersey number after the player's name.

|  | MINT | EXC | G-VG |
|---|---|---|---|
| COMPLETE SET (10) | 30.00 | 12.00 | 3.00 |
| COMMON CARD (1-10) | 2.50 | 1.00 | .25 |
| ☐ 1 George Allen CO | 7.50 | 3.00 | .75 |
| ☐ 2 Luther Bradley 27 | 3.50 | 1.40 | .35 |
| ☐ 3 Trumaine Johnson 2 | 3.50 | 1.40 | .35 |
| ☐ 4 Greg Landry 11 | 6.00 | 2.40 | .60 |
| ☐ 5 Kit Lathrop 70 | 2.50 | 1.00 | .25 |
| ☐ 6 John Lee 64 | 2.50 | 1.00 | .25 |
| ☐ 7 Keith Long 33 | 2.50 | 1.00 | .25 |
| ☐ 8 Alan Risher 7 | 3.50 | 1.40 | .35 |
| ☐ 9 Tim Spencer 46 | 3.50 | 1.40 | .35 |
| ☐ 10 Lenny Willis 89 | 2.50 | 1.00 | .25 |

# 1993 Air Force Smokey

These 16 standard-size (2 1/2" by 3 1/2") cards feature on their fronts color player action shots set within gray borders with white diagonal stripes. The player's name and position appear on the left side underneath the photo. The team name and logo appear above the photo. The plain white back carries the player's name and position at the top, followed by a Smokey safety tip, and the player's career highlights. The cards are unnumbered and checklisted below in alphabetical order.

| | MINT | EXC | G-VG |
|---|---|---|---|
| COMPLETE SET (16) | 10.00 | 4.00 | 1.00 |
| COMMON PLAYER (1-16) | .50 | .20 | .05 |
| ☐ 1 Fisher DeBerry CO | 1.00 | .40 | .10 |
| ☐ 2 Dee Dowis | 2.00 | .80 | .20 |
| ☐ 3 Chad Hennings | 2.00 | .80 | .20 |
| ☐ 4 Carlton MacDonald | .75 | .30 | .07 |
| ☐ 5 Terry Maki | .75 | .30 | .07 |
| ☐ 6 Reggie Minton CO | .75 | .30 | .07 |
| ☐ 7 Air Force Falcon | .50 | .20 | .05 |
| ☐ 8 Air Force Thunderbirds | .50 | .20 | .05 |
| ☐ 9 Cadet Field House | .50 | .20 | .05 |
| ☐ 10 Chapel | .50 | .20 | .05 |
| ☐ 11 Color Guard | .50 | .20 | .05 |
| ☐ 12 Commander-in-Chief's Trophy | .50 | .20 | .05 |
| ☐ 13 Drum and Bugle Corp | .50 | .20 | .05 |
| ☐ 14 Falcon Stadium | .50 | .20 | .05 |
| ☐ 15 Parachute Team | .50 | .20 | .05 |
| ☐ 16 Talon T-38 | .50 | .20 | .05 |

# 1972 Alabama

This 54-card standard-size (2 1/2" by 3 1/2") set was issued in a box as if it were a playing card deck. The cards have rounded corners and the typical playing card finish. The fronts feature black-and-white posed action photos of helmetless players in their uniforms. A white border surrounds each picture and contains the card number and suit designation in the upper left corner and again, but inverted, in the lower right. The player's name and hometown appear just beneath the photo. The white-bordered crimson backs all have the Alabama "A" logo in white and the year of issue, 1972. The name Alabama Crimson Tide also appears on the backs. Since the set is similar to a playing card set, the set is arranged just like a card deck and checklisted below accordingly. In the checklist below S means Spades, D means Diamonds, C means Clubs, H means Hearts, and JK means Joker. The cards are checklisted below in playing card order by suits and numbers are assigned to Aces (1), Jacks (11), Queens (12), and Kings (13). The jokers are unnumbered and listed at the end. Key cards in

the set are early cards of coaching legend Paul "Bear" Bryant and lineman John Hannah.

| | NRMT | VG-E | GOOD |
|---|---|---|---|
| COMPLETE SET (54) | 60.00 | 24.00 | 6.00 |
| COMMON PLAYER | 1.50 | .60 | .15 |
| ☐ 1C Skip Kubelius | 1.50 | .60 | .15 |
| ☐ 1D Terry Davis | 2.00 | .80 | .20 |
| ☐ 1H Robert Fraley | 1.50 | .60 | .15 |
| ☐ 1S Paul(Bear) Bryant CO | 20.00 | 8.00 | 2.00 |
| ☐ 2C David Watkins | 1.50 | .60 | .15 |
| ☐ 2D Bobby McKinney | 1.50 | .60 | .15 |
| ☐ 2H Dexter Wood | 1.50 | .60 | .15 |
| ☐ 2S Chuck Strickland | 1.50 | .60 | .15 |
| ☐ 3C John Hannah | 12.00 | 5.00 | 1.20 |
| ☐ 3D Tom Lusk | 1.50 | .60 | .15 |
| ☐ 3H Jim Krapf | 1.50 | .60 | .15 |
| ☐ 3S Warren Dyar | 1.50 | .60 | .15 |
| ☐ 4C Greg Gantt | 3.00 | 1.20 | .30 |
| ☐ 4D Johnny Sharpless | 1.50 | .60 | .15 |
| ☐ 4H Steve Wade | 1.50 | .60 | .15 |
| ☐ 4S John Rogers | 1.50 | .60 | .15 |
| ☐ 5C Doug Faust | 1.50 | .60 | .15 |
| ☐ 5D Jeff Rouzie | 1.50 | .60 | .15 |
| ☐ 5H Buddy Brown | 1.50 | .60 | .15 |
| ☐ 5S Randy Moore | 1.50 | .60 | .15 |
| ☐ 6C David Knapp | 2.00 | .80 | .20 |
| ☐ 6D Lanny Norris | 1.50 | .60 | .15 |
| ☐ 6H Paul Spivey | 1.50 | .60 | .15 |
| ☐ 6S Pat Raines | 1.50 | .60 | .15 |
| ☐ 7C Pete Pappas | 1.50 | .60 | .15 |
| ☐ 7D Ed Hines | 1.50 | .60 | .15 |
| ☐ 7H Mike Washington | 1.50 | .60 | .15 |
| ☐ 7S David McMakin | 1.50 | .60 | .15 |
| ☐ 8C Steve Dean | 1.50 | .60 | .15 |
| ☐ 8D Joe LaBue | 1.50 | .60 | .15 |
| ☐ 8H John Croyle | 1.50 | .60 | .15 |
| ☐ 8S Noah Miller | 1.50 | .60 | .15 |
| ☐ 9C Bobby Stanford | 1.50 | .60 | .15 |
| ☐ 9D Sylvester Croom | 2.50 | 1.00 | .25 |
| ☐ 9H Wilbur Jackson | 5.00 | 2.00 | .50 |
| ☐ 9S Ellis Beck | 1.50 | .60 | .15 |
| ☐ 10C Steve Bisceglia | 1.50 | .60 | .15 |
| ☐ 10D Andy Cross | 1.50 | .60 | .15 |
| ☐ 10H John Mitchell | 1.50 | .60 | .15 |
| ☐ 10S Bill Davis | 1.50 | .60 | .15 |
| ☐ 11C Gary Rutledge | 2.00 | .80 | .20 |
| ☐ 11D Randy Billingsley | 1.50 | .60 | .15 |
| ☐ 11H Randy Hall | 1.50 | .60 | .15 |
| ☐ 11S Ralph Stokes | 1.50 | .60 | .15 |
| ☐ 12C Jeff Blitz | 1.50 | .60 | .15 |
| ☐ 12D Robby Rowan | 1.50 | .60 | .15 |
| ☐ 12H Mike Raines | 1.50 | .60 | .15 |
| ☐ 12S Wayne Wheeler | 1.50 | .60 | .15 |
| ☐ 13C Steve Sprayberry | 1.50 | .60 | .15 |
| ☐ 13D Wayne Hall | 2.00 | .80 | .20 |
| ☐ 13H Morris Hunt | 1.50 | .60 | .15 |
| ☐ 13S Butch Norman | 1.50 | .60 | .15 |
| ☐ JK Denny Stadium | 1.50 | .60 | .15 |
| ☐ JK Memorial Coliseum | 1.50 | .60 | .15 |

# 1973 Alabama

These 54 standard-size (2 1/2" by 3 1/2") playing cards have rounded corners and the typical playing card finish. The fronts feature black-and-white posed action photos of helmetless players in their uniforms. A white border surrounds each picture and contains the card number and suit designation in the upper left corner and again, but inverted, in the lower right. The player's name and hometown appear just beneath the photo. The white-bordered crimson backs all have the Alabama "A" logo in white and the year of issue, 1973. The name Alabama Crimson Tide also appears on the backs. Since this is a set of playing cards, the set is checklisted below accordingly. In the checklist below

S means Spades, D means Diamonds, C means Clubs, H means Hearts, and JK means Joker. The cards are in playing card order by suits and numbers are assigned to Aces (1), Jacks (11), Queens (12), and Kings (13). The jokers are unnumbered and listed at the end.

| | NRMT | VG-E | GOOD |
|---|---|---|---|
| COMPLETE SET (54) | 60.00 | 24.00 | 6.00 |
| COMMON PLAYER | 1.50 | .60 | .15 |
| ☐ 1C Skip Kubelius | 1.50 | .60 | .15 |
| ☐ 1D Mark Prudhomme | 1.50 | .60 | .15 |
| ☐ 1H Robert Fraley | 1.50 | .60 | .15 |
| ☐ 1S Paul(Bear) Bryant CO | 20.00 | 8.00 | 2.00 |
| ☐ 2C David Watkins | 1.50 | .60 | .15 |
| ☐ 2D Richard Todd | 9.00 | 3.75 | .90 |
| ☐ 2H Buddy Pope | 1.50 | .60 | .15 |
| ☐ 2S Chuck Strickland | 1.50 | .60 | .15 |
| ☐ 3C Bob Bryan | 1.50 | .60 | .15 |
| ☐ 3D Gary Hanrahan | 1.50 | .60 | .15 |
| ☐ 3H Greg Montgomery | 1.50 | .60 | .15 |
| ☐ 3S Warren Dyar | 1.50 | .60 | .15 |
| ☐ 4C Greg Gantt | 3.00 | 1.20 | .30 |
| ☐ 4D Johnny Sharpless | 1.50 | .60 | .15 |
| ☐ 4H Rick Watson | 1.50 | .60 | .15 |
| ☐ 4S John Rogers | 1.50 | .60 | .15 |
| ☐ 5C George Pugh | 2.50 | 1.00 | .25 |
| ☐ 5D Jeff Rouzie | 1.50 | .60 | .15 |
| ☐ 5H Buddy Brown | 1.50 | .60 | .15 |
| ☐ 5S Randy Moore | 1.50 | .60 | .15 |
| ☐ 6C Ray Maxwell | 1.50 | .60 | .15 |
| ☐ 6D Alan Pizzitola | 1.50 | .60 | .15 |
| ☐ 6H Paul Spivey | 1.50 | .60 | .15 |
| ☐ 6S Ron Robertson | 1.50 | .60 | .15 |
| ☐ 7C Pete Pappas | 1.50 | .60 | .15 |
| ☐ 7D Steve Kulback | 1.50 | .60 | .15 |
| ☐ 7H Mike Washington | 1.50 | .60 | .15 |
| ☐ 7S David McMakin | 1.50 | .60 | .15 |
| ☐ 8C Steve Dean | 1.50 | .60 | .15 |
| ☐ 8D Jerry Brown | 1.50 | .60 | .15 |
| ☐ 8H John Croyle | 1.50 | .60 | .15 |
| ☐ 8S Noah Miller | 1.50 | .60 | .15 |
| ☐ 9C Leroy Cook | 1.50 | .60 | .15 |
| ☐ 9D Sylvester Croom | 2.50 | 1.00 | .25 |
| ☐ 9H Wilbur Jackson | 5.00 | 2.00 | .50 |
| ☐ 9S Ellis Beck | 1.50 | .60 | .15 |
| ☐ 10C Tyrone King | 1.50 | .60 | .15 |
| ☐ 10D Mike Stock | 1.50 | .60 | .15 |
| ☐ 10H Mike Dubose | 1.50 | .60 | .15 |
| ☐ 10S Bill Davis | 1.50 | .60 | .15 |
| ☐ 11C Gary Rutledge | 2.00 | .80 | .20 |
| ☐ 11D Randy Billingsley | 1.50 | .60 | .15 |
| ☐ 11H Randy Hall | 1.50 | .60 | .15 |
| ☐ 11S Ralph Stokes | 1.50 | .60 | .15 |
| ☐ 12C Woodrow Lowe | 5.00 | 2.00 | .50 |
| ☐ 12D Marvin Barron | 1.50 | .60 | .15 |
| ☐ 12H Mike Raines | 1.50 | .60 | .15 |
| ☐ 12S Wayne Wheeler | 1.50 | .60 | .15 |
| ☐ 13C Steve Sprayberry | 1.50 | .60 | .15 |
| ☐ 13D Wayne Hall | 2.00 | .80 | .20 |
| ☐ 13H Morris Hunt | 1.50 | .60 | .15 |
| ☐ 13S Butch Norman | 1.50 | .60 | .15 |
| ☐ JK Denny Stadium | 1.50 | .60 | .15 |
| ☐ JK Memorial Coliseum | 1.50 | .60 | .15 |

## 1988 Alabama Winners

The 1988 Alabama Winners set contains 73 standard-size (2 1/2" by 3 1/2") cards. The fronts have color portrait photos with "Alabama" and name banners in school colors; the vertically oriented backs have brief profiles and Crimson Tide highlights from specific seasons. The card numbering is essentially in order alphabetically by subject's name. The set features an early card of Derrick Thomas.

| | MINT | EXC | G-VG |
|---|---|---|---|
| COMPLETE SET (73) | 10.00 | 4.00 | 1.00 |
| COMMON CARD (1-73) | .15 | .06 | .01 |
| ☐ 1 Title Card | .35 | .14 | .03 |
| (Schedule on back) | | | |
| ☐ 2 Charlie Abrams | .15 | .06 | .01 |
| ☐ 3 Sam Atkins | .15 | .06 | .01 |
| ☐ 4 Marco Battle | .15 | .06 | .01 |
| ☐ 5 George Bethune | .15 | .06 | .01 |
| ☐ 6 Scott Bolt | .15 | .06 | .01 |
| ☐ 7 Tommy Bowden | .25 | .10 | .02 |
| ☐ 8 Danny Cash | .15 | .06 | .01 |
| ☐ 9 John Cassimus | .15 | .06 | .01 |
| ☐ 10 David Casteal | .15 | .06 | .01 |
| ☐ 11 Terrill Chatman | .15 | .06 | .01 |
| ☐ 12 Andy Christoff | .15 | .06 | .01 |
| ☐ 13 Tommy Cole | .15 | .06 | .01 |
| ☐ 14 Tony Cox | .15 | .06 | .01 |
| ☐ 15 Howard Cross | .25 | .10 | .02 |
| ☐ 16 Bill Curry CO | .35 | .14 | .03 |
| ☐ 17 John Davis | .25 | .10 | .02 |
| ☐ 18 Vantreise Davis | .15 | .06 | .01 |
| ☐ 19 Joe Demos | .15 | .06 | .01 |
| ☐ 20 Philip Doyle | .15 | .06 | .01 |
| ☐ 21 Jeff Dunn | .15 | .06 | .01 |
| ☐ 22 Johh Fruhmorgen | .15 | .06 | .01 |
| ☐ 23 Jim Fuller | .15 | .06 | .01 |
| ☐ 24 Greg Gilbert | .15 | .06 | .01 |
| ☐ 25 Pierre Goode | .25 | .10 | .02 |
| ☐ 26 John Guy | .15 | .06 | .01 |
| ☐ 27 Spencer Hammond | .15 | .06 | .01 |
| ☐ 28 Stacy Harrison | .15 | .06 | .01 |
| ☐ 29 Murry Hill | .15 | .06 | .01 |
| ☐ 30 Byron Holdbrooks | .15 | .06 | .01 |
| ☐ 31 Ben Holt | .15 | .06 | .01 |
| ☐ 32 Bobby Humphrey | .50 | .20 | .05 |
| ☐ 33 Gene Jelks | .35 | .14 | .03 |
| ☐ 34 Kermit Kendrick | .15 | .06 | .01 |
| ☐ 35 William Kent | .15 | .06 | .01 |
| ☐ 36 David Lenoir | .15 | .06 | .01 |
| ☐ 37 Butch Lewis | .15 | .06 | .01 |
| ☐ 38 Don Lindsey | .15 | .06 | .01 |
| ☐ 39 John Mangum | .15 | .06 | .01 |
| ☐ 40 Tim Matheny | .15 | .06 | .01 |
| ☐ 41 Mac McWhorter | .15 | .06 | .01 |
| ☐ 42 Chris Mohr | .25 | .10 | .02 |
| ☐ 43 Larry New | .15 | .06 | .01 |
| ☐ 44 Gene Newberry | .15 | .06 | .01 |
| ☐ 45 Lee Ozmint | .15 | .06 | .01 |
| ☐ 46 Trent Patterson | .15 | .06 | .01 |
| ☐ 47 Greg Payne | .15 | .06 | .01 |
| ☐ 48 Thomas Rayam | .15 | .06 | .01 |
| ☐ 49 Chris Robinette | .15 | .06 | .01 |
| ☐ 50 Larry Rose | .15 | .06 | .01 |
| ☐ 51 Derrick Rushton | .15 | .06 | .01 |
| ☐ 52 Lamonde Russell | .15 | .06 | .01 |
| ☐ 53 Craig Sanderson | .15 | .06 | .01 |
| ☐ 54 Wayne Shaw | .15 | .06 | .01 |
| ☐ 55 Willie Shephard | .15 | .06 | .01 |
| ☐ 56 Roger Shultz | .15 | .06 | .01 |
| ☐ 57 David Smith | .15 | .06 | .01 |
| ☐ 58 Homer Smith | .15 | .06 | .01 |
| ☐ 59 Mike Smith | .15 | .06 | .01 |
| ☐ 60 Byron Sneed | .15 | .06 | .01 |
| ☐ 61 Robert Stewart | .15 | .06 | .01 |
| ☐ 62 Vince Strickland | .15 | .06 | .01 |
| ☐ 63 Brian Stutson | .15 | .06 | .01 |
| ☐ 64 Vince Sutton | .15 | .06 | .01 |
| ☐ 65 Derrick Thomas | 4.00 | 1.60 | .40 |
| ☐ 66 Steve Turner | .15 | .06 | .01 |
| ☐ 67 Alan Ward | .15 | .06 | .01 |
| ☐ 68 Lorenzo Ward | .15 | .06 | .01 |
| ☐ 69 Steve Webb | .15 | .06 | .01 |
| ☐ 70 Woody Wilson | .15 | .06 | .01 |
| ☐ 71 Chip Wisdom | .15 | .06 | .01 |
| ☐ 72 Willie Wyatt | .15 | .06 | .01 |
| ☐ 73 Mike Zuga | .15 | .06 | .01 |

## 1989 Alabama Coke 20

The 1989 Coke University of Alabama football set contains 20 standard-size (2 1/2" by 3 1/2") cards, depicting former Crimson Tide greats. The fronts have vintage photos; the horizontally oriented backs feature player profiles. Both sides have crimson borders. These cards were printed on very thin stock. The set is numbered C1 to C20.

| | MINT | EXC | G-VG |
|---|---|---|---|
| COMPLETE SET (20) | 10.00 | 4.00 | 1.00 |
| COMMON CARD (C1-C20) | .35 | .14 | .03 |
| ☐ C1 Paul(Bear) Bryant CO | 1.50 | .60 | .15 |
| ☐ C2 John Hannah | .75 | .30 | .07 |
| ☐ C3 Fred Sington | .35 | .14 | .03 |
| ☐ C4 Derrick Thomas | 1.50 | .60 | .15 |

| | | | |
|---|---|---|---|
| ☐ C5 Dwight Stephenson | .50 | .20 | .05 |
| ☐ C6 Cornelius Bennett | 1.00 | .40 | .10 |
| ☐ C7 Ozzie Newsome | 1.00 | .40 | .10 |
| ☐ C8 Joe Namath (Art) | 2.00 | .80 | .20 |
| ☐ C9 Steve Sloan | .60 | .24 | .06 |
| ☐ C10 Bill Curry CO | .50 | .20 | .05 |
| ☐ C11 Paul(Bear) Bryant CO | 1.50 | .60 | .15 |
| ☐ C12 Big Al (Mascot) | .35 | .14 | .03 |
| ☐ C13 Scott Hunter | .50 | .20 | .05 |
| ☐ C14 Lee Roy Jordan | .75 | .30 | .07 |
| ☐ C15 Walter Lewis | .50 | .20 | .05 |
| ☐ C16 Bobby Humphrey | .35 | .14 | .03 |
| ☐ C17 John Mitchell | .35 | .14 | .03 |
| ☐ C18 Johnny Musso | .75 | .30 | .07 |
| ☐ C19 Pat Trammell | .50 | .20 | .05 |
| ☐ C20 Ray Perkins CO | .60 | .24 | .06 |

## 1989 Alabama Coke 580

The 1989 Coke University of Alabama football set contains 580 standard-size (2 1/2" by 3 1/2") cards, depicting former Crimson Tide greats. The fronts contain vintage photos; the horizontally oriented backs feature player profiles. Both sides have crimson borders. The cards were distributed in sets and in poly packs. These cards were printed on very thin stock.

| | MINT | EXC | G-VG |
|---|---|---|---|
| COMPLETE SET (580) | 30.00 | 12.00 | 3.00 |
| COMMON CARD (1-580) | .08 | .03 | .01 |

| | | | |
|---|---|---|---|
| ☐ 1 Paul(Bear) Bryant CO | .75 | .30 | .07 |
| ☐ 2 W.T. Van De Graff | .08 | .03 | .01 |
| ☐ 3 A.T.S. Hubert | .08 | .03 | .01 |
| ☐ 4 Bill Buckler | .08 | .03 | .01 |
| ☐ 5 Hoyt(Wu) Winslett | .08 | .03 | .01 |
| ☐ 6 Tony Holm | .08 | .03 | .01 |
| ☐ 7 Fred Sington Sr. | .15 | .06 | .01 |
| ☐ 8 John Suther | .08 | .03 | .01 |
| ☐ 9 Johnny Cain | .08 | .03 | .01 |
| ☐ 10 Tom Hupke | .08 | .03 | .01 |
| ☐ 11 Millard Howell | .20 | .08 | .02 |
| ☐ 12 Steve Wright | .08 | .03 | .01 |
| ☐ 13 Bill Searcey | .08 | .03 | .01 |
| ☐ 14 Riley Smith | .08 | .03 | .01 |
| ☐ 15 Arthur White | .08 | .03 | .01 |
| ☐ 16 Joe Kilgrow | .08 | .03 | .01 |
| ☐ 17 Leroy Monsky | .08 | .03 | .01 |
| ☐ 18 James Ryba | .08 | .03 | .01 |
| ☐ 19 Carey Cox | .08 | .03 | .01 |
| ☐ 20 Holt Rast | .08 | .03 | .01 |
| ☐ 21 Joe Domnanovich | .08 | .03 | .01 |
| ☐ 22 Don Whitmire | .08 | .03 | .01 |
| ☐ 23 Harry Gilmer | .20 | .08 | .02 |
| ☐ 24 Vaughn Mancha | .08 | .03 | .01 |

| | | | |
|---|---|---|---|
| ☐ 25 Ed Salem | .08 | .03 | .01 |
| ☐ 26 Bobby Marlow | .30 | .12 | .03 |
| ☐ 27 George Mason | .08 | .03 | .01 |
| ☐ 28 Billy Neighbors | .20 | .08 | .02 |
| ☐ 29 Lee Roy Jordan | .50 | .20 | .05 |
| ☐ 30 Wayne Freeman | .08 | .03 | .01 |
| ☐ 31 Dan Kearley | .08 | .03 | .01 |
| ☐ 32 Joe Namath | 1.00 | .40 | .10 |
| ☐ 33 David Ray | .15 | .06 | .01 |
| ☐ 34 Paul Crane | .08 | .03 | .01 |
| ☐ 35 Steve Sloan | .30 | .12 | .03 |
| ☐ 36 Richard Cole | .08 | .03 | .01 |
| ☐ 37 Cecil Dowdy | .15 | .06 | .01 |
| ☐ 38 Bobby Johns | .08 | .03 | .01 |
| ☐ 39 Ray Perkins | .30 | .12 | .03 |
| ☐ 40 Dennis Homan | .20 | .08 | .02 |
| ☐ 41 Kenny Stabler | .50 | .20 | .05 |
| ☐ 42 Robert W. Boylston | .08 | .03 | .01 |
| ☐ 43 Mike Hall | .08 | .03 | .01 |
| ☐ 44 Alvin Samples | .08 | .03 | .01 |
| ☐ 45 Johnny Musso | .20 | .08 | .02 |
| ☐ 46 Bryant-Denney Stadium | .08 | .03 | .01 |
| ☐ 47 Tom Surlas | .08 | .03 | .01 |
| ☐ 48 John Hannah | .30 | .12 | .03 |
| ☐ 49 Jim Krapf | .08 | .03 | .01 |
| ☐ 50 John Mitchell | .15 | .06 | .01 |
| ☐ 51 Buddy Brown | .08 | .03 | .01 |
| ☐ 52 Woodrow Lowe | .15 | .06 | .01 |
| ☐ 53 Wayne Wheeler | .08 | .03 | .01 |
| ☐ 54 Leroy Cook | .08 | .03 | .01 |
| ☐ 55 Sylvester Croom | .15 | .06 | .01 |
| ☐ 56 Mike Washington | .08 | .03 | .01 |
| ☐ 57 Ozzie Newsome | .50 | .20 | .05 |
| ☐ 58 Barry Krauss | .15 | .06 | .01 |
| ☐ 59 Marty Lyons | .20 | .08 | .02 |
| ☐ 60 Jim Bunch | .08 | .03 | .01 |
| ☐ 61 Don McNeal | .15 | .06 | .01 |
| ☐ 62 Dwight Stephenson | .20 | .08 | .02 |
| ☐ 63 Bill Davis | .08 | .03 | .01 |
| ☐ 64 E.J. Junior | .15 | .06 | .01 |
| ☐ 65 Tommy Wilcox | .15 | .06 | .01 |
| ☐ 66 Jeremiah Castille | .15 | .06 | .01 |
| ☐ 67 Bobby Swafford | .08 | .03 | .01 |
| ☐ 68 Cornelius Bennett | .50 | .20 | .05 |
| ☐ 69 David Knapp | .08 | .03 | .01 |
| ☐ 70 Bobby Humphrey | .30 | .12 | .03 |
| ☐ 71 Van Tiffin | .08 | .03 | .01 |
| ☐ 72 Sid Smith | .08 | .03 | .01 |
| ☐ 73 Pat Trammell | .20 | .08 | .02 |
| ☐ 74 Mickey Andrews | .08 | .03 | .01 |
| ☐ 75 Steve Bowman | .08 | .03 | .01 |
| ☐ 76 Bob Baumhower | .20 | .08 | .02 |
| ☐ 77 Bob Cryder | .08 | .03 | .01 |
| ☐ 78 Bryon Braggs | .15 | .06 | .01 |
| ☐ 79 Warren Lyles | .08 | .03 | .01 |
| ☐ 80 Steve Mott | .08 | .03 | .01 |
| ☐ 81 Walter Lewis | .15 | .06 | .01 |
| ☐ 82 Ricky Moore | .08 | .03 | .01 |
| ☐ 83 Wes Neighbors | .08 | .03 | .01 |
| ☐ 84 Derrick Thomas | .75 | .30 | .07 |
| ☐ 85 Kermit Kendrick | .08 | .03 | .01 |
| ☐ 86 Larry Rose | .08 | .03 | .01 |
| ☐ 87 Charlie Marr | .08 | .03 | .01 |
| ☐ 88 James Whatley | .08 | .03 | .01 |
| ☐ 89 Erin Warren | .08 | .03 | .01 |
| ☐ 90 Charlie Holm | .08 | .03 | .01 |
| ☐ 91 Fred Davis | .08 | .03 | .01 |
| ☐ 92 John Wyhonic | .08 | .03 | .01 |
| ☐ 93 Jimmy Nelson | .08 | .03 | .01 |
| ☐ 94 Rebel Steiner | .15 | .06 | .01 |
| ☐ 95 Tom Whitley | .08 | .03 | .01 |
| ☐ 96 John Wozniak | .08 | .03 | .01 |
| ☐ 97 Ed Holdnak | .08 | .03 | .01 |
| ☐ 98 Al Lary | .08 | .03 | .01 |
| ☐ 99 Mike Mizerany | .08 | .03 | .01 |
| ☐ 100 Pat O'Sullivan | .08 | .03 | .01 |
| ☐ 101 Jerry Watford | .08 | .03 | .01 |
| ☐ 102 Cecil Ingram | .15 | .06 | .01 |
| ☐ 103 Mike Fracchia | .08 | .03 | .01 |
| ☐ 104 Benny Nelson | .08 | .03 | .01 |
| ☐ 105 Tommy Tolleson | .08 | .03 | .01 |
| ☐ 106 Creed Gilmer | .08 | .03 | .01 |
| ☐ 107 John Calvert | .08 | .03 | .01 |
| ☐ 108 Derrick Slaughter | .08 | .03 | .01 |
| ☐ 109 Mike Ford | .08 | .03 | .01 |
| ☐ 110 Bruce Stephens | .08 | .03 | .01 |
| ☐ 111 Danny Ford | .20 | .08 | .02 |
| ☐ 112 Jimmy Grammer | .08 | .03 | .01 |
| ☐ 113 Steve Higginbotham | .08 | .03 | .01 |
| ☐ 114 David Bailey | .08 | .03 | .01 |
| ☐ 115 Greg Gantt | .20 | .08 | .02 |
| ☐ 116 Terry Davis | .15 | .06 | .01 |
| ☐ 117 Chuck Strickland | .08 | .03 | .01 |
| ☐ 118 Bobby McKinney | .08 | .03 | .01 |
| ☐ 119 Wilbur Jackson | .25 | .10 | .02 |
| ☐ 120 Mike Raines | .08 | .03 | .01 |
| ☐ 121 Steve Sprayberry | .08 | .03 | .01 |

| | | | |
|---|---|---|---|
| ☐ 122 David McMakin | .08 | .03 | .01 |
| ☐ 123 Ben Smith | .08 | .03 | .01 |
| ☐ 124 Steadman Shealy | .20 | .08 | .02 |
| ☐ 125 John Rogers | .08 | .03 | .01 |
| ☐ 126 Ricky Davis | .15 | .06 | .01 |
| ☐ 127 Conley Duncan | .08 | .03 | .01 |
| ☐ 128 Wayne Rhodes | .08 | .03 | .01 |
| ☐ 129 Buddy Seay | .08 | .03 | .01 |
| ☐ 130 Alan Pizzitola | .08 | .03 | .01 |
| ☐ 131 Richard Todd | .20 | .08 | .02 |
| ☐ 132 Charlie Ferguson | .08 | .03 | .01 |
| ☐ 133 Charlie Hannah | .15 | .06 | .01 |
| ☐ 134 Wiley Barnes | .08 | .03 | .01 |
| ☐ 135 Mike Brock | .08 | .03 | .01 |
| ☐ 136 Murray Legg | .08 | .03 | .01 |
| ☐ 137 Wayne Hamilton | .08 | .03 | .01 |
| ☐ 138 David Hannah | .08 | .03 | .01 |
| ☐ 139 Jim Bob Harris | .08 | .03 | .01 |
| ☐ 140 Bart Krout | .08 | .03 | .01 |
| ☐ 141 Bob Cayavec | .08 | .03 | .01 |
| ☐ 142 Joe Beazley | .08 | .03 | .01 |
| ☐ 143 Mike Adcock | .08 | .03 | .01 |
| ☐ 144 Albert Bell | .08 | .03 | .01 |
| ☐ 145 Mike Shula | .35 | .14 | .03 |
| ☐ 146 Curt Jarvis | .08 | .03 | .01 |
| ☐ 147 Freddie Robinson | .08 | .03 | .01 |
| ☐ 148 Bill Condon | .08 | .03 | .01 |
| ☐ 149 Howard Cross | .20 | .08 | .02 |
| ☐ 150 Joe Demyanovich | .08 | .03 | .01 |
| ☐ 151 Major Ogilvie | .20 | .08 | .02 |
| ☐ 152 Perron Shoemaker | .08 | .03 | .01 |
| ☐ 153 Ralph Jones | .08 | .03 | .01 |
| ☐ 154 Vic Bradford | .08 | .03 | .01 |
| ☐ 155 Ed Hickerson | .08 | .03 | .01 |
| ☐ 156 Mitchell Olenski | .08 | .03 | .01 |
| ☐ 157 George Hecht | .08 | .03 | .01 |
| ☐ 158 Russ Craft | .08 | .03 | .01 |
| ☐ 159 Joey Jones | .20 | .08 | .02 |
| ☐ 160 Jack Green | .08 | .03 | .01 |
| ☐ 161 Lowell Tew | .15 | .06 | .01 |
| ☐ 162 Lamar Moye | .08 | .03 | .01 |
| ☐ 163 Jesse Richardson | .15 | .06 | .01 |
| ☐ 164 Harold Lutz | .08 | .03 | .01 |
| ☐ 165 Travis Hunt | .08 | .03 | .01 |
| ☐ 166 Ed Culpepper | .08 | .03 | .01 |
| ☐ 167 Nick Germanos | .08 | .03 | .01 |
| ☐ 168 Billy Rains | .08 | .03 | .01 |
| ☐ 169 Don Cochran | .08 | .03 | .01 |
| ☐ 170 Cotton Clark | .08 | .03 | .01 |
| ☐ 171 Gaylon McCollogh | .08 | .03 | .01 |
| ☐ 172 Tim Bates | .08 | .03 | .01 |
| ☐ 173 Wayne Cook | .08 | .03 | .01 |
| ☐ 174 Jerry Duncan | .08 | .03 | .01 |
| ☐ 175 Steve Davis | .08 | .03 | .01 |
| ☐ 176 Donnie Sutton | .08 | .03 | .01 |
| ☐ 177 Randy Barron | .08 | .03 | .01 |
| ☐ 178 Frank Mann | .08 | .03 | .01 |
| ☐ 179 Jeff Rouzie | .08 | .03 | .01 |
| ☐ 180 John Croyle | .08 | .03 | .01 |
| ☐ 181 Skip Kubelius | .08 | .03 | .01 |
| ☐ 182 Steve Bisceglia | .15 | .06 | .01 |
| ☐ 183 Gary Rutledge | .08 | .03 | .01 |
| ☐ 184 Mike Dubose | .20 | .08 | .02 |
| ☐ 185 Johnny Davis | .08 | .03 | .01 |
| ☐ 186 K.J. Lazenby | .08 | .03 | .01 |
| ☐ 187 Jeff Rutledge | .25 | .10 | .02 |
| ☐ 188 Mike Tucker | .08 | .03 | .01 |
| ☐ 189 Tony Nathan | .25 | .10 | .02 |
| ☐ 190 Buddy Aydelette | .08 | .03 | .01 |
| ☐ 191 Steve Whitman | .08 | .03 | .01 |
| ☐ 192 Ricky Tucker | .08 | .03 | .01 |
| ☐ 193 Randy Scott | .08 | .03 | .01 |
| ☐ 194 Warren Averitte | .08 | .03 | .01 |
| ☐ 195 Doug Vickers | .08 | .03 | .01 |
| ☐ 196 Jackie Cline | .08 | .03 | .01 |
| ☐ 197 Wayne Davis | .08 | .03 | .01 |
| ☐ 198 Hardy Walker | .08 | .03 | .01 |
| ☐ 199 Paul Ott Carruth | .15 | .06 | .01 |
| ☐ 200 Paul(Bear) Bryant CO | .75 | .30 | .07 |
| ☐ 201 Randy Rockwell | .08 | .03 | .01 |
| ☐ 202 Chris Mohr | .15 | .06 | .01 |
| ☐ 203 Walter Merrill | .08 | .03 | .01 |
| ☐ 204 Johnny Sullivan | .08 | .03 | .01 |
| ☐ 205 Harold Newman | .08 | .03 | .01 |
| ☐ 206 Erskine Walker | .08 | .03 | .01 |
| ☐ 207 Ted Cook | .08 | .03 | .01 |
| ☐ 208 Charles Compton | .08 | .03 | .01 |
| ☐ 209 Bill Cadenhead | .08 | .03 | .01 |
| ☐ 210 Butch Avinger | .08 | .03 | .01 |
| ☐ 211 Bobby Wilson | .08 | .03 | .01 |
| ☐ 212 Sid Youngelman | .20 | .08 | .02 |
| ☐ 213 Leon Fuller | .08 | .03 | .01 |
| ☐ 214 Tommy Brooker | .15 | .06 | .01 |
| ☐ 215 Richard Williamson | .25 | .10 | .02 |
| ☐ 216 Riggs Stephenson | .20 | .08 | .02 |
| ☐ 217 Al Clemens | .08 | .03 | .01 |
| ☐ 218 Grant Gillis | .08 | .03 | .01 |
| ☐ 219 Johnny Mack Brown | .30 | .12 | .03 |
| ☐ 220 Major Ogilvie | .20 | .08 | .02 |
| ☐ 221 Fred Pickhard | .08 | .03 | .01 |
| ☐ 222 Herschel Caldwell | .08 | .03 | .01 |
| ☐ 223 Emile Barnes | .08 | .03 | .01 |
| ☐ 224 Mike McQueen | .08 | .03 | .01 |
| ☐ 225 Ray Abruzzese | .15 | .06 | .01 |
| ☐ 226 Jesse Bendross | .20 | .08 | .02 |
| ☐ 227 Lew Bostick | .08 | .03 | .01 |
| ☐ 228 Jimmy Bowdoin | .08 | .03 | .01 |
| ☐ 229 Dave Brown | .08 | .03 | .01 |
| ☐ 230 Tom Calvin | .08 | .03 | .01 |
| ☐ 231 Ken Emerson | .08 | .03 | .01 |
| ☐ 232 Calvin Frey | .08 | .03 | .01 |
| ☐ 233 Thornton Chandler | .15 | .06 | .01 |
| ☐ 234 George Weeks | .08 | .03 | .01 |
| ☐ 235 Randy Edwards | .08 | .03 | .01 |
| ☐ 236 Phillip Brown | .08 | .03 | .01 |
| ☐ 237 Clay Whitehurst | .08 | .03 | .01 |
| ☐ 238 Chris Goode | .08 | .03 | .01 |
| ☐ 239 Preston Gothard | .08 | .03 | .01 |
| ☐ 240 Herb Hannah | .08 | .03 | .01 |
| ☐ 241 John M. Snoderly | .08 | .03 | .01 |
| ☐ 242 Scott Hunter | .20 | .08 | .02 |
| ☐ 243 Bobby Jackson | .08 | .03 | .01 |
| ☐ 244 Bruce Jones | .08 | .03 | .01 |
| ☐ 245 Robbie Jones | .08 | .03 | .01 |
| ☐ 246 Terry Jones | .08 | .03 | .01 |
| ☐ 247 Leslie Kelley | .08 | .03 | .01 |
| ☐ 248 Larry Lauer | .08 | .03 | .01 |
| ☐ 249 '61 National Champs | .30 | .12 | .03 |
| (Tommy Brooker, | | | |
| Pat Trammell, | | | |
| Lee Roy Jordan, | | | |
| Paul(Bear) Bryant, | | | |
| Mike Fracchia, and | | | |
| Billy Neighbors) | | | |
| ☐ 250 Bobby Luna | .08 | .03 | .01 |
| ☐ 251 Keith Pugh | .08 | .03 | .01 |
| ☐ 252 Alan McElroy | .08 | .03 | .01 |
| ☐ 253 '25 National Champs | .15 | .06 | .01 |
| (Team Photo) | | | |
| ☐ 254 Curtis McGriff | .20 | .08 | .02 |
| ☐ 255 Norman Mosley | .08 | .03 | .01 |
| ☐ 256 Herky Mosley | .08 | .03 | .01 |
| ☐ 257 Ray Ogden | .15 | .06 | .01 |
| ☐ 258 Pete Jilleba | .08 | .03 | .01 |
| ☐ 259 Benny Perrin | .08 | .03 | .01 |
| ☐ 260 Claude Perry | .08 | .03 | .01 |
| ☐ 261 Tommy Cole | .08 | .03 | .01 |
| ☐ 262 Ed Versprille | .08 | .03 | .01 |
| ☐ 263 '30 National Champs | .15 | .06 | .01 |
| (Team Photo) | | | |
| ☐ 264 Don Jacobs | .08 | .03 | .01 |
| ☐ 265 Robert Skelton | .08 | .03 | .01 |
| ☐ 266 Joe Curtis | .08 | .03 | .01 |
| ☐ 267 Bart Starr | .60 | .24 | .06 |
| ☐ 268 Young Boozer | .08 | .03 | .01 |
| ☐ 269 Tommy Lewis | .15 | .06 | .01 |
| ☐ 270 Woody Umphrey | .08 | .03 | .01 |
| ☐ 271 Carney Laslie | .08 | .03 | .01 |
| ☐ 272 Russ Wood | .08 | .03 | .01 |
| ☐ 273 David Smith | .08 | .03 | .01 |
| ☐ 274 Paul Spivey | .08 | .03 | .01 |
| ☐ 275 Linnie Patrick | .08 | .03 | .01 |
| ☐ 276 Ron Durby | .08 | .03 | .01 |
| ☐ 277 '26 National Champs | .15 | .06 | .01 |
| (Team Photo) | | | |
| ☐ 278 Robert Higginbotham | .08 | .03 | .01 |
| ☐ 279 William Oliver | .08 | .03 | .01 |
| ☐ 280 Stan Moss | .08 | .03 | .01 |
| ☐ 281 Eddie Propst | .08 | .03 | .01 |
| ☐ 282 Laurien Stapp | .08 | .03 | .01 |
| ☐ 283 Clem Gryska | .08 | .03 | .01 |
| ☐ 284 Clark Pearce | .08 | .03 | .01 |
| ☐ 285 Pete Cavan | .08 | .03 | .01 |
| ☐ 286 Tom Newton | .08 | .03 | .01 |
| ☐ 287 Rich Wingo | .15 | .06 | .01 |
| ☐ 288 Rickey Gilliland | .08 | .03 | .01 |
| ☐ 289 Conrad Fowler | .08 | .03 | .01 |
| ☐ 290 Rick Neal | .08 | .03 | .01 |
| ☐ 291 James Blevins | .08 | .03 | .01 |
| ☐ 292 Dick Flowers | .08 | .03 | .01 |
| ☐ 293 Marshall Brown | .08 | .03 | .01 |
| ☐ 294 Jeff Beard | .08 | .03 | .01 |
| ☐ 295 Pete Moore | .08 | .03 | .01 |
| ☐ 296 Vince Boothe | .08 | .03 | .01 |
| ☐ 297 Charley Boswell | .08 | .03 | .01 |
| ☐ 298 Van Marcus | .08 | .03 | .01 |
| ☐ 299 Randy Billingsley | .08 | .03 | .01 |
| ☐ 300 Paul(Bear) Bryant CO | .75 | .30 | .07 |
| ☐ 301 Gene Blackwell | .08 | .03 | .01 |
| ☐ 302 Johnny Mosley | .08 | .03 | .01 |
| ☐ 303 Ray Perkins CO | .25 | .10 | .02 |
| ☐ 304 Harold Drew CO | .08 | .03 | .01 |
| ☐ 305 Frank Thomas CO | .20 | .08 | .02 |
| (Not the Frank Thomas | | | |

that went to Auburn)

| | | | |
|---|---|---|---|
| ☐ 306 Wallace Wade | .15 | .06 | .01 |
| ☐ 307 Newton Godfree | .08 | .03 | .01 |
| ☐ 308 Steve Williams | .08 | .03 | .01 |
| ☐ 309 Al Lewis | .08 | .03 | .01 |
| ☐ 310 Fred Grant | .08 | .03 | .01 |
| ☐ 311 Jerry Brown | .08 | .03 | .01 |
| ☐ 312 Mal Moore | .15 | .06 | .01 |
| ☐ 313 Tilden Campbell | .08 | .03 | .01 |
| ☐ 314 Jack Smalley | .08 | .03 | .01 |
| ☐ 315 Paul(Bear) Bryant CO | .75 | .30 | .07 |
| ☐ 316 C.B. Clements | .08 | .03 | .01 |
| ☐ 317 Billy Piper | .08 | .03 | .01 |
| ☐ 318 Robert Lee Hamner | .08 | .03 | .01 |
| ☐ 319 Donnie Faust | .08 | .03 | .01 |
| ☐ 320 Gary Bramblett | .08 | .03 | .01 |
| ☐ 321 Peter Kim | .08 | .03 | .01 |
| ☐ 322 Fred Berrey | .08 | .03 | .01 |
| ☐ 323 Paul(Bear) Bryant CO | .75 | .30 | .07 |
| ☐ 324 John Fruhmorgen | .08 | .03 | .01 |
| ☐ 325 Jimmy Fuller | .08 | .03 | .01 |
| ☐ 326 Doug Allen | .08 | .03 | .01 |
| ☐ 327 Russ Mosley | .08 | .03 | .01 |
| ☐ 328 Ricky Thomas | .08 | .03 | .01 |
| ☐ 329 Vince Sutton | .08 | .03 | .01 |
| ☐ 330 Larry Roberts | .15 | .06 | .01 |
| ☐ 331 Rick McLain | .08 | .03 | .01 |
| ☐ 332 Charles Eckerly | .08 | .03 | .01 |
| ☐ 333 '34 National Champs | .15 | .06 | .01 |
| (Team Photo) | | | |
| ☐ 334 Eddie McCombs | .08 | .03 | .01 |
| ☐ 335 Scott Allison | .08 | .03 | .01 |
| ☐ 336 Vince Cowell | .08 | .03 | .01 |
| ☐ 337 David Watkins | .08 | .03 | .01 |
| ☐ 338 Jim Duke | .08 | .03 | .01 |
| ☐ 339 Don Harris | .08 | .03 | .01 |
| ☐ 340 Lanny Norris | .08 | .03 | .01 |
| ☐ 341 Thad Flanagan | .08 | .03 | .01 |
| ☐ 342 Albert Elmore Jr. | .08 | .03 | .01 |
| ☐ 343 Alan Gray | .08 | .03 | .01 |
| ☐ 344 David Gilmer | .08 | .03 | .01 |
| ☐ 345 Hal Self | .08 | .03 | .01 |
| ☐ 346 Ben McLeod | .08 | .03 | .01 |
| ☐ 347 Clell(Butch) Hobson | .60 | .24 | .06 |
| ☐ 348 Jimmy Carroll | .08 | .03 | .01 |
| ☐ 349 Frank Canterbury | .08 | .03 | .01 |
| ☐ 350 John Byrd Williams | .08 | .03 | .01 |
| ☐ 351 Marvin Barron | .08 | .03 | .01 |
| ☐ 352 William J. Stone | .08 | .03 | .01 |
| ☐ 353 Barry Smith | .08 | .03 | .01 |
| ☐ 354 Jerrill Sprinkle | .08 | .03 | .01 |
| ☐ 355 Hank Crisp CO | .08 | .03 | .01 |
| ☐ 356 Bobby Smith | .08 | .03 | .01 |
| ☐ 357 Charles Gray | .08 | .03 | .01 |
| ☐ 358 Marlin Dyess | .08 | .03 | .01 |
| ☐ 359 '41 National Champs | .15 | .06 | .01 |
| (Team Photo) | | | |
| ☐ 360 Robert Moore | .08 | .03 | .01 |
| ☐ 361 1961 National Champs | .15 | .06 | .01 |
| (Billy Neighbors, | | | |
| Pat Trammell, and | | | |
| Darwin Holt) | | | |
| Team Photo) | | | |
| ☐ 362 Tommy White | .08 | .03 | .01 |
| ☐ 363 Earl Wesley | .08 | .03 | .01 |
| ☐ 364 John O'Linger | .08 | .03 | .01 |
| ☐ 365 Bill Battle | .08 | .03 | .01 |
| ☐ 366 Butch Wilson | .08 | .03 | .01 |
| ☐ 367 Tim Davis | .08 | .03 | .01 |
| ☐ 368 Larry Wall | .08 | .03 | .01 |
| ☐ 369 Hudson Harris | .08 | .03 | .01 |
| ☐ 370 Mike Hopper | .08 | .03 | .01 |
| ☐ 371 Jackie Sherrill | .30 | .12 | .03 |
| ☐ 372 Tom Somerville | .08 | .03 | .01 |
| ☐ 373 David Chatwood | .08 | .03 | .01 |
| ☐ 374 George Ranager | .08 | .03 | .01 |
| ☐ 375 Tommy Wade | .15 | .06 | .01 |
| ☐ 376 '64 National Champs | .60 | .24 | .06 |
| (Joe Namath) | | | |
| ☐ 377 Reid Drinkard | .08 | .03 | .01 |
| ☐ 378 Mike Hand | .08 | .03 | .01 |
| ☐ 379 Ed White | .20 | .08 | .02 |
| ☐ 380 Angelo Stafford | .08 | .03 | .01 |
| ☐ 381 Ellis Beck | .08 | .03 | .01 |
| ☐ 382 Wayne Hall | .15 | .06 | .01 |
| ☐ 383 Randy Lee Hall | .08 | .03 | .01 |
| ☐ 384 Jack O'Rear | .08 | .03 | .01 |
| ☐ 385 Colenzo Hubbard | .08 | .03 | .01 |
| ☐ 386 Gus White | .08 | .03 | .01 |
| ☐ 387 Rich Watson | .08 | .03 | .01 |
| ☐ 388 Steve Allen | .08 | .03 | .01 |
| ☐ 389 John David Crow Jr. | .15 | .06 | .01 |
| ☐ 390 Britton Cooper | .08 | .03 | .01 |
| ☐ 391 Mike Rodriguez | .08 | .03 | .01 |
| ☐ 392 Steve Wade | .08 | .03 | .01 |
| ☐ 393 William J. Rice | .08 | .03 | .01 |
| ☐ 394 Greg Richardson | .08 | .03 | .01 |
| ☐ 395 Joe Jones | .15 | .06 | .01 |

| | | | |
|---|---|---|---|
| ☐ 396 Todd Richardson | .08 | .03 | .01 |
| ☐ 397 Anthony Smiley | .08 | .03 | .01 |
| ☐ 398 Duff Morrison | .08 | .03 | .01 |
| ☐ 399 Jay Grogan | .08 | .03 | .01 |
| ☐ 400 Steve Booker | .08 | .03 | .01 |
| ☐ 401 Larry Abney | .08 | .03 | .01 |
| ☐ 402 Bill Abston | .08 | .03 | .01 |
| ☐ 403 Wayne Adkinson | .08 | .03 | .01 |
| ☐ 404 Charles Allen | .08 | .03 | .01 |
| ☐ 405 Phil Allman | .08 | .03 | .01 |
| ☐ 406 1965 National Champs | .25 | .10 | .02 |
| (1965 Seniors) | | | |
| ☐ 407 James Angelich | .08 | .03 | .01 |
| ☐ 408 Troy Barker | .08 | .03 | .01 |
| ☐ 409 George Bethune | .08 | .03 | .01 |
| ☐ 410 Bill Blair | .08 | .03 | .01 |
| ☐ 411 Clark Boler | .08 | .03 | .01 |
| ☐ 412 Duffy Boles | .08 | .03 | .01 |
| ☐ 413 Ray Bolden | .08 | .03 | .01 |
| ☐ 414 Bruce Bolton | .08 | .03 | .01 |
| ☐ 415 Alvin Davis | .08 | .03 | .01 |
| ☐ 416 Baxter Booth | .08 | .03 | .01 |
| ☐ 417 Paul Boschung | .08 | .03 | .01 |
| ☐ 418 1979 National Champs | .20 | .08 | .02 |
| (Team Photo) | | | |
| ☐ 419 Richard Brewer | .08 | .03 | .01 |
| ☐ 420 Jack Brown | .08 | .03 | .01 |
| ☐ 421 Larry Brown | .08 | .03 | .01 |
| ☐ 422 David Brungard | .08 | .03 | .01 |
| ☐ 423 Jim Burkett | .08 | .03 | .01 |
| ☐ 424 Auxford Burks | .08 | .03 | .01 |
| ☐ 425 Jim Cain | .08 | .03 | .01 |
| ☐ 426 Dick Turpin | .08 | .03 | .01 |
| ☐ 427 Neil Callaway | .08 | .03 | .01 |
| ☐ 428 David Casteal | .08 | .03 | .01 |
| ☐ 429 Phil Chaffin | .08 | .03 | .01 |
| ☐ 430 Howard Chappell | .08 | .03 | .01 |
| ☐ 431 Bob Childs | .08 | .03 | .01 |
| ☐ 432 Knute Rockne Christian | .08 | .03 | .01 |
| ☐ 433 Richard Ciemny | .08 | .03 | .01 |
| ☐ 434 J.B. Whitworth | .08 | .03 | .01 |
| ☐ 435 Mike Clements | .08 | .03 | .01 |
| ☐ 436 1973 National Champs | .20 | .08 | .02 |
| (Coaching Staff) | | | |
| ☐ 437 Rocky Colburn | .08 | .03 | .01 |
| ☐ 438 Danny Collins | .08 | .03 | .01 |
| ☐ 439 James Taylor | .08 | .03 | .01 |
| ☐ 440 Joe Compton | .08 | .03 | .01 |
| ☐ 441 Bob Conway | .08 | .03 | .01 |
| ☐ 442 Charlie Stephens | .08 | .03 | .01 |
| ☐ 443 Kerry Goode | .15 | .06 | .01 |
| ☐ 444 Joe LaBue | .08 | .03 | .01 |
| ☐ 445 Allen Crumbley | .08 | .03 | .01 |
| ☐ 446 Bill Curry CO | .15 | .06 | .01 |
| ☐ 447 David Bedwell | .08 | .03 | .01 |
| ☐ 448 Jim Davis | .08 | .03 | .01 |
| ☐ 449 Mike Dean | .08 | .03 | .01 |
| ☐ 450 Steve Dean | .08 | .03 | .01 |
| ☐ 451 Vince DeLaurentis | .08 | .03 | .01 |
| ☐ 452 Gary Deniro | .08 | .03 | .01 |
| ☐ 453 Jim Dildy | .08 | .03 | .01 |
| ☐ 454 Joe Dildy | .08 | .03 | .01 |
| ☐ 455 Jimmy Dill | .08 | .03 | .01 |
| ☐ 456 Joe Dismuke | .08 | .03 | .01 |
| ☐ 457 Junior Davis | .08 | .03 | .01 |
| ☐ 458 Warren Dyar | .08 | .03 | .01 |
| ☐ 459 Hugh Morrow | .08 | .03 | .01 |
| ☐ 460 Grady Elmore | .08 | .03 | .01 |
| ☐ 461 1978 National Champs | .20 | .08 | .02 |
| (Jeff Rutledge, | | | |
| Tony Nathan, | | | |
| Barry Krauss, | | | |
| Marty Lyons, | | | |
| and Rich Wingo) | | | |
| ☐ 462 Ed Hines | .08 | .03 | .01 |
| ☐ 463 D. Joe Gambrell | .08 | .03 | .01 |
| ☐ 464 Kavanaugh(Kay) Francis | .08 | .03 | .01 |
| ☐ 465 Robert Fraley | .08 | .03 | .01 |
| ☐ 466 Milton Frank | .08 | .03 | .01 |
| ☐ 467 Jim Franko | .08 | .03 | .01 |
| ☐ 468 Buddy French | .08 | .03 | .01 |
| ☐ 469 Wayne Rhoads | .08 | .03 | .01 |
| ☐ 470 Ralph Gandy | .08 | .03 | .01 |
| ☐ 471 Danny Gilbert | .08 | .03 | .01 |
| ☐ 472 Greg Gilbert | .08 | .03 | .01 |
| ☐ 473 Joe Godwin | .08 | .03 | .01 |
| ☐ 474 Richard Grammer | .08 | .03 | .01 |
| ☐ 475 Louis Green | .08 | .03 | .01 |
| ☐ 476 Gary Martin | .08 | .03 | .01 |
| ☐ 477 Bill Hannah | .08 | .03 | .01 |
| ☐ 478 Allen Harpole | .08 | .03 | .01 |
| ☐ 479 Neb Hayden | .08 | .03 | .01 |
| ☐ 480 Butch Henry | .08 | .03 | .01 |
| ☐ 481 Norwood Hodges | .08 | .03 | .01 |
| ☐ 482 Earl Smith | .08 | .03 | .01 |
| ☐ 483 Darwin Holt | .08 | .03 | .01 |
| ☐ 484 Scott Homan | .08 | .03 | .01 |

| | | | |
|---|---|---|---|
| ☐ 485 Nathan Rustin | .08 | .03 | .01 |
| ☐ 486 Gene Raburn | .08 | .03 | .01 |
| ☐ 487 Ellis Houston | .08 | .03 | .01 |
| ☐ 488 Frank Howard | .08 | .03 | .01 |
| ☐ 489 Larry Hughes | .08 | .03 | .01 |
| ☐ 490 Joe Kelley | .08 | .03 | .01 |
| ☐ 491 Charlie Harris | .08 | .03 | .01 |
| ☐ 492 Legion Field | .08 | .03 | .01 |
| ☐ 493 Tim Hurst | .08 | .03 | .01 |
| ☐ 494 Hunter Husband | .08 | .03 | .01 |
| ☐ 495 Lou Ikner | .08 | .03 | .01 |
| ☐ 496 Craig Epps | .08 | .03 | .01 |
| ☐ 497 Jug Jenkins | .08 | .03 | .01 |
| ☐ 498 Billy Johnson | .08 | .03 | .01 |
| ☐ 499 David Johnson | .08 | .03 | .01 |
| ☐ 500 Jon Hand | .30 | .12 | .03 |
| ☐ 501 Max Kelley | .08 | .03 | .01 |
| ☐ 502 Terry Killgore | .08 | .03 | .01 |
| ☐ 503 Eddie Lowe | .08 | .03 | .01 |
| ☐ 504 Noah Langdale | .08 | .03 | .01 |
| ☐ 505 Ed Lary | .08 | .03 | .01 |
| ☐ 506 Foy Leach | .08 | .03 | .01 |
| ☐ 507 Harry Lee | .08 | .03 | .01 |
| ☐ 508 Jim Loftin | .08 | .03 | .01 |
| ☐ 509 Curtis Lynch | .08 | .03 | .01 |
| ☐ 510 John Mauro | .08 | .03 | .01 |
| ☐ 511 Ray Maxwell | .08 | .03 | .01 |
| ☐ 512 Frank McClendon | .08 | .03 | .01 |
| ☐ 513 Tom McCrary | .08 | .03 | .01 |
| ☐ 514 Sonny McGahey | .08 | .03 | .01 |
| ☐ 515 John McIntosh | .08 | .03 | .01 |
| ☐ 516 David McIntyre | .08 | .03 | .01 |
| ☐ 517 Wes Thompson | .08 | .03 | .01 |
| ☐ 518 James Melton | .08 | .03 | .01 |
| ☐ 519 John Miller | .08 | .03 | .01 |
| ☐ 520 Fred Mims | .08 | .03 | .01 |
| ☐ 521 Dewey Mitchell | .08 | .03 | .01 |
| ☐ 522 Lydell Mitchell (Linebacker) | .08 | .03 | .01 |
| ☐ 523 Greg Montgomery | .15 | .06 | .01 |
| ☐ 524 Jimmie Moore | .08 | .03 | .01 |
| ☐ 525 Randy Moore | .08 | .03 | .01 |
| ☐ 526 Ed Morgan | .08 | .03 | .01 |
| ☐ 527 Norris Hamer | .08 | .03 | .01 |
| ☐ 528 Frank Mosely | .08 | .03 | .01 |
| ☐ 529 Sidney Neighbors | .08 | .03 | .01 |
| ☐ 530 Rod Nelson | .08 | .03 | .01 |
| ☐ 531 James Nisbet | .08 | .03 | .01 |
| ☐ 532 Mark Nix | .08 | .03 | .01 |
| ☐ 533 L.W. Noonan | .08 | .03 | .01 |
| ☐ 534 Louis Thompson | .08 | .03 | .01 |
| ☐ 535 William Oliver | .08 | .03 | .01 |
| ☐ 536 Gary Otten | .08 | .03 | .01 |
| ☐ 537 Wayne Owen | .08 | .03 | .01 |
| ☐ 538 Steve Patterson | .08 | .03 | .01 |
| ☐ 539 Charley Pell | .25 | .10 | .02 |
| ☐ 540 Bob Pettee | .08 | .03 | .01 |
| ☐ 541 Gordon Pettus | .08 | .03 | .01 |
| ☐ 542 Gary Phillips | .08 | .03 | .01 |
| ☐ 543 Clay Walls | .08 | .03 | .01 |
| ☐ 544 Douglas Potts | .08 | .03 | .01 |
| ☐ 545 Mike Stock | .08 | .03 | .01 |
| ☐ 546 John Mark Prudhomme | .08 | .03 | .01 |
| ☐ 547 George Pugh | .15 | .06 | .01 |
| ☐ 548 Pat Raines | .08 | .03 | .01 |
| ☐ 549 Joe Riley | .08 | .03 | .01 |
| ☐ 550 Wayne Trimble | .08 | .03 | .01 |
| ☐ 551 Darryl White | .08 | .03 | .01 |
| ☐ 552 Bill Richardson | .08 | .03 | .01 |
| ☐ 553 Ray Richeson | .08 | .03 | .01 |
| ☐ 554 Danny Ridgeway | .08 | .03 | .01 |
| ☐ 555 Terry Sanders | .08 | .03 | .01 |
| ☐ 556 Kenneth Roberts | .08 | .03 | .01 |
| ☐ 557 Jimmy Watts | .08 | .03 | .01 |
| ☐ 558 Ronald Robertson | .08 | .03 | .01 |
| ☐ 559 Norbie Ronsonet | .08 | .03 | .01 |
| ☐ 560 Jimmy Lynn Rosser | .08 | .03 | .01 |
| ☐ 561 Terry Rowell | .08 | .03 | .01 |
| ☐ 562 Larry Joe Ruffin | .08 | .03 | .01 |
| ☐ 563 Jack Rutledge | .08 | .03 | .01 |
| ☐ 564 Al Sabo | .08 | .03 | .01 |
| ☐ 565 David Sadler | .08 | .03 | .01 |
| ☐ 566 Donald Sanford | .08 | .03 | .01 |
| ☐ 567 Hayward Sanford | .08 | .03 | .01 |
| ☐ 568 Paul Tripoli | .08 | .03 | .01 |
| ☐ 569 Lou Scales | .08 | .03 | .01 |
| ☐ 570 Kurt Schmissrauter | .08 | .03 | .01 |
| ☐ 571 Willard Scissum | .08 | .03 | .01 |
| ☐ 572 Joe Sewell | .15 | .06 | .01 |
| ☐ 573 Jimmy Sharpe | .08 | .03 | .01 |
| ☐ 574 Willie Shepherd | .08 | .03 | .01 |
| ☐ 575 Jack Smalley Jr. | .08 | .03 | .01 |
| ☐ 576 Jim Simmons (Tight End) | | | |
| ☐ 577 Jim Simmons (Tackle) | .08 | .03 | .01 |
| ☐ 578 Malcolm Simmons | .08 | .03 | .01 |

| | | | |
|---|---|---|---|
| ☐ 579 Dave Sington | .08 | .03 | .01 |
| ☐ 580 Fred Sington Jr. | .15 | .06 | .01 |

# 1992 Alabama Greats Hoby

This 42-card standard-size (2 1/2" by 3 1/2") set was issued to commemorate a special Centennial Festival weekend. It features 42 Team of the Century candidates as selected by the fans. The fronts display a mix of glossy black and white or color player photos with rounded corners on a crimson card face. The "Century of Champions" logo is superimposed at the bottom of the picture over a white and crimson stripe pattern. On the crimson-colored backs, "Bama" appears in large block lettering at the top, with the player's name and brief biographical information presented below. The cards are numbered on the back and checklisted below accordingly.

| | MINT | EXC | G-VG |
|---|---|---|---|
| COMPLETE SET (42) | 10.00 | 4.00 | 1.00 |
| COMMON CARD (1-42) | .25 | .10 | .02 |
| ☐ 1 Bob Baumhower | .50 | .20 | .05 |
| ☐ 2 Cornelius Bennett | .75 | .30 | .07 |
| ☐ 3 Buddy Brown | .25 | .10 | .02 |
| ☐ 4 Paul(Bear) Bryant CO | .75 | .30 | .07 |
| ☐ 5 Johnny Cain | .25 | .10 | .02 |
| ☐ 6 Jeremiah Castille | .35 | .14 | .03 |
| ☐ 7 Leroy Cook | .25 | .10 | .02 |
| ☐ 8 Paul Crane | .35 | .14 | .03 |
| ☐ 9 Philip Doyle | .25 | .10 | .02 |
| ☐ 10 Harry Gilmer | .35 | .14 | .03 |
| ☐ 11 Jon Hand | .50 | .20 | .05 |
| ☐ 12 Herb Hannah | .25 | .10 | .02 |
| ☐ 13 John Hannah | .75 | .30 | .07 |
| ☐ 14 Dennis Homan | .35 | .14 | .03 |
| ☐ 15 Dixie Howell | .35 | .14 | .03 |
| ☐ 16 Bobby Humphrey | .35 | .14 | .03 |
| ☐ 17 Don Hutson | .75 | .30 | .07 |
| ☐ 18 Curt Jarvis | .35 | .14 | .03 |
| ☐ 19 Lee Roy Jordan | .75 | .30 | .07 |
| ☐ 20 Barry Krauss | .35 | .14 | .03 |
| ☐ 21 Woodrow Lowe | .35 | .14 | .03 |
| ☐ 22 Marty Lyons | .35 | .14 | .03 |
| ☐ 23 Vaughn Mancha | .25 | .10 | .02 |
| ☐ 24 John Mangum | .25 | .10 | .02 |
| ☐ 25 Bobby Marlow | .35 | .14 | .03 |
| ☐ 26 Don McNeal | .35 | .14 | .03 |
| ☐ 27 Chris Mohr | .35 | .14 | .03 |
| ☐ 28 Johnny Musso | .50 | .20 | .05 |
| ☐ 29 Billy Neighbors | .35 | .14 | .03 |
| ☐ 30 Ozzie Newsome | .75 | .30 | .07 |
| ☐ 31 Ray Perkins | .50 | .20 | .05 |
| ☐ 32 Fred Sington | .25 | .10 | .02 |
| ☐ 33 Kenny Stabler | .75 | .30 | .07 |
| ☐ 34 Siran Stacy | .35 | .14 | .03 |
| ☐ 35 Dwight Stephenson | .35 | .14 | .03 |
| ☐ 36 Robert Stewart | .25 | .10 | .02 |
| ☐ 37 Derrick Thomas | 1.00 | .40 | .10 |
| ☐ 38 Van Tiffin | .25 | .10 | .02 |
| ☐ 39 Mike Washington | .25 | .10 | .02 |
| ☐ 40 Tarzan White | .25 | .10 | .02 |
| ☐ 41 Tommy Wilcox | .35 | .14 | .03 |
| ☐ 42 Willie Wyatt | .25 | .10 | .02 |

# 1980 Arizona Police

The 1980 University of Arizona Police set contains 24 cards measuring approximately 2 7/16" by 3 3/4". The fronts have borderless color player photos, with the player's name and jersey number in a white stripe beneath the picture. The backs have brief biographical information and safety tips. The cards are unnumbered and

JOHN RAMSEYER • #94

**JOHN RAMSEYER #94**

is a 21 year old Junior Offensive Line Backer, he is 6'1" tall and weighs 218 pounds and is from La Canada, California.

**EQUIPMENT**

Player safety is a major concern in football. Equipment such as helmets are designed to prevent injury.

When riding a motorcycle, common sense dictates the use of safety equipment. Get a good helmet and use it.

A service to the community from
**Golden Eagle Distributors, Inc.**
705 E. Ajo Way
Bill Clements, President

checklisted below in alphabetical order. Reportedly the Reggie Ware card is very difficult to find.

|  | MINT | EXC | G-VG |
|---|---|---|---|
| COMPLETE SET (24) | 75.00 | 30.00 | 7.50 |
| COMMON CARD (1-24) | 2.50 | 1.00 | .25 |
| ☐ 1 Brian Clifford | 2.50 | 1.00 | .25 |
| ☐ 2 Mark Fulcher | 2.50 | 1.00 | .25 |
| ☐ 3 Bob Gareeb | 2.50 | 1.00 | .25 |
| ☐ 4 Marcellus Green | 3.50 | 1.40 | .35 |
| ☐ 5 Drew Hardville | 2.50 | 1.00 | .25 |
| ☐ 6 Neal Harris | 2.50 | 1.00 | .25 |
| ☐ 7 Richard Hersey | 2.50 | 1.00 | .25 |
| ☐ 8 Alfondia Hill | 2.50 | 1.00 | .25 |
| ☐ 9 Tim Holmes | 2.50 | 1.00 | .25 |
| ☐ 10 Jack Housley | 2.50 | 1.00 | .25 |
| ☐ 11 Glenn Hutchinson | 2.50 | 1.00 | .25 |
| ☐ 12 Bill Jensen | 2.50 | 1.00 | .25 |
| ☐ 13 Frank Kalil | 2.50 | 1.00 | .25 |
| ☐ 14 Dave Liggins | 2.50 | 1.00 | .25 |
| ☐ 15 Tom Manno | 2.50 | 1.00 | .25 |
| ☐ 16 Bill Nettling | 2.50 | 1.00 | .25 |
| ☐ 17 Hubert Oliver | 6.00 | 2.40 | .60 |
| ☐ 18 Glenn Perkins | 2.50 | 1.00 | .25 |
| ☐ 19 John Ramseyer | 2.50 | 1.00 | .25 |
| ☐ 20 Mike Robinson | 2.50 | 1.00 | .25 |
| ☐ 21 Chris Schultz | 3.50 | 1.40 | .35 |
| ☐ 22 Larry Smith CO | 3.50 | 1.40 | .35 |
| ☐ 23 Reggie Ware SP | 25.00 | 10.00 | 2.50 |
| ☐ 24 Bill Zivic | 2.50 | 1.00 | .25 |

## 1981 Arizona Police

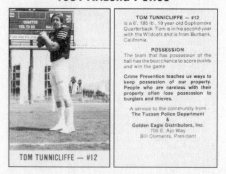

TOM TUNNICLIFFE — #12

**TOM TUNNICLIFFE — #12**

is a 6', 185 lb., 19 year old Sophomore Quarterback. Tom is in his second year with the Wildcats and is from Burbank, California.

**POSSESSION**

The team that has possession of the ball has the best chance to score points and win the game.

Crime Prevention teaches us ways to keep possession of our property. People who are careless with their property often lose possession to burglars and thieves.

A service to the community from
**The Tucson Police Department**
&
**Golden Eagle Distributors, Inc.**
705 E. Ajo Way
Bill Clements, President

The 1981 University of Arizona Police set contains 27 cards measuring approximately 2 3/8" by 3 1/2". The fronts have borderless color player photos, with the player's name and jersey number in a white stripe beneath the picture. The backs have brief biographical information and safety tips. The cards are unnumbered and checklisted below in alphabetical order.

|  | MINT | EXC | G-VG |
|---|---|---|---|
| COMPLETE SET (27) | 40.00 | 16.00 | 4.00 |
| COMMON CARD (1-27) | 2.00 | .80 | .20 |
| ☐ 1 Moe Ankney ACO | 2.50 | 1.00 | .25 |
| ☐ 2 Van Brandon | 2.00 | .80 | .20 |
| ☐ 3 Bob Carter | 2.00 | .80 | .20 |
| ☐ 4 Brian Christiansen | 2.00 | .80 | .20 |
| ☐ 5 Mark Fulcher | 2.00 | .80 | .20 |
| ☐ 6 Bob Gareeb | 2.00 | .80 | .20 |
| ☐ 7 Gary Gibson | 2.00 | .80 | .20 |

| ☐ 8 Mark Gobel | 2.00 | .80 | .20 |
|---|---|---|---|
| ☐ 9 Alfred Gross | 2.00 | .80 | .20 |
| ☐ 10 Kevin Hardcastle | 2.00 | .80 | .20 |
| ☐ 11 Neal Harris | 2.00 | .80 | .20 |
| ☐ 12 Brian Holland | 2.00 | .80 | .20 |
| ☐ 13 Ricky Hunley | 4.00 | 1.60 | .40 |
| ☐ 14 Frank Kalil | 2.00 | .80 | .20 |
| ☐ 15 Jeff Kiewel | 2.00 | .80 | .20 |
| ☐ 16 Chris Knudsen | 2.00 | .80 | .20 |
| ☐ 17 Ivan Lesnik | 2.00 | .80 | .20 |
| ☐ 18 Tony Neely | 2.00 | .80 | .20 |
| ☐ 19 Glenn Perkins | 2.00 | .80 | .20 |
| ☐ 20 Randy Robbins | 2.00 | .80 | .20 |
| ☐ 21 Gerald Roper | 2.00 | .80 | .20 |
| ☐ 22 Chris Schultz | 3.00 | 1.20 | .30 |
| ☐ 23 Gary Shaw | 2.00 | .80 | .20 |
| ☐ 24 Larry Smith CO | 3.00 | 1.20 | .30 |
| ☐ 25 Tom Tunnicliffe | 3.00 | 1.20 | .30 |
| ☐ 26 Sergio Vega | 2.00 | .80 | .20 |
| ☐ 27 Brett Weber | 2.50 | 1.00 | .25 |

## 1982 Arizona Police

The 1982 University of Arizona Police set contains 26 cards. The fronts have borderless color player photos, with the player's name and jersey number in a white stripe beneath the picture. The backs have brief biographical information and safety tips. The cards are unnumbered and checklisted below in alphabetical order.

|  | MINT | EXC | G-VG |
|---|---|---|---|
| COMPLETE SET (26) | 35.00 | 14.00 | 3.50 |
| COMMON CARD (1-26) | 1.50 | .60 | .15 |
| ☐ 1 Brad Anderson | 1.50 | .60 | .15 |
| ☐ 2 Steve Boadway | 1.50 | .60 | .15 |
| ☐ 3 Bruce Bush | 1.50 | .60 | .15 |
| ☐ 4 Mike Freeman | 1.50 | .60 | .15 |
| ☐ 5 Marsharne Graves | 1.50 | .60 | .15 |
| ☐ 6 Courtney Griffin | 1.50 | .60 | .15 |
| ☐ 7 Al Gross | 2.00 | .80 | .20 |
| ☐ 8 Julius Holt | 1.50 | .60 | .15 |
| ☐ 9 Lamonte Hunley | 2.00 | .80 | .20 |
| ☐ 10 Ricky Hunley | 3.00 | 1.20 | .30 |
| ☐ 11 Vance Johnson | 5.00 | 2.00 | .50 |
| ☐ 12 Chris Kaesman | 1.50 | .60 | .15 |
| ☐ 13 John Kaiser | 1.50 | .60 | .15 |
| ☐ 14 Mark Keel | 1.50 | .60 | .15 |
| ☐ 15 Jeff Kiewell | 1.50 | .60 | .15 |
| ☐ 16 Ivan Lesnik | 1.50 | .60 | .15 |
| ☐ 17 Glenn McCormick | 1.50 | .60 | .15 |
| ☐ 18 Ray Moret | 1.50 | .60 | .15 |
| ☐ 19 Tony Neely | 1.50 | .60 | .15 |
| ☐ 20 Byron Nelson | 2.00 | .80 | .20 |
| ☐ 21 Glenn Perkins | 1.50 | .60 | .15 |
| ☐ 22 Randy Robbins | 1.50 | .60 | .15 |
| ☐ 23 Larry Smith CO | 2.50 | 1.00 | .25 |
| ☐ 24 Tom Tunnicliffe | 2.00 | .80 | .20 |
| ☐ 25 Kevin Ward | 1.50 | .60 | .15 |
| ☐ 26 David Wood | 1.50 | .60 | .15 |

## 1983 Arizona Police

The 1983 University of Arizona Police set contains 24 cards. The fronts have borderless color player photos, with the player's name and jersey number in a white stripe beneath the picture. The backs have brief biographical information and safety tips. The cards are unnumbered and checklisted below in alphabetical order.

|  | MINT | EXC | G-VG |
|---|---|---|---|
| COMPLETE SET (24) | 30.00 | 12.00 | 3.00 |
| COMMON CARD (1-24) | 1.50 | .60 | .15 |
| ☐ 1 John Barthalt | 1.50 | .60 | .15 |
| ☐ 2 Steve Boadway | 1.50 | .60 | .15 |
| ☐ 3 Chris Brewer | 1.50 | .60 | .15 |
| ☐ 4 Lynnden Brown | 1.50 | .60 | .15 |
| ☐ 5 Charlie Dickey | 1.50 | .60 | .15 |
| ☐ 6 Jay Dobins | 1.50 | .60 | .15 |
| ☐ 7 Joe Drake | 1.50 | .60 | .15 |
| ☐ 8 Allan Durden | 1.50 | .60 | .15 |
| ☐ 9 Byron Evans | 3.00 | 1.20 | .30 |
| ☐ 10 Nils Fox | 1.50 | .60 | .15 |
| ☐ 11 Mike Freeman | 1.50 | .60 | .15 |
| ☐ 12 Marsharne Graves | 1.50 | .60 | .15 |
| ☐ 13 Lamonte Hunley | 2.00 | .80 | .20 |
| ☐ 14 Vance Johnson | 4.00 | 1.60 | .40 |
| ☐ 15 John Kaiser | 1.50 | .60 | .15 |
| ☐ 16 Ivan Lesnik | 1.50 | .60 | .15 |
| ☐ 17 Byron Nelson | 2.00 | .80 | .20 |
| ☐ 18 Randy Robbins | 1.50 | .60 | .15 |
| ☐ 19 Craig Schiller | 1.50 | .60 | .15 |
| ☐ 20 Larry Smith CO | 2.50 | 1.00 | .25 |

| | | | |
|---|---|---|---|
| ☐ 21 Tom Tunnicliffe | 2.00 | .80 | .20 |
| ☐ 22 Mark Walczak | 1.50 | .60 | .15 |
| ☐ 23 David Wood | 1.50 | .60 | .15 |
| ☐ 24 Max Zendejas | 2.00 | .80 | .20 |

## 1984 Arizona Police

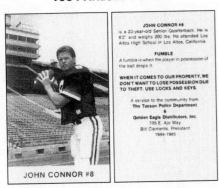

JOHN CONNOR #8

is a 23-year-old Senior Quarterback. He is 6'2" and weighs 200 lbs. He attended Los Altos High School in Los Altos, California.

**FUMBLE**
A fumble is when the player in possession of the ball drops it.

WHEN IT COMES TO OUR PROPERTY, WE DON'T WANT TO LOSE POSSESSION DUE TO THEFT. USE LOCKS AND KEYS.

A service to the community from
The Tucson Police Department
&
Golden Eagle Distributors, Inc.
705 E. Ajo Way
Bill Clements, President
1984-1985

JOHN CONNOR #8

The 1984 University of Arizona Police set contains 25 cards measuring approximately 2 1/4" by 3 5/8". The fronts have borderless color photos; the vertically oriented backs have brief bios and safety tips. The cards are unnumbered, so are listed by jersey numbers. These cards are printed on very thin stock. The set is described on the back of each card as 1984-85.

| | MINT | EXC | G-VG |
|---|---|---|---|
| COMPLETE SET (25) | 15.00 | 6.00 | 1.50 |
| COMMON CARD | .75 | .30 | .07 |
| | | | |
| ☐ 1 Alfred Jenkins | 2.00 | .80 | .20 |
| ☐ 8 John Connor | 1.00 | .40 | .10 |
| ☐ 13 Max Zendejas | 1.25 | .50 | .12 |
| ☐ 15 Gordon Bunch | .75 | .30 | .07 |
| ☐ 19 Allen Durden | .75 | .30 | .07 |
| ☐ 23 Lynnden Brown | .75 | .30 | .07 |
| ☐ 25 Vance Johnson | 2.50 | 1.00 | .25 |
| ☐ 28 Tom Bayse | .75 | .30 | .07 |
| ☐ 35 Brent Wood | .75 | .30 | .07 |
| ☐ 40 Greg Turner | .75 | .30 | .07 |
| ☐ 47 Steve Boadway | .75 | .30 | .07 |
| ☐ 52 Nils Fox | .75 | .30 | .07 |
| ☐ 54 Craig Vesling | .75 | .30 | .07 |
| ☐ 62 David Connor | .75 | .30 | .07 |
| ☐ 67 Charlie Dickey | .75 | .30 | .07 |
| ☐ 71 Brian Denton | .75 | .30 | .07 |
| ☐ 78 John DuBose | .75 | .30 | .07 |
| ☐ 79 Joe Drake | .75 | .30 | .07 |
| ☐ 82 Joy Dobyns | .75 | .30 | .07 |
| ☐ 85 Mark Walczak | .75 | .30 | .07 |
| ☐ 86 Jon Horton | .75 | .30 | .07 |
| ☐ 92 David Wood | .75 | .30 | .07 |
| ☐ 98 Lamonte Hunley | 1.00 | .40 | .10 |
| ☐ 99 John Barthalt | .75 | .30 | .07 |
| ☐ xx Larry Smith CO | 1.25 | .50 | .12 |

## 1985 Arizona Police

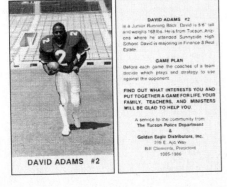

DAVID ADAMS #2

is a Junior Running Back. David is 5'6" tall and weighs 168 lbs. He is from Tucson, Arizona where he attended Sunnyside High School. David is majoring in Finance & Real Estate.

**GAME PLAN**
Before each game the coaches of a team decide which plays and strategy to use against the opponent.

FIND OUT WHAT INTERESTS YOU AND PUT TOGETHER A GAME FOR LIFE. YOUR FAMILY, TEACHERS, AND MINISTERS WILL BE GLAD TO HELP YOU.

A service to the community from
The Tucson Police Department
&
Golden Eagle Distributors, Inc.
705 E. Ajo Way
Bill Clements, President
1985-1986

DAVID ADAMS #2

The 1985 University of Arizona Police set contains 23 cards measuring 2 1/4" by 3 5/8". The fronts have borderless color photos; the vertically oriented backs have brief bios and safety tips. The cards are unnumbered, so are listed by jersey numbers. These cards are printed on very thin stock. The set is described on the back of each card as 1985-86.

| | MINT | EXC | G-VG |
|---|---|---|---|
| COMPLETE SET (23) | 15.00 | 6.00 | 1.50 |
| COMMON CARD | .75 | .30 | .07 |
| | | | |
| ☐ 1 Alfred Jenkins | 1.50 | .60 | .15 |
| ☐ 2 David Adams | .75 | .30 | .07 |
| ☐ 6 Chuck Cecil | 2.00 | .80 | .20 |
| ☐ 13 Max Zendejas | 1.25 | .50 | .12 |
| ☐ 15 Gordon Bunch | .75 | .30 | .07 |
| ☐ 18 Jeff Fairholm | 1.50 | .60 | .15 |
| ☐ 19 Allen Durden | .75 | .30 | .07 |
| ☐ 29 Don Be'ans | .75 | .30 | .07 |
| ☐ 32 Joe Prior | .75 | .30 | .07 |
| ☐ 42 Blake Custer | .75 | .30 | .07 |
| ☐ 44 Boomer Gibson | .75 | .30 | .07 |
| ☐ 48 Byron Evans | 1.50 | .60 | .15 |
| ☐ 50 Val Bichekas | .75 | .30 | .07 |
| ☐ 52 Joe Tofflemire | 1.00 | .40 | .10 |
| ☐ 54 Craig Vesling | .75 | .30 | .07 |
| ☐ 59 Jim Birmingham | .75 | .30 | .07 |
| ☐ 72 Curt DiGiacomo | .75 | .30 | .07 |
| ☐ 73 Lee Brunelli | .75 | .30 | .07 |
| ☐ 78 John DuBose | .75 | .30 | .07 |
| ☐ 83 Gary Parrish | .75 | .30 | .07 |
| ☐ 95 Cliff Thorpe | .75 | .30 | .07 |
| ☐ 96 Glenn Howell | .75 | .30 | .07 |
| ☐ xx Larry Smith CO | 1.25 | .50 | .12 |

## 1986 Arizona Police

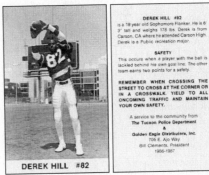

DEREK HILL #82

is a 19 year old Sophomore Flanker. He is 6'3" tall and weighs 178 lbs. Derek is from Carson, CA where he attended Carson High. Derek is a Public recreation major.

**SAFETY**
This occurs when a player with the ball is tackled behind his own goal line. The other team earns two points for a safety.

REMEMBER WHEN CROSSING THE STREET TO CROSS AT THE CORNER OR IN A CROSSWALK. YIELD TO ALL ONCOMING TRAFFIC AND MAINTAIN YOUR OWN LANE.

A service to the community from
The Tucson Police Department
&
Golden Eagle Distributors, Inc.
705 E. Ajo Way
Bill Clements, President
1986-1987

DEREK HILL #82

This 24-card set was cosponsored by the Tucson Police Department and Golden Eagle Distributors. The cards measure approximately 2 1/4" by 3 5/8". The fronts feature borderless posed color player photos, with the player's name and uniform number in the white stripe beneath the picture. The backs present player profile, a discussion or definition of some aspect of football, and a safety message. The cards are unnumbered and checklisted below in alphabetical order. The set is described on the back of each card as 1986-87.

| | MINT | EXC | G-VG |
|---|---|---|---|
| COMPLETE SET (24) | 15.00 | 6.00 | 1.50 |
| COMMON CARD (1-24) | .75 | .30 | .07 |
| | | | |
| ☐ 1 David Adams | .75 | .30 | .07 |
| ☐ 2 Frank Arriola | .75 | .30 | .07 |
| ☐ 3 Val Biehekas | .75 | .30 | .07 |
| ☐ 4 Jim Birmingham | .75 | .30 | .07 |
| ☐ 5 Chuck Cecil | 1.50 | .60 | .15 |
| ☐ 6 James Debow | .75 | .30 | .07 |
| ☐ 7 Brian Denton | .75 | .30 | .07 |
| ☐ 8 Byron Evans | 1.50 | .60 | .15 |
| ☐ 9 Jeff Fairholm | 1.25 | .50 | .12 |
| ☐ 10 Boomer Gibson | .75 | .30 | .07 |
| ☐ 11 Eugene Hardy | .75 | .30 | .07 |
| ☐ 12 Derek Hill | 1.50 | .60 | .15 |
| ☐ 13 Jon Horton | .75 | .30 | .07 |
| ☐ 14 Alfred Jenkins | 1.25 | .50 | .12 |
| ☐ 15 Danny Lockett | 1.25 | .50 | .12 |
| ☐ 16 Stan Mataele | .75 | .30 | .07 |
| ☐ 17 Chris McLemore | .75 | .30 | .07 |
| ☐ 18 Jeff Rinehart | .75 | .30 | .07 |
| ☐ 19 Ruben Rodriguez | 1.25 | .50 | .12 |
| ☐ 20 Martin Rudolph | .75 | .30 | .07 |
| ☐ 21 Larry Smith CO | 1.25 | .50 | .12 |

| | MINT | EXC | G-VG |
|---|---|---|---|
| ☐ 22 Joe Tofflemire | 1.00 | .40 | .10 |
| ☐ 23 Dana Wells | .75 | .30 | .07 |
| ☐ 24 Brent Wood | .75 | .30 | .07 |

## 1987 Arizona Police

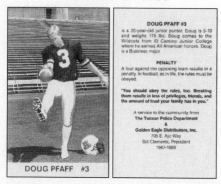

### DOUG PFAFF #3

is a 20-year-old junior punter. Doug is 5-10 and weighs 175 lbs. Doug comes to the Wildcats from El Camino Junior College where he earned All American honors. Doug is a Business major.

### PENALTY

A foul against the opposing team results in a penalty. In football, as in life, the rules must be obeyed.

"You should obey the rules, too. Breaking them results in loss of privileges, friends, and the amount of trust your family has in you."

A service to the community from
The Tucson Police Department
&
Golden Eagle Distributors, Inc.
705 E. Ajo Way
Bill Clements, President
1987-1988

DOUG PFAFF #3

The 1987 University of Arizona Police set contains 23 cards measuring approximately 2 1/4" by 3 5/8". The fronts have borderless color photos; the vertically oriented backs have brief bios and safety tips. The cards are unnumbered, so they are listed by jersey numbers. These cards are printed on very thin stock. The set is described on the back of each card as 1987-88.

| | MINT | EXC | G-VG |
|---|---|---|---|
| COMPLETE SET (23) | 15.00 | 6.00 | 1.50 |
| COMMON CARD | .75 | .30 | .07 |
| | | | |
| ☐ 2 Bobby Watters | 1.00 | .40 | .10 |
| ☐ 3 Doug Pfaff | .75 | .30 | .07 |
| ☐ 6 Chuck Cecil | 1.50 | .60 | .15 |
| ☐ 11 Gary Coston | .75 | .30 | .07 |
| ☐ 18 Jeff Fairholm | 1.25 | .50 | .12 |
| ☐ 22 Eugene Hardy | .75 | .30 | .07 |
| ☐ 26 Troy Cephers | .75 | .30 | .07 |
| ☐ 34 Charles Webb | .75 | .30 | .07 |
| ☐ 38 James Debow | .75 | .30 | .07 |
| ☐ 40 Art Greathouse | .75 | .30 | .07 |
| ☐ 43 Jerry Beasley | .75 | .30 | .07 |
| ☐ 44 Boomer Gibson | .75 | .30 | .07 |
| ☐ 47 Gallen Allen | .75 | .30 | .07 |
| ☐ 52 Joe Tofflemire | 1.00 | .40 | .10 |
| ☐ 60 Jeff Rinehart | .75 | .30 | .07 |
| ☐ 64 Kevin McKinney | .75 | .30 | .07 |
| ☐ 68 Tom Lynch | .75 | .30 | .07 |
| ☐ 82 Derek Hill | 1.25 | .50 | .12 |
| ☐ 84 Kevin Singleton | 1.25 | .50 | .12 |
| ☐ 87 Chris Singleton | 2.50 | 1.00 | .25 |
| ☐ 97 George Hinkle | .75 | .30 | .07 |
| ☐ 99 Dana Wells | .75 | .30 | .07 |
| ☐ xx Dick Tomey CO | 1.00 | .40 | .10 |

## 1988 Arizona Police

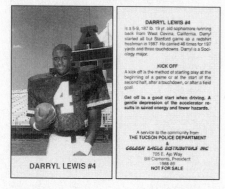

### DARRYL LEWIS #4

is a 5-9, 187 lb. 19 yr. old sophomore running back from West Covina, California. Darryl started all but Stanford game as a redshirt freshman in 1987. He carried 46 times for 197 yards and three touchdowns. Darryl is a Sociology major.

### KICK OFF

A kick off is the method of starting play at the beginning of a game or at the start of the second half, after a touchdown, or after a field goal.

Get off to a good start when driving. A gentle depression of the accelerator results in saved energy and fewer hazards.

A service to the community from
THE TUCSON POLICE DEPARTMENT
&
GOLDEN EAGLE DISTRIBUTORS INC
705 E. Ajo Way
Bill Clements, President
1988-89
NOT FOR SALE

DARRYL LEWIS #4

The 1988 University of Arizona Police set contains 25 cards measuring approximately 2 5/16" by 3 3/4". The fronts have borderless color photos; the vertically oriented backs have brief bios and safety tips.

The cards are unnumbered, so they are listed by jersey numbers. These cards are printed on very thin stock. The set is described on the back of each card as 1988-89.

| | MINT | EXC | G-VG |
|---|---|---|---|
| COMPLETE SET (25) | 15.00 | 6.00 | 1.50 |
| COMMON CARD | .75 | .30 | .07 |
| | | | |
| ☐ 2 Bobby Watters | 1.00 | .40 | .10 |
| ☐ 4 Darryl Lewis | 2.00 | .80 | .20 |
| ☐ 5 Durrell Jones | .75 | .30 | .07 |
| ☐ 8 Reggie McGill | .75 | .30 | .07 |
| ☐ 10 Ronald Veal | 1.25 | .50 | .12 |
| ☐ 15 Jeff Hammerschmidt | .75 | .30 | .07 |
| ☐ 22 Scott Geyer | .75 | .30 | .07 |
| ☐ 24 R. Groppenbacher | .75 | .30 | .07 |
| ☐ 25 David Eldridge | .75 | .30 | .07 |
| ☐ 35 Mario Hampton | .75 | .30 | .07 |
| ☐ 38 James Debow | .75 | .30 | .07 |
| ☐ 40 Art Greathouse | .75 | .30 | .07 |
| ☐ 50 Darren Case | .75 | .30 | .07 |
| ☐ 51 Doug Penner | .75 | .30 | .07 |
| ☐ 52 Joe Tofflemire | 1.00 | .40 | .10 |
| ☐ 63 John Brandom | .75 | .30 | .07 |
| ☐ 65 Ken Hakes | .75 | .30 | .07 |
| ☐ 74 Glenn Parker | .75 | .30 | .07 |
| ☐ 78 Rob Woods | .75 | .30 | .07 |
| ☐ 82 Derek Hill | 1.25 | .50 | .12 |
| ☐ 84 Kevin Singleton | 1.00 | .40 | .10 |
| ☐ 87 Chris Singleton | 2.00 | .80 | .20 |
| ☐ 96 Brad Henke | .75 | .30 | .07 |
| ☐ 99 Dana Wells | .75 | .30 | .07 |
| ☐ xx Dick Tomey CO | 1.00 | .40 | .10 |

## 1989 Arizona Police

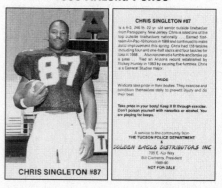

### CHRIS SINGLETON #87

is a 6-3, 246 lb. 22 yr. old senior outside linebacker from Parsippany, New Jersey. Chris is rated one of the top outside linebackers nationally. Earned first-team All-Pac-10 honors in 1988 and continued to make good improvement this spring. Chris had 118 tackles including four and one-half sacks and four tackles for loss in 1988. Also recovered a fumble and broke up a pass. Tied an Arizona record established by Ricky Hunley in 1983 by causing five fumbles. Chris is a General Studies major.

### PRIDE

Wildcats take pride in their bodies. They exercise and condition themselves daily to prevent injury and do their best.

Take pride in your body! Keep it fit through exercise. Don't poison yourself with narcotics or alcohol. You are playing for keeps.

A service to the community from
THE TUCSON POLICE DEPARTMENT
&
GOLDEN EAGLE DISTRIBUTORS INC
705 E. Ajo Way
Bill Clements, President
1989-90
NOT FOR SALE

CHRIS SINGLETON #87

This 26-card set was cosponsored by the Tucson Police Department and Golden Eagle Distributors. The cards measure approximately 2 1/4" by 3 3/4". The fronts feature borderless posed color player photos, with the player's name and uniform number in the white stripe beneath the picture. The backs present player profile, a discussion or definition of some aspect of football, and a safety message. The cards are unnumbered and checklisted below in alphabetical order. The set is described on the back of each card as 1989-90.

| | MINT | EXC | G-VG |
|---|---|---|---|
| COMPLETE SET (26) | 12.00 | 5.00 | 1.20 |
| COMMON CARD (1-26) | .60 | .24 | .06 |
| | | | |
| ☐ 1 Zeno Alexander | .60 | .24 | .06 |
| ☐ 2 John Brandom | .60 | .24 | .06 |
| ☐ 3 Todd Burden | .60 | .24 | .06 |
| ☐ 4 Darren Case | .60 | .24 | .06 |
| ☐ 5 David Eldridge | .60 | .24 | .06 |
| ☐ 6 Nick Fineanganofo | .60 | .24 | .06 |
| ☐ 7 Scott Geyer | .60 | .24 | .06 |
| ☐ 8 Art Greathouse | .60 | .24 | .06 |
| ☐ 9 Richard Griffith | .60 | .24 | .06 |
| ☐ 10 Ken Hakes | .60 | .24 | .06 |
| ☐ 11 Jeff Hammerschmidt | .60 | .24 | .06 |
| ☐ 12 Mario Hampton | .60 | .24 | .06 |
| ☐ 13 Darryll Lewis | 1.25 | .50 | .12 |
| ☐ 14 Kip Lewis | .60 | .24 | .06 |
| ☐ 15 George Malauulu | .75 | .30 | .07 |
| ☐ 16 Reggie McGill | .60 | .24 | .06 |
| ☐ 17 John Nies | .60 | .24 | .06 |
| ☐ 18 Glenn Parker | .60 | .24 | .06 |
| ☐ 19 Mike Parker | .60 | .24 | .06 |
| ☐ 20 Doug Pfaff | .60 | .24 | .06 |
| ☐ 21 David Roney | .60 | .24 | .06 |
| ☐ 22 Pete Russell | .60 | .24 | .06 |

| | MINT | EXC | G-VG |
|---|---|---|---|
| ☐ 23 Chris Singleton | 1.00 | .40 | .10 |
| ☐ 24 Paul Tofflemire | .60 | .24 | .06 |
| ☐ 25 Dick Tomey CO | .75 | .30 | .07 |
| ☐ 26 Ronald Veal | 1.00 | .40 | .10 |

## 1992 Arizona Police

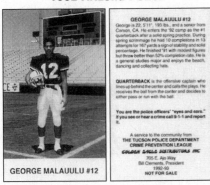

**GEORGE MALAUULU #12**

George is 22, 5'11", 193 lbs., and a senior from Carson, CA. He enters the '92 camp as the #1 quarterback after a solid spring practice. During spring scrimmage he had 10 completions in 13 attempts for 167 yards a sign of stability and solid percentage. He finished '91 with modest figures but threw better than 52% completion rate. He is a general studies major and enjoys the beach, dancing and collecting hats.

QUARTERBACK is the offensive captain who lines up behind the center and calls the plays. He receives the ball from the center and decides to either pass or run with the ball.

You are the police officers' "eyes and ears." If you see or hear a crime call 9-1-1 and report it.

A service to the community from
THE TUCSON POLICE DEPARTMENT
CRIME PREVENTION LEAGUE
GOLDEN EAGLE DISTRIBUTORS INC
705 E. Ajo Way
Bill Clements, President
1992-93
NOT FOR SALE

This 21-card set was sponsored by the Tucson Police Department and Golden Eagle Distributors. The cards measure approximately 2" by 3 3/4". The fronts feature borderless color photos of the players posed at the football stadium, with bleaches and scoreboard in the background. The player's name and jersey number are printed in the white stripe at the bottom. The backs are white and carry player information, an explanation of some aspect of football, and a safety message. The cards are unnumbered and checklisted below in alphabetical order.

| | MINT | EXC | G-VG |
|---|---|---|---|
| COMPLETE SET (21) | 10.00 | 4.00 | 1.00 |
| COMMON CARD (1-21) | .50 | .20 | .05 |
| | | | |
| ☐ 1 Tony Bouie | .60 | .24 | .06 |
| ☐ 2 Heath Bray | .50 | .20 | .05 |
| ☐ 3 Charlie Camp | .50 | .20 | .05 |
| ☐ 4 Ontiwaun Carter | 1.00 | .40 | .10 |
| ☐ 5 Richard Griffith | .50 | .20 | .05 |
| ☐ 6 Sean Harris | .60 | .24 | .06 |
| ☐ 7 Mike Heemsbergen | .50 | .20 | .05 |
| ☐ 8 Jimmy Hopkins | .50 | .20 | .05 |
| ☐ 9 Billy Johnson | .50 | .20 | .05 |
| ☐ 10 Keshon Johnson | .50 | .20 | .05 |
| ☐ 11 Chuck Levy | 1.50 | .60 | .15 |
| ☐ 12 Richard Maddox | .50 | .20 | .05 |
| ☐ 13 George Malauulu | .75 | .30 | .07 |
| ☐ 14 Darryl Morrison | .50 | .20 | .05 |
| ☐ 15 Mani Ott | .50 | .20 | .05 |
| ☐ 16 Ty Parten | .50 | .20 | .05 |
| ☐ 17 Mike Scurlock | .60 | .24 | .06 |
| ☐ 18 Warner Smith | .50 | .20 | .05 |
| ☐ 19 Dick Tomey CO | .75 | .30 | .07 |
| ☐ 20 Terry Vaughn | .50 | .20 | .05 |
| ☐ 21 Rob Waldrop | 1.00 | .40 | .10 |

## 1993 Army Smokey

Printed on thin card stock, this 15-card standard-size (2 1/2" by 3 1/2") set was sponsored by the USDA, the Forest Service, other state and federal agencies, Pepsi, Freihofer's, and The Times Herald Record.

Smokey sets issued in 1993 have a special 50th year anniversary logo on the front. The fronts feature color player action shots framed by thin white and black lines and with gold-colored borders highlighted by oblique white stripes. The team's name appears within the upper margin, and the player's name and position, along with the Smokey 50-year celebration logo, rest in the lower margin. The white backs carry player profile and a fire prevention cartoon starring Smokey. The cards are unnumbered and checklisted below in alphabetical order.

| | MINT | EXC | G-VG |
|---|---|---|---|
| COMPLETE SET (15) | 10.00 | 4.00 | 1.00 |
| COMMON PLAYER (1-15) | .75 | .30 | .07 |
| | | | |
| ☐ 1 Paul Andrzejewski | .75 | .30 | .07 |
| ☐ 2 Kevin Czarnecki | .75 | .30 | .07 |
| ☐ 3 Chad Davis | .75 | .30 | .07 |
| ☐ 4 Glenn Davis | 2.00 | .80 | .20 |
| ☐ 5 Mark Escobedo | .75 | .30 | .07 |
| ☐ 6 Gary Graves | .75 | .30 | .07 |
| ☐ 7 Leamon Hall | 1.50 | .60 | .15 |
| ☐ 8 Jason Miller | 1.00 | .40 | .10 |
| ☐ 9 Mike Plaia | .75 | .30 | .07 |
| ☐ 10 Rick Roper | 1.00 | .40 | .10 |
| ☐ 11 Jim Slomka | .75 | .30 | .07 |
| ☐ 12 Bob Sutton CO | .75 | .30 | .07 |
| ☐ 13 Jason Sutton | .75 | .30 | .07 |
| ☐ 14 Pat Zelley | .75 | .30 | .07 |
| ☐ 15 Army Mule (Mascot) | .75 | .30 | .07 |

## 1972 Auburn Tigers

This 54-card standard-size (2 1/2" by 3 1/2") set was issued in a playing card deck box. The cards have rounded corners and the typical playing card finish. The fronts feature black-and-white posed photos of helmetless players in their uniforms. A white border surrounds each picture and contains the card number and suit designation in the upper left corner and again, but inverted, in the lower right. The player's name and hometown appear just beneath the photo. The white-bordered orange backs all have the Auburn "AU" logo in navy blue and orange and white outlines. The the year of issue, 1972, and the name "Auburn Tigers" also appears on the backs. Since the set is similar to a playing card set, it is arranged just like a card deck and checklisted below accordingly. In the checklist below C means Clubs, D means Diamonds, H means Hearts, S means Spades and JK means Joker. Numbers are assigned to Aces (1), Jacks (11), Queens (12), and Kings (13). The jokers are unnumbered and listed at the end.

| | NRMT | VG-E | GOOD |
|---|---|---|---|
| COMPLETE SET (54) | 50.00 | 20.00 | 5.00 |
| COMMON PLAYER (1-54) | 1.50 | .60 | .15 |
| | | | |
| ☐ 1C Ken Calleja | 1.50 | .60 | .15 |
| ☐ 1D James Owens | 1.50 | .60 | .15 |
| ☐ 1H Mac Lorendo | 1.50 | .60 | .15 |
| ☐ 1S Ralph(Shug) Jordan CO | 5.00 | 2.00 | .50 |
| ☐ 2C Rick Neel | 1.50 | .60 | .15 |
| ☐ 2D Ted Smith | 1.50 | .60 | .15 |
| ☐ 2H Eddie Welch | 1.50 | .60 | .15 |
| ☐ 2S Mike Neel | 1.50 | .60 | .15 |
| ☐ 3C Larry Taylor | 1.50 | .60 | .15 |
| ☐ 3D Rett Davis | 1.50 | .60 | .15 |
| ☐ 3H Rusty Fuller | 1.50 | .60 | .15 |
| ☐ 3S Lee Gross | 1.50 | .60 | .15 |
| ☐ 4C Bruce Evans | 1.50 | .60 | .15 |
| ☐ 4D Rusty Deen | 1.50 | .60 | .15 |
| ☐ 4H Johnny Simmons | 1.50 | .60 | .15 |
| ☐ 4S Bill Newton | 1.50 | .60 | .15 |
| ☐ 5C David Beverly | 1.50 | .60 | .15 |
| ☐ 5D Dave Lyon | 1.50 | .60 | .15 |
| ☐ 5H Mike Fuller | 2.50 | 1.00 | .25 |
| ☐ 5S Bill Luka | 1.50 | .60 | .15 |
| ☐ 6C Ken Bernich | 1.50 | .60 | .15 |

| | MINT | EXC | G-VG |
|---|---|---|---|
| ☐ 6D Andy Steele...... | 1.50 | .60 | .15 |
| ☐ 6H Wade Whatley...... | 1.50 | .60 | .15 |
| ☐ 6S Bob Newton...... | 1.50 | .60 | .15 |
| ☐ 7C Benny Sivley...... | 2.00 | .80 | .20 |
| ☐ 7D Gardner Jett...... | 2.00 | .80 | .20 |
| ☐ 7H Rob Spivey...... | 2.00 | .80 | .20 |
| ☐ 7S Jay Casey...... | 1.50 | .60 | .15 |
| ☐ 8C David Langner...... | 1.50 | .60 | .15 |
| ☐ 8D Terry Henley...... | 1.50 | .60 | .15 |
| ☐ 8H Thomas Gossom...... | 1.50 | .60 | .15 |
| ☐ 8S Joe Tanory...... | 1.50 | .60 | .15 |
| ☐ 9C Chris Linderman...... | 1.50 | .60 | .15 |
| ☐ 9D Harry Unger...... | 1.50 | .60 | .15 |
| ☐ 9H Kenny Burks...... | 1.50 | .60 | .15 |
| ☐ 9S Sandy Cannon...... | 1.50 | .60 | .15 |
| ☐ 10C Roger Mitchell...... | 1.50 | .60 | .15 |
| ☐ 10D Jim McKinney...... | 1.50 | .60 | .15 |
| ☐ 10H Gaines Lanier...... | 1.50 | .60 | .15 |
| ☐ 10S Dave Beck...... | 1.50 | .60 | .15 |
| ☐ 11C Bob Farrior...... | 1.50 | .60 | .15 |
| ☐ 11D Miles Jones...... | 1.50 | .60 | .15 |
| ☐ 11H Tres Rogers...... | 1.50 | .60 | .15 |
| ☐ 11S David Hughes...... | 1.50 | .60 | .15 |
| ☐ 12C Sherman Moon...... | 1.50 | .60 | .15 |
| ☐ 12D Danny Sanspree...... | 1.50 | .60 | .15 |
| ☐ 12H Steve Taylor...... | 1.50 | .60 | .15 |
| ☐ 12S Randy Walls...... | 1.50 | .60 | .15 |
| ☐ 13C Steve Wilson...... | 1.50 | .60 | .15 |
| ☐ 13D Bobby Davis...... | 1.50 | .60 | .15 |
| ☐ 13H Hamlin Caldwell...... | 1.50 | .60 | .15 |
| ☐ 13S Dan Nugent...... | 1.50 | .60 | .15 |
| ☐ JK Joker...... | 1.50 | .60 | .15 |
|    Auburn Memorial Coliseum | | | |
| ☐ JK Joker...... | 1.50 | .60 | .15 |
|    Cliff Hare Stadium | | | |

# 1973 Auburn Tigers

This 54-card standard-size (2 1/2" by 3 1/2") set was issued in a playing card deck box. The cards have rounded corners and the typical playing card finish. The fronts feature black-and-white posed photos of helmetless players in their uniforms. A white border surrounds each picture and contains the card number and suit designation in the upper left corner and again, but inverted, in the lower right. The player's name and hometown appear just beneath the photo. The white-bordered navy blue backs all have the Auburn "AU" logo in navy blue and orange and white outlines. The the year of issue, 1973, and the name "Auburn Tigers" also appears on the backs. Since the set is similar to a playing card set, it is arranged just like a card deck and checklisted below accordingly. In the checklist below C means Clubs, D means Diamonds, H means Hearts, S means Spades and JK means Joker. Numbers are assigned to Aces (1), Jacks (11), Queens (12), and Kings (13). The jokers are unnumbered and listed at the end.

| | MINT | EXC | G-VG |
|---|---|---|---|
| COMPLETE SET (54)...... | 50.00 | 20.00 | 5.00 |
| COMMON PLAYER...... | 1.50 | .60 | .15 |
| | | | |
| ☐ 1C Ken Calleja...... | 1.50 | .60 | .15 |
| ☐ 1D Chris Wilson...... | 1.50 | .60 | .15 |
| ☐ 1H Lee Hayley...... | 1.50 | .60 | .15 |
| ☐ 1S Ralph(Shug) Jordan CO...... | 5.00 | 2.00 | .50 |
| ☐ 2C Rick Neel...... | 1.50 | .60 | .15 |
| ☐ 2D Johnny Sumner...... | 1.50 | .60 | .15 |
| ☐ 2H Mitzi Jackson...... | 1.50 | .60 | .15 |
| ☐ 2S Jim Pitts...... | 1.50 | .60 | .15 |
| ☐ 3C Steve Stanaland...... | 1.50 | .60 | .15 |
| ☐ 3D Rett Davis...... | 1.50 | .60 | .15 |
| ☐ 3H Rusty Fuller...... | 1.50 | .60 | .15 |
| ☐ 3S Lee Gross...... | 1.50 | .60 | .15 |
| ☐ 4C Bruce Evans...... | 1.50 | .60 | .15 |
| ☐ 4D Rusty Deen...... | 1.50 | .60 | .15 |
| ☐ 4H Liston Eddins...... | 1.50 | .60 | .15 |

| | MINT | EXC | G-VG |
|---|---|---|---|
| ☐ 4S Bill Newton...... | 1.50 | .60 | .15 |
| ☐ 5C Jimmy Sirmans...... | 1.50 | .60 | .15 |
| ☐ 5D Harry Ward...... | 1.50 | .60 | .15 |
| ☐ 5H Mike Fuller...... | 2.50 | 1.00 | .25 |
| ☐ 5S Bill Luka...... | 1.50 | .60 | .15 |
| ☐ 6C Ken Bernich...... | 1.50 | .60 | .15 |
| ☐ 6D Andy Steele...... | 1.50 | .60 | .15 |
| ☐ 6H Wade Whatley...... | 1.50 | .60 | .15 |
| ☐ 6S Bob Newton...... | 1.50 | .60 | .15 |
| ☐ 7C Benny Sivley...... | 2.00 | .80 | .20 |
| ☐ 7D Rick Telhiard...... | 2.00 | .80 | .20 |
| ☐ 7H Rob Spivey...... | 2.00 | .80 | .20 |
| ☐ 7S David Williams...... | 1.50 | .60 | .15 |
| ☐ 8C David Langner...... | 1.50 | .60 | .15 |
| ☐ 8D Chuck Fletcher...... | 1.50 | .60 | .15 |
| ☐ 8H Thomas Gossom...... | 1.50 | .60 | .15 |
| ☐ 8S Holley Caldwell...... | 1.50 | .60 | .15 |
| ☐ 9C Chris Linderman...... | 1.50 | .60 | .15 |
| ☐ 9D Ed Butler...... | 1.50 | .60 | .15 |
| ☐ 9H Kenny Burks...... | 1.50 | .60 | .15 |
| ☐ 9S Mike Flynn...... | 1.50 | .60 | .15 |
| ☐ 10C Roger Mitchell...... | 1.50 | .60 | .15 |
| ☐ 10D Jim McKinney...... | 1.50 | .60 | .15 |
| ☐ 10H Gaines Lanier...... | 1.50 | .60 | .15 |
| ☐ 10S Carl Hubbard...... | 1.50 | .60 | .15 |
| ☐ 11C Bob Farrior...... | 1.50 | .60 | .15 |
| ☐ 11D Ronnie Jones...... | 1.50 | .60 | .15 |
| ☐ 11H Billy Woods...... | 1.50 | .60 | .15 |
| ☐ 11S David Hughes...... | 1.50 | .60 | .15 |
| ☐ 12C Sherman Moon...... | 1.50 | .60 | .15 |
| ☐ 12D Mike Gates...... | 1.50 | .60 | .15 |
| ☐ 12H Steve Taylor...... | 1.50 | .60 | .15 |
| ☐ 12S Randy Walls...... | 1.50 | .60 | .15 |
| ☐ 13C Roger Pruett...... | 1.50 | .60 | .15 |
| ☐ 13D Bobby Davis...... | 1.50 | .60 | .15 |
| ☐ 13H Hamlin Caldwell...... | 1.50 | .60 | .15 |
| ☐ 13S Dan Nugent...... | 1.50 | .60 | .15 |
| ☐ JK Joker...... | 1.50 | .60 | .15 |
|    Auburn Memorial Coliseum | | | |
| ☐ JK Jocker...... | 1.50 | .60 | .15 |
|    Cliff Hare Stadium | | | |

# 1989 Auburn Coke 20

The 1989 Coke Auburn University football set contains 20 standard-size (2 1/2" by 3 1/2") cards, depicting former Auburn greats. The fronts contain vintage photos; the horizontally oriented backs feature player profiles. Both sides have navy borders. These cards were printed on very thin stock. The set is numbered C1 to C20.

| | MINT | EXC | G-VG |
|---|---|---|---|
| COMPLETE SET (20)...... | 9.00 | 3.75 | .90 |
| COMMON CARD (C1-C20)...... | .35 | .14 | .03 |
| | | | |
| ☐ C1 Pat Dye CO...... | .50 | .20 | .05 |
| ☐ C2 Zeke Smith...... | .35 | .14 | .03 |
| ☐ C3 War Eagle (Mascot)...... | .50 | .20 | .05 |
| ☐ C4 Tucker Frederickson...... | .50 | .20 | .05 |
| ☐ C5 John Heisman...... | .50 | .20 | .05 |
| ☐ C6 Ralph(Shug) Jordan CO...... | .50 | .20 | .05 |
| ☐ C7 Pat Sullivan...... | .50 | .20 | .05 |
| ☐ C8 Terry Beasley...... | .35 | .14 | .03 |
| ☐ C9 Punt Bama Punt...... | .50 | .20 | .05 |
|    Ralph(Shug) Jordan | | | |
|    and Paul(Bear) Bryant | | | |
| ☐ C10 Retired Jerseys...... | .50 | .20 | .05 |
|    (Pat Sullivan and | | | |
|    Terry Beasley) | | | |
| ☐ C11 Bo Jackson...... | 2.50 | 1.00 | .25 |
| ☐ C12 Lawyer Tillman...... | .75 | .30 | .07 |
| ☐ C13 Gregg Carr...... | .35 | .14 | .03 |
| ☐ C14 Lionel James...... | .50 | .20 | .05 |
| ☐ C15 Joe Cribbs...... | .60 | .24 | .06 |
| ☐ C16 Heisman Winners...... | 1.00 | .40 | .10 |
|    (Pat Sullivan, | | | |

|  | MINT | EXC | G-VG |
|---|---|---|---|
| Bo Jackson, and Pat Dye CO) | | | |
| ☐ C17 Aundray Bruce | .35 | .14 | .03 |
| ☐ C18 Aubie (Mascot) | .35 | .14 | .03 |
| ☐ C19 Tracy Rocker | .35 | .14 | .03 |
| ☐ C20 James Brooks | 1.00 | .40 | .10 |

## 1989 Auburn Coke 580

The 1989 Coke Auburn University football set contains 580 standard-size (2 1/2" by 3 1/2") cards, depicting former Auburn greats. The fronts contain vintage photos; the horizontally oriented backs feature player profiles. Both sides have navy borders. The cards were distributed in sets and in poly packs. These cards were printed on very thin stock. This set is notable for its inclusion of several Bo Jackson cards.

|  | MINT | EXC | G-VG |
|---|---|---|---|
| COMPLETE SET (580) | 25.00 | 10.00 | 2.50 |
| COMMON CARD (1-580) | .07 | .03 | .01 |
| ☐ 1 Pat Dye CO | .20 | .08 | .02 |
| (His First Game) | | | |
| ☐ 2 Auburn's First Team | .15 | .06 | .01 |
| (1892 Team Photo) | | | |
| ☐ 3 Pat Sullivan | .20 | .08 | .02 |
| ☐ 4 Bo (Jackson) | .75 | .30 | .07 |
| Over The Top | | | |
| ☐ 5 Jimmy Hitchcock | .07 | .03 | .01 |
| ☐ 6 Walter Gilbert | .07 | .03 | .01 |
| ☐ 7 Monk Gafford | .07 | .03 | .01 |
| ☐ 8 Frank D'Agostino | .07 | .03 | .01 |
| ☐ 9 Joe Childress | .15 | .06 | .01 |
| ☐ 10 Jim Pyburn | .15 | .06 | .01 |
| ☐ 11 Tex Warrington | .07 | .03 | .01 |
| ☐ 12 Travis Tidwell | .15 | .06 | .01 |
| ☐ 13 Fob James | .07 | .03 | .01 |
| ☐ 14 Jimmy Phillips | .15 | .06 | .01 |
| ☐ 15 Zeke Smith | .07 | .03 | .01 |
| ☐ 16 Mike Fuller | .07 | .03 | .01 |
| ☐ 17 Ed Dyas | .07 | .03 | .01 |
| ☐ 18 Jack Thornton | .07 | .03 | .01 |
| ☐ 19 Ken Rice | .07 | .03 | .01 |
| ☐ 20 Freddie Hyatt | .20 | .08 | .02 |
| ☐ 21 Jackie Burkett | .20 | .08 | .02 |
| ☐ 22 Jimmy Sidle | .07 | .03 | .01 |
| ☐ 23 Buddy McClinton | .15 | .06 | .01 |
| ☐ 24 Larry Willingham | .07 | .03 | .01 |
| ☐ 25 Bob Harris | .07 | .03 | .01 |
| ☐ 26 Bill Cody | .07 | .03 | .01 |
| ☐ 27 Lewis Colbert | .20 | .08 | .02 |
| ☐ 28 Brent Fullwood | .15 | .06 | .01 |
| ☐ 29 Tracy Rocker | .07 | .03 | .01 |
| ☐ 30 Kurt Grain | .15 | .06 | .01 |
| ☐ 31 Walter Reeves | .07 | .03 | .01 |
| ☐ 32 Jordan-Hare Stadium | .07 | .03 | .01 |
| ☐ 33 Ben Tamburello | .07 | .03 | .01 |
| ☐ 34 Benji Roland | .07 | .03 | .01 |
| ☐ 35 Chris Knapp | .07 | .03 | .01 |
| ☐ 36 Dowe Aughtman | .07 | .03 | .01 |
| ☐ 37 Auburn Tigers Logo | .07 | .03 | .01 |
| ☐ 38 Tommie Agee | .15 | .06 | .01 |
| ☐ 39 Bo Jackson | .75 | .30 | .07 |
| ☐ 40 Freddy Weygand | .15 | .06 | .01 |
| ☐ 41 Rodney Garner | .07 | .03 | .01 |
| ☐ 42 Brian Shulman | .07 | .03 | .01 |
| ☐ 43 Jim Thompson | .07 | .03 | .01 |
| ☐ 44 Shan Morris | .07 | .03 | .01 |
| ☐ 45 Ralph(Shug) Jordan CO | .15 | .06 | .01 |
| ☐ 46 Stacy Searels | .07 | .03 | .01 |
| ☐ 47 1957 Champs | .15 | .06 | .01 |
| (Team Photo) | | | |
| ☐ 48 Mike Kolen | .07 | .03 | .01 |
| ☐ 49 A Challenge Met | .15 | .06 | .01 |
| (Pat Dye) | | | |
| ☐ 50 Mark Dorminey | .07 | .03 | .01 |
| ☐ 51 Greg Staples | .07 | .03 | .01 |
| ☐ 52 Randy Campbell | .07 | .03 | .01 |
| ☐ 53 Duke Donaldson | .07 | .03 | .01 |
| ☐ 54 Yann Cowart | .07 | .03 | .01 |
| ☐ 55 Second Blocked Punt | .15 | .06 | .01 |
| (Vs. Alabama 1972) | | | |
| ☐ 56 Keith Uecker | .15 | .06 | .01 |
| ☐ 57 David Jordan | .07 | .03 | .01 |
| ☐ 58 Tim Drinkard | .07 | .03 | .01 |
| ☐ 59 Connie Frederick | .07 | .03 | .01 |
| ☐ 60 Pat Arrington | .07 | .03 | .01 |
| ☐ 61 Willie Howell | .07 | .03 | .01 |
| ☐ 62 Terry Page | .07 | .03 | .01 |
| ☐ 63 Ben Thomas | .15 | .06 | .01 |
| ☐ 64 Ron Stallworth | .07 | .03 | .01 |
| ☐ 65 Charlie Trotman | .07 | .03 | .01 |
| ☐ 66 Ed West | .15 | .06 | .01 |
| ☐ 67 James Brooks | .50 | .20 | .05 |
| ☐ 68 Changing of the Guard | .15 | .06 | .01 |
| Doug Barfield and | | | |
| Ralph(Shug) Jordan | | | |
| ☐ 69 Ken Bernich | .07 | .03 | .01 |
| ☐ 70 Chris Woods | .07 | .03 | .01 |
| ☐ 71 Ralph(Shug) Jordan CO | .15 | .06 | .01 |
| ☐ 72 Steve Dennis CO | .07 | .03 | .01 |
| ☐ 73 Reggie Herring CO | .07 | .03 | .01 |
| ☐ 74 Al Del Greco | .15 | .06 | .01 |
| ☐ 75 Wayne Hall CO | .07 | .03 | .01 |
| ☐ 76 Langdon Hall | .07 | .03 | .01 |
| ☐ 77 Donnie Humphrey | .07 | .03 | .01 |
| ☐ 78 Jeff Burger | .20 | .08 | .02 |
| ☐ 79 Vernon Blackard | .07 | .03 | .01 |
| ☐ 80 Larry Blakeney CO | .07 | .03 | .01 |
| ☐ 81 Doug Smith | .07 | .03 | .01 |
| ☐ 82 Two Eras Meet | .15 | .06 | .01 |
| Ralph(Shug) Jordan | | | |
| and Vince Dooley | | | |
| ☐ 83 Kyle Collins | .07 | .03 | .01 |
| ☐ 84 Bobby Freeman | .07 | .03 | .01 |
| ☐ 85 Pat Sullivan CO | .25 | .10 | .02 |
| ☐ 86 Neil Callaway CO | .07 | .03 | .01 |
| ☐ 87 William Andrews | .20 | .08 | .02 |
| ☐ 88 Curtis Kuykendall | .07 | .03 | .01 |
| ☐ 89 David Campbell | .07 | .03 | .01 |
| ☐ 90 Seniors of '83 | .25 | .10 | .02 |
| ☐ 91 Bud Casey CO | .07 | .03 | .01 |
| ☐ 92 Jay Jacobs CO | .07 | .03 | .01 |
| ☐ 93 Al Del Greco | .15 | .06 | .01 |
| ☐ 94 Pate Mote | .07 | .03 | .01 |
| ☐ 95 Rob Shuler | .07 | .03 | .01 |
| ☐ 96 Jerry Beasley | .07 | .03 | .01 |
| ☐ 97 Pat Washington | .07 | .03 | .01 |
| ☐ 98 Ed Graham | .07 | .03 | .01 |
| ☐ 99 Leon Myers | .07 | .03 | .01 |
| ☐ 100 Paul Davis CO | .15 | .06 | .01 |
| ☐ 101 Tom Banks Jr | .07 | .03 | .01 |
| ☐ 102 Mike Simmons | .07 | .03 | .01 |
| ☐ 103 Alex Bowden | .07 | .03 | .01 |
| ☐ 104 Jim Bone | .07 | .03 | .01 |
| ☐ 105 Wincent Harris | .07 | .03 | .01 |
| ☐ 106 James Daniel CO | .07 | .03 | .01 |
| ☐ 107 Jimmy Carter | .20 | .08 | .02 |
| ☐ 108 Leading Passers | .20 | .08 | .02 |
| (Pat Sullivan) | | | |
| ☐ 109 Alvin Mitchell | .07 | .03 | .01 |
| ☐ 110 Mark Clement | .07 | .03 | .01 |
| ☐ 111 Bob Brown | .07 | .03 | .01 |
| ☐ 112 Shot Senn | .07 | .03 | .01 |
| ☐ 113 Loran Carter | .07 | .03 | .01 |
| ☐ 114 Pat Dye's First Team | .15 | .06 | .01 |
| (Team Photo) | | | |
| ☐ 115 Bob Hix | .07 | .03 | .01 |
| ☐ 116 Torrance Russell | .07 | .03 | .01 |
| ☐ 117 Mike Mann | .07 | .03 | .01 |
| ☐ 118 Mike Shirey | .07 | .03 | .01 |
| ☐ 119 Pat Dye CO | .15 | .06 | .01 |
| ☐ 120 Kevin Greene | .20 | .08 | .02 |
| ☐ 121 Auburn Creed | .07 | .03 | .01 |
| ☐ 122 Jordan's All-Americans | .20 | .08 | .02 |
| (Ralph(Shug) Jordan, | | | |
| Tucker Frederickson, | | | |
| and Jimmy Sidle) | | | |
| ☐ 123 Dave Blanks | .07 | .03 | .01 |
| ☐ 124 Scott Bolton | .07 | .03 | .01 |
| ☐ 125 Vince Dooley | .15 | .06 | .01 |
| ☐ 126 Tim Jessie | .07 | .03 | .01 |
| ☐ 127 Joe Davis | .07 | .03 | .01 |
| ☐ 128 Clayton Beauford | .07 | .03 | .01 |
| ☐ 129 Wilbur Hutsell AD | .07 | .03 | .01 |
| ☐ 130 Joe Whit CO | .07 | .03 | .01 |
| ☐ 131 Gary Kelley | .07 | .03 | .01 |
| ☐ 132 Bo Jackson | .75 | .30 | .07 |
| ☐ 133 Aundray Bruce | .20 | .08 | .02 |
| ☐ 134 Ronny Bellew | .07 | .03 | .01 |
| ☐ 135 Hindman Wall | .07 | .03 | .01 |
| ☐ 136 Frank Warren | .07 | .03 | .01 |

| | | | |
|---|---|---|---|
| ☐ 137 Abb Chrietzberg | .07 | .03 | .01 |
| ☐ 138 Collis Campbell | .07 | .03 | .01 |
| ☐ 139 Randy Stokes | .07 | .03 | .01 |
| ☐ 140 Teedy Faulk | .07 | .03 | .01 |
| ☐ 141 Reese McCall | .15 | .06 | .01 |
| ☐ 142 Jeff Jackson | .07 | .03 | .01 |
| ☐ 143 Bill Burgess | .07 | .03 | .01 |
| ☐ 144 Willie Huntley | .07 | .03 | .01 |
| ☐ 145 Doug Huntley | .07 | .03 | .01 |
| ☐ 146 Bacardi Bowl | .07 | .03 | .01 |
| (Walter Gilbert) | | | |
| ☐ 147 Russ Carreker | .07 | .03 | .01 |
| ☐ 148 Joe Moon | .07 | .03 | .01 |
| ☐ 149 A Look Ahead | .15 | .06 | .01 |
| (Pat Dye CO) | | | |
| ☐ 150 Joe Sullivan | .07 | .03 | .01 |
| ☐ 151 Scott Riley | .07 | .03 | .01 |
| ☐ 152 Larry Ellis | .07 | .03 | .01 |
| ☐ 153 Jeff Parks | .07 | .03 | .01 |
| ☐ 154 Gerald Williams | .07 | .03 | .01 |
| ☐ 155 Lee Griffith | .07 | .03 | .01 |
| ☐ 156 First Blocked Punt | .15 | .06 | .01 |
| (Vs. Alabama 1972) | | | |
| ☐ 157 Bill Beckwith ADMIN | .07 | .03 | .01 |
| ☐ 158 Celebration | .15 | .06 | .01 |
| (1957 Action Photo) | | | |
| ☐ 159 Tommy Carroll | .15 | .06 | .01 |
| ☐ 160 John Dailey | .07 | .03 | .01 |
| ☐ 161 George Stephenson | .07 | .03 | .01 |
| ☐ 162 Danny Arnold | .07 | .03 | .01 |
| ☐ 163 Mike Edwards | .07 | .03 | .01 |
| ☐ 164 1894 Auburn-Alabama | .15 | .06 | .01 |
| Trophy | | | |
| ☐ 165 Don Anderson | .07 | .03 | .01 |
| ☐ 166 Alvin Briggs | .07 | .03 | .01 |
| ☐ 167 Herb Waldrop CO | .07 | .03 | .01 |
| ☐ 168 Jim Skuthan | .07 | .03 | .01 |
| ☐ 169 Alan Hardin | .07 | .03 | .01 |
| ☐ 170 Coaching Generations | .15 | .06 | .01 |
| (Pat Sullivan | | | |
| and Bobby Freeman) | | | |
| ☐ 171 Georgia Celebration | .07 | .03 | .01 |
| (1971 Locker Room) | | | |
| ☐ 172 Auburn 17, Alabama 16 | .15 | .06 | .01 |
| (1972) | | | |
| ☐ 173 Nat Ceasar | .07 | .03 | .01 |
| ☐ 174 Billy Hitchcock | .15 | .06 | .01 |
| ☐ 175 SEC Championship | .15 | .06 | .01 |
| Trophy | | | |
| ☐ 176 Dr. James E. Martin | .07 | .03 | .01 |
| PRES | | | |
| ☐ 177 Ricky Westbrook | .15 | .06 | .01 |
| ☐ 178 Fob James | .07 | .03 | .01 |
| ☐ 179 Stacy Dunn | .07 | .03 | .01 |
| ☐ 180 Tracy Turner | .07 | .03 | .01 |
| ☐ 181 Pat Dye CO | .15 | .06 | .01 |
| ☐ 182 Terry Beasley in the | .07 | .03 | .01 |
| Record Book | | | |
| ☐ 183 Ed(Foots) Bauer | .07 | .03 | .01 |
| ☐ 184 1984 Sugar Bowl | .07 | .03 | .01 |
| Scoreboard | | | |
| ☐ 185 Mark Robbins | .07 | .03 | .01 |
| ☐ 186 Paul White CO | .07 | .03 | .01 |
| ☐ 187 Hindman Wall AD | .07 | .03 | .01 |
| ☐ 188 David Beverly | .15 | .06 | .01 |
| ☐ 189 Sugar Bowl Trophy | .07 | .03 | .01 |
| ☐ 190 Edmund Nelson | .07 | .03 | .01 |
| ☐ 191 Edmund Nelson | .07 | .03 | .01 |
| ☐ 192 Cliff Hare | .07 | .03 | .01 |
| ☐ 193 Byron Franklin | .15 | .06 | .01 |
| ☐ 194 Richard Manry | .07 | .03 | .01 |
| ☐ 195 Malcolm McCary | .07 | .03 | .01 |
| ☐ 196 Patrick Waters ADMIN | .07 | .03 | .01 |
| ☐ 197 Chester Willis | .07 | .03 | .01 |
| ☐ 198 Alex Dudchock | .07 | .03 | .01 |
| ☐ 199 Pat Sullivan in the | .15 | .06 | .01 |
| Record Book | | | |
| ☐ 200 Victory Ride | .15 | .06 | .01 |
| (Pat Dye CO) | | | |
| ☐ 201 Dr. George Petrie CO | .07 | .03 | .01 |
| ☐ 202 D.M. Balliet CO | .07 | .03 | .01 |
| ☐ 203 G.H. Harvey CO | .07 | .03 | .01 |
| ☐ 204 F.M. Hall CO | .07 | .03 | .01 |
| ☐ 205 John Heisman CO | .20 | .08 | .02 |
| ☐ 206 Billy Watkins CO | .07 | .03 | .01 |
| ☐ 207 J.R. Kent CO | .07 | .03 | .01 |
| ☐ 208 Mike Harvey CO | .07 | .03 | .01 |
| ☐ 209 Billy Bates CO | .07 | .03 | .01 |
| ☐ 210 Mike Donahue CO | .07 | .03 | .01 |
| ☐ 211 W.S. Kienholz CO | .07 | .03 | .01 |
| ☐ 212 Mike Donahue CO | .07 | .03 | .01 |
| ☐ 213 Boozer Pitts CO | .07 | .03 | .01 |
| ☐ 214 Dave Morey CO | .07 | .03 | .01 |
| ☐ 215 George Bohler CO | .07 | .03 | .01 |
| ☐ 216 John Floyd CO | .07 | .03 | .01 |
| ☐ 217 Chet Wynne CO | .07 | .03 | .01 |
| ☐ 218 Jack Meagher CO | .07 | .03 | .01 |
| ☐ 219 Carl Voyles CO | .07 | .03 | .01 |
| ☐ 220 Earl Brown CO | .07 | .03 | .01 |
| ☐ 221 Ralph(Shug) Jordan CO | .15 | .06 | .01 |
| ☐ 222 Doug Barfield CO | .15 | .06 | .01 |
| ☐ 223 Most Career Points | .35 | .14 | .03 |
| (Bo Jackson) | | | |
| ☐ 224 Sonny Ferguson | .07 | .03 | .01 |
| ☐ 225 Ronnie Ross | .07 | .03 | .01 |
| ☐ 226 Gardner Jett | .15 | .06 | .01 |
| ☐ 227 Jerry Wilson | .07 | .03 | .01 |
| ☐ 228 Dick Schmalz | .07 | .03 | .01 |
| ☐ 229 Morris Savage | .07 | .03 | .01 |
| ☐ 230 James Owens | .07 | .03 | .01 |
| ☐ 231 Eddie Welch | .07 | .03 | .01 |
| ☐ 232 Lee Hayley | .07 | .03 | .01 |
| ☐ 233 Dick Hayley | .07 | .03 | .01 |
| ☐ 234 Jeff McCollum | .07 | .03 | .01 |
| ☐ 235 Rick Freeman | .07 | .03 | .01 |
| ☐ 236 Bobby Freeman CO | .07 | .03 | .01 |
| ☐ 237 Auburn 32, Alabama 22 | .15 | .06 | .01 |
| (Trophy) | | | |
| ☐ 238 Chip Powell | .07 | .03 | .01 |
| ☐ 239 Nick Ardillo | .07 | .03 | .01 |
| ☐ 240 Don Bristow | .07 | .03 | .01 |
| ☐ 241 Bucky Waid | .07 | .03 | .01 |
| ☐ 242 Greg Robert | .07 | .03 | .01 |
| ☐ 243 Ray Rollins | .07 | .03 | .01 |
| ☐ 244 Tommy Hicks | .07 | .03 | .01 |
| ☐ 245 Steve Wallace | .15 | .06 | .01 |
| ☐ 246 David Hughes | .07 | .03 | .01 |
| ☐ 247 Chuck Hurston | .07 | .03 | .01 |
| ☐ 248 Jimmy Long | .07 | .03 | .01 |
| ☐ 249 John Cochran AD | .07 | .03 | .01 |
| ☐ 250 Bobby Davis | .07 | .03 | .01 |
| ☐ 251 G.W. Clapp | .07 | .03 | .01 |
| ☐ 252 Jere Colley | .07 | .03 | .01 |
| ☐ 253 Tim James | .07 | .03 | .01 |
| ☐ 254 Joe Dolan | .07 | .03 | .01 |
| ☐ 255 Jerry Gordon | .07 | .03 | .01 |
| ☐ 256 Billy Edge | .07 | .03 | .01 |
| ☐ 257 Lawyer Tillman | .25 | .10 | .02 |
| ☐ 258 John McAfee | .07 | .03 | .01 |
| ☐ 259 Scotty Long | .07 | .03 | .01 |
| ☐ 260 Billy Austin | .07 | .03 | .01 |
| ☐ 261 Tracy Rocker | .15 | .06 | .01 |
| ☐ 262 Mickey Sutton | .07 | .03 | .01 |
| ☐ 263 Tommy Traylor | .07 | .03 | .01 |
| ☐ 264 Bill Van Dyke | .07 | .03 | .01 |
| ☐ 265 Sam McClurkin | .07 | .03 | .01 |
| ☐ 266 Mike Flynn | .07 | .03 | .01 |
| ☐ 267 Jim Sirmans | .07 | .03 | .01 |
| ☐ 268 Reggie Ware | .15 | .06 | .01 |
| ☐ 269 Bill Luke | .07 | .03 | .01 |
| ☐ 270 Don Machen | .07 | .03 | .01 |
| ☐ 271 Bill Grisham | .07 | .03 | .01 |
| ☐ 272 Bruce Evans | .07 | .03 | .01 |
| ☐ 273 Hank Hall | .07 | .03 | .01 |
| ☐ 274 Tommy Lunceford | .07 | .03 | .01 |
| ☐ 275 Pat Thomas | .07 | .03 | .01 |
| ☐ 276 Marvin Trott | .07 | .03 | .01 |
| ☐ 277 Brad Everett | .07 | .03 | .01 |
| ☐ 278 Frank Reeves | .07 | .03 | .01 |
| ☐ 279 Bishop Reeves | .07 | .03 | .01 |
| ☐ 280 Carver Reeves | .07 | .03 | .01 |
| ☐ 281 Billy Haas | .07 | .03 | .01 |
| ☐ 282 Dye's First AU Bowl | .15 | .06 | .01 |
| (Pat Dye CO) | | | |
| ☐ 283 Nate Hill | .07 | .03 | .01 |
| ☐ 284 Bucky Howard | .07 | .03 | .01 |
| ☐ 285 Tim Christian | .07 | .03 | .01 |
| ☐ 286 Tim Christian CO | .07 | .03 | .01 |
| ☐ 287 Tom Nettleman | .07 | .03 | .01 |
| ☐ 288 Carl Hubbard | .07 | .03 | .01 |
| ☐ 289 Auburn's Biggest Wins | .07 | .03 | .01 |
| (Chart) | | | |
| ☐ 290 Jay Jacobs | .07 | .03 | .01 |
| ☐ 291 Jimmy Pettus | .07 | .03 | .01 |
| ☐ 292 Cliff Hare Stadium | .07 | .03 | .01 |
| ☐ 293 Richard Wood | .15 | .06 | .01 |
| ☐ 294 Sandy Cannon | .07 | .03 | .01 |
| ☐ 295 Bill Braswell | .07 | .03 | .01 |
| ☐ 296 Foy Thompson | .07 | .03 | .01 |
| ☐ 297 Robert Margeson | .07 | .03 | .01 |
| ☐ 298 Pipeline to the Pros | .20 | .08 | .02 |
| (Seven Pro Players) | | | |
| ☐ 299 Bill Evans | .07 | .03 | .01 |
| ☐ 300 Marvin Tucker | .07 | .03 | .01 |
| ☐ 301 Jack Locklear | .07 | .03 | .01 |
| ☐ 302 Mike Locklear | .07 | .03 | .01 |
| ☐ 303 Harry Unger | .07 | .03 | .01 |
| ☐ 304 Lee Marke Sellers | .07 | .03 | .01 |
| ☐ 305 Ted Foret | .07 | .03 | .01 |
| ☐ 306 Bobby Foret | .07 | .03 | .01 |
| ☐ 307 Mike Neel | .07 | .03 | .01 |
| ☐ 308 Rick Neel | .07 | .03 | .01 |
| ☐ 309 Mike Alford | .07 | .03 | .01 |
| ☐ 310 Mac Crawford | .07 | .03 | .01 |

| | | | | | | |
|---|---|---|---|---|---|---|
| ☐ 311 Bill Cunningham | .07 | .03 | .01 | ☐ 391 Lee Gross | .07 | .03 | .01 |
| ☐ 312 Legends | .20 | .08 | .02 | ☐ 392 Jerry Popwell | .07 | .03 | .01 |
| (Pat Sullivan | | | | ☐ 393 Tommy Groat | .07 | .03 | .01 |
| and Jeff Burger) | | | | ☐ 394 Neal Dettmering | .07 | .03 | .01 |
| ☐ 313 Frank LaRussa | .07 | .03 | .01 | ☐ 395 Dr. W.S. Bailey ADMIN | .07 | .03 | .01 |
| ☐ 314 Chris Vacarella | .07 | .03 | .01 | ☐ 396 Jim Pitts | .07 | .03 | .01 |
| ☐ 315 Gerald Robinson | .15 | .06 | .01 | ☐ 397 College Football | .07 | .03 | .01 |
| ☐ 316 Ronnie Baynes | .07 | .03 | .01 | History | | | |
| ☐ 317 Dave Edwards | .07 | .03 | .01 | (Cliff Hare Stadium) | | | |
| ☐ 318 Steve Taylor | .07 | .03 | .01 | ☐ 398 Doc Griffith | .07 | .03 | .01 |
| ☐ 319 Phillip Gilchrist | .07 | .03 | .01 | ☐ 399 Liston Eddins | .07 | .03 | .01 |
| ☐ 320 Ben McCurdy | .07 | .03 | .01 | ☐ 400 Woody Woodall | .07 | .03 | .01 |
| ☐ 321 David Hill | .07 | .03 | .01 | ☐ 401 Auburn Helmet | .07 | .03 | .01 |
| ☐ 322 Jimmy Reynolds | .07 | .03 | .01 | ☐ 402 Skip Johnston | .07 | .03 | .01 |
| ☐ 323 Chuck Fletcher | .07 | .03 | .01 | ☐ 403 Trey Gainous | .07 | .03 | .01 |
| ☐ 324 Bogue Miller | .07 | .03 | .01 | ☐ 404 Randy Walls | .07 | .03 | .01 |
| ☐ 325 Dave Beck | .07 | .03 | .01 | ☐ 405 Jimmy Partin | .07 | .03 | .01 |
| ☐ 326 Johnny Simmons | .07 | .03 | .01 | ☐ 406 Dick Ingwerson | .07 | .03 | .01 |
| ☐ 327 Howard Simpson | .07 | .03 | .01 | ☐ 407 David Shelby | .07 | .03 | .01 |
| ☐ 328 Benny Sivley | .15 | .06 | .01 | ☐ 408 Harry Ward | .07 | .03 | .01 |
| ☐ 329 1987 SEC Champions | .15 | .06 | .01 | ☐ 409 Thomas Gossom | .07 | .03 | .01 |
| (Team Photo) | | | | ☐ 410 Samford T. Gower | .07 | .03 | .01 |
| ☐ 330 Frank Cox | .07 | .03 | .01 | ☐ 411 Architects of the | .15 | .06 | .01 |
| ☐ 331 Phil Gargis | .07 | .03 | .01 | Future | | | |
| ☐ 332 Don Webb | .07 | .03 | .01 | (Jeff Beard and | | | |
| ☐ 333 Dan Presley | .07 | .03 | .01 | Ralph(Shug) Jordan) | | | |
| ☐ 334 Al Giffin | .07 | .03 | .01 | ☐ 412 Ed Butler | .07 | .03 | .01 |
| ☐ 335 Don Lewis | .07 | .03 | .01 | ☐ 413 Bob Butler | .07 | .03 | .01 |
| ☐ 336 Eric Floyd | .15 | .06 | .01 | ☐ 414 Ben Strickland | .07 | .03 | .01 |
| ☐ 337 Jordan and Stadium | .15 | .06 | .01 | ☐ 415 Jeff Lott | .07 | .03 | .01 |
| (Ralph(Shug) Jordan) | | | | ☐ 416 Harris Rabren | .07 | .03 | .01 |
| ☐ 338 Terry Hendly | .07 | .03 | .01 | ☐ 417 Mike McQuaig | .07 | .03 | .01 |
| ☐ 339 Billy Atkins | .07 | .03 | .01 | ☐ 418 Steve Wilson | .07 | .03 | .01 |
| ☐ 340 Tony Long | .07 | .03 | .01 | ☐ 419 Jorge Portela | .07 | .03 | .01 |
| ☐ 341 Jimmy Clemmer | .07 | .03 | .01 | ☐ 420 Dave Middleton | .15 | .06 | .01 |
| ☐ 342 John Valentine | .07 | .03 | .01 | ☐ 421 Tommy Yearout | .07 | .03 | .01 |
| ☐ 343 Bruce Bylsma | .07 | .03 | .01 | ☐ 422 Gusty Yearout | .07 | .03 | .01 |
| ☐ 344 Merrill Shirley | .07 | .03 | .01 | ☐ 423 The Auburn Stadium | .07 | .03 | .01 |
| ☐ 345 Kenny Howard CO | .07 | .03 | .01 | ☐ 424 Cliff Hare Stadium | .07 | .03 | .01 |
| ☐ 346 Hal Hamrick | .07 | .03 | .01 | ☐ 425 Oscar Burford | .07 | .03 | .01 |
| ☐ 347 Greg Zipp | .07 | .03 | .01 | ☐ 426 Cliff Hare Stadium | .07 | .03 | .01 |
| ☐ 348 Mac Champion | .07 | .03 | .01 | ☐ 427 Cliff Hare Stadium | .07 | .03 | .01 |
| ☐ 349 Most Tackles in | .07 | .03 | .01 | ☐ 428 Jordan-Hare Stadium | .07 | .03 | .01 |
| One Game | | | | ☐ 429 Jack Meagher CO | .07 | .03 | .01 |
| (Kurt Crain) | | | | ☐ 430 Jeff Beard AD | .07 | .03 | .01 |
| ☐ 350 Leading Career | .35 | .14 | .03 | ☐ 431 Frank Young ADMIN | .07 | .03 | .01 |
| Rushers | | | | ☐ 432 Frank Riley | .07 | .03 | .01 |
| (Bo Jackson) | | | | ☐ 433 Ernie Warren | .07 | .03 | .01 |
| ☐ 351 Homer Williams | .07 | .03 | .01 | ☐ 434 Brian Atkins | .07 | .03 | .01 |
| ☐ 352 Mike Gates | .07 | .03 | .01 | ☐ 435 George Atkins | .07 | .03 | .01 |
| ☐ 353 Rusty Fuller | .07 | .03 | .01 | ☐ 436 Ricky Sanders | .35 | .14 | .03 |
| ☐ 354 Rusty Deen | .07 | .03 | .01 | ☐ 437 George Kenmore | .07 | .03 | .01 |
| ☐ 355 Stalwart Defenders | .07 | .03 | .01 | ☐ 438 Don Heller | .07 | .03 | .01 |
| (Bob Harris and | | | | ☐ 439 Pat Meagher | .07 | .03 | .01 |
| Mark Dorminey) | | | | ☐ 440 Tim Davis | .07 | .03 | .01 |
| ☐ 356 Heroes of '56 | .15 | .06 | .01 | ☐ 441 Tiger Meat (Cooks) | .07 | .03 | .01 |
| (Ralph(Shug) Jordan, | | | | ☐ 442 Joe Connally CO | .07 | .03 | .01 |
| Jerry Elliott, and | | | | ☐ 443 Bob Newton | .07 | .03 | .01 |
| Frank Reeves) | | | | ☐ 444 Bill Newton | .07 | .03 | .01 |
| ☐ 357 Road to the Top | .15 | .06 | .01 | ☐ 445 David Langner | .07 | .03 | .01 |
| (Cartoon) | | | | ☐ 446 Charlie Langner | .07 | .03 | .01 |
| ☐ 358 Cleve Wester | .07 | .03 | .01 | ☐ 447 Brownie Flournoy ADMIN | .07 | .03 | .01 |
| ☐ 359 Line Stars | .15 | .06 | .01 | ☐ 448 Mike Hicks | .07 | .03 | .01 |
| (Jackie Burkett | | | | ☐ 449 Larry Hill | .07 | .03 | .01 |
| and Zeke Smith) | | | | ☐ 450 Tim Baker | .07 | .03 | .01 |
| ☐ 360 Bob Scarbrough | .07 | .03 | .01 | ☐ 451 Danny Bentley | .07 | .03 | .01 |
| ☐ 361 Jimmy Speigner | .07 | .03 | .01 | ☐ 452 Tommy Lowry | .07 | .03 | .01 |
| ☐ 362 Danny Speigner | .07 | .03 | .01 | ☐ 453 Jim Price | .07 | .03 | .01 |
| ☐ 363 Alvin Bresler | .07 | .03 | .01 | ☐ 454 Lloyd Nix | .07 | .03 | .01 |
| ☐ 364 Wade Whatley | .07 | .03 | .01 | ☐ 455 Kenny Burks | .07 | .03 | .01 |
| ☐ 365 Lance Hill | .07 | .03 | .01 | ☐ 456 Rusty and Sallie Deen | .07 | .03 | .01 |
| ☐ 366 Andy Steele | .07 | .03 | .01 | ADMIN | | | |
| ☐ 367 John Whatley | .07 | .03 | .01 | ☐ 457 Johnny Sumner | .07 | .03 | .01 |
| ☐ 368 Alton Shell | .07 | .03 | .01 | ☐ 458 Scott Blackmon | .07 | .03 | .01 |
| ☐ 369 Larry Blakeney | .07 | .03 | .01 | ☐ 459 Chuck Maxime | .07 | .03 | .01 |
| ☐ 370 Mickey Zofko | .07 | .03 | .01 | ☐ 460 Big SEC Wins (Chart) | .07 | .03 | .01 |
| ☐ 371 Gene Lorendo CO | .07 | .03 | .01 | ☐ 461 Bo Davis | .07 | .03 | .01 |
| ☐ 372 Mac Lorendo | .07 | .03 | .01 | ☐ 462 George Rose | .07 | .03 | .01 |
| ☐ 373 Buddy Davidson AD | .07 | .03 | .01 | ☐ 463 Bob Bradley | .07 | .03 | .01 |
| ☐ 374 Dave Woodward | .07 | .03 | .01 | ☐ 464 Steve Osburne | .07 | .03 | .01 |
| ☐ 375 Richard Guthrie | .07 | .03 | .01 | ☐ 465 George Gross | .07 | .03 | .01 |
| ☐ 376 George Rose | .07 | .03 | .01 | ☐ 466 Andy Gross | .07 | .03 | .01 |
| ☐ 377 Alan Bollinger | .07 | .03 | .01 | ☐ 467 M.L. Brackett | .07 | .03 | .01 |
| ☐ 378 Danny Sanspree | .07 | .03 | .01 | ☐ 468 Herman Wilkes | .07 | .03 | .01 |
| ☐ 379 Winky Giddens | .07 | .03 | .01 | ☐ 469 Roger Mitchell | .07 | .03 | .01 |
| ☐ 380 Franklin Fuller | .07 | .03 | .01 | ☐ 470 Bobby Beaird | .07 | .03 | .01 |
| ☐ 381 Charles Collins | .07 | .03 | .01 | ☐ 471 Sammy Oates | .07 | .03 | .01 |
| ☐ 382 Auburn, 23-22 | .07 | .03 | .01 | ☐ 472 Jimmy Ricketts | .07 | .03 | .01 |
| (Scoreboard) | | | | ☐ 473 Bucky Ayters | .07 | .03 | .01 |
| ☐ 383 Jeff Weekley | .07 | .03 | .01 | ☐ 474 Bill James | .07 | .03 | .01 |
| ☐ 384 Larry Haynie | .07 | .03 | .01 | ☐ 475 Johnny Wallis | .07 | .03 | .01 |
| ☐ 385 Miles Jones | .07 | .03 | .01 | ☐ 476 Chris Jornson | .07 | .03 | .01 |
| ☐ 386 Bobby Wilson | .15 | .06 | .01 | ☐ 477 Joe Overton | .07 | .03 | .01 |
| ☐ 387 Bobby Lauder | .07 | .03 | .01 | ☐ 478 Tommy Lorino | .07 | .03 | .01 |
| ☐ 388 Charlie Glenn | .07 | .03 | .01 | ☐ 479 James Warren | .07 | .03 | .01 |
| ☐ 389 Claude Saia | .07 | .03 | .01 | ☐ 480 Lynn Johnson | .07 | .03 | .01 |
| ☐ 390 Tom Bryan | .07 | .03 | .01 | ☐ 481 Sam Mitchell | .07 | .03 | .01 |

| | | | |
|---|---|---|---|
| ☐ 482 Sedrick McIntyre | .07 | .03 | .01 |
| ☐ 483 Mike Holtzclaw | .07 | .03 | .01 |
| ☐ 484 Dave Ostrowski | .07 | .03 | .01 |
| ☐ 485 Jim Walsh | .07 | .03 | .01 |
| ☐ 486 Mike Henley | .07 | .03 | .01 |
| ☐ 487 Roy Tatum | .07 | .03 | .01 |
| ☐ 488 Al Parks | .07 | .03 | .01 |
| ☐ 489 Billy Wilson | .15 | .06 | .01 |
| ☐ 490 Ken Luke | .07 | .03 | .01 |
| ☐ 491 Phillip Hall | .07 | .03 | .01 |
| ☐ 492 Bruce Yates | .07 | .03 | .01 |
| ☐ 493 Dan Hataway | .07 | .03 | .01 |
| ☐ 494 Joe Leichtnam | .07 | .03 | .01 |
| ☐ 495 Danny Fulford | .07 | .03 | .01 |
| ☐ 496 Ken Hardy | .07 | .03 | .01 |
| ☐ 497 Rob Spivey | .07 | .03 | .01 |
| ☐ 498 Rick Telhiard | .07 | .03 | .01 |
| ☐ 499 Ron Yarbrough | .07 | .03 | .01 |
| ☐ 500 Leo Sexton | .07 | .03 | .01 |
| ☐ 501 Dick McGowen CO | .07 | .03 | .01 |
| ☐ 502 Lee Kidd | .07 | .03 | .01 |
| ☐ 503 Rex McKissick | .07 | .03 | .01 |
| ☐ 504 Fagen Canzoneri and Zach Jenkins | .07 | .03 | .01 |
| ☐ 505 Jim Bouchillon | .07 | .03 | .01 |
| ☐ 506 Forrest Blue | .20 | .08 | .02 |
| ☐ 507 Mike Helms | .07 | .03 | .01 |
| ☐ 508 Bobby Hunt | .15 | .06 | .01 |
| ☐ 509 John Liptak | .07 | .03 | .01 |
| ☐ 510 James McKinney | .07 | .03 | .01 |
| ☐ 511 Ed Baker | .07 | .03 | .01 |
| ☐ 512 Heisman Trophies | .25 | .10 | .02 |
| ☐ 513 Eddy Jackson | .07 | .03 | .01 |
| ☐ 514 Jimmy Powell | .07 | .03 | .01 |
| ☐ 515 Jerry Elliott | .07 | .03 | .01 |
| ☐ 516 Jimmy Jones | .07 | .03 | .01 |
| ☐ 517 Jimmy Laster | .07 | .03 | .01 |
| ☐ 518 Larry Laster | .07 | .03 | .01 |
| ☐ 519 Jerry Sansom | .07 | .03 | .01 |
| ☐ 520 Don Downs | .07 | .03 | .01 |
| ☐ 521 Danny Skutack | .07 | .03 | .01 |
| ☐ 522 Keith Green | .07 | .03 | .01 |
| ☐ 523 Spence McCracken | .07 | .03 | .01 |
| ☐ 524 Lloyd Cheattom | .07 | .03 | .01 |
| ☐ 525 Mike Shows | .07 | .03 | .01 |
| ☐ 526 Spec Kelley | .07 | .03 | .01 |
| ☐ 527 Dick McGowen | .07 | .03 | .01 |
| ☐ 528 Jon Kilgore | .07 | .03 | .01 |
| ☐ 529 Frank Gatski | .30 | .12 | .03 |
| ☐ 530 Joel Eaves | .07 | .03 | .01 |
| ☐ 531 John Adcock | .07 | .03 | .01 |
| ☐ 532 Jimmy Fenton | .07 | .03 | .01 |
| ☐ 533 Mike McCartney | .07 | .03 | .01 |
| ☐ 534 Harrison McCraw | .07 | .03 | .01 |
| ☐ 535 Mailon Kent | .07 | .03 | .01 |
| ☐ 536 Dickie Flournoy | .07 | .03 | .01 |
| ☐ 537 Coker Barton | .07 | .03 | .01 |
| ☐ 538 Scotty Elam | .07 | .03 | .01 |
| ☐ 539 Tim Wood | .07 | .03 | .01 |
| ☐ 540 Terry Fuller | .07 | .03 | .01 |
| ☐ 541 Johnny Kern | .07 | .03 | .01 |
| ☐ 542 Mike Currier | .07 | .03 | .01 |
| ☐ 543 Richard Cheek | .07 | .03 | .01 |
| ☐ 544 Dan Dickerson | .07 | .03 | .01 |
| ☐ 545 Arnold Fagen | .07 | .03 | .01 |
| ☐ 546 John "Rat" Riley | .15 | .06 | .01 |
| ☐ 547 Jimmy Burson | .15 | .06 | .01 |
| ☐ 548 Bob Fleming | .07 | .03 | .01 |
| ☐ 549 Mike Fitzhugh | .07 | .03 | .01 |
| ☐ 550 Jim Patton | .20 | .08 | .02 |
| ☐ 551 Bryant Harvard | .07 | .03 | .01 |
| ☐ 552 Leon Cochran | .07 | .03 | .01 |
| ☐ 553 Wayne Frazier | .07 | .03 | .01 |
| ☐ 554 Philip Dembowski | .07 | .03 | .01 |
| ☐ 555 Alex Spurlin and Ed Spurlin | .07 | .03 | .01 |
| ☐ 556 Bill Kilpatrick | .07 | .03 | .01 |
| ☐ 557 Gaines Lanier | .07 | .03 | .01 |
| ☐ 558 Johnny McDonald | .07 | .03 | .01 |
| ☐ 559 Ray Powell | .07 | .03 | .01 |
| ☐ 560 Jimmy Putman | .07 | .03 | .01 |
| ☐ 561 Bobby Wasden | .07 | .03 | .01 |
| ☐ 562 Roger Pruett | .07 | .03 | .01 |
| ☐ 563 Don Braswell | .07 | .03 | .01 |
| ☐ 564 Jim Jeffery | .07 | .03 | .01 |
| ☐ 565 Auburn-A TV Favorite (Pat Dye CO) | .15 | .06 | .01 |
| ☐ 566 Lamar Rawson | .07 | .03 | .01 |
| ☐ 567 Larry Rawson | .07 | .03 | .01 |
| ☐ 568 David Rawson | .07 | .03 | .01 |
| ☐ 569 Hal Herring CO | .07 | .03 | .01 |
| ☐ 570 Pat Sullivan | .20 | .08 | .02 |
| ☐ 571 John Cochran | .07 | .03 | .01 |
| ☐ 572 Jerry Gulledge | .07 | .03 | .01 |
| ☐ 573 Steve Stanaland | .15 | .06 | .01 |
| ☐ 574 Greg Zipp | .07 | .03 | .01 |
| ☐ 575 John Trotman | .07 | .03 | .01 |

| | | | |
|---|---|---|---|
| ☐ 576 Clyde Baumgartner | .07 | .03 | .01 |
| ☐ 577 Jay Casey | .07 | .03 | .01 |
| ☐ 578 Ralph O'Gwynne | .07 | .03 | .01 |
| ☐ 579 Sid Scarborough | .07 | .03 | .01 |
| ☐ 580 Tom Banks Sr. | .15 | .06 | .01 |

# 1991 Auburn Hoby

This 42-card set was produced by Hoby and features the 1991 Auburn football team. Five hundred uncut press sheets were also produced, and they were signed and numbered by Pat Dye. The standard size (2 1/2" by 3 1/2") cards feature on the fronts a mix of posed and action color photos, with thin white borders on a royal blue card face. The school logo occurs in the lower left corner in an orange circle, with the player's name in a gold stripe extending to the right. On a light orange background, the backs carry biography, player profile, or statistics. The cards are numbered on the back.

| | MINT | EXC | G-VG |
|---|---|---|---|
| COMPLETE SET (42) | 9.00 | 3.75 | .90 |
| COMMON CARD (523-564) | .25 | .10 | .02 |

| | | | |
|---|---|---|---|
| ☐ 523 Thomas Bailey | .25 | .10 | .02 |
| ☐ 524 Corey Barlow | .35 | .14 | .03 |
| ☐ 525 Reggie Barlow | .35 | .14 | .03 |
| ☐ 526 Fred Baxter | .35 | .14 | .03 |
| ☐ 527 Eddie Blake | .35 | .14 | .03 |
| ☐ 528 Herbert Casey | .25 | .10 | .02 |
| ☐ 529 Pedro Cherry | .25 | .10 | .02 |
| ☐ 530 Darrel Crawford | .35 | .14 | .03 |
| ☐ 531 Tim Cromartie | .35 | .14 | .03 |
| ☐ 532 Juan Crum | .25 | .10 | .02 |
| ☐ 533 Karekin Cunningham | .25 | .10 | .02 |
| ☐ 534 Alonzo Etheridge | .25 | .10 | .02 |
| ☐ 535 Joe Frazier | .25 | .10 | .02 |
| ☐ 536 Pat Dye AD/CO | .35 | .14 | .03 |
| ☐ 537 Thery George | .25 | .10 | .02 |
| ☐ 538 Chris Gray | .35 | .14 | .03 |
| ☐ 539 Victor Hall | .25 | .10 | .02 |
| ☐ 540 Randy Hart | .25 | .10 | .02 |
| ☐ 541 Chris Holland | .25 | .10 | .02 |
| ☐ 542 Chuckie Johnson | .25 | .10 | .02 |
| ☐ 543 Anthony Judge | .25 | .10 | .02 |
| ☐ 544 Corey Lewis | .25 | .10 | .02 |
| ☐ 545 Reid McMilion | .25 | .10 | .02 |
| ☐ 546 Bob Meeks | .25 | .10 | .02 |
| ☐ 547 Dale Overton | .25 | .10 | .02 |
| ☐ 548 Mike Pelton | .25 | .10 | .02 |
| ☐ 549 Bennie Pierce | .25 | .10 | .02 |
| ☐ 550 Mike Pina | .25 | .10 | .02 |
| ☐ 551 Anthony Redmon | .25 | .10 | .02 |
| ☐ 552 Tony Richardson | .25 | .10 | .02 |
| ☐ 553 Richard Shea | .25 | .10 | .02 |
| ☐ 554 Fred Smith | .25 | .10 | .02 |
| ☐ 555 Otis Mounds | .25 | .10 | .02 |
| ☐ 556 Ricky Sutton | .25 | .10 | .02 |
| ☐ 557 Alex Thomas | .25 | .10 | .02 |
| ☐ 558 Greg Thompson | .25 | .10 | .02 |
| ☐ 559 Jim Tillman | .25 | .10 | .02 |
| ☐ 560 Jim Von Wyl | .25 | .10 | .02 |
| ☐ 561 Stan White | .50 | .20 | .05 |
| ☐ 562 Darrell Williams | .25 | .10 | .02 |
| ☐ 563 James Willis | .25 | .10 | .02 |
| ☐ 564 Jon Wilson | .25 | .10 | .02 |

# 1993 Baylor

Sponsored by First Waco National Bank, the 21 cards comprising this set were issued as perforated game program insert sheets. The three perforated sheets measure approximately 7 5/8" by 11". Each sheet consists of seven player cards and a sponsor card, which is the size of

two player cards. Each perforated player card measures approximately 2 7/16" by 3 5/16" and features green-bordered posed color head shots of helmetless players. The player's name and position appear within an orange banner at the bottom. The team name, Baylor Bears, appears in white lettering within a black bar at the upper right. The player's uniform number is shown in white within a black circle at the upper left. The white back carries the player's name, position, and biography in bold black lettering at the upper right. Previous season highlights follow below. The player's uniform number appears in white within a black icon of a bear's paw at the upper left, but otherwise the cards are unnumbered and so checklisted below in alphabetical order.

|  | MINT | EXC | G-VG |
|---|---|---|---|
| COMPLETE SET (21) | 12.00 | 5.00 | 1.20 |
| COMMON PLAYER (1-21) | .60 | .24 | .06 |
| ☐ 1 Lamone Alexander | .60 | .24 | .06 |
| ☐ 2 Joseph Asbell | .60 | .24 | .06 |
| ☐ 3 Marvin Callies | .60 | .24 | .06 |
| ☐ 4 Todd Crawford | .60 | .24 | .06 |
| ☐ 5 Earnest Crownover | .60 | .24 | .06 |
| ☐ 6 Will Davidson | 1.00 | .40 | .10 |
| ☐ 7 Chris Dull | .60 | .24 | .06 |
| ☐ 8 Raynor Finley | .60 | .24 | .06 |
| ☐ 9 J.J. Joe | 2.00 | .80 | .20 |
| ☐ 10 Phillip Kent | .60 | .24 | .06 |
| ☐ 11 David Leaks | .60 | .24 | .06 |
| ☐ 12 Scotty Lewis | 1.00 | .40 | .10 |
| ☐ 13 Fred Miller | 1.00 | .40 | .10 |
| ☐ 14 Bruce Nowak | .60 | .24 | .06 |
| ☐ 15 Mike Oatis | .60 | .24 | .06 |
| ☐ 16 Chuck Pope | .60 | .24 | .06 |
| ☐ 17 Adrian Robinson | .60 | .24 | .06 |
| ☐ 18 Tyrone Smith | .60 | .24 | .06 |
| ☐ 19 Andrew Swasey | .60 | .24 | .06 |
| ☐ 20 Byron Thompson | .60 | .24 | .06 |
| ☐ 21 Tony Tubbs | .60 | .24 | .06 |

## 1984 BYU All-Time Greats

This 15-card set features BYU's all-time great football players since 1958. The sets were sold in a plastic bag, and the back of the attached paper tab indicated that additional sets could be purchased for 2.00 plus 75 cents for postage and handling. The cards measure the standard size (2 1/2" by 3 1/2"). On a white card face, the fronts display both close-up and action player photos that have a purple tint. The top reads "All-Time Cougar Greats B.Y.U.," with the words "Cougar Greats" in a purple banner. The player's name is printed in purple in the bottom white border. The horizontal backs are gray and carry biography, BYU career statistics, and a career summary. The cards are numbered on the back.

|  | MINT | EXC | G-VG |
|---|---|---|---|
| COMPLETE SET (15) | 15.00 | 6.00 | 1.50 |
| COMMON PLAYER (1-15) | .50 | .20 | .05 |
| ☐ 1 Steve Young | 9.00 | 3.75 | .90 |
| ☐ 2 Eldon Fortie | .50 | .20 | .05 |
| ☐ 3 Bart Oates | 1.50 | .60 | .15 |
| ☐ 4 Pete VanValkenburg | .50 | .20 | .05 |
| ☐ 5 Mike Mees | .50 | .20 | .05 |
| ☐ 6 Wayne Baker | .50 | .20 | .05 |
| ☐ 7 Gordon Gravelle | .75 | .30 | .07 |
| ☐ 8 Gordon Hudson | 1.00 | .40 | .10 |
| ☐ 9 Kurt Gunther | .50 | .20 | .05 |
| ☐ 10 Todd Shell | 1.00 | .40 | .10 |
| ☐ 11 Chris Farasopoulos | 1.00 | .40 | .10 |
| ☐ 12 Paul Howard | .50 | .20 | .05 |
| ☐ 13 Dave Atkinson | .50 | .20 | .05 |
| ☐ 14 Paul Linford | .50 | .20 | .05 |
| ☐ 15 Phil Odle | .75 | .30 | .07 |

## 1990 BYU Safety

This 12-card standard size (2 1/2" by 3 1/2") set was issued in Utah in conjunction with three area hospitals to promote safety. The fronts of the cards feature the hospitals' names on the top while underneath them are full-color action shots framed in the blue and white colors of the Cougars. The word "Cougars" is on top of the photo with the year "1990" on the right side and the player's name and position on the bottom of the card. The backs have biographical information as well as various safety tips. The set was issued in three strips of four cards; since the cards are unnumbered, we are listing them in alphabetical order. This set features an early card of 1990 Heisman trophy winner Ty Detmer.

|  | MINT | EXC | G-VG |
|---|---|---|---|
| COMPLETE SET (12) | 15.00 | 6.00 | 1.50 |
| COMMON PLAYER (1-12) | 1.00 | .40 | .10 |
| ☐ 1 Rocky Beigel | 1.00 | .40 | .10 |
| ☐ 2 Matt Bellini | 1.00 | .40 | .10 |
| ☐ 3 Tony Crutchfield | 1.00 | .40 | .10 |
| ☐ 4 Ty Detmer | 6.00 | 2.40 | .60 |
| ☐ 5 Norm Dixon | 1.00 | .40 | .10 |
| ☐ 6 Earl Kauffman | 1.00 | .40 | .10 |
| ☐ 7 Rich Kaufusi | 1.50 | .60 | .15 |
| ☐ 8 Bryan May | 1.00 | .40 | .10 |
| ☐ 9 Brent Nyberg | 1.00 | .40 | .10 |
| ☐ 10 Chris Smith | 2.00 | .80 | .20 |
| ☐ 11 Mark Smith | 1.00 | .40 | .10 |
| ☐ 12 Robert Stephens | 1.00 | .40 | .10 |

## 1991 BYU Safety

This 16-card set was sponsored by Orem Community Hospital, Utah Valley Regional Medical Center, and American Fork Hospital. The cards measure the standard size (2 1/2" by 3 1/2") and were issued in four-card perforated strips at four different home games. The fronts feature a full-color action shot enclosed by a three-sided blue drop border and a small white border at the left. The name "Cougars" is in white reversed-out letters in the top blue border, while 1991 runs down the right side, and the player's name and position are in the bottom border. Sponsor logos appear in aqua lettering at the top, while the school logo is in blue in the lower left corner. Card backs feature player profile, "Tips from the Cougars" (anti-drug or alcohol messages), and sponsor names. The cards are unnumbered and checklisted below in alphabetical order.

| | MINT | EXC | G-VG |
|---|---|---|---|
| COMPLETE SET (16) | 10.00 | 4.00 | 1.00 |
| COMMON CARD (1-16) | .75 | .30 | .07 |
| ☐ 1 Josh Arnold | .75 | .30 | .07 |
| ☐ 2 Rocky Biegel | .75 | .30 | .07 |
| ☐ 3 Scott Charlton | .75 | .30 | .07 |
| ☐ 4 Tony Crutchfield | .75 | .30 | .07 |
| ☐ 5 Ty Detmer | 3.00 | 1.20 | .30 |
| ☐ 6 LaVell Edwards CO | 1.25 | .50 | .12 |
| ☐ 7 Scott Giles | .75 | .30 | .07 |
| ☐ 8 Derwin Gray | 1.00 | .40 | .10 |
| ☐ 9 Shad Hansen | .75 | .30 | .07 |
| ☐ 10 Brad Hunter | .75 | .30 | .07 |
| ☐ 11 Earl Kauffman | .75 | .30 | .07 |
| ☐ 12 Jared Leavitt | .75 | .30 | .07 |
| ☐ 13 Micah Matsuzaki | .75 | .30 | .07 |
| ☐ 14 Bryan May | .75 | .30 | .07 |
| ☐ 15 Peter Tuipulotu | .75 | .30 | .07 |
| ☐ 16 Matt Zundel | .75 | .30 | .07 |

## 1992 BYU Safety

This 16-card set was sponsored by Fillmore Medical Center, an Intermountain Health Care facility. The cards measure the standard size (2 1/2" by 3 1/2") and were issued in four-card perforated strips. The fronts feature a glossy full-color action shot enclosed by a three-sided blue border and a small white border at the left. The name "Cougars" is in white lettering in the top blue border, "1992" runs down the right side, and the player's name and position are in the bottom border. The sponsor logo appears in blue lettering at the top, while the school logo is in blue at the lower left corner. The card backs feature a player profile, "Tips from the Cougars" (anti-drug or alcohol messages), and sponsor names. The cards are unnumbered and checklisted below in alphabetical order.

| | MINT | EXC | G-VG |
|---|---|---|---|
| COMPLETE SET (16) | 10.00 | 4.00 | 1.00 |
| COMMON CARD (1-16) | .60 | .24 | .06 |
| ☐ 1 Tyler Anderson | .60 | .24 | .06 |
| ☐ 2 Randy Brock | .75 | .30 | .07 |
| ☐ 3 Brad Clark | .60 | .24 | .06 |
| ☐ 4 Eric Drage | 1.00 | .40 | .10 |
| ☐ 5 LaVell Edwards CO | 1.00 | .40 | .10 |
| ☐ 6 Mike Empey | .60 | .24 | .06 |
| ☐ 7 Lenny Gomes | .75 | .30 | .07 |
| ☐ 8 Derwin Gray | 1.00 | .40 | .10 |
| ☐ 9 Shad Hansen | .60 | .24 | .06 |
| ☐ 10 Eli Herring | .75 | .30 | .07 |
| ☐ 11 Micah Matsuzaki | .60 | .24 | .06 |
| ☐ 12 Patrick Mitchell | .75 | .30 | .07 |
| ☐ 13 Garry Pay | .60 | .24 | .06 |
| ☐ 14 Greg Pitts | .60 | .24 | .06 |
| ☐ 15 Byron Rex | 1.00 | .40 | .10 |
| ☐ 16 Jamal Willis | 1.00 | .40 | .10 |

## 1993 BYU

These 20 cards measure 2 3/4" by 3 3/4" and feature on their fronts blue-bordered color player action shots. These photos are offset slightly toward the upper right, making the margins on the top and right narrower. In the wide left margin appears the words "Brigham Young Football '93" in black lettering. The player's name, position, and uniform number rest in the wide lower margin. The gray and white horizontal back carries player biography, career highlights, and statistics. A paper tag on the cello pack carries a handwritten set number out of a total production run of 3,000 sets. The cards are unnumbered and checklisted below in alphabetical order.

| | MINT | EXC | G-VG |
|---|---|---|---|
| COMPLETE SET (20) | 12.00 | 5.00 | 1.20 |
| COMMON PLAYER (1-20) | .50 | .20 | .05 |
| ☐ 1 Tyler Anderson | .50 | .20 | .05 |
| ☐ 2 Randy Brock | .75 | .30 | .07 |
| ☐ 3 Frank Christianson | .50 | .20 | .05 |
| ☐ 4 Eric Drage | 1.00 | .40 | .10 |
| ☐ 5 LaVell Edwards CO | .75 | .30 | .07 |
| ☐ 6 Mike Empey | .50 | .20 | .05 |
| ☐ 7 Lenny Gomes | .75 | .30 | .07 |
| ☐ 8 Kalin Hall | .50 | .20 | .05 |
| ☐ 9 Nathan Hall | .50 | .20 | .05 |
| ☐ 10 Hema Heimuli | .50 | .20 | .05 |
| ☐ 11 Todd Herget | .50 | .20 | .05 |
| ☐ 12 Eli Herring | .75 | .30 | .07 |
| ☐ 13 Micah Matsuzaki | .50 | .20 | .05 |
| ☐ 14 Casey Mazzota | .50 | .20 | .05 |
| ☐ 15 Patrick Mitchell | .75 | .30 | .07 |
| ☐ 16 Evan Pilgrim | .75 | .30 | .07 |
| ☐ 17 Greg Pitts | .50 | .20 | .05 |
| ☐ 18 Vic Tarleton | .50 | .20 | .05 |
| ☐ 19 John Walsh | 2.00 | .80 | .20 |
| ☐ 20 Jamal Willis | 1.00 | .40 | .10 |

## 1988 California Smokey

The 1988 California Bears Smokey set contains 12 standard-size (2 1/2" by 3 1/2") cards. The fronts feature color action photos with name, position, and jersey number. The vertically oriented backs have brief career highlights. The cards are unnumbered, so they are listed in alphabetical order by subject's name. The card fronts contain a yellow stripe on the top and bottom that includes the team and player names.

| | MINT | EXC | G-VG |
|---|---|---|---|
| COMPLETE SET (12) | 12.00 | 5.00 | 1.20 |
| COMMON CARD (1-12) | 1.25 | .50 | .12 |

| | MINT | EXC | G-VG |
|---|---|---|---|
| ☐ 1 Rob Bimson | 1.25 | .50 | .12 |
| ☐ 2 Joel Dickson | 1.25 | .50 | .12 |
| ☐ 3 Robert DosRemedios | 1.25 | .50 | .12 |
| ☐ 4 Mike Ford | 1.25 | .50 | .12 |
| ☐ 5 Darryl Ingram | 1.25 | .50 | .12 |
| ☐ 6 David Ortega | 1.25 | .50 | .12 |
| ☐ 7 Chris Richards | 1.25 | .50 | .12 |
| ☐ 8 Bruce Snyder CO | 1.50 | .60 | .15 |
| ☐ 9 Troy Taylor | 2.50 | 1.00 | .25 |
| ☐ 10 Natu Tuatagaloa | 2.00 | .80 | .20 |
| ☐ 11 Majett Whiteside | 1.25 | .50 | .12 |
| ☐ 12 Dave Zawatson | 1.25 | .50 | .12 |

## 1989 California Smokey

The 1989 California Bears Smokey set contains 16 standard-size (2 1/2" by 3 1/2") cards. The fronts feature color action photos with name, position, and jersey number. The vertically oriented backs have brief career highlights. The cards are unnumbered, so they are listed by jersey numbers. The card fronts contain a player photo bordered on the left by a yellow stripe and a blue stripe on the right and below the photo.

| | MINT | EXC | G-VG |
|---|---|---|---|
| COMPLETE SET (16) | 12.00 | 5.00 | 1.20 |
| COMMON CARD | 1.00 | .40 | .10 |
| ☐ 1 John Hardy | 1.00 | .40 | .10 |
| ☐ 2 Mike Ford | 1.00 | .40 | .10 |
| ☐ 10 Robbie Keen | 1.00 | .40 | .10 |
| ☐ 11 Troy Taylor | 1.50 | .60 | .15 |
| ☐ 20 Dwayne Jones | 1.00 | .40 | .10 |
| ☐ 21 Travis Oliver | 1.00 | .40 | .10 |
| ☐ 34 Darrin Greer | 1.00 | .40 | .10 |
| ☐ 40 David Ortega | 1.00 | .40 | .10 |
| ☐ 41 Dan Slevin | 1.00 | .40 | .10 |
| ☐ 52 Troy Auzenne | 2.00 | .80 | .20 |
| ☐ 69 Tony Smith | 1.00 | .40 | .10 |
| ☐ 80 Junior Tagaloa | 1.00 | .40 | .10 |
| ☐ 83 Michael Smith | 1.00 | .40 | .10 |
| ☐ 95 DeWayne Odom | 1.00 | .40 | .10 |
| ☐ 99 Joel Dickson | 1.00 | .40 | .10 |
| ☐ xx Bruce Snyder CO | 1.25 | .50 | .12 |

## 1990 California Smokey

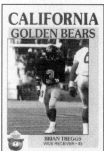

The 1990 California Bears Smokey set contains 16 standard-size (2 1/2" by 3 1/2") cards. The fronts feature a color action photo bordered in yellow on three sides, with the player's name, position, and jersey number below the picture. The backs have brief career highlights and a fire prevention cartoon starring Smokey the Bear. These

unnumbered cards are listed in alphabetical order below for convenience. The card fronts contain a player photo bordered on three sides by a yellow stripe.

| | MINT | EXC | G-VG |
|---|---|---|---|
| COMPLETE SET (16) | 10.00 | 4.00 | 1.00 |
| COMMON CARD (1-16) | .75 | .30 | .07 |
| ☐ 1 Troy Auzenne 52 | 1.50 | .60 | .15 |
| ☐ 2 John Belli 61 | .75 | .30 | .07 |
| ☐ 3 Joel Dickson 99 | .75 | .30 | .07 |
| ☐ 4 Ron English 42 | .75 | .30 | .07 |
| ☐ 5 Rhett Hall 57 | .75 | .30 | .07 |
| ☐ 6 John Hardy 1 | .75 | .30 | .07 |
| ☐ 7 Robbie Keen 10 | .75 | .30 | .07 |
| ☐ 8 DeWayne Odom 95 | .75 | .30 | .07 |
| ☐ 9 Mike Pawlawski 9 | 1.50 | .60 | .15 |
| ☐ 10 Castle Redmond 37 | .75 | .30 | .07 |
| ☐ 11 James Richards 64 | .75 | .30 | .07 |
| ☐ 12 Ernie Rogers 68 | .75 | .30 | .07 |
| ☐ 13 Bruce Snyder CO | 1.25 | .50 | .12 |
| ☐ 14 Brian Treggs 3 | 1.25 | .50 | .12 |
| ☐ 15 Anthony Wallace 6 | .75 | .30 | .07 |
| ☐ 16 Greg Zomalt 28 | .75 | .30 | .07 |

## 1991 California Smokey

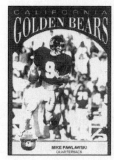

This 16-card set was sponsored by the USDA Forest Service and other agencies. The cards measure the standard size (2 1/2" by 3 1/2") and are printed on thin cardboard stock. The card fronts are accented in the team's colors (dark blue and yellow) and have glossy color action player photos. The top of the pictures is curved to resemble an archway, and the team name follows the curve of the arch. The player's name and position appear in a stripe below the picture. The backs present player profile and a fire prevention cartoon starring Smokey. The cards are unnumbered and checklisted below in alphabetical order.

| | MINT | EXC | G-VG |
|---|---|---|---|
| COMPLETE SET (16) | 15.00 | 6.00 | 1.50 |
| COMMON CARD (1-16) | .75 | .30 | .07 |
| ☐ 1 Troy Auzenne | 1.50 | .60 | .15 |
| ☐ 2 Chris Cannon | .75 | .30 | .07 |
| ☐ 3 Cornell Collier | .75 | .30 | .07 |
| ☐ 4 Sean Dawkins | 4.00 | 1.60 | .40 |
| ☐ 5 Steve Gordon | .75 | .30 | .07 |
| ☐ 6 Mike Pawlawski | 1.25 | .50 | .12 |
| ☐ 7 Bruce Snyder CO | 1.25 | .50 | .12 |
| ☐ 8 Todd Steussie | 1.25 | .50 | .12 |
| ☐ 9 Mack Travis | .75 | .30 | .07 |
| ☐ 10 Brian Treggs | 1.25 | .50 | .12 |
| ☐ 11 Russell White | 3.00 | 1.20 | .30 |
| ☐ 12 Jason Wilborn | .75 | .30 | .07 |
| ☐ 13 David Wilson | .75 | .30 | .07 |
| ☐ 14 Brent Woodall | .75 | .30 | .07 |
| ☐ 15 Eric Zomalt | 1.25 | .50 | .12 |
| ☐ 16 Greg Zomalt | .75 | .30 | .07 |

## 1992 California Smokey

This 16-card set was sponsored by the USDA Forest Service and other state and federal agencies. The cards measure the standard size (2 1/2" by 3 1/2") and are printed on thin card stock. The fronts carry a color action player photo on a navy blue card face. The team name and year appear above the photo in yellow print on a navy blue bar that partially rests on a yellow bar with notched ends. Below the photo, the player's name and sponsor logos appear in a yellow border stripe. The backs carry player profile and a fire prevention cartoon starring Smokey. The cards are unnumbered and checklisted below in alphabetical order.

| | MINT | EXC | G-VG |
|---|---|---|---|
| COMPLETE SET (16) | 10.00 | 4.00 | 1.00 |
| COMMON CARD (1-16) | .60 | .24 | .06 |
| ☐ 1 Chidi Ahanotu | .60 | .24 | .06 |
| ☐ 2 Wolf Barber | .60 | .24 | .06 |
| ☐ 3 Mick Barsala | .60 | .24 | .06 |
| ☐ 4 Doug Brien | .75 | .30 | .07 |
| ☐ 5 Al Casner | .60 | .24 | .06 |
| ☐ 6 Lindsey Chapman | 1.00 | .40 | .10 |
| ☐ 7 Sean Dawkins | 3.00 | 1.20 | .30 |
| ☐ 8 Keith Gilbertson CO | .75 | .30 | .07 |
| ☐ 9 Eric Mahlum | 1.00 | .40 | .10 |
| ☐ 10 Chris Noonan | .60 | .24 | .06 |
| ☐ 11 Todd Steussie | 1.00 | .40 | .10 |
| ☐ 12 Mack Travis | .75 | .30 | .07 |
| ☐ 13 Russell White | 2.00 | .80 | .20 |
| ☐ 14 Jerrott Willard | 1.25 | .50 | .12 |
| ☐ 15 Eric Zomalt | 1.00 | .40 | .10 |
| ☐ 16 Greg Zomalt | .60 | .24 | .06 |

## 1993 California Smokey

Printed on thin card stock, this 16-card standard-size (2 1/2" by 3 1/2") set was sponsored by the USDA, the Forest Service, and other state and federal agencies. The fronts feature color player action shots framed by thin white and black lines and with gold-colored borders highlighted by oblique white stripes. The team's name appears within the upper margin, and the player's name and position, along with the Smokey 50-year celebration logo, rest in the lower margin. The white backs carry player profile and a fire prevention cartoon starring Smokey. The cards are unnumbered and checklisted below in alphabetical order.

| | MINT | EXC | G-VG |
|---|---|---|---|
| COMPLETE SET (16) | 10.00 | 4.00 | 1.00 |
| COMMON PLAYER (1-16) | .60 | .24 | .06 |
| ☐ 1 Dave Barr | 1.00 | .40 | .10 |
| ☐ 2 Doug Brien | .75 | .30 | .07 |
| ☐ 3 Mike Caldwell | .60 | .24 | .06 |
| ☐ 4 Lindsey Chapman | .75 | .30 | .07 |
| ☐ 5 Jerod Cherry | .60 | .24 | .06 |
| ☐ 6 Michael Davis | .60 | .24 | .06 |
| ☐ 7 Tyrone Edwards | .60 | .24 | .06 |
| ☐ 8 Keith Gilbertson CO | .75 | .30 | .07 |
| ☐ 9 Jody Graham | .60 | .24 | .06 |
| ☐ 10 Marty Holly | .60 | .24 | .06 |
| ☐ 11 Paul Joiner | .75 | .30 | .07 |
| ☐ 12 Eric Mahlum | .75 | .30 | .07 |
| ☐ 13 Damien Semien | .60 | .24 | .06 |
| ☐ 14 Todd Steussie | .75 | .30 | .07 |
| ☐ 15 Jerrott Willard | 1.00 | .40 | .10 |
| ☐ 16 Eric Zomalt | .75 | .30 | .07 |

## 1989 Clemson

This 32-card set commemorates the Clemson Tigers as the 1989 Mazda Gator Bowl Champions. It was sponsored by Carolina Pride and measures the standard size, 2 1/2" by 3 1/2". The front presents either a posed or action color photo. Two orange bands with black lettering on the top and bottom have the school, player's name, number, classification, and position. The Carolina Pride logo appears in the lower left hand corner and the Tiger pawprint appears in the upper left hand corner. The back has biographical information and a tip from the Tigers in the form of an anti-drug or alcohol message. The cards are unnumbered and are listed below in alphabetical order by subject.

| | MINT | EXC | G-VG |
|---|---|---|---|
| COMPLETE SET (32) | 20.00 | 8.00 | 2.00 |
| COMMON CARD (1-32) | .75 | .30 | .07 |
| ☐ 1 Wally Ake CO | .75 | .30 | .07 |
| ☐ 2 Larry Beckman CO | .75 | .30 | .07 |
| ☐ 3 Mitch Belton 32 | .75 | .30 | .07 |
| ☐ 4 Scott Beville 61 | .75 | .30 | .07 |
| ☐ 5 Doug Brewster 92 | .75 | .30 | .07 |
| ☐ 6 Larry Brinson CO | 1.25 | .50 | .12 |
| ☐ 7 Reggie Demps 30 | .75 | .30 | .07 |
| ☐ 8 Robin Eaves 44 | .75 | .30 | .07 |
| ☐ 9 Barney Farrar CO | .75 | .30 | .07 |
| ☐ 10 Stacy Fields 46 | .75 | .30 | .07 |
| ☐ 11 Vance Hammond 90 | .75 | .30 | .07 |
| ☐ 12 Eric Harmon 76 | .75 | .30 | .07 |
| ☐ 13 Ken Hatfield CO | 1.50 | .60 | .15 |
| ☐ 14 Jerome Henderson 36 | 1.50 | .60 | .15 |
| ☐ 15 Les Herrin CO | .75 | .30 | .07 |
| ☐ 16 Roger Hinshaw CO | .75 | .30 | .07 |
| ☐ 17 John Johnson 12 | 1.50 | .60 | .15 |
| ☐ 18 Reggie Lawrence 34 | .75 | .30 | .07 |
| ☐ 19 Stacy Long 67 | .75 | .30 | .07 |
| ☐ 20 Eric Mader 82 | .75 | .30 | .07 |
| ☐ 21 Arlington Nunn 39 | .75 | .30 | .07 |
| ☐ 22 David Puckett 68 | .75 | .30 | .07 |
| ☐ 23 Danny Sizer 54 | .75 | .30 | .07 |
| ☐ 24 Robbie Spector 2 | .75 | .30 | .07 |
| ☐ 25 Rick Stockstill CO | 1.00 | .40 | .10 |
| ☐ 26 Bruce Taylor 6 | .75 | .30 | .07 |
| ☐ 27 Doug Thomas 41 | .75 | .30 | .07 |
| ☐ 28 The Tiger (Mascot) | .75 | .30 | .07 |
| ☐ 29 Tiger Paw Title Card | .75 | .30 | .07 |
| ☐ 30 Bob Trott CO | .75 | .30 | .07 |
| ☐ 31 Larry VanDerHeyden CO | .75 | .30 | .07 |
| ☐ 32 Richard Wilson CO | .75 | .30 | .07 |

## 1950 C.O.P. Betsy Ross

Subtitled C.O.P.'s Player of the Week, this six-card set features outstanding players from College of the Pacific. The date of the set is fixed by the Eddie LeBaron card, which listed him as a senior. The oversized cards measure approximately 5" by 7" and are printed on thin paper stock. The fronts feature black-and-white posed action shots that are tilted slightly to the left and have rounded corners. The top stripe carries brief biographical information and career highlights. The bottom stripe notes that these cards were distributed "as a public service by your neighborhood Grocer and Betsy Ross Bread." The bread company's logo at the lower right corner rounds out the back. Other cards may belong to this set. The backs are blank and the unnumbered cards are listed below in alphabetical order.

|  | NRMT | VG-E | GOOD |
|---|---|---|---|
| COMPLETE SET (6) | 75.00 | 30.00 | 7.50 |
| COMMON PLAYER (1-6) | 10.00 | 4.00 | 1.00 |
| ☐ 1 Don Campora | 10.00 | 4.00 | 1.00 |
| ☐ 2 Don Hardey | 10.00 | 4.00 | 1.00 |
| ☐ 3 Robert Klein | 10.00 | 4.00 | 1.00 |
| ☐ 4 Eddie LeBaron | 30.00 | 12.00 | 3.00 |
| ☐ 5 Eddie Macon | 15.00 | 6.00 | 1.50 |
| ☐ 6 John Rohde | 10.00 | 4.00 | 1.00 |

## 1990 Colorado Smokey

This 16-card standard size (2 1/2" by 3 1/2") set was issued to honor the eventual co-National Champion Colorado Buffaloes as well as to promote fire safety. This set was distributed at the final Colorado home game of the 1990 season at Folsom Field. Featured are some of the leading players on the Buffaloes including Eric Bieniemy, Darian Hagan, Charles Johnson, and Butkus Award winner Alfred Williams. The set was issued in a sheet of 16 cards which, when perforated, measure the standard size. The cards feature full-color action photos of the players on the front and a brief biography along with a safety tip featuring the popular safety figure, Smokey the Bear. This unnumbered set has been checklisted below in alphabetical order.

|  | MINT | EXC | G-VG |
|---|---|---|---|
| COMPLETE SET (16) | 20.00 | 8.00 | 2.00 |
| COMMON CARD (1-16) | 1.00 | .40 | .10 |
| ☐ 1 Eric Bieniemy | 3.00 | 1.20 | .30 |
| ☐ 2 Joe Garten | 1.50 | .60 | .15 |
| ☐ 3 Darian Hagan | 2.50 | 1.00 | .25 |
| ☐ 4 George Hemingway | 1.00 | .40 | .10 |
| ☐ 5 Garry Howe | 1.00 | .40 | .10 |
| ☐ 6 Tim James | 1.00 | .40 | .10 |
| ☐ 7 Charles Johnson | 4.00 | 1.60 | .40 |
| ☐ 8 Bill McCartney CO | 2.00 | .80 | .20 |
| ☐ 9 Dave McCloughan | 2.00 | .80 | .20 |
| ☐ 10 Kanavis McGhee | 2.00 | .80 | .20 |
| ☐ 11 Mike Pritchard | 6.00 | 2.40 | .60 |
| ☐ 12 Tom Rouen | 1.50 | .60 | .15 |
| ☐ 13 Michael Simmons | 1.00 | .40 | .10 |
| ☐ 14 Mark Vander Poel | 1.50 | .60 | .15 |
| ☐ 15 Alfred Williams | 2.50 | 1.00 | .25 |
| ☐ 16 Ralphie (Mascot) | 1.00 | .40 | .10 |

## 1992 Colorado Pepsi

Originally issued in perforated sheets, these 12 standard-size (2 1/2" by 3 1/2") cards feature on their fronts color player posed and action shots set within black borders and framed by a yellowish line. The player's name and position, along with the Pepsi logo, appear underneath the photo. The team name and logo appear above the photo. The plain white back carries the player's name and jersey number at the top, followed below by position, height, weight, class, hometown, major, and career highlights. The cards are unnumbered and checklisted below in alphabetical order.

|  | MINT | EXC | G-VG |
|---|---|---|---|
| COMPLETE SET (12) | 15.00 | 6.00 | 1.50 |
| COMMON PLAYER (1-12) | 1.25 | .50 | .12 |
| ☐ 1 Greg Biekert | 1.25 | .50 | .12 |
| ☐ 2 Pat Blottiaux | 1.25 | .50 | .12 |
| ☐ 3 Ronnie Bradford | 2.00 | .80 | .20 |
| ☐ 4 Chad Brown | 2.00 | .80 | .20 |
| ☐ 5 Marcellous Elder | 1.50 | .60 | .15 |
| ☐ 6 Deon Figures | 2.50 | 1.00 | .25 |
| ☐ 7 Jim Hansen | 1.25 | .50 | .12 |
| ☐ 8 Jack Keys | 1.25 | .50 | .12 |
| ☐ 9 Bill McCartney CO | 2.00 | .80 | .20 |
| ☐ 10 Clint Moles | 1.25 | .50 | .12 |
| ☐ 11 Jason Perkins | 1.25 | .50 | .12 |
| ☐ 12 Scott Starr | 1.25 | .50 | .12 |

## 1993 Colorado Smokey

Originally issued in perforated sheets, these 16 standard-size (2 1/2" by 3 1/2") cards feature on their fronts color player action shots set within yellowish borders with white diagonal stripes. The player's name and position appear on the left side underneath the photo. The team name and logo appear above the photo. The plain white back carries the player's name, jersey number, and position at the top, followed by a Smokey cartoon safety tip. The cards are unnumbered and checklisted below in alphabetical order.

|  | MINT | EXC | G-VG |
|---|---|---|---|
| COMPLETE SET (16) | 15.00 | 6.00 | 1.50 |
| COMMON PLAYER (1-16) | 1.25 | .50 | .12 |
| ☐ 1 Craig Anderson | 1.25 | .50 | .12 |
| ☐ 2 Mitch Berger | 1.25 | .50 | .12 |
| ☐ 3 Jeff Brunner | 1.25 | .50 | .12 |
| ☐ 4 Dennis Collier | 1.25 | .50 | .12 |
| ☐ 5 Dwayne Davis | 1.25 | .50 | .12 |
| ☐ 6 Brian Dyet | 1.25 | .50 | .12 |
| ☐ 7 Sean Embree | 1.25 | .50 | .12 |
| ☐ 8 Garrett Ford | 1.25 | .50 | .12 |
| ☐ 9 James Hill | 1.25 | .50 | .12 |
| ☐ 10 Charles Johnson | 3.50 | 1.40 | .35 |
| ☐ 11 Greg Lindsey | 1.25 | .50 | .12 |
| ☐ 12 Sam Rogers | 1.25 | .50 | .12 |
| ☐ 13 Mark Smith | 1.25 | .50 | .12 |
| ☐ 14 Duke Tobin | 1.25 | .50 | .12 |
| ☐ 15 Ron Woolfork | 2.50 | 1.00 | .25 |
| ☐ 16 Derek Agnew | 1.25 | .50 | .12 |

## 1973 Colorado State

The 1973 Colorado State football set consists of eight cards, measuring approximately 2 1/2" by 3 3/4". The set was sponsored by Poudre Valley Dairy Foods. The fronts display green-tinted posed action shots with rounded corners and green borders. The words "1973 CSU Football" appear in the top border while the player's name and position are printed in the bottom border. The horizontal backs present the 1973 football schedule. Reportedly, the Stuebbe and Simpson cards are more difficult to obtain because they were given out to the public before hobbyists began to collect the set. Best known among the players is Willie Miller, who played for the Los Angeles Rams. The cards are unnumbered and checklisted below in alphabetical order.

|  | NRMT | VG-E | GOOD |
|---|---|---|---|
| COMPLETE SET (8) | 50.00 | 20.00 | 5.00 |
| COMMON PLAYER (1-8) | 6.00 | 2.40 | .60 |
| □ 1 Wes Cerveny | 6.00 | 2.40 | .60 |
| □ 2 Mark Driscoll | 6.00 | 2.40 | .60 |
| □ 3 Jim Kennedy | 6.00 | 2.40 | .60 |
| □ 4 Greg Kuhn | 6.00 | 2.40 | .60 |
| □ 5 Willie Miller | 15.00 | 6.00 | 1.50 |
| □ 6 Al Simpson SP | 12.00 | 5.00 | 1.20 |
| □ 7 Jan Stuebbe SP | 12.00 | 5.00 | 1.20 |
| □ 8 Tom Wallace | 6.00 | 2.40 | .60 |

## 1987 Duke Police

This 16-card, standard-size (2 1/2" by 3 1/2") set features players on Duke University's 1987 Blue Devils football team. The set was distributed to elementary school children in North Carolina by local law enforcement representatives as part of a drug education program. The front has a color action player photo, with Adolescent CareUnit logos in the upper corners and the player's name, uniform number, and position centered beneath the picture. The back has two Duke helmet logos in the upper corners, biographical information, and an anti-drug tip. The cards are unnumbered and checklisted below in alphabetical order.

|  | MINT | EXC | G-VG |
|---|---|---|---|
| COMPLETE SET (16) | 25.00 | 10.00 | 2.50 |
| COMMON CARD (1-16) | 1.50 | .60 | .15 |
| □ 1 Andy Andreasik 60 | 1.50 | .60 | .15 |
| □ 2 Brian Bernard 93 | 1.50 | .60 | .15 |
| □ 3 Bob Calamari 31 | 1.50 | .60 | .15 |
| □ 4 Jason Cooper 22 | 1.50 | .60 | .15 |
| □ 5 Dave Demore 92 | 1.50 | .60 | .15 |

| □ 6 Mike Diminick 21 | 1.50 | .60 | .15 |
|---|---|---|---|
| □ 7 Jim Godfrey 56 | 1.50 | .60 | .15 |
| □ 8 Doug Green 5 | 1.50 | .60 | .15 |
| □ 9 Stanley Monk 24 | 1.50 | .60 | .15 |
| □ 10 Chris Port 73 | 2.50 | 1.00 | .25 |
| □ 11 Steve Ryan 61 | 1.50 | .60 | .15 |
| □ 12 Steve Slayden 7 | 2.50 | 1.00 | .25 |
| □ 13 Steve Spurrier CO | 6.00 | 2.40 | .60 |
| □ 14 Dewayne Terry 27 | 1.50 | .60 | .15 |
| □ 15 Fonda Williams 19 | 1.50 | .60 | .15 |
| □ 16 Blue Devil (Mascot) | 2.50 | 1.00 | .25 |

## 1988 Florida Burger King

This 16-card set features then-current football players at the University of Florida. The cards are numbered on the back in the lower right corner. The cards measure approximately 2 1/2" by 3 1/2". The set was produced by McDag Productions and sponsored by Burger King. The set is also considered to be a police/safety set due to the "Tip from the Gators" on each card back. The Emmitt Smith card from this set has been illegally reprinted; all known reprints (counterfeits) are missing the Burger King logo on the card front.

|  | MINT | EXC | G-VG |
|---|---|---|---|
| COMPLETE SET (16) | 25.00 | 10.00 | 2.50 |
| COMMON CARD (1-16) | .75 | .30 | .07 |
| □ 1 Florida Gators Team | 2.50 | 1.00 | .25 |
| □ 2 Emmitt Smith 22 | 15.00 | 6.00 | 1.50 |
| □ 3 David Williams 73 | 1.00 | .40 | .10 |
| □ 4 Jeff Roth 96 | .75 | .30 | .07 |
| □ 5 Rhondy Weston 68 | 1.00 | .40 | .10 |
| □ 6 Stacey Simmons 25 | 1.25 | .50 | .12 |
| □ 7 Huey Richardson 90 | 1.00 | .40 | .10 |
| □ 8 Wayne Williams 23 | 1.00 | .40 | .10 |
| □ 9 Charlie Wright 79 | .75 | .30 | .07 |
| □ 10 Tracy Daniels 63 | .75 | .30 | .07 |
| □ 11 Ernie Mills 14 | 2.00 | .80 | .20 |
| □ 12 Willie McGrady 38 | .75 | .30 | .07 |
| □ 13 Chris Bromley 52 | .75 | .30 | .07 |
| □ 14 Louis Oliver 18 | 2.00 | .80 | .20 |
| □ 15 Galen Hall CO | 1.25 | .50 | .12 |
| □ 16 Albert the Alligator (Mascot) | .75 | .30 | .07 |

## 1989 Florida

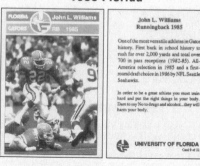

The 1989 Florida Gators football set contains 22 standard-size (2 1/2" by 3 1/2") cards of past players, i.e., all-time Gators. The fronts have vintage or color action photos with white borders; the vertically oriented backs have player profiles. These cards were distributed as a complete set. A safety message is included near the bottom of each reverse along with a card number.

| | MINT | EXC | G-VG |
|---|---|---|---|
| COMPLETE SET (22) | 10.00 | 4.00 | 1.00 |
| COMMON CARD (1-22) | .40 | .16 | .04 |
| ☐ 1 Dale VanSickle | .40 | .16 | .04 |
| ☐ 2 Cris Collinsworth | 1.25 | .50 | .12 |
| ☐ 3 Wilber Marshall | 1.25 | .50 | .12 |
| ☐ 4 Jack Youngblood | 1.25 | .50 | .12 |
| ☐ 5 Steve Spurrier | 1.50 | .60 | .15 |
| ☐ 6 David Little | .75 | .30 | .07 |
| ☐ 7 Bruce Bennett | .40 | .16 | .04 |
| ☐ 8 Charlie LaPradd | .40 | .16 | .04 |
| ☐ 9 John L. Williams | 1.25 | .50 | .12 |
| ☐ 10 Steve Tannen | .60 | .24 | .06 |
| ☐ 11 Neal Anderson | 1.25 | .50 | .12 |
| ☐ 12 Larry Dupree | .40 | .16 | .04 |
| ☐ 13 Guy Dennis | .40 | .16 | .04 |
| ☐ 14 Jarvis Williams | .60 | .24 | .06 |
| ☐ 15 Bill Carr | .40 | .16 | .04 |
| ☐ 16 Clifford Charlton | .60 | .24 | .06 |
| ☐ 17 Wes Chandler | 1.00 | .40 | .10 |
| ☐ 18 David Galloway | .60 | .24 | .06 |
| ☐ 19 Carlos Alvarez | .60 | .24 | .06 |
| ☐ 20 Lomas Brown | 1.00 | .40 | .10 |
| ☐ 21 Larry Smith | .40 | .16 | .04 |
| ☐ 22 Ricky Nattiel | .75 | .30 | .07 |

## 1989 Florida Smokey

This 16-card set measures the standard card size, 2 1/2" by 3 1/2". This set was issued with the cooperation of the USDA Forest Service, the Florida Division of Forestry, and the BDA and features members of the 1989 Florida Gators including a college card of future NFL player Emmitt Smith. The cards feature the words "Florida Gators 1989" on top of an action photo and a biography of the player and a fire prevention cartoon on the back. We have checklisted this set in alphabetical order and put the uniform number next to the player's name. Sets are sometimes found with only 15 cards, missing the Galen Hall card, which was apparently withdrawn after his termination as coach of the Gators.

| | MINT | EXC | G-VG |
|---|---|---|---|
| COMPLETE SET (16) | 25.00 | 10.00 | 2.50 |
| COMMON CARD (1-16) | 1.00 | .40 | .10 |
| ☐ 1 Chris Bromley 52 | 1.00 | .40 | .10 |
| ☐ 2 Richard Fain 28 | 1.25 | .50 | .12 |
| ☐ 3 John David Francis 7 | 1.00 | .40 | .10 |
| ☐ 4 Galen Hall CO SP | 6.00 | 2.40 | .60 |
| ☐ 5 Tony Lomack 20 | 1.00 | .40 | .10 |
| ☐ 6 Willie McClendon 5 | 2.00 | .80 | .20 |
| ☐ 7 Pat Moorer 45 | 1.00 | .40 | .10 |
| ☐ 8 Kyle Morris 1 | 1.00 | .40 | .10 |
| ☐ 9 Huey Richardson 90 | 1.25 | .50 | .12 |
| ☐ 10 Stacey Simmons 25 | 1.25 | .50 | .12 |
| ☐ 11 Emmitt Smith 22 | 12.50 | 5.00 | 1.25 |
| ☐ 12 Richard Starowesky 75 | 1.00 | .40 | .10 |
| ☐ 13 Kerry Watkins 4 | 1.00 | .40 | .10 |
| ☐ 14 Albert (Mascot) | 1.00 | .40 | .10 |
| ☐ 15 Cheerleaders | 1.50 | .60 | .15 |
| ☐ 16 Gator Helmet | 1.00 | .40 | .10 |

## 1990 Florida Smokey

This 12-card set was sponsored by the USDA Forest Service in conjunction with several other federal agencies. The standard size (2 1/2" by 3 1/2") cards have color action shots, with orange lettering and borders on a purple card face. The back has two Florida helmet icons

at the top and features a player profile and a fire prevention cartoon starring Smokey. The cards are unnumbered and checklisted below in alphabetical order, with the uniform number after the name.

| | MINT | EXC | G-VG |
|---|---|---|---|
| COMPLETE SET (12) | 15.00 | 6.00 | 1.50 |
| COMMON CARD (1-12) | 1.00 | .40 | .10 |
| ☐ 1 Terence Barber 3 | 1.00 | .40 | .10 |
| ☐ 2 Chris Bromley 52 | 1.00 | .40 | .10 |
| ☐ 3 Richard Fain 28 | 1.25 | .50 | .12 |
| ☐ 4 Willie McClendon 5 | 1.50 | .60 | .15 |
| ☐ 5 Dexter McNabb 21 | 1.50 | .60 | .15 |
| ☐ 6 Ernie Mills 14 | 2.00 | .80 | .20 |
| ☐ 7 Mark Murray 54 | 1.00 | .40 | .10 |
| ☐ 8 Jerry Odom 57 | 1.00 | .40 | .10 |
| ☐ 9 Huey Richardson 90 | 1.25 | .50 | .12 |
| ☐ 10 Steve Spurrier CO | 3.00 | 1.20 | .30 |
| ☐ 11 Albert and Alberta (Mascots) | 1.00 | .40 | .10 |
| ☐ 12 Mr. Two-Bits (Fan) | 1.00 | .40 | .10 |

## 1991 Florida Smokey

This 12-card set was sponsored by the USDA Forest Service and other agencies. The cards measure the standard size (2 1/2" by 3 1/2") and are printed on thin cardboard stock. The card fronts are accented in the team's colors (blue and red-orange) and have glossy color action player photos. The top of the pictures is curved to resemble an archway, and the team name follows the curve of the arch. The player's name and position appear in a stripe below the picture. The backs present a player profile and a fire prevention cartoon starring Smokey the Bear. The cards are unnumbered and checklisted below in alphabetical order.

| | MINT | EXC | G-VG |
|---|---|---|---|
| COMPLETE SET (12) | 12.00 | 5.00 | 1.20 |
| COMMON CARD (1-12) | 1.00 | .40 | .10 |
| ☐ 1 Ephesians Bartley | 1.25 | .50 | .12 |
| ☐ 2 Mike Brandon | 1.00 | .40 | .10 |
| ☐ 3 Brad Culpepper | 1.50 | .60 | .15 |
| ☐ 4 Arden Czyzewski | 1.00 | .40 | .10 |
| ☐ 5 Cal Dixon | 1.50 | .60 | .15 |
| ☐ 6 Tre Everett | 1.00 | .40 | .10 |
| ☐ 7 Hesham Ismail | 1.00 | .40 | .10 |
| ☐ 8 Shane Matthews | 3.50 | 1.40 | .35 |
| ☐ 9 Steve Spurrier CO | 3.00 | 1.20 | .30 |
| ☐ 10 Mark White | 1.00 | .40 | .10 |
| ☐ 11 Will White | 1.00 | .40 | .10 |
| ☐ 12 Albert and Alberta (Mascots) | 1.00 | .40 | .10 |

## 1993 Florida State

These six football "credit" cards each contained 10.00 of food and merchandise value at FSU concession stands specially equipped with scanners to read the value in the cards. The cards were sold for 15.00 each exclusively through the Florida State Athletic Department and could be purchased individually or as a six-card set. Charlie Ward was the first card issued (for the Seminoles' home opener against Clemson) with an additional card issued at each successive home game. Reportedly only 12,000 sets were produced. The cards were manufactured by CollectorCard of America in Minneapolis. The cards have rounded corners and measure 2 1/8" by 3 3/8". The fronts feature borderless color player cutouts superposed upon a background of sky and clouds. The player's name and position appear within a light blue rectangle at the bottom. The horizontal back has a borderless ghosted color photo of an FSU campus building as the background. At the top are shown the FSU opponent and date for the game at which the card was first available. The player's name, position, height, weight, class, hometown, and 1992 season highlights appear on the left side; his career statistics appear on the right. The black scanning stripe appears across the back near the bottom. The cards are unnumbered and checklisted below in alphabetical order.

|  | MINT | EXC | G-VG |
|---|---|---|---|
| COMPLETE SET (6) | 75.00 | 30.00 | 7.50 |
| COMMON PLAYER (1-6) | 5.00 | 2.00 | .50 |
| ☐ 1 Bobby Bowden CO | 15.00 | 6.00 | 1.50 |
| ☐ 2 Derrick Brooks | 15.00 | 6.00 | 1.50 |
| ☐ 3 Corey Sawyer | 10.00 | 4.00 | 1.00 |
| ☐ 4 Tamarick Vanover | 10.00 | 4.00 | 1.00 |
| ☐ 5 Charlie Ward | 50.00 | 20.00 | 5.00 |
| ☐ 6 Chief Osceola (Mascot) | 5.00 | 2.00 | .50 |

## 1987 Fresno State Burger King

This 16-card, standard-size (2 1/2" by 3 1/2") set features past and then-current football players at Fresno State University. The cards are unnumbered and hence are listed below in uniform number order. The set was produced by Sports Marketing Inc. and sponsored by Burger King. The set is also considered to be a police/safety set due to the "Tip from the Bulldogs" on each card back.

|  | MINT | EXC | G-VG |
|---|---|---|---|
| COMPLETE SET (16) | 25.00 | 10.00 | 2.50 |
| COMMON CARD | 1.50 | .60 | .15 |
| ☐ 1 Gene Taylor | 1.50 | .60 | .15 |
| ☐ 5 Michael Stewart | 2.00 | .80 | .20 |
| ☐ 9 Kevin Sweeney | 2.50 | 1.00 | .25 |

| ☐ 12 Eric Buechele | 1.50 | .60 | .15 |
|---|---|---|---|
| ☐ 19 Rod Webster | 1.50 | .60 | .15 |
| ☐ 26 Kelly Skipper | 1.50 | .60 | .15 |
| ☐ 27 Barry Belli | 1.50 | .60 | .15 |
| ☐ 32 Kelly Brooks | 1.50 | .60 | .15 |
| ☐ 45 David Grayson | 2.00 | .80 | .20 |
| ☐ 67 Jethro Franklin | 1.50 | .60 | .15 |
| ☐ 71 Jeff Truschel | 1.50 | .60 | .15 |
| ☐ 80 John O'Leary | 1.50 | .60 | .15 |
| ☐ 81 Stephen Baker | 2.50 | 1.00 | .25 |
| ☐ 83 Henry Ellard | 4.50 | 1.80 | .45 |
| ☐ 86 Stephone Paige | 4.50 | 1.80 | .45 |
| ☐ xx Jim Sweeney CO | 2.00 | .80 | .20 |

## 1990 Fresno State Smokey

This unnumbered, 15-card set measures the standard card size, 2 1/2" by 3 1/2". The set was sponsored by the USDA Forest Service and issued with the cooperation of Grandy's and the BDA. The front features an action color photo, bounded on top and bottom by red and purple strips. At the bottom the player's name, position, and jersey number are sandwiched between the Smokey the Bear picture and Grandy's logo. The back has biographical information and a public service announcement (with cartoon) concerning fire prevention. Future NFL players included in this set are Ron Cox, Aaron Craver, Marquez Pope, and James Williams.

|  | MINT | EXC | G-VG |
|---|---|---|---|
| COMPLETE SET (16) | 15.00 | 6.00 | 1.50 |
| COMMON PLAYER (1-16) | 1.00 | .40 | .10 |
| ☐ 1 Mark Barsotti | 1.25 | .50 | .12 |
| ☐ 2 Ron Cox | 1.50 | .60 | .15 |
| ☐ 3 Aaron Craver | 1.50 | .60 | .15 |
| ☐ 4 DeVonne Edwards | 1.00 | .40 | .10 |
| ☐ 5 Courtney Griffin | 1.00 | .40 | .10 |
| ☐ 6 Jesse Hardwick | 1.00 | .40 | .10 |
| ☐ 7 Melvin Johnson | 1.00 | .40 | .10 |
| ☐ 8 Brian Lasho | 1.00 | .40 | .10 |
| ☐ 9 Kelvin Means | 1.00 | .40 | .10 |
| ☐ 10 Marquez Pope | 1.50 | .60 | .15 |
| ☐ 11 Zack Rix | 1.00 | .40 | .10 |
| ☐ 12 Nick Ruggeroli | 1.00 | .40 | .10 |
| ☐ 13 Jim Sweeney CO | 1.25 | .50 | .12 |
| ☐ 14 Erick Tanuvasa | 1.00 | .40 | .10 |
| ☐ 15 Jeff Thiesen | 1.00 | .40 | .10 |
| ☐ 16 James Williams | 1.50 | .60 | .15 |

## 1988 Georgia McDag

This 16-card set features then-current football players at the University of Georgia. The cards are numbered on the back in the lower right corner. The cards measure approximately 2 1/2" by 3 1/2". The set was produced by McDag Productions. The set is also considered to be a police/safety set due to the "Tip from the Bulldogs" on each card back. The key card in the set is Rodney Hampton.

| | MINT | EXC | G-VG |
|---|---|---|---|
| COMPLETE SET (16) | 20.00 | 8.00 | 2.00 |
| COMMON CARD (1-16) | .75 | .30 | .07 |

| | | MINT | EXC | G-VG |
|---|---|---|---|---|
| ☐ | 1 UGA IV (Mascot) | .75 | .30 | .07 |
| ☐ | 2 Vince Dooley AD/CO | 1.00 | .40 | .10 |
| ☐ | 3 Steve Crumley | 1.00 | .40 | .10 |
| ☐ | 4 Aaron Chubb | .75 | .30 | .07 |
| ☐ | 5 Keith Henderson | 2.00 | .80 | .20 |
| ☐ | 6 Steve Harmon | .75 | .30 | .07 |
| ☐ | 7 Terrie Webster | .75 | .30 | .07 |
| ☐ | 8 John Kasay | 2.00 | .80 | .20 |
| ☐ | 9 Wayne Johnson | .75 | .30 | .07 |
| ☐ | 10 Tim Worley | 3.00 | 1.20 | .30 |
| ☐ | 11 Wycliffe Lovelace | .75 | .30 | .07 |
| ☐ | 12 Brent Collins | .75 | .30 | .07 |
| ☐ | 13 Vince Guthrie | .75 | .30 | .07 |
| ☐ | 14 Todd Wheeler | .75 | .30 | .07 |
| ☐ | 15 Bill Goldberg | .75 | .30 | .07 |
| ☐ | 16 Rodney Hampton | 10.00 | 4.00 | 1.00 |

## 1989 Georgia 200

The 1989 University of Georgia football set contains 200 standard-size (2 1/2" by 3 1/2") cards, depicting former Bulldog greats. The fronts contain vintage photos; the horizontally oriented backs feature player profiles. Both sides have red borders. The cards were distributed in sets and in poly packs. These cards were printed on very thin stock. This set is notable for its inclusion of several Herschel Walker cards.

| | MINT | EXC | G-VG |
|---|---|---|---|
| COMPLETE SET (200) | 18.00 | 7.25 | 1.80 |
| COMMON CARD (1-200) | .10 | .04 | .01 |

| | | MINT | EXC | G-VG |
|---|---|---|---|---|
| ☐ | 1 Vince Dooley AD | .20 | .08 | .02 |
| ☐ | 2 Ivy M. Shiver | .10 | .04 | .01 |
| ☐ | 3 Vince Dooley CO | .15 | .06 | .01 |
| ☐ | 4 Vince Dooley CO | .15 | .06 | .01 |
| ☐ | 5 Ray Goff CO | .15 | .06 | .01 |
| ☐ | 6 Ray Goff CO | .15 | .06 | .01 |
| ☐ | 7 Wally Butts CO | .15 | .06 | .01 |
| ☐ | 8 Wally Butts CO | .15 | .06 | .01 |
| ☐ | 9 Herschel Walker | .75 | .30 | .07 |
| ☐ | 10 Frank Sinkwich | .15 | .06 | .01 |
| ☐ | 11 Bob McWhorter | .10 | .04 | .01 |
| ☐ | 12 Joe Bennett | .10 | .04 | .01 |
| ☐ | 13 Dan Edwards | .10 | .04 | .01 |
| ☐ | 14 Tom A. Nash | .10 | .04 | .01 |
| ☐ | 15 Herb Maffett | .10 | .04 | .01 |
| ☐ | 16 Ralph Maddox | .10 | .04 | .01 |
| ☐ | 17 Vernon Smith | .10 | .04 | .01 |
| ☐ | 18 Bill Hartman Jr. | .10 | .04 | .01 |
| ☐ | 19 Frank Sinkwich | .20 | .08 | .02 |
| ☐ | 20 Joe O'Malley | .10 | .04 | .01 |
| ☐ | 21 Mike Castronis | .10 | .04 | .01 |
| ☐ | 22 Aschel M. Day | .10 | .04 | .01 |
| ☐ | 23 Herb St. John | .10 | .04 | .01 |
| ☐ | 24 Craig Hertwig | .10 | .04 | .01 |
| ☐ | 25 Johnny Rauch | .15 | .06 | .01 |
| ☐ | 26 Harry Babcock | .10 | .04 | .01 |
| ☐ | 27 Bruce Kemp | .15 | .06 | .01 |
| ☐ | 28 Pat Dye | .75 | .30 | .07 |
| ☐ | 29 Fran Tarkenton | .75 | .30 | .07 |
| ☐ | 30 Larry Kohn | .10 | .04 | .01 |
| ☐ | 31 Ray Rissmiller | .10 | .04 | .01 |
| ☐ | 32 George Patton | .15 | .06 | .01 |
| ☐ | 33 Mixon Robinson | .10 | .04 | .01 |
| ☐ | 34 Lynn Hughes | .10 | .04 | .01 |
| ☐ | 35 Bill Stanfill | .20 | .08 | .02 |
| ☐ | 36 Robert Dicks | .10 | .04 | .01 |
| ☐ | 37 Lynn Hunnicutt | .10 | .04 | .01 |
| ☐ | 38 Tommy Lyons | .10 | .04 | .01 |
| ☐ | 39 Royce Smith | .10 | .04 | .01 |
| ☐ | 40 Steve Greer | .15 | .06 | .01 |
| ☐ | 41 Randy Johnson | .15 | .06 | .01 |
| ☐ | 42 Mike Wilson | .15 | .06 | .01 |
| ☐ | 43 Joel Parrish | .10 | .04 | .01 |
| ☐ | 44 Ben Zambiasi | .20 | .08 | .02 |
| ☐ | 45 Allan Leavitt | .10 | .04 | .01 |
| ☐ | 46 George Collins | .10 | .04 | .01 |
| ☐ | 47 Rex Robinson | .15 | .06 | .01 |
| ☐ | 48 Scott Woerner | .15 | .06 | .01 |
| ☐ | 49 Herschel Walker | .75 | .30 | .07 |
| ☐ | 50 Bob Burns | .10 | .04 | .01 |
| ☐ | 51 Jimmy Payne | .10 | .04 | .01 |
| ☐ | 52 Fred Brown | .10 | .04 | .01 |
| ☐ | 53 Kevin Butler | .20 | .08 | .02 |
| ☐ | 54 Don Porterfield | .10 | .04 | .01 |
| ☐ | 55 Mac McWhorter | .15 | .06 | .01 |
| ☐ | 56 John Little | .10 | .04 | .01 |
| ☐ | 57 Marion Campbell | .20 | .08 | .02 |
| ☐ | 58 Zeke Bratkowski | .25 | .10 | .02 |
| ☐ | 59 Buck Belue | .20 | .08 | .02 |
| ☐ | 60 Duward Pennington | .10 | .04 | .01 |
| ☐ | 61 Lamar Davis | .10 | .04 | .01 |
| ☐ | 62 Steve Wilson | .10 | .04 | .01 |
| ☐ | 63 Leman L. Rosenberg | .10 | .04 | .01 |
| ☐ | 64 Dennis Hughes | .10 | .04 | .01 |
| ☐ | 65 Wayne Radloff | .10 | .04 | .01 |
| ☐ | 66 Lindsay Scott | .20 | .08 | .02 |
| ☐ | 67 Wayne Swinford | .10 | .04 | .01 |
| ☐ | 68 Kim Stephens | .10 | .04 | .01 |
| ☐ | 69 Willie McClendon | .20 | .08 | .02 |
| ☐ | 70 Ron Jenkins | .10 | .04 | .01 |
| ☐ | 71 Jeff Lewis | .10 | .04 | .01 |
| ☐ | 72 Larry Rakestraw | .15 | .06 | .01 |
| ☐ | 73 Spike Jones | .15 | .06 | .01 |
| ☐ | 74 Tom Nash Jr. | .10 | .04 | .01 |
| ☐ | 75 Vassa Cate | .10 | .04 | .01 |
| ☐ | 76 Theron Sapp | .15 | .06 | .01 |
| ☐ | 77 Claude Hipps | .15 | .06 | .01 |
| ☐ | 78 Charley Trippi | .40 | .16 | .04 |
| ☐ | 79 Mike Weaver | .10 | .04 | .01 |
| ☐ | 80 Anderson Johnson | .10 | .04 | .01 |
| ☐ | 81 Matt Robinson | .20 | .08 | .02 |
| ☐ | 82 Bill Krug | .10 | .04 | .01 |
| ☐ | 83 Todd Wheeler | .10 | .04 | .01 |
| ☐ | 84 Mack Guest | .10 | .04 | .01 |
| ☐ | 85 Frank Ros | .10 | .04 | .01 |
| ☐ | 86 Jeff Hipp | .15 | .06 | .01 |
| ☐ | 87 Milton Leathers | .10 | .04 | .01 |
| ☐ | 88 George Morton | .10 | .04 | .01 |
| ☐ | 89 Jim Broadway | .10 | .04 | .01 |
| ☐ | 90 Tim Morrison | .10 | .04 | .01 |
| ☐ | 91 Homer Key | .10 | .04 | .01 |
| ☐ | 92 Richard Tardits | .20 | .08 | .02 |
| ☐ | 93 Tommy Thurson | .10 | .04 | .01 |
| ☐ | 94 Bob Kelley | .10 | .04 | .01 |
| ☐ | 95 Bob McWhorter | .10 | .04 | .01 |
| ☐ | 96 Vernon Smith | .10 | .04 | .01 |
| ☐ | 97 Eddie Weaver | .10 | .04 | .01 |
| ☐ | 98 Bill Stanfill | .20 | .08 | .02 |
| ☐ | 99 Scott Williams | .10 | .04 | .01 |
| ☐ | 100 Checklist Card | .15 | .06 | .01 |
| ☐ | 101 Len Hauss | .20 | .08 | .02 |
| ☐ | 102 Jim Griffith | .10 | .04 | .01 |
| ☐ | 103 Nat Dye | .10 | .04 | .01 |
| ☐ | 104 Quinton Lumpkin | .10 | .04 | .01 |
| ☐ | 105 Mike Garrett | .10 | .04 | .01 |
| ☐ | 106 Glynn Harrison | .10 | .04 | .01 |
| ☐ | 107 Aaron Chubb | .10 | .04 | .01 |
| ☐ | 108 John Brantley | .15 | .06 | .01 |
| ☐ | 109 Pat Hodgson | .10 | .04 | .01 |
| ☐ | 110 Guy McIntyre | .20 | .08 | .02 |
| ☐ | 111 Keith Harris | .10 | .04 | .01 |
| ☐ | 112 Mike Cavan | .10 | .04 | .01 |
| ☐ | 113 Kevin Jackson | .10 | .04 | .01 |
| ☐ | 114 Jim Cagle | .10 | .04 | .01 |
| ☐ | 115 Charles Whittemore | .10 | .04 | .01 |
| ☐ | 116 Graham Batchelor | .10 | .04 | .01 |
| ☐ | 117 Art DeCarlo | .10 | .04 | .01 |
| ☐ | 118 Kendall Keith | .10 | .04 | .01 |
| ☐ | 119 Jeff Pyburn | .20 | .08 | .02 |
| ☐ | 120 James Ray | .10 | .04 | .01 |
| ☐ | 121 Mack Burroughs | .10 | .04 | .01 |
| ☐ | 122 Jimmy Vickers | .10 | .04 | .01 |
| ☐ | 123 Charley Britt | .15 | .06 | .01 |
| ☐ | 124 Matt Braswell | .10 | .04 | .01 |
| ☐ | 125 Jake Richardson | .10 | .04 | .01 |
| ☐ | 126 Ronnie Stewart | .10 | .04 | .01 |
| ☐ | 127 Tim Crowe | .10 | .04 | .01 |
| ☐ | 128 Troy Sadowski | .10 | .04 | .01 |
| ☐ | 129 Robert Honeycutt | .10 | .04 | .01 |
| ☐ | 130 Warren Gray | .10 | .04 | .01 |
| ☐ | 131 David Guthrie | .10 | .04 | .01 |
| ☐ | 132 John Lastinger | .20 | .08 | .02 |

| □ 133 Chip Wisdom | .10 | .04 | .01 |
|---|---|---|---|
| □ 134 Butch Box | .10 | .04 | .01 |
| □ 135 Tony Cushenberry | .10 | .04 | .01 |
| □ 136 Vince Guthrie | .10 | .04 | .01 |
| □ 137 Floyd Reid Jr. | .15 | .06 | .01 |
| □ 138 Mark Hodge | .10 | .04 | .01 |
| □ 139 Joe Happe | .10 | .04 | .01 |
| □ 140 Al Bodine | .10 | .04 | .01 |
| □ 141 Gene Chandler | .10 | .04 | .01 |
| □ 142 Tommy Lawhorne | .10 | .04 | .01 |
| □ 143 Bobby Walden | .15 | .06 | .01 |
| □ 144 Douglas McFalls | .10 | .04 | .01 |
| □ 145 Jim Milo | .10 | .04 | .01 |
| □ 146 Billy Payne | .10 | .04 | .01 |
| □ 147 Paul Holmes | .10 | .04 | .01 |
| □ 148 Bob Clemens | .10 | .04 | .01 |
| □ 149 Kenny Sims | .10 | .04 | .01 |
| □ 150 Reid Moseley Jr. | .10 | .04 | .01 |
| □ 151 Tim Callaway | .10 | .04 | .01 |
| □ 152 Rusty Russell | .10 | .04 | .01 |
| □ 153 Jim McCollough | .10 | .04 | .01 |
| □ 154 Wally Williamson | .10 | .04 | .01 |
| □ 155 John Bond | .10 | .04 | .01 |
| □ 156 Charley Trippi | .40 | .16 | .04 |
| □ 157 The Play | .20 | .08 | .02 |
| (Lindsay Scott) | | | |
| □ 158 Joe Boland | .10 | .04 | .01 |
| □ 159 Michael Babb | .10 | .04 | .01 |
| □ 160 Jimmy Poulos | .10 | .04 | .01 |
| □ 161 Chris McCarthy | .10 | .04 | .01 |
| □ 162 Billy Mixon | .10 | .04 | .01 |
| □ 163 Dicky Clark | .10 | .04 | .01 |
| □ 164 David Rholetter | .10 | .04 | .01 |
| □ 165 Chuck Heard | .10 | .04 | .01 |
| □ 166 Pat Field | .10 | .04 | .01 |
| □ 167 Preston Ridlehuber | .10 | .04 | .01 |
| □ 168 Heyward Allen | .10 | .04 | .01 |
| □ 169 Kirby Moore | .10 | .04 | .01 |
| □ 170 Chris Welton | .10 | .04 | .01 |
| □ 171 Bill McKenny | .10 | .04 | .01 |
| □ 172 Steve Boswell | .10 | .04 | .01 |
| □ 173 Bob Towns | .10 | .04 | .01 |
| □ 174 Anthony Towns | .10 | .04 | .01 |
| □ 175 Porter Payne | .10 | .04 | .01 |
| □ 176 Bobby Garrard | .10 | .04 | .01 |
| □ 177 Jack Griffith | .10 | .04 | .01 |
| □ 178 Herschel Walker | .75 | .30 | .07 |
| □ 179 Andy Perhach | .10 | .04 | .01 |
| □ 180 Dr. Charles Herty CO | .10 | .04 | .01 |
| □ 181 Kent Lawrence | .25 | .10 | .02 |
| □ 182 David McKnight | .10 | .04 | .01 |
| □ 183 Joe Tereshinski Jr. | .15 | .06 | .01 |
| □ 184 Cicero Lucas | .10 | .04 | .01 |
| □ 185 Glenn(Pop) Warner CO | .20 | .08 | .02 |
| □ 186 Tony Flack | .10 | .04 | .01 |
| □ 187 Kevin Butler | .20 | .08 | .02 |
| □ 188 Bill Mitchell | .10 | .04 | .01 |
| □ 189 Poulos vs. Tech | .10 | .04 | .01 |
| (Jimmy Poulos) | | | |
| □ 190 Pete Case | .15 | .06 | .01 |
| □ 191 Pete Tinsley | .10 | .04 | .01 |
| □ 192 Joe Tereshinski | .15 | .06 | .01 |
| □ 193 Jimmy Harper | .10 | .04 | .01 |
| □ 194 Don Leebern | .10 | .04 | .01 |
| □ 195 Harry Mehre CO | .10 | .04 | .01 |
| □ 196 Retired Jerseys | .25 | .10 | .02 |
| (Herschel Walker, | | | |
| Theron Sapp, | | | |
| Charley Trippi, | | | |
| and Frank Sinkwich) | | | |
| □ 197 Terrie Webster | .10 | .04 | .01 |
| □ 198 George Woodruff CO | .10 | .04 | .01 |
| □ 199 First Georgia Team | .15 | .06 | .01 |
| (1892 Team Photo) | | | |
| □ 200 Checklist Card | .15 | .06 | .01 |

## 1989 Georgia Police

This 16-card set was sponsored by Charter Winds Hospital. The cards were issued on an uncut sheet with four rows of four cards each; if cut, the cards would measure the standard size (2 1/2" by 3 1/2"). The color action photos on the fronts are bordered in gray, and card face itself is red. The words "UGA Bulldogs '89" appear in white lettering above the picture. The backs have biography, career summary, and "Tips from the Bulldogs" in the form of anti-drug or alcohol messages. The cards are unnumbered and checklisted below in alphabetical order, with the uniform number after the name.

| | MINT | EXC | G-VG |
|---|---|---|---|
| COMPLETE SET (16) | 15.00 | 6.00 | 1.50 |
| COMMON CARD (1-16) | .75 | .30 | .07 |
| □ 1 Hiawatha Berry 58 | .75 | .30 | .07 |
| □ 2 Brian Cleveland 37 | .75 | .30 | .07 |

| □ 3 Demetrius Douglas 53 | .75 | .30 | .07 |
|---|---|---|---|
| □ 4 Alphonso Ellis 33 | .75 | .30 | .07 |
| □ 5 Ray Goff CO | 1.25 | .50 | .12 |
| □ 6 Bill Goldberg 95 | .75 | .30 | .07 |
| □ 7 Rodney Hampton 7 | 7.50 | 3.00 | .75 |
| □ 8 David Hargett 25 | .75 | .30 | .07 |
| □ 9 Joey Hester 1 | .75 | .30 | .07 |
| □ 10 John Kasay 3 | 2.00 | .80 | .20 |
| □ 11 Mo Lewis 57 | 2.50 | 1.00 | .25 |
| □ 12 Arthur Marshall 12 | 2.50 | 1.00 | .25 |
| □ 13 Curt Mull 50 | .75 | .30 | .07 |
| □ 14 Ben Smith 26 | 2.00 | .80 | .20 |
| □ 15 Greg Talley 11 | .75 | .30 | .07 |
| □ 16 Kirk Warner 83 | .75 | .30 | .07 |

## 1990 Georgia Police

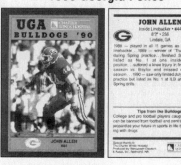

This 14-card standard size (2 1/2" by 3 1/2") set was sponsored by Charter Winds Hospital and features the University of Georgia Bulldogs. The front design has red stripes above and below the color action player photo, with gray borders on a black card face. The back has biographical information, player profile, and "Tips from the Bulldogs" in the form of anti-drug and alcohol messages. The cards are unnumbered and checklisted below in alphabetical order, with the uniform number after the name.

| | MINT | EXC | G-VG |
|---|---|---|---|
| COMPLETE SET (14) | 10.00 | 4.00 | 1.00 |
| COMMON CARD (1-14) | .75 | .30 | .07 |
| □ 1 John Allen 44 | .75 | .30 | .07 |
| □ 2 Brian Cleveland 37 | .75 | .30 | .07 |
| □ 3 Norman Cowins 59 | .75 | .30 | .07 |
| □ 4 Alphonso Ellis 33 | .75 | .30 | .07 |
| □ 5 Ray Goff CO | 1.25 | .50 | .12 |
| □ 6 David Hargett 25 | .75 | .30 | .07 |
| □ 7 Sean Hunnings 6 | .75 | .30 | .07 |
| □ 8 Preston Jones 14 | 1.00 | .40 | .10 |
| □ 9 John Kasay 3 | 1.50 | .60 | .15 |
| □ 10 Arthur Marshall 12 | 2.00 | .80 | .20 |
| □ 11 Jack Swan 76 | .75 | .30 | .07 |
| □ 12 Greg Talley 11 | .75 | .30 | .07 |
| □ 13 Lemonte Tellis 77 | .75 | .30 | .07 |
| □ 14 Chris Wilson 16 | .75 | .30 | .07 |

## 1991 Georgia Police

The 1991 Georgia Bulldog set was sponsored by Charter Winds Hospital, and its company logo appears on both sides of the cards. The cards measure the standard size (2 1/2" by 3 1/2") and were issued on an unperforated sheet. Fronts feature a mix of glossy color

action or posed player photos, with a gray border stripe on a red card face. The words "UGA Bulldogs '91" appear in a black stripe above the picture, while player identification is given in a black stripe below the picture. The backs have biography, career summary, and "Tips from the Bulldogs" in the form of anti-drug or alcohol messages. The cards are unnumbered and checklisted below in alphabetical order. The key card in the set is Garrison Hearst.

|  | MINT | EXC | G-VG |
|---|---|---|---|
| COMPLETE SET (16) | 12.00 | 5.00 | 1.20 |
| COMMON CARD (1-16) | .75 | .30 | .07 |
| ☐ 1 John Allen | .75 | .30 | .07 |
| ☐ 2 Chuck Carswell | .75 | .30 | .07 |
| ☐ 3 Russell DeFoor | .75 | .30 | .07 |
| ☐ 4 Ray Goff CO | 1.25 | .50 | .12 |
| ☐ 5 David Hargett | .75 | .30 | .07 |
| ☐ 6 Andre Hastings | 2.00 | .80 | .20 |
| ☐ 7 Garrison Hearst | 6.00 | 2.40 | .60 |
| ☐ 8 Arthur Marshall | 2.00 | .80 | .20 |
| ☐ 9 Kevin Maxwell | .75 | .30 | .07 |
| ☐ 10 DeWayne Simmons | .75 | .30 | .07 |
| ☐ 11 Jack Swan | .75 | .30 | .07 |
| ☐ 12 Greg Talley | .75 | .30 | .07 |
| ☐ 13 Lemonte Tellis | .75 | .30 | .07 |
| ☐ 14 Chris Wilson | .75 | .30 | .07 |
| ☐ 15 George Wynn | .75 | .30 | .07 |
| ☐ 16 UGA V (Mascot) | .75 | .30 | .07 |

## 1992 Georgia Police

This 15-card set was sponsored by Charter Winds Hospital and produced by BD and A cards. The cards measure the standard size (2 1/2" by 3 1/2"). The fronts feature color action player photos against a black card face. The top of the picture is arched, and the year and words "Georgia Bulldogs" are printed in red above the arch. The player's name is printed in a gray stripe at the bottom. The backs are white with black print and contain career highlights and "Tips from the Bulldogs." Sponsor logos appear at the bottom. The set features Garrison Hearst in his second college card.

|  | MINT | EXC | G-VG |
|---|---|---|---|
| COMPLETE SET (15) | 10.00 | 4.00 | 1.00 |
| COMMON CARD (1-15) | .50 | .20 | .05 |
| ☐ 1 Mitch Davis | .75 | .30 | .07 |
| ☐ 2 Damon Evans | .50 | .20 | .05 |
| ☐ 3 Torrey Evans | .50 | .20 | .05 |
| ☐ 4 Ray Goff CO | 1.00 | .40 | .10 |
| ☐ 5 Andre Hastings | 1.50 | .60 | .15 |
| ☐ 6 Garrison Hearst | 4.00 | 1.60 | .40 |
| ☐ 7 Donnie Maib | .50 | .20 | .05 |
| ☐ 8 Alec Millen | .50 | .20 | .05 |

| ☐ 9 Shannon Mitchell | .50 | .20 | .05 |
|---|---|---|---|
| ☐ 10 Mack Strong | .50 | .20 | .05 |
| ☐ 11 Jack Swan | .50 | .20 | .05 |
| ☐ 12 UGA (Mascot) | .50 | .20 | .05 |
| ☐ 13 Bernard Williams | .75 | .30 | .07 |
| ☐ 14 Chris Wilson | .50 | .20 | .05 |
| ☐ 15 Eric Zeier | 2.50 | 1.00 | .25 |

## 1993 Georgia Police

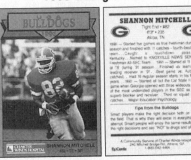

Originally issued in perforated sheets, this 16-card set was sponsored by Charter Winds Hospital and produced by BD and A cards. The cards measure the standard size (2 1/2" by 3 1/2"). The fronts feature color action and posed player photos against a red card face. The year and words "Georgia Bulldogs" are printed in gray lettering above the photo. The player's name, jersey number, position, and class are printed in a gray stripe at the bottom. The plain white backs carry the player's name, position, jersey number, height, weight, and hometown at the top, followed below by career highlights and "Tips from the Bulldogs." The cards are unnumbered and checklisted below in alphabetical order.

|  | MINT | EXC | G-VG |
|---|---|---|---|
| COMPLETE SET (16) | 8.00 | 3.25 | .80 |
| COMMON PLAYER (1-16) | .50 | .20 | .05 |
| ☐ 1 Scot Armstrong | .50 | .20 | .05 |
| ☐ 2 Brian Bohannon | .50 | .20 | .05 |
| ☐ 3 Carlo Butler | .50 | .20 | .05 |
| ☐ 4 Charlie Clemons | .50 | .20 | .05 |
| ☐ 5 Mitch Davis | .75 | .30 | .07 |
| ☐ 6 Terrell Davis | .50 | .20 | .05 |
| ☐ 7 Randall Godfrey | .50 | .20 | .05 |
| ☐ 8 Ray Goff CO | 1.00 | .40 | .10 |
| ☐ 9 Frank Harvey | .50 | .20 | .05 |
| ☐ 10 Travis Jones | .50 | .20 | .05 |
| ☐ 11 Shannon Mitchell | .50 | .20 | .05 |
| ☐ 12 Greg Tremble | .50 | .20 | .05 |
| ☐ 13 Bernard Williams | .75 | .30 | .07 |
| ☐ 14 Chad Wilson | .50 | .20 | .05 |
| ☐ 15 Eric Zeier | 2.00 | .80 | .20 |
| ☐ 16 UGA (Mascot) | .50 | .20 | .05 |

## 1991 Georgia Southern

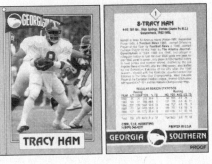

Produced by TJR Marketing, this 45-card set features All-American players and school record holders from Georgia Southern University. Twenty-five hundred numbered sets were printed and sold to the public; each set was accompanied by a certificate of limited edition. One hundred numbered and uncut sheets were also offered. An additional 275 proof sets and another 100 unnumbered uncut sheets with different backs were produced. The 275 proof sets differ from the 2500 limited sets in that the former have a light blue (rather than a dark blue) back border and the word "proof" on the card backs. The fronts feature a full-color photo within a small yellow border enclosed in a turquoise border. A yellow flag pole with a Georgia Southern flag highlights the left side of the card while the player's name is in a white box beneath the photo. The back contains biography, career summary, and statistics. The cards are numbered on the back.

|  | MINT | EXC | G-VG |
|---|---|---|---|
| COMPLETE SET (45) | 30.00 | 12.00 | 3.00 |
| COMMON CARD (1-45) | .60 | .24 | .06 |

| | | MINT | EXC | G-VG |
|---|---|---|---|---|
| ☐ 1 | Tracey Ham | 5.00 | 2.00 | .50 |
| ☐ 2 | Tim Foley | 1.25 | .50 | .12 |
| ☐ 3 | Vance Pike | .60 | .24 | .06 |
| ☐ 4 | Dennis Franklin | .60 | .24 | .06 |
| ☐ 5 | Ernest Thompson | .60 | .24 | .06 |
| ☐ 6 | Giff Smith | .60 | .24 | .06 |
| ☐ 7 | Flint Matthews | .60 | .24 | .06 |
| ☐ 8 | Joe Ross | .60 | .24 | .06 |
| ☐ 9 | Gerald Harris | .60 | .24 | .06 |
| ☐ 10 | Monty Sharpe | .60 | .24 | .06 |
| ☐ 11 | The Beginning | 1.00 | .40 | .10 |
| | Erskine(Erk) Russell CO | | | |
| ☐ 12 | Mike West | .60 | .24 | .06 |
| ☐ 13 | Jessie Jenkins | .60 | .24 | .06 |
| ☐ 14 | '85 Championship (Ring) | .60 | .24 | .06 |
| ☐ 15 | Erskine(Erk) Russell CO | 1.00 | .40 | .10 |
| ☐ 16 | Tim Brown | .75 | .30 | .07 |
| ☐ 17 | Taz Dixon | .60 | .24 | .06 |
| ☐ 18 | '86 Championship | .60 | .24 | .06 |
| ☐ 19 | Sean Gainey | .60 | .24 | .06 |
| ☐ 20 | James(Peanut) Carter | .75 | .30 | .07 |
| ☐ 21 | Ricky Harris | .75 | .30 | .07 |
| ☐ 22 | Fred Stokes | 1.25 | .50 | .12 |
| ☐ 23 | Randell Boone | .60 | .24 | .06 |
| ☐ 24 | Ronald Warnock | .60 | .24 | .06 |
| ☐ 25 | Raymond Gross | .60 | .24 | .06 |
| ☐ 26 | Robert Underwood | .60 | .24 | .06 |
| ☐ 27 | Frank Johnson | .60 | .24 | .06 |
| ☐ 28 | Darren Alford | .60 | .24 | .06 |
| ☐ 29 | Darrell Hendrix | .60 | .24 | .06 |
| ☐ 30 | Raymond Gross | .60 | .24 | .06 |
| ☐ 31 | Hugo Rossignol | .60 | .24 | .06 |
| ☐ 32 | Charles Carper | .60 | .24 | .06 |
| ☐ 33 | Melvin Bell | .60 | .24 | .06 |
| ☐ 34 | The Catch | 1.25 | .50 | .12 |
| | (Tracey Ham to Frank Johnson) | | | |
| ☐ 35 | Karl Miller | .60 | .24 | .06 |
| ☐ 36 | Our House | .60 | .24 | .06 |
| | Allen E. Paulson Stadium | | | |
| ☐ 37 | Danny Durham | .60 | .24 | .06 |
| ☐ 38 | '89 Championship | .60 | .24 | .06 |
| ☐ 39 | Tony Belser | .60 | .24 | .06 |
| ☐ 40 | Nay Young | .60 | .24 | .06 |
| ☐ 41 | Steve Bussoletti | .60 | .24 | .06 |
| ☐ 42 | Tim Stowers CO | .60 | .24 | .06 |
| ☐ 43 | Rodney Oglesby | .60 | .24 | .06 |
| ☐ 44 | '90 Championship | .60 | .24 | .06 |
| ☐ 45 | Tracey Ham | 5.00 | 2.00 | .50 |

# 1989 Hawaii

This 25-card set features current football players at the University of Hawaii. The cards are unnumbered, so they are listed below according to uniform number, which is prominently displayed on both sides of the card. The cards measure approximately 2 1/2" by 3 1/2". The set was sponsored by Longs Drugs and Kodak.

|  | MINT | EXC | G-VG |
|---|---|---|---|
| COMPLETE SET (25) | 10.00 | 4.00 | 1.00 |
| COMMON CARD | .50 | .20 | .05 |

| | | MINT | EXC | G-VG |
|---|---|---|---|---|
| ☐ 3 | Michael Coulson | .50 | .20 | .05 |
| ☐ 4 | Walter Briggs | .50 | .20 | .05 |
| ☐ 5 | Gavin Robertson | .50 | .20 | .05 |
| ☐ 7 | Jason Elam | 2.00 | .80 | .20 |
| ☐ 16 | Clayton Mahuka | .50 | .20 | .05 |
| ☐ 18 | Garrett Gabriel | .50 | .20 | .05 |
| ☐ 19 | Kim McCloud | .50 | .20 | .05 |
| ☐ 27 | Kyle Ah Loo | .50 | .20 | .05 |
| ☐ 28 | Dane McArthur | .50 | .20 | .05 |
| ☐ 30 | Travis Sims | .50 | .20 | .05 |
| ☐ 31 | David Maeva | .50 | .20 | .05 |
| ☐ 37 | Mike Tresler | .50 | .20 | .05 |
| ☐ 43 | Jamal Farmer | 1.00 | .40 | .10 |
| ☐ 56 | Mark Odom | .50 | .20 | .05 |
| ☐ 61 | Allen Smith | .50 | .20 | .05 |
| ☐ 66 | Manly Williams | .50 | .20 | .05 |
| ☐ 67 | Larry Jones | .50 | .20 | .05 |
| ☐ 71 | Sean Robinson | .50 | .20 | .05 |
| ☐ 72 | Shawn Alivado | .50 | .20 | .05 |
| ☐ 79 | Leo Goeas | .75 | .30 | .07 |
| ☐ 86 | Larry Khan-Smith | .50 | .20 | .05 |
| ☐ 89 | Chris Roscoe | .50 | .20 | .05 |
| ☐ 91 | Augie Apelu | .50 | .20 | .05 |
| ☐ 97 | Dana Directo | .50 | .20 | .05 |
| ☐ xx | Bob Wagner CO | .75 | .30 | .07 |

# 1990 Hawaii 7-Eleven

This 50-card standard size (2 1/2" by 3 1/2") set features members of the 1990 Hawaii Rainbow Warriors Football team. The cards have white borders framing a full-color photo on the front and biographical information on the back of the card. We have checklisted this set in alphabetical order and placed the uniform number of the player next to the name of the player.

|  | MINT | EXC | G-VG |
|---|---|---|---|
| COMPLETE SET (50) | 15.00 | 6.00 | 1.50 |
| COMMON CARD (1-50) | .35 | .14 | .03 |

| | | MINT | EXC | G-VG |
|---|---|---|---|---|
| ☐ 1 | Sean Abreu 40 | .35 | .14 | .03 |
| ☐ 2 | Joaquin Barnett 53 | .35 | .14 | .03 |
| ☐ 3 | Darrick Branch 87 | .35 | .14 | .03 |
| ☐ 4 | David Brantley 9 | .35 | .14 | .03 |
| ☐ 5 | Akili Calhoun 98 | .35 | .14 | .03 |
| ☐ 6 | Michael Carter 3 | .35 | .14 | .03 |
| ☐ 7 | Shawn Ching 72 | .35 | .14 | .03 |
| ☐ 8 | Jason Elam 7 | 1.50 | .60 | .15 |
| ☐ 9 | Jamal Farmer 43 | .75 | .30 | .07 |
| ☐ 10 | Garrett Gabriel 18 | .35 | .14 | .03 |
| ☐ 11 | Brian Gordon 15 | .35 | .14 | .03 |
| ☐ 12 | Kenny Harper 6 | .35 | .14 | .03 |
| ☐ 13 | Mitchell Kaaialii 57 | .35 | .14 | .03 |
| ☐ 14 | Larry Kahn-Smith 86 | .35 | .14 | .03 |
| ☐ 15 | Haku Kahoano 95 | .35 | .14 | .03 |
| ☐ 16 | Nuuanu Kaulia 94 | .35 | .14 | .03 |
| ☐ 17 | Eddie Kealoha 38 | .35 | .14 | .03 |
| ☐ 18 | Zerin Khan 14 | .35 | .14 | .03 |
| ☐ 19 | David Maeva 31 | .35 | .14 | .03 |
| ☐ 20 | Dane McArthur 28 | .35 | .14 | .03 |
| ☐ 21 | Kim McCloud 19 | .35 | .14 | .03 |
| ☐ 22 | Jeff Newman 1 | .35 | .14 | .03 |
| ☐ 23 | Mark Odom 56 | .35 | .14 | .03 |
| ☐ 24 | Louis Randall 51 | .35 | .14 | .03 |
| ☐ 25 | Gavin Robertson 5 | .35 | .14 | .03 |
| ☐ 26 | Sean Robinson 71 | .35 | .14 | .03 |
| ☐ 27 | Tavita Sagapolu 77 | .35 | .14 | .03 |
| ☐ 28 | Lyno Samana 45 | .35 | .14 | .03 |
| ☐ 29 | Walter Santiago 12 | .35 | .14 | .03 |
| ☐ 30 | Joe Sardo 21 | .35 | .14 | .03 |
| ☐ 31 | Travis Sims 30 | .35 | .14 | .03 |
| ☐ 32 | Allen Smith 61 | .35 | .14 | .03 |
| ☐ 33 | Jeff Sydner 26 | 1.25 | .50 | .12 |
| ☐ 34 | Richard Stevenson 33 | .35 | .14 | .03 |
| ☐ 35 | David Tanuvasa 44 | .35 | .14 | .03 |

| | MINT | EXC | G-VG |
|---|---|---|---|
| ☐ 36 Mike Tresler 37 | .35 | .14 | .03 |
| ☐ 37 Lemoe Tua 60 | .35 | .14 | .03 |
| ☐ 38 Peter Viliamu 69 | .35 | .14 | .03 |
| ☐ 39 Bob Wagner CO | .50 | .20 | .05 |
| ☐ 40 Terry Whitaker 2 | .35 | .14 | .03 |
| ☐ 41 Manly Williams 66 | .35 | .14 | .03 |
| ☐ 42 Jerry Winfrey 90 | .35 | .14 | .03 |
| ☐ 43 Aloha Stadium | .35 | .14 | .03 |
| ☐ 44 Assistant Coaches | .35 | .14 | .03 |
| (Nuuanu Kaulia) | | | |
| ☐ 45 Defense | .35 | .14 | .03 |
| ☐ 46 Offense | .50 | .20 | .05 |
| (Jamal Farmer) | | | |
| ☐ 47 Special Teams | .75 | .30 | .07 |
| (Jason Elam) | | | |
| ☐ 48 BYU Victory | .50 | .20 | .05 |
| (Jamal Farmer) | | | |
| ☐ 49 UH Logo | .35 | .14 | .03 |
| ☐ 50 WAC Logo | .50 | .20 | .05 |

## 1992 Houston Motion Sports

Produced by Motion Sports Inc., these 66 standard-size (2 1/2" by 3 1/2") cards feature on their fronts black-bordered color player photos, mostly posed, with the player's name and uniform number appearing in white lettering within a red stripe at the top. The back carries a borderless action photo, upon which are ghosted panels that contain the player's biography and Houston highlights. The cards are numbered on the back.

| | MINT | EXC | G-VG |
|---|---|---|---|
| COMPLETE SET (66) | 25.00 | 10.00 | 2.50 |
| COMMON PLAYER (1-62) | .35 | .14 | .03 |
| | | | |
| ☐ 1 Freddie Gilbert | .50 | .20 | .05 |
| ☐ 2 Lorenzo Dickson | .35 | .14 | .03 |
| ☐ 3 Sherman Smith | .50 | .20 | .05 |
| ☐ 4 Brad Whigham | .35 | .14 | .03 |
| ☐ 5 Allen Aldridge | 1.00 | .40 | .10 |
| ☐ 6 Truett Akin | .35 | .14 | .03 |
| ☐ 7 Nahala Johnson | .50 | .20 | .05 |
| ☐ 8 1980 Garden State Bowl | .35 | .14 | .03 |
| Terald Clark | | | |
| ☐ 9 1977 Cotton Bowl | .50 | .20 | .05 |
| ☐ 10 Tyrone Davis | .35 | .14 | .03 |
| ☐ 11 Kevin Bleier | .35 | .14 | .03 |
| ☐ 12 Nigel Ventress | .35 | .14 | .03 |
| ☐ 13 Darren Woods | .35 | .14 | .03 |
| ☐ 14 Linton Weatherspoon | .35 | .14 | .03 |
| ☐ 15 John R. Morris | .35 | .14 | .03 |
| ☐ 16 Kevin Batiste | .50 | .20 | .05 |
| ☐ 17 Kelvin McKnight | .35 | .14 | .03 |
| ☐ 18 Stewart Carpenter | .35 | .14 | .03 |
| ☐ 19 Ron Peters | .35 | .14 | .03 |
| ☐ 20 Stephen Dixon | .50 | .20 | .05 |
| ☐ 21 Chandler Evans | .35 | .14 | .03 |
| ☐ 22 Tyler Mucho | .35 | .14 | .03 |
| ☐ 23 Kevin Labay | .35 | .14 | .03 |
| ☐ 24 Steve Clarke | .35 | .14 | .03 |
| ☐ 25 Keith Jack | .35 | .14 | .03 |
| ☐ 26 Steve Matejka | .35 | .14 | .03 |
| ☐ 27 The Astrodome | .35 | .14 | .03 |
| ☐ 28 Roman Anderson | .35 | .14 | .03 |
| ☐ 29 Quarterback U. | 1.50 | .60 | .15 |
| Andre Ware | | | |
| David Klingler | | | |
| ☐ 30 Cougar Pride | 1.50 | .60 | .15 |
| Andre Ware | | | |
| David Klingler | | | |
| ☐ 31 Bayou Bucket | .35 | .14 | .03 |
| (Annual Houston | | | |
| vs. Rice game) | | | |
| ☐ 32 Jeff Tait | .35 | .14 | .03 |
| ☐ 33 Donald Douglas | .35 | .14 | .03 |

| | MINT | EXC | G-VG |
|---|---|---|---|
| ☐ 34 Victor Mamich | .35 | .14 | .03 |
| ☐ 35 John W.Brown | .35 | .14 | .03 |
| ☐ 36 Zach Chatman | .35 | .14 | .03 |
| ☐ 37 Jason Youngblood | .35 | .14 | .03 |
| ☐ 38 David Klingler | 2.50 | 1.00 | .25 |
| ☐ 39 John H.Brown | .35 | .14 | .03 |
| ☐ 40 Tommy Guy | .35 | .14 | .03 |
| ☐ 41 1980 Cotton Bowl | .50 | .20 | .05 |
| (Game action) | | | |
| ☐ 42 1973 Bluebonnet Bowl | .35 | .14 | .03 |
| (Game action) | | | |
| ☐ 43 Chris Pezman | .35 | .14 | .03 |
| ☐ 44 Tracy Good | .35 | .14 | .03 |
| ☐ 45 Stephen Harris | .35 | .14 | .03 |
| ☐ 46 Ryan McCoy | .50 | .20 | .05 |
| ☐ 47 Michael Newhouse | .35 | .14 | .03 |
| ☐ 48 Jimmy Klingler | 1.25 | .50 | .12 |
| ☐ 49 Joe Wheeler | .35 | .14 | .03 |
| ☐ 50 Eric Harrison | .35 | .14 | .03 |
| ☐ 51 Craig Hall | .35 | .14 | .03 |
| ☐ 52 Shasta (Mascot) | .35 | .14 | .03 |
| ☐ 53 NCAA Records | .35 | .14 | .03 |
| (Passing and Receiving) | | | |
| ☐ 54 Darrell Clapp | .50 | .20 | .05 |
| ☐ 55 Eric Blount | .35 | .14 | .03 |
| ☐ 56 Tiandre Sanders | .35 | .14 | .03 |
| ☐ 57 Kyle Allen | .35 | .14 | .03 |
| ☐ 58 Brisket Howard | .35 | .14 | .03 |
| ☐ 59 Greg Thornburgh | .35 | .14 | .03 |
| ☐ 60 Wilson Whitley | .75 | .30 | .07 |
| ☐ 61 Andre Ware | 1.25 | .50 | .12 |
| ☐ 62 John Jenkins CO | .50 | .20 | .05 |
| ☐ NNO Ad Card Motion Sports | .35 | .14 | .03 |
| ☐ NNO Front Card | .35 | .14 | .03 |
| ☐ NNO Back Card | .35 | .14 | .03 |
| ☐ NNO Checklist | .35 | .14 | .03 |

## 1988 Humboldt State Smokey

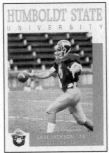 

This unnumbered, 11-card set was issued by the Humboldt State University football team and sponsored by the U. S. Forest Service. The cards measure the standard size (2 1/2" by 3 1/2") and feature posed color photos on the front. The cards are bordered right and below in green, with player information below the photo in gold lettering. The Smokey Bear logo is in the lower left corner. The backs have biographical information on the player and a cartoon concerning fire prevention.

| | MINT | EXC | G-VG |
|---|---|---|---|
| COMPLETE SET (1-11) | 18.00 | 7.25 | 1.80 |
| COMMON PLAYER (11) | 2.00 | .80 | .20 |
| | | | |
| ☐ 1 Richard Ashe 1 | 2.00 | .80 | .20 |
| ☐ 2 Darin Bradbury 64 | 2.00 | .80 | .20 |
| ☐ 3 Rodney Dorsett 7 | 2.00 | .80 | .20 |
| ☐ 4 Dave Harper 55 | 2.00 | .80 | .20 |
| ☐ 5 Earl Jackson 6 | 2.00 | .80 | .20 |
| ☐ 6 Derek Mallard 82 | 2.00 | .80 | .20 |
| ☐ 7 Scott Reagan 60 | 2.00 | .80 | .20 |
| ☐ 8 Wesley White 1 | 2.00 | .80 | .20 |
| ☐ 9 Paul Wienecke 40 | 2.00 | .80 | .20 |
| ☐ 10 William Williams 14 | 2.00 | .80 | .20 |
| ☐ 11 Kelvin Windham 30 | 2.00 | .80 | .20 |

## 1989 Idaho

This 12-card set features then-current football players at the University of Idaho. The cards are unnumbered, so they are listed below according to uniform number, which is displayed on both sides of the card. The photos are in black and white. The cards in the set contain "Tips from the Vandals" on the reverses and measure approximately 2 1/2" by 3 1/2".

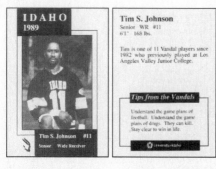

|  | MINT | EXC | G-VG |
|---|---|---|---|
| COMPLETE SET (12) | 12.00 | 5.00 | 1.20 |
| COMMON PLAYER | .75 | .30 | .07 |
| ☐ 3 Brian Smith | .75 | .30 | .07 |
| ☐ 11 Tim S. Johnson | .75 | .30 | .07 |
| ☐ 16 Lee Allen | .75 | .30 | .07 |
| ☐ 17 John Friesz | 6.00 | 2.40 | .60 |
| ☐ 20 Todd Hoiness | .75 | .30 | .07 |
| ☐ 25 David Jackson | .75 | .30 | .07 |
| ☐ 53 Steve Unger | .75 | .30 | .07 |
| ☐ 58 John Rust | .75 | .30 | .07 |
| ☐ 63 Troy Wright | .75 | .30 | .07 |
| ☐ 67 Todd Neu | .75 | .30 | .07 |
| ☐ 83 Michael Davis | .75 | .30 | .07 |
| ☐ 93 Mike Zeller | .75 | .30 | .07 |

## 1990 Illinois Centennial

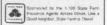

This 45-card set measures 2 1/2" by 3 1/2" and was issued to celebrate 100 years of football at the University of Illinois. The set was produced by College Classics and the State Farm Insurance agents in Illinois. The front features either a color or black and white photo of the player with a dark blue border on an orange background. The back has biographical information as well as the card number.

|  | MINT | EXC | G-VG |
|---|---|---|---|
| COMPLETE SET (45) | 15.00 | 6.00 | 1.50 |
| COMMON CARD (1-45) | .35 | .14 | .03 |
| ☐ 1 Harold(Red) Grange | 1.50 | .60 | .15 |
| ☐ 2 Dick Butkus | 1.50 | .60 | .15 |
| ☐ 3 Ray Nitschke | .75 | .30 | .07 |
| ☐ 4 Jim Grabowski | .50 | .20 | .05 |
| ☐ 5 Alex Agase | .50 | .20 | .05 |
| ☐ 6 Claude Young | .50 | .20 | .05 |
| ☐ 7 Scott Studwell | .50 | .20 | .05 |
| ☐ 8 Tony Eason | .50 | .20 | .05 |
| ☐ 9 John Mackovic | .50 | .20 | .05 |
| ☐ 10 Jack Trudeau | .50 | .20 | .05 |
| ☐ 11 Jeff George | 1.50 | .60 | .15 |
| ☐ 12 Rose Bowl Coaches | .35 | .14 | .03 |
|    Ray Eliot | | | |
|    Pete Elliott | | | |
|    Mike White | | | |
| ☐ 13 George Huff | .35 | .14 | .03 |
| ☐ 14 David Williams | .35 | .14 | .03 |
| ☐ 15 Bob Zuppke | .50 | .20 | .05 |
| ☐ 16 George Halas | 1.00 | .40 | .10 |
| ☐ 17 Dike Eddleman | .35 | .14 | .03 |
| ☐ 18 Dave Wilson | .35 | .14 | .03 |
| ☐ 19 Tab Bennett | .35 | .14 | .03 |
| ☐ 20 Jim Juriga | .35 | .14 | .03 |
| ☐ 21 John Karras | .35 | .14 | .03 |
| ☐ 22 Bobby Mitchell | .75 | .30 | .07 |
| ☐ 23 Dan Beaver | .35 | .14 | .03 |
| ☐ 24 Joe Rutgens | .50 | .20 | .05 |
| ☐ 25 Bill Burrell | .35 | .14 | .03 |
| ☐ 26 J.C. Caroline | .50 | .20 | .05 |
| ☐ 27 Al Brosky | .35 | .14 | .03 |
| ☐ 28 Don Thorp | .35 | .14 | .03 |
| ☐ 29 First Football Team | .35 | .14 | .03 |
| ☐ 30 Red Grange Retired | .75 | .30 | .07 |
| ☐ 31 Memorial Stadium | .35 | .14 | .03 |
| ☐ 32 Chris White | .35 | .14 | .03 |
| ☐ 33 Early Stars | .35 | .14 | .03 |
|    Ralph Chapman | | | |
|    Perry Graves | | | |
|    Bart Macomber | | | |
| ☐ 34 Early Stars | .35 | .14 | .03 |
|    John Depler | | | |
|    Charles Carney | | | |
|    Jim McMillen | | | |
| ☐ 35 Early Stars | .35 | .14 | .03 |
|    Burt Ingwerson | | | |
|    Butch Nowack | | | |
|    Bernie Shively | | | |
| ☐ 36 Great Quarterbacks | .35 | .14 | .03 |
|    Fred Custardo | | | |
|    Mike Wells | | | |
|    Tom O'Connell | | | |
| ☐ 37 Great Running Backs | .50 | .20 | .05 |
|    Thomas Rooks | | | |
|    Abe Woodson | | | |
|    Keith Jones | | | |
| ☐ 38 Great Receivers | .50 | .20 | .05 |
|    Mike Bellamy | | | |
|    Doug Dieken | | | |
|    John Wright | | | |
| ☐ 39 Great Offensive | .35 | .14 | .03 |
|    Forrest Van Hook | | | |
|    Larry McCarren | | | |
|    Chris Babyar | | | |
| ☐ 40 Great Defensive Backs | .35 | .14 | .03 |
|    Craig Swope | | | |
|    George Donnelly | | | |
|    Mike Gower | | | |
| ☐ 41 Great Linebackers | .35 | .14 | .03 |
|    Charles Boerlo | | | |
|    Don Hansen | | | |
|    John Sullivan | | | |
| ☐ 42 Defensive Linemen | .35 | .14 | .03 |
|    Archie Sutton | | | |
|    Chuck Studley | | | |
|    Scott Davis | | | |
| ☐ 43 Great Kickers | .35 | .14 | .03 |
|    Mike Bass | | | |
|    Bill Brown | | | |
|    Frosty Peters | | | |
| ☐ 44 Retired Numbers | 1.00 | .40 | .10 |
|    Dick Butkus | | | |
| ☐ 45 Football Centennial | .35 | .14 | .03 |
|    Logo | | | |

## 1992 Illinois

Produced by Flying Color Graphics Inc. and sponsored by WDWS radio station (AM 1400), this 48-card set features the University of Illinois football team. The cards measure the standard size (2 1/2" by 3 1/2") and are printed on thin card stock. The fronts feature a mix of posed or action color player photos. The pictures are bordered on the left by an orange stripe and at the bottom by a purple stripe. The player's name and position are printed in the purple stripe. The backs carry biographical information, the producer's logo, and a brief public service announcement. The cards are unnumbered and checklisted below in alphabetical order.

|  | MINT | EXC | G-VG |
|---|---|---|---|
| COMPLETE SET (48) | 15.00 | 6.00 | 1.50 |
| COMMON PLAYER (1-48) | .35 | .14 | .03 |
| ☐ 1 Derek Allen | .35 | .14 | .03 |
| ☐ 2 Jeff Arneson | .35 | .14 | .03 |
| ☐ 3 Randy Bierman | .35 | .14 | .03 |
| ☐ 4 Darren Boyer | .35 | .14 | .03 |
| ☐ 5 Rod Boykin | .35 | .14 | .03 |
| ☐ 6 Mike Cole | .35 | .14 | .03 |
| ☐ 7 Chad Copher | .35 | .14 | .03 |
| ☐ 8 Fred Cox | .35 | .14 | .03 |
| ☐ 9 Robert Crumpton | .60 | .24 | .06 |
| ☐ 10 Ken Dilger | .35 | .14 | .03 |
| ☐ 11 Jason Edwards | .35 | .14 | .03 |
| ☐ 12 Greg Engel | .50 | .20 | .05 |
| ☐ 13 Steve Feagin | .35 | .14 | .03 |
| ☐ 14 Erik Foggey | .35 | .14 | .03 |
| ☐ 15 Kevin Hardy | .35 | .14 | .03 |
| ☐ 16 Jeff Hasenstab | .50 | .20 | .05 |
| ☐ 17 John Holecek | .50 | .20 | .05 |
| ☐ 18 Brad Hopkins | .75 | .30 | .07 |
| ☐ 19 John Horn | .35 | .14 | .03 |
| ☐ 20 Dana Howard | 1.00 | .40 | .10 |
| ☐ 21 Filmel Johnson | .50 | .20 | .05 |
| ☐ 22 Jon Kerr | .35 | .14 | .03 |
| ☐ 23 Jeff Kinney | .50 | .20 | .05 |
| ☐ 24 Jim Klein | .35 | .14 | .03 |
| ☐ 25 Todd Leach | .35 | .14 | .03 |
| ☐ 26 Wagner Lester | .35 | .14 | .03 |
| ☐ 27 Lashon Ludington | .35 | .14 | .03 |
| ☐ 28 Clinton Lynch | .35 | .14 | .03 |
| ☐ 29 Tim McCloud | .35 | .14 | .03 |
| ☐ 30 David Olson | .35 | .14 | .03 |
| ☐ 31 Antwoine Patton | .50 | .20 | .05 |
| ☐ 32 Jim Pesek | .35 | .14 | .03 |
| ☐ 33 Alfred Pierce | .35 | .14 | .03 |
| ☐ 34 Mark Qualls | .35 | .14 | .03 |
| ☐ 35 Phil Rathke | .35 | .14 | .03 |
| ☐ 36 Chris Richardson | .50 | .20 | .05 |
| ☐ 37 Derrick Rucker | .35 | .14 | .03 |
| ☐ 38 Aaron Shelby | .35 | .14 | .03 |
| ☐ 39 John Sidari | .35 | .14 | .03 |
| ☐ 40 J.J. Strong | .35 | .14 | .03 |
| ☐ 41 Mike Suarez | .35 | .14 | .03 |
| ☐ 42 Lou Tepper CO | .35 | .14 | .03 |
| ☐ 43 Scott Turner | .35 | .14 | .03 |
| ☐ 44 Jason Verduzco | 1.50 | .60 | .15 |
| ☐ 45 Tyrone Washington | .35 | .14 | .03 |
| ☐ 46 Forry Wells | .35 | .14 | .03 |
| ☐ 47 Pat Wendt | .35 | .14 | .03 |
| ☐ 48 John Wright | .35 | .14 | .03 |

## 1982 Indiana State Police

This 64-card police set was sponsored by First National Bank (Terre Haute), 7-Up, and WTHI/TV (Channel 10). The cards measure approximately 2 5/8" by 4 1/8". A white diagonal cutting across the bottom of the card face has a drawing of the school mascot (an Indian with tomahawk in hand) and the words "Sycamore Rampage." The backs have brief biographical information, a trivia feature about the player, an anti-drug or alcohol message, and sponsor logos. The cards are unnumbered and checklisted below in alphabetical order by subject.

|  | NRMT | VG-E | GOOD |
|---|---|---|---|
| COMPLETE SET (64) | 150.00 | 60.00 | 15.00 |
| COMMON CARD (1-64) | 2.50 | 1.00 | .25 |
| ☐ 1 David Allen | 2.50 | 1.00 | .25 |
| ☐ 2 Doug Arnold | 2.50 | 1.00 | .25 |
| ☐ 3 James Banks | 2.50 | 1.00 | .25 |
| ☐ 4 Scott Bartel | 2.50 | 1.00 | .25 |
| ☐ 5 Kurt Bell | 2.50 | 1.00 | .25 |
| ☐ 6 Terry Bell | 2.50 | 1.00 | .25 |
| ☐ 7 Steve Bidwell | 2.50 | 1.00 | .25 |
| ☐ 8 Keith Bonney | 2.50 | 1.00 | .25 |
| ☐ 9 Mark Boster | 2.50 | 1.00 | .25 |
| ☐ 10 Bobby Boyce | 2.50 | 1.00 | .25 |
| ☐ 11 Steve Brickey CO | 2.50 | 1.00 | .25 |
| ☐ 12 Mark Bryson | 2.50 | 1.00 | .25 |
| ☐ 13 Steve Buxton | 2.50 | 1.00 | .25 |
| ☐ 14 Ed Campbell | 2.50 | 1.00 | .25 |
| ☐ 15 Jeff Campbell | 3.50 | 1.40 | .35 |
| ☐ 16 Tom Chapman | 2.50 | 1.00 | .25 |
| ☐ 17 Cheerleaders | 3.50 | 1.40 | .35 |
| (Ruth Ann Medworth DIR) | | | |
| ☐ 18 Darrold Clardy | 2.50 | 1.00 | .25 |
| ☐ 19 Wayne Davis | 2.50 | 1.00 | .25 |
| ☐ 20 Herbert Dawson | 2.50 | 1.00 | .25 |
| ☐ 21 Richard Dawson | 3.50 | 1.40 | .35 |
| ☐ 22 Chris Delaplaine | 2.50 | 1.00 | .25 |
| ☐ 23 Max Dillon | 2.50 | 1.00 | .25 |
| ☐ 24 Rick Dwenger | 2.50 | 1.00 | .25 |

|  |  | | |
|---|---|---|---|
| ☐ 25 Ed Foggs | 2.50 | 1.00 | .25 |
| ☐ 26 Allen Hartwig | 2.50 | 1.00 | .25 |
| ☐ 27 Pat Henderson CO | 2.50 | 1.00 | .25 |
| ☐ 28 Don Hitz | 2.50 | 1.00 | .25 |
| ☐ 29 Pete Hoener CO | 2.50 | 1.00 | .25 |
| ☐ 30 Bob Hopkins | 2.50 | 1.00 | .25 |
| ☐ 31 Kris Huber | 3.50 | 1.40 | .35 |
| Baton Twirler | | | |
| ☐ 32 Leroy Irvin | 15.00 | 6.00 | 1.50 |
| ☐ 33 Mike Johannes | 2.50 | 1.00 | .25 |
| ☐ 34 Anthony Kimball | 2.50 | 1.00 | .25 |
| ☐ 35 Gregg Kimbrough | 2.50 | 1.00 | .25 |
| ☐ 36 Bob Koehne | 2.50 | 1.00 | .25 |
| ☐ 37 Jerry Lasko CO | 2.50 | 1.00 | .25 |
| ☐ 38 Kevin Lynch | 2.50 | 1.00 | .25 |
| ☐ 39 Dan Maher | 2.50 | 1.00 | .25 |
| ☐ 40 Ed Martin | 2.50 | 1.00 | .25 |
| ☐ 41 Regis Mason | 2.50 | 1.00 | .25 |
| ☐ 42 Rob McIntyre | 2.50 | 1.00 | .25 |
| ☐ 43 Quintin Mikell | 2.50 | 1.00 | .25 |
| ☐ 44 Jeff Miller | 2.50 | 1.00 | .25 |
| ☐ 45 Mark Miller | 2.50 | 1.00 | .25 |
| ☐ 46 Mike Osborne | 2.50 | 1.00 | .25 |
| ☐ 47 Max Payne CO | 2.50 | 1.00 | .25 |
| ☐ 48 Scott Piercy | 2.50 | 1.00 | .25 |
| ☐ 49 Dennis Raetz CO | 2.50 | 1.00 | .25 |
| ☐ 50 Kevin Ramsey | 2.50 | 1.00 | .25 |
| ☐ 51 Dean Reader | 2.50 | 1.00 | .25 |
| ☐ 52 Eric Robinson | 2.50 | 1.00 | .25 |
| ☐ 53 Walter Seaphus | 3.50 | 1.40 | .35 |
| ☐ 54 Sparkettes | 2.50 | 1.00 | .25 |
| (Marthann Markler DIR) | | | |
| ☐ 55 John Spradley | 2.50 | 1.00 | .25 |
| ☐ 56 Manual Studway | 2.50 | 1.00 | .25 |
| ☐ 57 Sam Suggs | 2.50 | 1.00 | .25 |
| ☐ 58 Larry Swart | 2.50 | 1.00 | .25 |
| ☐ 59 Bob Tyree | 2.50 | 1.00 | .25 |
| ☐ 60 Bob Turner CO | 2.50 | 1.00 | .25 |
| ☐ 61 Brad Verdun | 2.50 | 1.00 | .25 |
| ☐ 62 Keith Ward | 2.50 | 1.00 | .25 |
| ☐ 63 Sean Whiten | 2.50 | 1.00 | .25 |
| ☐ 64 Perry Willett | 2.50 | 1.00 | .25 |

## 1984 Iowa

The 1984 Iowa Hawkeyes set contains 60 standard-size (2 1/2" by 3 1/2") cards. The fronts feature color portrait photos bordered in black. The backs provide brief profiles. The cards are unnumbered and so they are listed in alphabetical order by player name.

|  | MINT | EXC | G-VG |
|---|---|---|---|
| COMPLETE SET (60) | 40.00 | 16.00 | 4.00 |
| COMMON CARD (1-60) | .75 | .30 | .07 |
| ☐ 1 Kevin Angel | .75 | .30 | .07 |
| ☐ 2 Kerry Burt | .75 | .30 | .07 |
| ☐ 3 Fred Bush | .75 | .30 | .07 |
| ☐ 4 Craig Clark | .75 | .30 | .07 |
| ☐ 5 Zane Corbin | .75 | .30 | .07 |
| ☐ 6 Nate Creer | .75 | .30 | .07 |
| ☐ 7 Dave Croston | .75 | .30 | .07 |
| ☐ 8 George Davis | .75 | .30 | .07 |
| ☐ 9 Jeff Drost | .75 | .30 | .07 |
| ☐ 10 Quinn Early | 2.50 | 1.00 | .25 |
| ☐ 11 Mike Flagg | .75 | .30 | .07 |
| ☐ 12 Hayden Fry CO | 2.00 | .80 | .20 |
| ☐ 13 Bruce Gear | .75 | .30 | .07 |
| ☐ 14 Owen Gill | 1.50 | .60 | .15 |
| ☐ 15 Bill Glass | 1.00 | .40 | .10 |
| ☐ 16 Mike Haight | 1.50 | .60 | .15 |
| ☐ 17 Bill Happel | .75 | .30 | .07 |
| ☐ 18 Kevin Harmon | 1.00 | .40 | .10 |
| ☐ 19 Ronnie Harmon | 3.00 | 1.20 | .30 |
| ☐ 20 Craig Hartman | .75 | .30 | .07 |
| ☐ 21 Jon Hayes | 2.00 | .80 | .20 |
| ☐ 22 Erric Hedgeman | .75 | .30 | .07 |
| ☐ 23 Scott Helverson | .75 | .30 | .07 |
| ☐ 24 Mike Hooks | .75 | .30 | .07 |
| ☐ 25 Paul Hufford | .75 | .30 | .07 |
| ☐ 26 Keith Hunter | .75 | .30 | .07 |
| ☐ 27 George Little | .75 | .30 | .07 |
| ☐ 28 Chuck Long | 2.00 | .80 | .20 |
| ☐ 29 J.C. Love-Jordan | .75 | .30 | .07 |
| ☐ 30 George Millett | .75 | .30 | .07 |
| ☐ 31 Devon Mitchell | 1.00 | .40 | .10 |
| ☐ 32 Tom Nichol | .75 | .30 | .07 |
| ☐ 33 Kelly O'Brien | .75 | .30 | .07 |
| ☐ 34 Hap Peterson | .75 | .30 | .07 |
| ☐ 35 Joe Schuster | .75 | .30 | .07 |
| ☐ 36 Tim Sennott | .75 | .30 | .07 |
| ☐ 37 Ken Sims | .75 | .30 | .07 |
| ☐ 38 Mark Sindlinger | .75 | .30 | .07 |
| ☐ 39 Robert Smith | .75 | .30 | .07 |
| ☐ 40 Kevin Spitzig | .75 | .30 | .07 |
| ☐ 41 Larry Station | .75 | .30 | .07 |

| | MINT | EXC | G-VG |
|---|---|---|---|
| ☐ 42 Mike Stoops | .75 | .30 | .07 |
| ☐ 43 Dave Strobel | .75 | .30 | .07 |
| ☐ 44 Mark Vlasic | 2.50 | 1.00 | .25 |
| ☐ 45 Jon Vrieze | .75 | .30 | .07 |
| ☐ 46 Tony Wancket | .75 | .30 | .07 |
| ☐ 47 Herb Webster | .75 | .30 | .07 |
| ☐ 48 Coaching Staff | 1.00 | .40 | .10 |
| ☐ 49 Captains | 1.00 | .40 | .10 |
| ☐ 50 Bowl Players | .75 | .30 | .07 |
| ☐ 51 Harmon Brothers | 1.25 | .50 | .12 |
| (Kevin and Ronnie) | | | |
| ☐ 52 Cheerleaders | 1.00 | .40 | .10 |
| ☐ 53 Pompons | 1.00 | .40 | .10 |
| ☐ 54 Kinnick Stadium | .75 | .30 | .07 |
| ☐ 55 Herky the Hawk | .75 | .30 | .07 |
| (Mascot) | | | |
| ☐ 56 Rose Bowl Ring | .75 | .30 | .07 |
| ☐ 57 Peach Bowl Trophy | .75 | .30 | .07 |
| ☐ 58 Gator Bowl Stadium | .75 | .30 | .07 |
| ☐ 59 Floyd of Rosedale | .75 | .30 | .07 |
| (Trophy) | | | |
| ☐ 60 Checklist Card | .75 | .30 | .07 |

## 1987 Iowa

The 1987 Iowa football set contains 63 cards measuring approximately 2 1/2" by 3 9/16". Inside a black border, the fronts display color posed photos shot from the waist up. The Hawkeye helmet appears in the lower left corner, with player information in a yellow stripe extending to the right. The horizontally oriented backs have biographical information, player profile, and bowl game emblems. The cards are unnumbered and checklisted below in alphabetical order, with non-player cards listed at the end.

| | MINT | EXC | G-VG |
|---|---|---|---|
| COMPLETE SET (63) | 35.00 | 14.00 | 3.50 |
| COMMON CARD (1-63) | .60 | .24 | .06 |
| ☐ 1 Mark Adams | .60 | .24 | .06 |
| ☐ 2 Dave Alexander | 1.00 | .40 | .10 |
| ☐ 3 Bill Anderson | .60 | .24 | .06 |
| ☐ 4 Tim Anderson | .60 | .24 | .06 |
| ☐ 5 Rick Bayless | .60 | .24 | .06 |
| ☐ 6 Jeff Beard | .60 | .24 | .06 |
| ☐ 7 Mike Burke | .60 | .24 | .06 |
| ☐ 8 Kerry Burt | .60 | .24 | .06 |
| ☐ 9 Malcolm Christie | .60 | .24 | .06 |
| ☐ 10 Craig Clark | .60 | .24 | .06 |
| ☐ 11 Marv Cook | 2.00 | .80 | .20 |
| ☐ 12 Jeff Croston | .60 | .24 | .06 |
| ☐ 13 Greg Divis | .60 | .24 | .06 |
| ☐ 14 Quinn Early | 2.00 | .80 | .20 |
| ☐ 15 Greg Fedders | .60 | .24 | .06 |
| ☐ 16 Mike Flagg | .60 | .24 | .06 |
| ☐ 17 Melvin Foster | .60 | .24 | .06 |
| ☐ 18 Hayden Fry CO | 1.50 | .60 | .15 |
| ☐ 19 Grant Goodman | .60 | .24 | .06 |
| ☐ 20 Dave Haight | 1.00 | .40 | .10 |
| ☐ 21 Merton Hanks | 1.50 | .60 | .15 |
| ☐ 22 Deven Harbers | .60 | .24 | .06 |
| ☐ 23 Kevin Harmon | .75 | .30 | .07 |
| ☐ 24 Chuck Hartlieb | 1.25 | .50 | .12 |
| ☐ 25 Tork Hook | .60 | .24 | .06 |
| ☐ 26 Rob Houghtlin | .60 | .24 | .06 |
| ☐ 27 David Hudson | .60 | .24 | .06 |
| ☐ 28 Myron Keppy | .60 | .24 | .06 |
| ☐ 29 Jeff Koeppel | .60 | .24 | .06 |
| ☐ 30 Bob Kratch | 1.50 | .60 | .15 |
| ☐ 31 Peter Marciano | .60 | .24 | .06 |
| ☐ 32 Jim Mauro | .60 | .24 | .06 |
| ☐ 33 Marc Mazzeri | .60 | .24 | .06 |
| ☐ 34 Dan McGwire | 2.00 | .80 | .20 |
| ☐ 35 Mike Miller | .60 | .24 | .06 |
| ☐ 36 Joe Mott | 1.00 | .40 | .10 |

| | MINT | EXC | G-VG |
|---|---|---|---|
| ☐ 37 James Pipkins | .60 | .24 | .06 |
| ☐ 38 Tom Poholsky | .75 | .30 | .07 |
| ☐ 39 Jim Poynton | .60 | .24 | .06 |
| ☐ 40 J.J. Puk | .60 | .24 | .06 |
| ☐ 41 Brad Quast | .60 | .24 | .06 |
| ☐ 42 Jim Reilly | .60 | .24 | .06 |
| ☐ 43 Matt Ruhland | .60 | .24 | .06 |
| ☐ 44 Bob Schmitt | .60 | .24 | .06 |
| ☐ 45 Joe Schuster | .75 | .30 | .07 |
| ☐ 46 Dwight Sistrunk | .60 | .24 | .06 |
| ☐ 47 Mark Stoops | .60 | .24 | .06 |
| ☐ 48 Steve Thomas | .60 | .24 | .06 |
| ☐ 49 Kent Thompson | .60 | .24 | .06 |
| ☐ 50 Travis Watkins | .60 | .24 | .06 |
| ☐ 51 Herb Wester | .60 | .24 | .06 |
| ☐ 52 Anthony Wright | .60 | .24 | .06 |
| ☐ 53 Big 10 Championship | .60 | .24 | .06 |
| Ring and Rose Bowl Ring | | | |
| ☐ 54 Cheerleaders | .75 | .30 | .07 |
| ☐ 55 Floyd of Rosedale | .60 | .24 | .06 |
| (Trophy) | | | |
| ☐ 56 Freedom Bowl | .60 | .24 | .06 |
| (Game Action Photo) | | | |
| ☐ 57 Herky the Hawk | .60 | .24 | .06 |
| (Mascot) | | | |
| ☐ 58 Holiday Bowl | .60 | .24 | .06 |
| (Game Action Photo) | | | |
| ☐ 59 Indoor Practice Facility | .60 | .24 | .06 |
| ☐ 60 Iowa Team Captains | 1.00 | .40 | .10 |
| (Quinn Early and five others) | | | |
| ☐ 61 Kinnick Stadium | .60 | .24 | .06 |
| ☐ 62 Peach Bowl | .60 | .24 | .06 |
| (Game Action Photo) | | | |
| ☐ 63 Pom Pons | 1.00 | .40 | .10 |
| (Cheerleaders) | | | |

## 1988 Iowa

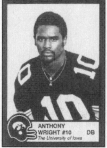

The 1988 Iowa Hawkeyes set contains 64 standard-size (2 1/2" by 3 1/2") cards. The fronts feature color portrait photos bordered in black. The horizontally oriented backs show brief profiles. The cards are unnumbered, so are listed by jersey numbers.

| | MINT | EXC | G-VG |
|---|---|---|---|
| COMPLETE SET (64) | 30.00 | 12.00 | 3.00 |
| COMMON CARD | .50 | .20 | .05 |
| ☐ 2 Travis Watkins | .75 | .30 | .07 |
| ☐ 4 James Pipkins | .50 | .20 | .05 |
| ☐ 5 Mike Burke | .50 | .20 | .05 |
| ☐ 8 Chuck Hartlieb | 1.00 | .40 | .10 |
| ☐ 10 Anthony Wright | .50 | .20 | .05 |
| ☐ 14 Tom Poholsky | .60 | .24 | .06 |
| ☐ 16 Deven Harberts | .50 | .20 | .05 |
| ☐ 18 Leroy Smith | .50 | .20 | .05 |
| ☐ 20 David Hudson | .50 | .20 | .05 |
| ☐ 21 Tony Stewart | .50 | .20 | .05 |
| ☐ 22 Sean Smith | .50 | .20 | .05 |
| ☐ 23 Richard Bass | .50 | .20 | .05 |
| ☐ 26 Peter Marciano | .50 | .20 | .05 |
| ☐ 29 Greg Brown | .50 | .20 | .05 |
| ☐ 30 Grant Goodman | .50 | .20 | .05 |
| ☐ 31 John Derby | .50 | .20 | .05 |
| ☐ 32 Mike Saunders | 1.00 | .40 | .10 |
| ☐ 35 Brad Quast | .50 | .20 | .05 |
| ☐ 38 Chet Davis | .50 | .20 | .05 |
| ☐ 40 Marc Mazzeri | .50 | .20 | .05 |
| ☐ 41 Mark Stoops | .50 | .20 | .05 |
| ☐ 42 Tork Hook | .50 | .20 | .05 |
| ☐ 44 Keaton Smiley | .50 | .20 | .05 |
| ☐ 45 Merton Hanks | 1.25 | .50 | .12 |
| ☐ 48 Tyrone Berrie | .50 | .20 | .05 |

| | | | |
|---|---|---|---|
| ☐ 50 Bill Anderson | .50 | .20 | .05 |
| ☐ 51 Jeff Koeppel | .50 | .20 | .05 |
| ☐ 53 Greg Fedders | .50 | .20 | .05 |
| ☐ 57 Matt Ruhland | .50 | .20 | .05 |
| ☐ 58 Greg Davis | .50 | .20 | .05 |
| ☐ 60 Bob Schmitt | .50 | .20 | .05 |
| ☐ 61 Dave Turner | .50 | .20 | .05 |
| ☐ 64 Dave Haight | .75 | .30 | .07 |
| ☐ 66 Melvin Foster | .50 | .20 | .05 |
| ☐ 67 Jim Poynton | .50 | .20 | .05 |
| ☐ 68 Tim Anderson | .50 | .20 | .05 |
| ☐ 70 Bob Kratch | 1.00 | .40 | .10 |
| ☐ 71 Jim Johnson | .50 | .20 | .05 |
| ☐ 74 George Hawthorne | .50 | .20 | .05 |
| ☐ 75 Greg Aegerter | .50 | .20 | .05 |
| ☐ 77 Paul Glonek | .50 | .20 | .05 |
| ☐ 80 Steve Green | .50 | .20 | .05 |
| ☐ 81 Brian Wise | .50 | .20 | .05 |
| ☐ 82 Jon Filloon | .50 | .20 | .05 |
| ☐ 84 Marv Cook | 1.50 | .60 | .15 |
| ☐ 85 John Palmer | .60 | .24 | .06 |
| ☐ 87 Jeff Skillett | .50 | .20 | .05 |
| ☐ 88 Tom Ward | .50 | .20 | .05 |
| ☐ 95 Jim Reilly | .50 | .20 | .05 |
| ☐ 96 Ron Geater | .50 | .20 | .05 |
| ☐ 97 Joe Mott | .75 | .30 | .07 |
| ☐ 99 Moses Santos | .50 | .20 | .05 |
| ☐ xx Team Captains | 1.00 | .40 | .10 |
| (Marv Cook and four others) | | | |
| ☐ xx Hayden Fry CO | 1.00 | .40 | .10 |
| ☐ xx Holiday Bowl 1987 | .75 | .30 | .07 |
| Hayden Fry CO) | | | |
| ☐ xx Peach Bowl | .50 | .20 | .05 |
| (Game Action Photo) | | | |
| ☐ xx Holiday Bowl 1986 | .50 | .20 | .05 |
| (Game Action Photo) | | | |
| ☐ xx Herky the Hawk(Mascot) | .50 | .20 | .05 |
| ☐ xx Cheerleaders | .75 | .30 | .07 |
| ☐ xx Kinnick Stadium | .50 | .20 | .05 |
| ☐ xx Pom Pons | .75 | .30 | .07 |
| (Cheerleaders) | | | |
| ☐ xx Championship Rings | .50 | .20 | .05 |
| ☐ xx Indoor Practice | .50 | .20 | .05 |
| Facility | | | |
| ☐ xx Symbolic Tiger Hawk | .60 | .24 | .06 |
| (Helmet) | | | |

## 1989 Iowa

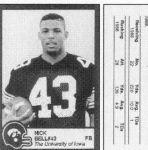

NICK BELL #43 FB
The University of Iowa

The 1989 Iowa football set contains 90 cards measuring approximately 2 1/2" by 3 9/16". Inside a black border, the fronts display color posed photos shot from the waist up. The team helmet appears in the lower left corner, with player information in a yellow stripe extending to the right. The horizontally oriented backs have biographical information, player profile, and bowl game emblems. The cards are unnumbered and checklisted below in alphabetical order, with non-player cards listed at the end.

| | MINT | EXC | G-VG |
|---|---|---|---|
| COMPLETE SET (90) | 30.00 | 12.00 | 3.00 |
| COMMON CARD (1-90) | .40 | .16 | .04 |
| | | | |
| ☐ 1 Greg Aegerter | .40 | .16 | .04 |
| ☐ 2 Kevin Allendorf | .40 | .16 | .04 |
| ☐ 3 Bill Anderson | .40 | .16 | .04 |
| ☐ 4 Richard Bass | .40 | .16 | .04 |
| ☐ 5 Rob Baxley | .40 | .16 | .04 |
| ☐ 6 Nick Bell | 2.50 | 1.00 | .25 |
| ☐ 7 Phil Bradley | .40 | .16 | .04 |
| ☐ 8 Greg Brown | .40 | .16 | .04 |
| ☐ 9 Doug Buch | .40 | .16 | .04 |
| ☐ 10 Gary Clark | .40 | .16 | .04 |
| ☐ 11 Roderick Davis | .40 | .16 | .04 |
| ☐ 12 Scott Davis | .75 | .30 | .07 |

| | | | |
|---|---|---|---|
| ☐ 13 John Derby | .50 | .20 | .05 |
| ☐ 14 Mike Devlin | .40 | .16 | .04 |
| ☐ 15 Jason Dumont | .40 | .16 | .04 |
| ☐ 16 Mike Ertz | .40 | .16 | .04 |
| ☐ 17 Ted Faley | .40 | .16 | .04 |
| ☐ 18 Greg Fedders | .40 | .16 | .04 |
| ☐ 19 Mike Ferroni | .50 | .20 | .05 |
| ☐ 20 Jon Filloon | .40 | .16 | .04 |
| ☐ 21 Melvin Foster | .50 | .20 | .05 |
| ☐ 22 Hayden Fry CO | 1.00 | .40 | .10 |
| ☐ 23 Ron Geater | .40 | .16 | .04 |
| ☐ 24 Ed Gochenour | .40 | .16 | .04 |
| ☐ 25 Merton Hanks | .75 | .30 | .07 |
| ☐ 26 Jim Hartlieb | .50 | .20 | .05 |
| ☐ 27 George Hawthorne | .40 | .16 | .04 |
| ☐ 28 Tork Hook | .40 | .16 | .04 |
| ☐ 29 Danan Hughes | .75 | .30 | .07 |
| ☐ 30 Jim Johnson | .40 | .16 | .04 |
| ☐ 31 Jeff Koeppel | .40 | .16 | .04 |
| ☐ 32 Marvin Lampkin | .40 | .16 | .04 |
| ☐ 33 Peter Marciano | .40 | .16 | .04 |
| ☐ 34 Ed Marshall | .40 | .16 | .04 |
| ☐ 35 Kirk McGowan | .40 | .16 | .04 |
| ☐ 36 Mike Miller | .40 | .16 | .04 |
| ☐ 37 Lew Montgomery | .40 | .16 | .04 |
| ☐ 38 George Murphy | .40 | .16 | .04 |
| ☐ 39 John Palmer | .50 | .20 | .05 |
| ☐ 40 James Pipkens | .40 | .16 | .04 |
| ☐ 41 Tom Poholsky | .50 | .20 | .05 |
| ☐ 42 Eddie Polly | .40 | .16 | .04 |
| ☐ 43 Jim Poynton | .40 | .16 | .04 |
| ☐ 44 Brad Quast | .40 | .16 | .04 |
| ☐ 45 Matt Rodgers | .75 | .30 | .07 |
| ☐ 46 Matt Ruhland | .40 | .16 | .04 |
| ☐ 47 Ron Ryan | .40 | .16 | .04 |
| ☐ 48 Moses Santos | .40 | .16 | .04 |
| ☐ 49 Mike Saunders | .75 | .30 | .07 |
| ☐ 50 Doug Scott | .40 | .16 | .04 |
| ☐ 51 Jeff Skillett | .40 | .16 | .04 |
| ☐ 52 Leroy Smith | .40 | .16 | .04 |
| ☐ 53 Sean Smith | .40 | .16 | .04 |
| ☐ 54 Sean Snyder | .40 | .16 | .04 |
| ☐ 55 Tony Stewart | .40 | .16 | .04 |
| ☐ 56 Mark Stoops | .40 | .16 | .04 |
| ☐ 57 Dave Turner | .40 | .16 | .04 |
| ☐ 58 Darin Vande Zande | .40 | .16 | .04 |
| ☐ 59 Ted Velicer | .40 | .16 | .04 |
| ☐ 60 Travis Watkins | .40 | .16 | .04 |
| ☐ 61 Dusty Weiland | .40 | .16 | .04 |
| ☐ 62 Ladd Wessels | .40 | .16 | .04 |
| ☐ 63 Matt Whitaker | .40 | .16 | .04 |
| ☐ 64 Brian Wise | .40 | .16 | .04 |
| ☐ 65 Anthony Wright | .40 | .16 | .04 |
| ☐ 66 100 Years of Iowa Football (Logo) | .40 | .16 | .04 |
| ☐ 67 The Tigerhawk (School Logo) | .40 | .16 | .04 |
| ☐ 68 Herky The Hawk (Mascot) | .40 | .16 | .04 |
| ☐ 69 Kinnick Stadium | .40 | .16 | .04 |
| ☐ 70 Hawkeye Fans | .40 | .16 | .04 |
| ☐ 71 NFL Tradition (Logo) | .40 | .16 | .04 |
| ☐ 72 1982 Peach Bowl (Logo) | .40 | .16 | .04 |
| ☐ 73 1982 Rose Bowl (Logo) | .40 | .16 | .04 |
| ☐ 74 1983 Gator Bowl (Logo) | .40 | .16 | .04 |
| ☐ 75 1984 Freedom Bowl (Logo) | .40 | .16 | .04 |
| ☐ 76 1986 Holiday Bowl (Logo) | .40 | .16 | .04 |
| ☐ 77 1986 Rose Bowl (Logo) | .40 | .16 | .04 |
| ☐ 78 1987 Holiday Bowl (Logo) | .40 | .16 | .04 |
| ☐ 79 1988 Peach Bowl (Logo) | .40 | .16 | .04 |
| ☐ 80 Big Ten Conference (Logo) | .40 | .16 | .04 |
| ☐ 81 Iowa Marching Band | .40 | .16 | .04 |
| ☐ 82 Indoor Practice Facility | .40 | .16 | .04 |
| ☐ 83 Iowa Locker Rooms | .40 | .16 | .04 |
| ☐ 84 Iowa Weight Room | .40 | .16 | .04 |
| ☐ 85 Iowa Class Rooms | .40 | .16 | .04 |
| ☐ 86 Players' Lounge | .40 | .16 | .04 |
| ☐ 87 Floyd of Rosedale (Trophy) | .40 | .16 | .04 |
| ☐ 88 Medical Facilities | .40 | .16 | .04 |
| ☐ 89 Media Coverage | .40 | .16 | .04 |
| ☐ 90 Television Coverage (Camera) | .50 | .20 | .05 |

## 1993 Iowa

The 1993 Iowa set consists of 64 standard-size (2 1/2" by 3 1/2") cards. The fronts feature black-bordered color player photos, mostly posed, with the player's name and uniform number appearing in gold-colored lettering within the top margin. The team name and the

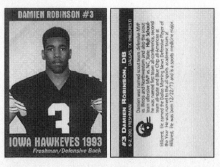

player's postion are shown in gold-colored lettering within the bottom margin. The yellow horizontal back carries the player's name, position, and biography in white lettering within the black stripe across the top. Below are the player's high school and college football highlights. The cards are unnumbered and checklisted below in alphabetical order, with nonplayer cards listed at the end.

|  | MINT | EXC | G-VG |
|---|---|---|---|
| COMPLETE SET (64) | 25.00 | 10.00 | 2.50 |
| COMMON PLAYER (1-64) | .35 | .14 | .03 |
| ☐ 1 Ryan Abraham | .50 | .20 | .05 |
| ☐ 2 Greg Allen | .35 | .14 | .03 |
| ☐ 3 Jeff Andrews | .35 | .14 | .03 |
| ☐ 4 Jeff Anttila | .35 | .14 | .03 |
| ☐ 5 Jefferson Bates | .35 | .14 | .03 |
| ☐ 6 George Bennett | .35 | .14 | .03 |
| ☐ 7 Lloyd Bickham | .35 | .14 | .03 |
| ☐ 8 Larry Blue | .50 | .20 | .05 |
| ☐ 9 Pat Boone | .35 | .14 | .03 |
| ☐ 10 Tyrone Boudreaux | .35 | .14 | .03 |
| ☐ 11 Paul Burmeister | .75 | .30 | .07 |
| ☐ 12 Tyler Casey | .35 | .14 | .03 |
| ☐ 13 Billy Coats | .35 | .14 | .03 |
| ☐ 14 Maurea Crain | .50 | .20 | .05 |
| ☐ 15 Ernest Crank | .75 | .30 | .07 |
| ☐ 16 Mike Dailey | .50 | .20 | .05 |
| ☐ 17 Anthony Dean | .75 | .30 | .07 |
| ☐ 18 Bobby Diaco | .35 | .14 | .03 |
| ☐ 19 Mike Duprey | .35 | .14 | .03 |
| ☐ 20 Billy Ennis-Inge | .35 | .14 | .03 |
| ☐ 21 Matt Eyde | .35 | .14 | .03 |
| ☐ 22 Fritz Fequiere | .35 | .14 | .03 |
| ☐ 23 Hayden Fry CO | 1.00 | .40 | .10 |
| ☐ 24 Willie Guy | .35 | .14 | .03 |
| ☐ 25 John Hartlieb | .50 | .20 | .05 |
| ☐ 26 Jason Henlon | .35 | .14 | .03 |
| ☐ 27 Matt Hilliard | .35 | .14 | .03 |
| ☐ 28 Mike Hornaday | .35 | .14 | .03 |
| ☐ 29 Rob Huber | .35 | .14 | .03 |
| ☐ 30 Chris Jackson | .35 | .14 | .03 |
| ☐ 31 Harold Jasper | .75 | .30 | .07 |
| ☐ 32 Jamar Jones | .35 | .14 | .03 |
| ☐ 33 Kent Kahl | .35 | .14 | .03 |
| ☐ 34 Cliff King | .50 | .20 | .05 |
| ☐ 35 John Kline | .35 | .14 | .03 |
| ☐ 36 Tom Knight | .35 | .14 | .03 |
| ☐ 37 Aaron Kooiker | .35 | .14 | .03 |
| ☐ 38 Andy Kreider | .35 | .14 | .03 |
| ☐ 39 Bill Lange | .50 | .20 | .05 |
| ☐ 40 Doug Laufenberg | .35 | .14 | .03 |
| ☐ 41 Hal Mady | .75 | .30 | .07 |
| ☐ 42 Brian McCullouch | .35 | .14 | .03 |
| ☐ 43 Jason Olejniczak | .50 | .20 | .05 |
| ☐ 44 Chris Palmer | .35 | .14 | .03 |
| ☐ 45 Scott Plate | .50 | .20 | .05 |
| ☐ 46 Marquis Porter | .50 | .20 | .05 |
| ☐ 47 Matt Purdy | .35 | .14 | .03 |
| ☐ 48 Matt Quest | .35 | .14 | .03 |
| ☐ 49 Damien Robinson | .50 | .20 | .05 |
| ☐ 50 Todd Romano | .35 | .14 | .03 |
| ☐ 51 Mark Roussell | .35 | .14 | .03 |
| ☐ 52 Ted Serama | .35 | .14 | .03 |
| ☐ 53 Scott Sether | .35 | .14 | .03 |
| ☐ 54 Sedrick Shaw | .50 | .20 | .05 |
| ☐ 55 Scott Slutzker | .75 | .30 | .07 |
| ☐ 56 Ryan Terry | .75 | .30 | .07 |
| ☐ 57 Mike Wells | .50 | .20 | .05 |
| ☐ 58 Casey Wiegmann | .35 | .14 | .03 |
| ☐ 59 Parker Wildeman | .35 | .14 | .03 |
| ☐ 60 Big Ten Conference (Logo card) | .35 | .14 | .03 |
| ☐ 61 Hawkeyes Schedule | .35 | .14 | .03 |
| ☐ 62 Herky (Mascot) | .35 | .14 | .03 |
| ☐ 63 Indoor Practice Facility | .35 | .14 | .03 |
| ☐ 64 Kinnick Stadium | .50 | .20 | .05 |

## 1989 Kansas

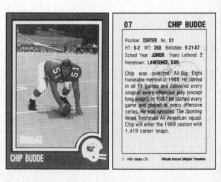

The 1989 University of Kansas set contains 40 standard-size (2 1/2" by 3 1/2") cards. The fronts feature color photos bordered in blue. The vertically oriented backs show brief profiles. The cards are numbered on the back in the upper left corner. The set was produced by Leesley, Ltd. for the University of Kansas. The set was originally available from the KU Bookstore for 6.00 plus 1.50 for postage.

|  | MINT | EXC | G-VG |
|---|---|---|---|
| COMPLETE SET (40) | 12.00 | 5.00 | 1.20 |
| COMMON CARD (1-40) | .35 | .14 | .03 |
| ☐ 1 Kelly Donohoe | .75 | .30 | .07 |
| ☐ 2 Roger Robben | .35 | .14 | .03 |
| ☐ 3 Tony Sands | .35 | .14 | .03 |
| ☐ 4 Paul Zaffaroni | .35 | .14 | .03 |
| ☐ 5 Lance Flachsbarth | .35 | .14 | .03 |
| ☐ 6 Brad Fleeman | .35 | .14 | .03 |
| ☐ 7 Chip Budde | .50 | .20 | .05 |
| ☐ 8 Bill Hundelt | .35 | .14 | .03 |
| ☐ 9 Dan Newbrough | .35 | .14 | .03 |
| ☐ 10 Gary Oatis | .35 | .14 | .03 |
| ☐ 11 B.J. Lohsen | .50 | .20 | .05 |
| ☐ 12 John Fritch | .35 | .14 | .03 |
| ☐ 13 Russ Bowen | .35 | .14 | .03 |
| ☐ 14 Smith Holland | .35 | .14 | .03 |
| ☐ 15 Jason Priest | .50 | .20 | .05 |
| ☐ 16 Scott McCabe | .35 | .14 | .03 |
| ☐ 17 Jason Tyrer | .35 | .14 | .03 |
| ☐ 18 Mongo Allen | .35 | .14 | .03 |
| ☐ 19 Glen Mason CO | .50 | .20 | .05 |
| ☐ 20 Deral Boykin | .35 | .14 | .03 |
| ☐ 21 Quintin Smith | .35 | .14 | .03 |
| ☐ 22 Mark Koncz | .35 | .14 | .03 |
| ☐ 23 John Baker | .50 | .20 | .05 |
| ☐ 24 Football Staff (schedule on back) | .35 | .14 | .03 |
| ☐ 25 Maurice Hooks | .35 | .14 | .03 |
| ☐ 26 Frank Hatchett | .35 | .14 | .03 |
| ☐ 27 Paul Friday | .35 | .14 | .03 |
| ☐ 28 Doug Terry | .35 | .14 | .03 |
| ☐ 29 Kenny Drayton | .35 | .14 | .03 |
| ☐ 30 Jim New | .35 | .14 | .03 |
| ☐ 31 Chris Perez | .35 | .14 | .03 |
| ☐ 32 Maurice Douglas | .75 | .30 | .07 |
| ☐ 33 Curtis Moore | .35 | .14 | .03 |
| ☐ 34 David Gordon | .35 | .14 | .03 |
| ☐ 35 Matt Nolen | .35 | .14 | .03 |
| ☐ 36 Dave Walton | .35 | .14 | .03 |
| ☐ 37 King Dixon | .50 | .20 | .05 |
| ☐ 38 Memorial Stadium | .35 | .14 | .03 |
| ☐ 39 Jayhawks in Action (Kelly Donohue) | .50 | .20 | .05 |
| ☐ 40 Jayhawks in Action (John Baker) | .50 | .20 | .05 |
| ☐ NNO Title Card | .75 | .30 | .07 |

## 1992 Kansas

This 52-card set measures the standard size (2 1/2" by 3 1/2") and features the 1992 Kansas Jayhawks football team. The fronts display either posed or action color player photos inside green and blue borders. The green border has white yard markers as found on a football field. The team helmet, player's name, position, and uniform number are presented in a red bar beneath the picture. The horizontal backs carry a black-and-white head shot, biographical information, player profile, or statistics. The cards are unnumbered and checklisted below in alphabetical order.

|  | MINT | EXC | G-VG |
|---|---|---|---|
| COMPLETE SET (52) | 20.00 | 8.00 | 2.00 |
| COMMON CARD (1-50) | .40 | .16 | .04 |
| ☐ 1 Mark Allison | .40 | .16 | .04 |
| ☐ 2 Hassan Bailey | .40 | .16 | .04 |
| ☐ 3 Greg Ballard | .40 | .16 | .04 |
| ☐ 4 Marlin Blakeney | .40 | .16 | .04 |
| ☐ 5 Khristopher Booth | .40 | .16 | .04 |
| ☐ 6 Charley Bowen | .40 | .16 | .04 |
| ☐ 7 Gilbert Brown | .75 | .30 | .07 |
| ☐ 8 Dwayne Chandler | .40 | .16 | .04 |
| ☐ 9 Brian Christian | .40 | .16 | .04 |
| ☐ 10 David Converse | .40 | .16 | .04 |
| ☐ 11 Monte Cozzens | .40 | .16 | .04 |
| ☐ 12 Don Davis | .40 | .16 | .04 |
| ☐ 13 Maurice Douglas | .60 | .24 | .06 |
| ☐ 14 Dan Eichloff | .60 | .24 | .06 |
| ☐ 15 Chad Fette | .40 | .16 | .04 |
| ☐ 16 Matt Gay | .40 | .16 | .04 |
| ☐ 17 Harold Harris | .40 | .16 | .04 |
| ☐ 18 Rodney Harris | .60 | .24 | .06 |
| ☐ 19 Steve Harvey | .40 | .16 | .04 |
| ☐ 20 Hessley Hempstead | .40 | .16 | .04 |
| ☐ 21 Chip Hilleary | 1.00 | .40 | .10 |
| ☐ 22 Dick Holt | .40 | .16 | .04 |
| ☐ 23 Guy Howard | .40 | .16 | .04 |
| ☐ 24 Chaka Johnson | .40 | .16 | .04 |
| ☐ 25 John Jones | .40 | .16 | .04 |
| ☐ 26 Rod Jones | .40 | .16 | .04 |
| ☐ 27 Kwamie Lassiter | .40 | .16 | .04 |
| ☐ 28 Rob Licursi | .40 | .16 | .04 |
| ☐ 29 Trace Liggett | .40 | .16 | .04 |
| ☐ 30 Keith Loneker | .40 | .16 | .04 |
| ☐ 31 Dave Marcum | .40 | .16 | .04 |
| ☐ 32 Glen Mason CO | .60 | .24 | .06 |
| ☐ 33 Chris Maumalanga | .40 | .16 | .04 |
| ☐ 34 Gerald McBurrows | .40 | .16 | .04 |
| ☐ 35 Robert Mitchell | .40 | .16 | .04 |
| ☐ 36 Ty Moeder | .40 | .16 | .04 |
| ☐ 37 Kyle Moore | .40 | .16 | .04 |
| ☐ 38 Ron Page | .40 | .16 | .04 |
| ☐ 39 Chris Powell | .40 | .16 | .04 |
| ☐ 40 Dan Schmidt | .40 | .16 | .04 |
| ☐ 41 Ashaundai Smith | .40 | .16 | .04 |
| ☐ 42 Mike Steele | .40 | .16 | .04 |
| ☐ 43 Dana Stubblefield | 1.50 | .60 | .15 |
| ☐ 44 Wes Swinford | .40 | .16 | .04 |
| ☐ 45 Larry Thiel | .40 | .16 | .04 |
| ☐ 46 Fredrick Thomas | .60 | .24 | .06 |
| ☐ 47 Pete Vang | .40 | .16 | .04 |
| ☐ 48 Robert Vaughn | .40 | .16 | .04 |
| ☐ 49 George White | .60 | .24 | .06 |
| ☐ 50 Sylvester Wright | .40 | .16 | .04 |
| ☐ NNO Schedule Card | .40 | .16 | .04 |
| ☐ NNO Coaching Staff | .40 | .16 | .04 |

## 1981 Louisville Police

This 64-card set, which measures approximately 2 5/8" by 4 1/8", was sponsored by Pepsi-Cola (Take the Pepsi Challenge), The Louisville Area Chamber of Commerce, and the Greater Louisville Police Departments. The card front features red borders surrounding a black-and-white photo of the player. The backs feature definitions of football terms and a brief safety tip. This set features future professional star Mark Clayton in one of his earliest card appearances. Reportedly the Title/Logo card is very difficult to find. The cards are numbered on the back by safety tips.

|  | MINT | EXC | G-VG |
|---|---|---|---|
| COMPLETE SET (64) | 100.00 | 40.00 | 10.00 |
| COMMON CARD (1-64) | 1.00 | .40 | .10 |
| ☐ 1 Title Card SP | 30.00 | 12.00 | 3.00 |

| (Catch That Cardinal Spirit) |  |  |  |
|---|---|---|---|
| ☐ 2 Bob Weber CO | 1.00 | .40 | .10 |
| ☐ 3 Assistant Coaches | 1.00 | .40 | .10 |
| ☐ 4 Jay Trautwein | 1.00 | .40 | .10 |
| ☐ 5 Darrell Wimberly | 1.00 | .40 | .10 |
| ☐ 6 Jeff Van Camp | 1.00 | .40 | .10 |
| ☐ 7 Joe Welch | 1.00 | .40 | .10 |
| ☐ 8 Fred Blackmon | 1.00 | .40 | .10 |
| ☐ 9 Lamar(Toot) Evans | 1.00 | .40 | .10 |
| ☐ 10 Tom Blair | 1.00 | .40 | .10 |
| ☐ 11 Joe Kader | 1.00 | .40 | .10 |
| ☐ 12 Mike Trainor | 1.00 | .40 | .10 |
| ☐ 13 Richard Tharpe | 1.00 | .40 | .10 |
| ☐ 14 Gene Hagan | 1.00 | .40 | .10 |
| ☐ 15 Greg Jones | 1.00 | .40 | .10 |
| ☐ 16 Leon Williams | 1.00 | .40 | .10 |
| ☐ 17 Ellsworth Larkins | 1.00 | .40 | .10 |
| ☐ 18 Sebastian Curry | 1.00 | .40 | .10 |
| ☐ 19 Frank Minnifield | 5.00 | 2.00 | .50 |
| ☐ 20 Roger Clay | 1.00 | .40 | .10 |
| ☐ 21 Mark Blasinsky | 1.00 | .40 | .10 |
| ☐ 22 Mike Cruz | 1.00 | .40 | .10 |
| ☐ 23 David Arthur | 1.00 | .40 | .10 |
| ☐ 24 Johnny Unitas | 15.00 | 6.00 | 1.50 |
| (In front background, list of Cardinals who played pro ball) |  |  |  |
| ☐ 25 John DeMarco | 1.00 | .40 | .10 |
| ☐ 26 Eric Rollins | 1.00 | .40 | .10 |
| ☐ 27 Jack Pok | 1.00 | .40 | .10 |
| ☐ 28 Pete McCartney | 1.00 | .40 | .10 |
| ☐ 29 Mark Clayton | 15.00 | 6.00 | 1.50 |
| ☐ 30 Jeff Hortert | 1.00 | .40 | .10 |
| ☐ 31 Pete Bowen | 1.00 | .40 | .10 |
| ☐ 32 Robert Niece | 1.00 | .40 | .10 |
| ☐ 33 Todd McMahan | 1.00 | .40 | .10 |
| ☐ 34 John Wall | 1.00 | .40 | .10 |
| ☐ 35 Kelly Stickrod | 1.00 | .40 | .10 |
| ☐ 36 Jim Miller | 1.00 | .40 | .10 |
| ☐ 37 Tom Moore | 1.00 | .40 | .10 |
| ☐ 38 Kurt Knop | 1.00 | .40 | .10 |
| ☐ 39 Mark Musgrave | 1.00 | .40 | .10 |
| ☐ 40 Tony Campbell | 1.00 | .40 | .10 |
| ☐ 41 Mark Wilson | 1.00 | .40 | .10 |
| ☐ 42 Robert Mitchell | 1.00 | .40 | .10 |
| ☐ 43 Courtney Jeter | 1.00 | .40 | .10 |
| ☐ 44 Wayne Taylor | 1.00 | .40 | .10 |
| ☐ 45 Jeff Speedy | 1.00 | .40 | .10 |
| ☐ 46 Donald Craft | 1.00 | .40 | .10 |
| ☐ 47 Glenn Hunter | 1.00 | .40 | .10 |
| ☐ 48 1981 Louisville Schedule | 1.00 | .40 | .10 |
| ☐ 49 Greg Hickman | 1.00 | .40 | .10 |
| ☐ 50 Nate Dozier | 1.00 | .40 | .10 |
| ☐ 51 Pat Patterson | 1.00 | .40 | .10 |
| ☐ 52 Scott Gannon | 1.00 | .40 | .10 |
| ☐ 53 Dean May | 1.00 | .40 | .10 |
| ☐ 54 David Hatfield | 1.00 | .40 | .10 |
| ☐ 55 Mike Nuzzolese | 1.00 | .40 | .10 |
| ☐ 56 John Ayers | 1.00 | .40 | .10 |
| ☐ 57 Lamar Cummins | 1.00 | .40 | .10 |
| ☐ 58 Bill Olsen AD | 1.00 | .40 | .10 |
| ☐ 59 Tailgating | 1.00 | .40 | .10 |
| ☐ 60 Football Complex | 1.00 | .40 | .10 |
| ☐ 61 Marching Band | 1.00 | .40 | .10 |
| ☐ 62 Cheerleaders | 1.50 | .60 | .15 |
| ☐ 63 Administration Bldg. | 1.00 | .40 | .10 |
| ☐ 64 Cardinal Bird | 1.50 | .60 | .15 |

# 1990 Louisville Smokey

This 16-card set was sponsored by the USDA Forest Service in cooperation with several other federal agencies. The cards measure the standard size (2 1/2" by 3 1/2"). On white card stock, the fronts display color action player photos with rounded bottom corners. The player's name and position appear between two Cardinal logos in a red stripe above the picture. The backs have brief biographical information and a safety cartoon featuring Smokey the Bear. The cards are unnumbered and checklisted below in alphabetical order.

|  | MINT | EXC | G-VG |
|---|---|---|---|
| COMPLETE SET (16) | 25.00 | 10.00 | 2.50 |
| COMMON CARD (1-16) | 1.25 | .50 | .12 |
|  |  |  |  |
| ☐ 1 Greg Brohm | 1.25 | .50 | .12 |
| ☐ 2 Jeff Brohm | 1.25 | .50 | .12 |
| ☐ 3 Pete Burkey | 1.25 | .50 | .12 |
| ☐ 4 Mike Flores | 1.25 | .50 | .12 |
| ☐ 5 Dan Gangwer | 1.25 | .50 | .12 |
| ☐ 6 Reggie Johnson | 2.00 | .80 | .20 |
| ☐ 7 Scott McAllister | 1.25 | .50 | .12 |
| ☐ 8 Ken McKay | 1.25 | .50 | .12 |
| ☐ 9 Browning Nagle | 4.00 | 1.60 | .40 |
| ☐ 10 Ed Reynolds | 1.25 | .50 | .12 |
| ☐ 11 Mark Sander | 1.25 | .50 | .12 |
| ☐ 12 Howard Schnellenberger CO | 3.00 | 1.20 | .30 |
| ☐ 13 Ted Washington | 3.00 | 1.20 | .30 |
| ☐ 14 Klaus Wilmsmeyer | 2.00 | .80 | .20 |
| ☐ 15 Cardinal Bird Mascot | 1.25 | .50 | .12 |
| ☐ 16 Cardinal Stadium | 1.25 | .50 | .12 |

# 1992 Louisville Kraft

Originally issued in perforated sheets, this 30-card set was sponsored by Kraft. The cards measure the standard size (2 1/2" by 3 1/2"). The fronts feature color posed player photos against a white card face. The team's name appears in red above the photo. Below the photo are team helmet, two horizonal red stripes, and the player's name, jersey number, position, and class. The plain white backs carry the player's name, position, jersey number, height, weight, and hometown at the top, followed below by career highlights. The cards are unnumbered and checklisted below in alphabetical order.

|  | MINT | EXC | G-VG |
|---|---|---|---|
| COMPLETE SET (30) | 15.00 | 6.00 | 1.50 |
| COMMON PLAYER (1-30) | .60 | .24 | .06 |
|  |  |  |  |
| ☐ 1 Jamie Asher | .75 | .30 | .07 |
| ☐ 2 Xzavia Atkins | .60 | .24 | .06 |
| ☐ 3 Kevin Blumeier | .60 | .24 | .06 |

| ☐ 4 Greg Brohm | .75 | .30 | .07 |
|---|---|---|---|
| ☐ 5 Jeff Brohm | .75 | .30 | .07 |
| ☐ 6 Brandon Brookfield | .60 | .24 | .06 |
| ☐ 7 Ray Buchanan | .60 | .24 | .06 |
| ☐ 8 Rawle Bynoe | .60 | .24 | .06 |
| ☐ 9 Tom Cavallo | .60 | .24 | .06 |
| ☐ 10 Kevin Cook | .60 | .24 | .06 |
| ☐ 11 Andy Culley | .60 | .24 | .06 |
| ☐ 12 Ralph Dawkins | .60 | .24 | .06 |
| ☐ 13 Dave Debold | .60 | .24 | .06 |
| ☐ 14 Chris Fitzpatrick | .60 | .24 | .06 |
| ☐ 15 Kevin Gaines | .60 | .24 | .06 |
| ☐ 16 Jose Gonzalez | .60 | .24 | .06 |
| ☐ 17 Jim Hanna | .60 | .24 | .06 |
| ☐ 18 Ken Harnden | .60 | .24 | .06 |
| ☐ 19 Ivey Henderson | .60 | .24 | .06 |
| ☐ 20 Joe Johnson | .75 | .30 | .07 |
| ☐ 21 Robert Knuutila | .60 | .24 | .06 |
| ☐ 22 Marty Lowe | .60 | .24 | .06 |
| ☐ 23 Roman Oben | .75 | .30 | .07 |
| ☐ 24 Garin Patrick | .60 | .24 | .06 |
| ☐ 25 Leonard Ray | .60 | .24 | .06 |
| ☐ 26 Shawn Rodriguez | .60 | .24 | .06 |
| ☐ 27 Anthony Shelman | .60 | .24 | .06 |
| ☐ 28 Brevin Smith | .60 | .24 | .06 |
| ☐ 29 Jason Stinson | .75 | .30 | .07 |
| ☐ 30 Ben Sumpter | .75 | .30 | .07 |

# 1993 Louisville Kraft

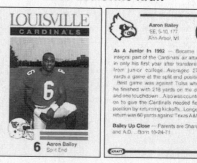

Originally issued in perforated sheets, this 30-card set was sponsored by Kraft. The cards measure the standard size (2 1/2" by 3 1/2"). The fronts feature color posed player photos against a white card face. The team's name appears in red above the photo. Below the photo are team helmet, two horizonal red stripes, and the player's name, jersey number, position, and class. The plain white backs carry the player's name, position, jersey number, height, weight, and hometown at the top, followed below by career highlights. The cards are unnumbered and checklisted below in alphabetical order.

|  | MINT | EXC | G-VG |
|---|---|---|---|
| COMPLETE SET (30) | 15.00 | 6.00 | 1.50 |
| COMMON PLAYER (1-30) | .60 | .24 | .06 |
|  |  |  |  |
| ☐ 1 Jamie Asher | .75 | .30 | .07 |
| ☐ 2 Aaron Bailey | .60 | .24 | .06 |
| ☐ 3 Zoe Barney | .60 | .24 | .06 |
| ☐ 4 Anthony Bridges | .60 | .24 | .06 |
| ☐ 5 Jeff Brohm | .75 | .30 | .07 |
| ☐ 6 Brandon Brookfield | .60 | .24 | .06 |
| ☐ 7 Kendall Brown | .60 | .24 | .06 |
| ☐ 8 Tom Carrol | .60 | .24 | .06 |
| ☐ 9 Tom Cavallo | .60 | .24 | .06 |
| ☐ 10 Kevin Cook | .60 | .24 | .06 |
| ☐ 11 Ralph Dawkins | .60 | .24 | .06 |
| ☐ 12 Dave Debold | .60 | .24 | .06 |
| ☐ 13 Reggie Ferguson | .60 | .24 | .06 |
| ☐ 14 Chris Fitzpatrick | .60 | .24 | .06 |
| ☐ 15 Johnny Frost | .60 | .24 | .06 |
| ☐ 16 Jim Hanna | .60 | .24 | .06 |
| ☐ 17 Ivey Henderson | .60 | .24 | .06 |
| ☐ 18 Marcus Hill | .60 | .24 | .06 |
| ☐ 19 Shawn Jackson | .60 | .24 | .06 |
| ☐ 20 Joe Johnson | .75 | .30 | .07 |
| ☐ 21 Marty Lowe | .60 | .24 | .06 |
| ☐ 22 Vertis McKinney | .60 | .24 | .06 |
| ☐ 23 Greg Minnis | .60 | .24 | .06 |
| ☐ 24 Roman Oben | .75 | .30 | .07 |
| ☐ 25 Garin Patrick | .60 | .24 | .06 |
| ☐ 26 Terry Quinn | .75 | .30 | .07 |
| ☐ 27 Leonard Ray | .60 | .24 | .06 |
| ☐ 28 Anthony Shelman | .60 | .24 | .06 |
| ☐ 29 Jason Stinson | .75 | .30 | .07 |
| ☐ 30 Ben Sumpter | .75 | .30 | .07 |

## 1983 LSU Sunbeam

This set features 100 cards remembering ex-football players from Louisiana State University (LSU). Cards are numbered on the back and measure 2 1/2" by 3 1/2". The posed pictures on the front are black and white, bordered on the top and sides by a goal post in the school's colors, purple and gold. The horizontally oriented backs feature purple printing with biographical information and the card number in the upper left hand corner. Some of the former and current NFL stars included in this set are Billy Cannon, Carlos Carson, Tommy Casanova, Tommy Davis, Sid Fournet, Bo Harris, Bert Jones, Leonard Marshall, Jim Taylor, Y.A. Tittle, Steve Van Buren, Roy Winston, and David Woodley. The set was sponsored by Sunbeam Bread in conjunction with McDAG Productions.

|  | MINT | EXC | G-VG |
|---|---|---|---|
| COMPLETE SET (100) | 9.00 | 3.75 | .90 |
| COMMON CARD (1-100) | .10 | .04 | .01 |
| ☐ 1 1958 LSU National Championship Team | .20 | .08 | .02 |
| ☐ 2 Abe Mickal | .10 | .04 | .01 |
| ☐ 3 Carlos Carson | .20 | .08 | .02 |
| ☐ 4 Charles Alexander | .15 | .06 | .01 |
| ☐ 5 Steve Ensminger | .10 | .04 | .01 |
| ☐ 6 Ken Kavanaugh Sr. | .20 | .08 | .02 |
| ☐ 7 Bert Jones | .50 | .20 | .05 |
| ☐ 8 David Woodley | .25 | .10 | .02 |
| ☐ 9 Jerry Marchand | .10 | .04 | .01 |
| ☐ 10 Clyde Lindsey | .10 | .04 | .01 |
| ☐ 11 James Britt | .10 | .04 | .01 |
| ☐ 12 Warren Rabb | .15 | .06 | .01 |
| ☐ 13 Mike Hillman | .10 | .04 | .01 |
| ☐ 14 Nelson Stokley | .10 | .04 | .01 |
| ☐ 15 Abner Wimberly | .10 | .04 | .01 |
| ☐ 16 Terry Robiskie | .10 | .04 | .01 |
| ☐ 17 Steve Van Buren | .30 | .12 | .03 |
| ☐ 18 Doug Moreau | .15 | .06 | .01 |
| ☐ 19 George Tarasovic | .10 | .04 | .01 |
| ☐ 20 Billy Cannon | .30 | .12 | .03 |
| ☐ 21 Jerry Stovall | .25 | .10 | .02 |
| ☐ 22 Joe Labruzzo | .10 | .04 | .01 |
| ☐ 23 Mickey Mangham | .10 | .04 | .01 |
| ☐ 24 Craig Burns | .10 | .04 | .01 |
| ☐ 25 Y.A. Tittle | .60 | .24 | .06 |
| ☐ 26 Wendell Harris | .10 | .04 | .01 |
| ☐ 27 Leroy Labat | .10 | .04 | .01 |
| ☐ 28 Hokie Gajan | .15 | .06 | .01 |
| ☐ 29 Mike Williams | .10 | .04 | .01 |
| ☐ 30 Sammy Grezaffi | .15 | .06 | .01 |
| ☐ 31 Clinton Burrell | .10 | .04 | .01 |
| ☐ 32 Orlando McDaniel | .10 | .04 | .01 |
| ☐ 33 George Bevan | .10 | .04 | .01 |
| ☐ 34 Johnny Robinson | .20 | .08 | .02 |
| ☐ 35 Billy Masters | .10 | .04 | .01 |
| ☐ 36 J.W. Brodnax | .10 | .04 | .01 |
| ☐ 37 Tommy Casanova | .20 | .08 | .02 |
| ☐ 38 Fred Miller | .10 | .04 | .01 |
| ☐ 39 George Rice | .10 | .04 | .01 |
| ☐ 40 Earl Gros | .20 | .08 | .02 |
| ☐ 41 Lynn LeBlanc | .10 | .04 | .01 |
| ☐ 42 Jim Taylor | .40 | .16 | .04 |
| ☐ 43 Joe Tumenello | .10 | .04 | .01 |
| ☐ 44 Tommy Davis | .20 | .08 | .02 |
| ☐ 45 Alvin Dark | .30 | .12 | .03 |
| ☐ 46 Richard Picou | .10 | .04 | .01 |
| ☐ 47 Chaille Percy | .10 | .04 | .01 |
| ☐ 48 John Garlington | .20 | .08 | .02 |
| ☐ 49 Mike Morgan | .10 | .04 | .01 |
| ☐ 50 Charles(Bo) Strange | .10 | .04 | .01 |
| ☐ 51 Max Fugler | .25 | .10 | .02 |
| ☐ 52 Don Schwab | .10 | .04 | .01 |
| ☐ 53 Dennis Gaubatz | .15 | .06 | .01 |
| ☐ 54 Jimmy Field | .10 | .04 | .01 |
| ☐ 55 Warren Capone | .10 | .04 | .01 |
| ☐ 56 Albert Richardson | .10 | .04 | .01 |
| ☐ 57 Charley Cusiman | .10 | .04 | .01 |
| ☐ 58 Brad Davis | .10 | .04 | .01 |
| ☐ 59 Gaynell(Gus) Kinchen | .10 | .04 | .01 |
| ☐ 60 Roy(Moonie) Winston | .20 | .08 | .02 |
| ☐ 61 Mike Anderson | .10 | .04 | .01 |
| ☐ 62 Jesse Fatherree | .10 | .04 | .01 |
| ☐ 63 Gene"Red" Knight | .10 | .04 | .01 |
| ☐ 64 Tyler LaFauci | .10 | .04 | .01 |
| ☐ 65 Emile Fournet | .10 | .04 | .01 |
| ☐ 66 Gaynell"Gus" Tinsley | .10 | .04 | .01 |
| ☐ 67 Remi Prudhomme | .15 | .06 | .01 |
| ☐ 68 Marvin"Moose"Stewart | .10 | .04 | .01 |
| ☐ 69 Jerry Guillot | .10 | .04 | .01 |
| ☐ 70 Steve Cassidy | .10 | .04 | .01 |
| ☐ 71 Bo Harris | .15 | .06 | .01 |
| ☐ 72 Robert Dugas | .10 | .04 | .01 |
| ☐ 73 Malcolm Scott | .10 | .04 | .01 |
| ☐ 74 Charles(Pinky) Rohm | .10 | .04 | .01 |
| ☐ 75 Gerald Keigley | .10 | .04 | .01 |
| ☐ 76 Don Alexander | .10 | .04 | .01 |
| ☐ 77 A.J. Duhe | .20 | .08 | .02 |
| ☐ 78 Ronnie Estay | .10 | .04 | .01 |
| ☐ 79 John Wood | .10 | .04 | .01 |
| ☐ 80 Andy Hamilton | .20 | .08 | .02 |
| ☐ 81 Jay Michaelson | .10 | .04 | .01 |
| ☐ 82 Kenny Konz | .15 | .06 | .01 |
| ☐ 83 Tracy Porter | .10 | .04 | .01 |
| ☐ 84 Billy Truax | .20 | .08 | .02 |
| ☐ 85 Alan Risher | .15 | .06 | .01 |
| ☐ 86 John Adams | .10 | .04 | .01 |
| ☐ 87 Tommy Neck | .10 | .04 | .01 |
| ☐ 88 Brad Boyd | .10 | .04 | .01 |
| ☐ 89 Greg LaFluer | .10 | .04 | .01 |
| ☐ 90 Bill Elko | .10 | .04 | .01 |
| ☐ 91 Binks Miciotto | .10 | .04 | .01 |
| ☐ 92 Lew Sibley | .10 | .04 | .01 |
| ☐ 93 Willie Teal | .15 | .06 | .01 |
| ☐ 94 Lyman White | .10 | .04 | .01 |
| ☐ 95 Chris Williams | .10 | .04 | .01 |
| ☐ 96 Sid Fournet | .10 | .04 | .01 |
| ☐ 97 Leonard Marshall | .20 | .08 | .02 |
| ☐ 98 Ramsey Dardar | .10 | .04 | .01 |
| ☐ 99 Kenny Bordelon | .10 | .04 | .01 |
| ☐ 100 Fred(Skinny) Hall | .15 | .06 | .01 |

## 1985 LSU Police

The 1985 LSU Police set contains 16 standard-size (2 1/2" by 3 1/2") cards. The fronts have color action photos bordered in white; the vertically oriented backs have brief career highlights and safety tips. The cards are unnumbered, so they are listed below alphabetically by subject's name. These cards are printed on very thin stock. The set was produced by McDag Productions. Card backs contain "Tips from the Tigers," while card fronts contain a blue Louisiana Savings logo.

|  | MINT | EXC | G-VG |
|---|---|---|---|
| COMPLETE SET (16) | 7.00 | 2.80 | .70 |
| COMMON CARD (1-16) | .50 | .20 | .05 |
| ☐ 1 Mitch Andrews | .50 | .20 | .05 |
| ☐ 2 Bill Arnsparger CO | .75 | .30 | .07 |
| ☐ 3 Roland Barbay | .50 | .20 | .05 |
| ☐ 4 Michael Brooks | .75 | .30 | .07 |
| ☐ 5 Shawn Burks | .50 | .20 | .05 |
| ☐ 6 Tommy Clapp | .50 | .20 | .05 |
| ☐ 7 Matt DeFrank | .50 | .20 | .05 |
| ☐ 8 Kevin Guidry | .60 | .24 | .06 |
| ☐ 9 Dalton Hilliard | 1.50 | .60 | .15 |
| ☐ 10 Garry James | .75 | .30 | .07 |
| ☐ 11 Norman Jefferson | .50 | .20 | .05 |
| ☐ 12 Rogie Magee | .50 | .20 | .05 |
| ☐ 13 Mike the Tiger(Mascot) | .50 | .20 | .05 |
| ☐ 14 Craig Rathjen | .50 | .20 | .05 |

| | MINT | EXC | G-VG |
|---|---|---|---|
| ☐ 15 Jeff Wickersham | .75 | .30 | .07 |
| ☐ 16 Karl Wilson | .60 | .24 | .06 |

# 1986 LSU Police

The 1986 LSU Police set contains 16 standard-size (2 1/2" by 3 1/2") cards. The fronts have color action photos bordered in white; the vertically oriented backs have brief career highlights and safety tips. The cards are unnumbered, so they are listed below alphabetically by subject's name. These cards are printed on thin stock. The set was produced by McDag Productions. Card backs contain "Tips from the Tigers," while card fronts contain logos for The General and the Chemical Dependency Unit of Baton Rouge.

| | MINT | EXC | G-VG |
|---|---|---|---|
| COMPLETE SET (16) | 8.00 | 3.25 | .80 |
| COMMON CARD (1-16) | .50 | .20 | .05 |
| | | | |
| ☐ 1 Nacho Albergamo | .50 | .20 | .05 |
| ☐ 2 Eric Andolsek | .75 | .30 | .07 |
| ☐ 3 Bill Arnsparger CO | .75 | .30 | .07 |
| ☐ 4 Roland Barbay | .50 | .20 | .05 |
| ☐ 5 Michael Brooks | 1.00 | .40 | .10 |
| ☐ 6 Chris Carrier | .50 | .20 | .05 |
| ☐ 7 Toby Caston | 1.00 | .40 | .10 |
| ☐ 8 Wendell Davis | 2.00 | .80 | .20 |
| ☐ 9 Kevin Guidry | .60 | .24 | .06 |
| ☐ 10 John Hazard | .50 | .20 | .05 |
| ☐ 11 Oliver Lawrence | .50 | .20 | .05 |
| ☐ 12 Rogie Magee | .50 | .20 | .05 |
| ☐ 13 Sam Martin | .75 | .30 | .07 |
| ☐ 14 Darrell Phillips | .50 | .20 | .05 |
| ☐ 15 Steve Rehage | .50 | .20 | .05 |
| ☐ 16 Ron Sancho | .75 | .30 | .07 |

# 1987 LSU Police

The 1987 LSU Police set contains 16 standard-size (2 1/2" by 3 1/2") cards. The fronts have color action photos bordered in white; the vertically oriented backs have brief career highlights and safety tips. These cards are printed on very thin stock. This set was distributed at the Oct. 17, 1987 game vs. Kentucky. The set was produced by McDag Productions. Card backs contain "Tips from the Tigers". The cards are unnumbered, so they are listed below alphabetically by subject's name. The key card in the set is Harvey Williams' first card.

| | MINT | EXC | G-VG |
|---|---|---|---|
| COMPLETE SET (16) | 9.00 | 3.75 | .90 |
| COMMON CARD (1-16) | .50 | .20 | .05 |
| | | | |
| ☐ 1 Nacho Albergamo | .50 | .20 | .05 |

| | MINT | EXC | G-VG |
|---|---|---|---|
| ☐ 2 Eric Andolsek | .75 | .30 | .07 |
| ☐ 3 Mike Archer CO | .75 | .30 | .07 |
| ☐ 4 David Browndyke | .60 | .24 | .06 |
| ☐ 5 Chris Carrier | .50 | .20 | .05 |
| ☐ 6 Wendell Davis | 1.50 | .60 | .15 |
| ☐ 7 Matt DeFrank | .50 | .20 | .05 |
| ☐ 8 Nicky Hazard | .50 | .20 | .05 |
| ☐ 9 Eric Hill | .75 | .30 | .07 |
| ☐ 10 Tommy Hodson | 1.50 | .60 | .15 |
| ☐ 11 Greg Jackson | .75 | .30 | .07 |
| ☐ 12 Brian Kinchen | .75 | .30 | .07 |
| ☐ 13 Darren Malbrough | .50 | .20 | .05 |
| ☐ 14 Sam Martin | .75 | .30 | .07 |
| ☐ 15 Ron Sancho | .75 | .30 | .07 |
| ☐ 16 Harvey Williams | 2.50 | 1.00 | .25 |

# 1988 LSU Police

The 1988 LSU football set contains 16 standard-size (2 1/2" by 3 1/2") cards. The fronts have color action photos with white borders and black lettering; the vertically oriented backs have career highlights. These cards were distributed as a set, which was produced by McDag Productions. Card backs contain "Tips from the Tigers" and card number.

| | MINT | EXC | G-VG |
|---|---|---|---|
| COMPLETE SET (16) | 7.50 | 3.00 | .75 |
| COMMON CARD (1-16) | .50 | .20 | .05 |
| | | | |
| ☐ 1 Mike The Tiger (Mascot) | .50 | .20 | .05 |
| ☐ 2 Mike Archer CO | .75 | .30 | .07 |
| ☐ 3 Tommy Hodson | 1.25 | .50 | .12 |
| ☐ 4 Harvey Williams | 2.00 | .80 | .20 |
| ☐ 5 David Browndyke | .60 | .24 | .06 |
| ☐ 6 Karl Dunbar | .50 | .20 | .05 |
| ☐ 7 Eddie Fuller | .60 | .24 | .06 |
| ☐ 8 Mickey Guidry | .60 | .24 | .06 |
| ☐ 9 Greg Jackson | .75 | .30 | .07 |
| ☐ 10 Clint James | .50 | .20 | .05 |
| ☐ 11 Victor Jones | .50 | .20 | .05 |
| ☐ 12 Tony Moss | .50 | .20 | .05 |
| ☐ 13 Ralph Norwood | .50 | .20 | .05 |
| ☐ 14 Darrell Phillips | .50 | .20 | .05 |
| ☐ 15 Ruffin Rodrigue | .50 | .20 | .05 |
| ☐ 16 Ron Sancho | .60 | .24 | .06 |

# 1989 LSU Police

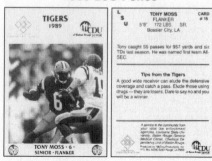

The 1989 LSU football set contains 16 standard-size (2 1/2" by 3 1/2") cards. The fronts have color action photos with white borders and black lettering; the vertically oriented backs have career highlights. These cards were distributed as a set, which was produced by McDag

Productions. Card backs contain "Tips from the Tigers" and the card number in the upper right hand corner.

| | MINT | EXC | G-VG |
|---|---|---|---|
| COMPLETE SET (16) | 7.50 | 3.00 | .75 |
| COMMON CARD (1-16) | .50 | .20 | .05 |

| | | MINT | EXC | G-VG |
|---|---|---|---|---|
| ☐ 1 | Mike the Tiger(Mascot) | .50 | .20 | .05 |
| ☐ 2 | David Browndyke 4 | .60 | .24 | .06 |
| ☐ 3 | Mike Archer CO | .75 | .30 | .07 |
| ☐ 4 | Ruffin Rodrigue 68 | .50 | .20 | .05 |
| ☐ 5 | Marc Boutte 95 | .75 | .30 | .07 |
| ☐ 6 | Clint James 70 | .50 | .20 | .05 |
| ☐ 7 | Jimmy Young 5 | .50 | .20 | .05 |
| ☐ 8 | Alvin Lee 26 | .60 | .24 | .06 |
| ☐ 9 | Eddie Fuller 33 | .60 | .24 | .06 |
| ☐ 10 | Tiger Stadium | .50 | .20 | .05 |
| ☐ 11 | Harvey Williams 22 | 1.50 | .60 | .15 |
| ☐ 12 | Verge Ausberry 98 | .50 | .20 | .05 |
| ☐ 13 | Karl Dunbar 63 | .50 | .20 | .05 |
| ☐ 14 | Tommy Hodson 13 | 1.00 | .40 | .10 |
| ☐ 15 | Tony Moss 6 | .50 | .20 | .05 |
| ☐ 16 | The Golden Girls (Cheerleaders) | .75 | .30 | .07 |

## 1992 LSU McDag

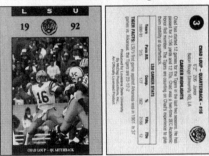

This 16-card set, which measures the standard size (2 1/2" by 3 1/2"), was produced for Louisiana State University by McDag Productions Inc. The cards are printed on thin stock and feature on the fronts action color player shots framed in purple on a mustard background. A purple bar at the top contains "LSU" in white lettering with the year and team logo (a tiger's head) immediately below on the mustard top border. The white backs are printed in purple and feature biography, career highlights, statistics, and "Tiger Facts". The cards are numbered on the back.

| | MINT | EXC | G-VG |
|---|---|---|---|
| COMPLETE SET (16) | 6.00 | 2.40 | .60 |
| COMMON CARD (1-16) | .50 | .20 | .05 |

| | | MINT | EXC | G-VG |
|---|---|---|---|---|
| ☐ 1 | Curley Hallman CO | .75 | .30 | .07 |
| ☐ 2 | Ray Adams | .50 | .20 | .05 |
| ☐ 3 | Chad Loup | .75 | .30 | .07 |
| ☐ 4 | Odell Beckham | .50 | .20 | .05 |
| ☐ 5 | Wesley Jacob | .50 | .20 | .05 |
| ☐ 6 | Kevin Mawae | .75 | .30 | .07 |
| ☐ 7 | Clayton Mouton | .50 | .20 | .05 |
| ☐ 8 | Roovelroe Swan | .50 | .20 | .05 |
| ☐ 9 | Ricardo Washington | .50 | .20 | .05 |
| ☐ 10 | David Walkup | .50 | .20 | .05 |
| ☐ 11 | Jessie Daigle | .50 | .20 | .05 |
| ☐ 12 | Carlton Buckles | .50 | .20 | .05 |
| ☐ 13 | Anthony Williams | .50 | .20 | .05 |
| ☐ 14 | Darron Landry | .50 | .20 | .05 |
| ☐ 15 | Frank Godfrey | .50 | .20 | .05 |
| ☐ 16 | Pedro Suarez | .50 | .20 | .05 |

## 1991 Maryland HS Big 33

This 34-card standard-size (2 1/2" by 3 1/2") high school football set was issued to commemorate the Big 33 Football Classic, an annual high school football game begun in 1958 and featuring Pennsylvania versus Maryland for the past seven games. The fronts feature a posed black and white player photo enclosed in a white border. State name appears at top. Player number and position appear as white reversed-out lettering within a black bar. The Big 33 logo and The Super Bowl of High School Football appear at the bottom. The backs feature biographical information and honors received within a thin black border. The cards are numbered on the back.

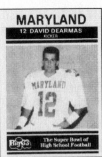

| | MINT | EXC | G-VG |
|---|---|---|---|
| COMPLETE SET (34) | 15.00 | 6.00 | 1.50 |
| COMMON PLAYER (MD1-MD34) | .75 | .30 | .07 |

| | | MINT | EXC | G-VG |
|---|---|---|---|---|
| ☐ MD1 | Asim Penny — Bishop Namara High | 1.00 | .40 | .10 |
| ☐ MD2 | Louis Jason — DeMatha High | .75 | .30 | .07 |
| ☐ MD3 | Mark McCain — Oxon Hill High | 1.00 | .40 | .10 |
| ☐ MD4 | Matthew Byrne — Damascus High | .75 | .30 | .07 |
| ☐ MD5 | Mike Gillespie — Springbrook High | .75 | .30 | .07 |
| ☐ MD6 | Ricky Rowe — Wilde Lake High | .75 | .30 | .07 |
| ☐ MD7 | David DeArmas — DeMatha High | 1.00 | .40 | .10 |
| ☐ MD8 | Duane Ashman — Paint Branch High | .75 | .30 | .07 |
| ☐ MD9 | James Cunningham — Crossland High | .75 | .30 | .07 |
| ☐ MD10 | Keith Kormanik — Gilman High | .75 | .30 | .07 |
| ☐ MD11 | Leonard Green — Springbrook High | .75 | .30 | .07 |
| ☐ MD12 | Larry Washington — Randallstown High | .75 | .30 | .07 |
| ☐ MD13 | Raphael Wall — Wilde Lake High | .75 | .30 | .07 |
| ☐ MD14 | Kai Hebron — Quince Orchard High | .75 | .30 | .07 |
| ☐ MD15 | Coy Gibbs — DeMatha High | 1.00 | .40 | .10 |
| ☐ MD16 | Lenard Marcus — Baltimore Polytech | .75 | .30 | .07 |
| ☐ MD17 | John Taliaferro — DeMatha High | .75 | .30 | .07 |
| ☐ MD18 | J.C. Price — Northern High | .75 | .30 | .07 |
| ☐ MD19 | Jamal Cox — Gilman High | 1.50 | .60 | .15 |
| ☐ MD20 | Rick Budd — Fort Hill High | .75 | .30 | .07 |
| ☐ MD21 | Shaun Marshall — Bladensburg High | .75 | .30 | .07 |
| ☐ MD22 | Allan Jenkins — High Point High | .75 | .30 | .07 |
| ☐ MD23 | Bryon Turner — Aberdeen High | .75 | .30 | .07 |
| ☐ MD24 | Ryan Foran — DeMatha High | .75 | .30 | .07 |
| ☐ MD25 | John Summerday — Great Mills High | .75 | .30 | .07 |
| ☐ MD26 | Joshua Austin — Forest Park High | .75 | .30 | .07 |
| ☐ MD27 | Emile Palmer — Fairmont Heights High | .75 | .30 | .07 |
| ☐ MD28 | John Teter — DeMatha High | .75 | .30 | .07 |
| ☐ MD29 | John Kennedy — Springbrook High | .75 | .30 | .07 |
| ☐ MD30 | Clarence Collins — Bishop McNamara High | .75 | .30 | .07 |
| ☐ MD31 | Daryl Smith — C.M. Wright High | .75 | .30 | .07 |
| ☐ MD32 | David Wilkins — James M. Bennett High | .75 | .30 | .07 |
| ☐ MD33 | David Thomas — Good Counsel High | .75 | .30 | .07 |
| ☐ MD34 | Russell Thomas — Oxon Hill High | 1.00 | .40 | .10 |

# 1988 McNeese State McDag/Police

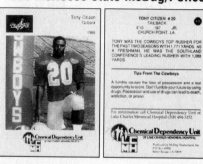

This 16-card standard-size (2 1/2" by 3 1/2") set is printed on thin card stock. It is sponsored by the Behavioral Health and Chemical Dependency Units of Lake Charles Memorial Hospital. Card front has a posed picture enclosed in a white border. Team logo appears in upper left while player's name, position, and the year appear in upper right corner. The sponsor logos appear at the bottom. Horizontally oriented backs present biography, player profile, "Tips From the Cowboys" in the form of anti-drug messages, and sponsor logos at the bottom. The cards are numbered on the back.

|  | MINT | EXC | G-VG |
|---|---|---|---|
| COMPLETE SET (16) | 7.00 | 2.80 | .70 |
| COMMON CARD (1-16) | .50 | .20 | .05 |
| ☐ 1 Sonny Jackson CO | .50 | .20 | .05 |
| ☐ 2 Lance Wiley | .50 | .20 | .05 |
| ☐ 3 Brian McZeal | .50 | .20 | .05 |
| ☐ 4 Berwick Davenport | .50 | .20 | .05 |
| ☐ 5 Gary Irvin | .50 | .20 | .05 |
| ☐ 6 Glenn Koch | .50 | .20 | .05 |
| ☐ 7 Chad Habetz | .50 | .20 | .05 |
| ☐ 8 Pete Sinclair | .50 | .20 | .05 |
| ☐ 9 Tony Citizen | .50 | .20 | .05 |
| ☐ 10 Scott Dieterich | .50 | .20 | .05 |
| ☐ 11 Hud Jackson | .50 | .20 | .05 |
| ☐ 12 Darrin Andrus | .50 | .20 | .05 |
| ☐ 13 Jeff Mathews | .50 | .20 | .05 |
| ☐ 14 Devin Babineaux | .50 | .20 | .05 |
| ☐ 15 Jeff Delhomme | .50 | .20 | .05 |
| ☐ 16 Eric LeBlanc | .50 | .20 | .05 |
| Mike Pierce | | | |

# 1989 McNeese State McDag/Police

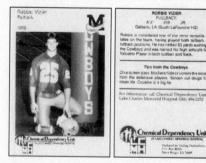

This 16-card standard-size (2 1/2" by 3 1/2") set is printed on thin card stock. It is sponsored by the Behavioral Health and Chemical Dependency Units of Lake Charles Memorial Hospital. The fronts feature color posed photos enclosed by light blue borders. The player's name, position, year, and school logo are in the top border while the sponsor logo appears beneath the picture. The backs carry biography, player profile, and "Tips From The Cowboys" in the form of anti-drug or mental health messages. The cards are numbered on the back in the upper right corner.

|  | MINT | EXC | G-VG |
|---|---|---|---|
| COMPLETE SET (16) | 7.00 | 2.80 | .70 |
| COMMON PLAYER (1-16) | .50 | .20 | .05 |
| ☐ 1 Marc Stampley | .50 | .20 | .05 |

| | | | |
|---|---|---|---|
| ☐ 2 Mark LeBlanc | .50 | .20 | .05 |
| ☐ 3 Kip Texada | .50 | .20 | .05 |
| ☐ 4 Brian Champagne | .50 | .20 | .05 |
| ☐ 5 Ronald Scott | .50 | .20 | .05 |
| ☐ 6 Jimmy Poirier | .50 | .20 | .05 |
| ☐ 7 Cliff Buckner | .50 | .20 | .05 |
| ☐ 8 Jericho Loupe | .50 | .20 | .05 |
| ☐ 9 Vaughn Calbert | .50 | .20 | .05 |
| ☐ 10 Rodney Burks | .50 | .20 | .05 |
| ☐ 11 Troy Jones | .50 | .20 | .05 |
| ☐ 12 Chris Andrus | .50 | .20 | .05 |
| ☐ 13 Robbie Vizier | .50 | .20 | .05 |
| ☐ 14 Kenneth Pierce | .50 | .20 | .05 |
| ☐ 15 Bobby Smith | .50 | .20 | .05 |
| ☐ 16 Trent Lee | .50 | .20 | .05 |

# 1990 McNeese State McDag/Police

The 1990 McNeese State Cowboys football set contains 16 standard-size (2 1/2" by 3 1/2") cards and is basically the same design as previous years. The card front features a posed player photo, with rounded corners and enclosed by a light blue border. The player's name, position, year, and school logo are in the top border while the sponsor's name and logo (Lake Charles Memorial Hospital) are beneath the picture. Backs feature biography, player profile, and "Tips From The Cowboys" in the form of anti-drug or mental health messages. The cards are numbered in a black football in the upper right corner.

|  | MINT | EXC | G-VG |
|---|---|---|---|
| COMPLETE SET (16) | 7.00 | 2.80 | .70 |
| COMMON PLAYER (1-16) | .50 | .20 | .05 |
| ☐ 1 Hud Jackson | .50 | .20 | .05 |
| ☐ 2 Wes Watts | .50 | .20 | .05 |
| ☐ 3 Mark LeBlanc | .50 | .20 | .05 |
| ☐ 4 Jeff Delhomme | .50 | .20 | .05 |
| ☐ 5 Mike Reed | .50 | .20 | .05 |
| ☐ 6 Chuck Esponge | .50 | .20 | .05 |
| ☐ 7 Ronald Scott | .50 | .20 | .05 |
| ☐ 8 Ken Naquin | .50 | .20 | .05 |
| ☐ 9 Steve Aultman | .50 | .20 | .05 |
| ☐ 10 Sean Judge | .50 | .20 | .05 |
| ☐ 11 Greg Rayson | .50 | .20 | .05 |
| ☐ 12 Kip Texada | .50 | .20 | .05 |
| ☐ 13 Mike Pierce | .50 | .20 | .05 |
| ☐ 14 Jimmy Poirier | .50 | .20 | .05 |
| ☐ 15 Ronald Solomon | .50 | .20 | .05 |
| ☐ 16 Eric Foster | .50 | .20 | .05 |

# 1991 McNeese State McDag/Police

This 16-card set was produced by McDag Productions and sponsored by Lake Charles Memorial Hospital. The print run was reportedly limited to 3,500 sets. Each of the standard-size (2 1/2" by 3 1/2") cards features a posed color photo of the player kneeling beside the goalpost, with the stadium in the background. The pictures have rounded corners and light blue borders. Player information appears above the picture, while the sponsor's logo adorns the bottom of the card. The backs have biography, player profile, and "Tips from the Cowboys" in the form of anti-drug and alcohol messages. The cards are numbered on the back.

|  | MINT | EXC | G-VG |
|---|---|---|---|
| COMPLETE SET (16)......................... | 7.00 | 2.80 | .70 |
| COMMON CARD (1-16) .................... | .50 | .20 | .05 |
| ☐ 1 Eric Roberts .............................. | .50 | .20 | .05 |
| ☐ 2 Erwin Brown ............................. | .50 | .20 | .05 |
| ☐ 3 Marcus Bowie .......................... | .50 | .20 | .05 |
| ☐ 4 Wes Watts................................. | .50 | .20 | .05 |
| ☐ 5 Brian Brumfield ........................ | .50 | .20 | .05 |
| ☐ 6 Marc Stampley ......................... | .50 | .20 | .05 |
| ☐ 7 Sean Judge............................... | .50 | .20 | .05 |
| ☐ 8 Joey Bernard............................. | .50 | .20 | .05 |
| ☐ 9 Ken Naquin ............................... | .50 | .20 | .05 |
| ☐ 10 Bobby Smith ........................... | .50 | .20 | .05 |
| ☐ 11 Sam Breaux............................. | .50 | .20 | .05 |
| ☐ 12 Ronald Scott ........................... | .50 | .20 | .05 |
| ☐ 13 Edward Dyer ........................... | .50 | .20 | .05 |
| ☐ 14 Greg Rayson ........................... | .50 | .20 | .05 |
| ☐ 15 Eric Kidd ................................. | .50 | .20 | .05 |
| ☐ 16 Bobby Keasler CO ................... | .50 | .20 | .05 |

## 1992 McNeese State McDag/Police

This 16-card set was produced by McDag Productions and sponsored by Lake Charles Memorial Hospital. The set is printed on thin card stock and measures the standard size (2 1/2" by 3 1/2"). The fronts feature rounded-corner posed color player photos on a mustard card face. The player's name and position appear below the picture. The backs have a white background and carry biographical information, player profile, and anti-drug or alcohol messages under the heading "Tips from the Cowboys." The cards are numbered on the back.

|  | MINT | EXC | G-VG |
|---|---|---|---|
| COMPLETE SET (16)......................... | 7.00 | 2.80 | .70 |
| COMMON PLAYER (1-16)................. | .50 | .20 | .05 |
| ☐ 1 Eric Acheson ............................ | .50 | .20 | .05 |
| ☐ 2 Pat Neck.................................... | .50 | .20 | .05 |
| ☐ 3 Marcus Bowie .......................... | .50 | .20 | .05 |
| ☐ 4 Marty Posey ............................. | .50 | .20 | .05 |
| ☐ 5 Brian Brumfield ........................ | .50 | .20 | .05 |
| ☐ 6 Terry Irving .............................. | .75 | .30 | .07 |
| ☐ 7 Eric Fleming ............................. | .50 | .20 | .05 |
| ☐ 8 Lance Guidry............................. | .50 | .20 | .05 |
| ☐ 9 Ken Naquin ............................... | .50 | .20 | .05 |
| ☐ 10 Chris Fontenette...................... | .50 | .20 | .05 |
| ☐ 11 Sam Breaux............................. | .50 | .20 | .05 |
| ☐ 12 Dana Scott .............................. | .50 | .20 | .05 |
| ☐ 13 Edward Dyer ........................... | .50 | .20 | .05 |
| ☐ 14 Blayne Rush ............................ | .50 | .20 | .05 |
| ☐ 15 Ronald Solomon ..................... | .50 | .20 | .05 |
| ☐ 16 Steve Aultman......................... | .50 | .20 | .05 |

## 1990 Miami Smokey

The 1990 Miami Hurricanes Smokey set was issued in a sheet of 16 cards which, when perforated, measure the standard size (2 1/2" by 3 1/2"). The fronts feature color action photos bordered in orange on green background, with the player's name, position, and jersey

number below the picture. The backs have biographical information (in English and Spanish) and a fire prevention cartoon starring Smokey. The cards are unnumbered, so they are listed below alphabetically by subject's name.

|  | MINT | EXC | G-VG |
|---|---|---|---|
| COMPLETE SET (16)...................... | 20.00 | 8.00 | 2.00 |
| COMMON CARD (1-16) .................. | 1.00 | .40 | .10 |
| ☐ 1 Randy Bethel 93 ....................... | 1.25 | .50 | .12 |
| ☐ 2 Wesley Carroll 81 ..................... | 2.00 | .80 | .20 |
| ☐ 3 Rob Chudzinski 84 .................... | 1.00 | .40 | .10 |
| ☐ 4 Leonard Conley 28 .................... | 1.50 | .60 | .15 |
| ☐ 5 Luis Cristobal 59 ...................... | 1.25 | .50 | .12 |
| ☐ 6 Maurice Crum 49 ...................... | 1.00 | .40 | .10 |
| ☐ 7 Shane Curry 44 ........................ | 1.50 | .60 | .15 |
| ☐ 8 Craig Erickson 7 ....................... | 3.00 | 1.20 | .30 |
| ☐ 9 Dennis Erickson CO .................. | 2.00 | .80 | .20 |
| ☐ 10 Darren Handy 66 ..................... | 1.00 | .40 | .10 |
| ☐ 11 Randal Hill 3........................... | 5.00 | 2.00 | .50 |
| ☐ 12 Carlos Huerta 27 ..................... | 1.25 | .50 | .12 |
| ☐ 13 Russell Maryland 67 ................ | 3.00 | 1.20 | .30 |
| ☐ 14 Stephen McGuire 30 ................ | 1.50 | .60 | .15 |
| ☐ 15 Roland Smith 16 ...................... | 1.00 | .40 | .10 |
| ☐ 16 Mike Sullivan 79...................... | 1.25 | .50 | .12 |

## 1991 Miami Police

This 16-card standard-size (2 1/2" by 3 1/2") set was sponsored by Bounty. Approximately 5,000 sets were issued, and they were given away at the Nov. 9 game against West Virginia at the Orange Bowl. The player action photos on the fronts are enclosed in black, orange, and green borders. College and team name are printed inside top borders while player information appears between the team helmet and Bounty logo at the bottom of the card face. Horizontally oriented backs provide player profile (in English and Spanish), biographical information, a head shot, and "Tips from the Hurricanes" in form of public service announcements. Sponsor logo and photo credits also appear on the back. The cards are unnumbered and checklisted below in alphabetical order.

|  | MINT | EXC | G-VG |
|---|---|---|---|
| COMPLETE SET (16)......................... | 15.00 | 6.00 | 1.50 |
| COMMON CARD (1-16) .................... | 1.00 | .40 | .10 |
| ☐ 1 Jessie Armstead......................... | 1.50 | .60 | .15 |
| ☐ 2 Micheal Barrow ......................... | 1.50 | .60 | .15 |
| ☐ 3 Hurlie Brown ............................. | 1.00 | .40 | .10 |
| ☐ 4 Dennis Erickson CO .................. | 1.50 | .60 | .15 |
| ☐ 5 Anthony Hamlet ........................ | 1.25 | .50 | .12 |
| ☐ 6 Carlos Huerta ........................... | 1.25 | .50 | .12 |
| ☐ 7 Herbert James........................... | 1.00 | .40 | .10 |
| ☐ 8 Claude Jones............................. | 1.00 | .40 | .10 |

| | | | |
|---|---|---|---|
| ☐ 9 Stephen McGuire | 1.50 | .60 | .15 |
| ☐ 10 Eric Miller | 1.00 | .40 | .10 |
| ☐ 11 Joe Moore | 1.00 | .40 | .10 |
| ☐ 12 Charles Pharms | 1.00 | .40 | .10 |
| ☐ 13 Leon Searcy | 1.25 | .50 | .12 |
| ☐ 14 Darrin Smith | 2.00 | .80 | .20 |
| ☐ 15 Lamar Thomas | 2.50 | 1.00 | .25 |
| ☐ 16 Gino Torretta | 3.00 | 1.20 | .30 |

## 1992 Miami Safety

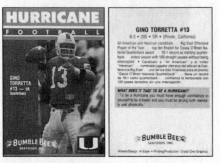

This 16-card safety set was sponsored by Bumble Bee Seafoods Inc., and its company logo is found at the bottom of both sides of the card. The cards were issued as an unperforated sheet with four rows of four cards each. If the cards were cut, they would measure the standard size (2 1/2" by 3 1/2"). The color player photos on the fronts bleed off the bottom and right side but are edged by a thick green stripe on the left. The words "Hurricane Football" are printed in orange and green stripes that cut across the top of the front. The backs present biography, career summary, and "What Does It Take to Be a Hurricane" feature, which consists of a quote stressing a positive mental attitude. The cards are unnumbered and checklisted below in alphabetical order. The set features the second collegiate card of 1992 Heismann Trophy winner Gino Torretta.

| | MINT | EXC | G-VG |
|---|---|---|---|
| COMPLETE SET (16) | 15.00 | 6.00 | 1.50 |
| COMMON CARD (1-16) | .75 | .30 | .07 |

| | | | |
|---|---|---|---|
| ☐ 1 Jessie Armstead | 1.25 | .50 | .12 |
| ☐ 2 Micheal Barrow | 1.25 | .50 | .12 |
| ☐ 3 Coleman Bell | .75 | .30 | .07 |
| ☐ 4 Mark Caesar | .75 | .30 | .07 |
| ☐ 5 Horace Copeland UER | 2.00 | .80 | .20 |
| (Name misspelled Horrace on front) | | | |
| ☐ 6 Mario Cristobal | .75 | .30 | .07 |
| ☐ 7 Dennis Erickson CO | 1.25 | .50 | .12 |
| ☐ 8 Casey Greer | .75 | .30 | .07 |
| ☐ 9 Stephen McGuire | 1.25 | .50 | .12 |
| ☐ 10 Ryan McNeil | 1.50 | .60 | .15 |
| ☐ 11 Rusty Medearis | 1.00 | .40 | .10 |
| ☐ 12 Darrin Smith | 1.50 | .60 | .15 |
| ☐ 13 Darryl Spencer | .75 | .30 | .07 |
| ☐ 14 Lamar Thomas | 2.00 | .80 | .20 |
| ☐ 15 Gino Torretta | 2.50 | 1.00 | .25 |
| ☐ 16 Kevin Williams | 3.00 | 1.20 | .30 |

## 1993 Miami Bumble Bee

Sponsored by Bumble Bee, the 16 cards comprising this set were issued in one 16-card perforated sheet. The sheet measures approximately 10" by 14" and consists of four rows of four cards each. Each card measures the standard size (2 1/2" by 3 1/2") and carries on its front a black-bordered color player action shot. The player's name, uniform number, and position appear vertically in white lettering within the orange stripe at the upper left. The Hurricanes' logo is displayed within a lower corner of the player photo. The Bumble Bee logo in white lettering rests in the lower black margin. The white back carries the player's name, uniform number, biography, highlights in both English and Spanish, and the player's "Most memorable moment as a Hurricane." The Bumble Bee logo at the bottom rounds out the card. The cards are unnumbered and checklisted below in alphabetical order.

| | MINT | EXC | G-VG |
|---|---|---|---|
| COMPLETE SET (16) | 12.00 | 5.00 | 1.20 |
| COMMON PLAYER (1-16) | .60 | .24 | .06 |

| | | | |
|---|---|---|---|
| ☐ 1 Rudy Barber | .75 | .30 | .07 |
| ☐ 2 Robert Bass | .75 | .30 | .07 |
| ☐ 3 Donnell Bennett | 2.00 | .80 | .20 |
| ☐ 4 Jason Budroni | .60 | .24 | .06 |
| ☐ 5 Marcus Carey | .60 | .24 | .06 |
| ☐ 6 Ryan Collins | 1.00 | .40 | .10 |
| ☐ 7 Frank Costa | 1.00 | .40 | .10 |
| ☐ 8 Dennis Erickson CO | 1.00 | .40 | .10 |
| ☐ 9 Terris Harris | .75 | .30 | .07 |
| ☐ 10 Chris T. Jones | 1.00 | .40 | .10 |
| ☐ 11 Larry Jones | .60 | .24 | .06 |
| ☐ 12 Darren Krein | .75 | .30 | .07 |
| ☐ 13 Kenny Lopez | .75 | .30 | .07 |
| ☐ 14 Kevin Patrick | .75 | .30 | .07 |
| ☐ 15 Dexter Seigler | .75 | .30 | .07 |
| ☐ 16 Paul White | .75 | .30 | .07 |

## 1977 Michigan

Produced by Stommen Enterprises, this 21-card postcard size (approximately 3 1/2" by 5 1/2") set features the 1977 Michigan Wolverines. Bordered in blue, the fronts divide into three registers. The top register is pale yellow and carries "Michigan" in block lettering. The middle register displays a color posed photo of the player in uniform holding his helmet. The bottom register is pale yellow and has the player's name, position, and a drawing of the mascot, all in blue. The horizontal backs are divided down the middle by two thin bluish-purple stripes, and Michigan's 1977 schedule appears in the same color ink on the upper left. Three cards, those of Giesler, Stephenson, and Szara, have an additional feature on their backs, an order blank printed on the right side. The order blank speaks of the "entire set of 18" and goes on to state "also available at the gates before and after the games." It appears that these three cards may have been produced or distributed later than the other eighteen. The cards are numbered on the back.

| | NRMT | VG-E | GOOD |
|---|---|---|---|
| COMPLETE SET (21) | 20.00 | 8.00 | 2.00 |
| COMMON PLAYER (1-21) | 1.00 | .40 | .10 |

| | | | |
|---|---|---|---|
| ☐ 1 John Anderson | 1.50 | .60 | .15 |
| ☐ 2 Russell Davis | 1.50 | .60 | .15 |
| ☐ 3 Mark Donahue | 1.00 | .40 | .10 |
| ☐ 4 Walt Downing | 1.00 | .40 | .10 |
| ☐ 5 Bill Dufek | 1.50 | .60 | .15 |
| ☐ 6 Jon Giesler SP | 2.00 | .80 | .20 |
| ☐ 7 Steve Graves | 1.00 | .40 | .10 |
| ☐ 8 Curtis Greer | 2.50 | 1.00 | .25 |
| ☐ 9 Dwight Hicks | 3.00 | 1.20 | .30 |
| ☐ 10 Derek Howard | 1.00 | .40 | .10 |

| | | | |
|---|---|---|---|
| ☐ 11 Harlan Huckleby | 3.00 | 1.20 | .30 |
| ☐ 12 Gene Johnson | 1.00 | .40 | .10 |
| ☐ 13 Dale Keitz | 1.00 | .40 | .10 |
| ☐ 14 Mike Kenn | 3.00 | 1.20 | .30 |
| ☐ 15 Rick Leach | 3.00 | 1.20 | .30 |
| ☐ 16 Mark Schmerge | 1.00 | .40 | .10 |
| ☐ 17 Ron Simpkins | 1.50 | .60 | .15 |
| ☐ 18 Curt Stephenson SP | 2.00 | .80 | .20 |
| ☐ 19 Gerry Szara SP | 2.00 | .80 | .20 |
| ☐ 20 Rick White | 1.00 | .40 | .10 |
| ☐ 21 Gregg Willner | 1.00 | .40 | .10 |

## 1989 Michigan

JIM HARBAUGH
Quarterback 1983-86

The 1989 Michigan football set contains 22 standard-size (2 1/2" by 3 1/2") cards. The fronts have vintage or color action photos with white borders; the vertically oriented backs have detailed profiles. These cards were distributed as a set. The cards are numbered on the back in the lower right corner.

| | MINT | EXC | G-VG |
|---|---|---|---|
| COMPLETE SET (22) | 10.00 | 4.00 | 1.00 |
| COMMON CARD (1-22) | .50 | .20 | .05 |
| | | | |
| ☐ 1 H.O.(Fritz) Crisler CO | .60 | .24 | .06 |
| ☐ 2 Anthony Carter | 1.25 | .50 | .12 |
| ☐ 3 William M. Heston | .50 | .20 | .05 |
| ☐ 4 Reggie McKenzie | .50 | .20 | .05 |
| ☐ 5 Bo Schembechler CO | 1.25 | .50 | .12 |
| ☐ 6 Dan Dierdorf | 1.25 | .50 | .12 |
| ☐ 7 Jim Harbaugh | 1.25 | .50 | .12 |
| ☐ 8 Bennie Oosterbaan | .50 | .20 | .05 |
| ☐ 9 Jamie Morris | .50 | .20 | .05 |
| ☐ 10 Gerald R. Ford | 1.50 | .60 | .15 |
| ☐ 11 Curtis Greer | .60 | .24 | .06 |
| ☐ 12 Ron Kramer | .60 | .24 | .06 |
| ☐ 13 Calvin O'Neal | .50 | .20 | .05 |
| ☐ 14 Bob Chappuis | .50 | .20 | .05 |
| ☐ 15 Fielding H. Yost CO | .60 | .24 | .06 |
| ☐ 16 Dennis Franklin | .50 | .20 | .05 |
| ☐ 17 Benny Friedman | .60 | .24 | .06 |
| ☐ 18 Jim Mandich | .60 | .24 | .06 |
| ☐ 19 Rob Lytle | .60 | .24 | .06 |
| ☐ 20 Bump Elliott | .60 | .24 | .06 |
| ☐ 21 Harry Kipke | .50 | .20 | .05 |
| ☐ 22 Dave Brown | .60 | .24 | .06 |

## 1991 Mississippi Hoby

TOM LUKE
6-1•195 lbs •Junior•QB
Gulfport, Miss.

This 42-card set was produced by Hoby and features the 1991 Ole Miss football team. Five hundred uncut press sheets were also produced, and they were signed and numbered by Billy Brewer. The

standard size (2 1/2" by 3 1/2") cards feature on the fronts color head and shoulders shots, with thin white borders on a royal blue card face. The school logo occurs in the lower left corner in a red circle, with the player's name in a gold stripe extending to the right. On a light red background, the backs carry biography, player profile, and statistics. The cards are numbered on the back and are ordered alphabetically by player's name.

| | MINT | EXC | G-VG |
|---|---|---|---|
| COMPLETE SET (42) | 9.00 | 3.75 | .90 |
| COMMON CARD (439-480) | .25 | .10 | .02 |
| | | | |
| ☐ 439 Gary Abide | .25 | .10 | .02 |
| ☐ 440 Dwayne Amos | .25 | .10 | .02 |
| ☐ 441 Tyji Armstrong | .75 | .30 | .07 |
| ☐ 442 Tyrone Ashley | .25 | .10 | .02 |
| ☐ 443 Darron Billings | .25 | .10 | .02 |
| ☐ 444 Danny Boyd | .25 | .10 | .02 |
| ☐ 445 Billy Brewer CO | .35 | .14 | .03 |
| ☐ 446 Chad Brown | .50 | .20 | .05 |
| ☐ 447 Tony Brown | .25 | .10 | .02 |
| ☐ 448 Vincent Brownlee | .25 | .10 | .02 |
| ☐ 449 Jeff Carter | .35 | .14 | .03 |
| ☐ 450 Richard Chisolm | .25 | .10 | .02 |
| ☐ 451 Clint Conlee | .25 | .10 | .02 |
| ☐ 452 Marvin Courtney | .25 | .10 | .02 |
| ☐ 453 Cliff Dew | .25 | .10 | .02 |
| ☐ 454 Johnny Dixon | .25 | .10 | .02 |
| ☐ 455 Artis Ford | .25 | .10 | .02 |
| ☐ 456 Chauncey Godwin | .25 | .10 | .02 |
| ☐ 457 Brian Harper | .25 | .10 | .02 |
| ☐ 458 David Harris | .25 | .10 | .02 |
| ☐ 459 Pete Harris | .25 | .10 | .02 |
| ☐ 460 David Herring | .25 | .10 | .02 |
| ☐ 461 James Holcombe | .25 | .10 | .02 |
| ☐ 462 Kevin Ingram | .25 | .10 | .02 |
| ☐ 463 Phillip Kent | .35 | .14 | .03 |
| ☐ 464 Derrick King | .25 | .10 | .02 |
| ☐ 465 Brian Lee | .25 | .10 | .02 |
| ☐ 466 Jim Lentz | .25 | .10 | .02 |
| ☐ 467 Everett Lindsay | .25 | .10 | .02 |
| ☐ 468 Tom Luke | .25 | .10 | .02 |
| ☐ 469 Thomas McLeish | .25 | .10 | .02 |
| ☐ 470 Wesley Melton | .25 | .10 | .02 |
| ☐ 471 Tyrone Montgomery | .50 | .20 | .05 |
| ☐ 472 Deano Orr | .25 | .10 | .02 |
| ☐ 473 Darrick Owens | .35 | .14 | .03 |
| ☐ 474 Lynn Ross | .25 | .10 | .02 |
| ☐ 475 Russ Shows | .25 | .10 | .02 |
| ☐ 476 Eddie Small | .35 | .14 | .03 |
| ☐ 477 Trea Southerland | .25 | .10 | .02 |
| ☐ 478 Gerald Vaughn | .25 | .10 | .02 |
| ☐ 479 Abner White | .25 | .10 | .02 |
| ☐ 480 Sebastian Williams | .25 | .10 | .02 |

## 1991 Mississippi State Hoby

TONY JAMES
5-9•184 lbs •Junior•WR
Clinton, Miss.

This 42-card set was produced by Hoby and features the 1991 Mississippi State football team. The standard size (2 1/2" by 3 1/2") cards feature on the fronts color head shots, with thin white borders on a royal blue card face. The school logo occurs in the lower left corner in a maroon circle, with the player's name in a gold stripe extending to the right. On a light maroon background, the backs carry biography, player profile, and statistics. The cards are numbered on the back and are ordered alphabetically by player's name.

| | MINT | EXC | G-VG |
|---|---|---|---|
| COMPLETE SET (42) | 9.00 | 3.75 | .90 |
| COMMON CARD (481-522) | .25 | .10 | .02 |
| | | | |
| ☐ 481 Lance Aldridge | .25 | .10 | .02 |
| ☐ 482 Treddis Anderson | .25 | .10 | .02 |
| ☐ 483 Shea Bell | .25 | .10 | .02 |

| | | | |
|---|---|---|---|
| ☐ 484 Chris Bosarge | .25 | .10 | .02 |
| ☐ 485 Daniel Boyd | .25 | .10 | .02 |
| ☐ 486 Jerome Brown | .25 | .10 | .02 |
| ☐ 487 Torrance Brown | .25 | .10 | .02 |
| ☐ 488 Keith Carr | .25 | .10 | .02 |
| ☐ 489 Herman Carroll | .25 | .10 | .02 |
| ☐ 490 Keo Coleman | .50 | .20 | .05 |
| ☐ 491 Michael Davis | .25 | .10 | .02 |
| ☐ 492 Trenell Edwards | .25 | .10 | .02 |
| ☐ 493 Chris Firle | .25 | .10 | .02 |
| ☐ 494 Lee Ford | .25 | .10 | .02 |
| ☐ 495 Tay Galloway | .25 | .10 | .02 |
| ☐ 496 Chris Gardner | .25 | .10 | .02 |
| ☐ 497 Arleye Gibson | .25 | .10 | .02 |
| ☐ 498 Tony Harris | .25 | .10 | .02 |
| ☐ 499 Willie Harris | .25 | .10 | .02 |
| ☐ 500 Kevin Henry | .35 | .14 | .03 |
| ☐ 501 Jackie Sherrill CO | .50 | .20 | .05 |
| ☐ 502 John James | .25 | .10 | .02 |
| ☐ 503 Tony James | .25 | .10 | .02 |
| ☐ 504 Todd Jordan | .25 | .10 | .02 |
| ☐ 505 Keith Joseph | .25 | .10 | .02 |
| ☐ 506 Kelvin Knight | .25 | .10 | .02 |
| ☐ 507 Lee Lipscomb | .25 | .10 | .02 |
| ☐ 508 Juan Long | .25 | .10 | .02 |
| ☐ 509 Kyle McCoy | .25 | .10 | .02 |
| ☐ 510 Tommy Morrell | .25 | .10 | .02 |
| ☐ 511 Kelly Ray | .25 | .10 | .02 |
| ☐ 512 Mike Riley | .25 | .10 | .02 |
| ☐ 513 Kenny Roberts | .25 | .10 | .02 |
| ☐ 514 William Robinson | .25 | .10 | .02 |
| ☐ 515 Bill Sartin | .25 | .10 | .02 |
| ☐ 516 Kenny Stewart | .25 | .10 | .02 |
| ☐ 517 Rodney Stowers | .50 | .20 | .05 |
| ☐ 518 Anthony Thames | .25 | .10 | .02 |
| ☐ 519 Edward Williams | .25 | .10 | .02 |
| ☐ 520 Nate Williams | .25 | .10 | .02 |
| ☐ 521 Karl Williamson | .25 | .10 | .02 |
| ☐ 522 Marc Woodard | .25 | .10 | .02 |

# 1989 Nebraska 100

This 100-card set was sponsored and produced by Leesley Ltd. The set is sometimes subtitled as "100 Years of Nebraska Football" as it features past University of Nebraska football players. Many of the pictures are actually color portrait drawings rather than photos. The cards are standard size, 2 1/2" by 3 1/2", and have thick red borders. The vertically oriented backs have detailed profiles. These cards were distributed as a complete set and as eight-card cello packs. The cards are numbered on the back in the upper left corner.

| | MINT | EXC | G-VG |
|---|---|---|---|
| COMPLETE SET (100) | 40.00 | 16.00 | 4.00 |
| COMMON CARD (1-100) | .35 | .14 | .03 |

| | | | |
|---|---|---|---|
| ☐ 1 Tony Davis | .50 | .20 | .05 |
| ☐ 2 Keith Jones | .35 | .14 | .03 |
| ☐ 3 Turner Gill | 1.00 | .40 | .10 |
| ☐ 4 Dave Butterfield | .35 | .14 | .03 |
| ☐ 5 Wonder Monds | .75 | .30 | .07 |
| ☐ 6 Dave Rimington | .75 | .30 | .07 |
| ☐ 7 John Dutton | .75 | .30 | .07 |
| ☐ 8 Irving Fryar | 1.50 | .60 | .15 |
| ☐ 9 Dean Steinkuhler | .75 | .30 | .07 |
| ☐ 10 Mike Rozier | 1.25 | .50 | .12 |
| ☐ 11 Jarvis Redwine | .75 | .30 | .07 |
| ☐ 12 Randy Schleusener | .35 | .14 | .03 |
| ☐ 13 Junior Miller | .50 | .20 | .05 |
| ☐ 14 Broderick Thomas | 1.25 | .50 | .12 |
| ☐ 15 Steve Taylor | .60 | .24 | .06 |
| ☐ 16 Neil Smith | 1.25 | .50 | .12 |
| ☐ 17 John McCormick | .35 | .14 | .03 |
| ☐ 18 Danny Noonan | .60 | .24 | .06 |
| ☐ 19 Mike Fultz | .35 | .14 | .03 |

| | | | |
|---|---|---|---|
| ☐ 20 Vince Ferragamo | 1.00 | .40 | .10 |
| ☐ 21 Jerry Tagge | 1.00 | .40 | .10 |
| ☐ 22 Jeff Kinney | .50 | .20 | .05 |
| ☐ 23 Rich Glover | .50 | .20 | .05 |
| ☐ 24 Johnny Rodgers | 1.25 | .50 | .12 |
| ☐ 25 Rik Bonness | .60 | .24 | .06 |
| ☐ 26 Dave Humm | .50 | .20 | .05 |
| ☐ 27 Mark Traynowicz | .50 | .20 | .05 |
| ☐ 28 Harry Grimminger | .35 | .14 | .03 |
| ☐ 29 Bill Lewis | .50 | .20 | .05 |
| ☐ 30 Jim Skow | .50 | .20 | .05 |
| ☐ 31 Larry Kramer | .35 | .14 | .03 |
| ☐ 32 Tony Jeter | .50 | .20 | .05 |
| ☐ 33 Robert Brown | .35 | .14 | .03 |
| ☐ 34 Larry Wachholtz | .35 | .14 | .03 |
| ☐ 35 Wayne Meylan | .50 | .20 | .05 |
| ☐ 36 Bob Newton | .35 | .14 | .03 |
| ☐ 37 Willie Harper | .50 | .20 | .05 |
| ☐ 38 Bob Martin | .35 | .14 | .03 |
| ☐ 39 Jerry Murtaugh | .50 | .20 | .05 |
| ☐ 40 Daryl White | .35 | .14 | .03 |
| ☐ 41 Larry Jacobson | .35 | .14 | .03 |
| ☐ 42 Joe Armstrong | .35 | .14 | .03 |
| ☐ 43 Laverne Allers | .35 | .14 | .03 |
| ☐ 44 Freeman White | .50 | .20 | .05 |
| ☐ 45 Marvin Crenshaw | .50 | .20 | .05 |
| ☐ 46 Forrest Behm | .35 | .14 | .03 |
| ☐ 47 Jerry Minnick | .35 | .14 | .03 |
| ☐ 48 Tom Davis | .35 | .14 | .03 |
| ☐ 49 Kelvin Clark | .50 | .20 | .05 |
| ☐ 50 Tom Rathman | 1.25 | .50 | .12 |
| ☐ 51 Sam Francis | .35 | .14 | .03 |
| ☐ 52 Joe Orduna | .50 | .20 | .05 |
| ☐ 53 Ed Weir | .35 | .14 | .03 |
| ☐ 54 Bill Thornton | .35 | .14 | .03 |
| ☐ 55 Bob Devaney CO | .60 | .24 | .06 |
| ☐ 56 Bret Clark | .35 | .14 | .03 |
| ☐ 57 Frank Solich | .35 | .14 | .03 |
| ☐ 58 Tim Smith | .35 | .14 | .03 |
| ☐ 59 George Andrews | .35 | .14 | .03 |
| ☐ 60 Rick Berns | .50 | .20 | .05 |
| ☐ 61 Monte Johnson | .50 | .20 | .05 |
| ☐ 62 Walt Barnes | .35 | .14 | .03 |
| ☐ 63 Jim McFarland | .35 | .14 | .03 |
| ☐ 64 Jimmy Williams | .35 | .14 | .03 |
| ☐ 65 Vic Halligan | .35 | .14 | .03 |
| ☐ 66 Guy Chamberlain | .35 | .14 | .03 |
| ☐ 67 Hugh Rhea | .35 | .14 | .03 |
| ☐ 68 George Sauer | .50 | .20 | .05 |
| ☐ 69 E.O. Stiehm CO | .35 | .14 | .03 |
| ☐ 70 Walter G. Booth CO | .35 | .14 | .03 |
| ☐ 71 First Night Game (Memorial Stadium) | .35 | .14 | .03 |
| ☐ 72 Memorial Stadium | .35 | .14 | .03 |
| ☐ 73 M-Stadium Expansions | .35 | .14 | .03 |
| ☐ 74 Andra Franklin | .75 | .30 | .07 |
| ☐ 75 Ron McDole | .50 | .20 | .05 |
| ☐ 76 Pat Fischer | .60 | .24 | .06 |
| ☐ 77 Dan McMullen | .35 | .14 | .03 |
| ☐ 78 Charles Brock | .35 | .14 | .03 |
| ☐ 79 Verne Lewellen | .35 | .14 | .03 |
| ☐ 80 Bob Nelson | .50 | .20 | .05 |
| ☐ 81 Roger Craig | 2.00 | .80 | .20 |
| ☐ 82 Fred Shirey | .35 | .14 | .03 |
| ☐ 83 Tom Novak | .35 | .14 | .03 |
| ☐ 84 Ray Richards | .35 | .14 | .03 |
| ☐ 85 Warren Alfson | .35 | .14 | .03 |
| ☐ 86 Lawrence Ely | .35 | .14 | .03 |
| ☐ 87 Mike Rozier | 1.25 | .50 | .12 |
| ☐ 88 Dean Steinkuhler | .75 | .30 | .07 |
| ☐ 89 John Dutton | .75 | .30 | .07 |
| ☐ 90 Dave Rimington | .75 | .30 | .07 |
| ☐ 91 Johnny Rodgers | 1.25 | .50 | .12 |
| ☐ 92 Herbie Husker (Mascot) | .35 | .14 | .03 |
| ☐ 93 Tom Osborne CO | .75 | .30 | .07 |
| ☐ 94 Broderick Thomas | 1.25 | .50 | .12 |
| ☐ 95 Bobby Reynolds | .35 | .14 | .03 |
| ☐ 96 Mick Tingelhoff UER (Name misspelled Tinglehoff) | .75 | .30 | .07 |
| ☐ 97 Lloyd Cardwell | .35 | .14 | .03 |
| ☐ 98 Johnny Rodgers | 1.25 | .50 | .12 |
| ☐ 99 '70 National Champs (Team Photo) | .50 | .20 | .05 |
| ☐ 100 '71 National Champs (Team Photo) | .50 | .20 | .05 |
| ☐ NNO Title Card (Contest on back) | .50 | .20 | .05 |

# 1982 North Carolina Schedules

This eight-card set was apparently issued by the Department of Athletics at North Carolina (Chapel Hill). The cards measure approximately 2 3/8" by 3 3/8". The card front features a full-bleed head shot of the player, with the player's name and jersey number

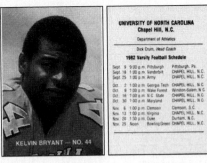

KELVIN BRYANT — NO. 44

burned into the bottom portion of the picture. The backs carry the 1982 varsity football schedule. The cards are unnumbered and checklisted below in alphabetical order.

|  | NRMT | VG-E | GOOD |
|---|---|---|---|
| COMPLETE SET (8) | 20.00 | 8.00 | 2.00 |
| COMMON PLAYER (1-8) | 2.50 | 1.00 | .25 |
| □ 1 Kelvin Bryant | 6.00 | 2.40 | .60 |
| □ 2 Alan Burrus | 2.50 | 1.00 | .25 |
| □ 3 David Drechsler | 2.50 | 1.00 | .25 |
| □ 4 Rod Elkins | 2.50 | 1.00 | .25 |
| □ 5 Jack Parry | 2.50 | 1.00 | .25 |
| □ 6 Greg Poole | 2.50 | 1.00 | .25 |
| □ 7 Ron Spruill | 2.50 | 1.00 | .25 |
| □ 8 Mike Wilcher | 3.50 | 1.40 | .35 |

## 1993 North Carolina State

These 56 standard-size (2 1/2" by 3 1/2") cards were produced by Action Graphics. They feature on their fronts color tilted player action and posed shots set within red borders. The team's name appears reversed out of a black bar above the photo. The player's name appears in white lettering within a black bar near the bottom of the photo. The gray-bordered back carries the team name and year at the top. The player's name, position, number, biography, and career highlights follow within a white area below. The cards are unnumbered and checklisted below in alphabetical order.

|  | MINT | EXC | G-VG |
|---|---|---|---|
| COMPLETE SET (56) | 25.00 | 10.00 | 2.50 |
| COMMON PLAYER (1-56) | .50 | .20 | .05 |
| □ 1 John Akins | .75 | .30 | .07 |
| □ 2 Darryl Beard | .50 | .20 | .05 |
| □ 3 Ricky Bell | .50 | .20 | .05 |
| □ 4 Geoff Bender | .50 | .20 | .05 |
| □ 5 Chuck Browning | .50 | .20 | .05 |
| □ 6 Chuck Cole | .50 | .20 | .05 |
| □ 7 Chris Cotton | .50 | .20 | .05 |
| □ 8 Eric Counts | .50 | .20 | .05 |
| □ 9 Damien Covington | .75 | .30 | .07 |
| □ 10 Dallas Dickerson | .50 | .20 | .05 |
| □ 11 Gary Downs | .50 | .20 | .05 |
| □ 12 Brian Fitzgerald | .50 | .20 | .05 |
| □ 13 Ed Gallon | .50 | .20 | .05 |
| □ 14 Ledel George | .50 | .20 | .05 |
| □ 15 Walt Gerard | .50 | .20 | .05 |
| □ 16 Gregg Giannamore | .50 | .20 | .05 |
| □ 17 Eddie Goines | 1.00 | .40 | .10 |
| □ 18 Ray Griffis | .50 | .20 | .05 |
| □ 19 Mike Harrison | .50 | .20 | .05 |
| □ 20 Terry Harvey | .50 | .20 | .05 |
| □ 21 George Hegamin | .50 | .20 | .05 |
| □ 22 Chris Hennie-Roed | .50 | .20 | .05 |
| □ 23 Adrian Hill | .50 | .20 | .05 |
| □ 24 Robert Hinton | .50 | .20 | .05 |
| □ 25 David Inman | .50 | .20 | .05 |
| □ 26 Dave Janik | .50 | .20 | .05 |
| □ 27 Shawn Johnson | .50 | .20 | .05 |
| □ 28 Tyler Lawrence | .50 | .20 | .05 |
| □ 29 Miller Lawson | .50 | .20 | .05 |
| □ 30 Sean Maguire | .50 | .20 | .05 |
| □ 31 Drea Major | .50 | .20 | .05 |
| □ 32 Mike Moore | .50 | .20 | .05 |
| □ 33 James Newsome | .50 | .20 | .05 |
| □ 34 Mike O'Cain CO | .50 | .20 | .05 |
| □ 35 Loren Pinkney | .50 | .20 | .05 |
| □ 36 Carlos Pruitt | .50 | .20 | .05 |
| □ 37 Carl Reeves | .75 | .30 | .07 |
| □ 38 Jon Rissler | .50 | .20 | .05 |
| □ 39 Chad Robinson | .50 | .20 | .05 |
| □ 40 Ryan Schultz | .50 | .20 | .05 |
| □ 41 William Strong | .50 | .20 | .05 |
| □ 42 Jimmy Sziksai | .50 | .20 | .05 |
| □ 43 Eric Taylor | .50 | .20 | .05 |
| □ 44 Pat Threatt | .50 | .20 | .05 |
| □ 45 Steve Videtich | .75 | .30 | .07 |
| □ 46 James Walker | .75 | .30 | .07 |
| □ 47 Todd Ward | .75 | .30 | .07 |
| □ 48 Dewayne Washington | .75 | .30 | .07 |
| □ 49 Heath Names | .50 | .20 | .05 |
| □ 50 Scott Woods | .50 | .20 | .05 |
| □ 51 Defensive Coaches | .50 | .20 | .05 |
| Buddy Green | | | |
| Kent Briggs | | | |
| Ken Pettus | | | |
| Jeff Snipes | | | |
| Henry Trevathan | | | |
| □ 52 Offensive Coaches | .50 | .20 | .05 |
| Ted Cain | | | |
| Robbie Caldwell | | | |
| Jimmy Kiser | | | |
| Brette Simmons | | | |
| Dick Portee | | | |
| □ 53 Tri-Captains | .50 | .20 | .05 |
| John Akins | | | |
| Todd Ward | | | |
| Dewayne Washington | | | |
| □ 54 Carter-Finley Stadium | .50 | .20 | .05 |
| □ 55 Checklist | .50 | .20 | .05 |
| □ 56 Title Card | .75 | .30 | .07 |

## 1989 North Texas McDag

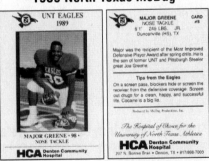

The 1989 University of North Texas McdDag set contains 16 standard-size (2 1/2" by 3 1/2") cards. The fronts have color portrait photos bordered in white; the vertically oriented backs have brief career highlights and safety tips. These cards are printed on very thin stock and are numbered on the back in the upper right corner. The cards were produced by McDag Productions and the set was co-sponsored by the Denton Community Hospital. Each card back contains "Tips from the Eagles".

|  | MINT | EXC | G-VG |
|---|---|---|---|
| COMPLETE SET (16) | 7.00 | 2.80 | .70 |
| COMMON PLAYER (1-16) | .50 | .20 | .05 |
| □ 1 Clay Bode | .50 | .20 | .05 |
| □ 2 Scott Bowles | .50 | .20 | .05 |
| □ 3 Keith Chapman | .50 | .20 | .05 |
| □ 4 Darrin Collins | .50 | .20 | .05 |
| □ 5 Tony Cook | .50 | .20 | .05 |
| □ 6 Scott Davis | 1.25 | .50 | .12 |
| □ 7 Byron Gross | .50 | .20 | .05 |
| □ 8 Larry Green | .50 | .20 | .05 |
| □ 9 Major Greene | 1.25 | .50 | .12 |
| □ 10 Carl Brewer | .50 | .20 | .05 |

| | | | |
|---|---|---|---|
| ☐ 11 J.D. Martinez | .50 | .20 | .05 |
| ☐ 12 Charles Monroe | .50 | .20 | .05 |
| ☐ 13 Kregg Sanders | .50 | .20 | .05 |
| ☐ 14 Lou Smith | .50 | .20 | .05 |
| ☐ 15 Jeff Tutson | .50 | .20 | .05 |
| ☐ 16 Trent Touchstone | .50 | .20 | .05 |

## 1990 North Texas McDag

This 16-card set was sponsored by the HCA Denton Community Hospital, whose company name appears at the bottom on both sides of the card. The cards measure the standard size (2 1/2" by 3 1/2"). The front features a color posed photo, with the player in a kneeling posture and the football in his hand. The picture is framed by a thin dark green border on a white card face, with the player's name and position below the picture. In the lower left corner a North Texas Eagles' helmet appears in the school's colors, green and white. The back has biographical information and a tip from the Eagles in the form of an anti-drug or alcohol message. The cards are numbered on the back. The set features an early card of running back Erric Pegram.

| | MINT | EXC | G-VG |
|---|---|---|---|
| COMPLETE SET (16) | 9.00 | 3.75 | .90 |
| COMMON PLAYER (1-16) | .50 | .20 | .05 |
| ☐ 1 Scott Davis | 1.00 | .40 | .10 |
| ☐ 2 Byron Gross | .50 | .20 | .05 |
| ☐ 3 Tony Cook | .50 | .20 | .05 |
| ☐ 4 Walter Casey | .50 | .20 | .05 |
| ☐ 5 Erric Pegram | 3.00 | 1.20 | .30 |
| ☐ 6 Clay Bode | .50 | .20 | .05 |
| ☐ 7 Scott Bowles | .50 | .20 | .05 |
| ☐ 8 Shawn Wash | .50 | .20 | .05 |
| ☐ 9 Isaac Barnett | .50 | .20 | .05 |
| ☐ 10 Paul Gallamore | .50 | .20 | .05 |
| ☐ 11 J.D. Martinez | .50 | .20 | .05 |
| ☐ 12 Velton Morgan | .50 | .20 | .05 |
| ☐ 13 Major Greene | 1.00 | .40 | .10 |
| ☐ 14 Bart Helsley | .50 | .20 | .05 |
| ☐ 15 Jeff Tutson | .50 | .20 | .05 |
| ☐ 16 Tony Walker | .50 | .20 | .05 |

## 1992 Northwestern Louisiana State

This 13-card set was sponsored by the USDA Forest Service, the National Association of State Foresters, and Northwestern State University of Louisiana. The cards measure 2 5/8" by 3 5/8" and are printed on thin card stock. The fronts feature posed color player photos (from the waist up) that are bordered in the team's colors (purple and orange). Player information and the Smokey logo appear in a white box superimposed toward the bottom. In black on white, the backs present basic player information and a fire prevention cartoon starring Smokey. The cards are unnumbered and checklisted below in alphabetical order.

| | MINT | EXC | G-VG |
|---|---|---|---|
| COMPLETE SET (13) | 7.00 | 2.80 | .70 |
| COMMON PLAYER (1-13) | .50 | .20 | .05 |
| ☐ 1 Darius Adams | .50 | .20 | .05 |
| ☐ 2 Paul Arevalo | .50 | .20 | .05 |
| ☐ 3 Brad Brown | .50 | .20 | .05 |
| ☐ 4 Steve Brown | .60 | .24 | .06 |
| ☐ 5 J.J. Eldridge | .50 | .20 | .05 |
| ☐ 6 Adrian Hardy | .60 | .24 | .06 |
| ☐ 7 Guy Hedrick | .50 | .20 | .05 |
| ☐ 8 Brad Laird | .75 | .30 | .07 |
| ☐ 9 Lawann Latson | .50 | .20 | .05 |
| ☐ 10 Deon Ridgell | .50 | .20 | .05 |
| ☐ 11 Bryan Roussell | .50 | .20 | .05 |
| ☐ 12 Brannon Rowlett | .50 | .20 | .05 |
| ☐ 13 Marcus Spears | .75 | .30 | .07 |
| ☐ 14 Carlos Treadway | .60 | .24 | .06 |
| ☐ 15 Vic (Team Mascot) | .50 | .20 | .05 |

## 1988 Notre Dame

The 1988 Notre Dame football set contains 60 standard-size (2 1/2" by 3 1/2") cards depicting the 1988 National Champions. The fronts have sharp color action photos with dark blue borders and gold lettering; the vertically oriented backs have biographical information. These cards were distributed as a complete set. There are 58 cards of players from the National Championship team, plus one coach card and one for the Golden Dome. The key card in the set is Raghib Ismail, his first known card.

| | MINT | EXC | G-VG |
|---|---|---|---|
| COMPLETE SET (60) | 25.00 | 10.00 | 2.50 |
| COMMON CARD (1-60) | .60 | .24 | .06 |
| ☐ 1 Golden Dome | 1.25 | .50 | .12 |
| ☐ 2 Lou Holtz CO | 3.00 | 1.20 | .30 |
| ☐ 3 Mark Green | .60 | .24 | .06 |
| ☐ 4 Andy Heck | 1.25 | .50 | .12 |
| ☐ 5 Ned Bolcar | 1.00 | .40 | .10 |
| ☐ 6 Anthony Johnson | 1.25 | .50 | .12 |
| ☐ 7 Flash Gordon | .60 | .24 | .06 |
| ☐ 8 Pat Eilers | .60 | .24 | .06 |
| ☐ 9 Raghib(Rocket) Ismail | 10.00 | 4.00 | 1.00 |
| ☐ 10 Ted FitzGerald | .60 | .24 | .06 |
| ☐ 11 Ted Healy | .60 | .24 | .06 |
| ☐ 12 Braxston Banks | 1.00 | .40 | .10 |
| ☐ 13 Steve Belles | .60 | .24 | .06 |
| ☐ 14 Steve Alaniz | .60 | .24 | .06 |
| ☐ 15 Chris Zorich | 3.00 | 1.20 | .30 |
| ☐ 16 Kent Graham | 1.25 | .50 | .12 |
| ☐ 17 Mike Brennan | .60 | .24 | .06 |
| ☐ 18 Marty Lippincott | .60 | .24 | .06 |
| ☐ 19 Rod West | .60 | .24 | .06 |
| ☐ 20 Dean Brown | .60 | .24 | .06 |
| ☐ 21 Tom Gorman | .60 | .24 | .06 |
| ☐ 22 Tony Rice | 2.00 | .80 | .20 |
| ☐ 23 Steve Roddy | .60 | .24 | .06 |
| ☐ 24 Reggie Ho | .75 | .30 | .07 |
| ☐ 25 Pat Terrell | 1.25 | .50 | .12 |
| ☐ 26 Joe Jarosz | .60 | .24 | .06 |
| ☐ 27 Mike Stonebreaker | 1.00 | .40 | .10 |
| ☐ 28 David Jandric | .60 | .24 | .06 |
| ☐ 29 Jeff Alm | 1.25 | .50 | .12 |
| ☐ 30 Pete Graham | .60 | .24 | .06 |
| ☐ 31 Corny Southall | .60 | .24 | .06 |
| ☐ 32 Joe Allen | .60 | .24 | .06 |
| ☐ 33 Jim Sexton | .60 | .24 | .06 |
| ☐ 34 Michael Crounse | .60 | .24 | .06 |
| ☐ 35 Kurt Zackrison | .60 | .24 | .06 |

| | MINT | EXC | G-VG |
|---|---|---|---|
| ☐ 36 Stan Smagala | 1.00 | .40 | .10 |
| ☐ 37 Mike Heldt | .60 | .24 | .06 |
| ☐ 38 Frank Stams | 1.00 | .40 | .10 |
| ☐ 39 D'Juan Francisco | .75 | .30 | .07 |
| ☐ 40 Tim Ryan | 1.25 | .50 | .12 |
| ☐ 41 Arnold Ale | .60 | .24 | .06 |
| ☐ 42 Andre Jones | .60 | .24 | .06 |
| ☐ 43 Wes Pritchett | .60 | .24 | .06 |
| ☐ 44 Tim Grunhard | 1.25 | .50 | .12 |
| ☐ 45 Chuck Killian | .60 | .24 | .06 |
| ☐ 46 Scott Kowalkowski | .75 | .30 | .07 |
| ☐ 47 George Streeter | .60 | .24 | .06 |
| ☐ 48 Donn Grimm | .60 | .24 | .06 |
| ☐ 49 Ricky Watters | 10.00 | 4.00 | 1.00 |
| ☐ 50 Ryan Mihalko | .60 | .24 | .06 |
| ☐ 51 Tony Brooks | 1.50 | .60 | .15 |
| ☐ 52 Todd Lyght | 2.00 | .80 | .20 |
| ☐ 53 Winston Sandri | .60 | .24 | .06 |
| ☐ 54 Aaron Robb | .60 | .24 | .06 |
| ☐ 55 Derek Brown | 3.00 | 1.20 | .30 |
| ☐ 56 Bryan Flannery | .60 | .24 | .06 |
| ☐ 57 Kevin McShane | .60 | .24 | .06 |
| ☐ 58 Billy Hackett | .60 | .24 | .06 |
| ☐ 59 George Williams | .60 | .24 | .06 |
| ☐ 60 Frank Jacobs | .60 | .24 | .06 |

# 1988 Notre Dame Smokey *

This 14-card set was sponsored by the U. S. Forestry Service and measures the standard size 2 1/2" by 3 1/2". The front features a color action photo, with orange and green borders on a purple background. The back has biographical information (or a schedule) and a fire prevention cartoon starring Smokey the Bear. These unnumbered cards are ordered alphabetically within type for convenience.

| | MINT | EXC | G-VG |
|---|---|---|---|
| COMPLETE SET (14) | 25.00 | 10.00 | 2.50 |
| COMMON CARD (1-10) | 1.25 | .50 | .12 |
| COMMON SPORT (11-14) | 1.25 | .50 | .12 |
| | | | |
| ☐ 1 Braxton Banks 39 | 2.00 | .80 | .20 |
| ☐ 2 Ned Bolcar 47 | 2.00 | .80 | .20 |
| ☐ 3 Tom Gorman 87 | 1.25 | .50 | .12 |
| ☐ 4 Mark Green 24 | 1.25 | .50 | .12 |
| ☐ 5 Andy Heck 66 | 2.00 | .80 | .20 |
| ☐ 6 Lou Holtz CO | 3.00 | 1.20 | .30 |
| ☐ 7 Anthony Johnson 22 | 2.50 | 1.00 | .25 |
| ☐ 8 Wes Pritchett 34 | 1.25 | .50 | .12 |
| ☐ 9 George Streeter 27 | 1.25 | .50 | .12 |
| ☐ 10 Ricky Watters 12 | 7.50 | 3.00 | .75 |
| ☐ 11 Men's Soccer | 1.25 | .50 | .12 |
| ☐ 12 Volleyball | 1.25 | .50 | .12 |
| ☐ 13 Women's Basketball | 1.25 | .50 | .12 |
| ☐ 14 Women's Tennis | 1.25 | .50 | .12 |

# 1989 Notre Dame 1903-32

The 1989 Notre Dame Football I set contains 22 standard-size (2 1/2" by 3 1/2") cards depicting the Irish stars from 1903-32. The fronts have vintage photos with white borders and gold lettering; the vertically oriented backs have detailed profiles. These cards were distributed as a set.

| | MINT | EXC | G-VG |
|---|---|---|---|
| COMPLETE SET (22) | 6.00 | 2.50 | .50 |
| COMMON CARD (1-22) | .50 | .20 | .05 |
| | | | |
| ☐ 1 Hunk Anderson | .60 | .24 | .06 |
| ☐ 2 Bert Metzger | .50 | .20 | .05 |
| ☐ 3 Roger Kiley | .50 | .20 | .05 |
| ☐ 4 Nordy Hoffman | .50 | .20 | .05 |
| ☐ 5 Knute Rockne CO | 1.50 | .60 | .15 |

| | | |
|---|---|---|
| **George Gipp** | | |
| Halfback - 1920 | | |

Consensus All-American halfback who led the Irish in passing, scoring and rushing for three seasons while also punting and returning kicks. Still holds the record for best yards-per-carry average for a season, 8.1 yards per carry in 1920. His final season was cut short by strep throat — he later died of complications (pneumonia) at age 25 on December 14, 1920 just two weeks after being named Walter Camp's Player of the Year for 1920. His deathbed plea to Rockne led 1928 Irish to "Win One For The Gipper" in come-from-behind 12-6 upset over unbeaten Army. Gipp was a native of Laurium, Michigan.

GEORGE GIPP
HALFBACK 1920

Card 21 of 22

| | MINT | EXC | G-VG |
|---|---|---|---|
| ☐ 6 Elmer Layden | .75 | .30 | .07 |
| ☐ 7 Gus Dorais | .60 | .24 | .06 |
| ☐ 8 Ray Eichenlaub | .50 | .20 | .05 |
| ☐ 9 Don Miller | .60 | .24 | .06 |
| ☐ 10 Moose Krause | .75 | .30 | .07 |
| ☐ 11 Jesse Harper | .50 | .20 | .05 |
| ☐ 12 Jack Cannon | .50 | .20 | .05 |
| ☐ 13 Eddie Anderson | .50 | .20 | .05 |
| ☐ 14 Louis Salmon | .50 | .20 | .05 |
| ☐ 15 John Smith | .50 | .20 | .05 |
| ☐ 16 Harry Stuhldreher | .75 | .30 | .07 |
| ☐ 17 Joe Kurth | .50 | .20 | .05 |
| ☐ 18 Frank Carideo | .50 | .20 | .05 |
| ☐ 19 Marchy Schwartz | .50 | .20 | .05 |
| ☐ 20 Adam Walsh | .50 | .20 | .05 |
| ☐ 21 George Gipp | 1.50 | .60 | .15 |
| ☐ 22 Jim Crowley | .75 | .30 | .07 |

# 1989 Notre Dame 1935-59

| | | |
|---|---|---|
| **Jim Martin** | | |
| Tackle - 1949 | | |

Consensus All-American tackle for the 1949 national champions. A four year starter, along with Emil Sitko during the Glory Years of Notre Dame football when the Irish won three national championships in four seasons, never losing a game. Along with Leon Hart, helped pave the way for running back Emil Sitko.

My fondest memories were "first, attending the University of Notre Dame, [and] second, playing football for the University of Notre Dame. The fondest memory was playing four years of football and never losing a game. Starting and playing both offense and defense in 36 of those games. To be on three national championships, to co-captain the 1949 national champion team, and [to] go unbeaten in 10 games — this is the greatest and fondest memory of all."
Jim Martin

JIM MARTIN
TACKLE 1949

Card 3 of 22

The 1989 Notre Dame Football II set contains 22 standard-size (2 1/2" by 3 1/2") cards depicting the Irish stars from 1935-59. The fronts have vintage photos with white borders and gold lettering; the vertically oriented backs have detailed profiles. These cards were distributed as a set.

| | MINT | EXC | G-VG |
|---|---|---|---|
| COMPLETE SET (22) | 6.00 | 2.50 | .60 |
| COMMON CARD (1-22) | .50 | .20 | .05 |
| | | | |
| ☐ 1 Frank Leahy CO | .75 | .30 | .07 |
| ☐ 2 John Lattner | .75 | .30 | .07 |
| ☐ 3 Jim Martin | .75 | .30 | .07 |
| ☐ 4 Joe Heap | .50 | .20 | .05 |
| ☐ 5 Paul Hornung | 1.50 | .60 | .15 |
| ☐ 6 Bill Shakespeare | .75 | .30 | .07 |
| ☐ 7 Bob Dove | .50 | .20 | .05 |
| ☐ 8 Bob Williams | .50 | .20 | .05 |
| ☐ 9 Al Ecuyer | .50 | .20 | .05 |
| ☐ 10 George Connor | 1.00 | .40 | .10 |
| ☐ 11 Leon Hart | 1.00 | .40 | .10 |
| ☐ 12 Joe Beinor | .50 | .20 | .05 |
| ☐ 13 Bill Fischer | .50 | .20 | .05 |
| ☐ 14 Angelo Bertelli | 1.00 | .40 | .10 |
| ☐ 15 Ralph Guglielmi | .60 | .24 | .06 |
| ☐ 16 Pat Filley | .50 | .20 | .05 |
| ☐ 17 Emil Sitko | .60 | .24 | .06 |
| ☐ 18 Don Schaefer | .50 | .20 | .05 |
| ☐ 19 Monty Stickles | .60 | .24 | .06 |
| ☐ 20 Creighton Miller | .60 | .24 | .06 |
| ☐ 21 Chuck Sweeney | .50 | .20 | .05 |
| ☐ 22 John Lujack | 1.00 | .40 | .10 |

# 1989 Notre Dame 1964-87

**Tim Brown**
**Flanker - 1987**

Unanimous consensus first team All-American flanker, Brown won the Heisman Trophy and Walter Camp Trophy in 1987 in the second year of Lou Holtz's renewal of Irish football success. He was Notre Dame's seventh Heisman winner, the most of any school, and its first in 23 years. He is all-time Notre Dame leader in career pass reception yards with 2493, and led the team in receptions for three seasons. As a senior he averaged 168 all-purpose yards per game as a receiver, kick returner and occasionally a rusher. As a junior he had 45 receptions for 910 yards and five touchdowns, capping the season off with a 252-yard all-purpose performance in a season-ending come-from-behind 38-37 win over Southern Cal. Averaged 42.3 yards on his 22 career touchdown plays, including six punt or kickoff returns for touchdowns. A native of Dallas, Texas.

Card 4 of 22

The 1989 Notre Dame Football III set contains 22 standard-size (2 1/2" by 3 1/2") cards depicting the Irish stars from 1964-87. The fronts have vintage and color photos with white borders and gold lettering; the vertically oriented backs have detailed profiles. These cards were distributed as a set.

|  | MINT | EXC | G-VG |
|---|---|---|---|
| COMPLETE SET (22) | 6.00 | 2.50 | .50 |
| COMMON CARD (1-22) | .50 | .20 | .05 |
| ☐ 1 Dan Devine CO | .60 | .24 | .06 |
| ☐ 2 Joe Theismann | 1.25 | .50 | .12 |
| ☐ 3 Tom Gatewood | .75 | .30 | .07 |
| ☐ 4 Tim Brown | 1.25 | .50 | .12 |
| ☐ 5 Ara Parseghian CO | .75 | .30 | .07 |
| ☐ 6 Jim Lynch | .60 | .24 | .06 |
| ☐ 7 Luther Bradley | .50 | .20 | .05 |
| ☐ 8 Ross Browner | .60 | .24 | .06 |
| ☐ 9 John Huarte | 1.00 | .40 | .10 |
| ☐ 10 Bob Crable | .60 | .24 | .06 |
| ☐ 11 Ken MacAfee | .60 | .24 | .06 |
| ☐ 12 Alan Page | 1.00 | .40 | .10 |
| ☐ 13 Vagas Ferguson | .60 | .24 | .06 |
| ☐ 14 Dick Arrington | .50 | .20 | .05 |
| ☐ 15 Bob Golic | .75 | .30 | .07 |
| ☐ 16 Mike Tonsend | .50 | .20 | .05 |
| ☐ 17 Walt Patulski | .60 | .24 | .06 |
| ☐ 18 Allen Pinkett | .75 | .30 | .07 |
| ☐ 19 Terry Hanratty | .75 | .30 | .07 |
| ☐ 20 Dave Casper | .75 | .30 | .07 |
| ☐ 21 Jack Snow | .75 | .30 | .07 |
| ☐ 22 Nick Eddy | .60 | .24 | .06 |

# 1990 Notre Dame Promos

**JOE MONTANA**
QUARTERBACK • 1975, 1977-78
FIGHTING IRISH CAREER

This ten-card standard size (2 1/2" by 3 1/2") set was issued by Collegiate Collection to honor some of the leading figures in Fighting Irish history. This set has a mix of the most famous Notre Dame coaches and some of the offensive stars of Notre Dame's long history. The featured subjects active after 1960 are shown in color photos.

|  | MINT | EXC | G-VG |
|---|---|---|---|
| COMPLETE SET (10) | 6.00 | 2.40 | .60 |
| COMMON PLAYER (1-10) | .50 | .20 | .05 |
| ☐ 1 Knute Rockne CO | 1.00 | .40 | .10 |
| ☐ 2 Joe Theismann | 1.00 | .40 | .10 |
| ☐ 3 Joe Montana | 3.00 | 1.20 | .30 |
| ☐ 4 George Gipp | 1.00 | .40 | .10 |
| ☐ 5 Notre Dame Stadium | .50 | .20 | .05 |
| ☐ 6 Ara Parseghian CO | .60 | .24 | .06 |

| ☐ 7 Frank Leahy CO | .50 | .20 | .05 |
|---|---|---|---|
| ☐ 8 Lou Holtz CO | .60 | .24 | .06 |
| ☐ 9 Tony Rice | .75 | .30 | .07 |
| ☐ 10 Rocky Bleier | .75 | .30 | .07 |

# 1990 Notre Dame 200

**RALPH GUGLIELMI**
QUARTERBACK • 1951-54
FIGHTING IRISH CAREER

A consensus All-American in 1954, Ralph Guglielmi still holds the Notre Dame record for passing for three consecutive games. He led the team in passing four years from 1952-54. He won the Walter Camp Trophy as the nation's top back in 1954 while finishing fourth in the Heisman Trophy balloting. A native of Columbus, OH.

**35**

This 200-card standard size set (2 1/2" by 3 1/2") was issued by Collegiate Collection in 1990 and features many of the great players and figures of Notre Dame history. The set was available in wax packs and features a mixture of black and white or color photos, posed and action, with a yellow border against a blue background. The horizontally oriented backs are numbered in the upper right hand corner and provide career highlights. There were 2000 special George Gipp cards randomly inserted in wax packs as a bonus.

|  | MINT | EXC | G-VG |
|---|---|---|---|
| COMPLETE SET (200) | 20.00 | 8.00 | 2.00 |
| COMMON CARD (1-200) | .10 | .04 | .01 |
| ☐ 1 Joe Montana | 1.25 | .50 | .12 |
| ☐ 2 Tim Brown | .50 | .20 | .05 |
| ☐ 3 Reggie Barnett | .25 | .10 | .02 |
| ☐ 4 Joe Theismann | .50 | .20 | .05 |
| ☐ 5 Bob Clasby | .15 | .06 | .01 |
| ☐ 6 Dave Casper | .25 | .10 | .02 |
| ☐ 7 George Kunz | .20 | .08 | .02 |
| ☐ 8 Vince Phelan | .10 | .04 | .01 |
| ☐ 9 Tom Gibbons | .10 | .04 | .01 |
| ☐ 10 Tom Thayer | .15 | .06 | .01 |
| ☐ 11 Notre Dame Helmet | .10 | .04 | .01 |
| ☐ 12 John Scully | .10 | .04 | .01 |
| ☐ 13 Lou Holtz CO | .25 | .10 | .02 |
| ☐ 14 Larry Dinardo | .10 | .04 | .01 |
| ☐ 15 Greg Marx | .10 | .04 | .01 |
| ☐ 16 Greg Dingens | .10 | .04 | .01 |
| ☐ 17 Jim Seymour | .15 | .06 | .01 |
| ☐ 18 1979 Cotton Bowl | .10 | .04 | .01 |
| (Program) | | | |
| ☐ 19 Mike Kadish | .15 | .06 | .01 |
| ☐ 20 Bob Crable | .20 | .08 | .02 |
| ☐ 21 Tony Rice | .25 | .10 | .02 |
| ☐ 22 Phil Carter | .10 | .04 | .01 |
| ☐ 23 Ken MacAfee | .15 | .06 | .01 |
| ☐ 24 Nick Eddy | .20 | .08 | .02 |
| ☐ 25 1988 National Champs | .15 | .06 | .01 |
| (Trophies) | | | |
| ☐ 26 Clarence Ellis | .20 | .08 | .02 |
| ☐ 27 Joe Restic | .15 | .06 | .01 |
| ☐ 28 Dan Devine CO | .15 | .06 | .01 |
| ☐ 29 John K. Carney | .10 | .04 | .01 |
| ☐ 30 Stacey Toran | .15 | .06 | .01 |
| ☐ 31 47th Sugar Bowl | .10 | .04 | .01 |
| (Program) | | | |
| ☐ 32 J. Heavens | .10 | .04 | .01 |
| ☐ 33 Mike Fanning | .10 | .04 | .01 |
| ☐ 34 Dave Vinson | .10 | .04 | .01 |
| ☐ 35 Ralph Gugliemi | .15 | .06 | .01 |
| ☐ 36 Reggie Ho | .10 | .04 | .01 |
| ☐ 37 Allen Pinkett | .20 | .08 | .02 |
| ☐ 38 Jim Browner | .25 | .10 | .02 |
| ☐ 39 Blair Kiel | .25 | .10 | .02 |
| ☐ 40 Joe Montana | 1.25 | .50 | .12 |
| ☐ 41 Rocky Bleier | .30 | .12 | .03 |
| ☐ 42 Terry Hanratty | .25 | .10 | .02 |
| ☐ 43 Tom Regner | .15 | .06 | .01 |
| ☐ 44 Pete Holohan | .15 | .06 | .01 |
| ☐ 45 Greg Bell | .20 | .08 | .02 |
| ☐ 46 Dave Duerson | .15 | .06 | .01 |
| ☐ 47 Frank Varrichione | .10 | .04 | .01 |
| ☐ 48 1988 Championship | .15 | .06 | .01 |
| (Team Photo) | | | |
| ☐ 49 Ted Burgmeier | .10 | .04 | .01 |
| ☐ 50 Ara Parseghian CO | .20 | .08 | .02 |

| | | | |
|---|---|---|---|
| ☐ 51 Mike Townsend | .10 | .04 | .01 |
| ☐ 52 Liberty Bowl 1983 | .10 | .04 | .01 |
| (Program) | | | |
| ☐ 53 Tony Furjanic | .10 | .04 | .01 |
| ☐ 54 Luther Bradley | .15 | .06 | .01 |
| ☐ 55 Steve Niehaus | .15 | .06 | .01 |
| ☐ 56 56th Orange Bowl | .10 | .04 | .01 |
| (Program) | | | |
| ☐ 57 32nd Gator Bowl | .10 | .04 | .01 |
| (Program) | | | |
| ☐ 58 40th Sugar Bowl | .10 | .04 | .01 |
| (Program) | | | |
| ☐ 59 52nd Cotton Bowl | .10 | .04 | .01 |
| (Program) | | | |
| ☐ 60 1975 Orange Bowl | .10 | .04 | .01 |
| (Program) | | | |
| ☐ 61 Wayne Bullock | .10 | .04 | .01 |
| ☐ 62 Larry Moriarty | .10 | .04 | .01 |
| ☐ 63 Jim Lynch | .20 | .08 | .02 |
| ☐ 64 Mike McCoy | .20 | .08 | .02 |
| ☐ 65 Tony Hunter | .20 | .08 | .02 |
| ☐ 66 1984 Aloha Bowl | .10 | .04 | .01 |
| (Program) | | | |
| ☐ 67 Dave Huffman | .10 | .04 | .01 |
| ☐ 68 John Lattner | .20 | .08 | .02 |
| ☐ 69 Tom Gatewood | .20 | .08 | .02 |
| ☐ 70 Knute Rockne CO | .35 | .14 | .03 |
| ☐ 71 Phil Pozderac | .10 | .04 | .01 |
| ☐ 72 Ross Browner | .20 | .08 | .02 |
| ☐ 73 Pete Demmerle | .10 | .04 | .01 |
| ☐ 74 Sunkist Fiesta Bowl | .10 | .04 | .01 |
| (Program) | | | |
| ☐ 75 Walt Patulski | .20 | .08 | .02 |
| ☐ 76 George Gipp | .50 | .20 | .05 |
| ☐ 77 LeRoy Leopold | .10 | .04 | .01 |
| ☐ 78 John Huarte | .30 | .12 | .03 |
| ☐ 79 Tony Yelovich CO | .10 | .04 | .01 |
| ☐ 80 John Lujack | .30 | .12 | .03 |
| ☐ 81 Cotton Bowl Classic | .10 | .04 | .01 |
| (Program) | | | |
| ☐ 82 Tim Huffman | .10 | .04 | .01 |
| ☐ 83 Bob Golic | .20 | .08 | .02 |
| ☐ 84 Tom Clements | .25 | .10 | .02 |
| ☐ 85 39th Orange Bowl | .10 | .04 | .01 |
| (Program) | | | |
| ☐ 86 James J. White ADMIN | .10 | .04 | .01 |
| ☐ 87 Frank Carideo | .10 | .04 | .01 |
| ☐ 88 Vinny Cerrato | .10 | .04 | .01 |
| ☐ 89 Louis Salmon | .10 | .04 | .01 |
| ☐ 90 Bob Burger | .10 | .04 | .01 |
| ☐ 91 Gerry Dinardo | .10 | .04 | .01 |
| ☐ 92 Mike Creaney | .10 | .04 | .01 |
| ☐ 93 John Krimm | .10 | .04 | .01 |
| ☐ 94 Vagas Ferguson | .15 | .06 | .01 |
| ☐ 95 Kris Haines | .10 | .04 | .01 |
| ☐ 96 Gus Dorais | .20 | .08 | .02 |
| ☐ 97 Tom Schoen | .10 | .04 | .01 |
| ☐ 98 Jack Robinson | .10 | .04 | .01 |
| ☐ 99 Joe Heap | .10 | .04 | .01 |
| ☐ 100 Checklist 1-99 | .15 | .06 | .01 |
| ☐ 101 Gary Darnell CO | .10 | .04 | .01 |
| ☐ 102 Peter Vaas CO | .10 | .04 | .01 |
| ☐ 103 1924 National Champs | .15 | .06 | .01 |
| (Team Photo) | | | |
| ☐ 104 Wayne Millner | .25 | .10 | .02 |
| ☐ 105 Moose Krause | .20 | .08 | .02 |
| ☐ 106 Jack Cannon | .10 | .04 | .01 |
| ☐ 107 Christy Flanagan | .10 | .04 | .01 |
| ☐ 108 Bob Lehmann | .10 | .04 | .01 |
| ☐ 109 1947 Champions | .15 | .06 | .01 |
| (Team Photo) | | | |
| ☐ 110 Joe Kurth | .10 | .04 | .01 |
| ☐ 111 Tommy Yarr | .10 | .04 | .01 |
| ☐ 112 Nick Buoniconti | .35 | .14 | .03 |
| ☐ 113 Jim Smithberger | .10 | .04 | .01 |
| ☐ 114 Joe Beinor | .10 | .04 | .01 |
| ☐ 115 Pete Cordelli CO | .10 | .04 | .01 |
| ☐ 116 Daryle Lamonica | .30 | .12 | .03 |
| ☐ 117 Kevin Hardy | .15 | .06 | .01 |
| ☐ 118 Creighton Miller | .20 | .08 | .02 |
| ☐ 119 Bob Gladieux | .15 | .06 | .01 |
| ☐ 120 Fred Miller | .25 | .10 | .02 |
| (Later Miller Brewing) | | | |
| ☐ 121 Gary Potempa | .10 | .04 | .01 |
| ☐ 122 Bob Kuechenberg | .20 | .08 | .02 |
| ☐ 123 Jesse Harper CO | .10 | .04 | .01 |
| ☐ 124 1929 National Champs | .15 | .06 | .01 |
| (Team Photo) | | | |
| ☐ 125 Alan Page | .30 | .12 | .03 |
| ☐ 126 Don Miller | .10 | .04 | .01 |
| ☐ 127 1943 National Champs | .15 | .06 | .01 |
| (Team Photo) | | | |
| ☐ 128 Bob Wetoska | .10 | .04 | .01 |
| ☐ 129 Skip Holtz CO | .10 | .04 | .01 |
| ☐ 130 Hunk Anderson CO | .10 | .04 | .01 |
| ☐ 131 Bob Williams | .10 | .04 | .01 |
| ☐ 132 1966 National Champs | .15 | .06 | .01 |
| ☐ 133 Jim Reilly | .10 | .04 | .01 |
| ☐ 134 Earl(Curly) Lambeau | .20 | .08 | .02 |
| ☐ 135 Ernie Hughes | .10 | .04 | .01 |
| ☐ 136 Dick Bumpas CO | .10 | .04 | .01 |
| ☐ 137 Jay Haynes CO | .10 | .04 | .01 |
| ☐ 138 Harry Stuhldreher | .20 | .08 | .02 |
| ☐ 139 1971 Cotton Bowl | .15 | .06 | .01 |
| (Game Photo) | | | |
| ☐ 140 1930 National Champs | .15 | .06 | .01 |
| (Team Photo) | | | |
| ☐ 141 Larry Conjar | .20 | .08 | .02 |
| ☐ 142 1977 National Champs | .15 | .06 | .01 |
| (Team Photo) | | | |
| ☐ 143 Pete Duranko | .20 | .08 | .02 |
| ☐ 144 Heisman Winners | .30 | .12 | .03 |
| (Seven Trophy Winners) | | | |
| ☐ 145 Bill Fisher | .10 | .04 | .01 |
| ☐ 146 Marchy Schwartz | .10 | .04 | .01 |
| ☐ 147 Chuck Heater CO | .10 | .04 | .01 |
| ☐ 148 Bert Metzger | .10 | .04 | .01 |
| ☐ 149 Bill Shakespeare | .25 | .10 | .02 |
| ☐ 150 Adam Walsh | .10 | .04 | .01 |
| ☐ 151 Nordy Hoffman | .10 | .04 | .01 |
| ☐ 152 Ted Gradel | .10 | .04 | .01 |
| ☐ 153 Monty Stickles | .15 | .06 | .01 |
| ☐ 154 Neil Worden | .10 | .04 | .01 |
| ☐ 155 Pat Filley | .10 | .04 | .01 |
| ☐ 156 Angelo Bertelli | .25 | .10 | .02 |
| ☐ 157 Nick Pietrosante | .20 | .08 | .02 |
| ☐ 158 Art Hunter | .10 | .04 | .01 |
| ☐ 159 Ziggy Czarobski | .15 | .06 | .01 |
| ☐ 160 1925 Rose Bowl | .10 | .04 | .01 |
| (Program) | | | |
| ☐ 161 Al Ecuyer | .10 | .04 | .01 |
| ☐ 162 1949 Notre Dame Champs | .15 | .06 | .01 |
| (Team Photo) | | | |
| ☐ 163 Elmer Layden | .25 | .10 | .02 |
| ☐ 164 Joe Moore CO | .10 | .04 | .01 |
| ☐ 165 1946 National Champs | .15 | .06 | .01 |
| (Team Photo) | | | |
| ☐ 166 Frank Rydzewski | .10 | .04 | .01 |
| ☐ 167 Bud Boeringer | .10 | .04 | .01 |
| ☐ 168 Jerry Groom | .10 | .04 | .01 |
| ☐ 169 Jack Snow | .20 | .08 | .02 |
| ☐ 170 Joe Montana | 1.25 | .50 | .12 |
| ☐ 171 John Smith | .10 | .04 | .01 |
| ☐ 172 Frank Leahy CO | .20 | .08 | .02 |
| ☐ 173 Emil Sitko | .15 | .06 | .01 |
| ☐ 174 Dick Arrington | .15 | .06 | .01 |
| ☐ 175 Eddie Anderson | .10 | .04 | .01 |
| ☐ 176 1928 Army | .10 | .04 | .01 |
| (Logo and score) | | | |
| ☐ 177 1913 Army | .10 | .04 | .01 |
| (Logo and score) | | | |
| ☐ 178 1935 Ohio State | .10 | .04 | .01 |
| (Logo and game score) | | | |
| ☐ 179 1946 Army | .10 | .04 | .01 |
| (Logo and game score) | | | |
| ☐ 180 1953 Georgia Tech | .10 | .04 | .01 |
| (Logo and game score) | | | |
| ☐ 181 Don Schaefer | .10 | .04 | .01 |
| ☐ 182 1973 Football Team | .15 | .06 | .01 |
| (Team Photo) | | | |
| ☐ 183 Bob Dove | .10 | .04 | .01 |
| ☐ 184 Dick Szymanski | .10 | .04 | .01 |
| ☐ 185 Jim Martin | .15 | .06 | .01 |
| ☐ 186 1957 Oklahoma | .10 | .04 | .01 |
| (Logo and game score) | | | |
| ☐ 187 1966 Michigan State | .10 | .04 | .01 |
| (Logo and game score) | | | |
| ☐ 188 1973 USC | .10 | .04 | .01 |
| (Logo and game score) | | | |
| ☐ 189 1980 Michigan | .10 | .04 | .01 |
| (Logo and game score) | | | |
| ☐ 190 1982 Michigan | .10 | .04 | .01 |
| (Logo and game score) | | | |
| ☐ 191 Chuck Sweeney | .10 | .04 | .01 |
| ☐ 192 Notre Dame Stadium | .10 | .04 | .01 |
| ☐ 193 Roger Kiley | .10 | .04 | .01 |
| ☐ 194 Ray Eichenlaub | .10 | .04 | .01 |
| ☐ 195 George Connor | .25 | .10 | .02 |
| ☐ 196 1982 Pittsburgh | .10 | .04 | .01 |
| (Logo and game score) | | | |
| ☐ 197 1986 USC | .10 | .04 | .01 |
| (Logo and game score) | | | |
| ☐ 198 1988 Miami | .10 | .04 | .01 |
| (Logo and game score) | | | |
| ☐ 199 1988 USC | .10 | .04 | .01 |
| (Logo and game score) | | | |
| ☐ 200 Checklist 101-199 | .15 | .06 | .01 |

## 1990 Notre Dame 60

This 60-card set measures 2 1/2" by 3 1/2" and was issued to celebrate the 1990 Notre Dame football team. The key cards in this set feature Reggie Brooks, Raghib "Rocket" Ismail, Rick Mirer, and Ricky Watters. There is a full color photo on the front, with the Notre Dame logo in the lower right-hand corner of the card. The back has biographical information about the player. The set was produced by College Classics; reportedly 10,000 sets were produced and distributed.

| | MINT | EXC | G-VG |
|---|---|---|---|
| COMPLETE SET (60) | 25.00 | 10.00 | 2.50 |
| COMMON CARD (1-60) | .35 | .14 | .03 |
| | | | |
| ☐ 1 Joe Allen | .35 | .14 | .03 |
| ☐ 2 William Pollard | .35 | .14 | .03 |
| ☐ 3 Tony Smith | .35 | .14 | .03 |
| ☐ 4 Tony Brooks | .75 | .30 | .07 |
| ☐ 5 Kenny Spears | .35 | .14 | .03 |
| ☐ 6 Mike Heldt | .35 | .14 | .03 |
| ☐ 7 Derek Brown | 1.50 | .60 | .15 |
| ☐ 8 Rodney Culver | 1.25 | .50 | .12 |
| ☐ 9 Ricky Watters | 3.50 | 1.40 | .35 |
| ☐ 10 Raghib(Rocket) Ismail | 3.50 | 1.40 | .35 |
| ☐ 11 Lou Holtz CO | 1.25 | .50 | .12 |
| ☐ 12 Chris Zorich | 1.50 | .60 | .15 |
| ☐ 13 Erik Simien | .35 | .14 | .03 |
| ☐ 14 Shawn Davis | .35 | .14 | .03 |
| ☐ 15 Greg Davis | .35 | .14 | .03 |
| ☐ 16 Walter Boyd | .35 | .14 | .03 |
| ☐ 17 Tim Ryan | .75 | .30 | .07 |
| ☐ 18 Lindsay Knapp | .35 | .14 | .03 |
| ☐ 19 Junior Bryant | .35 | .14 | .03 |
| ☐ 20 Michael Stonebreaker | .60 | .24 | .06 |
| ☐ 21 Randy Scianna | .35 | .14 | .03 |
| ☐ 22 Rick Mirer | 10.00 | 4.00 | 1.00 |
| ☐ 23 Ryan Mihalko | .35 | .14 | .03 |
| ☐ 24 Todd Lyght | 1.25 | .50 | .12 |
| ☐ 25 Andre Jones | .35 | .14 | .03 |
| ☐ 26 Rod Smith | .60 | .24 | .06 |
| ☐ 27 Winston Sandri | .35 | .14 | .03 |
| ☐ 28 Bob Dahl | .60 | .24 | .06 |
| ☐ 29 Stuart Tyner | .35 | .14 | .03 |
| ☐ 30 Brian Shannon | .35 | .14 | .03 |
| ☐ 31 Shawn Smith | .35 | .14 | .03 |
| ☐ 32 Jim Sexton | .35 | .14 | .03 |
| ☐ 33 Dorsey Levens | .35 | .14 | .03 |
| ☐ 34 Lance Johnson | .35 | .14 | .03 |
| ☐ 35 George Poorman | .35 | .14 | .03 |
| ☐ 36 Irv Smith | 1.25 | .50 | .12 |
| ☐ 37 George Williams | .35 | .14 | .03 |
| ☐ 38 George Marshall | .50 | .20 | .05 |
| ☐ 39 Reggie Brooks | 5.00 | 2.00 | .50 |
| ☐ 40 Scott Kowalkowski | .50 | .20 | .05 |
| ☐ 41 Jerry Bodine | .35 | .14 | .03 |
| ☐ 42 Karmeeleyah McGill | .35 | .14 | .03 |
| ☐ 43 Donn Grimm | .35 | .14 | .03 |
| ☐ 44 Billy Hackett | .35 | .14 | .03 |
| ☐ 45 Jordan Halter | .35 | .14 | .03 |
| ☐ 46 Mirko Jurkovic | .75 | .30 | .07 |
| ☐ 47 Mike Callan | .35 | .14 | .03 |
| ☐ 48 Justin Hall | .35 | .14 | .03 |
| ☐ 49 Nick Smith | .35 | .14 | .03 |
| ☐ 50 Brian Ratigan | .35 | .14 | .03 |
| ☐ 51 Eric Jones | .35 | .14 | .03 |
| ☐ 52 Todd Norman | .35 | .14 | .03 |
| ☐ 53 Devon McDonald | .60 | .24 | .06 |
| ☐ 54 Marc deManigold | .35 | .14 | .03 |
| ☐ 55 Bret Hankins | .35 | .14 | .03 |
| ☐ 56 Aaron Jarrell | .35 | .14 | .03 |
| ☐ 57 Craig Hentrich | .60 | .24 | .06 |
| ☐ 58 Demetrius DuBose | 1.00 | .40 | .10 |
| ☐ 59 Gene McGuire | .75 | .30 | .07 |
| ☐ 60 Ray Griggs | .35 | .14 | .03 |

## 1990 Notre Dame Greats

This 22-card standard size (2 1/2" by 3 1/2") set celebrates 22 of the All-Americans and past greats who attended Notre Dame. The cards have a mix of color and black and white photos on the front of the card and the back of the card has a biography of the player which describes his career at Notre Dame.

| | MINT | EXC | G-VG |
|---|---|---|---|
| COMPLETE SET (22) | 6.00 | 2.50 | .50 |
| COMMON PLAYER (1-22) | .50 | .20 | .05 |
| | | | |
| ☐ 1 Clarence Ellis | .50 | .20 | .05 |
| ☐ 2 Rocky Bleier | 1.00 | .40 | .10 |
| ☐ 3 Tom Regner | .50 | .20 | .05 |
| ☐ 4 Jim Seymour | .50 | .20 | .05 |
| ☐ 5 Joe Montana | 4.00 | 1.60 | .40 |
| ☐ 6 Art Hunter | .50 | .20 | .05 |
| ☐ 7 Mike McCoy | .50 | .20 | .05 |
| ☐ 8 Bud Boeringer | .50 | .20 | .05 |
| ☐ 9 Greg Marx | .50 | .20 | .05 |
| ☐ 10 Nick Buoniconti | 1.00 | .40 | .10 |
| ☐ 11 Pete Demmerle | .50 | .20 | .05 |
| ☐ 12 Fred Miller | .50 | .20 | .05 |
| ☐ 13 Tommy Yarr | .50 | .20 | .05 |
| ☐ 14 Frank Rydzewski | .50 | .20 | .05 |
| ☐ 15 Dave Duerson | .50 | .20 | .05 |
| ☐ 16 Ziggy Czarobski | .60 | .24 | .06 |
| ☐ 17 Jim White | .50 | .20 | .05 |
| ☐ 18 Larry DiNardo | .50 | .20 | .05 |
| ☐ 19 George Kunz | .60 | .24 | .06 |
| ☐ 20 Jack Robinson | .50 | .20 | .05 |
| ☐ 21 Steve Niehaus | .50 | .20 | .05 |
| ☐ 22 John Scully | .60 | .24 | .06 |

## 1992 Notre Dame

This 59-card set measures the standard size (2 1/2" by 3 1/2") and features color action player photos bordered on the left or right edge by a gray stripe containing the team name. The player's name appears in gold lettering on a white stripe at the bottom. The horizontal backs feature close-up player pictures with shadow box borders. The white background is printed with a profile of the player. The school logo and biographical information appear at the top. The cards are numbered on the back and are arranged alphabetically (with a few exceptions) after leading off with Coach Holtz, Rick Mirer, and Demetrius DuBose. Other noteworthy cards in the set are Jerome Bettis and Reggie Brooks.

| | MINT | EXC | G-VG |
|---|---|---|---|
| COMPLETE SET (59) | 30.00 | 12.00 | 3.00 |
| COMMON CARD (1-59) | .35 | .14 | .03 |

| | | | |
|---|---|---|---|
| ☐ 1 Lou Holtz CO | 1.50 | .60 | .15 |
| ☐ 2 Rick Mirer | 8.00 | 3.25 | .80 |
| ☐ 3 Demetrius DuBose | 1.00 | .40 | .10 |
| ☐ 4 Lee Becton | 2.00 | .80 | .20 |
| ☐ 5 Pete Bercich | .50 | .20 | .05 |
| ☐ 6 Jerome Bettis | 10.00 | 4.00 | 1.00 |
| ☐ 7 Reggie Brooks | 4.00 | 1.60 | .40 |
| ☐ 8 Junior Bryant | .35 | .14 | .03 |
| ☐ 9 Jeff Burris | 2.50 | 1.00 | .25 |
| ☐ 10 Tom Carter | 2.00 | .80 | .20 |
| ☐ 11 Willie Clark | .35 | .14 | .03 |
| ☐ 12 John Covington | .50 | .20 | .05 |
| ☐ 13 Travis Davis | .35 | .14 | .03 |
| ☐ 14 Lake Dawson | 2.50 | 1.00 | .25 |
| ☐ 15 Mark Zataveski | .35 | .14 | .03 |
| ☐ 16 Paul Failla | 1.00 | .40 | .10 |
| ☐ 17 Jim Flanigan | 1.00 | .40 | .10 |
| ☐ 18 Oliver Gibson | .50 | .20 | .05 |
| ☐ 19 Justin Goheen | .50 | .20 | .05 |
| ☐ 20 Tracey Graham | .35 | .14 | .03 |
| ☐ 21 Ray Griggs | .35 | .14 | .03 |
| ☐ 22 Justin Hall | .35 | .14 | .03 |
| ☐ 23 Jordan Halter | .35 | .14 | .03 |
| ☐ 24 Brian Hamilton | .50 | .20 | .05 |
| ☐ 25 Craig Hentrich | .60 | .24 | .06 |
| ☐ 26 Germaine Holden | .35 | .14 | .03 |
| ☐ 27 Adrian Jarrell | .35 | .14 | .03 |
| ☐ 28 Clint Johnson | .50 | .20 | .05 |
| ☐ 29 Lance Johnson | .35 | .14 | .03 |
| ☐ 30 Lindsay Knapp | .60 | .24 | .06 |
| ☐ 31 Ryan Leahy | .50 | .20 | .05 |
| (Not alphabetical order) | | | |
| ☐ 32 Greg Lane | .50 | .20 | .05 |
| ☐ 33 Dean Lytle | .35 | .14 | .03 |
| ☐ 34 Bernard Mannelly | .35 | .14 | .03 |
| ☐ 35 Oscar McBride | .35 | .14 | .03 |
| ☐ 36 Devon McDonald | .60 | .24 | .06 |
| ☐ 37 Kevin McDougal | 1.25 | .50 | .12 |
| ☐ 38 Karl McGill | .35 | .14 | .03 |
| ☐ 39 Mike McGlinn | .35 | .14 | .03 |
| ☐ 40 Mike Miller | 1.00 | .40 | .10 |
| ☐ 41 Jeremy Nau | .35 | .14 | .03 |
| ☐ 42 Todd Norman | .50 | .20 | .05 |
| ☐ 43 Tim Ruddy | .50 | .20 | .05 |
| (Not alphabetical order) | | | |
| ☐ 44 William Pollard | .35 | .14 | .03 |
| ☐ 45 Brian Ratigan | .35 | .14 | .03 |
| ☐ 46 Leshane Saddler | .35 | .14 | .03 |
| ☐ 47 Jeremy Sample | .35 | .14 | .03 |
| ☐ 48 Irv Smith | 1.25 | .50 | .12 |
| ☐ 49 Laron Moore | .35 | .14 | .03 |
| (Not alphabetical order) | | | |
| ☐ 50 Anthony Peterson | .50 | .20 | .05 |
| (Not alphabetical order) | | | |
| ☐ 51 Charles Stafford | .35 | .14 | .03 |
| ☐ 52 Nick Smith | .35 | .14 | .03 |
| ☐ 53 Greg Stec | .35 | .14 | .03 |
| ☐ 54 John Taliaferro | .35 | .14 | .03 |
| ☐ 55 Aaron Taylor | 1.25 | .50 | .12 |
| ☐ 56 Stuart Tyner | .35 | .14 | .03 |
| ☐ 57 Ray Zellars | .75 | .30 | .07 |
| (Not alphabetical order) | | | |
| ☐ 58 Tyler Young | .35 | .14 | .03 |
| (Not alphabetical order) | | | |
| ☐ 59 Bryant Young | 1.50 | .60 | .15 |

## 1993 Notre Dame

These 72 standard-size (2 1/2" by 3 1/2") cards feature on their fronts color player action shots. These photos are bordered in either blue, gold, green, or white, and each variety has its own checklist. All the cards have gold-colored outer borders. The player's name appears vertically in multicolored lettering within a photo of a football stadium near the left side. The horizontal back is bordered in the same color as

its front, and carries a color player head shot within a diamond at the upper left, which is framed by a gold-colored line. The player's name, class, position, uniform number, and biography appear within a grayish rectangle at the top. His Notre Dame highlights and stats follow within the greenish panel below. The cards are unnumbered and checklisted below in alphabetical order.

| | MINT | EXC | G-VG |
|---|---|---|---|
| COMPLETE SET (72) | 25.00 | 10.00 | 2.50 |
| COMMON PLAYER (1-72) | .25 | .10 | .02 |
| ☐ 1 Jeremy Akers | .35 | .14 | .03 |
| ☐ 2 Joe Babey | .25 | .10 | .02 |
| ☐ 3 Huntley Bakich | .25 | .10 | .02 |
| ☐ 4 Jason Beckwith | .25 | .10 | .02 |
| ☐ 5 Lee Becton | 1.50 | .60 | .15 |
| ☐ 6 Pete Bercich | .35 | .14 | .03 |
| ☐ 7 Jeff Burris | 2.00 | .80 | .20 |
| ☐ 8 Pete Chryplewicz | .25 | .10 | .02 |
| ☐ 9 Willie Clark | .25 | .10 | .02 |
| ☐ 10 John Covington | .35 | .14 | .03 |
| ☐ 11 Travis Davis | .25 | .10 | .02 |
| ☐ 12 Lake Dawson | 2.00 | .80 | .20 |
| ☐ 13 Paul Failla | .75 | .30 | .07 |
| ☐ 14 Jim Flanigan | .75 | .30 | .07 |
| ☐ 15 Reggie Fleurima | .25 | .10 | .02 |
| ☐ 16 Ben Foos | .25 | .10 | .02 |
| ☐ 17 Herbert Gibson | .25 | .10 | .02 |
| ☐ 18 Oliver Gibson | .35 | .14 | .03 |
| ☐ 19 Justin Goheen | .35 | .14 | .03 |
| ☐ 20 Tracy Graham | .25 | .10 | .02 |
| ☐ 21 Paul Grasmanis | .25 | .10 | .02 |
| ☐ 22 Jordan Halter | .25 | .10 | .02 |
| ☐ 23 Brian Hamilton | .35 | .14 | .03 |
| ☐ 24 Germaine Holden | .25 | .10 | .02 |
| ☐ 25 Lou Holtz CO | 1.50 | .60 | .15 |
| ☐ 26 Robert Hughes | .25 | .10 | .02 |
| ☐ 27 Adrian Jarrell | .25 | .10 | .02 |
| ☐ 28 Clint Johnson | .35 | .14 | .03 |
| ☐ 29 Lance Johnson | .25 | .10 | .02 |
| ☐ 30 Thomas Knight | .35 | .14 | .03 |
| ☐ 31 Jim Kordas | .25 | .10 | .02 |
| ☐ 32 Greg Lane | .35 | .14 | .03 |
| ☐ 33 Ryan Leahy | .35 | .14 | .03 |
| ☐ 34 Will Lyell | .35 | .14 | .03 |
| ☐ 35 Dean Lytle | .25 | .10 | .02 |
| ☐ 36 Brian Magee | .25 | .10 | .02 |
| ☐ 37 Alton Maiden | .25 | .10 | .02 |
| ☐ 38 Derrick Mayes | .60 | .24 | .06 |
| ☐ 39 Oscar McBride | .25 | .10 | .02 |
| ☐ 40 Mike McCullough | .35 | .14 | .03 |
| ☐ 41 Kevin McDougal | 1.00 | .40 | .10 |
| ☐ 42 Mike McGlinn | .25 | .10 | .02 |
| ☐ 43 Brian Meter | .25 | .10 | .02 |
| ☐ 44 Mike Miller | .75 | .30 | .07 |
| ☐ 45 Steve Misetic | .25 | .10 | .02 |
| ☐ 46 Jeremy Nau | .25 | .10 | .02 |
| ☐ 47 Todd Norman | .35 | .14 | .03 |
| ☐ 48 Kevin Pendergast | .35 | .14 | .03 |
| ☐ 49 Anthony Peterson | .25 | .10 | .02 |
| ☐ 50 David Quist | .25 | .10 | .02 |
| ☐ 51 Jeff Riney | .25 | .10 | .02 |
| ☐ 52 Tim Ruddy | .35 | .14 | .03 |
| ☐ 53 LeShane Saddler | .25 | .10 | .02 |
| ☐ 54 Jeremy Sample | .25 | .10 | .02 |
| ☐ 55 Charles Stafford | .25 | .10 | .02 |
| ☐ 56 Greg Stec | .25 | .10 | .02 |
| ☐ 57 Cliff Stroud | .25 | .10 | .02 |
| ☐ 58 John Taliaferro | .25 | .10 | .02 |
| ☐ 59 Aaron Taylor | 1.00 | .40 | .10 |
| ☐ 60 Bobby Taylor | .75 | .30 | .07 |
| ☐ 61 Bill Wagasy | .25 | .10 | .02 |
| ☐ 62 Leon Wallace | .25 | .10 | .02 |
| ☐ 63 Shawn Wooden | .25 | .10 | .02 |
| ☐ 64 Renaldo Wynn | .35 | .14 | .03 |
| ☐ 65 Bryant Young | 1.25 | .50 | .12 |
| ☐ 66 Mark Zataveski | .35 | .14 | .03 |
| ☐ 67 Dusty Zeigler | .25 | .10 | .02 |
| ☐ 68 Ray Zellars | .50 | .20 | .05 |
| ☐ 69 Blue Roster Checklist | .25 | .10 | .02 |
| ☐ 70 Gold Roster Checklist | .25 | .10 | .02 |
| ☐ 71 Green Roster Checklist | .25 | .10 | .02 |
| ☐ 72 White Roster Checklist | .25 | .10 | .02 |

## 1991 Oberlin College Heisman Club

This five-card set was issued to commemorate 100 years of Oberlin football. The cards measure the standard size (2 1/2" by 3 1/2") and feature black-and-white posed and action photos of coaches and players significant to Oberlin's history. The front picture rests on a white card face, and a thin maroon line frames the photo and forms a box around the player's name at the bottom. A football icon in the upper left corner contains the years 1891-1991, and a maroon banner emanating from the football is printed with the words "Celebrating

Oberlin Football". The backs are plain cardboard. A thin maroon line forms a box containing information about the front photos. In a smaller box is information about Oberlin College, including the Oberlin Office of Communications' phone number. The cards are unnumbered and checklisted below in alphabetical order.

|  | MINT | EXC | G-VG |
|---|---|---|---|
| COMPLETE SET (5) | 5.00 | 2.00 | .50 |
| COMMON CARD (1-5) | 1.00 | .40 | .10 |
|  |  |  |  |
| ☐ 1 50 Years, Two Careers | 1.00 | .40 | .10 |
| C.W.(Doc) Savage |  |  |  |
| J.H. Nichols |  |  |  |
| (Athletic Directors) |  |  |  |
| ☐ 2 John W. Heisman CO | 2.00 | .80 | .20 |
| ☐ 3 Oberlin's 1892 Team | 1.00 | .40 | .10 |
| ☐ 4 Oberlin's Fauver Twins | 1.00 | .40 | .10 |
| Doc Edgar Fauver |  |  |  |
| Doc Edwin Fauver |  |  |  |
| ☐ 5 Oberlin's Four Horsemen | 1.00 | .40 | .10 |
| Carl Semple |  |  |  |
| Carl Williams |  |  |  |
| H.K. Regal |  |  |  |
| C.W.(Doc) Savage |  |  |  |

## 1979 Ohio State Greats

This 53-card set contains all the Ohio State football players and coaches who obtained All-American or National Football Hall of Fame status through 1978. The cards were issued in the playing card format, and each card measures approximately 2 1/2" by 3 1/4". The fronts feature a close-up photograph of the player in an octagon frame. Those cards with two stars in the octagon frame indicate those players voted into the National Football Hall of Fame. The backs feature a collage of Ohio State players within an octagon border with "All-Americans, National Football Hall of Famers" at the bottom. Because this set is similar to a playing card set, the set is arranged just like a card deck and checklisted as follows: C means Clubs, D means Diamonds, H means Hearts, S means Spades, and JK means Joker. The cards are checklisted below in playing card order by suits and numbers are assigned to Aces (1), Jacks (11), Queens (12), and Kings (13). The joker is listed at the end.

|  | NRMT | VG-E | GOOD |
|---|---|---|---|
| COMPLETE SET (53) | 30.00 | 12.00 | 3.00 |
| COMMON CARD | .75 | .30 | .07 |
|  |  |  |  |
| ☐ 1C Chris Ward | .75 | .30 | .07 |
| ☐ 1D Jan White | 1.00 | .40 | .10 |
| ☐ 1H Ernest R. Godfrey ACO | .75 | .30 | .07 |
| ☐ 1S Ray Pryor | .75 | .30 | .07 |
| ☐ 2C Ray Griffin | 1.00 | .40 | .10 |
| ☐ 2D Tom Deleone | .75 | .30 | .07 |
| ☐ 2H Francis A. Schmidt CO | .75 | .30 | .07 |
| ☐ 2S Dave Foley | 1.00 | .40 | .10 |
| ☐ 3C Tom Cousineau | 1.50 | .60 | .15 |
| ☐ 3D Randy Gradishar | 2.00 | .80 | .20 |
| ☐ 3H Jim Parker | 2.00 | .80 | .20 |
| ☐ 3S Rufus Mayes | 1.00 | .40 | .10 |
| ☐ 4C Aaron Brown | 1.00 | .40 | .10 |
| ☐ 4D John Hicks | 1.25 | .50 | .12 |
| ☐ 4H Vic Janowicz | 1.50 | .60 | .15 |
| ☐ 4S Rex Kern | 1.50 | .60 | .15 |
| ☐ 5C Chris Ward | .75 | .30 | .07 |
| ☐ 5D Van Decree | .75 | .30 | .07 |
| ☐ 5H Les Horvath | 1.25 | .50 | .12 |
| ☐ 5S Jim Otis | 1.50 | .60 | .15 |
| ☐ 6C Tom Skladany | 1.00 | .40 | .10 |
| ☐ 6D Randy Gradishar | 2.00 | .80 | .20 |
| ☐ 6H Bill Willis | 1.25 | .50 | .12 |
| ☐ 6S Ted Provost | .75 | .30 | .07 |
| ☐ 7C Bob Brudzinski | 1.00 | .40 | .10 |
| ☐ 7D Archie Griffin | 2.50 | 1.00 | .25 |
| ☐ 7H James Daniell | .75 | .30 | .07 |
| ☐ 7S Jim Stillwagon | 1.25 | .50 | .12 |
| ☐ 8C Ted Smith | .75 | .30 | .07 |
| ☐ 8D John Hicks | 1.25 | .50 | .12 |
| ☐ 8H Gust Zarnas | .75 | .30 | .07 |
| ☐ 8S Jack Tatum | 1.50 | .60 | .15 |
| ☐ 9C Tom Skladany | 1.00 | .40 | .10 |
| ☐ 9D Neal Colzie | 1.00 | .40 | .10 |
| ☐ 9H Gomer Jones | .75 | .30 | .07 |
| ☐ 9S Tim Anderson | .75 | .30 | .07 |
| ☐ 10C Archie Griffin | 2.50 | 1.00 | .25 |
| ☐ 10D Pete Cusick | .75 | .30 | .07 |
| ☐ 10H Wes Fesler | .75 | .30 | .07 |
| ☐ 10S John Brockington | 1.50 | .60 | .15 |
| ☐ 11C Tim Fox | 1.00 | .40 | .10 |
| ☐ 11D Van Decree | .75 | .30 | .07 |
| ☐ 11H Gaylord Stinchcomb | .75 | .30 | .07 |
| ☐ 11S Mike Sensibaugh | 1.00 | .40 | .10 |
| ☐ 12C Tom Skladany | 1.00 | .40 | .10 |
| ☐ 12D Archie Griffin | 2.50 | 1.00 | .25 |

| ☐ 12H Chic Harley | .75 | .30 | .07 |
| ☐ 12S Jim Stillwagon | 1.25 | .50 | .12 |
| ☐ 13C Kurt Schumacher | 1.00 | .40 | .10 |
| ☐ 13D Steve Meyers | 1.00 | .40 | .10 |
| ☐ 13H Tom Cousineau | 1.50 | .60 | .15 |
| ☐ 13S Jack Tatum | 1.50 | .60 | .15 |
| ☐ JK Howard Jones CO | .75 | .30 | .07 |

## 1988 Ohio State

**KEITH BYARS**
**RUNNING BACK 1982-85**

This versatile running back ranks third in career rushing (3,200 yards) at Ohio State and is second in scoring (300 points) and touchdowns (50), also ranked eighth in receptions (75) and total offense (3,308 yards), averaged 5.7 yards per carry in four varsity seasons, the Big Ten's leading rusher in 1983 and 1984, enjoyed incredible junior campaign, leading the nation in rushing, scoring, and all-purpose running, consensus All-American, runner-up in Heisman Trophy balloting and voted Big Ten player of the year in 1984, when he set an Ohio State single-season record with 1,764 yards rushing, established Buckeye single-game record with 274 yards or memorable 1984 win over Illinois, four-year letter winner, three-year starter and team captain as a senior, slowed by a foot injury most of his 1985 campaign, native of Dayton, Ohio.

If no one else is around at night or when your cards come from school, play it safe. That means keeping doors and windows locked. Never let anyone in unless it's someone you know.
Message sponsored by OSU Police Dept.

KEITH BYARS
RUNNING BACK

Kroger     wbns 10 TV

The 1988 Ohio State University football set contains 22 standard-size (2 1/2" by 3 1/2") cards. The fronts have vintage or color action photos with white borders; the vertically oriented backs have detailed profiles. These cards were distributed as a set. The set is unnumbered, so the cards are listed alphabetically.

|  | MINT | EXC | G-VG |
|---|---|---|---|
| COMPLETE SET (22) | 15.00 | 6.00 | 1.50 |
| COMMON CARD (1-22) | .60 | .24 | .06 |
|  |  |  |  |
| ☐ 1 Bob Brudzinski | 1.00 | .40 | .10 |
| ☐ 2 Keith Byars | 2.00 | .80 | .20 |
| ☐ 3 Hopalong Cassady | 1.25 | .50 | .12 |
| ☐ 4 Arnold Chonko | .75 | .30 | .07 |
| ☐ 5 Wes Fesler | .60 | .24 | .06 |
| ☐ 6 Randy Gradishar | 1.50 | .60 | .15 |
| ☐ 7 Archie Griffin | 2.00 | .80 | .20 |
| ☐ 8 Chic Harley | .60 | .24 | .06 |
| ☐ 9 Woody Hayes CO | 1.50 | .60 | .15 |
| ☐ 10 John Hicks | .75 | .30 | .07 |
| ☐ 11 Les Horvath | 1.50 | .60 | .15 |
| ☐ 12 Jim Houston | .75 | .30 | .07 |
| ☐ 13 Vic Janowicz | 1.00 | .40 | .10 |
| ☐ 14 Pepper Johnson | .75 | .30 | .07 |
| ☐ 15 Ike Kelley | .60 | .24 | .06 |
| ☐ 16 Rex Kern | 1.00 | .40 | .10 |
| ☐ 17 Jim Lachey | 1.25 | .50 | .12 |
| ☐ 18 Jim Parker | 1.25 | .50 | .12 |
| ☐ 19 Tom Skladany | .75 | .30 | .07 |
| ☐ 20 Chris Spielman | 1.25 | .50 | .12 |
| ☐ 21 Jim Stillwagon | .75 | .30 | .07 |
| ☐ 22 Jack Tatum | 1.00 | .40 | .10 |

## 1989 Ohio State

OHIO STATE

**MARCUS MAREK**
**LINEBACKER 1979-82**

OSU's all-time leader in total tackles, a mainstay in the Buckeye lineup for four years, starting every contest after the third game of his freshman season...earned the first of his three all-Big Ten honors his sophomore year and also was an Academic All-American that year...earned second-team Associated Press All-America honors his junior year by turning in performances such as the one he had against Stanford when he recorded 13 solo tackles...first team UPI and Kodak All-American as a senior...a tri-captain on that squad, Marek was instrumental in the 24-14 win over Michigan, recording 21 total tackles on the day.

Friends who pressure you into breaking the law aren't really friends.
Message sponsored by The Ohio State University Police Department.

Card 16 of 22

MARCUS MAREK
LINEBACKER 1979-82

The 1989 Ohio State University football set contains 22 standard-size (2 1/2" by 3 1/2") cards. The fronts have vintage or color action photos with white borders; the vertically oriented backs have detailed profiles. These cards were distributed as a set and are numbered on the backs.

|  | MINT | EXC | G-VG |
|---|---|---|---|
| COMPLETE SET (22) | 6.00 | 2.50 | .50 |
| COMMON CARD (1-22) | .40 | .16 | .04 |

| | MINT | EXC | G-VG |
|---|---|---|---|
| ☐ 1 Mike Tomczak | 1.25 | .50 | .12 |
| ☐ 2 Paul Warfield | 1.50 | .60 | .15 |
| ☐ 3 Kirk Lowdermilk | .50 | .20 | .05 |
| ☐ 4 Bob Ferguson | .75 | .30 | .07 |
| ☐ 5 Jack Graf | .40 | .16 | .04 |
| ☐ 6 Tim Fox | .50 | .20 | .05 |
| ☐ 7 Eric Kumerow | .50 | .20 | .05 |
| ☐ 8 Neal Colzie | .50 | .20 | .05 |
| ☐ 9 Jim Otis | 1.00 | .40 | .10 |
| ☐ 10 John Brockington | 1.00 | .40 | .10 |
| ☐ 11 Cornelius Greene | .40 | .16 | .04 |
| ☐ 12 Jim Marshall | 1.25 | .50 | .12 |
| ☐ 13 Tim Spencer | .50 | .20 | .05 |
| ☐ 14 Don Scott | .40 | .16 | .04 |
| ☐ 15 Chris Ward | .50 | .20 | .05 |
| ☐ 16 Marcus Marek | .50 | .20 | .05 |
| ☐ 17 Dave Foley | .50 | .20 | .05 |
| ☐ 18 Bill Willis | .75 | .30 | .07 |
| ☐ 19 John Frank | .60 | .24 | .06 |
| ☐ 20 Rufus Mayes | .60 | .24 | .06 |
| ☐ 21 Tom Tupa | .75 | .30 | .07 |
| ☐ 22 Jan White | .50 | .20 | .05 |

## 1990 Ohio State

This 22-card set measures 2 1/2" by 3 1/2". There is a full color photograph on the front, and the Ohio State logo on the lower right-hand corner. The back has biographical information about the player. The set was produced by College Classics and features past and current players.

| | MINT | EXC | G-VG |
|---|---|---|---|
| COMPLETE SET (22) | 9.00 | 3.75 | .90 |
| COMMON CARD (1-22) | .40 | .16 | .04 |
| | | | |
| ☐ 1 Jeff Uhlenhake | .60 | .24 | .06 |
| ☐ 2 Ray Ellis | .40 | .16 | .04 |
| ☐ 3 Todd Bell | .60 | .24 | .06 |
| ☐ 4 Jeff Logan | .40 | .16 | .04 |
| ☐ 5 Pete Johnson | .75 | .30 | .07 |
| ☐ 6 Van DeCree | .40 | .16 | .04 |
| ☐ 7 Ted Provost | .40 | .16 | .04 |
| ☐ 8 Mike Lanese | .40 | .16 | .04 |
| ☐ 9 Aaron Brown | .60 | .24 | .06 |
| ☐ 10 Pete Cusick | .40 | .16 | .04 |
| ☐ 11 Vlade Janakievski | .40 | .16 | .04 |
| ☐ 12 Steve Myers | .40 | .16 | .04 |
| ☐ 13 Ted Smith | .40 | .16 | .04 |
| ☐ 14 Doug Donley | .60 | .24 | .06 |
| ☐ 15 Ron Springs | .60 | .24 | .06 |
| ☐ 16 Ken Fritz | .40 | .16 | .04 |
| ☐ 17 Jeff Davidson | .40 | .16 | .04 |
| ☐ 18 Art Schlichter | .75 | .30 | .07 |
| ☐ 19 Tom Cousineau | .75 | .30 | .07 |
| ☐ 20 Call Murray | .40 | .16 | .04 |
| ☐ 21 Brian Baschnagel | .60 | .24 | .06 |
| ☐ 22 Joe Staysniak | .40 | .16 | .04 |

## 1982 Oklahoma

Manufactured for OU by TransMedia, these 56 playing cards measure approximately 2 3/8" by 3 3/8" and have rounded corners and the typical playing card finish. Some of the fronts feature color action shots, some carry black-and-white head shots, and still others have no photos at all, just text. The red backs carry the white OU logo. The set is checklisted below in playing card order by suits, with numbers assigned for Aces (1), Jacks (11), Queens (12), and Kings (13).

| | MINT | EXC | G-VG |
|---|---|---|---|
| COMPLETE SET (56) | 30.00 | 12.00 | 3.00 |
| COMMON CARD | .75 | .30 | .07 |

| | MINT | EXC | G-VG |
|---|---|---|---|
| ☐ C1 Action shot | .75 | .30 | .07 |
| ☐ C2 Coaches 1895-1934 | .75 | .30 | .07 |
| ☐ C3 All-Americans 1946-48 | 1.00 | .40 | .10 |
| ☐ C4 All-Americans 1953-54 | 1.00 | .40 | .10 |
| ☐ C5 All-Americans 1963-69 | 1.00 | .40 | .10 |
| ☐ C6 All-Americans 1974-75 | 1.00 | .40 | .10 |
| ☐ C7 Jim Weatherall 1951 | 1.00 | .40 | .10 |
| ☐ C8 Billy Vessels 1952 | 1.00 | .40 | .10 |
| ☐ C9 NCAA Champions 1955 | 1.00 | .40 | .10 |
| ☐ C10 Action shot | .75 | .30 | .07 |
| ☐ C11 Action shot | .75 | .30 | .07 |
| ☐ C12 Action shot | .75 | .30 | .07 |
| ☐ C13 Action shot | .75 | .30 | .07 |
| ☐ D1 Action shot | .75 | .30 | .07 |
| ☐ D2 Coaches 1935-1982 | .75 | .30 | .07 |
| ☐ D3 All-Americans 1949 | 1.00 | .40 | .10 |
| ☐ D4 All-Americans 1955-56 | 1.00 | .40 | .10 |
| ☐ D5 All-Americans 1966-71 | 1.00 | .40 | .10 |
| ☐ D6 All-Americans 1975-76 | 1.00 | .40 | .10 |
| ☐ D7 J.D. Roberts 1953 | 1.00 | .40 | .10 |
| ☐ D8 Steve Owens 1969 | 1.50 | .60 | .15 |
| ☐ D9 NCAA Champions 1956 | 1.00 | .40 | .10 |
| ☐ D10 Barry Switzer CO | 3.00 | 1.20 | .30 |
| ☐ D11 Action shot | .75 | .30 | .07 |
| ☐ D12 Action shot | .75 | .30 | .07 |
| ☐ D13 Action shot | .75 | .30 | .07 |
| ☐ H1 Action shot | .75 | .30 | .07 |
| ☐ H2 All-Americans 1913-34 | 1.00 | .40 | .10 |
| ☐ H3 All-Americans 1949-51 | 1.00 | .40 | .10 |
| ☐ H4 All-Americans 1957-59 | 1.00 | .40 | .10 |
| ☐ H5 All-Americans 1971-74 | 1.00 | .40 | .10 |
| ☐ H6 All-Americans 1976-78 | 1.00 | .40 | .10 |
| ☐ H7 Lee Roy Selmon 1975 | 1.25 | .50 | .12 |
| ☐ H8 Billy Sims 1978 | 1.50 | .60 | .15 |
| ☐ H9 NCAA Champions 1974 | 1.00 | .40 | .10 |
| ☐ H10 Action shot | .75 | .30 | .07 |
| ☐ H11 Action shot | .75 | .30 | .07 |
| ☐ H12 Action shot | .75 | .30 | .07 |
| ☐ H13 Action shot | .75 | .30 | .07 |
| ☐ JK Sooner Schooner | .75 | .30 | .07 |
| ☐ JK Sooner Schooner | .75 | .30 | .07 |
| ☐ NNO Mail order card | .75 | .30 | .07 |
| ☐ NNO Mail order card | .75 | .30 | .07 |
| ☐ S1 Action shot | .75 | .30 | .07 |
| ☐ S2 All-Americans 1938-46 | 1.00 | .40 | .10 |
| ☐ S3 All-Americans 1951-52 | 1.00 | .40 | .10 |
| ☐ S4 All-Americans 1962-63 | 1.00 | .40 | .10 |
| ☐ S5 All-Americans 1973-75 | 1.00 | .40 | .10 |
| ☐ S6 All-Americans 1978-81 | 1.00 | .40 | .10 |
| ☐ S7 Greg Roberts 1978 | 1.00 | .40 | .10 |
| ☐ S8 NCAA Champions 1950 | 1.00 | .40 | .10 |
| ☐ S9 NCAA Champions 1975 | 1.00 | .40 | .10 |
| ☐ S10 Action shot | .75 | .30 | .07 |
| ☐ S11 Action shot | .75 | .30 | .07 |
| ☐ S12 Action shot | .75 | .30 | .07 |
| ☐ S13 Action shot | .75 | .30 | .07 |

## 1986 Oklahoma

The 1986 Oklahoma National Championship set contains 16 unnumbered, standard-size (2 1/2" by 3 1/2") cards. The fronts are "pure" with color photos, thin white borders and no printing; the backs describe the front photos. These cards were printed on very thin stock. This set sports several unusual and/or attractive pictures.

| | MINT | EXC | G-VG |
|---|---|---|---|
| COMPLETE SET (16) | 8.00 | 3.25 | .80 |
| COMMON CARD (1-16) | .50 | .20 | .05 |
| | | | |
| ☐ 1 Championship Ring | .60 | .24 | .06 |
|    1985 National Champs | | | |
| ☐ 2 Orange Bowl | .50 | .20 | .05 |
|    (In Bowl Play) | | | |
| ☐ 3 On the Road to Record | .50 | .20 | .05 |
| ☐ 4 Graduation Record | .50 | .20 | .05 |

| | | MINT | EXC | G-VG |
|---|---|---|---|---|
| ☐ 5 | Lawrence G. Rawl | .60 | .24 | .06 |
| | President of Exxon | | | |
| ☐ 6 | Barry Switzer | 1.50 | .60 | .15 |
| | (Winners) | | | |
| ☐ 7 | Win Streaks Hold | .50 | .20 | .05 |
| | Records | | | |
| ☐ 8 | Brian Bosworth | 1.00 | .40 | .10 |
| ☐ 9 | Heisman Trophy | .75 | .30 | .07 |
| | Billy Vessels 1952 | | | |
| | Steve Owens 1969 | | | |
| | Billy Sims 1978 | | | |
| ☐ 10 | All-America Sooners | .75 | .30 | .07 |
| | (Tony Casillas) | | | |
| ☐ 11 | Jamelle Holieway | .60 | .24 | .06 |
| ☐ 12 | Sooner Strength | .50 | .20 | .05 |
| ☐ 13 | Sooner Support | .50 | .20 | .05 |
| ☐ 14 | Go Sooners | .50 | .20 | .05 |
| | (Crimson and Cream) | | | |
| ☐ 15 | Border Battle | .50 | .20 | .05 |
| | (Oklahoma vs. Texas) | | | |
| ☐ 16 | Barry Switzer CO SP | 3.00 | 1.20 | .30 |
| | (Caricature; "I Want You ...; '86 OU foot-ball schedule on back) | | | |

## 1986 Oklahoma McDag

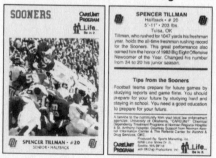

The 1986 Oklahoma McDag set contains 16 standard-size (2 1/2" by 3 1/2") cards printed on very thin stock. The fronts have color action photos bordered in white; the vertically oriented backs have brief career highlights and safety tips. The cards are unnumbered, so they are listed alphabetically by player's name. The key card in the set features tight end Keith Jackson.

| | | MINT | EXC | G-VG |
|---|---|---|---|---|
| | COMPLETE SET (16) | 20.00 | 8.00 | 2.00 |
| | COMMON PLAYER (1-16) | 1.00 | .40 | .10 |
| ☐ 1 | Brian Bosworth | 2.00 | .80 | .20 |
| ☐ 2 | Sonny Brown | 1.00 | .40 | .10 |
| ☐ 3 | Steve Bryan | 1.00 | .40 | .10 |
| ☐ 4 | Lydell Carr | 1.50 | .60 | .15 |
| ☐ 5 | Patrick Collins | 1.50 | .60 | .15 |
| ☐ 6 | Jamelle Holieway | 2.00 | .80 | .20 |
| ☐ 7 | Mark Hutson | 1.00 | .40 | .10 |
| ☐ 8 | Keith Jackson | 8.00 | 3.25 | .80 |
| ☐ 9 | Troy Johnson | 1.00 | .40 | .10 |
| ☐ 10 | Dante Jones | 3.00 | 1.20 | .30 |
| ☐ 11 | Tim Lashar | 1.00 | .40 | .10 |
| ☐ 12 | Paul Migliazzo | 1.00 | .40 | .10 |
| ☐ 13 | Anthony Phillips | 1.00 | .40 | .10 |
| ☐ 14 | Darrell Reed | 1.00 | .40 | .10 |
| ☐ 15 | Derrick Shepard | 1.50 | .60 | .15 |
| ☐ 16 | Spencer Tillman | 1.50 | .60 | .15 |

## 1987 Oklahoma Police

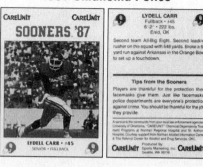

The 1987 Oklahoma Police set consists of 16 standard-size (2 1/2" by 3 1/2") cards printed on thin card stock. The fronts feature color action player photos on a white card face. CareUnit logos and the words "Sooners '87" are printed in the top margin, while player information between two helmets fill the bottom margin. The backs carry biography, career highlights, and "Tips from the Sooners" in the form of anti-crime messages. The cards are unnumbered and checklisted below according to uniform number.

| | | MINT | EXC | G-VG |
|---|---|---|---|---|
| | COMPLETE SET (16) | 15.00 | 6.00 | 1.50 |
| | COMMON CARD | .75 | .30 | .07 |
| ☐ 1 | Eric Mitchel | 1.50 | .60 | .15 |
| ☐ 4 | Jamelle Holieway | 2.00 | .80 | .20 |
| ☐ 10 | David Vickers | .75 | .30 | .07 |
| ☐ 25 | Anthony Stafford | 1.50 | .60 | .15 |
| ☐ 29 | Rickey Dixon | 2.00 | .80 | .20 |
| ☐ 33 | Patrick Collins | 1.50 | .60 | .15 |
| ☐ 40 | Darrell Reed | .75 | .30 | .07 |
| ☐ 45 | Lydell Carr | 1.50 | .60 | .15 |
| ☐ 50 | Dante Jones | 2.50 | 1.00 | .25 |
| ☐ 66 | Jon Phillips and 68 Anthony Phillips | .75 | .30 | .07 |
| ☐ 75 | Greg Johnson | .75 | .30 | .07 |
| ☐ 79 | Mark Hutson | .75 | .30 | .07 |
| ☐ 80 | Troy Johnson | .75 | .30 | .07 |
| ☐ 88 | Keith Jackson | 6.00 | 2.40 | .60 |
| ☐ 98 | Dante Williams | .75 | .30 | .07 |
| ☐ xx | Barry Switzer CO | 2.00 | .80 | .20 |

## 1988 Oklahoma Greats

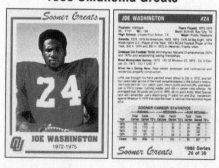

The 1988 Oklahoma Greats set features 30 standard-size (2 1/2" by 3 1/2") cards. The fronts have color photos bordered in white and red. The vertically oriented backs feature detailed biographical information, statistics, and highlights.

| | | MINT | EXC | G-VG |
|---|---|---|---|---|
| | COMPLETE SET (30) | 5.00 | 2.00 | .50 |
| | COMMON CARD (1-30) | .20 | .08 | .02 |
| ☐ 1 | Jerry Anderson | .20 | .08 | .02 |
| ☐ 2 | Dee Andros | .30 | .12 | .03 |
| ☐ 3 | Dean Blevins | .20 | .08 | .02 |
| ☐ 4 | Rick Bryan | .50 | .20 | .05 |
| ☐ 5 | Paul(Buddy) Burris | .20 | .08 | .02 |
| ☐ 6 | Eddie Crowder | .30 | .12 | .03 |
| ☐ 7 | Jack Ging | .20 | .08 | .02 |
| ☐ 8 | Jim Grisham | .30 | .12 | .03 |
| ☐ 9 | Jimmy Harris | .30 | .12 | .03 |

| | MINT | EXC | G-VG |
|---|---|---|---|
| ☐ 10 Scott Hill | .20 | .08 | .02 |
| ☐ 11 Eddie Hinton | .30 | .12 | .03 |
| ☐ 12 Earl Johnson | .20 | .08 | .02 |
| ☐ 13 Don Key | .20 | .08 | .02 |
| ☐ 14 Tim Lashar | .20 | .08 | .02 |
| ☐ 15 Granville Liggins | .50 | .20 | .05 |
| ☐ 16 Thomas Lott | .40 | .16 | .04 |
| ☐ 17 Carl McAdams | .30 | .12 | .03 |
| ☐ 18 Jack Mitchell | .30 | .12 | .03 |
| ☐ 19 Billy Pricer | .20 | .08 | .02 |
| ☐ 20 John Roush | .20 | .08 | .02 |
| ☐ 21 Darrell Royal | .60 | .24 | .06 |
| ☐ 22 Lucious Selmon | .30 | .12 | .03 |
| ☐ 23 Ron Shotts | .20 | .08 | .02 |
| ☐ 24 Jerry Tubbs | .30 | .12 | .03 |
| ☐ 25 Bob Warmack | .30 | .12 | .03 |
| ☐ 26 Joe Washington | .50 | .20 | .05 |
| ☐ 27 Jim Weatherall | .30 | .12 | .03 |
| ☐ 28 '86 Sooner Great Game | .20 | .08 | .02 |
| ☐ 29 '75 Sooners | .20 | .08 | .02 |
| ☐ 30 Checklist Card | .30 | .12 | .03 |

## 1988 Oklahoma Police

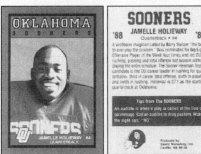

This 16-card set was produced by Sports Marketing (Seattle, WA). The cards measure the standard size (2 1/2" by 3 1/2") and are printed on thin card stock. On a red card face, the fronts display posed color head and shoulders shots accented by black borders. The school and team name are printed above the picture, with player information below the picture. In black print on a white background, the backs have player profile and "Tips from The Sooners," which consist of anti-drug and alcohol messages. The cards are unnumbered and checklisted below in alphabetical order.

| | MINT | EXC | G-VG |
|---|---|---|---|
| COMPLETE SET (16) | 15.00 | 6.00 | 1.50 |
| COMMON CARD (1-16) | 1.00 | .40 | .10 |
| | | | |
| ☐ 1 Rotnei Anderson | 1.50 | .60 | .15 |
| ☐ 2 Eric Bross | 1.00 | .40 | .10 |
| ☐ 3 Mike Gaddis | 2.00 | .80 | .20 |
| ☐ 4 Scott Garl | 1.00 | .40 | .10 |
| ☐ 5 James Goode | 1.00 | .40 | .10 |
| ☐ 6 Jamelle Holieway | 2.00 | .80 | .20 |
| ☐ 7 Bob Latham | 1.00 | .40 | .10 |
| ☐ 8 Ken McMichel | 1.00 | .40 | .10 |
| ☐ 9 Eric Mitchel | 1.50 | .60 | .15 |
| ☐ 10 Leon Perry | 1.50 | .60 | .15 |
| ☐ 11 Anthony Phillips | 1.00 | .40 | .10 |
| ☐ 12 Anthony Stafford | 1.25 | .50 | .12 |
| ☐ 13 Barry Switzer CO | 2.00 | .80 | .20 |
| ☐ 14 Mark Vankeirsbilck | 1.00 | .40 | .10 |
| ☐ 15 Curtice Williams | 1.00 | .40 | .10 |
| ☐ 16 Dante Williams | 1.00 | .40 | .10 |

## 1989 Oklahoma Police

This 16-card set features members of the Oklahoma Sooners football team. The cards are unnumbered and checklisted below in alphabetical order.

| | MINT | EXC | G-VG |
|---|---|---|---|
| COMPLETE SET (16) | 12.00 | 5.00 | 1.20 |
| COMMON PLAYER (1-16) | .75 | .30 | .07 |
| | | | |
| ☐ 1 Tom Backes | .75 | .30 | .07 |
| ☐ 2 Frank Blevins | .75 | .30 | .07 |
| ☐ 3 Eric Bross | .75 | .30 | .07 |
| ☐ 4 Adrian Cooper | 2.50 | 1.00 | .25 |
| ☐ 5 Scott Evans | .75 | .30 | .07 |
| ☐ 6 Mike Gaddis | 1.50 | .60 | .15 |
| ☐ 7 Gary Gibbs CO | 1.25 | .50 | .12 |

| | MINT | EXC | G-VG |
|---|---|---|---|
| ☐ 8 James Goode | .75 | .30 | .07 |
| ☐ 9 Ken McMichel | .75 | .30 | .07 |
| ☐ 10 Leon Perry | 1.25 | .50 | .12 |
| ☐ 11 Mike Sawatzky | .75 | .30 | .07 |
| ☐ 12 Don Smitherman | .75 | .30 | .07 |
| ☐ 13 Kevin Thompson | .75 | .30 | .07 |
| ☐ 14 Mark VanKeirsbilck | .75 | .30 | .07 |
| ☐ 15 Mike Wise | .75 | .30 | .07 |
| ☐ 16 Dante Williams | .75 | .30 | .07 |

## 1991 Oklahoma Police

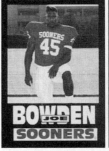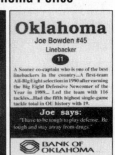

This 16-card Police set was sponsored by the Bank of Oklahoma and given away during the season. The cards were issued on an uncut sheet measuring approximately 10 1/2" by 17". If the cards were cut, each would measure approximately 2 1/2" by 4 1/4". The fronts feature color player photos with the players posed with one knee on the ground. The borders are black. The player's name and team name are printed in large block lettering beneath the picture. The backs list career highlights and a player quote in the form of anti-drug messages. The cards are numbered on the back in a black oval.

| | MINT | EXC | G-VG |
|---|---|---|---|
| COMPLETE SET (16) | 12.00 | 5.00 | 1.20 |
| COMMON CARD (1-16) | .75 | .30 | .07 |
| | | | |
| ☐ 1 Gary Gibbs CO | 1.25 | .50 | .12 |
| ☐ 2 Cale Gundy | 3.00 | 1.20 | .30 |
| ☐ 3 Charles Franks | .75 | .30 | .07 |
| ☐ 4 Mike Gaddis | 1.25 | .50 | .12 |
| ☐ 5 Brad Reddell | .75 | .30 | .07 |
| ☐ 6 Brandon Houston | .75 | .30 | .07 |
| ☐ 7 Chris Wilson | .75 | .30 | .07 |
| ☐ 8 Darnell Walker | .75 | .30 | .07 |
| ☐ 9 Mike McKinley | .75 | .30 | .07 |
| ☐ 10 Kenyon Rasheed | 1.25 | .50 | .12 |
| ☐ 11 Joe Bowden | 1.25 | .50 | .12 |
| ☐ 12 Jason Belser | .75 | .30 | .07 |
| ☐ 13 Steve Collins | .75 | .30 | .07 |
| ☐ 14 Reggie Barnes | .75 | .30 | .07 |
| ☐ 15 Randy Wallace | .75 | .30 | .07 |
| ☐ 16 Proctor Land | .75 | .30 | .07 |

## 1953 Oregon

This 20-card set measures the standard size (2 1/2" by 3 1/2"). The fronts feature a posed action photo, with player information appearing in handwritten script in a white box toward the bottom of the picture. Below the motto "Football is Fun," the backs have a list of locations where adult tickets can be purchased and a Knothole Gang membership offer. The cards are unnumbered and checklisted below in alphabetical order.

| | NRMT | VG-E | GOOD |
|---|---|---|---|
| COMPLETE SET (20) | 225.00 | 90.00 | 22.00 |
| COMMON PLAYER (1-20) | 12.00 | 5.00 | 1.20 |
| | | | |
| ☐ 1 Farrell Albright | 12.00 | 5.00 | 1.20 |
| ☐ 2 Ted Anderson | 12.00 | 5.00 | 1.20 |
| ☐ 3 Len Berrie | 12.00 | 5.00 | 1.20 |
| ☐ 4 Tom Elliott | 12.00 | 5.00 | 1.20 |
| ☐ 5 Tim Flaherty | 12.00 | 5.00 | 1.20 |
| ☐ 6 Cecil Hodges | 12.00 | 5.00 | 1.20 |
| ☐ 7 Barney Holland | 12.00 | 5.00 | 1.20 |
| ☐ 8 Dick James | 18.00 | 7.25 | 1.80 |
| ☐ 9 Harry Johnson | 12.00 | 5.00 | 1.20 |
| ☐ 10 Dave Lowe | 12.00 | 5.00 | 1.20 |
| ☐ 11 Jack Patera | 25.00 | 10.00 | 2.50 |
| ☐ 12 Ron Pheister | 15.00 | 6.00 | 1.50 |
| ☐ 13 John Reed | 12.00 | 5.00 | 1.20 |
| ☐ 14 Hal Reeve | 15.00 | 6.00 | 1.50 |

| | NRMT | VG-E | GOOD |
|---|---|---|---|
| ☐ 15 Larry Rose | 12.00 | 5.00 | 1.20 |
| ☐ 16 George Shaw | 18.00 | 7.25 | 1.80 |
| ☐ 17 Lon Stiner Jr. | 12.00 | 5.00 | 1.20 |
| ☐ 18 Ken Sweitzer | 12.00 | 5.00 | 1.20 |
| ☐ 19 Keith Tucker | 12.00 | 5.00 | 1.20 |
| ☐ 20 Dean Van Leuven | 12.00 | 5.00 | 1.20 |

## 1956 Oregon

This 19-card set measures the standard size (2 1/2" by 3 1/2"). The fronts feature a posed action photo, with player information appearing in a white box toward the bottom of the picture. Below the motto "Follow the Ducks," the backs have schedule information and a list of locations where adult tickets can be purchased. The cards are unnumbered and checklisted below in alphabetical order.

| | NRMT | VG-E | GOOD |
|---|---|---|---|
| COMPLETE SET (19) | 200.00 | 80.00 | 20.00 |
| COMMON PLAYER (1-19) | 12.00 | 5.00 | 1.20 |
| | | | |
| ☐ 1 Bruce Brenn | 12.00 | 5.00 | 1.20 |
| ☐ 2 Jack Brown | 12.00 | 5.00 | 1.20 |
| ☐ 3 Reanous Cochran | 12.00 | 5.00 | 1.20 |
| ☐ 4 Jack Crabtree | 15.00 | 6.00 | 1.50 |
| ☐ 5 Tom Crabtree | 12.00 | 5.00 | 1.20 |
| ☐ 6 Tom Hale | 12.00 | 5.00 | 1.20 |
| ☐ 7 Spike Hillstrom | 12.00 | 5.00 | 1.20 |
| ☐ 8 Jim Linden | 12.00 | 5.00 | 1.20 |
| ☐ 9 Hank Loumena | 12.00 | 5.00 | 1.20 |
| ☐ 10 Nick Markulis | 12.00 | 5.00 | 1.20 |
| ☐ 11 Phil McHugh | 12.00 | 5.00 | 1.20 |
| ☐ 13 Harry Mondale | 12.00 | 5.00 | 1.20 |
| ☐ 14 Leroy Phelps | 12.00 | 5.00 | 1.20 |
| ☐ 15 Jack Pocock | 12.00 | 5.00 | 1.20 |
| ☐ 16 John Roventos | 12.00 | 5.00 | 1.20 |
| ☐ 17 Jim Shanley | 12.00 | 5.00 | 1.20 |
| ☐ 18 Ron Stover | 15.00 | 6.00 | 1.50 |
| ☐ 19 J.C. Wheeler | 12.00 | 5.00 | 1.20 |

## 1958 Oregon

This 20-card set measures approximately 2 1/4" by 3 9/16". The fronts feature a posed action player photo with player information in the white border beneath the picture. The cards are unnumbered and checklisted below in alphabetical order.

| | NRMT | VG-E | GOOD |
|---|---|---|---|
| COMPLETE SET (20) | 200.00 | 80.00 | 20.00 |
| COMMON PLAYER (1-20) | 12.00 | 5.00 | 1.20 |
| | | | |
| ☐ 1 Greg Altenhofen | 12.00 | 5.00 | 1.20 |
| ☐ 2 Darrel Aschbacher | 15.00 | 6.00 | 1.50 |
| ☐ 3 Dave Fish | 12.00 | 5.00 | 1.20 |
| ☐ 4 Sandy Fraser | 12.00 | 5.00 | 1.20 |
| ☐ 5 Dave Grosz | 15.00 | 6.00 | 1.50 |
| ☐ 6 Bob Grottkau | 15.00 | 6.00 | 1.50 |
| ☐ 7 Marlan Holland | 12.00 | 5.00 | 1.20 |
| ☐ 8 Tom Keele | 12.00 | 5.00 | 1.20 |
| ☐ 9 Alden Kimbrough | 12.00 | 5.00 | 1.20 |
| ☐ 10 Don Laudenslager | 12.00 | 5.00 | 1.20 |
| ☐ 11 Riley Mattson | 20.00 | 8.00 | 2.00 |
| ☐ 12 Bob Peterson | 12.00 | 5.00 | 1.20 |
| ☐ 13 Dave Powell | 12.00 | 5.00 | 1.20 |
| ☐ 14 Len Read | 12.00 | 5.00 | 1.20 |
| ☐ 15 Will Reeve | 12.00 | 5.00 | 1.20 |
| ☐ 16 Joe Schaffeld | 12.00 | 5.00 | 1.20 |
| ☐ 17 Charlie Tourville | 12.00 | 5.00 | 1.20 |
| ☐ 18 Dave Urell | 12.00 | 5.00 | 1.20 |
| ☐ 19 Pete Welch | 12.00 | 5.00 | 1.20 |
| ☐ 20 Willie West | 20.00 | 8.00 | 2.00 |

## 1991 Oregon Smokey

This 12-card (approximately 3" by 4") set was issued as a perforated sheet. Distinctive green and gold fronts feature player action photos printed on white card stock. Oregon appears at the top of each picture while the Smokey logo, player name, position, and number are reversed-out white letters in the green bar at the bottom. The backs have biographical information and a fire prevention cartoon starring Smokey the Bear. The cards are unnumbered and checklisted below in alphabetical order.

| | MINT | EXC | G-VG |
|---|---|---|---|
| COMPLETE SET (12) | 10.00 | 4.00 | 1.00 |
| COMMON CARD (1-12) | 1.00 | .40 | .10 |
| | | | |
| ☐ 1 Bud Bowie | 1.00 | .40 | .10 |
| ☐ 2 Rich Brooks CO | 1.50 | .60 | .15 |
| ☐ 3 Sean Burwell | 1.00 | .40 | .10 |

Eric Castle
6'-3" • 206

Eric led the Ducks with 101 tackles last season. In addition, he had four interceptions and deflected 13 other passes, another team high. After the season, Castle was honored as a second team all-league performer.

ERIC CASTLE
Free Safety #12

| | MINT | EXC | G-VG |
|---|---|---|---|
| ☐ 4 Eric Castle | 1.00 | .40 | .10 |
| ☐ 5 Andy Conner | 1.00 | .40 | .10 |
| ☐ 6 Joe Farwell | 1.00 | .40 | .10 |
| ☐ 7 Matt LaBounty | 1.50 | .60 | .15 |
| ☐ 8 Gregg McCallum | 1.00 | .40 | .10 |
| ☐ 9 Daryle Smith | 1.00 | .40 | .10 |
| ☐ 10 Jeff Thomason | 1.00 | .40 | .10 |
| ☐ 11 Tommy Thompson | 1.00 | .40 | .10 |
| ☐ 12 Marcus Woods | 1.50 | .60 | .15 |

## 1988 Oregon State Smokey

OREGON STATE
UNIVERSITY

ROBB THOMAS
5'-11" • 173

This second team All Pac-10 selection returns for his senior season trying to better last season's total of 58 receptions (second highest total in the Pac-10). Thomas led the Pac-10 in 1987 with 887 receiving yards. Robb also had 10 TDs in '87.

DON'T GET BURNED BY—

ROBB THOMAS
WIDE RECEIVER • #18

The 1988 Oregon State Smokey set contains 12 standard-size (2 1/2" by 3 1/2") cards. The fronts feature color action photos with name, position, and jersey number. The vertically oriented backs have brief career highlights as well as a brief message from Smokey. The cards are unnumbered, but listed alphabetically below.

| | MINT | EXC | G-VG |
|---|---|---|---|
| COMPLETE SET (12) | 12.00 | 5.00 | 1.20 |
| COMMON CARD (1-12) | 1.25 | .50 | .12 |
| | | | |
| ☐ 1 Troy Bussanich | 1.25 | .50 | .12 |
| ☐ 2 Andre Harris | 1.25 | .50 | .12 |
| ☐ 3 Teddy Johnson | 1.25 | .50 | .12 |
| ☐ 4 Jason Kent | 1.25 | .50 | .12 |
| ☐ 5 Dave Kragthorpe CO | 1.25 | .50 | .12 |
| ☐ 6 Mike Matthews | 1.25 | .50 | .12 |
| ☐ 7 Phil Ross | 1.25 | .50 | .12 |
| ☐ 8 Brian Taylor | 1.25 | .50 | .12 |
| ☐ 9 Robb Thomas | 2.50 | 1.00 | .25 |
| ☐ 10 Esera Tuaolo | 2.50 | 1.00 | .25 |
| ☐ 11 Erik Wilhelm | 3.00 | 1.20 | .30 |
| ☐ 12 Dowell Williams | 1.25 | .50 | .12 |

## 1990 Oregon State Smokey

This 16-card set was sponsored by the USDA Forest Service in cooperation with other federal and state agencies. The cards were issued on a sheet with four rows of four cards each; after perforation, they measure the standard size (2 1/2" by 3 1/2"). The fronts feature a mix of color action or posed shots of the players, with black lettering and borders on an orange card face. The backs have player information and a fire prevention cartoon starring Smokey. The cards are unnumbered and checklisted below in alphabetical order.

| | MINT | EXC | G-VG |
|---|---|---|---|
| COMPLETE SET (16) | 12.00 | 5.00 | 1.20 |
| COMMON CARD (1-16) | 1.00 | .40 | .10 |
| | | | |
| ☐ 1 Brian Beck | 1.00 | .40 | .10 |
| ☐ 2 Martin Billings | 1.00 | .40 | .10 |

| | MINT | EXC | G-VG |
|---|---|---|---|
| ☐ 3 Matt Booher | 1.00 | .40 | .10 |
| ☐ 4 George Breland | 1.00 | .40 | .10 |
| ☐ 5 Brad D'Ancona | 1.00 | .40 | .10 |
| ☐ 6 Dennis Edwards | 1.00 | .40 | .10 |
| ☐ 7 Brent Huff | 1.00 | .40 | .10 |
| ☐ 8 James Jones | 1.00 | .40 | .10 |
| ☐ 9 Dave Kragthorpe CO | 1.00 | .40 | .10 |
| ☐ 10 Todd McKinney | 1.00 | .40 | .10 |
| ☐ 11 Torey Overstreet | 1.00 | .40 | .10 |
| ☐ 12 Reggie Pitchford | 1.00 | .40 | .10 |
| ☐ 13 Todd Sahlfeld | 1.00 | .40 | .10 |
| ☐ 14 Scott Thompson | 1.00 | .40 | .10 |
| ☐ 15 Esera Tuaolo | 2.00 | .80 | .20 |
| ☐ 16 Maurice Wilson | 1.00 | .40 | .10 |

## 1991 Oregon State Smokey

This 12-card set was sponsored by Prime Sports Northwest and other companies to promote fire safety in Oregon. The oversized cards were issued as a perforated sheet and measure approximately 3" by 4". The fronts feature action player photos banded by a black stripe above and an orange stripe below. A Smokey logo and player information are given in the bottom orange stripe. Horizontally oriented backs present career summary and a fire prevention cartoon starring Smokey. The cards are unnumbered and checklisted below in alphabetical order.

| | MINT | EXC | G-VG |
|---|---|---|---|
| COMPLETE SET (12) | 9.00 | 3.75 | .90 |
| COMMON CARD (1-12) | .75 | .30 | .07 |
| ☐ 1 Adam Albaugh | .75 | .30 | .07 |
| ☐ 2 Jamie Burke | .75 | .30 | .07 |
| ☐ 3 Chad de Sully | .75 | .30 | .07 |
| ☐ 4 Dennis Edwards | .75 | .30 | .07 |
| ☐ 5 James Jones | .75 | .30 | .07 |
| ☐ 6 Fletcher Keister | .75 | .30 | .07 |
| ☐ 7 Tom Nordquist | .75 | .30 | .07 |
| ☐ 8 Tony O'Billovich | .75 | .30 | .07 |
| ☐ 9 Jerry Pettibone CO | 1.00 | .40 | .10 |
| ☐ 10 Mark Price | .75 | .30 | .07 |
| ☐ 11 Todd Sahlfeld | .75 | .30 | .07 |
| ☐ 12 Earl Zackery | .75 | .30 | .07 |

## 1992 Oregon State Smokey

Sponsored by Prime Sports Northwest, this 12-card set was issued on thin card stock as a perforated sheet; after perforation, each card would measure approximately 3" by 4". The fronts show color player photos bordered in white. The school and team name appear in a black bar above the picture, while the player's name, jersey number, and position are printed on a orange bar beneath the picture. In black

print on a white background, the backs feature a player profile and a fire prevention cartoon starring Smokey. The cards are unnumbered and checklisted below in alphabetical order.

| | MINT | EXC | G-VG |
|---|---|---|---|
| COMPLETE SET (12) | 9.00 | 3.75 | .90 |
| COMMON CARD (1-12) | .75 | .30 | .07 |
| ☐ 1 Zechariah Davis | .75 | .30 | .07 |
| ☐ 2 Chad De Sully | .75 | .30 | .07 |
| ☐ 3 Michael Hale | .75 | .30 | .07 |
| ☐ 4 Fletcher Keister | .75 | .30 | .07 |
| ☐ 5 Chad Paulson | .75 | .30 | .07 |
| ☐ 6 Rico Petrini | .75 | .30 | .07 |
| ☐ 7 Jerry Pettibone CO | 1.00 | .40 | .10 |
| ☐ 8 Sailusi Poulivaati | .75 | .30 | .07 |
| ☐ 9 Tony O'Billovich | .75 | .30 | .07 |
| ☐ 10 Dwayne Owens | .75 | .30 | .07 |
| ☐ 11 J.J. Young | 2.00 | .80 | .20 |
| ☐ 12 Maurice Wilson | .75 | .30 | .07 |

## 1988 Penn State Police

The 1988 Penn State University police/safety set contains 12 standard-size (2 1/2" by 3 1/2") cards. The fronts feature color action photos with name, position, and jersey number. The vertically oriented backs have brief career highlights and "Nittany Lion Tips". The set was produced by McDag Productions. The set is subtitled "The Second Mile" on the front and back of each card. The cards are unnumbered and hence are numbered by uniform number which is given on both sides of each player's card.

| | MINT | EXC | G-VG |
|---|---|---|---|
| COMPLETE SET (12) | 20.00 | 8.00 | 2.00 |
| COMMON CARD | 1.00 | .40 | .10 |
| ☐ 5 Michael Timpson | 3.00 | 1.20 | .30 |
| ☐ 20 John Greene | 1.00 | .40 | .10 |
| ☐ 28 Brian Chizmar | 1.00 | .40 | .10 |
| ☐ 31 Andre Collins | 3.00 | 1.20 | .30 |
| ☐ 32 Blair Thomas | 3.00 | 1.20 | .30 |
| ☐ 39 Eddie Johnson | 1.00 | .40 | .10 |
| ☐ 66 Steve Wisniewski | 3.00 | 1.20 | .30 |
| ☐ 75 Rich Schonewolf | 1.00 | .40 | .10 |
| ☐ 78 Roger Duffy | 1.00 | .40 | .10 |
| ☐ 84 Keith Karpinski | 1.00 | .40 | .10 |
| ☐ xx Joe Paterno CO | 4.00 | 1.60 | .40 |
| ☐ xx Penn State Mascot | 1.50 | .60 | .15 |
| The Nittany Lion | | | |

# 1989 Penn State Police

This 15-card standard-size (2 1/2" by 3 1/2") set was sponsored by "The Second Mile" (a non-profit organization) in conjunction with IBM. The fronts feature a mix of action and posed player photos, with the player's name and position listed below the picture. The backs carry career highlights and "Nittany Lion Tips." The cards are unnumbered and checklisted below in alphabetical order.

|  | MINT | EXC | G-VG |
|---|---|---|---|
| COMPLETE SET (15) | 20.00 | 8.00 | 2.00 |
| COMMON CARD (1-15) | 1.00 | .40 | .10 |
| ☐ 1 Brian Chizmar | 1.00 | .40 | .10 |
| ☐ 2 Andre Collins | 2.50 | 1.00 | .25 |
| ☐ 3 David Daniels | 2.00 | .80 | .20 |
| ☐ 4 Roger Duffy | 1.00 | .40 | .10 |
| ☐ 5 Tim Freeman | 1.00 | .40 | .10 |
| ☐ 6 Scott Gob | 1.00 | .40 | .10 |
| ☐ 7 David Jakob | 1.00 | .40 | .10 |
| ☐ 8 Geoff Japchen | 1.00 | .40 | .10 |
| ☐ 9 Joe Paterno CO | 4.00 | 1.60 | .40 |
| ☐ 10 Sherrod Rainge | 1.00 | .40 | .10 |
| ☐ 11 Rich Schonewolf | 1.00 | .40 | .10 |
| ☐ 12 Dave Szott | 2.00 | .80 | .20 |
| ☐ 13 Blair Thomas | 2.50 | 1.00 | .25 |
| ☐ 14 Leroy Thompson | 4.00 | 1.60 | .40 |
| ☐ 15 Nittany Lion (Mascot) | 1.50 | .60 | .15 |

# 1990 Penn State Police

The 16-card police/safety set was sponsored by "The Second Mile," a nonprofit organization that helps needy children. The set was underwritten in part by the Mellon Family Foundation. The cards measure the standard size (2 1/2" by 3 1/2") and are printed on thin card stock. The fronts display a mix of posed or action color photos, with solid blue borders above and below, and blue and white striped borders on the sides. The school logo and name are printed in the top blue border while the sponsor's name and player information appear beneath the picture. The backs have brief biographical information, player profile, and "Nittany Lion Tips" in the form of player quotes. A sponsor advertisement at the bottom rounds out the card back. The cards are unnumbered and checklisted below in alphabetical order.

|  | MINT | EXC | G-VG |
|---|---|---|---|
| COMPLETE SET (16) | 15.00 | 6.00 | 1.50 |
| COMMON CARD (1-16) | .75 | .30 | .07 |
| ☐ 1 Gerry Collins | .75 | .30 | .07 |
| ☐ 2 David Daniels | 1.25 | .50 | .12 |
| ☐ 3 Jim Deter | .75 | .30 | .07 |
| ☐ 4 Mark D'Onofrio | 1.50 | .60 | .15 |
| ☐ 5 Sam Gash | 1.50 | .60 | .15 |
| ☐ 6 Frank Giannetti | .75 | .30 | .07 |
| ☐ 7 Keith Goganious | 1.25 | .50 | .12 |
| ☐ 8 Doug Helkowski | .75 | .30 | .07 |
| ☐ 9 Hernon Henderson | .75 | .30 | .07 |
| ☐ 10 Matt McCartin | .75 | .30 | .07 |
| ☐ 11 Joe Paterno CO | 3.00 | 1.20 | .30 |
| ☐ 12 Darren Perry | 1.50 | .60 | .15 |
| ☐ 13 Tony Sacca | 2.50 | 1.00 | .25 |
| ☐ 14 Terry Smith | .75 | .30 | .07 |
| ☐ 15 Willie Thomas | .75 | .30 | .07 |
| ☐ 16 Leroy Thompson | 3.00 | 1.20 | .30 |

# 1991-92 Penn State Legends

This 50-card standard-size (2 1/2" by 3 1/2") set was produced by Front Row for "The Second Mile," a non-profit organization that helps needy children. The set spotlights All-Americans who played at Penn State from 1923 to 1991. The production run was limited to 20,000

sets. The fronts feature a mix of color and black and white, as well as posed and action, player photos with white borders. Card top carries Penn State in white on a blue border while the bottom has the player's name in a blue border and All-American in red. Front Row's logo appears at the bottom right. Horizontally printed backs have statistics and biography within a red border. An unnumbered insert has a checklist on one side and acknowledgments on the other. The cards are numbered on the back, with the player cards arranged in alphabetical order. Front Row also produced two promo cards prior to the general release of the set; they are distinguished by the fact that "Promo" is stamped diagonally across the back.

|  | MINT | EXC | G-VG |
|---|---|---|---|
| COMPLETE SET (50) | 15.00 | 6.00 | 1.50 |
| COMMON CARD (1-50) | .35 | .14 | .03 |
| ☐ 1 Joe Paterno CO | 1.50 | .60 | .15 |
| ☐ 2 Kurt Allerman | .50 | .20 | .05 |
| ☐ 3 Chris Bahr | .50 | .20 | .05 |
| ☐ 4 Matt Bahr | .50 | .20 | .05 |
| ☐ 5 Bruce Bannon | .35 | .14 | .03 |
| ☐ 6 Greg Buttle | .50 | .20 | .05 |
| ☐ 7 John Capelletti | .75 | .30 | .07 |
| ☐ 8 Bruce Clark | .50 | .20 | .05 |
| ☐ 9 Andre Collins | .75 | .30 | .07 |
| ☐ 10 Shane Conlan | .75 | .30 | .07 |
| ☐ 11 Chris Conlin | .35 | .14 | .03 |
| ☐ 12 Randy Crowder | .35 | .14 | .03 |
| ☐ 13 Keith Dorney | .35 | .14 | .03 |
| ☐ 14 D.J. Dozier | .75 | .30 | .07 |
| ☐ 15 Bill Dugan | .35 | .14 | .03 |
| ☐ 16 Chuck Fusina | .50 | .20 | .05 |
| ☐ 17 Leon Gajecki | .35 | .14 | .03 |
| ☐ 18 Jack Ham | 1.25 | .50 | .12 |
| ☐ 19 Bob Higgins | .35 | .14 | .03 |
| ☐ 20 John Hufnagel | .60 | .24 | .06 |
| ☐ 21 Kenny Jackson | .50 | .20 | .05 |
| ☐ 22 Tim Johnson | .35 | .14 | .03 |
| ☐ 23 Dave Joyner | .35 | .14 | .03 |
| ☐ 24 Roger Kochman | .35 | .14 | .03 |
| ☐ 25 Ted Kwalick | .50 | .20 | .05 |
| ☐ 26 Rich Lucas | .60 | .24 | .06 |
| ☐ 27 Matt Millen | .60 | .24 | .06 |
| ☐ 28 Lydell Mitchell | .75 | .30 | .07 |
| ☐ 29 Bob Mitinger | .35 | .14 | .03 |
| ☐ 30 John Nessel | .35 | .14 | .03 |
| ☐ 31 Ed O'Neil | .50 | .20 | .05 |
| ☐ 32 Dennis Onkotz | .50 | .20 | .05 |
| ☐ 33 Darren Perry | .60 | .24 | .06 |
| ☐ 34 Charlie Pittman | .60 | .24 | .06 |
| ☐ 35A Tom Rafferty ERR | 1.25 | .50 | .12 |
| (Photo actually T. Quinn) | | | |
| ☐ 35B Tom Rafferty COR | 1.25 | .50 | .12 |
| ☐ 36 Mike Reid UER | 1.25 | .50 | .12 |
| (Reversed negative) | | | |
| ☐ 37 Glenn Ressler | .50 | .20 | .05 |
| ☐ 38 Dave Robinson | .60 | .24 | .06 |
| ☐ 39 Mark Robinson | .35 | .14 | .03 |
| ☐ 40 Randy Sidler | .35 | .14 | .03 |
| ☐ 41 John Skorupan | .50 | .20 | .05 |
| ☐ 42 Neal Smith | .35 | .14 | .03 |
| ☐ 43 Steve Suhey | .60 | .24 | .06 |
| ☐ 44 Sam Tamburo | .35 | .14 | .03 |
| ☐ 45 Blair Thomas | 1.50 | .60 | .15 |
| ☐ 46 Curt Warner | 1.50 | .60 | .15 |
| ☐ 47 Steve Wisniewski | .75 | .30 | .07 |
| ☐ 48 Charlie Zapiec | .50 | .20 | .05 |
| ☐ 49 Mike Zordich | .50 | .20 | .05 |
| ☐ 50 Harry Wilson and Joe Bedenk | .35 | .14 | .03 |
| ☐ NNO Checklist Card | .35 | .14 | .03 |
| ☐ P10 Shane Conlan (Promo) | 2.00 | .80 | .20 |
| ☐ P18 Jack Ham (Promo) | 2.50 | 1.00 | .25 |

## 1992 Penn State Police

Sponsored by The Second Mile, this 16-card set measures the standard size (2 1/2" by 3 1/2") and features posed and action color player photos against a royal blue background that is also edged in light blue. White banners, outlined with red and light blue, run across the top and bottom, and behind the middle of the picture. The banners contain the player's position, jersey number, and name. The backs have biographical information, a player profile, and "Nittany Lion Tips" in the form of player quotes. A sponsor message at the bottom rounds out the card back. The cards are unnumbered and checklisted below in alphabetical order. The key card in the set features O.J. McDuffie.

|  | MINT | EXC | G-VG |
|---|---|---|---|
| COMPLETE SET (16) | 12.00 | 5.00 | 1.20 |
| COMMON PLAYER (1-16) | .60 | .24 | .06 |
| ☐ 1 Richie Anderson | 2.00 | .80 | .20 |
| ☐ 2 Lou Benfatti | .60 | .24 | .06 |
| ☐ 3 Derek Bochna | .60 | .24 | .06 |
| ☐ 4 Kyle Brady | 1.00 | .40 | .10 |
| ☐ 5 Kerry Collins | 1.25 | .50 | .12 |
| ☐ 6 Troy Drayton | 2.00 | .80 | .20 |
| ☐ 7 John Gerak | 1.00 | .40 | .10 |
| ☐ 8 Reggie Givens | 1.00 | .40 | .10 |
| ☐ 9 Shelly Hammonds | .60 | .24 | .06 |
| ☐ 10 Greg Huntington | .60 | .24 | .06 |
| ☐ 11 Tyoka Jackson | 1.00 | .40 | .10 |
| ☐ 12 O.J. McDuffie | 5.00 | 2.00 | .50 |
| ☐ 13 Lee Rubin | .60 | .24 | .06 |
| ☐ 14 E.J. Sandusky | .60 | .24 | .06 |
| ☐ 15 Tisen Thomas | .60 | .24 | .06 |
| ☐ 16 Brett Wright | .60 | .24 | .06 |

## 1993 Penn State

These 25 standard-size (2 1/2" by 3 1/2") cards feature on their fronts color player action and posed shots set within blue and red borders with white paw tracks within the right margin. The school name appears in white lettering within the blue margin above the photo. The player's name, number, and position appear in blue lettering in a white rectangle below the photo. The white back carries the player's name, number, and profile at the top. Below is a Nittany Lions tip given by each player. The cards are unnumbered and checklisted below in alphabetical order.

|  | MINT | EXC | G-VG |
|---|---|---|---|
| COMPLETE SET (25) | 12.00 | 5.00 | 1.20 |
| COMMON PLAYER (1-25) | .50 | .20 | .05 |
| ☐ 1 Mike Archie | .50 | .20 | .05 |
| Ki-Jana Carter | | | |

| | | | |
|---|---|---|---|
| Stephen Pitts | | | |
| ☐ 2 Lou Benfatti | .50 | .20 | .05 |
| ☐ 3 Derek Bochna | .50 | .20 | .05 |
| ☐ 4 Kyle Brady | .75 | .30 | .07 |
| ☐ 5 Kerry Collins | 1.00 | .40 | .10 |
| ☐ 6 Criag Fayak | .50 | .20 | .05 |
| ☐ 7 Marlon Forbes | .50 | .20 | .05 |
| ☐ 8 Brian Gelzheiser | .75 | .30 | .07 |
| ☐ 9 Bucky Greeley | .50 | .20 | .05 |
| ☐ 10 Ryan Grube | .75 | .30 | .07 |
| ☐ 11 Shelly Hammonds | .50 | .20 | .05 |
| ☐ 12 Jeff Hartings | .75 | .30 | .07 |
| ☐ 13 Rob Holmberg | .75 | .30 | .07 |
| ☐ 14 Tyoka Jackson | .75 | .30 | .07 |
| ☐ 15 Mike Malinoski | .75 | .30 | .07 |
| ☐ 16 Brian Monaghan | .50 | .20 | .05 |
| ☐ 17 Brian O'Neal | .75 | .30 | .07 |
| ☐ 18 Jeff Perry | .50 | .20 | .05 |
| ☐ 19 Derick Pickett | .50 | .20 | .05 |
| ☐ 20 Tony Pittman | .50 | .20 | .05 |
| ☐ 21 Eric Ravotti | .50 | .20 | .05 |
| ☐ 22 Lee Rubin | .50 | .20 | .05 |
| ☐ 23 Vin Stewart | .50 | .20 | .05 |
| ☐ 24 Tisen Thomas | .50 | .20 | .05 |
| ☐ 25 Phil Yeboah-Kodie | .50 | .20 | .05 |

## 1991 Pennsylvania HS Big 33

This 36-card standard-size (2 1/2" by 3 1/2") high school football set was issued to commemorate the Big 33 Football Classic, an annual high school football game begun in 1958 and featuring Pennsylvania versus Maryland for the past seven games. The fronts feature posed black and white player photos enclosed by a white border. State name appears at top of card while player name, number, and position appear in white reversed-out lettering in black. The Big 33 logo and The Super Bowl of High School Football appear in same reverse-out fashion at bottom. The backs feature player's biographical information enclosed within a thin black border.

|  | MINT | EXC | G-VG |
|---|---|---|---|
| COMPLETE SET (36) | 15.00 | 6.00 | 1.50 |
| COMMON PLAYER (PA1-PA36) | .75 | .30 | .07 |
| ☐ PA1 Dietrich Jells | 1.00 | .40 | .10 |
| Tech Memorial High | | | |
| ☐ PA2 Mike Archie | .75 | .30 | .07 |
| Sharon High | | | |
| ☐ PA3 Tony Miller | .75 | .30 | .07 |
| Coatsville High | | | |
| ☐ PA4 Edmund Robinson | .75 | .30 | .07 |
| Bensalem High | | | |
| ☐ PA5 Brian Miller | .75 | .30 | .07 |
| Ringgold High | | | |
| ☐ PA6 Marvin Harrison | .75 | .30 | .07 |
| Roman Catholic High | | | |
| ☐ PA7 Mike Cawley | .75 | .30 | .07 |
| Mount Lebanon High | | | |
| ☐ PA8 Thomas Marchese | .75 | .30 | .07 |
| Dunmore High | | | |
| ☐ PA9 Scott Milanovich | 2.00 | .80 | .20 |
| Butler High | | | |
| ☐ PA10 Shawn Wooden | .75 | .30 | .07 |
| Abington High | | | |
| ☐ PA11 Curtis Martin | .75 | .30 | .07 |
| Allderdice High | | | |
| ☐ PA12 William Khayat | .75 | .30 | .07 |
| York Catholic High | | | |
| ☐ PA13 Jermell Fleming | .75 | .30 | .07 |
| Stelton-Highspire High | | | |
| ☐ PA14 Raymond Zellars | 2.00 | .80 | .20 |
| David B. Oliver High | | | |
| ☐ PA15 Jon Witman | .75 | .30 | .07 |
| Eastern York High | | | |
| ☐ PA16 Chris McCartney | .75 | .30 | .07 |
| Bellwood-Antis High | | | |

| | | | |
|---|---|---|---|
| ☐ PA17 David Rebar | .75 | .30 | .07 |
| Mid-Valley High | | | |
| ☐ PA18 Mark Zataveski | 1.00 | .40 | .10 |
| Bishop McDevitt High | | | |
| ☐ PA19 Todd Atkins | .75 | .30 | .07 |
| Laural High | | | |
| ☐ PA20 Shannon Stevens | .75 | .30 | .07 |
| Glen Mills High | | | |
| ☐ PA21 Keith Conlin | .75 | .30 | .07 |
| LaSalle High | | | |
| ☐ PA22 John Bowman | .75 | .30 | .07 |
| Berwick High | | | |
| ☐ PA23 Maurice Lawrence | .75 | .30 | .07 |
| Wilkinsburg High | | | |
| ☐ PA24 Mike Halapin | .75 | .30 | .07 |
| Kiski Area High | | | |
| ☐ PA25 Steve Keim | .75 | .30 | .07 |
| Red Land High | | | |
| ☐ PA26 Dennis Martin | .75 | .30 | .07 |
| Perry Traditional High | | | |
| ☐ PA27 Keith Morris | .75 | .30 | .07 |
| Elizabethtown Area High | | | |
| ☐ PA28 Chris Villarrial | .75 | .30 | .07 |
| Hershey High | | | |
| ☐ PA29 Thomas Tumulty | .75 | .30 | .07 |
| Penn Hills High | | | |
| ☐ PA30 Jason Augustino | .75 | .30 | .07 |
| North Allegheny High | | | |
| ☐ PA31 Gregory Delong | .75 | .30 | .07 |
| Parkland High | | | |
| ☐ PA32 James Moore | .75 | .30 | .07 |
| Towanda High | | | |
| ☐ PA33 Eric Clair | .75 | .30 | .07 |
| Elizabethtown Area High | | | |
| ☐ PA34 Tyler Young | .75 | .30 | .07 |
| Liberty High | | | |
| ☐ PA35 Jeffrey Sauve | .75 | .30 | .07 |
| Cumberland Valley High | | | |
| ☐ PA36 Terry Hammons | .75 | .30 | .07 |
| Upper St. Clair High | | | |

## 1989 Pittsburgh

The 1989 Pitt football set contains 22 standard-size (2 1/2" by 3 1/2") cards. The fronts have vintage or color action photos with white borders; the vertically oriented backs have detailed profiles. These cards were distributed as a set. The cards are numbered on the back in the lower right corner.

| | MINT | EXC | G-VG |
|---|---|---|---|
| COMPLETE SET (22) | 6.00 | 2.50 | .50 |
| COMMON CARD (1-22) | .40 | .16 | .04 |
| | | | |
| ☐ 1 Tony Dorsett | 2.00 | .80 | .20 |
| ☐ 2 Pop Warner CO | .60 | .24 | .06 |
| ☐ 3 Hugh Green | .75 | .30 | .07 |
| ☐ 4 Matt Cavanaugh | .60 | .24 | .06 |
| ☐ 5 Mike Gottfried | .40 | .16 | .04 |
| ☐ 6 Jimbo Covert | .60 | .24 | .06 |
| ☐ 7 Bob Peck | .40 | .16 | .04 |
| ☐ 8 Gibby Welch | .40 | .16 | .04 |
| ☐ 9 Bill Daddio | .40 | .16 | .04 |
| ☐ 10 Jock Sutherland CO | .60 | .24 | .06 |
| ☐ 11 Joe Walton | .40 | .16 | .04 |
| ☐ 12 Dan Marino | 4.00 | 1.60 | .40 |
| ☐ 13 Russ Grimm | .60 | .24 | .06 |
| ☐ 14 Mike Ditka | 2.00 | .80 | .20 |
| ☐ 15 Marshall Goldberg | .60 | .24 | .06 |
| ☐ 16 Bill Fralic | .75 | .30 | .07 |
| ☐ 17 Paul Martha | .60 | .24 | .06 |
| ☐ 18 Joe Schmidt | .75 | .30 | .07 |
| ☐ 19 Rickey Jackson | .75 | .30 | .07 |
| ☐ 20 Ave Daniell | .40 | .16 | .04 |
| ☐ 21 Bill Maas | .60 | .24 | .06 |
| ☐ 22 Mark May | .60 | .24 | .06 |

## 1990 Pitt Foodland

This 12-card set, which measures the standard size (2 1/2" by 3 1/2"), was sponsored by Foodland to promote anti-drug involvement in the Pittsburgh area. This set features members of the 1990 Pittsburgh Panthers football team. The front features a color action photo, with the team name, player's name, and position at the top. The Pitt helmet appears at the bottom left hand corner and the Foodland logo below the picture. The back contains biographical information and a tip from the Panthers in the form of an anti-drug message. The set was produced by Bensussen-Deutsch and Association from Redmond, Washington. For convenient reference, these unnumbered cards are checklisted below in alphabetical order.

| | MINT | EXC | G-VG |
|---|---|---|---|
| COMPLETE SET (12) | 9.00 | 3.75 | .90 |
| COMMON CARD (1-12) | .75 | .30 | .07 |
| | | | |
| ☐ 1 Curtis Bray | .75 | .30 | .07 |
| ☐ 2 Craig Gob | .75 | .30 | .07 |
| ☐ 3 Paul Hackett CO | 1.25 | .50 | .12 |
| ☐ 4 Keith Hamilton | 2.00 | .80 | .20 |
| ☐ 5 Ricardo McDonald | 1.25 | .50 | .12 |
| ☐ 6 Ronald Redmon | .75 | .30 | .07 |
| ☐ 7 Curvin Richards | 1.00 | .40 | .10 |
| ☐ 8 Louis Riddick | .75 | .30 | .07 |
| ☐ 9 Chris Sestili | .75 | .30 | .07 |
| ☐ 10 Olanda Truitt | 1.50 | .60 | .15 |
| ☐ 11 Alex Van Pelt | 1.50 | .60 | .15 |
| ☐ 12 Nelson Walker | .75 | .30 | .07 |

## 1991 Pitt Foodland

This 12-card set was sponsored by Foodland and features the 1991 Pittsburgh Panthers. The cards measure the standard size (2 1/2" by 3 1/2") and are printed on thin cardboard stock. The set was issued as individual cards or as an unperforated sheet. The card fronts are accented in the team's colors (blue and yellow) and have glossy color action player photos. The top of the pictures is curved to resemble an archway, and the team name follows the curve of the arch. The player's name and position appear in a yellow stripe below the picture. In black print on white, the backs have the team logo, biography, player profile, and "Tips from the Panthers" in the form of anti-drug messages. The cards are unnumbered and checklisted below in alphabetical order.

| | MINT | EXC | G-VG |
|---|---|---|---|
| COMPLETE SET (12) | 7.00 | 2.80 | .70 |
| COMMON CARD (1-12) | .75 | .30 | .07 |
| | | | |
| ☐ 1 Richard Allen | .75 | .30 | .07 |

|  |  |  |  |
|---|---|---|---|
| ☐ 2 Curtis Bray | .75 | .30 | .07 |
| ☐ 3 Jeff Christy | .75 | .30 | .07 |
| ☐ 4 Steven Israel | 1.25 | .50 | .12 |
| ☐ 5 Scott Kaplan | .75 | .30 | .07 |
| ☐ 6 Ricardo McDonald | 1.00 | .40 | .10 |
| ☐ 7 David Moore | .75 | .30 | .07 |
| ☐ 8 Eric Seaman | .75 | .30 | .07 |
| ☐ 9 Chris Sestili | .75 | .30 | .07 |
| ☐ 10 Alex Van Pelt | 1.25 | .50 | .12 |
| ☐ 11 Nelson Walker | .75 | .30 | .07 |
| ☐ 12 Kevin Williams | .75 | .30 | .07 |

## 1991 Pitt State

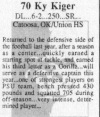

70 Ky Kiger
DL...6-2...250...SR...
Catoosa, OK/Union HS

Returned to the defensive side of the football last year, after a season as a center...quickly earned a starting spot at tackle, and earned his third letter as a Gorilla...will serve as a defensive captain this year...one of strongest players on PSU team, bench pressed 430 pounds and squatted 705 during off-season...very intense, determined player...

Ky Kiger          DL

The 1991 Pitt State Gorillas set consists of 18 standard-size (2 1/2" by 3 1/2") cards. Printed on thin white card stock, fronts show player in either a posed or an action photo placed within an arch design. College and team name appears at top of each card while player's name is in a gold bar at bottom next to a picture of the mascot. The backs present biography and player profile superimposed over a drawing of the mascot. A checklist is included with the set on a paper insert. The key player in this set is NFL running back Ron Moore. Also appearing in the set is Ronnie West, who was the Gorillas' Harlon Hill Award candidate. The cards are unnumbered and listed alphabetically below.

|  | MINT | EXC | G-VG |
|---|---|---|---|
| COMPLETE SET (18) | 12.00 | 5.00 | 1.20 |
| COMMON CARD (1-18) | .60 | .24 | .06 |
| ☐ 1 Chuck Broyles CO | .75 | .30 | .07 |
| ☐ 2 Darren Dawson | .60 | .24 | .06 |
| ☐ 3 Kendall Gammon | .60 | .24 | .06 |
| ☐ 4 Jamie Goodson | .60 | .24 | .06 |
| ☐ 5 Brian Hoover | .60 | .24 | .06 |
| ☐ 6 James Jenkins | .60 | .24 | .06 |
| ☐ 7 Ky Kiger | .60 | .24 | .06 |
| ☐ 8 Phil McCoy | .60 | .24 | .06 |
| ☐ 9 Kline Minniefield | .60 | .24 | .06 |
| ☐ 10 Ron Moore | 4.00 | 1.60 | .40 |
| ☐ 11 Jeff Mundhenke | .60 | .24 | .06 |
| ☐ 12 Brian Pinamonti | .60 | .24 | .06 |
| ☐ 13 Michael Rose | .60 | .24 | .06 |
| ☐ 14 Shane Tafoya | .60 | .24 | .06 |
| ☐ 15 Ronnie West | 1.25 | .50 | .12 |
| ☐ 16 Michael Wilber | .60 | .24 | .06 |
| ☐ 17 Troy Wilson | .60 | .24 | .06 |
| ☐ 18 Team Photo | 1.25 | .50 | .12 |

## 1992 Pitt State

96 - Troy Wilson          DE
Height: 6'4"     Weight: 235     Senior
Topeka, Kan./Shawnee Heights HS

1991 NCAA Division II Champions

Initiated by Students in Free Enterprise (SIFE), this 18-card set was produced to raise funds for the Pitt State athletic department. The cards could be purchased at football games, the University Post Office, or Kelce room 220. The production run figures were 3,000 numbered packaged sets and 750 uncut sheets. One thousand of the packaged sets contained a Ronnie West bonus card. In addition to the 18 cards, the set included one paper insert providing card history, a checklist, and set serial number, and another paper insert with cartoons about four different "Isms" (socialism, communism, nazism, and capitalism) and a list of examples of "Big Government" waste in spending. This 18-card set measures the standard size (2 1/2" by 3 1/2"). The set features full-bleed color action player photos. The backs are plain white card stock printed with black and contain biographies and player profiles. Some cards also carry Pitt State trivia, while others have statistics. The cards are numbered on the back and checklisted below accordingly. The key card in the set features running back Ron Moore.

|  | MINT | EXC | G-VG |
|---|---|---|---|
| COMPLETE SET (18) | 10.00 | 4.00 | 1.00 |
| COMMON CARD (1-18) | .60 | .24 | .06 |
| ☐ 1 Ron Moore | 3.00 | 1.20 | .30 |
| ☐ 2 Craig Jordan | .60 | .24 | .06 |
| ☐ 3 Joel Thornton | .60 | .24 | .06 |
| ☐ 4 Don Tolar | .60 | .24 | .06 |
| ☐ 5 Andy Kesinger | .60 | .24 | .06 |
| ☐ 6 Mike Brockel | .60 | .24 | .06 |
| ☐ 7 Troy Wilson | .60 | .24 | .06 |
| ☐ 8 Brian Hutchins | .60 | .24 | .06 |
| ☐ 9 Chris Hanna | .60 | .24 | .06 |
| ☐ 10 Coaching Staff | .60 | .24 | .06 |
| ☐ 11 Gus Gorilla (Mascot) | .60 | .24 | .06 |
| ☐ 12 Lance Gosch | .60 | .24 | .06 |
| ☐ 13 Jerry Boone / Chad Watskey | .60 | .24 | .06 |
| ☐ 14 Jeff Moreland / Scott Lutz | .60 | .24 | .06 |
| ☐ 15 Ronnie Fuller / Mickey Beagle | .60 | .24 | .06 |
| ☐ 16 Todd Hafner / Kevin Duncan | .60 | .24 | .06 |
| ☐ 17 Duke Palmer / Eric Perks | .60 | .24 | .06 |
| ☐ 18 Kris Mengarelli | .60 | .24 | .06 |

## 1989 Purdue Legends Smokey

PURDUE
BOILERMAKERS

STEVE JACKSON
DEFENSIVE BACK - #1

STEVE JACKSON
Defensive Back - #1
5' 9" - 180 - Junior
Houston, Texas
Steve is a speedy defender who won UPI honorable mention All-Big Ten in 1988.

KEEP IT GREEN around your House!

A Public Service in Wildfire Prevention, 1989, in cooperation with USDA Forest Service, Indiana Department of Natural Resources and BDA.

This 16-card set features members of the 1989 Purdue Boilermakers as well as some stars of the past. These sets were distributed at the Purdue/Iowa game in 1989 and have a full-color action photo on the front underneath the Purdue Boilermaker name on top and the player's name, uniform number, and position underneath his photo. The card backs have biographical information as well as a fire safety tip. This set was sponsored by the USDA Forest Service, Indiana Department of Natural Resources, and BDA. We have checklisted this set in alphabetical order and put the initials LEG next to the alumni.

|  | MINT | EXC | G-VG |
|---|---|---|---|
| COMPLETE SET (16) | 20.00 | 8.00 | 2.00 |
| COMMON CARD (1-16) | 1.00 | .40 | .10 |
| ☐ 1 Fred Akers CO | 1.25 | .50 | .12 |
| ☐ 2 Jim Everett LEG | 2.50 | 1.00 | .25 |
| ☐ 3 Bob Griese LEG | 5.00 | 2.00 | .50 |
| ☐ 4 Mark Herrmann LEG | 1.50 | .60 | .15 |
| ☐ 5 Bill Hitchcock | 1.00 | .40 | .10 |
| ☐ 6 Steve Jackson | 1.25 | .50 | .12 |
| ☐ 7 Derrick Kelson | 1.00 | .40 | .10 |
| ☐ 8 Leroy Keyes LEG | 2.00 | .80 | .20 |

| | MINT | EXC | G-VG |
|---|---|---|---|
| ☐ 9 Shawn McCarthy | 1.25 | .50 | .12 |
| ☐ 10 Dwayne O'Connor | 1.00 | .40 | .10 |
| ☐ 11 Mike Phipps LEG | 1.50 | .60 | .15 |
| ☐ 12 Darren Trieb | 1.00 | .40 | .10 |
| ☐ 13 Tony Vinson | 1.00 | .40 | .10 |
| ☐ 14 Calvin Williams | 2.50 | 1.00 | .25 |
| ☐ 15 Rod Woodson LEG | 3.00 | 1.20 | .30 |
| ☐ 16 Dave Young LEG | 1.00 | .40 | .10 |

## 1990 Rice Aetna

This 12-card set, which measures the standard size (2 1/2" by 3 1/2"), was sponsored by The Houston Post and Aetna Life and Casualty. The cards feature color action player photos with a navy-blue shadow border on a white card face. The player's name, uniform number, position, and classification appear in the shadow border at the bottom. The team name and sponsor logos are at the top. The backs feature navy-blue print on a white background and include biographical information, player profile, and anti-drug or alcohol messages under the heading "Tips from the Owls". The cards are unnumbered and checklisted below in alphabetical order. The sole distribution of the cards was as giveaways to fans at the Owls' home game against Texas; reportedly 25,000 sets were given away.

| | MINT | EXC | G-VG |
|---|---|---|---|
| COMPLETE SET (12) | 10.00 | 4.00 | 1.00 |
| COMMON CARD (1-12) | .75 | .30 | .07 |
| ☐ 1 O.J. Brigance | .75 | .30 | .07 |
| ☐ 2 Trevor Cobb | 3.00 | 1.20 | .30 |
| ☐ 3 Tim Fitzpatrick | .75 | .30 | .07 |
| ☐ 4 Fred Goldsmith CO | 1.25 | .50 | .12 |
| ☐ 5 David Griffin | .75 | .30 | .07 |
| ☐ 6 Eric Henley | 1.25 | .50 | .12 |
| ☐ 7 Donald Hollas | 2.00 | .80 | .20 |
| ☐ 8 Richard Segina | .75 | .30 | .07 |
| ☐ 9 Matt Sign | .75 | .30 | .07 |
| ☐ 10 Bill Stone | .75 | .30 | .07 |
| ☐ 11 Trey Teichelman UER (Misspelled Tichelman on front and back) | .75 | .30 | .07 |
| ☐ 12 Alonzo Williams | .75 | .30 | .07 |

## 1991 Rice Aetna

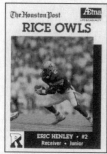 

Sponsored by the Houston Post and Aetna Life and Casualty, these 12 cards measure the standard size (2 1/2" by 3 1/2"). The fronts feature color action player photos with gray inner borders and white outer borders. The player's name, uniform number, position, and class appear within a navy blue stripe below the photo. The words "Rice

Owls '91" appear within a navy blue stripe above the picture. The backs feature navy-colored lettering on a white background and include biographical information, player profile, and anti-drug and alcohol messages under the heading "Tips from the Owls." At the lower right corner the cards are labeled "series 2." The cards are unnumbered and checklisted below in alphabetical order. The sole distribution of the cards was as giveaways to fans at the Owls' home game against Texas A and M; reportedly 25,000 sets were given away.

| | MINT | EXC | G-VG |
|---|---|---|---|
| COMPLETE SET (12) | 10.00 | 4.00 | 1.00 |
| COMMON PLAYER (1-12) | .75 | .30 | .07 |
| ☐ 1 Mike Appelbaum | .75 | .30 | .07 |
| ☐ 2 Louis Balady | .75 | .30 | .07 |
| ☐ 3 Nathan Bennett | .75 | .30 | .07 |
| ☐ 4 Trevor Cobb | 2.50 | 1.00 | .25 |
| ☐ 5 Herschel Crowe | .75 | .30 | .07 |
| ☐ 6 David Griffin | .75 | .30 | .07 |
| ☐ 7 Eric Henley | 1.25 | .50 | .12 |
| ☐ 8 Matt Sign | .75 | .30 | .07 |
| ☐ 9 Larry Stuppy | .75 | .30 | .07 |
| ☐ 10 Trey Teichelman | .75 | .30 | .07 |
| ☐ 11 Alonzo Williams | .75 | .30 | .07 |
| ☐ 12 Greg Willig | .75 | .30 | .07 |

## 1992 Rice Taco Cabana

This 12-card set was sponsored by The Houston Post and Taco Cabana, and their company logos appear in the top white border. The fronts feature color action player photos bordered in white. A navy blue bar above the picture carries the words "Rice Owls '92", while a navy blue bar below the picture has the school logo and player information. The backs feature navy-blue print on a white background and include biographical information, player profile, and anti-drug or alcohol messages under the heading "Tips from the Owls". The cards are unnumbered and checklisted below in alphabetical order. The sole distribution of the cards was as giveaways to fans at the Owls' home game against Texas; reportedly 25,000 sets were given away.

| | MINT | EXC | G-VG |
|---|---|---|---|
| COMPLETE SET (12) | 10.00 | 4.00 | 1.00 |
| COMMON PLAYER (1-12) | .75 | .30 | .07 |
| ☐ 1 Shawn Alberding | .75 | .30 | .07 |
| ☐ 2 Mike Appelbaum | .75 | .30 | .07 |
| ☐ 3 Louis Balady | .75 | .30 | .07 |
| ☐ 4 Nathan Bennett | .75 | .30 | .07 |
| ☐ 5 Trevor Cobb | 2.00 | .80 | .20 |
| ☐ 6 Josh LaRocca | .75 | .30 | .07 |
| ☐ 7 Jimmy Lee | 1.25 | .50 | .12 |
| ☐ 8 Corey Seymour | .75 | .30 | .07 |
| ☐ 9 Matt Sign | .75 | .30 | .07 |
| ☐ 10 Emmett Waldron | 1.50 | .60 | .15 |
| ☐ 11 Alonzo Williams | .75 | .30 | .07 |
| ☐ 12 Taco Cabana (Advertisement) | .75 | .30 | .07 |

## 1993 Rice Taco Cabana

This 12-card set was sponsored by The Houston Post and Taco Cabana. The cards measure the standard size (2 1/2" by 3 1/2"). The fronts feature color action player photos within a gray card face. The year and team name are shown in white lettering within a blue bar above the photo. The player's name, jersey number, position, and class are printed in white lettering within a blue bar at the bottom. The horizontal white backs carry the player's name, position, jersey number, height, weight, and hometown at the top, followed below by career highlights and "Tips from the Owls." The cards are unnumbered and checklisted below in alphabetical order.

|  | MINT | EXC | G-VG |
|---|---|---|---|
| COMPLETE SET (12) | 10.00 | 4.00 | 1.00 |
| COMMON PLAYER (1-12) | .75 | .30 | .07 |
| ☐ 1 Nathan Bennett | .75 | .30 | .07 |
| ☐ 2 Cris Cooley | .75 | .30 | .07 |
| ☐ 3 Bert Emanuel | 2.50 | 1.00 | .25 |
| ☐ 4 Jimmy Golden | .75 | .30 | .07 |
| ☐ 5 Tom Hetherington | .75 | .30 | .07 |
| ☐ 6 Ed Howard | .75 | .30 | .07 |
| ☐ 7 Jimmy Lee | 1.25 | .50 | .12 |
| ☐ 8 Corey Seymour | .75 | .30 | .07 |
| ☐ 9 Clemente Torres | .75 | .30 | .07 |
| ☐ 10 Emmett Waldron | 1.25 | .50 | .12 |
| ☐ 11 Sean Washington | .75 | .30 | .07 |
| ☐ 12 Taco Cabana Ad Card | 1.00 | .40 | .10 |

## 1990 San Jose State Smokey

This 15-card set measures the standard 2 1/2" by 3 1/2" and features members of the 1990 San Jose State football team. The front has a color action photo, with the school name above the picture and the player's name, uniform number, and school year below. The picture is enframed by an orange border on a blue background. The back provides information on the player and features a fire prevention cartoon starring Smokey the Bear. For convenient reference, these unnumbered cards are checklisted below in alphabetical order.

|  | MINT | EXC | G-VG |
|---|---|---|---|
| COMPLETE SET (15) | 9.00 | 3.75 | .90 |
| COMMON CARD (1-15) | .75 | .30 | .07 |
| ☐ 1 Bob Bleisch 90 | .75 | .30 | .07 |
| ☐ 2 Sheldon Canley 20 | .75 | .30 | .07 |
| ☐ 3 Paul Franklin 37 | .75 | .30 | .07 |
| ☐ 4 Anthony Gallegos 72 | .75 | .30 | .07 |
| ☐ 5 Steve Hieber 48 | .75 | .30 | .07 |
| ☐ 6 Everett Lampkins 43 | .75 | .30 | .07 |
| ☐ 7 Kelly Liebengood 21 | .75 | .30 | .07 |
| ☐ 8 Ralph Martini 9 | .75 | .30 | .07 |
| ☐ 9 Lyneil Mayo 62 | .75 | .30 | .07 |
| ☐ 10 Mike Powers 57 | .75 | .30 | .07 |
| ☐ 11 Mike Scialabba 46 | .75 | .30 | .07 |
| ☐ 12 Terry Shea CO | .75 | .30 | .07 |
| ☐ 13 Freddie Smith 4 | .75 | .30 | .07 |
| ☐ 14 Eddie Thomas 26 | .75 | .30 | .07 |
| ☐ 15 Brian Woods 64 | .75 | .30 | .07 |

## 1974 Southern Cal Discs

This 30-disc set was issued inside a miniature plastic football display holder, sitting on a red stand that reads "Trojans 1974". The discs measure approximately 2 5/16" in diameter and feature borderless color glossy player photos, shot from the waist up. The backs have biographical information, including the high school attended in the player's hometown. The discs are unnumbered and are listed alphabetically below. The set was reportedly sold during Southern Cal's homecoming week during the Fall of 1974.

|  | NRMT | VG-E | GOOD |
|---|---|---|---|
| COMPLETE SET (30) | 75.00 | 30.00 | 7.50 |
| COMMON DISC (1-30) | 2.00 | .80 | .20 |
| ☐ 1 Bill Bain | 2.50 | 1.00 | .25 |
| ☐ 2 Otha Bradley | 2.50 | 1.00 | .25 |
| ☐ 3 Kevin Bruce | 2.00 | .80 | .20 |
| ☐ 4 Mario Celotto | 2.00 | .80 | .20 |
| ☐ 5 Marvin Cobb | 3.00 | 1.20 | .30 |
| ☐ 6 Anthony Davis | 7.50 | 3.00 | .75 |
| ☐ 7 Joe Davis | 2.00 | .80 | .20 |
| ☐ 8 Shelton Diggs | 3.00 | 1.20 | .30 |
| ☐ 9 Dave Farmer | 2.00 | .80 | .20 |
| ☐ 10 Pat Haden | 9.00 | 3.75 | .90 |
| ☐ 11 Donnie Hickman | 2.00 | .80 | .20 |
| ☐ 12 Doug Hogan | 2.00 | .80 | .20 |
| ☐ 13 Mike Howell | 2.00 | .80 | .20 |
| ☐ 14 Gary Jeter | 3.50 | 1.40 | .35 |
| ☐ 15 Steve Knutson | 2.00 | .80 | .20 |
| ☐ 16 Chris Limahelu | 2.50 | 1.00 | .25 |
| ☐ 17 Bob McCaffrey | 2.00 | .80 | .20 |
| ☐ 18 J.K. McKay | 3.50 | 1.40 | .35 |
| ☐ 19 John McKay CO | 5.00 | 2.00 | .50 |
| ☐ 20 Jim O'Bradovich | 2.50 | 1.00 | .25 |
| ☐ 21 Charles Phillips | 2.50 | 1.00 | .25 |
| ☐ 22 Ed Powell | 2.00 | .80 | .20 |
| ☐ 23 Marvin Powell | 3.50 | 1.40 | .35 |
| ☐ 24 Danny Reece | 2.50 | 1.00 | .25 |
| ☐ 25 Art Riley | 2.00 | .80 | .20 |
| ☐ 26 Traveller II and Richard Sako | 2.50 | 1.00 | .25 |
| ☐ 27 Tommy Trojan Trojan Statue | 2.50 | 1.00 | .25 |
| ☐ 28 USC Song Girls | 3.00 | 1.20 | .30 |
| ☐ 29 USC Song Girls | 3.00 | 1.20 | .30 |
| ☐ 30 Richard Wood | 3.00 | 1.20 | .30 |

## 1988 Southern Cal Smokey

The 1988 Southern Cal Smokey set contains 17 standard-size (2 1/2" by 3 1/2") cards. The fronts feature color photos with name, position, and jersey number. The vertically oriented backs have brief career highlights. The cards are unnumbered, so they are listed alphabetically by subject's name.

|  | MINT | EXC | G-VG |
|---|---|---|---|
| COMPLETE SET (17) | 12.00 | 5.00 | 1.20 |
| COMMON CARD | .75 | .30 | .07 |
| ☐ 1 Erik Affholter | 1.25 | .50 | .12 |
| ☐ 2 Gene Arrington | .75 | .30 | .07 |
| ☐ 3 Scott Brennan | .75 | .30 | .07 |
| ☐ 4 Jeff Brown | .75 | .30 | .07 |
| ☐ 5 Tracy Butts | .75 | .30 | .07 |
| ☐ 6 Martin Chesley | .75 | .30 | .07 |
| ☐ 7 Paul Green | .75 | .30 | .07 |
| ☐ 8 John Guerrero | .75 | .30 | .07 |
| ☐ 9 Chris Hale | .75 | .30 | .07 |
| ☐ 10 Rodney Peete | 4.00 | 1.60 | .40 |
| ☐ 11 Dave Powroznik | .75 | .30 | .07 |
| ☐ 12 Mark Sager | .75 | .30 | .07 |
| ☐ 13 Mike Serpa | .75 | .30 | .07 |
| ☐ 14 Larry Smith CO | 1.00 | .40 | .10 |
| ☐ 15 Chris Sperle | .75 | .30 | .07 |
| ☐ 16 Joe Walshe | .75 | .30 | .07 |
| ☐ 17 Steven Webster | .75 | .30 | .07 |

## 1988 Southern Cal Winners

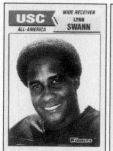

The 1988 Southern Cal Winners set contains 73 standard-size (2 1/2" by 3 1/2") cards. The fronts have black and white mugshots with USC and name banners in school colors; the vertically oriented backs have brief profiles and Trojan highlights from specific seasons. The set was sold by the USC bookstore. The cards are unnumbered, so they are listed alphabetically by type.

|  | MINT | EXC | G-VG |
|---|---|---|---|
| COMPLETE SET (73) | 12.00 | 5.00 | 1.20 |
| COMMON CARD (1-73) | .15 | .06 | .01 |
| ☐ 1 Title Card | .25 | .10 | .02 |
| (schedule on back) |  |  |  |
| ☐ 2 George Achica | .25 | .10 | .02 |
| ☐ 3 Marcus Allen | 1.50 | .60 | .15 |
| ☐ 4 Jon Arnett | .25 | .10 | .02 |
| ☐ 5 Johnny Baker | .15 | .06 | .01 |
| ☐ 6 Damon Bame | .25 | .10 | .02 |
| ☐ 7 Chip Banks | .35 | .14 | .03 |
| ☐ 8 Mike Battle | .25 | .10 | .02 |
| ☐ 9 Hal Bedsole | .25 | .10 | .02 |
| ☐ 10 Ricky Bell | .35 | .14 | .03 |
| ☐ 11 Jeff Bregel | .15 | .06 | .01 |
| ☐ 12 Tay Brown | .15 | .06 | .01 |
| ☐ 13 Brad Budde | .25 | .10 | .02 |
| ☐ 14 Dave Cadigan | .25 | .10 | .02 |
| ☐ 15 Pat Cannamela | .15 | .06 | .01 |
| ☐ 16 Paul Cleary | .15 | .06 | .01 |
| ☐ 17 Sam Cunningham | .35 | .14 | .03 |
| ☐ 18 Anthony Davis | .35 | .14 | .03 |
| ☐ 19 Clarence Davis | .25 | .10 | .02 |
| ☐ 20 Morley Drury | .15 | .06 | .01 |
| ☐ 21 John Ferraro | .15 | .06 | .01 |
| ☐ 22 Bill Fisk | .15 | .06 | .01 |
| ☐ 23 Roy Foster | .25 | .10 | .02 |
| ☐ 24 Mike Garrett | .35 | .14 | .03 |
| ☐ 25 Frank Gifford | 1.00 | .40 | .10 |
| ☐ 26 Ralph Heywood | .15 | .06 | .01 |
| ☐ 27 Pat Howell | .15 | .06 | .01 |
| ☐ 28 Gary Jeter | .25 | .10 | .02 |
| ☐ 29 Dennis Johnson | .15 | .06 | .01 |
| ☐ 30 Mort Kaer | .15 | .06 | .01 |
| ☐ 31 Grenny Lansdell | .15 | .06 | .01 |
| ☐ 32 Ronnie Lott | 1.00 | .40 | .10 |
| ☐ 33 Paul McDonald | .25 | .10 | .02 |
| ☐ 34 Tim McDonald | .50 | .20 | .05 |
| ☐ 35 Ron Mix | .35 | .14 | .03 |
| ☐ 36 Don Mosebar | .25 | .10 | .02 |
| ☐ 37 Artimus Parker | .25 | .10 | .02 |
| ☐ 38 Charles Phillips | .15 | .06 | .01 |

|  | MINT | EXC | G-VG |
|---|---|---|---|
| ☐ 39 Erny Pinckert | .15 | .06 | .01 |
| ☐ 40 Marvin Powell | .25 | .10 | .02 |
| ☐ 41 Aaron Rosenberg | .15 | .06 | .01 |
| ☐ 42 Tim Rossovich | .25 | .10 | .02 |
| ☐ 43 Jim Sears | .15 | .06 | .01 |
| ☐ 44 Gus Shaver | .15 | .06 | .01 |
| ☐ 45 Nate Shaw | .15 | .06 | .01 |
| ☐ 46 O.J. Simpson | 4.00 | 1.60 | .40 |
| ☐ 47 Ernie Smith | .15 | .06 | .01 |
| ☐ 48 Harry Smith | .15 | .06 | .01 |
| ☐ 49 Larry Stevens | .15 | .06 | .01 |
| ☐ 50 Lynn Swann | .75 | .30 | .07 |
| ☐ 51 Brice Taylor | .15 | .06 | .01 |
| ☐ 52 Dennis Thurman | .25 | .10 | .02 |
| ☐ 53 Keith Van Horne | .25 | .10 | .02 |
| ☐ 54 Cotton Warburton | .15 | .06 | .01 |
| ☐ 55 Charles White | .35 | .14 | .03 |
| ☐ 56 Elmer Willhoite | .15 | .06 | .01 |
| ☐ 57 Richard Wood | .25 | .10 | .02 |
| ☐ 58 Ron Yary | .35 | .14 | .03 |
| ☐ 59 Adrian Young | .15 | .06 | .01 |
| ☐ 60 Charles Young UER | .25 | .10 | .02 |
| (listed as Adrian |  |  |  |
| Young on card front) |  |  |  |
| ☐ 61 Pete Adams and | .15 | .06 | .01 |
| John Grant |  |  |  |
| ☐ 62 Bill Bain and | .25 | .10 | .02 |
| Jim O'Bradovich |  |  |  |
| ☐ 63 Nate Barrager and | .15 | .06 | .01 |
| Francis Tappan |  |  |  |
| ☐ 64 Booker Brown and | .15 | .06 | .01 |
| Steve Riley |  |  |  |
| ☐ 65 Al Cowlings, | .50 | .20 | .05 |
| Jimmy Gunn, and |  |  |  |
| Charles Weaver |  |  |  |
| ☐ 66 Jack Del Rio and | .35 | .14 | .03 |
| Duane Bickett |  |  |  |
| ☐ 67 Clay Matthews and | .50 | .20 | .05 |
| Bruce Matthews |  |  |  |
| ☐ 68 Marlin McKeever and | .35 | .14 | .03 |
| Mike McKeever |  |  |  |
| ☐ 69 Orv Mohler and | .15 | .06 | .01 |
| Garrett Arbelbide |  |  |  |
| ☐ 70 Sid Smith and | .15 | .06 | .01 |
| Marv Montgomery |  |  |  |
| ☐ 71 John Vella and | .15 | .06 | .01 |
| Willie Hall |  |  |  |
| ☐ 72 Don Williams and | .15 | .06 | .01 |
| Jesse Hibbs |  |  |  |
| ☐ 73 Stan Williamson and | .15 | .06 | .01 |
| Tony Slaton |  |  |  |

## 1989 Southern Cal Smokey

The 1989 Smokey USC football set contains 23 standard-size (2 1/2" by 3 1/2") cards. The fronts have color action photos with maroon borders; the vertically oriented backs have fire prevention tips. These cards were distributed as a set. The cards are unnumbered, so the cards are listed below alphabetically by subject.

|  | MINT | EXC | G-VG |
|---|---|---|---|
| COMPLETE SET (23) | 10.00 | 4.00 | 1.00 |
| COMMON CARD (1-23) | .60 | .24 | .06 |
| ☐ 1 Dan Barnes | .60 | .24 | .06 |
| ☐ 2 Dwight Carner | .60 | .24 | .06 |
| ☐ 3 Delmar Chesley | .60 | .24 | .06 |
| ☐ 4 Cleveland Colter | .60 | .24 | .06 |
| ☐ 5 Aaron Emanuel | 1.00 | .40 | .10 |
| ☐ 6 Scott Galbraith | .75 | .30 | .07 |
| ☐ 7 Leroy Holt | .75 | .30 | .07 |
| ☐ 8 Randy Hord | .60 | .24 | .06 |
| ☐ 9 John Jackson | 1.00 | .40 | .10 |
| ☐ 10 Brad Leggett | .60 | .24 | .06 |

| | | | |
|---|---|---|---|
| ☐ 11 Marching Band | .60 | .24 | .06 |
| ☐ 12 Dan Owens | 1.25 | .50 | .12 |
| ☐ 13 Brent Parkinson | .60 | .24 | .06 |
| ☐ 14 Tim Ryan | 1.25 | .50 | .12 |
| ☐ 15 Bill Schultz | .60 | .24 | .06 |
| ☐ 16 Larry Smith CO | .75 | .30 | .07 |
| ☐ 17 Ernest Spears | .60 | .24 | .06 |
| ☐ 18 J.P. Sullivan | .60 | .24 | .06 |
| ☐ 19 Cordell Sweeney | .60 | .24 | .06 |
| ☐ 20 Traveler | .60 | .24 | .06 |
| (Horse Mascot) | | | |
| ☐ 21 Marlon Washington | .60 | .24 | .06 |
| ☐ 22 Michael Williams | .60 | .24 | .06 |
| ☐ 23 Yell Leaders and | .75 | .30 | .07 |
| Song Girls | | | |

# 1991 Southern Cal College Classics*

Anthony Davis

ANTHONY DAVIS
TAILBACK
1972-74

Produced by College Classics Inc., this 100-card standard-size (2 1/2"
by 3 1/2") set honors former Trojan athletes. The white-bordered
fronts feature color and black-and-white player photos, mostly action
shots, which are framed by red lines. The player's name appears in
red lettering within a yellow rectangle at the bottom. The white back
carries the player's name, position (or sport if not football), and the
years he or she played for USC, all in red lettering within the yellow
rectangle at the top. Career highlights follow below. The complete set
comes with a blank-backed white card that carries the set's production
number out of a total of 20,000 produced. The cards are numbered on
the back.

| | MINT | EXC | G-VG |
|---|---|---|---|
| COMPLETE SET (100) | 30.00 | 12.00 | 3.00 |
| COMMON PLAYER (1-100) | .25 | .10 | .02 |
| | | | |
| ☐ 1 Charles White | .50 | .20 | .05 |
| ☐ 2 Anthony Davis | .50 | .20 | .05 |
| ☐ 3 Clay Matthews | .75 | .30 | .07 |
| ☐ 4 Hoby Brenner | .35 | .14 | .03 |
| ☐ 5 Mike Garrett | .50 | .20 | .05 |
| ☐ 6 Bill Sharman | 1.00 | .40 | .10 |
| (Basketball) | | | |
| ☐ 7 Bob Seagren | .35 | .14 | .03 |
| (Track) | | | |
| ☐ 8 Mike McKeever | .35 | .14 | .03 |
| ☐ 9 Celso Kalache | .25 | .10 | .02 |
| (Volleyball) | | | |
| ☐ 10 John Williams CO | .25 | .10 | .02 |
| (Water polo) | | | |
| ☐ 11 John Naber | .50 | .20 | .05 |
| (Swimming) | | | |
| ☐ 12 Brad Budde | .35 | .14 | .03 |
| ☐ 13 Tim Ryan | .35 | .14 | .03 |
| ☐ 14 Mark Tucker | .25 | .10 | .02 |
| ☐ 15 Rodney Peete | .75 | .30 | .07 |
| ☐ 16 Art Mazmanian | .25 | .10 | .02 |
| (Baseball) | | | |
| ☐ 17 Red Badgro | .35 | .14 | .03 |
| (Baseball) | | | |
| ☐ 18 Sue Habernigg | .25 | .10 | .02 |
| (Women's swimming) | | | |
| ☐ 19 Craig Fertig | .25 | .10 | .02 |
| ☐ 20 John Block | .35 | .14 | .03 |
| (Basketball) | | | |
| ☐ 21 Jen-Kai Liu | .25 | .10 | .02 |
| (Volleyball) | | | |
| ☐ 22 Kim Ruddins | .25 | .10 | .02 |
| (Women's volleyball) | | | |
| ☐ 23 Al Cowlings | .75 | .30 | .07 |
| ☐ 24 Ronnie Lott | 1.00 | .40 | .10 |
| ☐ 25 Adam Johnson | .75 | .30 | .07 |
| (Volleyball) | | | |
| ☐ 26 Fred Lynn | .50 | .20 | .05 |
| (Baseball) | | | |

| | | | |
|---|---|---|---|
| ☐ 27 Rick Leach | .35 | .14 | .03 |
| (Tennis) | | | |
| ☐ 28 Tim Rossovich | .50 | .20 | .05 |
| ☐ 29 Marvin Powell | .35 | .14 | .03 |
| ☐ 30 Ron Yary | .50 | .20 | .05 |
| ☐ 31 Ken Ruettgers | .35 | .14 | .03 |
| ☐ 32 Bob Yoder CO | .25 | .10 | .02 |
| (Men's volleyball) | | | |
| ☐ 33 Megan McCallister | .25 | .10 | .02 |
| (Women's volleyball) | | | |
| ☐ 34 Dave Cadigan | .35 | .14 | .03 |
| ☐ 35 Jeff Bregel | .25 | .10 | .02 |
| ☐ 36 Michael Wayman | .25 | .10 | .02 |
| (Tennis) | | | |
| ☐ 37 Sippy Woodhead-Kantzer | .35 | .14 | .03 |
| (Women's swimming) | | | |
| ☐ 38 Tim Hovland | .50 | .20 | .05 |
| (Volleyball) | | | |
| ☐ 39 Steve Busby | .35 | .14 | .03 |
| (Baseball) | | | |
| ☐ 40 Tom Seaver | 1.50 | .60 | .15 |
| (Baseball) | | | |
| ☐ 41 Anthony Colorito | .25 | .10 | .02 |
| ☐ 42 Wayne Carlander | .35 | .14 | .03 |
| (Basketball) | | | |
| ☐ 43 Erik Affholter | .35 | .14 | .03 |
| ☐ 44 Jim Obradovich | .35 | .14 | .03 |
| ☐ 45 Duane Bickett | .50 | .20 | .05 |
| ☐ 46 Leslie Daland | .25 | .10 | .02 |
| (Women's swimming) | | | |
| ☐ 47 Ole Oleson | .35 | .14 | .03 |
| (Track) | | | |
| ☐ 48 Ed Putnam | .25 | .10 | .02 |
| (Baseball) | | | |
| ☐ 49 Stan Smith | .50 | .20 | .05 |
| (Tennis) | | | |
| ☐ 50 Jeff Hart | .25 | .10 | .02 |
| (Golf) | | | |
| ☐ 51 Jack Del Rio | .35 | .14 | .03 |
| ☐ 52 Bob Boyd CO | .35 | .14 | .03 |
| (Basketball) | | | |
| ☐ 53 Pat Haden | .75 | .30 | .07 |
| ☐ 54 John Lambert | .35 | .14 | .03 |
| (Basketball) | | | |
| ☐ 55 Pete Beathard | .50 | .20 | .05 |
| ☐ 56 Anna-Maria Fernandez | .50 | .20 | .05 |
| (Women's tennis) | | | |
| ☐ 57 Marta Figueras-Dotti | .25 | .10 | .02 |
| (Women's golf) | | | |
| ☐ 58 Don Mosebar | .35 | .14 | .03 |
| ☐ 59 Don Doll | .35 | .14 | .03 |
| ☐ 60 Dave Stockton | .50 | .20 | .05 |
| (Golf) | | | |
| ☐ 61 Trisha Laux | .35 | .14 | .03 |
| (Women's tennis) | | | |
| ☐ 62 Roy Foster | .35 | .14 | .03 |
| ☐ 63 Bruce Matthews | .35 | .14 | .03 |
| ☐ 64 Steve Sogge | .35 | .14 | .03 |
| ☐ 65 Tracy Nakamura | .35 | .14 | .03 |
| (Women's golf) | | | |
| ☐ 66 Marv Montgomery | .25 | .10 | .02 |
| ☐ 67 Jack Tingley | .25 | .10 | .02 |
| (Swimming) | | | |
| ☐ 68 Larry Stevens | .25 | .10 | .02 |
| ☐ 69 Harry Smith | .25 | .10 | .02 |
| ☐ 70 Bill Bain | .25 | .10 | .02 |
| ☐ 71 Mark McGwire | .75 | .30 | .07 |
| (Baseball) | | | |
| ☐ 72 Brad Brink | .35 | .14 | .03 |
| (Baseball) | | | |
| ☐ 73 Richard Wood | .35 | .14 | .03 |
| ☐ 74 Rod Dedeaux CO | .50 | .20 | .05 |
| (Baseball) | | | |
| ☐ 75 Paul Westphal | 1.00 | .40 | .10 |
| (Basketball) | | | |
| ☐ 76 Al Krueger | .25 | .10 | .02 |
| ☐ 77 James McConica | .25 | .10 | .02 |
| (Swimming) | | | |
| ☐ 78 Rod Martin | .35 | .14 | .03 |
| ☐ 79 Bill Yardley | .25 | .10 | .02 |
| (Volleyball) | | | |
| ☐ 80 Bill Stetson | .25 | .10 | .02 |
| (Volleyball) | | | |
| ☐ 81 Ray Looze | .25 | .10 | .02 |
| (Swimming) | | | |
| ☐ 82 Dan Jorgensen | .25 | .10 | .02 |
| (Swimming) | | | |
| ☐ 83 Anna-Lucia Fernandez | .35 | .14 | .03 |
| (Women's tennis) | | | |
| ☐ 84 Terri O'Loughlin | .25 | .10 | .02 |
| (Women's swimming) | | | |
| ☐ 85 John Grant | .25 | .10 | .02 |
| ☐ 86 Chris Lewis | .25 | .10 | .02 |
| (Tennis) | | | |
| ☐ 87 Steve Timmons | 1.50 | .60 | .15 |
| (Volleyball) | | | |
| ☐ 88 Dr. Dallas Long | .35 | .14 | .03 |

| | MINT | EXC | G-VG |
|---|---|---|---|
| (Track) | | | |
| ☐ 89 John McKay CO | .50 | .20 | .05 |
| ☐ 90 Joe Bottom | .25 | .10 | .02 |
| (Swimming) | | | |
| ☐ 91 John Jackson | .25 | .10 | .02 |
| ☐ 92 Paul McDonald | .35 | .14 | .03 |
| ☐ 93 Jimmy Gunn | .35 | .14 | .03 |
| ☐ 94 Rod Sherman | .35 | .14 | .03 |
| ☐ 95 Cecilia Fernandez | .35 | .14 | .03 |
| (Women's tennis) | | | |
| ☐ 96 Doug Adler | .25 | .10 | .02 |
| (Tennis) | | | |
| ☐ 97 Ron Orr | .25 | .10 | .02 |
| (Swimming) | | | |
| ☐ 98 Debbie Landreth Brown | .25 | .10 | .02 |
| (Women's volleyball) | | | |
| ☐ 99 Debbie Green | .25 | .10 | .02 |
| (Women's volleyball) | | | |
| ☐ 100 Pat Harrison | .25 | .10 | .02 |
| (Baseball) | | | |

## 1991 Southern Cal Smokey

This 16-card standard-size (2 1/2" by 3 1/2") set was sponsored by the USDA Forest Service as well as other federal and state agencies. The front features color action player photos bordered in maroon. The top of the pictures is curved to resemble an archway, and the team name follows the curve of the arch. Player information and logos appear in a mustard stripe beneath the picture. In black on white, the backs carry player profile and a fire prevention cartoon starring Smokey. The cards are unnumbered and checklisted below in alphabetical order.

| | MINT | EXC | G-VG |
|---|---|---|---|
| COMPLETE SET (16) | 8.00 | 3.25 | .80 |
| COMMON CARD (1-16) | .60 | .24 | .06 |
| | | | |
| ☐ 1 Kurt Barber | 1.25 | .50 | .12 |
| ☐ 2 Ron Dale | .60 | .24 | .06 |
| ☐ 3 Derrick Deese | .60 | .24 | .06 |
| ☐ 4 Michael Gaytan | .60 | .24 | .06 |
| ☐ 5 Matt Gee | .60 | .24 | .06 |
| ☐ 6 Calvin Holmes | 1.00 | .40 | .10 |
| ☐ 7 Scott Lockwood | 1.25 | .50 | .12 |
| ☐ 8 Michael Moody | .60 | .24 | .06 |
| ☐ 9 Marvin Pollard | .60 | .24 | .06 |
| ☐ 10 Mark Raab | .60 | .24 | .06 |
| ☐ 11 Larry Smith CO | .75 | .30 | .07 |
| ☐ 12 Raoul Spears | .60 | .24 | .06 |
| ☐ 13 Matt Willig | .60 | .24 | .06 |
| ☐ 14 Alan Wilson | .60 | .24 | .06 |
| ☐ 15 James Wilson | .60 | .24 | .06 |
| ☐ 16 Traveler | .60 | .24 | .06 |
| (The Trojan Horse) | | | |

## 1992 Southern Cal Smokey

This 16-card set was sponsored by the USDA Forest Service and other state and federal agencies. The cards measure the standard size (2 1/2" by 3 1/2") and are printed on thin card stock. The fronts carry a color action player photo on a brick-red card face. The team name and year appear above the photo in gold print on a brick-red bar that partially rests on a gold bar with notched ends. Below the photo, the player's name and sponsor logos appear in a gold border stripe. The backs carry player profile and a fire prevention cartoon starring Smokey. The cards are unnumbered and checklisted below in alphabetical order.

| | MINT | EXC | G-VG |
|---|---|---|---|
| COMPLETE SET (16) | 8.00 | 3.25 | .80 |
| COMMON CARD (1-16) | .60 | .24 | .06 |

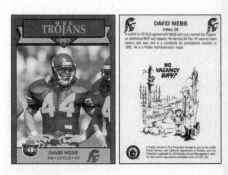

| | MINT | EXC | G-VG |
|---|---|---|---|
| ☐ 1 Wes Bender | .60 | .24 | .06 |
| ☐ 2 Estrus Crayton | .60 | .24 | .06 |
| ☐ 3 Eric Dixon | .60 | .24 | .06 |
| ☐ 4 Travis Hannah | 1.00 | .40 | .10 |
| ☐ 5 Zuri Hector | .60 | .24 | .06 |
| ☐ 6 Lamont Hollinquest | .60 | .24 | .06 |
| ☐ 7 Yonnie Jackson | .60 | .24 | .06 |
| ☐ 8 Bruce Luizzi | .60 | .24 | .06 |
| ☐ 9 Mike Mooney | .60 | .24 | .06 |
| ☐ 10 Stephon Pace | .60 | .24 | .06 |
| ☐ 11 Joel Scott | .60 | .24 | .06 |
| ☐ 12 DeNail Sparks | .60 | .24 | .06 |
| ☐ 13 Titus Tuiasosopo | .60 | .24 | .06 |
| ☐ 14 Larry Wallace | .60 | .24 | .06 |
| ☐ 15 David Webb | .60 | .24 | .06 |
| ☐ 16 Title Card ART | .75 | .30 | .07 |

## 1988 Southwestern Louisiana McDag*

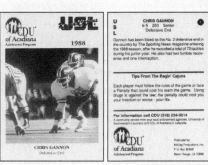

Produced by McDag, this standard-size (2 1/2" by 3 1/2") card set features USL action player photos printed on white card stock. Card numbers 1-10 are player cards; cards 11 and 12 feature dance team members. The CDU of Acadiana Adolescent Program logo appears at the top of each card as well as USL Ragin' Cajuns and year. Player's name appears at bottom in white border. The backs carry biographical information, "Tips from the Ragin' Cajuns" in the form of anti-drug messages, and sponsor advertisement. The cards are numbered on the back.

| | MINT | EXC | G-VG |
|---|---|---|---|
| COMPLETE SET (12) | 6.00 | 2.40 | .60 |
| COMMON CARD (1-12) | .50 | .20 | .05 |
| | | | |
| ☐ 1 Brian Mitchell | 1.50 | .60 | .15 |
| (QB rolling out) | | | |
| ☐ 2 Brian Mitchell | 1.50 | .60 | .15 |
| (QB over center) | | | |
| ☐ 3 Chris Gannon | .50 | .20 | .05 |
| (DE signalling sideline) | | | |
| ☐ 4 Chris Gannon | .50 | .20 | .05 |
| (DE awaiting snap) | | | |
| ☐ 5 Willie Culpepper | .75 | .30 | .07 |
| ☐ 6 Greg Eagles | .50 | .20 | .05 |
| ☐ 7 Steve McKinney | .50 | .20 | .05 |
| ☐ 8 Pat Decuir | .50 | .20 | .05 |
| ☐ 9 Leslie Luquette | .50 | .20 | .05 |
| ☐ 10 Robert Johnson | .50 | .20 | .05 |
| ☐ 11 Lisa McCoy | .75 | .30 | .07 |
| (Cheerleader) | | | |
| ☐ 12 Michelle Aubert | .75 | .30 | .07 |
| (Cheerleader) | | | |

## 1991 Stanford All-Century

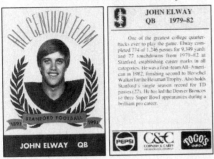

**JOHN ELWAY**
QB     1979–82

One of the greatest college quarterbacks ever to play the game. Elway completed 774 of 1,246 passes for 9,349 yards and 77 touchdowns from 1979–82 at Stanford, establishing career marks in all categories. He was a first-team All-American in 1982, finishing second to Herschel Walker for the Heisman Trophy. Also holds Stanford's single season record for TD passes (27). He has led the Denver Broncos to three Super Bowl appearances during a brilliant pro career.

JOHN ELWAY     QB

This 100-card standard-size (2 1/2" by 3 1/2") set is an All-Century commemorative set issued to honor outstanding players at Stanford during the past 100 years. The set was issued in perforated strips of six cards each. The first card of each strip, redeemable at Togo's for a free Pepsi with any purchase, lists the 1991 home schedule on back. It is claimed that only 5,000 sets were produced. Card fronts are pale yellow and feature a close-up black and white player photo in a circle surrounded by palm branches. A gold banner with the words "1891 Stanford Football 1991" appears at bottom of picture while "All-Century Team" rounds out the top of picture. The player's name appears in a red stripe at the bottom of the card face. In mauve print on white, card backs have biographical information and sponsor logos at the bottom. The cards are unnumbered and checklisted below in alphabetical order.

|  | MINT | EXC | G-VG |
|---|---|---|---|
| COMPLETE SET (100) | 75.00 | 30.00 | 7.50 |
| COMMON CARD (1-100) | .75 | .30 | .07 |
| ☐ 1 Frankie Albert | 1.00 | .40 | .10 |
| ☐ 2 Lester Archambeau | .75 | .30 | .07 |
| ☐ 3 Bruno Banducci | .75 | .30 | .07 |
| ☐ 4 Benny Barnes | 1.00 | .40 | .10 |
| ☐ 5 Guy Benjamin | 2.00 | .80 | .20 |
| ☐ 6 Mike Boryla | 1.25 | .50 | .12 |
| ☐ 7 Marty Brill | .75 | .30 | .07 |
| ☐ 8 John Brodie | 6.00 | 2.40 | .60 |
| ☐ 9 Jackie Brown | .75 | .30 | .07 |
| ☐ 10 George Buehler | .75 | .30 | .07 |
| ☐ 11 Don Bunce | 1.25 | .50 | .12 |
| ☐ 12 Chris Burford | 1.25 | .50 | .12 |
| ☐ 13 Walter Camp CO | 2.00 | .80 | .20 |
| ☐ 14 Gordy Ceresino | .75 | .30 | .07 |
| ☐ 15 Jack Chapple | .75 | .30 | .07 |
| ☐ 16 Toi Cook | 1.25 | .50 | .12 |
| ☐ 17 Bill Corbus | .75 | .30 | .07 |
| ☐ 18 Steve Dils | 2.00 | .80 | .20 |
| ☐ 19 Pat Donovan | 1.50 | .60 | .15 |
| ☐ 20 John Elway | 20.00 | 8.00 | 2.00 |
| ☐ 21 Chuck Evans | .75 | .30 | .07 |
| ☐ 22 Skip Face | .75 | .30 | .07 |
| ☐ 23 Hugh Gallarneau | .75 | .30 | .07 |
| ☐ 24 Rod Garcia | .75 | .30 | .07 |
| ☐ 25 Bob Garrett | .75 | .30 | .07 |
| ☐ 26 Rick Gervais | .75 | .30 | .07 |
| ☐ 27 John Gillory | .75 | .30 | .07 |
| ☐ 28 Bobby Grayson | 1.00 | .40 | .10 |
| ☐ 29 Bones Hamilton | 1.00 | .40 | .10 |
| ☐ 30 Ray Handley | 1.50 | .60 | .15 |
| ☐ 31 Mark Harmon | 1.50 | .60 | .15 |
| ☐ 32 Marv Harris | .75 | .30 | .07 |
| ☐ 33 Emile Harry | 1.00 | .40 | .10 |
| ☐ 34 Tony Hill | 2.00 | .80 | .20 |
| ☐ 35 Brian Holloway | 1.25 | .50 | .12 |
| ☐ 36 John Hopkins | .75 | .30 | .07 |
| ☐ 37 Dick Horn | .75 | .30 | .07 |
| ☐ 38 Jeff James | 1.00 | .40 | .10 |
| ☐ 39 Gary Kerkorian | .75 | .30 | .07 |
| ☐ 40 Gordon King | 1.00 | .40 | .10 |
| ☐ 41 Younger Klippert | .75 | .30 | .07 |
| ☐ 42 Pete Kmetovic | .75 | .30 | .07 |
| ☐ 43 Jim Lawson | .75 | .30 | .07 |
| ☐ 44 Pete Lazetich | .75 | .30 | .07 |
| ☐ 45 Dave Lewis | 1.00 | .40 | .10 |
| ☐ 46 Vic Lindskog | .75 | .30 | .07 |
| ☐ 47 James Lofton | 6.00 | 2.40 | .60 |
| ☐ 48 Ken Margerum | 1.25 | .50 | .12 |
| ☐ 49 Ed McCaffrey | 2.00 | .80 | .20 |
| ☐ 50 Charles McCloud | .75 | .30 | .07 |
| ☐ 51 Bill McColl | 1.00 | .40 | .10 |
| ☐ 52 Duncan McColl | .75 | .30 | .07 |
| ☐ 53 Milt McColl | .75 | .30 | .07 |
| ☐ 54 Jim Merlo | 1.00 | .40 | .10 |
| ☐ 55 Phil Moffatt | .75 | .30 | .07 |
| ☐ 56 Bob Moore | 1.00 | .40 | .10 |
| ☐ 57 Sam Morley | .75 | .30 | .07 |
| ☐ 58 Monk Moscrip | .75 | .30 | .07 |
| ☐ 59 Brad Muster | 2.50 | 1.00 | .25 |
| ☐ 60 Ken Naber | .75 | .30 | .07 |
| ☐ 61 Darrin Nelson | 2.00 | .80 | .20 |
| ☐ 62 Ernie Nevers | 3.00 | 1.20 | .30 |
| ☐ 63 Dick Norman | .75 | .30 | .07 |
| ☐ 64 Blaine Nye | 1.25 | .50 | .12 |
| ☐ 65 Don Parish | .75 | .30 | .07 |
| ☐ 66 John Paye | 2.00 | .80 | .20 |
| ☐ 67 Gary Pettigrew | .75 | .30 | .07 |
| ☐ 68 Jim Plunkett | 5.00 | 2.00 | .50 |
| ☐ 69 Randy Poltl | .75 | .30 | .07 |
| ☐ 70 Seraphim Post | .75 | .30 | .07 |
| ☐ 71 John Ralston CO | 1.25 | .50 | .12 |
| ☐ 72 Bob Reynolds | .75 | .30 | .07 |
| ☐ 73 Don Robesky | .75 | .30 | .07 |
| ☐ 74 Doug Robison | .75 | .30 | .07 |
| ☐ 75 Greg Sampson | .75 | .30 | .07 |
| ☐ 76 John Sande | .75 | .30 | .07 |
| ☐ 77 Turk Schonert | 2.00 | .80 | .20 |
| ☐ 78 Jack Schultz | .75 | .30 | .07 |
| ☐ 79 Clark Shaughnessy CO | 1.25 | .50 | .12 |
| ☐ 80 Ted Shipkey | .75 | .30 | .07 |
| ☐ 81 Jeff Siemon | 2.00 | .80 | .20 |
| ☐ 82 Andy Sinclair | .75 | .30 | .07 |
| ☐ 83 Malcolm Snider | 1.00 | .40 | .10 |
| ☐ 84 Norm Standlee | 1.00 | .40 | .10 |
| ☐ 85 Roger Stillwell | .75 | .30 | .07 |
| ☐ 86 Chuck Taylor CO | .75 | .30 | .07 |
| ☐ 87 Dink Templeton | .75 | .30 | .07 |
| ☐ 88 Tiny Thornhill CO | .75 | .30 | .07 |
| ☐ 89 Dave Tipton | .75 | .30 | .07 |
| ☐ 90 Keith Topping | .75 | .30 | .07 |
| ☐ 91 Randy Vataha | 1.50 | .60 | .15 |
| ☐ 92 Garin Veris | 1.25 | .50 | .12 |
| ☐ 93 Jon Volpe | 2.00 | .80 | .20 |
| ☐ 94 Bill Walsh CO | 4.00 | 1.60 | .40 |
| ☐ 95 Pop Warner CO | 2.00 | .80 | .20 |
| ☐ 96 Gene Washington | 2.00 | .80 | .20 |
| ☐ 97 Vincent White | .75 | .30 | .07 |
| ☐ 98 Paul Wiggin | 1.25 | .50 | .12 |
| ☐ 99 John Wilbur | 1.00 | .40 | .10 |
| ☐ 100 Dave Wyman | 1.25 | .50 | .12 |

## 1992 Stanford

5

**GLYN MILBURN**
Runningback

No. 5 – 6 NN, 175 Pounds, 9/19/71, Aurora, Santa Monica, CA Major: Poli. Sci.

A true All-America Candidate in 1992..."I expect to use Glyn as we used Darrin Nelson in 1977 and '78," said Bill Walsh. He added: Glyn is an excellent runner and receiver as well as being a great return man. He is without question one of the most talented players in college football." His 3,286 all-purpose yards place him fourth all-time at Stanford. He holds the single game all-purpose yards record at Stanford with 379 yards vs. California in 1990. In 1991 he was named Second-Team All-Pac-10 and First-Team Academic All-Pac-10. His cousin Rod Milburn won the gold medal in the 1972 Olympics.

| Year | Rushes | Yards | Average | TD's | Catches | Yards |
|---|---|---|---|---|---|---|
| 1990 | 152 | 729 | 4.8 | 5 | 48 | 632 |
| 1991 | 131 | 598 | 4.6 | 6 | 56 | 454 |
| TOTAL | 283 | 1,527 | 4.7 | 11 | 104 | 1,086 |

GLYN MILBURN     Runningback

This 35-card set was manufactured by High Step College Football Cards (Turlock, California) and measures the standard size (2 1/2" by 3 1/2"). The cards were given away individually at home games. Complete sets could be purchased for 10.00 at the Stanford Stadium, the Track House, or by mail order. Production was reportedly limited to 10,000 cards with only 7,500 being sold as complete sets. The cards were also available in five-card packs; the packs were .75 each and could only be purchased in lots of 20 for 15.00. The cards feature posed action color player photos with white borders. The player's name and position appear in the bottom border. The word "Stanford" is printed in brick-red with a white outline either at the top or bottom of the picture. The backs are white and carry biographical and statistical information and career highlights. The player's uniform number appears in a football icon at the upper right corner. The cards are unnumbered and checklisted below in alphabetical order. The key card in the set is Glyn Milburn.

|  | MINT | EXC | G-VG |
|---|---|---|---|
| COMPLETE SET (35) | 15.00 | 6.00 | 1.50 |
| COMMON CARD (1-35) | .35 | .14 | .03 |
| ☐ 1 Seyon Albert | .35 | .14 | .03 |
| ☐ 2 Estevan Avila | .50 | .20 | .05 |

| | | | |
|---|---|---|---|
| ☐ 3 Tyler Batson | .35 | .14 | .03 |
| ☐ 4 Guy Benjamin ACO | .60 | .24 | .06 |
| ☐ 5 David Calomese | .35 | .14 | .03 |
| ☐ 6 Mike Cook | .60 | .24 | .06 |
| ☐ 7 Chris Dalman | .35 | .14 | .03 |
| ☐ 8 Dave Garnett | .35 | .14 | .03 |
| ☐ 9 Ron George | .60 | .24 | .06 |
| ☐ 10 Darrien Gordon | 2.00 | .80 | .20 |
| ☐ 11 Tom Holmoe ACO | .60 | .24 | .06 |
| ☐ 12 Derron Klafter | .35 | .14 | .03 |
| ☐ 13 J.J. Lasley | .35 | .14 | .03 |
| ☐ 14 John Lynch | .50 | .20 | .05 |
| ☐ 15 Glyn Milburn | 6.00 | 2.40 | .60 |
| ☐ 16 Fernando Montes ACO | .35 | .14 | .03 |
| ☐ 17 Vince Otoupal | .35 | .14 | .03 |
| ☐ 18 Rick Pallow | .35 | .14 | .03 |
| ☐ 19 Ron Redell | .35 | .14 | .03 |
| ☐ 20 Aaron Rembisz | .35 | .14 | .03 |
| ☐ 21 Bill Ring ACO | .60 | .24 | .06 |
| ☐ 22 Ellery Roberts | .75 | .30 | .07 |
| ☐ 23 Scott Schuhmann ACO | .35 | .14 | .03 |
| ☐ 24 Terry Shea ACO | .35 | .14 | .03 |
| ☐ 25 Bill Singler ACO | .35 | .14 | .03 |
| ☐ 26 Paul Stonehouse | .35 | .14 | .03 |
| ☐ 27 Dave Tipton ACO | .35 | .14 | .03 |
| ☐ 28 Keena Turner ACO | .75 | .30 | .07 |
| ☐ 29 Fred vonAppen ACO | .35 | .14 | .03 |
| ☐ 30 Bill Walsh CO | 2.00 | .80 | .20 |
| ☐ 31 Ryan Wetnight | 2.00 | .80 | .20 |
| ☐ 32 Tom Williams | .35 | .14 | .03 |
| ☐ 33 Mike Wilson ACO | .50 | .20 | .05 |
| ☐ 34 Billy Wittman | .35 | .14 | .03 |
| ☐ 35 Checklist Card | .50 | .20 | .05 |

(J.J. Lasley)

## 1993 Stanford

These 18 standard-size (2 1/2" by 3 1/2") cards feature on their fronts color player action shots set within white borders. The player's name appears underneath the photo. The white horizonal back carries the player's name, position, number, and biography at the top. On the left is a player head shot, and on the right, the player's career highlights. The cards are unnumbered and checklisted below in alphabetical order.

| | MINT | EXC | G-VG |
|---|---|---|---|
| COMPLETE SET (18) | 10.00 | 4.00 | 1.00 |
| COMMON PLAYER (1-18) | .50 | .20 | .05 |
| | | | |
| ☐ 1 Jeff Bailey | .50 | .20 | .05 |
| ☐ 2 Parker Bailey | .50 | .20 | .05 |
| ☐ 3 Roger Boden | .50 | .20 | .05 |
| ☐ 4 Hartwell Brown | .50 | .20 | .05 |
| ☐ 5 Vaughn Bryant | .75 | .30 | .07 |
| ☐ 6 Brian Cassidy | .50 | .20 | .05 |
| ☐ 7 Glen Cavanaugh | .50 | .20 | .05 |
| ☐ 8 Kevin Garnett | .50 | .20 | .05 |
| ☐ 9 Mark Hatzenbuhler | .50 | .20 | .05 |
| ☐ 10 Steve Hoyem | .75 | .30 | .07 |
| ☐ 11 Mike Jerich | .50 | .20 | .05 |
| ☐ 12 Paul Nickel | .50 | .20 | .05 |
| ☐ 13 Toby Norwood | .75 | .30 | .07 |
| ☐ 14 Tyrone Parker | .75 | .30 | .07 |
| ☐ 15 Ellery Roberts | .75 | .30 | .07 |
| ☐ 16 David Shaw | .50 | .20 | .05 |
| ☐ 17 Bill Walsh CO | 1.50 | .60 | .15 |
| ☐ 18 Josh Wright | .50 | .20 | .05 |

## 1989 Syracuse Burger King

This 15-card set, featuring cards measuring approximately 2 1/2" by 3 1/2", was produced to honor members of the 1989 Syracuse football

team. This set includes an early card of Rob Moore. The fronts of the card have an action photo of the player along with the identification "Syracuse University 1989" and the players name while the back has biography and a safety tip. This set was sponsored by WYSR radio, Burger King, and Pepsi. Since the set is unnumbered, we have checklisted it in alphabetical order. The key card in the set is wide receiver Rob Moore.

| | MINT | EXC | G-VG |
|---|---|---|---|
| COMPLETE SET (15) | 15.00 | 6.00 | 1.50 |
| COMMON CARD (1-15) | 1.00 | .40 | .10 |
| | | | |
| ☐ 1 David Bavaro | 1.50 | .60 | .15 |
| ☐ 2 Blake Bednars | 1.00 | .40 | .10 |
| ☐ 3 Alban Brown | 1.00 | .40 | .10 |
| ☐ 4 Dan Burey | 1.00 | .40 | .10 |
| ☐ 5 Rob Burnett | 2.00 | .80 | .20 |
| ☐ 6 Fred DeRiggi | 1.00 | .40 | .10 |
| ☐ 7 John Flannery | 2.00 | .80 | .20 |
| ☐ 8 Duane Kinnon | 1.00 | .40 | .10 |
| ☐ 9 Dick MacPherson CO | 2.00 | .80 | .20 |
| ☐ 10 Rob Moore | 6.00 | 2.40 | .60 |
| ☐ 11 Michael Owens | 1.50 | .60 | .15 |
| ☐ 12 Bill Scharr | 1.00 | .40 | .10 |
| ☐ 13 Turnell Sims | 1.00 | .40 | .10 |
| ☐ 14 Sean Whiteman | 1.00 | .40 | .10 |
| ☐ 15 Terry Wooden | 2.00 | .80 | .20 |

## 1991 Syracuse Program Cards

The 1991 Syracuse football set was sponsored by Drumlins Travel and available as inserts in Syracuse University football game programs. Each perforated insert measures approximately 8" by 11" and displays three rows of three cards each. The top two rows consist of six approximately 2 5/8" by 3 1/2" player cards, while the third row has three cards with a sponsor advertisement, a 1991-92 basketball schedule, and the university's logo respectively. The player cards feature glossy color action photos bordered in white, with text reversed-out in white in a burnt orange stripe beneath the picture. The backs have biography, career summary, and an "Orange Tip" in the form of an anti-drug message. The cards are numbered on the back.

| | MINT | EXC | G-VG |
|---|---|---|---|
| COMPLETE SET (36) | 30.00 | 12.00 | 3.00 |
| COMMON CARD (1-36) | .75 | .30 | .07 |
| | | | |
| ☐ 1 George Rooks | .75 | .30 | .07 |
| ☐ 2 Marvin Graves | 4.00 | 1.60 | .40 |
| ☐ 3 Andrew Dees | .75 | .30 | .07 |
| ☐ 4 Glen Young | .75 | .30 | .07 |
| ☐ 5 Chris Gedney | 1.25 | .50 | .12 |
| ☐ 6 Paul Pasqualoni CO | 1.25 | .50 | .12 |
| ☐ 7 Terrence Wisdom | .75 | .30 | .07 |

| | MINT | EXC | G-VG |
|---|---|---|---|
| ☐ 8 John Biskup | .75 | .30 | .07 |
| ☐ 9 Mark McDonald | .75 | .30 | .07 |
| ☐ 10 Dan Conley | .75 | .30 | .07 |
| ☐ 11 Kevin Mitchell | .75 | .30 | .07 |
| ☐ 12 Qadry Ismail | 8.00 | 3.25 | .80 |
| ☐ 13 John Lusardi | .75 | .30 | .07 |
| ☐ 14 David Walker | .75 | .30 | .07 |
| ☐ 15 John Capachione | .75 | .30 | .07 |
| ☐ 16 Shelby Hill | 1.00 | .40 | .10 |
| ☐ 17 Dwayne Joseph | .75 | .30 | .07 |
| ☐ 18 Greg Walker | .75 | .30 | .07 |
| ☐ 19 Jerry Sharp | .75 | .30 | .07 |
| ☐ 20 Tim Sandquist | .75 | .30 | .07 |
| ☐ 21 Chuck Bull | .75 | .30 | .07 |
| ☐ 22 Jo Jo Wooden | .75 | .30 | .07 |
| ☐ 23 Terry Richardson | .75 | .30 | .07 |
| ☐ 24 Doug Womack | .75 | .30 | .07 |
| ☐ 25 Reggie Terry | .75 | .30 | .07 |
| ☐ 26 Garland Hawkins | .75 | .30 | .07 |
| ☐ 27 Tony Montemorra | .75 | .30 | .07 |
| ☐ 28 Chip Todd | .75 | .30 | .07 |
| ☐ 29 Pat O'Neill | .75 | .30 | .07 |
| ☐ 30 Kevin Barker | .75 | .30 | .07 |
| ☐ 31 John Reagan | .75 | .30 | .07 |
| ☐ 32 Pat O'Rourke | .75 | .30 | .07 |
| ☐ 33 Jim Wentworth | .75 | .30 | .07 |
| ☐ 34 Ernie Brown | .75 | .30 | .07 |
| ☐ 35 John Nilsen | .75 | .30 | .07 |
| ☐ 36 Al Wooten | .75 | .30 | .07 |

## 1980 Tennessee Police

John Warren
Punter

CRIME PREVENTION TIPS FROM THE VOLS

The 1980 Tennessee Police Set features 19 cards measuring approximately 2 5/8" by 4 3/16". The fronts have color photos bordered in white; the vertically oriented backs feature football terminology and safety tips. The cards are unnumbered, so they are listed alphabetically by subject's name.

| | MINT | EXC | G-VG |
|---|---|---|---|
| COMPLETE SET (19) | 45.00 | 18.00 | 4.50 |
| COMMON CARD (1-19) | 2.00 | .80 | .20 |
| | | | |
| ☐ 1 Bill Bates | 10.00 | 4.00 | 1.00 |
| ☐ 2 James Berry | 2.00 | .80 | .20 |
| ☐ 3 Chris Bolton | 2.00 | .80 | .20 |
| ☐ 4 Mike L. Cofer | 6.00 | 2.40 | .60 |
| ☐ 5 Glenn Ford | 2.00 | .80 | .20 |
| ☐ 6 Anthony Hancock | 5.00 | 2.00 | .50 |
| ☐ 7 Brian Ingram | 2.00 | .80 | .20 |
| ☐ 8 Tim Irwin | 3.00 | 1.20 | .30 |
| ☐ 9 Kenny Jones | 2.00 | .80 | .20 |
| ☐ 10 Wilbert Jones | 2.00 | .80 | .20 |
| ☐ 11 Johnny Majors CO | 4.00 | 1.60 | .40 |
| ☐ 12 Bill Marren | 2.00 | .80 | .20 |
| ☐ 13 Danny Martin | 2.00 | .80 | .20 |
| ☐ 14 Jim Noonan | 2.00 | .80 | .20 |
| ☐ 15 Lee North | 2.00 | .80 | .20 |
| ☐ 16 Hubert Simpson | 4.00 | 1.60 | .40 |
| ☐ 17 Danny Spradlin | 3.00 | 1.20 | .30 |
| ☐ 18 John Warren | 2.00 | .80 | .20 |
| ☐ 19 Brad White | 2.00 | .80 | .20 |

## 1990 Tennessee Centennial

The 1990 Tennessee Volunteers set contains 294 standard-size (2 1/2" by 3 1/2") cards. The fronts feature a mix of color or black and white player photos, enframed by orange borders. The player's name appears in a white stripe above the picture, and a Tennessee insignia with the words "100 Years of Volunteers" is superimposed at the

bottom of the picture. In a horizontal format, the backs have player profiles in black lettering overlaying an indistinct version of the same insignia as on the card fronts. The cards are numbered on the backs in both upper corners.

| | MINT | EXC | G-VG |
|---|---|---|---|
| COMPLETE SET (294) | 35.00 | 14.00 | 3.50 |
| COMMON CARD (1-294) | .10 | .04 | .01 |
| | | | |
| ☐ 1 Vince Moore | .25 | .10 | .02 |
| ☐ 2 Steve Matthews | .10 | .04 | .01 |
| ☐ 3 Joey Chapman | .10 | .04 | .01 |
| ☐ 4 Terence Cleveland | .10 | .04 | .01 |
| ☐ 5 Thomas Wood | .10 | .04 | .01 |
| ☐ 6 J.J. McCleskey | .10 | .04 | .01 |
| ☐ 7 Jason Julian | .25 | .10 | .02 |
| ☐ 8 Andy Kelly | .25 | .10 | .02 |
| ☐ 9 Derrick Folsom | .10 | .04 | .01 |
| ☐ 10 Chip McCallum | .10 | .04 | .01 |
| ☐ 11 Lloyd Kerr | .10 | .04 | .01 |
| ☐ 12 Cory Fleming | .50 | .20 | .05 |
| ☐ 13 Kevin Zurcher | .10 | .04 | .01 |
| ☐ 14 Lee England | .10 | .04 | .01 |
| ☐ 15 Carl Pickens | 1.50 | .60 | .15 |
| ☐ 16 Sterling Henton | .10 | .04 | .01 |
| ☐ 17 Lee Wood | .10 | .04 | .01 |
| ☐ 18 Kent Elmore | .10 | .04 | .01 |
| ☐ 19 Craig Faulkner | .10 | .04 | .01 |
| ☐ 20 Keith Denson | .10 | .04 | .01 |
| ☐ 21 Preston Warren | .10 | .04 | .01 |
| ☐ 22 Floyd Miley | .10 | .04 | .01 |
| ☐ 23 Earnest Fields | .10 | .04 | .01 |
| ☐ 24 Tony Thompson | .10 | .04 | .01 |
| ☐ 25 Jeremy Lincoln | .35 | .14 | .03 |
| ☐ 26 David Bennett | .10 | .04 | .01 |
| ☐ 27 Greg Burke | .10 | .04 | .01 |
| ☐ 28 Tavio Henson | .10 | .04 | .01 |
| ☐ 29 Kevin Wendelboe | .10 | .04 | .01 |
| ☐ 30 Cedric Kline | .10 | .04 | .01 |
| ☐ 31 Keith Jeter | .10 | .04 | .01 |
| ☐ 32 Chris Russ | .10 | .04 | .01 |
| ☐ 33 DeWayne Dotson | .10 | .04 | .01 |
| ☐ 34 Mike Rapien | .10 | .04 | .01 |
| ☐ 35 Clemons McCroskey | .10 | .04 | .01 |
| ☐ 36 Mark Fletcher | .10 | .04 | .01 |
| ☐ 37 Chuck Smith | .25 | .10 | .02 |
| ☐ 38 Jeff Tullis | .10 | .04 | .01 |
| ☐ 39 Kelly Days | .10 | .04 | .01 |
| ☐ 40 Shazzon Bradley | .10 | .04 | .01 |
| ☐ 41 Reggie Ingram | .10 | .04 | .01 |
| ☐ 42 Roland Poles | .10 | .04 | .01 |
| ☐ 43 Tracy Smith | .10 | .04 | .01 |
| ☐ 44 Chuck Webb | .50 | .20 | .05 |
| ☐ 45 Shon Walker | .25 | .10 | .02 |
| ☐ 46 Eric Riffer | .10 | .04 | .01 |
| ☐ 47 Greg Amsler | .10 | .04 | .01 |
| ☐ 48 J.J. Surlas | .10 | .04 | .01 |
| ☐ 49 Brian Bradley | .15 | .06 | .01 |
| ☐ 50 Tom Myslinski | .15 | .06 | .01 |
| ☐ 51 John Fisher | .10 | .04 | .01 |
| ☐ 52 Craig Martin | .10 | .04 | .01 |
| ☐ 53 Carey Bailey | .10 | .04 | .01 |
| ☐ 54 Houston Thomas | .10 | .04 | .01 |
| ☐ 55 Ryan Patterson | .10 | .04 | .01 |
| ☐ 56 Chad Goodin | .10 | .04 | .01 |
| ☐ 57 Brian Spivey | .10 | .04 | .01 |
| ☐ 58 Todd Kelly | .10 | .04 | .01 |
| ☐ 59 Mike Stowell | .10 | .04 | .01 |
| ☐ 60 Jim Fenwick | .10 | .04 | .01 |
| ☐ 61 Marc Jones | .10 | .04 | .01 |
| ☐ 62 Chris Ragan | .10 | .04 | .01 |
| ☐ 63 Rodney Gordon | .10 | .04 | .01 |
| ☐ 64 Mark Needham | .10 | .04 | .01 |
| ☐ 65 Patrick Lenoir | .10 | .04 | .01 |
| ☐ 66 Martin Williams | .10 | .04 | .01 |
| ☐ 67 Brad Seiber | .10 | .04 | .01 |
| ☐ 68 Larry Smith | .10 | .04 | .01 |

| | | | |
|---|---|---|---|
| ☐ 69 Jerry Teel | .10 | .04 | .01 |
| ☐ 70 Charles McRae | .50 | .20 | .05 |
| ☐ 71 Rex Hargrove | .10 | .04 | .01 |
| ☐ 72 James Wilson | .10 | .04 | .01 |
| ☐ 73 Doug Baird | .10 | .04 | .01 |
| ☐ 74 Mark Moore | .10 | .04 | .01 |
| ☐ 75 Lance Nelson | .10 | .04 | .01 |
| ☐ 76 Robert Todd | .10 | .04 | .01 |
| ☐ 77 Greg Gerardi | .10 | .04 | .01 |
| ☐ 78 Antone Davis | .50 | .20 | .05 |
| ☐ 79 Eric Still | .10 | .04 | .01 |
| ☐ 80 Anthony Morgan | .60 | .24 | .06 |
| ☐ 81 Alvin Harper | 2.00 | .80 | .20 |
| ☐ 82 Charles Longmire | .10 | .04 | .01 |
| ☐ 83 Mark Adams | .10 | .04 | .01 |
| ☐ 84 Chris Benson | .10 | .04 | .01 |
| ☐ 85 Horace Morris | .10 | .04 | .01 |
| ☐ 86 Harlan Davis | .10 | .04 | .01 |
| ☐ 87 Darryl Hardy | .10 | .04 | .01 |
| ☐ 88 Tracy Hayworth | .20 | .08 | .02 |
| ☐ 89 Von Reeves | .10 | .04 | .01 |
| ☐ 90 Marion Hobby | .10 | .04 | .01 |
| ☐ 91 John Ward ANN | .10 | .04 | .01 |
| ☐ 92 Roderick Lewis | .10 | .04 | .01 |
| ☐ 93 Orion McCants | .10 | .04 | .01 |
| ☐ 94 James Warren | .10 | .04 | .01 |
| ☐ 95 Mario Brunson | .10 | .04 | .01 |
| ☐ 96 Joe Davis | .10 | .04 | .01 |
| ☐ 97 Shawn Truss | .10 | .04 | .01 |
| ☐ 98 Keith Steed | .10 | .04 | .01 |
| ☐ 99 Kacy Rodgers | .10 | .04 | .01 |
| ☐ 100 Johnny Majors CO | .20 | .08 | .02 |
| ☐ 101 Phillip Fulmer CO | .25 | .10 | .02 |
| ☐ 102 Larry Lacewell CO | .15 | .06 | .01 |
| ☐ 103 Charlie Coe CO | .10 | .04 | .01 |
| ☐ 104 Tommy West CO | .10 | .04 | .01 |
| ☐ 105 David Cutcliffe CO | .10 | .04 | .01 |
| ☐ 106 Jack Sells CO | .10 | .04 | .01 |
| ☐ 107 Rex Norris CO | .10 | .04 | .01 |
| ☐ 108 John Chavis CO | .10 | .04 | .01 |
| ☐ 109 Tim Keane CO | .10 | .04 | .01 |
| ☐ 110 Tim Mingey | .10 | .04 | .01 |
| Recruiter | | | |
| ☐ 111 Bill Higdon | .10 | .04 | .01 |
| Sr. Admin. Asst. | | | |
| ☐ 112 Tim Kerin TR | .10 | .04 | .01 |
| ☐ 113 Bruno Pauletto CO | .10 | .04 | .01 |
| ☐ 114 Vols 17, Co.State 14 | .25 | .10 | .02 |
| (Chuck Webb) | | | |
| ☐ 115 Vols 24, UCLA 6 | .25 | .10 | .02 |
| (Chuck Webb) | | | |
| ☐ 116 Vols 28, Duke 6 | .10 | .04 | .01 |
| (Game action photo) | | | |
| ☐ 117 Vols 21, Auburn 14 | .10 | .04 | .01 |
| (Game action photo) | | | |
| ☐ 118 Vols 17, Georgia 14 | .10 | .04 | .01 |
| (Jason Julian) | | | |
| ☐ 119 Vols 30, Alabama 47 | .10 | .04 | .01 |
| (Roland Poles) | | | |
| ☐ 120 Vols 45, LSU 39 | .20 | .08 | .02 |
| (Charles McRae) | | | |
| ☐ 121 Vols 52, Akron 9 | .10 | .04 | .01 |
| (Brian Spivey) | | | |
| ☐ 122 Vols 33, Ole Miss 21 | .35 | .14 | .03 |
| (Alvin Harper) | | | |
| ☐ 123 Vols 31, Kentucky 10 | .10 | .04 | .01 |
| (Kelly Days) | | | |
| ☐ 124 Vols 17, Vanderbilt 10 | .10 | .04 | .01 |
| (Game action photo) | | | |
| ☐ 125 '90 Mobil Cotton | .10 | .04 | .01 |
| Bowl 1 (Jason Julian) | | | |
| ☐ 126 '90 Mobil Cotton | .15 | .06 | .01 |
| Bowl 2 (Andy Kelly) | | | |
| ☐ 127 '90 Mobil Cotton | .25 | .10 | .02 |
| Bowl 3 (Chuck Webb) | | | |
| ☐ 128 '90 Mobil Cotton | .10 | .04 | .01 |
| Bowl 4 (Scoreboard) | | | |
| ☐ 129 Eric Still | .10 | .04 | .01 |
| ☐ 130 Chris Benson | .10 | .04 | .01 |
| ☐ 131 Preston Warren | .10 | .04 | .01 |
| ☐ 132 Lee England | .10 | .04 | .01 |
| ☐ 133 Kent Elmore | .10 | .04 | .01 |
| ☐ 134 Eric Still | .10 | .04 | .01 |
| ☐ 135 Chuck Webb | .50 | .20 | .05 |
| ☐ 136 Marion Hobby | .10 | .04 | .01 |
| ☐ 137 Kent Elmore | .10 | .04 | .01 |
| ☐ 138 Antone Davis | .50 | .20 | .05 |
| ☐ 139 Thomas Woods | .10 | .04 | .01 |
| ☐ 140 Charles McRae | .50 | .20 | .05 |
| ☐ 141 Preston Warren | .10 | .04 | .01 |
| ☐ 142 Darryl Hardy | .10 | .04 | .01 |
| ☐ 143 Offense or Defense | .50 | .20 | .05 |
| (Carl Pickens) | | | |
| ☐ 144 Carl Pickens | 1.50 | .60 | .15 |
| ☐ 145 Chuck Webb | .50 | .20 | .05 |
| ☐ 146 Thomas Woods | .10 | .04 | .01 |
| ☐ 147 Total Offense Game | .15 | .06 | .01 |

| | | | |
|---|---|---|---|
| (Andy Kelly) | | | |
| ☐ 148 The TVA | .10 | .04 | .01 |
| (Offensive Line) | | | |
| ☐ 149 Smokey (Mascot) | .10 | .04 | .01 |
| ☐ 150 Doug Dickey | .15 | .06 | .01 |
| Director of Athletics | | | |
| ☐ 151 Neyland Stadium | .10 | .04 | .01 |
| ☐ 152 Neyland-Thompson Ctr | .10 | .04 | .01 |
| ☐ 153 Gibbs Hall | .10 | .04 | .01 |
| (Dormitory) | | | |
| ☐ 154 Academics and | .10 | .04 | .01 |
| Athletics | | | |
| (Carmen Tegano Asst.AD) | | | |
| ☐ 155 Gene McEver HOF | .10 | .04 | .01 |
| ☐ 156 Beattie Feathers HOF | .35 | .14 | .03 |
| ☐ 157 Robert Neyland HOF CO | .25 | .10 | .02 |
| ☐ 158 Herman Hickman HOF | .15 | .06 | .01 |
| ☐ 159 Bowden Wyatt HOF | .15 | .06 | .01 |
| ☐ 160 Hank Lauricella HOF | .15 | .06 | .01 |
| ☐ 161 Doug Atkins HOF | .35 | .14 | .03 |
| ☐ 162 Johnny Majors HOF | .25 | .10 | .02 |
| ☐ 163 Bobby Dodd HOF | .25 | .10 | .02 |
| ☐ 164 Bob Suffridge HOF | .15 | .06 | .01 |
| ☐ 165 Nathan Dougherty HOF | .15 | .06 | .01 |
| ☐ 166 George Cafego HOF | .15 | .06 | .01 |
| ☐ 167 Bob Johnson HOF | .20 | .08 | .02 |
| ☐ 168 Ed Molinski HOF | .15 | .06 | .01 |
| ☐ 169 Reggie White | 1.50 | .60 | .15 |
| ☐ 170 Willie Gault | .60 | .24 | .06 |
| ☐ 171 Doug Atkins | .35 | .14 | .03 |
| ☐ 172 Keith DeLong | .25 | .10 | .02 |
| ☐ 173 Ron Widby | .20 | .08 | .02 |
| ☐ 174 Bill Johnson | .20 | .08 | .02 |
| ☐ 175 Jack Reynolds | .30 | .12 | .03 |
| ☐ 176 Tim McGee | .40 | .16 | .04 |
| ☐ 177 Harry Galbreath | .20 | .08 | .02 |
| ☐ 178 Roland James | .20 | .08 | .02 |
| ☐ 179 Abe Shires | .10 | .04 | .01 |
| ☐ 180 Ted Daffer | .10 | .04 | .01 |
| ☐ 181 Bob Foxx | .10 | .04 | .01 |
| ☐ 182 Richmond Flowers | .25 | .10 | .02 |
| ☐ 183 Beattie Feathers | .25 | .10 | .02 |
| ☐ 184 Condredge Holloway | .35 | .14 | .03 |
| ☐ 185 Larry Sievers | .20 | .08 | .02 |
| ☐ 186 Johnnie Jones | .10 | .04 | .01 |
| ☐ 187 Carl Zander | .20 | .08 | .02 |
| ☐ 188 Dale Jones | .10 | .04 | .01 |
| ☐ 189 Bruce Wilkerson | .10 | .04 | .01 |
| ☐ 190 Terry McDaniel | .30 | .12 | .03 |
| ☐ 191 Craig Colquitt | .20 | .08 | .02 |
| ☐ 192 Stanley Morgan | .75 | .30 | .07 |
| ☐ 193 Curt Watson | .10 | .04 | .01 |
| ☐ 194 Bobby Majors | .10 | .04 | .01 |
| ☐ 195 Steve Kiner | .20 | .08 | .02 |
| ☐ 196 Paul Naumoff | .20 | .08 | .02 |
| ☐ 197 Bud Sherrod | .10 | .04 | .01 |
| ☐ 198 Murray Warmath | .20 | .08 | .02 |
| ☐ 199 Steve DeLong | .20 | .08 | .02 |
| ☐ 200 Bill Pearman | .10 | .04 | .01 |
| ☐ 201 Bobby Gordon | .10 | .04 | .01 |
| ☐ 202 John Michels | .10 | .04 | .01 |
| ☐ 203 Bill Mayo | .10 | .04 | .01 |
| ☐ 204 Andy Kozar | .10 | .04 | .01 |
| ☐ 205 1892 Volunteers | .15 | .06 | .01 |
| (Team photo) | | | |
| ☐ 206 1900 Volunteers | .15 | .06 | .01 |
| (Team photo) | | | |
| ☐ 207 1905 Volunteers | .15 | .06 | .01 |
| (Team photo) | | | |
| ☐ 208 1907 Volunteers | .15 | .06 | .01 |
| (Individual player photos) | | | |
| ☐ 209 1916 Volunteers | .15 | .06 | .01 |
| (Team photo) | | | |
| ☐ 210 1914 Volunteers | .15 | .06 | .01 |
| (Team photo) | | | |
| ☐ 211 1896 Volunteers | .15 | .06 | .01 |
| (Team photo) | | | |
| ☐ 212 1908 Volunteers | .15 | .06 | .01 |
| (Team photo) | | | |
| ☐ 213 1926 Volunteers | .15 | .06 | .01 |
| (Team photo) | | | |
| ☐ 214 1930 Volunteers | .15 | .06 | .01 |
| (Team photo) | | | |
| ☐ 215 1934 Volunteers | .15 | .06 | .01 |
| (Team photo) | | | |
| ☐ 216 1938 Volunteers | .15 | .06 | .01 |
| (Team photo) | | | |
| ☐ 217 1940 Volunteers | .15 | .06 | .01 |
| (Team photo) | | | |
| ☐ 218 1944 Volunteers | .15 | .06 | .01 |
| (Team photo) | | | |
| ☐ 219 1945 Volunteers | .15 | .06 | .01 |
| (Team photo) | | | |
| ☐ 220 1954 Volunteers | .15 | .06 | .01 |
| (Team photo) | | | |
| ☐ 221 1969 Volunteers | .15 | .06 | .01 |
| (Team photo) | | | |
| ☐ 222 1962 Volunteers | .15 | .06 | .01 |

| | | MINT | EXC | G-VG |
|---|---|---|---|---|

☐ 223 1976 Volunteers........................ .15 .06 .01
(Team photo)
☐ 224 1985 Volunteers........................ .15 .06 .01
(Team photo)
☐ 225 1978 Volunteers........................ .15 .06 .01
(Team photo)
☐ 226 1980 Volunteeeers.................... .15 .06 .01
(Team photo)
☐ 227 1984 Volunteers........................ .15 .06 .01
(Team photo)
☐ 228 1988 Volunteers........................ .15 .06 .01
(Team photo)
☐ 229 James Baird ............................ .10 .04 .01
☐ 230 Condredge Holloway ............. .35 .14 .03
☐ 231 J.G. Lowe ............................... .10 .04 .01
☐ 232 E.A. McLean............................ .10 .04 .01
☐ 233 Lemont Holt Jeffers ............... .10 .04 .01
☐ 234 Howard Johnson...................... .10 .04 .01
☐ 235 Malcolm Aiken ........................ .10 .04 .01
☐ 236 Toby Palmer............................ .10 .04 .01
☐ 237 Sam Bartholomew.................... .10 .04 .01
☐ 238 Ray Graves ............................. .10 .04 .01
☐ 239 Billy Bevis .............................. .10 .04 .01
☐ 240 Bert Rechichar........................ .20 .08 .02
☐ 241 Jim Beutel .............................. .10 .04 .01
☐ 242 Mike Lucci............................... .25 .10 .02
☐ 243 Hal Wantland............................ .10 .04 .01
☐ 244 Jackie Walker .......................... .10 .04 .01
☐ 245 Ron McCartney ........................ .10 .04 .01
☐ 246 Robert Shaw ........................... .25 .10 .02
☐ 247 Lee North ............................... .10 .04 .01
☐ 248 James Berry ............................ .10 .04 .01
☐ 249 Carl Zander ............................ .20 .08 .02
☐ 250 Chris White ............................ .10 .04 .01
☐ 251 Tommy Sims ........................... .10 .04 .01
☐ 252 Tim McGee .............................. .40 .16 .04
☐ 253 Keith DeLong .......................... .25 .10 .02
☐ 254 1931 NY Charity Game........... .10 .04 .01
(Program)
☐ 255 1941 Sugar Bowl ................... .10 .04 .01
(Program)
☐ 256 1945 Rose Bowl ..................... .10 .04 .01
(Program)
☐ 257 1957 Gator Bowl ................... .10 .04 .01
(Program)
☐ 258 1968 Orange Bowl ................. .10 .04 .01
(Program)
☐ 259 1972 Bluebonnet Bowl .......... .10 .04 .01
(Program)
☐ 260 1981 Garden State ................ .10 .04 .01
Bowl (Program)
☐ 261 1968 Sugar Bowl ................... .10 .04 .01
(Program)
☐ 262 Checklist 1-76 ....................... .15 .06 .01
☐ 263 Checklist 77-152 .................... .15 .06 .01
☐ 264 Checklist 153-228 .................. .15 .06 .01
☐ 265 Checklist 229-294 .................. .15 .06 .01
☐ 266 Chris White ............................ .10 .04 .01
☐ 267 Kelsey Finch ........................... .10 .04 .01
☐ 268 Johnnie Jones ......................... .10 .04 .01
☐ 269 Johnnie Jones ......................... .10 .04 .01
☐ 270 Curt Watson ........................... .10 .04 .01
☐ 271 William Howard ....................... .10 .04 .01
☐ 272 Bubba Wyche .......................... .60 .24 .06
☐ 273 Tony Robinson ........................ .35 .14 .03
☐ 274 Daryl Dickey ........................... .30 .12 .03
☐ 275 Alan Cockrell To ..................... .35 .14 .03
Willie Gault
☐ 276 Alan Cockrell .......................... .35 .14 .03
☐ 277 Bobby Scott ............................ .35 .14 .03
☐ 278 Tony Robinson ........................ .35 .14 .03
☐ 279 Jeff Francis ............................. .20 .08 .02
☐ 280 Alvin Harper ........................... 2.00 .80 .20
☐ 281 Johnny Mills ........................... .10 .04 .01
☐ 282 Thomas Woods ........................ .10 .04 .01
☐ 283 Bob Lund ................................ .10 .04 .01
☐ 284 Gene McEver .......................... .10 .04 .01
☐ 285 Stanley Morgan....................... .75 .30 .07
☐ 286 Fuad Reveiz ............................ .15 .06 .01
☐ 287 Kent Elmore ........................... .10 .04 .01
☐ 288 Jimmy Colquitt......................... .10 .04 .01
☐ 289 Willie Gault ............................ .60 .24 .06
☐ 290 100 Years ............................... .50 .20 .05
Celebration
(Reggie White)
☐ 291 The 100 Years Kickoff ........... .15 .06 .01
(Group photo)
☐ 292 Like Father, Like Son............. .25 .10 .02
Keith DeLong
Steve DeLong
☐ 293 Offense and Defense ............. .25 .10 .02
Raleigh McKenzie
Reggie McKenzie
☐ 294 It's Football Time ................. .15 .06 .01
(1990 schedule on back)

# 1991 Tennessee Hoby

This 42-card set was produced by Hoby and features the 1991 Tennessee football team. Five hundred uncut press sheets were also produced, and they were signed and numbered by Johnny Majors. The standard size (2 1/2" by 3 1/2") cards feature on the fronts a mix of posed and action color photos, with thin white borders on a royal blue card face. The school logo appears in the lower left corner in an orange circle, with the player's name in a gold stripe extending to the right. On a light orange background, the backs carry biography, player profile, or statistics. The cards are numbered on the back and are ordered alphabetically by player. Several NFL players make their first card appearance in this set: Dale Carter, Chris Mims, Carl Pickens, and Heath Shuler.

| | MINT | EXC | G-VG |
|---|---|---|---|
| COMPLETE SET (42)....................... | 20.00 | 8.00 | 2.00 |
| COMMON CARD (397-438)............. | .25 | .10 | .02 |
| ☐ 397 Mark Adams...................... | .25 | .10 | .02 |
| ☐ 398 Carey Bailey..................... | .25 | .10 | .02 |
| ☐ 399 David Bennett.................... | .25 | .10 | .02 |
| ☐ 400 Shazzon Bradley................ | .25 | .10 | .02 |
| ☐ 401 Kenneth Campbell.............. | .25 | .10 | .02 |
| ☐ 402 Dale Carter....................... | 1.00 | .40 | .10 |
| ☐ 403 Joey Chapman .................. | .25 | .10 | .02 |
| ☐ 404 Jerry Colquitt.................... | .25 | .10 | .02 |
| ☐ 405 Bernard Daffney................. | .35 | .14 | .03 |
| ☐ 406 Craig Faulkner................... | .25 | .10 | .02 |
| ☐ 407 Earnest Fields................... | .25 | .10 | .02 |
| ☐ 408 John Fisher....................... | .25 | .10 | .02 |
| ☐ 409 Cory Fleming..................... | .75 | .30 | .07 |
| ☐ 410 Mark Fletcher.................... | .25 | .10 | .02 |
| ☐ 411 Tom Fuhler........................ | .25 | .10 | .02 |
| ☐ 412 Johnny Majors CO.............. | .50 | .20 | .05 |
| ☐ 413 Darryl Hardy...................... | .25 | .10 | .02 |
| ☐ 414 Aaron Hayden.................... | .25 | .10 | .02 |
| ☐ 415 Tavio Henson..................... | .25 | .10 | .02 |
| ☐ 416 Reggie Ingram................... | .25 | .10 | .02 |
| ☐ 417 Andy Kelly........................ | .60 | .24 | .06 |
| ☐ 418 Todd Kelly........................ | .25 | .10 | .02 |
| ☐ 419 Patrick Lenoir.................... | .25 | .10 | .02 |
| ☐ 420 Roderick Lewis.................. | .25 | .10 | .02 |
| ☐ 421 Jeremy Lincoln.................. | .50 | .20 | .05 |
| ☐ 422 J.J. McCleskey................... | .25 | .10 | .02 |
| ☐ 423 Floyd Miley....................... | .25 | .10 | .02 |
| ☐ 424 Chris Mims....................... | 1.25 | .50 | .12 |
| ☐ 425 Tom Myslinski.................... | .35 | .14 | .03 |
| ☐ 426 Carl Pickens..................... | 2.00 | .80 | .20 |
| ☐ 427 Roc Powe.......................... | .25 | .10 | .02 |
| ☐ 428 Von Reeves....................... | .25 | .10 | .02 |
| ☐ 429 Eric Riffer......................... | .25 | .10 | .02 |
| ☐ 430 Kacy Rodgers.................... | .25 | .10 | .02 |
| ☐ 431 Steve Session................... | .25 | .10 | .02 |
| ☐ 432 Heath Shuler..................... | 10.00 | 4.00 | 1.00 |
| ☐ 433 Chuck Smith...................... | .25 | .10 | .02 |
| ☐ 434 James Stewart................... | .25 | .10 | .02 |
| ☐ 435 Mike Stowell...................... | .25 | .10 | .02 |
| ☐ 436 J.J. Surlas........................ | .25 | .10 | .02 |
| ☐ 437 Shon Walker ..................... | .35 | .14 | .03 |
| ☐ 438 James Wilson.................... | .25 | .10 | .02 |

# 1991 Texas HS Legends

This 25-card set was sponsored by Pepsi and issued by the Texas High School Football Hall of Fame. Apparently the set was sold in five five-card packs; each pack featured four player cards and a numbered cover card. The cards measure the standard size (2 1/2" by 3 1/2"). On a black card face, the fronts feature sepia-toned player photos. The words "Texas High School Football Legend" and logos adorn the top of the front, while the player's name, high school, and years attended are presented below the picture. In red and blue print on a white panel,

the backs carry biographical information, career summary under four subheadings (performance chart; college/pro honors; unforgettable moment; expert opinion), and the player's signature. The cards are unnumbered and checklisted below in alphabetical order, with the cover cards listed at the end.

|  | MINT | EXC | G-VG |
|---|---|---|---|
| COMPLETE SET (25) | 12.50 | 5.00 | 1.25 |
| COMMON CARD (1-25) | .50 | .20 | .05 |

| | | MINT | EXC | G-VG |
|---|---|---|---|---|
| ☐ 1 | Marty Akins | .50 | .20 | .05 |
| ☐ 2 | Gil Bartosh | .50 | .20 | .05 |
| ☐ 3 | Bill Bradley | .75 | .30 | .07 |
| ☐ 4 | Chris Gilbert | 1.00 | .40 | .10 |
| ☐ 5 | Glynn Gregory | .75 | .30 | .07 |
| ☐ 6 | Charlie Haas | .50 | .20 | .05 |
| ☐ 7 | Craig James | 1.50 | .60 | .15 |
| ☐ 8 | Boody Johnson | .50 | .20 | .05 |
| ☐ 9 | Ernie Koy Jr. | .75 | .30 | .07 |
| ☐ 10 | Glenn Lippman | .50 | .20 | .05 |
| ☐ 11 | Jack Pardee | 1.00 | .40 | .10 |
| ☐ 12 | Billy Patterson | .50 | .20 | .05 |
| ☐ 13 | Billy Sims | 2.00 | .80 | .20 |
| ☐ 14 | Byron Townsend | .50 | .20 | .05 |
| ☐ 15 | Doyle Traylor | .50 | .20 | .05 |
| ☐ 16 | Joe Washington Jr. | 1.00 | .40 | .10 |
| ☐ 17 | Allie White | .50 | .20 | .05 |
| ☐ 18 | Wilson Whitley | .75 | .30 | .07 |
| ☐ 19 | Gordon Wood | .75 | .30 | .07 |
| ☐ 20 | Willie Zapalac | .50 | .20 | .05 |
| ☐ 21 | Cover Card 1 | .50 | .20 | .05 |
| ☐ 22 | Cover Card 2 | .50 | .20 | .05 |
| ☐ 23 | Cover Card 3 | .50 | .20 | .05 |
| ☐ 24 | Cover Card 4 | .50 | .20 | .05 |
| ☐ 25 | Cover Card 5 | .50 | .20 | .05 |

| | | MINT | EXC | G-VG |
|---|---|---|---|---|
| ☐ 1 | Mike Adams | 1.50 | .60 | .15 |
| ☐ 2 | Thomas Baskin | .50 | .20 | .05 |
| ☐ 3 | Tony Brackens | .75 | .30 | .07 |
| ☐ 4 | Steve Bradley | .50 | .20 | .05 |
| ☐ 5 | Blake Brockermeyer | .75 | .30 | .07 |
| | (Wearing home jersey) | | | |
| ☐ 6 | Blake Brockermeyer | .75 | .30 | .07 |
| | (Wearing away jersey) | | | |
| ☐ 7 | Phil Brown | .50 | .20 | .05 |
| ☐ 8 | Chris Carter | .75 | .30 | .07 |
| ☐ 9 | Stonie Clark | .75 | .30 | .07 |
| ☐ 10 | Gerald Crawford | .50 | .20 | .05 |
| ☐ 12 | Trent Elliot | .50 | .20 | .05 |
| ☐ 13 | Joey Ellis | .75 | .30 | .07 |
| ☐ 14 | John Elmore | .75 | .30 | .07 |
| ☐ 15 | Jon Feick | .50 | .20 | .05 |
| ☐ 16 | Victor Frazier | .50 | .20 | .05 |
| ☐ 17 | Jimmy Hakes | .50 | .20 | .05 |
| ☐ 18 | Anthony Holmes | .50 | .20 | .05 |
| ☐ 19 | Brian Howard | .50 | .20 | .05 |
| ☐ 20 | Jon Hunter | .50 | .20 | .05 |
| ☐ 21 | Curtis Jackson | .75 | .30 | .07 |
| ☐ 22 | Eric Jackson | .50 | .20 | .05 |
| ☐ 23 | Bryan Johnson | .75 | .30 | .07 |
| ☐ 24 | James Lane | .50 | .20 | .05 |
| ☐ 25 | Doug Livingston | .50 | .20 | .05 |
| ☐ 26 | Chad Lucas | .50 | .20 | .05 |
| ☐ 27 | John Mackovic CO | 1.00 | .40 | .10 |
| ☐ 28 | Van Malone | .50 | .20 | .05 |
| ☐ 29 | Justin McLemore | .50 | .20 | .05 |
| ☐ 30 | Shea Morenz | 3.00 | 1.20 | .30 |
| ☐ 31 | Dan Neil | .75 | .30 | .07 |
| ☐ 32 | Cosmo Palmieri | .50 | .20 | .05 |
| ☐ 33 | Joe Phillips | .50 | .20 | .05 |
| ☐ 34 | Lovell Pinkney | 1.50 | .60 | .15 |
| ☐ 35 | Chris Rapp | .50 | .20 | .05 |
| ☐ 36 | Robert Reed | .50 | .20 | .05 |
| ☐ 37 | Jason Reeves | .50 | .20 | .05 |
| ☐ 38 | Troy Riemer | .50 | .20 | .05 |
| ☐ 39 | Scott Szeredy | .50 | .20 | .05 |
| ☐ 40 | Tre Thomas | .75 | .30 | .07 |
| ☐ 41 | Winfred Tubbs | .50 | .20 | .05 |
| ☐ 42 | Duane Vacek | .75 | .30 | .07 |
| ☐ 43 | Brian Vasek | .50 | .20 | .05 |
| ☐ 44 | Rodrick Walker | .75 | .30 | .07 |
| ☐ 45 | Norman Watkins | .50 | .20 | .05 |
| ☐ 46 | Kevin Watler | .75 | .30 | .07 |
| ☐ 47 | Pascal Watty | .50 | .20 | .05 |
| ☐ 48 | Bryant Westbrook | .75 | .30 | .07 |
| ☐ 49 | Longhorns Band | .50 | .20 | .05 |
| ☐ 50 | Taco Bell logo card | .50 | .20 | .05 |
| | 1993 Texas schedule | | | |

## 1993 Texas Taco Bell

Sponsored by Taco Bell, the 50 cards comprising this set were issued in perforated game program insert sheets. The sheets measure approximately 8" by 10 7/8". Each card measures approximately 2 3/8" by 3 3/8" and carries on its front a white-bordered color player action shot. The player's name and position appear in black lettering within the white border at the bottom. The words "Texas Longhorns" in white lettering, along with the team logo, appear within the vertical black bar along the photo's left side. Each back carries the player's name in orange lettering at the upper left, followed below by his class, position, hometown, and highlights. The Taco Bell logo at the lower left rounds out the card. The cards are unnumbered and checklisted below in alphabetical order.

|  | MINT | EXC | G-VG |
|---|---|---|---|
| COMPLETE SET (50) | 25.00 | 10.00 | 2.50 |
| COMMON PLAYER (1-50) | .50 | .20 | .05 |

## 1992 Texas A and M

Produced by Motions Sports Inc., this 64-card standard-size (2 1/2" by 3 1/2") set was sponsored by Pepsi Cola and Chili's restaurants. The cards were to be sold only at the campus bookstore of Texas A and M University. The fronts feature posed color player photos on a black card face. The photo is framed in black and has a white border at the right and bottom and a maroon border at the top and left. The player's name and number appear in the top maroon border and "Texas A and M University" appear in the bottom white border. On a ghosted player photo, the backs present a player profile in a transparent white box. The cards are numbered on the back.

|  | MINT | EXC | G-VG |
|---|---|---|---|
| COMPLETE SET (65) | 20.00 | 8.00 | 2.00 |
| COMMON CARD (1-62) | .35 | .14 | .03 |

| | | MINT | EXC | G-VG |
|---|---|---|---|---|
| ☐ 1 | Matt Miller | .50 | .20 | .05 |
| ☐ 2 | Steve Emerson | .35 | .14 | .03 |
| ☐ 3 | Brad Cooper | .35 | .14 | .03 |
| ☐ 4 | Mike Hendricks | .60 | .24 | .06 |

| | | | |
|---|---|---|---|
| ☐ 5 Dexter Wesley | .35 | .14 | .03 |
| ☐ 6 Darrell Red | .35 | .14 | .03 |
| ☐ 7 Antonio Shorter | 1.00 | .40 | .10 |
| ☐ 8 Larry Wallace | .35 | .14 | .03 |
| ☐ 9 Kefa Chatham | .35 | .14 | .03 |
| ☐ 10 Billy Mitchell | .35 | .14 | .03 |
| ☐ 11 Patrick Bates | 1.50 | .60 | .15 |
| ☐ 12 Greg Hill | 3.00 | 1.20 | .30 |
| ☐ 13 Tommy Preston | .35 | .14 | .03 |
| ☐ 14 Ryan Mathews | .35 | .14 | .03 |
| ☐ 15 Steve Kenney | .35 | .14 | .03 |
| ☐ 16 John Richard | .35 | .14 | .03 |
| ☐ 17 John Ellisor | .35 | .14 | .03 |
| ☐ 18 Ryan Kern | .35 | .14 | .03 |
| ☐ 19 Jeff Jones | .35 | .14 | .03 |
| ☐ 20 Chris Sanders | .35 | .14 | .03 |
| ☐ 21 Reggie Graham | .35 | .14 | .03 |
| ☐ 22 David Davis | .35 | .14 | .03 |
| ☐ 23 Tony Harrison | .50 | .20 | .05 |
| ☐ 24 Jason Mathews | .50 | .20 | .05 |
| ☐ 25 Otis Nealy | .35 | .14 | .03 |
| ☐ 26 Kent Petty | .35 | .14 | .03 |
| ☐ 27 Rodney Thomas | 1.50 | .60 | .15 |
| ☐ 28 Sam Adams | 1.50 | .60 | .15 |
| ☐ 29 Clif Groce | .35 | .14 | .03 |
| ☐ 30 Tyler Harrison | .35 | .14 | .03 |
| ☐ 31 Eric England | .50 | .20 | .05 |
| ☐ 32 Jason Atkinson | .35 | .14 | .03 |
| ☐ 33 Lance Teichelman | .35 | .14 | .03 |
| ☐ 34 Marcus Buckley | 1.50 | .60 | .15 |
| ☐ 35 Steve Solari | .35 | .14 | .03 |
| ☐ 36 Aggie Coaches | .50 | .20 | .05 |
| ☐ 37 Derrick Frazier | .50 | .20 | .05 |
| ☐ 38 James McKeehan | .60 | .24 | .06 |
| ☐ 39 Doug Carter | .35 | .14 | .03 |
| ☐ 40 Larry Jackson | .35 | .14 | .03 |
| ☐ 41 Brian Mitchell | .75 | .30 | .07 |
| ☐ 42 Greg Schorp | .50 | .20 | .05 |
| ☐ 43 Greg Cook | .35 | .14 | .03 |
| ☐ 44 Kyle Maxfield | .35 | .14 | .03 |
| ☐ 45 Todd Mathison | .35 | .14 | .03 |
| ☐ 46 Chris Dausin | .35 | .14 | .03 |
| ☐ 47 Junior White | .35 | .14 | .03 |
| ☐ 48 Wilbert Biggens | .35 | .14 | .03 |
| ☐ 49 Terry Venetoulias | .35 | .14 | .03 |
| ☐ 50 Jessie Cox | .35 | .14 | .03 |
| ☐ 51 R.C. Slocum CO | .75 | .30 | .07 |
| ☐ 52 Defensive Coaches | .35 | .14 | .03 |
|    Bob Davie | | | |
|    Kirk Doll | | | |
|    Bill Johnson | | | |
|    Trent Walters | | | |
| ☐ 53 Offensive Coaches | .50 | .20 | .05 |
|    Mike Sherman | | | |
|    Shawn Slocum | | | |
|    Bob Toledo | | | |
|    Gary Kubiak | | | |
|    David Culley | | | |
| ☐ 54 Tim Cassidy | .35 | .14 | .03 |
|    Recruiting Coordinator | | | |
| ☐ 55 Yell Leaders | .35 | .14 | .03 |
|    Steve Scanlon | | | |
|    Adin Pfeuffer | | | |
|    Tim Isgitt | | | |
|    Ronnie McDonald | | | |
|    Mark Rollins | | | |
| ☐ 56 A and M Band | .35 | .14 | .03 |
| ☐ 57 Reveille V | .35 | .14 | .03 |
|    Mascot | | | |
| ☐ 58 Twelfth Man | .50 | .20 | .05 |
|    Statue | | | |
| ☐ 59 Bonfire | .35 | .14 | .03 |
| ☐ 60 Training Facility | .35 | .14 | .03 |
| ☐ 61 Kyle Field | .35 | .14 | .03 |
| ☐ 62 Texas A and M Campus | .35 | .14 | .03 |
| ☐ NNO Front Card | .35 | .14 | .03 |
|    (Texas A and M logo) | | | |
| ☐ NNO Back Card | .35 | .14 | .03 |
| ☐ NNO Checklist Card | .35 | .14 | .03 |

## 1991 UNLV

This 12-card standard size (2 1/2" by 3 1/2") set was sponsored by KVVU TV (Fox 5), BDA, and Vons. The cards were printed on thin card stock and issued on a perforated sheet measuring approximately 10" by 10 1/2". The fronts feature color action photos bordered in red. The top of the pictures is curved to resemble an archway, and the team name follows the curve of the arch. The player's name and position appear in a gray stripe below the picture. The backs carry comments, "Drug Tips From The Rebels," sponsor logos, and a phone number for Junior Rebel Club Information. The cards are unnumbered and checklisted below in alphabetical order.

| | MINT | EXC | G-VG |
|---|---|---|---|
| COMPLETE SET (12) | 8.00 | 3.25 | .80 |
| COMMON CARDS (1-12) | .75 | .30 | .07 |
| ☐ 1 Cheerleaders | 1.00 | .40 | .10 |
|    and Songleaders | | | |
| ☐ 2 Gang Tackle | .75 | .30 | .07 |
| ☐ 3 Instant Offense | .75 | .30 | .07 |
|    Hernandez Cooper | | | |
| ☐ 4 No Escape | .75 | .30 | .07 |
| ☐ 5 On the Move | .75 | .30 | .07 |
| ☐ 6 Punching It In | .75 | .30 | .07 |
| ☐ 7 Ready to Fire | .75 | .30 | .07 |
|    Derek Stott | | | |
| ☐ 8 Rebel Fever | .75 | .30 | .07 |
| ☐ 9 Rebel Sack | .75 | .30 | .07 |
| ☐ 10 Sam Boyd Silver Bowl | .75 | .30 | .07 |
| ☐ 11 Jim Strong CO | .75 | .30 | .07 |
| ☐ 12 Team Photo | 1.25 | .50 | .12 |

## 1990 Versailles HS

This 20-card set features the Versailles Tigers, the 1990 State Champions of Division 4 Ohio Football. The set was issued as a perforated sheet consisting of five rows of four cards each; after perforation, each individual card measures the standard size (2 1/2" by 3 1/2"). On a white card face, the fronts feature black and white action game shots. The player's name team name above the photo and the player's name below it are printed in orange lettering; other information on the fronts is in black lettering. The backs are dominated by a black and white head shot with biography and a list of sponsors immediately below the pictures. The cards are unnumbered and checklisted below alphabetically.

| | MINT | EXC | G-VG |
|---|---|---|---|
| COMPLETE SET (20) | 8.00 | 3.25 | .80 |
| COMMON CARD (1-20) | .50 | .20 | .05 |
| ☐ 1 Kevin Bergman | .50 | .20 | .05 |
| ☐ 2 A.J. Bey | .50 | .20 | .05 |
| ☐ 3 Brad Bey | .50 | .20 | .05 |
| ☐ 4 Ed Dingman | .75 | .30 | .07 |
| ☐ 5 Brian Griesdorn | .50 | .20 | .05 |
| ☐ 6 Al Hetrick CO | .75 | .30 | .07 |
| ☐ 7 Garth Hoellrich | .50 | .20 | .05 |
| ☐ 8 Trent Huff | .50 | .20 | .05 |
| ☐ 9 Brian Keiser | .50 | .20 | .05 |
| ☐ 10 Lane Knore | .50 | .20 | .05 |
| ☐ 11 Brian Kunk | .50 | .20 | .05 |
| ☐ 12 Keenan Leichty | .50 | .20 | .05 |
| ☐ 13 Marc Litten | .50 | .20 | .05 |
| ☐ 14 Craig Oliver | .50 | .20 | .05 |
| ☐ 15 Jon Pothast | .50 | .20 | .05 |

| | MINT | EXC | G-VG |
|---|---|---|---|
| ☐ 16 Joe Rush | .50 | .20 | .05 |
| ☐ 17 Shane Schultz | .50 | .20 | .05 |
| ☐ 18 Mark Siekman | .50 | .20 | .05 |
| ☐ 19 Matt Stall | .50 | .20 | .05 |
| ☐ 20 Nathan Subler | .50 | .20 | .05 |

## 1990 Virginia

This 16-card standard size (2 1/2" by 3 1/2") set was issued to celebrate the 1990 Virginia Cavalier team, which contended for the National Title. This set features a good mix of action photography and portrait shots on the front with biographical information on the back. The set was issued as a perforated sheet with four rows of four cards each. This set was sponsored by the Charter Hospital of Charlottesville and was given out to those fans in attendance at the Sept. 29, 1990 game against William and Mary. The cards are unnumbered and listed below in alphabetical order. The key card in this set is wide receiver Herman Moore.

| | MINT | EXC | G-VG |
|---|---|---|---|
| COMPLETE SET (16) | 20.00 | 8.00 | 2.00 |
| COMMON CARD (1-16) | 1.00 | .40 | .10 |
| ☐ 1 Chris Borsari | 1.00 | .40 | .10 |
| ☐ 2 Ron Carey | 1.00 | .40 | .10 |
| ☐ 3 Paul Collins | 1.00 | .40 | .10 |
| ☐ 4 Tony Covington | 2.00 | .80 | .20 |
| ☐ 5 Derek Dooley | 1.00 | .40 | .10 |
| ☐ 6 Joe Hall | 1.00 | .40 | .10 |
| ☐ 7 Myron Martin | 1.00 | .40 | .10 |
| ☐ 8 Bruce McGonnigal | 1.50 | .60 | .15 |
| ☐ 9 Jake McInerney | 1.00 | .40 | .10 |
| ☐ 10 Keith McMeans | 1.00 | .40 | .10 |
| ☐ 11 Herman Moore | 10.00 | 4.00 | 1.00 |
| ☐ 12 Shawn Moore | 4.00 | 1.60 | .40 |
| ☐ 13 Trevor Ryals | 1.00 | .40 | .10 |
| ☐ 14 Chris Stearns | 1.00 | .40 | .10 |
| ☐ 15 Jason Wallace | 1.00 | .40 | .10 |
| ☐ 16 George Welsh CO | 1.50 | .60 | .15 |

## 1992 Virginia Coca-Cola

Sponsored by Coca-Cola, the 16 cards comprising this set were issued in one 16-card insert sheet. The perforated sheet measures approximately 10" by 14" and consists of four rows of four cards each. Each card measures the standard size (2 1/2" by 3 1/2") and carries on its front a blue-bordered color player action shot. The player's name and position appear in white lettering within a dark blue bar set off by white lines at the bottom of the player photo. "Virginia" appears in orange lettering within the blue border above the photo. The Cavaliers

logo is shown in one corner of the photo, and the word "Cavs" appears in orange lettering within a white rectangle at the lower left corner of the player photo. The Coca-Cola logo rests within the blue border at the bottom. The white back carries the player's name, position, biography, and highlights. The Coca-Cola logo at the bottom rounds out the card. The cards are unnumbered and checklisted below in alphabetical order.

| | MINT | EXC | G-VG |
|---|---|---|---|
| COMPLETE SET (16) | 15.00 | 6.00 | 1.50 |
| COMMON PLAYER (1-16) | 1.00 | .40 | .10 |
| ☐ 1 Bobby Goodman | 1.00 | .40 | .10 |
| ☐ 2 Michael Husted | 1.50 | .60 | .15 |
| ☐ 3 Greg Jeffries | 1.50 | .60 | .15 |
| ☐ 4 Charles Keiningham | 1.00 | .40 | .10 |
| ☐ 5 Terry Kirby | 6.00 | 2.40 | .60 |
| ☐ 6 Kenneth Miles | 1.00 | .40 | .10 |
| ☐ 7 Tim Samec | 1.00 | .40 | .10 |
| ☐ 8 Chris Slade | 3.00 | 1.20 | .30 |
| ☐ 9 Alvin Snead | 1.00 | .40 | .10 |
| ☐ 10 Gary Steele | 1.00 | .40 | .10 |
| ☐ 11 Jeff Tomlin | 1.00 | .40 | .10 |
| ☐ 12 Terrence Tomlin | 1.00 | .40 | .10 |
| ☐ 13 David Ware | 1.00 | .40 | .10 |
| ☐ 14 George Welsh CO | 1.50 | .60 | .15 |
| ☐ 15 Virginia 20, Clemson 7; Sept. 8, 1990 | 1.00 | .40 | .10 |
| ☐ 16 Virginia 20, N.Carolina 17; Nov. 14, 1987 | 1.00 | .40 | .10 |

## 1993 Virginia Coca-Cola

Sponsored by Coca-Cola, the 16 cards comprising this set were issued in one 16-card game program insert sheet. The perforated sheet measures approximately 10" by 14" and consists of four rows of four cards each. Each card measures the standard size (2 1/2" by 3 1/2") and carries on its front an elliptical color player action shot bordered in blue with black vertical stirpes. The player's name and position appear in white lettering within a dark blue stripe at the bottom. The team name appears in orange and white lettering above the photo. The Coca-Cola logo appears at the lower right. The white back carries the player's name, position, biography, and highlights. The Coca-Cola logo at the bottom rounds out the card. The cards are unnumbered and checklisted below in alphabetical order.

| | MINT | EXC | G-VG |
|---|---|---|---|
| COMPLETE SET (16) | 15.00 | 6.00 | 1.50 |
| COMMON PLAYER (1-16) | 1.00 | .40 | .10 |
| ☐ 1 Tom Burns | 1.25 | .50 | .12 |
| ☐ 2 Peter Collins | 1.25 | .50 | .12 |
| ☐ 3 Bill Curry | 1.00 | .40 | .10 |
| ☐ 4 Mark Dixon | 1.25 | .50 | .12 |
| ☐ 5 Bill Edwards | 1.00 | .40 | .10 |
| ☐ 6 P.J. Killian | 1.00 | .40 | .10 |
| ☐ 7 Keith Lyle | 1.25 | .50 | .12 |
| ☐ 8 Greg McClellan | 1.25 | .50 | .12 |
| ☐ 9 Matt Mikeska | 1.25 | .50 | .12 |
| ☐ 10 Aaron Mundy | 1.25 | .50 | .12 |
| ☐ 11 Jim Reid | 1.25 | .50 | .12 |
| ☐ 12 Josh Schrader | 1.00 | .40 | .10 |
| ☐ 13 Jerrod Washington | 1.25 | .50 | .12 |
| ☐ 14 George Welsh CO | 1.50 | .60 | .15 |
| ☐ 15 Cavalier Spirit (Cheerleaders) | 1.25 | .50 | .12 |
| ☐ 16 Cavalier Mascot | 1.00 | .40 | .10 |

## 1973 Washington KFC

Sponsored by Kentucky Fried Chicken and KIRO (Radio Northwest 710), these 30 cards measure approximately 3" by 4" and are printed on thick card stock. The fronts feature posed black-and-white head shots with white borders. The Kentucky Fried Chicken logo is in the top border, while player information is printed in the bottom border. The backs are blank. The cards are unnumbered and checklisted below in alphabetical order. The cards were given out by KFC with purchase of their product. Also distributed to purchasers of 5.00 or more was a color team photo or coaches picture measuring approximately 8" by 10".

|  | NRMT | VG-E | GOOD |
|---|---|---|---|
| COMPLETE SET (30)..................... | 200.00 | 80.00 | 20.00 |
| COMMON PLAYER (1-30)............... | 8.00 | 3.25 | .80 |
| ☐ 1 Jim Anderson..................... | 8.00 | 3.25 | .80 |
| ☐ 2 Jim Andrilenas .................... | 8.00 | 3.25 | .80 |
| ☐ 3 Glen Bonner ...................... | 12.00 | 5.00 | 1.20 |
| ☐ 4 Bob Boustead .................... | 8.00 | 3.25 | .80 |
| ☐ 5 Skip Boyd ........................ | 12.00 | 5.00 | 1.20 |
| ☐ 6 Gordie Bronson .................. | 8.00 | 3.25 | .80 |
| ☐ 7 Reggie Brown .................... | 8.00 | 3.25 | .80 |
| ☐ 8 Dan Celoni........................ | 8.00 | 3.25 | .80 |
| ☐ 9 Brian Daheny ..................... | 8.00 | 3.25 | .80 |
| ☐ 10 Fred Dean ....................... | 8.00 | 3.25 | .80 |
| ☐ 11 Pete Elswick ..................... | 8.00 | 3.25 | .80 |
| ☐ 12 Dennis Fitzpatrick............... | 8.00 | 3.25 | .80 |
| ☐ 13 Bob Graves ...................... | 8.00 | 3.25 | .80 |
| ☐ 14 Pedro Hawkins .................. | 8.00 | 3.25 | .80 |
| ☐ 15 Rick Hayes ...................... | 8.00 | 3.25 | .80 |
| ☐ 16 Barry Houlihan .................. | 8.00 | 3.25 | .80 |
| ☐ 17 Roberto Jourdan ................ | 8.00 | 3.25 | .80 |
| ☐ 18 Washington Keenan ............ | 8.00 | 3.25 | .80 |
| ☐ 19 Eddie King ...................... | 8.00 | 3.25 | .80 |
| ☐ 20 Jim Kristoff ..................... | 8.00 | 3.25 | .80 |
| ☐ 21 Murphy McFarland .............. | 8.00 | 3.25 | .80 |
| ☐ 22 Walter Oldes .................... | 8.00 | 3.25 | .80 |
| ☐ 23 Louis Quinn ..................... | 12.00 | 5.00 | 1.20 |
| ☐ 24 Frank Reed ...................... | 8.00 | 3.25 | .80 |
| ☐ 25 Dain Rodwell .................... | 8.00 | 3.25 | .80 |
| ☐ 26 Ron Stanley...................... | 8.00 | 3.25 | .80 |
| ☐ 27 Joe Tabor ....................... | 8.00 | 3.25 | .80 |
| ☐ 28 Pete Taggares ................... | 8.00 | 3.25 | .80 |
| ☐ 29 John Whitacre ................... | 8.00 | 3.25 | .80 |
| ☐ 30 Hans Woldseth .................. | 15.00 | 6.00 | 1.50 |
| ☐ xx Color Team Photo................ | 15.00 | 6.00 | 1.50 |
| (Large 8x10) | | | |
| ☐ xx Coaches Photo .................. | 25.00 | 10.00 | 2.50 |
| (Large 8x10) | | | |

## 1988 Washington Smokey

The 1988 University of Washington Smokey set contains 16 standard-size (2 1/2" by 3 1/2") cards. The fronts feature color photos bordered in deep purple, with name, position, and jersey number. The vertically oriented backs have fire prevention cartoons. The cards are unnumbered and are listed below in alphabetical order.

|  | MINT | EXC | G-VG |
|---|---|---|---|
| COMPLETE SET (16)........................ | 15.00 | 6.00 | 1.50 |
| COMMON CARD (1-16) ................... | 1.00 | .40 | .10 |
| ☐ 1 Ricky Andrews ......................... | 1.00 | .40 | .10 |
| ☐ 2 Bern Brostek ........................... | 1.50 | .60 | .15 |
| ☐ 3 Dennis Brown .......................... | 1.00 | .40 | .10 |
| ☐ 4 Cary Conklin............................ | 3.00 | 1.20 | .30 |
| ☐ 5 Tony Covington ........................ | 1.00 | .40 | .10 |
| ☐ 6 Darryl Hall .............................. | 1.50 | .60 | .15 |
| ☐ 7 Martin Harrison ........................ | 1.00 | .40 | .10 |
| ☐ 8 Don James CO ......................... | 2.00 | .80 | .20 |
| ☐ 9 Aaron Jenkins .......................... | 1.00 | .40 | .10 |
| ☐ 10 Le-Lo Lang ........................... | 2.50 | 1.00 | .25 |
| ☐ 11 Art Malone ........................... | 1.00 | .40 | .10 |
| ☐ 12 Andre Riley ........................... | 1.00 | .40 | .10 |
| ☐ 13 Brian Slater ........................... | 1.00 | .40 | .10 |
| ☐ 14 Vince Weathersby .................... | 1.00 | .40 | .10 |
| ☐ 15 Brett Wiese ........................... | 1.00 | .40 | .10 |
| ☐ 16 Mike Zandofsky ...................... | 1.50 | .60 | .15 |

## 1990 Washington Smokey *

This 16-card set, which measures the standard size (2 1/2" by 3 1/2"), was issued in conjunction with the Washington Huskies to promote fire safety. The fronts of the cards are purple bordered with "1990 Washington Huskies" on the top of the card. A full-color action photo is in the middle of the card and the player's name, uniform number, and position are underneath. On the lower left corner is the Smokey symbol and in the lower right-hand corner is the Washington Huskies logo. On the back is biographical information about the player and a fire safety tip. The set was issued with cooperation from the USDI Bureau of Land Management, the National Park Service, the National Association of State Foresters, Keep Washington Green, BDA, and KOMO Radio. We have checklisted this set alphabetically within player type and put the uniform number, where applicable, next to the player's name. The set was also issued in an unperforated sheet with four rows of four cards each. The last row of cards features women volleyball players.

|  | MINT | EXC | G-VG |
|---|---|---|---|
| COMPLETE SET (16)........................ | 15.00 | 6.00 | 1.50 |
| COMMON CARD (1-12) ................... | .75 | .30 | .07 |
| COMMON CARD (13-16) ................. | .75 | .30 | .07 |
| ☐ 1 Eric Briscoe 28......................... | .75 | .30 | .07 |
| ☐ 2 Mark Brunell 11 ....................... | 4.00 | 1.60 | .40 |
| ☐ 3 James Clifford 53...................... | .75 | .30 | .07 |
| ☐ 4 John Cook 93........................... | .75 | .30 | .07 |
| ☐ 5 Ed Cunningham 79..................... | 1.50 | .60 | .15 |
| ☐ 6 Dana Hall 5............................. | 3.00 | 1.20 | .30 |
| ☐ 7 Don James CO ......................... | 1.50 | .60 | .15 |
| ☐ 8 Donald Jones 48....................... | .75 | .30 | .07 |
| ☐ 9 Dean Kirkland 51...................... | .75 | .30 | .07 |
| ☐ 10 Greg Lewis 20 ........................ | 1.50 | .60 | .15 |
| ☐ 11 Orlando McKay 4 .................... | .75 | .30 | .07 |
| ☐ 12 Travis Richardson 58................ | .75 | .30 | .07 |
| ☐ 13 Kelley Larsen ......................... | .75 | .30 | .07 |
| (Women's volleyball) | | | |
| ☐ 14 Michelle Reid ......................... | .75 | .30 | .07 |
| (Women's volleyball) | | | |
| ☐ 15 Ashleigh Robertson .................. | .75 | .30 | .07 |
| (Women's volleyball) | | | |
| ☐ 16 Gail Thorpe ........................... | .75 | .30 | .07 |
| (Women's volleyball) | | | |

# 1991 Washington Smokey *

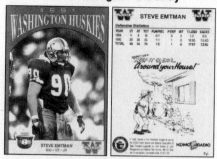

This 16-card set was sponsored by the USDA Forest Service and other federal agencies. The cards measure the standard size (2 1/2" by 3 1/2") and are printed on thin cardboard stock. The set was issued in two different forms. Ten thousand 12-card sets were distributed at the Huskies' home game against the University of Toledo. This set was also issued as a 16-card unperforated sheet, with the final row featuring four women volleyball players. The card fronts are accented in the team's colors (purple and gold) and have glossy color action player photos. The top of the pictures is curved to resemble an archway, and the team name follows the curve of the arch. The player's name and position appear in a stripe below the picture. The backs present statistics and a fire prevention cartoon starring Smokey. The cards are unnumbered and checklisted below in alphabetical order, with the women volleyball players listed at the end.

|  | MINT | EXC | G-VG |
|---|---|---|---|
| COMPLETE SET (16) | 15.00 | 6.00 | 1.50 |
| COMMON CARD (1-12) | .75 | .30 | .07 |
| COMMON CARD (13-16) | .75 | .30 | .07 |
| ☐ 1 Mario Bailey | 1.50 | .60 | .15 |
| ☐ 2 Beno Bryant | 1.25 | .50 | .12 |
| ☐ 3 Brett Collins | .75 | .30 | .07 |
| ☐ 4 Ed Cunningham | 1.25 | .50 | .12 |
| ☐ 5 Steve Emtman | 2.00 | .80 | .20 |
| ☐ 6 Dana Hall | 2.50 | 1.00 | .25 |
| ☐ 7 Billy Joe Hobert | 4.00 | 1.60 | .40 |
| ☐ 8 Dave Hoffmann | .75 | .30 | .07 |
| ☐ 9 Don James CO | 1.50 | .60 | .15 |
| ☐ 10 Donald Jones | .75 | .30 | .07 |
| ☐ 11 Siupeli Malamala | 1.25 | .50 | .12 |
| ☐ 12 Orlando McKay | .75 | .30 | .07 |
| ☐ 13 Diane Flick | .75 | .30 | .07 |
| (Women's volleyball) | | | |
| ☐ 14 Kelley Larsen | .75 | .30 | .07 |
| (Women's volleyball) | | | |
| ☐ 15 Ashleigh Robertson | .75 | .30 | .07 |
| (Women's volleyball) | | | |
| ☐ 16 Dana Thompson | .75 | .30 | .07 |
| (Women's volleyball) | | | |

# 1992 Washington Pay Less

This 16-card set was sponsored by Pay Less Drug Stores and Prime Sports Northwest. The cards measure the standard size (2 1/2" by 3 1/2") and are printed on thin card stock. The fronts carry a color action player photo on a purple card face. The team name and year appear above the photo in gold print on a purple bar that partially rests on a gold bar with notched ends. Below the photo, the player's name and

sponsor logos appear in a gold border stripe. The backs carry statistics and sponsor advertisements. The cards are unnumbered and checklisted below in alphabetical order. The Billy Joe Hobart card was reportedly pulled from circulation aaafter his suspension from the team.

|  | MINT | EXC | G-VG |
|---|---|---|---|
| COMPLETE SET (16) | 15.00 | 6.00 | 1.50 |
| COMMON CARD (1-16) | .75 | .30 | .07 |
| ☐ 1 Walter Bailey | .75 | .30 | .07 |
| ☐ 2 Jay Barry | .75 | .30 | .07 |
| ☐ 3 Mark Brunell | 3.00 | 1.20 | .30 |
| ☐ 4 Beno Bryant | 1.00 | .40 | .10 |
| ☐ 5 James Clifford | .75 | .30 | .07 |
| ☐ 6 Jamie Fields | 1.00 | .40 | .10 |
| ☐ 7 Travis Hanson | .75 | .30 | .07 |
| ☐ 8 Billy Joe Hobert | 5.00 | 2.00 | .50 |
| ☐ 9 Dave Hoffmann | .75 | .30 | .07 |
| ☐ 10 Matt Jones | .75 | .30 | .07 |
| ☐ 11 Lincoln Kennedy | 3.00 | 1.20 | .30 |
| ☐ 12 Andy Mason | .75 | .30 | .07 |
| ☐ 13 Shane Pahukoa | .75 | .30 | .07 |
| ☐ 14 Tommie Smith | .75 | .30 | .07 |
| ☐ 15 Darius Turner | .75 | .30 | .07 |
| ☐ 16 Team Photo | 1.00 | .40 | .10 |
| (Schedule) | | | |

# 1992 Washington Greats/Pacific

This 110-card standard-size (2 1/2" by 3 1/2") set highlights 100 years of Huskies football. The cards were produced by Pacific Trading Cards, who donated a portion of the proceeds from their sale to the University of Washington and the Don James Endowment Fund for athletic scholarships. Reportedly the production run was limited to 2,500 numbered cases; moreover, 1,000 serial numbered cards autographed by Hugh McElhenny were randomly inserted in the ten-card foil packs. On a white card face, the fronts display a mix of color or black and white player photos enclosed by thin gold and purple borders. The team helmet appears in the lower left corner, with the player's name and position in a gold stripe extending to the right. The backs carry biography and career summary. The cards are numbered on the back. The checklist card was randomly inserted at a reported rate of one every one or two wax boxes; it is not included in the complete set price listed below.

|  | MINT | EXC | G-VG |
|---|---|---|---|
| COMPLETE SET (110) | 15.00 | 6.00 | 1.50 |
| COMMON CARD (1-110) | .15 | .06 | .01 |
| ☐ 1 Don James CO | .50 | .20 | .05 |
| ☐ 2 Cary Conklin | .50 | .20 | .05 |
| ☐ 3 Tom Cowan | .15 | .06 | .01 |
| ☐ 4 Thane Cleland | .15 | .06 | .01 |
| ☐ 5 Steve Pelluer | .50 | .20 | .05 |
| ☐ 6 Sonny Sixkiller | .50 | .20 | .05 |
| ☐ 7 Koll Hagen | .15 | .06 | .01 |
| ☐ 8 Danny Greene | .15 | .06 | .01 |
| ☐ 9 George Black | .15 | .06 | .01 |
| ☐ 10 Mike Baldassin | .15 | .06 | .01 |
| ☐ 11 Bill Douglas | .15 | .06 | .01 |
| ☐ 12 Tom Flick | .25 | .10 | .02 |
| ☐ 13 Brian Slater | .15 | .06 | .01 |
| ☐ 14 Dick Sprague | .15 | .06 | .01 |
| ☐ 15 Bob Schloredt | .35 | .14 | .03 |
| ☐ 16 Bill Smith | .15 | .06 | .01 |
| ☐ 17 Marv Bergmann | .15 | .06 | .01 |
| ☐ 18 Sam Mitchell | .25 | .10 | .02 |
| ☐ 19 Bill Earley | .15 | .06 | .01 |
| ☐ 20 Clarence Dirks | .15 | .06 | .01 |
| ☐ 21 Jimmie Cain | .15 | .06 | .01 |
| ☐ 22 Don Heinrich | .35 | .14 | .03 |
| ☐ 23 Paul(Socko) Sulkosky | .15 | .06 | .01 |

| | | | |
|---|---|---|---|
| ☐ 24 By Haines | .15 | .06 | .01 |
| ☐ 25 Joe Steele | .15 | .06 | .01 |
| ☐ 26 Bob Monroe | .15 | .06 | .01 |
| ☐ 27 Roy McKasson | .15 | .06 | .01 |
| ☐ 28 Charlie Mitchell | .25 | .10 | .02 |
| ☐ 29 Ernie Steele | .15 | .06 | .01 |
| ☐ 30 Kyle Heinrich | .25 | .10 | .02 |
| ☐ 31 Travis Richardson | .15 | .06 | .01 |
| ☐ 32 Hugh McElhenny | 1.00 | .40 | .10 |
| ☐ 33 George Wilson | .15 | .06 | .01 |
| ☐ 34 Merle Hufford | .15 | .06 | .01 |
| ☐ 35 Steve Thompson | .15 | .06 | .01 |
| ☐ 36 Jim Krieg | .15 | .06 | .01 |
| ☐ 37 Chuck Olson | .15 | .06 | .01 |
| ☐ 38 Charley Russell | .15 | .06 | .01 |
| ☐ 39 Duane Wardlow | .15 | .06 | .01 |
| ☐ 40 Jay MacDowell | .15 | .06 | .01 |
| ☐ 41 Alf Hemstad | .15 | .06 | .01 |
| ☐ 42 Max Starcevich | .15 | .06 | .01 |
| ☐ 43 Ray Mansfield | .25 | .10 | .02 |
| ☐ 44 Brooks Biddle | .15 | .06 | .01 |
| ☐ 45 Toussaint Tyler | .35 | .14 | .03 |
| ☐ 46 Randy Van Diver | .15 | .06 | .01 |
| ☐ 47 John Cook | .15 | .06 | .01 |
| ☐ 48 Paul Skansi | .25 | .10 | .02 |
| ☐ 49 Tim Meamber | .15 | .06 | .01 |
| ☐ 50 Milt Bohart | .15 | .06 | .01 |
| ☐ 51 Curt Marsh | .15 | .06 | .01 |
| ☐ 52 Antowaine Richardson | .15 | .06 | .01 |
| ☐ 53 Jim Rodgers | .15 | .06 | .01 |
| ☐ 54 Mike Rohrbach | .15 | .06 | .01 |
| ☐ 55 Dan Agen | .15 | .06 | .01 |
| ☐ 56 Tom Turnure | .25 | .10 | .02 |
| ☐ 57 Ron Medved | .15 | .06 | .01 |
| ☐ 58 Vic Markov | .15 | .06 | .01 |
| ☐ 59 Carl(Bud) Ericksen | .15 | .06 | .01 |
| ☐ 60 Bill Kinnune | .15 | .06 | .01 |
| ☐ 61 Karsten(Corky) Lewis | .15 | .06 | .01 |
| ☐ 62 Sam Robinson | .25 | .10 | .02 |
| ☐ 63 Dave Nisbet | .15 | .06 | .01 |
| ☐ 64 Barry Bullard | .15 | .06 | .01 |
| ☐ 65 Norm Dicks | .15 | .06 | .01 |
| ☐ 66 Rick Redman | .25 | .10 | .02 |
| ☐ 67 Mark Jerue | .25 | .10 | .02 |
| ☐ 68 Jeff Toews | .15 | .06 | .01 |
| ☐ 69 Fletcher Jenkins | .25 | .10 | .02 |
| ☐ 70 Ray Horton | .15 | .06 | .01 |
| ☐ 71 Tom Erlandson | .15 | .06 | .01 |
| ☐ 72 Steve Alvord | .15 | .06 | .01 |
| ☐ 73 Dean Browning | .15 | .06 | .01 |
| ☐ 74 Scott Greenwood | .15 | .06 | .01 |
| ☐ 75 Bo Yates | .15 | .06 | .01 |
| ☐ 76 Jake Kupp | .25 | .10 | .02 |
| ☐ 77 Jim Owens CO | .15 | .06 | .01 |
| ☐ 78 Don McKeta | .15 | .06 | .01 |
| ☐ 79 Ben Davidson | .50 | .20 | .05 |
| ☐ 80 Tim Bullard | .15 | .06 | .01 |
| ☐ 81 Bill Albrecht | .15 | .06 | .01 |
| ☐ 82 Jim Cope | .15 | .06 | .01 |
| ☐ 83 Earl Monlux | .15 | .06 | .01 |
| ☐ 84 Paul Schwegler | .15 | .06 | .01 |
| ☐ 85 Steve Bramwell | .15 | .06 | .01 |
| ☐ 86 Ted Holzknecht | .15 | .06 | .01 |
| ☐ 87 Larry Hatch | .15 | .06 | .01 |
| ☐ 88 John Brady | .15 | .06 | .01 |
| ☐ 89 Bob Hivner | .15 | .06 | .01 |
| ☐ 90 Chuck Nelson | .25 | .10 | .02 |
| ☐ 91 Jeff Jaeger | .25 | .10 | .02 |
| ☐ 92 Rich Camarillo | .25 | .10 | .02 |
| ☐ 93 Jim Houston | .25 | .10 | .02 |
| ☐ 94 Jim Skaggs | .25 | .10 | .02 |
| ☐ 95 John Cherberg CO | .15 | .06 | .01 |
| ☐ 96 Bo Cornell | .25 | .10 | .02 |
| ☐ 97 Bill Cahill | .15 | .06 | .01 |
| ☐ 98 Dean McAdams | .15 | .06 | .01 |
| ☐ 99 Gil Dobie CO | .25 | .10 | .02 |
| ☐ 100 Walter Shiel | .15 | .06 | .01 |
| ☐ 101 Enoch Bagshaw CO | .15 | .06 | .01 |
| ☐ 102 Ray Eckmann | .15 | .06 | .01 |
| ☐ 103 Luther Carr | .15 | .06 | .01 |
| ☐ 104 Jimmy Bryan | .15 | .06 | .01 |
| ☐ 105 Darrell Royal | .35 | .14 | .03 |
| ☐ 106 Ray Frankowski | .15 | .06 | .01 |
| ☐ 107 Ray Pinney | .25 | .10 | .02 |
| ☐ 108 Skip Boyd | .15 | .06 | .01 |
| ☐ 109 Al Burleson | .15 | .06 | .01 |
| ☐ 110 Dennis Fitzpatrick | .25 | .10 | .02 |
| ☐ AU32 Hugh McElhenny | 50.00 | 20.00 | 5.00 |
| (Certified Autograph, serially numbered of 1000) | | | |
| ☐ NNO Checklist Card | 3.00 | 1.20 | .30 |

## 1993 Washington Safeway

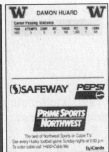

The 16 standard-size (2 1/2" by 3 1/2") cards comprising this Huskies set sponsored by Safeway food stores, Pepsi, and Prime Sports Northwest, were printed on thin card stock and feature on their fronts purple- and gold-bordered color player action shots. The player's name and position, along with the sponsors' logos, appear within the gold margin at the bottom. The words "Huskies 1993" appear in purple lettering within a gold bar at the upper left. The player's uniform number appears in white lettering at the upper right. The white back carries the player's name at the top, followed below by a stat table or player highlights. The sponsors' logos at the bottom round out the card. The cards are unnumbered and checklisted below in alphabetical order.

| | MINT | EXC | G-VG |
|---|---|---|---|
| COMPLETE SET (16) | 10.00 | 4.00 | 1.00 |
| COMMON PLAYER (1-16) | .75 | .30 | .07 |
| ☐ 1 Beno Bryant | 1.00 | .40 | .10 |
| ☐ 2 Hillary Butler | .75 | .30 | .07 |
| ☐ 3 D'Marco Farr | .75 | .30 | .07 |
| ☐ 4 Jamal Fountaine | .75 | .30 | .07 |
| ☐ 5 Tom Gallagher | .75 | .30 | .07 |
| ☐ 6 Travis Hanson | .75 | .30 | .07 |
| ☐ 7 Damon Huard | .75 | .30 | .07 |
| ☐ 8 Matt Jones | .75 | .30 | .07 |
| ☐ 9 Pete Kaligis | .75 | .30 | .07 |
| ☐ 10 Napoleon Kaufman | 3.50 | 1.40 | .35 |
| ☐ 11 Joe Kralik | .75 | .30 | .07 |
| ☐ 12 Andy Mason | .75 | .30 | .07 |
| ☐ 13 Jim Nevelle | .75 | .30 | .07 |
| ☐ 14 Pete Pierson | .75 | .30 | .07 |
| ☐ 15 Steve Springstead | .75 | .30 | .07 |
| ☐ 16 John Werdel | .75 | .30 | .07 |

## 1988 Washington State Smokey

The 1988 Washington State University Smokey set contains 12 standard-size (2 1/2" by 3 1/2") cards. The fronts feature color photos bordered in white and maroon, with name, position, and jersey number. The vertically oriented backs have fire prevention cartoons. The cards are unnumbered, so are listed by jersey numbers. The set is also noteworthy in that it contains one of the few cards of Mike Utley, the courageous Detroit Lions' lineman, who was paralyzed as a result of an on-field injury during a game in 1991.

| | MINT | EXC | G-VG |
|---|---|---|---|
| COMPLETE SET (12) | 18.00 | 7.25 | 1.80 |
| COMMON PLAYER | 1.00 | .40 | .10 |

| | | | |
|---|---|---|---|
| ☐ 3 Timm Rosenbach | 4.00 | 1.60 | .40 |
| ☐ 18 Shawn Landrum | 1.00 | .40 | .10 |
| ☐ 19 Artie Holmes | 1.00 | .40 | .10 |
| ☐ 31 Steve Broussard | 3.00 | 1.20 | .30 |
| ☐ 42 Ron Lee | 1.00 | .40 | .10 |
| ☐ 55 Tuineau Alipate | 1.00 | .40 | .10 |
| ☐ 60 Mike Utley | 6.00 | 2.40 | .60 |
| ☐ 68 Chris Dyko | 1.00 | .40 | .10 |
| ☐ 74 Jim Michalczik | 1.00 | .40 | .10 |
| ☐ 75 Tony Savage | 1.00 | .40 | .10 |
| ☐ 76 Ivan Cook | 1.00 | .40 | .10 |
| ☐ 82 Doug Wellsandt | 1.00 | .40 | .10 |

## 1990 Washington State Smokey *

This 16-card set was sponsored by the USDA Forest Service in cooperation with several other federal agencies. The cards measure the standard size, 2 1/2" by 3 1/2". Apart from four female volleyball players (2, 11, 13, and 14), the set features football players. The front presents an action color photo with text and borders in the school's colors maroon and silver. The Smokey the Bear picture appears in the lower left hand corner. The back includes biographical information and a public service announcement (with cartoon) concerning fire prevention. The cards are unnumbered, so they are listed alphabetically by subject's name.

| | MINT | EXC | G-VG |
|---|---|---|---|
| COMPLETE SET (16) | 10.00 | 4.00 | 1.00 |
| COMMON CARD (1-16) | .75 | .30 | .07 |
| | | | |
| ☐ 1 Lewis Bush 48 | .75 | .30 | .07 |
| ☐ 2 Carrie Couturier | .75 | .30 | .07 |
|   (Women's volleyball) | | | |
| ☐ 3 Steve Cromer 70 | .75 | .30 | .07 |
| ☐ 4 C.J. Davis 1 | .75 | .30 | .07 |
| ☐ 5 John Diggs 22 | .75 | .30 | .07 |
| ☐ 6 Alvin Dunn 27 | .75 | .30 | .07 |
| ☐ 7 Aaron Garcia 9 | .75 | .30 | .07 |
| ☐ 8 Bob Garman 74 | .75 | .30 | .07 |
| ☐ 9 Brad Gossen 12 | .75 | .30 | .07 |
| ☐ 10 Calvin Griggs 5 | .75 | .30 | .07 |
| ☐ 11 Kelly Hankins | .75 | .30 | .07 |
|   (Women's volleyball) | | | |
| ☐ 12 Jason Hanson 4 | 2.50 | 1.00 | .25 |
| ☐ 13 Kristen Hovde | .75 | .30 | .07 |
|   (Women's volleyball) | | | |
| ☐ 14 Keri Killebrew | .75 | .30 | .07 |
|   (Women's volleyball) | | | |
| ☐ 15 Chris Moton 6 | .75 | .30 | .07 |
| ☐ 16 Ron Ricard 26 | .75 | .30 | .07 |

## 1991 Washington State Smokey *

This 16-card set was sponsored by the USDA Forest Service and other federal agencies. The cards measure the standard size (2 1/2" by 3 1/2") and are printed on thin cardboard stock. The set was issued as a perforated sheet and as an uncut sheet without perforations. The final row of the sheet features four women volleyball players. The card fronts are accented in the team's colors (dark red and gray) and have either glossy color action or posed player photos. The top of the pictures is curved to resemble an archway, and the team name follows the curve of the arch. The player's name and position appear in a stripe below the picture. The backs present statistics and a fire prevention cartoon starring Smokey. The cards are unnumbered and checklisted below in alphabetical order, with the women volleyball players listed at the end.

| | MINT | EXC | G-VG |
|---|---|---|---|
| COMPLETE SET (16) | 9.00 | 3.75 | .90 |
| COMMON CARD (1-12) | .75 | .30 | .07 |
| COMMON CARD (13-16) | .75 | .30 | .07 |
| | | | |
| ☐ 1 Lewis Bush | .75 | .30 | .07 |
| ☐ 2 Chad Cushing | .75 | .30 | .07 |
| ☐ 3 C.J. Davis | .75 | .30 | .07 |
| ☐ 4 Bob Garman | .75 | .30 | .07 |
| ☐ 5 Jason Hanson | 2.00 | .80 | .20 |
| ☐ 6 Gabriel Oladipo | .75 | .30 | .07 |
| ☐ 7 Anthony Prior | 1.50 | .60 | .15 |
| ☐ 8 Jay Reyna | .75 | .30 | .07 |
| ☐ 9 Lee Tilleman | .75 | .30 | .07 |
| ☐ 10 Kirk Westerfield | .75 | .30 | .07 |
| ☐ 11 Butch Williams | .75 | .30 | .07 |
| ☐ 12 Michael Wright | .75 | .30 | .07 |
| ☐ 13 Carrie Couturier | .75 | .30 | .07 |
|   (Women's volleyball) | | | |
| ☐ 14 Kelly Hankins | .75 | .30 | .07 |
|   (Women's volleyball) | | | |
| ☐ 15 Kristen Hovde | .75 | .30 | .07 |
|   (Women's volleyball) | | | |
| ☐ 16 Keri Killebrew | .75 | .30 | .07 |
|   (Women's volleyball) | | | |

## 1992 Washington State Smokey *

This 20-card set was sponsored by the USDA Forest Service and other federal agencies. The cards measure the standard size (2 1/2" by 3 1/2") and are printed on thin cardboard stock. The set was issued as a perforated sheet. The last two rows of the sheet feature women volleyball players. The card fronts are accented in the team's colors (brick-red and gray) and have color action player photos. The team name and year appear above the photo in gray print on a brick-red bar that partially rests on a gray bar with notched ends. Below the photo, the player's name and sponsor logos appear in a gray border stripe. The cards are unnumbered and checklisted below in alphabetical order with the volleyball players listed at the end.

| | MINT | EXC | G-VG |
|---|---|---|---|
| COMPLETE SET (20) | 15.00 | 6.00 | 1.50 |
| COMMON PLAYER (1-12) | .60 | .24 | .06 |
| COMMON CARD (13-20) | .50 | .20 | .05 |
| | | | |
| ☐ 1 Drew Bledsoe | 10.00 | 4.00 | 1.00 |
| ☐ 2 Phillip Bobo | .75 | .30 | .07 |
| ☐ 3 Lewis Bush | .75 | .30 | .07 |
| ☐ 4 C.J. Davis | .75 | .30 | .07 |
| ☐ 5 Shaumbe Wright-Fair | .75 | .30 | .07 |
| ☐ 6 Bob Garman | .60 | .24 | .06 |
| ☐ 7 Ray Hall | .60 | .24 | .06 |
| ☐ 8 Torey Hunter | .75 | .30 | .07 |
| ☐ 9 Kurt Loertscher | .60 | .24 | .06 |
| ☐ 10 Anthony McClanahan | .75 | .30 | .07 |
| ☐ 11 John Rushing | .60 | .24 | .06 |
| ☐ 12 Clarence Williams | .75 | .30 | .07 |
| ☐ 13 Betty Bartram | .50 | .20 | .05 |
|   (Women's volleyball) | | | |

| | | | |
|---|---|---|---|
| ☐ 14 Krista Beightol (Women's volleyball) | .50 | .20 | .05 |
| ☐ 15 Carrie Gilley (Women's volleyball) | .50 | .20 | .05 |
| ☐ 16 Shannan Griffin (Women's volleyball) | .50 | .20 | .05 |
| ☐ 17 Becky Howlett (Women's volleyball) | .50 | .20 | .05 |
| ☐ 18 Kristen Hovde (Women's volleyball) | .50 | .20 | .05 |
| ☐ 19 Keri Killebrew (Women's volleyball) | .50 | .20 | .05 |
| ☐ 20 Cindy Fredrick CO M. Farokhmanesh ACO Gweyn Leabo ACO (Women's volleyball) | .50 | .20 | .05 |

| | | | |
|---|---|---|---|
| ☐ 10C Dwayne Woods | 1.00 | .40 | .10 |
| ☐ 10D Ben Williams | 2.00 | .80 | .20 |
| ☐ 10H John Adams | 1.00 | .40 | .10 |
| ☐ 10S Tom Florence | 1.00 | .40 | .10 |
| ☐ 11C Marcus Mauney | 1.00 | .40 | .10 |
| ☐ 11D John Spraggins | 1.00 | .40 | .10 |
| ☐ 11H Bruce Huffman | 1.00 | .40 | .10 |
| ☐ 11S Bernie Kirchner | 1.00 | .40 | .10 |
| ☐ 12C Artie Owens | 2.00 | .80 | .20 |
| ☐ 12D Charlie Miller | 1.00 | .40 | .10 |
| ☐ 12H 1974 Cheerleaders | 2.00 | .80 | .20 |
| ☐ 12S Eddie Russell | 1.00 | .40 | .10 |
| ☐ 13C Danny Buggs | 4.00 | 1.60 | .40 |
| ☐ 13D Marshall Mills | 1.00 | .40 | .10 |
| ☐ 13H John Everly | 1.00 | .40 | .10 |
| ☐ 13S Jeff Merrow | 3.00 | 1.20 | .30 |
| ☐ JK Student Foundation | 1.50 | .60 | .15 |

## 1974 West Virginia

This 53-card set was sponsored by the Student Foundation, a non-profit campus development group. The cards were issued in the playing card format, and each card measures approximately 2 1/8" by 3 1/8". The fronts feature either close-ups or posed action shots of the players. Card backs feature a line drawing of a West Virginia Mountaineer, with the four corners cut off to create triangles. There are two different card backs, same design, but either blue or gold. Because this set is similar to a playing card set, the set is arranged just like a card deck and checklisted below as follows: C means Clubs, D means Diamonds, H means Hearts, S means Spades, and JK means Joker. The cards are checklisted below in playing card order by suits and numbers are assigned to Aces (1), Jacks (11), Queens (12), and Kings (13). The joker is listed at the end. The key card in the set is coach Bobby Bowden.

| | NRMT | VG-E | GOOD |
|---|---|---|---|
| COMPLETE SET (53) | 50.00 | 20.00 | 5.00 |
| COMMON CARD | 1.00 | .40 | .10 |
| ☐ 1C Stu Wolpert | 1.00 | .40 | .10 |
| ☐ 1D Mountaineer Coaches | 4.00 | 1.60 | .40 |
| ☐ 1H Leland Byrd AD | 1.00 | .40 | .10 |
| ☐ 1S Bobby Bowden CO | 25.00 | 10.00 | 2.50 |
| ☐ 2C Jay Sheehan | 1.00 | .40 | .10 |
| ☐ 2D Tom Brandner | 1.00 | .40 | .10 |
| ☐ 2H Tom Bowden | 1.00 | .40 | .10 |
| ☐ 2S Chuck Smith | 1.00 | .40 | .10 |
| ☐ 3C Ray Marshall | 1.00 | .40 | .10 |
| ☐ 3D Randy Swinson | 1.00 | .40 | .10 |
| ☐ 3H Tom Loadman | 1.00 | .40 | .10 |
| ☐ 3S Bob Kaminski | 1.00 | .40 | .10 |
| ☐ 4C Ron Lee | 3.00 | 1.20 | .30 |
| ☐ 4D Kirk Lewis | 1.00 | .40 | .10 |
| ☐ 4H Greg Dorn | 1.00 | .40 | .10 |
| ☐ 4S Emil Ros | 1.00 | .40 | .10 |
| ☐ 5C Mark Burke | 1.00 | .40 | .10 |
| ☐ 5D Rory Fields | 1.00 | .40 | .10 |
| ☐ 5H Gary Lombard | 1.00 | .40 | .10 |
| ☐ 5S Brian Gates | 1.00 | .40 | .10 |
| ☐ 6C John Schell | 1.00 | .40 | .10 |
| ☐ 6D Paul Jordan | 1.00 | .40 | .10 |
| ☐ 6H Mike Hubbard | 1.00 | .40 | .10 |
| ☐ 6S Chuck Kelly | 1.00 | .40 | .10 |
| ☐ 7C Rick Pennypacker | 2.00 | .80 | .20 |
| ☐ 7D Heywood Smith | 1.00 | .40 | .10 |
| ☐ 7H Jack Eastwood | 1.00 | .40 | .10 |
| ☐ 7S Andy Peters | 1.00 | .40 | .10 |
| ☐ 8C Steve Dunlap | 1.00 | .40 | .10 |
| ☐ 8D Dave Wilcher | 1.00 | .40 | .10 |
| ☐ 8H Greg Anderson | 1.00 | .40 | .10 |
| ☐ 8S Ken Culbertson | 1.00 | .40 | .10 |
| ☐ 9C David Van Halanger | 1.00 | .40 | .10 |
| ☐ 9D Rick Shaffer | 1.00 | .40 | .10 |
| ☐ 9H Rich Lukowski | 1.00 | .40 | .10 |
| ☐ 9S Al Gluchoski | 1.00 | .40 | .10 |

## 1988 West Virginia

The 1988 West Virginia University set contains 16 standard-size (2 1/2" by 3 1/2") cards. The fronts feature color photos bordered in white, with name, position, and jersey number. The vertically oriented backs have brief biographical information and "Tips from the Mountaineers." The cards are unnumbered and are listed alphabetically by subject. The set was sponsored by West Virginia University Hospitals.

| | MINT | EXC | G-VG |
|---|---|---|---|
| COMPLETE SET (16) | 20.00 | 8.00 | 2.00 |
| COMMON CARD (1-16) | 1.00 | .40 | .10 |
| ☐ 1 Charlie Baumann | 2.00 | .80 | .20 |
| ☐ 2 Anthony Brown | 1.00 | .40 | .10 |
| ☐ 3 Willie Edwards | 1.00 | .40 | .10 |
| ☐ 4 Theron Ellis | 1.50 | .60 | .15 |
| ☐ 5 Chris Haering | 1.00 | .40 | .10 |
| ☐ 6 Major Harris | 5.00 | 2.00 | .50 |
| ☐ 7 Undra Johnson | 1.50 | .60 | .15 |
| ☐ 8 Kevin Koken | 1.00 | .40 | .10 |
| ☐ 9 Pat Marlatt | 1.00 | .40 | .10 |
| ☐ 10 Eugene Napoleon | 1.00 | .40 | .10 |
| ☐ 11 Don Nehlen CO | 2.50 | 1.00 | .25 |
| ☐ 12 Bo Orlando | 3.00 | 1.20 | .30 |
| ☐ 13 Chris Parker | 1.00 | .40 | .10 |
| ☐ 14 Robert Pickett | 1.00 | .40 | .10 |
| ☐ 15 Brian Smider | 1.00 | .40 | .10 |
| ☐ 16 John Stroia | 1.00 | .40 | .10 |

## 1990 West Virginia Program Cards

Sponsored by Gatorade Thirst Quencher, the 1990 West Virginia Mountaineers football set consists of 49 standard-size (2 1/2" by 3

1/2") cards printed on thin card stock. The set was available as a complete set or in seven-card perforated sheets featured in issues of Mountaineer Illustrated Magazine. The fronts feature posed color action shots bordered in white. The words "West Virginia Mountaineers" is shown in the team's colors above the picture. Below the picture are the team helmet, a green broken stripe, and player information. The back has biographical information, player profile, and "Mountaineer Tips" that consist of encouragements to stay in school. The cards are unnumbered and checklisted below in alphabetical order. Key cards in the set include James Jett and baseball's Darrell Whitmore.

|  | MINT | EXC | G-VG |
|---|---|---|---|
| COMPLETE SET (49) | 30.00 | 12.00 | 3.00 |
| COMMON CARD (1-49) | .75 | .30 | .07 |
| ☐ 1 Tarris Alexander | 1.00 | .40 | .10 |
| ☐ 2 Leroy Axem | .75 | .30 | .07 |
| ☐ 3 Michael Beasley | .75 | .30 | .07 |
| ☐ 4 Calvin Bell | .75 | .30 | .07 |
| ☐ 5 Matt Bland | .75 | .30 | .07 |
| ☐ 6 John Brown | 1.25 | .50 | .12 |
| ☐ 7 Brad Carroll | .75 | .30 | .07 |
| ☐ 8 Mike Collins | .75 | .30 | .07 |
| ☐ 9 Mike Compton | 1.50 | .60 | .15 |
| ☐ 10 Cecil Doggette | .75 | .30 | .07 |
| ☐ 11 Rick Dolly | .75 | .30 | .07 |
| ☐ 12 Theron Ellis | 1.25 | .50 | .12 |
| ☐ 13 Charlie Fedorco | .75 | .30 | .07 |
| ☐ 14 Garrett Ford | .75 | .30 | .07 |
| ☐ 15 Scott Gaskins | 1.00 | .40 | .10 |
| ☐ 16 Boris Graham | .75 | .30 | .07 |
| ☐ 17 Keith Graley | .75 | .30 | .07 |
| ☐ 18 Chris Gray | .75 | .30 | .07 |
| ☐ 19 Greg Hertzog | .75 | .30 | .07 |
| ☐ 20 Ed Hill | 1.00 | .40 | .10 |
| ☐ 21 Verne Howard | .75 | .30 | .07 |
| ☐ 22 James Jett | 5.00 | 2.00 | .50 |
| ☐ 23 Greg Jones | .75 | .30 | .07 |
| ☐ 24 Jon Jones | .75 | .30 | .07 |
| ☐ 25 Ted Kester | .75 | .30 | .07 |
| ☐ 26 Darroll Mitchell | .75 | .30 | .07 |
| ☐ 27 John Murphy | .75 | .30 | .07 |
| ☐ 28 Don Nehlen CO | 2.00 | .80 | .20 |
| ☐ 29 Tim Newsom | .75 | .30 | .07 |
| ☐ 30 Joe Pabian | .75 | .30 | .07 |
| ☐ 31 John Ray | .75 | .30 | .07 |
| ☐ 32 Steve Redd | .75 | .30 | .07 |
| ☐ 33 Joe Ruth | .75 | .30 | .07 |
| ☐ 34 Alex Shook | .75 | .30 | .07 |
| ☐ 35 Jeff Sniffen | .75 | .30 | .07 |
| ☐ 36 Ray Staten | .75 | .30 | .07 |
| ☐ 37 Rick Stead | .75 | .30 | .07 |
| ☐ 38 Darren Studstill | 2.50 | 1.00 | .25 |
| ☐ 39 Lorenzo Styles | .75 | .30 | .07 |
| ☐ 40 Gary Tillis | .75 | .30 | .07 |
| ☐ 41 Rico Tyler | .75 | .30 | .07 |
| ☐ 42 Darrell Whitmore | 4.00 | 1.60 | .40 |
| ☐ 43 E.J. Wheeler | .75 | .30 | .07 |
| ☐ 44 Darrick Wiley | 1.00 | .40 | .10 |
| ☐ 45 Tim Williams | .75 | .30 | .07 |
| ☐ 46 Sam Wilson | .75 | .30 | .07 |
| ☐ 47 Dale Wolfley | .75 | .30 | .07 |
| ☐ 48 Rob Yachini | .75 | .30 | .07 |
| ☐ 49 Mountaineer Field | .75 | .30 | .07 |

## 1991 West Virginia ATG

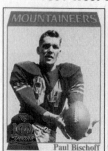

Paul Bischoff

The 1991 West Virginia All-Time Greats football set was produced by College Classics to celebrate the university's 100th year anniversary. It was sponsored and sold by 7-Eleven Stores. The 50 standard-size (2 1/2" by 3 1/2") cards display action photos, with the team name above and the player's name in the white border beneath the picture. A "100 Years" emblem is superimposed at the lower right corner. The backs

have biographical information, career statistics, and "Mountaineer Tips" in the form of "stay in school" messages.

|  | MINT | EXC | G-VG |
|---|---|---|---|
| COMPLETE SET (50) | 15.00 | 6.00 | 1.50 |
| COMMON CARD (1-50) | .35 | .14 | .03 |
| ☐ 1 Jeff Hostetler | 2.00 | .80 | .20 |
| ☐ 2 Tom Allman | .35 | .14 | .03 |
| ☐ 3 Russ Bailey | .35 | .14 | .03 |
| ☐ 4 Paul Bischoff | .35 | .14 | .03 |
| ☐ 5 Bruce Bosley | .50 | .20 | .05 |
| ☐ 6 Jim Braxton | .50 | .20 | .05 |
| ☐ 7 Danny Buggs | .50 | .20 | .05 |
| ☐ 8 Harry Clarke | .35 | .14 | .03 |
| ☐ 9 Ken Culbertson | .35 | .14 | .03 |
| ☐ 10 Willie Drewrey | .60 | .24 | .06 |
| ☐ 11 Steve Dunlap | .35 | .14 | .03 |
| ☐ 12 Garrett Ford | .35 | .14 | .03 |
| ☐ 13 Dennis Fowlkes | .35 | .14 | .03 |
| ☐ 14 Bob Gresham | .35 | .14 | .03 |
| ☐ 15 Chris Haering | .50 | .20 | .05 |
| ☐ 16 Major Harris | 1.00 | .40 | .10 |
| ☐ 17 Steve Hathaway | .35 | .14 | .03 |
| ☐ 18 Rick Hollins | .35 | .14 | .03 |
| ☐ 19 Chuck Howley | .75 | .30 | .07 |
| ☐ 20 Sam Huff | 1.25 | .50 | .12 |
| ☐ 21 Brian Jozwiak | .50 | .20 | .05 |
| ☐ 22 Gene Lamone | .35 | .14 | .03 |
| ☐ 23 Oliver Luck | .60 | .24 | .06 |
| ☐ 24 Kerry Marbury | .35 | .14 | .03 |
| ☐ 25 Joe Marconi | .50 | .20 | .05 |
| ☐ 26 Jeff Merrow | .50 | .20 | .05 |
| ☐ 27 Steve Newberry | .35 | .14 | .03 |
| ☐ 28 Bob Orders | .35 | .14 | .03 |
| ☐ 29 Artie Owens | .35 | .14 | .03 |
| ☐ 30 Tom Pridemore | .50 | .20 | .05 |
| ☐ 31 Mark Raugh | .35 | .14 | .03 |
| ☐ 32 Reggie Rembert | .60 | .24 | .06 |
| ☐ 33 Ira Rodgers | .35 | .14 | .03 |
| ☐ 34 Mike Sherwood | .35 | .14 | .03 |
| ☐ 35 Joe Stydahar | .60 | .24 | .06 |
| ☐ 36 Renaldo Turnbull | .75 | .30 | .07 |
| ☐ 37 Paul Woodside | .35 | .14 | .03 |
| ☐ 38 Fred Wyant | .35 | .14 | .03 |
| ☐ 39 Carl Leatherwood | .35 | .14 | .03 |
| ☐ 40 Darryl Talley | .75 | .30 | .07 |
| ☐ 41 David Grant | .35 | .14 | .03 |
| ☐ 42 Bobby Bowden CO | .75 | .30 | .07 |
| ☐ 43 Jim Carlen CO | .35 | .14 | .03 |
| ☐ 44 Frank Cignetti CO | .35 | .14 | .03 |
| ☐ 45 Gene Corum CO | .35 | .14 | .03 |
| ☐ 46 Art Lewis CO | .35 | .14 | .03 |
| ☐ 47 Don Nehlen CO | .60 | .24 | .06 |
| ☐ 48 New Mountaineer Field | .35 | .14 | .03 |
| ☐ 49 Old Mountaineer Field | .35 | .14 | .03 |
| ☐ 50 Lambert Trophy | .50 | .20 | .05 |

## 1991 West Virginia Program Cards

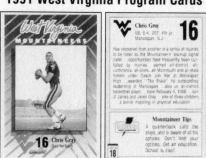

This 42-card standard-size (2 1/2" by 3 1/2") set was printed on thin card stock with white borders; the card fronts carry a posed action player image photo against a screened blue background with blue and gold diagonal lines. West Virginia Mountaineers is imprinted over blue background at top while jersey number, name, and position appear at bottom. The backs have biography, "Mountaineer Tips" consisting of school advice, and the Gatorade Thirst Quencher logo. The cards are numbered on the back; the numbering is essentially alphabetical by player's name. Seven different cards were featured in each of the team's six home game Mountaineer Illustrated programs.

|  | MINT | EXC | G-VG |
|---|---|---|---|
| COMPLETE SET (42) | 25.00 | 10.00 | 2.50 |
| COMMON PLAYER (1-42) | .75 | .30 | .07 |

| | | | |
|---|---|---|---|
| ☐ 1 Tarris Alexander | 1.00 | .40 | .10 |
| ☐ 2 Johnathan Allen | .75 | .30 | .07 |
| ☐ 3 Leroy Axem | .75 | .30 | .07 |
| ☐ 4 Joe Ayuso | .75 | .30 | .07 |
| ☐ 5 Michael Beasley | .75 | .30 | .07 |
| ☐ 6 Rich Braham | 1.00 | .40 | .10 |
| ☐ 7 Tom Briggs | .75 | .30 | .07 |
| ☐ 8 John Cappa | .75 | .30 | .07 |
| ☐ 9 Mike Collins | 1.00 | .40 | .10 |
| ☐ 10 Mike Compton | 1.25 | .50 | .12 |
| ☐ 11 Doug Cooley | .75 | .30 | .07 |
| ☐ 12 Cecil Doggette | .75 | .30 | .07 |
| ☐ 13 Rick Dolly | .75 | .30 | .07 |
| ☐ 14 Garrett Ford | 1.00 | .40 | .10 |
| ☐ 15 Scott Gaskins | .75 | .30 | .07 |
| ☐ 16 Boris Graham | .75 | .30 | .07 |
| ☐ 17 Keith Graley | .75 | .30 | .07 |
| ☐ 18 Chris Gray | .75 | .30 | .07 |
| ☐ 19 Barry Hawkins | .75 | .30 | .07 |
| ☐ 20 Ed Hill | 1.00 | .40 | .10 |
| ☐ 21 James Jett | 3.50 | 1.40 | .35 |
| ☐ 22 Jon Jones | .75 | .30 | .07 |
| ☐ 23 Jim LeBlanc | 1.00 | .40 | .10 |
| ☐ 24 David Mayfield | 1.25 | .50 | .12 |
| ☐ 25 Adrian Murrell | 2.50 | 1.00 | .25 |
| ☐ 26 Sam Mustipher | .75 | .30 | .07 |
| ☐ 27 Tim Newsom | .75 | .30 | .07 |
| ☐ 28 Tommy Orr | 1.00 | .40 | .10 |
| ☐ 29 Joe Pabian | .75 | .30 | .07 |
| ☐ 30 John Ray | .75 | .30 | .07 |
| ☐ 31 Wes Richardson | 1.00 | .40 | .10 |
| ☐ 32 Nate Rine | 1.00 | .40 | .10 |
| ☐ 33 Joe Ruth | .75 | .30 | .07 |
| ☐ 34 Alex Shook | .75 | .30 | .07 |
| ☐ 35 Kwame Smith | .75 | .30 | .07 |
| ☐ 36 Darren Studstill | 2.00 | .80 | .20 |
| ☐ 37 Lorenzo Styles | .75 | .30 | .07 |
| ☐ 38 Gary Tillis | .75 | .30 | .07 |
| ☐ 39 Ron Weaver | .75 | .30 | .07 |
| ☐ 40 Darrell Whitmore | 3.00 | 1.20 | .30 |
| ☐ 41 Darrick Wiley | 1.00 | .40 | .10 |
| ☐ 42 Rodney Woodard | .75 | .30 | .07 |

| | | | |
|---|---|---|---|
| ☐ 17 Scott Gaskins | 1.00 | .40 | .10 |
| ☐ 18 Boris Graham | .75 | .30 | .07 |
| ☐ 19 Dan Harless | 1.00 | .40 | .10 |
| ☐ 20 Barry Hawkins | 1.00 | .40 | .10 |
| ☐ 21 Ed Hill | 1.00 | .40 | .10 |
| ☐ 22 James Jett | 3.00 | 1.20 | .30 |
| ☐ 23 Mark Johnson | .75 | .30 | .07 |
| ☐ 24 Jon Jones | .75 | .30 | .07 |
| ☐ 25 Jake Kelchner | 2.50 | 1.00 | .25 |
| ☐ 26 Harold Kidd | 1.00 | .40 | .10 |
| ☐ 27 Jim LeBlanc | 1.00 | .40 | .10 |
| ☐ 28 David Mayfield | 1.00 | .40 | .10 |
| ☐ 29 Brian Moore | .75 | .30 | .07 |
| ☐ 30 Adrian Murrell | 2.50 | 1.00 | .25 |
| ☐ 31 Robert Nelson | .75 | .30 | .07 |
| ☐ 32 Tommy Orr | 1.00 | .40 | .10 |
| ☐ 33 Joe Pabian | .75 | .30 | .07 |
| ☐ 34 Brett Parise | .75 | .30 | .07 |
| ☐ 35 Steve Perkins | 1.00 | .40 | .10 |
| ☐ 36 Steve Redd | .75 | .30 | .07 |
| ☐ 37 Wes Richardson | 1.00 | .40 | .10 |
| ☐ 38 Nate Rine | 1.00 | .40 | .10 |
| ☐ 39 Tom Robsock | 1.00 | .40 | .10 |
| ☐ 40 Kwame Smith | .75 | .30 | .07 |
| ☐ 41 Darren Studstill | 2.00 | .80 | .20 |
| ☐ 42 Lorenzo Styles | .75 | .30 | .07 |
| ☐ 43 Matt Taffoni | 1.00 | .40 | .10 |
| ☐ 44 Mark Ulmer | .75 | .30 | .07 |
| ☐ 45 Mike Vanderjagt | .75 | .30 | .07 |
| ☐ 46 Darrick Wiley | 1.00 | .40 | .10 |
| ☐ 47 Dale Williams | 1.00 | .40 | .10 |
| ☐ 48 Rodney Woodard | .75 | .30 | .07 |
| ☐ 49 James Wright | .75 | .30 | .07 |

## 1993 West Virginia

These 49 standard-size (2 1/2" by 3 1/2") cards feature on their fronts posed color player photos set within blue marbleized borders. The player's name and position appear in a yellowish rectangle underneath the photo. The gray bordered back carries the player's name, position, uniform number and biography at the top, followed by the player's career highlights. The cards are numbered on the back.

| | MINT | EXC | G-VG |
|---|---|---|---|
| COMPLETE SET (49) | 20.00 | 8.00 | 2.00 |
| COMMON PLAYER (1-49) | .50 | .20 | .05 |
| ☐ 1 Zach Abraham | .75 | .30 | .07 |
| ☐ 2 Tarris Alexander | .50 | .20 | .05 |
| ☐ 3 Mike Baker | .75 | .30 | .07 |
| ☐ 4 Aaron Beasley | .50 | .20 | .05 |
| ☐ 5 Derrick Bell | .50 | .20 | .05 |
| ☐ 6 Mike Booth | .50 | .20 | .05 |
| ☐ 7 Rich Braham | .75 | .30 | .07 |
| ☐ 8 Tim Brown | .75 | .30 | .07 |
| ☐ 9 Mike Collins | .75 | .30 | .07 |
| ☐ 10 Doug Costin | .50 | .20 | .05 |
| ☐ 11 Calvin Edwards | .50 | .20 | .05 |
| ☐ 12 Jim Freeman | .50 | .20 | .05 |
| ☐ 13 Big East Trophy | .75 | .30 | .07 |
| ☐ 14 Jimmy Gary | .50 | .20 | .05 |
| ☐ 15 Scott Gaskins | .75 | .30 | .07 |
| ☐ 16 Buddy Hager | .50 | .20 | .05 |
| ☐ 17 Dan Harless | .75 | .30 | .07 |
| ☐ 18 John Harper | .50 | .20 | .05 |
| ☐ 19 Barry Hawkins | .75 | .30 | .07 |
| ☐ 20 Ed Hill | .75 | .30 | .07 |
| ☐ 21 Jon Jones | .50 | .20 | .05 |
| ☐ 22 Jay Kearney | .50 | .20 | .05 |
| ☐ 23 Jake Kelchner | 2.00 | .80 | .20 |
| ☐ 24 Harold Kidd | .75 | .30 | .07 |
| ☐ 25 Chris Klick | .50 | .20 | .05 |
| ☐ 26 Jim LeBlanc | .75 | .30 | .07 |
| ☐ 27 Chris Ling | .50 | .20 | .05 |
| ☐ 28 David Mayfield | .75 | .30 | .07 |

## 1992 West Virginia Program Cards

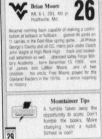

This 49-card set was available in the team's home game Mountaineer Illustrated Programs. The cards measure the standard-size (2 1/2" by 3 1/2") and were printed on thin stock. The white-bordered fronts carry a posed action player photo on an orange-yellow background with short diagonal maroon and gray lines. West Virginia Mountaineers is imprinted at the top above the player's photo. The jersey number, name and position appear at the bottom. The backs have biography, "Mountaineer Tips," consisting of school advice, and the Gatorade logo. The cards are numbered on the back.

| | MINT | EXC | G-VG |
|---|---|---|---|
| COMPLETE SET (49) | 25.00 | 10.00 | 2.50 |
| COMMON PLAYER (1-49) | .75 | .30 | .07 |
| ☐ 1 Tarris Alexander | 1.00 | .40 | .10 |
| ☐ 2 Joe Avila | .75 | .30 | .07 |
| ☐ 3 Leroy Axem | .75 | .30 | .07 |
| ☐ 4 Mike Baker | 1.00 | .40 | .10 |
| ☐ 5 Sean Biser | .75 | .30 | .07 |
| ☐ 6 Mike Booth | .75 | .30 | .07 |
| ☐ 7 Rich Braham | 1.00 | .40 | .10 |
| ☐ 8 Tom Briggs | .75 | .30 | .07 |
| ☐ 9 Tim Brown | 1.00 | .40 | .10 |
| ☐ 10 Darius Burwell | .75 | .30 | .07 |
| ☐ 11 John Cappa | .75 | .30 | .07 |
| ☐ 12 Matt Ceglie | .75 | .30 | .07 |
| ☐ 13 Mike Collins | 1.00 | .40 | .10 |
| ☐ 14 Mike Compton | 1.25 | .50 | .12 |
| ☐ 15 Rick Dolly | .75 | .30 | .07 |
| ☐ 16 Garrett Ford | .75 | .30 | .07 |

| | | | |
|---|---|---|---|
| ☐ 29 Keith Morris | .50 | .20 | .05 |
| ☐ 30 Tommy Orr | .75 | .30 | .07 |
| ☐ 31 Joe Pabian | .50 | .20 | .05 |
| ☐ 32 Ken Painter | .50 | .20 | .05 |
| ☐ 33 Steve Perkins | .75 | .30 | .07 |
| ☐ 34 Maurice Richards | .50 | .20 | .05 |
| ☐ 35 Wes Richardson | .75 | .30 | .07 |
| ☐ 36 Nate Rine | .75 | .30 | .07 |
| ☐ 37 Tom Robsock | .75 | .30 | .07 |
| ☐ 38 Todd Sauerbrun | 1.25 | .50 | .12 |
| ☐ 39 Darren Studstill | 2.00 | .80 | .20 |
| ☐ 40 Matt Taffoni | .75 | .30 | .07 |
| ☐ 41 Keith Taparausky | .50 | .20 | .05 |
| ☐ 42 Mark Ulmer | .50 | .20 | .05 |
| ☐ 43 Robert Walker | 1.25 | .50 | .12 |
| ☐ 44 Charles Washington | .50 | .20 | .05 |
| ☐ 45 Darrick Wiley | .75 | .30 | .07 |
| ☐ 46 Dale Williams | .75 | .30 | .07 |
| ☐ 47 James(Puppy) Wright | .50 | .20 | .05 |
| ☐ 48 Don Nehlen CO | 1.00 | .40 | .07 |
| ☐ 49 Mountaineer Field | .50 | .20 | .05 |

## 1992 Wisconsin Program Cards

This 27-card set of standard size (2 1/2" by 3 1/2") cards was issued in three Badger game programs in October 1992, each containing one nine-card sheet. The fronts feature former Badger football legends pictured in various poses, some in color, others in black-and-white, on a red-bordered card that has the red Wisconsin "W" logo in the top right. The player's name and uniform number appear in white in the bottom margin. The back has the player's name in white on a red stripe at the top. Another red stripe at the bottom contains the "W" logo and the logo of the sponsor, Bucky's Locker Room. Between the red stripes, a brief player biography appears in the white middle portion. The cards are numbered on the back.

| | MINT | EXC | G-VG |
|---|---|---|---|
| COMPLETE SET (27) | 20.00 | 8.00 | 2.00 |
| COMMON PLAYER (1-27) | .75 | .30 | .07 |
| ☐ 1 Troy Vincent | 2.50 | 1.00 | .25 |
| ☐ 2 Tim Krumrie | 1.25 | .50 | .12 |
| ☐ 3 Barry Alvarez CO | 1.25 | .50 | .12 |
| ☐ 4 Pat Richter | 1.25 | .50 | .12 |
| ☐ 5 Nate Odomes | 1.25 | .50 | .12 |
| ☐ 6 Ron Vander Kelen | 1.50 | .60 | .15 |
| ☐ 7 Don Davey | 1.25 | .50 | .12 |
| ☐ 8 Alan Ameche | 1.50 | .60 | .15 |
| ☐ 9 Randy Wright | 1.25 | .50 | .12 |
| ☐ 10 Ken Bowman | 1.00 | .40 | .10 |
| ☐ 11 Chuck Belin | .75 | .30 | .07 |
| ☐ 12 Elroy Hirsch | 1.50 | .60 | .15 |
| ☐ 13 Paul Gruber | 1.25 | .50 | .12 |
| ☐ 14 Al Toon | 1.25 | .50 | .12 |
| ☐ 15 Richard Johnson | 1.00 | .40 | .10 |
| ☐ 16 Pat Harder | 1.00 | .40 | .10 |
| ☐ 17 Gary Casper | .75 | .30 | .07 |
| ☐ 18 Rufus Ferguson | 1.00 | .40 | .10 |
| ☐ 19 Pat O'Donahue | .75 | .30 | .07 |
| ☐ 20 Dennis Lick | .75 | .30 | .07 |
| ☐ 21 Jeff Dellenbach | 1.00 | .40 | .10 |
| ☐ 22 Jim Bakken | 1.00 | .40 | .10 |
| ☐ 23 Milt Bruhn CO | .75 | .30 | .07 |
| ☐ 24 Mike Webster | 1.25 | .50 | .12 |
| ☐ 25 Dave McClain CO | .75 | .30 | .07 |
| ☐ 26 Bill Marek | .75 | .30 | .07 |
| ☐ 27 Rick Graf | 1.00 | .40 | .10 |

## 1990 Wyoming Smokey

The 1990 Wyoming Cowboys Smokey set was issued in a sheet of 16 cards which, when perforated, measure the standard size (2 1/2" by 3

1/2"). The fronts feature color photos with the player's name, position, and jersey number below the picture. The backs have biographical information and a fire prevention cartoon starring Smokey. The cards are unnumbered, so they are listed below in alphabetical order by subject.

| | MINT | EXC | G-VG |
|---|---|---|---|
| COMPLETE SET (16) | 20.00 | 8.00 | 2.00 |
| COMMON CARD (1-16) | 1.50 | .60 | .15 |
| ☐ 1 Tom Corontzos 18 | 1.50 | .60 | .15 |
| ☐ 2 Jay Daffer 34 | 1.50 | .60 | .15 |
| ☐ 3 Mitch Donahue 49 | 3.00 | 1.20 | .30 |
| ☐ 4 Sean Fleming 42 | 1.50 | .60 | .15 |
| ☐ 5 Pete Gosar 53 | 1.50 | .60 | .15 |
| ☐ 6 Robert Midgett 57 | 1.50 | .60 | .15 |
| ☐ 7 Bryan Mooney 9 | 1.50 | .60 | .15 |
| ☐ 8 Doug Rigby 77 | 1.50 | .60 | .15 |
| ☐ 9 Paul Roach CO | 2.00 | .80 | .20 |
| ☐ 10 Mark Timmer 48 | 1.50 | .60 | .15 |
| ☐ 11 Paul Wallace 29 | 1.50 | .60 | .15 |
| ☐ 12 Shawn Wiggins 15 | 1.50 | .60 | .15 |
| ☐ 13 Gordy Wood 95 | 1.50 | .60 | .15 |
| ☐ 14 Willie Wright 96 | 1.50 | .60 | .15 |
| ☐ 15 Cowboy Joe Mascot | 1.50 | .60 | .15 |
| ☐ 16 Title Card Cowboy logo | 1.50 | .60 | .15 |

## 1993 Wyoming Smokey

These 16 standard-size (2 1/2" by 3 1/2") cards feature on their fronts color player action shots set within yellow borders. The player's name and position appear on the left side beneath the photo; the team name and logo appear above the photo. The plain white back carries the player's name and position at the top, followed by a Smokey safety tip, and the player's career highlights. The cards are unnumbered and checklisted below in alphabetical order.

| | MINT | EXC | G-VG |
|---|---|---|---|
| COMPLETE SET (16) | 12.00 | 5.00 | 1.20 |
| COMMON PLAYER (1-16) | .75 | .30 | .07 |
| ☐ 1 John Burrough | .75 | .30 | .07 |
| ☐ 2 Wade Constance | .75 | .30 | .07 |
| ☐ 3 Mike Fitzgerald | 1.00 | .40 | .10 |
| ☐ 4 Jarrod Heidmann | 1.00 | .40 | .10 |
| ☐ 5 Joe Hughes | 1.00 | .40 | .10 |
| ☐ 6 Kenny Johnson | 1.00 | .40 | .10 |
| ☐ 7 Mike Jones | 1.00 | .40 | .10 |
| ☐ 8 Cody Kelly | 1.00 | .40 | .10 |
| ☐ 9 Rob Levin | 1.00 | .40 | .10 |
| ☐ 10 Prentice Rhone | .75 | .30 | .07 |
| ☐ 11 Greg Scanlan | 1.00 | .40 | .10 |

| | MINT | EXC | G-VG |
|---|---|---|---|
| ☐ 12 Cory Talich | 1.00 | .40 | .10 |
| ☐ 13 Kurt Whitehead | 1.00 | .40 | .10 |
| ☐ 14 Thomas Williams | .75 | .30 | .07 |
| ☐ 15 Tyrone Williams | .75 | .30 | .07 |
| ☐ 16 Ryan Yarborough | 3.00 | 1.20 | .30 |

## 1992 Youngstown State

These 54 standard-size (2 1/2" by 3 1/2") cards feature on their fronts posed black-and-white player photos set within red borders. The player's name, position, and jersey number appear beneath the photo. The gray-bordered back carries the player's name, position, uniform number and biography at the top, followed by the player's career highlights. The cards are unnumbered and checklisted below in alphabetical order.

| | MINT | EXC | G-VG |
|---|---|---|---|
| COMPLETE SET (54) | 20.00 | 8.00 | 2.00 |
| COMMON PLAYER (1-54) | .35 | .14 | .03 |
| | | | |
| ☐ 1 Ramon Amill | .35 | .14 | .03 |
| ☐ 2 Dan Black | .35 | .14 | .03 |
| ☐ 3 Trent Boykin | .35 | .14 | .03 |
| ☐ 4 Reginald Brown | .35 | .14 | .03 |
| ☐ 5 Mark Brungard | 1.00 | .40 | .10 |
| ☐ 6 Larry Bucciarelli | .35 | .14 | .03 |
| ☐ 7 David Burch | .35 | .14 | .03 |
| ☐ 8 Nick Cochran | .35 | .14 | .03 |
| ☐ 9 Brian Coman | .35 | .14 | .03 |
| ☐ 10 Ken Conatser ACO | .35 | .14 | .03 |
| ☐ 11 Darnell Clark | 1.00 | .40 | .10 |
| ☐ 12 Dave DelBoccio | .35 | .14 | .03 |
| ☐ 13 Tom Dillingham | .35 | .14 | .03 |
| ☐ 14 John Englehardt | .35 | .14 | .03 |
| ☐ 15 Marcus Evans | .35 | .14 | .03 |
| ☐ 16 Malcolm Everette | .35 | .14 | .03 |
| ☐ 17 Drew Gerber | .35 | .14 | .03 |
| ☐ 18 Michael Ghent | .35 | .14 | .03 |
| ☐ 19 Aaron Green | .35 | .14 | .03 |
| ☐ 20 Jon Heacock ACO | .35 | .14 | .03 |
| ☐ 21 Alfred Hill | .35 | .14 | .03 |
| ☐ 22 Terica Jones | .35 | .14 | .03 |
| ☐ 23 Craig Kertesz | .35 | .14 | .03 |
| ☐ 24 Paul Kokos Jr. | .35 | .14 | .03 |
| ☐ 25 Reginald Lee | .50 | .20 | .05 |
| ☐ 26 Raymond Miller | .50 | .20 | .05 |
| ☐ 27 Brian Moore ACO | .35 | .14 | .03 |
| ☐ 28 Mike Nezbeth | .35 | .14 | .03 |
| ☐ 29 William Norris | .35 | .14 | .03 |
| ☐ 30 James Panozzo | .35 | .14 | .03 |
| ☐ 31 Derek Pixley | .35 | .14 | .03 |
| ☐ 32 Jeff Powers | .35 | .14 | .03 |
| ☐ 33 David Quick | .35 | .14 | .03 |
| ☐ 34 John Quintana | .35 | .14 | .03 |
| ☐ 35 Mike Rekstis | .35 | .14 | .03 |
| ☐ 36 Demario Ridgeway | .35 | .14 | .03 |
| ☐ 37 Dave Roberts | .50 | .20 | .05 |
| ☐ 38 Chris Sammarone | .35 | .14 | .03 |
| ☐ 39 Randy Smith | .35 | .14 | .03 |
| ☐ 40 Tamron Smith | .75 | .30 | .07 |
| ☐ 41 John Steele | .35 | .14 | .03 |
| ☐ 42 Jim Tressel CO | .75 | .30 | .07 |
| ☐ 43 Chris Vecchione | .35 | .14 | .03 |
| ☐ 44 Lester Weaver | .50 | .20 | .05 |
| ☐ 45 Jeffrey Wilkins | .50 | .20 | .05 |
| ☐ 46 Herb Williams | .35 | .14 | .03 |
| ☐ 47 Ryan Wood | .35 | .14 | .03 |
| ☐ 48 Don Zwisler | .35 | .14 | .03 |
| ☐ 49 Penguin Pros Card 1 | .75 | .30 | .07 |
| ☐ 50 Penguin Pros Card 2 | .75 | .30 | .07 |
| ☐ 51 First-Team All-American | .75 | .30 | .07 |
| ☐ 52 Did You Know 1 | .35 | .14 | .03 |
| ☐ 53 Did You Know 2 | .35 | .14 | .03 |
| ☐ 54 Did You Know 3 | .35 | .14 | .03 |

## 1991 All World CFL Promo

This standard-size (2 1/2" by 3 1/2") promo card features Raghib "Rocket" Ismail, who was engaged by All World to serve as a spokesperson. The cards is lettered "P" on the back. The card front shows a blue and white striped border, i.e., the card is styled the same as the regular issue 1991 All World CFL cards.

| | MINT | EXC | G-VG |
|---|---|---|---|
| COMPLETE SET (1) | 1.00 | .40 | .10 |
| COMMON PLAYER | 1.00 | .40 | .10 |
| | | | |
| ☐ P Raghib Ismail | 1.00 | .40 | .10 |

## 1991 All World CFL

The premier edition of the 1991 All World Canadian Football set contains 110 cards measuring the standard size (2 1/2" by 3 1/2"). The cards were produced in both set and foil cases, and in both English and French versions. This set includes legends of the CFL (designated below by LEG) and an eight-card "Rocket" subset. In addition, 2,000 personally signed Rocket Ismail cards were randomly inserted in the packs: 1600 in the English foil cases and 400 in the French foil cases. The cards are numbered from 1-1600 in the English and 1-400 in the French. The front design has high gloss color action photos trimmed in red, on a royal blue background with diagonal white pinstripes. The player's name appears in red lettering in the lower left corner, and the CFL helmet logo is in the lower right corner. The backs are horizontally oriented and have royal blue borders. While the veteran player cards have head and shoulders color shots and player information on the backs, the rookie, coach, All Star, "Rocket," and legend cards omit the picture and have personal information framed by red borders. The cards are numbered on the back. The following cards are designated as "Rookie" on the card front: 4, 16, 28, 33, 53, 63, 66, 68, 78, 84, 92, 101, and 110. The premium for the French version is very slight, perhaps ten percent above the prices listed below.

| | MINT | EXC | G-VG |
|---|---|---|---|
| COMPLETE SET (110) | 4.00 | 1.60 | .40 |
| COMMON PLAYER (1-110) | .05 | .02 | .00 |
| | | | |
| ☐ 1 Raghib(Rocket) Ismail | .40 | .16 | .04 |
| Toronto Argonauts | | | |
| ☐ 2 Bruce McNall, Owner | .10 | .04 | .01 |
| Toronto Argonauts | | | |
| ☐ 3 Ray Alexander | .05 | .02 | .00 |
| British Columbia Lions | | | |
| ☐ 4 Matt Clark | .10 | .04 | .01 |
| British Columbia Lions | | | |
| ☐ 5 Bobby Jurasin | .10 | .04 | .01 |

Saskatchewan Roughriders
| | | | |
|---|---|---|---|
| ☐ 6 Dieter Brock LEG | .10 | .04 | .01 |
| ☐ 7 Doug Flutie | .50 | .20 | .05 |

British Columbia Lions
| | | | |
|---|---|---|---|
| ☐ 8 Stewart Hill | .05 | .02 | .00 |

British Columbia Lions
| | | | |
|---|---|---|---|
| ☐ 9 James Mills | .10 | .04 | .01 |

British Columbia Lions
| | | | |
|---|---|---|---|
| ☐ 10 Raghib(Rocket) Ismail | .25 | .10 | .02 |

Toronto Argonauts
(With Bruce McNall)
| | | | |
|---|---|---|---|
| ☐ 11 Tom Clements LEG | .15 | .06 | .01 |
| ☐ 12 Lui Passaglia | .10 | .04 | .01 |

British Columbia Lions
| | | | |
|---|---|---|---|
| ☐ 13 Ian Sinclair | .10 | .04 | .01 |

British Columbia Lions
| | | | |
|---|---|---|---|
| ☐ 14 Chris Skinner | .10 | .04 | .01 |

British Columbia Lions
| | | | |
|---|---|---|---|
| ☐ 15 Joe Theismann LEG | .20 | .08 | .02 |
| ☐ 16 Jon Volpe | .50 | .20 | .05 |

British Columbia Lions
| | | | |
|---|---|---|---|
| ☐ 17 Deatrich Wise | .05 | .02 | .00 |

British Columbia Lions
| | | | |
|---|---|---|---|
| ☐ 18 Danny Barrett | .10 | .04 | .01 |

Calgary Stampeders
| | | | |
|---|---|---|---|
| ☐ 19 Warren Moon LEG | .20 | .08 | .02 |
| ☐ 20 Leo Blanchard | .05 | .02 | .00 |

Calgary Stampeders
| | | | |
|---|---|---|---|
| ☐ 21 Derrick Crawford | .10 | .04 | .01 |

Calgary Stampeders
| | | | |
|---|---|---|---|
| ☐ 22 Lloyd Fairbanks | .10 | .04 | .01 |

Calgary Stampeders
| | | | |
|---|---|---|---|
| ☐ 23 David Beckman CO | .05 | .02 | .00 |

Hamilton Tiger-Cats
| | | | |
|---|---|---|---|
| ☐ 24 Matt Finlay | .05 | .02 | .00 |

Calgary Stampeders
| | | | |
|---|---|---|---|
| ☐ 25 Darryl Hall | .05 | .02 | .00 |

Calgary Stampeders
| | | | |
|---|---|---|---|
| ☐ 26 Ron Hopkins | .10 | .04 | .01 |

Calgary Stampeders
| | | | |
|---|---|---|---|
| ☐ 27 Wally Buono CO | .05 | .02 | .00 |

Calgary Stampeders
| | | | |
|---|---|---|---|
| ☐ 28 Kenton Leonard | .10 | .04 | .01 |

Calgary Stampeders
| | | | |
|---|---|---|---|
| ☐ 29 Brent Matich | .05 | .02 | .00 |

Calgary Stampeders
| | | | |
|---|---|---|---|
| ☐ 30 Greg Peterson | .05 | .02 | .00 |

Calgary Stampeders
| | | | |
|---|---|---|---|
| ☐ 31 Steve Goldman CO | .05 | .02 | .00 |

Ottawa Rough Riders
| | | | |
|---|---|---|---|
| ☐ 32 Allen Pitts | .50 | .20 | .05 |

Calgary Stampeders
| | | | |
|---|---|---|---|
| ☐ 33 Raghib(Rocket) Ismail | .25 | .10 | .02 |

Toronto Argonauts
| | | | |
|---|---|---|---|
| ☐ 34 Danny Bass | .10 | .04 | .01 |

Edmonton Eskimos
| | | | |
|---|---|---|---|
| ☐ 35 John Gregory CO | .05 | .02 | .00 |

Saskatchewan Roughriders
| | | | |
|---|---|---|---|
| ☐ 36 Rod Connop | .05 | .02 | .00 |

Edmonton Eskimos
| | | | |
|---|---|---|---|
| ☐ 37 Craig Ellis | .10 | .04 | .01 |

Edmonton Eskimos
| | | | |
|---|---|---|---|
| ☐ 38 Raghib(Rocket) Ismail | .25 | .10 | .02 |

Toronto Argonauts
Rookie
| | | | |
|---|---|---|---|
| ☐ 39 Ron Lancaster CO | .10 | .04 | .01 |

Edmonton Eskimos
| | | | |
|---|---|---|---|
| ☐ 40 Tracey Ham | .25 | .10 | .02 |

Edmonton Eskimos
| | | | |
|---|---|---|---|
| ☐ 41 Ray Macoritti | .10 | .04 | .01 |

Edmonton Eskimos
| | | | |
|---|---|---|---|
| ☐ 42 Willie Pless | .15 | .06 | .01 |

Edmonton Eskimos
| | | | |
|---|---|---|---|
| ☐ 43 Bob O'Billovich CO | .05 | .02 | .00 |

British Columbia Lions
| | | | |
|---|---|---|---|
| ☐ 44 Michael Soles | .10 | .04 | .01 |

Edmonton Eskimos
| | | | |
|---|---|---|---|
| ☐ 45 Reggie Taylor | .15 | .06 | .01 |

Edmonton Eskimos
| | | | |
|---|---|---|---|
| ☐ 46 Henry Williams | .30 | .12 | .03 |

Edmonton Eskimos
| | | | |
|---|---|---|---|
| ☐ 47 Adam Rita CO | .05 | .02 | .00 |

Toronto Argonauts
| | | | |
|---|---|---|---|
| ☐ 48 Larry Wruck | .10 | .04 | .01 |

Edmonton Eskimos
| | | | |
|---|---|---|---|
| ☐ 49 Grover Covington | .15 | .06 | .01 |

Hamilton Tiger-Cats
| | | | |
|---|---|---|---|
| ☐ 50 Rocky DiPietro | .15 | .06 | .01 |

Hamilton Tiger-Cats
| | | | |
|---|---|---|---|
| ☐ 51 Darryl Rogers CO | .05 | .02 | .00 |

Winnipeg Blue Bombers
| | | | |
|---|---|---|---|
| ☐ 52 Pete Giftopoulus | .10 | .04 | .01 |

Hamilton Tiger-Cats
| | | | |
|---|---|---|---|
| ☐ 53 Herman Heard | .15 | .06 | .01 |

Hamilton Tiger-Cats
| | | | |
|---|---|---|---|
| ☐ 54 Mike Kerrigan | .15 | .06 | .01 |

Hamilton Tiger-Cats
| | | | |
|---|---|---|---|
| ☐ 55 Reggie Barnes AS | .10 | .04 | .01 |

Ottawa Rough Riders
| | | | |
|---|---|---|---|
| ☐ 56 Derrick McAdoo | .15 | .06 | .01 |

Hamilton Tiger-Cats
| | | | |
|---|---|---|---|
| ☐ 57 Paul Osbaldiston | .10 | .04 | .01 |

Hamilton Tiger-Cats
| | | | |
|---|---|---|---|
| ☐ 58 Earl Winfield | .15 | .06 | .01 |

Hamilton Tiger-Cats
| | | | |
|---|---|---|---|
| ☐ 59 Greg Battle AS | .10 | .04 | .01 |

Winnipeg Blue Bombers
| | | | |
|---|---|---|---|
| ☐ 60 Damon Allen | .15 | .06 | .01 |

Ottawa Rough Riders
| | | | |
|---|---|---|---|
| ☐ 61 Reggie Barnes | .20 | .08 | .02 |

Ottawa Rough Riders
| | | | |
|---|---|---|---|
| ☐ 62 Bob Molle | .05 | .02 | .00 |

Winnipeg Blue Bombers
| | | | |
|---|---|---|---|
| ☐ 63 Raghib(Rocket) Ismail | .25 | .10 | .02 |

Toronto Argonauts
| | | | |
|---|---|---|---|
| ☐ 64 Irv Daymond | .05 | .02 | .00 |

Ottawa Rough Riders
| | | | |
|---|---|---|---|
| ☐ 65 Andre Francis | .05 | .02 | .00 |

Ottawa Rough Riders
| | | | |
|---|---|---|---|
| ☐ 66 Bart Hull | .15 | .06 | .01 |

Ottawa Rough Riders
| | | | |
|---|---|---|---|
| ☐ 67 Stephen Jones | .15 | .06 | .01 |

Ottawa Rough Riders
| | | | |
|---|---|---|---|
| ☐ 68 Raghib(Rocket) Ismail | .25 | .10 | .02 |

Toronto Argonauts
| | | | |
|---|---|---|---|
| ☐ 69 Glenn Kulka | .10 | .04 | .01 |

Ottawa Rough Riders
| | | | |
|---|---|---|---|
| ☐ 70 Loyd Lewis | .05 | .02 | .00 |

Ottawa Rough Riders
| | | | |
|---|---|---|---|
| ☐ 71 Rob Smith | .05 | .02 | .00 |

Ottawa Rough Riders
| | | | |
|---|---|---|---|
| ☐ 72 Roger Aldag | .10 | .04 | .01 |

Saskatchewan Roughriders
| | | | |
|---|---|---|---|
| ☐ 73 Kent Austin | .30 | .12 | .03 |

Saskatchewan Roughriders
| | | | |
|---|---|---|---|
| ☐ 74 Ray Elgaard | .15 | .06 | .01 |

Saskatchewan Roughriders
| | | | |
|---|---|---|---|
| ☐ 75 Mike Clemons AS | .20 | .08 | .02 |

Toronto Argonauts
| | | | |
|---|---|---|---|
| ☐ 76 Jeff Fairholm | .15 | .06 | .01 |

Saskatchewan Roughriders
| | | | |
|---|---|---|---|
| ☐ 77 Richie Hall | .05 | .02 | .00 |

Saskatchewan Roughriders
| | | | |
|---|---|---|---|
| ☐ 78 Willis Jacox | .15 | .06 | .01 |

Saskatchewan Roughriders
| | | | |
|---|---|---|---|
| ☐ 79 Eddie Lowe | .05 | .02 | .00 |

Saskatchewan Roughriders
| | | | |
|---|---|---|---|
| ☐ 80 Ray Elgaard AS | .10 | .04 | .01 |

Saskatchewan Roughriders
| | | | |
|---|---|---|---|
| ☐ 81 Donald Narcisse | .25 | .10 | .02 |

Saskatchewan Roughriders
| | | | |
|---|---|---|---|
| ☐ 82 James Mills AS | .10 | .04 | .01 |

British Columbia Lions
| | | | |
|---|---|---|---|
| ☐ 83 Dave Ridgway | .10 | .04 | .01 |

Saskatchewan Roughriders
| | | | |
|---|---|---|---|
| ☐ 84 Ted Wahl | .10 | .04 | .01 |

Saskatchewan Roughriders
| | | | |
|---|---|---|---|
| ☐ 85 Carl Brazley | .10 | .04 | .01 |

Toronto Argonauts
| | | | |
|---|---|---|---|
| ☐ 86 Mike Clemons | .30 | .12 | .03 |

Toronto Argonauts
| | | | |
|---|---|---|---|
| ☐ 87 Matt Dunigan | .30 | .12 | .03 |

Toronto Argonauts
| | | | |
|---|---|---|---|
| ☐ 88 Grey Cup | .10 | .04 | .01 |

Checklist 1
| | | | |
|---|---|---|---|
| ☐ 89 Harold Hallman | .10 | .04 | .01 |

Toronto Argonauts
| | | | |
|---|---|---|---|
| ☐ 90 Rodney Harding | .10 | .04 | .01 |

Toronto Argonauts
| | | | |
|---|---|---|---|
| ☐ 91 Don Moen | .10 | .04 | .01 |

Toronto Argonauts
| | | | |
|---|---|---|---|
| ☐ 92 Raghib(Rocket) Ismail | .25 | .10 | .02 |

Toronto Argonauts
| | | | |
|---|---|---|---|
| ☐ 93 Reggie Pleasant | .10 | .04 | .01 |

Toronto Argonauts
| | | | |
|---|---|---|---|
| ☐ 94 Darrell Smith UER | .20 | .08 | .02 |

Toronto Argonauts
(One L on front,
two on back)
| | | | |
|---|---|---|---|
| ☐ 95 Group Shot | .10 | .04 | .01 |

Checklist 2
| | | | |
|---|---|---|---|
| ☐ 96 Chris Schultz | .10 | .04 | .01 |

Toronto Argonauts
| | | | |
|---|---|---|---|
| ☐ 97 Don Wilson | .05 | .02 | .00 |

Toronto Argonauts
| | | | |
|---|---|---|---|
| ☐ 98 Greg Battle | .10 | .04 | .01 |

Winnipeg Blue Bombers
| | | | |
|---|---|---|---|
| ☐ 99 Lyle Bauer | .05 | .02 | .00 |

Winnipeg Blue Bombers
| | | | |
|---|---|---|---|
| ☐ 100 Less Browne | .10 | .04 | .01 |

Winnipeg Blue Bombers
| | | | |
|---|---|---|---|
| ☐ 101 Raghib(Rocket) Ismail | .25 | .10 | .02 |

Toronto Argonauts
| | | | |
|---|---|---|---|
| ☐ 102 Tom Burgess | .15 | .06 | .01 |

Winnipeg Blue Bombers
| | | | |
|---|---|---|---|
| ☐ 103 Mike Gray | .05 | .02 | .00 |

| | MINT | EXC | G-VG |
|---|---|---|---|
| Winnipeg Blue Bombers | | | |
| ☐ 104 Rod Hill | .10 | .04 | .01 |
| Winnipeg Blue Bombers | | | |
| ☐ 105 Warren Hudson | .10 | .04 | .01 |
| Winnipeg Blue Bombers | | | |
| ☐ 106 Tyrone Jones | .20 | .08 | .02 |
| Winnipeg Blue Bombers | | | |
| ☐ 107 Stan Mikawos | .05 | .02 | .00 |
| Winnipeg Blue Bombers | | | |
| ☐ 108 Robert Mimbs | .25 | .10 | .02 |
| Winnipeg Blue Bombers | | | |
| ☐ 109 James West | .15 | .06 | .01 |
| Winnipeg Blue Bombers | | | |
| ☐ 110 Raghib(Rocket) Ismail | .30 | .12 | .03 |
| Toronto Argonauts | | | |
| ☐ NNO Raghib(Rocket) Ismail | 50.00 | 20.00 | 5.00 |
| (Autographed card; AU/1600) | | | |

# 1992 All World CFL Promos

These two standard-size (2 1/2" by 3 1/2") promo cards feature Doug Flutie and Raghib "Rocket" Ismail, two of the Canadian Football League's outstanding players who were engaged by All World to serve as spokesmen. The color action player photos on the fronts are headlined by the colors of the Canadian flag, including a red maple leaf, which bleed off the top. Player information appears in a gray stripe bordering the bottom of the picture. In a horizontal format, the backs carry another color player photo as well as biography, statistics, career summary, and an import designation that indicates a player is not Canadian. The cards are lettered "P" on the back and checklisted below alphabetically.

| | MINT | EXC | G-VG |
|---|---|---|---|
| COMPLETE SET (2) | 4.00 | 1.60 | .40 |
| COMMON PLAYER | 2.00 | .80 | .20 |
| ☐ P Doug Flutie | 2.50 | 1.00 | .25 |
| Calgary Stampeders | | | |
| ☐ P Raghib(Rocket) Ismail | 2.00 | .80 | .20 |
| Toronto Argonauts | | | |

# 1992 All World CFL

The 1992 All World CFL set consists of 180 cards measuring the standard size (2 1/2" by 3 1/2"). The production run was 4,000 individually numbered foil cases and 8,000 numbered factory sets. Foil embossed maple leaf cards and 1,000 autographed Doug Flutie cards were randomly inserted into foil packs. Special insert sets focus on Rookies (eight cards), Trophy Winners (12 cards), Road to the Cup

(four cards), and Memorable Grey Cups (four cards). The color action player photos on the fronts are accented above by a Canadian flag that bleeds off the card top. The backs present statistics, another player photo, biography, and an import designation to indicate a player is non-Canadian. The cards are numbered on the back.

| | MINT | EXC | G-VG |
|---|---|---|---|
| COMPLETE SET (180) | 15.00 | 6.00 | 1.50 |
| COMMON PLAYER (1-180) | .10 | .04 | .01 |
| ☐ 1 Checklist 1-90 | .10 | .04 | .01 |
| ☐ 2 Draft Picks Checklist | .10 | .04 | .01 |
| ☐ 3 Western Final | .10 | .04 | .01 |
| ☐ 4 Eastern Final | .10 | .04 | .01 |
| ☐ 5 79th Grey Cup | .10 | .04 | .01 |
| ☐ 6 Grey Cup Most | .25 | .10 | .02 |
| Outstanding Player Raghib Ismail | | | |
| ☐ 7 Memorable Grey Cups 1909 | .10 | .04 | .01 |
| ☐ 8 Memorable Grey Cups 1969 | .10 | .04 | .01 |
| ☐ 9 Memorable Grey Cups 1982 | .10 | .04 | .01 |
| ☐ 10 Memorable Grey Cups 1989 | .10 | .04 | .01 |
| ☐ 11 Jeff Braswell | .10 | .04 | .01 |
| ☐ 12 Glenn Kulka | .10 | .04 | .01 |
| ☐ 13 Will Johnson | .10 | .04 | .01 |
| ☐ 14 Lance Chomyc | .25 | .10 | .02 |
| ☐ 15 Stan Mikawos | .10 | .04 | .01 |
| ☐ 16 Bobby Jurasin | .20 | .08 | .02 |
| ☐ 17 Terry Baker | .10 | .04 | .01 |
| ☐ 18 Tracey Ham | .35 | .14 | .03 |
| ☐ 19 Todd Wiseman | .10 | .04 | .01 |
| ☐ 20 Rob Crifo | .10 | .04 | .01 |
| ☐ 21 Chris Morris | .10 | .04 | .01 |
| ☐ 22 Jon Volpe | .50 | .20 | .05 |
| ☐ 23 Donald Narcisse | .25 | .10 | .02 |
| ☐ 24 David Williams | .25 | .10 | .02 |
| ☐ 25 Paul Clatney | .10 | .04 | .01 |
| ☐ 26 Willie Pless | .25 | .10 | .02 |
| ☐ 27 Rickey Foggie | .20 | .08 | .02 |
| ☐ 28 Denny Chronopoulos | .10 | .04 | .01 |
| ☐ 29 Darryl Sampson | .10 | .04 | .01 |
| ☐ 30 Patrick Wayne | .10 | .04 | .01 |
| ☐ 31 Terrence Jones | .25 | .10 | .02 |
| ☐ 32 Larry Wruck | .15 | .06 | .01 |
| ☐ 33 Angelo Snipes | .50 | .20 | .05 |
| ☐ 34 Tony Champion | .25 | .10 | .02 |
| ☐ 35 Steve Taylor | .20 | .08 | .02 |
| ☐ 36 Lorne King | .10 | .04 | .01 |
| ☐ 37 Roger Aldag | .15 | .06 | .01 |
| ☐ 38 Damon Allen | .30 | .12 | .03 |
| ☐ 39 Chris Walby | .20 | .08 | .02 |
| ☐ 40 Doug Davies | .10 | .04 | .01 |
| ☐ 41 Dan Rashovich | .10 | .04 | .01 |
| ☐ 42 Mark Scott | .10 | .04 | .01 |
| ☐ 43 Reggie Pleasant | .20 | .08 | .02 |
| ☐ 44 Bob Cameron | .10 | .04 | .01 |
| ☐ 45 Danny McManus | .20 | .08 | .02 |
| ☐ 46 Matt Clark | .20 | .08 | .02 |
| ☐ 47 Bart Hull | .20 | .08 | .02 |
| ☐ 48 Hank Ilesic | .10 | .04 | .01 |
| ☐ 49 Pee Wee Smith | .35 | .14 | .03 |
| ☐ 50 Irv Daymond | .10 | .04 | .01 |
| ☐ 51 Greg Battle | .15 | .06 | .01 |
| J.P. McCaffrey Trophy | | | |
| ☐ 52 Will Johnson | .15 | .06 | .01 |
| Norm Fieldgate Trophy | | | |
| ☐ 53 Lance Chomyc | .15 | .06 | .01 |
| Lew Hayman Trophy | | | |
| ☐ 54 Jim Mills | .15 | .06 | .01 |
| DeMarco-Becket Memorial Trophy | | | |
| ☐ 55 Jon Volpe | .25 | .10 | .02 |
| Jackie Parker Trophy | | | |
| ☐ 56 Raghib(Rocket) Ismail | .25 | .10 | .02 |
| Frank M. Gibson Trophy | | | |
| ☐ 57 David Ridgway | .15 | .06 | .01 |
| David Dryburgh Memorial Trophy | | | |
| ☐ 58 Chris Walby | .15 | .06 | .01 |
| Leo Dandurand Trophy | | | |
| ☐ 59 Doug Flutie | .35 | .14 | .03 |
| Jeff Nicklin Memorial Trophy | | | |
| ☐ 60 Robert Mimbs | .20 | .08 | .02 |
| Jeff Russell Memorial Trophy | | | |
| ☐ 61 Jon Volpe | .25 | .10 | .02 |
| Eddie James Memorial Trophy | | | |
| ☐ 62 Blake Marshall | .15 | .06 | .01 |
| Dr. Beattie Martin Trophy | | | |
| ☐ 63 Eric Streater | .20 | .08 | .02 |
| ☐ 64 Carl Brazley | .10 | .04 | .01 |

| | | | |
|---|---|---|---|
| ☐ 65 Kent Warnock | .10 | .04 | .01 |
| ☐ 66 Brian Bonner | .10 | .04 | .01 |
| ☐ 67 Tom Burgess | .25 | .10 | .02 |
| ☐ 68 Bob Gordon | .10 | .04 | .01 |
| ☐ 69 Milson Jones | .20 | .08 | .02 |
| ☐ 70 Todd Dillon | .10 | .04 | .01 |
| ☐ 71 Keyvan Jenkins | .20 | .08 | .02 |
| ☐ 72 Ken Evraire | .20 | .08 | .02 |
| ☐ 73 Willis Jacox | .20 | .08 | .02 |
| ☐ 74 Carl Bland | .10 | .04 | .01 |
| ☐ 75 Daniel Hunter | .10 | .04 | .01 |
| ☐ 76 Chris Schultz | .10 | .04 | .01 |
| ☐ 77 Earl Winfield | .20 | .08 | .02 |
| ☐ 78 Henry Williams | .40 | .16 | .04 |
| ☐ 79 Matt Dunigan | .50 | .20 | .05 |
| ☐ 80 Mark McLoughlin | .10 | .04 | .01 |
| ☐ 81 Craig Ellis | .10 | .04 | .01 |
| ☐ 82 Rodney Harding | .20 | .08 | .02 |
| ☐ 83 Scott Douglas | .10 | .04 | .01 |
| ☐ 84 Ray Elgaard | .20 | .08 | .02 |
| ☐ 85 Doug Flutie | .75 | .30 | .07 |
| ☐ 86 Gary Lewis | .10 | .04 | .01 |
| ☐ 87 Rod Hill | .15 | .06 | .01 |
| ☐ 88 Gregg Stumon | .10 | .04 | .01 |
| ☐ 89 Ray Alexander | .15 | .06 | .01 |
| ☐ 90 Blake Dermott | .10 | .04 | .01 |
| ☐ 91 Checklist 91-180 | .10 | .04 | .01 |
| ☐ 92 Trophy Winners CL | .20 | .08 | .02 |
| ☐ 93 British Columbia CL | .10 | .04 | .01 |
| ☐ 94 Calgary CL | .10 | .04 | .01 |
| ☐ 95 Edmonton CL | .10 | .04 | .01 |
| ☐ 96 Saskatchewan CL | .10 | .04 | .01 |
| ☐ 97 Hamilton CL | .10 | .04 | .01 |
| ☐ 98 Ottawa CL | .10 | .04 | .01 |
| ☐ 99 Toronto CL | .10 | .04 | .01 |
| ☐ 100 Winnipeg CL | .10 | .04 | .01 |
| ☐ 101 James West | .20 | .08 | .02 |
| ☐ 102 Jeff Fairholm | .25 | .10 | .02 |
| ☐ 103 Mike Campbell | .10 | .04 | .01 |
| ☐ 104 Darren Flutie | .25 | .10 | .02 |
| ☐ 105 Blake Marshall | .30 | .12 | .03 |
| ☐ 106 Loyd Lewis | .10 | .04 | .01 |
| ☐ 107 Enis Jackson | .10 | .04 | .01 |
| ☐ 108 John Motton | .40 | .16 | .04 |
| ☐ 109 Ken Walcott | .10 | .04 | .01 |
| ☐ 110 Richie Hall | .10 | .04 | .01 |
| ☐ 111 Greg Peterson | .10 | .04 | .01 |
| ☐ 112 Wally Zatylny | .10 | .04 | .01 |
| ☐ 113 Lui Passaglia | .20 | .08 | .02 |
| ☐ 114 Darryl Hall | .10 | .04 | .01 |
| ☐ 115 Michael Soles | .20 | .08 | .01 |
| ☐ 116 Doug Brewster | .10 | .04 | .01 |
| ☐ 117 Mike Gray | .10 | .04 | .01 |
| ☐ 118 Mike Trevathan | .10 | .04 | .01 |
| ☐ 119 Don Moen | .10 | .04 | .01 |
| ☐ 120 Chris Armstrong | .10 | .04 | .01 |
| ☐ 121 Lucius Floyd | .10 | .04 | .01 |
| ☐ 122 Ken Pettway | .10 | .04 | .01 |
| ☐ 123 Anthony Drawhorn | .30 | .12 | .03 |
| ☐ 124 Brian Walling | .10 | .04 | .01 |
| ☐ 125 Troy Westwood | .25 | .10 | .02 |
| ☐ 126 Reggie Barnes | .25 | .10 | .02 |
| ☐ 127 Raghib(Rocket) Ismail | .25 | .10 | .02 |
| ☐ 128 Rod Connop | .15 | .06 | .01 |
| ☐ 129 Chris Major | .20 | .08 | .02 |
| ☐ 130 David Bovell | .10 | .04 | .01 |
| ☐ 131 Quency Williams | .10 | .04 | .01 |
| ☐ 132 Michel Bourgeau | .10 | .04 | .01 |
| ☐ 133 Harold Hallman | .15 | .06 | .01 |
| ☐ 134 Junior Thurman | .30 | .12 | .03 |
| ☐ 135 Stewart Hill | .10 | .04 | .01 |
| ☐ 136 Brent Matich | .10 | .04 | .01 |
| ☐ 137 Leroy Blugh | .10 | .04 | .01 |
| ☐ 138 Nick Mazzoli | .10 | .04 | .01 |
| ☐ 139 David Ridgway | .20 | .08 | .02 |
| ☐ 140 Matt Finlay | .10 | .04 | .01 |
| ☐ 141 Mike Clemons | .50 | .20 | .05 |
| ☐ 142 Jason Riley | .10 | .04 | .01 |
| ☐ 143 Stacey Hairston | .10 | .04 | .01 |
| ☐ 144 Jim Mills | .20 | .08 | .02 |
| ☐ 145 Paul Randolph | .10 | .04 | .01 |
| ☐ 146 David Sapunjis | .25 | .10 | .02 |
| ☐ 147 Charles Gordon | .10 | .04 | .01 |
| ☐ 148 Chris Tsangaris | .10 | .04 | .01 |
| ☐ 149 Darrell K. Smith | .25 | .10 | .02 |
| ☐ 150 Leo Groenewegen | .10 | .04 | .01 |
| ☐ 151 Greg Battle | .20 | .08 | .02 |
| ☐ 152 Bruce Covernton | .10 | .04 | .01 |
| ☐ 153 Paul Osbaldiston | .20 | .08 | .02 |
| ☐ 154 Don Wilson | .10 | .04 | .01 |
| ☐ 155 Kent Austin | .35 | .14 | .03 |
| ☐ 156 Jamie Morris | .20 | .08 | .02 |
| ☐ 157 Andre Francis | .10 | .04 | .01 |
| ☐ 158 O.J. Brigance | .20 | .08 | .02 |
| ☐ 159 Less Browne | .20 | .08 | .02 |
| ☐ 160 Alondra Johnson | .10 | .04 | .01 |
| ☐ 161 Dexter Manley | .20 | .08 | .02 |

| | | | |
|---|---|---|---|
| ☐ 162 Bob Poley | .10 | .04 | .01 |
| ☐ 163 Ed Berry | .10 | .04 | .01 |
| ☐ 164 Peter Giftopoulos | .10 | .04 | .01 |
| ☐ 165 Glen Suitor | .10 | .04 | .01 |
| ☐ 166 Eddie Thomas | .10 | .04 | .01 |
| ☐ 167 Danny Barrett | .25 | .10 | .02 |
| ☐ 168 Robert Mimbs | .30 | .12 | .03 |
| ☐ 169 Jim Sandusky | .20 | .08 | .02 |
| ☐ 170 Maurice Smith | .10 | .04 | .01 |
| ☐ 171 David Conrad | .10 | .04 | .01 |
| ☐ 172 Larry Willis | .10 | .04 | .01 |
| ☐ 173 Ian Sinclair | .10 | .04 | .01 |
| ☐ 174 Allen Pitts | .60 | .24 | .06 |
| ☐ 175 Don McPherson | .25 | .10 | .02 |
| ☐ 176 Ray Bernard | .10 | .04 | .01 |
| ☐ 177 Dale Sanderson | .10 | .04 | .01 |
| ☐ 178 Dan Ferrone | .15 | .06 | .01 |
| ☐ 179 Vic Stevenson | .10 | .04 | .01 |
| ☐ 180 Rob Smith | .10 | .04 | .01 |

# 1982 Bantam/FBI CFL Discs

The disks in this set measure approximately 2 7/8" in diameter and two were available on the bottoms of specially marked Bantam Orange Drink and FBI Juice product boxes. The disks were perforated for removal. Each disk carries a black-and-white photo of the player's face against a white background. The player's name and team are printed on either side of the photo, while the player's position is printed below. The players were paired on the packages as follows: Cutler/Rhino, Gregoire/Highbaugh, and Corrigall/Mofford. The card backs are blank. The cards are unnumbered and checklisted below in alphabetical order.

| | MINT | EXC | G-VG |
|---|---|---|---|
| COMPLETE SET (12) | 200.00 | 80.00 | 20.00 |
| COMMON PLAYER (1-12) | 15.00 | 6.00 | 1.50 |
| | | | |
| ☐ 1 Leon Bright | 20.00 | 8.00 | 2.00 |
| British Columbia Lions | | | |
| ☐ 2 Bob Cameron | 15.00 | 6.00 | 1.50 |
| Winnipeg Blue Bombers | | | |
| ☐ 3 Tom Clements | 50.00 | 20.00 | 5.00 |
| Hamilton Tiger-Cats | | | |
| ☐ 4 Jim Corrigall | 20.00 | 8.00 | 2.00 |
| Toronto Argonauts | | | |
| ☐ 5 Dave Cutler | 20.00 | 8.00 | 2.00 |
| Edmonton Eskimos | | | |
| ☐ 6 Vince Ferragamo | 30.00 | 12.00 | 3.00 |
| Montreal Alouettes | | | |
| ☐ 7 Gabriel Gregoire | 15.00 | 6.00 | 1.50 |
| Montreal Alouettes | | | |
| ☐ 8 Larry Highbaugh | 20.00 | 8.00 | 2.00 |
| Edmonton Eskimos | | | |
| ☐ 9 Marc Lacelle | 15.00 | 6.00 | 1.50 |
| Montreal Alouettes | | | |
| ☐ 10 Ian Mofford | 15.00 | 6.00 | 1.50 |
| ☐ 11 Gerry Organ | 20.00 | 8.00 | 2.00 |
| Ottawa Rough Riders | | | |
| ☐ 12 Randy Rhino | 25.00 | 10.00 | 2.50 |
| Ottawa Rough Riders | | | |

# 1954 Blue Ribbon Tea CFL

The 1954 Blue Ribbon Tea set contains 80 color cards of CFL players. The cards measure 2 1/4" by 4". The pictures on the front are obviously posed rather than actual action shots. The backs of the cards contain biographical data in both English and French. An album for this set exists as an offer for this album is listed on the back. The set is printed in Canada, presumably by a firm called Colorgraphic, as this firm's logo appears at the bottom on the back of the card. Cards are numbered in team order, i.e., Winnipeg Blue Bombers (1-19), Ottawa Rough Riders (20-29), Hamilton Tiger-Cats (30-39), Edmonton Eskimos (40-50), Calgary Stampeders (51-60), and Montreal Alouettes (61-80).

| | NRMT | VG-E | GOOD |
|---|---|---|---|
| COMPLETE SET (80) | 9000.00 | 4000.00 | 1000.00 |
| COMMON PLAYER (1-80) | 100.00 | 40.00 | 10.00 |

| | | | |
|---|---|---|---|
| ☐ 1 Jack Jacobs | 250.00 | 100.00 | 25.00 |
| ☐ 2 Neil Armstrong | 150.00 | 60.00 | 15.00 |
| ☐ 3 Lorne Benson | 100.00 | 40.00 | 10.00 |
| ☐ 4 Tom Casey | 125.00 | 50.00 | 12.50 |
| ☐ 5 Vincent Drake | 100.00 | 40.00 | 10.00 |
| ☐ 6 Tommy Ford | 100.00 | 40.00 | 10.00 |
| ☐ 7 Bud Grant | 500.00 | 200.00 | 50.00 |
| ☐ 8 Dick Huffman | 125.00 | 50.00 | 12.50 |
| ☐ 9 Gerry James | 150.00 | 60.00 | 15.00 |
| ☐ 10 Bud Korchak | 100.00 | 40.00 | 10.00 |
| ☐ 11 Thomas Lumsden | 100.00 | 40.00 | 10.00 |
| ☐ 12 Steve Patrick | 100.00 | 40.00 | 10.00 |
| ☐ 13 Keith Pearce | 100.00 | 40.00 | 10.00 |
| ☐ 14 Jesse Thomas | 100.00 | 40.00 | 10.00 |
| ☐ 15 Buddy Tinsley | 125.00 | 50.00 | 12.50 |
| ☐ 16 Alan Scott Wiley | 100.00 | 40.00 | 10.00 |
| ☐ 17 Winty Young | 100.00 | 40.00 | 10.00 |
| ☐ 18 Joseph Zaleski | 100.00 | 40.00 | 10.00 |
| ☐ 19 Ron Vaccher | 100.00 | 40.00 | 10.00 |
| ☐ 20 John Gramling | 100.00 | 40.00 | 10.00 |
| ☐ 21 Bob Simpson | 150.00 | 60.00 | 15.00 |
| ☐ 22 Bruno Bitkowski | 125.00 | 50.00 | 12.50 |
| ☐ 23 Kaye Vaughan | 125.00 | 50.00 | 12.50 |
| ☐ 24 Don Carter | 100.00 | 40.00 | 10.00 |
| ☐ 25 Gene Roberts | 100.00 | 40.00 | 10.00 |
| ☐ 26 Howie Turner | 100.00 | 40.00 | 10.00 |
| ☐ 27 Avatus Stone | 100.00 | 40.00 | 10.00 |
| ☐ 28 Tom McHugh | 100.00 | 40.00 | 10.00 |
| ☐ 29 Clyde Bennett | 100.00 | 40.00 | 10.00 |
| ☐ 30 Bill Berezowski | 100.00 | 40.00 | 10.00 |
| ☐ 31 Eddie Bevan | 100.00 | 40.00 | 10.00 |
| ☐ 32 Dick Brown | 100.00 | 40.00 | 10.00 |
| ☐ 33 Bernie Custis | 125.00 | 50.00 | 12.50 |
| ☐ 34 Merle Hapes | 100.00 | 40.00 | 10.00 |
| ☐ 35 Tip Logan | 100.00 | 40.00 | 10.00 |
| ☐ 36 Vince Mazza | 125.00 | 50.00 | 12.50 |
| ☐ 37 Pete Neumann | 125.00 | 50.00 | 12.50 |
| ☐ 38 Vince Scott | 125.00 | 50.00 | 12.50 |
| ☐ 39 Ralph Toohy | 100.00 | 40.00 | 10.00 |
| ☐ 40 Frank Anderson | 100.00 | 40.00 | 10.00 |
| ☐ 41 Bob Dean | 100.00 | 40.00 | 10.00 |
| ☐ 42 Leon Manley | 100.00 | 40.00 | 10.00 |
| ☐ 43 Bill Zock | 125.00 | 50.00 | 12.50 |
| ☐ 44 Frank Morris | 150.00 | 60.00 | 15.00 |
| ☐ 45 Jim Quondamatteo | 100.00 | 40.00 | 10.00 |
| ☐ 46 Eagle Keys | 150.00 | 60.00 | 15.00 |
| ☐ 47 Bernie Faloney | 400.00 | 160.00 | 40.00 |
| ☐ 48 Jackie Parker | 500.00 | 200.00 | 50.00 |
| ☐ 49 Ray Willsey | 100.00 | 40.00 | 10.00 |
| ☐ 50 Mike King | 100.00 | 40.00 | 10.00 |
| ☐ 51 Johnny Bright | 300.00 | 120.00 | 30.00 |
| ☐ 52 Gene Brito | 150.00 | 60.00 | 15.00 |
| ☐ 53 Stan Heath | 100.00 | 40.00 | 10.00 |
| ☐ 54 Roy Jenson | 100.00 | 40.00 | 10.00 |
| ☐ 55 Don Loney | 100.00 | 40.00 | 10.00 |
| ☐ 56 Eddie Macon | 100.00 | 40.00 | 10.00 |
| ☐ 57 Peter Maxwell-Muir | 100.00 | 40.00 | 10.00 |
| ☐ 58 Tom Miner | 100.00 | 40.00 | 10.00 |
| ☐ 59 Jim Prewett | 100.00 | 40.00 | 10.00 |
| ☐ 60 Lowell Wagner | 100.00 | 40.00 | 10.00 |
| ☐ 61 Red O'Quinn | 125.00 | 50.00 | 12.50 |
| ☐ 62 Ray Poole | 125.00 | 50.00 | 12.50 |
| ☐ 63 Jim Staton | 100.00 | 40.00 | 10.00 |
| ☐ 64 Alex Webster | 150.00 | 60.00 | 15.00 |
| ☐ 65 Al Dekdebrun | 100.00 | 40.00 | 10.00 |
| ☐ 66 Ed Bradley | 100.00 | 40.00 | 10.00 |
| ☐ 67 Tex Coulter | 125.00 | 50.00 | 12.50 |
| ☐ 68 Sam Etcheverry | 500.00 | 200.00 | 50.00 |
| ☐ 69 Larry Grigg | 100.00 | 40.00 | 10.00 |
| ☐ 70 Tom Hugo | 100.00 | 40.00 | 10.00 |
| ☐ 71 Chuck Hunsinger | 100.00 | 40.00 | 10.00 |
| ☐ 72 Herb Trawick | 125.00 | 50.00 | 12.50 |
| ☐ 73 Virgil Wagner | 125.00 | 50.00 | 12.50 |
| ☐ 74 Phil Adrian | 100.00 | 40.00 | 10.00 |
| ☐ 75 Bruce Coulter | 100.00 | 40.00 | 10.00 |
| ☐ 76 Jim Miller | 100.00 | 40.00 | 10.00 |
| ☐ 77 Jim Mitchener | 100.00 | 40.00 | 10.00 |
| ☐ 78 Tom Moran | 100.00 | 40.00 | 10.00 |
| ☐ 79 Doug McNichol | 100.00 | 40.00 | 10.00 |
| ☐ 80 Joey Pal | 100.00 | 40.00 | 10.00 |

## 1988 Bootlegger B.C. Lions

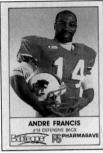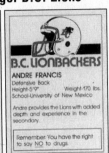

This 13-card safety set features members of the British Columbia Lions and was co-sponsored by Bootlegger and PS Pharmasave, whose company logos adorn the bottom of the card face. The standard-size (2 1/2" by 3 1/2") cards display posed color player photos, shot from the waist up against a sky blue background. The photos are framed by white borders, with player information immediately below the pictures. The backs have an icon of the team helmet, biography, and an anti-drug message. A different "Just Say No To Drugs" message is included on each card. The sponsor title card lists a total of 36 different companies who financed the drug awareness program. The cards are unnumbered and checklisted below in alphabetical order.

| | MINT | EXC | G-VG |
|---|---|---|---|
| COMPLETE SET (13) | 15.00 | 6.00 | 1.50 |
| COMMON PLAYER (1-12) | 1.00 | .40 | .10 |

| | | | |
|---|---|---|---|
| ☐ 1 Jamie Buis | 1.00 | .40 | .10 |
| ☐ 2 Jan Carinci | 1.00 | .40 | .10 |
| ☐ 3 Dwayne Derban | 1.00 | .40 | .10 |
| ☐ 4 Roy Dewalt | 3.00 | 1.20 | .30 |
| ☐ 5 Andre Francis | 1.50 | .60 | .15 |
| ☐ 6 Rick Klassen | 2.00 | .80 | .20 |
| ☐ 7 Kevin Konar | 1.50 | .60 | .15 |
| ☐ 8 Scott Lecky | 1.00 | .40 | .10 |
| ☐ 9 James(Quick) Parker | 3.00 | 1.20 | .30 |
| ☐ 10 John Ulmer | 1.00 | .40 | .10 |
| ☐ 11 Pieter Vanden Bos | 1.00 | .40 | .10 |
| ☐ 12 Todd Wiseman | 1.00 | .40 | .10 |
| ☐ NNO Title Card | 1.25 | .50 | .12 |
| Corporate Sponsors | | | |

## 1971 Chiquita CFL All-Stars

This set of CFL All-Stars actually consists of 13 slides which were intended to be viewed by a special yellow Chiquita viewer. Each slide measures approximately 1 3/4" by 3 5/8" and contains four small color slides showing two views of each player. Each slide has a player summary on its middle portion, with two small color action slides at each end stacked one above the other. When the slide is placed in the viewer, the two bottom slides, which are identical, reveal the first player. Flipping the slide over reveals the other player biography and enables one to view the other two slides, which show the second player. Each side of the slides is numbered as listed below. The set is considered complete without the yellow viewer.

| | NRMT | VG-E | GOOD |
|---|---|---|---|
| COMPLETE SET (13) | 200.00 | 80.00 | 20.00 |
| COMMON PAIR | 15.00 | 6.00 | 1.50 |
| ☐ 1 Bill Baker | 20.00 | 8.00 | 2.00 |
|    Saskatchewan Roughriders | | | |
|    2 Ken Sugarman | | | |
|    British Columbia Lions | | | |
| ☐ 3 Wayne Giardino | 15.00 | 6.00 | 1.50 |
|    Ottawa Rough Riders | | | |
|    4 Peter Dalla Riva | | | |
|    Montreal Alouettes | | | |
| ☐ 5 Leon McQuay | 20.00 | 8.00 | 2.00 |
|    Toronto Argonauts | | | |
|    6 Jim Thorpe | | | |
|    Winnipeg Blue Bombers | | | |
| ☐ 7 George Reed | 20.00 | 8.00 | 2.00 |
|    Saskatchewan Roughriders | | | |
|    8 Jerry Campbell | | | |
|    Ottawa Rough Riders | | | |
| ☐ 9 Tommy Joe Coffey | 25.00 | 10.00 | 2.50 |
|    Hamilton Tiger-Cats | | | |
|    10 Terry Evanshen | | | |
|    Montreal Alouettes | | | |
| ☐ 11 Jim Young | 20.00 | 8.00 | 2.00 |
|    Winnipeg Blue Bombers | | | |
|    12 Mark Kosmos | | | |
|    Montreal Alouettes | | | |
| ☐ 13 Ron Forwick | 15.00 | 6.00 | 1.50 |
|    Edmonton Eskimos | | | |
|    14 Jack Abendschan | | | |
|    Saskatchewan Roughriders | | | |
| ☐ 15 Don Jonas | 20.00 | 8.00 | 2.00 |
|    Winnipeg Blue Bombers | | | |
|    16 Al Marcellin | | | |
|    Ottawa Rough Riders | | | |
| ☐ 17 Joe Theismann | 50.00 | 20.00 | 5.00 |
|    Toronto Argonauts | | | |
|    18 Jim Corrigall | | | |
|    Toronto Argonauts | | | |
| ☐ 19 Ed George | 15.00 | 6.00 | 1.50 |
|    Montreal Alouettes | | | |
|    20 Dick Dupuis | | | |
|    Edmonton Eskimos | | | |
| ☐ 21 Ted Dushinski | 15.00 | 6.00 | 1.50 |
|    Saskatchewan Roughriders | | | |
|    22 Bob Swift | | | |
|    Winnipeg Blue Bombers | | | |
| ☐ 23 John Lagrone | 15.00 | 6.00 | 1.50 |
|    Edmonton Eskimos | | | |
|    24 Bill Danychuk | | | |
|    Hamilton Tiger-Cats | | | |
| ☐ 25 Garney Henley | 20.00 | 8.00 | 2.00 |
|    Hamilton Tiger-Cats | | | |
|    26 John Williams | | | |
|    Hamilton Tiger-Cats | | | |
| ☐ xx Yellow Viewer | 40.00 | 16.00 | 4.00 |

## 1961 CKNW B.C. Lions

Each of these photos measure approximately 3 7/8" by 5 1/2". Inside white borders, the fronts feature black-and-white posed action photos. The player's facsimile autograph is written across the picture; on most of the cards it is in red ink. Immediately below the picture in small print are player information and "Graphic Industries Limited Photo." The wider white bottom border also carries sponsor information and a five- or six-digit serial number. Apparently the photos were primarily sponsored by CKNW (a radio station), which appears on every photo, and various other co-sponsors that may vary from card to card. Since the photos show signs of perforation, they may have originally been issued in game programs. The backs display various advertisements. The photos are unnumbered and checklisted below in alphabetical order. The co-sponsors (listed on the card front) are also listed below. The set can be distinguished from the set of the following year by the presence of the set's date in the lower left corner of the obverse.

| | NRMT | VG-E | GOOD |
|---|---|---|---|
| COMPLETE SET (9) | 100.00 | 40.00 | 10.00 |
| COMMON PLAYER (1-9) | 12.00 | 5.00 | 1.20 |
| ☐ 1 Bob Belak | 12.00 | 5.00 | 1.20 |
|    Kings Drive-In | | | |
| ☐ 2 Bill Britton | 12.00 | 5.00 | 1.20 |
|    Nestle's Quik | | | |
| ☐ 3 Tom Brown | 20.00 | 8.00 | 2.00 |
|    Kings Drive-In | | | |
| ☐ 4 Lonnie Dennis | 12.00 | 5.00 | 1.20 |
|    Nestle's Quik | | | |
| ☐ 5 Sonny Homer | 15.00 | 6.00 | 1.50 |
|    Nestle's Quik | | | |
| ☐ 6 Rae Ross | 12.00 | 5.00 | 1.20 |
|    Nestle's Quik | | | |
| ☐ 7 Mel Semenko | 12.00 | 5.00 | 1.20 |
|    Kings Drive-In | | | |
| ☐ 8 Barney Therrien | 12.00 | 5.00 | 1.20 |
|    Nestle's Quik | | | |
| ☐ 9 Ron Watton | 12.00 | 5.00 | 1.20 |
|    Unknown | | | |

## 1962 CKNW B.C. Lions

Each of these photos measure approximately 3 7/8" by 5 1/2". Inside white borders, the fronts feature black-and-white posed action photos. The player's facsimile autograph is written across the picture; on most of the cards it is in red ink. Immediately below the picture in small print are player information and "Graphic Industries Limited Photo." The wider white bottom border also carries sponsor information and a five- or six-digit serial number. Apparently the photos were primarily sponsored by CKNW (a radio station), which appears on every photo, and various other co-sponsors that may vary from card to card. Since the photos show signs of perforation, they may have originally been issued in game programs. The backs display various advertisements. The photos are unnumbered and checklisted below in alphabetical order. The co-sponsors are also listed below. The set can be distinguished from the set of the previous year by the presence of the set's date in the lower left corner of the obverse.

| | NRMT | VG-E | GOOD |
|---|---|---|---|
| COMPLETE SET (4) | 60.00 | 24.00 | 6.00 |
| COMMON PLAYER (1-4) | 12.00 | 5.00 | 1.20 |
| ☐ 1 Tom Brown | 20.00 | 8.00 | 2.00 |
|    Shop-Easy | | | |
| ☐ 2 Mack Burton | 15.00 | 6.00 | 1.50 |
|    Shop-Easy | | | |
| ☐ 3 Willie Fleming | 30.00 | 12.00 | 3.00 |
|    Shop-Easy | | | |
| ☐ 4 Vic Kristopaitis | 12.00 | 5.00 | 1.20 |
|    Shop-Easy | | | |

## 1965 Coke Caps CFL

This set of 230 Coke caps was issued on bottled soft drinks and featured CFL players. The caps measure approximately one inch in diameter. The outside of the cap exhibits a black-and-white photo of the player's face, with a Coke (or Sprite) advertisement below the picture. Sprite caps are harder to find and are valued with a 50 percent premium over the prices listed below. The player's team name is written vertically on the left side, following the curve of the bottle cap, and likewise for the player's name on the right side. The players are listed in alphabetical order within their teams, and the teams are arranged alphabetically as follows: British Columbia Lions (1-24), Calgary Stampeders (25-48), Edmonton Eskimos (49-76), Hamilton Tigercats (77-100), Montreal Alouettes (101-126), Ottawa Rough

Riders (127-150), Saskatchewan Roughriders (151-175), Toronto Argonauts (176-205), and Winnipeg Blue Bombers (206-230). Three players appear twice with two different teams, Don Fuell, Hal Ledyard, and L. Tomlinson. A plastic holder measuring approximately 14" by 16" was also available.

|  | NRMT | VG-E | GOOD |
|---|---|---|---|
| COMPLETE SET (230) | 500.00 | 200.00 | 50.00 |
| COMMON PLAYER (1-230) | 2.50 | 1.00 | .25 |
|  |  |  |  |
| ☐ 1 Neal Beaumont | 2.50 | 1.00 | .25 |
| ☐ 2 Tom Brown | 5.00 | 2.00 | .50 |
| ☐ 3 Mack Burton | 2.50 | 1.00 | .25 |
| ☐ 4 Mike Cacic | 2.50 | 1.00 | .25 |
| ☐ 5 Pat Claridge | 2.50 | 1.00 | .25 |
| ☐ 6 Steve Cotter | 2.50 | 1.00 | .25 |
| ☐ 7 Norm Fieldgate | 5.00 | 2.00 | .50 |
| ☐ 8 Greg Findlay | 2.50 | 1.00 | .25 |
| ☐ 9 Willie Fleming | 6.00 | 2.40 | .60 |
| ☐ 10 Dick Fouts | 2.50 | 1.00 | .25 |
| ☐ 11 Tom Hinton | 5.00 | 2.00 | .50 |
| ☐ 12 Sonny Homer | 2.50 | 1.00 | .25 |
| ☐ 13 Joe Kapp | 15.00 | 6.00 | 1.50 |
| ☐ 14 G. Kasapis | 2.50 | 1.00 | .25 |
| ☐ 15 P. Kempf | 2.50 | 1.00 | .25 |
| ☐ 16 B. Lasseter | 2.50 | 1.00 | .25 |
| ☐ 17 M. Martin | 2.50 | 1.00 | .25 |
| ☐ 18 R. Morris | 2.50 | 1.00 | .25 |
| ☐ 19 Bill Munsey | 2.50 | 1.00 | .25 |
| ☐ 20 Paul Seale | 2.50 | 1.00 | .25 |
| ☐ 21 Steve Shafer | 2.50 | 1.00 | .25 |
| ☐ 22 Ken Sugerman | 2.50 | 1.00 | .25 |
| ☐ 23 Bob Swift | 2.50 | 1.00 | .25 |
| ☐ 24 J. Williams | 2.50 | 1.00 | .25 |
| ☐ 25 Ron Allbright | 2.50 | 1.00 | .25 |
| ☐ 26 Lu Bain | 2.50 | 1.00 | .25 |
| ☐ 27 F. Budd | 2.50 | 1.00 | .25 |
| ☐ 28 Lovell Coleman | 3.50 | 1.40 | .35 |
| ☐ 29 Eagle Day | 5.00 | 2.00 | .50 |
| ☐ 30 P. Dudley | 2.50 | 1.00 | .25 |
| ☐ 31 Jim Furlong | 2.50 | 1.00 | .25 |
| ☐ 32 G. Hansen | 2.50 | 1.00 | .25 |
| ☐ 33 Wayne Harris | 7.50 | 3.00 | .75 |
| ☐ 34 Herman Harrison | 5.00 | 2.00 | .50 |
| ☐ 35 Pat Holmes | 2.50 | 1.00 | .25 |
| ☐ 36 A. Johnson | 2.50 | 1.00 | .25 |
| ☐ 37 Jerry Keeling | 5.00 | 2.00 | .50 |
| ☐ 38 Roger Kramer | 3.50 | 1.40 | .35 |
| ☐ 39 Hal Krebs | 2.50 | 1.00 | .25 |
| ☐ 40 Don Luzzi | 5.00 | 2.00 | .50 |
| ☐ 41 Pete Manning | 2.50 | 1.00 | .25 |
| ☐ 42 D. Parsons | 2.50 | 1.00 | .25 |
| ☐ 43 R. Payne | 2.50 | 1.00 | .25 |
| ☐ 44 Larry Robinson | 2.50 | 1.00 | .25 |
| ☐ 45 Gerry Shaw | 2.50 | 1.00 | .25 |
| ☐ 46 D. Stephenson | 2.50 | 1.00 | .25 |
| ☐ 47 Bobby Taylor | 2.50 | 1.00 | .25 |
| ☐ 48 Ted Woods | 2.50 | 1.00 | .25 |
| ☐ 49 Jon Anabo | 2.50 | 1.00 | .25 |
| ☐ 50 R. Ash | 2.50 | 1.00 | .25 |
| ☐ 51 Jim Battle | 2.50 | 1.00 | .25 |
| ☐ 52 Charley Brown | 2.50 | 1.00 | .25 |
| ☐ 53 Tommy Joe Coffey | 7.50 | 3.00 | .75 |
| ☐ 54 Marcel Deleeuw | 2.50 | 1.00 | .25 |
| ☐ 55 Al Ecuyer | 2.50 | 1.00 | .25 |
| ☐ 56 Ron Forwick | 2.50 | 1.00 | .25 |
| ☐ 57 Jim Higgins | 2.50 | 1.00 | .25 |
| ☐ 58 H. Huth | 2.50 | 1.00 | .25 |
| ☐ 59 R. Kerbow | 2.50 | 1.00 | .25 |
| ☐ 60 Oscar Kruger | 2.50 | 1.00 | .25 |
| ☐ 61 T. Machan | 2.50 | 1.00 | .25 |
| ☐ 62 G. McKee | 2.50 | 1.00 | .25 |
| ☐ 63 B. Mitchell | 2.50 | 1.00 | .25 |
| ☐ 64 Barry Mitchelson | 2.50 | 1.00 | .25 |
| ☐ 65 Roger Nelson | 5.00 | 2.00 | .50 |
| ☐ 66 Bill Redell | 2.50 | 1.00 | .25 |
| ☐ 67 M. Rohliser | 2.50 | 1.00 | .25 |
| ☐ 68 H. Schumm | 2.50 | 1.00 | .25 |
| ☐ 69 E.A. Sims | 2.50 | 1.00 | .25 |
| ☐ 70 J. Sklopan | 2.50 | 1.00 | .25 |
| ☐ 71 Jim Stinnette | 2.50 | 1.00 | .25 |
| ☐ 72 B. Therrien | 2.50 | 1.00 | .25 |
| ☐ 73 Jim Thomas | 2.50 | 1.00 | .25 |
| ☐ 74 N. Thomas | 2.50 | 1.00 | .25 |
| ☐ 75 B. Tobin | 2.50 | 1.00 | .25 |
| ☐ 76 Terry Wilson | 2.50 | 1.00 | .25 |
| ☐ 77 Art Baker | 2.50 | 1.00 | .25 |
| ☐ 78 John Barrow | 5.00 | 2.00 | .50 |
| ☐ 79 Gene Ceppetelli | 2.50 | 1.00 | .25 |
| ☐ 80 J. Cimba | 2.50 | 1.00 | .25 |
| ☐ 81 Dick Cohee | 2.50 | 1.00 | .25 |
| ☐ 82 Frank Cosentino | 3.50 | 1.40 | .35 |
| ☐ 83 Johnny Counts | 2.50 | 1.00 | .25 |
| ☐ 84 Stan Crisson | 2.50 | 1.00 | .25 |
| ☐ 85 Tommy Grant | 3.50 | 1.40 | .35 |
| ☐ 86 Garney Henley | 6.00 | 2.40 | .60 |
| ☐ 87 E. Hoerster | 2.50 | 1.00 | .25 |
| ☐ 88 Zeno Karcz | 2.50 | 1.00 | .25 |
| ☐ 89 Ellison Kelly | 6.00 | 2.40 | .60 |
| ☐ 90 Bob Krouse | 2.50 | 1.00 | .25 |
| ☐ 91 Billy Ray Locklin | 2.50 | 1.00 | .25 |
| ☐ 92 Chet Miksza | 2.50 | 1.00 | .25 |
| ☐ 93 Angelo Mosca | 12.00 | 5.00 | 1.20 |
| ☐ 94 Bronko Nagurski | 7.50 | 3.00 | .75 |
| ☐ 95 T. Page | 2.50 | 1.00 | .25 |
| ☐ 96 Don Sutherin | 5.00 | 2.00 | .50 |
| ☐ 97 Dave Viti | 2.50 | 1.00 | .25 |
| ☐ 98 D. Walton | 2.50 | 1.00 | .25 |
| ☐ 99 Billy Wayte | 2.50 | 1.00 | .25 |
| ☐ 100 Joe Zuger | 2.50 | 1.00 | .25 |
| ☐ 101 Jim Andreotti | 2.50 | 1.00 | .25 |
| ☐ 102 John Baker | 3.50 | 1.40 | .35 |
| ☐ 103 G. Beretta | 2.50 | 1.00 | .25 |
| ☐ 104 B. Bewley | 2.50 | 1.00 | .25 |
| ☐ 105 Garland Boyette | 3.50 | 1.40 | .35 |
| ☐ 106 D. Daigneault | 2.50 | 1.00 | .25 |
| ☐ 107 George Dixon | 6.00 | 2.40 | .60 |
| ☐ 108 D. Dolatri | 2.50 | 1.00 | .25 |
| ☐ 109 Ted Elsby | 2.50 | 1.00 | .25 |
| ☐ 110 D. Estes | 2.50 | 1.00 | .25 |
| ☐ 111 Terry Evenshen | 7.50 | 3.00 | .75 |
| ☐ 112 Clare Exelby | 2.50 | 1.00 | .25 |
| ☐ 113 Larry Fairholm | 3.50 | 1.40 | .35 |
| ☐ 114 Bernie Faloney | 15.00 | 6.00 | 1.50 |
| ☐ 115 Don Fuell | 2.50 | 1.00 | .25 |
| ☐ 116 M. Gibbons | 2.50 | 1.00 | .25 |
| ☐ 117 Ralph Goldston | 2.50 | 1.00 | .25 |
| ☐ 118 Al Irwin | 2.50 | 1.00 | .25 |
| ☐ 119 J. Kenerson | 2.50 | 1.00 | .25 |
| ☐ 120 Ed Learn | 2.50 | 1.00 | .25 |
| ☐ 121 Moe Levesque | 2.50 | 1.00 | .25 |
| ☐ 122 Bob Minihane | 2.50 | 1.00 | .25 |
| ☐ 123 Jim Reynolds | 2.50 | 1.00 | .25 |
| ☐ 124 Billy Roy | 2.50 | 1.00 | .25 |
| ☐ 125 L. Tomlinson | 2.50 | 1.00 | .25 |
| ☐ 126 Ernie White | 2.50 | 1.00 | .25 |
| ☐ 127 R. Black | 2.50 | 1.00 | .25 |
| ☐ 128 Mike Blum | 2.50 | 1.00 | .25 |
| ☐ 129 Billy Joe Booth | 2.50 | 1.00 | .25 |
| ☐ 130 Jim Cain | 2.50 | 1.00 | .25 |
| ☐ 131 B. Cline | 2.50 | 1.00 | .25 |
| ☐ 132 M. Collins | 2.50 | 1.00 | .25 |
| ☐ 133 Jim Conroy | 2.50 | 1.00 | .25 |
| ☐ 134 Larry DeGraw | 2.50 | 1.00 | .25 |
| ☐ 135 Jim Dillard | 2.50 | 1.00 | .25 |
| ☐ 136 Gene Gaines | 5.00 | 2.00 | .50 |
| ☐ 137 D. Gilbert | 2.50 | 1.00 | .25 |
| ☐ 138 Russ Jackson | 15.00 | 6.00 | 1.50 |
| ☐ 139 Ken Lehmann | 2.50 | 1.00 | .25 |
| ☐ 140 Bob O'Billovich | 2.50 | 1.00 | .25 |
| ☐ 141 John Pentecost | 2.50 | 1.00 | .25 |
| ☐ 142 Joe Poirier | 2.50 | 1.00 | .25 |
| ☐ 143 Moe Racine | 2.50 | 1.00 | .25 |
| ☐ 144 S. Scoccia | 2.50 | 1.00 | .25 |
| ☐ 145 Bo Scott | 6.00 | 2.40 | .60 |
| ☐ 146 Jerry Selinger | 2.50 | 1.00 | .25 |
| ☐ 147 Marshall Shirk | 2.50 | 1.00 | .25 |
| ☐ 148 Bill Siekierski | 2.50 | 1.00 | .25 |
| ☐ 149 Ron Stewart | 6.00 | 2.40 | .60 |
| ☐ 150 Whit Tucker | 5.00 | 2.00 | .50 |
| ☐ 151 Ron Atchison | 5.00 | 2.00 | .50 |
| ☐ 152 Al Benecick | 2.50 | 1.00 | .25 |
| ☐ 153 Clyde Brock | 2.50 | 1.00 | .25 |
| ☐ 154 Ed Buchanan | 2.50 | 1.00 | .25 |
| ☐ 155 R. Cameron | 2.50 | 1.00 | .25 |
| ☐ 156 Hugh Campbell | 7.50 | 3.00 | .75 |
| ☐ 157 Henry Dorsch | 2.50 | 1.00 | .25 |
| ☐ 158 L. Dumelie | 2.50 | 1.00 | .25 |
| ☐ 159 Garner Ekstran | 2.50 | 1.00 | .25 |
| ☐ 160 Martin Fabi | 2.50 | 1.00 | .25 |
| ☐ 161 Bob Good | 2.50 | 1.00 | .25 |
| ☐ 162 Bob Kosid | 2.50 | 1.00 | .25 |
| ☐ 163 Ron Lancaster | 7.50 | 3.00 | .75 |
| ☐ 164 Hal Ledyard | 2.50 | 1.00 | .25 |
| ☐ 165 Len Legault | 2.50 | 1.00 | .25 |
| ☐ 166 R. Meadmore | 2.50 | 1.00 | .25 |
| ☐ 167 Bob Ptacek | 2.50 | 1.00 | .25 |
| ☐ 168 George Reed | 7.50 | 3.00 | .75 |
| ☐ 169 D. Schnell | 2.50 | 1.00 | .25 |

| | NRMT | VG-E | GOOD |
|---|---|---|---|
| ☐ 170 Wayne Shaw | 2.50 | 1.00 | .25 |
| ☐ 171 Ted Urness | 5.00 | 2.00 | .50 |
| ☐ 172 Dale West | 2.50 | 1.00 | .25 |
| ☐ 173 Reg Whitehouse | 2.50 | 1.00 | .25 |
| ☐ 174 G. Wlasiuk | 2.50 | 1.00 | .25 |
| ☐ 175 Jim Worden | 2.50 | 1.00 | .25 |
| ☐ 176 D. Aldridge | 2.50 | 1.00 | .25 |
| ☐ 177 W. Balasiuk | 2.50 | 1.00 | .25 |
| ☐ 178 Ron Brewer | 2.50 | 1.00 | .25 |
| ☐ 179 W. Dickey | 2.50 | 1.00 | .25 |
| ☐ 180 B. Dugan | 2.50 | 1.00 | .25 |
| ☐ 181 L. Ferguson | 2.50 | 1.00 | .25 |
| ☐ 182 Don Fuell | 2.50 | 1.00 | .25 |
| ☐ 183 Ed Harrington | 2.50 | 1.00 | .25 |
| ☐ 184 Ron Howell | 2.50 | 1.00 | .25 |
| ☐ 185 F. Laroue | 2.50 | 1.00 | .25 |
| ☐ 186 Sherman Lewis | 6.00 | 2.40 | .60 |
| ☐ 187 Marv Luster | 5.00 | 2.00 | .50 |
| ☐ 188 Dave Mann | 3.50 | 1.40 | .35 |
| ☐ 189 P. Martin | 2.50 | 1.00 | .25 |
| ☐ 190 Marty Martinello | 2.50 | 1.00 | .25 |
| ☐ 191 Lamar McHan | 5.00 | 2.00 | .50 |
| ☐ 192 Danny Nykoluk | 2.50 | 1.00 | .25 |
| ☐ 193 Jackie Parker | 18.00 | 7.25 | 1.80 |
| ☐ 194 Dave Pivec | 2.50 | 1.00 | .25 |
| ☐ 195 Jim Rountree | 2.50 | 1.00 | .25 |
| ☐ 196 Dick Shatto | 6.00 | 2.40 | .60 |
| ☐ 197 Billy Shipp | 2.50 | 1.00 | .25 |
| ☐ 198 Len Sparks | 2.50 | 1.00 | .25 |
| ☐ 199 D. Still | 2.50 | 1.00 | .25 |
| ☐ 200 Norm Stoneburgh | 2.50 | 1.00 | .25 |
| ☐ 201 Dave Thelan | 5.00 | 2.00 | .50 |
| ☐ 202 J. Vilanus | 2.50 | 1.00 | .25 |
| ☐ 203 J. Walter | 2.50 | 1.00 | .25 |
| ☐ 204 P. Watson | 2.50 | 1.00 | .25 |
| ☐ 205 John Wydareny | 2.50 | 1.00 | .25 |
| ☐ 206 Billy Cooper | 2.50 | 1.00 | .25 |
| ☐ 207 Wayne Dennis | 2.50 | 1.00 | .25 |
| ☐ 208 P. Desjardins | 2.50 | 1.00 | .25 |
| ☐ 209 N. Dunford | 2.50 | 1.00 | .25 |
| ☐ 210 Farrell Funston | 2.50 | 1.00 | .25 |
| ☐ 211 Herb Gray | 6.00 | 2.40 | .60 |
| ☐ 212 R. Hamelin | 2.50 | 1.00 | .25 |
| ☐ 213 B. Hansen | 2.50 | 1.00 | .25 |
| ☐ 214 Henry Janzen | 2.50 | 1.00 | .25 |
| ☐ 215 Hal Ledyard | 2.50 | 1.00 | .25 |
| ☐ 216 Leo Lewis | 6.00 | 2.40 | .60 |
| ☐ 217 Brian Palmer | 2.50 | 1.00 | .25 |
| ☐ 218 Art Perkins | 2.50 | 1.00 | .25 |
| ☐ 219 Cornel Piper | 2.50 | 1.00 | .25 |
| ☐ 220 Ernie Pitts | 2.50 | 1.00 | .25 |
| ☐ 221 Ken Ploen | 6.00 | 2.40 | .60 |
| ☐ 222 Dave Raimey | 3.50 | 1.40 | .35 |
| ☐ 223 Norm Rauhaus | 2.50 | 1.00 | .25 |
| ☐ 224 Frank Rigney | 5.00 | 2.00 | .50 |
| ☐ 225 Roger Savoie | 2.50 | 1.00 | .25 |
| ☐ 226 Jackie Simpson | 5.00 | 2.00 | .50 |
| ☐ 227 Dick Thornton | 3.50 | 1.40 | .35 |
| ☐ 228 Sherwyn Thorson | 2.50 | 1.00 | .25 |
| ☐ 229 Ed Ulmer | 2.50 | 1.00 | .25 |
| ☐ 230 Bill Whisler | 2.50 | 1.00 | .25 |

## 1953 Crown Brand

This set of 48 pictures was distributed by Crown Brand Corn Syrup. The collection of the complete set of pictures involved a mail-in offer: one label or cone top from a tin of Crown Brand Corn Syrup and 10 cents for two pictures; or two labels and 25 cents for seven pictures. The photos measure approximately 7" by 8 1/4" and feature a posed photo of the player, with player information below. The back has a checklist of all 48 players included in the set. Hall of Famers included in this set are Tom Casey, Dick Huffman, Jack Jacobs, Martin Ruby, Buddy Tinsley, and Frank Morris. The photos are listed below in alphabetical order according to their teams: Winnipeg Blue Bombers (1-12), Saskatchewan Roughriders (13-24), Calgary Stampeders (25-36), and Edmonton Eskimos (37-48).

| | NRMT | VG-E | GOOD |
|---|---|---|---|
| COMPLETE SET (48) | 2000.00 | 900.00 | 225.00 |
| COMMON PLAYER (1-48) | 50.00 | 20.00 | 5.00 |
| ☐ 1 John Brown | 50.00 | 20.00 | 5.00 |
| ☐ 2 Tom Casey | 75.00 | 30.00 | 7.50 |
| ☐ 3 Tommy Ford | 50.00 | 20.00 | 5.00 |
| ☐ 4 Ian Gibb | 50.00 | 20.00 | 5.00 |
| ☐ 5 Dick Huffman | 75.00 | 30.00 | 7.50 |
| ☐ 6 Jack Jacobs | 100.00 | 40.00 | 10.00 |
| ☐ 7 Thomas Lumsden | 50.00 | 20.00 | 5.00 |
| ☐ 8 George McPhail | 50.00 | 20.00 | 5.00 |
| ☐ 9 Jim McPherson | 50.00 | 20.00 | 5.00 |
| ☐ 10 Buddy Tinsley | 75.00 | 30.00 | 7.50 |
| ☐ 11 Ron Vaccher | 50.00 | 20.00 | 5.00 |
| ☐ 12 Al Wiley | 50.00 | 20.00 | 5.00 |
| ☐ 13 Ken Charlton | 75.00 | 30.00 | 7.50 |
| ☐ 14 Glenn Dobbs | 60.00 | 24.00 | 6.00 |
| ☐ 15 Sully Glasser | 50.00 | 20.00 | 5.00 |
| ☐ 16 Nelson Greene | 50.00 | 20.00 | 5.00 |
| ☐ 17 Bert Iannone | 50.00 | 20.00 | 5.00 |
| ☐ 18 Art McEwan | 50.00 | 20.00 | 5.00 |
| ☐ 19 Jimmy McFaul | 50.00 | 20.00 | 5.00 |
| ☐ 20 Bob Pelling | 50.00 | 20.00 | 5.00 |
| ☐ 21 Chuck Radley | 50.00 | 20.00 | 5.00 |
| ☐ 22 Martin Ruby | 75.00 | 30.00 | 7.50 |
| ☐ 23 Jack Russell | 50.00 | 20.00 | 5.00 |
| ☐ 24 Roy Wright | 50.00 | 20.00 | 5.00 |
| ☐ 25 Paul Alford | 50.00 | 20.00 | 5.00 |
| ☐ 26 Sugarfoot Anderson | 50.00 | 20.00 | 5.00 |
| ☐ 27 Dick Bradley | 50.00 | 20.00 | 5.00 |
| ☐ 28 Bob Bryant | 50.00 | 20.00 | 5.00 |
| ☐ 29 Cliff Cyr | 50.00 | 20.00 | 5.00 |
| ☐ 30 Cal Green | 50.00 | 20.00 | 5.00 |
| ☐ 31 Stan Heath | 50.00 | 20.00 | 5.00 |
| ☐ 32 Stan Kaluznick | 50.00 | 20.00 | 5.00 |
| ☐ 33 Guss Knickerhm | 50.00 | 20.00 | 5.00 |
| ☐ 34 Paul Salata | 50.00 | 20.00 | 5.00 |
| ☐ 35 Murry Sullivan | 50.00 | 20.00 | 5.00 |
| ☐ 36 Dave West | 50.00 | 20.00 | 5.00 |
| ☐ 37 Joe Aguirre | 50.00 | 20.00 | 5.00 |
| ☐ 38 Claude Arnold | 50.00 | 20.00 | 5.00 |
| ☐ 39 Bill Briggs | 50.00 | 20.00 | 5.00 |
| ☐ 40 Mario DeMarco | 60.00 | 24.00 | 6.00 |
| ☐ 41 Mike King | 50.00 | 20.00 | 5.00 |
| ☐ 42 Donald Lord | 50.00 | 20.00 | 5.00 |
| ☐ 43 Frank Morris | 75.00 | 30.00 | 7.50 |
| ☐ 44 Gayle Pace | 50.00 | 20.00 | 5.00 |
| ☐ 45 Rod Pantages | 50.00 | 20.00 | 5.00 |
| ☐ 46 Rollin Prather | 50.00 | 20.00 | 5.00 |
| ☐ 47 Chuck Quilter | 50.00 | 20.00 | 5.00 |
| ☐ 48 Jim Quondamatteo | 60.00 | 24.00 | 6.00 |

## 1993 Dairy Lids Saskatchewan Roughriders

Issued in Saskatchewan and featuring 1993 Roughriders players, these six 1993 Dairy Producers Ice Cream collector lids were issued on four-litre ice cream cartons. Each white plastic lid measures approximately 8 1/4" in diameter. Inside a black border, the circular lids display a head shot, team helmet, and facsimile autograph on the upper portion, with information about the ice cream on the lower portion. The lids are unnumbered and checklisted below in alphabetical order.

| | MINT | EXC | G-VG |
|---|---|---|---|
| COMPLETE SET (6) | 20.00 | 8.00 | 2.00 |
| COMMON PLAYER (1-6) | 3.00 | 1.20 | .30 |
| ☐ 1 Kent Austin | 8.00 | 3.25 | .80 |
| ☐ 2 Ray Elgaard | 6.00 | 2.40 | .60 |
| ☐ 3 Jeff Fairholm | 6.00 | 2.40 | .60 |
| ☐ 4 Bobby Jurasin | 5.00 | 2.00 | .50 |
| ☐ 5 Dave Ridgway UER (Misspelled Ridgeway) | 4.00 | 1.60 | .40 |
| ☐ 6 Glen Suitor | 3.00 | 1.20 | .30 |

## 1993 Dream Cards Winnipeg Bombers

Printed on thin card stock, these 12 standard-size (2 1/2" by 3 1/2") cards feature on their fronts white-bordered color player action shots. The player's name and position appear in black lettering within the wide upper margin. The white-bordered horizontal back is framed by a blue line and carries a color player head shot at the upper left. The player's name and biography appear below, and his career highlights are shown to the right. The cards are numbered on the back.

| | MINT | EXC | G-VG |
|---|---|---|---|
| COMPLETE SET (12) | 10.00 | 4.00 | 1.00 |
| COMMON PLAYER (1-12) | .75 | .30 | .07 |
| ☐ 1 Matt Dunigan | 3.00 | 1.20 | .30 |
| ☐ 2 Greg Battle | 1.50 | .60 | .15 |
| ☐ 3 Nathaniel Bolton | .75 | .30 | .07 |
| ☐ 4 Stan Mikawos | .75 | .30 | .07 |
| ☐ 5 Miles Gorrell | .75 | .30 | .07 |
| ☐ 6 Troy Westwood | 1.00 | .40 | .10 |
| ☐ 7 Michael Richardson | 3.00 | 1.20 | .30 |
| ☐ 8 David Black | .75 | .30 | .07 |
| ☐ 9 Chris Walby | 1.00 | .40 | .10 |
| ☐ 10 David Wiliams | 1.50 | .60 | .15 |
| ☐ 11 Blaise Bryant | 1.50 | .60 | .15 |
| ☐ 12 Bob Cameron | .75 | .30 | .07 |

## 1981 Edmonton Journal Eskimos

This 16-card set measures approximately 3" by 5" and was sponsored by the Edmonton Journal. The set features black-and-white posed player photos with white borders. The player's name and position is printed at the bottom. The Edmonton helmet icon is printed at the bottom. The backs are blank. The cards are unnumbered and checklisted below in alphabetical order.

| | MINT | EXC | G-VG |
|---|---|---|---|
| COMPLETE SET (16) | 200.00 | 80.00 | 20.00 |
| COMMON PLAYER (1-16) | 5.00 | 2.00 | .50 |
| ☐ 1 Dave Fennell | 7.50 | 3.00 | .75 |
| ☐ 2 Brian Fryer | 5.00 | 2.00 | .50 |
| ☐ 3 Jim Germany | 6.00 | 2.40 | .60 |
| ☐ 4 Gary Hayes | 5.00 | 2.00 | .50 |
| ☐ 5 Larry Highbaugh | 10.00 | 4.00 | 1.00 |
| ☐ 6 Joe Hollimon | 5.00 | 2.00 | .50 |
| ☐ 7 Ed Jones | 5.00 | 2.00 | .50 |
| ☐ 8 Dan Kearns | 5.00 | 2.00 | .50 |
| ☐ 9 Brian Kelly | 15.00 | 6.00 | 1.50 |
| ☐ 10 Dan Kepley | 10.00 | 4.00 | 1.00 |
| ☐ 11 Neil Lumsden | 6.00 | 2.40 | .60 |
| ☐ 12 Warren Moon | 100.00 | 40.00 | 10.00 |
| ☐ 13 James Parker | 15.00 | 6.00 | 1.50 |
| ☐ 14 Tom Scott | 10.00 | 4.00 | 1.00 |
| ☐ 15 Waddell Smith | 5.00 | 2.00 | .50 |
| ☐ 16 Bill Stevenson | 6.00 | 2.40 | .60 |

## 1984 Edmonton Journal Eskimos

This 13-card set measures approximately 3" by 5" and was sponsored by the Edmonton Journal. The set features black-and-white posed player photos with white borders. The player's name and position is printed at the bottom. The sponsor's logo and a Edmonton helmet icon are printed at the top. The backs are blank. The cards are unnumbered and checklisted below in alphabetical order.

| | MINT | EXC | G-VG |
|---|---|---|---|
| COMPLETE SET (13) | 40.00 | 16.00 | 4.00 |
| COMMON PLAYER (1-13) | 3.50 | 1.40 | .35 |
| ☐ 1 Leo Blanchard | 3.50 | 1.40 | .35 |
| ☐ 2 Marco Cyncar | 5.00 | 2.00 | .50 |
| ☐ 3 Blake Dermott | 3.50 | 1.40 | .35 |
| ☐ 4 Brian Fryer | 3.50 | 1.40 | .35 |
| ☐ 5 Joe Hollimon | 3.50 | 1.40 | .35 |
| ☐ 6 James Hunter | 3.50 | 1.40 | .35 |
| ☐ 7 Greg Marshall | 6.00 | 2.40 | .60 |
| ☐ 8 Mike Nelson CO | 3.50 | 1.40 | .35 |
| ☐ 9 Hector Pothier | 3.50 | 1.40 | .35 |
| ☐ 10 Paul G. Rudzinski ACO | 3.50 | 1.40 | .35 |
| ☐ 11 Bill Stevenson | 5.00 | 2.00 | .50 |
| ☐ 12 Tom Towns | 3.50 | 1.40 | .35 |
| ☐ 13 Eric Upton | 3.50 | 1.40 | .35 |

## 1981 JOGO CFL B/W

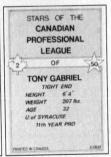

This Canadian Football League set consists of 50 numbered black and white cards with blue printing on the backs of the cards. Cards were printed in Canada and measure 3 1/2" by 5". J.C. Watts (card number 4) was added to the set after he was the MVP of the Grey Cup in 1981 replacing Greg Marshall. According to the producer, there were three press runs (500 sets, 500 sets, and 300 sets) for this set; only the third contained the J.C. Watts card. The set price below includes both number 4's. The key card in the set is Warren Moon, representing his first card of any kind.

| | MINT | EXC | G-VG |
|---|---|---|---|
| COMPLETE SET (51) | 200.00 | 80.00 | 20.00 |
| COMMON PLAYER (1-50) | 1.00 | .40 | .10 |
| ☐ 1 Richard Crump | 2.00 | .80 | .20 |
| ☐ 2 Tony Gabriel | 7.50 | 3.00 | .75 |
| ☐ 3 Gerry Organ | 1.00 | .40 | .10 |
| ☐ 4A Greg Marshall | 2.00 | .80 | .20 |
| ☐ 4B J.C. Watts | 20.00 | 8.00 | 2.00 |
| ☐ 5 Mike Raines | 1.00 | .40 | .10 |

| | | | |
|---|---|---|---|
| ☐ 6 Larry Brune | 1.00 | .40 | .10 |
| ☐ 7 Randy Rhino | 2.00 | .80 | .20 |
| ☐ 8 Bruce Clark | 4.00 | 1.60 | .40 |
| ☐ 9 Condredge Holloway | 6.00 | 2.40 | .60 |
| ☐ 10 Dave Newman | 1.00 | .40 | .10 |
| ☐ 11 Cedric Minter | 1.00 | .40 | .10 |
| ☐ 12 Peter Muller | 1.00 | .40 | .10 |
| ☐ 13 Vince Ferragamo | 7.50 | 3.00 | .75 |
| ☐ 14 James Scott | 2.00 | .80 | .20 |
| ☐ 15 Billy Johnson ("White Shoes") | 5.00 | 2.00 | .50 |
| ☐ 16 David Overstreet | 6.00 | 2.40 | .60 |
| ☐ 17 Keith Gary | 1.50 | .60 | .15 |
| ☐ 18 Tom Clements | 10.00 | 4.00 | 1.00 |
| ☐ 19 Keith Baker | 1.00 | .40 | .10 |
| ☐ 20 David Shaw | 1.00 | .40 | .10 |
| ☐ 21 Ben Zambiasi | 2.50 | 1.00 | .25 |
| ☐ 22 John Priestner | 1.00 | .40 | .10 |
| ☐ 23 Warren Moon | 125.00 | 50.00 | 12.50 |
| ☐ 24 Tom Wilkinson | 3.00 | 1.20 | .30 |
| ☐ 25 Brian Kelly | 6.00 | 2.40 | .60 |
| ☐ 26 Dan Kepley | 2.00 | .80 | .20 |
| ☐ 27 Larry Highbaugh | 2.50 | 1.00 | .25 |
| ☐ 28 David Boone | 1.00 | .40 | .10 |
| ☐ 29 John Henry White | 1.00 | .40 | .10 |
| ☐ 30 Joe Paopao | 3.00 | 1.20 | .30 |
| ☐ 31 Larry Key | 1.00 | .40 | .10 |
| ☐ 32 Glen Jackson | 1.00 | .40 | .10 |
| ☐ 33 Joe Hollimon | 1.00 | .40 | .10 |
| ☐ 34 Dieter Brock | 6.00 | 2.40 | .60 |
| ☐ 35 Mike Holmes | 1.00 | .40 | .10 |
| ☐ 36 William Miller | 1.00 | .40 | .10 |
| ☐ 37 John Helton | 3.00 | 1.20 | .30 |
| ☐ 38 Joe Poplawski | 1.50 | .60 | .15 |
| ☐ 39 Joe Barnes | 4.00 | 1.60 | .40 |
| ☐ 40 John Hufnagel | 5.00 | 2.00 | .50 |
| ☐ 41 Bobby Thompson | 1.00 | .40 | .10 |
| ☐ 42 Steve Stapler | 1.00 | .40 | .10 |
| ☐ 43 Tom Cousineau | 5.00 | 2.00 | .50 |
| ☐ 44 Bruce Threadgill | 1.00 | .40 | .10 |
| ☐ 45 Ed McAleney | 1.00 | .40 | .10 |
| ☐ 46 Leif Petterson | 1.50 | .60 | .15 |
| ☐ 47 Paul Bennett | 1.00 | .40 | .10 |
| ☐ 48 James Reed | 1.00 | .40 | .10 |
| ☐ 49 Gerry Dattilio | 1.50 | .60 | .15 |
| ☐ 50 Checklist Card | 3.00 | 1.20 | .30 |

| | | | |
|---|---|---|---|
| ☐ 12 Kelvin Kirk | .50 | .20 | .05 |
| ☐ 13 Gerry Organ | .60 | .24 | .06 |
| ☐ 14 Carl Brazley | .75 | .30 | .07 |
| ☐ 15 William Mitchell | .50 | .20 | .05 |
| ☐ 16 Billy Hardee | .50 | .20 | .05 |
| ☐ 17 Jonathan Sutton | .50 | .20 | .05 |
| ☐ 18 Doug Seymour | .50 | .20 | .05 |
| ☐ 19 Pat Staub | .50 | .20 | .05 |
| ☐ 20 Larry Tittley | .50 | .20 | .05 |
| ☐ 21 Pat Stoqua | .50 | .20 | .05 |
| ☐ 22 Sam Platt | .50 | .20 | .05 |
| ☐ 23 Gary Dulin | .50 | .20 | .05 |
| ☐ 24 John Holland | .60 | .24 | .06 |

## 1982-84 JOGO Ottawa Stars of the Past

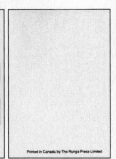

This set consists of 22 black and white numbered cards distributed between 1982 and 1984. Cards measure approximately 3 1/2" by 5" and are subtitled "Stars of the Past." These large black and white cards feature ex-Ottawa players; the front of the card also gives the position and years that the player played for the Ottawa Rough Riders; cards are numbered on the front in the lower right corner and are in black and white; backs are blank except for "Printed in Canada by The Runge Press Limited". The first series (1-12) was issued as an insert to the 1982 color set of Rough Riders; the next series of four (13-16) were added to the original 12; then in 1984 an additional six cards were issued as inserts in the Ottawa Rough Rider program. The cards of the last series contain write-up on the back, as well as different sponsor advertising. In the first series, six of the cards were double printed; these are designated with a DP in the checklist below. There are recognizable differences in the original and program insert Whit Tucker and Russ Jackson photos.

| | MINT | EXC | G-VG |
|---|---|---|---|
| COMPLETE 1982 (1-16) | 25.00 | 10.00 | 2.50 |
| COMPLETE 1984 (17-22) | 60.00 | 24.00 | 6.00 |
| COMMON PLAYER (1-12) | 1.00 | .40 | .10 |
| COMMON PLAYER (13-16) | 2.00 | .80 | .20 |
| COMMON PLAYER (17-22) | 12.00 | 5.00 | 1.20 |

| | | | |
|---|---|---|---|
| ☐ 1 Tony Gabriel | 3.00 | 1.20 | .30 |
| ☐ 2 Whit Tucker DP | 2.00 | .80 | .20 |
| ☐ 3 Dave Thelen | 2.00 | .80 | .20 |
| ☐ 4 Ron Stewart DP | 2.00 | .80 | .20 |
| ☐ 5 Russ Jackson DP | 4.00 | 1.60 | .40 |
| ☐ 6 Kaye Vaughan | 2.00 | .80 | .20 |
| ☐ 7 Bob Simpson | 2.00 | .80 | .20 |
| ☐ 8 Ken Lehmann | 1.25 | .50 | .12 |
| ☐ 9 Lou Bruce | 1.00 | .40 | .10 |
| ☐ 10 Wayne Giardino DP | 1.00 | .40 | .10 |
| ☐ 11 Moe Racine | 1.00 | .40 | .10 |
| ☐ 12 Gary Schreider | 1.00 | .40 | .10 |
| ☐ 13 Don Sutherin | 4.00 | 1.60 | .40 |
| ☐ 14 Mark Kosmos DP | 2.00 | .80 | .20 |
| ☐ 15 Jim Foley DP | 2.50 | 1.00 | .25 |
| ☐ 16 Jim Conroy | 2.00 | .80 | .20 |
| ☐ 17 George Brancato | 12.00 | 5.00 | 1.20 |
| ☐ 18 Art Green | 12.00 | 5.00 | 1.20 |
| ☐ 19 Rudy Sims | 12.00 | 5.00 | 1.20 |
| ☐ 20 Jim Coode | 12.00 | 5.00 | 1.20 |
| ☐ 21 Jerry Campbell | 12.00 | 5.00 | 1.20 |
| ☐ 22 Jim Piaskoski | 15.00 | 6.00 | 1.50 |

## 1982 JOGO Ottawa

These 24 large (approximately 3 1/2" by 5") cards featuring the Ottawa Rough Riders of the CFL have full color fronts while the backs are printed in red and black on white stock. Cards are numbered inside a leaf in the middle of the back of the card; player's uniform number is also given on the back of the card. A sample card of Rick Sowieta (with blank back) is also available with overstruck "Collector's Series" in red ink diagonally across the front of the card. These cards were endorsed by the CFL Players Association and produced by JOGO and were available for sale in some confectionary stores.

| | MINT | EXC | G-VG |
|---|---|---|---|
| COMPLETE SET (24) | 10.00 | 4.00 | 1.00 |
| COMMON PLAYER (1-24) | .50 | .20 | .05 |

| | | | |
|---|---|---|---|
| ☐ 1 Jordan Case | .60 | .24 | .06 |
| ☐ 2 Larry Brune | .60 | .24 | .06 |
| ☐ 3 Val Belcher | .60 | .24 | .06 |
| ☐ 4 Greg Marshall | .75 | .30 | .07 |
| ☐ 5 Mike Raines | .50 | .20 | .05 |
| ☐ 6 Rick Sowieta | .50 | .20 | .05 |
| ☐ 7 John Glassford | .50 | .20 | .05 |
| ☐ 8 Bruce Walker | .50 | .20 | .05 |
| ☐ 9 Jim Reid | .60 | .24 | .06 |
| ☐ 10 Kevin Powell | .50 | .20 | .05 |
| ☐ 11 Jim Piaskoski | .60 | .24 | .06 |

## 1983 JOGO Quarterbacks

This nine-card black and white (with red border) set contains several well-known quarterbacks performing in the CFL. The cards are unnumbered although each player's uniform number is given on the

back of his card. The cards are numbered in alphabetical order in the checklist below for convenience. Cards measure 2 1/2" by 3 1/2". Cards were produced by JOGO Novelties.

|  | MINT | EXC | G-VG |
|---|---|---|---|
| COMPLETE SET (9) | 60.00 | 24.00 | 6.00 |
| COMMON PLAYER (1-9) | 1.50 | .60 | .15 |
| ☐ 1 Dieter Brock | 6.00 | 2.40 | .60 |
| Winnipeg Blue Bombers |  |  |  |
| ☐ 2 Tom Clements | 7.50 | 3.00 | .75 |
| Hamilton Tiger-Cats |  |  |  |
| ☐ 3 Gerry Dattilio | 1.50 | .60 | .15 |
| Calgary Stampeders |  |  |  |
| ☐ 4 Roy DeWalt | 3.00 | 1.20 | .30 |
| British Columbia Lions |  |  |  |
| ☐ 5 Johnny Evans | 1.50 | .60 | .15 |
| Montreal Alouettes |  |  |  |
| ☐ 6 Condredge Holloway | 4.00 | 1.60 | .40 |
| Toronto Argonauts |  |  |  |
| ☐ 7 John Hufnagel | 5.00 | 2.00 | .50 |
| Saskatchewan Roughriders |  |  |  |
| ☐ 8 Warren Moon | 40.00 | 16.00 | 4.00 |
| Edmonton Eskimos |  |  |  |
| ☐ 9 J.C. Watts | 4.00 | 1.60 | .40 |
| Ottawa Rough Riders |  |  |  |

## 1983 JOGO Hall of Fame A

This 25-card set features members of the Canadian Football Hall of Fame. Cards measure 2 1/2" by 3 1/2". Cards were produced by JOGO Novelties. These black and white standard sized cards have a red border. On the back they are numbered (with the prefix A) and contain biographical information.

|  | MINT | EXC | G-VG |
|---|---|---|---|
| COMPLETE SET (25) | 25.00 | 10.00 | 2.50 |
| COMMON PLAYER (A1-A25) | 1.00 | .40 | .10 |
| ☐ A1 Russ Jackson | 5.00 | 2.00 | .50 |
| Ottawa |  |  |  |
| ☐ A2 Harvey Wylie | 1.00 | .40 | .10 |
| Calgary |  |  |  |
| ☐ A3 Kenny Ploen | 2.00 | .80 | .20 |
| Winnipeg |  |  |  |
| ☐ A4 Garney Henley | 2.00 | .80 | .20 |
| Hamilton |  |  |  |
| ☐ A5 Hal Patterson | 2.50 | 1.00 | .25 |
| Hamilton/Montreal |  |  |  |
| ☐ A6 Carl Cronin | 1.00 | .40 | .10 |
| Winnipeg |  |  |  |
| ☐ A7 Bob Simpson | 1.25 | .50 | .12 |
| Ottawa |  |  |  |

| ☐ A8 Dick Shatto | 1.25 | .50 | .12 |
|---|---|---|---|
| Toronto |  |  |  |
| ☐ A9 John Red O'Quinn | 1.00 | .40 | .10 |
| Montreal |  |  |  |
| ☐ A10 Johnny Bright | 2.00 | .80 | .20 |
| Edmonton |  |  |  |
| ☐ A11 Ernest Cox | 1.00 | .40 | .10 |
| Hamilton |  |  |  |
| ☐ A12 Rollie Miles | 1.00 | .40 | .10 |
| Edmonton |  |  |  |
| ☐ A13 Leo Lewis | 2.00 | .80 | .20 |
| Winnipeg |  |  |  |
| ☐ A14 Bud Grant | 7.50 | 3.00 | .75 |
| Winnipeg |  |  |  |
| ☐ A15 Herb Trawick | 1.00 | .40 | .10 |
| Montreal |  |  |  |
| ☐ A16 Wayne Harris | 1.25 | .50 | .12 |
| Calgary |  |  |  |
| ☐ A17 Earl Lunsford | 1.00 | .40 | .10 |
| Calgary |  |  |  |
| ☐ A18 Tony Golab | 1.00 | .40 | .10 |
| Ottawa |  |  |  |
| ☐ A19 George Reed | 2.50 | 1.00 | .25 |
| Saskatchewan |  |  |  |
| ☐ A20 By Bailey | 1.00 | .40 | .10 |
| British Columbia |  |  |  |
| ☐ A21 Harry Batstone | 1.00 | .40 | .10 |
| Toronto |  |  |  |
| ☐ A22 Ron Atchison | 1.25 | .50 | .12 |
| Saskatchewan |  |  |  |
| ☐ A23 Willie Fleming | 1.25 | .50 | .12 |
| British Columbia |  |  |  |
| ☐ A24 Frank Leadlay | 1.00 | .40 | .10 |
| Hamilton |  |  |  |
| ☐ A25 Lionel Conacher | 2.00 | .80 | .20 |
| Toronto |  |  |  |

## 1983 JOGO Hall of Fame B

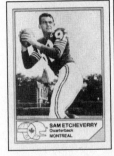

This 25-card set features members of the Canadian Football Hall of Fame. Cards measure 2 1/2" by 3 1/2". Cards were produced by JOGO Novelties. These black and white standard-sized cards have a red border. On the back they are numbered (with the prefix B) and contain biographical information. The title card is not required (or considered below) as part of the complete set as priced below; however the title card is indeed somewhat harder to find separately as there were reportedly only half as many title cards printed as there were cards for each player.

|  | MINT | EXC | G-VG |
|---|---|---|---|
| COMPLETE SET (25) | 25.00 | 10.00 | 2.50 |
| COMMON PLAYER (B1-B25) | 1.00 | .40 | .10 |
| ☐ B1 Bernie Faloney | 4.00 | 1.60 | .40 |
| Hamilton |  |  |  |
| ☐ B2 George Dixon | 2.00 | .80 | .20 |
| Montreal |  |  |  |
| ☐ B3 John Barrow | 2.00 | .80 | .20 |
| Hamilton |  |  |  |
| ☐ B4 Jackie Parker | 6.00 | 2.40 | .60 |
| Edmonton/Toronto |  |  |  |
| ☐ B5 Jack Jacobs | 1.50 | .60 | .15 |
| Winnipeg |  |  |  |
| ☐ B6 Sam (The Rifle) | 6.00 | 2.40 | .60 |
| Etcheverry Montreal |  |  |  |
| ☐ B7 Norm Fieldgate | 1.25 | .50 | .12 |
| British Columbia |  |  |  |
| ☐ B8 John Ferrard | 1.00 | .40 | .10 |
| Hamilton |  |  |  |
| ☐ B9 Tommy Joe Coffey | 2.50 | 1.00 | .25 |
| Edmonton/Hamilton |  |  |  |
| ☐ B10 Martin Ruby | 1.00 | .40 | .10 |
| Saskatchewan |  |  |  |

| | | | |
|---|---|---|---|
| ☐ B11 Ted Reeve | 1.00 | .40 | .10 |
| Toronto | | | |
| ☐ B12 Kaye Vaughan | 1.00 | .40 | .10 |
| Ottawa | | | |
| ☐ B13 Ron Lancaster | 3.00 | 1.20 | .30 |
| Saskatchewan | | | |
| ☐ B14 Smirle Lawson | 1.00 | .40 | .10 |
| Toronto | | | |
| ☐ B15 Fritz Hanson | 1.00 | .40 | .10 |
| Winnipeg | | | |
| ☐ B16 Vince Scott | 1.00 | .40 | .10 |
| Hamilton | | | |
| ☐ B17 Frank Morris | 1.00 | .40 | .10 |
| Toronto/Edmonton | | | |
| ☐ B18 Normie Kwong | 2.50 | 1.00 | .25 |
| Edmonton | | | |
| ☐ B19 Dr. Tom Casey | 1.25 | .50 | .12 |
| Winnipeg | | | |
| ☐ B20 Herb Gray | 2.50 | 1.00 | .25 |
| Winnipeg | | | |
| ☐ B21 Gerry James | 1.25 | .50 | .12 |
| Winnipeg | | | |
| ☐ B22 Pete Neumann | 1.00 | .40 | .10 |
| Hamilton | | | |
| ☐ B23 Joe Krol | 1.00 | .40 | .10 |
| Toronto | | | |
| ☐ B24 Ron Stewart | 1.50 | .60 | .15 |
| Ottawa | | | |
| ☐ B25 Buddy Tinsley | 1.00 | .40 | .10 |
| Winnipeg | | | |
| ☐ NNO Title Card SP | 6.00 | 2.40 | .60 |
| (Map to HOF on back) | | | |

# 1983 JOGO CFL Limited

This unnumbered set of 110 color cards was printed in very limited quantities (only 600 sets of which 500 were numbered according to the producer) and features players in the Canadian Football League. The backs of the cards appear to be on off-white card stock. The checklist below is organized in alphabetical order within each team, although the player's uniform number is given on the back of the cards. Team order is as follows: Toronto Argonauts (1-22), Ottawa Rough Riders (23-42), Hamilton Tiger-Cats (43-51), Montreal Concordes (52-57), British Columbia Lions (58-69), Winnipeg Blue Bombers (70-84), Edmonton Eskimos (85-96), Calgary Stampeders (97-104 and 110), and Saskatchewan Roughriders (105-109). Cards of Warren Moon and Dieter Brock are especially difficult to find since both of these players purchased quantities of their own card directly from the producer for distribution to their fans. Each of the registered sets is numbered on the Darrell Moir (Calgary number 110) card.

| | MINT | EXC | G-VG |
|---|---|---|---|
| COMPLETE SET (110) | 1100.00 | 500.00 | 125.00 |
| COMMON PLAYER (1-110) | 4.50 | 1.80 | .45 |
| | | | |
| ☐ 1 Steve Ackroyd | 4.50 | 1.80 | .45 |
| ☐ 2 Joe Barnes | 12.00 | 5.00 | 1.20 |
| ☐ 3 Bob Bronk | 4.50 | 1.80 | .45 |
| ☐ 4 Jan Carinci | 4.50 | 1.80 | .45 |
| ☐ 5 Gordon Elser | 4.50 | 1.80 | .45 |
| ☐ 6 Dan Ferrone | 6.00 | 2.40 | .60 |
| ☐ 7 Terry Greer | 12.00 | 5.00 | 1.20 |
| ☐ 8 Mike Hameluck | 4.50 | 1.80 | .45 |
| ☐ 9 Condredge Holloway | 15.00 | 6.00 | 1.50 |
| ☐ 10 Greg Holmes | 4.50 | 1.80 | .45 |
| ☐ 11 Hank Ilesic | 10.00 | 4.00 | 1.00 |
| ☐ 12 John Malinosky | 4.50 | 1.80 | .45 |
| ☐ 13 Cedric Minter | 4.50 | 1.80 | .45 |
| ☐ 14 Don Moen | 4.50 | 1.80 | .45 |
| ☐ 15 Rick Mohr | 4.50 | 1.80 | .45 |
| ☐ 16 Darrell Nicholson | 4.50 | 1.80 | .45 |
| ☐ 17 Paul Pearson | 6.00 | 2.40 | .60 |

| | | | |
|---|---|---|---|
| ☐ 18 Matthew Teague | 4.50 | 1.80 | .45 |
| ☐ 19 Geoff Townsend | 4.50 | 1.80 | .45 |
| ☐ 20 Tom Trifaux | 4.50 | 1.80 | .45 |
| ☐ 21 Darrell Wilson | 4.50 | 1.80 | .45 |
| ☐ 22 Earl Wilson | 4.50 | 1.80 | .45 |
| ☐ 23 Ricky Barden | 4.50 | 1.80 | .45 |
| ☐ 24 Roger Cattelan | 4.50 | 1.80 | .45 |
| ☐ 25 Michael Collymore | 4.50 | 1.80 | .45 |
| ☐ 26 Charles Cornelius | 4.50 | 1.80 | .45 |
| ☐ 27 Mariet Ford | 4.50 | 1.80 | .45 |
| ☐ 28 Tyron Gray | 6.00 | 2.40 | .60 |
| ☐ 29 Steve Harrison | 4.50 | 1.80 | .45 |
| ☐ 30 Tim Hook | 4.50 | 1.80 | .45 |
| ☐ 31 Greg Marshall | 6.00 | 2.40 | .60 |
| ☐ 32 Ken Miller | 4.50 | 1.80 | .45 |
| ☐ 33 Dave Newman | 4.50 | 1.80 | .45 |
| ☐ 34 Rudy Phillips | 4.50 | 1.80 | .45 |
| ☐ 35 Jim Reid | 4.50 | 1.80 | .45 |
| ☐ 36 Junior Robinson | 4.50 | 1.80 | .45 |
| ☐ 37 Mark Seale | 4.50 | 1.80 | .45 |
| ☐ 38 Rick Sowieta | 4.50 | 1.80 | .45 |
| ☐ 39 Pat Stoqua | 4.50 | 1.80 | .45 |
| ☐ 40 Skip Walker | 10.00 | 4.00 | 1.00 |
| ☐ 41 Al Washington | 4.50 | 1.80 | .45 |
| ☐ 42 J.C. Watts | 12.00 | 5.00 | 1.20 |
| ☐ 43 Keith Baker | 4.50 | 1.80 | .45 |
| ☐ 44 Dieter Brock | 50.00 | 20.00 | 5.00 |
| ☐ 45 Rocky DiPietro | 30.00 | 12.00 | 3.00 |
| ☐ 46 Howard Fields | 4.50 | 1.80 | .45 |
| ☐ 47 Ron Johnson | 7.50 | 3.00 | .75 |
| ☐ 48 John Priestner | 4.50 | 1.80 | .45 |
| ☐ 49 Johnny Shepherd | 4.50 | 1.80 | .45 |
| ☐ 50 Mike Walker | 7.50 | 3.00 | .75 |
| ☐ 51 Ben Zambiasi | 12.00 | 5.00 | 1.20 |
| ☐ 52 Nick Arakgi | 6.00 | 2.40 | .60 |
| ☐ 53 Brian DeRoo | 4.50 | 1.80 | .45 |
| ☐ 54 Denny Ferdinand | 4.50 | 1.80 | .45 |
| ☐ 55 Willie Hampton | 4.50 | 1.80 | .45 |
| ☐ 56 Kevin Starkey | 4.50 | 1.80 | .45 |
| ☐ 57 Glen Weir | 4.50 | 1.80 | .45 |
| ☐ 58 Larry Crawford | 7.50 | 3.00 | .75 |
| ☐ 59 Tyrone Crews | 4.50 | 1.80 | .45 |
| ☐ 60 James Curry | 10.00 | 4.00 | 1.00 |
| ☐ 61 Roy DeWalt | 12.00 | 5.00 | 1.20 |
| ☐ 62 Mervyn Fernandez | 50.00 | 20.00 | 5.00 |
| ☐ 63 Sammy Green | 4.50 | 1.80 | .45 |
| ☐ 64 Glen Jackson | 4.50 | 1.80 | .45 |
| ☐ 65 Glen Leonhard | 4.50 | 1.80 | .45 |
| ☐ 66 Nelson Martin | 4.50 | 1.80 | .45 |
| ☐ 67 Joe Paopao | 10.00 | 4.00 | 1.00 |
| ☐ 68 Lui Passaglia | 12.00 | 5.00 | 1.20 |
| ☐ 69 Al Wilson | 4.50 | 1.80 | .45 |
| ☐ 70 Nick Bastaja | 4.50 | 1.80 | .45 |
| ☐ 71 Paul Bennett | 4.50 | 1.80 | .45 |
| ☐ 72 John Bonk | 4.50 | 1.80 | .45 |
| ☐ 73 Aaron Brown | 4.50 | 1.80 | .45 |
| ☐ 74 Bob Cameron | 4.50 | 1.80 | .45 |
| ☐ 75 Tom Clements | 50.00 | 20.00 | 5.00 |
| ☐ 76 Rick House | 6.00 | 2.40 | .60 |
| ☐ 77 John Hufnagel | 10.00 | 4.00 | 1.00 |
| ☐ 78 Sean Kehoe | 4.50 | 1.80 | .45 |
| ☐ 79 James Murphy | 12.00 | 5.00 | 1.20 |
| ☐ 80 Tony Norman | 4.50 | 1.80 | .45 |
| ☐ 81 Joe Poplawski | 4.50 | 1.80 | .45 |
| ☐ 82 Willard Reaves | 15.00 | 6.00 | 1.50 |
| ☐ 83 Bobby Thompson | 4.50 | 1.80 | .45 |
| ☐ 84 Wylie Turner | 4.50 | 1.80 | .45 |
| ☐ 85 Dave Fennell | 7.50 | 3.00 | .75 |
| ☐ 86 Jim Germany | 6.00 | 2.40 | .60 |
| ☐ 87 Larry Highbaugh | 7.50 | 3.00 | .75 |
| ☐ 88 Joe Holliman | 4.50 | 1.80 | .45 |
| ☐ 89 Dan Kepley | 10.00 | 4.00 | 1.00 |
| ☐ 90 Neil Lumsden | 4.50 | 1.80 | .45 |
| ☐ 91 Warren Moon | 600.00 | 240.00 | 60.00 |
| ☐ 92 James Parker | 15.00 | 6.00 | 1.50 |
| ☐ 93 Dale Potter | 4.50 | 1.80 | .45 |
| ☐ 94 Angelo Santucci | 4.50 | 1.80 | .45 |
| ☐ 95 Tom Towns | 4.50 | 1.80 | .45 |
| ☐ 96 Tom Tuinei | 4.50 | 1.80 | .45 |
| ☐ 97 Danny Bass | 15.00 | 6.00 | 1.50 |
| ☐ 98 Ray Crouse | 4.50 | 1.80 | .45 |
| ☐ 99 Gerry Dattilio | 7.50 | 3.00 | .75 |
| ☐ 100 Tom Forzani | 4.50 | 1.80 | .45 |
| ☐ 101 Mike Levenseller | 4.50 | 1.80 | .45 |
| ☐ 102 Mike McTague | 6.00 | 2.40 | .60 |
| ☐ 103 Bernie Morrison | 4.50 | 1.80 | .45 |
| ☐ 104 Darrell Toussaint | 4.50 | 1.80 | .45 |
| ☐ 105 Chris DeFrance | 4.50 | 1.80 | .45 |
| ☐ 106 Dwight Edwards | 6.00 | 2.40 | .60 |
| ☐ 107 Vince Goldsmith | 10.00 | 4.00 | 1.00 |
| ☐ 108 Homer Jordan | 4.50 | 1.80 | .45 |
| ☐ 109 Mike Washington | 4.50 | 1.80 | .45 |
| ☐ 110A Darrell Moir | 12.00 | 5.00 | 1.20 |
| (Set number on back) | | | |
| ☐ 110B Darrell Moir | 50.00 | 20.00 | 5.00 |
| (Without set number) | | | |

# 1984 JOGO CFL

This full-color set of 160 cards produced by JOGO consists of two series: the first series is 1-110 and the second series runs from 111-160. According to the producer, there were 400 more sets of the first series printed than were printed of the second series; hence the second series is slightly more valuable per card. The cards are numbered on the back; the backs contain printing in red and black ink. The second series was printed on a gray cardboard stock whereas the first series is on a cream-colored stock. Photos were taken by F. Scott Grant, who is credited on the fronts of the cards. The cards feature players in the Canadian Football League. Cards in both series measure the standard 2 1/2" by 3 1/2". Some players are featured in both series.

|  | MINT | EXC | G-VG |
|---|---|---|---|
| COMPLETE SET (160) | 300.00 | 120.00 | 30.00 |
| COMPLETE SERIES 1 (110) | 150.00 | 60.00 | 15.00 |
| COMPLETE SERIES 2 (50) | 150.00 | 60.00 | 15.00 |
| COMMON PLAYER (1-110) | 1.00 | .40 | .10 |
| COMMON PLAYER (111-160) | 2.00 | .80 | .20 |

| | | | |
|---|---|---|---|
| ☐ 1 Mike Hameluck | 1.50 | .60 | .15 |
| ☐ 2 Bob Bronk | 1.00 | .40 | .10 |
| ☐ 3 Paul Pearson | 1.00 | .40 | .10 |
| ☐ 4 Dan Ferrone | 1.50 | .60 | .15 |
| ☐ 5 Paul Bennett | 1.00 | .40 | .10 |
| ☐ 6 Joe Barnes | 4.00 | 1.60 | .40 |
| ☐ 7 Condredge Holloway | 5.00 | 2.00 | .50 |
| ☐ 8 Terry Greer | 5.00 | 2.00 | .50 |
| ☐ 9 Vince Goldsmith | 3.00 | 1.20 | .30 |
| ☐ 10 Darrell Wilson | 1.00 | .40 | .10 |
| ☐ 11 Tom Trifaux | 1.00 | .40 | .10 |
| ☐ 12 Kelvin Pruenster | 1.00 | .40 | .10 |
| ☐ 13 Earl Wilson | 1.00 | .40 | .10 |
| ☐ 14 Hank Ilesic | 2.50 | 1.00 | .25 |
| ☐ 15 Stephen Del Col | 1.00 | .40 | .10 |
| ☐ 16 Lamont Meacham | 1.00 | .40 | .10 |
| ☐ 17 Lester Brown | 1.00 | .40 | .10 |
| ☐ 18 Rob Forbes | 1.00 | .40 | .10 |
| ☐ 19 Darrell Nicholson | 1.00 | .40 | .10 |
| ☐ 20 James Curry | 2.50 | 1.00 | .25 |
| ☐ 21 Skip Walker | 2.50 | 1.00 | .25 |
| ☐ 22 J.C. Watts | 5.00 | 2.00 | .50 |
| ☐ 23 Kevin Powell | 1.00 | .40 | .10 |
| ☐ 24 Dean Dorsey | 2.00 | .80 | .20 |
| ☐ 25 Tyron Gray | 2.00 | .80 | .20 |
| ☐ 26 Mike Hudson | 1.50 | .60 | .15 |
| ☐ 27 Dan Rashovich | 1.00 | .40 | .10 |
| ☐ 28 Rudy Phillips | 1.50 | .60 | .15 |
| ☐ 29 Larry Tittley | 1.00 | .40 | .10 |
| ☐ 30 Ricky Barden UER | 1.00 | .40 | .10 |
| (Number missing) | | | |
| ☐ 31 Mark Seale | 1.00 | .40 | .10 |
| ☐ 32 Prince McJunkins | 1.25 | .50 | .12 |
| ☐ 33 Kevin Dalliday | 1.00 | .40 | .10 |
| ☐ 34 Rick Sowieta | 1.00 | .40 | .10 |
| ☐ 35 Roger Cattelan | 1.00 | .40 | .10 |
| ☐ 36 Damir Dupin | 1.00 | .40 | .10 |
| ☐ 37 Jack Williams | 1.00 | .40 | .10 |
| ☐ 38 Dave Newman | 1.00 | .40 | .10 |
| ☐ 39 Maurice Doyle | 1.00 | .40 | .10 |
| ☐ 40 Tim Hook | 1.00 | .40 | .10 |
| ☐ 41 Dieter Brock | 10.00 | 4.00 | 1.00 |
| ☐ 42 Rufus Crawford | 5.00 | 2.00 | .50 |
| ☐ 43 Steve Kearns | 1.00 | .40 | .10 |
| ☐ 44 Ross Francis | 1.00 | .40 | .10 |
| ☐ 45 Henry Waszczuk | 1.00 | .40 | .10 |
| ☐ 46 Mark Streeter | 1.00 | .40 | .10 |
| ☐ 47 Mike McIntyre | 1.00 | .40 | .10 |
| ☐ 48 John Priestner | 1.00 | .40 | .10 |
| ☐ 49 Paul Palma | 1.00 | .40 | .10 |
| ☐ 50 Mike Walker | 1.50 | .60 | .15 |
| ☐ 51 Mike Barker | 1.00 | .40 | .10 |
| ☐ 52 Todd Brown | 1.00 | .40 | .10 |
| ☐ 53 Andre Francis | 2.00 | .80 | .20 |
| ☐ 54 Glenn Keeble | 1.00 | .40 | .10 |
| ☐ 55 Turner Gill | 7.50 | 3.00 | .75 |
| ☐ 56 Eugene Belliveau | 1.00 | .40 | .10 |
| ☐ 57 Willie Hampton | 1.00 | .40 | .10 |
| ☐ 58 Ken Ciancone | 1.00 | .40 | .10 |
| ☐ 59 Preston Young | 1.00 | .40 | .10 |
| ☐ 60 Stanley Washington | 1.00 | .40 | .10 |
| ☐ 61 Denny Ferdinand | 1.00 | .40 | .10 |
| ☐ 62 Steve Smith | 1.00 | .40 | .10 |
| ☐ 63 Rick Klassen | 1.50 | .60 | .15 |
| ☐ 64 Larry Crawford | 1.50 | .60 | .15 |
| ☐ 65 John Henry White | 1.00 | .40 | .10 |
| ☐ 66 Bernie Glier | 1.00 | .40 | .10 |
| ☐ 67 Don Taylor | 1.00 | .40 | .10 |
| ☐ 68 Roy DeWalt | 3.00 | 1.20 | .30 |
| ☐ 69 Mervyn Fernandez | 25.00 | 10.00 | 2.50 |
| ☐ 70 John Blain | 1.00 | .40 | .10 |
| ☐ 71 James Parker | 4.00 | 1.60 | .40 |
| ☐ 72 Henry Vereen | 1.00 | .40 | .10 |
| ☐ 73 Gerald Roper | 1.00 | .40 | .10 |
| ☐ 74 Jim Sandusky | 12.00 | 5.00 | 1.20 |
| ☐ 75 John Pankratz | 1.00 | .40 | .10 |
| ☐ 76 Tom Clements | 7.50 | 3.00 | .75 |
| ☐ 77 Vernon Pahl | 1.00 | .40 | .10 |
| ☐ 78 Trevor Kennerd | 2.50 | 1.00 | .25 |
| ☐ 79 Stan Mikawos | 1.00 | .40 | .10 |
| ☐ 80 Ken Hailey | 1.00 | .40 | .10 |
| ☐ 81 James Murphy | 4.00 | 1.60 | .40 |
| ☐ 82 Jeff Boyd | 2.00 | .80 | .20 |
| ☐ 83 Bob Cameron | 1.50 | .60 | .15 |
| ☐ 84 Jerome Erdman | 1.00 | .40 | .10 |
| ☐ 85 Tyrone Jones | 2.50 | 1.00 | .25 |
| ☐ 86 John Bonk | 1.00 | .40 | .10 |
| ☐ 87 John Sturdivant | 1.00 | .40 | .10 |
| ☐ 88 Dan Huclack | 1.00 | .40 | .10 |
| ☐ 89 Tony Norman | 1.00 | .40 | .10 |
| ☐ 90 Kevin Neiles | 1.00 | .40 | .10 |
| ☐ 91 Dave Kirzinger | 1.00 | .40 | .10 |
| ☐ 92 Kevin Molle | 1.00 | .40 | .10 |
| ☐ 93 Jerry DeBrouolny | 1.00 | .40 | .10 |
| ☐ 94 Larry Hogue | 1.00 | .40 | .10 |
| ☐ 95 Ken Moore | 1.00 | .40 | .10 |
| ☐ 96 Jerry Friesen | 1.00 | .40 | .10 |
| ☐ 97 Mike McTague | 1.00 | .40 | .10 |
| ☐ 98 Jason Riley | 1.00 | .40 | .10 |
| ☐ 99 Roger Aldag | 2.00 | .80 | .20 |
| ☐ 100 Dave Ridgway | 4.00 | 1.60 | .40 |
| ☐ 101 Eric Upton | 1.00 | .40 | .10 |
| ☐ 102 Laurent DesLauriers | 1.00 | .40 | .10 |
| ☐ 103 Brian Fryer | 1.00 | .40 | .10 |
| ☐ 104 Brian DeRoo | 1.00 | .40 | .10 |
| ☐ 105 Neil Lumsden | 1.00 | .40 | .10 |
| ☐ 106 Hector Pothier | 1.00 | .40 | .10 |
| ☐ 107 Brian Kelly | 12.00 | 5.00 | 1.20 |
| ☐ 108 Dan Kepley | 3.00 | 1.20 | .30 |
| ☐ 109 Danny Bass | 5.00 | 2.00 | .50 |
| ☐ 110 Nick Arakgi | 1.50 | .60 | .15 |
| ☐ 111 Lyle Bauer | 2.00 | .80 | .20 |
| ☐ 112 Al Washington | 2.00 | .80 | .20 |
| ☐ 113 Michel Bourgeau | 2.50 | 1.00 | .25 |
| ☐ 114 Keith Gooch | 2.00 | .80 | .20 |
| ☐ 115 Sean Kehoe | 2.00 | .80 | .20 |
| ☐ 116 Ken Clark | 3.00 | 1.20 | .30 |
| ☐ 117 Orlando Flanagan | 2.00 | .80 | .20 |
| ☐ 118 Greg Vavra | 2.00 | .80 | .20 |
| ☐ 119 Mark Bragagnolo | 2.00 | .80 | .20 |
| ☐ 120 Dave Cutler | 6.00 | 2.40 | .60 |
| ☐ 121 Nick Hebeler | 2.00 | .80 | .20 |
| ☐ 122 Harry Skipper | 5.00 | 2.00 | .50 |
| ☐ 123 Frank Robinson | 3.00 | 1.20 | .30 |
| ☐ 124 DeWayne Jett | 3.00 | 1.20 | .30 |
| ☐ 125 Mark Young | 2.00 | .80 | .20 |
| ☐ 126 Felix Wright | 25.00 | 10.00 | 2.50 |
| ☐ 127 Bob Poley | 2.00 | .80 | .20 |
| ☐ 128 Leo Ezerins | 2.00 | .80 | .20 |
| ☐ 129 Johnny Shepherd | 3.00 | 1.20 | .30 |
| ☐ 130 Jeff Inglis | 2.00 | .80 | .20 |
| ☐ 131 Dwaine Wilson | 2.00 | .80 | .20 |
| ☐ 132 Aaron Hill | 2.00 | .80 | .20 |
| ☐ 133 Brian Dudley | 2.00 | .80 | .20 |
| ☐ 134 Ned Armour | 2.00 | .80 | .20 |
| ☐ 135 Darryl Hall | 2.00 | .80 | .20 |
| ☐ 136 Vince Phason | 2.00 | .80 | .20 |
| ☐ 137 Terry Lymon | 2.00 | .80 | .20 |
| ☐ 138 Jerry Dobrovolny | 2.00 | .80 | .20 |
| ☐ 139 Richard Nemeth | 2.00 | .80 | .20 |
| ☐ 140 Matt Dunigan | 60.00 | 24.00 | 6.00 |
| ☐ 141 Rick Mohr | 2.00 | .80 | .20 |
| ☐ 142 Lawrie Skolrood | 2.00 | .80 | .20 |
| ☐ 143 Craig Ellis | 6.00 | 2.40 | .60 |
| ☐ 144 Steve Johnson | 2.00 | .80 | .20 |
| ☐ 145 Glen Suitor | 2.50 | 1.00 | .25 |
| ☐ 146 Jeff Roberts | 2.00 | .80 | .20 |
| ☐ 147 Greg Fieger | 2.00 | .80 | .20 |
| ☐ 148 Sterling Hinds | 2.00 | .80 | .20 |
| ☐ 149 Willard Reaves | 7.50 | 3.00 | .75 |

| | | | | |
|---|---|---|---|---|
| ☐ 150 | John Pitts | 2.00 | .80 | .20 |
| ☐ 151 | Delbert Fowler | 3.00 | 1.20 | .30 |
| ☐ 152 | Mark Hopkins | 2.00 | .80 | .20 |
| ☐ 153 | Pat Cantner | 2.00 | .80 | .20 |
| ☐ 154 | Scott Flagel | 2.50 | 1.00 | .25 |
| ☐ 155 | Donovan Rose | 2.00 | .80 | .20 |
| ☐ 156 | David Shaw | 2.00 | .80 | .20 |
| ☐ 157 | Mark Moors | 2.00 | .80 | .20 |
| ☐ 158 | Chris Walby | 7.50 | 3.00 | .75 |
| ☐ 159 | Eugene Belliveau | 2.00 | .80 | .20 |
| ☐ 160 | Trevor Kennerd | 7.50 | 3.00 | .75 |

## 1985 JOGO CFL

The 1985 JOGO CFL set is standard size (2 1/2" by 3 1/2") and was distributed as a single series of 110 cards, numbered 1-110. With some exceptions, the number ordering of the set is by teams, e.g., Toronto Argonauts (1, 25-27, 29-35), Ottawa Rough Riders (2-19), Montreal (20, 56-74), Hamilton Tiger-Cats (21-24), Saskatchewan Roughriders (28, 75-90, 104, 107), British Columbia Lions (36-47), Edmonton Eskimos (48-55), Winnipeg Blue Bombers (91-103, 105, 109-110), and Calgary Stampeders (106, 108).

| | MINT | EXC | G-VG |
|---|---|---|---|
| COMPLETE SET (110) | 150.00 | 60.00 | 15.00 |
| COMMON PLAYER (1-110) | 1.00 | .40 | .10 |

| | | | | |
|---|---|---|---|---|
| ☐ 1 | Mike Hameluck | 1.50 | .60 | .15 |
| ☐ 2 | Michel Bourgeau | 1.25 | .50 | .12 |
| ☐ 3 | Waymon Alridge | 1.00 | .40 | .10 |
| ☐ 4 | Daric Zeno | 1.25 | .50 | .12 |
| ☐ 5 | J.C. Watts | 7.50 | 3.00 | .75 |
| ☐ 6 | Kevin Gray | 1.00 | .40 | .10 |
| ☐ 7 | Steve Harrison | 1.00 | .40 | .10 |
| ☐ 8 | Ralph Dixon | 1.00 | .40 | .10 |
| ☐ 9 | Jo Jo Heath | 1.00 | .40 | .10 |
| ☐ 10 | Rick Sowieta | 1.00 | .40 | .10 |
| ☐ 11 | Brad Fawcett | 1.00 | .40 | .10 |
| ☐ 12 | Lamont Meacham | 1.00 | .40 | .10 |
| ☐ 13 | Dean Dorsey | 1.50 | .60 | .15 |
| ☐ 14 | Bernard Quarles | 1.00 | .40 | .10 |
| ☐ 15 | Mike Caterbone | 1.00 | .40 | .10 |
| ☐ 16 | Bob Stephen | 1.00 | .40 | .10 |
| ☐ 17 | Nick Benjamin | 1.50 | .60 | .15 |
| ☐ 18 | Tim McCray | 1.50 | .60 | .15 |
| ☐ 19 | Chris Sigler | 1.00 | .40 | .10 |
| ☐ 20 | Tony Johns | 1.00 | .40 | .10 |
| ☐ 21 | Jason Riley | 1.00 | .40 | .10 |
| ☐ 22 | Ralph Scholz | 1.00 | .40 | .10 |
| ☐ 23 | Ken Hobart | 2.50 | 1.00 | .25 |
| ☐ 24 | Paul Bennett | 1.00 | .40 | .10 |
| ☐ 25 | Dan Ferrone | 1.50 | .60 | .15 |
| ☐ 26 | Jim Kalafat | 1.00 | .40 | .10 |
| ☐ 27 | William Mitchell | 1.00 | .40 | .10 |
| ☐ 28 | Denny Ferdinand | 1.00 | .40 | .10 |
| ☐ 29 | James Curry | 2.50 | 1.00 | .25 |
| ☐ 30 | Jeff Inglis | 1.00 | .40 | .10 |
| ☐ 31 | Bob Bronk | 1.00 | .40 | .10 |
| ☐ 32 | Dan Petschenig | 1.00 | .40 | .10 |
| ☐ 33 | Terry Greer | 4.00 | 1.60 | .40 |
| ☐ 34 | Condredge Holloway | 4.00 | 1.60 | .40 |
| ☐ 35 | Ian Beckstead | 1.00 | .40 | .10 |
| ☐ 36 | James Parker | 3.00 | 1.20 | .30 |
| ☐ 37 | Tim Cowan | 1.50 | .60 | .15 |
| ☐ 38 | Roy DeWalt | 2.50 | 1.00 | .25 |
| ☐ 39 | Mervyn Fernandez | 15.00 | 6.00 | 1.50 |
| ☐ 40 | Bernie Glier | 1.00 | .40 | .10 |
| ☐ 41 | Keyvan Jenkins | 3.00 | 1.20 | .30 |
| ☐ 42 | Melvin Byrd | 2.00 | .80 | .20 |
| ☐ 43 | Ron Robinson | 2.00 | .80 | .20 |
| ☐ 44 | Andre Jones | 1.00 | .40 | .10 |
| ☐ 45 | Jim Sandusky | 6.00 | 2.40 | .60 |
| ☐ 46 | Darnell Clash | 2.50 | 1.00 | .25 |
| ☐ 47 | Rick Klassen | 1.50 | .60 | .15 |

| | | | | |
|---|---|---|---|---|
| ☐ 48 | Brian Kelly | 6.00 | 2.40 | .60 |
| ☐ 49 | Rick House | 1.50 | .60 | .15 |
| ☐ 50 | Stewart Hill | 3.00 | 1.20 | .30 |
| ☐ 51 | Chris Woods | 3.00 | 1.20 | .30 |
| ☐ 52 | Darryl Hall | 1.00 | .40 | .10 |
| ☐ 53 | Laurent DesLauriers | 1.00 | .40 | .10 |
| ☐ 54 | Larry Cowan | 1.00 | .40 | .10 |
| ☐ 55 | Matt Dunigan | 12.00 | 5.00 | 1.20 |
| ☐ 56 | Andre Francis | 1.50 | .60 | .15 |
| ☐ 57 | Roy Kurtz | 1.00 | .40 | .10 |
| ☐ 58 | Steve Raquet | 1.00 | .40 | .10 |
| ☐ 59 | Turner Gill | 3.50 | 1.40 | .35 |
| ☐ 60 | Sandy Armstrong | 1.00 | .40 | .10 |
| ☐ 61 | Nick Arakgi | 1.50 | .60 | .15 |
| ☐ 62 | Mike McTague | 1.00 | .40 | .10 |
| ☐ 63 | Aaron Hill | 1.00 | .40 | .10 |
| ☐ 64 | Brett Williams | 2.00 | .80 | .20 |
| ☐ 65 | Trevor Bowles | 1.00 | .40 | .10 |
| ☐ 66 | Mark Hopkins | 1.00 | .40 | .10 |
| ☐ 67 | Frank Kosec | 1.00 | .40 | .10 |
| ☐ 68 | Ken Ciancone | 1.00 | .40 | .10 |
| ☐ 69 | Dwaine Wilson | 1.00 | .40 | .10 |
| ☐ 70 | Mark Stevens | 1.00 | .40 | .10 |
| ☐ 71 | George Voelk | 1.00 | .40 | .10 |
| ☐ 72 | Doug Scott | 1.00 | .40 | .10 |
| ☐ 73 | Rob Smith | 1.00 | .40 | .10 |
| ☐ 74 | Alan Reid | 1.00 | .40 | .10 |
| ☐ 75 | Rick Mohr | 1.00 | .40 | .10 |
| ☐ 76 | Dave Ridgway | 3.50 | 1.40 | .35 |
| ☐ 77 | Homer Jordan | 1.00 | .40 | .10 |
| ☐ 78 | Terry Leschuk | 1.00 | .40 | .10 |
| ☐ 79 | Rick Goltz | 1.00 | .40 | .10 |
| ☐ 80 | Neil Quilter | 1.00 | .40 | .10 |
| ☐ 81 | Joe Paopao | 2.50 | 1.00 | .25 |
| ☐ 82 | Stephen Jones | 2.50 | 1.00 | .25 |
| ☐ 83 | Scott Redl | 1.00 | .40 | .10 |
| ☐ 84 | Tony Dennis | 1.00 | .40 | .10 |
| ☐ 85 | Glen Suitor | 1.50 | .60 | .15 |
| ☐ 86 | Mike Anderson | 1.00 | .40 | .10 |
| ☐ 87 | Stewart Fraser | 1.00 | .40 | .10 |
| ☐ 88 | Fran McDermott | 1.00 | .40 | .10 |
| ☐ 89 | Craig Ellis | 3.00 | 1.20 | .30 |
| ☐ 90 | Eddie Ray Walker | 2.00 | .80 | .20 |
| ☐ 91 | Trevor Kennerd | 2.50 | 1.00 | .25 |
| ☐ 92 | Pat Cantner | 1.00 | .40 | .10 |
| ☐ 93 | Tom Clements | 7.50 | 3.00 | .75 |
| ☐ 94 | Glen Steele | 1.00 | .40 | .10 |
| ☐ 95 | Willard Reaves | 4.00 | 1.60 | .40 |
| ☐ 96 | Tony Norman | 1.00 | .40 | .10 |
| ☐ 97 | Tyrone Jones | 2.50 | 1.00 | .25 |
| ☐ 98 | Jerome Erdman | 1.00 | .40 | .10 |
| ☐ 99 | Sean Kehoe | 1.00 | .40 | .10 |
| ☐ 100 | Kevin Neiles | 1.00 | .40 | .10 |
| ☐ 101 | Ken Hailey | 1.00 | .40 | .10 |
| ☐ 102 | Scott Flagel | 1.25 | .50 | .12 |
| ☐ 103 | Mark Moors | 1.00 | .40 | .10 |
| ☐ 104 | Gerry McGrath | 1.00 | .40 | .10 |
| ☐ 105 | James Hood | 1.00 | .40 | .10 |
| ☐ 106 | Randy Ambrosie | 1.00 | .40 | .10 |
| ☐ 107 | Terry Irvin | 1.00 | .40 | .10 |
| ☐ 108 | Joe Barnes | 3.00 | 1.20 | .30 |
| ☐ 109 | Richard Nemeth | 1.00 | .40 | .10 |
| ☐ 110 | Darrell Patterson | 2.00 | .80 | .20 |

## 1985 JOGO Ottawa Program Inserts

These inserts were featured in Ottawa home game programs. The cards are black-and-white with a white border and measure approximately 3 3/8" by 5 1/8". They are numbered in the lower right hand corner.

| | MINT | EXC | G-VG |
|---|---|---|---|
| COMPLETE SET (9) | 40.00 | 16.00 | 4.00 |
| COMMON PLAYER (1-9) | 4.00 | 1.60 | .40 |

| | | | | |
|---|---|---|---|---|
| ☐ 1 | 1960 Grey Cup Team | 7.50 | 3.00 | .75 |
| ☐ 2 | Russ Jackson | 10.00 | 4.00 | 1.00 |
| ☐ 3 | Angelo Mosca | 9.00 | 3.75 | .90 |
| ☐ 4 | Joe Poirier | 4.00 | 1.60 | .40 |
| ☐ 5 | Sam Scoccia | 4.00 | 1.60 | .40 |
| ☐ 6 | Gilles Archambault | 4.00 | 1.60 | .40 |
| ☐ 7 | Ron Lancaster | 7.50 | 3.00 | .75 |
| ☐ 8 | Tom Jones | 4.00 | 1.60 | .40 |
| ☐ 9 | Gerry Nesbitt | 4.00 | 1.60 | .40 |

## 1986 JOGO CFL

The 1986 JOGO CFL set is standard size, 2 1/2" by 3 1/2". These numbered cards were issued in two different series, 1-110 and 111-169. A few players appear in both series. This year's set from JOGO has a distinctive black border on the front of the card. Card backs are printed in red and black on white card stock. The player's name and

CARD 57
MERVYN FERNANDEZ #24

RECEIVER
Ht: 6'3"    Wt: 200 lbs.    Import
San Jose State
Years Pro: 5

MERVYN FERNANDEZ #24

JOGO INC. '86

uniform number are given on the front of the card. The player's team is not explicitly listed anywhere on the card.

| | MINT | EXC | G-VG |
|---|---|---|---|
| COMPLETE SET (169) | 150.00 | 60.00 | 15.00 |
| COMPLETE SERIES 1 (110) | 90.00 | 36.00 | 9.00 |
| COMPLETE SERIES 2 (59) | 60.00 | 24.00 | 6.00 |
| COMMON PLAYER (1-110) | .75 | .30 | .07 |
| COMMON PLAYER (111-169) | .75 | .30 | .07 |

| | MINT | EXC | G-VG |
|---|---|---|---|
| ☐ 1 Ken Hobart | 2.00 | .80 | .20 |
| ☐ 2 Tom Porras | 1.50 | .60 | .15 |
| ☐ 3 Jason Riley | .75 | .30 | .07 |
| ☐ 4 Ron Ingram | .75 | .30 | .07 |
| ☐ 5 Steve Stapler | 1.50 | .60 | .15 |
| ☐ 6 Mike Derks | .75 | .30 | .07 |
| ☐ 7 Grover Covington | 5.00 | 2.00 | .50 |
| ☐ 8 Lance Shields | 1.25 | .50 | .12 |
| ☐ 9 Mike Robinson | .75 | .30 | .07 |
| ☐ 10 Mark Napiorkowski | .75 | .30 | .07 |
| ☐ 11 Romel Andrews | .75 | .30 | .07 |
| ☐ 12 Ed Gataveckas | .75 | .30 | .07 |
| ☐ 13 Tony Champion | 5.00 | 2.00 | .50 |
| ☐ 14 Dale Sanderson | .75 | .30 | .07 |
| ☐ 15 Mark Barousse | .75 | .30 | .07 |
| ☐ 16 Nick Benjamin | 1.25 | .50 | .12 |
| ☐ 17 Reginal Butts | .75 | .30 | .07 |
| ☐ 18 Tom Burgess | 6.00 | 2.40 | .60 |
| ☐ 19 Todd Dillon | 3.00 | 1.20 | .30 |
| ☐ 20 Jim Reid | 1.00 | .40 | .10 |
| ☐ 21 Robert Reid | .75 | .30 | .07 |
| ☐ 22 Roger Cattelan | .75 | .30 | .07 |
| ☐ 23 Kevin Powell | .75 | .30 | .07 |
| ☐ 24 Randy Fabi | .75 | .30 | .07 |
| ☐ 25 Gerry Hornett | .75 | .30 | .07 |
| ☐ 26 Rick Sowieta | .75 | .30 | .07 |
| ☐ 27 Warren Hudson | 1.25 | .50 | .12 |
| ☐ 28 Steven Cox | .75 | .30 | .07 |
| ☐ 29 Dean Dorsey | 1.00 | .40 | .10 |
| ☐ 30 Michel Bourgeau | 1.25 | .50 | .12 |
| ☐ 31 Ken Joiner | .75 | .30 | .07 |
| ☐ 32 Mark Seale | .75 | .30 | .07 |
| ☐ 33 Condredge Holloway | 3.50 | 1.40 | .35 |
| ☐ 34 Bob Bronk | .75 | .30 | .07 |
| ☐ 35 Jeff Inglis | .75 | .30 | .07 |
| ☐ 36 Lance Chomyc | 2.00 | .80 | .20 |
| ☐ 37 Craig Ellis | 2.00 | .80 | .20 |
| ☐ 38 Marcellus Greene | 1.25 | .50 | .12 |
| ☐ 39 David Marshall | .75 | .30 | .07 |
| ☐ 40 Kerry Parker | .75 | .30 | .07 |
| ☐ 41 Darrell Wilson | .75 | .30 | .07 |
| ☐ 42 Walter Lewis | 3.50 | 1.40 | .35 |
| ☐ 43 Sandy Armstrong | .75 | .30 | .07 |
| ☐ 44 Ken Ciancone | .75 | .30 | .07 |
| ☐ 45 Steve Raquet | .75 | .30 | .07 |
| ☐ 46 Lemont Jeffers | .75 | .30 | .07 |
| ☐ 47 Paul Gray | .75 | .30 | .07 |
| ☐ 48 Jacques Chapdelaine | .75 | .30 | .07 |
| ☐ 49 Rick Ryan | .75 | .30 | .07 |
| ☐ 50 Mark Hopkins | .75 | .30 | .07 |
| ☐ 51 Glenn Keeble | .75 | .30 | .07 |
| ☐ 52 Roy Kurtz | .75 | .30 | .07 |
| ☐ 53 Brian Dudley | .75 | .30 | .07 |
| ☐ 54 Mike Gray | .75 | .30 | .07 |
| ☐ 55 Tyrone Crews | .75 | .30 | .07 |
| ☐ 56 Roy DeWalt | 2.50 | 1.00 | .25 |
| ☐ 57 Mervyn Fernandez | 6.00 | 2.40 | .60 |
| ☐ 58 Bernie Glier | .75 | .30 | .07 |
| ☐ 59 James Parker | 3.00 | 1.20 | .30 |
| ☐ 60 Bruce Barnett | .75 | .30 | .07 |
| ☐ 61 Keyvan Jenkins | 2.50 | 1.00 | .25 |
| ☐ 62 Alan Wilson | .75 | .30 | .07 |
| ☐ 63 Delbert Fowler | 1.25 | .50 | .12 |
| ☐ 64 James Jefferson | 5.00 | 2.00 | .50 |
| ☐ 65 James West | 7.50 | 3.00 | .75 |
| ☐ 66 Laurent DesLauriers | .75 | .30 | .07 |
| ☐ 67 Damon Allen | 10.00 | 4.00 | 1.00 |

| | MINT | EXC | G-VG |
|---|---|---|---|
| ☐ 68 Roy Bennett | 3.00 | 1.20 | .30 |
| ☐ 69 Hasson Arbubakrr | .75 | .30 | .07 |
| ☐ 70 Tom Clements | 6.00 | 2.40 | .60 |
| ☐ 71 Trevor Kennerd | 1.50 | .60 | .15 |
| ☐ 72 Perry Tuttle | 3.50 | 1.40 | .35 |
| ☐ 73 Pat Cantner | .75 | .30 | .07 |
| ☐ 74 Mike Hameluck | .75 | .30 | .07 |
| ☐ 75 Rob Prodanovic | .75 | .30 | .07 |
| ☐ 76 James Bell | 1.00 | .40 | .10 |
| ☐ 77 Hector Pothier | .75 | .30 | .07 |
| ☐ 78 Milson Jones | 3.00 | 1.20 | .30 |
| ☐ 79 Craig Shaffer | .75 | .30 | .07 |
| ☐ 80 Chris Skinner | 1.25 | .50 | .12 |
| ☐ 81 Matt Dunigan | 7.50 | 3.00 | .75 |
| ☐ 82 Tom Dixon | .75 | .30 | .07 |
| ☐ 83 Brian Pillman | .75 | .30 | .07 |
| ☐ 84 Randy Ambrosie | .75 | .30 | .07 |
| ☐ 85 Rick Johnson | 3.50 | 1.40 | .35 |
| ☐ 86 Larry Hogue | .75 | .30 | .07 |
| ☐ 87 Garrett Doll | .75 | .30 | .07 |
| ☐ 88 Stu Laird | 1.25 | .50 | .12 |
| ☐ 89 Greg Fieger | .75 | .30 | .07 |
| ☐ 90 Sean McKeown | .75 | .30 | .07 |
| ☐ 91 Rob Bresciani | .75 | .30 | .07 |
| ☐ 92 Harold Hallman | 2.50 | 1.00 | .25 |
| ☐ 93 Jamie Harris | .75 | .30 | .07 |
| ☐ 94 Dan Rashovich | .75 | .30 | .07 |
| ☐ 95 David Conrad | .75 | .30 | .07 |
| ☐ 96 Glen Suitor | 1.00 | .40 | .10 |
| ☐ 97 Mike Siroishka | .75 | .30 | .07 |
| ☐ 98 Mike McGruder | 3.00 | 1.20 | .30 |
| ☐ 99 Brad Calip | .75 | .30 | .07 |
| ☐ 100 Mike Anderson | .75 | .30 | .07 |
| ☐ 101 Trent Bryant | .75 | .30 | .07 |
| ☐ 102 Gary Lewis | .75 | .30 | .07 |
| ☐ 103 Tony Dennis | .75 | .30 | .07 |
| ☐ 104 Paul Tripoli | .75 | .30 | .07 |
| ☐ 105 Daric Zeno | .75 | .30 | .07 |
| ☐ 106 Michael Elarms | .75 | .30 | .07 |
| ☐ 107 Donohue Grant | .75 | .30 | .07 |
| ☐ 108 Ray Elgaard | 15.00 | 6.00 | 1.50 |
| ☐ 109 Joe Paopao | 2.00 | .80 | .20 |
| ☐ 110 Dave Ridgway | 2.50 | 1.00 | .25 |
| ☐ 111 Rudy Phillips | 1.50 | .60 | .15 |
| ☐ 112 Carl Brazley | 1.25 | .50 | .12 |
| ☐ 113 Andre Francis | 1.00 | .40 | .10 |
| ☐ 114 Mitchell Price | 1.50 | .60 | .15 |
| ☐ 115 Wayne Lee | .75 | .30 | .07 |
| ☐ 116 Tim McCray | 1.50 | .60 | .15 |
| ☐ 117 Scott Virkus | .75 | .30 | .07 |
| ☐ 118 Nick Hebeler | .75 | .30 | .07 |
| ☐ 119 Eddie Ray Walker | 1.25 | .50 | .12 |
| ☐ 120 Bobby Johnson | .75 | .30 | .07 |
| ☐ 121 Mike McTague | 1.00 | .40 | .10 |
| ☐ 122 Jeff Inglis | .75 | .30 | .07 |
| ☐ 123 Joe Fuller | .75 | .30 | .07 |
| ☐ 124 Steve Crane | .75 | .30 | .07 |
| ☐ 125 Bill Henry | .75 | .30 | .07 |
| ☐ 126 Ron Brown | .75 | .30 | .07 |
| ☐ 127 Henry Taylor | .75 | .30 | .07 |
| ☐ 128 Greg Holmes | .75 | .30 | .07 |
| ☐ 129 Steve Harrison | .75 | .30 | .07 |
| ☐ 130 Paul Osbaldiston | 5.00 | 2.00 | .50 |
| ☐ 131 Craig Walls | .75 | .30 | .07 |
| ☐ 132 Clorindo Grilli | .75 | .30 | .07 |
| ☐ 133 Marty Palazeti | .75 | .30 | .07 |
| ☐ 134 Darryl Hall | .75 | .30 | .07 |
| ☐ 135 David Black | .75 | .30 | .07 |
| ☐ 136 Bennie Thompson | 2.50 | 1.00 | .25 |
| ☐ 137 Darryl Sampson | .75 | .30 | .07 |
| ☐ 138 Danny Murphy | 2.50 | 1.00 | .25 |
| ☐ 139 Scott Flagel | .75 | .30 | .07 |
| ☐ 140 Trevor Kennerd | 2.00 | .80 | .20 |
| ☐ 141 Bob Molle | .75 | .30 | .07 |
| ☐ 142 Darrell Patterson | .75 | .30 | .07 |
| ☐ 143 Stan Mikawos | .75 | .30 | .07 |
| ☐ 144 John Sturdivant | .75 | .30 | .07 |
| ☐ 145 Tyrone Jones | 2.00 | .80 | .20 |
| ☐ 146 Jim Zorn | 15.00 | 6.00 | 1.50 |
| ☐ 147 Steve Howlett | .75 | .30 | .07 |
| ☐ 148 Jeff Volpe | .75 | .30 | .07 |
| ☐ 149 Jerome Erdman | .75 | .30 | .07 |
| ☐ 150 Ned Armour | .75 | .30 | .07 |
| ☐ 151 Rick Klassen | 1.50 | .60 | .15 |
| ☐ 152 Brett Williams | 2.00 | .80 | .20 |
| ☐ 153 Richie Hall | .75 | .30 | .07 |
| ☐ 154 Ray Alexander | 2.50 | 1.00 | .25 |
| ☐ 155 Willie Pless | 5.00 | 2.00 | .50 |
| ☐ 156 Marlon Jones | .75 | .30 | .07 |
| ☐ 157 Danny Bass | 3.50 | 1.40 | .35 |
| ☐ 158 Frank Balkovec | .75 | .30 | .07 |
| ☐ 159 Less Browne | 4.00 | 1.60 | .40 |
| ☐ 160 Paul Osbaldiston | 2.50 | 1.00 | .25 |
| ☐ 161 Trevor Bowles | .75 | .30 | .07 |
| ☐ 162 David Daniels | .75 | .30 | .07 |
| ☐ 163 Kevin Konar | 2.00 | .80 | .20 |
| ☐ 164 Gary Allen | 2.00 | .80 | .20 |

| | MINT | EXC | G-VG |
|---|---|---|---|
| ☐ 165 Karlton Watson | .75 | .30 | .07 |
| ☐ 166 Ron Hopkins | 1.25 | .50 | .12 |
| ☐ 167 Rob Smith | .75 | .30 | .07 |
| ☐ 168 Garrett Doll | .75 | .30 | .07 |
| ☐ 169 Rod Skillman | 2.00 | .80 | .20 |

## 1987 JOGO CFL

The 1987 JOGO CFL set is standard size, 2 1/2" by 3 1/2". These numbered cards were issued essentially in team order as follows: Ottawa Rough Riders (1-5, 7, 9-18), Calgary Stampeders (6, 50, 74-84), British Columbia Lions (8, 33, 52, 64, 71-73), Toronto Argonauts (19-32), Winnipeg Blue Bombers (34-49, 51), Hamilton Tiger-Cats (53-63, 65-70, 90-93), Edmonton Eskimos (85-89), Saskatchewan Roughriders (94-110). A color photo is framed by a blue border. Card backs are printed in black on white card stock except for the CFLPA (Canadian Football League Players' Association) logo in the upper right corner which is red and black.

| | MINT | EXC | G-VG |
|---|---|---|---|
| COMPLETE SET (110) | 100.00 | 40.00 | 10.00 |
| COMMON PLAYER (1-110) | .75 | .30 | .07 |

| | MINT | EXC | G-VG |
|---|---|---|---|
| ☐ 1 Jim Reid | 2.00 | .80 | .20 |
| ☐ 2 Nick Benjamin | 1.00 | .40 | .10 |
| ☐ 3 Dean Dorsey | 1.00 | .40 | .10 |
| ☐ 4 Hasson Arbubakrr | .75 | .30 | .07 |
| ☐ 5 Gerald Alphin | 6.00 | 2.40 | .60 |
| ☐ 6 Larry Willis | 3.00 | 1.20 | .30 |
| ☐ 7 Rick Wolkensperg | .75 | .30 | .07 |
| ☐ 8 Roy DeWalt | 2.00 | .80 | .20 |
| ☐ 9 Michel Bourgeau | 1.00 | .40 | .10 |
| ☐ 10 Anthony Woodson | .75 | .30 | .07 |
| ☐ 11 Marv Allemang | .75 | .30 | .07 |
| ☐ 12 Jerry Dobrovolny | .75 | .30 | .07 |
| ☐ 13 Larry Mohr | .75 | .30 | .07 |
| ☐ 14 Kyle Hall | .75 | .30 | .07 |
| ☐ 15 Irv Daymond | .75 | .30 | .07 |
| ☐ 16 Ken Ford | .75 | .30 | .07 |
| ☐ 17 Leo Groenewegen | .75 | .30 | .07 |
| ☐ 18 Michael Cline | .75 | .30 | .07 |
| ☐ 19 Gilbert Renfroe | 4.00 | 1.60 | .40 |
| ☐ 20 Danny Barrett | 6.00 | 2.40 | .60 |
| ☐ 21 Dan Petschenig | .75 | .30 | .07 |
| ☐ 22 Gill Fenerty UER | 9.00 | 3.75 | .90 |
| (Misspelled Gil on card front) | | | |
| ☐ 23 Lance Chomyc | 1.50 | .60 | .15 |
| ☐ 24 Jake Vaughan | .75 | .30 | .07 |
| ☐ 25 John Congemi | 3.00 | 1.20 | .30 |
| ☐ 26 Kelvin Pruenster | .75 | .30 | .07 |
| ☐ 27 Mike Siroishka | .75 | .30 | .07 |
| ☐ 28 Dwight Edwards | 1.00 | .40 | .10 |
| ☐ 29 Darnell Clash | 1.50 | .60 | .15 |
| ☐ 30 Glenn Kulka | 2.00 | .80 | .20 |
| ☐ 31 Jim Kardash | .75 | .30 | .07 |
| ☐ 32 Selwyn Drain | .75 | .30 | .07 |
| ☐ 33 Ian Sinclair | 1.00 | .40 | .10 |
| ☐ 34 Pat Cantner | .75 | .30 | .07 |
| ☐ 35 Trevor Kennerd | 2.50 | 1.00 | .25 |
| ☐ 36 Bob Cameron | 1.00 | .40 | .10 |
| ☐ 37 Willard Reaves | 3.00 | 1.20 | .30 |
| ☐ 38 Jeff Treftlin | .75 | .30 | .07 |
| ☐ 39 David Black | .75 | .30 | .07 |
| ☐ 40 Chris Walby | 2.00 | .80 | .20 |
| ☐ 41 Tom Clements | 3.50 | 1.40 | .35 |
| ☐ 42 Mike Gray | .75 | .30 | .07 |
| ☐ 43 Bennie Thompson | 1.50 | .60 | .15 |
| ☐ 44 Tyrone Jones | 2.00 | .80 | .20 |
| ☐ 45 Ken Winey | .75 | .30 | .07 |
| ☐ 46 Nick Arakgi | 1.00 | .40 | .10 |
| ☐ 47 James West | 2.50 | 1.00 | .25 |
| ☐ 48 Ken Pettway | .75 | .30 | .07 |
| ☐ 49 James Murphy | 2.50 | 1.00 | .25 |

| | MINT | EXC | G-VG |
|---|---|---|---|
| ☐ 50 Carl Fodor | .75 | .30 | .07 |
| ☐ 51 Tom Muecke | 3.00 | 1.20 | .30 |
| ☐ 52 Alvis Satele | .75 | .30 | .07 |
| ☐ 53 Grover Covington | 2.00 | .80 | .20 |
| ☐ 54 Tom Porras | 1.50 | .60 | .15 |
| ☐ 55 Jason Riley | .75 | .30 | .07 |
| ☐ 56 Jed Tommy | .75 | .30 | .07 |
| ☐ 57 Bernie Ruoff | 1.00 | .40 | .10 |
| ☐ 58 Ed Gataveckas | .75 | .30 | .07 |
| ☐ 59 Wayne Lee | .75 | .30 | .07 |
| ☐ 60 Ken Hobart | 1.50 | .60 | .15 |
| ☐ 61 Frank Robinson | 1.00 | .40 | .10 |
| ☐ 62 Mike Robinson | .75 | .30 | .07 |
| ☐ 63 Ben Zambiasi UER | 2.00 | .80 | .20 |
| (No team listed on front of card) | | | |
| ☐ 64 Byron Williams | .75 | .30 | .07 |
| ☐ 65 Lance Shields | 1.00 | .40 | .10 |
| ☐ 66 Ralph Scholz | .75 | .30 | .07 |
| ☐ 67 Earl Winfield | 5.00 | 2.00 | .50 |
| ☐ 68 Terry Lehne | .75 | .30 | .07 |
| ☐ 69 Alvin Bailey | .75 | .30 | .07 |
| ☐ 70 David Sauve | .75 | .30 | .07 |
| ☐ 71 Bernie Glier | .75 | .30 | .07 |
| ☐ 72 Nelson Martin | .75 | .30 | .07 |
| ☐ 73 Kevin Konar | 1.00 | .40 | .10 |
| ☐ 74 Greg Peterson | .75 | .30 | .07 |
| ☐ 75 Harold Hallman | 1.50 | .60 | .15 |
| ☐ 76 Sandy Armstrong | .75 | .30 | .07 |
| ☐ 77 Glenn Harper | .75 | .30 | .07 |
| ☐ 78 Rick Worman | 1.50 | .60 | .15 |
| ☐ 79 Darrell Toussaint | .75 | .30 | .07 |
| ☐ 80 Larry Hogue | .75 | .30 | .07 |
| ☐ 81 Rick Johnson | 2.50 | 1.00 | .25 |
| ☐ 82 Richie Hall | .75 | .30 | .07 |
| ☐ 83 Stu Laird | 1.00 | .40 | .10 |
| ☐ 84 Mike Emery | .75 | .30 | .07 |
| ☐ 85 Cliff Toney | .75 | .30 | .07 |
| ☐ 86 Matt Dunigan | 5.00 | 2.00 | .50 |
| ☐ 87 Hector Pothier | .75 | .30 | .07 |
| ☐ 88 Stewart Hill | 1.50 | .60 | .15 |
| ☐ 89 Stephen Jones | 1.50 | .60 | .15 |
| ☐ 90 Dan Huclack | .75 | .30 | .07 |
| ☐ 91 Mark Napiorkowski | .75 | .30 | .07 |
| ☐ 92 Mike Derks | .75 | .30 | .07 |
| ☐ 93 Mike Walker | 1.50 | .60 | .15 |
| ☐ 94 Mike McGruder | 2.00 | .80 | .20 |
| ☐ 95 Terry Baker | 3.00 | 1.20 | .30 |
| ☐ 96 Bobby Jurasin | 4.00 | 1.60 | .40 |
| ☐ 97 James Curry | 2.50 | 1.00 | .25 |
| ☐ 98 Tracey Mack | .75 | .30 | .07 |
| ☐ 99 Tom Burgess | 3.50 | 1.40 | .35 |
| ☐ 100 Steve Crane | .75 | .30 | .07 |
| ☐ 101 Glen Suitor | 1.00 | .40 | .10 |
| ☐ 102 Walter Bender | .75 | .30 | .07 |
| ☐ 103 Jeff Bentrim | 2.00 | .80 | .20 |
| ☐ 104 Eric Florence | .75 | .30 | .07 |
| ☐ 105 Terry Cochrane | .75 | .30 | .07 |
| ☐ 106 Tony Dennis | .75 | .30 | .07 |
| ☐ 107 David Albright | .75 | .30 | .07 |
| ☐ 108 David Sidoo | .75 | .30 | .07 |
| ☐ 109 Harry Skipper | 1.00 | .40 | .10 |
| ☐ 110 Dave Ridgway | 2.00 | .80 | .20 |

## 1988 JOGO CFL

The 1988 JOGO CFL set is standard size, 2 1/2" by 3 1/2". These numbered cards were issued essentially in team order. A color photo is framed by a blue border with a white inner outline. Card backs are printed in black on white card stock, except for the CFLPA (Canadian Football League Players' Association) logo in the upper right corner which is red and black. The cards are arranged according to teams as follows: Ottawa Rough Riders (1-6, 8-16), Winnipeg Blue Bombers (7, 17, 72, 87, 90, 98-109), Edmonton Eskimos (18-20, 45-48, 86),

Hamilton Tiger-Cats (21-44), Saskatchewan Roughriders (49-55), Toronto Argonauts (56-71, 73-80), Calgary Stampeders (81-85, 88-89, 91-92), and British Columbia Lions (93-97, 100).

| | MINT | EXC | G-VG |
|---|---|---|---|
| COMPLETE SET (110) | 90.00 | 36.00 | 9.00 |
| COMMON PLAYER (1-110) | .60 | .24 | .06 |
| □ 1 Roy DeWalt | 2.00 | .80 | .20 |
| □ 2 Jim Reid | 1.25 | .50 | .12 |
| □ 3 Patrick Wayne | .60 | .24 | .06 |
| □ 4 Jerome Erdman | .60 | .24 | .06 |
| □ 5 Tom Dixon | .60 | .24 | .06 |
| □ 6 Brad Fawcett | .60 | .24 | .06 |
| □ 7 Tom Muecke | 1.50 | .60 | .15 |
| □ 8 Mike Hudson | .60 | .24 | .06 |
| □ 9 Orville Lee | 2.00 | .80 | .20 |
| □ 10 Michel Bourgeau | .75 | .30 | .07 |
| □ 11 Dan Sellers | .60 | .24 | .06 |
| □ 12 Rob Pavan | .60 | .24 | .06 |
| □ 13 Rae Robirtis | .60 | .24 | .06 |
| □ 14 Rod Brown | .60 | .24 | .06 |
| □ 15 Ken Evraire | .75 | .30 | .07 |
| □ 16 Irv Daymond | .60 | .24 | .06 |
| □ 17 Tim Jessie | 1.00 | .40 | .10 |
| □ 18 Jim Sandusky | 4.00 | 1.60 | .40 |
| □ 19 Blake Dermott | 1.00 | .40 | .10 |
| □ 20 Brian Warren | .60 | .24 | .06 |
| □ 21 Mike Walker | 3.00 | 1.20 | .30 |
| □ 22 Tom Porras | 1.25 | .50 | .12 |
| □ 23 Less Browne | 1.25 | .50 | .12 |
| □ 24 Paul Osbaldiston | 1.25 | .50 | .12 |
| □ 25 Vernell Quinn | .60 | .24 | .06 |
| □ 26 Mike Derks | .60 | .24 | .06 |
| □ 27 Arnold Grevious | .60 | .24 | .06 |
| □ 28 Jim Lorenz | .60 | .24 | .06 |
| □ 29 Mike Robinson | .60 | .24 | .06 |
| □ 30 Doug Davies | .60 | .24 | .06 |
| □ 31 Earl Winfield | 3.00 | 1.20 | .30 |
| □ 32 Wally Zatylny | 2.00 | .80 | .20 |
| □ 33 Martin Sartin | .75 | .30 | .07 |
| □ 34 Lee Knight | .60 | .24 | .06 |
| □ 35 Jason Riley | .60 | .24 | .06 |
| □ 36 Darrell Gorbin | .60 | .24 | .06 |
| □ 37 Tony Champion | 2.50 | 1.00 | .25 |
| □ 38 Steve Stapler | 1.00 | .40 | .10 |
| □ 39 Scott Flagel | .75 | .30 | .07 |
| □ 40 Grover Covington | 1.50 | .60 | .15 |
| □ 41 Mark Napiorkowski | .60 | .24 | .06 |
| □ 42 Jacques Chapdelaine | 1.00 | .40 | .10 |
| □ 43 Lance Shields | .60 | .24 | .06 |
| □ 44 Donohue Grant | .60 | .24 | .06 |
| □ 45 Henry Williams | 25.00 | 10.00 | 2.50 |
| □ 46 Trevor Bowles | .60 | .24 | .06 |
| □ 47 Don Wilson | .60 | .24 | .06 |
| □ 48 Tracey Ham | 15.00 | 6.00 | 1.50 |
| □ 49 Richie Hall | 1.00 | .40 | .10 |
| □ 50 Rob Bresciani | .60 | .24 | .06 |
| □ 51 James Curry | 1.25 | .50 | .12 |
| □ 52 Kent Austin | 15.00 | 6.00 | 1.50 |
| □ 53 Jeff Bentrim | 1.25 | .50 | .12 |
| □ 54 Dave Ridgway | 1.25 | .50 | .12 |
| □ 55 Terry Baker | 1.25 | .50 | .12 |
| □ 56 Lance Chomyc | 1.25 | .50 | .12 |
| □ 57 Paul Sandor | .60 | .24 | .06 |
| □ 58 Kevin Cummings | .60 | .24 | .06 |
| □ 59 John Congemi | 1.50 | .60 | .15 |
| □ 60 Gilbert Renfroe | 2.00 | .80 | .20 |
| □ 61 Jake Vaughan | .60 | .24 | .06 |
| □ 62 Doran Major | .60 | .24 | .06 |
| □ 63 Dwight Edwards | 1.00 | .40 | .10 |
| □ 64 Bruce Elliott | .60 | .24 | .06 |
| □ 65 Lorenzo Graham | .60 | .24 | .06 |
| □ 66 Jim Kardash | .60 | .24 | .06 |
| □ 67 Reggie Pleasant | 1.50 | .60 | .15 |
| □ 68 Carl Brazley | 1.50 | .60 | .15 |
| □ 69 Gill Fenerty | 5.00 | 2.00 | .50 |
| □ 70 Selwyn Drain | .60 | .24 | .06 |
| □ 71 Warren Hudson | 1.00 | .40 | .10 |
| □ 72 Willie Fears | .75 | .30 | .07 |
| □ 73 Randy Ambrosie | .60 | .24 | .06 |
| □ 74 George Ganas | .60 | .24 | .06 |
| □ 75 Glenn Kulka | .75 | .30 | .07 |
| □ 76 Kelvin Pruenster | .60 | .24 | .06 |
| □ 77 Darrell Smith | 2.50 | 1.00 | .25 |
| □ 78 Jearld Baylis | 1.50 | .60 | .15 |
| □ 79 Blaine Schmidt | .60 | .24 | .06 |
| □ 80 Tony Visco | 1.25 | .50 | .12 |
| □ 81 Carl Fodor | .60 | .24 | .06 |
| □ 82 Rudy Phillips | 1.25 | .50 | .12 |
| □ 83 Craig Watson | .60 | .24 | .06 |
| □ 84 Kent Warnock | 1.00 | .40 | .10 |
| □ 85 Ken Ford | .60 | .24 | .06 |
| □ 86 Blake Marshall | 2.00 | .80 | .20 |
| □ 87 Terry Cochrane | .60 | .24 | .06 |
| □ 88 Shawn Faulkner | .60 | .24 | .06 |
| □ 89 Marshall Toner | .60 | .24 | .06 |
| □ 90 Darren Yewshyn | .60 | .24 | .06 |
| □ 91 Eugene Belliveau | .75 | .30 | .07 |
| □ 92 Jay Christensen | .75 | .30 | .07 |
| □ 93 Anthony Parker | 1.25 | .50 | .12 |
| □ 94 Walter Ballard | .60 | .24 | .06 |
| □ 95 Matt Dunigan | 5.00 | 2.00 | .50 |
| □ 96 Andre Francis | .75 | .30 | .07 |
| □ 97 Rickey Foggie | 7.50 | 3.00 | .75 |
| □ 98 Delbert Fowler | .75 | .30 | .07 |
| □ 99 Michael Allen | .60 | .24 | .06 |
| □ 100 Greg Battle | 6.00 | 2.40 | .60 |
| □ 101 Mike Gray | .60 | .24 | .06 |
| □ 102 Dan Wicklum | .60 | .24 | .06 |
| □ 103 Paul Shorten | .60 | .24 | .06 |
| □ 104 Paul Clatney | .60 | .24 | .06 |
| □ 105 Rod Hill | 3.00 | 1.20 | .30 |
| □ 106 Steve Rodehutskors | .75 | .30 | .07 |
| □ 107 Sean Salisbury | 5.00 | 2.00 | .50 |
| □ 108 Vernon Pahl | .60 | .24 | .06 |
| □ 109 Trevor Kennerd | 1.25 | .50 | .12 |
| □ 110 David Williams | 4.00 | 1.60 | .40 |

## 1988 JOGO CFL League

Nick Arakgi #78

This 106-card set was produced and distributed before the CFL season started. The set was produced expressly for the league. There were to be 13 players for each of the eight teams with, reportedly, 3000 complete sets printed. Since the cards were intended for promotional purposes, each team was responsible for distributing their own cards making complete sets rather difficult. After the cards were printed, roster changes caused some of the cards to be withdrawn. All the cards were distributed by the players and teams except for three cards: Tom Clements number 105 (retired), Nick Arakgi number 54 (retired), and the checklist number 106, which were only available from hobby distributors of JOGO products. In addition, players who were victims of early trades or injuries, are also more difficult to find, e.g., Kevin Powell (traded to Edmonton), Greg Marshall (injured and retired), Willard Reaves (signed with Washington Redskins), Milson Jones (traded to Saskatchewan), Scott Flagel (traded to Hamilton), and Jim Sandusky (traded to Edmonton). Cards are unnumbered except for uniform number which is prominently displayed on both sides of the card. The cards are ordered below alphabetically within team. Teams are ordered as follows, British Columbia Lions (1-13), Calgary Stampeders (14-26), Edmonton Eskimos (27-39), Hamilton Tiger-Cats (40-52), Ottawa Rough Riders (53-65), Saskatchewan Roughriders (66-78), Toronto Argonauts (79-91), Winnipeg Blue Bombers (92-105), and the Checklist (106).

| | MINT | EXC | G-VG |
|---|---|---|---|
| COMPLETE SET (106) | 350.00 | 140.00 | 35.00 |
| COMMON PLAYER (1-106) | 1.50 | .60 | .15 |
| □ 1 Walter Ballard | 1.50 | .60 | .15 |
| □ 2 Jan Carinci | 1.50 | .60 | .15 |
| □ 3 Larry Crawford | 2.50 | 1.00 | .25 |
| □ 4 Tyrone Crews | 1.50 | .60 | .15 |
| □ 5 Andre Francis | 2.00 | .80 | .20 |
| □ 6 Bernie Glier | 1.50 | .60 | .15 |
| □ 7 Keith Gooch | 1.50 | .60 | .15 |
| □ 8 Kevin Konar | 2.00 | .80 | .20 |
| □ 9 Scott Lecky | 1.50 | .60 | .15 |
| □ 10 James Parker | 4.00 | 1.60 | .40 |
| □ 11 Jim Sandusky (Traded) | 10.00 | 4.00 | 1.00 |
| □ 12 Gregg Stumon | 2.50 | 1.00 | .25 |
| □ 13 Todd Wiseman (Not listed on checklist card) | 1.50 | .60 | .15 |
| □ 14 Gary Allen | 2.50 | 1.00 | .25 |
| □ 15 Scott Flagel (Traded) | 3.50 | 1.40 | .35 |
| □ 16 Harold Hallman | 2.50 | 1.00 | .25 |

| | | | |
|---|---|---|---|
| ☐ 17 Larry Hogue UER | 1.50 | .60 | .15 |
| (Misspelled Hoque) | | | |
| ☐ 18 Ron Hopkins | 2.00 | .80 | .20 |
| ☐ 19 Stu Laird | 2.00 | .80 | .20 |
| ☐ 20 Andy McVey | 1.50 | .60 | .15 |
| ☐ 21 Bernie Morrison | 1.50 | .60 | .15 |
| ☐ 22 Tim Petros | 2.50 | 1.00 | .25 |
| ☐ 23 Bob Poley | 1.50 | .60 | .15 |
| ☐ 24 Tom Spoletini | 1.50 | .60 | .15 |
| ☐ 25 Emanuel Tolbert | 6.00 | 2.40 | .60 |
| ☐ 26 Larry Willis | 2.50 | 1.00 | .25 |
| ☐ 27 Damon Allen | 7.50 | 3.00 | .75 |
| ☐ 28 Danny Bass | 5.00 | 2.00 | .50 |
| ☐ 29 Stanley Blair | 2.00 | .80 | .20 |
| ☐ 30 Marco Cyncar | 2.00 | .80 | .20 |
| ☐ 31 Tracey Ham | 30.00 | 12.00 | 3.00 |
| ☐ 32 Milson Jones | 5.00 | 2.00 | .50 |
| (Traded) | | | |
| ☐ 33 Stephen Jones | 3.50 | 1.40 | .35 |
| ☐ 34 Jerry Kauric | 3.50 | 1.40 | .35 |
| ☐ 35 Hector Pothier | 1.50 | .60 | .15 |
| ☐ 36 Tom Richards | 3.50 | 1.40 | .35 |
| ☐ 37 Chris Skinner | 2.00 | .80 | .20 |
| ☐ 38 Henry Williams | 40.00 | 16.00 | 4.00 |
| ☐ 39 Larry Wruck | 2.00 | .80 | .20 |
| ☐ 40 Pat Brady | 1.50 | .60 | .15 |
| ☐ 41 Grover Covington | 4.00 | 1.60 | .40 |
| ☐ 42 Rocky DiPietro | 5.00 | 2.00 | .50 |
| ☐ 43 Howard Fields | 1.50 | .60 | .15 |
| ☐ 44 Miles Gorrell | 1.50 | .60 | .15 |
| ☐ 45 Johnnie Jones | 1.50 | .60 | .15 |
| ☐ 46 Tom Porras | 2.50 | 1.00 | .25 |
| ☐ 47 Jason Riley | 1.50 | .60 | .15 |
| ☐ 48 Dale Sanderson | 1.50 | .60 | .15 |
| ☐ 49 Ralph Scholz | 1.50 | .60 | .15 |
| ☐ 50 Lance Shields | 1.50 | .60 | .15 |
| ☐ 51 Steve Stapler | 2.00 | .80 | .20 |
| ☐ 52 Mike Walker | 3.00 | 1.20 | .30 |
| ☐ 53 Gerald Alphin | 6.00 | 2.40 | .60 |
| ☐ 54 Nick Arakgi SP | 25.00 | 10.00 | 2.50 |
| (Retired before season) | | | |
| ☐ 55 Nick Benjamin | 2.50 | 1.00 | .25 |
| ☐ 56 Tom Dixon | 1.50 | .60 | .15 |
| ☐ 57 Leo Groenewegen | 1.50 | .60 | .15 |
| ☐ 58 Will Lewis | 1.50 | .60 | .15 |
| ☐ 59 Greg Marshall | 6.00 | 2.40 | .60 |
| (Injured and retired) | | | |
| ☐ 60 Larry Mohr | 1.50 | .60 | .15 |
| ☐ 61 Kevin Powell | 3.50 | 1.40 | .35 |
| (Traded) | | | |
| ☐ 62 Jim Reid | 2.50 | 1.00 | .25 |
| ☐ 63 Art Schlichter | 15.00 | 6.00 | 1.50 |
| ☐ 64 Rick Wolkensperg | 1.50 | .60 | .15 |
| ☐ 65 Anthony Woodson | 1.50 | .60 | .15 |
| ☐ 66 David Albright | 1.50 | .60 | .15 |
| ☐ 67 Roger Aldag | 2.00 | .80 | .20 |
| ☐ 68 Mike Anderson | 1.50 | .60 | .15 |
| ☐ 69 Kent Austin | 30.00 | 12.00 | 3.00 |
| ☐ 70 Tom Burgess | 7.50 | 3.00 | .75 |
| ☐ 71 James Curry | 3.50 | 1.40 | .35 |
| ☐ 72 Ray Elgaard | 5.00 | 2.00 | .50 |
| ☐ 73 Denny Ferdinand | 1.50 | .60 | .15 |
| ☐ 74 Bobby Jurasin | 7.50 | 3.00 | .75 |
| ☐ 75 Gary Lewis | 1.50 | .60 | .15 |
| ☐ 76 Dave Ridgway | 3.00 | 1.20 | .30 |
| ☐ 77 Harry Skipper | 2.00 | .80 | .20 |
| ☐ 78 Glen Suitor | 2.00 | .80 | .20 |
| ☐ 79 Ian Beckstead | 1.50 | .60 | .15 |
| ☐ 80 Lance Chomyc | 2.50 | 1.00 | .25 |
| ☐ 81 John Congemi | 3.50 | 1.40 | .35 |
| ☐ 82 Gill Fenerty | 10.00 | 4.00 | 1.00 |
| ☐ 83 Dan Ferrone | 2.50 | 1.00 | .25 |
| ☐ 84 Warren Hudson | 2.50 | 1.00 | .25 |
| ☐ 85 Hank Ilesic | 3.50 | 1.40 | .35 |
| ☐ 86 Jim Kardash | 1.50 | .60 | .15 |
| ☐ 87 Glenn Kulka | 2.00 | .80 | .20 |
| ☐ 88 Don Moen | 1.50 | .60 | .15 |
| ☐ 89 Gilbert Renfroe | 5.00 | 2.00 | .50 |
| ☐ 90 Chris Schultz | 2.50 | 1.00 | .25 |
| ☐ 91 Darrell Smith | 5.00 | 2.00 | .50 |
| ☐ 92 Lyle Bauer | 1.50 | .60 | .15 |
| ☐ 93 Nick Bastaja | 1.50 | .60 | .15 |
| ☐ 94 David Black | 1.50 | .60 | .15 |
| ☐ 95 Bob Cameron | 2.00 | .80 | .20 |
| ☐ 96 Randy Fabi | 1.50 | .60 | .15 |
| ☐ 97 James Jefferson | 7.50 | 3.00 | .75 |
| ☐ 98 Stan Mikawos | 1.50 | .60 | .15 |
| ☐ 99 James Murphy | 3.50 | 1.40 | .35 |
| ☐ 100 Ken Pettway | 1.50 | .60 | .15 |
| ☐ 101 Willard Reaves | 15.00 | 6.00 | 1.50 |
| (Signed with Redskins) | | | |
| ☐ 102 Darryl Sampson | 1.50 | .60 | .15 |
| ☐ 103 Chris Walby | 5.00 | 2.00 | .50 |
| ☐ 104 James West | 6.00 | 2.40 | .60 |
| ☐ 105 Tom Clements SP | 30.00 | 12.00 | 3.00 |
| (Retired before season) | | | |
| ☐ 106 Checklist Card SP | 10.00 | 4.00 | 1.00 |

# 1989 JOGO CFL

The 1989 JOGO CFL set contains 160 standard-size (2 1/2" by 3 1/2") cards. The cards were issued in two series, 1-110 and 111-160. Except for the card numbering, the two series are indistinguishable. The fronts have color action photos with dark blue borders and yellow lettering; the vertically oriented backs have biographical information and career highlights. The first 200 sets of the first series cards came out with purple borders; these rather scarce color variations are valued at approximately triple the values listed below. The cards are numbered on the back and checklisted below according to teams as follows: Hamilton Tiger-Cats (1, 15-25, 30-31, 112-113, 145, 157-158), Toronto Argonauts (2-14, 26-29, 152), Ottawa Rough Riders (32-40, 78, 122, 125, 127-130, 135, 138-140, 143-144, 146), Saskatchewan Roughriders (41-50, 74, 93, 156), Edmonton Eskimos (51-54, 56-67, 71-72, 114-115, 119, 126), Calgary Stampeders (55, 68-70, 73, 75-77, 111, 116, 118, 120-121, 123, 141-142, 148-151, 153-155, 159-160), British Columbia (79-90, 117, 124, 132-134, 136-137, 147), and Winnipeg Blue Bombers (91-92, 94-110, 131).

| | MINT | EXC | G-VG |
|---|---|---|---|
| COMPLETE SET (160) | 100.00 | 40.00 | 10.00 |
| COMPLETE SERIES 1 (110) | 65.00 | 26.00 | 6.50 |
| COMPLETE SERIES 2 (50) | 35.00 | 14.00 | 3.50 |
| COMMON PLAYER (1-110) | .50 | .20 | .05 |
| COMMON PLAYER (111-160) | .50 | .20 | .05 |
| | | | |
| ☐ 1 Mike Kerrigan | 3.00 | 1.20 | .30 |
| ☐ 2 Ian Beckstead | .50 | .20 | .05 |
| ☐ 3 Lance Chomyc | .75 | .30 | .07 |
| ☐ 4 Gill Fenerty | 3.00 | 1.20 | .30 |
| ☐ 5 Lee Morris | .50 | .20 | .05 |
| ☐ 6 Todd Wiseman | .50 | .20 | .05 |
| ☐ 7 John Congemi | 1.00 | .40 | .10 |
| ☐ 8 Harold Hallman | .75 | .30 | .07 |
| ☐ 9 Jim Kardash | .50 | .20 | .05 |
| ☐ 10 Kelvin Pruenster | .50 | .20 | .05 |
| ☐ 11 Blaine Schmidt | .50 | .20 | .05 |
| ☐ 12 Bruce Holmes | .50 | .20 | .05 |
| ☐ 13 Ed Berry | .50 | .20 | .05 |
| ☐ 14 Bobby McAllister | 2.50 | 1.00 | .25 |
| ☐ 15 Frank Robinson | .75 | .30 | .07 |
| ☐ 16 Darrell Corbin | .50 | .20 | .05 |
| ☐ 17 Jason Riley | .50 | .20 | .05 |
| ☐ 18 Darrell Patterson | .50 | .20 | .05 |
| ☐ 19 Darrell Harle | .50 | .20 | .05 |
| ☐ 20 Mark Napiorkowski | .50 | .20 | .05 |
| ☐ 21 Derrick McAdoo | 2.50 | 1.00 | .25 |
| ☐ 22 Sam Loucks | .50 | .20 | .05 |
| ☐ 23 Ronnie Glanton | .50 | .20 | .05 |
| ☐ 24 Lance Shields | .75 | .30 | .07 |
| ☐ 25 Tony Champion | 2.00 | .80 | .20 |
| ☐ 26 Floyd Salazar | .50 | .20 | .05 |
| ☐ 27 Tony Visco | .75 | .30 | .07 |
| ☐ 28 Glenn Kulka | .75 | .30 | .07 |
| ☐ 29 Reggie Pleasant | .75 | .30 | .07 |
| ☐ 30 Rod Skillman | .50 | .20 | .05 |
| ☐ 31 Grover Covington | 1.50 | .60 | .15 |
| ☐ 32 Gerald Alphin | 2.00 | .80 | .20 |
| ☐ 33 Gerald Wilcox | .50 | .20 | .05 |
| ☐ 34 Daniel Hunter | .50 | .20 | .05 |
| ☐ 35 Tony Kimbrough | .75 | .30 | .07 |
| ☐ 36 Willie Fears | .75 | .30 | .07 |
| ☐ 37 Tyrone Thurman | 4.00 | 1.60 | .40 |
| ☐ 38 Dean Dorsey | .50 | .20 | .05 |
| ☐ 39 Tom Schimmer | .50 | .20 | .05 |
| ☐ 40 Ken Evraire | .75 | .30 | .07 |
| ☐ 41 Steve Wiggins | .50 | .20 | .05 |
| ☐ 42 Donovan Wright | .50 | .20 | .05 |
| ☐ 43 Tuineau Alipate | .50 | .20 | .05 |
| ☐ 44 Richie Hall | .50 | .20 | .05 |
| ☐ 45 Rob Bresciani | .50 | .20 | .05 |
| ☐ 46 Tom Burgess | 1.50 | .60 | .15 |
| ☐ 47 Jeff Fairholm | 4.00 | 1.60 | .40 |

| | | | |
|---|---|---|---|
| ☐ 48 John Hoffman | .50 | .20 | .05 |
| ☐ 49 Dave Ridgway | 1.25 | .50 | .12 |
| ☐ 50 Terry Baker | .75 | .30 | .07 |
| ☐ 51 Mike Hildebrand | .50 | .20 | .05 |
| ☐ 52 Danny Bass | 2.50 | 1.00 | .25 |
| ☐ 53 Jeff Braswell | .50 | .20 | .05 |
| ☐ 54 Michel Bourgeau | .50 | .20 | .05 |
| ☐ 55 Ken Ford | .50 | .20 | .05 |
| ☐ 56 Enis Jackson | .50 | .20 | .05 |
| ☐ 57 Tony Hunter | 1.25 | .50 | .12 |
| ☐ 58 Andre Francis | .75 | .30 | .07 |
| ☐ 59 Larry Wruck | .75 | .30 | .07 |
| ☐ 60 Pierre Vercheval | 1.00 | .40 | .10 |
| ☐ 61 Keith Wright | .50 | .20 | .05 |
| ☐ 62 Andrew McConnell | .50 | .20 | .05 |
| ☐ 63 Gregg Stumon | .75 | .30 | .07 |
| ☐ 64 Steve Taylor | 3.00 | 1.20 | .30 |
| ☐ 65 Brett Williams | .75 | .30 | .07 |
| ☐ 66 Tracey Ham | 5.00 | 2.00 | .50 |
| ☐ 67 Stewart Hill | 1.00 | .40 | .10 |
| ☐ 68 Eugene Belliveau | .50 | .20 | .05 |
| ☐ 69 Tom Porras | 1.00 | .40 | .10 |
| ☐ 70 Jay Christensen | .50 | .20 | .05 |
| ☐ 71 Michael Soles | 1.00 | .40 | .10 |
| ☐ 72 John Mandarich | 1.25 | .50 | .12 |
| ☐ 73 Dan Wicklum | .50 | .20 | .05 |
| ☐ 74 Shawn Daniels | .50 | .20 | .05 |
| ☐ 75 Marshall Toner | .50 | .20 | .05 |
| ☐ 76 Kent Warnock | .75 | .30 | .07 |
| ☐ 77 Terrence Jones | 4.00 | 1.60 | .40 |
| ☐ 78 Damon Allen | 3.00 | 1.20 | .30 |
| ☐ 79 Kevin Konar | .75 | .30 | .07 |
| ☐ 80 Phillip Smith | .50 | .20 | .05 |
| ☐ 81 Marcus Thomas | .50 | .20 | .05 |
| ☐ 82 Jamie Taras | .50 | .20 | .05 |
| ☐ 83 Rob Moretto | .50 | .20 | .05 |
| ☐ 84 Eugene Mingo | .50 | .20 | .05 |
| ☐ 85 Matt Dunigan | 5.00 | 2.00 | .50 |
| ☐ 86 Jan Carinci | .50 | .20 | .05 |
| ☐ 87 Anthony Parker | 1.00 | .40 | .10 |
| ☐ 88 Keith Gooch | .50 | .20 | .05 |
| ☐ 89 Ron Howard | .50 | .20 | .05 |
| ☐ 90 David Williams | 2.50 | 1.00 | .25 |
| ☐ 91 Less Browne | 1.00 | .40 | .10 |
| ☐ 92 Quency Williams | .50 | .20 | .05 |
| ☐ 93 Tim McCray | 1.00 | .40 | .10 |
| ☐ 94 Jeff Croonen | .50 | .20 | .05 |
| ☐ 95 Greg Battle | 2.00 | .80 | .20 |
| ☐ 96 Moustafa Ali | .50 | .20 | .05 |
| ☐ 97 Michael Allen | .50 | .20 | .05 |
| ☐ 98 David Black | .50 | .20 | .05 |
| ☐ 99 Paul Randolph | .50 | .20 | .05 |
| ☐ 100 Trevor Kennerd | 1.00 | .40 | .10 |
| ☐ 101 Ken Pettway | .50 | .20 | .05 |
| ☐ 102 Sean Salisbury | 3.00 | 1.20 | .30 |
| ☐ 103 Bob Cameron | .50 | .20 | .05 |
| ☐ 104 Tim Jessie | 1.00 | .40 | .10 |
| ☐ 105 Leon Hatziioannou | .50 | .20 | .05 |
| ☐ 106 Matt Pearce | .50 | .20 | .05 |
| ☐ 107 Paul Clatney | .50 | .20 | .05 |
| ☐ 108 Randy Fabi | .50 | .20 | .05 |
| ☐ 109 Mike Gray | .50 | .20 | .05 |
| ☐ 110 James Murphy | 2.00 | .80 | .20 |
| ☐ 111 Danny Barrett | 1.50 | .60 | .15 |
| ☐ 112 Wally Zatylny | .75 | .30 | .07 |
| ☐ 113 Tony Truelove | .50 | .20 | .05 |
| ☐ 114 Leroy Blugh | .50 | .20 | .05 |
| ☐ 115 Reggie Taylor | 1.50 | .60 | .15 |
| ☐ 116 Mark Zeno | 2.50 | 1.00 | .25 |
| ☐ 117 Paul Wetmore | .50 | .20 | .05 |
| ☐ 118 Mark McLoughlin | .50 | .20 | .05 |
| ☐ 119 Randy Ambrosie | .50 | .20 | .05 |
| ☐ 120 Will Johnson | .50 | .20 | .05 |
| ☐ 121 Brock Smith | .50 | .20 | .05 |
| ☐ 122 Willie Gillus | .50 | .20 | .05 |
| ☐ 123 Andy McVey | .50 | .20 | .05 |
| ☐ 124 Wes Cooper | .50 | .20 | .05 |
| ☐ 125 Tyrone Pope | .50 | .20 | .05 |
| ☐ 126 Craig Ellis | 1.50 | .60 | .15 |
| ☐ 127 Darrel Hopper | .50 | .20 | .05 |
| ☐ 128 Brad Fawcett | .50 | .20 | .05 |
| ☐ 129 Pat Miller | .50 | .20 | .05 |
| ☐ 130 Irv Daymond | .50 | .20 | .05 |
| ☐ 131 Bob Molle | .50 | .20 | .05 |
| ☐ 132 James Mills | 3.00 | 1.20 | .30 |
| ☐ 133 Darrell Wallace | .75 | .30 | .07 |
| ☐ 134 Jerry Beasley | .50 | .20 | .05 |
| ☐ 135 Loyd Lewis | .50 | .20 | .05 |
| ☐ 136 Bernie Glier | .50 | .20 | .05 |
| ☐ 137 Eric Streater | 2.00 | .80 | .20 |
| ☐ 138 Gerald Roper | .50 | .20 | .05 |
| ☐ 139 Brad Tierney | .50 | .20 | .05 |
| ☐ 140 Patrick Wayne | .50 | .20 | .05 |
| ☐ 141 Craig Watson | .50 | .20 | .05 |
| ☐ 142 Doug(Tank) Landry | 3.50 | 1.40 | .35 |
| ☐ 143 Orville Lee | 1.50 | .60 | .15 |
| ☐ 144 Rocco Romano | .50 | .20 | .05 |

| | | | |
|---|---|---|---|
| ☐ 145 Todd Dillon | 1.00 | .40 | .10 |
| ☐ 146 Michel Lamy | .50 | .20 | .05 |
| ☐ 147 Tony Cherry | 3.50 | 1.40 | .35 |
| ☐ 148 Flint Fleming | .50 | .20 | .05 |
| ☐ 149 Kennard Martin | .50 | .20 | .05 |
| ☐ 150 Lorenzo Graham | .50 | .20 | .05 |
| ☐ 151 Junior Thurman | 1.50 | .60 | .15 |
| ☐ 152 Darnell Graham | .50 | .20 | .05 |
| ☐ 153 Dan Ferrone | .75 | .30 | .07 |
| ☐ 154 Matt Finlay | .50 | .20 | .05 |
| ☐ 155 Brent Matich | .50 | .20 | .05 |
| ☐ 156 Kent Austin | 5.00 | 2.00 | .50 |
| ☐ 157 Will Lewis | .50 | .20 | .05 |
| ☐ 158 Mike Walker | 1.50 | .60 | .15 |
| ☐ 159 Tim Petros | 1.00 | .40 | .10 |
| ☐ 160 Stu Laird | 1.50 | .60 | .15 |

# 1990 JOGO CFL

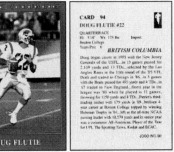

This 220-card standard-size (2 1/2" by 3 1/2") set of JOGO Canadian Football League cards was issued in two series of 110 cards. The first series card fronts feature an action shot of the player, enframed by a thin red border on blue background, with team name above the photo and player's name below. The second series card fronts feature solid blue borders surrounding an action shot of the player with the team's name on the top of the card and the player's name underneath. The card number and player information are found on the back. Three British Columbia players featured in the set that are of interest to American collectors are Doug Flutie, Mark Gastineau, and Major Harris. The complete set price below includes only one of the variations of card 84. First series cards are arranged according to teams as follows: Saskatchewan Roughriders (1-14), Hamilton Tiger-Cats (15-29), Calgary Stampeders (30-42), Toronto Argonauts (43-56, 92), Winnipeg Blue Bombers (57-70), Edmonton Eskimos (71-84), British Columbia Lions (85-91, 93-94), and Ottawa Rough Riders (95-110).

| | MINT | EXC | G-VG |
|---|---|---|---|
| COMPLETE SET (220) | 70.00 | 28.00 | 7.00 |
| COMPLETE SERIES 1 (110) | 40.00 | 16.00 | 4.00 |
| COMPLETE SERIES 2 (110) | 30.00 | 12.00 | 3.00 |
| COMMON PLAYER (1-110) | .25 | .10 | .02 |
| COMMON PLAYER (111-220) | .25 | .10 | .02 |

| | | | |
|---|---|---|---|
| ☐ 1 1989 Grey Cup Champs | 1.00 | .40 | .10 |
| (Saskatchewan) | | | |
| ☐ 2 Kent Austin | 2.50 | 1.00 | .25 |
| ☐ 3 James Ellingson | .50 | .20 | .05 |
| ☐ 4 Vince Goldsmith | .50 | .20 | .05 |
| ☐ 5 Gary Lewis | .25 | .10 | .02 |
| ☐ 6 Bobby Jurasin | .75 | .30 | .07 |
| ☐ 7 Tim McCray | .35 | .14 | .03 |
| ☐ 8 Chuck Klingbeil | .75 | .30 | .07 |
| ☐ 9 Albert Brown | .25 | .10 | .02 |
| ☐ 10 Dave Ridgway | .75 | .30 | .07 |
| ☐ 11 Tony Rice | 3.00 | 1.20 | .30 |
| ☐ 12 Richie Hall | .25 | .10 | .02 |
| ☐ 13 Jeff Fairholm | 1.00 | .40 | .10 |
| ☐ 14 Ray Elgaard | 1.25 | .50 | .12 |
| ☐ 15 Sonny Gordon | .25 | .10 | .02 |
| ☐ 16 Peter Giftopoulos | .75 | .30 | .07 |
| ☐ 17 Mike Kerrigan | 1.00 | .40 | .10 |
| ☐ 18 Jason Riley | .25 | .10 | .02 |
| ☐ 19 Wally Zatylny | .35 | .14 | .03 |
| ☐ 20 Derrick McAdoo | .75 | .30 | .07 |
| ☐ 21 Dale Sanderson | .25 | .10 | .02 |
| ☐ 22 Paul Osbaldiston | .50 | .20 | .05 |
| ☐ 23 Todd Dillon | .50 | .20 | .05 |
| ☐ 24 Miles Gorrell | .25 | .10 | .02 |
| ☐ 25 Earl Winfield | .75 | .30 | .07 |
| ☐ 26 Bill Henry | .25 | .10 | .02 |
| ☐ 27 Darrell Harle | .25 | .10 | .02 |
| ☐ 28 Ernie Schramayr | .25 | .10 | .02 |

| | | | |
|---|---|---|---|
| ☐ 29 Greg Peterson | .25 | .10 | .02 |
| ☐ 30 Marshall Toner | .25 | .10 | .02 |
| ☐ 31 Danny Barrett | 1.50 | .60 | .15 |
| ☐ 32 Mike Palumbo | .25 | .10 | .02 |
| ☐ 33 Ken Ford | .25 | .10 | .02 |
| ☐ 34 Brock Smith | .25 | .10 | .02 |
| ☐ 35 Tom Spoletini | .25 | .10 | .02 |
| ☐ 36 Will Johnson | .25 | .10 | .02 |
| ☐ 37 Terrence Jones | 1.50 | .60 | .15 |
| ☐ 38 Darcy Kopp | .25 | .10 | .02 |
| ☐ 39 Tim Petros | .35 | .14 | .03 |
| ☐ 40 Mitchell Price | .35 | .14 | .03 |
| ☐ 41 Junior Thurman | 1.00 | .40 | .10 |
| ☐ 42 Kent Warnock | .35 | .14 | .03 |
| ☐ 43 Darrell Smith | 1.00 | .40 | .10 |
| ☐ 44 Chris Schultz UER | .35 | .14 | .03 |
| (No team on back) | | | |
| ☐ 45 Kelvin Pruenster | .25 | .10 | .02 |
| ☐ 46 Matt Dunigan | 3.00 | 1.20 | .30 |
| ☐ 47 Lance Chomyc | .50 | .20 | .05 |
| ☐ 48 John Congemi | .75 | .30 | .07 |
| ☐ 49 Mike Clemons | 9.00 | 3.75 | .90 |
| ☐ 50 Glenn Harper | .25 | .10 | .02 |
| ☐ 51 Branko Vincic | .25 | .10 | .02 |
| ☐ 52 Tom Porras | .50 | .20 | .05 |
| ☐ 53 Reggie Pleasant | .50 | .20 | .05 |
| ☐ 54 Randy Marriott | .25 | .10 | .02 |
| ☐ 55 James Parker | .75 | .30 | .07 |
| ☐ 56 Don Moen | .35 | .14 | .03 |
| ☐ 57 James West | 1.00 | .40 | .10 |
| ☐ 58 Trevor Kennerd | .75 | .30 | .07 |
| ☐ 59 Warren Hudson | .35 | .14 | .03 |
| ☐ 60 Tom Burgess | 1.50 | .60 | .15 |
| ☐ 61 David Black | .25 | .10 | .02 |
| ☐ 62 Matt Pearce | .25 | .10 | .02 |
| ☐ 63 Steve Rodehutskors | .35 | .14 | .03 |
| ☐ 64 Rod Hill | .75 | .30 | .07 |
| ☐ 65 Nick Benjamin | .35 | .14 | .03 |
| ☐ 66 Bob Cameron | .35 | .14 | .03 |
| ☐ 67 Leon Hatziioannou | .25 | .10 | .02 |
| ☐ 68 Robert Mimbs | 2.50 | 1.00 | .25 |
| ☐ 69 Mike Gray | .25 | .10 | .02 |
| ☐ 70 Ken Winey | .25 | .10 | .02 |
| ☐ 71 Mike Hildebrand | .25 | .10 | .02 |
| ☐ 72 Brett Williams | .35 | .14 | .03 |
| ☐ 73 Tracey Ham | 2.50 | 1.00 | .25 |
| ☐ 74 Danny Bass | .75 | .30 | .07 |
| ☐ 75 Mark Norman | .25 | .10 | .02 |
| ☐ 76 Andre Francis | .35 | .14 | .03 |
| ☐ 77 Todd Storme | .25 | .10 | .02 |
| ☐ 78 Henry Williams | 4.00 | 1.60 | .40 |
| ☐ 79 Kevin Clark | .75 | .30 | .07 |
| ☐ 80 Enis Jackson | .25 | .10 | .02 |
| ☐ 81 Leroy Blugh | .25 | .10 | .02 |
| ☐ 82 Jeff Braswell | .35 | .14 | .03 |
| ☐ 83 Larry Wruck | .35 | .14 | .03 |
| ☐ 84A Mike McLean ERR | 3.00 | 1.20 | .30 |
| (Photo actually | | | |
| 24 Mike Hildebrand) | | | |
| ☐ 84B Mike McLean COR | 5.00 | 2.00 | .50 |
| (Two players shown) | | | |
| ☐ 85 Leo Groenewegen UER | .25 | .10 | .02 |
| (Misspelled Groenewegan | | | |
| on card back) | | | |
| ☐ 86 Mark Gastineau | 1.50 | .60 | .15 |
| ☐ 87 Larry Clarkson | .25 | .10 | .02 |
| ☐ 88 Major Harris | 2.50 | 1.00 | .25 |
| ☐ 89 Ray Alexander | .35 | .14 | .03 |
| ☐ 90 Joe Paopao | .50 | .20 | .05 |
| ☐ 91 Ian Sinclair | .35 | .14 | .03 |
| ☐ 92 Tony Visco UER | .25 | .10 | .02 |
| (British Columbia on front, | | | |
| correctly has team as | | | |
| Toronto on front) | | | |
| ☐ 93 Lui Passaglia | .75 | .30 | .07 |
| ☐ 94 Doug Flutie | 15.00 | 6.00 | 1.50 |
| ☐ 95 Glenn Kulka | .35 | .14 | .03 |
| ☐ 96 Bruce Holmes | .25 | .10 | .02 |
| ☐ 97 Stacey Dawsey | .25 | .10 | .02 |
| ☐ 98 Damon Allen | 1.25 | .50 | .12 |
| ☐ 99 Ken Evraire | .35 | .14 | .03 |
| ☐ 100 David Williams | 1.00 | .40 | .10 |
| ☐ 101 Gregg Stumon | .35 | .14 | .03 |
| ☐ 102 Scott Flagel | .35 | .14 | .03 |
| ☐ 103 Gerald Roper | .25 | .10 | .02 |
| ☐ 104 Tony Cherry | 1.00 | .40 | .10 |
| ☐ 105 Pat Miller | .50 | .20 | .05 |
| ☐ 106 Dean Dorsey | .35 | .14 | .03 |
| ☐ 107 Patrick Wayne | .25 | .10 | .02 |
| ☐ 108 Reggie Barnes | 2.00 | .80 | .20 |
| ☐ 109 Kari Yli-Renko | .25 | .10 | .02 |
| ☐ 110 Ken Hobart | .75 | .30 | .07 |
| ☐ 111 Doug Flutie | 10.00 | 4.00 | 1.00 |
| British Columbia Lions | | | |
| ☐ 112 Grover Covington | .75 | .30 | .07 |
| Hamilton Tiger-Cats | | | |
| ☐ 113 Michael Allen | .25 | .10 | .02 |

| | | | |
|---|---|---|---|
| Winnipeg Blue Bombers | | | |
| ☐ 114 Mike Walker | .75 | .30 | .07 |
| Edmonton Eskimos | | | |
| ☐ 115 Danny McManus | 2.50 | 1.00 | .25 |
| Winnipeg Blue Bombers | | | |
| ☐ 116 Greg Battle | 1.25 | .50 | .12 |
| Winnipeg Blue Bombers | | | |
| ☐ 117 Quency Williams | .25 | .10 | .02 |
| Winnipeg Blue Bombers | | | |
| ☐ 118 Jeff Croonen | .25 | .10 | .02 |
| Winnipeg Blue Bombers | | | |
| ☐ 119 Paul Randolph | .25 | .10 | .02 |
| Winnipeg Blue Bombers | | | |
| ☐ 120 Rick House | .35 | .14 | .03 |
| Winnipeg Blue Bombers | | | |
| ☐ 121 Rob Smith | .50 | .20 | .05 |
| Ottawa Rough Riders | | | |
| ☐ 122 Mark Napiorkowski | .25 | .10 | .02 |
| Hamilton Tiger-Cats | | | |
| ☐ 123 Ed Berry | .25 | .10 | .02 |
| Toronto Argonauts | | | |
| ☐ 124 Rob Crifo | .25 | .10 | .02 |
| Winnipeg Blue Bombers | | | |
| ☐ 125 Gord Weber | .25 | .10 | .02 |
| Ottawa Rough Riders | | | |
| ☐ 126 Jeff Boyd | .50 | .20 | .05 |
| Toronto Argonauts | | | |
| ☐ 127 Paul McGowan | .50 | .20 | .05 |
| Ottawa Rough Riders | | | |
| ☐ 128 Reggie Taylor | .75 | .30 | .07 |
| Edmonton Eskimos | | | |
| ☐ 129 Warren Jones | .25 | .10 | .02 |
| Edmonton Eskimos | | | |
| ☐ 130 Blake Marshall | .50 | .20 | .05 |
| Edmonton Eskimos | | | |
| ☐ 131 Darrell Corbin | .25 | .10 | .02 |
| Hamilton Tiger-Cats | | | |
| ☐ 132 Jim Rockford | .50 | .20 | .05 |
| Hamilton Tiger-Cats | | | |
| ☐ 133 Richard Nurse | .25 | .10 | .02 |
| Hamilton Tiger-Cats | | | |
| ☐ 134 Bryan Illerbrun | .25 | .10 | .02 |
| Ottawa Rough Riders | | | |
| ☐ 135 Mark Waterman | .25 | .10 | .02 |
| Hamilton Tiger-Cats | | | |
| ☐ 136 Doug(Tank) Landry | 1.25 | .50 | .12 |
| British Columbia Lions | | | |
| ☐ 137 Ronnie Glanton | .25 | .10 | .02 |
| Hamilton Tiger-Cats | | | |
| ☐ 138 Mark Guy | .35 | .14 | .03 |
| Saskatchewan Roughriders | | | |
| ☐ 139 Mike Anderson | .25 | .10 | .02 |
| Saskatchewan Roughriders | | | |
| ☐ 140 Remi Trudell | .25 | .10 | .02 |
| British Columbia Lions | | | |
| ☐ 141 Stephen Jones | .60 | .24 | .06 |
| Ottawa Rough Riders | | | |
| ☐ 142 Mike Derks | .25 | .10 | .02 |
| Hamilton Tiger-Cats | | | |
| ☐ 143 Michel Bourgeau | .35 | .14 | .03 |
| Edmonton Oilers | | | |
| ☐ 144 Jeff Bentrim | .50 | .20 | .05 |
| Saskatchewan Roughriders | | | |
| ☐ 145 Roger Aldag | .35 | .14 | .03 |
| Saskatchewan Roughriders | | | |
| ☐ 146 Donald Narcisse | 2.50 | 1.00 | .25 |
| Saskatchewan Roughriders | | | |
| ☐ 147 Troy Wilson | .25 | .10 | .02 |
| Ottawa Rough Riders | | | |
| ☐ 148 Glen Suitor | .35 | .14 | .03 |
| Saskatchewan Roughriders | | | |
| ☐ 149 Stewart Hill | 1.00 | .40 | .10 |
| Edmonton Eskimos | | | |
| ☐ 150 Chris Johnstone | .25 | .10 | .02 |
| Edmonton Eskimos | | | |
| ☐ 151 Mark Mathis | .25 | .10 | .02 |
| Edmonton Eskimos | | | |
| ☐ 152 Blaine Schmidt | .25 | .10 | .02 |
| Toronto Argonauts | | | |
| ☐ 153 Craig Ellis | .75 | .30 | .07 |
| Edmonton Eskimos | | | |
| ☐ 154 John Mandarich | .50 | .20 | .05 |
| Ottawa Rough Riders | | | |
| ☐ 155 Steve Zatylny | .25 | .10 | .02 |
| Winnipeg Blue Bombers | | | |
| ☐ 156 Michel Lamy | .25 | .10 | .02 |
| Ottawa Rough Riders | | | |
| ☐ 157 Irv Daymond | .25 | .10 | .02 |
| Ottawa Rough Riders | | | |
| ☐ 158 Tom Porras | .50 | .20 | .05 |
| Calgary Stampeders | | | |
| ☐ 159 Rick Worman | .50 | .20 | .05 |
| Calgary Stampeders | | | |
| ☐ 160 Major Harris | 1.50 | .60 | .15 |
| British Columbia Lions | | | |
| ☐ 161 Darryl Hall | .50 | .20 | .05 |
| Calgary Stampeders | | | |
| ☐ 162 Terry Andrysiak | .35 | .14 | .03 |

| | | MINT | EXC | G-VG |
|---|---|---|---|---|
| Hamilton Tiger-Cats | | | | |
| ☐ 163 Harold Hallman | .50 | .20 | .05 | |
| Toronto Argonauts | | | | |
| ☐ 164 Carl Brazley | .60 | .24 | .06 | |
| Toronto Argonauts | | | | |
| ☐ 165 Kevin Smellie | .25 | .10 | .02 | |
| Toronto Argonauts | | | | |
| ☐ 166 Mark Campbell | .50 | .20 | .05 | |
| Toronto Argonauts | | | | |
| ☐ 167 Andy McVey | .25 | .10 | .02 | |
| Calgary Stampeders | | | | |
| ☐ 168 Derrick Crawford | .75 | .30 | .07 | |
| Calgary Stampeders | | | | |
| ☐ 169 Howard Dell | .25 | .10 | .02 | |
| Toronto Argonauts | | | | |
| ☐ 170 Dave Van Belleghem | .25 | .10 | .02 | |
| Toronto Argonauts | | | | |
| ☐ 171 Don Wilson | .25 | .10 | .02 | |
| Toronto Argonauts | | | | |
| ☐ 172 Robert Smith | .25 | .10 | .02 | |
| Toronto Argonauts | | | | |
| ☐ 173 Keith Browner | .50 | .20 | .05 | |
| Toronto Argonauts | | | | |
| ☐ 174 Chris Munford | .25 | .10 | .02 | |
| Toronto Argonauts | | | | |
| ☐ 175 Gary Wilkerson | .25 | .10 | .02 | |
| Hamilton Tiger-Cats | | | | |
| ☐ 176 Rickey Foggie UER | 1.25 | .50 | .12 | |
| (Misspelled Foogie on card front) | | | | |
| Toronto Argonauts | | | | |
| ☐ 177 Robin Belanger | .25 | .10 | .02 | |
| British Columbia Lions | | | | |
| ☐ 178 Andrew Murray | .25 | .10 | .02 | |
| Toronto Argonauts | | | | |
| ☐ 179 Paul Masotti | .50 | .20 | .05 | |
| Toronto Argonauts | | | | |
| ☐ 180 Chris Gaines | .25 | .10 | .02 | |
| Toronto Argonauts | | | | |
| ☐ 181 Joe Clausi | .25 | .10 | .02 | |
| Calgary Stampeders | | | | |
| ☐ 182 Greg Harris | .25 | .10 | .02 | |
| Saskatchewan Roughriders | | | | |
| ☐ 183 Dave Bovell | .25 | .10 | .02 | |
| Winnipeg Blue Bombers | | | | |
| ☐ 184 Eric Streater | .50 | .20 | .05 | |
| Winnipeg Blue Bombers | | | | |
| ☐ 185 Larry Hogue | .25 | .10 | .02 | |
| Saskatchewan Roughriders | | | | |
| ☐ 186 Jan Carinci | .25 | .10 | .02 | |
| British Columbia Lions | | | | |
| ☐ 187 Floyd Salazar | .25 | .10 | .02 | |
| Hamilton Tiger-Cats | | | | |
| ☐ 188 Alondra Johnson | .50 | .20 | .05 | |
| British Columbia Lions | | | | |
| ☐ 189 Jay Christensen UER | .35 | .14 | .03 | |
| (Misspelled Christenson on card front) | | | | |
| British Columbia Lions | | | | |
| ☐ 190 Rick Ryan | .25 | .10 | .02 | |
| British Columbia Lions | | | | |
| ☐ 191 Willie Pless | 1.00 | .40 | .10 | |
| British Columbia Lions | | | | |
| ☐ 192 Walter Ballard | .25 | .10 | .02 | |
| Calgary Stampeders | | | | |
| ☐ 193 Lee Knight | .25 | .10 | .02 | |
| Hamilton Tiger-Cats | | | | |
| ☐ 194 Ray Macoritti | .35 | .14 | .03 | |
| Edmonton Eskimos | | | | |
| ☐ 195 Dan Payne | .25 | .10 | .02 | |
| British Columbia Lions | | | | |
| ☐ 196 Dan Sellers | .25 | .10 | .02 | |
| Hamilton Tiger-Cats | | | | |
| ☐ 197 Rae Robirts | .25 | .10 | .02 | |
| Hamilton Tiger-Cats | | | | |
| ☐ 198 Dave Mossman | .25 | .10 | .02 | |
| Hamilton Tiger-Cats | | | | |
| ☐ 199 Sam Loucks | .25 | .10 | .02 | |
| Hamilton Tiger-Cats | | | | |
| ☐ 200 Derek MacCready | .25 | .10 | .02 | |
| British Columbia Lions | | | | |
| ☐ 201 Tony Cherry | .75 | .30 | .07 | |
| Calgary Stampeders | | | | |
| ☐ 202 Moustafa Ali | .35 | .14 | .03 | |
| Calgary Stampeders | | | | |
| ☐ 203 Terry Baker | .50 | .20 | .05 | |
| Ottawa Rough Riders | | | | |
| ☐ 204 Matt Finlay | .25 | .10 | .02 | |
| Calgary Stampeders | | | | |
| ☐ 205 Daniel Hunter | .25 | .10 | .02 | |
| Ottawa Rough Riders | | | | |
| ☐ 206 Chris Major | 1.50 | .60 | .15 | |
| British Columbia Lions | | | | |
| ☐ 207 Henry Smith | .25 | .10 | .02 | |
| Calgary Stampeders | | | | |
| ☐ 208 David Sapunjis | 2.50 | 1.00 | .25 | |
| Calgary Stampeders | | | | |
| ☐ 209 Darrell Wallace | .35 | .14 | .03 | |

| | | MINT | EXC | G-VG |
|---|---|---|---|---|
| Calgary Stampeders | | | | |
| ☐ 210 Mark Singer | .25 | .10 | .02 | |
| Calgary Stampeders | | | | |
| ☐ 211 Tuineau Alipate | .25 | .10 | .02 | |
| Saskatchewan Roughriders | | | | |
| ☐ 212 Tony Champion | 1.25 | .50 | .12 | |
| Hamilton Tiger-Cats | | | | |
| ☐ 213 Mike Lazecki | .25 | .10 | .02 | |
| Saskatchewan Roughriders | | | | |
| ☐ 214 Larry Clarkson | .25 | .10 | .02 | |
| British Columbia Lions | | | | |
| ☐ 215 Lorenzo Graham | .25 | .10 | .02 | |
| British Columbia Lions | | | | |
| ☐ 216 Tony Martino | .25 | .10 | .02 | |
| British Columbia Lions | | | | |
| ☐ 217 Ken Watson | .25 | .10 | .02 | |
| British Columbia Lions | | | | |
| ☐ 218 Paul Clatney | .25 | .10 | .02 | |
| Calgary Stampeders | | | | |
| ☐ 219 Ken Pettway | .25 | .10 | .02 | |
| Winnipeg Blue Bombers | | | | |
| ☐ 220 Tyrone Jones | 1.00 | .40 | .10 | |
| Winnipeg Blue Bombers | | | | |

# 1991 JOGO Ismail Promo

The front design of this promo card has a high gloss color photo trimmed in red, on a royal blue background with diagonal white pinstripes. Ismail is pictured in his Argonaut uniform, holding his helmet in his right hand. His name appears in red lettering in the lower left corner, and the CFL helmet logo is in the lower right corner. The horizontally oriented back has a second color photo, biography, and college statistics (all-purpose yardage). The card is numbered on the back. The card is standard size, 2 1/2" by 3 1/2".

| | MINT | EXC | G-VG |
|---|---|---|---|
| COMPLETE SET (1) | 2.00 | .80 | .20 |
| COMMON PLAYER | 2.00 | .80 | .20 |
| | | | |
| ☐ P Raghib(Rocket) Ismail | 2.00 | .80 | .20 |

# 1991 JOGO CFL

The 1991 JOGO CFL football set contains 220 cards measuring the standard size (2 1/2" by 3 1/2"). The set was released in two series, 1-110 and 111-220. The set was distributed in factory sets and in foil packs (10 cards per pack). The front design has glossy color action shots, with thin gray and red borders against a royal blue card face. The team name appears above the picture, while the CFL helmet logo and the player's name appear at the bottom of the card face. The backs have red, green, and yellow lettering on a black background. They feature biography and career summary. The team logo and card number round out the back. The cards are numbered on the back and checklisted below according to teams as follows: Edmonton Eskimos (1-27), Ottawa Rough Riders (28-54), Calgary Stampeders (55-81), Hamilton Tiger-Cats (82-109), Saskatchewan Roughriders (111-137), Winnipeg Blue Bombers (138-164, 199), British Columbia Lions (165-191), and Toronto Argonauts (192-198, 200-219). It is estimated that 30,000 sets were produced. Raghib(Rocket) Ismail was originally planned for inclusion in the set, but was removed based on litigation. Ismail had apparently signed an exclusive with All World, which apparently took precedence over JOGO's attempt to include him in the set based on his membership in the CFL Players' Association.

| | MINT | EXC | G-VG |
|---|---|---|---|
| COMPLETE SET (220) | 8.00 | 3.25 | .80 |
| COMPLETE SERIES 1 (110) | 4.00 | 1.60 | .40 |
| COMPLETE SERIES 2 (110) | 4.00 | 1.60 | .40 |
| COMMON PLAYER (1-110) | .05 | .02 | .00 |
| COMMON PLAYER (111-220) | .05 | .02 | .00 |

| | | | |
|---|---|---|---|
| ☐ 1 Tracey Ham | .35 | .14 | .03 |
| ☐ 2 Larry Wruck | .05 | .02 | .00 |
| ☐ 3 Pierre Vercheval | .10 | .04 | .01 |
| ☐ 4 Rod Connop | .05 | .02 | .00 |
| ☐ 5 Michel Bourgeau | .10 | .04 | .01 |
| ☐ 6 Leroy Blugh | .05 | .02 | .00 |
| ☐ 7 Mike Walker | .15 | .06 | .01 |
| ☐ 8 Ray Macoritti | .10 | .04 | .01 |
| ☐ 9 Michael Soles | .20 | .08 | .02 |
| ☐ 10 Brett Williams | .15 | .06 | .01 |
| ☐ 11 Blake Marshall | .15 | .06 | .01 |
| ☐ 12 David Williams | .20 | .08 | .02 |
| ☐ 13 Enis Jackson | .05 | .02 | .00 |
| ☐ 14 Craig Ellis | .15 | .06 | .01 |
| ☐ 15 Reggie Taylor | .15 | .06 | .01 |
| ☐ 16 Mike McLean | .05 | .02 | .00 |
| ☐ 17 Blake Dermott | .10 | .04 | .01 |
| ☐ 18 Henry Williams | .50 | .20 | .05 |
| ☐ 19 Jordan Gaertner | .05 | .02 | .00 |
| ☐ 20 Willie Pless | .15 | .06 | .01 |
| ☐ 21 Danny Bass | .20 | .08 | .02 |
| ☐ 22 Trevor Bowles | .05 | .02 | .00 |
| ☐ 23 Rob Davidson | .05 | .02 | .00 |
| ☐ 24 Mark Norman | .05 | .02 | .00 |
| ☐ 25 Ron Lancaster CO | .10 | .04 | .01 |
| ☐ 26 Chris Johnstone | .10 | .04 | .01 |
| ☐ 27 Randy Ambrosie | .05 | .02 | .00 |
| ☐ 28 Glenn Kulka | .10 | .04 | .01 |
| ☐ 29 Gerald Wilcox | .05 | .02 | .00 |
| ☐ 30 Kari Yli-Renko | .05 | .02 | .00 |
| ☐ 31 Daniel Hunter | .05 | .02 | .00 |
| ☐ 32 Bryan Illerbrun | .05 | .02 | .00 |
| ☐ 33 Terry Baker | .10 | .04 | .01 |
| ☐ 34 Jeff Braswell | .10 | .04 | .01 |
| ☐ 35 Andre Francis | .10 | .04 | .01 |
| ☐ 36 Irv Daymond | .05 | .02 | .00 |
| ☐ 37 Sean Foudy | .05 | .02 | .00 |
| ☐ 38 Brad Tierney | .05 | .02 | .00 |
| ☐ 39 Gregg Stumon | .10 | .04 | .01 |
| ☐ 40 Scott Flagel | .05 | .02 | .00 |
| ☐ 41 Gerald Roper | .05 | .02 | .00 |
| ☐ 42 Charles Wright | .05 | .02 | .00 |
| ☐ 43 Rob Smith | .05 | .02 | .00 |
| ☐ 44 James Ellingson | .10 | .04 | .01 |
| ☐ 45 Damon Allen | .25 | .10 | .02 |
| ☐ 46 John Congemi | .10 | .04 | .01 |
| ☐ 47 Reggie Barnes | .30 | .12 | .03 |
| ☐ 48 Stephen Jones | .20 | .08 | .02 |
| ☐ 49 Rob Prodanovic | .05 | .02 | .00 |
| ☐ 50 Steve Goldman | .05 | .02 | .00 |
| ☐ 51 Patrick Wayne | .05 | .02 | .00 |
| ☐ 52 David Conrad | .05 | .02 | .00 |
| ☐ 53 John Krupke | .05 | .02 | .00 |
| ☐ 54 Loyd Lewis | .05 | .02 | .00 |
| ☐ 55 Tony Cherry | .20 | .08 | .02 |
| ☐ 56 Terrence Jones | .30 | .12 | .03 |
| ☐ 57 Dan Wicklum | .05 | .02 | .00 |
| ☐ 58 Allen Pitts | 1.50 | .60 | .15 |
| ☐ 59 Junior Thurman | .20 | .08 | .02 |
| ☐ 60 Ron Hopkins | .10 | .04 | .01 |
| ☐ 61 Andy McVey | .05 | .02 | .00 |
| ☐ 62 Leo Blanchard | .05 | .02 | .00 |
| ☐ 63 Mark Singer | .05 | .02 | .00 |
| ☐ 64 Darryl Hall | .05 | .02 | .00 |
| ☐ 65 David McCrary | .05 | .02 | .00 |
| ☐ 66 Mark Guy | .10 | .04 | .01 |
| ☐ 67 Marshall Toner | .05 | .02 | .00 |
| ☐ 68 Derrick Crawford | .15 | .06 | .01 |
| ☐ 69 Danny Barrett | .25 | .10 | .02 |
| ☐ 70 Kent Warnock | .05 | .02 | .00 |
| ☐ 71 Brent Matich | .05 | .02 | .00 |
| ☐ 72 Mark McLoughlin | .10 | .04 | .01 |
| ☐ 73 Joe Clausi | .05 | .02 | .00 |
| ☐ 74 Wally Buono CO | .05 | .02 | .00 |
| ☐ 75 Will Johnson | .10 | .04 | .01 |
| ☐ 76 Walter Ballard | .05 | .02 | .00 |
| ☐ 77 Matt Finlay | .05 | .02 | .00 |
| ☐ 78 David Sapunjis | .25 | .10 | .02 |
| ☐ 79 Greg Peterson | .05 | .02 | .00 |
| ☐ 80 Paul Clatney | .05 | .02 | .00 |
| ☐ 81 Lloyd Fairbanks | .10 | .04 | .01 |
| ☐ 82 Herman Heard | .20 | .08 | .02 |
| ☐ 83 Richard Nurse | .05 | .02 | .00 |
| ☐ 84 Dave Richardson | .05 | .02 | .00 |
| ☐ 85 Ernie Schramayr | .05 | .02 | .00 |
| ☐ 86 Todd Dillon | .10 | .04 | .01 |
| ☐ 87 Tuineau Alipate | .05 | .02 | .00 |
| ☐ 88 Peter Giftopoulos | .10 | .04 | .01 |
| ☐ 89 Miles Gorrell | .05 | .02 | .00 |
| ☐ 90 Earl Winfield | .25 | .10 | .02 |
| ☐ 91 Paul Osbaldiston | .10 | .04 | .01 |
| ☐ 92 Dale Sanderson | .05 | .02 | .00 |
| ☐ 93 Jason Riley | .05 | .02 | .00 |
| ☐ 94 Ken Evraire | .10 | .04 | .01 |
| ☐ 95 Lee Knight | .05 | .02 | .00 |
| ☐ 96 Tim Lorenz | .05 | .02 | .00 |
| ☐ 97 Derrick McAdoo | .20 | .08 | .02 |
| ☐ 98 Bobby Dawson | .05 | .02 | .00 |
| ☐ 99 Rickey Royal | .05 | .02 | .00 |
| ☐ 100 Ronald Veal | .30 | .12 | .03 |
| ☐ 101 Grover Covington | .20 | .08 | .02 |
| ☐ 102 Mike Kerrigan | .35 | .14 | .03 |
| ☐ 103 Rocky DiPietro | .30 | .12 | .03 |
| ☐ 104 Mark Dennis | .05 | .02 | .00 |
| ☐ 105 Tony Champion | .25 | .10 | .02 |
| ☐ 106 Tony Visco | .05 | .02 | .00 |
| ☐ 107 Darrell Harle | .05 | .02 | .00 |
| ☐ 108 Wally Zatylny | .10 | .04 | .01 |
| ☐ 109 David Beckman CO | .05 | .02 | .00 |
| ☐ 110 Checklist 1-110 | .10 | .04 | .01 |
| ☐ 111 Jeff Fairholm | .20 | .08 | .02 |
| ☐ 112 Roger Aldag | .10 | .04 | .01 |
| ☐ 113 David Albright | .05 | .02 | .00 |
| ☐ 114 Gary Lewis | .05 | .02 | .00 |
| ☐ 115 Dan Rashovich | .05 | .02 | .00 |
| ☐ 116 Lucius Floyd | .15 | .06 | .01 |
| ☐ 117 Bob Poley | .05 | .02 | .00 |
| ☐ 118 Donald Narcisse | .25 | .10 | .02 |
| ☐ 119 Bobby Jurasin | .15 | .06 | .01 |
| ☐ 120 Orville Lee | .15 | .06 | .01 |
| ☐ 121 Stacey Hairston | .05 | .02 | .00 |
| ☐ 122 Richie Hall | .05 | .02 | .00 |
| ☐ 123 John Gregory CO | .05 | .02 | .00 |
| ☐ 124 Rick Worman | .10 | .04 | .01 |
| ☐ 125 Dave Ridgway | .10 | .04 | .01 |
| ☐ 126 Wayne Drinkwalter | .05 | .02 | .00 |
| ☐ 127 Eddie Lowe | .05 | .02 | .00 |
| ☐ 128 Mike Hogue | .05 | .02 | .00 |
| ☐ 129 Larry Hogue | .05 | .02 | .00 |
| ☐ 130 Milson Jones | .15 | .06 | .01 |
| ☐ 131 Ray Elgaard | .30 | .12 | .03 |
| ☐ 132 David Pitcher | .05 | .02 | .00 |
| ☐ 133 Vic Stevenson | .05 | .02 | .00 |
| ☐ 134 Albert Brown | .05 | .02 | .00 |
| ☐ 135 Mike Anderson | .05 | .02 | .00 |
| ☐ 136 Glen Suitor | .05 | .02 | .00 |
| ☐ 137 Kent Austin | .35 | .14 | .03 |
| ☐ 138 Mike Gray | .05 | .02 | .00 |
| ☐ 139 Steve Rodehutskors | .10 | .04 | .01 |
| ☐ 140 Eric Streater | .10 | .04 | .01 |
| ☐ 141 David Black | .05 | .02 | .00 |
| ☐ 142 James West | .20 | .08 | .02 |
| ☐ 143 Danny McManus | .40 | .16 | .04 |
| ☐ 144 Darryl Sampson | .05 | .02 | .00 |
| ☐ 145 Bob Cameron | .05 | .02 | .00 |
| ☐ 146 Tom Burgess | .35 | .14 | .03 |
| ☐ 147 Rick House | .10 | .04 | .01 |
| ☐ 148 Chris Walby | .20 | .08 | .02 |
| ☐ 149 Michael Allen | .05 | .02 | .00 |
| ☐ 150 Warren Hudson | .10 | .04 | .01 |
| ☐ 151 Dave Bovell | .05 | .02 | .00 |
| ☐ 152 Rob Crifo | .05 | .02 | .00 |
| ☐ 153 Lyle Bauer | .05 | .02 | .00 |
| ☐ 154 Trevor Kennerd | .20 | .08 | .02 |
| ☐ 155 Troy Johnson | .10 | .04 | .01 |
| ☐ 156 Less Browne | .10 | .04 | .01 |
| ☐ 157 Nick Benjamin | .10 | .04 | .01 |
| ☐ 158 Matt Pearce | .05 | .02 | .00 |
| ☐ 159 Tyrone Jones | .20 | .08 | .02 |
| ☐ 160 Rod Hill | .15 | .06 | .01 |
| ☐ 161 Bob Molle | .05 | .02 | .00 |
| ☐ 162 Lee Hull | .10 | .04 | .01 |
| ☐ 163 Greg Battle | .25 | .10 | .02 |
| ☐ 164 Robert Mimbs | .50 | .20 | .05 |
| ☐ 165 Giulio Caravatta | .15 | .06 | .01 |
| ☐ 166 James Mills | .25 | .10 | .02 |
| ☐ 167 Ian Sinclair | .10 | .04 | .01 |
| ☐ 168 Robin Belanger | .05 | .02 | .00 |
| ☐ 169 Deatrich Wise | .05 | .02 | .00 |
| ☐ 170 Chris Skinner | .10 | .04 | .01 |
| ☐ 171 Norman Jefferson | .05 | .02 | .00 |
| ☐ 172 Larry Clarkson | .05 | .02 | .00 |
| ☐ 173 Chris Major | .25 | .10 | .02 |
| ☐ 174 Stewart Hill | .20 | .08 | .02 |
| ☐ 175 Tony Hunter | .15 | .06 | .01 |
| ☐ 176 Stacey Dawsey | .05 | .02 | .00 |
| ☐ 177 Doug Flutie | 1.25 | .50 | .12 |
| ☐ 178 Mike Trevathan | .15 | .06 | .01 |
| ☐ 179 Jearld Baylis | .15 | .06 | .01 |
| ☐ 180 Matt Clark | .35 | .14 | .03 |
| ☐ 181 Ken Pettway | .05 | .02 | .00 |
| ☐ 182 Lloyd Joseph | .05 | .02 | .00 |
| ☐ 183 Jon Volpe | 1.00 | .40 | .10 |
| ☐ 184 Leo Groenewegen | .05 | .02 | .00 |
| ☐ 185 Carl Coulter | .05 | .02 | .00 |
| ☐ 186 O.J. Brigance | .30 | .12 | .03 |
| ☐ 187 Ryan Hanson | .10 | .04 | .01 |
| ☐ 188 Rocco Romano | .05 | .02 | .00 |
| ☐ 189 Ray Alexander | .10 | .04 | .01 |
| ☐ 190 Bob O'Billovich CO | .05 | .02 | .00 |
| ☐ 191 Paul Wetmore | .05 | .02 | .00 |
| ☐ 192 Harold Hallman | .10 | .04 | .01 |
| ☐ 193 Ed Berry | .05 | .02 | .00 |
| ☐ 194 Brian Warren | .05 | .02 | .00 |

| | MINT | EXC | G-VG |
|---|---|---|---|
| ☐ 195 Matt Dunigan | .50 | .20 | .05 |
| ☐ 196 Kelvin Pruenster | .05 | .02 | .00 |
| ☐ 197 Ian Beckstead | .05 | .02 | .00 |
| ☐ 198 Carl Brazley | .10 | .04 | .01 |
| ☐ 199 Trevor Kennerd | .15 | .06 | .01 |
| ☐ 200 Reggie Pleasant | .10 | .04 | .01 |
| ☐ 201 Kevin Smellie | .05 | .02 | .00 |
| ☐ 202 Don Moen | .10 | .04 | .01 |
| ☐ 203 Blaine Schmidt | .05 | .02 | .00 |
| ☐ 204 Chris Schultz | .10 | .04 | .01 |
| ☐ 205 Lance Chomyc | .10 | .04 | .01 |
| ☐ 206 Darrell Smith | .25 | .10 | .02 |
| ☐ 207 Dan Ferrone | .10 | .04 | .01 |
| ☐ 208 Chris Gaines | .05 | .02 | .00 |
| ☐ 209 Keith Castello | .05 | .02 | .00 |
| ☐ 210 Chris Munford | .05 | .02 | .00 |
| ☐ 211 Rodney Harding | .25 | .10 | .02 |
| ☐ 212 Darryl Ford | .05 | .02 | .00 |
| ☐ 213 Rickey Foggie | .30 | .12 | .03 |
| ☐ 214 Don Wilson | .05 | .02 | .00 |
| ☐ 215 Andrew Murray | .05 | .02 | .00 |
| ☐ 216 Jim Kardash | .05 | .02 | .00 |
| ☐ 217 Mike Clemons | .75 | .30 | .07 |
| ☐ 218 Bruce Elliott | .05 | .02 | .00 |
| ☐ 219 Mike McCarthy | .05 | .02 | .00 |
| ☐ 220 Checklist Card | .15 | .06 | .01 |

## 1991 JOGO CFL Stamp Card Inserts

These three standard-size (2 1/2" by 3 1/2") insert cards have photos on their fronts within a white postage stamp border. In red, green, and yellow print on a black background, the backs present commentary to the front pictures. The first two cards are numbered on the back, while the card picturing the Grey Cup Trophy is unnumbered.

| | MINT | EXC | G-VG |
|---|---|---|---|
| COMPLETE SET (3) | 45.00 | 18.00 | 4.50 |
| COMMON PLAYER | 15.00 | 6.00 | 1.50 |
| | | | |
| ☐ 1 Albert Henry George Grey | 15.00 | 6.00 | 1.50 |
| ☐ 2 Trevor Kennerd | 15.00 | 6.00 | 1.50 |
| Winnipeg Blue Bombers | | | |
| ☐ NNO Grey Cup Trophy | 25.00 | 10.00 | 2.50 |
| (Grey Cup Winners | | | |
| listed on card back) | | | |

## 1992 JOGO CFL Promos

These three promo cards were produced by JOGO and measure the standard size (2 1/2" by 3 1/2"). The first two feature color action player photos on a silver card face. The team helmet and player's name appear in the bottom silver border. In yellow, red, and green

print on a silver background, the back has biography and player profile. The third card features Rocket Rat, the JOGO Card Company "mascot." The back presents his biography and closes with an educational message ("Education Equals More Freedom"). The cards are numbered on the back. Reportedly only 6,000 of each card were released.

| | MINT | EXC | G-VG |
|---|---|---|---|
| COMPLETE SET (3) | 5.00 | 2.00 | .50 |
| COMMON PLAYER (A1-A3) | 2.00 | .80 | .20 |
| | | | |
| ☐ A1 Mike Pinball Clemons | 2.00 | .80 | .20 |
| Toronto Argonauts | | | |
| ☐ A2 Jon Volpe | 2.00 | .80 | .20 |
| British Columbia Lions | | | |
| ☐ A3 Rocket Rat | 2.00 | .80 | .20 |
| (Cartoon character) | | | |

## 1992 JOGO CFL Charlton Inserts

These two promo cards were produced by JOGO and, when cut, measure the standard size (2 1/2" by 3 1/2"). The cards were bound into the center of copies of the second edition of the Charlton CFL Football Card Guide. Reportedly 5500 card sheets were produced. The cards are numbered on the back and clearly marked as promo cards.

| | MINT | EXC | G-VG |
|---|---|---|---|
| COMPLETE SET (2) | 5.00 | 2.00 | .50 |
| COMMON PLAYER (P1-P2) | 3.00 | 1.20 | .30 |
| | | | |
| ☐ P1 Mike Pinball Clemons | 3.00 | 1.20 | .30 |
| Toronto Argonauts | | | |
| ☐ P2 Jon Volpe | 3.00 | 1.20 | .30 |
| British Columbia Lions | | | |

## 1992 JOGO CFL

The 1992 JOGO CFL set contains 220 standard-size (2 1/2" by 3 1/2") cards. Reportedly there were less than 1200 cases produced. The cards feature color action player photos on a silver card face. The team helmet and player's name appear in the bottom silver border. In yellow, red, and green print on a silver background, the back has biography and player profile. The cards are numbered on the back and checklisted below according to teams as follows: Toronto Argonauts (1-27), Calgary Stampeders (28-54), Ottawa Rough Riders (55-82, 110), Edmonton Eskimos (83-107), Winnipeg Blue Bombers (111-139), Saskatchewan Roughriders (140-164), Hamilton Tiger-Cats (165-191), British Columbia Lions (192-219).

| | MINT | EXC | G-VG |
|---|---|---|---|
| COMPLETE SET (220) | 20.00 | 8.00 | 2.00 |
| COMMON PLAYER (1-220) | .07 | .03 | .01 |

| | | | |
|---|---|---|---|
| ☐ 1 Dave Bovell | .10 | .04 | .01 |
| ☐ 2 Don Moen | .10 | .04 | .01 |
| ☐ 3 Ian Beckstead | .07 | .03 | .01 |
| ☐ 4 David Williams | .25 | .10 | .02 |
| ☐ 5 Hank Ilesic | .15 | .06 | .01 |
| ☐ 6 Brian Warren | .07 | .03 | .01 |
| ☐ 7 Paul Masotti | .10 | .04 | .01 |
| ☐ 8 Kelvin Pruenster | .07 | .03 | .01 |
| ☐ 9 Mike Clemons | .75 | .30 | .07 |
| ☐ 10 Chris Schultz | .10 | .04 | .01 |
| ☐ 11 Andrew Murray | .07 | .03 | .01 |
| ☐ 12 Lance Chomyc | .15 | .06 | .01 |
| ☐ 13 Ed Berry | .07 | .03 | .01 |
| ☐ 14 Harold Hallman | .10 | .04 | .01 |
| ☐ 15 Dave Van Belleghem | .07 | .03 | .01 |
| ☐ 16 Rodney Harding | .15 | .06 | .01 |
| ☐ 17 Rickey Foggie | .25 | .10 | .02 |
| ☐ 18 Darrell Smith | .30 | .12 | .03 |
| ☐ 19 Bob Skemp | .07 | .03 | .01 |
| ☐ 20 Carl Brazley | .15 | .06 | .01 |
| ☐ 21 J.P. Izquierdo | .07 | .03 | .01 |
| ☐ 22 Mike Campbell | .10 | .04 | .01 |
| ☐ 23 Reggie Pleasant | .10 | .04 | .01 |
| ☐ 24 Dan Ferrone | .10 | .04 | .01 |
| ☐ 25 Kevin Smellie | .07 | .03 | .01 |
| ☐ 26 Don Wilson | .07 | .03 | .01 |
| ☐ 27 Adam Rita CO | .07 | .03 | .01 |
| ☐ 28 Greg Peterson | .07 | .03 | .01 |
| ☐ 29 David Sapunjis | .35 | .14 | .03 |
| ☐ 30 Srecko Zizakovic | .07 | .03 | .01 |
| ☐ 31 Carl Bland | .07 | .03 | .01 |
| ☐ 32 Errol Tucker | .07 | .03 | .01 |
| ☐ 33 Allen Pitts | .75 | .30 | .07 |
| ☐ 34 Pee Wee Smith | .35 | .14 | .03 |
| ☐ 35 Will Johnson | .30 | .12 | .03 |
| ☐ 36 Kent Warnock | .10 | .04 | .01 |
| ☐ 37 Brent Matich | .07 | .03 | .01 |
| ☐ 38 Stu Laird | .10 | .04 | .01 |
| ☐ 39 Sean Beals | .07 | .03 | .01 |
| ☐ 40 Darcy Kopp | .07 | .03 | .01 |
| ☐ 41 Ken Moore | .07 | .03 | .01 |
| ☐ 42 Alondra Johnson | .10 | .04 | .01 |
| ☐ 43 Matt Finlay | .07 | .03 | .01 |
| ☐ 44 Andy McVey | .07 | .03 | .01 |
| ☐ 45 Paul Clatney | .07 | .03 | .01 |
| ☐ 46 Karl Anthony | .07 | .03 | .01 |
| ☐ 47 Bruce Covernton | .35 | .14 | .03 |
| ☐ 48 Mark McLoughlin UER | .10 | .04 | .01 |
| (Name misspelled several | | | |
| times on the card back) | | | |
| ☐ 49 Pat Hinds | .07 | .03 | .01 |
| ☐ 50 Eric Mitchel UER | .20 | .08 | .02 |
| (Misspelled Mitchell | | | |
| on both sides) | | | |
| ☐ 51 Dan Wicklum | .07 | .03 | .01 |
| ☐ 52 Tim Cofield | .07 | .03 | .01 |
| ☐ 53 Steve Taylor | .35 | .14 | .03 |
| ☐ 54 Darryl Hall | .07 | .03 | .01 |
| ☐ 55 Angelo Snipes | .75 | .30 | .07 |
| ☐ 56 Shawn Daniels | .07 | .03 | .01 |
| ☐ 57 Terrence Jones | .25 | .10 | .02 |
| ☐ 58 Brian Bonner | .07 | .03 | .01 |
| ☐ 59 Kari Yli-Renko | .07 | .03 | .01 |
| ☐ 60 Denny Chronopoulos | .07 | .03 | .01 |
| ☐ 61 Damon Allen | .40 | .16 | .04 |
| ☐ 62 Reggie Barnes | .40 | .16 | .04 |
| ☐ 63 Andre Francis UER | .10 | .04 | .01 |
| (Misspelled Frances | | | |
| on card front) | | | |
| ☐ 64 Rob Smith | .25 | .10 | .02 |
| ☐ 65 Anthony Drawhorn | .25 | .10 | .02 |
| ☐ 66 David Conrad UER | .07 | .03 | .01 |
| (Back text says team | | | |
| is Green Riders) | | | |
| ☐ 67 Irv Daymond | .07 | .03 | .01 |
| ☐ 68 Terry Baker | .15 | .06 | .01 |
| ☐ 69 Daniel Hunter | .07 | .03 | .01 |
| ☐ 70 Gord Weber | .07 | .03 | .01 |
| ☐ 71 Tom Burgess | .25 | .10 | .02 |
| ☐ 72 Charles Gordon | .07 | .03 | .01 |
| ☐ 73 Bob Gordon | .07 | .03 | .01 |
| ☐ 74 Jock Climie | .35 | .14 | .03 |
| ☐ 75 Patrick Wayne | .07 | .03 | .01 |
| ☐ 76 Sean Foudy | .07 | .03 | .01 |
| ☐ 77 James Ellingson | .10 | .04 | .01 |
| ☐ 78 Gregg Stumon | .15 | .06 | .01 |
| ☐ 79 John Kropke | .07 | .03 | .01 |
| ☐ 80 Stephen Jones | .25 | .10 | .02 |
| ☐ 81 Ron Smeltzer | .07 | .03 | .01 |
| ☐ 82 Scott Campbell | .50 | .20 | .05 |
| ☐ 83 Henry Williams | 1.00 | .40 | .10 |
| ☐ 84 Willie Pless | .30 | .12 | .03 |
| ☐ 85 Dan Murphy | .07 | .03 | .01 |
| ☐ 86 Chris Armstrong | .07 | .03 | .01 |
| ☐ 87 Tracey Ham | .60 | .24 | .06 |
| ☐ 88 Larry Wruck | .10 | .04 | .01 |
| ☐ 89 Rod Connop | .07 | .03 | .01 |
| ☐ 90 Jim Sandusky | .25 | .10 | .02 |
| ☐ 91 Randy Ambrosie | .07 | .03 | .01 |
| ☐ 92 Michel Bourgeau | .10 | .04 | .01 |
| ☐ 93 Bennie Goods UER | .10 | .04 | .01 |
| (Misspelled Benny) | | | |
| ☐ 94 Rob Davidson | .07 | .03 | .01 |
| ☐ 95 Leroy Blugh | .07 | .03 | .01 |
| ☐ 96 Brian Walling | .07 | .03 | .01 |
| ☐ 97 Michael Soles | .25 | .10 | .02 |
| ☐ 98 Craig Ellis | .25 | .10 | .02 |
| ☐ 99 Pierre Vercheval | .25 | .10 | .02 |
| ☐ 100 Matt Dunigan | .40 | .16 | .04 |
| ☐ 101 Enis Jackson | .07 | .03 | .01 |
| ☐ 102 Tom Muecke | .25 | .10 | .02 |
| ☐ 103 Jed Roberts | .07 | .03 | .01 |
| ☐ 104 Stephen Krupey | .07 | .03 | .01 |
| ☐ 105 Blake Marshall | .35 | .14 | .03 |
| ☐ 106 Trevor Bowles | .07 | .03 | .01 |
| ☐ 107 Eddie Thomas | .07 | .03 | .01 |
| ☐ 108 Rocket Rat | .25 | .10 | .02 |
| (JOGO Mascot) | | | |
| ☐ 109 Checklist 1-110 UER | .20 | .08 | .02 |
| (50 Eric Mitchell | | | |
| 93 Benny Goods) | | | |
| ☐ 110 Tom Burgess | .35 | .14 | .03 |
| ☐ 111 Bob Cameron | .10 | .04 | .01 |
| ☐ 112 James West | .25 | .10 | .02 |
| ☐ 113 Chris Walby | .20 | .08 | .02 |
| ☐ 114 David Black | .07 | .03 | .01 |
| ☐ 115 Nick Benjamin | .10 | .04 | .01 |
| ☐ 116 Matt Pearce | .07 | .03 | .01 |
| ☐ 117 Bob Molle | .07 | .03 | .01 |
| ☐ 118 Rod Hill | .15 | .06 | .01 |
| ☐ 119 Kyle Hall | .07 | .03 | .01 |
| ☐ 120 Danny McManus | .35 | .14 | .03 |
| ☐ 121 Cal Murphy | .15 | .06 | .01 |
| ☐ 122 Stan Mikawos | .07 | .03 | .01 |
| ☐ 123 Bobby Evans | .07 | .03 | .01 |
| ☐ 124 Larry Willis | .15 | .06 | .01 |
| ☐ 125 Eric Streater | .15 | .06 | .01 |
| ☐ 126 Perry Tuttle | .25 | .10 | .02 |
| ☐ 127 Leon Hatziioannou | .07 | .03 | .01 |
| ☐ 128 Sammy Garza | .07 | .03 | .01 |
| ☐ 129 Greg Battle | .30 | .12 | .03 |
| ☐ 130 Elfrid Payton | .07 | .03 | .01 |
| ☐ 131 Troy Westwood | .25 | .10 | .02 |
| ☐ 132 Mike Gray | .07 | .03 | .01 |
| ☐ 133 Dave Vankoughnett | .07 | .03 | .01 |
| ☐ 134 Paul Randolph | .07 | .03 | .01 |
| ☐ 135 Darryl Sampson | .07 | .03 | .01 |
| ☐ 136 Less Browne | .20 | .08 | .02 |
| ☐ 137 Quency Williams | .07 | .03 | .01 |
| ☐ 138 Robert Mimbs | .40 | .16 | .04 |
| ☐ 139 Matt Dunigan | .60 | .24 | .06 |
| ☐ 140 Dan Rashovich | .07 | .03 | .01 |
| ☐ 141 Dan Farthing | .07 | .03 | .01 |
| ☐ 142 Bruce Boyko | .07 | .03 | .01 |
| ☐ 143 Kim McCloud | .07 | .03 | .01 |
| ☐ 144 Richie Hall | .07 | .03 | .01 |
| ☐ 145 Paul Vajda | .07 | .03 | .01 |
| ☐ 146 Willis Jacox | .30 | .12 | .03 |
| ☐ 147 Glen Scrivener | .07 | .03 | .01 |
| ☐ 148 Dave Ridgway | .15 | .06 | .01 |
| ☐ 149 Lucius Floyd | .20 | .08 | .02 |
| ☐ 150 James King | .07 | .03 | .01 |
| ☐ 151 Kent Austin | .50 | .20 | .05 |
| ☐ 152 Jeff Fairholm | .20 | .08 | .02 |
| ☐ 153 Roger Aldag | .10 | .04 | .01 |
| ☐ 154 Albert Brown | .07 | .03 | .01 |
| ☐ 155 Chris Gioskos | .07 | .03 | .01 |
| ☐ 156 Stacey Hairston | .07 | .03 | .01 |
| ☐ 157 Glen Suitor | .10 | .04 | .01 |
| ☐ 158 Milson Jones | .15 | .06 | .01 |
| ☐ 159 Vic Stevenson | .07 | .03 | .01 |
| ☐ 160 Bob Poley | .07 | .03 | .01 |
| ☐ 161 Bobby Jurasin | .20 | .08 | .02 |
| ☐ 162 Gary Lewis | .07 | .03 | .01 |
| ☐ 163 Donald Narcisse | .30 | .12 | .03 |
| ☐ 164 Mike Anderson | .07 | .03 | .01 |
| ☐ 165 Nick Mazzoli | .07 | .03 | .01 |
| ☐ 166 Lance Trumble | .07 | .03 | .01 |
| ☐ 167 Dale Sanderson | .07 | .03 | .01 |
| ☐ 168 Todd Wiseman | .07 | .03 | .01 |
| ☐ 169 Mark Dennis | .07 | .03 | .01 |
| ☐ 170 Peter Giftopoulos | .15 | .06 | .01 |
| ☐ 171 Ken Evraire | .20 | .08 | .02 |
| ☐ 172 Darrell Harle | .07 | .03 | .01 |
| ☐ 173 Terry Wright | .07 | .03 | .01 |
| ☐ 174 Jamie Morris | .25 | .10 | .02 |
| ☐ 175 Corris Ervin | .07 | .03 | .01 |
| ☐ 176 Don McPherson | .50 | .20 | .05 |
| ☐ 177 Jason Riley | .07 | .03 | .01 |
| ☐ 178 Tim Jackson | .07 | .03 | .01 |
| ☐ 179 Todd Dillon | .15 | .06 | .01 |
| ☐ 180 Lee Knight | .07 | .03 | .01 |
| ☐ 181 Scott Douglas | .07 | .03 | .01 |
| ☐ 182 Dave Richardson | .07 | .03 | .01 |

| | | | |
|---|---|---|---|
| ☐ 183 Wally Zatylny | .10 | .04 | .01 |
| ☐ 184 Rickey Martin | .07 | .03 | .01 |
| ☐ 185 John Motton | .60 | .24 | .06 |
| ☐ 186 Mark Waterman | .07 | .03 | .01 |
| ☐ 187 Ernie Schramayr | .07 | .03 | .01 |
| ☐ 188 Miles Gorrell | .07 | .03 | .01 |
| ☐ 189 Tony Champion | .20 | .08 | .02 |
| ☐ 190 Earl Winfield | .30 | .12 | .03 |
| ☐ 191 John Zajdel | .07 | .03 | .01 |
| ☐ 192 Danny Barrett | .50 | .20 | .05 |
| ☐ 193 Ian Sinclair | .10 | .04 | .01 |
| ☐ 194 Norman Jefferson | .07 | .03 | .01 |
| ☐ 195 Ryan Hanson | .07 | .03 | .01 |
| ☐ 196 Matt Clark | .25 | .10 | .02 |
| ☐ 197 Leo Groenewegen | .07 | .03 | .01 |
| ☐ 198 Ray Alexander | .15 | .06 | .01 |
| ☐ 199 James Mills | .25 | .10 | .02 |
| ☐ 200 Jon Volpe | .75 | .30 | .07 |
| ☐ 201 Doug Hockings | .07 | .03 | .01 |
| ☐ 202 Tony Kimbrough | .07 | .03 | .01 |
| ☐ 203 Lui Passaglia | .15 | .06 | .01 |
| ☐ 204 Bruce Holmes | .07 | .03 | .01 |
| ☐ 205 Jamie Taras | .07 | .03 | .01 |
| ☐ 206 Derek MacCready | .07 | .03 | .01 |
| ☐ 207 Jay Christensen | .10 | .04 | .01 |
| ☐ 208 O.J. Brigance | .25 | .10 | .02 |
| ☐ 209 Robin Belanger | .07 | .03 | .01 |
| ☐ 210 Stewart Hill | .15 | .06 | .01 |
| ☐ 211 Mike Marasco | .07 | .03 | .01 |
| ☐ 212 Mike Trevathan | .10 | .04 | .01 |
| ☐ 213 Chris Major | .25 | .10 | .02 |
| ☐ 214 Steve Rodehutskors | .10 | .04 | .01 |
| ☐ 215 Paul Wetmore | .07 | .03 | .01 |
| ☐ 216 Ken Pettway | .07 | .03 | .01 |
| ☐ 217 Darren Flutie | .50 | .20 | .05 |
| ☐ 218 Giulio Caravatta | .07 | .03 | .01 |
| ☐ 219 Murray Pezim | .10 | .04 | .01 |
| ☐ 220 Checklist 111-220 | .20 | .08 | .02 |
| ☐ CC1 Ken Danby SP | .75 | .30 | .07 |
|     Collector's Classics (Artwork) | | | |
| ☐ CC2 Ken Danby SP | .75 | .30 | .07 |
|     Collector's Classics (Artwork) | | | |

# 1992 JOGO CFL Missing Years

Since no CFL cards were produced from 1972 to 1981, JOGO created this set of "Missing Years" players to provide CFL fans with memories of their favorite players of the 70's. This 22-card set was randomly inserted in the packs and measures the standard size (2 1/2" by 3 1/2"). The fronts carry action black-and-white player photos on a gold metallic face. A red, blue, and orange stripe borders the bottom of the picture. A blue helmet with the JOGO "J" is in the lower left corner and the player's name appears in red in the bottom border. The backs are metallic gold with red and green print. They carry biographical information and a player profile. The cards are numbered on the back with an "A" suffix.

| | MINT | EXC | G-VG |
|---|---|---|---|
| COMPLETE SET (22) | 25.00 | 10.00 | 2.50 |
| COMMON PLAYER (1-22) | 1.00 | .40 | .10 |
| ☐ 1 Larry Smith | 2.50 | 1.00 | .25 |
| ☐ 2 Mike Nelms | 2.00 | .80 | .20 |
| ☐ 3 John Sciarra | 2.50 | 1.00 | .25 |
| ☐ 4 Ed Chalupka | 1.00 | .40 | .10 |
| ☐ 5 Mike Rae | 2.00 | .80 | .20 |
| ☐ 6 Terry Metcalf UER | 3.00 | 1.20 | .30 |
|     (His CFL years were 78-80, not 78-90) | | | |
| ☐ 7 Chuck Ealey | 5.00 | 2.00 | .50 |
| ☐ 8 Junior Ah-You | 2.00 | .80 | .20 |
| ☐ 9 Mike Samples | 1.00 | .40 | .10 |

| | | | |
|---|---|---|---|
| ☐ 10 Ray Nettles | 1.00 | .40 | .10 |
| ☐ 11 Dickie Harris | 1.00 | .40 | .10 |
| ☐ 12 Willie Burden | 4.00 | 1.60 | .40 |
| ☐ 13 Johnny Rodgers | 5.00 | 2.00 | .50 |
| ☐ 14 Anthony Davis | 5.00 | 2.00 | .50 |
| ☐ 15 Joe Pisarcik UER | 1.50 | .60 | .15 |
|     (His CFL years were 74-76, not 74-75) | | | |
| ☐ 16 Jim Washington | 1.00 | .40 | .10 |
| ☐ 17 Tom Scott UER | 1.50 | .60 | .15 |
|     (11 years in CFL, not 10) | | | |
| ☐ 18 Butch Norman | 1.00 | .40 | .10 |
| ☐ 19 Steve Molnar | 1.00 | .40 | .10 |
| ☐ 20 Jerry Tagge | 2.50 | 1.00 | .25 |
| ☐ 21 Leon Bright UER | 2.50 | 1.00 | .25 |
|     (His CFL years were 77-80, not 77-79) | | | |
| ☐ 22 Waddell Smith | 2.00 | .80 | .20 |

# 1992 JOGO CFL Stamp Cards

This five-card set measures the standard size (2 1/2" by 3 1/2"), and was randomly inserted in foil packs. There were only two sets per foil case and only 1,200 cases of foil made according to JOGO. The fronts feature color photos with white postage stamp borders. In green, yellow, and red print on a silver metallic background, the backs provide information about the pictures on the front. The cards are numbered on the back.

| | MINT | EXC | G-VG |
|---|---|---|---|
| COMPLETE SET (5) | 50.00 | 20.00 | 5.00 |
| COMMON PLAYER (1-5) | 10.00 | 4.00 | 1.00 |
| ☐ 1 CFL Hall of Fame | 12.00 | 5.00 | 1.20 |
|     Museum and Statue | | | |
| ☐ 2 Toronto Argonauts | 12.00 | 5.00 | 1.20 |
|     1991 Grey Cup Champs | | | |
| ☐ 3 Tom Pate Memorial | 10.00 | 4.00 | 1.00 |
|     Trophy | | | |
| ☐ 4 Russ Jackson MVP | 20.00 | 8.00 | 2.00 |
| ☐ 5 Oldest Trophy in | 10.00 | 4.00 | 1.00 |
|     The Hall of Fame (Montreal Football Challenge Cup) | | | |

# 1993 JOGO CFL

The 1993 JOGO CFL set consists of 220 standard-size (2 1/2" by 3 1/2") cards. Just 1,300 numbered sets and 440 sets for the players were produced. The fronts feature color action player photos on a light gray card face with ghosted JOGO CFL lettering. A team-color coded stripe highlights the bottom edge of the picture. The team helmet and player's name appear in the bottom border. The white backs contain biography and player profiles which are printed in red and black. The cards are numbered on the back according to teams as follows: Ottawa Rough Riders (1-14, 113-126, 139), Winnipeg Blue Bombers (15-26, 111-112, 154-156, 169), Toronto Argonauts (27-38, 127, 157, 169, 173, 192, 209, 211-216, 218-219), Hamilton Tiger-Cats (39-51, 137-138, 140-149), Saskatchewan Roughriders (52-60, 129-132, 134-136, 158-165), Calgary Stampeders (61-74, 166, 186, 193-207, 220), Edmonton Eskimos (75-88, 128, 133, 150-153, 170, 178, 181, 210, 217), British Columbia Lions (89-99, 171-172, 174-177, 179-180, 182-185, 187-191, 208), and Sacramento Gold Miners (100-110, 167-168).

|  | MINT | EXC | G-VG |
|---|---|---|---|
| COMPLETE SET (220) | 50.00 | 20.00 | 5.00 |
| COMPLETE SERIES 1 (110) | 30.00 | 12.00 | 3.00 |
| COMPLETE SERIES 2 (110) | 20.00 | 8.00 | 2.00 |
| COMMON PLAYER (1-110) | .20 | .08 | .02 |
| COMMON PLAYER (111-220) | .20 | .08 | .02 |

| | | | |
|---|---|---|---|
| ☐ 1 Stephen Jones | .50 | .20 | .05 |
| ☐ 2 Chris Gioskos | .20 | .08 | .02 |
| ☐ 3 Treamelle Taylor | .20 | .08 | .02 |
| ☐ 4 Irv Daymond | .20 | .08 | .02 |
| ☐ 5 Gord Weber | .20 | .08 | .02 |
| ☐ 6 James Ellingson | .20 | .08 | .02 |
| ☐ 7 Lybrant Robinson | .20 | .08 | .02 |
| ☐ 8 Michael Allen | .40 | .16 | .04 |
| ☐ 9 Gregg Stumon | .30 | .12 | .03 |
| ☐ 10 Darren Joseph | .50 | .20 | .05 |
| ☐ 11 Terry Baker | .40 | .16 | .04 |
| ☐ 12 Denny Chronopoulos | .20 | .08 | .02 |
| ☐ 13 Tom Burgess | .60 | .24 | .06 |
| ☐ 14 Wayne Walker | .50 | .20 | .05 |
| ☐ 15 Brendan Rogers | .20 | .08 | .02 |
| ☐ 16 Matt Pearce | .20 | .08 | .02 |
| ☐ 17 Chris Tsangaris | .20 | .08 | .02 |
| ☐ 18 Leon Hatziioannou | .20 | .08 | .02 |
| ☐ 19 Bob Cameron | .20 | .08 | .02 |
| ☐ 20 Donald Smith | .20 | .08 | .02 |
| ☐ 21 Michael Richardson | 3.00 | 1.20 | .30 |
| ☐ 22 Jayson Dzikowicz | .20 | .08 | .02 |
| ☐ 23 Matt Dunigan | .75 | .30 | .07 |
| ☐ 24 Steve Grant | .20 | .08 | .02 |
| ☐ 25 Rob Crifo | .20 | .08 | .02 |
| ☐ 26 Dave Vankoughnett | .20 | .08 | .02 |
| ☐ 27 Paul Masotti | .30 | .12 | .03 |
| ☐ 28 Blaine Schmidt | .20 | .08 | .02 |
| ☐ 29 Dave Van Belleghem | .20 | .08 | .02 |
| ☐ 30 Brian Warren | .20 | .08 | .02 |
| ☐ 31 Reggie Pleasant | .30 | .12 | .03 |
| ☐ 32 Tracy Ham | .75 | .30 | .07 |
| ☐ 33 Mike Clemons | 1.00 | .40 | .10 |
| ☐ 34 Lance Chomyc | .40 | .16 | .04 |
| ☐ 35 Ken Benson | .20 | .08 | .02 |
| ☐ 36 Chris Green | .20 | .08 | .02 |
| ☐ 37 Mike Campbell | .30 | .12 | .03 |
| ☐ 38 Chris Schultz | .30 | .12 | .03 |
| ☐ 39 Reggie Rogers | .30 | .12 | .03 |
| ☐ 40 John Hood | .20 | .08 | .02 |
| ☐ 41 Dave Richardson | .30 | .12 | .03 |
| ☐ 42 Mike Jovanovich | .30 | .12 | .03 |
| ☐ 43 Joey Jauch | .20 | .08 | .02 |
| ☐ 44 Lubo Zizakovic | .20 | .08 | .02 |
| ☐ 45 Don McPherson | .50 | .20 | .05 |
| ☐ 46 Brett Williams | .40 | .16 | .04 |
| ☐ 47 Todd Wiseman | .20 | .08 | .02 |
| ☐ 48 Jim Jauch | .20 | .08 | .02 |
| ☐ 49 Eros Sanchez | .20 | .08 | .02 |
| ☐ 50 Scott Walker | .20 | .08 | .02 |
| ☐ 51 Roger Hennig | .20 | .08 | .02 |
| ☐ 52 Glen Suitor | .30 | .12 | .03 |
| ☐ 53 Bobby Jurasin | .40 | .16 | .04 |
| ☐ 54 Scott Hendrickson | .20 | .08 | .02 |
| ☐ 55 Ventson Donelson | .20 | .08 | .02 |
| ☐ 56 Dan Rashovich | .20 | .08 | .02 |
| ☐ 57 Kent Austin | .75 | .30 | .07 |
| ☐ 58 Ray Elgaard | .50 | .20 | .05 |
| ☐ 59 Dave Ridgeway | .40 | .16 | .04 |
| ☐ 60 Byron K. Williams | .20 | .08 | .02 |
| ☐ 61 Larry Ryckman PRES | .20 | .08 | .02 |
| ☐ 62 Karl Anthony | .20 | .08 | .02 |
| ☐ 63 Greg Knox | .20 | .08 | .02 |
| ☐ 64 Ken Moore | .20 | .08 | .02 |
| ☐ 65 Allen Pitts | .75 | .30 | .07 |
| ☐ 66 Matt Finlay | .30 | .12 | .03 |
| ☐ 67 Tony Martino | .20 | .08 | .02 |
| ☐ 68 Harald Hasselback | .30 | .12 | .03 |
| ☐ 69 David Sapunjis | .50 | .20 | .05 |
| ☐ 70 Andy McVey | .20 | .08 | .02 |
| ☐ 71 Stu Laird | .30 | .12 | .03 |
| ☐ 72 Derrick Crawford | .30 | .12 | .03 |
| ☐ 73 Mark McLoughlin | .20 | .08 | .02 |
| ☐ 74A Will Johnson ERR | .75 | .30 | .07 |
| (Eskimo logo) | | | |
| ☐ 74B Will Johnson COR | .75 | .30 | .07 |
| (Stampeder logo) | | | |
| ☐ 75 Don Wilson | .20 | .08 | .02 |
| ☐ 76 J.P. Izquierdo | .20 | .08 | .02 |
| ☐ 77 Henry Williams | 1.00 | .40 | .10 |
| ☐ 78 Larry Wruck | .30 | .12 | .03 |
| ☐ 79 David Shelton | .30 | .12 | .03 |
| ☐ 80 Damion Lyons | .20 | .08 | .02 |
| ☐ 81 Jed Roberts | .20 | .08 | .02 |
| ☐ 82 Trent Brown | .20 | .08 | .02 |
| ☐ 83 Michel Bourgeau | .30 | .12 | .03 |
| ☐ 84 Blake Dermott | .20 | .08 | .02 |
| ☐ 85 Willie Pless | .40 | .16 | .04 |
| ☐ 86 Leroy Blugh | .20 | .08 | .02 |
| ☐ 87 Steve Krupey | .20 | .08 | .02 |
| ☐ 88 Jim Sandusky | .40 | .16 | .04 |
| ☐ 89 Danny Barrett | .50 | .20 | .05 |
| ☐ 90 James West | .40 | .16 | .04 |
| ☐ 91 Glen Scrivener | .20 | .08 | .02 |
| ☐ 92 Tyrone Jones | .40 | .16 | .04 |
| ☐ 93A Jon Volpe ERR | 2.00 | .80 | .20 |
| (Photo has poor color) | | | |
| ☐ 93B Jon Volpe COR | .75 | .30 | .07 |
| ☐ 94 Less Browne | .30 | .12 | .03 |
| ☐ 95 Matt Clark | .30 | .12 | .03 |
| ☐ 96 Andre Francis | .30 | .12 | .03 |
| ☐ 97 Darren Flutie | .50 | .20 | .05 |
| ☐ 98 Ray Alexander | .30 | .12 | .03 |
| ☐ 99 Rob Smith | 1.00 | .40 | .10 |
| ☐ 100 Fred Anderson | .30 | .12 | .03 |
| Managing General Partner | | | |
| ☐ 101 Rob White | .20 | .08 | .02 |
| ☐ 102 Bobby Humphery | .30 | .12 | .03 |
| ☐ 103 Willie Bouyer | .20 | .08 | .02 |
| ☐ 104 Titus Dixon | .30 | .12 | .03 |
| ☐ 105 John Wiley | .20 | .08 | .02 |
| ☐ 106 Kerwin Bell | .40 | .16 | .04 |
| ☐ 107 Carl Parker | .20 | .08 | .02 |
| ☐ 108 Mike Oliphant | .60 | .24 | .06 |
| ☐ 109 David Archer | .75 | .30 | .07 |
| ☐ 110 Freeman Baysinger | .60 | .24 | .06 |
| ☐ 111 Gerald Alphin | .30 | .12 | .03 |
| ☐ 112 Gerald Wilcox | .30 | .12 | .03 |
| ☐ 113 Reggie Barnes | .50 | .20 | .05 |
| ☐ 114 Michel Raby | .20 | .08 | .02 |
| ☐ 115 Charles Wright | .20 | .08 | .02 |
| ☐ 116 Brett Young | .20 | .08 | .02 |
| ☐ 117 Charles Gordon | .20 | .08 | .02 |
| ☐ 118 Anthony Drawhorn | .30 | .12 | .03 |
| ☐ 119 Daved Benefield | .30 | .12 | .03 |
| ☐ 120 Patrick Burke | .20 | .08 | .02 |
| ☐ 121 Joe Sardo | .20 | .08 | .02 |
| ☐ 122 Dexter Manley | .50 | .20 | .05 |
| ☐ 123 Bruce Beaton | .20 | .08 | .02 |
| ☐ 124 Joe Fuller | .20 | .08 | .02 |
| ☐ 125 Michel Lamy | .20 | .08 | .02 |
| ☐ 126 Terrence Jones | .40 | .16 | .04 |
| ☐ 127 Jeff Croonen | .20 | .08 | .02 |
| ☐ 128 Leonard Johnson | .20 | .08 | .02 |
| ☐ 129 Dan Payne | .20 | .08 | .02 |
| ☐ 130 Carlton Lance | .20 | .08 | .02 |
| ☐ 131 Errol Brown | .20 | .08 | .02 |
| ☐ 132 Wayne Drinkwalter | .20 | .08 | .02 |
| ☐ 133 Malvin Hunter | .20 | .08 | .02 |
| ☐ 134 Maurice Crum | .20 | .08 | .02 |
| ☐ 135 Brooks Findlay | .20 | .08 | .02 |
| ☐ 136 Ray Bernard | .20 | .08 | .02 |
| ☐ 137 Paul Osbaldiston | .30 | .12 | .03 |
| ☐ 138 Mark Dennis | .30 | .12 | .03 |
| ☐ 139 Glenn Kulka | .30 | .12 | .03 |
| ☐ 140 Lee Knight | .20 | .08 | .02 |
| ☐ 141 Mike O'Shea | .30 | .12 | .03 |
| ☐ 142 Paul Bushey | .20 | .08 | .02 |
| ☐ 143 Nick Mazzoli | .20 | .08 | .02 |
| ☐ 144 Earl Winfield | .40 | .16 | .04 |
| ☐ 145 Gary Wilkerson | .20 | .08 | .02 |
| ☐ 146 Jason Riley | .20 | .08 | .02 |
| ☐ 147 Bob MacDonald | .30 | .12 | .03 |
| ☐ 148 Dale Sanderson | .20 | .08 | .02 |
| ☐ 149 Bobby Dawson | .30 | .12 | .03 |
| ☐ 150 Rod Connop | .20 | .08 | .02 |
| ☐ 151 Tony Woods | .30 | .12 | .03 |
| ☐ 152 Dan Murphy | .20 | .08 | .02 |
| ☐ 153 Mike DuMaresq | .20 | .08 | .02 |
| ☐ 154 Allan Boyko | .20 | .08 | .02 |
| ☐ 155 Vaughn Booker | .20 | .08 | .02 |
| ☐ 156 Elfrid Payton | .50 | .20 | .05 |
| ☐ 157 Mike Kerrigan | .20 | .08 | .02 |
| ☐ 158 Charles Anthony | .20 | .08 | .02 |
| ☐ 159 Brent Matich | .20 | .08 | .02 |
| ☐ 160 Craig Hendrickson | .20 | .08 | .02 |
| ☐ 161 Dave Pitcher | .20 | .08 | .02 |
| ☐ 162 Stewart Hill | .40 | .16 | .04 |
| ☐ 163 Terryl Ulmer | .20 | .08 | .02 |
| ☐ 164 Paul Cranmer | .20 | .08 | .02 |
| ☐ 165 Mike Saunders | .40 | .16 | .04 |
| ☐ 166 Doug Flutie | 2.00 | .80 | .20 |

| | | | |
|---|---|---|---|
| ☐ 167 Keilan Matthews | .20 | .08 | .02 |
| ☐ 168 Kip Texada | .20 | .08 | .02 |
| ☐ 169 Johnathan Wilson | .20 | .08 | .02 |
| ☐ 170 Bruce Dickson | .20 | .08 | .02 |
| ☐ 171 Mike Trevathan | .20 | .08 | .02 |
| ☐ 172 Vic Stevenson | .20 | .08 | .02 |
| ☐ 173 Keith Powe | .20 | .08 | .02 |
| ☐ 174 Eddie Taylor | .20 | .08 | .02 |
| ☐ 175 Tim Lorenz | .20 | .08 | .02 |
| ☐ 176 Sean Millington | .20 | .08 | .02 |
| ☐ 177 Ryan Hanson | .20 | .08 | .02 |
| ☐ 178 Ed Berry | .20 | .08 | .02 |
| ☐ 179 Kent Warnock | .30 | .12 | .03 |
| ☐ 180 Spencer McLennan | .20 | .08 | .02 |
| ☐ 181 Brian Walling | .20 | .08 | .02 |
| ☐ 182 Danny McManus | .40 | .16 | .04 |
| ☐ 183 Donovan Wright | .20 | .08 | .02 |
| ☐ 184 Giulio Caravatta | .20 | .08 | .02 |
| ☐ 185 Derek MacCready | .20 | .08 | .02 |
| ☐ 186 Greg Eaglin | .20 | .08 | .02 |
| ☐ 187 Jim Mills | .40 | .16 | .04 |
| ☐ 188 Tom Europe | .20 | .08 | .02 |
| ☐ 189 Zock Allen | .20 | .08 | .02 |
| ☐ 190 Ian Sinclair | .30 | .12 | .03 |
| ☐ 191 O.J. Brigance | .30 | .12 | .03 |
| ☐ 192 Steve Rodehutskors | .30 | .12 | .03 |
| ☐ 193 Lou Cafazzo | .20 | .08 | .02 |
| ☐ 194 Mark Dube | .20 | .08 | .02 |
| ☐ 195 Srecko Zizakovic | .20 | .08 | .02 |
| ☐ 196 Alondra Johnson | .30 | .12 | .03 |
| ☐ 197 Rocco Romano | .20 | .08 | .02 |
| ☐ 198 Raymond Biggs | .20 | .08 | .02 |
| ☐ 199 Frank Marof | .20 | .08 | .02 |
| ☐ 200 Brian Wiggins | .20 | .08 | .02 |
| ☐ 201 Marvin Pope | .20 | .08 | .02 |
| ☐ 202 Gerald Vaughn | .20 | .08 | .02 |
| ☐ 203 Todd Storme | .20 | .08 | .02 |
| ☐ 204 Blair Zerr | .20 | .08 | .02 |
| ☐ 205 Eric Johnson | .30 | .12 | .03 |
| ☐ 206 Mark Pearce | .20 | .08 | .02 |
| ☐ 207 Will Moore | .40 | .16 | .04 |
| ☐ 208 Bruce Plummer | .20 | .08 | .02 |
| ☐ 209 Kari Yli-Renko | .20 | .08 | .02 |
| ☐ 210 Doug Parrish | .20 | .08 | .02 |
| ☐ 211 Warren Hudson | .30 | .12 | .03 |
| ☐ 212 Kevin Whitley | .20 | .08 | .02 |
| ☐ 213 Enis Jackson | .20 | .08 | .02 |
| ☐ 214 Wally Zatylny | .30 | .12 | .03 |
| ☐ 215 Bruce Elliott | .20 | .08 | .02 |
| ☐ 216 Harold Hallman | .30 | .12 | .03 |
| ☐ 217 Glenn Rogers | .20 | .08 | .02 |
| ☐ 218 Manny Hazard | .40 | .16 | .04 |
| ☐ 219 Robert Clark | .30 | .12 | .03 |
| ☐ 220 Doug Flutie UER | 1.50 | .60 | .15 |
| (Three misspelled Tree on back) | | | |

## 1993 JOGO CFL Missing Years

For the second year, JOGO created a "Missing Years" set to provide CFL fans with memories of their favorite players of the '70s, since no CFL cards were produced from 1972 to 1981. These cards were randomly inserted in packs. The 22 cards measure the standard size (2 1/2" by 3 1/2") and feature on their fronts black-and-white player photos with metallic gold borders. Blue, white, and orange stripes border the bottom of the picture. A blue helmet with the JOGO "J" is in the lower left corner, and the player's name appears in red lettering within the lower gold margin. The white back has black and red lettering and carries the player's name, uniform number, position, biography, team name, and career highlights. The cards are numbered on the back with a "B" suffix.

| | MINT | EXC | G-VG |
|---|---|---|---|
| COMPLETE SET (22) | 15.00 | 6.00 | 1.50 |
| COMMON PLAYER (B1-B22) | .50 | .20 | .05 |

| | | | |
|---|---|---|---|
| ☐ B1 Jimmy Edwards | .75 | .30 | .07 |
| ☐ B2 Lou Harris | .75 | .30 | .07 |
| ☐ B3 George Mira | 1.25 | .50 | .12 |
| ☐ B4 Fred Biletnikoff | 3.00 | 1.20 | .30 |
| ☐ B5 Randy Halsall | .50 | .20 | .05 |
| ☐ B6 Don Sweet | .50 | .20 | .05 |
| ☐ B7 Jim Coode | .50 | .20 | .05 |
| ☐ B8 Steve Mazurak | .75 | .30 | .07 |
| ☐ B9 Wayne Allison | .50 | .20 | .05 |
| ☐ B10 Paul Williams | .50 | .20 | .05 |
| ☐ B11 Eric Allen | 1.00 | .40 | .10 |
| ☐ B12 M.L. Harris | .75 | .30 | .07 |
| ☐ B13 James Sykes | 1.50 | .60 | .15 |
| ☐ B14 Chuck Zapiec | .75 | .30 | .07 |
| ☐ B15 George McGowan | .50 | .20 | .05 |
| ☐ B16 Bob Macoritti | .75 | .30 | .07 |
| ☐ B17 Chuck Walton | .50 | .20 | .05 |
| ☐ B18 Willie Armstead | .75 | .30 | .07 |
| ☐ B19 Rocky Long | .50 | .20 | .05 |
| ☐ B20 Gene Mack | .50 | .20 | .05 |
| ☐ B21 David Green | 1.25 | .50 | .12 |
| ☐ B22 Don Warrington | .75 | .30 | .07 |

## 1994 JOGO CFL Caravan

These 22 standard-size (2 1/2" by 3 1/2") cards feature white-bordered color player action shots framed by a black line. Black, white, and red stripes border the bottom of the picture. The player's name appears in red lettering within the bottom white margin; his team helmet rests at the lower left. The white back has black and red lettering and carries the player's name, uniform number, position, biography, nationality, and team name. Below is the show schedule that lists the North American cities and dates for "Caravan 1994." The cards are numbered on the back as "X of 22." The cards are organized as follows: Ottawa Rough Riders (1-4), Toronto Argonauts (5-6), Hamilton Tiger-Cats (7-11), Sacramento Surge (12), Winnipeg Blue Bombers (13-14), Baltimore Colts (15), Shreveport (16), Saskatchewan Roughriders (17), Calgary Stampeders (18-19), Edmonton Eskimos (20-21), and British Columbia Lions (22).

| | MINT | EXC | G-VG |
|---|---|---|---|
| COMPLETE SET (22) | 15.00 | 6.00 | 1.50 |
| COMMON PLAYER (1-22) | .60 | .24 | .06 |

| | | | |
|---|---|---|---|
| ☐ 1 Glenn Kulka | .75 | .30 | .07 |
| ☐ 2 Jock Climie | 1.00 | .40 | .10 |
| ☐ 3 Danny Barrett | 1.50 | .60 | .15 |
| ☐ 4 Stephen Jones | 1.00 | .40 | .10 |
| ☐ 5 Mike Clemons | 2.00 | .80 | .20 |
| ☐ 6 Pierre Vercheval | .75 | .30 | .07 |
| ☐ 7 Ken Evraire | .75 | .30 | .07 |
| ☐ 8 Brett Williams UER | .75 | .30 | .07 |
| (Misspelled Willians on card front) | | | |
| ☐ 9 Wally Zatylny | .75 | .30 | .07 |
| ☐ 10 Mike O'Shea | .75 | .30 | .07 |
| ☐ 11 Earl Winfield | 1.00 | .40 | .10 |
| ☐ 12 Mike Oliphant | 1.00 | .40 | .10 |
| ☐ 13 Matt Dunigan | 2.00 | .80 | .20 |
| ☐ 14 Chris Walby | 1.00 | .40 | .10 |
| ☐ 15 Tracy Ham | 1.50 | .60 | .15 |
| ☐ 16 Darrell K. Smith | 1.00 | .40 | .10 |
| ☐ 17 Glen Suitor | .60 | .24 | .06 |
| ☐ 18 Mark McLoughlin | .60 | .24 | .06 |
| ☐ 19 Bruce Covernton | .75 | .30 | .07 |
| ☐ 20 Willie Pless | 1.00 | .40 | .10 |
| ☐ 21 Henry Williams | 2.00 | .80 | .20 |
| ☐ 22 Lui Passaglia | .75 | .30 | .07 |

# 1989 KFC Calgary

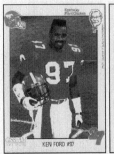

KEN FORD #97

The 1989 KFC Calgary Stampeders set contains 24 cards measuring approximately 2 7/16" by 3 5/16". The fronts have color portrait photos bordered in white; the vertically oriented backs have detailed profiles and statistics. The cards come as perforated strips of four player cards and one discount card for 2.00 off any 1989 Stampeder home game ticket purchase. The cards are ordered on the strips by uniform number such that by looking at the reverse of each strip, the cards are in almost perfect numerical order. The only exception is that card 9 comes before 8.

|  | MINT | EXC | G-VG |
|---|---|---|---|
| COMPLETE SET (24) | 9.00 | 3.75 | .90 |
| COMMON PLAYER | .40 | .16 | .04 |
| ☐ 3 David McCrary | .40 | .16 | .04 |
| ☐ 4 Brent Matich | .40 | .16 | .04 |
| ☐ 8 Danny Barrett | 1.25 | .50 | .12 |
| ☐ 9 Terrence Jones | 1.25 | .50 | .12 |
| ☐ 12 Tim Petros | .75 | .30 | .07 |
| ☐ 13 Mark McLoughlin | .40 | .16 | .04 |
| ☐ 15 Ron Hopkins | .50 | .20 | .05 |
| ☐ 20 Chris Major | 1.00 | .40 | .10 |
| ☐ 24 Greg Peterson | .40 | .16 | .04 |
| ☐ 25 Shawn Faulkner | .40 | .16 | .04 |
| ☐ 32 Darcy Kopp | .40 | .16 | .04 |
| ☐ 34 Andy McVey | .40 | .16 | .04 |
| ☐ 39 Doug(Tank) Landry | 1.00 | .40 | .10 |
| ☐ 59 Leo Blanchard | .40 | .16 | .04 |
| ☐ 61 Tom Spoletini | .40 | .16 | .04 |
| ☐ 65 Mike Palumbo | .40 | .16 | .04 |
| ☐ 66 Dan Ferrone | .50 | .20 | .05 |
| ☐ 74 Mitchell Price | .50 | .20 | .05 |
| ☐ 76 Marshall Toner | .40 | .16 | .04 |
| ☐ 84 Eugene Belliveau | .50 | .20 | .05 |
| ☐ 85 Brock Smith | .40 | .16 | .04 |
| ☐ 89 Larry Willis | .75 | .30 | .07 |
| ☐ 93 Kent Warnock | .50 | .20 | .05 |
| ☐ 97 Ken Ford | .40 | .16 | .04 |

# 1990 KFC Calgary

The 1990 KFC Calgary Stampeders set contains 24 cards measuring approximately 2 7/16" by 3 5/16". The fronts have color portrait photos bordered in white. The cards come as perforated strips of four player cards and one discount card for 2.00 off any 1990 Stampeder home game ticket purchase. The cards are ordered alphabetically in the list below.

|  | MINT | EXC | G-VG |
|---|---|---|---|
| COMPLETE SET (24) | 10.00 | 4.00 | 1.00 |
| COMMON PLAYER (1-24) | .50 | .20 | .05 |
| ☐ 1 Walter Ballard | .50 | .20 | .05 |
| ☐ 2 Danny Barrett | 1.25 | .50 | .12 |
| ☐ 3 Eddie Brown | .50 | .20 | .05 |
| ☐ 4 Joe Clausi | .50 | .20 | .05 |
| ☐ 5 Lloyd Fairbanks | .75 | .30 | .07 |
| ☐ 6 Matt Finlay | .50 | .20 | .05 |
| ☐ 7 Ken Ford | .50 | .20 | .05 |
| ☐ 8 Ron Hopkins | .75 | .30 | .07 |
| ☐ 9 Keyvan Jenkins | 1.25 | .50 | .12 |
| ☐ 10 Will Johnson | .75 | .30 | .07 |
| ☐ 11 Terrence Jones | 1.25 | .50 | .12 |
| ☐ 12 David McCrary | .50 | .20 | .05 |
| ☐ 13 Mark McLoughlin | .50 | .20 | .05 |
| ☐ 14 Andy McVey | .50 | .20 | .05 |
| ☐ 15 Brent Matich | .50 | .20 | .05 |
| ☐ 16 Mike Palumbo | .50 | .20 | .05 |
| ☐ 17 Greg Peterson | .50 | .20 | .05 |

| | | | |
|---|---|---|---|
| ☐ 18 Tim Petros | .75 | .30 | .07 |
| ☐ 19 Mitchell Price | .60 | .24 | .06 |
| ☐ 20 Brock Smith | .50 | .20 | .05 |
| ☐ 21 Tom Spoletini | .50 | .20 | .05 |
| ☐ 22 Junior Thurman | 1.25 | .50 | .12 |
| ☐ 23 Marshall Toner | .50 | .20 | .05 |
| ☐ 24 Kent Warnock | .60 | .24 | .06 |

# 1984 McDonald's Ottawa

This 12-card full-color set was issued in panels of three over a four-week period as a promotion of McDonald's and radio station CFRA 58 AM. It was reported that 210,000 panels were given away at McDonald's. Cards were produced in conjunction with JOGO Novelties. The cards can be separated as they are perforated. The cards are unnumbered although the player's uniform number is given on the back of the card. The numbering below refers to the week (of the promotion) during which the panel was distributed. Photos were taken by F. Scott Grant, who is credited on the fronts of the cards. The cards measure approximately 2 1/2" by 3 1/2".

|  | MINT | EXC | G-VG |
|---|---|---|---|
| COMPLETE SET (4) | 9.00 | 3.75 | .90 |
| COMMON PANEL (1-4) | 2.50 | 1.00 | .25 |
| ☐ 1 Ken Miller | 2.50 | 1.00 | .25 |
| Rudy Phillips |  |  |  |
| Jim Reid |  |  |  |
| ☐ 2 Gary Dulin | 2.50 | 1.00 | .25 |
| Greg Marshall |  |  |  |
| Junior Robinson |  |  |  |
| ☐ 3 Kevin Powell | 2.50 | 1.00 | .25 |
| Tyron Gray |  |  |  |
| Skip Walker |  |  |  |
| ☐ 4 Rick Sowieta | 3.00 | 1.20 | .30 |
| Bruce Walker |  |  |  |
| J.C. Watts |  |  |  |

# 1983 Mohawk B.C. Lions

This 24-card set of the CFL's British Columbia Lions was only issued in British Columbia by Mohawk Oil as a premium at its gas stations. Posed color player's photos appear on a white card face. The cards measure approximately 2 1/2" by 3 5/8". A thin black line forms a box at the bottom that contains the player's name, jersey number, position, team logo, and sponsor logo. Each card has a facsimile autograph of the player on the front. The backs have biographical information and career notes printed in blue. The cards are unnumbered and checklisted below in alphabetical order.

|  | MINT | EXC | G-VG |
|---|---|---|---|
| COMPLETE SET (24) | 15.00 | 6.00 | 1.50 |
| COMMON PLAYER (1-24) | .60 | .24 | .06 |

| | | | | |
|---|---|---|---|---|
| ☐ 1 John Blain | | .60 | .24 | .06 |
| ☐ 2 Tim Cowan | | .60 | .24 | .06 |
| ☐ 3 Larry Crawford | | .75 | .30 | .07 |
| ☐ 4 Tyrone Crews | | .60 | .24 | .06 |
| ☐ 5 James Curry | | 1.00 | .40 | .10 |
| ☐ 6 Roy Dewalt | | 1.50 | .60 | .15 |
| ☐ 7 Mervyn Fernandez | | 3.00 | 1.20 | .30 |
| ☐ 8 Sammy Greene | | .60 | .24 | .06 |
| ☐ 9 Jo Jo Heath | | .60 | .24 | .06 |
| ☐ 10 Nick Hebeler | | .60 | .24 | .06 |
| ☐ 11 Glen Jackson | | .60 | .24 | .06 |
| ☐ 12 Tim Kearse | | .60 | .24 | .06 |
| ☐ 13 Rick Klassen | | .75 | .30 | .07 |
| ☐ 14 Kevin Konar | | .75 | .30 | .07 |
| ☐ 15 Glenn Leonhard | | .60 | .24 | .06 |
| ☐ 16 Nelson Martin | | .60 | .24 | .06 |
| ☐ 17 Mack Moore | | .60 | .24 | .06 |
| ☐ 18 John Pankratz | | .60 | .24 | .06 |
| ☐ 19 Joe Paopao | | 1.25 | .50 | .12 |
| ☐ 20 Lui Passaglia | | 1.50 | .60 | .15 |
| ☐ 21 Don Taylor | | .60 | .24 | .06 |
| ☐ 22 Mike Washburn | | .60 | .24 | .06 |
| ☐ 23 John Henry White | | .60 | .24 | .06 |
| ☐ 24 Al Wilson | | .60 | .24 | .06 |

## 1984 Mohawk B.C. Lions

This 32-card set was co-sponsored by Mohawk and Old Dutch, and only issued in British Columbia by Mohawk Oil as a premium at its gas stations. The set features members of the British Columbia Lions of the CFL. The cards measure approximately 2 1/2" by 3 5/8". The front features a posed color player photo, with white borders and a facsimile autograph across the picture. Player information and sponsors' logos appear in a rectangle below the picture. In blue print on white, the back has biography and player profile. The cards are unnumbered and checklisted below in alphabetical order.

|  | MINT | EXC | G-VG |
|---|---|---|---|
| COMPLETE SET (32) | 15.00 | 6.00 | 1.50 |
| COMMON PLAYER (1-32) | .50 | .20 | .05 |

| | | | | |
|---|---|---|---|---|
| ☐ 1 Ned Armour | | .50 | .20 | .05 |
| ☐ 2 John Blain | | .50 | .20 | .05 |
| ☐ 3 Melvin Byrd | | .75 | .30 | .07 |
| ☐ 4 Darnell Clash | | 1.00 | .40 | .10 |
| ☐ 5 Tim Cowan | | .50 | .20 | .05 |
| ☐ 6 Larry Crawford | | .75 | .30 | .07 |
| ☐ 7 Tyrone Crews | | .50 | .20 | .05 |
| ☐ 8 Roy DeWalt | | 1.50 | .60 | .15 |
| ☐ 9 Mervyn Fernandez | | 3.00 | 1.20 | .30 |
| ☐ 10 Bernie Glier | | .50 | .20 | .05 |
| ☐ 11 Dennis Guevin | | .50 | .20 | .05 |
| ☐ 12 Nick Hebeler | | .50 | .20 | .05 |
| ☐ 13 Bryan Illerbrun | | .50 | .20 | .05 |
| ☐ 14 Glen Jackson | | .50 | .20 | .05 |
| ☐ 15 Andre Jones | | .50 | .20 | .05 |
| ☐ 16 Rick Klassen | | .75 | .30 | .07 |
| ☐ 17 Kevin Konar | | .75 | .30 | .07 |
| ☐ 18 Glenn Leonhard | | .50 | .20 | .05 |
| ☐ 19 Nelson Martin | | .50 | .20 | .05 |
| ☐ 20 Billy McBride | | .50 | .20 | .05 |
| ☐ 21 Mack Moore | | .50 | .20 | .05 |
| ☐ 22 John Pankratz | | .50 | .20 | .05 |
| ☐ 23 James Parker | | 1.50 | .60 | .15 |
| ☐ 24 Lui Passaglia | | 1.50 | .60 | .15 |
| ☐ 25 Ryan Potter | | .50 | .20 | .05 |
| ☐ 26 Gerald Roper | | .50 | .20 | .05 |
| ☐ 27 Jim Sandusky | | 2.00 | .80 | .20 |
| ☐ 28 Don Taylor | | .50 | .20 | .05 |
| ☐ 29 John Henry White | | .50 | .20 | .05 |

| | | | | |
|---|---|---|---|---|
| ☐ 30 Al Wilson | | .50 | .20 | .05 |
| ☐ 31 Team Card | | 1.00 | .40 | .10 |
| ☐ 32 Checklist | | 1.00 | .40 | .10 |

## 1985 Mohawk B.C. Lions

This 32-card set was co-sponsored by Mohawk and Old Dutch, and only issued in British Columbia by Mohawk Oil as a premium at its gas stations. Measuring approximately 2 1/2" by 3 5/8", the card fronts feature posed, color player photos with white borders. A facsimile autograph is inscribed across the picture. At the bottom, a white box that is outlined by a thin black line carries the player's name, jersey number, position, and sponsor logos. In blue print, the backs carry biographical information and a player profile. The cards are unnumbered and checklisted below in alphabetical order.

|  | MINT | EXC | G-VG |
|---|---|---|---|
| COMPLETE SET (32) | 15.00 | 6.00 | 1.50 |
| COMMON PLAYER (1-32) | .50 | .20 | .05 |

| | | | | |
|---|---|---|---|---|
| ☐ 1 John Blain | | .50 | .20 | .05 |
| ☐ 2 Jamie Buis | | .50 | .20 | .05 |
| ☐ 3 Melvin Byrd | | .75 | .30 | .07 |
| ☐ 4 Darnell Clash | | 1.00 | .40 | .10 |
| ☐ 5 Tim Cowan | | .75 | .30 | .07 |
| ☐ 6 Tyrone Crews | | .50 | .20 | .05 |
| ☐ 7 Mark DeBrueys | | .50 | .20 | .05 |
| ☐ 8 Roy Dewalt | | 1.50 | .60 | .15 |
| ☐ 9 Mervyn Fernandez | | 3.00 | 1.20 | .30 |
| ☐ 10 Bernie Glier | | .50 | .20 | .05 |
| ☐ 11 Keith Gooch | | .50 | .20 | .05 |
| ☐ 12 Dennis Guevin | | .50 | .20 | .05 |
| ☐ 13 Nick Hebeler | | .50 | .20 | .05 |
| ☐ 14 Bryan Illerbrun | | .50 | .20 | .05 |
| ☐ 15 Glen Jackson | | .50 | .20 | .05 |
| ☐ 16 Keyvan Jenkins | | 1.00 | .40 | .10 |
| ☐ 17 Andre Jones | | .50 | .20 | .05 |
| ☐ 18 Rick Klassen | | .75 | .30 | .07 |
| ☐ 19 Kevin Konar | | .75 | .30 | .07 |
| ☐ 20 Glenn Leonhard | | .50 | .20 | .05 |
| ☐ 21 Nelson Martin | | .50 | .20 | .05 |
| ☐ 22 John Pankratz | | .50 | .20 | .05 |
| ☐ 23 James Parker | | 1.50 | .60 | .15 |
| ☐ 24 Lui Passaglia | | 1.50 | .60 | .15 |
| ☐ 25 Ryan Potter | | .50 | .20 | .05 |
| ☐ 26 Ron Robinson | | .75 | .30 | .07 |
| ☐ 27 Gerald Roper | | .50 | .20 | .05 |
| ☐ 28 Jim Sandusky | | 2.00 | .80 | .20 |
| ☐ 29 John Henry White | | .50 | .20 | .05 |
| ☐ 30 Al Wilson | | .50 | .20 | .05 |
| ☐ 31 Team Photo | | 1.00 | .40 | .10 |
| ☐ 32 Checklist | | 1.00 | .40 | .10 |

## 1963 Nalley's Coins

This 160-coin set is difficult to complete due to the fact that within every team grouping, the last ten coins are much tougher to find. The back of the coin is not hard plastic, but is see-through. The coins can be found with sponsors Nalley's Potato Chips, Hunter's Potato Chips, Krun-Chee Potato Chips, and Humpty Dumpty Potato Chips. The set numbering is in team order, i.e., Toronto Argonauts (1-20), Ottawa Rough Riders (21-40), Hamilton Tiger-Cats (41-60), Montreal Alouettes (61-80), Winnipeg Blue Bombers (81-100), Edmonton Eskimos (101-120), Calgary Stampeders (121-140), and British Columbia Lions (141-160). The coins measure approximately 1 3/8" in diameter. Shields to hold the coins were also issued; these shields are also very collectible and are listed at the end of the list below, with the prefix S. The shields are not included in the complete set price.

| | NRMT | VG-E | GOOD |
|---|---|---|---|
| COMPLETE SET (160) | 2500.00 | 1100.00 | 275.00 |
| COMMON PLAYER (1-160) | 4.00 | 1.60 | .40 |
| ☐ 1 Jackie Parker | 20.00 | 8.00 | 2.00 |
| ☐ 2 Dick Shatto | 8.00 | 3.25 | .80 |
| ☐ 3 Dave Mann | 5.00 | 2.00 | .50 |
| ☐ 4 Danny Nykoluk | 4.00 | 1.60 | .40 |
| ☐ 5 Billy Shipp | 4.00 | 1.60 | .40 |
| ☐ 6 Doug McNichol | 4.00 | 1.60 | .40 |
| ☐ 7 Jim Rountree | 4.00 | 1.60 | .40 |
| ☐ 8 Art Johnson | 4.00 | 1.60 | .40 |
| ☐ 9 Walt Radzick | 4.00 | 1.60 | .40 |
| ☐ 10 Jim Andreotti | 4.00 | 1.60 | .40 |
| ☐ 11 Gerry Philip | 20.00 | 8.00 | 2.00 |
| ☐ 12 Lynn Bottoms | 20.00 | 8.00 | 2.00 |
| ☐ 13 Ron Morris SP | 90.00 | 36.00 | 9.00 |
| ☐ 14 Nobby Wirkowski CO | 20.00 | 8.00 | 2.00 |
| ☐ 15 John Wydareny | 20.00 | 8.00 | 2.00 |
| ☐ 16 Gerry Wilson | 20.00 | 8.00 | 2.00 |
| ☐ 17 Gerry Patrick SP | 40.00 | 16.00 | 4.00 |
| ☐ 18 Aubrey Linne | 20.00 | 8.00 | 2.00 |
| ☐ 19 Norm Stoneburgh | 20.00 | 8.00 | 2.00 |
| ☐ 20 Ken Beck | 20.00 | 8.00 | 2.00 |
| ☐ 21 Russ Jackson | 15.00 | 6.00 | 1.50 |
| ☐ 22 Kaye Vaughan | 8.00 | 3.25 | .80 |
| ☐ 23 Dave Thelen | 8.00 | 3.25 | .80 |
| ☐ 24 Ron Stewart | 8.00 | 3.25 | .80 |
| ☐ 25 Moe Racine | 4.00 | 1.60 | .40 |
| ☐ 26 Jim Conroy | 4.00 | 1.60 | .40 |
| ☐ 27 Joe Poirier | 4.00 | 1.60 | .40 |
| ☐ 28 Mel Seminko | 4.00 | 1.60 | .40 |
| ☐ 29 Whit Tucker | 8.00 | 3.25 | .80 |
| ☐ 30 Ernie White | 4.00 | 1.60 | .40 |
| ☐ 31 Frank Clair CO | 20.00 | 8.00 | 2.00 |
| ☐ 32 Marv Bevan | 20.00 | 8.00 | 2.00 |
| ☐ 33 Jerry Selinger | 20.00 | 8.00 | 2.00 |
| ☐ 34 Jim Cain | 20.00 | 8.00 | 2.00 |
| ☐ 35 Mike Snodgrass | 20.00 | 8.00 | 2.00 |
| ☐ 36 Ted Smale | 20.00 | 8.00 | 2.00 |
| ☐ 37 Billy Joe Booth | 20.00 | 8.00 | 2.00 |
| ☐ 38 Len Chandler | 20.00 | 8.00 | 2.00 |
| ☐ 39 Rick Black | 20.00 | 8.00 | 2.00 |
| ☐ 40 Allen Schau | 20.00 | 8.00 | 2.00 |
| ☐ 41 Bernie Faloney | 15.00 | 6.00 | 1.50 |
| ☐ 42 Bobby Kuntz | 4.00 | 1.60 | .40 |
| ☐ 43 Joe Zuger | 4.00 | 1.60 | .40 |
| ☐ 44 Hal Patterson | 12.00 | 5.00 | 1.20 |
| ☐ 45 Bronko Nagurski | 10.00 | 4.00 | 1.00 |
| ☐ 46 Zeno Karcz | 4.00 | 1.60 | .40 |
| ☐ 47 Hardiman Cureton | 4.00 | 1.60 | .40 |
| ☐ 48 John Barrow | 8.00 | 3.25 | .80 |
| ☐ 49 Tommy Grant | 4.00 | 1.60 | .40 |
| ☐ 50 Garney Henley | 8.00 | 3.25 | .80 |
| ☐ 51 Dick Easterly | 20.00 | 8.00 | 2.00 |
| ☐ 52 Frank Cosentino | 20.00 | 8.00 | 2.00 |
| ☐ 53 Geno DeNobile | 20.00 | 8.00 | 2.00 |
| ☐ 54 Ralph Goldston | 20.00 | 8.00 | 2.00 |
| ☐ 55 Chet Miksza | 20.00 | 8.00 | 2.00 |
| ☐ 56 Bob Minihane | 20.00 | 8.00 | 2.00 |
| ☐ 57 Don Sutherin | 40.00 | 16.00 | 4.00 |
| ☐ 58 Ralph Sazio CO | 20.00 | 8.00 | 2.00 |
| ☐ 59 Dave Viti SP | 30.00 | 12.00 | 3.00 |
| ☐ 60 Angelo Mosca SP | 75.00 | 30.00 | 7.50 |
| ☐ 61 Sandy Stephens | 8.00 | 3.25 | .80 |
| ☐ 62 George Dixon | 8.00 | 3.25 | .80 |
| ☐ 63 Don Clark | 4.00 | 1.60 | .40 |
| ☐ 64 Don Paquette | 4.00 | 1.60 | .40 |
| ☐ 65 Billy Wayte | 4.00 | 1.60 | .40 |
| ☐ 66 Ed Nickla | 4.00 | 1.60 | .40 |
| ☐ 67 Marv Luster | 8.00 | 3.25 | .80 |
| ☐ 68 Joe Stracina | 4.00 | 1.60 | .40 |
| ☐ 69 Bobby Jack Oliver | 4.00 | 1.60 | .40 |
| ☐ 70 Ted Elsby | 4.00 | 1.60 | .40 |
| ☐ 71 Jim Trimble CO | 20.00 | 8.00 | 2.00 |
| ☐ 72 Bob Leblanc | 20.00 | 8.00 | 2.00 |
| ☐ 73 Dick Schnell | 20.00 | 8.00 | 2.00 |
| ☐ 74 Milt Crain | 20.00 | 8.00 | 2.00 |
| ☐ 75 Dick Dalatri | 20.00 | 8.00 | 2.00 |
| ☐ 76 Billy Roy | 20.00 | 8.00 | 2.00 |
| ☐ 77 Dave Hoppmann | 20.00 | 8.00 | 2.00 |
| ☐ 78 Billy Ray Locklin | 20.00 | 8.00 | 2.00 |
| ☐ 79 Ed Learn SP | 100.00 | 40.00 | 10.00 |
| ☐ 80 Meco Poliziani SP | 40.00 | 16.00 | 4.00 |
| ☐ 81 Leo Lewis | 8.00 | 3.25 | .80 |
| ☐ 82 Kenny Ploen | 8.00 | 3.25 | .80 |
| ☐ 83 Steve Patrick | 4.00 | 1.60 | .40 |
| ☐ 84 Farrell Funston | 4.00 | 1.60 | .40 |
| ☐ 85 Charlie Shepard | 4.00 | 1.60 | .40 |
| ☐ 86 Ronnie Latourelle | 4.00 | 1.60 | .40 |
| ☐ 87 Gord Rowland | 4.00 | 1.60 | .40 |
| ☐ 88 Frank Rigney | 5.00 | 2.00 | .50 |
| ☐ 89 Cornel Piper | 4.00 | 1.60 | .40 |
| ☐ 90 Ernie Pitts | 4.00 | 1.60 | .40 |
| ☐ 91 Roger Hagberg | 30.00 | 12.00 | 3.00 |
| ☐ 92 Herb Gray | 50.00 | 20.00 | 5.00 |
| ☐ 93 Jack Delveaux | 20.00 | 8.00 | 2.00 |
| ☐ 94 Roger Savoie | 20.00 | 8.00 | 2.00 |
| ☐ 95 Nick Miller | 20.00 | 8.00 | 2.00 |
| ☐ 96 Norm Rauhaus | 20.00 | 8.00 | 2.00 |
| ☐ 97 Cec Luining | 20.00 | 8.00 | 2.00 |
| ☐ 98 Hal Ledyard | 20.00 | 8.00 | 2.00 |
| ☐ 99 Neil Thomas | 20.00 | 8.00 | 2.00 |
| ☐ 100 Bud Grant CO | 75.00 | 30.00 | 7.50 |
| ☐ 101 Eagle Keys CO | 8.00 | 3.25 | .80 |
| ☐ 102 Mike Wicklum | 4.00 | 1.60 | .40 |
| ☐ 103 Bill Mitchell | 4.00 | 1.60 | .40 |
| ☐ 104 Mike Lashuk | 4.00 | 1.60 | .40 |
| ☐ 105 Tommy Joe Coffey | 8.00 | 3.25 | .80 |
| ☐ 106 Zeke Smith | 4.00 | 1.60 | .40 |
| ☐ 107 Joe Hernandez | 4.00 | 1.60 | .40 |
| ☐ 108 Johnny Bright | 8.00 | 3.25 | .80 |
| ☐ 109 Don Getty | 8.00 | 3.25 | .80 |
| ☐ 110 Nat Dye | 4.00 | 1.60 | .40 |
| ☐ 111 James Earl Wright | 20.00 | 8.00 | 2.00 |
| ☐ 112 Mike Volcan SP | 30.00 | 12.00 | 3.00 |
| ☐ 113 Jon Rechner | 20.00 | 8.00 | 2.00 |
| ☐ 114 Len Vella | 20.00 | 8.00 | 2.00 |
| ☐ 115 Ted Frechette | 20.00 | 8.00 | 2.00 |
| ☐ 116 Larry Fleisher | 20.00 | 8.00 | 2.00 |
| ☐ 117 Oscar Kruger | 20.00 | 8.00 | 2.00 |
| ☐ 118 Ken Peterson | 20.00 | 8.00 | 2.00 |
| ☐ 119 Bobby Walden | 30.00 | 12.00 | 3.00 |
| ☐ 120 Mickey Ording | 20.00 | 8.00 | 2.00 |
| ☐ 121 Pete Manning | 4.00 | 1.60 | .40 |
| ☐ 122 Harvey Wylie | 4.00 | 1.60 | .40 |
| ☐ 123 Tony Pajaczkowski | 8.00 | 3.25 | .80 |
| ☐ 124 Wayne Harris | 10.00 | 4.00 | 1.00 |
| ☐ 125 Earl Lunsford | 8.00 | 3.25 | .80 |
| ☐ 126 Don Luzzi | 4.00 | 1.60 | .40 |
| ☐ 127 Ed Buckanan | 4.00 | 1.60 | .40 |
| ☐ 128 Lovell Coleman | 5.00 | 2.00 | .50 |
| ☐ 129 Hal Krebs | 4.00 | 1.60 | .40 |
| ☐ 130 Eagle Day | 8.00 | 3.25 | .80 |
| ☐ 131 Bobby Dobbs CO | 20.00 | 8.00 | 2.00 |
| ☐ 132 George Hansen | 20.00 | 8.00 | 2.00 |
| ☐ 133 Roy Jokanovich SP | 60.00 | 24.00 | 6.00 |
| ☐ 134 Jerry Keeling | 40.00 | 16.00 | 4.00 |
| ☐ 135 Larry Anderson | 20.00 | 8.00 | 2.00 |
| ☐ 136 Bill Crawford | 20.00 | 8.00 | 2.00 |
| ☐ 137 Ron Albright | 20.00 | 8.00 | 2.00 |
| ☐ 138 Bill Britton | 20.00 | 8.00 | 2.00 |
| ☐ 139 Jim Dillard | 20.00 | 8.00 | 2.00 |
| ☐ 140 Jim Furlong | 20.00 | 8.00 | 2.00 |
| ☐ 141 Dave Skrien CO | 6.00 | 2.40 | .60 |
| ☐ 142 Willie Fleming | 10.00 | 4.00 | 1.00 |
| ☐ 143 Nub Beamer | 4.00 | 1.60 | .40 |
| ☐ 144 Norm Fieldgate | 8.00 | 3.25 | .80 |
| ☐ 145 Joe Kapp | 40.00 | 16.00 | 4.00 |
| ☐ 146 Tom Hinton | 8.00 | 3.25 | .80 |
| ☐ 147 Pat Claridge | 4.00 | 1.60 | .40 |
| ☐ 148 Bill Munsey | 4.00 | 1.60 | .40 |
| ☐ 149 Mike Martin | 4.00 | 1.60 | .40 |
| ☐ 150 Tom Brown | 8.00 | 3.25 | .80 |
| ☐ 151 Ian Hagemoen | 20.00 | 8.00 | 2.00 |
| ☐ 152 Jim Carphin | 20.00 | 8.00 | 2.00 |
| ☐ 153 By Bailey | 40.00 | 16.00 | 4.00 |
| ☐ 154 Steve Cotter | 20.00 | 8.00 | 2.00 |
| ☐ 155 Mike Cacic | 20.00 | 8.00 | 2.00 |
| ☐ 156 Neil Beaumont | 20.00 | 8.00 | 2.00 |
| ☐ 157 Lonnie Dennis | 20.00 | 8.00 | 2.00 |
| ☐ 158 Barney Therrien | 20.00 | 8.00 | 2.00 |
| ☐ 159 Sonny Homer | 20.00 | 8.00 | 2.00 |
| ☐ 160 Walt Bilicki | 20.00 | 8.00 | 2.00 |
| ☐ S1 Toronto Shield | 50.00 | 20.00 | 5.00 |
| ☐ S2 Ottawa Shield | 50.00 | 20.00 | 5.00 |
| ☐ S3 Hamilton Shield | 50.00 | 20.00 | 5.00 |
| ☐ S4 Montreal Shield | 50.00 | 20.00 | 5.00 |
| ☐ S5 Winnipeg Shield | 50.00 | 20.00 | 5.00 |
| ☐ S6 Edmonton Shield | 50.00 | 20.00 | 5.00 |
| ☐ S7 Calgary Shield | 50.00 | 20.00 | 5.00 |
| ☐ S8 British Columbia Shield | 50.00 | 20.00 | 5.00 |

# 1964 Nalley's Coins

This 100-coin set is very similar to the set from the previous year except that there are no real distribution scarcities this year. The backs of the coins are plastic, not see-through, with no specific information

about the player as in the previous year. The coins were sponsored by Nalley's Potato Chips. The set numbering is in team order, i.e., British Columbia Lions (1-20), Calgary Stampeders (21-40), Edmonton Eskimos (41-60), Saskatchewan Roughriders (61-80), and Winnipeg Blue Bombers (81-100). The coins measure approximately 1 3/8" in diameter. Shields to hold the coins were also issued; these shields are also very collectible and are listed at the end of the list below with the prefix S. The shields are not included in the complete set price.

| | NRMT | VG-E | GOOD |
|---|---|---|---|
| COMPLETE SET (100) | 450.00 | 180.00 | 45.00 |
| COMMON PLAYER (1-100) | 4.00 | 1.60 | .40 |
| ☐ 1 Joe Kapp | 30.00 | 12.00 | 3.00 |
| ☐ 2 Willie Fleming | 10.00 | 4.00 | 1.00 |
| ☐ 3 Norm Fieldgate | 8.00 | 3.25 | .80 |
| ☐ 4 Bill Murray | 4.00 | 1.60 | .40 |
| ☐ 5 Tom Brown | 8.00 | 3.25 | .80 |
| ☐ 6 Neil Beaumont | 4.00 | 1.60 | .40 |
| ☐ 7 Sonny Homer | 4.00 | 1.60 | .40 |
| ☐ 8 Lonnie Dennis | 4.00 | 1.60 | .40 |
| ☐ 9 Dave Skrien | 4.00 | 1.60 | .40 |
| ☐ 10 Dick Fouts CO | 4.00 | 1.60 | .40 |
| ☐ 11 Paul Seale | 4.00 | 1.60 | .40 |
| ☐ 12 Peter Kempf | 4.00 | 1.60 | .40 |
| ☐ 13 Steve Shafer | 4.00 | 1.60 | .40 |
| ☐ 14 Tom Hinton | 8.00 | 3.25 | .80 |
| ☐ 15 Pat Claridge | 4.00 | 1.60 | .40 |
| ☐ 16 By Bailey | 8.00 | 3.25 | .80 |
| ☐ 17 Nub Beamer | 4.00 | 1.60 | .40 |
| ☐ 18 Steve Cotter | 4.00 | 1.60 | .40 |
| ☐ 19 Mike Cacic | 4.00 | 1.60 | .40 |
| ☐ 20 Mike Martin | 4.00 | 1.60 | .40 |
| ☐ 21 Eagle Day | 8.00 | 3.25 | .80 |
| ☐ 22 Jim Dillard | 4.00 | 1.60 | .40 |
| ☐ 23 Pete Murray | 4.00 | 1.60 | .40 |
| ☐ 24 Tony Pajaczkowski | 8.00 | 3.25 | .80 |
| ☐ 25 Don Luzzi | 4.00 | 1.60 | .40 |
| ☐ 26 Wayne Harris | 10.00 | 4.00 | 1.00 |
| ☐ 27 Harvey Wylie | 4.00 | 1.60 | .40 |
| ☐ 28 Bill Crawford | 4.00 | 1.60 | .40 |
| ☐ 29 Jim Furlong | 4.00 | 1.60 | .40 |
| ☐ 30 Lovell Coleman | 5.00 | 2.00 | .50 |
| ☐ 31 Pat Haines | 4.00 | 1.60 | .40 |
| ☐ 32 Bob Taylor | 4.00 | 1.60 | .40 |
| ☐ 33 Ernie Danjean | 4.00 | 1.60 | .40 |
| ☐ 34 Jerry Keeling | 8.00 | 3.25 | .80 |
| ☐ 35 Larry Robinson | 4.00 | 1.60 | .40 |
| ☐ 36 George Hansen | 4.00 | 1.60 | .40 |
| ☐ 37 Ron Albright | 4.00 | 1.60 | .40 |
| ☐ 38 Larry Anderson | 4.00 | 1.60 | .40 |
| ☐ 39 Bill Miller | 4.00 | 1.60 | .40 |
| ☐ 40 Bill Britton | 4.00 | 1.60 | .40 |
| ☐ 41 Lynn Amadee | 8.00 | 3.25 | .80 |
| ☐ 42 Mike Lashuk | 4.00 | 1.60 | .40 |
| ☐ 43 Tommy Joe Coffey | 8.00 | 3.25 | .80 |
| ☐ 44 Junior Hawthorne | 4.00 | 1.60 | .40 |
| ☐ 45 Nat Dye | 4.00 | 1.60 | .40 |
| ☐ 46 Al Ecuyer | 4.00 | 1.60 | .40 |
| ☐ 47 Howie Schumm | 4.00 | 1.60 | .40 |
| ☐ 48 Zeke Smith | 4.00 | 1.60 | .40 |
| ☐ 49 Mike Wicklum | 4.00 | 1.60 | .40 |
| ☐ 50 Mike Volcan | 4.00 | 1.60 | .40 |
| ☐ 51 E.A. Sims | 4.00 | 1.60 | .40 |
| ☐ 52 Bill Mitchell | 4.00 | 1.60 | .40 |
| ☐ 53 Ken Reed | 4.00 | 1.60 | .40 |
| ☐ 54 Len Vella | 4.00 | 1.60 | .40 |
| ☐ 55 Johnny Bright | 8.00 | 3.25 | .80 |
| ☐ 56 Don Getty | 8.00 | 3.25 | .80 |
| ☐ 57 Oscar Kruger | 4.00 | 1.60 | .40 |
| ☐ 58 Ted Frechette | 4.00 | 1.60 | .40 |
| ☐ 59 James Earl Wright | 4.00 | 1.60 | .40 |
| ☐ 60 Roger Nelson | 4.00 | 1.60 | .40 |
| ☐ 61 Ron Lancaster | 10.00 | 4.00 | 1.00 |
| ☐ 62 Bill Clarke | 4.00 | 1.60 | .40 |
| ☐ 63 Bob Shaw | 4.00 | 1.60 | .40 |
| ☐ 64 Ray Purdin | 4.00 | 1.60 | .40 |
| ☐ 65 Ron Atchison | 8.00 | 3.25 | .80 |
| ☐ 66 Ted Urness | 8.00 | 3.25 | .80 |
| ☐ 67 Bob Ptacek | 4.00 | 1.60 | .40 |
| ☐ 68 Neil Habig | 4.00 | 1.60 | .40 |
| ☐ 69 Garner Ekstran | 4.00 | 1.60 | .40 |
| ☐ 70 Gene Wlasiuk | 4.00 | 1.60 | .40 |
| ☐ 71 Jack Gotta | 4.00 | 1.60 | .40 |
| ☐ 72 Dick Cohee | 4.00 | 1.60 | .40 |
| ☐ 73 Ron Meadmore | 4.00 | 1.60 | .40 |
| ☐ 74 Martin Fabi | 4.00 | 1.60 | .40 |
| ☐ 75 Bob Good | 4.00 | 1.60 | .40 |
| ☐ 76 Len Legault | 4.00 | 1.60 | .40 |
| ☐ 77 Al Benecick | 4.00 | 1.60 | .40 |
| ☐ 78 Dale West | 4.00 | 1.60 | .40 |
| ☐ 79 Reg Whitehouse | 4.00 | 1.60 | .40 |
| ☐ 80 George Reed | 10.00 | 4.00 | 1.00 |
| ☐ 81 Kenny Ploen | 8.00 | 3.25 | .80 |
| ☐ 82 Leo Lewis | 8.00 | 3.25 | .80 |
| ☐ 83 Dick Thornton | 5.00 | 2.00 | .50 |
| ☐ 84 Steve Patrick | 4.00 | 1.60 | .40 |
| ☐ 85 Frank Rigney | 5.00 | 2.00 | .50 |
| ☐ 86 Cornel Piper | 4.00 | 1.60 | .40 |
| ☐ 87 Sherwyn Thorson | 4.00 | 1.60 | .40 |
| ☐ 88 Ernie Pitts | 4.00 | 1.60 | .40 |
| ☐ 89 Roger Hagberg | 5.00 | 2.00 | .50 |
| ☐ 90 Bud Grant CO | 30.00 | 12.00 | 3.00 |
| ☐ 91 Jack Delveaux | 4.00 | 1.60 | .40 |
| ☐ 92 Farrell Funston | 4.00 | 1.60 | .40 |
| ☐ 93 Ronnie Latourelle | 4.00 | 1.60 | .40 |
| ☐ 94 Roger Hamelin | 4.00 | 1.60 | .40 |
| ☐ 95 Gord Rowland | 4.00 | 1.60 | .40 |
| ☐ 96 Herb Gray | 10.00 | 4.00 | 1.00 |
| ☐ 97 Nick Miller | 4.00 | 1.60 | .40 |
| ☐ 98 Norm Rauhaus | 4.00 | 1.60 | .40 |
| ☐ 99 Bill Whisler | 4.00 | 1.60 | .40 |
| ☐ 100 Hal Ledyard | 4.00 | 1.60 | .40 |
| ☐ S1 British Columbia Shield | 45.00 | 18.00 | 4.50 |
| ☐ S2 Calgary Shield | 45.00 | 18.00 | 4.50 |
| ☐ S3 Edmonton Shield | 45.00 | 18.00 | 4.50 |
| ☐ S4 Saskatchewan Shield | 45.00 | 18.00 | 4.50 |
| ☐ S5 Winnipeg Shield | 45.00 | 18.00 | 4.50 |

# 1976 Nalley's Chips CFL

This 30-card set was distributed in Western Canada in boxes of Nalley's potato chips. The cards measure approximately 3 3/8" by 5 1/2" and feature posed color photos of the player, with the Nalley company name and player's signature below the picture. These blank-backed, unnumbered cards are listed below in alphabetical order according to their teams: British Columbia Lions (1-10), Edmonton Eskimos (11-20), and Calgary Stampeders (21-30).

| | NRMT | VG-E | GOOD |
|---|---|---|---|
| COMPLETE SET (30) | 250.00 | 100.00 | 25.00 |
| COMMON PLAYER (1-30) | 8.00 | 3.25 | .80 |
| ☐ 1 Bill Baker | 20.00 | 8.00 | 2.00 |
| ☐ 2 Eric Guthrie | 8.00 | 3.25 | .80 |
| ☐ 3 Lou Harris | 10.00 | 4.00 | 1.00 |
| ☐ 4 Layne McDowell | 8.00 | 3.25 | .80 |
| ☐ 5 Ray Nettles | 8.00 | 3.25 | .80 |
| ☐ 6 Lui Passaglia | 20.00 | 8.00 | 2.00 |
| ☐ 7 John Sciarra | 15.00 | 6.00 | 1.50 |
| ☐ 8 Wayne Smith | 8.00 | 3.25 | .80 |
| ☐ 9 Michael Strickland | 8.00 | 3.25 | .80 |
| ☐ 10 Jim Young | 20.00 | 8.00 | 2.00 |
| ☐ 11 Dave Cutler | 15.00 | 6.00 | 1.50 |
| ☐ 12 Larry Highbaugh | 12.00 | 5.00 | 1.20 |
| ☐ 13 John Konihowski | 8.00 | 3.25 | .80 |
| ☐ 14 Bruce Lemmerman | 8.00 | 3.25 | .80 |
| ☐ 15 George McGowan | 12.00 | 5.00 | 1.20 |
| ☐ 16 Dale Potter | 8.00 | 3.25 | .80 |
| ☐ 17 Charlie Turner | 8.00 | 3.25 | .80 |
| ☐ 18 Tyrone Walls | 8.00 | 3.25 | .80 |
| ☐ 19 Don Warrington | 8.00 | 3.25 | .80 |
| ☐ 20 Tom Wilkinson | 25.00 | 10.00 | 2.50 |

| | | | |
|---|---|---|---|
| ☐ 21 Willie Burden | 30.00 | 12.00 | 3.00 |
| ☐ 22 Larry Cates | 8.00 | 3.25 | .80 |
| ☐ 23 Lloyd Fairbanks | 12.00 | 5.00 | 1.20 |
| ☐ 24 Joe Forzani | 8.00 | 3.25 | .80 |
| ☐ 25 Tom Forzani | 8.00 | 3.25 | .80 |
| ☐ 26 Rick Galbos | 8.00 | 3.25 | .80 |
| ☐ 27 John Helton | 15.00 | 6.00 | 1.50 |
| ☐ 28 Harold Holton | 8.00 | 3.25 | .80 |
| ☐ 29 Rudy Linterman | 12.00 | 5.00 | 1.20 |
| ☐ 30 Joe Pisarcik | 15.00 | 6.00 | 1.50 |

## 1968 O-Pee-Chee CFL

The 1968 O-Pee-Chee CFL set of 132 cards received limited distribution and is considered by some to be a test set. The card backs are written in English and French in green ink on yellowish card stock. The cards measure the standard 2 1/2" by 3 1/2". Cards are ordered by teams: Montreal Alouettes (1-13), Ottawa Rough Riders (14-27), Toronto Argonauts (28-42), Hamilton Tiger-Cats (43-57), Winnipeg Blue Bombers (58-72), Calgary Stampeders (73-85), Saskatchewan Roughriders (86-103), Edmonton Eskimos (104-117), and British Columbia Lions (118-131). A complete checklist is given on card number 132. The card front design is similar to the design of the 1968 Topps NFL set.

| | NRMT | VG-E | GOOD |
|---|---|---|---|
| COMPLETE SET (132) | 1000.00 | 450.00 | 125.00 |
| COMMON PLAYER (1-132) | 7.50 | 3.00 | .75 |

| | | | |
|---|---|---|---|
| ☐ 1 Roger Murphy | 15.00 | 6.00 | 1.50 |
| ☐ 2 Charlie Parker | 7.50 | 3.00 | .75 |
| ☐ 3 Mike Webster | 7.50 | 3.00 | .75 |
| ☐ 4 Carroll Williams | 7.50 | 3.00 | .75 |
| ☐ 5 Phil Brady | 7.50 | 3.00 | .75 |
| ☐ 6 Dave Lewis | 7.50 | 3.00 | .75 |
| ☐ 7 John Baker | 7.50 | 3.00 | .75 |
| ☐ 8 Basil Bark | 7.50 | 3.00 | .75 |
| ☐ 9 Donnie Davis | 7.50 | 3.00 | .75 |
| ☐ 10 Pierre Desjardins | 7.50 | 3.00 | .75 |
| ☐ 11 Larry Fairholm | 7.50 | 3.00 | .75 |
| ☐ 12 Peter Paquette | 7.50 | 3.00 | .75 |
| ☐ 13 Ray Lychak | 7.50 | 3.00 | .75 |
| ☐ 14 Ted Collins | 7.50 | 3.00 | .75 |
| ☐ 15 Margene Adkins | 15.00 | 6.00 | 1.50 |
| ☐ 16 Ron Stewart | 20.00 | 8.00 | 2.00 |
| ☐ 17 Russ Jackson | 35.00 | 14.00 | 3.50 |
| ☐ 18 Bo Scott | 15.00 | 6.00 | 1.50 |
| ☐ 19 Joe Poirier | 7.50 | 3.00 | .75 |
| ☐ 20 Wayne Giardino | 7.50 | 3.00 | .75 |
| ☐ 21 Gene Gaines | 15.00 | 6.00 | 1.50 |
| ☐ 22 Billy Joe Booth | 7.50 | 3.00 | .75 |
| ☐ 23 Whit Tucker | 15.00 | 6.00 | 1.50 |
| ☐ 24 Rick Black | 7.50 | 3.00 | .75 |
| ☐ 25 Ken Lehmann | 12.00 | 5.00 | 1.20 |
| ☐ 26 Bob Brown | 7.50 | 3.00 | .75 |
| ☐ 27 Moe Racine | 7.50 | 3.00 | .75 |
| ☐ 28 Dick Thornton | 10.00 | 4.00 | 1.00 |
| ☐ 29 Bob Taylor | 7.50 | 3.00 | .75 |
| ☐ 30 Mel Profit | 12.00 | 5.00 | 1.20 |
| ☐ 31 Dave Mann | 10.00 | 4.00 | 1.00 |
| ☐ 32 Marv Luster | 12.00 | 5.00 | 1.20 |
| ☐ 33 Ed Buchanan | 7.50 | 3.00 | .75 |
| ☐ 34 Ed Harrington | 10.00 | 4.00 | 1.00 |
| ☐ 35 Jim Dillard | 7.50 | 3.00 | .75 |
| ☐ 36 Bobby Taylor | 7.50 | 3.00 | .75 |
| ☐ 37 Ron Arends | 7.50 | 3.00 | .75 |
| ☐ 38 Mike Wadsworth | 7.50 | 3.00 | .75 |
| ☐ 39 Wally Gabler | 12.00 | 5.00 | 1.20 |
| ☐ 40 Pete Martin | 7.50 | 3.00 | .75 |
| ☐ 41 Danny Nykoluk | 7.50 | 3.00 | .75 |
| ☐ 42 Bill Frank | 7.50 | 3.00 | .75 |
| ☐ 43 Gordon Christian | 7.50 | 3.00 | .75 |
| ☐ 44 Tommy Joe Coffey | 20.00 | 8.00 | 2.00 |
| ☐ 45 Ellison Kelly | 20.00 | 8.00 | 2.00 |

| | | | |
|---|---|---|---|
| ☐ 46 Angelo Mosca | 30.00 | 12.00 | 3.00 |
| ☐ 47 John Barrow | 20.00 | 8.00 | 2.00 |
| ☐ 48 Bill Danychuk | 12.00 | 5.00 | 1.20 |
| ☐ 49 Jon Hohman | 7.50 | 3.00 | .75 |
| ☐ 50 Bill Redell | 7.50 | 3.00 | .75 |
| ☐ 51 Joe Zuger | 10.00 | 4.00 | 1.00 |
| ☐ 52 Willie Bethea | 12.00 | 5.00 | 1.20 |
| ☐ 53 Dick Cohee | 7.50 | 3.00 | .75 |
| ☐ 54 Tommy Grant | 10.00 | 4.00 | 1.00 |
| ☐ 55 Garney Henley | 20.00 | 8.00 | 2.00 |
| ☐ 56 Ted Page | 7.50 | 3.00 | .75 |
| ☐ 57 Bob Krouse | 7.50 | 3.00 | .75 |
| ☐ 58 Phil Minnick | 7.50 | 3.00 | .75 |
| ☐ 59 Butch Pressley | 7.50 | 3.00 | .75 |
| ☐ 60 Dave Raimey | 10.00 | 4.00 | 1.00 |
| ☐ 61 Sherwyn Thorson | 7.50 | 3.00 | .75 |
| ☐ 62 Bill Whisler | 7.50 | 3.00 | .75 |
| ☐ 63 Roger Hamelin | 7.50 | 3.00 | .75 |
| ☐ 64 Chuck Harrison | 7.50 | 3.00 | .75 |
| ☐ 65 Ken Nielsen | 12.00 | 5.00 | 1.20 |
| ☐ 66 Ernie Pitts | 7.50 | 3.00 | .75 |
| ☐ 67 Mitch Zainasky | 7.50 | 3.00 | .75 |
| ☐ 68 John Schneider | 7.50 | 3.00 | .75 |
| ☐ 69 Ron Kirkland | 7.50 | 3.00 | .75 |
| ☐ 70 Paul Desjardins | 7.50 | 3.00 | .75 |
| ☐ 71 Luther Selbo | 7.50 | 3.00 | .75 |
| ☐ 72 Don Gilbert | 7.50 | 3.00 | .75 |
| ☐ 73 Bob Lueck | 7.50 | 3.00 | .75 |
| ☐ 74 Gerry Shaw | 7.50 | 3.00 | .75 |
| ☐ 75 Chuck Zickefoose | 7.50 | 3.00 | .75 |
| ☐ 76 Frank Andruski | 7.50 | 3.00 | .75 |
| ☐ 77 Lanny Boleski | 7.50 | 3.00 | .75 |
| ☐ 78 Terry Evanshen | 20.00 | 8.00 | 2.00 |
| ☐ 79 Jim Furlong | 7.50 | 3.00 | .75 |
| ☐ 80 Wayne Harris | 20.00 | 8.00 | 2.00 |
| ☐ 81 Jerry Keeling | 15.00 | 6.00 | 1.50 |
| ☐ 82 Roger Kramer | 10.00 | 4.00 | 1.00 |
| ☐ 83 Pete Liske | 20.00 | 8.00 | 2.00 |
| ☐ 84 Dick Suderman | 12.00 | 5.00 | 1.20 |
| ☐ 85 Granville Liggins | 20.00 | 8.00 | 2.00 |
| ☐ 86 George Reed | 30.00 | 12.00 | 3.00 |
| ☐ 87 Ron Lancaster | 30.00 | 12.00 | 3.00 |
| ☐ 88 Alan Ford | 7.50 | 3.00 | .75 |
| ☐ 89 Gordon Barwell | 7.50 | 3.00 | .75 |
| ☐ 90 Wayne Shaw | 7.50 | 3.00 | .75 |
| ☐ 91 Bruce Bennett | 15.00 | 6.00 | 1.50 |
| ☐ 92 Henry Dorsch | 7.50 | 3.00 | .75 |
| ☐ 93 Ken Reed | 7.50 | 3.00 | .75 |
| ☐ 94 Ron Atchison | 15.00 | 6.00 | 1.50 |
| ☐ 95 Clyde Brock | 7.50 | 3.00 | .75 |
| ☐ 96 Alex Benecick | 7.50 | 3.00 | .75 |
| ☐ 97 Ted Urness | 12.00 | 5.00 | 1.20 |
| ☐ 98 Wally Dempsey | 7.50 | 3.00 | .75 |
| ☐ 99 Don Gerhardt | 7.50 | 3.00 | .75 |
| ☐ 100 Ted Dushinski | 7.50 | 3.00 | .75 |
| ☐ 101 Ed McQuarters | 12.00 | 5.00 | 1.20 |
| ☐ 102 Bob Kosid | 7.50 | 3.00 | .75 |
| ☐ 103 Gary Brandt | 7.50 | 3.00 | .75 |
| ☐ 104 John Wydareny | 7.50 | 3.00 | .75 |
| ☐ 105 Jim Thomas | 7.50 | 3.00 | .75 |
| ☐ 106 Art Perkins | 7.50 | 3.00 | .75 |
| ☐ 107 Frank Cosentino | 12.00 | 5.00 | 1.20 |
| ☐ 108 Earl Edwards | 10.00 | 4.00 | 1.00 |
| ☐ 109 Garry Lefebvre | 7.50 | 3.00 | .75 |
| ☐ 110 Greg Pipes | 10.00 | 4.00 | 1.00 |
| ☐ 111 Ian MacLeod | 7.50 | 3.00 | .75 |
| ☐ 112 Dick Dupuis | 7.50 | 3.00 | .75 |
| ☐ 113 Ron Forwick | 7.50 | 3.00 | .75 |
| ☐ 114 Jerry Griffin | 7.50 | 3.00 | .75 |
| ☐ 115 John LaGrone | 12.00 | 5.00 | 1.20 |
| ☐ 116 E.A. Sims | 7.50 | 3.00 | .75 |
| ☐ 117 Greenard Poles | 7.50 | 3.00 | .75 |
| ☐ 118 Leroy Sledge | 7.50 | 3.00 | .75 |
| ☐ 119 Ken Sugarman | 7.50 | 3.00 | .75 |
| ☐ 120 Jim Young | 30.00 | 12.00 | 3.00 |
| ☐ 121 Garner Ekstran | 12.00 | 5.00 | 1.20 |
| ☐ 122 Jim Evenson | 12.00 | 5.00 | 1.20 |
| ☐ 123 Greg Findlay | 7.50 | 3.00 | .75 |
| ☐ 124 Ted Gerela | 7.50 | 3.00 | .75 |
| ☐ 125 Lach Heron | 10.00 | 4.00 | 1.00 |
| ☐ 126 Mike Martin | 7.50 | 3.00 | .75 |
| ☐ 127 Craig Murray | 7.50 | 3.00 | .75 |
| ☐ 128 Pete Ohler | 7.50 | 3.00 | .75 |
| ☐ 129 Sonny Homer | 7.50 | 3.00 | .75 |
| ☐ 130 Bill Lasseter | 7.50 | 3.00 | .75 |
| ☐ 131 John McDowell | 7.50 | 3.00 | .75 |
| ☐ 132 Checklist Card | 60.00 | 10.00 | 2.00 |

## 1968 O-Pee-Chee CFL Poster Inserts

This 16-card set of color posters featuring all-stars of the Canadian Football League was inserted in wax packs along with the regular issue of 1968 O-Pee-Chee CFL cards. These (approximately) 5" by 7" posters were folded twice in order to fit in the wax packs. They are unnumbered and are blank on the back. They were printed on very thin

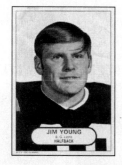

JIM YOUNG
B.C. LIONS
HALFBACK

paper. These posters are similar in appearance to the 1967 Topps baseball and 1968 Topps football poster inserts.

| | NRMT | VG-E | GOOD |
|---|---|---|---|
| COMPLETE SET (16) | 300.00 | 120.00 | 30.00 |
| COMMON PLAYER (1-16) | 15.00 | 6.00 | 1.50 |

| | | NRMT | VG-E | GOOD |
|---|---|---|---|---|
| ☐ 1 | Margene Adkins<br>Ottawa Rough Riders | 20.00 | 8.00 | 2.00 |
| ☐ 2 | Tommy Joe Coffey<br>Hamilton Tiger-Cats | 25.00 | 10.00 | 2.50 |
| ☐ 3 | Frank Cosentino<br>Edmonton Eskimos | 18.00 | 7.25 | 1.80 |
| ☐ 4 | Terry Evanshen<br>Montreal Alouettes | 25.00 | 10.00 | 2.50 |
| ☐ 5 | Larry Fairholm<br>Montreal Alouettes | 15.00 | 6.00 | 1.50 |
| ☐ 6 | Wally Gabler<br>Toronto Argonauts | 15.00 | 6.00 | 1.50 |
| ☐ 7 | Russ Jackson<br>Ottawa Rough Riders | 35.00 | 14.00 | 3.50 |
| ☐ 8 | Ron Lancaster<br>Saskatchewan Roughriders | 30.00 | 12.00 | 3.00 |
| ☐ 9 | Pete Liske<br>Calgary Stampeders | 25.00 | 10.00 | 2.50 |
| ☐ 10 | Dave Mann<br>Toronto Argonauts | 18.00 | 7.25 | 1.80 |
| ☐ 11 | Ken Nielsen<br>Winnipeg Blue Bombers | 18.00 | 7.25 | 1.80 |
| ☐ 12 | Dave Raimey<br>Winnipeg Blue Bombers | 18.00 | 7.25 | 1.80 |
| ☐ 13 | George Reed<br>Saskatchewan Roughriders | 30.00 | 12.00 | 3.00 |
| ☐ 14 | Carroll Williams<br>Montreal Alouettes | 15.00 | 6.00 | 1.50 |
| ☐ 15 | Jim Young<br>B.C. Lions | 30.00 | 12.00 | 3.00 |
| ☐ 16 | Joe Zuger<br>Hamilton Tiger-Cats | 15.00 | 6.00 | 1.50 |

## 1970 O-Pee-Chee CFL

Terry
EVANSHEN
Montreal Alouettes • Flanker

The 1970 O-Pee-Chee CFL set features 115 cards ordered by teams: Toronto Argonauts (1-12), Hamilton Tiger-Cats (13-24), British Columbia Lions (25-36), Ottawa Rough Riders (37-48), Edmonton Eskimos (49-60), Winnipeg Blue Bombers (61-72), Saskatchewan Roughriders (73-85), Calgary Stampeders (86-97) and Montreal Alouettes (98-109). The cards measure 2 1/2" by 3 1/2". The design of these cards is very similar to the 1969 Topps NFL football issue. The card backs are written in French and English; the card back is predominantly black with white lettering and green accent. Six miscellaneous special feature cards comprise cards numbered 110-115.

| | NRMT | VG-E | GOOD |
|---|---|---|---|
| COMPLETE SET (115) | 275.00 | 110.00 | 27.00 |
| COMMON PLAYER (1-115) | 2.25 | .90 | .22 |

| | | NRMT | VG-E | GOOD |
|---|---|---|---|---|
| ☐ 1 | Ed Harrington | 5.00 | 2.00 | .50 |
| ☐ 2 | Danny Nykoluk | 2.25 | .90 | .22 |
| ☐ 3 | Marv Luster | 4.00 | 1.60 | .40 |
| ☐ 4 | Dave Raimey | 3.00 | 1.20 | .30 |
| ☐ 5 | Bill Symons | 3.00 | 1.20 | .30 |
| ☐ 6 | Tom Wilkinson | 20.00 | 8.00 | 2.00 |
| ☐ 7 | Mike Wadsworth | 2.25 | .90 | .22 |
| ☐ 8 | Dick Thornton | 3.00 | 1.20 | .30 |
| ☐ 9 | Jim Tomlin | 2.25 | .90 | .22 |
| ☐ 10 | Mel Profit | 3.00 | 1.20 | .30 |
| ☐ 11 | Bobby Taylor | 4.00 | 1.60 | .40 |
| ☐ 12 | Dave Mann | 3.00 | 1.20 | .30 |
| ☐ 13 | Tommy Joe Coffey | 5.00 | 2.00 | .50 |
| ☐ 14 | Angelo Mosca | 15.00 | 6.00 | 1.50 |
| ☐ 15 | Joe Zuger | 3.00 | 1.20 | .30 |
| ☐ 16 | Garney Henley | 10.00 | 4.00 | 1.00 |
| ☐ 17 | Mike Strofolino | 2.25 | .90 | .22 |
| ☐ 18 | Billy Ray Locklin | 2.25 | .90 | .22 |
| ☐ 19 | Ted Page | 2.25 | .90 | .22 |
| ☐ 20 | Bill Danychuk | 3.00 | 1.20 | .30 |
| ☐ 21 | Bob Krouse | 2.25 | .90 | .22 |
| ☐ 22 | John Reid | 2.25 | .90 | .22 |
| ☐ 23 | Dick Wesolowski | 2.25 | .90 | .22 |
| ☐ 24 | Willie Bethea | 3.00 | 1.20 | .30 |
| ☐ 25 | Ken Sugarman | 3.00 | 1.20 | .30 |
| ☐ 26 | Rich Robinson | 2.25 | .90 | .22 |
| ☐ 27 | Dave Tobey | 2.25 | .90 | .22 |
| ☐ 28 | Paul Brothers | 2.25 | .90 | .22 |
| ☐ 29 | Charlie Brown | 2.25 | .90 | .22 |
| ☐ 30 | Jerry Bradley | 2.25 | .90 | .22 |
| ☐ 31 | Ted Gerela | 2.25 | .90 | .22 |
| ☐ 32 | Jim Young | 8.00 | 3.25 | .80 |
| ☐ 33 | Gary Robinson | 2.25 | .90 | .22 |
| ☐ 34 | Bob Howes | 2.25 | .90 | .22 |
| ☐ 35 | Greg Findlay | 2.25 | .90 | .22 |
| ☐ 36 | Trevor Ekdahl | 3.00 | 1.20 | .30 |
| ☐ 37 | Ron Stewart | 6.00 | 2.40 | .60 |
| ☐ 38 | Joe Poirier | 3.00 | 1.20 | .30 |
| ☐ 39 | Wayne Giardino | 2.25 | .90 | .22 |
| ☐ 40 | Tom Schuette | 2.25 | .90 | .22 |
| ☐ 41 | Roger Perdrix | 2.25 | .90 | .22 |
| ☐ 42 | Jim Mankins | 2.25 | .90 | .22 |
| ☐ 43 | Jay Roberts | 2.25 | .90 | .22 |
| ☐ 44 | Ken Lehmann | 3.00 | 1.20 | .30 |
| ☐ 45 | Jerry Campbell | 2.25 | .90 | .22 |
| ☐ 46 | Billy Joe Booth | 3.00 | 1.20 | .30 |
| ☐ 47 | Whit Tucker | 5.00 | 2.00 | .50 |
| ☐ 48 | Moe Racine | 2.25 | .90 | .22 |
| ☐ 49 | Corey Colehour | 3.00 | 1.20 | .30 |
| ☐ 50 | Dave Gasser | 2.25 | .90 | .22 |
| ☐ 51 | Jerry Griffin | 2.25 | .90 | .22 |
| ☐ 52 | Greg Pipes | 3.00 | 1.20 | .30 |
| ☐ 53 | Roy Shatzko | 2.25 | .90 | .22 |
| ☐ 54 | Ron Forwick | 2.25 | .90 | .22 |
| ☐ 55 | Ed Molstad | 2.25 | .90 | .22 |
| ☐ 56 | Ken Ferguson | 2.25 | .90 | .22 |
| ☐ 57 | Terry Swarn | 5.00 | 2.00 | .50 |
| ☐ 58 | Tom Nettles | 2.25 | .90 | .22 |
| ☐ 59 | John Wydareny | 2.25 | .90 | .22 |
| ☐ 60 | Bayne Norrie | 2.25 | .90 | .22 |
| ☐ 61 | Wally Gabler | 3.00 | 1.20 | .30 |
| ☐ 62 | Paul Desjardins | 2.25 | .90 | .22 |
| ☐ 63 | Peter Francis | 2.25 | .90 | .22 |
| ☐ 64 | Bill Frank | 2.25 | .90 | .22 |
| ☐ 65 | Chuck Harrison | 2.25 | .90 | .22 |
| ☐ 66 | Gene Lakusiak | 2.25 | .90 | .22 |
| ☐ 67 | Phil Minnick | 2.25 | .90 | .22 |
| ☐ 68 | Doug Strong | 2.25 | .90 | .22 |
| ☐ 69 | Glen Schapansky | 2.25 | .90 | .22 |
| ☐ 70 | Ed Ulmer | 2.25 | .90 | .22 |
| ☐ 71 | Bill Whisler | 2.25 | .90 | .22 |
| ☐ 72 | Ted Collins | 2.25 | .90 | .22 |
| ☐ 73 | Larry DeGraw | 2.25 | .90 | .22 |
| ☐ 74 | Henry Dorsch | 2.25 | .90 | .22 |
| ☐ 75 | Alan Ford | 2.25 | .90 | .22 |
| ☐ 76 | Ron Lancaster | 20.00 | 8.00 | 2.00 |
| ☐ 77 | Bob Kosid | 2.25 | .90 | .22 |
| ☐ 78 | Bobby Thompson | 2.25 | .90 | .22 |
| ☐ 79 | Ted Dushinski | 2.25 | .90 | .22 |
| ☐ 80 | Bruce Bennett | 4.00 | 1.60 | .40 |
| ☐ 81 | George Reed | 15.00 | 6.00 | 1.50 |
| ☐ 82 | Wayne Shaw | 2.25 | .90 | .22 |
| ☐ 83 | Cliff Shaw | 2.25 | .90 | .22 |
| ☐ 84 | Jack Abendschan | 2.25 | .90 | .22 |
| ☐ 85 | Ed McQuarters | 5.00 | 2.00 | .50 |
| ☐ 86 | Jerry Keeling | 5.00 | 2.00 | .50 |
| ☐ 87 | Gerry Shaw | 2.25 | .90 | .22 |
| ☐ 88 | Basil Bark UER<br>(Misspelled Back) | 2.25 | .90 | .22 |
| ☐ 89 | Wayne Harris | 6.00 | 2.40 | .60 |
| ☐ 90 | Jim Furlong | 2.25 | .90 | .22 |
| ☐ 91 | Larry Robinson | 2.50 | 1.00 | .25 |
| ☐ 92 | John Helton | 10.00 | 4.00 | 1.00 |
| ☐ 93 | Dave Cranmer | 2.25 | .90 | .22 |

| | NRMT | VG-E | GOOD |
|---|---|---|---|
| ☐ 94 Lanny Boleski UER | 2.25 | .90 | .22 |
| (Misspelled Larry) | | | |
| ☐ 95 Herman Harrison | 5.00 | 2.00 | .50 |
| ☐ 96 Granville Liggins | 5.00 | 2.00 | .50 |
| ☐ 97 Joe Forzani | 3.00 | 1.20 | .30 |
| ☐ 98 Terry Evanshen | 8.00 | 3.25 | .80 |
| ☐ 99 Sonny Wade | 6.00 | 2.40 | .60 |
| ☐ 100 Dennis Duncan | 2.25 | .90 | .22 |
| ☐ 101 Al Phaneuf | 2.25 | .90 | .22 |
| ☐ 102 Larry Fairholm | 2.25 | .90 | .22 |
| ☐ 103 Moses Denson | 4.00 | 1.60 | .40 |
| ☐ 104 Gino Baretta | 2.25 | .90 | .22 |
| ☐ 105 Gene Ceppetelli | 2.25 | .90 | .22 |
| ☐ 106 Dick Smith | 2.25 | .90 | .22 |
| ☐ 107 Gordon Judges | 2.25 | .90 | .22 |
| ☐ 108 Harry Olszewski | 2.25 | .90 | .22 |
| ☐ 109 Mike Webster | 2.25 | .90 | .22 |
| ☐ 110 Checklist 1-115 | 30.00 | 5.00 | 1.00 |
| ☐ 111 Outstanding Player | 8.00 | 3.25 | .80 |
| (list from 1953-1969) | | | |
| ☐ 112 Player of the Year | 8.00 | 3.25 | .80 |
| (list from 1954-1969) | | | |
| ☐ 113 Lineman of the Year | 6.00 | 2.40 | .60 |
| (list from 1955-1969) | | | |
| ☐ 114 CFL Coaches | 6.00 | 2.40 | .60 |
| (listed on card front) | | | |
| ☐ 115 Identifying Player | 15.00 | 6.00 | 1.50 |
| (explanation of uni- | | | |
| form numbering system) | | | |

# 1970 O-Pee-Chee CFL Push-Out Inserts

This attractive set of 16 push-out inserts features players in the Canadian Football League. The cards are standard size, 2 1/2" by 3 1/2", but are actually stickers, if the backs are moistened. The cards are numbered at the bottom and the backs are blank. Instructions on the front (upper left corner) are written in both English and French. Each player's team is identified on his card under his name. The player is shown superimposed over a football; the push-out area is essentially the football.

| | NRMT | VG-E | GOOD |
|---|---|---|---|
| COMPLETE SET (16) | 200.00 | 80.00 | 20.00 |
| COMMON PLAYER (1-16) | 10.00 | 4.00 | 1.00 |
| ☐ 1 Ed Harrington | 10.00 | 4.00 | 1.00 |
| Toronto Argonauts | | | |
| ☐ 2 Danny Nykoluk | 10.00 | 4.00 | 1.00 |
| Toronto Argonauts | | | |
| ☐ 3 Tommy Joe Coffey | 25.00 | 10.00 | 2.50 |
| Toronto Argonauts | | | |
| ☐ 4 Angelo Mosca | 30.00 | 12.00 | 3.00 |
| Hamilton Tiger-Cats | | | |
| ☐ 5 Ken Sugarman | 12.00 | 5.00 | 1.20 |
| British Columbia Lions | | | |
| ☐ 6 Jay Roberts | 10.00 | 4.00 | 1.00 |
| Ottawa Rough Riders | | | |
| ☐ 7 Joe Poirier | 12.00 | 5.00 | 1.20 |
| Ottawa Rough Riders | | | |
| ☐ 8 Corey Colehour | 10.00 | 4.00 | 1.00 |
| Edmonton Eskimos | | | |
| ☐ 9 Dave Gasser | 10.00 | 4.00 | 1.00 |
| Edmonton Eskimos | | | |
| ☐ 10 Wally Gabler | 10.00 | 4.00 | 1.00 |
| Winnipeg Blue Bombers | | | |
| ☐ 11 Paul Desjardins | 10.00 | 4.00 | 1.00 |
| Winnipeg Blue Bombers | | | |
| ☐ 12 Larry DeGraw | 10.00 | 4.00 | 1.00 |
| Saskatchewan Roughriders | | | |
| ☐ 13 Jerry Keeling | 20.00 | 8.00 | 2.00 |
| Calgary Stampeders | | | |
| ☐ 14 Gerry Shaw | 10.00 | 4.00 | 1.00 |

| | NRMT | VG-E | GOOD |
|---|---|---|---|
| Calgary Stampeders | | | |
| ☐ 15 Terry Evanshen | 25.00 | 10.00 | 2.50 |
| Montreal Alouettes | | | |
| ☐ 16 Sonny Wade | 12.00 | 5.00 | 1.20 |
| Montreal Alouettes | | | |

# 1971 O-Pee-Chee CFL

The 1971 O-Pee-Chee CFL set features 132 cards ordered by teams: Toronto Argonauts (1-15), Winnipeg Blue Bombers (16-30), British Columbia Lions (31-45), Edmonton Eskimos (46-60), Hamilton Tiger-Cats (61-75), Ottawa Rough Riders (76-89), Saskatchewan Roughriders (90-103), Montreal Alouettes (104-117), and Calgary Stampeders (118-131). The cards measure 2 1/2" by 3 1/2". The card fronts feature a bright red border. The card backs are written in French and English. A complete checklist is given on card number 132. The key card in the set is Joe Theismann, his first professional football card, predating his later entry into the NFL.

| | NRMT | VG-E | GOOD |
|---|---|---|---|
| COMPLETE SET (132) | 275.00 | 110.00 | 27.00 |
| COMMON PLAYER (1-132) | 1.25 | .50 | .12 |
| ☐ 1 Bill Symons | 5.00 | 1.50 | .30 |
| ☐ 2 Mel Profit | 2.00 | .80 | .20 |
| ☐ 3 Jim Tomlin | 1.25 | .50 | .12 |
| ☐ 4 Ed Harrington | 2.00 | .80 | .20 |
| ☐ 5 Jim Corrigall | 4.00 | 1.60 | .40 |
| ☐ 6 Chip Barrett | 1.25 | .50 | .12 |
| ☐ 7 Marv Luster | 3.00 | 1.20 | .30 |
| ☐ 8 Ellison Kelly | 4.00 | 1.60 | .40 |
| ☐ 9 Charlie Bray | 1.25 | .50 | .12 |
| ☐ 10 Pete Martin | 1.25 | .50 | .12 |
| ☐ 11 Tony Moro | 1.25 | .50 | .12 |
| ☐ 12 Dave Raimey | 2.00 | .80 | .20 |
| ☐ 13 Joe Theismann | 125.00 | 50.00 | 12.50 |
| ☐ 14 Greg Barton | 6.00 | 2.40 | .60 |
| ☐ 15 Leon McQuay | 6.00 | 2.40 | .60 |
| ☐ 16 Don Jonas | 6.00 | 2.40 | .60 |
| ☐ 17 Doug Strong | 1.25 | .50 | .12 |
| ☐ 18 Paul Brule | 1.25 | .50 | .12 |
| ☐ 19 Bill Frank | 1.25 | .50 | .12 |
| ☐ 20 Joe Critchlow | 1.25 | .50 | .12 |
| ☐ 21 Chuck Liebrock | 1.25 | .50 | .12 |
| ☐ 22 Rob McLaren | 1.25 | .50 | .12 |
| ☐ 23 Bob Swift | 1.25 | .50 | .12 |
| ☐ 24 Rick Shaw | 1.25 | .50 | .12 |
| ☐ 25 Ross Richardson | 1.25 | .50 | .12 |
| ☐ 26 Benji Dial | 1.25 | .50 | .12 |
| ☐ 27 Jim Heighton | 1.25 | .50 | .12 |
| ☐ 28 Ed Ulmer | 1.25 | .50 | .12 |
| ☐ 29 Glen Schapansky | 1.25 | .50 | .12 |
| ☐ 30 Larry Slagle | 1.25 | .50 | .12 |
| ☐ 31 Tom Cassese | 1.25 | .50 | .12 |
| ☐ 32 Ted Gerela | 1.25 | .50 | .12 |
| ☐ 33 Bob Howes | 1.25 | .50 | .12 |
| ☐ 34 Ken Sugarman | 2.00 | .80 | .20 |
| ☐ 35 A.D. Whitfield | 2.00 | .80 | .20 |
| ☐ 36 Jim Young | 6.00 | 2.40 | .60 |
| ☐ 37 Tom Wilkinson | 8.00 | 3.25 | .80 |
| ☐ 38 Lefty Hendrickson | 1.25 | .50 | .12 |
| ☐ 39 Dave Golinsky | 1.25 | .50 | .12 |
| ☐ 40 Gerry Herron | 1.25 | .50 | .12 |
| ☐ 41 Jim Evenson | 2.00 | .80 | .20 |
| ☐ 42 Greg Findlay | 1.25 | .50 | .12 |
| ☐ 43 Garrett Hunsperger | 1.25 | .50 | .12 |
| ☐ 44 Jerry Bradley | 1.25 | .50 | .12 |
| ☐ 45 Trevor Ekdahl | 2.00 | .80 | .20 |
| ☐ 46 Bayne Norrie | 1.25 | .50 | .12 |
| ☐ 47 Henry King | 1.25 | .50 | .12 |
| ☐ 48 Terry Swarn | 2.00 | .80 | .20 |
| ☐ 49 Jim Thomas | 2.00 | .80 | .20 |
| ☐ 50 Bob Houmard | 1.25 | .50 | .12 |
| ☐ 51 Don Trull | 3.00 | 1.20 | .30 |

| | | | |
|---|---|---|---|
| ☐ 52 Dave Cutler | 10.00 | 4.00 | 1.00 |
| ☐ 53 Mike Law | 1.25 | .50 | .12 |
| ☐ 54 Dick Dupuis | 2.00 | .80 | .20 |
| ☐ 55 Dave Gasser | 1.25 | .50 | .12 |
| ☐ 56 Ron Forwick | 1.25 | .50 | .12 |
| ☐ 57 John LaGrone | 2.00 | .80 | .20 |
| ☐ 58 Greg Pipes | 2.00 | .80 | .20 |
| ☐ 59 Ted Page | 1.25 | .50 | .12 |
| ☐ 60 John Wydareny | 2.00 | .80 | .20 |
| ☐ 61 Joe Zuger | 2.00 | .80 | .20 |
| ☐ 62 Tommy Joe Coffey | 6.00 | 2.40 | .60 |
| ☐ 63 Rensi Perdoni | 1.25 | .50 | .12 |
| ☐ 64 Bobby Taylor | 2.50 | 1.00 | .25 |
| ☐ 65 Garney Henley | 6.00 | 2.40 | .60 |
| ☐ 66 Dick Wesolowski | 1.25 | .50 | .12 |
| ☐ 67 Dave Fleming | 1.25 | .50 | .12 |
| ☐ 68 Bill Danychuk | 2.00 | .80 | .20 |
| ☐ 69 Angelo Mosca | 12.00 | 5.00 | 1.20 |
| ☐ 70 Bob Krouse | 1.25 | .50 | .12 |
| ☐ 71 Tony Gabriel | 20.00 | 8.00 | 2.00 |
| ☐ 72 Wally Gabler | 2.00 | .80 | .20 |
| ☐ 73 Bob Steiner | 1.25 | .50 | .12 |
| ☐ 74 John Reid | 1.25 | .50 | .12 |
| ☐ 75 Jon Hohman | 1.25 | .50 | .12 |
| ☐ 76 Barry Ardern | 1.25 | .50 | .12 |
| ☐ 77 Jerry Campbell | 1.25 | .50 | .12 |
| ☐ 78 Billy Cooper | 1.25 | .50 | .12 |
| ☐ 79 Dave Braggins | 1.25 | .50 | .12 |
| ☐ 80 Tom Schuette | 1.25 | .50 | .12 |
| ☐ 81 Dennis Duncan | 1.25 | .50 | .12 |
| ☐ 82 Moe Racine | 1.25 | .50 | .12 |
| ☐ 83 Rod Woodward | 1.25 | .50 | .12 |
| ☐ 84 Al Marcelin | 2.00 | .80 | .20 |
| ☐ 85 Garry Wood | 5.00 | 2.00 | .50 |
| ☐ 86 Wayne Giardino | 1.25 | .50 | .12 |
| ☐ 87 Roger Perdrix | 1.25 | .50 | .12 |
| ☐ 88 Hugh Oldham | 1.25 | .50 | .12 |
| ☐ 89 Rick Cassatta | 2.50 | 1.00 | .25 |
| ☐ 90 Jack Abendschan | 2.00 | .80 | .20 |
| ☐ 91 Don Bahnuik | 1.25 | .50 | .12 |
| ☐ 92 Bill Baker | 10.00 | 4.00 | 1.00 |
| ☐ 93 Gordon Barwell | 1.25 | .50 | .12 |
| ☐ 94 Gary Brandt | 1.25 | .50 | .12 |
| ☐ 95 Henry Dorsch | 1.25 | .50 | .12 |
| ☐ 96 Ted Dushinski | 1.25 | .50 | .12 |
| ☐ 97 Alan Ford | 1.25 | .50 | .12 |
| ☐ 98 Ken Frith | 1.25 | .50 | .12 |
| ☐ 99 Ralph Galloway | 1.25 | .50 | .12 |
| ☐ 100 Bob Kosid | 1.25 | .50 | .12 |
| ☐ 101 Ron Lancaster | 12.00 | 5.00 | 1.20 |
| ☐ 102 Silas McKinnie | 1.25 | .50 | .12 |
| ☐ 103 George Reed | 10.00 | 4.00 | 1.00 |
| ☐ 104 Gene Ceppetelli | 1.25 | .50 | .12 |
| ☐ 105 Merl Code | 1.25 | .50 | .12 |
| ☐ 106 Peter Dalla Riva | 10.00 | 4.00 | 1.00 |
| ☐ 107 Moses Denson | 2.50 | 1.00 | .25 |
| ☐ 108 Pierre Desjardins | 1.25 | .50 | .12 |
| ☐ 109 Terry Evanshen | 6.00 | 2.40 | .60 |
| ☐ 110 Larry Fairholm | 2.00 | .80 | .20 |
| ☐ 111 Gene Gaines | 5.00 | 2.00 | .50 |
| ☐ 112 Ed George | 2.00 | .80 | .20 |
| ☐ 113 Gordon Judges | 1.25 | .50 | .12 |
| ☐ 114 Garry Lefebvre | 1.25 | .50 | .12 |
| ☐ 115 Al Phaneuf | 2.00 | .80 | .20 |
| ☐ 116 Steve Smear | 5.00 | 2.00 | .50 |
| ☐ 117 Sonny Wade | 3.00 | 1.20 | .30 |
| ☐ 118 Frank Andruski | 1.25 | .50 | .12 |
| ☐ 119 Basil Bark | 1.25 | .50 | .12 |
| ☐ 120 Lanny Boleski | 1.25 | .50 | .12 |
| ☐ 121 Joe Forzani | 2.00 | .80 | .20 |
| ☐ 122 Jim Furlong | 1.25 | .50 | .12 |
| ☐ 123 Wayne Harris | 6.00 | 2.40 | .60 |
| ☐ 124 Herman Harrison | 5.00 | 2.00 | .50 |
| ☐ 125 John Helton | 5.00 | 2.00 | .50 |
| ☐ 126 Wayne Holm | 1.25 | .50 | .12 |
| ☐ 127 Fred James | 1.25 | .50 | .12 |
| ☐ 128 Jerry Keeling | 5.00 | 2.00 | .50 |
| ☐ 129 Rudy Linterman | 2.00 | .80 | .20 |
| ☐ 130 Larry Robinson | 2.00 | .80 | .20 |
| ☐ 131 Gerry Shaw | 1.25 | .50 | .12 |
| ☐ 132 Checklist Card | 25.00 | 4.00 | .80 |

## 1971 O-Pee-Chee CFL Poster Inserts

This 16-card set of posters featuring all-stars of the Canadian Football League was inserted in wax packs along with the regular issue of O-Pee-Chee cards. These 5" by 7" posters were folded twice in order to fit in the wax packs. They are numbered at the bottom and are blank on the back. These posters are somewhat similar in appearance to the Topps football poster inserts of 1971.

| | NRMT | VG-E | GOOD |
|---|---|---|---|
| COMPLETE SET (16) | 125.00 | 50.00 | 12.50 |
| COMMON PLAYER (1-16) | 5.00 | 2.00 | .50 |

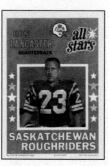

| | | | |
|---|---|---|---|
| ☐ 1 Tommy Joe Coffey | 15.00 | 6.00 | 1.50 |
| Hamilton Tiger-Cats | | | |
| ☐ 2 Herman Harrison | 10.00 | 4.00 | 1.00 |
| Calgary Stampeders | | | |
| ☐ 3 Bill Frank | 5.00 | 2.00 | .50 |
| Winnipeg Blue Bombers | | | |
| ☐ 4 Ellison Kelly | 10.00 | 4.00 | 1.00 |
| Toronto Argonauts | | | |
| ☐ 5 Charlie Bray | 5.00 | 2.00 | .50 |
| Toronto Argonauts | | | |
| ☐ 6 Bill Danychuk | 6.00 | 2.40 | .60 |
| Hamilton Tiger-Cats | | | |
| ☐ 7 Ron Lancaster | 20.00 | 8.00 | 2.00 |
| Saskatchewan Roughriders | | | |
| ☐ 8 Bill Symons | 6.00 | 2.40 | .60 |
| Toronto Argonauts | | | |
| ☐ 9 Steve Smear | 10.00 | 4.00 | 1.00 |
| Montreal Alouettes | | | |
| ☐ 10 Angelo Mosca | 18.00 | 7.25 | 1.80 |
| Hamilton Tiger-Cats | | | |
| ☐ 11 Wayne Harris | 15.00 | 6.00 | 1.50 |
| Calgary Stampeders | | | |
| ☐ 12 Greg Findlay | 5.00 | 2.00 | .50 |
| British Columbia Lions | | | |
| ☐ 13 John Wydareny | 6.00 | 2.40 | .60 |
| Edmonton Eskimos | | | |
| ☐ 14 Garney Henley | 15.00 | 6.00 | 1.50 |
| Hamilton Tiger-Cats | | | |
| ☐ 15 Al Phaneuf | 6.00 | 2.40 | .60 |
| Montreal Alouettes | | | |
| ☐ 16 Ed Harrington | 5.00 | 2.00 | .50 |
| Toronto Argonauts | | | |

## 1972 O-Pee-Chee CFL

The 1972 O-Pee-Chee CFL set of 132 cards is the last O-Pee-Chee CFL issue to date. Cards are ordered by teams: Hamilton Tiger-Cats (1-13), Montreal Alouettes (14-26), Toronto Argonauts (27-39), British Columbia Lions (40-52), Calgary Stampeders (53-65), Ottawa Rough Riders (66-78), Saskatchewan Roughriders (79-91), Edmonton Eskimos (92-104), and Winnipeg Blue Bombers (105-117). The cards measure 2 1/2" by 3 1/2". The card backs are written in French and English; card back is blue and green print on white card stock. Fourteen Pro-Action cards (118-131) and a checklist card (132) complete the set. The key card in the set is Joe Theismann. The cards were originally sold in ten-cent wax packs with eight cards and a piece of bubble gum.

| | NRMT | VG-E | GOOD |
|---|---|---|---|
| COMPLETE SET (132) | 175.00 | 70.00 | 18.00 |
| COMMON PLAYER (1-132) | 1.25 | .50 | .12 |

| | | | |
|---|---|---|---|
| ☐ 1 Bob Krouse | 2.50 | 1.00 | .25 |
| ☐ 2 John Williams | 1.25 | .50 | .12 |
| ☐ 3 Garney Henley | 6.00 | 2.40 | .60 |
| ☐ 4 Dick Wesolowski | 1.25 | .50 | .12 |
| ☐ 5 Paul McKay | 1.25 | .50 | .12 |
| ☐ 6 Bill Danychuk | 2.00 | .80 | .20 |
| ☐ 7 Angelo Mosca | 10.00 | 4.00 | 1.00 |
| ☐ 8 Tommy Joe Coffey | 5.00 | 2.00 | .50 |
| ☐ 9 Tony Gabriel | 10.00 | 4.00 | 1.00 |
| ☐ 10 Mike Blum | 1.25 | .50 | .12 |
| ☐ 11 Doug Mitchell | 1.25 | .50 | .12 |
| ☐ 12 Emery Hicks | 1.25 | .50 | .12 |
| ☐ 13 Max Anderson | 1.25 | .50 | .12 |
| ☐ 14 Ed George | 2.00 | .80 | .20 |
| ☐ 15 Mark Kosmos | 2.00 | .80 | .20 |
| ☐ 16 Ted Collins | 1.25 | .50 | .12 |
| ☐ 17 Peter Dalla Riva | 5.00 | 2.00 | .50 |
| ☐ 18 Pierre Desjardins | 1.25 | .50 | .12 |
| ☐ 19 Terry Evanshen | 6.00 | 2.40 | .60 |
| ☐ 20 Larry Fairholm | 2.00 | .80 | .20 |
| ☐ 21 Jim Foley | 2.00 | .80 | .20 |
| ☐ 22 Gordon Judges | 1.25 | .50 | .12 |
| ☐ 23 Barry Randall | 1.25 | .50 | .12 |
| ☐ 24 Brad Upshaw | 1.25 | .50 | .12 |
| ☐ 25 Jorma Kuisma | 1.25 | .50 | .12 |
| ☐ 26 Mike Widger | 1.25 | .50 | .12 |
| ☐ 27 Joe Theismann | 50.00 | 20.00 | 5.00 |
| ☐ 28 Greg Barton | 4.00 | 1.60 | .40 |
| ☐ 29 Bill Symons | 3.00 | 1.20 | .30 |
| ☐ 30 Leon McQuay | 4.00 | 1.60 | .40 |
| ☐ 31 Jim Corrigall | 4.00 | 1.60 | .40 |
| ☐ 32 Jim Stillwagon | 4.00 | 1.60 | .40 |
| ☐ 33 Dick Thornton | 2.00 | .80 | .20 |
| ☐ 34 Marv Luster | 4.00 | 1.60 | .40 |
| ☐ 35 Paul Desjardins | 1.25 | .50 | .12 |
| ☐ 36 Mike Eben | 1.25 | .50 | .12 |
| ☐ 37 Eric Allen | 5.00 | 2.00 | .50 |
| ☐ 38 Chip Barrett | 1.25 | .50 | .12 |
| ☐ 39 Noah Jackson | 3.00 | 1.20 | .30 |
| ☐ 40 Jim Young | 6.00 | 2.40 | .60 |
| ☐ 41 Trevor Ekdahl | 2.00 | .80 | .20 |
| ☐ 42 Garrett Hunsperger | 1.25 | .50 | .12 |
| ☐ 43 Willie Postler | 1.25 | .50 | .12 |
| ☐ 44 George Anderson | 1.25 | .50 | .12 |
| ☐ 45 Ron Estay | 1.25 | .50 | .12 |
| ☐ 46 Johnny Musso | 20.00 | 8.00 | 2.00 |
| ☐ 47 Eric Guthrie | 1.25 | .50 | .12 |
| ☐ 48 Monroe Eley | 1.25 | .50 | .12 |
| ☐ 49 Don Bunce | 5.00 | 2.00 | .50 |
| ☐ 50 Jim Evenson | 2.00 | .80 | .20 |
| ☐ 51 Ken Sugarman | 2.00 | .80 | .20 |
| ☐ 52 Dave Golinsky | 1.25 | .50 | .12 |
| ☐ 53 Wayne Harris | 5.00 | 2.00 | .50 |
| ☐ 54 Jerry Keeling | 4.00 | 1.60 | .40 |
| ☐ 55 Herman Harrison | 4.00 | 1.60 | .40 |
| ☐ 56 Larry Robinson | 2.00 | .80 | .20 |
| ☐ 57 John Helton | 4.00 | 1.60 | .40 |
| ☐ 58 Gerry Shaw | 1.25 | .50 | .12 |
| ☐ 59 Frank Andruski | 1.25 | .50 | .12 |
| ☐ 60 Basil Bark | 1.25 | .50 | .12 |
| ☐ 61 Joe Forzani | 2.00 | .80 | .20 |
| ☐ 62 Jim Furlong | 1.25 | .50 | .12 |
| ☐ 63 Rudy Linterman | 2.00 | .80 | .20 |
| ☐ 64 Granville Liggins | 4.00 | 1.60 | .40 |
| ☐ 65 Lanny Boleski | 1.25 | .50 | .12 |
| ☐ 66 Hugh Oldham | 1.25 | .50 | .12 |
| ☐ 67 Dave Braggins | 1.25 | .50 | .12 |
| ☐ 68 Jerry Campbell | 1.25 | .50 | .12 |
| ☐ 69 Al Marcelin | 2.00 | .80 | .20 |
| ☐ 70 Tom Pullen | 1.25 | .50 | .12 |
| ☐ 71 Rudy Sims | 1.25 | .50 | .12 |
| ☐ 72 Marshall Shirk | 1.25 | .50 | .12 |
| ☐ 73 Tom Laputka | 1.25 | .50 | .12 |
| ☐ 74 Barry Ardern | 1.25 | .50 | .12 |
| ☐ 75 Billy Cooper | 1.25 | .50 | .12 |
| ☐ 76 Dan Deever | 1.25 | .50 | .12 |
| ☐ 77 Wayne Giardino | 1.25 | .50 | .12 |
| ☐ 78 Terry Wellesley | 1.25 | .50 | .12 |
| ☐ 79 Ron Lancaster | 12.00 | 5.00 | 1.20 |
| ☐ 80 George Reed | 10.00 | 4.00 | 1.00 |
| ☐ 81 Bobby Thompson | 1.25 | .50 | .12 |
| ☐ 82 Jack Abendschan | 1.25 | .50 | .12 |
| ☐ 83 Ed McQuarters | 3.00 | 1.20 | .30 |
| ☐ 84 Bruce Bennett | 3.00 | 1.20 | .30 |
| ☐ 85 Bill Baker | 5.00 | 2.00 | .50 |
| ☐ 86 Don Bahnuik | 1.25 | .50 | .12 |
| ☐ 87 Gary Brandt | 1.25 | .50 | .12 |
| ☐ 88 Henry Dorach | 1.25 | .50 | .12 |
| ☐ 89 Ted Dushinski | 1.25 | .50 | .12 |
| ☐ 90 Alan Ford | 1.25 | .50 | .12 |
| ☐ 91 Bob Kosid | 1.25 | .50 | .12 |
| ☐ 92 Greg Pipes | 2.00 | .80 | .20 |
| ☐ 93 John LaGrone | 2.00 | .80 | .20 |
| ☐ 94 Dave Gasser | 1.25 | .50 | .12 |
| ☐ 95 Bobby Taylor | 2.50 | 1.00 | .25 |
| ☐ 96 Dave Cutler | 5.00 | 2.00 | .50 |
| ☐ 97 Dick Dupuis | 1.50 | .60 | .15 |
| ☐ 98 Ron Forwick | 1.25 | .50 | .12 |
| ☐ 99 Bayne Norrie | 1.25 | .50 | .12 |
| ☐ 100 Jim Henshall | 1.25 | .50 | .12 |
| ☐ 101 Charlie Turner | 1.25 | .50 | .12 |
| ☐ 102 Fred Dunn | 1.25 | .50 | .12 |
| ☐ 103 Sam Scarber | 1.25 | .50 | .12 |
| ☐ 104 Bruce Lemmerman | 5.00 | 2.00 | .50 |
| ☐ 105 Don Jonas | 5.00 | 2.00 | .50 |
| ☐ 106 Doug Strong | 1.25 | .50 | .12 |
| ☐ 107 Ed Williams | 1.25 | .50 | .12 |
| ☐ 108 Paul Markle | 1.25 | .50 | .12 |
| ☐ 109 Gene Lakusiak | 1.25 | .50 | .12 |
| ☐ 110 Bob LaRose | 1.25 | .50 | .12 |
| ☐ 111 Rob McLaren | 1.25 | .50 | .12 |
| ☐ 112 Pete Ribbins | 1.25 | .50 | .12 |
| ☐ 113 Bill Frank | 1.25 | .50 | .12 |
| ☐ 114 Bob Swift | 1.25 | .50 | .12 |
| ☐ 115 Chuck Liebrock | 1.25 | .50 | .12 |
| ☐ 116 Joe Critchlow | 1.25 | .50 | .12 |
| ☐ 117 Paul Williams | 1.25 | .50 | .12 |
| ☐ 118 Pro Action | 1.25 | .50 | .12 |
| ☐ 119 Pro Action | 1.25 | .50 | .12 |
| ☐ 120 Pro Action | 1.25 | .50 | .12 |
| ☐ 121 Pro Action | 1.25 | .50 | .12 |
| ☐ 122 Pro Action | 1.25 | .50 | .12 |
| ☐ 123 Pro Action | 1.25 | .50 | .12 |
| ☐ 124 Pro Action | 1.25 | .50 | .12 |
| ☐ 125 Pro Action | 1.25 | .50 | .12 |
| ☐ 126 Pro Action | 1.25 | .50 | .12 |
| ☐ 127 Pro Action | 1.25 | .50 | .12 |
| ☐ 128 Pro Action | 1.25 | .50 | .12 |
| ☐ 129 Pro Action | 1.25 | .50 | .12 |
| ☐ 130 Pro Action | 1.25 | .50 | .12 |
| ☐ 131 Pro Action | 1.25 | .50 | .12 |
| ☐ 132 Checklist Card | 25.00 | 4.00 | .80 |

## 1972 O-Pee-Chee CFL Trio Sticker Inserts

Issued with the 1972 CFL regular cards was this 24-card set of trio peel-off sticker inserts. These blank-backed panels of three small stickers are 2 1/2" by 3 1/2" and have a distinctive black border around an inner white border. Each individual player is numbered in the upper corner of his card; the player's name and team are given below the player's picture in the black border. The copyright notation (O.P.C. Printed in Canada) is overprinted in the picture area of the card.

| | NRMT | VG-E | GOOD |
|---|---|---|---|
| COMPLETE SET (24) | 250.00 | 100.00 | 25.00 |
| COMMON PANEL (1-72) | 10.00 | 4.00 | 1.00 |
| | | | |
| ☐ 1 Johnny Musso | 40.00 | 16.00 | 4.00 |
|    2 Ron Lancaster | | | |
|    3 Don Jonas | | | |
| ☐ 4 Jerry Campbell | 10.00 | 4.00 | 1.00 |
|    5 Bill Symons | | | |
|    6 Ted Collins | | | |
| ☐ 7 Dave Cutler | 10.00 | 4.00 | 1.00 |
|    8 Paul McKay | | | |
|    9 Rudy Sims | | | |
| ☐ 10 Wayne Harris | 25.00 | 10.00 | 2.50 |
|    11 Greg Pipes | | | |
|    12 Chuck Ealey | | | |
| ☐ 13 Ron Estay | 10.00 | 4.00 | 1.00 |
|    14 Jack Abendschan | | | |
|    15 Paul Markle | | | |
| ☐ 16 Jim Stillwagon | 15.00 | 6.00 | 1.50 |
|    17 Terry Evanshen | | | |
|    18 Willie Postler | | | |
| ☐ 19 Hugh Oldham | 40.00 | 16.00 | 4.00 |
|    20 Joe Theismann | | | |
|    21 Ed George | | | |

| | | | |
|---|---|---|---|
| ☐ 22 Larry Robinson | 15.00 | 6.00 | 1.50 |
| 23 Bruce Lemmerman | | | |
| 24 Garney Henley | | | |
| ☐ 25 Bill Baker | 12.00 | 5.00 | 1.20 |
| 26 Bob LaRose | | | |
| 27 Frank Andruski | | | |
| ☐ 28 Don Bunce | 18.00 | 7.25 | 1.80 |
| 29 George Reed | | | |
| 30 Doug Strong | | | |
| ☐ 31 Al Marcelin | 12.00 | 5.00 | 1.20 |
| 32 Leon McQuay | | | |
| 33 Peter Dalla Riva | | | |
| ☐ 34 Dick Dupuis | 10.00 | 4.00 | 1.00 |
| 35 Bill Danychuk | | | |
| 36 Marshall Shirk | | | |
| ☐ 37 Jerry Keeling | 15.00 | 6.00 | 1.50 |
| 38 John LaGrone | | | |
| 39 Bob Krouse | | | |
| ☐ 40 Jim Young | 15.00 | 6.00 | 1.50 |
| 41 Ed McQuarters | | | |
| 42 Gene Lakusiak | | | |
| ☐ 43 Dick Thornton | 10.00 | 4.00 | 1.00 |
| 44 Larry Fairholm | | | |
| 45 Garrett Hunsperger | | | |
| ☐ 46 Dave Braggins | 12.00 | 5.00 | 1.20 |
| 47 Greg Barton | | | |
| 48 Mark Kosmos | | | |
| ☐ 49 John Helton | 12.00 | 5.00 | 1.20 |
| 50 Bobby Taylor | | | |
| 51 Dick Wesolowski | | | |
| ☐ 52 Don Bahnuik | 10.00 | 4.00 | 1.00 |
| 53 Rob McLaren | | | |
| 54 Granville Liggins | | | |
| ☐ 55 Monroe Eley | 10.00 | 4.00 | 1.00 |
| 56 Bob Thompson | | | |
| 57 Ed Williams | | | |
| ☐ 58 Tom Pullen | 10.00 | 4.00 | 1.00 |
| 59 Jim Corrigall | | | |
| 60 Pierre Desjardins | | | |
| ☐ 61 Ron Forwick | 18.00 | 7.25 | 1.80 |
| 62 Angelo Mosca | | | |
| 63 Tom Laputka | | | |
| ☐ 64 Herman Harrison | 10.00 | 4.00 | 1.00 |
| 65 Dave Gasser | | | |
| 66 John Williams | | | |
| ☐ 67 Trevor Ekdahl | 10.00 | 4.00 | 1.00 |
| 68 Bruce Bennett | | | |
| 69 Gerry Shaw | | | |
| ☐ 70 Jim Foley | 10.00 | 4.00 | 1.00 |
| 71 Pete Ribbins | | | |
| 72 Marv Luster | | | |

## 1952 Parkhurst CFL

Peter Neumann
Hamilton Tiger-Cats

Peter Neumann was born in St. Catharines, Ontario, on August 10th, 1932. 5' 11½" tall, Pete plays end and has earned himself the reputation of being one of the better young players. Great things are expected of him on the gridiron in the future. This blue eyed, brown haired footballer played with the Tiger-Cats last year.

SAVE THE COMPLETE SET OF 100 PARKIES 1952 FOOTBALL CARDS

The 1952 Parkhurst CFL set of 100 cards is the earliest known CFL issue. Features include the four Eastern teams: Toronto Argonauts (20-40), Montreal Alouettes (41-61), Ottawa Rough Riders (63-78, 100), and Hamilton Tiger-Cats (79-99), as well as 19 instructional artwork cards (1-19). These small cards measure approximately 1 7/8" by 2 3/4". There are two different number 58's and card number 62 does not exist.

| | NRMT | VG-E | GOOD |
|---|---|---|---|
| COMPLETE SET (100) | 3000.00 | 1350.00 | 325.00 |
| COMMON CARD (1-19) | 20.00 | 8.00 | 2.00 |
| COMMON PLAYER (20-100) | 30.00 | 12.00 | 3.00 |

| | | | |
|---|---|---|---|
| ☐ 1 Watch the games | 50.00 | 12.00 | 2.50 |
| ☐ 2 Teamwork | 20.00 | 8.00 | 2.00 |
| ☐ 3 Football Equipment | 20.00 | 8.00 | 2.00 |
| ☐ 4 Hang onto the ball | 20.00 | 8.00 | 2.00 |
| ☐ 5 The head on tackle | 20.00 | 8.00 | 2.00 |
| ☐ 6 The football field | 20.00 | 8.00 | 2.00 |

| | | | |
|---|---|---|---|
| ☐ 7 The Lineman's Stance | 20.00 | 8.00 | 2.00 |
| ☐ 8 Centre's spiral pass | 20.00 | 8.00 | 2.00 |
| ☐ 9 The lineman | 20.00 | 8.00 | 2.00 |
| ☐ 10 The place kick | 20.00 | 8.00 | 2.00 |
| ☐ 11 The cross-body block | 20.00 | 8.00 | 2.00 |
| ☐ 12 T formation | 20.00 | 8.00 | 2.00 |
| ☐ 13 Falling on the ball | 20.00 | 8.00 | 2.00 |
| ☐ 14 The throw | 20.00 | 8.00 | 2.00 |
| ☐ 15 Breaking from tackle | 20.00 | 8.00 | 2.00 |
| ☐ 16 How to catch a pass | 20.00 | 8.00 | 2.00 |
| ☐ 17 The punt | 20.00 | 8.00 | 2.00 |
| ☐ 18 Shifting the ball | 20.00 | 8.00 | 2.00 |
| ☐ 19 Penalty signals | 20.00 | 8.00 | 2.00 |
| ☐ 20 Leslie Ascott | 30.00 | 12.00 | 3.00 |
| ☐ 21 Robert Marshall | 30.00 | 12.00 | 3.00 |
| ☐ 22 Tom Harpley | 30.00 | 12.00 | 3.00 |
| ☐ 23 Robert McClelland | 30.00 | 12.00 | 3.00 |
| ☐ 24 Rod Smylie | 30.00 | 12.00 | 3.00 |
| ☐ 25 Bill Bass | 30.00 | 12.00 | 3.00 |
| ☐ 26 Fred Black | 30.00 | 12.00 | 3.00 |
| ☐ 27 Jack Carpenter | 30.00 | 12.00 | 3.00 |
| ☐ 28 Bob Hack | 30.00 | 12.00 | 3.00 |
| ☐ 29 Ulysses Curtis | 30.00 | 12.00 | 3.00 |
| ☐ 30 Nobby Wirkowski | 50.00 | 20.00 | 5.00 |
| ☐ 31 George Arnett | 30.00 | 12.00 | 3.00 |
| ☐ 32 Lorne Parkin | 30.00 | 12.00 | 3.00 |
| ☐ 33 Alex Toogood | 30.00 | 12.00 | 3.00 |
| ☐ 34 Marshall Haymes | 30.00 | 12.00 | 3.00 |
| ☐ 35 Shanty McKenzie | 30.00 | 12.00 | 3.00 |
| ☐ 36 Byron Karrys | 30.00 | 12.00 | 3.00 |
| ☐ 37 George Rooks | 30.00 | 12.00 | 3.00 |
| ☐ 38 Red Ettinger | 30.00 | 12.00 | 3.00 |
| ☐ 39 Al Bruno | 40.00 | 16.00 | 4.00 |
| ☐ 40 Stephen Karrys | 30.00 | 12.00 | 3.00 |
| ☐ 41 Herb Trawick | 50.00 | 20.00 | 5.00 |
| ☐ 42 Sam Etcheverry | 300.00 | 120.00 | 30.00 |
| ☐ 43 Marv Melrowitz | 30.00 | 12.00 | 3.00 |
| ☐ 44 John O'Quinn | 50.00 | 20.00 | 5.00 |
| ☐ 45 Jim Ostendarp | 30.00 | 12.00 | 3.00 |
| ☐ 46 Tom Tofaute | 30.00 | 12.00 | 3.00 |
| ☐ 47 Joey Pal | 30.00 | 12.00 | 3.00 |
| ☐ 48 Ray Cicia | 30.00 | 12.00 | 3.00 |
| ☐ 49 Bruce Coulter | 35.00 | 14.00 | 3.50 |
| ☐ 50 Jim Mitchener | 30.00 | 12.00 | 3.00 |
| ☐ 51 Lally Lalonde | 30.00 | 12.00 | 3.00 |
| ☐ 52 Jim Staton | 30.00 | 12.00 | 3.00 |
| ☐ 53 Glenn Douglas | 30.00 | 12.00 | 3.00 |
| ☐ 54 Dave Tomlinson | 30.00 | 12.00 | 3.00 |
| ☐ 55 Ed Salem | 30.00 | 12.00 | 3.00 |
| ☐ 56 Virgil Wagner | 50.00 | 20.00 | 5.00 |
| ☐ 57 Dawson Tilley | 30.00 | 12.00 | 3.00 |
| ☐ 58A Cec Findlay | 40.00 | 16.00 | 4.00 |
| ☐ 58B Tommy Manastersky | 40.00 | 16.00 | 4.00 |
| ☐ 59 Frank Nable | 30.00 | 12.00 | 3.00 |
| ☐ 60 Chuck Anderson | 30.00 | 12.00 | 3.00 |
| ☐ 61 Charlie Hubbard | 30.00 | 12.00 | 3.00 |
| ☐ 63 Benny MacDonnell | 30.00 | 12.00 | 3.00 |
| ☐ 64 Peter Karpuk | 30.00 | 12.00 | 3.00 |
| ☐ 65 Tom O'Malley | 30.00 | 12.00 | 3.00 |
| ☐ 66 Bill Stanton | 30.00 | 12.00 | 3.00 |
| ☐ 67 Matt Anthony | 30.00 | 12.00 | 3.00 |
| ☐ 68 John Morneau | 30.00 | 12.00 | 3.00 |
| ☐ 69 Howie Turner | 30.00 | 12.00 | 3.00 |
| ☐ 70 Alton Baldwin | 30.00 | 12.00 | 3.00 |
| ☐ 71 John Bovey | 30.00 | 12.00 | 3.00 |
| ☐ 72 Bruno Bitkowski | 35.00 | 14.00 | 3.50 |
| ☐ 73 Gene Roberts | 30.00 | 12.00 | 3.00 |
| ☐ 74 John Wagoner | 30.00 | 12.00 | 3.00 |
| ☐ 75 Ted MacLarty | 30.00 | 12.00 | 3.00 |
| ☐ 76 Jerry Lefebvre | 30.00 | 12.00 | 3.00 |
| ☐ 77 Buck Rogers | 30.00 | 12.00 | 3.00 |
| ☐ 78 Bruce Cummings | 30.00 | 12.00 | 3.00 |
| ☐ 79 Hal Wagner | 40.00 | 16.00 | 4.00 |
| ☐ 80 Joe Shinn | 30.00 | 12.00 | 3.00 |
| ☐ 81 Eddie Bevan | 30.00 | 12.00 | 3.00 |
| ☐ 82 Ralph Sazio | 50.00 | 20.00 | 5.00 |
| ☐ 83 Bob McDonald | 30.00 | 12.00 | 3.00 |
| ☐ 84 Vince Scott | 40.00 | 16.00 | 4.00 |
| ☐ 85 Jack Stewart | 30.00 | 12.00 | 3.00 |
| ☐ 86 Ralph Bartolini | 30.00 | 12.00 | 3.00 |
| ☐ 87 Blake Taylor | 30.00 | 12.00 | 3.00 |
| ☐ 88 Richard Brown | 30.00 | 12.00 | 3.00 |
| ☐ 89 Douglas Gray | 30.00 | 12.00 | 3.00 |
| ☐ 90 Alex Muzyka | 30.00 | 12.00 | 3.00 |
| ☐ 91 Pete Neumann | 50.00 | 20.00 | 5.00 |
| ☐ 92 Jack Rogers | 30.00 | 12.00 | 3.00 |
| ☐ 93 Bernie Custis | 40.00 | 16.00 | 4.00 |
| ☐ 94 Cam Fraser | 30.00 | 12.00 | 3.00 |
| ☐ 95 Vince Mazza | 40.00 | 16.00 | 4.00 |
| ☐ 96 Peter Wooley | 30.00 | 12.00 | 3.00 |
| ☐ 97 Earl Valiquette | 30.00 | 12.00 | 3.00 |
| ☐ 98 Floyd Cooper | 30.00 | 12.00 | 3.00 |
| ☐ 99 Louis DiFrancisco | 30.00 | 12.00 | 3.00 |
| ☐ 100 Robert Simpson | 125.00 | 25.00 | 5.00 |

## 1956 Parkhurst CFL

ROLLIE MILES—Halfback
Edmonton Eskimos

Rollie is the most popular player on the team. Made the Western Conference All Stars, 1951-55. He is 26 years old, 5'10" and weighs 182 lbs.

The 1956 Parkhurst CFL set of 50 cards features ten players from each of five teams: Edmonton Eskimos (1-10), Saskatchewan Roughriders (11-20), Calgary Stampeders (21-30), Winnipeg Blue Bombers (31-40), and Montreal Alouettes (41-50). Cards are numbered on the front. The cards measure approximately 1 3/4" by 1 7/8". The cards were sold in wax boxes of 48 five-cent wax packs each containing cards and gum. The set features an early card of Bud Grant, who later coached the Minnesota Vikings.

|  | NRMT | VG-E | GOOD |
|---|---|---|---|
| COMPLETE SET (50) | 3500.00 | 1500.00 | 400.00 |
| COMMON PLAYER (1-50) | 40.00 | 16.00 | 4.00 |
| ☐ 1 Art Walker | 80.00 | 32.00 | 8.00 |
| ☐ 2 Frank Anderson | 40.00 | 16.00 | 4.00 |
| ☐ 3 Normie Kwong | 150.00 | 60.00 | 15.00 |
| ☐ 4 Johnny Bright | 150.00 | 60.00 | 15.00 |
| ☐ 5 Jackie Parker | 500.00 | 200.00 | 50.00 |
| ☐ 6 Bob Dean | 40.00 | 16.00 | 4.00 |
| ☐ 7 Don Getty | 125.00 | 50.00 | 12.50 |
| ☐ 8 Rollie Miles | 100.00 | 40.00 | 10.00 |
| ☐ 9 Ted Tully | 40.00 | 16.00 | 4.00 |
| ☐ 10 Frank Morris | 90.00 | 36.00 | 9.00 |
| ☐ 11 Martin Ruby | 80.00 | 32.00 | 8.00 |
| ☐ 12 Mel Beckett | 80.00 | 32.00 | 8.00 |
| ☐ 13 Bill Clarke | 40.00 | 16.00 | 4.00 |
| ☐ 14 John Wozniak | 40.00 | 16.00 | 4.00 |
| ☐ 15 Larry Isbell | 40.00 | 16.00 | 4.00 |
| ☐ 16 Ken Carpenter | 80.00 | 32.00 | 8.00 |
| ☐ 17 Sully Glasser | 40.00 | 16.00 | 4.00 |
| ☐ 18 Bobby Marlow | 90.00 | 36.00 | 9.00 |
| ☐ 19 Paul Anderson | 40.00 | 16.00 | 4.00 |
| ☐ 20 Gord Sturtridge | 80.00 | 32.00 | 8.00 |
| ☐ 21 Alex Macklin | 40.00 | 16.00 | 4.00 |
| ☐ 22 Duke Cook | 40.00 | 16.00 | 4.00 |
| ☐ 23 Bill Stevenson | 40.00 | 16.00 | 4.00 |
| ☐ 24 Lynn Bottoms | 80.00 | 32.00 | 8.00 |
| ☐ 25 Aramis Dandoy | 40.00 | 16.00 | 4.00 |
| ☐ 26 Peter Muir | 40.00 | 16.00 | 4.00 |
| ☐ 27 Harvey Wylie | 80.00 | 32.00 | 8.00 |
| ☐ 28 Joe Yamauchi | 40.00 | 16.00 | 4.00 |
| ☐ 29 John Alderton | 40.00 | 16.00 | 4.00 |
| ☐ 30 Bill McKenna | 40.00 | 16.00 | 4.00 |
| ☐ 31 Edward Kotowich | 40.00 | 16.00 | 4.00 |
| ☐ 32 Herb Gray | 100.00 | 40.00 | 10.00 |
| ☐ 33 Calvin Jones | 100.00 | 40.00 | 10.00 |
| ☐ 34 Herman Day | 40.00 | 16.00 | 4.00 |
| ☐ 35 Buddy Leake | 40.00 | 16.00 | 4.00 |
| ☐ 36 Robert McNamara | 40.00 | 16.00 | 4.00 |
| ☐ 37 Bud Grant | 300.00 | 120.00 | 30.00 |
| ☐ 38 Gord Rowland | 80.00 | 32.00 | 8.00 |
| ☐ 39 Glen McWhinney | 40.00 | 16.00 | 4.00 |
| ☐ 40 Lorne Benson | 40.00 | 16.00 | 4.00 |
| ☐ 41 Sam Etcheverry | 300.00 | 120.00 | 30.00 |
| ☐ 42 Joey Pal | 40.00 | 16.00 | 4.00 |
| ☐ 43 Tom Hugo | 40.00 | 16.00 | 4.00 |
| ☐ 44 Tex Coulter | 80.00 | 32.00 | 8.00 |
| ☐ 45 Doug McNichol | 40.00 | 16.00 | 4.00 |
| ☐ 46 Tom Moran | 40.00 | 16.00 | 4.00 |
| ☐ 47 Red O'Quinn | 80.00 | 32.00 | 8.00 |
| ☐ 48 Hal Patterson | 200.00 | 80.00 | 20.00 |
| ☐ 49 Jacques Belec | 40.00 | 16.00 | 4.00 |
| ☐ 50 Pat Abruzzi | 100.00 | 35.00 | 7.00 |

## 1982 Police Hamilton

This 35-card safety set was co-sponsored by the Hamilton Tiger-Cats, The Spectator (newspaper), and the Hamilton Fire Department. These standard-size (2 1/2" by 3 1/2") cards were printed on thin cardboard stock and feature posed color player photos, shot from the waist up against a light blue background. The surrounding card face is gold, with player information in black below the picture. The backs have biography, a fire safety tip in the form of a player quote, as well as team and sponsor logos. The cards are unnumbered and checklisted below in alphabetical order. Four additional cards were produced but

TOM CLEMENTS
QUARTERBACK
HAMILTON TIGER-CATS, 1982

TOM CLEMENTS
QUARTERBACK
6'0" 183 lbs., Age 28
Import
University of Notre Dame

FIRE SAFETY TIP
Tom Clements says: "Pass the word — fire destroys life, property and jobs."

The 1982 Hamilton Tiger-Cat trading card program is a community project co-sponsored by the Hamilton Tiger-Cats, The Spectator and the Hamilton Fire Department. This program is endorsed by the CFL Player's Association.

The Spectator
IT'S YOUR NEWSPAPER

not released as part of the set and hence are not included below. These four cards (Horton, Kuklo, Martel, and Mathews) are quite scarce as they were only issued to press members and a few distinguished guests at a Hamilton Tiger-Cat game.

|  | MINT | EXC | G-VG |
|---|---|---|---|
| COMPLETE SET (35) | 20.00 | 8.00 | 2.00 |
| COMMON PLAYER (1-35) | .50 | .20 | .05 |
| ☐ 1 Marv Allemang | .50 | .20 | .05 |
| ☐ 2 Jeff Arp | .50 | .20 | .05 |
| ☐ 3 Keith Baker | .50 | .20 | .05 |
| ☐ 4 Gerald Bess | .75 | .30 | .07 |
| ☐ 5 Mark Bragagnolo | .50 | .20 | .05 |
| ☐ 6 Carmelo Carteri | .50 | .20 | .05 |
| ☐ 7 Tom Clements | 7.50 | 3.00 | .75 |
| ☐ 8 Grover Covington | 3.00 | 1.20 | .30 |
| ☐ 9 Rocky DiPietro | 4.00 | 1.60 | .40 |
| ☐ 10 Howard Fields | .50 | .20 | .05 |
| ☐ 11 Ross Francis | .50 | .20 | .05 |
| ☐ 12 Ed Fulton | .50 | .20 | .05 |
| ☐ 13 Peter Gales | .50 | .20 | .05 |
| ☐ 14 Ed Gataveckas | .50 | .20 | .05 |
| ☐ 15 Dave Graffi | .50 | .20 | .05 |
| ☐ 16 Obie Graves | .50 | .20 | .05 |
| ☐ 17 Hazen Henderson | .50 | .20 | .05 |
| ☐ 18 Ron Johnson | 1.25 | .50 | .12 |
| ☐ 19 Dave Marler | .75 | .30 | .07 |
| ☐ 20 Jim Muller | .50 | .20 | .05 |
| ☐ 21 Leroy Paul | .50 | .20 | .05 |
| ☐ 22 John Priestner | .75 | .30 | .07 |
| ☐ 23 Dave Purves | .50 | .20 | .05 |
| ☐ 24 James Ramey | .50 | .20 | .05 |
| ☐ 25 Doug Redl | .50 | .20 | .05 |
| ☐ 26 Bernie Ruoff | .75 | .30 | .07 |
| ☐ 27 David Sauve | .50 | .20 | .05 |
| ☐ 28 David Shaw | .50 | .20 | .05 |
| ☐ 29 Kerry Smith | .50 | .20 | .05 |
| ☐ 30 Steve Stapler | 1.00 | .40 | .10 |
| ☐ 31 Kyle Stevens | .50 | .20 | .05 |
| ☐ 32 Mike Walker | 2.00 | .80 | .20 |
| ☐ 33 Henry Waszczuk | .50 | .20 | .05 |
| ☐ 34 Harold Woods | .50 | .20 | .05 |
| ☐ 35 Ben Zambiasi | 2.50 | 1.00 | .25 |

## 1982 Police Saskatchewan

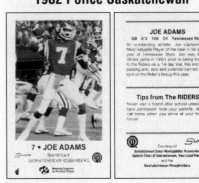

7 • JOE ADAMS
SASKATCHEWAN ROUGHRIDERS

JOE ADAMS
QB 6'3 190 24 Tennessee State

An outstanding athlete, Joe captured the Most Valuable Player of the Year in his senior year at Tennessee State. Joe was in the 49'ers camp in 1981 prior to being brought to the Riders on a 14 day trial. His excellent passing arm, size and potential earned him a spot on the Rider's lineup this year.

Tips from The RIDERS
Never visit a friend after school unless you have permission from your parents. Always call home when you arrive at your friend's house.

Courtesy of
Saskatchewan Urban Municipalities Association, Optimist Clubs of Saskatchewan, Your Local Police and the Saskatchewan Roughriders

The 1982 Police SUMA (Saskatchewan Urban Municipalities Association) Saskatchewan Roughriders set contains 16 cards measuring approximately 2 5/8" by 4 1/8". The fronts have color action photos bordered in white; the vertically oriented backs have career highlights and safety tips. The card backs have black printing with green accent on white card stock. The cards are printed on thin stock. The cards are unnumbered, so they are listed below by uniform number.

| | MINT | EXC | G-VG |
|---|---|---|---|
| COMPLETE SET (16) | 12.00 | 5.00 | 1.20 |
| COMMON PLAYER | .75 | .30 | .07 |
| ☐ 2 Greg Fieger | .75 | .30 | .07 |
| ☐ 7 Joe Adams | 1.00 | .40 | .10 |
| ☐ 12 John Hufnagel | 4.00 | 1.60 | .40 |
| ☐ 17 Joey Walters | .75 | .30 | .07 |
| ☐ 20 Ken McEachern | .75 | .30 | .07 |
| ☐ 21 Marcellus Greene | 1.00 | .40 | .10 |
| ☐ 25 Steve Dennis | .75 | .30 | .07 |
| ☐ 29 Fran McDermott | .75 | .30 | .07 |
| ☐ 37 Frank Robinson | 1.00 | .40 | .10 |
| ☐ 44 Roger Aldag | 1.25 | .50 | .12 |
| ☐ 57 Bob Poley | .75 | .30 | .07 |
| ☐ 66 Mike Samples | .75 | .30 | .07 |
| ☐ 69 Don Swafford | .75 | .30 | .07 |
| ☐ 74 Chris DeFrance | .75 | .30 | .07 |
| ☐ 76 Lyall Woznesensky | .75 | .30 | .07 |
| ☐ 78 Vince Goldsmith | 1.50 | .60 | .15 |

## 1982 Police Winnipeg

This 24-card Police set was sponsored by the Union of Manitoba Municipalities, all Police Forces in Manitoba, and The Optimist Clubs of Manitoba. The cards measure approximately 2 5/8" by 3 7/8" and were issued in two-card perforated panels. The panel pairs were Kennerd/Phason, Jackson/Walby, Pierson/House, Miller/Mikawos, Goodlow/Bennett, Bonk/Helton, Catan/Ezerins, Norman/Jones, Smith/Williams, Thompson/Poplawski, Bastaja/Reed, and Jauch/Brock. The fronts have posed color player photos, bordered in white with player information below the picture. The backs have "Bomber Tips" that consist of public safety announcements. These thin-stock cards are unnumbered and checklisted below in alphabetical order.

| | MINT | EXC | G-VG |
|---|---|---|---|
| COMPLETE SET (24) | 12.00 | 5.00 | 1.20 |
| COMMON CARD (1-24) | .50 | .20 | .05 |
| ☐ 1 Nick Bastaja | .50 | .20 | .05 |
| ☐ 2 Paul Bennett | .50 | .20 | .05 |
| ☐ 3 John Bonk | .50 | .20 | .05 |
| ☐ 4 Dieter Brock | 3.00 | 1.20 | .30 |
| ☐ 5 Peter Catan | .50 | .20 | .05 |
| ☐ 6 Leo Ezerins | .50 | .20 | .05 |
| ☐ 7 Eugene Goodlow | .50 | .20 | .05 |
| ☐ 8 John Helton | 2.00 | .80 | .20 |
| ☐ 9 Rick House | .75 | .30 | .07 |
| ☐ 10 Mark Jackson | .60 | .24 | .06 |
| ☐ 11 Ray Jauch CO | .50 | .20 | .05 |
| ☐ 12 Milson Jones | 1.00 | .40 | .10 |
| ☐ 13 Trevor Kennerd | 1.50 | .60 | .15 |
| ☐ 14 Stan Mikawos | .50 | .20 | .05 |
| ☐ 15 William Miller | .60 | .24 | .06 |
| ☐ 16 Tony Norman | .50 | .20 | .05 |
| ☐ 17 Vince Phason | .50 | .20 | .05 |
| ☐ 18 Reggie Pierson | .50 | .20 | .05 |
| ☐ 19 Joe Poplawski | .75 | .30 | .07 |
| ☐ 20 James Reed | .50 | .20 | .05 |
| ☐ 21 Franky Smith | .50 | .20 | .05 |
| ☐ 22 Bobby Thompson | .50 | .20 | .05 |
| ☐ 23 Chris Walby | 1.50 | .60 | .15 |
| ☐ 24 Charles Williams | .50 | .20 | .05 |

## 1983 Police Hamilton

This 37-card police set was jointly sponsored by the Hamilton Tiger-Cats, The Spectator (a newspaper), and the Hamilton Fire Department. The standard-size (2 1/2" by 3 1/2") cards are printed on thin card stock and feature posed color player photos, shot from the waist up against a black background. The surrounding card face is gold, with player information in black print below the picture. The backs have biographical information, a fire safety tip in the form of a player quote, as well as team and sponsor logos. The cards are unnumbered and checklisted below in alphabetical order.

| | MINT | EXC | G-VG |
|---|---|---|---|
| COMPLETE SET (37) | 20.00 | 8.00 | 2.00 |
| COMMON PLAYER (1-37) | .50 | .20 | .05 |
| ☐ 1 Marv Allemang | .50 | .20 | .05 |
| ☐ 2 Jeff Arp | .50 | .20 | .05 |
| ☐ 3 Keith Baker | .50 | .20 | .05 |
| ☐ 4 Harold E. Ballard PRES | 2.50 | 1.00 | .25 |
| ☐ 5 Mike Barker | .50 | .20 | .05 |
| ☐ 6 Gerald Bess | .75 | .30 | .07 |
| ☐ 7 Pat Brady | .50 | .20 | .05 |
| ☐ 8 Mark Bragagnolo | .50 | .20 | .05 |
| ☐ 9 Tom Clements | 7.50 | 3.00 | .75 |
| ☐ 10 Grover Covington | 3.00 | 1.20 | .30 |
| ☐ 11 Rufus Crawford | 1.50 | .60 | .15 |
| ☐ 12 Rocky DiPietro | 4.00 | 1.60 | .40 |
| ☐ 13 Leo Ezerins | .50 | .20 | .05 |
| ☐ 14 Howard Fields | .50 | .20 | .05 |
| ☐ 15 Ross Francis | .50 | .20 | .05 |
| ☐ 16 Peter Gales | .50 | .20 | .05 |
| ☐ 17 Ed Gataveckas | .50 | .20 | .05 |
| ☐ 18 Paul Gohier | .50 | .20 | .05 |
| ☐ 19 Dave Graffi | .50 | .20 | .05 |
| ☐ 20 Ron Johnson | 1.25 | .50 | .12 |
| ☐ 21 Steve Kearns | .50 | .20 | .05 |
| ☐ 22 Wayne Lee | .50 | .20 | .05 |
| ☐ 23 Mike McIntyre | .50 | .20 | .05 |
| ☐ 24 Paul Palma | .50 | .20 | .05 |
| ☐ 25 George Piva | .50 | .20 | .05 |
| ☐ 26 Mitchell Price | .75 | .30 | .07 |
| ☐ 27 John Priestner | .75 | .30 | .07 |
| ☐ 28 Bernie Ruoff | .75 | .30 | .07 |
| ☐ 29 David Sauve | .50 | .20 | .05 |
| ☐ 30 Johnny Shepherd | .50 | .20 | .05 |
| ☐ 31 Steve Stapler | 1.00 | .40 | .10 |
| ☐ 32 Mark Streeter | .50 | .20 | .05 |
| ☐ 33 Jeff Tedford | .50 | .20 | .05 |
| ☐ 34 Mike Walker | 2.00 | .80 | .20 |
| ☐ 35 Henry Waszczuk | .50 | .20 | .05 |
| ☐ 36 Felix Wright | 2.50 | 1.00 | .25 |
| ☐ 37 Ben Zambiasi | 2.50 | 1.00 | .25 |

## 1983 Police Saskatchewan

The 1983 Police SUMA (Saskatchewan Urban Municipalities Association) Saskatchewan Roughriders set contains 16 cards measuring approximately 2 5/8" by 4 1/8". The fronts have color action photos bordered in white; the vertically oriented backs have career highlights and safety tips. The card backs have black printing with green accent on white card stock. The cards are printed on thin stock. The cards are unnumbered, so they are listed below by uniform number. The 1983 set is distinguished from the similar 1982 SUMA set by the presence of facsimile autographs on the 1983 version.

| | MINT | EXC | G-VG |
|---|---|---|---|
| COMPLETE SET (16) | 12.00 | 5.00 | 1.20 |
| COMMON PLAYER | .75 | .30 | .07 |

| | | | |
|---|---|---|---|
| ☐ 9 Ron Robinson | 1.00 | .40 | .10 |
| ☐ 12 John Hufnagel | 3.00 | 1.20 | .30 |
| ☐ 13 Ken Clark | 1.00 | .40 | .10 |
| ☐ 18 Mike Washington | 1.00 | .40 | .10 |
| ☐ 24 Marshall Hamilton | .75 | .30 | .07 |
| ☐ 25 Mike Emery | .75 | .30 | .07 |
| ☐ 30 Duane Galloway | .75 | .30 | .07 |
| ☐ 33 Dwight Edwards | 1.00 | .40 | .10 |
| ☐ 36 Dave Ridgway | 2.00 | .80 | .20 |
| ☐ 42 Eddie Lowe | .75 | .30 | .07 |
| ☐ 58 J.C. Pelusi | .75 | .30 | .07 |
| ☐ 60 Karl Morgan | .75 | .30 | .07 |
| ☐ 61 Bryan Illerbrun | .75 | .30 | .07 |
| ☐ 65 Neil Quilter | .75 | .30 | .07 |
| ☐ 72 Ray Elgaard | 3.00 | 1.20 | .30 |
| ☐ 74 Chris DeFrance | .75 | .30 | .07 |

# 1984 Police Ottawa

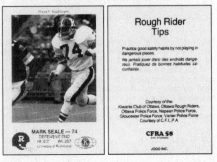

This ten-card full-color set was given away over a ten-week period. The sponsors were Kiwanis, several Police Forces, and radio station CFRA 58 AM. Cards were produced in conjunction with JOGO Inc. The cards are unnumbered although the player's uniform number is given on the front of the card. The numbering below is in alphabetical order for convenience. The cards measure approximately 2 1/2" by 3 1/2". Photos were taken by F. Scott Grant, who is credited on the fronts of the cards. Mark Seale was the card for the tenth and final week; he was printed in a much smaller quantity than the other cards. It was reported that 6,000 of each of the first nine players were given away, whereas only 500 Mark Seale cards were given out.

| | MINT | EXC | G-VG |
|---|---|---|---|
| COMPLETE SET (10) | 25.00 | 10.00 | 2.50 |
| COMMON PLAYER (1-10) | .75 | .30 | .07 |
| | | | |
| ☐ 1 Greg Marshall | 1.50 | .60 | .15 |
| ☐ 2 Dave Newman | .75 | .30 | .07 |
| ☐ 3 Rudy Phillips | 1.25 | .50 | .12 |
| ☐ 4 Jim Reid | 1.25 | .50 | .12 |
| ☐ 5 Mark Seale SP | 18.00 | 7.25 | 1.80 |
| ☐ 6 Rick Sowieta | 1.25 | .50 | .12 |
| ☐ 7 Pat Stoqua | 1.00 | .40 | .10 |
| ☐ 8 Skip Walker | 2.50 | 1.00 | .25 |
| ☐ 9 Al Washington | .75 | .30 | .07 |
| ☐ 10 J.C. Watts | 4.00 | 1.60 | .40 |

# 1985 Police Ottawa

This ten-card set was also sponsored by Burger King as indicated on the front of each card and JOGO Inc. as indicated on the back. The cards measure approximately 2 1/2" by 3 1/2". Card photos (by

photographer F. Scott Grant) all show Ottawa Rough Riders in game action. The numbering below is in alphabetical order for convenience.

| | MINT | EXC | G-VG |
|---|---|---|---|
| COMPLETE SET (10) | 6.00 | 2.40 | .60 |
| COMMON PLAYER (1-10) | .50 | .20 | .05 |
| | | | |
| ☐ 1 Ricky Barden | .50 | .20 | .05 |
| ☐ 2 Michel Bourgeau | .75 | .30 | .07 |
| ☐ 3 Roger Cattelan | .50 | .20 | .05 |
| ☐ 4 Ken Clark | .75 | .30 | .07 |
| ☐ 5 Dean Dorsey | .75 | .30 | .07 |
| ☐ 6 Greg Marshall | .75 | .30 | .07 |
| ☐ 7 Kevin Powell | .50 | .20 | .05 |
| ☐ 8 Jim Reid | .75 | .30 | .07 |
| ☐ 9 Rick Sowieta | .75 | .30 | .07 |
| ☐ 10 J.C. Watts | 1.50 | .60 | .15 |

# 1962 Post Cereal CFL

The 1962 Post Cereal CFL set is the first of two Post Cereal Canadian Football issues. The cards measure the standard 2 1/2" by 3 1/2". The cards were issued on the backs of boxes of Post Cereals distributed in Canada. Cards were not available directly from the company via a send-in offer as with other Post Cereal issues. Cards which are marked as SP are considered somewhat shorter printed and more limited in supply. Many of these short-printed cards have backs that are not the typical brown color but rather white. The cards are arranged according to teams as follows: Montreal Alouettes (1-16), Ottawa Rough Riders (17-34), Toronto Argonauts (35-54), Hamilton Tiger-Cats (55-69), Winnipeg Blue Bombers (70-87), Saskatchewan Roughriders (88-97), Calgary Stampeders (98-107), Edmonton Eskimos (108-121), and British Columbia Lions (122-137).

| | NRMT | VG-E | GOOD |
|---|---|---|---|
| COMPLETE SET (137) | 1500.00 | 650.00 | 165.00 |
| COMMON PLAYER (1-137) | 7.50 | 3.00 | .75 |
| | | | |
| ☐ 1A Don Clark | 20.00 | 8.00 | 2.00 |
| (Brown back) | | | |
| ☐ 1B Don Clark SP | 60.00 | 24.00 | 6.00 |
| (White back) | | | |
| ☐ 2 Ed Meadows | 7.50 | 3.00 | .75 |
| ☐ 3 Meco Poliziani | 7.50 | 3.00 | .75 |
| ☐ 4 George Dixon | 20.00 | 8.00 | 2.00 |
| ☐ 5 Bobby Jack Oliver | 9.00 | 3.75 | .90 |
| ☐ 6 Ross Buckle | 7.50 | 3.00 | .75 |
| ☐ 7 Jack Espenship | 7.50 | 3.00 | .75 |
| ☐ 8 Howard Cissell | 7.50 | 3.00 | .75 |
| ☐ 9 Ed Nickla | 7.50 | 3.00 | .75 |
| ☐ 10 Ed Learn | 7.50 | 3.00 | .75 |
| ☐ 11 Billy Ray Locklin | 7.50 | 3.00 | .75 |
| ☐ 12 Don Paquette | 7.50 | 3.00 | .75 |
| ☐ 13 Milt Crain | 7.50 | 3.00 | .75 |
| ☐ 14 Dick Schnell | 7.50 | 3.00 | .75 |
| ☐ 15 Dick Cohee | 7.50 | 3.00 | .75 |
| ☐ 16 Joe Francis | 7.50 | 3.00 | .75 |
| ☐ 17 Gilles Archambeault | 7.50 | 3.00 | .75 |
| ☐ 18 Angelo Mosca | 25.00 | 10.00 | 2.50 |
| ☐ 19 Ernie White | 7.50 | 3.00 | .75 |
| ☐ 20 George Brancato | 7.50 | 3.00 | .75 |
| ☐ 21 Ron Lancaster | 30.00 | 12.00 | 3.00 |
| ☐ 22 Jim Cain | 7.50 | 3.00 | .75 |
| ☐ 23 Gerry Nesbitt | 7.50 | 3.00 | .75 |
| ☐ 24 Russ Jackson | 30.00 | 12.00 | 3.00 |
| ☐ 25 Bob Simpson | 18.00 | 7.25 | 1.80 |
| ☐ 26 Sam Scoccia | 7.50 | 3.00 | .75 |
| ☐ 27 Tom Jones | 7.50 | 3.00 | .75 |
| ☐ 28 Kaye Vaughan | 15.00 | 6.00 | 1.50 |
| ☐ 29 Chuck Stanley | 7.50 | 3.00 | .75 |
| ☐ 30 Dave Thelen | 15.00 | 6.00 | 1.50 |
| ☐ 31 Gary Schreider | 7.50 | 3.00 | .75 |
| ☐ 32 Jim Reynolds | 7.50 | 3.00 | .75 |

| | | | |
|---|---|---|---|
| ☐ 33 Doug Daigneault | 7.50 | 3.00 | .75 |
| ☐ 34 Joe Poirier | 9.00 | 3.75 | .90 |
| ☐ 35 Clare Exelby | 7.50 | 3.00 | .75 |
| ☐ 36 Art Johnson | 7.50 | 3.00 | .75 |
| ☐ 37 Menan Schriewer | 7.50 | 3.00 | .75 |
| ☐ 38 Art Darch | 7.50 | 3.00 | .75 |
| ☐ 39 Cookie Gilchrist | 25.00 | 10.00 | 2.50 |
| ☐ 40 Brian Aston | 7.50 | 3.00 | .75 |
| ☐ 41 Bobby Kuntz SP | 50.00 | 20.00 | 5.00 |
| ☐ 42 Gerry Patrick | 7.50 | 3.00 | .75 |
| ☐ 43 Norm Stoneburgh | 7.50 | 3.00 | .75 |
| ☐ 44 Billy Shipp | 7.50 | 3.00 | .75 |
| ☐ 45 Jim Andreotti | 15.00 | 6.00 | 1.50 |
| ☐ 46 Tobin Rote | 20.00 | 8.00 | 2.00 |
| ☐ 47 Dick Shatto | 15.00 | 6.00 | 1.50 |
| ☐ 48 Dave Mann | 9.00 | 3.75 | .90 |
| ☐ 49 Ron Morris | 7.50 | 3.00 | .75 |
| ☐ 50 Lynn Bottoms | 9.00 | 3.75 | .90 |
| ☐ 51 Jim Rountree | 7.50 | 3.00 | .75 |
| ☐ 52 Bill Mitchell | 7.50 | 3.00 | .75 |
| ☐ 53 Wes Gideon SP | 50.00 | 20.00 | 5.00 |
| ☐ 54 Boyd Carter | 7.50 | 3.00 | .75 |
| ☐ 55 Ron Howell | 9.00 | 3.75 | .90 |
| ☐ 56 John Barrow | 15.00 | 6.00 | 1.50 |
| ☐ 57 Bernie Faloney | 30.00 | 12.00 | 3.00 |
| ☐ 58 Ron Ray | 7.50 | 3.00 | .75 |
| ☐ 59 Don Sutherin | 15.00 | 6.00 | 1.50 |
| ☐ 60 Frank Cosentino | 9.00 | 3.75 | .90 |
| ☐ 61 Hardiman Cureton | 7.50 | 3.00 | .75 |
| ☐ 62 Hal Patterson | 20.00 | 8.00 | 2.00 |
| ☐ 63 Ralph Goldston | 7.50 | 3.00 | .75 |
| ☐ 64 Tommy Grant | 9.00 | 3.75 | .90 |
| ☐ 65 Larry Hickman | 7.50 | 3.00 | .75 |
| ☐ 66 Zeno Karcz | 9.00 | 3.75 | .90 |
| ☐ 67 Garney Henley | 20.00 | 8.00 | 2.00 |
| ☐ 68 Gerry McDougall | 9.00 | 3.75 | .90 |
| ☐ 69 Vince Scott | 12.00 | 5.00 | 1.20 |
| ☐ 70 Gerry James | 15.00 | 6.00 | 1.50 |
| ☐ 71 Roger Hagberg | 9.00 | 3.75 | .90 |
| ☐ 72 Gord Rowland | 9.00 | 3.75 | .90 |
| ☐ 73 Ernie Pitts | 7.50 | 3.00 | .75 |
| ☐ 74 Frank Rigney | 12.00 | 5.00 | 1.20 |
| ☐ 75 Norm Rauhaus | 12.00 | 5.00 | 1.20 |
| ☐ 76 Leo Lewis | 20.00 | 8.00 | 2.00 |
| ☐ 77 Mike Wright | 7.50 | 3.00 | .75 |
| ☐ 78 Jack Delveaux | 7.50 | 3.00 | .75 |
| ☐ 79 Steve Patrick | 7.50 | 3.00 | .75 |
| ☐ 80 Dave Burkholder | 7.50 | 3.00 | .75 |
| ☐ 81 Charlie Shepard | 7.50 | 3.00 | .75 |
| ☐ 82 Kenny Ploen | 20.00 | 8.00 | 2.00 |
| ☐ 83 Ronnie Latourelle | 7.50 | 3.00 | .75 |
| ☐ 84 Herb Gray | 15.00 | 6.00 | 1.50 |
| ☐ 85 Hal Ledyard | 7.50 | 3.00 | .75 |
| ☐ 86 Cornel Piper SP | 50.00 | 20.00 | 5.00 |
| ☐ 87 Farrell Funston | 7.50 | 3.00 | .75 |
| ☐ 88 Ray Smith | 7.50 | 3.00 | .75 |
| ☐ 89 Clair Branch | 7.50 | 3.00 | .75 |
| ☐ 90 Fred Burket | 7.50 | 3.00 | .75 |
| ☐ 91 Dave Grosz | 7.50 | 3.00 | .75 |
| ☐ 92 Bob Golic | 9.00 | 3.75 | .90 |
| ☐ 93 Billy Gray | 7.50 | 3.00 | .75 |
| ☐ 94 Neil Habig | 7.50 | 3.00 | .75 |
| ☐ 95 Reg Whitehouse | 7.50 | 3.00 | .75 |
| ☐ 96 Jack Gotta | 9.00 | 3.75 | .90 |
| ☐ 97 Bob Ptacek | 9.00 | 3.75 | .90 |
| ☐ 98 Jerry Keeling | 15.00 | 6.00 | 1.50 |
| ☐ 99 Ernie Danjean | 7.50 | 3.00 | .75 |
| ☐ 100 Don Luzzi | 12.00 | 5.00 | 1.20 |
| ☐ 101 Wayne Harris | 20.00 | 8.00 | 2.00 |
| ☐ 102 Tony Pajaczkowski | 15.00 | 6.00 | 1.50 |
| ☐ 103 Earl Lunsford | 15.00 | 6.00 | 1.50 |
| ☐ 104 Ernie Warlick | 12.00 | 5.00 | 1.20 |
| ☐ 105 Gene Filipski | 12.00 | 5.00 | 1.20 |
| ☐ 106 Eagle Day | 15.00 | 6.00 | 1.50 |
| ☐ 107 Bill Crawford | 7.50 | 3.00 | .75 |
| ☐ 108 Oscar Kruger | 7.50 | 3.00 | .75 |
| ☐ 109 Gino Fracas | 9.00 | 3.75 | .90 |
| ☐ 110 Don Stephenson | 7.50 | 3.00 | .75 |
| ☐ 111 Jim Letcavits | 7.50 | 3.00 | .75 |
| ☐ 112 Howie Schumm | 7.50 | 3.00 | .75 |
| ☐ 113 Jackie Parker | 40.00 | 16.00 | 4.00 |
| ☐ 114 Rollie Miles | 15.00 | 6.00 | 1.50 |
| ☐ 115 Johnny Bright | 20.00 | 8.00 | 2.00 |
| ☐ 116 Don Getty | 15.00 | 6.00 | 1.50 |
| ☐ 117 Bobby Walden | 9.00 | 3.75 | .90 |
| ☐ 118 Roger Nelson | 15.00 | 6.00 | 1.50 |
| ☐ 119 Al Ecuyer | 7.50 | 3.00 | .75 |
| ☐ 120 Ed Gray | 7.50 | 3.00 | .75 |
| ☐ 121 Vic Chapman SP | 50.00 | 20.00 | 5.00 |
| ☐ 122 Earl Keeley | 7.50 | 3.00 | .75 |
| ☐ 123 Sonny Homer | 7.50 | 3.00 | .75 |
| ☐ 124 Bob Jeter | 20.00 | 8.00 | 2.00 |
| ☐ 125 Jim Carphin | 7.50 | 3.00 | .75 |
| ☐ 126 By Bailey | 15.00 | 6.00 | 1.50 |
| ☐ 127 Norm Fieldgate | 15.00 | 6.00 | 1.50 |
| ☐ 128 Vic Kristopaitis | 7.50 | 3.00 | .75 |
| ☐ 129 Willie Fleming | 20.00 | 8.00 | 2.00 |

| | | | |
|---|---|---|---|
| ☐ 130 Don Vicic | 7.50 | 3.00 | .75 |
| ☐ 131 Tom Brown SP | 50.00 | 20.00 | 5.00 |
| ☐ 132 Tom Hinton SP | 50.00 | 20.00 | 5.00 |
| ☐ 133 Pat Claridge | 7.50 | 3.00 | .75 |
| ☐ 134 Bill Britton | 7.50 | 3.00 | .75 |
| ☐ 135 Neal Beaumont | 9.00 | 3.75 | .90 |
| ☐ 136 Nub Beamer SP | 50.00 | 20.00 | 5.00 |
| ☐ 137 Joe Kapp | 60.00 | 24.00 | 6.00 |

## 1963 Post Cereal CFL

The 1963 Post Cereal CFL set was issued on backs of boxes of Post Cereals in Canada. The cards measure 2 1/2" by 3 1/2". Cards could also be obtained from an order-by-number offer during 1963 from Post's Canadian affiliate. Cards are numbered and ordered within the set according to the team each player played for, i.e., Montreal Alouettes (1-18), Ottawa Rough Riders (19-36), Toronto Argonauts (37-54), Hamilton Tiger-Cats (55-72), Winnipeg Blue Bombers (73-90), Saskatchewan Roughriders (91-106), Calgary Stampeders (107-124), Edmonton Eskimos (125-142), and British Columbia Lions (143-160).

| | NRMT | VG-E | GOOD |
|---|---|---|---|
| COMPLETE SET (160) | 750.00 | 300.00 | 75.00 |
| COMMON PLAYER (1-160) | 4.00 | 1.60 | .40 |
| ☐ 1 Larry Hickman | 7.50 | 3.00 | .75 |
| ☐ 2 Dick Schnell | 4.00 | 1.60 | .40 |
| ☐ 3 Don Clark | 5.00 | 2.00 | .50 |
| ☐ 4 Ted Page | 4.00 | 1.60 | .40 |
| ☐ 5 Milt Crain | 5.00 | 2.00 | .50 |
| ☐ 6 George Dixon | 10.00 | 4.00 | 1.00 |
| ☐ 7 Ed Nickla | 4.00 | 1.60 | .40 |
| ☐ 8 Barrie Hansen | 4.00 | 1.60 | .40 |
| ☐ 9 Ed Learn | 4.00 | 1.60 | .40 |
| ☐ 10 Billy Ray Locklin | 4.00 | 1.60 | .40 |
| ☐ 11 Bobby Jack Oliver | 5.00 | 2.00 | .50 |
| ☐ 12 Don Paquette | 4.00 | 1.60 | .40 |
| ☐ 13 Sandy Stephens | 12.00 | 5.00 | 1.20 |
| ☐ 14 Billy Wayte | 4.00 | 1.60 | .40 |
| ☐ 15 Jim Reynolds | 4.00 | 1.60 | .40 |
| ☐ 16 Ross Buckle | 4.00 | 1.60 | .40 |
| ☐ 17 Bob Geary | 4.00 | 1.60 | .40 |
| ☐ 18 Bobby Lee Thompson | 4.00 | 1.60 | .40 |
| ☐ 19 Mike Snodgrass | 4.00 | 1.60 | .40 |
| ☐ 20 Billy Joe Booth | 5.00 | 2.00 | .50 |
| ☐ 21 Jim Cain | 4.00 | 1.60 | .40 |
| ☐ 22 Kaye Vaughan | 10.00 | 4.00 | 1.00 |
| ☐ 23 Doug Daigneault | 4.00 | 1.60 | .40 |
| ☐ 24 Millard Flemming | 4.00 | 1.60 | .40 |
| ☐ 25 Russ Jackson | 20.00 | 8.00 | 2.00 |
| ☐ 26 Joe Poirier | 5.00 | 2.00 | .50 |
| ☐ 27 Moe Racine | 4.00 | 1.60 | .40 |
| ☐ 28 Norb Roy | 4.00 | 1.60 | .40 |
| ☐ 29 Ted Smale | 4.00 | 1.60 | .40 |
| ☐ 30 Ernie White | 4.00 | 1.60 | .40 |
| ☐ 31 Whit Tucker | 10.00 | 4.00 | 1.00 |
| ☐ 32 Dave Thelen | 10.00 | 4.00 | 1.00 |
| ☐ 33 Len Chandler | 4.00 | 1.60 | .40 |
| ☐ 34 Jim Conroy | 5.00 | 2.00 | .50 |
| ☐ 35 Jerry Selinger | 4.00 | 1.60 | .40 |
| ☐ 36 Ron Stewart | 12.00 | 5.00 | 1.20 |
| ☐ 37 Jim Andreotti | 5.00 | 2.00 | .50 |
| ☐ 38 Jackie Parker | 25.00 | 10.00 | 2.50 |
| ☐ 39 Lynn Bottoms | 5.00 | 2.00 | .50 |
| ☐ 40 Gerry Patrick | 4.00 | 1.60 | .40 |
| ☐ 41 Gerry Philip | 4.00 | 1.60 | .40 |
| ☐ 42 Art Johnson | 4.00 | 1.60 | .40 |
| ☐ 43 Aubrey Linne | 4.00 | 1.60 | .40 |
| ☐ 44 Dave Mann | 5.00 | 2.00 | .50 |
| ☐ 45 Marty Martinello | 4.00 | 1.60 | .40 |
| ☐ 46 Doug McNichol | 4.00 | 1.60 | .40 |
| ☐ 47 Ron Morris | 4.00 | 1.60 | .40 |
| ☐ 48 Walt Radzick | 4.00 | 1.60 | .40 |

| | | | |
|---|---|---|---|
| ☐ 49 Jim Rountree | 4.00 | 1.60 | .40 |
| ☐ 50 Dick Shatto | 10.00 | 4.00 | 1.00 |
| ☐ 51 Billy Shipp | 4.00 | 1.60 | .40 |
| ☐ 52 Norm Stoneburgh | 4.00 | 1.60 | .40 |
| ☐ 53 Gerry Wilson | 4.00 | 1.60 | .40 |
| ☐ 54 Danny Nykoluk | 4.00 | 1.60 | .40 |
| ☐ 55 John Barrow | 10.00 | 4.00 | 1.00 |
| ☐ 56 Frank Cosentino | 5.00 | 2.00 | .50 |
| ☐ 57 Hardiman Cureton | 5.00 | 2.00 | .50 |
| ☐ 58 Bobby Kuntz | 5.00 | 2.00 | .50 |
| ☐ 59 Bernie Faloney | 20.00 | 8.00 | 2.00 |
| ☐ 60 Garney Henley | 12.00 | 5.00 | 1.20 |
| ☐ 61 Zeno Karcz | 5.00 | 2.00 | .50 |
| ☐ 62 Dick Easterly | 4.00 | 1.60 | .40 |
| ☐ 63 Bronko Nagurski | 12.00 | 5.00 | 1.20 |
| ☐ 64 Hal Patterson | 15.00 | 6.00 | 1.50 |
| ☐ 65 Ron Ray | 4.00 | 1.60 | .40 |
| ☐ 66 Don Sutherin | 8.00 | 3.25 | .80 |
| ☐ 67 Dave Viti | 4.00 | 1.60 | .40 |
| ☐ 68 Joe Zuger | 5.00 | 2.00 | .50 |
| ☐ 69 Angelo Mosca | 15.00 | 6.00 | 1.50 |
| ☐ 70 Ralph Goldston | 4.00 | 1.60 | .40 |
| ☐ 71 Tommy Grant | 5.00 | 2.00 | .50 |
| ☐ 72 Geno DeNobile | 4.00 | 1.60 | .40 |
| ☐ 73 Dave Burkholder | 4.00 | 1.60 | .40 |
| ☐ 74 Jack Delveaux | 4.00 | 1.60 | .40 |
| ☐ 75 Farrell Funston | 4.00 | 1.60 | .40 |
| ☐ 76 Herb Gray | 10.00 | 4.00 | 1.00 |
| ☐ 77 Roger Hagberg | 5.00 | 2.00 | .50 |
| ☐ 78 Henry Janzen | 5.00 | 2.00 | .50 |
| ☐ 79 Ronnie Latourelle | 4.00 | 1.60 | .40 |
| ☐ 80 Leo Lewis | 10.00 | 4.00 | 1.00 |
| ☐ 81 Cornel Piper | 4.00 | 1.60 | .40 |
| ☐ 82 Ernie Pitts | 4.00 | 1.60 | .40 |
| ☐ 83 Kenny Ploen | 10.00 | 4.00 | 1.00 |
| ☐ 84 Norm Rauhaus | 5.00 | 2.00 | .50 |
| ☐ 85 Charlie Shepard | 4.00 | 1.60 | .40 |
| ☐ 86 Gar Warren | 4.00 | 1.60 | .40 |
| ☐ 87 Dick Thornton | 5.00 | 2.00 | .50 |
| ☐ 88 Hal Ledyard | 4.00 | 1.60 | .40 |
| ☐ 89 Frank Rigney | 6.00 | 2.40 | .60 |
| ☐ 90 Gord Rowland | 5.00 | 2.00 | .50 |
| ☐ 91 Don Walsh | 4.00 | 1.60 | .40 |
| ☐ 92 Bill Burrell | 4.00 | 1.60 | .40 |
| ☐ 93 Ron Atchison | 8.00 | 3.25 | .80 |
| ☐ 94 Billy Gray | 4.00 | 1.60 | .40 |
| ☐ 95 Neil Habig | 4.00 | 1.60 | .40 |
| ☐ 96 Bob Ptacek | 5.00 | 2.00 | .50 |
| ☐ 97 Ray Purdin | 4.00 | 1.60 | .40 |
| ☐ 98 Ted Urness | 8.00 | 3.25 | .80 |
| ☐ 99 Dale West | 5.00 | 2.00 | .50 |
| ☐ 100 Reg Whitehouse | 4.00 | 1.60 | .40 |
| ☐ 101 Clair Branch | 4.00 | 1.60 | .40 |
| ☐ 102 Bill Clarke | 4.00 | 1.60 | .40 |
| ☐ 103 Garner Ekstran | 5.00 | 2.00 | .50 |
| ☐ 104 Jack Gotta | 5.00 | 2.00 | .50 |
| ☐ 105 Len Legault | 4.00 | 1.60 | .40 |
| ☐ 106 Larry Dumelie | 4.00 | 1.60 | .40 |
| ☐ 107 Bill Britton | 4.00 | 1.60 | .40 |
| ☐ 108 Ed Buchanan | 4.00 | 1.60 | .40 |
| ☐ 109 Lovell Coleman | 5.00 | 2.00 | .50 |
| ☐ 110 Bill Crawford | 4.00 | 1.60 | .40 |
| ☐ 111 Ernie Danjean | 4.00 | 1.60 | .40 |
| ☐ 112 Eagle Day | 8.00 | 3.25 | .80 |
| ☐ 113 Jim Furlong | 4.00 | 1.60 | .40 |
| ☐ 114 Wayne Harris | 12.00 | 5.00 | 1.20 |
| ☐ 115 Roy Jakanovich | 4.00 | 1.60 | .40 |
| ☐ 116 Phil Lohmann | 4.00 | 1.60 | .40 |
| ☐ 117 Earl Lunsford | 8.00 | 3.25 | .80 |
| ☐ 118 Don Luzzi | 8.00 | 3.25 | .80 |
| ☐ 119 Tony Pajaczkowski | 8.00 | 3.25 | .80 |
| ☐ 120 Pete Manning | 5.00 | 2.00 | .50 |
| ☐ 121 Harvey Wylie | 8.00 | 3.25 | .80 |
| ☐ 122 George Hansen | 4.00 | 1.60 | .40 |
| ☐ 123 Pat Holmes | 4.00 | 1.60 | .40 |
| ☐ 124 Larry Robinson | 5.00 | 2.00 | .50 |
| ☐ 125 Johnny Bright | 12.00 | 5.00 | 1.20 |
| ☐ 126 Jon Rechner | 4.00 | 1.60 | .40 |
| ☐ 127 Al Ecuyer | 4.00 | 1.60 | .40 |
| ☐ 128 Don Getty | 12.00 | 5.00 | 1.20 |
| ☐ 129 Ed Gray | 4.00 | 1.60 | .40 |
| ☐ 130 Oscar Kruger | 4.00 | 1.60 | .40 |
| ☐ 131 Jim Letcavits | 4.00 | 1.60 | .40 |
| ☐ 132 Mike Lashuk | 5.00 | 2.00 | .50 |
| ☐ 133 Don Duncalfe | 4.00 | 1.60 | .40 |
| ☐ 134 Bobby Walden | 6.00 | 2.40 | .60 |
| ☐ 135 Tommy Joe Coffey | 12.00 | 5.00 | 1.20 |
| ☐ 136 Nat Dye | 4.00 | 1.60 | .40 |
| ☐ 137 Roy Stevenson | 4.00 | 1.60 | .40 |
| ☐ 138 Howie Schumm | 4.00 | 1.60 | .40 |
| ☐ 139 Roger Nelson | 8.00 | 3.25 | .80 |
| ☐ 140 Larry Fleisher | 5.00 | 2.00 | .50 |
| ☐ 141 Dunc Harvey | 4.00 | 1.60 | .40 |
| ☐ 142 James Earl Wright | 5.00 | 2.00 | .50 |
| ☐ 143 By Bailey | 8.00 | 3.25 | .80 |
| ☐ 144 Nub Beamer | 4.00 | 1.60 | .40 |
| ☐ 145 Neal Beaumont | 5.00 | 2.00 | .50 |

| | | | |
|---|---|---|---|
| ☐ 146 Tom Brown | 8.00 | 3.25 | .80 |
| ☐ 147 Pat Claridge | 4.00 | 1.60 | .40 |
| ☐ 148 Lonnie Dennis | 5.00 | 2.00 | .50 |
| ☐ 149 Norm Fieldgate | 8.00 | 3.25 | .80 |
| ☐ 150 Willie Fleming | 12.00 | 5.00 | 1.20 |
| ☐ 151 Dick Fouts | 5.00 | 2.00 | .50 |
| ☐ 152 Tom Hinton | 8.00 | 3.25 | .80 |
| ☐ 153 Sonny Homer | 5.00 | 2.00 | .50 |
| ☐ 154 Joe Kapp | 30.00 | 12.00 | 3.00 |
| ☐ 155 Tom Larscheid | 4.00 | 1.60 | .40 |
| ☐ 156 Mike Martin | 4.00 | 1.60 | .40 |
| ☐ 157 Mel Mein | 4.00 | 1.60 | .40 |
| ☐ 158 Mike Cacic | 4.00 | 1.60 | .40 |
| ☐ 159 Walt Bilicki | 4.00 | 1.60 | .40 |
| ☐ 160 Earl Keeley | 6.00 | 2.40 | .60 |

## 1991 Queen's University

This 52-card standard-size (2 1/2" by 3 1/2") set, produced by Breakaway Graphics, Inc., commemorates the sesquicentennial year of Queen's University. This Golden Gaels football set is the first ever to be issued by a Canadian college football organization. Reportedly only 5,725 sets and 275 uncut sheets were printed. The card fronts feature color player photos inside a gold border, with a pale green strip running down the left side of the picture. On a pale green background, the backs have a color head shot, biography, player profile, and statistics. Five special promotional cards were also included with this commemorative set. Five hundred autographed promo cards were randomly inserted in the production run, including 100 by Mike Schad and Jock Climie and 300 by Ron Stewart. The cards are numbered on the back.

| | MINT | EXC | G-VG |
|---|---|---|---|
| COMPLETE SET (52) | 15.00 | 6.00 | 1.50 |
| COMMON CARD (1-51) | .35 | .14 | .03 |
| COMMON CARD (P1-P5) | 3.00 | 1.20 | .30 |
| | | | |
| ☐ 1 First Rugby Team | .75 | .30 | .07 |
|     Team photo | | | |
| ☐ 2 Grey Cup Years | .75 | .30 | .07 |
|     Harry Batstone | | | |
|     Frank R. Leadlay | | | |
| ☐ 3 1978 Vanier Cup Champs | .35 | .14 | .03 |
| ☐ 4 1978 Vanier Cup Champs | .35 | .14 | .03 |
| ☐ 5 Tim Pendergast | .35 | .14 | .03 |
| ☐ 6 Brad Elberg | .35 | .14 | .03 |
| ☐ 7 Ken Kirkwood | .35 | .14 | .03 |
| ☐ 8 Kyle Wanzel | .35 | .14 | .03 |
| ☐ 9 Brian Alford | .35 | .14 | .03 |
| ☐ 10 Paul Kozan | .35 | .14 | .03 |
| ☐ 11 Paul Beresford | .35 | .14 | .03 |
| ☐ 12 Ron Herman | .35 | .14 | .03 |
| ☐ 13 Mike Ross | .35 | .14 | .03 |
| ☐ 14 Tom Black | .35 | .14 | .03 |
| ☐ 15 Steve Yovetich | .35 | .14 | .03 |
| ☐ 16 Mark Robinson | .35 | .14 | .03 |
| ☐ 17 Don Rorwick | .35 | .14 | .03 |
| ☐ 18 Ed Kidd | .35 | .14 | .03 |
| ☐ 19 Jamie Galloway | .35 | .14 | .03 |
| ☐ 20 Dan Wright | .35 | .14 | .03 |
| ☐ 21 Scott Gray | .35 | .14 | .03 |
| ☐ 22 Dan McCullough | .35 | .14 | .03 |
| ☐ 23 Steve Othen | .35 | .14 | .03 |
| ☐ 24 Doug Hargreaves CO | .35 | .14 | .03 |
| ☐ 25 Sue Bolton CO | .35 | .14 | .03 |
| ☐ 26 Coaching Staff | .50 | .20 | .05 |
| ☐ 27 Joel Dagnone | .35 | .14 | .03 |
| ☐ 28 Mark Morrison | .35 | .14 | .03 |
| ☐ 29 Rob Krog | .35 | .14 | .03 |
| ☐ 30 Dan Pawliw | .35 | .14 | .03 |
| ☐ 31 Greg Bryk | .35 | .14 | .03 |
| ☐ 32 Eric Dell | .35 | .14 | .03 |
| ☐ 33 Mike Boone | .35 | .14 | .03 |

| | | | |
|---|---|---|---|
| ☐ 34 James Paterson | .35 | .14 | .03 |
| ☐ 35 Jeff Yach | .35 | .14 | .03 |
| ☐ 36 Peter Pain | .35 | .14 | .03 |
| ☐ 37 Aron Campbell | .35 | .14 | .03 |
| ☐ 38 Chris McCormick | .35 | .14 | .03 |
| ☐ 39 Jason Moller | .35 | .14 | .03 |
| ☐ 40 Terry Huhtala | .35 | .14 | .03 |
| ☐ 41 Matt Zarowny | .35 | .14 | .03 |
| ☐ 42 David St. Amour | .35 | .14 | .03 |
| ☐ 43 Frank Tindall | .35 | .14 | .03 |
| ☐ 44 Ron Stewart | 1.00 | .40 | .10 |
| ☐ 45 Jim Young | 1.00 | .40 | .10 |
| ☐ 46 Bob Howes | .35 | .14 | .03 |
| ☐ 47 Stu Lang | .50 | .20 | .05 |
| ☐ 48 Mike Schad | .75 | .30 | .07 |
| (In college uniform) | | | |
| ☐ 49 Mike Schad | .75 | .30 | .07 |
| (In Philadelphia Eagles uniform) | | | |
| ☐ 50 Jock Climie | 1.00 | .40 | .10 |
| ☐ 51 Checklist | .75 | .30 | .07 |
| ☐ NNO Title Card | .75 | .30 | .07 |
| ☐ P1 Jock Climie | 3.00 | 1.20 | .30 |
| ☐ P1AU Jock Climie AU/100 | 30.00 | 12.00 | 3.00 |
| ☐ P2 Ron Stewart | 4.00 | 1.60 | .40 |
| ☐ P2AU Ron Stewart AU/300 | 30.00 | 12.00 | 3.00 |
| ☐ P3 Jim Young | 4.00 | 1.60 | .40 |
| ☐ P4 Stu Lang | 3.00 | 1.20 | .30 |
| ☐ P5 Mike Schad | 3.00 | 1.20 | .30 |
| ☐ P5AU Mike Schad AU/100 | 30.00 | 12.00 | 3.00 |

# 1981 Red Rooster
# Calgary Stampeders

This 40-card set measures 2 3/4" by 3 5/8" and features posed, color player photos with rounded corners on a white card face. Since the card edges are perforated, the cards were apparently issued as a sheet. The player's name is printed below the photo, as is the team name and a CFL Players Association endorsement. (Some of the cards have a serial number below the endorsement). The backs carry biographical information and a player profile. Sponsor logos and names are printed at the bottom. The cards are unnumbered and checklisted below in alphabetical order.

| | MINT | EXC | G-VG |
|---|---|---|---|
| COMPLETE SET (40) | 25.00 | 10.00 | 2.50 |
| COMMON PLAYER (1-40) | .60 | .24 | .06 |
| | | | |
| ☐ 1 Willie Armstead | .60 | .24 | .06 |
| ☐ 2 Doug Battershill | .60 | .24 | .06 |
| ☐ 3 Willie Burden | 3.00 | 1.20 | .30 |
| (From waist up) | | | |
| ☐ 4 Willie Burden | 3.00 | 1.20 | .30 |
| (Head and shoulders) | | | |
| ☐ 5 Scott Burk UER | .60 | .24 | .06 |
| (Misspelled Burke 4th line of bio) | | | |
| ☐ 6 Al Burleson | .60 | .24 | .06 |
| ☐ 7 Ken Dombrowski | .60 | .24 | .06 |
| ☐ 8 Lloyd Fairbanks | 1.00 | .40 | .10 |
| ☐ 9 Rob Forbes | .60 | .24 | .06 |
| ☐ 10 Tom Forzani | .75 | .30 | .07 |
| ☐ 11 Miles Gorrell | .60 | .24 | .06 |
| ☐ 12 J.T. Hay | .60 | .24 | .06 |
| ☐ 13 John Holland | 1.00 | .40 | .10 |
| ☐ 14 Norm Hopely | .60 | .24 | .06 |
| ☐ 15 Jeff Inglis | .60 | .24 | .06 |
| ☐ 16 Lepoleon Ingram | .60 | .24 | .06 |
| ☐ 17 Terry Irvin | .60 | .24 | .06 |
| ☐ 18 Ken Johnson | .60 | .24 | .06 |
| ☐ 19 Franklin King | .60 | .24 | .06 |
| ☐ 20 Dave Kirzinger | .60 | .24 | .06 |
| ☐ 21 Frank Kosec | .60 | .24 | .06 |

| | | | |
|---|---|---|---|
| ☐ 22 Tom Krebs | .60 | .24 | .06 |
| ☐ 23 Reggie Lewis | .60 | .24 | .06 |
| ☐ 24 Robert Lubig | .60 | .24 | .06 |
| ☐ 25 Scott MacArthur | .60 | .24 | .06 |
| ☐ 26 Ed McAleney | .60 | .24 | .06 |
| ☐ 27 Mike McTague | .75 | .30 | .07 |
| ☐ 28 Mark Moors | .60 | .24 | .06 |
| ☐ 29 Bernie Morrison | .60 | .24 | .06 |
| ☐ 30 Mark Nelson | .60 | .24 | .06 |
| ☐ 31 Ray Odums | .60 | .24 | .06 |
| ☐ 32 Ronnie Paggett | .60 | .24 | .06 |
| ☐ 33 John Palazeti | .60 | .24 | .06 |
| ☐ 34 John Prassas | .60 | .24 | .06 |
| ☐ 35 Tom Reimer | .60 | .24 | .06 |
| ☐ 36 James Sykes | 3.00 | 1.20 | .30 |
| (Close-up) | | | |
| ☐ 37 James Sykes | 3.00 | 1.20 | .30 |
| (From waist up) | | | |
| ☐ 38 Bruce Threadgill | .60 | .24 | .06 |
| ☐ 39 Bob Viccars | .60 | .24 | .06 |
| ☐ 40 Merv Walker | .60 | .24 | .06 |

# 1981 Red Rooster
# Edmonton Eskimos

This 40-card set measures approximately 2 3/4" by 3 1/2" and features posed, color player photos with rounded corners on a white card face. Since the card edges are perforated, the cards were apparently issued as a sheet. The player's name is printed below the photo, as is the team name and a CFL Players Association endorsement. The backs carry biographical information and a player profile. Sponsor logos and names are printed at the bottom. The cards are unnumbered and checklisted below in alphabetical order.

| | MINT | EXC | G-VG |
|---|---|---|---|
| COMPLETE SET (40) | 50.00 | 20.00 | 5.00 |
| COMMON PLAYER (1-40) | .60 | .24 | .06 |
| | | | |
| ☐ 1 Leo Blanchard | .60 | .24 | .06 |
| ☐ 2 David Boone | .60 | .24 | .06 |
| ☐ 3 Brian Broomell | .60 | .24 | .06 |
| ☐ 4 Hugh Campbell CO | 1.25 | .50 | .12 |
| ☐ 5 Dave Cutler | 2.50 | 1.00 | .25 |
| ☐ 6 Marco Cyncar | 1.00 | .40 | .10 |
| ☐ 7 Ron Estay | .60 | .24 | .06 |
| ☐ 8 Dave Fennell | 1.00 | .40 | .10 |
| ☐ 9 Emilio Fraietta | .60 | .24 | .06 |
| ☐ 10 Brian Fryer | .60 | .24 | .06 |
| ☐ 11 Jim Germany | 1.00 | .40 | .10 |
| ☐ 12 Gary Hayes | .60 | .24 | .06 |
| ☐ 13 Larry Highbaugh | 1.25 | .50 | .12 |
| ☐ 14 Joe Hollimon | .60 | .24 | .06 |
| ☐ 15 Hank Ilesic | 1.25 | .50 | .12 |
| ☐ 16 Ed Jones | .60 | .24 | .06 |
| ☐ 17 Dan Kearns | .60 | .24 | .06 |
| ☐ 18 Sean Kehoe | .60 | .24 | .06 |
| ☐ 19 Brian Kelly | 2.50 | 1.00 | .25 |
| ☐ 20 Dan Kepley | 1.25 | .50 | .12 |
| ☐ 21 Stu Lang | .60 | .24 | .06 |
| ☐ 22 Pete Lavorato | .60 | .24 | .06 |
| ☐ 23 Neil Lumsden | .75 | .30 | .07 |
| ☐ 24 Bill Manchuk | .60 | .24 | .06 |
| ☐ 25 Mike McLeod | .60 | .24 | .06 |
| ☐ 26 Ted Milian | .60 | .24 | .06 |
| ☐ 27 Warren Moon | 30.00 | 12.00 | 3.00 |
| ☐ 28 James Parker | 2.00 | .80 | .20 |
| ☐ 29 John Pointer | .60 | .24 | .06 |
| ☐ 30 Hector Pothier | .60 | .24 | .06 |
| ☐ 31 Dale Potter | .60 | .24 | .06 |
| ☐ 32 Angelo Santucci | .60 | .24 | .06 |
| ☐ 33 Tom Scott | 1.00 | .40 | .10 |
| ☐ 34 Waddell Smith | .75 | .30 | .07 |
| ☐ 35 Bill Stevenson | .75 | .30 | .07 |
| ☐ 36 Tom Towns | .60 | .24 | .06 |

| | | | |
|---|---|---|---|
| ☐ 37 Eric Upton | .60 | .24 | .06 |
| ☐ 38 Mark Wald | .60 | .24 | .06 |
| ☐ 39 Ken Walter | .60 | .24 | .06 |
| ☐ 40 Tom Wilkinson | 3.00 | 1.20 | .30 |

## 1971 Royal Bank B.C. Lions

This 16-photo set of the CFL's British Columbia Lions was sponsored by Royal Bank. Each black-and-white, blank-backed picture measures approximately 5" by 7" and features a white-bordered posed action photo and a facsimile autograph inscribed across it. The sponsor logo appears in black in each corner of the bottom margin. The photos are unnumbered and checklisted below in alphabetical order.

| | NRMT | VG-E | GOOD |
|---|---|---|---|
| COMPLETE SET (16) | 50.00 | 20.00 | 5.00 |
| COMMON PLAYER (1-16) | 3.00 | 1.20 | .30 |
| | | | |
| ☐ 1 George Anderson | 3.00 | 1.20 | .30 |
| ☐ 2 Paul Brothers | 3.00 | 1.20 | .30 |
| ☐ 3 Brian Donnelly | 3.00 | 1.20 | .30 |
| ☐ 4 Dave Easley | 3.00 | 1.20 | .30 |
| ☐ 5 Trevor Ekdahl | 4.00 | 1.60 | .40 |
| ☐ 6 Jim Evenson | 4.00 | 1.60 | .40 |
| ☐ 7 Greg Findlay | 3.00 | 1.20 | .30 |
| ☐ 8 Lefty Hendrickson | 3.00 | 1.20 | .30 |
| ☐ 9 Bob Howes | 3.00 | 1.20 | .30 |
| ☐ 10 Garrett Hunsperger | 3.00 | 1.20 | .30 |
| ☐ 11 Wayne Matherne | 3.00 | 1.20 | .30 |
| ☐ 12 Don Moorhead | 3.00 | 1.20 | .30 |
| ☐ 13 Ken Phillips | 3.00 | 1.20 | .30 |
| ☐ 14 Ken Sugarman | 4.00 | 1.60 | .40 |
| ☐ 15 Tom Wilkinson | 10.00 | 4.00 | 1.00 |
| ☐ 16 Jim Young | 10.00 | 4.00 | 1.00 |

## 1972 Royal Bank B.C. Lions

This set of 16 photos was sponsored by Royal Bank. They measure approximately 5" by 7" and are printed on thin glossy paper. The color posed player photos are bordered in white. A facsimile autograph is inscribed across the picture. At the bottom of the front, the words "Royal Leaders, B.C. Lions Player of the Week" are printed between the sponsor's logo and the Lions' logo. The backs are blank. The photos are unnumbered and checklisted below in alphabetical order. One noteworthy card in the set is Carl Weathers, who went on to acting fame as Apollo Creed in Sylvester Stallone's popular "Rocky" movies.

| | NRMT | VG-E | GOOD |
|---|---|---|---|
| COMPLETE SET (16) | 50.00 | 20.00 | 5.00 |
| COMMON PLAYER (1-16) | 2.50 | 1.00 | .25 |

| | | | |
|---|---|---|---|
| ☐ 1 George Anderson | 2.50 | 1.00 | .25 |
| ☐ 2 Brian Donnelly | 2.50 | 1.00 | .25 |
| ☐ 3 Dave Easley | 2.50 | 1.00 | .25 |
| ☐ 4 Trevor Ekdahl | 3.50 | 1.40 | .35 |
| ☐ 5 Ron Estay | 2.50 | 1.00 | .25 |
| ☐ 6 Jim Evenson | 3.50 | 1.40 | .35 |
| ☐ 7 Dave Golinsky | 2.50 | 1.00 | .25 |
| ☐ 8 Larry Highbaugh | 3.50 | 1.40 | .35 |
| ☐ 9 Garrett Hunsperger | 2.50 | 1.00 | .25 |
| ☐ 10 Don Moorhead | 2.50 | 1.00 | .25 |
| ☐ 11 Johnny Musso | 7.50 | 3.00 | .75 |
| ☐ 12 Ray Nettles | 2.50 | 1.00 | .25 |
| ☐ 13 Willie Postler | 2.50 | 1.00 | .25 |
| ☐ 14 Carl Weathers | 10.00 | 4.00 | 1.00 |
| ☐ 15 Jim Young | 7.50 | 3.00 | .75 |
| ☐ 16 Coaching Staff | 3.50 | 1.40 | .35 |
|    Bud Tynes | | | |
|    Ken McCullough | | | |
|    Owen Dejanovich | | | |
|    Eagle Keys | | | |

## 1973 Royal Bank B.C. Lions

This set of 16 photos was sponsored by Royal Bank. They measure approximately 5" by 7" and are printed on thin glossy paper. The color posed action shots are bordered in white. A facsimile autograph is inscribed across the picture. At the bottom of the front, the words "Royal Leaders, B.C. Lions Player of the Week" are printed between the sponsor's logo and the Lions' logo. The set includes two Moorhead cards, and only these have borders around the picture. Moreover, one has a black border, while the other has a silver border. Only the Matherne photo has a black stripe at the bottom. This black stripe appears to be covering up a wrong signature, that of Don Moorhead. The backs are blank. The photos are unnumbered and checklisted below in alphabetical order.

| | NRMT | VG-E | GOOD |
|---|---|---|---|
| COMPLETE SET (16) | 50.00 | 20.00 | 5.00 |
| COMMON PLAYER (1-15) | 2.50 | 1.00 | .25 |

| | | | |
|---|---|---|---|
| ☐ 1 Barry Ardern | 2.50 | 1.00 | .25 |
| ☐ 2 Monroe Eley | 3.50 | 1.40 | .35 |
| ☐ 3 Bob Friend | 2.50 | 1.00 | .25 |
| ☐ 4 Eric Guthrie | 2.50 | 1.00 | .25 |
| ☐ 5 Garrett Hunsperger | 2.50 | 1.00 | .25 |
| ☐ 6 Wayne Matherne | 2.50 | 1.00 | .25 |
| ☐ 7A Don Moorhead | 2.50 | 1.00 | .25 |
|    (Black border) | | | |
| ☐ 7B Don Moorhead | 2.50 | 1.00 | .25 |
|    (Silver border) | | | |
| ☐ 8 Johnny Musso | 7.50 | 3.00 | .75 |
| ☐ 9 Ray Nettles | 2.50 | 1.00 | .25 |
| ☐ 10 Pete Palmer | 2.50 | 1.00 | .25 |
| ☐ 11 Gary Robinson SP | 20.00 | 8.00 | 2.00 |
| ☐ 12 Al Wilson | 2.50 | 1.00 | .25 |
| ☐ 13 Mike Wilson | 2.50 | 1.00 | .25 |
| ☐ 14 Jim Young | 7.50 | 3.00 | .75 |
| ☐ 15 Coaches | 3.50 | 1.40 | .35 |
|    Bud Tynes | | | |
|    Ken McCullough | | | |
|    Owen Dejanovich | | | |
|    Eagle Keys | | | |

## 1974 Royal Bank B.C. Lions

This blank-backed 14-photo color set was sponsored by Royal Bank. Each posed and bordered CFL Lions player's photo measures approximately 5" by 7" and carries a facsimile autograph across it. The

sponsor logo appears in the lower left corner while the team logo is in the lower right corner. The photos are unnumbered and checklisted below in alphabetical order.

| | NRMT | VG-E | GOOD |
|---|---|---|---|
| COMPLETE SET (14) | 40.00 | 16.00 | 4.00 |
| COMMON PLAYER (1-14) | 2.50 | 1.00 | .25 |
| | | | |
| ☐ 1 Bill Baker | 7.50 | 3.00 | .75 |
| ☐ 2 Karl Douglas | 2.50 | 1.00 | .25 |
| ☐ 3 Layne McDowell | 2.50 | 1.00 | .25 |
| ☐ 4 Ivan MacMillan | 2.50 | 1.00 | .25 |
| ☐ 5 Bud Magrum | 2.50 | 1.00 | .25 |
| ☐ 6 Don Moorhead | 2.50 | 1.00 | .25 |
| ☐ 7 Johnny Musso | 7.50 | 3.00 | .75 |
| ☐ 8 Ray Nettles | 2.50 | 1.00 | .25 |
| ☐ 9 Brian Sopatyk | 2.50 | 1.00 | .25 |
| ☐ 10 Curtis Wester | 3.50 | 1.40 | .35 |
| ☐ 11 Slade Willis | 2.50 | 1.00 | .25 |
| ☐ 12 Al Wilson | 2.50 | 1.00 | .25 |
| ☐ 13 Jim Young | 7.50 | 3.00 | .75 |
| ☐ 14 Coaching Staff | 3.50 | 1.40 | .35 |

## 1975 Royal Bank B.C. Lions

Royal Bank sponsored this 14-photo set. Each photo measures approximately 5 1/4" by 6". The photos are unnumbered and checklisted below in alphabetical order.

| | NRMT | VG-E | GOOD |
|---|---|---|---|
| COMPLETE SET (14) | 40.00 | 16.00 | 4.00 |
| COMMON PLAYER (1-14) | 2.50 | 1.00 | .25 |
| | | | |
| ☐ 1 Brock Ansley | 2.50 | 1.00 | .25 |
| ☐ 2 Terry Bailey | 2.50 | 1.00 | .25 |
| ☐ 3 Bill Baker | 7.50 | 3.00 | .75 |
| ☐ 4 Elton Brown | 2.50 | 1.00 | .25 |
| ☐ 5 Grady Cavness | 3.50 | 1.40 | .35 |
| ☐ 6 Ross Clarkson | 2.50 | 1.00 | .25 |
| ☐ 7 Joe Fourqurean | 2.50 | 1.00 | .25 |
| ☐ 8 Lou Harris | 3.50 | 1.40 | .35 |
| ☐ 9 Layne McDowell | 2.50 | 1.00 | .25 |
| ☐ 10 Don Moorhead | 2.50 | 1.00 | .25 |
| ☐ 11 Tony Moro | 2.50 | 1.00 | .25 |
| ☐ 12 Ray Nettles | 2.50 | 1.00 | .25 |
| ☐ 13 Curtis Wester | 3.50 | 1.40 | .35 |
| ☐ 14 Jim Young | 7.50 | 3.00 | .75 |

## 1976 Royal Bank B.C. Lions

This set of 15 photos was sponsored by Royal Bank. They measure approximately 5 1/4" by 6" and are printed on thin glossy paper. The color posed player shots (from the waist up) are bordered in white. A facsimile autograph is inscribed across the picture. At the bottom of the front, the words "1976 Royal Leaders, B.C. Lions Player of the

Week" are printed between the sponsor's logo and the Lions' logo. The backs are blank. The photos are unnumbered and checklisted below in alphabetical order.

| | NRMT | VG-E | GOOD |
|---|---|---|---|
| COMPLETE SET (15) | 40.00 | 16.00 | 4.00 |
| COMMON PLAYER (1-15) | 2.50 | 1.00 | .25 |
| | | | |
| ☐ 1 Terry Bailey | 2.50 | 1.00 | .25 |
| ☐ 2 Bill Baker | 7.50 | 3.00 | .75 |
| ☐ 3 Ted Dushinski | 2.50 | 1.00 | .25 |
| ☐ 4 Eric Guthrie | 2.50 | 1.00 | .25 |
| ☐ 5 Lou Harris | 3.50 | 1.40 | .35 |
| ☐ 6 Glen Jackson | 2.50 | 1.00 | .25 |
| ☐ 7 Rocky Long | 2.50 | 1.00 | .25 |
| ☐ 8 Layne McDowell | 2.50 | 1.00 | .25 |
| ☐ 9 Ray Nettles | 2.50 | 1.00 | .25 |
| ☐ 10 Gary Robinson | 2.50 | 1.00 | .25 |
| ☐ 11 John Sciarra | 6.00 | 2.40 | .60 |
| ☐ 12 Wayne Smith | 2.50 | 1.00 | .25 |
| ☐ 13 Michael Strickland | 2.50 | 1.00 | .25 |
| ☐ 14 Al Wilson | 2.50 | 1.00 | .25 |
| ☐ 15 Jim Young | 7.50 | 3.00 | .75 |

## 1977 Royal Bank B.C. Lions

This set of 12 photos was sponsored by Royal Bank. They measure approximately 4 3/4" by 5 3/8" and are printed on thin glossy paper. The color head and shoulders shots are bordered in white. A facsimile autograph is inscribed across the picture. At the bottom of the front, the words "Royal Leaders, B.C. Lions Player of the Week" are printed between the Lions' logo and the sponsor's logo. The backs are blank. The photos are unnumbered and checklisted below in alphabetical order.

| | NRMT | VG-E | GOOD |
|---|---|---|---|
| COMPLETE SET (12) | 40.00 | 16.00 | 4.00 |
| COMMON PLAYER (1-12) | 2.50 | 1.00 | .25 |
| | | | |
| ☐ 1 Doug Carlson | 2.50 | 1.00 | .25 |
| ☐ 2 Sam Cvijanovich | 2.50 | 1.00 | .25 |
| ☐ 3 Ted Dushinski | 2.50 | 1.00 | .25 |
| ☐ 4 Paul Giroday | 2.50 | 1.00 | .25 |
| ☐ 5 Glen Jackson | 2.50 | 1.00 | .25 |
| ☐ 6 Frank Landy | 2.50 | 1.00 | .25 |
| ☐ 7 Lui Passaglia | 7.50 | 3.00 | .75 |
| ☐ 8 John Sciarra | 6.00 | 2.40 | .60 |
| ☐ 9 Michael Strickland | 2.50 | 1.00 | .25 |
| ☐ 10 Jerry Tagge | 7.50 | 3.00 | .75 |
| ☐ 11 Al Wilson | 2.50 | 1.00 | .25 |
| ☐ 12 Jim Young | 7.50 | 3.00 | .75 |

## 1978 Royal Bank B.C. Lions

Royal Bank sponsored this 12-photo set. Each photo measures approximately 4 1/4" by 5 1/2". The photos are unnumbered and checklisted below in alphabetical order.

| | NRMT | VG-E | GOOD |
|---|---|---|---|
| COMPLETE SET (12) | 40.00 | 16.00 | 4.00 |
| COMMON PLAYER (1-12) | 2.50 | 1.00 | .25 |
| | | | |
| ☐ 1 Terry Bailey | 2.50 | 1.00 | .25 |
| ☐ 2 Leon Bright | 5.00 | 2.00 | .50 |
| ☐ 3 Doug Carlson | 2.50 | 1.00 | .25 |
| ☐ 4 Grady Cavness | 3.50 | 1.40 | .35 |
| ☐ 5 Al Charuk | 2.50 | 1.00 | .25 |
| ☐ 6 Paul Giroday | 2.50 | 1.00 | .25 |
| ☐ 7 Larry Key | 2.50 | 1.00 | .25 |
| ☐ 8 Frank Landy | 2.50 | 1.00 | .25 |
| ☐ 9 Lui Passaglia | 6.00 | 2.40 | .60 |
| ☐ 10 Jerry Tagge | 7.50 | 3.00 | .75 |
| ☐ 11 Al Wilson | 2.50 | 1.00 | .25 |
| ☐ 12 Jim Young | 7.50 | 3.00 | .75 |

# 1971 Sargent Promotions Stamps

JOE THEISMANN    TOR.

This photo album, measuring approximately 10 3/4" by 13", features 225 players from nine Canadian Football League teams. The set was sponsored by Eddie Sargent Promotions and is completely bi-lingual. The collector completed the set by purchasing a different picture packet from a participating food store each week. There were 16 different picture packets, with 14 color stickers per packet. After a general introduction, the album is divided into team sections, with two pages devoted to each team. A brief history of each team is presented, followed by 25 numbered sticker slots. Each sticker measures 2" by 2 1/2" and has a posed color player photo with white borders. The player's name and team affiliation are indicated in the bottom white border. Biographical information and career summary appear below each sticker slot on the page itself. The stickers are numbered on the front and checklisted below alphabetically according to teams as follows: British Columbia Lions (1-25), Calgary Stampeders (26-50), Edmonton Eskimos (51-75), Hamilton Tiger-Cats (76-100), Montreal Alouettes (101-125), Ottawa Rough Riders (126-150), Saskatchewan Roughriders (151-175), Toronto Argonauts (176-200), and Winnipeg Blue Bombers (201-225).

| | NRMT | VG-E | GOOD |
|---|---|---|---|
| COMPLETE SET (225) | 200.00 | 80.00 | 20.00 |
| COMMON PLAYER (1-225) | .75 | .30 | .07 |

| | | NRMT | VG-E | GOOD |
|---|---|---|---|---|
| ☐ 1 Jim Young | | 7.50 | 3.00 | .75 |
| ☐ 2 Trevor Ekdahl | | 1.25 | .50 | .12 |
| ☐ 3 Ted Gerela | | .75 | .30 | .07 |
| ☐ 4 Jim Evenson | | 1.25 | .50 | .12 |
| ☐ 5 Ray Lychak | | .75 | .30 | .07 |
| ☐ 6 Dave Golinsky | | .75 | .30 | .07 |
| ☐ 7 Ted Warkentin | | .75 | .30 | .07 |
| ☐ 8 A.D. Whitfield | | 1.25 | .50 | .12 |
| ☐ 9 Lach Heron | | 1.00 | .40 | .10 |
| ☐ 10 Ken Phillips | | .75 | .30 | .07 |
| ☐ 11 Lefty Hendrickson | | .75 | .30 | .07 |
| ☐ 12 Paul Brothers | | .75 | .30 | .07 |
| ☐ 13 Eagle Keys CO | | 1.50 | .60 | .15 |
| ☐ 14 Garrett Hunsperger | | .75 | .30 | .07 |
| ☐ 15 Greg Findlay | | .75 | .30 | .07 |
| ☐ 16 Dave Easley | | .75 | .30 | .07 |
| ☐ 17 Barrie Hansen | | .75 | .30 | .07 |
| ☐ 18 Wayne Dennis | | .75 | .30 | .07 |
| ☐ 19 Jerry Bradley | | .75 | .30 | .07 |
| ☐ 20 Gerry Herron | | .75 | .30 | .07 |
| ☐ 21 Gary Robinson | | .75 | .30 | .07 |
| ☐ 22 Bill Whisler | | .75 | .30 | .07 |
| ☐ 23 Bob Howes | | .75 | .30 | .07 |
| ☐ 24 Tom Wilkinson | | 6.00 | 2.40 | .60 |
| ☐ 25 Tom Cassese | | .75 | .30 | .07 |
| ☐ 26 Dick Suderman | | 1.25 | .50 | .12 |
| ☐ 27 Jerry Keeling | | 4.00 | 1.60 | .40 |
| ☐ 28 John Helton | | 4.00 | 1.60 | .40 |
| ☐ 29 Jim Furlong | | .75 | .30 | .07 |
| ☐ 30 Fred James | | .75 | .30 | .07 |
| ☐ 31 Howard Starks | | .75 | .30 | .07 |
| ☐ 32 Craig Koinzan | | .75 | .30 | .07 |
| ☐ 33 Frank Andruski | | .75 | .30 | .07 |
| ☐ 34 Joe Forzani | | 1.25 | .50 | .12 |
| ☐ 35 Herb Schumm | | .75 | .30 | .07 |
| ☐ 36 Gerry Shaw | | .75 | .30 | .07 |
| ☐ 37 Lanny Boleski | | .75 | .30 | .07 |
| ☐ 38 Jim Duncan CO | | .75 | .30 | .07 |
| ☐ 39 Hugh McKinnis | | .75 | .30 | .07 |
| ☐ 40 Basil Bark | | .75 | .30 | .07 |
| ☐ 41 Herman Harrison | | 4.00 | 1.60 | .40 |
| ☐ 42 Larry Robinson | | 1.25 | .50 | .12 |
| ☐ 43 Larry Lawrence | | .75 | .30 | .07 |
| ☐ 44 Granville Liggins | | 2.00 | .80 | .20 |
| ☐ 45 Wayne Harris | | 4.00 | 1.60 | .40 |
| ☐ 46 John Atamian | | .75 | .30 | .07 |
| ☐ 47 Wayne Holm | | .75 | .30 | .07 |
| ☐ 48 Rudy Linterman | | 1.25 | .50 | .12 |
| ☐ 49 Jim Sillye | | .75 | .30 | .07 |

| | | NRMT | VG-E | GOOD |
|---|---|---|---|---|
| ☐ 50 Terry Wilson | | .75 | .30 | .07 |
| ☐ 51 Don Trull | | 2.00 | .80 | .20 |
| ☐ 52 Rusty Clark | | .75 | .30 | .07 |
| ☐ 53 Ted Page | | .75 | .30 | .07 |
| ☐ 54 Ken Ferguson | | .75 | .30 | .07 |
| ☐ 55 Alan Pitcaithley | | .75 | .30 | .07 |
| ☐ 56 Bayne Norrie | | .75 | .30 | .07 |
| ☐ 57 Dave Gasser | | .75 | .30 | .07 |
| ☐ 58 Jim Thomas | | .75 | .30 | .07 |
| ☐ 59 Terry Swarn | | 1.25 | .50 | .12 |
| ☐ 60 Ron Forwick | | .75 | .30 | .07 |
| ☐ 61 Henry King | | .75 | .30 | .07 |
| ☐ 62 John Wydareny | | 1.00 | .40 | .10 |
| ☐ 63 Ray Jauch CO | | 1.00 | .40 | .10 |
| ☐ 64 Jim Henshall | | .75 | .30 | .07 |
| ☐ 65 Dave Cutler | | 4.00 | 1.60 | .40 |
| ☐ 66 Fred Dunn | | .75 | .30 | .07 |
| ☐ 67 Dick Dupuis | | 1.25 | .50 | .12 |
| ☐ 68 Fritz Greenlee | | .75 | .30 | .07 |
| ☐ 69 Jerry Griffin | | 1.25 | .50 | .12 |
| ☐ 70 Allen Ische | | .75 | .30 | .07 |
| ☐ 71 John LaGrone | | 1.25 | .50 | .12 |
| ☐ 72 Mike Law | | .75 | .30 | .07 |
| ☐ 73 Ed Molstad | | .75 | .30 | .07 |
| ☐ 74 Greg Pipes | | 1.25 | .50 | .12 |
| ☐ 75 Roy Shatzko | | .75 | .30 | .07 |
| ☐ 76 Joe Zuger | | 1.25 | .50 | .12 |
| ☐ 77 Wally Gabler | | 1.25 | .50 | .12 |
| ☐ 78 Tony Gabriel | | 6.00 | 2.40 | .60 |
| ☐ 79 John Reid | | .75 | .30 | .07 |
| ☐ 80 Dave Fleming | | .75 | .30 | .07 |
| ☐ 81 Jon Hohman | | .75 | .30 | .07 |
| ☐ 82 Tommy Joe Coffey | | 5.00 | 2.00 | .50 |
| ☐ 83 Dick Wesolowski | | .75 | .30 | .07 |
| ☐ 84 Gordon Christian | | .75 | .30 | .07 |
| ☐ 85 Steve Worster | | 6.00 | 2.40 | .60 |
| ☐ 86 Bobby Taylor | | 1.50 | .60 | .15 |
| ☐ 87 Doug Mitchell | | .75 | .30 | .07 |
| ☐ 88 Al Dorow CO | | 1.25 | .50 | .12 |
| ☐ 89 Angelo Mosca | | 7.50 | 3.00 | .75 |
| ☐ 90 Bill Danychuk | | 1.00 | .40 | .10 |
| ☐ 91 Mike Blum | | .75 | .30 | .07 |
| ☐ 92 Garney Henley | | 6.00 | 2.40 | .60 |
| ☐ 93 Bob Steiner | | .75 | .30 | .07 |
| ☐ 94 John Manel | | .75 | .30 | .07 |
| ☐ 95 Bob Krouse | | .75 | .30 | .07 |
| ☐ 96 John Williams | | .75 | .30 | .07 |
| ☐ 97 Scott Henderson | | .75 | .30 | .07 |
| ☐ 98 Ed Chalupka | | .75 | .30 | .07 |
| ☐ 99 Paul McKay | | .75 | .30 | .07 |
| ☐ 100 Rensi Perdoni | | .75 | .30 | .07 |
| ☐ 101 Ed George | | 1.25 | .50 | .12 |
| ☐ 102 Al Phaneuf | | 1.25 | .50 | .12 |
| ☐ 103 Sonny Wade | | 2.00 | .80 | .20 |
| ☐ 104 Moses Denson | | 2.00 | .80 | .20 |
| ☐ 105 Terry Evanshen | | 6.00 | 2.40 | .60 |
| ☐ 106 Pierre Desjardins | | .75 | .30 | .07 |
| ☐ 107 Larry Fairholm | | .75 | .30 | .07 |
| ☐ 108 Gene Gaines | | 4.00 | 1.60 | .40 |
| ☐ 109 Bobby Lee Thompson | | .75 | .30 | .07 |
| ☐ 110 Mike Widger | | .75 | .30 | .07 |
| ☐ 111 Gene Ceppetelli | | .75 | .30 | .07 |
| ☐ 112 Barry Randall | | .75 | .30 | .07 |
| ☐ 113 Sam Etcheverry CO | | 2.50 | 1.00 | .25 |
| ☐ 114 Mark Kosmos | | 1.25 | .50 | .12 |
| ☐ 115 Peter Dalla Riva | | 4.00 | 1.60 | .40 |
| ☐ 116 Ted Collins | | .75 | .30 | .07 |
| ☐ 117 John Couture | | .75 | .30 | .07 |
| ☐ 118 Tony Passander | | .75 | .30 | .07 |
| ☐ 119 Garry Lefebvre | | .75 | .30 | .07 |
| ☐ 120 George Springate | | .75 | .30 | .07 |
| ☐ 121 Gordon Judges | | .75 | .30 | .07 |
| ☐ 122 Steve Smear | | 2.50 | 1.00 | .25 |
| ☐ 123 Tom Pullen | | .75 | .30 | .07 |
| ☐ 124 Merl Code | | .75 | .30 | .07 |
| ☐ 125 Steve Booras | | .75 | .30 | .07 |
| ☐ 126 Hugh Oldham | | .75 | .30 | .07 |
| ☐ 127 Moe Racine | | .75 | .30 | .07 |
| ☐ 128 John Kruspe | | .75 | .30 | .07 |
| ☐ 129 Ken Lehmann | | 1.25 | .50 | .12 |
| ☐ 130 Billy Cooper | | .75 | .30 | .07 |
| ☐ 131 Marshall Shirk | | .75 | .30 | .07 |
| ☐ 132 Tom Schuette | | .75 | .30 | .07 |
| ☐ 133 Doug Specht | | .75 | .30 | .07 |
| ☐ 134 Dennis Duncan | | .75 | .30 | .07 |
| ☐ 135 Jerry Campbell | | .75 | .30 | .07 |
| ☐ 136 Wayne Giardino | | .75 | .30 | .07 |
| ☐ 137 Roger Perdrix | | .75 | .30 | .07 |
| ☐ 138 Jack Gotta CO | | .75 | .30 | .07 |
| ☐ 139 Terry Wellesley | | .75 | .30 | .07 |
| ☐ 140 Dave Braggins | | .75 | .30 | .07 |
| ☐ 141 Dave Pivec | | .75 | .30 | .07 |
| ☐ 142 Rod Woodward | | .75 | .30 | .07 |
| ☐ 143 Garry Wood | | 2.00 | .80 | .20 |
| ☐ 144 Al Marcelin | | 1.25 | .50 | .12 |
| ☐ 145 Dan Dever | | .75 | .30 | .07 |
| ☐ 146 Ivan MacMillan | | .75 | .30 | .07 |

| | | | | |
|---|---|---|---|---|
| ☐ 147 Wayne Smith | .75 | .30 | .07 |
| ☐ 148 Barry Ardern | .75 | .30 | .07 |
| ☐ 149 Rick Cassatta | 1.25 | .50 | .12 |
| ☐ 150 Bill Van Burkleo | .75 | .30 | .07 |
| ☐ 151 Ron Lancaster | 5.00 | 2.00 | .50 |
| ☐ 152 Wayne Shaw | .75 | .30 | .07 |
| ☐ 153 Bob Kosid | .75 | .30 | .07 |
| ☐ 154 George Reed | 7.50 | 3.00 | .75 |
| ☐ 155 Don Bahnuik | .75 | .30 | .07 |
| ☐ 156 Gordon Barwell | .75 | .30 | .07 |
| ☐ 157 Clyde Brock | .75 | .30 | .07 |
| ☐ 158 Alan Ford | .75 | .30 | .07 |
| ☐ 159 Jack Abendschan | .75 | .30 | .07 |
| ☐ 160 Steve Molnar | .75 | .30 | .07 |
| ☐ 161 Al Rankin | .75 | .30 | .07 |
| ☐ 162 Bobby Thompson | .75 | .30 | .07 |
| ☐ 163 Dave Skrien CO | .75 | .30 | .07 |
| ☐ 164 Nolan Bailey | .75 | .30 | .07 |
| ☐ 165 Bill Baker | 5.00 | 2.00 | .50 |
| ☐ 166 Bruce Bennett | 1.50 | .60 | .15 |
| ☐ 167 Gary Brandt | .75 | .30 | .07 |
| ☐ 168 Charlie Collins | .75 | .30 | .07 |
| ☐ 169 Henry Dorsch | .75 | .30 | .07 |
| ☐ 170 Ted Dushinski | .75 | .30 | .07 |
| ☐ 171 Bruce Gainer | .75 | .30 | .07 |
| ☐ 172 Ralph Galloway | .75 | .30 | .07 |
| ☐ 173 Ken Frith | .75 | .30 | .07 |
| ☐ 174 Cliff Shaw | .75 | .30 | .07 |
| ☐ 175 Silas McKinnie | .75 | .30 | .07 |
| ☐ 176 Mike Eben | .75 | .30 | .07 |
| ☐ 177 Greg Barton | 2.00 | .80 | .20 |
| ☐ 178 Joe Theismann | 20.00 | 8.00 | 2.00 |
| ☐ 179 Charlie Bray | .75 | .30 | .07 |
| ☐ 180 Roger Scales | .75 | .30 | .07 |
| ☐ 181 Bob Hudspeth | .75 | .30 | .07 |
| ☐ 182 Bill Symons | 1.50 | .60 | .15 |
| ☐ 183 Dave Raimey | 1.25 | .50 | .12 |
| ☐ 184 Dave Cranmer | 1.25 | .50 | .12 |
| ☐ 185 Mel Profit | 1.25 | .50 | .12 |
| ☐ 186 Paul Desjardins | .75 | .30 | .07 |
| ☐ 187 Tony Moro | .75 | .30 | .07 |
| ☐ 188 Leo Cahill CO | .75 | .30 | .07 |
| ☐ 189 Chip Barrett | .75 | .30 | .07 |
| ☐ 190 Pete Martin | .75 | .30 | .07 |
| ☐ 191 Walt Balasiuk | .75 | .30 | .07 |
| ☐ 192 Jim Corrigall | 1.50 | .60 | .15 |
| ☐ 193 Ellison Kelly | 5.00 | 2.00 | .50 |
| ☐ 194 Jim Tomlin | .75 | .30 | .07 |
| ☐ 195 Marv Luster | 2.00 | .80 | .20 |
| ☐ 196 Jim Thorpe | 2.00 | .80 | .20 |
| ☐ 197 Jim Stillwagon | 4.00 | 1.60 | .40 |
| ☐ 198 Ed Harrington | .75 | .30 | .07 |
| ☐ 199 Jim Dye | .75 | .30 | .07 |
| ☐ 200 Leon McQuay | 2.50 | 1.00 | .25 |
| ☐ 201 Rob McLaren | .75 | .30 | .07 |
| ☐ 202 Benji Dial | .75 | .30 | .07 |
| ☐ 203 Chuck Liebrock | .75 | .30 | .07 |
| ☐ 204 Glen Schapansky | .75 | .30 | .07 |
| ☐ 205 Ed Ulmer | .75 | .30 | .07 |
| ☐ 206 Ross Richardson | .75 | .30 | .07 |
| ☐ 207 Lou Andrus | .75 | .30 | .07 |
| ☐ 208 Paul Robson | .75 | .30 | .07 |
| ☐ 209 Paul Brule | .75 | .30 | .07 |
| ☐ 210 Doug Strong | .75 | .30 | .07 |
| ☐ 211 Dick Smith | .75 | .30 | .07 |
| ☐ 212 Bill Frank | .75 | .30 | .07 |
| ☐ 213 Jim Spavital CO | .75 | .30 | .07 |
| ☐ 214 Rick Shaw | .75 | .30 | .07 |
| ☐ 215 Joe Critchlow | .75 | .30 | .07 |
| ☐ 216 Don Jonas | 2.50 | 1.00 | .25 |
| ☐ 217 Bob Swift | .75 | .30 | .07 |
| ☐ 218 Larry Kerychuk | .75 | .30 | .07 |
| ☐ 219 Bob McCarthy | .75 | .30 | .07 |
| ☐ 220 Gene Lakusiak | .75 | .30 | .07 |
| ☐ 221 Jim Heighton | .75 | .30 | .07 |
| ☐ 222 Chuck Harrison | .75 | .30 | .07 |
| ☐ 223 Lance Fletcher | .75 | .30 | .07 |
| ☐ 224 Larry Slagle | .75 | .30 | .07 |
| ☐ 225 Wayne Giesbrecht | .75 | .30 | .07 |

## 1956 Shredded Wheat CFL

The 1956 Shredded Wheat CFL football card set contains 105 cards portraying CFL players. The cards measure 2 1/2" by 3 1/2". The fronts of the cards contain a black and white portrait photo of the player on a one-color striped background. The lower 1/2" of the front contains the card number and the player's name below a dashed line. This lower portion of the card was presumably connected with a premium offer, as the back indicates such an offer, in both English and French, on the bottom. The backs contain brief biographical data in both English and French. Each letter prefix corresponds to a team, e.g., A: Calgary Stampeders, B: Edmonton Eskimos, C: Winnipeg Blue Bombers, D: Hamilton Tiger-Cats, E: Toronto Argonauts, F: Saskatchewan Roughriders, and G: Ottawa Rough Riders.

**12 B    JACK PARKER**

| | NRMT | VG-E | GOOD |
|---|---|---|---|
| COMPLETE SET (105) | 9000.00 | 4000.00 | 1000.00 |
| COMMON PLAYER | 80.00 | 32.00 | 8.00 |
| ☐ A1 Peter Muir | 80.00 | 32.00 | 8.00 |
| ☐ A2 Harry Langford | 80.00 | 32.00 | 8.00 |
| ☐ A3 Tony Pajaczkowski | 150.00 | 60.00 | 15.00 |
| ☐ A4 Bob Morgan | 80.00 | 32.00 | 8.00 |
| ☐ A5 Baz Nagle | 80.00 | 32.00 | 8.00 |
| ☐ A6 Alex Macklin | 80.00 | 32.00 | 8.00 |
| ☐ A7 Bob Geary | 80.00 | 32.00 | 8.00 |
| ☐ A8 Don Klosterman | 125.00 | 50.00 | 12.50 |
| ☐ A9 Bill McKenna | 80.00 | 32.00 | 8.00 |
| ☐ A10 Bill Stevenson | 80.00 | 32.00 | 8.00 |
| ☐ A11 Charles Baillie | 80.00 | 32.00 | 8.00 |
| ☐ A12 Berdett Hess | 90.00 | 36.00 | 9.00 |
| ☐ A13 Lynn Bottoms | 80.00 | 32.00 | 8.00 |
| ☐ A14 Doug Brown | 80.00 | 32.00 | 8.00 |
| ☐ A15 Jack Hennemier | 80.00 | 32.00 | 8.00 |
| ☐ B1 Frank Anderson | 80.00 | 32.00 | 8.00 |
| ☐ B2 Don Barry | 80.00 | 32.00 | 8.00 |
| ☐ B3 Johnny Bright | 200.00 | 80.00 | 20.00 |
| ☐ B4 Kurt Burris | 80.00 | 32.00 | 8.00 |
| ☐ B5 Bob Dean | 80.00 | 32.00 | 8.00 |
| ☐ B6 Don Getty | 150.00 | 60.00 | 15.00 |
| ☐ B7 Normie Kwong | 200.00 | 80.00 | 20.00 |
| ☐ B8 Earl Lindley | 80.00 | 32.00 | 8.00 |
| ☐ B9 Art Walker | 100.00 | 40.00 | 10.00 |
| ☐ B10 Rollie Miles | 125.00 | 50.00 | 12.50 |
| ☐ B11 Frank Morris | 125.00 | 50.00 | 12.50 |
| ☐ B12 Jackie Parker | 300.00 | 120.00 | 30.00 |
| ☐ B13 Ted Tully | 80.00 | 32.00 | 8.00 |
| ☐ B14 Frank Ivy | 80.00 | 32.00 | 8.00 |
| ☐ B15 Bill Rowekamp | 80.00 | 32.00 | 8.00 |
| ☐ C1 Al Sherman | 80.00 | 32.00 | 8.00 |
| ☐ C2 Larry Cabrelli | 80.00 | 32.00 | 8.00 |
| ☐ C3 Ron Kelly | 80.00 | 32.00 | 8.00 |
| ☐ C4 Edward Kotowich | 80.00 | 32.00 | 8.00 |
| ☐ C5 Buddy Leake | 80.00 | 32.00 | 8.00 |
| ☐ C6 Thomas Lumsden | 80.00 | 32.00 | 8.00 |
| ☐ C7 Bill Smitiuk | 80.00 | 32.00 | 8.00 |
| ☐ C8 Buddy Tinsley | 125.00 | 50.00 | 12.50 |
| ☐ C9 Ron Vaccher | 80.00 | 32.00 | 8.00 |
| ☐ C10 Eagle Day | 125.00 | 50.00 | 12.50 |
| ☐ C11 Buddy Allison | 80.00 | 32.00 | 8.00 |
| ☐ C12 Bob Haas | 90.00 | 36.00 | 9.00 |
| ☐ C13 Steve Patrick | 80.00 | 32.00 | 8.00 |
| ☐ C14 Keith Pearce UER (Misspelled Pierce on front) | 80.00 | 32.00 | 8.00 |
| ☐ C15 Lorne Benson | 80.00 | 32.00 | 8.00 |
| ☐ D1 George Arnett | 80.00 | 32.00 | 8.00 |
| ☐ D2 Eddie Bevan | 80.00 | 32.00 | 8.00 |
| ☐ D3 Art Darch | 80.00 | 32.00 | 8.00 |
| ☐ D4 John Fedosoff | 80.00 | 32.00 | 8.00 |
| ☐ D5 Cam Fraser | 80.00 | 32.00 | 8.00 |
| ☐ D6 Ron Howell | 90.00 | 36.00 | 9.00 |
| ☐ D7 Alex Muzyka | 80.00 | 32.00 | 8.00 |
| ☐ D8 Chet Miksza | 80.00 | 32.00 | 8.00 |
| ☐ D9 Walt Nikorak | 80.00 | 32.00 | 8.00 |
| ☐ D10 Pete Neumann | 125.00 | 50.00 | 12.50 |
| ☐ D11 Steve Oneschuk | 80.00 | 32.00 | 8.00 |
| ☐ D12 Vince Scott | 125.00 | 50.00 | 12.50 |
| ☐ D13 Ralph Toohy | 80.00 | 32.00 | 8.00 |
| ☐ D14 Ray Truant | 80.00 | 32.00 | 8.00 |
| ☐ D15 Nobby Wirkowski | 100.00 | 40.00 | 10.00 |
| ☐ E1 Pete Bennett | 80.00 | 32.00 | 8.00 |
| ☐ E2 Fred Black | 80.00 | 32.00 | 8.00 |
| ☐ E3 Jim Copeland | 80.00 | 32.00 | 8.00 |
| ☐ E4 Al Pfeifer | 90.00 | 36.00 | 9.00 |
| ☐ E5 Ron Albright | 80.00 | 32.00 | 8.00 |
| ☐ E6 Tom Dublinski | 125.00 | 50.00 | 12.50 |
| ☐ E7 Billy Shipp | 80.00 | 32.00 | 8.00 |
| ☐ E8 Baz Mackie | 80.00 | 32.00 | 8.00 |
| ☐ E9 Bill McFarlane | 80.00 | 32.00 | 8.00 |
| ☐ E10 John Sopinka | 100.00 | 40.00 | 10.00 |
| ☐ E11 Dick Brown | 80.00 | 32.00 | 8.00 |
| ☐ E12 Gerry Doucette | 80.00 | 32.00 | 8.00 |

| | | | |
|---|---|---|---|
| ☐ E13 Dan Shaw | 80.00 | 32.00 | 8.00 |
| ☐ E14 Dick Shatto | 150.00 | 60.00 | 15.00 |
| ☐ E15 Bill Swiacki | 100.00 | 40.00 | 10.00 |
| ☐ F1 Ray Syrnyk | 80.00 | 32.00 | 8.00 |
| ☐ F2 Martin Ruby | 125.00 | 50.00 | 12.50 |
| ☐ F3 Bobby Marlow | 125.00 | 50.00 | 12.50 |
| ☐ F4 Doug Kiloh | 80.00 | 32.00 | 8.00 |
| ☐ F5 Gord Sturtridge | 90.00 | 36.00 | 9.00 |
| ☐ F6 Stan Williams | 80.00 | 32.00 | 8.00 |
| ☐ F7 Larry Isbell | 80.00 | 32.00 | 8.00 |
| ☐ F8 Ken Casner | 80.00 | 32.00 | 8.00 |
| ☐ F9 Mel Becket | 100.00 | 40.00 | 10.00 |
| ☐ F10 Reg Whitehouse | 80.00 | 32.00 | 8.00 |
| ☐ F11 Harry Lampman | 80.00 | 32.00 | 8.00 |
| ☐ F12 Mario DeMarco | 90.00 | 36.00 | 9.00 |
| ☐ F13 Ken Carpenter | 100.00 | 40.00 | 10.00 |
| ☐ F14 Frank Filchock | 90.00 | 36.00 | 9.00 |
| ☐ F15 Frank Tripucka | 125.00 | 50.00 | 12.50 |
| ☐ G1 Tom Tracy | 125.00 | 50.00 | 12.50 |
| ☐ G2 Pete Ladygo | 80.00 | 32.00 | 8.00 |
| ☐ G3 Sam Scoccia | 80.00 | 32.00 | 8.00 |
| ☐ G4 Joe Upton | 80.00 | 32.00 | 8.00 |
| ☐ G5 Bob Simpson | 150.00 | 60.00 | 15.00 |
| ☐ G6 Bruno Bitkowski | 90.00 | 36.00 | 9.00 |
| ☐ G7 Joe Stracini UER | 80.00 | 32.00 | 8.00 |
| (Misspelled Straccini on card front) | | | |
| ☐ G8 Hal Ledyard | 80.00 | 32.00 | 8.00 |
| ☐ G9 Milt Graham | 80.00 | 32.00 | 8.00 |
| ☐ G10 Bill Sowalski | 80.00 | 32.00 | 8.00 |
| ☐ G11 Avatus Stone | 80.00 | 32.00 | 8.00 |
| ☐ G12 Boick | 80.00 | 32.00 | 8.00 |
| ☐ G13 Don Pinhey UER | 80.00 | 32.00 | 8.00 |
| (Misspelled Bob Pinkney on card front) | | | |
| ☐ G14 Peter Karpuk | 80.00 | 32.00 | 8.00 |
| ☐ G15 Frank Clair | 125.00 | 50.00 | 12.50 |

## 1958 Topps CFL

BERNIE FALONEY
QUARTERBACK    HAMILTON TIGER-CATS

The 1958 Topps CFL set features eight of the nine Canadian Football League teams, excluding Montreal. The cards measure 2 1/2" by 3 1/2". This first Topps Canadian issue is very similar in format to the 1958 Topps NFL issue. The cards were sold in wax boxes containing 36 five-cent wax packs. The card backs feature a "Rub-a-coin" quiz along with the typical biographical and statistical information. The set features the first card of Cookie Gilchrist, who later led the AFL in rushing twice.

| | NRMT | VG-E | GOOD |
|---|---|---|---|
| COMPLETE SET (88) | 600.00 | 240.00 | 60.00 |
| COMMON PLAYER (1-88) | 6.00 | 2.40 | .60 |

| | | | |
|---|---|---|---|
| ☐ 1 Paul Anderson | 12.00 | 5.00 | 1.20 |
| ☐ 2 Leigh McMillan | 6.00 | 2.40 | .60 |
| ☐ 3 Vic Chapman | 6.00 | 2.40 | .60 |
| ☐ 4 Bobby Marlow | 12.00 | 5.00 | 1.20 |
| ☐ 5 Mike Cacic | 6.00 | 2.40 | .60 |
| ☐ 6 Ron Pawlowski | 6.00 | 2.40 | .60 |
| ☐ 7 Frank Morris | 9.00 | 3.75 | .90 |
| ☐ 8 Earl Keeley | 7.50 | 3.00 | .75 |
| ☐ 9 Don Walsh | 6.00 | 2.40 | .60 |
| ☐ 10 Bryan Engram | 6.00 | 2.40 | .60 |
| ☐ 11 Bobby Kuntz | 7.50 | 3.00 | .75 |
| ☐ 12 Jerry Janes | 6.00 | 2.40 | .60 |
| ☐ 13 Don Bingham | 6.00 | 2.40 | .60 |
| ☐ 14 Paul Fedor | 6.00 | 2.40 | .60 |
| ☐ 15 Tommy Grant | 7.50 | 3.00 | .75 |
| ☐ 16 Don Getty | 20.00 | 8.00 | 2.00 |
| ☐ 17 George Brancato | 6.00 | 2.40 | .60 |
| ☐ 18 Jackie Parker | 35.00 | 14.00 | 3.50 |
| ☐ 19 Alan Valdes | 6.00 | 2.40 | .60 |
| ☐ 20 Paul Dekker | 6.00 | 2.40 | .60 |
| ☐ 21 Frank Tripucka | 12.00 | 5.00 | 1.20 |

| | | | |
|---|---|---|---|
| ☐ 22 Gerry McDougall | 9.00 | 3.75 | .90 |
| ☐ 23 Duke Dewveall | 7.50 | 3.00 | .75 |
| ☐ 24 Ted Smale | 6.00 | 2.40 | .60 |
| ☐ 25 Tony Pajaczkowski | 12.00 | 5.00 | 1.20 |
| ☐ 26 Don Pinhey | 6.00 | 2.40 | .60 |
| ☐ 27 Buddy Tinsley | 12.00 | 5.00 | 1.20 |
| ☐ 28 Cookie Gilchrist | 30.00 | 12.00 | 3.00 |
| ☐ 29 Larry Isbell | 6.00 | 2.40 | .60 |
| ☐ 30 Bob Kelley | 6.00 | 2.40 | .60 |
| ☐ 31 Thomas(Corky) Tharp | 7.50 | 3.00 | .75 |
| ☐ 32 Steve Patrick | 6.00 | 2.40 | .60 |
| ☐ 33 Hardiman Cureton | 6.00 | 2.40 | .60 |
| ☐ 34 Joe Mobra | 6.00 | 2.40 | .60 |
| ☐ 35 Harry Lunn | 6.00 | 2.40 | .60 |
| ☐ 36 Gord Rowland | 7.50 | 3.00 | .75 |
| ☐ 37 Herb Gray | 15.00 | 6.00 | 1.50 |
| ☐ 38 Bob Simpson | 15.00 | 6.00 | 1.50 |
| ☐ 39 Cam Fraser | 6.00 | 2.40 | .60 |
| ☐ 40 Kenny Ploen | 15.00 | 6.00 | 1.50 |
| ☐ 41 Lynn Bottoms | 7.50 | 3.00 | .75 |
| ☐ 42 Bill Stevenson | 6.00 | 2.40 | .60 |
| ☐ 43 Jerry Selinger | 6.00 | 2.40 | .60 |
| ☐ 44 Oscar Kruger | 9.00 | 3.75 | .90 |
| ☐ 45 Gerry James | 15.00 | 6.00 | 1.50 |
| ☐ 46 Dave Mann | 12.00 | 5.00 | 1.20 |
| ☐ 47 Tom Dimitroff | 6.00 | 2.40 | .60 |
| ☐ 48 Vince Scott | 12.00 | 5.00 | 1.20 |
| ☐ 49 Fran Rogel | 7.50 | 3.00 | .75 |
| ☐ 50 Henry Hair | 6.00 | 2.40 | .60 |
| ☐ 51 Bob Brady | 6.00 | 2.40 | .60 |
| ☐ 52 Gerry Doucette | 6.00 | 2.40 | .60 |
| ☐ 53 Ken Carpenter | 7.50 | 3.00 | .75 |
| ☐ 54 Bernie Faloney | 25.00 | 10.00 | 2.50 |
| ☐ 55 John Barrow | 20.00 | 8.00 | 2.00 |
| ☐ 56 George Druxman | 6.00 | 2.40 | .60 |
| ☐ 57 Rollie Miles | 12.00 | 5.00 | 1.20 |
| ☐ 58 Jerry Cornelison | 6.00 | 2.40 | .60 |
| ☐ 59 Harry Langford | 6.00 | 2.40 | .60 |
| ☐ 60 Johnny Bright | 20.00 | 8.00 | 2.00 |
| ☐ 61 Ron Clinkscale | 6.00 | 2.40 | .60 |
| ☐ 62 Jack Hill | 6.00 | 2.40 | .60 |
| ☐ 63 Ron Quillian | 6.00 | 2.40 | .60 |
| ☐ 64 Ted Tully | 6.00 | 2.40 | .60 |
| ☐ 65 Pete Neft | 6.00 | 2.40 | .60 |
| ☐ 66 Arvyd Buntins | 6.00 | 2.40 | .60 |
| ☐ 67 Normie Kwong | 20.00 | 8.00 | 2.00 |
| ☐ 68 Matt Phillips | 6.00 | 2.40 | .60 |
| ☐ 69 Pete Bennett | 6.00 | 2.40 | .60 |
| ☐ 70 Vern Lofstrom | 6.00 | 2.40 | .60 |
| ☐ 71 Norm Stoneburgh | 6.00 | 2.40 | .60 |
| ☐ 72 Danny Nykoluk | 6.00 | 2.40 | .60 |
| ☐ 73 Chuck Dubuque | 6.00 | 2.40 | .60 |
| ☐ 74 John Varone | 6.00 | 2.40 | .60 |
| ☐ 75 Bob Kimoff | 6.00 | 2.40 | .60 |
| ☐ 76 John Pyeatt | 6.00 | 2.40 | .60 |
| ☐ 77 Pete Neumann | 12.00 | 5.00 | 1.20 |
| ☐ 78 Ernie Pitts | 9.00 | 3.75 | .90 |
| ☐ 79 Steve Oneschuk | 6.00 | 2.40 | .60 |
| ☐ 80 Kaye Vaughan | 12.00 | 5.00 | 1.20 |
| ☐ 81 Joe Yamauchi | 6.00 | 2.40 | .60 |
| ☐ 82 Harvey Wylie | 9.00 | 3.75 | .90 |
| ☐ 83 Berdett Hess | 6.00 | 2.40 | .60 |
| ☐ 84 Dick Shatto | 20.00 | 8.00 | 2.00 |
| ☐ 85 Floyd Harrawood | 6.00 | 2.40 | .60 |
| ☐ 86 Ron Atchison | 12.00 | 5.00 | 1.20 |
| ☐ 87 Bobby Judd | 6.00 | 2.40 | .60 |
| ☐ 88 Keith Pearce | 9.00 | 3.75 | .90 |

## 1959 Topps CFL

DAVE THELAN
FULLBACK    OTTAWA ROUGH RIDERS

The 1959 Topps CFL set features cards grouped by teams, i.e., Winnipeg Blue Bombers (1-7), British Columbia Lions (8-19), Calgary Stampeders (20-29), Montreal Alouettes (30-37), Edmonton Eskimos (38-48), Ottawa Rough Riders (49-58), Toronto Argonauts (59-69), Hamilton Tiger-Cats (70-78), and Saskatchewan Roughriders (79-88).

The cards measure 2 1/2" by 3 1/2". Checklists are given on the backs of card number 15 (1-44) and card number 44 (45-88). The issue is very similar to the Topps 1959 NFL issue. The cards were originally sold in five-cent wax packs with gum.

| | NRMT | VG-E | GOOD |
|---|---|---|---|
| COMPLETE SET (88) | 500.00 | 200.00 | 50.00 |
| COMMON PLAYER (1-88) | 5.00 | 2.00 | .50 |
| ☐ 1 Norm Rauhaus | 10.00 | 4.00 | 1.00 |
| ☐ 2 Cornel Piper UER | 5.00 | 2.00 | .50 |
| (Name spelled Cornell on both sides) | | | |
| ☐ 3 Leo Lewis | 20.00 | 8.00 | 2.00 |
| ☐ 4 Roger Savoie | 5.00 | 2.00 | .50 |
| ☐ 5 Jim Van Pelt | 10.00 | 4.00 | 1.00 |
| ☐ 6 Herb Gray | 10.00 | 4.00 | 1.00 |
| ☐ 7 Gerry James | 10.00 | 4.00 | 1.00 |
| ☐ 8 By Bailey | 12.00 | 5.00 | 1.20 |
| ☐ 9 Tom Hinton | 10.00 | 4.00 | 1.00 |
| ☐ 10 Chuck Quilter | 5.00 | 2.00 | .50 |
| ☐ 11 M. Gillett | 5.00 | 2.00 | .50 |
| ☐ 12 Ted Hunt | 5.00 | 2.00 | .50 |
| ☐ 13 Sonny Homer | 6.00 | 2.40 | .60 |
| ☐ 14 Bill Jessup | 5.00 | 2.00 | .50 |
| ☐ 15 Al Dorow | 20.00 | 5.00 | 1.00 |
| (Checklist 1-44 back) | | | |
| ☐ 16 Norm Fieldgate | 12.00 | 5.00 | 1.20 |
| ☐ 17 Urban Henry | 6.00 | 2.40 | .60 |
| ☐ 18 Paul Cameron | 5.00 | 2.00 | .50 |
| ☐ 19 Bruce Claridge | 5.00 | 2.00 | .50 |
| ☐ 20 Jim Bakhtiar | 5.00 | 2.00 | .50 |
| ☐ 21 Earl Lunsford | 12.00 | 5.00 | 1.20 |
| ☐ 22 Walt Radzick | 5.00 | 2.00 | .50 |
| ☐ 23 Ron Albright | 5.00 | 2.00 | .50 |
| ☐ 24 Art Scullion | 5.00 | 2.00 | .50 |
| ☐ 25 Ernie Warlick | 6.00 | 2.40 | .60 |
| ☐ 26 Nobby Wirkowski | 7.50 | 3.00 | .75 |
| ☐ 27 Harvey Wylie | 9.00 | 3.75 | .90 |
| ☐ 28 Gordon Brown | 5.00 | 2.00 | .50 |
| ☐ 29 Don Luzzi | 10.00 | 4.00 | 1.00 |
| ☐ 30 Hal Patterson | 15.00 | 6.00 | 1.50 |
| ☐ 31 Jackie Simpson | 15.00 | 6.00 | 1.50 |
| ☐ 32 Doug McNichol | 5.00 | 2.00 | .50 |
| ☐ 33 B. Maclellan | 5.00 | 2.00 | .50 |
| ☐ 34 Ted Elsby | 5.00 | 2.00 | .50 |
| ☐ 35 Mike Kovac | 5.00 | 2.00 | .50 |
| ☐ 36 Bob Leary | 5.00 | 2.00 | .50 |
| ☐ 37 Hal Krebs | 5.00 | 2.00 | .50 |
| ☐ 38 Steve Jennings | 5.00 | 2.00 | .50 |
| ☐ 39 Don Getty | 12.00 | 5.00 | 1.20 |
| ☐ 40 Normie Kwong | 12.00 | 5.00 | 1.20 |
| ☐ 41 Johnny Bright | 15.00 | 6.00 | 1.50 |
| ☐ 42 Art Walker | 7.50 | 3.00 | .75 |
| ☐ 43 Jackie Parker UER | 30.00 | 12.00 | 3.00 |
| (Incorrectly listed as Tackle on card front) | | | |
| ☐ 44 Don Barry | 20.00 | 5.00 | 1.00 |
| (Checklist 45-88 back) | | | |
| ☐ 45 Tommy Joe Coffey | 25.00 | 10.00 | 2.50 |
| ☐ 46 Mike Volcan | 5.00 | 2.00 | .50 |
| ☐ 47 S. Renning | 5.00 | 2.00 | .50 |
| ☐ 48 Gino Fracas | 9.00 | 3.75 | .90 |
| ☐ 49 Ted Smale | 5.00 | 2.00 | .50 |
| ☐ 50 Mack Yoho | 6.00 | 2.40 | .60 |
| ☐ 51 B. Gravens | 5.00 | 2.00 | .50 |
| ☐ 52 Milt Graham | 5.00 | 2.00 | .50 |
| ☐ 53 Lou Bruce | 5.00 | 2.00 | .50 |
| ☐ 54 Bob Simpson | 12.00 | 5.00 | 1.20 |
| ☐ 55 Bill Sowalski | 5.00 | 2.00 | .50 |
| ☐ 56 Russ Jackson | 35.00 | 14.00 | 3.50 |
| ☐ 57 Don Clark | 5.00 | 2.00 | .50 |
| ☐ 58 Dave Thelen | 9.00 | 3.75 | .90 |
| ☐ 59 Larry Cowart | 5.00 | 2.00 | .50 |
| ☐ 60 Dave Mann | 7.50 | 3.00 | .75 |
| ☐ 61 Norm Stoneburgh UER | 5.00 | 2.00 | .50 |
| (Misspelled Stoneburg) | | | |
| ☐ 62 Ronnie Knox | 9.00 | 3.75 | .90 |
| ☐ 63 Dick Shatto | 12.00 | 5.00 | 1.20 |
| ☐ 64 Bobby Kuntz | 6.00 | 2.40 | .60 |
| ☐ 65 P. Muntz | 5.00 | 2.00 | .50 |
| ☐ 66 Gerry Doucette | 5.00 | 2.00 | .50 |
| ☐ 67 Sam DeLuca | 6.00 | 2.40 | .60 |
| ☐ 68 Boyd Carter | 5.00 | 2.00 | .50 |
| ☐ 69 Vic Kristopaitis | 9.00 | 3.75 | .90 |
| ☐ 70 Gerry McDougall UER | 7.50 | 3.00 | .75 |
| (Misspelled Jerry) | | | |
| ☐ 71 Vince Scott | 10.00 | 4.00 | 1.00 |
| ☐ 72 Angelo Mosca | 35.00 | 14.00 | 3.50 |
| ☐ 73 Chet Miksza | 5.00 | 2.00 | .50 |
| ☐ 74 Eddie Macon | 6.00 | 2.40 | .60 |
| ☐ 75 Harry Lampman | 5.00 | 2.00 | .50 |
| ☐ 76 B. Graham | 5.00 | 2.00 | .50 |
| ☐ 77 Ralph Goldston | 7.50 | 3.00 | .75 |
| ☐ 78 Cam Fraser | 5.00 | 2.00 | .50 |
| ☐ 79 Ron Dundas | 5.00 | 2.00 | .50 |
| ☐ 80 Bill Clarke | 5.00 | 2.00 | .50 |
| ☐ 81 Len Legault | 5.00 | 2.00 | .50 |
| ☐ 82 Reg Whitehouse | 5.00 | 2.00 | .50 |
| ☐ 83 Dale Parsons | 5.00 | 2.00 | .50 |
| ☐ 84 Doug Kiloh | 5.00 | 2.00 | .50 |
| ☐ 85 T. Whitehouse | 5.00 | 2.00 | .50 |
| ☐ 86 Mike Hagler | 5.00 | 2.00 | .50 |
| ☐ 87 Paul Anderson | 5.00 | 2.00 | .50 |
| ☐ 88 Danny Banda | 7.50 | 3.00 | .75 |

# 1960 Topps CFL

The 1960 Topps CFL set features cards grouped by teams, i.e., British Columbia Lions (1-10), Edmonton Eskimos (11-20), Calgary Stampeders (21-30), Hamilton Tiger-Cats (31-40), Montreal Alouettes (41-50), Saskatchewan Roughriders (51-59), Ottawa Rough Riders (60-68), Toronto Argonauts (69-78), and Winnipeg Blue Bombers (79-88). The cards measure 2 1/2" by 3 1/2". Checklists are given on the backs of card number 14 (1-44) and card number 45 (45-88). The issue is very similar in format to the Topps NFL issue of 1960. The set features a card of Gerry James, who also played in the National Hockey League.

| | NRMT | VG-E | GOOD |
|---|---|---|---|
| COMPLETE SET (88) | 500.00 | 200.00 | 50.00 |
| COMMON PLAYER (1-88) | 5.00 | 2.00 | .50 |
| ☐ 1 By Bailey | 12.00 | 5.00 | 1.00 |
| ☐ 2 Paul Cameron | 5.00 | 2.00 | .50 |
| ☐ 3 Bruce Claridge | 5.00 | 2.00 | .50 |
| ☐ 4 Chuck Dubuque | 5.00 | 2.00 | .50 |
| ☐ 5 Randy Duncan | 12.00 | 5.00 | 1.20 |
| ☐ 6 Norm Fieldgate | 10.00 | 4.00 | 1.00 |
| ☐ 7 Urban Henry | 6.00 | 2.40 | .60 |
| ☐ 8 Ted Hunt | 5.00 | 2.00 | .50 |
| ☐ 9 Bill Jessup | 5.00 | 2.00 | .50 |
| ☐ 10 Ted Tully | 5.00 | 2.00 | .50 |
| ☐ 11 Vic Chapman | 5.00 | 2.00 | .50 |
| ☐ 12 Gino Fracas | 7.50 | 3.00 | .75 |
| ☐ 13 Don Getty | 10.00 | 4.00 | 1.00 |
| ☐ 14 Ed Gray | 5.00 | 2.00 | .50 |
| ☐ 15 Oscar Kruger | 20.00 | 5.00 | 1.00 |
| (Checklist 1-44 back) | | | |
| ☐ 16 Rollie Miles | 10.00 | 4.00 | 1.00 |
| ☐ 17 Jackie Parker | 25.00 | 10.00 | 2.50 |
| ☐ 18 Joe-Bob Smith UER | 5.00 | 2.00 | .50 |
| (Name spelled Bob-Joe on both sides of card) | | | |
| ☐ 19 Mike Volcan | 5.00 | 2.00 | .50 |
| ☐ 20 Art Walker | 7.50 | 3.00 | .75 |
| ☐ 21 Ron Albright | 5.00 | 2.00 | .50 |
| ☐ 22 Jim Bakhtiar | 5.00 | 2.00 | .50 |
| ☐ 23 Lynn Bottoms | 6.00 | 2.40 | .60 |
| ☐ 24 Jack Gotta | 9.00 | 3.75 | .90 |
| ☐ 25 Joe Kapp | 50.00 | 20.00 | 5.00 |
| ☐ 26 Earl Lunsford | 9.00 | 3.75 | .90 |
| ☐ 27 Don Luzzi | 9.00 | 3.75 | .90 |
| ☐ 28 Art Scullion | 5.00 | 2.00 | .50 |
| ☐ 29 H. Simpson | 5.00 | 2.00 | .50 |
| ☐ 30 Ernie Warlick | 9.00 | 3.75 | .90 |
| ☐ 31 John Barrow | 12.00 | 5.00 | 1.20 |
| ☐ 32 Paul Dekker | 5.00 | 2.00 | .50 |
| ☐ 33 Bernie Faloney | 20.00 | 8.00 | 2.00 |
| ☐ 34 Cam Fraser | 5.00 | 2.00 | .50 |
| ☐ 35 Ralph Goldston | 7.50 | 3.00 | .75 |
| ☐ 36 Ron Howell | 7.50 | 3.00 | .75 |
| ☐ 37 Gerry McDougall UER | 5.00 | 2.00 | .50 |
| (Misspelled Jerry) | | | |
| ☐ 38 Angelo Mosca | 20.00 | 8.00 | 2.00 |
| ☐ 39 Pete Neumann | 9.00 | 3.75 | .90 |
| ☐ 40 Vince Scott | 9.00 | 3.75 | .90 |
| ☐ 41 Ted Elsby | 5.00 | 2.00 | .50 |
| ☐ 42 Sam Etcheverry | 20.00 | 8.00 | 2.00 |
| ☐ 43 Mike Kovac | 5.00 | 2.00 | .50 |
| ☐ 44 Ed Learn | 5.00 | 2.00 | .50 |

| | NRMT | VG-E | GOOD |
|---|---|---|---|
| ☐ 45 I. Livingstone | 20.00 | 5.00 | 1.00 |
| (Checklist 45-88 back) | | | |
| ☐ 46 Hal Patterson | 15.00 | 6.00 | 1.50 |
| ☐ 47 Jackie Simpson | 12.00 | 5.00 | 1.20 |
| ☐ 48 Veryl Switzer | 5.00 | 2.00 | .50 |
| ☐ 49 Bill Bewley | 9.00 | 3.75 | .90 |
| ☐ 50 J. Wells | 5.00 | 2.00 | .50 |
| ☐ 51 Ron Atchison | 9.00 | 3.75 | .90 |
| ☐ 52 Ken Carpenter | 6.00 | 2.40 | .60 |
| ☐ 53 Bill Clarke | 5.00 | 2.00 | .50 |
| ☐ 54 Ron Dundas | 5.00 | 2.00 | .50 |
| ☐ 55 Mike Hagler | 5.00 | 2.00 | .50 |
| ☐ 56 Jack Hill | 5.00 | 2.00 | .50 |
| ☐ 57 Doug Kiloh | 5.00 | 2.00 | .50 |
| ☐ 58 Bobby Marlow | 10.00 | 4.00 | 1.00 |
| ☐ 59 B. Mulgado | 5.00 | 2.00 | .50 |
| ☐ 60 George Brancato | 7.50 | 3.00 | .75 |
| ☐ 61 Lou Bruce | 5.00 | 2.00 | .50 |
| ☐ 62 Hardiman Cureton | 6.00 | 2.40 | .60 |
| ☐ 63 Russ Jackson | 20.00 | 8.00 | 2.00 |
| ☐ 64 Gerry Nesbitt | 5.00 | 2.00 | .50 |
| ☐ 65 Bob Simpson | 10.00 | 4.00 | 1.00 |
| ☐ 66 Ted Smale | 5.00 | 2.00 | .50 |
| ☐ 67 Dave Thelen | 9.00 | 3.75 | .90 |
| ☐ 68 Kaye Vaughan | 9.00 | 3.75 | .90 |
| ☐ 69 Pete Bennett | 5.00 | 2.00 | .50 |
| ☐ 70 Boyd Carter | 5.00 | 2.00 | .50 |
| ☐ 71 Gerry Doucette | 5.00 | 2.00 | .50 |
| ☐ 72 Bobby Kuntz | 6.00 | 2.40 | .60 |
| ☐ 73 A. Panton | 5.00 | 2.00 | .50 |
| ☐ 74 Tobin Rote | 15.00 | 6.00 | 1.50 |
| ☐ 75 Jim Rountree | 7.50 | 3.00 | .75 |
| ☐ 76 Dick Shatto | 10.00 | 4.00 | 1.00 |
| ☐ 77 Norm Stoneburgh | 5.00 | 2.00 | .50 |
| ☐ 78 Thomas(Corky) Tharp | 6.00 | 2.40 | .60 |
| ☐ 79 George Druxman | 5.00 | 2.00 | .50 |
| ☐ 80 Herb Gray | 10.00 | 4.00 | 1.00 |
| ☐ 81 Gerry James | 12.00 | 5.00 | 1.20 |
| ☐ 82 Leo Lewis | 10.00 | 4.00 | 1.00 |
| ☐ 83 Ernie Pitts | 5.00 | 2.00 | .50 |
| ☐ 84 Kenny Ploen | 12.00 | 5.00 | 1.20 |
| ☐ 85 Norm Rauhaus | 5.00 | 2.00 | .50 |
| ☐ 86 Gord Rowland | 5.00 | 2.00 | .50 |
| ☐ 87 Charlie Shepard | 7.50 | 3.00 | .75 |
| ☐ 88 Don Clark | 10.00 | 3.00 | .60 |

## 1961 Topps CFL

The 1961 Topps CFL set features cards grouped by teams with the team picture last in the sequence: British Columbia Lions (1-15), Calgary Stampeders (16-29), Edmonton Eskimos (30-43), Hamilton Tiger-Cats (44-58), Montreal Alouettes (59-73), Ottawa Rough Riders (74-88), Saskatchewan Roughriders (89-101), Toronto Argonauts (103-117), and Winnipeg Blue Bombers (118-132). The cards measure 2 1/2" by 3 1/2". Card number 102 gives the full set checklist. Although the T.C.G. trademark appears on these cards, they were printed in Canada by O-Pee-Chee.

| | NRMT | VG-E | GOOD |
|---|---|---|---|
| COMPLETE SET (132) | 1000.00 | 450.00 | 100.00 |
| COMMON PLAYER (1-132) | 7.00 | 2.80 | .70 |
| ☐ 1 By Bailey | 15.00 | 6.00 | 1.50 |
| ☐ 2 Bruce Claridge | 7.00 | 2.80 | .70 |
| ☐ 3 Norm Fieldgate | 12.00 | 5.00 | 1.20 |
| ☐ 4 Willie Fleming | 20.00 | 8.00 | 2.00 |
| ☐ 5 Urban Henry | 9.00 | 3.75 | .90 |
| ☐ 6 Bill Herron | 7.00 | 2.80 | .70 |
| ☐ 7 Tom Hinton | 12.00 | 5.00 | 1.20 |
| ☐ 8 Sonny Homer | 9.00 | 3.75 | .90 |
| ☐ 9 Bob Jeter | 15.00 | 6.00 | 1.50 |
| ☐ 10 Vic Kristopaitis | 7.00 | 2.80 | .70 |
| ☐ 11 Baz Nagle | 7.00 | 2.80 | .70 |
| ☐ 12 Ron Watton | 7.00 | 2.80 | .70 |
| ☐ 13 Joe Yamauchi | 7.00 | 2.80 | .70 |
| ☐ 14 Bob Schloredt | 15.00 | 6.00 | 1.50 |
| ☐ 15 B.C. Lions Team | 12.00 | 5.00 | 1.20 |
| ☐ 16 Ron Albright | 7.00 | 2.80 | .70 |
| ☐ 17 Gordon Brown | 7.00 | 2.80 | .70 |
| ☐ 18 Gerry Doucette | 7.00 | 2.80 | .70 |
| ☐ 19 Gene Filipski | 12.00 | 5.00 | 1.20 |
| ☐ 20 Joe Kapp | 25.00 | 10.00 | 2.50 |
| ☐ 21 Earl Lunsford | 12.00 | 5.00 | 1.20 |
| ☐ 22 Don Luzzi | 12.00 | 5.00 | 1.20 |
| ☐ 23 Bill McKenna | 7.00 | 2.80 | .70 |
| ☐ 24 Ron Morris | 7.00 | 2.80 | .70 |
| ☐ 25 Tony Pajaczkowski | 12.00 | 5.00 | 1.20 |
| ☐ 26 Lorne Reid | 7.00 | 2.80 | .70 |
| ☐ 27 Art Scullion | 7.00 | 2.80 | .70 |
| ☐ 28 Ernie Warlick | 10.00 | 4.00 | 1.00 |
| ☐ 29 Stampeders Team | 12.00 | 5.00 | 1.20 |
| ☐ 30 Johnny Bright | 15.00 | 6.00 | 1.50 |
| ☐ 31 Vic Chapman | 7.00 | 2.80 | .70 |
| ☐ 32 Gino Fracas | 9.00 | 3.75 | .90 |
| ☐ 33 Tommy Joe Coffey | 15.00 | 6.00 | 1.50 |
| ☐ 34 Don Getty | 15.00 | 6.00 | 1.50 |
| ☐ 35 Ed Gray | 7.00 | 2.80 | .70 |
| ☐ 36 Oscar Kruger | 9.00 | 3.75 | .90 |
| ☐ 37 Rollie Miles | 12.00 | 5.00 | 1.20 |
| ☐ 38 Roger Nelson | 12.00 | 5.00 | 1.20 |
| ☐ 39 Jackie Parker | 30.00 | 12.00 | 3.00 |
| ☐ 40 Howie Schumm | 7.00 | 2.80 | .70 |
| ☐ 41 Joe-Bob Smith UER | 7.00 | 2.80 | .70 |
| (Name misspelled Bob-Joe) | | | |
| ☐ 42 Art Walker | 9.00 | 3.75 | .90 |
| ☐ 43 Eskimos Team | 12.00 | 5.00 | 1.20 |
| ☐ 44 John Barrow | 15.00 | 6.00 | 1.50 |
| ☐ 45 Paul Dekker | 7.00 | 2.80 | .70 |
| ☐ 46 Tom Dublinski | 7.00 | 2.80 | .70 |
| ☐ 47 Bernie Faloney | 25.00 | 10.00 | 2.50 |
| ☐ 48 Cam Fraser | 7.00 | 2.80 | .70 |
| ☐ 49 Ralph Goldston | 9.00 | 3.75 | .90 |
| ☐ 50 Ron Howell | 9.00 | 3.75 | .90 |
| ☐ 51 Gerry McDougall | 9.00 | 3.75 | .90 |
| ☐ 52 Pete Neumann | 12.00 | 5.00 | 1.20 |
| ☐ 53 Bronko Nagurski | 15.00 | 6.00 | 1.50 |
| ☐ 54 Vince Scott | 12.00 | 5.00 | 1.20 |
| ☐ 55 Steve Oneschuk | 9.00 | 3.75 | .90 |
| ☐ 56 Hal Patterson | 20.00 | 8.00 | 2.00 |
| ☐ 57 Jim Taylor | 9.00 | 3.75 | .90 |
| ☐ 58 Tiger-Cats Team | 12.00 | 5.00 | 1.20 |
| ☐ 59 Ted Elsby | 7.00 | 2.80 | .70 |
| ☐ 60 Don Clark | 9.00 | 3.75 | .90 |
| ☐ 61 Dick Cohee | 10.00 | 4.00 | 1.00 |
| ☐ 62 George Dixon | 20.00 | 8.00 | 2.00 |
| ☐ 63 Wes Gideon | 7.00 | 2.80 | .70 |
| ☐ 64 Harry Lampman | 7.00 | 2.80 | .70 |
| ☐ 65 Meco Poliziani | 7.00 | 2.80 | .70 |
| ☐ 66 Charles Baillie | 7.00 | 2.80 | .70 |
| ☐ 67 Howard Cissell | 7.00 | 2.80 | .70 |
| ☐ 68 Ed Learn | 7.00 | 2.80 | .70 |
| ☐ 69 Tom Moran | 7.00 | 2.80 | .70 |
| ☐ 70 Jack Simpson | 12.00 | 5.00 | 1.20 |
| ☐ 71 Bill Bewley | 9.00 | 3.75 | .90 |
| ☐ 72 Tom Hugo | 7.00 | 2.80 | .70 |
| ☐ 73 Alouettes Team | 12.00 | 5.00 | 1.20 |
| ☐ 74 Gilles Archambeault | 7.00 | 2.80 | .70 |
| ☐ 75 Lou Bruce | 7.00 | 2.80 | .70 |
| ☐ 76 Russ Jackson | 25.00 | 10.00 | 2.50 |
| ☐ 77 Tom Jones | 7.00 | 2.80 | .70 |
| ☐ 78 Gerry Nesbitt | 7.00 | 2.80 | .70 |
| ☐ 79 Ron Lancaster | 40.00 | 16.00 | 4.00 |
| ☐ 80 Joe Kelly | 7.00 | 2.80 | .70 |
| ☐ 81 Joe Poirier | 9.00 | 3.75 | .90 |
| ☐ 82 Doug Daigneault | 7.00 | 2.80 | .70 |
| ☐ 83 Kaye Vaughan | 12.00 | 5.00 | 1.20 |
| ☐ 84 Dave Thelen | 15.00 | 6.00 | 1.50 |
| ☐ 85 Ron Stewart | 20.00 | 8.00 | 2.00 |
| ☐ 86 Ted Smale | 7.00 | 2.80 | .70 |
| ☐ 87 Bob Simpson | 15.00 | 6.00 | 1.50 |
| ☐ 88 Ottawa Rough Riders Team | 12.00 | 5.00 | 1.20 |
| ☐ 89 Don Allard | 7.00 | 2.80 | .70 |
| ☐ 90 Ron Atchison | 12.00 | 5.00 | 1.20 |
| ☐ 91 Bill Clarke | 7.00 | 2.80 | .70 |
| ☐ 92 Ron Dundas | 7.00 | 2.80 | .70 |
| ☐ 93 Jack Gotta | 10.00 | 4.00 | 1.00 |
| ☐ 94 Bob Golic | 7.00 | 2.80 | .70 |
| ☐ 95 Jack Hill | 7.00 | 2.80 | .70 |
| ☐ 96 Doug Kiloh | 9.00 | 3.75 | .90 |
| ☐ 97 Len Legault | 7.00 | 2.80 | .70 |
| ☐ 98 Doug McKenzie | 7.00 | 2.80 | .70 |
| ☐ 99 Bob Ptacek | 7.00 | 2.80 | .70 |
| ☐ 100 Roy Smith | 7.00 | 2.80 | .70 |
| ☐ 101 Saskatchewan Roughriders Team | 12.00 | 5.00 | 1.20 |
| ☐ 102 Checklist 1-132 | 90.00 | 10.00 | 2.00 |
| ☐ 103 Jim Andreotti | 9.00 | 3.75 | .90 |
| ☐ 104 Boyd Carter | 7.00 | 2.80 | .70 |
| ☐ 105 Dick Fouts | 9.00 | 3.75 | .90 |
| ☐ 106 Cookie Gilchrist | 20.00 | 8.00 | 2.00 |

| | | | |
|---|---|---|---|
| 107 Bobby Kuntz | 9.00 | 3.75 | .90 |
| 108 Jim Rountree | 7.00 | 2.80 | .70 |
| 109 Dick Shatto | 15.00 | 6.00 | 1.50 |
| 110 Norm Stoneburgh | 7.00 | 2.80 | .70 |
| 111 Dave Mann | 10.00 | 4.00 | 1.00 |
| 112 Ed Ochiena | 7.00 | 2.80 | .70 |
| 113 Bill Stribling | 7.00 | 2.80 | .70 |
| 114 Tobin Rote | 15.00 | 6.00 | 1.50 |
| 115 Stan Wallace | 7.00 | 2.80 | .70 |
| 116 Billy Shipp | 9.00 | 3.75 | .90 |
| 117 Argonauts Team | 12.00 | 5.00 | 1.20 |
| 118 Dave Burkholder | 7.00 | 2.80 | .70 |
| 119 Jack Delveaux | 7.00 | 2.80 | .70 |
| 120 George Druxman | 7.00 | 2.80 | .70 |
| 121 Farrell Funston | 9.00 | 3.75 | .90 |
| 122 Herb Gray | 15.00 | 6.00 | 1.50 |
| 123 Gerry James | 15.00 | 6.00 | 1.50 |
| 124 Ronnie Latourelle | 7.00 | 2.80 | .70 |
| 125 Leo Lewis | 15.00 | 6.00 | 1.50 |
| 126 Steve Patrick | 7.00 | 2.80 | .70 |
| 127 Ernie Pitts | 7.00 | 2.80 | .70 |
| 128 Kenny Ploen | 15.00 | 6.00 | 1.50 |
| 129 Norm Rauhaus | 9.00 | 3.75 | .90 |
| 130 Gord Rowland | 9.00 | 3.75 | .90 |
| 131 Charlie Shepard | 9.00 | 3.75 | .90 |
| 132 Winnipeg Blue Bombers Team Card | 20.00 | 8.00 | 2.00 |

## 1962 Topps CFL

This 1962 Topps CFL set features 169 different numbered cards in perforated pairs. The cards measure 1 1/4" by 2 1/2" individually and 2 1/2" by 3 1/2" as a pair. The team cards contain a team checklist on the reverse side. The players preceding the team cards belong to the respective teams. Teams are in alphabetical order and players within teams are also in alphabetical order. The cards are ordered as follows: British Columbia Lions (1-20), Calgary Stampeders (21-37), Edmonton Eskimos (38-58), Hamilton Tiger-Cats (59-78), Montreal Alouettes (77-94), Ottawa Rough Riders (95-113), Saskatchewan Roughriders (114-130), Toronto Argonauts (131-148), Winnipeg Blue Bombers (149-169). Although the T.C.G. trademark appears on the cards, they were printed in Canada by O-Pee-Chee.

| | NRMT | VG-E | GOOD |
|---|---|---|---|
| COMPLETE SET (169) | 500.00 | 200.00 | 50.00 |
| COMMON PLAYER (1-169) | 2.00 | .80 | .20 |

| | | | |
|---|---|---|---|
| 1 By Bailey | 6.00 | 2.00 | .40 |
| 2 Nub Beamer | 2.00 | .80 | .20 |
| 3 Tom Brown | 8.00 | 3.25 | .80 |
| 4 Mack Burton | 2.00 | .80 | .20 |
| 5 Mike Cacic | 2.00 | .80 | .20 |
| 6 Pat Claridge | 2.00 | .80 | .20 |
| 7 Steve Cotter | 2.00 | .80 | .20 |
| 8 Lonnie Dennis | 2.00 | .80 | .20 |
| 9 Norm Fieldgate | 4.00 | 1.60 | .40 |
| 10 Willie Fleming | 8.00 | 3.25 | .80 |
| 11 Tom Hinton | 4.00 | 1.60 | .40 |
| 12 Sonny Homer | 2.50 | 1.00 | .25 |
| 13 Joe Kapp | 12.00 | 5.00 | 1.20 |
| 14 Tom Larscheid | 2.00 | .80 | .20 |
| 15 Gordie Mitchell | 2.00 | .80 | .20 |
| 16 Baz Nagle | 2.00 | .80 | .20 |
| 17 Norris Stevenson | 2.00 | .80 | .20 |
| 18 Barney Therrien UER | 2.00 | .80 | .20 |
| (Name misspelled Therien on front of card) | | | |
| 19 Don Vicic | 2.00 | .80 | .20 |
| 20 B.C. Lions Team | 8.00 | 3.25 | .80 |
| 21 Ed Buchanan | 2.00 | .80 | .20 |
| 22 Joe Carruthers | 2.00 | .80 | .20 |
| 23 Lovell Coleman | 3.00 | 1.20 | .30 |
| 24 Barrie Cyr | 2.00 | .80 | .20 |
| 25 Ernie Danjean | 2.00 | .80 | .20 |

| | | | |
|---|---|---|---|
| 26 Gene Filipski | 3.00 | 1.20 | .30 |
| 27 George Hansen | 2.00 | .80 | .20 |
| 28 Earl Lunsford | 4.00 | 1.60 | .40 |
| 29 Don Luzzi | 4.00 | 1.60 | .40 |
| 30 Bill McKenna | 2.00 | .80 | .20 |
| 31 Tony Pajaczkowski | 4.00 | 1.60 | .40 |
| 32 Chuck Quilter | 2.00 | .80 | .20 |
| 33 Lorne Reid | 2.00 | .80 | .20 |
| 34 Art Scullion | 2.00 | .80 | .20 |
| 35 Jim Walden | 2.00 | .80 | .20 |
| 36 Harvey Wylie | 4.00 | 1.60 | .40 |
| 37 Calgary Stampeders Team | 8.00 | 3.25 | .80 |
| 38 Johnny Bright | 10.00 | 4.00 | 1.00 |
| 39 Vic Chapman | 2.00 | .80 | .20 |
| 40 Marion Drew Deese | 2.00 | .80 | .20 |
| 41 Al Ecuyer | 2.00 | .80 | .20 |
| 42 Gino Fracas | 3.00 | 1.20 | .30 |
| 43 Don Getty | 6.00 | 2.40 | .60 |
| 44 Ed Gray | 2.00 | .80 | .20 |
| 45 Urban Henry | 2.00 | .80 | .20 |
| 46 Bill Hill | 2.00 | .80 | .20 |
| 47 Mike Kmeche | 2.00 | .80 | .20 |
| 48 Oscar Kruger | 2.50 | 1.00 | .25 |
| 49 Mike Lashuk | 2.00 | .80 | .20 |
| 50 Jim Letcavits | 2.00 | .80 | .20 |
| 51 Roger Nelson | 4.00 | 1.60 | .40 |
| 52 Jackie Parker | 15.00 | 6.00 | 1.50 |
| 53 Howie Schumm | 2.00 | .80 | .20 |
| 54 Jim Shipka | 2.00 | .80 | .20 |
| 55 Bill Smith | 2.00 | .80 | .20 |
| 56 Joe-Bob Smith | 2.00 | .80 | .20 |
| 57 Art Walker | 3.00 | 1.20 | .30 |
| 58 Edmonton Eskimos Team card | 8.00 | 3.25 | .80 |
| 59 John Barrow | 8.00 | 3.25 | .80 |
| 60 Hardiman Cureton | 2.00 | .80 | .20 |
| 61 Geno DeNobile | 2.00 | .80 | .20 |
| 62 Tom Dublinski | 2.00 | .80 | .20 |
| 63 Bernie Faloney | 12.00 | 5.00 | 1.20 |
| 64 Cam Fraser | 2.00 | .80 | .20 |
| 65 Ralph Goldston | 2.50 | 1.00 | .25 |
| 66 Tommy Grant | 2.50 | 1.00 | .25 |
| 67 Garney Henley | 15.00 | 6.00 | 1.50 |
| 68 Ron Howell | 2.50 | 1.00 | .25 |
| 69 Zeno Karcz | 2.50 | 1.00 | .25 |
| 70 Gerry McDougall UER | 3.00 | 1.20 | .30 |
| (Name spelled Jerry) | | | |
| 71 Chet Miksza | 2.00 | .80 | .20 |
| 72 Bronko Nagurski | 5.00 | 2.00 | .50 |
| 73 Hal Patterson | 10.00 | 4.00 | 1.00 |
| 74 George Scott | 2.00 | .80 | .20 |
| 75 Vince Scott | 4.00 | 1.60 | .40 |
| 76 Hamilton Tiger-Cats Team card | 8.00 | 3.25 | .80 |
| 77 Ron Brewer | 2.50 | 1.00 | .25 |
| 78 Ron Brooks | 2.00 | .80 | .20 |
| 79 Howard Cissell | 2.00 | .80 | .20 |
| 80 Don Clark | 2.50 | 1.00 | .25 |
| 81 Dick Cohee | 2.50 | 1.00 | .25 |
| 82 John Conroy | 2.00 | .80 | .20 |
| 83 Milt Crain | 2.50 | 1.00 | .25 |
| 84 Ted Elsby | 2.00 | .80 | .20 |
| 85 Joe Francis | 2.00 | .80 | .20 |
| 86 Gene Gaines | 8.00 | 3.25 | .80 |
| 87 Barrie Hansen | 2.00 | .80 | .20 |
| 88 Mike Kovac | 2.00 | .80 | .20 |
| 89 Ed Learn | 2.00 | .80 | .20 |
| 90 Billy Ray Locklin | 2.00 | .80 | .20 |
| 91 Marv Luster | 6.00 | 2.40 | .60 |
| 92 Bobby Jack Oliver | 2.50 | 1.00 | .25 |
| 93 Sandy Stephens | 8.00 | 3.25 | .80 |
| 94 Montreal Alouettes Team Card | 8.00 | 3.25 | .80 |
| 95 Gilles Archambeault | 2.00 | .80 | .20 |
| 96 Bruno Bitkowski | 2.50 | 1.00 | .25 |
| 97 Jim Conroy | 2.50 | 1.00 | .25 |
| 98 Doug Daigneault | 2.00 | .80 | .20 |
| 99 Dick Desmarais | 2.00 | .80 | .20 |
| 100 Russ Jackson | 15.00 | 6.00 | 1.50 |
| 101 Tom Jones | 2.00 | .80 | .20 |
| 102 Ron Lancaster | 20.00 | 8.00 | 2.00 |
| 103 Angelo Mosca | 15.00 | 6.00 | 1.50 |
| 104 Gerry Nesbitt | 2.00 | .80 | .20 |
| 105 Joe Poirier | 2.50 | 1.00 | .25 |
| 106 Moe Racine | 2.00 | .80 | .20 |
| 107 Gary Schreider | 2.00 | .80 | .20 |
| 108 Bob Simpson | 6.00 | 2.40 | .60 |
| 109 Ted Smale | 2.00 | .80 | .20 |
| 110 Ron Stewart | 6.00 | 2.40 | .60 |
| 111 Dave Thelen | 5.00 | 2.00 | .50 |
| 112 Kaye Vaughan | 4.00 | 1.60 | .40 |
| 113 Ottawa Rough Riders Team card | 8.00 | 3.25 | .80 |
| 114 Ron Atchison UER | 4.00 | 1.60 | .40 |
| (Name spelled Atcheson on front of card) | | | |

| | | | |
|---|---|---|---|
| ☐ 115 Danny Banda | 2.00 | .80 | .20 |
| ☐ 116 Al Benecick | 2.00 | .80 | .20 |
| ☐ 117 Clair Branch | 2.00 | .80 | .20 |
| ☐ 118 Fred Burket | 2.00 | .80 | .20 |
| ☐ 119 Bill Clarke | 2.00 | .80 | .20 |
| ☐ 120 Jim Copeland | 2.00 | .80 | .20 |
| ☐ 121 Ron Dundas | 2.00 | .80 | .20 |
| ☐ 122 Bob Golic | 2.00 | .80 | .20 |
| ☐ 123 Jack Gotta | 3.00 | 1.20 | .30 |
| ☐ 124 Dave Grosz | 2.00 | .80 | .20 |
| ☐ 125 Neil Habig | 2.00 | .80 | .20 |
| ☐ 126 Jack Hill | 2.00 | .80 | .20 |
| ☐ 127 Len Legault | 2.00 | .80 | .20 |
| ☐ 128 Bob Ptacek | 2.00 | .80 | .20 |
| ☐ 129 Roy Smith | 2.00 | .80 | .20 |
| ☐ 130 Saskatchewan Rough- riders Team Card | 8.00 | 3.25 | .80 |
| ☐ 131 Lynn Bottoms | 2.50 | 1.00 | .25 |
| ☐ 132 Dick Fouts | 2.50 | 1.00 | .25 |
| ☐ 133 Wes Gideon | 2.00 | .80 | .20 |
| ☐ 134 Cookie Gilchrist | 10.00 | 4.00 | 1.00 |
| ☐ 135 Art Johnson | 2.00 | .80 | .20 |
| ☐ 136 Bobby Kuntz | 2.50 | 1.00 | .25 |
| ☐ 137 Dave Mann | 3.00 | 1.20 | .30 |
| ☐ 138 Marty Martinello | 2.00 | .80 | .20 |
| ☐ 139 Doug McNichol | 2.00 | .80 | .20 |
| ☐ 140 Bill Mitchell | 2.00 | .80 | .20 |
| ☐ 141 Danny Nykoluk | 2.00 | .80 | .20 |
| ☐ 142 Walt Radzick | 2.50 | 1.00 | .25 |
| ☐ 143 Tobin Rote | 8.00 | 3.25 | .80 |
| ☐ 144 Jim Rountree | 2.00 | .80 | .20 |
| ☐ 145 Dick Shatto | 6.00 | 2.40 | .60 |
| ☐ 146 Billy Shipp | 2.50 | 1.00 | .25 |
| ☐ 147 Norm Stoneburgh | 2.00 | .80 | .20 |
| ☐ 148 Toronto Argonauts Team Card | 8.00 | 3.25 | .80 |
| ☐ 149 Dave Burkholder | 2.00 | .80 | .20 |
| ☐ 150 Jack Delveaux | 2.00 | .80 | .20 |
| ☐ 151 George Druxman | 2.00 | .80 | .20 |
| ☐ 152 Farrell Funston | 2.50 | 1.00 | .25 |
| ☐ 153 Herb Gray | 5.00 | 2.00 | .50 |
| ☐ 154 Roger Hagberg | 2.50 | 1.00 | .25 |
| ☐ 155 Gerry James | 5.00 | 2.00 | .50 |
| ☐ 156 Henry Janzen | 2.50 | 1.00 | .25 |
| ☐ 157 Ronnie Latourelle | 2.00 | .80 | .20 |
| ☐ 158 Hal Ledyard | 2.00 | .80 | .20 |
| ☐ 159 Leo Lewis | 6.00 | 2.40 | .60 |
| ☐ 160 Steve Patrick | 2.00 | .80 | .20 |
| ☐ 161 Cornel Piper | 2.00 | .80 | .20 |
| ☐ 162 Ernie Pitts | 2.00 | .80 | .20 |
| ☐ 163 Kenny Ploen | 6.00 | 2.40 | .60 |
| ☐ 164 Norm Rauhaus | 2.50 | 1.00 | .25 |
| ☐ 165 Frank Rigney | 6.00 | 2.40 | .60 |
| ☐ 166 Gord Rowland | 2.50 | 1.00 | .25 |
| ☐ 167 Roger Savoie | 2.00 | .80 | .20 |
| ☐ 168 Charlie Shepard | 2.50 | 1.00 | .25 |
| ☐ 169 Winnipeg Blue Bombers Team Card | 15.00 | 6.00 | 1.50 |

## 1963 Topps CFL

JOE KAPP

The 1963 Topps CFL set features cards ordered by teams (which are in alphabetical order) with players preceding their respective team cards; for example, British Columbia Lions (1-10), Calgary Stampeders (11-20), Edmonton Eskimos (21-29), Hamilton Tiger-Cats (30-39), Montreal Alouettes (40-49), Ottawa Rough Riders (50-58), Saskatchewan Roughriders (59-67), Toronto Argonauts (68-77), and Winnipeg Blue Bombers (78-87). The cards measure 2 1/2" by 3 1/2". Although the T.C.G. trademark appears on the cards, they were printed in Canada by O-Pee-Chee.

| | NRMT | VG-E | GOOD |
|---|---|---|---|
| COMPLETE SET (88) | 275.00 | 110.00 | 27.00 |
| COMMON PLAYER (1-88) | 2.50 | 1.00 | .25 |

| | | | |
|---|---|---|---|
| ☐ 1 Willie Fleming | 10.00 | 4.00 | 1.00 |
| ☐ 2 Dick Fouts | 3.00 | 1.20 | .30 |
| ☐ 3 Joe Kapp | 15.00 | 6.00 | 1.50 |
| ☐ 4 Nub Beamer | 2.50 | 1.00 | .25 |
| ☐ 5 By Bailey | 6.00 | 2.40 | .60 |
| ☐ 6 Tom Walker | 2.50 | 1.00 | .25 |
| ☐ 7 Sonny Homer | 3.00 | 1.20 | .30 |
| ☐ 8 Tom Hinton | 5.00 | 2.00 | .50 |
| ☐ 9 Lonnie Dennis | 2.50 | 1.00 | .25 |
| ☐ 10 British Columbia Lions Team Card | 7.50 | 3.00 | .75 |
| ☐ 11 Ed Buchanan | 2.50 | 1.00 | .25 |
| ☐ 12 Ernie Danjean | 2.50 | 1.00 | .25 |
| ☐ 13 Eagle Day | 6.00 | 2.40 | .60 |
| ☐ 14 Earl Lunsford | 5.00 | 2.00 | .50 |
| ☐ 15 Don Luzzi | 5.00 | 2.00 | .50 |
| ☐ 16 Tony Pajaczkowski | 5.00 | 2.00 | .50 |
| ☐ 17 Jerry Keeling | 15.00 | 6.00 | 1.50 |
| ☐ 18 Pat Holmes | 2.50 | 1.00 | .25 |
| ☐ 19 Wayne Harris | 15.00 | 6.00 | 1.50 |
| ☐ 20 Calgary Stampeders Team Card | 7.50 | 3.00 | .75 |
| ☐ 21 Tommy Joe Coffey | 7.50 | 3.00 | .75 |
| ☐ 22 Mike Lashuk | 2.50 | 1.00 | .25 |
| ☐ 23 Bobby Walden | 5.00 | 2.00 | .50 |
| ☐ 24 Don Getty | 10.00 | 4.00 | 1.00 |
| ☐ 25 Len Vella | 2.50 | 1.00 | .25 |
| ☐ 26 Ted Frechette | 2.50 | 1.00 | .25 |
| ☐ 27 E.A. Sims | 2.50 | 1.00 | .25 |
| ☐ 28 Nat Dye | 2.50 | 1.00 | .25 |
| ☐ 29 Edmonton Eskimos Team Card | 7.50 | 3.00 | .75 |
| ☐ 30 Bernie Faloney | 10.00 | 4.00 | 1.00 |
| ☐ 31 Hal Patterson | 9.00 | 3.75 | .90 |
| ☐ 32 John Barrow | 6.00 | 2.40 | .60 |
| ☐ 33 Sam Fernandez | 2.50 | 1.00 | .25 |
| ☐ 34 Garney Henley | 12.00 | 5.00 | 1.20 |
| ☐ 35 Joe Zuger | 5.00 | 2.00 | .50 |
| ☐ 36 Hardiman Cureton | 2.50 | 1.00 | .25 |
| ☐ 37 Zeno Karcz | 3.00 | 1.20 | .30 |
| ☐ 38 Bobby Kuntz | 3.00 | 1.20 | .30 |
| ☐ 39 Hamilton Tiger-Cats Team Card | 7.50 | 3.00 | .75 |
| ☐ 40 George Dixon | 6.00 | 2.40 | .60 |
| ☐ 41 Don Clark | 3.00 | 1.20 | .30 |
| ☐ 42 Marv Luster | 6.00 | 2.40 | .60 |
| ☐ 43 Bobby Jack Oliver | 3.00 | 1.20 | .30 |
| ☐ 44 Billy Ray Locklin | 2.50 | 1.00 | .25 |
| ☐ 45 Sandy Stephens | 6.00 | 2.40 | .60 |
| ☐ 46 Milt Crain | 3.00 | 1.20 | .30 |
| ☐ 47 Meco Poliziani | 2.50 | 1.00 | .25 |
| ☐ 48 Ted Elsby | 2.50 | 1.00 | .25 |
| ☐ 49 Montreal Alouettes Team Card | 7.50 | 3.00 | .75 |
| ☐ 50 Russ Jackson | 15.00 | 6.00 | 1.50 |
| ☐ 51 Ron Stewart | 7.50 | 3.00 | .75 |
| ☐ 52 Dave Thelen | 6.00 | 2.40 | .60 |
| ☐ 53 Kaye Vaughan | 5.00 | 2.00 | .50 |
| ☐ 54 Joe Poirier | 3.00 | 1.20 | .30 |
| ☐ 55 Moe Racine | 2.50 | 1.00 | .25 |
| ☐ 56 Whit Tucker | 10.00 | 4.00 | 1.00 |
| ☐ 57 Ernie White | 2.50 | 1.00 | .25 |
| ☐ 58 Ottawa Rough Riders Team Card | 7.50 | 3.00 | .75 |
| ☐ 59 Bob Ptacek | 2.50 | 1.00 | .25 |
| ☐ 60 Ray Purdin | 2.50 | 1.00 | .25 |
| ☐ 61 Dale West | 3.00 | 1.20 | .30 |
| ☐ 62 Neil Habig | 2.50 | 1.00 | .25 |
| ☐ 63 Jack Gotta | 3.00 | 1.20 | .30 |
| ☐ 64 Billy Gray | 2.50 | 1.00 | .25 |
| ☐ 65 Don Walsh | 2.50 | 1.00 | .25 |
| ☐ 66 Bill Clarke | 2.50 | 1.00 | .25 |
| ☐ 67 Saskatchewan Rough- riders Team Card | 7.50 | 3.00 | .75 |
| ☐ 68 Jackie Parker | 15.00 | 6.00 | 1.50 |
| ☐ 69 Dave Mann | 4.00 | 1.60 | .40 |
| ☐ 70 Dick Shatto | 6.00 | 2.40 | .60 |
| ☐ 71 Norm Stoneburgh UER (Name spelled Stoneburg on front of card) | 2.50 | 1.00 | .25 |
| ☐ 72 Clare Exelby | 2.50 | 1.00 | .25 |
| ☐ 73 Art Johnson | 2.50 | 1.00 | .25 |
| ☐ 74 Doug McNichol | 2.50 | 1.00 | .25 |
| ☐ 75 Danny Nykoluk | 2.50 | 1.00 | .25 |
| ☐ 76 Walt Radzick | 2.50 | 1.00 | .25 |
| ☐ 77 Toronto Argonauts Team Card | 7.50 | 3.00 | .75 |
| ☐ 78 Leo Lewis | 6.00 | 2.40 | .60 |
| ☐ 79 Kenny Ploen | 6.00 | 2.40 | .60 |
| ☐ 80 Henry Janzen | 3.00 | 1.20 | .30 |
| ☐ 81 Charlie Shepard | 3.00 | 1.20 | .30 |
| ☐ 82 Roger Hagberg | 3.00 | 1.20 | .30 |
| ☐ 83 Herb Gray | 6.00 | 2.40 | .60 |
| ☐ 84 Frank Rigney | 5.00 | 2.00 | .50 |
| ☐ 85 Jack Delveaux | 2.50 | 1.00 | .25 |
| ☐ 86 Ronnie Latourelle | 2.50 | 1.00 | .25 |
| ☐ 87 Winnipeg Blue Bombers | 7.50 | 3.00 | .75 |

Team Card
☐ 88 Checklist Card ......................... 40.00 6.00 1.25

# 1964 Topps CFL

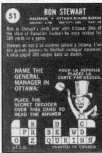

The 1964 Topps CFL set features cards ordered by teams (which are in alphabetical order) with players preceding their respective team cards, for example, British Columbia Lions (1-10), Calgary Stampeders (11-20), Edmonton Eskimos (21-29), Hamilton Tiger-Cats (30-39), Montreal Alouettes (40-49), Ottawa Rough Riders (50-58), Saskatchewan Roughriders (59-67), Toronto Argonauts (68-77), and Winnipeg Blue Bombers (78-87). The cards measure 2 1/2" by 3 1/2". Although the T.C.G. trademark appears on the cards, they were printed in Canada by O-Pee-Chee.

|  | NRMT | VG-E | GOOD |
|---|---|---|---|
| COMPLETE SET (88) ...................... | 275.00 | 110.00 | 27.00 |
| COMMON PLAYER (1-88) ................ | 2.50 | 1.00 | .25 |

| | | | |
|---|---|---|---|
| ☐ 1 Willie Fleming ......................... | 10.00 | 4.00 | 1.00 |
| ☐ 2 Dick Fouts ............................. | 3.00 | 1.20 | .30 |
| ☐ 3 Joe Kapp ............................... | 15.00 | 6.00 | 1.50 |
| ☐ 4 Nub Beamer ........................... | 2.50 | 1.00 | .25 |
| ☐ 5 Tom Brown ............................ | 5.00 | 2.00 | .50 |
| ☐ 6 Tom Walker ........................... | 2.50 | 1.00 | .25 |
| ☐ 7 Sonny Homer ......................... | 3.00 | 1.20 | .30 |
| ☐ 8 Tom Hinton ............................ | 5.00 | 2.00 | .50 |
| ☐ 9 Lonnie Dennis ........................ | 2.50 | 1.00 | .25 |
| ☐ 10 B.C. Lions Team .................... | 7.50 | 3.00 | .75 |
| ☐ 11 Lovell Coleman ...................... | 4.00 | 1.60 | .40 |
| ☐ 12 Ernie Danjean ....................... | 2.50 | 1.00 | .25 |
| ☐ 13 Eagle Day ............................ | 5.00 | 2.00 | .50 |
| ☐ 14 Jim Furlong .......................... | 2.50 | 1.00 | .25 |
| ☐ 15 Don Luzzi ............................. | 5.00 | 2.00 | .50 |
| ☐ 16 Tony Pajaczkowski ................. | 5.00 | 2.00 | .50 |
| ☐ 17 Jerry Keeling ........................ | 6.00 | 2.40 | .60 |
| ☐ 18 Pat Holmes .......................... | 2.50 | 1.00 | .25 |
| ☐ 19 Wayne Harris ........................ | 7.50 | 3.00 | .75 |
| ☐ 20 Calgary Stampeders Team Card | 7.50 | 3.00 | .75 |
| ☐ 21 Tommy Joe Coffey ................. | 7.50 | 3.00 | .75 |
| ☐ 22 Al Ecuyer ............................ | 2.50 | 1.00 | .25 |
| ☐ 23 Checklist Card ...................... | 30.00 | 5.00 | 1.00 |
| ☐ 24 Don Getty ............................ | 7.50 | 3.00 | .75 |
| ☐ 25 Len Vella ............................. | 2.50 | 1.00 | .25 |
| ☐ 26 Ted Frechette ....................... | 2.50 | 1.00 | .25 |
| ☐ 27 E.A. Sims ............................ | 2.50 | 1.00 | .25 |
| ☐ 28 Nat Dye .............................. | 2.50 | 1.00 | .25 |
| ☐ 29 Edmonton Eskimos Team Card | 7.50 | 3.00 | .75 |
| ☐ 30 Bernie Faloney ...................... | 15.00 | 6.00 | 1.50 |
| ☐ 31 Hal Patterson ....................... | 9.00 | 3.75 | .90 |
| ☐ 32 John Barrow ......................... | 6.00 | 2.40 | .60 |
| ☐ 33 Tommy Grant ....................... | 3.00 | 1.20 | .30 |
| ☐ 34 Garney Henley ...................... | 9.00 | 3.75 | .90 |
| ☐ 35 Joe Zuger ........................... | 3.50 | 1.40 | .35 |
| ☐ 36 Hardiman Cureton ................. | 2.50 | 1.00 | .25 |
| ☐ 37 Zeno Karcz ......................... | 3.00 | 1.20 | .30 |
| ☐ 38 Bobby Kuntz ........................ | 3.00 | 1.20 | .30 |
| ☐ 39 Hamilton Tiger-Cats Team Card | 7.50 | 3.00 | .75 |
| ☐ 40 George Dixon ....................... | 7.50 | 3.00 | .75 |
| ☐ 41 Dave Hoppmann .................... | 2.50 | 1.00 | .25 |
| ☐ 42 Dick Walton ......................... | 2.50 | 1.00 | .25 |
| ☐ 43 Jim Andreotti ....................... | 3.00 | 1.20 | .30 |
| ☐ 44 Billy Ray Locklin ................... | 2.50 | 1.00 | .25 |
| ☐ 45 Fred Burket .......................... | 2.50 | 1.00 | .25 |
| ☐ 46 Milt Crane ........................... | 3.00 | 1.20 | .30 |
| ☐ 47 Meco Poliziani ...................... | 2.50 | 1.00 | .25 |
| ☐ 48 Ted Elsby ............................ | 2.50 | 1.00 | .25 |
| ☐ 49 Montreal Alouettes Team Card | 7.50 | 3.00 | .75 |
| ☐ 50 Russ Jackson ....................... | 15.00 | 6.00 | 1.50 |
| ☐ 51 Ron Stewart ......................... | 9.00 | 3.75 | .90 |
| ☐ 52 Dave Thelen ......................... | 5.00 | 2.00 | .50 |
| ☐ 53 Kaye Vaughan ...................... | 5.00 | 2.00 | .50 |
| ☐ 54 Joe Poirier .......................... | 3.00 | 1.20 | .30 |
| ☐ 55 Moe Racine .......................... | 2.50 | 1.00 | .25 |
| ☐ 56 Whit Tucker ......................... | 6.00 | 2.40 | .60 |
| ☐ 57 Ernie White ......................... | 2.50 | 1.00 | .25 |
| ☐ 58 Ottawa Rough Riders Team Card | 7.50 | 3.00 | .75 |
| ☐ 59 Bob Ptacek ......................... | 2.50 | 1.00 | .25 |
| ☐ 60 Ray Purdin .......................... | 2.50 | 1.00 | .25 |
| ☐ 61 Dale West ........................... | 3.00 | 1.20 | .30 |
| ☐ 62 Neil Habig ........................... | 2.50 | 1.00 | .25 |
| ☐ 63 Jack Gotta .......................... | 3.00 | 1.20 | .30 |
| ☐ 64 Billy Gray ........................... | 2.50 | 1.00 | .25 |
| ☐ 65 Don Walsh .......................... | 2.50 | 1.00 | .25 |
| ☐ 66 Bill Clarke ........................... | 2.50 | 1.00 | .25 |
| ☐ 67 Saskatchewan Rough- riders Team Card | 7.50 | 3.00 | .75 |
| ☐ 68 Jackie Parker ....................... | 20.00 | 8.00 | 2.00 |
| ☐ 69 Dave Mann .......................... | 3.50 | 1.40 | .35 |
| ☐ 70 Dick Shatto ......................... | 6.00 | 2.40 | .60 |
| ☐ 71 Norm Stoneburgh ................. | 2.50 | 1.00 | .25 |
| ☐ 72 Clare Exelby ........................ | 2.50 | 1.00 | .25 |
| ☐ 73 Jim Christopherson ............... | 2.50 | 1.00 | .25 |
| ☐ 74 Sherman Lewis ..................... | 6.00 | 2.40 | .60 |
| ☐ 75 Danny Nykoluk ..................... | 2.50 | 1.00 | .25 |
| ☐ 76 Walt Radzick ........................ | 2.50 | 1.00 | .25 |
| ☐ 77 Toronto Argonauts Team Card | 7.50 | 3.00 | .75 |
| ☐ 78 Leo Lewis ........................... | 6.00 | 2.40 | .60 |
| ☐ 79 Kenny Ploen ........................ | 6.00 | 2.40 | .60 |
| ☐ 80 Henry Janzen ....................... | 3.00 | 1.20 | .30 |
| ☐ 81 Charlie Shepard .................... | 3.00 | 1.20 | .30 |
| ☐ 82 Roger Hagberg ..................... | 3.00 | 1.20 | .30 |
| ☐ 83 Herb Gray ........................... | 6.00 | 2.40 | .60 |
| ☐ 84 Frank Rigney ....................... | 5.00 | 2.00 | .50 |
| ☐ 85 Jack Delveaux ...................... | 2.50 | 1.00 | .25 |
| ☐ 86 Ronnie Latourelle .................. | 2.50 | 1.00 | .25 |
| ☐ 87 Winnipeg Blue Bombers Team Card | 7.50 | 3.00 | .75 |
| ☐ 88 Checklist Card ...................... | 40.00 | 6.00 | 1.25 |

# 1965 Topps CFL

The 1965 Topps CFL set features 132 cards ordered by teams (which are in alphabetical order) with players also in alphabetical order, for example, British Columbia Lions (1-15), Calgary Stampeders (16-29), Edmonton Eskimos (30-44), Hamilton Tiger-Cats (45-59), Montreal Alouettes (60-73), Ottawa Rough Riders (74-88), Saskatchewan Roughriders (89-102), Toronto Argonauts (103-117), and Winnipeg Blue Bombers (118-131). The cards measure 2 1/2" by 3 1/2". Card numbers 60 (1-60) and 132 (61-132) are checklist cards. Don Sutherlin, number 57, has number 51 on the back. Although the T.C.G. trademark appears on the cards, they were printed in Canada by O-Pee-Chee.

|  | NRMT | VG-E | GOOD |
|---|---|---|---|
| COMPLETE SET (132) ...................... | 325.00 | 150.00 | 35.00 |
| COMMON PLAYER (1-132) ............... | 1.75 | .70 | .17 |

| | | | |
|---|---|---|---|
| ☐ 1 Neal Beaumont ....................... | 6.00 | 2.40 | .60 |
| ☐ 2 Tom Brown ............................ | 6.00 | 2.40 | .60 |
| ☐ 3 Mike Cacic ............................ | 1.75 | .70 | .17 |
| ☐ 4 Pat Claridge .......................... | 1.75 | .70 | .17 |
| ☐ 5 Steve Cotter .......................... | 1.75 | .70 | .17 |
| ☐ 6 Lonnie Dennis ........................ | 1.75 | .70 | .17 |
| ☐ 7 Norm Fieldgate ...................... | 4.00 | 1.60 | .40 |
| ☐ 8 Willie Fleming ........................ | 6.00 | 2.40 | .60 |
| ☐ 9 Dick Fouts ............................ | 2.50 | 1.00 | .25 |
| ☐ 10 Tom Hinton .......................... | 4.00 | 1.60 | .40 |
| ☐ 11 Sonny Homer ....................... | 2.50 | 1.00 | .25 |
| ☐ 12 Joe Kapp ............................ | 12.00 | 5.00 | 1.20 |
| ☐ 13 Paul Seale ........................... | 1.75 | .70 | .17 |
| ☐ 14 Steve Shafer ........................ | 1.75 | .70 | .17 |

| | | | |
|---|---|---|---|
| ☐ 15 Bob Swift | 1.75 | .70 | .17 |
| ☐ 16 Larry Anderson | 1.75 | .70 | .17 |
| ☐ 17 Lu Bain | 1.75 | .70 | .17 |
| ☐ 18 Lovell Coleman | 2.50 | 1.00 | .25 |
| ☐ 19 Eagle Day | 4.00 | 1.60 | .40 |
| ☐ 20 Jim Furlong | 1.75 | .70 | .17 |
| ☐ 21 Wayne Harris | 6.00 | 2.40 | .60 |
| ☐ 22 Herman Harrison | 12.00 | 5.00 | 1.20 |
| ☐ 23 Jerry Keeling | 5.00 | 2.00 | .50 |
| ☐ 24 Hal Krebs | 1.75 | .70 | .17 |
| ☐ 25 Don Luzzi | 4.00 | 1.60 | .40 |
| ☐ 26 Tony Pajaczkowski | 4.00 | 1.60 | .40 |
| ☐ 27 Larry Robinson | 4.00 | 1.60 | .40 |
| ☐ 28 Bobby Taylor | 2.50 | 1.00 | .25 |
| ☐ 29 Ted Woods | 1.75 | .70 | .17 |
| ☐ 30 Jon Anabo | 1.75 | .70 | .17 |
| ☐ 31 Jim Battle | 1.75 | .70 | .17 |
| ☐ 32 Charley Brown | 1.75 | .70 | .17 |
| ☐ 33 Tommy Joe Coffey | 7.50 | 3.00 | .75 |
| ☐ 34 Marcel Deleeuw | 1.75 | .70 | .17 |
| ☐ 35 Al Ecuyer | 1.75 | .70 | .17 |
| ☐ 36 Jim Higgins | 1.75 | .70 | .17 |
| ☐ 37 Oscar Kruger | 2.50 | 1.00 | .25 |
| ☐ 38 Barry Mitchelson | 1.75 | .70 | .17 |
| ☐ 39 Roger Nelson | 4.00 | 1.60 | .40 |
| ☐ 40 Bill Redell | 1.75 | .70 | .17 |
| ☐ 41 E.A. Sims | 1.75 | .70 | .17 |
| ☐ 42 Jim Stinnette | 1.75 | .70 | .17 |
| ☐ 43 Jim Thomas | 1.75 | .70 | .17 |
| ☐ 44 Terry Wilson | 1.75 | .70 | .17 |
| ☐ 45 Art Baker | 1.75 | .70 | .17 |
| ☐ 46 John Barrow | 6.00 | 2.40 | .60 |
| ☐ 47 Dick Cohee | 2.50 | 1.00 | .25 |
| ☐ 48 Frank Cosentino | 4.00 | 1.60 | .40 |
| ☐ 49 Johnny Counts | 1.75 | .70 | .17 |
| ☐ 50 Tommy Grant | 2.50 | 1.00 | .25 |
| ☐ 51 Garney Henley | 9.00 | 3.75 | .90 |
| (See also number 57) | | | |
| ☐ 52 Zeno Karcz | 2.50 | 1.00 | .25 |
| ☐ 53 Ellison Kelly | 12.00 | 5.00 | 1.20 |
| ☐ 54 Bobby Kuntz | 2.50 | 1.00 | .25 |
| ☐ 55 Angelo Mosca | 12.00 | 5.00 | 1.20 |
| ☐ 56 Bronko Nagurski | 6.00 | 2.40 | .60 |
| ☐ 57 Don Sutherin UER | 12.00 | 5.00 | 1.20 |
| (number 51 on back) | | | |
| ☐ 58 Dave Viti | 1.75 | .70 | .17 |
| ☐ 59 Joe Zuger | 3.00 | 1.20 | .30 |
| ☐ 60 Checklist 1-60 | 25.00 | 3.50 | .75 |
| ☐ 61 Jim Andreotti | 2.50 | 1.00 | .25 |
| ☐ 62 Harold Cooley | 1.75 | .70 | .17 |
| ☐ 63 Nat Craddock | 1.75 | .70 | .17 |
| ☐ 64 George Dixon | 6.00 | 2.40 | .60 |
| ☐ 65 Ted Elsby | 1.75 | .70 | .17 |
| ☐ 66 Clare Exelby | 1.75 | .70 | .17 |
| ☐ 67 Bernie Faloney | 12.00 | 5.00 | 1.20 |
| ☐ 68 Al Irwin | 1.75 | .70 | .17 |
| ☐ 69 Ed Learn | 1.75 | .70 | .17 |
| ☐ 70 Moe Levesque | 1.75 | .70 | .17 |
| ☐ 71 Bob Minihane | 1.75 | .70 | .17 |
| ☐ 72 Jim Reynolds | 1.75 | .70 | .17 |
| ☐ 73 Billy Roy | 1.75 | .70 | .17 |
| ☐ 74 Billy Joe Booth | 2.50 | 1.00 | .25 |
| ☐ 75 Jim Cain | 1.75 | .70 | .17 |
| ☐ 76 Larry DeGraw | 1.75 | .70 | .17 |
| ☐ 77 Don Estes | 1.75 | .70 | .17 |
| ☐ 78 Gene Gaines | 5.00 | 2.00 | .50 |
| ☐ 79 John Kennerson | 1.75 | .70 | .17 |
| ☐ 80 Roger Kramer | 2.50 | 1.00 | .25 |
| ☐ 81 Ken Lehmann | 2.50 | 1.00 | .25 |
| ☐ 82 Bob O'Billovich | 1.75 | .70 | .17 |
| ☐ 83 Joe Poirier | 2.50 | 1.00 | .25 |
| ☐ 84 Bill Quinter | 1.75 | .70 | .17 |
| ☐ 85 Jerry Selinger | 1.75 | .70 | .17 |
| ☐ 86 Bill Siekierski | 1.75 | .70 | .17 |
| ☐ 87 Len Sparks | 1.75 | .70 | .17 |
| ☐ 88 Whit Tucker | 4.00 | 1.60 | .40 |
| ☐ 89 Ron Atchison | 4.00 | 1.60 | .40 |
| ☐ 90 Ed Buchanan | 1.75 | .70 | .17 |
| ☐ 91 Hugh Campbell | 10.00 | 4.00 | 1.00 |
| ☐ 92 Henry Dorsch | 1.75 | .70 | .17 |
| ☐ 93 Garner Ekstran | 2.50 | 1.00 | .25 |
| ☐ 94 Martin Fabi | 1.75 | .70 | .17 |
| ☐ 95 Bob Good | 1.75 | .70 | .17 |
| ☐ 96 Ron Lancaster | 12.00 | 5.00 | 1.20 |
| ☐ 97 Bob Ptacek | 1.75 | .70 | .17 |
| ☐ 98 George Reed | 25.00 | 10.00 | 2.50 |
| ☐ 99 Wayne Shaw | 1.75 | .70 | .17 |
| ☐ 100 Dale West | 2.50 | 1.00 | .25 |
| ☐ 101 Reg Whitehouse | 1.75 | .70 | .17 |
| ☐ 102 Jim Worden | 1.75 | .70 | .17 |
| ☐ 103 Ron Brewer | 2.50 | 1.00 | .25 |
| ☐ 104 Don Fuell | 1.75 | .70 | .17 |
| ☐ 105 Ed Harrington | 2.50 | 1.00 | .25 |
| ☐ 106 George Hughley | 1.75 | .70 | .17 |
| ☐ 107 Dave Mann | 3.00 | 1.20 | .30 |
| ☐ 108 Marty Martinello | 1.75 | .70 | .17 |
| ☐ 109 Danny Nykoluk | 1.75 | .70 | .17 |

| | | | |
|---|---|---|---|
| ☐ 110 Jackie Parker | 15.00 | 6.00 | 1.50 |
| ☐ 111 Dave Pivec | 1.75 | .70 | .17 |
| ☐ 112 Walt Radzick | 1.75 | .70 | .17 |
| ☐ 113 Lee Sampson | 1.75 | .70 | .17 |
| ☐ 114 Dick Shatto | 5.00 | 2.00 | .50 |
| ☐ 115 Norm Stoneburgh | 1.75 | .70 | .17 |
| ☐ 116 Jim Vollenweider | 1.75 | .70 | .17 |
| ☐ 117 John Wydareny | 2.50 | 1.00 | .25 |
| ☐ 118 Billy Cooper | 1.75 | .70 | .17 |
| ☐ 119 Farrell Funston | 2.50 | 1.00 | .25 |
| ☐ 120 Herb Gray | 5.00 | 2.00 | .50 |
| ☐ 121 Henry Janzen | 2.50 | 1.00 | .25 |
| ☐ 122 Leo Lewis | 6.00 | 2.40 | .60 |
| ☐ 123 Brian Palmer | 1.75 | .70 | .17 |
| ☐ 124 Cornel Piper | 1.75 | .70 | .17 |
| ☐ 125 Ernie Pitts | 1.75 | .70 | .17 |
| ☐ 126 Kenny Ploen | 6.00 | 2.40 | .60 |
| ☐ 127 Norm Rauhaus | 2.50 | 1.00 | .25 |
| ☐ 128 Frank Rigney | 4.00 | 1.60 | .40 |
| ☐ 129 Roger Savoie | 1.75 | .70 | .17 |
| ☐ 130 Dick Thornton | 4.00 | 1.60 | .40 |
| ☐ 131 Bill Whisler | 1.75 | .70 | .17 |
| ☐ 132 Checklist 61-132 | 40.00 | 5.00 | 1.00 |

## 1988 Vachon CFL

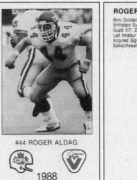

ROGER ALDAG

Born: October 6, 1953
Birthplace: Gull Lake, Saskatchewan
Guard, 6'0", 235 lbs, Non-import
Last Amateur Club: Regina Rams Juniors (PJFC)
Acquired: Signed as a free agent by the
Saskatchewan Roughriders in March 1976

#44 ROGER ALDAG
1988

The 1988 Vachon CFL set contains 160 cards measuring 2" by 3 1/2", that is, standard business card size. The fronts have color action photos bordered in white; the vertically oriented backs have brief biographies and career highlights. These cards were printed on very thin stock. Since the cards are unnumbered, they have been ordered below alphabetically for reference. The card fronts contain the Vachon logo and the CFL logo.

| | MINT | EXC | G-VG |
|---|---|---|---|
| COMPLETE SET (160) | 125.00 | 50.00 | 12.50 |
| COMMON PLAYER (1-160) | .75 | .30 | .07 |
| | | | |
| ☐ 1 David Albright | 1.00 | .40 | .10 |
| ☐ 2 Roger Aldag | 1.00 | .40 | .10 |
| ☐ 3 Marv Allemang | .75 | .30 | .07 |
| ☐ 4 Damon Allen | 4.00 | 1.60 | .40 |
| ☐ 5 Gary Allen | 1.00 | .40 | .10 |
| ☐ 6 Randy Ambrosie | .75 | .30 | .07 |
| ☐ 7 Mike Anderson | .75 | .30 | .07 |
| ☐ 8 Kent Austin | 4.00 | 1.60 | .40 |
| ☐ 9 Terry Baker | 1.00 | .40 | .10 |
| ☐ 10 Danny Bass | 3.00 | 1.20 | .30 |
| ☐ 11 Nick Bastaja | .75 | .30 | .07 |
| ☐ 12 Greg Battle | 2.50 | 1.00 | .25 |
| ☐ 13 Lyle Bauer | .75 | .30 | .07 |
| ☐ 14 Jearld Baylis | 2.00 | .80 | .20 |
| ☐ 15 Ian Beckstead | .75 | .30 | .07 |
| ☐ 16 Walter Bender | 1.50 | .60 | .15 |
| ☐ 17 Nick Benjamin | 1.00 | .40 | .10 |
| ☐ 18 David Black | .75 | .30 | .07 |
| ☐ 19 Leo Blanchard | .75 | .30 | .07 |
| ☐ 20 Trevor Bowles | .75 | .30 | .07 |
| ☐ 21 Ken Braden | .75 | .30 | .07 |
| ☐ 22 Rod Brown | .75 | .30 | .07 |
| ☐ 23 Less Browne | 1.25 | .50 | .12 |
| ☐ 24 Jamie Buis | .75 | .30 | .07 |
| ☐ 25 Tom Burgess | 3.00 | 1.20 | .30 |
| ☐ 26 Bob Cameron | 1.00 | .40 | .10 |
| ☐ 27 Jan Carinci | .75 | .30 | .07 |
| ☐ 28 Tony Champion | 2.50 | 1.00 | .25 |
| ☐ 29 Jacques Chapdelaine | .75 | .30 | .07 |
| ☐ 30 Tony Cherry | 2.50 | 1.00 | .25 |
| ☐ 31 Lance Chomyc | 1.50 | .60 | .15 |

| | MINT | EXC | G-VG |
|---|---|---|---|
| ☐ 32 John Congemi | 2.00 | .80 | .20 |
| ☐ 33 Rod Connop | .75 | .30 | .07 |
| ☐ 34 David Conrad | .75 | .30 | .07 |
| ☐ 35 Grover Covington | 2.00 | .80 | .20 |
| ☐ 36 Larry Crawford | 1.25 | .50 | .12 |
| ☐ 37 James Curry | 2.00 | .80 | .20 |
| ☐ 38 Marco Cyncar | 1.00 | .40 | .10 |
| ☐ 39 Gabriel DeLaGarza | .75 | .30 | .07 |
| ☐ 40 Mike Derks | .75 | .30 | .07 |
| ☐ 41 Blake Dermott | 1.00 | .40 | .10 |
| ☐ 42 Roy DeWalt SP | 4.00 | 1.60 | .40 |
| ☐ 43 Todd Dillon | 1.25 | .50 | .12 |
| ☐ 44 Rocky DiPietro | 2.00 | .80 | .20 |
| ☐ 45 Kevin Dixon SP | 1.50 | .60 | .15 |
| ☐ 46 Tom Dixon | .75 | .30 | .07 |
| ☐ 47 Selwyn Drain | .75 | .30 | .07 |
| ☐ 48 Matt Dunigan | 6.00 | 2.40 | .60 |
| ☐ 49 Ray Elgaard | 3.00 | 1.20 | .30 |
| ☐ 50 Jerome Erdman | .75 | .30 | .07 |
| ☐ 51 Randy Fabi | .75 | .30 | .07 |
| ☐ 52 Gill Fenerty | 3.00 | 1.20 | .30 |
| ☐ 53 Denny Ferdinand | 1.00 | .40 | .10 |
| ☐ 54 Dan Ferrone | 1.00 | .40 | .10 |
| ☐ 55 Howard Fields | .75 | .30 | .07 |
| ☐ 56 Matt Finlay | .75 | .30 | .07 |
| ☐ 57 Rickey Foggie | 2.00 | .80 | .20 |
| ☐ 58 Delbert Fowler | 1.00 | .40 | .10 |
| ☐ 59 Ed Gataveckas | .75 | .30 | .07 |
| ☐ 60 Keith Gooch | .75 | .30 | .07 |
| ☐ 61 Miles Gorrell | .75 | .30 | .07 |
| ☐ 62 Mike Gray | .75 | .30 | .07 |
| ☐ 63 Leo Groenewegen | .75 | .30 | .07 |
| ☐ 64 Ken Hailey | .75 | .30 | .07 |
| ☐ 65 Harold Hallman | 1.00 | .40 | .10 |
| ☐ 66 Tracey Ham | 4.00 | 1.60 | .40 |
| ☐ 67 Rodney Harding | 2.00 | .80 | .20 |
| ☐ 68 Glenn Harper | .75 | .30 | .07 |
| ☐ 69 J.T. Hay | .75 | .30 | .07 |
| ☐ 70 Larry Hogue | .75 | .30 | .07 |
| ☐ 71 Ron Hopkins SP | 2.00 | .80 | .20 |
| ☐ 72 Hank Ilesic | 2.00 | .80 | .20 |
| ☐ 73 Bryan Illerbrun | .75 | .30 | .07 |
| ☐ 74 Lemont Jeffers | .75 | .30 | .07 |
| ☐ 75 James Jefferson | 2.00 | .80 | .20 |
| ☐ 76 Rick Johnson | 2.00 | .80 | .20 |
| ☐ 77 Chris Johnstone | .75 | .30 | .07 |
| ☐ 78 Johnnie Jones | .75 | .30 | .07 |
| ☐ 79 Milson Jones | 1.50 | .60 | .15 |
| ☐ 80 Stephen Jones | 2.00 | .80 | .20 |
| ☐ 81 Bobby Jurasin | 2.00 | .80 | .20 |
| ☐ 82 Jerry Kauric | 1.25 | .50 | .12 |
| ☐ 83 Dan Kearns | .75 | .30 | .07 |
| ☐ 84 Trevor Kennerd | 2.00 | .80 | .20 |
| ☐ 85 Mike Kerrigan | 3.00 | 1.20 | .30 |
| ☐ 86 Rick Klassen | 2.00 | .80 | .20 |
| ☐ 87 Lee Knight | .75 | .30 | .07 |
| ☐ 88 Kevin Konar | 1.00 | .40 | .10 |
| ☐ 89 Glenn Kulka | 1.25 | .50 | .12 |
| ☐ 90 Doug(Tank) Landry | 2.00 | .80 | .20 |
| ☐ 91 Scott Lecky | .75 | .30 | .07 |
| ☐ 92 Orville Lee | 1.50 | .60 | .15 |
| ☐ 93 Marc Lewis | 1.00 | .40 | .10 |
| ☐ 94 Eddie Lowe | .75 | .30 | .07 |
| ☐ 95 Lynn Madsen | .75 | .30 | .07 |
| ☐ 96 Chris Major | 2.00 | .80 | .20 |
| ☐ 97 Doran Major | .75 | .30 | .07 |
| ☐ 98 Tony Martino | .75 | .30 | .07 |
| ☐ 99 Tim McCray | 1.25 | .50 | .12 |
| ☐ 100 Mike McGruder | 1.25 | .50 | .12 |
| ☐ 101 Sean McKeown SP | 4.00 | 1.60 | .40 |
| ☐ 102 Andy McVey | .75 | .30 | .07 |
| ☐ 103 Stan Mikawos | .75 | .30 | .07 |
| ☐ 104 James Mills | 2.00 | .80 | .20 |
| ☐ 105 Larry Mohr | .75 | .30 | .07 |
| ☐ 106 Bernie Morrison | .75 | .30 | .07 |
| ☐ 107 James Murphy | 2.00 | .80 | .20 |
| ☐ 108 Paul Osbaldiston | 1.50 | .60 | .15 |
| ☐ 109 Anthony Parker | 1.25 | .50 | .12 |
| ☐ 110 James Parker | 2.00 | .80 | .20 |
| ☐ 111 Greg Peterson | .75 | .30 | .07 |
| ☐ 112 Tim Petros | 1.25 | .50 | .12 |
| ☐ 113 Reggie Pleasant | 1.25 | .50 | .12 |
| ☐ 114 Willie Pless | 2.00 | .80 | .20 |
| ☐ 115 Bob Poley | .75 | .30 | .07 |
| ☐ 116 Tom Porras | 1.50 | .60 | .15 |
| ☐ 117 Hector Pothier | .75 | .30 | .07 |
| ☐ 118 Jim Reid | 1.50 | .60 | .15 |
| ☐ 119 Robert Reid | .75 | .30 | .07 |
| ☐ 120 Gilbert Renfroe | 2.00 | .80 | .20 |
| ☐ 121 Tom Richards | 1.25 | .50 | .12 |
| ☐ 122 Dave Ridgway | 2.00 | .80 | .20 |
| ☐ 123 Rae Robirtis | .75 | .30 | .07 |
| ☐ 124 Gerald Roper | .75 | .30 | .07 |
| ☐ 125 Darryl Sampson | .75 | .30 | .07 |
| ☐ 126 Jim Sandusky | 2.50 | 1.00 | .25 |
| ☐ 127 David Sauve | .75 | .30 | .07 |
| ☐ 128 Art Schlichter | 3.00 | 1.20 | .30 |
| ☐ 129 Ralph Scholz | .75 | .30 | .07 |
| ☐ 130 Mark Seale | .75 | .30 | .07 |
| ☐ 131 Dan Sellers | .75 | .30 | .07 |
| ☐ 132 Lance Shields | 1.00 | .40 | .10 |
| ☐ 133 Ian Sinclair | 1.25 | .50 | .12 |
| ☐ 134 Mike Siroishka | .75 | .30 | .07 |
| ☐ 135 Chris Skinner | .75 | .30 | .07 |
| ☐ 136 Harry Skipper | 1.00 | .40 | .10 |
| ☐ 137 Darrell Smith | 3.00 | 1.20 | .30 |
| ☐ 138 Tom Spoletini | .75 | .30 | .07 |
| ☐ 139 Steve Stapler | 1.00 | .40 | .10 |
| ☐ 140 Bill Stevenson | .75 | .30 | .07 |
| ☐ 141 Gregg Stumon | 1.00 | .40 | .10 |
| ☐ 142 Glen Suitor | .75 | .30 | .07 |
| ☐ 143 Emanuel Tolbert | 2.50 | 1.00 | .25 |
| ☐ 144 Perry Tuttle SP | 4.00 | 1.60 | .40 |
| ☐ 145 Peter VandenBos | .75 | .30 | .07 |
| ☐ 146 Jake Vaughan | .75 | .30 | .07 |
| ☐ 147 Chris Walby | 2.00 | .80 | .20 |
| ☐ 148 Mike Walker | 1.50 | .60 | .15 |
| ☐ 149 Patrick Wayne | .75 | .30 | .07 |
| ☐ 150 James West | 2.00 | .80 | .20 |
| ☐ 151 Brett Williams | 1.50 | .60 | .15 |
| ☐ 152 David Williams | 3.00 | 1.20 | .30 |
| ☐ 153 Henry Williams | 10.00 | 4.00 | 1.00 |
| ☐ 154 Tommie Williams | .75 | .30 | .07 |
| ☐ 155 Larry Willis | 1.25 | .50 | .12 |
| ☐ 156 Don Wilson | .75 | .30 | .07 |
| ☐ 157 Earl Winfield | 2.50 | 1.00 | .25 |
| ☐ 158 Rick Worman | 2.00 | .80 | .20 |
| ☐ 159 Larry Wruck | .75 | .30 | .07 |
| ☐ 160 Kari Yli-Renko | .75 | .30 | .07 |

## 1989 Vachon CFL

The 1989 Vachon CFL set consists of 160 cards, measuring approximately 2" by 3 1/2". The set was issued in panels of five inside specially marked packages of Vachon Cakes as part of a contest. The front features posed or action color photos, with the CFL football helmet logo and Vachon's logo at the bottom of the card. The back has biographical information, the team helmet logo, and the card number.

| | MINT | EXC | G-VG |
|---|---|---|---|
| COMPLETE SET (160) | 100.00 | 40.00 | 10.00 |
| COMMON PLAYER (1-160) | .75 | .30 | .07 |
| ☐ 1 Tony Williams | 1.00 | .40 | .10 |
| ☐ 2 Sean Foudy | .75 | .30 | .07 |
| ☐ 3 Tom Schimmer | .75 | .30 | .07 |
| ☐ 4 Ken Evraire | 1.25 | .50 | .12 |
| ☐ 5 Gerald Wilcox | .75 | .30 | .07 |
| ☐ 6 Damon Allen | 2.50 | 1.00 | .25 |
| ☐ 7 Tony Kimbrough | .75 | .30 | .07 |
| ☐ 8 Dean Dorsey | 1.00 | .40 | .10 |
| ☐ 9 Rocco Romano | .75 | .30 | .07 |
| ☐ 10 Ken Braden | .75 | .30 | .07 |
| ☐ 11 Kari Yli-Renko | .75 | .30 | .07 |
| ☐ 12 Darrel Hopper | .75 | .30 | .07 |
| ☐ 13 Irv Daymond | .75 | .30 | .07 |
| ☐ 14 Orville Lee | 1.25 | .50 | .12 |
| ☐ 15 Steve Howlett | .75 | .30 | .07 |
| ☐ 16 Kyle Hall | .75 | .30 | .07 |
| ☐ 17 Reggie Ward | .75 | .30 | .07 |
| ☐ 18 Gerald Alphin | 2.00 | .80 | .20 |
| ☐ 19 Troy Wilson | .75 | .30 | .07 |
| ☐ 20 Patrick Wayne | .75 | .30 | .07 |
| ☐ 21 Harold Hallman | 1.25 | .50 | .12 |
| ☐ 22 John Congemi | 1.50 | .60 | .15 |
| ☐ 23 Doran Major | .75 | .30 | .07 |
| ☐ 24 Hank Ilesic | 1.50 | .60 | .15 |
| ☐ 25 Gilbert Renfroe | 2.00 | .80 | .20 |
| ☐ 26 Rodney Harding | 1.25 | .50 | .12 |
| ☐ 27 Todd Wisemen | .75 | .30 | .07 |
| ☐ 28 Chris Schultz | 1.00 | .40 | .10 |
| ☐ 29 Carl Brazley | 1.25 | .50 | .12 |
| ☐ 30 Darrell Smith | 2.50 | 1.00 | .25 |
| ☐ 31 Glenn Kulka | 1.00 | .40 | .10 |
| ☐ 32 Bob Skemp | .75 | .30 | .07 |
| ☐ 33 Don Moen | 1.00 | .40 | .10 |
| ☐ 34 Jearld Baylis | 1.50 | .60 | .15 |
| ☐ 35 Lorenzo Graham | .75 | .30 | .07 |
| ☐ 36 Lance Chomyc | 1.25 | .50 | .12 |
| ☐ 37 Warren Hudson | .75 | .30 | .07 |
| ☐ 38 Gill Fenerty | 2.50 | 1.00 | .25 |
| ☐ 39 Paul Masotti | 1.00 | .40 | .10 |
| ☐ 40 Reggie Pleasant | 1.25 | .50 | .12 |
| ☐ 41 Scott Flagel | .75 | .30 | .07 |
| ☐ 42 Mike Kerrigan | 2.00 | .80 | .20 |
| ☐ 43 Frank Robinson | 1.00 | .40 | .10 |
| ☐ 44 Jacques Chapdelaine | .75 | .30 | .07 |
| ☐ 45 Miles Gorrell | .75 | .30 | .07 |
| ☐ 46 Mike Walker | 1.50 | .60 | .15 |

| | | | |
|---|---|---|---|
| ☐ 47 Jason Riley | .75 | .30 | .07 |
| ☐ 48 Grover Covington | 1.50 | .60 | .15 |
| ☐ 49 Ralph Scholz | .75 | .30 | .07 |
| ☐ 50 Mike Derks | .75 | .30 | .07 |
| ☐ 51 Derrick McAdoo | 1.50 | .60 | .15 |
| ☐ 52 Rocky DiPietro | 2.00 | .80 | .20 |
| ☐ 53 Lance Shields | 1.00 | .40 | .10 |
| ☐ 54 Dale Sanderson | .75 | .30 | .07 |
| ☐ 55 Tim Lorenz | .75 | .30 | .07 |
| ☐ 56 Rod Skillman | .75 | .30 | .07 |
| ☐ 57 Jed Tommy | .75 | .30 | .07 |
| ☐ 58 Paul Osbaldiston | 1.25 | .50 | .12 |
| ☐ 59 Darrell Corbin | .75 | .30 | .07 |
| ☐ 60 Tony Champion | 1.50 | .60 | .15 |
| ☐ 61 Romel Andrews | .75 | .30 | .07 |
| ☐ 62 Bob Cameron | 1.00 | .40 | .10 |
| ☐ 63 Greg Battle | 2.00 | .80 | .20 |
| ☐ 64 Rod Hill | 1.50 | .60 | .15 |
| ☐ 65 Steve Rodehutskors | 1.00 | .40 | .10 |
| ☐ 66 Trevor Kennerd | 1.50 | .60 | .15 |
| ☐ 67 Moustafa Ali | 1.00 | .40 | .10 |
| ☐ 68 Mike Gray | .75 | .30 | .07 |
| ☐ 69 Bob Molle | .75 | .30 | .07 |
| ☐ 70 Tim Jessie | 1.00 | .40 | .10 |
| ☐ 71 Matt Pearce | .75 | .30 | .07 |
| ☐ 72 Will Lewis | .75 | .30 | .07 |
| ☐ 73 Sean Salisbury | 2.50 | 1.00 | .25 |
| ☐ 74 Chris Walby | 1.50 | .60 | .15 |
| ☐ 75 Jeff Croonen | .75 | .30 | .07 |
| ☐ 76 David Black | .75 | .30 | .07 |
| ☐ 77 Buster Rhymes | 2.00 | .80 | .20 |
| ☐ 78 James Murphy | 1.50 | .60 | .15 |
| ☐ 79 Stan Mikawos | .75 | .30 | .07 |
| ☐ 80 Lee Saltz | 2.00 | .80 | .20 |
| ☐ 81 Bryan Illerbrun | .75 | .30 | .07 |
| ☐ 82 Donald Narcisse | 3.00 | 1.20 | .30 |
| ☐ 83 Milson Jones | 1.00 | .40 | .10 |
| ☐ 84 Dave Ridgway | 1.50 | .60 | .15 |
| ☐ 85 Glen Suitor | .75 | .30 | .07 |
| ☐ 86 Terry Baker | 1.00 | .40 | .10 |
| ☐ 87 James Curry | 1.50 | .60 | .15 |
| ☐ 88 Harry Skipper | 1.00 | .40 | .10 |
| ☐ 89 Bobby Jurasin | 1.50 | .60 | .15 |
| ☐ 90 Gary Lewis | .75 | .30 | .07 |
| ☐ 91 Roger Aldag | 1.00 | .40 | .10 |
| ☐ 92 Jeff Fairholm | 2.00 | .80 | .20 |
| ☐ 93 David Albright | .75 | .30 | .07 |
| ☐ 94 Ray Elgaard | 2.50 | 1.00 | .25 |
| ☐ 95 Kent Austin | 3.00 | 1.20 | .30 |
| ☐ 96 Tom Burgess | 2.50 | 1.00 | .25 |
| ☐ 97 Richie Hall | .75 | .30 | .07 |
| ☐ 98 Eddie Lowe | .75 | .30 | .07 |
| ☐ 99 Vince Goldsmith | 1.00 | .40 | .10 |
| ☐ 100 Tim McCray | 1.00 | .40 | .10 |
| ☐ 101 Leo Blanchard | .75 | .30 | .07 |
| ☐ 102 Tom Spoletini | .75 | .30 | .07 |
| ☐ 103 Dan Ferrone | 1.00 | .40 | .10 |
| ☐ 104 Doug(Tank) Landry | 1.50 | .60 | .15 |
| ☐ 105 Chris Major | 1.50 | .60 | .15 |
| ☐ 106 Mike Palumbo | .75 | .30 | .07 |
| ☐ 107 Terrence Jones | 2.00 | .80 | .20 |
| ☐ 108 Larry Willis | 1.25 | .50 | .12 |
| ☐ 109 Kent Warnock | .75 | .30 | .07 |
| ☐ 110 Tim Petros | 1.00 | .40 | .10 |
| ☐ 111 Marshall Toner | .75 | .30 | .07 |
| ☐ 112 Ken Ford | .75 | .30 | .07 |
| ☐ 113 Ron Hopkins | .75 | .30 | .07 |
| ☐ 114 Erik Kramer | 4.00 | 1.60 | .40 |
| ☐ 115 Stu Laird | 1.25 | .50 | .12 |
| ☐ 116 Vernell Quinn | .75 | .30 | .07 |
| ☐ 117 Lemont Jeffers | .75 | .30 | .07 |
| ☐ 118 Derrick Taylor | .75 | .30 | .07 |
| ☐ 119 Jay Christensen | 1.00 | .40 | .10 |
| ☐ 120 Mitchell Price | .75 | .30 | .07 |
| ☐ 121 Rod Connop | .75 | .30 | .07 |
| ☐ 122 Mark Norman | .75 | .30 | .07 |
| ☐ 123 Andre Francis | 1.00 | .40 | .10 |
| ☐ 124 Reggie Taylor | 1.50 | .60 | .15 |
| ☐ 125 Rick Worman | 1.25 | .50 | .12 |
| ☐ 126 Marco Cyncar | 1.00 | .40 | .10 |
| ☐ 127 Blake Dermott | .75 | .30 | .07 |
| ☐ 128 Jerry Kauric | 1.00 | .40 | .10 |
| ☐ 129 Steve Taylor | 2.00 | .80 | .20 |
| ☐ 130 Dave Richardson | .75 | .30 | .07 |
| ☐ 131 John Mandarich | 1.00 | .40 | .10 |
| ☐ 132 Gregg Stumon | 1.00 | .40 | .10 |
| ☐ 133 Tracey Ham | 3.00 | 1.20 | .30 |
| ☐ 134 Danny Bass | 2.00 | .80 | .20 |
| ☐ 135 Blake Marshall | 1.50 | .60 | .15 |
| ☐ 136 Jeff Braswell | 1.00 | .40 | .10 |
| ☐ 137 Larry Wruck | 1.00 | .40 | .10 |
| ☐ 138 Warren Jones | .75 | .30 | .07 |
| ☐ 139 Stephen Jones | 1.50 | .60 | .15 |
| ☐ 140 Tom Richards | 1.00 | .40 | .10 |
| ☐ 141 Tony Cherry | 1.50 | .60 | .15 |
| ☐ 142 Anthony Parker | 1.25 | .50 | .12 |
| ☐ 143 Gerald Roper | .75 | .30 | .07 |

| | | | |
|---|---|---|---|
| ☐ 144 Lui Passaglia | 1.50 | .60 | .15 |
| ☐ 145 Mack Moore | .75 | .30 | .07 |
| ☐ 146 Jamie Taras | .75 | .30 | .07 |
| ☐ 147 Rickey Foggie | 1.50 | .60 | .15 |
| ☐ 148 Matt Dunigan | 5.00 | 2.00 | .50 |
| ☐ 149 Anthony Drawhorn | 1.25 | .50 | .12 |
| ☐ 150 Eric Streater | 1.25 | .50 | .12 |
| ☐ 151 Marcus Thomas | .75 | .30 | .07 |
| ☐ 152 Wes Cooper | .75 | .30 | .07 |
| ☐ 153 James Mills | 1.50 | .60 | .15 |
| ☐ 154 Peter VandenBos | .75 | .30 | .07 |
| ☐ 155 Ian Sinclair | 1.00 | .40 | .10 |
| ☐ 156 James Parker | 1.50 | .60 | .15 |
| ☐ 157 Andrew Murray | .75 | .30 | .07 |
| ☐ 158 Larry Crawford | 1.25 | .50 | .12 |
| ☐ 159 Kevin Konar | 1.00 | .40 | .10 |
| ☐ 160 David Williams | 2.50 | 1.00 | .25 |

# 1959 Wheaties CFL

The 1959 Wheaties CFL set contains 48 cards, each measuring 2 1/2" by 3 1/2". The fronts contain a black and white photo on a one-colored striped field, with the player's name and team in black within a white rectangle at the lower portion. The back contains the player's name and team, his position, and brief biographical data in both English and French. The cards are quite similar in appearance to the 1956 Shredded Wheat set. These unnumbered cards are ordered below in alphabetical order. Every 1959 CFL game program contained a full-page ad for the Wheaties Grey Cup Game Contest. The ad detailed the card program which indicated that each specially marked package of Wheaties contained four cards.

| | NRMT | VG-E | GOOD |
|---|---|---|---|
| COMPLETE SET (48) | 4000.00 | 1800.00 | 450.00 |
| COMMON PLAYER (1-48) | 60.00 | 24.00 | 6.00 |
| | | | |
| ☐ 1 Ron Adam | 60.00 | 24.00 | 6.00 |
| ☐ 2 Bill Bewley | 75.00 | 30.00 | 7.50 |
| ☐ 3 Lynn Bottoms | 75.00 | 30.00 | 7.50 |
| ☐ 4 Johnny Bright | 150.00 | 60.00 | 15.00 |
| ☐ 5 Ken Carpenter | 75.00 | 30.00 | 7.50 |
| ☐ 6 Tony Curcillo | 60.00 | 24.00 | 6.00 |
| ☐ 7 Sam Etcheverry | 250.00 | 100.00 | 25.00 |
| ☐ 8 Bernie Faloney | 200.00 | 80.00 | 20.00 |
| ☐ 9 Cam Fraser | 75.00 | 30.00 | 7.50 |
| ☐ 10 Don Getty | 125.00 | 50.00 | 12.50 |
| ☐ 11 Jack Gotta | 75.00 | 30.00 | 7.50 |
| ☐ 12 Milt Graham | 60.00 | 24.00 | 6.00 |
| ☐ 13 Jack Hill | 60.00 | 24.00 | 6.00 |
| ☐ 14 Ron Howell | 75.00 | 30.00 | 7.50 |
| ☐ 15 Russ Jackson | 200.00 | 80.00 | 20.00 |
| ☐ 16 Gerry James | 125.00 | 50.00 | 12.50 |
| ☐ 17 Doug Kiloh | 60.00 | 24.00 | 6.00 |
| ☐ 18 Ronnie Knox | 75.00 | 30.00 | 7.50 |
| ☐ 19 Vic Kristopaitis | 60.00 | 24.00 | 6.00 |
| ☐ 20 Oscar Kruger | 60.00 | 24.00 | 6.00 |
| ☐ 21 Bobby Kuntz | 75.00 | 30.00 | 7.50 |
| ☐ 22 Normie Kwong | 150.00 | 60.00 | 15.00 |
| ☐ 23 Leo Lewis | 125.00 | 50.00 | 12.50 |
| ☐ 24 Harry Lunn | 60.00 | 24.00 | 6.00 |
| ☐ 25 Don Luzzi | 90.00 | 36.00 | 9.00 |
| ☐ 26 Dave Mann | 75.00 | 30.00 | 7.50 |
| ☐ 27 Bobby Marlow | 90.00 | 36.00 | 9.00 |
| ☐ 28 Gerry McDougall | 75.00 | 30.00 | 7.50 |
| ☐ 29 Doug McNichol | 60.00 | 24.00 | 6.00 |
| ☐ 30 Rollie Miles | 100.00 | 40.00 | 10.00 |
| ☐ 31 Red O'Quinn | 90.00 | 36.00 | 9.00 |
| ☐ 32 Jackie Parker | 250.00 | 100.00 | 25.00 |
| ☐ 33 Hal Patterson | 150.00 | 60.00 | 15.00 |
| ☐ 34 Don Pinhey | 60.00 | 24.00 | 6.00 |
| ☐ 35 Kenny Ploen | 125.00 | 50.00 | 12.50 |
| ☐ 36 Gord Rowland | 75.00 | 30.00 | 7.50 |
| ☐ 37 Vince Scott | 90.00 | 36.00 | 9.00 |
| ☐ 38 Art Scullion | 60.00 | 24.00 | 6.00 |
| ☐ 39 Dick Shatto | 125.00 | 50.00 | 12.50 |
| ☐ 40 Bob Simpson | 125.00 | 50.00 | 12.50 |
| ☐ 41 Jackie Simpson UER | 100.00 | 40.00 | 10.00 |
| (Misspelled Jacki) | | | |
| ☐ 42 Bill Sowalski | 60.00 | 24.00 | 6.00 |
| ☐ 43 Norm Stoneburgh | 60.00 | 24.00 | 6.00 |
| ☐ 44 Buddy Tinsley | 90.00 | 36.00 | 9.00 |
| ☐ 45 Frank Tripucka | 90.00 | 36.00 | 9.00 |
| ☐ 46 Jim Van Pelt | 60.00 | 24.00 | 6.00 |
| ☐ 47 Ernie Warlick | 75.00 | 30.00 | 7.50 |
| ☐ 48 Nobby Wirkowski | 75.00 | 30.00 | 7.50 |